Eight Translation New Testament

King James Version
The Living Bible
Phillips Modern English
Revised Standard Version
Today's English Version
New International Version
Jerusalem Bible
New English Bible

Eight Translation New Testament

King James Version
The Living Bible
Phillips Modern English
Revised Standard Version
Today's English Version
New International Version
Jerusalem Bible
New English Bible

Tyndale House Publishers, Inc.
Wheaton, Illinois

Fifth Printing 1983

Library of Congress Catalog Card Number 74-21060
ISBN 0-8423-4690-2, Cloth
ISBN 0-8423-4691-0, Paper

175 Fifth Ave., New York, N.Y. 10010
Printed in the United States of America

CONTENTS

INTRODUCTION

If you are confused by the plethora of Scripture translations on the market today, perhaps you wonder why we have put eight different ones together in the same volume. The reason is simple: we believe if you have only one version of the Bible, you are missing much of the richness of God's Word.

Although nearly everyone owns a Bible, until recently that Bible was most likely the King James or Douay-Rheims Version. The King James Version has been revered by Protestants for more than three centuries. First published in 1611, it was the best possible translation at that time and is still a masterpiece of seventeenth century English literature. The Douay-Rheims Version dates back to 1582 (New Testament) and 1609-10 (Old Testament). It was the work of exiled English priests and educators who had been banned from England when the Roman Catholic Church was outlawed in 1560. Hence, like the King James Version, it presents God's Word in seventeenth century Elizabethian English.

But the English language has so changed that the contemporary reader of the Bible either needs study helps to clarify these texts, or a modern translation utilizing today's English. In addition, better resource materials and greater knowledge make these new translations necessities, not luxuries.

We believe the many Bible translations and paraphrases available today can help you understand the more exact meaning of various passages, can make them "come alive" for you. To read the Scriptures in any of these translations which speak in our kind of English is an exciting experience. For the first time you may feel that Moses or Paul or Isaiah or Christ is speaking directly to you, about your problems, in clear, straightforward terms that are relevant to life here and now.

This clarity of meaning and new adventure in Scripture reading have been our primary concern and motive in producing this volume. We trust that each translation selected contributes in some way to your understanding of God's Word and brings new joy to your study of Scripture.

THE
NEW TESTAMENT
OF OUR LORD AND SAVIOUR JESUS CHRIST

Translated out of the original Greek and with the former translations diligently compared and revised

Set forth in 1611
And commonly known as the

KING JAMES VERSION

THE EPISTLE DEDICATORY

TO THE MOST HIGH *and* MIGHTY PRINCE JAMES *by the Grace of God* KING OF GREAT BRITAIN, FRANCE, *and* IRELAND, DEFENDER OF THE FAITH, &C. *The Translators of this Bible wish Grace, Mercy, and Peace, through* JESUS CHRIST *our Lord*

Great and manifold were the blessings, most dread Sovereign, which Almighty God, the Father of all mercies, bestowed upon us the people of England, when first he sent Your Majesty's Royal Person to rule and reign over us. For whereas it was the expectation of many, who wished not well unto our Sion, that upon the setting of that bright Occidental Star, Queen Elizabeth of most happy memory, some thick and palpable clouds of darkness would so have overshadowed this Land, that men should have been in doubt which way they were to walk; and that it should hardly be known, who was to direct the unsettled State; the appearance of Your Majesty, as of the Sun in his strength, instantly dispelled those supposed and surmised mists, and gave unto all that were well affected exceeding cause of comfort; especially when we beheld the Government established in Your Highness, and Your hopeful Seed, by an undoubted Title, and this also accompanied with peace and tranquillity at home and abroad.

But among all our joys, there was no one that more filled our hearts, than the blessed continuance of the preaching of God's sacred Word among us; which is that inestimable treasure, which excelleth all the riches of the earth; because the fruit thereof extendeth itself, not only to the time spent in this transitory world, but directeth and disposeth men unto that eternal happiness which is above in heaven.

Then not to suffer this to fall to the ground, but rather to take it up, and to continue it in that state, wherein the famous Predecessor of Your Highness did leave it: nay, to go forward with the confidence and resolution of a Man in maintaining the truth of Christ, and propagating it far and near, is that which hath so bound and firmly knit the hearts of all Your Majesty's loyal and religious people unto You, that Your very name is precious among them: their eye doth behold You with comfort, and they bless You in their hearts, as that sanctified Person, who, under God, is the immediate Author of their true happiness. And this their contentment doth not diminish or decay, but every day increaseth and taketh strength, when they observe, that the zeal of Your Majesty toward the house of God doth not slack or go backward, but is more and more kindled, manifesting itself abroad in the farthest parts of Christendom, by writing in defence of the Truth, (which hath given such a blow unto that man of sin, as will not be healed,) and every day at home, by religious and learned discourse, by frequenting the house of God, by hearing the Word preached, by cherishing the Teachers thereof, by caring for the Church, as a most tender and loving nursing Father.

There are infinite arguments of this right Christian and religious affection in Your Majesty; but none is more forcible to declare it to others than the vehement and perpetuated desire of accomplishing and publishing of this work, which now with all humility we present unto Your Majesty. For when Your Highness had once out of deep judgment apprehended how convenient it was, that out of the Original Sacred Tongues, together with comparing of the labours, both in our own, and other foreign Languages, of many worthy men who went before us, there should be one more exact Translation of the Holy Scriptures into the English Tongue; Your Majesty did never desist to urge and to excite those to whom it was commended, that the work might be hastened, and that the business might be expedited in so decent a manner, as a matter of such importance might justly require.

And now at last, by the mercy of God, and the continuance of our labours, it being brought unto such a conclusion, as that we have great hopes that the Church of England shall reap good fruit thereby; we hold it our duty to offer it to Your Majesty, not only as to our King and Sovereign, but as to the principal Mover and Author of the work: humbly craving of Your most Sacred Majesty, that since things of this quality have ever been subject to the censures of illmeaning and discontented persons, it may receive approbation and patronage from so learned and judicious a Prince as Your Highness is, whose allowance and acceptance of our labours shall more honour and encourage us, than all the calumniations and hard interpretations of other men shall dismay us. So that if, on the one side, we shall be traduced by Popish Persons at home or abroad, who therefore will malign us, because we are poor instruments to make God's holy Truth to be yet more and more known unto the people, whom they desire still to keep in ignorance and darkness; or if, on the other side, we shall be maligned by selfconceited Brethren, who run their own ways, and give liking unto nothing, but what is framed by themselves, and hammered on their anvil; we may rest secure, supported within by the truth and innocency of a good conscience, having walked the ways of simplicity and integrity, as before the Lord; and sustained without by the powerful protection of Your Majesty's grace and favour, which will ever give countenance to honest and Christian endeavours against bitter censures and uncharitable imputations.

The Lord of heaven and earth bless Your Majesty with many and happy days, that, as his heavenly hand hath enriched Your Highness with many singular and extraordinary graces, so You may be the wonder of the world in this latter age for happiness and true felicity, to the honour of that great GOD, and the good of his Church, through Jesus Christ our Lord and only Saviour.

THE

LIVING BIBLE

PARAPHRASED

NEW TESTAMENT

TYNDALE HOUSE PUBLISHERS
Wheaton, Illinois

The Living Bible is a compilation of the Scripture paraphrases previously published by Tyndale House Publishers under the following titles:
Living Letters, 1962; *Living Prophecies,* 1965; *Living Gospels,* 1966; *Living Psalms and Proverbs,* 1967; *Living Lessons of Life and Love,* 1968; *Living Books of Moses,* 1969; *Living History of Israel,* 1970.

From Wm. Tyndale's Prologue
to the first printed English New Testament:

I have here translated, brethren and sisters most dear and tenderly beloved in Christ, the New Testament for your spiritual edifying, consolation and solace, exhortynge instantly and besechynge those that are better sene in the tongues than I, and that have higher gifts of grace to interpret the sense of Scripture, and meaning of the Spirit, than I, to consider and ponder my labor, and that with the spirit of meekness. And if they perceive in any places that I have not attained the very sense of the tongue, or meaning of the Scripture, or have not given the right English word, that they put to their hands to amend it, remembering that so is their duty to do. For we have not received the gifts of God for ourselves only, or for to hide them; but for to bestow them unto the honoring of God and Christ and edifying of the congregation, which is the body of Christ.

PREFACE

In this wonderful day of many new translations and revisions we can greet another new one with either dread or joy! Dread that "people will become confused" or joy that some will understand more perfectly what the Bible is talking about. We choose the way of joy! For each new presentation of God's World will find its circle, large or small, of those to whom it will minister strength and blessing.

This book, though arriving late on the current translation scene, has been underway for many years. It has undergone several major manuscript revisions and has been under the careful scrutiny of a team of Greek and Hebrew experts to check content, and of English critics for style. Their many suggestions have been largely followed, though none of those consulted feels entirely satisfied with the present result. This is therefore a tentative edition. Further suggestions as to both renderings and style will be gladly considered as future printings are called for.

A word should be said here about paraphrases. What are they? To paraphrase is to say something in different words than the author used. It is a restatement of an author's thoughts, using different words than he did. This book is a paraphrase of the Old and New Testaments. Its purpose is to say as exactly as possible what the writers of the Scriptures meant, and to say it simply, expanding where necessary for a clear understanding by the modern reader.

The Bible writers often used idioms and patterns of thought that are hard for us to follow today. Frequently the thought sequence is fast-moving, leaving gaps for the reader to understand and fill in, or the thought jumps ahead or backs up to something said before (as one would do in conversation) without clearly stating the antecedent reference. Sometimes the result for us, with our present-day stress on careful sentence construction and sequential logic, is that we are left far behind.

Then too, the writers often have compressed enormous thoughts into single technical words that are full of meaning, but need expansion and amplification if we are to be sure of understanding what the author meant to include in such words as "justification," "righteousness," "redemption," "baptism for the dead," "elect," and "saints." Such amplification is permitted in a paraphrase but exceeds the responsibilities of a strict translation.

There are dangers in paraphrases, as well as values. For whenever the author's exact words are not translated from the original languages, there is a possibility that the translator, however honest, may be giving the English reader something that the original writer did not mean to say. This is because a paraphrase is guided not only by the translator's skill in simplifying but also by the clarity of his understanding of what the author meant and by his theology. For when the Greek or Hebrew is not clear, then the theology of the translator is his guide, along with his sense of logic, unless perchance the translation is allowed to stand without any clear meaning at all. The theological lodestar in this book has been a rigid evangelical position.

If this paraphrase helps to simplify the deep and often complex thoughts of the Word of God, and if it makes the Bible easier to understand and follow, deepening the Christian lives of its readers and making it easier for them to follow their Lord, then the book has achieved its goal.

—Adapted from the preface to
the first edition of
Living Letters

THE

NEW TESTAMENT in Modern English

TRANSLATED BY J. B. PHILLIPS

Revised Edition

THE MACMILLAN COMPANY
New York, New York

I DEDICATE THIS TRANSLATION TO VERA,

MY WIFE AND FINEST CRITIC

INTRODUCTION TO THIS NEW EDITION

I would like to make it clear to my readers that this new edition is in fact a new translation from the latest and best Greek text published by the United Bible Societies in 1966 and recognised by scholars of all denominations as the best source available. Naturally some considerable parts of the former translation reappear, but that is only because after considerable thought I did not think I could improve upon their wording. However, the reader may rest assured that every single Greek word was read and considered. This rather exacting task took me more than two years.

I fear that a little personal history must be part of the explanation of why I have now been able to start completely afresh. I began the work of translation as long ago as 1941, and the work was undertaken primarily for the benefit of my Youth Club, and members of my congregation, in a much-bombed parish in S.E. London. I had almost no tools to work with apart from my own Greek Testament and no friends who could help me in this particular field. I felt then that since much of the New Testament was written to Christians in danger, it should be particularly appropriate for us who, for many months, lived in a different, but no less real, danger. I began with the Epistles since most of my Christian members had at least a nodding acquaintance with the Gospels, but regarded the Epistles as obscure and difficult and therefore largely unread. In those days of danger and emergency I was not over-concerned with minute accuracy, I wanted above all to convey the vitality and radiant faith as well as the courage of the early Church. The attempt succeeded and, as I have mentioned in the Translator's Preface to earlier editions, the strong encouragement of C. S. Lewis led me to continue the task. The war was over and I had been moved to a large and scattered country parish in Surrey before the translation of the Epistles was completed. I revised the typescript as well as I could with many other demands on my hands, and after many rejections succeeded in finding a publisher in the late Mr. Geoffrey Bles. The work, under the title *Letters to Young Churches,* appeared in 1947.

Within five years and not without trepidation I had completed *The Gospels in Modern English,* and this was similarly well received. I then began the Acts, which I renamed *The Young Church in Action.* But before I could complete this I realised that the work of translation plus the many duties of a large parish were proving too formidable a task for me. I therefore purchased a small house in a quiet part of Dorset where I could continue my translation and other writing, and attend properly to the huge volume of correspondence that was beginning to arrive from all over the English-speaking world. Thus it happened that *The Young Church in Action* and *The Book of Revelation* were both published after I had left parish work.

In 1958 the books were collected together in one volume and published under the title of *The New Testament in Modern English.* During the years from 1947 to 1958 I had been able to make some minor alterations and to correct some errors, many of which were pointed out to me by kind friends. The edition of my complete translation issued in 1960 incorporated a large number of small but significant emendations.

Now, more than ten years later, I offer this translation as a wholly new book. Having by this time done much collateral reading and learned more of the usages of the N.T. Greek, I felt that now, faced with a completely clean sheet, as it were, I could do a better job. Quite apart from my own feelings there were good reasons for tackling this rather daunting task. The most important by far was the fact, which perhaps I had been slow to grasp, that "Phillips" was being used as an authoritative version by Bible Study Groups in various parts of the world. I still feel that the most important "object of the exercise" is communication. I see it as my job as one who knows Greek pretty well and ordinary English very well to convey the living quality of the N.T. documents. I want above all to create in my readers the same emotions as the original writings evoked nearly 2,000 years ago. This passion of mine for communication, for I can hardly call it less, has led me sometimes into paraphrase and sometimes to interpolate clarifying remarks which are certainly not in the Greek. But being now regarded as "an authority", I felt I must curb my youthful enthusiasms and keep as close as I possibly could to the Greek text. Thus most of my conversationally-worded additions in the Letters of Paul had to go. Carried away sometimes by the intensity of his argument or by his passion for the welfare of his new converts I found I had inserted things like, "as I am sure you realise" or "you must know by now" and many extra words which do not occur in the Greek text at all. I must say that it was not without some pangs of regret that I deleted nearly all of them!

There was a further reason for making the translation not merely readable but as accurate as I could make it. It has been proposed that a Commentary on the Phillips translation should be undertaken. I felt it essential that the scholars who would contribute to such work should have before them the best translation of which I am capable. I certainly did not want them to waste time in pointing out errors which I had in fact by now corrected!

The last, but not least important, reason for making a fresh translation was to check the English itself. It must be current and easily understood, and I must confess that I thought that the twenty-five years since the publication of *Letters to Young Churches* might have seriously "dated" the English I used then. With the help of my wife, several friends, including some critical young people, we scrutinised the English very carefully. Rather to my surprise only a few alterations were necessary, and this showed me that the ordinary English which we use in communication changes far more slowly than I had imagined. I knew, however, that slang and colloquialisms change rapidly, but since I had used few of these there was not much to alter. A couple of examples may illustrate my meaning. The "little tin gods" of I Peter 5, *3* (an expression no longer current) have become "dictators". The colloquial use of the word "plutocrats" of James 5, *1* has been changed to "men of affluence".

The essential principles of translation

There seem to be three necessary tests which any work of transference from one language to another must pass before it can be classed as good translation. The first is simply that it must not sound like a translation at all. If it is skilfully done, and we are not previously informed, we should be quite unaware that it *is* a translation, even though the work we are reading is far distant from us in both time and place. That is a first, and indeed fundamental test, but it is not by itself sufficient. For the translator himself may be a skilful writer, and although he may have conveyed the essential meaning, characterisation and plot of the original author, he may have so strong a style of his own that he completely changes that of the original author. The example of this kind of translation which springs most readily to my mind is Fitzgerald's *Rubáiyát of Omar Khayyám*. I would therefore make this the second test: that a translator does his work with the least possible obtrusion of his own personality. The third and final test which a good translator should be able to pass is that of being able to produce in the hearts and minds of his readers an effect equivalent to that produced by the author upon his original readers. Of course no translator living would claim that his work successfully achieved these three ideals. But he must bear them in mind constantly as principles for his guidance.

Translation as interpretation

As I have frequently said, a translator is not a commentator. He is usually well aware of the different connotations which a certain passage may bear, but unless his work is to be cluttered with footnotes he is bound, after careful consideration, to set down what is the most likely meaning. Occasionally one is driven into what appears to be a paraphrase, simply because a literal translation of the original Greek would prove unintelligible. But where this has proved necessary I have always been careful to avoid giving any slant or flavour which is purely of my own making. That is why I have been reluctant to accept the suggestion that my translation is "interpretation"! If the word interpretation is used in a bad sense, that is, if it means that a work is tendentious, or that there has been a manipulation of the words of New Testament Scripture to fit some private point of view, then I would still strongly repudiate the charge! But "interpretation" can also mean transmitting meaning from one language to another, and skilled interpreters in world affairs do not intentionally inject any meaning of their own. In this sense I gladly accept the word interpretation to describe my work. For, as I see it, the translator's function is to understand as fully and deeply as possible what the New Testament writers had to say and then, after a process of what might be called reflective digestion, to write it down in the language of the people today. And here I must say that it is essential for the interpreter to know the language of both parties. He may be a first-class scholar in New Testament Greek and know the significance of every traditional crux, and yet be abysmally ignorant of how his contemporaries outside his scholastic world are thinking and feeling.

Words and their context

After reading a large number of commentaries I have a feeling that some scholars, at least, have lived so close to the Greek Text that they have lost their sense of proportion. I doubt very much whether the New Testament writers were as subtle or as selfconscious as some commentators would make them appear. For the most part I am convinced that they had no idea that they were writing Holy Scripture. They would be, or indeed perhaps are, amazed to learn what meanings are sometimes read back into their simple utterances! Paul, for instance, writing in haste and urgency to some of his wayward and difficult Christians, was not tremendously concerned about dotting the "i's" and crossing the "t's" of his message. I doubt very much whether he was even concerned about being completely consistent with what he had already written. Consequently, it seems to me quite beside the point to study his writings microscopically, as it were, and deduce hidden meanings of which almost certainly he was unaware. His letters are alive, and they are moving—in both senses of that word—and their meaning can no more be appreciated by cold minute examination than can the beauty of a bird's flight be appreciated by dissection after its death. We have to take these living New Testament documents in their context, a context of supreme urgency and often of acute danger. But a word is modified very considerably by the context in which it appears, and where a translator fails to realise this, we are not far away from the use of a computer! The translators of the Authorised Version were certainly not unaware of this modification, even though they had an extreme reverence for the actual words of Holy Writ. Three hundred years ago they did not hesitate to translate the Greek word EKBALLO by such varying expressions as *put out, drive forth, bring forth, send out, tear out, take out, leave out, cast out,* etc., basing their decision on the context. And as a striking example of their translational freedom, in Matthew 27, *44* we read that the thieves who were crucified with Jesus "cast the same in his teeth", where the Greek words mean simply, "abused him".

The translator must be flexible

I feel strongly that a translator, although he must make himself as familiar as possible with New Testament Greek usage, must steadfastly refuse to be driven by the bogey of consistency. He must be guided both by the context in which a word appears, and by the sensibilities of modern English readers. In the story of the raising of Lazarus, for example, Martha's objection to opening the grave would be natural enough to an Eastern mind. But to put into her lips the words, "by this time he's stinking", would sound to Western ears unpleasantly out of key with the rest of that moving story. Similarly, we know that the early Christians greeted one another with "an holy kiss". Yet to introduce such an expression into a modern English translation immediately reveals the gulf between the early Christians and ourselves, the very thing which I as a translator am trying to bridge. Again, it is perfectly true, if we are to translate literally, that Jesus said, "Blessed are the beggars in spirit". In an Eastern land, where the disparity between rich and poor was very great, beggars were common. But it is to my mind extremely doubtful whether the word "beggar" in our Welfare State, or indeed in most English-speaking countries, conjures up the mental image which Jesus intended to convey to his hearers. It was not the social misfit or the work-shy, but the one who was spiritually speaking obviously and consciously in need whom Jesus describes as "blessed" or "happy".

The use of insight and sympathy

I have found imaginative sympathy, not so much with words as with people, to be essential. If it is not presumptuous to say so, I attempted, as far as I could, to think myself into the heart and mind of Paul, for example, or of Mark or of John the Divine. Then I tried further to imagine myself as each of the New Testament authors writing his particular message for the people of today. No one could succeed in doing this superlatively well, if only because of the scantiness of our knowledge of the first century A.D. But this has been my ideal, and that is why consistency and meticulous accuracy have sometimes both been sacrificed in the attempt to transmit freshness and life across the centuries. By the use of cross-headings, solid and rather forbidding slabs of continuous writing (such as appear in the Greek Text) are made more digestible to the modern reader, whose reading habits have already been "conditioned" by the comparatively recent usage of clear punctuation, intelligent paragraphing and good printer's type.

Acknowledgments

It would be ungracious to forget the very many people who have made the work possible. I think first of the textual critics, whose patient work gives us a text to work from which is as near as possible to that of the original writers. I am most grateful to them, as all translators must be, and I should also like to express my thanks to the numerous commentators whose works I have consulted. As will be gathered from what I have said above, I have not always agreed with them, but they have informed my mind and stimulated my thoughts many times. Again, although it would be impossible to supply a full list, I am extremely grateful to the many people—including first-rate scholars, hard-working parish priests, busy ministers, doctors, scientists, missionaries, educationists, elderly saints and lively young people—who have, over the years, written me hundreds of letters, the great majority of which were constructive and useful. Their help has been invaluable.

I find myself therefore indebted to all kinds of people of different denominations. The assurance has grown within me that here in the New Testament, at the very heart and core of our Faith, Christians are far more at one than their outward divisions would imply. From this unquestionable evidence of fundamental unity I derive not only great comfort but a great hope for the future.

J. B. PHILLIPS

SWANAGE, DORSET
1972

THE NEW COVENANT

COMMONLY CALLED

THE

NEW TESTAMENT

OF OUR LORD AND SAVIOR
JESUS CHRIST

REVISED STANDARD VERSION

TRANSLATED FROM THE GREEK
BEING THE VERSION SET FORTH A.D. 1611
REVISED A.D. 1881 AND A.D. 1901
COMPARED WITH THE MOST ANCIENT AUTHORITIES
AND REVISED A.D. 1946

New York and Glasgow
COLLINS' CLEAR-TYPE PRESS
Licensee
London • Toronto • Sydney • Aukland

PREFACE

The Revised Standard Version of the New Testament is an authorized revision of the American Standard Version, published in 1901, which was a revision of the King James Version, published in 1611.

The King James Version was itself a revision rather than a new translation. The first English version of the New Testament made by translation from the Greek was that of William Tyndale, 1525; and this became the foundation for successive versions, notably those of Coverdale, 1535; the Great Bible, 1539; Geneva, 1560; and the Bishops' Bible, 1568. In 1582 a translation of the New Testament, made from the Latin Vulgate by Roman Catholic scholars, was published at Rheims. The translators of the King James Version took into account all of these preceding versions; and comparison shows that it owes something to each of them. It kept felicitous turns of phrase and apt expressions, from whatever source, which had stood the test of public usage.

As a result of the discovery of manuscripts of the New Testament more ancient than those used by translators in 1611, together with a marked development in Biblical studies, a demand for the revision of the King James Version arose in the middle of the nineteenth century. The task was undertaken, by authority of the Church of England, in 1870. The English Revised Version was published in 1881-1885; and the American Standard Version, its variant embodying the preferences of the American scholars associated in the work, was published in 1901.

Because of unhappy experience with unauthorized publications in the two decades between 1881 and 1901, which tampered with the text of the English Revised Version in the supposed interest of the American public, the American Standard Version was copyrighted, to protect the text from unauthorized changes. In 1928 this copyright was acquired by the International Council of Religious Education, and thus passed into the ownership of the churches of the United States and Canada which were associated in this Council through their boards of education and publication.

The Council appointed a Committee of scholars to have charge of the text of the American Standard Version; and in 1937 it authorized this Committee to undertake a further revision, on the ground that there is need for a version which will "embody the best results of modern scholarship as to the meaning of the Scriptures, and express this meaning in English diction which is designed for use in public and private worship and preserves those qualities which have given to the King James Version a supreme place in English literature."

Thirty-two scholars have served as members of the Committee charged with making the revision; and they have secured the review and counsel of an Advisory Board of fifty representatives of the cooperating denominations. The Committee has worked in two sections, one dealing with the Old Testament and one with the New Testament. Each section has submitted its work to the scrutiny of the members of the other section, however; and the charter of the Committee requires that all changes be agreed upon by a two-thirds vote of the total membership of the Committee. The publication of the Revised Standard Version of the Bible, containing the Old and New Testaments, was authorized by vote of the National Council of the Churches of Christ in the U.S.A. in 1951.

The King James Version of the New Testament was based upon a Greek text that was marred by mistakes, containing the accumulated errors of fourteen centuries of manuscript copying. It was essentially the Greek text of the New Testament as edited by Beza, 1589, who closely followed that published by Erasmus, 1516-1535, which was based upon a few medieval manuscripts. The earliest and best of the eight manuscripts which Erasmus consulted was from the tenth century, and he made the least use of it because it differed most from the commonly received text; Beza had access to two manuscripts of great value, dating from the fifth and sixth centuries, but he made very little use of them because they differed from the text published by Erasmus.

We now possess many more ancient manuscripts of the New Testament, and are far better equipped to seek to recover the original wording of the Greek text. The evidence for the text of the books of the New Testament is better than for any other ancient book, both in the number of extant manuscripts and in the nearness of the date of some of these manuscripts to the date when the book was originally written.

The revisers in the 1870's had most of the evidence that we now have for the Greek text, though the most ancient of all extant manuscripts of the Greek New Testament were not discovered until 1931. But they lacked the resources which discoveries within the past eighty years have afforded for understanding the vocabulary, grammar, and idioms of the Greek New Testament. An amazing body of Greek papyri has been unearthed in Egypt since the 1870's—private letters, official reports, wills, business accounts, petitions, and other such trivial, every-day recordings of the ongoing activities of human beings. In 1895 appeared the first of Adolf Deissmann's studies of these ordinary materials. He proved that many words which had hitherto been assumed to belong to what was called "Biblical Greek" were current in the spoken vernacular of the first century A.D. The New Testament was written in the Koiné, the common Greek which was spoken and understood practically everywhere throughout the Roman Empire in the early centuries of the Christian era. This development in the study of New Testament Greek has come since the work on the English Revised Version and the American Standard Version was done, and at many points sheds new light upon the meaning of the Greek text.

Another reason for revision of the King James Version is afforded by changes in English usage. The problem is presented, not so much by its archaic forms or obsolete words, as by the English words which are still in constant use but now convey different meanings from those which they had in 1611 and in the King James Version. These words were once accurate translations of the Hebrew and Greek Scriptures; but now, having changed in meaning, they have become misleading. They no longer say what the King James translators meant them to say. Thus, the King James Version uses the word "let" in the sense of "hinder," "prevent" to mean "precede," "allow" in the sense of "approve," "communicate" for "share," "conversation" for "conduct," "comprehend" for "overcome," "ghost" for "spirit," "wealth" for "well-being," "allege" for "prove," "demand" for "ask," "take no thought" for "be not anxious," etc.

This preface does not undertake to set forth in detail the lines along which the revision proceeded. That is done in pamphlets entitled *An Introduction to the Revised Standard Version of the Old Testament* and *An Introduction to the Revised Standard Version of the New Testament,* written by members of the Committee and designed to help the general public to understand the main principles which have guided this comprehensive revision of the King James and American Standard versions.

These principles were reaffirmed by the Committee in 1959 in connection with a study of criticisms and suggestions from various readers. As a result, a few changes were authorized for subsequent editions, most of them corrections of punctuation, capitalization, or footnotes. Some of them are changes of words or phrases made in the interest of consistency, clarity, or accuracy of translation.

The Revised Standard Version Bible Committee is a continuing body, holding its meetings at regular intervals. It has become both ecumenical and international, with Protestant and Catholic active members, who come from Great Britain, Canada, and the United States.

The Second Edition of the translation of the New Testament (1971) profits from textual and linguistic studies published since the Revised Standard Version New Testament was first issued in 1946. Many proposals for modification were submitted to the Committee by individuals and by two denominational committees. All of these were given careful attention by the Committee.

Two passages, the longer ending of Mark (16.9-20) and the account of the woman caught in adultery (Jn 7.53—8.11), are restored to the text, separated from it by a blank space and accompanied by informative notes describing the various arrangements of the text in the ancient authorities. With new manuscript support two passages, Lk 22.19b-20 and 24.51b, are restored to the text, and one passage, Lk 22.43-44, is placed in the note, as is a phrase in Lk 12.39. Notes are added which indicate significant variations, additions, or omissions in the ancient authorities (Mt 9.34; Mk 3.16; 7.4; Lk 24.32,51; etc.). Among the new notes are those giving the equivalence of ancient coinage with the contemporary day's or year's wages of a laborer (Mt 18.24,28; 20.2; etc.). Some of the revisions clarify the meaning through rephrasing or reordering the text (see Mk 5.42; Lk 22.29-30; Jn 10.33; 1 Cor 3.9; 2 Cor 5.19; Heb 13.13). Even when the changes appear to be largely matters of English style, they have the purpose of presenting to the reader more adequately the meaning of the text (see Mt 10.8; 12.1; 15.29; 17.20; Lk 7.36; 11.17; 12.40; Jn 16.9; Rom 10.16; 1 Cor 12.24; 2 Cor 2.3; 3.5,6; etc.).

The Revised Standard Version Bible seeks to preserve all that is best in the English Bible as it has been known and used through the years. It is intended for use in public and private worship, not merely for reading and instruction. We have resisted the temptation to use phrases that are merely current usage, and have sought to put the message of the Bible in simple, enduring words that are worthy to stand in the great Tyndale-King James tradition. We are glad to say, with the King James translators: "Truly (good Christian Reader) we never thought from the beginning, that we should need to make a new Translation, nor yet to make of a bad one a good one . . . but to make a good one better."

The Bible is more than a historical document to be preserved. And it is more than a classic of English literature to be cherished and admired. It is a record of God's dealing with men, of God's revelation of Himself and His will. It records the life and work of Him in whom the Word of God became flesh and dwelt among men. The Bible carries its full message, not to those who regard it simply as a heritage of the past or praise its literary style, but to those who read it that they may discern and understand God's Word to men. That Word must not be disguised in phrases that are no longer clear, or hidden under words that have changed or lost their meaning. It must stand forth in language that is direct and plain and meaningful to people today. It is our hope and our earnest prayer that this Revised Standard Version of the Bible may be used by God to speak to men in these momentous times, and to help them to understand and believe and obey His Word.

GOOD NEWS
for
Modern Man

NEW TESTAMENT

in

Today's English Version

Third Edition

AMERICAN BIBLE SOCIETY
New York, N.Y.

PREFACE

The New Testament is the book about Jesus Christ. Its name means that it is the record of God's new covenant with his people. This covenant, or agreement, is the good news of God's promise to save those who believe in Jesus Christ as Lord and Savior. The New Testament does not merely inform; it demands decision and calls for commitment on the part of those who read this Good News.

The twenty-seven books which make up the New Testament were written by perhaps as many as twelve different authors over a period of some fifty years. Although the books differ in content, a constant theme runs through all of them and joins them into a unity—God's love for man revealed in the person of Jesus Christ.

The four Gospels tell the story of the life, teaching, deeds, death, and resurrection of Jesus. They are followed by the Acts of the Apostles, which traces the spread of the gospel for some thirty years, from Jerusalem to Rome, the capital of the Empire. The letters of Paul were all written to meet specific needs faced by early Christians. The eight books that follow, known as the General Letters, are varied: some of them are addressed in general terms to believers everywhere, while others are written to individual churches or persons.

The last book in the New Testament is different from all the others. Its teaching concerning the victory of the Kingdom of God and the lordship of Christ is conveyed by means of visions, images, and symbols, many of which are very difficult for the modern reader to understand. But its central message, which may also be taken as the theme of the whole New Testament, is clearly proclaimed: "The power to rule over the world belongs now to our Lord and his Messiah, and he will rule forever and ever!" (Revelation 11.15).

This translation of the New Testament has been prepared by the American Bible Society for people who speak English either as their mother tongue or as an acquired language. As a distinctly new translation, it does not conform to traditional vocabulary or style, but seeks to express the meaning of the Greek text in words and forms accepted as standard by people everywhere who employ English as a means of communication. *Today's English Version* of the New Testament attempts to follow, in this century, the example set by the authors of the New Testament books who, for the most part, wrote in the standard, or common, form of the Greek language used throughout the Roman Empire. As much as possible, words and forms of English not in current use have been avoided; but no rigid limit has been set to the vocabulary employed.

A *Word List* at the end of the volume explains technical terms and rarely used words, and identifies a number of places and persons mentioned in the New Testament, in order to enable the reader to understand the text better in its historical setting. Some of the more important variations in Greek manuscripts and ancient versions, and some of the passages in the text which may be translated in more than one way, are listed in *Other Readings and Renderings*. An *Index* is provided which locates, by page numbers, some of the more important subjects, persons, places, and events in the New Testament. Finally there are a few line *Maps* designed to help the reader visualize the geographic setting of the countries and places mentioned in the New Testament.

The text from which this translation was made is the Greek New Testament prepared by an international committee of New Testament scholars, sponsored by several members of the United Bible Societies, and published in 1966. Verses marked with brackets [ ] are not in the oldest and best manuscripts of the New Testament.

The basic draft of this translation was prepared by Dr. Robert G. Bratcher. It was submitted to a panel of specialists for study and finally reviewed and approved by the Translations Committee of the American Bible Society.

NEW INTERNATIONAL VERSION
OF THE
NEW TESTAMENT

ZONDERVAN BIBLE PUBLISHERS
Grand Rapids, Michigan

PREFACE

This New Testament is the first portion of The New International Version of the Holy Bible. It is a completely new translation made by many scholars working directly from the Greek.

The New International Version had its beginning in 1965, when, after many years of exploratory study, a group of biblical scholars met in Chicago and concurred in the need for a new translation of the Holy Scriptures. This group, though not made up of official church representatives, was nevertheless transdenominational in character. Their conclusion was subsequently endorsed by a large gathering of Christian leaders from many denominations in North America. Final responsibility for the new version was delegated to a body of fifteen, the Committee on Bible Translation, composed for the most part of biblical specialists from universities, colleges and theological seminaries. In 1967 the New York Bible Society International generously undertook financial sponsorship of the project—a sponsorship that has made it possible to enlist the help of many distinguished scholars. The fact that participants from the United States, Canada, England, Australia and New Zealand are working together gives the project its international scope. That they come from various denominations, including Baptist, Brethren, Church of Christ, Episcopal, Lutheran, Mennonite, Methodist, Nazarene, Presbyterian, and Reformed churches, safeguards it from sectarian bias.

Because the distinctive nature of the New International Version is derived so largely from the working procedures, an explanation of these is in order. The translation of each book was assigned to a team of scholars. Next, an Intermediate Editorial Committee revised the initial translation, with constant reference to the Greek. Their work then went to a General Editorial Committee, which rechecked it in relation to the Greek and made another thorough revision. This revision in turn was carefully reviewed by the Committee on Bible Translation, which made further changes and then issued the final version. In this way the entire New Testament underwent three revisions, during each of which the translation was examined for its faithfulness to the original Greek and for its English style.

A sensitive feeling for style does not always go with scholarship in biblical languages. Accordingly the Committee on Bible Translation submitted the developing version to a number of literary consultants. Two of them read every word of the completed New Testament twice—once before the last major revision and once afterward—making invaluable suggestions. During the process, it was also tested for clarity and idiom by various kinds of people—young and old, educated and uneducated, ministers and laymen.

The Greek text used in the work of translation was an eclectic one. No other piece of ancient literature has so much manuscript support as does the New Testament. Where existing texts differ, the translators made their choice of readings in accord with sound principles of textual criticism. Footnotes call attention to places where there is uncertainty about what constitutes the original text. These have been introduced by the phrase "Some MSS add (*or* omit *or* read)."

As in all translations of the Scriptures, the precise meaning of the original text could not in every case be determined. In important instances of this kind, footnotes introduced by "Or" suggest an alternate rendering of the text. In the translation itself, brackets are occasionally used to indicate words or phrases supplied for clarification.

Certain convictions and aims have guided the translators. They are all committed to the full authority and complete trustworthiness of the Scriptures, which they believe to be God's Word in written form. They are agreed that the Bible contains the answer to man's deepest needs and sets forth the way to his eternal well-being. Therefore their first concern has been the accuracy of the translation and its fidelity to the thought of the New Testament writers. While they have weighed the significance of the lexical and grammatical details of the Greek text, they have striven for more than a word-for-word translation. Because thought patterns and syntax differ from language to language, faithful communication of the meaning of the writers of the New Testament demands frequent modifications in sentence structure and constant regard for the contextual meanings of words.

Concern for clarity of style—that it should be idiomatic without being idiosyncratic, contemporary without being dated—has also motivated the translators and their consultants. They have consistently aimed at simplicity of expression, with sensitive attention to the connotation and sound of the chosen word. At the same time, they have endeavored to avoid a sameness of style in order to reflect the varied styles and moods of the New Testament writers. These aims the translators and consultants have tried to embody in language that will speak not only to people today but also to those of future decades. And they trust that the wide use of the New International Version will encourage the wholesome practice of memorizing Scripture.

Among the languages of the world, English stands first in international use. The translators of this version, coming as they do from major English-speaking nations, have sought to recognize the world-wide character of the language by avoiding overt Americanisms on the one hand and overt Anglicisms on the other hand.

As for the omission of the pronouns "thou," "thee," and "thine" in reference to the Deity, the translators remind the reader that to retain these archaisms (along with the strange verb forms, such as *doest, wouldest* and *hadst*) would have violated their aim of faithful translation. The Greek text uses no special pronouns to express reverence for God and Christ. Scripture is not enhanced by keeping, as a special mode of addressing Deity, forms that in the days of the King James Bible were simply the regular pronouns and verbs used in everyday speech, whether referring to God or to man.

Like all translations of the Bible, made as they are by imperfect men, this one undoubtedly falls short of its aims. Yet we are grateful to God for the extent to which he has enabled us to realize our aims and for the strength he has given us to complete this part of our task. We offer this version of the New Testament to him in whose name and for whose glory it has been made. We pray that it will lead many into a better understanding of the Holy Scriptures and a fuller knowledge of Jesus Christ the Incarnate Word, of whom the Scriptures so faithfully testify.

The Committee on Bible Translation
Names of the translators and editors may be secured
from the New York Bible Society International,
5 East 48th Street, New York, New York 10017

THE JERUSALEM BIBLE

NEW TESTAMENT

READERS EDITION

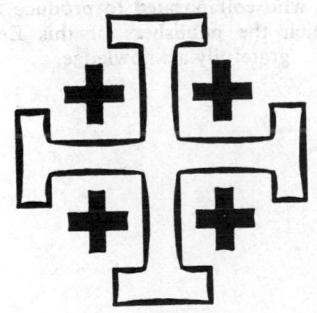

DOUBLEDAY & COMPANY, INC.
Garden City, New York

The abridged introductions and notes of this Bible are based on those which appear in *La Bible de Jérusalem* (one volume edition) published by Les Editions du Cerf, Paris. The English text, though translated from the ancient texts, owes a large debt to the work of the many scholars who collaborated to produce *La Bible de Jérusalem*, which the publishers of this English Bible gratefully acknowledge.

READER'S EDITION

La Bible de Jérusalem, originally published in France, was the culmination of decades of research and biblical scholarship. It was immediately recognized the world over as one of the greatest Bible achievements of our times. The publication of the English translation in 1966 was equally enthusiastically received by scholars and readers of all faiths for its vigorous, contemporary literary style. It is truly the modern Bible for the modern reader seeking a greater understanding and appreciation of the scriptures in the language and imagery of today.

In response to popular demand, this *Reader's Edition* has been designed to provide the general reader with an edition that is suited to his needs. It contains the complete text of THE JERUSALEM BIBLE in a translation that employs all the beauty and majesty of the English language—but always as a living language of the twentieth century. It includes many of the features of the Regular Edition: single-column pages for easy reading, verse numbers in the margin for ready and convenient reference; 8 pages of nine maps—four in color, five in black-and-white; a Chronological Table; and Tables of Measures and Money. The notes and introductions were carefully gone over by Alexander Jones, the General Editor, and abridged to relieve the average reader of burdensome detail while retaining necessary and helpful information for a fuller understanding and appreciation of the scriptures.

In preparing this translation, the translators made full use of the ancient Greek, Aramaic and Hebrew texts. How this was done while still retaining the interpretations and insights of the French edition is explained by Father Jones:

> "The translation of the biblical text itself could clearly not be made from the French. In the case of a few books the initial draft was made from the French and then compared word for word with the Hebrew or Aramaic . . . and amended where necessary to ensure complete conformity with the ancient text. For the much greater part, the initial drafts were made from the Hebrew or Greek and simultaneously compared with the French when questions of variant reading or interpretation arose. Whichever system was used, therefore, the same intended result was achieved, that is, an entirely faithful version of the ancient texts which, in doubtful points, preserves the text established and (for the most part) the interpretation adopted by the French scholars in the light of the most recent researches in the fields of history, archaeology and literary criticism."

THE JERUSALEM BIBLE has been acclaimed by biblical scholars and readers of all denominations for its vigorous and vital translation, faithful in all respects to the original sources—a translation that captures for contemporary man the vitality and immediacy that the Bible had for the first Christians.

EDITOR'S FOREWORD TO THE READER'S EDITION

When the Jerusalem Bible was first published in English in 1966, the Foreword to the complete Standard edition announced its objects: to serve two pressing needs facing the Church, the need to keep abreast of the times and the need to deepen theological thought. This double program was carried out by translating the ancient texts into the language we use today, and by providing notes to the texts which were neither sectarian nor superficial. In that Foreword also, the dependence of the translators on the original pioneer work of the School of Biblical Studies in Jerusalem was acknowledged, and the English version was offered as an entirely faithful rendering of the original texts which, in doubtful points, preserved the text established and (for the most part) the interpretation adopted by the School in the light of the most recent researches in the fields of history, archaeology and literary criticism. With the text, the Standard edition presents the full explanatory notes that would enable any student to confirm for himself the interpretations that were adopted, to appreciate the theological implications drawn from them, and to understand the complex relations between different parts of the Bible.

However the Bible is not only for students undergoing a formal course of study, and there has been an immediate demand for an edition of the Jerusalem Bible which would bring the modern clarity of the text before the ordinary reader, and open to him the results of modern researches without either justifying them at length in literary and historical notes or linking them with doctrinal studies. For this reason, the present Reader's Edition has been prepared. The full Introductions of the Standard edition are here greatly abridged, to serve simply as brief explanations of the character of each book or group of books, their dates and their authorship; and the full Notes of the Standard edition have been greatly reduced in number and length, to restrict them to the minimum which are necessary for understanding the primary, literal meaning of the text; to explain terms, places, people and customs; to specify dates, and to identify the sources of quotations. In short, the brief Introductions and Notes are here only to help the ordinary reader to understand what he is reading and do not assume in him any wide literary, historical or theological knowledge or interests.

Christ's College, Liverpool — Alexander Jones
March 1, 1968 — GENERAL EDITOR

THE

NEW ENGLISH BIBLE

NEW TESTAMENT

A NEW ENGLISH TRANSLATION

OXFORD UNIVERSITY PRESS
CAMBRIDGE UNIVERSITY PRESS

PREFACE

In May 1946 the General Assembly of the Church of Scotland received an overture from the Presbytery of Stirling and Dunblane, where it had been initiated by the Reverend G. S. Hendry, recommending that a translation of the Bible be made in the language of the present day, inasmuch as the language of the Authorized Version, already archaic when it was made, had now become even more definitely archaic and less generally understood. The General Assembly resolved to make an approach to other Churches, and, as a result, delegates of the Church of England, the Church of Scotland, and the Methodist, Baptist, and Congregational Churches met in conference in October. They recommended that the work should be undertaken; that a completely new translation should be made, rather than a revision, such as had earlier been contemplated by the University Presses of Oxford and Cambridge; and that the translators should be free to employ a contemporary idiom rather than reproduce the traditional 'biblical' English.

In January 1947 a second conference, held like the first in the Central Hall, Westminster, included representatives of the University Presses. At the request of this conference, the Churches named above appointed representatives to form the Joint Committee on the New Translation of the Bible. This Committee met for the first time in July of the same year. By January 1948, when its third meeting was held, invitations to be represented had been sent to the Presbyterian Church of England, the Society of Friends, the Churches in Wales, the Churches in Ireland, the British and Foreign Bible Society, and the National Bible Society of Scotland: these invitations were accepted. At a much later stage the hierarchies of the Roman Catholic Church in England and Scotland accepted an invitation to appoint representatives, and these attended as observers.

The Joint Committee provided for the actual work of translation from the original tongues by appointing three panels, to deal, respectively, with the Old Testament, the Apocrypha, and the New Testament. Their members were scholars drawn from various British universities, whom the Committee believed to be representative of competent biblical scholarship at the present time. Apprehending, however, that sound scholarship does not necessarily carry with it a delicate sense of English style, the Committee appointed a fourth panel, of trusted literary advisers, to whom all the work of the translating panels was to be submitted for scrutiny. It should be said that denominational considerations played no part in the appointment of the panels.

The Joint Committee issued general directions to the panels, in pursuance of the aims which the enterprise had in view. The translating panels adopted the following procedure. An individual was invited to submit a draft translation of a particular book, or group of books. Normally he would be a member of the panel concerned. Very occasionally a draft translation was invited from a scholar outside the panel, who was known to have worked specially on the book in question. The draft was circulated in typescript to members of the panel for their consideration. They then met together and discussed the draft round a table, verse by verse, sentence by sentence. Each member brought his view about the meaning of the original to the judgement of his fellows, and discussion went on until they reached a common mind. There are passages where, in the present state of our knowledge, no one could say with certainty which of two (or even more) possible meanings is intended. In such cases, after careful discussion, alternative meanings have been recorded in footnotes, but only where they seemed of sufficient importance. There is probably no member of a panel who has not found himself obliged to give up, perhaps with lingering regret, a cherished view about the meaning of this or that difficult passage, but in the end the panel accepted corporate responsibility for the interpretation set forth in the translation adopted.

The resultant draft was now remitted to the panel of literary advisers. They scrutinized it, once again, verse by verse, sentence by sentence, and took pains to secure, as best they could, the tone and level of language appropriate to the different kinds of writing to be found in the Bible, whether narrative, familiar discourse, argument, law, rhetoric or poetry. The translation thus amended was returned to the translating panel, who examined it to make sure that the meaning intended had not been in any way misunderstood. Passages of peculiar difficulty might on occasion pass repeatedly between the panels. The final form of the version was reached by agreement between the translators concerned and the literary advisers. It was then ready for submission to the Joint Committee.

Since January 1948 the Joint Committee has met regularly twice a year in the Jerusalem Chamber, Westminster Abbey, with four exceptions during 1954-5 when the Langham Room in the precincts of the Abbey was kindly made available. At these meetings the Committee has received reports on the progress of the work from the Conveners of the four panels, and its members have had in their hands typescripts of the books so far translated and revised. They have made such comments and given such advice or decisions as they judged to be necessary, and from time to time they have met members of the panels in conference.

Of the original members of the panels most have happily been able to stay with the work all through, though some have been lost, through death or otherwise, and their places have been filled by fresh appointments.

The Committee has warmly appreciated the courteous hospitality of the Dean of Westminster and of the Trustees of the Central Hall. We owe a great debt to the support and the experienced counsel of the University Presses of Oxford and Cambridge. We recognize gratefully the service rendered to the enterprise by the Reverend Dr G. S. Hendry and the Reverend Professor J. K. S. Reid, who have successively held the office of Secretary to the Committee. To those who have borne special responsibility, as Chairmen of the Joint Committee, we owe more than could readily be told. Dr J. W. Hunkin, Bishop of Truro, our first Chairman, brought to the work an exuberant vigour and initiative without which the formidable project might hardly have got off the ground at all. On his lamented death in 1950 he was succeeded by Dr A. T. P. Williams, then Bishop of Durham and subsequently Bishop of Winchester, who for eighteen years guided our enterprise with judicious wisdom, tact, and benign firmness, but who to our sorrow died when the end of the task was in sight. To both of these we would put on record the gratitude of the Committee and of all engaged in the enterprise.

If we embarked on mentioning the names of those who have served on the various committees and panels, the list would be a long one; and if we mentioned some and not others, the selection would be an invidious one. There are, nevertheless, three names the omission of which would be utterly wrong. As Vice-Chairman and Director, Dr C. H. Dodd has from start to finish given outstanding leadership and guidance to the project, bringing to the work scholarship, sensitivity, and an ever watchful eye. Professor Sir Godfrey Driver, Joint Director since 1965, has also brought to the work a wealth of knowledge and wisdom; to his enthusiasm, tenacity of purpose, and unflagging devotion the whole enterprise is greatly indebted. Professor W. D. McHardy, Deputy Director since 1968, has made an invaluable contribution particularly, but by no means exclusively, in the sphere of the Apocrypha. It is right that the names of these three scholars should always be associated with The New English Bible. Our debt to them is incalculably great.

DONALD EBOR:
Chairman of the Joint Committee

INTRODUCTION

This translation of the New Testament was undertaken with the object of providing English readers, whether familiar with the Bible or not, with a faithful rendering of the best available Greek text into the current speech of our own time, and a rendering which should harvest the gains of recent biblical scholarship.

It is now some three centuries and a half since King James's men put out what we have come to know as the Authorized Version. Two hundred and seventy years later the New Testament was revised. The Revised Version of the New Testament, which appeared in 1881, marked a new departure especially in that it abandoned the so-called Received Text, which had reigned ever since printed editions of the New Testament began, but which the advance of textual criticism had antiquated. The Revisers no longer followed (as their predecessors had done) the text of the majority of manuscripts, which, being for the most part of late date, had been exposed not only to the accidental corruptions of long-continued copying, but also in part to deliberate correction and 'improvement.' Instead, they followed a very small group of manuscripts, the earliest, and in their judgement the best, of those which had survived. During the years which have passed since their time, textual criticism has not stood still. Manuscripts have been discovered of substantially earlier date than any which the Revisers knew. Other important sources of evidence have been either freshly discovered or made more fully available. Meanwhile the methods of textual criticism have themselves been refined and estimates of the value of particular manuscripts have sometimes been reconsidered. The problem of restoring a form of text as near as possible to the vanished autographs now appears less simple than it did to our predecessors. There is not at the present time any critical text which would command the same degree of general acceptance as the Revisers' text did in its day. Nor has the time come, in the judgment of most scholars, to construct such a text, since new material constantly comes to light, and the debate continues. The present translators therefore could do no other than consider variant readings on their merits, and, having weighed the evidence for themselves, select for translation in each passage the reading which to the best of their judgement seemed most likely to represent what the author wrote. Where other readings seemed to deserve serious consideration they have been recorded in footnotes. In assessing the evidence, the translators have taken into account (*a*) ancient manuscripts of the New Testament in Greek, (*b*) manuscripts of early translations into other languages, and (*c*) quotations from the New Testament by early Christian writers. These three sources of evidence are collectively referred to as 'witnesses'. A large number of variants, however, are such as could make no appreciable difference to the meaning so far as it could be represented in translation, and these have been passed over in silence. The translators are well aware that their judgement is at best provisional, but they believe the text they have followed to be an improvement on that underlying the earlier translations. This text can now be read in *The Greek New Testament,* edited by R. V. G. Tasker (Oxford and Cambridge University Presses, 1964).

So much for the text. The next step was the effort to understand the original as accurately as possible, as a preliminary to turning it into English. The Revisers of 1881 believed that a better knowledge of the Greek language made it possible to correct a number of mistranslations in the older version, though in doing so they were somewhat limited by the instruction 'to introduce as few alterations as possible . . . . consistently with faithfulness'. Since their time the study of the Greek language has no more stood still than has textual criticism. In particular, our knowledge of the kind of Greek used by most of the New Testament writers has been greatly enriched since 1881 by the discovery of many thousands of papyrus documents in popular or non-literary Greek of about the same period as the New Testament. It would be wrong to suggest that they lead to any far-reaching change in our understanding of the Greek of the New Testament period, but they have often made possible a better appreciation of the finer shades of idiom, which sometimes clarifies the meaning of passages in the New Testament. Its language is indeed in many respects more flexible and easy-going than the Revisers were ready to allow, and invites the translator to use a larger freedom.

Our task, however, differed in an important respect from that of the Revisers of 1881. They were instructed not only to introduce as few alterations as possible, but also 'to limit, as far as possible, the expression of such alterations to the language of the Authorised and earlier English Versions'. The present translators were subject to no such limitation. In accordance with the original decision of the Joint Committee they were to make the attempt to use consistently the idiom of contemporary English to convey the meaning of the Greek.

The older translators, on the whole, considered that fidelity to the original demanded that they should reproduce, as far as possible, characteristic features of the language in which it was written, such as the syntactical order of words, the structure and division of sentences, and even such irregularities of grammar as were indeed natural enough to authors writing in the easy idiom of popular Hellenistic Greek, but less natural when turned into English. The present translators were enjoined to replace Greek constructions and idioms by those of contemporary English.

This meant a different theory and practice of translation, and one which laid a heavier burden on the translators. Fidelity in translation was not to mean keeping the general framework of the original intact while replacing Greek words by Englsh words more or less equivalent. A word, indeed, in one language is seldom the exact equivalent of a word in a different language. Each word is the centre of a whole cluster of meanings and associations, and in different languages these clusters overlap but do not often coincide. The place of a word in the clause or sentence, or even in a larger unit of thought, will determine what aspect of its total meaning is in the foreground. The translator can hardly hope to convey in another language every shade of meaning that attaches to the word in the original, but if he is free to exploit a wide range of English words covering a similar area of meaning and association he may hope to carry over the meaning of the sentence as a whole. Thus we have not felt obliged (as did the Revisers of 1881) to make an effort to render the same Greek word everywhere by the same English word. We have in this respect returned to the wholesome practice of King James's men, who (as they expressly state in their preface) recognized no such obligation.

We have conceived our task to be that of understanding the original as precisely as we could (using all available aids), and then saying again in our own native idiom what we believed the author to be saying in his. We have found that in practice this frequently compelled us to make decisions where the older method of translation allowed a comfortable ambiguity. In such places we have been aware that we take a risk, but we have thought it our duty to take the risk rather than remain on the fence.

In doing our work, we have constantly striven to follow our instructions and render the Greek, as we understood it, into the English of the present day, that is, into the natural vocabulary, constructions, and rhythms of contemporary speech. We have sought to avoid archaism, jargon, and all that is either stilted or slipshod.

It should be said that our intention has been to offer a translation in the strict sense, and not a paraphrase, and we have not wished to encroach on the field of the commentator. But if the best commentary is a good translation, it is also true that every intelligent translation is in a sense a paraphrase. The line between translation and paraphrase is a fine one. But we have had recourse to deliberate paraphrase with great caution, and only in a few passages where without it we could see no way to attain our aim of making the meaning as clear as it could be made. Taken as a whole, our version claims to be a translation, free, it may be, rather than literal, but a faithful translation nevertheless, so far as we could compass it.

For this edition, the translation of the New Testament has been given a careful revision, in which account has been taken of numerous criticisms and suggestions which have come in from various quarters. It is hoped that the modifications introduced, mostly in minor details and seldom reflecting any substantial change of view about the meaning of a passage, will be found to be in the direction of improvement.

In the course of revision, consideration has been given to passages from the Old Testament quoted in the New. These have now been harmonized with the present version of the Old Testament, where this seemed desirable, and practicable. But the quotations are in Greek, and the Greek is by no means always an exact equivalent of the Hebrew. Where it is not, we have deemed it our duty to render the Greek as it lay before us, and not to attempt to reproduce the underlying Hebrew. On this point there has been consultation between representatives of the Old and the New Testament panels.

The translators are as conscious as anyone can be of the limitations and imperfections of their work. No one who has not tried it can know how impossible an art translation is. Only those who have meditated long upon the Greek original are aware of the richness and subtlety of meaning that may lie even within the most apparently simple sentence, or know the despair that attends all efforts to bring it out through the medium of a different language. Yet we may hope that we have been able to convey to our readers something at least of what the New Testament has said to us during these years of work, and trust that under the providence of Almighty God this translation may open the truth of the Scriptures to many who have been hindered in their approach to it by barriers of language.

C.H.D.

The conventional verse divisions in the New Testament date only from 1551 and have no basis in the manuscripts. Any system of division into numbered verses is foreign to the spirit of this translation, which is intended to convey the meaning in continuous natural English rather than to correspond sentence by sentence with the Greek.

Eight Translation New Testament

King James Version

THE GOSPEL
ACCORDING TO

SAINT MATTHEW

1 The book of the generation of Jesus Christ,
the son of David, the son of Abraham. 2Abra-
ham begat Isaac; and Isaac begat Jacob; and
Jacob begat Judas and his brethren; 3And Judas
begat Phares and Zara of Thamar; and Phares
begat Esrom; and Esrom begat Aram; 4And
Aram begat Aminadab; and Aminadab begat
Naasson; and Naasson begat Salmon; 5And
Salmon begat Booz of Rachab; and Booz begat

Living Bible

MATTHEW

1 These are the ancestors of Jesus Christ, a
descendant of King David and of Abraham:
2 Abraham was the father of Isaac; Isaac was
the father of Jacob; Jacob was the father
of Judah and his brothers.
3 Judah was the father of Perez and Zerah
(Tamar was their mother); Perez was the
father of Hezron; Hezron was the father
of Aram;
4 Aram was the father of Amminadab; Amminadab was the father of Nahshon; Nahshon was the father of Salmon;
5 Salmon was the father of Boaz (Rahab was

Today's English Version

THE
GOSPEL OF

MATTHEW

The family record of Jesus Christ

1 This is the family record of Jesus Christ,
who was a descendant of David, who was a
descendant of Abraham.
2 Abraham was the father of Isaac; Isaac was
the father of Jacob; Jacob was the father of
Judah and his brothers; 3 Judah was the father
of Perez and Zerah (their mother was Tamar);
Perez was the father of Hezron; Hezron was the
father of Ram; 4 Ram was the father of Amminadab; Amminadab was the father of Nahshon; Nahshon was the father of Salmon; 5 Salmon was the father of Boaz (Rahab was his

New International Version

MATTHEW

The genealogy of Jesus

1 A record of the genealogy of Jesus Christ,
son of David, son of Abraham:
2 Abraham was the father of Isaac,
Isaac the father of Jacob,
Jacob the father of Judah and his brothers,
3 Judah the father of Perez and Zerah, whose mother was Tamar,
Perez the father of Hezron,
Hezron the father of Ram,
4 Ram the father of Amminadab,
Amminadab the father of Nahshon,
Nahshon the father of Salmon,
5 Salmon the father of Boaz, whose mother was Rahab,

Phillips Modern English

THE GOSPEL OF MATTHEW

1.1 ***The ancestry of Jesus Christ***

This is the record of the ancestry of Jesus Christ who was the descendant of both David and Abraham:

Abraham was the father of Isaac, who was the father of Jacob, who was the father of Judah and his brothers, who was the father of Perez and Zerah (whose mother was Tamar). Perez was the father of Hezron, who was the father of Ram, who was the father of Amminadab, who was the father of Nahshon, who was the father of Salmon, who was the father of Boaz (whose

Revised Standard Version

THE GOSPEL ACCORDING TO MATTHEW

1 The book of the genealogy of Jesus Christ,
the son of David, the son of Abraham.
2 Abraham was the father of Isaac, and
Isaac the father of Jacob, and Jacob the father
of Judah and his brothers, 3 and Judah the father of Perez and Zerah by Tamar, and Perez
the father of Hezron, and Hezron the father of
Ram,[a] 4 and Ram[a] the father of Amminadab,
and Amminadab the father of Nahshon, and
Nahshon the father of Salmon, 5 and Salmon the
father of Boaz by Rahab, and Boaz the father of

[a] Greek *Aram.*

Jerusalem Bible

THE GOSPEL ACCORDING TO SAINT MATTHEW

I. The birth and infancy of Jesus

The ancestry of Jesus

1 A genealogy of Jesus Christ, son of David, son of Abraham[a]:

2 Abraham was the father of Isaac,
Isaac the father of Jacob,
Jacob the father of Judah and his brothers,
3 Judah was the father of Perez and Zerah,
Tamar being their mother,
Perez was the father of Hezron,
Hezron the father of Ram,
4 Ram was the father of Amminadab,
Amminadab, the father of Nahshon,
Nahshon the father of Salmon,
5 Salmon was the father of Boaz, Rahab being his mother,

[a] Showing the descent of Joseph, legally the father of Jesus, from Abraham and David, to whom the messianic promises were made.

New English Bible

THE GOSPEL ACCORDING TO MATTHEW

The coming of Christ

1 A table of the descent of Jesus Christ, son of David, son of Abraham.
Abraham was the father of Isaac, Isaac of Jacob, Jacob of Judah and his brothers, Judah of Perez and Zarah (their mother was Tamar), Perez of Hezron, Hezron of Ram, Ram of Amminadab, Amminadab of Nahshon, Nahshon of Salma, Salma of Boaz (his mother was Rahab),

King James Version

Obed of Ruth; and Obed begat Jesse; 6 And Jesse
begat David the king; and David the king begat
Solomon of her *that had been the wife* of Urias;
7 And Solomon begat Roboam; and Roboam begat Abia; and Abia begat Asa; 8 And Asa begat
Josaphat; and Josaphat begat Joram; and Joram
begat Ozias; 9 And Ozias begat Joatham; and
Joatham begat Achaz; and Achaz begat Ezekias; 10 And Ezekias begat Manasses; and Manasses begat Amon; and Amon begat Josias;
11 And Josias begat Jechonias and his brethren,
about the time they were carried away to Babylon: 12 And after they were brought to Babylon,
Jechonias begat Salathiel; and Salathiel begat
Zorobabel; 13 And Zorobabel begat Abiud; and
Abiud begat Eliakim; and Eliakim begat Azor;
14 And Azor begat Sadoc; and Sadoc begat
Achim; and Achim begat Eliud; 15 And Eliud
begat Eleazar; and Eleazar begat Matthan; and
Matthan begat Jacob; 16 And Jacob begat Joseph
the husband of Mary, of whom was born Jesus,

Living Bible

his mother); Boaz was the father of Obed (Ruth was his mother); Obed was the father of Jesse;

6 Jesse was the father of King David. David was the father of Solomon (his mother was the widow of Uriah);

7 Solomon was the father of Rehoboam; Rehoboam was the father of Abijah; Abijah was the father of Asa;

8 Asa was the father of Jehoshaphat; Jehoshaphat was the father of Joram; Joram was the father of Uzziah;

9 Uzziah was the father of Jotham; Jotham was the father of Ahaz; Ahaz was the father of Hezekiah;

10 Hezekiah was the father of Manasseh; Manasseh was the father of Amos; Amos was the father of Josiah;

11 Josiah was the father of Jechoniah and his brothers (born at the time of the exile to Babylon).

12 After the exile:
Jechoniah was the father of Shealtiel;
Shealtiel was the father of Zerubbabel;

13 Zerubbabel was the father of Abiud; Abiud was the father of Eliakim; Eliakim was the father of Azor;

14 Azor was the father of Zadok; Zadok was the father of Achim; Achim was the father of Eliud;

15 Eliud was the father of Eleazar; Eleazar was the father of Matthan; Matthan was the father of Jacob;

16 Jacob was the father of Joseph (who was the husband of Mary, the mother of Je-

Today's English Version

mother); Boaz was the father of Obed (Ruth
was his mother); Obed was the father of Jesse;
6 Jesse was the father of King David.
David was the father of Solomon (his mother
had been Uriah's wife); 7 Solomon was the father of Rehoboam; Rehoboam was the father of
Abijah; Abijah was the father of Asa; 8 Asa was
the father of Jehoshaphat; Jehoshaphat was the
father of Joram; Joram was the father of Uzziah;
9 Uzziah was the father of Jotham; Jotham was
the father of Ahaz; Ahaz was the father of
Hezekiah; 10 Hezekiah was the father of Manasseh; Manasseh was the father of Amon; Amon
was the father of Josiah; 11 Josiah was the father of Jechoniah and his brothers, at the time
when the people of Israel were carried away to
Babylon.
12 After the people were carried away to Babylon: Jechoniah was the father of Shealtiel; Shealtiel was the father of Zerubbabel; 13 Zerubbabel was the father of Abiud; Abiud was the
father of Eliakim; Eliakim was the father of
Azor; 14 Azor was the father of Zadok; Zadok
was the father of Achim; Achim was the father
of Eliud; 15 Eliud was the father of Eleazar;
Eleazar was the father of Matthan; Matthan
was the father of Jacob; 16 Jacob was the father
of Joseph, the husband of Mary, who was the

New International Version

Boaz the father of Obed, whose mother was Ruth,
Obed the father of Jesse,
6 and Jesse the father of King David.
David was the father of Solomon, whose mother had been Uriah's wife,
7 Solomon the father of Rehoboam,
Rehoboam the father of Abijah,
Abijah the father of Asa,
8 Asa the father of Jehoshaphat,
Jehoshaphat the father of Joram,
Joram the father of Uzziah,
9 Uzziah the father of Jotham,
Jotham the father of Ahaz,
Ahaz the father of Hezekiah,
10 Hezekiah the father of Manasseh,
Manasseh the father of Amon,
Amon the father of Josiah,
11 and Josiah the father of Jeconiah and his brothers at the time of the exile to Babylon.
12 After the exile to Babylon:
Jeconiah was the father of Shealtiel,
Shealtiel the father of Zerubbabel,
13 Zerubbabel the father of Abiud,
Abiud the father of Eliakim,
Eliakim the father of Azor,
14 Azor the father of Zadok,
Zadok the father of Achim,
Achim the father of Eliud,
15 Eliud the father of Eleazar,
Eleazar the father of Matthan,
Matthan the father of Jacob,
16 and Jacob the father of Joseph, the husband of Mary, of whom was born

Phillips Modern English

mother was Rahab). Boaz was the father of Obed (whose mother was Ruth), and Obed was the father of Jesse, who was the father of King David, who was the father of Solomon (whose mother had been Uriah's wife). Solomon was the father of Rehoboam, who was the father of Abijah, who was the father of Asa, who was the father of Jehoshaphat, who was the father of Joram, who was the father of Uzziah, who was the father of Jotham, who was the father of Ahaz, who was the father of Hezekiah, who was the father of Manasseh, who was the father of Amon, who was the father of Josiah, who was the father of Jechoniah and his brothers, at the time of the deportation to Babylon.

After the Babylonian exile Jechoniah was the father of Shealtiel, who was the father of Zerubbabel, who was the father of Abiud, who was the father of Eliakim, who was the father of Azor, who was the father of Sadoc, who was the father of Achim, who was the father of Eliud, who was the father of Eleazar, who was the father of Matthan, who was the father of Jacob, who was the father of Joseph, who was

Revised Standard Version

Obed by Ruth, and Obed the father of Jesse,
6 and Jesse the father of David the king.
And David was the father of Solomon by the
wife of Uriah, 7 and Solomon the father of
Rehoboam, and Rehoboam the father of Abijah,
and Abijah the father of Asa,[b] 8 and Asa[b] the
father of Jehoshaphat, and Jehoshaphat the father of Joram, and Joram the father of Uzziah,
9 and Uzziah the father of Jotham, and Jotham
the father of Ahaz, and Ahaz the father of Hezekiah, 10 and Hezekiah the father of Manasseh,
and Manasseh the father of Amos,[c] and Amos[c]
the father of Josiah, 11 and Josiah the father of
Jechoniah and his brothers, at the time of the deportation to Babylon.
12 And after the deportation to Babylon:
Jechoniah was the father of Shealtiel,[d] and Shealtiel[d] the father of Zerubbabel, 13 and Zerubbabel the father of Abiud, and Abiud the father
of Eliakim, and Eliakim the father of Azor,
14 and Azor the father of Zadok, and Zadok
the father of Achim, and Achim the father of
Eliud, 15 and Eliud the father of Eleazar, and
Eleazar the father of Matthan, and Matthan the
father of Jacob, 16 and Jacob the father of

[b] Greek *Asaph*. [c] Other authorities read *Amon*.
[d] Greek *Salathiel*.

Jerusalem Bible

Boaz was the father of Obed, Ruth being his mother,
Obed was the father of Jesse;
6 and Jesse was the father of King David.

David was the father of Solomon, whose mother had been Uriah's wife,
7 Solomon was the father of Rehoboam,
Rehoboam the father of Abijah,
Abijah the father of Asa,
8 Asa was the father of Jehoshaphat,
Jehoshaphat the father of Joram,
Joram the father of Azariah,
9 Azariah was the father of Jotham,
Jotham the father of Ahaz,
Ahaz the father of Hezekiah,
10 Hezekiah was the father of Manasseh,
Manasseh the father of Amon,
Amon the father of Josiah;
11 and Josiah was the father of Jechoniah and his brothers.
Then the deportation to Babylon took place.

12 After the deportation to Babylon:
Jechoniah was the father of Shealtiel,
Shealtiel the father of Zerubbabel,
13 Zerubbabel was the father of Abiud,
Abiud the father of Eliakim,
Eliakim the father of Azor,
14 Azor was the father of Zadok,
Zadok the father of Achim,
Achim the father of Eliud,
15 Eliud was the father of Eleazar,
Eleazar the father of Matthan,
Matthan the father of Jacob;
16 and Jacob was the father of Joseph the husband of Mary;

New English Bible

Boaz of Obed (his mother was Ruth), Obed of Jesse; and Jesse was the father of King David.

David was the father of Solomon (his mother had been the wife of Uriah), Solomon of Rehoboam, Rehoboam of Abijah, Abijah of Asa, Asa of Jehoshaphat, Jehoshaphat of Joram, Joram of Azariah, Azariah of Jotham, Jotham of Ahaz, Ahaz of Hezekiah, Hezekiah of Manasseh, Manasseh of Amon, Amon of Josiah; and Josiah was the father of Jeconiah and his brothers at the time of the deportation to Babylon.

After the deportation Jeconiah was the father of Shealtiel, Shealtiel of Zerubbabel, Zerubbabel of Abiud, Abiud of Eliakim, Eliakim of Azor, Azor of Zadok, Zadok of Achim, Achim of Eliud, Eliud of Eleazar, Eleazar of Matthan, Matthan of Jacob, Jacob of Joseph, the husband

King James Version

who is called Christ. 17 So all the generations
from Abraham to David *are* fourteen generations; and from David until the carrying away
into Babylon *are* fourteen generations; and from
the carrying away into Babylon unto Christ *are*
fourteen generations.
18 Now the birth of Jesus Christ was on this
wise: When as his mother Mary was espoused
to Joseph, before they came together, she was
found with child of the Holy Ghost. 19 Then
Joseph her husband, being a just *man,* and not
willing to make her a public example, was
minded to put her away privily. 20 But while
he thought on these things, behold, the angel of
the Lord appeared unto him in a dream, saying,
Joseph, thou son of David, fear not to take unto
thee Mary thy wife: for that which is conceived
in her is of the Holy Ghost. 21 And she shall
bring forth a son, and thou shalt call his name
JESUS: for he shall save his people from their
sins. 22 Now all this was done, that it might be
fulfilled which was spoken of the Lord by the
prophet, saying, 23 Behold, a virgin shall be with
child, and shall bring forth a son, and they shall
call his name Emmanuel, which being inter-

Living Bible

sus Christ the Messiah).
17 These are[a] fourteen of the generations from
Abraham to King David; and fourteen
from King David's time to the exile; and
fourteen from the exile to Christ.
18 These are the facts concerning the birth of
Jesus Christ: His mother, Mary, was engaged to
be married to Joseph. But while she was still a
virgin she became pregnant by the Holy Spirit.
19 Then Joseph, her fiancé,[b] being a man of stern
principle,[c] decided to break the engagement but
to do it quietly, as he didn't want to publicly
disgrace her.
20 As he lay awake[d] considering this, he fell
into a dream, and saw an angel standing beside
him. "Joseph, son of David," the angel said,
"don't hesitate to take Mary as your wife! For
the child within her has been conceived by the
Holy Spirit. 21 And she will have a Son, and you
shall name him Jesus (meaning 'Savior'), for he
will save his people from their sins. 22 This will
fulfill God's message through his prophets—
23 '*Listen! The virgin shall conceive a child!*
She shall give birth to a Son, and he shall
be called "Emmanuel" (meaning "God is
with us").' "

[*a*] Literally, "So all the generations from Abraham unto David are fourteen." [*b*] Literally, "her husband." [*c*] Literally, "a just man." [*d*] Implied in remainder of verse.

Today's English Version

mother of Jesus, called the Messiah.
17 So then, there were fourteen sets of fathers
and sons from Abraham to David, and fourteen
from David to the time when the people were
carried away to Babylon, and fourteen from
then to the birth of the Messiah.

The birth of Jesus Christ

18 This was the way that Jesus Christ was
born. His mother Mary was engaged to Joseph,
but before they were married she found out that
she was going to have a baby by the Holy Spirit.
19 Joseph, to whom she was engaged, was a man
who always did what was right; but he did not
want to disgrace Mary publicly, so he made
plans to break the engagement secretly. 20 While
he was thinking about this, an angel of the Lord
appeared to him in a dream and said, "Joseph,
descendant of David, do not be afraid to take
Mary to be your wife. For it is by the Holy
Spirit that she has conceived. 21 She will give
birth to a son and you will name him Jesus—
because he will save his people from their sins."
22 Now all this happened in order to make
come true what the Lord had said through the
prophet, 23 "The virgin will become pregnant
and give birth to a son, and he will be called
Emmanuel" (which means, "God is with us").

New International Version

Jesus, who is called Christ.
17 Thus there were fourteen generations in all
from Abraham to David, fourteen from David to
the exile to Babylon, and fourteen from the exile
to the Christ.[a]

The birth of Jesus Christ

18 This is how the birth of Jesus Christ came
about. His mother Mary was pledged to be married to Joseph, but before they came together,
she was found to be with child through the
Holy Spirit. 19 Because Joseph her husband was
a righteous man and did not want to expose her
to public disgrace, he had in mind to divorce
her quietly.
20 But after he had considered this, an angel
of the Lord appeared to him in a dream and
said, "Joseph son of David, do not be afraid to
take Mary home as your wife, because what is
conceived in her is from the Holy Spirit. 21 She
will give birth to a son, and you are to give him
the name Jesus, because he will save his people
from their sins."
22 All this took place to fulfill what the Lord
had said through the prophet: 23 "The virgin
will be with child and will give birth to a son,
and they will call him Immanuel"[b]—which
means, "God with us."

[*a*] Or *Messiah*. "The Christ" (Greek) and "the Messiah" (Hebrew) both mean "the Anointed One." [*b*] Isaiah 7:14.

Phillips Modern English

the husband of Mary, who gave birth to Jesus called Christ.

The genealogy of Jesus Christ may thus be traced for fourteen generations from Abraham to David, fourteen from David to the deportation to Babylon, and fourteen more from the deportation to Christ.

1.18 His birth in human history

The birth of Jesus Christ happened like this. When Mary was engaged to Joseph, before their marriage, she was discovered to be pregnant—by the Holy Spirit. Whereupon Joseph, her future husband, who was a good man and did not want to see her disgraced, planned to break off the engagement quietly. But while he was turning the matter over in his mind an angel of the Lord appeared to him in a dream and said, "Joseph, son of David, do not be afraid to take Mary as your wife! What she has conceived is conceived through the Holy Spirit, and she will give birth to a son, whom you will call Jesus ('the Saviour') for it is he who will save his people from their sins."

All this happened to fulfil what the Lord had said through the prophet—

Behold, the virgin shall be with child, and shall bring forth a son, and they shall call his name Immanuel. ("Immanuel" means "God with us.")

Revised Standard Version

Joseph the husband of Mary, of whom Jesus was
born, who is called Christ.
17 So all the generations from Abraham to
David were fourteen generations, and from
David to the deportation to Babylon fourteen
generations, and from the deportation to Babylon to the Christ fourteen generations.

18 Now the birth of Jesus Christ[f] took place
in this way. When his mother Mary had been
betrothed to Joseph, before they came together
she was found to be with child of the Holy
Spirit; 19 and her husband Joseph, being a just
man and unwilling to put her to shame, resolved
to divorce her quietly. 20 But as he considered
this, behold, an angel of the Lord appeared to
him in a dream, saying, "Joseph, son of David,
do not fear to take Mary your wife, for that
which is conceived in her is of the Holy Spirit;
21 she will bear a son, and you shall call his
name Jesus, for he will save his people from
their sins." 22 All this took place to fulfil what
the Lord had spoken by the prophet:
23 "Behold, a virgin shall conceive and bear
a son,
and his name shall be called Emmanuel"

[*f*] Other ancient authorities read *of the Christ.*

Jerusalem Bible

of her was born Jesus who is called Christ.

17 The sum of generations is therefore: fourteen from Abraham to David; fourteen from
David to the Babylonian deportation; and fourteen from the Babylonian deportation to Christ.

The virginal conception of Christ

18 This is how Jesus Christ came to be born.
His mother Mary was betrothed to Joseph[b]; but
before they came to live together she was found
to be with child through the Holy Spirit. 19 Her
husband Joseph, being a man of honor and
wanting to spare her publicity, decided to divorce her informally. 20 He had made up his
mind to do this when the angel of the Lord appeared to him in a dream and said, "Joseph son
of David, do not be afraid to take Mary home
as your wife, because she has conceived what is
in her by the Holy Spirit. 21 She will give birth
to a son and you must name him Jesus, because
he is the one who is to save[c] his people from
their sins." 22 Now all this took place to fulfill
the words spoken by the Lord through the
prophet:
23 *The virgin will conceive and give birth to a
son
and they will call him Immanuel,*[d]

[*b*] In a Jewish betrothal the man was already called the "husband" of the woman, and he could release himself from the engagement only by an act of repudiation, v. 19. [*c*] "Jesus" (Hebrew Yehoshua) means "Yahweh saves." [*d*] Is. 7:14

New English Bible

of Mary, who gave birth to[a] Jesus called Messiah.

There were thus fourteen generations in all from Abraham to David, fourteen from David until the deportation to Babylon, and fourteen from the deportation until the Messiah.

This is the story of the birth of the Messiah. Mary his mother was betrothed to Joseph; before their marriage she found that she was with child by the Holy Spirit. Being a man of principle, and at the same time wanting to save her from exposure, Joseph desired to have the marriage contract set aside quietly. He had resolved on this, when an angel of the Lord appeared to him in a dream. 'Joseph son of David,' said the angel, 'do not be afraid to take Mary home with you as your wife. It is by the Holy Spirit that she has conceived this child. She will bear a son; and you shall give him the name Jesus (Saviour), for he will save his people from their sins.' All this happened in order to fulfil what the Lord declared through the prophet: 'The virgin will conceive and bear a son, and he shall be called Emmanuel', a name which means 'God is with

[*a*] *Some witnesses read* Joseph, to whom was betrothed Mary, a virgin, who gave birth to . . . ; *one witness has* Joseph, and Joseph, to whom Mary, a virgin, was betrothed, was the father of . . .

King James Version

preted is, God with us. 24 Then Joseph being
raised from sleep did as the angel of the Lord
had bidden him, and took unto him his wife:
25 And knew her not till she had brought forth
her firstborn son: and he called his name JESUS.

2 Now when Jesus was born in Bethlehem of
Judea in the days of Herod the king, behold,
there came wise men from the east to Jerusalem,
2 Saying, Where is he that is born King of the
Jews? for we have seen his star in the east, and
are come to worship him. 3 When Herod the
king had heard *these things,* he was troubled, and
all Jerusalem with him. 4 And when he had gathered all the chief priests and scribes of the people together, he demanded of them where Christ
should be born. 5 And they said unto him, In
Bethlehem of Judea: for thus it is written by
the prophet, 6 And thou Bethlehem, *in* the land
of Juda, art not the least among the princes of
Juda: for out of thee shall come a Governor,

Living Bible

24 When Joseph awoke, he did as the angel commanded, and brought Mary home to be his wife,
25 but she remained a virgin until her Son was
born; and Joseph named him "Jesus."

2 Jesus was born in the town of Bethlehem,
in Judea, during the reign of King Herod.
At about that time some astrologers from eastern lands arrived in Jerusalem, asking, 2 "Where
is the newborn King of the Jews? for we have
seen his star in far-off eastern lands, and have
come to worship him."
3 King Herod was deeply disturbed by their
question, and all Jerusalem was filled with rumors.[a] 4 He called a meeting of the Jewish religious leaders.
"Did the prophets tell us where the Messiah
would be born?" he asked.
5 "Yes, in Bethlehem," they said, "for this is
what the prophet Micah[b] wrote:
6 'O little town of Bethlehem, you are not just
an unimportant Judean village, for a Governor shall rise from you to rule my people
Israel.' "

[a] Literally, "and all Jerusalem with him." [b] Implied. Micah 5:2.

Today's English Version

24 So when Joseph woke up he did what the
angel of the Lord had told him to do and married Mary. 25 But he had no sexual relations
with her before she gave birth to her son. And
Joseph named him Jesus.

Visitors from the east

2 Jesus was born in the town of Bethlehem,
in the land of Judea, during the time when
Herod was king. Soon afterwards some men
who studied the stars came from the east to
Jerusalem 2 and asked, "Where is the baby born
to be the king of the Jews? We saw his star
when it came up in the east, and we have come
to worship him."
3 When King Herod heard about this he was
very upset, and so was everyone else in Jerusalem. 4 He called together all the chief priests
and the teachers of the Law and asked them,
"Where will the Messiah be born?"
5 "In the town of Bethlehem, in Judea," they
answered. "This is what the prophet wrote,

6 'Bethlehem, in the land of Judah,
you are by no means the least among the
rulers of Judah;
for from you will come a leader
who will guide my people Israel.' "

New International Version

24 When Joseph woke up, he did what the
angel of the Lord had commanded him and took
Mary home as his wife. 25 But he had no union
with her until she gave birth to a son. And he
gave him the name Jesus.

The visit of the Magi

2 After Jesus was born in Bethlehem in Judea, during the time of King Herod, Magi
from the east came to Jerusalem 2 and asked,
"Where is the one who has been born king of
the Jews? We saw his star in the east[c] and have
come to worship him."
3 When King Herod heard this he was disturbed, and all Jerusalem with him. 4 When he
had called together all the chief priests and
teachers of the law, he asked them where the
Christ[d] was to be born. 5 "In Bethlehem in Judea," they replied, "for this is what the prophet
has written:
6 'And you, Bethlehem, in the land of Judah,
are by no means least among the rulers of
Judah;
for out of you will come a ruler
who will be the shepherd of my people
Israel.'[e] "

[c] Or *star when it rose.* [d] Or *Messiah.* [e] Micah 5:2.

Phillips Modern English

When Joseph woke up he did what the angel had told him. He married Mary, but had no intercourse with her until she had given birth to a son. Then he gave him the name Jesus.

2.1 *Herod, suspicious of the new-born king, takes vindictive precautions*

Jesus was born in Bethlehem, in Judaea, in the days when Herod was king of the province. After his birth there came from the east a party of astrologers making for Jerusalem and enquiring as they went, "Where is the child born to be king of the Jews? For we saw his star in the east and we have come to pay homage to him."

When King Herod heard about this he was deeply perturbed, as indeed were all the other people living in Jerusalem. So he summoned all the Jewish chief priests and scribes together and asked them where "Christ" should be born. Their reply was: "In Bethlehem, in Judaea, for this is what the prophet wrote about the matter—

And thou Bethlehem, land of Judah,
Art in no wise least among the princes of Judah:
For out of thee shall come forth a governor,
Which shall be shepherd of my people Israel."

Revised Standard Version

(which means, God with us). 24 When Joseph
woke from sleep, he did as the angel of the Lord
commanded him; he took his wife, 25 but knew
her not until she had borne a son; and he called
his name Jesus.

2 Now when Jesus was born in Bethlehem of
Judea in the days of Herod the king, behold,
wise men from the East came to Jerusalem, saying, 2 "Where is he who has been born king of
the Jews? For we have seen his star in the East,
and have come to worship him." 3 When Herod
the king heard this, he was troubled, and all
Jerusalem with him; 4 and assembling all the
chief priests and scribes of the people, he inquired of them where the Christ was to be born.
5 They told him, "In Bethlehem of Judea; for so
it is written by the prophet:
6 'And you, O Bethlehem, in the land of Judah,
are by no means least among the rulers of Judah;
for from you shall come a ruler
who will govern my people Israel.' "

Jerusalem Bible

a name which means "God-is-with-us." 24 When
Joseph woke up he did what the angel of the
Lord had told him to do: he took his wife to
his home 25 and, though he had not had intercourse with her, she gave birth to a son; and he
named him Jesus.

The visit of the Magi

2 After Jesus had been born at Bethlehem in
Judaea during the reign of King Herod,[e]
some wise men came to Jerusalem from the east.
2 "Where is the infant king of the Jews?" they
asked. "We saw his star as it rose[f] and have
come to do him homage." 3 When King Herod
heard this he was perturbed, and so was the
whole of Jerusalem. 4 He called together all the
chief priests and the scribes of the people, and
inquired of them where the Christ was to be
born. 5 "At Bethlehem in Judaea," they told
him, "for this is what the prophet wrote:

6 *And you, Bethlehem, in the land of Judah,*
you are by no means least among the leaders of Judah,
for out of you will come a leader
who will shepherd my people Israel." [g]

[*e*] About 5 or 4 B.C. Herod was king of Judaea, Idumaea and Samaria from 37-4 B.C. [*f*] "In the east" is an alternative translation, here and in v. 9. [*g*] Mi. 5:1.

New English Bible

us'. Rising from sleep Joseph did as the angel had directed him; he took Mary home to be his wife, but had no intercourse with her until her son was born. And he named the child Jesus.

2 Jesus was born at Bethlehem in Judaea during the reign of Herod. After his birth astrologers from the east arrived in Jerusalem, asking, 'Where is the child who is born to be king of the Jews? [a] We observed the rising of his star, and we have come to pay him homage.' King Herod was greatly perturbed when he heard this; and so was the whole of Jerusalem. He called a meeting of the chief priests and lawyers of the Jewish people, and put before them the question: 'Where is it that the Messiah is to be born?' 'At Bethlehem in Judaea', they replied; and they referred him to the prophecy which reads: 'Bethlehem in the land of Judah, you are far from least in the eyes of [b] the rulers of Judah; for out of you shall come a leader to be the shepherd of my people Israel.'

[*a*] *Or* Where is the king of the Jews who has just been born? [*b*] *Or* least among.

King James Version

that shall rule my people Israel. 7 Then Herod, when he had privily called the wise men, inquired of them diligently what time the star appeared. 8And he sent them to Bethlehem, and said, Go and search diligently for the young child; and when ye have found *him,* bring me word again, that I may come and worship him also. 9 When they had heard the king, they departed; and, lo, the star, which they saw in the east, went before them, till it came and stood over where the young child was. 10 When they saw the star, they rejoiced with exceeding great joy.

11 And when they were come into the house, they saw the young child with Mary his mother, and fell down, and worshipped him: and when they had opened their treasures, they presented unto him gifts; gold, and frankincense, and myrrh. 12And being warned of God in a dream that they should not return to Herod, they departed into their own country another way. 13And when they were departed, behold, the angel of the Lord appeareth to Joseph in a dream, saying, Arise, and take the young child and his mother, and flee into Egypt, and be thou there until I bring thee word: for Herod will seek the young child to destroy him. 14 When he arose, he took the young child and his mother by night, and departed into Egypt: 15And was there until the death of Herod: that it might be fulfilled which was spoken of the Lord by the

Living Bible

7 Then Herod sent a private message to the astrologers, asking them to come to see him; at this meeting he found out from them the exact time when they first saw the star. Then he told them, 8 "Go to Bethlehem and search for the child. And when you find him, come back and tell me so that I can go and worship him too!"

9 After this interview the astrologers started out again. And look! The star appeared to them again, standing over Bethlehem.[c] 10 Their joy knew no bounds!

11 Entering the house where the baby and Mary his mother were, they threw themselves down before him, worshiping. Then they opened their presents and gave him gold, frankincense and myrrh. 12 But when they returned to their own land, they didn't go through Jerusalem to report to Herod, for God had warned them in a dream to go home another way.

13 After they were gone, an angel of the Lord appeared to Joseph in a dream. "Get up and flee to Egypt with the baby and his mother," the angel said, "and stay there until I tell you to return, for King Herod is going to try to kill the child." 14 That same[d] night he left for Egypt with Mary and the baby, 15 and stayed there until King Herod's death. This fulfilled the prophet's prediction,

[c] Literally, "went before them until it came and stood over where the baby was." [d] Implied.

Today's English Version

7 So Herod called the visitors from the east to a secret meeting and found out from them the exact time the star had appeared. 8 Then he sent them to Bethlehem with these instructions: "Go and make a careful search for the child, and when you find him let me know, so that I may go and worship him too."

9 With this they left, and on their way they saw the star—the same one they had seen in the east—and it went ahead of them until it came and stopped over the place where the child was. 10 How happy they were, what joy was theirs, when they saw the star! 11 They went into the house and saw the child with his mother Mary. They knelt down and worshiped him; then they opened their bags and offered him presents: gold, frankincense, and myrrh.

12 God warned them in a dream not to go back to Herod; so they went back to their country by another road.

The escape to Egypt

13 After they had left, an angel of the Lord appeared in a dream to Joseph and said, "Get up, take the child and his mother and run away to Egypt, and stay there until I tell you to leave. Herod will be looking for the child to kill him."

14 Joseph got up, took the child and his mother, and left during the night for Egypt, 15 where he stayed until Herod died.

This was done to make come true what the

New International Version

7 Then Herod called the Magi secretly and found out from them the exact time the star had appeared. 8 He sent them to Bethlehem and said, "Go and make a careful search for the child. As soon as you find him, report to me, so that I too may go and worship him."

9 After they had heard the king, they went on their way, and the star they had seen in the east[f] went ahead of them until it stopped over the place where the child was. 10 When they saw the star, they were overjoyed. 11 On coming to the house, they saw the child with his mother Mary, and they bowed down and worshiped him. Then they opened their treasures and presented him with gifts of gold and of incense and of myrrh. 12And having been warned in a dream not to go back to Herod, they returned to their country by another route.

The escape to Egypt

13 When they had gone, an angel of the Lord appeared to Joseph in a dream. "Get up," he said, "take the child and his mother and escape to Egypt. Stay there until I tell you, for Herod is going to search for the child to kill him."

14 So he got up, took the child and his mother during the night and left for Egypt, 15 where he stayed until the death of Herod. And so was fulfilled what the Lord had said through the

[f] Or *seen when it rose.*

Phillips Modern English

Then Herod invited the wise men to meet him privately and found out from them the exact time when the star appeared. Then he sent them off to Bethlehem saying, "When you get there, search for this little child with the utmost care. And when you have found him report back to me—so that I may go and worship him too."

The wise men listened to the king and then went on their way, to Bethlehem. And now the star, which they had seen in the east, went in front of them until at last it shone immediately above the place where the little child lay. The sight of the star filled them with indescribable joy.

So they went into the house and saw the little child with his mother Mary. And they fell on their knees and worshipped him. Then they opened their treasures and presented him with gifts—gold, incense and myrrh.

Then, since they were warned in a dream not to return to Herod, they went back to their own country by a different route.

But after they had gone the angel of the Lord appeared to Joseph in a dream and said, "Get up now, take the little child and his mother and escape to Egypt. Stay there until I tell you. For Herod means to seek out the child and kill him."

So Joseph got up, and taking the child and his mother with him set off for Egypt that same night, where he remained until Herod's death.

This again is a fulfilment of the Lord's word spoken through the prophet—

Revised Standard Version

7 Then Herod summoned the wise men secretly and ascertained from them what time the
star appeared; 8 and he sent them to Bethlehem,
saying, "Go and search diligently for the child,
and when you have found him bring me word,
that I too may come and worship him." 9 When
they had heard the king they went their way;
and lo, the star which they had seen in the East
went before them, till it came to rest over the
place where the child was. 10 When they saw
the star, they rejoiced exceedingly with great
joy; 11 and going into the house they saw the
child with Mary his mother, and they fell down
and worshiped him. Then, opening their treasures, they offered him gifts, gold and frankincense and myrrh. 12 And being warned in a
dream not to return to Herod, they departed to
their own country by another way.
13 Now when they had departed, behold, an
angel of the Lord appeared to Joseph in a dream
and said, "Rise, take the child and his mother,
and flee to Egypt, and remain there till I tell you;
for Herod is about to search for the child, to
destroy him." 14 And he rose and took the child
and his mother by night, and departed to Egypt,
15 and remained there until the death of Herod.
This was to fulfil what the Lord had spoken by

Jerusalem Bible

7 Then Herod summoned the wise men to see
him privately. He asked them the exact date on
which the star had appeared, 8 and sent them on
to Bethlehem. "Go and find out all about the
child," he said, "and when you have found him,
let me know, so that I too may go and do him
homage." 9 Having listened to what the king
had to say, they set out. And there in front of
them was the star they had seen rising; it went
forward and halted over the place where the
child was. 10 The sight of the star filled them
with delight, 11 and going into the house they
saw the child with his mother Mary, and falling
to their knees they did him homage. Then, opening their treasures, they offered him gifts of
gold and frankincense and myrrh.[h] 12 But they
were warned in a dream not to go back to
Herod, and returned to their own country by
a different way.

The flight into Egypt. The massacre of the Innocents

13 After they had left, the angel of the Lord
appeared to Joseph in a dream and said, "Get
up, take the child and his mother with you, and
escape into Egypt, and stay there until I tell
you, because Herod intends to search for the
child and do away with him." 14 So Joseph got
up and, taking the child and his mother with
him, left that night for Egypt, 15 where he
stayed until Herod was dead. This was to fulfill
what the Lord had spoken through the prophet:

[*h*] The wealth and perfumes of Arabia.

New English Bible

Herod next called the astrologers to meet him in private, and ascertained from them the time when the star had appeared. He then sent them on to Bethlehem, and said, 'Go and make a careful inquiry for the child. When you have found him, report to me, so that I may go myself and pay him homage.'

They set out at the king's bidding; and the star which they had seen at its rising went ahead of them until it stopped above the place where the child lay. At the sight of the star they were overjoyed. Entering the house, they saw the child with Mary his mother, and bowed to the ground in homage to him; then they opened their treasures and offered him gifts: gold, frankincense, and myrrh. And being warned in a dream not to go back to Herod, they returned home another way.

After they had gone, an angel of the Lord appeared to Joseph in a dream, and said to him, 'Rise up, take the child and his mother and escape with them to Egypt, and stay there until I tell you; for Herod is going to search for the child to do away with him.' So Joseph rose from sleep, and taking mother and child by night he went away with them to Egypt, and there he stayed till Herod's death. This was to fulfil what the Lord had declared through the prophet: 'I

King James Version

prophet, saying, Out of Egypt have I called my
son.
16 Then Herod, when he saw that he was
mocked of the wise men, was exceeding wroth,
and sent forth, and slew all the children that
were in Bethlehem, and in all the coasts thereof,
from two years old and under, according to the
time which he had diligently inquired of the wise
men. 17 Then was fulfilled that which was spoken
by Jeremy the prophet, saying, 18 In Rama was
there a voice heard, lamentation, and weeping,
and great mourning, Rachel weeping *for* her children, and would not be comforted, because they
are not.
19 But when Herod was dead, behold, an angel
of the Lord appeareth in a dream to Joseph in
Egypt, 20 Saying, Arise, and take the young child
and his mother, and go into the land of Israel:
for they are dead which sought the young child's
life. 21 And he arose, and took the young child
and his mother, and came into the land of Israel.
22 But when he heard that Archelaus did reign
in Judea in the room of his father Herod, he
was afraid to go thither: notwithstanding, being

Living Bible

"I have called my Son from Egypt." [e]
16 Herod was furious when he learned that the
astrologers had disobeyed him. Sending soldiers
to Bethlehem, he ordered them to kill every baby
boy two years old and under, both in the town
and on the nearby farms, for the astrologers had
told him the star first appeared to them two
years before. 17 This brutal action of Herod's
fulfilled the prophecy of Jeremiah,[f]
18 "Screams of anguish come from Ramah,[g]
Weeping unrestrained;
Rachel weeping for her children,
Uncomforted—
For they are dead."
19 When Herod died, an angel of the Lord appeared in a dream to Joseph in Egypt, and told
him, 20 "Get up and take the baby and his
mother back to Israel, for those who were trying
to kill the child are dead."
21 So he returned immediately to Israel with
Jesus and his mother. 22 But on the way he was
frightened to learn that the new king was Herod's
son, Archelaus. Then, in another dream, he was

[*e*] Hosea 11:1. [*f*] Jeremiah 31:15. [*g*] Or, "the region of Ramah."

Today's English Version

Lord had said through the prophet, "I called
my Son out of Egypt."

The killing of the children

16 When Herod realized that the visitors from
the east had tricked him, he was furious. He
gave orders to kill all the boys in Bethlehem and
its neighborhood who were two years old and
younger—in accordance with what he had
learned from the visitors about the time when
the star had appeared.
17 In this way what the prophet Jeremiah had
said came true:

18 "A sound is heard in Ramah,
the sound of bitter crying and weeping.
Rachel weeps for her children;
she weeps and will not be comforted,
because they are all dead."

The return from Egypt

19 After Herod had died, an angel of the
Lord appeared in a dream to Joseph, in Egypt,
20 and said, "Get up, take the child and his
mother, and go back to the land of Israel, because those who tried to kill the child are dead."
21 So Joseph got up, took the child and his
mother, and went back to Israel.
22 When he heard that Archelaus had succeeded his father Herod as king of Judea, Joseph
was afraid to settle there. He was given more

New International Version

prophet: "I called my son out of Egypt." [g]
16 When Herod realized that he had been outwitted by the Magi, he was furious, and he gave
orders to kill all the boys in Bethlehem and its
vicinity who were two years old and under, in
accordance with the time he had learned from
the Magi. 17 Then what was said through the
prophet Jeremiah was fulfilled:
18 "A voice was heard in Ramah,
weeping and great mourning,
Rachel weeping for her children
and refusing to be comforted,
because they were no more." [h]

The return to Nazareth

19 After Herod died, an angel of the Lord
appeared in a dream to Joseph in Egypt 20 and
said, "Get up, take the child and his mother and
go to the land of Israel, for those who were
trying to take the child's life are dead."
21 So he got up, took the child and his
mother and went to the land of Israel. 22 But
when he heard that Archelaus was reigning in
Judea in place of his father Herod, he was
afraid to go there. Having been warned in a

[*g*] Hosea 11:1. [*h*] Jer. 31:15.

Phillips Modern English

Out of Egypt did I call my son.

When Herod saw that he had been fooled by the wise men he was furiously angry. He issued orders for the execution of all male children of two years and under in Bethlehem and the surrounding district—basing his calculation on his careful questioning of the wise men.

Then Jeremiah's prophecy was fulfilled:

A voice was heard in Ramah,
Weeping and great mourning,
Rachel weeping for her children;
And she would not be comforted, because they are not.

2.19 Jesus is brought to Nazareth

But after Herod's death an angel of the Lord appeared in a dream to Joseph in Egypt and said, "Now get up and take the infant and his mother with you and go into the land of Israel. For those who sought the child's life are dead."

So Joseph got up and took the little child and his mother with him and journeyed towards the land of Israel. But when he heard that Archelaus was now reigning as king of Judaea in the place of his father Herod, he was afraid to enter the country. Then he received warning in a dream

Revised Standard Version

the prophet, "Out of Egypt have I called my son."
16 Then Herod, when he saw that he had been tricked by the wise men, was in a furious rage, and he sent and killed all the male children in Bethlehem and in all that region who were two years old or under, according to the time which he had ascertained from the wise men.
17 Then was fulfilled what was spoken by the prophet Jeremiah:
18 "A voice was heard in Ramah,
wailing and loud lamentation,
Rachel weeping for her children;
she refused to be consoled,
because they were no more."
19 But when Herod died, behold, an angel of the Lord appeared in a dream to Joseph in Egypt, saying, 20 "Rise, take the child and his mother, and go to the land of Israel, for those who sought the child's life are dead." 21 And he rose and took the child and his mother, and went to the land of Israel. 22 But when he heard that Archelaus reigned over Judea in place of his father Herod, he was afraid to go there, and be-

Jerusalem Bible

I called my son out of Egypt.[i]

16 Herod was furious when he realized that he had been outwitted by the wise men, and in Bethlehem and its surrounding district he had all the male children killed who were two years old or under, reckoning by the date he had been careful to ask the wise men. 17 It was then that the words spoken through the prophet Jeremiah were fulfilled:

18 *A voice was heard in Ramah,*
sobbing and loudly lamenting:
it was Rachel weeping for her children,
refusing to be comforted
because they were no more.[j]

From Egypt to Nazareth

19 After Herod's death, the angel of the Lord appeared in a dream to Joseph in Egypt 20 and said, "Get up, take the child and his mother with you and go back to the land of Israel, for those who wanted to kill the child are dead."
21 So Joseph got up and, taking the child and his mother with him, went back to the land of Israel. 22 But when he learned that Archelaus[k] had succeeded his father Herod as ruler of Judaea he was afraid to go there, and being

[i] Ho. 11:1. [j] Jr. 31:15. [k] Ethnarch of Judaea, 4 B.C. to A.D. 6.

New English Bible

called my son out of Egypt.'

When Herod saw how the astrologers had tricked him he fell into a passion, and gave orders for the massacre of all children in Bethlehem and its neighbourhood, of the age of two years or less, corresponding with the time he had ascertained from the astrologers. So the words spoken through Jeremiah the prophet were fulfilled: 'A voice was heard in Rama, wailing and loud laments; it was Rachel weeping for her children, and refusing all consolation, because they were no more.'

The time came that Herod died; and an angel of the Lord appeared in a dream to Joseph in Egypt and said to him, 'Rise up, take the child and his mother, and go with them to the land of Israel, for the men who threatened the child's life are dead.' So he rose, took mother and child with him, and came to the land of Israel. Hearing, however, that Archelaus had succeeded his father Herod as king of Judaea, he was afraid to go there. And being warned by a dream, he

King James Version

warned of God in a dream, he turned aside into the parts of Galilee: 23And he came and dwelt in a city called Nazareth: that it might be fulfilled which was spoken by the prophets, He shall be called a Nazarene.

3 In those days came John the Baptist, preaching in the wilderness of Judea, 2And saying, Repent ye: for the kingdom of heaven is at hand. 3 For this is he that was spoken of by the prophet Esaias, saying, The voice of one crying in the wilderness, Prepare ye the way of the Lord, make his paths straight. 4And the same John had his raiment of camel's hair, and a leathern girdle about his loins; and his meat was locusts and wild honey. 5 Then went out to him Jerusalem, and all Judea, and all the region

Living Bible

warned not to go to Judea, so they went to Galilee instead, 23 and lived in Nazareth. This fulfilled the prediction of the prophets concerning the Messiah,

"He shall be called a Nazarene."

3 While they were living in Nazareth,[a] John the Baptist began preaching out in the Judean wilderness. His constant theme was, 2 "Turn from your sins . . . turn to God . . . for the Kingdom of Heaven is coming soon." [b] 3 Isaiah the prophet had told about John's ministry centuries before! He had written,

"I hear[c] a shout from the wilderness, 'Prepare a road for the Lord—straighten out the path where he will walk.' "

4 John's clothing was woven from camel's hair and he wore a leather belt; his food was locusts and wild honey. 5 People from Jerusalem and from all over the Jordan Valley, and, in fact, from every section of Judea went out to the

[a] Literally, "in those days." [b] Or, "has arrived." Literally, "is at hand." [c] Implied. Isaiah 40:3.

Today's English Version

instructions in a dream, and so he went to the province of Galilee 23 and made his home in a town named Nazareth. He did this to make come true what the prophets had said, "He will be called a Nazarene."

The preaching of John the Baptist

3 At that time John the Baptist came and started preaching in the desert of Judea. 2 "Turn away from your sins," he said, "because the Kingdom of heaven is near!" 3 John was the one that the prophet Isaiah was talking about when he said,

"Someone is shouting in the desert,
'Get the Lord's road ready for him;
make a straight path for him to travel!' "

4 John's clothes were made of camel's hair; he wore a leather belt around his waist, and ate locusts and wild honey. 5 People came to him from Jerusalem, from the whole province of Judea, and from all the country around the

New International Version

dream, he withdrew to the district of Galilee, 23 and he went and lived in a town called Nazareth. So was fulfilled what was said through the prophets: "He will be called a Nazarene."

John the Baptist prepares the way

3 In those days John the Baptist came, preaching in the desert of Judea 2 and saying, "Repent, for the kingdom of heaven is near." 3 This is he who was spoken of through the prophet Isaiah:

"A voice of one calling in the desert,
'Prepare the way for the Lord,
make straight paths for him.' "[i]

4 John's clothes were made of camel's hair, and he had a leather belt around his waist. His food was locusts and wild honey. 5 People went out to him from Jerusalem and all Judea and

[i] Isaiah 40:3.

Phillips Modern English

to turn aside into the district of Galilee and came to live in a small town called Nazareth—thus fulfilling the old prophecy, that he should be called a Nazarene.

3.1 The prophesied "Elijah": John the Baptist

In due course John the Baptist arrived, preaching in the Judaean desert: "You must change your hearts and minds—for the kingdom of Heaven has arrived!"

This was the man whom the prophet Isaiah spoke about in the words:

The voice of one crying in the wilderness,
Make ye ready the way of the Lord,
Make his paths straight.

John wore clothes of camel-hair with a leather belt round his waist, and lived on locusts and wild honey. The people of Jerusalem and of all Judaea and the Jordan district flocked to him,

Revised Standard Version

ing warned in a dream he withdrew to the district of Galilee. 23And he went and dwelt in a city called Nazareth, that what was spoken by the prophets might be fulfilled, "He shall be called a Nazarene."

3 In those days came John the Baptist, preaching in the wilderness of Judea, 2 "Repent, for the kingdom of heaven is at hand." 3 For this is he who was spoken of by the prophet Isaiah when he said,

"The voice of one crying in the wilderness:
Prepare the way of the Lord,
make his paths straight."

4 Now John wore a garment of camel's hair, and a leather girdle around his waist; and his food was locusts and wild honey. 5 Then went out to him Jerusalem and all Judea and all the region

Jerusalem Bible

warned in a dream he left for the region of Galilee. [l] 23 There he settled in a town called Nazareth. In this way the words spoken through the prophets were to be fulfilled:

He will be called a Nazarene.

II. The kingdom of heaven proclaimed

A. Narrative section

The preaching of John the Baptist

3 In due course John the Baptist appeared; he preached in the wilderness of Judaea and this was his message: 2 "Repent for the kingdom of heaven[m] is close at hand." 3 This was the man the prophet Isaiah spoke of when he said:

A voice cries in the wilderness:
prepare a way for the Lord,
make his paths straight.[n]

4 This man John wore a garment made of camel hair with a leather belt around his waist, and his food was locusts and wild honey. 5 Then Jerusalem and all Judaea and the whole Jordan

[*l*] The territory of Herod Antipas. [*m*] "kingdom of God"; Matthew's phrase reflects the Jewish scruple against using the name of God. [*n*] Is. 40:3.

New English Bible

withdrew to the region of Galilee; there he settled in a town called Nazareth. This was to fulfil the words spoken through the prophets: 'He shall be called a Nazarene.'

3 About that time John the Baptist appeared as a preacher in the Judaean wilderness; his theme was: 'Repent; for the kingdom of Heaven is upon you!' It is of him that the prophet Isaiah spoke when he said, 'A voice crying aloud in the wilderness, "Prepare a way for the Lord; clear a straight path for him." '

John's clothing was a rough coat of camel's hair, with a leather belt round his waist, and his food was locusts and wild honey. They flocked to him from Jerusalem, from all Judaea, and the

King James Version

round about Jordan, 6And were baptized of him in Jordan, confessing their sins.

7 But when he saw many of the Pharisees and Sadducees come to his baptism, he said unto them, O generation of vipers, who hath warned you to flee from the wrath to come? 8 Bring forth therefore fruits meet for repentance: 9And think not to say within yourselves, We have Abraham to *our* father: for I say unto you, that God is able of these stones to raise up children unto Abraham. 10And now also the axe is laid unto the root of the trees: therefore every tree which bringeth not forth good fruit is hewn down, and cast into the fire. 11 I indeed baptize you with water unto repentance: but he that cometh after me is mightier than I, whose shoes I am not worthy to bear: he shall baptize you with the Holy Ghost, and *with* fire: 12 Whose fan *is* in his hand, and he will thoroughly purge his floor, and gather his wheat into the garner; but he will burn up the chaff with unquenchable fire.

13 Then cometh Jesus from Galilee to Jordan unto John, to be baptized of him. 14 But John forbade him, saying, I have need to be baptized of thee, and comest thou to me? 15And Jesus answering said unto him, Suffer *it to be so* now:

Living Bible

wilderness to hear him preach, 6 and when they confessed their sins, he baptized them in the Jordan River.

7 But when he saw many Pharisees[d] and Sadducees[e] coming to be baptized, he denounced them.

"You sons of snakes!" he warned. "Who said that you could escape the coming wrath of God? 8 Before being baptized, prove that you have turned from sin by doing worthy deeds. 9 Don't try to get by as you are, thinking, 'We are safe for we are Jews—descendants of Abraham.' That proves nothing. God can change these stones here into Jews! [f]

10 "And even now the axe of God's judgment is poised to chop down every unproductive tree. They will be chopped and burned.

11 "With[g] water I baptize those who repent of their sins; but someone else is coming, far greater than I am, so great that I am not worthy to carry his shoes! He shall baptize you with[h] the Holy Spirit and with fire. 12 He will separate the chaff from the grain, burning the chaff with never-ending fire, and storing away the grain."

13 Then Jesus went from Galilee to the Jordan River to be baptized there by John. 14 John didn't want to do it.

"This isn't proper," he said. "I am the one who needs to be baptized by you."

15 But Jesus said, "Please do it, for I must

[*d*] Jewish religious leaders who strictly followed the letter of the law but often violated its intent. [*e*] Jewish political leaders. [*f*] Literally, "God is able of these stones to raise up children unto Abraham." [*g*] Or, "in water." [*h*] Or, "in the Holy Spirit and in fire."

Today's English Version

Jordan River. 6 They confessed their sins and he baptized them in the Jordan.

7 When John saw many Pharisees and Sadducees coming to him to be baptized, he said to them, "You snakes—who told you that you could escape from God's wrath that is about to come? 8 Do the things that will show that you have turned from your sins. 9And don't think you can excuse yourselves by saying, 'Abraham is our ancestor.' I tell you that God can take these rocks and make descendants for Abraham! 10 The ax is ready to cut down the trees at the roots; every tree that does not bear good fruit will be cut down and thrown in the fire. 11 I baptize you with water to show that you have repented; but the one who will come after me will baptize you with the Holy Spirit and fire. He is much greater than I am; I am not good enough even to carry his sandals. 12 He has his winnowing shovel with him, to thresh out all the grain; he will gather his wheat into his barn, but burn the chaff in a fire that never goes out."

The baptism of Jesus

13 At that time Jesus went from Galilee to the Jordan, and came to John to be baptized by him. 14 But John tried to make him change his mind. "I ought to be baptized by you," John said, "yet you come to me!"

15 But Jesus answered him, "Let it be so for now. For in this way we shall do all that God

New International Version

the whole region of the Jordan. 6 Confessing their sins, they were baptized by him in the Jordan River.

7 But when he saw many of the Pharisees and Sadducees coming to where he was baptizing, he said to them: "You brood of vipers! Who warned you to flee from the coming wrath? 8 Produce fruit in keeping with repentance. 9And do not think you can say to yourselves, 'We have Abraham as our father.' I tell you that out of these stones God can raise up children for Abraham. 10 The ax is already at the root of the trees, and every tree that does not produce good fruit will be cut down and thrown into the fire.

11 "I baptize you with[j] water for repentance. But after me will come one who is more powerful than I, whose sandals I am not fit to carry. He will baptize you with the Holy Spirit and with fire. 12 His winnowing fork is in his hand, and he will clear his threshing floor, gathering the wheat into his barn and burning up the chaff with unquenchable fire."

The baptism of Jesus

13 Then Jesus came from Galilee to the Jordan to be baptized by John. 14 But John tried to deter him, saying, "I need to be baptized by you, and do you come to me?"

15 Jesus replied, "Let it be so now; it is proper for us to do this to fulfill all righteous-

[*j*] Or *in*.

Phillips Modern English

and were baptised by him in the river Jordan, publicly confessing their sins.

But when he saw many Pharisees and Sadducees coming for baptism he said: "Who warned you, you serpent's brood, to escape from the wrath to come? Go and do something to show that your hearts are really changed. Don't suppose that you can say to yourselves, 'We are Abraham's children', for I tell you that God could produce children of Abraham out of these stones!

"The axe already lies at the root of the tree, and the tree that fails to produce good fruit will be cut down and thrown into the fire. It is true that I baptise you with water as a sign of your repentance, but the one who follows me is far stronger than I am—indeed, I am not fit to carry his shoes. He will baptise you with the fire of the Holy Spirit. He comes all ready to separate the wheat from the chaff and very thoroughly will he clear his threshing-floor—the wheat he will collect into the granary and the chaff he will burn with a fire that can never be put out."

3.13 John baptises Jesus

Then Jesus came from Galilee to the Jordan to be baptised by John. But John tried to prevent him. "I need you to baptise *me*", he said. "Surely *you* do not come to me?" But Jesus replied, "It is right for us to meet all the Law's

Revised Standard Version

about the Jordan, 6 and they were baptized by
him in the river Jordan, confessing their sins.
7 But when he saw many of the Pharisees and
Sadducees coming for baptism, he said to them,
"You brood of vipers! Who warned you to flee
from the wrath to come? 8 Bear fruit that befits
repentance, 9 and do not presume to say to yourselves, 'We have Abraham as our father'; for I
tell you, God is able from these stones to raise
up children to Abraham. 10 Even now the axe
is laid to the root of the trees; every tree therefore that does not bear good fruit is cut down
and thrown into the fire.
11 "I baptize you with water for repentance,
but he who is coming after me is mightier than
I, whose sandals I am not worthy to carry; he
will baptize you with the Holy Spirit and with
fire. 12 His winnowing fork is in his hand, and
he will clear his threshing floor and gather his
wheat into the granary, but the chaff he will
burn with unquenchable fire."
13 Then Jesus came from Galilee to the Jordan to John, to be baptized by him. 14 John
would have prevented him, saying, "I need to be
baptized by you, and do you come to me?"
15 But Jesus answered him, "Let it be so now;

Jerusalem Bible

district made their way to him, 6 and as they
were baptized by him in the river Jordan they
confessed their sins. 7 But when he saw a number
of Pharisees and Sadducees[o] coming for baptism he said to them, 8 "Brood of vipers, who
warned you to fly from the retribution that is
coming? But if you are repentant, produce the
appropriate fruit, 9 and do not presume to tell
yourselves, 'We have Abraham for our father,'
because, I tell you, God can raise children
for Abraham from these stones. 10 Even now
the ax is laid to the roots of the trees, so that
any tree which fails to produce good fruit will
be cut down and thrown on the fire. 11 I baptize
you in water for repentance, but the one who
follows me is more powerful than I am, and I
am not fit to carry his sandals; he will baptize
you with the Holy Spirit and fire. 12 His winnowing fan is in his hand; he will clear his threshing
floor and gather his wheat into the barn; but the
chaff he will burn in a fire that will never go
out."

Jesus is baptized

13 Then Jesus appeared: he came from
Galilee to the Jordan to be baptized by John.
14 John tried to dissuade him. "It is I who
need baptism from you," he said, "and yet you
come to me!" 15 But Jesus replied, "Leave it
like this for the time being; it is fitting that we

[o] Pharisees: members of a Jewish sect known for its strict observance of the Law as it was interpreted and developed by their rabbis. Sadducees: conservatives who observed the written form of the Law in the Scriptures.

New English Bible

whole Jordan valley, and were baptized by him in the River Jordan, confessing their sins.

When he saw many of the Pharisees and Sadducees coming for baptism he said to them: 'You vipers' brood! Who warned you to escape from the coming retribution? Then prove your repentance by the fruit it bears; and do not presume to say to yourselves, "We have Abraham for our father." I tell you that God can make children for Abraham out of these stones here. Already the axe is laid to the roots of the trees; and every tree that fails to produce good fruit is cut down and thrown on the fire. I baptize you with water, for repentance; but the one who comes after me is mightier than I. I am not fit to take off his shoes. He will baptize you with the Holy Spirit and with fire. His shovel is ready in his hand and he will winnow his threshing-floor; the wheat he will gather into his granary, but he will burn the chaff on a fire that can never go out.'

Then Jesus arrived at the Jordan from Galilee, and came to John to be baptized by him. John tried to dissuade him. 'Do you come to me?' he said; 'I need rather to be baptized by you.' Jesus replied, 'Let it be so for the present; we do well

King James Version

for thus it becometh us to fulfil all righteousness. Then he suffered him. 16And Jesus, when he was baptized, went up straightway out of the water: and, lo, the heavens were opened unto him, and he saw the Spirit of God descending like a dove, and lighting upon him: 17And lo a voice from heaven, saying, This is my beloved Son, in whom I am well pleased.

4 Then was Jesus led up of the Spirit into the wilderness to be tempted of the devil. 2And when he had fasted forty days and forty nights, he was afterward a hungered. 3And when the tempter came to him, he said, If thou be the Son of God, command that these stones be made bread. 4 But he answered and said, It is written, Man shall not live by bread alone, but by every word that proceedeth out of the mouth of God. 5 Then the devil taketh him up into the holy city, and setteth him on a pinnacle of the temple, 6And saith unto him, If thou be the Son of God, cast thyself down: for it is written, He shall give his angels charge concerning thee: and in *their* hands they shall bear thee up, lest at any time thou dash thy foot against a stone. 7 Jesus said unto him, It is written again, Thou shalt not

Living Bible

do all that is right." [i] So then John baptized him.

16 After his baptism, as soon as Jesus came up out of the water, the heavens were opened to him and he saw the Spirit of God coming down in the form of a dove. 17And a voice from heaven said, "This is my beloved Son, and I am wonderfully pleased with him."

4 Then Jesus was led out into the wilderness by the Holy Spirit, to be tempted there by Satan. 2 For forty days and forty nights he ate nothing and became very hungry. 3 Then Satan tempted him to get food by changing stones into loaves of bread.

"It will prove you are the Son of God," he said.

4 But Jesus told him, "No! For the Scriptures tell us that bread won't feed men's souls: obedience to every word of God is what we need."

5 Then Satan took him to Jerusalem to the roof of the Temple. 6 "Jump off," he said, "and prove you are the Son of God; for the Scriptures declare, 'God will send his angels to keep you from harm,'. . . they will prevent you from smashing on the rocks below."

7 Jesus retorted, "It also says not to put the

[*i*] Literally, "to fulfill all righteousness."

Today's English Version

requires."

So John agreed. 16As soon as he was baptized, Jesus came up out of the water. Then heaven was opened to him, and he saw the Spirit of God coming down like a dove and lighting on him. 17And then a voice said from heaven, "This is my own dear Son, with whom I am well pleased."

The temptation of Jesus

4 Then the Spirit led Jesus into the desert to be tempted by the Devil. 2After spending forty days and nights without food, Jesus was hungry. 3 The Devil came to him and said, "If you are God's Son, order these stones to turn into bread."

4 Jesus answered, "The scripture says, 'Man cannot live on bread alone, but on every word that God speaks.'"

5 Then the Devil took Jesus to the Holy City, set him on the highest point of the temple, 6 and said to him, "If you are God's Son, throw yourself down to the ground; because the scripture says,

'God will give orders to his angels about you;
they will hold you up with their hands,
so that not even your feet will be hurt on the stones.'"

7 Jesus answered, "But the scripture also says,

New International Version

ness." Then John consented.

16 As soon as Jesus was baptized, he went up out of the water. At that moment heaven was opened, and he saw the Spirit of God descending on him like a dove. 17And a voice from heaven said, "This is my Son, whom I love; with him I am well-pleased."

The temptation of Jesus

4 Then Jesus was led by the Spirit into the desert to be tempted by the devil. 2After fasting forty days and nights, he was hungry. 3 The tempter came to him and said, "If you are the Son of God, tell these stones to become bread."

4 Jesus answered, "It is written:
'Man does not live on bread alone,
but on every word that comes from the mouth of God.' [k]"

5 Then the devil took him to the holy city and had him stand on the highest point of the temple. 6 "If you are the Son of God," he said, "throw yourself down. For it is written:
'He will command his angels concerning you,
and they will lift you up in their hands,
so that you will not strike your foot against a stone.' [l]"

7 Jesus answered him, "It is also written: 'Do

[*k*] Deut. 8:3. [*l*] Psalm 91:11,12.

Phillips Modern English

demands—let it be so now."

Then John agreed to baptise him. Jesus came straight out of the water afterwards, and suddenly the heavens opened and he saw the Spirit of God coming down like a dove and resting upon him. And a voice came out of Heaven saying, "This is my dearly-loved Son, in whom I am well pleased."

4.1 Jesus faces temptation alone in the desert

Then Jesus was led by the Spirit up into the desert, to be tempted by the devil. After a fast of forty days and nights he was very hungry.

"If you are the Son of God," said the tempter, coming to him, "tell these stones to turn into loaves."

Jesus answered, "The scripture says 'Man shall not live by bread alone, but by every word that proceedeth out of the mouth of God'."

Then the devil took him to the holy city, and set him on the highest pinnacle of the Temple. "If you are the Son of God," he said, "throw yourself down. For the scripture says—

He shall give his angels charge concerning thee:
And on their hands they shall bear thee up,
Lest haply thou dash thy foot against a stone."

"Yes," retorted Jesus, "and the scripture also

Revised Standard Version

for thus it is fitting for us to fulfil all righteousness." Then he consented. 16And when Jesus
was baptized, he went up immediately from the
water, and behold, the heavens were opened[g]
and he saw the Spirit of God descending like a
dove, and alighting on him; 17 and lo, a voice
from heaven, saying, "This is my beloved Son,[h]
with whom I am well pleased."

4 Then Jesus was led up by the Spirit into
the wilderness to be tempted by the devil.
2And he fasted forty days and forty nights, and
afterward he was hungry. 3And the tempter came
and said to him, "If you are the Son of God,
command these stones to become loaves of
bread." 4 But he answered, "It is written,
'Man shall not live by bread alone,
but by every word that proceeds from the
mouth of God.' "
5 Then the devil took him to the holy city, and
set him on the pinnacle of the temple, 6 and said
to him, "If you are the Son of God, throw yourself down; for it is written,
'He will give his angels charge of you,'
and
'On their hands they will bear you up,
lest you strike your foot against a stone.' "
7 Jesus said to him, "Again it is written, 'You

[g] Other ancient anthorities add *to him*. [h] Or *my Son, my* (or *the*) *Beloved*.

Jerusalem Bible

should, in this way, do all that righteousness
demands." At this, John gave in to him.
16 As soon as Jesus was baptized he came
up from the water, and suddenly the heavens
opened and he saw the Spirit of God descending like a dove and coming down on him. 17And
a voice spoke from heaven, "This is my Son,
the Beloved; my favor rests on him."

Temptation in the wilderness

4 Then Jesus was led by the Spirit out into
the wilderness to be tempted by the devil.
2 He fasted for forty days and forty nights, after
which he was very hungry, 3 and the tempter
came and said to him, "If you are the Son of
God, tell these stones to turn into loaves." 4 But
he replied, "Scripture says:

Man does not live on bread alone
but on every word that comes from the mouth
of God." [p]

5 The devil then took him to the holy city and
made him stand on the parapet of the Temple.
6 "If you are the Son of God," he said, "throw
yourself down; for Scripture says:

He will put you in his angels' charge,
and they will support you on their hands
in case you hurt your foot against a stone." [q]

7 Jesus said to him, "Scripture also says:

[p] Dt. 8:3. [q] Ps. 91:11-12.

New English Bible

to conform in this way with all that God requires.' John then allowed him to come. After baptism Jesus came up out of the water at once, and at that moment heaven opened; he saw the Spirit of God descending like a dove to alight upon him; and a voice from heaven was heard saying, 'This is my Son, my Beloved,[a] on whom my favour rests.'

4 Jesus was then led away by the Spirit into the wilderness, to be tempted by the devil.

For forty days and nights he fasted, and at the end of them he was famished. The tempter approached him and said, 'If you are the Son of God, tell these stones to become bread.' Jesus answered, 'Scripture says, "Man cannot live on bread alone; he lives on every word that God utters." '

The devil then took him to the Holy City and set him on the parapet of the temple. 'If you are the Son of God,' he said, 'throw yourself down; for Scripture says, "He will put his angels in charge of you, and they will support you in their arms, for fear you should strike your foot against a stone." ' Jesus answered him, 'Scripture

[a] *Or* This is my only Son.

King James Version

tempt the Lord thy God. 8Again, the devil taketh
him up into an exceeding high mountain, and
sheweth him all the kingdoms of the world, and
the glory of them; 9And saith unto him, All
these things will I give thee, if thou wilt fall
down and worship me. 10 Then saith Jesus unto
him, Get thee hence, Satan: for it is written,
Thou shalt worship the Lord thy God, and him
only shalt thou serve. 11 Then the devil leaveth
him, and, behold, angels came and ministered
unto him.
12 Now when Jesus had heard that John was
cast into prison, he departed into Galilee; 13And
leaving Nazareth, he came and dwelt in Capernaum,
which is upon the sea coast, in the borders
of Zabulon and Nephthalim: 14 That it might be
fulfilled which was spoken by Esaias the prophet,
saying, 15 The land of Zabulon, and the land of
Nephthalim, *by* the way of the sea, beyond Jordan,
Galilee of the Gentiles; 16 The people which
sat in darkness saw great light; and to them
which sat in the region and shadow of death
light is sprung up.

Living Bible

Lord your God to a foolish test!"
8 Next Satan took him to the peak of a very
high mountain and showed him the nations of
the world and all their glory. 9 "I'll give it all
to you," he said, "if you will only kneel and
worship me."
10 "Get out of here, Satan," Jesus told him.
"The Scriptures say, 'Worship only the Lord
God. Obey only him.'"
11 Then Satan went away, and angels came
and cared for Jesus.
12, 13 When Jesus heard that John had been
arrested, he left Judea and returned home[a] to
Nazareth in Galilee; but soon he moved to
Capernaum, beside the Lake of Galilee, close to
Zebulun and Naphtali. 14 This fulfilled Isaiah's
prophecy:

15, 16 "The land of Zebulun and the land of
Naphtali, beside the Lake, and the
countryside beyond the Jordan River,
and Upper Galilee where so many foreigners
live—there the people who sat
in darkness have seen a great Light;
they sat in the land of death, and the
Light broke through upon them." [b]

[a] Implied. [b] Isaiah 9:1,2.

Today's English Version

'You must not put the Lord your God to the
test.'"
8 Then the Devil took Jesus to a very high
mountain and showed him all the kingdoms of
the world, in all their greatness. 9 "All this I
will give you," the Devil said, "if you kneel
down and worship me."
10 Then Jesus answered, "Go away, Satan!
The scripture says, 'Worship the Lord your God
and serve only him!'"
11 Then the Devil left him; and angels came
and helped Jesus.

Jesus begins his work in Galilee

12 When Jesus heard that John had been put
in prison, he went away to Galilee. 13 He did
not settle down in Nazareth, but went and lived
in Capernaum, a town by Lake Galilee, in the
territory of Zebulun and Naphtali. 14 This was
done to make come true what the prophet Isaiah
had said,

15 "Land of Zebulun, and land of Naphtali,
in the direction of the sea, on the other
side of the Jordan,
Galilee of the Gentiles!
16 The people who live in darkness
will see a great light.
On those who live in the dark land of death
the light will shine."

New International Version

not put the Lord your God to the test.'[m]"
8 Again, the devil took him to a very high
mountain and showed him all the kingdoms of
the world and their splendor. 9 "All this I will
give you," he said, "if you will bow down and
worship me."
10 Jesus said to him, "Away from me, Satan!
For it is written: 'Worship the Lord your God,
and serve him only.'[n]"
11 Then the devil left him, and angels came
and attended him.

Jesus begins to preach

12 When Jesus heard that John had been put
in prison, he returned to Galilee. 13 Leaving
Nazareth, he went and lived in Capernaum,
which was by the lake in the area of Zebulun
and Naphtali—14 to fulfill what was said through
the prophet Isaiah:

15 "Land of Zebulun and land of Naphtali,
the way to the sea, along the Jordan,
Galilee of the Gentiles—
16 the people living in darkness
have seen a great light;
on those living in the land of the shadow
of death
a light has dawned."[o]

[m] Deut. 6:16. [n] Deut. 6:13. [o] Isaiah 9:1,2.

Phillips Modern English

says 'Thou shalt not tempt the Lord thy God'."
Once again the devil took him to a very high mountain, and from there showed him all the kingdoms of the world and their magnificence. "Everything there I will give you," he said to him, "if you will fall down and worship me."
"Away with you, Satan!" replied Jesus, "the scripture says,

Thou shalt worship the Lord thy God, and him only shalt thou serve."

Then the devil let him alone, and angels came to him and took care of him.

4.12 Jesus begins his ministry, in Galilee, and calls his first disciples

Now when Jesus heard that John had been arrested he went back to Galilee. He left Nazareth and came to live in Capernaum, a lake-side town in the Zebulun-Naphtali territory. In this way Isaiah's prophecy came true:

The land of Zebulun and the land of Naphtali,
Toward the sea, beyond Jordan,
Galilee of the Gentiles,
The people which sat in darkness
Saw a great light,
And to them which sat in the region and shadow of death,
To them did light spring up.

Revised Standard Version

shall not tempt the Lord your God.'" 8 Again,
the devil took him to a very high mountain, and
showed him all the kingdoms of the world and
the glory of them; 9 and he said to him, "All
these I will give you, if you will fall down and
worship me." 10 Then Jesus said to him, "Begone, Satan! for it is written,
'You shall worship the Lord your God
and him only shall you serve.'"
11 Then the devil left him, and behold, angels
came and ministered to him.
12 Now when he heard that John had been
arrested, he withdrew into Galilee; 13 and leaving Nazareth he went and dwelt in Capernaum
by the sea, in the territory of Zebulun and
Naphtali, 14 that what was spoken by the
prophet Isaiah might be fulfilled:
15 "The land of Zebulun and the land of Naphtali,
toward the sea, across the Jordan,
Galilee of the Gentiles—
16 the people who sat in darkness
have seen a great light,
and for those who sat in the region and shadow of death
light has dawned."

Jerusalem Bible

You must not put the Lord your God to the test." [r]

8 Next, taking him to a very high mountain, the
devil showed him all the kingdoms of the world
and their splendor. 9 "I will give you all these,"
he said, "if you fall at my feet and worship me."
10 Then Jesus replied, "Be off, Satan! For Scripture says:

You must worship the Lord your God, and serve him alone." [s]

11 Then the devil left him, and angels appeared
and looked after him.

Return to Galilee

12 Hearing that John had been arrested he
went back to Galilee, 13 and leaving Nazareth
he went and settled in Capernaum, a lakeside
town on the borders of Zebulun and Naphtali.
14 In this way the prophecy of Isaiah was to be
fulfilled:

15 *Land of Zebulun! Land of Naphtali!*
Way of the sea on the far side of Jordan,
Galilee of the nations!
16 *The people that lived in darkness*
has seen a great light;
on those who dwell in the land and shadow of death
a light has dawned. [t]

[r] Dt. 6:16. [s] Dt. 6:13. [t] Is. 8:23-9:1.

New English Bible

says again, "You are not to put the Lord your God to the test."'
Once again, the devil took him to a very high mountain, and showed him all the kingdoms of the world in their glory. 'All these', he said, 'I will give you, if you will only fall down and do me homage.' But Jesus said, 'Begone, Satan! Scripture says, "You shall do homage to the Lord your God and worship him alone."'
Then the devil left him; and angels appeared and waited on him.
When he heard that John had been arrested, Jesus withdrew to Galilee; and leaving Nazareth he went and settled at Capernaum on the Sea of Galilee, in the district of Zebulun and Naphtali. This was to fulfil the passage in the prophet Isaiah which tells of 'the land of Zebulun, the land of Naphtali, the Way of the Sea, the land beyond Jordan, heathen Galilee', and says:

'The people that lived in darkness saw a great light;
light dawned on the dwellers in the land of death's dark shadow.'

King James Version

17 From that time Jesus began to preach, and
to say, Repent: for the kingdom of heaven is at
hand.
18 And Jesus, walking by the sea of Galilee,
saw two brethren, Simon called Peter, and Andrew his brother, casting a net into the sea: for
they were fishers. 19And he saith unto them,
Follow me, and I will make you fishers of men.
20And they straightway left *their* nets, and followed him. 21And going on from thence, he saw
other two brethren, James *the son* of Zebedee,
and John his brother, in a ship with Zebedee
their father, mending their nets; and he called
them. 22And they immediately left the ship and
their father, and followed him.
23 And Jesus went about all Galilee, teaching
in their synagogues, and preaching the gospel
of the kingdom, and healing all manner of sickness and all manner of disease among the people.
24And his fame went throughout all Syria: and
they brought unto him all sick people that were
taken with divers diseases and torments, and
those which were possessed with devils, and those
which were lunatic, and those that had the palsy;
and he healed them. 25And there followed him

Living Bible

17 From then on, Jesus began to preach, "Turn
from sin, and turn to God, for the Kingdom of
Heaven is near." [c]
18 One day as he was walking along the
beach beside the Lake of Galilee, he saw two
brothers—Simon, also called Peter, and Andrew
—out in a boat[d] fishing with a net, for they were
commercial fishermen.
19 Jesus called out, "Come along with me
and I will show you how to fish for the souls
of men!" 20And they left their nets at once and
went with him.
21 A little farther up the beach he saw two
other brothers, James and John, sitting in a
boat with their father Zebedee, mending their
nets; and he called to them to come too. 22At
once they stopped their work and, leaving their
father behind, went with him.
23 Jesus traveled all through Galilee teaching
in the Jewish synagogues, everywhere preaching
the Good News about the Kingdom of Heaven.
And he healed every kind of sickness and disease. 24 The report of his miracles spread far
beyond the borders of Galilee so that sick folk
were soon coming to be healed from as far away
as Syria. And whatever their illness and pain, or
if they were possessed by demons, or were insane, or paralyzed—he healed them all. 25 Enor-

[*c*] Or, "is at hand," or, "has arrived." [*d*] Literally, "with your brother."

Today's English Version

17 From that time Jesus began to preach his
message, "Turn away from your sins, because
the Kingdom of heaven is near!"

Jesus calls four fishermen

18 As Jesus walked by Lake Galilee, he saw
two brothers who were fishermen, Simon (called
Peter) and his brother Andrew, catching fish in
the lake with a net. 19 Jesus said to them, "Come
with me and I will teach you to catch men."
20At once they left their nets and went with him.
21 He went on and saw two other brothers,
James and John, the sons of Zebedee. They were
in their boat with their father Zebedee, getting
their nets ready. Jesus called them; 22 at once
they left the boat and their father, and went
with Jesus.

Jesus teaches, preaches, and heals

23 Jesus went all over Galilee, teaching in
their synagogues, preaching the Good News of
the Kingdom, and healing people from every kind
of disease and sickness. 24 The news about him
spread through the whole country of Syria, so
that people brought him all those who were sick
with all kinds of diseases, and afflicted with all
sorts of troubles: people with demons, and epileptics, and paralytics—Jesus healed them all.
25 Great crowds followed him from Galilee and

New International Version

17 From that time on Jesus began to preach,
"Repent, for the kingdom of heaven is near."

The calling of the first disciples

18 As Jesus was walking beside the Sea of
Galilee, he saw two brothers, Simon called Peter
and his brother Andrew. They were casting a
net into the lake, for they were fishermen.
19 "Come, follow me," Jesus said, "and I will
make you fishers of men." 20At once they left
their nets and followed him.
21 Going on from there, he saw two other
brothers, James son of Zebedee and his brother
John. They were in a boat with their father
Zebedee, preparing their nets. Jesus called them,
22 and immediately they left the boat and their
father and followed him.

Jesus heals the sick

23 Jesus went throughout Galilee teaching in
their synagogues, preaching the good news of the
kingdom, and healing every disease and sickness
among the people. 24 News about him spread
all over Syria, and people brought to him all who
were ill with various diseases, those suffering
severe pain, the demon-possessed, the epileptics
and the paralytics, and he healed them. 25 Large

Phillips Modern English

From that time Jesus began to preach and to say, "You must change your hearts and minds—for the kingdom of Heaven has arrived."

While he was walking by the lake of Galilee he saw two brothers, Simon (Peter) and Andrew, casting their net into the water. They were fishermen, so Jesus said to them,

"Follow me and I will teach you to catch men!"

At once they left their nets and followed him.

Then he went further on and saw two more men, also brothers, James and John. They were aboard the boat with their father Zebedee repairing their nets, and he called them. At once they left the boat, and their father, and followed him.

4.23 Jesus teaches, preaches and heals

Jesus now moved about through the whole of Galilee, teaching in their synagogues and preaching the good news about the kingdom, and healing every disease and disability among the people. His reputation spread throughout Syria, and people brought to him all those who were ill, suffering from all kinds of diseases and pains—including the devil-possessed, the insane and the paralysed. He healed them, and was followed

Revised Standard Version

17 From that time Jesus began to preach, saying, "Repent, for the kingdom of heaven is at
hand."
18 As he walked by the Sea of Galilee, he
saw two brothers, Simon who is called Peter and
Andrew his brother, casting a net into the sea;
for they were fishermen. 19 And he said to them,
"Follow me, and I will make you fishers of
men." 20 Immediately they left their nets and
followed him. 21 And going on from there he
saw two other brothers, James the son of Zebedee and John his brother, in the boat with
Zebedee their father, mending their nets, and he
called them. 22 Immediately they left the boat
and their father, and followed him.

23 And he went about all Galilee, teaching in
their synagogues and preaching the gospel of the
kingdom and healing every disease and every infirmity among the people. 24 So his fame spread
throughout all Syria, and they brought him all
the sick, those afflicted with various diseases and
pains, demoniacs, epileptics, and paralytics, and
he healed them. 25 And great crowds followed

Jerusalem Bible

17 From that moment Jesus began his preaching
with the message, "Repent, for the kingdom of
heaven is close at hand."

The first four disciples are called

18 As he was walking by the Sea of Galilee
he saw two brothers, Simon, who was called
Peter, and his brother Andrew; they were making
a cast in the lake with their net, for they were
fishermen. 19 And he said to them, "Follow me
and I will make you fishers of men." 20 And they
left their nets at once and followed him.
21 Going on from there he saw another pair
of brothers, James son of Zebedee and his
brother John; they were in their boat with their
father Zebedee, mending their nets, and he called
them. 22 At once, leaving the boat and their
father, they followed him.

Jesus preaches and heals the sick

23 He went around the whole of Galilee
teaching in their synagogues, proclaiming the
Good News of the kingdom and curing all
kinds of diseases and sickness among the people. 24 His fame spread throughout Syria,[u]
and those who were suffering from diseases and
painful complaints of one kind or another, the
possessed, epileptics, the paralyzed, were all
brought to him, and he cured them. 25 Large

[u] I.e., Galilee and the districts listed in v. 25.

New English Bible

From that day Jesus began to proclaim the message: 'Repent; for[a] the kingdom of Heaven is upon you.'

Jesus was walking by the Sea of Galilee when he saw two brothers, Simon called Peter and his brother Andrew, casting a net into the lake; for they were fishermen. Jesus said to them, 'Come with me, and I will make you fishers of men.' And at once they left their nets and followed him.

He went on, and saw another pair of brothers, James son of Zebedee and his brother John; they were in the boat with their father Zebedee, overhauling their nets. He called them, and at once they left the boat and their father, and followed him.

He went round the whole of Galilee, teaching in the synagogues, preaching the gospel of the Kingdom, and curing whatever illness or infirmity there was among the people. His fame reached the whole of Syria; and sufferers from every kind of illness, racked with pain, possessed by devils, epileptic, or paralysed, were all brought to him, and he cured them. Great

[a] *Some witnesses omit* Repent; for.

King James Version

great multitudes of people from Galilee, and
from Decapolis, and *from* Jerusalem, and *from*
Judea, and *from* beyond Jordan.

5 And seeing the multitudes, he went up into
a mountain: and when he was set, his disciples came unto him: 2 And he opened his mouth,
and taught them, saying, 3 Blessed *are* the poor
in spirit: for theirs is the kingdom of heaven.
4 Blessed *are* they that mourn: for they shall be
comforted. 5 Blessed *are* the meek: for they shall
inherit the earth. 6 Blessed *are* they which do
hunger and thirst after righteousness: for they
shall be filled. 7 Blessed *are* the merciful: for
they shall obtain mercy. 8 Blessed *are* the pure

Living Bible

mous crowds followed him wherever he went—
people from Galilee, and the Ten Cities, and
Jerusalem, and from all over Judea, and even
from across the Jordan River.

5 One day as the crowds were gathering, he
went up the hillside with his disciples and
sat down and taught them there.
3 "Humble men are very fortunate!" he told
them, "for the Kingdom of Heaven is given to
them. 4 Those who mourn are fortunate! for
they shall be comforted. 5 The meek and lowly
are fortunate! for the whole wide world belongs
to them.
6 "Happy are those who long to be just and
good, for they shall be completely satisfied.
7 Happy are the kind and merciful, for they shall
be shown mercy. 8 Happy are those whose hearts

Today's English Version

the Ten Towns, from Jerusalem, Judea, and the
land on the other side of the Jordan.

The sermon on the mount

5 Jesus saw the crowds and went up a hill,
where he sat down. His disciples gathered
around him, 2 and he began to teach them:

True happiness

3 "Happy are those who know they are spiritually poor;
the Kingdom of heaven belongs to them!
4 "Happy are those who mourn;
God will comfort them!
5 "Happy are the meek;
they will receive what God has promised!
6 "Happy are those whose greatest desire is
to do what God requires;
God will satisfy them fully!
7 "Happy are those who are merciful to
others;
God will be merciful to them!
8 "Happy are the pure in heart;
they will see God!

New International Version

crowds from Galilee, the Decapolis,[p] Jerusalem,
Judea and the region across the Jordan followed
him.

The beatitudes

5 Now when he saw the crowds, he went up
on a mountainside and sat down. His disciples came to him, 2 and he began to teach
them, saying:
3 "Blessed are the poor in spirit,
for theirs is the kingdom of heaven.
4 Blessed are those who mourn,
for they will be comforted.
5 Blessed are the meek,
for they will inherit the earth.
6 Blessed are those who hunger and thirst for
righteousness,
for they will be filled.
7 Blessed are the merciful,
for they will be shown mercy.
8 Blessed are the pure in heart,
for they will see God.

[p] That is, *the Ten Cities.*

Phillips Modern English

by enormous crowds from Galilee, the Ten Towns, Jerusalem, Judaea, and from beyond the river Jordan.

5.1 *Jesus proclaims the new values of the kingdom*

When Jesus saw the vast crowds he went up the hill-side and after he had sat down his disciples came to him.

Then he began his teaching by saying to them, "How happy are those who know their need for God, for the kingdom of Heaven is theirs!

"How happy are those who know what sorrow means, for they will be given courage and comfort!

"Happy are those who claim nothing, for the whole earth will belong to them!

"Happy are those who are hungry and thirsty for true goodness, for they will be fully satisfied!

"Happy are the merciful, for they will have mercy shown to them!

"Happy are the utterly sincere, for they will see God!

Revised Standard Version

him from Galilee and the Decapolis and Jerusalem and Judea and from beyond the Jordan.

5 Seeing the crowds, he went up on the mountain, and when he sat down his disciples came to him. 2And he opened his mouth and taught them, saying:
3 "Blessed are the poor in spirit, for theirs is the kingdom of heaven.
4 "Blessed are those who mourn, for they shall be comforted.
5 "Blessed are the meek, for they shall inherit the earth.
6 "Blessed are those who hunger and thirst for righteousness, for they shall be satisfied.
7 "Blessed are the merciful, for they shall obtain mercy.
8 "Blessed are the pure in heart, for they shall see God.

Jerusalem Bible

crowds followed him, coming from Galilee, the Decapolis,[v] Jerusalem, Judaea and Transjordania.

B. The sermon on the mount[w]

The Beatitudes

5 Seeing the crowds, he went up the hill. There he sat down and was joined by his disciples. 2 Then he began to speak. This is what he taught them:

3 "How happy are the poor in spirit;
theirs is the kingdom of heaven.
4 Happy *the gentle*[x]*:*
they shall have the earth for their heritage.
5 Happy those who mourn:
they shall be comforted.
6 Happy those who hunger and thirst for what is right:
they shall be satisfied.
7 Happy the merciful:
they shall have mercy shown them.
8 Happy the pure in heart:
they shall see God.

[v] The "ten towns," a region southeast of Galilee. [w] In this discourse, which occupies three chapters of this gospel, Matthew has included sayings which probably originated on other occasions (cf. their parallels in Luke). [x] Or "the lowly"; the word comes from the Greek version of Ps. 37.

New English Bible

crowds also followed him, from Galilee and the Ten Towns,[b] from Jerusalem and Judaea, and from Transjordan.

The Sermon on the Mount

5 When he saw the crowds he went up the hill. There he took his seat, and when his disciples had gathered round him he began to address them. And this is the teaching he gave:

'How blest are those who know their need of God;
the kingdom of Heaven is theirs.
How blest are the sorrowful;
they shall find consolation.
How blest are those of a gentle spirit;
they shall have the earth for their possession.
How blest are those who hunger and thirst to see right prevail;[c]
they shall be satisfied.
How blest are those who show mercy;
mercy shall be shown to them.
How blest are those whose hearts are pure;
they shall see God.

[b] *Greek* Decapolis. [c] *Or* to do what is right.

King James Version

in heart: for they shall see God. 9 Blessed *are*
the peacemakers: for they shall be called the
children of God. 10 Blessed *are* they which are
persecuted for righteousness' sake: for theirs is
the kingdom of heaven. 11 Blessed are ye, when
men shall revile you, and persecute *you*, and
shall say all manner of evil against you falsely,
for my sake. 12 Rejoice, and be exceeding glad:
for great *is* your reward in heaven: for so persecuted they the prophets which were before you.
13 Ye are the salt of the earth: but if the
salt have lost his savour, wherewith shall it be
salted? It is thenceforth good for nothing, but to
be cast out, and to be trodden under foot of
men. 14 Ye are the light of the world. A city
that is set on a hill cannot be hid. 15 Neither do
men light a candle, and put it under a bushel,
but on a candlestick; and it giveth light unto
all that are in the house. 16 Let your light so
shine before men, that they may see your good
works, and glorify your Father which is in
heaven.
17 Think not that I am come to destroy the
law, or the prophets: I am not come to destroy,

Living Bible

are pure, for they shall see God. 9 Happy are
those who strive for peace—they shall be called
the sons of God. 10 Happy are those who are
persecuted because they are good, for the Kingdom of Heaven is theirs.
11 "When you are reviled and persecuted and
lied about because you are my followers—wonderful! 12 Be *happy* about it! Be *very glad!* for
a *tremendous reward* awaits you up in heaven.
And remember, the ancient prophets were persecuted too.
13 "You are the world's seasoning, to make
it tolerable. If you lose your flavor, what will
happen to the world? And you yourselves will
be thrown out and trampled underfoot as worthless. 14 You are the world's light—a city on a hill,
glowing in the night for all to see. 15, 16 Don't
hide your light! Let it shine for all; let your
good deeds glow for all to see, so that they will
praise your heavenly Father.
17 "Don't misunderstand why I have come—
it isn't to cancel the laws of Moses and the

Today's English Version

9 "Happy are those who work for peace
among men;
God will call them his sons!
10 "Happy are those who are persecuted because they do what God requires;
the Kingdom of heaven belongs to them!

11 "Happy are you when men insult you, and
persecute you, and tell all kinds of evil lies
against you because you are my followers. 12 Be
glad and happy, because a great reward is kept
for you in heaven. This is how men persecuted
the prophets who lived before you."

Salt and light

13 "You are like salt for all mankind. But if
salt loses its taste, there is no way to make it
salty again. It has become worthless, so it is
thrown away and people walk on it.
14 "You are like light for the whole world.
A city built on a hill cannot be hid. 15 No one
lights a lamp to put it under a bowl; instead he
puts it on the lampstand, where it gives light
for everyone in the house. 16 In the same way
your light must shine before people, so that they
will see the good things you do and give praise
to your Father in heaven."

Teaching about the law

17 "Do not think that I have come to do
away with the Law of Moses and the teachings

New International Version

9 Blessed are the peacemakers,
for they will be called sons of God.
10 Blessed are those who are persecuted because of righteousness,
for theirs is the kingdom of heaven.
11 "Blessed are you when people insult you,
persecute you and falsely say all kinds of evil
against you because of me. 12 Rejoice and be
glad, because great is your reward in heaven, for
in the same way they persecuted the prophets
who were before you.

Salt and light

13 "You are the salt of the earth. But if the
salt loses its saltiness, how can it be made salty
again? It is no longer good for anything, except
to be thrown out and trampled by men.
14 "You are the light of the world. A city on
a hill cannot be hidden. 15 Neither do people
light a lamp and put it under a bowl. Instead
they put it on its stand, and and it gives light to
everyone in the house. 16 In the same way, let
your light shine before men, that they may see
your good deeds and praise your Father in
heaven.

The fulfillment of the Law

17 "Do not think that I have come to abolish
the Law or the Prophets; I have not come to

Phillips Modern English

"Happy are those who make peace, for they will be known as sons of God!

"Happy are those who have suffered persecution for the cause of goodness, for the kingdom of Heaven is theirs!

"And what happiness will be yours when people blame you and ill-treat you and say all kinds of slanderous things against you for my sake! Be glad then, yes, be tremendously glad—for your reward in Heaven is magnificent. They persecuted the prophets before your time in exactly the same way.

"You are the earth's salt. But if the salt should become tasteless, what can make it salt again? It is completely useless and can only be thrown out of doors and stamped under foot.

"You are the world's light—it is impossible to hide a town built on the top of a hill. Men do not light a lamp and put it under a bucket. They put it on a lamp-stand and it gives light for everybody in the house.

"Let your light shine like that in the sight of men. Let them see the good things you do and praise your Father in Heaven.

5.17 Christ's authority surpasses that of the Law

"You must not think that I have come to abolish the Law or the Prophets; I have not

Revised Standard Version

9 "Blessed are the peacemakers, for they shall
be called sons of God.
10 "Blessed are those who are persecuted for
righteousness' sake, for theirs is the kingdom of
heaven.
11 "Blessed are you when men revile you and
persecute you and utter all kinds of evil against
you falsely on my account. 12 Rejoice and be
glad, for your reward is great in heaven, for so
men persecuted the prophets who were before
you.
13 "You are the salt of the earth; but if salt
has lost its taste, how shall its saltiness be restored? It is no longer good for anything except
to be thrown out and trodden under foot by
men.
14 "You are the light of the world. A city set
on a hill cannot be hid. 15 Nor do men light a
lamp and put it under a bushel, but on a stand,
and it gives light to all in the house. 16 Let your
light so shine before men, that they may see your
good works and give glory to your Father who
is in heaven.
17 "Think not that I have come to abolish
the law and the prophets; I have come not to

Jerusalem Bible

9 Happy the peacemakers:
they shall be called sons of God.
10 Happy those who are persecuted in the
cause of right:
theirs is the kingdom of heaven.

11 "Happy are you when people abuse you and
persecute you and speak all kinds of calumny
against you on my account. 12 Rejoice and be
glad, for your reward will be great in heaven;
this is how they persecuted the prophets before
you.

Salt of the earth and light of the world

13 "You are the salt of the earth. But if salt
becomes tasteless, what can make it salty again?
It is good for nothing, and can only be thrown
out to be trampled underfoot by men.
14 "You are the light of the world. A city
built on a hilltop cannot be hidden. 15 No one
lights a lamp to put it under a tub; they put
it on the lampstand where it shines for everyone
in the house. 16 In the same way your light
must shine in the sight of men, so that, seeing
your good works, they may give the praise to
your Father in heaven.

The fulfillment of the Law

17 "Do not imagine that I have come to
abolish the Law or the Prophets. I have come

New English Bible

How blest are the peacemakers;
God shall call them his sons.
How blest are those who have suffered persecution for the cause of right;
the kingdom of Heaven is theirs.

'How blest you are, when you suffer insults and persecution and every kind of calumny for my sake. Accept it with gladness and exultation, for you have a rich reward in heaven; in the same way they persecuted the prophets before you.

'You are salt to the world. And if salt becomes tasteless, how is its saltiness to be restored? It is now good for nothing but to be thrown away and trodden underfoot.

'You are light for all the world. A town that stands on a hill cannot be hidden. When a lamp is lit, it is not put under the meal-tub, but on the lamp-stand, where it gives light to everyone in the house. And you, like the lamp, must shed light among your fellows, so that, when they see the good you do, they may give praise to your Father in heaven.

'Do not suppose that I have come to abolish the Law and the prophets; I did not come to

King James Version

but to fulfil. 18 For verily I say unto you, Till heaven and earth pass, one jot or one tittle shall in no wise pass from the law, till all be fulfilled. 19 Whosoever therefore shall break one of these least commandments, and shall teach men so, he shall be called the least in the kingdom of heaven: but whosoever shall do and teach *them*, the same shall be called great in the kingdom of heaven. 20 For I say unto you, That except your righteousness shall exceed *the righteousness* of the scribes and Pharisees, ye shall in no case enter into the kingdom of heaven.

21 Ye have heard that it was said by them of old time, Thou shalt not kill; and whosoever shall kill shall be in danger of the judgment: 22 But I say unto you, That whosoever is angry with his brother without a cause shall be in danger of the judgment: and whosoever shall say to his brother, Raca, shall be in danger of the council: but whosoever shall say, Thou fool, shall be in danger of hell fire. 23 Therefore if thou bring thy gift to the altar, and there rememberest that thy brother hath aught against thee; 24 Leave there thy gift before the altar, and go thy way; first be reconciled to thy brother, and then come and offer thy gift. 25 Agree with thine adversary quickly, while thou art in the

Living Bible

warnings of the prophets. No, I came to fulfill them, and to make them all come true. 18 With all the earnestness I have I say: Every law in the Book will continue until its purpose is achieved.[a] 19 And so if anyone breaks the least commandment, and teaches others to, he shall be the least in the Kingdom of Heaven. But those who teach God's laws *and obey them* shall be great in the Kingdom of Heaven.

20 "But I warn you—unless your goodness[b] is greater than that of the Pharisees and other Jewish leaders, you can't get into the Kingdom of Heaven at all!

21 "Under the laws of Moses the rule was, 'If you murder, you must die.' 22 But I have added to that rule,[c] and tell you that if you are only *angry*, even in your own home,[d] you are in danger of judgment! If you call your friend an idiot, you are in danger of being brought before the court. And if you curse him, you are in danger of the fires of hell.[e]

23 "So if you are standing before the altar in the Temple, offering a sacrifice to God, and suddenly remember that a friend has something against you, 24 leave your sacrifice there beside the altar and go and apologize and be reconciled to him, and then come and offer your sacrifice to God. 25 Come to terms quickly with your enemy before it is too late and he drags you into

[*a*] Literally, "until all things be accomplished." [*b*] Literally, "righteousness." [*c*] Literally, "But I say." [*d*] Literally, "with your brother." [*e*] Literally, "the hell of fire."

Today's English Version

of the prophets. I have not come to do away with them, but to make their teachings come true. 18 Remember this! As long as heaven and earth last, the least point or the smallest detail of the Law will not be done away with—not until the end of all things. 19 So then, whoever disobeys even the smallest of the commandments, and teaches others to do the same, will be least in the Kingdom of heaven. On the other hand, whoever obeys the Law, and teaches others to do the same, will be great in the Kingdom of heaven. 20 I tell you, then, that you will be able to enter the Kingdom of heaven only if you are more faithful than the teachers of the Law and the Pharisees in doing what God requires."

Teaching about anger

21 "You have heard that men were told in the past, 'Do not murder; anyone who commits murder will be brought before the judge.' 22 But now I tell you: whoever is angry with his brother will be brought before the judge; whoever calls his brother 'You good-for-nothing!' will be brought before the Council; and whoever calls his brother a worthless fool will be in danger of going to the fire of hell. 23 So if you are about to offer your gift to God at the altar and there you remember that your brother has something against you, 24 leave your gift there in front of the altar and go at once to make peace with your brother; then come back and offer your gift to God.

25 "If a man brings a lawsuit against you and takes you to court, be friendly with him while

New International Version

abolish them but to fulfill them. 18 I tell you the truth, until heaven and earth disappear, not the smallest letter, not the least stroke of a pen, will by any means disappear from the Law until everything is accomplished. 19 Anyone who breaks one of the least of these commandments and teaches others to do the same will be called least in the kingdom of heaven, but whoever practices and teaches these commands will be called great in the kingdom of heaven. 20 For I tell you that unless your righteousness surpasses that of the Pharisees and the teachers of the law, you will certainly not enter the kingdom of heaven.

Murder

21 "You have heard that it was said to the people long ago, 'Do not murder,[q] and anyone who murders will be subject to judgment.' 22 But I tell you that anyone who is angry with his brother[r] will be subject to judgment. Again, anyone who says to his brother, 'Raca,'[s] is answerable to the Sanhedrin. But anyone who says, 'You fool!' will be in danger of the fire of hell.

23 "Therefore, if you are offering your gift at the altar and there remember that your brother has something against you, 24 leave your gift there in front of the altar. First go and be reconciled to your brother; then come and offer your gift.

25 "Settle matters quickly with your adversary who is taking you to court. Do it while you are

[*q*] Exodus 20:13. [*r*] Some MSS add *without cause.* [*s*] An Aramaic term of contempt.

Phillips Modern English

come to abolish them but to complete them. Indeed, I assure you that, while Heaven and earth last, the Law will not lose a single dot or comma until its purpose is complete. This means that whoever now relaxes one of the least of these commandments and teaches men to do the same will himself be called least in the kingdom of Heaven. But whoever teaches and practises them will be called great in the kingdom of Heaven. For I tell you that your goodness must be a far better thing than the goodness of the scribes and Pharisees before you can set foot in the kingdom of Heaven at all!

"You have heard that it was said to the people in the old days, 'Thou shalt not murder', and anyone who does so must stand his trial. But I say to you that anyone who is angry with his brother must stand his trial; anyone who contemptuously calls his brother a fool must face the supreme court; and anyone who looks down on his brother as a lost soul is himself heading straight for the fire of destruction.

"So that if, while you are offering your gift at the altar, you should remember that your brother has something against you, you must leave your gift there before the altar and go away. Make your peace with your brother first, then come and offer your gift. Come to terms quickly with your opponent at law while you are on the way

Revised Standard Version

abolish them but to fulfil them. 18 For truly, I
say to you, till heaven and earth pass away, not
an iota, not a dot, will pass from the law until all
is accomplished. 19 Whoever then relaxes one of
the least of these commandments and teaches
men so, shall be called least in the kingdom of
heaven; but he who does them and teaches them
shall be called great in the kingdom of heaven.
20 For I tell you, unless your righteousness exceeds that of the scribes and Pharisees, you will
never enter the kingdom of heaven.
21 "You have heard that it was said to the
men of old, 'You shall not kill; and whoever
kills shall be liable to judgment.' 22 But I say
to you that every one who is angry with his
brother[i] shall be liable to judgment; whoever
insults[j] his brother shall be liable to the council, and whoever says, 'You fool!' shall be liable
to the hell [k] of fire. 23 So if you are offering your
gift at the altar, and there remember that your
brother has something against you, 24 leave your
gift there before the altar and go; first be reconciled to your brother, and then come and offer
your gift. 25 Make friends quickly with your
accuser, while you are going with him to court,

[i] Other ancient authorities insert *without cause*.
[j] Greek *says Raca to* (an obscure term of abuse).
[k] Greek *Gehenna*.

Jerusalem Bible

not to abolish but to complete them. 18 I tell
you solemnly, till heaven and earth disappear,
not one dot, not one little stroke, shall disappear
from the Law until its purpose is achieved.
19 Therefore, the man who infringes even one of
the least of these commandments and teaches
others to do the same will be considered the least
in the kingdom of heaven; but the man who
keeps them and teaches them will be considered
great in the kingdom of heaven.

The new standard higher than the old

20 "For I tell you, if your virtue goes no
deeper than that of the scribes and Pharisees, you
will never get into the kingdom of heaven.
21 "You have learned how it was said to
our ancestors: *You must not kill*[y]; and if anyone does kill he must answer for it before the
court. 22 But I say this to you: anyone who is
angry with his brother will answer for it before
the court; if a man calls his brother 'Fool' [z] he
will answer for it before the Sanhedrin[a]; and if
a man calls him 'Renegade' [b] he will answer for
it in hell fire. 23 So then, if you are bringing
your offering to the altar and there remember
that your brother has something against you,
24 leave your offering there before the altar, go
and be reconciled with your brother first, and
then come back and present your offering.
25 Come to terms with your opponent in good
time while you are still on the way to the court

[y] Ex. 20:13. [z] Translating an Aramaic term of contempt. [a] The High Court at Jerusalem. [b] Apostasy was the most repulsive of all sins.

New English Bible

abolish, but to complete. I tell you this: so long as heaven and earth endure, not a letter, not a stroke, will disappear from the Law until all that must happen has happened.[a] If any man therefore sets aside even the least of the Law's demands, and teaches others to do the same, he will have the lowest place in the kingdom of Heaven, whereas anyone who keeps the Law, and teaches others so, will stand high in the kingdom of Heaven. I tell you, unless you show yourselves far better men than the Pharisees and the doctors of the law, you can never enter the kingdom of Heaven.

'You have learned that our forefathers were told, "Do not commit murder; anyone who commits murder must be brought to judgement." But what I tell you is this: Anyone who nurses anger against his brother[b] must be brought to judgement. If he abuses his brother he must answer for it to the court; if he sneers at him he will have to answer for it in the fires of hell.

'If, when you are bringing your gift to the altar, you suddenly remember that your brother has a grievance against you, leave your gift where it is before the altar. First go and make your peace with your brother, and only then come back and offer your gift.

'If someone sues you, come to terms with him promptly while you are both on your way to

[a] *Or* before all that it stands for is achieved.
[b] *Some witnesses insert* without good cause.

King James Version

way with him; lest at any time the adversary deliver thee to the judge, and the judge deliver thee to the officer, and thou be cast into prison. 26 Verily I say unto thee, Thou shalt by no means come out thence, till thou hast paid the uttermost farthing.

27 Ye have heard that it was said by them of old time, Thou shalt not commit adultery: 28 But I say unto you, That whosoever looketh on a woman to lust after her hath committed adultery with her already in his heart. 29 And if thy right eye offend thee, pluck it out, and cast *it* from thee: for it is profitable for thee that one of thy members should perish, and not *that* thy whole body should be cast into hell. 30 And if thy right hand offend thee, cut it off, and cast *it* from thee: for it is profitable for thee that one of thy members should perish, and not *that* thy whole body should be cast into hell. 31 It hath been said, Whosoever shall put away his wife, let him give her a writing of divorcement: 32 But I say unto you, That whosoever shall put away his wife, saving for the cause of fornication, causeth her to commit adultery: and whosoever shall marry her that is divorced committeth adultery.

Living Bible

court and you are thrown into a debtor's cell, 26 for you will stay there until you have paid the last penny.

27 "The laws of Moses said, 'You shall not commit adultery.' 28 But I say: Anyone who even looks at a woman with lust in his eye has already committed adultery with her in his heart. 29 So if your eye—even if it is your best[f] eye!—causes you to lust, gouge it out and throw it away. Better for part of you to be destroyed than for all of you to be cast into hell. 30 And if your hand—even your right hand—causes you to sin, cut it off and throw it away. Better that than find yourself in hell.

31 "The law of Moses says, 'If anyone wants to be rid of his wife, he can divorce her merely by giving her a letter of dismissal.' 32 But I say that a man who divorces his wife, except for fornication, causes her to commit adultery if she marries again. And he who marries her commits adultery.

[f] Literally, "your right eye."

Today's English Version

there is time, before you get to court; once you are there he will turn you over to the judge, who will hand you over to the police, and you will be put in jail. 26 There you will stay, I tell you, until you pay the last penny of your fine."

Teaching about adultery

27 "You have heard that it was said, 'Do not commit adultery.' 28 But now I tell you: anyone who looks at a woman and wants to possess her is guilty of committing adultery with her in his heart. 29 So if your right eye causes you to sin, take it out and throw it away! It is much better for you to lose a part of your body than to have your whole body thrown into hell. 30 If your right hand causes you to sin, cut it off and throw it away! It is much better for you to lose one of your limbs than to have your whole body go off to hell."

Teaching about divorce

31 "It was also said, 'Anyone who divorces his wife must give her a written notice of divorce.' 32 But now I tell you: if a man divorces his wife, and she has not been unfaithful, then he is guilty of making her commit adultery if she marries again; and the man who marries her also commits adultery."

New International Version

still with him on the way, or he may hand you over to the judge, and the judge may hand you over to the officer, and you may be thrown into prison. 26 I tell you the truth, you will not get out until you have paid the last penny.

Adultery

27 "You have heard that it was said, 'Do not commit adultery.'[t] 28 But I tell you that anyone who looks at a woman lustfully has already committed adultery with her in his heart. 29 If your right eye causes you to sin, gouge it out and throw it away. It is better for you to lose one part of your body than for your whole body to be thrown into hell. 30 And if your right hand causes you to sin, cut it off and throw it away. It is better for you to lose one part of your body than for your whole body to go into hell.

31 "It has been said, 'Anyone who divorces his wife must give her a certificate of divorce.'[u] 32 But I tell you that anyone who divorces his wife, except for marital unfaithfulness, causes her to commit adultery, and anyone who marries a woman so divorced commits adultery.

[t] Exodus 20:14. [u] Deut. 24:1.

Phillips Modern English

to court. Otherwise he may hand you over to the judge and the judge in turn hand you over to the officer of the court and you will be thrown into prison. Believe me, you will never get out again till you have paid your last farthing!

"You have heard that it was said to the people in the old days, 'Thou shalt not commit adultery.' But I say to you that every man who looks at a woman lustfully has already committed adultery with her—in his heart.

"Yes, if your right eye leads you astray pluck it out and throw it away; it is better for you to lose one of your members than that your whole body should be thrown on to the rubbish-heap.

"Yes, if your right hand leads you astray cut it off and throw it away; it is better for you to lose one of your members than that your whole body should go to the rubbish-heap.

"It also used to be said that whoever divorces his wife must give her a proper certificate of divorce. But I say to you that whoever divorces his wife except on the ground of unfaithfulness is making her an adulteress. And whoever marries the woman who has been divorced also commits adultery.

Revised Standard Version

lest your accuser hand you over to the judge, and the judge to the guard, and you be put in prison; 26 truly, I say to you, you will never get out till you have paid the last penny.
27 "You have heard that it was said, 'You shall not commit adultery.' 28 But I say to you that every one who looks at a woman lustfully has already committed adultery with her in his heart. 29 If your right eye causes you to sin, pluck it out and throw it away; it is better that you lose one of your members than that your whole body be thrown into hell.[k] 30 And if your right hand causes you to sin, cut it off and throw it away; it is better that you lose one of your members than that your whole body go into hell.[k]
31 "It was also said, 'Whoever divorces his wife, let him give her a certificate of divorce.' 32 But I say to you that every one who divorces his wife, except on the ground of unchastity, makes her an adulteress; and whoever marries a divorced woman commits adultery.

[k] Greek *Gehenna.*

Jerusalem Bible

with him, or he may hand you over to the judge and the judge to the officer, and you will be thrown into prison. 26 I tell you solemnly, you will not get out till you have paid the last penny.
27 "You have learned how it was said: *You must not commit adultery.*[c] 28 But I say this to you: if a man looks at a woman lustfully, he has already committed adultery with her in his heart. 29 If your right eye should cause you to sin, tear it out and throw it away; for it will do you less harm to lose one part of you than to have your whole body thrown into hell. 30 And if your right hand should cause you to sin, cut it off and throw it away; for it will do you less harm to lose one part of you than to have your whole body go to hell.
31 "It has also been said: *Anyone who divorces his wife must give her a writ of dismissal.*[d] 32 But I say this to you: everyone who divorces his wife, except for the case of fornication, makes her an adulteress; and anyone who marries a divorced woman commits adultery.

[c] Ex. 20:14. [d] Dt. 24:1.

New English Bible

court; otherwise he may hand you over to the judge, and the judge to the constable, and you will be put in jail. I tell you, once you are there you will not be let out till you have paid the last farthing.

'You have learned that they were told, "Do not commit adultery." But what I tell you is this: If a man looks on a woman with a lustful eye, he has already committed adultery with her in his heart.

'If your right eye is your undoing, tear it out and fling it away; it is better for you to lose one part of your body than for the whole of it to be thrown into hell. And if your right hand is your undoing, cut it off and fling it away; it is better for you to lose one part of your body than for the whole of it to go to hell.

'They were told, "A man who divorces his wife must give her a note of dismissal." But what I tell you is this: If a man divorces his wife for any cause other than unchastity he involves her in adultery; and anyone who marries a divorced woman commits adultery.

King James Version

33 Again, ye have heard that it hath been said
by them of old time, Thou shalt not forswear
thyself, but shalt perform unto the Lord thine
oaths: 34 But I say unto you, Swear not at all;
neither by heaven; for it is God's throne: 35 Nor
by the earth; for it is his footstool: neither by
Jerusalem; for it is the city of the great King.
36 Neither shalt thou swear by thy head, because
thou canst not make one hair white or black.
37 But let your communication be, Yea, yea;
Nay, nay: for whatsoever is more than these
cometh of evil.
38 Ye have heard that it hath been said, An
eye for an eye, and a tooth for a tooth: 39 But
I say unto you, That ye resist not evil: but whosoever shall smite thee on thy right cheek, turn
to him the other also. 40 And if any man will
sue thee at the law, and take away thy coat, let
him have *thy* cloak also. 41 And whosoever shall
compel thee to go a mile, go with him twain.
42 Give to him that asketh thee, and from him
that would borrow of thee turn not thou away.

Living Bible

33 "Again, the law of Moses says, 'You shall
not break your vows to God, but must fulfill
them all.' 34 But I say: Don't make any vows!
And even to say, 'By heavens!' is a sacred vow
to God, for the heavens are God's throne. 35 And
if you say 'By the earth!' it is a sacred vow, for
the earth is his footstool. And don't swear 'By
Jerusalem!' for Jerusalem is the capital of the
great King. 36 Don't even swear 'By my head!'
for you can't turn one hair white or black.
37 Say just a simple 'Yes, I will' or 'No, I won't.'
Your word is enough. To strengthen your promise with a vow shows that something is wrong.
38 "The law of Moses says, 'If a man gouges
out another's eye, he must pay with his own eye.
If a tooth gets knocked out, knock out the tooth
of the one who did it.' [g] 39 But I say: Don't resist violence! If you are slapped on one cheek,
turn the other too. 40 If you are ordered to
court, and your shirt is taken from you, give
your coat too. 41 If the military demand that you
carry their gear for a mile, carry it two. 42 Give
to those who ask, and don't turn away from
those who want to borrow.

[g] Literally, "an eye for an eye and a tooth for a tooth."

Today's English Version

Teaching about vows

33 "You have also heard that men were told
in the past, 'Do not break your promise, but do
what you have sworn to the Lord to do.' 34 But
now I tell you: do not use any vow when you
make a promise; do not swear by heaven, because it is God's throne; 35 nor by earth, because
it is the resting place for his feet; nor by Jerusalem, because it is the city of the great King.
36 Do not even swear by your head, because you
cannot make a single hair white or black. 37 Just
say 'Yes' or 'No'—anything else you have to say
comes from the Evil One."

Teaching about revenge

38 "You have heard that it was said, 'An eye
for an eye, and a tooth for a tooth.' 39 But now
I tell you: do not take revenge on someone who
does you wrong. If anyone slaps you on the right
cheek, let him slap your left cheek too. 40 And
if someone takes you to court to sue you for
your shirt, let him have your coat as well. 41 And
if one of the occupation troops forces you to
carry his pack one mile, carry it another mile.
42 When someone asks you for something, give
it to him; when someone wants to borrow something, lend it to him."

New International Version

Oaths

33 "Again, you have heard that it was said to
the people long ago, 'Do not break your oath,
but keep the oaths you have made to the Lord.'
34 But I tell you, Do not swear at all: either by
heaven, for it is God's throne; 35 or by the earth,
for it is his footstool; or by Jerusalem, for it is
the city of the great King. 36 And do not swear
by your head, for you cannot make even one
hair white or black. 37 Simply let your 'Yes' be
'Yes,' and your 'No,' 'No'; anything beyond this
comes from the evil one.

An eye for an eye

38 "You have heard that it was said, 'An eye
for an eye, and a tooth for a tooth.' [v] 39 But I
tell you, Do not resist an evil person. If someone strikes you on the right cheek, turn to him
the other also. 40 And if someone wants to sue
you and take your tunic, let him have your cloak
as well. 41 If someone forces you to go one
mile, go with him two miles. 42 Give to the one
who asks you, and do not turn away from the
one who wants to borrow from you.

[v] Exodus 21:24; Lev. 24:20; Deut. 19:21.

Phillips Modern English

"Again, you have heard that the people in the old days were told—'Thou shalt not forswear thyself, but shalt perform unto the Lord thine oaths', but I say to you, don't use an oath at all. Don't swear by Heaven for it is God's throne, nor by the earth for it is his footstool, nor by Jerusalem for it is the city of the great King. No, and don't swear by your own head, for you cannot make a single hair white or black! Whatever you have to say let your 'yes' be a plain 'yes' and your 'no' be a plain 'no'—anything more than this has a taint of evil.

"You have heard that it used to be said 'An eye for an eye and a tooth for a tooth', but I tell you, don't resist evil. If a man hits your right cheek, turn the other one to him as well. If a man wants to sue you for your coat, let him have it and your cloak as well. If anybody forces you to go a mile with him, do more—go two miles with him. Give to the man who asks anything from you, and don't turn away from the man who wants to borrow.

Revised Standard Version

33 "Again you have heard that it was said to the men of old, 'You shall not swear falsely, but shall perform to the Lord what you have sworn.' 34 But I say to you, Do not swear at all, either by heaven, for it is the throne of God, 35 or by the earth, for it is his footstool, or by Jerusalem, for it is the city of the great King. 36And do not swear by your head, for you cannot make one hair white or black. 37 Let what you say be simply 'Yes' or 'No'; anything more than this comes from evil.[l]

38 "You have heard that it was said, 'An eye for an eye and a tooth for a tooth.' 39 But I say to you, Do not resist one who is evil. But if any one strikes you on the right cheek, turn to him the other also; 40 and if any one would sue you and take your coat, let him have your cloak as well; 41 and if any one forces you to go one mile, go with him two miles. 42 Give to him who begs from you, and do not refuse him who would borrow from you.

[*l*] Or *the evil one.*

Jerusalem Bible

33 "Again, you have learned how it was said to our ancestors: *You must not break your oath, but must fulfill your oaths to the Lord.*[e] 34 But I say this to you: do not swear at all, either by *heaven,* since that is God's throne; 35 or by *the earth,* since that is *his footstool;* or by Jerusalem, since that is *the city of the great king.* 36 Do not swear by your own head either, since you cannot turn a single hair white or black. 37All you need say is 'Yes' if you mean yes, 'No' if you mean no; anything more than this comes from the evil one.

38 "You have learned how it was said: *Eye for eye and tooth for tooth.*[f] 39 But I say this to you: offer the wicked man no resistance. On the contrary, if anyone hits you on the right cheek, offer him the other as well; 40 if a man takes you to law and would have your tunic, let him have your cloak as well. 41And if anyone orders you to go one mile, go two miles with him. 42 Give to anyone who asks, and if anyone wants to borrow, do not turn away.

[*e*] Ex. 20:7. [*f*] Ex. 21:24.

New English Bible

'Again, you have learned that our forefathers were told, "Do not break your oath", and, "Oaths sworn to the Lord must be kept." But what I tell you is this: You are not to swear at all—not by heaven, for it is God's throne, nor by earth, for it is his footstool, nor by Jerusalem, for it is the city of the great King, nor by your own head, because you cannot turn one hair of it white or black. Plain "Yes" or "No" is all you need to say; anything beyond that comes from the devil.

'You have learned that they were told, "Eye for eye, tooth for tooth." But what I tell you is this: Do not set yourself against the man who wrongs you. If someone slaps you on the right cheek, turn and offer him your left. If a man wants to sue you for your shirt, let him have your coat as well. If a man in authority makes you go one mile, go with him two. Give when you are asked to give; and do not turn your back on a man who wants to borrow.

King James Version

43 Ye have heard that it hath been said, Thou
shalt love thy neighbour, and hate thine enemy.
44 But I say unto you, Love your enemies, bless
them that curse you, do good to them that hate
you, and pray for them which despitefully use
you, and persecute you; 45 That ye may be the
children of your Father which is in heaven: for
he maketh his sun to rise on the evil and on
the good, and sendeth rain on the just and on
the unjust. 46 For if ye love them which love you,
what reward have ye? do not even the publicans
the same? 47 And if ye salute your brethren only,
what do ye more *than others?* do not even the
publicans so? 48 Be ye therefore perfect, even
as your Father which is in heaven is perfect.

6 Take heed that ye do not your alms before
men, to be seen of them: otherwise ye have
no reward of your Father which is in heaven.
2 Therefore when thou doest *thine* alms, do not
sound a trumpet before thee, as the hypocrites
do in the synagogues and in the streets, that
they may have glory of men. Verily I say unto
you, They have their reward. 3 But when thou
doest alms, let not thy left hand know what thy
right hand doeth: 4 That thine alms may be in
secret: and thy Father which seeth in secret himself shall reward thee openly.

Living Bible

43 "There is a saying, 'Love your *friends* and
hate your enemies.' 44 But I say: Love your
enemies! Pray for those who *persecute* you! 45 In
that way you will be acting as true sons of your
Father in heaven. For he gives his sunlight to
both the evil and the good, and sends rain on
the just and on the unjust too. 46 If you love
only those who love you, what good is that?
Even scoundrels do that much. 47 If you are
friendly only to your friends, how are you different from anyone else? Even the heathen do
that. 48 But you are to be perfect, even as your
Father in heaven is perfect.

6 "Take care! Don't do your good deeds
publicly, to be admired, for then you will
lose the reward from your Father in heaven.
2 When you give a gift to a beggar, don't shout
about it as the hypocrites do—blowing trumpets
in the synagogues and streets to call attention
to their acts of charity! I tell you in all earnestness, they have received all the reward they will
ever get. 3 But when you do a kindness to someone, do it secretly—don't tell your left hand
what your right hand is doing. 4 And your Father
who knows all secrets will reward you.

Today's English Version

Love for enemies

43 "You have heard that it was said, 'Love
your friends, hate your enemies.' 44 But now I
tell you: love your enemies, and pray for those
who persecute you, 45 so that you will become
the sons of your Father in heaven. For he makes
his sun to shine on bad and good people alike,
and gives rain to those who do good and those
who do evil. 46 Why should God reward you if
you love only the people who love you? Even the
tax collectors do that! 47 And if you speak only
to your friends, have you done anything out of
the ordinary? Even the pagans do that! 48 You
must be perfect—just as your Father in heaven
is perfect."

Teaching about charity

6 "Be careful not to perform your religious
duties in public so that people will see what
you do. If you do these things publicly you will
not have any reward from your Father in
heaven.
2 "So when you give something to a needy
person, do not make a big show of it, as the
hypocrites do in the synagogues and on the
streets. They do it so that people will praise
them. Remember this! They have already been
paid in full. 3 But when you help a needy person, do it in such a way that even your closest
friend will not know about it, 4 but it will be
a private matter. And your Father, who sees
what you do in private, will reward you."

New International Version

Love for enemies

43 "You have heard that it was said, 'Love
your neighbor[w] and hate your enemy.' 44 But I
tell you, Love your enemies[x] and pray for those
who persecute you, 45 that you may be sons of
your Father in heaven. He causes his sun to rise
on the evil and the good, and sends rain on the
righteous and the unrighteous. 46 If you love
those who love you, what reward will you get?
Are not even the tax collectors doing that?
47 And if you greet only your brothers, what are
you doing more than others? Do not even pagans
do that? 48 Be perfect, therefore, as your heavenly Father is perfect.

Giving to the needy

6 "Be careful not to do your 'acts of righteousness' before men, to be seen by them.
If you do, you will have no reward from your
Father in heaven.
2 "So when you give to the needy, do not
announce it with trumpets, as the hypocrites do
in the synagogues and on the streets, to be
honored by men. I tell you the truth, they have
received their reward in full. 3 But when you
give to the needy, do not let your left hand know
what your right hand is doing, 4 so that your
giving may be in secret. Then your Father, who
sees what is done in secret, will reward you.

[*w*] Lev. 19:18. [*x*] Some late MSS add *bless those who curse you, do good to those who hate you.*

Phillips Modern English

"You have heard that it used to be said 'Thou shalt love thy neighbour and hate thine enemy', but I tell you, 'Love your enemies, and pray for those who persecute you,' so that you may be sons of your Heavenly Father. For he makes his sun rise upon evil men as well as good, and he sends his rain upon honest and dishonest men alike.

"For if you love only those who love you, what credit is that to you? Even tax-collectors do that! And if you exchange greetings only with your own circle, are you doing anything exceptional? Even the pagans do that much. No, you will be perfect as your Heavenly Father is perfect.

6.1 The new life is not a matter of outward show

"Beware of doing your good deeds conspicuously to catch men's eyes or you will miss the reward of your Heavenly Father.

"So, when you do good to other people, don't hire a trumpeter to go in front of you—like those play-actors in the synagogues and streets who make sure that men admire them. Believe me, they have had all the reward they are going to get! No, when you give to charity, don't even let your left hand know what your right hand is doing, so that your giving may be secret. Your Father who knows all secrets will reward you.

Revised Standard Version

43 "You have heard that it was said, 'You shall love your neighbor and hate your enemy.' 44 But I say to you, Love your enemies and pray for those who persecute you, 45 so that you may be sons of your Father who is in heaven; for he makes his sun rise on the evil and on the good, and sends rain on the just and on the unjust. 46 For if you love those who love you, what reward have you? Do not even the tax collectors do the same? 47 And if you salute only your brethren, what more are you doing than others? Do not even the Gentiles do the same? 48 You, therefore, must be perfect, as your heavenly Father is perfect.

6 "Beware of practicing your piety before men in order to be seen by them; for then you will have no reward from your Father who is in heaven.

2 "Thus, when you give alms, sound no trumpet before you, as the hypocrites do in the synagogues and in the streets, that they may be praised by men. Truly, I say to you, they have received their reward. 3 But when you give alms, do not let your left hand know what your right hand is doing, 4 so that your alms may be in secret; and your Father who sees in secret will reward you.

Jerusalem Bible

43 "You have learned how it was said: *You must love your neighbor* and hate your enemy.[g] 44 But I say this to you: love your enemies and pray for those who persecute you; 45 in this way you will be sons of your Father in heaven, for he causes his sun to rise on bad men as well as good, and his rain to fall on honest and dishonest men alike. 46 For if you love those who love you, what right have you to claim any credit? Even the tax collectors[h] do as much, do they not? 47 And if you save your greetings for your brothers, are you doing anything exceptional? Even the pagans do as much, do they not? 48 You must therefore be perfect just as your heavenly Father is perfect.

Almsgiving in secret

6 "Be careful not to parade your good deeds before men to attract their notice; by doing this you will lose all reward from your Father in heaven. 2 So when you give alms, do not have it trumpeted before you; this is what the hypocrites do in the synagogues and in the streets to win men's admiration. I tell you solemnly, they have had their reward. 3 But when you give alms, your left hand must not know what your right is doing; 4 your almsgiving must be secret, and your Father who sees all that is done in secret will reward you.

[g] The quotation is from Lv. 19:18; the second part of this commandment, not in the written Law, is an Aramaic way of saying "You do not have to love your enemy." [h] They were employed by the occupying power and this earned them popular contempt.

New English Bible

'You have learned that they were told, "Love your neighbour, hate your enemy." But what I tell you is this: Love your enemies[a] and pray for your persecutors;[b] only so can you be children of your heavenly Father, who makes his sun rise on good and bad alike, and sends the rain on the honest and the dishonest. If you love only those who love you, what reward can you expect? Surely the tax-gatherers do as much as that. And if you greet only your brothers, what is there extraordinary about that? Even the heathen do as much. There must be no limit to your goodness, as your heavenly Father's goodness knows no bounds.

6 'Be careful not to make a show of your religion before men; if you do, no reward awaits you in your Father's house in heaven.

'Thus, when you do some act of charity, do not announce it with a flourish of trumpets, as the hypocrites do in synagogue and in the streets to win admiration from men. I tell you this: they have their reward already. No; when you do some act of charity, do not let your left hand know what your right is doing; your good deed must be secret, and your Father who sees what is done in secret will reward you.[c]

[a] *Some witnesses insert* bless those who curse you, do good to those who hate you. [b] *Some witnesses insert* and those who treat you spitefully. [c] *Some witness add* openly.

King James Version

5 And when thou prayest, thou shalt not be
as the hypocrites *are:* for they love to pray
standing in the synagogues and in the corners of
the streets, that they may be seen of men. Verily
I say unto you, They have their reward. 6 But
thou, when thou prayest, enter into thy closet,
and when thou hast shut thy door, pray to thy
Father which is in secret; and thy Father which
seeth in secret shall reward thee openly. 7 But
when ye pray, use not vain repetitions, as the
heathen *do:* for they think that they shall be
heard for their much speaking. 8 Be not ye therefore like unto them: for your Father knoweth
what things ye have need of, before ye ask him.
9 After this manner therefore pray ye: Our Father
which art in heaven, Hallowed be thy name.
10 Thy kingdom come. Thy will be done in earth,
as *it is* in heaven. 11 Give us this day our daily
bread. 12 And forgive us our debts, as we forgive
our debtors. 13 And lead us not into temptation,
but deliver us from evil: For thine is the kingdom, and the power, and the glory, for ever.

Living Bible

5 "And now about prayer. When you pray,
don't be like the hypocrites who pretend piety
by praying publicly on street corners and in the
synagogues where everyone can see them. Truly,
that is all the reward they will ever get. 6 But
when you pray, go away by yourself, all alone,
and shut the door behind you and pray to your
Father secretly, and your Father, who knows
your secrets, will reward you.
7, 8 "Don't recite the same prayer over and
over as the heathen do, who think prayers are
answered only by repeating them again and again.
Remember, your Father knows exactly what you
need even before you ask him!
9 "Pray along these lines: 'Our Father in
heaven, we honor your holy name. 10 We ask
that your kingdom will come now. May your will
be done here on earth, just as it is in heaven.
11 Give us our food again today, as usual, 12 and
forgive us our sins, just as we have forgiven
those who have sinned against us. 13 Don't bring
us into temptation, but deliver us from the Evil

Today's English Version

Teaching about prayer

5 "When you pray, do not be like the hypocrites! They love to stand up and pray in the
synagogues and on the street corners so that
everyone will see them. Remember this! They
have already been paid in full. 6 But when you
pray, go to your room and close the door, and
pray to your Father, who is unseen. And your
Father, who sees what you do in private, will reward you.
7 "In your prayers do not use a lot of meaningless words, as the pagans do, who think that
God will hear them because of their long prayers. 8 Do not be like them; your Father already
knows what you need before you ask him. 9 This,
then, is how you should pray:

'Our Father in heaven:
May your holy name be honored;
10 may your Kingdom come;
may your will be done on earth as it is
in heaven.
11 Give us today the food we need.
12 Forgive us the wrongs that we have done,
as we forgive the wrongs that others
have done us.
13 Do not bring us to hard testing,
but keep us safe from the Evil One.'

New International Version

Prayer

5 "When you pray, do not be like the hypocrites, for they love to pray standing in the
synagogues and on the street corners to be seen
by men. I tell you the truth, they have received
their reward in full. 6 When you pray, go into
your room, close the door and pray to your
Father, who is unseen. Then your Father, who
sees what is done in secret, will reward you.
7 And when you pray, do not keep on babbling
like pagans, for they think they will be heard
because of their many words. 8 Do not be like
them, for your Father knows what you need
before you ask him.
9 "This is how you should pray:
'Our Father in heaven,
hallowed be your name,
10 your kingdom come,
your will be done
on earth as it is in heaven.
11 Give us today our daily bread.
12 Forgive us our debts,
as we also have forgiven our debtors.
13 And lead us not into temptation,
but deliver us from the evil one.' [y]

[y] Or *from evil.* Some late MSS add *for yours is the kingdom and the power and the glory forever. Amen.*

Phillips Modern English

"And then, when you pray, don't be like the play-actors. They love to stand and pray in the synagogues and at street-corners so that people may see them at it. Believe me, they have had all the reward they are going to get. But when you pray, go into your own room, shut your door and pray to your Father privately. Your Father who sees all private things will reward you. And when you pray don't rattle off long prayers like the pagans who think they will be heard because they use so many words. Don't be like them. For your Father knows your needs before you ask him. Pray then like this—

Our Heavenly Father, may your name be honoured;
May your kingdom come, and your will be done on earth as it is in Heaven.
Give us each day the bread we need for the day,
Forgive us what we owe to you, as we have also forgiven those who owe anything to us.
Keep us clear of temptation, and save us from evil.

Revised Standard Version

5 "And when you pray, you must not be like
the hypocrites; for they love to stand and pray
in the synagogues and at the street corners, that
they may be seen by men. Truly, I say to you,
they have received their reward. 6 But when you
pray, go into your room and shut the door and
pray to your Father who is in secret; and your
Father who sees in secret will reward you.
7 "And in praying do not heap up empty
phrases as the Gentiles do; for they think that
they will be heard for their many words. 8 Do
not be like them, for your Father knows what
you need before you ask him. 9 Pray then like
this:

Our Father who art in heaven,
Hallowed be thy name.
10 Thy kingdom come,
Thy will be done,
On earth as it is in heaven.
11 Give us this day our daily bread;[m]
12 And forgive us our debts,
As we also have forgiven our debtors;
13 And lead us not into temptation,
But deliver us from evil.[n]

[m] Or *our bread for the morrow.* [n] Or *the evil one.* Other authorities, some ancient, add, in some form, *For thine is the kingdom and the power and the glory, for ever. Amen.*

Jerusalem Bible

Prayer in secret

5 "And when you pray, do not imitate the
hypocrites: they love to say their prayers standing up in the synagogues and at the street corners for people to see them. I tell you solemnly,
they have had their reward. 6 But when you
pray, *go to your private room and, when you have shut your door, pray*[i] to your Father who
is in that secret place, and your Father who
sees all that is done in secret will reward you.

How to pray. The Lord's Prayer

7 "In your prayers do not babble as the pagans do, for they think that by using many
words they will make themselves heard. 8 Do
not be like them; your Father knows what you
need before you ask him. 9 So you should pray
like this:

"Our Father in heaven,
may your name be held holy,
10 your kingdom come,
your will be done,
on earth as in heaven.
11 Give us today our daily bread.
12 And forgive us our debts,
as we have forgiven those who are in debt to us.
13 And do not put us to the test,
but save us from the evil one.

[i] Not a direct quotation but an allusion to the practice common in the Old Testament, see 2 K. 4:33.

New English Bible

'Again, when you pray, do not be like the hypocrites; they love to say their prayers standing up in synagogue and at the street-corners, for everyone to see them. I tell you this: they have their reward already. But when you pray, go into a room by yourself, shut the door, and pray to your Father who is there in the secret place; and your Father who sees what is secret will reward you.[c]

'In your prayers do not go babbling on like the heathen, who imagine that the more they say the more likely they are to be heard. Do not imitate them. Your Father knows what your needs are before you ask him.

'This is how you should pray:

"Our Father in heaven,
thy name be hallowed;
thy kingdom come,
thy will be done,
on earth as in heaven.
Give us today our daily bread.[d]
Forgive us the wrong we have done,
as we have forgiven those who have wronged us.
And do not bring us to the test,
but save us from the evil one." [a, b]

[c] *Some witnesses add* openly. [d] *Or* our bread for the morrow. [a] *Or* from evil. [b] *Some witnesses add* For thine is the kingdom and the power and the glory, for ever. Amen.

King James Version

Amen. 14 For if ye forgive men their trespasses, your heavenly Father will also forgive you: 15 But if ye forgive not men their trespasses, neither will your Father forgive your trespasses.

16 Moreover when ye fast, be not, as the hypocrites, of a sad countenance: for they disfigure their faces, that they may appear unto men to fast. Verily I say unto you, They have their reward. 17 But thou, when thou fastest, anoint thine head, and wash thy face; 18 That thou appear not unto men to fast, but unto thy Father which is in secret: and thy Father which seeth in secret shall reward thee openly.

19 Lay not up for yourselves treasures upon earth, where moth and rust doth corrupt, and where thieves break through and steal: 20 But lay up for yourselves treasures in heaven, where neither moth nor rust doth corrupt, and where thieves do not break through nor steal: 21 For where your treasure is, there will your heart be

Living Bible

One.[a] Amen.' 14, 15 Your heavenly Father will forgive you if you forgive those who sin against you; but if *you* refuse to forgive *them, he* will not forgive *you.*

16 "And now about fasting. When you fast, declining your food for a spiritual purpose, don't do it publicly, as the hypocrites do, who try to look wan and disheveled so people will feel sorry for them. Truly, that is the only reward they will ever get. 17 But when you fast, put on festive clothing, 18 so that no one will suspect you are hungry, except your Father who knows every secret. And he will reward you.

19 "Don't store up treasures here on earth where they can erode away or may be stolen. 20 Store them in heaven where they will never lose their value, and are safe from thieves. 21 If your profits are in heaven your heart will be there too.

[a] Or, "from evil." Some manuscripts add here, "For yours is the kingdom and the power and the glory forever. Amen."

Today's English Version

14 "If you forgive others the wrongs they have done you, your Father in heaven will also forgive you. 15 But if you do not forgive the wrongs of others, then your Father in heaven will not forgive the wrongs you have done."

Teaching about fasting

16 "And when you fast, do not put on a sad face as the hypocrites do. They go around with a hungry look so that everyone will see that they are fasting. Remember this! They have already been paid in full. 17 When you go without food, wash your face and comb your hair, 18 so that others cannot know that you are fasting—only your Father, who is unseen, will know. And your Father, who sees what you do in private, will reward you."

Riches in heaven

19 "Do not save riches for yourselves here on earth, where moths and rust destroy, and robbers break in and steal. 20 Instead, save riches for yourselves in heaven, where moths and rust cannot destroy, and robbers cannot break in and steal. 21 For your heart will always be where your riches are."

New International Version

14 For if you forgive men when they sin against you, your heavenly Father will also forgive you. 15 But if you do not forgive men their sins, your Father will not forgive your sins.

Fasting

16 "When you fast, do not look somber as the hypocrites do, for they disfigure their faces to show men they are fasting. I tell you the truth, they have received their reward in full. 17 But when you fast, put oil on your head and wash your face, 18 so that it will not be obvious to men that you are fasting, but only to your Father, who is unseen; and your Father, who sees what is done in secret, will reward you.

Treasures in heaven

19 "Do not store up for yourselves treasures on earth, where moth and rust destroy, and where thieves break in and steal. 20 But store up for yourselves treasures in heaven, where moth and rust do not destroy, and where thieves do not break in and steal. 21 For where your treasure is, there your heart will be also.

Phillips Modern English

6.14 Forgiveness of fellow-man is essential

"For if you forgive other people their failures, your Heavenly Father will also forgive you. But if you will not forgive other people, neither will your Father forgive you your failures.

"Then, when you fast, don't look like those miserable play-actors! For they deliberately disfigure their faces so that people may see that they are fasting. Believe me, they have had all their reward. No, when you fast, anoint your head and wash your face so that nobody knows that you are fasting—let it be a secret between you and your Father. And your Father who knows all secrets will reward you.

6.19 Put your trust in God alone

"Don't pile up treasures on earth, where moth and rust can spoil them and thieves can break in and steal. But keep your treasure in Heaven where there is neither moth nor rust to spoil it and nobody can break in and steal. For wherever your treasure is, your heart will be there too!

Revised Standard Version

14 For if you forgive men their trespasses, your heavenly Father also will forgive you; 15 but if you do not forgive men their trespasses, neither will your Father forgive your trespasses.

16 "And when you fast, do not look dismal, like the hypocrites, for they disfigure their faces that their fasting may be seen by men. Truly, I say to you, they have received their reward. 17 But when you fast, anoint your head and wash your face, 18 that your fasting may not be seen by men but by your Father who is in secret; and your Father who sees in secret will reward you.

19 "Do not lay up for yourselves treasures on earth, where moth and rust[o] consume and where thieves break in and steal, 20 but lay up for yourselves treasures in heaven, where neither moth nor rust[o] consumes and where thieves do not break in and steal. 21 For where your treasure is, there will your heart be also.

[o] Or *worm*.

Jerusalem Bible

14 Yes, if you forgive others their failings, your heavenly Father will forgive you yours; 15 but if you do not forgive others, your Father will not forgive your failings either.

Fasting in secret

16 "When you fast do not put on a gloomy look as the hypocrites do: they pull long faces to let men know they are fasting. I tell you solemnly, they have had their reward. 17 But when you fast, put oil on your head and wash your face, 18 so that no one will know you are fasting except your Father who sees all that is done in secret; and your Father who sees all that is done in secret will reward you.

True treasures

19 "Do not store up treasures for yourselves on earth, where moths and woodworms destroy them and thieves can break in and steal. 20 But store up treasures for yourselves in heaven, where neither moth nor woodworms destroy them and thieves cannot break in and steal. 21 For where your treasure is, there will your heart be also.

New English Bible

For if you forgive others the wrongs they have done, your heavenly Father will also forgive you; but if you do not forgive others, then the wrongs you have done will not be forgiven by your Father.

'So too when you fast, do not look gloomy like the hypocrites: they make their faces unsightly so that other people may see that they are fasting. I tell you this: they have their reward already. But when you fast, anoint your head and wash your face, so that men may not see that you are fasting, but only your Father who is in the secret place; and your Father who sees what is secret will give you your reward.

'Do not store up for yourselves treasure on earth, where it grows rusty and moth-eaten, and thieves break in to steal it. Store up treasure in heaven, where there is no moth and no rust to spoil it, no thieves to break in and steal. For where your treasure is, there will your heart be also.

King James Version

also. 22 The light of the body is the eye: if
therefore thine eye be single, thy whole body
shall be full of light. 23 But if thine eye be evil,
thy whole body shall be full of darkness. If
therefore the light that is in thee be darkness,
how great *is* that darkness!
24 No man can serve two masters: for either
he will hate the one, and love the other; or else
he will hold to the one, and despise the other.
Ye cannot serve God and mammon. 25 Therefore I say unto you, Take no thought for your
life, what ye shall eat, or what ye shall drink; nor
yet for your body, what ye shall put on. Is not
the life more than meat, and the body than raiment? 26 Behold the fowls of the air: for they
sow not, neither do they reap, nor gather into
barns; yet your heavenly Father feedeth them.
Are ye not much better than they? 27 Which of
you by taking thought can add one cubit unto
his stature? 28 And why take ye thought for raiment? Consider the lilies of the field, how they
grow; they toil not, neither do they spin: 29 And
yet I say unto you, That even Solomon in all

Living Bible

22 "If your eye is pure, there will be sunshine
in your soul. 23 But if your eye is clouded with
evil thoughts and desires, you are in deep spiritual darkness. And oh, how deep that darkness
can be!
24 "You cannot serve two masters: God and
money. For you will hate one and love the other,
or else the other way around.
25 "So my counsel is: Don't worry about
things—food, drink, and clothes. For you already have life and a body—and they are far
more important than what to eat and wear.
26 Look at the birds! They don't worry about
what to eat—they don't need to sow or reap or
store up food—for your heavenly Father feeds
them. And you are far more valuable to him
than they are. 27 Will all your worries add a
single moment to your life?
28 "And why worry about your clothes? Look
at the field lilies! They don't worry about theirs.
29 Yet King Solomon in all his glory was not

Today's English Version

The light of the body

22 "The eyes are like a lamp for the body. If
your eyes are clear, your whole body will be full
of light; 23 but if your eyes are bad, your body
will be in darkness. So if the light in you is
darkness, how terribly dark it will be!"

God and possessions

24 "No one can be a slave to two masters; he
will hate one and love the other; he will be loyal
to one and despise the other. You cannot serve
both God and money.
25 "This is why I tell you: do not be worried
about the food and drink you need to stay alive,
or about clothes for your body. After all, isn't
life worth more than food? And isn't the body
worth more than clothes? 26 Look at the birds
flying around: they do not plant seeds, gather a
harvest, and put it in barns; your Father in
heaven takes care of them! Aren't you worth
much more than birds? 27 Which one of you can
live a few more years by worrying about it?
28 "And why worry about clothes? Look how
the wild flowers grow: they do not work or make
clothes for themselves. 29 But I tell you that not

New International Version

22 "The eye is the lamp of the body. If your
eyes are good, your whole body will be full of
light. 23 But if your eyes are bad, your whole
body will be full of darkness. If then the light
within you is darkness, how great is that darkness!
24 "No one can serve two masters. Either he
will hate the one and love the other, or he will
be devoted to the one and despise the other.
You cannot serve both God and Money.

Do not worry

25 "Therefore I tell you, do not worry about
your life, what you will eat or drink; or about
your body, what you will wear. Is not life more
important than food, and the body more important than clothes? 26 Look at the birds of
the air; they do not sow or reap or store away
in barns, and yet your heavenly Father feeds
them. Are you not much more valuable than
they? 27 Who of you by worrying can add a
single hour to his life? [z]
28 "And why do you worry about clothes?
See how the lilies of the field grow. They do
not labor or spin. 29 Yet I tell you that not

[z] Or *single cubit to his height.*

Phillips Modern English

"The lamp of the body is the eye. If your eye is sound, your whole body will be full of light. But if your eye is evil, your whole body will be full of darkness. If all the light you have is darkness, it is dark indeed!

"No one can fully serve two masters. He is bound to hate one and love the other, or be loyal to one and despise the other. You cannot serve both God and the power of money. That is why I say to you, don't worry about living—wondering what you are going to eat or drink, or what you are going to wear. Surely life is more important than food, and the body more important than the clothes you wear. Look at the birds in the sky. They never sow nor reap nor store away in barns, and yet your Heavenly Father feeds them. Aren't you much more valuable to him than they are? Can any of you, however much he worries, make himself even a few inches taller? And why do you worry about clothes? Consider how the wild flowers grow. They neither work nor weave, but I tell you that even Solomon in all his glory was not ar-

Revised Standard Version

22 "The eye is the lamp of the body. So, if
your eye is sound, your whole body will be full
of light; 23 but if your eye is not sound, your
whole body will be full of darkness. If then the
light in you is darkness, how great is the darkness!
24 "No one can serve two masters; for either
he will hate the one and love the other, or he
will be devoted to the one and despise the other.
You cannot serve God and mammon.[x]
25 "Therefore I tell you, do not be anxious
about your life, what you shall eat or what you
shall drink, nor about your body, what you shall
put on. Is not life more than food, and the body
more than clothing? 26 Look at the birds of the
air: they neither sow nor reap nor gather into
barns, and yet your heavenly Father feeds them.
Are you not of more value than they? 27 And
which of you by being anxious can add one
cubit to his span of life?[p] 28 And why are you
anxious about clothing? Consider the lilies of
the field, how they grow; they neither toil nor
spin; 29 yet I tell you, even Solomon in all his

[x] *Mammon* is a Semitic word for money or riches.
[p] Or *to his stature*.

Jerusalem Bible

The eye, the lamp of the body

22 "The lamp of the body is the eye. It follows that if your eye is sound, your whole body
will be filled with light. 23 But if your eye is
diseased, your whole body will be all darkness.
If then, the light inside you is darkness, what
darkness that will be!

God and money

24 "No one can be the slave of two masters:
he will either hate the first and love the second,
or treat the first with respect and the second
with scorn. You cannot be the slave both of
God and of money.

Trust in Providence

25 "That is why I am telling you not to worry
about your life and what you are to eat, nor
about your body and how you are to clothe it.
Surely life means more than food, and the body
more than clothing! 26 Look at the birds in the
sky. They do not sow or reap or gather into
barns; yet your heavenly Father feeds them.
Are you not worth much more than they are?
27 Can any of you, for all his worrying, add
one single cubit to his span of life? 28 And why
worry about clothing? Think of the flowers
growing in the fields; they never have to work
or spin; 29 yet I assure you that not even Solo-

New English Bible

'The lamp of the body is the eye. If your eyes are sound, you will have light for your whole body; if the eyes are bad, your whole body will be in darkness. If then the only light you have is darkness, the darkness is doubly dark.

'No servant can be the slave of two masters; for either he will hate the first and love the second, or he will be devoted to the first and think nothing of the second. You cannot serve God and Money.

'Therefore I bid you put away anxious thoughts about food and drink to keep you alive, and clothes to cover your body. Surely life is more than food, the body more than clothes. Look at the birds of the air; they do not sow and reap and store in barns, yet your heavenly Father feeds them. You are worth more than the birds! Is there a man of you who by anxious thought can add a foot to his height[c]? And why be anxious about clothes? Consider how the lilies grow in the fields; they do not work, they do not spin;[d] and yet, I tell you, even Solomon in all his

[c] *Or* a day to his life. [d] *One witness reads* Consider the lilies: they neither card nor spin, nor labour.

King James Version

his glory was not arrayed like one of these. 30 Wherefore, if God so clothe the grass of the field, which to day is, and to morrow is cast into the oven, *shall he* not much more *clothe* you, O ye of little faith? 31 Therefore take no thought, saying, What shall we eat? or, What shall we drink? or, Wherewithal shall we be clothed? 32 (For after all these things do the Gentiles seek:) for your heavenly Father knoweth that ye have need of all these things. 33 But seek ye first the kingdom of God, and his righteousness; and all these things shall be added unto you. 34 Take therefore no thought for the morrow: for the morrow shall take thought for the things of itself. Sufficient unto the day *is* the evil thereof.

7 Judge not, that ye be not judged. 2 For with what judgment ye judge, ye shall be judged: and with what measure ye mete, it shall be measured to you again. 3 And why beholdest thou the mote that is in thy brother's eye, but considerest not the beam that is in thine own eye? 4 Or how wilt thou say to thy brother, Let me pull out the mote out of thine eye; and, behold, a beam *is* in thine own eye? 5 Thou hypocrite, first cast out the beam out of thine own eye; and then shalt thou see clearly to cast out the mote out of thy brother's eye.

Living Bible

clothed as beautifully as they. 30 And if God cares so wonderfully for flowers that are here today and gone tomorrow, won't he more surely care for you, O men of little faith?

31, 32 "So don't worry at all about having enough food and clothing. Why be like the heathen? For they take pride in all these things and are deeply concerned about them. But your heavenly Father already knows perfectly well that you need them, 33 and he will give them to you if you give him first place in your life and live as he wants you to.

34 "So don't be anxious about tomorrow. God will take care of your tomorrow too. Live one day at a time.[b]

7 "Don't criticize, and then you won't be criticized. 2 For others will treat you as you treat them. 3 And why worry about a speck in the eye of a brother when you have a board in your own? 4 Should you say, 'Friend, let me help you get that speck out of your eye,' when you can't even see because of the board in your own? 5 Hypocrite! First get rid of the board. Then you can see to help your brother.

[*b*] Literally, "sufficient unto the day is the evil thereof."

Today's English Version

even Solomon, as rich as he was, had clothes as beautiful as one of these flowers. 30 It is God who clothes the wild grass—grass that is here today, gone tomorrow, burned up in the oven. Won't he be all the more sure to clothe you? How little faith you have! 31 So do not start worrying: 'Where will my food come from? or my drink? or my clothes?' 32 (These are the things the heathen are always concerned about.) Your Father in heaven knows that you need all these things. 33 Instead, be concerned above everything else with his Kingdom and with what he requires, and he will provide you with all these other things. 34 So do not worry about tomorrow; it will have enough worries of its own. There is no need to add to the troubles each day brings."

Judging others

7 "Do not judge others, so that God will not judge you—2 because God will judge you in the same way you judge others, and he will apply to you the same rules you apply to others. 3 Why, then, do you look at the speck in your brother's eye, and pay no attention to the log in your own eye? 4 How dare you say to your brother, 'Please, let me take that speck out of your eye,' when you have a log in your own eye? 5 You hypocrite! Take the log out of your own eye first, and then you will be able to see and take the speck out of your brother's eye.

New International Version

even Solomon in all his splendor was dressed like one of these. 30 If that is how God clothes the grass of the field, which is here today and tomorrow is thrown into the fire, will he not much more clothe you, O you of little faith? 31 So do not worry, saying, 'What shall we eat?' or 'What shall we drink?' or 'What shall we wear?' 32 For the pagans run after all these things, and your heavenly Father knows that you need them. 33 But seek first his kingdom and his righteousness, and all these things will be given to you as well. 34 Therefore do not worry about tomorrow, for tomorrow will worry about itself. Each day has enough trouble of its own.

Judging others

7 "Do not judge, or you too will be judged. 2 For in the same way you judge others, you will be judged, and with the measure you use, it will be measured to you.

3 "Why do you look at the speck of sawdust in your brother's eye and pay no attention to the plank in your own eye? 4 How can you say to your brother, 'Let me take the speck out of your eye,' when all the time there is a plank in your own eye? 5 You hypocrite, first take the plank out of your own eye, and then you will see clearly to remove the speck from your brother's eye.

Phillips Modern English

rayed like one of these! Now if God so clothes the flowers of the field, which are alive today and burnt in the stove tomorrow, is he not much more likely to clothe you, you 'little-faiths'?

"So don't worry and don't keep saying, 'What shall we eat, what shall we drink or what shall we wear?' That is what pagans are always looking for; your Heavenly Father knows that you need them all. Set your heart first on his kingdom and his goodness, and all these things will come to you as a matter of course.

"Don't worry at all then about tomorrow. Tomorrow can worry about itself! One day's trouble is enough for one day.

7.1 The common sense behind right behaviour

"Don't criticise people, and you will not be criticised. For you will be judged by the way you criticise others, and the measure you give will be the measure you receive.

"Why do you look at the speck of sawdust in your brother's eye and fail to notice the plank in your own? How can you say to your brother, 'Let me get the speck out of your eye', when there is a plank in your own? You hypocrite! Take the plank out of your own eye first, and then you can see clearly enough to remove your brother's speck of dust.

Revised Standard Version

glory was not arrayed like one of these. 30 But
if God so clothes the grass of the field, which
today is alive and tomorrow is thrown into the
oven, will he not much more clothe you, O men
of little faith? 31 Therefore do not be anxious,
saying, 'What shall we eat?' or 'What shall we
drink?' or 'What shall we wear?' 32 For the Gentiles seek all these things; and your heavenly
Father knows that you need them all. 33 But seek
first his kingdom and his righteousness, and all
these things shall be yours as well.

34 "Therefore do not be anxious about tomorrow, for tomorrow will be anxious for itself. Let
the day's own trouble be sufficient for the day.

7 "Judge not, that you be not judged. 2 For
with the judgment you pronounce you will
be judged, and the measure you give will be the
measure you get. 3 Why do you see the speck
that is in your brother's eye, but do not notice
the log that is in your own eye? 4 Or how can
you say to your brother, 'Let me take the speck
out of your eye,' when there is the log in your
own eye? 5 You hypocrite, first take the log out
of your own eye, and then you will see clearly
to take the speck out of your brother's eye.

Jerusalem Bible

mon in all his regalia was robed like one of
these. 30 Now if that is how God clothes the
grass in the field which is there today and
thrown into the furnace tomorrow, will he not
much more look after you, you men of little
faith? 31 So do not worry; do not say, 'What
are we to eat? What are we to drink? How are
we to be clothed?' 32 It is the pagans who set
their hearts on all these things. Your heavenly
Father knows you need them all. 33 Set your
hearts on his kingdom first, and on his righteousness, and all these other things will be given you
as well. 34 So do not worry about tomorrow:
tomorrow will take care of itself. Each day has
enough trouble of its own.

Do not judge

7 "Do not judge, and you will not be judged;
2 because the judgments you give are the
judgments you will get, and the amount you
measure out is the amount you will be given.
3 Why do you observe the splinter in your
brother's eye and never notice the plank in your
own? 4 How dare you say to your brother, 'Let
me take the splinter out of your eye,' when all
the time there is a plank in your own? 5 Hypocrite! Take the plank out of your own eye first,
and then you will see clearly enough to take
the splinter out of your brother's eye.

New English Bible

splendour was not attired like one of these. But if that is how God clothes the grass in the fields, which is there today, and tomorrow is thrown on the stove, will he not all the more clothe you? How little faith you have! No, do not ask anxiously, "What are we to eat? What are we to drink? What shall we wear?" All these are things for the heathen to run after, not for you, because your heavenly Father knows that you need them all. Set your mind on God's kingdom and his justice before everything else, and all the rest will come to you as well. So do not be anxious about tomorrow; tomorrow will look after itself. Each day has troubles enough of its own.

7 'Pass no judgement, and you will not be judged. For as you judge others, so you will yourselves be judged, and whatever measure you deal out to others will be dealt back to you. Why do you look at the speck of sawdust in your brother's eye, with never a thought for the great plank in your own? Or how can you say to your brother, "Let me take the speck out of your eye", when all the time there is that plank in your own? You hypocrite! First take the plank out of your own eye, and then you will see clearly to take the speck out of your brother's.

King James Version

6 Give not that which is holy unto the dogs,
neither cast ye your pearls before swine, lest
they trample them under their feet, and turn
again and rend you.
7 Ask, and it shall be given you; seek, and ye
shall find; knock, and it shall be opened unto
you: 8 For every one that asketh receiveth; and
he that seeketh findeth; and to him that knocketh it shall be opened. 9 Or what man is there
of you, whom if his son ask bread, will he give
him a stone? 10 Or if he ask a fish, will he give
him a serpent? 11 If ye then, being evil, know
how to give good gifts unto your children, how
much more shall your Father which is in heaven
give good things to them that ask him? 12 Therefore all things whatsoever ye would that men
should do to you, do ye even so to them: for
this is the law and the prophets.

Living Bible

6 "Don't give holy things to depraved men.
Don't give pearls to swine! They will trample the
pearls and turn and attack you.
7 "Ask, and you will be given what you ask
for. Seek, and you will find. Knock, and the
door will be opened. 8 For everyone who asks,
receives. Anyone who seeks, finds. If only you
will knock, the door will open. 9 If a child asks
his father for a loaf of bread, will he be given a
stone instead? 10 If he asks for fish, will he be
given a poisonous snake? Of course not! 11 And
if you hardhearted, sinful men know how to give
good gifts to your children, won't your Father in
heaven even more certainly give good gifts to
those who ask him for them?
12 "Do for others what you want them to do
for you. This is the teaching of the laws of
Moses in a nutshell.[a]

[a] Literally, "this is the law and the prophets."

Today's English Version

6 "Do not give what is holy to dogs—they
will only turn and attack you; do not throw your
pearls in front of pigs—they will only trample
them underfoot."

Ask, seek, knock

7 "Ask, and you will receive; seek, and you
will find; knock, and the door will be opened to
you. 8 For everyone who asks will receive, and
he who seeks will find, and the door will be
opened to him who knocks. 9 Would any of you
who are fathers give your son a stone, when he
asks you for bread? 10 Or would you give him a
snake, when he asks you for fish? 11 As bad as
you are, you know how to give good things to
your children. How much more, then, your Father in heaven will give good things to those who
ask him!
12 "Do for others what you want them to do
for you: this is the meaning of the Law of Moses
and the teaching of the prophets."

New International Version

6 "Do not give dogs what is sacred; do not
throw your pearls to pigs. If you do, they may
trample them under their feet, and then turn
and tear you to pieces.

Ask, seek, knock

7 "Ask and it will be given to you; seek and
you will find; knock and the door will be
opened to you. 8 For everyone who asks receives; he who seeks finds; and to him who
knocks, the door will be opened.
9 "Which of you, if his son asks for bread,
will give him a stone? 10 Or if he asks for a fish,
will give him a snake? 11 If you, then, though
you are evil, know how to give good gifts to
your children, how much more will your Father
in heaven give good gifts to those who ask him!
12 In everything do to others what you would
have them do to you, for this sums up the Law
and the Prophets.

Phillips Modern English

"You must not give holy things to dogs, nor must you throw your pearls before pigs—or they may trample them underfoot and turn and attack you.

"Ask and it will be given to you. Search and you will find. Knock and the door will be opened for you. The one who asks will always receive; the one who is searching will always find, and the door is opened to the man who knocks.

"If any of you were asked by his son for bread would you give him a stone, or if he asks for a fish would you give him a snake? If you then, for all your evil, quite naturally give good things to your children, how much more likely is it that your Heavenly Father will give good things to those who ask him?

"Treat other people exactly as you would like to be treated by them—this is the meaning of the Law and the Prophets.

Revised Standard Version

6 "Do not give dogs what is holy; and do
not throw your pearls before swine, lest they
trample them under foot and turn to attack you.
7 "Ask, and it will be given you; seek, and
you will find; knock, and it will be opened to
you. 8 For every one who asks receives, and he
who seeks finds, and to him who knocks it will
be opened. 9 Or what man of you, if his son
asks him for bread, will give him a stone? 10 Or
if he asks for a fish, will give him a serpent?
11 If you then, who are evil, know how to give
good gifts to your children, how much more will
your Father who is in heaven give good things
to those who ask him! 12 So whatever you wish
that men would do to you, do so to them; for
this is the law and the prophets.

Jerusalem Bible

Do not profane sacred things

6 "Do not give dogs what is holy[j]; and do
not throw your pearls in front of pigs, or they
may trample them and then turn on you and
tear you to pieces.

Effective prayer

7 "Ask, and it will be given to you; search,
and you will find; knock, and the door will be
opened to you. 8 For the one who asks always
receives; the one who searches always finds; the
one who knocks will always have the door
opened to him. 9 Is there a man among you who
would hand his son a stone when he asked for
bread? 10 Or would hand him a snake when he
asked for a fish? 11 If you, then, who are evil,
know how to give your children what is good,
how much more will your Father in heaven give
good things to those who ask him!

The golden rule

12 "So always treat others as you would like
them to treat you; that is the meaning of the
Law and the Prophets.

[j] The meat of animals which have been offered in sacrifice in the Temple; the application is to the parading of holy beliefs and practices in front of those who cannot understand them.

New English Bible

'Do not give dogs what is holy; do not throw your pearls to the pigs: they will only trample on them, and turn and tear you to pieces.

'Ask, and you will receive; seek, and you will find; knock, and the door will be opened. For everyone who asks receives, he who seeks finds, and to him who knocks, the door will be opened.

'Is there a man among you who will offer his son a stone when he asks for bread, or a snake when he asks for fish? If you, then, bad as you are, know how to give your children what is good for them, how much more will your heavenly Father give good things to those who ask him!

'Always treat others as you would like them to treat you: that is the Law and the prophets.

King James Version

13 Enter ye in at the strait gate: for wide *is*
the gate, and broad *is* the way, that leadeth to
destruction, and many there be which go in
thereat: 14 Because strait *is* the gate, and narrow *is* the way, which leadeth unto life, and
few there be that find it.
15 Beware of false prophets, which come to
you in sheep's clothing, but inwardly they are
ravening wolves. 16 Ye shall know them by their
fruits. Do men gather grapes of thorns, or figs
of thistles? 17 Even so every good tree bringeth
forth good fruit; but a corrupt tree bringeth
forth evil fruit. 18A good tree cannot bring forth
evil fruit, neither *can* a corrupt tree bring forth
good fruit. 19 Every tree that bringeth not forth
good fruit is hewn down, and cast into the fire.
20 Wherefore by their fruits ye shall know them.
21 Not every one that saith unto me, Lord,
Lord, shall enter into the kingdom of heaven;
but he that doeth the will of my Father which
is in heaven. 22 Many will say to me in that day,
Lord, Lord, have we not prophesied in thy
name? and in thy name have cast out devils?
and in thy name done many wonderful works?

Living Bible

13 "Heaven can be entered only through the
narrow gate! The highway to hell [b] is broad, and
its gate is wide enough for all the multitudes
who choose its easy way. 14 But the Gateway to
Life is small, and the road is narrow, and only
a few ever find it.
15 "Beware of false teachers who come disguised as harmless sheep, but are wolves and
will tear you apart. 16 You can detect them by
the way they act, just as you can identify a tree
by its fruit. You need never confuse grapevines
with thorn bushes or figs with thistles. 17 Different kinds of fruit trees can quickly be identified
by examining their fruit. 18A variety that produces delicious fruit never produces an inedible
kind. And a tree producing an inedible kind
can't produce what is good. 19 So the trees having the inedible fruit are chopped down and
thrown on the fire. 20 Yes, the way to identify a
tree or a person[c] is by the kind of fruit produced.
21 "Not all who sound religious are really
godly people. They may refer to me as 'Lord,'
but still won't get to heaven. For the decisive
question is whether they obey my Father in
heaven. 22At the Judgment[d] many will tell me,
'Lord, Lord, we told others about you and used
your name to cast out demons and to do many

[*b*] Literally, "the way that leads to destruction." [*c*] Implied. [*d*] Literally, "in that day."

Today's English Version

The narrow gate

13 "Go in through the narrow gate, because
the gate is wide and the road is easy that leads
to hell, and there are many who travel it. 14 The
gate is narrow and the way is hard that leads to
life, and few people find it."

A tree and its fruit

15 "Watch out for false prophets; they come
to you looking like sheep on the outside, but
they are really like wild wolves on the inside.
16 You will know them by the way they act.
Thorn bushes do not bear grapes, and briers do
not bear figs. 17A healthy tree bears good fruit,
while a poor tree bears bad fruit. 18A healthy
tree cannot bear bad fruit, and a poor tree cannot bear good fruit. 19Any tree that does not
bear good fruit is cut down and thrown in the
fire. 20 So, then, you will know the false prophets
by the way they act."

I never knew you

21 "Not everyone who calls me 'Lord, Lord,'
will enter into the Kingdom of heaven, but only
those who do what my Father in heaven wants
them to do. 22 When that Day comes, many will
say to me, 'Lord, Lord! In your name we spoke
God's message, by your name we drove out
many demons and performed many miracles!'

New International Version

The narrow and wide gates

13 "Enter through the narrow gate. For wide
is the gate and broad is the road that leads to
destruction, and many enter through it. 14 But
small is the gate and narrow the road that leads
to life, and only a few find it.

A tree and its fruit

15 "Watch out for false prophets. They come
to you in sheep's clothing, but inwardly they are
ferocious wolves. 16 By their fruit you will recognize them. Do people pick grapes from thorn-
bushes, or figs from thistles? 17 Likewise every
good tree bears good fruit, but a bad tree bears
bad fruit. 18A good tree cannot bear bad fruit,
and a bad tree cannot bear good fruit. 19 Every
tree that does not bear good fruit is cut down
and thrown into the fire. 20 Thus, by their fruit
you will recognize them.
21 "Not everyone who says to me, 'Lord,
Lord,' will enter the kingdom of heaven, but
only he who does the will of my Father who is
in heaven. 22 Many will say to me on that day,
'Lord, Lord, did we not prophesy in your name,
and in your name drive out demons and per-

Phillips Modern English

"Go in by the narrow gate. For the wide gate has a broad road which leads to disaster and there are many people going that way. The narrow gate and the hard road lead out into life and only a few are finding it.

7.15 Living, not professing, is what matters

"Be on your guard against false religious teachers, who come to you dressed up as sheep but are really greedy wolves. You can tell them by their fruits. Do you pick a bunch of grapes from a thorn-bush or figs from a clump of thistles? Every good tree produces sound fruit, but a rotten tree produces bad fruit. A good tree cannot produce bad fruit, and a rotten tree cannot produce good fruit. The tree that fails to produce good fruit is cut down and burnt. So you may know the quality of men by what they produce.

"It is not everyone who keeps saying to me 'Lord, Lord' who will enter the kingdom of Heaven, but the man who actually does my Heavenly Father's will.

"In 'that day' many will say to me, 'Lord, Lord, didn't we preach in your name, didn't we cast out devils in your name, and do many great

Revised Standard Version

13 "Enter by the narrow gate; for the gate is wide and the way is easy,[q] that leads to destruction, and those who enter by it are many.
14 For the gate is narrow and the way is hard, that leads to life, and those who find it are few.

15 "Beware of false prophets, who come to you in sheep's clothing but inwardly are ravenous wolves.
16 You will know them by their fruits. Are grapes gathered from thorns, or figs from thistles?
17 So, every sound tree bears good fruit, but the bad tree bears evil fruit.
18 A sound tree cannot bear evil fruit, nor can a bad tree bear good fruit.
19 Every tree that does not bear good fruit is cut down and thrown into the fire.
20 Thus you will know them by their fruits.

21 "Not every one who says to me, 'Lord, Lord,' shall enter the kingdom of heaven, but he who does the will of my Father who is in heaven.
22 On that day many will say to me, 'Lord, Lord, did we not prophesy in your name, and cast out demons in your name, and do many

[q] Other ancient authorities read *for the way is wide and easy.*

Jerusalem Bible

The two ways

13 "Enter by the narrow gate, since the road that leads to perdition is wide and spacious, and many take it;
14 but it is a narrow gate and a hard road that leads to life, and only a few find it.

False prophets

15 "Beware of false prophets[k] who come to you disguised as sheep but underneath are ravenous wolves.
16 You will be able to tell them by their fruits. Can people pick grapes from thorns, or figs from thistles?
17 In the same way, a sound tree produces good fruit but a rotten tree bad fruit.
18 A sound tree cannot bear bad fruit, nor a rotten tree bear good fruit.
19 Any tree that does not produce good fruit is cut down and thrown on the fire.
20 I repeat, you will be able to tell them by their fruits.

The true disciple

21 "It is not those who say to me, 'Lord, Lord,' who will enter the kingdom of heaven, but the person who does the will of my Father in heaven.
22 When the day[l] comes many will say to me, 'Lord, Lord, did we not prophesy in your name, cast out demons in your name, work

[k] Lying teachers of religion. [l] The day of Judgment.

New English Bible

'Enter by the narrow gate. The gate is wide that leads to perdition, there is plenty of room on the road,[a] and many go that way; but the gate that leads to life is small and the road is narrow,[b] and those who find it are few.

'Beware of false prophets, men who come to you dressed up as sheep while underneath they are savage wolves. You will recognize them by the fruits they bear. Can grapes be picked from briars, or figs from thistles? In the same way, a good tree always yields good fruit, and a poor tree bad fruit. A good tree cannot bear bad fruit, or a poor tree good fruit. And when a tree does not yield good fruit it is cut down and burnt. That is why I say you will recognize them by their fruits.

'Not everyone who calls me "Lord, Lord" will enter the kingdom of Heaven, but only those who do the will of my heavenly Father. When that day comes, many will say to me, "Lord, Lord, did we not prophesy in your name, cast out devils in your name, and in your name per-

[a] *Some witnesses read* The road that leads to perdition is wide with plenty of room. [b] *Some witnesses read* but the road that leads to life is small and narrow.

King James Version

23And then will I profess unto them, I never knew you: depart from me, ye that work iniquity.
24 Therefore whosoever heareth these sayings of mine, and doeth them, I will liken him unto a wise man, which built his house upon a rock:
25And the rain descended, and the floods came, and the winds blew, and beat upon that house; and it fell not: for it was founded upon a rock.
26And every one that heareth these sayings of mine, and doeth them not, shall be likened unto a foolish man, which built his house upon the
sand: 27And the rain descended, and the floods came, and the winds blew, and beat upon that house; and it fell: and great was the fall of it.
28And it came to pass, when Jesus had ended these sayings, the people were astonished at his doctrine: 29 For he taught them as *one* having authority, and not as the scribes.

Living Bible

other great miracles.' 23 But I will reply, 'You have never been mine.[e] Go away, for your deeds are evil.'

24 "All who listen to my instructions and follow them are wise, like a man who builds his house on solid rock. 25 Though the rain comes in torrents, and the floods rise and the storm winds beat against his house, it won't collapse, for it is built on rock.

26 "But those who hear my instructions and ignore them are foolish, like a man who builds his house on sand. 27 For when the rains and floods come, and storm winds beat against his house, it will fall with a mighty crash." 28 The crowds were amazed at Jesus' sermons, 29 for he taught as one who had great authority, and not as their Jewish leaders.[f]

[*e*] Literally, "I never knew you." [*f*] Literally, "not as the scribes." These leaders only quoted others, and did not presume to present any fresh revelation.

Today's English Version

23 Then I will say to them, 'I never knew you. Away from me, you evildoers!'"

The two house builders

24 "So then, everyone who hears these words of mine and obeys them will be like a wise man who built his house on the rock. 25 The rain poured down, the rivers flooded over, and the winds blew hard against that house. But it did not fall, because it had been built on the rock.
26 "But everyone who hears these words of mine and does not obey them will be like a foolish man who built his house on the sand.
27 The rain poured down, the rivers flooded over, the winds blew hard against that house, and it fell. What a terrible fall that was!"

The authority of Jesus

28 Jesus finished saying these things, and the crowd was amazed at the way he taught. 29 He wasn't like their teachers of the Law; instead, he taught with authority.

New International Version

form many miracles?' 23 Then I will tell them plainly, 'I never knew you. Away from me, you evildoers!'

The wise and foolish builders

24 "Therefore, everyone who hears these words of mine and puts them into practice is like a wise man who built his house on the rock.
25 The rain came down, the streams rose, and the winds blew and beat against that house; yet it did not fall, because it had its foundation on the rock. 26 But everyone who hears these words of mine and does not put them into practice is like a foolish man who built his house on sand.
27 The rain came down, the streams rose, and the winds blew and beat against that house, and it fell with a great crash."
28 When Jesus had finished saying these things, the crowds were amazed at his teaching,
29 because he taught as one who had authority, and not as their teachers of the law.

Phillips Modern English

things in your name?' Then I shall tell them plainly, 'I have never known you. Go away from me, you have worked on the side of evil!'

7.24 To follow Christ's teaching means the only real security

"Everyone then who hears these words of mine and puts them into practice is like a sensible man who builds his house on rock. Down came the rain and up came the floods, while the winds blew and roared upon that house—and it did not fall because its foundations were on rock.

"And everyone who hears these words of mine and does not follow them can be compared with a foolish man who built his house on sand. Down came the rain and up came the floods, while the winds blew and battered that house till it collapsed, and fell with a great crash."

When Jesus had finished these words the crowd were astonished at the power behind his teaching. For his words had the ring of authority, quite unlike those of their scribes.

Revised Standard Version

mighty works in your name?' 23And then will I
declare to them, 'I never knew you; depart from
me, you evildoers.'
24 "Every one then who hears these words of
mine and does them will be like a wise man who
built his house upon the rock; 25 and the rain
fell, and the floods came, and the winds blew
and beat upon that house, but it did not fall,
because it had been founded on the rock. 26And
every one who hears these words of mine and
does not do them will be like a foolish man who
built his house upon the sand; 27 and the rain
fell, and the floods came, and the winds blew
and beat against that house, and it fell; and
great was the fall of it."
28 And when Jesus finished these sayings, the
crowds were astonished at his teaching, 29 for he
taught them as one who had authority, and not
as their scribes.

Jerusalem Bible

many miracles in your name?' 23 Then I shall
tell them to their faces: I have never known
you; *away from me, you evil men!*"
24 "Therefore, everyone who listens to these
words of mine and acts on them will be like a
sensible man who built his house on rock.
25 Rain came down, floods rose, gales blew and
hurled themselves against that house, and it did
not fall: it was founded on rock. 26 But everyone who listens to these words of mine and does
not act on them will be like a stupid man who
built his house on sand. 27 Rain came down,
floods rose, gales blew and struck that house,
and it fell; and what a fall it had!"

The amazement of the crowds

28 Jesus had now finished what he wanted to
say, and his teaching made a deep impression on
the people 29 because he taught them with authority, and not like their own scribes.[m]

[m] Doctors of the law, who buttressed their teaching by quotation from the Scriptures and traditions.

New English Bible

form many miracles?" Then I will tell them to their face, "I never knew you; out of my sight, you and your wicked ways!"

'What then of the man who hears these words of mine and acts upon them? He is like a man who had the sense to build his house on rock. The rain came down, the floods rose, the wind blew, and beat upon that house; but it did not fall, because its foundations were on rock. But what of the man who hears these words of mine and does not act upon them? He is like a man who was foolish enough to build his house on sand. The rain came down, the floods rose, the wind blew, and beat upon that house; down it fell with a great crash.'

When Jesus had finished this discourse the people were astounded at his teaching; unlike their own teachers he taught with a note of authority.

King James Version

8 When he was come down from the mountain, great multitudes followed him. 2And, behold, there came a leper and worshipped him, saying, Lord, if thou wilt, thou canst make me clean. 3And Jesus put forth *his* hand, and touched him, saying, I will; be thou clean. And immediately his leprosy was cleansed. 4And Jesus saith unto him, See thou tell no man; but go thy way, shew thyself to the priest, and offer the gift that Moses commanded, for a testimony unto them.

5 And when Jesus was entered into Capernaum, there came unto him a centurion, beseeching him, 6And saying, Lord, my servant lieth at home sick of the palsy, grievously tormented. 7And Jesus saith unto him, I will come and heal him. 8 The centurion answered and said, Lord, I am not worthy that thou shouldest come under my roof: but speak the word only,

Living Bible

8 Large crowds followed Jesus as he came down the hillside.

2 *Look! A leper is approaching. He kneels before him, worshiping. "Sir," the leper pleads, "if you want to, you can heal me."*

3 *Jesus touches the man. "I want to," he says; "be healed." And instantly the leprosy disappears.*

4 *Then Jesus says to him, "Don't stop to talk[a] to anyone; go right over to the priest to be examined; and take with you the offering required by Moses' law for lepers who are healed —a public testimony of your cure."*

5, 6 When Jesus arrived in Capernaum, a Roman army captain came and pled with him to come to his home and heal his servant boy who was in bed paralyzed and racked with pain.

7 "Yes," Jesus said, "I will come and heal him."

8, 9 Then the officer said, "Sir, I am not worthy to have you in my home; [and it isn't necessary for you to come[b]]. If you will only stand here and say, 'Be healed,' my servant will

[*a*] Literally, "See you tell no man." [*b*] Implied.

Today's English Version

Jesus makes a leper clean

8 Jesus came down from the hill, and large crowds followed him. 2 Then a leper came to him, knelt down before him, and said, "Sir, if you want to, you can make me clean."

3 Jesus reached out and touched him. "I do want to," he answered. "Be clean!" At once he was clean from his leprosy. 4 Then Jesus said to him, "Listen! Don't tell anyone, but go straight to the priest and let him examine you; then offer the sacrifice that Moses ordered, to prove to everyone that you are now clean."

Jesus heals a Roman officer's servant

5 When Jesus entered Capernaum, a Roman officer met him and begged for help: 6 "Sir, my servant is at home, sick in bed, unable to move and suffering terribly."

7 "I will go and make him well," Jesus said.

8 "Oh no, sir," answered the officer. "I do not deserve to have you come into my house. Just

New International Version

The man with leprosy

8 When he came down from the mountainside, large crowds followed him. 2A man with leprosy[a] came and knelt before him and said, "Lord, if you are willing, you can make me clean."

3 Jesus reached out his hand and touched the man. "I am willing," he said. "Be clean!" Immediately he was cured [b] of his leprosy. 4 Then Jesus said to him, "See that you don't tell anyone. But go, show yourself to the priest and offer the gift Moses commanded, as a testimony to them."

The faith of the centurion

5 When Jesus had entered Capernaum, a centurion came to him, asking for help. 6 "Lord," he said, "my servant lies at home paralyzed and in terrible suffering."

7 Jesus said to him, "I will go and heal him."

8 The centurion replied, "Lord, I do not deserve to have you come under my roof. But just say the word, and my servant will be healed.

[*a*] The Greek word probably designated other related diseases also. [*b*] Greek *made clean*.

Phillips Modern English

8.1 *Jesus cures leprosy, and heals many other people*

Large crowds followed him when he came down from the hill-side. There was a leper who came and knelt in front of him. "Sir," he said, "if you want to, you can make me clean." Jesus stretched out his hand and placed it on the leper saying, "Of course I want to. Be clean!" And at once he was clear of the leprosy.

"Mind you say nothing to anybody," Jesus told him. "Go straight off and show yourself to the priest and make the offering for your recovery that Moses prescribed, as evidence to the authorities."

Then as he was coming into Capernaum a centurion approached. "Sir," he implored him, "my servant is in bed at home paralysed and in dreadful pain."

"I will come and heal him," said Jesus to him.

"Sir," replied the centurion, "I'm not important enough for you to come under my roof. You have only to give the order and my servant

Revised Standard Version

8 When he came down from the mountain,
great crowds followed him; 2 and behold, a
leper came to him and knelt before him, saying,
"Lord, if you will, you can make me clean."
3 And he stretched out his hand and touched
him, saying, "I will; be clean." And immediately
his leprosy was cleansed. 4 And Jesus said to him,
"See that you say nothing to any one; but go,
show yourself to the priest, and offer the gift
that Moses commanded, for a proof to the people."[r]
5 As he entered Capernaum, a centurion came
forward to him, beseeching him 6 and saying,
"Lord, my servant is lying paralyzed at home, in
terrible distress." 7 And he said to him, "I will
come and heal him." 8 But the centurion answered him, "Lord, I am not worthy to have
you come under my roof; but only say the word,

[r] Greek *to them.*

Jerusalem Bible

III. The kingdom of heaven is preached

A. Narrative section: Ten miracles

Cure of a leper

8 After he had come down from the mountain large crowds followed him. 2 A leper
now came up and bowed low in front of him.
"Sir," he said, "if you want to, you can cure
me." 3 Jesus stretched out his hand, touched him
and said, "Of course I want to! Be cured!" And
his leprosy was cured at once. 4 Then Jesus said
to him, "Mind you do not tell anyone, but go
and show yourself to the priest and make the
offering prescribed by Moses, as evidence for
them."

Cure of the centurion's servant

5 When he went into Capernaum a centurion
came up and pleaded with him. 6 "Sir," he said,
"my servant is lying at home paralyzed, and in
great pain." 7 "I will come myself and cure
him," said Jesus. 8 The centurion replied, "Sir,
I am not worthy to have you under my roof;
just give the word and my servant will be cured.

New English Bible

Teaching and healing

8 After he had come down from the hill he was followed by a great crowd. And now a leper[a] approached him, bowed low, and said, 'Sir, if only you will, you can cleanse me.' Jesus stretched out his hand, touched him, and said, 'Indeed I will; be clean again.' And his leprosy was cured immediately. Then Jesus said to him, 'Be sure you tell nobody; but go and show yourself to the priest, and make the offering laid down by Moses for your cleansing; that will certify the cure.'

When he had entered Capernaum a centurion came up to ask his help. 'Sir,' he said, 'a boy of mine lies at home paralysed and racked with pain.' Jesus said, 'I will come and cure him.'[b] But the centurion replied, 'Sir, who am I to have you under my roof? You need only say the word

[a] *The words* leper, leprosy, *as used in this translation, refer to some disfiguring skin disease which entailed ceremonial defilement. It is different from what is now called leprosy.* [b] *Or* Am I to come and cure him?

King James Version

and my servant shall be healed. 9 For I am a man under authority, having soldiers under me: and I say to this *man,* Go, and he goeth; and to another, Come, and he cometh; and to my servant, Do this, and he doeth *it.* 10 When Jesus heard *it,* he marvelled, and said to them that followed, Verily I say unto you, I have not found so great faith, no, not in Israel. 11 And I say unto you, That many shall come from the east and west, and shall sit down with Abraham, and Isaac, and Jacob, in the kingdom of heaven: 12 But the children of the kingdom shall be cast out into outer darkness: there shall be weeping and gnashing of teeth. 13 And Jesus said unto the centurion, Go thy way; and as thou hast believed, *so* be it done unto thee. And his servant was healed in the selfsame hour.

14 And when Jesus was come into Peter's house, he saw his wife's mother laid, and sick of a fever. 15 And he touched her hand, and the fever left her: and she arose, and ministered unto them.

16 When the even was come, they brought unto him many that were possessed with devils: and he cast out the spirits with *his* word, and healed all that were sick: 17 That it might be fulfilled which was spoken by Esaias the prophet,

Living Bible

get well! I know, because I am under the authority of my superior officers and I have authority over my soldiers, and I say to one, 'Go,' and he goes, and to another, 'Come,' and he comes, and to my slave boy, 'Do this or that,' and he does it. And I know you have authority to tell his sickness to go—and it will go!"

10 Jesus stood there amazed! Turning to the crowd he said, "I haven't seen faith like this in all the land of Israel! 11 And I tell you this, that many Gentiles [like this Roman officer[b]], shall come from all over the world and sit down in the Kingdom of Heaven with Abraham, Isaac, and Jacob. 12 And many an Israelite—those for whom the Kingdom was prepared—shall be cast into outer darkness, into the place of weeping and torment."

13 Then Jesus said to the Roman officer, "Go on home. What you have believed has happened!" And the boy was healed that same hour!

14 When Jesus arrived at Peter's house, Peter's mother-in-law was in bed with a high fever. 15 But when Jesus touched her hand, the fever left her; and she got up and prepared a meal[c] for them!

16 That evening several demon-possessed people were brought to Jesus; and when he spoke a single word, all the demons fled; and all the sick were healed. 17 This fulfilled the prophecy of

[*b*] Implied. [*c*] Literally, "ministered unto them."

Today's English Version

give the order and my servant will get well. 9 I, too, am a man under the authority of superior officers, and I have soldiers under me. I order this one, 'Go!' and he goes; and I order that one, 'Come!' and he comes; and I order my slave, 'Do this!' and he does it."

10 Jesus was surprised when he heard this, and said to the people who were following him, "I tell you, I have never seen such faith as this in anyone in Israel. 11 Remember this! Many will come from the east and the west and sit down at the table in the Kingdom of heaven with Abraham, Isaac, and Jacob. 12 But those who should be in the Kingdom will be thrown out into the darkness outside, where they will cry and gnash their teeth." 13 And Jesus said to the officer, "Go home, and what you believe will be done for you."

And the officer's servant was healed that very hour.

Jesus heals many people

14 Jesus went to Peter's home, and there he saw Peter's mother-in-law sick in bed with a fever. 15 He touched her hand; the fever left her, and she got up and began to wait on him.

16 When evening came, people brought to Jesus many who had demons in them. Jesus drove out the evil spirits with a word and healed all who were sick. 17 He did this to make come

New International Version

9 For I myself am a man under authority, with soldiers under me. I tell this one, 'Go,' and he goes; and that one, 'Come,' and he comes. I say to my servant, 'Do this,' and he does it."

10 When Jesus heard this, he was astonished and said to those following him, "I tell you the truth, I have not found anyone in Israel with such great faith. 11 I say to you that many will come from the east and the west, and will take their places at the feast with Abraham, Isaac and Jacob in the kingdom of heaven. 12 But the subjects of the kingdom will be thrown outside, into the darkness, where there will be weeping and grinding of teeth."

13 Then Jesus said to the centurion, "Go! It will be done just as you believed it would." And his servant was healed at that very hour.

Jesus heals many

14 When Jesus came into Peter's house, he saw Peter's mother-in-law lying in bed with a fever. 15 He touched her hand and the fever left her, and she got up and began to wait on him.

16 When evening came, many who were demon-possessed were brought to him, and he drove out the spirits with a word and healed all the sick. 17 This was to fulfill what was spoken through the prophet Isaiah:

Phillips Modern English

will recover. I'm a man under authority myself, and I have soldiers under me. I can say to one man 'Go' and I know he'll go, or I can say 'Come here' to another and I know he'll come—or I can say to my slave 'Do this' and he'll do it."

When Jesus heard this, he was astonished. "Believe me," he said to those who were following him, "I have never found faith like this, even in Israel! I tell you that many people will come from east and west and be fellow-guests with Abraham, Isaac and Jacob in the kingdom of Heaven. But those who should have belonged to the kingdom will be banished to the darkness outside, where there will be tears and bitter regret."

Then he said to the centurion, "Go home now, and everything will happen as you have believed it will."

And his servant was healed at that actual moment.

Then, on coming into Peter's house Jesus saw that Peter's mother-in-law had been put to bed with a high fever. He touched her hand and the fever left her. And then she got up and began to see to his needs.

When evening came they brought to him many who were possessed by evil spirits, which he expelled with a word. Indeed, he healed all who were ill. Thus was fulfilled Isaiah's prophecy—

Revised Standard Version

and my servant will be healed. 9 For I am a
man under authority, with soldiers under me;
and I say to one, 'Go,' and he goes, and to
another, 'Come,' and he comes, and to my slave,
'Do this,' and he does it." 10 When Jesus heard
him, he marveled, and said to those who followed him, "Truly, I say to you, not even[s] in
Israel have I found such faith. 11 I tell you,
many will come from east and west and sit at
table with Abraham, Isaac, and Jacob in the
kingdom of heaven, 12 while the sons of the
kingdom will be thrown into the outer darkness;
there men will weep and gnash their teeth."
13 And to the centurion Jesus said, "Go; be it
done for you as you have believed." And the
servant was healed at that very moment.

14 And when Jesus entered Peter's house, he
saw his mother-in-law lying sick with a fever;
15 he touched her hand, and the fever left her,
and she rose and served him. 16 That evening
they brought to him many who were possessed
with demons; and he cast out the spirits with
a word, and healed all who were sick. 17 This
was to fulfil what was spoken by the prophet

[s] Other ancient authorities read *with no one*.

Jerusalem Bible

9 For I am under authority myself, and have
soldiers under me; and I say to one man: Go,
and he goes; to another: Come here, and he
comes; to my servant: Do this, and he does it."
10 When Jesus heard this he was astonished and
said to those following him, "I tell you solemnly,
nowhere in Israel have I found faith like this.
11 And I tell you that many will come from east
and west to take their places with Abraham and
Isaac and Jacob at the feast in the kingdom of
heaven; 12 but the subjects of the kingdom[n] will
be turned out into the dark, where there will be
weeping and grinding of teeth." 13 And to the
centurion Jesus said, "Go back, then; you have
believed, so let this be done for you." And the
servant was cured at that moment.

Cure of Peter's mother-in-law

14 And going into Peter's house Jesus found
Peter's mother-in-law in bed with fever. 15 He
touched her hand and the fever left her, and
she got up and began to wait on him.

A number of cures

16 That evening they brought him many who
were possessed by devils. He cast out the spirits
with a word and cured all who were sick. 17 This
was to fulfill the prophecy of Isaiah:

[n] The Jews, natural heirs of the promises.

New English Bible

and the boy will be cured. I know, for I am myself under orders, with soldiers under me. I say to one, "Go", and he goes; to another, "Come here", and he comes; and to my servant, "Do this", and he does it.' Jesus heard him with astonishment, and said to the people who were following him, 'I tell you this: nowhere, even in Israel, have I found such faith.

'Many, I tell you, will come from east and west to feast with Abraham, Isaac, and Jacob in the kingdom of Heaven. But those who were born to the kingdom will be driven out into the dark, the place of wailing and grinding of teeth.'

Then Jesus said to the centurion, 'Go home now; because of your faith, so let it be.' At that moment the boy recovered.

Jesus then went to Peter's house and found Peter's mother-in-law in bed with fever. So he took her by the hand; the fever left her, and she got up and waited on him.

When evening fell, they brought to him many who were possessed by devils; and he drove the spirits out with a word and healed all who were

King James Version

saying, Himself took our infirmities, and bare *our* sicknesses.
18 Now when Jesus saw great multitudes about him, he gave commandment to depart unto the other side.
19And a certain scribe came, and said unto him, Master, I will follow thee whithersoever thou goest.
20And Jesus saith unto him, The foxes have holes, and the birds of the air *have* nests; but the Son of man hath not where to lay *his* head.
21And another of his disciples said unto him, Lord, suffer me first to go and bury my father.
22 But Jesus said unto him, Follow me; and let the dead bury their dead.
23 And when he was entered into a ship, his disciples followed him.
24And, behold, there arose a great tempest in the sea, insomuch that the ship was covered with the waves: but he was asleep.
25And his disciples came to *him*, and awoke him, saying, Lord, save us: we perish.
26And he saith unto them, Why are ye fearful, O ye of little faith? Then he arose, and rebuked the winds and the sea; and there was

Living Bible

Isaiah, "He took our sicknesses and bore our diseases." [d]
18 When Jesus noticed how large the crowd was growing, he instructed his disciples to get ready to cross to the other side of the lake.
19 Just then[e] one of the Jewish religious teachers[f] said to him, "Teacher, I will follow you no matter where you go!"
20 But Jesus said, "Foxes have dens and birds have nests, but I, the Messiah,[g] have no home of my own—no place to lay my head."
21 Another of his disciples said, "Sir, when my father is dead, then I will follow you." [h]
22 But Jesus told him, "Follow me *now!* [e] Let those who are spiritually[e] dead care for their own dead."
23 Then he got into a boat and started across the lake with his disciples.
24 Suddenly a terrible storm came up, with waves higher than the boat. But Jesus was asleep.
25 The disciples went to him and wakened him, shouting, "Lord, save us! We're sinking!"
26 But Jesus answered, "O you men of little faith! Why are you so frightened?" Then he stood up and rebuked the wind and waves, and

[*d*] Isaiah 53:4. [*e*] Implied. [*f*] Literally, "a scribe." [*g*] Literally, "the Son of Man." [*h*] Or, "Let me first go and bury my father."

Today's English Version

true what the prophet Isaiah had said, "He himself took our illnesses and carried away our diseases."

The would-be followers of Jesus

18 Jesus noticed the crowd around him and ordered his disciples to go to the other side of the lake.
19A teacher of the Law came to him. "Teacher," he said, "I am ready to go with you wherever you go."
20 Jesus answered him, "Foxes have holes, and birds have nests, but the Son of Man has no place to lie down and rest."
21 Another man, who was a disciple, said, "Sir, first let me go back and bury my father."
22 "Follow me," Jesus answered, "and let the dead bury their own dead."

Jesus calms a storm

23 Jesus got into the boat, and his disciples went with him.
24 Suddenly a fierce storm hit the lake, so that the waves covered the boat. But Jesus was asleep.
25 The disciples went to him and woke him up. "Save us, Lord!" they said. "We are about to die!"
26 "Why are you so frightened?" Jesus answered. "How little faith you have!" Then he got up and gave a command to the winds and to the waves, and there was a great calm.

New International Version

"He took up our diseases
and carried our illnesses." [c]

The cost of following Jesus

18 When Jesus saw the crowd around him, he gave orders to cross to the other side of the lake.
19 Then a teacher of the law came to him and said, "Teacher, I will follow you wherever you go."
20 Jesus replied, "Foxes have holes and birds of the air have nests, but the Son of Man has no place to lay his head."
21 Another man, one of his disciples, said to him, "Lord, first let me go and bury my father."
22 But Jesus told him, "Follow me, and let the dead bury their own dead."

Jesus calms the storm

23 Then he got into the boat and his disciples followed him.
24 Without warning, a furious storm came up on the lake, so that the waves swept over the boat. But Jesus was sleeping.
25 The disciples went and woke him, saying, "Lord, save us! We're going to drown!"
26 He replied, "You of little faith, why are you so afraid?" Then he got up and rebuked the winds and the waves, and it was completely calm.

[*c*] Isaiah 53:4.

Phillips Modern English

Himself took our infirmities and bare our diseases.

When Jesus had seen the great crowds around him he gave orders to cross over to the other side of the lake. But before they started, one of the scribes came up to Jesus and said to him, "Master, I will follow you wherever you go."

"Foxes have earths, birds in the sky have nests, but the Son of Man has nowhere that he can call his own," replied Jesus.

Another of his disciples said, "Lord, let me first go and bury my father."

But Jesus said to him, "Follow me, and leave the dead to bury their own dead."

8.23 Jesus shows his mastery over the forces of nature

Then he went aboard the boat, and his disciples followed him. Before long a terrific storm sprang up and the boat was awash with the waves. Jesus was sleeping soundly and the disciples went forward and woke him up.

"Lord, save us!" they cried. "We are drowning!"

"Why are you so frightened, you little-faiths?" he replied.

Then he got to his feet and rebuked the wind

Revised Standard Version

Isaiah, "He took our infirmities and bore our diseases."
18 Now when Jesus saw great crowds around
him, he gave orders to go over to the other side.
19 And a scribe came up and said to him,
"Teacher, I will follow you wherever you go."
20 And Jesus said to him, "Foxes have holes, and
birds of the air have nests; but the Son of man
has nowhere to lay his head." 21 Another of the
disciples said to him, "Lord, let me first go and
bury my father." 22 But Jesus said to him, "Follow me, and leave the dead to bury their own dead."
23 And when he got into the boat, his disciples followed him.
24 And behold, there arose a
great storm on the sea, so that the boat was being swamped by the waves; but he was asleep.
25 And they went and woke him, saying, "Save,
Lord; we are perishing." 26 And he said to them,
"Why are you afraid, O men of little faith?"
Then he rose and rebuked the winds and the

Jerusalem Bible

He took our sicknesses away and carried our diseases for us.[o]

Hardships of the apostolic calling

18 When Jesus saw the great crowds all about
him he gave orders to leave for the other side.[p]
19 One of the scribes then came up and said to
him, "Master, I will follow you wherever you
go." 20 Jesus replied, "Foxes have holes and the
birds of the air have nests, but the Son of Man
has nowhere to lay his head."
21 Another man, one of his disciples, said to
him, "Sir, let me go and bury my father first."
22 But Jesus replied, "Follow me, and leave the
dead to bury their dead."

The calming of the storm

23 Then he got into the boat followed by his
disciples. 24 Without warning a storm broke over
the lake, so violent that the waves were breaking
right over the boat. But he was asleep. 25 So
they went to him and woke him saying, "Save
us, Lord, we are going down!" 26 And he said
to them, "Why are you so frightened, you men
of little faith?" And with that he stood up and
rebuked the winds and the sea; and all was calm

[o] Is. 53:4. [p] The east bank of Lake Tiberias.

New English Bible

sick, to fulfil the prophecy of Isaiah: 'He took away our illnesses and lifted our diseases from us.'[c]

At the sight of the crowds surrounding him Jesus gave word to cross to the other shore. A doctor of the law came up, and said, 'Master, I will follow you wherever you go.' Jesus replied, 'Foxes have their holes, the birds their roosts; but the Son of Man has nowhere to lay his head.' Another man, one of his disciples, said to him, 'Lord, let me go and bury my father first.' Jesus replied, 'Follow me, and leave the dead to bury their dead.'

Jesus then got into the boat, and his disciples followed. All at once a great storm arose on the lake, till the waves were breaking right over the boat; but he went on sleeping. So they came and woke him up, crying: 'Save us, Lord; we are sinking!' 'Why are you such cowards?' he said; 'how little faith you have!' Then he stood up and rebuked the wind and the sea, and there

[c] *Or* and bore the burden of our diseases.

King James Version

a great calm. 27 But the men marvelled, saying,
What manner of man is this, that even the winds
and the sea obey him!
28 And when he was come to the other side
into the country of the Gergesenes, there met
him two possessed with devils, coming out of
the tombs, exceeding fierce, so that no man
might pass by that way. 29And behold, they cried
out, saying, What have we to do with thee, Jesus, thou Son of God? art thou come hither to
torment us before the time? 30And there was a
good way off from them a herd of many swine
feeding. 31 So the devils besought him, saying,
If thou cast us out, suffer us to go away into
the herd of swine. 32And he said unto them,
Go. And when they were come out, they went
into the herd of swine: and, behold, the whole
herd of swine ran violently down a steep place
into the sea, and perished in the waters. 33And
they that kept them fled, and went their ways
into the city, and told every thing, and what was
befallen to the possessed of the devils. 34And,
behold, the whole city came out to meet Jesus:
and when they saw him, they besought *him* that
he would depart out of their coasts.

Living Bible

the storm subsided and all was calm. 27 The disciples just sat there, awed! "Who is this," they
asked themselves, "that even the winds and the
sea obey him?"
28 When they arrived on the other side of
the lake, in the country of the Gadarenes, two
men with demons in them met him. They lived in
a cemetery and were so dangerous that no one
could go through that area.
29 They began screaming at him, "What do
you want with us, O Son of God? You have no
right to torment us yet." [i]
30 A herd of pigs was feeding in the distance,
31 so the demons begged, "If you cast us out,
send us into that herd of pigs."
32 "All right," Jesus told them. "Begone."
And they came out of the men and entered
the pigs, and the whole herd rushed over a cliff
and drowned in the water below. 33 The herdsmen fled to the nearest city with the story of
what had happened, 34 and the entire population
came rushing out to see Jesus, and begged him to
go away and leave them alone.

[*i*] Literally, "Have you come here to torment us before the time?"

Today's English Version

27 Everyone was amazed. "What kind of man
is this?" they said. "Even the winds and the
waves obey him!"

Jesus heals two men with demons

28 Jesus came to the territory of the Gadarenes, on the other side of the lake, and was
met by two men who came out of the burial
caves. These men had demons in them and were
so fierce that no one dared travel on that road.
29At once they screamed, "What do you want
with us, Son of God? Have you come to punish
us before the right time?"
30 Not far away a large herd of pigs was
feeding. 31 The demons begged Jesus, "If you
are going to drive us out, send us into that herd
of pigs."
32 "Go," Jesus told them; so they left and
went off into the pigs. The whole herd rushed
down the side of the cliff into the lake and were
drowned.
33 The men who had been taking care of the
pigs ran away and went to the town, where they
told the whole story, and what had happened to
the men with the demons. 34 So everyone from
the town went out to meet Jesus; and when they
saw him they begged him to leave their territory.

New International Version

27 The men were amazed and asked, "What
kind of man is this? Even the winds and the
waves obey him!"

The healing of two demon-possessed men

28 When he arrived at the other side in the
region of the Gadarenes,[d] two demon-possessed
men coming from the tombs met him. They were
so violent that no one could pass that way.
29 "What do you want with us, Son of God?"
they shouted. "Have you come here to torture
us before the appointed time?"
30 Some distance from them a large herd of
pigs was feeding. 31 The demons begged Jesus,
"If you drive us out, send us into the herd of
pigs."
32 He said to them, "Go!" So they came out
and went into the pigs, and the whole herd
rushed down the steep bank into the lake and
died in the water. 33 Those tending the pigs ran
off, went into the town, and reported all this,
including what had happened to the demon-
possessed men. 34 Then the whole town went
out to meet Jesus. And when they saw him,
they pleaded with him to leave their region.

[*d*] Some MSS read *Gergesenes;* others read *Gerasenes.*

Phillips Modern English

and the waters and there was a great calm. The men were filled with astonishment and kept saying, "Whatever sort of man is this—why, even the winds and the waters do what he tells them!"

When he arrived on the other side (which is the Gadarenes' country) he was met by two devil-possessed men who came out from among the tombs. They were so violent that nobody dared to use that road.

"What have you got to do with us, you Son of God?" they screamed at him. "Have you come here to torture us before our time?"

It happened that in the distance there was a large herd of pigs feeding. So the devils implored him, "If you throw us out, send us into the herd of pigs!"

"Then go!" said Jesus to them.

And the devils came out and went into the pigs. Then quite suddenly the whole herd stampeded down the steep cliff into the lake and were drowned.

The swineherds took to their heels, and ran to the town. There they poured out the whole story of what had happened to the two men who had been devil-possessed. Whereupon the whole town came out to meet Jesus, and as soon as they saw him implored him to leave their territory.

Revised Standard Version

sea; and there was a great calm. 27And the men
marveled, saying, "What sort of man is this, that
even winds and sea obey him?"
28 And when he came to the other side, to
the country of the Gadarenes,[t] two demoniacs
met him, coming out of the tombs, so fierce that
no one could pass that way. 29And behold, they
cried out, "What have you to do with us, O Son
of God? Have you come here to torment us before the time?" 30 Now a herd of many swine
was feeding at some distance from them. 31And
the demons begged him, "If you cast us out,
send us away into the herd of swine." 32And
he said to them, "Go." So they came out and
went into the swine; and behold, the whole herd
rushed down the steep bank into the sea, and
perished in the waters. 33 The herdsmen fled,
and going into the city they told everything, and
what had happened to the demoniacs. 34And behold, all the city came out to meet Jesus; and
when they saw him, they begged him to leave
their neighborhood.

[t] Other ancient authorities read *Gergesenes;* some, *Gerasenes.*

Jerusalem Bible

again. 27 The men were astounded and said,
"Whatever kind of man is this? Even the winds
and the sea obey him."

The demoniacs of Gadara

28 When he reached the country of the Gadarenes on the other side, two demoniacs came
toward him out of the tombs—creatures so fierce
that no one could pass that way. 29 They stood
there shouting, "What do you want with us, Son
of God? Have you come here to torture us before the time?"[q] 30 Now some distance away
there was a large herd of pigs feeding, 31 and
the devils pleaded with Jesus, "If you cast us
out, send us into the herd of pigs." 32And he
said to them, "Go then," and they came out
and made for the pigs; and at that the whole
herd charged down the cliff into the lake and
perished in the water. 33 The swineherds ran off
and made for the town, where they told the
whole story, including what had happened to
the demoniacs. 34At this the whole town set out
to meet Jesus; and as soon as they saw him they
implored him to leave the neighborhood.

[q] The day of Judgment, when the reign of God would banish all demons.

New English Bible

was a dead calm. The men were astonished at what had happened, and exclaimed, 'What sort of man is this? Even the wind and the sea obey him.'

When he reached the other side, in the country of the Gadarenes, he was met by two men who came out from the tombs; they were possessed by devils, and so violent that no one dared pass that way. 'You son of God,' they shouted, 'what do you want with us? Have you come here to torment us before our time?' In the distance a large herd of pigs was feeding; and the devils begged him: 'If you drive us out, send us into that herd of pigs.' 'Begone!' he said. Then they came out and went into the pigs; the whole herd rushed over the edge into the lake, and perished in the water.

The men in charge of them took to their heels, and made for the town, where they told the whole story, and what had happened to the madmen. Thereupon all the town came out to meet Jesus; and when they saw him they begged him to leave the district and go.

King James Version

9 And he entered into a ship, and passed over,
and came into his own city. 2And, behold,
they brought to him a man sick of the palsy,
lying on a bed: and Jesus seeing their faith said
unto the sick of the palsy; Son, be of good
cheer; thy sins be forgiven thee. 3And, behold,
certain of the scribes said within themselves,
This *man* blasphemeth. 4And Jesus knowing their
thoughts said, Wherefore think ye evil in your
hearts? 5 For whether is easier, to say, *Thy* sins
be forgiven thee; or to say, Arise, and walk?
6 But that ye may know that the Son of man
hath power on earth to forgive sins, (then saith
he to the sick of the palsy,) Arise, take up thy
bed, and go unto thine house. 7And he arose,
and departed to his house. 8 But when the multitudes saw *it*, they marvelled, and glorified God,
which had given such power unto men.

9 And as Jesus passed forth from thence, he
saw a man, named Matthew, sitting at the receipt of custom: and he saith unto him, Follow
me. And he arose, and followed him.

10 And it came to pass, as Jesus sat at meat

Living Bible

9 So Jesus climbed into a boat and went
across the lake to Capernaum, his home
town.[a]

2 Soon some men brought him a paralyzed
boy on a mat. When Jesus saw their faith, he
said to the sick boy, "Cheer up, son! For I have
forgiven your sins!"

3 "Blasphemy! This man is saying he is God!"
exclaimed some of the religious leaders to themselves.

4 Jesus knew what they were thinking and
asked them, "Why are you thinking such evil
thoughts? 5, 6 I, the Messiah,[b] have the authority
on earth to forgive sins. But talk is cheap—anybody could say that. So I'll prove it to you by
healing this man." Then, turning to the paralyzed
man, he commanded, "Pick up your stretcher
and go on home, for you are healed."

7 And the boy jumped up and left!

8 A chill of fear swept through the crowd as
they saw this happen right before their eyes. How
they praised God for giving such authority to a
man!

9 As Jesus was going on down the road, he
saw a tax collector, Matthew,[c] sitting at a tax
collection booth. "Come and be my disciple,"
Jesus said to him, and Matthew jumped up and
went along with him.

10 Later, as Jesus and his disciples were eat-

[*a*] Literally, "his own city." [*b*] Literally, "the Son of Man." [*c*] The Matthew who wrote this book.

Today's English Version

Jesus heals a paralyzed man

9 Jesus got into the boat, went back across
the lake, and came to his own town. 2 Some
people brought him a paralyzed man, lying on a
bed. Jesus saw how much faith they had, and
said to the paralyzed man, "Courage, my son!
Your sins are forgiven."

3 Then some teachers of the Law said to themselves, "This man is talking against God!"

4 Jesus knew what they were thinking and
said, "Why are you thinking such evil things?
5 Is it easier to say, 'Your sins are forgiven,' or
to say, 'Get up and walk'? 6 I will prove to you,
then, that the Son of Man has authority on
earth to forgive sins." So he said to the paralyzed man, "Get up, pick up your bed, and go
home!"

7 The man got up and went home. 8 When the
people saw it, they were afraid, and praised God
for giving such authority as this to men.

Jesus calls Matthew

9 Jesus left that place, and as he walked along
he saw a tax collector, named Matthew, sitting
in his office. He said to him, "Follow me."
Matthew got up and followed him.

10 While Jesus was having dinner at his house,

New International Version

Jesus heals a paralytic

9 Jesus stepped into a boat, crossed over and
came to his own town. 2 Some men brought
to him a paralytic, lying on a mat. When Jesus
saw their faith, he said to the paralytic, "Take
heart, son; your sins are forgiven."

3 At this, some of the teachers of the law
said to themselves, "This fellow is blaspheming!"

4 Knowing their thoughts, Jesus said, "Why
do you entertain evil thoughts in your hearts?
5 Which is easier: to say, 'Your sins are forgiven,' or to say, 'Get up and walk'? 6 But so
that you may know that the Son of Man has
authority on earth to forgive sins. . . ." Then
he said to the paralytic, "Get up, take your mat
and go home." 7And the man got up and went
home. 8 When the crowd saw this, they were
filled with awe; and they praised God, who had
given such authority to men.

The calling of Matthew

9 As Jesus went on from there, he saw a man
named Matthew sitting at the tax collector's
booth. "Follow me," he told him, and Matthew
got up and followed him.

10 While Jesus was having dinner at Mat-

Phillips Modern English

9.1 Jesus heals in his own town

So Jesus re-embarked on the boat, crossed the lake, and came to his own town. Immediately some people arrived bringing him a paralytic lying flat on his bed. When Jesus saw the faith of those who brought him he said to the paralytic, "Cheer up, my son! Your sins are forgiven."

At once some of the scribes said to themselves, "This man is blaspheming." But Jesus realised what they were thinking, and said to them, "Why must you have such evil thoughts in your minds? Do you think it is easier to say, 'Your sins are forgiven' or 'Get up and walk'? But to make it quite plain that the Son of Man has full authority on earth to forgive sins"—and here he spoke to the paralytic—"Get up, pick up your bed and go home." And the man sprang to his feet and went home. When the crowds saw what had happened they were filled with awe and praised God for giving such power to men.

9.9 Jesus calls a "sinner" to be his disciple

Jesus left there and as he passed on he saw a man called Matthew sitting at his desk in the tax-collector's office.

"Follow me!" he said to him—and the man got to his feet and followed him.

Later, as Jesus was in a house sitting at the

Revised Standard Version

9 And getting into a boat he crossed over and came to his own city. 2 And behold, they brought to him a paralytic, lying on his bed; and when Jesus saw their faith he said to the paralytic, "Take heart, my son; your sins are forgiven." 3 And behold, some of the scribes said to themselves, "This man is blaspheming." 4 But Jesus, knowing[u] their thoughts, said, "Why do you think evil in your hearts? 5 For which is easier, to say, 'Your sins are forgiven,' or to say, 'Rise and walk'? 6 But that you may know that the Son of man has authority on earth to forgive sins"—he then said to the paralytic—"Rise, take up your bed and go home." 7 And he rose and went home. 8 When the crowds saw it, they were afraid, and they glorified God, who had given such authority to men.

9 As Jesus passed on from there, he saw a man called Matthew sitting at the tax office; and he said to him, "Follow me." And he rose and followed him.

10 And as he sat at table[v] in the house, be-

[*u*] Other ancient authorities read *seeing*. [*v*] Greek *reclined*.

Jerusalem Bible

Cure of a paralytic

9 He got back in the boat, crossed the water and came to his own town.[r] 2 Then some people appeared, bringing him a paralytic stretched out on a bed. Seeing their faith, Jesus said to the paralytic, "Courage, my child, your sins are forgiven." 3 And at this some scribes said to themselves, "This man is blaspheming." 4 Knowing what was in their minds Jesus said, "Why do you have such wicked thoughts in your hearts? 5 Now, which of these is easier: to say, 'Your sins are forgiven,' or to say, 'Get up and walk?' 6 But to prove to you that the Son of Man has authority on earth to forgive sins," —he said to the paralytic—"get up, and pick up your bed and go off home." 7 And the man got up and went home. 8 A feeling of awe came over the crowd when they saw this, and they praised God for giving such power to men.

The call of Matthew

9 As Jesus was walking on from there he saw a man named Matthew[s] sitting by the customs house, and he said to him, "Follow me." And he got up and followed him.

Eating with sinners

10 While he was at dinner in the house it

[*r*] Capernaum, cf. 4:13. [*s*] Called Levi by Mark and Luke.

New English Bible

9 So he got into the boat and crossed over, and came to his own town.

And now some men brought him a paralysed man lying on a bed. Seeing their faith Jesus said to the man, 'Take heart, my son; your sins are forgiven.' At this some of the lawyers said to themselves, 'This is blasphemous talk.' Jesus knew what they were thinking, and said, 'Why do you harbour these evil thoughts? Is it easier to say, "Your sins are forgiven", or to say, "Stand up and walk"? But to convince you that the Son of Man has the right on earth to forgive sins'—he turned to the paralysed man—'stand up, take your bed, and go home.' Thereupon the man got up, and went off home. The people were filled with awe at the sight, and praised God for granting such authority to men.

As he passed on from there Jesus saw a man named Matthew at his seat in the custom-house, and said to him, 'Follow me'; and Matthew rose and followed him.

When Jesus was at table in the house, many

King James Version

in the house, behold, many publicans and sinners came and sat down with him and his disciples. 11And when the Pharisees saw *it,* they said unto his disciples, Why eateth your master with publicans and sinners? 12 But when Jesus heard *that* he said unto them, They that be whole need not a physician, but they that are sick. 13 But go ye and learn what *that* meaneth, I will have mercy, and not sacrifice: for I am not come to call the righteous, but sinners to repentance.

14 Then came to him the disciples of John, saying, Why do we and the Pharisees fast oft, but thy disciples fast not? 15And Jesus said unto them, Can the children of the bridechamber mourn, as long as the bridegroom is with them? but the days will come, when the bridegroom shall be taken from them, and then shall they fast. 16 No man putteth a piece of new cloth unto an old garment; for that which is put in to fill it up taketh from the garment, and the rent is made worse. 17 Neither do men put new wine into old bottles: else the bottles break, and the wine runneth out, and the bottles perish: but they put new wine into new bottles, and both are preserved.

Living Bible

ing dinner [at Matthew's house[d]], there were many notorious swindlers there as guests!

11 The Pharisees were indignant. "Why does your teacher associate with men like that?"

12 "Because people who are well don't need a doctor! It's the sick people who do!" was Jesus' reply. 13 Then he added, "Now go away and learn the meaning of this verse of Scripture,

'It isn't your sacrifices and your gifts I want—I want you to be merciful.' [e]

For I have come to urge sinners, not the self-righteous, back to God."

14 One day the disciples of John the Baptist came to Jesus and asked him, "Why don't your disciples fast as we do and as the Pharisees do?"

15 "Should the bridegroom's friends mourn and go without food while he is with them?" Jesus asked. "But the time is coming when I [f] will be taken from them. Time enough then for them to refuse to eat.

16 "And who would patch an old garment with unshrunk cloth? For the patch would tear away and make the hole worse. 17And who would use old wineskins[g] to store new wine? For the old skins would burst with the pressure, and the wine would be spilled and the skins ruined. Only new wineskins are used to store new wine. That way both are preserved."

[*d*] Implied. [*e*] Hosea 6:6. [*f*] Literally, "the Bridegroom." [*g*] These were leather bags for storing wine.

Today's English Version

many tax collectors and outcasts came and joined him and his disciples at the table. 11 Some Pharisees saw this and said to his disciples, "Why does your teacher eat with tax collectors and outcasts?"

12 Jesus heard them and answered, "People who are well do not need a doctor, but only those who are sick. 13 Go and find out what this scripture means, 'I do not want animal sacrifices, but kindness.' I have not come to call the respectable people, but the outcasts."

The question about fasting

14 Then the followers of John the Baptist came to Jesus, asking, "Why is it that we and the Pharisees fast often, but your disciples don't fast at all?"

15 Jesus answered, "Do you expect the guests at a wedding party to be sad as long as the bridegroom is with them? Of course not! But the time will come when the bridegroom will be taken away from them, and then they will go without food.

16 "No one patches up an old coat with a piece of new cloth, because such a patch tears off from the coat, making an even bigger hole. 17 Nor does anyone pour new wine into used wineskins. If he does, the skins will burst, and then the wine pours out and the skins will be ruined. Instead, new wine is poured into fresh wineskins, and both will keep in good condition."

New International Version

thew's house, many tax collectors and "sinners" came and ate with him and his disciples. 11 When the Pharisees saw this, they asked his disciples, "Why does your teacher eat with tax collectors and 'sinners'?"

12 On hearing this, Jesus said, "It is not the healthy who need a doctor, but the sick. 13 But go and learn what this means: 'I desire mercy, not sacrifice.' [e] For I have not come to call the righteous, but sinners."

Jesus questioned about fasting

14 Then John's disciples came and asked him, "How is it that we and the Pharisees fast, but your disciples do not fast?"

15 Jesus answered, "How can the guests of the bridegroom mourn while he is with them? The time will come when the bridegroom will be taken from them; then they will fast.

16 "No one sews a patch of unshrunk cloth on an old garment, for the patch will pull away from the garment, making the tear worse. 17 Neither do men pour new wine into old wineskins. If they do, the skins will burst, the wine will run out and the wineskins will be ruined. No, they pour new wine into new wineskins, and both are preserved."

[*e*] Hosea 6:6.

Phillips Modern English

dinner-table, many tax-collectors and other disreputable people came and joined him and his disciples. The Pharisees noticed this and said to the disciples, "Why does your master have his meals with tax-collectors and sinners?" But Jesus heard this and replied,

"It is not the fit and flourishing who need the doctor, but those who are ill! You should go and learn what this text means: 'I desire mercy and not sacrifice.' In any case I did not come to invite the 'righteous' but the 'sinners'."

9.14 *He explains the joy and strength of the new order*

Then John's disciples approached him with the question, "Why is it that we and the Pharisees observe the fasts, but your disciples do not?"

"Can you expect wedding-guests to mourn while they have the bridegroom with them?" replied Jesus. "The day will come when the bridegroom will be taken away from them—they will certainly fast then!

"Nobody sews a patch of unshrunk cloth on to an old coat, for the patch will pull away from the coat and the hole will be worse than ever. Nor do people put new wine into old wineskins—otherwise the skins burst, the wine is spilt and the skins are ruined. But they put new wine into new skins and both are preserved."

Revised Standard Version

hold, many tax collectors and sinners came and
sat down with Jesus and his disciples. 11 And
when the Pharisees saw this, they said to his disciples, "Why does your teacher eat with tax collectors and sinners?" 12 But when he heard it,
he said, "Those who are well have no need of a
physician, but those who are sick. 13 Go and
learn what this means, 'I desire mercy, and not
sacrifice.' For I came not to call the righteous,
but sinners."

14 Then the disciples of John came to him,
saying, "Why do we and the Pharisees fast,[w]
but your disciples do not fast?" 15 And Jesus
said to them, "Can the wedding guests mourn
as long as the bridegroom is with them? The
days will come, when the bridegroom is taken
away from them, and then they will fast. 16 And
no one puts a piece of unshrunk cloth on an
old garment, for the patch tears away from the
garment, and a worse tear is made. 17 Neither
is new wine put into old wineskins; if it is, the
skins burst, and the wine is spilled, and the skins
are destroyed; but new wine is put into fresh
wineskins, and so both are preserved."

[w] Other ancient authorities add *much* or *often*.

Jerusalem Bible

happened that a number of tax collectors and
sinners[t] came to sit at the table with Jesus and
his disciples. 11 When the Pharisees saw this,
they said to his disciples, "Why does your master eat with tax collectors and sinners?" 12 When
he heard this he replied, "It is not the healthy
who need the doctor, but the sick. 13 Go and
learn the meaning of the words: *What I want is mercy, not sacrifice.*[u] And indeed I did not
come to call the virtuous, but sinners."

A discussion on fasting

14 Then John's[v] disciples came to him and
said, "Why is it that we and the Pharisees fast,
but your disciples do not?" 15 Jesus replied,
"Surely the bridegroom's attendants would never
think of mourning as long as the bridegroom is
still with them? But the time will come for the
bridegroom to be taken away from them, and
then they will fast. 16 No one puts a piece of
unshrunken cloth onto an old cloak, because the
patch pulls away from the cloak and the tear
gets worse. 17 Nor do people put new wine into
old wineskins; if they do, the skins burst, the
wine runs out, and the skins are lost. No; they
put new wine into fresh skins and both are preserved." [w]

[t] Social outcasts, made "unclean" by breaking religious laws or following a disreputable profession. [u] Ho. 6:6. [v] John the Baptist. [w] New devotional exercises, like those which John and the Pharisees add to the religion of the old order, will not preserve it.

New English Bible

bad characters—tax-gatherers and others—were seated with him and his disciples. The Pharisees noticed this, and said to his disciples, 'Why is it that your master eats with tax-gatherers and sinners?' Jesus heard it and said, 'It is not the healthy that need a doctor, but the sick. Go and learn what that text means, "I require mercy, not sacrifice." I did not come to invite virtuous people, but sinners.'

Then John's disciples came to him with the question: 'Why do we and the Pharisees fast, but your disciples do not?' Jesus replied, 'Can you expect the bridegroom's friends to go mourning while the bridegroom is with them? The time will come when the bridegroom will be taken away from them; that will be the time for them to fast.

'No one sews a patch of unshrunk cloth on to an old coat; for then the patch tears away from the coat, and leaves a bigger hole. Neither do you put new wine into old wine-skins; if you do, the skins burst, and then the wine runs out and the skins are spoilt. No, you put new wine into fresh skins; then both are preserved.'

King James Version

18 While he spake these things unto them,
behold, there came a certain ruler, and worshipped him, saying, My daughter is even now
dead: but come and lay thy hand upon her, and
she shall live. 19And Jesus arose, and followed
him, and *so did* his disciples.
20 And, behold, a woman, which was diseased
with an issue of blood twelve years, came behind
him, and touched the hem of his garment: 21 For
she said within herself, If I may but touch his
garment, I shall be whole. 22 But Jesus turned
him about, and when he saw her, he said, Daughter, be of good comfort; thy faith hath made
thee whole. And the woman was made whole
from that hour. 23And when Jesus came into
the ruler's house, and saw the minstrels and the
people making a noise, 24 He said unto them,
Give place: for the maid is not dead, but sleepeth. And they laughed him to scorn. 25 But
when the people were put forth, he went in,
and took her by the hand, and the maid arose.
26And the fame hereof went abroad into all that
land.

Living Bible

18 As he was saying this, the rabbi of the
local synagogue came and worshiped him. "My
little daughter has just died," he said, "but you
can bring her back to life again if you will only
come and touch her."
19 As Jesus and the disciples were going to
the rabbi's home, 20 a woman who had been
sick for twelve years with internal bleeding came
up behind him and touched a tassel of his robe,
21 for she thought, "If I only touch him, I will
be healed."
22 Jesus turned around and spoke to her.
"Daughter," he said, "all is well! Your faith has
healed you." And the woman was well from
that moment.
23 When Jesus arrived at the rabbi's home
and saw the noisy crowds and heard the funeral
music, 24 he said, "Get them out, for the little
girl isn't dead; she is only sleeping!" Then how
they all scoffed and sneered at him!
25 When the crowd was finally outside, Jesus
went in where the little girl was lying and took
her by the hand, and she jumped up and was all
right again! 26 The report of this wonderful
miracle swept the entire countryside.

Today's English Version

The official's daughter and the woman who touched Jesus' cloak

18 While Jesus was saying this to them, a
Jewish official came to him, knelt down before
him, and said, "My daughter has just died; but
come and place your hand on her and she will
live."
19 So Jesus got up and followed him, and his
disciples went with him.
20 A certain woman, who had had severe
bleeding for twelve years, came up behind Jesus
and touched the edge of his cloak. 21 She said
to herself, "If only I touch his cloak I will get
well."
22 Jesus turned around and saw her, and said,
"Courage, my daughter! Your faith has made
you well." At that very moment the woman became well.
23 So Jesus went into the official's house.
When he saw the musicians for the funeral, and
the people all stirred up, 24 he said, "Get out,
everybody! The little girl is not dead—she is only
sleeping!"
They all started making fun of him. 25As soon
as the people had been put out, Jesus went into
the girl's room and took hold of her hand, and
she got up. 26 The news about this spread all
over that part of the country.

New International Version

A dead girl and a sick woman

18 While he was saying this, a ruler of the
synagogue came and knelt before him and said,
"My daughter is at the point of death. But
come and put your hand on her, and she will
live." 19 Jesus got up and went with him, and so
did his disciples.
20 Just then a woman who had been subject
to bleeding for twelve years came up behind
him and touched the edge of his cloak. 21 She
said to herself, "If I only touch his cloak, I will
be healed."
22 Jesus turned and saw her. "Take heart,
daughter," he said, "your faith has healed you."
And the woman was healed from that moment.
23 When Jesus entered the ruler's house and
saw the flute-players and the noisy crowd, 24 he
said, "Go away. The girl is not dead but asleep."
But they laughed at him. 25After the crowd had
been put outside, he went in and took the girl by
the hand, and she got up. 26 News of this spread
through all that region.

Phillips Modern English

9.18 Jesus heals a young girl, and several others in need

While he was saying these things to them an official came up to him and, bowing low before him, said,

"My daughter has just this moment died. Please come and lay your hand on her and she will come back to life!"

At this Jesus got to his feet and followed him, accompanied by his disciples. And on the way a woman who had had a haemorrhage for twelve years approached him from behind and touched the edge of his cloak.

"If I can only touch his cloak," she kept saying to herself, "I shall be all right."

But Jesus turned round and saw her.

"Cheer up, my daughter," he said, "your faith has made you well!" And the woman was completely cured from that moment.

Then when Jesus came into the official's house and noticed the flute-players and the noisy crowd he said, "You must all go outside; the little girl is not dead, she is fast asleep."

This was met with scornful laughter. But when the crowd had been turned out, he came right into the room, took hold of her hand, and the girl got up. And this became the talk of the whole district.

Revised Standard Version

18 While he was thus speaking to them, behold, a ruler came in and knelt before him, saying, "My daughter has just died; but come and lay your hand on her, and she will live." 19And Jesus rose and followed him, with his disciples. 20And behold, a woman who had suffered from a hemorrhage for twelve years came up behind him and touched the fringe of his garment; 21 for she said to herself, "If I only touch his garment, I shall be made well." 22 Jesus turned, and seeing her he said, "Take heart, daughter; your faith has made you well." And instantly the woman was made well. 23And when Jesus came to the ruler's house, and saw the flute players, and the crowd making a tumult, 24 he said, "Depart; for the girl is not dead but sleeping." And they laughed at him. 25 But when the crowd had been put outside, he went in and took her by the hand, and the girl arose. 26And the report of this went through all that district.

Jerusalem Bible

Cure of the woman with a hemorrhage. The official's daughter raised to life

18 While he was speaking to them, up came one of the officials, who bowed low in front of him and said, "My daughter has just died, but come and lay your hand on her and her life will be saved." 19 Jesus rose and, with his disciples, followed him.

20 Then from behind him came a woman, who had suffered from a hemorrhage for twelve years, and she touched the fringe of his cloak, 21 for she said to herself, "If I can only touch his cloak I shall be well again." 22 Jesus turned around and saw her and he said to her, "Courage, my daughter, your faith has restored you to health." And from that moment the woman was well again.

23 When Jesus reached the official's house and saw the flute players, with the crowd making a commotion[x] he said, 24 "Get out of here; the little girl is not dead, she is asleep." And they laughed at him. 25 But when the people had been turned out he went inside and took the little girl by the hand; and she stood up. 26And the news spread all around the countryside.

[x] The loud wailing of the oriental mourner.

New English Bible

Even as he spoke, there came a president of the synagogue, who bowed low before him and said, 'My daughter has just died; but come and lay your hand on her, and she will live.' Jesus rose and went with him, and so did his disciples.

Then a woman who had suffered from haemorrhages for twelve years came up from behind, and touched the edge of his cloak; for she said to herself, 'If I can only touch his cloak, I shall be cured.' But Jesus turned and saw her, and said, 'Take heart, my daughter; your faith has cured you.' And from that moment she recovered.

When Jesus arrived at the president's house and saw the flute-players and the general commotion, he said, 'Be off! The girl is not dead: she is asleep'; and they only laughed at him. But, when everyone had been turned out, he went into the room and took the girl by the hand, and she got up. This story became the talk of all the country round.

King James Version

27 And when Jesus departed thence, two blind
men followed him, crying, and saying, *Thou*
Son of David, have mercy on us. 28And when
he was come into the house, the blind men
came to him: and Jesus saith unto them, Believe
ye that I am able to do this? They said unto
him, Yea, Lord. 29 Then touched he their eyes,
saying, According to your faith be it unto you.
30And their eyes were opened; and Jesus straitly
charged them, saying, See *that* no man know *it*.
31 But they, when they were departed, spread
abroad his fame in all that country.
32 As they went out, behold, they brought to
him a dumb man possessed with a devil. 33And
when the devil was cast out, the dumb spake:
and the multitudes marvelled, saying, It was
never so seen in Israel. 34 But the Pharisees said,
He casteth out devils through the prince of the
devils. 35And Jesus went about all the cities
and villages, teaching in their synagogues, and

Living Bible

27 As Jesus was leaving her home, two blind
men followed along behind, shouting, "O Son of
King David, have mercy on us."
28 They went right into the house where he
was staying, and Jesus asked them, "Do you
believe I can make you see?"
"Yes, Lord," they told him, "we do."
29 Then he touched their eyes and said, "Because of your faith it will happen."
30 And suddenly they could see! Jesus sternly
warned them not to tell anyone about it, 31 but
instead they spread his fame all over the town.[h]
32 Leaving that place, Jesus met a man who
couldn't speak because a demon was inside him.
33 So Jesus cast out the demon, and instantly
the man could talk. How the crowds marveled!
"Never in all our lives have we seen anything
like this," they exclaimed.
34 But the Pharisees said, "The reason he can
cast out demons is that he is demon-possessed
himself—possessed by Satan, the demon king!"
35 Jesus traveled around through all the cities
and villages of that area, teaching in the Jewish

[*h*] Literally, "in all that land."

Today's English Version

Jesus heals two blind men

27 Jesus left that place, and as he walked
along two blind men started following him.
"Have mercy on us, Son of David!" they shouted.
28 When Jesus had gone indoors, the two
blind men came to him and he asked them, "Do
you believe that I can do this?"
"Yes, sir!" they answered.
29 Then Jesus touched their eyes and said,
"May it happen, then, just as you believe!"—
30 and their sight was restored. Jesus spoke
harshly to them, "Don't tell this to anyone!"
31 But they left and spread the news about
Jesus all over that part of the country.

Jesus heals a dumb man

32 As the men were leaving, some people
brought to Jesus a man who could not talk because he had a demon. 33As soon as the demon
was driven out, the man started talking. Everyone was amazed. "We never saw the like in Israel!" they exclaimed.
34 But the Pharisees said, "It is the chief of
the demons who gives him the power to drive
them out."

Jesus has pity for the people

35 So Jesus went around visiting all the towns
and villages. He taught in their synagogues,

New International Version

Jesus heals the blind and dumb

27 As Jesus went on from there, two blind men
followed him, calling out, "Have mercy on us,
Son of David!"
28 When he had gone indoors, the blind men
came to him, and he asked them, "Do you believe that I am able to do this?"
"Yes, Lord," they replied.
29 Then he touched their eyes and said, "According to your faith will it be done to you";
30 and their sight was restored. Jesus warned
them sternly, "See that no one knows about
this." 31 But they went out and spread the news
about him all over that region.
32 While they were going out, a man who was
demon-possessed and could not talk was brought
to Jesus. 33And when the demon was driven out,
the man who had been dumb spoke. The crowd
was amazed and said, "Nothing like this has
ever been seen in Israel."
34 But the Pharisees said, "It is by the prince
of demons that he drives out demons."

The workers are few

35 Jesus went through all the towns and villages, teaching in their synagogues, preaching

Phillips Modern English

As Jesus passed on his way two blind men followed him with the cry, "Have pity on us, Son of David!" And when he had gone inside the house these two came up to him.

"Do you believe I can do it?" he said to them.

"Yes, Lord," they replied.

Then he touched their eyes, saying, "You have believed and so it shall be."

Then their sight returned, but Jesus sternly warned them,

"Don't let anyone know about this." Yet they went outside and spread the story throughout the whole district.

Later, when Jesus and his party were coming out, they brought to him a dumb man who was possessed by a devil. As soon as the devil had been ejected the dumb man began to talk. The crowds were simply amazed and said, "Nothing like this has ever been seen in Israel." But the Pharisees' comment was, "He throws out these devils because he is in league with the devil himself."

9.35 Jesus is touched by the people's need

Jesus now travelled through all the towns and villages, teaching in their synagogues, proclaim-

Revised Standard Version

27 And as Jesus passed on from there, two
blind men followed him, crying aloud, "Have
mercy on us, Son of David." 28 When he entered
the house, the blind men came to him; and Jesus
said to them, "Do you believe that I am able to
do this?" They said to him, "Yes, Lord."
29 Then he touched their eyes, saying, "According to your faith be it done to you." 30 And their
eyes were opened. And Jesus sternly charged
them, "See that no one knows it." 31 But they
went away and spread his fame through all that
district.

32 As they were going away, behold, a dumb
demoniac was brought to him. 33 And when the
demon had been cast out, the dumb man spoke;
and the crowds marveled, saying, "Never was
anything like this seen in Israel." 34 But the
Pharisees said, "He casts out demons by the
prince of demons." [a]

35 And Jesus went about all the cities and
villages, teaching in their synagogues and preach-

[a] Other ancient authorities omit this verse.

Jerusalem Bible

Cure of two blind men

27 As Jesus went on his way two blind men
followed him shouting, "Take pity on us, Son of
David." 28 And when Jesus reached the house
the blind men came up with him and he said
to them, "Do you believe I can do this?" They
said, "Sir, we do." 29 Then he touched their eyes
saying, "Your faith deserves it, so let this be
done for you." 30 And their sight returned. Then
Jesus sternly warned them, "Take care that no
one learns about this." 31 But when they had
gone, they talked about him all over the countryside.

Cure of a dumb demoniac

32 They had only just left when a man was
brought to him, a dumb demoniac. 33 And when
the devil was cast out, the dumb man spoke and
the people were amazed. "Nothing like this has
ever been seen in Israel," they said. 34 But the
Pharisees said, "It is through the prince of
devils that he casts out devils."

The distress of the crowds

35 Jesus made a tour through all the towns
and villages, teaching in their synagogues, pro-

New English Bible

As he passed on Jesus was followed by two blind men, who cried out, 'Son of David, have pity on us!' And when he had gone indoors they came to him. Jesus asked, 'Do you believe that I have the power to do what you want?' 'Yes, sir,' they said. Then he touched their eyes, and said, 'As you have believed, so let it be'; and their sight was restored. Jesus said to them sternly, 'See that no one hears about this.' But as soon as they had gone out they talked about him all over the country-side.

They were on their way out when a man was brought to him, who was dumb and possessed by a devil; the devil was cast out and the patient recovered his speech. Filled with amazement the onlookers said, 'Nothing like this has ever been seen in Israel.' [a]

So Jesus went round all the towns and villages teaching in their synagogues, announcing the

[a] *Some witnesses add* (34) But the Pharisees said, 'He casts out devils by the prince of devils.'

King James Version

preaching the gospel of the kingdom, and healing
every sickness and every disease among the people.
36 But when he saw the multitudes, he was
moved with compassion on them, because they
fainted, and were scattered abroad, as sheep having no shepherd. 37 Then saith he unto his disciples, The harvest truly *is* plenteous, but the
labourers *are* few; 38 Pray ye therefore the Lord
of the harvest, that he will send forth labourers
into his harvest.

10 And when he had called unto *him* his
twelve disciples, he gave them power *against*
unclean spirits, to cast them out, and to heal
all manner of sickness and all manner of disease.
2 Now the names of the twelve apostles are
these; The first, Simon, who is called Peter, and
Andrew his brother; James *the son* of Zebedee,
and John his brother; 3 Philip, and Bartholomew; Thomas, and Matthew the publican;
James *the son* of Alpheus, and Lebbeus, whose
surname was Thaddeus; 4 Simon the Canaanite,
and Judas Iscariot, who also betrayed him.
5 These twelve Jesus sent forth, and commanded

Living Bible

synagogues and announcing the Good News
about the Kingdom. And wherever he went he
healed people of every sort of illness. 36And
what pity he felt for the crowds that came, because their problems were so great and they
didn't know what to do or where to go for help.
They were like sheep without a shepherd.
37 "The harvest is so great, and the workers
are so few," he told his disciples. 38 "So pray
to the one in charge of the harvesting, and ask
him to recruit more workers for his harvest
fields."

10 Jesus called his twelve disciples to him,
and gave them authority to cast out evil
spirits and to heal every kind of sickness and
disease.
2, 3, 4 Here are the names of his twelve disciples:

Simon (also called Peter),
Andrew (Peter's brother),
James (Zebedee's son),
John (James' brother),
Philip,
Bartholomew,
Thomas,
Matthew (the tax collector),
James (Alphaeus' son),
Thaddaeus,
Simon (a member of "The Zealots," a sub-
versive political party),
Judas Iscariot (the one who betrayed him).

5 Jesus sent them out with these instructions:

Today's English Version

preached the Good News of the Kingdom, and
healed people from every kind of disease and
sickness. 36As he saw the crowds, his heart was
filled with pity for them, because they were worried and helpless, like sheep without a shepherd.
37 So he said to his disciples, "There is a large
harvest, but few workers to gather it in. 38 Pray
to the owner of the harvest that he will send
out workers to gather in his harvest."

The twelve apostles

10 Jesus called his twelve disciples together
and gave them authority to drive out the
evil spirits and to heal every disease and every
sickness. 2 These are the names of the twelve
apostles: first, Simon (called Peter) and his
brother Andrew; James and his brother John, the
sons of Zebedee; 3 Philip and Bartholomew;
Thomas and Matthew, the tax collector; James,
the son of Alphaeus, and Thaddaeus; 4 Simon
the Patriot, and Judas Iscariot, who betrayed
Jesus.

The mission of the twelve

5 Jesus sent these twelve men out with the

New International Version

the good news of the kingdom and healing every
kind of disease and sickness. 36 When he saw
the crowds, he had compassion on them, because they were harassed and helpless, like sheep
without a shepherd. 37 Then he said to his disciples, "The harvest is plentiful but the workers
are few. 38Ask the Lord of the harvest, therefore, to send out workers into his harvest field."

Jesus sends out the twelve

10 He called his twelve disciples to him and
gave them authority to drive out evil[f]
spirits and to cure every kind of disease and
sickness.
2 These are the names of the twelve apostles:
first, Simon (who is called Peter) and his
brother Andrew; James son of Zebedee, and his
brother John; 3 Philip and Bartholomew; Thomas
and Matthew the tax collector; James son of
Alphaeus, and Thaddaeus; 4 Simon the Zealot
and Judas Iscariot, who betrayed him.
5 These twelve Jesus sent out with the fol-

[f] Greek *unclean.*

Phillips Modern English

ing the gospel of the kingdom, and healing all kinds of illness and disability. As he looked at the vast crowds he was deeply moved with pity for them, for they were as bewildered and miserable as a flock of sheep with no shepherd.

"The harvest is great enough," he remarked to his disciples, "but the reapers are few. So you must pray to the Lord of the harvest to send men out to bring it in."

10.1 Jesus sends out the twelve with divine power

Jesus called his twelve disciples to him and gave them authority to expel evil spirits and heal all kinds of disease and infirmity. The names of the twelve apostles are:

First, Simon, called Peter, with his brother Andrew;
James and his brother John, sons of Zebedee;
Philip and Bartholomew,
Thomas, and Matthew the tax-collector,
James, the son of Alphaeus, and Thaddaeus,
Simon the Patriot, and Judas Iscariot, who later turned traitor.

These were the twelve whom Jesus sent out,

Revised Standard Version

ing the gospel of the kingdom, and healing every
disease and every infirmity. 36 When he saw the
crowds, he had compassion for them, because
they were harassed and helpless, like sheep without a shepherd. 37 Then he said to his disciples,
"The harvest is plentiful, but the laborers are
few; 38 pray therefore the Lord of the harvest to
send out laborers into his harvest."

10 And he called to him his twelve disciples
and gave them authority over unclean
spirits, to cast them out, and to heal every disease and every infirmity. 2 The names of the
twelve apostles are these: first, Simon, who is
called Peter, and Andrew his brother; James the
son of Zebedee, and John his brother; 3 Philip
and Batholomew; Thomas and Matthew the tax
collector; James the son of Alphaeus, and Thaddaeus;[x] 4 Simon the Cananaean, and Judas Iscariot, who betrayed him.
5 These twelve Jesus sent out, charging them,

[x] Other ancient authorities read ***Lebbaeus*** or ***Lebbaeus called Thaddaeus.***

Jerusalem Bible

claiming the Good News of the kingdom and
curing all kinds of diseases and sickness.
36 And when he saw the crowds he felt sorry
for them because they were harassed and de-
jected, like sheep without a shepherd. 37 Then
he said to his disciples, "The harvest is rich but
the laborers are few, so ask the Lord of the
harvest to send laborers to his harvest."

B. The instruction of the apostles

The mission of the Twelve

10 He summoned his twelve disciples, and
gave them authority over unclean spirits
with power to cast them out and to cure all
kinds of diseases and sickness.
2 These are the names of the twelve apostles: first, Simon who is called Peter, and his
brother Andrew; James the son of Zebedee, and
his brother John; 3 Philip and Bartholomew;
Thomas, and Matthew the tax collector; James
the son of Alphaeus, and Thaddaeus; 4 Simon
the Zealot and Judas Iscariot, the one who was
to betray him. 5 These twelve Jesus sent out, in-

New English Bible

good news of the Kingdom, and curing every kind of ailment and disease. The sight of the people moved him to pity: they were like sheep without a shepherd, harassed and helpless; and he said to his disciples, 'The crop is heavy, but labourers are scarce; you must therefore beg the owner to send labourers to harvest his crop.'

10 Then he called his twelve disciples to him and gave them authority to cast out unclean spirits and to cure every kind of ailment and disease.

These are the names of the twelve apostles: first Simon, also called Peter, and his brother Andrew; James son of Zebedee, and his brother John; Philip and Bartholomew, Thomas and Matthew the tax-gatherer, James son of Alphaeus, Lebbaeus,[b] Simon, a member of the Zealot party, and Judas Iscariot, the man who betrayed him.

These twelve Jesus sent out with the follow-

[b] *Some witnesses read* Thaddaeus.

King James Version

them, saying, Go not into the way of the Gentiles, and into *any* city of the Samaritans enter
ye not: 6 But go rather to the lost sheep of the
house of Israel. 7And as ye go, preach, saying,
The kingdom of heaven is at hand. 8 Heal the
sick, cleanse the lepers, raise the dead, cast out
devils: freely ye have received, freely give.
9 Provide neither gold, nor silver, nor brass in
your purses; 10 Nor scrip for *your* journey,
neither two coats, neither shoes, nor yet staves:
for the workman is worthy of his meat. 11And
into whatsoever city or town ye shall enter, inquire who in it is worthy; and there abide till ye
go thence. 12And when ye come into a house,
salute it. 13And if the house be worthy, let your
peace come upon it: but if it be not worthy,
let your peace return to you. 14And whosoever
shall not receive you, nor hear your words, when
ye depart out of that house or city, shake off
the dust of your feet. 15 Verily I say unto you,
It shall be more tolerable for the land of Sodom
and Gomorrah in the day of judgment, than for
that city.

16 Behold, I send you forth as sheep in the
midst of wolves: be ye therefore wise as serpents,
and harmless as doves. 17 But beware of men:
for they will deliver you up to the councils, and
they will scourge you in their synagogues; 18And
ye shall be brought before governors and kings

Living Bible

"Don't go to the Gentiles or the Samaritans,
6 but only to the people of Israel—God's lost
sheep. 7 Go and announce to them that the
Kingdom of Heaven is near.[a] 8 Heal the sick,
raise the dead, cure the lepers, and cast out
demons. Give as freely as you have received!

9 "Don't take any money with you; 10 don't
even carry a duffle bag with extra clothes and
shoes, or even a walking stick; for those you
help should feed and care for you. 11 Whenever
you enter a city or village, search for a godly
man and stay in his home until you leave for
the next town. 12 When you ask permission to
stay, be friendly, 13 and if it turns out to be a
godly home, give it your blessing; if not, keep
the blessing. 14Any city or home that doesn't
welcome you—shake off the dust of that place
from your feet as you leave. 15 Truly, the wicked
cities of Sodom and Gomorrah will be better off
at Judgment Day than they.

16 "I am sending you out as sheep among
wolves. Be as wary as serpents and harmless as
doves. 17 But beware! For you will be arrested
and tried, and whipped in the synagogues.
18 Yes, and you must stand trial before governors

[a] Or, "at hand," or, "has arrived."

Today's English Version

following instructions: "Do not go to any Gentile territory or any Samaritan towns. 6 Go, instead, to the lost sheep of the people of Israel.
7 Go and preach, 'The Kingdom of heaven is
near!' 8 Heal the sick, raise the dead, make the
lepers clean, drive out demons. You have received without paying, so give without being
paid. 9 Do not carry any gold, silver, or copper
money in your pockets; 10 do not carry a beggar's bag for the trip, or an extra shirt, or shoes,
or a walking stick. A worker should be given
what he needs.

11 "When you come to a town or village, go
in and look for someone who is willing to welcome you, and stay with him until you leave that
place. 12 When you go into a house say, 'Peace
be with you.' 13 If the people in that house welcome you, let your greeting of peace remain; but
if they do not welcome you, then take back
your greeting. 14And if some home or town will
not welcome you or listen to you, then leave that
place and shake the dust off your feet. 15 Remember this! On the Judgment Day God will
show more mercy to the people of Sodom and
Gomorrah than to the people of that town!"

Coming persecutions

16 "Listen! I am sending you just like sheep
to a pack of wolves. You must be as cautious as
snakes and as gentle as doves. 17 Watch out, for
there will be men who will arrest you and take
you to court, and they will whip you in their
synagogues. 18 You will be brought to trial be-

New International Version

lowing instructions: "Do not go among the
Gentiles or enter any town of the Samaritans.
6 Go rather to the lost sheep of Israel. 7As you
go, preach this message: 'The kingdom of heaven
is near.' 8 Heal the sick, raise the dead, cleanse
those who have leprosy,[g] drive out demons.
Freely you have received, freely give. 9 Do not
take along any gold or silver or copper in your
belts; 10 take no bag for the journey, or extra
tunic, or sandals or a staff; for the worker is
worth his keep.

11 "Whatever city or village you enter, search
for some worthy person there and stay at his
house until you leave. 12As you enter the home,
give it your greeting. 13 If the home is deserving,
let your peace rest on it; if it is not, let your
peace return to you. 14 If anyone will not welcome you or listen to your words, shake the dust
off your feet when you leave that home or town.
15 I tell you the truth, it will be more bearable
for Sodom and Gomorrah on the day of judgment than for that town.

16 "I am sending you out like sheep among
wolves. Therefore be as shrewd as snakes and
as innocent as doves. 17 But be on your guard
against men; they will hand you over to the
local councils and flog you in their synagogues.
18 On my account you will be brought before

[g] The Greek word probably designated other related diseases also.

Phillips Modern English

with the instructions: "Don't turn off into any of the heathen roads, and don't go into any Samaritan town. Go rather to the lost sheep of the house of Israel. As you go proclaim that the kingdom of Heaven has arrived. Heal the sick, raise the dead, cure the lepers, drive out devils—give, as you have received, without any charge whatever.

"Don't take any gold or silver or even coppers to put in your purse; nor a knapsack for the journey, nor even a second coat, nor sandals nor staff—the workman deserves his keep!

"Wherever you go, whether it is into a town or a village, find out someone who is respected, and stay with him until you leave. As you enter his house give it your blessing. If the house deserves it, the peace of your blessing will come to it. But if it doesn't, your peace will return to you.

"And if no one will welcome you or even listen to what you have to say, leave that house or town, and once outside it shake off the dust of that place from your feet. Believe me, it will be easier for Sodom and Gomorrah in the day of judgment than for that town.

10.16 He warns them of troubles that lie ahead

"Here am I sending you out like sheep with wolves all round you; so be as wise as serpents and harmless as doves. But be on your guard against men. For they will take you to the courts and flog you in the synagogues. You will be brought into the presence of governors and kings

Revised Standard Version

"Go nowhere among the Gentiles, and enter no
town of the Samaritans, 6 but go rather to the
lost sheep of the house of Israel. 7 And preach
as you go, saying, 'The kingdom of heaven is
at hand.' 8 Heal the sick, raise the dead, cleanse
lepers, cast out demons. You received without
paying, give without pay. 9 Take no gold, nor
silver, nor copper in your belts, 10 no bag for
your journey, nor two tunics, nor sandals, nor
a staff; for the laborer deserves his food. 11 And
whatever town or village you enter, find out
who is worthy in it, and stay with him until you
depart. 12 As you enter the house, salute it.
13 And if the house is worthy, let your peace
come upon it; but if it is not worthy, let your
peace return to you. 14 And if any one will not
receive you or listen to your words, shake off
the dust from your feet as you leave that house
or town. 15 Truly, I say to you, it shall be more
tolerable on the day of judgment for the land
of Sodom and Gomorrah than for that town.
16 "Behold, I send you out as sheep in the
midst of wolves; so be wise as serpents and innocent as doves. 17 Beware of men; for they
will deliver you up to councils, and flog you in
their synagogues, 18 and you will be dragged

Jerusalem Bible

structing them as follows:
"Do not turn your steps to pagan territory,
and do not enter any Samaritan town; 6 go
rather to the lost sheep of the House of Israel.
7 And as you go, proclaim that the kingdom of
heaven is close at hand. 8 Cure the sick, raise
the dead, cleanse the lepers, cast out devils. You
received without charge, give without charge.
9 Provide yourselves with no gold or silver, not
even with a few coppers for your purses, 10 with
no haversack for the journey or spare tunic or
footwear or a staff, for the workman deserves
his keep.
11 "Whatever town or village you go into,
ask for someone trustworthy and stay with him
until you leave. 12 As you enter his house, salute
it, 13 and if the house deserves it, let your peace
descend upon it; if it does not, let your peace
come back to you. 14 And if anyone does not
welcome you or listen to what you have to say,
as you walk out of the house or town, shake
the dust from your feet. 15 I tell you solemnly,
on the day of Judgment it will not go as hard
with the land of Sodom and Gomorrah as with
that town. 16 Remember, I am sending you out
like sheep among wolves; so be cunning as serpents and yet as harmless as doves.

The missionaries will be persecuted [y]

17 "Beware of men: they will hand you over
to Sanhedrins and scourge you in their synagogues. 18 You will be dragged before governors

[y] The conditions described in vv. 17-39 are those of a later time than this first mission of the Twelve.

New English Bible

ing instructions: 'Do not take the road to gentile lands, and do not enter any Samaritan town; but go rather to the lost sheep of the house of Israel. And as you go proclaim the message: "The kingdom of Heaven is upon you." Heal the sick, raise the dead, cleanse lepers, cast out devils. You received without cost; give without charge.

'Provide no gold, silver, or copper to fill your purse, no pack for the road, no second coat, no shoes, no stick; the worker earns his keep.

'When you come to any town or village, look for some worthy person in it, and make your home there until you leave. Wish the house peace as you enter it, so that, if it is worthy, your peace may descend on it; if it is not worthy, your peace can come back to you. If anyone will not receive you or listen to what you say, then as you leave that house or that town shake the dust of it off your feet. I tell you this: on the day of judgement it will be more bearable for the land of Sodom and Gomorrah than for that town.

'Look, I send you out like sheep among wolves; be wary as serpents, innocent as doves.

'And be on your guard, for men will hand you over to their courts, they will flog you in the synagogues, and you will be brought before governors and kings, for my sake, to testify

King James Version

for my sake, for a testimony against them and
the Gentiles. 19 But when they deliver you up,
take no thought how or what ye shall speak: for
it shall be given you in that same hour what ye
shall speak. 20 For it is not ye that speak, but the
Spirit of your Father which speaketh in you.
21 And the brother shall deliver up the brother to
death, and the father the child: and the children
shall rise up against *their* parents, and cause
them to be put to death. 22 And ye shall be hated
of all *men* for my name's sake: but he that endureth to the end shall be saved. 23 But when
they persecute you in this city, flee ye into another: for verily I say unto you, Ye shall not
have gone over the cities of Israel, till the Son
of man be come. 24 The disciple is not above
his master, nor the servant above his lord. 25 It
is enough for the disciple that he be as his
master, and the servant as his lord. If they have
called the master of the house Beelzebub, how
much more *shall they call* them of his household? 26 Fear them not therefore: for there is
nothing covered, that shall not be revealed; and
hid, that shall not be known. 27 What I tell you
in darkness, *that* speak ye in light: and what ye
hear in the ear, *that* preach ye upon the house-

Living Bible

and kings for my sake. This will give you the
opportunity to tell them about me, yes, to witness to the world.
19 "When you are arrested, don't worry about
what to say at your trial, for you will be
given the right words at the right time. 20 For
it won't be you doing the talking—it will be the
Spirit of your heavenly Father speaking through
you!
21 "Brother shall betray brother to death, and
fathers shall betray their own children. And children shall rise against their parents and cause
their deaths. 22 Everyone shall hate you because
you belong to me. But all of you who endure to
the end shall be saved.
23 "When you are persecuted in one city, flee
to the next! I [b] will return before you have
reached them all! 24 A student is not greater than
his teacher. A servant is not above his master.
25 The student shares his teacher's fate. The
servant shares his master's! And since I, the
master of the household, have been called 'Satan,' [c] how much more will you! 26 But don't be
afraid of those who threaten you. For the time
is coming when the truth will be revealed: their
secret plots will become public information.
27 "What I tell you now in the gloom, shout
abroad when daybreak comes. What I whisper
in your ears, proclaim from the housetops!

[*b*] Literally, "the Son of Man." [*c*] See Matthew 9:34, where they called him this.

Today's English Version

fore rulers and kings for my sake, to tell the
Good News to them and to the Gentiles. 19 When
they bring you to trial, do not worry about what
you are going to say or how you will say it;
when the time comes, you will be given what you
will say. 20 For the words you speak will not be
yours; they will come from the Spirit of your
Father speaking in you.
21 "Men will hand over their own brothers to
be put to death, and fathers will do the same to
their children; children will turn against their
parents and have them put to death. 22 Everyone will hate you, because of me. But whoever
holds out to the end will be saved. 23 And when
they persecute you in one town, run away to
another one. I tell you, you will not finish your
work in all the towns of Israel before the Son
of Man comes.
24 "No pupil is greater than his teacher; no
slave is greater than his master. 25 So a pupil
should be satisfied to become like his teacher,
and a slave like his master. If the head of the
family is called Beelzebul, the members of the
family will be called by even worse names!"

Whom to fear

26 "Do not be afraid of men, then. Whatever
is covered up will be uncovered, and every secret
will be made known. 27 What I am telling you
in the dark you must repeat in broad daylight,
and what you have heard in private you must

New International Version

governors and kings as witnesses to them and
to the Gentiles. 19 But when they arrest you, do
not worry about what to say or how to say it.
At that time you will be given what to say,
20 for it will not be you speaking, but the
Spirit of your Father speaking through you.
21 "Brother will betray brother to death, and
a father his child; children will rebel against
their parents and have them put to death. 22 All
men will hate you because of me, but he who
stands firm to the end will be saved. 23 When
you are persecuted in one place, flee to another.
I tell you the truth, you will not finish going
through the cities of Israel before the Son of
Man comes.
24 "A student is not above his teacher, nor
a servant above his master. 25 It is enough for
the student to be like his teacher, and the servant like his master. If the head of the house
has been called Beelzebub,[h] how much more the
members of his household!
26 "So do not be afraid of them. There is
nothing concealed that will not be disclosed, or
hidden that will not be made known. 27 What
I tell you in the dark, speak in the daylight;
what is whispered in your ear, proclaim from

[*h*] Greek MSS *Beelzeboul* or *Beezeboul*.

Phillips Modern English

because of me—to give your witness to them and to the heathen.

"But when they do arrest you, never worry about how you are to speak or what you are to say. You will be told at the time what you are to say. For it will not be really you who are speaking but the Spirit of your Father speaking through you.

"Brother will betray brother to death, and a father his children. Children will turn against their parents and have them executed. You yourselves will be universally hated because of my name. But the man who endures to the very end will be safe and sound.

"But when they persecute you in one town make your escape to the next. Believe me, you will not have covered the towns of Israel before the Son of Man arrives. The disciple is not superior to his teacher any more than the servant is superior to his master, for what is good enough for the teacher is good enough for the disciple, and the servant will not fare better than his master. If men call the master of the household the 'Prince of Evil', what sort of names will they give to his servants? But never let them frighten you, for there is nothing covered up which is not going to be exposed nor anything private which will not be made public. The things I tell you in the dark you must say in the daylight, and the things you hear in your private ear you must proclaim from the housetops.

Revised Standard Version

before governors and kings for my sake, to bear testimony before them and the Gentiles. 19 When they deliver you up, do not be anxious how you are to speak or what you are to say; for what you are to say will be given to you in that hour; 20 for it is not you who speak, but the Spirit of your Father speaking through you. 21 Brother will deliver up brother to death, and the father his child, and children will rise against parents and have them put to death; 22 and you will be hated by all for my name's sake. But he who endures to the end will be saved. 23 When they persecute you in one town, flee to the next; for truly, I say to you, you will not have gone through all the towns of Israel, before the Son of man comes.

24 "A disciple is not above his teacher, nor a servant[y] above his master; 25 it is enough for the disciple to be like his teacher, and the servant[y] like his master. If they have called the master of the house Beelzebul, how much more will they malign those of his household.

26 "So have no fear of them; for nothing is covered that will not be revealed, or hidden that will not be known. 27 What I tell you in the dark, utter in the light; and what you hear whispered,

[y] Or *slave*.

Jerusalem Bible

and kings for my sake, to bear witness before them and the pagans. 19 But when they hand you over, do not worry about how to speak or what to say; what you are to say will be given to you when the time comes; 20 because it is not you who will be speaking; the Spirit of your Father will be speaking in you.

21 "Brother will betray brother to death, and the father his child; children will rise against their parents and have them put to death. 22 You will be hated by all men on account of my name; but the man who stands firm to the end will be saved. 23 If they persecute you in one town, take refuge in the next; and if they persecute you in that, take refuge in another. I tell you solemnly, you will not have gone the round of the towns of Israel before the Son of Man comes.

24 "The disciple is not superior to his teacher, nor the slave to his master. 25 It is enough for the disciple that he should grow to be like his teacher, and the slave like his master. If they have called the master of the house Beelzebul, what will they not say of his household?

Open and fearless speech

26 "Do not be afraid of them therefore. For everything that is now covered will be uncovered, and everything now hidden will be made clear. 27 What I say to you in the dark, tell in the daylight; what you hear in whispers, proclaim from the housetops.

New English Bible

before them and the heathen. But when you are arrested, do not worry about what you are to say; when the time comes, the words you need will be given you; for it is not you who will be speaking: it will be the Spirit of your Father speaking in you.

'Brother will betray brother to death, and the father his child; children will turn against their parents and send them to their death. All will hate you for your allegiance to me; but the man who holds out to the end will be saved. When you are persecuted in one town, take refuge in another; I tell you this: before you have gone through all the towns of Israel the Son of Man will have come.

'A pupil does not rank above his teacher, or a servant above his master. The pupil should be content to share his teacher's lot, the servant to share his master's. If the master has been called Beelzebub, how much more his household!

'So do not be afraid of them. There is nothing covered up that will not be uncovered, nothing hidden that will not be made known. What I say to you in the dark you must repeat in broad daylight; what you hear whispered you must

King James Version

tops. 28And fear not them which kill the body,
but are not able to kill the soul: but rather fear
him which is able to destroy both soul and body
in hell. 29Are not two sparrows sold for a
farthing? and one of them shall not fall on the
ground without your Father. 30 But the very
hairs of your head are all numbered. 31 Fear ye
not therefore, ye are of more value than many
sparrows. 32 Whosoever therefore shall confess
me before men, him will I confess also before
my Father which is in heaven. 33 But whosoever shall deny me before men, him will I also
deny before my Father which is in heaven.
34 Think not that I am come to send peace on
earth: I came not to send peace, but a sword.
35 For I am come to set a man at variance
against his father, and the daughter against her
mother, and the daughter in law against her
mother in law. 36And a man's foes *shall be* they
of his own household. 37 He that loveth father
or mother more than me is not worthy of me:
and he that loveth son or daughter more than
me is not worthy of me. 38And he that taketh

Living Bible

28 "Don't be afraid of those who can kill
only your bodies—but can't touch your souls!
Fear only God who can destroy both soul and
body in hell. 29 Not one sparrow (What do
they cost? Two for a penny?) can fall to the
ground without your Father knowing it. 30And
the very hairs of your head are all numbered.
31 So don't worry! You are more valuable to
him than many sparrows.

32 "If anyone publicly acknowledges me as
his friend, I will openly acknowledge him as my
friend before my Father in heaven. 33 But if
anyone publicly denies me, I will openly deny
him before my Father in heaven.

34 "Don't imagine that I came to bring peace
to the earth! No, rather, a sword. 35 I have come
to set a man against his father, and a daughter
against her mother, and a daughter-in-law against
her mother-in-law—36 a man's worst enemies will
be right in his own home! 37 If you love your
father and mother more than you love me, you
are not worthy of being mine; or if you love
your son or daughter more than me, you are
not worthy of being mine. 38 If you refuse to

Today's English Version

tell from the housetops. 28 Do not be afraid of
those who kill the body but cannot kill the soul;
rather be afraid of God, who can destroy both
body and soul in hell. 29 You can buy two sparrows for a penny; yet not a single one of them
falls to the ground without your Father's consent. 30As for you, even the hairs of your head
have all been counted. 31 So do not be afraid;
you are worth much more than many sparrows!"

Confessing and denying Christ

32 "Whoever declares publicly that he belongs
to me, I will do the same for him before my
Father in heaven. 33 But whoever denies publicly
that he belongs to me, then I will deny him before my Father in heaven."

Not peace, but a sword

34 "Do not think that I have come to bring
peace to the world; no, I did not come to bring
peace, but a sword. 35 I came to set sons against
their fathers, daughters against their mothers,
daughters-in-law against their mothers-in-law;
36 a man's worst enemies will be the members
of his own family.

37 "Whoever loves his father or mother more
than me is not worthy of me; whoever loves his
son or daughter more than me is not worthy of
me. 38 Whoever does not take up his cross and

New International Version

the housetops. 28 Do not be afraid of those who
kill the body but cannot kill the soul. Rather,
be afraid of the one who can destroy both soul
and body in hell. 29Are not two sparrows sold
for a penny? Yet not one of them will fall to
the ground apart from the will of your Father.
30And even the very hairs of your head are all
numbered. 31 So don't be afraid; you are worth
more than many sparrows.

32 "Whoever acknowledges me before men, I
will also acknowledge him before my Father in
heaven. 33 But whoever disowns me before men,
I will disown him before my Father in heaven.

34 "Do not suppose that I have come to bring
peace to the earth. I did not come to bring
peace, but a sword. 35 For I have come to turn
'a man against his father,
a daughter against her mother,
and a daughter-in-law against her mother-in-law.
36 A man's enemies will be the members of
his own household.' [i]

37 "Anyone who loves his father or mother
more than me is not worthy of me; anyone who
loves his son or daughter more than me is not
worthy of me; 38 and anyone who does not take

[i] Micah 7:6.

Phillips Modern English

10.28 They should reverence God but have no fear of man

"Never be afraid of those who can kill the body but are powerless to kill the soul! Far better to stand in awe of the one who has the power to destroy body and soul in the fires of destruction!

"Two sparrows are sold for a farthing, aren't they? Yet not a single sparrow falls to the ground without your father's knowledge. The very hairs of your head are all numbered. Never be afraid, then—you are far more valuable than sparrows.

"Every man who publicly acknowledges me I shall acknowledge in the presence of my Father in Heaven, but the man who disowns me before men I shall disown before my Father in Heaven.

10.34 The Prince of Peace comes to bring division

"Never think I have come to bring peace upon the earth. No, I have not come to bring peace but a sword! For I have come to set a man against his own father, a daughter against her own mother, and a daughter-in-law against her mother-in-law. A man's enemies will be those who live in his own house.

"Anyone who puts his love for father or mother above his love for me does not deserve to be mine, and he who loves son or daughter more than me is not worthy of me, and neither is the man who refuses to take up his cross and fol-

Revised Standard Version

proclaim upon the housetops.
28And do not fear those who kill the body but cannot kill the soul; rather fear him who can destroy both soul and body in hell.[z]
29Are not two sparrows sold for a penny? And not one of them will fall to the ground without your Father's will.
30 But even the hairs of your head are all numbered.
31 Fear not, therefore; you are of more value than many sparrows.
32 So every one who acknowledges me before men, I also will acknowledge before my Father who is in heaven;
33 but whoever denies me before men, I also will deny before my Father who is in heaven.

34 "Do not think that I have come to bring peace on earth; I have not come to bring peace, but a sword.
35 For I have come to set a man against his father, and a daughter against her mother, and a daughter-in-law against her mother-in-law;
36 and a man's foes will be those of his own household.
37 He who loves father or mother more than me is not worthy of me; and he who loves son or daughter more than me is not worthy of me;
38 and he who does

[z] Greek *Gehenna*.

Jerusalem Bible

28 "Do not be afraid of those who kill the body but cannot kill the soul; fear him rather who can destroy both body and soul in hell.
29 Can you not buy two sparrows for a penny? And yet not one falls to the ground without your Father knowing.
30 Why, every hair on your head has been counted.
31 So there is no need to be afraid; you are worth more than hundreds of sparrows.

32 "So if anyone declares himself for me in the presence of men, I will declare myself for him in the presence of my Father in heaven.
33 But the one who disowns me in the presence of men, I will disown in the presence of my Father in heaven.

Jesus, the cause of dissension

34 "Do not suppose that I have come to bring peace to the earth: it is not peace I have come to bring, but a sword.
35 For I have come to set *a man against his father, a daughter against her mother, a daughter-in-law against her mother-in-law.*
36*A man's enemies will be those of his own household.*[z]

Renouncing self to follow Jesus

37 "Anyone who prefers father or mother to me is not worthy of me. Anyone who prefers son or daughter to me is not worthy of me.
38Anyone who does not take his cross and fol-

[z] Mi. 7:6.

New English Bible

shout from the house-tops. Do not fear those who kill the body, but cannot kill the soul. Fear him rather who is able to destroy both soul and body in hell.

'Are not sparrows two a penny? Yet without your Father's leave not one of them can fall to the ground. As for you, even the hairs of your head have all been counted. So have no fear; you are worth more than any number of sparrows.

'Whoever then will acknowledge me before men, I will acknowledge him before my Father in heaven; and whoever disowns me before men, I will disown him before my Father in heaven.

'You must not think that I have come to bring peace to the earth; I have not come to bring peace, but a sword. I have come to set a man against his father, a daughter against her mother, a son's wife against her mother-in-law; and a man will find his enemies under his own roof.

'No man is worthy of me who cares more for father or mother than for me; no man is worthy of me who cares more for son or daughter; no man is worthy of me who does not take up his

King James Version

not his cross, and followeth after me, is not worthy of me. 39 He that findeth his life shall lose it: and he that loseth his life for my sake shall find it.

40 He that receiveth you receiveth me; and he that receiveth me receiveth him that sent me. 41 He that receiveth a prophet in the name of a prophet shall receive a prophet's reward; and he that receiveth a righteous man in the name of a righteous man shall receive a righteous man's reward. 42And whosoever shall give to drink unto one of these little ones a cup of cold *water* only in the name of a disciple, verily I say unto you, he shall in no wise lose his reward.

11 And it came to pass, when Jesus had made an end of commanding his twelve disciples, he departed thence to teach and to preach in

Living Bible

take up your cross and follow me, you are not worthy of being mine.

39 "If you cling to your life, you will lose it; but if you give it up for me, you will save it.

40 "Those who welcome you are welcoming me. And when they welcome me they are welcoming God who sent me. 41 If you welcome a prophet because he is a man of God, you will be given the same reward a prophet gets. And if you welcome good and godly men because of their godliness, you will be given a reward like theirs.

42 "And if, as my representatives, you give even a cup of cold water to a little child, you will surely be rewarded."

11 When Jesus had finished giving these instructions to his twelve disciples, he went off preaching in the cities where they were scheduled to go.[a]

[a] Literally, "to teach and preach in their cities." Luke 10:1 remarks, "The Lord appointed seventy others and sent them two and two before his face, into every city and place where he himself was about to come."

Today's English Version

follow in my steps is not worthy of me. 39 Whoever tries to gain his own life will lose it; whoever loses his life for my sake will gain it."

Rewards

40 "Whoever welcomes you, welcomes me; and whoever welcomes me, welcomes the one who sent me. 41 Whoever welcomes God's messenger because he is God's messenger will share in his reward; and whoever welcomes a truly good man, because he is that, will share in his reward. 42And remember this! Whoever gives even a drink of cold water to one of the least of these my followers, because he is my follower, will certainly receive his reward."

The messengers from John the Baptist

11 When Jesus finished giving these instructions to his twelve disciples, he left that place and went on to teach and preach in the towns near there.

New International Version

his cross and follow me is not worthy of me. 39 Whoever finds his life will lose it, and whoever loses his life for my sake will find it.

40 "He who receives you receives me, and he who receives me receives the one who sent me. 41Anyone who receives a prophet because he is a prophet will receive a prophet's reward, and anyone who receives a righteous man because he is a righteous man will receive a righteous man's reward. 42And if anyone gives a cup of cold water to one of these little ones because he is my disciple, I tell you the truth, he will certainly not lose his reward."

Jesus and John the Baptist

11 After Jesus had finished instructing his twelve disciples, he went on from there to teach and preach in the towns of Galilee.[j]

[j] Greek *in their towns.*

Phillips Modern English

low my way. The man who has found his own life will lose it, but the man who has lost it for my sake will find it.

"Whoever welcomes you, welcomes me; and whoever welcomes me is welcoming him who sent me.

"Whoever welcomes a prophet because he is a prophet will get a prophet's reward. And whoever welcomes a good man because he is a good man will get a good man's reward. Believe me, anyone who gives even a cup of cold water to one of these little ones, just because he is my disciple, will by no means lose his reward."

When Jesus had finished giving his twelve disciples these instructions he went on from there to teach and preach in the towns in which they lived.

Revised Standard Version

not take his cross and follow me is not worthy
of me. 39 He who finds his life will lose it, and
he who loses his life for my sake will find it.
40 "He who receives you receives me, and
he who receives me receives him who sent me.
41 He who receives a prophet because he is a
prophet shall receive a prophet's reward, and he
who receives a righteous man because he is a
righteous man shall receive a righteous man's
reward. 42 And whoever gives to one of these
little ones even a cup of cold water because he
is a disciple, truly, I say to you, he shall not
lose his reward."

11 And when Jesus had finished instructing his twelve disciples, he went on from there to teach and preach in their cities.

Jerusalem Bible

low in my footsteps is not worthy of me. 39 Anyone who finds his life will lose it; anyone who
loses his life for my sake will find it.

Conclusion

40 "Anyone who welcomes you welcomes me; and those who welcome me welcome the one who sent me.

41 "Anyone who welcomes a prophet because he is a prophet will have a prophet's reward; and anyone who welcomes a holy man because he is a holy man will have a holy man's reward.

42 "If anyone gives so much as a cup of cold water to one of these little ones because he is a disciple, then I tell you solemnly, he will most certainly not lose his reward."

IV. The mystery of the kingdom of heaven

A. Narrative section

11 When Jesus had finished instructing his twelve disciples he moved on from there to teach and preach in their towns.[a]

[a] I.e., the Jews' towns.

New English Bible

cross and walk in my footsteps. By gaining his life a man will lose it; by losing his life for my sake, he will gain it.

'To receive you is to receive me, and to receive me is to receive the One who sent me. Whoever receives a prophet as a prophet will be given a prophet's reward, and whoever receives a good man because he is a good man will be given a good man's reward. And if anyone gives so much as a cup of cold water to one of these little ones, because he is a disciple of mine, I tell you this: that man will assuredly not go unrewarded.'

11 When Jesus had finished giving his twelve disciples their instructions, he left that place and went to teach and preach in the neighbouring towns.

King James Version

their cities. 2 Now when John had heard in the
prison the works of Christ, he sent two of his
disciples, 3 And said unto him, Art thou he that
should come, or do we look for another? 4 Jesus
answered and said unto them, Go and shew
John again those things which ye do hear and
see: 5 The blind receive their sight, and the
lame walk, the lepers are cleansed, and the deaf
hear, the dead are raised up, and the poor have
the gospel preached to them. 6 And blessed is *he*,
whosoever shall not be offended in me.
7 And as they departed, Jesus began to say
unto the multitudes concerning John, What went
ye out into the wilderness to see? A reed shaken
with the wind? 8 But what went ye out for to
see? A man clothed in soft raiment? behold, they
that wear soft *clothing* are in kings' houses.
9 But what went ye out for to see? A prophet?
yea, I say unto you, and more than a prophet.
10 For this is *he*, of whom it is written, Behold,
I send my messenger before thy face, which shall
prepare thy way before thee. 11 Verily I say unto
you, Among them that are born of women there
hath not risen a greater than John the Baptist:
notwithstanding, he that is least in the kingdom
of heaven is greater than he. 12 And from the
days of John the Baptist until now the kingdom

Living Bible

2 John the Baptist, who was now in prison,
heard about all the miracles the Messiah was
doing, so he sent his disciples to ask Jesus,
3 "Are you really the one we are waiting for,
or shall we keep on looking?"
4 Jesus told them, "Go back to John and tell
him about the miracles you've seen me do—
5 the blind people I've healed, and the lame
people now walking without help, and the cured
lepers, and the deaf who hear, and the dead
raised to life; and tell him about my preaching
the Good News to the poor. 6 Then give him
this message, 'Blessed are those who don't doubt
me.' "
7 When John's disciples had gone, Jesus began
talking about him to the crowds. "When you
went out into the barren wilderness to see John,
what did you expect him to be like? Grass blowing in the wind? 8 Or were you expecting to see
a man dressed as a prince in a palace? 9 Or a
prophet of God? Yes, and he is more than just
a prophet. 10 For John is the man mentioned in
the Scriptures—a messenger to precede me, to
announce my coming, and prepare people to
receive me.[b]
11 "Truly, of all men ever born, none shines
more brightly than John the Baptist. And yet,
even the lesser lights in the Kingdom of Heaven
will be greater than he is! 12 And from the time
John the Baptist began preaching and baptizing

[*b*] Literally, "prepare your way before you."

Today's English Version

2 When John the Baptist heard in prison
about Christ's works, he sent some of his disciples to him. 3 "Tell us," they asked Jesus, "are
you the one John said was going to come, or
should we expect someone else?"
4 Jesus answered, "Go back and tell John
what you are hearing and seeing: 5 the blind can
see, the lame can walk, the lepers are made
clean, the deaf hear, the dead are raised to life,
and the Good News is preached to the poor.
6 How happy is he who has no doubts about me!"
7 While John's disciples were going back, Jesus spoke about John to the crowds, "When you
went out to John in the desert, what did you
expect to see? A blade of grass bending in the
wind? 8 What did you go out to see? A man
dressed up in fancy clothes? People who dress
like that live in palaces! 9 Tell me, what did you
go out to see? A prophet? Yes, I tell you—you
saw much more than a prophet. 10 For John is
the one of whom the scripture says: 'Here is my
messenger, says God; I will send him ahead of
you to open the way for you.' 11 Remember this!
John the Baptist is greater than any man who
has ever lived. But he who is least in the Kingdom of heaven is greater than he. 12 From the
time John preached his message until this very

New International Version

2 When John heard in prison what Christ was
doing, he sent his disciples 3 to ask him, "Are
you the one who was to come, or should we expect someone else?"
4 Jesus replied, "Go back and report to John
what you hear and see: 5 The blind receive sight,
the lame walk, those who have leprosy[k] are
cured, the deaf hear, the dead are raised, and
the good news is preached to the poor. 6 Blessed
is the man who does not fall away on account of
me."
7 As John's disciples were leaving, Jesus began to speak to the crowd about John: "What
did you go out into the desert to see? A reed
swayed by the wind? 8 If not, what did you go
out to see? A man dressed in fine clothes? No,
those who wear fine clothes are in kings' palaces.
9 Then what did you go out to see? A prophet?
Yes, I tell you, and more than a prophet. 10 This
is the one about whom it is written:

'I will send my messenger ahead of you,
who will prepare your way before you.'[l]

11 I tell you the truth: Among those born of
women there has not risen anyone greater than
John the Baptist; yet he who is least in the
kingdom of heaven is greater than he. 12 From
the days of John the Baptist until now, the king-

[*k*] The Greek word probably designated other related diseases also. [*l*] Mal. 3:1.

Phillips Modern English

11.2 John enquires about Christ: Christ speaks about John

John the Baptist was in prison when he heard what Christ was doing, and he sent a message through his own disciples asking the question, "Are you the one who was to come or are we to look for somebody else?"

Jesus gave them this reply, "Go and tell John what you hear and see—that blind men are recovering their sight, cripples are walking, lepers being healed, the deaf hearing, the dead being raised to life and the good news is being given to those in need. And happy is the man who never loses his faith in me."

As John's disciples were going away Jesus began talking to the crowd about John:

"What did you go out into the desert to look at? A reed waving in the breeze? No? Then *what* was it you went out to see?—a man dressed in fine clothes? But the men who wear fine clothes live in the courts of kings! But what did you really go to see—a prophet? Yes, I tell you, a prophet and far more than a prophet! This is the man of whom the scripture says—

Behold, I send my messenger before thy face,
Who shall prepare thy way before thee.

"Believe me, no one greater than John the Baptist has ever been born of all mankind, and yet a humble member of the kingdom of Heaven is greater than he.

"From the days of John the Baptist until now

Revised Standard Version

2 Now when John heard in prison about the deeds of the Christ, he sent word by his disciples 3 and said to him, "Are you he who is to come, or shall we look for another?" 4 And Jesus answered them, "Go and tell John what you hear and see: 5 the blind receive their sight and the lame walk, lepers are cleansed and the deaf hear, and the dead are raised up, and the poor have good news preached to them. 6 And blessed is he who takes no offense at me."

7 As they went away, Jesus began to speak to the crowds concerning John: "What did you go out into the wilderness to behold? A reed shaken by the wind? 8 Why then did you go out? To see a man[a] clothed in soft raiment? Behold, those who wear soft raiment are in kings' houses. 9 Why then did you go out? To see a prophet? [b] Yes, I tell you, and more than a prophet. 10 This is he of whom it is written,

'Behold, I send my messenger before thy face,
who shall prepare thy way before thee.'

11 Truly, I say to you, among those born of women there has risen no one greater than John the Baptist; yet he who is least in the kingdom of heaven is greater than he. 12 From the days of John the Baptist until now the kingdom of

[a] Or *What then did you go out to see? A man . . .*
[b] Other ancient authorities read *What then did you go out to see? A prophet?*

Jerusalem Bible

The Baptist's question. Jesus commends him

2 Now John in his prison had heard what Christ was doing and he sent his disciples to ask him, 3 "Are you the one who is to come, or have we got to wait for someone else?" 4 Jesus answered, "Go back and tell John what you hear and see; 5 the blind see again, and the lame walk, lepers are cleansed, and the deaf hear, and the dead are raised to life and the Good News is proclaimed to the poor[b]; 6 and happy is the man who does not lose faith in me."

7 As the messengers were leaving, Jesus began to talk to the people about John: "What did you go out into the wilderness to see? A reed swaying in the breeze? No? 8 Then what did you go out to see? A man wearing fine clothes? Oh no, those who wear fine clothes are to be found in palaces. 9 Then what did you go out for? To see a prophet? Yes, I tell you, and much more than a prophet: 10 he is the one of whom scripture says:

Look, I am going to send my messenger before you;
he will prepare your way before you.[c]

11 "I tell you solemnly, of all the children born of women, a greater than John the Baptist has never been seen; yet the least in the kingdom of heaven is greater than he is. 12 Since John the Baptist came, up to this present time,

[b] These are signs of the messianic age in the prophecies of Isaiah. [c] Ml. 3:1.

New English Bible

John, who was in prison, heard what Christ was doing, and sent his own disciples to him with this message: 'Are you the one who is to come, or are we to expect some other?' Jesus answered, 'Go and tell John what you hear and see: the blind recover their sight, the lame walk, the lepers are made clean, the deaf hear, the dead are raised to life, the poor are hearing the good news—and happy is the man who does not find me a stumbling-block.'

When the messengers were on their way back, Jesus began to speak to the people about John: 'What was the spectacle that drew you to the wilderness? A reed-bed swept by the wind? No? Then what did you go out to see? A man dressed in silks and satins? Surely you must look in palaces for that. But why did you go out? To see a prophet? Yes indeed, and far more than a prophet. He is the man of whom Scripture says,

"Here is my herald, whom I send on ahead of you,
and he will prepare your way before you."

I tell you this: never has there appeared on earth a mother's son greater than John the Baptist, and yet the least in the kingdom of Heaven is greater than he.

'Ever since the coming of John the Baptist the

King James Version

of heaven suffereth violence, and the violent take it by force. 13 For all the prophets and the law prophesied until John. 14 And if ye will receive *it*, this is Elias, which was for to come. 15 He that hath ears to hear, let him hear.

16 But whereunto shall I liken this generation? It is like unto children sitting in the markets, and calling unto their fellows, 17 And saying, We have piped unto you, and ye have not danced; we have mourned unto you, and ye have not lamented. 18 For John came neither eating nor drinking, and they say, He hath a devil. 19 The Son of man came eating and drinking, and they say, Behold a man gluttonous, and a winebibber, a friend of publicans and sinners. But wisdom is justified of her children.

20 Then began he to upbraid the cities wherein most of his mighty works were done, because they repented not: 21 Woe unto thee, Chorazin!

Living Bible

until now, ardent multitudes have been crowding toward the Kingdom of Heaven,[c] 13 for all the laws and prophets looked forward [to the Messiah[d]]. Then John appeared, 14 and if you are willing to understand what I mean, he is Elijah, the one the prophets said would come [at the time the Kingdom begins[d]]. 15 If ever you were willing to listen, listen now!

16 "What shall I say about this nation? These people are like children playing, who say to their little friends, 17 'We played wedding and you weren't happy, so we played funeral but you weren't sad.' 18 For John the Baptist doesn't even drink wine and often goes without food, and you say, 'He's crazy.'[e] 19 And I, the Messiah,[f] feast and drink, and you complain that I am 'a glutton and a drinking man, and hang around with the worst sort of sinners!' But brilliant men like you can justify your every inconsistency!"[g]

20 Then he began to pour out his denunciations against the cities where he had done most of his miracles, because they hadn't turned to God.

21 "Woe to you, Chorazin, and woe to you,

[c] Literally, "the Kingdom of Heaven suffers violence and men of violence take it by force." [d] Implied. [e] Literally, "he has a demon." [f] Literally, "the Son of Man." [g] Literally, "wisdom is justified by her children."

Today's English Version

day the Kingdom of heaven has suffered violent attacks, and violent men try to seize it. 13 All the prophets and the Law of Moses, until the time of John, spoke about the Kingdom; 14 and if you are willing to believe their message, John is Elijah, whose coming was predicted. 15 Listen, then, if you have ears!

16 "Now, to what can I compare the people of this day? They are like children sitting in the market place. One group shouts to the other, 17 'We played wedding music for you, but you would not dance! We sang funeral songs, but you would not cry!' 18 John came, and he fasted and drank no wine, and everyone said, 'He has a demon in him!' 19 The Son of Man came, and he ate and drank, and everyone said, 'Look at this man! He is a glutton and wine-drinker, a friend of tax collectors and outcasts!' God's wisdom, however, is shown to be true by its results."

The unbelieving towns

20 Then Jesus began to reproach the towns where he had performed most of his miracles, because the people had not turned from their sins. 21 "How terrible it will be for you, Cho-

New International Version

dom of heaven has been forcefully advancing, and forceful men lay hold of it. 13 For all the Prophets and the Law prophesied until John. 14 And if you are willing to accept it, he is the Elijah who was to come. 15 He who has ears, let him hear.

16 "To what can I compare this generation? They are like children sitting in the marketplaces and calling out to others:

17 'We played the flute for you, and you did not dance;
we sang a dirge, and you did not mourn.'

18 For John came neither eating nor drinking, and they say, 'He has a demon.' 19 The Son of Man came eating and drinking, and they say, 'Here is a glutton and a drunkard, a friend of tax collectors and "sinners."' But wisdom is proved right by her actions."

Woes on unrepentant cities

20 Then Jesus began to denounce the cities in which most of his miracles had been performed, because they did not repent. 21 "Woe to you, Chorazin! Woe to you, Bethsaida! If the

Phillips Modern English

the kingdom of Heaven has been subject to force and violent men are trying to seize it. For the Law and all the Prophets foretold it till the time of John and—if you can believe it—John himself is the 'Elijah' who must come before the kingdom. The man who has ears to hear must use them!

"But how can I show what the people of this generation are like? They are like children sitting in the market-place calling out to their friends, 'We played at weddings for you but you wouldn't dance, and we played at funerals and you wouldn't cry!' For John came in the strictest austerity and people say, 'He's crazy!' Then the Son of Man came, enjoying life, and people say, 'Look, a drunkard and a glutton—the bosom-friend of the tax-collector and the sinner.' Ah, well, wisdom stands or falls by her results."

11.20 Jesus denounces apathy—and thanks God that simple men understand his message

Then Jesus began reproaching the towns where most of his miracles had taken place because their hearts were unchanged.

"Alas for you, Chorazin! Alas for you, Beth-

Revised Standard Version

heaven has suffered violence,[c] and men of violence take it by force. 13 For all the prophets
and the law prophesied until John; 14 and if you
are willing to accept it, he is Elijah who is to
come. 15 He who has ears to hear,[d] let him
hear.
16 "But to what shall I compare this generation? It is like children sitting in the market
places and calling to their playmates,
17 'We piped to you, and you did not dance;
we wailed, and you did not mourn.'
18 For John came neither eating nor drinking,
and they say, 'He has a demon'; 19 the Son of
man came eating and drinking, and they say,
'Behold, a glutton and a drunkard, a friend of
tax collectors and sinners!' Yet wisdom is justified by her deeds." [e]
20 Then he began to upbraid the cities where
most of his mighty works had been done, because they did not repent. 21 "Woe to you,
Chorazin! woe to you, Bethsaida! for if the

[c] Or *has been coming violently.* [d] Other ancient authorities omit *to hear.* [e] Other ancient authorities read *children* (Lk. 7.35).

Jerusalem Bible

the kingdom of heaven has been subjected to
violence and the violent are taking it by storm.
13 Because it was toward John that all the
prophecies of the prophets and of the Law were
leading; 14 and he, if you will believe me, is the
Elijah who was to return.[d] 15 If anyone has ears
to hear, let him listen!

Jesus condemns his contemporaries

16 "What description can I find for this generation? It is like children shouting to each
other as they sit in the market place:

17 'We played the pipes for you,
and you wouldn't dance;
we sang dirges,
and you wouldn't be mourners.'

18 "For John came, neither eating nor drinking,
and they say, 'He is possessed.' 19 The Son of
Man came, eating and drinking, and they say,
'Look, a glutton and a drunkard, a friend of tax
collectors and sinners.' Yet wisdom has been
proved right by her actions."

Lament over the lake towns

20 Then he began to reproach the towns in
which most of his miracles had been worked,
because they refused to repent.
21 "Alas for you, Chorazin! Alas for you,

[d] According to the last of the prophets, Mi. 3:23.

New English Bible

kingdom of Heaven has been subjected to violence and violent men[a] are seizing it. For all the prophets and the Law foretold things to come until John appeared, and John is the destined Elijah, if you will but accept it. If you have ears, then hear.

'How can I describe this generation? They are like children sitting in the market-place and shouting at each other,

"We piped for you and you would not dance."
"We wept and wailed, and you would not mourn."

For John came, neither eating nor drinking, and they say, "He is possessed." The Son of Man came eating and drinking, and they say, "Look at him! a glutton and a drinker, a friend of tax-gatherers and sinners!" And yet God's wisdom is proved right by its results.'

Then he spoke of the towns in which most of his miracles had been performed, and denounced them for their impenitence. 'Alas for you, Chorazin!' he said; 'alas for you, Beth-

[a] *Or* has been forcing its way forward, and men of force . . .

King James Version

woe unto thee, Bethsaida! for if the mighty
works, which were done in you, had been done
in Tyre and Sidon, they would have repented
long ago in sackcloth and ashes. 22 But I say
unto you, It shall be more tolerable for Tyre and
Sidon at the day of judgment, than for you.
23 And thou, Capernaum, which art exalted unto
heaven, shalt be brought down to hell: for if the
mighty works, which have been done in thee,
had been done in Sodom, it would have remained until this day. 24 But I say unto you,
That it shall be more tolerable for the land of
Sodom in the day of judgment, than for thee.
25 At that time Jesus answered and said, I
thank thee, O Father, Lord of heaven and earth,
because thou hast hid these things from the wise
and prudent, and hast revealed them unto babes.
26 Even so, Father; for so it seemed good in thy
sight. 27 All things are delivered unto me of my
Father: and no man knoweth the Son, but the
Father; neither knoweth any man the Father,
save the Son, and *he* to whomsoever the Son
will reveal *him*.
28 Come unto me, all *ye* that labour and are
heavy laden, and I will give you rest. 29 Take my
yoke upon you, and learn of me; for I am meek

Living Bible

Bethsaida! For if the miracles I did in your
streets had been done in wicked Tyre and Sidon[h]
their people would have repented long ago in
shame and humility. 22 Truly, Tyre and Sidon
will be better off on the Judgment Day than you!
23 And Capernaum, though highly honored,[i] shall
go down to hell! For if the marvelous miracles
I did in you had been done in Sodom,[h] it would
still be here today. 24 Truly, Sodom will be better
off at the Judgment Day than you."
25 And Jesus prayed this prayer: "O Father,
Lord of heaven and earth, thank you for hiding
the truth from those who think themselves so
wise, and for revealing it to little children. 26 Yes,
Father, for it pleased you to do it this way! . . .
27 "Everything has been entrusted to me by
my Father. Only the Father knows the Son, and
the Father is known only by the Son and by
those to whom the Son reveals him. 28 Come to
me and I will give you rest—all of you who
work so hard beneath a heavy yoke. 29, 30 Wear
my yoke—for it fits perfectly—and let me teach

[h] Cities destroyed by God for their wickedness.
[i] Highly honored by Christ's being there.

Today's English Version

razin! How terrible for you too, Bethsaida! If the
miracles which were performed in you had been
performed in Tyre and Sidon, long ago the people there would have put on sackcloth, and
sprinkled ashes on themselves to show they had
turned from their sins! 22 Remember, then, that
on the Judgment Day God will show more mercy
to the people of Tyre and Sidon than to you!
23 And as for you, Capernaum! You wanted to
lift yourself up to heaven? You will be thrown
down to hell! If the miracles which were performed in you had been performed in Sodom, it
would still be in existence today! 24 Remember,
then, that on the Judgment Day God will show
more mercy to Sodom than to you!"

Come to me and rest

25 At that time Jesus said, "Father, Lord of
heaven and earth! I thank you because you have
shown to the unlearned what you have hidden
from the wise and learned. 26 Yes, Father, this
was done by your own choice and pleasure.
27 "My Father has given me all things. No
one knows the Son except the Father, and no
one knows the Father except the Son, and those
to whom the Son wants to reveal him.
28 "Come to me, all of you who are tired
from carrying your heavy loads, and I will give
you rest. 29 Take my yoke and put it on you,

New International Version

miracles that were performed in you had been
performed in Tyre and Sidon, they would have
repented long ago in sackcloth and ashes. 22 But
I tell you, it will be more bearable for Tyre and
Sidon on the day of judgment than for you.
23 And you, Capernaum, will you be lifted up to
the skies? No, you will go down to the depths.[m]
If the miracles that were performed in you had
been performed in Sodom, it would have remained to this day. 24 But I tell you that it will
be more bearable for Sodom on the day of
judgment than for you."

Rest for the weary

25 At that time Jesus said, "I praise you,
Father, Lord of heaven and earth, because you
have hidden these things from the wise and
learned, and revealed them to little children.
26 Yes, Father, for this was your good pleasure.
27 "All things have been committed to me by
my Father. No one knows the Son except the
Father, and no one knows the Father except the
Son and those to whom the Son chooses to
reveal him.
28 "Come to me, all you who are weary and
burdened, and I will give you rest. 29 Take my
yoke upon you and learn from me, for I am

[m] Greek *Hades*.

Phillips Modern English

saida! For if Tyre and Sidon had seen the demonstrations of God's power which you have seen they would have repented long ago in sackcloth and ashes. Yet I tell you this, that it will be more bearable for Tyre and Sidon in the day of judgment than for you.

"And as for you, Capernaum, are you on your way up to heaven? I tell you you will go hurtling down among the dead! If Sodom had seen the miracles that you have seen, Sodom would be standing today Yet I tell you now that it will be more bearable for the land of Sodom in the day of judgment than for you."

At this same time Jesus said, "O Father, Lord of Heaven and earth, I thank you for hiding these things from the clever and intelligent and for showing them to mere children. Yes, I thank you, Father, that this was your will."

Then he said: "Everything has been put into my hands by my Father, and nobody knows the Son except the Father. Nor does anyone know the Father except the Son—and the man to whom the Son chooses to reveal him.

"Come to me, all of you who are weary and over-burdened, and I will give you rest! Put on my yoke and learn from me. For I am gentle

Revised Standard Version

mighty works done in you had been done in Tyre
and Sidon, they would have repented long ago
in sackcloth and ashes. 22 But I tell you, it shall
be more tolerable on the day of judgment for
Tyre and Sidon than for you. 23And you, Capernaum,
will you be exalted to heaven? You
shall be brought down to Hades. For if the
mighty works done in you had been done in
Sodom, it would have remained until this day.
24 But I tell you that it shall be more tolerable
on the day of judgment for the land of Sodom
than for you."

25 At that time Jesus declared, "I thank thee,
Father, Lord of heaven and earth, that thou
hast hidden these things from the wise and
understanding and revealed them to babes;
26 yea, Father, for such was thy gracious will.[f]
27All things have been delivered to me by my
Father; and no one knows the Son except the
Father, and no one knows the Father except the
Son and any one to whom the Son chooses to
reveal him. 28 Come to me, all who labor and
are heavy laden, and I will give you rest. 29 Take
my yoke upon you, and learn from me; for I

[f] Or *so it was well-pleasing before thee.*

Jerusalem Bible

Bethsaida! For if the miracles done in you had
been done in Tyre and Sidon, they would have
repented long ago in sackcloth and ashes. 22And
still, I tell you that it will not go as hard on
Judgment day with Tyre and Sidon as with you.
23And as for you, Capernaum, did you want to
be exalted as high as heaven? *You shall be
thrown down to hell.*[e] For if the miracles done
in you had been done in Sodom, it would have
been standing yet. 24And still, I tell you that it
will not go as hard with the land of Sodom on
Judgment day as with you."

The Good News revealed to the simple. The Father and the Son

25 At that time Jesus exclaimed, "I bless you,
Father, Lord of heaven and of earth, for hiding
these things from the learned and the clever and
revealing them to mere children. 26 Yes, Father,
for that is what it pleased you to do. 27 Everything has been entrusted to me by my Father;
and no one knows the Son except the Father,
just as no one knows the Father except the Son
and those to whom the Son chooses to reveal
him.

The gentle mastery of Christ

28 "Come to me, all you who labor and are
overburdened, and I will give you rest. 29 Shoulder my yoke and learn from me, for I am gentle

[e] Is. 14.

New English Bible

saida! If the miracles that were performed in you had been performed in Tyre and Sidon, they would have repented long ago in sackcloth and ashes. But it will be more bearable, I tell you, for Tyre and Sidon on the day of judgement than for you. And as for you, Capernaum, will you be exalted to the skies? No, brought down to the depths! For if the miracles had been performed in Sodom which were performed in you, Sodom would be standing to this day. But it will be more bearable, I tell you, for the land of Sodom on the day of judgement than for you.'

At that time Jesus spoke these words: 'I thank thee, Father, Lord of heaven and earth, for hiding these things from the learned and wise, and revealing them to the simple. Yes, Father, such[b] was thy choice. Everything is entrusted to me by my Father; and no one knows the Son but the Father, and no one knows the Father but the Son and those to whom the Son may choose to reveal him.

'Come to me, all whose work is hard, whose load is heavy; and I will give you relief. Bend your necks to my yoke, and learn from me, for

[b] *Or* Yes, I thank thee, Father, that such . . .

King James Version

and lowly in heart: and ye shall find rest unto
your souls. 30 For my yoke *is* easy, and my
burden is light.

12 At that time Jesus went on the sabbath
day through the corn; and his disciples
were a hungered, and began to pluck the ears of
corn, and to eat. 2 But when the Pharisees saw
it, they said unto him, Behold, thy disciples do
that which is not lawful to do upon the sabbath
day. 3 But he said unto them, Have ye not read
what David did, when he was a hungered, and
they that were with him; 4 How he entered into
the house of God, and did eat the shewbread,
which was not lawful for him to eat, neither for
them which were with him, but only for the
priests? 5 Or have ye not read in the law, how
that on the sabbath days the priests in the
temple profane the sabbath, and are blameless?
6 But I say unto you, That in this place is *one*
greater than the temple. 7 But if ye had known
what *this* meaneth, I will have mercy, and not
sacrifice, ye would not have condemned the
guiltless. 8 For the Son of man is Lord even of

Living Bible

you; for I am gentle and humble, and you shall
find rest for your souls; for I give you only light
burdens."

12 About that time, Jesus was walking one
day through some grainfields with his disciples. It was on the Sabbath, the Jewish day of
worship, and his disciples were hungry; so they
began breaking off heads of wheat and eating
the grain.
2 But some Pharisees saw them do it and
protested, "Your disciples are breaking the law.
They are harvesting on the Sabbath."
3 But Jesus said to them, "Haven't you ever
read what King David did when he and his
friends were hungry? 4 He went into the Temple
and they ate the special bread permitted to the
priests alone. That was breaking the law too.
5 And haven't you ever read in the law of Moses
how the priests on duty in the Temple may work
on the Sabbath? 6 And truly, one is here who is
greater than the Temple! 7 But if you had known
the meaning of this Scripture verse, 'I want you
to be merciful more than I want your offerings,'
you would not have condemned those who aren't
guilty! 8 For I, the Messiah,[a] am master even
of the Sabbath."

[*a*] Literally, "the Son of Man."

Today's English Version

and learn from me, because I am gentle and
humble in spirit; and you will find rest. 30 The
yoke I will give you is easy, and the load I will
put on you is light."

The question about the Sabbath

12 Not long afterward Jesus was walking
through the wheat fields on a Sabbath day.
His disciples were hungry, so they began to pick
heads of wheat and eat the grain. 2 When the
Pharisees saw this, they said to Jesus, "Look, it
is against our Law for your disciples to do this
on the Sabbath!"
3 Jesus answered, "Have you never read what
David did that time when he and his men were
hungry? 4 He went into the house of God, and
he and his men ate the bread offered to God,
even though it was against the Law for them to
eat that bread—only the priests were allowed to
eat it. 5 Or have you not read in the Law of
Moses that every Sabbath the priests in the temple actually break the Sabbath law, yet they are
not guilty? 6 There is something here, I tell you,
greater than the temple. 7 The scripture says, 'I
do not want animal sacrifices, but kindness.' If
you really knew what this means, you would not
condemn people who are not guilty; 8 because
the Son of Man is Lord of the Sabbath."

New International Version

gentle and humble in heart, and you will find
rest for your souls. 30 For my yoke is easy and
my burden is light."

Lord of the Sabbath

12 At that time Jesus went through the grainfields on the Sabbath. His disciples were
hungry and began to pick some heads of grain
and eat them. 2 When the Pharisees saw this,
they said to him, "Look! Your disciples are
doing what is unlawful on the Sabbath."
3 He answered, "Haven't you read what
David did when he and his companions were
hungry? 4 He entered the house of God, and he
and his companions ate the consecrated bread—
which was not lawful for them to do, but only
for the priests. 5 Or haven't you read in the Law
that on the Sabbath the priests in the temple
desecrate the day and yet are innocent? 6 I tell
you that one greater than the temple is here.
7 If you had known what these words mean, 'I
desire mercy, not sacrifice,'[n] you would not
have condemned the innocent. 8 For the Son of
Man is Lord of the Sabbath."

[*n*] Hosea 6:6.

Phillips Modern English

and humble in heart and you will find rest for your souls. For my yoke is easy and my burden is light."

12.1 Jesus rebukes the sabbatarians

It happened then that Jesus passed through the cornfields on the Sabbath day. His disciples were hungry and began picking the ears of wheat and eating them. But the Pharisees saw them do it.

"There, you see," they remarked to Jesus, "your disciples are doing what the Law forbids them to do on the Sabbath."

"Haven't any of you read what David did when he and his companions were hungry?" replied Jesus, "—how he went into the house of God and ate the presentation loaves, which he and his followers were not allowed to eat since only priests can do so?

"Haven't any of you read in the Law that every Sabbath day priests in the Temple can break the Sabbath and yet remain blameless? I tell you that there is something more important than the Temple here. If you had grasped the meaning of the scripture 'I desire mercy and not sacrifice', you would not have been so quick to condemn the innocent! For the Son of Man is master even of the Sabbath."

Revised Standard Version

am gentle and lowly in heart, and you will find
rest for your souls. 30 For my yoke is easy, and
my burden is light."

12 At that time Jesus went through the
grainfields on the sabbath; his disciples
were hungry, and they began to pluck heads of
grain and to eat. 2 But when the Pharisees saw it,
they said to him, "Look, your disciples are doing what is not lawful to do on the sabbath."
3 He said to them, "Have you not read what
David did, when he was hungry, and those who
were with him: 4 how he entered the house of
God and ate the bread of the Presence, which it
was not lawful for him to eat nor for those who
were with him, but only for the priests? 5 Or
have you not read in the law how on the sabbath the priests in the temple profane the sabbath, and are guiltless? 6 I tell you, something
greater than the temple is here. 7 And if you had
known what this means, 'I desire mercy, and not
sacrifice,' you would not have condemned the
guiltless. 8 For the Son of man is lord of the
sabbath."

Jerusalem Bible

and humble in heart, *and you will find rest for
your souls.*[f] 30 Yes, my yoke is easy and my
burden light."

Picking corn on the sabbath

12 At that time Jesus took a walk one sabbath day through the cornfields. His disciples were hungry and began to pick ears of
corn and eat them. 2 The Pharisees noticed it
and said to him, "Look, your disciples are doing something that is forbidden on the sabbath."
3 But he said to them, "Have you not read what
David did when he and his followers were hungry—4 how he went into the house of God and
how they ate the loaves of offering which neither
he nor his followers were allowed to eat, but
which were for the priests alone? 5 Or again,
have you not read in the Law that on the sabbath day the Temple priests break the sabbath
without being blamed for it? 6 Now here, I tell
you, is something greater than the Temple. 7 And
if you had understood the meaning of the words:
What I want is mercy, not sacrifice, you would
not have condemned the blameless. 8 For the
Son of Man is master of the sabbath."

[f] Jr. 6:16.

New English Bible

I am gentle and humble-hearted; and your souls will find relief. For my yoke is good to bear, my load is light.'

Controversy

12 Once about that time Jesus went through the cornfields on the Sabbath; and his disciples, feeling hungry, began to pluck some ears of corn and eat them. The Pharisees noticed this, and said to him, 'Look, your disciples are doing something which is forbidden on the Sabbath.' He answered, 'Have you not read what David did when he and his men were hungry? He went into the House of God and ate the sacred bread, though neither he nor his men had a right to eat it, but only the priests. Or have you not read in the Law that on the Sabbath the priests in the temple break the Sabbath and it is not held against them? I tell you, there is something greater than the temple here. If you had known what that text means, "I require mercy, not sacrifice", you would not have condemned the innocent. For the Son of Man is sovereign over the Sabbath.'

King James Version

the sabbath day. 9And when he was departed
thence, he went into their synagogue:
10 And, behold, there was a man which had
his hand withered. And they asked him, saying,
Is it lawful to heal on the sabbath days? that
they might accuse him. 11And he said unto them,
What man shall there be among you, that shall
have one sheep, and if it fall into a pit on the
sabbath day, will he not lay hold on it, and lift
it out? 12 How much then is a man better than a
sheep? Wherefore it is lawful to do well on the
sabbath days. 13 Then saith he to the man,
Stretch forth thine hand. And he stretched *it*
forth; and it was restored whole, like as the
other.
14 Then the Pharisees went out, and held a
council against him, how they might destroy
him. 15 But when Jesus knew *it,* he withdrew
himself from thence: and great multitudes followed him, and he healed them all; 16And
charged them that they should not make him
known: 17 That it might be fulfilled which was
spoken by Esaias the prophet, saying, 18 Behold
my servant, whom I have chosen; my beloved, in
whom my soul is well pleased: I will put my
Spirit upon him, and he shall shew judgment

Living Bible

9 Then he went over to the synagogue, 10 and
noticed there a man with a deformed hand. The
Pharisees[b] asked Jesus, "Is it legal to work by
healing on the Sabbath day?" (They were, of
course, hoping he would say "Yes," so they could
arrest[c] him!) 11 This was his answer: "If you
had just one sheep, and it fell into a well on
the Sabbath, would you work to rescue it that
day? Of course you would.[b] 12And how much
more valuable is a person than a sheep! Yes, it
is right to do good on the Sabbath." 13 Then he
said to the man, "Stretch out your arm." And
as he did, his hand became normal, just like the
other one!
14 Then the Pharisees called a meeting to
plot Jesus' arrest and death. 15 But he knew
what they were planning, and left the synagogue,
with many following him. He healed all the sick
among them, 16 but he cautioned them against
spreading the news about his miracles. 17 This
fulfilled the prophecy of Isaiah concerning him:
18 "Look at my Servant.
See my Chosen One.
He is my Beloved, in whom my soul delights.
I will put my Spirit upon him,
And he will judge the nations.

[b] Implied. [c] Literally, "accuse."

Today's English Version

The man with a crippled hand

9 Jesus left that place and went to one of their
synagogues. 10A man was there who had a crippled hand. There were some men present who
wanted to accuse Jesus of wrongdoing; so they
asked him, "Is it against our Law to cure on the
Sabbath?"
11 Jesus answered, "What if one of you has a
sheep and it falls into a deep hole on the Sabbath? Will you not take hold of it and lift it
out? 12And a man is worth much more than a
sheep! So then, our Law does allow us to help
someone on the Sabbath." 13 Then he said to the
man, "Stretch out your hand."
He stretched it out, and it became well again,
just like the other one. 14 The Pharisees left and
made plans against Jesus to kill him.

God's chosen servant

15 When Jesus heard about it, he went away
from that place; and many people followed him.
He healed all the sick, 16 and gave them orders
not to tell others about him, 17 to make come
true what God had said through the prophet
Isaiah,

18 "Here is my servant, whom I have chosen,
the one I love, with whom I am well
pleased.
I will put my Spirit on him,
and he will announce my judgment to all
peoples.

New International Version

9 Going on from that place, he went into their
synagogue, 10 and a man with a shriveled hand
was there. Looking for a reason to accuse Jesus,
they asked him, "Is it lawful to heal on the
Sabbath?"
11 He said to them, "If any of you has a
sheep and it falls into a pit on the Sabbath, will
you not take hold of it and lift it out? 12 How
much more valuable is a man than a sheep!
Therefore, it is lawful to do good on the Sabbath."
13 Then he said to the man, "Stretch out your
hand." So he stretched it out and it was completely restored, just as sound as the other.
14 But the Pharisees went out and plotted how
they might kill Jesus.

God's chosen servant

15 Aware of this, Jesus withdrew from that
place. Many followed him, and he healed all
their sick, 16 warning them not to tell who he
was. 17 This was to fulfill what was spoken
through the prophet Isaiah:
18 "Here is my servant whom I have chosen,
the one I love and in whom I delight;
I will put my Spirit on him,
and he will proclaim justice to the nations.

Phillips Modern English

Leaving there he went into their synagogue, where there happened to be a man with a shrivelled hand.

"Is it right to heal anyone on the Sabbath day?" they asked him—hoping to bring a charge against him.

"If any of you had a sheep which fell into a ditch on the Sabbath day, would he not take hold of it and pull it out?" replied Jesus. "How much more valuable is a man than a sheep? You see, it is right to do good on the Sabbath day."

Then Jesus said to the man, "Stretch out your hand!" He did stretch it out, and it was restored as sound as the other.

But the Pharisees went out and held a meeting against Jesus and discussed how they could get rid of him altogether.

12.15 Jesus retires to continue his work

But Jesus knew of this and he left the place. Large crowds followed him and he healed them all, with the strict injunction that they should not make him conspicuous by their talk, thus fulfilling Isaiah's prophecy:

Behold, my servant whom I have chosen;
My beloved in whom my soul is well pleased:
I will put my Spirit upon him,
And he shall declare judgment to the gentiles.

Revised Standard Version

9 And he went on from there, and entered
their synagogue. 10 And behold, there was a
man with a withered hand. And they asked him,
"Is it lawful to heal on the sabbath?" so that
they might accuse him. 11 He said to them,
"What man of you, if he has one sheep and it
falls into a pit on the sabbath, will not lay hold
of it and lift it out? 12 Of how much more value
is a man than a sheep! So it is lawful to do good
on the sabbath." 13 Then he said to the man,
"Stretch out your hand." And the man stretched
it out, and it was restored, whole like the other.
14 But the Pharisees went out and took counsel
against him, how to destroy him.
15 Jesus, aware of this, withdrew from there.
And many followed him, and he healed them all,
16 and ordered them not to make him known.
17 This was to fulfil what was spoken by the
prophet Isaiah:
18 "Behold, my servant whom I have chosen,
my beloved with whom my soul is well pleased.
I will put my Spirit upon him,
and he shall proclaim justice to the Gentiles.

Jerusalem Bible

Cure of the man with a withered hand

9 He moved on from there and went to their
synagogue, 10 and a man was there at the time
who had a withered hand. They asked him, "Is
it against the law to cure a man on the sabbath
day?" hoping for something to use against him.
11 But he said to them, "If any one of you here
had only one sheep and it fell down a hole on
the sabbath day, would he not get hold of it and
lift it out? 12 Now a man is far more important
than a sheep, so it follows that it is permitted
to do good on the sabbath day." 13 Then he
said to the man, "Stretch out your hand." He
stretched it out and his hand was better, as
sound as the other one. 14 At this the Pharisees
went out and began to plot against him, discussing how to destroy him.

Jesus the "servant of Yahweh"

15 Jesus knew this and withdrew from the
district. Many followed him and he cured them
all, 16 but warned them not to make him known.
17 This was to fulfill the prophecy of Isaiah:

18 *Here is my servant whom I have chosen,*
my beloved, the favorite of my soul.
I will endow him with my spirit,
and he will proclaim the true faith to the nations.

New English Bible

He went on to another place, and entered their synagogue. A man was there with a withered arm, and they asked Jesus, 'Is it permitted to heal on the Sabbath?' (They wanted to frame a charge against him.) But he said to them, 'Suppose you had one sheep, which fell into a ditch on the Sabbath; is there one of you who would not catch hold of it and lift it out? And surely a man is worth far more than a sheep! It is therefore permitted to do good on the Sabbath.' Turning to the man he said, 'Stretch out your arm.' He stretched it out, and it was made sound again like the other. But the Pharisees, on leaving the synagogue, laid a plot to do away with him.

Jesus was aware of it and withdrew. Many followed, and he cured all who were ill; and he gave strict injunctions that they were not to make him known. This was to fulfil Isaiah's prophecy:

'Here is my servant, whom I have chosen,
my beloved, on whom my favour rests;
I will put my Spirit upon him,
and he will proclaim judgement among the nations.

King James Version

to the Gentiles. 19 He shall not strive, nor cry;
neither shall any man hear his voice in the
streets. 20 A bruised reed shall he not break,
and smoking flax shall he not quench, till he
send forth judgment unto victory. 21 And in his
name shall the Gentiles trust.
22 Then was brought unto him one possessed
with a devil, blind, and dumb: and he healed
him, insomuch that the blind and dumb both
spake and saw. 23 And all the people were
amazed, and said, Is not this the Son of David?
24 But when the Pharisees heard *it*, they said,
This *fellow* doth not cast out devils, but by
Beelzebub the prince of the devils. 25 And Jesus
knew their thoughts, and said unto them, Every
kingdom divided against itself is brought to
desolation; and every city or house divided
against itself shall not stand: 26 And if Satan
cast out Satan, he is divided against himself;
how shall then his kingdom stand? 27 And if I
by Beelzebub cast out devils, by whom do your
children cast *them* out? therefore they shall be
your judges. 28 But if I cast out devils by the
Spirit of God, then the kingdom of God is come

Living Bible

19 He does not fight nor shout;
He does not raise his voice!
20 He does not crush the weak,
Or quench the smallest hope;
He will end all conflict with his final victory,
21 And his name shall be the hope
Of all the world."[d]
22 Then a demon-possessed man—he was both
blind and unable to talk—was brought to Jesus,
and Jesus healed him so that he could both
speak and see. 23 The crowd was amazed.
"Maybe Jesus is the Messiah!"[e] they exclaimed.
24 But when the Pharisees heard about the
miracle they said, "He can cast out demons because he is Satan,[f] king of devils."
25 Jesus knew their thoughts and replied, "A
divided kingdom ends in ruin. A city or home
divided against itself cannot stand. 26 And if
Satan is casting out Satan, he is fighting himself,
and destroying his own kingdom. 27 And if, as you
claim, I am casting out demons by invoking the
powers of Satan, then what power do your own
people use when they cast them out? Let them
answer your accusation! 28 But if I am casting
out demons by the Spirit of God, then the King-

[*d*] Isaiah 42:1-4. [*e*] Literally, "the Son of David."
[*f*] Literally, "Beelzebub."

Today's English Version

19 But he will not argue or shout,
nor make loud speeches in the streets.
20 He will not break off a bent reed,
nor put out a flickering lamp.
He will persist until he causes justice to triumph;
21 and all peoples will put their hope in him."

Jesus and Beelzebul

22 Then some people brought to Jesus a man
who was blind and could not talk because he
had a demon. Jesus healed the man, so that he
was able to talk and see. 23 The crowds were all
amazed. "Could he be the Son of David?" they
asked.
24 When the Pharisees heard this they replied,
"He drives out demons only because their ruler
Beelzebul gives him power to do so."
25 Jesus knew what they were thinking and
said to them, "Any country that divides itself
into groups that fight each other will not last
very long. And any town or family that divides
itself into groups that fight each other will fall
apart. 26 So if one group is fighting another in
Satan's kingdom, this means that it is already
divided into groups and will soon fall apart!
27 You say that I drive out demons because
Beelzebul gives me the power to do so. Well,
then, who gives your followers the power to
drive them out? Your own followers prove that
you are wrong! 28 No, it is God's Spirit who
gives me the power to drive out demons, which

New International Version

19 He will not quarrel or cry out;
no one will hear his voice in the streets.
20 A bruised reed he will not break,
and a smoldering wick he will not quench,
till he leads justice to victory.
21 In his name the nations will put their hope."[o]

Jesus and Beelzebub

22 Then they brought him a demon-possessed
man who was blind and mute, and Jesus healed
him, so that he could both talk and see. 23 All
the people were astonished and said, "Could
this be the Son of David?"
24 But when the Pharisees heard this, they
said, "It is only by Beelzebub,[p] the prince of
demons, that this fellow drives out demons."
25 Jesus knew their thoughts and said to
them, "Every kingdom divided against itself will
be ruined, and every city or household divided
against itself will not stand. 26 If Satan drives
out Satan, he is divided against himself. How
then can his kingdom stand? 27 And if I drive
out demons by Beelzebub,[p] by whom do your
people drive them out? So then, they will be
your judges. 28 But if I drive out demons by
the Spirit of God, then the kingdom of God

[*o*] Isaiah 42:1-4. [*p*] Greek MSS *Beelzeboul* or *Beezeboul*.

Phillips Modern English

He shall not strive, nor cry aloud;
Neither shall anyone hear his voice in the streets.
A bruised reed shall he not break,
And smoking flax shall he not quench,
Till he send forth judgment unto victory.
And in his name shall the gentiles hope.

Then a devil-possessed man who could neither see nor speak was brought to Jesus. He healed him, so that the dumb man could both speak and see. At this the whole crowd went wild with excitement, and people kept saying, "Can this be the Son of David?"

12.24 The Pharisees draw an evil conclusion, and Jesus rebukes them

But the Pharisees on hearing this remark said, "This man is only expelling devils because he is in league with Beelzebub, the prince of devils."

Jesus knew what they were thinking and said to them, "Any kingdom divided against itself is bound to collapse, and no town or household divided against itself can last for long. If it is Satan who is expelling Satan, then he is divided against himself—so how do you suppose that his kingdom can continue? And if I expel devils because I am an ally of Beelzebub, what alliance do your sons make when they do the same thing? They can settle that question for you. But if I am expelling devils by the Spirit of God, then

Revised Standard Version

19 He will not wrangle or cry aloud,
nor will any one hear his voice in the streets;
20 he will not break a bruised reed
or quench a smoldering wick,
till he brings justice to victory;
21 and in his name will the Gentiles hope."
22 Then a blind and dumb demoniac was
brought to him, and he healed him, so that the
dumb man spoke and saw. 23 And all the people
were amazed, and said, "Can this be the Son of
David?" 24 But when the Pharisees heard it they
said, "It is only by Beelzebul, the prince of demons, that this man casts out demons." 25 Knowing their thoughts, he said to them, "Every
kingdom divided against itself is laid waste, and
no city or house divided against itself will stand;
26 and if Satan casts out Satan, he is divided
against himself; how then will his kingdom
stand? 27 And if I cast out demons by Beelzebul,
by whom do your sons cast them out? Therefore
they shall be your judges. 28 But if it is by the
Spirit of God that I cast out demons, then the

Jerusalem Bible

19 *He will not brawl or shout,*
nor will anyone hear his voice in the streets.
20 *He will not break the crushed reed,*
nor put out the smoldering wick
till he has led the truth to victory:
21 *in his name the nations will put their hope.*[g]

Jesus and Beelzebul

22 Then they brought to him a blind and
dumb demoniac; and he cured him, so that the
dumb man could speak and see. 23 All the people were astounded and said, "Can this be the
Son of David?" 24 But when the Pharisees heard
this they said. "The man casts out devils only
through Beelzebul,[h] the prince of devils."
25 Knowing what was in their minds he said
to them, "Every kingdom divided against itself
is heading for ruin; and no town, no household
divided against itself can stand. 26 Now if Satan
casts out Satan, he is divided against himself;
so how can his kingdom stand? 27 And if it is
through Beelzebul that I cast out devils, through
whom do your own experts cast them out? Let
them be your judges, then. 28 But if it is through
the Spirit of God that I cast devils out, then

[g] Is. 42:1-4. [h] "Prince Baal," often contemptuously changed (e.g., 2 K. 1:2f) to "Beelzebub," "Lord of the flies."

New English Bible

He will not strive, he will not shout,
nor will his voice be heard in the streets.
He will not snap off the broken reed,
nor snuff out the smouldering wick,
until he leads justice on to victory.
In him the nations shall place their hope.'

Then they brought him a man who was possessed; he was blind and dumb; and Jesus cured him, restoring both speech and sight. The bystanders were all amazed, and the word went round: 'Can this be the Son of David?' But when the Pharisees heard it they said, 'It is only by Beelzebub prince of devils that this man drives the devils out.'

He knew what was in their minds; so he said to them, 'Every kingdom divided against itself goes to ruin; and no town, no household, that is divided against itself can stand. And if it is Satan who casts out Satan, Satan is divided against himself; how then can his kingdom stand? And if it is by Beelzebub that I cast out devils, by whom do your own people drive them out? If this is your argument, they themselves will refute you. But if it is by the Spirit of God that I drive out the devils, then be sure the king-

King James Version

unto you. 29 Or else, how can one enter into a
strong man's house, and spoil his goods, except
he first bind the strong man? and then he will
spoil his house. 30 He that is not with me is
against me; and he that gathereth not with me
scattereth abroad.
31 Wherefore I say unto you, All manner of
sin and blasphemy shall be forgiven unto men:
but the blasphemy *against* the *Holy* Ghost shall
not be forgiven unto men. 32And whosoever
speaketh a word against the Son of man, it shall
be forgiven him: but whosoever speaketh against
the Holy Ghost, it shall not be forgiven him,
neither in this world, neither in the *world* to
come. 33 Either make the tree good, and his
fruit good; or else make the tree corrupt, and
his fruit corrupt: for the tree is known by *his*
fruit. 34 O generation of vipers, how can ye, being evil, speak good things? for out of the
abundance of the heart the mouth speaketh.
35A good man out of the good treasure of the
heart bringeth forth good things: and an evil
man out of the evil treasure bringeth forth evil
things. 36 But I say unto you, That every idle
word that men shall speak, they shall give account thereof in the day of judgment. 37 For by
thy words thou shalt be justified, and by thy
words thou shalt be condemned.

Living Bible

dom of God has arrived among you. 29 One cannot rob Satan's kingdom without first binding
Satan.[g] Only then can his demons be cast out![h]
30Anyone who isn't helping me is harming me.
31, 32 "Even blasphemy against me[a] or any
other sin, can be forgiven—all except one: speaking against the Holy Spirit shall never be forgiven, either in this world or in the world to
come.
33 "A tree is identified by its fruit. A tree
from a select variety produces good fruit; poor
varieties don't. 34 You brood of snakes! How
could evil men like you speak what is good and
right? For a man's heart determines his speech.
35A good man's speech reveals the rich treasures
within him. An evil-hearted man is filled with
venom, and his speech reveals it. 36And I tell
you this, that you must give account on Judgment Day for every idle word you speak. 37 Your
words now reflect your fate then: either you
will be justified by them or you will be condemned."

[g] Literally, "the strong." [h] Literally, "then will he spoil his house." [a] Literally, "the Son of Man."

Today's English Version

proves that the Kingdom of God has already
come upon you.
29 "No one can break into a strong man's
house and take away his belongings unless he
ties up the strong man first; then he can plunder
his house.
30 "Anyone who is not for me is really against
me; anyone who does not help me gather is
really scattering. 31 For this reason I tell you:
men can be forgiven any sin and any evil thing
they say; but whoever says evil things against
the Holy Spirit will not be forgiven. 32Anyone
who says something against the Son of Man can
be forgiven; but whoever says something against
the Holy Spirit will not be forgiven—now or
ever."

A tree and its fruit

33 "To have good fruit you must have a
healthy tree; if you have a poor tree you will
have bad fruit. For a tree is known by the kind
of fruit it bears. 34 You snakes—how can you
say good things when you are evil? For the
mouth speaks what the heart is full of. 35A good
man brings good things out of his treasure of
good things; a bad man brings bad things out of
his treasure of bad things.
36 "I tell you this: on the Judgment Day everyone will have to give account of every useless word he has ever spoken. 37 For your words
will be used to judge you, either to declare you
innocent or to declare you guilty."

New International Version

has come upon you.
29 "Or again, how can anyone enter a strong
man's house and carry off his possessions unless he first ties up the strong man? Then he can
rob his house.
30 "He who is not with me is against me, and
he who does not gather with me scatters. 31And
so I tell you, every sin and blasphemy will be
forgiven men, but the blasphemy against the
Spirit will not be forgiven. 32Anyone who speaks
a word against the Son of Man will be forgiven,
but anyone who speaks against the Holy Spirit
will not be forgiven, either in this age or in the
age to come.
33 "Make a tree good and its fruit will be
good, or make a tree bad and its fruit will be
bad, for a tree is recognized by its fruit. 34 You
brood of vipers, how can you who are evil say
anything good? For out of the overflow of the
heart the mouth speaks. 35 The good man brings
good things out of the good stored up in him,
and the evil man brings evil things out of the
evil stored up in him. 36 But I tell you that men
will have to give account on the day of judgment
for every careless word they have spoken. 37 For
by your words you will be acquitted, and by
your words you will be condemned."

Phillips Modern English

the kingdom of God has already swept over you! How do you suppose anyone could get into a strong man's house and steal his property unless he first tied up the strong man? But if he did that, he could ransack his whole house.

"The man who is not on my side is against me, and the man who does not gather with me is really scattering. That is why I tell you that men may be forgiven for every sin and blasphemy, but blasphemy against the Spirit cannot be forgiven. A man may say a word against the Son of Man and be forgiven, but whoever speaks against the Holy Spirit cannot be forgiven either in this world or in the world to come.

"You must choose between having a good tree with good fruit and a rotten tree with rotten fruit. For you can tell a tree at once by its fruit.

"You serpent's brood, how can you say anything good out of your evil hearts? For a man's words flow out of what fills his heart. A good man gives out good—from the goodness stored in his heart; a bad man gives out evil—from his store of evil. I tell you that men will have to answer at the day of judgment for every careless word they utter—for it is your words that will acquit you, and your words that will condemn you."

Revised Standard Version

kingdom of God has come upon you. 29 Or how
can one enter a strong man's house and plunder
his goods, unless he first binds the strong man?
Then indeed he may plunder his house. 30 He
who is not with me is against me, and he who
does not gather with me scatters. 31 Therefore
I tell you, every sin and blasphemy will be forgiven men, but the blasphemy against the Spirit
will not be forgiven. 32And whoever says a word
against the Son of man will be forgiven; but
whoever speaks against the Holy Spirit will not
be forgiven, either in this age or in the age to
come.

33 "Either make the tree good, and its fruit
good; or make the tree bad, and its fruit bad;
for the tree is known by its fruit. 34 You brood
of vipers! how can you speak good, when you
are evil? For out of the abundance of the heart
the mouth speaks. 35 The good man out of his
good treasure brings forth good, and the evil
man out of his evil treasure brings forth evil.
36 I tell you, on the day of judgment men will
render account for every careless word they utter; 37 for by your words you will be justified,
and by your words you will be condemned."

Jerusalem Bible

know that the kingdom of God has overtaken you.

29 "Or again, how can anyone make his way
into a strong man's house and burgle his property unless he has tied up the strong man first?
Only then can he burgle his house.

30 "He who is not with me is against me, and
he who does not gather with me scatters. 31And
so I tell you, every one of men's sins and blasphemies will be forgiven, but blasphemy against
the Spirit will not be forgiven. 32And anyone
who says a word against the Son of Man will
be forgiven; but let anyone speak against the
Holy Spirit and he will not be forgiven either in
this world or in the next.

Words betray the heart

33 "Make a tree sound and its fruit will be
sound; make a tree rotten and its fruit will be
rotten. For the tree can be told by its fruit.
34 Brood of vipers, how can your speech be good
when you are evil? For a man's words flow out
of what fills his heart. 35A good man draws
good things from his store of goodness; a bad
man draws bad things from his store of badness. 36 So I tell you this, that for every unfounded word men utter they will answer on
Judgment day, 37 since it is by your words you
will be acquitted, and by your words condemned."

New English Bible

dom of God has already come upon you.

'Or again, how can anyone break into a strong man's house and make off with his goods, unless he has first tied the strong man up before ransacking the house?

'He who is not with me is against me, and he who does not gather with me scatters.

'And so I tell you this: no sin, no slander, is beyond forgiveness for men, except slander spoken against the Spirit, and that will not be forgiven. Any man who speaks a word against the Son of Man will be forgiven; but if anyone speaks against the Holy Spirit, for him there is no forgiveness, either in this age or in the age to come.

'Either make the tree good and its fruit good, or make the tree bad and its fruit bad; you can tell a tree by its fruit. You vipers' brood! How can your words be good when you yourselves are evil? For the words that the mouth utters come from the overflowing of the heart. A good man produces good from the store of good within himself; and an evil man from evil within produces evil.

'I tell you this: there is not a thoughtless word that comes from men's lips but they will have to account for it on the day of judgement. For out of your own mouth you will be acquitted; out of your own mouth you will be condemned.'

King James Version

38 Then certain of the scribes and of the Pharisees answered, saying, Master, we would see a sign from thee. 39 But he answered and said unto them, An evil and adulterous generation seeketh after a sign; and there shall no sign be given to it, but the sign of the prophet Jonas: 40 For as Jonas was three days and three nights in the whale's belly; so shall the Son of man be three days and three nights in the heart of the earth. 41 The men of Nineveh shall rise in judgment with this generation, and shall condemn it: because they repented at the preaching of Jonas; and, behold, a greater than Jonas *is* here. 42 The queen of the south shall rise up in the judgment with this generation, and shall condemn it: for she came from the uttermost parts of the earth to hear the wisdom of Solomon; and, behold, a greater than Solomon *is* here. 43 When the unclean spirit is gone out of a man, he walketh through dry places, seeking rest, and findeth none. 44 Then he saith, I will return into my house from whence I came out; and when he is come, he findeth *it* empty, swept, and garnished. 45 Then goeth he, and taketh with himself seven other spirits more wicked than himself, and they enter in and dwell there: and the last *state* of

Living Bible

38 One day some of the Jewish leaders, including some Pharisees, came to Jesus asking him to show them a miracle.

39, 40 But Jesus replied, "Only an evil, faithless nation would ask for further proof; and none will be given except what happened to Jonah the prophet! For as Jonah was in the great fish for three days and three nights, so I, the Messiah,[i] shall be in the heart of the earth three days and three nights. 41 The men of Nineveh shall arise against this nation at the judgment and condemn you. For when Jonah preached to them, they repented and turned to God from all their evil ways. And now a greater than Jonah is here—and you refuse to believe him.[j] 42 The Queen of Sheba shall rise against this nation in the judgment, and condemn it; for she came from a distant land to hear the wisdom of Solomon; and now a greater than Solomon is here—and you refuse to believe him.[j]

43, 44, 45 "This evil nation is like a man possessed by a demon. For if the demon leaves, it goes into the deserts[k] for a while, seeking rest but finding none. Then it says, 'I will return to the man I came from.' So it returns and finds the man's heart clean but empty! Then the demon finds seven other spirits more evil than itself, and all enter the man and live in him. And so he

[*i*] Literally, "the Son of Man." [*j*] Implied. [*k*] Literally, "passes through waterless places."

Today's English Version

The demand for a miracle

38 Then some teachers of the Law and some Pharisees spoke up. "Teacher," they said, "we want to see you perform a miracle."

39 "How evil and godless are the people of this day!" Jesus exclaimed. "You ask me for a miracle? No! The only miracle you will be given is the miracle of the prophet Jonah. 40 In the same way that Jonah spent three days and nights in the belly of the big fish, so will the Son of Man spend three days and nights in the depths of the earth. 41 On the Judgment Day the people of Nineveh will stand up and accuse you, because they turned from their sins when they heard Jonah preach; and there is something here, I tell you, greater than Jonah! 42 On the Judgment Day the Queen from the South will stand up and accuse you, because she traveled halfway around the world to listen to Solomon's wise teaching; and there is something here, I tell you, greater than Solomon!"

The return of the evil spirit

43 "When an evil spirit goes out of a man, it travels over dry country looking for a place to rest. If it can't find one, 44 it says to itself, 'I will go back to my house which I left.' So it goes back and finds the house empty, clean, and all fixed up. 45 Then it goes out and brings along seven other spirits even worse than itself, and they come and live there. So that man is in

New International Version

The sign of Jonah

38 Then some of the Pharisees and teachers of the law said to him, "Teacher, we want to see a miraculous sign from you."

39 He answered, "A wicked and adulterous generation asks for a miraculous sign! But none will be given it except the sign of the prophet Jonah. 40 For as Jonah was three days and three nights in the belly of a huge fish, so the Son of Man will be three days and three nights in the heart of the earth. 41 The men of Nineveh will stand up at the judgment with this generation and condemn it; for they repented at the preaching of Jonah, and now one greater than Jonah is here. 42 The Queen of the South will rise at the judgment with this generation and condemn it; for she came from the ends of the earth to listen to Solomon's wisdom; and now one greater than Solomon is here.

43 "When an evil [q] spirit comes out of a man, it goes through arid places seeking rest and does not find it. 44 Then it says, 'I will return to the house I left.' When it arrives, it finds the house unoccupied, swept clean and put in order. 45 Then it goes and takes with it seven other spirits more wicked than itself, and they go in and live there. And the final condition of that

[*q*] Greek *unclean*.

Phillips Modern English

12.38 Jesus refuses to give a sign

Then some of the scribes and Pharisees said, "Master, we want to see a sign from you." But Jesus told them,

"It is an evil and unfaithful generation that craves for a sign, and no sign will be given to it—except the sign of the prophet Jonah. For just as Jonah was in the belly of that great sea-monster for three days and nights, so will the Son of Man be in the heart of the earth for three days and nights. The men of Nineveh will stand up with this generation in the judgment and will condemn it. For they did repent when Jonah preached to them, and you have more than Jonah's preaching with you now! The Queen of the South will stand up in the judgment with this generation and will condemn it. For she came from the ends of the earth to listen to the wisdom of Solomon, and you have more than the wisdom of Solomon with you now!

12.43 The danger of spiritual emptiness

"When the evil spirit goes out of a man it wanders through waterless places looking for rest and never finding it. Then it says, 'I will go back to my house from which I came.' When it arrives it finds it unoccupied, but cleaned and all in order. Then it goes and collects seven other spirits more evil than itself to keep it company, and they all go in and make them-

Revised Standard Version

38 Then some of the scribes and Pharisees
said to him, "Teacher, we wish to see a sign
from you." 39 But he answered them, "An evil
and adulterous generation seeks for a sign; but
no sign shall be given to it except the sign of
the prophet Jonah. 40 For as Jonah was three
days and three nights in the belly of the whale,
so will the Son of man be three days and three
nights in the heart of the earth. 41 The men of
Nineveh will arise at the judgment with this
generation and condemn it; for they repented
at the preaching of Jonah, and behold, something greater than Jonah is here. 42 The queen
of the South will arise at the judgment with
this generation and condemn it; for she came
from the ends of the earth to hear the wisdom
of Solomon, and behold, something greater than
Solomon is here.

43 "When the unclean spirit has gone out of
a man, he passes through waterless places seeking rest, but he finds none. 44 Then he says, 'I
will return to my house from which I came.'
And when he comes he finds it empty, swept,
and put in order. 45 Then he goes and brings
with him seven other spirits more evil than
himself, and they enter and dwell there; and

Jerusalem Bible

The sign of Jonah

38 Then some of the scribes and Pharisees
spoke up. "Master," they said, "we should like
to see a sign[i] from you." 39 He replied, "It is an
evil and unfaithful generation that asks for a
sign! The only sign it will be given is the sign
of the prophet Jonah. 40 For as Jonah *was in
the belly of the sea monster for three days and
three nights,*[j] so will the Son of Man be in the
heart of the earth for three days and three
nights. 41 On Judgment day the men of Nineveh
will stand up with this generation and condemn
it, because when Jonah preached they repented;
and there is something greater than Jonah here.
42 On Judgment day the Queen of the South
will rise up with this generation and condemn
it, because she came from the ends of the earth
to hear the wisdom of Solomon; and there is
something greater than Solomon here.

The return of the unclean spirit

43 "When an unclean spirit goes out of a man
it wanders through waterless country looking for
a place to rest, and cannot find one. 44 Then it
says, 'I will return to the home I came from.'
But on arrival, finding it unoccupied, swept and
tidied, 45 it then goes off and collects seven other
spirits more evil than itself, and they go in and
set up house there, so that the man ends up by

[i] A miracle to prove his authority. [j] Jon. 2:1.

New English Bible

At this some of the doctors of the law and the Pharisees said, 'Master, we should like you to show us a sign.' He answered: 'It is a wicked, godless generation that asks for a sign; and the only sign that will be given it is the sign of the prophet Jonah. Jonah was in the sea-monster's belly for three days and three nights, and in the same way the Son of Man will be three days and three nights in the bowels of the earth. At the Judgement, when this generation is on trial, the men of Nineveh will appear against it[a] and ensure its condemnation, for they repented at the preaching of Jonah; and what is here is greater than Jonah. The Queen of the South will appear at the Judgement when this generation is on trial,[b] and ensure its condemnation, for she came from the ends of the earth to hear the wisdom of Solomon; and what is here is greater than Solomon.

'When an unclean spirit comes out of a man it wanders over the deserts seeking a resting-place, and finds none. Then it says, "I will go back to the home I left." So it returns and finds the house unoccupied, swept clean, and tidy. Off it goes and collects seven other spirits more wicked than itself, and they all come in and settle down; and in the end the man's plight is

[a] *Or* will rise again together with it. [b] *Or* At the Judgement the Queen of the South will be raised to life together with this generation.

King James Version

that man is worse than the first. Even so shall it
be also unto this wicked generation.
46 While he yet talked to the people, behold,
his mother and his brethren stood without, desiring to speak with him. 47 Then one said unto
him, Behold, thy mother and thy brethren stand
without, desiring to speak with thee. 48 But he
answered and said unto him that told him, Who
is my mother? and who are my brethren? 49And
he stretched forth his hand toward his disciples,
and said, Behold my mother and my brethren!
50 For whosoever shall do the will of my Father
which is in heaven, the same is my brother, and
sister, and mother.

13 The same day went Jesus out of the house,
and sat by the sea side. 2And great multitudes were gathered together unto him, so that
he went into a ship, and sat; and the whole
multitude stood on the shore. 3And he spake
many things unto them in parables, saying, Be-

Living Bible

is worse off than before."
46, 47 As Jesus was speaking in a crowded
house[l] his mother and brothers were outside,
wanting to talk with him. When someone told
him they were there, 48 he remarked, "Who is
my mother? Who are my brothers?" 49 He
pointed to his disciples. "Look!" he said, "these
are my mother and brothers." 50 Then he added,
"Anyone who obeys my Father in heaven is my
brother, sister and mother!"

13 Later that same day, Jesus left the house
and went down to the shore, 2, 3 where an
immense crowd soon gathered. He got into a
boat and taught from it while the people listened
on the beach. He used many illustrations such
as this one in his sermon:

[*l*] Implied in Mark 3:32.

Today's English Version

worse shape, when it is all over, than he was at
the beginning. This is the way it will happen to
the evil people of this day."

Jesus' mother and brothers

46 Jesus was still talking to the people when
his mother and brothers arrived. They stood
outside, asking to speak with him. 47 So one of
the people there said to him, "Look, your mother
and brothers are standing outside, and they want
to speak with you."
48 Jesus answered, "Who is my mother? Who
are my brothers?" 49 Then he pointed to his disciples and said, "Look! Here are my mother and
my brothers! 50 Whoever does what my Father
in heaven wants him to do is my brother, my
sister, my mother."

The parable of the sower

13 That same day Jesus left the house and
went to the lakeside, where he sat down to
teach. 2 The crowd that gathered around him
was so large that he got into a boat and sat in
it, while the crowd stood on the shore. 3 He used
parables to tell them many things.

New International Version

man is worse than the first. That is how it will
be with this wicked generation."

Jesus' mother and brothers

46 While Jesus was still talking to the crowd,
his mother and brothers stood outside, wanting
to speak to him. 47 Someone told him, "Your
mother and brothers are standing outside, wanting to speak to you."[r]
48 He replied, "Who is my mother, and who
are my brothers?" 49 Pointing to his disciples,
he said, "Here are my mother and my brothers.
50 For whoever does the will of my Father in
heaven is my brother and sister and mother."

The parable of the sower

13 That same day Jesus went out of the
house and sat by the lake. 2 Such large
crowds gathered around him that he got into a
boat and sat in it, while all the people stood on
the shore. 3 Then he told them many things in

[*r*] Some MSS omit verse 47.

Phillips Modern English

selves at home. The last state of that man is worse than the first—and that is just what will happen to this evil generation."

12.46 Jesus and his relations

While he was still talking to the crowds, his mother and his brothers happened to be standing outside wanting to speak to him. Somebody said to him, "Look, your mother and your brothers are outside wanting to speak to you." But Jesus replied to the man who had told him, "Who is my mother, and who are my brothers?"; then with a gesture of his hand towards his disciples he went on, "There are my mother and brothers! For whoever does the will of my Heavenly Father is brother and sister and mother to me."

13.1 Jesus tells the parable of the seed

It was on the same day that Jesus went out of the house and sat down by the lake-side. Such great crowds collected round him that he went aboard a small boat and sat down while all the people stood on the beach. He told them a great deal in parables, and began:

Revised Standard Version

the last state of that man becomes worse than the first. So shall it be also with this evil generation."
46 While he was still speaking to the people, behold, his mother and his brothers stood outside, asking to speak to him.[g] 48 But he replied to the man who told him, "Who is my mother, and who are my brothers?" 49And stretching out his hand toward his disciples, he said, "Here are my mother and my brothers! 50 For whoever does the will of my Father in heaven is my brother, and sister, and mother."

13 That same day Jesus went out of the house and sat beside the sea. 2And great crowds gathered about him, so that he got into a boat and sat there; and the whole crowd stood on the beach. 3And he told them many things

[g] Other ancient authorities insert verse 47, *Some one told him, "Your mother and your brothers are standing outside, asking to speak to you."*

Jerusalem Bible

being worse than he was before. That is what will happen to this evil generation."

The true kinsmen of Jesus

46 He was still speaking to the crowds when his mother and his brothers[k] appeared; they were standing outside and were anxious to have a word with him.[l] 48 But to the man who told him this Jesus replied, "Who is my mother? Who are my brothers?" 49And stretching out his hand toward his disciples he said, "Here are my mother and my brothers. 50Anyone who does the will of my Father in heaven, he is my brother and sister and mother."

B. The sermon of parables

Introduction

13 That same day, Jesus left the house and sat by the lakeside, 2 but such crowds gathered around him that he got into a boat and sat there. The people all stood on the beach, 3 and he told them many things in parables.

[k] In Hebrew and Aramaic (and many other languages), "brothers" is the word used for cousins or even more distant relations of the same generation. [l] V. 47 ("someone said to him: your mother and brothers are standing outside and want to speak to you") is omitted by some important textual witnesses. It is probably a restatement of v. 46 modeled on Mk. and Lk.

New English Bible

worse than before. That is how it will be with this wicked generation.'

He was still speaking to the crowd when his mother and brothers appeared; they stood outside, wanting to speak to him. Someone said, 'Your mother and your brothers are here outside; they want to speak to you.' Jesus turned to the man who brought the message, and said, 'Who is my mother? Who are my brothers?'; and pointing to the disciples, he said, 'Here are my mother and my brothers. Whoever does the will of my heavenly Father is my brother, my sister, my mother.'

13 That same day Jesus went out and sat by the lake-side, where so many people gathered round him that he had to get into a boat. He sat there, and all the people stood on the shore. He spoke to them in parables, at some length.

King James Version

hold, a sower went forth to sow; 4And when he
sowed, some *seeds* fell by the way side, and the
fowls came and devoured them up: 5 Some fell
upon stony places, where they had not much
earth: and forthwith they sprung up, because
they had no deepness of earth: 6And when the
sun was up, they were scorched; and because
they had no root, they withered away. 7And
some fell among thorns; and the thorns sprung
up, and choked them: 8 But other fell into good
ground, and brought forth fruit, some a hundredfold, some sixtyfold, some thirtyfold. 9 Who
hath ears to hear, let him hear. 10And the disciples came, and said unto him, Why speakest thou
unto them in parables? 11 He answered and said
unto them, Because it is given unto you to know
the mysteries of the kingdom of heaven, but to
them it is not given. 12 For whosoever hath, to
him shall be given, and he shall have more
abundance: but whosoever hath not, from him
shall be taken away even that he hath. 13 Therefore speak I to them in parables: because they
seeing see not; and hearing they hear not, neither
do they understand. 14And in them is fulfilled
the prophecy of Esaias, which saith, By hearing
ye shall hear, and shall not understand; and see-

Living Bible

"A farmer was sowing grain in his fields. 4As
he scattered the seed across the ground, some
fell beside a path, and the birds came and ate
it. 5And some fell on rocky soil where there was
little depth of earth; the plants sprang up quickly
enough in the shallow soil, 6 but the hot sun
soon scorched them and they withered and died,
for they had so little root. 7 Other seeds fell
among thorns, and the thorns choked out the
tender blades. 8 But some fell on good soil, and
produced a crop that was thirty, sixty, and even
a hundred times as much as he had planted. 9 If
you have ears, listen!"

10 His disciples came and asked him, "Why
do you always use these hard-to-understand [a]
illustrations?"

11 Then he explained to them that only they
were permitted to understand about the Kingdom of Heaven, and others were not.

12, 13 "For to him who has will more be
given," he told them, "and he will have great
plenty; but from him who has not, even the
little he has will be taken away. That is why I
use these illustrations, so people will hear and
see but not understand.[b]

14 "This fulfills the prophecy of Isaiah:
'They hear, but don't understand;

[*a*] Implied. [*b*] Those who were receptive to spiritual truth understood the illustrations. To others they were only stories without meaning.

Today's English Version

"There was a man who went out to sow. 4As
he scattered the seed in the field, some of it fell
along the path, and the birds came and ate it
up. 5 Some of it fell on rocky ground, where
there was little soil. The seeds soon sprouted,
because the soil wasn't deep. 6 When the sun
came up it burned the young plants, and because the roots had not grown deep enough the
plants soon dried up. 7 Some of the seed fell
among thorns, which grew up and choked the
plants. 8 But some seeds fell in good soil, and
bore grain: some had one hundred grains, others
sixty, and others thirty."

9 And Jesus concluded, "Listen, then, if you
have ears!"

The purpose of the parables

10 Then the disciples came to Jesus and asked
him, "Why do you use parables when you talk
to them?"

11 Jesus answered, "The knowledge of the secrets of the Kingdom of heaven has been given
to you, but not to them. 12 For the man who
has something will be given more, so that he
will have more than enough; but the man who
has nothing will have taken away from him even
the little he has. 13 The reason that I use parables to talk to them is this: they look, but do
not see, and they listen, but do not hear or understand. 14 So the prophecy of Isaiah comes true
in their case:

'You will listen and listen, but not understand;

New International Version

parables, saying: "A farmer went out to sow
his seed. 4As he was scattering the seed, some
fell along the path, and the birds came and ate
it up. 5 Some fell on rocky places, where it did
not have much soil. It sprang up quickly, because the soil was shallow. 6 But when the sun
came up, the plants were scorched, and they
withered because they had no root. 7 Other seed
fell among thorns, which grew up and choked
the plants. 8 Still other seed fell on good soil,
where it produced a crop, a hundred, sixty or
thirty times what was sown. 9 He who has ears,
let him hear."

10 The disciples came to him and asked,
"Why do you speak to the people in parables?"

11 He replied, "The knowledge of the secrets
of the kingdom of heaven has been given to
you, but not to them. 12 Whoever has will be
given more, and he will have an abundance.
Whoever does not have, even what he has will
be taken from him. 13 This is why I speak to
them in parables:

Though seeing, they do not see;
though hearing, they do not hear or understand.

14 In them is fulfilled the prophecy of Isaiah:
'You will be ever hearing but never understanding;

Phillips Modern English

"There was once a man who went out to sow. In his sowing some of the seeds fell by the roadside and the birds swooped down and gobbled them up. Some fell on stony patches where they had very little soil. They sprang up quickly in the shallow soil, but when the sun came up they were scorched by the heat and withered away because they had no roots. Some seeds fell among thorn-bushes and the thorns grew up and choked the life out of them. But some fell on good soil and produced a crop—some a hundred times what had been sown, some sixty and some thirty times. The man who has ears to hear should use them!"

At this the disciples approached him and asked, "Why do you talk to them in parables?"

"Because you have been given the privilege of understanding the secrets of the kingdom of Heaven," replied Jesus, "but they have not. For when a man has something, more is given to him till he has plenty. But if he has nothing even his nothing will be taken away from him. This is why I speak to them in these parables; because they go through life with their eyes open, but see nothing, and with their ears open, but understand nothing of what they hear. They are the living fulfilment of Isaiah's prophecy which says:

By hearing ye shall hear, and shall in no wise understand;

Revised Standard Version

in parables, saying: "A sower went out to sow.
4And as he sowed, some seeds fell along the
path, and the birds came and devoured them.
5 Other seeds fell on rocky ground, where they
had not much soil, and immediately they sprang
up, since they had no depth of soil, 6 but when
the sun rose they were scorched; and since they
had no root they withered away. 7 Other seeds
fell upon thorns, and the thorns grew up and
choked them. 8 Other seeds fell on good soil
and brought forth grain, some a hundredfold,
some sixty, some thirty. 9 He who has ears,[h] let
him hear."

10 Then the disciples came and said to him,
"Why do you speak to them in parables?"
11And he answered them, "To you it has been
given to know the secrets of the kingdom of
heaven, but to them it has not been given. 12 For
to him who has will more be given, and he will
have abundance; but from him who has not,
even what he has will be taken away. 13 This
is why I speak to them in parables, because seeing they do not see, and hearing they do not
hear, nor do they understand. 14 With them indeed is fulfilled the prophecy of Isaiah which
says:

'You shall indeed hear but never understand,

[h] Other ancient authorities add here and in verse 43 *to hear.*

Jerusalem Bible

Parable of the sower

He said, "Imagine a sower going out to sow.
4As he sowed, some seeds fell on the edge of
the path, and the birds came and ate them up.
5 Others fell on patches of rock where they
found little soil and sprang up straight away, because there was no depth of earth; 6 but as soon
as the sun came up they were scorched and, not
having any roots, they withered away. 7 Others
fell among thorns, and the thorns grew up and
choked them. 8 Others fell on rich soil and produced their crop, some a hundredfold, some
sixty, some thirty. 9 Listen, anyone who has
ears!"

Why Jesus speaks in parables

10 Then the disciples went up to him and
asked, "Why do you talk to them in parables?"
11 "Because," he replied, "the mysteries of the
kingdom of heaven are revealed to you, but they
are not revealed to them. 12 For anyone who
has will be given more, and he will have more
than enough; but from anyone who has not,
even what he has will be taken away. 13 The
reason I talk to them in parables is that they
look without seeing and listen without hearing
or understanding. 14 So in their case this prophecy of Isaiah is being fulfilled:

You will listen and listen again, but not understand,

New English Bible

He said: 'A sower went out to sow. And as he sowed, some seed fell along the footpath; and the birds came and ate it up. Some seed fell on rocky ground, where it had little soil, and it sprouted quickly because it had no depth of earth; but when the sun rose the young corn was scorched, and as it had no root it withered away. Some seed fell among thistles; and the thistles shot up, and choked the corn. And some of the seed fell into good soil, where it bore fruit, yielding a hundredfold or, it might be, sixtyfold or thirtyfold. If you have ears, then hear.'

The disciples went up to him and asked, 'Why do you speak to them in parables?' He replied, 'It has been granted to you to know the secrets of the kingdom of Heaven; but to those others it has not been granted. For the man who has will be given more, till he has enough and to spare; and the man who has not will forfeit even what he has. That is why I speak to them in parables; for they look without seeing, and listen without hearing or understanding. There is a prophecy of Isaiah which is being fulfilled for them: "You may hear and hear, but you will never understand; you may

King James Version

ing ye shall see, and shall not perceive: 15 For
this people's heart is waxed gross, and *their* ears
are dull of hearing, and their eyes they have
closed; lest at any time they should see with
their eyes, and hear with *their* ears, and should
understand with *their* heart, and should be converted, and I should heal them. 16 But blessed
are your eyes, for they see: and your ears, for
they hear. 17 For verily I say unto you, That
many prophets and righteous *men* have desired
to see *those things* which ye see, and have not
seen *them;* and to hear *those things* which ye
hear, and have not heard *them.*
18 Hear ye therefore the parable of the sower.
19 When any one heareth the word of the
kingdom, and understandeth *it* not, then cometh
the wicked one, and catcheth away that which
was sown in his heart. This is he which received
seed by the way side. 20 But he that received the
seed into stony places, the same is he that
heareth the word, and anon with joy receiveth it;
21 Yet hath he not root in himself, but dureth for
a while: for when tribulation or persecution
ariseth because of the word, by and by he is
offended. 22 He also that received seed among
the thorns is he that heareth the word; and the
care of this world, and the deceitfulness of
riches, choke the word, and he becometh un-

Living Bible

they look, but don't see!
15 For their hearts are fat
and heavy, and their ears
are dull, and they have
closed their eyes in sleep,
16 so they won't see and hear
and understand and turn to God
again, and let me heal them.'
But blessed are your eyes, for they see; and
your ears, for they hear. 17 Many a prophet
and godly man has longed to see what you have
seen, and hear what you have heard, but couldn't.
18 "Now here is the explanation of the story
I told about the farmer planting grain: 19 The
hard path where some of the seeds fell represents
the heart of a person who hears the Good News
about the Kingdom and doesn't understand it;
then Satan[c] comes and snatches away the seeds
from his heart. 20 The shallow, rocky soil represents the heart of a man who hears the message
and receives it with real joy, 21 but he doesn't
have much depth in his life, and the seeds don't
root very deeply, and after a while when trouble
comes, or persecution begins because of his beliefs, his enthusiasm fades, and he drops out.
22 The ground covered with thistles represents a
man who hears the message, but the cares of this
life and his longing for money choke out God's

[c] Literally, "the evil."

Today's English Version

you will look and look, but not see,
15 because this people's minds are dull,
and they have stopped up their ears,
and have closed their eyes.
Otherwise, their eyes would see,
their ears would hear,
their minds would understand,
and they would turn to me, says God,
and I would heal them.

16 "As for you, how fortunate you are! Your
eyes see and your ears hear. 17 Remember this!
Many prophets and many of God's people
wanted very much to see what you see, but they
could not, and to hear what you hear, but they
did not."

Jesus explains the parable of the sower

18 "Listen, then, and learn what the parable
of the sower means. 19 Those who hear the message about the Kingdom but do not understand
it are like the seed that fell along the path. The
Evil One comes and snatches away what was
sown in them. 20 The seed that fell on rocky
ground stands for those who receive the message
gladly as soon as they hear it. 21 But it does not
sink deep in them, and they don't last long. So
when trouble or persecution comes because of
the message, they give up at once. 22 The seed
that fell among thorns stands for those who
hear the message, but the worries about this life
and the love for riches choke the message, and

New International Version

you will be ever seeing but never perceiving.
15 For this people's heart has become calloused;
they hardly hear with their ears,
and they have closed their eyes.
Otherwise they might see with their eyes,
hear with their ears,
understand with their hearts
and turn, and I would heal them.' [s]
16 But blessed are your eyes because they see,
and your ears because they hear. 17 For I tell
you the truth, many prophets and righteous men
longed to see what you see but did not see it,
and to hear what you hear but did not hear it.
18 "Listen then to what the parable of the
sower means: 19 When anyone hears the message
about the kingdom and does not understand it,
the evil one comes and snatches away what was
sown in his heart. This is the seed sown along
the path. 20 What was sown on rocky places is
the man who hears the word and at once receives
it with joy. 21 But since he has no root, he lasts
only a short time. When trouble or persecution
comes because of the word, he quickly falls
away. 22 What was sown among the thorns is
the man who hears the word, but the worries of
this life and the deceitfulness of wealth choke it,

[s] Isaiah 6:9,10.

Phillips Modern English

And seeing ye shall see, and shall in no wise
perceive:
For this people's heart is waxed gross,
And their ears are dull of hearing,
And their eyes they have closed;
Lest haply they should perceive with their
eyes,
And hear with their ears,
And understand with their heart,
And should turn again,
And I should heal them.

"But how fortunate you are to have eyes that see and ears that hear! Believe me, a great many prophets and good men have longed to see what you are seeing and they never saw it. Yes, and they longed to hear what you are hearing and they never heard it.

"Now listen to the parable of the sower. When a man hears the message of the kingdom and does not grasp it, the evil one comes and snatches away what was sown in his heart. This is like the seed sown by the road-side. The seed sown on the stony patches represents the man who hears the message and eagerly accepts it. But it has not taken root in him and does not last long—the moment trouble or persecution arises through the message he gives up his faith at once. The seed sown among the thorns represents the man who hears the message, and then the worries of this life and the illusions of wealth choke it to death and so it produces no

Revised Standard Version

and you shall indeed see but never perceive.
15 For this people's heart has grown dull,
and their ears are heavy of hearing,
and their eyes they have closed,
lest they should perceive with their eyes,
and hear with their ears,
and understand with their heart,
and turn for me to heal them.'
16 But blessed are your eyes, for they see, and
your ears, for they hear. 17 Truly, I say to you,
many prophets and righteous men longed to see
what you see, and did not see it, and to hear
what you hear, and did not hear it.
18 "Hear then the parable of the sower.
19 When any one hears the word of the kingdom and does not understand it, the evil one
comes and snatches away what is sown in his
heart; this is what was sown along the path.
20 As for what was sown on rocky ground, this
is he who hears the word and immediately receives it with joy; 21 yet he has no root in himself, but endures for a while, and when tribulation or persecution arises on account of the
word, immediately he falls away.[i] 22 As for what
was sown among thorns, this is he who hears
the word, but the cares of the world and the delight in riches choke the word, and it proves un-

[i] Or *stumbles.*

Jerusalem Bible

see and see again, but not perceive.
15 *For the heart of this nation has grown*
coarse,
their ears are dull of hearing, and they have
shut their eyes,
for fear they should see with their eyes,
hear with their ears,
understand with their heart,
and be converted
and be healed by me.[m]

16 "But happy are your eyes because they see,
your ears because they hear! 17 I tell you solemnly, many prophets and holy men longed to
see what you see, and never saw it; to hear
what you hear, and never heard it.

The parable of the sower explained

18 "You, therefore, are to hear the parable of
the sower. 19 When anyone hears the word of
the kingdom without understanding, the evil one
comes and carries off what was sown in his
heart: this is the man who received the seed on
the edge of the path. 20 The one who received
it on patches of rock is the man who hears the
word and welcomes it at once with joy. 21 But
he has no root in him, he does not last; let some
trial come, or some persecution on account of
the word, and he falls away at once. 22 The one
who received the seed in thorns is the man who
hears the word, but the worries of this world
and the lure of riches choke the word and so

[m] Is. 6:9-10.

New English Bible

look and look, but you will never see. For this people's mind has become gross; their ears are dulled, and their eyes are closed. Otherwise, their eyes might see, their ears hear, and their mind understand, and then they might turn again, and I would heal them."

'But happy are your eyes because they see, and your ears because they hear! Many prophets and saints, I tell you, desired to see what you now see, yet never saw it; to hear what you hear, yet never heard it.

'You, then, may hear the parable of the sower. When a man hears the word that tells of the Kingdom but fails to understand it, the evil one comes and carries off what has been sown in his heart. There you have the seed sown along the footpath. The seed sown on rocky ground stands for the man who, on hearing the word, accepts it at once with joy; but as it strikes no root in him he has no staying-power, and when there is trouble or persecution on account of the word he falls away at once. The seed sown among thistles represents the man who hears the word, but worldly cares and the false glamour

King James Version

fruitful. 23 But he that received seed into the good ground is he that heareth the word, and understandeth *it;* which also beareth fruit, and bringeth forth, some a hundredfold, some sixty, some thirty.

24 Another parable put he forth unto them, saying, The kingdom of heaven is likened unto a man which sowed good seed in his field: 25 But while men slept, his enemy came and sowed tares among the wheat, and went his way. 26 But when the blade was sprung up, and brought forth fruit, then appeared the tares also. 27 So the servants of the householder came and said unto him, Sir, didst not thou sow good seed in thy field? from whence then hath it tares? 28 He said unto them, An enemy hath done this. The servants said unto him, Wilt thou then that we go and gather them up? 29 But he said, Nay; lest while ye gather up the tares, ye root up also the wheat with them. 30 Let both grow together until the harvest: and in the time of harvest I will say to the reapers, Gather ye together first the tares, and bind them in bundles to burn them: but gather the wheat into my barn.

31 Another parable put he forth unto them,

Living Bible

Word, and he does less and less for God. 23 The good ground represents the heart of a man who listens to the message and understands it and goes out and brings thirty, sixty, or even a hundred others into the Kingdom." [d]

24 Here is another illustration Jesus used: "The Kingdom of Heaven is like a farmer sowing good seed in his field; 25 but one night as he slept, his enemy came and sowed thistles among the wheat. 26 When the crop began to grow, the thistles grew too.

27 "The farmer's men came and told him, 'Sir, the field where you planted that choice seed is full of thistles!'

28 " 'An enemy has done it,' he exclaimed.

" 'Shall we pull out the thistles?' they asked.

29 " 'No,' he replied. 'You'll hurt the wheat if you do. 30 Let both grow together until the harvest, and I will tell the reapers to sort out the thistles and burn them, and put the wheat in the barn.' " 31, 32 Here is another of his il-

[*d*] Literally, "produces a crop many times greater than the amount planted—thirty, sixty, or even a hundred times as much."

Today's English Version

they don't bear fruit. 23 And the seed sown in the good soil stands for those who hear the message and understand it: they bear fruit, some as much as one hundred, others sixty, and others thirty."

The parable of the weeds

24 Jesus told them another parable, "The Kingdom of heaven is like a man who sowed good seed in his field. 25 One night, when everyone was asleep, an enemy came and sowed weeds among the wheat, and went away. 26 When the plants grew and the heads of grain began to form, then the weeds showed up. 27 The man's servants came to him and said, 'Sir, it was good seed you sowed in your field; where did the weeds come from?' 28 'It was some enemy who did this,' he answered. 'Do you want us to go and pull up the weeds?' they asked him. 29 'No,' he answered, 'because as you gather the weeds you might pull up some of the wheat along with them. 30 Let the wheat and the weeds both grow together until harvest, and then I will tell the harvest workers: Pull up the weeds first and tie them in bundles to throw in the fire; then gather in the wheat and put it in my barn.' "

The parable of the mustard seed

31 Jesus told them another parable, "The

New International Version

making it unfruitful. 23 But what was sown on good soil is the man who hears the word and understands it. He produces a crop, yielding a hundred, sixty or thirty times what was sown."

The parable of the weeds

24 Jesus told them another parable: "The kingdom of heaven is like a man who sowed good seed in his field. 25 But while everyone was sleeping, his enemy came and sowed weeds among the wheat, and went away. 26 When the wheat sprouted and formed heads, then the weeds also appeared.

27 "The owner's servants came to him and said, 'Sir, didn't you sow good seed in your field? Where then did the weeds come from?'

28 " 'An enemy did this,' he replied.

"The servants asked him, 'Do you want us to go and pull them up?'

29 " 'No,' he answered, 'because while you are pulling the weeds, you may root up the wheat with them. 30 Let both grow together until the harvest. At that time I will tell the harvesters: First collect the weeds and tie them in bundles to be burned, then gather the wheat and bring it into my barn.' "

The parables of the mustard seed and the yeast

31 He told them another parable: "The king-

Phillips Modern English

'crop' in his life. But the seed sown on good soil is the man who both hears and understands the message. His life shows a good crop, a hundred, sixty or thirty times what was sown."

13.24 Good and evil grow side by side in this present world

Then he put another parable before them. "The kingdom of Heaven," he said, "is like a man who sowed good seed in his field. But while his men were asleep his enemy came and sowed weeds among the wheat, and went away. When the crop came up and began to ripen, the weeds appeared as well. Then the owner's servants came up to him and said, "Sir, didn't you sow good seed in your field? Where did all these weeds come from?' 'Some enemy of mine has done this,' he replied. 'Do you want us then to go out and pull them all up?' said the servants. 'No,' he returned, 'if you pull up the weeds now, you would pull up the wheat with them. Let them both grow together till the harvest. And at harvest-time I shall tell the reapers, 'Collect all the weeds first and tie them up in bundles ready to burn, but collect the wheat and store it in my barn.' "

13.31 The kingdom's power of growth, and widespread influence

Then he put another parable before them.

Revised Standard Version

fruitful. 23 As for what was sown on good soil,
this is he who hears the word and understands
it; he indeed bears fruit, and yields, in one case
a hundredfold, in another sixty, and in another
thirty."
24 Another parable he put before them, saying, "The kingdom of heaven may be compared to a man who sowed good seed in his
field; 25 but while men were sleeping, his enemy
came and sowed weeds among the wheat, and
went away. 26 So when the plants came up and
bore grain, then the weeds appeared also. 27 And
the servants[j] of the householder came and said
to him, 'Sir, did you not sow good seed in your
field? How then has it weeds?' 28 He said to
them, 'An enemy has done this.' The servants[j]
said to him, 'Then do you want us to go and
gather them?' 29 But he said, 'No; lest in gathering the weeds you root up the wheat along with
them. 30 Let both grow together until the harvest; and at harvest time I will tell the reapers,
Gather the weeds first and bind them in bundles to be burned, but gather the wheat into my
barn.' "
31 Another parable he put before them, say-

[j] Or *slaves*.

Jerusalem Bible

he produces nothing. 23 And the one who received the seed in rich soil is the man who hears
the word and understands it; he is the one who
yields a harvest and produces now a hundredfold, now sixty, now thirty."

Parable of the darnel

24 He put another parable before them, "The
kingdom of heaven may be compared to a man
who sowed good seed in his field. 25 While everybody was asleep his enemy came, sowed darnel
all among the wheat, and made off. 26 When
the new wheat sprouted and ripened, the darnel
appeared as well. 27 The owner's servants went
to him and said, 'Sir, was it not good seed that
you sowed in your field? If so, where does the
darnel come from?' 28 'Some enemy has done
this,' he answered. And the servants said, 'Do
you want us to go and weed it out?' 29 But he
said, 'No, because when you weed out the darnel
you might pull up the wheat with it. 30 Let them
both grow till the harvest; and at harvest time I
shall say to the reapers: First collect the darnel
and tie it in bundles to be burned, then gather
the wheat into my barn.' "

Parable of the mustard seed

31 He put another parable before them, "The

New English Bible

of wealth choke it, and it proves barren. But the seed that fell into good soil is the man who hears the word and understands it, who accordingly bears fruit, and yields a hundredfold or, it may be, sixtyfold or thirtyfold.'

Here is another parable that he put before them: 'The kingdom of Heaven is like this. A man sowed his field with good seed; but while everyone was asleep his enemy came, sowed darnel among the wheat, and made off. When the corn sprouted and began to fill out, the darnel could be seen among it. The farmer's men went to their master and said, "Sir, was it not good seed that you sowed in your field? Then where has the darnel come from?" "This is an enemy's doing", he replied. "Well then," they said, "shall we go and gather the darnel?" "No," he answered; "in gathering it you might pull up the wheat at the same time. Let them both grow together till harvest; and at harvest-time I will tell the reapers, 'Gather the darnel first, and tie it in bundles for burning; then collect the wheat into my barn.' " '

And this is another parable that he put before

King James Version

saying, The kingdom of heaven is like to a grain of mustard seed, which a man took, and sowed in his field: 32 Which indeed is the least of all seeds: but when it is grown, it is the greatest among herbs, and becometh a tree, so that the birds of the air come and lodge in the branches thereof.

33 Another parable spake he unto them; The kingdom of heaven is like unto leaven, which a woman took, and hid in three measures of meal, till the whole was leavened. 34 All these things spake Jesus unto the multitude in parables; and without a parable spake he not unto them: 35 That it might be fulfilled which was spoken by the prophet, saying, I will open my mouth in parables; I will utter things which have been kept secret from the foundation of the world. 36 Then Jesus sent the multitude away, and went into the house: and his disciples came unto him,

Living Bible

lustrations: "The Kingdom of Heaven is like a tiny mustard seed planted in a field. It is the smallest of all seeds, but becomes the largest of plants, and grows into a tree where birds can come and find shelter."

33 He also used this example:

"The Kingdom of Heaven can be compared to a woman making bread. She takes a measure of flour and mixes in the yeast until it permeates every part of the dough."

34, 35 Jesus constantly used these illustrations when speaking to the crowds. In fact, because the prophets said that he would use so many, he never spoke to them without at least one illustration. For it had been prophesied, "I will talk in parables; I will explain mysteries hidden since the beginning of time." [e] 36 Then, leaving the crowds outside, he went into the house. His

[e] Psalm 78:2.

Today's English Version

Kingdom of heaven is like a mustard seed, which a man takes and sows in his field. 32 It is the smallest of all seeds, but when it grows up it is the biggest of all plants. It becomes a tree, so that the birds come and make their nests in its branches."

The parable of the yeast

33 Jesus told them another parable, "The Kingdom of heaven is like yeast. A woman takes it and mixes it with a bushel of flour, until the whole batch of dough rises."

Jesus' use of parables

34 Jesus used parables to tell all these things to the crowds; he would not say a thing to them without using a parable. 35 He did this to make come true what the prophet had said,

"I will use parables when I speak to them;
I will tell them things unknown since
the creation of the world."

Jesus explains the parable of the weeds

36 Then Jesus left the crowd and went indoors. His disciples came to him and said, "Tell

New International Version

dom of heaven is like a mustard seed, which a man took and planted in his field. 32 Though it is the smallest of all your seeds, yet when it grows, it is the largest of garden plants and becomes a tree, so that the birds of the air come and perch in its branches."

33 He told them still another parable: "The kingdom of heaven is like yeast that a woman took and mixed into a large amount[t] of flour until it worked all through the dough."

34 Jesus spoke all these things to the crowd in parables, and he did not say anything to them without using a parable. 35 So was fulfilled what was spoken through the prophet:

"I will open my mouth in parables;
I will utter things hidden since the creation of the world."[u]

The parable of the weeds explained

36 Then he left the crowd and went into the house. His disciples came to him and said, "Ex-

[t] Greek *three satas* (about a bushel). [u] Psalm 78:2.

Phillips Modern English

"The kingdom of Heaven is like a tiny grain of mustard-seed which a man took and sowed in his field. As a seed it is the smallest of them all, but it grows to be the biggest of all plants. It becomes a tree, big enough for birds to come and nest in its branches."

This is another of the parables he told them: "The kingdom of Heaven is like yeast, taken by a woman and put into three measures of flour until the whole had risen."

All these things Jesus spoke to the crowd in parables, and he did not speak to them at all without using parables—to fulfil the prophecy:

I will open my mouth in parables;
I will utter things hidden from the foundation of the world.

13.36 Jesus again explains a parable to his disciples

Later, he left the crowds and went indoors, where his disciples came and said, "Please ex-

Revised Standard Version

ing, "The kingdom of heaven is like a grain of mustard seed which a man took and sowed in his field; 32 it is the smallest of all seeds, but when it has grown it is the greatest of shrubs and becomes a tree, so that the birds of the air come and make nests in its branches."

33 He told them another parable. "The kingdom of heaven is like leaven which a woman took and hid in three measures of flour, till it was all leavened."

34 All this Jesus said to the crowds in parables; indeed he said nothing to them without a parable. 35 This was to fulfil what was spoken by the prophet:[k]

"I will open my mouth in parables,
I will utter what has been hidden since the foundation of the world."

36 Then he left the crowds and went into the house. And his disciples came to him, saying,

[k] Other ancient authorities read *the prophet Isaiah.*

Jerusalem Bible

kingdom of heaven is like a mustard seed which a man took and sowed in his field. 32 It is the smallest of all the seeds, but when it has grown it is the biggest shrub of all and becomes a tree so that the birds of the air come and shelter in its branches."

Parable of the yeast

33 He told them another parable, "The kingdom of heaven is like the yeast a woman took and mixed in with three measures of flour till it was leavened all through."

The people are taught only in parables

34 In all this Jesus spoke to the crowds in parables; indeed, he would never speak to them except in parables. 35 This was to fulfill the prophecy:

I will speak to you in parables
and expound things hidden since the foundation of the world.[n]

The parable of the darnel explained

36 Then, leaving the crowds, he went to the house; and his disciples came to him and said,

[n] Ps. 78:2.

New English Bible

them: 'The kingdom of Heaven is like a mustard-seed, which a man took and sowed in his field. As a seed, mustard is smaller than any other; but when it has grown it is bigger than any garden-plant; it becomes a tree, big enough for the birds to come and roost among its branches.'

He told them also this parable: 'The kingdom of Heaven is like yeast, which a woman took and mixed with half a hundredweight of flour till it was all leavened.'

In all this teaching to the crowds Jesus spoke in parables; in fact he never spoke to them without a parable. This was to fulfil the prophecy of Isaiah:[a]

'I will open my mouth in parables;
I will utter things kept secret since the world was made.'

He then dismissed the people, and went into the house, where his disciples came to him and

[a] *Some witnesses omit* of Isaiah.

King James Version

saying, Declare unto us the parable of the tares
of the field. 37 He answered and said unto them,
He that soweth the good seed is the Son of man;
38 The field is the world; the good seed are the
children of the kingdom; but the tares are the
children of the wicked one; 39 The enemy that
sowed them is the devil; the harvest is the end
of the world; and the reapers are the angels.
40 As therefore the tares are gathered and burned
in the fire; so shall it be in the end of this world.
41 The Son of man shall send forth his angels,
and they shall gather out of his kingdom all
things that offend, and them which do iniquity;
42 And shall cast them into a furnace of fire:
there shall be wailing and gnashing of teeth.
43 Then shall the righteous shine forth as the
sun in the kingdom of their Father. Who hath
ears to hear, let him hear.

44 Again, the kingdom of heaven is like unto
treasure hid in a field; the which when a man
hath found, he hideth, and for joy thereof goeth
and selleth all that he hath, and buyeth that
field.

45 Again, the kingdom of heaven is like unto
a merchantman, seeking goodly pearls: 46 Who,

Living Bible

disciples asked him to explain to them the illustration of the thistles and the wheat.

37 "All right," he said, "I[f] am the farmer
who sows the choice seed. 38 The field is the
world, and the seed represents the people of the
Kingdom; the thistles are the people belonging
to Satan. 39 The enemy who sowed the thistles
among the wheat is the devil; the harvest is the
end of the world,[g] and the reapers are the angels.

40 "Just as in this story the thistles are separated and burned, so shall it be at the end of
the world:[g] 41 I[f] will send my angels and they
will separate out of the Kingdom every temptation and all who are evil, 42 and throw them
into the furnace and burn them. There shall be
weeping and gnashing of teeth. 43 Then the godly
shall shine as the sun in their Father's Kingdom.
Let those with ears, listen!

44 "The Kingdom of Heaven is like a treasure
a man discovered in a field. In his excitement,
he sold everything he owned to get enough
money to buy the field—and get the treasure,
too!

45 "Again, the Kingdom of Heaven is like a
pearl merchant on the lookout for choice pearls.
46 He discovered a real bargain—a pearl of great

[f] Literally, "the Son of Man." [g] Or, "age."

Today's English Version

us what the parable of the weeds in the field
means."

37 Jesus answered, "The man who sowed the
good seed is the Son of Man; 38 the field is the
world; the good seed is the people who belong
to the Kingdom; the weeds are the people who
belong to the Evil One; 39 and the enemy who
sowed the weeds is the Devil. The harvest is the
end of the age, and the harvest workers are
angels. 40 Just as the weeds are gathered up and
burned in the fire, so it will be at the end of the
age: 41 the Son of Man will send out his angels
and they will gather up out of his Kingdom all
who cause people to sin, and all other evildoers,
42 and throw them into the fiery furnace, where
they will cry and gnash their teeth. 43 Then
God's people will shine like the sun in their
Father's Kingdom. Listen, then, if you have ears!"

The parable of the hidden treasure

44 "The Kingdom of heaven is like a treasure
hidden in a field. A man happens to find it, so
he covers it up again. He is so happy that he
goes and sells everything he has, and then goes
back and buys the field."

The parable of the pearl

45 "Also, the Kingdom of heaven is like a
buyer looking for fine pearls. 46 When he finds

New International Version

plain to us the parable of the weeds in the field."

37 He answered, "The one who sowed the
good seed is the Son of Man. 38 The field is the
world, and the good seed stands for the sons of
the kingdom. The weeds are the sons of the evil
one, 39 and the enemy who sows them is the
devil. The harvest is the end of the age, and the
harvesters are angels.

40 "As the weeds are pulled up and burned
in the fire, so it will be at the end of the age.
41 The Son of Man will send out his angels, and
they will weed out of his kingdom everything
that causes sin and all who do evil. 42 They will
throw them into the fiery furnace, where there
will be weeping and grinding of teeth. 43 Then
the righteous will shine like the sun in the kingdom of their Father. He who has ears, let him
hear.

The parables of the hidden treasure and the pearl

44 "The kingdom of heaven is like treasure
hidden in a field. When a man found it, he hid
it again, and then in his joy went and sold all
he had and bought that field.

45 "Again, the kingdom of heaven is like a
merchant looking for fine pearls. 46 When he

Phillips Modern English

plain to us the parable of the weeds in the field."

"The one who sows the good seed is the Son of Man," replied Jesus. "The field is the whole world. The good seed? That is the sons of the kingdom, while the weeds are the sons of the evil one. The enemy who sowed them is the devil. The harvest is the end of this world. The reapers are angels.

"Just as weeds are gathered up and burned in the fire so will it happen at the end of this world. The Son of Man will send out his angels and they will uproot from the kingdom everything that is spoiling it, and all those who live in defiance of its laws, and will throw them into the blazing furnace, where there will be tears and bitter regret. Then the good will shine out like the sun in their Father's kingdom. The man who has ears should use them!

13.44 More pictures of the kingdom of Heaven

"Again, the kingdom of Heaven is like some treasure which has been buried in a field. A man finds it and buries it again, and goes off overjoyed to sell all his possessions to buy himself that field.

"Or again, the kingdom of Heaven is like a merchant searching for fine pearls. When he has

Revised Standard Version

"Explain to us the parable of the weeds of the
field." 37 He answered, "He who sows the good
seed is the Son of man; 38 the field is the world,
and the good seed means the sons of the kingdom; the weeds are the sons of the evil one,
39 and the enemy who sowed them is the devil;
the harvest is the close of the age, and the reapers are angels. 40 Just as the weeds are gathered
and burned with fire, so will it be at the close
of the age. 41 The Son of man will send his
angels, and they will gather out of his kingdom
all causes of sin and all evildoers, 42 and throw
them into the furnace of fire; there men will
weep and gnash their teeth. 43 Then the righteous
will shine like the sun in the kingdom of their
Father. He who has ears, let him hear.
44 "The kingdom of heaven is like treasure
hidden in a field, which a man found and covered up; then in his joy he goes and sells all
that he has and buys that field.
45 "Again, the kingdom of heaven is like a
merchant in search of fine pearls, 46 who, on

Jerusalem Bible

"Explain the parable about the darnel in the
field to us." 37 He said in reply, "The sower of
the good seed is the Son of Man. 38 The field is
the world; the good seed is the subjects of the
kingdom; the darnel, the subjects of the evil one;
39 the enemy who sowed them, the devil; the
harvest is the end of the world; the reapers are
the angels. 40 Well then, just as the darnel is
gathered up and burned in the fire, so it will be
at the end of time. 41 The Son of Man will send
his angels and they will gather out of his kingdom all things that provoke offenses and all who
do evil, 42 and throw them into the blazing
furnace, where there will be weeping and grinding of teeth. 43 Then the virtuous will shine like
the sun in the kingdom of their father.[o] Listen,
anyone who has ears!

Parables of the treasure and of the pearl

44 "The kingdom of heaven is like treasure
hidden in a field which someone has found; he
hides it again, goes off happy, sells everything he
owns and buys the field.
45 "Again, the kingdom of heaven is like a
merchant looking for fine pearls; 46 when he

[o] The kingdom of the Son, v. 41, is succeeded by the kingdom of the Father.

New English Bible

said, 'Explain to us the parable of the darnel in the field.' And this was his answer: 'The sower of the good seed is the Son of Man. The field is the world; the good seed stands for the children of the Kingdom, the darnel for the children of the evil one. The enemy who sowed the darnel is the devil. The harvest is the end of time. The reapers are angels. As the darnel, then, is gathered up and burnt, so at the end of time the Son of Man will send out his angels, who will gather out of his kingdom whatever makes men stumble, and all whose deeds are evil, and these will be thrown into the blazing furnace, the place of wailing and grinding of teeth. And then the righteous will shine as brightly as the sun in the kingdom of their Father. If you have ears, then hear.

'The kingdom of Heaven is like treasure lying buried in a field. The man who found it, buried it again; and for sheer joy went and sold everything he had, and bought that field.

'Here is another picture of the kingdom of Heaven. A merchant looking out for fine pearls found one of very special value; so he went and

King James Version

when he had found one pearl of great price,
went and sold all that he had, and bought it.
47 Again, the kingdom of heaven is like unto
a net, that was cast into the sea, and gathered
of every kind: 48 Which, when it was full, they
drew to shore, and sat down, and gathered the
good into vessels, but cast the bad away. 49 So
shall it be at the end of the world: the angels
shall come forth, and sever the wicked from
among the just, 50 And shall cast them into the
furnace of fire: there shall be wailing and
gnashing of teeth. 51 Jesus saith unto them, Have
ye understood all these things? They say unto
him, Yea, Lord. 52 Then said he unto them,
Therefore every scribe *which is* instructed unto
the kingdom of heaven, is like unto a man *that
is* a householder, which bringeth forth out of his
treasure *things* new and old.

Living Bible

value—and sold everything he owned to purchase it!
47, 48 "Again, the Kingdom of Heaven can be
illustrated by a fisherman—he casts a net into
the water and gathers in fish of every kind,
valuable and worthless. When the net is full, he
drags it up onto the beach and sits down and
sorts out the edible ones into crates and throws
the others away. 49 That is the way it will be at
the end of the world [h]—the angels will come
and separate the wicked people from the godly,
50 casting the wicked into the fire; there shall be
weeping and gnashing of teeth. 51 Do you understand?"
"Yes," they said, "we do."
52 Then he added, "Those experts in Jewish
law who are now my disciples have double treasures—from the Old Testament as well as from
the New!" [i]

[*h*] Or, "age." [*i*] Literally, "brings back out of his treasure things both new and old." The paraphrase is of course highly anachronistic!

Today's English Version

one that is unusually fine, he goes and sells everything he has, and buys the pearl."

The parable of the net

47 "Also, the Kingdom of heaven is like a net
thrown out in the lake, which catches all kinds
of fish. 48 When it is full, the fishermen pull it
to shore and sit down to divide the fish: the
good ones go into their buckets, the worthless
ones are thrown away. 49 It will be like this at
the end of the age: the angels will go out and
gather up the evil people from among the good,
50 and throw them into the fiery furnace. There
they will cry and gnash their teeth."

New and old truths

51 "Do you understand these things?" Jesus
asked them.
"Yes," they answered.
52 So he replied, "This means, then, that every
teacher of the Law who becomes a disciple in
the Kingdom of heaven is like a homeowner
who takes new and old things out of his storage
room."

New International Version

found one of great value, he went away and
sold everything he had and bought it.

The parable of the net

47 "Once again, the kingdom of heaven is
like a net that was let down into the lake and
caught all kinds of fish. 48 When it was full, the
fishermen pulled it up on the shore. Then they
sat down and collected the good fish in baskets,
but threw the bad away. 49 This is how it will be
at the end of the age. The angels will come and
separate the wicked from the righteous 50 and
throw them into the fiery furnace, where there
will be weeping and grinding of teeth."
51 "Have you understood all these things?"
Jesus asked.
"Yes," they replied.
52 He said to them, "Therefore every teacher
of the law who has been instructed about the
kingdom of heaven is like the owner of a house
who brings out of his storeroom new treasures as
well as old."

Phillips Modern English

found a single pearl of great value, he goes and sells all his possessions and buys it.

"Or the kingdom of Heaven is like a big net thrown into the sea collecting all kinds of fish. When it is full, the fishermen haul it ashore and sit down and pick out the good ones for the barrels, but they throw away the bad. That is how it will be at the end of this world. The angels will go out and pick out the wicked from among the good and throw them into the blazing furnace, where there will be tears and bitter regret.

"Have you grasped all this?"

"Yes," they replied.

"You can see, then," returned Jesus, "how everyone who knows the Law and becomes a disciple of the kingdom of Heaven is like a householder who can produce from his store both the new and the old."

Revised Standard Version

finding one pearl of great value, went and sold
all that he had and bought it.
47 "Again, the kingdom of heaven is like a
net which was thrown into the sea and gathered
fish of every kind; 48 when it was full, men drew
it ashore and sat down and sorted the good into
vessels but threw away the bad. 49 So it will be
at the close of the age. The angels will come
out and separate the evil from the righteous,
50 and throw them into the furnace of fire; there
men will weep and gnash their teeth.
51 "Have you understood all this?" They said
to him, "Yes." 52 And he said to them, "Therefore every scribe who has been trained for the
kingdom of heaven is like a householder who
brings out of his treasure what is new and what
is old."

Jerusalem Bible

finds one of great value he goes and sells everything he owns and buys it.

Parable of the dragnet

47 "Again, the kingdom of heaven is like a
dragnet cast into the sea that brings in a haul
of all kinds. 48 When it is full, the fishermen
haul it ashore; then, sitting down, they collect
the good ones in a basket and throw away those
that are no use. 49 This is how it will be at the
end of time: the angels will appear and separate the wicked from the just 50 to throw them
into the blazing furnace where there will be
weeping and grinding of teeth.

Conclusion

51 "Have you understood all this?" They said,
"Yes." 52 And he said to them, "Well then, every
scribe who becomes a disciple of the kingdom
of heaven is like a householder who brings out
from his storeroom things both new and old." [p]

[p] Perhaps a saying of particular significance to Matthew, a "scribe who became a disciple."

New English Bible

sold everything he had, and bought it.

'Again the kingdom of Heaven is like a net let down into the sea, where fish of every kind were caught in it. When it was full, it was dragged ashore. Then the men sat down and collected the good fish into pails and threw the worthless away. That is how it will be at the end of time. The angels will go forth, and they will separate the wicked from the good, and throw them into the blazing furnace, the place of wailing and grinding of teeth.

'Have you understood all this?' he asked; and they answered, 'Yes.' He said to them, 'When, therefore, a teacher of the law has become a learner in the kingdom of Heaven, he is like a householder who can produce from his store both the new and the old.'

King James Version

53 And it came to pass, *that* when Jesus had finished these parables, he departed thence. 54And when he was come into his own country, he taught them in their synagogue, insomuch that they were astonished, and said, Whence hath this *man* this wisdom, and *these* mighty works? 55 Is not this the carpenter's son? is not his mother called Mary? and his brethren, James, and Joses, and Simon, and Judas? 56And his sisters, are they not all with us? Whence then hath this *man* all these things? 57And they were offended in him. But Jesus said unto them, A prophet is not without honour, save in his own country, and in his own house. 58And he did not many mighty works there because of their unbelief.

14 At that time Herod the tetrarch heard of the fame of Jesus, 2And said unto his servants, This is John the Baptist; he is risen from the dead; and therefore mighty works do shew forth themselves in him.

Living Bible

53, 54 When Jesus had finished giving these illustrations, he returned to his home town, Nazareth in Galilee,[j] and taught there in the synagogue and astonished everyone with his wisdom and his miracles.

55 "How is this possible?" the people exclaimed. "He's just a carpenter's son, and we know Mary his mother and his brothers—James, Joseph, Simon, and Judas. 56And his sisters—they all live here. How can he be so great?" 57And they became angry with him!

Then Jesus told them, "A prophet is honored everywhere except in his own country, and among his own people!" 58And so he did only a few great miracles there, because of their unbelief.

14 When King[a] Herod heard about Jesus, 2 he said to his men, "This must be John the Baptist, come back to life again. That is

[j] Implied. [a] Literally, "the Tetrarch"—he was one of four "kings" over the area, his sovereignty being Galilee and Peraea.

Today's English Version

Jesus rejected at Nazareth

53 When Jesus finished telling these parables, he left that place 54 and went back to his home town. He taught in their synagogue, and those who heard him were amazed. "Where did he get such wisdom?" they asked. "And what about his miracles? 55 Isn't he the carpenter's son? Isn't Mary his mother, and aren't James, Joseph, Simon, and Judas his brothers? 56Aren't all his sisters living here? Where did he get all this?" 57And so they rejected him.

Jesus said to them, "A prophet is respected everywhere except in his home town and by his own family." 58 He did not perform many miracles there because they did not have faith.

The death of John the Baptist

14 It was at that time that Herod, the ruler of Galilee, heard about Jesus. 2 "He is really John the Baptist, who has come back to life," he told his officials. "That is why these powers are at work in him."

New International Version

A prophet without honor

53 When Jesus had finished these parables, he moved on from there. 54 Coming to his home town, he began teaching the people in their synagogue, and they were amazed. "Where did this man get this wisdom and these miraculous powers?" they asked. 55 "Isn't this the carpenter's son? Isn't his mother's name Mary, and aren't his brothers James, Joseph, Simon and Judas? 56 Aren't all his sisters with us? Where then did this man get all these things?" 57And they took offense at him.

But Jesus said to them, "Only in his home town and in his own house is a prophet without honor."

58 And he did not do many miracles there because of their lack of faith.

John the Baptist beheaded

14 At that time Herod the tetrarch heard the reports about Jesus, 2 and he said to his attendants, "This is John the Baptist; he has risen from the dead! That is why miraculous powers are at work in him."

Phillips Modern English

13.53 Jesus is not appreciated in his native town

When Jesus had finished these parables he left the place, and came into his own country. Here he taught the people in their own synagogue, till in their amazement they said, "Where does this man get this wisdom and these powers? He's only the carpenter's son. Isn't Mary his mother, and aren't James, Joseph, Simon and Judas his brothers? And aren't all his sisters living here with us? Where did he get all this?" And they were deeply offended with him.

But Jesus said to them, "No prophet goes unhonoured except in his own country and in his own home!"

And he performed very few miracles there because of their lack of faith.

14.1 Herod's guilty conscience

About this time Herod, governor of the province, heard the reports about Jesus and said to his men, "This must be John the Baptist: he has risen from the dead. That is why miraculous powers are at work in him."

Revised Standard Version

53 And when Jesus had finished these parables, he went away from there, 54 and coming to his own country he taught them in their synagogue, so that they were astonished, and said, "Where did this man get this wisdom and these mighty works? 55 Is not this the carpenter's son? Is not his mother called Mary? And are not his brothers James and Joseph and Simon and Judas? 56And are not all his sisters with us? Where then did this man get all this?" 57And they took offense at him. But Jesus said to them, "A prophet is not without honor except in his own country and in his own house." 58And he did not do many mighty works there, because of their unbelief.

14 At that time Herod the tetrarch heard about the fame of Jesus; 2 and he said to his servants, "This is John the Baptist, he has been raised from the dead; that is why these

Jerusalem Bible

V. The church, first fruits of the kingdom of heaven

A. Narrative section

A visit to Nazareth

53 When Jesus had finished these parables he left the district; 54 and, coming to his home town,[q] he taught the people in their synagogue in such a way that they were astonished and said, "Where did the man get this wisdom and these miraculous powers? 55 This is the carpenter's son, surely? Is not his mother the woman called Mary, and his brothers James and Joseph and Simon and Jude? 56 His sisters, too, are they not all here with us? So where did the man get it all?" 57And they would not accept him. But Jesus said to them, "A prophet is only despised in his own country and in his own house," 58 and he did not work many miracles there because of their lack of faith.

Herod and Jesus

14 At that time Herod the tetrarch heard about the reputation of Jesus, 2 and said to his court, "This is John the Baptist himself; he has risen from the dead, and that is why miraculous powers are at work in him."

[q] Nazareth, see 2:23.

New English Bible

When he had finished these parables Jesus left that place, and came to his home town, where he taught the people in their synagogue. In amazement they asked, 'Where does he get this wisdom from, and these miraculous powers? Is he not the carpenter's son? Is not his mother called Mary, his brothers James, Joseph, Simon, and Judas? And are not all his sisters here with us? Where then has he got all this from?' So they fell foul of him, and this led him to say, 'A prophet will always be held in honour, except in his home town, and in his own family.' And he did not work many miracles there: such was their want of faith.

14 It was at that time that reports about Jesus reached the ears of Prince Herod. 'This is John the Baptist,' he said to his attendants; 'John has been raised to life, and that is why these miraculous powers are at work in him.'

King James Version

3 For Herod had laid hold on John, and
bound him, and put *him* in prison for Herodias'
sake, his brother Philip's wife. 4 For John said
unto him, It is not lawful for thee to have her.
5 And when he would have put him to death, he
feared the multitude, because they counted him
as a prophet. 6 But when Herod's birthday was
kept, the daughter of Herodias danced before
them, and pleased Herod. 7 Whereupon he promised with an oath to give her whatsoever she
would ask. 8 And she, being before instructed of
her mother, said, Give me here John Baptist's
head in a charger. 9 And the king was sorry:
nevertheless for the oath's sake, and them which
sat with him at meat, he commanded *it* to be
given *her*. 10 And he sent, and beheaded John in
the prison. 11 And his head was brought in a
charger, and given to the damsel: and she
brought *it* to her mother. 12 And his disciples
came, and took up the body, and buried it, and
went and told Jesus.
13 When Jesus heard *of it*, he departed thence
by ship into a desert place apart: and when the
people had heard *thereof*, they followed him on
foot out of the cities. 14 And Jesus went forth,
and saw a great multitude, and was moved with
compassion toward them, and he healed their
sick.
15 And when it was evening, his disciples

Living Bible

why he can do these miracles." 3 For Herod had
arrested John and chained him in prison at the
demand of[b] his wife Herodias, his brother Philip's
ex-wife, 4 because John had told him it was
wrong for him to marry her. 5 He would have
killed John but was afraid of a riot, for all the
people believed John was a prophet.
6 But at a birthday party for Herod, Herodias' daughter performed a dance that greatly
pleased him, 7 so he vowed to give her anything
she wanted. 8 Consequently, at her mother's
urging, the girl asked for John the Baptist's head
on a tray.
9 The king was grieved, but because of his
oath, and because he didn't want to back down
in front of his guests, he issued the necessary
orders.
10 So John was beheaded in the prison, 11 and
his head was brought on a tray and given to the
girl, who took it to her mother.
12 Then John's disciples came for his body
and buried it, and came to tell Jesus what had
happened.
13 As soon as Jesus heard the news, he went
off by himself in a boat to a remote area to be
alone. But the crowds saw where he was headed,
and followed by land from many villages.
14 So when Jesus came out of the wilderness,
a vast crowd was waiting for him and he pitied
them and healed their sick.
15 That evening the disciples came to him

[*b*] Literally, "on account of."

Today's English Version

3 For Herod had ordered John's arrest, and
had him tied up and put in prison. He did this
because of Herodias, his brother Philip's wife.
4 John the Baptist kept telling Herod, "It isn't
right for you to marry her!" 5 Herod wanted to
kill him, but he was afraid of the Jewish people,
because they considered John to be a prophet.
6 On Herod's birthday the daughter of Herodias danced in front of the whole group. Herod
was so pleased 7 that he promised her, "I swear
that I will give you anything you ask for!"
8 At her mother's suggestion she asked him,
"Give me right here the head of John the Baptist
on a plate!"
9 The king was sad, but because of the promise he had made in front of all his guests he
gave orders that her wish be granted. 10 So he
had John beheaded in prison. 11 The head was
brought in on a plate and given to the girl, who
took it to her mother. 12 John's disciples came,
got his body, and buried it; then they went and
told Jesus.

Jesus feeds the five thousand

13 When Jesus heard the news, he left that
place in a boat and went to a lonely place by
himself. The people heard about it, left their
towns, and followed him by land. 14 Jesus got
out of the boat, and when he saw the large
crowd his heart was filled with pity for them,
and he healed their sick.
15 That evening his disciples came to him and

New International Version

3 Now Herod had arrested John and bound
him and put him in prison because of Herodias,
his brother Philip's wife, 4 for John had been
saying to him: "It is not lawful for you to have
her." 5 Herod wanted to kill John, but he was
afraid of the people, because they considered
him a prophet.
6 On Herod's birthday the daughter of
Herodias danced for them and pleased Herod
so much 7 that he promised with an oath to give
her whatever she asked. 8 Prompted by her
mother, she said, "Give me here on a platter the
head of John the Baptist." 9 The king was distressed, but because of his oaths and his dinner
guests, he ordered that her request be granted
10 and had John beheaded in the prison. 11 His
head was brought in on a platter and given to
the girl, who carried it to her mother. 12 John's
disciples came and took his body and buried it.
Then they went and told Jesus.

Jesus feeds the five thousand

13 When Jesus heard what had happened, he
withdrew by boat privately to a solitary place.
Hearing of this, the crowds followed him on
foot from the towns. 14 When Jesus landed and
saw a large crowd, he had compassion on them
and healed their sick.
15 As evening approached, the disciples came

Phillips Modern English

For previously Herod had arrested John and had him bound and put in prison, all on account of Herodias, the wife of his brother Philip. For John had said to him, "It is not right for you to have this woman." Herod wanted to kill him for this, but he was afraid of the people, since they all thought John was a prophet. But during Herod's birthday celebrations Herodias' daughter delighted him by dancing before his guests, so much so that he swore to give her anything she liked to ask. And she, prompted by her mother, said, "I want you to give me, here and now, on a dish, the head of John the Baptist!" Herod was appalled at this, but because he had sworn in front of his guests, he gave orders that she should be given what she had asked. So he sent men and had John beheaded in the prison. Then his head was carried in on a dish and presented to the young girl who handed it to her mother. Later, John's disciples came, took his body and buried it. Then they went and told the news to Jesus. When he heard it he went away by boat to a deserted place, quite alone.

14.13b Jesus feeds a tired and hungry crowd

Then the crowds heard of his departure and followed him out of the towns on foot. When Jesus emerged from his retreat he saw a vast crowd and was very deeply moved and healed the sick among them. As evening fell his disciples came to him and said, "We are right in

Revised Standard Version

powers are at work in him." 3 For Herod had seized John and bound him and put him in prison, for the sake of Herodias, his brother Philip's wife;[l] 4 because John said to him, "It is not lawful for you to have her." 5 And though he wanted to put him to death, he feared the people, because they held him to be a prophet. 6 But when Herod's birthday came, the daughter of Herodias danced before the company, and pleased Herod, 7 so that he promised with an oath to give her whatever she might ask. 8 Prompted by her mother, she said, "Give me the head of John the Baptist here on a platter." 9 And the king was sorry; but because of his oaths and his guests he commanded it to be given; 10 he sent and had John beheaded in the prison, 11 and his head was brought on a platter and given to the girl, and she brought it to her mother. 12 And his disciples came and took the body and buried it; and they went and told Jesus.

13 Now when Jesus heard this, he withdrew from there in a boat to a lonely place apart. But when the crowds heard it, they followed him on foot from the towns. 14 As he went ashore he saw a great throng; and he had compassion on them, and healed their sick. 15 When it was evening, the disciples came to him and said, "This

[l] Other ancient authorities read *his brother's wife.*

Jerusalem Bible

John the Baptist beheaded

3 Now it was Herod who had arrested John, chained him up and put him in prison because of Herodias, his brother Philip's[r] wife. 4 For John had told him, "It is against the Law for you to have her." 5 He had wanted to kill him but was afraid of the people, who regarded John as a prophet. 6 Then, during the celebrations for Herod's birthday, the daugher of Herodias[s] danced before the company, and so delighted Herod 7 that he promised on oath to give her anything she asked. 8 Prompted by her mother she said, "Give me John the Baptist's head, here, on a dish." 9 The king was distressed but, thinking of the oaths he had sworn and of his guests, he ordered it to be given her, 10 and sent and had John beheaded in the prison. 11 The head was brought in on a dish and given to the girl who took it to her mother. 12 John's disciples came and took the body and buried it; then they went off to tell Jesus.

First miracle of the loaves

13 When Jesus received this news he withdrew by boat to a lonely place where they could be by themselves. But the people heard of this and, leaving the towns, went after him on foot. 14 So as he stepped ashore he saw a large crowd; and he took pity on them and healed their sick.
15 When evening came, the disciples went to

[r] Philip, Herod's half brother, was still alive. [s] According to Josephus, the girl's name was Salome.

New English Bible

Now Herod had arrested John, put him in chains, and thrown him into prison, on account of Herodias, his brother Philip's wife; for John had told him: 'You have no right to her.' Herod would have liked to put him to death, but he was afraid of the people, in whose eyes John was a prophet. But at his birthday celebrations the daughter of Herodias danced before the guests, and Herod was so delighted that he took an oath to give her anything she cared to ask. Prompted by her mother, she said, 'Give me here on a dish the head of John the Baptist.' The king was distressed when he heard it; but out of regard for his oath and for his guests, he ordered the request to be granted, and had John beheaded in prison. The head was brought in on a dish and given to the girl; and she carried it to her mother. Then John's disciples came and took away the body, and buried it; and they went and told Jesus.

When he heard what had happened Jesus withdrew privately by boat to a lonely place; but people heard of it, and came after him in crowds by land from the towns. When he came ashore, he saw a great crowd; his heart went out to them, and he cured those of them who were sick. When it grew late the disciples came

King James Version

came to him, saying, This is a desert place, and the time is now past; send the multitude away, that they may go into the villages, and buy themselves victuals. 16 But Jesus said unto them, They need not depart; give ye them to eat. 17And they say unto him, We have here but five loaves, and two fishes. 18 He said, Bring them hither to me. 19And he commanded the multitude to sit down on the grass, and took the five loaves, and the two fishes, and looking up to heaven, he blessed, and brake, and gave the loaves to *his* disciples, and the disciples to the multitude. 20And they did all eat, and were filled: and they took up of the fragments that remained twelve baskets full. 21And they that had eaten were about five thousand men, beside women and children.

22 And straightway Jesus constrained his disciples to get into a ship, and to go before him unto the other side, while he sent the multitudes away. 23And when he had sent the multitudes away, he went up into a mountain apart to pray: and when the evening was come, he was there alone. 24 But the ship was now in the midst of the sea, tossed with waves: for the wind was contrary. 25And in the fourth watch of the night Jesus went unto them, walking on the sea. 26And when the disciples saw him walking on the sea, they were troubled, saying, It is a spirit;

Living Bible

and said, "It is already past time for supper, and there is nothing to eat here in the desert; send the crowds away so they can go to the villages and buy some food."

16 But Jesus replied, "That isn't necessary—you feed them!"

17 "What!" they exclaimed. "We have exactly five small loaves of bread and two fish!"

18 "Bring them here," he said.

19 Then he told the people to sit down on the grass; and he took the five loaves and two fish, looked up into the sky and asked God's blessing on the meal, then broke the loaves apart and gave them to the disciples to place before the people. 20And everyone ate until full! And when the scraps were picked up afterwards, there were twelve basketfuls left over! 21 (About 5,000 men were in the crowd that day, besides all the women and children.) 22 Immediately after this, Jesus told his disciples to get into their boat and cross to the other side of the lake while he stayed to get the people started home.

23, 24 Then afterwards he went up into the hills to pray. Night fell, and out on the lake the disciples were in trouble. For the wind had risen and they were fighting heavy seas.

25 About four o'clock in the morning Jesus came to them, walking on the water! 26 They screamed in terror, for they thought he was a ghost.

Today's English Version

said, "It is already very late, and this is a lonely place. Send the people away and let them go to the villages and buy food for themselves."

16 "They don't have to leave," answered Jesus. "You yourselves give them something to eat."

17 "All we have here are five loaves and two fish," they replied.

18 "Bring them here to me," Jesus said. 19 He ordered the people to sit down on the grass; then he took the five loaves and the two fish, looked up to heaven, and gave thanks to God. He broke the loaves and gave them to the disciples, and the disciples gave them to the people. 20 Everyone ate and had enough. Then the disciples took up twelve baskets full of what was left over. 21 The number of men who ate was about five thousand, not counting the women and children.

Jesus walks on the water

22 Then Jesus made the disciples get into the boat and go ahead of him to the other side of the lake, while he sent the people away. 23After sending the people away, he went up a hill by himself to pray. When evening came, Jesus was there alone; 24 by this time the boat was far out in the lake, tossed about by the waves, because the wind was blowing against it. 25 Between three and six o'clock in the morning Jesus came to them, walking on the water. 26 When the disciples saw him walking on the water they were terrified. "It's a ghost!" they said, and screamed with fear.

New International Version

to him and said, "This is a remote place, and it's already getting late. Send the crowds away, so they can go to the villages and buy themselves some food."

16 Jesus replied, "They do not need to go away. You give them something to eat."

17 "We have here only five loaves of bread and two fish," they answered.

18 "Bring them here to me," he said. 19And he directed the people to sit down on the grass. Taking the five loaves and the two fish and looking up to heaven, he gave thanks and broke the loaves. Then he gave them to the disciples, and the disciples gave them to the people. 20 They all ate and were satisfied, and the disciples picked up twelve basketfuls of broken pieces that were left over. 21 The number of those who ate was about five thousand men, besides women and children.

Jesus walks on the water

22 Immediately Jesus made the disciples get into the boat and go on ahead of him to the other side, while he dismissed the crowd. 23After he had dismissed them, he went up into the hills by himself to pray. When evening came, he was there alone, 24 but the boat was already a considerable distance from land, buffeted by the waves because the wind was against it.

25 During the fourth watch of the night Jesus went out to them, walking on the lake. 26 When the disciples saw him walking on the lake, they were terrified. "It's a ghost," they said, and cried out in fear.

Phillips Modern English

the wilds here and it is very late. Send away these crowds now, so that they can go into the villages and buy themselves food."

"There's no need for them to go away," returned Jesus. "You give them something to eat!"

"But we haven't anything here," they told him, "except five loaves and two fish." To which Jesus replied, "Bring them here to me."

He told the crowd to sit down on the grass. Then he took the five loaves and the two fish in his hands, and, looking up to Heaven, he thanked God, broke the loaves and passed them to his disciples who handed them to the crowd. Everybody ate and was satisfied. Afterwards they collected twelve baskets full of the pieces which were left over. Those who ate numbered about five thousand men, apart from the women and children.

14.22 Jesus again shows his power over the forces of nature

Directly after this Jesus insisted on his disciples' getting aboard their boat and going on ahead to the other side, while he himself sent the crowds home. And when he had sent them away he went up the hill-side quite alone, to pray. When it grew late he was there by himself while the boat was by now a good way from the shore at the mercy of the waves, for the wind was dead against them. In the small hours Jesus went out to them, walking on the lake. When the disciples caught sight of him walking on the water they were terrified. "It's a ghost!" they

Revised Standard Version

is a lonely place, and the day is now over; send
the crowds away to go into the villages and buy
food for themselves." 16 Jesus said, "They need
not go away; you give them something to eat."
17 They said to him, "We have only five loaves
here and two fish." 18 And he said, "Bring them
here to me." 19 Then he ordered the crowds to sit
down on the grass; and taking the five loaves
and the two fish he looked up to heaven, and
blessed, and broke and gave the loaves to the
disciples, and the disciples gave them to the
crowds. 20 And they all ate and were satisfied.
And they took up twelve baskets full of the
broken pieces left over. 21 And those who ate
were about five thousand men, besides women
and children.
22 Then he made the disciples get into the
boat and go before him to the other side, while
he dismissed the crowds. 23 And after he had
dismissed the crowds, he went up on the mountain by himself to pray. When evening came, he
was there alone, 24 but the boat by this time
was many furlongs distant from the land,[m]
beaten by the waves; for the wind was against
them. 25 And in the fourth watch of the night
he came to them, walking on the sea. 26 But
when the disciples saw him walking on the sea,
they were terrified, saying, "It is a ghost!" and

[*m*] Other ancient authorities read *was out on the sea.*

Jerusalem Bible

him and said, "This is a lonely place, and the
time has slipped by; so send the people away,
and they can go to the villages to buy themselves
some food." 16 Jesus replied, "There is no need
for them to go: give them something to eat
yourselves." 17 But they answered, "All we have
with us is five loaves and two fish." 18 "Bring
them here to me," he said. 19 He gave orders
that the people were to sit down on the grass;
then he took the five loaves and the two fish,
raised his eyes to heaven and said the blessing.
And breaking the loaves he handed them to his
disciples who gave them to the crowds. 20 They
all ate as much as they wanted, and they collected the scraps remaining, twelve baskets full.
21 Those who ate numbered about five thousand
men, to say nothing of women and children.

Jesus walks on the water and, with him, Peter

22 Directly after this he made the disciples get
into the boat and go on ahead to the other side
while he would send the crowds away. 23 After
sending the crowds away he went up into the
hills by himself to pray. When evening came, he
was there alone, 24 while the boat, by now far
out on the lake, was battling with a heavy sea,
for there was a head wind. 25 In the fourth
watch of the night[t] he went toward them, walking on the lake, 26 and when the disciples saw
him walking on the lake they were terrified. "It
is a ghost," they said, and cried out in fear.

[*t*] 3 to 6 A.M.

New English Bible

up to him and said, 'This is a lonely place, and the day has gone; send the people off to the villages to buy themselves food.' He answered, 'There is no need for them to go; give them something to eat yourselves.' 'All we have here', they said, 'is five loaves and two fishes.' 'Let me have them', he replied. So he told the people to sit down on the grass; then, taking the five loaves and the two fishes, he looked up to heaven, said the blessing, broke the loaves, and gave them to the disciples; and the disciples gave them to the people. They all ate to their hearts' content; and the scraps left over, which they picked up, were enough to fill twelve great baskets. Some five thousand men shared in this meal, to say nothing of women and children.

Then he made the disciples embark and go on ahead to the other side, while he sent the people away; after doing that, he went up the hill-side to pray alone. It grew late, and he was there by himself. The boat was already some furlongs from the shore,[a] battling with a head-wind and a rough sea. Between three and six in the morning he came to them, walking over the lake. When the disciples saw him walking on the lake they were so shaken that they cried out in

[*a*] *Some witnesses read* already well out on the water.

King James Version

and they cried out for fear. 27 But straightway
Jesus spake unto them, saying, Be of good cheer;
it is I; be not afraid. 28 And Peter answered him
and said, Lord, if it be thou, bid me come unto
thee on the water. 29 And he said, Come. And
when Peter was come down out of the ship, he
walked on the water, to go to Jesus. 30 But when
he saw the wind boisterous, he was afraid; and
beginning to sink, he cried, saying, Lord, save
me. 31 And immediately Jesus stretched forth *his*
hand, and caught him, and said unto him, O
thou of little faith, wherefore didst thou doubt?
32 And when they were come into the ship, the
wind ceased. 33 Then they that were in the ship
came and worshipped him, saying, Of a truth
thou art the Son of God.
34 And when they were gone over, they came
into the land of Gennesaret. 35 And when the
men of that place had knowledge of him, they
sent out into all that country round about, and
brought unto him all that were diseased; 36 And
besought him that they might only touch the
hem of his garment: and as many as touched
were made perfectly whole.

Living Bible

27 But Jesus immediately spoke to them, reassuring them. "Don't be afraid!" he said.
28 Then Peter called to him: "Sir, if it is
really you, tell me to come over to you, walking
on the water."
29 "All right," the Lord said, "come along!"
So Peter went over the side of the boat and
walked on the water toward Jesus. 30 But when
he looked around at the high waves, he was
terrified and began to sink. "Save me, Lord!"
he shouted.
31 Instantly Jesus reached out his hand and
rescued him. "O man of little faith," Jesus said.
"Why did you doubt me?" 32 And when they
had climbed back into the boat, the wind
stopped.
33 The others sat there, awestruck. "You
really are the Son of God!" they exclaimed.
34 They landed at Gennesaret. 35 The news
of their arrival spread quickly throughout the
city, and soon people were rushing around,
telling everyone to bring in their sick to be
healed. 36 The sick begged him to let them touch
even the tassel of his robe, and all who did were
healed.

Today's English Version

27 Jesus spoke to them at once. "Courage!"
he said. "It is I. Don't be afraid!"
28 Then Peter spoke up. "Lord," he said, "if
it is really you, order me to come out on the
water to you."
29 "Come!" answered Jesus. So Peter got out
of the boat and started walking on the water to
Jesus. 30 When he noticed the wind, however,
he was afraid, and started to sink down in the
water. "Save me, Lord!" he cried.
31 At once Jesus reached out and grabbed
him and said, "How little faith you have! Why
did you doubt?"
32 They both got into the boat, and the wind
died down. 33 The disciples in the boat worshiped Jesus. "Truly you are the Son of God!"
they exclaimed.

Jesus heals the sick in Gennesaret

34 They crossed the lake and came to land
at Gennesaret, 35 where the people recognized
Jesus. So they sent for the sick people in all the
surrounding country and brought them to Jesus.
36 They begged him to let the sick at least touch
the edge of his cloak; and all who touched it
were made well.

New International Version

27 But Jesus immediately said to them: "Take
courage! It is I. Don't be afraid."
28 "Lord, if it's you," Peter replied, "tell me
to come to you on the water."
29 "Come," he said.
Then Peter got down out of the boat and
walked on the water to Jesus. 30 But when he
saw the wind, he was afraid and, beginning to
sink, cried out, "Lord, save me!"
31 Immediately Jesus reached out his hand
and caught him. "You of little faith," he said,
"why did you doubt?"
32 And when they climbed into the boat, the
wind died down. 33 Then those who were in
the boat worshiped him, saying, "Truly you are
the Son of God."
34 When they had crossed over, they landed
at Gennesaret. 35 And when the men of that
place recognized Jesus, they sent word to all
the surrounding country. People brought all
their sick to him 36 and begged him to let the
sick just touch the edge of his cloak, and all
who touched him were healed.

Phillips Modern English

said, and screamed with fear. But at once Jesus spoke to them. "It's all right! It's I myself, don't be afraid!"

"Lord, if it's really you," said Peter, "tell me to come to you on the water."

"Come on, then," replied Jesus.

Peter stepped down from the boat and began to walk on the water, making for Jesus. But when he saw the fury of the wind he panicked and began to sink, calling out, "Lord save me!" At once Jesus reached out his hand and caught him, saying, "You little-faith! What made you lose your nerve like that?" Then, when they were both aboard the boat, the wind dropped. The whole crew came and knelt down before Jesus, crying, "You are indeed the Son of God!"

When they had crossed over to the other side of the lake, they landed at Gennesaret, and when the men of that place had recognised him, they sent word to the whole surrounding country and brought all the diseased to him. They implored him to let them "touch just the edge of his cloak", and all those who did so were completely cured.

Revised Standard Version

they cried out for fear. 27 But immediately he
spoke to them, saying, "Take heart, it is I;
have no fear."
28 And Peter answered him, "Lord, if it is
you, bid me come to you on the water." 29 He
said, "Come." So Peter got out of the boat and
walked on the water and came to Jesus; 30 but
when he saw the wind,[n] he was afraid, and beginning to sink he cried out, "Lord, save me."
31 Jesus immediately reached out his hand and
caught him, saying to him, "O man of little faith,
why did you doubt?" 32 And when they got into
the boat, the wind ceased. 33 And those in the
boat worshiped him, saying, "Truly you are the
Son of God."
34 And when they had crossed over, they
came to land at Gennesaret. 35 And when the
men of that place recognized him, they sent
round to all that region and brought to him all
that were sick, 36 and besought him that they
might only touch the fringe of his garment; and
as many as touched it were made well.

[n] Other ancient authorities read *strong wind*.

Jerusalem Bible

27 But at once Jesus called out to them, saying,
"Courage! It is I! Do not be afraid." 28 It was
Peter who answered. "Lord," he said, "if it is
you, tell me to come to you across the water."
29 "Come," said Jesus. Then Peter got out of
the boat and started walking toward Jesus across
the water, 30 but as soon as he felt the force of
the wind, he took fright and began to sink.
"Lord! Save me!" he cried. 31 Jesus put out his
hand at once and held him. "Man of little faith,"
he said, "why did you doubt?" 32 And as they
got into the boat the wind dropped. 33 The men
in the boat bowed down before him and said,
"Truly, you are the Son of God."

Cures at Gennesaret

34 Having made the crossing, they came to
land at Gennesaret. 35 When the local people
recognized him they spread the news through the
whole neighborhood and took all that were sick
to him, 36 begging him just to let them touch
the fringe of his cloak. And all those who
touched it were completely cured.

New English Bible

terror: 'It is a ghost!' But at once he spoke to them: 'Take heart! It is I; do not be afraid.'

Peter called to him: 'Lord, if it is you, tell me to come to you over the water.' 'Come', said Jesus. Peter stepped down from the boat, and walked over the water towards Jesus. But when he saw the strength of the gale he was seized with fear; and beginning to sink, he cried, 'Save me, Lord.' Jesus at once reached out and caught hold of him, and said, 'Why did you hesitate? How little faith you have!' They then climbed into the boat; and the wind dropped. And the men in the boat fell at his feet, exclaiming, 'Truly you are the Son of God.'

So they finished the crossing and came to land at Gennesaret. There Jesus was recognized by the people of the place, who sent out word to all the country round. And all who were ill were brought to him, and he was begged to allow them simply to touch the edge of his cloak. And everyone who touched it was completely cured.

King James Version

15 Then came to Jesus scribes and Pharisees, which were of Jerusalem, saying, 2 Why do thy disciples transgress the tradition of the elders? for they wash not their hands when they eat bread. 3 But he answered and said unto them, Why do ye also transgress the commandment of God by your tradition? 4 For God commanded, saying, Honour thy father and mother: and, He that curseth father or mother, let him die the death. 5 But ye say, Whosoever shall say to *his* father or *his* mother, *It is* a gift, by whatsoever thou mightest be profited by me; 6 And honour not his father or his mother, *he shall be free*. Thus have ye made the commandment of God of none effect by your tradition. 7 *Ye* hypocrites, well did Esaias prophesy of you, saying, 8 This people draweth nigh unto me with their mouth, and honoureth me with *their* lips; but their heart is far from me. 9 But in vain they do worship me, teaching *for* doctrines the commandments of men.

10 And he called the multitude, and said unto

Living Bible

15 Some Pharisees and other Jewish leaders now arrived from Jerusalem to interview Jesus.

2 "Why do your disciples disobey the ancient Jewish traditions?" they demanded. "For they ignore our ritual of ceremonial hand washing before they eat." 3 He replied, "And why do your traditions violate the direct commandments of God? 4 For instance, God's law is 'Honor your father and mother; anyone who reviles his parents must die.' 5, 6 But you say, 'Even if your parents are in need, you may give their support money to the church[a] instead.' And so, by your man-made rule, you nullify the direct command of God to honor and care for your parents. 7 You hypocrites! Well did Isaiah prophesy of you, 8 'These people say they honor me, but their hearts are far away. 9 Their worship is worthless, for they teach their man-made laws instead of those from God.' "[b]

10 Then Jesus called to the crowds and said,

[*a*] Literally, "to God." [*b*] Isaiah 29:13.

Today's English Version

The teaching of the ancestors

15 Then some Pharisees and teachers of the Law came to Jesus from Jerusalem and asked him, 2 "Why is it that your disciples disobey the teaching handed down by our ancestors? They don't wash their hands in the proper way before they eat!"

3 Jesus answered, "And why do you disobey God's command and follow your own teaching? 4 For God said, 'Honor your father and mother,' and 'Anyone who says bad things about his father or mother must be put to death.' 5 But you teach that if a person has something he could use to help his father or mother, but says, 'This belongs to God,' 6 he does not need to honor his father. This is how you disregard God's word to follow your own teaching. 7 You hypocrites! How right Isaiah was when he prophesied about you!

8 'These people, says God, honor me with their words,
but their heart is really far away from me.
9 It is no use for them to worship me,
because they teach man-made commandments as though they were God's rules!' "

The things that make a person unclean

10 Then Jesus called the crowd to him and

New International Version

Clean and unclean

15 Then some Pharisees and teachers of the law came to Jesus from Jerusalem and asked, 2 "Why do your disciples break the tradition of the elders? They don't wash their hands before they eat!"

3 Jesus replied, "And why do you break the command of God for the sake of your tradition? 4 For God said, 'Honor your father and mother,'[v] and, 'Anyone who curses his father or mother must be put to death.'[w] 5 But you say that if a man says to his father or mother, 'Whatever help you might otherwise have received from me is a gift devoted to God,' 6 he is not to 'honor his father'[x] with it. Thus you nullify the word of God for the sake of your tradition. 7 You hypocrites! Isaiah was right when he prophesied about you:

8 'These people honor me with their lips,
but their hearts are far from me.
9 They worship me in vain;
their teachings are but rules made by man.'[y] "

10 Jesus called the crowd to him and said,

[*v*] Exodus 20:12; Deut. 5:16. [*w*] Exodus 21:17. [*x*] Some MSS add *or his mother*. [*y*] Isaiah 29:13.

Phillips Modern English

15.1 The dangers of tradition

Then some of the scribes and Pharisees from Jerusalem came and asked Jesus, "Why do your disciples break our ancient tradition and eat their food without washing their hands properly first?"

"Tell me," replied Jesus, "why do you break God's commandment through your tradition? For God said, 'Honour thy father and thy mother', and 'He that speaketh evil of father or mother, let him die the death.' But you say that if a man tells his father or his mother, 'Whatever duty I might have owed you is now given to God,' then he will never honour his father again. And so your tradition makes the commandment of God ineffectual. You hypocrites! Isaiah described you beautifully when he said:

This people honoureth me with their lips;
But their heart is far from me.
But in vain do they worship me,
Teaching as their doctrines the precepts of men."

15.10 Superficial and true cleanliness

Then he called the crowd to him and said,

Revised Standard Version

15 Then Pharisees and scribes came to Jesus
from Jerusalem and said, 2 "Why do your
disciples transgress the tradition of the elders?
For they do not wash their hands when they
eat." 3 He answered them, "And why do you
transgress the commandment of God for the
sake of your tradition? 4 For God commanded,
'Honor your father and your mother,' and, 'He
who speaks evil of father or mother, let him
surely die.' 5 But you say, 'If any one tells his
father or his mother, What you would have
gained from me is given to God,[o] he need not
honor his father.' 6 So, for the sake of your
tradition, you have made void the word[p] of
God. 7 You hypocrites! Well did Isaiah prophesy
of you, when he said:
8 'This people honors me with their lips,
but their heart is far from me;
9 in vain do they worship me,
teaching as doctrines the precepts of men.'"
10 And he called the people to him and said

[o] Or *an offering*. [p] Other ancient authorities read *law*.

Jerusalem Bible

The traditions of the Pharisees

15 Pharisees and scribes from Jerusalem then
came to Jesus and said, 2 "Why do your
disciples break away from the tradition of the
elders?[u] They do not wash their hands when
they eat food." 3 "And why do you," he answered, "break away from the commandment of
God for the sake of your tradition? 4 For God
said: *Do your duty to*[v] *your father and mother*
and: *Anyone who curses father or mother must*
be put to death.[w] 5 But you say, 'If anyone says
to his father or mother: Anything I have that I
might have used to help you is dedicated to
God,' 6 he is rid of his duty to father or mother.[x]
In this way you have made God's word null
and void by means of your tradition. 7 Hypocrites! It was you Isaiah meant when he so
rightly prophesied:

8 *This people honors me only with lip service,*
while their hearts are far from me.
9 *The worship they offer me is worthless;*
the doctrines they teach are only human
regulations."[y]

On clean and unclean

10 He called the people to him and said,

[u] The traditional teaching, including many additions to and extensions of the Law. [v] Often translated "honor," but the word implies a respect expressed in practical ways, Ex. 20:12. [w] Lv. 20:9. [x] Property dedicated in this way could not be passed to another person. [y] Is. 29:13.

New English Bible

15 Then Jesus was approached by a group of Pharisees and lawyers from Jerusalem, with the question: 'Why do your disciples break the ancient tradition? They do not wash their hands before meals.' He answered them: 'And what of you? Why do you break God's commandment in the interest of your tradition? For God said, "Honour your father and mother", and, "The man who curses his father or mother must suffer death." But you say, "If a man says to his father or mother, 'Anything of mine which might have been used for your benefit is set apart for God', then he must not honour his father or his mother." You have made God's law null and void out of respect for your tradition. What hypocrisy! Isaiah was right when he prophesied about you: "This people pays me lip-service, but their heart is far from me; their worship of me is in vain, for they teach as doctrines the commandments of men." '

He called the crowd and said to them, 'Listen

King James Version

them, Hear, and understand: 11 Not that which
goeth into the mouth defileth a man; but that
which cometh out of the mouth, this defileth a
man. 12 Then came his disciples, and said unto
him, Knowest thou that the Pharisees were offended, after they heard this saying? 13 But he
answered and said, Every plant, which my heavenly Father hath not planted, shall be rooted up.
14 Let them alone: they be blind leaders of the
blind. And if the blind lead the blind, both shall
fall into the ditch. 15 Then answered Peter and
said unto him, Declare unto us this parable.
16 And Jesus said, Are ye also yet without understanding? 17 Do not ye yet understand, that
whatsoever entereth in at the mouth goeth into
the belly, and is cast out into the draught?
18 But those things which proceed out of the
mouth come forth from the heart; and they defile
the man. 19 For out of the heart proceed evil
thoughts, murders, adulteries, fornications, thefts,
false witness, blasphemies: 20 These are *the
things* which defile a man: but to eat with unwashen hands defileth not a man.
21 Then Jesus went thence, and departed into
the coasts of Tyre and Sidon. 22 And, behold, a
woman of Canaan came out of the same coasts,
and cried unto him, saying, Have mercy on me,
O Lord, *thou* Son of David; my daughter is

Living Bible

"Listen to what I say and try to understand:
11 You aren't made unholy by eating non-kosher
food! It is what you *say* and *think*[c] that makes
you unclean."
12 Then the disciples came and told him,
"You offended the Pharisees by that remark."
13, 14 Jesus replied, "Every plant not planted
by my Father shall be rooted up, so ignore them.
They are blind guides leading the blind, and both
will fall into a ditch."
15 Then Peter asked Jesus to explain what he
meant when he said that people are not defiled
by non-kosher food.
16 "Don't you understand?" Jesus asked him.
17 "Don't you see that anything you eat passes
through the digestive tract and out again? 18 But
evil words come from an evil heart, and defile
the man who says them. 19 For from the heart
come evil thoughts, murder, adultery, fornication, theft, lying and slander. 20 These are what
defile; but there is no spiritual defilement from
eating without first going through the ritual of
ceremonial handwashing!"
21 Jesus then left that part of the country
and walked the fifty miles[d] to Tyre and Sidon.
22 A woman from Canaan who was living
there came to him, pleading, "Have mercy on
me, O Lord, King David's Son! For my daughter
has a demon within her, and it torments her
constantly."

[*c*] Implied. Literally, "what comes out of a man defiles a man." [*d*] Implied. Literally, "withdraw into the parts of Tyre and Sidon."

Today's English Version

said to them, "Listen, and understand! 11 It is
not what goes into a person's mouth that makes
him unclean; rather, what comes out of it makes
him unclean."
12 Then the disciples came to him and said,
"Do you know that the Pharisees had their feelings hurt by what you said?"
13 "Every plant which my Father in heaven
did not plant will be pulled up," answered Jesus.
14 "Don't worry about them! They are blind
leaders; and when one blind man leads another
one, both fall into a ditch."
15 Peter spoke up, "Tell us what this parable
means."
16 Jesus said to them, "You are still no more
intelligent than the others. 17 Don't you understand? Anything that goes into a person's mouth
goes into his stomach and then on out of the
body. 18 But the things that come out of the
mouth come from the heart; such things make a
man unclean. 19 For from his heart come the
evil ideas which lead him to kill, commit adultery, and do other immoral things; to rob, lie,
and slander others. 20 These are the things that
make a man unclean. But to eat without washing
your hands as they say you should—this does
not make a man unclean."

A woman's faith

21 Jesus left that place and went off to the
territory near the cities of Tyre and Sidon. 22 A
Canaanite woman who lived in that region came
to him. "Son of David, sir!" she cried. "Have
mercy on me! My daughter has a demon and is
in a terrible condition."

New International Version

"Listen and understand. 11 What goes into a
man's mouth does not make him 'unclean,' but
what comes out of his mouth, that is what makes
him 'unclean.' "
12 Then the disciples came to him and asked,
"Do you know that the Pharisees were offended
when they heard this?"
13 He replied, "Every plant that my heavenly
Father has not planted will be pulled up by the
roots. 14 Leave them; they are blind guides.[z] If
a blind man leads a blind man, both will fall
into a pit."
15 Peter said, "Explain the parable to us."
16 "Are you still so dull?" Jesus asked them.
17 "Don't you see that whatever enters the
mouth goes into the stomach and then out of
the body? 18 But the things that come out of the
mouth come from the heart, and these make a
man 'unclean.' 19 For out of the heart come evil
thoughts, murder, adultery, sexual immorality,
theft, false testimony, slander. 20 These are what
make a man 'unclean'; but eating with unwashed
hands does not make him 'unclean.' "

The faith of the Canaanite woman

21 Leaving that place, Jesus withdrew to the
region of Tyre and Sidon. 22 A Canaanite woman
from that vicinity came to him, crying out,
"Lord, Son of David, have mercy on me! My
daughter is suffering terribly from demon-posses-
sion."

[*z*] Some MSS add *of the blind.*

Phillips Modern English

"Listen, and understand this thoroughly! It is not what goes *into* a man's mouth that makes him common or unclean. It is what comes *out* of a man's mouth that makes him unclean."

Later his disciples came to him and said, "Do you know that the Pharisees are deeply offended by what you said?"

"Every plant which my Heavenly Father did not plant will be pulled up by the roots," returned Jesus. "Let them alone. They are blind guides, and when one blind man leads another blind man they will both fall into the ditch!"

"Explain this parable to us," broke in Peter.

"Are you still as dull as the others?" asked Jesus. "Don't you see that whatever goes *into* the mouth passes into the stomach and then out of the body altogether? But the things that come *out* of a man's mouth come from his heart and mind, and it is they that really make a man unclean. For it is from a man's mind that evil thoughts arise—murder, adultery, lust, theft, perjury and slander. These are the things which make a man unclean, not eating without washing his hands properly!"

15.21 A gentile's faith in Jesus

Jesus then left that place and retired into the Tyre and Sidon district. There a Canaanite woman from those parts came to him crying at the top of her voice,

"Lord, son of David, have pity on me! My daughter is in a terrible state—a devil has got into her!"

Revised Standard Version

to them, "Hear and understand: 11 not what
goes into the mouth defiles a man, but what
comes out of the mouth, this defiles a man."
12 Then the disciples came and said to him, "Do
you know that the Pharisees were offended when
they heard this saying?" 13 He answered, "Every
plant which my heavenly Father has not planted
will be rooted up. 14 Let them alone; they are
blind guides. And if a blind man leads a blind
man, both will fall into a pit." 15 But Peter said
to him, "Explain the parable to us." 16 And he
said, "Are you also still without understanding?
17 Do you not see that whatever goes into the
mouth passes into the stomach, and so passes
on? [q] 18 But what comes out of the mouth proceeds from the heart, and this defiles a man.
19 For out of the heart come evil thoughts,
murder, adultery, fornication, theft, false witness, slander. 20 These are what defile a man;
but to eat with unwashed hands does not defile
a man."
21 And Jesus went away from there and
withdrew to the district of Tyre and Sidon.
22 And behold, a Canaanite woman from that
region came out and cried, "Have mercy on me,
O Lord, Son of David; my daughter is severely

[q] Or *is evacuated.*

Jerusalem Bible

"Listen, and understand. 11 What goes into the
mouth does not make a man unclean; it is what
comes out of the mouth that makes him unclean."
12 Then the disciples came to him and said,
"Do you know that the Pharisees were shocked
when they heard what you said?" 13 He replied,
"Any plant my heavenly Father has not planted
will be pulled up by the roots. 14 Leave them
alone. They are blind men leading blind men;
and if one blind man leads another, both will
fall into a pit."
15 At this, Peter said to him, "Explain the
parable for us." 16 Jesus replied, "Do even you
not yet understand? 17 Can you not see that
whatever goes into the mouth passes through the
stomach and is discharged into the sewer? 18 But
the things that come out of the mouth come
from the heart, and it is these that make a man
unclean. 19 For from the heart come evil intentions: murder, adultery, fornication, theft, perjury, slander. 20 These are the things that make
a man unclean. But to eat with unwashed hands
does not make a man unclean."

The daughter of the Canaanite woman healed

21 Jesus left that place and withdrew to the
region of Tyre and Sidon. 22 Then out came a
Canaanite woman from that district and started
shouting, "Sir, Son of David, take pity on me.

New English Bible

to me, and understand this: a man is not defiled by what goes into his mouth, but by what comes out of it.'

Then the disciples came to him and said, 'Do you know that the Pharisees have taken great offence at what you have been saying?' His answer was: 'Any plant that is not of my heavenly Father's planting will be rooted up. Leave them alone; they are blind guides,[a] and if one blind man guides another they will both fall into the ditch.'

Then Peter said, 'Tell us what that parable means.' Jesus answered, 'Are you still as dull as the rest? Do you not see that whatever goes in by the mouth passes into the stomach and so is discharged into the drain? But what comes out of the mouth has its origins in the heart; and that is what defiles a man. Wicked thoughts, murder, adultery, fornication, theft, perjury, slander—these all proceed from the heart; and these are the things that defile a man; but to eat without first washing his hands, that cannot defile him.'

Jesus and his disciples

Jesus then left that place and withdrew to the region of Tyre and Sidon. And a Canaanite woman from those parts came crying out, 'Sir! have pity on me, Son of David; my daughter is

[a] *Some witnesses insert* of blind men.

King James Version

grievously vexed with a devil. 23 But he answered her not a word. And his disciples came and besought him, saying, Send her away; for she crieth after us. 24 But he answered and said, I am not sent but unto the lost sheep of the house of Israel. 25 Then came she and worshipped him, saying, Lord, help me. 26 But he answered and said, It is not meet to take the children's bread, and to cast *it* to dogs. 27And she said, Truth, Lord: yet the dogs eat of the crumbs which fall from their masters' table. 28 Then Jesus answered and said unto her, O woman, great *is* thy faith: be it unto thee even as thou wilt. And her daughter was made whole from that very hour. 29And Jesus departed from thence, and came nigh unto the sea of Galilee; and went up into a mountain, and sat down there. 30And great multitudes came unto him, having with them *those that were* lame, blind, dumb, maimed, and many others, and cast them down at Jesus' feet; and he healed them: 31 Insomuch that the multitude wondered, when they saw the dumb to speak, the maimed to be whole, the lame to walk, and the blind to see: and they glorified the God of Israel.

Living Bible

23 But Jesus gave her no reply—not even a word. Then his disciples urged him to send her away. "Tell her to get going," they said, "for she is bothering us with all her begging."

24 Then he said to the woman, "I was sent to help the Jews—the lost sheep of Israel—not the Gentiles."

25 But she came and worshiped him and pled again, "Sir, help me!"

26 "It doesn't seem right to take bread from the children and throw it to the dogs," he said.

27 "Yes, it is!" she replied, "for even the puppies beneath the table are permitted to eat the crumbs that fall."

28 "Woman," Jesus told her, "your faith is large, and your request is granted." And her daughter was healed right then.

29 Jesus now returned to the Sea of Galilee, and climbed a hill and sat there. 30And a vast crowd brought him their lame, blind, maimed, and those who couldn't speak, and many others, and laid them before Jesus, and he healed them all. 31 What a spectacle it was! Those who hadn't been able to say a word before were talking excitedly, and those with missing arms and legs had new ones; the crippled were walking and jumping around, and those who had been blind were gazing about them! The crowds just marveled, and praised the God of Israel.

Today's English Version

23 But Jesus did not say a word to her. His disciples came to him and begged him, "Send her away! She is following us and making all this noise!"

24 Then Jesus replied, "I have been sent only to the lost sheep of the people of Israel."

25 At this the woman came and fell at his feet. "Help me, sir!" she said.

26 Jesus answered, "It isn't right to take the children's food and throw it to the dogs."

27 "That is true, sir," she answered; "but even the dogs eat the leftovers that fall from their masters' table."

28 So Jesus answered her, "You are a woman of great faith! What you want will be done for you." And at that very moment her daughter was healed.

Jesus heals many people

29 Jesus left that place and went along by Lake Galilee. He climbed a hill and sat down. 30 Large crowds came to him, bringing with them the lame, the blind, the crippled, the dumb, and many other sick people, whom they placed at Jesus' feet; and he healed them. 31 The people were amazed as they saw the dumb speaking, the crippled whole, the lame walking, and the blind seeing; and they praised the God of Israel.

New International Version

23 Jesus did not answer a word. So his disciples came to him and urged him, "Send her away, for she keeps crying out after us."

24 He answered, "I was sent only to the lost sheep of Israel."

25 The woman came and knelt before him. "Lord, help me!" she said.

26 He replied, "It is not right to take the children's bread and toss it to their dogs."

27 "Yes, Lord," she said, "but even the dogs eat the crumbs that fall from their masters' table."

28 Then Jesus answered, "Woman, you have great faith! Your request is granted." And her daughter was healed from that very hour.

Jesus feeds the four thousand

29 Jesus left there and went along the Sea of Galilee. Then he went up into the hills and sat down. 30 Great crowds came to him, bringing the lame, the blind, the crippled, the dumb and many others, and laid them at his feet; and he healed them. 31 The people were amazed when they saw the dumb speaking, the crippled made well, the lame walking and the blind seeing. And they praised the God of Israel.

Phillips Modern English

Jesus made no answer, and the disciples came up to him and said, "Do send her away—she's still following us and calling out."

"I was only sent," replied Jesus, "to the lost sheep of the house of Israel."

Then the woman came and knelt at his feet. "Lord, help me," she said.

"It is not right, you know," Jesus replied, "to take the children's food and throw it to the dogs."

"Yes, Lord, I know, but even the dogs live on the scraps that fall from their master's table!"

"You certainly don't lack faith," returned Jesus, "it shall be as you wish."

And at that moment her daughter was healed.

15.29 Jesus heals and feeds vast crowds of people

Jesus left there, walked along the shore of the lake of Galilee, then climbed the hill and sat down. And great crowds came to him, bringing with them people who were lame, blind, crippled, dumb and many others. They simply laid them at his feet and he healed them. The result was that the people were astonished at seeing dumb men speak, crippled men healed, lame men walking about and blind men having recovered their sight. And they praised the God of Israel.

Revised Standard Version

possessed by a demon." 23 But he did not answer
her a word. And his disciples came and begged
him, saying, "Send her away, for she is crying
after us." 24 He answered, "I was sent only to
the lost sheep of the house of Israel." 25 But she
came and knelt before him, saying, "Lord, help
me." 26 And he answered, "It is not fair to take
the children's bread and throw it to the dogs."
27 She said, "Yes, Lord, yet even the dogs eat
the crumbs that fall from their masters' table."
28 Then Jesus answered her, "O woman, great
is your faith! Be it done for you as you desire."
And her daughter was healed instantly.

29 And Jesus went on from there and passed
along the Sea of Galilee. And he went up on
the mountain, and sat down there. 30 And great
crowds came to him, bringing with them the
lame, the maimed, the blind, the dumb, and
many others, and they put them at his feet, and
he healed them, 31 so that the throng wondered,
when they saw the dumb speaking, the maimed
whole, the lame walking, and the blind seeing;
and they glorified the God of Israel.

Jerusalem Bible

My daughter is tormented by a devil." 23 But he
answered her not a word. And his disciples went
and pleaded with him. "Give her what she
wants," they said, "because she is shouting after
us." 24 He said in reply, "I was sent only to the
lost sheep of the House of Israel." 25 But the
woman had come up and was kneeling at his
feet. "Lord," she said, "help me." 26 He replied, "It is not fair to take the children's food
and throw it to the house dogs." 27 She retorted,
"Ah yes, sir; but even house dogs can eat the
scraps that fall from their master's table."
28 Then Jesus answered her, "Woman, you have
great faith. Let your wish be granted." And from
that moment her daughter was well again.

Cures near the lake

29 Jesus went on from there and reached the
shores of the Sea of Galilee, and he went up
into the hills. He sat there, 30 and large crowds
came to him bringing the lame, the crippled, the
blind, the dumb and many others; these they put
down at his feet, and he cured them. 31 The
crowds were astonished to see the dumb speaking, the cripples whole again, the lame walking
and the blind with their sight, and they praised
the God of Israel.

New English Bible

tormented by a devil.' But he said not a word in reply. His disciples came and urged him: 'Send her away; see how she comes shouting after us.' Jesus replied, 'I was sent to the lost sheep of the house of Israel, and to them alone.' But the woman came and fell at his feet and cried, 'Help me, sir.' To this Jesus replied, 'It is not right to take the children's bread and throw it to the dogs.' 'True, sir,' she answered; 'and yet the dogs eat the scraps that fall from their masters' table.' Hearing this Jesus replied, 'Woman, what faith you have! Be it as you wish!' And from that moment her daughter was restored to health.

After leaving that region Jesus took the road by the Sea of Galilee and went up to the hills. When he was seated there, crowds flocked to him, bringing with them the lame, blind, dumb, and crippled, and many other sufferers; they threw them down at his feet, and he healed them. Great was the amazement of the people when they saw the dumb speaking, the crippled strong, the lame walking, and sight restored to the blind; and they gave praise to the God of Israel.

King James Version

32 Then Jesus called his disciples *unto him,*
and said, I have compassion on the multitude,
because they continue with me now three days,
and have nothing to eat: and I will not send
them away fasting, lest they faint in the way.
33And his disciples say unto him, Whence should
we have so much bread in the wilderness, as to
fill so great a multitude? 34And Jesus saith unto
them, How many loaves have ye? And they said,
Seven, and a few little fishes. 35And he commanded the multitude to sit down on the ground.
36And he took the seven loaves and the fishes,
and gave thanks, and brake *them,* and gave to
his disciples, and the disciples to the multitude.
37And they did all eat, and were filled: and they
took up of the broken *meat* that was left seven
baskets full. 38And they that did eat were four
thousand men, beside women and children.
39And he sent away the multitude, and took ship,
and came into the coasts of Magdala.

16 The Pharisees also with the Sadducees
came, and tempting desired him that he
would shew them a sign from heaven. 2 He
answered and said unto them, When it is eve-

Living Bible

32 Then Jesus called his disciples to him and
said, "I pity these people—they've been here with
me for three days now, and have nothing left to
eat; I don't want to send them away hungry or
they will faint along the road."

33 The disciples replied, "And where would
we get enough here in the desert for all this
mob to eat?"

34 Jesus asked them, "How much food do
you have?" And they replied, "Seven loaves of
bread and a few small fish!"

35 Then Jesus told all of the people to sit
down on the ground, 36 and he took the seven
loaves and the fish, and gave thanks to God for
them, and divided them into pieces, and gave
them to the disciples who presented them to the
crowd. 37, 38And everyone ate until full—4,000
men besides the women and children! And afterwards, when the scraps were picked up, there
were seven basketfuls left over!

39 Then Jesus sent the people home and got
into the boat and crossed to Magadan.

16 One day the Pharisees and Sadducees[a]
came to test Jesus' claim of being the Messiah by asking him to show them some great
demonstrations in the skies.

2, 3 He replied, "You are good at reading the

[a] Jewish politico-religious leaders of two different parties.

Today's English Version

Jesus feeds the four thousand

32 Jesus called his disciples to him and said,
"I feel sorry for these people, because they have
been with me for three days and now have nothing to eat. I don't want to send them away without feeding them, because they might faint on
their way home."

33 The disciples asked him, "Where will we
find enough food in this desert to feed this
crowd?"

34 "How much bread do you have?" Jesus
asked.

"Seven loaves," they answered, "and a few
small fish."

35 So Jesus ordered the crowd to sit down on
the ground. 36 Then he took the seven loaves
and the fish, gave thanks to God, broke them
and gave them to the disciples, and the disciples
gave them to the people. 37 They all ate and
had enough. The disciples took up seven baskets
full of pieces left over. 38 The number of men
who ate was four thousand, not counting the
women and children.

39 Then Jesus sent the people away, got into
the boat, and went to the territory of Magadan.

The demand for a miracle

16 Some Pharisees and Sadducees came to
Jesus. They wanted to trap him, so they
asked him to perform a miracle for them, to
show God's approval. 2 But Jesus answered,

New International Version

32 Jesus called his disciples to him and said,
"I have compassion for these people; they have
already been with me three days and have nothing to eat. I do not want to send them away
hungry, or they may collapse on the way."

33 His disciples answered, "Where could we
get enough bread in this remote place to feed
such a crowd?"

34 "How many loaves do you have?" Jesus
asked.

"Seven," they replied, "and a few small fish."

35 He told the crowd to sit down on the
ground. 36 Then he took the seven loaves and
the fish, and when he had given thanks, he broke
them and gave them to the disciples, and they
in turn to the people. 37 They all ate and were
satisfied. Afterward the disciples picked up seven
basketfuls of broken pieces that were left over.
38 The number of those who ate was four thousand, besides women and children. 39After Jesus
had sent the crowd away, he got into the boat
and went to the vicinity of Magadan.

The demand for a sign

16 The Pharisees and Sadducees came to Jesus and tested him by asking him to show
them a sign from heaven.

2 He replied,[a] "When evening comes, you say,

[a] Some early MSS omit the rest of verse 2 and all of verse 3.

Phillips Modern English

But Jesus quietly called his disciples to him. "My heart goes out to this crowd," he said. "They've stayed with me three days now and have no more food. I don't want to send them home without anything to eat or they will collapse on the way."

"Where could we find enough food to feed such a crowd in this deserted spot?" said the disciples.

"How many loaves have you?" asked Jesus.

"Seven, and a few small fish," they replied.

Then Jesus told the crowd to sit down comfortably on the ground. And when he had taken the seven loaves and the fish into his hands, he broke them with a prayer of thanksgiving and gave them to the disciples to pass on to the people. Everybody ate and was satisfied, and they picked up seven baskets full of the pieces left over. Those who ate numbered four thousand men, apart from women and children. Then Jesus sent the crowds home, boarded the boat and arrived at the district of Magadan.

16.1 Jesus again refuses to give a sign

Once the Pharisees and the Sadducees arrived together to test him, and asked him to give them a sign from Heaven. But he replied, "When the

Revised Standard Version

32 Then Jesus called his disciples to him and said, "I have compassion on the crowd, because they have been with me now three days, and have nothing to eat; and I am unwilling to send them away hungry, lest they faint on the way." 33 And the disciples said to him, "Where are we to get bread enough in the desert to feed so great a crowd?" 34 And Jesus said to them, "How many loaves have you?" They said, "Seven, and a few small fish." 35 And commanding the crowd to sit down on the ground, 36 he took the seven loaves and the fish, and having given thanks he broke them and gave them to the disciples, and the disciples gave them to the crowds. 37 And they all ate and were satisfied; and they took up seven baskets full of the broken pieces left over. 38 Those who ate were four thousand men, besides women and children. 39 And sending away the crowds, he got into the boat and went to the region of Magadan.

16 And the Pharisees and Sadducees came, and to test him they asked him to show them a sign from heaven. 2 He answered them,[r]

[r] Other ancient authorities omit the following words to the end of verse 3.

Jerusalem Bible

Second miracle of the loaves

32 But Jesus called his disciples to him and said, "I feel sorry for all these people; they have been with me for three days now and have nothing to eat. I do not want to send them off hungry, they might collapse on the way." 33 The disciples said to him, "Where could we get enough bread in this deserted place to feed such a crowd?" 34 Jesus said to them, "How many loaves have you?" "Seven," they said, "and a few small fish." 35 Then he instructed the crowd to sit down on the ground, 36 and he took the seven loaves and the fish, and he gave thanks and broke them and handed them to the disciples who gave them to the crowds. 37 They all ate as much as they wanted, and they collected what was left of the scraps, seven baskets full. 38 Now four thousand men had eaten, to say nothing of women and children. 39 And when he had sent the crowds away he got into the boat and went to the district of Magadan.

The Pharisees ask for a sign from heaven

16 The Pharisees and Sadducees came, and to test him they asked if he would show them a sign from heaven. 2 He replied, "In the

New English Bible

Jesus called his disciples and said to them, 'I feel sorry for all these people; they have been with me now for three days and have nothing to eat. I do not want to send them away unfed; they might turn faint on the way.' The disciples replied, 'Where in this lonely place can we find bread enough to feed such a crowd?' 'How many loaves have you?' Jesus asked. 'Seven,' they replied; 'and there are a few small fishes.' So he ordered the people to sit down on the ground; then he took the seven loaves and the fishes, and after giving thanks to God he broke them and gave to the disciples, and the disciples gave to the people. They all ate to their hearts' content; and the scraps left over, which they picked up, were enough to fill seven baskets. Four thousand men shared in this meal, to say nothing of women and children. He then dismissed the crowds, got into a boat, and went to the neighbourhood of Magadan.

16 The Pharisees and Sadducees came, and to test him they asked him to show them

King James Version

ning, ye say, *It will be* fair weather: for the sky is red. 3And in the morning, *It will be* foul weather to day: for the sky is red and lowering. O *ye* hypocrites, ye can discern the face of the sky; but can ye not *discern* the signs of the times? 4A wicked and adulterous generation seeketh after a sign; and there shall no sign be given unto it, but the sign of the prophet Jonas. And he left them, and departed. 5And when his disciples were come to the other side, they had forgotten to take bread.

6 Then Jesus said unto them, Take heed and beware of the leaven of the Pharisees and of the Sadducees. 7And they reasoned among themselves, saying, *It is* because we have taken no bread. 8 *Which* when Jesus perceived, he said unto them, O ye of little faith, why reason ye among yourselves, because ye have brought no bread? 9 Do ye not yet understand, neither remember the five loaves of the five thousand, and how many baskets ye took up? 10 Neither the seven loaves of the four thousand, and how many baskets ye took up? 11 How is it that ye do not understand that I spake *it* not to you concerning bread, that ye should beware of the leaven of the Pharisees and of the Sadducees?

Living Bible

weather signs of the skies—red sky tonight means fair weather tomorrow; red sky in the morning means foul weather all day—but you can't read the obvious signs of the times! 4 This evil, unbelieving nation is asking for some strange sign in the heavens, but no further proof will be given except the miracle that happened to Jonah." Then Jesus walked out on them.

5 Arriving across the lake, the disciples discovered they had forgotten to bring any food.

6 "Watch out!" Jesus warned them; "beware of the yeast of the Pharisees and Sadducees."

7 They thought he was saying this because they had forgotten to bring bread.

8 Jesus knew what they were thinking and told them, "O men of little faith! Why are you so worried about having no food? 9 Won't you ever understand? Don't you remember at all the 5,000 I fed with five loaves, and the basketfuls left over? 10 Don't you remember the 4,000 I fed, and all that was left? 11 How could you even think I was talking about food? But again I say, 'Beware of the yeast of the Pharisees and Sadducees.' "

Today's English Version

"When the sun is setting you say, 'We are going to have fine weather, because the sky is red.' 3And early in the morning you say, 'It is going to rain, because the sky is red and dark.' You can predict the weather by looking at the sky; but you cannot interpret the signs concerning these times! 4 How evil and godless are the people of this day! You ask me for a miracle? No! The only miracle you will be given is the miracle of Jonah."

So he left them and went away.

The yeast of the Pharisees and Sadducees

5 When the disciples crossed over to the other side of the lake, they forgot to take any bread. 6 Jesus said to them, "Look out, and be on your guard against the yeast of the Pharisees and Sadducees."

7 They started discussing among themselves, "He says this because we didn't bring any bread."

8 Jesus knew what they were saying, so he asked them, "Why are you discussing among yourselves about not having any bread? How little faith you have! 9 Don't you understand yet? Don't you remember when I broke the five loaves for the five thousand men? How many baskets did you fill? 10And what about the seven loaves for the four thousand men? How many baskets did you fill? 11 How is it that you don't understand that I was not talking to you about bread? Guard yourselves from the yeast of the Pharisees and Sadducees!"

New International Version

'It will be fair weather, for the sky is red,' 3 and in the morning, 'Today it will be stormy, for the sky is red and overcast.' You know how to interpret the appearance of the sky, but you cannot interpret the signs of the times. 4A wicked and adulterous generation looks for a miraculous sign, but none will be given it except the sign of Jonah." Jesus then left them and went away.

The yeast of the Pharisees and Sadducees

5 But when they went across the lake, the disciples forgot to take bread. 6 "Be careful," Jesus said to them. "Be on your guard against the yeast of the Pharisees and Sadducees."

7 They discussed this among themselves and said, "It is because we didn't bring any bread."

8 Aware of their discussion, Jesus asked, "You of little faith, why are you talking among yourselves about having no bread? 9 Do you still not understand? Don't you remember the five loaves for the five thousand, and how many basketfuls you gathered? 10 Or the seven loaves for the four thousand, and how many basketfuls you gathered? 11 How is it you don't understand that I was not talking to you about bread? But be on your guard against the yeast of the Phari-

Phillips Modern English

evening comes you say, 'Ah, fine weather—the sky is red.' In the morning you say, 'There will be a storm today, the sky is red and threatening.' Yes, you know how to interpret the look of the sky but you have no idea how to interpret the signs of the times! A wicked and unfaithful age insists on a sign; and it will not be given any sign at all but that of the prophet Jonah." And he turned on his heel and left them.

16.5 He is misunderstood by the disciples

Then his disciples came to him on the other side of the lake, forgetting to bring any bread with them. "Keep your eyes open," said Jesus to them, "and be on your guard against the 'yeast' of the Pharisees and Sadducees!" But they were arguing with each other, and saying, "We forgot to bring the bread." When Jesus saw this he said to them, "Why all this argument among yourselves about not bringing any bread, you little-faiths? Don't you understand yet, or have you forgotten the five loaves and the five thousand, and how many baskets you took up afterwards; or the seven loaves and the four thousand and how many baskets you took up then? I wonder why you don't yet understand that I wasn't talking about bread at all—I told you to beware of the yeast of the Pharisees and Sad-

Revised Standard Version

"When it is evening, you say, 'It will be fair weather; for the sky is red.' 3And in the morning, 'It will be stormy today, for the sky is red and threatening.' You know how to interpret the appearance of the sky, but you cannot interpret the signs of the times. 4An evil and adulterous generation seeks for a sign, but no sign shall be given to it except the sign of Jonah." So he left them and departed.

5 When the disciples reached the other side, they had forgotten to bring any bread. 6 Jesus said to them, "Take heed and beware of the leaven of the Pharisees and Sadducees." 7And they discussed it among themselves, saying, "We brought no bread." 8 But Jesus, aware of this, said, "O men of little faith, why do you discuss among yourselves the fact that you have no bread? 9 Do you not yet perceive? Do you not remember the five loaves of the five thousand, and how many baskets you gathered? 10 Or the seven loaves of the four thousand, and how many baskets you gathered? 11 How is it that you fail to perceive that I did not speak about bread? Beware of the leaven of the Pharisees and

Jerusalem Bible

evening you say, 'It will be fine; there is a red sky,' 3 and in the morning, 'Stormy weather today; the sky is red and overcast.' You know how to read the face of the sky, but you cannot read the signs of the times. 4 It is an evil and unfaithful generation that asks for a sign! The only sign it will be given is the sign of Jonah." And leaving them standing there, he went away.

The yeast of the Pharisees and Sadducees

5 The disciples, having crossed to the other shore, had forgotten to take any food. 6 Jesus said to them, "Keep your eyes open, and be on your guard against the yeast of the Pharisees and Sadducees." 7And they said to themselves, "It is because we have not brought any bread." 8 Jesus knew it, and he said, "Men of little faith, why are you talking among yourselves about having no bread? 9 Do you not yet understand? Do you not remember the five loaves for the five thousand and the number of baskets you collected? 10 Or the seven loaves for the four thousand and the number of baskets you collected? 11 How could you fail to understand that I was not talking about bread? What I said was: Beware of the yeast of the Pharisees and Sad-

New English Bible

a sign from heaven. His answer was: [a] 'It is a wicked generation that asks for a sign; and the only sign that will be given it is the sign of Jonah.' So he went off and left them.

In crossing to the other side the disciples had forgotten to take bread with them. So, when Jesus said to them, 'Beware, be on your guard against the leaven of the Pharisees and Sadducees', they began to say among themselves, 'It is because we have brought no bread!' Knowing what was in their minds, Jesus said to them: 'Why do you talk about bringing no bread? Where is your faith? Do you not understand even yet? Do you not remember the five loaves for the five thousand, and how many basketfuls you picked up? Or the seven loaves for the four thousand, and how many basketfuls you picked up? How can you fail to see that I was not speaking about bread? Be on your guard, I said, against the leaven of the Pharisees and

[a] *Some witnesses here insert* 'In the evening you say, "It will be fine weather, for the sky is red"; (3) and in the morning you say, "It will be stormy today; the sky is red and lowering." You know how to interpret the appearance of the sky; can you not interpret the signs of the times?'

King James Version

12 Then understood they how that he bade *them*
not beware of the leaven of bread, but of the
doctrine of the Pharisees and of the Sadducees.
13 When Jesus came into the coasts of Cesarea Philippi, he asked his disciples, saying,
Whom do men say that I, the Son of man, am?
14 And they said, Some *say that thou art* John
the Baptist; some, Elias; and others, Jeremias, or
one of the prophets. 15 He saith unto them, But
whom say ye that I am? 16 And Simon Peter
answered and said, Thou art the Christ, the Son
of the living God. 17 And Jesus answered and
said unto him, Blessed art thou, Simon Bar-jona:
for flesh and blood hath not revealed *it* unto
thee, but my Father which is in heaven. 18 And I
say also unto thee, That thou art Peter, and
upon this rock I will build my church; and the
gates of hell shall not prevail against it. 19 And
I will give unto thee the keys of the kingdom of
heaven: and whatsoever thou shalt bind on earth
shall be bound in heaven; and whatsoever thou
shalt loose on earth shall be loosed in heaven.
20 Then charged he his disciples that they should
tell no man that he was Jesus the Christ.

Living Bible

12 Then at last they understood that by
"yeast" he meant the *wrong teaching* of the
Pharisees and Sadducees.

13 When Jesus came to Caesarea Philippi, he
asked his disciples, "Who are the people saying
I [b] am?"

14 "Well," they replied, "some say John the
Baptist; some, Elijah; some, Jeremiah or one of
the other prophets."

15 Then he asked them, "Who do *you* think
I am?"

16 Simon Peter answered, "The Christ, the
Messiah, the Son of the living God."

17 "God has blessed you, Simon, son of Jonah," Jesus said, "for my Father in heaven has
personally revealed this to you—this is not from
any human source. 18 You are Peter, a stone;
and upon this rock I will build my church; and
all the powers of hell shall not prevail against it.
19 And I will give you the keys of the Kingdom
of Heaven; whatever doors you lock on earth
shall be locked in heaven; and whatever doors
you open on earth shall be open in heaven!"

20 Then he warned the disciples against telling
others that he was the Messiah.

[b] Literally, "the Son of Man."

Today's English Version

12 Then the disciples understood that he was
not telling them to guard themselves from the
yeast used in bread, but from the teaching of the
Pharisees and Sadducees.

Peter's declaration about Jesus

13 Jesus went to the territory near the town
of Caesarea Philippi, where he asked his disciples, "Who do men say the Son of Man is?"

14 "Some say John the Baptist," they answered. "Others say Elijah, while others say
Jeremiah or some other prophet."

15 "What about you?" he asked them. "Who
do you say I am?"

16 Simon Peter answered, "You are the Messiah, the Son of the living God."

17 "Good for you, Simon, son of John!" answered Jesus. "Because this truth did not come
to you from any human being, but it was given
to you directly by my Father in heaven. 18 And
so I tell you: you are a rock, Peter, and on this
rock foundation I will build my church, which
not even death will ever be able to overcome.
19 I will give you the keys of the Kingdom of
heaven; what you prohibit on earth will be prohibited in heaven; what you permit on earth will
be permitted in heaven."

20 Then Jesus ordered his disciples not to tell
anyone that he was the Messiah.

New International Version

sees and Sadducees." 12 Then they understood
that he was not telling them to guard against the
yeast used in bread, but against the teaching of
the Pharisees and Sadducees.

Peter's confession of Christ

13 When Jesus came to the region of Caesarea
Philippi, he asked his disciples, "Who do people
say the Son of Man is?"

14 They replied, "Some say John the Baptist;
others say Elijah; and still others, Jeremiah or
one of the prophets."

15 "But what about you?" he asked. "Who do
you say I am?"

16 Simon Peter answered, "You are the
Christ,[b] the Son of the living God."

17 Jesus replied, "Blessed are you, Simon son
of Jonah, for this was not revealed to you by
man, but by my Father in heaven. 18 And I tell
you that you are Peter,[c] and on this rock I will
build my church, and the gates of Hades will
not overcome it.[d] 19 I will give you the keys of
the kingdom of heaven; whatever you bind on
earth will be bound in heaven, and whatever you
loose on earth will be loosed in heaven." 20 Then
he warned his disciples not to tell anyone that
he was the Christ.[b]

[b] Or *Messiah*. [c] *Peter* means *rock*. [d] Or *not prove stronger than it*.

Phillips Modern English

ducees." Then they grasped the fact that he
had not told them to beware of yeast in the
ordinary sense but of the influence of the teaching of the Pharisees and Sadducees.

16.13 Peter's bold affirmation

When Jesus reached the Caesarea-Philippi district he asked his disciples a question. "Who do
people say the Son of Man is?"
"Well, some say John the Baptist," they told
him. "Some say Elijah, others Jeremiah or one
of the prophets."
"But what about you?" he said to them. "Who
do you say that I am?"
Simon Peter answered, "You? You are Christ,
the Son of the living God!"
"Simon, son of Jonah, you are a fortunate
man indeed!" said Jesus, "for it was not your
own nature but my Heavenly Father who revealed this truth to you! Now I tell you that
you are Peter the rock, and it is on this rock
that I am going to found my Church, and the
powers of death will never have the power to
destroy it. I will give you the keys of the kingdom of Heaven; whatever you forbid on earth
will be what is forbidden in Heaven and whatever you permit on earth will be what is permitted in Heaven!" Then he impressed on his
disciples that they should not tell anyone that
he was Christ.

Revised Standard Version

Sadducees." 12 Then they understood that he did
not tell them to beware of the leaven of bread,
but of the teaching of the Pharisees and Sadducees.
13 Now when Jesus came into the district of
Caesarea Philippi, he asked his disciples, "Who
do men say that the Son of man is?" 14 And they
said, "Some say John the Baptist, others say
Elijah, and others Jeremiah or one of the prophets." 15 He said to them, "But who do you say
that I am?" 16 Simon Peter replied, "You are
the Christ, the Son of the living God." 17 And
Jesus answered him, "Blessed are you, Simon
Bar-Jona! For flesh and blood has not revealed
this to you, but my Father who is in heaven.
18 And I tell you, you are Peter,[s] and on this
rock[t] I will build my church, and the powers of
death[u] shall not prevail against it. 19 I will give
you the keys of the kingdom of heaven, and
whatever you bind on earth shall be bound in
heaven, and whatever you loose on earth shall
be loosed in heaven." 20 Then he strictly charged
the disciples to tell no one that he was the Christ.

[s] Greek *Petros.* [t] Greek *petra.* [u] Greek *the gates of Hades.*

Jerusalem Bible

ducees." 12 Then they understood that he was
telling them to be on their guard, not against
the yeast for making bread, but against the
teaching of the Pharisees and Sadducees.[z]

Peter's profession of faith; his pre-eminence

13 When Jesus came to the region of Caesarea
Philippi he put this question to his disciples,
"Who do people say the Son of Man is?" 14 And
they said, "Some say he is John the Baptist, some
Elijah, and others Jeremiah or one of the
prophets." 15 "But you," he said, "who do you
say I am?" 16 Then Simon Peter spoke up, "You
are the Christ," he said, "the Son of the living
God." 17 Jesus replied, "Simon son of Jonah,
you are a happy man! Because it was not flesh
and blood that revealed this to you but my
Father in heaven. 18 So I now say to you: You
are Peter[a] and on this rock I will build my
Church. And the gates of the underworld[b] can
never hold out against it. 19 I will give you the
keys of the kingdom of heaven: whatever you
bind on earth shall be considered bound in
heaven; whatever you loose on earth shall be
considered loosed in heaven."[c] 20 Then he gave
the disciples strict orders not to tell anyone that
he was the Christ.

[z] Yeast, here, is regarded as adulterating pure flour. [a] Not, until now, a proper name: Greek *petros* (as in English saltpeter) represents Aramaic *kepha,* rock. [b] The gates symbolize the power of the underworld to hold captives. [c] The keys have become the traditional insignia of Peter.

New English Bible

Sadducees.' Then they understood: they were
to be on their guard, not against baker's leaven,
but against the teaching of the Pharisees and
Sadducees.
When he came to the territory of Caesarea
Philippi, Jesus asked his disciples, 'Who do men
say that the Son of Man is[b]?' They answered,
'Some say John the Baptist, others Elijah, others
Jeremiah, or one of the prophets.' 'And you,' he
asked, 'who do you say I am?' Simon Peter
answered: 'You are the Messiah, the Son of the
living God.' Then Jesus said: 'Simon son of
Jonah, you are favoured indeed! You did not
learn that from mortal man; it was revealed to
you by my heavenly Father. And I say this to
you: You are Peter, the Rock; and on this rock
I will build my church, and the power of death
shall never conquer it.[a] I will give you the keys
of the kingdom of Heaven; what you forbid
on earth shall be forbidden in heaven, and what
you allow on earth shall be allowed in heaven.'
He then gave his disciples strict orders not to
tell anyone that he was the Messiah.

[b] *Some witnesses read* that I, the Son of Man, am.
[a] *Or* the gates of death shall never close upon it.

King James Version

21 From that time forth began Jesus to shew
unto his disciples, how that he must go unto
Jerusalem, and suffer many things of the elders
and chief priests and scribes, and be killed, and
be raised again the third day. 22 Then Peter took
him, and began to rebuke him, saying, Be it far
from thee, Lord: this shall not be unto thee.
23 But he turned, and said unto Peter, Get thee
behind me, Satan: thou art an offence unto me:
for thou savourest not the things that be of
God, but those that be of men.
24 Then said Jesus unto his disciples, If any
man will come after me, let him deny himself,
and take up his cross, and follow me. 25 For
whosoever will save his life shall lose it: and
whosoever will lose his life for my sake shall
find it. 26 For what is a man profited, if he shall
gain the whole world, and lose his own soul? or
what shall a man give in exchange for his soul?
27 For the Son of man shall come in the glory of
his Father with his angels; and then he shall
reward every man according to his works.
28 Verily I say unto you, There be some standing
here, which shall not taste of death, till they see
the Son of man coming in his kingdom.

Living Bible

21 From then on Jesus began to speak plainly
to his disciples about going to Jerusalem, and
what would happen to him there—that he would
suffer at the hands of the Jewish leaders,[c] that
he would be killed, and that three days later he
would be raised to life again.
22 But Peter took him aside to remonstrate
with him. "Heaven forbid, sir," he said. "This
is not going to happen to you!"
23 Jesus turned on Peter and said, "Get away
from me, you Satan! You are a dangerous trap
to me. You are thinking merely from a human
point of view, and not from God's."
24 Then Jesus said to the disciples, "If anyone wants to be a follower of mine, let him deny
himself and take up his cross and follow me.
25 For anyone who keeps his life for himself
shall lose it; and anyone who loses his life for
me shall find it again. 26 What profit is there if
you gain the whole world—and lose eternal life?
What can be compared with the value of eternal
life? 27 For I, the Son of Mankind, shall come
with my angels in the glory of my Father and
judge each person according to his deeds. 28And
some of you standing right here now will certainly live to see me coming in my Kingdom."

[*c*] Literally, "of the elders, and chief priests, and scribes."

Today's English Version

Jesus speaks about his suffering and death

21 From that time on Jesus began to say
plainly to his disciples, "I must go to Jerusalem
and suffer much from the elders, the chief priests,
and the teachers of the Law. I will be put to
death, and on the third day I will be raised to
life."
22 Peter took him aside and began to rebuke
him. "God forbid it, Lord!" he said. "This must
never happen to you!"
23 Jesus turned around and said to Peter, "Get
away from me, Satan! You are an obstacle in
my way, because these thoughts of yours are
men's thoughts, not God's!"
24 Then Jesus said to his disciples, "If anyone
wants to come with me, he must forget himself,
carry his cross, and follow me. 25 For whoever
wants to save his own life will lose it; but whoever loses his life for my sake will find it. 26 Will
a man gain anything if he wins the whole world
but loses his life? Of course not! There is nothing
a man can give to regain his life. 27 For the
Son of Man is about to come in the glory of his
Father with his angels, and then he will repay
everyone according to his deeds. 28 Remember
this! There are some here who will not die until
they have seen the Son of Man come as King."

New International Version

Jesus predicts his death

21 From that time on Jesus began to explain
to his disciples that he must go to Jerusalem
and suffer many things at the hands of the elders, chief priests and teachers of the law, and
that he must be killed and on the third day be
raised to life.
22 Peter took him aside and began to rebuke
him. "Perish the thought, Lord!" he said. "This
shall never happen to you!"
23 Jesus turned and said to Peter, "Out of my
sight, Satan! You are a stumbling block to me;
you do not have in mind the things of God, but
the things of men."
24 Then Jesus said to his disciples, "If anyone would come after me, he must deny himself
and take up his cross and follow me. 25 For
whoever wants to save his life[e] will lose it, but
whoever loses his life for me will find it. 26 What
good will it be for a man if he gains the whole
world, yet forfeits his soul? [e] Or what can a man
give in exchange for his soul? 27 For the Son of
Man is going to come in his Father's glory with
his angels, and then he will reward each person
according to what he has done. 28 I tell you the
truth, some who are standing here will not taste
death before they see the Son of Man coming in
his kingdom."

[*e*] The Greek word means either *life* or *soul.*

Phillips Modern English

16.21 Jesus speaks about his passion, and the cost of following him

From that time onwards Jesus began to explain to his disciples that he would have to go to Jerusalem, and endure much suffering from the elders, chief priests and scribes, and finally be killed; and be raised to life again on the third day.

Then Peter took him on one side and started to remonstrate with him over this. "God bless you, Master! Nothing like this must happen to you!" Then Jesus turned round and said to Peter, "Out of my way, Satan! . . . . you stand right in my path, Peter, when you think the thoughts of man and not those of God."

Then Jesus said to his disciples, "If anyone wants to follow in my footsteps he must give up all right to himself, take up his cross and follow me. For the man who wants to save his life will lose it; but the man who loses his life for my sake will find it. For what good is it for a man to gain the whole world at the price of his real life? What could a man offer to buy back that life once he has lost it?

"For the Son of Man will come in the glory of his Father and in the company of his angels and then he will repay every man for what he has done. Believe me, there are some standing here today who will know nothing of death till they have seen the Son of Man coming as king."

Revised Standard Version

21 From that time Jesus began to show his
disciples that he must go to Jerusalem and suffer many things from the elders and chief priests
and scribes, and be killed, and on the third day
be raised. 22And Peter took him and began to
rebuke him, saying, "God forbid, Lord! This
shall never happen to you." 23 But he turned and
said to Peter, "Get behind me, Satan! You are
a hindrance[v] to me; for you are not on the side
of God, but of men."
24 Then Jesus told his disciples, "If any man
would come after me, let him deny himself and
take up his cross and follow me. 25 For whoever
would save his life will lose it, and whoever
loses his life for my sake will find it. 26 For what
will it profit a man, if he gains the whole world
and forfeits his life? Or what shall a man give
in return for his life? 27 For the Son of man
is to come with his angels in the glory of his
Father, and then he will repay every man for
what he has done. 28 Truly, I say to you, there
are some standing here who will not taste death
before they see the Son of man coming in his
kingdom."

[v] Greek *stumbling block.*

Jerusalem Bible

First prophecy of the Passion

21 From that time Jesus began to make it
clear to his disciples that he was destined to go
to Jerusalem and suffer grievously at the hands
of the elders and chief priests and scribes, to
be put to death and to be raised up on the third
day. 22 Then, taking him aside, Peter started to
remonstrate with him. "Heaven preserve you,
Lord"; he said, "this must not happen to you."
23 But he turned and said to Peter, "Get behind
me, Satan! You are an obstacle in my path, because the way you think is not God's way but
man's."

The condition of following Christ

24 Then Jesus said to his disciples, "If anyone wants to be a follower of mine, let him
renounce himself and take up his cross and follow me. 25 For anyone who wants to save his
life will lose it; but anyone who loses his life
for my sake will find it. 26 What, then, will a
man gain if he wins the whole world and ruins
his life? Or what has a man to offer in exchange
for his life?
27 "For the Son of Man is going to come in
the glory of his Father with his angels, and,
when he does, he will reward each one according to his behavior. 28 I tell you solemnly, there
are some of these standing here who will not
taste death before they see the Son of Man
coming with his kingdom." [d]

[d] In vv. 27-28, two different sayings have been combined because both refer to the coming of the kingdom; but the first is about Judgment day, and the second is about the destruction of Jerusalem, the sign of "the last days."

New English Bible

From that time Jesus began to make it clear to his disciples that he had to go to Jerusalem, and there to suffer much from the elders, chief priests, and doctors of the law; to be put to death and to be raised again on the third day. At this Peter took him by the arm and began to rebuke him: 'Heaven forbid!' he said. 'No, Lord, this shall never happen to you.' Then Jesus turned and said to Peter, 'Away with you, Satan; you are a stumbling-block to me. You think as men think, not as God thinks.'

Jesus then said to his disciples, 'If anyone wishes to be a follower of mine, he must leave self behind; he must take up his cross and come with me. Whoever cares for his own safety is lost; but if a man will let himself be lost for my sake, he will find his true self. What will a man gain by winning the whole world, at the cost of his true self? Or what can he give that will buy that self back? For the Son of Man is to come in the glory of his Father with his angels, and then he will give each man the due reward for what he has done. I tell you this: there are some of those standing here who will not taste death before they have seen the Son of Man coming in his kingdom.'

King James Version

17 And after six days Jesus taketh Peter, James, and John his brother, and bringeth them up into a high mountain apart, 2And was transfigured before them: and his face did shine as the sun, and his raiment was white as the light. 3And, behold, there appeared unto them Moses and Elias talking with him. 4 Then answered Peter, and said unto Jesus, Lord, it is good for us to be here: if thou wilt, let us make here three tabernacles; one for thee, and one for Moses, and one for Elias. 5 While he yet spake, behold, a bright cloud overshadowed them: and behold a voice out of the cloud, which said, This is my beloved Son, in whom I am well pleased; hear ye him. 6And when the disciples heard *it*, they fell on their face, and were sore afraid. 7And Jesus came and touched them, and said, Arise, and be not afraid. 8And when they had lifted up their eyes, they saw no man, save Jesus only. 9And as they came down from the mountain, Jesus charged them, saying, Tell the vision to no man, until the Son of man be risen again from the dead. 10And his disciples asked him, saying, Why then say the scribes that Elias must first come? 11And Jesus answered and said unto them, Elias truly shall first come, and restore all

Living Bible

17 Six days later Jesus took Peter, James, and his brother John to the top of a high and lonely hill, 2 and as they watched, his appearance changed so that his face shone like the sun and his clothing became dazzling white.

3 Suddenly Moses and Elijah appeared and were talking with him. 4 Peter blurted out, "Sir, it's wonderful that we can be here! If you want me to, I'll make three shelters,[a] one for you and one for Moses and one for Elijah."

5 But even as he said it, a bright cloud came over them, and a voice from the cloud said, *"This* is my beloved Son, and I am wonderfully pleased with him. Obey[b] *him."*

6 At this the disciples fell face downward to the ground, terribly frightened. 7 Jesus came over and touched them. "Get up," he said, "don't be afraid."

8 And when they looked, only Jesus was with them.

9 As they were going down the mountains, Jesus commanded them not to tell anyone what they had seen until after he had risen from the dead.

10 His disciples asked, "Why do the Jewish leaders insist Elijah must return before the Messiah comes?" [c]

11 Jesus replied, "They are right. Elijah must

[*a*] Literally, "three tabernacles" or "tents." What was in Peter's mind is not explained. [*b*] Literally, "hear him." [*c*] Implied. Literally, "what Elijah must come first."

Today's English Version

The transfiguration

17 Six days later Jesus took with him Peter and the brothers James and John, and led them up a high mountain by themselves. 2As they looked on, a change came over him: his face became as bright as the sun, and his clothes as white as light. 3 Then the three disciples saw Moses and Elijah talking with Jesus. 4 So Peter spoke up and said to Jesus, "Lord, it is a good thing that we are here; if you wish, I will make three tents here, one for you, one for Moses, and one for Elijah."

5 While he was talking, a shining cloud came over them and a voice said from the cloud: "This is my own dear Son, with whom I am well pleased—listen to him!"

6 When the disciples heard the voice they were so terrified that they threw themselves face down to the ground. 7 Jesus came to them and touched them. "Get up," he said. "Don't be afraid!" 8 So they looked up and saw no one else except Jesus.

9 As they came down the mountain Jesus ordered them, "Don't tell anyone about this vision you have seen until the Son of Man has been raised from death."

10 Then the disciples asked Jesus, "Why do the teachers of the Law say that Elijah has to come first?"

11 "Elijah does indeed come first," answered

New International Version

The transfiguration

17 After six days Jesus took with him Peter, James, and John the brother of James, and led them up a high mountain by themselves. 2 There he was transfigured before them. His face shone like the sun, and his clothes became as white as the light. 3 Just then there appeared before them Moses and Elijah, talking with Jesus.

4 Peter said to Jesus, "Lord, it is good for us to be here. If you wish, I will put up three shelters[f]—one for you, one for Moses and one for Elijah."

5 While he was still speaking, a bright cloud enveloped them, and a voice from the cloud said, "This is my Son, whom I love; with him I am well-pleased. Listen to him!"

6 When the disciples heard this, they fell face down to the ground, terrified. 7 But Jesus came and touched them. "Get up," he said. "Don't be afraid." 8 When they looked up, they saw no one except Jesus.

9 As they were coming down the mountain, Jesus instructed them, "Don't tell anyone what you have seen, until the Son of Man has been raised from the dead."

10 The disciples asked him, "Why then do the teachers of the law say that Elijah must come first?"

11 Jesus replied, "To be sure, Elijah comes

[*f*] Or *sanctuaries.*

Phillips Modern English

17.1 Three disciples glimpse the glory of Christ

Six days later Jesus chose Peter, James and his brother John, to accompany him high up on the hill-side where they were quite alone. There his whole appearance changed before their eyes, his face shining like the sun and his clothes as white as light. Then Moses and Elijah were seen talking to Jesus.

"Lord," exclaimed Peter, "it is wonderful for us to be here! If you like I could put up three shelters, one each for you and Moses and Elijah——"

But while he was still talking a bright cloud overshadowed them and a voice came out of the cloud:

"This is my dearly loved Son in whom I am well pleased. Listen to him!"

When they heard this voice the disciples fell on their faces, overcome with fear. Then Jesus came up to them and touched them.

"Get up and don't be frightened," he said. And as they raised their eyes there was no one to be seen but Jesus himself.

On their way down the hill-side Jesus warned them not to tell anyone about what they had seen until after the Son of Man had been raised from the dead. Then the disciples demanded, "Why is it, then, that the scribes always say Elijah must come first?"

"Yes, Elijah does come first," replied Jesus,

Revised Standard Version

17 And after six days Jesus took with him Peter and James and John his brother, and led them up a high mountain apart. 2And he was transfigured before them, and his face shone like the sun, and his garments became white as light. 3And behold, there appeared to them Moses and Elijah, talking with him. 4And Peter said to Jesus, "Lord, it is well that we are here; if you wish, I will make three booths here, one for you and one for Moses and one for Elijah." 5 He was still speaking, when lo, a bright cloud overshadowed them, and a voice from the cloud said, "This is my beloved Son,[w] with whom I am well pleased; listen to him." 6 When the disciples heard this, they fell on their faces, and were filled with awe. 7 But Jesus came and touched them, saying, "Rise, and have no fear." 8And when they lifted up their eyes, they saw no one but Jesus only.

9 And as they were coming down the mountain, Jesus commanded them, "Tell no one the vision, until the Son of man is raised from the dead." 10And the disciples asked him, "Then why do the scribes say that first Elijah must come?" 11 He replied, "Elijah does come, and

[w] Or *my Son, my* (or *the*) *Beloved.*

Jerusalem Bible

The transfiguration

17 Six days later, Jesus took with him Peter and James and his brother John and led them up a high mountain where they could be alone. 2 There in their presence he was transfigured: his face shone like the sun and his clothes became as white as the light. 3 Suddenly Moses and Elijah[e] appeared to them; they were talking with him. 4 Then Peter spoke to Jesus. "Lord," he said, "it is wonderful for us to be here; if you wish, I will make three tents here, one for you, one for Moses and one for Elijah." 5 He was still speaking when suddenly a bright cloud covered them with shadow, and from the cloud there came a voice which said, "This is my Son, the Beloved; he enjoys my favor. Listen to him." 6 When they heard this, the disciples fell on their faces, overcome with fear. 7 But Jesus came up and touched them. "Stand up," he said, "do not be afraid." 8And when they raised their eyes they saw no one but only Jesus.

The question about Elijah

9 As they came down from the mountain Jesus gave them this order, "Tell no one about the vision until the Son of Man has risen from the dead." 10And the disciples put this question to him, "Why do the scribes say then that Elijah has to come first?" 11 "True," he replied, "Elijah is to come to see that everything is once more

[e] Representing the Law and the prophets.

New English Bible

17 Six days later Jesus took Peter, James, and John the brother of James, and led them up a high mountain where they were alone; and in their presence he was transfigured; his face shone like the sun, and his clothes became white as the light. And they saw Moses and Elijah appear, conversing with him. Then Peter spoke: 'Lord,' he said, 'how good it is that we are here! If you wish it, I will make three shelters here, one for you, one for Moses, and one for Elijah.' While he was still speaking, a bright cloud suddenly overshadowed them, and a voice called from the cloud: 'This is my Son, my Beloved,[b] on whom my favour rests; listen to him.' At the sound of the voice the disciples fell on their faces in terror. Jesus then came up to them, touched them, and said, 'Stand up; do not be afraid.' And when they raised their eyes they saw no one, but only Jesus.

On their way down the mountain, Jesus enjoined them not to tell anyone of the vision until the Son of Man had been raised from the dead. The disciples put a question to him: 'Why then do our teachers say that Elijah must come first?' He replied, 'Yes, Elijah will come and set

[b] *Or* This is my only Son.

King James Version

things. 12 But I say unto you, That Elias is come
already, and they knew him not, but have done
unto him whatsoever they listed. Likewise shall
also the Son of man suffer of them. 13 Then the
disciples understood that he spake unto them of
John the Baptist.
14 And when they were come to the multitude, there came to him a *certain* man, kneeling
down to him, and saying, 15 Lord, have mercy
on my son; for he is lunatic, and sore vexed: for
ofttimes he falleth into the fire, and oft into the
water. 16 And I brought him to thy disciples, and
they could not cure him. 17 Then Jesus answered
and said, O faithless and perverse generation,
how long shall I be with you? how long shall I
suffer you? bring him hither to me. 18 And Jesus
rebuked the devil; and he departed out of him:
and the child was cured from that very hour.
19 Then came the disciples to Jesus apart, and
said, Why could not we cast him out? 20 And
Jesus said unto them, Because of your unbelief:
for verily I say unto you, If ye have faith as a
grain of mustard seed, ye shall say unto this
mountain, Remove hence to yonder place; and
it shall remove: and nothing shall be impossible unto you. 21 Howbeit this kind goeth not out
but by prayer and fasting.

Living Bible

come and set everything in order. 12 And, in fact,
he has already come, but he wasn't recognized,
and was badly mistreated by many. And I, the
Messiah[d], shall also suffer at their hands."
13 Then the disciples realized he was speaking of John the Baptist.
14 When they arrived at the bottom of the
hill, a huge crowd was waiting for them. A man
came and knelt before Jesus and said, 15 "Sir,
have mercy on my son, for he is mentally de-
ranged, and in great trouble, for he often falls
into the fire or into the water; 16 so I brought
him to your disciples, but they couldn't cure
him."
17 Jesus replied, "Oh, you stubborn, faithless
people! How long shall I bear with you? Bring
him here to me." 18 Then Jesus rebuked the
demon in the boy and it left him, and from that
moment the boy was well.
19 Afterwards the disciples asked Jesus privately, "Why couldn't we cast that demon out?"
20 "Because of your little faith," Jesus told
them. "For if you had faith even as small as a
tiny mustard seed you could say to this mountain, 'Move!' and it would go far away. Nothing
would be impossible. 21 But this kind of demon
won't leave unless you have prayed and gone
without food." [e]

[d] Literally, "the Son of Man." [e] This verse is omitted in many of the ancient manuscripts.

Today's English Version

Jesus, "and he will get everything ready. 12 But
I tell you this: Elijah has already come and people did not recognize him, but treated him just
as they pleased. In the same way the Son of Man
will also be mistreated by them."
13 Then the disciples understood that he was
talking to them about John the Baptist.

Jesus heals a boy with a demon

14 When they returned to the crowd, a man
came to Jesus, knelt before him, 15 and said,
"Sir, have mercy on my son! He is epileptic and
has such terrible fits that he often falls in the fire
or in the water. 16 I brought him to your disciples, but they could not heal him."
17 Jesus answered, "How unbelieving and
wrong you people are! How long must I stay
with you? How long do I have to put up with
you? Bring the boy here to me!" 18 Jesus commanded the demon and it went out, so that the
boy was healed at that very moment.
19 Then the disciples came to Jesus in private
and asked him, "Why couldn't we drive the
demon out?"
20 "It was because you do not have enough
faith," answered Jesus. "Remember this! If you
have faith as big as a mustard seed, you can say
to this hill, 'Go from here to there!' and it will
go. You could do anything! [21 But only prayer
and fasting can drive this kind out; nothing else
can.]"

New International Version

and will restore all things. 12 But I tell you,
Elijah has already come, and they did not recognize him, but have done to him everything
they wished. In the same way the Son of Man
is going to suffer at their hands." 13 Then the
disciples understood that he was talking to them
about John the Baptist.

The healing of an epileptic boy

14 When they came to the crowd, a man approached Jesus and knelt before him. 15 "Lord,
have mercy on my son," he said. "He is an epileptic and is suffering greatly. He often falls into
the fire or into the water. 16 I brought him to
your disciples, but they could not heal him."
17 "O unbelieving and perverse generation,"
Jesus replied, "how long shall I stay with you?
How long shall I put up with you? Bring the
boy here to me." 18 Jesus rebuked the demon,
and it came out of the boy, and he was healed
from that moment.
19 Then the disciples came to Jesus in private
and asked, "Why couldn't we drive it out?"
20 He replied, "Because you have so little
faith. I tell you the truth, if you have faith as
small as a mustard seed, you can say to this
mountain, 'Move from here to there' and it will
move. Nothing will be impossible for you." [g]

[g] Some MSS add verse 21: *But this kind does not go out except by prayer and fasting.*

Phillips Modern English

"and begins the world's reformation. But I tell you that Elijah has come already and men did not recognise him. They did what they liked with him, and the Son of Man will also suffer at their hands."

Then the disciples realised that he had been referring to John the Baptist.

17.14 Jesus heals an epileptic boy

When they returned to the crowd again a man came and knelt in front of Jesus. "Lord, have pity on my son," he said, "for he is a lunatic and suffers terribly. He is always falling into the fire or into the water. I did bring him to your disciples but they couldn't cure him."

"You really are an unbelieving and difficult people," Jesus returned. "How long must I be with you, and how long must I put up with you? Bring him here to me!"

Then Jesus spoke sternly to the evil spirit and it went out of the boy, who was cured from that moment.

Afterwards the disciples approached Jesus privately and asked, "Why weren't we able to get rid of it?"

"Because you have so little faith," replied Jesus. "I assure you that if you have faith the size of a mustard-seed you can say to this hill, 'Up you get and move over there!' and it will move—you will find nothing is impossible."

Revised Standard Version

he is to restore all things; 12 but I tell you that
Elijah has already come, and they did not
know him, but did to him whatever they pleased.
So also the Son of man will suffer at their
hands." 13 Then the disciples understood that
he was speaking to them of John the Baptist.
14 And when they came to the crowd, a man
came up to him and kneeling before him said,
15 "Lord, have mercy on my son, for he is an
epileptic and he suffers terribly; for often he
falls into the fire, and often into the water.
16 And I brought him to your disciples, and they
could not heal him." 17 And Jesus answered, "O
faithless and perverse generation, how long am I
to be with you? How long am I to bear with
you? Bring him here to me." 18 And Jesus rebuked him, and the demon came out of him,
and the boy was cured instantly. 19 Then the disciples came to Jesus privately and said, "Why
could we not cast it out?" 20 He said to them,
"Because of your little faith. For truly, I say
to you, if you have faith as a grain of mustard
seed, you will say to this mountain, 'Move from
here to there,' and it will move; and nothing will
be impossible to you." [x]

[x] Other ancient authorities insert verse 21, *"But this kind never comes out except by prayer and fasting."*

Jerusalem Bible

as it should be; 12 however, I tell you that Elijah
has come already and they did not recognize him
but treated him as they pleased; and the Son
of Man will suffer similarly at their hands."
13 The disciples understood then that he had
been speaking of John the Baptist.

The epileptic demoniac

14 As they were rejoining the crowd a man
came up to him and went down on his knees
before him. 15 "Lord," he said, "take pity on
my son: he is a lunatic and in a wretched state;
he is always falling into the fire or into the
water. 16 I took him to your disciples and they
were unable to cure him." 17 "Faithless and perverse generation!" Jesus said in reply. "How
much longer must I be with you? How much
longer must I put up with you? Bring him here
to me." 18 And when Jesus rebuked it the devil
came out of the boy who was cured from that
moment.
19 Then the disciples came privately to Jesus.
"Why were we unable to cast it out?" they
asked. 20 He answered, "Because you have little
faith. I tell you solemnly, if your faith were the
size of a mustard seed you could say to this
mountain, 'Move from here to there,' and it
would move; nothing would be impossible for
you." [f]

[f] Add. v. 21 "As for this kind (of devil), it is cast out only by prayer and fasting," cf. Mk. 9:29.

New English Bible

everything right. But I tell you that Elijah has already come, and they failed to recognize him, and worked their will upon him; and in the same way the Son of Man is to suffer at their hands.' Then the disciples understood that he meant John the Baptist.

When they returned to the crowd, a man came up to Jesus, fell on his knees before him, and said, 'Have pity, sir, on my son: he is an epileptic and has bad fits, and he keeps falling about, often into the fire, often into water. I brought him to your disciples, but they could not cure him.' Jesus answered, 'What an unbelieving and perverse generation! How long shall I be with you? How long must I endure you? Bring him here to me.' Jesus then spoke sternly to the boy; the devil left him, and from that moment he was cured.

Afterwards the disciples came to Jesus and asked him privately, 'Why could not we cast it out?' He answered, 'Your faith is too small. I tell you this: if you have faith no bigger even than a mustard-seed, you will say to this mountain, "Move from here to there!", and it will move; nothing will prove impossible for you.' [a]

[a] *Some witnesses add* (21) But there is no means of casting out this sort but prayer and fasting.

King James Version

22 And while they abode in Galilee, Jesus
said unto them, The Son of man shall be betrayed into the hands of men: 23 And they shall
kill him, and the third day he shall be raised
again. And they were exceeding sorry.
24 And when they were come to Capernaum,
they that received tribute *money* came to Peter,
and said, Doth not your master pay tribute?
25 He saith, Yes. And when he was come into
the house, Jesus prevented him, saying, What
thinkest thou, Simon? of whom do the kings of
the earth take custom or tribute? of their own
children, or of strangers? 26 Peter saith unto him,
Of strangers. Jesus saith unto him, Then are the
children free. 27 Notwithstanding, lest we should
offend them, go thou to the sea, and cast a hook,
and take up the fish that first cometh up; and
when thou hast opened his mouth, thou shalt
find a piece of money: that take, and give unto
them for me and thee.

Living Bible

22, 23 One day while they were still in Galilee, Jesus told them, "I am going to be betrayed
into the power of those who will kill me, and on
the third day afterwards I will be brought back
to life again." And the disciples' hearts were
filled with sorrow and dread.
24 On their arrival in Capernaum, the Temple
tax collectors came to Peter and asked him,
"Doesn't your master pay taxes?"
25 "Of course he does," Peter replied.
Then he went into the house to talk to Jesus
about it, but before he had a chance to speak,
Jesus asked him, "What do you think, Peter? Do
kings levy assessments against their own people,
or against conquered foreigners?"
26, 27 "Against the foreigners," Peter replied.
"Well, then," Jesus said, "the citizens are free!
However, we don't want to offend them, so go
down to the shore and throw in a line, and open
the mouth of the first fish you catch. You will
find a coin to cover the taxes for both of us;
take it and pay them."

Today's English Version

Jesus speaks again about his death

22 When the disciples all came together in
Galilee, Jesus said to them, "The Son of Man is
about to be handed over to men 23 who will kill
him; but on the third day he will be raised to
life."
The disciples became very sad.

Payment of the temple tax

24 When Jesus and his disciples came to Capernaum, the collectors of the temple tax came to
Peter and asked, "Does your teacher pay the
temple tax?"
25 "Of course," Peter answered.
When Peter went into the house, Jesus spoke
up first, "Simon, what is your opinion? Who
pays duties or taxes to the kings of this world?
The citizens of the country or the foreigners?"
26 "The foreigners," answered Peter.
"Well, then," replied Jesus, "that means that
the citizens don't have to pay. 27 But we don't
want to offend these people. So go to the lake
and drop in a line; pull up the first fish you
hook, and in its mouth you will find a coin
worth enough for my temple tax and yours; take
it and pay them our taxes."

New International Version

22 When they came together in Galilee, he
said to them, "The Son of Man is going to be
betrayed into the hands of men. 23 They will kill
him, and on the third day he will be raised to
life." And the disciples were filled with grief.

The temple tax

24 After Jesus and his disciples arrived in
Capernaum, the collectors of the two-drachma
tax came to Peter and asked, "Doesn't your
teacher pay the temple tax[h] ?"
25 "Yes, he does," he replied.
When Peter came into the house, Jesus was
the first to speak. "What do you think, Simon?"
he asked. "From whom do the kings of the earth
collect duty and taxes—from their own sons or
from others?"
26 "From others," Peter answered.
"Then the sons are exempt," Jesus said to him.
27 "But so that we may not offend them, go to
the lake and throw out your line. Take the first
fish you catch; open its mouth and you will find
a four-drachma coin. Take it and give it to them
for my tax and yours."

[h] Greek *the two drachmas.*

Phillips Modern English

As they went about together in Galilee, Jesus told them, "The Son of Man is going to be handed over to the power of men, and they will kill him. And on the third day he will be raised to life again." This greatly distressed the disciples.

17.24 Jesus pays the Temple-tax—in an unusual way

Then when they arrived at Capernaum the Temple tax-collectors came up and said to Peter, "Your master doesn't pay Temple-tax, we presume?"

"Oh, yes, he does!" replied Peter. Later when he went into the house Jesus anticipated what he was going to say. "What do *you* think, Simon?" he said. "Whom do the kings of this world get their tolls and taxes from—their own family or from others?"

"From others," replied Peter

"Then the family is exempt," Jesus told him. "Yet we don't want to give offence to these people, so go down to the lake and throw in your hook. Take the first fish that bites, open his mouth and you'll find a silver coin. Take that and give it to them, for both of us."

Revised Standard Version

22 As they were gathering[y] in Galilee, Jesus
said to them, "The Son of man is to be delivered
into the hands of men, 23 and they will kill him,
and he will be raised on the third day." And
they were greatly distressed.
24 When they came to Capernaum, the collectors of the half-shekel tax went up to Peter and
said, "Does not your teacher pay the tax?" 25 He
said, "Yes." And when he came home, Jesus
spoke to him first, saying, "What do you think,
Simon? From whom do kings of the earth take
toll or tribute? From their sons or from others?"
26And when he said, "From others," Jesus said
to him, "Then the sons are free. 27 However,
not to give offense to them, go to the sea and
cast a hook, and take the first fish that comes up,
and when you open its mouth you will find a
shekel; take that and give it to them for me and
for yourself."

[y] Other ancient authorities read *abode*.

Jerusalem Bible

Second prophecy of the Passion

22 One day when they were together in Galilee, Jesus said to them, "The Son of Man is
going to be handed over into the power of men;
23 they will put him to death, and on the third
day he will be raised to life again." And a great
sadness came over them.

The Temple tax paid by Jesus and Peter

24 When they reached Capernaum, the collectors of the half shekel[g] came to Peter and
said, "Does your master not pay the half shekel?"
25 "Oh yes," he replied, and went into the house.
But before he could speak, Jesus said, "Simon,
what is your opinion? From whom do the kings
of the earth take toll or tribute? From their
sons or from foreigners?" 26And when he replied, "From foreigners," Jesus said, "Well then,
the sons are exempt. 27 However, so as not to
offend these people, go to the lake and cast a
hook; take the first fish that bites, open its
mouth and there you will find a shekel; take it
and give it to them for me and for you."

[g] A tax for the upkeep of the Temple.

New English Bible

They were going about together in Galilee when Jesus said to them, 'The Son of Man is to be given up into the power of men, and they will kill him; then on the third day he will be raised again.' And they were filled with grief.

On their arrival at Capernaum the collectors of the temple-tax came up to Peter and asked, 'Does your master not pay temple-tax?' 'He does', said Peter. When he went indoors Jesus forestalled him by asking, 'What do you think about this, Simon? From whom do earthly monarchs collect tax or toll? From their own people, or from aliens?' 'From aliens', said Peter. 'Why then,' said Jesus, 'their own people are exempt! But as we do not want to cause offence, go and cast a line in the lake; take the first fish that comes to the hook, open its mouth, and you will find a silver coin; take that and pay it in; it will meet the tax for us both.'

King James Version

18 At the same time came the disciples unto Jesus, saying, Who is the greatest in the kingdom of heaven? 2And Jesus called a little child unto him, and set him in the midst of them, 3And said, Verily I say unto you, Except ye be converted, and become as little children, ye shall not enter into the kingdom of heaven. 4 Whosoever therefore shall humble himself as this little child, the same is greatest in the kingdom of heaven. 5And whoso shall receive one such little child in my name receiveth me. 6 But whoso shall offend one of these little ones which believe in me, it were better for him that a millstone were hanged about his neck, and *that* he were drowned in the depth of the sea.

7 Woe unto the world because of offences! for it must needs be that offences come; but woe to that man by whom the offence cometh! 8 Wherefore if thy hand or thy foot offend thee, cut them off, and cast *them* from thee: it is better for thee to enter into life halt or maimed, rather than having two hands or two feet to be cast into everlasting fire. 9And if thine eye offend thee, pluck it out, and cast *it* from thee: it is

Living Bible

18 About that time the disciples came to Jesus to ask which of them would be greatest in the Kingdom of Heaven!

2 Jesus called a small child over to him and set the little fellow down among them, 3 and said, "Unless you turn to God from your sins and become as little children, you will never get into the Kingdom of Heaven. 4 Therefore anyone who humbles himself as this little child, is the greatest in the Kingdom of Heaven. 5And any of you who welcomes a little child like this because you are mine, is welcoming me and caring for me. 6 But if any of you causes one of these little ones who trusts in me to lose his faith,[a] it would be better for you to have a rock tied to your neck and be thrown into the sea.

7 "Woe upon the world for all of its evils.[b] Temptation to do wrong is inevitable, but woe to the man who does the tempting. 8 So if your hand or foot causes you to sin, cut it off and throw it away. Better to enter heaven crippled than to be in hell with both of your hands and feet. 9And if your eye causes you to sin, gouge it out and throw it away. Better to enter heaven

[*a*] Literally, "cause to stumble." [*b*] Literally, "because of occasions of stumbling."

Today's English Version

Who is the greatest?

18 At that moment the disciples came to Jesus, asking, "Who is the greatest in the Kingdom of heaven?"

2 Jesus called a child, had him stand in front of them, 3 and said, "Remember this! Unless you change and become like children, you will never enter the Kingdom of heaven. 4 The greatest in the Kingdom of heaven is the one who humbles himself and becomes like this child. 5And whoever welcomes in my name one such child as this, welcomes me."

Temptations to sin

6 "If anyone should cause one of these little ones to turn away from his faith in me, it would be better for that man to have a large millstone tied around his neck and be drowned in the deep sea. 7 How terrible for the world that there are things that make people turn away! Such things will always happen—but how terrible for the one who causes them!

8 "If your hand or your foot makes you turn away, cut it off and throw it away! It is better for you to enter life without a hand or a foot than to keep both hands and both feet and be thrown into the eternal fire. 9And if your eye makes you turn away, take it out and throw it away! It is better for you to enter life with only

New International Version

The greatest in the kingdom of heaven

18 At that time the disciples came to Jesus and asked, "Who is the greatest in the kingdom of heaven?"

2 He called a little child and had him stand among them. 3And he said: "I tell you the truth, unless you change and become like little children, you will never enter the kingdom of heaven. 4 Therefore, whoever humbles himself like this child is the greatest in the kingdom of heaven. 5And whoever welcomes a little child like this in my name welcomes me.

6 "But if anyone causes one of these little ones who believe in me to sin, it would be better for him to have a large millstone hung around his neck and to be drowned in the depths of the sea. 7 Woe to the world because of the things that cause people to sin! Such things must come, but woe to the man through whom they come! 8 If your hand or your foot causes you to sin, cut it off and throw it away. It is better for you to enter life maimed or crippled than to have two hands or two feet and be thrown into eternal fire. 9And if your eye causes you to sin, gouge it out and throw it away. It is better for

Phillips Modern English

18.1 *Jesus commends the simplicity of children*

It was at this time that the disciples came to Jesus with the question, "Who is really greatest in the kingdom of Heaven?" Jesus called a little child to his side and set him on his feet in the middle of them all. "Believe me," he said, "unless you change your whole outlook and become like little children you will never enter the kingdom of Heaven. It is the man who can be as humble as this little child who is greatest in the kingdom of Heaven.

"Anyone who welcomes one child like this for my sake is welcoming me. But if anyone leads astray one of these little children who believe in me he would be better off thrown into the depths of the sea with a mill-stone hung round his neck! Alas for the world with its pitfalls! In the nature of things there must be pitfalls, yet alas for the man who is responsible for them!

18.8 *The right way may mean costly sacrifice*

"If your hand or your foot leads you astray, cut it off and throw it away. It is a good thing to go into life maimed or crippled—rather than to have both hands and feet and be thrown on to the everlasting fire. Yes, and if your eye leads you astray, tear it out and throw it away. It is a good thing to go one-eyed into life—rather than

Revised Standard Version

18 At that time the disciples came to Jesus,
saying, "Who is the greatest in the kingdom of heaven?" 2And calling to him a child,
he put him in the midst of them, 3 and said,
"Truly, I say to you, unless you turn and become like children, you will never enter the
kingdom of heaven. 4 Whoever humbles himself like this child, he is the greatest in the
kingdom of heaven.
5 "Whoever receives one such child in my
name receives me; 6 but whoever causes one of
these little ones who believe in me to sin,[z] it
would be better for him to have a great millstone fastened round his neck and to be drowned
in the depth of the sea.
7 "Woe to the world for temptations to sin![a]
For it is necessary that temptations come, but woe
to the man by whom the temptation comes!
8And if your hand or your foot causes you to
sin,[z] cut it off and throw it away; it is better for
you to enter life maimed or lame than with two
hands or two feet to be thrown into the eternal
fire. 9And if your eye causes you to sin,[z] pluck
it out and throw it away; it is better for you to

[z] Greek *causes . . . to stumble.* [a] Greek *stumbling blocks.*

Jerusalem Bible

B. The discourse on the church

Who is the greatest?

18 At this time the disciples came to Jesus
and said, "Who is the greatest in the kingdom of heaven?" 2 So he called a little child to
him and set the child in front of them. 3 Then
he said, "I tell you solemnly, unless you change
and become like little children you will never
enter the kingdom of heaven. 4And so, the one
who makes himself as little as this little child is
the greatest in the kingdom of heaven.

On leading others astray

5 "Anyone who welcomes a little child like
this in my name welcomes me. 6 But anyone
who is an obstacle to bring down one of these
little ones who have faith in me would be better
drowned in the depths of the sea with a great
millstone around his neck. 7Alas for the world
that there should be such obstacles! Obstacles
indeed there must be, but alas for the man who
provides them!
8 "If your hand or your foot should cause
you to sin, cut it off and throw it away: it is
better for you to enter into life crippled or lame,
than to have two hands or two feet and be
thrown into eternal fire. 9And if your eye should
cause you to sin, tear it out and throw it away:
it is better for you to enter into life with one

New English Bible

18 At that time the disciples came to Jesus and asked, 'Who is the greatest in the kingdom of Heaven?' He called a child, set him in front of them, and said, 'I tell you this: unless you turn round and become like children, you will never enter the kingdom of Heaven. Let a man humble himself till he is like this child, and he will be the greatest in the kingdom of Heaven. Whoever receives one such child in my name receives me. But if a man is a cause of stumbling to one of these little ones who have faith in me, it would be better for him to have a millstone hung round his neck and be drowned in the depths of the sea. Alas for the world that such causes of stumbling arise! Come they must, but woe betide the man through whom they come!

'If your hand or your foot is your undoing, cut it off and fling it away; it is better for you to enter into life maimed or lame, than to keep two hands or two feet and be thrown into the eternal fire. If it is your eye that is your undoing, tear it out and fling it away; it is

King James Version

better for thee to enter into life with one eye,
rather than having two eyes to be cast into hell
fire. 10 Take heed that ye despise not one of
these little ones; for I say unto you, That in
heaven their angels do always behold the face of
my Father which is in heaven. 11 For the Son of
man is come to save that which was lost.
12 How think ye? if a man have a hundred
sheep, and one of them be gone astray, doth he
not leave the ninety and nine, and goeth into
the mountains, and seeketh that which is gone
astray? 13 And if so be that he find it, verily I say
unto you, he rejoiceth more of that *sheep,* than
of the ninety and nine which went not astray.
14 Even so it is not the will of your Father
which is in heaven, that one of these little ones
should perish.
15 Moreover if thy brother shall trespass
against thee, go and tell him his fault between
thee and him alone: if he shall hear thee, thou
hast gained thy brother. 16 But if he will not
hear *thee, then* take with thee one or two more,
that in the mouth of two or three witnesses every
word may be established. 17 And if he shall
neglect to hear them, tell *it* unto the church: but
if he neglect to hear the church, let him be unto

Living Bible

with one eye than to be in hell with two.
10 "Beware that you don't look down upon
a single one of these little children. For I tell
you that in heaven their angels have constant
access[c] to my Father. 11 And I, the Messiah,[d]
came to save the lost.[e]
12 "If a man has a hundred sheep, and one
wanders away and is lost, what will he do?
Won't he leave the ninety-nine others and go
out into the hills to search for the lost one?
13 And if he finds it, he will rejoice over it more
than over the ninety-nine others safe at home!
14 Just so, it is not my Father's will that even
one of these little ones should perish.
15 "If a brother sins against you, go to him
privately and confront him with his fault. If
he listens and confesses it, you have won back
a brother. 16 But if not, then take one or two
others with you and go back to him again, proving everything you say by these witnesses. 17 If
he still refuses to listen, then take your case to
the church, and if the church's verdict favors
you, but he won't accept it, then the church

[c] "Do always behold . . ." [d] Literally, "the Son of Man." [e] This verse is omitted in many manuscripts, some ancient.

Today's English Version

one eye than to keep both eyes and be thrown
into the fire of hell."

The parable of the lost sheep

10 "See that you don't despise any of these
little ones. Their angels in heaven, I tell you, are
always in the presence of my Father in heaven.
[11 For the Son of Man came to save the lost.]
12 "What do you think? What will a man do
who has one hundred sheep and one of them
gets lost? He will leave the other ninety-nine
grazing on the hillside and go to look for the
lost sheep. 13 When he finds it, I tell you, he
feels far happier over this one sheep than over
the ninety-nine that did not get lost. 14 In just
the same way your Father in heaven does not
want any of these littles ones to be lost."

A brother who sins

15 "If your brother sins against you, go to
him and show him his fault. But do it privately,
just between yourselves. If he listens to you, you
have won your brother back. 16 But if he will
not listen to you, take one or two other persons
with you, so that 'every accusation may be upheld by the testimony of two or three witnesses,'
as the scripture says. 17 But if he will not listen
to them, then tell the whole thing to the church.
And then, if he will not listen to the church, treat
him as though he were a foreigner or a tax
collector."

New International Version

you to enter life with one eye than to have two
eyes and be thrown into the fire of hell.

The parable of the lost sheep

10 "See that you do not look down on one of
these little ones. For I tell you that their angels
in heaven always see the face of my Father in
heaven.[i]
12 "What do you think? If a man owns a
hundred sheep, and one of them wanders away,
will he not leave the ninety-nine on the hills and
go to look for the one that wandered off? 13 And
if he finds it, I tell you the truth, he is happier
about that one sheep than about the ninety-nine
that did not wander off. 14 In the same way your
Father in heaven is not willing that any of these
little ones should be lost.

A brother who sins against you

15 "If your brother sins against you, go and
show him his fault, just between the two of you.
If he listens to you, you have won your brother
over. 16 But if he will not listen, take one or
two others along, so that 'every matter may be
established by the testimony of two or three
witnesses.'[j] 17 If he refuses to listen to them, tell
it to the church; and if he refuses to listen even
to the church, treat him as you would a pagan
or a tax collector.

[i] Some MSS add verse 11: *The Son of Man came to save what was lost.* [j] Deut. 19:15.

Phillips Modern English

to have both your eyes and be thrown on the fire of the rubbish-heap.

"Be careful that you never despise a single one of these little ones—for I tell you that they have angels who see my Father's face continually in Heaven.

"What do you think? If a man has a hundred sheep and one wanders away from the rest, won't he leave the ninety-nine on the hill-side and set out to look for the one who has wandered away? Yes, and if he should chance to find it I assure you he is more delighted over that one than he is over the ninety-nine who never wandered away. You can understand then that it is never the will of your Father in Heaven that a single one of these little ones should be lost.

18.15 Reconciliation must always be attempted

"But if your brother wrongs you, go and have it out with him at once—just between the two of you. If he will listen to you, you have won him back as your brother. But if he will not listen to you, take one or two others with you so that everything that is said may have the support of two or three witnesses. And if he still won't pay any attention, tell the matter to the church. And if he won't even listen to the church then he must be to you just like a pagan —or a tax-collector!

Revised Standard Version

enter life with one eye than with two eyes to
be thrown into the hell [b] of fire.
10 "See that you do not despise one of these
little ones; for I tell you that in heaven their
angels always behold the face of my Father
who is in heaven.[c] 12 What do you think? If a
man has a hundred sheep, and one of them has
gone astray, does he not leave the ninety-nine
on the mountains and go in search of the one
that went astray? 13 And if he finds it, truly, I
say to you, he rejoices over it more than over
the ninety-nine that never went astray. 14 So it
is not the will of my[d] Father who is in heaven
that one of these little ones should perish.
15 "If your brother sins against you, go and
tell him his fault, between you and him alone.
If he listens to you, you have gained your
brother. 16 But if he does not listen, take one
or two others along with you, that every word
may be confirmed by the evidence of two or
three witnesses. 17 If he refuses to listen to them,
tell it to the church; and if he refuses to listen
even to the church, let him be to you as a Gen-

[*b*] Greek *Gehenna*. [*c*] Other ancient authorities add verse 11, *For the Son of man came to save the lost.* [*d*] Other ancient authorities read *your*.

Jerusalem Bible

eye, than to have two eyes and be thrown into
the hell of fire.
10 "See that you never despise any of these
little ones, for I tell you that their angels in
heaven are continually in the presence of my
Father in heaven.[h]

The lost sheep

12 "Tell me. Suppose a man has a hundred
sheep and one of them strays; will he not leave
the ninety-nine on the hillside and go in search
of the stray? 13 I tell you solemnly, if he finds
it, it gives him more joy than do the ninety-nine
that did not stray at all. 14 Similarly, it is never
the will of your Father in heaven that one of
these little ones should be lost.

Brotherly correction

15 "If your brother does something wrong,
go and have it out with him alone, between
your two selves. If he listens to you, you have
won back your brother. 16 If he does not listen,
take one or two others along with you: *the evidence of two or three witnesses is required to
sustain any charge.* 17 But if he refuses to listen
to these, report it to the community[i]; and if he
refuses to listen to the community, treat him like
a pagan or a tax collector.

[*h*] V. 11, at the time when verse numbers were added, consisted of a sentence which is not now accepted as part of the original text. [*i*] The community of the brothers (the Church).

New English Bible

better to enter into life with one eye than to keep both eyes and be thrown into the fires of hell.

'Never despise one of these little ones; I tell you, they have their guardian angels in heaven, who look continually on the face of my heavenly Father.[a]

'What do you think? Suppose a man has a hundred sheep. If one of them strays, does he not leave the other ninety-nine on the hillside and go in search of the one that strayed? And if he should find it, I tell you this: he is more delighted over that sheep than over the ninety-nine that never strayed. In the same way, it is not your heavenly Father's will that one of these little ones should be lost.

'If your brother commits a sin,[b] go and take the matter up with him, strictly between yourselves, and if he listens to you, you have won your brother over. If he will not listen, take one or two others with you, so that all facts may be duly established on the evidence of two or three witnesses. If he refuses to listen to them, report the matter to the congregation; and if he will not listen even to the congregation, you must then treat him as you would a pagan or a taxgatherer.

[*a*] *Some witnesses add* (11) For the Son of Man came to save the lost. [*b*] *Some witnesses insert* against you.

King James Version

thee as a heathen man and a publican. 18 Verily
I say unto you, Whatsoever ye shall bind on
earth shall be bound in heaven; and whatsoever
ye shall loose on earth shall be loosed in heaven.
19 Again I say unto you, That if two of you shall
agree on earth as touching any thing that they
shall ask, it shall be done for them of my Father
which is in heaven. 20 For where two or three
are gathered together in my name, there am I
in the midst of them.
21 Then came Peter to him, and said, Lord,
how oft shall my brother sin against me, and I
forgive him? till seven times? 22 Jesus saith unto
him, I say not unto thee, Until seven times: but,
Until seventy times seven.
23 Therefore is the kingdom of heaven likened
unto a certain king, which would take account
of his servants. 24 And when he had begun to
reckon, one was brought unto him, which owed
him ten thousand talents. 25 But forasmuch as
he had not to pay, his lord commanded him to

Living Bible

should excommunicate him.[f] 18 And I tell you
this—whatever you bind on earth is bound in
heaven, and whatever you free on earth will be
freed in heaven.
19 "I also tell you this—if two of you agree
down here on earth concerning anything you ask
for, my Father in heaven will do it for you.
20 For where two or three gather together because they are mine, I will be right there among
them."
21 Then Peter came to him and asked, "Sir,
how often should I forgive a brother who sins
against me? Seven times?"
22 "No!" Jesus replied, "seventy times seven!
23 "The Kingdom of Heaven can be compared
to a king who decided to bring his accounts up
to date. 24 In the process, one of his debtors was
brought in who owed him $10,000,000! [g] 25 He
couldn't pay, so the king ordered him sold for

[*f*] Literally, "let him be to you as the Gentile and the publican." [*g*] Literally, "10,000 talents." Approximately £3,000,000.

Today's English Version

Prohibiting and permitting

18 "And so I tell all of you: what you prohibit
on earth will be prohibited in heaven; what you
permit on earth will be permitted in heaven.
19 "And I tell you more: whenever two of you
on earth agree about anything you pray for, it
will be done for you by my Father in heaven.
20 For where two or three come together in my
name, I am there with them."

The parable of the unforgiving servant

21 Then Peter came to Jesus and asked, "Lord,
how many times can my brother sin against me
and I have to forgive him? Seven times?"
22 "No, not seven times," answered Jesus, "but
seventy times seven. 23 Because the Kingdom of
heaven is like a king who decided to check on
his servants' accounts. 24 He had just begun to
do so when one of them was brought in who
owed him millions of dollars. 25 The servant did
not have enough to pay his debt, so his master
ordered him to be sold as a slave, with his wife

New International Version

18 "I tell you the truth, whatever you bind
on earth will be bound in heaven, and whatever you loose on earth will be loosed in heaven.
19 "Again, I tell you that if two of you on
earth agree about anything you ask for, it will
be done for you by my Father in heaven. 20 For
where two or three come together in my name,
there am I with them."

The parable of the unmerciful servant

21 Then Peter came to Jesus and asked,
"Lord, how many times shall I forgive my brother
when he sins against me? Up to seven times?"
22 Jesus answered, "I tell you, not seven
times, but seventy-seven times.[k]
23 "Therefore, the kingdom of heaven is like
a king who wanted to settle accounts with his
servants. 24 As he began the settlement, a man
who owed him ten thousand talents[l] was brought
to him. 25 Since he was not able to pay, the
master ordered that he and his wife and his

[*k*] Or *seventy times seven.* [*l*] That is, several million dollars.

Phillips Modern English

18.18 The connection between earthly conduct and spiritual reality

"Believe me, whatever you forbid upon earth will be what is forbidden in Heaven, and whatever you permit on earth will be what is permitted in Heaven.

"And I tell you once more that if two of you on earth agree in asking for anything it will be granted to you by my Heavenly Father. For wherever two or three people have come together in my name, I am there, right among them!"

18.21 The necessity for forgiveness

Then Peter approached him with the question, "Master, if my brother goes on wronging me how often should I forgive him? Would seven times be enough?"

"No," replied Jesus, "not seven times, but seventy times seven! For the kingdom of Heaven is like a king who decided to settle his accounts with his servants. When he had started calling in his accounts, a man was brought to him who owed him millions of pounds. As he had no means of repaying the debt, his master gave orders for him to be sold as a slave, and his wife

Revised Standard Version

tile and a tax collector. 18 Truly, I say to you, whatever you bind on earth shall be bound in heaven, and whatever you loose on earth shall be loosed in heaven. 19Again I say to you, if two of you agree on earth about anything they ask, it will be done for them by my Father in heaven. 20 For where two or three are gathered in my name, there am I in the midst of them."

21 Then Peter came up and said to him, "Lord, how often shall my brother sin against me, and I forgive him? As many as seven times?" 22 Jesus said to him, "I do not say to you seven times, but seventy times seven.[e]

23 "Therefore the kingdom of heaven may be compared to a king who wished to settle accounts with his servants. 24 When he began the reckoning, one was brought to him who owed him ten thousand talents;[f] 25 and as he could not pay, his lord ordered him to be sold, with

[e] Or *seventy-seven times.* [f] This talent was more than fifteen years' wages of a laborer.

Jerusalem Bible

18 "I tell you solemnly, whatever you bind on earth shall be considered bound in heaven; whatever you loose on earth shall be considered loosed in heaven.

Prayer in common

19 "I tell you solemnly once again, if two of you on earth agree to ask anything at all, it will be granted to you by my Father in heaven. 20 For where two or three meet in my name, I shall be there with them."

Forgiveness of injuries

21 Then Peter went up to him and said, "Lord, how often must I forgive my brother if he wrongs me? As often as seven times?" 22 Jesus answered, "Not seven, I tell you, but seventy-seven times.

Parable of the unforgiving debtor

23 "And so the kingdom of heaven may be compared to a king who decided to settle his accounts with his servants. 24 When the reckoning began, they brought him a man who owed ten thousand talents[j]; 25 but he had no means of paying, so his master gave orders that he should be sold, together with his wife and chil-

[j] "Millions of dollars"—about $7,000,000.

New English Bible

'I tell you this: whatever you forbid on earth shall be forbidden in heaven, and whatever you allow on earth shall be allowed in heaven.

'Again I tell you this: if two of you agree on earth about any request you have to make, that request will be granted by my heavenly Father. For where two or three have met together in my name, I am there among them.'

Then Peter came up and asked him, 'Lord, how often am I to forgive my brother if he goes on wronging me? As many as seven times?' Jesus replied, 'I do not say seven times; I say seventy times seven.[a]

'The kingdom of Heaven, therefore, should be thought of in this way: There was once a king who decided to settle accounts with the men who served him. At the outset there appeared before him a man whose debt ran into millions.[b] Since he had no means of paying, his master ordered him to be sold to meet the debt,

[a] *Or* seventy-seven times. [b] *Literally* who owed 10,000 talents.

King James Version

be sold, and his wife, and children, and all that he had, and payment to be made. 26 The servant therefore fell down, and worshipped him, saying, Lord, have patience with me, and I will pay thee all. 27 Then the lord of that servant was moved with compassion, and loosed him, and forgave him the debt. 28 But the same servant went out, and found one of his fellow servants, which owed him a hundred pence: and he laid hands on him, and took *him* by the throat, saying, Pay me that thou owest. 29 And his fellow servant fell down at his feet, and besought him, saying, Have patience with me, and I will pay thee all. 30 And he would not: but went and cast him into prison, till he should pay the debt. 31 So when his fellow servants saw what was done, they were very sorry, and came and told unto their lord all that was done. 32 Then his lord, after that he had called him, said unto him, O thou wicked servant, I forgave thee all that debt, because thou desiredst me: 33 Shouldest not thou also have had compassion on thy fellow servant, even as I had pity on thee? 34 And his lord was wroth, and delivered him to the tormentors, till he should pay all that was due unto him. 35 So likewise shall my heavenly Father do also unto you, if ye from your hearts forgive not every one his brother their trespasses.

Living Bible

the debt, also his wife and children and everything he had.

26 "But the man fell down before the king, his face in the dust, and said, 'Oh, sir, be patient with me and I will pay it all.'

27 "Then the king was filled with pity for him and released him and forgave his debt.

28 "But when the man left the king, he went to a man who owed him $2,000 [h] and grabbed him by the throat and demanded instant payment.

29 "The man fell down before him and begged him to give him a little time. 'Be patient and I will pay it,' he pled.

30 "But his creditor wouldn't wait. He had the man arrested and jailed until the debt would be paid in full.

31 "Then the man's friends went to the king and told him what had happened. 32 And the king called before him the man he had forgiven and said, 'You evil-hearted wretch! Here I forgave you all that tremendous debt, just because you asked me to—33 shouldn't you have mercy on others, just as I had mercy on you?'

34 "Then the angry king sent the man to the torture chamber until he had paid every last penny due. 35 So shall my heavenly Father do to you if you refuse to truly forgive your brothers."

[*h*] Approximately £700.

Today's English Version

and his children and all that he had, in order to pay the debt. 26 The servant fell on his knees before his master. 'Be patient with me,' he begged, 'and I will pay you everything!' 27 The master felt sorry for him, so he forgave him the debt and let him go.

28 "The man went out and met one of his fellow servants who owed him a few dollars. He grabbed him and started choking him. 'Pay back what you owe me!' he said. 29 His fellow servant fell down and begged him, 'Be patient with me and I will pay you back!' 30 But he would not; instead, he had him thrown into jail until he should pay the debt. 31 When the other servants saw what had happened, they were very upset, and went to their master and told him everything. 32 So the master called the servant in. 'You worthless slave!' he said. 'I forgave you the whole amount you owed me, just because you asked me to. 33 You should have had mercy on your fellow servant, just as I had mercy on you.' 34 The master was very angry, and he sent the servant to jail to be punished until he should pay back the whole amount."

35 And Jesus concluded, "That is how my Father in heaven will treat you if you do not forgive your brother, every one of you, from your heart."

New International Version

children and all that he had be sold to repay the debt.

26 "The servant fell on his knees before him. 'Be patient with me,' he begged, 'and I will pay back everything.' 27 The servant's master took pity on him, canceled the debt and let him go.

28 "But when that servant went out, he found one of his fellow servants who owed him a hundred denarii.[m] He grabbed him and began to choke him. 'Pay back what you owe me!' he demanded.

29 "His fellow servant fell to his knees and begged him, 'Be patient with me, and I will pay you back.'

30 "But he refused. Instead, he went off and had the man thrown in prison until he could pay the debt. 31 When the other servants saw what had happened, they were greatly distressed and went and told their master everything that had happened.

32 "Then the master called the servant in. 'You wicked servant,' he said, 'I canceled all that debt of yours because you begged me to. 33 Shouldn't you have had mercy on your fellow servant just as I had on you?' 34 In anger his master turned him over to the jailers until he should pay back all he owed.

35 "This is how my heavenly Father will treat each of you unless you forgive your brother from your heart."

[*m*] That is, a few dollars.

Phillips Modern English

and children and all his possessions as well, and the money to be paid over. At this the servant fell on his knees before his master, 'Oh, be patient with me!' he cried, 'and I will pay you back every penny!' Then his master was moved with pity for him, set him free and cancelled his debt.

"But when this same servant had left his master's presence, he found one of his fellow-servants who owed him a few shillings. He grabbed him and seized him by the throat, crying, 'Pay up what you owe me!' At this his fellow-servant fell down at his feet, and implored him, 'Oh, be patient with me, and I will pay you back!' But he refused and went out and had him put in prison until he should repay the debt.

"When the other fellow-servants saw what had happened, they were horrified and went and told their master the whole incident. Then his master called him in.

" 'You wicked servant!' he said. 'Didn't I cancel all that debt when you begged me to do so? Oughtn't you to have taken pity on your fellow-servant as I, your master, took pity on you?' And his master in anger handed him over to the jailers till he should repay the whole debt. This is how my Heavenly Father will treat you unless you each forgive your brother from your heart."

Revised Standard Version

his wife and children and all that he had, and
payment to be made. 26 So the servant fell on
his knees, imploring him, 'Lord, have patience
with me, and I will pay you everything.' 27 And
out of pity for him the lord of that servant released him and forgave him the debt. 28 But that
same servant, as he went out, came upon one of
his fellow servants who owed him a hundred
denarii;[g] and seizing him by the throat he said,
'Pay what you owe.' 29 So his fellow servant fell
down and besought him, 'Have patience with
me, and I will pay you.' 30 He refused and went
and put him in prison till he should pay the
debt. 31 When his fellow servants saw what had
taken place, they were greatly distressed, and
they went and reported to their lord all that had
taken place. 32 Then his lord summoned him
and said to him, 'You wicked servant! I forgave
you all that debt because you besought me;
33 and should not you have had mercy on your
fellow servant, as I had mercy on you?' 34 And
in anger his lord delivered him to the jailers,[h]
till he should pay all his debt. 35 So also my
heavenly Father will do to every one of you, if
you do not forgive your brother from your
heart."

[g] The denarius was a day's wage for a laborer.
[h] Greek *torturers*.

Jerusalem Bible

dren and all his possessions, to meet the debt.
26 At this, the servant threw himself down at his
master's feet. 'Give me time,' he said, 'and I
will pay the whole sum.' 27 And the servant's
master felt so sorry for him that he let him go
and canceled the debt. 28 Now as this servant
went out, he happened to meet a fellow servant
who owed him one hundred denarii[k]; and he
seized him by the throat and began to throttle
him. 'Pay what you owe me,' he said. 29 His fellow servant fell at his feet and implored him,
saying, 'Give me time and I will pay you.' 30 But
the other would not agree; on the contrary, he
had him thrown into prison till he should pay
the debt. 31 His fellow servants were deeply distressed when they saw what had happened, and
they went to their master and reported the whole
affair to him. 32 Then the master sent for him.
'You wicked servant,' he said, 'I canceled all
that debt of yours when you appealed to me.
33 Were you not bound, then, to have pity on
your fellow servant just as I had pity on you?'
34 And in his anger the master handed him over
to the torturers till he should pay all his debt.
35 And that is how my heavenly Father will deal
with you unless you each forgive your brother
from your heart."

[k] Under $12.

New English Bible

with his wife, his children, and everything he had. The man fell prostrate at his master's feet. "Be patient with me," he said, "and I will pay in full"; and the master was so moved with pity that he let the man go and remitted the debt. But no sooner had the man gone out than he met a fellow-servant who owed him a few pounds;[c] and catching hold of him he gripped him by the throat and said, "Pay me what you owe." The man fell at his fellow-servant's feet, and begged him, "Be patient with me, and I will pay you"; but he refused, and had him jailed until he should pay the debt. The other servants were deeply distressed when they saw what had happened, and they went to their master and told him the whole story. He accordingly sent for the man. "You scoundrel!" he said to him; "I remitted the whole of your debt when you appealed to me; were you not bound to show your fellow-servant the same pity as I showed you?" And so angry was the master that he condemned the man to torture until he should pay the debt in full. And that is how my heavenly Father will deal with you, unless you each forgive your brother from your hearts.'

[c] *Literally* owed him 100 denarii.

King James Version

19 And it came to pass, *that* when Jesus had
finished these sayings, he departed from
Galilee, and came into the coasts of Judea beyond Jordan; 2 And great multitudes followed
him; and he healed them there.
3 The Pharisees also came unto him, tempting
him, and saying unto him, Is it lawful for a man
to put away his wife for every cause? 4 And he
answered and said unto them, Have ye not read,
that he which made *them* at the beginning made
them male and female, 5 And said, For this cause
shall a man leave father and mother, and shall
cleave to his wife: and they twain shall be one
flesh? 6 Wherefore they are no more twain, but
one flesh. What therefore God hath joined together, let not man put asunder. 7 They say unto
him, Why did Moses then command to give a
writing of divorcement, and to put her away?
8 He saith unto them, Moses because of the
hardness of your hearts suffered you to put away
your wives: but from the beginning it was not
so. 9 And I say unto you, Whosoever shall put
away his wife, except *it be* for fornication, and
shall marry another, committeth adultery: and
whoso marrieth her which is put away doth commit adultery.

Living Bible

19 After Jesus had finished this address, he
left Galilee and circled back to Judea from
across the Jordan River. 2 Vast crowds followed
him, and he healed their sick. 3 Some Pharisees
came to interview him, and tried to trap him
into saying something that would ruin him.
"Do you permit divorce?" they asked.
4 "Don't you read the Scriptures?" he replied.
"In them it is written that at the beginning God
created man and woman, 5, 6 and that a man
should leave his father and mother, and be forever united to his wife. The two shall become
one—no longer two, but one! And no man may
divorce what God has joined together."
7 "Then, why," they asked, "did Moses say a
man may divorce his wife by merely writing her
a letter of dismissal?"
8 Jesus replied, "Moses did that in recognition
of your hard and evil hearts, but it was not what
God had originally intended. 9 And I tell you
this, that anyone who divorces his wife, except
for fornication, and marries another, commits
adultery." [a]

[a] "And the man who marries a divorced woman commits adultery." This sentence is added in some ancient manuscripts.

Today's English Version

Jesus teaches about divorce

19 When Jesus finished saying these things,
he left Galilee and went to the territory of
Judea, on the other side of the Jordan River.
2 Large crowds followed him, and he healed
them there.
3 Some Pharisees came to him and tried to
trap him by asking, "Does our Law allow a man
to divorce his wife for any reason he wishes?"
4 Jesus answered, "Haven't you read this
scripture? 'In the beginning the Creator made
them male and female, 5 and said, "For this reason a man will leave his father and mother and
unite with his wife, and the two will become
one." ' 6 So they are no longer two, but one. Man
must not separate, then, what God has joined
together."
7 The Pharisees asked him, "Why, then, did
Moses give the commandment for a man to give
his wife a divorce notice and send her away?"
8 Jesus answered, "Moses gave you permission to divorce your wives because you are so
hard to teach. But it was not this way at the
time of creation. 9 I tell you, then, that any man
who divorces his wife, and she has not been unfaithful, commits adultery if he marries some
other woman."

New International Version

Divorce

19 When Jesus had finished saying these
things, he left Galilee and went into the
region of Judea to the other side of the Jordan.
2 Large crowds followed him, and he healed
them there.
3 Some Pharisees came to him to test him.
They asked, "Is it lawful for a man to divorce
his wife for any and every reason?"
4 "Haven't you read," he replied, "that at the
beginning the Creator 'made them male and female,' [n] 5 and said, 'For this reason a man will
leave his father and mother and be united to his
wife, and the two will become one flesh' [o]?
6 So they are no longer two, but one. Therefore
what God has joined together, let man not
separate."
7 "Why then," they asked, "did Moses command that a man give his wife a certificate of
divorce and send her away?"
8 Jesus replied, "Moses permitted you to divorce your wives because your hearts were hard.
But it was not this way from the beginning. 9 I
tell you that anyone who divorces his wife, except for marital unfaithfulness, and marries another woman commits adultery."

[n] Gen. 1:27. [o] Gen. 2:24.

Phillips Modern English

19.1 The divine principle of marriage

When Jesus had finished talking on these matters, he left Galilee and went on to the district of Judaea on the far side of the Jordan. Vast crowds followed him, and he healed them there.

Then the Pharisees arrived with a test-question. "Is it right," they asked, "for a man to divorce his wife on any grounds whatever?"

"Haven't you read," he answered, "that the one who created them from the beginning made them male and female and said: 'For this cause shall a man leave his father and mother, and shall cleave to his wife; and the twain shall become one flesh'? So they are no longer two separate people but one. No man therefore must separate what God has joined together."

"Then why," they retorted, "did Moses command us to give a written divorce-notice and dismiss the woman?"

"It was because you knew so little of the meaning of love that Moses allowed you to divorce your wives! But that was not the original principle. I tell you that anyone who divorces his wife on any grounds except her unfaithfulness and marries some other woman commits adultery."

Revised Standard Version

19 Now when Jesus had finished these sayings, he went away from Galilee and entered the region of Judea beyond the Jordan;
2 and large crowds followed him, and he healed them there.
3 And Pharisees came up to him and tested him by asking, "Is it lawful to divorce one's wife for any cause?" 4 He answered, "Have you not read that he who made them from the beginning made them male and female, 5 and said, 'For this reason a man shall leave his father and mother and be joined to his wife, and the two shall become one flesh'? 6 So they are no longer two but one flesh. What therefore God has joined together, let not man put asunder."
7 They said to him, "Why then did Moses command one to give a certificate of divorce, and to put her away?" 8 He said to them, "For your hardness of heart Moses allowed you to divorce your wives, but from the beginning it was not so. 9 And I say to you: whoever divorces his wife, except for unchastity,[j] and marries another, commits adultery." [k]

[j] Other ancient authorities, after *unchastity*, read *makes her commit adultery*. [k] Other ancient authorities insert *and he who marries a divorced woman commits adultery*.

Jerusalem Bible

VI. The approaching advent of the kingdom of heaven

A. Narrative section

The question about divorce

19 Jesus had now finished what he wanted to say, and he left Galilee and came into the part of Judaea which is on the far side of the Jordan. 2 Large crowds followed him and he healed them there.
3 Some Pharisees approached him, and to test him they said, "Is it against the Law for a man to divorce his wife on any pretext whatever?"
4 He answered, "Have you not read that the creator from the beginning *made them male and female* 5 and that he said: *This is why a man must leave father and mother, and cling to his wife, and the two become one body?* 6 They are no longer two, therefore, but one body. So then, what God has united, man must not divide."
7 They said to him, "Then why did Moses command that a writ of dismissal should be given in cases of divorce?" 8 "It was because you were so unteachable," he said, "that Moses allowed you to divorce your wives, but it was not like this from the beginning. 9 Now I say this to you: the man who divorces his wife—I am not speaking of fornication—and marries another, is guilty of adultery."

New English Bible

19 When Jesus had finished this discourse he left Galilee and came into the region of Judaea across Jordan. Great crowds followed him, and he healed them there.

Some Pharisees came and tested him by asking, 'Is it lawful for a man to divorce his wife on any and every ground?' [d] He asked in return, 'Have you never read that the Creator made them from the beginning male and female?'; and he added, 'For this reason a man shall leave his father and mother, and be made one with his wife; and the two shall become one flesh. It follows that they are no longer two individuals: they are one flesh. What God has joined together, man must not separate.' 'Why then', they objected, 'did Moses lay it down that a man might divorce his wife by note of dismissal?' He answered, 'It was because your minds were closed that Moses gave you permission to divorce your wives; but it was not like that when all began. I tell you, if a man divorces his wife for any cause other than unchastity, and marries another, he commits adultery.' [a]

[d] *Or* Is there any ground on which it is lawful for a man to divorce his wife? [a] *Some witnesses add* And the man who marries a woman so divorced commits adultery.

King James Version

10 His disciples say unto him, If the case of the man be so with *his* wife, it is not good to marry. 11 But he said unto them, All *men* cannot receive this saying, save *they* to whom it is given. 12 For there are some eunuchs, which were so born from *their* mother's womb: and there are some eunuchs, which were made eunuchs of men: and there be eunuchs, which have made themselves eunuchs for the kingdom of heaven's sake. He that is able to receive *it*, let him receive *it*.

13 Then were there brought unto him little children, that he should put *his* hands on them, and pray: and the disciples rebuked them. 14 But Jesus said, Suffer little children, and forbid them not, to come unto me; for of such is the kingdom of heaven. 15 And he laid *his* hands on them, and departed thence.

16 And, behold, one came and said unto him, Good Master, what good thing shall I do, that I may have eternal life? 17 And he said unto him, Why callest thou me good? *there is* none good but one, *that is*, God: but if thou wilt enter into

Living Bible

10 Jesus' diciples then said to him, "If that is how it is, it is better not to marry!"

11 "Not everyone can accept this statement," Jesus said. "Only those whom God helps. 12 Some are born without the ability to marry,[b] and some are disabled by men, and some refuse to marry for the sake of the Kingdom of Heaven. Let anyone who can, accept my statement."

13 Little children were brought for Jesus to lay his hands on them and pray. But the disciples scolded those who brought them. "Don't bother him," they said.

14 But Jesus said, "Let the little children come to me, and don't prevent them. For of such is the Kingdom of Heaven." 15 And he put his hands on their heads and blessed them before he left.

16 Someone came to Jesus with this question: "Good master, what must I do to have eternal life?"

17 "When you call me good you are calling me God," Jesus replied, "for God alone is truly good.[c] But to answer your question, you can get to heaven if you keep the commandments."

[b] Literally, "born eunuchs," or, "born emasculated." [c] Implied from Luke 18:19.

Today's English Version

10 His disciples said to him, "If this is the way it is between a man and his wife, it is better not to marry."

11 Jesus answered, "This teaching does not apply to everyone, but only to those to whom God has given it. 12 For there are different reasons why men cannot marry: some, because they were born that way; others, because men made them that way; and others do not marry because of the Kingdom of heaven. Let him who can do it accept this teaching."

Jesus blesses little children

13 Some people brought children to Jesus for him to place his hands on them and pray, but the disciples scolded those people. 14 Jesus said, "Let the children come to me, and do not stop them, because the Kingdom of heaven belongs to such as these."

15 He placed his hands on them and left.

The rich young man

16 Once a man came to Jesus. "Teacher," he asked, "what good thing must I do to receive eternal life?"

17 "Why do you ask me concerning what is good?" answered Jesus. "There is only One who is good. Keep the commandments if you want to enter life."

New International Version

10 The disciples said to him, "If this is the situation between a husband and wife, it is better not to marry."

11 Jesus replied, "Not everyone can accept this teaching, but only those to whom it has been given. 12 For some are eunuchs because they were born that way; others were made that way by men; and others have renounced marriage[p] because of the kingdom of heaven. The one who can accept this should accept it."

The little children and Jesus

13 Then little children were brought to Jesus for him to place his hands on them and pray for them. But the disciples rebuked those who brought them.

14 Jesus said, "Let the little children come to me, and do not hinder them, for the kingdom of heaven belongs to such as these." 15 When he had placed his hands on them, he went on from there.

The rich young man

16 Now a man came up to Jesus and asked, "Teacher, what good thing must I do to get eternal life?"

17 "Why do you ask me about what is good?" Jesus replied. "There is only One who is good. If you want to enter life, obey the commandments."

[p] Or *have made themselves eunuchs.*

Phillips Modern English

His disciples said to him, "If that is a man's position with his wife, it is not worth getting married!"

"It is not everybody who can accept this principle," replied Jesus, "—only those who have a special gift. For some are incapable of marriage from birth, some are made incapable by the action of men, and some have made themselves so for the sake of the kingdom of Heaven. Let the man who can accept what I have said accept it."

19.13 Jesus welcomes children

Then some little children were brought to him, so that he could put his hands on them and pray for them. The disciples strongly disapproved of this but Jesus said,

"You must let little children come to me, and you must never stop them. The kingdom of Heaven belongs to little children like these!" Then he laid his hands on them and walked away.

19.16 Jesus shows that keeping the commandments is not enough

Then it happened that a man came up to him and said, "Master what good thing must I do to secure eternal life?"

"I wonder why you ask me about what is good?" Jesus answered him. "Only One is good.

Revised Standard Version

10 The disciples said to him, "If such is the
case of a man with his wife, it is not expedient
to marry." 11 But he said to them, "Not all men
can receive this saying, but only those to whom
it is given. 12 For there are eunuchs who have
been so from birth, and there are eunuchs who
have been made eunuchs by men, and there are
eunuchs who have made themselves eunuchs for
the sake of the kingdom of heaven. He who is
able to receive this, let him receive it."
13 Then children were brought to him that
he might lay his hands on them and pray. The
disciples rebuked the people; 14 but Jesus said,
"Let the children come to me, and do not hinder
them; for to such belongs the kingdom of
heaven." 15 And he laid his hands on them and
went away.
16 And behold, one came up to him, saying,
"Teacher, what good deed must I do, to have
eternal life?" 17 And he said to him, "Why do
you ask me about what is good? One there is
who is good. If you would enter life, keep the

Jerusalem Bible

Continence

10 The disciples said to him, "If that is how
things are between husband and wife, it is not
advisable to marry." 11 But he replied, "It is not
everyone who can accept what I have said, but
only those to whom it is granted. 12 There are
eunuchs born that way from their mother's
womb, there are eunuchs made so by men and
there are eunuchs who have made themselves
that way for the sake of the kingdom of heaven.
Let anyone accept this who can."

Jesus and the children

13 People brought little children to him, for
him to lay his hands on them and say a prayer.
The disciples turned them away, 14 but Jesus
said, "Let the little children alone, and do not
stop them coming to me; for it is to such as
these that the kingdom of heaven belongs."
15 Then he laid his hands on them and went on
his way.

The rich young man

16 And there was a man who came to him
and asked, "Master, what good deed must I do
to possess eternal life?" 17 Jesus said to him,
"Why do you ask me about what is good? There
is one alone who is good. But if you wish to

New English Bible

The disciples said to him, 'If that is the position with husband and wife, it is better not to marry.' To this he replied, 'That is something which not everyone can accept, but only those for whom God has appointed it. For while some are incapable of marriage because they were born so, or were made so by men, there are others who have themselves renounced marriage for the sake of the kingdom of Heaven. Let those accept it who can.'

They brought children for him to lay his hands on them with prayer. The disciples rebuked them, but Jesus said to them, 'Let the children come to me; do not try to stop them; for the kingdom of Heaven belongs to such as these.' And he laid his hands on the children, and went his way.

And now a man came up and asked him, 'Master, what good must I do to gain eternal life?' 'Good?' said Jesus. 'Why do you ask me about that? One alone is good. But if you wish to enter into life, keep the commandments.'

King James Version

life, keep the commandments. 18 He saith unto
him, Which? Jesus said, Thou shalt do no
murder, Thou shalt not commit adultery, Thou
shalt not steal, Thou shalt not bear false witness, 19 Honour thy father and *thy* mother: and,
Thou shalt love thy neighbour as thyself. 20 The
young man saith unto him, All these things have
I kept from my youth up: what lack I yet?
21 Jesus said unto him, If thou wilt be perfect,
go *and* sell that thou hast, and give to the poor,
and thou shalt have treasure in heaven: and
come *and* follow me. 22 But when the young
man heard that saying, he went away sorrowful:
for he had great possessions.
23 Then said Jesus unto his disciples, Verily
I say unto you, That a rich man shall hardly
enter into the kingdom of heaven. 24 And again
I say unto you, It is easier for a camel to go
through the eye of a needle, than for a rich
man to enter into the kingdom of God. 25 When
his disciples heard *it*, they were exceedingly
amazed, saying, Who then can be saved? 26 But
Jesus beheld *them*, and said unto them, With
men this is impossible; but with God all things
are possible.
27 Then answered Peter and said unto him,
Behold, we have forsaken all, and followed thee;

Living Bible

18 "Which ones?" the man asked.
And Jesus replied, "Don't kill, don't commit
adultery, don't steal, don't lie, 19 honor your
father and mother, and love your neighbor as
yourself!"
20 "I've always obeyed every one of them,"
the youth replied. "What else must I do?"
21 Jesus told him, "If you want to be perfect,
go and sell everything you have and give the
money to the poor, and you will have treasure in
heaven; and come, follow me." 22 But when the
young man heard this, he went away sadly, for
he was very rich.
23 Then Jesus said to his disciples, "It is almost impossible for a rich man to get into the
Kingdom of Heaven. 24 I say it again—it is
easier for a camel to go through the eye of a
needle than for a rich man to enter the Kingdom of God!"
25 This remark confounded the disciples.
"Then who in the world can be saved?" they
asked.
26 Jesus looked at them intently and said,
"Humanly speaking, no one. But with God,
everything is possible."
27 Then Peter said to him, "We left everything to follow you. What will we get out of it?"

Today's English Version

18 "What commandments?" he asked.
Jesus answered, "Do not murder; do not commit adultery; do not steal; do not lie; 19 honor
your father and mother; and love your fellow-
man as yourself."
20 "I have obeyed all these commandments,"
the young man replied. "What else do I need?"
21 Jesus said to him, "If you want to be perfect, go and sell all you have and give the money
to the poor, and you will have riches in heaven;
then come and follow me."
22 When the young man heard this he went
away sad, because he was very rich.
23 Jesus then said to his disciples, "It will be
very hard, I tell you, for a rich man to enter the
Kingdom of heaven. 24 I tell you something else:
it is much harder for a rich man to enter the
Kingdom of God than for a camel to go through
the eye of a needle."
25 When the disciples heard this they were
completely amazed. "Who can be saved, then?"
they asked.
26 Jesus looked straight at them and answered,
"This is impossible for men; but for God everything is possible."
27 Then Peter spoke up. "Look," he said, "we
have left everything and followed you. What will
we have?"

New International Version

18 "Which ones?" the man inquired.
Jesus replied, " 'Do not murder, do not commit
adultery, do not steal, do not give false testimony, 19 honor your father and mother,'[q] and
'love your neighbor as yourself.'[r] "
20 "All these I have kept," the young man
said. "What do I still lack?"
21 Jesus answered, "If you want to be perfect, go, sell your possessions and give to the
poor, and you will have treasure in heaven.
Then come, follow me."
22 When the young man heard this, he went
away sad, because he had great wealth.
23 Then Jesus said to his disciples, "I tell you
the truth, it is hard for a rich man to enter the
kingdom of heaven. 24 Again I tell you, it is
easier for a camel to go through the eye of a
needle than for a rich man to enter the kingdom of God."
25 When the disciples heard this, they were
greatly astonished and asked, "Who then can
be saved?"
26 Jesus looked at them and said, "With man
this is impossible, but with God all things are
possible."
27 Peter answered him, "We have left everything to follow you! What then will there be
for us?"

[q] Exodus 20:12-16; Deut. 5:16-20. [r] Lev. 19:18.

Phillips Modern English

But if you want to enter that life you must keep the commandments."

"Which ones?" he asked.

"Thou shalt do no murder, Thou shalt not commit adultery, Thou shalt not steal, Thou shalt not bear false witness, Honour thy father and thy mother; and Thou shalt love thy neighbour as thyself," replied Jesus.

"I have carefully kept all these," returned the young man. "What is still missing in my life?"

Then Jesus told him, "If you want to be perfect, go now and sell your possessions and give the money to the poor—you will have riches in Heaven. Then come and follow me!"

When the young man heard that he turned away crestfallen, for he was very wealthy.

Then Jesus remarked to his disciples, "Believe me, a rich man will find it very difficult to enter the kingdom of Heaven. Yes, I repeat, a camel could more easily squeeze through the eye of a needle than a rich man get into the kingdom of God!"

The disciples were simply amazed to hear this, and said, "Then who can possibly be saved?"

Jesus looked steadily at them and replied, "Humanly speaking it is impossible; but with God anything is possible!"

19.27 Jesus declares that sacrifice for the kingdom will be repaid

At this Peter exclaimed, "Look, we have left everything and followed you. What will that be worth to us?"

Revised Standard Version

commandments." 18 He said to him, "Which?"
And Jesus said, "You shall not kill, You shall
not commit adultery, You shall not steal, You
shall not bear false witness, 19 Honor your father and mother, and, You shall love your
neighbor as yourself." 20 The young man said
to him, "All these I have observed; what do I
still lack?" 21 Jesus said to him, "If you would
be perfect, go, sell what you possess and give to
the poor, and you will have treasure in heaven;
and come, follow me." 22 When the young man
heard this he went away sorrowful; for he had
great possessions.
23 And Jesus said to his disciples, "Truly, I
say to you, it will be hard for a rich man to
enter the kingdom of heaven. 24Again I tell you,
it is easier for a camel to go through the eye of
a needle than for a rich man to enter the kingdom of God." 25 When the disciples heard this
they were greatly astonished, saying, "Who then
can be saved?" 26 But Jesus looked at them and
said to them, "With men this is impossible, but
with God all things are possible." 27 Then Peter
said in reply, "Lo, we have left everything and
followed you. What then shall we have?"

Jerusalem Bible

enter into life, keep the commandments." 18 He
said, "Which?" "These": Jesus replied, *"You
must not kill. You must not commit adultery.
You must not steal. You must not bring false
witness.* 19 *Honor your father and mother,* and:
you must love your neighbor as yourself." [l]
20 The young man said to him, "I have kept all
these. What more do I need to do?" 21 Jesus
said, "If you wish to be perfect, go and sell
what you own and give the money to the poor,
and you will have treasure in heaven; then
come, follow me." 22 But when the young man
heard these words he went away sad, for he
was a man of great wealth.

The danger of riches

23 Then Jesus said to his disciples, "I tell you
solemnly, it will be hard for a rich man to enter
the kingdom of heaven. 24 Yes, I tell you again,
it is easier for a camel to pass through the eye
of a needle than for a rich man to enter the
kingdom of heaven." 25 When the disciples heard
this they were astonished. "Who can be saved,
then?" they said. 26 Jesus gazed at them. "For
men," he told them, "this is impossible; for God
everything is possible."

The reward of renunciation

27 Then Peter spoke. "What about us?" he
said to him. "We have left everything and fol-

[l] Ex. 20:12-16; Dt. 5:16 20.

New English Bible

'Which commandments?' he asked. Jesus answered, 'Do not murder; do not commit adultery; do not steal; do not give false evidence; honour your father and mother; and love your neighbour as yourself.' The young man answered, 'I have kept all these. Where do I still fall short?' Jesus said to him, 'If you wish to go the whole way, go, sell your possessions, and give to the poor, and then you will have riches in heaven; and come, follow me.' When the young man heard this, he went away with a heavy heart; for he was a man of great wealth.

Jesus said to his disciples, 'I tell you this: a rich man will find it hard to enter the kingdom of Heaven. I repeat, it is easier for a camel to pass through the eye of a needle than for a rich man to enter the kingdom of God.' The disciples were amazed to hear this. 'Then who can be saved?' they asked. Jesus looked at them, and said, 'For men this is impossible; but everything is possible for God.'

At this Peter said, 'We here have left everything to become your followers. What will

King James Version

what shall we have therefore? 28And Jesus said unto them, Verily I say unto you, That ye which have followed me, in the regeneration when the Son of man shall sit in the throne of his glory, ye also shall sit upon twelve thrones, judging the twelve tribes of Israel. 29And every one that hath forsaken houses, or brethren, or sisters, or father, or mother, or wife, or children, or lands, for my name's sake, shall receive a hundredfold, and shall inherit everlasting life. 30 But many *that are* first shall be last; and the last *shall be* first.

20 For the kingdom of heaven is like unto a man *that is* a householder, which went out early in the morning to hire labourers into his vineyard. 2And when he had agreed with the labourers for a penny a day, he sent them into his vineyard. 3And he went out about the third hour, and saw others standing idle in the marketplace, 4And said unto them; Go ye also into the vineyard, and whatsoever is right I will give you. And they went their way. 5Again he went out about the sixth and ninth hour, and did likewise. 6And about the eleventh hour he went out, and found others standing idle, and saith unto them,

Living Bible

28 And Jesus replied, "When I, the Messiah,[d] shall sit upon my glorious throne in the Kingdom,[e] you my disciples shall certainly sit on twelve thrones judging the twelve tribes of Israel. 29And anyone who gives up his home, brothers, sisters, father, mother, wife,[f] children, or property, to follow me, shall receive a hundred times as much in return, and shall have eternal life. 30 But many who are first now will be last then; and some who are last now will be first then."

20 Here is another illustration of the Kingdom of Heaven. "The owner of an estate went out early one morning to hire workers for his harvest field. 2 He agreed to pay them $20 a day[a] and sent them out to work.

3 "A couple of hours later he was passing a hiring hall and saw some men standing around waiting for jobs, 4 so he sent them also into his fields, telling them he would pay them whatever was right at the end of the day. 5At noon and again around three o'clock in the afternoon he did the same thing.

6 "At five o'clock that evening he was in town again and saw some more men standing around and asked them, 'Why haven't you been working today?'

[*d*] Literally, "the Son of Man." [*e*] Literally, "in the regeneration." [*f*] Omitted here in many manuscripts, but included in Luke 18:29. [*a*] Literally, "a denarius," the payment for a day's labor; equivalent to $20 in modern times, or £7.

Today's English Version

28 Jesus said to them, "I tell you this: when the Son of Man sits on his glorious throne in the New Age, then you twelve followers of mine will also sit on thrones, to judge the twelve tribes of Israel. 29And every one who has left houses or brothers or sisters or father or mother or children or fields for my sake, will receive a hundred times more, and will be given eternal life. 30 But many who now are first will be last, and many who now are last will be first."

The workers in the vineyard

20 "The Kingdom of heaven is like the owner of a vineyard who went out early in the morning to hire some men to work in his vineyard. 2 He agreed to pay them the regular wage, a silver coin a day, and sent them to work in his vineyard. 3 He went out again to the market place at nine o'clock and saw some men standing there doing nothing, 4 so he told them, 'You also go to work in the vineyard, and I will pay you a fair wage.' 5 So they went. Then at twelve o'clock and again at three o'clock he did the same thing. 6 It was nearly five o'clock when he went to the market place and saw some other men still standing there. 'Why are you wasting the whole day

New International Version

28 Jesus said to them, "I tell you the truth, at the renewal of all things, when the Son of Man sits on his throne in heavenly glory, you who have followed me will also sit on twelve thrones, judging the twelve tribes of Israel. 29And everyone who has left houses or brothers or sisters or father or mother or children or fields for my sake will receive a hundred times as much and will inherit eternal life. 30 But many who are first will be last, and many who are last will be first.

The parable of the workers in the vineyard

20 "The kingdom of heaven is like a landowner who went out early in the morning to hire men to work in his vineyard. 2 He agreed to pay them a denarius for the day and sent them into his vineyard.

3 "About the third hour he went out and saw others standing in the marketplace doing nothing. 4 He told them, 'You also go and work in my vineyard, and I will pay you whatever is right.' 5 So they went.

"He went out again about the sixth hour and the ninth hour and did the same thing. 6About the eleventh hour he went out and found still others standing around. He asked them, 'Why have you been standing here all day long doing nothing?'

Phillips Modern English

"Believe me," said Jesus, "when I tell you
that in the new world, when the Son of Man
shall take his seat on his glorious throne, you
who have followed me will also be seated on
twelve thrones as judges of the twelve tribes of
Israel. Every man who has left houses or brothers
or sisters or father or mother or children or
land for my sake will get them back many times
over, and will inherit eternal life. But many
who are first now will be last then—and the last
first!

20.1 But God's generosity may appear unfair

"For the kingdom of Heaven is like a householder going out early in the morning to hire
labourers for his vineyard. He agreed with them
on a wage of a silver coin a day and sent them
to work. About nine o'clock he went and saw
some others standing about in the market-place
with nothing to do. 'You go to the vineyard too,'
he said to them, 'and I will pay you a fair
wage.' And off they went. At about mid-day and
again at about three o'clock in the afternoon
he went out and did the same thing. Then about
five o'clock he went out and found some others
standing about. 'Why are you standing about

Revised Standard Version

28 Jesus said to them, "Truly, I say to you, in
the new world, when the Son of man shall sit on
his glorious throne, you who have followed me
will also sit on twelve thrones, judging the
twelve tribes of Israel. 29 And every one who
has left houses or brothers or sisters or father
or mother or children or lands, for my name's
sake, will receive a hundredfold,[l] and inherit
eternal life. 30 But many that are first will be
last, and the last first.

20 "For the kingdom of heaven is like a
householder who went out early in the
morning to hire laborers for his vineyard. 2After
agreeing with the laborers for a denarius[m] a day,
he sent them into his vineyard. 3And going out
about the third hour he saw others standing idle
in the market place; 4 and to them he said, 'You
go into the vineyard too, and whatever is right
I will give you.' So they went. 5 Going out again
about the sixth hour and the ninth hour, he
did the same. 6And about the eleventh hour he
went out and found others standing; and he
said to them, 'Why do you stand here idle all

[l] Other ancient authorities read *manifold.* [m] The denarius was a day's wage for a laborer.

Jerusalem Bible

lowed you. What are we to have, then?" 28 Jesus
said to him, "I tell you solemnly, when all is
made new and the Son of Man sits on his throne
of glory, you will yourselves sit on twelve
thrones to judge[m] the twelve tribes of Israel.
29And everyone who has left houses, brothers,
sisters, father, mother, children or land for the
sake of my name will be repaid a hundred
times over, and also inherit eternal life.
30 "Many who are first will be last, and the
last, first.

Parable of the vineyard laborers

20 "Now the kingdom of heaven is like a
landowner going out at daybreak to hire
workers for his vineyard. 2 He made an agreement
with the workers for one denarius a day, and
sent them to his vineyard. 3 Going out at about
the third hour he saw others standing idle in
the market place 4 and said to them, 'You go to
my vineyard too and I will give you a fair wage.'
5 So they went. At about the sixth hour and
again at about the ninth hour, he went out and
did the same. 6 Then at about the eleventh hour
he went out and found more men standing
around, and he said to them, 'Why have you

[m] I.e., to govern.

New English Bible

there be for us?' Jesus replied, 'I tell you this:
in the world that is to be, when the Son of Man
is seated on his throne in heavenly splendour,
you my followers will have thrones of your own,
where you will sit as judges of the twelve tribes
of Israel. And anyone who has left brothers or
sisters, father, mother, or children, land or
houses for the sake of my name will be repaid
many times over, and gain eternal life. But many
who are first will be last, and the last first.

20 'The kingdom of Heaven is like this.
There was once a landowner who went out
early one morning to hire labourers for his vineyard; and after agreeing to pay them the usual
day's wage[a] he sent them off to work. Going out
three hours later he saw some more men standing idle in the market-place. "Go and join the
others in the vineyard," he said, "and I will pay
you a fair wage"; so off they went. At midday
he went out again, and at three in the afternoon,
and made the same arrangement as before. An
hour before sunset he went out and found another group standing there; so he said to them,
"Why are you standing about like this all day

[a] *Literally* one denarius for the day.

King James Version

Why stand ye here all the day idle? 7 They say unto him, Because no man hath hired us. He saith unto them, Go ye also into the vineyard; and whatsoever is right, *that* shall ye receive. 8 So when even was come, the lord of the vineyard saith unto his steward, Call the labourers, and give them *their* hire, beginning from the last unto the first. 9 And when they came that *were hired* about the eleventh hour, they received every man a penny. 10 But when the first came, they supposed that they should have received more; and they likewise received every man a penny. 11 And when they had received *it*, they murmured against the goodman of the house, 12 Saying, These last have wrought *but* one hour, and thou hast made them equal unto us, which have borne the burden and heat of the day. 13 But he answered one of them, and said, Friend, I do thee no wrong: didst not thou agree with me for a penny? 14 Take *that* thine *is*, and go thy way: I will give unto this last, even as unto thee. 15 Is it not lawful for me to do what I will with mine own? Is thine eye evil, because I am good? 16 So the last shall be first, and the first last: for many be called, but few chosen.

17 And Jesus going up to Jerusalem took the

Living Bible

7 " 'Because no one hired us,' they replied. " 'Then go on out and join the others in my fields,' he told them.

8 "That evening he told the paymaster to call the men in and pay them, beginning with the last men first. 9 When the men hired at five o'clock were paid, each received $20. 10 So when the men hired earlier came to get theirs, they assumed they would receive much more. But they, too, were paid $20.

11, 12 "They protested, 'Those fellows worked only one hour, and yet you've paid them just as much as those of us who worked all day in the scorching heat.'

13 " 'Friend,' he answered one of them, 'I did you no wrong! Didn't you agree to work all day for $20? 14 Take it and go. It is my desire to pay all the same; 15 is it against the law to give away my money if I want to? Should you be angry because I am kind?' 16 And so it is that the last shall be first, and the first, last."

17 As Jesus was on the way to Jerusalem, he

Today's English Version

here doing nothing?' he asked them. 7 'It is because no one hired us,' they answered. 'Well, then, you also go to work in the vineyard,' he told them.

8 "When evening came, the owner told his foreman, 'Call the workers and pay them their wages, starting with those who were hired last, and ending with those who were hired first.' 9 The men who had begun to work at five o'clock were paid a silver coin each. 10 So when the men who were the first to be hired came to be paid, they thought they would get more; but they too were given a silver coin each. 11 They took their money and started grumbling against the employer. 12 'These men who were hired last worked only one hour,' they said, 'while we put up with a whole day's work in the hot sun—yet you paid them the same as you paid us!' 13 'Listen, friend,' the owner answered one of them. 'I have not cheated you. After all, you agreed to do a day's work for a silver coin. 14 Now, take your pay and go home. I want to give this man who was hired last as much as I have given you. 15 Don't I have the right to do as I wish with my own money? Or are you jealous because I am generous?' "

16 And Jesus concluded, "So those who are last will be first, and those who are first will be last."

Jesus speaks a third time about his death

17 As Jesus was going up to Jerusalem he took

New International Version

7 " 'Because no one has hired us,' they answered.

"He said to them, 'You also go and work in my vineyard.'

8 "When evening came, the owner of the vineyard said to his foreman, 'Call the workers and pay them their wages, beginning with the last ones hired and going on to the first.'

9 "The workers who were hired about the eleventh hour came and each received a denarius. 10 So when those came who were hired first, they expected to receive more. But each one of them also received a denarius. 11 When they received it, they began to grumble against the landowner. 12 'These men who were hired last worked only one hour,' they said, 'and you have made them equal to us who have borne the burden of the work and the heat of the day.'

13 "But he answered one of them, 'Friend, I am not being unfair to you. Didn't you agree to work for a denarius? 14 Take your pay and go. I want to give the man who was hired last the same as I gave you. 15 Don't I have the right to do what I want with my own money? Or are you envious because I am generous?'

16 "So the last will be first, and the first will be last."

Jesus again predicts his death

17 Now as Jesus was going up to Jerusalem,

Phillips Modern English

here all day doing nothing?' he asked them. 'Because no one has employed us,' they replied. 'You go off into the vineyard as well, then,' he said.

"When evening came the owner of the vineyard said to his foreman, 'Call the labourers and pay them their wages, beginning with the last and ending with the first.' So those who were engaged at five o'clock came up and each man received a silver coin. But when the first to be employed came they reckoned they would get more; yet they also received a silver coin each. As they took their money they grumbled at the householder and said, 'These last fellows have only put in one hour's work and you've treated them exactly the same as us who have gone through all the hard work and heat of the day!'

"But he replied to one of them, 'My friend, I'm not being unjust to you. Wasn't our agreement for a silver coin a day? Take your money and go home. It is my wish to give the late-comers as much as I give you. May I not do what I like with what belongs to me? Must you be jealous because I am generous?'

"So, many who are the last now will be first then and the first last."

20.17 Jesus' final journey to Jerusalem

Then, as he was on his way up to Jerusalem,

Revised Standard Version

day?' 7 They said to him, 'Because no one has
hired us.' He said to them, 'You go into the
vineyard too.' 8And when evening came, the
owner of the vineyard said to his steward, 'Call
the laborers and pay them their wages, beginning
with the last, up to the first.' 9And when those
hired about the eleventh hour came, each of
them received a denarius. 10 Now when the first
came, they thought they would receive more;
but each of them also received a denarius. 11And
on receiving it they grumbled at the householder,
12 saying, 'These last worked only one hour, and
you have made them equal to us who have borne
the burden of the day and the scorching heat.'
13 But he replied to one of them, 'Friend, I am
doing you no wrong; did you not agree with me
for a denarius? 14 Take what belongs to you,
and go; I choose to give to this last as I give to
you. 15Am I not allowed to do what I choose
with what belongs to me? Or do you begrudge
my generosity?" [n] 16 So the last will be first, and
the first last."
17 And as Jesus was going up to Jerusalem,

[n] Or *is your eye evil because I am good?*

Jerusalem Bible

been standing here idle all day?' 7 'Because no
one has hired us,' they answered. He said to
them, 'You go into my vineyard too.' 8 In the
evening, the owner of the vineyard said to his
bailiff, 'Call the workers and pay them their
wages, starting with the last arrivals and ending
with the first.' 9 So those who were hired at
about the eleventh hour came forward and received one denarius each. 10 When the first
came, they expected to get more, but they too
received one denarius each. 11 They took it,
but grumbled at the landowner. 12 'The men
who came last,' they said, 'have done only one
hour, and you have treated them the same as
us, though we have done a heavy day's work in
all the heat.' 13 He answered one of them and
said, 'My friend, I am not being unjust to you;
did we not agree on one denarius? 14 Take your
earnings and go. I choose to pay the last comer
as much as I pay you. 15 Have I no right to do
what I like with my own? Why be envious because I am generous?' 16 Thus the last will be
first, and the first, last."

Third prophecy of the Passion

17 Jesus was going up to Jerusalem, and on

New English Bible

with nothing to do?" "Because no one has hired us", they replied; so he told them, "Go and join the others in the vineyard." When evening fell, the owner of the vineyard said to his steward, "Call the labourers and give them their pay, beginning with those who came last and ending with the first." Those who had started work an hour before sunset came forward, and were paid the full day's wage.[b] When it was the turn of the men who had come first, they expected something extra, but were paid the same amount as the others. As they took it, they grumbled at their employer: "These late-comers have done only one hour's work, yet you have put them on a level with us, who have sweated the whole day long in the blazing sun!" The owner turned to one of them and said, "My friend, I am not being unfair to you. You agreed on the usual wage for the day,[c] did you not? Take your pay and go home. I choose to pay the last man the same as you. Surely I am free to do what I like with my own money. Why be jealous because I am kind?" Thus will the last be first, and the first last.'

Challenge to Jerusalem

Jesus was journeying towards Jerusalem, and

[b] *Literally* one denarius each. [c] *Literally* You agreed on a denarius.

King James Version

twelve disciples apart in the way, and said unto them, 18 Behold, we go up to Jerusalem; and the Son of man shall be betrayed unto the chief priests and unto the scribes, and they shall condemn him to death, 19 And shall deliver him to the Gentiles to mock, and to scourge, and to crucify *him:* and the third day he shall rise again.

20 Then came to him the mother of Zebedee's children with her sons, worshipping *him,* and desiring a certain thing of him. 21 And he said unto her, What wilt thou? She saith unto him, Grant that these my two sons may sit, the one on thy right hand, and the other on the left, in thy kingdom. 22 But Jesus answered and said, Ye know not what ye ask. Are ye able to drink of the cup that I shall drink of, and to be baptized with the baptism that I am baptized with? They say unto him, We are able. 23 And he saith unto them, Ye shall drink indeed of my cup, and be baptized with the baptism that I am baptized with: but to sit on my right hand, and on my left, is not mine to give, but *it shall be given to them* for whom it is prepared of my Father.

Living Bible

took the twelve disciples aside, 18 and talked to them about what would happen to him when they arrived.

"I [b] will be betrayed to the chief priests and other Jewish leaders, and they will condemn me to die. 19 And they will hand me over to the Roman government, and I will be mocked and crucified, and the third day I will rise to life again."

20 Then the mother of James and John, the sons of Zebedee, brought them to Jesus and respectfully asked a favor.

21 "What is your request?" he asked. She replied, "In your Kingdom, will you let my two sons sit on two thrones[c] next to yours?"

22 But Jesus told her, "You don't know what you are asking!" Then he turned to James and John and asked them, "Are you able to drink from the terrible cup I am about to drink from?"

"Yes," they replied, "we are able!"

23 "You shall indeed drink from it," he told them. "But I have no right to say who will sit on the thrones[c] next to mine. Those places are reserved for the persons my Father selects."

[*b*] Literally, "the Son of Man." [*c*] Implied.

Today's English Version

the twelve disciples aside and spoke to them privately, as they walked along. 18 "Listen," he told them, "we are going up to Jerusalem, where the Son of Man will be handed over to the chief priests and the teachers of the Law. They will condemn him to death 19 and then hand him over to the Gentiles, who will make fun of him, whip him, and nail him to the cross; and on the third day he will be raised to life."

A mother's request

20 Then the mother of Zebedee's sons came to Jesus with her sons, bowed before him, and asked him for a favor.

21 "What do you want?" Jesus asked her.

She answered, "Promise that these two sons of mine will sit at your right and your left when you are King."

22 "You don't know what you are asking for," Jesus answered them. "Can you drink the cup that I am about to drink?"

"We can," they answered.

23 "You will indeed drink from my cup," Jesus told them, "but I do not have the right to choose who will sit at my right and my left. These places belong to those for whom my Father has prepared them."

New International Version

he took the twelve disciples aside and said to them, 18 "We are going up to Jerusalem, and the Son of Man will be betrayed to the chief priests and the teachers of the law. They will condemn him to death 19 and will turn him over to the Gentiles to be mocked and flogged and crucified. On the third day he will be raised to life!"

A mother's request

20 Then the mother of Zebedee's sons came to Jesus with her sons and, kneeling down, asked a favor of him.

21 "What is it you want?" he asked.

She said, "Grant that one of these two sons of mine may sit at your right and the other at your left in your kingdom."

22 "You don't know what you are asking," Jesus said to them. "Can you drink the cup I am going to drink?"

"We can," they answered.

23 Jesus said to them, "You will indeed drink from my cup, but to sit at my right or left is not for me to grant. These places belong to those for whom they have been prepared by my Father."

Phillips Modern English

Jesus took the twelve disciples aside and spoke to them as they walked along. "Listen, we are now going up to Jerusalem and the Son of Man will be handed over to the chief priests and the scribes—and they will condemn him to death. They will hand him over to the heathen to ridicule and flog and crucify. And on the third day he will be raised again!"

At this point the mother of the sons of Zebedee arrived with her sons and knelt in front of Jesus to ask him a favour.

"What is it you want?" he asked her.

"Please say that these two sons of mine may sit one on each side of you when you are king!" she said.

"You don't know what it is you are asking," replied Jesus. "Can you two drink what I have to drink?"

"Yes, we can," they answered.

"Ah, you will indeed 'drink my drink'," Jesus told them, "but as for sitting on either side of me, that is not for me to grant—that is reserved for those for whom it has been prepared by my Father."

Revised Standard Version

he took the twelve disciples aside, and on the way he said to them, 18 "Behold, we are going up to Jerusalem; and the Son of man will be delivered to the chief priests and scribes, and they will condemn him to death, 19 and deliver him to the Gentiles to be mocked and scourged and crucified, and he will be raised on the third day."

20 Then the mother of the sons of Zebedee came up to him, with her sons, and kneeling before him she asked him for something. 21 And he said to her, "What do you want?" She said to him, "Command that these two sons of mine may sit, one at your right hand and one at your left, in your kingdom." 22 But Jesus answered, "You do not know what you are asking. Are you able to drink the cup that I am to drink?" They said to him, "We are able." 23 He said to them, "You will drink my cup, but to sit at my right hand and at my left is not mine to grant, but it is for those for whom it has been pre-

Jerusalem Bible

the way he took the Twelve to one side and said to them, 18 "Now we are going up to Jerusalem, and the Son of Man is about to be handed over to the chief priests and scribes. They will condemn him to death 19 and will hand him over to the pagans to be mocked and scourged and crucified; and on the third day he will rise again."

The mother of Zebedee's sons makes her request

20 Then the mother of Zebedee's sons came with her sons to make a request of him, and bowed low; 21 and he said to her, "What is it you want?" She said to him, "Promise that these two sons of mine may sit one at your right hand and the other at your left in your kingdom." 22 "You do not know what you are asking," Jesus answered. "Can you drink the cup that I am going to drink?" They replied, "We can." 23 "Very well," he said, "you shall drink my cup,[n] but as for seats at my right hand and my left, these are not mine to grant; they belong to those to whom they have been allotted by my Father."

[*n*] Perhaps a prophecy of the martyrdom of James and John; James was certainly put to death by Herod Agrippa about 44 A.D., Ac. 12:2.

New English Bible

on the way he took the Twelve aside, and said to them, 'We are now going to Jerusalem, and the Son of Man will be given up to the chief priests and the doctors of the law; they will condemn him to death and hand him over to the foreign power, to be mocked and flogged and crucified, and on the third day he will be raised to life again.'

The mother of Zebedee's sons then came before him, with her sons. She bowed low and begged a favour. 'What is it you wish?' asked Jesus. 'I want you', she said, 'to give orders that in your kingdom my two sons here may sit next to you, one at your right, and the other at your left.' Jesus turned to the brothers and said, 'You do not understand what you are asking. Can you drink the cup that I am to drink?' 'We can', they replied. Then he said to them, 'You shall indeed share my cup; but to sit at my right or left is not for me to grant; it is for those to whom it has already been assigned by my Father.'

King James Version

24And when the ten heard *it,* they were moved
with indignation against the two brethren. 25 But
Jesus called them *unto him,* and said, Ye know
that the princes of the Gentiles exercise dominion over them, and they that are great exercise
authority upon them. 26 But it shall not be so
among you: but whosoever will be great among
you, let him be your minister; 27And whosoever
will be chief among you, let him be your servant:
28 Even as the Son of man came not to be ministered unto, but to minister, and to give his life
a ransom for many. 29And as they departed from
Jericho, a great multitude followed him.
30 And, behold, two blind men sitting by the
way side, when they heard that Jesus passed by,
cried out, saying, Have mercy on us, O Lord,
thou Son of David. 31And the multitude rebuked
them, because they should hold their peace: but
they cried the more, saying, Have mercy on us,
O Lord, *thou* Son of David. 32And Jesus stood
still, and called them, and said, What will ye
that I shall do unto you? 33 They say unto him,
Lord, that our eyes may be opened. 34 So Jesus
had compassion *on them,* and touched their eyes:
and immediately their eyes received sight, and
they followed him.

Living Bible

24 The other ten disciples were indignant when
they heard what James and John had asked for.
25 But Jesus called them together and said,
"Among the heathen, kings are tyrants and
each minor official lords it over those beneath
him. 26 But among you it is quite different. Anyone wanting to be a leader among you must be
your servant. 27And if you want to be right at
the top, you must serve like a slave. 28 Your
attitude[d] must be like my own, for I, the Messiah,[e] did not come to be served, but to serve,
and to give my life as a ransom for many."
29 As Jesus and the disciples left the city of
Jericho, a vast crowd surged along behind.
30 Two blind men were sitting beside the road
and when they heard that Jesus was coming
that way, they began shouting, "Sir, King David's
Son, have mercy on us!"
31 The crowd told them to be quiet, but they
only yelled the louder.
32, 33 When Jesus came to the place where
they were he stopped in the road and called,
"What do you want me to do for you?"
"Sir," they said, "we want to see!"
34 Jesus was moved with pity for them and
touched their eyes. And instantly they could see,
and followed him.

[*d*] Implied. [*e*] Literally, "the Son of Man."

Today's English Version

24 When the other ten disciples heard about
this they became angry with the two brothers.
25 So Jesus called them all together to him and
said, "You know that the rulers have power
over the people, and their leaders rule over them.
26 This, however, is not the way it shall be among
you. If one of you wants to be great, he must be
the servant of the rest; 27 and if one of you wants
to be first, he must be your slave—28 like the
Son of Man, who did not come to be served, but
to serve and to give his life to redeem many
people."

Jesus heals two blind men

29 As they were leaving Jericho a large crowd
followed Jesus. 30 Two blind men who were sitting by the road heard that Jesus was passing by,
so they began to shout, "Son of David! Have
mercy on us, sir!"
31 The crowd scolded them and told them to
be quiet. But they shouted even more loudly,
"Son of David! Have mercy on us, sir!"
32 Jesus stopped and called them. "What do
you want me to do for you?" he asked them.
33 "Sir," they answered, "we want you to open
our eyes!"
34 Jesus had pity on them and touched their
eyes; at once they were able to see, and followed
him.

New International Version

24 When the ten heard about this, they were
indignant with the two brothers. 25 Jesus called
them together and said, "You know that the
rulers of the Gentiles lord it over them, and
their high officials exercise authority over them.
26 Not so with you. Instead, whoever wants to
become great among you must be your servant,
27 and whoever wants to be first must be your
slave—28 just as the Son of Man did not come
to be served, but to serve, and to give his life
a ransom for many."

Two blind men receive sight

29 As Jesus and his disciples were leaving
Jericho, a large crowd followed him. 30 Two
blind men were sitting by the roadside, and
when they heard that Jesus was going by, they
shouted, "Lord, Son of David, have mercy on
us!"
31 The crowd rebuked them and told them
to be quiet, but they shouted all the louder,
"Lord, Son of David, have mercy on us!"
32 Jesus stopped and called them. "What do
you want me to do for you?" he asked.
33 "Lord," they answered, "we want our
sight."
34 Jesus had compassion on them and touched
their eyes. Immediately they received their sight
and followed him.

Phillips Modern English

When the other ten heard of this incident they were highly indignant with the two brothers.

But Jesus called them to him and said,

"You know that the rulers of the heathen lord it over them and that their great ones have absolute power? But it must not be so among you. No, whoever among you wants to be great must become your servant, and if he wants to be first among you he must be your slave—just as the Son of Man has not come to be served but to serve, and to give his life to set many others free."

20.29 He restores sight to two blind men

A great crowd followed them as they were leaving Jericho, and two blind men who were sitting by the roadside, hearing that it was Jesus who was passing, cried out, "Have pity on us, Lord, you Son of David!" The crowd told them sharply to be quiet, but this only made them cry out more loudly still, "Have pity on us, Lord, you Son of David!"

Jesus stood quite still and called out to them, "What do you want me to do for you?"

"Lord, let us see again!"

And Jesus, deeply moved with pity, touched their eyes. At once their sight was restored, and they followed him.

Revised Standard Version

pared by my Father." 24And when the ten heard
it, they were indignant at the two brothers.
25 But Jesus called them to him and said, "You
know that the rulers of the Gentiles lord it over
them, and their great men exercise authority
over them. 26 It shall not be so among you; but
whoever would be great among you must be
your servant, 27 and whoever would be first
among you must be your slave; 28 even as the
Son of man came not to be served but to serve,
and to give his life as a ransom for many."

29 And as they went out of Jericho, a great
crowd followed him. 30And behold, two blind
men sitting by the roadside, when they heard
that Jesus was passing by, cried out,[o] "Have
mercy on us, Son of David!" 31 The crowd rebuked them, telling them to be silent; but they
cried out the more, "Lord, have mercy on us,
Son of David!" 32And Jesus stopped and
called them, saying, "What do you want me to
do for you?" 33 They said to him, "Lord, let
our eyes be opened." 34And Jesus in pity
touched their eyes, and immediately they received their sight and followed him.

[o] Other ancient authorities insert *Lord*.

Jerusalem Bible

Leadership with service

24 When the other ten heard this they were
indignant with the two brothers. 25 But Jesus
called them to him and said, "You know that
among the pagans the rulers lord it over them,
and their great men make their authority felt.
26 This is not to happen among you. No; anyone
who wants to be great among you must be your
servant, 27 and anyone who wants to be first
among you must be your slave, 28 just as the
Son of Man came not to be served but to serve,
and to give his life as a ransom for many."

The two blind men of Jericho

29 As they left Jericho a large crowd followed him. 30 Now there were two blind men
sitting at the side of the road. When they heard
that it was Jesus who was passing by, they
shouted, "Lord! Have pity on us, Son of David."
31And the crowd scolded them and told them
to keep quiet, but they only shouted more loudly,
"Lord! Have pity on us, Son of David." 32 Jesus
stopped, called them over and said, "What do
you want me to do for you?" 33 They said to
him, "Lord, let us have our sight back." 34 Jesus
felt pity for them and touched their eyes, and
immediately their sight returned and they followed him.

New English Bible

When the other ten heard this, they were indignant with the two brothers. So Jesus called them to him and said, 'You know that in the world, rulers lord it over their subjects, and their great men make them feel the weight of authority; but it shall not be so with you. Among you, whoever wants to be great must be your servant, and whoever wants to be first must be the willing slave of all—like the Son of Man; he did not come to be served, but to serve, and to give up his life as a ransom for many.'

As they were leaving Jericho he was followed by a great crowd of people. At the roadside sat two blind men. When they heard it said that Jesus was passing they shouted, 'Have pity on us; Son of David.' The people told them sharply to be quiet. But they shouted all the more, 'Sir, have pity on us, have pity on us, Son of David.' Jesus stopped and called the men. 'What do you want me to do for you?' he asked. 'Sir,' they answered, 'we want our sight.' Jesus was deeply moved, and touched their eyes. At once their sight came back, and they followed him.

King James Version

21 And when they drew nigh unto Jerusalem, and were come to Bethphage, unto the mount of Olives, then sent Jesus two disciples, 2 Saying unto them, Go into the village over against you, and straightway ye shall find an ass tied, and a colt with her: loose *them,* and bring *them* unto me. 3And if any *man* say aught unto you, ye shall say, The Lord hath need of them; and straightway he will send them. 4All this was done, that it might be fulfilled which was spoken by the prophet, saying, 5 Tell ye the daughter of Sion, Behold, thy King cometh unto thee, meek, and sitting upon an ass, and a colt the foal of an ass. 6And the disciples went, and did as Jesus commanded them, 7And brought the ass, and the colt, and put on them their clothes, and they set *him* thereon. 8And a very great multitude spread their garments in the way; others cut down branches from the trees, and strewed *them* in the way. 9And the multitudes that went before, and that followed, cried, saying, Hosanna to the Son of David: Blessed *is* he that cometh in the name of the Lord; Hosanna in the highest.

Living Bible

21 As Jesus and the disciples approached Jerusalem, and were near the town of Bethphage on the Mount of Olives, Jesus sent two of them into the village ahead.

2 "Just as you enter," he said, "you will see a donkey tied there, with its colt beside it. Untie them and bring them here. 3 If anyone asks you what you are doing, just say, 'The Master needs them,' and there will be no trouble."

4 This was done to fulfill the ancient prophecy, 5 "Tell Jerusalem her King is coming to her, riding humbly on a donkey's colt!"

6 The two disciples did as Jesus said, 7 and brought the animals to him and threw their garments over the colt[a] for him to ride on. 8And some in the crowd threw down their coats along the road ahead of him, and others cut branches from the trees and spread them out before him.

9 Then the crowds surged on ahead and pressed along behind, shouting, "God bless King David's Son!" . . . "God's Man is here! [b] . . . Bless him, Lord!" . . . "Praise God in highest heaven!"

[a] Implied. [b] Literally, "Blessed is he who comes in the name of the Lord."

Today's English Version

The triumphant entry into Jerusalem

21 As they approached Jerusalem, they came to Bethphage, at the Mount of Olives. There Jesus sent two of the disciples on ahead 2 with these instructions, "Go to the village there ahead of you, and at once you will find a donkey tied up and her colt with her. Untie them and bring them to me. 3And if anyone says anything, tell him, 'The Master needs them'; and he will let them go at once."

4 This happened to make come true what the prophet had said:

5 "Tell the city of Zion,
Now your king is coming to you.
He is gentle and rides on a donkey,
on a colt, the foal of a donkey."

6 So the disciples went ahead and did what Jesus had told them to do: 7 they brought the donkey and the colt, threw their cloaks over them, and Jesus got on. 8A great crowd of people spread their cloaks on the road, while others cut branches from the trees and spread them on the road. 9 The crowds walking in front of Jesus and the crowds walking behind began to shout, "Praise to David's Son! God bless him who comes in the name of the Lord! Praise be to God!"

New International Version

The triumphal entry

21 As they approached Jerusalem and came to Bethphage on the Mount of Olives, Jesus sent two disciples, 2 saying to them, "Go to the village ahead of you, and at once you will find a donkey tied there, with her colt by her. Untie them and bring them to me. 3 If anyone says anything to you, tell him that the Lord needs them, and he will send them right away."

4 This took place to fulfill what was spoken through the prophet:

5 "Say to the daughter of Zion,
'See, your king comes to you,
gentle and riding on a donkey,
on a colt, the foal of a donkey.' " [s]

6 The disciples went and did as Jesus had instructed them. 7 They brought the donkey and the colt, placed their cloaks on them, and Jesus sat on them. 8A very large crowd spread their cloaks on the road, while others cut branches from the trees and spread them on the road. 9 The crowds that went ahead of him and those that followed shouted,

"Hosanna[t] to the Son of David!
Blessed is he who comes in the name of the Lord! [u]
Hosanna[t] in the highest!"

[s] Zech. 9:9. [t] A Hebrew expression meaning "Save!" which became an exclamation of praise. [u] Psalm 118:26.

Phillips Modern English

21.1 Jesus' final entry into Jerusalem

As they approached Jerusalem and came to Bethphage and the Mount of Olives, Jesus sent two disciples ahead telling them, "Go into the village in front of you and you will at once find there a donkey tethered, and a colt with her. Untie them and bring them to me. Should anyone say anything to you, you are to say, 'The Lord needs them', and he will send them immediately."

All this happened to fulfil the prophet's saying—

Tell ye the daughter of Zion,
Behold, thy King cometh unto thee,
Meek, and riding upon an ass,
And upon a colt the foal of an ass.

So the disciples went off and followed Jesus' instructions. They brought the donkey and the colt, and put their cloaks on them, and Jesus took his seat upon them. Then a vast crowd spread their cloaks on the road, while others cut down branches from the trees and spread them in his path. The crowds who went in front of him and the crowds who followed behind him all shouted, "God save the Son of David! Blessed is the man who comes in the name of the Lord! God save him from on high!"

Revised Standard Version

21 And when they drew near to Jerusalem
and came to Bethphage, to the Mount of
Olives, then Jesus sent two disciples, 2 saying to
them, "Go into the village opposite you, and
immediately you will find an ass tied, and a colt
with her; untie them and bring them to me.
3 If any one says anything to you, you shall say,
'The Lord has need of them,' and he will send
them immediately." 4 This took place to fulfil
what was spoken by the prophet, saying,
5 "Tell the daughter of Zion,
Behold, your king is coming to you,
humble, and mounted on an ass,
and on a colt, the foal of an ass."
6 The disciples went and did as Jesus had directed them; 7 they brought the ass and the colt,
and put their garments on them, and he sat
thereon. 8 Most of the crowd spread their garments on the road, and others cut branches from
the trees and spread them on the road. 9 And the
crowds that went before him and that followed
him shouted, "Hosanna to the Son of David!
Blessed is he who comes in the name of the

Jerusalem Bible

The Messiah enters Jerusalem

21 When they were near Jerusalem and had
come in sight of Bethphage on the Mount of
Olives, Jesus sent two disciples, 2 saying to them,
"Go to the village facing you, and you will immediately find a tethered donkey and a colt
with her. Untie them and bring them to me.
3 If anyone says anything to you, you are to
say, 'The Master needs them and will send them
back directly.'" 4 This took place to fulfill the
prophecy:

5 *Say to the daughter of Zion:*
Look, your king comes to you;
he is humble, he rides on a donkey
and on a colt, the foal of a beast of burden.[o]

6 So the disciples went out and did as Jesus had
told them. 7 They brought the donkey and the
colt, then they laid their cloaks on their backs
and he sat on them. 8 Great crowds of people
spread their cloaks on the road, while others
were cutting branches from the trees and spreading them in his path. 9 The crowds who went in
front of him and those who followed were all
shouting:

"*Hosanna*[p] to the Son of David!
Blessings on him who comes in the name of the Lord! [q]
Hosanna in the highest heavens!"

[o] Is. 62:11; Zc. 9:9. [p] Conventional shout of acclaim, like a cheer. [q] Ps. 118:26.

New English Bible

21 They were now nearing Jerusalem; and when they reached Bethphage at the Mount of Olives, Jesus sent two disciples with these instructions: 'Go to the village opposite, where you will at once find a donkey tethered with her foal beside her; untie them, and bring them to me. If anyone speaks to you, say, "Our Master needs them"; and he will let you take them at once.' [a] This was to fulfil the prophecy which says, 'Tell the daughter of Zion, "Here is your king, who comes to you in gentleness, riding on an ass, riding on the foal of a beast of burden."'

The disciples went and did as Jesus had directed, and brought the donkey and her foal; they laid their cloaks on them and Jesus mounted. Crowds of people carpeted the road with their cloaks, and some cut branches from the trees to spread in his path. Then the crowd that went ahead and the others that came behind raised the shout: 'Hosanna to the Son of David! Blessings on him who comes in the name of the Lord! Hosanna in the heavens!'

[a] *Or* "Our Master needs them and will send them back straight away."

King James Version

10 And when he was come into Jerusalem, all the city was moved, saying, Who is this? 11 And the multitude said, This is Jesus the prophet of Nazareth of Galilee.

12 And Jesus went into the temple of God, and cast out all them that sold and bought in the temple, and overthrew the tables of the money changers, and the seats of them that sold doves, 13 And said unto them, It is written, My house shall be called the house of prayer; but ye have made it a den of thieves. 14 And the blind and the lame came to him in the temple; and he healed them. 15 And when the chief priests and scribes saw the wonderful things that he did, and the children crying in the temple, and saying, Hosanna to the Son of David; they were sore displeased, 16 And said unto him, Hearest thou what these say? And Jesus saith unto them, Yea; have ye never read, Out of the mouth of babes and sucklings thou hast perfected praise?

17 And he left them, and went out of the city

Living Bible

10 The entire city of Jerusalem was stirred as he entered. "Who is this?" they asked.

11 And the crowds replied, "It's Jesus, the prophet from Nazareth up in Galilee."

12 Jesus went into the Temple, drove out the merchants, and knocked over the money-changers' tables and the stalls of those selling doves.

13 "The Scriptures say my Temple is a place of prayer," he declared, "but you have turned it into a den of thieves."

14 And now the blind and crippled came to him and he healed them there in the Temple. 15 But when the chief priests and other Jewish leaders saw these wonderful miracles, and heard even the little children in the Temple shouting, "God bless the Son of David," they were disturbed and indignant and asked him, "Do you hear what these children are saying?"

16 "Yes," Jesus replied. "Didn't you ever read the Scriptures? For they say, 'Even little babies shall praise him!' "

17 Then he returned to Bethany, where he stayed overnight.

Today's English Version

10 When Jesus entered Jerusalem the whole city was thrown in an uproar. "Who is he?" the people asked.

11 "This is the prophet Jesus, from Nazareth of Galilee," the crowds answered.

Jesus goes to the temple

12 Jesus went into the temple and drove out all those who bought and sold in the temple; he overturned the tables of the moneychangers and the stools of those who sold pigeons, 13 and said to them, "It is written in the Scriptures that God said, 'My house will be called a house of prayer.' But you are making it a hideout for thieves!"

14 The blind and the crippled came to him in the temple and he healed them. 15 The chief priests and the teachers of the Law became angry when they saw the wonderful things he was doing, and the children shouting and crying in the temple, "Praise to David's Son!"

16 So they said to Jesus, "Do you hear what they are saying?"

"Indeed I do," answered Jesus. "Haven't you ever read this scripture? 'You have trained children and babies to offer perfect praise.' "

17 Jesus left them and went out of the city to Bethany, where he spent the night.

New International Version

10 When Jesus entered Jerusalem, the whole city was stirred and asked, "Who is this?"

11 The crowds answered, "This is Jesus, the prophet from Nazareth in Galilee."

Jesus at the temple

12 Jesus entered the temple area and drove out all who were buying and selling there. He overturned the tables of the money-changers and the benches of those selling doves. 13 "It is written," he said to them, " 'My house will be called a house of prayer,' [v] but you are making it a 'den of robbers.' [w] "

14 The blind and the lame came to him at the temple, and he healed them. 15 But when the chief priests and the teachers of the law saw the wonderful things he did and the children shouting in the temple area, "Hosanna[x] to the Son of David," they were indigant.

16 "Do you hear what these children are saying?" they asked him.

"Yes," replied Jesus, "have you never read,
'From the lips of children and infants
you have raised up praise' [y] ?"

17 And he left them and went out of the city to Bethany, where he spent the night.

[v] Isaiah 56:7. [w] Jer. 7:11. [x] A Hebrew expression meaning "Save!" which became an exclamation of praise. [y] Psalm 8:2.

Phillips Modern English

And as he entered Jerusalem a shock ran through the whole city. "Who *is* this?" men cried. "This is Jesus the prophet," replied the crowd, "the man from Nazareth in Galilee!"

Then Jesus went into the Temple-precincts and drove out all the buyers and sellers there. He overturned the tables of the money-changers and the benches of those who sold doves, crying—

"It is written, 'My house shall be called a house of prayer.' But you have turned it into a thieves' kitchen!"

And there in the Temple the blind and the lame came to him, and he healed them. But when the chief priests and the scribes saw the wonderful things he did, and that children were shouting in the Temple the words, "God save the Son of David", they were highly indignant. "Can't you hear what these children are saying?" they asked Jesus.

"Yes," he replied, "and haven't you ever read the words, 'Out of the mouth of babes and sucklings thou hast perfected praise'?" And he turned on his heel and went out of the city to Bethany, where he spent the night.

Revised Standard Version

Lord! Hosanna in the highest!"
10 And when he entered Jerusalem, all the city was stirred, saying, "Who is this?"
11 And the crowds said, "This is the prophet Jesus from Nazareth of Galilee."

12 And Jesus entered the temple of God[p] and drove out all who sold and bought in the temple, and he overturned the tables of the money-changers and the seats of those who sold pigeons.
13 He said to them, "It is written, 'My house shall be called a house of prayer'; but you make it a den of robbers."

14 And the blind and the lame came to him in the temple, and he healed them.
15 But when the chief priests and the scribes saw the wonderful things that he did, and the children crying out in the temple, "Hosanna to the Son of David!" they were indignant;
16 and they said to him, "Do you hear what these are saying?" And Jesus said to them, "Yes; have you never read,

'Out of the mouth of babes and sucklings
thou hast brought perfect praise'?"

17 And leaving them, he went out of the city to Bethany and lodged there.

[p] Other ancient authorities omit *of God.*

Jerusalem Bible

10 And when he entered Jerusalem, the whole city was in turmoil. "Who is this?" people asked,
11 and the crowds answered, "This is the prophet Jesus from Nazareth in Galilee."

The expulsion of the dealers from the Temple

12 Jesus then went into the Temple and drove out all those who were selling and buying there; he upset the tables of the money changers and the chairs of those who were selling pigeons.[r]
13 "According to scripture," he said, *"my house will be called a house of prayer*[s]; but you are turning it into a *robbers' den."*[t]
14 There were also blind and lame people who came to him in the Temple, and he cured them.
15 At the sight of the wonderful things he did and of the children shouting, "Hosanna to the Son of David" in the Temple, the chief priests and the scribes were indignant.
16 "Do you hear what they are saying?" they said to him. "Yes," Jesus answered, "have you never read this:

By the mouths of children, babes in arms,
you have made sure of praise?"[u]

17 With that he left them and went out of the city to Bethany where he spent the night.

[r] Money changers provided Temple currency, and the traders the animals, for making sacrificial offerings. [s] Is. 56:7. [t] Jr. 7:11. [u] Ps. 8:2 (LXX); Wisdom 10:21.

New English Bible

When he entered Jerusalem the whole city went wild with excitement. 'Who is this?' people asked, and the crowd replied, 'This is the prophet Jesus, from Nazareth in Galilee.'

Jesus then went into the temple and drove out all who were buying and selling in the temple precincts; he upset the tables of the money-changers and the seats of the dealers in pigeons; and said to them, 'Scripture says, "My house shall be called a house of prayer"; but you are making it a robbers' cave.'

In the temple blind men and cripples came to him, and he healed them. The chief priests and doctors of the law saw the wonderful things he did, and heard the boys in the temple shouting, 'Hosanna to the Son of David!', and they asked him indignantly, 'Do you hear what they are saying?' Jesus answered, 'I do; have you never read that text, "Thou hast made children and babes at the breast sound aloud thy praise"?' Then he left them and went out of the city to Bethany, where he spent the night.

King James Version

into Bethany; and he lodged there. 18 Now in the morning, as he returned into the city, he hungered. 19And when he saw a fig tree in the way, he came to it, and found nothing thereon, but leaves only, and said unto it, Let no fruit grow on thee henceforward for ever. And presently the fig tree withered away. 20And when the disciples saw *it,* they marvelled, saying, How soon is the fig tree withered away! 21 Jesus answered and said unto them, Verily I say unto you, If ye have faith, and doubt not, ye shall not only do this *which is done* to the fig tree, but also if ye shall say unto this mountain, Be thou removed, and be thou cast into the sea; it shall be done. 22And all things, whatsoever ye shall ask in prayer, believing, ye shall receive.

23 And when he was come into the temple, the chief priests and the elders of the people came unto him as he was teaching, and said, By what authority doest thou these things? and who gave thee this authority? 24And Jesus answered and said unto them, I also will ask you one thing, which if ye tell me, I in like wise will tell you by what authority I do these things. 25 The baptism of John, whence was it? from heaven, or of men? And they reasoned with themselves, saying, If we shall say, From heaven; he will say unto us, Why did ye not then believe

Living Bible

18 In the morning, as he was returning to Jerusalem, he was hungry, 19 and noticed a fig tree beside the road. He went over to see if there were any figs, but there were only leaves. Then he said to it, "Never bear fruit again!" And soon[c] the fig tree withered up.

20 The disciples were utterly amazed and asked, "How did the fig tree wither so quickly?"

21 Then Jesus told them, "Truly, if you have faith, and don't doubt, you can do things like this and much more. You can even say to this Mount of Olives, 'Move over into the ocean,' and it will. 22 You can get anything—*anything* you ask for in prayer—if you believe."

23 When he had returned to the Temple and was teaching, the chief priests and other Jewish leaders came up to him and demanded to know by whose authority he had thrown out the merchants the day before.[d]

24 "I'll tell you if you answer one question first," Jesus replied. 25 "Was John the Baptist sent from God, or not?"

They talked it over among themselves. "If we say, 'From God,'" they said, "then he will ask

[*c*] Or, "immediately." [*d*] Literally, "By what authority do you do these things?"

Today's English Version

Jesus curses the fig tree

18 On his way back to the city, early next morning, Jesus was hungry. 19 He saw a fig tree by the side of the road and went to it, but found nothing on it except leaves. So he said to the tree, "You will never again bear fruit!" At once the fig tree dried up.

20 The disciples saw this and were astounded. "How did the fig tree dry up so quickly?" they asked.

21 "Remember this!" Jesus answered. "If you believe, and do not doubt, you will be able to do what I have done to this fig tree; not only this, you will even be able to say to this hill, 'Get up and throw yourself in the sea,' and it will. 22 If you believe, you will receive whatever you ask for in prayer."

The question about Jesus' authority

23 Jesus came back to the temple; and as he taught, the chief priests and the Jewish elders came to him and asked, "What right do you have to do these things? Who gave you this right?"

24 Jesus answered them, "I will ask you just one question, and if you give me an answer I will tell you what right I have to do these things. 25 Where did John's right to baptize come from: from God or from men?"

They started to argue among themselves, "What shall we say? If we answer, 'From God,' he will say to us, 'Why, then, did you not believe

New International Version

The fig tree withers

18 Early the next morning, as he was on his way back to the city, he was hungry. 19 Seeing a fig tree by the road, he went up to it but found nothing on it except leaves. Then he said to it, "May you never bear fruit again!" Immediately the tree withered.

20 When the disciples saw this, they were amazed. "How did the fig tree wither so quickly?" they asked.

21 Jesus replied, "I tell you the truth, if you have faith and do not doubt, not only can you do what was done to the fig tree, but also you can say to this mountain, 'Go, throw yourself into the sea,' and it will be done. 22 If you believe, you will receive whatever you ask for in prayer."

The authority of Jesus questioned

23 Jesus entered the temple courts, and, while he was teaching, the chief priests and the elders of the people came to him. "By what authority are you doing these things?" they asked. "And who gave you this authority?"

24 Jesus replied, "I will also ask you one question. If you answer me, I will tell you by what authority I am doing these things. 25 John's baptism—where did it come from? Was it from heaven, or from men?"

They discussed it among themselves and said, "If we say, 'From heaven,' he will ask, 'Then

Phillips Modern English

21.18 His strange words to the fig-tree

In the morning he came back early to the city and felt hungry. He saw a fig-tree growing by the side of the road, but when he got to it he discovered there was nothing on it but leaves. "No more fruit shall ever grow on you!" he said to it, and all at once the fig-tree withered away. When the disciples saw this happen they were simply amazed. "How on earth did the fig-tree wither away as suddenly as that?" they asked.

"Believe me," replied Jesus, "if you have faith and have no doubts in your heart, you will not only do this to a fig-tree but even if you should say to this hill, 'Be uprooted and thrown into the sea', it will happen! Everything you ask for in prayer, if you have faith, you will receive."

21.23 Jesus meets a question with a counter-question

Then when he had entered the Temple and was in the act of teaching, the chief priests and Jewish elders came up to him and said, "What authority have you for what you're doing, and who gave you that authority?"

"I am also going to ask you one question," Jesus replied to them, "and if you answer it I will tell you what authority I have for what I do. John's baptism, now, did it come from Heaven or was it purely human?"

At this they began arguing among themselves, "If we say, 'It came from Heaven', he will say to

Revised Standard Version

18 In the morning, as he was returning to the city, he was hungry. 19And seeing a fig tree by the wayside he went to it, and found nothing on it but leaves only. And he said to it, "May no fruit ever come from you again!" And the fig tree withered at once. 20 When the disciples saw it they marveled, saying, "How did the fig tree wither at once?" 21And Jesus answered them, "Truly, I say to you, if you have faith and never doubt, you will not only do what has been done to the fig tree, but even if you say to this mountain, 'Be taken up and cast into the sea,' it will be done. 22And whatever you ask in prayer, you will receive, if you have faith."

23 And when he entered the temple, the chief priests and the elders of the people came up to him as he was teaching, and said, "By what authority are you doing these things, and who gave you this authority?" 24 Jesus answered them, "I also will ask you a question; and if you tell me the answer, then I also will tell you by what authority I do these things. 25 The baptism of John, whence was it? From heaven or from men?" And they argued with one another, "If we say, 'From heaven,' he will say to us, 'Why

Jerusalem Bible

The barren fig tree withers.
Faith and prayer

18 As he was returning to the city in the early morning, he felt hungry. 19 Seeing a fig tree by the road, he went up to it and found nothing on it but leaves. And he said to it, "May you never bear fruit again"; and at that instant the fig tree withered. 20 The disciples were amazed when they saw it. "What happened to the tree," they said, "that it withered there and then?" 21 Jesus answered, "I tell you solemnly, if you have faith and do not doubt at all, not only will you do what I have done to the fig tree, but even if you say to this mountain, 'Get up and throw yourself into the sea,' it will be done. 22And if you have faith, everything you ask for in prayer you will receive."

The authority of Jesus is questioned

23 He had gone into the Temple and was teaching, when the chief priests and the elders of the people came to him and said, "What authority have you for acting like this? And who gave you this authority?" 24 "And I," replied Jesus, "will ask you a question, only one; if you tell me the answer to it, I will then tell you my authority for acting like this. 25 John's baptism: where did it come from: heaven or man?" And they argued it out this way among themselves, "If we say from heaven, he will retort, 'Then

New English Bible

Next morning on his way to the city he felt hungry; and seeing a fig-tree at the roadside he went up to it, but found nothing on it but leaves. He said to the tree, 'You shall never bear fruit any more!'; and the tree withered away at once. The disciples were amazed at the sight. 'How is it', they asked, 'that the tree has withered so suddenly?' Jesus answered them, 'I tell you this: if only you have faith and have no doubts, you will do what has been done to the fig-tree; and more than that, you need only say to this mountain, "Be lifted from your place and hurled into the sea", and what you say will be done. And whatever you pray for in faith you will receive.'

He entered the temple, and the chief priests and elders of the nation came to him with the question: 'By what authority are you acting like this? Who gave you this authority?' Jesus replied, 'I have a question to ask you too; answer it, and I will tell you by what authority I act. The baptism of John: was it from God, or from men?' This set them arguing among themselves: 'If we say, "from God", he will say, "Then why

King James Version

him? 26 But if we shall say, Of men; we fear
the people; for all hold John as a prophet. 27 And
they answered Jesus, and said, We cannot tell.
And he said unto them, Neither tell I you by
what authority I do these things.
28 But what think ye? A *certain* man had two
sons; and he came to the first, and said, Son, go
work to day in my vineyard. 29 He answered
and said, I will not; but afterward he repented,
and went. 30 And he came to the second, and
said likewise. And he answered and said, I *go,*
sir; and went not. 31 Whether of them twain
did the will of *his* father? They say unto him,
The first. Jesus saith unto them, Verily I say
unto you, That the publicans and the harlots go
into the kingdom of God before you. 32 For
John came unto you in the way of righteousness,
and ye believed him not; but the publicans and
the harlots believed him: and ye, when ye had
seen *it,* repented not afterward, that ye might
believe him.
33 Hear another parable: There was a cer-

Living Bible

why we didn't believe what John said. 26 And if
we deny that God sent him, we'll be mobbed,
for the crowd all think he was a prophet." 27 So
they finally replied, "We don't know!"
And Jesus said, "Then I won't answer your
question either.
28 "But what do you think about this? A man
with two sons told the older boy, 'Son, go out
and work on the farm today.' 29 'I won't,' he answered, but later he changed his mind and went.
30 Then the father told the youngest, 'You go!'
and he said, 'Yes, sir, I will.' But he didn't.
31 Which of the two was obeying his father?"
They replied, "The first, of course."
Then Jesus explained his meaning: "Surely
evil men and prostitutes will get into the Kingdom before you do. 32 For John the Baptist told
you to repent and turn to God, and you
wouldn't, while very evil men and prostitutes did.
And even when you saw this happening, you refused to repent, and so you couldn't believe.
33 "Now listen to this story: A certain land-

Today's English Version

John?' 26 But if we say, 'From men,' we are
afraid of what the people might do, because they
are all convinced that John was a prophet." 27 So
they answered Jesus, "We don't know."
And he said to them, "Neither will I tell you,
then, by what right I do these things."

The parable of the two sons

28 "Now, what do you think? There was a
man who had two sons. He went to the older one
and said, 'Son, go work in the vineyard today.'
29 'I don't want to,' he answered, but later he
changed his mind and went to the vineyard.
30 Then the father went to the other son and
said the same thing. 'Yes, sir,' he answered, but
he did not go. 31 Which one of the two did what
his father wanted?"
"The older one," they answered.
"And I tell you this," Jesus said to them. "The
tax collectors and the prostitutes are going into
the Kingdom of God ahead of you. 32 For John
the Baptist came to you showing you the right
path to take, and you would not believe him; but
the tax collectors and the prostitutes believed
him. Even when you saw this you did not change
your minds later on and believe him."

The parable of the tenants in the vineyard

33 "Listen to another parable," Jesus said.

New International Version

why didn't you believe him?' 26 But if we say,
'From men'—we are afraid of the people, for
they all hold that John was a prophet."
27 So they answered Jesus, "We don't know."
Then he said, "Neither will I tell you by
what authority I am doing these things.

The parable of the two sons

28 "What do you think? There was a man
who had two sons. He went to the first and said,
'Son, go and work today in the vineyard.'
29 " 'I will not,' he answered, but later he
changed his mind and went.
30 "Then the father went to the other son and
said the same thing. He answered, 'I will, sir,' but
he did not go.
31 "Which of the two did what his father
wanted?"
"The first," they answered.
Jesus said to them, "I tell you the truth, the
tax collectors and the prostitutes are entering
the kingdom of God ahead of you. 32 For John
came to you to show you the way of righteousness, and you did not believe him, but the tax
collectors and the prostitutes did. And even
after you saw this, you did not repent and believe him.

The parable of the tenants

33 "Listen to another parable: There was a

Phillips Modern English

us, 'Then why didn't you believe in him?' But if we should say, 'It was purely human'—well, we are afraid of the people—for all of them consider John was a prophet."

So they answered Jesus, "We do not know."

"Then I will not tell you by what authority I do these things!" returned Jesus. "But what is your opinion about this? There was a man with two sons. He went to the first and said, 'Go and work in my vineyard today, my son.' He said, 'I won't'. But afterwards he changed his mind and went. Then the father approached the second son with the same request. He said, 'All right, sir'—but he never went. Which of these two did what his father wanted?"

"The first one," they replied.

"Yes," retorted Jesus, "and I tell you that tax-collectors and prostitutes are going into the kingdom of God in front of you!" "For John came to you as a truly good man, and you did not believe in him—yet the tax-collectors and the prostitutes did! And, even after seeing that, you would not change your minds and believe him."

21.33 Jesus tells a pointed story

"Now listen to another parable. There was

Revised Standard Version

then did you not believe him?' 26 But if we say,
'From men,' we are afraid of the multitude; for
all hold that John was a prophet." 27 So they
answered Jesus, "We do not know." And he
said to them, "Neither will I tell you by what
authority I do these things.
28 "What do you think? A man had two sons;
and he went to the first and said, 'Son, go and
work in the vineyard today.' 29 And he answered,
'I will not'; but afterward he repented and went.
30 And he went to the second and said the same;
and he answered, 'I go, sir,' but did not go.
31 Which of the two did the will of his father?"
They said, "The first." Jesus said to them,
"Truly, I say to you, the tax collectors and the
harlots go into the kingdom of God before you.
32 For John came to you in the way of righteousness, and you did not believe him, but the
tax collectors and the harlots believed him; and
even when you saw it, you did not afterward
repent and believe him.
33 "Hear another parable. There was a

Jerusalem Bible

why did you refuse to believe him?'; 26 but if
we say from man, we have the people to fear,
for they all hold that John was a prophet." 27 So
their reply to Jesus was, "We do not know."
And he retorted, "Nor will I tell you my authority for acting like this.

Parable of the two sons

28 "What is your opinion? A man had two
sons. He went and said to the first, 'My boy,
you go and work in the vineyard today.' 29 He
answered, 'I will not go,' but afterward thought
better of it and went. 30 The man then went
and said the same thing to the second who answered, 'Certainly, sir,' but did not go. 31 Which
of the two did the father's will?" "The first,"
they said. Jesus said to them, "I tell you solemnly, tax collectors and prostitutes are making
their way into the kingdom of God before you.
32 For John came to you, a pattern of true
righteousness, but you did not believe him, and
yet the tax collectors and prostitutes did. Even
after seeing that, you refused to think better of
it and believe in him.

Parable of the wicked husbandmen

33 "Listen to another parable. There was a

New English Bible

did you not believe him?" But if we say, "from men", we are afraid of the people, for they all take John for a prophet.' So they answered, 'We do not know.' And Jesus said: 'Then neither will I tell you by what authority I act.

'But what do you think about this? A man had two sons. He went to the first, and said, "My boy, go and work today in the vineyard." "I will, sir", the boy replied; but he never went. The father came to the second and said the same. "I will not", he replied, but afterwards he changed his mind and went. Which of these two did as his father wished?' 'The second', they said. Then Jesus answered, 'I tell you this: tax-gatherers and prostitutes are entering the kingdom of God ahead of you. For when John came to show you the right way to live, you did not believe him, but the tax-gatherers and prostitutes did; and even when you had seen that, you did not change your minds and believe him.

'Listen to another parable. There was a land-

King James Version

tain householder, which planted a vineyard, and
hedged it round about, and digged a winepress
in it, and built a tower, and let it out to husbandmen, and went into a far country: 34And
when the time of the fruit drew near, he sent
his servants to the husbandmen, that they might
receive the fruits of it. 35And the husbandmen
took his servants, and beat one, and killed another, and stoned another. 36Again, he sent other
servants more than the first: and they did unto
them likewise. 37 But last of all he sent unto
them his son, saying, They will reverence my
son. 38 But when the husbandmen saw the son,
they said among themselves, This is the heir;
come, let us kill him, and let us seize on his
inheritance. 39And they caught him, and cast
him out of the vineyard, and slew *him*. 40 When
the lord therefore of the vineyard cometh, what
will he do unto those husbandmen? 41 They say
unto him, He will miserably destroy those wicked
men, and will let out *his* vineyard unto other
husbandmen, which shall render him the fruits
in their seasons. 42 Jesus saith unto them, Did
ye never read in the Scriptures, The stone which
the builders rejected, the same is become the
head of the corner: this is the Lord's doing, and
it is marvellous in our eyes? 43 Therefore say I
unto you, The kingdom of God shall be taken
from you, and given to a nation bringing forth
the fruits thereof. 44And whosoever shall fall on

Living Bible

owner planted a vineyard with a hedge around
it, and built a platform for the watchman, then
leased the vineyard to some farmers on a share-
crop basis, and went away to live in another
country.

34 "At the time of the grape harvest he sent
his agents to the farmers to collect his share.
35 But the farmers attacked his men, beat one,
killed one and stoned another.

36 "Then he sent a larger group of his men
to collect for him, but the results were the same.
37 Finally the owner sent his son, thinking they
would surely respect him.

38 "But when these farmers saw the son coming they said among themselves, 'Here comes
the heir to this estate; come on, let's kill him
and get it for ourselves!' 39 So they dragged him
out of the vineyard and killed him.

40 "When the owner returns, what do you
think he will do to those farmers?"

41 The Jewish leaders replied, "He will put the
wicked men to a horrible death, and lease the
vineyard to others who will pay him promptly."

42 Then Jesus asked them, "Didn't you ever
read in the Scriptures: 'The stone rejected by
the builders has been made the honored corner-
stone;[e] how remarkable! what an amazing thing
the Lord has done'?

43 "What I mean is that the Kingdom of God
shall be taken away from you, and given to a
nation that will give God his share of the crop.[f]
44All who stumble on this rock of truth[g] shall

[*e*] Literally, "the head of the corner." [*f*] Literally, "bringing forth the fruits." [*g*] Literally, "on this stone."

Today's English Version

"There was a landowner who planted a vineyard, put a fence around it, dug a hole for the
winepress, and built a watchtower. Then he
rented the vineyard to tenants and left home on
a trip. 34 When the time came to harvest the
grapes he sent his slaves to the tenants to receive his share. 35 The tenants grabbed his slaves,
beat one, killed another, and stoned another.
36Again the man sent other slaves, more than
the first time, and the tenants treated them the
same way. 37 Last of all he sent them his son.
'Surely they will respect my son,' he said. 38 But
when the tenants saw the son they said to themselves, 'This is the owner's son. Come on, let us
kill him, and we will get his property!' 39 So
they grabbed him, threw him out of the vineyard,
and killed him.

40 "Now, when the owner of the vineyard
comes, what will he do to those tenants?" Jesus
asked.

41 "He will certainly kill those evil men," they
answered, "and rent the vineyard out to other
tenants, who will give him his share of the harvest at the right time."

42 Jesus said to them, "Haven't you ever read
what the Scriptures say?

'The very stone which the builders rejected
turned out to be the most important stone.
This was done by the Lord;
how wonderful it is!'

43 "And so I tell you," added Jesus, "the
Kingdom of God will be taken away from you
and be given to a people who will produce the
proper fruits. [44 Whoever falls on this stone will

New International Version

landowner who planted a vineyard. He put a
wall around it, dug a wine press in it and built
a tower. Then he rented the vineyard to some
farmers and went away on a journey. 34 When
the harvest time approached, he sent his servants to the tenants to collect his fruit.

35 "The tenants seized his servants; they
beat one, killed another, and stoned a third.
36 Then he sent other servants to them, more
than the first time, and the tenants treated them
the same way. 37 Last of all, he sent his son to
them. 'They will respect my son,' he said.

38 "But when the tenants saw the son, they
said to one another, 'This is the heir. Come,
let's kill him and take his inheritance.' 39 So
they took him and threw him out of the vineyard and killed him.

40 "Therefore, when the owner of the vineyard comes, what will he do to those tenants?"

41 "He will bring those wretches to a
wretched end," they replied, "and he will rent
the vineyard to other tenants, who will give him
his share of the crop at harvest time."

42 Jesus said to them, "Have you never read
in the Scriptures:

'The stone the builders rejected
has become the capstone;
the Lord has done this,
and it is marvelous in our eyes'[z]?

43 "Therefore I tell you that the kingdom of
God will be taken away from you and given to a
people who will produce its fruit. 44 He who falls

[*z*] Psalm 118:22,23.

Phillips Modern English

once a man, a land-owner, who planted a vineyard, fenced it round, dug out a hole for the wine-press and built a watch-tower. Then he let it out to farm-workers and went abroad. When the vintage-time approached he sent his servants to the farm-workers to receive his share of the crop. But they took his servants, beat up one, killed another, and stoned a third. Then he sent some more servants, a larger party than the first, but they treated them in just the same way. Finally he sent his own son, saying, 'They will respect my son.' Yet when the farm-workers saw the son they said to each other, 'This fellow is the future owner. Come on, let's kill him and we shall get everything that he would have had!' So they took him, threw him out of the vineyard and killed him. Now when the owner of the vineyard returns, what will he do to those farm-workers?"

"He will kill those scoundrels without mercy," they replied, "and will let the vineyard out to other tenants, who will give him the produce at the right season."

"And have you never read these words of scripture," said Jesus to them:

The stone which the builders rejected,
The same was made the head of the corner:
This was from the Lord,
And it is marvellous in our eyes?

"Here, I tell you, lies the reason why the kingdom of God is going to be taken away from you and given to a people who will produce its proper fruit.
(Any man who falls on this stone will be shat-

Revised Standard Version

householder who planted a vineyard, and set a
hedge around it, and dug a wine press in it, and
built a tower, and let it out to tenants, and went
into another country. 34 When the season of
fruit drew near, he sent his servants to the tenants, to get his fruit; 35 and the tenants took his
servants and beat one, killed another, and stoned
another. 36 Again he sent other servants, more
than the first; and they did the same to them.
37 Afterward he sent his son to them, saying,
'They will respect my son.' 38 But when the
tenants saw the son, they said to themselves,
'This is the heir; come, let us kill him and have
his inheritance.' 39 And they took him and cast
him out of the vineyard, and killed him. 40 When
therefore the owner of the vineyard comes, what
will he do to those tenants?" 41 They said to
him, "He will put those wretches to a miserable
death, and let out the vineyard to other tenants
who will give him the fruits in their seasons."
42 Jesus said to them, "Have you never read
in the scriptures:
'The very stone which the builders rejected
has become the head of the corner;
this was the Lord's doing,
and it is marvelous in our eyes'?
43 Therefore I tell you, the kingdom of God will
be taken away from you and given to a nation
producing the fruits of it." [q]

[q] Other ancient authorities add verse 44, *"And he who falls on this stone will be broken to pieces; but when it falls on any one, it will crush him."*

Jerusalem Bible

man, a landowner, who planted a vineyard; he
fenced it around, dug a winepress in it and built
a tower; then he leased it to tenants and went
abroad. 34 When vintage time drew near he sent
his servants to the tenants to collect his produce.
35 But the tenants seized his servants, thrashed
one, killed another and stoned a third. 36 Next
he sent some more servants, this time a larger
number, and they dealt with them in the same
way. 37 Finally he sent his son to them. 'They
will respect my son,' he said. 38 But when the
tenants saw the son, they said to each other,
'This is the heir. Come on, let us kill him and
take over his inheritance.' 39 So they seized him
and threw him out of the vineyard and killed
him. 40 Now when the owner of the vineyard
comes, what will he do to those tenants?"
41 They answered, "He will bring those wretches
to a wretched end and lease the vineyard to
other tenants who will deliver the produce to
him when the season arrives." 42 Jesus said to
them, "Have you never read in the scriptures:

It was the stone rejected by the builders
that became the keystone.
This was the Lord's doing
and it is wonderful to see? [v]

43 I tell you, then, that the kingdom of God
will be taken from you and given to a people
who will produce its fruit."

[v] Ps. 118:22-23.

New English Bible

owner who planted a vineyard: he put a wall round it, hewed out a winepress, and built a watch-tower; then he let it out to vine-growers and went abroad. When the vintage season approached, he sent his servants to the tenants to collect the produce due to him. But they took his servants and thrashed one, killed another, and stoned a third. Again, he sent other servants, this time a larger number; and they did the same to them. At last he sent to them his son. "They will respect my son", he said. But when they saw the son the tenants said to one another, "This is the heir; come on, let us kill him, and get his inheritance." And they took him, flung him out of the vineyard, and killed him. When the owner of the vineyard comes, how do you think he will deal with those tenants?' 'He will bring those bad men to a bad end', they answered, 'and hand the vineyard over to other tenants, who will let him have his share of the crop when the season comes.' Then Jesus said to them, 'Have you never read in the scriptures: "The stone which the builders rejected has become the main corner-stone. This is the Lord's doing, and it is wonderful in our eyes"? Therefore, I tell you, the kingdom of God will be taken away from you, and given to a nation that yields the proper fruit.' [a]

[a] *Some witnesses add* (44) Any man who falls on this stone will be dashed to pieces; and if it falls on a man he will be crushed by it.

King James Version

this stone shall be broken: but on whomsoever
it shall fall, it will grind him to powder. 45 And
when the chief priests and Pharisees had heard
his parables, they perceived that he spake of
them. 46 But when they sought to lay hands on
him, they feared the multitude, because they
took him for a prophet.

22 And Jesus answered and spake unto them
again by parables, and said, 2 The kingdom
of heaven is like unto a certain king, which made
a marriage for his son, 3 And sent forth his servants to call them that were bidden to the wedding: and they would not come. 4 Again, he sent
forth other servants, saying, Tell them which
are bidden, Behold, I have prepared my dinner:
my oxen and *my* fatlings *are* killed, and all
things *are* ready: come unto the marriage. 5 But
they made light of *it,* and went their ways, one
to his farm, another to his merchandise: 6 And
the remnant took his servants, and entreated
them spitefully, and slew *them.* 7 But when the
king heard *thereof,* he was wroth: and he sent
forth his armies, and destroyed those murderers,
and burned up their city. 8 Then saith he to his
servants, The wedding is ready, but they which
were bidden were not worthy. 9 Go ye therefore
into the highways, and as many as ye shall find,
bid to the marriage. 10 So those servants went

Living Bible

be broken, but those it falls on will be scattered
as dust."
45 When the chief priests and other Jewish
leaders realized that Jesus was talking about
them—that they were the farmers in his story—
46 they wanted to get rid of him, but were afraid
to try because of the crowds, for they accepted
Jesus as a prophet.

22 Jesus told several other stories to show
what the Kingdom of Heaven is like.
"For instance," he said, "it can be illustrated by the story of a king who prepared a
great wedding dinner for his son. 3 Many guests
were invited, and when the banquet was ready
he sent messengers to notify everyone that it
was time to come. But all refused! 4 So he sent
other servants to tell them, 'Everything is ready
and the roast is in the oven. Hurry!'
5 "But the guests he had invited merely
laughed and went on about their business, one
to his farm, another to his store; 6 others beat
up his messengers and treated them shamefully,
even killing some of them.
7 "Then the angry king sent out his army
and destroyed the murderers and burned their
city. 8 And he said to his servants, 'The wedding
feast is ready, and the guests I invited aren't
worthy of the honor. 9 Now go out to the street
corners and invite everyone you see.'
10 "So the servants did, and brought in all

Today's English Version

be broken to pieces; and if the stone falls on
someone it will crush him to dust.]"
45 The chief priests and the Pharisees heard
Jesus' parables and knew that he was talking
about them, 46 so they tried to arrest him. But
they were afraid of the crowds, who considered
Jesus to be a prophet.

The parable of the wedding feast

22 Jesus again used parables in talking to
the people. 2 "The Kingdom of heaven is
like a king who prepared a wedding feast for his
son. 3 He sent his servants to tell the invited
guests to come to the feast, but they did not
want to come. 4 So he sent other servants with
the message: 'Tell the guests, "My feast is ready
now; my steers and prize calves have been
butchered, and everything is ready. Come to the
wedding feast!"' 5 But the invited guests paid no
attention and went about their business: one
went to his farm, the other to his store, 6 while
others grabbed the servants, beat them, and killed
them. 7 The king was very angry; he sent his soldiers, who killed those murderers and burned
down their city. 8 Then he called his servants.
'My wedding feast is ready,' he said, 'but the
people I invited did not deserve it. 9 Now go to
the main streets and invite to the feast as many
people as you find.' 10 So the servants went out

New International Version

on this stone will be broken to pieces, but he on
whom it falls will be crushed." [a]
45 When the chief priests and the Pharisees
heard Jesus' parables, they knew he was talking
about them. 46 They looked for a way to arrest
him, but they were afraid of the crowd because
the people held that he was a prophet.

The parable of the wedding banquet

22 Jesus spoke to them again in parables,
saying: 2 "The kingdom of heaven is like
a king who prepared a wedding banquet for his
son. 3 He sent his servants to those who had
been invited to the banquet to tell them to
come, but they refused to come.
4 "Then he sent some more servants and said,
'Tell those who have been invited that I have
prepared my dinner: My oxen and fattened cattle have been butchered, and everything is ready.
Come to the wedding banquet.'
5 "But they paid no attention and went off—
one to his field, another to his business. 6 The
rest seized his servants, mistreated them and
killed them. 7 The king was enraged. He sent
his army and destroyed those murderers and
burned their city.
8 "Then he said to his servants, 'The wedding
banquet is ready, but those I invited did not
deserve to come. 9 Go to the street corners and
invite to the banquet anyone you find.' 10 So
the servants went out into the streets and gath-

[a] Some MSS omit verse 44.

Phillips Modern English

tered, and any man upon whom it falls will be ground into dust)."

When the chief priests and the Pharisees heard his parables they realised that he was speaking about them. They longed to get their hands on him, but they were afraid of the crowds, who regarded him as a prophet.

22.1 The kingdom is not to be lightly disregarded

Then Jesus began to talk to them again in parables.

"The kingdom of Heaven," he said, "is like a king who arranged a wedding-feast for his son. He sent his servants to summon those who had been invited to the festivities, but they refused to come. Then he tried again; he sent some more servants, saying to them, 'Tell those who have been invited, "Here is my banquet all ready, my bullocks and fat cattle have been slaughtered and everything is prepared. Come along to the wedding."' But they took no notice of this and went off, one to his farm, and another to his business. As for the rest, they got hold of the servants, treated them with insults, and finally killed them. At this the king was very angry and sent his troops and killed those murderers and burned down their city. Then he said to his servants, 'The wedding-feast is all ready, but those who were invited were not good enough for it. So go off now to all the street corners and invite everyone you find there to the feast.' So the servants went out on to the

Revised Standard Version

45 When the chief priests and the Pharisees heard his parables, they perceived that he was speaking about them. 46 But when they tried to arrest him, they feared the multitudes, because they held him to be a prophet.

22 And again Jesus spoke to them in parables, saying, 2 "The kingdom of heaven may be compared to a king who gave a marriage feast for his son, 3 and sent his servants to call those who were invited to the marriage feast; but they would not come. 4 Again he sent other servants, saying, 'Tell those who are invited, Behold, I have made ready my dinner, my oxen and my fat calves are killed, and everything is ready; come to the marriage feast.' 5 But they made light of it and went off, one to his farm, another to his business, 6 while the rest seized his servants, treated them shamefully, and killed them. 7 The king was angry, and he sent his troops and destroyed those murderers and burned their city. 8 Then he said to his servants, 'The wedding is ready, but those invited were not worthy. 9 Go therefore to the thoroughfares, and invite to the marriage feast as many as you find.' 10 And those servants went out into the

Jerusalem Bible

45 When they heard his parables, the chief priests and the scribes realized he was speaking about them, 46 but though they would have liked to arrest him they were afraid of the crowds, who looked on him as a prophet.

Parable of the wedding feast

22 Jesus began to speak to them in parables once again, 2 "The kingdom of heaven may be compared to a king who gave a feast for his son's wedding. 3 He sent his servants to call those who had been invited, but they would not come. 4 Next he sent some more servants. 'Tell those who have been invited,' he said, 'that I have my banquet all prepared, my oxen and fattened cattle have been slaughtered, everything is ready. Come to the wedding.' 5 But they were not interested: one went off to his farm, another to his business, 6 and the rest seized his servants, maltreated them and killed them. 7 The king was furious. He dispatched his troops, destroyed those murderers and burned their town. 8 Then he said to his servants, 'The wedding is ready; but as those who were invited proved to be unworthy, 9 go to the crossroads in the town and invite everyone you can find to the wedding.' 10 So these servants went out on to the

New English Bible

When the chief priests and Pharisees heard his parables, they saw that he was referring to them; they wanted to arrest him, but they were afraid of the people, who looked on Jesus as a prophet.

22 Then Jesus spoke to them again in parables: 'The kingdom of Heaven is like this. There was a king who prepared a feast for his son's wedding; but when he sent his servants to summon the guests he had invited, they would not come. He sent others again, telling them to say to the guests, "See now! I have prepared this feast for you. I have had my bullocks and fatted beasts slaughtered; everything is ready; come to the wedding at once." But they took no notice; one went off to his farm, another to his business, and the others seized the servants, attacked them brutally, and killed them. The king was furious; he sent troops to kill those murderers and set their town on fire. Then he said to his servants, "The wedding-feast is ready; but the guests I invited did not deserve the honour. Go out to the main thoroughfares, and invite everyone you can find to the wedding." The servants went out into

King James Version

out into the highways, and gathered together all
as many as they found, both bad and good: and
the wedding was furnished with guests.
11 And when the king came in to see the
guests, he saw there a man which had not on a
wedding garment: 12And he saith unto him,
Friend, how camest thou in hither not having
a wedding garment? And he was speechless.
13 Then said the king to the servants, Bind him
hand and foot, and take him away, and cast
him into outer darkness; there shall be weeping
and gnashing of teeth. 14 For many are called,
but few *are* chosen.
15 Then went the Pharisees, and took counsel
how they might entangle him in *his* talk. 16And
they sent out unto him their disciples with the
Herodians, saying, Master, we know that thou
art true, and teachest the way of God in truth,
neither carest thou for any *man:* for thou regardest not the person of men. 17 Tell us therefore, What thinkest thou? Is it lawful to give
tribute unto Cesar, or not? 18 But Jesus perceived their wickedness, and said, Why tempt
ye me, *ye* hypocrites? 19 Shew me the tribute
money. And they brought unto him a penny.
20And he saith unto them, Whose *is* this image
and superscription? 21 They say unto him, Ce-

Living Bible

they could find, good and bad alike; and the
banquet hall was filled with guests. 11 But when
the king came in to meet the guests he noticed
a man who wasn't wearing the wedding robe
[provided for him[a]].
12 " 'Friend,' he asked, 'how does it happen
that you are here without a wedding robe?' And
the man had no reply.
13 "Then the king said to his aides, 'Bind
him hand and foot and throw him out into the
outer darkness where there is weeping and gnashing of teeth.' 14 For many are called, but few
are chosen."
15 Then the Pharisees met together to try to
think of some way to trap Jesus into saying
something for which they could arrest him.
16 They decided to send some of their men along
with the Herodians[b] to ask him this question:
"Sir, we know you are very honest and teach
the truth regardless of the consequences, without
fear or favor. 17 Now tell us, is it right to pay
taxes to the Roman government or not?"
18 But Jesus saw what they were after. "You
hypocrites!" he exclaimed. "Who are you trying
to fool with your trick questions? 19 Here, show
me a coin." And they handed him a penny.
20 "Whose picture is stamped on it?" he asked
them. "And whose name is this beneath the
picture?"
21 "Caesar's," they replied.

[a] Implied. [b] The Herodians were a Jewish political party.

Today's English Version

into the streets and gathered all the people they
could find, good and bad alike; and the wedding
hall was filled with people.
11 "The king went in to look at the guests and
he saw a man who was not wearing wedding
clothes. 12 'Friend, how did you get in here
without wedding clothes?' the king asked him.
But the man said nothing. 13 Then the king told
the servants, 'Tie him up hand and foot and
throw him outside in the dark. There he will
cry and gnash his teeth.' "
14 And Jesus concluded, "For many are invited, but few are chosen."

The question about paying taxes

15 The Pharisees went off and made a plan
to trap Jesus with questions. 16 Then they sent
some of their disciples and some members of
Herod's party to Jesus. "Teacher," they said, "we
know that you tell the truth. You teach the truth
about God's will for man, without worrying
about what people think, because you pay no
attention to a man's status. 17 Tell us, then, what
do you think? Is it against our Law to pay taxes
to the Roman Emperor, or not?"
18 Jesus was aware of their evil plan, however,
and so he said, "You hypocrites! Why are you
trying to trap me? 19 Show me the coin to pay
the tax!"
They brought him the coin, 20 and he asked
them, "Whose face and name are these?"
21 "The Emperor's," they answered.

New International Version

ered all the people they could find, both good
and bad, and the wedding hall was filled with
guests.
11 "But when the king came in to see the
guests, he noticed a man there who was not
wearing wedding clothes. 12 'Friend,' he asked,
'how did you get in here without wedding
clothes?' The man was speechless.
13 "Then the king told the attendants, 'Tie
him hand and foot, and throw him outside, into
the darkness, where there will be weeping and
grinding of teeth.'
14 "For many are invited, but few are
chosen."

Paying taxes to Caesar

15 Then the Pharisees went out and laid plans
to trap him in his words. 16 They sent their disciples to him along with the Herodians.
"Teacher," they said, "we know you are a man
of integrity and that you teach the way of God
in accordance with the truth. You aren't
swayed by men, because you pay no attention to
who they are. 17 Tell us then, what is your opinion? Is it right to pay taxes to Caesar or not?"
18 But Jesus, knowing their evil intent, said,
"You hypocrites, why are you trying to trap me?
19 Show me the coin used for paying the tax."
They brought him a denarius, 20 and he asked
them, "Whose portrait is this? And whose inscription?"
21 "Caesar's," they replied.

Phillips Modern English

streets and collected together all those whom they found, bad and good alike. And the hall became filled with guests. But when the king came in to inspect the guests, he noticed among them a man not dressed for a wedding. 'How did you come in here, my friend,' he said to him, 'without being properly dressed for the wedding?' And the man had nothing to say. Then the king said to the ushers, 'Tie him up and throw him into the darkness outside, where there will be tears and bitter regret!' For many are invited but few are chosen."

22.15 A clever trap—and a penetrating answer

Then the Pharisees went off and discussed how they could trap him in argument. Eventually they sent their disciples with some of the Herod-party to say this, "Master, we know that you are an honest man who teaches the way of God faithfully and that you are not swayed by men's opinion of you. Obviously you don't care for human approval. Now tell us—'Is it right to pay taxes to Caesar or not?' "

But Jesus knowing their evil intention said, "Why try this trick one me, you frauds? Show me the money you pay the tax with." They handed him a silver coin, and he said to them, "Whose head is this and whose name is in the inscription?"

"Caesar's," they said.

Revised Standard Version

streets and gathered all whom they found, both
bad and good; so the wedding hall was filled
with guests.
11 "But when the king came in to look at the
guests, he saw there a man who had no wedding
garment; 12 and he said to him, 'Friend, how did
you get in here without a wedding garment?'
And he was speechless. 13 Then the king said to
the attendants, 'Bind him hand and foot, and
cast him into the outer darkness; there men will
weep and gnash their teeth.' 14 For many are
called, but few are chosen."
15 Then the Pharisees went and took counsel how to entangle him in his talk. 16And they
sent their disciples to him, along with the Herodians, saying, "Teacher, we know that you are
true, and teach the way of God truthfully, and
care for no man; for you do not regard the
position of men. 17 Tell us, then, what you
think. Is it lawful to pay taxes to Caesar, or
not?" 18 But Jesus, aware of their malice, said,
"Why put me to the test, you hypocrites?
19 Show me the money for the tax." And they
brought him a coin.[r] 20And Jesus said to them,
"Whose likeness and inscription is this?" 21 They

[r] Greek *a denarius.*

Jerusalem Bible

roads and collected together everyone they could
find, bad and good alike; and the wedding hall
was filled with guests. 11 When the king came in
to look at the guests he noticed one man who
was not wearing a wedding garment, 12 and said
to him, 'How did you get in here, my friend,
without a wedding garment?' And the man was
silent. 13 Then the king said to the attendants,
'Bind him hand and foot and throw him out
into the dark, where there will be weeping and
grinding of teeth.' 14 For many are called, but
few are chosen."

On tribute to Caesar

15 Then the Pharisees went away to work out
between them how to trap him in what he said.
16And they sent their disciples to him, together
with the Herodians,[w] to say, "Master, we know
that you are an honest man and teach the way
of God in an honest way, and that you are not
afraid of anyone, because a man's rank means
nothing to you. 17 Tell us your opinion, then.
Is it permissible to pay taxes to Caesar or not?"
18 But Jesus was aware of their malice and replied, "You hypocrites! Why do you set this
trap for me? 19 Let me see the money you pay
the tax with." They handed him a denarius,
20 and he said, "Whose head is this? Whose
name?" 21 "Caesar's," they replied. He then said

[w] Supporters of the ruling family, hoping to find a cause for denouncing Jesus to the Romans.

New English Bible

the streets, and collected all they could find, good and bad alike. So the hall was packed with guests.

'When the king came in to see the company at table, he observed one man who was not dressed for a wedding. "My friend," said the king, "how do you come to be here without your wedding clothes?" He had nothing to say. The king then said to his attendants, "Bind him hand and foot; turn him out into the dark, the place of wailing and grinding of teeth." For though many are invited, few are chosen.'

Then the Pharisees went away and agreed on a plan to trap him in his own words. Some of their followers were sent to him in company with men of Herod's party. They said, 'Master, you are an honest man, we know; you teach in all honesty the way of life that God requires, truckling to no man, whoever he may be. Give us your ruling on this: are we or are we not permitted to pay taxes to the Roman Emperor?' Jesus was aware of their malicious intention and said to them, 'You hypocrites! Why are you trying to catch me out? Show me the money in which the tax is paid.' They handed him a silver piece. Jesus asked, 'Whose head is this, and whose inscription?' 'Caesar's', they replied. He said to them,

King James Version

sar's. Then saith he unto them, Render therefore unto Cesar the things which are Cesar's;
and unto God the things that are God's. 22 When
they had heard *these words,* they marvelled, and
left him, and went their way.
23 The same day came to him the Sadducees,
which say that there is no resurrection, and
asked him, 24 Saying, Master, Moses said, If a
man die, having no children, his brother shall
marry his wife, and raise up seed unto his
brother. 25 Now there were with us seven brethren: and the first, when he had married a wife,
deceased, and, having no issue, left his wife unto
his brother: 26 Likewise the second also, and the
third, unto the seventh. 27 And last of all the
woman died also. 28 Therefore in the resurrection, whose wife shall she be of the seven? for
they all had her. 29 Jesus answered and said
unto them, Ye do err, not knowing the Scriptures, nor the power of God. 30 For in the resurrection they neither marry, nor are given in
marriage, but are as the angels of God in heaven.
31 But as touching the resurrection of the dead,
have ye not read that which was spoken unto
you by God, saying, 32 I am the God of Abraham, and the God of Isaac, and the God of
Jacob? God is not the God of the dead, but of

Living Bible

"Well, then," he said, "give it to Caesar if it
is his, and give God everything that belongs to
God."
22 His reply surprised and baffled them and
they went away.
23 But that same day some of the Sadducees,
who say there is no resurrection after death,
came to him and asked, 24 "Sir, Moses said that
if a man died without children, his brother
should marry the widow and their children
would get all the dead man's property. 25 Well,
we had among us a family of seven brothers.
The first of these men married and then died,
without children, so his widow became the second brother's wife. 26 This brother also died
without children, and the wife was passed to the
next brother, and so on until she had been the
wife of each of them. 27 And then she also died.
28 So whose wife will she be in the resurrection?
For she was the wife of all seven of them!"
29 But Jesus said, "Your error is caused by
your ignorance of the Scriptures and of God's
power! 30 For in the resurrection there is no
marriage; everyone is as the angels in heaven.
31 But now, as to whether there is a resurrection
of the dead—don't you ever read the Scriptures?
Don't you realize that God was speaking directly to you when he said, 32 'I *am* the God of
Abraham, Isaac, and Jacob'? So God is not the
God of the dead, but of the *living.*" [c]

[c] i.e., if Abraham, Isaac, and Jacob, long dead, were not alive in the presence of God, then God would have said, "I *was* the God of Abraham, etc."

Today's English Version

So Jesus said to them, "Well, then, pay to the
Emperor what belongs to him, and pay to God
what belongs to God."
22 When they heard this, they were filled with
wonder; and they left him and went away.

The question about rising from death

23 That same day some Sadducees came to
Jesus. (They are the ones who say that people
will not rise from death.) 24 "Teacher," they
said, "Moses taught: 'If a man who has no children dies, his brother must marry the widow so
they can have children for the dead man.'
25 Now, there were seven brothers who used to
live here. The oldest got married, and died without having children, so he left his widow to his
brother. 26 The same thing happened to the second brother, to the third, and finally to all seven.
27 Last of all, the woman died. 28 Now, on the
day when the dead rise to life, whose wife will
she be? All of them had married her."
29 Jesus answered them, "How wrong you are!
It is because you don't know the Scriptures or
God's power. 30 For when the dead rise to life
they will be like the angels in heaven, and men
and women will not marry. 31 Now, as for the
dead rising to life: haven't you ever read what
God has told you? He said, 32 'I am the God of
Abraham, the God of Isaac, and the God of
Jacob.' This means that he is the God of the living, not of the dead."

New International Version

Then he said to them, "Give to Caesar what
is Caesar's, and to God what is God's."
22 When they heard this, they were amazed.
So they left him and went away.

Marriage at the resurrection

23 That same day the Sadducees, who say
there is no resurrection, came to him with a
question. 24 "Teacher," they said, "Moses told
us that if a man dies without having children,
his brother must marry the widow and have
children for him. 25 Now there were seven
brothers among us. The first one married and
died, and since he had no children, he left his
wife to his brother. 26 The same thing happened
to the second and third brother, right on down
to the seventh. 27 Finally, the woman died.
28 Now then, at the resurrection, whose wife will
she be of the seven, since all of them were married to her?"
29 Jesus replied, "You are in error because
you do not know the Scriptures or the power of
God. 30 At the resurrection people will neither
marry nor be given in marriage; they will be like
the angels in heaven. 31 But about the resurrection of the dead—have you not read what God
said to you, 32 'I am the God of Abraham, the
God of Isaac, and the God of Jacob' [b]? He is
not the God of the dead but of the living."

[b] Exodus 3:6.

Phillips Modern English

"Then give to Caesar," he replied, "what belongs to Caesar and to God what belongs to God!"

This reply astonished them and they went away and let him alone.

22.23 Jesus exposes the ignorance of the Sadducees

On the same day some Sadducees (who deny that there is any resurrection) approached Jesus with this question: "Master, Moses said if a man should die without any children, his brother should marry his widow and raise up a family for him. Now, we had a case of seven brothers. The first one married and died, and since he had no family he left his wife to his brother. The same thing happened with the second and the third, right up to the seventh. Last of all the woman herself died. Now in this 'resurrection', whose wife will she be of these seven men—for she belonged to all of them?"

"You are very wide of the marks" replied Jesus to them, "for you are ignorant of both the scriptures and the power of God. For in the resurrection there is no such thing as marrying or being given in marriage—men live like the angels in Heaven. And as for the matter of the resurrection of the dead, haven't you ever read what was said to you by God himself, 'I am the God of Abraham, the God of Isaac and the God of Jacob'? God is not God of the dead

Revised Standard Version

said, "Caesar's." Then he said to them, "Render therefore to Caesar the things that are Caesar's, and to God the things that are God's." 22 When they heard it, they marveled; and they left him and went away.

23 The same day Sadducees came to him, who say that there is no resurrection; and they asked him a question, 24 saying, "Teacher, Moses said, 'If a man dies, having no children, his brother must marry the widow, and raise up children for his brother.' 25 Now there were seven brothers among us; the first married, and died, and having no children left his wife to his brother. 26 So too the second and third, down to the seventh. 27 After them all, the woman died. 28 In the resurrection, therefore, to which of the seven will she be wife? For they all had her."

29 But Jesus answered them, "You are wrong, because you know neither the scriptures nor the power of God. 30 For in the resurrection they neither marry nor are given in marriage, but are like angels[s] in heaven. 31 And as for the resurrection of the dead, have you not read what was said to you by God, 32 'I am the God of Abraham, and the God of Isaac, and the God of Jacob'? He is not God of the dead, but of the

[s] Other ancient authorities add *of God.*

Jerusalem Bible

to them, "Very well, give back to Caesar what belongs to Caesar—and to God what belongs to God." 22 This reply took them by surprise, and they left him alone and went away.

The resurrection of the dead

23 That day some Sadducees—who deny that there is a resurrection—approached him and they put this question to him, 24 "Master, Moses said that if a man dies childless, his brother is to marry the widow, his sister-in-law, to raise children for his brother. 25 Now we had a case involving seven brothers; the first married and then died without children, leaving his wife to his brother; 26 the same thing happened with the second and third and so on to the seventh, 27 and then last of all the woman herself died. 28 Now at the resurrection to which of those seven will she be wife, since she had been married to them all?" 29 Jesus answered them, "You are wrong, because you understand neither the scriptures nor the power of God. 30 For at the resurrection men and women do not marry; no, they are like the angels in heaven. 31 And as for the resurrection of the dead, have you never read what God himself said to you: 32 *I am the God of Abraham, the God of Isaac and the God of Jacob?* [x] God is God, not of the

[x] Ex. 3:6.

New English Bible

'Then pay Caesar what is due to Caesar, and pay God what is due to God.' This answer took them by surprise, and they went away and left him alone.

The same day Sadducees came to him, maintaining that there is no resurrection. Their question was this: 'Master, Moses said, "If a man should die childless, his brother shall marry the widow and carry on his brother's family." Now we knew of seven brothers. The first married and died, and as he was without issue his wife was left to his brother. The same thing happened with the second, and the third, and so on with all seven. Last of all the woman died. At the resurrection, then, whose wife will she be, for they had all married her?' Jesus answered: 'You are mistaken, because you know neither the scriptures nor the power of God. At the resurrection men and women do not marry; they are like angels in heaven.

'But about the resurrection of the dead, have you never read what God himself said to you: "I am the God of Abraham, the God of Isaac, and the God of Jacob"? He is not God of the

King James Version

the living. 33And when the multitude heard *this,*
they were astonished at his doctrine.
34 But when the Pharisees had heard that he
had put the Sadducees to silence, they were
gathered together. 35 Then one of them, *which*
was a lawyer, asked *him a question,* tempting
him, and saying, 36 Master, which *is* the great
commandment in the law? 37 Jesus said unto
him, Thou shalt love the Lord thy God with
all thy heart, and with all thy soul, and with all
thy mind. 38 This is the first and great commandment. 39And the second *is* like unto it,
Thou shalt love thy neighbour as thyself. 40 On
these two commandments hang all the law and
the prophets.
41 While the Pharisees were gathered together,
Jesus asked them, 42 Saying, What think ye of
Christ? whose son is he? They say unto him,
The son of David. 43 He saith unto them, How
then doth David in spirit call him Lord, saying,
44 The Lord said unto my Lord, Sit thou on my

Living Bible

33 The crowds were profoundly impressed by
his answers—34, 35 but not the Pharisees! When
they heard that he had routed the Sadducees
with his reply, they thought up a fresh question
of their own to ask him.

One of them, a lawyer, spoke up: 36 "Sir,
which is the most important command in the
laws of Moses?"
37 Jesus replied, " 'Love the Lord your God
with all your heart, soul, and mind.' 38, 39 This
is the first and greatest commandment. The second most important is similar: 'Love your neighbor as much as you love yourself.' 40All the
other commandments and all the demands of the
prophets stem from these two laws and are fulfilled if you obey them. Keep only these and you
will find that you are obeying all the others."
41 Then, surrounded by the Pharisees, he
asked them a question: 42 "What about the Messiah? Whose son is he?" "The son of David,"
they replied.
43 "Then why does David, speaking under the
inspiration of the Holy Spirit, call him 'Lord'?"
Jesus asked. "For David said,
44 'God said to my Lord, Sit at my right hand

Today's English Version

33 When the crowds heard this they were
amazed at his teaching.

The great commandment

34 When the Pharisees heard that Jesus had
silenced the Sadducees, they came together,
35 and one of them, a teacher of the Law, tried
to trap him with a question. 36 "Teacher," he
asked, "which is the greatest commandment in
the Law?"
37 Jesus answered, " 'You must love the Lord
your God with all your heart, with all your soul,
and with all your mind.' 38 This is the greatest
and the most important commandment. 39 The
second most important commandment is like it:
'You must love your fellow-man as yourself.'
40 The whole Law of Moses and the teachings
of the prophets depend on these two commandments."

The question about the Messiah

41 When the Pharisees gathered together, Jesus asked them, 42 "What do you think about the
Messiah? Whose descendant is he?"
"He is David's descendant," they answered.
43 "Why, then," Jesus asked, "did the Spirit
inspire David to call him 'Lord'? Because David
said,

44 'The Lord said to my Lord:

New International Version

33 When the crowds heard this, they were
astonished at his teaching.

The greatest commandment

34 Hearing that Jesus had silenced the Sadducees, the Pharisees got together. 35 One of them,
an expert in the law, tested him with this question: 36 "Teacher, which is the greatest commandment in the Law?"
37 Jesus replied: " 'Love the Lord your God
with all your heart, with all your soul and with
all your mind.' [c] 38 This is the first and greatest
commandment. 39And the second is like it:
'Love your neighbor as yourself.' [d] 40All the Law
and the Prophets hang on these two commandments."

Whose son is the Christ?

41 While the Pharisees were gathered together,
Jesus asked them, 42 "What do you think about
the Christ? [e] Whose son is he?"
"The son of David," they replied.
43 He said to them, "How is it then that
David, speaking by the Spirit, calls him 'Lord'?
For he says,
44 'The Lord said to my Lord:

[c] Deut. 6:5. [d] Lev. 19:18. [e] Or *Messiah.*

Phillips Modern English

but of living men!" When the crowds heard this they were astounded at his teaching.

22.34 *The greatest commandments in the Law*

When the Pharisees heard that he had silenced the Sadducees they came up to him in a body and one of them, an expert in the Law, put this test-question: "Master, which is the Law's greatest commandment?"

Jesus answered him, "'Thou shalt love the Lord thy God with all thy heart, and with all thy soul, and with all thy mind.' This is the first and great commandment. And there is a second like it: 'Thou shalt love thy neighbour as thyself.' The whole of the Law and the Prophets depends on these two commandments."

22.41 *Jesus puts an unanswerable question*

Then Jesus asked the assembled Pharisees this question: "What is your opinion about Christ? Whose son is he?"

"The Son of David," they answered.

"How then," returned Jesus, "does David when inspired by the Spirit call him Lord? He says—

The Lord said unto my *Lord,*

Revised Standard Version

living." 33And when the crowd heard it, they
were astonished at his teaching.
34 But when the Pharisees heard that he had
silenced the Sadducees, they came together.
35And one of them, a lawyer, asked him a question, to test him. 36 "Teacher, which is the great
commandment in the law?" 37And he said to
him, "You shall love the Lord your God with
all your heart, and with all your soul, and with
all your mind. 38 This is the great and first commandment. 39And a second is like it, You shall
love your neighbor as yourself. 40 On these two
commandments depend all the law and the
prophets."
41 Now while the Pharisees were gathered
together, Jesus asked them a question, 42 saying,
"What do you think of the Christ? Whose son
is he?" They said to him, "The son of David."
43 He said to them, "How is it then that David,
inspired by the Spirit,[t] calls him Lord, saying,
44 'The Lord said to my Lord,

[t] Or *David in the Spirit.*

Jerusalem Bible

dead, but of the living." 33And his teaching
made a deep impression on the people who
heard it.

The greatest commandment of all

34 But when the Pharisees heard that he had
silenced the Sadducees they got together 35 and,
to disconcert him, one of them put a question,
36 "Master, which is the greatest commandment
of the Law?" 37 Jesus said, "*You must love the
Lord your God with all your heart, with all
your soul, and with all your mind.* 38 This is
the greatest and the first commandment. 39 The
second resembles it: *You must love your neighbor as yourself.* 40 On these two commandments
hang the whole Law, and the Prophets also."

Christ not only son but also Lord of David

41 While the Pharisees were gathered around,
Jesus put to them this question, 42 "What is
your opinion about the Christ? Whose son is
he?" "David's," they told him. 43 "Then how is
it," he said, "that David, moved by the Spirit,
calls him Lord, where he says:

44 *The Lord said to my Lord:*

New English Bible

dead but of the living.' The people heard what he said, and were astounded at his teaching.

Hearing that he had silenced the Sadducees, the Pharisees met together; and one of their number[a] tested him with this question: 'Master, which is the greatest commandment in the Law?' He answered, '"Love the Lord your God with all your heart, with all your soul, with all your mind." That is the greatest commandment. It comes first. The second is like it: "Love your neighbour as yourself." Everything in the Law and the prophets hangs on these two commandments.'

Turning to the assembled Pharisees Jesus asked them, 'What is your opinion about the Messiah? Whose son is he?' 'The son of David', they replied. 'How then is it', he asked, 'that David by inspiration calls him "Lord"? For he says, "The Lord said to my Lord, 'Sit at my

[a] *Some witnesses insert* a lawyer.

King James Version

right hand, till I make thine enemies thy footstool? 45 If David then call him Lord, how is he his son? 46 And no man was able to answer him a word, neither durst any *man* from that day forth ask him any more *questions.*

23 Then spake Jesus to the multitude, and to his disciples, 2 Saying, The scribes and the Pharisees sit in Moses' seat: 3 All therefore whatsoever they bid you observe, *that* observe and do; but do not ye after their works: for they say, and do not. 4 For they bind heavy burdens and grievous to be borne, and lay *them* on men's shoulders; but they *themselves* will not move them with one of their fingers. 5 But all their works they do for to be seen of men: they make broad their phylacteries, and enlarge the borders of their garments, 6 And love the uppermost rooms at feasts, and the chief seats in the synagogues, 7 And greetings in the markets, and to be called of men, Rabbi, Rabbi. 8 But be not

Living Bible

until I put your enemies beneath your feet.' 45 Since David called him 'Lord,' how can he be merely his son?"

46 They had no answer. And after that no one dared ask him any more questions.

23 Then Jesus said to the crowds, and to his disciples, 2 "You would think these Jewish leaders and these Pharisees were Moses, the way they keep making up so many laws![a] 3 And of course you should obey their every whim! It may be all right to do what they say, but above anything else, *don't follow their example.* For they don't do what they tell you to do. 4 They load you with impossible demands that they themselves don't even try to keep.

5 "Everything they do is done for show. They act holy[b] by wearing on their arms little prayer boxes with Scripture verses inside,[c] and by lengthening the memorial fringes of their robes. 6 And how they love to sit at the head table at banquets, and in the reserved pews in the synagogue! 7 How they enjoy the deference paid them on the streets, and to be called 'Rabbi' and 'Master'! 8 Don't ever let anyone call you that.

[*a*] Literally, "sit on Moses' seat." [*b*] Implied. [*c*] Literally, "enlarge their phylacteries."

Today's English Version

Sit here at my right side,
until I put your enemies under your feet.'

45 If, then, David called him 'Lord,' how can the Messiah be David's descendant?"

46 No one was able to answer Jesus a single word, and from that day on no one dared ask him any more questions.

Jesus warns against the teachers of the law and the Pharisees

23 Then Jesus spoke to the crowds and to his disciples. 2 "The teachers of the Law and the Pharisees," he said, "are the authorized interpreters of Moses' Law. 3 So you must obey and follow everything they tell you to do; do not, however, imitate their actions, because they do not practice what they preach. 4 They fix up heavy loads and tie them on men's backs, yet they aren't willing even to lift a finger to help them carry those loads. 5 They do everything just so people will see them. See how big are the containers with scripture verses on their foreheads and arms, and notice how long are the hems of their cloaks! 6 They love the best places at feasts and the reserved seats in the synagogues; 7 they love to be greeted with respect in the market places and have people call them 'Teacher.' 8 You must not be called 'Teacher,' because you

New International Version

Sit at my right hand
until I put your enemies under your feet.'[f]

45 If then David calls him 'Lord,' how can he be his son?" 46 No one could say a word in reply, and from that day on no one dared to ask him any more questions.

Seven woes

23 Then Jesus said to the crowds and to his disciples: 2 "The teachers of the law and the Pharisees sit in Moses' seat. 3 So you must obey them and do everything they tell you. But do not do what they do, for they do not practice what they preach. 4 They tie up heavy loads and put them on men's shoulders, but they themselves are not willing to lift a finger to move them.

5 "Everything they do is done for men to see: They make their phylacteries[g] wide and the tassels of their prayer shawls long; 6 they love the place of honor at banquets and the most important seats in the synagogues; 7 they love to be greeted in the marketplaces and to have men call them 'Rabbi.'

8 "But you are not to be called 'Rabbi,' for

[*f*] Psalm 110:1. [*g*] That is, boxes containing Scripture verses, which were worn on the forehead and arms.

Phillips Modern English

Sit thou on my right hand,
Till I put thine enemies underneath thy feet?

If David then calls them Lord, how can he be his son?"

Nobody was able to answer this and from that day on no one dared to ask him any further questions.

23.1 He publicly warns the people against their religious leaders

Then Jesus addressed the crowds and his disciples. "The scribes and the Pharisees speak with the authority of Moses," he told them, "so you must do what they tell you and follow their instructions. But you must not imitate their lives! For they preach but do not practise. They pile up back-breaking burdens and lay them on other men's shoulders—yet they themselves will not raise a finger to move them. Their whole lives are planned with an eye to effect. They increase the size of their phylacteries* and lengthen the tassels of their robes; they love seats of honour at dinner parties and front places in the synagogues. They love to be greeted with respect in public places and to have men call them 'rabbi!' Don't you ever be called 'rabbi'—

* Phylacteries: Strips of parchment inscribed with texts from the Law, worn on the arm or forehead.

Revised Standard Version

Sit at my right hand,
till I put thy enemies under thy feet'?
45 If David thus calls him Lord, how is he his
son?" 46And no one was able to answer him a
word, nor from that day did any one dare to ask
him any more questions.

23 Then said Jesus to the crowds and to his
disciples, 2 "The scribes and the Pharisees
sit on Moses' seat; 3 so practice and observe
whatever they tell you, but not what they do;
for they preach, but do not practice. 4 They bind
heavy burdens, hard to bear,[u] and lay them on
men's shoulders; but they themselves will not
move them with their finger. 5 They do all their
deeds to be seen by men; for they make their
phylacteries broad and their fringes long, 6 and
they love the place of honor at feasts and the
best seats in the synagogues, 7 and salutations
in the market places, and being called rabbi by
men. 8 But you are not to be called rabbi, for

[u] Other ancient authorities omit *hard to bear*.

Jerusalem Bible

Sit at my right hand
and I will put your enemies
under your feet? [y]

45 "If David can call him Lord, then how can
he be his son?" 46 Not one could think of anything to say in reply, and from that day no one
dared to ask him any further questions.

The scribes and Pharisees: their hypocrisy and vanity

23 Then addressing the people and his disciples Jesus said, 2 "The scribes and the
Pharisees occupy the chair of Moses. 3 You
must therefore do what they tell you and listen
to what they say; but do not be guided by what
they do: since they do not practice what they
preach. 4 They tie up heavy burdens and lay
them on men's shoulders, but will they lift a
finger to move them? Not they! 5 Everything
they do is done to attract attention, like wearing
broader phylacteries and longer tassels,[z] 6 like
wanting to take the place of honor at banquets
and the front seats in the synagogues, 7 being
greeted obsequiously in the market squares and
having people call them Rabbi.
8 "You, however, must not allow yourselves

[y] Ps. 110:1. [z] Phylacteries: containers for short texts taken from the Law; they were worn on the arm or the forehead in obedience to Ex. 13:9,16 and Dt. 6:8. The tassels were sewn to the corners of the cloak.

New English Bible

right hand until I put your enemies under your feet.'" If David calls him "Lord", how can he be David's son?' Not a man could say a word in reply; and from that day forward no one dared ask him another question.

23 Jesus then addressed the people and his disciples in these words: 'The doctors of the law and the Pharisees sit in the chair of Moses; therefore do what they tell you; pay attention to their words. But do not follow their practice; for they say one thing and do another. They make up heavy packs and pile them on men's shoulders, but will not raise a finger to lift the load themselves. Whatever they do is done for show. They go about with broad phylacteries[a] and with large tassels on their robes; they like to have places of honour at feasts and the chief seats in synagogues, to be greeted respectfully in the street, and to be addressed as "rabbi".

'But you must not be called "rabbi"; for you

[a] *See Deuteronomy 6. 8-9 & Exodus 13. 9.*

King James Version

ye called Rabbi: for one is your Master, *even* Christ; and all ye are brethren. 9And call no *man* your father upon the earth: for one is your Father, which is in heaven. 10 Neither be ye called masters: for one is your Master, *even* Christ. 11 But he that is greatest among you shall be your servant. 12And whosoever shall exalt himself shall be abased; and he that shall humble himself shall be exalted.

13 But woe unto you, scribes and Pharisees, hypocrites! for ye shut up the kingdom of heaven against men: for ye neither go in *yourselves,* neither suffer ye them that are entering to go in. 14 Woe unto you, scribes and Pharisees, hypocrites! for ye devour widows' houses, and for a pretence make long prayer: therefore ye shall receive the greater damnation. 15 Woe unto you, scribes and Pharisees, hypocrites! for ye compass sea and land to make one proselyte; and when he is made, ye make him twofold more the child of hell than yourselves. 16 Woe unto you, *ye* blind guides, which say, Whosoever shall swear by the temple, it is nothing; but whosoever shall swear by the gold of the temple, he is a debtor! 17 *Ye* fools and blind: for whether is greater, the gold, or the temple that sanctifieth the gold? 18And, Whosoever shall swear by the

Living Bible

For only God is your Rabbi and all of you are on the same level, as brothers. 9And don't address anyone here on earth as 'Father,' for only God in heaven should be addressed like that. 10And don't be called 'Master,' for only one is your master, even the Messiah.

11 "The more lowly your service to others, the greater you are. To be the greatest, be a servant. 12 But those who think themselves great shall be disappointed and humbled; and those who humble themselves shall be exalted.

13, 14 "Woe to you, Pharisees, and you other religious leaders. Hypocrites! For you won't let others enter the Kingdom of Heaven, and won't go in yourselves. And you pretend to be holy, with all your long, public prayers in the streets, while you are evicting widows from their homes. Hypocrites! 15 Yes, woe upon you hypocrites. For you go to all lengths to make one convert, and then turn him into twice the son of hell you are yourselves. 16 Blind guides! Woe upon you! For your rule is that to swear 'By God's Temple' means nothing—you can break that oath, but to swear 'By the gold in the Temple' is binding! 17 Blind fools! Which is greater, the gold, or the Temple that sanctifies the gold? 18And you say

Today's English Version

are all brothers of one another and have only one Teacher. 9And you must not call anyone here on earth 'Father,' because you have only the one Father in heaven. 10 Nor should you be called 'Leader,' because your one and only leader is the Messiah. 11 The greatest one among you must be your servant. 12 Whoever makes himself great will be humbled, and whoever humbles himself will be made great."

Jesus condemns their hypocrisy

13 "How terrible for you, teachers of the Law and Pharisees! Hypocrites! You lock the door to the Kingdom of heaven in men's faces, but you yourselves will not go in, and neither will you let people in who are trying to go in!

[14 "How terrible for you, teachers of the Law and Pharisees! Hypocrites! You take advantage of widows and rob them of their homes, and then make a show of saying long prayers! Because of this your punishment will be all the worse!]

15 "How terrible for you, teachers of the Law and Pharisees! Hypocrites! You sail the seas and cross whole countries to win one convert; and when you succeed, you make him twice as deserving of going to hell as you yourselves are!

16 "How terrible for you, blind guides! You teach, 'If a man swears by the temple he isn't bound by his vow; but if he swears by the gold in the temple, he is bound.' 17 Blind fools! Which is more important, the gold or the temple which makes the gold holy? 18 You also teach, 'If a man

New International Version

you have only one Master and you are all brothers. 9And do not call anyone on earth 'father,' for you have one Father, and he is in heaven. 10 Nor are you to be called 'teacher,' for you have one Teacher, the Christ.[h] 11 The greatest among you will be your servant. 12 For whoever exalts himself will be humbled, and whoever humbles himself will be exalted.

13 "Woe to you, teachers of the law and Pharisees, you hypocrites! You shut the kingdom of heaven in men's faces. You yourselves do not enter, nor will you let those enter who are trying to.[i]

15 "Woe to you, teachers of the law and Pharisees, you hypocrites! You travel over land and sea to win a single convert, and when he becomes one, you make him twice as much a son of hell as you are.

16 "Woe to you, blind guides! You say, 'If anyone swears by the temple, it means nothing; but if anyone swears by the gold of the temple, he is bound by his oath.' 17 You blind fools! Which is greater: the gold, or the temple that makes the gold sacred? 18 You also say, 'If any-

[h] Or *Messiah.* [i] Some MSS add verse 14: *Woe to you, teachers of the law and Pharisees, you hypocrites! You devour widows' houses and for a show make lengthy prayers. Therefore you will be punished more severely.*

Phillips Modern English

you have only one teacher, and all of you are brothers. And don't call any human being 'father'—for you have one Father and he is in Heaven. And you must not let people call you 'leaders'—you have only one leader, Christ! The only 'superior' among you is the one who serves the others. For every man who promotes himself will be humbled, and every man who learns to be humble will find promotion.

"But alas for you, you scribes and Pharisees, play-actors that you are! You lock the doors of the kingdom of Heaven in men's faces; you will not go in yourselves neither will you allow those at the door to go inside.

"Alas for you, you scribes and Pharisees, play-actors! You scour sea and land to make a single convert, and then you make him twice as ripe for destruction as you are yourselves.

"Alas for you, you blind leaders! You say, 'If anyone swears by the Temple it amounts to nothing, but if he swears by the gold of the Temple he is bound by his oath.' You blind fools, which is the more important, the gold or the Temple which sanctifies the gold? And you

Revised Standard Version

you have one teacher, and you are all brethren.
9 And call no man your father on earth, for you
have one Father, who is in heaven. 10 Neither
be called masters, for you have one master, the
Christ. 11 He who is greatest among you shall
be your servant; 12 whoever exalts himself will
be humbled, and whoever humbles himself will
be exalted.
13 "But woe to you, scribes and Pharisees,
hypocrites! because you shut the kingdom of
heaven against men; for you neither enter yourselves, nor allow those who would enter to go
in.[v] 15 Woe to you, scribes and Pharisees, hypo-
crites! for you traverse sea and land to make a
single proselyte, and when he becomes a proselyte, you make him twice as much a child of
hell [w] as yourselves.
16 "Woe to you, blind guides, who say, 'If
any one swears by the temple, it is nothing; but
if any one swears by the gold of the temple, he
is bound by his oath.' 17 You blind fools! For
which is greater, the gold or the temple that has
made the gold sacred? 18 And you say, 'If any

[v] Other authorities add here (or after verse 12) verse 14, *Woe to you, scribes and Pharisees, hypocrites! for you devour widows' houses and for a pretense you make long prayers; therefore you will receive the greater condemnation.* [w] Greek *Gehenna.*

Jerusalem Bible

to be called Rabbi, since you have only one
Master, and you are all brothers. 9 You must
call no one on earth your father, since you have
only one Father, and he is in heaven. 10 Nor
must you allow yourselves to be called teachers,
for you have only one Teacher, the Christ.
11 The greatest among you must be your servant.
12 Anyone who exalts himself will be humbled,
and anyone who humbles himself will be exalted.

The sevenfold indictment of the scribes and Pharisees

13 "Alas for you, scribes and Pharisees, you
hypocrites! You who shut up the kingdom of
heaven in men's faces, neither going in yourselves nor allowing others to go in[a] who want to.
15 "Alas for you, scribes and Pharisees, you
hypocrites! You who travel over sea and land
to make a single proselyte, and when you have
him you make him twice as fit for hell as you
are.
16 "Alas for you, blind guides! You who say,
'If a man swears by the Temple, it has no force;
but if a man swears by the gold of the Temple,
he is bound.' 17 Fools and blind! For which is
of greater worth, the gold or the Temple that
makes the gold sacred? 18 Or else, 'If a man

[a] By interpreting the Law so strictly that nobody could obey all of it.

New English Bible

have one Rabbi, and you are all brothers. Do not call any man on earth "father"; for you have one Father, and he is in heaven. Nor must you be called "teacher"; you have one Teacher, the Messiah. The greatest among you must be your servant. For whoever exalts himself will be humbled; and whoever humbles himself will be exalted.

'Alas, alas for you, lawyers and Pharisees, hypocrites that you are! You shut the door of the kingdom of Heaven in men's faces; you do not enter yourselves, and when others are entering, you stop them.[b]

'Alas for you, lawyers and Pharisees, hypocrites! You travel over sea and land to win one convert; and when you have won him you make him twice as fit for hell as you are yourselves.

'Alas for you, blind guides! You say, "If a man swears by the sanctuary, that is nothing; but if he swears by the gold in the sanctuary, he is bound by his oath." Blind fools! Which is the more important, the gold, or the sanctuary which sanctifies the gold? Or you say, "If a man swears

[b] *Some witnesses add* (14) Alas for you, lawyers and Pharisees, hypocrites! You eat up the property of widows, while you say long prayers for appearance' sake. You will receive the severest sentence.

King James Version

altar, it is nothing; but whosoever sweareth by
the gift that is upon it, he is guilty. 19 *Ye* fools
and blind: for whether *is* greater, the gift, or the
altar that sanctifieth the gift? 20 Whoso therefore shall swear by the altar, sweareth by it,
and by all things thereon. 21 And whoso shall
swear by the temple, sweareth by it, and by
him that dwelleth therein. 22 And he that shall
swear by heaven, sweareth by the throne of God,
and by him that sitteth thereon. 23 Woe unto
you, scribes and Pharisees, hypocrites! for ye
pay tithe of mint and anise and cummin, and
have omitted the weightier *matters* of the law,
judgment, mercy, and faith: these ought ye to
have done, and not to leave the other undone.
24 *Ye* blind guides, which strain at a gnat, and
swallow a camel. 25 Woe unto you, scribes and
Pharisees, hypocrites! for ye make clean the
outside of the cup and of the platter, but within
they are full of extortion and excess. 26 *Thou*
blind Pharisee, cleanse first that *which is* within
the cup and platter, that the outside of them
may be clean also. 27 Woe unto you, scribes and
Pharisees, hypocrites! for ye are like unto whited
sepulchres, which indeed appear beautiful outward, but are within full of dead *men's* bones,
and of all uncleanness. 28 Even so ye also outwardly appear righteous unto men, but within ye

Living Bible

that to take an oath 'By the altar' can be broken,
but to swear 'By the gifts on the altar' is binding!
19 Blind! For which is greater, the gift on the
altar, or the altar itself that sanctifies the gift?
20 When you swear 'By the altar' you are swearing by it and everything on it, 21 and when you
swear 'By the Temple' you are swearing by it,
and by God who lives in it. 22 And when you
swear 'By heavens' you are swearing by the
Throne of God and by God himself.

23 "Yes, woe upon you, Pharisees, and you
other religious leaders—hypocrites! For you tithe
down to the last mint leaf in your garden, but
ignore the important things—justice and mercy
and faith. Yes, you should tithe, but you
shouldn't leave the more important things undone. 24 Blind guides! You strain out a gnat and
swallow a camel.

25 "Woe to you, Pharisees, and you religious
leaders—hypocrites! You are so careful to polish
the outside of the cup, but the inside is foul
with extortion and greed. 26 Blind Pharisees!
First cleanse the inside of the cup, and then the
whole cup will be clean.

27 "Woe to you, Pharisees, and you religious
leaders! You are like beautiful mausoleums—
full of dead men's bones, and of foulness and
corruption. 28 You try to look like saintly men,
but underneath those pious robes of yours are
hearts besmirched with every sort of hypocrisy
and sin.

Today's English Version

swears by the altar he isn't bound by his vow; but
if he swears by the gift on the altar, he is bound.'
19 How blind you are! Which is more important,
the gift or the altar which makes the gift holy?
20 So then, when a man swears by the altar he
is swearing by it and by all the gifts on it;
21 and when a man swears by the temple he is
swearing by it and by God, the one who lives
there; 22 and when a man swears by heaven he
is swearing by God's throne and by him who sits
on it.

23 "How terrible for you, teachers of the Law
and Pharisees! Hypocrites! You give to God one
tenth even of the seasoning herbs, such as mint,
dill, and cummin, but you neglect to obey the
really important teachings of the Law, such as
justice and mercy and honesty. These you should
practice, without neglecting the others. 24 Blind
guides! You strain a fly out of your drink, but
swallow a camel!

25 "How terrible for you, teachers of the Law
and Pharisees! Hypocrites! You clean the outside of your cup and plate, while the inside is full
of things you have gotten by violence and selfishness. 26 Blind Pharisee! Clean what is inside
the cup first, and then the outside will be clean
too!

27 "How terrible for you, teachers of the Law
and Pharisees! Hypocrites! You are like whitewashed tombs, which look fine on the outside,
but are full of dead men's bones and rotten stuff
on the inside. 28 In the same way, on the outside
you appear to everybody as good, but inside
you are full of hypocrisy and sins."

New International Version

one swears by the altar, it means nothing; but if
anyone swears by the gift on it, he is bound by
his oath.' 19 You blind men! Which is greater:
the gift, or the altar that makes the gift sacred?
20 Therefore, he who swears by the altar swears
by it and by everything on it. 21 And he who
swears by the temple swears by it and by the one
who dwells in it. 22 And he who swears by heaven
swears by God's throne and by the one who
sits on it.

23 "Woe to you, teachers of the law and
Pharisees, you hypocrites! You give a tenth of
your spices—mint, dill and cummin. But you have
neglected the more important matters of the law
—justice, mercy and faithfulness. You ought to
have practiced the latter, without neglecting the
former. 24 You blind guides! You strain out a
gnat but swallow a camel.

25 "Woe to you, teachers of the law and
Pharisees, you hypocrites! You clean the outside
of the cup and dish, but inside they are full of
greed and self-indulgence. 26 Blind Pharisee!
First clean the inside of the cup and dish, and
then the outside also will be clean.

27 "Woe to you, teachers of the law and
Pharisees, you hypocrites! You are like whitewashed tombs, which look beautiful on the outside but on the inside are full of dead men's
bones and everything unclean. 28 In the same
way, on the outside you appear to people as
righteous but on the inside you are full of
hypocrisy and wickedness.

Phillips Modern English

say, 'If anyone swears by the altar it doesn't matter, but if he swears by the gift placed on the altar he is bound by his oath.' Have you no eyes—which is more important, the gift, or the altar which sanctifies the gift? Any man who swears by the altar is swearing by the altar and whatever is offered upon it; and anyone who swears by the Temple is swearing by the Temple and by him who dwells in it; and anyone who swears by Heaven is swearing by the throne of God and by the One who sits upon that throne.

"Alas for you, scribes and Pharisees, you utter frauds! For you pay your tithe on mint and dill and cummin, and neglect the things which carry far more weight in the Law—justice, mercy and good faith. These are the things you should have observed—without neglecting the others. You are blind leaders, for you filter out a mosquito yet swallow a camel.

"What miserable frauds you are, you scribes and Pharisees! You clean the outside of the cup and the dish, while the inside is full of greed and self-indulgence. Can't you see, Pharisee? First wash the inside of a cup, and then you can clean the outside.

"Alas for you, you hypocritical scribes and Pharisees! You are like white-washed tombs, which look fine on the outside but inside are full of dead men's bones and all kinds of rottenness. For you appear like good men on the outside—but inside you are a mass of pretence and wickedness.

Revised Standard Version

one swears by the altar, it is nothing; but if any one swears by the gift that is on the altar, he is bound by his oath.' 19 You blind men! For which is greater, the gift or the altar that makes the gift sacred? 20 So he who swears by the altar, swears by it and by everything on it; 21 and he who swears by the temple, swears by it and by him who dwells in it; 22 and he who swears by heaven, swears by the throne of God and by him who sits upon it.

23 "Woe to you, scribes and Pharisees, hypocrites! for you tithe mint and dill and cummin, and have neglected the weightier matters of the law, justice and mercy and faith; these you ought to have done, without neglecting the others. 24 You blind guides, straining out a gnat and swallowing a camel!

25 "Woe to you, scribes and Pharisees, hypocrites! for you cleanse the outside of the cup and of the plate, but inside they are full of extortion and rapacity. 26 You blind Pharisee! first cleanse the inside of the cup and of the plate, that the outside also may be clean.

27 "Woe to you, scribes and Pharisees, hypocrites! for you are like whitewashed tombs, which outwardly appear beautiful, but within they are full of dead men's bones and all uncleanness. 28 So you also outwardly appear righteous to men, but within you are full of hypocrisy and iniquity.

Jerusalem Bible

swears by the altar it has no force; but if a man swears by the offering that is on the altar, he is bound.' 19 You blind men! For which is of greater worth, the offering or the altar that makes the offering sacred? 20 Therefore, when a man swears by the altar he is swearing by that and by everything on it. 21 And when a man swears by the Temple he is swearing by that and by the One who dwells in it. 22 And when a man swears by heaven he is swearing by the throne of God and by the One who is seated there.

23 "Alas for you, scribes and Pharisees, you hypocrites! You who pay your tithe of mint and dill and cummin[b] and have neglected the weightier matters of the Law—justice, mercy, good faith! These you should have practiced, without neglecting the others. 24 You blind guides! Straining out gnats and swallowing camels!

25 "Alas for you, scribes and Pharisees, you hypocrites! You who clean the outside of cup and dish and leave the inside full of extortion and intemperance. 26 Blind Pharisee! Clean the inside of cup and dish first so that the outside may become clean as well.

27 "Alas for you, scribes and Pharisees, you hypocrites! You who are like whitewashed tombs that look handsome on the outside, but inside are full of dead men's bones and every kind of corruption. 28 In the same way you appear to people from the outside like good honest men, but inside you are full of hypocrisy and lawlessness.

[*b*] The law of paying tithes on crops was extended to include herbs and plants grown for flavoring.

New English Bible

by the altar, that is nothing; but if he swears by the offering that lies on the altar, he is bound by his oath." What blindness! Which is the more important, the offering, or the altar which sanctifies it? To swear by the altar, then, is to swear both by the altar and by whatever lies on it; to swear by the sanctuary is to swear both by the sanctuary and by him who dwells there; and to swear by heaven is to swear both by the throne of God and by him who sits upon it.

'Alas for you, lawyers and Pharisees, hypocrites! You pay tithes of mint and dill and cummin; but you have overlooked the weightier demands of the Law, justice, mercy, and good faith. It is these you should have practised, without neglecting the others. Blind guides! You strain off a midge, yet gulp down a camel!

'Alas for you, lawyers and Pharisees, hypocrites! You clean the outside of cup and dish, which you have filled inside by robbery and self-indulgence! Blind Pharisee! Clean the inside of the cup first; then the outside will be clean also.

'Alas for you, lawyers and Pharisees, hypocrites! You are like tombs covered with whitewash; they look well from outside, but inside they are full of dead men's bones and all kinds of filth. So it is with you: outside you look like honest men, but inside you are brim-full of hypocrisy and crime.

King James Version

are full of hypocrisy and iniquity. 29 Woe unto you, scribes and Pharisees, hypocrites! because ye build the tombs of the prophets, and garnish the sepulchres of the righteous, 30 And say, If we had been in the days of our fathers, we would not have been partakers with them in the blood of the prophets. 31 Wherefore ye be witnesses unto yourselves, that ye are the children of them which killed the prophets. 32 Fill ye up then the measure of your fathers. 33 *Ye* serpents, *ye* generation of vipers, how can ye escape the damnation of hell?

34 Wherefore, behold, I send unto you prophets, and wise men, and scribes: and *some* of them ye shall kill and crucify; and *some* of them shall ye scourge in your synagogues, and persecute *them* from city to city: 35 That upon you may come all the righteous blood shed upon the earth, from the blood of righteous Abel unto the blood of Zacharias son of Barachias, whom ye slew between the temple and the altar. 36 Verily I say unto you, All these things shall come upon this generation. 37 O Jerusalem, Jerusalem, *thou* that killest the prophets, and stonest

Living Bible

29, 30 "Yes, woe to you, Pharisees, and you religious leaders—hypocrites! For you build monuments to the prophets killed by your fathers and lay flowers on the graves of the godly men they destroyed, and say, 'We certainly would never have acted as our fathers did.'

31 "In saying that, you are accusing yourselves of being the sons of wicked men. 32 And you are following in their steps, filling up the full measure of their evil. 33 Snakes! Sons of vipers! How shall you escape the judgment of hell?

34 "I will send you prophets, and wise men, and inspired writers, and you will kill some by crucifixion, and rip open the backs of others with whips in your synagogues, and hound them from city to city, 35 so that you will become guilty of all the blood of murdered godly men from righteous Abel to Zechariah (son of Barachiah), slain by you in the Temple between the altar and the sanctuary. 36 Yes, all the accumulated judgment of the centuries shall break upon the heads of this very generation.

37 "O Jerusalem, Jerusalem, the city that kills the prophets, and stones all those God sends to

Today's English Version

Jesus predicts their punishment

29 "How terrible for you, teachers of the Law and Pharisees! Hypocrites! You make fine tombs for the prophets, and decorate the monuments of those who lived good lives, 30 and you say, 'If we had lived long ago in the time of our ancestors, we would not have done what they did and killed the prophets.' 31 So you actually admit that you are the descendants of those who murdered the prophets! 32 Go on, then, and finish up what your ancestors started! 33 Snakes, and sons of snakes! How do you expect to escape from being condemned to hell? 34 And so I tell you: I will send you prophets and wise men and teachers; you will kill some of them, nail others to the cross, and whip others in your synagogues and chase them from town to town. 35 As a result, the punishment for the murder of all innocent men will fall on you, from the murder of innocent Abel to the murder of Zechariah, Barachiah's son, whom you murdered between the temple and the altar. 36 I tell you indeed: the punishment for all these will fall on the people of this day!"

Jesus' love for Jerusalem

37 "Jerusalem, Jerusalem! You kill the prophets and stone the messengers God has sent you!

New International Version

29 "Woe to you, teachers of the law and Pharisees, you hypocrites! You build tombs for the prophets and decorate the graves of the righteous. 30 And you say, 'If we had lived in the days of our forefathers, we would not have taken part with them in shedding the blood of the prophets.' 31 So you testify against yourselves that you are the descendants of those who murdered the prophets. 32 Fill up, then, the measure of the sin of your forefathers!

33 "You snakes! You brood of vipers! How will you escape being condemned to hell? 34 Therefore I am sending you prophets and wise men and teachers. Some of them you will kill and crucify; others you will flog in your synagogues and pursue from town to town. 35 And so upon you will come all the righteous blood that has been shed on earth, from the blood of righteous Abel to the blood of Zechariah son of Berachiah, whom you murdered between the temple and the altar. 36 I tell you the truth, all this will come upon this generation.

37 "O Jerusalem, Jerusalem, you who kill the prophets and stone those sent to you, how

Phillips Modern English

"What miserable frauds you are, you scribes and Pharisees! You build tombs for the prophets, and decorate monuments for good men of the past, and then say, 'If we had lived in the times of our ancestors we should never have joined in the killing of the prophets.' Yes, 'your ancestors'—*that* shows you to be sons indeed of those who murdered the prophets. Go ahead then, and finish off what your ancestors tried to do! You serpents, you viper's brood, how do you think you are going to avoid being condemned to the fires of destruction? Listen now to the reason why I send you prophets and wise and learned men; some of these you will kill and crucify, others you will flog in your synagogues and hunt from town to town. So that on your hands is all the innocent blood spilt on this earth, from the blood of Abel the good to the blood of Zachariah, Barachiah's son, whom you murdered between the sanctuary and the altar. Yes, I tell you that all this will be laid at the doors of this generation.

23.37 Jesus mourns over Jerusalem, and foretells its destruction

"Oh, Jerusalem, Jerusalem! You murder the prophets and stone the messengers that are sent

Revised Standard Version

29 "Woe to you, scribes and Pharisees, hypocrites! for you build the tombs of the prophets
and adorn the monuments of the righteous,
30 saying, 'If we had lived in the days of our
fathers, we would not have taken part with
them in shedding the blood of the prophets.'
31 Thus you witness against yourselves, that you
are sons of those who murdered the prophets.
32 Fill up, then, the measure of your fathers.
33 You serpents, you brood of vipers, how are
you to escape being sentenced to hell? [w]
34 Therefore I send you prophets and wise men
and scribes, some of whom you will kill and
crucify, and some you will scourge in your synagogues and persecute from town to town, 35 that
upon you may come all the righteous blood shed
on earth, from the blood of innocent Abel to
the blood of Zechariah the son of Barachiah,
whom you murdered between the sanctuary and
the altar. 36 Truly, I say to you, all this will
come upon this generation.
37 "O Jerusalem, Jerusalem, killing the prophets and stoning those who are sent to you! How

[w] Greek *Gehenna*

Jerusalem Bible

29 "Alas for you, scribes and Pharisees, you
hypocrites! You who build the sepulchers of the
prophets and decorate the tombs of holy men,
30 saying, 'We would never have joined in
shedding the blood of the prophets, had we
lived in our fathers' day.' 31 So! Your own evidence tells against you! You are the sons of
those who murdered the prophets! 32 Very well
then, finish off the work that your fathers began.

Their crimes and approaching punishment

33 "Serpents, brood of vipers, how can you
escape being condemned to hell? 34 This is why,
in my turn, I am sending you prophets and wise
men and scribes: some you will slaughter and
crucify, some you will scourge in your synagogues and hunt from town to town; 35 and so
you will draw down on yourselves the blood of
every holy man that has been shed on earth,
from the blood of Abel the Holy to the blood
of Zechariah son of Barachiah[c] whom you murdered between the sanctuary and the altar. 36 I
tell you solemnly, all of this will recoil on this
generation.

Jerusalem admonished

37 "Jerusalem, Jerusalem, you that kill the
prophets and stone those who are sent to you!

[c] Possibly Zechariah, the last of the prophets to be killed, according to the Jewish scriptures (2 Ch. 24: 20-22).

New English Bible

'Alas for you, lawyers and Pharisees, hypocrites! You build up the tombs of the prophets and embellish the monuments of the saints, and you say, "If we had been alive in our fathers' time, we should never have taken part with them in the murder of the prophets." So you acknowledge that you are the sons of the men who killed the prophets. Go on then, finish off what your fathers began! [c]

'You snakes, you vipers' brood, how can you escape being condemned to hell? I send you therefore prophets, sages, and teachers; some of them you will kill and crucify, others you will flog in your synagogues and hound from city to city. And so, on you will fall the guilt of all the innocent blood spilt on the ground, from innocent Abel to Zechariah son of Berachiah, whom you murdered between the sanctuary and the altar. Believe me, this generation will bear the guilt of it all.

'O Jerusalem, Jerusalem, the city that murders the prophets and stones the messengers sent to

[c] *Or* You too must come up to your fathers' standards.

King James Version

them which are sent unto thee, how often would I have gathered thy children together, even as a hen gathereth her chickens under *her* wings, and ye would not! 38 Behold, your house is left unto you desolate. 39 For I say unto you, Ye shall not see me henceforth, till ye shall say, Blessed *is* he that cometh in the name of the Lord.

24 And Jesus went out, and departed from the temple: and his disciples came to *him* for to shew him the buildings of the temple. 2And Jesus said unto them, See ye not all these things? verily I say unto you, There shall not be left here one stone upon another, that shall not be thrown down.

3 And as he sat upon the mount of Olives, the disciples came unto him privately, saying, Tell us, when shall these things be? and what *shall be* the sign of thy coming, and of the end of the world? 4And Jesus answered and said unto them, Take heed that no man deceive you. 5 For many shall come in my name, saying, I

Living Bible

her! How often I have wanted to gather your children together as a hen gathers her chicks beneath her wings, but you wouldn't let me. 38And now your house is left to you, desolate. 39 For I tell you this, you will never see me again until you are ready to welcome the one sent to you from God." [d]

24 As Jesus was leaving the Temple grounds, his disciples came along and wanted to take him on a tour of the various Temple buildings.

2 But he told them, "All these buildings will be knocked down, with not one stone left on top of another!"

3 "When will this happen?" the disciples asked him later, as he sat on the slopes of the Mount of Olives. "What events will signal your return, and the end of the world?" [a]

4 Jesus told them, "Don't let anyone fool you. 5 For many will come claiming to be the Mes-

[d] Literally, "in the name of the Lord." [a] Literally "age."

Today's English Version

How many times have I wanted to put my arms around all your people, just as a hen gathers her chicks under her wings, but you would not let me! 38 Now your home will be completely forsaken. 39 From now on you will never see me again, I tell you, until you say, 'God bless him who comes in the name of the Lord.' "

Jesus speaks of the destruction of the temple

24 Jesus left and was going away from the temple when his disciples came to him to show him the temple's buildings. 2 "Yes," he said, "you may well look at all these. I tell you this: not a single stone here will be left in its place; every one of them will be thrown down."

Troubles and persecutions

3 As Jesus sat on the Mount of Olives, the disciples came to him in private. "Tell us when all this will be," they asked, "and what will happen to show that it is the time for your coming and the end of the age."

4 Jesus answered, "Watch out, and do not let anyone fool you. 5 Because many men will come

New International Version

often I have longed to gather your children together, as a hen gathers her chicks under her wings, but you were not willing. 38 Look, your house is left to you desolate. 39 For I tell you, you will not see me again until you say, 'Blessed is he who comes in the name of the Lord.' [j] "

Signs of the end of the age

24 Jesus left the temple and was walking away when his disciples came up to him to call his attention to its buildings. 2 "Do you see all these things?" he asked. "I tell you the truth, not one stone here will be left on another; every one will be thrown down."

3 As Jesus was sitting on the Mount of Olives, the disciples came to him privately. "Tell us," they said, "when will this happen, and what will be the sign of your coming and of the end of the age?"

4 Jesus answered: "Watch out that no one deceives you. 5 For many will come in my name,

[j] Psalm 118:26.

Phillips Modern English

to you. How often have I longed to gather your children round me like a bird gathering her brood together under her wings—and you would never have it. Now all you have left is your house—desolate. I tell you that you will never see me again till the day when you cry, 'Blessed is he who comes in the name of the Lord!' "

Then Jesus went out of the Temple and was walking away when his disciples came up and drew his attention to its buildings. "You see all these?" replied Jesus. "I tell you every stone will be thrown down till there is not a single one left standing upon another."

And as he was sitting on the slope of the Mount of Olives his disciples came to him privately and said, "Tell us, when will this happen? What will be the signal for your coming and the end of this world?"

"Be careful that no one misleads you," returned Jesus, "for many men will come in my

Revised Standard Version

often would I have gathered your children together as a hen gathers her brood under her
wings, and you would not! 38 Behold, your house
is forsaken and desolate.[x] 39 For I tell you, you
will not see me again, until you say, 'Blessed is he who comes in the name of the Lord.' "

24 Jesus left the temple and was going away, when his disciples came to point out to him the buildings of the temple.
2 But he answered them, "You see all these, do you not? Truly, I say to you, there will not be left here one stone upon another, that will not be thrown down."
3 As he sat on the Mount of Olives, the disciples came to him privately, saying, "Tell us, when will this be, and what will be the sign of your coming and of the close of the age?"
4 And Jesus answered them, "Take heed that no one leads you astray.
5 For many will come in my

[x] Other ancient authorities omit *and desolate.*

Jerusalem Bible

How often have I longed to gather your children, as a hen gathers her chicks under her
wings, and you refused! 38 So be it! Your house
will be left to you desolate, 39 for, I promise, you shall not see me any more until you say:

Blessings on him who comes in the name of the Lord!" [d]

B. The sermon on the end

Introduction

24 Jesus left the Temple, and as he was going away his disciples came up to draw his attention to the Temple buildings.
2 He said to them in reply, "You see all these? I tell you solemnly, not a single stone here will be left on another: everything will be destroyed."
3 And when he was sitting on the Mount of Olives the disciples came and asked him privately, "Tell us, when is this going to happen, and what will be the sign of your coming and of the end of the world?"

The beginning of sorrows

4 And Jesus answered them, "Take care that no one deceives you;
5 because many will come

[d] Ps. 118:26.

New English Bible

her! How often have I longed to gather your children, as a hen gathers her brood under her wings; but you would not let me. Look, look! there is your temple, forsaken by God.[a] [b] And I tell you, you shall never see me until the time when you say, "Blessings on him who comes in the name of the Lord." '

Prophecies and warnings

24 Jesus was leaving the temple when his disciples came and pointed to the temple buildings. He answered, 'Yes, look at it all. I tell you this: not one stone will be left upon another; all will be thrown down.'

When he was sitting on the Mount of Olives the disciples came to speak to him privately. 'Tell us,' they said, 'when will this happen? And what will be the signal for your coming and the end of the age?'

Jesus replied: 'Take care that no one misleads you. For many will come claiming my name and

[a] *Or* Look, your home is desolate. [b] *Some witnesses add* and laid waste.

King James Version

am Christ; and shall deceive many. 6 And ye shall
hear of wars and rumours of wars: see that ye
be not troubled: for all *these things* must come
to pass, but the end is not yet. 7 For nation shall
rise against nation, and kingdom against kingdom: and there shall be famines, and pestilences,
and earthquakes, in divers places. 8 All these *are*
the beginning of sorrows. 9 Then shall they deliver you up to be afflicted, and shall kill you:
and ye shall be hated of all nations for my
name's sake. 10 And then shall many be offended,
and shall betray one another, and shall hate one
another. 11 And many false prophets shall rise,
and shall deceive many. 12 And because iniquity
shall abound, the love of many shall wax cold.
13 But he that shall endure unto the end, the
same shall be saved. 14 And this gospel of the
kingdom shall be preached in all the world for
a witness unto all nations; and then shall the
end come. 15 When ye therefore shall see the
abomination of desolation, spoken of by Daniel
the prophet, stand in the holy place, (whoso
readeth, let him understand,) 16 Then let them
which be in Judea flee into the mountains: 17 Let
him which is on the housetop not come down
to take any thing out of his house: 18 Neither
let him which is in the field return back to take

Living Bible

siah, and will lead many astray. 6 When you hear
of wars beginning, this does not signal my return; these must come, but the end is not yet.
7 The nations and kingdoms of the earth will
rise against each other and there will be famines
and earthquakes in many places. 8 But all this
will be only the beginning of the horrors to
come.

9 "Then you will be tortured and killed and
hated all over the world because you are mine,
10 and many of you shall fall back into sin and
betray and hate each other. 11 And many false
prophets will appear and lead many astray. 12 Sin
will be rampant everywhere and will cool the
love of many. 13 But those enduring to the end
shall be saved.

14 "And the Good News about the Kingdom
will be preached throughout the whole world,
so that all nations will hear it, and then, finally,
the end will come.

15 "So, when you see the horrible thing[b]
(told about by Daniel[c] the prophet) standing
in a holy place (Note to the reader: You know
what is meant!),[d] 16 then those in Judea must
flee into the Judean hills. 17 Those on their
porches[e] must not even go inside to pack before
they flee. 18 Those in the fields should not re-

[b] Literally, "the abomination of desolation." [c] Daniel 9:27, 11:31, 12:11. [d] Literally, "Let the reader take note." [e] Literally, "roof tops" which, being flat, were used as porches at that time. See Acts 10:9.

Today's English Version

in my name, saying, 'I am the Messiah!' and fool
many people. 6 You are going to hear the noise
of battles close by and the news of battles far
away; but, listen, do not be troubled. Such things
must happen, but they do not mean that the end
has come. 7 Countries will fight each other, kingdoms will attack one another. There will be
famines and earthquakes everywhere. 8 All these
things are like the first pains of childbirth.

9 "Then you will be arrested and handed over
to be punished, and be put to death. All mankind
will hate you because of me. 10 Many will give
up their faith at that time; they will betray each
other and hate each other. 11 Then many false
prophets will appear and fool many people.
12 Such will be the spread of evil that many people's love will grow cold. 13 But whoever holds
out to the end will be saved. 14 And this Good
News about the Kingdom will be preached
through all the world, for a witness to all mankind; and then will come the end."

The awful horror

15 "You will see 'The Awful Horror,' of
which the prophet Daniel spoke, standing in the
holy place." (Note to the reader: understand
what this means!) 16 "Then those who are in
Judea must run away to the hills. 17 The man
who is on the roof of his house must not take
the time to go down and get his belongings from
the house. 18 The man who is in the field must

New International Version

claiming, 'I am the Christ,[k]' and will deceive
many. 6 You will hear of wars and rumors of
wars, but see to it that you are not alarmed. Such
things must happen, but the end is still to come.
7 Nation will rise against nation, and kingdom
against kingdom. There will be famines and
earthquakes in various places. 8 All these are the
beginning of birth pains.

9 "Then you will be handed over to be persecuted and put to death, and you will be hated
by all nations because of me. 10 At that time
many will turn away from the faith and will
betray and hate each other, 11 and many false
prophets will appear and deceive many people.
12 Because of the increase of wickedness, the
love of most will grow cold, 13 but he who
stands firm to the end will be saved. 14 And this
gospel of the kingdom will be preached in the
whole world as a testimony to all nations, and
then the end will come.

15 "So when you see standing in the holy
place 'the abomination that causes desolation,'[l]
spoken of through the prophet Daniel—let the
reader understand—16 then let those who are
in Judea flee to the mountains. 17 Let no one on
the roof of his house go down to take anything
out of the house. 18 Let no one in the field go

[k] Or *Messiah.* [l] Daniel 9:27; 11:31; 12:11.

Phillips Modern English

name saying 'I am Christ', and they will mislead many. You will certainly hear of wars and rumours of wars—but don't be alarmed. Such things must indeed happen, but that is not the end. For one nation will rise in arms against another, and one kingdom against another, and there will be famines and earthquakes in different parts of the world. But all that is only the beginning of the birth-pangs. For then comes the time when men will hand you over to persecution, and kill you. And all nations will hate you because you bear my name. Then comes the time when many will lose their faith and will betray and hate each other. Yes, and many false prophets will arise, and will mislead many people. Because of the spread of wickedness the love of most men will grow cold, though the man who holds out to the end will be saved. This good news of the kingdom will be proclaimed to men all over the world as a witness to all the nations, and then the end will come.

24.15 *Jesus prophesies a future of suffering*

"When the time comes, then, that you see the 'abomination of desolation' prophesied by Daniel 'standing in the sacred place'—the reader should note this—then is the time for those in Judaea to take to the hills. A man on his house-top must not waste time going into his house to collect anything; a man at work in the fields must

Revised Standard Version

name, saying, 'I am the Christ,' and they will lead
many astray. 6And you will hear of wars and
rumors of wars; see that you are not alarmed;
for this must take place, but the end is not yet.
7 For nation will rise against nation, and kingdom against kingdom, and there will be famines
and earthquakes in various places: 8 all this is
but the beginning of the birth-pangs.
9 "Then they will deliver you up to tribulation, and put you to death; and you will be hated
by all nations for my name's sake. 10And then
many will fall away,[y] and betray one another, and hate one another. 11And many false
prophets will arise and lead many astray. 12And
because wickedness is multiplied, most men's
love will grow cold. 13 But he who endures to
the end will be saved. 14And this gospel of the
kingdom will be preached throughout the whole
world, as a testimony to all nations; and then
the end will come.
15 "So when you see the desolating sacrilege
spoken of by the prophet Daniel, standing in
the holy place (let the reader understand),
16 then let those who are in Judea flee to the
mountains; 17 let him who is on the housetop
not go down to take what is in his house; 18 and
let him who is in the field not turn back to take

[y] Or *stumble.*

Jerusalem Bible

using my name and saying, 'I am the Christ,'
and they will deceive many. 6 You will hear of
wars and rumors of wars; do not be alarmed,
for this is something that must happen, but the
end will not be yet. 7 For nation will fight
against nation, and kingdom against kingdom.
There will be famines and earthquakes here and
there. 8All this is only the beginning of the birth
pangs.
9 "Then they will hand you over to be tortured and put to death; and you will be hated
by all the nations on account of my name.
10And then many will fall away; men will betray one another and hate one another. 11 Many
false prophets will arise; they will deceive many,
12 and with the increase of lawlessness, love in
most men will grow cold; 13 but the man who
stands firm to the end will be saved.
14 "This Good News of the kingdom will be
proclaimed to the whole world[e] as a witness to
all the nations. And then the end[f] will come.

The great tribulation of Jerusalem

15 "So when you see *the disastrous abomination,* of which the prophet Daniel spoke, set up
in the Holy Place (let the reader understand),
16 then those in Judaea must escape to the
mountains; 17 if a man is on the housetop, he
must not come down to collect his belongings;
18 if a man is in the fields, he must not turn

[e] The "inhabited world" as it was known. [f] The fall and destruction of Jerusalem. A prophecy of this is combined, in this discourse, with descriptions of the "last days."

New English Bible

saying, "I am the Messiah"; and many will be misled by them. The time is coming when you will hear the noise of battle near at hand and the news of battles far away; see that you are not alarmed. Such things are bound to happen; but the end is still to come. For nation will make war upon nation, kingdom upon kingdom; there will be famines and earthquakes in many places. With all these things the birth-pangs of the new age begin.

'You will then be handed over for punishment and execution; and men of all nations will hate you for your allegiance to me. Many will fall from their faith; they will betray one another and hate one another. Many false prophets will arise, and will mislead many; and as lawlessness spreads, men's love for one another will grow cold. But the man who holds out to the end will be saved. And this gospel of the Kingdom will be proclaimed throughout the earth as a testimony to all nations; and then the end will come.

'So when you see "the abomination of desolation", of which the prophet Daniel spoke, standing in the holy place (let the reader understand), then those who are in Judaea must take to the hills. If a man is on the roof, he must not come down to fetch his goods from the house; if in the field, he must not turn back for his coat.

King James Version

his clothes. 19 And woe unto them that are with child, and to them that give suck in those days! 20 But pray ye that your flight be not in the winter, neither on the sabbath day: 21 For then shall be great tribulation, such as was not since the beginning of the world to this time, no, nor ever shall be. 22 And except those days should be shortened, there should no flesh be saved: but for the elect's sake those days shall be shortened. 23 Then if any man shall say unto you, Lo, here *is* Christ, or there; believe *it* not. 24 For there shall arise false Christs, and false prophets, and shall shew great signs and wonders; insomuch that, if *it were* possible, they shall deceive the very elect. 25 Behold, I have told you before. 26 Wherefore if they shall say unto you, Behold, he is in the desert; go not forth: behold, *he is* in the secret chambers; believe *it* not. 27 For as the lightning cometh out of the east, and shineth even unto the west; so shall also the coming of the Son of man be. 28 For wheresoever the carcass is, there will the eagles be gathered together.

29 Immediately after the tribulation of those

Living Bible

turn to their homes for their clothes.

19 "And woe to pregnant women and to those with babies in those days. 20 And pray that your flight will not be in winter, or on the Sabbath.[f] 21 For there will be persecution such as the world has never before seen in all its history, and will never see again.

22 "In fact, unless those days are shortened, all mankind will perish. But they will be shortened for the sake of God's chosen[g] people.

23 "Then if anyone tells you, 'The Messiah has arrived at such and such a place, or has appeared here or there,' don't believe it. 24 For false Christs shall arise, and false prophets, and will do wonderful miracles, so that if it were possible, even God's chosen[g] ones would be deceived. 25 See, I have warned you.

26 "So if someone tells you the Messiah has returned and is out in the desert, don't bother to go and look. Or, that he is hiding at a certain place, don't believe it! 27 For as the lightning flashes across the sky from east to west, so shall my coming be, when I, the Messiah,[h] return. 28 And wherever the carcass is, there the vultures will gather.

29 "Immediately after the persecution of those

[*f*] The city gates were closed on the Sabbath. [*g*] Literally, "the elect." [*h*] Literally, "the Son of Man."

Today's English Version

not go back to get his cloak. 19 How terrible it will be in those days for women who are pregnant, and for mothers who have little babies! 20 Pray to God that you will not have to run away during the winter or on a Sabbath! 21 For the trouble at that time will be far more terrible than any there has ever been, from the beginning of the world to this very day. Nor will there ever be anything like it. 22 But God has already reduced the number of days; had he not done so, nobody would survive. For the sake of his chosen people, however, God will reduce the days.

23 "Then, if anyone says to you, 'Look, here is the Messiah!' or 'There he is!'—do not believe him. 24 For false Messiahs and false prophets will appear; they will perform great signs and wonders for the purpose of deceiving God's chosen people, if possible. 25 Listen! I have told you this ahead of time.

26 "Or, if people should tell you, 'Look, he is out in the desert!'—don't go there; or if they say, 'Look, he is hiding here!'—don't believe it. 27 For the Son of Man will come like the lightning which flashes across the whole sky from the east to the west.

28 "Wherever there is a dead body the vultures will gather."

The coming of the Son of Man

29 "Soon after the trouble of those days the

New International Version

back to get his cloak. 19 How dreadful it will be in those days for pregnant women and nursing mothers! 20 Pray that your flight will not take place in winter or on the Sabbath. 21 For then there will be great distress, unequaled from the beginning of the world until now—and never to be equaled again. 22 If those days had not been cut short, no one would survive, but for the sake of the elect those days will be shortened. 23 At that time if anyone says to you, 'Look, here is the Christ![m]' or, 'There he is!' do not believe it. 24 For false Christs and false prophets will appear and perform great signs and miracles to deceive even the elect—if that were possible. 25 See, I have told you ahead of time.

26 "So if anyone tells you, 'There he is, out in the desert,' do not go out; or, 'Here he is, in the inner rooms,' do not believe it. 27 For as the lightning comes from the east and flashes to the west, so will be the coming of the Son of Man. 28 Wherever there is a carcass, there the vultures will gather.

29 "Immediately after the distress of those days,

[*m*] Or *Messiah.*

Phillips Modern English

not go back home to fetch his clothes. Alas for the pregnant, alas for those with babes at their breasts at that time! Pray God that you may not have to make your escape in the winter or on the Sabbath day, for then there will be great misery, such as has never happened from the beginning of the world until now, and will never happen again! Yes, if those days had not been cut short no human being would survive. But for the sake of God's people those days are to be shortened.

"If anyone says to you then, 'Look, here is Christ!' or 'There he is!' don't believe it. False christs and false prophets are going to appear and will produce great signs and wonders to mislead, if it were possible, even God's own people. Listen, I am warning you. So that if people say to you, 'There he is, in the desert!' you are not to go out there. If they say, 'Here he is, in this inner room!' don't believe it. For as lightning flashes across from east to west so will the Son of Man's coming be. 'Wherever there is a dead body, there the vultures will flock.'

24.29 At the end of time the Son of Man will return

"Immediately after the misery of those days

Revised Standard Version

his mantle. 19And alas for those who are with
child and for those who give suck in those days!
20 Pray that your flight may not be in winter or
on a sabbath. 21 For then there will be great
tribulation, such as has not been from the beginning of the world until now, no, and never
will be. 22And if those days had not been
shortened, no human being would be saved; but
for the sake of the elect those days will be
shortened. 23 Then if any one says to you, 'Lo,
here is the Christ!' or 'There he is!' do not believe it. 24 For false Christs and false prophets
will arise and show great signs and wonders, so
as to lead astray, if possible, even the elect.
25 Lo, I have told you beforehand. 26 So, if they
say to you, 'Lo, he is in the wilderness,' do not
go out; if they say, 'Lo, he is in the inner rooms,'
do not believe it. 27 For as the lightning comes
from the east and shines as far as the west, so
will be the coming of the Son of man. 28 Wherever the body is, there the eagles[z] will be gathered together.
29 "Immediately after the tribulation of those

[z] Or *vultures*.

Jerusalem Bible

back to fetch his cloak. 19Alas for those with
child, or with babies at the breast, when those
days come! 20 Pray that you will not have to
escape in winter or on a sabbath. 21 For then
there will be *great distress such as, until now,*
since the world began, there never *has been,* nor
ever will be again. 22And if that time had not
been shortened, no one would have survived;
but shortened that time shall be, for the sake
of those who are chosen.
23 "If anyone says to you then, 'Look, here
is the Christ' or, 'He is there,' do not believe it;
24 for false Christs and false prophets will arise
and produce great signs and portents, enough to
deceive even the chosen, if that were possible.
25 There; I have forewarned you.

The coming of the Son of Man will be evident

26 "If, then, they say to you, 'Look, he is in
the desert,' do not go there; 'Look, he is in
some hiding place,' do not believe it; 27 because
the coming of the Son of Man will be like
lightning striking in the east and flashing far
into the west. 28 Wherever the corpse is, there
will the vultures gather.

The universal significance of this coming

29 "Immediately after the distress of those

New English Bible

Alas for women with child in those days, and for those who have children at the breast! Pray that it may not be winter when you have to make your escape, or Sabbath. It will be a time of great distress; there has never been such a time from the beginning of the world until now, and will never be again. If that time of troubles were not cut short, no living thing could survive; but for the sake of God's chosen it will be cut short.

'Then, if anyone says to you, "Look, here is the Messiah", or, "There he is", do not believe it. Impostors will come claiming to be messiahs or prophets, and they will produce great signs and wonders to mislead even God's chosen, if such a thing were possible. See, I have forewarned you. If they tell you, "He is there in the wilderness", do not go out; or if they say, "He is there in the inner room", do not believe it. Like lightning from the east, flashing as far as the west, will be the coming of the Son of Man.

'Wherever the corpse is, there the vultures will gather.

'As soon as the distress of those days has

King James Version

days shall the sun be darkened, and the moon shall not give her light, and the stars shall fall from heaven, and the powers of the heavens shall be shaken: 30 And then shall appear the sign of the Son of man in heaven: and then shall all the tribes of the earth mourn, and they shall see the Son of man coming in the clouds of heaven with power and great glory. 31 And he shall send his angels with a great sound of a trumpet, and they shall gather together his elect from the four winds, from one end of heaven to the other. 32 Now learn a parable of the fig tree; When his branch is yet tender, and putteth forth leaves, ye know that summer *is* nigh: 33 So likewise ye, when ye shall see all these things, know that it is near, *even* at the doors. 34 Verily I say unto you, This generation shall not pass, till all these things be fulfilled. 35 Heaven and earth shall pass away, but my words shall not pass away.

36 But of that day and hour knoweth no *man*, no, not the angels of heaven, but my Father only. 37 But as the days of Noe *were*, so shall also the coming of the Son of man be. 38 For

Living Bible

days the sun will be darkened, and the moon will not give light, and the stars will seem[i] to fall from the heavens, and the powers overshadowing the earth will be convulsed.[j]

30 "And then at last the signal of my coming[k] will appear in the heavens and there will be deep mourning all around the earth. And the nations of the world will see me arrive in the clouds of heaven, with power and great glory. 31 And I shall send forth my angels with the sound of a mighty trumpet blast, and they shall gather my chosen ones from the farthest ends of the earth and heaven.[l]

32 "Now learn a lesson from the fig tree. When her branch is tender and the leaves begin to sprout, you know that summer is almost here. 33 Just so, when you see all these things beginning to happen, you can know that my[m] return is near, even at the doors. 34 Then at last this age will come to its close.[n]

35 "Heaven and earth will disappear, but my words remain forever. 36 But no one knows the date and hour when the end will be—not even the angels. No, nor even God's Son.[o] Only the Father knows.

37, 38 "The world will be at ease[p]—banquets and parties and weddings—just as it was in

[*i*] Literally, "the stars shall fall from heaven." [*j*] Literally, "the powers of the heavens shall be shaken." See Ephesians 6:12. [*k*] Literally, "of the coming of the Son of Man." [*l*] "From the four winds, from one end of heaven to the other." [*m*] Literally, "He is nigh." [*n*] Or, "after all these things take place, this generation shall pass away." [*o*] Literally, "neither the Son." Many ancient manuscripts omit this phrase. [*p*] Implied.

Today's English Version

sun will grow dark, the moon will no longer shine, the stars will fall from heaven, and the powers in space will be driven from their courses. 30 Then the sign of the Son of Man will appear in the sky; then all the tribes of earth will weep, and they will see the Son of Man coming on the clouds of heaven with power and great glory. 31 The great trumpet will sound, and he will send out his angels to the four corners of the earth, and they will gather his chosen people from one end of the world to the other."

The lesson of the fig tree

32 "Let the fig tree teach you a lesson. When its branches become green and tender, and it starts putting out leaves, you know that summer is near. 33 In the same way, when you see all these things, you will know that the time is near, ready to begin. 34 Remember this! All these things will happen before the people now living have all died. 35 Heaven and earth will pass away; my words will never pass away."

No one knows the day and hour

36 "No one knows, however, when that day and hour will come—neither the angels in heaven, nor the Son; the Father alone knows. 37 The coming of the Son of Man will be like what happened in the time of Noah. 38 Just as in

New International Version

'the sun will be darkened,
and the moon will not give its light;
the stars will fall from the sky,
and the heavenly bodies will be shaken.'[n]

30 "At that time the sign of the Son of Man will appear in the sky, and all the nations of the earth will mourn. They will see the Son of Man coming on the clouds of the sky, with power and great glory. 31 And he will send his angels with a loud trumpet call, and they will gather his elect from the four winds, from one end of the heavens to the other.

32 "Now learn this lesson from the fig tree: As soon as its twigs get tender and its leaves come out, you know that summer is near. 33 Even so, when you see all these things, you know that it[o] is near, right at the door. 34 I tell you the truth, this generation[p] will certainly not pass away until all these things have happened. 35 Heaven and earth will pass away, but my words will never pass away.

The day and hour unknown

36 "No one knows about that day or hour, not even the angels in heaven, nor the Son,[q] but only the Father. 37 As it was in the days of Noah, so it will be at the coming of the Son of Man. 38 For in the days before the flood, people

[*n*] Isaiah 13:10; 34:4. [*o*] Or *he*. [*p*] Or *race*. [*q*] Some MSS omit *nor the Son*.

Phillips Modern English

the sun will be darkened, the moon will fail to give her light, the stars will fall from the sky, and the powers of heaven will be shaken. Then the sign of the Son of Man will appear in the sky, and all the nations of the earth will wring their hands as they see the Son of Man coming on the clouds of the sky in power and great splendour. And he will send out his angels with a loud trumpet-call and they will gather together his chosen from the four winds—from one end of the heavens to the other.

"Learn what the fig-tree can teach you. As soon as its branches grow full of sap and produce leaves you know that summer is near. So when you see all these things happening you may know that he is near, at your very door! Believe me, this generation will not disappear till all this has taken place. Heaven and earth will pass away, but my words will never pass away! But about that actual day and time no one knows—not even the angels of Heaven, nor the Son, only the Father. For just as life went on in the days of Noah so will it be at the coming of the Son of Man. In those days before

Revised Standard Version

days the sun will be darkened, and the moon will
not give its light, and the stars will fall from
heaven, and the powers of the heavens will be
shaken; 30 then will appear the sign of the Son
of man in heaven, and then all the tribes of the
earth will mourn, and they will see the Son of
man coming on the clouds of heaven with
power and great glory; 31 and he will send out
his angels with a loud trumpet call, and they
will gather his elect from the four winds, from
one end of heaven to the other.
32 "From the fig tree learn its lesson: as soon
as its branch becomes tender and puts forth its
leaves, you know that summer is near. 33 So
also, when you see all these things, you know
that he is near, at the very gates. 34 Truly, I say
to you, this generation will not pass away till all
these things take place. 35 Heaven and earth will
pass away, but my words will not pass away.
36 "But of that day and hour no one knows,
not even the angels of heaven, nor the Son,[a] but
the Father only. 37 As were the days of Noah,
so will be the coming of the Son of man. 38 For

[a] Other ancient authorities omit *nor the Son.*

Jerusalem Bible

days[g] the sun will be darkened, the moon will
lose its brightness, the stars will fall from the
sky and the powers of heaven will be shaken.
30 And then the sign of the Son of Man will appear in heaven; then too all the peoples of the
earth will beat their breasts; and they will see
the Son of Man coming on the clouds of
heaven with power and great glory.[h] 31 And he
will send his angels with a loud trumpet to
gather his chosen from the four winds, from
one end of heaven to the other.

The time of this coming

32 "Take the fig tree as a parable: as soon
as its twigs grow supple and its leaves come out,
you know that summer is near. 33 So with you
when you see all these things: know that he is
near, at the very gates. 34 I tell you solemnly,
before this generation has passed away all these
things will have taken place.[i] 35 Heaven and
earth will pass away, but my words will never
pass away. 36 But as for that day and hour, nobody knows it, neither the angels of heaven, nor
the Son, no one but the Father only.

Be on the alert

37 "As it was in Noah's day, so will it be
when the Son of Man comes. 38 For in those

[g] Join with v. 22. Vv. 23-28 are a digression. [h] As foretold in Dn. 7:14. [i] Meaning the fall and destruction of Jerusalem.

New English Bible

passed, the sun will be darkened, the moon will not give her light, the stars will fall from the sky, the celestial powers will be shaken. Then will appear in heaven the sign that heralds the Son of Man. All the peoples of the world will make lamentation, and they will see the Son of Man coming on the clouds of heaven with great power and glory. With a trumpet blast he will send out his angels, and they will gather his chosen from the four winds, from the farthest bounds of heaven on every side.

'Learn a lesson from the fig-tree. When its tender shoots appear and are breaking into leaf, you know that summer is near. In the same way, when you see all these things, you may know that the end is near,[a] at the very door. I tell you this: the present generation will live to see it all. Heaven and earth will pass away; my words will never pass away.

'But about that day and hour no one knows, not even the angels in heaven, not even the Son; only the Father.

'As things were in Noah's days, so will they be when the Son of Man comes. In the days be-

[a] *Or* that he is near.

King James Version

as in the days that were before the flood they
were eating and drinking, marrying and giving
in marriage, until the day that Noe entered into
the ark, 39 And knew not until the flood came,
and took them all away; so shall also the coming
of the Son of man be. 40 Then shall two be in
the field; the one shall be taken, and the other
left. 41 Two *women shall be* grinding at the mill;
the one shall be taken, and the other left.
42 Watch therefore; for ye know not what
hour your Lord doth come. 43 But know this,
that if the goodman of the house had known in
what watch the thief would come, he would
have watched, and would not have suffered his
house to be broken up. 44 Therefore be ye also
ready: for in such an hour as ye think not the
Son of man cometh. 45 Who then is a faithful
and wise servant, whom his lord hath made ruler
over his household, to give them meat in due
season? 46 Blessed *is* that servant, whom his lord
when he cometh shall find so doing. 47 Verily
I say unto you, That he shall make him ruler
over all his goods. 48 But and if that evil servant shall say in his heart, My lord delayeth his
coming; 49 And shall begin to smite *his* fellow
servants, and to eat and drink with the drunken;
50 The lord of that servant shall come in a day

Living Bible

Noah's time before the sudden coming of the
flood; 39 people wouldn't believe[q] what was going to happen until the flood actually arrived
and took them all away. So shall my coming be.
40 "Two men will be working together in the
fields, and one will be taken, the other left.
41 Two women will be going about their household tasks; one will be taken, the other left.
42 "So be prepared, for you don't know what
day your Lord is coming.
43 "Just as a man can prevent trouble from
thieves by keeping watch for them, 44 so you
can avoid trouble by always being ready for my
unannounced return.
45 "Are you a wise and faithful servant of the
Lord? Have I given you the task of managing
my household, to feed my children day by day?
46 Blessings on you if I return and find you faithfully doing your work. 47 I will put such faithful
ones in charge of everything I own!
48 "But if you are evil and say to yourself,
'My Lord won't be coming for a while,' 49 and
begin oppressing your fellow servants, partying
and getting drunk, 50 your Lord will arrive un-

[q] Literally, "knew not."

Today's English Version

the days before the Flood, people ate and drank,
men and women married, up to the very day
Noah went into the ark; 39 yet they did not
know what was happening until the Flood came
and swept them all away. That is how it will be
when the Son of Man comes. 40 At that time two
men will be working in the field: one will be
taken away, the other will be left behind. 41 Two
women will be at the mill grinding meal: one will
be taken away, the other will be left behind.
42 Watch out, then, because you do not know
what day your Lord will come. 43 Remember
this: if the man of the house knew the time when
the thief would come, he would stay awake and
not let the thief break into his house. 44 For this
reason, then, you also must be always ready, because the Son of Man will come at an hour when
you are not expecting him."

The faithful or the unfaithful servant

45 "Who, then, is the faithful and wise servant? He is the one whom his master has placed
in charge of the other servants, to give them
their food at the proper time. 46 How happy is
that servant if his master finds him doing this
when he comes home! 47 Indeed, I tell you, the
master will put that servant in charge of all his
property. 48 But if he is a bad servant, he will
tell himself, 'My master will not come back
for a long time,' 49 and he will begin to beat his
fellow servants, and eat and drink with drunkards. 50 Then that servant's master will come

New International Version

were eating and drinking, marrying and giving in
marriage, up to the day Noah entered the ark;
39 and they knew nothing about what would happen until the flood came and took them all away.
That is how it will be at the coming of the Son
of Man. 40 Two men will be in the field; one
will be taken and the other left. 41 Two women
will be grinding with a hand mill; one will be
taken and the other left.
42 "Therefore keep watch, because you do
not know on what day your Lord will come.
43 But understand this: If the owner of the house
had known at what time of night the thief was
coming, he would have kept watch and would
not have let his house be broken into. 44 So you
also must be ready, because the Son of Man
will come at an hour when you do not expect
him.
45 "Who then is the faithful and wise servant, whom the master has put in charge of the
servants in his household to give them their food
at the proper time? 46 It will be good for that
servant whose master finds him doing so when
he returns. 47 I tell you the truth, he will put
him in charge of all his possessions. 48 But suppose that servant is wicked and says to himself,
'My master is staying away a long time,' 49 and
he then begins to beat his fellow servants and to
eat and drink with drunkards. 50 The master of

Phillips Modern English

the flood people were eating, drinking, marrying and being given in marriage until the very day that Noah went into the ark, and knew nothing about the flood until it came and destroyed them all. So will it be at the coming of the Son of Man. Two men will be in the field; one is taken and one is left behind. Two women will be grinding at the hand-mill; one is taken and one is left behind. You must be on the alert then, for you do not know on what day your master is coming. You can be sure of this, however, that if the householder had known what time of night the burglar would arrive, he would have been ready for him and would not have allowed his house to be broken into. That is why you must always be ready, for you do not know when to expect the Son of Man to arrive.

24.45 Vigilance is essential

"Who then is the faithful and sensible servant, whom his master put in charge of his household to give the others their food at the proper time? Well, he is fortunate if his master finds him doing that duty on his return! Believe me, he will promote him to look after all his property. But if he should be a bad servant who says to himself, 'My master takes his time about returning', and should begin to beat his fellow-servants and eat and drink with drunkards, that servant's master will return on a day which he

Revised Standard Version

as in those days before the flood they were eating and drinking, marrying and giving in marriage, until the day when Noah entered the ark,
39 and they did not know until the flood came
and swept them all away, so will be the coming
of the Son of man. 40 Then two men will be in
the field; one is taken and one is left. 41 Two
women will be grinding at the mill; one is taken
and one is left. 42 Watch therefore, for you do
not know on what day your Lord is coming.
43 But know this, that if the householder had
known in what part of the night the thief was
coming, he would have watched and would not
have let his house be broken into. 44 Therefore
you also must be ready; for the Son of man is
coming at an hour you do not expect.
45 "Who then is the faithful and wise servant,
whom his master has set over his household, to
give them their food at the proper time?
46 Blessed is that servant whom his master when
he comes will find so doing. 47 Truly, I say to
you, he will set him over all his possessions.
48 But if that wicked servant says to himself,
'My master is delayed,' 49 and begins to beat
his fellow servants, and eats and drinks with the
drunken, 50 the master of that servant will come

Jerusalem Bible

days before the Flood people were eating, drinking, taking wives, taking husbands, right up to
the day Noah went into the ark, 39 and they
suspected nothing till the Flood came and swept
all away. It will be like this when the Son of
Man comes. 40 Then of two men in the fields
one is taken, one left; 41 of two women at the
millstone grinding, one is taken, one left.
42 "So stay awake, because you do not know
the day when your master is coming. 43 You
may be quite sure of this that if the householder
had known at what time of the night the burglar
would come, he would have stayed awake and
would not have allowed anyone to break through
the wall of his house. 44 Therefore, you too
must stand ready because the Son of Man is
coming at an hour you do not expect.

Parable of the conscientious steward

45 "What sort of servant, then, is faithful and
wise enough for the master to place him over
his household to give them their food at the
proper time? 46 Happy that servant if his master's arrival finds him at this employment. 47 I
tell you solemnly, he will place him over everything he owns. 48 But as for the dishonest servant who says to himself, 'My master is taking
his time,' 49 and sets about beating his fellow
servants and eating and drinking with drunkards, 50 his master will come on a day he does

New English Bible

fore the flood they ate and drank and married, until the day that Noah went into the ark, and they knew nothing until the flood came and swept them all away. That is how it will be when the Son of Man comes. Then there will be two men in the field; one will be taken, the other left; two women grinding at the mill; one will be taken, the other left.

'Keep awake, then; for you do not know on what day your Lord is to come. Remember, if the householder had known at what time of night the burglar was coming, he would have kept awake and not have let his house be broken into. Hold yourselves ready, therefore, because the Son of Man will come at the time you least expect him.

'Who is the trusty servant, the sensible man charged by his master to manage his household staff and issue their rations at the proper time? Happy that servant who is found at his task when his master comes! I tell you this: he will be put in charge of all his master's property. But if he is a bad servant and says to himself, "The master is a long time coming", and begins to bully the other servants and to eat and drink with his drunken friends, then the master will arrive on

King James Version

when he looketh not for *him*, and in an hour
that he is not aware of, 51 And shall cut him
asunder, and appoint *him* his portion with the
hypocrites: there shall be weeping and gnashing
of teeth.

25 Then shall the kingdom of heaven be
likened unto ten virgins, which took their
lamps, and went forth to meet the bridegroom.
2 And five of them were wise, and five *were* foolish. 3 They that *were* foolish took their lamps,
and took no oil with them: 4 But the wise took
oil in their vessels with their lamps. 5 While the
bridegroom tarried, they all slumbered and slept.
6 And at midnight there was a cry made, Behold,
the bridegroom cometh; go ye out to meet him.
7 Then all those virgins arose, and trimmed their
lamps. 8 And the foolish said unto the wise, Give
us of your oil; for our lamps are gone out. 9 But
the wise answered, saying, *Not so;* lest there be
not enough for us and you: but go ye rather to
them that sell, and buy for yourselves. 10 And
while they went to buy, the bridegroom came;
and they that were ready went in with him to
the marriage: and the door was shut. 11 Afterward came also the other virgins, saying, Lord,
Lord, open to us. 12 But he answered and said,

Living Bible

announced and unexpected, 51 and severely whip
you and send you off to the judgment of the
hypocrites; there will be weeping and gnashing
of teeth.

25 "The kingdom of Heaven can be illustrated by the story of ten bridesmaids[a]
who took their lamps and went to meet the
bridegroom. 2, 3, 4 But only five of them were
wise enough to fill their lamps with oil, while
the other five were foolish and forgot.

5, 6 "So, when the bridegroom was delayed,
they lay down to rest until midnight, when they
were roused by the shout, 'The bridegroom is
coming! Come out and welcome him!'

7, 8 "All the girls jumped up and trimmed
their lamps. Then the five who hadn't any oil
begged the others to share with them, for their
lamps were going out.

9 "But the others replied, 'We haven't enough.
Go instead to the shops and buy some for yourselves.'

10 "But while they were gone, the bridegroom
came, and those who were ready went in with
him to the marriage feast, and the door was
locked.

11 "Later, when the other five returned, they
stood outside, calling, 'Sir, open the door for us!'

12 "But he called back, 'Go away! It is too
late!'[b]

[a] Literally, "virgins." [b] Literally, "I know you not!"

Today's English Version

back some day when he does not expect him and
at a time he does not know. 51 The master will
cut him to pieces, and make him share the fate
of the hypocrites. There he will cry and gnash
his teeth."

The parable of the ten girls

25 "On that day the Kingdom of heaven
will be like ten girls who took their oil
lamps and went out to meet the bridegroom.
2 Five of them were foolish, and the other five
were wise. 3 The foolish ones took their lamps
but did not take any extra oil with them, 4 while
the wise ones took containers full of oil with
their lamps. 5 The bridegroom was late in coming, so the girls began to nod and fall asleep.

6 "It was already midnight when the cry rang
out, 'Here is the bridegroom! Come and meet
him!' 7 The ten girls woke up and trimmed their
lamps. 8 Then the foolish ones said to the wise
ones, 'Let us have some of your oil, because our
lamps are going out.' 9 'No, indeed,' the wise
ones answered back, 'there is not enough for you
and us. Go to the store and buy some for yourselves.' 10 So the foolish girls went off to buy
some oil, and while they were gone the bridegroom arrived. The five girls who were ready
went in with him to the wedding feast, and the
door was closed.

11 "Later the other girls arrived. 'Sir, sir! Let
us in!' they cried. 12 'But I really don't know
you,' the bridegroom answered."

New International Version

that servant will come on a day when he does
not expect him and at an hour he is not aware
of. 51 He will cut him to pieces and assign him
a place with the hypocrites, where there will be
weeping and grinding of teeth.

The parable of the ten virgins

25 "At that time the kingdom of heaven will
be like ten virgins who took their lamps
and went out to meet the bridegroom. 2 Five of
them were foolish and five were wise. 3 The foolish ones took their lamps but did not take any
oil with them. 4 The wise, however, took oil in
jars along with their lamps. 5 The bridegroom
was late, and they all became drowsy and fell
asleep.

6 "At midnight the cry rang out: 'Here's the
bridegroom! Come out to meet him!'

7 "Then all the virgins woke up and trimmed
their lamps. 8 The foolish ones said to the wise,
'Give us some of your oil; our lamps are going
out.'

9 " 'No,' they replied, 'there may not be
enough for both us and you. Instead, go to those
who sell oil and buy some for yourselves.'

10 "But while they were on their way to buy
the oil, the bridegroom arrived. The virgins who
were ready went in with him to the wedding banquet. And the door was shut.

11 "Later the others also came. 'Sir! Sir!' they
said. 'Open the door for us!'

12 "But he replied, 'I tell you the truth, I
don't know you.'

Phillips Modern English

does not expect and at a time which he does not know, and will punish him severely and send him off to share the penalty of the unfaithful—to the place of tears and bitter regret!

"In those days the kingdom of Heaven will be like ten bridesmaids who took their lamps and went out to meet the bridegroom. Five of them were foolish and five were sensible. The foolish ones took their lamps but did not take any oil with them. But the sensible ones brought their lamps and oil in their flasks as well. Then, as the bridegroom was a very long time, they all grew drowsy and fell asleep. But in the middle of the night there came a shout, 'Wake up, here comes the bridegroom! Out you go to meet him!' Then up got all the bridesmaids and attended to their lamps. The foolish ones said to the sensible ones, 'Please give us some of your oil—our lamps are going out!' 'Oh, no,' returned the sensible ones, 'there might not be enough for all of us. Better go to the oil-shop and buy some for yourselves.' But while they had gone off to buy the oil the bridegroom arrived, and those bridesmaids who were ready went in with him for the festivities and the door was shut behind them. Later on the rest of the bridesmaids came and said, 'Oh, please, sir, open the door for us!' But he replied, 'I tell you I don't

Revised Standard Version

on a day when he does not expect him and at
an hour he does not know, 51 and will punish[b]
him, and put him with the hypocrites; there
men will weep and gnash their teeth.

25 "Then the kingdom of heaven shall be
compared to ten maidens who took their
lamps and went to meet the bridegroom.[c] 2 Five
of them were foolish, and five were wise. 3 For
when the foolish took their lamps, they took no
oil with them; 4 but the wise took flasks of oil
with their lamps. 5 As the bridegroom was delayed, they all slumbered and slept. 6 But at
midnight there was a cry, 'Behold, the bridegroom! Come out to meet him.' 7 Then all those
maidens rose and trimmed their lamps. 8 And the
foolish said to the wise, 'Give us some of your
oil, for our lamps are going out.' 9 But the wise
replied, 'Perhaps there will not be enough for
us and for you; go rather to the dealers and buy
for yourselves.' 10 And while they went to buy,
the bridegroom came, and those who were ready
went in with him to the marriage feast; and the
door was shut. 11 Afterward the other maidens
came also, saying, 'Lord, lord, open to us.'
12 But he replied, 'Truly, I say to you, I do not

[b] Or *cut him in pieces.* [c] Other ancient authorities add *and the bride.*

Jerusalem Bible

not expect and at an hour he does not know.
51 The master will cut him off and send him to
the same fate as the hypocrites, where there
will be weeping and grinding of teeth.

Parable of the ten bridesmaids

25 "Then the kingdom of heaven will be
like this: Ten bridesmaids took their lamps
and went to meet the bridegroom. 2 Five of
them were foolish and five were sensible: 3 the
foolish ones did take their lamps, but they
brought no oil, 4 whereas the sensible ones took
flasks of oil as well as their lamps. 5 The bridegroom was late, and they all grew drowsy and
fell asleep. 6 But at midnight there was a cry,
'The bridegroom is here! Go out and meet him.'
7 At this, all those bridesmaids woke up and
trimmed their lamps, 8 and the foolish ones
said to the sensible ones, 'Give us some of your
oil: our lamps are going out.' 9 But they replied, 'There may not be enough for us and
you; you had better go to those who sell it and
buy some for yourselves.' 10 They had gone off
to buy it when the bridegroom arrived. Those
who were ready went in with him to the wedding hall and the door was closed. 11 The other
bridesmaids arrived later. 'Lord, Lord,' they said,
'open the door for us.' 12 But he replied, 'I

New English Bible

a day that servant does not expect, at a time he does not know, and will cut him in pieces. Thus he will find his place among the hypocrites, where there is wailing and grinding of teeth.

25 'When that day comes, the kingdom of Heaven will be like this. There were ten girls, who took their lamps and went out to meet the bridegroom. Five of them were foolish, and five prudent; when the foolish ones took their lamps, they took no oil with them, but the others took flasks of oil with their lamps. As the bridegroom was late in coming they all dozed off to sleep. But at midnight a cry was heard: "Here is the bridegroom! Come out to meet him." With that the girls all got up and trimmed their lamps. The foolish said to the prudent, "Our lamps are going out; give us some of your oil." "No," they said; "there will never be enough for all of us. You had better go to the shop and buy some for yourselves." While they were away the bridegroom arrived; those who were ready went in with him to the wedding; and the door was shut. And then the other five came back. "Sir, sir," they cried, "open the door for us." But he

King James Version

Verily I say unto you, I know you not. 13 Watch therefore; for ye know neither the day nor the hour wherein the Son of man cometh.

14 For *the kingdom of heaven is* as a man travelling into a far country, *who* called his own servants, and delivered unto them his goods. 15And unto one he gave five talents, to another two, and to another one; to every man according to his several ability; and straightway took his journey. 16 Then he that had received the five talents went and traded with the same, and made *them* other five talents. 17And likewise he that *had received* two, he also gained other two. 18 But he that had received one went and digged in the earth, and hid his lord's money. 19After a long time the lord of those servants cometh, and reckoneth with them. 20And so he that had received five talents came and brought other five talents, saying, Lord, thou deliveredst unto me five talents: behold, I have gained beside them five talents more. 21 His lord said unto him, Well done, *thou* good and faithful servant: thou hast been faithful over a few things, I will make thee ruler over many things: enter thou into the joy of thy lord. 22 He also that had received two talents came and said, Lord, thou deliveredst

Living Bible

13 "So stay awake and be prepared, for you do not know the date or moment of my return.[c]

14 "Again, the Kingdom of Heaven can be illustrated by the story of a man going into another country, who called together his servants and loaned them money to invest for him while he was gone.

15 "He gave $5,000 to one, $2,000 to another, and $1,000 to the last—dividing it in proportion to their abilities—and then left on his trip. 16 The man who received the $5,000 began immediately to buy and sell with it and soon earned another $5,000. 17 The man with $2,000 went right to work, too, and earned another $2,000.

18 "But the man who received the $1,000 dug a hole in the ground and hid the money for safekeeping.

19 "After a long time their master returned from his trip and called them to him to account for his money. 20 The man to whom he had entrusted the $5,000 brought him $10,000.

21 "His master praised him for good work. 'You have been faithful in handling this small amount,' he told him, 'so now I will give you many more responsibilities. Begin the joyous tasks I have assigned to you.'

22 "Next came the man who had received the $2,000, with the report, 'Sir, you gave me $2,000

[*c*] Implied.

Today's English Version

13 And Jesus concluded, "Watch out, then, because you do not know the day or hour."

The parable of the three servants

14 "It will be like a man who was about to leave home on a trip; he called his servants and put them in charge of his property. 15 He gave to each one according to his ability: to one he gave five thousand dollars, to the other two thousand dollars, and to the other one thousand dollars. Then he left on his trip. 16 The servant who had received five thousand dollars went at once and invested his money and earned another five thousand dollars. 17 In the same way the servant who received two thousand dollars earned another two thousand dollars. 18 But the servant who received one thousand dollars went off, dug a hole in the ground, and hid his master's money.

19 "After a long time the master of those servants came back and settled accounts with them. 20 The servant who had received five thousand dollars came in and handed over the other five thousand dollars. 'You gave me five thousand dollars, sir,' he said. 'Look! Here are another five thousand dollars that I have earned.' 21 'Well done, good and faithful servant!' said his master. 'You have been faithful in managing small amounts, so I will put you in charge of large amounts. Come on in and share my happiness!' 22 Then the servant who had been given two thousand dollars came in and said, 'You gave me two thousand dollars, sir. Look! Here are an-

New International Version

13 "Therefore keep watch, because you do not know the day or the hour.

The parable of the talents

14 "Again, it will be like a man going on a journey, who called his servants and entrusted his property to them. 15 To one he gave five talents[r] of money, to another two talents, and to another one talent, each according to his ability. Then he went on his journey. 16 The man who had received the five talents went at once and put his money to work and gained five more. 17 So also, the one with the two talents gained two more. 18 But the man who had received the one talent went off, dug a hole in the ground and hid his master's money.

19 "After a long time the master of those servants returned and settled accounts with them. 20 The man who had received the five talents brought the other five. 'Master,' he said, 'you entrusted me with five talents. See, I have gained five more.'

21 "His master replied, 'Well done, good and faithful servant! You have been faithful with a few things; I will put you in charge of many things. Come and share your master's happiness!'

22 "The man with the two talents also came. 'Master,' he said, 'you entrusted me with two

[*r*] A talent was worth more than a thousand dollars.

Phillips Modern English

know you!' So be on the alert—for you do not know the day or the time.

25.14 Life is hard for the faint-hearted

"It is just like a man leaving home who called his household servants together before he went and handed his possessions over to them to manage. He gave one five thousand pounds, another two thousand and another one thousand—according to the man's ability. Then he went away.

"The man who had received five thousand pounds went out at once and by doing business with this sum he made another five thousand. Similarly the man with two thousand pounds made another two thousand. But the man who had received one thousand pounds went off and dug a hole in the ground and hid his master's money.

"Some years later the master of these servants arrived and went into the accounts with them. The one who had the five thousand pounds came in and brought him an additional five thousand with the words, 'You gave me five thousand pounds, sir; look, I've increased it by another five thousand.' 'Well done!' said his master, 'you're a sound, reliable servant. You've been trustworthy over a few things, now I'm going to put you in charge of many more. Come in and share your master's rejoicing.' Then the servant who had received two thousand pounds came in and said, 'You gave me two thousand pounds, sir; look, here's two thousand more that

Revised Standard Version

know you.' 13 Watch therefore, for you know
neither the day nor the hour.
14 "For it will be as when a man going on a
journey called his servants and entrusted to them
his property; 15 to one he gave five talents,[d] to
another two, to another one, to each according
to his ability. Then he went away. 16 He who
had received the five talents went at once and
traded with them; and he made five talents more.
17 So also, he who had the two talents made two
talents more. 18 But he who had received the
one talent went and dug in the ground and hid
his master's money. 19 Now after a long time
the master of those servants came and settled
accounts with them. 20 And he who had received
the five talents came forward, bringing five
talents more, saying, 'Master, you delivered to
me five talents; here I have made five talents
more.' 21 His master said to him, 'Well done,
good and faithful servant; you have been faithful over a little, I will set you over much; enter
into the joy of your master.' 22 And he also who
had the two talents came forward, saying, 'Mas-

[d] This talent was more than fifteen years' wages of a laborer.

Jerusalem Bible

tell you solemnly, I do not know you.' 13 So
stay awake, because you do not know either the
day or the hour.

Parable of the talents

14 "It is like a man on his way abroad who
summoned his servants and entrusted his property to them. 15 To one he gave five talents, to
another two, to a third one; each in proportion
to his ability. Then he set out. 16 The man who
had received the five talents promptly went and
traded with them and made five more. 17 The
man who had received two made two more in
the same way. 18 But the man who had received
one went off and dug a hole in the ground and
hid his master's money. 19 Now a long time
after, the master of those servants came back
and went through his accounts with them. 20 The
man who had received the five talents came
forward bringing five more. 'Sir,' he said, 'you
entrusted me with five talents; here are five
more that I have made.' 21 His master said to
him, 'Well done, good and faithful servant; you
have shown you can be faithful in small things,
I will trust you with greater; come and join in
your master's happiness.' 22 Next the man with
the two talents came forward. 'Sir,' he said, 'you
entrusted me with two talents; here are two

New English Bible

answered, "I declare, I do not know you." Keep awake then; for you never know the day or the hour.

'It is like a man going abroad, who called his servants and put his capital in their hands; to one he gave five bags of gold, to another two, to another one, each according to his capacity. Then he left the country. The man who had the five bags went at once and employed them in business, and made a profit of five bags, and the man who had the two bags made two. But the man who had been given one bag of gold went off and dug a hole in the ground, and hid his master's money. A long time afterwards their master returned, and proceeded to settle accounts with them. The man who had been given the five bags of gold came and produced the five he had made: "Master," he said, "you left five bags with me; look, I have made five more." "Well done, my good and trusty servant!" said the master. "You have proved trustworthy in a small way; I will now put you in charge of something big. Come and share your master's delight." The man with the two bags then came and said, "Master, you left two bags with me;

King James Version

unto me two talents: behold, I have gained two
other talents beside them. 23 His lord said unto
him, Well done, good and faithful servant; thou
hast been faithful over a few things, I will make
thee ruler over many things: enter thou into
the joy of thy lord. 24 Then he which had received the one talent came and said, Lord, I
knew thee that thou art a hard man, reaping
where thou hast not sown, and gathering where
thou hast not strewed: 25And I was afraid, and
went and hid thy talent in the earth: lo, *there*
thou hast *that is* thine. 26 His lord answered and
said unto him, *Thou* wicked and slothful servant,
thou knewest that I reap where I sowed not,
and gather where I have not strewed: 27 Thou
oughtest therefore to have put my money to the
exchangers, and *then* at my coming I should
have received mine own with usury. 28 Take
therefore the talent from him, and give *it* unto
him which hath ten talents. 29 For unto every
one that hath shall be given, and he shall have
abundance: but from him that hath not shall
be taken away even that which he hath. 30And
cast ye the unprofitable servant into outer darkness: there shall be weeping and gnashing of
teeth.
31 When the Son of man shall come in his
glory, and all the holy angels with him, then
shall he sit upon the throne of his glory: 32And
before him shall be gathered all nations: and he
shall separate them one from another, as a shep-

Living Bible

to use, and I have doubled it.'
23 " 'Good work,' his master said. 'You are a
good and faithful servant. You have been faithful over this small amount, so now I will give
you much more.'
24, 25 "Then the man with the $1,000 came
and said, 'Sir, I knew you were a hard man,
and I was afraid you would rob me of what I
earned,[d] so I hid your money in the earth and
here it is!'
26 "But his master replied, 'Wicked man! Lazy
slave! Since you knew I would demand your
profit, 27 you should at least have put my money
into the bank so I could have some interest.
28 Take the money from this man and give it to
the man with the $10,000. 29 For the man who
uses well what he is given shall be given more,
and he shall have abundance. But from the man
who is unfaithful, even what little responsibility
he has shall be taken from him. 30And throw
the useless servant out into outer darkness:
there shall be weeping and gnashing of teeth.'
31 "But when I, the Messiah,[e] shall come in
my glory, and all the angels with me, then I shall
sit upon my throne of glory. 32And all the nations shall be gathered before me. And I will
separate the people[f] as a shepherd separates the

[*d*] Literally, "reaping where you didn't sow, and gathering where you didn't scatter, and I was afraid . . ." [*e*] Literally, "the Son of Man." [*f*] Or, "separate the nations."

Today's English Version

other two thousand dollars that I have earned.'
23 'Well done, good and faithful servant!' said
his master. 'You have been faithful in managing
small amounts, so I will put you in charge of
large amounts. Come on in and share my happiness!' 24 Then the servant who had received
one thousand dollars came in and said, 'Sir, I
know you are a hard man; you reap harvests
where you did not plant, and gather crops where
you did not scatter seed. 25 I was afraid, so I
went off and hid your money in the ground.
Look! Here is what belongs to you.' 26 'You bad
and lazy servant!' his master said. 'You knew,
did you, that I reap harvests where I did not
plant, and gather crops where I did not scatter
seed? 27 Well, then, you should have deposited
my money in the bank, and I would have received it all back with interest when I returned.
28 Now, take the money away from him and give
it to the one who has ten thousand dollars. 29 For
to every one who has, even more will be given,
and he will have more than enough; but the
one who has nothing, even the little he has will
be taken away from him. 30As for this useless
servant—throw him outside in the darkness; there
he will cry and gnash his teeth.' "

The final judgment

31 "When the Son of Man comes as King, and
all the angels with him, he will sit on his royal
throne, 32 and all the earth's people will be gathered before him. Then he will divide them into
two groups, just as a shepherd separates the sheep

New International Version

talents; see, I have gained two more.'
23 "His master replied, 'Well done, good and
faithful servant! You have been faithful with a
few things; I will put you in charge of many
things. Come and share your master's happiness!'
24 "Then the man who had received the one
talent came. 'Master,' he said, 'I knew that you
are a hard man, harvesting where you have not
sown and gathering where you have not scattered
seed. 25 So I was afraid and went out and hid
your talent in the ground. See, here is what belongs to you.'
26 "His master replied, 'You wicked, lazy
servant! So you knew that I harvest where I
have not sown and gather where I have not scattered seed? 27 Well then, you should have put
my money on deposit with the bankers, so that
when I returned I would have received it back
with interest.
28 " 'Take the talent from him and give it to
the one who has the ten talents. 29 For everyone
who has will be given more, and he will have an
abundance. Whoever does not have, even what
he has will be taken from him. 30And throw
that worthless servant outside, into the darkness,
where there will be weeping and grinding of
teeth.'

The sheep and the goats

31 "When the Son of Man comes in his glory,
and all the angels with him, he will sit on his
throne in heavenly glory. 32All the nations will
be gathered before him, and he will separate
the people one from another as a shepherd sepa-

Phillips Modern English

I've managed to make by it.' 'Well done!' said his master, 'you're a sound, reliable servant. You've been trustworthy over a few things, now I'm going to put you in charge of many. Come in and share your master's pleasure.'

"Then the man who had received the one thousand pounds came in and said, 'Sir, I always knew you were a hard man, reaping where you never sowed and collecting where you never laid out—so I was scared and I went off and hid your thousand pounds in the ground. Here is your money, intact.'

"'You're a wicked, lazy servant!' his master told him. 'You say you knew that I reap where I never sowed and collect where I never laid out? Then you ought to have put my money in the bank, and when I came I should at any rate have received what belongs to me with interest. Take his thousand pounds away from him and give it to the man who now has the ten thousand!' (For the man who has something will have more given to him and will have plenty. But as for the man who has nothing, even his 'nothing' will be taken away.) 'And throw this useless servant into the darkness outside, where there will be tears and bitter regret.'

25.31 The final judgment

"But when the Son of Man comes in his splendour with all his angels with him, then he will take his seat on his glorious throne. All the nations will be assembled before him and he will separate men from each other like a shep-

Revised Standard Version

ter, you delivered to me two talents; here I
have made two talents more.' 23 His master said
to him, 'Well done, good and faithful servant;
you have been faithful over a little, I will set
you over much; enter into the joy of your master.' 24 He also who had received the one talent
came forward, saying, 'Master, I knew you to
be a hard man, reaping where you did not sow,
and gathering where you did not winnow; 25 so
I was afraid, and I went and hid your talent in
the ground. Here you have what is yours.' 26 But
his master answered him, 'You wicked and
slothful servant! You knew that I reap where I
have not sowed, and gather where I have not
winnowed? 27 Then you ought to have invested
my money with the bankers, and at my coming
I should have received what was my own with
interest. 28 So take the talent from him, and
give it to him who has the ten talents. 29 For to
every one who has will more be given, and he
will have abundance; but from him who has
not, even what he has will be taken away.
30 And cast the worthless servant into the outer
darkness; there men will weep and gnash their
teeth.'

31 "When the Son of man comes in his glory,
and all the angels with him, then he will sit on
his glorious throne. 32 Before him will be gathered all the nations, and he will separate them
one from another as a shepherd separates the

Jerusalem Bible

more that I have made.' 23 His master said to
him, 'Well done, good and faithful servant; you
have shown you can be faithful in small things,
I will trust you with greater; come and join in
your master's happiness.' 24 Last came forward
the man who had the one talent. 'Sir,' said he, 'I
had heard you were a hard man, reaping where
you have not sown and gathering where you
have not scattered; 25 so I was afraid, and I
went off and hid your talent in the ground.
Here it is; it was yours, you have it back.' 26 But
his master answered him, 'You wicked and lazy
servant! So you knew that I reap where I have
not sown and gather where I have not scattered?
27 Well then, you should have deposited my
money with the bankers, and on my return I
would have recovered my capital with interest.
28 So now, take the talent from him and give
it to the man who has the five talents. 29 For to
everyone who has will be given more, and he
will have more than enough; but from the man
who has not, even what he has will be taken
away. 30 As for this good-for-nothing servant,
throw him out into the dark, where there will
be weeping and grinding of teeth.'

The Last Judgment

31 "When the Son of Man comes in his
glory, escorted by all the angels, then he will
take his seat on his throne of glory. 32 All the
nations will be assembled before him and he
will separate men one from another as the shep-

New English Bible

look, I have made two more." "Well done, my good and trusty servant!" said the master. "You have proved trustworthy in a small way; I will now put you in charge of something big. Come and share your master's delight." Then the man who had been given one bag came and said, "Master, I knew you to be a hard man: you reap where you have not sown, you gather where you have not scattered; so I was afraid, and I went and hid your gold in the ground. Here it is—you have what belongs to you." "You lazy rascal!" said the master. "You knew that I reap where I have not sown, and gather where I have not scattered? Then you ought to have put my money on deposit, and on my return I should have got it back with interest. Take the bag of gold from him, and give it to the one with the ten bags. For the man who has will always be given more, till he has enough and to spare; and the man who has not will forfeit even what he has. Fling the useless servant out into the dark, the place of wailing and grinding of teeth!"

'When the Son of Man comes in his glory and all the angels with him, he will sit in state on his throne, with all the nations gathered before him. He will separate men into two groups, as a shep-

King James Version

herd divideth *his* sheep from the goats: 33 And
he shall set the sheep on his right hand, but
the goats on the left. 34 Then shall the King say
unto them on his right hand, Come, ye blessed
of my Father, inherit the kingdom prepared for
you from the foundation of the world: 35 For
I was a hungered, and ye gave me meat: I was
thirsty, and ye gave me drink: I was a stranger,
and ye took me in: 36 Naked, and ye clothed
me: I was sick, and ye visited me: I was in
prison, and ye came unto me. 37 Then shall the
righteous answer him, saying, Lord, when saw
we thee a hungered, and fed *thee?* or thirsty,
and gave *thee* drink? 38 When saw we thee a
stranger, and took *thee* in? or naked, and clothed
thee? 39 Or when saw we thee sick, or in prison,
and came unto thee? 40 And the King shall answer and say unto them, Verily I say unto you,
Inasmuch as ye have done *it* unto one of the
least of these my brethren, ye have done *it* unto
me. 41 Then shall he say also unto them on the
left hand, Depart from me, ye cursed, into everlasting fire, prepared for the devil and his angels:
42 For I was a hungered, and ye gave me no
meat: I was thirsty, and ye gave me no drink:
43 I was a stranger, and ye took me not in:
naked, and ye clothed me not: sick, and in
prison, and ye visited me not. 44 Then shall they
also answer him, saying, Lord, when saw we
thee a hungered, or athirst, or a stranger, or
naked, or sick, or in prison, and did not minister

Living Bible

sheep from the goats, 33 and place the sheep at
my right hand, and the goats at my left.
34 "Then I, the King, shall say to those at
my right, 'Come, blessed of my Father, into the
Kingdom prepared for you from the founding of
the world. 35 For I was hungry and you fed me;
I was thirsty and you gave me water; I was a
stranger and you invited me into your homes;
36 naked and you clothed me; sick and in prison,
and you visited me.'
37 "Then these righteous ones will reply, 'Sir,
when did we ever see you hungry and feed you?
Or thirsty and give you anything to drink? 38 Or
a stranger, and help you? Or naked, and clothe
you? 39 When did we ever see you sick or in
prison, and visit you?'
40 "And I, the King, will tell them, 'When
you did it to these my brothers you were doing
it to me!' 41 Then I will turn to those on my
left and say, 'Away with you, you cursed ones,
into the eternal fire prepared for the devil and
his demons. 42 For I was hungry and you
wouldn't feed me; thirsty, and you wouldn't
give me anything to drink; 43 a stranger, and
you refused me hospitality; naked, and you
wouldn't clothe me; sick, and in prison, and you
didn't visit me.'
44 "Then they will reply, 'Lord, when did we
ever see you hungry or thirsty or a stranger or
naked or sick or in prison, and not help you?'

Today's English Version

from the goats: 33 he will put the sheep at his
right and the goats at his left. 34 Then the King
will say to the people on his right, 'You that are
blessed by my Father: come! Come and receive
the kingdom which has been prepared for you
ever since the creation of the world. 35 I was
hungry and you fed me, thirsty and you gave me
drink; I was a stranger and you received me in
your homes, 36 naked and you clothed me; I was
sick and you took care of me, in prison and you
visited me.' 37 The righteous will then answer
him, 'When, Lord, did we ever see you hungry
and feed you, or thirsty and give you drink?
38 When did we ever see you a stranger and welcome you in our homes, or naked and clothe
you? 39 When did we ever see you sick or in
prison, and visit you?' 40 The King will answer
back, 'I tell you, indeed, whenever you did this
for one of the least important of these brothers
of mine, you did it for me!'
41 "Then he will say to those on his left,
'Away from me, you that are under God's curse!
Away to the eternal fire which has been prepared
for the Devil and his angels! 42 I was hungry
but you would not feed me, thirsty but you would
not give me drink; 43 I was a stranger but you
would not welcome me in your homes, naked but
you would not clothe me; I was sick and in
prison but you would not take care of me.'
44 Then they will answer him, 'When, Lord, did
we ever see you hungry, or thirsty, or a stranger,
or naked, or sick, or in prison, and we would

New International Version

rates the sheep from the goats. 33 He will put the
sheep on his right and the goats on his left.
34 "Then the King will say to those on his
right, 'Come, you who are blessed by my Father; take your inheritance, the kingdom prepared for you since the creation of the world.
35 For I was hungry and you gave me something to eat, I was thirsty and you gave me
something to drink, I was a stranger and you
invited me in, 36 I needed clothes and you
clothed me, I was sick and you looked after
me, I was in prison and you came to visit me.'
37 "Then the righteous will answer him, 'Lord,
when did we see you hungry and feed you,
or thirsty and give you something to drink?
38 When did we see you a stranger and invite
you in, or needing clothes and clothe you?
39 When did we see you sick or in prison and
go to visit you?'
40 "The King will reply, 'I tell you the truth,
whatever you did for one of the least of these
brothers of mine, you did for me.'
41 "Then he will say to those on his left, 'Depart from me, you who are cursed, into the eternal fire prepared for the devil and his angels.
42 For I was hungry and you gave me nothing
to eat, I was thirsty and you gave me nothing to
drink, 43 I was a stranger and you did not invite me in, I needed clothes and you did not
clothe me, I was sick and in prison and you did
not look after me.'
44 "They also will answer, 'Lord, when did
we see you hungry or thirsty or a stranger or
needing clothes or sick or in prison, and did not
help you?'

Phillips Modern English

herd separating sheep from goats. He will place the sheep on his right hand and the goats on his left.

"Then the king will say to those on his right: 'Come, you who have won my Father's blessing! Take your inheritance—the kingdom reserved for you since the foundation of the world! For I was hungry and you gave me food. I was thirsty and you gave me a drink. I was a stranger and you made me welcome. I was naked and you clothed me. I was ill and you came and looked after me. I was in prison and you came to see me there.'

"Then the true men will answer him, 'Lord, when did we see *you* hungry and give you food? When did we see *you* thirsty and give you something to drink? When did we see *you* a stranger and make you welcome, or see *you* naked and clothe you, or see *you* ill or in prison and go to see you?'

"And the king will reply, 'I assure you that whatever you did for the humblest of my brothers you did for me.'

"Then he will say to those on his left, 'Out of my presence, cursed as you are, into the eternal fire prepared for the devil and his angels! For I was hungry and you gave me nothing to eat. I was thirsty and you gave me nothing to drink. I was a stranger and you never made me welcome. When I was naked you did nothing to clothe me; when I was sick and in prison you never cared to visit me.'

"Then they too will answer him, 'Lord, when did we ever see *you* hungry, or thirsty, or a stranger, or naked, or sick or in prison, and fail to look after you?'

Revised Standard Version

sheep from the goats, 33 and he will place the sheep at his right hand, but the goats at the left. 34 Then the King will say to those at his right hand, 'Come, O blessed of my Father, inherit the kingdom prepared for you from the foundation of the world; 35 for I was hungry and you gave me food, I was thirsty and you gave me drink, I was a stranger and you welcomed me, 36 I was naked and you clothed me, I was sick and you visited me, I was in prison and you came to me.' 37 Then the righteous will answer him, 'Lord, when did we see thee hungry and feed thee, or thirsty and give thee drink? 38 And when did we see thee a stranger and welcome thee, or naked and clothe thee? 39 And when did we see thee sick or in prison and visit thee?' 40 And the King will answer them, 'Truly, I say to you, as you did it to one of the least of these my brethren, you did it to me.' 41 Then he will say to those at his left hand, 'Depart from me, you cursed, into the eternal fire prepared for the devil and his angels; 42 for I was hungry and you gave me no food, I was thirsty and you gave me no drink, 43 I was a stranger and you did not welcome me, naked and you did not clothe me, sick and in prison and you did not visit me.' 44 Then they also will answer, 'Lord, when did we see thee hungry or thirsty or a stranger or naked or sick or in prison, and did

Jerusalem Bible

herd separates sheep from goats. 33 He will place the sheep on his right hand and the goats on his left. 34 Then the King will say to those on his right hand, 'Come, you whom my Father has blessed, take for your heritage the kingdom prepared for you since the foundation of the world. 35 For I was hungry and you gave me food; I was thirsty and you gave me drink; I was a stranger and you made me welcome; 36 naked and you clothed me, sick and you visited me, in prison and you came to see me.' 37 Then the virtuous will say to him in reply, 'Lord, when did we see you hungry and feed you; or thirsty and give you drink? 38 When did we see you a stranger and make you welcome; naked and clothe you; 39 sick or in prison and go to see you?' 40 And the King will answer, 'I tell you solemnly, in so far as you did this to one of the least of these brothers of mine, you did it to me.' 41 Next he will say to those on his left hand, 'Go away from me, with your curse upon you, to the eternal fire prepared for the devil and his angels. 42 For I was hungry and you never gave me food; I was thirsty and you never gave me anything to drink; 43 I was a stranger and you never made me welcome, naked and you never clothed me, sick and in prison and you never visited me.' 44 Then it will be their turn to ask, 'Lord, when did we see you hungry or thirsty, a stranger or naked, sick or in prison,

New English Bible

herd separates the sheep from the goats, and he will place the sheep on his right hand and the goats on his left. Then the king will say to those on his right hand, "You have my Father's blessing; come, enter and possess the kingdom that has been ready for you since the world was made. For when I was hungry, you gave me food; when thirsty, you gave me drink; when I was a stranger you took me into your home, when naked you clothed me; when I was ill you came to my help, when in prison you visited me." Then the righteous will reply, "Lord, when was it that we saw you hungry and fed you, or thirsty and gave you drink, a stranger and took you home, or naked and clothed you? When did we see you ill or in prison, and come to visit you?" And the king will answer, "I tell you this: anything you did for one of my brothers here, however humble, you did for me." Then he will say to those on his left hand, "The curse is upon you; go from my sight to the eternal fire that is ready for the devil and his angels. For when I was hungry you gave me nothing to eat, when thirsty nothing to drink; when I was a stranger you gave me no home, when naked you did not clothe me; when I was ill and in prison you did not come to my help." And they too will reply, "Lord, when was it that we saw you hungry or thirsty or a stranger or naked or ill or in prison,

King James Version

unto thee? 45 Then shall he answer them, saying,
Verily I say unto you, Inasmuch as ye did *it*
not to one of the least of these, ye did *it* not to
me. 46And these shall go away into everlasting
punishment: but the righteous into life eternal.

26 And it came to pass, when Jesus had
finished all these sayings, he said unto his
disciples, 2 Ye know that after two days is *the*
feast of the passover, and the Son of man is betrayed to be crucified. 3 Then assembled together
the chief priests, and the scribes, and the elders
of the people, unto the palace of the high priest,
who was called Caiaphas, 4And consulted that
they might take Jesus by subtilty, and kill *him*.
5 But they said, Not on the feast *day*, lest there
be an uproar among the people.
6 Now when Jesus was in Bethany, in the
house of Simon the leper, 7 There came unto
him a woman having an alabaster box of very

Living Bible

45 "And I will answer, 'When you refused to
help the least of these my brothers, you were
refusing help to me.'
46 "And they shall go away into eternal punishment; but the righteous into everlasting life."

26 When Jesus had finished this talk with his
disciples, he told them,
2 "As you know, the Passover celebration begins in two days, and I [a] shall be betrayed and
crucified."
3 At that very moment the chief priests and
other Jewish officials were meeting at the residence of Caiaphas the High Priest, 4 to discuss
ways of capturing Jesus quietly, and killing him.
5 "But not during the Passover celebration," they
agreed, "for there would be a riot."
6 Jesus now proceeded to Bethany, to the
home of Simon the leper. 7 While he was eating,
a woman came in with a bottle of very expen-

[*a*] Literally, "the Son of Man."

Today's English Version

not help you?' 45 The King will answer them
back, 'I tell you, indeed, whenever you refused
to help one of these least important ones, you
refused to help me.' 46 These, then, will be sent
off to eternal punishment; the righteous will go
to eternal life."

The plot against Jesus

26 When Jesus had finished teaching all these
things, he said to his disciples, 2 "In two
days, as you know, it will be the Feast of Passover, and the Son of Man will be handed over to
be nailed to the cross."
3 Then the chief priests and the Jewish elders
met together in the palace of Caiaphas, the High
Priest, 4 and made plans to arrest Jesus secretly
and put him to death. 5 "We must not do it during the feast," they said, "or the people will riot."

Jesus anointed at Bethany

6 While Jesus was at the house of Simon the
leper, in Bethany, 7 a woman came to him with
an alabaster jar filled with an expensive perfume,

New International Version

45 "He will reply, 'I tell you the truth, whatever you did not do for one of the least of these,
you did not do for me.'
46 "Then they will go away to eternal punishment, but the righteous to eternal life."

The plot against Jesus

26 When Jesus had finished saying all these
things, he said to his disciples, 2 "As you
know, the Passover is two days away—and the
Son of Man will be handed over to be crucified."
3 Then the chief priests and the elders of the
people assembled in the palace of the high priest,
whose name was Caiaphas, 4 and they plotted to
arrest Jesus in some sly way and kill him. 5 "But
not during the feast," they said, "or there may
be a riot among the people."

Jesus anointed at Bethany

6 While Jesus was in Bethany in the home of
a man known as Simon the Leper, 7 a woman
came to him with an alabaster jar of very ex-

Phillips Modern English

"Then the king will answer them with these words, 'I assure you that whatever you failed to do to the humblest of my brothers you failed to do to me.'

"And these will go off to eternal punishment, but the true men to eternal life."

26.1 Jesus announces his coming death

When Jesus had finished all this teaching he spoke to his disciples, "Do you realise that the Passover will begin in two days' time; and the Son of Man is going to be betrayed and crucified?"

26.3 An evil plot—and an act of love

At that very time the chief priests and elders of the people had assembled in the court of Caiaphas, the High Priest, and were discussing together how they might get hold of Jesus by some trick and kill him. But they kept saying, "It must not be during the festival or there might be a riot."

Back in Bethany, while Jesus was in the house of Simon the leper, a woman came to him with an alabaster flask of most expensive perfume,

Revised Standard Version

not minister to thee?' 45 Then he will answer
them, 'Truly, I say to you, as you did it not to
one of the least of these, you did it not to me.'
46 And they will go away into eternal punishment, but the righteous into eternal life."

26 When Jesus had finished all these sayings, he said to his disciples, 2 "You
know that after two days the Passover is coming, and the Son of man will be delivered up to
be crucified."
3 Then the chief priests and the elders of the
people gathered in the palace of the high priest,
who was called Caiaphas, 4 and took counsel
together in order to arrest Jesus by stealth and
kill him. 5 But they said, "Not during the feast,
lest there be a tumult among the people."
6 Now when Jesus was at Bethany in the
house of Simon the leper, 7 a woman came up
to him with an alabaster flask of very expensive

Jerusalem Bible

and did not come to your help?' 45 Then he
will answer, 'I tell you solemnly, in so far as
you neglected to do this to one of the least of
these, you neglected to do it to me.' 46 And they
will go away to eternal punishment, and the
virtuous to eternal life."

VII. Passion and resurrection

The conspiracy against Jesus

26 Jesus had now finished all he wanted to
say, and he told his disciples, 2 "It will be
Passover, as you know, in two days' time, and
the Son of Man will be handed over to be crucified."
3 Then the chief priests and the elders of the
people assembled in the palace of the high priest,
whose name was Caiaphas, 4 and made plans to
arrest Jesus by some trick and have him put to
death. 5 They said, however, "It must not be
during the festivities; there must be no disturbance among the people."

The anointing at Bethany

6 Jesus was at Bethany in the house of Simon
the leper, when 7 a woman came to him with an
alabaster jar of the most expensive ointment,

New English Bible

and did nothing for you?" And he will answer, "I tell you this: anything you did not do for one of these, however humble, you did not do for me." And they will go away to eternal punishment, but the righteous will enter eternal life.'

The final conflict

26 When Jesus had finished this discourse he said to his disciples, 'You know that in two days' time it will be Passover, and the Son of Man is to be handed over for crucifixion.'

Then the chief priests and the elders of the nation met in the palace of the High Priest, Caiaphas; and there they conferred together on a scheme to have Jesus arrested by some trick and put to death. 'It must not be during the festival,' they said, 'or there may be rioting among the people.'

Jesus was at Bethany in the house of Simon the leper, when a woman came to him with a small bottle of fragrant oil, very costly; and as

King James Version

precious ointment, and poured it on his head, as he sat at meat. 8 But when his disciples saw *it,* they had indignation, saying, To what purpose *is* this waste? 9 For this ointment might have been sold for much, and given to the poor. 10 When Jesus understood *it,* he said unto them, Why trouble ye the woman? for she hath wrought a good work upon me. 11 For ye have the poor always with you; but me ye have not always. 12 For in that she hath poured this ointment on my body, she did *it* for my burial. 13 Verily I say unto you, Wheresoever this gospel shall be preached in the whole world, *there* shall also this, that this woman hath done, be told for a memorial of her.

14 Then one of the twelve, called Judas Iscariot, went unto the chief priests, 15 And said *unto them,* What will ye give me, and I will deliver him unto you? And they covenanted with him for thirty pieces of silver. 16 And from that time he sought opportunity to betray him.

17 Now the first *day* of the *feast of* unleavened bread the disciples came to Jesus, say-

Living Bible

sive perfume, and poured it over his head.

8, 9 The disciples were indignant. "What a waste of good money," they said. "Why, she could have sold it for a fortune and given it to the poor."

10 Jesus knew what they were thinking, and said, "Why are you criticizing her? For she has done a good thing to me. 11 You will always have the poor among you, but you won't always have me. 12 She has poured this perfume on me to prepare my body for burial. 13 And she will always be remembered for this deed. The story of what she has done will be told throughout the whole world, wherever the Good News is preached."

14 Then Judas Iscariot, one of the twelve apostles, went to the chief priests, 15 and asked, "How much will you pay me to get Jesus into your hands?" And they gave him thirty silver coins. 16 From that time on, Judas watched for an opportunity to betray Jesus to them.

17 On the first day of the Passover ceremonies, when bread made with yeast was purged

Today's English Version

which she poured on Jesus' head as he was eating. 8 The disciples saw this and became angry. "Why all this waste?" they asked. 9 "This perfume could have been sold for a large amount and the money given to the poor!"

10 Jesus knew what they were saying and said to them, "Why are you bothering this woman? It is a fine and beautiful thing that she has done for me. 11 You will always have poor people with you, but I will not be with you always. 12 What she did was to pour this perfume on my body to get me ready for burial. 13 Now, remember this! Wherever this gospel is preached, all over the world, what she has done will be told in memory of her."

Judas agrees to betray Jesus

14 Then one of the twelve disciples—the one named Judas Iscariot—went to the chief priests 15 and said, "What will you give me if I hand Jesus over to you?" They counted out thirty silver coins and gave them to him. 16 From then on Judas was looking for a good chance to betray Jesus.

Jesus eats the Passover meal with his disciples

17 On the first day of the Feast of Unleavened Bread the disciples came to Jesus and

New International Version

pensive perfume, which she poured on his head as he was reclining at the table.

8 When the disciples saw this, they were indignant. "Why this waste?" they asked. 9 "This perfume could have been sold at a high price and the money given to the poor."

10 Aware of this, Jesus said to them, "Why are you bothering this woman? She has done a beautiful thing to me. 11 The poor you will always have with you, but you will not always have me. 12 When she poured this perfume on my body, she did it to prepare me for burial. 13 I tell you the truth, wherever this gospel is preached throughout the world, what she has done will also be told, in memory of her."

Judas agrees to betray Jesus

14 Then one of the Twelve—the one called Judas Iscariot—went to the chief priests 15 and asked, "What are you willing to give me if I hand him over to you?" So they counted out for him thirty silver coins. 16 From then on Judas watched for an opportunity to hand him over.

The Lord's Supper

17 On the first day of the Feast of Unleavened Bread, the disciples came to Jesus and

Phillips Modern English

and poured it on his head as he was at table. The disciples were indignant when they saw this, and said, "What is the point of such wicked waste? Couldn't this perfume have been sold for a lot of money which could be given to the poor?" Jesus knew what they were saying and spoke to them, "Why must you make this woman feel uncomfortable? She has done a beautiful thing for me. You have the poor with you always, but you will not always have me. When she poured this perfume on my body, she was preparing it for my burial. I assure you that wherever the gospel is preached throughout the whole world, what she has done will also be told, as her memorial to me."

26.14 The betrayal is arranged

After this, one of the twelve, Judas Iscariot by name, approached the chief priests. "What will you give me," he said to them, "if I hand him over to you?" They settled with him for thirty silver coins, and from then on he looked for a convenient opportunity to betray Jesus.

26.17 The last supper

On the first day of unleavened bread the disciples came to Jesus with the question, "Where

Revised Standard Version

ointment, and she poured it on his head, as he sat at table. 8 But when the disciples saw it, they were indignant, saying, "Why this waste? 9 For this ointment might have been sold for a large sum, and given to the poor." 10 But Jesus, aware of this, said to them, "Why do you trouble the woman? For she has done a beautiful thing to me. 11 For you always have the poor with you, but you will not always have me. 12 In pouring this ointment on my body she has done it to prepare me for burial. 13 Truly, I say to you, wherever this gospel is preached in the whole world, what she has done will be told in memory of her."

14 Then one of the twelve, who was called Judas Iscariot, went to the chief priests 15 and said, "What will you give me if I deliver him to you?" And they paid him thirty pieces of silver. 16 And from that moment he sought an opportunity to betray him.

17 Now on the first day of Unleavened Bread the disciples came to Jesus, saying, "Where will

Jerusalem Bible

and poured it on his head as he was at table. 8 When they saw this, the disciples were indignant. "Why this waste?" they said. 9 "This could have been sold at a high price and the money given to the poor." 10 Jesus noticed this. "Why are you upsetting the woman?" he said to them. "What she has done for me is one of the good works[j] indeed! 11 You have the poor with you always, but you will not always have me. 12 When she poured this ointment on my body, she did it to prepare me for burial. 13 I tell you solemnly, wherever in all the world this Good News is proclaimed, what she has done will be told also, in remembrance of her."

Judas betrays Jesus

14 Then one of the Twelve, the man called Judas Iscariot, went to the chief 15 priests and said, "What are you prepared to give me if I hand him over to you?" 16 They paid him thirty silver pieces,[k] and from that moment he looked for an opportunity to betray him.

Preparations for the Passover supper

17 Now on the first day of Unleavened Bread[l] the disciples came to Jesus to say, "Where do

[j] As "good works," charitable deeds were reckoned superior to almsgiving. [k] Thirty shekels, the price fixed for a slave's life, Ex. 21:32. [l] Unleavened bread was normally to be eaten during the seven days which followed the Passover supper; here the writer appears to mean the first day of the whole Passover celebration.

New English Bible

he sat at table she began to pour it over his head. The disciples were indignant when they saw it. 'Why this waste?' they said; 'it could have been sold for a good sum and the money given to the poor.' Jesus was aware of this, and said to them, 'Why must you make trouble for the woman? It is a fine thing she has done for me. You have the poor among you always; but you will not always have me. When she poured this oil on my body it was her way of preparing me for burial. I tell you this: wherever in all the world this gospel is proclaimed, what she has done will be told as her memorial.'

Then one of the Twelve, the man called Judas Iscariot, went to the chief priests and said, 'What will you give me to betray him to you?' They weighed him out[a] thirty silver pieces. From that moment he began to look out for an opportunity to betray him.

On the first day of Unleavened Bread the disciples came to ask Jesus, 'Where would you

[a] *Or* agreed to pay him . . .

King James Version

ing unto him, Where wilt thou that we prepare
for thee to eat the passover? 18 And he said, Go
into the city to such a man, and say unto him,
The Master saith, My time is at hand; I will
keep the passover at thy house with my disciples. 19 And the disciples did as Jesus had appointed them; and they made ready the passover. 20 Now when the even was come, he sat
down with the twelve. 21 And as they did eat, he
said, Verily I say unto you, that one of you
shall betray me. 22 And they were exceeding sorrowful, and began every one of them to say
unto him, Lord, is it I? 23 And he answered and
said, He that dippeth *his* hand with me in the
dish, the same shall betray me. 24 The Son of
man goeth as it is written of him: but woe unto
that man by whom the Son of man is betrayed!
it had been good for that man if he had not been
born. 25 Then Judas, which betrayed him, answered and said, Master, is it I? He said unto
him, Thou hast said.

26 And as they were eating, Jesus took bread,
and blessed *it,* and brake it, *and* gave *it* to the
disciples, and said, Take, eat; this is my body.

Living Bible

from every Jewish home, the disciples came to Jesus and asked, "Where shall we plan to eat the Passover?"

18 He replied, "Go into the city and see Mr. So-and-So, and tell him, 'Our Master says, my time has come, and I will eat the Passover meal with my disciples at your house.' " 19 So the disciples did as he told them, and prepared the supper there.

20, 21 That evening as he sat eating with the Twelve, he said, "One of you will betray me."

22 Sorrow chilled their hearts, and each one asked, "Am I the one?"

23 He replied, "It is the one I served first.[b] 24 For I must die[c] just as was prophesied, but woe to the man by whom I am betrayed. Far better for that one if he had never been born."

25 Judas, too, had asked him, "Rabbi, am I the one?" And Jesus had told him, "Yes."

26 As they were eating, Jesus took a small loaf of bread and blessed it and broke it apart and gave it to the disciples and said, "Take it and eat it, for this is my body."

[*b*] Literally, "he that dipped his hand with me in the dish." [*c*] Literally, "the Son of Man goes."

Today's English Version

asked him, "Where do you want us to get the Passover meal ready for you?"

18 "Go to a certain man in the city," he said to them, "and tell him: 'The Teacher says, My hour has come; my disciples and I will celebrate the Passover at your house.' "

19 The disciples did as Jesus had told them and prepared the Passover meal.

20 When it was evening Jesus and the twelve disciples sat down to eat. 21 During the meal Jesus said, "I tell you, one of you will betray me."

22 The disciples were very upset and began to ask him, one after the other, "Surely you don't mean me, Lord?"

23 Jesus answered, "One who dips his bread in the dish with me will betray me. 24 The Son of Man will die as the Scriptures say he will, but how terrible for that man who will betray the Son of Man! It would have been better for that man if he had never been born!"

25 Judas, the traitor, spoke up. "Surely you don't mean me, Teacher?" he asked.

Jesus answered, "So you say."

The Lord's supper

26 While they were eating, Jesus took the bread, gave a prayer of thanks, broke it, and gave it to his disciples. "Take and eat it," he said; "this is my body."

New International Version

asked, "Where do you want us to make preparations for you to eat the Passover?"

18 He replied, "Go into the city to a certain man and tell him, 'The Teacher says: My appointed time is near. I am going to celebrate the Passover with my disciples at your house.' " 19 So the disciples did as Jesus had directed them and prepared the Passover.

20 When evening came, Jesus was reclining at the table with the Twelve. 21 And while they were eating, he said, "I tell you the truth, one of you will betray me."

22 They were very sad and began to say to him one after the other, "Surely not I, Lord?"

23 Jesus replied, "The one who has dipped his hand into the bowl with me will betray me. 24 The Son of Man will go just as it is written about him. But woe to that man who betrays the Son of Man! It would be better for him if he had not been born."

25 Then Judas, the one who would betray him, said, "Surely not I, Rabbi?"

Jesus answered, "Yes, it is you."[s]

26 While they were eating, Jesus took bread, gave thanks and broke it, and gave it to his disciples, saying, "Take and eat; this is my body."

[*s*] Or *You yourself have said it.*

Phillips Modern English

do you want us to make our preparations for you to eat the Passover?"

"Go into the city," Jesus replied, "to a certain man there and say to him, 'The Master says, "My time is near. I am going to keep the Passover with my disciples at your house." ' " The disciples did as Jesus had instructed them and prepared the Passover. Then late in the evening he took his place at table with the twelve and during the meal he said, "I tell you plainly that one of you is going to betray me." They were deeply distressed at this and each began to say to him in turn, "Surely, Lord, I am not the one?" And his answer was, "A man who has dipped his hand into the dish with me is the man who will betray me. It is true that the Son of Man will follow the road foretold by the scriptures, but alas for the man through whom he is betrayed! It would be better for that man if he had never been born." And Judas, who actually betrayed him, said, "Master, surely I am not the one?"

"You have said it!" replied Jesus.

In the middle of the meal Jesus took a loaf and after blessing it he broke it into pieces and gave it to the disciples. "Take and eat this," he

Revised Standard Version

you have us prepare for you to eat the passover?" 18 He said, "Go into the city to a certain
one, and say to him, 'The Teacher says, My time
is at hand; I will keep the passover at your
house with my disciples.' " 19And the disciples
did as Jesus had directed them, and they prepared the passover.
20 When it was evening, he sat at table with
the twelve disciples;[e] 21 and as they were eating,
he said, "Truly, I say to you, one of you will
betray me." 22And they were very sorrowful,
and began to say to him one after another, "Is
it I, Lord?" 23 He answered, "He who has dipped
his hand in the dish with me, will betray me.
24 The Son of man goes as it is written of him,
but woe to that man by whom the Son of man is
betrayed! It would have been better for that man
if he had not been born." 25 Judas, who betrayed him, said, "Is it I, Master?"[f] He said
to him, "You have said so."
26 Now as they were eating, Jesus took bread,
and blessed, and broke it, and gave it to the
disciples and said, "Take, eat; this is my body."

[*e*] Other authorities omit *disciples.* [*f*] Or *Rabbi.*

Jerusalem Bible

you want us to make the preparations for you
to eat the passover?" 18 "Go to so-and-so in the
city," he replied, "and say to him, 'The Master
says: My time is near. It is at your house that
I am keeping Passover with my disciples.' "
19 The disciples did what Jesus told them and
prepared the passover.

The treachery of Judas foretold

20 When evening came he was at table with
the twelve disciples. 21And while they were eating he said, "I tell you solemnly, one of you is
about to betray me." 22 They were greatly distressed and started asking him in turn, "Not I,
Lord, surely?" 23 He answered, "Someone, who
has dipped his hand into the dish with me, will
betray me. 24 The Son of Man is going to his
fate, as the scriptures say he will, but alas for
that man by whom the Son of Man is betrayed!
Better for that man if he had never been born!"
25 Judas, who was to betray him, asked in his
turn, "Not I, Rabbi, surely?" "They are your
own words," answered Jesus.

The institution of the Eucharist

26 Now as they were eating,[m] Jesus took
some bread, and when he had said the blessing
he broke it and gave it to the disciples. "Take it

[*m*] The Passover supper itself, for which exact rules for the blessing of bread and wine were laid down. The "eating" of v. 21 is the first course, which came before the passover itself.

New English Bible

like us to prepare for your Passover supper?' He answered, 'Go to a certain man in the city, and tell him, "The Master says, 'My appointed time is near; I am to keep Passover with my disciples at your house.' " ' The disciples did as Jesus directed them and prepared for Passover.

In the evening he sat down with the twelve disciples; and during supper he said, 'I tell you this: one of you will betray me.' In great distress they exclaimed one after the other, 'Can you mean me, Lord?' He answered, 'One who has dipped his hand into this bowl with me will betray me. The Son of Man is going the way appointed for him in the scriptures; but alas for that man by whom the Son of Man is betrayed! It would be better for that man if he had never been born.' Then Judas spoke, the one who was to betray him: 'Rabbi, can you mean me?' Jesus replied, 'The words are yours.'[b]

During supper Jesus took bread, and having said the blessing he broke it and gave it to the disciples with the words: 'Take this and eat; this

[*b*] *Or* It is as you say.

King James Version

27 And he took the cup, and gave thanks, and gave *it* to them, saying, Drink ye all of it; 28 For this is my blood of the new testament, which is shed for many for the remission of sins. 29 But I say unto you, I will not drink henceforth of this fruit of the vine, until that day when I drink it new with you in my Father's kingdom. 30 And when they had sung a hymn, they went out into the mount of Olives. 31 Then saith Jesus unto them, All ye shall be offended because of me this night: for it is written, I will smite the Shepherd, and the sheep of the flock shall be scattered abroad. 32 But after I am risen again, I will go before you into Galilee. 33 Peter answered and said unto him, Though all *men* shall be offended because of thee, *yet* will I never be offended. 34 Jesus said unto him, Verily I say unto thee, That this night, before the cock crow, thou shalt deny me thrice. 35 Peter said unto him, Though I should die with thee, yet will I not deny thee. Likewise also said all the disciples.

Living Bible

27 And he took a cup of wine and gave thanks for it and gave it to them and said, "Each one drink from it, 28 for this is my blood, sealing the New Covenant. It is poured out to forgive the sins of multitudes. 29 Mark my words—I will not drink this wine again until the day I drink it new with you in my Father's Kingdom."

30 And when they had sung a hymn, they went out to the Mount of Olives.

31 Then Jesus said to them, "Tonight you will all desert me. For it is written in the Scriptures[d] that God will smite the Shepherd, and the sheep of the flock will be scattered. 32 But after I have been brought back to life again I will go to Galilee, and meet you there."

33 Peter declared, "If everyone else deserts you, I won't."

34 Jesus told him, "The truth is that this very night, before the cock crows at dawn, you will deny me three times!"

35 "I would die first!" Peter insisted. And all the other disciples said the same thing.

[d] Zechariah 13:7.

Today's English Version

27 Then he took the cup, gave thanks to God, and gave it to them. "Drink it, all of you," he said; 28 "this is my blood, which seals God's covenant, my blood poured out for many for the forgiveness of sins. 29 I tell you, I will never again drink this wine until the day I drink the new wine with you in my Father's Kingdom."

30 Then they sang a hymn and went out to the Mount of Olives.

Jesus predicts Peter's denial

31 Then Jesus said to them, "This very night all of you will run away and leave me, because the scripture says, 'God will kill the shepherd and the sheep of the flock will be scattered.' 32 But after I am raised to life I will go to Galilee ahead of you."

33 Peter spoke up and said to Jesus, "I will never leave you, even though all the rest do!"

34 "Remember this!" Jesus said to Peter. "Before the rooster crows tonight you will say three times that you do not know me."

35 Peter answered, "I will never say I do not know you, even if I have to die with you!"

And all the disciples said the same thing.

New International Version

27 Then he took the cup, gave thanks and offered it to them, saying, "Drink from it, all of you. 28 This is my blood of the[t] covenant, which is poured out for many for the forgiveness of sins. 29 I tell you, I will not drink from this fruit of the vine from now on until that day when I drink it anew with you in my Father's kingdom."

30 When they had sung a hymn, they went out to the Mount of Olives.

Jesus predicts Peter's denial

31 Then Jesus told them, "This very night you will all fall away on account of me, for it is written:

'I will strike the shepherd,
and the sheep of the flock will be scattered.' [u]

32 But after I have risen, I will go ahead of you into Galilee."

33 Peter replied, "Even if all fall away on account of you, I never will."

34 "I tell you the truth," Jesus answered, "this very night, before the rooster crows, you will disown me three times."

35 But Peter declared, "Even if I have to die with you, I will never disown you." And all the other disciples said the same.

[t] Some MSS add *new*. [u] Zech. 13:7.

Phillips Modern English

said, "it is my body." Then he took a cup and, after thanking God, he gave it to them with the words, "Drink this, all of you, for it is my blood, the blood of the new agreement shed to set many free from their sins. I tell you I will drink no more wine until I drink it afresh with you in my Father's kingdom." Then they sang a hymn together and went out to the Mount of Olives. There Jesus said to them, "Tonight every one of you will lose his faith in me. For the scripture says, 'I will smite the shepherd, and the sheep of the flock shall be scattered abroad.' But after I am raised I shall go before you into Galilee!"

At this Peter exclaimed, "Even if everyone should lose his faith in you, I never will!"

"I tell you, Peter," replied Jesus, "that tonight, before the cock crows, you will disown me three times."

"Even if it means dying with you I will never disown you," said Peter. And all the disciples made the same protest.

Revised Standard Version

27 And he took a cup, and when he had given thanks he gave it to them, saying, "Drink of it, all of you; 28 for this is my blood of the[g] covenant, which is poured out for many for the forgiveness of sins. 29 I tell you I shall not drink again of this fruit of the vine until that day when I drink it new with you in my Father's kingdom."

30 And when they had sung a hymn, they went out to the Mount of Olives. 31 Then Jesus said to them, "You will all fall away because of me this night; for it is written, 'I will strike the shepherd, and the sheep of the flock will be scattered.' 32 But after I am raised up, I will go before you to Galilee." 33 Peter declared to him, "Though they all fall away because of you, I will never fall away." 34 Jesus said to him, "Truly, I say to you, this very night, before the cock crows, you will deny me three times." 35 Peter said to him, "Even if I must die with you, I will not deny you." And so said all the disciples.

[g] Other ancient authorities insert *new*.

Jerusalem Bible

and eat"; he said, "this is my body." 27 Then he took a cup, and when he had returned thanks he gave it to them. "Drink all of you from this," he said, 28 "for this is my blood, the blood of the covenant, which is to be poured out for many for the forgiveness of sins. 29 From now on, I tell you, I shall not drink wine until the day I drink the new wine with you in the kingdom of my Father."

Peter's denial foretold

30 After psalms had been sung[n] they left for the Mount of Olives. 31 Then Jesus said to them, "You will all lose faith in me this night,[o] for the scripture says: *I shall strike the shepherd and the sheep of the flock will be scattered,*[p] 32 but after my resurrection I shall go before you to Galilee." 33 At this, Peter said, "Though all lose faith in you, I will never lose faith." 34 Jesus answered him, "I tell you solemnly, this very night, before the cock crows, you will have disowned me three times." 35 Peter said to him, "Even if I have to die with you, I will never disown you." And all the disciples said the same.

[n] The psalms of praise which end the Passover supper. [o] "be brought down": the regular expression for the losing of faith through a difficulty or blow to it. [p] Zc. 13:7.

New English Bible

is my body.' Then he took a cup, and having offered thanks to God he gave it to them with the words: 'Drink from it, all of you. For this is my blood, the blood of the covenant, shed for many for the forgiveness of sins. I tell you, never again shall I drink from the fruit of the vine until that day when I drink it new with you in the kingdom of my Father.'

After singing the Passover Hymn, they went out to the Mount of Olives. Then Jesus said to them, 'Tonight you will all fall from your faith on my account; for it stands written: "I will strike the shepherd down and the sheep of his flock will be scattered." But after I am raised again, I will go on before you into Galilee.' Peter replied, 'Everyone else may fall away on your account, but I never will.' Jesus said to him, 'I tell you, tonight before the cock crows you will disown me three times.' Peter said, 'Even if I must die with you, I will never disown you.' And all the disciples said the same.

King James Version

36 Then cometh Jesus with them unto a place called Gethsemane, and saith unto the disciples, Sit ye here, while I go and pray yonder. 37And he took with him Peter and the two sons of Zebedee, and began to be sorrowful and very heavy. 38 Then saith he unto them, My soul is exceeding sorrowful, even unto death: tarry ye here, and watch with me. 39And he went a little further, and fell on his face, and prayed, saying, O my Father, if it be possible, let this cup pass from me: nevertheless, not as I will, but as thou *wilt.* 40And he cometh unto the disciples, and findeth them asleep, and saith unto Peter, What, could ye not watch with me one hour? 41Watch and pray, that ye enter not into temptation: the spirit indeed *is* willing, but the flesh *is* weak. 42 He went away again the second time, and prayed, saying, O my Father, if this cup may not pass away from me, except I drink it, thy will be done. 43And he came and found them asleep again: for their eyes were heavy. 44And he left them, and went away again, and prayed the third time, saying the same words. 45 Then cometh he to his disciples, and saith unto them, Sleep on now, and take *your* rest: behold, the hour is at hand, and the Son of man is betrayed into the hands of sinners. 46 Rise, let us be going: behold, he is at hand that doth betray me.

Living Bible

36 Then Jesus brought them to a garden grove, Gethsemane, and told them to sit down and wait while he went on ahead to pray. 37 He took Peter with him and Zebedee's two sons James and John, and began to be filled with anguish and despair.

38 Then he told them, "My soul is crushed with horror and sadness to the point of death . . . stay here . . . stay awake with me."

39 He went forward a little, and fell face downward on the ground, and prayed, "My Father! If it is possible, let this cup be taken away from me. But I want your will, not mine."

40 Then he returned to the three disciples and found them asleep. "Peter," he called, "couldn't you even stay awake with me one hour? 41 Keep alert and pray. Otherwise temptation will overpower you. For the spirit indeed is willing, but how weak the body is!"

42 Again he left them and prayed, "My Father! If this cup cannot go away until I drink it all, your will be done."

43 He returned to them again and found them sleeping, for their eyes were heavy, 44 so he went back to prayer the third time, saying the same things again.

45 Then he came to the disciples and said, "Sleep on now and take your rest . . . but no! The time has come! I[e] am betrayed into the hands of evil men! 46 Up! Let's be going! Look! Here comes the man who is betraying me!"

[*e*] Literally, "the Son of Man."

Today's English Version

Jesus prays in Gethsemane

36 Then Jesus went with his disciples to a place called Gethsemane, and he said to them, "Sit here while I go over there and pray." 37 He took with him Peter, and Zebedee's two sons. Grief and anguish came over him, 38 and he said to them, "The sorrow in my heart is so great that it almost crushes me. Stay here and watch with me."

39 He went a little farther on, threw himself face down to the ground, and prayed, "My Father, if it is possible; take this cup away from me! But not what I want, but what you want."

40 Then he returned to the three disciples and found them asleep; and he said to Peter, "How is it that you three were not able to watch with me for one hour? 41 Keep watch, and pray so that you will not fall into temptation. The spirit is willing, but the flesh is weak."

42 Again a second time Jesus went away and prayed, "My Father, if this cup cannot be taken away unless I drink it, your will be done." 43 He returned once more and found the disciples asleep; they could not keep their eyes open.

44 Again Jesus left them, went away, and prayed the third time, saying the same words. 45 Then he returned to the disciples and said, "Are you still sleeping and resting? Look! The hour has come for the Son of Man to be handed over to the power of sinful men. 46 Get up, let us go. Look, here is the man who is betraying me!"

New International Version

Gethsemane

36 Then Jesus went with his disciples to a place called Gethsemane, and he said to them, "Sit here while I go over there and pray." 37 He took Peter and the two sons of Zebedee along with him, and he began to be sorrowful and troubled. 38 Then he said to them, "My soul is overwhelmed with sorrow to the point of death. Stay here and keep watch with me."

39 Going a little farther, he fell with his face to the ground and prayed, "My Father, if it is possible, may this cup be taken from me. Yet not as I will, but as you will."

40 Then he returned to his disciples and found them sleeping. "Could you men not keep watch with me for one hour?" he asked Peter. 41 "Watch and pray so that you will not fall into temptation. The spirit is willing, but the body is weak."

42 He went away a second time and prayed, "My Father, if it is not possible for this cup to be taken away unless I drink it, may your will be done."

43 When he came back, he again found them sleeping, because their eyes were heavy. 44 So he left them and went away once more and prayed the third time, saying the same thing.

45 Then he returned to the disciples and said to them, "Are you still sleeping and resting? Look, the hour is near, and the Son of Man is betrayed into the hands of sinners. 46 Rise, let us go! Here comes my betrayer!"

Phillips Modern English

26.36 The prayer in Gethsemane

Then Jesus came with the disciples to a place called Gethsemane and said to them, "Sit down here while I go over there and pray." Then he took with him Peter and the two sons of Zebedee and began to be in terrible pain and agony of mind. "My heart is breaking with a deathlike grief," he told them, "stay here and keep watch with me." Then he walked on a little way and fell on his face and prayed, "My Father, if it is possible let this cup pass from me—yet it must not be what I want, but what you want."

Then he came back to the disciples and found them fast asleep. He spoke to Peter, "Couldn't you three keep awake with me for a single hour? Watch and pray, all of you, that you may not have to face temptation. Your spirit is willing, but human nature is weak."

Then he went away a second time and prayed, "My Father, if it is not possible for this cup to pass from me without my drinking it, then your will must be done."

And he came and found them asleep again, for they could not keep their eyes open. So he left them and went away again and prayed for the third time using the same words as before. Then he came back to his disciples and spoke to them, "Are you still sleeping and taking your ease? In a moment you will see the Son of Man betrayed into the hands of evil men. Wake up, let us be going! Look, here comes my betrayer!"

Revised Standard Version

36 Then Jesus went with them to a place called
Gethsemane, and he said to his disciples, "Sit
here, while I go yonder and pray." 37And taking with him Peter and the two sons of Zebedee,
he began to be sorrowful and troubled. 38 Then
he said to them, "My soul is very sorrowful,
even to death; remain here, and watch[h] with
me." 39And going a little farther he fell on his
face and prayed, "My Father, if it be possible,
let this cup pass from me; nevertheless, not as I
will, but as thou wilt." 40And he came to the
disciples and found them sleeping; and he said
to Peter, "So, could you not watch[h] with me one
hour? 41 Watch[h] and pray that you may not enter into temptation; the spirit indeed is willing,
but the flesh is weak." 42Again, for the second
time, he went away and prayed, "My Father, if
this cannot pass unless I drink it, thy will be
done." 43And again he came and found them
sleeping, for their eyes were heavy. 44 So, leaving them again, he went away and prayed for
the third time, saying the same words. 45 Then
he came to the disciples and said to them, "Are
you still sleeping and taking your rest? Behold,
the hour is at hand, and the Son of man is
betrayed into the hands of sinners. 46 Rise, let
us be going; see, my betrayer is at hand."

[h] Or *keep awake.*

Jerusalem Bible

Gethsemane

36 Then Jesus came with them to a small
estate called Gethsemane; and he said to his disciples, "Stay here while I go over there to pray."
37 He took Peter and the two sons of Zebedee
with him. And sadness came over him, and great
distress. 38 Then he said to them, "My soul is
sorrowful to the point of death. Wait here and
keep awake with me." 39And going on a little
further he fell on his face and prayed. "My
Father," he said, "if it is possible, let this cup
pass me by. Nevertheless, let it be as you, not
I, would have it." 40 He came back to the disciples and found them sleeping, and he said to
Peter, "So you had not the strength to keep
awake with me one hour? 41 You should be
awake, and praying not to be put to the test.
The spirit is willing, but the flesh is weak."
42Again, a second time, he went away and
prayed: "My Father," he said, "if this cup cannot pass by without my drinking it, your will
be done!" 43And he came back again and found
them sleeping, their eyes were so heavy.
44 Leaving them there, he went away again and
prayed for the third time, repeating the same
words. 45 Then he came back to the disciples
and said to them, "You can sleep on now and
take your rest. Now the hour has come when
the Son of Man is to be betrayed into the hands
of sinners. 46 Get up! Let us go! My betrayer is
already close at hand."

New English Bible

Jesus then came with his disciples to a place called Gethsemane. He said to them, 'Sit here while I go over there to pray.' He took with him Peter and the two sons of Zebedee. Anguish and dismay came over him, and he said to them, 'My heart is ready to break with grief. Stop here, and stay awake with me.' He went on a little, fell on his face in prayer, and said, 'My Father, if it is possible, let this cup pass me by. Yet not as I will, but as thou wilt.'

He came to the disciples and found them asleep; and he said to Peter, 'What! Could none of you stay awake with me one hour? Stay awake, and pray that you may be spared the test. The spirit is willing, but the flesh is weak.'

He went away a second time, and prayed: 'My Father, if it is not possible for this cup to pass me by without my drinking it, thy will be done.' He came again and found them asleep, for their eyes were heavy. So he left them and went away again; and he prayed the third time, using the same words as before.

Then he came to the disciples and said to them, 'Still sleeping? Still taking your ease? The hour has come! The Son of Man is betrayed to sinful men. Up, let us go forward; the traitor is upon us.'

King James Version

47 And while he yet spake, lo, Judas, one of
the twelve, came, and with him a great multitude with swords and staves, from the chief
priests and elders of the people. 48 Now he that
betrayed him gave them a sign, saying, Whomsoever I shall kiss, that same is he; hold him fast.
49And forthwith he came to Jesus, and said,
Hail, Master; and kissed him. 50And Jesus said
unto him, Friend, wherefore art thou come?
Then came they, and laid hands on Jesus, and
took him. 51And, behold, one of them which
were with Jesus stretched out *his* hand, and
drew his sword, and struck a servant of the high
priest, and smote off his ear. 52 Then said Jesus
unto him, Put up again thy sword into his place:
for all they that take the sword shall perish with
the sword. 53 Thinkest thou that I cannot now
pray to my Father, and he shall presently give
me more than twelve legions of angels? 54 But
how then shall the Scriptures be fulfilled, that
thus it must be? 55 In that same hour said Jesus
to the multitudes, Are ye come out as against a
thief with swords and staves for to take me? I
sat daily with you teaching in the temple, and ye
laid no hold on me. 56 But all this was done,
that the Scriptures of the prophets might be fulfilled. Then all the disciples forsook him, and
fled.

Living Bible

47 At that very moment while he was still
speaking, Judas, one of the Twelve, arrived with
a great crowd armed with swords and clubs, sent
by the Jewish leaders. 48 Judas had told them to
arrest the man he greeted, for that would be the
one they were after. 49 So now Judas came
straight to Jesus and said, "Hello, Master!" and
embraced [f] him in friendly fashion.
50 Jesus said, "My friend, go ahead and do
what you have come for." Then the others
grabbed him.
51 One of the men with Jesus pulled out a
sword and slashed off the ear of the High Priest's
servant.
52 "Put away your sword," Jesus told him.
"Those using swords will get killed. 53 Don't you
realize that I could ask my Father for thousands
of angels to protect us, and he would send them
instantly? 54 But if I did, how would the Scriptures be fulfilled that describe what is happening
now?" 55 Then Jesus spoke to the crowd. "Am I
some dangerous criminal," he asked, "that you
had to arm yourselves with swords and clubs
before you could arrest me? I was with you
teaching daily in the Temple and you didn't
stop me then. 56 But this is all happening to
fulfill the words of the prophets as recorded in
the Scriptures."

At that point, all the disciples deserted him
and fled.

[f] Literally, "kissed," the greeting still used among men in Eastern lands.

Today's English Version

The arrest of Jesus

47 Jesus was still speaking when Judas, one of
the twelve disciples, arrived. With him was a
large crowd carrying swords and clubs, sent by
the chief priests and the Jewish elders. 48 The
traitor had given the crowd a signal: "The man
I kiss is the one you want. Arrest him!"
49 When Judas arrived he went straight to
Jesus and said, "Peace be with you, Teacher,"
and kissed him.
50 Jesus answered, "Be quick about it, friend!"
Then they came up, arrested Jesus, and held
him tight. 51 One of those who were with Jesus
drew his sword and struck at the High Priest's
slave, cutting off his ear. 52 Then Jesus said to
him, "Put your sword back in its place, because
all who take the sword will die by the sword.
53 Don't you know that I could call on my Father for help and at once he would send me
more than twelve armies of angels? 54 But in that
case, how could the Scriptures come true that
say it must happen in this way?"
55 Then Jesus spoke to the crowd, "Did you
have to come with swords and clubs to capture
me, as though I were an outlaw? Every day I
sat down and taught in the temple, and you did
not arrest me. 56 But all this has happened to
make come true what the prophets wrote in the
Scriptures."

Then all the disciples left him and ran away.

New International Version

Jesus arrested

47 While he was still speaking, Judas, one of
the Twelve, arrived. With him was a large
crowd armed with swords and clubs, sent from
the chief priests and the elders of the people.
48 Now the betrayer had arranged a signal with
them: "The one I kiss is the man; arrest him."
49 Going at once to Jesus, Judas said, "Greetings, Rabbi!" and kissed him.
50 Jesus replied, "Friend, do what you came
for." [v]

Then the men stepped forward, seized Jesus
and arrested him. 51 With that, one of Jesus'
companions reached for his sword, drew it out
and struck the servant of the high priest, cutting off his ear.
52 "Put your sword back in its place," Jesus
said to him, "for all who draw the sword will
die by the sword. 53 Do you think I cannot call
on my Father, and he will at once put at my
disposal more than twelve legions of angels?
54 But how then would the Scriptures be fulfilled
that say it must happen in this way?"
55 At that time Jesus said to the crowd, "Am
I leading a rebellion, that you have come out
with swords and clubs to capture me? Every day
I sat in the temple courts teaching, and you did
not arrest me. 56 But this has all taken place
that the writings of the prophets might be fulfilled." Then all the disciples deserted him and
fled.

[v] Or *"Friend, why have you come?"*

Phillips Modern English

26.47 The betrayal

And while the words were still on his lips Judas, one of the twelve, appeared with a great crowd armed with swords and staves, sent by the chief priests and Jewish elders. (The traitor himself had given them a sign, "The one I kiss will be the man. Get him!")

Without any hesitation he walked up to Jesus. "Greetings, Master!" he cried and kissed him affectionately. "Judas, my friend," replied Jesus, "why are you here?"

Then the others came up, seized hold of Jesus and held him. Suddenly one of Jesus' disciples drew his sword, slashed at the High Priest's servant and cut off his ear. At this Jesus said to him, "Put your sword back into its proper place. All those who take the sword die by the sword. Do you imagine that I could not appeal to my Father, and he would at once send more than twelve legions of angels to defend me? But then, how would the scriptures be fulfilled which say that all this must take place?"

And then Jesus spoke to the crowds around him: "So you've come out with your swords and staves to capture me like a bandit, have you? Day after day I sat teaching in the Temple and you never laid a finger on me. But all this is happening as the prophets said it would." And at this point all the disciples deserted him and made their escape.

Revised Standard Version

47 While he was still speaking, Judas came,
one of the twelve, and with him a great crowd
with swords and clubs, from the chief priests and
the elders of the people. 48 Now the betrayer had
given them a sign, saying, "The one I shall kiss
is the man; seize him." 49 And he came up to
Jesus at once and said, "Hail, Master!" [i] And he
kissed him. 50 Jesus said to him, "Friend, why
are you here?" [j] Then they came up and laid
hands on Jesus and seized him. 51 And behold,
one of those who were with Jesus stretched out
his hand and drew his sword, and struck the
slave of the high priest, and cut off his ear.
52 Then Jesus said to him, "Put your sword
back into its place; for all who take the sword
will perish by the sword. 53 Do you think that
I cannot appeal to my Father, and he will at
once send me more than twelve legions of angels? 54 But how then should the scriptures be
fulfilled, that it must be so?" 55 At that hour
Jesus said to the crowds, "Have you come out
as against a robber, with swords and clubs to
capture me? Day after day I sat in the temple
teaching, and you did not seize me. 56 But all
this has taken place, that the scriptures of the
prophets might be fulfilled." Then all the disciples forsook him and fled.

[i] Or *Rabbi.* [j] Or *do that for which you have come.*

Jerusalem Bible

The arrest

47 He was still speaking when Judas, one of
the Twelve, appeared, and with him a large
number of men armed with swords and clubs,
sent by the chief priests and elders of the people. 48 Now the traitor had arranged a sign with
them. "The one I kiss," he had said, "he is the
man. Take him in charge." 49 So he went
straight up to Jesus and said, "Greetings, Rabbi,"
and kissed him. 50 Jesus said to him, "My friend,
do what you are here for." Then they came forward, seized Jesus and took him in charge. 51 At
that, one of the followers of Jesus grasped his
sword and drew it; he struck out at the high
priest's servant, and cut off his ear. 52 Jesus then
said, "Put your sword back, for all who draw
the sword will die by the sword. 53 Or do you
think that I cannot appeal to my Father who
would promptly send more than twelve legions
of angels to my defense? 54 But then, how would
the scriptures be fulfilled that say this is the
way it must be?" 55 It was at this time that
Jesus said to the crowds, "Am I a brigand, that
you had to set out to capture me with swords
and clubs? I sat teaching in the Temple day
after day and you never laid hands on me."
56 Now all this happened to fulfill the prophecies
in scripture. Then all the disciples deserted him
and ran away.

New English Bible

While he was still speaking, Judas, one of the Twelve, appeared; with him was a great crowd armed with swords and cudgels, sent by the chief priests and the elders of the nation. The traitor gave them this sign: 'The one I kiss is your man; seize him'; and stepping forward at once, he said, 'Hail, Rabbi!', and kissed him. Jesus replied, 'Friend, do what you are here to do.' [a] They then came forward, seized Jesus, and held him fast.

At that moment one of those with Jesus reached for his sword and drew it, and he struck at the High Priest's servant and cut off his ear. But Jesus said to him, 'Put up your sword. All who take the sword die by the sword. Do you suppose that I cannot appeal to my Father, who would at once send to my aid more than twelve legions of angels? But how then could the scriptures be fulfilled, which say that this must be?'

At the same time Jesus spoke to the crowd: 'Do you take me for a bandit, that you have come out with swords and cudgels to arrest me? Day after day I sat teaching in the temple, and you did not lay hands on me. But this has all happened to fulfil what the prophets wrote.'

Then the disciples all deserted him and ran away.

[a] *Or* Friend, what are you here for?

King James Version

57 And they that had laid hold on Jesus led *him* away to Caiaphas the high priest, where the scribes and the elders were assembled. 58 But Peter followed him afar off unto the high priest's palace, and went in, and sat with the servants, to see the end. 59 Now the chief priests, and elders, and all the council, sought false witness against Jesus, to put him to death; 60 But found none: yea, though many false witnesses came, *yet* found they none. At the last came two false witnesses, 61 And said, This *fellow* said, I am able to destroy the temple of God, and to build it in three days. 62 And the high priest arose, and said unto him, Answerest thou nothing? what *is it which* these witness against thee? 63 But Jesus held his peace. And the high priest answered and said unto him, I adjure thee by the living God, that thou tell us whether thou be the Christ, the Son of God. 64 Jesus saith unto him, Thou hast said: nevertheless I say unto you, Hereafter shall ye see the Son of man sitting on the right hand of power, and coming in the clouds of heaven. 65 Then the high priest rent his clothes, saying, He hath spoken blasphemy; what further need have we of witnesses? behold, now ye have heard his blasphemy. 66 What think ye? They answered and said, He is guilty of death. 67 Then did they spit in his face, and buffeted him: and others smote *him* with the palms of their hands, 68 Saying, Prophesy unto us, thou Christ, Who is he that smote thee?

Living Bible

57 Then the mob led him to the home of Caiaphas the High Priest, where all the Jewish leaders were gathering. 58 Meanwhile, Peter was following far to the rear, and came to the courtyard of the High Priest's house and went in and sat with the soldiers, and waited to see what was going to be done to Jesus.

59 The chief priests and, in fact, the entire Jewish Supreme Court assembled there and looked for witnesses who would lie about Jesus, in order to build a case against him that would result in a death sentence. 60, 61 But even though they found many who agreed to be false witnesses, these always contradicted each other.

Finally two men were found who declared, "This man said, 'I am able to destroy the Temple of God and rebuild it in three days.'"

62 Then the High Priest stood up and said to Jesus, "Well, what about it? Did you say that, or didn't you?" 63 But Jesus remained silent.

Then the High Priest said to him, "I demand in the name of the living God that you tell us whether you claim to be the Messiah, the Son of God."

64 "Yes," Jesus said, "I am. And in the future you will see me, the Messiah,[e] sitting at the right hand of God and returning on the clouds of heaven."

65, 66 Then the High Priest tore at his own clothing, shouting, "Blasphemy! What need have we for other witnesses? You have all heard him say it! What is your verdict?"

They shouted, "Death!—Death!—Death!"

67 Then they spat in his face and struck him and some slapped him, 68 saying, "Prophesy to us, you Messiah! Who struck you that time?"

Today's English Version

Jesus before the council

57 Those who had arrested Jesus took him to the house of Caiaphas, the High Priest, where the teachers of the Law and the elders had gathered together. 58 Peter followed him from a distance, as far as the courtyard of the High Priest's house. He went into the courtyard and sat down with the guards, to see how it would all come out. 59 The chief priests and the whole Council tried to find some false evidence against Jesus, to put him to death; 60 but they could not find any, even though many came up and told lies about him. Finally two men stepped forward 61 and said, "This man said, 'I am able to tear down God's temple and three days later build it back up.'"

62 The High Priest stood up and said to Jesus, "Have you no answer to give to this accusation against you?" 63 But Jesus kept quiet. Again the High Priest spoke to him, "In the name of the living God, I now put you on oath: tell us if you are the Messiah, the Son of God."

64 Jesus answered him, "So you say. But I tell all of you: from this time on you will see the Son of Man sitting at the right side of the Almighty, and coming on the clouds of heaven!"

65 At this the High Priest tore his clothes and said, "Blasphemy! We don't need any more witnesses! Right here you have heard his wicked words! 66 What do you think?"

They answered, "He is guilty, and must die."

67 Then they spat in his face and beat him; and those who slapped him 68 said, "Prophesy for us, Messiah! Guess who hit you!"

New International Version

Before the Sanhedrin

57 Those who had arrested Jesus took him to Caiaphas, the high priest, where the teachers of the law and the elders had assembled. 58 But Peter followed him at a distance, right up to the courtyard of the high priest. He entered and sat down with the guards to see the outcome.

59 The chief priests and the whole Sanhedrin were looking for false evidence against Jesus so that they could put him to death. 60 But they did not find any, though many false witnesses came forward.

Finally two came forward 61 and declared, "This fellow said, 'I am able to destroy the temple of God and rebuild it in three days.'"

62 Then the high priest stood up and said to Jesus, "Are you not going to answer? What is this testimony that these men are bringing against you?" 63 But Jesus remained silent.

The high priest said to him, "I charge you under oath by the living God: Tell us if you are the Christ,[w] the Son of God."

64 "Yes, it is as you say," Jesus replied. "But I say to all of you: In the future you will see the Son of Man sitting at the right hand of the Mighty One and coming on the clouds of heaven."

65 Then the high priest tore his clothes and said, "He has spoken blasphemy! Why do we need any more witnesses? Look, now you have heard the blasphemy. 66 What do you think?"

"He is worthy of death," they answered.

67 Then they spit in his face and struck him with their fists. Others slapped him 68 and said, "Prophesy to us, Christ.[w] Who hit you?"

[w] Or *Messiah*.

Phillips Modern English

26.57 Jesus before the High Priest

The men who had seized Jesus took him off to Caiaphas the High Priest in whose house the scribes and elders were assembled. Peter followed him at a distance right up to the High Priest's courtyard. Then he went inside and sat down with the servants and waited to see the end.

Meanwhile the chief priests and the whole Council did all they could to find false evidence against Jesus to get him condemned to death. They failed completely, even after a number of perjurers came forward. In the end two men stood up and said, "This man said, 'I can pull down the Temple of God and rebuild it in three days.'" Then the High Priest rose to his feet and addressed Jesus. "Have you no answer? What about the evidence of these men against you?" But Jesus was silent. Then the High Priest said to him, "I command you by the living God, to tell us on your oath if you are Christ, the Son of God." Jesus said to him, "You have said so. Yes, and I tell you that in the future you will see the Son of Man sitting at the right hand of power and coming on the clouds of Heaven."

At this the High Priest tore his robes and cried, "That was blasphemy! Where is the need for further witnesses? Look, you've heard the blasphemy—what's your verdict now?" And they replied, "He deserves to die."

Then they spat in his face and knocked him about, and some slapped him, crying, "Prophesy, you Christ, who was that who hit you?"

Revised Standard Version

57 Then those who had seized Jesus led him
to Caiaphas the high priest, where the scribes
and the elders had gathered. 58 But Peter followed him at a distance, as far as the courtyard
of the high priest, and going inside he sat with
the guards to see the end. 59 Now the chief
priests and the whole council sought false testimony against Jesus that they might put him to
death, 60 but they found none, though many
false witnesses came forward. At last two came
forward 61 and said, "This fellow said, 'I am
able to destroy the temple of God, and to build
it in three days.'" 62 And the high priest stood
up and said, "Have you no answer to make?
What is it that these men testify against you?"
63 But Jesus was silent. And the high priest said
to him, "I adjure you by the living God, tell us
if you are the Christ, the Son of God." 64 Jesus
said to him, "You have said so. But I tell you,
hereafter you will see the Son of man seated at
the right hand of Power, and coming on the
clouds of heaven." 65 Then the high priest tore
his robes, and said, "He has uttered blasphemy.
Why do we still need witnesses? You have now
heard his blasphemy. 66 What is your judgment?"
They answered, "He deserves death." 67 Then
they spat in his face, and struck him; and some
slapped him, 68 saying, "Prophesy to us, you
Christ! Who is it that struck you?"

Jerusalem Bible

Jesus before the Sanhedrin

57 The men who had arrested Jesus led him
off to Caiaphas the high priest, where the scribes
and the elders were assembled. 58 Peter followed
him at a distance, and when he reached the high
priest's palace, he went in and sat down with
the attendants to see what the end would be.
59 The chief priests and the whole Sanhedrin
were looking for evidence against Jesus, however false, on which they might pass the death
sentence. 60 But they could not find any, though
several lying witnesses came forward. Eventually
two stepped forward 61 and made a statement,
"This man said, 'I have power to destroy the
Temple of God and in three days build it up.'"
62 The high priest then stood up and said to him,
"Have you no answer to that? What is this evidence these men are bringing against you?"
63 But Jesus was silent. And the high priest said
to him, "I put you on oath by the living God
to tell us if you are the Christ, the Son of God."
64 "The words are your own," answered Jesus.
"Moreover, I tell you that from this time onward you will see the *Son of Man seated at the*
right hand of the Power and *coming on the*
clouds of heaven." 65 At this, the high priest tore
his clothes and said, "He has blasphemed. What
need of witnesses have we now? There! You
have just heard the blasphemy. 66 What is your
opinion?" They answered, "He deserves to die."
67 Then they spat in his face and hit him
with their fists; others said as they struck him,
68 "Play the prophet, Christ! Who hit you then?"

New English Bible

Jesus was led off under arrest to the house of Caiaphas the High Priest, where the lawyers and elders were assembled. Peter followed him at a distance till he came to the High Priest's courtyard, and going in he sat down there among the attendants, meaning to see the end of it all.

The chief priests and the whole Council tried to find some allegation against Jesus on which a death-sentence could be based; but they failed to find one, though many came forward with false evidence. Finally two men alleged that he had said, 'I can pull down the temple of God, and rebuild it in three days.' At this the High Priest rose and said to him, 'Have you no answer to the charge that these witnesses bring against you?' But Jesus kept silence. The High Priest then said, 'By the living God I charge you to tell us: Are you the Messiah, the Son of God?' Jesus replied, 'The words are yours.[a] But I tell you this: from now on, you will see the Son of Man seated at the right hand of God [b] and coming on the clouds of heaven.' At these words the High Priest tore his robes and exclaimed, 'Blasphemy! Need we call further witnesses? You have heard the blasphemy. What is your opinion?' 'He is guilty,' they answered; 'he should die.'

Then they spat in his face and struck him with their fists; and others said, as they beat him, 'Now, Messiah, if you are a prophet, tell us who hit you.'

[a] *Or* It is as you say. [b] *Literally* of the Power.

King James Version

69 Now Peter sat without in the palace: and
a damsel came unto him, saying, Thou also wast
with Jesus of Galilee. 70 But he denied before
them all, saying, I know not what thou sayest.
71 And when he was gone out into the porch,
another *maid* saw him, and said unto them that
were there, This *fellow* was also with Jesus of
Nazareth. 72 And again he denied with an oath, I
do not know the man. 73 And after a while came
unto *him* they that stood by, and said to Peter,
Surely thou also art *one* of them; for thy speech
bewrayeth thee. 74 Then began he to curse and
to swear, *saying*, I know not the man. And immediately the cock crew. 75 And Peter remembered the word of Jesus, which said unto him,
Before the cock crow, thou shalt deny me thrice.
And he went out, and wept bitterly.

27 When the morning was come, all the chief
priests and elders of the people took coun-

Living Bible

69 Meanwhile, as Peter was sitting in the
courtyard a girl came over and said to him, "You
were with Jesus, for both of you are from Galilee." [g]

70 But Peter denied it loudly. "I don't even
know what you are talking about," he angrily
declared.

71 Later, out by the gate, another girl noticed
him and said to those standing around, "This
man was with Jesus—from Nazareth."

72 Again Peter denied it, this time with an
oath. "I don't even know the man," he said.

73 But after a while the men who had been
standing there came over to him and said, "We
know you are one of his disciples, for we can
tell by your Galilean[h] accent."

74 Peter began to curse and swear. "I don't
even know the man," he said.

And immediately the cock crowed. 75 Then
Peter remembered what Jesus had said, "Before
the cock crows, you will deny me three times."
And he went away, crying bitterly.

27 When it was morning, the chief priests
and Jewish leaders met again to discuss

[g] Literally, "with Jesus the Galilean." [h] Implied.

Today's English Version

Peter denies Jesus

69 Peter was sitting outside in the courtyard,
when one of the High Priest's servant girls came
to him and said, "You, too, were with Jesus of
Galilee."

70 But he denied it in front of them all. "I
don't know what you are talking about," he
answered, 71 and went on out to the entrance of
the courtyard. Another servant girl saw him and
said to the men there, "He was with Jesus of
Nazareth."

72 Again Peter denied it, and answered, "I
swear that I don't know that man!"

73 After a little while the men standing there
came to Peter. "Of course you are one of them,"
they said. "After all, the way you speak gives you
away!"

74 Then Peter made a vow: "May God punish
me if I am not telling the truth! I do not know
that man!"

Just then a rooster crowed, 75 and Peter remembered what Jesus had told him, "Before the
rooster crows, you will say three times that you
do not know me." He went out and wept bitterly.

Jesus taken to Pilate

27 Early in the morning all the chief priests
and the Jewish elders made their plan

New International Version

Peter disowns Jesus

69 Now Peter was sitting out in the courtyard,
and a servant girl came to him. "You also were
with Jesus of Galilee," she said.

70 But he denied it before them all. "I don't
know what you're talking about," he said.

71 Then he went out to the gateway, where
another girl saw him and said to the people
there, "This fellow was with Jesus of Nazareth."

72 He denied it again, with an oath: "I don't
know the man!"

73 After a little while, those standing there
went up to Peter and said, "Surely you are one
of them, for your accent gives you away."

74 Then he began to call down curses on
himself and he swore to them, "I don't know
the man!"

Immediately a rooster crowed. 75 Then Peter
remembered the word Jesus had spoken: "Before the rooster crows, you will disown me three
times." And he went outside and wept bitterly.

Judas hangs himself

27 Early in the morning, all the chief priests
and the elders of the people came to the

Phillips Modern English

26.69 Peter disowns his master

All this time Peter was sitting outside in the courtyard, and a maidservant came up to him and said, "Weren't you too with Jesus, the man from Galilee?" But he denied it before them all, saying, "I don't know what you're talking about." Then when he had gone out into the porch, another maid caught sight of him and said to those who were there, "This man was with Jesus of Nazareth." And again he denied it with an oath—"I don't know the man!" A few minutes later those who were standing about came up to Peter and said to him, "You certainly are one of them, it's obvious from your accent." At that he began to curse and swear—"I tell you I don't know the man!" Immediately the cock crew, and the words of Jesus came back into Peter's mind—"Before the cock crows you will disown me three times." And he went outside and wept bitterly.

When the morning came, all the chief priests and elders of the people met in council to de-

Revised Standard Version

69 Now Peter was sitting outside in the courtyard. And a maid came up to him, and said,
"You also were with Jesus the Galilean." 70 But
he denied it before them all, saying, "I do not
know what you mean." 71 And when he went out
to the porch, another maid saw him, and she
said to the bystanders, "This man was with
Jesus of Nazareth." 72 And again he denied it
with an oath, "I do not know the man." 73 After
a little while the bystanders came up and said
to Peter, "Certainly you are also one of them,
for your accent betrays you." 74 Then he began
to invoke a curse on himself and to swear, "I
do not know the man." And immediately the
cock crowed. 75 And Peter remembered the saying of Jesus, "Before the cock crows, you will
deny me three times." And he went out and wept
bitterly.

27 When morning came, all the chief priests and the elders of the people took counsel

Jerusalem Bible

Peter's denials

69 Meanwhile Peter was sitting outside in the
courtyard, and a servant girl came up to him
and said, "You too were with Jesus the Galilean." 70 But he denied it in front of them all.
"I do not know what you are talking about,"
he said. 71 When he went out to the gateway
another servant girl saw him and said to the
people there, "This man was with Jesus the
Nazarene." 72 And again, with an oath, he denied
it, "I do not know the man." 73 A little later the
bystanders came up and said to Peter, "You are
one of them for sure! Why, your accent gives
you away." 74 Then he started calling down
curses on himself and swearing, "I do not know
the man." At that moment the cock crew, 75 and
Peter remembered what Jesus had said, "Before
the cock crows you will have disowned me three
times." And he went outside and wept bitterly.

Jesus is taken before Pilate

27 When morning came, all the chief priests and the elders of the people met in coun-

New English Bible

Meanwhile Peter was sitting outside in the courtyard when a serving-maid accosted him and said, 'You were there too with Jesus the Galilean.' Peter denied it in face of them all. 'I do not know what you mean', he said. He then went out to the gateway, where another girl, seeing him, said to the people there, 'This fellow was with Jesus of Nazareth.' Once again he denied it, saying with an oath, 'I do not know the man.' Shortly afterwards the bystanders came up and said to Peter, 'Surely you are another of them; your accent gives you away!' At this he broke into curses and declared with an oath: 'I do not know the man.' At that moment a cock crew; and Peter remembered how Jesus had said, 'Before the cock crows you will disown me three times.' He went outside, and wept bitterly.

27 When morning came, the chief priests and the elders of the nation met in conference

King James Version

sel against Jesus to put him to death: 2And
when they had bound him, they led *him* away,
and delivered him to Pontius Pilate the governor.
3 Then Judas, which had betrayed him, when
he saw that he was condemned, repented himself, and brought again the thirty pieces of silver to the chief priests and elders, 4 Saying, I
have sinned in that I have betrayed the innocent
blood. And they said, What *is that* to us? see
thou *to that.* 5And he cast down the pieces of
silver in the temple, and departed, and went and
hanged himself. 6And the chief priests took the
silver pieces, and said, It is not lawful for to put
them into the treasury, because it is the price of
blood. 7And they took counsel, and bought with
them the potter's field, to bury strangers in.
8 Wherefore that field was called, The field of
blood, unto this day. 9 Then was fulfilled that
which was spoken by Jeremy the prophet, saying, And they took the thirty pieces of silver,
the price of him that was valued, whom they of
the children of Israel did value; 10And gave
them for the potter's field, as the Lord appointed

Living Bible

how to induce the Roman government to sentence Jesus to death.[a] 2 Then they sent him in
chains to Pilate, the Roman governor.
3 About that time Judas, who betrayed him,
when he saw that Jesus had been condemned to
die, changed his mind and deeply regretted what
he had done,[b] and brought back the money to
the chief priests and other Jewish leaders.
4 "I have sinned," he declared, "for I have
betrayed an innocent man."
"That's your problem," they retorted.
5 Then he threw the money onto the floor of
the Temple and went out and hanged himself.
6 The chief priests picked the money up. "We
can't put it in the collection," they said, "since
it's against our laws to accept money paid for
murder."
7 They talked it over and finally decided to
buy a certain field where the clay was used by
potters, and to make it into a cemetery for
foreigners who died in Jerusalem. 8 That is why
the cemetery is still called "The Field of Blood."
9 This fulfilled the prophecy of Jeremiah
which says,
"They took the thirty pieces of silver—the
price at which he was valued by the people
of Israel—10 and purchased a field from the
potters as the Lord directed me."

[a] Literally, "took counsel against Jesus to put him to death." They did not have the authority themselves. [b] Literally, "repented himself."

Today's English Version

against Jesus to put him to death. 2 They put him
in chains, took him, and handed him over to
Pilate, the Roman governor.

The death of Judas

3 When Judas, the traitor, saw that Jesus had
been condemned, he repented and took back the
thirty silver coins to the chief priests and the elders. 4 "I have sinned by betraying an innocent
man to death!" he said.
"What do we care about that?" they answered.
"That is your business!"
5 Judas threw the money into the sanctuary
and left them; then he went off and hanged himself.
6 The chief priests picked up the money and
said, "This is blood money, and it is against our
Law to put it in the temple treasury." 7After
reaching an agreement about it, they used the
money to buy Potter's Field, as a cemetery for
foreigners. 8 That is why that field is called
"Field of Blood" to this very day.
9 Then what the prophet Jeremiah had said
came true, "They took the thirty silver coins, the
amount the people of Israel had agreed to pay
for him, 10 and used them to buy the potter's
field, as the Lord commanded me."

New International Version

decision to put Jesus to death. 2 They bound
him, led him away and handed him over to
Pilate, the governor.
3 When Judas, who betrayed him, saw that
Jesus was condemned, he was seized with remorse and returned the thirty silver coins to the
chief priests and the elders. 4 "I have sinned," he
said, "for I have betrayed innocent blood."
"What is that to us?" they replied. "That's
your responsibility."
5 So Judas threw the money into the temple
and left. Then he went away and hanged himself.
6 The chief priests picked up the coins and
said, "It is against the law to put this into the
treasury, since it is blood money." 7 So they decided to use the money to buy the potter's field
as a burial place for foreigners. 8 That is why it
has been called the Field of Blood to this day.
9 Then what was spoken by Jeremiah the prophet
was fulfilled: "They took the thirty silver coins,
the price set on him by the people of Israel,
10 and they used them to buy the potter's field,
as the Lord commanded me." [x]

[x] Zech. 11:12,13; Jer. 32:6-9.

Phillips Modern English

cide how they could get Jesus executed. Then they marched him off with his hands tied, and handed him over to Pilate the governor.

27.3 The remorse of Judas

When Judas, who had betrayed him, saw that Jesus was condemned, he was overcome with remorse. He returned the thirty silver coins to the chief priests and elders, with the words, "I have done wrong—I have betrayed an innocent man to death."

"And what has that got to do with us?" they replied. "That's your affair."

And Judas flung down the silver in the Temple, left and went away and hanged himself. But the chief priests picked up the money and said, "It is not right to put this into the Temple treasury, for it is the price of a man's life." So, after a further consultation, they purchased with it the Potter's Field to be a burial-ground for foreigners, which is why it is called "the Field of Blood" to this day. And so the words of Jeremiah the prophet came true:

And they took the thirty pieces of silver, the price of him that was priced, whom certain of the children of Israel did price; and they gave them for the potter's field, as the Lord appointed me.

Revised Standard Version

against Jesus to put him to death; 2 and they bound him and led him away and delivered him to Pilate the governor.

3 When Judas, his betrayer, saw that he was condemned, he repented and brought back the thirty pieces of silver to the chief priests and the elders, 4 saying, "I have sinned in betraying innocent blood." They said, "What is that to us? See to it yourself." 5 And throwing down the pieces of silver in the temple, he departed; and he went and hanged himself. 6 But the chief priests, taking the pieces of silver, said, "It is not lawful to put them into the treasury, since they are blood money." 7 So they took counsel, and bought with them the potter's field, to bury strangers in. 8 Therefore that field has been called the Field of Blood to this day. 9 Then was fulfilled what had been spoken by the prophet Jeremiah, saying, "And they took the thirty pieces of silver, the price of him on whom a price had been set by some of the sons of Israel, 10 and they gave them for the potter's field, as the Lord directed me."

Jerusalem Bible

cil to bring about the death of Jesus. 2 They had him bound, and led him away to hand him over to Pilate[q] the governor.

The death of Judas

3 When he found that Jesus had been condemned, Judas his betrayer was filled with remorse and took the thirty silver pieces back to the chief priests and elders. 4 "I have sinned"; he said, "I have betrayed innocent blood." "What is that to us?" they replied. "That is your concern." 5 And flinging down the silver pieces in the sanctuary he made off, and went and hanged himself. 6 The chief priests picked up the silver pieces and said, "It is against the Law to put this into the treasury; it is blood money." 7 So they discussed the matter and bought the potter's field with it as a graveyard for foreigners, 8 and this is why the field is called the Field of Blood today. 9 The words of the prophet Jeremiah[r] were then fulfilled: *And they took the thirty silver pieces, the sum at which the precious One was priced by children of Israel,* 10 *and they gave them for the potter's field, just as the Lord directed me.*

[q] The Jews had to approach the Roman governor for confirmation and execution of any sentence of death. [r] Actually a free quotation from Zc. 11:12-13.

New English Bible

to plan the death of Jesus. They then put him in chains and led him away, to hand him over to Pilate, the Roman Governor.

When Judas the traitor saw that Jesus had been condemned, he was seized with remorse, and returned the thirty silver pieces to the chief priests and elders. 'I have sinned,' he said; 'I have brought an innocent man to his death.' But they said, 'What is that to us? See to that yourself.' So he threw the money down in the temple and left them, and went and hanged himself.

Taking up the money, the chief priests argued: 'This cannot be put into the temple fund; it is blood-money.' So after conferring they used it to buy the Potter's Field, as a burial-place for foreigners. This explains the name 'Blood Acre', by which that field has been known ever since; and in this way fulfilment was given to the prophetic utterance of Jeremiah: 'They took[a] the thirty silver pieces, the price set on a man's head (for that was his price among the Israelites), and gave the money for the potter's field, as the Lord directed me.'

[a] *Or* I took.

King James Version

me. 11 And Jesus stood before the governor: and
the governor asked him, saying, Art thou the
King of the Jews? And Jesus said unto him,
Thou sayest. 12 And when he was accused of the
chief priests and elders, he answered nothing.
13 Then said Pilate unto him, Hearest thou not
how many things they witness against thee?
14 And he answered him to never a word; insomuch that the governor marvelled greatly.
15 Now at *that* feast the governor was wont to
release unto the people a prisoner, whom they
would. 16 And they had then a notable prisoner,
called Barabbas. 17 Therefore when they were
gathered together, Pilate said unto them, Whom
will ye that I release unto you? Barabbas, or Jesus which is called Christ? 18 For he knew that
for envy they had delivered him.
19 When he was set down on the judgment
seat, his wife sent unto him, saying, Have thou
nothing to do with that just man: for I have
suffered many things this day in a dream because
of him. 20 But the chief priests and elders persuaded the multitude that they should ask
Barabbas, and destroy Jesus. 21 The governor
answered and said unto them, Whether of the
twain will ye that I release unto you? They said,

Living Bible

11 Now Jesus was standing before Pilate, the Roman governor. "Are you the Jews' Messiah?" [c] the governor asked him.

"Yes," Jesus replied.

12 But when the chief priests and other Jewish leaders made their many accusations against him, Jesus remained silent.

13 "Don't you hear what they are saying?" Pilate demanded.

14 But Jesus said nothing, much to the governor's surprise.

15 Now the governor's custom was to release one Jewish prisoner each year during the Passover celebration—anyone they wanted. 16 This year there was a particularly notorious criminal in jail named Barabbas, 17 and as the crowds gathered before Pilate's house that morning he asked them, "Which shall I release to you—Barabbas, or Jesus your Messiah?" [d] 18 For he knew very well that the Jewish leaders had arrested Jesus out of envy because of his popularity with the people.

19 Just then, as he was presiding over the court, Pilate's wife sent him this message: "Leave that good man alone; for I had a terrible nightmare concerning him last night."

20 Meanwhile the chief priests and Jewish officials persuaded the crowds to ask for Barabbas' release, and for Jesus' death. 21 So when the governor asked again,[e] "Which of these two shall I release to you?" the crowd shouted back their reply: "Barabbas!"

[*c*] Literally, " 'King' of the Jews." [*d*] Literally, "Jesus who is called Christ." [*e*] Implied.

Today's English Version

Pilate questions Jesus

11 Jesus stood before the Governor, who questioned him. "Are you the king of the Jews?" he asked.

"So you say," answered Jesus. 12 He said nothing, however, to the accusations of the chief priests and elders.

13 So Pilate said to him, "Don't you hear all these things they accuse you of?"

14 But Jesus refused to answer a single word, so that the Governor was greatly surprised.

Jesus sentenced to death

15 At every Passover Feast the Governor was in the habit of setting free any prisoner the crowd asked for. 16 At that time there was a well-known prisoner named Jesus Barabbas. 17 So when the crowd gathered, Pilate asked them, "Which one do you want me to set free for you? Jesus Barabbas or Jesus called the Christ?" 18 He knew very well that they had handed Jesus over to him because they were jealous.

19 While Pilate was sitting in the judgment hall, his wife sent him a message: "Have nothing to do with that innocent man, because in a dream last night I suffered much on account of him."

20 The chief priests and the elders persuaded the crowds to ask Pilate to set Barabbas free and have Jesus put to death. 21 But the Governor asked them, "Which one of these two do you want me to set free for you?"

"Barabbas!" they answered.

New International Version

Jesus before Pilate

11 Meanwhile Jesus stood before the governor, and the governor asked him, "Are you the king of the Jews?"

"Yes, it is as you say," Jesus replied.

12 When he was accused by the chief priests and the elders, he gave no answer. 13 Then Pilate asked him, "Don't you hear how many things they are accusing you of?" 14 But Jesus made no reply, not even to a single charge—to the great amazement of the governor.

15 Now it was the governor's custom at the Feast to release a prisoner chosen by the crowd. 16 At that time they had a notorious prisoner, called Barabbas. 17 So when the crowd had gathered, Pilate asked them, "Which one do you want me to release to you: Barabbas, or Jesus who is called Christ?" 18 For he knew it was out of envy that they had handed Jesus over to him.

19 While Pilate was sitting on the judge's seat, his wife sent him this message: "Don't have anything to do with that innocent man, because I have suffered a great deal today in a dream on account of him."

20 But the chief priests and the elders persuaded the crowd to ask for Barabbas and to have Jesus executed.

21 "Which of the two do you want me to release to you?" asked the governor.

"Barabbas," they answered.

Phillips Modern English

27.11 Jesus before Pilate

Meanwhile Jesus stood in front of the governor, who asked him, "Well, you—*are* you the King of the Jews?"

"That is what you are saying," replied Jesus. But while the chief priests and elders were making their accusations, he made no reply at all. So Pilate said to him, "Can you not hear the evidence they're bringing against you?" But to the governor's amazement, Jesus did not answer a single one of their accusations.

Now it was the custom at festival-time for the governor to release any one prisoner whom the people chose. And it happened that at this time they had a notorious prisoner called Barabbas. So when they were assembled, Pilate said to them, "Which one do you want me to set free, Barabbas or Jesus called Christ?" For he knew very well that the latter had been handed over to him through sheer malice. And indeed while he was actually sitting on the Bench his wife sent a message to him—"Don't have anything to do with that good man! I had terrible dreams about him last night!" But the chief priests and elders persuaded the mob to ask for Barabbas and demand Jesus' execution. Then the governor asked them directly, "Which of these two are you asking me to release?"

"Barabbas!" they cried.

Revised Standard Version

11 Now Jesus stood before the governor; and
the governor asked him, "Are you the King of
the Jews?" Jesus said, "You have said so." 12 But
when he was accused by the chief priests and
elders, he made no answer. 13 Then Pilate said to
him, "Do you not hear how many things they
testify against you?" 14 But he gave him no
answer, not even to a single charge; so the governor wondered greatly.
15 Now at the feast the governor was accustomed to release for the crowd any one prisoner
whom they wanted. 16And they had then a notorious prisoner, called Barabbas.[k] 17 So when
they had gathered, Pilate said to them, "Whom
do you want me to release for you, Barabbas[k]
or Jesus who is called Christ?" 18 For he knew
that it was out of envy that they had delivered
him up. 19 Besides, while he was sitting on the
judgment seat, his wife sent word to him, "Have
nothing to do with that righteous man, for I
have suffered much over him today in a dream."
20 Now the chief priests and the elders persuaded the people to ask for Barabbas and destroy Jesus. 21 The governor again said to them,
"Which of two do you want me to release for

[k] Other ancient authorities read *Jesus Barabbas*.

Jerusalem Bible

Jesus before Pilate

11 Jesus, then, was brought before the governor, and the governor put to him this question,
"Are you the king of the Jews?" Jesus replied,
"It is you who say it." 12 But when he was accused by the chief priests and the elders he refused to answer at all. 13 Pilate then said to him,
"Do you not hear how many charges they have
brought against you?" 14 But to the governor's
complete amazement, he offered no reply to any
of the charges.
15 At festival time it was the governor's practice to release a prisoner for the people, anyone they chose. 16 Now there was at that time
a notorious prisoner whose name was Barabbas.
17 So when the crowd gathered, Pilate said to
them, "Which do you want me to release for
you: Barabbas, or Jesus who is called Christ?"
18 For Pilate knew it was out of jealousy that
they had handed him over.
19 Now as he was seated in the chair of
judgment, his wife sent him a message, "Have
nothing to do with that man; I have been upset
all day by a dream I had about him."
20 The chief priests and the elders, however,
had persuaded the crowd to demand the release
of Barabbas and the execution of Jesus. 21 So
when the governor spoke and asked them,
"Which of the two do you want me to release

New English Bible

Jesus was now brought before the Governor; and as he stood there the Governor asked him, 'Are you the king of the Jews?' 'The words are yours',[b] said Jesus; and to the charges laid against him by the chief priests and elders he made no reply. Then Pilate said to him, 'Do you not hear all this evidence that is brought against you?'; but he still refused to answer one word, to the Governor's great astonishment.

At the festival season it was the Governor's custom to release one prisoner chosen by the people. There was then in custody a man of some notoriety, called Jesus[c] Bar-Abbas. When they were assembled Pilate said to them, 'Which would you like me to release to you—Jesus[c] Bar-Abbas, or Jesus called Messiah?' For he knew that it was out of malice that they had brought Jesus before him.

While Pilate was sitting in court a message came to him from his wife: 'Have nothing to do with that innocent man; I was much troubled on his account in my dreams last night.'

Meanwhile the chief priests and elders had persuaded the crowd to ask for the release of Bar-Abbas and to have Jesus put to death. So when the Governor asked, 'Which of the two do you wish me to release to you?', they said, 'Bar-

[b] *Or* It is as you say. [c] *Some witnesses omit* Jesus.

King James Version

Barabbas. 22 Pilate saith unto them, What shall I do then with Jesus which is called Christ? *They* all say unto him, Let him be crucified. 23 And the governor said, Why, what evil hath he done? But they cried out the more, saying, Let him be crucified.

24 When Pilate saw that he could prevail nothing, but *that* rather a tumult was made, he took water, and washed *his* hands before the multitude, saying, I am innocent of the blood of this just person: see ye *to it*. 25 Then answered all the people, and said, His blood *be* on us, and on our children.

26 Then released he Barabbas unto them: and when he had scourged Jesus, he delivered *him* to be crucified. 27 Then the soldiers of the governor took Jesus into the common hall, and gathered unto him the whole band *of soldiers*. 28 And they stripped him, and put on him a scarlet robe.

29 And when they had platted a crown of thorns, they put *it* upon his head, and a reed in his right hand: and they bowed the knee before him, and mocked him, saying, Hail, King of the Jews! 30 And they spit upon him, and took the reed, and smote him on the head. 31 And after that they had mocked him, they took the robe off from him, and put his own raiment on him,

Living Bible

22 "Then what shall I do with Jesus, your Messiah?" Pilate asked.

And they shouted, "Crucify him!"

23 "Why?" Pilate demanded. "What has he done wrong?" But they kept shouting, "Crucify! Crucify!"

24 When Pilate saw that he wasn't getting anywhere, and that a riot was developing, he sent for a bowl of water and washed his hands before the crowd, saying, "I am innocent of the blood of this good man. The responsibility is yours!"

25 And the mob yelled back, "His blood be on us and on our children!"

26 Then Pilate released Barabbas to them. And after he had whipped Jesus, he gave him to the Roman soldiers to take away and crucify. 27 But first they took him into the armory and called out the entire contingent. 28 They stripped him and put a scarlet robe on him, 29 and made a crown from long thorns and put it on his head, and placed a stick in his right hand as a scepter and knelt before him in mockery. "Hail, King of the Jews," they yelled. 30 And they spat on him and grabbed the stick and beat him on the head with it.

31 After the mockery, they took off the robe and put his own garment on him again, and took

Today's English Version

22 "What, then, shall I do with Jesus called the Christ?" Pilate asked them.

"Nail him to the cross!" they all answered.

23 But Pilate asked, "What crime has he committed?"

Then they started shouting at the top of their voices, "Nail him to the cross!"

24 When Pilate saw it was no use to go on, but that a riot might break out, he took some water, washed his hands in front of the crowd, and said, "I am not responsible for the death of this man! This is your doing!"

25 The whole crowd answered back, "Let the punishment for his death fall on us and on our children!"

26 Then Pilate set Barabbas free for them; he had Jesus whipped and handed him over to be nailed to the cross.

The soldiers make fun of Jesus

27 Then Pilate's soldiers took Jesus into the Governor's palace, and the whole company gathered around him. 28 They stripped off his clothes and put a scarlet robe on him. 29 Then they made a crown out of thorny branches and placed it on his head, and put a stick in his right hand; then they knelt before him and made fun of him. "Long live the King of the Jews!" they said. 30 They spat on him, and took the stick and hit him over the head. 31 When they had finished making fun of him, they took the robe off and put his own clothes back on him. Then they led him out to nail him to the cross.

New International Version

22 "What shall I do, then, with Jesus who is called Christ?" Pilate asked.

They all answered, "Crucify him!"

23 "Why? What crime has he committed?" asked Pilate.

But they shouted all the louder, "Crucify him!"

24 When Pilate saw that he was getting nowhere, but that instead an uproar was starting, he took water and washed his hands in front of the crowd. "I am innocent of this man's blood," he said. "It is your responsibility!"

25 All the people answered, "Let his blood be on us and on our children!"

26 Then he released Barabbas to them. But he had Jesus flogged, and handed him over to be crucified.

The soldiers mock Jesus

27 Then the governor's soldiers took Jesus into the Praetorium and gathered the whole company of soldiers around him. 28 They stripped him and put a scarlet robe on him, 29 and then wove a crown of thorns and set it on his head. They put a staff in his right hand and knelt in front of him and mocked him. "Hail, king of the Jews!" they said. 30 They spit on him, and took the staff and struck him on the head again and again. 31 After they had mocked him, they took off the robe and put his own clothes on him. Then they led him away to crucify him.

Phillips Modern English

"Then what am I to do with Jesus who is called Christ?" asked Pilate.

"Have him crucified!" they all cried. At this Pilate said, "Why, what is his crime?" But their voices rose to a roar, "Have him crucified!" When Pilate realised that nothing more could be done but that there would soon be a riot, he took a bowl of water and washed his hands before the crowd, saying, "I take no responsibility for the death of this man. You must see to that yourselves." To this the whole crowd replied, "Let his blood be on us and on our children!" Whereupon Pilate released Barabbas for them, but he had Jesus flogged and handed over for crucifixion.

Then the governor's soldiers took Jesus into the governor's palace and collected the whole guard around him. There they stripped him and put a scarlet cloak upon him. They twisted some thorn-twigs into a crown and put it on his head and put a stick into his right hand. They bowed low before him and jeered at him with the words, "Hail, your majesty, king of the Jews!" Then they spat on him, took the stick and hit him on the head with it. And when they had finished their fun, they stripped the cloak off again, put his own clothes upon him and led

Revised Standard Version

you?" And they said, "Barabbas." 22 Pilate said to them, "Then what shall I do with Jesus who is called Christ?" They all said, "Let him be crucified." 23 And he said, "Why, what evil has he done?" But they shouted all the more, "Let him be crucified."

24 So when Pilate saw that he was gaining nothing, but rather that a riot was beginning, he took water and washed his hands before the crowd, saying, "I am innocent of this man's blood;[l] see to it yourselves." 25 And all the people answered, "His blood be on us and on our children!" 26 Then he released for them Barabbas, and having scourged Jesus, delivered him to be crucified.

27 Then the soldiers of the governor took Jesus into the praetorium, and they gathered the whole battalion before him. 28 And they stripped him and put a scarlet robe upon him, 29 and plaiting a crown of thorns they put it on his head, and put a reed in his right hand. And kneeling before him they mocked him, saying, "Hail, King of the Jews!" 30 And they spat upon him, and took the reed and struck him on the head. 31 And when they had mocked him, they stripped him of the robe, and put his own clothes on him, and led him away to crucify him.

[l] Other authorities read *this righteous blood* or *this righteous man's blood.*

Jerusalem Bible

for you?" they said, "Barabbas." 22 "But in that case," Pilate said to them, "what am I to do with Jesus who is called Christ?" They all said, "Let him be crucified!" 23 "Why?" he asked. "What harm has he done?" But they shouted all the louder, "Let him be crucified!" 24 Then Pilate saw that he was making no impression, that in fact a riot was imminent. So he took some water, washed his hands in front of the crowd and said, "I am innocent of this man's blood. It is your concern." 25 And the people to a man, shouted back, "His blood be on us and on our children!" 26 Then he released Barabbas for them. He ordered Jesus to be first scourged[s] and then handed over to be crucified.

Jesus is crowned with thorns

27 The governor's soldiers took Jesus with them into the Praetorium and collected the whole cohort around him. 28 Then they stripped him and made him wear a scarlet cloak, 29 and having twisted some thorns into a crown they put this on his head and placed a reed in his right hand. To make fun of him they knelt to him saying, "Hail, king of the Jews!" 30 And they spat on him and took the reed and struck him on the head with it. 31 And when they had finished making fun of him, they took off the cloak and dressed him in his own clothes and led him away to crucify him.

[s] The normal prelude to crucifixion.

New English Bible

Abbas.' 'Then what am I to do with Jesus called Messiah?' asked Pilate; and with one voice they answered, 'Crucify him!' 'Why, what harm has he done?' Pilate asked; but they shouted all the louder, 'Crucify him!'

Pilate could see that nothing was being gained, and a riot was starting; so he took water and washed his hands in full view of the people, saying, 'My hands are clean of this man's blood; see to that yourselves.' And with one voice the people cried, 'His blood be on us, and on our children.' He then released Bar-Abbas to them; but he had Jesus flogged, and handed him over to be crucified.

Pilate's soldiers then took Jesus into the Governor's headquarters, where they collected the whole company round him. They stripped him and dressed him in a scarlet mantle; and plaiting a crown of thorns they placed it on his head, with a cane in his right hand. Falling on their knees before him they jeered at him: 'Hail, King of the Jews!' They spat on him, and used the cane to beat him about the head. When they had finished their mockery, they took off the mantle and dressed him in his own clothes.

King James Version

and led him away to crucify *him*. 32And as they
came out, they found a man of Cyrene, Simon
by name: him they compelled to bear his cross.
33And when they were come unto a place called
Golgotha, that is to say, a place of a skull,
34 They gave him vinegar to drink mingled
with gall: and when he had tasted *thereof*, he
would not drink. 35And they crucified him, and
parted his garments, casting lots: that it might
be fulfilled which was spoken by the prophet,
They parted my garments among them, and
upon my vesture did they cast lots. 36And sitting
down they watched him there; 37And set up
over his head his accusation written, THIS IS
JESUS THE KING OF THE JEWS. 38 Then
were there two thieves crucified with him; one
on the right hand, and another on the left.
39 And they that passed by reviled him, wagging their heads, 40And saying, Thou that destroyest the temple, and buildest *it* in three days,
save thyself. If thou be the Son of God, come
down from the cross. 41 Likewise also the chief
priests mocking *him*, with the scribes and elders,
said, 42 He saved others; himself he cannot save.
If he be the King of Israel, let him now come
down from the cross, and we will believe him.

Living Bible

him out to crucify him. 32As they were on the
way to the execution grounds they came across
a man from Cyrene, in Africa—Simon was his
name—and forced him to carry Jesus' cross.
33 Then they went out to an area known as
Golgotha, that is, "Skull Hill," 34 where the soldiers gave him drugged wine to drink; but when
he had tasted it, he refused.
35 After the crucifixion, the soldiers threw
dice to divide up his clothes among themselves.
36 Then they sat around and watched him as he
hung there. 37And they put a sign above his
head, "This is Jesus, the King of the Jews."
38 Two robbers were also crucified there that
morning, one on either side of him. 39And the
people passing by hurled abuse, shaking their
heads at him and saying, 40 "So! You can destroy the Temple and build it again in three days,
can you? Well, then, come on down from the
cross if you are the Son of God!"
41, 42, 43 And the chief priests and Jewish
leaders also mocked him. "He saved others,"
they scoffed, "but he can't save himself! So you
are the King of Israel, are you? Come down

Today's English Version

Jesus nailed to the cross

32 As they were going out they met a man
from Cyrene named Simon, and they forced him
to carry Jesus' cross. 33 They came to a place
called Golgotha, which means "The Place of the
Skull." 34 There they offered him wine to drink,
mixed with gall; after tasting it, however, he
would not drink it.
35 They nailed him to the cross, and then
divided his clothes among them by throwing dice.
36After that they sat there and watched him.
37Above his head they put the written notice of
the accusation against him: "This is Jesus, the
King of the Jews." 38 Then they nailed two
bandits to crosses with Jesus, one on his right
and the other on his left.
39 People passing by shook their heads and
hurled insults at Jesus: 40 "You were going to
tear down the temple and build it back up in
three days! Save yourself, if you are God's Son!
Come on down from the cross!"
41 In the same way the chief priests and the
teachers of the Law and the elders made fun of
him: 42 "He saved others but he cannot save
himself! Isn't he the King of Israel? If he will
come down off the cross now, we will believe in

New International Version

The crucifixion

32 As they were going out, they met a man
from Cyrene, named Simon, and they forced him
to carry the cross. 33 They came to a place
called Golgotha (which means The Place of the
Skull). 34 There they offered him wine to drink,
mixed with gall; but after tasting it, he refused
to drink it. 35 When they had crucified him, they
divided up his clothes by casting lots.[y] 36And
sitting down, they kept watch over him there.
37Above his head they placed the written charge
against him: THIS IS JESUS, THE KING OF THE
JEWS. 38 Two robbers were crucified with him,
one on his right and one on his left. 39 Those
who passed by hurled insults at him, shaking
their heads 40 and saying, "You who are going
to destroy the temple and build it in three days,
save yourself! Come down from the cross, if you
are the Son of God!"
41 In the same way the chief priests, the
teachers of the law and the elders mocked him.
42 "He saved others," they said, "but he can't
save himself! He's the king of Israel! Let him
come down now from the cross, and we will be-

[y] A few late MSS add *that the word spoken by the prophet might be fulfilled: "They divided my garments among themselves and cast lots for my clothing"* (Psalm 22:18).

Phillips Modern English

him off for crucifixion. On their way out of the city they met a man called Simon, a native of Cyrene in Africa, and they compelled him to carry Jesus' cross.

27.33 The crucifixion

Then when they came to a place called Golgotha (which means Skull Hill) they offered him a drink of wine mixed with some bitter drug, but when he had tasted it he refused to drink. And when they had crucified him they shared out his clothes by drawing lots.

Then they sat down to keep guard over him. And over his head they put a placard with the charge against him:

THIS IS JESUS, THE KING OF THE JEWS

Now two bandits were crucified with Jesus at the same time, one on either side of him. The passers-by nodded their heads knowingly and called out to him in mockery, "Hi, you who could pull down the Temple and build it up again in three days—why don't you save yourself? If you are the Son of God, step down from the cross!" The chief priests also joined the scribes and elders in jeering at him, saying, "He saved others, but he can't save himself! If this is the king of Israel, why doesn't he come down from the cross now, and we will believe

Revised Standard Version

32 As they went out, they came upon a man of Cyrene, Simon by name; this man they compelled to carry his cross. 33And when they came to a place called Golgotha (which means the place of a skull), 34 they offered him wine to drink, mingled with gall; but when he tasted it, he would not drink it. 35And when they had crucified him, they divided his garments among them by casting lots; 36 then they sat down and kept watch over him there. 37And over his head they put the charge against him, which read, "This is Jesus the King of the Jews." 38 Then two robbers were crucified with him, one on the right and one on the left. 39And those who passed by derided him, wagging their heads 40 and saying, "You who would destroy the temple and build it in three days, save yourself! If you are the Son of God, come down from the cross." 41 So also the chief priests, with the scribes and elders, mocked him, saying, 42 "He saved others; he cannot save himself. He is the King of Israel; let him come down now from the

Jerusalem Bible

The crucifixion

32 On their way out, they came across a man from Cyrene, Simon by name, and enlisted him to carry his cross. 33 When they had reached a place called Golgotha,[t] that is, the place of the skull, 34 they gave him wine to drink mixed with gall, which he tasted but refused to drink. 35 When they had finished crucifying him they shared out his clothing by casting lots, 36 and then sat down and stayed there keeping guard over him.

37 Above his head was placed the charge against him; it read: "This is Jesus, the King of the Jews." 38At the same time two robbers were crucified with him, one on the right and one on the left.

The crucified Christ is mocked

39 The passers-by jeered at him; they shook their heads 40 and said, "So you would destroy the Temple and rebuild it in three days! Then save yourself! If you are God's son, come down from the cross!" 41 The chief priests with the scribes and elders mocked him in the same way. 42 "He saved others," they said, "he cannot save himself. He is the king of Israel; let him come down from the cross now, and we will

[t] The Aramaic form of the name of which Calvary is the more familiar Latin equivalent.

New English Bible

Then they led him away to be crucified. On their way out they met a man from Cyrene, Simon by name, and pressed him into service to carry his cross.

So they came to a place called Golgotha (which means 'Place of a skull') and there he was offered a draught of wine mixed with gall; but when he had tasted it he would not drink.

After fastening him to the cross they divided his clothes among them by casting lots, and then sat down there to keep watch. Over his head was placed the inscription giving the charge: 'This is Jesus the king of the Jews.'

Two bandits were crucified with him, one on his right and the other on his left.

The passers-by hurled abuse at him: they wagged their heads and cried, 'You would pull the temple down, would you, and build it in three days? Come down from the cross and save yourself, if you are indeed the Son of God.' So too the chief priests with the lawyers and elders mocked at him: 'He saved others,' they said, 'but he cannot save himself. King of Israel, indeed! Let him come down now from the cross,

King James Version

43 He trusted in God; let him deliver him now,
if he will have him: for he said, I am the Son
of God. 44 The thieves also, which were crucified
with him, cast the same in his teeth. 45 Now
from the sixth hour there was darkness over all
the land unto the ninth hour. 46And about the
ninth hour Jesus cried with a loud voice, saying,
Eli, Eli, lama sabachthani? that is to say, My
God, my God, why hast thou forsaken me?
47 Some of them that stood there, when they
heard *that,* said, This *man* calleth for Elias.
48And straightway one of them ran, and took a
sponge, and filled *it* with vinegar, and put *it* on
a reed, and gave him to drink. 49 The rest said,
Let be, let us see whether Elias will come to save
him.
50 Jesus, when he had cried again with a loud
voice, yielded up the ghost. 51And, behold, the
vail of the temple was rent in twain from the top
to the bottom; and the earth did quake, and the
rocks rent; 52And the graves were opened; and
many bodies of the saints which slept arose,
53And came out of the graves after his resurrection, and went into the holy city, and appeared unto many. 54 Now when the centurion,
and they that were with him, watching Jesus,
saw the earthquake, and those things that were
done, they feared greatly, saying, Truly this was

Living Bible

from the cross and we'll believe you! He trusted God—let God show his approval by delivering him! Didn't he say, 'I am God's Son'?"

44 And the robbers also threw the same in his teeth.

45 That afternoon, the whole earth[f] was covered with darkness for three hours, from noon until three o'clock.

46 About three o'clock, Jesus shouted, "Eli, Eli, lama sabachthani," which means, "My God, my God, why have you forsaken me?"

47 Some of the bystanders misunderstood and
thought he was calling for Elijah. 48 One of
them ran and filled a sponge with sour wine and
put it on a stick and held it up to him to drink.
49 But the rest said, "Leave him alone. Let's see
whether Elijah will come and save him."

50 Then Jesus shouted out again, dismissed
his spirit, and died. 51And look! The curtain
secluding the Holiest Place[g] in the Temple was
split apart from top to bottom; and the earth
shook, and rocks broke, 52 and tombs opened,
and many godly men and women who had died
came back to life again. 53After Jesus' resurrection, they left the cemetery and went into Jerusalem, and appeared to many people there.

54 The soldiers at the crucifixion and their sergeant were terribly frightened by the earthquake and all that happened. They exclaimed, "Surely this was God's Son."[h]

[f] Or, "land." [g] Implied. [h] Or, "a godly man."

Today's English Version

him! 43 He trusts in God and says he is God's Son. Well, then, let us see if God wants to save him now!"

44 Even the bandits who had been crucified with him insulted him in the same way.

The death of Jesus

45 At noon the whole country was covered
with darkness, which lasted for three hours. 46At
about three o'clock Jesus cried out with a loud
shout, *"Eli, Eli, lema sabachthani?"* which means,
"My God, my God, why did you abandon me?"

47 Some of the people standing there heard
him and said, "He is calling for Elijah!" 48 One
of them ran up at once, took a sponge, soaked it
in cheap wine, put it on the end of a stick, and
tried to make him drink it.

49 But the others said, "Wait, let us see if Elijah is coming to save him!"

50 Jesus again gave a loud cry, and breathed his last.

51 Then the curtain hanging in the temple was
torn in two, from top to bottom. The earth
shook, the rocks split apart, 52 the graves broke
open, and many of God's people who had died
were raised to life. 53 They left the graves; and
after Jesus rose from death they went into the
Holy City, where many people saw them.

54 When the army officer and the soldiers with him who were watching Jesus saw the earthquake and everything else that happened, they were terrified and said, "He really was the Son of God!"

New International Version

lieve in him. 43 He trusts in God. Let God
rescue him now if he wants him, for he said,
'I am the Son of God.' " 44 In the same way
the robbers who were crucified with him also
heaped insults on him.

The death of Jesus

45 From the sixth hour until the ninth hour
darkness came over all the land. 46About the
ninth hour Jesus cried out in a loud voice, *"Eloi,
Eloi, lama sabachthani?"*—which means, "My
God, my God, why have you forsaken me?"[z]

47 When some of those standing there heard this, they said, "He's calling Elijah."

48 Immediately one of them ran and got a
sponge. He filled it with wine vinegar, put it
on a stick, and offered it to Jesus to drink.
49 But the rest said, "Leave him alone. Let's
see if Elijah comes to save him."

50 And when Jesus had cried out again in a loud voice, he gave up his spirit.

51 At that moment the curtain of the temple
was torn in two from top to bottom. The earth
shook and the rocks split. 52 The tombs broke
open and the bodies of many holy people who
had died were raised to life. 53 They came out
of the tombs, and after Jesus' resurrection they
went into the holy city and appeared to many
people.

54 When the centurion and those with him who were guarding Jesus saw the earthquake and all that had happened, they were terrified, and exclaimed, "Surely he was the Son[a] of God!"

[z] Psalm 22:1. [a] Or *a son.*

Phillips Modern English

him! He trusted in God . . . let God rescue him if He wants to. For he said, 'I am God's son'." Even the bandits who were crucified with him hurled the same abuse at him.

Then from midday until three o'clock darkness spread over the whole countryside, and about then Jesus cried with a loud voice, "My God, my God, why did you forsake me?" Some of those who were standing there heard these words which Jesus spoke in Aramaic (*Eli, Eli lama sabachthani?*), and said, "This man is calling for Elijah!" And one of them ran off and fetched a sponge, soaked it in vinegar and put it on a stick and held it up for him to drink. But the others said, "Let him alone! Let's see if Elijah will come and save him." But Jesus uttered one more great cry, and gave up his spirit.

And the sanctuary curtain in the Temple was torn in two from top to bottom. The ground shook, rocks split and graves were opened. (A number of bodies of holy men who were asleep in death rose again. They left their graves after Jesus' resurrection and entered the holy city and appeared to many people.) When the centurion and his company who were keeping guard over Jesus saw the earthquake and all that was happening they were terrified. "Indeed this man was a son of God!" they said.

Revised Standard Version

cross, and we will believe in him. 43 He trusts in
God; let God deliver him now, if he desires him;
for he said, 'I am the Son of God.' " 44And the
robbers who were crucified with him also reviled
him in the same way.
45 Now from the sixth hour there was darkness over all the land [m] until the ninth hour.
46And about the ninth hour Jesus cried with a
loud voice, "Eli, Eli, lama sabach-thani?" that
is, "My God, my God, why hast thou forsaken
me?" 47And some of the bystanders hearing it
said, "This man is calling Elijah." 48And one of
them at once ran and took a sponge, filled it
with vinegar, and put it on a reed, and gave it
to him to drink. 49 But the others said, "Wait,
let us see whether Elijah will come to save
him." [n] 50And Jesus cried again with a loud
voice and yielded up his spirit.
51 And behold, the curtain of the temple was
torn in two, from top to bottom; and the earth
shook, and the rocks were split; 52 the tombs
also were opened, and many bodies of the
saints who had fallen asleep were raised, 53 and
coming out of the tombs after his resurrection
they went into the holy city and appeared to
many. 54 When the centurion and those who
were with him, keeping watch over Jesus, saw
the earthquake and what took place, they were
filled with awe, and said, "Truly this was the
Son[x] of God!"

[*m*] Or *earth.* [*n*] Other ancient authorities insert *And another took a spear and pierced his side, and out came water and blood.* [*x*] Or *a son.*

Jerusalem Bible

believe in him. 43 He puts his trust in God; now
let God rescue him if he wants him. For he did
say, 'I am the son of God.' " 44 Even the robbers
who were crucified with him taunted him in the
same way.

The death of Jesus

45 From the sixth hour there was darkness
over all the land until the ninth hour.[u] 46And
about the ninth hour, Jesus cried out in a loud
voice, "Eli, Eli, lama sabachthani?" that is, *"My
God, my God, why have you deserted me?"* [v]
47 When some of those who stood there heard
this, they said, "The man is calling on Elijah,"
48 and one of them quickly ran to get a sponge
which he dipped in vinegar[w] and, putting it on
a reed, gave it him to drink. 49 "Wait!" said the
rest of them, "and see if Elijah will come to
save him." 50 But Jesus, again crying out in a
loud voice, yielded up his spirit.
51 At that, the veil of the Temple[x] was torn
in two from top to bottom; the earth quaked;
the rocks were split; 52 the tombs opened and
the bodies of many holy men rose from the
dead, 53 and these, after his resurrection, came
out of the tombs, entered the Holy City and
appeared to a number of people. 54 Meanwhile
the centurion, together with the others guarding
Jesus, had seen the earthquake and all that was
taking place, and they were terrified and said,
"In truth this was a son of God."

[*u*] From midday to 3 P.M. [*v*] Ps. 22:1. [*w*] The rough wine drunk by Roman soldiers. [*x*] There were two curtains in the Temple; most probably this was the inner curtain which guarded the Most Holy Place.

New English Bible

and then we will believe him. Did he trust in God? Let God rescue him, if he wants him—for he said he was God's Son.' Even the bandits who were crucified with him taunted him in the same way.

From midday a darkness fell over the whole land, which lasted until three in the afternoon; and about three Jesus cried aloud, *'Eli, Eli, lema sabachthani?'*, which means, 'My God, my God, why hast thou forsaken me?' Some of the bystanders, on hearing this, said, 'He is calling Elijah.' One of them ran at once and fetched a sponge, which he soaked in sour wine, and held it to his lips on the end of a cane. But the others said, 'Let us see if Elijah will come to save him.'

Jesus again gave a loud cry, and breathed his last. At that moment the curtain of the temple was torn in two from top to bottom. There was an earthquake, the rocks split and the graves opened, and many of God's saints were raised from sleep; and coming out of their graves after his resurrection they entered the Holy City, where many saw them. And when the centurion and his men who were keeping watch over Jesus saw
the earthquake and all that was happening, they were filled with awe, and they said, 'Truly this man was a son of God.'[a]

[*a*] Or the Son of God.

King James Version

the Son of God. 55And many women were there beholding afar off, which followed Jesus from Galilee, ministering unto him: 56Among which was Mary Magdalene, and Mary the mother of James and Joses, and the mother of Zebedee's children. 57 When the even was come, there came a rich man of Arimathea, named Joseph, who also himself was Jesus' disciple: 58 He went to Pilate, and begged the body of Jesus. Then Pilate commanded the body to be delivered. 59And when Joseph had taken the body, he wrapped it in a clean linen cloth, 60And laid it in his own new tomb, which he had hewn out in the rock: and he rolled a great stone to the door of the sepulchre, and departed. 61And there was Mary Magdalene, and the other Mary, sitting over against the sepulchre.

62 Now the next day, that followed the day of the preparation, the chief priests and Pharisees came together unto Pilate, 63 Saying, Sir, we remember that that deceiver said, while he was yet alive, After three days I will rise again. 64 Command therefore that the sepulchre be made sure until the third day, lest his disciples come by night, and steal him away, and say unto

Living Bible

55 And many women who had come down from Galilee with Jesus to care for him were watching from a distance. 56Among them were Mary Magdalene and Mary the mother of James and Joseph, and the mother of James and John (the sons of Zebedee).

57 When evening came, a rich man from Arimathea named Joseph, one of Jesus' followers, 58 went to Pilate and asked for Jesus' body. And Pilate issued an order to release it to him. 59 Joseph took the body and wrapped it in a clean linen cloth, 60 and placed it in his own new rock-hewn tomb, and rolled a great stone across the entrance as he left. 61 Both Mary Magdalene and the other Mary were sitting nearby watching.

62 The next day—at the close of the first day of the Passover ceremonies[i]—the chief priests and Pharisees went to Pilate, 63 and told him, "Sir, that liar once said, 'After three days I will come back to life again.' 64 So we request an order from you sealing the tomb until the third day, to prevent his disciples from coming and stealing his body and then telling everyone he

[i] Implied; literally, "on the morrow, which is after the Preparation."

Today's English Version

55 There were many women there, looking on from a distance, who had followed Jesus from Galilee and helped him. 56Among them were Mary Magdalene, Mary the mother of James and Joseph, and the mother of Zebedee's sons.

The burial of Jesus

57 When it was evening, a rich man from Arimathea arrived; his name was Joseph, and he also was a disciple of Jesus. 58 He went into the presence of Pilate and asked for the body of Jesus. Pilate gave orders for the body to be given to Joseph. 59 So Joseph took it, wrapped it in a new linen sheet, 60 and placed it in his own grave, which he had just recently dug out of the rock. Then he rolled a large stone across the entrance to the grave and went away. 61 Mary Magdalene and the other Mary were sitting there, facing the grave.

The guard at the grave

62 On the next day—that is, the day following Friday—the chief priests and the Pharisees met with Pilate 63 and said, "Sir, we remember that while that liar was still alive he said, 'I will be raised to life after three days.' 64 Give orders, then, for the grave to be safely guarded until the third day, so that his disciples will not be able to go and steal him, and then tell the people, 'He

New International Version

55 Many women were there, watching from a distance. They had followed Jesus from Galilee to care for his needs. 56Among them were Mary Magdalene, Mary the mother of James and Joseph, and the mother of Zebedee's sons.

The burial of Jesus

57 As evening approached, there came a rich man from Arimathea, named Joseph, who had himself become a disciple of Jesus. 58 Going to Pilate, he asked for Jesus' body, and Pilate ordered that it be given to him. 59 Joseph took the body, wrapped it in a clean linen cloth, 60 and placed it in his own new tomb that he had cut out of the rock. He rolled a big stone in front of the entrance to the tomb and went away. 61 Mary Magdalene and the other Mary were sitting there across from the tomb.

The guard at the tomb

62 The next day, the one after Preparation Day, the chief priests and the Pharisees went to Pilate. 63 "Sir," they said, "we remember that while he was still alive that impostor said, 'After three days I will rise again.' 64 So give the order for the tomb to be made secure until the third day. Otherwise, his disciples may come and steal the body and tell the people that he has

Phillips Modern English

There were many women at the scene watching from a distance. They had followed Jesus from Galilee to look after his needs. Among them were Mary of Magdala, Mary the mother of James and Joseph, and the mother of Zebedee's sons.

27.57 Jesus is buried and the tomb is guarded

When evening fell, Joseph, a wealthy man from Arimathaea, who was himself a disciple of Jesus, went to Pilate and asked for the body of Jesus, and Pilate gave orders for the body to be handed over to him. So Joseph took it, wrapped it in clean linen and placed it in his own new tomb which had been hewn out of the rock. Then he rolled a large stone to the doorway of the tomb and went away. Mary from Magdala and the other Mary were there, sitting in front of the tomb.

Next day, which was the day after the Preparation, the chief priests and the Pharisees went in a body to Pilate and said, "Sir, we have remembered that while this impostor was alive, he said, 'After three days I shall be raised again.' Will you give the order then to have the grave closely guarded until the third day, so that there can be no chance of his disciples' coming and stealing the body and telling people that he has

Revised Standard Version

55 There were also many women there, looking on from afar, who had followed Jesus from Galilee, ministering to him; 56 among whom were Mary Magdalene, and Mary the mother of James and Joseph, and the mother of the sons of Zebedee.
57 When it was evening, there came a rich man from Arimathea, named Joseph, who also was a disciple of Jesus. 58 He went to Pilate and asked for the body of Jesus. Then Pilate ordered it to be given to him. 59 And Joseph took the body, and wrapped it in a clean linen shroud, 60 and laid it in his own new tomb, which he had hewn in the rock; and he rolled a great stone to the door of the tomb, and departed. 61 Mary Magdalene and the other Mary were there, sitting opposite the sepulchre.
62 Next day, that is, after the day of Preparation, the chief priests and the Pharisees gathered before Pilate 63 and said, "Sir, we remember how that imposter said, while he was still alive, 'After three days I will rise again.' 64 Therefore order the sepulchre to be made secure until the third day, lest his disciples go and steal him

Jerusalem Bible

55 And many women were there, watching from a distance, the same women who had followed Jesus from Galilee and looked after him.
56 Among them were Mary of Magdala, Mary the mother of James and Joseph, and the mother of Zebedee's sons.

The burial

57 When it was evening, there came a rich man of Arimathaea, called Joseph, who had himself become a disciple of Jesus. 58 This man went to Pilate and asked for the body of Jesus. Pilate thereupon ordered it to be handed over.
59 So Joseph took the body, wrapped it in a clean shroud 60 and put it in his own new tomb which he had hewn out of the rock. He then rolled a large stone across the entrance of the tomb and went away. 61 Now Mary of Magdala and the other Mary were there, sitting opposite the sepulcher.

The guard at the tomb

62 Next day, that is, when Preparation Day[y] was over, the chief priests and the Pharisees went in a body to Pilate 63 and said to him, "Your Excellency, we recall that this impostor said, while he was still alive, 'After three days I shall rise again.' 64 Therefore give the order to have the sepulcher kept secure until the third day, for fear his disciples come and steal him away and

[y] The day before the sabbath.

New English Bible

A number of women were also present, watching from a distance; they had followed Jesus from Galilee and waited on him. Among them were Mary of Magdala, Mary the mother of James and Joseph, and the mother of the sons of Zebedee.

When evening fell, there came a man of Arimathaea, Joseph by name, who was a man of means, and had himself become a disciple of Jesus. He approached Pilate, and asked for the body of Jesus; and Pilate gave orders that he should have it. Joseph took the body, wrapped it in a clean linen sheet, and laid it in his own unused tomb, which he had cut out of the rock; he then rolled a large stone against the entrance, and went away. Mary of Magdala was there, and the other Mary, sitting opposite the grave.

Next day, the morning after that Friday, the chief priests and the Pharisees came in a body to Pilate. 'Your Excellency,' they said, 'we recall how that impostor said while he was still alive, "I am to be raised again after three days." So will you give orders for the grave to be made secure until the third day? Otherwise his disciples may come, steal the body, and then tell

King James Version

the people, He is risen from the dead: so the last error shall be worse than the first. 65 Pilate said unto them, Ye have a watch: go your way, make *it* as sure as ye can. 66 So they went, and made the sepulchre sure, sealing the stone, and setting a watch.

28 In the end of the sabbath, as it began to dawn toward the first *day* of the week, came Mary Magdalene and the other Mary to see the sepulchre. 2 And, behold, there was a great earthquake: for the angel of the Lord descended from heaven, and came and rolled back the stone from the door, and sat upon it. 3 His countenance was like lightning, and his raiment white as snow: 4 And for fear of him the keepers did shake, and became as dead *men*. 5 And the angel answered and said unto the women, Fear not ye: for I know that ye seek Jesus, which was crucified. 6 He is not here: for he is risen, as he said. Come, see the place where the Lord lay. 7 And go quickly, and tell his disciples that he is risen from the dead; and, behold, he goeth before you into Galilee; there shall ye see him: lo, I have told you. 8 And they departed quickly from the sepulchre with fear and great joy; and did run to bring his disciples word.

Living Bible

came back to life! If that happens we'll be worse off than we were at first."

65 "Use your own Temple police," Pilate told them. "They can guard it safely enough."

66 So they sealed [j] the stone and posted guards to protect it from intrusion.

28 Early on Sunday morning, as the new day was dawning, Mary Magdalene and the other Mary went out to the tomb.

2 Suddenly there was a great earthquake; for an angel of the Lord came down from heaven and rolled aside the stone and sat on it. 3 His face shone like lightning and his clothing was a brilliant white. 4 The guards shook with fear when they saw him, and fell into a dead faint.

5 Then the angel spoke to the women. "Don't be frightened!" he said. "I know you are looking for Jesus, who was crucified, 6 but he isn't here! For he has come back to life again, just as he said he would. Come in and see where his body was lying. . . . 7 And now, go quickly and tell his disciples that he has risen from the dead, and that he is going to Galilee to meet them there. That is my message to them."

8 The women ran from the tomb, badly frightened, but also filled with joy, and rushed to find the disciples to give them the angel's

[j] This was done by stringing a cord across the rock, the cord being sealed at each end with clay.

Today's English Version

was raised from death.' This last lie would be even worse than the first one."

65 "Take a guard," Pilate told them; "go and guard the grave as best you can."

66 So they left, and made the grave secure by putting a seal on the stone and leaving the guard on watch.

The resurrection

28 After the Sabbath, as Sunday morning was dawning, Mary Magdalene and the other Mary went to look at the grave. 2 Suddenly there was a strong earthquake; an angel of the Lord came down from heaven, rolled the stone away, and sat on it. 3 His appearance was like lightning and his clothes were white as snow. 4 The guards were so afraid that they trembled and became like dead men.

5 The angel spoke to the women. "You must not be afraid," he said. "I know you are looking for Jesus, who was nailed to the cross. 6 He is not here; he has been raised, just as he said. Come here and see the place where he lay. 7 Quickly, now, go and tell his disciples, 'He has been raised from death, and now he is going to Galilee ahead of you; there you will see him!' Remember what I have told you."

8 So they left the grave in a hurry, afraid and yet filled with joy, and ran to tell his disciples.

New International Version

been raised from the dead. This last deception will be worse than the first."

65 "Take a guard," Pilate answered. "Go, make the tomb as secure as you know how." 66 So they went and made the tomb secure by putting a seal on the stone and posting the guard.

The resurrection

28 After the Sabbath, at dawn on the first day of the week, Mary Magdalene and the other Mary went to look at the tomb.

2 There was a violent earthquake, for an angel of the Lord came down from heaven and, going to the tomb, rolled back the stone and sat on it. 3 His appearance was like lightning, and his clothes were white as snow. 4 The guards were so afraid of him that they shook and became like dead men.

5 The angel said to the women, "Do not be afraid, for I know that you are looking for Jesus, who was crucified. 6 He is not here; he has risen, just as he said. Come and see the place where he lay. 7 Then go quickly and tell his disciples: 'He has risen from the dead and is going ahead of you into Galilee. There you will see him.' Now I have told you."

8 So the women hurried away from the tomb, afraid yet filled with joy, and ran to tell his

Phillips Modern English

been raised from the dead? We should then be faced with a worse fraud than the first one." "You have a guard," Pilate told them. "Go and make it as safe as you think necessary." And they went and made the grave secure, putting a seal on the stone and leaving it under guard.

28.1 The first Lord's day: Jesus rises

When the Sabbath was over, just as the first day of the week was dawning, Mary from Magdala and the other Mary went to look at the tomb. At that moment there was a great earthquake, for an angel of the Lord came down from Heaven, went forward and rolled back the stone, and sat down upon it. His appearance shone like lightning and his clothes were white as snow. The guards shook with terror at the sight of him and collapsed like dead men. But the angel spoke to the women, "Do not be afraid. I know that you are looking for Jesus who was crucified. He is not here—he has been raised, just as he said. Come and look at the place where he was lying. Then go quickly and tell his disciples that he has been raised from the dead. And, listen, he goes before you into Galilee; you will see him there! Now I have told you my message." Then the women went away quickly from the tomb, their hearts filled with awe and great joy, and ran to give the news to

Revised Standard Version

away, and tell the people, 'He has risen from
the dead,' and the last fraud will be worse than
the first." 65 Pilate said to them, "You have a
guard [o] of soldiers; go, make it as secure as you
can." [p] 66 So they went and made the sepulchre
secure by sealing the stone and setting a guard.

28 Now after the sabbath, toward the dawn
of the first day of the week, Mary Magdalene and the other Mary went to see the sepulchre. 2 And behold, there was a great earthquake;
for an angel of the Lord descended from heaven
and came and rolled back the stone, and sat
upon it. 3 His appearance was like lightning, and
his raiment white as snow. 4 And for fear of
him the guards trembled and became like dead
men. 5 But the angel said to the women, "Do
not be afraid; for I know that you seek Jesus
who was crucified. 6 He is not here; for he has
risen, as he said. Come, see the place where he[q]
lay. 7 Then go quickly and tell his disciples that
he has risen from the dead, and behold, he is
going before you to Galilee; there you will see
him. Lo, I have told you." 8 So they departed
quickly from the tomb with fear and great joy,

[o] Or *Take a guard.* [p] Greek *know.* [q] Other ancient authorities read *the Lord.*

Jerusalem Bible

tell the people, 'He has risen from the dead.'
This last piece of fraud would be worse than
what went before." 65 "You may have your
guard," said Pilate to them. "Go and make all
as secure as you know how." 66 So they went
and made the sepulcher secure, putting seals on
the stone and mounting a guard.

The empty tomb. The angel's message

28 After the sabbath, and toward dawn on
the first day of the week, Mary of Magdala and the other Mary went to visit the sepulcher. 2 And all at once there was a violent earthquake, for the angel of the Lord, descending
from heaven, came and rolled away the stone
and sat on it. 3 His face was like lightning, his
robe white as snow. 4 The guards were so shaken,
so frightened of him, that they were like dead
men. 5 But the angel spoke; and he said to the
women, "There is no need for you to be afraid.
I know you are looking for Jesus, who was
crucified. 6 He is not here, for he has risen, as
he said he would. Come and see the place where
he lay, 7 then go quickly and tell his disciples,
'He has risen from the dead and now he is going before you to Galilee; it is there you will
see him.' Now I have told you." 8 Filled with
awe and great joy the women came quickly
away from the tomb and ran to tell the disciples.

New English Bible

the people that he has been raised from the dead; and the final deception will be worse than the first.' 'You may have your guard,' said Pilate; 'go and make it secure as best you can.' So they went and made the grave secure; they sealed the stone, and left the guard in charge.

28 The Sabbath was over, and it was about daybreak on Sunday, when Mary of Magdala and the other Mary came to look at the grave. Suddenly there was a violent earthquake; an angel of the Lord descended from heaven; he came to the stone and rolled it away, and sat himself down on it. His face shone like lightning; his garments were white as snow. At the sight of him the guards shook with fear and lay like the dead.

The angel then addressed the women: 'You', he said, 'have nothing to fear. I know you are looking for Jesus who was crucified. He is not here; he has been raised again, as he said he would be. Come and see the place where he was laid, and then go quickly and tell his disciples: "He has been raised from the dead and is going on before you into Galilee; there you will see him." That is what I had to tell you.'

They hurried away from the tomb in awe and

King James Version

9 And as they went to tell his disciples, behold, Jesus met them, saying, All hail. And they came and held him by the feet, and worshipped him. 10 Then said Jesus unto them, Be not afraid: go tell my brethren that they go into Galilee, and there shall they see me.
11 Now when they were going, behold, some of the watch came into the city, and shewed unto the chief priests all the things that were done. 12 And when they were assembled with the elders, and had taken counsel, they gave large money unto the soldiers, 13 Saying, Say ye, His disciples came by night, and stole him *away* while we slept. 14 And if this come to the governor's ears, we will persuade him, and secure you. 15 So they took the money, and did as they were taught: and this saying is commonly reported among the Jews until this day.
16 Then the eleven disciples went away into Galilee, into a mountain where Jesus had ap-

Living Bible

message. 9 And as they were running, suddenly Jesus was there in front of them!
"Good morning!" [a] he said. And they fell to the ground before him, holding his feet and worshiping him.
10 Then Jesus said to them, "Don't be frightened! Go tell my brothers to leave at once for Galilee, to meet me there."
11 As the women were on the way into the city, some of the Temple police who had been guarding the tomb went to the chief priests and told them what had happened. 12, 13 A meeting of all the Jewish leaders was called, and it was decided to bribe the police to say they had all been asleep when Jesus' disciples came during the night and stole his body.
14 "If the governor hears about it," the Council promised, "we'll stand up for you and everything will be all right."
15 So the police accepted the bribe and said what they were told to. Their story spread widely among the Jews, and is still believed by them to this very day.
16 Then the eleven disciples left for Galilee, going to the mountain where Jesus had said

[*a*] Literally, "All hail!"

Today's English Version

9 Suddenly Jesus met them and said, "Peace be with you." They came up to him, took hold of his feet, and worshiped him. 10 "Do not be afraid," Jesus said to them. "Go and tell my brothers to go to Galilee, and there they will see me."

The report of the guard

11 While the women went on their way, some of the soldiers guarding the grave went back to the city and told the chief priests everything that had happened. 12 The chief priests met with the elders and made their plan; they gave a large sum of money to the soldiers 13 and said, "You are to say that his disciples came during the night and stole his body while you were asleep. 14 And if the Governor should hear of this, we will convince him and you will have nothing to worry about."
15 The guards took the money and did what they were told to do. To this very day that is the report spread around by the Jews.

Jesus appears to his disciples

16 The eleven disciples went to the hill in Galilee where Jesus had told them to go. 17 When

New International Version

disciples. 9 Suddenly Jesus met them. "Greetings," he said. They came to him, clasped his feet and worshiped him. 10 Then Jesus said to them, "Do not be afraid. Go and tell my brothers to go to Galilee; there they will see me."

The guards' report

11 While the women were on their way, some of the guards went into the city and reported to the chief priests everything that had happened. 12 When the chief priests had met with the elders, they devised a plan. They gave the soldiers a large sum of money, 13 telling them, "You are to say, 'His disciples came during the night and stole him away while we were asleep.' 14 If this report gets to the governor, we will satisfy him and keep you out of trouble." 15 So the soldiers took the money and did as they were instructed. And this story has been widely circulated among the Jews to this very day.

The great commission

16 Then the eleven disciples went to Galilee, to the mountain where Jesus had told them to

Phillips Modern English

his disciples. But quite suddenly, Jesus stood before them in their path, and said, "Peace be with you!" and they went forward to meet him, and clasping his feet, worshipped him. Then Jesus said to them, "Do not be afraid. Go and tell my brothers to go off now into Galilee and they shall see me there."

And while they were on their way, some of the sentries went into the city and reported to the chief priests everything that had happened. They then joined the elders, and after consultation gave the soldiers a considerable sum of money and told them, "Your story must be that his disciples came after dark, and stole him away while you were asleep. If by any chance this reaches the governor's ears, we will put it right with him and see that you do not suffer for it." So they took the money and obeyed their instructions. The story was spread and is current among the Jews to this day.

28.16 Jesus gives his final commission

But the eleven went to the hill-side in Galilee where Jesus had arranged to meet them, and

Revised Standard Version

and ran to tell his disciples. 9And behold, Jesus met them and said, "Hail!" And they came up and took hold of his feet and worshiped him. 10 Then Jesus said to them, "Do not be afraid; go and tell my brethren to go to Galilee, and there they will see me."

11 While they were going, behold, some of the guard went into the city and told the chief priests all that had taken place. 12And when they had assembled with the elders and taken counsel, they gave a sum of money to the soldiers 13 and said, "Tell people, 'His disciples came by night and stole him away while we were asleep.' 14And if this comes to the governor's ears, we will satisfy him and keep you out of trouble." 15 So they took the money and did as they were directed; and this story has been spread among the Jews to this day.

16 Now the eleven disciples went to Galilee, to the mountain to which Jesus had directed

Jerusalem Bible

Appearance to the women

9 And there, coming to meet them, was Jesus. "Greetings," he said. And the women came up to him and, falling down before him, clasped his feet. 10 Then Jesus said to them, "Do not be afraid; go and tell my brothers that they must leave for Galilee; they will see me there."

Precautions taken by the leaders of the people

11 While they were on their way, some of the guard went off into the city to tell the chief priests all that had happened. 12 These held a meeting with the elders and, after some discussion, handed a considerable sum of money to the soldiers 13 with these instructions, "This is what you must say, 'His disciples came during the night and stole him away while we were asleep.' 14And should the governor come to hear of this, we undertake to put things right with him ourselves and to see that you do not get into trouble." 15 The soldiers took the money and carried out their instructions, and to this day that is the story among the Jews.

Appearance in Galilee. The mission to the world

16 Meanwhile the eleven disciples set out for Galilee, to the mountain where Jesus had ar-

New English Bible

great joy, and ran to tell the disciples. Suddenly Jesus was there in their path. He gave them his greeting, and they came up and clasped his feet, falling prostrate before him. Then Jesus said to them, 'Do not be afraid. Go and take word to my brothers that they are to leave for Galilee. They will see me there.'

The women had started on their way when some of the guard went into the city and reported to the chief priests everything that had happened. After meeting with the elders and conferring together, the chief priests offered the soldiers a substantial bribe and told them to say, 'His disciples came by night and stole the body while we were asleep.' They added, 'If this should reach the Governor's ears, we will put matters right with him and see that you do not suffer.' So they took the money and did as they were told. This story became widely known, and is current in Jewish circles to this day.

The eleven disciples made their way to Galilee, to the mountain where Jesus had told them to

King James Version

pointed them. 17And when they saw him, they worshipped him: but some doubted. 18And Jesus came and spake unto them, saying, All power is given unto me in heaven and in earth.
19 Go ye therefore, and teach all nations, baptizing them in the name of the Father, and of the Son, and of the Holy Ghost: 20 Teaching them to observe all things whatsoever I have commanded you: and, lo, I am with you alway, *even* unto the end of the world. Amen.

Living Bible

they would find him. 17 There they met him and worshiped him—but some of them weren't sure it really was Jesus!

18 He told his disciples, "I have been given all authority in heaven and earth. 19 Therefore go and make disciples in[b] all the nations, baptizing them into the name of the Father and of the Son and of the Holy Spirit, 20 and then teach these new disciples to obey all the commands I have given you; and be sure of this—that I am with you always, even to the end of the world." [c]

[*b*] Literally, "of." [*c*] Or, "age."

Today's English Version

they saw him they worshiped him, even though some of them doubted. 18 Jesus drew near and said to them, "I have been given all authority in heaven and on earth. 19 Go, then, to all peoples everywhere and make them my disciples: baptize them in the name of the Father, the Son, and the Holy Spirit, 20 and teach them to obey everything I have commanded you. And remember! I will be with you always, to the end of the age."

New International Version

go. 17 When they saw him, they worshiped him; but some doubted. 18 Then Jesus came to them and said, "All authority in heaven and on earth has been given to me. 19 Therefore go and make disciples of all nations, baptizing them in[b] the name of the Father and of the Son and of the Holy Spirit, 20 and teaching them to obey everything I have commanded you. And surely I will be with you always, to the very end of the age."

[*b*] Or *into*. See Acts 8:16; 19:5; Rom. 6:3; 1 Cor. 1:13; 10:2; Gal. 3:27.

Phillips Modern English

when they had seen him they worshipped him, though some of them were doubtful. But Jesus came and spoke these words to them, "All power in Heaven and on earth has been given to me. You, then, are to go and make disciples of all the nations and baptise them in the name of the Father and of the Son and of the Holy Spirit. Teach them to observe all that I have commanded you and, remember, I am with you always, even to the end of the world."

Revised Standard Version

them. 17 And when they saw him they worshiped him; but some doubted. 18 And Jesus came and said to them, "All authority in heaven and on earth has been given to me. 19 Go therefore and make disciples of all nations, baptizing them in the name of the Father and of the Son and of the Holy Spirit, 20 teaching them to observe all that I have commanded you; and lo, I am with you always, to the close of the age."

Jerusalem Bible

ranged to meet them. 17 When they saw him they fell down before him, though some hesitated. 18 Jesus came up and spoke to them. He said, "All authority in heaven and on earth has been given to me. 19 Go, therefore, make disciples of all the nations; baptize them in the name of the Father and of the Son and of the Holy Spirit,[z] 20 and teach them to observe all the commands I gave you. And know that I am with you always; yes, to the end of time."

[z] This formula is perhaps a reflection of the liturgical usage of the writer's own time.

New English Bible

meet him. When they saw him, they fell prostrate before him, though some were doubtful. Jesus then came up and spoke to them. He said: 'Full authority in heaven and on earth has been committed to me. Go forth therefore and make all nations my disciples; baptize men everywhere in the name of the Father and the Son and the Holy Spirit, and teach them to observe all that I have commanded you. And be assured, I am with you always, to the end of time.'

King James Version

THE GOSPEL ACCORDING TO SAINT MARK

1 The beginning of the gospel of Jesus Christ,
the Son of God; 2 As it is written in the
prophets, Behold, I send my messenger before
thy face, which shall prepare thy way before
thee. 3 The voice of one crying in the wilderness,
Prepare ye the way of the Lord, make his paths
straight. 4 John did baptize in the wilderness,
and preach the baptism of repentance for the

Living Bible

MARK

1 Here begins the wonderful story of Jesus the Messiah, the Son of God.

2 In the book written by the prophet Isaiah, God announced that he would send his Son[a] to earth, and that a special messenger would arrive first to prepare the world for his coming.

3 This messenger will live out in the barren wilderness," Isaiah[b] said, "and will proclaim that everyone must straighten out his life to be ready for the Lord's arrival." [c]

4 This messenger was John the Baptist. He lived in the wilderness and taught that all should be baptized as a public announcement of their decision to turn their backs on sin, so that God

[a] Implied. [b] Some ancient manuscripts read, "the prophets said." This quotation, unrecorded in the book of Isaiah, appears in Malachi 3:1. [c] Literally, "make ready the way of the Lord; make his paths straight."

Today's English Version

THE GOSPEL OF MARK

The preaching of John the Baptist

1 This is the Good News about Jesus Christ, the Son of God. 2 It began as the prophet Isaiah had written:

" 'Here is my messenger,' says God; 'I will send him ahead of you to open the way for you.'
3 Someone is shouting in the desert,
'Get the Lord's road ready for him;
make a straight path for him to travel!' "

4 So John appeared in the desert, baptizing people and preaching his message. "Turn away from your sins and be baptized," he told the peo-

New International Version

MARK

John the Baptist prepares the way

1 The beginning of the gospel about Jesus Christ, the Son of God.[a]

2 It is written in Isaiah the prophet:
"I will send my messenger ahead of you,
who will prepare your way" [b]—
3 "a voice of one calling in the desert,
'Prepare the way for the Lord,
make straight paths for him.' [c] "
4 And so John came, baptizing in the desert region and preaching repentance and baptism for

[a] Some MSS omit *the Son of God*. [b] 2 Mal. 3:1. [c] Isaiah 40:3.

Phillips Modern English

THE GOSPEL OF MARK

1.1 *How it began*

The Gospel of Jesus Christ, the Son of God, begins with the fulfilment of this prophecy of Isaiah—

Behold, I send my messenger before thy face,
Who shall prepare thy way;
The voice of one crying in the wilderness,
Make ye ready the way of the Lord,
Make his paths straight.

For John came and began to baptise men in the desert, proclaiming baptism as the mark of a complete change of heart and of the forgive-

Revised Standard Version

THE GOSPEL ACCORDING TO MARK

1 The beginning of the gospel of Jesus Christ,
the Son of God.[a]
2 As it is written in Isaiah the prophet,[b]
"Behold, I send my messenger before thy
face,
who shall prepare thy way;
3 the voice of one crying in the wilderness:
Prepare the way of the Lord,
make his paths straight—"
4 John the baptizer appeared [c] in the wilderness,
preaching a baptism of repentance for the for-

[a] Other ancient authorities omit *the Son of God.*
[b] Other ancient authorities read *in the prophets.*
[c] Other ancient authorities read *John was baptizing.*

Jerusalem Bible

THE GOSPEL ACCORDING TO SAINT MARK

I. Prelude to the public ministry of Jesus

The preaching of John the Baptist

1 The beginning of the Good News about
Jesus Christ, the Son of God. 2 It is written
in the book of the prophet Isaiah:

Look, I am going to send my messenger before you;
he will prepare your way.
3 *A voice cries in the wilderness:*
Prepare a way for the Lord,
make his paths straight,[a]

4 and so it was that John the Baptist appeared
in the wilderness, proclaiming a baptism of re-

[a] Is. 40:3.

New English Bible

THE GOSPEL ACCORDING TO MARK

The coming of Christ

1 Here begins the gospel of Jesus Christ the Son of God.[a] In the prophet Isaiah it stands written: 'Here is my herald whom I send on ahead of you, and he will prepare your way. A voice crying aloud in the wilderness, "Prepare a way for the Lord; clear a straight path for him."' And so it was that John the Baptist appeared in the wilderness proclaiming a baptism in token of repentance,

[a] *Some witnesses omit* the Son of God.

King James Version

remission of sins. 5And there went out unto him all the land of Judea, and they of Jerusalem, and were all baptized of him in the river of Jordan, confessing their sins. 6And John was clothed with camel's hair, and with a girdle of a skin about his loins; and he did eat locusts and wild honey; 7And preached, saying, There cometh one mightier than I after me, the latchet of whose shoes I am not worthy to stoop down and unloose. 8 I indeed have baptized you with water: but he shall baptize you with the Holy Ghost. 9And it came to pass in those days, that Jesus came from Nazareth of Galilee, and was baptized of John in Jordan. 10And straightway coming up out of the water, he saw the heavens opened, and the Spirit like a dove descending upon him: 11And there came a voice from heaven, *saying,* Thou art my beloved Son, in whom I am well pleased. 12And immediately the Spirit driveth him into the wilderness. 13And he was there in the wilderness forty days tempted of Satan; and was with the wild beasts; and the

Living Bible

could forgive them.[d] 5 People from Jerusalem and from all over Judea traveled out into the Judean wastelands to see and hear John, and when they confessed their sins he baptized them in the Jordan River. 6 His clothes were woven from camel's hair and he wore a leather belt; locusts and wild honey were his food. 7 Here is a sample of his preaching:

"Someone is coming soon who is far greater than I am, so much greater that I am not even worthy to be his slave.[e] 8 I baptize you with[f] water but he will baptize you with[f] God's Holy Spirit!"

9 Then one day Jesus came from Nazareth in Galilee, and was baptized by John there in the Jordan River. 10 The moment Jesus came up out of the water, he saw the heavens open and the Holy Spirit in the form of a dove descending on him, 11 and a voice from heaven said, "You are my beloved Son; you are my Delight."

12, 13 Immediately the Holy Spirit urged Jesus into the desert. There, for forty days, alone except for desert animals, he was subjected to Satan's temptations to sin. And afterwards[g] the angels came and cared for him.

[*d*] Literally, "preaching a baptism of repentance for the forgiveness of sins." [*e*] Literally, "Whose shoes I am not worthy to unloose." [*f*] Or, "in." The Greek word is not clear on this controversial point. [*g*] Implied in parallel passages.

Today's English Version

ple, "and God will forgive your sins." 5 Everybody from the region of Judea and the city of Jerusalem went out to hear John. They confessed their sins and he baptized them in the Jordan River.

6 John wore clothes made of camel's hair, with a leather belt around his waist; he ate locusts and wild honey. 7 He announced to the people, "The man who will come after me is much greater than I am; I am not good enough even to bend down and untie his sandals. 8 I baptize you with water, but he will baptize you with the Holy Spirit."

The baptism and temptation of Jesus

9 Not long afterward Jesus came from Nazareth, in the region of Galilee, and John baptized him in the Jordan. 10As soon as Jesus came up out of the water he saw heaven opening and the Spirit coming down on him like a dove. 11And a voice came from heaven, "You are my own dear Son. I am well pleased with you."

12 At once the Spirit made him go into the desert. 13 He was there forty days, being tempted by Satan. Wild animals were there also, but angels came and helped him.

New International Version

the forgiveness of sins. 5 The whole Judean countryside and all the people of Jerusalem went out to him. Confessing their sins, they were baptized by him in the Jordan River. 6 John wore clothing made of camel's hair, with a leather belt around his waist, and he ate locusts and wild honey. 7And this was his message: "After me will come one more powerful than I, the thongs of whose sandals I am not worthy to stoop down and untie. 8 I baptize you with water, but he will baptize you with the Holy Spirit."

The baptism and temptation of Jesus

9 At that time Jesus came from Nazareth in Galilee and was baptized by John in the Jordan. 10As Jesus was coming up out of the water, he saw heaven torn open and the Spirit descend on him like a dove. 11And a voice came from heaven: "You are my Son, whom I love; with you I am well-pleased."

12 At once the Spirit sent him out into the desert, 13 and he was in the desert forty days, being tempted by Satan. He was with the wild animals, and angels attended him.

Phillips Modern English

ness of sins. All the people of the Judaean countryside and everyone in Jerusalem went out to him in the desert and received his baptism in the river Jordan, publicly confessing their sins.

John himself was dressed in camel-hair, with a leather belt round his waist, and he lived on locusts and wild honey. The burden of his preaching was, "There is someone coming after me who is stronger than I—indeed I am not good enough to kneel down and undo his shoes. I have baptised you with water, but he will baptise you with the Holy Spirit."

1.9 The arrival of Jesus

It was in those days that Jesus arrived from the Galilean village of Nazareth and was baptised by John in the Jordan. All at once, as he came up out of the water, he saw the heavens split open, and the Spirit coming down upon him like a dove. A voice came out of Heaven, saying,

"You are my dearly-beloved Son, in whom I am well pleased!"

Then the Spirit sent him out at once into the desert, and there he remained for forty days while Satan tempted him. During this time no one was with him but wild animals, and only the angels were there to care for him.

Revised Standard Version

giveness of sins. 5And there went out to him all
the country of Judea, and all the people of
Jerusalem; and they were baptized by him in the
river Jordan, confessing their sins. 6 Now John
was clothed with camel's hair, and had a leather
girdle around his waist, and ate locusts and wild
honey. 7And he preached, saying, "After me
comes he who is mightier than I, the thong of
whose sandals I am not worthy to stoop down
and untie. 8 I have baptized you with water; but
he will baptize you with the Holy Spirit."
9 In those days Jesus came from Nazareth
of Galilee and was baptized by John in the
Jordan. 10And when he came up out of the
water, immediately he saw the heavens opened
and the Spirit descending upon him like a dove;
11 and a voice came from heaven, "Thou art
my beloved son;[d] with thee I am well pleased."
12 The Spirit immediately drove him out into
the wilderness. 13And he was in the wilderness
forty days, tempted by Satan; and he was with
the wild beasts; and the angels ministered to him.

[d] Or *my Son, my* (or *the*) *Beloved.*

Jerusalem Bible

pentance for the forgiveness of sins. 5All Judaea and all the people of Jerusalem made their
way to him, and as they were baptized by him
in the river Jordan they confessed their sins.
6 John wore a garment of camel skin, and he
lived on locusts and wild honey. 7 In the course
of his preaching he said, "Someone is following
me, someone who is more powerful than I am,
and I am not fit to kneel down and undo the
strap of his sandals. 8 I have baptized you with
water, but he will baptize you with the Holy
Spirit."

Jesus is baptized

9 It was at this time that Jesus came from
Nazareth in Galilee and was baptized in the
Jordan by John. 10 No sooner had he come up
out of the water than he saw the heavens torn
apart and the Spirit, like a dove, descending on
him. 11And a voice came from heaven, "You
are my Son, the Beloved; my favor rests on
you."

Temptation in the wilderness

12 Immediately afterward the Spirit drove
him out into the wilderness 13 and he remained
there for forty days, and was tempted by Satan.
He was with the wild beasts, and the angels
looked after him.

New English Bible

for the forgiveness of sins; and they flocked to him from the whole Judaean country-side and the city of Jerusalem, and were baptized by him in the River Jordan, confessing their sins.

John was dressed in a rough coat of camel's hair, with a leather belt round his waist, and he fed on locusts and wild honey. His proclamation ran: 'After me comes one who is mightier than I. I am not fit to unfasten his shoes. I have baptized you with water; he will baptize you with the Holy Spirit.'

It happened at this time that Jesus came from Nazareth in Galilee and was baptized in the Jordan by John. At the moment when he came up out of the water, he saw the heavens torn open and the Spirit, like a dove, descending upon him. And a voice spoke from heaven: 'Thou art my Son, my Beloved;[b] on thee my favour rests.'

Thereupon the Spirit sent him away into the wilderness, and there he remained for forty days tempted by Satan. He was among the wild beasts; and the angels waited on him.

[b] *Or* Thou art my only Son.

King James Version

angels ministered unto him. 14 Now after that
John was put in prison, Jesus came into Galilee,
preaching the gospel of the kingdom of God,
15 And saying, The time is fulfilled, and the kingdom of God is at hand: repent ye, and believe
the gospel. 16 Now as he walked by the sea of
Galilee, he saw Simon and Andrew his brother
casting a net into the sea: for they were fishers.
17 And Jesus said unto them, Come ye after me,
and I will make you to become fishers of men.
18 And straightway they forsook their nets, and
followed him. 19 And when he had gone a little
further thence, he saw James the *son* of Zebedee,
and John his brother, who also were in the ship
mending their nets. 20 And straightway he called
them: and they left their father Zebedee in the
ship with the hired servants, and went after him.
21 And they went into Capernaum; and straightway on the sabbath day he entered into the synagogue, and taught. 22 And they were astonished at

Living Bible

14 Later on, after John was arrested by King
Herod,[h] Jesus went to Galilee to preach God's
Good News.
15 "At last the time has come!" he announced. "God's Kingdom is near! Turn from
your sins and act on this glorious news!"
16 One day as Jesus was walking along the
shores of the Sea of Galilee, he saw Simon and
his brother Andrew fishing with nets, for they
were commercial fishermen.
17 Jesus called out to them, "Come, follow
me! And I will make you fishermen for the souls
of men!" 18 At once they left their nets and went
along with him.
19 A little farther up the beach, he saw
Zebedee's sons, James and John, in a boat mending their nets. 20 He called them too, and immediately they left their father Zebedee in the
boat with the hired men and went with him.
21 Jesus and his companions now arrived at
the town of Capernaum and on Saturday morning went into the Jewish place of worship—the
synagogue—where he preached. 22 The congrega-

[*h*] Implied.

Today's English Version

Jesus calls four fishermen

14 After John had been put in prison, Jesus
went to Galilee and preached the Good News
from God. 15 "The right time has come," he
said, "and the Kingdom of God is near! Turn
away from your sins and believe the Good
News!"
16 As Jesus walked by Lake Galilee, he saw
two fishermen, Simon and his brother Andrew,
catching fish in the lake with a net. 17 Jesus said
to them, "Come with me and I will teach you to
catch men." 18 At once they left their nets and
went with him.
19 He went a little farther on and saw two
other brothers, James and John, the sons of
Zebedee. They were in their boat getting their
nets ready. 20 As soon as Jesus saw them he
called them; they left their father Zebedee in the
boat with the hired men and went with Jesus.

A man with an evil spirit

21 They came to the town of Capernaum, and
on the next Sabbath day Jesus went into the
synagogue and began to teach. 22 The people

New International Version

The calling of the first disciples

14 After John was put in prison, Jesus went
into Galilee, proclaiming the good news of God.
15 "The time has come," he said. "The kingdom
of God is near. Repent and believe the good
news!"
16 As Jesus walked beside the Sea of Galilee,
he saw Simon and his brother Andrew casting a
net into the lake, for they were fishermen.
17 "Come, follow me," Jesus said, "and I will
make you fishers of men." 18 At once they left
their nets and followed him.
19 When he had gone a little farther, he saw
James son of Zebedee and his brother John in
a boat, preparing their nets. 20 Without delay
he called them, and they left their father Zebedee
in the boat with the hired men and followed
him.

Jesus drives out an evil spirit

21 They went to Capernaum, and when the
Sabbath came, Jesus went into the synagogue
and began to teach. 22 The people were amazed

Phillips Modern English

1.14 Jesus begins to preach the gospel, and to call men to follow him

It was after John's arrest that Jesus came into Galilee, proclaiming the gospel of God, saying, "The time has come at last—the kingdom of God has arrived. You must change your hearts and minds and believe the good news."

As he walked along the shore of the Lake of Galilee, he saw two fishermen, Simon and his brother Andrew, casting their nets into the water. "Come and follow me, and I will teach you to catch men!" he cried.

At once they dropped their nets, and followed him.

Then he went a little further along the shore and saw James the son of Zebedee, aboard a boat with his brother John, overhauling their nets. At once he called them, and they left their father Zebedee in the boat with the hired men, and went off after him.

1.21 Jesus begins healing the sick

They arrived at Capernaum, and on the Sabbath day Jesus walked straight into the synagogue and began teaching. They were amazed

Revised Standard Version

14 Now after John was arrested, Jesus came into Galilee, preaching the gospel of God, 15 and saying, "The time is fulfilled, and the kingdom of God is at hand; repent, and believe in the gospel."

16 And passing along by the Sea of Galilee, he saw Simon and Andrew the brother of Simon casting a net in the sea; for they were fishermen. 17And Jesus said to them, "Follow me and I will make you become fishers of men." 18And immediately they left their nets and followed him. 19And going on a little farther, he saw James the son of Zebedee and John his brother, who were in their boat mending the nets. 20And immediately he called them; and they left their father Zebedee in the boat with the hired servants, and followed him.

21 And they went into Capernaum; and immediately on the sabbath he entered the synagogue and taught. 22And they were astonished

Jerusalem Bible

II. The Galilean ministry

Jesus begins to preach

14 After John had been arrested, Jesus went into Galilee. There he proclaimed the Good News from God. 15 "The time has come," he said, "and the kingdom of God is close at hand. Repent, and believe the Good News."

The first four disciples are called

16 As he was walking along by the Sea of Galilee he saw Simon and his brother Andrew casting a net in the lake—for they were fishermen. 17And Jesus said to them, "Follow me and I will make you into fishers of men." 18And at once they left their nets and followed him.

19 Going on a little further, he saw James son of Zebedee and his brother John; they too were in their boat, mending their nets. He called them at once 20 and, leaving their father Zebedee in the boat with the men he employed, they went after him.

Jesus teaches in Capernaum and cures a demoniac

21 They went as far as Capernaum, and as soon as the sabbath came he went to the synagogue and began to teach. 22And his teaching

New English Bible

In Galilee: success and opposition

After John had been arrested, Jesus came into Galilee proclaiming the Gospel of God: 'The time has come; the kingdom of God is upon you; repent, and believe the Gospel.'

Jesus was walking by the Sea of Galilee when he saw Simon and his brother Andrew on the lake at work with a casting-net; for they were fishermen. Jesus said to them, 'Come with me, and I will make you fishers of men.' And at once they left their nets and followed him.

When he had gone a little further he saw James son of Zebedee and his brother John, who were in the boat overhauling their nets. He called them; and, leaving their father Zebedee in the boat with the hired men, they went off to follow him.

They came to Capernaum, and on the Sabbath he went to synagogue and began to teach. The people were astounded at his teaching, for,

King James Version

his doctrine: for he taught them as one that had authority, and not as the scribes. 23And there was in their synagogue a man with an unclean spirit; and he cried out, 24 Saying, Let *us* alone; what have we to do with thee, thou Jesus of Nazareth? art thou come to destroy us? I know thee who thou art, the Holy One of God. 25And Jesus rebuked him, saying, Hold thy peace, and come out of him. 26And when the unclean spirit had torn him, and cried with a loud voice, he came out of him. 27And they were all amazed, insomuch that they questioned among themselves, saying, What thing is this? what new doctrine *is* this? for with authority commandeth he even the unclean spirits, and they do obey him. 28And immediately his fame spread abroad throughout all the region round about Galilee. 29And forthwith, when they were come out of the synagogue, they entered into the house of Simon and Andrew, with James and John. 30 But Simon's wife's mother lay sick of a fever; and anon they tell him of her. 31And he came and took her by the hand, and lifted her up; and immediately the fever left her, and she ministered unto them. 32And at even, when the sun did set, they brought unto him all that were diseased, and them that were possessed with devils. 33And all the city was gathered together

Living Bible

tion was surprised at his sermon because he spoke as an authority, and didn't try to prove his points by quoting others—quite unlike what they were used to hearing! [i]

23 A man possessed by a demon was present and began shouting, 24 "Why are you bothering us, Jesus of Nazareth—have you come to destroy us demons? I know who you are—the holy Son of God!"

25 Jesus curtly commanded the demon to say no more and to come out of the man. 26At that the evil spirit screamed and convulsed the man violently and left him. 27Amazement gripped the audience and they began discussing what had happened.

"What sort of new religion is this?" they asked excitedly. "Why, even evil spirits obey his orders!"

28 The news of what he had done spread quickly through that entire area of Galilee.

29, 30 Then, leaving the synagogue, he and his disciples went over to Simon and Andrew's home, where they found Simon's mother-in-law sick in bed with a high fever. They told Jesus about her right away. 31 He went to her bedside, and as he took her by the hand and helped her to sit up, the fever suddenly left, and she got up and prepared dinner for them!

32, 33 By sunset the courtyard was filled with the sick and demon-possessed, brought to him for healing; and a huge crowd of people from all

[i] Literally, "not as the scribes."

Today's English Version

who heard him were amazed at the way he taught. He wasn't like the teachers of the Law; instead, he taught with authority.

23 Just then a man with an evil spirit in him came into the synagogue and screamed, 24 "What do you want with us, Jesus of Nazareth? Are you here to destroy us? I know who you are: you are God's holy messenger!"

25 Jesus commanded the spirit, "Be quiet, and come out of the man!"

26 The evil spirit shook the man hard, gave a loud scream, and came out of him. 27 The people were all so amazed that they started saying to each other, "What is this? Some kind of new teaching? This man has authority to give orders to the evil spirits, and they obey him!"

28 And so the news about Jesus spread quickly everywhere in the region of Galilee.

Jesus heals many people

29 They left the synagogue and went straight to the home of Simon and Andrew; and James and John went with them. 30 Simon's mother-in-law was sick in bed with a fever, and as soon as Jesus got there he was told about her. 31 He went to her, took her by the hand, and helped her up. The fever left her and she began to wait on them.

32 When evening came, after the sun had set, people brought to Jesus all the sick and those who had demons. 33All the people of the town

New International Version

at his teaching, because he taught them as one who had authority, not as the teachers of the law. 23 Just then a man in their synagogue who was possessed by an evil [d] spirit cried out, 24 "What do you want with us, Jesus of Nazareth? Have you come to destroy us? I know who you are—the Holy One of God!"

25 "Be quiet!" said Jesus sternly. "Come out of him!" 26 The evil [d] spirit shook the man violently and came out of him with a shriek.

27 The people were all so amazed that they asked each other, "What is this? A new teaching —and with authority! He even gives orders to evil [e] spirits and they obey him." 28 News about him spread quickly over the whole region of Galilee.

Jesus heals many

29 As soon as they left the synagogue, they went with James and John to the home of Simon and Andrew. 30 Simon's mother-in-law was in bed with a fever, and they told Jesus about her. 31 So he went to her, took her hand and helped her up. The fever left her and she began to wait on them.

32 That evening after sunset the people brought to Jesus all the sick and demon-possessed. 33 The whole town gathered at the door,

[d] Greek *unclean.* [e] Greek *unclean.*

Phillips Modern English

at his way of teaching, for he taught with the ring of authority—quite unlike the scribes. All at once, a man in the grip of an evil spirit appeared in the synagogue shouting out,

"What have you got to do with us, Jesus from Nazareth? Have you come to kill us? I know who you are—you're God's holy one!"

But Jesus cut him short and spoke sharply,

"Hold your tongue and get out of him!"

At this the evil spirit convulsed the man, let out a loud scream and left him. Everyone present was so astounded that people kept saying to each other,

"What on earth has happened? This new teaching has authority behind it. Why, he even gives orders to evil spirits and they obey him!"

And his reputation spread like wild-fire through the whole Galilean district.

Then he got up and went straight from the synagogue to the house of Simon and Andrew, accompanied by James and John. Simon's mother-in-law was in bed with a high fever, and they lost no time in telling Jesus about her. He went up to her, took her hand and helped her to her feet. The fever left her, and she began to see to their needs.

Late that evening, after sunset, they kept bringing to him all who were sick or troubled by evil spirits. The whole population of the

Revised Standard Version

at his teaching, for he taught them as one who
had authority, and not as the scribes. 23And
immediately there was in their synagogue a man
with an unclean spirit; 24 and he cried out,
"What have you to do with us, Jesus of Nazareth? Have you come to destroy us? I know
who you are, the Holy One of God." 25 But
Jesus rebuked him, saying, "Be silent, and come
out of him!" 26And the unclean spirit, convulsing
him and crying with a loud voice, came out of
him. 27And they were all amazed, so that they
questioned among themselves, saying, "What is
this? A new teaching! With authority he commands even the unclean spirits, and they obey
him." 28And at once his fame spread everywhere throughout all the surrounding region of
Galilee.
29 And immediately he[e] left the synagogue,
and entered the house of Simon and Andrew,
with James and John. 30 Now Simon's mother-in-
law lay sick with a fever, and immediately they
told him of her. 31And he came and took her
by the hand and lifted her up, and the fever left
her; and she served them.
32 That evening, at sundown, they brought
to him all who were sick or possessed with
demons. 33And the whole city was gathered to-

[e] Other ancient authorities read *they*.

Jerusalem Bible

made a deep impression on them because, unlike the scribes, he taught them with authority.
23 In their synagogue just then there was a
man possessed by an unclean spirit, and it
shouted, 24 "What do you want with us, Jesus
of Nazareth? Have you come to destroy us? I
know who you are: the Holy One of God."
25 But Jesus said sharply, "Be quiet! Come out
of him!" 26And the unclean spirit threw the man
into convulsions and with a loud cry went out
of him. 27 The people were so astonished that
they started asking each other what it all meant.
"Here is a teaching that is new," they said, "and
with authority behind it: he gives orders even to
unclean spirits and they obey him." 28And his
reputation rapidly spread everywhere, through all
the surrounding Galilean countryside.

Cure of Simon's mother-in-law

29 On leaving the synagogue, he went with
James and John straight to the house of Simon
and Andrew. 30 Now Simon's mother-in-law had
gone to bed with fever, and they told him about
her straightaway. 31 He went to her, took her by
the hand and helped her up. And the fever left
her and she began to wait on them.

A number of cures

32 That evening, after sunset, they brought to
him all who were sick and those who were possessed by devils. 33 The whole town came crowd-

New English Bible

unlike the doctors of the law, he taught with a note of authority. Now there was a man in the synagogue possessed by an unclean spirit. He shrieked: 'What do you want with us, Jesus of Nazareth? Have you[a] come to destroy us? I know who you are—the Holy One of God.' Jesus rebuked him: 'Be silent', he said, 'and come out of him.' And the unclean spirit threw the man into convulsions and with a loud cry left him. They were all dumbfounded and began to ask one another, 'What is this? A new kind of teaching! He speaks with authority. When he gives orders, even the unclean spirits submit.' The news spread rapidly, and he was soon spoken of all over the district of Galilee.

On leaving the synagogue they went straight to the house of Simon and Andrew; and James and John went with them. Simon's mother-in-law was ill in bed with fever. They told him about her at once. He came forward, took her by the hand, and helped her to her feet. The fever left her and she waited upon them.

That evening after sunset they brought to him all who were ill or possessed by devils; and the

[a] *Or* You have.

King James Version

at the door. 34And he healed many that were sick of divers diseases, and cast out many devils; and suffered not the devils to speak, because they knew him. 35And in the morning, rising up a great while before day, he went out, and departed into a solitary place, and there prayed. 36And Simon and they that were with him followed after him. 37And when they had found him, they said unto him, All *men* seek for thee. 38And he said unto them, Let us go into the next towns, that I may preach there also: for therefore came I forth. 39And he preached in their synagogues throughout all Galilee, and cast out devils. 40And there came a leper to him, beseeching him, and kneeling down to him, and saying unto him, If thou wilt, thou canst make me clean. 41And Jesus, moved with compassion, put forth *his* hand, and touched him, and saith unto him, I will; be thou clean. 42And as soon as he had spoken, immediately the leprosy departed from him, and he was cleansed. 43And

Living Bible

over the city of Capernaum gathered outside the door to watch. 34 So Jesus healed great numbers of sick folk that evening and ordered many demons to come out of their victims. (But he refused to allow the demons to speak, because they knew who he was.)

35 The next morning he was up long before daybreak and went out alone into the wilderness to pray.

36, 37 Later, Simon and the others went out to find him, and told him, "Everyone is asking for you."

38 But he replied, "We must go on to other towns as well, and give my message to them too, for that is why I came."

39 So he traveled throughout the province of Galilee, preaching in the synagogues and releasing many from the power of demons. 40 Once a leper came and knelt in front of him and begged to be healed. "If you want to, you can make me well again," he pled.

41 And Jesus, moved with pity, touched him and said, "I want to! Be healed!" 42 Immediately the leprosy was gone—the man was healed!

43, 44 Jesus then told him sternly, "Go and

Today's English Version

gathered in front of the house. 34 Jesus healed many who were sick with all kinds of diseases and drove out many demons. He would not let the demons say anything, because they knew who he was.

Jesus preaches in Galilee

35 Very early the next morning, long before daylight, Jesus got up and left the house. He went out of town to a lonely place, where he prayed. 36 But Simon and his companions went out searching for him; 37 when they found him they said, "Everyone is looking for you."

38 But Jesus answered, "We must go on to the other villages around here. I have to preach in them also, because that is why I came."

39 So he traveled all over Galilee, preaching in the synagogues and driving out demons.

Jesus makes a leper clean

40 A leper came to Jesus, knelt down, and begged him for help. "If you want to," he said, "you can make me clean."

41 Jesus was filled with pity, and reached out and touched him. "I do want to," he answered. "Be clean!" 42At once the leprosy left the man and he was clean. 43 Then Jesus spoke harshly

New International Version

34 and Jesus healed many who had various diseases. He also drove out many demons, but he would not let the demons speak because they knew who he was.

Jesus prays in a solitary place

35 Very early in the morning, while it was still dark, Jesus got up, left the house and went off to a solitary place, where he prayed. 36 Simon and his companions went to look for him, 37 and when they found him, they exclaimed: "Everyone is looking for you!"

38 Jesus replied, "Let's go somewhere else—to the nearby villages—so I can preach there also. That is why I have come." 39 So he traveled throughout Galilee, preaching in their synagogues and driving out demons.

A man with leprosy

40 A man with leprosy[f] came to him and begged him on his knees, "If you are willing, you can make me clean."

41 Filled with compassion, Jesus reached out his hand and touched the man. "I am willing," he said. "Be clean!" 42 Immediately the leprosy left him and he was cured.

43 Jesus sent him away at once with a strong

[f] The Greek word probably designated other related diseases also.

Phillips Modern English

town gathered round the doorway. And he healed great numbers of people who were suffering from various forms of disease. In many cases he expelled evil spirits; but he would not allow them to say a word, for they knew perfectly well who he was.

1.35 He retires for private prayer

Then, in the early morning, while it was still dark, Jesus got up, left the house and went off to a deserted place, and there he prayed. Simon and his companions went in search of him, and when they found him, they said,

"Everyone is looking for you."

"Then we will go somewhere else, to the neighbouring towns," he replied, "so that I may give my message there too—that is why I have come."

So he continued preaching in their synagogues and expelling evil spirits throughout the whole of Galilee.

1.40 Jesus cures leprosy

Then a leper came to Jesus, knelt in front of him and appealed to him,

"If you want to, you can make me clean."

Jesus was filled with pity for him, and stretched out his hand and placed it on the leper, saying, "Of course I want to—*be clean!*"

At once the leprosy left him and he was quite clean. Jesus sent him away there and then with

Revised Standard Version

gether about the door. 34And he healed many
who were sick with various diseases, and cast
out many demons; and he would not permit the
demons to speak, because they knew him.
35 And in the morning, a great while before
day, he rose and went out to a lonely place, and
there he prayed. 36And Simon and those who
were with him pursued him, 37 and they found
him and said to him, "Every one is searching
for you." 38And he said to them, "Let us go on
to the next towns, that I may preach there also;
for that is why I came out." 39And he went
throughout all Galilee, preaching in their synagogues and casting out demons.
40 And a leper came to him beseeching him,
and kneeling said to him, "If you will, you can
make me clean." 41 Moved with pity, he stretched
out his hand and touched him, and said to him,
"I will; be clean." 42And immediately the leprosy
left him, and he was made clean. 43And he

Jerusalem Bible

ing around the door, 34 and he cured many who
were suffering from diseases of one kind or another; he also cast out many devils, but he
would not allow them to speak, because they
knew who he was.[b]

Jesus quietly leaves Capernaum and travels through Galilee

35 In the morning, long before dawn, he got
up and left the house, and went off to a lonely
place and prayed there. 36 Simon and his companions set out in search for him, 37 and when
they found him they said, "Everybody is looking
for you." 38 He answered, "Let us go elsewhere,
to the neighboring country towns, so that I can
preach there too, because that is why I came."
39And he went all through Galilee, preaching in
their synagogues and casting out devils.

Cure of a leper

40 A leper came to him and pleaded on his
knees: "If you want to," he said, "you can cure
me." 41 Feeling sorry for him, Jesus stretched
out his hand and touched him. "Of course I
want to!" he said. "Be cured!" 42And the leprosy
left him at once and he was cured. 43 Jesus im-

[*b*] Throughout this gospel, Jesus never explicitly claims to be the Messiah and he forbids others to speak of the fact.

New English Bible

whole town was there, gathered at the door. He healed many who suffered from various diseases, and drove out many devils. He would not let the devils speak, because they knew who he was.

Very early next morning he got up and went out. He went away to a lonely spot and remained there in prayer. But Simon and his companions searched him out, found him, and said, 'They are all looking for you.' He answered, 'Let us move on to the country towns in the neighbourhood; I have to proclaim my message there also; that is what I came out to do.' So all through Galilee he went, preaching in the synagogues and casting out the devils.

Once he was approached by a leper, who knelt before him begging his help. 'If only you will,' said the man, 'you can cleanse me.' In warm indignation Jesus stretched out his hand,[b] touched him, and said, 'Indeed I will; be clean again.' The leprosy left him immediately, and he was clean. Then he dismissed him with this stern

[*b*] *Some witnesses read* Jesus was sorry for him and stretched out his hand; *one witness has simply* He stretched out his hand.

King James Version

he straitly charged him, and forthwith sent him away; 44And saith unto him, See thou say nothing to any man: but go thy way, shew thyself to the priest, and offer for thy cleansing those things which Moses commanded, for a testimony unto them. 45 But he went out, and began to publish *it* much, and to blaze abroad the matter, insomuch that Jesus could no more openly enter into the city, but was without in desert places: and they came to him from every quarter.

2 And again he entered into Capernaum after *some* days; and it was noised that he was in the house. 2And straightway many were gathered together, insomuch that there was no room to receive *them*, no, not so much as about the door: and he preached the word unto them. 3And they come unto him, bringing one sick of the palsy, which was borne of four. 4And when they could not come nigh unto him for the press, they uncovered the roof where he was: and when they had broken *it* up, they let down the bed wherein the sick of the palsy lay. 5 When Jesus saw their faith, he said unto the sick of the palsy, Son, thy sins be forgiven thee. 6 But there were certain of the scribes sitting there, and reasoning in their hearts, 7 Why doth this *man* thus speak blasphemies? who can forgive

Living Bible

be examined immediately by the Jewish priest. Don't stop to speak to anyone along the way. Take along the offering prescribed by Moses for a leper who is healed, so that everyone will have proof that you are well again."

45 But as the man went on his way he began to shout the good news that he was healed; as a result, such throngs soon surrounded Jesus that he couldn't publicly enter a city anywhere, but had to stay out in the barren wastelands. And people from everywhere came to him there.

2 Several days later he returned to Capernaum, and the news of his arrival spread quickly through the city. 2 Soon the house where he was staying was so packed with visitors that there wasn't room for a single person more, not even outside the door. And he preached the Word to them. 3 Four men arrived carrying a paralyzed man on a stretcher. 4 They couldn't get to Jesus through the crowd, so they dug through the clay roof above his head and lowered the sick man on his stretcher, right down in front of Jesus.[a]

5 When Jesus saw how strongly they believed that he would help, Jesus said to the sick man, "Son, your sins are forgiven!"

6 But some of the Jewish religious leaders[b] said to themselves as they sat there, 7 "What? This is blasphemy! Does he think he is God? For only God can forgive sins."

[*a*] Implied. [*b*] Literally, "scribes."

Today's English Version

with him and sent him away at once. 44 "Listen," he said, "don't tell this to anyone. But go straight to the priest and let him examine you; then offer the sacrifice that Moses ordered, to prove to everyone that you are now clean."

45 But the man went away and began to spread the news everywhere. Indeed, he talked so much that Jesus could not go into a town publicly. Instead, he stayed out in lonely places, and people came to him from everywhere.

Jesus heals a paralyzed man

2 A few days later Jesus came back to Capernaum, and the news spread that he was at home. 2 So many people came together that there wasn't any room left, not even out in front of the door. Jesus was preaching the message to them, 3 when a paralyzed man, carried by four men, was brought to him. 4 Because of the crowd, however, they could not get the man to Jesus. So they made a hole in the roof right above the place where Jesus was. When they had made an opening, they let the man down, lying on his mat. 5 Jesus saw how much faith they had, and said to the paralyzed man, "My son, your sins are forgiven."

6 Some teachers of the Law who were sitting there thought to themselves, 7 "How does he dare talk against God like this? No man can forgive sins; only God can!"

New International Version

warning: 44 "See that you don't tell this to anyone. But go, show yourself to the priest and offer the sacrifices that Moses commanded for your cleansing, as a testimony to them." 45 Instead he went out and began to talk freely, spreading the news. As a result, Jesus could no longer enter a town openly but stayed outside in lonely places. Yet the people still came to him from everywhere.

Jesus heals a paralytic

2 A few days later, when Jesus again entered Capernaum, the people heard that he had come home. 2 So many gathered that there was no room left, not even outside the door, and he preached to them. 3 Some men came, bringing to him a paralytic, carried by four of them. 4 Since they could not get him to Jesus because of the crowd, they made an opening in the roof above Jesus and having dug through, lowered the mat the paralyzed man was lying on. 5 When Jesus saw their faith, he said to the paralytic, "Son, your sins are forgiven."

6 Now some teachers of the law were sitting there, thinking to themselves, 7 "Why does this fellow talk like that? He's blaspheming! Who can forgive sins but God alone?"

Phillips Modern English

the strict injunction,

"Mind you say nothing at all to anybody. Go straight off and show yourself to the priest, and make the offerings for your cleansing which Moses prescribed, as public proof of your recovery."

But he went off and began to talk a great deal about it in public, spreading his story far and wide. Consequently, it became impossible for Jesus to show his face in the towns and he had to stay outside in lonely places. Yet the people still came to him from all quarters.

2.1 Faith at Capernaum

When he re-entered Capernaum some days later, a rumour spread that he was in somebody's house. Such a large crowd collected that while he was giving them his message it was impossible even to get near the doorway. Meanwhile, a group of people arrived to see him, bringing with them a paralytic whom four of them were carrying. And when they found it was impossible to get near him because of the crowd, they removed the tiles from the roof over Jesus' head and let down the paralytic's bed through the opening. And when Jesus saw their faith, he said to the man who was paralysed,

"My son, your sins are forgiven."

But some of the scribes were sitting there silently asking themselves,

"Why does this man talk such blasphemy? Who can forgive sins but God alone?"

Revised Standard Version

sternly charged him, and sent him away at once,
44 and said to him, "See that you say nothing
to any one; but go, show yourself to the priest,
and offer for your cleansing what Moses commanded, for a proof to the people." [f] 45 But he
went out and began to talk freely about it, and
to spread the news, so that Jesus[g] could no
longer openly enter a town, but was out in the
country; and people came to him from every
quarter.

2 And when he returned to Capernaum after
some days, it was reported that he was at
home. 2 And many were gathered together, so
that there was no longer room for them, not
even about the door; and he was preaching the
word to them. 3 And they came, bringing to him
a paralytic carried by four men. 4 And when
they could not get near him because of the
crowd, they removed the roof above him; and
when they had made an opening, they let down
the pallet on which the paralytic lay. 5 And when
Jesus saw their faith, he said to the paralytic,
"My son, your sins are forgiven." 6 Now some
of the scribes were sitting there, questioning in
their hearts, 7 "Why does this man speak thus?
It is blasphemy! Who can forgive sins but God

[f] Greek *to them.* [g] Greek *he.*

Jerusalem Bible

mediately sent him away and sternly ordered
him, 44 Mind you say nothing to anyone, but go
and show yourself to the priest, and make the
offering for your healing prescribed by Moses as
evidence of your recovery." 45 The man went
away, but then started talking about it freely and
telling the story everywhere, so that Jesus could
no longer go openly into any town, but had to
stay outside in places where nobody lived. Even
so, people from all around would come to him.

Cure of a paralytic

2 When he returned to Capernaum some time
later, word went around that he was back;
2 and so many people collected that there was
no room left, even in front of the door. He was
preaching the word to them 3 when some people
came bringing him a paralytic carried by four
men, 4 but as the crowd made it impossible to
get the man to him, they stripped the roof over
the place where Jesus was; and when they had
made an opening, they lowered the stretcher on
which the paralytic lay. 5 Seeing their faith, Jesus
said to the paralytic, "My child, your sins are
forgiven." 6 Now some scribes were sitting there,
and they thought to themselves, 7 "How can this
man talk like that? He is blaspheming. Who can

New English Bible

warning: 'Be sure you say nothing to anybody. Go and show yourself to the priest, and make the offering laid down by Moses for your cleansing; that will certify the cure.' But the man went out and made the whole story public; he spread it far and wide, until Jesus could no longer show himself in any town, but stayed outside in the open country. Even so, people kept coming to him from all quarters.

2 When after some days he returned to Capernaum, the news went round that he was at home; and such a crowd collected that the space in front of the door was not big enough to hold them. And while he was proclaiming the message to them, a man was brought who was paralysed. Four men were carrying him, but because of the crowd they could not get him near. So they opened up the roof over the place where Jesus was, and when they had broken through they lowered the stretcher on which the paralysed man was lying. When Jesus saw their faith, he said to the paralysed man, 'My son, your sins are forgiven.'

Now there were some lawyers sitting there and they thought to themselves, 'Why does the fellow talk like that? This is blasphemy! Who but

King James Version

sins but God only? 8And immediately, when Jesus perceived in his spirit that they so reasoned within themselves, he said unto them, Why reason ye these things in your hearts? 9 Whether is it easier to say to the sick of the palsy, *Thy* sins be forgiven thee; or to say, Arise, and take up thy bed, and walk? 10 But that ye may know that the Son of man hath power on earth to forgive sins, (he saith to the sick of the palsy,) 11 I say unto thee, Arise, and take up thy bed, and go thy way into thine house. 12And immediately he arose, took up the bed, and went forth before them all; insomuch that they were all amazed, and glorified God, saying, We never saw it on this fashion. 13And he went forth again by the sea side; and all the multitude resorted unto him, and he taught them. 14And as he passed by, he saw Levi the *son* of Alpheus sitting at the receipt of custom, and said unto him, Follow me. And he arose and followed him. 15And it came to pass, that, as Jesus sat at meat in his house, many publicans and sinners sat also together with Jesus and his disciples; for there were many, and they followed him. 16And when the scribes and Pharisees saw him eat with publicans and sinners, they said unto his disciples, How is it that he eateth and drinketh with

Living Bible

8 Jesus could read their minds and said to them at once, "Why does this bother you? 9, 10, 11 I, the Messiah,[c] have the authority on earth to forgive sins. But talk is cheap—anybody could say that. So I'll prove it to you by healing this man." Then, turning to the paralyzed man, he commanded, "Pick up your stretcher and go on home, for you are healed!"[a]

12 The man jumped up, took the stretcher, and pushed his way through the stunned onlookers! Then how they praised God. "We've never seen anything like this before!" they all exclaimed.

13 Then Jesus went out to the seashore again, and preached to the crowds that gathered around him. 14As he was walking up the beach he saw Levi, the son of Alphaeus, sitting at his tax collection booth. "Come with me," Jesus told him. "Come be my disciple."

And Levi jumped to his feet and went along.

15 That night Levi invited his fellow tax collectors and many other notorious sinners to be his dinner guests so that they could meet Jesus and his disciples. (There were many men of this type among the crowds that followed him.) 16 But when some of the Jewish religious leaders[d] saw him eating with these men of ill repute, they said to his disciples, "How can he stand it, to eat with such scum?"

[*c*] Literally, "Son of Man." [*a*] Implied. [*d*] Literally, "the scribes of the Pharisees."

Today's English Version

8 At once Jesus knew their secret thoughts, so he said to them, "Why do you think such things? 9 Is it easier to say to this paralyzed man, 'Your sins are forgiven,' or to say, 'Get up, pick up your mat, and walk'? 10 I will prove to you, then, that the Son of Man has authority on earth to forgive sins." So he said to the paralyzed man, 11 "I tell you, get up, pick up your mat, and go home!"

12 While they all watched, the man got up, picked up his mat, and hurried away. They were all completely amazed and praised God, saying, "We have never seen anything like this!"

Jesus calls Levi

13 Jesus went back again to the shore of Lake Galilee. A crowd came to him and he started teaching them. 14As he walked along he saw a tax collector, Levi, the son of Alphaeus, sitting in his office. Jesus said to him, "Follow me." Levi got up and followed him.

15 Later on Jesus was having a meal in Levi's house. A large number of tax collectors and outcasts was following Jesus, and many of them joined him and his disciples at the table. 16 Some teachers of the Law, who were Pharisees, saw that Jesus was eating with these outcasts and tax collectors; so they asked his disciples, "Why does he eat with such people?"

New International Version

8 Immediately Jesus knew in his spirit that this was what they were thinking in their hearts, and he said to them, "Why are you thinking these things? 9 Which is easier: to say to the paralytic, 'Your sins are forgiven,' or to say, 'Get up, take your mat and walk'? 10 But that you may know that the Son of Man has authority on earth to forgive sins . . . ." He said to the paralytic, 11 "I tell you, get up, take your mat and go home." 12 He got up, took his mat and walked out in full view of them all. This amazed everyone and they praised God, saying, "We have never seen anything like this!"

The calling of Matthew

13 Once again Jesus went out beside the lake. A large crowd came to him, and he began to teach them. 14As he walked along, he saw Levi son of Alphaeus sitting at the tax collector's booth. "Follow me," Jesus told him, and Levi got up and followed him.

15 While Jesus was having dinner at Levi's house, many tax collectors and "sinners" were eating with him and his disciples, for there were many who followed him. 16 When the teachers of the law who were Pharisees saw him eating with the "sinners" and tax collectors, they asked his disciples: "Why does he eat with tax collectors and 'sinners'?"

Phillips Modern English

Jesus realised instantly what they were thinking, and said to them,

"Why must you argue like this in your minds? Which do you suppose is easier—to say to a paralysed man, 'Your sins are forgiven', or 'Get up, pick up your bed and walk'? But to prove to you that the Son of Man has full authority to forgive sins on earth, I say to you,"—and here he spoke to the paralytic—"Get up, pick up your bed and go home."

At once the man sprang to his feet, picked up his bed and walked off in full view of them all. Everyone was amazed, praised God and said,

"We have never seen anything like this before."

Then Jesus went out again by the lake-side and the whole crowd came to him, and he continued to teach them.

2.14 Jesus now calls "a sinner" to follow him

As Jesus went on his way, he saw Levi the son of Alphaeus sitting at his desk in the tax-office, and he said to him,

"Follow me!"

Levi got up and followed him. Later, when Jesus was sitting at dinner in Levi's house, a large number of tax-collectors and disreputable folk came in and joined him and his disciples. For there were many such people among his followers. When the scribes who were Pharisees saw him eating in the company of tax-collectors and outsiders, they remarked to his disciples,

"So he eats with tax-collectors and sinners!"

Revised Standard Version

alone?" 8And immediately Jesus, perceiving in
his spirit that they thus questioned within themselves, said to them, "Why do you question thus
in your hearts? 9 Which is easier, to say to the
paralytic, 'Your sins are forgiven,' or to say,
'Rise, take up your pallet and walk'? 10 But that
you may know that the Son of man has authority
on earth to forgive sins"—he said to the paralytic—11 "I say to you, rise, take up your pallet
and go home." 12And he rose, and immediately
took up the pallet and went out before them all;
so that they were all amazed and glorified God,
saying, "We never saw anything like this!"
13 He went out again beside the sea; and all
the crowd gathered about him, and he taught
them. 14And as he passed on, he saw Levi the
son of Alphaeus sitting at the tax office, and he
said to him, "Follow me." And he rose and
followed him.
15 And as he sat at table in his house, many
tax collectors and sinners were sitting with Jesus
and his disciples; for there were many who followed him. 16And the scribes of[h] the Pharisees,
when they saw that he was eating with sinners
and tax collectors, said to his disciples, "Why
does he eat[i] with tax collectors and sinners?"

[h] Other ancient authorities read *and*.

Jerusalem Bible

forgive sins but God?" 8 Jesus, inwardly aware
that this was what they were thinking, said to
them, "Why do you have these thoughts in your
hearts? 9 Which of these is easier: to say to the
paralytic, 'Your sins are forgiven' or to say, 'Get
up, pick up your stretcher and walk'? 10 But to
prove to you that the Son of Man has authority
on earth to forgive sins,"—11 he said to the paralytic—"I order you: get up, pick up your
stretcher, and go off home." 12And the man got
up, picked up his stretcher at once and walked
out in front of everyone, so that they were all
astounded and praised God saying, "We have
never seen anything like this."

The call of Levi

13 He went out again to the shore of the
lake[c]; and all the people came to him, and he
taught them. 14As he was walking on he saw
Levi the son of Alphaeus, sitting by the customs house, and he said to him, "Follow me."
And he got up and followed him.

Eating with sinners

15 When Jesus was at dinner in his house, a
number of tax collectors and sinners were also
sitting at the table with Jesus and his disciples;
for there were many of them among his followers. 16 When the scribes of the Pharisee party
saw him eating with sinners and tax collectors,
they said to his disciples, "Why does he eat with

[c] Tiberias, the "Sea of Galilee."

New English Bible

God alone can forgive sins?' Jesus knew in his own mind that this was what they were thinking, and said to them: 'Why do you harbour thoughts like these? Is it easier to say to this paralysed man, "Your sins are forgiven", or to say, "Stand up, take your bed, and walk"? But to convince you that the Son of Man has the right on earth to forgive sins'—he turned to the paralysed man—'I say to you, stand up, take your bed, and go home.' And he got up, and at once took his stretcher and went out in full view of them all, so that they were astounded and praised God. 'Never before', they said, 'have we seen the like.'

Once more he went away to the lake-side. All the crowd came to him, and he taught them there. As he went along, he saw Levi son of Alphaeus at his seat in the custom-house, and said to him, 'Follow me'; and Levi rose and followed him.

When Jesus was at table in his house, many bad characters—tax-gatherers and others—were seated with him and his disciples; for there were many who followed him. Some doctors of the law who were Pharisees noticed him eating in this bad company, and said to his disciples, 'He

King James Version

publicans and sinners? 17 When Jesus heard *it,* he saith unto them, They that are whole have no need of the physician, but they that are sick: I came not to call the righteous, but sinners to repentance. 18And the disciples of John and of the Pharisees used to fast: and they come and say unto him, Why do the disciples of John and of the Pharisees fast, but thy disciples fast not? 19And Jesus said unto them, Can the children of the bridechamber fast, while the bridegroom is with them? as long as they have the bridegroom with them, they cannot fast. 20 But the days will come, when the bridegroom shall be taken away from them, and then shall they fast in those days. 21 No man also seweth a piece of new cloth on an old garment; else the new piece that filled it up taketh away from the old, and the rent is made worse. 22And no man putteth new wine into old bottles; else the new wine doth burst the bottles, and the wine is spilled, and the bottles will be marred: but new wine must be put into new bottles. 23And it came to pass, that he went through the corn fields on the sabbath day; and his disciples began, as they went,

Living Bible

17 When Jesus heard what they were saying, he told them, "Sick people need the doctor, not healthy ones! I haven't come to tell good people to repent, but the bad ones."

18 John's disciples and the Jewish leaders sometimes fasted, that is, went without food as part of their religion. One day some people came to Jesus and asked why his disciples didn't do this too.

19 Jesus replied, "Do friends of the bridegroom refuse to eat at the wedding feast? Should they be sad while he is with them? 20 But some day he will be taken away from them, and then they will mourn. 21 [Besides, going without food is part of the old way of doing things.[a]] It is like patching an old garment with unshrunk cloth! What happens? The patch pulls away and leaves the hole worse than before. 22 You know better than to put new wine into old wineskins. They would burst. The wine would be spilled out and the wineskins ruined. New wine needs fresh wineskins."

23 Another time, on a Sabbath day as Jesus and his disciples were walking through the fields, the disciples were breaking off heads of wheat and eating the grain.[a]

[*a*] Implied.

Today's English Version

17 Jesus heard them and answered, "People who are well do not need a doctor, but only those who are sick. I have not come to call the respectable people, but the outcasts."

The question about fasting

18 On one occasion the followers of John the Baptist and the Pharisees were fasting. Some people came to Jesus and asked him, "Why is it that the disciples of John the Baptist and the disciples of the Pharisees fast, but yours do not?"

19 Jesus answered, "Do you expect the guests at a wedding party to go without food? Of course not! As long as the bridegroom is with them they will not do that. 20 But the time will come when the bridegroom will be taken away from them; when that day comes then they will go without food.

21 "No one uses a piece of new cloth to patch up an old coat. If he does, the new patch will tear off some of the old cloth, making an even bigger hole. 22 Nor does anyone pour new wine into used wineskins. If he does, the wine will burst the skins, and both the wine and the skins will be ruined. No! Fresh skins for new wine!"

The question about the Sabbath

23 Jesus was walking through some wheat fields on a Sabbath day. As his disciples walked along with him, they began to pick the heads of

New International Version

17 On hearing this, Jesus said to them, "It is not the healthy who need a doctor, but the sick. I have not come to call the righteous, but sinners."

Jesus questioned about fasting

18 Now John's disciples and the Pharisees were fasting. Some people came and asked Jesus, "How is it that John's disciples and the disciples of the Pharisees are fasting, but yours are not?"

19 Jesus answered, "How can the guests of the bridegroom fast while he is with them? They cannot, so long as they have him with them. 20 But the time will come when the bridegroom will be taken from them, and on that day they will fast.

21 "No one sews a patch of unshrunk cloth on an old garment. If he does, the new piece will pull away from the old, making the tear worse. 22And no one pours new wine into old wineskins. If he does, the wine will burst the skins, and both the wine and the wineskins will be ruined. No, he pours new wine into new wineskins."

Lord of the Sabbath

23 One Sabbath Jesus was going through the grainfields, and as his disciples walked along,

Phillips Modern English

When Jesus heard this, he said to them,
"It is not the fit and flourishing who need the doctor, but those who are ill. I did not come to invite the 'righteous', but the 'sinners'."

2.18 The question of fasting

The disciples of John and the Pharisees were fasting. They came and said to Jesus,
"Why do those who follow John or the Pharisees keep fasts but your disciples do nothing of the kind?"
Jesus told them,
"Can you expect wedding-guests to fast in the bridegroom's presence? Fasting is out of the question as long as they have the bridegroom with them. But the day will come when the bridegroom will be taken away from them—that will be the time for them to fast.
"Nobody," he continued, "sews a patch of unshrunk cloth on to an old coat. If he does, the new patch tears away from the old and the hole is worse than ever. And nobody puts new wine into old wineskins. If he does, the new wine bursts the skins, the wine is spilt and the skins are ruined. No, new wine must go into new wineskins."

2.23 Jesus rebukes the sabbatarians

One day he happened to be going through the cornfields on the Sabbath day. And his disciples, as they made their way along, began to

Revised Standard Version

17 And when Jesus heard it, he said to them, "Those who are well have no need of a physician, but those who are sick; I came not to call the righteous, but sinners."
18 Now John's disciples and the Pharisees were fasting; and people came and said to him, "Why do John's disciples and the disciples of the Pharisees fast, but your disciples do not fast?"
19 And Jesus said to them, "Can the wedding guests fast while the bridegroom is with them? As long as they have the bridegroom with them, they cannot fast.
20 The days will come, when the bridegroom is taken away from them, and then they will fast in that day.
21 No one sews a piece of unshrunk cloth on an old garment; if he does, the patch tears away from it, the new from the old, and a worse tear is made.
22 And no one puts new wine into old wineskins; if he does, the wine will burst the skins, and the wine is lost, and so are the skins; but new wine is for fresh skins." [j]
23 One sabbath he was going through the grainfields; and as they made their way his dis-

[i] Other ancient authorities add *and drink*. [j] Other ancient authorities omit *but new wine is for fresh skins*.

Jerusalem Bible

tax collectors and sinners?"
17 When Jesus heard this he said to them, "It is not the healthy who need the doctor, but the sick. I did not come to call the virtuous, but sinners."

A discussion on fasting

18 One day when John's disciples and the Pharisees were fasting, some people came and said to him, "Why is it that John's disciples and the disciples of the Pharisees fast, but your disciples do not?"
19 Jesus replied, "Surely the bridegroom's attendants would never think of fasting while the bridegroom is still with them? As long as they have the bridegroom with them, they could not think of fasting.
20 But the time will come for the bridegroom to be taken away from them, and then, on that day, they will fast.
21 No one sews a piece of unshrunken cloth on an old cloak; if he does, the patch pulls away from it, the new from the old, and the tear gets worse.
22 And nobody puts new wine into old wineskins; if he does, the wine will burst the skins, and the wine is lost and the skins too. No! New wine, fresh skins!"

Picking corn on the sabbath

23 One sabbath day he happened to be taking a walk through the cornfields, and his disciples began to pick ears of corn as they went along.

New English Bible

eats with tax-gatherers and sinners!' Jesus heard it and said to them, 'It is not the healthy that need a doctor, but the sick; I did not come to invite virtuous people, but sinners.'

Once, when John's disciples and the Pharisees were keeping a fast, some people came to him and said, 'Why is it that John's disciples and the disciples of the Pharisees are fasting, but yours are not?' Jesus said to them, 'Can you expect the bridegroom's friends to fast while the bridegroom is with them? As long as they have the bridegroom with them, there can be no fasting. But the time will come when the bridegroom will be taken away from them, and on that day they will fast.

'No one sews a patch of unshrunk cloth on to an old coat; if he does, the patch tears away from it, the new from the old, and leaves a bigger hole. No one puts new wine into old wineskins; if he does, the wine will burst the skins, and then wine and skins are both lost. Fresh skins for new wine!'

One Sabbath he was going through the cornfields; and his disciples, as they went, began to

King James Version

to pluck the ears of corn. 24And the Pharisees said unto him, Behold, why do they on the sabbath day that which is not lawful? 25And he said unto them, Have ye never read what David did, when he had need, and was a hungered, he, and they that were with him? 26 How he went into the house of God in the days of Abiathar the high priest, and did eat the shewbread, which is not lawful to eat but for the priests, and gave also to them which were with him? 27And he said unto them, The sabbath was made for man, and not man for the sabbath: 28 Therefore the Son of man is Lord also of the sabbath.

3 And he entered again into the synagogue; and there was a man there which had a withered hand. 2And they watched him, whether he would heal him on the sabbath day; that they might accuse him. 3And he saith unto the man which had the withered hand, Stand forth. 4And he saith unto them, Is it lawful to do good on the sabbath days, or to do evil? to save life, or to kill? But they held their peace. 5And when

Living Bible

24 Some of the Jewish religious leaders said to Jesus, "They shouldn't be doing that! It's against our laws to work by harvesting grain on the Sabbath."

25, 26 But Jesus replied, "Didn't you ever hear about the time King David and his companions were hungry, and he went into the house of God—Abiathar was High Priest then—and they ate the special bread[f] only priests were allowed to eat? That was against the law too. 27 But the Sabbath was made to benefit man, and not man to benefit the Sabbath. 28And I, the Messiah,[g] have authority even to decide what men can do on Sabbath days!"

3 While in Capernaum Jesus went over to the synagogue again, and noticed a man there with a deformed hand.

2 Since it was the Sabbath, Jesus' enemies watched him closely. Would he heal the man's hand? If he did, they planned to arrest him!

3 Jesus asked the man to come and stand in front of the congregation. 4 Then turning to his enemies he asked, "Is it all right to do kind deeds on Sabbath days? Or is this a day for doing harm? Is it a day to save lives or to destroy them?" But they wouldn't answer him. 5 Look-

[f] Literally, "shewbread." [g] Literally, "the Son of Man."

Today's English Version

wheat. 24 So the Pharisees said to Jesus, "Look, it is against our Law for your disciples to do this on the Sabbath!"

25 Jesus answered, "Have you never read what David did that time when he needed something to eat? He and his men were hungry, 26 so he went into the house of God and ate the bread offered to God. This happened when Abiathar was the High Priest. According to our Law only the priests may eat this bread—but David ate it, and even gave it to his men."

27 And Jesus concluded, "The Sabbath was made for the good of man; man was not made for the Sabbath. 28 So the Son of Man is Lord even of the Sabbath."

The man with a crippled hand

3 Then Jesus went back to the synagogue, where there was a man who had a crippled hand. 2 Some people were there who wanted to accuse Jesus of doing wrong; so they watched him very closely, to see whether he would cure him on the Sabbath. 3 Jesus said to the man with the crippled hand, "Come up here to the front." 4 Then he asked the people, "What does our Law allow us to do on the Sabbath? To help, or to harm? To save a man's life, or to destroy it?"

But they did not say a thing. 5 Jesus was angry

New International Version

they began to pick some heads of grain. 24 The Pharisees said to him, "Look, why are they doing what is unlawful on the Sabbath?"

25 He answered, "Have you never read what David did when he and his companions were hungry and in need? 26 In the time of Abiathar the high priest, he entered the house of God and ate the consecrated bread, which is only lawful for priests to eat. And he also gave some to his companions."

27 Then he said to them, "The Sabbath was made for man, not man for the Sabbath. 28 So the Son of Man is Lord even of the Sabbath."

3 Another time he went into the synagogue, and a man with a shriveled hand was there. 2 Some of them were looking for a reason to accuse Jesus, so they watched him closely to see if he would heal him on the Sabbath. 3 Jesus said to the man with the shriveled hand, "Stand up in front of everyone."

4 Then Jesus asked them, "Which is lawful on the Sabbath: to do good or to do evil, to save life or to kill?" But they remained silent.

5 He looked around at them in anger and,

Phillips Modern English

pick the ears of corn. The Pharisees said to him, "Look at that! Why should they do what is forbidden on the Sabbath day?"

Then he spoke to them.

"Have you never read what David did, when there was no food and he and his companions were famished? He went into the house of God when Abiathar was High Priest, and ate the presentation loaves, which nobody is allowed to eat, except the priests—and even gave some of the bread to his companions? The Sabbath," he continued, "was made for man's sake; man was not made for the sake of the Sabbath. That is why the Son of Man is master even of the Sabbath."

On another occasion when he went into the synagogue, there was a man there whose hand was shrivelled, and they were watching Jesus closely to see whether he would heal him on the Sabbath day, so that they might bring a charge against him. Jesus said to the man with the shrivelled hand,

"Stand up and come out here in front!"

Then he said to them,

"Is it right to do good on the Sabbath day, or to do harm? Is it right to save life or to kill?"

There was a dead silence. Then Jesus, deeply

Revised Standard Version

ciples began to pluck heads of grain. 24And the
Pharisees said to him, "Look, why are they doing what is not lawful on the sabbath?" 25And
he said to them, "Have you never read what
David did, when he was in need and was hungry,
he and those who were with him: 26 how he
entered the house of God, when Abiathar was
high priest, and ate the bread of the Presence,
which it is not lawful for any but the priests to
eat, and also gave it to those who were with
him?" 27And he said to them, "The sabbath
was made for man, not man for the sabbath;
28 so the Son of man is lord even of the sabbath."

3 Again he entered the synagogue, and a
man was there who had a withered hand.
2And they watched him, to see whether he would
heal him on the sabbath, so that they might accuse him. 3And he said to the man who had the
withered hand, "Come here." 4And he said to
them, "Is it lawful on the sabbath to do good or
to do harm, to save life or to kill?" But they
were silent. 5And he looked around at them with

Jerusalem Bible

24And the Pharisees said to him, "Look, why are
they doing something on the sabbath day that
is forbidden?" 25And he replied, "Did you never
read what David did in his time of need when he
and his followers were hungry—26 how he went
into the house of God when Abiathar[d] was high
priest, and ate the loaves of offering which only
the priests are allowed to eat, and how he also
gave some to the men with him?"
27 And he said to them, "The sabbath was
made for man, not man for the sabbath; 28 so
the Son of Man is master even of the sabbath."

Cure of the man with a withered hand

3 He went again into a synagogue, and there
was a man there who had a withered hand.
2And they were watching him to see if he would
cure him on the sabbath day, hoping for something to use against him. 3 He said to the man
with the withered hand, "Stand up out in the
middle!" 4 Then he said to them, "Is it against
the law on the sabbath day to do good, or to do
evil; to save life, or to kill?" But they said
nothing. 5 Then, grieved to find them so obsti-

[d] See 1 S. 21:1-7. Abiathar was the better known as high priest in David's reign, but Ahimelech is named in this source.

New English Bible

pluck ears of corn. The Pharisees said to him, 'Look, why are they doing what is forbidden on the Sabbath?' He answered, 'Have you never read what David did when he and his men were hungry and had nothing to eat? He went into the House of God, in the time of Abiathar the High Priest, and ate the sacred bread, though no one but a priest is allowed to eat it, and even gave it to his men.'

He also said to them, 'The Sabbath was made for the sake of man and not man for the Sabbath: therefore the Son of Man is sovereign even over the Sabbath.'

3 On another occasion when he went to synagogue, there was a man in the congregation who had a withered arm; and they were watching to see whether Jesus would cure him on the Sabbath, so that they could bring a charge against him. He said to the man with the withered arm, 'Come and stand out here.' Then he turned to them: 'Is it permitted to do good or to do evil on the Sabbath, to save life or to kill?' They had nothing to say; and, looking round at

King James Version

he had looked round about on them with anger,
being grieved for the hardness of their hearts, he
saith unto the man, Stretch forth thine hand.
And he stretched *it* out: and his hand was restored whole as the other. 6And the Pharisees
went forth, and straightway took counsel with
the Herodians against him, how they might destroy him. 7 But Jesus withdrew himself with his
disciples to the sea: and a great multitude from
Galilee followed him, and from Judea, 8And
from Jerusalem, and from Idumea, and *from* beyond Jordan; and they about Tyre and Sidon, a
great multitude, when they had heard what great
things he did, came unto him. 9And he spake to
his disciples, that a small ship should wait on
him because of the multitude, lest they should
throng him. 10 For he had healed many; insomuch that they pressed upon him for to touch
him, as many as had plagues. 11And unclean
spirits, when they saw him, fell down before him,
and cried, saying, Thou art the Son of God.
12And he straitly charged them that they should

Living Bible

ing around at them angrily, for he was deeply
disturbed by their indifference to human need,
he said to the man, "Reach out your hand." He
did, and instantly his hand was healed!
6 At once the Pharisees[a] went away and met
with the Herodians[b] to discuss plans for killing
Jesus. 7, 8 Meanwhile, Jesus and his disciples
withdrew to the beach, followed by a huge
crowd from all over Galilee, Judea, Jerusalem,
Idumea, from beyond the Jordan River, and
even from as far away as Tyre and Sidon. For
the news about his miracles had spread far and
wide and vast numbers came to see him for
themselves.
9 He instructed his disciples to bring around
a boat and to have it standing ready to rescue
him in case he was crowded off the beach. 10 For
there had been many healings that day and as a
result great numbers of sick people were crowding around him, trying to touch him.
11 And whenever those possessed by demons
caught sight of him they would fall down before
him shrieking, "You are the Son of God!" 12 But
he strictly warned them not to make him known.

[a] The Pharisees were a religious sect of the Jews.
[b] A pro-Roman political party.

Today's English Version

as he looked around at them, but at the same
time he felt sorry for them, because they were
so stubborn and wrong. Then he said to the man,
"Stretch out your hand." He stretched it out and
it became well again. 6 So the Pharisees left the
synagogue and met at once with some members
of Herod's party; and they made plans against
Jesus to kill him.

A crowd by the lake

7 Jesus and his disciples went away to Lake
Galilee, and a large crowd followed him. They
came from Galilee, from Judea, 8 from Jerusalem, from the territory of Idumea, from the
territory on the other side of the Jordan, and
from the neighborhood of the cities of Tyre and
Sidon. This large crowd came to Jesus because
they heard of the things he was doing. 9 The
crowd was so large that Jesus told his disciples
to get a boat ready for him, so the people would
not crush him. 10 He had healed many people,
and all the sick kept pushing their way to him
in order to touch him. 11And whenever the people who had evil spirits in them saw him they
would fall down before him and scream, "You
are the Son of God!"
12 Jesus gave a stern command to the evil
spirits not to tell who he was.

New International Version

deeply distressed at their stubborn hearts, said
to the man, "Stretch out your hand." He
stretched it out, and his hand was completely
restored. 6 Then the Pharisees went out and began to plot with the Herodians how they might
kill Jesus.

Crowds follow Jesus

7 Jesus withdrew with his disciples to the lake,
and a large crowd from Galilee followed. 8 When
they heard all he was doing, many people came
to him from Judea, Jerusalem, Idumea, and the
regions across the Jordan and around Tyre and
Sidon. 9 Because of the crowd he told his disciples to have a small boat ready for him, to keep
the people from crowding him. 10 For he had
healed many, so that those with diseases were
pushing forward to touch him. 11 Whenever the
evil [g] spirits saw him, they fell down before him
and cried out, "You are the Son of God." 12 But
he gave them strict orders not to tell who he
was.

[g] Greek *unclean.*

Phillips Modern English

hurt as he sensed their inhumanity, looked round in anger at the faces surrounding him, and said to the man,

"Stretch out your hand!"

And he stretched it out and the hand was restored. The Pharisees walked straight out and discussed with Herod's party how they could get rid of Jesus.

3.7 Jesus' enormous popularity

Jesus now retired to the lake-side with his disciples. A huge crowd of people followed him, not only from Galilee, but from Judaea, Jerusalem and Idumaea, some from the district beyond the Jordan and from the neighbourhood of Tyre and Sidon. This vast crowd came to him because they had heard about the sort of things he was doing. So Jesus told his disciples to have a small boat kept in readiness for him, in case the people should crowd him too closely. For he healed so many people that all those who were in pain kept pressing forward to touch him with their hands. Evil spirits, as soon as they saw him, acknowledged his authority and screamed,

"You are the Son of God!"

But he warned them repeatedly that they must not make him known.

Revised Standard Version

anger, grieved at their hardness of heart, and
said to the man, "Stretch out your hand." He
stretched it out, and his hand was restored.
6 The Pharisees went out, and immediately held
counsel with the Herodians against him, how to
destroy him.

7 Jesus withdrew with his disciples to the sea,
and a great multitude from Galilee followed;
also from Judea 8 and Jerusalem and Idumea
and from beyond the Jordan and from about
Tyre and Sidon a great multitude, hearing all
that he did, came to him. 9 And he told his disciples to have a boat ready for him because of
the crowd, lest they should crush him; 10 for he
had healed many, so that all who had diseases
pressed upon him to touch him. 11 And whenever the unclean spirits beheld him, they fell
down before him and cried out, "You are the
Son of God." 12 And he strictly ordered them
not to make him known.

Jerusalem Bible

nate, he looked angrily around at them, and said
to the man, "Stretch out your hand." He
stretched it out and his hand was better. 6 The
Pharisees went out and at once began to plot
with the Herodians against him, discussing how
to destroy him.

The crowds follow Jesus

7 Jesus withdrew with his disciples to the lake-
side, and great crowds from Galilee followed
him. From Judaea, 8 Jerusalem, Idumaea, Transjordania and the region of Tyre and Sidon, great
numbers who had heard of all he was doing
came to him. 9 And he asked his disciples to
have a boat ready for him because of the crowd,
to keep him from being crushed. 10 For he had
cured so many that all who were afflicted in any
way were crowding forward to touch him. 11 And
the unclean spirits, whenever they saw him, would
fall down before him and shout, "You are the
Son of God!" 12 But he warned them strongly
not to make him known.

New English Bible

them with anger and sorrow at their obstinate stupidity, he said to the man, 'Stretch out your arm.' He stretched it out and his arm was restored. But the Pharisees, on leaving the synagogue, began plotting against him with the partisans of Herod to see how they could make away with him.

Jesus went away to the lake-side with his disciples. Great numbers from Galilee, Judaea and Jerusalem, Idumaea and Transjordan, and the neighbourhood of Tyre and Sidon, heard what he was doing and came to see him. So he told his disciples to have a boat ready for him, to save him from being crushed by the crowd. For he cured so many that sick people of all kinds came crowding in upon him to touch him. The unclean spirits too, when they saw him, would fall at his feet and cry aloud, 'You are the Son of God'; but he insisted that they should not make him known.

King James Version

not make him known. 13 And he goeth up into a mountain, and called *unto him* whom he would: and they came unto him. 14 And he ordained twelve, that they should be with him, and that he might send them forth to preach, 15 And to have power to heal sicknesses, and to cast out devils: 16 And Simon he surnamed Peter; 17 And James the *son* of Zebedee, and John the brother of James; and he surnamed them Boanerges, which is, The sons of thunder: 18 And Andrew, and Philip, and Bartholomew, and Matthew, and Thomas, and James the *son* of Alpheus, and Thaddeus, and Simon the Canaanite, 19 And Judas Iscariot, which also betrayed him: and they went into a house. 20 And the multitude cometh together again, so that they could not so much as eat bread. 21 And when his friends heard *of it*, they went out to lay hold on him: for they said, He is beside himself.

22 And the scribes which came down from Jerusalem said, He hath Beelzebub, and by the prince of the devils casteth he out devils. 23 And he called them *unto him*, and said unto them in parables, How can Satan cast out Satan? 24 And

Living Bible

13 Afterwards he went up into the hills and summoned certain ones he chose, inviting them to come and join him there; and they did. 14, 15 Then he selected twelve of them to be his regular companions and to go out to preach and to cast out demons. 16–19 These are the names of the twelve he chose:

Simon (he renamed him "Peter"),
James and John (the sons of Zebedee, but Jesus called them "Sons of Thunder"),
Andrew,
Philip,
Bartholomew,
Matthew,
Thomas,
James (the son of Alphaeus),
Thaddaeus,
Simon (a member of a political party advocating violent overthrow of the Roman government),
Judas Iscariot (who later betrayed him).

20 When he returned to the house where he was staying, the crowds began to gather again, and soon it was so full of visitors that he couldn't even find time to eat. 21 When his friends heard what was happening they came to try to take him home with them.

"He's out of his mind," they said.

22 But the Jewish teachers of religion who had arrived from Jerusalem said, "His trouble is that he's possessed by Satan, king of demons. That's why demons obey him."

23 Jesus summoned these men and asked them (using proverbs they all understood), "How can Satan cast out Satan? 24 A kingdom

Today's English Version

Jesus chooses the twelve apostles

13 Then Jesus went up a hill and called to himself the men he wanted. They came to him 14 and he chose twelve, whom he named apostles. "I have chosen you to be with me," he told them; "I will also send you out to preach, 15 and you will have authority to drive out demons."

16 These are the twelve he chose: Simon (Jesus gave him the name Peter); 17 James and his brother John, the sons of Zebedee (Jesus gave them the name Boanerges, which means "Men of Thunder"); 18 Andrew, Philip, Bartholomew, Matthew, Thomas, James, the son of Alphaeus, Thaddaeus, Simon the Patriot, 19 and Judas Iscariot, who betrayed Jesus.

Jesus and Beelzebul

20 Then Jesus went home. Again such a large crowd gathered that Jesus and his disciples had no time to eat. 21 When his family heard about this they set out to get him, because people were saying, "He's gone mad!"

22 Some teachers of the Law who had come from Jerusalem were saying, "He has Beelzebul in him!"

Others said, "It is the chief of the demons who gives him the power to drive them out."

23 So Jesus called the people to him and told them some parables: "How can Satan drive out Satan? 24 If a country divides itself into groups

New International Version

The appointing of the twelve apostles

13 Jesus went up into the hills and called to him those he wanted, and they came to him. 14 He appointed twelve—designating them apostles[h]—that they might be with him and that he might send them out to preach 15 and to have authority to drive out demons. 16 These are the twelve he appointed: Simon (to whom he gave the name Peter); 17 James son of Zebedee and his brother John (to them he gave the name Boanerges, which means Sons of Thunder); 18 Andrew, Philip, Bartholomew, Matthew, Thomas, James son of Alphaeus, Thaddaeus, Simon the Zealot, 19 and Judas Iscariot, who betrayed him.

Jesus and Beelzebub

20 Then Jesus entered a house, and again a crowd gathered, so that he and his disciples were not even able to eat. 21 When his family heard about this, they went to take charge of him, for they said, "He is out of his mind."

22 And the teachers of the law who came down from Jerusalem said, "He is possessed by Beelzebub! [i] By the prince of demons he is driving out demons."

23 So Jesus called them and spoke to them in parables: "How can Satan drive out Satan? 24 If a kingdom is divided against itself, that

[*h*] Some MSS omit *designating them apostles.* [*i*] Greek MSS *Beelzeboul* or *Beezeboul.*

Phillips Modern English

3.13 Jesus chooses the twelve apostles

Later he went up on to the hill-side and summoned the men whom he wanted, and they went up to him. He appointed a band of twelve to be his companions, whom he could send out to preach, with power to drive out evil spirits. These were the twelve he appointed:

Peter (which was the new name he gave Simon), James the son of Zebedee, and John his brother, (He gave them the name of Boanerges, which means the "Thunderers"); Andrew, Philip, Bartholomew, Matthew, Thomas, James the son of Alphaeus, Thaddaeus, Simon the Patriot, and Judas Iscariot, who betrayed him.

3.20 Jesus exposes an absurd accusation

Then he went indoors, but again such a crowd collected that it was impossible for them even to eat a meal. When his relatives heard of this, they set out to take charge of him, for people were saying, "He must be mad!"

The scribes who had come down from Jerusalem were saying that he was possessed by Beelzebub, and that he drove out devils because he was in league with the prince of devils. So Jesus called them to him and spoke to them in parables—

"How can Satan be the one who drives out Satan? If a kingdom is divided against itself,

Revised Standard Version

13 And he went up on the mountain, and
called to him those whom he desired; and they
came to him. 14 And he appointed twelve,[k] to
be with him, and to be sent out to preach 15 and
have authority to cast out demons: 16 Simon[x]
whom he surnamed Peter; 17 James the son of
Zebedee and John the brother of James, whom
he surnamed Boanerges, that is, sons of thunder;
18 Andrew, and Philip, and Bartholomew, and
Matthew, and Thomas, and James the son of
Alphaeus, and Thaddaeus, and Simon the Cananaean, 19 and Judas Iscariot, who betrayed him.
Then he went home; 20 and the crowd came
together again, so that they could not even eat.
21 And when his family heard it, they went out
to seize him, for people were saying, "He is
beside himself." 22 And the scribes who came
down from Jerusalem said, "He is possessed by
Beelzebul, and by the prince of demons he casts
out the demons." 23 And he called them to him,
and said to them in parables, "How can Satan
cast out Satan? 24 If a kingdom is divided

[k] Other ancient authorities add *whom also he named apostles.* [x] Other authorities read *demons.* 16 *So he appointed the twelve: Simon.*

Jerusalem Bible

The appointment of the Twelve

13 He now went up into the hills and summoned those he wanted. So they came to him
14 and he appointed twelve; they were to be his
companions and to be sent out to preach, 15 with
power to cast out devils. 16 And so he appointed
the Twelve: Simon to whom he gave the name
Peter, 17 James the son of Zebedee and John the
brother of James, to whom he gave the name
Boanerges or "Sons of Thunder"; 18 then Andrew, Philip, Bartholomew, Matthew, Thomas,
James the son of Alphaeus, Thaddaeus, Simon
the Zealot 19 and Judas Iscariot, the man who
was to betray him.

His relatives are concerned about Jesus

20 He went home again, and once more such
a crowd collected that they could not even have
a meal. 21 When his relatives heard of this, they
set out to take charge of him, convinced he was
out of his mind.

Allegations of the scribes

22 The scribes who had come down from
Jerusalem were saying, "Beelzebul is in him" and,
"It is through the prince of devils that he cast
devils out." 23 So he called them to him and
spoke to them in parables. "How can Satan cast
out Satan? 24 If a kingdom is divided against

New English Bible

He then went up into the hill-country and called the men he wanted; and they went and joined him. He appointed twelve as his companions, whom he would send out to proclaim the Gospel, with a commission to drive out devils. So he appointed the Twelve: to Simon he gave the name Peter; then came the sons of Zebedee, James and his brother John, to whom he gave the name Boanerges, Sons of Thunder; then Andrew and Philip and Bartholomew and Matthew and Thomas and James the son of Alphaeus and Thaddaeus and Simon, a member of the Zealot party, and Judas Iscariot, the man who betrayed him.

He entered a house; and once more such a crowd collected round them that they had no chance to eat. When his family heard of this, they set out to take charge of him; for people were saying that he was out of his mind.[a]

The doctors of the law, too, who had come down from Jerusalem, said, 'He is possessed by Beelzebub', and, 'He drives out devils by the prince of devils.' So he called them to come forward, and spoke to them in parables: 'How can Satan drive out Satan? If a kingdom is divided

[a] *Or* of him. 'He is out of his mind', they said.

King James Version

if a kingdom be divided against itself, that kingdom cannot stand. 25And if a house be divided against itself, that house cannot stand. 26And if Satan rise up against himself, and be divided, he cannot stand, but hath an end. 27 No man can enter into a strong man's house, and spoil his goods, except he will first bind the strong man; and then he will spoil his house. 28 Verily I say unto you, All sins shall be forgiven unto the sons of men, and blasphemies wherewith soever they shall blaspheme: 29 But he that shall blaspheme against the Holy Ghost hath never forgiveness, but is in danger of eternal damnation: 30 Because they said, He hath an unclean spirit.

31 There came then his brethren and his mother, and, standing without, sent unto him, calling him. 32And the multitude sat about him, and they said unto him, Behold, thy mother and thy brethren without seek for thee. 33And he answered them, saying, Who is my mother, or my brethren? 34And he looked round about on them which sat about him, and said, Behold my mother and my brethren! 35 For whosoever shall do the will of God, the same is my brother, and my sister, and mother.

Living Bible

divided against itself will collapse. 25A home filled with strife and division destroys itself. 26And if Satan is fighting against himself, how can he accomplish anything? He would never survive. 27 [Satan must be bound before his demons are cast out[c]], just as a strong man must be tied up before his house can be ransacked and his property robbed.

28 "I solemnly declare that any sin of man can be forgiven, even blasphemy against me; 29 but blasphemy against the Holy Spirit can never be forgiven. It is an eternal sin."

30 He told them this because they were saying he did his miracles by Satan's power [instead of acknowledging it was by the Holy Spirit's power[c]].

31, 32 Now his mother and brothers arrived at the crowded house where he was teaching, and they sent word for him to come out and talk with them. "Your mother and brothers are outside and want to see you," he was told.

33 He replied, "Who is my mother? Who are my brothers?" 34 Looking at those around him he said, "These are my mother and brothers! 35Anyone who does God's will is my brother, and my sister, and my mother."

[c] Implied.

Today's English Version

that fight each other, that country will fall apart. 25 If a family divides itself into groups that fight each other, that family will fall apart. 26 So if Satan's kingdom divides into groups, it cannot last, but will fall apart and come to an end.

27 "No one can break into a strong man's house and take away his belongings unless he ties up the strong man first; then he can plunder his house.

28 "Remember this! Men can be forgiven all their sins and all the evil things they may say. 29 But whoever says evil things against the Holy Spirit will never be forgiven, because he has committed an eternal sin." 30 (Jesus said this because some had said, "He has an evil spirit in him.")

Jesus' mother and brothers

31 Then Jesus' mother and brothers arrived. They stood outside the house and sent in a message, asking for him. 32A crowd was sitting around Jesus, and they told him, "Look, your mother and brothers are outside, and they want you."

33 Jesus answered, "Who is my mother? Who are my brothers?" 34 He looked over the people sitting around him and said, "Look! Here are my mother and my brothers! 35 Whoever does what God wants him to do is my brother, my sister, my mother."

New International Version

kingdom cannot stand. 25 If a house is divided against itself, that house cannot stand. 26And if Satan opposes himself and is divided, he cannot stand; his end has come. 27 In fact, no one can enter a strong man's house and carry off his possessions unless he first ties up the strong man. Then he can rob his house. 28 I tell you the truth, all the sins and blasphemies of men will be forgiven them. 29 But whoever blasphemes against the Holy Spirit will never be forgiven; he is guilty of an eternal sin."

30 He said this because they were saying, "He has an evil [j] spirit."

Jesus' mother and brothers

31 Then Jesus' mother and brothers arrived. Standing outside, they sent someone in to call him. 32A crowd was sitting around him, and they told him, "Your mother and brothers are outside looking for you."

33 "Who are my mother and my brothers?" he asked.

34 Then he looked at those seated in a circle around him and said, "Here are my mother and my brothers! 35 Whoever does God's will is my brother and sister and mother."

[j] Greek *unclean.*

Phillips Modern English

then that kingdom cannot last, and if a household is divided against itself, it cannot last either. And if Satan leads a rebellion against Satan then his ranks are split, he cannot survive and his end is near. No one can break into a strong man's house and steal his property, without first tying up the strong man hand and foot. But if he did that, he could ransack the whole house.

"Believe me, all men's sins can be forgiven and all their blasphemies. But there can never be any forgiveness for blasphemy against the Holy Spirit. That is an eternal sin."

He said this because they were saying, "He is in the power of an evil spirit."

3.31 The new relationships in the kingdom

Then his mother and his brothers arrived. They stood outside the house and sent a message asking him to come out to them. There was a crowd sitting round him when the message was brought telling him, "Your mother and your brothers are outside looking for you."

Jesus replied, "And who are really my mother and my brothers?"

And he looked round at the faces of those sitting in a circle about him.

"Look!" he said, "my mother and my brothers are here. Anyone who does the will of God is brother and sister and mother to me."

Revised Standard Version

against itself, that kingdom cannot stand. 25 And if a house is divided against itself, that house will not be able to stand. 26 And if Satan has risen up against himself and is divided, he cannot stand, but is coming to an end. 27 But no one can enter a strong man's house and plunder his goods, unless he first binds the strong man; then indeed he may plunder his house.

28 "Truly, I say to you, all sins will be forgiven the sons of men, and whatever blasphemies they utter; 29 but whoever blasphemes against the Holy Spirit never has forgiveness, but is guilty of an eternal sin"—30 for they had said, "He has an unclean spirit."

31 And his mother and his brothers came; and standing outside they sent to him and called him. 32 And a crowd was sitting about him; and they said to him, "Your mother and your brothers[l] are outside, asking for you." 33 And he replied, "Who are my mother and my brothers?" 34 And looking around on those who sat about him, he said, "Here are my mother and my brothers! 35 Whoever does the will of God is my brother, and sister, and mother."

[l] Other early authorities add *and your sisters.*

Jerusalem Bible

itself, that kingdom cannot last. 25 And if a household is divided against itself, that household can never stand. 26 Now if Satan has rebelled against himself and is divided, he cannot stand either—it is the end of him. 27 But no one can make his way into a strong man's house and burgle his property unless he has tied up the strong man first. Only then can he burgle his house.

28 "I tell you solemnly, all men's sins will be forgiven, and all their blasphemies; 29 but let anyone blaspheme against the Holy Spirit and he will never have forgiveness: he is guilty of an eternal sin." 30 This was because they were saying, "An unclean spirit is in him."

The true kinsmen of Jesus

31 His mother and brothers now arrived and, standing outside, sent in a message asking for him. 32 A crowd was sitting around him at the time the message was passed to him, "Your mother and brothers and sisters are outside asking for you." 33 He replied, "Who are my mother and my brothers?" 34 And looking around at those sitting in a circle about him, he said, "Here are my mother and my brothers. 35 Anyone who does the will of God, that person is my brother and sister and mother."

New English Bible

against itself, that kingdom cannot stand; if a household is divided against itself, that house will never stand; and if Satan is in rebellion against himself, he is divided and cannot stand; and that is the end of him.

'On the other hand, no one can break into a strong man's house and make off with his goods unless he has first tied the strong man up; then he can ransack the house.

'I tell you this: no sin, no slander, is beyond forgiveness for men; but whoever slanders the Holy Spirit can never be forgiven; he is guilty of eternal sin.' He said this because they had declared that he was possessed by an unclean spirit.

Then his mother and his brothers arrived, and remaining outside sent in a message asking him to come out to them. A crowd was sitting round and word was brought to him: 'Your mother and your brothers are outside asking for you.' He replied, 'Who is my mother? Who are my brothers?' And looking round at those who were sitting in the circle about him he said, 'Here are my mother and my brothers. Whoever does the will of God is my brother, my sister, my mother.'

King James Version

4 And he began again to teach by the sea
side: and there was gathered unto him a
great multitude, so that he entered into a ship,
and sat in the sea; and the whole multitude was
by the sea on the land. 2And he taught them
many things by parables, and said unto them in
his doctrine, 3 Hearken; Behold, there went out
a sower to sow: 4And it came to pass, as he
sowed, some fell by the way side, and the fowls
of the air came and devoured it up. 5And some
fell on stony ground, where it had not much
earth; and immediately it sprang up, because it
had no depth of earth: 6 But when the sun was
up, it was scorched; and because it had no root,
it withered away. 7And some fell among thorns,
and the thorns grew up, and choked it, and it
yielded no fruit. 8And other fell on good ground,
and did yield fruit that sprang up and increased,
and brought forth, some thirty, and some sixty,
and some a hundred. 9And he said unto them,
He that hath ears to hear, let him hear. 10And
when he was alone, they that were about him
with the twelve asked of him the parable. 11And
he said unto them, Unto you it is given to know
the mystery of the kingdom of God: but unto
them that are without, all *these* things are done

Living Bible

4 Once again an immense crowd gathered
around him on the beach as he was teaching,
so he got into a boat and sat down and talked
from there. 2 His usual method of teaching was
to tell the people stories. One of them went like
this:
3 "Listen! A farmer decided to sow some
grain. As he scattered it across his field, 4 some
of it fell on a path, and the birds came and
picked it off the hard ground and ate it.
5, 6 Some fell on thin soil with underlying rock.
It grew up quickly enough, but soon wilted beneath the hot sun and died because the roots
had no nourishment in the shallow soil. 7 Other
seeds fell among thorns that shot up and
crowded the young plants so that they produced
no grain. 8 But some of the seeds fell into good
soil and yielded thirty times as much as he had
planted—some of it even sixty or a hundred
times as much! 9 If you have ears, listen!"
10 Afterwards, when he was alone with the
Twelve and with his other disciples, they asked
him, "What does your story mean?"
11, 12 He replied, "You are permitted to know
some truths about the Kingdom of God that are
hidden to those outside the Kingdom:

Today's English Version

The parable of the sower

4 Again Jesus began to teach by Lake Galilee.
The crowd that gathered around him was so
large that he got into a boat and sat in it. The
boat was out in the water, while the crowd stood
on the shore, at the water's edge. 2 He used parables to teach them many things, and in his teaching said to them,
3 "Listen! There was a man who went out to
sow. 4As he scattered the seed in the field, some
of it fell along the path, and the birds came and
ate it up. 5 Some of it fell on rocky ground,
where there was little soil. The seeds soon
sprouted, because the soil wasn't deep. 6 Then
when the sun came up it burned the young
plants, and because the roots had not grown deep
enough the plants soon dried up. 7 Some of the
seed fell among thorns, which grew up and
choked the plants, and they didn't bear grain.
8 But some seeds fell in good soil, and the plants
sprouted, grew, and bore grain: some had thirty
grains, others sixty, and others one hundred."
9 And Jesus concluded, "Listen, then, if you
have ears to hear with!"

The purpose of the parables

10 When Jesus was alone, some of those who
had heard him came to him with the twelve disciples and asked him to explain the parables.
11 "You have been given the secret of the Kingdom of God," Jesus answered. "But the others,
who are on the outside, hear all things by means

New International Version

The parable of the sower

4 On another occasion Jesus began to teach
by the lake. The crowd that gathered
around him was so large that he got into a boat
and sat in it out on the lake, while all the people were along the shore at the water's edge.
2 He taught them many things by parables, and
in his teaching said: 3 "Listen! A farmer went
out to sow his seed. 4As he was scattering the
seed, some fell along the path, and the birds
came and ate it up. 5 Some fell on rocky places,
where it did not have much soil. It sprang up
quickly, because the soil was shallow. 6 But when
the sun came up, the plants were scorched, and
they withered because they had no root. 7 Other
seed fell among thorns, which grew up and
choked the plants, so that they did not bear
grain. 8 Still other seed fell on good soil. It
came up, grew and produced a crop, multiplying
thirty, sixty, or even a hundred times."
9 Then Jesus said, "He who has ears to hear,
let him hear."
10 When he was alone, the Twelve and the
others around him asked him about the parables.
11 He told them, "The secret of the kingdom of
God has been given to you. But to those on the

Phillips Modern English

4.1 The story of the sower

Then once again he began to teach them by the lake-side. A bigger crowd than ever collected around him so that he got into the small boat on the lake and sat down, while the crowd covered the ground right down to the water's edge. He taught them a great deal in parables, and in the course of his teaching he said,

"Listen! A man once went out to sow his seed and as he sowed, some seed fell by the roadside and the birds came and gobbled it up. Some of the seed fell among the rocks where there was not much soil, and sprang up very quickly because there was no depth of earth. But when the sun rose it was scorched, and because it had no root, it withered away. And some of the seed fell among thorn-bushes and the thorns grew up and choked the life out of it, and it bore no crop. And there was some seed which fell on good soil, and when it sprang up and grew, produced a crop which yielded thirty or sixty or even a hundred times as much as the seed."

Then he added,

"Every man who has ears should use them!"

Then when they were by themselves, his close followers and the twelve asked him about the parables, and he told them.

"The secret of the kingdom of God has been given to you. But to those who do not know the

Revised Standard Version

4 Again he began to teach beside the sea.
And a very large crowd gathered about him,
so that he got into a boat and sat in it on the
sea; and the whole crowd was beside the sea on
the land. 2 And he taught them many things in
parables, and in his teaching he said to them:
3 "Listen! A sower went out to sow. 4 And as he
sowed, some seed fell along the path, and the
birds came and devoured it. 5 Other seed fell
on rocky ground, where it had not much soil,
and immediately it sprang up, since it had no
depth of soil; 6 and when the sun rose it was
scorched, and since it had no root it withered
away. 7 Other seed fell among thorns and the
thorns grew up and choked it, and it yielded no
grain. 8 And other seeds fell into good soil and
brought forth grain, growing up and increasing
and yielding thirtyfold and sixtyfold and a hundredfold." 9 And he said, "He who has ears to
hear, let him hear."
10 And when he was alone, those who were
about him with the twelve asked him concerning the parables. 11 And he said to them, "To you
has been given the secret of the kingdom of God,
but for those outside everything is in parables;

Jerusalem Bible

Parable of the sower

4 Again he began to teach by the lakeside,
but such a huge crowd gathered around him
that he got into a boat on the lake and sat there.
The people were all along the shore, at the
water's edge. 2 He taught them many things in
parables, and in the course of his teaching he
said to them, 3 "Listen! Imagine a sower going
out to sow. 4 Now it happened that, as he sowed,
some of the seed fell on the edge of the path,
and the birds came and ate it up. 5 Some seed
fell on rocky ground where it found little soil
and sprang up straightaway, because there was
no depth of earth; 6 and when the sun came up
it was scorched and, not having any roots, it
withered away. 7 Some seed fell into thorns, and
the thorns grew up and choked it, and it produced no crop. 8 And some seeds fell into rich
soil and, growing tall and strong, produced crop;
and yielded thirty, sixty, even a hundredfold."
9 And he said, "Listen, anyone who has ears to
hear!"

Why Jesus speaks in parables

10 When he was alone, the Twelve, together
with the others who formed his company, asked
what the parables meant. 11 He told them, "The
secret of the kingdom of God is given to you,
but to those who are outside everything comes

New English Bible

4 On another occasion he began to teach by the lake-side. The crowd that gathered round him was so large that he had to get into a boat on the lake, and there he sat, with the whole crowd on the beach right down to the water's edge. And he taught them many things by parables.

As he taught he said:

'Listen! A sower went out to sow. And it happened that as he sowed, some seed fell along the footpath; and the birds came and ate it up. Some seed fell on rocky ground, where it had little soil, and it sprouted quickly because it had no depth of earth; but when the sun rose the young corn was scorched, and as it had no root it withered away. Some seed fell among thistles; and the thistles shot up and choked the corn, and it yielded no crop. And some of the seed fell into good soil, where it came up and grew, and bore fruit; and the yield was thirtyfold, sixtyfold, even a hundredfold.' He added, 'If you have ears to hear, then hear.'

When he was alone, the Twelve and others who were round him questioned him about the parables. He replied, 'To you the secret of the kingdom of God has been given; but to those who are outside everything comes by way of

King James Version

in parables: 12 That seeing they may see, and
not perceive; and hearing they may hear, and
not understand; lest at any time they should be
converted, and *their* sins should be forgiven
them. 13 And he said unto them, Know ye not
this parable? and how then will ye know all
parables?

14 The sower soweth the word. 15 And these
are they by the way side, where the word is
sown; but when they have heard, Satan cometh
immediately, and taketh away the word that was
sown in their hearts. 16 And these are they likewise which are sown on stony ground; who,
when they have heard the word, immediately receive it with gladness; 17 And have no root in
themselves, and so endure but for a time: afterward, when affliction or persecution ariseth for
the word's sake, immediately they are offended.
18 And these are they which are sown among
thorns; such as hear the word, 19 And the cares
of this world, and the deceitfulness of riches,
and the lusts of other things entering in, choke
the word, and it becometh unfruitful. 20 And
these are they which are sown on good ground;
such as hear the word, and receive *it,* and bring
forth fruit, some thirtyfold, some sixty, and some
a hundred.

Living Bible

'Though they see and hear, they will not understand or turn to God, or be forgiven for
their sins.'
13 But if you can't understand *this* simple illustration, what will you do about all the others I
am going to tell?

14 "The farmer I talked about is anyone
who brings God's message to others, trying to
plant good seed within their lives. 15 The hard
pathway, where some of the seed fell, represents
the hard hearts of some of those who hear God's
message; Satan comes at once to try to make
them forget it. 16 The rocky soil represents the
hearts of those who hear the message with joy,
17 but, like young plants in such soil, their roots
don't go very deep, and though at first they get
along fine, as soon as persecution begins, they
wilt.

18 "The thorny ground represents the hearts
of people who listen to the Good News and receive it, 19 but all too quickly the attractions of
this world and the delights of wealth, and the
search for success and lure of nice things come
in and crowd out God's message from their
hearts, so that no crop is produced.

20 "But the good soil represents the hearts of
those who truly accept God's message and produce a plentiful harvest for God—thirty, sixty,
or even a hundred times as much as was planted

Today's English Version

of parables, 12 so that,

'They may look and look, yet not see,
they may listen and listen, yet not understand;
for if they did, they would turn to God
and he would forgive them.' "

Jesus explains the parable of the sower

13 Then Jesus asked them, "Don't you understand this parable? How, then, will you ever
understand any parable? 14 The sower sows
God's message. 15 Sometimes the message falls
along the path; these people hear it, but as soon
as they hear it Satan comes and takes away the
message sown in them. 16 Other people are like
the seeds that fall on rocky ground. As soon as
they hear the message they receive it gladly.
17 But it does not sink deep into them, and they
don't last long. So when trouble or persecution
comes because of the message, they give up at
once. 18 Other people are like the seeds sown
among the thorns. These are the ones who hear
the message, 19 but the worries about this life,
the love for riches, and all other kinds of desires
crowd in and choke the message, and they don't
bear fruit. 20 But other people are like the seeds
sown in good soil. They hear the message, accept it, and bear fruit: some thirty, some sixty,
and some one hundred."

New International Version

outside everything is said in parables 12 so that,
'they may be ever seeing but never perceiving,
and ever hearing but never understanding;
otherwise they might turn and be forgiven!' [k] "
13 Then Jesus said to them, "Don't you understand this parable? How then will you understand any parable? 14 The farmer sows the
word. 15 Some people are like seed along the
path, where the word is sown. As soon as they
hear it, Satan comes and takes away the word
that was sown in them. 16 Others, like seed
sown on rocky places, hear the word and at
once receive it with joy. 17 But since they have
no root, they last only a short time. When trouble or persecution comes because of the word,
they quickly fall away. 18 Still others, like seed
sown among thorns, hear the word; 19 but the
worries of this life, the deceitfulness of wealth
and the desires for other things come in and
choke the word, making it unfruitful. 20 Others,
like seed sown on good soil, hear the word, accept it, and produce a crop—thirty, sixty, or
even a hundred times what was sown."

[*k*] Isaiah 6:9,10.

Phillips Modern English

secret, everything remains in parables, so that,

> Seeing they may see, and not perceive;
> and hearing they may hear, and not understand;
> lest haply they should turn again, and it should be forgiven them."

Then he continued,

"Do you really not understand this parable? Then how are you going to understand all the other parables? The man who sows, sows the message. As for those who are by the roadside where the message is sown, as soon as they hear it Satan comes at once and takes away what has been sown in their minds. Similarly, the seed sown among the rocks represents those who hear the message without hesitation and accept it joyfully. But they have no real roots and do not last—when trouble or persecution arises because of the message, they give up their faith at once. Then there are the seeds which were sown among thorn-bushes. These are the people who hear the message, but the worries of this world and the false glamour of riches and all sorts of other ambitions creep in and choke the life out of what they have heard, and it produces no crop in their lives. As for the seed sown on good soil, this means the men who hear the message and accept it and do produce a crop—thirty, sixty, even a hundred times as much as they received."

Revised Standard Version

12 so that they may indeed see but not perceive,
and may indeed hear but not understand; lest
they should turn again, and be forgiven." 13 And
he said to them, "Do you not understand this
parable? How then will you understand all the
parables? 14 The sower sows the word. 15 And
these are the ones along the path, where the
word is sown; when they hear, Satan immediately comes and takes away the word which is
sown in them. 16 And these in like manner are
the ones sown upon rocky ground, who, when
they hear the word, immediately receive it with
joy; 17 and they have no root in themselves, but
endure for a while; then, when tribulation or
persecution arises on account of the word, immediately they fall away.[m] 18 And others are the
ones sown among thorns; they are those who
hear the word, 19 but the cares of the world, and
the delight in riches, and the desire for other
things, enter in and choke the word, and it
proves unfruitful. 20 But those that were sown
upon the good soil are the ones who hear the
word and accept it and bear fruit, thirtyfold
and sixtyfold and a hundredfold."

[m] Or *stumble*.

Jerusalem Bible

in parables, 12 so that *they may see and see
again, but not perceive; may hear and hear
again, but not understand; otherwise they might
be converted and be forgiven.*"[e]

The parable of the sower explained

13 He said to them, "Do you not understand
this parable? Then how will you understand any
of the parables? 14 What the sower is sowing is
the word. 15 Those on the edge of the path
where the word is sown are people who have no
sooner heard it than Satan comes and carries
away the word that was sown in them. 16 Similarly, those who receive the seed on patches of
rock are people who, when first they hear the
word, welcome it at once with joy. 17 But they
have no root in them, they do not last; should
some trial come, or some persecution on account
of the word, they fall away at once. 18 Then
there are others who receive the seed in thorns.
These have heard the word, 19 but the worries
of this world, the lure of riches and all the other
passions come in to choke the word, and so it
produces nothing. 20 And there are those who
have received the seed in rich soil: they hear the
word and accept it and yield a harvest, thirty and
sixty and a hundredfold."

[e] Is. 6:9-10.

New English Bible

parables, so that (as Scripture says) they may look and look, but see nothing; they may hear and hear, but understand nothing; otherwise they might turn to God and be forgiven.'

So he said, 'You do not understand this parable? How then are you to understand any parable? The sower sows the word. Those along the footpath are people in whom the word is sown, but no sooner have they heard it than Satan comes and carries off the word which has been sown in them. It is the same with those who receive the seed on rocky ground; as soon as they hear the word, they accept it with joy, but it strikes no root in them; they have no staying-power; then, when there is trouble or persecution on account of the word, they fall away at once. Others again receive the seed among thistles; they hear the word, but worldly cares and the false glamour of wealth and all kinds of evil desire come in and choke the word, and it proves barren. And there are those who receive the seed in good soil; they hear the word and welcome it; and they bear fruit thirtyfold, sixtyfold, or a hundredfold.'.

King James Version

21 And he said unto them, Is a candle brought to be put under a bushel, or under a bed? and not to be set on a candlestick? 22 For there is nothing hid, which shall not be manifested; neither was any thing kept secret, but that it should come abroad. 23 If any man have ears to hear, let him hear. 24And he said unto them, Take heed what ye hear. With what measure ye mete, it shall be measured to you; and unto you that hear shall more be given. 25 For he that hath, to him shall be given; and he that hath not, from him shall be taken even that which he hath.

26 And he said, So is the kingdom of God, as if a man should cast seed into the ground; 27And should sleep, and rise night and day, and the seed should spring and grow up, he knoweth not how. 28 For the earth bringeth forth fruit of herself; first the blade, then the ear, after that the full corn in the ear. 29 But when the fruit is brought forth, immediately he putteth in the sickle, because the harvest is come.

Living Bible

in their hearts." 21 Then he asked them, "When someone lights a lamp, does he put a box over it to shut out the light? Of course not! The light couldn't be seen or used. A lamp is placed on a stand to shine and be useful.

22 "All that is now hidden will someday come to light. 23 If you have ears, listen! 24And be sure to put into practice what you hear. The more you do this, the more you will understand what I tell you. 25 To him who has shall be given; from him who has not shall be taken away even what he has.

26 "Here is another story illustrating what the Kingdom of God is like:

"A farmer sowed his field, 27 and went away, and as the days went by, the seeds grew and grew without his help. 28 For the soil made the seeds grow. First a leaf-blade pushed through, and later the wheat-heads formed and finally the grain ripened, 29 and then the farmer came at once with his sickle and harvested it."

Today's English Version

A lamp under a bowl

21 Jesus continued, "Does anyone ever bring in a lamp and put it under a bowl or under the bed? Doesn't he put it on the lampstand? 22 Whatever is hidden away will be brought out into the open, and whatever is covered up will be uncovered. 23 Listen, then, if you have ears to hear with!"

24 He also said to them, "Pay attention to what you hear! The same rules you use to judge others will be used by God to judge you—but with even greater severity. 25 The man who has something will be given more; the man who has nothing will have taken away from him even the little he has."

The parable of the growing seed

26 Jesus went on to say, "The Kingdom of God is like a man who scatters seed in his field. 27 He sleeps at night, is up and about during the day, and all the while the seeds are sprouting and growing. Yet he does not know how it happens. 28 The soil itself makes the plants grow and bear fruit: first the tender stalk appears, then the head, and finally the head full of grain. 29 When the grain is ripe the man starts working with his sickle, because harvest time has come."

New International Version

A lamp on a stand

21 He said to them, "Do you bring in a lamp to put it under a bowl or a bed? Instead, don't you put it on its stand? 22 For whatever is hidden is meant to be disclosed, and whatever is concealed is meant to be brought out into the open. 23 If anyone has ears to hear, let him hear."

24 "Consider carefully what you hear," he continued. "With the measure you use it will be measured to you—and even more. 25 Whoever has will be given more; whoever does not have, even what he has will be taken from him."

The parable of the growing seed

26 He also said, "This is what the kingdom of God is like. A man scatters seed on the ground. 27 Night and day, whether he sleeps or gets up, the seed sprouts and grows, though he does not know how. 28All by itself the soil produces grain —first the stalk, then the head, then the full kernel in the head. 29As soon as the grain is ripe, he puts the sickle to it, because the harvest has come."

Phillips Modern English

4.21 *Truth is meant to be used*

Then he said to them,

"Is a lamp brought into the room to be put under a bucket or underneath the bed? Surely its place is on the lamp-stand! There is nothing hidden which is not meant to be made perfectly plain one day, and there are no secrets which are not meant one day to be common knowledge. If a man has ears he should use them!

"Pay attention to what you hear," he said to them. "Whatever measure you use will be used towards you, and even more than that. For the man who has something will receive more. As for the man who has nothing, even his 'nothing' will be taken away."

4.26 *Jesus gives pictures of the kingdom's growth*

Then he said,

"The kingdom of God is like a man scattering seed on the ground and then going to bed each night and getting up every morning, while the seed sprouts and grows up, though he has no idea how it happens. The earth produces a crop without any help from anyone: first a blade, then the ear of corn, then the full-grown grain in the ear. And as soon as the crop is ready, he sends the reapers in without delay, for the harvest-time has come."

Revised Standard Version

21 And he said to them, "Is a lamp brought
in to be put under a bushel, or under a bed, and
not on a stand? 22 For there is nothing hid, except to be made manifest; nor is anything secret, except to come to light. 23 If any man has
ears to hear, let him hear." 24 And he said to
them, "Take heed what you hear; the measure
you give will be the measure you get, and still
more will be given you. 25 For to him who has
will more be given; and from him who has not,
even what he has will be taken away."
26 And he said, "The kingdom of God is as
if a man should scatter seed upon the ground,
27 and should sleep and rise night and day, and
the seed should sprout and grow, he knows not
how. 28 The earth produces of itself, first the
blade, then the ear, then the full grain in the ear.
29 But when the grain is ripe, at once he puts in
the sickle, because the harvest has come."

Jerusalem Bible

Parable of the lamp

21 He also said to them, "Would you bring
in a lamp to put it under a tub or under the bed?
Surely you will put it on the lampstand? 22 For
there is nothing hidden but it must be disclosed,
nothing kept secret except to be brought to light.
23 If anyone has ears to hear, let him listen to
this."

Parable of the measure

24 He also said to them, "Take notice of what
you are hearing. The amount you measure out
is the amount you will be given—and more besides; 25 for the man who has will be given more;
from the man who has not, even what he has
will be taken away."

Parable of the seed growing by itself

26 He also said, "This is what the kingdom of
God is like. A man throws seed on the land.
27 Night and day, while he sleeps, when he is
awake, the seed is sprouting and growing; how,
he does not know. 28 Of its own accord the land
produces first the shoot, then the ear, then the
full grain in the ear. 29 And when the crop is
ready, he loses no time: he starts to reap because
the harvest has come."

New English Bible

He said to them, 'Do you bring in the lamp to put it under the meal-tub, or under the bed? Surely it is brought to be set on the lamp-stand. For nothing is hidden unless it is to be disclosed, and nothing put under cover unless it is to come into the open. If you have ears to hear, then hear.'

He also said, 'Take note of what you hear; the measure you give is the measure you will receive, with something more besides. For the man who has will be given more, and the man who has not will forfeit even what he has.'

He said, 'The kingdom of God is like this. A man scatters seed on the land; he goes to bed at night and gets up in the morning, and the seed sprouts and grows—how, he does not know. The ground produces a crop by itself, first the blade, then the ear, then full-grown corn in the ear; but as soon as the crop is ripe, he plies the sickle, because harvest-time has come.'

King James Version

30 And he said, Whereunto shall we liken the
kingdom of God? or with what comparison
shall we compare it? 31 *It is* like a grain of mustard seed, which, when it is sown in the earth, is
less than all the seeds that be in the earth:
32 But when it is sown, it groweth up, and becometh greater than all herbs, and shooteth out
great branches; so that the fowls of the air may
lodge under the shadow of it. 33And with many
such parables spake he the word unto them, as
they were able to hear *it*. 34 But without a parable spake he not unto them: and when they
were alone, he expounded all things to his disciples. 35And the same day, when the even was
come, he saith unto them, Let us pass over unto
the other side. 36And when they had sent away
the multitude, they took him even as he was in
the ship. And there were also with him other
little ships. 37And there arose a great storm of
wind, and the waves beat into the ship, so that
it was now full. 38And he was in the hinder part
of the ship, asleep on a pillow: and they awake
him, and say unto him, Master, carest thou not
that we perish? 39And he arose, and rebuked the

Living Bible

30 Jesus asked, "How can I describe the Kingdom of God? What story shall I use to illustrate
it? 31, 32 It is like a tiny mustard seed! Though
this is one of the smallest of seeds, yet it grows
to become one of the largest of plants, with long
branches where birds can build their nests and
be sheltered."
33 He used many such illustrations to teach
the people as much as they were ready to understand.[a] 34 In fact, he taught only by illustrations
in his public teaching, but afterwards, when he
was alone with his disciples, he would explain
his meaning to them.
35 As evening fell, Jesus said to his disciples,
"Let's cross to the other side of the lake." 36 So
they took him just as he was and started out,
leaving the crowds behind (though other boats
followed). 37 But soon a terrible storm arose.
High waves began to break into the boat until it
was nearly full of water and about to sink.
38 Jesus was asleep at the back of the boat with
his head on a cushion. Frantically they wakened
him, shouting, "Teacher, don't you even care
that we are all about to drown?"
39 Then he rebuked the wind and said to the

[*a*] Literally, "as they were able to hear."

Today's English Version

The parable of the mustard seed

30 "What shall we say the Kingdom of God
is like?" asked Jesus. "What parable shall we
use to explain it? 31 It is like a mustard seed, the
smallest seed in the world. A man takes it and
plants it in the ground; 32 after a while it grows
up and becomes the biggest of all plants. It puts
out such large branches that the birds come and
make their nests in its shade."
33 Jesus preached his message to the people,
using many other parables like these; he told
them as much as they could understand. 34 He
would not speak to them without using parables;
but when he was alone with his disciples he would
explain everything to them.

Jesus calms a storm

35 On the evening of that same day Jesus
said to his disciples, "Let us go across to the
other side of the lake." 36 So they left the crowd;
the disciples got into the boat that Jesus was already in, and took him with them. Other boats
were there too. 37A very strong wind blew up
and the waves began to spill over into the boat,
so that it was about to fill with water. 38 Jesus
was in the back of the boat, sleeping with his
head on a pillow. The disciples woke him up and
said, "Teacher, don't you care that we are about
to die?"
39 Jesus got up and commanded the wind,

New International Version

The parable of the mustard seed

30 Again he said, "What shall we say the
kingdom of God is like, or what parable shall
we use to describe it? 31 It is like a mustard
seed, which is the smallest seed you plant in
the ground. 32 Yet when planted, it grows and
becomes the largest of all garden plants, with
such big branches that the birds of the air can
perch in its shade."
33 With many similar parables Jesus spoke
the word to them, as much as they could understand. 34 He did not say anything to them without using a parable. But when he was alone with
his own disciples, he explained everything.

Jesus calms the storm

35 That day when evening came, he said to
his disciples, "Let's go over to the other side."
36 Leaving the crowd behind, they took him
along, just as he was, in the boat. There were
also other boats with him. 37A furious squall
came up, and the waves broke over the boat, so
that it was nearly swamped. 38 Jesus was in the
stern, sleeping on a cushion. The disciples woke
him and said to him, "Teacher, don't you care
if we drown?"
39 He got up, rebuked the wind and said to

Phillips Modern English

Then he continued,
"What can we say the kingdom of God is like? How shall we put it in a parable? It is like a tiny grain of mustard-seed which, when it is sown, is smaller than any seed that is ever sown. But after it is sown in the earth, it grows up and becomes bigger than any other plant. It shoots out great branches so that birds can come and nest in its shelter."

So he taught them his message with many parables like these, as far as their minds could understand it. He did not speak to them at all without using parables, although in private he explained everything to his disciples.

4.35 Jesus shows himself master of natural forces

On the evening of that day, he said to them, "Let us cross over to the other side of the lake."

So they sent the crowd home and took him with them in the small boat in which he had been sitting, accompanied by other small craft. Then came a violent squall of wind which drove the waves aboard the boat until it was almost swamped. Jesus was in the stern asleep on the cushion. They awoke him with the words,
"Master, don't you care that we're drowning?"
And he woke up, rebuked the wind, and said to the waves,

Revised Standard Version

30 And he said, "With what can we compare the kingdom of God, or what parable shall we use for it? 31 It is like a grain of mustard seed, which, when sown upon the ground, is the smallest of all the seeds on earth; 32 yet when it is sown it grows up and becomes the greatest of all shrubs, and puts forth large branches, so that the birds of the air can make nests in its shade."
33 With many such parables he spoke the word to them, as they were able to hear it; 34 he did not speak to them without a parable, but privately to his own disciples he explained everything.
35 On that day, when evening had come, he said to them, "Let us go across to the other side." 36 And leaving the crowd, they took him with them in the boat, just as he was. And other boats were with him. 37 And a great storm of wind arose, and the waves beat into the boat, so that the boat was already filling. 38 But he was in the stern, asleep on the cushion; and they woke him and said to him, "Teacher, do you not care if we perish?" 39 And he awoke and

Jerusalem Bible

Parable of the mustard seed

30 He also said, "What can we say the kingdom of God is like? What parable can we find for it? 31 It is like a mustard seed which at the time of its sowing in the soil is the smallest of all the seeds on earth; 32 yet once it is sown it grows into the biggest shrub of them all and puts out big branches so that the birds of the air can shelter in its shade."

The use of parables

33 Using many parables like these, he spoke the word to them, so far as they were capable of understanding it. 34 He would not speak to them except in parables, but he explained everything to his disciples when they were alone.

The calming of the storm

35 With the coming of evening that same day, he said to them, "Let us cross over to the other side." 36 And leaving the crowd behind they took him, just as he was, in the boat; and there were other boats with him. 37 Then it began to blow a gale and the waves were breaking into the boat so that it was almost swamped. 38 But he was in the stern, his head on the cushion, asleep. 39 They woke him and said to him, "Master, do you not care? We are going down!" And he woke up and rebuked the wind and said to the

New English Bible

He said also, 'How shall we picture the kingdom of God, or by what parable shall we describe it? It is like the mustard-seed, which is smaller than any seed in the ground at its sowing. But once sown, it springs up and grows taller than any other plant, and forms branches so large that the birds can settle in its shade.'

With many such parables he would give them his message, so far as they were able to receive it. He never spoke to them except in parables; but privately to his disciples he explained everything.

Miracles of Christ

That day, in the evening, he said to them, 'Let us cross over to the other side of the lake.' So they left the crowd and took him with them in the boat where he had been sitting; and there were other boats accompanying him. A heavy squall came on and the waves broke over the boat until it was all but swamped. Now he was in the stern asleep on a cushion; they roused him and said, 'Master, we are sinking! Do you not care?' He awoke, rebuked the wind, and

King James Version

wind, and said unto the sea, Peace, be still. And the wind ceased, and there was a great calm. 40 And he said unto them, Why are ye so fearful? how is it that ye have no faith? 41 And they feared exceedingly, and said one to another, What manner of man is this, that even the wind and the sea obey him?

5 And they came over unto the other side of the sea, into the country of the Gadarenes. 2 And when he was come out of the ship, immediately there met him out of the tombs a man with an unclean spirit, 3 Who had *his* dwelling among the tombs; and no man could bind him, no, not with chains: 4 Because that he had been often bound with fetters and chains, and the chains had been plucked asunder by him, and the fetters broken in pieces: neither could any *man* tame him. 5 And always, night and day, he was in the mountains, and in the tombs, crying, and cutting himself with stones. 6 But when he saw Jesus afar off, he ran and worshipped him, 7 And cried with a loud voice, and said, What have I to do with thee, Jesus, *thou* Son of the most high God? I adjure thee by God, that thou torment me not. 8 (For he said unto him, Come

Living Bible

sea, "Quiet down!" And the wind fell, and there was a great calm!

40 And he asked them, "Why were you so fearful? Don't you even yet have confidence in me?"

41 And they were filled with awe and said among themselves, "Who is this man, that even the winds and seas obey him?"

5 When they arrived at the other side of the lake a demon-possessed man ran out from a graveyard, just as Jesus was climbing from the boat.

3, 4 This man lived among the gravestones, and had such strength that whenever he was put into handcuffs and shackles—as he often was—he snapped the handcuffs from his wrists and smashed the shackles and walked away. No one was strong enough to control him. 5 All day long and through the night he would wander among the tombs and in the wild hills, screaming and cutting himself with sharp pieces of stone.

6 When Jesus was still far out on the water, the man had seen him and had run to meet him, and fell down before him.

7, 8 Then Jesus spoke to the demon within the man and said, "Come out, you evil spirit."

It gave a terrible scream, shrieking, "What are you going to do to me, Jesus, Son of the Most High God? For God's sake, don't torture me!"

Today's English Version

"Be quiet!" and said to the waves, "Be still!" The wind died down, and there was a great calm. 40 Then Jesus said to his disciples, "Why are you frightened? Are you still without faith?"

41 But they were terribly afraid, and began to say to each other, "Who is this man? Even the wind and the waves obey him!"

Jesus heals a man with evil spirits

5 They arrived on the other side of Lake Galilee, at the territory of the Gerasenes. 2 As soon as Jesus got out of the boat he was met by a man who came out of the burial caves. 3 This man had an evil spirit in him and lived among the graves. Nobody could keep him tied with chains any more; 4 many times his feet and hands had been tied, but every time he broke the chains, and smashed the irons on his feet. He was too strong for anyone to stop him. 5 Day and night he wandered among the graves and through the hills, screaming and cutting himself with stones.

6 He was some distance away when he saw Jesus; so he ran, fell on his knees before him, 7 and screamed in a loud voice, "Jesus, Son of the Most High God! What do you want with me? For God's sake, I beg you, don't punish me!" 8 (He said this because Jesus was saying to him, "Evil spirit, come out of this man!")

New International Version

the waves, "Quiet! Be still!" Then the wind died down and it was completely calm.

40 He said to his disciples, "Why are you so afraid? Have you still no faith?"

41 They were terrified and asked each other, "Who is this? Even the wind and the waves obey him!"

The healing of a demon-possessed man

5 They went across the lake to the region of the Gerasenes.[l] 2 When Jesus got out of the boat, a man with an evil [m] spirit came from the tombs to meet him. 3 This man lived in the tombs, and no one could bind him any more, not even with a chain. 4 For he had often been chained hand and foot, but he tore the chains apart and broke the irons on his feet. No one was strong enough to subdue him. 5 Night and day among the tombs and in the hills he would cry out and cut himself with stones.

6 When he saw Jesus from a distance, he ran and fell on his knees in front of him. 7 He shouted at the top of his voice, "What do you want with me, Jesus, Son of the Most High God? Swear to God that you won't torture me!" 8 For Jesus was saying to him, "Come out of this man, you evil [m] spirit!"

[*l*] Some MSS read *Gadarenes;* others read *Gergesenes.* [*m*] Greek *unclean.*

Phillips Modern English

"Hush now! be still!"

The wind dropped and there was a dead calm.

"Why are you so frightened? Do you not trust me even yet?" he asked them.

But sheer awe swept over them, and they kept saying to each other,

"Who ever can he be?—even the wind and the waves do what he tells them!"

5.1 Jesus meets a violent lunatic

So they arrived on the other side of the lake in the country of the Gerasenes. As Jesus was getting out of the boat, a man in the grip of an evil spirit rushed out to meet him from among the tombs where he was living. It was no longer possible for any human being to restrain him even with a chain. Indeed he had frequently been secured with fetters and lengths of chain, but he had simply snapped the chains and broken the fetters in pieces. No one could do anything with him. All through the night as well as in the day-time he screamed among the tombs and on the hill-side, and cut himself with stones. Now, as soon as he saw Jesus in the distance, he ran and knelt before him, yelling at the top of his voice,

"What have you got to do with me, Jesus, Son of the Most High God? For God's sake, don't torture me!"

For Jesus had already said, "Come out of this man, you evil spirit!"

Revised Standard Version

rebuked the wind, and said to the sea, "Peace!
Be still!" And the wind ceased, and there was a
great calm. 40 He said to them, "Why are you
afraid? Have you no faith?" 41 And they were
filled with awe, and said to one another, "Who
then is this, that even wind and sea obey him?"

5 They came to the other side of the sea, to
the country of the Gerasenes.[n] 2 And when
he had come out of the boat, there met him out
of the tombs a man with an unclean spirit, 3 who
lived among the tombs; and no one could bind
him any more, even with a chain; 4 for he had
often been bound with fetters and chains, but
the chains he wrenched apart, and the fetters
he broke in pieces; and no one had the strength
to subdue him. 5 Night and day among the
tombs and on the mountains he was always crying out, and bruising himself with stones. 6 And
when he saw Jesus from afar, he ran and worshiped him; 7 and crying out with a loud voice,
he said, "What have you to do with me, Jesus,
Son of the Most High God? I adjure you by
God, do not torment me." 8 For he had said to
him, "Come out of the man, you unclean spirit!"

[*n*] Other ancient authorities read *Gergesenes,* some *Gadarenes.*

Jerusalem Bible

sea, "Quiet now! Be calm!" And the wind
dropped, and all was calm again. 40 Then he said
to them, "Why are you so frightened? How is it
that you have no faith?" 41 They were filled with
awe and said to one another, "Who can this
be? Even the wind and the sea obey him."

The Gerasene demoniac

5 They reached the country of the Gerasenes[f]
on the other side of the lake, 2 and no sooner
had he left the boat than a man with an unclean
spirit came out from the tombs toward him.
3 The man lived in the tombs and no one could
secure him any more, even with a chain; 4 because he had often been secured with fetters and
chains but had snapped the chains and broken
the fetters, and no one had the strength to control him. 5 All night and all day, among the
tombs and in the mountains, he would howl and
gash himself with stones. 6 Catching sight of
Jesus from a distance, he ran up and fell at his
feet 7 and shouted at the top of his voice, "What
do you want with me, Jesus, son of the Most
High God? Swear by God you will not torture
me!" 8—For Jesus had been saying to him,

[*f*] "Gadarenes" in some versions.

New English Bible

said to the sea, 'Hush! Be still!' The wind dropped and there was a dead calm. He said to them, 'Why are you such cowards? Have you no faith even now?' They were awestruck and said to one another, 'Who can this be? Even the wind and the sea obey him.'

5 So they came to the other side of the lake, into the country of the Gerasenes. As he stepped ashore, a man possessed by an unclean spirit came up to him from among the tombs where he had his dwelling. He could no longer be controlled; even chains were useless; he had often been fettered and chained up, but he had snapped his chains and broken the fetters. No one was strong enough to master him. And so, unceasingly, night and day, he would cry aloud among the tombs and on the hill-sides and cut himself with stones. When he saw Jesus in the distance, he ran and flung himself down before him, shouting loudly, 'What do you want with me, Jesus, son of the Most High God? In God's name do not torment me.' (For Jesus was already saying to him, 'Out, unclean spirit, come

King James Version

out of the man, *thou* unclean spirit.) 9 And he
asked him, What *is* thy name? And he answered,
saying, My name *is* Legion: for we are many.
10 And he besought him much that he would not
send them away out of the country. 11 Now
there was there nigh unto the mountains a great
herd of swine feeding. 12 And all the devils besought him, saying, Send us into the swine, that
we may enter into them. 13 And forthwith Jesus
gave them leave. And the unclean spirits went
out, and entered into the swine; and the herd
ran violently down a steep place into the sea,
(they were about two thousand,) and were
choked in the sea. 14 And they that fed the swine
fled, and told *it* in the city, and in the country.
And they went out to see what it was that was
done. 15 And they come to Jesus, and see him
that was possessed with the devil, and had the legion, sitting, and clothed, and in his right mind;
and they were afraid. 16 And they that saw *it* told
them how it befell to him that was possessed
with the devil, and *also* concerning the swine.
17 And they began to pray him to depart out of
their coasts. 18 And when he was come into the
ship, he that had been possessed with the devil
prayed him that he might be with him. 19 Howbeit Jesus suffered him not, but saith unto him,
Go home to thy friends, and tell them how
great things the Lord hath done for thee, and
hath had compassion on thee. 20 And he departed, and began to publish in Decapolis how
great things Jesus had done for him: and all

Living Bible

9 "What is your name?" Jesus asked, and the
demon replied, "Legion, for there are many of
us here within this man."

10 Then the demons begged him again and
again not to send them to some distant land.

11 Now as it happened there was a huge herd
of hogs rooting around on the hill above the
lake. 12 "Send us into those hogs," the demons
begged.

13 And Jesus gave them permission. Then the
evil spirits came out of the man and entered the
hogs, and the entire herd plunged down the
steep hillside into the lake and drowned.

14 The herdsmen fled to the nearby towns
and countryside, spreading the news as they ran.
Everyone rushed out to see for themselves.
15 And a large crowd soon gathered where Jesus
was; but as they saw the man sitting there, fully
clothed and perfectly sane, they were frightened.
16 Those who saw what happened were telling
everyone about it, 17 and the crowd began pleading with Jesus to go away and leave them alone!
18 So he got back into the boat. The man who
had been possessed by the demons begged Jesus
to let him go along. 19 But Jesus said no.

"Go home to your friends," he told him,
"and tell them what wonderful things God has
done for you; and how merciful he has been."

20 So the man started off to visit the Ten
Towns[a] of that region and began to tell everyone about the great things Jesus had done for
him; and they were awestruck by his story.

[*a*] Or, "to visit Decapolis."

Today's English Version

9 So Jesus asked him, "What is your name?"
The man answered, "My name is 'Mob'—there
are so many of us!" 10 And he kept begging Jesus not to send the evil spirits out of that territory.

11 A large herd of pigs was near by, feeding
on the hillside. 12 The spirits begged Jesus,
"Send us to the pigs, and let us go into them."
13 So he let them. The evil spirits went out of
the man and went into the pigs. The whole herd
—about two thousand pigs in all—rushed down
the side of the cliff into the lake and were
drowned.

14 The men who had been taking care of the
pigs ran away and spread the news in the town
and among the farms. The people went out to
see what had happened. 15 They came to Jesus
and saw the man who used to have the mob of
demons in him. He was sitting there, clothed
and in his right mind; and they were all afraid.
16 Those who had seen it told the people what
had happened to the man with the demons, and
about the pigs. 17 So they began to ask Jesus to
leave their territory.

18 As Jesus was getting into the boat, the man
who had had the demons begged him, "Let me
go with you!"

19 But Jesus would not let him. Instead he
told him, "Go back home to your family and tell
them how much the Lord has done for you, and
how kind he has been to you."

20 So the man left and went all through the
Ten Towns telling what Jesus had done for him;
and all who heard it were filled with wonder.

New International Version

9 Then Jesus asked him, "What is your
name?"

"My name is Legion," he replied, "for we are
many." 10 And he begged Jesus again and again
not to send them out of the area.

11 A large herd of pigs was feeding on the
nearby hillside. 12 The demons begged Jesus,
"Send us among the pigs; allow us to go into
them." 13 He gave them permission, and the
evil[m] spirits came out and went into the pigs.
The herd, about two thousand in number, rushed
down the steep bank into the lake and were
drowned.

14 Those tending the pigs ran off and reported
this in the town and countryside, and the people
went out to see what had happened. 15 When
they came to Jesus, they saw the man who had
been possessed by the legion of demons, sitting
there, dressed and in his right mind; and they
were afraid. 16 Those who had seen it told the
people what had happened to the demon-possessed man—and told about the pigs as well.
17 Then the people began to plead with Jesus to
leave their region.

18 As Jesus was getting into the boat, the
man who had been demon-possessed begged to
go with him. 19 Jesus did not let him, but said,
"Go home to your family and tell them how
much the Lord has done for you, and how he
has had mercy on you." 20 So the man went
away and began to tell in the Decapolis[n] how
much Jesus had done for him. And all the people were amazed.

[*m*] Greek *unclean.* [*n*] That is, *the Ten Cities.*

Phillips Modern English

Then he asked him,
"What is your name?"

"My name is legion," he replied, "for there are many of us."

Then he begged and prayed him not to send "them" out of the country.

A large herd of pigs was grazing there on the hill-side, and the evil spirits implored him, "Send us over to the pigs and we'll get into them!"

So Jesus allowed them to do this, and they came out of the man, and made off and went into the pigs. The whole herd of about two thousand stampeded down the cliff into the lake and was drowned. The swineherds took to their heels and spread their story in the city and all over the countryside. Then the people came to see what had happened. As they approached Jesus, they saw the man who had been devil-possessed sitting there properly clothed and perfectly sane—the same man who had been possessed by "legion"—and they were really frightened. Those who had seen the incident told them what had happened to the devil-possessed man and about the disaster to the pigs. Then they began to implore Jesus to leave their district. As he was embarking on the small boat, the man who had been possessed begged that he might go with him. But Jesus would not allow this.

"Go home to your own people," he told him, "and tell them what the Lord has done for you, and how kind he has been to you!"

So the man went off and began to spread throughout the Ten Towns the story of what Jesus had done for him. And they were all simply amazed.

Revised Standard Version

9 And Jesus[o] asked him, "What is your name?" He replied, "My name is Legion; for we are many." 10 And he begged him eagerly not to send them out of the country. 11 Now a great herd of swine was feeding there on the hillside; 12 and they begged him, "Send us to the swine, let us enter them." 13 So he gave them leave. And the unclean spirits came out, and entered the swine; and the herd, numbering about two thousand, rushed down the steep bank into the sea, and were drowned in the sea.

14 The herdsmen fled, and told it in the city and in the country. And people came to see what it was that had happened. 15 And they came to Jesus, and saw the demoniac sitting there, clothed and in his right mind, the man who had had the legion; and they were afraid. 16 And those who had seen it told what had happened to the demoniac and to the swine. 17 And they began to beg Jesus[p] to depart from their neighborhood. 18 And as he was getting into the boat, the man who had been possessed with demons begged him that he might be with him. 19 But he refused, and said to him, "Go home to your friends, and tell them how much the Lord has done for you, and how he has had mercy on you." 20 And he went away and began to proclaim in the Decapolis how much Jesus had done for him; and all men marveled.

[*o*] Greek ***he***. [*p*] Greek ***him***.

Jerusalem Bible

"Come out of the man, unclean spirit." 9 "What is your name?" Jesus asked. "My name is legion," he answered, "for there are many of us." 10 And he begged him earnestly not to send them out of the district. 11 Now there was there on the mountainside a great herd of pigs feeding, 12 and the unclean spirits begged him, "Send us to the pigs, let us go into them." 13 So he gave them leave. With that, the unclean spirits came out and went into the pigs, and the herd of about two thousand pigs charged down the cliff into the lake, and there they were drowned. 14 The swineherds ran off and told their story in the town and in the country around about; and the people came to see what had really happened. 15 They came to Jesus and saw the demoniac sitting there, clothed and in his full senses—the very man who had had the legion in him before—and they were afraid. 16 And those who had witnessed it reported what had happened to the demoniac and what had become of the pigs. 17 Then they began to implore Jesus to leave the neighborhood. 18 As he was getting into the boat, the man who had been possessed begged to be allowed to stay with him. 19 Jesus would not let him but said to him, "Go home to your people and tell them all that the Lord in his mercy has done for you." 20 So the man went off and proceeded to spread throughout the Decapolis all that Jesus had done for him. And everyone was amazed.

New English Bible

out of this man!') Jesus asked him, 'What is your name?' 'My name is Legion,' he said, 'there are so many of us.' And he begged hard that Jesus would not send them out of the country.

Now there happened to be a large herd of pigs feeding on the hill-side, and the spirits begged him, 'Send us among the pigs and let us go into them.' He gave them leave; and the unclean spirits came out and went into the pigs; and the herd, of about two thousand, rushed over the edge into the lake and were drowned.

The men in charge of them took to their heels and carried the news to the town and country-side; and the people came out to see what had happened. They came to Jesus and saw the mad-man who had been possessed by the legion of devils, sitting there clothed and in his right mind; and they were afraid. The spectators told them how the madman had been cured and what had happened to the pigs. Then they begged Jesus to leave the district.

As he was stepping into the boat, the man who had been possessed begged to go with him. Jesus would not allow it, but said to him, 'Go home to your own folk and tell them what the Lord in his mercy has done for you.' The man went off and spread the news in the Ten Towns[a] of all that Jesus had done for him; and they were all amazed.

[*a*] *Greek* Decapolis.

King James Version

men did marvel. 21And when Jesus was passed over again by ship unto the other side, much people gathered unto him; and he was nigh unto the sea. 22And, behold, there cometh one of the rulers of the synagogue, Jairus by name; and when he saw him, he fell at his feet, 23And besought him greatly, saying, My little daughter lieth at the point of death: *I pray thee,* come and lay thy hands on her, that she may be healed; and she shall live. 24And *Jesus* went with him; and much people followed him, and thronged him. 25And a certain woman, which had an issue of blood twelve years, 26And had suffered many things of many physicians, and had spent all that she had, and was nothing bettered, but rather grew worse, 27 When she had heard of Jesus, came in the press behind, and touched his garment. 28 For she said, If I may touch but his clothes, I shall be whole. 29And straightway the fountain of her blood was dried up; and she felt in *her* body that she was healed of that plague. 30And Jesus, immediately knowing in himself that virtue had gone out of him, turned him about in the press, and said, Who touched my clothes? 31And his disciples said unto him, Thou seest the multitude thronging thee, and sayest thou, Who touched me? 32And he looked round about to see her that had done this thing. 33 But the woman fearing and trem-

Living Bible

21 When Jesus had gone across by boat to the other side of the lake, a vast crowd gathered around him on the shore.

22 The leader of the local synagogue, whose name was Jairus, came and fell down before him, 23 pleading with him to heal his little daughter.

"She is at the point of death," he said in desperation. "Please come and place your hands on her and make her live."

24 Jesus went with him, and the crowd thronged behind. 25 In the crowd was a woman who had been sick for twelve years with a hemorrhage. 26 She had suffered much from many doctors through the years and had become poor from paying them, and was no better but, in fact, was worse. 27 She had heard all about the wonderful miracles Jesus did, and that is why she came up behind him through the crowd and touched his clothes.

28 For she thought to herself, "If I can just touch his clothing, I will be healed." 29And sure enough, as soon as she had touched him, the bleeding stopped and she knew she was well!

30 Jesus realized at once that healing power had gone out from him, so he turned around in the crowd and asked, "Who touched my clothes?"

31 His disciples said to him, "All this crowd pressing around you, and you ask who touched you?"

32 But he kept on looking around to see who it was who had done it. 33 Then the frightened

Today's English Version

Jairus' daughter and the woman who touched Jesus' cloak

21 Jesus went back across to the other side of the lake. There at the lakeside a large crowd gathered around him. 22 Jairus, an official of the local synagogue, came up, and when he saw Jesus he threw himself down at his feet 23 and begged him with all his might, "My little daughter is very sick. Please come and place your hands on her, so that she will get well and live!"

24 Then Jesus started off with him. So many people were going along with him that they were crowding him from every side.

25 There was a woman who had suffered terribly from severe bleeding for twelve years, 26 even though she had been treated by many doctors. She had spent all her money, but instead of getting better she got worse all the time. 27 She had heard about Jesus, so she came in the crowd behind him. 28 "If I touch just his clothes," she said to herself, "I shall get well."

29 She touched his cloak and her bleeding stopped at once; and she had the feeling inside herself that she was cured of her trouble. 30At once Jesus knew that power had gone out of him. So he turned around in the crowd and said, "Who touched my clothes?"

31 His disciples answered, "You see how the people are crowding you; why do you ask who touched you?"

32 But Jesus kept looking around to see who had done it. 33 The woman realized what had

New International Version

A dead girl and a sick woman

21 When Jesus had again crossed over by boat to the other side of the lake, a large crowd gathered around him. While he was by the lake, 22 one of the synagogue rulers, named Jairus, came there. Seeing Jesus, he fell at his feet 23 and pleaded earnestly with him, "My little daughter is dying. Please come and put your hands on her so that she will be healed and live." 24 So Jesus went with him.

A large crowd followed and pressed around him. 25And a woman was there who had been subject to bleeding for twelve years. 26 She had suffered a great deal under the care of many doctors and had spent all she had, yet instead of getting better she grew worse. 27 When she heard about Jesus, she came up behind him in the crowd and touched his cloak, 28 because she thought, "If I just touch his clothes, I will be healed." 29 Immediately her bleeding stopped and she felt in her body that she was freed from her suffering.

30 At once Jesus realized that power had gone out from him. He turned around in the crowd and asked, "Who touched my clothes?"

31 "You see the people crowding against you," his disciples answered, "and yet you can ask, 'Who touched me?' "

32 But Jesus kept looking around to see who had done it. 33 Then the woman, knowing what

Phillips Modern English

5.21 Faith is followed by healing

When Jesus had crossed again in the boat to the other side of the lake, a great crowd collected around him as he stood on the shore. Then came a man called Jairus, one of the synagogue presidents. And when he saw Jesus, he knelt before him, pleading desperately for his help.

"My little girl is dying," he said. "Will you come and put your hands on her—then she will get better and live."

Jesus went off with him, followed by a large crowd jostling at his elbow. Among them was a woman who had suffered from haemorrhages for twelve years and who had gone through a great deal at the hands of many doctors, spending all her money in the process. She had derived no benefit from them but, on the contrary, was getting worse. This woman had heard about Jesus and came up behind him under cover of the crowd, and touched his cloak,

"For if I can only touch his clothes," she kept saying, "I shall be all right."

The haemorrhage was stopped immediately, and she knew in herself that she was cured of her trouble. At once Jesus knew intuitively that power had gone out of him, and he turned round in the middle of the crowd and said,

"Who touched my clothes?"

His disciples replied,

"You can see this crowd jostling you. How can you ask, 'Who touched me?' "

But he looked all round at their faces to see who had done so. Then the women, scared and

Revised Standard Version

21 And when Jesus had crossed again in the
boat to the other side, a great crowd gathered
about him; and he was beside the sea. 22 Then
came one of the rulers of the synagogue, Jairus
by name; and seeing him, he fell at his feet,
23 and besought him, saying, "My little daughter
is at the point of death. Come and lay your
hands on her, so that she may be made well, and
live." 24 And he went with him.
And a great crowd followed him and thronged
about him. 25 And there was a woman who had
had a flow of blood for twelve years, 26 and who
had suffered much under many physicians, and
had spent all that she had, and was no better
but rather grew worse. 27 She had heard the
reports about Jesus, and came up behind him in
the crowd and touched his garment. 28 For she
said, "If I touch even his garments, I shall be
made well." 29 And immediately the hemorrhage
ceased; and she felt in her body that she was
healed of her disease. 30 And Jesus, perceiving in
himself that power had gone forth from him,
immediately turned about in the crowd, and
said, "Who touched my garments?" 31 And his
disciples said to him, "You see the crowd pressing around you, and yet you say, 'Who touched
me?' " 32 And he looked around to see who had
done it. 33 But the woman, knowing what had

Jerusalem Bible

Cure of the woman with a hemorrhage. The daughter of Jairus raised to life

21 When Jesus had crossed again in the boat
to the other side, a large crowd gathered around
him and he stayed by the lakeside. 22 Then one
of the synagogue officials came up, Jairus by
name, and seeing him, fell at his feet 23 and
pleaded with him earnestly, saying, "My little
daughter is desperately sick. Do come and lay
your hands on her to make her better and save
her life." 24 Jesus went with him and a large
crowd followed him; they were pressing all
around him.
25 Now there was a woman who had suffered
from a hemorrhage for twelve years; 26 after
long and painful treatment under various doctors, she had spent all she had without being
any the better for it, in fact, she was getting
worse. 27 She had heard about Jesus, and she
came up behind him through the crowd and
touched his cloak. 28 "If I can touch even his
clothes," she had told herself, "I shall be well
again." 29 And the source of the bleeding dried
up instantly, and she felt in herself that she was
cured of her complaint. 30 Immediately aware
that power had gone out from him, Jesus turned
around in the crowd and said, "Who touched my
clothes?" 31 His disciples said to him, "You see
how the crowd is pressing around you and yet
you say, 'Who touched me?' " 32 But he continued to look all around to see who had done it.
33 Then the woman came forward, frightened

New English Bible

As soon as Jesus had returned by boat to the other shore, a great crowd once more gathered round him. While he was by the lake-side, the president of one of the synagogues came up, Jairus by name, and, when he saw him, threw himself down at his feet and pleaded with him. 'My little daughter', he said, 'is at death's door. I beg you to come and lay your hands on her to cure her and save her life.' So Jesus went with him, accompanied by a great crowd which pressed upon him.

Among them was a woman who had suffered from haemorrhages for twelve years; and in spite of long treatment by many doctors, on which she had spent all she had, there had been no improvement; on the contrary, she had grown worse. She had heard what people were saying about Jesus, so she came up from behind in the crowd and touched his cloak; for she said to herself, 'If I touch even his clothes, I shall be cured.' And there and then the source of her haemorrhages dried up and she knew in herself that she was cured of her trouble. At the same time Jesus, aware that power had gone out of him, turned round in the crowd and asked, 'Who touched my clothes?' His disciples said to him, 'You see the crowd pressing upon you and yet you ask, "Who touched me?" ' Meanwhile he was looking round to see who had done it. And

King James Version

bling, knowing what was done in her, came and fell down before him, and told him all the truth. 34 And he said unto her, Daughter, thy faith hath made thee whole; go in peace, and be whole of thy plague. 35 While he yet spake, there came from the ruler of the synagogue's *house certain* which said, Thy daughter is dead; why troublest thou the Master any further? 36 As soon as Jesus heard the word that was spoken, he saith unto the ruler of the synagogue, Be not afraid, only believe. 37 And he suffered no man to follow him, save Peter, and James, and John the brother of James. 38 And he cometh to the house of the ruler of the synagogue, and seeth the tumult, and them that wept and wailed greatly. 39 And when he was come in, he saith unto them, Why make ye this ado, and weep? the damsel is not dead, but sleepeth. 40 And they laughed him to scorn. But when he had put them all out, he taketh the father and the mother of the damsel, and them that were with him, and entereth in where the damsel was lying. 41 And he took the damsel by the hand, and said unto her, Talitha cumi; which is, being interpreted, Damsel, (I say unto thee,) arise. 42 And straightway the damsel arose, and walked; for she was *of the age* of twelve years. And they were astonished with a great astonishment. 43 And he charged them straitly that no man should know it; and commanded that something should be given her to eat.

Living Bible

woman, trembling at the realization of what had happened to her, came and fell at his feet and told him what she had done. 34 And he said to her, "Daughter, your faith has made you well; go in peace, healed of your disease."

35 While he was still talking to her, messengers arrived from Jairus' home with the news that it was too late—his daughter was dead and there was no point in Jesus' coming now. 36 But Jesus ignored their comments and said to Jairus, "Don't be afraid. Just trust me."

37 Then Jesus halted the crowd and wouldn't let anyone go on with him to Jairus' home except Peter and James and John. 38 When they arrived, Jesus saw that all was in great confusion, with unrestrained weeping and wailing. 39 He went inside and spoke to the people.

"Why all this weeping and commotion?" he asked. "The child isn't dead; she is only asleep!"

40 They laughed at him in bitter derision, but he told them all to leave, and taking the little girl's father and mother and his three disciples, he went into the room where she was lying.

41, 42 Taking her by the hand he said to her, "Get up, little girl!" (She was twelve years old.) And she jumped up and walked around! Her parents just couldn't get over it. 43 Jesus instructed them very earnestly not to tell what had happened, and told them to give her something to eat.

Today's English Version

happened to her; so she came, trembling with fear, fell at his feet, and told him the whole truth. 34 Jesus said to her, "My daughter, your faith has made you well. Go in peace, and be healed from your trouble."

35 While Jesus was saying this, some messengers came from Jairus' house and told him, "Your daughter has died. Why should you bother the Teacher any longer?"

36 Jesus paid no attention to what they said, but told him, "Don't be afraid, only believe." 37 Then he did not let anyone else go on with him except Peter and James and his brother John. 38 They arrived at the official's house, where Jesus saw the confusion and heard all the loud crying and wailing. 39 He went in and said to them, "Why all this confusion? Why are you crying? The child is not dead—she is only sleeping!"

40 They started making fun of him, so he put them all out, took the child's father and mother, and his three disciples, and went into the room where the child was lying. 41 He took her by the hand and said to her, *"Talitha, koum,"* which means, "Little girl! Get up, I tell you!"

42 She got up at once and started walking around. (She was twelve years old.) When this happened they were completely amazed! 43 But Jesus gave them strict orders not to tell anyone, and said, "Give her something to eat."

New International Version

had happened to her, came and fell at his feet and, trembling with fear, told him the whole truth. 34 He said to her, "Daughter, your faith has healed you. Go in peace, and be freed from your suffering."

35 While Jesus was still speaking, some men came from the house of Jairus, the synagogue ruler. "Your daughter is dead," they said. "Why bother the teacher any more?"

36 Ignoring what they said, Jesus told the synagogue ruler, "Don't be afraid; just believe."

37 He did not let anyone follow him except Peter, James and John, the brother of James. 38 When they came to the home of the synagogue ruler, Jesus saw a commotion, with people crying and wailing loudly. 39 He went in and said to them, "Why all this commotion and wailing? The child is not dead but asleep." 40 But they laughed at him.

After he put them all out, he took the child's father and mother and the disciples who were with him, and went in where the child was. 41 He took her by the hand and said to her, *"Talitha koum!"* (which means, "Little girl, I say to you, get up!"). 42 She stood right up and walked around (she was twelve years old). At this they were completely astonished. 43 He gave strict orders not to let anyone know about this, and told them to give her something to eat.

Phillips Modern English

shaking all over because she knew that she was the one to whom this thing had happened, came and flung herself before him and told him the whole story. But he said to her,

"Daughter, it is your faith that has healed you. Go home in peace, and be free from your trouble."

While he was still speaking, messengers arrived from the synagogue president's house, saying,

"Your daughter is dead—there is no need to bother the master any further."

But when Jesus heard this message, he said to the president of the synagogue,

"Now don't be afraid, just go on believing!"

Then he allowed no one to follow him except Peter and James and John, James's brother. They arrived at the president's house and Jesus noticed the hubbub and all the weeping and wailing, and as he went in, he said to the people in the house,

"Why are you making such a noise with your crying? The child is not dead; she is fast asleep."

They greeted this with a scornful laugh. But Jesus turned them all out, and taking only the father and mother and his own companions with him, went into the room where the child was. Then he took the little girl's hand and said to her in Aramaic,

"Little girl, I tell you to get up!"

At once she jumped to her feet and walked round the room, for she was twelve years old. This sight sent the others nearly out of their minds with joy. But Jesus gave them strict instructions not to let anyone know what had happened—and ordered food to be given to the little girl.

Revised Standard Version

been done to her, came in fear and trembling
and fell down before him, and told him the
whole truth. 34And he said to her, "Daughter,
your faith has made you well; go in peace, and
be healed of your disease."
35 While he was still speaking, there came
from the ruler's house some who said, "Your
daughter is dead. Why trouble the Teacher any
further?" 36 But ignoring[q] what they said, Jesus
said to the ruler of the synagogue, "Do not fear,
only believe." 37And he allowed no one to follow him except Peter and James and John the
brother of James. 38 When they came to the
house of the ruler of the synagogue, he saw a
tumult, and people weeping and wailing loudly.
39And when he had entered, he said to them,
"Why do you make a tumult and weep? The
child is not dead but sleeping." 40And they
laughed at him. But he put them all outside, and
took the child's father and mother and those
who were with him, and went in where the child
was. 41 Taking her by the hand he said to her,
"Talitha cumi"; which means, "Little girl, I say
to you, arise." 42And immediately the girl got
up and walked (she was twelve years of age),
and they were immediately overcome with
amazement. 43And he strictly charged them that
no one should know this, and told them to give
her something to eat.

[q] Or *overhearing*. Other ancient authorities read *hearing*.

Jerusalem Bible

and trembling[g] because she knew what had happened to her, and she fell at his feet and told
him the whole truth. 34 "My daughter," he said,
"your faith has restored you to health; go in
peace and be free from your complaint."
35 While he was still speaking some people
arrived from the house of the synagogue official
to say, "Your daughter is dead: why put the
Master to any further trouble?" 36 But Jesus had
overheard this remark of theirs and he said to
the official, "Do not be afraid; only have faith."
37And he allowed no one to go with him except
Peter and James and John the brother of James.
38 So they came to the official's house and Jesus
noticed all the commotion, with people weeping
and wailing unrestrainedly. 39 He went in and
said to them, "Why all this commotion and crying? The child is not dead, but asleep." 40 But
they laughed at him. So he turned them all out
and, taking with him the child's father and
mother and his own companions, he went into
the place where the child lay. 41And taking the
child by the hand he said to her, "Talitha, kum!"
which means, "Little girl, I tell you to get up."
42 The little girl got up at once and began to
walk about, for she was twelve years old. At this
they were overcome with astonishment, and he
ordered them strictly not to let anyone know
about it, and told them to give her something to
eat.

[g] According to the Law, she was unclean, and to be touched by her would be defilement.

New English Bible

the woman, trembling with fear when she grasped what had happened to her, came and fell at his feet and told him the whole truth. He said to her, 'My daughter, your faith has cured you. Go in peace, free for ever from this trouble.'

While he was still speaking, a message came from the president's house, 'Your daughter is dead; why trouble the Rabbi further?' But Jesus, overhearing the message as it was delivered, said to the president of the synagogue, 'Do not be afraid; only have faith.' After this he allowed no one to accompany him except Peter and James and James's brother John. They came to the president's house, where he found a great commotion, with loud crying and wailing. So he went in and said to them, 'Why this crying and commotion? The child is not dead: she is asleep'; and they only laughed at him. But after turning all the others out, he took the child's father and mother and his own companions and went in where the child was lying. Then, taking hold of her hand, he said to her, *'Talitha cum'*, which means, 'Get up, my child.' Immediately the girl got up and walked about—she was twelve years old. At that they were beside themselves with amazement. He gave them strict orders to let no one hear about it, and told them to give her something to eat.

King James Version

6 And he went out from thence, and came into his own country; and his disciples follow him. 2And when the sabbath day was come, he began to teach in the synagogue: and many hearing *him* were astonished, saying, From whence hath this *man* these things? and what wisdom *is* this which is given unto him, that even such mighty works are wrought by his hands? 3 Is not this the carpenter, the son of Mary, the brother of James, and Joses, and of Juda, and Simon? and are not his sisters here with us? And they were offended at him. 4 But Jesus said unto them, A prophet is not without honour, but in his own country, and among his own kin, and in his own house. 5And he could there do no mighty work, save that he laid his hands upon a few sick folk, and healed *them*. 6And he marvelled because of their unbelief. And he went round about the villages, teaching.
7 And he called *unto him* the twelve, and began to send them forth by two and two; and gave them power over unclean spirits; 8And commanded them that they should take nothing for *their* journey, save a staff only; no scrip, no bread, no money in *their* purse: 9 But *be* shod with sandals; and not put on two coats. 10And

Living Bible

6 Soon afterwards he left that section of the country and returned with his disciples to Nazareth, his home town. 2, 3 The next Sabbath he went to the synagogue to teach, and the people were astonished at his wisdom and his miracles because he was just a local man like themselves.

"He's no better than we are," they said. "He's just a carpenter, Mary's boy, and a brother of James and Joseph, Judas and Simon. And his sisters live right here among us." And they were offended!

4 Then Jesus told them, "A prophet is honored everywhere except in his home town and among his relatives and by his own family." 5And because of their unbelief he couldn't do any mighty miracles among them except to place his hands on a few sick people and heal them. 6And he could hardly accept the fact that they wouldn't believe in him.

Then he went out among the villages, teaching. 7And he called his twelve disciples together and sent them out two by two, with power to cast out demons. 8, 9 He told them to take nothing with them except their walking sticks—no food, no knapsack, no money, not even an extra pair of shoes or a change of clothes.

10 "Stay at one home in each village—don't

Today's English Version

Jesus rejected at Nazareth

6 Jesus left that place and went back to his home town, followed by his disciples. 2 On the Sabbath day he began to teach in the synagogue. Many people were there, and when they heard him they were all amazed. "Where did he get all this?" they asked. "What wisdom is this that has been given him? How does he perform miracles? 3 Isn't he the carpenter, the son of Mary, and the brother of James, Joses, Judas, and Simon? Aren't his sisters living here?" And so they rejected him.

4 Jesus said to them, "A prophet is respected everywhere except in his home town, and by his relatives and his family."

5 He was not able to perform any miracles there, except that he placed his hands on a few sick people and healed them. 6 He was greatly surprised, because they did not have faith.

Jesus sends out the twelve disciples

Then Jesus went to the villages around there, teaching the people. 7 He called the twelve disciples together and sent them out two by two. He gave them authority over the evil spirits 8 and ordered them, "Don't take anything with you on the trip except a walking stick; no bread, no beggar's bag, no money in your pockets. 9 Wear sandals, but don't wear an extra shirt." 10 He also

New International Version

A prophet without honor

6 Jesus left there and went to his home town, accompanied by his disciples. 2 When the Sabbath came, he began to teach in the synagogue, and many who heard him were amazed.

"Where did this man get these things?" they asked. "What's this wisdom that has been given him, that he even does miracles! 3 Isn't this the carpenter? Isn't this Mary's son and the brother of James, Joses, Judas and Simon? Aren't his sisters here with us?" And they took offense at him.

4 Jesus said to them, "Only in his home town, among his relatives and in his own house is a prophet without honor." 5 He could not do any miracles there, except lay his hands on a few sick people and heal them. 6And he was amazed at their lack of faith.

Jesus sends out the Twelve

Then Jesus went around teaching from village to village. 7 Calling the Twelve to him, he sent them out two by two and gave them authority over evil [o] spirits.

8 These were his instructions: "Take nothing for the journey except a staff—no bread, no bag, no money in your belts. 9 Wear sandals but not an extra tunic. 10 Whenever you enter a

[o] Greek *unclean*.

Phillips Modern English

6.1 *The "prophet without honour"*

Then he left that district and came into his own native town, followed by his disciples. When the Sabbath day came, he began to teach in the synagogue. The congregation were astonished at what they heard, and remarked,

"Where does he get all this? What is this wisdom that he has been given—and what about these marvellous things that he can do? He's only the carpenter, Mary's son, the brother of James, Joses, Judas and Simon; and his sisters are living here with us!"

And they were deeply offended with him. But Jesus said to them,

"No prophet goes unhonoured—except in his native town or with his own relations or in his own home!"

And he could do nothing miraculous there apart from laying his hands on a few sick people and healing them; their lack of faith astonished him.

6.6b *The twelve are sent out to preach the gospel*

Then he made his way round the villages, continuing his teaching. He summoned the twelve, and began to send them out in twos, giving them power over evil spirits. He instructed them to take nothing for the road except a staff—no bread, no satchel and no money in their pockets. They were to wear sandals and not to take more than one coat. And he told them,

Revised Standard Version

6 He went away from there and came to his own country; and his disciples followed him. 2And on the sabbath he began to teach in the synagogue; and many who heard him were astonished, saying, "Where did this man get all this? What is the wisdom given to him? What mighty works are wrought by his hands! 3 Is not this the carpenter, the son of Mary and brother of James and Joses and Judas and Simon, and are not his sisters here with us?" And they took offense[r] at him. 4And Jesus said to them, "A prophet is not without honor, except in his own country, and among his own kin, and in his own house." 5And he could do no mighty work there, except that he laid his hands upon a few sick people and healed them. 6And he marveled because of their unbelief.

And he went about among the villages teaching.

7 And he called to him the twelve, and began to send them out two by two, and gave them authority over the unclean spirits. 8 He charged them to take nothing for their journey except a staff; no bread, no bag, no money in their belts; 9 but to wear sandals and not put on two tunics. 10And he said to them, "Where you

[r] Or *stumbled.*

Jerusalem Bible

A visit to Nazareth

6 Going from that district, he went to his home town and his disciples accompanied him. 2 With the coming of the sabbath he began teaching in the synagogue and most of them were astonished when they heard him. They said, "Where did the man get all this? What is this wisdom that has been granted him, and these miracles that are worked through him? 3 This is the carpenter, surely, the son of Mary, the brother of James and Joset[h] and Jude and Simon? His sisters, too, are they not here with us?" And they would not accept him. 4And Jesus said to them, "A prophet is only despised in his own country, among his own relations and in his own house"; 5 and he could work no miracle there, though he cured a few sick people by laying his hands on them. 6 He was amazed at their lack of faith.

The mission of the Twelve

He made a tour around the villages, teaching. 7 Then he summoned the Twelve and began to send them out in pairs giving them authority over the unclean spirits. 8And he instructed them to take nothing for the journey except a staff—no bread, no haversack, no coppers for their purses. 9 They were to wear sandals but, he added, "Do not take a spare tunic." 10And he

[h] Var. "Jose" or "Joseph."

New English Bible

6 He left that place and went to his home town accompanied by his disciples. When the Sabbath came he began to teach in the synagogue; and the large congregation who heard him were amazed and said, 'Where does he get it from?', and, 'What wisdom is this that has been given him?', and, 'How does he work such miracles? Is not this the carpenter, the son of Mary,[a] the brother of James and Joseph and Judas and Simon? And are not his sisters here with us?' So they fell foul of him. Jesus said to them, 'A prophet will always be held in honour except in his home town, and among his kinsmen and family.' He could work no miracle there, except that he put his hands on a few sick people and healed them; and he was taken aback by their want of faith.

On one of his teaching journeys round the villages he summoned the Twelve and sent them out in pairs on a mission. He gave them authority over unclean spirits, and instructed them to take nothing for the journey beyond a stick: no bread, no pack, no money in their belts. They might wear sandals, but not a second coat. 'When you are admitted to a house,' he added,

[a] *Some witnesses read* Is not this the son of the carpenter and Mary . . .

King James Version

he said unto them, In what place soever ye enter into a house, there abide till ye depart from that place. 11And whosoever shall not receive you, nor hear you, when ye depart thence, shake off the dust under your feet for a testimony against them. Verily I say unto you, It shall be more tolerable for Sodom and Gomorrah in the day of judgment, than for that city. 12And they went out, and preached that men should repent. 13And they cast out many devils, and anointed with oil many that were sick, and healed *them.* 14And king Herod heard *of him;* (for his name was spread abroad;) and he said, That John the Baptist was risen from the dead, and therefore mighty works do shew forth themselves in him. 15 Others said, That it is Elias. And others said, That it is a prophet, or as one of the prophets. 16 But when Herod heard *thereof,* he said, It is John, whom I beheaded: he is risen from the dead. 17 For Herod himself had sent forth and laid hold upon John, and bound him in prison for Herodias' sake, his brother Philip's wife; for he had married her. 18 For John had said unto Herod, It is not lawful for thee to have thy brother's wife. 19 Therefore Herodias had a quarrel against him, and would have killed him; but she could not: 20 For Herod feared John, knowing that he was a just man and a holy, and

Living Bible

shift around from house to house while you are there," he said. 11 "And whenever a village won't accept you or listen to you, shake off the dust from your feet as you leave; it is a sign that you have abandoned it to its fate."

12 So the disciples went out, telling everyone they met to turn from sin. 13And they cast out many demons, and healed many sick people, anointing them with olive oil.

14 King Herod soon heard about Jesus, for his miracles were talked about everywhere. The king thought Jesus was John the Baptist come back to life again. So the people were saying, "No wonder he can do such miracles." 15 Others thought Jesus was Elijah the ancient prophet, now returned to life again; still others claimed he was a new prophet like the great ones of the past.

16 "No," Herod said, "it is John, the man I beheaded. He has come back from the dead."

17, 18 For Herod had sent soldiers to arrest and imprison John because he kept saying it was wrong for the king to marry Herodias, his brother Philip's wife. 19 Herodias wanted John killed in revenge, but without Herod's approval she was powerless. 20And Herod respected John, knowing that he was a good and holy man, and

Today's English Version

told them, "Wherever you are welcomed, stay in the same house until you leave that town. 11 If you come to a place where people do not welcome you or will not listen to you, leave it and shake the dust off your feet. This will be a warning to them!"

12 So they went out and preached that people should turn away from their sins. 13 They drove out many demons, and rubbed oil on many sick people and healed them.

The death of John the Baptist

14 Now King Herod heard about all this, because Jesus' reputation had spread everywhere. Some people were saying, "John the Baptist has come back to life! That is why these powers are at work in him."

15 Others, however, said, "He is Elijah."

Others said, "He is a prophet, like one of the prophets of long ago."

16 When Herod heard it he said, "He is John the Baptist! I had his head cut off, but he has come back to life!" 17 Herod himself had ordered John's arrest, and had him tied up and put in prison. Herod did this because of Herodias, whom he had married, even though she was the wife of his brother Philip. 18 John the Baptist kept telling Herod, "It isn't right for you to marry your brother's wife!"

19 So Herodias held a grudge against John and wanted to kill him, but she could not because of Herod. 20 Herod was afraid of John because he knew that John was a good and

New International Version

house, stay there until you leave that town. 11And if any place will not welcome you or listen to you, shake the dust off your feet when you leave, as a testimony against them."

12 They went out and preached that people should repent. 13 They drove out many demons and anointed many sick people with oil and healed them.

John the Baptist beheaded

14 King Herod heard about this, for Jesus' name had become well-known. Some were saying,[p] "John the Baptist has been raised from the dead, and that is why miraculous powers are at work in him."

15 Others said, "He is Elijah."

And still others claimed, "He is a prophet, like one of the prophets of long ago."

16 But when Herod heard this, he said, "John, the man I beheaded, has been raised from the dead!"

17 For Herod himself had given orders to have John arrested and put in prison. He did this because of Herodias, his brother Philip's wife, whom he had married. 18 For John had been saying to Herod, "It is not lawful for you to have your brother's wife." 19 So Herodias nursed a grudge against John and wanted to kill him. But she was not able to, 20 because Herod feared John and protected him, knowing him to be a

[p] Some early MSS read *He was saying.*

Phillips Modern English

"Wherever you are, when you go into a house, stay there until you leave that place. And wherever people will not welcome you or listen to what you have to say, leave them and shake the dust off your feet as a protest against them!"

So they went out and preached publicly that men should change their whole outlook. They expelled many evil spirits and anointed many sick people with oil and healed them.

6.14 Herod's guilty conscience

All this came to the ears of king Herod, for Jesus' reputation was spreading, and people were saying that John the Baptist had risen from the dead, and that was why he was showing such miraculous powers. Others maintained that he was Elijah, and others that he was one of the prophets of the old days come back again. But when Herod heard of all this, he said,

"It must be John whom I beheaded, risen from the dead!"

For Herod himself had sent and arrested John and had him bound in prison, all on account of Herodias, wife of his brother Philip. He had married her, though John used to say to Herod, "It is not right for you to possess your own brother's wife." Herodias herself nursed a grudge against John for this and wanted to have him executed, but she could not do it, for Herod had a deep respect for John, knowing that he was a

Revised Standard Version

enter a house, stay there until you leave the place. 11 And if any place will not receive you and they refuse to hear you, when you leave, shake off the dust that is on your feet for a testimony against them." 12 So they went out and preached that men should repent. 13 And they cast out many demons, and anointed with oil many that were sick and healed them.

14 King Herod heard of it; for Jesus'[s] name had become known. Some[t] said, "John the baptizer has been raised from the dead; that is why these powers are at work in him." 15 But others said, "It is Elijah." And others said, "It is a prophet, like one of the prophets of old." 16 But when Herod heard of it he said, "John, whom I beheaded, has been raised." 17 For Herod had sent and seized John, and bound him in prison for the sake of Herodias, his brother Philip's wife; because he had married her. 18 For John said to Herod, "It is not lawful for you to have your brother's wife." 19 And Herodias had a grudge against him, and wanted to kill him. But she could not, 20 for Herod feared John, knowing that he was a righteous and holy man, and

[*s*] Greek ***his***. [*t*] Other ancient authorities read ***he***.

Jerusalem Bible

said to them, "If you enter a house anywhere, stay there until you leave the district. 11 And if any place does not welcome you and people refuse to listen to you, as you walk away shake off the dust from under your feet as a sign to them." 12 So they set off to preach repentance; 13 and they cast out many devils, and anointed many sick people with oil and cured them.

Herod and Jesus

14 Meanwhile King Herod had heard about him, since by now his name was well-known. Some were saying, "John the Baptist has risen from the dead, and that is why miraculous powers are at work in him." 15 Others said, "He is Elijah"; others again, "He is a prophet, like the prophets we used to have." 16 But when Herod heard this he said, "It is John whose head I cut off; he has risen from the dead."

John the Baptist beheaded

17 Now it was this same Herod who had sent to have John arrested, and had him chained up in prison because of Herodias, his brother Philip's wife whom he had married. 18 For John had told Herod, "It is against the law for you to have your brother's wife." 19 As for Herodias, she was furious with him and wanted to kill him; but she was not able to, 20 because Herod was afraid of John, knowing him to be a good and

New English Bible

'stay there until you leave those parts. At any place where they will not receive you or listen to you, shake the dust off your feet as you leave, as a warning to them.' So they set out and called publicly for repentance. They drove out many devils, and many sick people they anointed with oil and cured.

Now King Herod heard of it, for the fame of Jesus had spread; and people were saying,[a] 'John the Baptist has been raised to life, and that is why these miraculous powers are at work in him.' Others said, 'It is Elijah.' Others again, 'He is a prophet like one of the old prophets.' But Herod, when he heard of it, said, 'This is John, whom I beheaded, raised from the dead.'

For this same Herod had sent and arrested John and put him in prison on account of his brother Philip's wife, Herodias, whom he had married. John had told Herod, 'You have no right to your brother's wife.' Thus Herodias nursed a grudge against him and would willingly have killed him, but she could not; for Herod went in awe of John, knowing him to be a good

[*a*] *Some witnesses read* and he said . . .

King James Version

observed him; and when he heard him, he did
many things, and heard him gladly. 21And when
a convenient day was come, that Herod on his
birthday made a supper to his lords, high captains, and chief *estates* of Galilee; 22And when
the daughter of the said Herodias came in, and
danced, and pleased Herod and them that sat
with him, the king said unto the damsel, Ask of
me whatsoever thou wilt, and I will give *it* thee.
23And he sware unto her, Whatsoever thou shalt
ask of me, I will give *it* thee, unto the half of my
kingdom. 24And she went forth, and said unto
her mother, What shall I ask? And she said, The
head of John the Baptist. 25And she came in
straightway with haste unto the king, and asked,
saying, I will that thou give me by and by in a
charger the head of John the Baptist. 26And the
king was exceeding sorry; *yet* for his oath's sake,
and for their sakes which sat with him, he would
not reject her. 27And immediately the king sent
an executioner, and commanded his head to be
brought: and he went and beheaded him in the
prison, 28And brought his head in a charger,
and gave it to the damsel; and the damsel gave
it to her mother. 29And when his disciples heard
of it, they came and took up his corpse, and laid

Living Bible

so he kept him under his protection. Herod was
disturbed whenever he talked with John, but
even so he liked to listen to him.
21 Herodias' chance finally came. It was Herod's birthday and he gave a stag party for his
palace aides, army officers, and the leading citizens of Galilee. 22, 23 Then Herodias' daughter
came in and danced before them and greatly
pleased them all.

"Ask me for anything you like," the king
vowed, "even half of my kingdom, and I will
give it to you!"

24 She went out and consulted her mother,
who told her, "Ask for John the Baptist's head!"
25 So she hurried back to the king and told
him, "I want the head of John the Baptist—
right now—on a tray!"
26 Then the king was sorry, but he was embarrassed to break his oath in front of his guests.
27 So he sent one of his bodyguards to the prison
to cut off John's head and bring it to him. The
soldier killed John in the prison, 28 and brought
back his head on a tray, and gave it to the girl
and she took it to her mother.
29 When John's disciples heard what had happened, they came for his body and buried it in
a tomb.

Today's English Version

holy man, and so he kept him safe. He liked to
listen to him, even though he became greatly
disturbed every time he heard him.
21 Finally Herodias got her chance. It was
on Herod's birthday, when he gave a feast for
all the top government officials, the military
chiefs, and the leading citizens of Galilee. 22 The
daughter of Herodias came in and danced, and
pleased Herod and his guests. So the king said
to the girl, "What would you like to have? I will
give you anything you want." 23 With many
vows he said to her, "I promise that I will give
you anything you ask for, even as much as half
my kingdom!"
24 So the girl went out and asked her mother,
"What shall I ask for?"

"The head of John the Baptist," she answered.
25 The girl hurried back at once to the king
and demanded, "I want you to give me right
now the head of John the Baptist on a plate!"
26 This made the king very sad; but he could
not refuse her, because of the vows he had made
in front of all his guests. 27 So he sent off a guard
at once with orders to bring John's head. The
guard left, went to the prison, and cut John's
head off; 28 then he brought it on a plate and
gave it to the girl, who gave it to her mother.
29 When John's disciples heard about this, they
came and got his body and laid it in a grave.

New International Version

righteous and holy man. When Herod heard
John, he was greatly puzzled;[q] yet he liked to
listen to him.
21 Finally the opportune time came. On his
birthday Herod gave a banquet for his high officials and military commanders and the leading
men of Galilee. 22 When the daughter of Herodias came in and danced, she pleased Herod
and his dinner guests.

The king said to the girl, "Ask me for anything you want, and I'll give it to you." 23And
he promised her with an oath, "Whatever you
ask I will give you, up to half my kingdom."
24 She went out and said to her mother,
"What shall I ask for?"

"The head of John the Baptist," she answered.
25 At once the girl hurried in to the king with
the request: "I want you to give me right now
the head of John the Baptist on a platter."
26 The king was greatly distressed, but because of his oaths and his dinner guests, he did
not want to refuse her. 27 So he immediately
sent an executioner with orders to bring John's
head. The man went, beheaded John in the
prison, 28 and brought back his head on a platter. He presented it to the girl, and she gave it
to her mother. 29 On hearing of this, John's disciples came and took his body and laid it in a
tomb.

[q] Some early MSS read *he did many things.*

Phillips Modern English

just and holy man, and kept him under his protection. He used to listen to him and be profoundly disturbed, and yet he enjoyed hearing him.

Then a good opportunity came, for Herod gave a birthday party for his courtiers and army commanders and for the leading people in Galilee. Herodias' daughter came in and danced, to the great delight of Herod and his guests. The king said to the girl,

"Ask me anything you like and I will give it to you!"

And he swore to her,

"I will give you whatever you ask me, up to half my kingdom!"

And she went out and spoke to her mother,

"What shall I ask for?"

And she said,

"The head of John the Baptist!"

The girl rushed back to the king's presence, and made her request.

"I want you to give me, this minute, the head of John the Baptist on a dish!" she said.

Herod was aghast, but because of his oath and the presence of his guests, he did not like to refuse her. So he sent the executioner straightaway to bring him John's head. He went off and beheaded him in the prison, brought back his head on the dish, and gave it to the girl who handed it to her mother. When his disciples heard what had happened, they came and took away his body and put it in a tomb.

Revised Standard Version

kept him safe. When he heard him, he was much perplexed; and yet he heard him gladly. 21 But an opportunity came when Herod on his birthday gave a banquet for his courtiers and officers and the leading men of Galilee. 22 For when Herodias' daughter came in and danced, she pleased Herod and his guests; and the king said to the girl, "Ask me for whatever you wish, and I will grant it." 23 And he vowed to her, "Whatever you ask me, I will give you, even half of my kingdom." 24 And she went out, and said to her mother, "What shall I ask?" And she said, "The head of John the baptizer." 25 And she came in immediately with haste to the king, and asked, saying, "I want you to give me at once the head of John the Baptist on a platter." 26 And the king was exceedingly sorry; but because of his oaths and his guests he did not want to break his word to her. 27 And immediately the king sent a soldier of the guard and gave orders to bring his head. He went and beheaded him in the prison, 28 and brought his head on a platter, and gave it to the girl; and the girl gave it to her mother. 29 When his disciples heard of it, they came and took his body, and laid it in a tomb.

Jerusalem Bible

holy man, and gave him his protection. When he had heard him speak he was greatly perplexed, and yet he liked to listen to him.

21 An opportunity came on Herod's birthday when he gave a banquet for the nobles of his court, for his army officers and for the leading figures in Galilee. 22 When the daughter of this same Herodias came in and danced, she delighted Herod and his guests; so the king said to the girl, "Ask me anything you like and I will give it you." 23 And he swore her an oath, "I will give you anything you ask, even half my kingdom." 24 She went out and said to her mother, "What shall I ask for?" She replied, "The head of John the Baptist." 25 The girl hurried straight back to the king and made her request, "I want you to give me John the Baptist's head, here and now, on a dish." 26 The king was deeply distressed but, thinking of the oaths he had sworn and of his guests, he was reluctant to break his word to her. 27 So the king at once sent one of the bodyguard with orders to bring John's head. 28 The man went off and beheaded him in prison; then he brought the head on a dish and gave it to the girl, and the girl gave it to her mother. 29 When John's disciples heard about this, they came and took his body and laid it in a tomb.

New English Bible

and holy man; so he kept him in custody. He liked to listen to him, although the listening left him greatly perplexed.

Herodias found her opportunity when Herod on his birthday gave a banquet to his chief officials and commanders and the leading men of Galilee. Her daughter came in[b] and danced, and so delighted Herod and his guests that the king said to the girl, 'Ask what you like and I will give it you.' And he swore an oath to her: 'Whatever you ask I will give you, up to half my kingdom.' She went out and said to her mother, 'What shall I ask for?' She replied, 'The head of John the Baptist.' The girl hastened back at once to the king with her request: 'I want you to give me here and now, on a dish, the head of John the Baptist.' The king was greatly distressed, but out of regard for his oath and for his guests he could not bring himself to refuse her. So the king sent a soldier of the guard with orders to bring John's head. The soldier went off and beheaded him in the prison, brought the head on a dish, and gave it to the girl; and she gave it to her mother.

When John's disciples heard the news, they came and took his body away and laid it in a tomb.

[b] *Or* A festive occasion came when Herod on his birthday gave . . . of Galilee. The daughter of Herodias came in . . .

King James Version

it in a tomb. 30And the apostles gathered themselves together unto Jesus, and told him all
things, both what they had done, and what they
had taught. 31And he said unto them, Come ye
yourselves apart into a desert place, and rest a
while: for there were many coming and going,
and they had no leisure so much as to eat. 32And
they departed into a desert place by ship
privately. 33And the people saw them departing,
and many knew him, and ran afoot thither out
of all cities, and outwent them, and came together unto him. 34And Jesus, when he came
out, saw much people, and was moved with
compassion toward them, because they were as
sheep not having a shepherd: and he began to
teach them many things. 35And when the day
was now far spent, his disciples came unto him,
and said, This is a desert place, and now the
time *is* far passed: 36 Send them away, that they
may go into the country round about, and into
the villages, and buy themselves bread: for they
have nothing to eat. 37 He answered and said
unto them, Give ye them to eat. And they say
unto him, Shall we go and buy two hundred
pennyworth of bread, and give them to eat?
38 He saith unto them, How many loaves have
ye? go and see. And when they knew, they say,

Living Bible

30 The apostles now returned to Jesus from
their tour and told him all they had done and
what they had said to the people they visited.
31 Then Jesus suggested, "Let's get away from
the crowds for a while and rest." For so many
people were coming and going that they scarcely
had time to eat. 32 So they left by boat for a
quieter spot. 33 But many people saw them
leaving and ran on ahead along the shore and
met them as they landed. 34 So the usual vast
crowd was there as he stepped from the boat;
and he had pity on them because they were like
sheep without a shepherd, and he taught them
many things they needed to know.
35, 36 Late in the afternoon his disciples came
to him and said, "Tell the people to go away to
the nearby villages and farms and buy themselves some food, for there is nothing to eat
here in this desolate spot, and it is getting late."
37 But Jesus said, "*You* feed them."
"With what?" they asked. "It would take a
fortune[a] to buy food for all this crowd!"
38 "How much food do we have?" he asked.
"Go and find out."
They came back to report that there were

[*a*] Literally, "200 denarii," a year's wage.

Today's English Version

Jesus feeds the five thousand

30 The apostles returned and met with Jesus,
and told him all they had done and taught.
31 There were so many people coming and going that Jesus and his disciples didn't even have
time to eat. So he said to them, "Let us go off
by ourselves to some place where we will be
alone and you can rest a while." 32 So they
started out in the boat by themselves to a lonely
place.
33 Many people, however, saw them leave and
knew at once who they were; so they went from
all the towns and ran ahead by land and got to
the place ahead of Jesus and his disciples.
34 When Jesus got out of the boat, he saw this
large crowd, and his heart was filled with pity
for them, because they were like sheep without
a shepherd. So he began to teach them many
things. 35 When it was getting late, his disciples
came to him and said, "It is already very late,
and this is a lonely place. 36 Send the people
away, and let them go to the nearby farms and
villages and buy themselves something to eat."
37 "You yourselves give them something to
eat," Jesus answered.
They asked, "Do you want us to go and buy
two hundred dollars' worth of bread and feed
them?"
38 So Jesus asked them, "How much bread
do you have? Go and see."
When they found out they told him, "Five
loaves, and two fish also."

New International Version

Jesus feeds the five thousand

30 The apostles gathered around Jesus and
reported to him all they had done and taught.
31 Then, because so many people were coming
and going that they did not even have a chance
to eat, he said to them, "Come with me by yourselves to a quiet place and get some rest."
32 So they went away by themselves in a
boat to a solitary place. 33 But many who saw
them leaving recognized them and ran on foot
from all the towns and got there ahead of them.
34 When Jesus landed and saw a large crowd, he
had compassion on them, because they were like
sheep without a shepherd. So he began teaching
them many things.
35 By this time it was late in the day, so his
disciples came to him. "This is a remote place,"
they said, "and it's already very late. 36 Send
the people away so they can go to the surrounding countryside and villages and buy themselves something to eat."
37 But he answered, "You give them something to eat."
They said to him, "That would take eight
months of a man's wages! [r] Are we to go and
spend that much on bread and give it to them
to eat?"
38 "How many loaves do you have?" he
asked. "Go and see."
When they found out, they said, "Five—and
two fish."

[*r*] Greek *take 200 denarii.*

Phillips Modern English

6.30 *The apostles return: the huge crowds make rest impossible*

The apostles returned to Jesus and reported to him every detail of what they had done and taught.

"Now come along to some quiet place by yourselves, and rest for a little while," said Jesus, for there were people coming and going incessantly so that they had not even time for meals. They went off in the boat to a quiet place by themselves, but a great many saw them go and recognised them, and people from all the towns hurried on foot to get there first. When Jesus disembarked he saw the large crowd and his heart was touched with pity for them because they seemed to him like sheep without a shepherd. And he settled down to teach them about many things. As the day wore on, his disciples came to him and said,

"We are right in the wilds here and it is getting late. Let them go now, so that they can buy themselves something to eat from the farms and villages around here."

But Jesus replied,

"You give them something to eat!"

"You mean we're to go and spend twenty pounds on bread? Is that how you want us to feed them?"

"What bread have you got?" asked Jesus. "Go and have a look."

And when they had found out, they told him, "We have five loaves and two fish."

Revised Standard Version

30 The apostles returned to Jesus, and told
him all that they had done and taught. 31And
he said to them, "Come away by yourselves to
a lonely place, and rest a while." For many
were coming and going, and they had no leisure
even to eat. 32And they went away in the boat
to a lonely place by themselves. 33 Now many
saw them going, and knew them, and they ran
there on foot from all the towns, and got there
ahead of them. 34As he went ashore he saw a
great throng, and he had compassion on them,
because they were like sheep without a shepherd; and he began to teach them many things.
35And when it grew late, his disciples came to
him and said, "This is a lonely place, and the
hour is now late; 36 send them away, to go into
the country and villages round about and buy
themselves something to eat." 37 But he answered them, "You give them something to eat."
And they said to him, "Shall we go and buy two
hundred denarii [u] worth of bread, and give it to
them to eat?" 38And he said to them, "How
many loaves have you? Go and see." And when
they had found out, they said, "Five, and two

[*u*] The denarius was a day's wage for a laborer.

Jerusalem Bible

First miracle of the loaves

30 The apostles rejoined Jesus and told him
all they had done and taught. 31 Then he said to
them, "You must come away to some lonely
place all by yourselves and rest for a while"; for
there were so many coming and going that the
apostles had no time even to eat. 32 So they went
off in a boat to a lonely place where they could
be by themselves. 33 But people saw them going,
and many could guess where; and from every
town they all hurried to the place on foot and
reached it before them. 34 So as he stepped ashore
he saw a large crowd; and he took pity on them
because they were like sheep without a shepherd,
and he set himself to teach them at some length.
35 By now it was getting very late, and his disciples came up to him and said, "This is a lonely
place and it is getting very late, 36 so send them
away, and they can go to the farms and villages
around about, to buy themselves something to
eat." 37 He replied, "Give them something to
eat yourselves." They answered, "Are we to go
and spend two hundred denarii on bread for
them to eat?" 38 "How many loaves have you?"
he asked. "Go and see." And when they had
found out they said, "Five, and two fish."

New English Bible

The apostles now rejoined Jesus and reported to him all that they had done and taught. He said to them, 'Come with me, by yourselves, to some lonely place where you can rest quietly.' (For they had no leisure even to eat, so many were coming and going.) Accordingly, they set off privately by boat for a lonely place. But many saw them leave and recognized them, and came round by land, hurrying from all the towns towards the place, and arrived there first. When he came ashore, he saw a great crowd; and his heart went out to them, because they were like sheep without a shepherd; and he had much to teach them. As the day wore on, his disciples came up to him and said, 'This is a lonely place and it is getting very late; send the people off to the farms and villages round about, to buy themselves something to eat.' 'Give them something to eat yourselves', he answered. They replied, 'Are we to go and spend twenty pounds[a] on bread to give them a meal?' 'How many loaves have you?' he asked; 'go and see.' They found out and told him, 'Five, and two fishes also.'

[*a*] *Literally* 200 denarii.

King James Version

Five, and two fishes. 39And he commanded them
to make all sit down by companies upon the
green grass. 40And they sat down in ranks, by
hundreds, and by fifties. 41And when he had
taken the five loaves and the two fishes, he
looked up to heaven, and blessed, and brake the
loaves, and gave *them* to his disciples to set before them; and the two fishes divided he among
them all. 42And they did all eat, and were filled.
43And they took up twelve baskets full of the
fragments, and of the fishes. 44And they that did
eat of the loaves were about five thousand men.
45And straightway he constrained his disciples to
get into the ship, and to go to the other side before unto Bethsaida, while he sent away the
people. 46And when he had sent them away, he
departed into a mountain to pray. 47And when
even was come, the ship was in the midst of the
sea, and he alone on the land. 48And he saw
them toiling in rowing; for the wind was contrary unto them: and about the fourth watch of
the night he cometh unto them, walking upon
the sea, and would have passed by them. 49 But
when they saw him walking upon the sea, they
supposed it had been a spirit, and cried out:
50 For they all saw him, and were troubled. And
immediately he talked with them, and saith unto

Living Bible

five loaves of bread and two fish. 39, 40 Then Jesus told the crowd to sit down, and soon color-
ful groups of fifty or a hundred each were sitting
on the green grass.
41 He took the five loaves and two fish and
looking up to heaven, gave thanks for the food.
Breaking the loaves into pieces, he gave some
of the bread and fish to each disciple to place
before the people. 42And the crowd ate until
they could hold no more!
43, 44 There were about 5,000 men there for
that meal, and afterwards twelve basketfuls of
scraps were picked up off the grass!
45 Immediately after this Jesus instructed his
disciples to get back into the boat and strike
out across the lake to Bethsaida, where he would
join them later. He himself would stay and tell
the crowds good-bye and get them started home.
46 Afterwards he went up into the hills to
pray. 47 During the night, as the disciples in
their boat were out in the middle of the lake,
and he was alone on land, 48 he saw that they
were in serious trouble, rowing hard and struggling against the wind and waves.
About three o'clock in the morning he walked
out to them on the water. He started past them,
49 but when they saw something walking along
beside them they screamed in terror, thinking it
was a ghost, 50 for they all saw him.
But he spoke to them at once. "It's all right,"

Today's English Version

39 Jesus then told his disciples to make all
the people divide into groups and sit down on
the green grass. 40 So the people sat down in
rows, in groups of a hundred and groups of fifty.
41 Then Jesus took the five loaves and the two
fish, looked up to heaven, and gave thanks to
God. He broke the loaves and gave them to his
disciples to distribute to the people. He also divided the two fish among them all. 42 Everyone
ate and had enough. 43 Then the disciples took
up twelve baskets full of what was left of the
bread and of the fish. 44 The number of men
who ate the bread was five thousand.

Jesus walks on the water

45 At once Jesus made his disciples get into
the boat and go ahead of him to Bethsaida, on
the other side of the lake, while he sent the
crowd away. 46After saying good-bye to the
disciples, he went away to a hill to pray. 47 When
evening came the boat was in the middle of the
lake, while Jesus was alone on land. 48 He saw
that his disciples were having trouble rowing
the boat, because the wind was blowing against
them; so sometime between three and six o'clock
in the morning he came to them, walking on the
water. He was going to pass them by. 49 But they
saw him walking on the water. "It's a ghost!"
they thought, and screamed. 50 For when they
all saw him they were terrified.
Jesus spoke to them at once, "Courage!" he

New International Version

39 Then Jesus directed them to have all the
people sit down in groups on the green grass.
40 So they sat down in groups of hundreds and
fifties. 41 Taking the five loaves and the two
fish and looking up to heaven, he gave thanks
and broke the loaves. Then he gave them to his
disciples to set before the people. He also divided the two fish among them all. 42 They all
ate and were satisfied, 43 and the disciples picked
up twelve basketfuls of broken pieces of bread
and fish. 44 The number of the men who had
eaten was five thousand.

Jesus walks on the water

45 Immediately Jesus made his disciples get
into the boat and go on ahead of him to Bethsaida, while he dismissed the crowd. 46After
leaving them, he went into the hills to pray.
47 When evening came, the boat was in the
middle of the lake, and he was alone on land.
48 He saw the disciples straining at the oars, because the wind was against them. About the
fourth watch of the night he went out to them,
walking on the lake. He was about to pass by
them, 49 but when they saw him walking on the
lake, they thought he was a ghost. They cried
out, 50 because they all saw him and were terrified.
Immediately he spoke to them and said, "Take

Phillips Modern English

6.39 Jesus miraculously feeds five thousand people

Then Jesus told them to arrange all the people in parties, sitting on the green grass. And they settled down, looking like flower-beds, in groups of fifty or a hundred. Then Jesus took the five loaves and the two fish, and looking up to Heaven, thanked God, broke the loaves and gave them to the disciples to distribute to the people. And he divided the two fish among them all. Everybody ate and was satisfied. Afterwards they collected twelve baskets full of pieces of bread and fish that were left over. There were five thousand men who ate the loaves.

6.45 Jesus' mastery over natural law

Directly after this, Jesus made his disciples get aboard the boat and go on ahead to Bethsaida on the other side of the lake, while he himself sent the crowds home. And when he had sent them all on their way, he went off to the hill-side to pray. When it grew late, the boat was in the middle of the lake, and he was by himself on land. He saw them straining at the oars, for the wind was dead against them, and in the small hours he went towards them, walking on the waters of the lake, intending to come alongside. But when they saw him walking on the water, they thought he was a ghost, and screamed out. For they all saw him and they were absolutely terrified. But Jesus at once spoke

Revised Standard Version

fish." 39 Then he commanded them all to sit down by companies upon the green grass. 40 So they sat down in groups, by hundreds and by fifties. 41 And taking the five loaves and the two fish he looked up to heaven, and blessed, and broke the loaves, and gave them to the disciples to set before the people; and he divided the two fish among them all. 42 And they all ate and were satisfied. 43 And they took up twelve baskets full of broken pieces and of the fish. 44 And those who ate the loaves were five thousand men.

45 Immediately he made his disciples get into the boat and go before him to the other side, to Bethsaida, while he dismissed the crowd. 46 And after he had taken leave of them, he went up on the mountain to pray. 47 And when evening came, the boat was out on the sea, and he was alone on the land. 48 And he saw that they were making headway painfully, for the wind was against them. And about the fourth watch of the night he came to them, walking on the sea. He meant to pass by them, 49 but when they saw him walking on the sea they thought it was a ghost, and cried out; 50 for they all saw him, and were terrified. But immediately he spoke to them

Jerusalem Bible

39 Then he ordered them to get all the people together in groups on the green grass, 40 and they sat down on the ground in squares of hundreds and fifties. 41 Then he took the five loaves and the two fish, raised his eyes to heaven and said the blessing; then he broke the loaves and handed them to his disciples to distribute among the people. He also shared out the two fish among them all. 42 They all ate as much as they wanted. 43 They collected twelve basketfuls of scraps of bread and pieces of fish. 44 Those who had eaten the loaves numbered five thousand men.

Jesus walks on the water

45 Directly after this he made his disciples get into the boat and go on ahead to Bethsaida, while he himself sent the crowd away. 46 After saying good-by to them he went off into the hills to pray. 47 When evening came, the boat was far out on the lake, and he was alone on the land. 48 He could see they were worn out with rowing, for the wind was against them; and about the fourth watch of the night he came toward them, walking on the lake. He was going to pass them by, 49 but when they saw him walking on the lake they thought it was a ghost and cried out; 50 for they had all seen him and were terrified. But he at once spoke to them, and said, "Cour-

New English Bible

He ordered them to make the people sit down in groups on the green grass, and they sat down in rows, a hundred rows of fifty each. Then, taking the five loaves and the two fishes, he looked up to heaven, said the blessing, broke the loaves, and gave them to the disciples to distribute. He also divided the two fishes among them. They all ate to their hearts' content; and twelve great basketfuls of scraps were picked up, with what was left of the fish. Those who ate the loaves numbered five thousand men.

As soon as it was over he made his disciples embark and cross to Bethsaida ahead of him, while he himself sent the people away. After taking leave of them, he went up the hill-side to pray. It grew late and the boat was already well out on the water, while he was alone on the land. Somewhere between three and six in the morning, seeing them labouring at the oars against a head-wind, he came towards them, walking on the lake. He was going to pass them by; but when they saw him walking on the lake, they thought it was a ghost and cried out; for they all saw him and were terrified. But at once

King James Version

them, Be of good cheer: it is I; be not afraid.
51And he went up unto them into the ship; and
the wind ceased: and they were sore amazed in
themselves beyond measure, and wondered.
52 For they considered not *the miracle* of the
loaves; for their heart was hardened. 53And
when they had passed over, they came into the
land of Gennesaret, and drew to the shore.
54And when they were come out of the ship,
straightway they knew him, 55And ran through
that whole region round about, and began to
carry about in beds those that were sick, where
they heard he was. 56And whithersoever he entered, into villages, or cities, or country, they
laid the sick in the streets, and besought him
that they might touch if it were but the border
of his garment: and as many as touched him
were made whole.

7 Then came together unto him the Pharisees,
and certain of the scribes, which came from
Jerusalem. 2And when they saw some of his disciples eat bread with defiled, that is to say, with
unwashen hands, they found fault. 3 For the
Pharisees, and all the Jews, except they wash

Living Bible

he said. "It is I! Don't be afraid." 51 Then he
climbed into the boat and the wind stopped!
They just sat there, unable to take it in! 52 For
they still didn't realize who he was, even after
the miracle the evening before! For they didn't
want to believe! [b]
53 When they arrived at Gennesaret on the
other side of the lake they moored the boat,
54 and climbed out.
The people standing around there recognized
him at once, 55 and ran throughout the whole
area to spread the news of his arrival, and began carrying sick folks to him on mats and
stretchers. 56 Wherever he went—in villages and
cities, and out on the farms—they laid the sick
in the market plazas and streets, and begged
him to let them at least touch the fringes of his
clothes; and as many as touched him were
healed.

7 One day some Jewish religious leaders arrived from Jerusalem to investigate him,
2 and noticed that some of his disciples failed
to follow the usual Jewish rituals before eating.
3 (For the Jews, especially the Pharisees, will
never eat until they have sprinkled their arms to

[b] Literally, "for their hearts were hardened," perhaps implying jealousy, as in Mark 6:2-6.

Today's English Version

said. "It is I. Don't be afraid!" 51 Then he got
into the boat with them, and the wind died down.
The disciples were completely amazed, 52 because
they had not understood what the loaves of bread
meant; their minds could not grasp it.

Jesus heals the sick in Gennesaret

53 They crossed the lake and came to land at
Gennesaret, where they tied up the boat. 54As
they left the boat, people recognized Jesus at
once. 55 So they ran throughout the whole region
and brought the sick lying on their mats to him,
wherever they heard he was. 56And everywhere
Jesus went, to villages, towns, or farms, people
would take their sick to the market places and
beg him to let the sick at least touch the edge
of his cloak; and all who touched it were made
well.

The teaching of the ancestors

7 The Pharisees and some teachers of the Law
who had come from Jerusalem gathered
around Jesus. 2 They noticed that some of his
disciples were eating their food with unclean
hands—that is, they had not washed them in the
way the Pharisees said people should.
3 For the Pharisees, as well as the rest of the
Jews, follow the teaching they received from

New International Version

courage! It is I. Don't be afraid." 51 Then he
climbed into the boat with them, and the wind
died down. They were completely amazed, 52 for
they had not understood about the loaves; their
minds were closed.
53 When they had crossed over, they landed
at Gennesaret and anchored there. 54As soon as
they got out of the boat, people recognized
Jesus. 55 They ran throughout that whole region
and carried the sick on mats to wherever they
heard he was. 56And everywhere he went, into
villages, towns or countryside, they placed the
sick in the marketplaces. They begged him to
let them touch even the edge of his cloak, and
all who touched him were healed.

Clean and unclean

7 The Pharisees and some of the teachers of
the law who had come from Jerusalem gathered around Jesus and 2 saw some of his disciples eating food with "unclean"—that is, ceremonially unwashed—hands. 3 (The Pharisees and
all the Jews do not eat unless they give their

Phillips Modern English

quietly to them,

"It's all right, it is I myself; don't be afraid!" And he climbed aboard the boat with them, and the wind dropped, But they were scared out of their wits. They had not had the sense to learn the lesson of the loaves; their minds were still in the dark.

And when they had crossed over to the other side of the lake, they landed at Gennesaret and tied up there. As soon as they came ashore, the people recognised Jesus and rushed all over the countryside and began to carry the sick around on their beds to wherever they heard that he was. Wherever he went, in villages or towns or hamlets, they laid down their sick right in the market-places and begged him that they might "just touch the edge of his cloak". And all those who touched him were healed.

7.1 Jesus exposes the danger of man-made traditions

And now Jesus was approached by the Pharisees and some of the scribes who had come from Jerusalem. They had noticed that his disciples ate their meals with "common" hands—meaning that they had not gone through a ceremonial washing. (The Pharisees, and indeed all the Jews, will never eat unless they have washed their

Revised Standard Version

and said, "Take heart, it is I; have no fear."
51 And he got into the boat with them and the
wind ceased. And they were utterly astounded,
52 for they did not understand about the loaves,
but their hearts were hardened.
53 And when they had crossed over, they
came to land at Gennesaret, and moored to the
shore. 54 And when they got out of the boat,
immediately the people recognized him, 55 and
ran about the whole neighborhood and began
to bring sick people on their pallets to any place
where they heard he was. 56 And wherever he
came, in villages, cities, or country, they laid the
sick in the market places, and besought him
that they might touch even the fringe of his
garment; and as many as touched it were made
well.

7 Now when the Pharisees gathered together
to him, with some of the scribes, who had
come from Jerusalem, 2 they saw that some of
his disciples ate with hands defiled, that is, unwashed. 3 (For the Pharisees, and all the Jews,
do not eat unless they wash their hands,[v] ob-

[v] One Greek word is of uncertain meaning and is not translated.

Jerusalem Bible

age! It is I! Do not be afraid." 51 Then he got
into the boat with them, and the wind dropped.
They were utterly and completely dumfounded,
52 because they had not seen what the miracle
of the loaves meant; their minds were closed.

Cures at Gennesaret

53 Having made the crossing, they came to
land at Gennesaret and tied up. 54 No sooner
had they stepped out of the boat than people
recognized him, 55 and started hurrying all
through the countryside and brought the sick on
stretchers to wherever they heard he was. 56 And
wherever he went, to village, or town, or farm,
they laid down the sick in the open spaces, begging him to let them touch even the fringe of his
cloak. And all those who touched him were
cured.

The traditions of the Pharisees

7 The Pharisees and some of the scribes who
had come from Jerusalem gathered around
him, 2 and they noticed that some of his disciples
were eating with unclean hands, that is, without
washing them. 3 For the Pharisees, and the Jews
in general, follow the tradition of the elders and

New English Bible

he spoke to them: 'Take heart! It is I; do not be afraid.' Then he climbed into the boat beside them, and the wind dropped. At this they were completely dumbfounded, for they had not understood the incident of the loaves; their minds were closed.

So they finished the crossing and came to land at Gennesaret, where they made fast. When they came ashore, he was immediately recognized; and the people scoured that whole country-side and brought the sick on stretchers to any place where he was reported to be. Wherever he went, to farmsteads, villages, or towns, they laid out the sick in the market-places and begged him to let them simply touch the edge of his cloak; and all who touched him were cured.

Growing tension

7 A group of Pharisees, with some doctors of the law who had come from Jerusalem, met him and noticed that some of his disciples were eating their food with 'defiled' hands—in other words, without washing them. (For the Pharisees and the Jews in general never eat without wash-

King James Version

their hands oft, eat not, holding the tradition of
the elders. 4And *when they come* from the
market, except they wash, they eat not. And
many other things there be, which they have received to hold, *as* the washing of cups, and pots,
brazen vessels, and of tables. 5 Then the Pharisees and scribes asked him, Why walk not thy
disciples according to the tradition of the elders,
but eat bread with unwashen hands? 6 He answered and said unto them, Well hath Esaias
prophesied of you hypocrites, as it is written,
This people honoureth me with *their* lips, but
their heart is far from me. 7 Howbeit in vain do
they worship me, teaching *for* doctrines the
commandments of men. 8 For laying aside the
commandment of God, ye hold the tradition of
men, *as* the washing of pots and cups: and many
other such like things ye do. 9And he said unto
them, Full well ye reject the commandment of
God, that ye may keep your own tradition.
10 For Moses said, Honour thy father and thy
mother; and, Whoso curseth father or mother,
let him die the death: 11 But ye say, If a man
shall say to his father or mother, *It is* Corban,
that is to say, a gift, by whatsoever thou mightest be profited by me; *he shall be free.* 12And ye
suffer him no more to do aught for his father or
his mother; 13 Making the word of God of none
effect through your tradition, which ye have de-

Living Bible

the elbows,[a] as required by their ancient traditions. 4 So when they come home from the
market they must always sprinkle themselves in
this way before touching any food. This is but
one of many examples of laws and regulations
they have clung to for centuries, and still follow,
such as their ceremony of cleansing for pots,
pans and dishes.)
5 So the religious leaders asked him, "Why
don't your disciples follow our age-old customs?
For they eat without first performing the washing ceremony."
6, 7 Jesus replied, "You bunch of hypocrites!
Isaiah the prophet described you very well when
he said, 'These people speak very prettily about
the Lord but they have no love for him at all.
Their worship is a farce, for they claim that
God commands the people to obey their petty
rules.' How right Isaiah was! 8 For you ignore
God's specific orders and substitute your own
traditions. 9 You are simply rejecting God's laws
and trampling them under your feet for the
sake of tradition.
10 For instance, Moses gave you this law
from God: 'Honor your father and mother.' And
he said that anyone who speaks against his father or mother must die. 11 But you say it is
perfectly all right for a man to disregard his
needy parents, telling them, 'Sorry, I can't help
you! For I have given to God what I could have
given to you.' 12, 13And so you break the law
of God in order to protect your man-made tra-

[a] Literally, "to wash with the fist."

Today's English Version

their ancestors: they do not eat unless they
wash their hands in the proper way, 4 nor do they
eat anything that comes from the market unless
they wash it first. And they follow many other
rules which they have received, such as the
proper way to wash cups, pots, copper bowls, and
beds.
5 So the Pharisees and the teachers of the Law
asked Jesus, "Why is it that your disciples do
not follow the teaching handed down by our ancestors, but instead eat with unclean hands?"
6 Jesus answered them, "How right Isaiah was
when he prophesied about you! You are hypocrites, just as he wrote:

'These people, says God, honor me with their
words,
but their heart is really far away from me.
7 It is no use for them to worship me,
because they teach man-made commandments as though they were God's rules!'

8 "You put aside the commandment of God
and obey the teachings of men."
9 And Jesus continued, "You have a clever
way of rejecting God's law in order to uphold
your own teaching. 10 For Moses commanded,
'Honor your father and mother,' and, 'Anyone
who says bad things about his father or mother
must be put to death.' 11 But you teach that if
a person has something he could use to help his
father or mother, but says, 'This is Corban'
(which means, it belongs to God), 12 he is excused from helping his father or mother. 13 In
this way you disregard the word of God with

New International Version

hands a ceremonial washing, holding to the tradition of the elders. 4 When they come from the
marketplace they do not eat unless they wash.
And they observe many other traditions, such as
the washing of cups, pitchers and kettles.[s])
5 So the Pharisees and teachers of the law
asked Jesus, "Why don't your disciples live according to the tradition of the elders instead of
eating their food with 'unclean' hands?"
6 He replied, "Isaiah was right when he
prophesied about you hypocrites; as it is written:
'These people honor me with their lips,
but their hearts are far from me.
7 They worship me in vain;
their teachings are but rules made by
men.' [t]
8 You have let go of the commands of God and
are holding on to the traditions of men."
9 And he said to them: "You have a fine way
of setting aside the commands of God in order
to observe[u] your own traditions! 10 For Moses
said, 'Honor your father and mother,' [v] and,
'Anyone who curses his father or mother must
be put to death.' [w] 11 But you say that if a man
says to his father or mother: 'Whatever help you
might otherwise have received from me is Corban' (that is, a gift devoted to God), 12 then you
no longer let him do anything for his father or
mother. 13 Thus you nullify the word of God
by your tradition that you have handed down.

[s] Some early MSS add *and dining couches.* [t] Isaiah 29:13. [u] Some MSS read *set up.* [v] Exodus 20:12; Deut. 5:16. [w] Exodus 21:17.

Phillips Modern English

hands in a particular way, following a traditional rule. And they will not eat anything bought in the market until they have first performed their "sprinkling". And there are many other things which they consider important, concerned with the washing of cups, jugs and basins.) So the Pharisees and the scribes put this question to Jesus,

"Why do your disciples refuse to follow the ancient tradition, and eat their bread with 'common' hands?"

Jesus replied,

"You hypocrites, Isaiah described you beautifully when he wrote—

This people honoureth me with their lips,
But their heart is far from me.
But in vain do they worship me,
Teaching as doctrines the precepts of men.

You are so busy holding on to the traditions of men that you let go the commandment of God!"

Then he went on,

"It is wonderful to see how you can set aside the commandment of God to preserve your own tradition! For Moses said, 'Honour thy father and thy mother' and 'He that speaketh evil of father or mother, let him die the death.' But you say, 'if a man says to his father or his mother, Korban—meaning, I have given God whatever duty I owed to you', then he need not lift a finger any longer for his father or mother, so making the word of God impotent for the sake of the tradition which you hold. And this

Revised Standard Version

serving the tradition of the elders; 4 and when
they come from the market place, they do not
eat unless they purify[w] themselves;[a] and there
are many other traditions which they observe,
the washing of cups and pots and vessels of
bronze.[x]) 5 And the Pharisees and the scribes
asked him, "Why do your disciples not live[y] according to the tradition of the elders, but eat
with hands defiled?" 6 And he said to them,
"Well did Isaiah prophesy of you hypocrites, as
it is written,

'This people honors me with their lips,
but their heart is far from me;
7 in vain do they worship me,
teaching as doctrines the precepts of men.'

8 You leave the commandment of God, and hold
fast the tradition of men."
9 And he said to them, "You have a fine
way of rejecting the commandment of God, in
order to keep your tradition! 10 For Moses said,
'Honor your father and your mother'; and, 'He
who speaks evil of father or mother, let him
surely die'; 11 but you say, 'If a man tells his
father or his mother, What you would have
gained from me is Corban' (that is, given to
God) [z]—12 then you no longer permit him to
do anything for his father or mother, 13 thus
making void the word of God through your tra-

[w] Other ancient authorities read *baptize.* [a] Other ancient authorities read *and they do not eat anything from the market unless they purify it.* [x] Other ancient authorities add *and beds.* [y] Greek *walk.* [z] Or *an offering.*

Jerusalem Bible

never eat without washing their arms as far as
the elbow; 4 and on returning from the market
place they never eat without first sprinkling
themselves. There are also many other observances which have been handed down to them
concerning the washing of cups and pots and
bronze dishes. 5 So these Pharisees and scribes
asked him, "Why do your disciples not respect
the tradition of the elders but eat their food
with unclean hands?" 6 He answered, "It was of
you hypocrites that Isaiah so rightly prophesied
in this passage of scripture:

This people honors me only with lip-service,
while their hearts are far from me.
7 *The worship they offer me is worthless,*
the doctrines they teach are only human regulations.[i]

8 You put aside the commandment of God to
cling to human traditions." 9 And he said to
them, "How ingeniously you get around the commandment of God in order to preserve your own
tradition! 10 For Moses said: *Do your duty to your father and your mother,* and, *Anyone who curses father or mother must be put to death.*
11 But you say, 'If a man says to his father or
mother: Anything I have that I might have used
to help you is Corban[j] (that is, dedicated to
God), 12 then he is forbidden from that moment
to do anything for his father or mother.' 13 In
this way you make God's word null and void for
the sake of your tradition which you have

[i] Is. 29:13. [j] See note on Mt. 15:6.

New English Bible

ing the hands,[a] in obedience to an old-established tradition; and on coming from the market-place they never eat without first washing. And there are many other points on which they have a traditional rule to maintain, for example, washing of cups and jugs and copper bowls.) Accordingly, these Pharisees and the lawyers asked him, 'Why do your disciples not conform to the ancient tradition, but eat their food with defiled hands?' He answered, 'Isaiah was right when he prophesied about you hypocrites in these words: "This people pays me lip-service, but their heart is far from me: their worship of me is in vain, for they teach as doctrines the commandments of men." You neglect the commandment of God, in order to maintain the tradition of men.'

He also said to them, 'How well you set aside the commandment of God in order to maintain[b] your tradition! Moses said, "Honour your father and your mother", and, "The man who curses his father or mother must suffer death." But you hold that if a man says to his father or mother, "Anything of mine which might have been used for your benefit is Corban"' (meaning, set apart for God), 'he is no longer permitted to do anything for his father or mother. Thus by your own tradition, handed down among you, you make

[a] *Some witnesses insert* with the fist; *others insert* frequently, *or* thoroughly. [b] *Some witnesses read* establish.

King James Version

livered: and many such like things do ye.
14 And when he had called all the people *unto him,* he said unto them, Hearken unto me every one *of you,* and understand: 15 There is nothing from without a man, that entering into him can defile him: but the things which come out of him, those are they that defile the man. 16 If any man have ears to hear, let him hear. 17 And when he was entered into the house from the people, his disciples asked him concerning the parable. 18 And he saith unto them, Are ye so without understanding also? Do ye not perceive, that whatsoever thing from without entereth into the man, *it* cannot defile him; 19 Because it entereth not into his heart, but into the belly, and goeth out into the draught, purging all meats? 20 And he said, That which cometh out of the man, that defileth the man. 21 For within, out of the heart of men, proceed evil thoughts, adulteries, fornications, murders, 22 Thefts, covetousness, wickedness, deceit, lasciviousness, an evil eye, blasphemy, pride, foolishness: 23 All these evil things come from within, and defile the man.

Living Bible

dition. And this is only one example. There are many, many others."

14 Then Jesus called to the crowd to come and hear. "All of you listen," he said, "and try to understand. 15, 16 [b] Your souls aren't harmed by what you eat, but by what you think and say!" [c]

17 Then he went into a house to get away from the crowds, and his disciples asked him what he meant by the statement he had just made.

18 "Don't you understand either?" he asked. "Can't you see that what you eat won't harm your soul? 19 For food doesn't come in contact with your heart, but only passes through the digestive system." (By saying this he showed that every kind of food is kosher.)

20 And then he added, "It is the thought-life that pollutes. 21 For from within, out of men's hearts, come evil thoughts of lust, theft, murder, adultery, 22 wanting what belongs to others, wickedness, deceit, lewdness, envy, slander, pride, and all other folly. 23 All these vile things come from within; they are what pollute you and make you unfit for God."

[b] Verse 16 is omitted in many of the ancient manuscripts. "If any man has ears to hear, let him hear."
[c] Literally, "what proceeds out of the man defiles the man."

Today's English Version

the teaching you pass on to others. And there are many other things like this that you do."

The things that make a person unclean

14 Then Jesus called the crowd to him once more and said to them, "Listen to me, all of you, and understand. 15 There is nothing that goes into a person from the outside which can make him unclean. Rather, it is what comes out of a person that makes him unclean. [16 Listen, then, if you have ears to hear with!]"

17 When he left the crowd and went into the house, his disciples asked him about this parable. 18 "You are no more intelligent than the others," Jesus said to them. "Don't you understand? Nothing that goes into a person from the outside can really make him unclean, 19 because it does not go into his heart but into his stomach and then goes on out of the body." (In saying this Jesus declared that all foods are fit to be eaten.)

20 And he went on to say, "It is what comes out of a person that makes him unclean. 21 For from the inside, from a man's heart, come the evil ideas which lead him to do immoral things, to rob, kill, 22 commit adultery, be greedy, and do all sorts of evil things; deceit, indecency, jealousy, slander, pride, and folly—23 all these evil things come from inside a man and make him unclean."

New International Version

And you do many things like that."

14 Again Jesus called the crowd to him and said, "Listen to me, everyone, and understand this. 15 Nothing outside a man can make him 'unclean' by going into him. Rather, it is what comes out of a man that makes him 'unclean.' " [x]

17 After he had left the crowd and entered the house, his disciples asked him about this parable. 18 "Are you so dull?" he asked. "Don't you see that nothing that enters a man from the outside can make him 'unclean'? 19 For it doesn't go into his heart but into his stomach, and then out of his body." (In saying this, Jesus declared all foods "clean.")

20 He went on: "What comes out of a man is what makes him 'unclean.' 21 For from within, out of men's hearts, come evil thoughts, sexual immorality, theft, murder, adultery, 22 greed, malice, deceit, lewdness, envy, slander, arrogance and folly. 23 All these evils come from inside and make a man 'unclean.' "

[x] Some early MSS add verse 16: *If anyone has ears to hear, let him hear.*

Phillips Modern English

is typical of much of what you do."

Then he called the crowd close to him again, and spoke to them,

"Listen to me now, all of you, and understand this. There is nothing outside a man which can enter into him and make him 'common'. It is the things which come out of a man that make him 'common'!"

Later, when he had gone indoors away from the crowd, his disciples asked him about this parable.

"Oh, are you as dull as they are?" he said. "Can't you see that anything that goes into a man from outside cannot make him 'common' or unclean? You see, it doesn't go into his heart, but into his stomach, and passes out of the body altogether, so that all food is clean enough. But," he went on, "whatever comes out of a man, that is what makes a man 'common' or unclean. For it is from inside, from men's hearts and minds, that evil thoughts arise—lust, theft, murder, adultery, greed, wickedness, deceit, sensuality, envy, slander, arrogance and folly! All these evil things come from inside a man and make him unclean!"

Revised Standard Version

dition which you hand on. And many such
things you do."
14 And he called the people to him again,
and said to them, "Hear me, all of you, and
understand: 15 there is nothing outside a man
which by going into him can defile him; but the
things which come out of a man are what defile
him." [a] 17And when he had entered the house,
and left the people, his disciples asked him about
the parable. 18And he said to them, "Then are
you also without understanding? Do you not see
that whatever goes into a man from outside
cannot defile him, 19 since it enters, not his
heart but his stomach, and so passes on?" [b]
(Thus he declared all foods clean.) 20And he
said, "What comes out of a man is what defiles
a man. 21 For from within, out of the heart of
man, come evil thoughts, fornication, theft, murder, adultery, 22 coveting, wickedness, deceit,
licentiousness, envy, slander, pride, foolishness.
23All these evil things come from within, and
they defile a man."

[a] Other ancient authorities add verse 16, *"If any man has ears to hear, let him hear."* [b] Or *is evacuated.*

Jerusalem Bible

handed down. And you do many other things like this."

On clean and unclean

14 He called the people to him again and said,
"Listen to me, all of you, and understand.
15 Nothing that goes into a man from outside
can make him unclean; it is the things that
come out of a man that make him unclean.
16 If anyone has ears to hear, let him listen to
this."
17 When he had gone back into the house,
away from the crowd, his disciples questioned
him about the parable. 18 He said to them, "Do
you not understand either? Can you not see that
whatever goes into a man from outside cannot
make him unclean, 19 because it does not go
into his heart but through his stomach and
passes out into the sewer?" (Thus he pronounced all foods clean.) 20And he went on,
"It is what comes out of a man that makes him
unclean. 21 For it is from within, from men's
hearts, that evil intentions emerge: fornication,
theft, murder, adultery, 22 avarice, malice, deceit, indecency, envy, slander, pride, folly. 23All
these evil things come from within and make a
man unclean."

New English Bible

God's word null and void. And many other things that you do are just like that.'

On another occasion he called the people and said to them, 'Listen to me, all of you, and understand this: nothing that goes into a man from outside can defile him; no, it is the things that come out of him that defile a man.' [c]

When he had left the people and gone indoors, his disciples questioned him about the parable. He said to them, 'Are you as dull as the rest? Do you not see that nothing that goes from outside into a man can defile him, because it does not enter into his heart but into his stomach, and so passes out into the drain?' Thus he declared all foods clean. He went on, 'It is what comes out of a man that defiles him. For from inside, out of a man's heart, come evil thoughts, acts of fornication, of theft, murder, adultery, ruthless greed, and malice; fraud, indecency, envy, slander, arrogance, and folly; these evil things all come from inside, and they defile the man.'

[c] *Some witnesses here add* (16) If you have ears to hear, then hear.

King James Version

24 And from thence he arose, and went into the borders of Tyre and Sidon, and entered into a house, and would have no man know *it:* but he could not be hid. 25 For a *certain* woman, whose young daughter had an unclean spirit, heard of him, and came and fell at his feet: 26 The woman was a Greek, a Syrophenician by nation; and she besought him that he would cast forth the devil out of her daughter. 27 But Jesus said unto her, Let the children first be filled: for it is not meet to take the children's bread, and to cast *it* unto the dogs. 28 And she answered and said unto him, Yes, Lord: yet the dogs under the table eat of the children's crumbs. 29 And he said unto her, For this saying go thy way; the devil is gone out of thy daughter. 30 And when she was come to her house, she found the devil gone out, and her daughter laid upon the bed.

31 And again, departing from the coasts of Tyre and Sidon, he came unto the sea of Galilee, through the midst of the coasts of De-

Living Bible

24 Then he left Galilee and went to the region of Tyre and Sidon,[d] and tried to keep it a secret that he was there, but couldn't. For as usual the news of his arrival spread fast.

25 Right away a woman came to him whose little girl was possessed by a demon. She had heard about Jesus and now she came and fell at his feet, 26 and pled with him to release her child from the demon's control. (But she was Syrophoenician—a "despised Gentile!")

27 Jesus told her, "First I should help my own family—the Jews.[e] It isn't right to take the children's food and throw it to the dogs."

28 She replied, "That's true, sir, but even the puppies under the table are given some scraps from the children's plates."

29 "Good!" he said, "You have answered well—so well that I have healed your little girl. Go on home, for the demon has left her!"

30 And when she arrived home, her little girl was lying quietly in bed, and the demon was gone.

31 From Tyre he went to Sidon, then back to the Sea of Galilee by way of the Ten Towns.

[d] About fifty miles away. [e] Literally, "Let the children eat first."

Today's English Version

A woman's faith

24 Then Jesus left and went away to the territory near the city of Tyre. He went into a house, and did not want anyone to know he was there; but he could not stay hidden. 25 A certain woman, whose daughter had an evil spirit in her, heard about Jesus and came to him at once and fell at his feet. 26 The woman was a foreigner, born in Phoenicia of Syria. She begged Jesus to drive the demon out of her daughter. 27 But Jesus answered, "Let us feed the children first; it isn't right to take the children's food and throw it to the dogs."

28 "Sir," she answered, "even the dogs under the table eat the children's leftovers!"

29 So Jesus said to her, "For such an answer you may go home; the demon has gone out of your daughter!"

30 She went back home and found her child lying on the bed; the demon had indeed gone out of her.

Jesus heals a deaf and dumb man

31 Jesus then left the neighborhood of Tyre and went on through Sidon to Lake Galilee, going by way of the territory of the Ten Towns.

New International Version

The faith of a Syrian Phoenician woman

24 Jesus left that place and went to the vicinity of Tyre.[y] He entered a house and did not want anyone to know it; yet he could not keep his presence secret. 25 In fact, as soon as she heard about him, a woman whose little daughter was possessed by an evil[z] spirit came and fell at his feet. 26 The woman was a Greek, born in Syrian Phoenicia. She begged Jesus to drive the demon out of her daughter.

27 "First let the children eat all they want," he told her, "for it is not right to take the children's bread and toss it to their dogs."

28 "Yes, Lord," she replied, "but even the dogs under the table eat the children's crumbs."

29 Then he told her, "For such a reply, you may go; the demon has left your daughter."

30 She went home and found her child lying on the bed, and the demon gone.

The healing of a deaf and dumb man

31 Then Jesus left the vicinity of Tyre and went through Sidon, down to the Sea of Galilee

[y] Many early MSS add *and Sidon.* [z] Greek *unclean.*

Phillips Modern English

7.24 The faith of a gentile is rewarded

Then he got up and left that place and went off to the neighbourhood of Tyre. There he went into a house and wanted no one to know where he was. But it proved impossible to remain hidden. For no sooner had he got there, than a woman who had heard about him, and who had a daughter possessed by an evil spirit, arrived and prostrated herself before him. She was a Greek, a Syrophoenician by birth, and she asked him to drive the evil spirit out of her daughter. Jesus said to her,

"You must let the children have all they want first. It is not right, you know, to take the children's food and throw it to the dogs."

But she replied,

"Yes, Lord, I know, but even the dogs under the table eat the scraps the children leave."

"If you can answer like that," Jesus said to her, "you can go home! The evil spirit has left your daughter."

And she went back to her home and found the child lying quietly on her bed, and the evil spirit gone.

7.31 Jesus restores speech and hearing

Once more Jesus left the neighbourhood of Tyre and passed through Sidon towards the Lake of Galilee, and crossed the Ten Towns territory.

Revised Standard Version

24 And from there he arose and went away
to the region of Tyre and Sidon.[c] And he entered a house, and would not have any one know
it; yet he could not be hid. 25 But immediately
a woman, whose little daughter was possessed by
an unclean spirit, heard of him, and came and
fell down at his feet. 26 Now the woman was
a Greek, a Syrophoenician by birth. And she
begged him to cast the demon out of her daughter. 27 And he said to her, "Let the children first
be fed, for it is not right to take the children's
bread and throw it to the dogs." 28 But she
answered him, "Yes, Lord; yet even the dogs
under the table eat the children's crumbs."
29 And he said to her, "For this saying you may
go your way; the demon has left your daughter."
30 And she went home, and found the child lying in bed, and the demon gone.
31 Then he returned from the region of Tyre,
and went through Sidon to the Sea of Galilee,

[c] Other ancient authorities omit *and Sidon.*

Jerusalem Bible

III. Journeys outside Galilee

The daughter of the Syrophoenician woman healed

24 He left that place and set out for the territory of Tyre. There he went into a house and
did not want anyone to know he was there but
he could not pass unrecognized. 25 A woman
whose little daughter had an unclean spirit heard
about him straightaway and came and fell at his
feet. 26 Now the woman was a pagan, by birth
a Syrophoenician, and she begged him to cast
the devil out of her daughter. 27 And he said to
her, "The children should be fed first, because
it is not fair to take the children's food and
throw it to the house dogs." 28 But she spoke
up: "Ah yes, sir," she replied, "but the house
dogs under the table can eat the children's
scraps." 29 And he said to her, "For saying this,
you may go home happy: the devil has gone
out of your daughter." 30 So she went off to her
home and found the child lying on the bed and
the devil gone.

Healing of the deaf man

31 Returning from the district of Tyre he
went by way of Sidon toward the Sea of Galilee,

New English Bible

Then he left that place and went away into the territory of Tyre. He found a house to stay in, and he would have liked to remain unrecognized, but this was impossible. Almost at once a woman whose young daughter was possessed by an unclean spirit heard of him, came in, and fell at his feet. (She was a Gentile, a Phoenician of Syria by nationality.) She begged him to drive the spirit out of her daughter. He said to her, 'Let the children be satisfied first; it is not fair to take the children's bread and throw it to the dogs.' 'Sir,' she answered, 'even the dogs under the table eat the children's scraps.' He said to her, 'For saying that, you may go home content; the unclean spirit has gone out of your daughter.' And when she returned home, she found the child lying in bed; the spirit had left her.

On his return journey from Tyrian territory he went by way of Sidon to the Sea of Galilee

King James Version

capolis. 32And they bring unto him one that was
deaf, and had an impediment in his speech; and
they beseech him to put his hand upon him.
33And he took him aside from the multitude,
and put his fingers into his ears, and he spit,
and touched his tongue; 34And looking up to
heaven, he sighed, and saith unto him, Ephphatha, that is, Be opened. 35And straightway his
ears were opened, and the string of his tongue
was loosed, and he spake plain. 36And he
charged them that they should tell no man: but
the more he charged them, so much the more a
great deal they published *it;* 37And were beyond
measure astonished, saying, He hath done all
things well: he maketh both the deaf to hear,
and the dumb to speak.

8 In those days the multitude being very
great and having nothing to eat, Jesus called
his disciples *unto him,* and saith unto them, 2 I
have compassion on the multitude, because they
have now been with me three days, and have
nothing to eat: 3And if I send them away fasting
to their own houses, they will faint by the way:
for divers of them came from far. 4And his disciples answered him, From whence can a man
satisfy these *men* with bread here in the wilder-

Living Bible

32A deaf man with a speech impediment was
brought to him, and everyone begged Jesus to
lay his hands on the man and heal him.
33 Jesus led him away from the crowd and
put his fingers into the man's ears, then spat
and touched the man's tongue with the spittle.
34 Then, looking up to heaven, he sighed and
commanded, "Open!" 35 Instantly the man could
hear perfectly and speak plainly!
36 Jesus told the crowd not to spread the
news, but the more he forbade them, the more
they made it known, 37 for they were overcome
with utter amazement. Again and again they
said, "Everything he does is wonderful; he even
corrects deafness and stammering!"

8 One day about this time as another great
crowd gathered, the people ran out of food
again. Jesus called his disciples to discuss the
situation.
"I pity these people," he said, "for they have
been here three days, and have nothing left to
eat. 3And if I send them home without feeding
them, they will faint along the road! For some
of them have come a long distance."
4 "Are we supposed to find food for them
here in the desert?" his disciples scoffed.

Today's English Version

32 Some people brought him a man who was
deaf and could hardly speak, and begged Jesus
to place his hand on him. 33 So Jesus took him
off alone, away from the crowd, put his fingers
in the man's ears, spat, and touched the man's
tongue. 34 Then Jesus looked up to heaven, gave
a deep groan, and said to the man, *"Ephphatha,"*
which means, "Open up!"
35 At once the man's ears were opened, his
tongue was set loose, and he began to talk without any trouble. 36 Then Jesus ordered them all
not to speak of it to anyone; but the more he
ordered them, the more they told it. 37And all
who heard were completely amazed. "How well
he does everything!" they exclaimed. "He even
makes the deaf to hear and the dumb to speak!"

Jesus feeds the four thousand

8 Not long afterward, another large crowd
came together. When they had nothing left to
eat, Jesus called the disciples to him and said,
2 "I feel sorry for these people, because they
have been with me for three days and now have
nothing to eat. 3 If I send them home without
feeding them they will faint as they go, because
some of them have come a long way."
4 His disciples asked him, "Where in this desert can anyone find enough food to feed all these
people?"

New International Version

and into the region of the Decapolis.[a] 32 There
some people brought a man to him who was
deaf and could hardly talk, and they begged
him to place his hand on the man.
33 After he took him aside, away from the
crowd, Jesus put his fingers into the man's ears.
Then he spit and touched the man's tongue.
34 He looked up to heaven and with a deep sigh
said to him, *"Ephphatha!"* (which means, "Be
opened!"). 35At this, the man's ears were opened,
his tongue was loosened and he began to speak
plainly.
36 Jesus commanded them not to tell anyone.
But the more he did so, the more they kept
talking about it. 37 People were overwhelmed
with amazement. "He has done everything well,"
they said. "He even makes the deaf hear and
the dumb speak."

Jesus feeds the four thousand

8 During those days another large crowd gathered. Since they had nothing to eat, Jesus
called his disciples to him and said, 2 "I have
compassion for these people; they have already
been with me three days and have nothing to
eat. 3 If I send them home hungry, they will collapse on the way, because some of them have
come a long distance."
4 His disciples answered, "But where in this
remote place can anyone get enough bread to
feed them?"

[a] That is, *the Ten Cities.*

Phillips Modern English

They brought to him a man who was deaf and unable to speak intelligibly, and they implored him to put his hand upon him. Jesus took him away from the crowd by himself. He put his fingers in the man's ears and touched his tongue with his own saliva. Then, looking up to Heaven, he gave a deep sigh and said to him in Aramaic, "Open!"

And his ears were opened and immediately whatever had tied his tongue came loose and he spoke quite plainly. Jesus gave instructions that they should tell no one about this happening, but the more he told them, the more they broadcast the news. People were absolutely amazed, and kept saying,

"How wonderfully he has done everything! He even makes the deaf hear and the dumb speak."

8.1 *He again feeds the people miraculously*

About this time it happened again that a large crowd collected and had nothing to eat. Jesus called the disciples over to him and said,

"My heart goes out to this crowd; they have been with me three days now and they have no food left. If I send them off home without anything, they will collapse on the way—and some of them have come from a distance."

His disciples replied,

"Where could anyone find the food to feed them here in this deserted spot?"

Revised Standard Version

through the region of the Decapolis. 32And they brought to him a man who was deaf and had an impediment in his speech; and they besought him to lay his hand upon him. 33And taking him aside from the multitude privately, he put his fingers into his ears, and he spat and touched his tongue; 34 and looking up to heaven, he sighed, and said to him, "Ephphatha," that is, "Be opened." 35And his ears were opened, his tongue was released, and he spoke plainly. 36And he charged them to tell no one; but the more he charged them, the more zealously they proclaimed it. 37And they were astonished beyond measure, saying, "He has done all things well; he even makes the deaf hear and the dumb speak."

8 In those days, when again a great crowd had gathered, and they had nothing to eat, he called his disciples to him, and said to them, 2 "I have compassion on the crowd, because they have been with me now three days, and have nothing to eat; 3 and if I send them away hungry to their homes, they will faint on the way; and some of them have come a long way." 4And his disciples answered him, "How can one feed these men with bread here in the

Jerusalem Bible

right through the Decapolis region. 32And they brought him a deaf man who had an impediment in his speech; and they asked him to lay his hand on him. 33 He took him aside in private, away from the crowd, put his fingers into the man's ears and touched his tongue with spittle. 34 Then looking up to heaven he sighed; and he said to him, "Ephphatha," that is, "Be opened." 35And his ears were opened, and the ligament of his tongue was loosened and he spoke clearly. 36And Jesus ordered them to tell no one about it, but the more he insisted, the more widely they published it. 37 Their admiration was unbounded. "He has done all things well," they said, "he makes the deaf hear and the dumb speak."

Second miracle of the loaves

8 And now once again a great crowd had gathered, and they had nothing to eat. So he called his disciples to him and said to them, 2 "I feel sorry for all these people; they have been with me for three days now and have nothing to eat. 3 If I send them off home hungry they will collapse on the way; some have come a great distance." 4 His disciples replied, "Where could anyone get bread to feed these people in a de-

New English Bible

through the territory of the Ten Towns.[a] They brought to him a man who was deaf and had an impediment in his speech, with the request that he would lay his hand on him. He took the man aside, away from the crowd, put his fingers into his ears, spat, and touched his tongue. Then, looking up to heaven, he sighed, and said to him, '*Ephphatha*', which means 'Be opened.' With that his ears were opened, and at the same time the impediment was removed and he spoke plainly. Jesus forbade them to tell anyone; but the more he forbade them, the more they published it. Their astonishment knew no bounds: 'All that he does, he does well,' they said; 'he even makes the deaf hear and the dumb speak.'

8 There was another occasion about this time when a huge crowd had collected, and, as they had no food, Jesus called his disciples and said to them, 'I feel sorry for all these people; they have been with me now for three days and have nothing to eat. If I send them home unfed, they will turn faint on the way; some of them have come from a distance.' The disciples answered, 'How can anyone provide all these

[a] *Greek* Decapolis.

King James Version

ness? 5And he asked them, How many loaves have ye? And they said, Seven. 6And he commanded the people to sit down on the ground: and he took the seven loaves, and gave thanks, and brake, and gave to his disciples to set before *them;* and they did set *them* before the people. 7And they had a few small fishes: and he blessed, and commanded to set them also before *them.* 8 So they did eat, and were filled: and they took up of the broken *meat* that was left seven baskets. 9And they that had eaten were about four thousand: and he sent them away.

10 And straightway he entered into a ship with his disciples, and came into the parts of Dalmanutha. 11And the Pharisees came forth, and began to question with him, seeking of him a sign from heaven, tempting him. 12And he sighed deeply in his spirit, and saith, Why doth this generation seek after a sign? verily I say unto you, There shall no sign be given unto this generation. 13And he left them, and entering into the ship again departed to the other side.

14 Now *the disciples* had forgotten to take

Living Bible

5 "How many loaves of bread do you have?" he asked.

"Seven," they replied. 6 So he told the crowd to sit down on the ground. Then he took the seven loaves, thanked God for them, broke them into pieces and passed them to his disciples; and the disciples placed them before the people. 7A few small fish were found, too, so Jesus also blessed these and told the disciples to serve them.

8, 9 And the whole crowd ate until they were full, and afterwards he sent them home. There were about 4,000 people in the crowd that day and when the scraps were picked up after the meal, there were seven very large basketfuls left over!

10 Immediately after this he got into a boat with his disciples and came to the region of Dalmanutha. 11 When the local Jewish leaders learned of his arrival they came to argue with him.

"Do a miracle for us," they said. "Make something happen in the sky. Then we will believe in you."[a]

12 He sighed deeply when he heard this and he said, "Certainly not. How many more miracles do you people need?"[b]

13 So he got back into the boat and left them, and crossed to the other side of the lake. 14 But the disciples had forgotten to stock up on

[*a*] Literally, "to test him." [*b*] Literally, "Why does this generation seek a sign?"

Today's English Version

5 "How much bread do you have?" Jesus asked.

"Seven loaves," they answered.

6 He ordered the crowd to sit down on the ground. Then he took the seven loaves, gave thanks to God, broke them, and gave them to his disciples to distribute to the crowd; and the disciples did so. 7 They also had a few small fish. Jesus gave thanks for these and told the disciples to distribute them too. 8 Everybody ate and had enough—there were about four thousand people. 9 Then the disciples took up seven baskets full of pieces left over. Jesus sent the people away, 10 and at once got into the boat with his disciples and went to the district of Dalmanutha.

The Pharisees ask for a miracle

11 Some Pharisees came to Jesus and started to argue with him. They wanted to trap him, so they asked him to perform a miracle to show God's approval. 12 Jesus gave a deep groan and said, "Why do the people of this day ask for a miracle? No, I tell you! No such proof will be given this people!"

13 He left them, got back into the boat, and started across to the other side of the lake.

The yeast of the Pharisees and of Herod

14 The disciples had forgotten to bring any

New International Version

5 "How many loaves do you have?" Jesus asked.

"Seven," they replied.

6 He told the crowd to sit down on the ground. When he had taken the seven loaves and given thanks, he broke them and gave them to his disciples to set before the people, and they did so. 7 They had a few small fish as well; he gave thanks for them also and told the disciples to distribute them. 8 The people ate and were satisfied. Afterward the disciples picked up seven basketfuls of broken pieces that were left over. 9About four thousand men were present. And having sent them away, 10 he got into the boat with his disciples and went to the region of Dalmanutha.

11 The Pharisees came and began to question Jesus. To test him, they asked him for a sign from heaven. 12 He sighed deeply and said, "Why does this generation ask for a miraculous sign? I tell you the truth, no sign will be given to it." 13 Then he left them, got back into the boat and crossed to the other side.

The yeast of the Pharisees and Herod

14 The disciples had forgotten to bring bread,

Phillips Modern English

"How many loaves have you got?" Jesus asked them.

"Seven," they replied.

So Jesus told the crowd to settle themselves on the ground. Then he took the seven loaves into his hands, and with a prayer of thanksgiving broke them, and gave them to the disciples to distribute to the people; and this they did. They had a few small fish as well, and after blessing them, Jesus told his disciples to give these also to the people. They ate and they were satisfied. Moreover, they picked up seven baskets full of pieces left over. The people numbered about four thousand. Jesus sent them home, and then he boarded the boat at once with his disciples and went on to the district of Dalmanutha.

8.11 Jesus refuses to give a sign

Now the Pharisees came out and began an argument with him. They were out to test him and wanted a sign from Heaven. Jesus gave a deep sigh, and then said,

"What makes this generation want a sign? I can tell you this, they will certainly not be given one!"

Then he left them and got aboard the boat again, and crossed the lake.

The disciples had forgotten to take any food

Revised Standard Version

desert?" 5And he asked them, "How many loaves have you?" They said, "Seven." 6And he commanded the crowd to sit down on the ground; and he took the seven loaves, and having given thanks he broke them and gave them to his disciples to set before the people; and they set them before the crowd. 7And they had a few small fish; and having blessed them, he commanded that these also should be set before them. 8And they ate, and were satisfied; and they took up the broken pieces left over, seven baskets full. 9And there were about four thousand people. 10And he sent them away; and immediately he got into the boat with his disciples, and went to the district of Dalmanutha.[d]

11 The Pharisees came and began to argue with him, seeking from him a sign from heaven, to test him. 12And he sighed deeply in his spirit, and said, "Why does this generation seek a sign? Truly, I say to you, no sign shall be given to this generation." 13And he left them, and getting into the boat again he departed to the other side.

14 Now they had forgotten to bring bread;

[d] Other ancient authorities read *Magadan* or *Magdala.*

Jerusalem Bible

serted place like this?" 5 He asked them, "How many loaves have you?" "Seven," they said. 6 Then he instructed the crowd to sit down on the ground, and he took the seven loaves, and after giving thanks he broke them and handed them to his disciples to distribute; and they distributed them among the crowd. 7 They had a few small fish as well, and over these he said a blessing and ordered them to be distributed also. 8 They ate as much as they wanted, and they collected seven basketfuls of the scraps left over. 9 Now there had been about four thousand people. He sent them away 10 and immediately, getting into the boat with his disciples, went to the region of Dalmanutha.

The Pharisees ask for a sign from heaven

11 The Pharisees came up and started a discussion with him; they demanded of him a sign from heaven, to test him. 12And with a sigh that came straight from the heart he said, "Why does this generation demand a sign? I tell you solemnly, no sign shall be given to this generation." 13And leaving them again and re-embarking he went away to the opposite shore.

The yeast of the Pharisees and of Herod

14 The disciples had forgotten to take any

New English Bible

people with bread in this lonely place?' 'How many loaves have you?' he asked; and they answered, 'Seven.' So he ordered the people to sit down on the ground; then he took the seven loaves, and, after giving thanks to God, he broke the bread and gave it to his disciples to distribute; and they served it out to the people. They had also a few small fishes, which he blessed and ordered them to distribute. They all ate to their hearts' content, and seven baskets were filled with the scraps that were left. The people numbered about four thousand. Then he dismissed them; and, without delay, got into the boat with his disciples and went to the district of Dalmanutha.[a]

Then the Pharisees came out and engaged him in discussion. To test him they asked him for a sign from heaven. He sighed deeply to himself and said, 'Why does this generation ask for a sign? I tell you this: no sign shall be given to this generation.' With that he left them, re-embarked, and went off to the other side of the lake.

Now they had forgotten to take bread with

[a] *Some witnesses give* Magedan; *others give* Magdala.

King James Version

bread, neither had they in the ship with them more than one loaf. 15And he charged them, saying, Take heed, beware of the leaven of the Pharisees, and *of* the leaven of Herod. 16And they reasoned among themselves, saying, *It is* because we have no bread. 17And when Jesus knew *it*, he saith unto them, Why reason ye, because ye have no bread? perceive ye not yet, neither understand? have ye your heart yet hardened? 18 Having eyes, see ye not? and having ears, hear ye not? and do ye not remember? 19 When I brake the five loaves among five thousand, how many baskets full of fragments took ye up? They say unto him, Twelve. 20And when the seven among four thousand, how many baskets full of fragments took ye up? And they said, Seven. 21And he said unto them, How is it that ye do not understand?

22 And he cometh to Bethsaida; and they bring a blind man unto him, and besought him to touch him. 23And he took the blind man by the hand, and led him out of the town; and when he had spit on his eyes, and put his hands upon him, he asked him if he saw aught. 24And he looked up, and said, I see men as trees,

Living Bible

food before they left, and had only one loaf of bread in the boat.

15 As they were crossing, Jesus said to them very solemnly, "Beware of the yeast of King Herod and of the Pharisees."

16 "What does he mean?" the disciples asked each other. They finally decided that he must be talking about their forgetting to bring bread.

17 Jesus realized what they were discussing and said, "No, that isn't it at all! Can't you understand? Are your hearts too hard to take it in? 18 'Your eyes are to see with—why don't you look? Why don't you open your ears and listen?' Don't you remember anything at all?

19 "What about the 5,000 men I fed with five loaves of bread? How many basketfuls of scraps did you pick up afterwards?"

"Twelve," they said.

20 "And when I fed the 4,000 with seven loaves, how much was left?"

"Seven basketfuls," they said.

21 "And yet you think I'm worried that we have no bread?" [c]

22 When they arrived at Bethsaida, some people brought a blind man to him and begged him to touch and heal him. 23 Jesus took the blind man by the hand and led him out of the village, and spat upon his eyes, and laid his hands over them.

"Can you see anything now?" Jesus asked him.

24 The man looked around. "Yes!" he said,

[c] Literally, "Do you not yet understand?"

Today's English Version

extra bread, and had only one loaf with them in the boat. 15 "Look out," Jesus warned them, "and be on your guard against the yeast of the Pharisees and the yeast of Herod."

16 They started discussing among themselves, "He says this because we don't have any bread."

17 Jesus knew what they were saying, so he asked them, "Why are you discussing about not having any bread? Don't you know or understand yet? Are your minds so dull? 18 You have eyes—can't you see? You have ears—can't you hear? Don't you remember 19 when I broke the five loaves for the five thousand people? How many baskets full of leftover pieces did you take up?"

"Twelve," they answered.

20 "And when I broke the seven loaves for the four thousand people," asked Jesus, "how many baskets full of leftover pieces did you take up?"

"Seven," they answered.

21 "And you still don't understand?" he asked them.

Jesus heals a blind man at Bethsaida

22 They came to Bethsaida, where some people brought a blind man to Jesus and begged him to touch him. 23 Jesus took the blind man by the hand and led him out of the village. After spitting on the man's eyes, Jesus placed his hands on him and asked him, "Can you see anything?"

24 The man looked up and said, "Yes, I can

New International Version

except for one loaf they had with them in the boat. 15 "Be careful," Jesus warned them. "Watch out for the yeast of the Pharisees and that of Herod."

16 They discussed this with one another and said, "It is because we have no bread."

17 Aware of their discussion, Jesus asked them: "Why are you talking about having no bread? Do you still not see or understand? Are your hearts hardened? 18 Do you have eyes but fail to see, and ears but fail to hear? And don't you remember? 19 When I broke the five loaves for the five thousand, how many basketfuls of pieces did you pick up?"

"Twelve," they replied.

20 "And when I broke the seven loaves for the four thousand, how many basketfuls of pieces did you pick up?"

They answered, "Seven."

21 He said to them, "Do you still not understand?"

The healing of a blind man at Bethsaida

22 They came to Bethsaida, and some people brought a blind man and begged Jesus to touch him. 23 He took the blind man by the hand and led him outside the village. When he had spit on the man's eyes and put his hands on him, Jesus asked, "Do you see anything?"

24 He looked up and said, "I see people; they

Phillips Modern English

and had only one loaf with them in the boat. Jesus spoke seriously to them, "Keep your eyes open! Be on your guard against the 'yeast' of the Pharisees and the 'yeast' of Herod!" And this sent them into an earnest consultation among themselves because they had brought no bread. Jesus knew it and said to them,

"Why all this discussion about bringing no bread? Don't you understand or grasp what I say even yet? Are your minds closed? Are you like the people who 'having eyes, do not see, and having ears, do not hear'? Have you forgotten—when I broke five loaves for five thousand people, how many baskets full of pieces did you pick up?"

"Twelve," they replied.

"And when there were seven loaves for four thousand people, how many baskets of pieces did you pick up?"

"Seven," they said.

"And does that still mean nothing to you?" he said.

8.22 Jesus restores sight

So they arrived at Bethsaida where a blind man was brought to him, with the earnest request that he should touch him. Jesus took the blind man's hand and led him outside the village. Then he moistened his eyes with saliva and putting his hands on him, asked,

"Can you see at all?"

The man looked up and said,

Revised Standard Version

and they had only one loaf with them in the boat. 15 And he cautioned them, saying, "Take heed, beware of the leaven of the Pharisees and the leaven of Herod." [e] 16 And they discussed it with one another, saying, "We have no bread." 17 And being aware of it, Jesus said to them, "Why do you discuss the fact that you have no bread? Do you not yet perceive or understand? Are your hearts hardened? 18 Having eyes do you not see, and having ears do you not hear? And do you not remember? 19 When I broke the five loaves for the five thousand, how many baskets full of broken pieces did you take up?" They said to him, "Twelve." 20 "And the seven for the four thousand, how many baskets full of broken pieces did you take up?" And they said to him, "Seven." 21 And he said to them, "Do you not yet understand?"

22 And they came to Bethsaida. And some people brought to him a blind man, and begged him to touch him. 23 And he took the blind man by the hand, and led him out of the village; and when he had spit on his eyes and laid his hands upon him, he asked him, "Do you see anything?" 24 And he looked up and said, "I see men; but

[e] Other ancient authorities read *the Herodians.*

Jerusalem Bible

food and they had only one loaf with them in the boat. 15 Then he gave them this warning, "Keep your eyes open; be on your guard against the yeast of the Pharisees and the yeast of Herod." 16 And they said to one another, "It is because we have no bread." 17 And Jesus knew it, and he said to them, "Why are you talking about having no bread? Do you not yet understand? Have you no perception? Are your minds closed? 18 Have you *eyes that do not see, ears that do not hear?* [k] Or do you not remember? 19 When I broke the five loaves among the five thousand, how many baskets full of scraps did you collect?" They answered, "Twelve." 20 "And when I broke the seven loaves for the four thousand, how many baskets full of scraps did you collect?" And they answered, "Seven." 21 Then he said to them, "Are you still without perception?"

Cure of a blind man at Bethsaida

22 They came to Bethsaida, and some people brought to him a blind man whom they begged him to touch. 23 He took the blind man by the hand and led him outside the village. Then putting spittle on his eyes and laying his hands on him, he asked, "Can you see anything?" 24 The man, who was beginning to see, replied, "I can

[k] Jr. 5:21; Ezk. 12:2.

New English Bible

them; they had no more than one loaf in the boat. He began to warn them: 'Beware,' he said, 'be on your guard against the leaven of the Pharisees and the leaven of Herod.' They said among themselves, 'It is because we have no bread.' Knowing what was in their minds, he asked them, 'Why do you talk about having no bread? Have you no inkling yet? Do you still not understand? Are your minds closed? You have eyes: can you not see? You have ears: can you not hear? Have you forgotten? When I broke the five loaves among five thousand, how many basketfuls of scraps did you pick up?' 'Twelve', they said. 'And how many when I broke the seven loaves among four thousand?' They answered, 'Seven.' He said, 'Do you still not understand?'

They arrived at Bethsaida. There the people brought a blind man to Jesus and begged him to touch him. He took the blind man by the hand and led him away out of the village. Then he spat on his eyes, laid his hands upon him, and asked whether he could see anything. The man's sight began to come back, and he said, 'I

King James Version

walking. 25 After that he put *his* hands again upon his eyes, and made him look up; and he was restored, and saw every man clearly. 26 And he sent him away to his house, saying, Neither go into the town, nor tell *it* to any in the town.

27 And Jesus went out, and his disciples, into the towns of Cesarea Philippi: and by the way he asked his disciples, saying unto them, Whom do men say that I am? 28 And they answered, John the Baptist: but some *say,* Elias; and others, One of the prophets. 29 And he saith unto them, But whom say ye that I am? And Peter answereth and saith unto him, Thou art the Christ. 30 And he charged them that they should tell no man of him. 31 And he began to teach them, that the Son of man must suffer many

Living Bible

"I see men! But I can't see them very clearly; they look like tree trunks walking around!"

25 Then Jesus placed his hands over the man's eyes again and as the man stared intently, his sight was completely restored, and he saw everything clearly, drinking in the sights around him.

26 Jesus sent him home to his family. "Don't even go back to the village first," he said.

27 Jesus and his disciples now left Galilee and went out to the villages of Caesarea Philippi. As they were walking along he asked them, "Who do the people think I am? What are they saying about me?"

28 "Some of them think you are John the Baptist," the disciples replied, "and others say you are Elijah or some other ancient prophet come back to life again."

29 Then he asked, "Who do you think I am?" Peter replied, "You are the Messiah." 30 But Jesus warned them not to tell anyone!

31 Then he began to tell them about the terrible things he[d] would suffer, and that he would

[*d*] Literally, "the Son of Man."

Today's English Version

see people, but they look like trees walking around."

25 Jesus again placed his hands on the man's eyes. This time the man looked hard, his eyesight came back, and he saw everything clearly. 26 Jesus then sent him home with the order, "Don't go back into the village."

Peter's declaration about Jesus

27 Then Jesus and his disciples went away to the villages of Caesarea Philippi. On the way he asked them, "Tell me, who do people say I am?"

28 "Some say that you are John the Baptist," they answered; "others say that you are Elijah, while others say that you are one of the prophets."

29 "What about you?" he asked them. "Who do you say I am?"

Peter answered, "You are the Messiah."

30 Then Jesus ordered them, "Do not tell anyone about me."

Jesus speaks about his suffering and death

31 Then Jesus began to teach his disciples: "The Son of Man must suffer much, and be re-

New International Version

look like trees walking around."

25 Once more Jesus put his hands on the man's eyes. Then his eyes were opened, his sight was restored, and he saw everything clearly. 26 Jesus sent him home, saying, "Don't go into the village." [b]

Peter's confession of Christ

27 Jesus and his disciples went on to the villages around Caesarea Philippi. On the way he asked them, "Who do people say I am?"

28 They replied, "Some say John the Baptist; others say Elijah; and still others, one of the prophets."

29 "But what about you?" he asked. "Who do you say I am?"

Peter answered, "You are the Christ." [c]

30 Jesus warned them not to tell anyone about him.

Jesus predicts his death

31 He then began to teach them that the Son of Man must suffer many things and be rejected

[*b*] Some MSS read ***Don't go and tell anyone in the village.*** [*c*] Or ***Messiah.*** "The Christ" (Greek) and "the Messiah" (Hebrew) both mean "the Anointed One."

Phillips Modern English

"I can see people. They look like trees—only they are walking about."

Then Jesus put his hands on his eyes once more and his sight came into focus, and he recovered and saw everything sharp and clear. And Jesus sent him off to his own house with the words,

"Don't even go into the village."

8.27 Jesus' question: Peter's inspired answer

Jesus then went away with his disciples to the villages of Caesarea Philippi. On the way he asked them,

"Who are men saying that I am?"

"John the Baptist," they answered. "But others say that you are Elijah or, some say, one of the prophets."

Then he asked them,

"But what about you—who do you say that I am?"

"You are Christ!" answered Peter.

Then Jesus impressed it upon them that they must not mention this to anyone.

8.31 Jesus speaks of the future and of the cost of discipleship

And he began to teach them that it was inevitable that the Son of Man should go through much suffering and be utterly repudiated by the

Revised Standard Version

they look like trees, walking." 25 Then again he
laid his hands upon his eyes; and he looked intently and was restored, and saw everything
clearly. 26 And he sent him away to his home,
saying, "Do not even enter the village."
27 And Jesus went on with his disciples, to
the villages of Caesarea Philippi; and on the way
he asked his disciples, "Who do men say that I
am?" 28 And they told him, "John the Baptist;
and others say, Elijah; and others one of the
prophets." 29 And he asked them, "But who do
you say that I am?" Peter answered him, "You
are the Christ." 30 And he charged them to tell
no one about him.
31 And he began to teach them that the Son
of man must suffer many things, and be re-

Jerusalem Bible

see people; they look like trees to me, but they
are walking about." 25 Then he laid his hands
on the man's eyes again and he saw clearly; he
was cured, and he could see everything plainly
and distinctly. 26 And Jesus sent him home, saying, "Do not even go into the village."

Peter's profession of faith

27 Jesus and his disciples left for the villages
around Caesarea Philippi. On the way he put
this question to his disciples, "Who do people
say I am?" 28 And they told him. "John the
Baptist," they said, "others Elijah; others again,
one of the prophets." 29 "But you," he asked,
"who do you say I am?" Peter spoke up and said
to him, "You are the Christ." 30 And he gave
them strict orders not to tell anyone about him.

First prophecy of the Passion

31 And he began to teach them that the Son
of Man was destined to suffer grievously, to be

New English Bible

see men; they look like trees, but they are walking about.' Jesus laid his hands on his eyes again; he looked hard, and now he was cured so that he saw everything clearly. Then Jesus sent him home, saying, 'Do not tell anyone in the village.' [b]

Jesus and his disciples set out for the villages of Caesarea Philippi. On the way he asked his disciples, 'Who do men say I am?' They answered, 'Some say John the Baptist, others Elijah, others one of the prophets.' 'And you,' he asked, 'who do you say I am?' Peter replied: 'You are the Messiah.' Then he gave them strict orders not to tell anyone about him; and he began to teach them that the Son of Man had to undergo great sufferings, and to be rejected

[b] *Some witnesses read* Do not go into the village.

King James Version

things, and be rejected of the elders, and *of* the
chief priests, and scribes, and be killed, and
after three days rise again. 32And he spake that
saying openly. And Peter took him, and began
to rebuke him. 33 But when he had turned about
and looked on his disciples, he rebuked Peter,
saying, Get thee behind me, Satan: for thou
savourest not the things that be of God, but the
things that be of men.
34 And when he had called the people *unto*
him with his disciples also, he said unto them,
Whosoever will come after me, let him deny
himself, and take up his cross, and follow me.
35 For whosoever will save his life shall lose it;
but whosoever shall lose his life for my sake
and the gospel's, the same shall save it. 36 For
what shall it profit a man, if he shall gain the
whole world, and lose his own soul? 37 Or what
shall a man give in exchange for his soul?
38 Whosoever therefore shall be ashamed of me
and of my words, in this adulterous and sinful
generation, of him also shall the Son of man be
ashamed, when he cometh in the glory of his
Father with the holy angels.

9 And he said unto them, Verily I say unto
you, That there be some of them that stand
here, which shall not taste of death, till they
have seen the kingdom of God come with
power.

Living Bible

be rejected by the elders and the Chief Priests
and the other Jewish leaders—and be killed, and
that he would rise again three days afterwards.
32 He talked about it quite frankly with them,
so Peter took him aside and chided him.[e] "You
shouldn't say things like that," he told Jesus.
33 Jesus turned and looked at his disciples
and then said to Peter very sternly, "Satan, get
behind me! You are looking at this only from a
human point of view and not from God's."
34 Then he called his disciples and the crowds
to come over and listen. "If any of you wants
to be my follower," he told them, "you must put
aside your own pleasures and shoulder your
cross, and follow me closely. 35 If you insist on
saving your life, you will lose it. Only those who
throw away their lives for my sake and for the
sake of the Good News will ever know what it
means to really live.
36 "And how does a man benefit if he gains
the whole world and loses his soul in the process? 37 For is anything worth more than his
soul? 38And anyone who is ashamed of me and
my message in these days of unbelief and sin, I,
the Messiah,[d] will be ashamed of him when I return in the glory of my Father, with the holy
angels."

9 Jesus went on to say to his disciples, "Some
of you who are standing here right now will
live to see the Kingdom of God arrive in great
power!"

[e] Literally, "Peter began to rebuke him." [d] Literally, "the Son of Man."

Today's English Version

jected by the elders, the chief priests, and the
teachers of the Law. He will be put to death, and
after three days he will rise to life." 32 He made
this very clear to them. So Peter took him aside
and began to rebuke him. 33 But Jesus turned
around, looked at his disciples, and rebuked
Peter. "Get away from me, Satan," he said.
"Your thoughts are men's thoughts, not God's!"
34 Then Jesus called the crowd and his disciples to him. "If anyone wants to come with me,"
he told them, "he must forget himself, carry his
cross, and follow me. 35 For whoever wants to
save his own life will lose it; but whoever loses
his life for me and for the gospel will save it.
36 Does a man gain anything if he wins the
whole world but loses his life? Of course not!
37 There is nothing a man can give to regain
his life. 38 If, then, a man is ashamed of me and
of my teaching in this godless and wicked day,
then the Son of Man will be ashamed of him
when he comes in the glory of his Father with
the holy angels."

9 And he went on to say, "Remember this!
There are some here who will not die until
they have seen the Kingdom of God come with
power."

New International Version

by the elders, chief priests and teachers of the
law, and that he must be killed and after three
days rise again. 32 He spoke plainly about this,
and Peter took him aside and began to rebuke
him.
33 But when Jesus turned and looked at his
disciples, he rebuked Peter. "Out of my sight,
Satan!" he said. "You do not have in mind the
things of God, but the things of men."
34 Then he called the crowd to him along
with his disciples and said: "If anyone would
come after me, he must deny himself and take
up his cross and follow me. 35 For whoever
wants to save his life[d] will lose it, but whoever
loses his life for me and for the gospel will save
it. 36 What good is it for a man to gain the
whole world, yet forfeit his soul? [d] 37 Or what
can a man give in exchange for his soul? 38 If
anyone is ashamed of me and my words in this
adulterous and sinful generation, the Son of
Man will be ashamed of him when he comes in
his Father's glory with the holy angels."

9 And he said to them, "I tell you the truth,
some who are standing here will not taste
death before they see the kingdom of God come
with power."

[d] The Greek word means either *life* or *soul*.

Phillips Modern English

elders and chief priests and scribes, and be killed, and after three days rise again. He told them all this quite bluntly.

This made Peter draw him on one side and take him to task about what he had said. But Jesus turned and faced his disciples and rebuked Peter.

"Out of my way, Satan!" he said. "Peter, your thoughts are not God's thoughts, but man's!"

Then he called his disciples and the people around him, and said to them,

"If anyone wants to follow in my footsteps, he must give up all right to himself, take up his cross and follow me. The man who tries to save his life will lose it; it is the man who loses his life for my sake and the gospel's who will save it. What good can it do a man to gain the whole world at the price of his own soul? What can a man offer to buy back his soul once he has lost it? If anyone is ashamed of me and my words in this unfaithful and sinful generation, the Son of Man will be ashamed of him when he comes in the Father's glory with the holy angels around him."

9.1 Jesus foretells his glory

Then he added,

"Believe me, there are some of you standing here who will know nothing of death until you have seen the kingdom of God already come in power!"

Revised Standard Version

jected by the elders and the chief priests and the scribes, and be killed, and after three days rise again. 32 And he said this plainly. And Peter took him, and began to rebuke him. 33 But turning and seeing his disciples, he rebuked Peter, and said, "Get behind me, Satan! For you are not on the side of God, but of men."

34 And he called to him the multitude with his disciples, and said to them, "If any man would come after me, let him deny himself and take up his cross and follow me. 35 For whoever would save his life will lose it; and whoever loses his life for my sake and the gospel's will save it. 36 For what does it profit a man, to gain the whole world and forfeit his life? 37 For what can a man give in return for his life? 38 For whoever is ashamed of me and of my words in this adulterous and sinful generation, of him will the Son of man also be ashamed, when he comes in the glory of his Father with the holy

9 angels." 1 And he said to them, "Truly, I say to you, there are some standing here who will not taste death before they see that the kingdom of God has come with power."

Jerusalem Bible

rejected by the elders and the chief priests and the scribes, and to be put to death, and after three days to rise again; 32 and he said all this quite openly. Then, taking him aside, Peter started to remonstrate with him. 33 But, turning and seeing his disciples, he rebuked Peter and said to him, "Get behind me Satan! Because the way you think is not God's way but man's."

The condition of following Christ

34 He called the people and his disciples to him and said, "If anyone wants to be a follower of mine, let him renounce himself and take up his cross and follow me. 35 For anyone who wants to save his life will lose it; but anyone who loses his life for my sake, and for the sake of the gospel, will save it. 36 What gain, then, is it for a man to win the whole world and ruin his life? 37 And indeed what can a man offer in exchange for his life? 38 For if anyone in this adulterous and sinful generation is ashamed of me and of my words, the Son of Man will also be ashamed of him when he comes in the glory of his Father with the holy angels."

9 And he said to them, "I tell you solemnly, there are some standing here who will not taste death before they see the kingdom of God come with power."

New English Bible

by the elders, chief priests, and doctors of the law; to be put to death, and to rise again three days afterwards. He spoke about it plainly. At this Peter took him by the arm and began to rebuke him. But Jesus turned round, and, looking at his disciples, rebuked Peter. 'Away with you, Satan,' he said; 'you think as men think, not as God thinks.'

Then he called the people to him, as well as his disciples, and said to them, 'Anyone who wishes to be a follower of mine must leave self behind; he must take up his cross, and come with me. Whoever cares for his own safety is lost; but if a man will let himself be lost for my sake and for the Gospel, that man is safe. What does a man gain by winning the whole world at the cost of his true self? What can he give to buy that self back? If anyone is ashamed of me and mine[a] in this wicked and godless age, the Son of Man will be ashamed of him, when he comes in the glory of his Father and of the holy angels.'[b]

9 He also said, 'I tell you this: there are some of those standing here who will not taste death before they have seen the kingdom of God already come in power.'

[a] *Some witnesses read* me and my words. [b] *Some witnesses read* Father with the holy angels.

King James Version

2 And after six days Jesus taketh *with him*
Peter, and James, and John, and leadeth them
up into a high mountain apart by themselves:
and he was transfigured before them. 3And his
raiment became shining, exceeding white as
snow; so as no fuller on earth can white them.
4And there appeared unto them Elias with
Moses: and they were talking with Jesus. 5And
Peter answered and said to Jesus, Master, it is
good for us to be here: and let us make three
tabernacles; one for thee, and one for Moses,
and one for Elias. 6 For he wist not what to say;
for they were sore afraid. 7And there was a
cloud that overshadowed them: and a voice
came out of the cloud, saying, This is my beloved Son: hear him. 8And suddenly, when they
had looked round about, they saw no man any
more, save Jesus only with themselves. 9And as
they came down from the mountain, he charged
them that they should tell no man what things
they had seen, till the Son of man were risen
from the dead. 10And they kept that saying with
themselves, questioning one with another what
the rising from the dead should mean.
11 And they asked him, saying, Why say the
scribes that Elias must first come? 12And he answered and told them, Elias verily cometh first,
and restoreth all things; and how it is written of

Living Bible

2 Six days later Jesus took Peter, James and
John to the top of a mountain. No one else was
there.
Suddenly his face began to shine with glory,
3 and his clothing became dazzling white, far
more glorious than any earthly process could
ever make it! 4 Then Elijah and Moses appeared
and began talking with Jesus!
5 "Teacher, this is wonderful!" Peter exclaimed. "We will make three shelters here, one
for each of you. . . .
6 He said this just to be talking, for he didn't
know what else to say and they were all terribly
frightened.
7 But while he was still speaking these words,
a cloud covered them, blotting out the sun, and
a voice from the cloud said, *"This* is my beloved
Son. Listen to *him."*
8 Then suddenly they looked around and
Moses and Elijah were gone, and only Jesus was
with them.
9 As they descended the mountainside he told
them never to mention what they had seen until
after he[a] had risen from the dead. 10 So they
kept it to themselves, but often talked about it,
and wondered what he meant by "rising from
the dead."
11 Now they began asking him about something the Jewish religious leaders often spoke of,
that Elijah must return [before the Messiah
could come[b]]. 12, 13 Jesus agreed that Elijah
must come first and prepare the way—and that
he had, in fact, already come! And that he had

[*a*] Literally, "the Son of Man." [*b*] Implied.

Today's English Version

The transfiguration

2 Six days later Jesus took Peter, James, and
John with him, and led them up a high mountain
by themselves. As they looked on, a change
came over him, 3 and his clothes became shining white, whiter than anyone in the world could
wash them. 4 Then the three disciples saw Elijah
and Moses, who were talking with Jesus. 5 Peter
spoke up and said to Jesus, "Teacher, it is a
good thing that we are here. We will make three
tents, one for you, one for Moses, and one for
Elijah." 6 He and the others were so frightened
that he did not know what to say.
7 A cloud appeared and covered them with
its shadow, and a voice came from the cloud,
"This is my own dear Son—listen to him!" 8 They
took a quick look around but did not see anyone else; only Jesus was with them.
9 As they came down the mountain Jesus ordered them, "Don't tell anyone what you have
seen, until the Son of Man has risen from death."
10 They obeyed his order, but among themselves they started discussing the matter, "What
does this 'rising from death' mean?" 11And
they asked Jesus, "Why do the teachers of the
Law say that Elijah has to come first?"
12 His answer was, "Elijah does indeed come
first to get everything ready. Yet why do the
Scriptures say that the Son of Man will suffer

New International Version

The transfiguration

2 After six days Jesus took Peter, James and
John with him and led them up a high mountain, where they were all alone. There he was
transfigured before them. 3 His clothes became
dazzling white, whiter than anyone in the world
could bleach them. 4And there appeared before
them Elijah and Moses, who were talking with
Jesus.
5 Peter said to Jesus, "Rabbi, it is good for
us to be here. Let us put up three shelters[e]—one
for you, one for Moses and one for Elijah."
6 (He did not know what to say, they were so
frightened.)
7 Then a cloud appeared and enveloped them,
and a voice came from the cloud: "This is my
Son, whom I love. Listen to him!"
8 Suddenly, when they looked around, they no
longer saw anyone with them except Jesus.
9 As they were coming down the mountain,
Jesus gave them orders not to tell anyone what
they had seen until the Son of Man had risen
from the dead. 10 They kept the matter to themselves, discussing what "rising from the dead"
meant.
11 And they asked him, "Why do the teachers
of the law say that Elijah must come first?"
12 Jesus replied, "To be sure, Elijah does come
first, and restores all things. Why then is it writ-

[*e*] Or *sanctuaries.*

Phillips Modern English

Six days later, Jesus took Peter and James and John with him and led them high up on a hill-side where they were entirely alone. His whole appearance changed before their eyes, while his clothes became white, dazzling white—whiter than any earthly bleaching could make them. Elijah and Moses appeared to the disciples and stood there in conversation with Jesus. Peter burst out to Jesus,

"Master, it is wonderful for us to be here! Shall we put up three shelters—one for you, one for Moses and one for Elijah?"

He really did not know what to say, for they were very frightened. Then came a cloud which overshadowed them and a voice spoke out of the cloud,

"This is my dearly-loved Son. Listen to him!"

Then, quite suddenly they looked all round them and saw nobody at all with them but Jesus. And as they came down the hill-side, he warned them not to tell anybody what they had seen till "the Son of Man should have risen again from the dead". They were deeply impressed by this remark and tried to puzzle out among themselves what "rising from the dead" could mean. Then they asked him this question,

"Why do the scribes say that Elijah must come before Christ?"

"It is quite true," he told them, "that Elijah does come first, and begins the restoration of all things. But what does the scripture say about the

Revised Standard Version

2 And after six days Jesus took with him Peter
and James and John, and led them up a high
mountain apart by themselves; and he was transfigured before them, 3 and his garments became
glistening, intensely white, as no fuller on earth
could bleach them. 4 And there appeared to
them Elijah with Moses; and they were talking
to Jesus. 5 And Peter said to Jesus, "Master,[f] it
is well that we are here; let us make three
booths, one for you and one for Moses and one
for Elijah." 6 For he did not know what to say,
for they were exceedingly afraid. 7 And a cloud
overshadowed them, and a voice came out of the
cloud, "This is my beloved Son;[g] listen to him."
8 And suddenly looking around they no longer
saw any one with them but Jesus only.
9 And as they were coming down the mountain, he charged them to tell no one what they
had seen, until the Son of man should have risen
from the dead. 10 So they kept the matter to
themselves, questioning what the rising from the
dead meant. 11 And they asked him, "Why do
the scribes say that first Elijah must come?"
12 And he said to them, "Elijah does come first
to restore all things; and how is it written of the

[f] Or *Rabbi*. [g] Or *my Son, my* (or *the*) *Beloved*.

Jerusalem Bible

The transfiguration

2 Six days later, Jesus took with him Peter
and James and John and led them up a high
mountain where they could be alone by themselves. There in their presence he was transfigured: 3 his clothes became dazzlingly white,
whiter than any earthly bleacher could make
them. 4 Elijah appeared to them with Moses; and
they were talking with Jesus. 5 Then Peter spoke
to Jesus: "Rabbi," he said, "it is wonderful for
us to be here; so let us make three tents, one
for you, one for Moses and one for Elijah."
6 He did not know what to say; they were so
frightened. 7 And a cloud came, covering them
in shadow; and there came a voice from the
cloud, "This is my Son, the Beloved. Listen
to him." 8 Then suddenly, when they looked
around, they saw no one with them any more
but only Jesus.

The question about Elijah

9 As they came down from the mountain he
warned them to tell no one what they had
seen, until after the Son of Man had risen from
the dead. 10 They observed the warning faithfully, though among themselves they discussed
what "rising from the dead" could mean. 11 And
they put this question to him, "Why do the
scribes say that Elijah has to come first?"
12 "True," he said, "Elijah is to come first and
to see that everything is as it should be; yet
how is it that the scriptures say about the Son

New English Bible

Six days later Jesus took Peter, James, and John with him and led them up a high mountain where they were alone; and in their presence he was transfigured; his clothes became dazzling white, with a whiteness no bleacher on earth could equal. They saw Elijah appear, and Moses with him, and there they were, conversing with Jesus. Then Peter spoke: 'Rabbi,' he said, 'how good it is that we are here! Shall we make three shelters, one for you, one for Moses, and one for Elijah?' (For he did not know what to say; they were so terrified.) Then a cloud appeared, casting its shadow over them, and out of the cloud came a voice: 'This is my Son, my Beloved;[a] listen to him.' And now suddenly, when they looked around, there was nobody to be seen but Jesus alone with themselves.

On their way down the mountain, he enjoined them not to tell anyone what they had seen until the Son of Man had risen from the dead. They seized upon those words, and discussed among themselves what this 'rising from the dead' could mean. And they put a question to him: 'Why do our teachers say that Elijah must come first?' He replied, 'Yes, Elijah does come first to set everything right. Yet how is it[b] that the scrip-

[a] *Or* This is my only Son. [b] *Or* Elijah, you say, comes first to set everything right: then how is it . . .

King James Version

the Son of man, that he must suffer many things, and be set at nought. 13 But I say unto you, That Elias is indeed come, and they have done unto him whatsoever they listed, as it is written of him.

14 And when he came to *his* disciples, he saw a great multitude about them, and the scribes questioning with them. 15And straightway all the people, when they beheld him, were greatly amazed, and running to *him* saluted him. 16And he asked the scribes, What question ye with them? 17And one of the multitude answered and said, Master, I have brought unto thee my son, which hath a dumb spirit; 18And wheresoever he taketh him, he teareth him; and he foameth, and gnasheth with his teeth, and pineth away: and I spake to thy disciples that they should cast him out; and they could not. 19 He answereth him, and saith, O faithless generation, how long shall I be with you? how long shall I suffer you? bring him unto me. 20And they brought him unto him: and when he saw him, straightway the spirit tare him; and he fell on the ground, and wallowed foaming. 21And he asked his father, How long is it ago since this came unto him? And he said, Of a child. 22And

Living Bible

been terribly mistreated, just as the prophets had predicted. Then Jesus asked them what the prophets could have been talking about when they predicted that the Messiah[a] would suffer and be treated with utter contempt.

14 At the bottom of the mountain they found a great crowd surrounding the other nine disciples, as some Jewish leaders argued with them. 15 The crowd watched Jesus in awe as he came toward them, and then ran to greet him. 16 "What's all the argument about?" he asked.

17 One of the men in the crowd spoke up and said, "Teacher, I brought my son for you to heal—he can't talk because he is possessed by a demon. 18And whenever the demon is in control of him it dashes him to the ground and makes him foam at the mouth and grind his teeth and become rigid.[c] So I begged your disciples to cast out the demon, but they couldn't do it."

19 Jesus said [to his disciples[b]], "Oh, what tiny faith you have;[d] how much longer must I be with you until you believe? How much longer must I be patient with you? Bring the boy to me."

20 So they brought the boy, but when he saw Jesus the demon convulsed the child horribly, and he fell to the ground writhing and foaming at the mouth.

21 "How long has he been this way?" Jesus asked the father.

And he repiled, "Since he was very small, 22 and the demon often makes him fall into the

[a] Literally, "the Son of Man." [c] Or, "is growing weaker day by day." [b] Implied. [d] Literally, "O unbelieving generation."

Today's English Version

much and be rejected? 13 I tell you, however, that Elijah has already come, and that people did to him what they wanted to, just as the Scriptures say about him."

Jesus heals a boy with an evil spirit

14 When they joined the rest of the disciples, they saw a large crowd there. Some teachers of the Law were arguing with the disciples. 15As soon as the people saw Jesus, they were greatly surprised and ran to him and greeted him. 16 Jesus asked his disciples, "What are you arguing with them about?"

17 A man in the crowd answered, "Teacher, I brought my son to you, because he has an evil spirit in him and cannot talk. 18 Whenever the spirit attacks him, it throws him to the ground, and he foams at the mouth, grits his teeth, and becomes stiff all over. I asked your disciples to drive the spirit out, but they could not."

19 Jesus said to them, "How unbelieving you people are! How long must I stay with you? How long do I have to put up with you? Bring the boy to me!" 20 They brought him to Jesus.

As soon as the spirit saw Jesus, it threw the boy into a fit, so that he fell on the ground and rolled around, foaming at the mouth. 21 "How long has he been like this?" Jesus asked the father.

"Ever since he was a child," he replied. 22 "Many times it has tried to kill him by throw-

New International Version

ten that the Son of Man must suffer much and be rejected? 13 But I tell you, Elijah has come, and they have done to him everything they wished, just as it is written about him."

The healing of a boy with an evil spirit

14 When they came to the other disciples, they saw a large crowd around them and the teachers of the law arguing with them. 15As soon as all the people saw Jesus, they were overwhelmed with wonder and ran to greet him.

16 "What are you arguing with them about?" he asked.

17 A man in the crowd answered, "Teacher, I brought you my son, who is possessed by a spirit that has robbed him of speech. 18 Whenever it seizes him, it throws him to the ground. He foams at the mouth, grinds his teeth and becomes rigid. I asked your disciples to drive out the spirit, but they could not."

19 "O unbelieving generation," Jesus replied, "how long shall I stay with you? How long shall I put up with you? Bring the boy to me."

20 So they brought him. When the spirit saw Jesus, it immediately threw the boy into a convulsion. He fell to the ground and rolled around, foaming at the mouth.

21 Jesus asked the boy's father, "How long has he been like this?"

"From childhood," he answered. 22 "It has

Phillips Modern English

Son of Man? This: that he must go through much suffering and be treated with contempt! I tell you that not only has Elijah come already but they have done to him exactly what they wanted—just as the scripture says of him."

9.14 Jesus heals an epileptic boy

Then as they rejoined the other disciples, they saw that they were surrounded by a large crowd and that some scribes were arguing with them. As soon as the people saw Jesus, they ran forward excitedly to welcome him.

"What is the trouble?" Jesus asked them.

A man from the crowd answered,

"Master, I brought my son to you because he has a dumb spirit. Wherever he is, it gets hold of him, throws him down on the ground and there he foams at the mouth and grinds his teeth. It's simply wearing him out. I did speak to your disciples to get them to drive it out, but they hadn't the power to do it."

Jesus answered them,

"Oh, what a faithless people you are! How long must I be with you, how long must I put up with you? Bring him here to me."

So they brought the boy to him, and as soon as the spirit saw Jesus, it convulsed the boy, who fell to the ground and writhed there, foaming at the mouth.

"How long has he been like this?" Jesus asked the father.

"Ever since he was a child," he replied. "Again and again it has thrown him into the fire or into

Revised Standard Version

Son of man, that he should suffer many things
and be treated with contempt? 13 But I tell you
that Elijah has come, and they did to him whatever they pleased, as it is written of him."

14 And when they came to the disciples, they
saw a great crowd about them, and scribes arguing with them. 15 And immediately all the crowd,
when they saw him, were greatly amazed, and
ran up to him and greeted him. 16 And he asked
them, "What are you discussing with them?"
17 And one of the crowd answered him, "Teacher,
I brought my son to you, for he has a dumb
spirit; 18 and wherever it seizes him, it dashes
him down; and he foams and grinds his teeth
and becomes rigid; and I asked your disciples to
cast it out, and they were not able." 19 And he
answered them, "O faithless generation, how
long am I to be with you? How long am I to
bear with you? Bring him to me." 20 And they
brought the boy to him; and when the spirit saw
him, immediately it convulsed the boy, and he
fell on the ground and rolled about, foaming at
the mouth. 21 And Jesus[h] asked his father, "How
long has he had this?" And he said, "From
childhood. 22 And it has often cast him into the

[h] Greek *he*.

Jerusalem Bible

of Man that he is to suffer grievously and be
treated with contempt? 13 However, I tell you
that Elijah has come and they have treated him
as they pleased, just as the scriptures say about
him."

The epileptic demoniac

14 When they rejoined the disciples they saw
a large crowd around them and some scribes
arguing with them. 15 The moment they saw
him the whole crowd were struck with amazement and ran to greet him. 16 "What are you
arguing about with them?" he asked. 17 A man
answered him from the crowd, "Master, I have
brought my son to you; there is a spirit of
dumbness in him, 18 and when it takes hold of
him it throws him to the ground, and he foams
at the mouth and grinds his teeth and goes
rigid. And I asked your disciples to cast it out
and they were unable to." 19 "You faithless
generation," he said to them in reply. "How
much longer must I be with you? How much
longer must I put up with you? Bring him to
me." 20 They brought the boy to him, and as
soon as the spirit saw Jesus it threw the boy
into convulsions, and he fell to the ground and
lay writhing there, foaming at the mouth. 21 Jesus asked the father, "How long has this been
happening to him?" "From childhood," he replied, 22 "and it has often thrown him into the

New English Bible

tures say of the Son of Man that he is to endure great sufferings and to be treated with contempt? However, I tell you, Elijah has already come and they have worked their will upon him, as the scriptures say of him.'

When they came back to the disciples they saw a large crowd surrounding them and lawyers arguing with them. As soon as they saw Jesus the whole crowd were overcome with awe, and they ran forward to welcome him. He asked them, 'What is this argument about?' A man in the crowd spoke up: 'Master, I brought my son to you. He is possessed by a spirit which makes him speechless. Whenever it attacks him, it dashes him to the ground, and he foams at the mouth, grinds his teeth, and goes rigid. I asked your disciples to cast it out, but they failed.' Jesus answered: 'What an unbelieving and perverse generation! How long shall I be with you? How long must I endure you? Bring him to me.' So they brought the boy to him; and as soon as the spirit saw him it threw the boy into convulsions, and he fell on the ground and rolled about foaming at the mouth. Jesus asked his father, 'How long has he been like this?' 'From childhood,' he replied; 'often it has tried

King James Version

ofttimes it hath cast him into the fire, and into
the waters, to destroy him: but if thou canst do
any thing, have compassion on us, and help us.
23 Jesus said unto him, If thou canst believe, all
things *are* possible to him that believeth. 24And
straightway the father of the child cried out, and
said with tears, Lord, I believe; help thou mine
unbelief. 25 When Jesus saw that the people
came running together, he rebuked the foul
spirit, saying unto him, *Thou* dumb and deaf
spirit, I charge thee, come out of him, and enter
no more into him. 26And *the spirit* cried, and
rent him sore, and came out of him: and he was
as one dead; insomuch that many said, He is
dead. 27 But Jesus took him by the hand, and
lifted him up; and he arose. 28And when he was
come into the house, his disciples asked him
privately, Why could not we cast him out? 29And
he said unto them, This kind can come forth by
nothing, but by prayer and fasting.
30 And they departed thence, and passed
through Galilee; and he would not that any man
should know *it*. 31 For he taught his disciples,
and said unto them, The Son of man is delivered
into the hands of men, and they shall kill him;
and after that he is killed, he shall rise the third
day. 32 But they understood not that saying, and
were afraid to ask him.

Living Bible

fire or into water to kill him. Oh, have mercy
on us and do something if you can."
23 "If I can?" Jesus asked. "*Anything* is possible if you have faith."
24 The father instantly replied, "I *do* have
faith; oh, help me to have *more!*"
25 When Jesus saw the crowd was growing he
rebuked the demon.
"O demon of deafness and dumbness," he
said, "I command you to come out of this child
and enter him no more!"
26 Then the demon screamed terribly and convulsed the boy again and left him; and the boy
lay there limp and motionless, to all appearance
dead. A murmur ran through the crowd—"He is
dead." 27 But Jesus took him by the hand and
helped him to his feet and he stood up and was
all right! 28Afterwards, when Jesus was alone in
the house with his disciples, they asked him,
"Why couldn't we cast that demon out?"
29 Jesus replied, "Cases like this require
prayer." [e]
30, 31 Leaving that region they traveled
through Galilee where he tried to avoid all publicity in order to spend more time with his disciples, teaching them. He would say to them, "I,
the Messiah,[a] am going to be betrayed and killed
and three days later I will return to life again."
32 But they didn't understand and were afraid
to ask him what he meant.

[*e*] "And fasting" is added in some manuscripts, but
not the most ancient. [*a*] Literally, "the Son of Man."

Today's English Version

ing him in the fire and in the water. Have pity on
us and help us, if you possibly can!"
23 "Yes," said Jesus, "if *you* can! Everything
is possible for the person who has faith."
24 The father at once cried out, "I do have
faith, but not enough. Help me have more!"
25 Jesus noticed that the crowd was closing
in on them, so he gave a command to the evil
spirit. "Deaf and dumb spirit," he said, "I order
you to come out of the boy and never go into
him again!"
26 The spirit screamed, threw the boy into a
bad fit, and came out. The boy looked like a
corpse, so that everyone said, "He is dead!"
27 But Jesus took the boy by the hand and
helped him rise, and he stood up.
28 After Jesus had gone indoors, his disciples
asked him privately, "Why couldn't we drive
the spirit out?"
29 "Only prayer can drive this kind out," answered Jesus; "nothing else can."

Jesus speaks again about his death

30 They left that place and went on through
Galilee. Jesus did not want anyone to know
where he was, 31 because he was teaching his
disciples, "The Son of Man will be handed over
to men who will kill him; three days later, however, he will rise to life."
32 They did not understand what this teaching meant, but they were afraid to ask him.

New International Version

often thrown him into fire or water to kill him.
But if you can do anything, take pity on us and
help us."
23 "What do you mean, 'If you can'?" said
Jesus. "Everything is possible for him who believes."
24 Immediately the boy's father exclaimed, "I
do believe; help me overcome my unbelief!"
25 When Jesus saw that a crowd was running to the scene, he rebuked the evil [f] spirit.
"You deaf and dumb spirit," he said, "I command you, come out of him and never enter him
again."
26 The spirit shrieked, convulsed him violently
and came out. The boy looked so much like a
corpse that many said, "He's dead." 27 But Jesus
took him by the hand and lifted him to his feet,
and he stood up.
28 After Jesus had gone indoors, his disciples
asked him privately, "Why couldn't we drive it
out?"
29 He replied, "This kind can come out only
by prayer." [g]
30 They left that place and passed through
Galilee. Jesus did not want anyone to know
where they were, 31 because he was teaching his
disciples. He said to them, "The Son of Man is
going to be betrayed into the hands of men.
They will kill him, and after three days he will
rise." 32 But they did not understand what he
meant and were afraid to ask him about it.

[*f*] Greek *unclean*. [*g*] Some MSS add *and fasting*.

Phillips Modern English

water to finish him off. But if you can do anything, please take pity on us and help us.",,

"If *I* can do anything!" retorted Jesus. "Everything is possible to the man who believes."

"I do believe," the boy's father burst out. "Help me to believe more!"

When Jesus noticed that a crowd was rapidly gathering, he spoke sharply to the evil spirit, with the words,

"I command you, deaf and dumb spirit, come out of this boy, and never go into him again!"

The spirit gave a loud scream and after a dreadful convulsion left him. The boy lay there like a corpse, so that most of the bystanders said, "He is dead."

But Jesus grasped his hands and lifted him up, and then he stood on his own feet. When he had gone home, Jesus' disciples asked him privately,

"Why were we unable to drive it out?"

"Nothing can drive out this kind of thing except prayer," replied Jesus.

9.30 Jesus privately warns his disciples of his own death

Then they left that district and went straight through Galilee. Jesus kept this journey secret for he was teaching his disciples that the Son of Man would be betrayed into the power of men, that they would kill him and that three days after his death he would rise again. But they were completely mystified by this saying, and were afraid to question him about it.

Revised Standard Version

fire and into the water, to destroy him; but if
you can do anything, have pity on us and help
us." 23 And Jesus said to him, "If you can! All
things are possible to him who believes." 24 Immediately the father of the child cried out[i] and
said, "I believe; help my unbelief!" 25 And when
Jesus saw that a crowd came running together,
he rebuked the unclean spirit, saying to it, "You
dumb and deaf spirit, I command you, come out
of him, and never enter him again." 26 And after
crying out and convulsing him terribly, it came
out, and the boy was like a corpse; so that most
of them said, "He is dead." 27 But Jesus took
him by the hand and lifted him up, and he arose.
28 And when he had entered the house, his disciples asked him privately, "Why could we not
cast it out?" 29 And he said to them, "This kind
cannot be driven out by anything but prayer."[j]
30 They went on from there and passed
through Galilee. And he would not have any
one know it; 31 for he was teaching his disciples,
saying to them, "The Son of man will be delivered
into the hands of men, and they will kill him;
and when he is killed, after three days he will
rise." 32 But they did not understand the saying,
and they were afraid to ask him.

[i] Other ancient authorities add *with tears.* [j] Other ancient authorities add *and fasting.*

Jerusalem Bible

fire and into the water, in order to destroy him.
But if you can do anything, have pity on us
and help us." 23 "If you can?" retorted Jesus.
"Everything is possible for anyone who has
faith." 24 Immediately the father of the boy
cried out, "I do have faith. Help the little faith
I have!" 25 And when Jesus saw how many people were pressing around him, he rebuked the
unclean spirit. "Deaf and dumb spirit," he said,
"I command you: come out of him and never
enter him again." 26 Then throwing the boy
into violent convulsions it came out shouting,
and the boy lay there so like a corpse that most
of them said, "He is dead." 27 But Jesus took
him by the hand and helped him up, and he was
able to stand. 28 When he had gone indoors
his disciples asked him privately, "Why were
we unable to cast it out?" 29 "This is the kind,"
he answered, "that can only be driven out by
prayer."

Second prophecy of the Passion

30 After leaving that place they made their
way through Galilee; and he did not want anyone to know, 31 because he was instructing his
disciples; he was telling them, "The Son of Man
will be delivered into the hands of men; they
will put him to death; and three days after he
has been put to death he will rise again." 32 But
they did not understand what he said and were
afraid to ask him.

New English Bible

to make an end of him by throwing him into the fire or into water. But if it is at all possible for you, take pity upon us and help us.' 'If it is possible!' said Jesus. 'Everything is possible to one who has faith.' 'I have faith,' cried the boy's father; 'help me where faith falls short.' Jesus saw then that the crowd was closing in upon them, so he rebuked the unclean spirit. 'Deaf and dumb spirit,' he said, 'I command you, come out of him and never go back!' After crying aloud and racking him fiercely, it came out; and the boy looked like a corpse; in fact, many said, 'He is dead.' But Jesus took his hand and raised him to his feet, and he stood up.

Then Jesus went indoors, and his disciples asked him privately, 'Why could not we cast it out?' He said, 'There is no means of casting out this sort but prayer.'[c]

They now left that district and made a journey through Galilee. Jesus wished it to be kept secret; for he was teaching his disciples, and telling them, 'The Son of Man is now to be given up into the power of men, and they will kill him, and three days after being killed, he will rise again.' But they did not understand what he said, and were afraid to ask.

[c] *Some witnesses add* and fasting.

King James Version

33 And he came to Capernaum: and being in
the house he asked them, What was it that ye
disputed among yourselves by the way? 34 But
they held their peace: for by the way they had
disputed among themselves, who *should be* the
greatest. 35 And he sat down, and called the
twelve, and saith unto them, If any man desire
to be first, *the same* shall be last of all, and servant of all. 36 And he took a child, and set him
in the midst of them: and when he had taken
him in his arms, he said unto them, 37 Whosoever shall receive one of such children in my
name, receiveth me; and whosoever shall receive
me, receiveth not me, but him that sent me.
38 And John answered him, saying, Master,
we saw one casting out devils in thy name, and
he followeth not us; and we forbade him, because he followeth not us. 39 But Jesus said, Forbid him not: for there is no man which shall do
a miracle in my name, that can lightly speak
evil of me. 40 For he that is not against us is on
our part. 41 For whosoever shall give you a cup
of water to drink in my name, because ye belong
to Christ, verily I say unto you, he shall not lose

Living Bible

33 And so they arrived at Capernaum. When
they were settled in the house where they were
to stay he asked them, "What were you discussing out on the road?"
34 But they were ashamed to answer, for they
had been arguing about which of them was the
greatest!
35 He sat down and called them around him
and said, "Anyone wanting to be the greatest
must be the least—the servant of all!"
36 Then he placed a little child among them;
and taking the child in his arms he said to
them, 37 "Anyone who welcomes a little child
like this in my name is welcoming me, and anyone who welcomes me is welcoming my Father
who sent me!"
38 One of his disciples, John, told him one
day, "Teacher, we saw a man using your name
to cast out demons; but we told him not to, for
he isn't one of our group."
39 "Don't forbid him!" Jesus said. "For no
one doing miracles in my name will quickly turn
against me.[f] 40 Anyone who isn't against us is for
us. 41 If anyone so much as gives you a cup of
water because you are Christ's—I say this sol-

[f] Literally, "will be able to speak evil of me."

Today's English Version

Who is the greatest?

33 They came to Capernaum, and after going indoors Jesus asked his disciples, "What
were you arguing about on the road?"
34 But they would not answer him, because
on the road they had been arguing among themselves about who was the greatest. 35 Jesus sat
down, called the twelve disciples, and said to
them, "Whoever wants to be first must place
himself last of all and be the servant of all."
36 He took a child and made him stand in front
of them. Then he put his arms around him and
said to them, 37 "Whoever in my name welcomes
one of these children, welcomes me; and whoever
welcomes me, welcomes not only me but also the
one who sent me."

Who is not against us is for us

38 John said to him, "Teacher, we saw a man
who was driving out demons in your name, and
we told him to stop, because he doesn't belong
to our group."
39 "Do not try to stop him," Jesus told them,
"because no one who performs a miracle in my
name will be able soon after to say bad things
about me. 40 For whoever is not against us is for
us. 41 Remember this! Anyone who gives you a
drink of water because you belong to Christ will
certainly receive his reward."

New International Version

Who is the greatest?

33 They came to Capernaum. When he was in
the house, he asked them, "What were you arguing about on the road?" 34 But they kept
quiet because on the way they had argued about
who was the greatest.
35 Sitting down, Jesus called the Twelve and
said, "If anyone wants to be first, he must be the
very last, and the servant of all."
36 He took a little child and had him stand
among them. Taking him in his arms, he said
to them, 37 "Whoever welcomes one of these
little children in my name welcomes me; and
whoever welcomes me does not welcome me but
the one who sent me."

Whoever is not against us is for us

38 "Teacher," said John, "we saw a man
driving out demons in your name and we told
him to stop, because he was not one of us."
39 "Do not stop him," Jesus said. "No one
who does a miracle in my name can in the next
moment say anything bad about me, 40 for whoever is not against us is for us. 41 I tell you the
truth, anyone who gives you a cup of water in
my name because you belong to Christ will certainly not lose his reward.

Phillips Modern English

9.33 Jesus defines the new "greatness"

So they came to Capernaum. And when they were indoors he asked them,
"What were you discussing as we came along the road?"
They were silent, for on the way they had been arguing about who should be the greatest. Jesus sat down and called the twelve, and said to them,
"If any man wants to be first, he must be last and servant of all."
Then he took a little child and stood him in front of them all, and putting his arm round him, said to them,
"Anyone who welcomes one little child like this for my sake is welcoming me. And the man who welcomes me is welcoming not only me but the one who sent me!"
Then John said to him,
"Master, we saw somebody driving out evil spirits in your name, and we tried to stop him, for he is not one who follows us."
But Jesus replied,
"You must not stop him. No one who exerts such power in my name would readily say anything against me. For the man who is not against us is on our side. In fact, I assure you that the man who gives you a mere drink of water in my name, because you are followers of mine, will

Revised Standard Version

33 And they came to Capernaum; and when
he was in the house he asked them, "What were
you discussing on the way?" 34 But they were
silent; for on the way they had discussed with
one another who was the greatest. 35 And he sat
down and called the twelve; and he said to them,
"If any one would be first, he must be last of
all and servant of all." 36 And he took a child,
and put him in the midst of them; and taking
him in his arms, he said to them, 37 "Whoever
receives one such child in my name receives me;
and whoever receives me, receives not me but
him who sent me."
38 John said to him, "Teacher, we saw a man
casting out demons in your name,[k] and we forbade him, because he was not following us."
39 But Jesus said, "Do not forbid him; for no
one who does a mighty work in my name will
be able soon after to speak evil of me. 40 For
he that is not against us is for us. 41 For truly, I
say to you, whoever gives you a cup of water to
drink because you bear the name of Christ, will
by no means lose his reward.

[k] Other ancient authorities add *who does not follow us.*

Jerusalem Bible

Who is the greatest?

33 They came to Capernaum, and when he
was in the house he asked them, "What were
you arguing about on the road?" 34 They said
nothing because they had been arguing which
of them was the greatest. 35 So he sat down,
called the Twelve to him and said, "If anyone
wants to be first, he must make himself last of
all and servant of all." 36 He then took a little
child, set him in front of them, put his arms
around him, and said to them, 37 "Anyone who
welcomes one of these little children in my
name, welcomes me; and anyone who welcomes
me welcomes not me but the one who sent me."

On using the name of Jesus

38 John said to him, "Master, we saw a man
who is not one of us casting out devils in your
name; and because he was not one of us we
tried to stop him." 39 But Jesus said, "You
must not stop him: no one who works a miracle
in my name is likely to speak evil of me. 40 Anyone who is not against us is for us.

Charity shown to Christ's disciples

41 "If anyone gives you a cup of water to
drink just because you belong to Christ, then
I tell you solemnly, he will most certainly not
lose his reward.

New English Bible

So they came to Capernaum; and when he was indoors, he asked them, 'What were you arguing about on the way?' They were silent, because on the way they had been discussing who was the greatest. He sat down, called the Twelve, and said to them, 'If anyone wants to be first, he must make himself last of all and servant of all.' Then he took a child, set him in front of them, and put his arm round him. 'Whoever receives one of these children in my name', he said, 'receives me; and whoever receives me, receives not me but the One who sent me.'

John said to him, 'Master, we saw a man driving out devils in your name, and as he was not one of us, we tried to stop him.' Jesus said, 'Do not stop him; no one who does a work of divine power in my name will be able the next moment to speak evil of me. For he who is not against us is on our side. I tell you this: if anyone gives you a cup of water to drink because you are followers of the Messiah, that man assuredly will not go unrewarded.

King James Version

his reward. 42And whosoever shall offend one of
these little ones that believe in me, it is better for
him that a millstone were hanged about his neck,
and he were cast into the sea. 43And if thy hand
offend thee, cut it off: it is better for thee to
enter into life maimed, than having two hands
to go into hell, into the fire that never shall be
quenched: 44 Where their worm dieth not, and
the fire is not quenched. 45And if thy foot offend
thee, cut it off: it is better for thee to enter halt
into life, than having two feet to be cast into
hell, into the fire that never shall be quenched:
46 Where their worm dieth not, and the fire is
not quenched. 47And if thine eye offend thee,
pluck it out: it is better for thee to enter into
the kingdom of God with one eye, than having
two eyes to be cast into hell fire: 48 Where their
worm dieth not, and the fire is not quenched.
49 For every one shall be salted with fire, and
every sacrifice shall be salted with salt. 50 Salt
is good: but if the salt have lost his saltness,
wherewith will ye season it? Have salt in yourselves, and have peace one with another.

Living Bible

emnly—he won't lose his reward. 42 But if someone causes one of these little ones who believe
in me to lose faith—it would be better for that
man if a huge millstone were tied around his
neck and he were thrown into the sea.

43, 44 [g] "If your hand does wrong, cut it off.
Better live forever with one hand than be thrown
into the unquenchable fires of hell with two!
45, 46 [g] If your foot carries you toward evil, cut
it off! Better be lame and live forever than have
two feet that carry you to hell.

47 "And if your eye is sinful, gouge it out.
Better enter the Kingdom of God half blind than
have two eyes and see the fires of hell, 48 where
the worm never dies, and the fire never goes out
—49 where all are salted with fire.[h]

50 "Good salt is worthless if it loses its saltiness; it can't season anything. So don't lose your
flavor! Live in peace with each other."

[g] Verses 44 and 46 (which are identical with verse 48) are omitted in some of the ancient manuscripts. [h] Literally, "For everyone shall be salted with fire."

Today's English Version

Temptations to sin

42 "If anyone should cause one of these little
ones to turn away from his faith in me, it would
be better for that man to have a large millstone
tied around his neck and be thrown into the sea.
43 So if your hand makes you turn away, cut it
off! It is better for you to enter life without a
hand than to keep both hands and go off to hell,
to the fire that never goes out. [44 There 'their
worms never die, and the fire is never put out.']
45And if your foot makes you turn away, cut it
off! It is better for you to enter life without a
foot than to keep both feet and be thrown into
hell. [46 There 'their worms never die, and the
fire is never put out.'] 47And if your eye makes
you turn away, take it out! It is better for you
to enter the Kingdom of God with only one eye,
than to keep both eyes and be thrown into hell.
48 There 'their worms never die, and the fire is
never put out.'

49 "For everyone will be salted with fire.
50 Salt is good; but if it loses its saltness, how
can you make it salty again? Have salt in yourselves, and be at peace with one another."

New International Version

Causing to sin

42 "And if anyone causes one of these little
ones who believe in me to sin, it would be better
for him to be thrown into the sea with a large
millstone tied around his neck. 43 If your hand
causes you to sin, cut it off. It is better for you
to enter life maimed than with two hands to go
into hell, where the fire never goes out.[h] 45And
if your foot causes you to sin, cut it off. It is
better for you to enter life crippled, than to
have two feet and be thrown into hell.[i] 47And
if your eye causes you to sin, pluck it out. It is
better for you to enter the kingdom of God
with one eye, than to have two eyes and be
thrown into hell, 48 where

'their worm does not die,
and the fire is not put out.'[j]

49 Everyone will be salted with fire.

50 "Salt is good, but if it loses its saltiness,
how can you make it salty again? Have salt in
yourselves, and be at peace with each other."

[h] Some MSS add verse 44, which reads the same as verse 48. [i] Some MSS add verse 46, which reads the same as verse 48. [j] Isaiah 66:24.

Phillips Modern English

most certainly be rewarded. And I tell you too, that the man who disturbs the faith of one of the humblest of those who believe in me would be better off if he were thrown into the sea with a great mill-stone hung round his neck!

9.43 Entering the kingdom may mean painful sacrifice

"Indeed, if it is your own hand that spoils your faith, you must cut it off. It is better for you to enter life maimed than to keep both your hands and go to the rubbish-heap, where the fire never dies. If your foot spoils your faith, you must cut it off. It is better for you to enter life on one foot than to keep both your feet and be thrown on to the rubbish-heap. And if your eye leads you astray, pluck it out. It is better for you to go one-eyed into the kingdom of God than to keep both eyes and be thrown on to the rubbish-heap, where decay never stops and the fire never goes out. For everyone will be salted with fire. Salt is a good thing; but if it should lose its saltiness, what can you do to restore its flavour? You must have salt in yourselves, and live at peace with each other."

Revised Standard Version

42 "Whoever causes one of these little ones
who believe in me to sin,[l] it would be better for
him if a great millstone were hung round his
neck and he were thrown into the sea. 43And
if your hand causes you to sin,[l] cut it off; it is
better for you to enter life maimed than with
two hands to go to hell,[m] to the unquenchable
fire.[n] 45And if your foot causes you to sin,[l]
cut it off; it is better for you to enter life lame
than with two feet to be thrown into hell.[m,n]
47And if your eye causes you to sin,[l] pluck it
out; it is better for you to enter the kingdom of
God with one eye than with two eyes to be
thrown into hell,[m] 48 where their worm does not
die, and the fire is not quenched. 49 For every
one will be salted with fire.[o] 50 Salt is good; but
if the salt has lost its saltness, how will you season it? Have salt in yourselves, and be at peace
with one another."

[l] Greek *stumble*. [m] Greek *Gehenna*. [n] Verses 44 and 46 (which are identical with verse 48) are omitted by the best ancient authorities. [o] Other ancient authorities add *and every sacrifice will be salted with salt*.

Jerusalem Bible

On leading others astray

42 "But anyone who is an obstacle to bring
down one of these little ones who have faith,
would be better thrown into the sea with a great
millstone around his neck. 43And if your hand
should cause you to sin, cut it off; it is better
for you to enter into life crippled, than to have
two hands and go to hell, into the fire that
cannot be put out.[l] 45And if your foot should
cause you to sin, cut it off; it is better for you
to enter into life lame, than to have two feet
and be thrown into hell. 47And if your eye
should cause you to sin, tear it out; it is better
for you to enter into the kingdom of God with
one eye, than to have two eyes and be thrown
into hell 48 where *their worm does not die nor
fire go out*.[m] 49 For everyone will be salted with
fire. 50 Salt is a good thing, but if salt has become insipid, how can you season it again?
Have salt in yourselves and be at peace with one
another."

[l] In the best MSS. vv. 44 and 46 (Vulg.) are omitted; merely repetitious of v. 48. [m] Is. 66:24.

New English Bible

'As for the man who is a cause of stumbling to one of these little ones who have faith, it would be better for him to be thrown into the sea with a millstone round his neck. If your hand is your undoing, cut it off; it is better for you to enter into life maimed than to keep both hands and go to hell and the unquenchable fire.[a] And if your foot is your undoing, cut it off; it is better to enter into life a cripple than to keep both your feet and be thrown into hell.[b] And if it is your eye, tear it out; it is better to enter into the kingdom of God with one eye than to keep both eyes and be thrown into hell, where the devouring worm never dies and the fire is not quenched.

'For everyone will be salted with fire.

'Salt is a good thing; but if the salt loses its saltness, what will you season it with?

'Have salt in yourselves; and be[c] at peace with one another.'

[a] *Some witnesses add* (44) where the devouring worm never dies and the fire is not quenched. [b] *Some witnesses add* (46) where the devouring worm never dies and the fire is not quenched. [c] *Or* Have the salt of fellowship and be . . . ; *or* You have the salt of fellowship between you; then be . . .

King James Version

10 And he arose from thence, and cometh into the coasts of Judea by the farther side of Jordan: and the people resort unto him again; and, as he was wont, he taught them again.

2 And the Pharisees came to him, and asked him, Is it lawful for a man to put away *his* wife? tempting him. 3 And he answered and said unto them, What did Moses command you? 4 And they said, Moses suffered to write a bill of divorcement, and to put *her* away. 5 And Jesus answered and said unto them, For the hardness of your heart he wrote you this precept. 6 But from the beginning of the creation God made them male and female. 7 For this cause shall a man leave his father and mother, and cleave to his wife; 8 And they twain shall be one flesh: so then they are no more twain, but one flesh. 9 What therefore God hath joined together, let not man put asunder. 10 And in the house his disciples asked him again of the same *matter*. 11 And he saith unto them, Whosoever shall put away his wife, and marry another, committeth adultery against her. 12 And if a woman shall put away her husband, and be married to another, she committeth adultery.

13 And they brought young children to him,

Living Bible

10 Then he left Capernaum[a] and went southward to the Judean borders and into the area east of the Jordan River. And as always there were the crowds; and as usual he taught them.

2 Some Pharisees came and asked him, "Do you permit divorce?" Of course they were trying to trap him.

3 "What did Moses say about divorce?" Jesus asked them.

4 "He said it was all right," they replied. "He said that all a man has to do is write his wife a letter of dismissal."

5 "And why did he say that?" Jesus asked. "I'll tell you why—it was a concession to your hardhearted wickedness. 6, 7 But it certainly isn't God's way. For from the very first he made man and woman to be joined together permanently in marriage; therefore a man is to leave his father and mother, 8 and he and his wife are united so that they are no longer two, but one. 9 And no man may separate what God has joined together."

10 Later, when he was alone with his disciples in the house, they brought up the subject again.

11 He told them, "When a man divorces his wife to marry someone else, he commits adultery against her. 12 And if a wife divorces her husband and remarries, she, too, commits adultery."

13 Once when some mothers[b] were bringing

[*a*] Literally, "and rising up, he went from there." Mentioned here so quietly, this was his final farewell to Galilee. He never returned until after his death and resurrection. [*b*] Implied.

Today's English Version

Jesus teaches about divorce

10 Then Jesus left that place, went to the region of Judea, and crossed the Jordan River. Crowds came flocking to him again and he taught them, as he always did.

2 Some Pharisees came to him and tried to trap him. "Tell us," they asked, "does our Law allow a man to divorce his wife?"

3 Jesus answered with a question, "What commandment did Moses give you?"

4 Their answer was, "Moses gave permission for a man to write a divorce notice and send his wife away."

5 Jesus said to them, "Moses wrote this commandment for you because you are so hard to teach. 6 But in the beginning, at the time of creation, it was said, 'God made them male and female. 7 And for this reason a man will leave his father and mother and unite with his wife, 8 and the two will become one.' So they are no longer two, but one. 9 Man must not separate, then, what God has joined together."

10 When they went back into the house, the disciples asked Jesus about this matter. 11 He said to them, "The man who divorces his wife and marries another woman commits adultery against his wife; 12 in the same way, the woman who divorces her husband and marries another man commits adultery."

Jesus blesses little children

13 Some people brought children to Jesus for

New International Version

Divorce

10 Jesus then left that place and went into the region of Judea and across the Jordan. Again crowds of people came to him, and as was his custom, he taught them.

2 Some Pharisees came and tested him by asking, "Is it lawful for a man to divorce his wife?"

3 "What did Moses command you?" he replied.

4 They said, "Moses permitted a man to write a certificate of divorce and send her away."

5 "It was because your hearts were hard that Moses wrote you this law," Jesus replied. 6 "But at the beginning of creation, God 'made them male and female.'[k] 7 'For this reason a man will leave his father and mother and be united to his wife,[l] 8 and the two will become one flesh.'[m] So they are no longer two, but one. 9 Therefore what God has joined together, let man not separate."

10 When they were in the house again, the disciples asked Jesus about this. 11 He answered, "Anyone who divorces his wife and marries another woman commits adultery against her. 12 And if she divorces her husband and marries another man, she commits adultery."

The little children and Jesus

13 People were bringing little children to Je-

[*k*] Gen. 1:27. [*l*] Some early MSS omit *and be united to his wife.* [*m*] Gen. 2:24.

Phillips Modern English

10.1 The divine purpose in marriage

Then he got up and left Galilee and went off to the borders of Judaea and beyond the Jordan. Again great crowds assembled to meet him, and again, according to his custom, he taught them. Then some Pharisees arrived to ask him this test-question.

"Is it right for a man to divorce his wife?"

Jesus replied by asking them,

"What has Moses commanded you to do?"

"Moses allows men to write a divorce-notice and then to dismiss her," they said.

"Moses gave you that commandment," returned Jesus, "because you know so little of the meaning of love. But from the beginning of the creation, God made them male and female. 'For this cause shall a man leave his father and mother, and shall cleave to his wife; and the twain shall become one flesh.' So that in body they are no longer two people but one. That is why man must never separate what God has joined together."

On reaching the house, his disciples questioned him again about this matter.

"Any man who divorces his wife and marries another woman," he told them, "commits adultery against his wife. And if she herself divorces her husband and marries someone else, she commits adultery."

10.13 He welcomes small children

Then some people came to him bringing little

Revised Standard Version

10 And he left there and went to the region
of Judea and beyond the Jordan, and
crowds gathered to him again; and again, as his
custom was, he taught them.
2 And Pharisees came up and in order to test
him asked, "Is it lawful for a man to divorce his
wife?" 3 He answered them, "What did Moses
command you?" 4 They said, "Moses allowed a
man to write a certificate of divorce, and to put
her away." 5 But Jesus said to them, "For your
hardness of heart he wrote you this commandment. 6 But from the beginning of creation, 'God
made them male and female.' 7 'For this reason
a man shall leave his father and mother and be
joined to his wife,[p] 8 and the two shall become
one flesh.' So they are no longer two but one
flesh. 9 What therefore God has joined together,
let not man put asunder."
10 And in the house the disciples asked him
again about this matter. 11 And he said to them,
"Whoever divorces his wife and marries another,
commits adultery against her; 12 and if she divorces her husband and marries another, she
commits adultery."
13 And they were bringing children to him,

[p] Other ancient authorities omit *and be joined to his wife.*

Jerusalem Bible

The question about divorce

10 Leaving there, he came to the district of
Judaea and the far side of the Jordan. And
again crowds gathered around him, and again he
taught them, as his custom was. 2 Some Pharisees approached him and asked, "Is it against
the law for a man to divorce his wife?" They
were testing him. 3 He answered them, "What
did Moses command you?" 4 "Moses allowed
us," they said, "to draw up a writ of dismissal
and so to divorce." 5 Then Jesus said to them,
"It was because you were so unteachable that
he wrote this commandment for you. 6 But from
the beginning of creation *God made them male
and female. 7 This is why a man must leave
father and mother, 8 and the two become one
body.*[n] They are no longer two, therefore, but
one body. 9 So then, what God has united, man
must not divide." 10 Back in the house the disciples questioned him again about this, 11 and
he said to them, "The man who divorces his
wife and marries another is guilty of adultery
against her. 12 And if a woman divorces her
husband and marries another she is guilty of
adultery too."

Jesus and the children

13 People were bringing little children to

[n] Gn. 1:27; 2:24.

New English Bible

10 On leaving those parts he came into the regions of Judaea and Transjordan; and when a crowd gathered round him once again, he followed his usual practice and taught them. The question was put to him:[a] 'Is it lawful for a man to divorce his wife?' This was to test him. He asked in return, 'What did Moses command you?' They answered, 'Moses permitted a man to divorce his wife by note of dismissal.' Jesus said to them. 'It was because your minds were closed that he made this rule for you; but in the beginning, at the creation, God made them male and female. For this reason a man shall leave his father and mother, and be made one with his wife;[b] and the two shall become one flesh. It follows that they are no longer two individuals: they are one flesh. What God has joined together, man must not separate.'

When they were indoors again the disciples questioned him about this matter; he said to them, 'Whoever divorces his wife and marries another commits adultery against her: so too, if she divorces her husband and marries another, she commits adultery.'

They brought children for him to touch. The

[a] *Some witnesses read* The Pharisees came forward and asked him the question . . . [b] *Some witnesses omit* and be made . . . wife.

King James Version

that he should touch them; and *his* disciples rebuked those that brought *them.* 14 But when
Jesus saw *it,* he was much displeased, and said
unto them, Suffer the little children to come unto
me, and forbid them not; for of such is the kingdom of God. 15 Verily I say unto you, Whosoever shall not receive the kingdom of God as a
little child, he shall not enter therein. 16And he
took them up in his arms, put *his* hands upon
them, and blessed them.
17 And when he was gone forth into the way,
there came one running, and kneeled to him, and
asked him, Good Master, what shall I do that I
may inherit eternal life? 18And Jesus said unto
him, Why callest thou me good? *there is* none
good but one, *that is,* God. 19 Thou knowest the
commandments, Do not commit adultery, Do
not kill, Do not steal, Do not bear false witness,
Defraud not, Honour thy father and mother.
20And he answered and said unto him, Master,
all these have I observed from my youth. 21 Then
Jesus beholding him loved him, and said unto
him, One thing thou lackest: go thy way, sell
whatsoever thou hast, and give to the poor, and
thou shalt have treasure in heaven: and come,
take up the cross, and follow me. 22And he was
sad at that saying, and went away grieved: for
he had great possessions.

Living Bible

their children to Jesus to bless them, the disciples shooed them away, telling them not to
bother him.
14 But when Jesus saw what was happening
he was very much displeased with his disciples
and said to them, "Let the children come to me,
for the Kingdom of God belongs to such as they.
Don't send them away! 15 I tell you as seriously
as I know how that anyone who refuses to come
to God as a little child will never be allowed
into his Kingdom."
16 Then he took the children into his arms
and placed his hands on their heads and he
blessed them.
17 As he was starting out on a trip, a man
came running to him and knelt down and asked,
"Good Teacher, what must I do to get to
heaven?"
18 "Why do you call me good?" Jesus asked.
"Only God is truly good! 19 But as for your
question—you know the commandments: don't
kill, don't commit adultery, don't steal, don't
lie, don't cheat, respect your father and mother."
20 "Teacher," the man replied, "I've never
once[c] broken a single one of those laws."
21 Jesus felt genuine love for this man as he
looked at him. "You lack only one thing," he
told him; "go and sell all you have and give the
money to the poor—and you shall have treasure
in heaven—and come, follow me."
22 Then the man's face fell, and he went
sadly away, for he was very rich.

[*c*] Literally, "from my youth."

Today's English Version

him to touch them, but the disciples scolded
those people. 14 When Jesus noticed it, he was
angry and said to his disciples, "Let the children come to me, and do not stop them, because
the Kingdom of God belongs to such as these.
15 Remember this! Whoever does not receive the
Kingdom of God like a child will never enter
it." 16 Then he took the children in his arms,
placed his hands on each of them, and blessed
them.

The rich man

17 As Jesus was starting again on his way, a
man ran up, knelt before him, and asked him,
"Good Teacher, what must I do to receive eternal
life?"
18 "Why do you call me good?" Jesus asked
him. "No one is good except God alone. 19 You
know the commandments: 'Do not murder; do
not commit adultery; do not steal; do not lie; do
not cheat; honor your father and mother.' "
20 "Teacher," the man said, "ever since I was
young I have obeyed all these commandments."
21 Jesus looked straight at him with love and
said, "You need only one thing. Go and sell all
you have and give the money to the poor, and
you will have riches in heaven; then come and
follow me." 22 When the man heard this, gloom
spread over his face and he went away sad, because he was very rich.

New International Version

sus to have him touch them, but the disciples
rebuked them. 14 When Jesus saw this, he was
indignant. He said to them, "Let the little children come to me, and do not hinder them, for
the kingdom of God belongs to such as these.
15 I tell you the truth, anyone who will not receive the kingdom of God like a little child
will never enter it." 16And he took the children
in his arms, put his hands on them and blessed
them.

The rich young man

17 As Jesus started on his way, a man ran
up to him and fell on his knees before him.
"Good teacher," he asked, "what must I do to
inherit eternal life?"
18 "Why do you call me good?" Jesus answered. "No one is good—except God alone.
19 You know the commandments: 'Do not murder, do not commit adultery, do not steal, do not
give false testimony, do not defraud, honor your
father and mother.'[n] "
20 "Teacher," he declared, "all these I have
kept since I was a boy."
21 Jesus looked at him and loved him. "One
thing you lack," he said. "Go, sell everything
you have and give to the poor, and you will
have treasure in heaven. Then come, follow me."
22 At this the man's face fell. He went away
sad, because he had great wealth.

[*n*] Exodus 20:12-16; Deut. 5:16-20.

Phillips Modern English

children for him to touch. The disciples tried to discourage them. When Jesus saw this, he was indignant and told them,

"You must let little children come to me—never stop them! For the kingdom of God belongs to such as these. Indeed, I assure you that the man who does not accept the kingdom of God like a little child will never enter it."

Then he took the children in his arms and laid his hands on them and blessed them.

10.17 Jesus shows the danger of riches

As he began to take the road again, a man came running up and fell at his feet, and asked him,

"Good Master, tell me, please, what must I do to be sure of eternal life?"

"Why do you call me good?" returned Jesus. "No one is good—only God. You know the commandments, 'Do no murder, Do not commit adultery, Do not steal, Do not bear false witness, Do not cheat, Honour thy father and mother'."

"Master," he replied, "I have carefully kept all these since I was quite young."

Jesus looked steadily at him, and his heart warmed towards him. Then he said,

"There is one thing you still need. Go and sell everything you have, give the money away to the poor—you will have riches in Heaven. And then come back and follow me."

At these words his face fell and he went away

Revised Standard Version

that he might touch them; and the disciples rebuked them. 14 But when Jesus saw it he was
indignant, and said to them, "Let the children
come to me, do not hinder them; for to such
belongs the kingdom of God. 15 Truly, I say to
you, whoever does not receive the kingdom of
God like a child shall not enter it." 16And he
took them in his arms and blessed them, laying
his hands upon them.
17 And as he was setting out on his journey,
a man ran up and knelt before him, and asked
him, "Good Teacher, what must I do to inherit
eternal life?" 18And Jesus said to him, "Why do
you call me good? No one is good but God
alone. 19 You know the commandments: 'Do
not kill, Do not commit adultery, Do not steal,
Do not bear false witness, Do not defraud,
Honor your father and mother.'" 20And he said
to him, "Teacher, all these I have observed from
my youth." 21And Jesus looking upon him loved
him, and said to him, "You lack one thing; go,
sell what you have, and give to the poor, and
you will have treasure in heaven; and come, follow me." 22At that saying his countenance fell,
and he went away sorrowful; for he had great
possessions.

Jerusalem Bible

him, for him to touch them. The disciples
turned them away, 14 but when Jesus saw this
he was indignant and said to them, "Let the little children come to me; do not stop them; for
it is to such as these that the kingdom of God
belongs. 15 I tell you solemnly, anyone who does
not welcome the kingdom of God like a little
child will never enter it." 16 Then he put his
arms around them, laid his hands on them and
gave them his blessing.

The rich young man

17 He was setting out on a journey when a
man ran up, knelt before him and put this question to him, "Good master, what must I do to
inherit eternal life?" 18 Jesus said to him, "Why
do you call me good? No one is good but God
alone. 19 You know the commandments: *You
must not kill; You must not commit adultery;
You must not steal; You must not bring false
witness;* You must not defraud; *Honor your
father and mother.*" 20And he said to him,
"Master, I have kept all these from my earliest
days." 21 Jesus looked steadily at him and loved
him, and he said, "There is one thing you lack.
Go and sell everything you own and give the
money to the poor, and you will have treasure
in heaven; then come, follow me." 22 But his
face fell at these words and he went away sad,
for he was a man of great wealth.

New English Bible

disciples rebuked them, but when Jesus saw this he was indignant, and said to them, 'Let the children come to me; do not try to stop them; for the kingdom of God belongs to such as these. I tell you, whoever does not accept the kingdom of God like a child will never enter it.' And he put his arms round them, laid his hands upon them, and blessed them.

As he was starting out on a journey, a stranger ran up, and, kneeling before him, asked, 'Good Master, what must I do to win eternal life?' Jesus said to him, 'Why do you call me good? No one is good except God alone. You know the commandments: "Do not murder; do not commit adultery; do not steal; do not give false evidence; do not defraud; honour your father and mother." ' 'But, Master,' he replied, 'I have kept all these since I was a boy.' Jesus looked straight at him; his heart warmed to him, and he said, 'One thing you lack: go, sell everything you have, and give to the poor, and you will have riches in heaven; and come, follow me.' At these words his face fell and he went away with a heavy heart; for he was a man of great wealth.

King James Version

23 And Jesus looked round about, and saith unto his disciples, How hardly shall they that have riches enter into the kingdom of God! 24And the disciples were astonished at his words. But Jesus answereth again, and saith unto them, Children, how hard is it for them that trust in riches to enter into the kingdom of God! 25 It is easier for a camel to go through the eye of a needle, than for a rich man to enter into the kingdom of God. 26And they were astonished out of measure, saying among themselves, Who then can be saved? 27And Jesus looking upon them saith, With men *it is* impossible, but not with God: for with God all things are possible.

28 Then Peter began to say unto him, Lo, we have left all, and have followed thee. 29And Jesus answered and said, Verily I say unto you, There is no man that hath left house, or brethren, or sisters, or father, or mother, or wife, or children, or lands, for my sake, and the gospel's, 30 But he shall receive a hundredfold now in this time, houses, and brethren, and sisters, and mothers, and children, and lands, with persecutions; and in the world to come eternal life. 31 But many *that are* first shall be last; and the last first.

Living Bible

23 Jesus watched him go, then turned around and said to his disciples, "It's almost impossible for the rich to get into the Kingdom of God!"

24 This amazed them. So Jesus said it again: "Dear children, how hard it is for those who trust in riches[d] to enter the Kingdom of God. 25 It is easier for a camel to go through the eye of a needle than for a rich man to enter the Kingdom of God."

26 The disciples were incredulous! "Then who in the world can be saved, if not a rich man?" they asked.

27 Jesus looked at them intently, then said, "Without God, it is utterly impossible. But with God everything is possible."

28 Then Peter began to mention all that he and the other disciples had left behind. "We've given up everything to follow you," he said.

29 And Jesus replied, "Let me assure you that no one has ever given up anything—home, brothers, sisters, mother, father, children, or property—for love of me and to tell others the Good News, 30 who won't be given back, a hundred times over, homes, brothers, sisters, mothers, children, and land—with persecutions!

"All these will be his here on earth, and in the world to come he shall have eternal life. 31 But many people who seem to be important now will be the least important then; and many who are considered least here shall be greatest there."

[*d*] Some of the ancient manuscripts do not contain the words, "for those who trust in riches."

Today's English Version

23 Jesus looked around at his disciples and said to them, "How hard it will be for rich people to enter the Kingdom of God!"

24 The disciples were shocked at these words, but Jesus went on to say, "My children, how hard it is to enter the Kingdom of God! 25 It is much harder for a rich man to enter the Kingdom of God than for a camel to go through the eye of a needle."

26 At this the disciples were completely amazed, and asked one another, "Who, then, can be saved?"

27 Jesus looked straight at them and answered, "This is impossible for men, but not for God; everything is possible for God."

28 Then Peter spoke up, "Look, we have left everything and followed you."

29 "Yes," Jesus said to them, "and I tell you this: anyone who leaves home or brothers or sisters or mother or father or children or fields for me, and for the gospel, 30 will receive much more in this present age. He will receive a hundred times more houses, brothers, sisters, mothers, children, and fields—and persecutions as well; and in the age to come he will receive eternal life. 31 But many who now are first will be last, and many who now are last will be first."

New International Version

23 Jesus looked around and said to his disciples, "How hard it is for the rich to enter the kingdom of God!"

24 The disciples were amazed at his words. But Jesus said again, "Children, how hard it is[o] to enter the kingdom of God! 25 It is easier for a camel to go through the eye of a needle than for a rich man to enter the kingdom of God."

26 The disciples were even more amazed, and said to each other, "Who then can be saved?"

27 Jesus looked at them and said, "With man this is impossible, but not with God; all things are possible with God."

28 Peter said to him, "We have left everything to follow you!"

29 "I tell you the truth," Jesus replied, "no one who has left home or brothers or sisters or mother or father or children or fields for me and the gospel 30 will fail to receive a hundred times as much in this present age (homes, brothers, sisters, mothers, children and fields—and with them, persecutions) and in the age to come, eternal life. 31 But many who are first will be last, and the last first."

[*o*] Some MSS add *for those who trust in riches.*

Phillips Modern English

in deep distress, for he was very rich. Then Jesus looked round at them all, and said to his disciples,

"How difficult it is for those who have great possessions to enter the kingdom of God!"

The disciples were staggered at these words, but Jesus continued,

"Children, you don't know how hard it is to get into the kingdom of God. Why, a camel could more easily pass through the eye of a needle than a rich man get into the kingdom of God."

At this their astonishment knew no bounds, and they said to each other,

"Then who can possibly be saved?"

Jesus looked straight at them and said,

"Humanly speaking it is impossible, but not with God. Everything is possible with God."

Then Peter burst out,

"But look, we have left everything and followed you!"

"I promise you," returned Jesus, "that nobody has left home or brothers or sisters or mother or father or children or land for my sake and the gospel's without getting back a hundred times over, now in this present life, homes and brothers and sisters, mothers and children and land—though not without persecution—and in the next world eternal life. But many who are first now will then be last, and the last now will then be first."

Revised Standard Version

23 And Jesus looked around and said to his disciples, "How hard it will be for those who have riches to enter the kingdom of God!" 24 And the disciples were amazed at his words. But Jesus said to them again, "Children, how hard it is[r] to enter the kingdom of God! 25 It is easier for a camel to go through the eye of a needle than for a rich man to enter the kingdom of God." 26 And they were exceedingly astonished, and said to him,[s] "Then who can be saved?" 27 Jesus looked at them and said, "With men it is impossible, but not with God; for all things are possible with God." 28 Peter began to say to him, "Lo, we have left everything and followed you." 29 Jesus said, "Truly, I say to you, there is no one who has left house or brothers or sisters or mother or father or children or lands, for my sake and for the gospel, 30 who will not receive a hundredfold now in this time, houses and brothers and sisters and mothers and children and lands, with persecutions, and in the age to come eternal life. 31 But many that are first will be last, and the last first."

[r] Other ancient authorities add *for those who trust in riches.* [s] Other ancient authorities read *to one another.*

Jerusalem Bible

The danger of riches

23 Jesus looked around and said to his disciples, "How hard it is for those who have riches to enter the kingdom of God!" 24 The disciples were astounded by these words, but Jesus insisted, "My children," he said to them, "how hard it is to enter the kingdom of God! 25 It is easier for a camel to pass through the eye of a needle than for a rich man to enter the kingdom of God." 26 They were more astonished than ever. "In that case," they said to one another, "who can be saved?" 27 Jesus gazed at them. "For men," he said, "it is impossible, but not for God: because everything is possible for God."

The reward of renunciation

28 Peter took this up. "What about us?" he asked him. "We have left everything and followed you." 29 Jesus said, "I tell you solemnly, there is no one who has left house, brothers, sisters, father, children or land for my sake and for the sake of the gospel 30 who will not be repaid a hundred times over, houses, brothers, sisters, mothers, children and land—not without persecutions—now in this present time and in the world to come, eternal life.

31 "Many who are first will be last, and the last first."

New English Bible

Jesus looked round at his disciples and said to them, 'How hard it will be for the wealthy to enter the kingdom of God!' They were amazed that he should say this, but Jesus insisted, 'Children, how hard it is[a] to enter the kingdom of God! It is easier for a camel to pass through the eye of a needle than for a rich man to enter the kingdom of God.' They were more astonished than ever, and said to one another, 'Then who can be saved?' Jesus looked at them and said, 'For men it is impossible, but not for God; everything is possible for God.'

At this Peter spoke. 'We here', he said, 'have left everything to become your followers.' Jesus said, 'I tell you this: there is no one who has given up home, brothers or sisters, mother, father or children, or land, for my sake and for the Gospel, who will not receive in this age a hundred times as much—houses, brothers and sisters, mothers and children, and land—and persecutions besides; and in the age to come eternal life. But many who are first will be last and the last first.'

[a] *Some witnesses insert* for those who trust in riches.

King James Version

32 And they were in the way going up to Jerusalem; and Jesus went before them: and they were amazed; and as they followed, they were afraid. And he took again the twelve, and began to tell them what things should happen unto him, 33 *Saying*, Behold, we go up to Jerusalem; and the Son of man shall be delivered unto the chief priests, and unto the scribes; and they shall condemn him to death, and shall deliver him to the Gentiles: 34 And they shall mock him, and shall scourge him, and shall spit upon him, and shall kill him; and the third day he shall rise again.

35 And James and John, the sons of Zebedee, come unto him, saying, Master, we would that thou shouldest do for us whatsoever we shall desire. 36 And he said unto them, What would ye that I should do for you? 37 They said unto him, Grant unto us that we may sit, one on thy right hand, and the other on thy left hand, in thy glory. 38 But Jesus said unto them, Ye know not what ye ask: can ye drink of the cup that I drink of? and be baptized with the baptism that I am baptized with? 39 And they said unto him,

Living Bible

32 Now they were on the way to Jerusalem, and Jesus was walking along ahead; and as the disciples were following they were filled with terror and dread.

Taking them aside, Jesus once more began describing all that was going to happen to him when they arrived at Jerusalem.

33 "When we get there," he told them, "I, the Messiah,[e] will be arrested and taken before the chief priests and the Jewish leaders, who will sentence me to die and hand me over to the Romans to be killed. 34 They will mock me and spit on me and flog me with their whips and kill me; but after three days I will come back to life again."

35 Then James and John, the sons of Zebedee, came over and spoke to him in a low voice.[f] "Master," they said, "we want you to do us a favor."

36 "What is it?" he asked.

37 "We want to sit on the thrones next to yours in your kingdom," they said, "one at your right and the other at your left!"

38 But Jesus answered, "You don't know what you are asking! Are you able to drink from the bitter cup of sorrow I must drink from? Or to be baptized with the baptism of suffering I must be baptized with?"

39 "Oh, yes," they said, "we are!"

[*e*] Literally, "the Son of Man." [*f*] Literally, "came up to him."

Today's English Version

Jesus speaks a third time about his death

32 They were now on the road going up to Jerusalem. Jesus was going ahead of the disciples, who were filled with alarm; the people who followed behind were afraid. Once again Jesus took the twelve disciples aside and spoke of the things that were going to happen to him. 33 "Listen," he told them, "we are going up to Jerusalem where the Son of Man will be handed over to the chief priests and the teachers of the Law. They will condemn him to death and then hand him over to the Gentiles. 34 These will make fun of him, spit on him, whip him, and kill him. And after three days he will rise to life."

The request of James and John

35 Then James and John, the sons of Zebedee, came to Jesus. "Teacher," they said, "there is something we want you to do for us."

36 "What do you want me to do for you?" Jesus asked them.

37 They answered, "When you sit on your throne in the glorious Kingdom, we want you to let us sit with you, one at your right and one at your left."

38 Jesus said to them, "You don't know what you are asking for. Can you drink the cup that I must drink? Can you be baptized in the way I must be baptized?"

39 "We can," they answered.

New International Version

Jesus again predicts his death

32 They were on their way up to Jerusalem, with Jesus leading the way, and the disciples were astonished, while those who followed were afraid. Again he took the Twelve aside and told them what was going to happen to him. 33 "We are going up to Jerusalem," he said, "and the Son of Man will be betrayed to the chief priests and teachers of the law. They will condemn him to death and will hand him over to the Gentiles, 34 who will mock him and spit on him, flog him and kill him. Three days later he will rise."

The request of James and John

35 Then James and John, the sons of Zebedee, came to him. "Teacher," they said, "we want you to do for us whatever we ask."

36 "What do you want me to do for you?" he asked.

37 They replied, "Let one of us sit at your right and the other at your left in your glory."

38 "You don't know what you are asking," Jesus said. "Can you drink the cup I drink or be baptized with the baptism I am baptized with?"

39 "We can," they answered.

Phillips Modern English

10.32 The last journey to Jerusalem begins

They were now on their way going up to Jerusalem and Jesus walked on ahead. The disciples were dismayed at this, and those who followed were afraid. Then once more he took the twelve aside and began to tell them what was going to happen to him.

"We are now going up to Jerusalem," he said, "as you can see. And the Son of Man will be betrayed into the power of the chief priests and scribes. They are going to condemn him to death and hand him over to pagans who will jeer at him and spit at him and flog him and kill him. But after three days he will rise again."

10.35 An ill-timed request

Then Zebedee's two sons James and John approached him, saying,

"Master, we want you to do for us whatever we ask."

"What do you want me to do for you?" answered Jesus.

"Give us permission to sit one on each side of you when you reign in your glory!"

"You don't know what you are asking," Jesus said to them. "Can you drink the cup I have to drink? Can you go through the baptism I have to bear?"

"Yes, we can," they replied.

Revised Standard Version

32 And they were on the road, going up to
Jerusalem, and Jesus was walking ahead of
them; and they were amazed, and those who followed were afraid. And taking the twelve again,
he began to tell them what was to happen to
him, 33 saying, "Behold, we are going up to
Jerusalem; and the Son of man will be delivered
to the chief priests and the scribes, and they will
condemn him to death, and deliver him to the
Gentiles; 34 and they will mock him, and spit
upon him, and scourge him, and kill him; and
after three days he will rise."

35 And James and John, the sons of Zebedee,
came forward to him, and said to him, "Teacher,
we want you to do for us whatever we ask of
you." 36 And he said to them, "What do you
want me to do for you?" 37 And they said to him,
"Grant us to sit, one at your right hand and
one at your left, in your glory." 38 But Jesus
said to them, "You do not know what you are
asking. Are you able to drink the cup that I
drink, or to be baptized with the baptism with
which I am baptized?" 39 And they said to him,

Jerusalem Bible

Third prophecy of the Passion

32 They were on the road, going up to Jerusalem; Jesus was walking on ahead of them;
they were in a daze, and those who followed
were apprehensive. Once more taking the Twelve
aside he began to tell them what was going to
happen to him: 33 "Now we are going up to
Jerusalem, and the Son of Man is about to be
handed over to the chief priests and the scribes.
They will condemn him to death and will hand
him over to the pagans, 34 who will mock him
and spit at him and scourge him and put him
to death; and after three days he will rise again."

The sons of Zebedee make their request

35 James and John, the sons of Zebedee, approached him. "Master," they said to him, "we
want you to do us a favor." 36 He said to them,
"What is it you want me to do for you?"
37 They said to him, "Allow us to sit one at your
right hand and the other at your left in your
glory." 38 "You do not know what you are asking," Jesus said to them. "Can you drink the
cup that I must drink, or be baptized with the
baptism with which I must be baptized?" 39 They
replied, "We can." Jesus said to them, "The

New English Bible

Challenge to Jerusalem

They were on the road, going up to Jerusalem, Jesus leading the way; and the disciples were filled with awe, while those who followed behind were afraid. He took the Twelve aside and began to tell them what was to happen to him. 'We are now going to Jerusalem,' he said; 'and the Son of Man will be given up to the chief priests and the doctors of the law; they will condemn him to death and hand him over to the foreign power. He will be mocked and spat upon, flogged and killed; and three days afterwards, he will rise again.'

James and John, the sons of Zebedee, approached him and said, 'Master, we should like you to do us a favour.' 'What is it you want me to do?' he asked. They answered, 'Grant us the right to sit in state with you, one at your right and the other at your left.' Jesus said to them, 'You do not understand what you are asking. Can you drink the cup that I drink, or be baptized with the baptism I am baptized with?' 'We can', they answered. Jesus said, 'The cup that

King James Version

We can. And Jesus said unto them, Ye shall indeed drink of the cup that I drink of; and with the baptism that I am baptized withal shall ye be baptized: 40 But to sit on my right hand and on my left hand is not mine to give; but *it shall be given to them* for whom it is prepared. 41 And when the ten heard *it*, they began to be much displeased with James and John. 42 But Jesus called them *to him*, and saith unto them, Ye know that they which are accounted to rule over the Gentiles exercise lordship over them; and their great ones exercise authority upon them. 43 But so shall it not be among you: but whosoever will be great among you, shall be your minister: 44 And whosoever of you will be the chiefest, shall be servant of all. 45 For even the Son of man came not to be ministered unto, but to minister, and to give his life a ransom for many.

46 And they came to Jericho: and as he went out of Jericho with his disciples and a great number of people, blind Bartimeus, the son of Timeus, sat by the highway side begging. 47 And when he heard that it was Jesus of Nazareth, he began to cry out, and say, Jesus, *thou* Son of David, have mercy on me. 48 And many charged him that he should hold his peace: but he cried the more a great deal, *Thou* Son of David, have

Living Bible

And Jesus said, "You shall indeed drink from my cup and be baptized with my baptism, 40 but I do not have the right to place you on thrones next to mine. Those appointments have already been made."

41 When the other disciples discovered what James and John had asked, they were very indignant. 42 So Jesus called them to him and said, "As you know, the kings and great men of the earth lord it over the people; 43 but among you it is different. Whoever wants to be great among you must be your servant. 44 And whoever wants to be greatest of all must be the slave of all. 45 For even I, the Messiah,[g] am not here to be served, but to help others, and to give my life as a ransom for many."

46 And so they reached Jericho. Later, as they left town, a great crowd was following. Now it happened that a blind beggar named Bartimaeus (the son of Timaeus) was sitting beside the road as Jesus was going by.

47 When Bartimaeus heard that Jesus from Nazareth was near, he began to shout out, "Jesus, Son of David, have mercy on me!"

48 "Shut up!" some of the people yelled at him.

But he only shouted the louder, again and again, "O Son of David, have mercy on me!"

[g] Literally, "the Son of Man."

Today's English Version

Jesus said to them, "You will indeed drink the cup I must drink and be baptized in the way I must be baptized. 40 But I do not have the right to choose who will sit at my right and my left. It is God who will give these places to those for whom he has prepared them."

41 When the other ten disciples heard about this they became angry with James and John. 42 So Jesus called them all together to him and said, "You know that the men who are considered rulers have power over the people, and their leaders rule over them. 43 This, however, is not the way it is among you. If one of you wants to be great, he must be the servant of the rest; 44 and if one of you wants to be first, he must be the slave of all. 45 For even the Son of Man did not come to be served; he came to serve and to give his life to redeem many people."

Jesus heals blind Bartimaeus

46 They came to Jericho. As Jesus was leaving with his disciples and a large crowd, a blind man named Bartimaeus, the son of Timaeus, was sitting by the road, begging. 47 When he heard that it was Jesus of Nazareth, he began to shout, "Jesus! Son of David! Have mercy on me!"

48 Many scolded him and told him to be quiet. But he shouted even more loudly, "Son of David, have mercy on me!"

New International Version

Jesus said to them, "You will drink the cup I drink and be baptized with the baptism I am baptized with, 40 but to sit at my right or left is not for me to grant. These places belong to those for whom they have been prepared."

41 When the ten heard about this, they became indignant with James and John. 42 Jesus called them together and said, "You know that those who are regarded as rulers of the Gentiles lord it over them, and their high officials exercise authority over them. 43 Not so with you. Instead, whoever wants to become great among you must be your servant, 44 and whoever wants to be first must be slave of all. 45 For even the Son of Man did not come to be served, but to serve, and to give his life a ransom for many."

Blind Bartimaeus receives his sight

46 Then they came to Jericho. As Jesus and his disciples, together with a large crowd, were leaving the city, a blind man, Bartimaeus (that is, the Son of Timaeus), was sitting by the roadside begging. 47 When he heard that it was Jesus of Nazareth, he began to shout, "Jesus, Son of David, have mercy on me!"

48 Many rebuked him and told him to be quiet, but he shouted all the more, "Son of David, have mercy on me!"

Phillips Modern English

Then Jesus told them,

"You will indeed drink the cup I am drinking, and you will undergo the baptism which I have to bear! But as for sitting on either side of me, that is not for me to give—such places belong to those for whom they are prepared."

When the other ten heard about this, they began to be highly indignant with James and John; so Jesus called them all to him, and said,

"You know that the so-called rulers of the heathen lord it over them, and their great men have absolute power. But it must not be so among you. No, whoever among you wants to be great must become the servant of you all, and if he wants to be first among you he must be the slave of all men! For the Son of Man himself has not come to be served but to serve, and to give his life to set many others free."

Then they came to Jericho, and as he was leaving it accompanied by his disciples and a large crowd, Bartimaeus (that is, the son of Timaeus), a blind beggar, was sitting by the side of the road. When he heard that it was Jesus of Nazareth he began to call out,

"Jesus, Son of David, have pity on me!"

Many of the people told him sharply to keep quiet, but he shouted all the more,

"Son of David, have pity on me!"

Revised Standard Version

"We are able." And Jesus said to them, "The
cup that I drink you will drink; and with the
baptism with which I am baptized, you will be
baptized; 40 but to sit at my right hand or at my
left is not mine to grant, but it is for those for
whom it has been prepared." 41 And when the
ten heard it, they began to be indignant at James
and John. 42 And Jesus called them to him and
said to them, "You know that those who are
supposed to rule over the Gentiles lord it over
them, and their great men exercise authority
over them. 43 But it shall not be so among you;
but whoever would be great among you must be
your servant, 44 and whoever would be first
among you must be slave of all. 45 For the Son
of man also came not to be served but to serve,
and to give his life as a ransom for many."

46 And they came to Jericho; and as he was
leaving Jericho with his disciples and a great
multitude, Bartimaeus, a blind beggar, the son
of Timaeus, was sitting by the roadside. 47 And
when he heard that it was Jesus of Nazareth, he
began to cry out and say, "Jesus, Son of David,
have mercy on me!" 48 And many rebuked him,
telling him to be silent; but he cried out all the

Jerusalem Bible

cup that I must drink you shall drink, and with
the baptism with which I must be baptized you
shall be baptized, 40 but as for seats at my right
hand or my left, these are not mine to grant;
they belong to those to whom they have been
allotted."

Leadership with service

41 When the other ten heard this they began
to feel indignant with James and John, 42 so Jesus called them to him and said to them, "You
know that among the pagans their so-called
rulers lord it over them, and their great men
make their authority felt. 43 This is not to happen among you. No; anyone who wants to become great among you must be your servant,
44 and anyone who wants to be first among you
must be slave to all. 45 For the Son of Man
himself did not come to be served but to serve,
and to give his life as a ransom for many."

The blind man of Jericho

46 They reached Jericho; and as he left Jericho with his disciples and a large crowd,
Bartimaeus (that is, the son of Timaeus), a blind
beggar, was sitting at the side of the road.
47 When he heard that it was Jesus of Nazareth,
he began to shout and to say, "Son of David,
Jesus, have pity on me." 48 And many of them
scolded him and told him to keep quiet, but he
only shouted all the louder, "Son of David, have

New English Bible

I drink you shall drink, and the baptism I am baptized with shall be your baptism; but to sit at my right or left is not for me to grant; it is for those to whom it has already been assigned.' [b]

When the other ten heard this, they were indignant with James and John. Jesus called them to him and said, 'You know that in the world the recognized rulers lord it over their subjects, and their great men make them feel the weight of authority. That is not the way with you; among you, whoever wants to be great must be your servant, and whoever wants to be first must be the willing slave of all. For even the Son of Man did not come to be served but to serve, and to give up his life as a ransom for many.'

They came to Jericho; and as he was leaving the town, with his disciples and a large crowd, Bartimaeus son of Timaeus, a blind beggar, was seated at the roadside. Hearing that it was Jesus of Nazareth, he began to shout, 'Son of David, Jesus, have pity on me!' Many of the people told him to hold his tongue; but he shouted all the more, 'Son of David, have pity on me.'

[b] *Some witnesses add* by my Father.

King James Version

mercy on me. 49And Jesus stood still, and commanded him to be called. And they call the blind man, saying unto him, Be of good comfort, rise; he calleth thee. 50And he, casting away his garment, rose, and came to Jesus. 51And Jesus answered and said unto him, What wilt thou that I should do unto thee? The blind man said unto him, Lord, that I might receive my sight. 52And Jesus said unto him, Go thy way; thy faith hath made thee whole. And immediately he received his sight, and followed Jesus in the way.

11 And when they came nigh to Jerusalem, unto Bethphage and Bethany, at the mount of Olives, he sendeth forth two of his disciples, 2And saith unto them, Go your way into the village over against you: and as soon as ye be entered into it, ye shall find a colt tied, whereon never man sat; loose him, and bring *him*. 3And if any man say unto you, Why do ye this? say ye that the Lord hath need of him; and straightway he will send him hither. 4And they went their way, and found the colt tied by the door without in a place where two ways met; and they loose him. 5And certain of them that stood there said unto them, What do ye, loosing the colt? 6And they said unto them even as Jesus

Living Bible

49 When Jesus heard him he stopped there in the road and said, "Tell him to come here."

So they called the blind man. "You lucky fellow,"[h] they said, "come on, he's calling you!" 50 Bartimaeus yanked off his old coat and flung it aside, jumped up and came to Jesus.

51 "What do you want me to do for you?" Jesus asked.

"O Teacher," the blind man said, "I want to see!"

52 And Jesus said to him, "All right, it's done.[i] Your faith has healed you."

And instantly the blind man could see, and followed Jesus down the road!

11 As they neared Bethphage and Bethany on the outskirts of Jerusalem and came to the Mount of Olives, Jesus sent two of his disciples on ahead.

2 "Go into that village over there," he told them, "and just as you enter you will see a colt tied up that has never been ridden. Untie him and bring him here. 3And if anyone asks you what you are doing, just say, 'Our Master needs him and will return him soon.' "

4, 5 Off went the two men and found the colt standing in the street, tied outside a house. As they were untying it, some who were standing there demanded, "What are you doing, untying that colt?"

6 So they said what Jesus had told them to,

[*h*] Literally, "Be of good cheer." [*i*] Literally, "Go your way."

Today's English Version

49 Jesus stopped and said, "Call him."

So they called the blind man. "Cheer up!" they said. "Get up, he is calling you."

50 He threw off his cloak, jumped up, and came to Jesus.

51 "What do you want me to do for you?" Jesus asked him.

"Teacher," the blind man answered, "I want to see again."

52 "Go," Jesus told him, "your faith has made you well."

At once he was able to see, and followed Jesus on the road.

The triumphant entry into Jerusalem

11 As they came near Jerusalem, at the towns of Bethphage and Bethany they came to the Mount of Olives. Jesus sent two of his disciples on ahead 2 with these instructions, "Go to the village there ahead of you. As soon as you get there you will find a colt tied up that has never been ridden. Untie it and bring it here. 3And if someone asks you, 'Why are you doing that?' tell him, 'The Master needs it and will send it back here at once.' "

4 So they went and found a colt out in the street, tied to the door of a house. As they were untying it, 5 some of the bystanders asked them, "What are you doing, untying that colt?"

6 They answered just as Jesus had told them,

New International Version

49 Jesus stopped and said, "Call him."

So they called to the blind man, "Cheer up! On your feet! He's calling you." 50 Throwing his cloak aside, he jumped to his feet and came to Jesus.

51 "What do you want me to do for you?" Jesus asked him.

The blind man said, "Rabbi, I want to see."

52 "Go," said Jesus, "your faith has healed you." Immediately he received his sight and followed Jesus along the road.

The triumphal entry

11 As they approached Jerusalem and came to Bethphage and Bethany at the Mount of Olives, Jesus sent two of his disciples, 2 saying to them, "Go to the village ahead of you, and just as you enter it, you will find a colt tied there, which no one has ever ridden. Untie it and bring it here. 3 If anyone asks you, 'Why are you doing this?' tell him, 'The Lord needs it and will send it back here shortly.' "

4 They went and found a colt outside in the street, tied at a doorway. As they untied it, 5 some people standing there asked, "What are you doing, untying that colt?" 6 They answered

Phillips Modern English

Jesus stood quite still and said,
"Call him here."

So they called the blind man, saying,
"It's all right now, get up, he's calling you!"

At this he threw off his coat, jumped to his feet and came to Jesus.

"What do you want me to do for you?" he asked him. The blind man answered,

"Oh, Master, let me see again!"

"Go on your way then," returned Jesus, "your faith has healed you."

And he recovered his sight at once and followed Jesus along the road.

11.1 Jesus arranges for his entry into the city

When they were approaching Jerusalem and had come to Bethphage and Bethany near the Mount of Olives, he sent off two of his disciples with these instructions,

"Go into the village just ahead of you and as soon as you enter it you will find a tethered colt on which no one has yet ridden. Untie it, and bring it here. If anybody asks you, 'Why are you doing this?', just say, 'His master needs him, and will send him back immediately.'"

So they went off and found the colt tethered by a doorway outside in the open street, and they untied it. Some of the bystanders did say, "What are you doing, untying this colt?", but they made the reply Jesus told them to make,

Revised Standard Version

more, "Son of David, have mercy on me!" 49 And Jesus stopped and said, "Call him." And they called the blind man, saying to him, "Take heart; rise, he is calling you." 50 And throwing off his mantle he sprang up and came to Jesus. 51 And Jesus said to him, "What do you want me to do for you?" And the blind man said to him, "Master,[t] let me receive my sight." 52 And Jesus said to him, "Go your way; your faith has made you well." And immediately he received his sight and followed him on the way.

11 And when they drew near to Jerusalem, to Bethphage and Bethany, at the Mount of Olives, he sent two of his disciples, 2 and said to them, "Go into the village opposite you, and immediately as you enter it you will find a colt tied, on which no one has ever sat; untie it and bring it. 3 If any one says to you, 'Why are you doing this?' say, 'The Lord has need of it and will send it back here immediately.'" 4 And they went away, and found a colt tied at the door out in the open street; and they untied it. 5 And those who stood there said to them, "What are you doing, untying the colt?" 6 And they told

[t] Or *Rabbi*.

Jerusalem Bible

pity on me." 49 Jesus stopped and said, "Call him here." So they called the blind man. "Courage," they said, "get up; he is calling you." 50 So throwing off his cloak, he jumped up and went to Jesus. 51 Then Jesus spoke, "What do you want me to do for you?" "Rabbuni,"[o] the blind man said to him, "Master, let me see again." 52 Jesus said to him, "Go; your faith has saved you." And immediately his sight returned and he followed him along the road.

IV. The Jerusalem ministry

The Messiah enters Jerusalem

11 When they were approaching Jerusalem, in sight of Bethphage and Bethany, close by the Mount of Olives, he sent two of his disciples 2 and said to them, "Go off to the village facing you, and as soon as you enter it you will find a tethered colt that no one has yet ridden. Untie it and bring it here. 3 If anyone says to you, 'What are you doing?' say, 'The Master needs it and will send it back here directly.'" 4 They went off and found a colt tethered near a door in the open street. As they untied it, 5 some men standing there said, "What are you doing, untying that colt?" 6 They gave the answer Jesus had told them, and the

[o] Aramaic: "My master."

New English Bible

Jesus stopped and said, 'Call him'; so they called the blind man and said, 'Take heart; stand up; he is calling you.' At that he threw off his cloak, sprang up, and came to Jesus. Jesus said to him, 'What do you want me to do for you?' 'Master,' the blind man answered, 'I want my sight back.' Jesus said to him, 'Go; your faith has cured you.' And at once he recovered his sight and followed him on the road.

11 They were now approaching Jerusalem, and when they reached Bethphage and Bethany, at the Mount of Olives, he sent two of his disciples with these instructions: 'Go to the village opposite, and, just as you enter, you will find tethered there a colt which no one has yet ridden. Untie it and bring it here. If anyone asks, "Why are you doing that?", say, "Our Master[a] needs it, and will send it back here without delay."' So they went off, and found the colt tethered at a door outside in the street. They were untying it when some of the bystanders asked, 'What are you doing, untying that colt?' They answered as Jesus had told them,

[a] *Or* Its owner.

King James Version

had commanded: and they let them go. 7And
they brought the colt to Jesus, and cast their
garments on him; and he sat upon him. 8And
many spread their garments in the way; and
others cut down branches off the trees, and
strewed *them* in the way. 9And they that went
before, and they that followed, cried, saying,
Hosanna; Blessed *is* he that cometh in the name
of the Lord: 10 Blessed *be* the kingdom of our
father David, that cometh in the name of the
Lord: Hosanna in the highest. 11And Jesus entered into Jerusalem, and into the temple: and
when he had looked round about upon all things,
and now the eventide was come, he went out
unto Bethany with the twelve.
12 And on the morrow, when they were come
from Bethany; he was hungry: 13And seeing a
fig tree afar off having leaves, he came, if haply
he might find any thing thereon: and when he
came to it, he found nothing but leaves; for the
time of figs was not *yet*. 14And Jesus answered
and said unto it, No man eat fruit of thee hereafter for ever. And his disciples heard *it*.
15 And they come to Jerusalem: and Jesus
went into the temple, and began to cast out

Living Bible

and then the men agreed.
7 So the colt was brought to Jesus and the
disciples threw their cloaks across its back for
him to ride on. 8 Then many in the crowd
spread out their coats along the road before
him, while others threw down leafy branches
from the fields.
9 He was in the center of the procession with
crowds ahead and behind, and all of them
shouting, "Hail to the King!" "Praise God for
him who comes in the name of the Lord!" . . .
10 "Praise God for the return of our father
David's kingdom . . ." "Hail to the King of the
universe!"
11 And so he entered Jerusalem and went into
the Temple. He looked around carefully at everything and then left—for now it was late in the
afternoon—and went out to Bethany with the
twelve disciples.
12 The next morning as they left Bethany, he
felt hungry. 13A little way off he noticed a fig
tree in full leaf, so he went over to see if he
could find any figs on it. But no, there were
only leaves, for it was too early in the season
for fruit.
14 Then Jesus said to the tree, "You shall
never bear fruit again!" And the disciples heard
him say it.
15 When they arrived back to Jerusalem he
went to the Temple and began to drive out the

Today's English Version

so the men let them go. 7 They brought the colt
to Jesus, threw their cloaks over the animal, and
Jesus got on. 8 Many people spread their cloaks
on the road, while others cut branches in the
fields and spread them on the road. 9 The people who were in front and those who followed
behind began to shout, "Praise God! God bless
him who comes in the name of the Lord! 10 God
bless the coming kingdom of our father David!
Praise be to God!"
11 Jesus entered Jerusalem, went into the
temple, and looked around at everything. But
since it was already late in the day, he went out
to Bethany with the twelve disciples.

Jesus curses the fig tree

12 The next day, as they were coming back
from Bethany, Jesus was hungry. 13 He saw in
the distance a fig tree covered with leaves, so
he went to it to see if he could find any figs on
it; but when he came to it he found only leaves,
because it was not the right time for figs. 14 Jesus said to the fig tree, "No one shall ever eat
figs from you again!"
And his disciples heard him.

Jesus goes to the temple

15 When they arrived in Jerusalem, Jesus
went to the temple and began to drive out all

New International Version

as Jesus had told them to, and the people let
them go. 7 When they brought the colt to Jesus
and threw their cloaks over it, he sat on it.
8 Many people spread their cloaks on the road,
while others spread branches they had cut in the
fields. 9 Those who went ahead and those who
followed shouted,
"Hosanna! [p]
Blessed is he who comes in the name of the
Lord! [q]
10 Blessed is the coming kingdom of our father
David!
Hosanna[p] in the highest!"
11 Jesus entered Jerusalem and went to the
temple. He looked around at everything, but
since it was already late, he went out to Bethany
with the Twelve.

Jesus clears the temple

12 The next day as they were leaving Bethany, Jesus was hungry. 13 Seeing in the distance
a fig tree in leaf, he went to find out if it had
any fruit. When he reached it, however, he found
nothing but leaves, because it was not the season
for figs. 14 Then he said to the tree, "May no
one ever eat fruit from you again." And his
disciples heard him say it.
15 On reaching Jerusalem, Jesus entered the
temple area and began driving out those who

[*p*] A Hebrew expression meaning "Save!" which became an exclamation of praise. [*q*] Psalm 118:25,26.

Phillips Modern English

and the men raised no objection. So they brought the colt to Jesus, threw their coats on its back, and he took his seat upon it.

Many of the people spread out their coats in his path as he rode along, and others put down rushes which they had cut from the fields. The whole crowd, both those who were in front and those who were behind Jesus, shouted,

"God save him!—God bless the one who comes in the name of the Lord! God bless the coming kingdom of our father David! God save him from on high!"

Jesus entered Jerusalem and went into the Temple and looked round on all that was going on. And then, since it was already late in the day, he went out to Bethany with the twelve.

On the following day, when they had left Bethany, Jesus felt hungry. He noticed a fig-tree in the distance covered with leaves, and he walked up to it to see if he could find any fruit on it. But when he got to it, he could find nothing but leaves, for it was not yet the season for figs. Then Jesus spoke to the tree,

"May nobody ever eat fruit from you!"

And the disciples heard him say it.

Then they came into Jerusalem and Jesus went into the Temple and began to drive out those

Revised Standard Version

them what Jesus had said; and they let them go.
7And they brought the colt to Jesus, and threw
their garments on it; and he sat upon it. 8And
many spread their garments on the road, and
others spread leafy branches which they had cut
from the fields. 9And those who went before and
those who followed cried out, "Hosanna!
Blessed is he who comes in the name of the Lord!
10 Blessed is the kingdom of our father David
that is coming! Hosanna in the highest!"
11 And he entered Jerusalem, and went into
the temple; and when he had looked round at
everything, as it was already late, he went out
to Bethany with the twelve.
12 On the following day, when they came
from Bethany, he was hungry. 13And seeing in
the distance a fig tree in leaf, he went to see if
he could find anything on it. When he came to
it, he found nothing but leaves, for it was not
the season for figs. 14And he said to it, "May
no one ever eat fruit from you again." And his
disciples heard it.
15 And they came to Jerusalem. And he entered the temple and began to drive out those

Jerusalem Bible

men let them go. 7 Then they took the colt to
Jesus and threw their cloaks on its back, and he
sat on it. 8 Many people spread their cloaks on
the road, others greenery which they had cut in
the fields. 9And those who went in front and
those who followed were all shouting, "*Hosanna! Blessings on him who comes in the name
of the Lord!* [p] 10 Blessings on the coming kingdom of our father David! *Hosanna* in the highest heavens!" 11 He entered Jerusalem and went
into the Temple. He looked all around him, but
as it was now late, he went out to Bethany
with the Twelve.

The barren fig tree

12 Next day as they were leaving Bethany,
he felt hungry. 13 Seeing a fig tree in leaf some
distance away, he went to see if he could find
any fruit on it, but when he came up to it he
found nothing but leaves; for it was not the
season for figs. 14And he addressed the fig tree.
"May no one ever eat fruit from you again,"
he said. And his disciples heard him say this.

The expulsion of the dealers from the Temple

15 So they reached Jerusalem and he went
into the Temple and began driving out those

[p] Ps. 118:25-26.

New English Bible

and were then allowed to take it. So they brought the colt to Jesus and spread their cloaks on it, and he mounted. And people carpeted the road with their cloaks, while others spread brushwood which they had cut in the fields; and those who went ahead and the others who came behind shouted, 'Hosanna! Blessings on him who comes in the name of the Lord! Blessings on the coming kingdom of our father David! Hosanna in the heavens!'

He entered Jerusalem and went into the temple, where he looked at the whole scene; but, as it was now late, he went out to Bethany with the Twelve.

On the following day, after they had left Bethany, he felt hungry, and, noticing in the distance a fig-tree in leaf, he went to see if he could find anything on it. But when he came there he found nothing but leaves; for it was not the season for figs. He said to the tree, 'May no one ever again eat fruit from you!' And his disciples were listening.

So they came to Jerusalem, and he went into the temple and began driving out those who

King James Version

them that sold and bought in the temple, and
overthrew the tables of the money changers, and
the seats of them that sold doves; 16 And would
not suffer that any man should carry *any* vessel
through the temple. 17 And he taught, saying unto
them, Is it not written, My house shall be called
of all nations the house of prayer? but ye have
made it a den of thieves. 18 And the scribes and
chief priests heard *it*, and sought how they might
destroy him: for they feared him, because all
the people was astonished at his doctrine. 19 And
when even was come, he went out of the city.
20 And in the morning, as they passed by,
they saw the fig tree dried up from the roots.
21 And Peter calling to remembrance saith unto
him, Master, behold, the fig tree which thou
cursedst is withered away. 22 And Jesus answering saith unto them, Have faith in God. 23 For
verily I say unto you, That whosoever shall say
unto this mountain, Be thou removed, and be
thou cast into the sea; and shall not doubt in
his heart, but shall believe that those things
which he saith shall come to pass; he shall have
whatsoever he saith. 24 Therefore I say unto you,
What things soever ye desire, when ye pray, believe that ye receive *them*, and ye shall have
them. 25 And when ye stand praying, forgive, if
ye have aught against any; that your Father also
which is in heaven may forgive you your tres-

Living Bible

merchants and their customers, and knocked
over the tables of the moneychangers and the
stalls of those selling doves, 16 and stopped
everyone from bringing in loads of merchandise.
17 He told them, "It is written in the Scriptures, 'My Temple is to be a place of prayer for
all nations,' but you have turned it into a den of
robbers."
18 When the chief priests and other Jewish
leaders heard what he had done they began planning how best to get rid of him. Their problem
was their fear of riots because the people were
so enthusiastic about Jesus' teaching.
19 That evening as usual they left the city.
20 Next morning, as the disciples passed the fig
tree he had cursed, they saw that it was withered
from the roots! 21 Then Peter remembered what
Jesus had said to the tree on the previous day,
and exclaimed, "Look, Teacher! The fig tree
you cursed has withered!"
22, 23 In reply Jesus said to the disciples,
"If you only have faith in God—this is the
absolute truth—you can say to this Mount of
Olives, 'Rise up and fall into the Mediterranean,'
and your command will be obeyed. All that's
required is that you really believe and have no
doubt! 24 Listen to me! You can pray for *anything,* and *if you believe, you have it;* it's yours!
25 But when you are praying, first forgive anyone you are holding a grudge against, so that
your Father in heaven will forgive you your sins
too."

Today's English Version

those who bought and sold in the temple. He
overturned the tables of the moneychangers and
the stools of those who sold pigeons, 16 and
would not let anyone carry anything through
the temple courts. 17 He then taught the people,
"It is written in the Scriptures that God said, 'My
house will be called a house of prayer for all
peoples.' But you have turned it into a hideout
for thieves!"
18 The chief priests and the teachers of the
Law heard of this, so they began looking for
some way to kill Jesus. They were afraid of him,
because the whole crowd was amazed at his
teaching.
19 When evening came, Jesus and his disciples left the city.

The lesson from the fig tree

20 Early next morning, as they walked along
the road, they saw the fig tree. It was dead all the
way down to its roots. 21 Peter remembered what
had happened and said to Jesus, "Look, Teacher,
the fig tree you cursed has died!"
22 Jesus answered them, "Remember this! If
you have faith in God, 23 you can say to this hill,
'Get up and throw yourself in the sea.' If you do
not doubt in your heart, but believe that what
you say will happen, it will be done for you.
24 For this reason I tell you: When you pray and
ask for something, believe that you have received
it, and you will be given whatever you ask for.
25 And when you stand praying, forgive anything
you may have against anyone, so that your Father

New International Version

were buying and selling there. He overturned
the tables of the money-changers and the
benches of those selling doves, 16 and would
not allow anyone to carry merchandise through
the temple courts. 17 And as he taught them, he
said, "Is it not written:
'My house will be called a house of prayer
for all nations'[r]?
But you have made it 'a den of robbers.'[s]"
18 The chief priests and the teachers of the
law heard this and began looking for a way to
kill him, for they feared him, because the whole
crowd was amazed at his teaching.
19 When evening came, they[t] went out of the
city.

The withered fig tree

20 In the morning, as they went along, they
saw the fig tree withered from the roots. 21 Peter
remembered and said to Jesus, "Rabbi, look!
The fig tree you cursed has withered!"
22 "Have[u] faith in God," Jesus answered.
23 "I tell you the truth, if anyone says to this
mountain, 'Go, throw yourself into the sea,' and
does not doubt in his heart but believes that
what he says will happen, it will be done for
him. 24 Therefore I tell you, whatever you ask
for in prayer, believe that you will receive it, and
it will be yours. 25 And when you stand praying,
if you hold anything against anyone, forgive him,
so that your Father in heaven may forgive you
your sins."[v]

[*r*] Isaiah 56:7. [*s*] Jer. 7:11. [*t*] Some early MSS read *he*. [*u*] Some early MSS read *If you have*. [*v*] Some MSS add verse 26: ***But if you do not forgive, neither will your Father who is in heaven forgive your sins.***

Phillips Modern English

who were buying and selling there. He overturned the tables of the money-changers and the benches of the dove-sellers, and he would not allow anyone to make a short cut through the Temple when carrying such things as water-pots. And he began to teach them and said,

"Doesn't the scripture say, 'My house shall be called a house of prayer for all nations'? But you have turned it into a thieves' kitchen!"

The chief priests and scribes heard him say this and tried to find a way of getting rid of him. But they were in fact afraid of him, for his teaching had captured the imagination of the people. And every evening they left the city.

11.20 Jesus talks of faith, prayer and forgiveness

One morning as they were walking along, they noticed that the fig-tree had withered away from the roots. Peter remembered it, and said,

"Master, look, the fig-tree that you cursed is all shrivelled up!"

"Have faith in God," replied Jesus to them. "I tell you that if anyone should say to this hill, 'Get up and throw yourself into the sea', and without any doubt in his heart believe that what he says will happen, then it *will* happen! That is why I tell you, whatever you pray about and ask for, believe that you have received it and it will be yours. And whenever you stand praying, you must forgive any grudge that you are holding against anyone else, and your Heavenly Father will forgive you *your* sins."

Revised Standard Version

who sold and those who bought in the temple,
and he overturned the tables of the money-
changers and the seats of those who sold pigeons;
16 and he would not allow any one to carry anything through the temple. 17And he taught, and
said to them, "Is it not written, 'My house shall
be called a house of prayer for all the nations'?
But you have made it a den of robbers." 18And
the chief priests and the scribes heard it and
sought a way to destroy him; for they feared
him, because all the multitude was astonished at
his teaching. 19And when evening came they[u]
went out of the city.
20 As they passed by in the morning, they saw
the fig tree withered away to its roots. 21And
Peter remembered and said to him, "Master,"[v]
look! The fig tree which you cursed has withered." 22And Jesus answered them, "Have faith in
God. 23 Truly, I say to you, whoever says to this
mountain, 'Be taken up and cast into the sea,'
and does not doubt in his heart, but believes that
what he says will come to pass, it will be done
for him. 24 Therefore I tell you, whatever you
ask in prayer, believe that you have received[a]
it, and it will be yours. 25And whenever you
stand praying, forgive, if you have anything
against any one; so that your Father also who
is in heaven may forgive you your trespasses."[w]

[u] Other ancient authorities read *he.* [v] Or *Rabbi.* [a] Other ancient authorities read *are receiving.* [w] Other ancient authorities add verse 26, *"But if you do not forgive, neither will your Father who is in heaven forgive your trespasses."*

Jerusalem Bible

who were selling and buying there; he upset the
tables of the money changers and the chairs of
those who were selling pigeons. 16 Nor would
he allow anyone to carry anything through the
Temple. 17And he taught them and said, "Does
not scripture say: *My house will be called a
house of prayer for all the peoples?*[q] But you
have turned it into *a robbers' den.*"[r] 18 This
came to the ears of the chief priests and the
scribes, and they tried to find some way of doing away with him; they were afraid of him
because the people were carried away by his
teaching. 19And when evening came he went
out of the city.

The fig tree withered. Faith and prayer

20 Next morning, as they passed by, they saw
the fig tree withered to the roots. 21 Peter remembered. "Look, Rabbi," he said to Jesus, "the
fig tree you cursed has withered away." 22 Jesus
answered, "Have faith in God. 23 I tell you solemnly, if anyone says to this mountain, 'Get up
and throw yourself into the sea,' with no hesitation in his heart but believing that what he
says will happen, it will be done for him. 24 I
tell you therefore: everything you ask and pray
for, believe that you have it already, and it will
be yours. 25And when you stand in prayer, forgive whatever you have against anybody, so that
your Father in heaven may forgive your failings
too."[s]

[q] Is. 56:7. [r] Jr. 7:11. [s] Add v. 26 "But if you do not forgive, your Father in heaven will not forgive your failings either." Cf. Mt. 6:15.

New English Bible

bought and sold in the temple. He upset the tables of the money-changers and the seats of the dealers in pigeons; and he would not allow anyone to use the temple court as a thoroughfare for carrying goods. Then he began to teach them, and said, 'Does not Scripture say, "My house shall be called a house of prayer for all the nations"? But you have made it a robbers' cave.' The chief priests and the doctors of the law heard of this and sought some means of making away with him; for they were afraid of him, because the whole crowd was spellbound by his teaching. And when evening came he went out of the city.

Early next morning, as they passed by, they saw that the fig-tree had withered from the roots up; and Peter, recalling what had happened, said to him, 'Rabbi, look, the fig-tree which you cursed has withered.' Jesus answered them, 'Have faith in God. I tell you this: if anyone says to this mountain, "Be lifted from your place and hurled into the sea", and has no inward doubts, but believes that what he says is happening, it will be done for him. I tell you, then, whatever you ask for in prayer, believe that you have received it and it will be yours.

'And when you stand praying, if you have a grievance against anyone, forgive him, so that your Father in heaven may forgive you the wrongs you have done.'[a]

[a] *Some witnesses add* (26) But if you do not forgive others, then the wrongs you have done will not be forgiven by your Father in heaven.

King James Version

passes. 26 But if ye do not forgive, neither will
your Father which is in heaven forgive your
trespasses.
27 And they come again to Jerusalem: and as
he was walking in the temple, there come to him
the chief priests, and the scribes, and the elders,
28And say unto him, By what authority doest
thou these things? and who gave thee this authority to do these things? 29And Jesus answered
and said unto them, I will also ask of you one
question, and answer me, and I will tell you by
what authority I do these things. 30 The baptism
of John, was *it* from heaven, or of men? answer
me. 31And they reasoned with themselves, saying, If we shall say, From heaven; he will say,
Why then did ye not believe him? 32 But if we
shall say, Of men; they feared the people: for
all *men* counted John, that he was a prophet
indeed. 33And they answered and said unto Jesus, We cannot tell. And Jesus answering saith
unto them, Neither do I tell you by what authority I do these things.

Living Bible

26,[a] 27, 28 By this time they had arrived in
Jerusalem again, and as he was walking through
the Temple area, the chief priests and other
Jewish leaders[b] came up to him demanding,
"What's going on here? Who gave you the authority to drive out the merchants?"
29 Jesus replied, "I'll tell you if you answer
one question! 30 What about John the Baptist?
Was he sent by God, or not? Answer me!"
31 They talked it over among themselves. "If
we reply that God sent him, then he will say,
'All right, why didn't you accept him?' 32 But if
we say God didn't send him, then the people
will start a riot." (For the people all believed
strongly that John was a prophet.)
33 So they said, "We can't answer. We don't
know."
To which Jesus replied, "Then I won't answer
your question either!"

[a] Many ancient authorities add verse 26, "but if you do not forgive, neither will your Father who is in heaven forgive your trespasses." All include this in Matthew 6:15. [b] Literally, "scribes and elders."

Today's English Version

in heaven will forgive your sins. [26 If you do
not forgive others, neither will your Father in
heaven forgive your sins.]"

The question about Jesus' authority

27 They came back to Jerusalem. As Jesus was
walking in the temple, the chief priests, the teachers of the Law, and the elders came to him
28 and asked him, "What right do you have to
do these things? Who gave you the right to do
them?"
29 Jesus answered them, "I will ask you just
one question, and if you give me an answer I
will tell you what right I have to do these things.
30 Tell me, where did John's right to baptize
come from: from God or from men?"
31 They started to argue among themselves,
"What shall we say? If we answer, 'From God,'
he will say, 'Why, then, did you not believe
John?' 32 But if we say, 'From men . . .'"
(They were afraid of the people, because everyone was convinced that John had been a
prophet.) 33 So their answer to Jesus was, "We
don't know."
Jesus said to them, "Neither will I tell you,
then, by what right I do these things."

New International Version

The authority of Jesus questioned

27 They arrived again in Jerusalem, and while
Jesus was walking in the temple courts, the
chief priests, the teachers of the law and the
elders came to him. 28 "By what authority are
you doing these things?" they asked. "And who
gave you authority to do this?"
29 Jesus replied, "I will ask you one question.
Answer me, and I will tell you by what authority I am doing these things. 30 John's baptism
—was it from heaven, or from men? Tell me!"
31 They discussed it among themselves and
said, "If we say, 'From heaven,' he will ask,
'Then why didn't you believe him?' 32 But if we
say, 'From men'. . . ." (They feared the people, for everyone held that John really was a
prophet.)
33 So they answered Jesus, "We don't know."
Jesus said, "Neither will I tell you by what
authority I am doing these things."

Phillips Modern English

11.27 Jesus' authority is directly challenged

So they came once more to Jerusalem, and while Jesus was walking in the Temple, the chief priests, scribes and elders approached him, and asked,

"What authority have you for what you're doing? And who gave you permission to do these things?"

"I am going to ask you a question," replied Jesus, "and if you answer me, I will tell you what authority I have for what I do. The baptism of John, now—did it come from Heaven or was it purely human? Tell me that."

At this they argued with each other, "If we say from Heaven, he will say, 'then why didn't you believe in him?' but if we say it was purely human, well . . ." For they were frightened of the people, since all of them believed that John was a real prophet. So they answered Jesus,

"We do not know."

"Then I cannot tell you by what authority I do these things," returned Jesus.

Revised Standard Version

27 And they came again to Jerusalem. And as he was walking in the temple, the chief priests and the scribes and the elders came to him,
28 and they said to him, "By what authority are you doing these things, or who gave you this authority to do them?" 29 Jesus said to them, "I will ask you a question; answer me, and I will tell you by what authority I do these things.
30 Was the baptism of John from heaven or from men? Answer me." 31 And they argued with one another, "If we say, 'From heaven,' he will say, 'Why then did you not believe him?' 32 But shall we say, 'From men'?"—they were afraid of the people, for all held that John was a real prophet. 33 So they answered Jesus, "We do not know." And Jesus said to them, "Neither will I tell you by what authority I do these things."

Jerusalem Bible

The authority of Jesus is questioned

27 They came to Jerusalem again, and as Jesus was walking in the Temple, the chief priests and the scribes and the elders came to him,
28 and they said to him, "What authority have you for acting like this? Or who gave you authority to do these things?" 29 Jesus said to them, "I will ask you a question, only one; answer me and I will tell you my authority for acting like this. 30 John's baptism: did it come from heaven, or from man? Answer me that." 31 And they argued it out this way among themselves: "If we say from heaven, he will say, 'Then why did you refuse to believe him?' 32 But dare we say from man?"—they had the people to fear, for everyone held that John was a real prophet.
33 So their reply to Jesus was, "We do not know." And Jesus said to them, "Nor will I tell you my authority for acting like this."

New English Bible

They came once more to Jerusalem. And as he was walking in the temple court the chief priests, lawyers, and elders came to him and said, 'By what authority are you acting like this? Who gave you authority to act in this way?' Jesus said to them, 'I have a question to ask you too; and if you give me an answer, I will tell you by what authority I act. The baptism of John: was it from God, or from men? Answer me.' This set them arguing among themselves: 'What shall we say? If we say, "from God", he will say, "Then why did you not believe him?" Shall we say, "from men"?'—but they were afraid of the people, for all held that John was in fact a prophet. So they answered, 'We do not know.' And Jesus said to them, 'Then neither will I tell you by what authority I act.'

King James Version

12 And he began to speak unto them by
parables. A *certain* man planted a vineyard,
and set a hedge about *it,* and digged *a place for*
the winefat, and built a tower, and let it out to
husbandmen, and went into a far country. 2And
at the season he sent to the husbandmen a servant, that he might receive from the husbandmen
of the fruit of the vineyard. 3And they caught
him, and beat him, and sent *him* away empty.
4And again he sent unto them another servant;
and at him they cast stones, and wounded *him*
in the head, and sent *him* away shamefully handled. 5And again he sent another; and him they
killed, and many others; beating some, and killing some. 6 Having yet therefore one son, his
well beloved, he sent him also last unto them,
saying, They will reverence my son. 7 But those
husbandmen said among themselves, This is the
heir; come, let us kill him, and the inheritance
shall be ours. 8And they took him, and killed
him, and cast *him* out of the vineyard. 9 What
shall therefore the lord of the vineyard do? he
will come and destroy the husbandmen, and will
give the vineyard unto others. 10And have ye
not read this Scripture; The stone which the
builders rejected is become the head of the corner: 11 This was the Lord's doing, and it is mar-

Living Bible

12 Here are some of the story-illustrations
Jesus gave to the people at that time:
"A man planted a vineyard and built a wall
around it and dug a pit for pressing out the
grape juice, and built a watchman's tower. Then
he leased the farm to tenant farmers and moved
to another country. 2 At grape-picking time he
sent one of his men to collect his share of the
crop. 3 But the farmers beat up the man and
sent him back empty-handed.
4 "The owner then sent another of his men,
who received the same treatment, only worse,
for his head was seriously injured. 5 The next
man he sent was killed; and later, others were
either beaten or killed, until 6 there was only
one left—his only son. He finally sent him,
thinking they would surely give him their full
respect.
7 "But when the farmers saw him coming they
said, 'He will own the farm when his father dies.
Come on, let's kill him—and then the farm will
be ours!' 8 So they caught him and murdered
him and threw his body out of the vineyard.
9 "What do you suppose the owner will do
when he hears what happened? He will come
and kill them all, and lease the vineyard to
others. 10 Don't you remember reading this verse
in the Scriptures? 'The Rock the builders threw
away became the cornerstone, the most honored
stone in the building! 11 This is the Lord's doing
and it is an amazing thing to see.' "

Today's English Version

The parable of the tenants in the vineyard

12 Then Jesus spoke to them in parables,
"There was a man who planted a vineyard,
put a fence around it, dug a hole for the winepress, and built a watchtower. Then he rented
the vineyard to tenants and left home on a trip.
2 When the time came for gathering the grapes,
he sent a slave to the tenants to receive from
them his share of the harvest. 3 The tenants
grabbed the slave, beat him, and sent him back
without a thing. 4 Then the owner sent another
slave; the tenants beat him over the head and
treated him shamefully. 5 The owner sent another
slave, and they killed him; and they treated many
others the same way, beating some and killing
others. 6 The only one left to send was the man's
own dear son. Last of all, then, he sent his son
to the tenants. 'I am sure they will respect my
son,' he said. 7 But those tenants said to one
another, 'This is the owner's son. Come on, let us
kill him, and his property will be ours!' 8 So they
took the son and killed him, and threw his body
out of the vineyard.
9 "What, then, will the owner of the vineyard
do?" asked Jesus. "He will come and kill those
men and turn over the vineyard to other tenants.
10 Surely you have read this scripture?

'The very stone which the builders rejected
turned out to be the most important stone.
11 This was done by the Lord;
how wonderful it is!' "

New International Version

The parable of the tenants

12 He then began to speak to them in parables: "A man planted a vineyard. He put
a wall around it, dug a pit for the winepress and
built a tower. Then he rented the vineyard to
some farmers and went away on a journey. 2At
harvest time he sent a servant to the tenants to
collect from them some of the fruit of the vineyard. 3 But they seized him, beat him and sent
him away empty-handed. 4 Then he sent another
servant to them; they struck this man on the
head and treated him shamefully. 5 He sent still
another, and that one they killed. He sent many
others; some of them they beat, others they
killed.
6 "He had one left to send, a son, whom he
loved. He sent him last of all, saying, 'They will
respect my son.'
7 "But the tenants said to one another, 'This
is the heir. Come, let's kill him, and the inheritance will be ours.' 8 So they took him and
killed him, and threw him out of the vineyard.
9 "What then will the owner of the vineyard
do? He will come and kill those tenants and give
the vineyard to others. 10 Haven't you read this
scripture:
'The stone the builders rejected
has become the capstone;
11 the Lord has done this,
and it is marvelous in our eyes' [w] ?"

[w] Psalm 118:22,23.

Phillips Modern English

12.1 Jesus tells a story, with a pointed application

Then he began to talk to them in parables. "A man once planted a vineyard," he said, "fenced it round, dug out the hole for the winepress and built a watch-tower. Then he let it out to some farm-workers and went abroad. At the end of the season he sent a servant to the tenants to receive his share of the vintage. But they got hold of him, knocked him about and sent him off empty-handed. The owner tried again. He sent another servant to them, but this one they knocked on the head and generally insulted. Once again he sent them another servant, but him they murdered. He sent many others and some they beat up and some they murdered. He had one man left—his own son who was very dear to him. He sent him last of all to the tenants, saying to himself, 'They will surely respect my own son.' But they said to each other, 'This fellow is the future owner—come on, let's kill him, and the property will be ours!' So they got hold of him and murdered him, and threw his body out of the vineyard. What do you suppose the owner of the vineyard is going to do? He will come and destroy the men who were working his vineyard and will hand it over to others. Have you never read this scripture—

The stone which the builders rejected,
The same was made the head of the corner;
This was from the Lord,
And it is marvellous in our eyes?"

Revised Standard Version

12 And he began to speak to them in parables. "A man planted a vineyard, and set
a hedge around it, and dug a pit for the wine
press, and built a tower, and let it out to tenants,
and went into another country. 2 When the time
came, he sent a servant to the tenants, to get
from them some of the fruit of the vineyard.
3 And they took him and beat him, and sent
him away empty-handed. 4 Again he sent to them
another servant, and they wounded him in the
head, and treated him shamefully. 5 And he sent
another, and him they killed; and so with many
others, some they beat and some they killed.
6 He had still one other, a beloved son; finally
he sent him to them, saying, 'They will respect
my son.' 7 But those tenants said to one another,
'This is the heir; come, let us kill him, and the
inheritance will be ours.' 8 And they took him
and killed him, and cast him out of the vineyard. 9 What will the owner of the vineyard do?
He will come and destroy the tenants, and give
the vineyard to others. 10 Have you not read this
scripture:
'The very stone which the builders rejected
has become the head of the corner;
11 this was the Lord's doing,
and it is marvelous in our eyes'?"

Jerusalem Bible

Parable of the wicked husbandmen

12 He went on to speak to them in parables,
"A man planted a vineyard; he fenced it
around, dug out a trough for the winepress and
built a tower; then he leased it to tenants and
went abroad. 2 When the time came, he sent a
servant to the tenants to collect from them his
share of the produce from the vineyard. 3 But
they seized the man, thrashed him and sent him
away empty-handed. 4 Next he sent another servant to them; him they beat about the head and
treated shamefully. 5 And he sent another and
him they killed; then a number of others,
and they thrashed some and killed the rest.
6 He had still someone left: his beloved son. He
sent him to them last of all. 'They will respect
my son,' he said. 7 But those tenants said to
each other, 'This is the heir. Come on, let us kill
him, and the inheritance will be ours.' 8 So they
seized him and killed him and threw him out of
the vineyard. 9 Now what will the owner of the
vineyard do? He will come and make an end of
the tenants and give the vineyard to others.
10 Have you not read this text of scripture:

It was the stone rejected by the builders
that became the keystone.
11 *This was the Lord's doing*
and it is wonderful to see?" [t]

[t] Ps. 118:22-23.

New English Bible

12 He went on to speak to them in parables: 'A man planted a vineyard and put a wall round it, hewed out a winepress, and built a watch-tower; then he let it out to vine-growers and went abroad. When the season came, he sent a servant to the tenants to collect from them his share of the produce. But they took him, thrashed him, and sent him away empty-handed. Again, he sent them another servant, whom they beat about the head and treated outrageously. So he sent another, and that one they killed; and many more besides, of whom they beat some, and killed others. He had now only one left to send, his own dear son.[a] In the end he sent him. "They will respect my son", he said. But the tenants said to one another, "This is the heir; come on, let us kill him, and the property will be ours." So they seized him and killed him, and flung his body out of the vineyard. What will the owner of the vineyard do? He will come and put the tenants to death and give the vineyard to others.

'Can it be that you have never read this text: "The stone which the builders rejected has become the main corner-stone. This is the Lord's doing, and it is wonderful in our eyes"?'

[a] *Or* his only son.

King James Version

vellous in our eyes? 12And they sought to lay hold on him, but feared the people; for they knew that he had spoken the parable against them: and they left him, and went their way.
13 And they send unto him certain of the Pharisees and of the Herodians, to catch him in *his* words. 14And when they were come, they say unto him, Master, we know that thou art true, and carest for no man; for thou regardest not the person of men, but teachest the way of God in truth: Is it lawful to give tribute to Cesar, or not? 15 Shall we give, or shall we not give? But he, knowing their hypocrisy, said unto them, Why tempt ye me? bring me a penny, that I may see *it*. 16And they brought *it*. And he saith unto them, Whose *is* this image and superscription? And they said unto him, Cesar's. 17And Jesus answering said unto them, Render to Cesar the things that are Cesar's, and to God the things that are God's. And they marvelled at him.

Living Bible

12 The Jewish leaders wanted to arrest him then and there for using this illustration, for they knew he was pointing at them—they were the wicked farmers in his story. But they were afraid to touch him for fear of a mob. So they left him and went away. 13 But they sent other religious and political leaders[a] to talk with him and try to trap him into saying something he could be arrested for.

14 "Teacher," these spies said, "we know you tell the truth no matter what! You aren't influenced by the opinions and desires of men, but sincerely teach the ways of God. Now tell us, is it right to pay taxes to Rome, or not?"

15 Jesus saw their trick and said, "Show me a coin and I'll tell you."

16 When they handed it to him he asked, "Whose picture and title is this on the coin?" They replied, "The emperor's."

17 "All right," he said, "if it is his, give it to him. But everything that belongs to God must be given to God!" And they scratched their heads in bafflement at his reply.

[a] Literally, "Pharisees and Herodians."

Today's English Version

12 The Jewish leaders tried to arrest Jesus, because they knew that he had told this parable against them. They were afraid of the crowd, however, so they left him and went away.

The question about paying taxes

13 Some Pharisees and some members of Herod's party were sent to Jesus to trap him with questions. 14 They came to him and said, "Teacher, we know that you tell the truth, without worrying about what people think. You pay no attention to a man's status, but teach the truth about God's will for man. Tell us, is it against our Law to pay taxes to the Roman Emperor? Should we pay them, or not?"

15 But Jesus saw through their trick and answered, "Why are you trying to trap me? Bring a silver coin, and let me see it."

16 They brought him one and he asked, "Whose face and name are these?"

"The Emperor's," they answered.

17 So Jesus said, "Well, then, pay to the Emperor what belongs to him, and pay to God what belongs to God."

And they were filled with wonder at him.

New International Version

12 Then they looked for a way to arrest him because they knew he had spoken the parable against them. But they were afraid of the crowd; so they left him and went away.

Paying taxes to Caesar

13 Later they sent some of the Pharisees and Herodians to Jesus to catch him in his words. 14 They came to him and said, "Teacher, we know you are a man of integrity. You aren't swayed by men, because you pay no attention to who they are; but you teach the way of God in accordance with the truth. Is it right to pay taxes to Caesar or not? 15 Should we pay or shouldn't we?"

But Jesus knew their hypocrisy. "Why are you trying to trap me?" he asked. "Bring me a denarius and let me look at it." 16 They brought the coin, and he asked them, "Whose portrait is this? And whose inscription?"

"Caesar's," they replied.

17 Then Jesus said to them, "Give to Caesar what is Caesar's and to God what is God's."

And they were amazed at him.

Phillips Modern English

At this they longed to get their hands on him, for they knew perfectly well that he had aimed this parable at them—but they were afraid of the people. So they left him and went away.

12.13 A test question

Later they sent some of the Pharisees and some of the Herod-party to trap him in an argument. They came up and said to him,

"Master, we know that you are an honest man and that you are not swayed by men's opinion of you. Obviously you don't care for human approval but teach the way of God with the strictest regard for truth—is it right to pay tribute to Caesar or not: are we to pay or not to pay?"

But Jesus saw through their hypocrisy and said to them,

"Why try this trick on me? Bring me a coin and let me look at it."

So they brought one to him.

"Whose face is this?" asked Jesus, "and whose name is in the inscription?"

"Caesar's," they replied. And Jesus said,

"Then pay to Caesar what belongs to Caesar, and to God what belongs to God!"—a reply which staggered them.

Revised Standard Version

12 And they tried to arrest him, but feared the multitude, for they perceived that he had told the parable against them; so they left him and went away.

13 And they sent to him some of the Pharisees and some of the Herodians, to entrap him in his
talk. 14 And they came and said to him,
"Teacher, we know that you are true, and care for no man; for you do not regard the position of men, but truly teach the way of God. Is it
lawful to pay taxes to Caesar, or not? 15 Should
we pay them, or should we not?" But knowing their hypocrisy, he said to them, "Why put me to the test? Bring me a coin,[x] and let me look at
it." 16 And they brought one. And he said to
them, "Whose likeness and inscription is this?"
They said to him, "Caesar's." 17 Jesus said to
them, "Render to Caesar the things that are Caesar's, and to God the things that are God's." And they were amazed at him.

[x] Greek *a denarius.*

Jerusalem Bible

12 And they would have liked to arrest him, because they realized that the parable was aimed at them, but they were afraid of the crowds. So they left him alone and went away.

On tribute to Caesar

13 Next they sent to him some Pharisees and some Herodians to catch him out in what he
said. 14 These came and said to him, "Master,
we know you are an honest man, that you are not afraid of anyone, because a man's rank means nothing to you, and that you teach the way of God in all honesty. Is it permissible to pay taxes to Caesar or not? Should we pay, yes
or no?" 15 Seeing through their hypocrisy he
said to them, "Why do you set this trap for me? Hand me a denarius and let me see it."
16 They handed him one and he said, "Whose
head is this? Whose name?" "Caesar's," they
told him. 17 Jesus said to them, "Give back to
Caesar what belongs to Caesar—and to God what belongs to God." This reply took them completely by surprise.

New English Bible

Then they began to look for a way to arrest him, for they saw that the parable was aimed at them; but they were afraid of the people, so they left him alone and went away.

A number of Pharisees and men of Herod's party were sent to trap him with a question. They came and said, 'Master, you are an honest man, we know, and truckle to no one, whoever he may be; you teach in all honesty the way of life that God requires. Are we or are we not permitted to pay taxes to the Roman Emperor? Shall we pay or not?' He saw how crafty their question was, and said, 'Why are you trying to catch me out? Fetch me a silver piece, and let me look at it.' They brought one, and he said to them, 'Whose head is this, and whose inscription?' 'Caesar's', they replied. Then Jesus said, 'Pay Caesar what is due to Caesar, and pay God what is due to God.' And they heard him with astonishment.

King James Version

18 Then come unto him the Sadducees, which say there is no resurrection; and they asked him, saying, 19 Master, Moses wrote unto us, If a man's brother die, and leave *his* wife *behind him,* and leave no children, that his brother should take his wife, and raise up seed unto his brother. 20 Now there were seven brethren: and the first took a wife, and dying left no seed. 21And the second took her, and died, neither left he any seed: and the third likewise. 22And the seven had her, and left no seed: last of all the woman died also. 23 In the resurrection therefore, when they shall rise, whose wife shall she be of them? for the seven had her to wife. 24And Jesus answering said unto them, Do ye not therefore err, because ye know not the Scriptures, neither the power of God? 25 For when they shall rise from the dead, they neither marry, nor are given in marriage; but are as the angels which are in heaven. 26And as touching the dead, that they rise; have ye not read in the book of Moses, how in the bush God spake unto him, saying, I *am* the God of Abraham, and the God of Isaac, and the God of Jacob? 27 He is not the God of the dead, but the God of the living: ye therefore do greatly err.

Living Bible

18 Then the Sadducees stepped forward—a group of men who say there is no resurrection. Here was their question:

19 "Teacher, Moses gave us a law that when a man dies without children, the man's brother should marry his widow and have children in his brother's name. 20, 21, 22 Well, there were seven brothers and the oldest married and died, and left no children. So the second brother married the widow, but soon he died too, and left no children. Then the next brother married her, and died without children, and so on until all were dead, and still there were no children; and last of all, the woman died too.

23 "What we want to know is this:[b] In the resurrection, whose wife will she be, for she had been the wife of each of them?"

24 Jesus replied, "Your trouble is that you don't know the Scriptures, and don't know the power of God. 25 For when these seven brothers and the woman rise from the dead, they won't be married—they will be like the angels.

26 "But now as to whether there will be a resurrection—have you never read in the book of Exodus about Moses and the burning bush? God said to Moses, 'I *am* the God of Abraham, and I *am* the God of Isaac, and I *am* the God of Jacob.'

27 "God was telling Moses that these men, though dead for hundreds of years,[b] were still very much alive, for he would not have said, 'I *am* the God' of those who don't exist! You have made a serious error."

[*b*] Implied.

Today's English Version

The question about rising from death

18 Some Sadducees came to Jesus. (They are the ones who say that people will not rise from death.) 19 "Teacher," they said, "Moses wrote this law for us: 'If a man dies and leaves a wife, but no children, that man's brother must marry the widow so they can have children for the dead man.' 20 Once there were seven brothers; the oldest got married, and died without having children. 21 Then the second one married the woman, and he died without having children. The same thing happened to the third brother, 22 and then to the rest: all seven brothers married the woman and died without having children. Last of all, the woman died. 23 Now, when all the dead rise to life on the day of resurrection, whose wife will she be? All seven of them had married her."

24 Jesus answered them, "How wrong you are! And do you know why? It is because you don't know the Scriptures or God's power. 25 For when the dead rise to life they will be like the angels in heaven, and men and women will not marry. 26 Now, as to the dead being raised: haven't you ever read in the book of Moses the passage about the burning bush? There it is written that God said to Moses, 'I am the God of Abraham, the God of Isaac, and the God of Jacob.' 27 That means that he is the God of the living, not of the dead. You are completely wrong!"

New International Version

Marriage at the resurrection

18 Then the Sadducees, who say there is no resurrection, came to him with a question. 19 "Teacher," they said, "Moses wrote for us that if a man's brother dies and leaves a wife but no children, the man must marry the widow and have children for his brother. 20 Now there were seven brothers. The first one married and died without leaving any children. 21 The second one married the widow, but he also died, leaving no child. It was the same with the third. 22 In fact, none of the seven left any children. Last of all, the woman died too. 23At the resurrection[x] whose wife will she be, since the seven were married to her?"

24 Jesus replied, "Are you not in error because you do not know the Scriptures or the power of God? 25 When the dead rise, they will neither marry nor be given in marriage; they will be like the angels in heaven. 26 Now about the dead rising—have you not read in the book of Moses, in the account of the bush, how God said to him, 'I am the God of Abraham, the God of Isaac, and the God of Jacob'[y]? 27 He is not the God of the dead, but of the living. You are badly mistaken!"

[*x*] Some MSS add *when men rise from the dead.*
[*y*] Exodus 3:6.

Phillips Modern English

12.18 Jesus reveals the ignorance of the Sadducees

Then some of the Sadducees (a party which maintains that there is no resurrection) approached him, and put this question to him, "Master, Moses instructed us that if a man's brother dies leaving a widow but no child, then the man should marry the woman and raise children for his brother. Now there were seven brothers, and the first one married and died without leaving issue. Then the second one married the widow and died leaving no issue behind him. The same thing happened with the third, and indeed the whole seven died without leaving any child behind them. Finally the woman herself died. Now in this 'resurrection', when men rise up again, whose wife is she going to be—for she was the wife of all seven of them?"

Jesus replied, "Does not this show where you go wrong—and how you fail to understand both the scriptures and the power of God? When people rise from the dead they neither marry nor are they given in marriage; they live like the angels in Heaven. But as for this matter of the dead being raised, have you never read in the book of Moses, in the passage about the bush, how God spoke to him in these words, 'I am the God of Abraham and the God of Isaac and the God of Jacob'? God is not God of the dead but of living men! That is where you make your great mistake"

Revised Standard Version

18 And Sadducees came to him, who say that
there is no resurrection; and they asked him a
question, saying, 19 "Teacher, Moses wrote for
us that if a man's brother dies and leaves a wife,
but leaves no child, the man[y] must take the wife,
and raise up children for his brother. 20 There
were seven brothers; the first took a wife, and
when he died left no children; 21 and the second
took her, and died, leaving no children; and the
third likewise; 22 and the seven left no children.
Last of all the woman also died. 23 In the resurrection whose wife will she be? For the seven
had her as wife."

24 Jesus said to them, "Is not this why you
are wrong, that you know neither the scriptures
nor the power of God? 25 For when they rise
from the dead, they neither marry nor are given
in marriage, but are like angels in heaven. 26 And
as for the dead being raised, have you not read
in the book of Moses, in the passage about the
bush, how God said to him, 'I am the God of
Abraham, and the God of Isaac, and the God
of Jacob'? 27 He is not God of the dead, but of
the living; you are quite wrong."

[y] Greek *his brother.*

Jerusalem Bible

The resurrection of the dead

18 Then some Sadducees—who deny that
there is a resurrection—came to him and they
put this question to him, 19 "Master, we have
it from Moses in writing, if a man's brother
dies leaving a wife but no child, the man must
marry the widow to raise up children for his
brother. 20 Now there were seven brothers. The
first married a wife and then died leaving no
children. 21 The second married the widow, and
he too died leaving no children; with the third
it was the same, 22 and none of the seven left
any children. Last of all the woman herself died.
23 Now at the resurrection, when they rise again,
whose wife will she be, since she had been married to all seven?"

24 Jesus said to them, "Is not the reason why
you go wrong, that you understand neither the
scriptures nor the power of God? 25 For when
they rise from the dead, men and women do
not marry; no, they are like the angels in heaven.
26 Now about the dead rising again, have you
never read in the Book of Moses, in the passage about the Bush, how God spoke to him and
said: *I am the God of Abraham, the God of
Isaac and the God of Jacob?*[u] 27 He is God,
not of the dead, but of the living. You are very
much mistaken."

[u] Ex. 3:6.

New English Bible

Next Sadducees came to him. (It is they who say that there is no resurrection.) Their question was this: 'Master, Moses laid it down for us that if there are brothers, and one dies leaving a wife but no child, then the next should marry the widow and carry on his brother's family. Now there were seven brothers. The first took a wife and died without issue. Then the second married her, and he too died without issue. So did the third. Eventually the seven of them died, all without issue. Finally the woman died. At the resurrection, when they come back to life, whose wife will she be, since all seven had married her?' Jesus said to them, 'You are mistaken, and surely this is the reason: you do not know either the scriptures or the power of God. When they rise from the dead, men and women do not marry; they are like angels in heaven.

'But about the resurrection of the dead, have you never read in the Book of Moses, in the story of the burning bush, how God spoke to him and said, "I am the God of Abraham, the God of Isaac, and the God of Jacob"? God is not God of the dead but of the living. You are greatly mistaken.'

King James Version

28 And one of the scribes came, and having heard them reasoning together, and perceiving that he had answered them well, asked him, Which is the first commandment of all? 29And Jesus answered him, The first of all the commandments *is,* Hear, O Israel; The Lord our God is one Lord: 30And thou shalt love the Lord thy God with all thy heart, and with all thy soul, and with all thy mind, and with all thy strength: this *is* the first commandment. 31And the second *is* like, *namely* this, Thou shalt love thy neighbour as thyself. There is none other commandment greater than these. 32And the scribe said unto him, Well, Master, thou hast said the truth: for there is one God; and there is none other but he: 33And to love him with all the heart, and with all the understanding, and with all the soul, and with all the strength, and to love *his* neighbour as himself, is more than all whole burnt offerings and sacrifices. 34And when Jesus saw that he answered discreetly, he said unto him, Thou art not far from the kingdom of God. And no man after that durst ask him *any question.*

Living Bible

28 One of the teachers of religion who was standing there listening to the discussion realized that Jesus had answered well. So he asked, "Of all the commandments, which is the most important?"

29 Jesus replied, "The one that says, 'Hear, O Israel! The Lord our God is the one and only God. 30And you must love him with all your heart and soul and mind and strength.'

31 "The second is: 'You must love others as much as yourself.' No other commandments are greater than these."

32 The teacher of religion replied, "Sir, you have spoken a true word in saying that there is only one God and no other. 33And I know it is far more important to love him with all my heart and understanding and strength, and to love others as myself, than to offer all kinds of sacrifices on the altar of the Temple."

34 Realizing this man's understanding, Jesus said to him, "You are not far from the Kingdom of God." And after that, no one dared ask him any more questions.

Today's English Version

The great commandment

28 A teacher of the Law was there who heard the discussion. He saw that Jesus had given the Sadducees a good answer, so he came to him with a question, "Which commandment is the most important of all?"

29 "This is the most important one," said Jesus. " 'Listen, Israel! The Lord our God is the only Lord. 30 You must love the Lord your God with all your heart, with all your soul, with all your mind, and with all your strength.' 31 The second most important commandment is this: 'You must love your fellow-man as yourself.' There is no other commandment more important than these two."

32 The teacher of the Law said to Jesus, "Well done, Teacher! It is true, as you say, that only the Lord is God, and that there is no other god but he. 33And man must love God with all his heart, and with all his mind, and with all his strength; and he must love his fellow-man as himself. It is more important to obey these two commandments than to offer animals and other sacrifices to God on the altar."

34 Jesus noticed how wise his answer was, and so he told him, "You are not far from the Kingdom of God."

After this nobody dared to ask Jesus any more questions.

New International Version

The greatest commandment

28 One of the teachers of the law came and heard them debating. Noticing that Jesus had given them a good answer, he asked him, "Of all the commandments, which is the most important?"

29 "The most important one," answered Jesus, "is this: 'Hear, O Israel, the Lord our God, the Lord is one;[z] 30 love the Lord your God with all your heart, with all your soul, with all your mind and with all your strength.'[a] 31 The second is this: 'Love your neighbor as yourself.'[b] There is no greater commandment than these."

32 "Well said, teacher," the man replied. "You are right in saying that God is one and there is no other but him. 33 To love him with all your heart, with all your understanding and with all your strength, and to love your neighbor as yourself is more important than all burnt offerings and sacrifices."

34 When Jesus saw that he had answered wisely, he said to him, "You are not far from the kingdom of God." And from then on no one dared ask him any more questions.

[z] Or *the Lord our God is the one Lord.* [a] Deut. 6:4,5. [b] Lev. 19:18.

Phillips Modern English

12.28 The most important commandments

Then one of the scribes approached him. He had been listening to the discussion, and had noticed how well Jesus had answered them, and he put this question to him,

"What are we to consider the greatest commandment of all?"

"The first and most important one is this," Jesus replied—" 'Hear, O Israel: The Lord our God, the Lord is one: and thou shalt love the Lord thy God with all thy heart, and with all thy soul, and with all thy mind, and with all thy strength.' The second is this, 'Thou shalt love thy neighbour as thyself.' No other commandment is greater than these."

"I am well answered, master," replied the scribe. "You are absolutely right when you say that there is one God and no other God exists but him; and to love him with the whole of our hearts, the whole of our intelligence and the whole of our strength, and to love our neighbours as ourselves is infinitely more important than all these burnt-offerings and sacrifices."

Then Jesus, noting the wisdom of his reply, said to him,

"You are not far from the kingdom of God!"

After this nobody felt they could ask him any more questions.

Revised Standard Version

28 And one of the scribes came up and heard
them disputing with one another, and seeing that
he answered them well, asked him, "Which
commandment is the first of all?" 29 Jesus answered, "The first is, 'Hear, O Israel: The Lord
our God, the Lord is one; 30 and you shall love
the Lord your God with all your heart, and with
all your soul, and with all your mind, and with
all your strength.' 31 The second is this, "You
shall love your neighbor as yourself.' There is
no other commandment greater than these."
32 And the scribe said to him, "You are right,
Teacher; you have truly said that he is one,
and there is no other but he; 33 and to love him
with all the heart, and with all the understanding, and with all the strength, and to love one's
neighbor as oneself, is much more than all whole
burnt offerings and sacrifices." 34 And when
Jesus saw that he answered wisely, he said to
him, "You are not far from the kingdom of
God." And after that no one dared to ask him
any question.

Jerusalem Bible

The greatest commandment of all

28 One of the scribes who had listened to
them debating and had observed how well Jesus
had answered them, now came up and put a
question to him, "Which is the first of all the
commandments?" 29 Jesus replied, "This is the
first: *Listen, Israel, the Lord our God is the one*
Lord, 30 *and you must love the Lord your God*
with all your heart, with all your soul, with all
your mind and *with all your strength.*[v] 31 The second is this: *You must love your neighbor as*
yourself.[w] There is no commandment greater
than these." 32 The scribe said to him, "Well
spoken, Master; what you have said is true:
that he is one and there is no other. 33 To love
him with all your heart, with all your understanding and strength, and to love your neighbor
as yourself, this is far more important than any
holocaust or sacrifice." 34 Jesus, seeing how
wisely he had spoken, said, "You are not far
from the kingdom of God." And after that no
one dared to question him any more.

[v] Dt. 6:4-5. [w] Lv. 19:18.

New English Bible

Then one of the lawyers, who had been listening to these discussions and had noted how well he answered, came forward and asked him, 'Which commandment is first of all?' Jesus answered, 'The first is, "Hear, O Israel: the Lord our God is the only Lord; love the Lord your God with all your heart, with all your soul, with all your mind, and with all your strength." The second is this: "Love your neighbour as yourself." There is no other commandment greater than these.' The lawyer said to him, 'Well said, Master. You are right in saying that God is one and beside him there is no other. And to love him with all your heart, all your understanding, and all your strength, and to love your neighbour as yourself—that is far more than any burnt offerings or sacrifices.' When Jesus saw how sensibly he answered, he said to him, 'You are not far from the kingdom of God.'

After that nobody ventured to put any more

King James Version

35 And Jesus answered and said, while he taught in the temple, How say the scribes that Christ is the son of David? 36 For David himself said by the Holy Ghost, The LORD said to my Lord, Sit thou on my right hand, till I make thine enemies thy footstool. 37 David therefore himself calleth him Lord; and whence is he *then* his son? And the common people heard him gladly.

38 And he said unto them in his doctrine, Beware of the scribes, which love to go in long clothing, and *love* salutations in the marketplaces, 39 And the chief seats in the synagogues, and the uppermost rooms at feasts: 40 Which devour widows' houses, and for a pretence make long prayers: these shall receive greater damnation.

Living Bible

35 Later, as Jesus was teaching the people in the Temple area, he asked them this question: "Why do your religious teachers claim that the Messiah must be a descendant of King David? 36 For David himself said—and the Holy Spirit was speaking through him when he said it—'God said to my Lord, sit at my right hand until I make your enemies your footstool.' 37 Since David called him his Lord, how can he be his *son?*"

(This sort of reasoning delighted the crowd and they listened to him with great interest.)

38 Here are some of the other things he taught them at this time:

"Beware of the teachers of religion! For they love to wear the robes of the rich and scholarly, and to have everyone bow to them as they walk through the markets. 39 They love to sit in the best seats in the synagogues, and at the places of honor at banquets— 40 but they shamelessly cheat widows out of their homes and then, to cover up the kind of men they really are, they pretend to be pious by praying long prayers in public. Because of this, their punishment will be greater."

Today's English Version

The question about the Messiah

35 As Jesus was teaching in the temple he asked the question, "How can the teachers of the Law say that the Messiah will be the descendant of David? 36 The Holy Spirit inspired David to say:

'The Lord said to my Lord:
Sit here at my right side,
until I put your enemies under your feet.'

37 David himself called him 'Lord'; how, then, can the Messiah be David's descendant?"

Jesus warns against the teachers of the law

The large crowd heard Jesus gladly. 38 As he taught them he said, "Watch out for the teachers of the Law, who like to walk around in their long robes and be greeted with respect in the market place; 39 who choose the reserved seats in the synagogues and the best places at feasts. 40 They take advantage of widows and rob them of their homes, and then make a show of saying long prayers. Their punishment will be all the worse!"

New International Version

Whose son is the Christ?

35 While Jesus was teaching in the temple courts, he asked, "How is it that the teachers of the law say that the Christ [c] is the son of David? 36 David himself, speaking by the Holy Spirit, declared:

'The Lord said to my Lord:
Sit at my right hand
until I put your enemies under your feet.' [d]

37 David himself calls him 'Lord.' How then can he be his son?"

The large crowd listened to him with delight.

38 As he taught, Jesus said, "Watch out for the teachers of the law. They like to walk around in flowing robes and be greeted in the marketplaces, 39 and have the most important seats in the synagogues and the places of honor at banquets. 40 They devour widows' houses and for a show make lengthy prayers. Such men will be punished most severely."

[c] Or *Messiah*. [d] Psalm 110:1.

Phillips Modern English

12.35 *Jesus criticises the scribes' teaching and behaviour*

Later, while Jesus was teaching in the Temple, he remarked,

"How can the scribes maintain that Christ is David's *son,* for David himself, inspired by the Holy Spirit, said,

The Lord said unto my *Lord,*
Sit thou on my right hand,
Till I make thine enemies the footstool of thy feet.

David is himself calling Christ 'Lord'—where do they get the idea that he is his son?"

The vast crowd heard this with great delight, and Jesus continued in his teaching,

"Be on your guard against these scribes who love to walk about in long robes and to be greeted respectfully in public and to have the front seats in the synagogue and the best places at dinner-parties! These are the men who grow fat on widows' property and cover up what they are doing by making lengthy prayers. They are only adding to the severity of their punishment!"

Revised Standard Version

35 And as Jesus taught in the temple, he
said, "How can the scribes say that the Christ
is the son of David? 36 David himself, inspired
by[z] the Holy Spirit, declared,
'The Lord said to my Lord,
Sit at my right hand,
till I put thy enemies under thy feet.'
37 David himself calls him Lord; so how is he
his son?" And the great throng heard him
gladly.
38 And in his teaching he said, "Beware of
the scribes, who like to go about in long robes,
and to have salutations in the market places
39 and the best seats in the synagogues and the
places of honor at feasts, 40 who devour widows'
houses and for a pretense make long prayers.
They will receive the greater condemnation."

[z] Or *himself, in.*

Jerusalem Bible

Christ not only son but also Lord of David

35 Later, while teaching in the Temple, Jesus
said, "How can the scribes maintain that the
Christ is the son of David? 36 David himself,
moved by the Holy Spirit, said:

The Lord said to my Lord:
Sit at my right hand
and I will put your enemies
under your feet.[x]

37 David himself calls him Lord, in what way
then can he be his son?" And the great majority
of the people heard this with delight.

The scribes condemned by Jesus

38 In his teaching he said, "Beware of the
scribes who like to walk about in long robes,
to be greeted obsequiously in the market squares,
39 to take the front seats in the synagogues and
the places of honor at banquets; 40 these are
the men who swallow the property of widows,
while making a show of lengthy prayers. The
more severe will be the sentence they receive."

[x] Ps. 110:1.

New English Bible

questions to him; and Jesus went on to say, as he taught in the temple, 'How can the teachers of the law maintain that the Messiah is "Son of David"? David himself said, when inspired by the Holy Spirit, "The Lord said to my Lord, 'Sit at my right hand until I put your enemies under your feet.'" David himself calls him "Lord"; how can he also be David's son?'

There was a great crowd and they listened eagerly.[a] He said as he taught them, 'Beware of the doctors of the law, who love to walk up and down in long robes, receiving respectful greetings in the street; and to have the chief seats in synagogues, and places of honour at feasts. These are the men who eat up the property of widows, while they say long prayers for appearance' sake, and they will receive the severest sentence.'[b]

[a] *Or* The mass of the people listened eagerly.
[b] *Or* As for those who eat up the property of widows, while they say long prayers for appearance' sake, they will have an even sterner judgement to face.

King James Version

41 And Jesus sat over against the treasury, and beheld how the people cast money into the treasury: and many that were rich cast in much. 42And there came a certain poor widow, and she threw in two mites, which make a farthing. 43And he called *unto him* his disciples, and saith unto them, Verily I say unto you, That this poor widow hath cast more in, than all they which have cast into the treasury: 44 For all *they* did cast in of their abundance; but she of her want did cast in all that she had, *even* all her living.

13 And as he went out of the temple, one of his disciples saith unto him, Master, see what manner of stones and what buildings *are here!* 2And Jesus answering said unto him, Seest thou these great buildings? there shall not be left one stone upon another, that shall not be thrown down. 3And as he sat upon the mount of Olives, over against the temple, Peter and James and John and Andrew asked him privately, 4 Tell us, when shall these things be? and what *shall be* the sign when all these things shall be ful-

Living Bible

41 Then he went over to the collection boxes in the Temple and sat and watched as the crowds dropped in their money. Some who were rich put in large amounts. 42 Then a poor widow came and dropped in two pennies.

43, 44 He called his disciples to him and remarked, "That poor widow has given more than all those rich men put together! For they gave a little of their extra fat,[c] while she gave up her last penny."

13 As he was leaving the Temple that day, one of his disciples said, "Teacher, what beautiful buildings these are! Look at the decorated stonework on the walls."

2 Jesus replied, "Yes, look! For not one stone will be left upon another, except as ruins."

3, 4 And as he sat on the slopes of the Mount of Olives across the valley from Jerusalem, Peter, James, John, and Andrew got alone with him and asked him, "Just when is all this going to happen to the Temple? Will there be some warning ahead of time?"

[*c*] Literally, "out of their surplus."

Today's English Version

The widow's offering

41 As Jesus sat near the temple treasury he watched the people as they dropped in their money. Many rich men dropped in much money; 42 then a poor widow came along and dropped in two little copper coins, worth about a penny. 43 He called his disciples together and said to them, "I tell you that this poor widow put more in the offering box than all the others. 44 For the others put in what they had to spare of their riches; but she, poor as she is, put in all she had —she gave all she had to live on."

Jesus speaks of the destruction of the temple

13 As Jesus was leaving the temple, one of his disciples said, "Look, Teacher! What wonderful stones and buildings!"

2 Jesus answered, "You see these great buildings? Not a single stone here will be left in its place; every one of them will be thrown down."

Troubles and persecutions

3 Jesus was sitting on the Mount of Olives, across from the temple, when Peter, James, John, and Andrew came to him in private. 4 "Tell us when this will be," they said, "and tell us what will happen to show that the time has come for all these things to take place."

New International Version

The widow's offering

41 Jesus sat down opposite the place where the offerings were put and watched the crowd putting their money into the temple treasury. Many rich people threw in large amounts. 42 But a poor widow came and put in two very small copper coins, worth only a fraction of a penny.

43 Calling his disciples to him, Jesus said, "I tell you the truth, this poor widow has put more into the treasury than all the others. 44 They all gave of their wealth; but she, out of her poverty, put in everything—all she had to live on."

Signs of the end of the age

13 As he was leaving the temple, one of his disciples said to him, "Look, Teacher! What massive stones! What magnificent buildings!"

2 "Do you see all these great buildings?" replied Jesus. "Not one stone here will be left on another; every one will be thrown down."

3 As Jesus was sitting on the Mount of Olives opposite the temple, Peter, James, John and Andrew asked him privately, 4 "Tell us, when will these things happen? And what will be the sign that they are all about to be fulfilled?"

Phillips Modern English

Then Jesus sat down opposite the Temple almsbox and watched the people putting their money into it. A great many rich people put in large sums. Then a poor widow came up and dropped in two little coins, worth together about a farthing. Jesus called his disciples to his side and said to them,

"Believe me, this poor widow has put in more than all the others. For they have all put in what they can easily afford, but she in her poverty who needs so much, has given away everything, her whole living!"

13.1 Jesus prophesies the ruin of the Temple

Then as Jesus was leaving the Temple, one of his disciples said to him,

"Look, Master, what wonderful stonework, what a size these buildings are!"

Jesus replied,

"You see these great buildings? Not a single stone will be left standing on another; every one will be thrown down!"

Then, while he was sitting on the slope of the Mount of Olives facing the Temple, Peter, James, John and Andrew asked him privately,

"Tell us, when will these things happen? What sign will there be that all these things are going to come to an end?"

Revised Standard Version

41 And he sat down opposite the treasury, and watched the multitude putting money into the treasury. Many rich people put in large sums. 42And a poor widow came, and put in two copper coins, which make a penny. 43And he called his disciples to him, and said to them, "Truly, I say to you, this poor widow has put in more than all those who are contributing to the treasury. 44 For they all contributed out of their abundance; but she out of her poverty has put in everything she had, her whole living."

13 And as he came out of the temple, one of his disciples said to him, "Look, Teacher, what wonderful stones and what wonderful buildings!" 2And Jesus said to him, "Do you see these great buildings? There will not be left here one stone upon another, that will not be thrown down."

3 And as he sat on the Mount of Olives opposite the temple, Peter and James and John and Andrew asked him privately, 4 "Tell us, when will this be, and what will be the sign when these things are all to be accomplished?"

Jerusalem Bible

The widow's mite

41 He sat down opposite the treasury and watched the people putting money into the treasury, and many of the rich put in a great deal. 42A poor widow came and put in two small coins, the equivalent of a penny. 43 Then he called his disciples and said to them, "I tell you solemnly, this poor widow has put more in than all who have contributed to the treasury; 44 for they have all put in money they had over, but she from the little she had has put in everything she possessed, all she had to live on."

The eschatological discourse: introduction

13 As he was leaving the Temple one of his disciples said to him, "Look at the size of those stones, Master! Look at the size of those buildings!" 2And Jesus said to him, "You see these great buildings? Not a single stone will be left on another: everything will be destroyed."

3 And while he was sitting facing the Temple, on the Mount of Olives, Peter, James, John and Andrew questioned him privately, 4 "Tell us when is this going to happen and what sign will there be that all this is about to be fulfilled?"

New English Bible

Once he was standing opposite the temple treasury, watching as people dropped their money into the chest. Many rich people were giving large sums. Presently there came a poor widow who dropped in two tiny coins, together worth a farthing. He called his disciples to him. 'I tell you this,' he said: 'this poor widow has given more than any of the others; for those others who have given had more than enough, but she, with less than enough, has given all that she had to live on.'

13 As he was leaving the temple, one of his disciples exclaimed, 'Look, Master, what huge stones! What fine buildings!' Jesus said to him, 'You see these great buildings? Not one stone will be left upon another; all will be thrown down.'

When he was sitting on the Mount of Olives facing the temple he was questioned privately by Peter, James, John, and Andrew. 'Tell us,' they said, 'when will this happen? What will be the sign when the fulfilment of all this is at hand?'

King James Version

filled? 5And Jesus answering them began to say, Take heed lest any *man* deceive you: 6 For many shall come in my name, saying, I am *Christ;* and shall deceive many. 7And when ye shall hear of wars and rumours of wars, be ye not troubled: for *such things* must needs be; but the end *shall* not *be* yet. 8 For nation shall rise against nation, and kingdom against kingdom: and there shall be earthquakes in divers places, and there shall be famines and troubles: these *are* the beginnings of sorrows.

9 But take heed to yourselves: for they shall deliver you up to councils; and in the synagogues ye shall be beaten: and ye shall be brought before rulers and kings for my sake, for a testimony against them. 10And the gospel must first be published among all nations. 11 But when they shall lead *you,* and deliver you up, take no thought beforehand what ye shall speak, neither do ye premeditate: but whatsoever shall be given you in that hour, that speak ye: for it is not ye that speak, but the Holy Ghost. 12 Now the brother shall betray the brother to death, and the father the son; and children shall rise up against *their* parents, and shall cause them to be put to death. 13And ye shall be hated of all *men* for my name's sake: but he that shall endure unto the end, the same shall be saved.

Living Bible

5 So Jesus launched into an extended reply. "Don't let anyone mislead you," he said, 6 "for many will come declaring themselves to be your Messiah, and will lead many astray. 7And wars will break out near and far, but this is not the signal of the end-time.

8 "For nations and kingdoms will proclaim war against each other, and there will be earthquakes in many lands, and famines. These herald only the early stages of the anguish ahead. 9 But when these things begin to happen, watch out! For you will be in great danger. You will be dragged before the courts, and beaten in the synagogues, and accused before governors and kings of being my followers. This is your opportunity to tell them the Good News. 10And the Good News must first be made known in every nation before the end-time finally comes.[a] 11 But when you are arrested and stand trial, don't worry about what to say in your defense. Just say what God tells you to. Then you will not be speaking, but the Holy Spirit will.

12 "Brothers will betray each other to death, fathers will betray their own children, and children will betray their parents to be killed. 13And everyone will hate you because you are mine. But all who endure to the end without renouncing me shall be saved.

[*a*] Implied.

Today's English Version

5 Jesus said to them, "Watch out, and don't let anyone fool you. 6 Many men will come in my name, saying, 'I am he!' and fool many people. 7And don't be troubled when you hear the noise of battles close by and news of battles far away. Such things must happen, but they do not mean that the end has come. 8 Countries will fight each other, kingdoms will attack one another. There will be earthquakes everywhere, and there will be famines. These things are like the first pains of childbirth.

9 "You yourselves must watch out. You will be arrested and taken to court. You will be beaten in the synagogues; you will stand before rulers and kings for my sake, to tell them the Good News. 10 The gospel must first be preached to all peoples. 11And when they arrest you and take you to court, do not worry ahead of time about what you are going to say; when the time comes, say whatever is given to you then. For the words you speak will not be yours; they will come from the Holy Spirit. 12 Men will hand over their own brothers to be put to death, and fathers will do the same to their children; children will turn against their parents and have them put to death. 13 Everyone will hate you because of me. But whoever holds out to the end will be saved."

New International Version

5 Jesus said to them: "Watch out that no one deceives you. 6 Many will come in my name, claiming, 'I am he,' and will deceive many. 7 When you hear of wars and rumors of wars, do not be alarmed. Such things must happen, but the end is still to come. 8 Nation will rise against nation, and kingdom against kingdom. There will be earthquakes in various places, and famines. These are the beginning of birth pains.

9 "You must be on your guard. You will be handed over to the local councils and flogged in the synagogues. On account of me you will stand before governors and kings as witnesses to them. 10And the gospel must first be preached to all nations. 11 Whenever you are arrested and brought to trial, do not worry beforehand about what to say. Just say whatever is given you at the time, for it is not you speaking, but the Holy Spirit.

12 "Brother will betray brother to death, and a father his child. Children will rebel against their parents and have them put to death. 13All men will hate you because of me, but he who stands firm to the end will be saved.

Phillips Modern English

So Jesus began to tell them:
"Be very careful that no one deceives you. Many are going to come in my name and say, 'I am he', and will lead many astray. When you hear of wars and rumours of wars, don't be alarmed. Such things are bound to happen, but the end is not yet. Nation will take up arms against nation and kingdom against kingdom. There will be earthquakes in different places and famines too. But these are only the beginning of birth-pangs. You yourselves must keep your wits about you, for men will hand you over to their councils, and will beat you in their synagogues. You will have to stand in front of rulers and kings for my sake to bear your witness to them. For before the end comes the gospel must be proclaimed to all nations. But when they are taking you off to trial, do not worry beforehand about what you are going to say—simply say the words you are given when the time comes. For it is not really you who will speak, but the Holy Spirit.

13.12 Jesus foretells utter misery

"A brother is going to betray his own brother to death, and a father his own child. Children will stand up against their parents and condemn them to death. There will come a time when the whole world will hate you because you are known as my followers. Yet the man who holds out to the end will be saved.

Revised Standard Version

5And Jesus began to say to them, "Take heed
that no one leads you astray. 6 Many will come
in my name, saying, 'I am he!' and they will lead
many astray. 7And when you hear of wars and
rumors of wars, do not be alarmed; this must
take place, but the end is not yet. 8 For nation
will rise against nation, and kingdom against
kingdom; there will be earthquakes in various
places, there will be famines; this is but the beginning of the birth-pangs.
9 "But take heed to yourselves; for they will
deliver you up to councils; and you will be
beaten in synagogues; and you will stand before
governors and kings for my sake, to bear testimony before them. 10And the gospel must first
be preached to all nations. 11And when they
bring you to trial and deliver you up, do not be
anxious beforehand what you are to say; but
say whatever is given you in that hour, for it is
not you who speak, but the Holy Spirit. 12And
brother will deliver up brother to death, and the
father his child, and children will rise against
parents and have them put to death; 13 and you
will be hated by all for my name's sake. But he
who endures to the end will be saved.

Jerusalem Bible

The beginning of sorrows

5 Then Jesus began to tell them, "Take care
that no one deceives you. 6 Many will come
using my name and saying, 'I am he,' and they
will deceive many. 7 When you hear of wars
and rumors of wars, do not be alarmed, this is
something that must happen, but the end will
not be yet. 8 For nation will fight against nation, and kingdom against kingdom. There will
be earthquakes here and there; there will be
famines. This is the beginning of the birth pangs.
9 "Be on your guard: they will hand you over
to sanhedrins; you will be beaten in synagogues;
and you will stand before governors and kings
for my sake, to bear witness before them,
10 since the Good News must first be proclaimed
to all the nations.
11 "And when they lead you away to hand
you over, do not worry beforehand about what
to say; no, say whatever is given to you when
the time comes, because it is not you who will
be speaking: it will be the Holy Spirit. 12 Brother
will betray brother to death, and the father his
child; children will rise against their parents and
have them put to death. 13 You will be hated
by all men on account of my name; but the man
who stands firm to the end will be saved.

New English Bible

Jesus began: 'Take care that no one misleads you. Many will come claiming my name, and saying, "I am he"; and many will be misled by them.

'When you hear the noise of battle near at hand and the news of battles far away, do not be alarmed. Such things are bound to happen; but the end is still to come. For nation will make war upon nation, kingdom upon kingdom; there will be earthquakes in many places; there will be famines. With these things the birth-pangs of the new age begin.

'As for you, be on your guard. You will be handed over to the courts. You will be flogged in synagogues. You will be summoned to appear before governors and kings on my account to testify in their presence. But before the end the Gospel must be proclaimed to all nations. So when you are arrested and taken away, do not worry beforehand about what you will say, but when the time comes say whatever is given you to say; for it is not you who will be speaking, but the Holy Spirit. Brother will betray brother to death, and the father his child; children will turn against their parents and send them to their death. All will hate you for your allegiance to me; but the man who holds out to the end will be saved.

King James Version

14 But when ye shall see the abomination of
desolation, spoken of by Daniel the prophet,
standing where it ought not, (let him that readeth understand,) then let them that be in Judea
flee to the mountains: 15And let him that is on
the housetop not go down into the house, neither
enter *therein,* to take any thing out of his house:
16And let him that is in the field not turn back
again for to take up his garment. 17 But woe to
them that are with child, and to them that give
suck in those days! 18And pray ye that your flight
be not in the winter. 19 For *in* those days shall
be affliction, such as was not from the beginning
of the creation which God created unto this
time, neither shall be. 20And except that the
Lord had shortened those days, no flesh should
be saved: but for the elect's sake, whom he hath
chosen, he hath shortened the days. 21And then
if any man shall say to you, Lo, here *is* Christ;
or, lo, *he is* there; believe *him* not: 22 For false
Christs and false prophets shall rise, and shall
shew signs and wonders, to seduce, if *it were*
possible, even the elect. 23 But take ye heed: behold, I have foretold you all things.
24 But in those days, after that tribulation,
the sun shall be darkened, and the moon shall

Living Bible

14 "When you see the horrible thing standing
in the Temple[b]—reader, pay attention!—flee, if
you can, to the Judean hills. 15, 16 Hurry! If you
are on your rooftop porch, don't even go back
into the house. If you are out in the fields, don't
even return for your money or clothes.
17 "Woe to pregnant women in those days,
and to mothers nursing their children. 18And
pray that your flight will not be in winter. 19 For
those will be days of such horror as have never
been since the beginning of God's creation, nor
will ever be again. 20And unless the Lord
shortens that time of calamity, not a soul in all
the earth will survive. But for the sake of his
chosen ones he will limit those days.
21 "And then if anyone tells you, 'This is the
Messiah,' or, 'That one is,' don't pay any attention. 22 For there will be many false Messiahs
and false prophets who will do wonderful miracles that would deceive, if possible, even God's
own children.[c] 23 Take care! I have warned you!
24 "After the tribulation ends, then the sun
will grow dim and the moon will not shine,

[*b*] Literally, "standing where he ought not." [*c*] Literally, "elect of God."

Today's English Version

The awful horror

14 "You will see 'The Awful Horror' standing in the place where he should not be." (Note
to the reader: understand what this means!)
"Then those who are in Judea must run away to
the hills. 15 The man who is on the roof of his
house must not lose time by going down into
the house to get anything to take with him. 16 The
man who is in the field must not go back to the
house for his cloak. 17 How terrible it will be in
those days for women who are pregnant, and for
mothers who have little babies! 18 Pray to God
that these things will not happen in wintertime!
19 For the trouble of those days will be far worse
than any the world has ever known, from the
very beginning when God created the world until
the present time. Nor will there ever again be
anything like it. 20 But the Lord has reduced the
number of those days; if he had not, nobody
would survive. For the sake of his chosen people,
however, he has reduced those days.
21 "Then, if anyone says to you, 'Look, here
is the Messiah!' or, 'Look, there he is!'—do not
believe him. 22 For false Messiahs and false
prophets will appear. They will perform signs
and wonders for the purpose of deceiving God's
chosen people, if possible. 23 Be on your guard! I
have told you everything ahead of time."

The coming of the Son of Man

24 "In the days after that time of trouble the
sun will grow dark, the moon will no longer

New International Version

14 "When you see 'the abomination that
causes desolation'[e] standing where it does not
belong—let the reader understand—then let
those who are in Judea flee to the mountains.
15 Let no one on the roof of his house go down
or enter the house to take anything out. 16 Let
no one in the field go back to get his cloak.
17 How dreadful it will be in those days for
pregnant women and nursing mothers! 18 Pray
that this will not take place in winter, 19 because those will be days of distress unequaled
from the beginning, when God created the world,
until now—and never to be equaled again. 20 If
the Lord had not cut short those days, no one
would survive. But for the sake of the elect,
whom he has chosen, he has shortened them.
21At that time if anyone says to you, 'Look,
here is the Christ!'[f] or, 'Look, there he is!' do
not believe it. 22 For false Christs and false
prophets will appear and perform signs and
miracles to deceive the elect—if that were possible. 23 So be on your guard; I have told you
everything ahead of time.
24 "But in those days, following that distress,
'the sun will be darkened,
and the moon will not give its light;

[*e*] Dan. 9:27; 11:31; 12:11. [*f*] Or *Messiah.*

Phillips Modern English

"But when you see 'the abomination of desolation' standing where it ought not—(let the reader take note of this)—then those who are in Judaea must take to the hills! The man on his house-top must not go down nor go into his house to fetch anything out of it, and the man in the field must not turn back to fetch his coat. Alas for the women who are pregnant at that time, and alas for those with babies at their breasts! Pray that it may not be winter when that time comes, for there will be such utter misery in those days as has never been from God's creation until now—and never will be again. Indeed, if the Lord did not shorten those days, no human being would survive. But for the sake of the people whom he has chosen he has shortened those days.

13.21 He warns against false christs, and commands vigilance

"If anyone tells you at that time, 'Look, here is Christ', or 'Look, there he is', don't believe it! For false christs and false prophets will arise and will perform signs and wonders, to deceive, if it be possible, even the men of God's choice. You must keep your eyes open! I am giving you this warning before all these things happen.

"But, in those days, when that misery is past, the light of the sun will be darkened and the

Revised Standard Version

14 "But when you see the desolating sacrilege set up where it ought not to be (let the
reader understand), then let those who are in
Judea flee to the mountains; 15 let him who is
on the housetop not go down, nor enter his
house, to take anything away; 16 and let him who
is in the field not turn back to take his mantle.
17 And alas for those who are with child and for
those who give suck in those days! 18 Pray that
it may not happen in winter. 19 For in those days
there will be such tribulation as has not been
from the beginning of the creation which God
created until now, and never will be. 20 And if
the Lord had not shortened the days, no human
being would be saved; but for the sake of the
elect, whom he chose, he shortened the days.
21 And then if any one says to you, 'Look, here
is the Christ!' or 'Look, there he is!' do not believe it. 22 False Christs and false prophets will
arise and show signs and wonders, to lead astray,
if possible, the elect. 23 But take heed; I have
told you all things beforehand.
24 "But in those days, after that tribulation,
the sun will be darkened, and the moon will not

Jerusalem Bible

The great tribulation of Jerusalem

14 "When you see the *disastrous abomination*[y] set up where it ought not to be (let the
reader understand), then those in Judaea must
escape to the mountains; 15 if a man is on the
housetop, he must not come down to go into
the house to collect any of his belongings; 16 if
a man is in the fields, he must not turn back
to fetch his cloak. 17 Alas for those with child,
or with babies at the breast, when those days
come! 18 Pray that this may not be in winter.
19 For in those days there will be *such distress
as, until now, has not been*[z] equaled since the
beginning when God created the world, nor ever
will be again. 20 And if the Lord had not
shortened that time, no one would have survived; but he did shorten the time, for the sake
of the elect whom he chose.
21 "And if anyone says to you then, 'Look,
here is the Christ' or, 'Look, he is there,' do
not believe it; 22 for false Christs and false
prophets will arise and produce signs and portents to deceive the elect, if that were possible.
23 You therefore must be on your guard. I have
forewarned you of everything.

The coming of the Son of Man

24 "But in those days, after that time of distress, the sun will be darkened, the moon will

[y] Dn. 9:27, and ch. 11,12. [z] Dn. 12:1.

New English Bible

'But when you see "the abomination of desolation" usurping a place which is not his (let the reader understand), then those who are in Judaea must take to the hills. If a man is on the roof, he must not come down into the house to fetch anything out; if in the field, he must not turn back for his coat. Alas for women with child in those days, and for those who have children at the breast! Pray that it may not come in winter. For those days will bring distress such as never has been until now since the beginning of the world which God created—and will never be again. If the Lord had not cut short that time of troubles, no living thing could survive. However, for the sake of his own, whom he has chosen, he has cut short the time.

'Then, if anyone says to you, "Look, here is the Messiah", or, "Look, there he is", do not believe it. Impostors will come claiming to be messiahs or prophets, and they will produce signs and wonders to mislead God's chosen, if such a thing were possible. But you be on your guard; I have forewarned you of it all.

'But in those days, after that distress, the sun will be darkened, the moon will not give her

King James Version

not give her light, 25And the stars of heaven shall fall, and the powers that are in heaven shall be shaken. 26And then shall they see the Son of man coming in the clouds with great power and glory. 27And then shall he send his angels, and shall gather together his elect from the four winds, from the uttermost part of the earth to the uttermost part of heaven. 28 Now learn a parable of the fig tree: When her branch is yet tender, and putteth forth leaves, ye know that summer is near: 29 So ye in like manner, when ye shall see these things come to pass, know that it is nigh, *even* at the doors. 30 Verily I say unto you, that this generation shall not pass, till all these things be done. 31 Heaven and earth shall pass away: but my words shall not pass away.

32 But of that day and *that* hour knoweth no man, no, not the angels which are in heaven, neither the Son, but the Father. 33 Take ye heed, watch and pray: for ye know not when the time is. 34 *For the Son of man is* as a man taking a far journey, who left his house, and gave authority to his servants, and to every man his work, and commanded the porter to watch. 35 Watch ye therefore: for ye know not when the master

Living Bible

25 and the stars will fall—the heavens will convulse.

26 "Then all mankind will see me, the Messiah,[d] coming in the clouds with great power and glory. 27And I will send out the angels to gather together my chosen ones from all over the world—from the farthest bounds of earth and heaven.

28 "Now, here is a lesson from a fig tree. When its buds become tender and its leaves begin to sprout, you know that spring has come. 29And when you see these things happening that I've described, you can be sure that my return is very near, that I am right at the door.

30 "Yes, these are the events that will signal the end of the age.[e] 31 Heaven and earth shall disappear, but my words stand sure forever.

32 "However, no one, not even the angels in heaven, nor I myself,[f] knows the day or hour when these things will happen; only the Father knows. 33And since you don't know when it will happen, stay alert. Be on the watch [for my return[a]].

34 "My coming[g] can be compared with that of a man who went on a trip to another country. He laid out his employees' work for them to do while he was gone, and told the gatekeeper to watch for his return.

35, 36, 37 "Keep a sharp lookout! For you do

[*d*] Literally, "the Son of Man." [*e*] Literally, "of this generation." [*f*] Literally, "the Son." [*a*] Implied. [*g*] Literally, "You do not know when the master of the house will come."

Today's English Version

shine, 25 the stars will fall from heaven, and the powers in space will be driven from their courses. 26 Then the Son of Man will appear, coming in the clouds with great power and glory. 27 He will send out the angels to the four corners of the earth and gather God's chosen people from one end of the world to the other."

The lesson of the fig tree

28 "Let the fig tree teach you a lesson. When its branches become green and tender, and it starts putting out leaves, you know that summer is near. 29 In the same way, when you see these things happening, you will know that the time is near, ready to begin. 30 Remember this! All these things will happen before the people now living have all died. 31 Heaven and earth will pass away; my words will never pass away."

No one knows the day or hour

32 "No one knows, however, when that day or hour will come—neither the angels in heaven, nor the Son; only the Father knows. 33 Be on watch, be alert, for you do not know when the time will be. 34 It will be like a man who goes away from home on a trip and leaves his servants in charge, each one with his own work to do; and he tells the doorkeeper to keep watch. 35 Watch, then, because you do not know when

New International Version

25 the stars will fall from the sky,
and the heavenly bodies will be shaken.'[g]

26 "At that time men will see the Son of Man coming in clouds with great power and glory. 27And he will send his angels and gather his elect from the four winds, from the ends of the earth to the ends of the heavens.

28 "Now learn this lesson from the fig tree: As soon as its twigs get tender and its leaves come out, you know that summer is near. 29 Even so, when you see these things happening, you know that it[h] is near, right at the door. 30 I tell you the truth, this generation[i] will certainly not pass away until all these things have happened. 31 Heaven and earth will pass away, but my words will never pass away.

The day and hour unknown

32 "No one knows about that day or hour, not even the angels in heaven, nor the Son, but only the Father. 33 Be on guard! Be alert![j] You do not know when that time will come. 34 It's like a man going away: He leaves his house in charge of his servants, each with his assigned task, and tells the one at the door to keep watch. 35 So you also must keep watch because you do

[*g*] Isaiah 13:10; 34:4. [*h*] Or *he*. [*i*] Or race. [*j*] Some MSS add *and pray*.

Phillips Modern English

moon will not give her light; stars will be falling from the sky and the powers of the heaven will rock on their foundations. Then men shall see the Son of Man coming in the clouds with great power and glory. And then shall he send out the angels to gather his chosen together from every quarter, from furthest earth to highest heaven. Let the fig-tree illustrate this for you: when its branches grow tender and produce leaves, you know that summer is near. So when you see these things happening, you may know that he is near, at your very doors! I tell you that this generation will not have passed until all these things have come true. Earth and sky will pass away, but what I have told you will never pass away! But no one knows the day or the hour of this happening, not even the angels in Heaven, no, not even the Son—only the Father. Keep your eyes open, keep on the alert, for you do not know when the time will be. It is as if a man who is travelling abroad had left his house and handed it over to be managed by his servants. He has given each one his work to do and has ordered the doorkeeper to be on the look-out. Just so must you keep a look-out, for you do

Revised Standard Version

give its light, 25 and the stars will be falling from
heaven, and the powers in the heavens will be
shaken. 26 And then they will see the Son of man
coming in clouds with great power and glory.
27 And then he will send out the angels, and
gather his elect from the four winds, from the
ends of the earth to the ends of heaven.
28 "From the fig tree learn its lesson: as soon
as its branch becomes tender and puts forth its
leaves, you know that summer is near. 29 So also,
when you see these things taking place, you
know that he is near, at the very gates. 30 Truly,
I say to you, this generation will not pass away
before all these things take place. 31 Heaven
and earth will pass away, but my words will not
pass away.
32 "But of that day or that hour no one
knows, not even the angels in heaven, nor the
Son, but only the Father. 33 Take heed, watch;[a]
for you do not know when the time will come.
34 It is like a man going on a journey, when he
leaves home and puts his servants in charge, each
with his work, and commands the doorkeeper to
be on the watch. 35 Watch therefore—for you do

[a] Other ancient authorities add *and pray*.

Jerusalem Bible

lose its brightness, 25 the stars will come falling
from heaven and the powers in the heavens will
be shaken. 26 And then they will see the Son of
Man coming in the clouds with great power and
glory; 27 then too he will send the angels to
gather his chosen from the four winds, from
the ends of the world to the ends of heaven.

The time of this coming

28 "Take the fig tree as a parable: as soon
as its twigs grow supple and its leaves come
out, you know that summer is near. 29 So with
you when you see these things happening: know
that he is near, at the very gates. 30 I tell you
solemnly, before this generation has passed away
all these things will have taken place. 31 Heaven
and earth will pass away, but my words will not
pass away.
32 "But as for that day or hour, nobody
knows it, neither the angels of heaven, nor the
Son; no one but the Father.

Be on the alert

33 "Be on your guard, stay awake, because
you never know when the time will come. 34 It
is like a man traveling abroad: he has gone
from home, and left his servants in charge, each
with his own task; and he has told the door-
keeper to stay awake. 35 So stay awake, because

New English Bible

light; the stars will come falling from the sky, the celestial powers will be shaken. Then they will see the Son of Man coming in the clouds with great power and glory, and he will send out the angels and gather his chosen from the four winds, from the farthest bounds of earth to the farthest bounds of heaven.

'Learn a lesson from the fig-tree. When its tender shoots appear and are breaking into leaf, you know that summer is near. In the same way, when you see all this happening, you may know that the end is near,[a] at the very door. I tell you this: the present generation will live to see it all. Heaven and earth will pass away; my words will never pass away.

'But about that day or that hour no one knows, not even the angels in heaven, not even the Son; only the Father.

'Be alert, be wakeful.[b] You do not know when the moment comes. It is like a man away from home: he has left his house and put his servants in charge, each with his own work to do, and he has ordered the door-keeper to stay awake. Keep awake, then, for you do not know

[a] *Or* that he is near. [b] *Some witnesses add* and pray.

King James Version

of the house cometh, at even, or at midnight, or at the cockcrowing, or in the morning: 36 Lest coming suddenly he find you sleeping. 37 And what I say unto you I say unto all, Watch.

14 After two days was *the feast of* the passover, and of unleavened bread: and the chief priests and the scribes sought how they might take him by craft, and put *him* to death. 2 But they said, Not on the feast *day*, lest there be an uproar of the people.

3 And being in Bethany, in the house of Simon the leper, as he sat at meat, there came a woman having an alabaster box of ointment of spikenard very precious; and she brake the box, and poured *it* on his head. 4 And there were some that had indignation within themselves, and said, Why was this waste of the ointment made? 5 For it might have been sold for more than three hundred pence, and have been given to the poor. And they murmured against her. 6 And Jesus said, Let her alone; why trouble

Living Bible

not know when I[h] will come, at evening, at midnight, early dawn or late daybreak. Don't let me find you sleeping. *Watch for my return!* This is my message to you and to everyone else."

14 The Passover observance began two days later—an annual Jewish holiday when no bread made with yeast was eaten. The chief priests and other Jewish leaders were still looking for an opportunity to arrest Jesus secretly and put him to death.

2 "But we can't do it during the Passover," they said, "or there will be a riot."

3 Meanwhile Jesus was in Bethany, at the home of Simon the leper; during supper a woman came in with a beautiful flask of expensive perfume. Then, breaking the seal, she poured it over his head.

4, 5 Some of those at the table were indignant among themselves about this "waste," as they called it.

"Why, she could have sold that perfume for a fortune and given the money to the poor!" they snarled.

6 But Jesus said, "Let her alone; why be-

[h] Implied.

Today's English Version

the master of the house is coming—it might be in the evening, or at midnight, or before dawn, or at sunrise. 36 If he comes suddenly, he must not find you asleep. 37 What I say to you, then, I say to all: Watch!"

The plot against Jesus

14 It was now two days before the Feast of Passover and Unleavened Bread. The chief priests and the teachers of the Law were looking for a way to arrest Jesus secretly and put him to death. 2 "We must not do it during the feast," they said, "or the people might riot."

Jesus anointed at Bethany

3 Jesus was in the house of Simon the leper, in Bethany; while he was eating, a woman came in with an alabaster jar full of a very expensive perfume, made of pure nard. She broke the jar and poured the perfume on Jesus' head. 4 Some of the people there became angry, and said to each other, "What was the use of wasting the perfume? 5 It could have been sold for more than three hundred dollars, and the money given to the poor!" And they criticized her harshly.

6 But Jesus said, "Leave her alone! Why are

New International Version

not know when the owner of the house will come back—whether in the evening, or at midnight, or when the rooster crows, or at dawn. 36 If he comes suddenly, don't let him find you sleeping. 37 What I say to you, I say to everyone: 'Watch!' "

Jesus anointed at Bethany

14 Now the Passover and the Feast of Unleavened Bread were only two days away, and the chief priests and the teachers of the law were looking for some sly way to arrest Jesus and kill him. 2 "But not during the feast," they said, "or the people may riot."

3 While he was in Bethany, reclining at the table in the home of a man known as Simon the Leper, a woman came with an alabaster jar of very expensive perfume, made of pure nard. She broke the jar and poured the perfume on his head.

4 Some of those present were saying indignantly to one another, "Why this waste of perfume? 5 It could have been sold for more than a year's wages[k] and the money given to the poor." And they rebuked her harshly.

6 "Leave her alone," said Jesus. "Why are

[k] Greek *300 denarii.*

Phillips Modern English

not know when the master of the house will come—it might be late evening, or midnight, or cock-crow, or early morning—otherwise he might come unexpectedly and find you sound asleep. What I am saying to you I am saying to all; keep on the alert!"

14.1 An act of love

In two days' time the festival of the Passover and of unleavened bread was due. Consequently, the chief priests and the scribes were trying to think of some trick by which they could get Jesus into their power and have him executed.

"But it must not be during the festival," they said, "or there will be a riot."

Jesus himself was now in Bethany in the house of Simon the leper. As he was sitting at table, a woman approached him with an alabaster flask of very costly spikenard perfume. She broke the neck of the flask and poured the perfume on Jesus' head. Some of those present were highly indignant and muttered,

"What is the point of such wicked waste of perfume? It could have been sold for over thirty pounds and the money given to the poor." And there was a murmur of resentment against her. But Jesus said,

"Let her alone, why must you make her feel

Revised Standard Version

not know when the master of the house will come, in the evening, or at midnight, or at cock-
crow, or in the morning—36 lest he come sud-
denly and find you asleep. 37 And what I say to you I say to all: Watch."

14 It was now two days before the Passover and the feast of Unleavened Bread. And the chief priests and the scribes were seeking how to arrest him by stealth, and kill him; 2 for
they said, "Not during the feast, lest there be a tumult of the people."
3 And while he was at Bethany in the house of Simon the leper, as he sat at table, a woman came with an alabaster flask of ointment of pure nard, very costly, and she broke the flask and poured it over his head. 4 But there were
some who said to themselves indignantly, "Why was the ointment thus wasted? 5 For this oint-
ment might have been sold for more than three hundred denarii,[b] and given to the poor." And
they reproached her. 6 But Jesus said, "Let her

[b] The denarius was a day's wage for a laborer.

Jerusalem Bible

you do not know when the master of the house is coming, evening, midnight, cockcrow, dawn;
36 if he comes unexpectedly he must not find
you asleep. 37 And what I say to you I say to all: Stay awake!"

V. Passion and resurrection

The conspiracy against Jesus

14 It was two days before the Passover and the feast of Unleavened Bread, and the chief priests and the scribes were looking for a way to arrest Jesus by some trick and have him
put to death. 2 For they said, "It must not be during the festivities, or there will be a disturbance among the people."

The anointing at Bethany

3 Jesus was at Bethany in the house of Simon the leper; he was at dinner when a woman came in with an alabaster jar of very costly ointment, pure nard. She broke the jar and poured the
ointment on his head. 4 Some who were there
said to one another indignantly, "Why this waste of ointment? 5 Ointment like this could have
been sold for over three hundred denarii and the money given to the poor"; and they were
angry with her. 6 But Jesus said, "Leave her

New English Bible

when the master of the house is coming. Evening or midnight, cock-crow or early dawn—if he comes suddenly, he must not find you asleep. And what I say to you, I say to everyone: Keep awake.'

The final conflict

14 Now the festival of Passover and Unleavened Bread was only two days off; and the chief priests and the doctors of the law were trying to devise some cunning plan to seize him and put him to death. 'It must not be during the festival,' they said, 'or we should have rioting among the people.'

Jesus was at Bethany, in the house of Simon the leper. As he sat at table, a woman came in carrying a small bottle of very costly perfume, pure oil of nard. She broke it open and poured the oil over his head. Some of those present said to one another angrily, 'Why this waste? The perfume might have been sold for thirty pounds[c] and the money given to the poor'; and they turned upon her with fury. But Jesus said, 'Let her alone. Why must you make trouble

[c] *Literally* 300 denarii; *some witnesses read* more than 300 denarii.

King James Version

ye her? she hath wrought a good work on me.
7 For ye have the poor with you always, and
whensoever ye will ye may do them good: but
me ye have not always. 8 She hath done what
she could: she is come aforehand to anoint
my body to the burying. 9 Verily I say unto
you, Wheresoever this gospel shall be preached
throughout the whole world, *this* also that she
hath done shall be spoken of for a memorial of
her.
10 And Judas Iscariot, one of the twelve,
went unto the chief priests, to betray him unto
them. 11 And when they heard *it*, they were glad,
and promised to give him money. And he sought
how he might conveniently betray him.
12 And the first day of unleavened bread,
when they killed the passover, his disciples said
unto him, Where wilt thou that we go and prepare that thou mayest eat the passover? 13 And
he sendeth forth two of his disciples, and saith
unto them, Go ye into the city, and there shall
meet you a man bearing a pitcher of water: follow him. 14 And wheresoever he shall go in, say
ye to the goodman of the house, The Master

Living Bible

rate her for doing a good thing? 7 You always
have the poor among you, and they badly need
your help, and you can aid them whenever you
want to; but I won't be here much longer.
8 "She has done what she could, and has
anointed my body ahead of time for burial.
9 And I tell you this in solemn truth, that wherever the Good News is preached throughout the
world, this woman's deed will be remembered
and praised."
10 Then Judas Iscariot, one of his disciples,
went to the chief priests to arrange to betray
Jesus to them.
11 When the chief priests heard why he had
come, they were excited and happy and promised him a reward. So he began looking for the
right time and place to betray Jesus.
12 On the first day of the Passover, the day
the lambs were sacrificed, his disciples asked him
where he wanted to go to eat the traditional
Passover supper. 13 He sent two of them into
Jerusalem to make the arrangements.
"As you are walking along," he told them,
"you will see a man coming towards you carrying a pot of water. Follow him. 14 At the house
he enters, tell the man in charge, 'Our Master
sent us to see the room you have ready for us,

Today's English Version

you bothering her? She has done a fine and
beautiful thing for me. 7 You will always have
poor people with you, and any time you want to
you can help them. But I shall not be with you
always. 8 She did what she could; she poured perfume on my body to prepare it ahead of time for
burial. 9 Now, remember this! Wherever the gospel is preached, all over the world, what she has
done will be told in memory of her."

Judas agrees to betray Jesus

10 Then Judas Iscariot, one of the twelve disciples, went off to the chief priests in order to hand
Jesus over to them. 11 They were greatly pleased
to hear what he had to say, and promised to give
him money. So Judas started looking for a good
chance to betray Jesus.

Jesus eats the Passover meal with his disciples

12 On the first day of the Feast of Unleavened
Bread, the day the lambs for the Passover meal
were killed, Jesus' disciples asked him, "Where do
you want us to go and get your Passover meal
ready?"
13 Then Jesus sent two of them out with these
instructions: "Go into the city, and a man carrying a jar of water will meet you. Follow him
14 to the house he enters, and say to the owner
of the house: 'The Teacher says, Where is my

New International Version

you bothering her? She has done a beautiful
thing to me. 7 The poor you will always have
with you, and you can help them any time you
want. But you will not always have me. 8 She
did what she could. She poured perfume on my
body beforehand to prepare for my burial. 9 I
tell you the truth, wherever the gospel is
preached throughout the world, what she has
done will also be told, in memory of her."
10 Then Judas Iscariot, one of the Twelve,
went to the chief priests to betray Jesus to them.
11 They were delighted to hear this and promised to give him money. So he watched for an
opportunity to hand him over.

The Lord's supper

12 On the first day of the Feast of Unleavened Bread, when it was customary to sacrifice the Passover lamb, Jesus' disciples asked
him, "Where do you want us to go and make
preparations for you to eat the Passover?"
13 So he sent two of his disciples, telling
them, "Go into the city, and a man carrying a
jar of water will meet you. Follow him. 14 Say
to the owner of the house he enters, 'The
Teacher asks: Where is my guest room, where

Phillips Modern English

uncomfortable? She has done a beautiful thing for me. You have the poor with you always and you can do good to them whenever you like, but you will not always have me. She has done all she could—for she has anointed my body in preparation for burial. I assure you that wherever the gospel is preached throughout the whole world, this deed of hers will also be recounted, as her memorial to me."

14.10 Judas volunteers to betray Jesus

Then Judas Iscariot, who was one of the twelve, went off to the chief priests to betray Jesus to them. And when they heard what he had to say, they were delighted and undertook to pay him money. So he looked for a convenient opportunity to betray him.

14.12 The Passover-supper prepared

On the first day of unleavened bread, the day when the Passover was sacrificed, Jesus' disciples said to him,

"Where do you want us to go and make the preparations for you to eat the Passover?"

Jesus sent off two of them with these instructions,

"Go into the town and you will meet a man carrying a pitcher of water. Follow him and say to the owner of the house which he enters, 'The master says, where is the room for me to eat the

Revised Standard Version

alone; why do you trouble her? She has done a
beautiful thing to me. 7 For you always have the
poor with you, and whenever you will, you can
do good to them; but you will not always have
me. 8 She has done what she could; she has
anointed my body beforehand for burying. 9 And
truly, I say to you, wherever the gospel is
preached in the whole world, what she has done
will be told in memory of her."
10 Then Judas Iscariot, who was one of the
twelve, went to the chief priests in order to betray him to them. 11 And when they heard it they
were glad, and promised to give him money. And
he sought an opportunity to betray him.
12 And on the first day of Unleavened Bread,
when they sacrificed the passover lamb, his disciples said to him, "Where will you have us go
and prepare for you to eat the passover?" 13 And
he sent two of his disciples, and said to them,
"Go into the city, and a man carrying a jar of
water will meet you; follow him, 14 and wherever he enters, say to the householder, 'The
Teacher says, Where is my guest room, where I

Jerusalem Bible

alone. Why are you upsetting her? What she
has done for me is one of the good works.
7 You have the poor with you always, and you
can be kind to them whenever you wish, but
you will not always have me. 8 She has done
what was in her power to do: she has anointed
my body beforehand for its burial. 9 I tell you
solemnly, wherever throughout all the world the
Good News is proclaimed, what she has done
will be told also, in remembrance of her."

Judas betrays Jesus

10 Judas Iscariot, one of the Twelve, approached the chief priests with an offer to hand
Jesus over to them. 11 They were delighted to
hear it, and promised to give him money; and he
looked for a way of betraying him when the
opportunity should occur.

Preparations for the Passover supper

12 On the first day of Unleavened Bread,
when the Passover lamb was sacrificed, his disciples said to him, "Where do you want us to
go and make the preparations for you to eat the
passover?" 13 So he sent two of his disciples,
saying to them, "Go into the city and you will
meet a man carrying a pitcher of water. Follow
him, 14 and say to the owner of the house which
he enters, 'The Master says: Where is my din-

New English Bible

for her? It is a fine thing she has done for me. You have the poor among you always, and you can help them whenever you like; but you will not always have me. She has done what lay in her power; she is beforehand with anointing my body for burial. I tell you this: wherever in all the world the Gospel is proclaimed, what she has done will be told as her memorial.'

Then Judas Iscariot, one of the Twelve, went to the chief priests to betray him to them. When they heard what he had come for, they were greatly pleased, and promised him money; and he began to look for a good opportunity to betray him.

Now on the first day of Unleavened Bread, when the Passover lambs were being slaughtered, his disciples said to him, 'Where would you like us to go and prepare for your Passover supper?' So he sent out two of his disciples with these instructions: 'Go into the city, and a man will meet you carrying a jar of water. Follow him, and when he enters a house give this message to the householder: "The Master says, 'Where is

King James Version

saith, Where is the guestchamber, where I shall eat the passover with my disciples? 15And he will shew you a large upper room furnished *and* prepared: there make ready for us. 16And his disciples went forth, and came into the city, and found as he had said unto them: and they made ready the passover. 17And in the evening he cometh with the twelve. 18And as they sat and did eat, Jesus said, Verily I say unto you, One of you which eateth with me shall betray me. 19And they began to be sorrowful, and to say unto him one by one, *Is* it I? and another *said, Is* it I? 20And he answered and said unto them, *It is* one of the twelve, that dippeth with me in the dish. 21 The Son of man indeed goeth, as it is written of him: but woe to that man by whom the Son of man is betrayed! good were it for that man if he had never been born.

22 And as they did eat, Jesus took bread, and blessed, and brake *it*, and gave to them, and said, Take, eat; this is my body. 23And he took the cup, and when he had given thanks, he gave *it* to them: and they all drank of it. 24And he said unto them, This is my blood of the new

Living Bible

where we will eat the Passover supper this evening!' 15 He will take you upstairs to a large room all set up. Prepare our supper there."

16 So the two disciples went on ahead into the city and found everything as Jesus had said, and prepared the Passover.

17 In the evening Jesus arrived with the other disciples, 18 and as they were sitting around the table eating, Jesus said, "I solemnly declare that one of you will betray me, one of you who is here eating with me."

19 A great sadness swept over them, and one by one they asked him, "Am I the one?"

20 He replied, "It is one of you twelve eating with me now. 21 I [a] must die, as the prophets declared long ago; but, oh, the misery ahead for the man by whom I [a] am betrayed. Oh, that he had never been born!"

22 As they were eating, Jesus took bread and asked God's blessing on it and broke it in pieces and gave it to them and said, "Eat it—this is my body."

23 Then he took a cup of wine and gave thanks to God for it and gave it to them; and they all drank from it. 24And he said to them, "This is my blood, poured out for many, sealing[b]

[*a*] Literally, "the Son of Man." [*b*] Literally, "This is my blood of the covenant." Some ancient manuscripts read, "new covenant."

Today's English Version

room where my disciples and I will eat the Passover meal?' 15 Then he will show you a large upstairs room, fixed up and furnished, where you will get everything ready for us."

16 The disciples left, went to the city, and found everything just as Jesus had told them; and they prepared the Passover meal.

17 When it was evening, Jesus came with the twelve disciples. 18 While they were at the table eating, Jesus said, "I tell you this: one of you will betray me—one who is eating with me."

19 The disciples were upset and began to ask him, one after the other, "Surely you don't mean me, do you?"

20 Jesus answered, "It will be one of you twelve, one who dips his bread in the dish with me. 21 The Son of Man will die as the Scriptures say he will; but how terrible for that man who will betray the Son of Man! It would have been better for that man if he had never been born!"

The Lord's supper

22 While they were eating, Jesus took the bread, gave a prayer of thanks, broke it, and gave it to his disciples. "Take it," he said, "this is my body."

23 Then he took the cup, gave thanks to God, and handed it to them; and they all drank from it. 24 Jesus said, "This is my blood which is poured out for many, my blood which seals

New International Version

I may eat the Passover with my disciples?' 15 He will show you a large upper room, furnished and ready. Make preparations for us there."

16 The disciples left, went into the city and found things just as Jesus had told them. So they prepared the Passover.

17 When evening came, Jesus arrived with the Twelve. 18 While they were reclining at the table eating, he said, "I tell you the truth, one of you will betray me—one who is eating with me."

19 They were saddened, and one by one they said to him, "Surely not I?"

20 "It is one of the Twelve," he replied, "one who dips bread into the bowl with me. 21 The Son of Man will go just as it is written about him. But woe to that man who betrays the Son of Man! It would be better for him if he had not been born."

22 While they were eating, Jesus took bread, gave thanks and broke it, and gave it to his disciples, saying, "Take it; this is my body."

23 Then he took the cup, gave thanks and offered it to them, and they all drank from it.

24 "This is my blood of the[l] covenant, which

[*l*] Some MSS add *new*.

Phillips Modern English

Passover with my disciples?' And he will show you a large upstairs room, set out and ready. That is where you must make our preparations."

So the disciples set off and went into the town, found everything as he had told them, and prepared for the Passover.

14.17 The last supper together: the mysterious bread and wine

Late in the evening he arrived with the twelve. And while they were sitting there, right in the middle of the meal, Jesus remarked,

"Believe me, one of you is going to betray me—someone who is now eating with me."

This deeply distressed them and one after another they began to say to him,

"Surely, I'm not the one?"

"It is one of the twelve," Jesus told them, "a man who is dipping his hand into the dish with me. It is true that the Son of Man will follow the road foretold by the scriptures, but alas for the man through whom he is betrayed! It would be better for that man if he had never been born."

And while they were still eating Jesus took a loaf, blessed it and broke it and gave it to them, with the words,

"Take this, it is my body."

Then he took a cup, and after thanking God, he gave it to them, and they all drank from it, and he said to them,

"This is my blood of the new agreement, and

Revised Standard Version

am to eat the passover with my disciples?' 15And
he will show you a large upper room furnished
and ready; there prepare for us." 16And the
disciples set out and went to the city, and found
it as he had told them; and they prepared the
passover.
17 And when it was evening he came with
the twelve. 18And as they were at table eating,
Jesus said, "Truly, I say to you, one of you will
betray me, one who is eating with me." 19 They
began to be sorrowful, and to say to him one
after another, "Is it I?" 20 He said to them, "It
is one of the twelve, one who is dipping bread
into the dish with me. 21 For the Son of man
goes as it is written of him, but woe to that
man by whom the Son of man is betrayed! It
would have been better for that man if he had
not been born."
22 And as they were eating, he took bread,
and blessed, and broke it, and gave it to them,
and said, "Take; this is my body." 23And he
took a cup, and when he had given thanks he
gave it to them, and they all drank of it. 24And
he said to them, "This is my blood of the[c] cove-

[c] Other ancient authorities insert *new*.

Jerusalem Bible

ing room in which I can eat the passover with
my disciples?' 15 He will show you a large upper
room furnished with couches, all prepared. Make
the preparations for us there." 16 The disciples
set out and went to the city and found everything as he had told them, and prepared the
passover.

The treachery of Judas foretold

17 When evening came he arrived with the
Twelve. 18And while they were at table eating,
Jesus said, "I tell you solemnly, one of you is
about to betray me, one of you eating with me."
19 They were distressed and asked him, one after
another, "Not I, surely?" 20 He said to them,
"It is one of the Twelve, one who is dipping
into the same dish with me. 21 Yes, the Son of
Man is going to his fate, as the scriptures say
he will, but alas for that man by whom the Son
of Man is betrayed! Better for that man if he
had never been born!"

The institution of the Eucharist

22 And as they were eating he took some
bread, and when he had said the blessing he
broke it and gave it to them. "Take it," he
said, "this is my body." 23 Then he took a cup,
and when he had returned thanks he gave it to
them, and all drank from it, 24 and he said to
them, "This is my blood, the blood of the cove-

New English Bible

the room reserved for me to eat the Passover with my disciples?' " He will show you a large room upstairs, set out in readiness. Make the preparations for us there.' Then the disciples went off, and when they came into the city they found everything just as he had told them. So they prepared for Passover.

In the evening he came to the house with the Twelve. As they sat at supper Jesus said, 'I tell you this: one of you will betray me—one who is eating with me.' At this they were dismayed; and one by one they said to him, 'Not I, surely?' 'It is one of the Twelve', he said, 'who is dipping into the same bowl with me. The Son of Man is going the way appointed for him in the scriptures; but alas for that man by whom the Son of Man is betrayed! It would be better for that man if he had never been born.'

During supper he took bread, and having said the blessing he broke it and gave it to them, with the words: 'Take this; this is my body.' Then he took a cup, and having offered thanks to God he gave it to them; and they all drank from it. And he said, 'This is my blood, the blood of the

King James Version

testament, which is shed for many. 25 Verily I
say unto you, I will drink no more of the fruit
of the vine, until that day that I drink it new
in the kingdom of God.
26 And when they had sung a hymn, they
went out into the mount of Olives. 27 And Jesus
saith unto them, All ye shall be offended because
of me this night: for it is written, I will smite
the Shepherd, and the sheep shall be scattered.
28 But after that I am risen, I will go before
you into Galilee. 29 But Peter said unto him,
Although all shall be offended, yet *will* not I.
30 And Jesus saith unto him, Verily I say unto
thee, That this day, *even* in this night, before
the cock crow twice, thou shalt deny me thrice.
31 But he spake the more vehemently, If I should
die with thee, I will not deny thee in any wise.
Likewise also said they all. 32 And they came to

Living Bible

the new agreement between God and man. 25 I
solemnly declare that I shall never again taste
wine until the day I drink a different kind [c] in
the Kingdom of God."
26 Then they sang a hymn and went out to
the Mount of Olives.
27 "All of you will desert me," Jesus told
them, "for God has declared through the prophets, 'I will kill the Shepherd, and the sheep will
scatter.' 28 But after I am raised to life again, I
will go to Galilee and meet you there."
29 Peter said to him, "I will never desert you
no matter what the others do!"
30 "Peter," Jesus said, "before the cock
crows a second time tomorrow morning you will
deny me three times."
31 "No!" Peter exploded. "Not even if I have
to die with you! I'll *never* deny you!" And all
the others vowed the same.
32 And now they came to an olive grove

[c] Literally, "drink it new."

Today's English Version

God's covenant. 25 I tell you, I will never again
drink this wine until the day I drink the new
wine in the Kingdom of God."
26 Then they sang a hymn and went out to
the Mount of Olives.

Jesus predicts Peter's denial

27 Jesus said to them, "All of you will run
away and leave me, because the scripture says,
'God will kill the shepherd and the sheep will all
be scattered.' 28 But after I am raised to life I
will go to Galilee ahead of you."
29 Peter answered, "I will never leave you,
even though all the rest do!"
30 "Remember this!" Jesus said to Peter. "Before the rooster crows two times tonight, you
will say three times that you do not know me."
31 Peter answered even more strongly, "I will
never say I do not know you, even if I have to
die with you!"
And all the disciples said the same thing.

Jesus prays in Gethsemane

32 They came to a place called Gethsemane,

New International Version

is poured out for many," he said. 25 "I tell you
the truth, I will not drink again from the fruit
of the vine until that day when I drink it anew
in the kingdom of God."
26 When they had sung a hymn, they went
out to the Mount of Olives.

Jesus predicts Peter's denial

27 "You will all fall away," Jesus told them,
"for it is written:
'I will strike the shepherd,
and the sheep will be scattered.' [m]
28 But after I have risen, I will go ahead of you
into Galilee."
29 Peter declared, "Even if all fall away, I will
not."
30 "I tell you the truth," Jesus answered,
"today—yes, tonight—before the rooster crows
twice[n] you yourself will disown me three times."
31 But Peter insisted emphatically, "Even if I
have to die with you, I will never disown you."
And all the others said the same.

Gethsemane

32 They went to a place called Gethsemane,

[m] Zech. 13:7. [n] Some early MSS omit *twice*.

Phillips Modern English

it is shed for many. I tell you truly I will drink no more wine until the day comes when I drink it fresh in the kingdom of God!"

Then they sang a hymn and went out to the Mount of Olives.

"Every one of you will lose your faith in me," Jesus told them, "as the scripture says:

I will smite the shepherd,
And the sheep shall be scattered abroad.

Yet after I have risen, I shall go before you into Galilee!"

14.29 Peter's bold words—and Jesus' reply

Then Peter said to him,

"Even if everyone should lose his faith, I never will."

"Believe me, Peter," returned Jesus, "this very night before the cock crows twice, you will disown me three times."

But Peter protested violently,

"Even if it means dying with you, I will never disown you!"

And they all made the same protest.

14.32 The last desperate prayer in Gethsemane

Then they arrived at a place called Gethsem-

Revised Standard Version

nant, which is poured out for many. 25 Truly, I
say to you, I shall not drink again of the fruit
of the vine until that day when I drink it new
in the kingdom of God."
26 And when they had sung a hymn, they
went out to the Mount of Olives. 27 And Jesus
said to them, "You will all fall away; for it is
written, 'I will strike the shepherd, and the sheep
will be scattered.' 28 But after I am raised up, I
will go before you to Galilee." 29 Peter said to
him, "Even though they all fall away, I will
not." 30 And Jesus said to him, "Truly, I say to
you, this very night, before the cock crows twice,
you will deny me three times." 31 But he said vehemently, "If I must die with you, I will not
deny you." And they all said the same.
32 And they went to a place which was called

Jerusalem Bible

nant, which is to be poured out for many. 25 I
tell you solemnly, I shall not drink any more
wine until the day I drink the new wine in the
kingdom of God."

Peter's denial foretold

26 After psalms had been sung they left for
the Mount of Olives. 27 And Jesus said to them,
"You will all lose faith, for the scripture says:
*I shall strike the shepherd and the sheep will be
scattered,*[a] 28 however after my resurrection I
shall go before you to Galilee." 29 Peter said,
"Even if all lose faith, I will not." 30 And Jesus
said to him, "I tell you solemnly, this day, this
very night, before 31 the cock crows twice, you
will have disowned me three times." But he repeated still more earnestly, "If I have to die with
you, I will never disown you." And they all
said the same.

Gethsemane

32 They came to a small estate called Geth-

[a] Zc. 13:7.

New English Bible

covenant, shed for many. I tell you this: never again shall I drink from the fruit of the vine until that day when I drink it new in the kingdom of God.'

After singing the Passover Hymn, they went out to the Mount of Olives. And Jesus said, 'You will all fall from your faith; for it stands written: "I will strike the shepherd down and the sheep will be scattered." Nevertheless, after I am raised again I will go on before you into Galilee.' Peter answered, 'Everyone else may fall away, but I will not.' Jesus said, 'I tell you this: today, this very night, before the cock crows twice, you yourself will disown me three times.' But he insisted and repeated: 'Even if I must die with you, I will never disown you.' And they all said the same.

When they reached a place called Gethsemane,

King James Version

a place which was named Gethsemane: and he saith to his disciples, Sit ye here, while I shall pray. 33And he taketh with him Peter and James and John, and began to be sore amazed, and to be very heavy; 34And saith unto them, My soul is exceeding sorrowful unto death: tarry ye here, and watch. 35And he went forward a little, and fell on the ground, and prayed that, if it were possible, the hour might pass from him. 36And he said, Abba, Father, all things *are* possible unto thee; take away this cup from me: nevertheless, not what I will, but what thou wilt. 37And he cometh, and findeth them sleeping, and saith unto Peter, Simon, sleepest thou? couldest not thou watch one hour? 38 Watch ye and pray, lest ye enter into temptation. The spirit truly *is* ready, but the flesh *is* weak. 39And again he went away, and prayed, and spake the same words. 40And when he returned, he found them asleep again, (for their eyes were heavy,) neither wist they what to answer him. 41And he cometh the third time, and saith unto them, Sleep on now, and take *your* rest: it is enough, the hour is come; behold, the Son of man is betrayed into the hands of sinners. 42 Rise up, let us go; lo, he that betrayeth me is at hand.

Living Bible

called the Garden of Gethsemane, and he instructed his disciples, "Sit here, while I go and pray."

33 He took Peter, James and John with him and began to be filled with horror and deepest distress. 34And he said to them, "My soul is crushed by sorrow to the point of death; stay here and watch with me."

35 He went on a little further and fell to the ground and prayed that if it were possible the awful hour awaiting him might never come.[d]

36 "Father, Father," he said, "everything is possible for you. Take away this cup from me. Yet I want your will, not mine."

37 Then he returned to the three disciples and found them asleep.

"Simon!" he said. "Asleep? Couldn't you watch with me even one hour? 38 Watch with me and pray lest the Tempter overpower you. For though the spirit is willing enough, the body is weak."

39 And he went away again and prayed, repeating his pleadings. 40Again he returned to them and found them sleeping, for they were very tired. And they didn't know what to say.

41 The third time when he returned to them he said, "Sleep on; get your rest! But no! The time for sleep has ended! Look! I[e] am betrayed into the hands of wicked men. 42 Come! Get up! We must go! Look! My betrayer is here!"

[*d*] Literally, "that the hour might pass away from him." [*e*] Literally, "the Son of Man."

Today's English Version

and Jesus said to his disciples, "Sit here while I pray."

33 Then he took Peter, James, and John with him. Distress and anguish came over him, 34 and he said to them, "The sorrow in my heart is so great that it almost crushes me. Stay here and watch."

35 He went a little farther on, threw himself on the ground, and prayed that, if possible, he might not have to go through the hour of suffering. 36 "Father!" he prayed, "my Father! All things are possible for you. Take this cup away from me. But not what I want, but what you want."

37 Then he returned and found the three disciples asleep, and said to Peter, "Simon, are you asleep? Weren't you able to stay awake for one hour?" 38And he said to them, "Keep watch, and pray that you will not fall into temptation. The spirit is willing, but the flesh is weak."

39 He went away once more and prayed, saying the same words. 40 Then he came back to the disciples and found them asleep; they could not keep their eyes open. And they did not know what to say to him.

41 When he came back the third time, he said to them, "Are you still sleeping and resting? Enough! The hour has come! Look, the Son of Man is now handed over to the power of sinful men. 42 Get up, let us go. Look, here is the man who is betraying me!"

New International Version

and Jesus said to his disciples, "Sit here while I pray." 33 He took Peter, James and John along with him, and he began to be deeply distressed and troubled. 34 "My soul is overwhelmed with sorrow to point of death," he said to them. "Stay here and keep watch."

35 Going a little farther, he fell to the ground and prayed that if possible the hour might pass from him. 36 "*Abba,*[o] Father," he said, "everything is possible for you. Take this cup from me. Yet not what I will, but what you will."

37 Then he returned to his disciples and found them sleeping. "Simon," he said to Peter, "are you asleep? Could you not keep watch for one hour? 38 Watch and pray so that you will not fall into temptation. The spirit is willing, but the body is weak."

39 Once more he went away and prayed the same thing. 40 When he came back, he again found them sleeping, because their eyes were heavy. They did not know what to say to him.

41 Returning the third time, he said to them, "Are you still sleeping and resting? Enough! The hour has come. Look, the Son of Man is betrayed into the hands of sinners. 42 Rise! Let us go! Here comes my betrayer!"

[*o*] Aramaic for *Father*.

Phillips Modern English

ane, and Jesus said to his disciples,

"Sit down here while I pray."

He took with him Peter, James and John, and began to be horror-stricken and desperately depressed.

"My heart is breaking with a death-like grief," he told them.

"Stay here and keep watch."

Then he walked forward a little way and flung himself on the ground, praying that, if it were possible, the hour might pass him by.

"Dear Father," he said, "all things are possible to you. Let me not have to drink this cup! Yet it is not what I want but what you want."

Then he came and found them fast asleep. He spoke to Peter,

"Are you asleep, Simon? Couldn't you manage to stay awake for a single hour? Stay awake and pray, all of you, that you may not have to face temptation. Your spirit is willing, but human nature is weak."

Then he went away again and prayed in the same words, and once more he came and found them asleep. They could not keep their eyes open and they did not know what to say for themselves. When he came back for the third time, he said,

"Are you still going to sleep and take your ease? All right—the moment has come; now you will see the Son of Man betrayed into the hands of evil men! Get up, let us be going! Look, here comes my betrayer!"

Revised Standard Version

Gethsemane; and he said to his disciples, "Sit here, while I pray." 33And he took with him Peter and James and John, and began to be greatly distressed and troubled. 34And he said to them, "My soul is very sorrowful, even to death; remain here, and watch." [d] 35And going a little farther, he fell on the ground and prayed that, if it were possible, the hour might pass from him. 36And he said, "Abba, Father, all things are possible to thee; remove this cup from me; yet not what I will, but what thou wilt." 37And he came and found them sleeping, and he said to Peter, "Simon, are you asleep? Could you not watch[d] one hour? 38 Watch[d] and pray that you may not enter into temptation; the spirit indeed is willing, but the flesh is weak." 39And again he went away and prayed, saying the same words. 40And again he came and found them sleeping, for their eyes were very heavy; and they did not know what to answer him. 41And he came the third time, and said to them, "Are you still sleeping and taking your rest? It is enough; the hour has come; the Son of man is betrayed into the hands of sinners. 42 Rise, let us be going; see, my betrayer is at hand."

[d] Or *keep awake.*

Jerusalem Bible

semane, and Jesus said to his disciples, "Stay here while I pray." 33 Then he took Peter and James and John with him. And a sudden fear came over him, and great distress. 34And he said to them, "My soul is sorrowful to the point of death. Wait here, and keep awake." 35And going on a little further he threw himself on the ground and prayed that, if it were possible, this hour might pass him by. 36 "Abba (Father)!" he said. "Everything is possible for you. Take this cup away from me. But let it be as you, not I, would have it." 37 He came back and found them sleeping, and he said to Peter, "Simon, are you asleep? Had you not the strength to keep awake one hour? 38 You should be awake, and praying not to be put to the test. The spirit is willing, but the flesh is weak." 39Again he went away and prayed, saying the same words. 40And once more he came back and found them sleeping, their eyes were so heavy; and they could find no answer for him. 41 He came back a third time and said to them, "You can sleep on now and take your rest. It is all over. The hour has come. Now the Son of Man is to be betrayed into the hands of sinners. 42 Get up! Let us go! My betrayer is close at hand already."

New English Bible

he said to his disciples, 'Sit here while I pray.' And he took Peter and James and John with him. Horror and dismay came over him, and he said to them, 'My heart is ready to break with grief; stop here, and stay awake.' Then he went forward a little, threw himself on the ground, and prayed that, if it were possible, this hour might pass him by. 'Abba, Father,' he said, 'all things are possible to thee; take this cup away from me. Yet not what I will, but what thou wilt.'

He came back and found them asleep; and he said to Peter, 'Asleep, Simon? Were you not able to stay awake for one hour? Stay awake, all of you; and pray that you may be spared the test. The spirit is willing, but the flesh is weak.' Once more he went away and prayed.[a] On his return he found them asleep again, for their eyes were heavy; and they did not know how to answer him.

The third time he came and said to them, 'Still sleeping? Still taking your ease? Enough! [b] The hour has come. The Son of Man is betrayed to sinful men. Up, let us go forward! My betrayer is upon us.'

[a] *Some witnesses add* using the same words.
[b] *The Greek is obscure; a possible meaning is* 'The money has been paid', 'The account is settled.'

King James Version

43 And immediately, while he yet spake, cometh Judas, one of the twelve, and with him a great multitude with swords and staves, from the chief priests and the scribes and the elders. 44And he that betrayed him had given them a token, saying, Whomsoever I shall kiss, that same is he; take him, and lead *him* away safely. 45And as soon as he was come, he goeth straightway to him, and saith, Master, Master; and kissed him.

46 And they laid their hands on him, and took him. 47And one of them that stood by drew a sword, and smote a servant of the high priest, and cut off his ear. 48And Jesus answered and said unto them, Are ye come out, as against a thief, with swords and *with* staves to take me? 49 I was daily with you in the temple teaching, and ye took me not: but the Scriptures must be fulfilled. 50And they all forsook him, and fled. 51And there followed him a certain young man, having a linen cloth cast about *his* naked *body;* and the young men laid hold on him: 52And he left the linen cloth, and fled from them naked.

53 And they led Jesus away to the high priest: and with him were assembled all the chief priests and the elders and the scribes. 54And Peter followed him afar off, even into the palace of the high priest: and he sat with the servants, and

Living Bible

43 And immediately, while he was still speaking, Judas (one of his disciples) arrived with a mob equipped with swords and clubs, sent out by the chief priests and other Jewish leaders.

44 Judas had told them, "You will know which one to arrest when I go over and greet[f] him. Then you can take him easily." 45 So as soon as they arrived he walked up to Jesus. "Master!" he exclaimed, and embraced him with a great show of friendliness. 46 Then the mob arrested Jesus and held him fast. 47 But someone[g] pulled a sword and slashed at the High Priest's servant, cutting off his ear.

48 Jesus asked them, "Am I some dangerous robber, that you come like this, armed to the teeth to capture me? 49 Why didn't you arrest me in the Temple? I was there teaching every day. But these things are happening to fulfill the prophecies about me."

50 Meanwhile, all his disciples had fled. 51, 52 There was, however, a young man following along behind, clothed only in a linen nightshirt.[h] When the mob tried to grab him, he escaped, though his clothes were torn off in the process, so that he ran away completely naked.

53 Jesus was led to the High Priest's home where all of the chief priests and other Jewish leaders soon gathered. 54 Peter followed far behind and then slipped inside the gates of the High Priest's residence and crouched beside a fire among the servants.

[*f*] Literally, "kiss"—the usual oriental greeting, even to this day. [*g*] It was Peter. John 18:10. [*h*] Implied. Literally, "wearing only a linen cloth."

Today's English Version

The arrest of Jesus

43 Jesus was still speaking when Judas, one of the twelve disciples, arrived. With him was a crowd carrying swords and clubs, sent by the chief priests, the teachers of the Law, and the elders. 44 The traitor had given the crowd a signal: "The man I kiss is the one you want. Arrest him and take him away under guard."

45 As soon as Judas arrived he went up to Jesus and said, "Teacher!" and kissed him. 46 So they arrested Jesus and held him tight. 47 But one of those standing by drew his sword and struck at the High Priest's slave, cutting off his ear. 48 Then Jesus spoke up and said to them, "Did you have to come with swords and clubs to capture me, as though I were an outlaw? 49 Day after day I was with you teaching in the temple, and you did not arrest me. But the Scriptures must come true."

50 Then all the disciples left him and ran away.

51 A certain young man, dressed only in a linen cloth, was following Jesus. They tried to arrest him, 52 but he ran away naked, leaving the linen cloth behind.

Jesus before the Council

53 Then they took Jesus to the High Priest's house, where all the chief priests, the elders, and the teachers of the Law were gathering. 54 Peter followed from a distance and went into the courtyard of the High Priest's house. There he sat down with the guards, keeping himself warm by

New International Version

Jesus arrested

43 Just as he was speaking, Judas, one of the Twelve, appeared. With him was a crowd armed with swords and clubs, sent from the chief priests, the teachers of the law, and the elders.

44 Now the betrayer had arranged a signal with them: "The one I kiss is the man; arrest him and lead him away under guard." 45 Going at once to Jesus, Judas said, "Rabbi!" and kissed him. 46 The men seized Jesus and arrested him. 47 Then one of those standing near drew his sword and struck the servant of the high priest, cutting off his ear.

48 "Am I leading a rebellion," said Jesus, "that you have come out with swords and clubs to capture me? 49 Every day I was with you, teaching in the temple courts, and you did not arrest me. But the Scriptures must be fulfilled." 50 Then everyone deserted him and fled.

51 A young man, wearing nothing but a linen garment, was following Jesus. When they seized him, 52 he fled naked, leaving his garment behind.

Before the Sanhedrin

53 They took Jesus to the high priest, and all the chief priests, elders and teachers of the law came together. 54 Peter followed him at a distance, right into the courtyard of the high priest. There he sat with the guards and warmed himself at the fire.

Phillips Modern English

14.43 Judas betrays Jesus

And suddenly, while the words were still on his lips, Judas, one of the twelve, arrived with a mob armed with swords and staves, sent by the chief priests and scribes and elders. The betrayer had given them a sign; he had said, "The one I kiss will be the man. Get hold of him and you can take him away without any trouble." So he walked straight up to Jesus, cried, "Master!" and kissed him affectionately. And so they got hold of him and held him. Somebody present drew his sword and struck at the High Priest's servant, slashing off his ear. Then Jesus spoke to them,

"So you've come out with your swords and staves to capture me like a bandit, have you? Day after day I was with you in the Temple, teaching, and you never laid a finger on me. But the scriptures must be fulfilled."

Then all the disciples deserted him and made their escape. There happened to be a young man among Jesus' followers who wore nothing but a linen shirt. They seized him, but he left the shirt in their hands and took to his heels stark naked.

14.53 Jesus before the High Priest

So they marched Jesus away to the High Priest in whose presence all the chief priests and elders and scribes had assembled. (Peter followed him at a distance, right into the High Priest's courtyard. There he sat in the firelight with the serv-

Revised Standard Version

43 And immediately, while he was still speaking, Judas came, one of the twelve, and with him a crowd with swords and clubs, from the chief priests and the scribes and the elders. 44 Now the betrayer had given them a sign, saying, "The one I shall kiss is the man; seize him and lead him away under guard." 45 And when he came, he went up to him at once, and said, "Master!" [e] And he kissed him. 46 And they laid hands on him and seized him. 47 But one of those who stood by drew his sword, and struck the slave of the high priest and cut off his ear. 48 And Jesus said to them, "Have you come out as against a robber, with swords and clubs to capture me? 49 Day after day I was with you in the temple teaching, and you did not seize me. But let the scriptures be fulfilled." 50 And they all forsook him, and fled.

51 And a young man followed him, with nothing but a linen cloth about his body; and they seized him, 52 but he left the linen cloth and ran away naked.

53 And they led Jesus to the high priest; and all the chief priests and the elders and the scribes were assembled. 54 And Peter had followed him at a distance, right into the courtyard of the high priest; and he was sitting with the

[*e*] Or *Rabbi*.

Jerusalem Bible

The arrest

43 Even while he was still speaking, Judas, one of the Twelve, came up with a number of men armed with swords and clubs, sent by the chief priests and the scribes and the elders. 44 Now the traitor had arranged a signal with them. "The one I kiss," he had said, "he is the man. Take him in charge, and see he is well guarded when you lead him away." 45 So when the traitor came, he went straight up to Jesus and said, "Rabbi!" and kissed him. 46 The others seized him and took him in charge. 47 Then one of the bystanders drew his sword and struck out at the high priest's servant, and cut off his ear.

48 Then Jesus spoke. "Am I a brigand," he said, "that you had to set out to capture me with swords and clubs? 49 I was among you teaching in the Temple day after day and you never laid hands on me. But this is to fulfill the scriptures." 50 And they all deserted him and ran away. 51 A young man who followed him had nothing on but a linen cloth. They caught hold of him, 52 but he left the cloth in their hands and ran away naked.

Jesus before the Sanhedrin

53 They led Jesus off to the high priest; and all the chief priests and the elders and the scribes assembled there. 54 Peter had followed him at a distance, right into the high priest's palace, and was sitting with the attendants warming himself at the fire.

New English Bible

Suddenly, while he was still speaking, Judas, one of the Twelve, appeared, and with him was a crowd armed with swords and cudgels, sent by the chief priests, lawyers, and elders. Now the traitor had agreed with them upon a signal: 'The one I kiss is your man; seize him and get him safely away.' When he reached the spot, he stepped forward at once and said to Jesus, 'Rabbi', and kissed him. Then they seized him and held him fast.

One of the party[a] drew his sword, and struck at the High Priest's servant, cutting off his ear. Then Jesus spoke: 'Do you take me for a bandit, that you have come out with swords and cudgels to arrest me? Day after day I was within your reach as I taught in the temple, and you did not lay hands on me. But let the scriptures be fulfilled.' Then the disciples all deserted him and ran away.

Among those following was a young man with nothing on but a linen cloth. They tried to seize him; but he slipped out of the linen cloth and ran away naked.

Then they led Jesus away to the High Priest's house, where the chief priests, elders, and doctors of the law were all assembling. Peter followed him at a distance right into the High Priest's courtyard; and there he remained, sitting among the attendants, warming himself at the fire.

[*a*] *Or* of the bystanders.

King James Version

warmed himself at the fire. 55 And the chief priests and all the council sought for witness against Jesus to put him to death; and found none. 56 For many bare false witness against him, but their witness agreed not together. 57 And there arose certain, and bare false witness against him, saying, 58 We heard him say, I will destroy this temple that is made with hands, and within three days I will build another made without hands. 59 But neither so did their witness agree together. 60 And the high priest stood up in the midst, and asked Jesus, saying, Answerest thou nothing? what *is it which* these witness against thee? 61 But he held his peace, and answered nothing. Again the high priest asked him, and said unto him, Art thou the Christ, the Son of the Blessed? 62 And Jesus said, I am: and ye shall see the Son of man sitting on the right hand of power, and coming in the clouds of heaven. 63 Then the high priest rent his clothes, and saith, What need we any further witnesses? 64 Ye have heard the blasphemy: what think ye? And they all condemned him to be guilty of death. 65 And some began to spit on him, and to cover his face, and to buffet him, and to say unto him, Prophesy: and the servants did strike him with the palms of their hands.

Living Bible

55 Inside, the chief priests and the whole Jewish Supreme Court were trying to find something against Jesus that would be sufficient to condemn him to death. But their efforts were in vain. 56 Many false witnesses volunteered, but they contradicted each other.

57 Finally some men stood up to lie about him and said, 58 "We heard him say, 'I will destroy this Temple made with human hands and in three days I will build another, made without human hands!' " 59 But even then they didn't get their stories straight!

60 Then the High Priest stood up before the Court and asked Jesus, "Do you refuse to answer this charge? What do you have to say for yourself?"

61 To this Jesus made no reply.

Then the High Priest asked him. "Are you the Messiah, the Son of God?"

62 Jesus said, "I am, and you will see me[e] sitting at the right hand of God, and returning to earth in the clouds of heaven."

63, 64 Then the High Priest tore at his clothes and said, "What more do we need? Why wait for witnesses? You have heard his blasphemy. What is your verdict?" And the vote for the death sentence was unanimous.

65 Then some of them began to spit at him, and they blindfolded him and began to hammer his face with their fists.

"Who hit you that time, you prophet?" they jeered. And even the bailiffs were using their fists on him as they led him away.

[e] Literally, "the Son of Man."

Today's English Version

the fire. 55 The chief priests and the whole Council tried to find some evidence against Jesus, in order to put him to death; but they could not find any. 56 Many witnesses told lies against Jesus, but their stories did not agree.

57 Then some men stood up and told this lie against Jesus, 58 "We heard him say, 'I will tear down this temple which men made, and after three days I will build one that is not made by men.' " 59 Not even they, however, could make their stories agree.

60 The High Priest stood up in front of them all and questioned Jesus, "Have you no answer to the accusation they bring against you?"

61 But Jesus kept quiet and would not say a word. Again the High Priest questioned him, "Are you the Messiah, the Son of the Blessed God?"

62 "I am," answered Jesus, "and you will all see the Son of Man seated at the right side of the Almighty, and coming with the clouds of heaven!"

63 The High Priest tore his robes and said, "We don't need any more witnesses! 64 You heard his wicked words. What is your decision?"

They all voted against him: he was guilty and should be put to death.

65 Some of them began to spit on Jesus, and they blindfolded him and hit him. "Guess who hit you!" they said. And the guards took him and slapped him.

New International Version

55 The chief priests and the whole Sanhedrin were looking for evidence against Jesus so that they could put him to death, but they did not find any. 56 Many testified falsely against him, but their statements did not agree.

57 Then some stood up and gave this false testimony against him: 58 "We heard him say, 'I will destroy this man-made temple and in three days will build another, not made by man.' " 59 Yet even then their testimony did not agree.

60 Then the high priest stood up before them and asked Jesus, "Are you not going to answer? What is this testimony that these men are bringing against you?" 61 But Jesus remained silent and gave no answer.

Again the high priest asked him, "Are you the Christ,[p] the Son of the Blessed One?"

62 "I am," said Jesus. "And you will see the Son of Man sitting at the right hand of the Mighty One and coming on the clouds of heaven."

63 The high priest tore his clothes. "Why do we need any more witnesses?" he asked. 64 "You have heard the blasphemy. What do you think?"

They all condemned him as worthy of death. 65 Then some began to spit at him; they blindfolded him, struck him with their fists, and said, "Prophesy!" And the guards took him and beat him.

[p] Or *Messiah.*

Phillips Modern English

ants, keeping himself warm.) Meanwhile, the chief priests and the whole council were trying to find some evidence against Jesus which would warrant the death penalty. But they failed completely. There were plenty of people ready to give false testimony against him, but their evidence was contradictory. Then some more perjurers stood up and said,

"We heard him say, 'I will destroy this Temple that was built by human hands and in three days I will build another made without human aid.'"

But even so their evidence conflicted. So the High Priest himself got up and took the centre of the floor.

"Have you no answer to make?" he asked Jesus. "What about all this evidence against you?"

But Jesus remained silent and offered no reply. Again the High Priest asked him,

"Are you Christ, Son of the blessed one?"

And Jesus said,

"I am! Yes, you will see the Son of Man sitting at the right hand of power, coming in the clouds of heaven."

Then the High Priest tore his robes and cried, "Why do we still need witnesses? You heard the blasphemy; what is your opinion now?"

Their unanimous verdict was that he deserved to die. Then some of them began to spit at him. They blindfolded him and then smacked him, saying,

"Now prophesy who hit you!"

Even the servants who took him away slapped his face.

Revised Standard Version

guards, and warming himself at the fire. 55 Now
the chief priests and the whole council sought
testimony against Jesus to put him to death; but
they found none. 56 For many bore false witness
against him, and their witness did not agree.
57 And some stood up and bore false witness
against him, saying, 58 "We heard him say, 'I
will destroy this temple that is made with hands,
and in three days I will build another, not made
with hands.'" 59 Yet not even so did their testimony agree. 60 And the high priest stood up in
the midst, and asked Jesus, "Have you no answer to make? What is it that these men testify
against you?" 61 But he was silent and made no
answer. Again the high priest asked him, "Are
you the Christ, the Son of the Blessed?" 62 And
Jesus said, "I am; and you will see the Son of
man seated at the right hand of Power, and coming with the clouds of heaven." 63 And the high
priest tore his garments, and said, "Why do we
still need witnesses? 64 You have heard his
blasphemy. What is your decision?" And they all
condemned him as deserving death. 65 And some
began to spit on him, and to cover his face, and
to strike him, saying to him, "Prophesy!" And
the guards received him with blows.

Jerusalem Bible

55 The chief priests and the whole Sanhedrin were
looking for evidence against Jesus on which they
might pass the death sentence. But they could not
find any. 56 Several, indeed, brought false evidence
against him, but their evidence was conflicting.
57 Some stood up and submitted this false evidence
against him, 58 "We heard him say, 'I am going to
destroy this Temple made by human hands, and in
three days build another, not made by human
hands.'" 59 But even on this point their evidence
was conflicting. 60 The high priest then stood up
before the whole assembly and put this question to
Jesus, "Have you no answer to that? What is this
evidence these men are bringing against you?"
61 But he was silent and made no answer at all. The
high priest put a second question to him, "Are you
the Christ," he said, "the Son of the Blessed One?"
62 "I am," said Jesus, "and you will see *the son of
Man seated at the right hand of the Power and coming with the clouds of heaven*." [b] 63 The high priest
tore his robes, "What need of witnesses have we
now?" he said. 64 "You heard the blasphemy. What
is your finding?" And they all gave their verdict: he
deserved to die.
65 Some of them started spitting at him and,
blindfolding him, began hitting him with their fists
and shouting, "Play the prophet!" And the attendants rained blows on him.

[b] Dn. 7:13; Ps. 110:1.

New English Bible

The chief priests and the whole Council tried to find some evidence against Jesus to warrant a death-sentence, but failed to find any. Many gave false evidence against him, but their statements did not tally. Some stood up and gave false evidence against him to this effect: 'We heard him say, "I will pull down this temple, made with human hands, and in three days I will build another, not made with hands."' But even on this point their evidence did not agree.

Then the High Priest stood up in his place and questioned Jesus: 'Have you no answer to the charges that these witnesses bring against you?' But he kept silence; he made no reply.

Again the High Priest questioned him: 'Are you the Messiah, the Son of the Blessed One?' Jesus said, 'I am; and you will see the Son of Man seated at the right hand of God [b] and coming with the clouds of heaven.' Then the High Priest tore his robes and said, 'Need we call further witnesses? You have heard the blasphemy. What is your opinion?' Their judgement was unanimous: that he was guilty and should be put to death.

Some began to spit on him, blindfolded him, and struck him with their fists, crying out, 'Prophesy!' [c] And the High Priest's men set upon him with blows.

[b] *Literally* of the Power. [c] *Some witnesses add* Who hit you? *as in Matthew and Luke.*

King James Version

66 And as Peter was beneath in the palace,
there cometh one of the maids of the high priest:
67And when she saw Peter warming himself, she
looked upon him, and said, And thou also wast
with Jesus of Nazareth. 68 But he denied, saying,
I know not, neither understand I what thou sayest. And he went out into the porch; and the
cock crew. 69And a maid saw him again, and
began to say to them that stood by, This is *one*
of them. 70And he denied it again. And a little
after, they that stood by said again to Peter,
Surely thou art *one* of them: for thou art a
Galilean, and thy speech agreeth *thereto.* 71 But
he began to curse and to swear, *saying,* I know
not this man of whom ye speak. 72And the
second time the cock crew. And Peter called to
mind the word that Jesus said unto him, Before
the cock crow twice, thou shalt deny me thrice.
And when he thought thereon, he wept.

Living Bible

66, 67 Meanwhile Peter was below in the courtyard. One of the maids who worked for the High Priest noticed Peter warming himself at the fire.

She looked at him closely and then announced, "*You* were with Jesus, the Nazarene."

68 Peter denied it. "I don't know what you're talking about!" he said, and walked over to the edge of the courtyard.

Just then, a rooster crowed.[i]

69 The maid saw him standing there and began telling the others, "There he is! There's that disciple of Jesus!"

70 Peter denied it again.

A little later others standing around the fire began saying to Peter, "You are, too, one of them, for you are from Galilee!"

71 He began to curse and swear. "I don't even know this fellow you are talking about," he said.

73 And immediately the rooster crowed the second time. Suddenly Jesus' words flashed through Peter's mind: "Before the cock crows twice, you will deny me three times." And he began to cry.

[*i*] This statement is found in only some of the manuscripts.

Today's English Version

Peter denies Jesus

66 Peter was still down in the courtyard when
one of the High Priest's servant girls came by.
67 When she saw Peter warming himself, she
looked straight at him and said, "You, too, were
with Jesus of Nazareth."

68 But he denied it. "I don't know . . . I don't understand what you are talking about," he answered, and went out into the passageway; just then a rooster crowed.

69 The servant girl saw him there and began
to repeat to the bystanders, "He is one of them!"
70 But Peter denied it again.

A little while later the bystanders accused Peter again, "You can't deny that you are one of them, because you, too, are from Galilee."

71 Then Peter made a vow: "May God punish me if I am not telling the truth! I do not know the man you are talking about!"

72 Just then a rooster crowed a second time, and Peter remembered how Jesus had said to him, "Before the rooster crows two times you will say three times that you do not know me." And he broke down and cried.

New International Version

Peter disowns Jesus

66 While Peter was below in the courtyard,
one of the servant girls of the high priest came
by. 67 When she saw Peter warming himself, she
looked closely at him.

"You also were with that Nazarene, Jesus," she said.

68 But he denied it. "I don't know or understand what you're talking about," he said, and went out into the entryway.[q]

69 When the servant girl saw him there, she
said again to those standing around, "This fellow
is one of them." 70Again he denied it.

After a little while, those standing near said to Peter, "Surely you are one of them, for you are a Galilean."

71 He began to call down curses on himself, and he swore to them, "I don't know this man you're talking about."

72 Immediately the rooster crowed the second time.[r] Then Peter remembered the word Jesus had spoken to him: "Before the rooster crows twice,[s] you will disown me three times." And he broke down and wept.

[*q*] Some early MSS add *and the rooster crowed.* [*r*] Some early MSS omit *the second time.* [*s*] Some early MSS omit *twice.*

Phillips Modern English

14.66 Peter, in fear, disowns his master

In the meantime, while Peter was in the courtyard below, one of the High Priest's maids came and saw him warming himself. She looked closely at him, and said,

"You were with the Nazarene too—with Jesus!"

But he denied it, saying,

"I neither know nor understand what you're talking about."

And he walked out into the gateway, and a cock crew.

Then the maid who had noticed him began to say again to the men standing there,

"This man is one of them!"

But he denied it again. A few minutes later the bystanders themselves said to Peter,

"You certainly are one of them. Why, you're a Galilean!"

But he started to curse and swear, saying,

"I tell you I don't know the man you're talking about!"

Immediately the cock crew for the second time, and back into Peter's mind came the words of Jesus, "Before the cock crows twice, you will disown me three times."

And as the truth broke upon him he burst into tears.

Revised Standard Version

66 And as Peter was below in the courtyard,
one of the maids of the high priest came; 67 and
seeing Peter warming himself, she looked at him,
and said, "You also were with the Nazarene,
Jesus." 68 But he denied it, saying, "I neither
know nor understand what you mean." And he
went out into the gateway.[f] 69And the maid
saw him, and began again to say to the bystanders, "This man is one of them." 70 But again
he denied it. And after a little while again the
bystanders said to Peter, "Certainly you are one
of them; for you are a Galilean." 71 But he began to invoke a curse on himself and to swear,
"I do not know this man of whom you speak."
72And immediately the cock crowed a second
time. And Peter remembered how Jesus had
said to him, "Before the cock crows twice, you
will deny me three times." And he broke down
and wept.

[f] Or *fore-court.* Other ancient authorities add *and the cock crowed.*

Jerusalem Bible

Peter's denials

66 While Peter was down below in the courtyard, one of the high priest's servant girls came
up. 67 She saw Peter warming himself there,
stared at him and said, "You too were with
Jesus, the man from Nazareth." 68 But he denied it. "I do not know, I do not understand,
what you are talking about," he said. And he
went out into the forecourt. 69 The servant girl
saw him and again started telling the bystanders, "This fellow is one of them." 70 But again
he denied it. A little later the bystanders themselves said to Peter, "You are one of them for
sure! Why, you are a Galilean." 71 But he started
calling down curses on himself and swearing,
"I do not know the man you speak of." 72At
that moment the cock crew for the second time,
and Peter recalled how Jesus had said to him,
"Before the cock crows twice, you will have
disowned me three times." And he burst into
tears.

New English Bible

Meanwhile Peter was still below in the courtyard. One of the High Priest's serving-maids came by and saw him there warming himself. She looked into his face and said, 'You were there too, with this man from Nazareth, this Jesus.' But he denied it: 'I know nothing,' he said; 'I do not understand what you mean.' Then he went outside into the porch;[d] and the maid saw him there again and began to say to the bystanders, 'He is one of them'; and again he denied it.

Again, a little later, the bystanders said to Peter, 'Surely you are one of them. You must be; you are a Galilean.' At this he broke out into curses, and with an oath he said, 'I do not know this man you speak of.' Then the cock crew a second time; and Peter remembered how Jesus had said to him, 'Before the cock crows twice you will disown me three times.' And he burst into tears.

[d] *Some witnesses insert* and a cock crew.

King James Version

15 And straightway in the morning the chief
priests held a consultation with the elders
and scribes and the whole council, and bound
Jesus, and carried *him* away, and delivered *him*
to Pilate. 2 And Pilate asked him, Art thou the
King of the Jews? And he answering said unto
him, Thou sayest *it.* 3 And the chief priests accused him of many things; but he answered
nothing. 4 And Pilate asked him again, saying,
Answerest thou nothing? behold how many things
they witness against thee. 5 But Jesus yet answered nothing; so that Pilate marvelled. 6 Now
at *that* feast he released unto them one prisoner,
whomsoever they desired. 7 And there was *one*
named Barabbas, *which lay* bound with them
that had made insurrection with him, who had
committed murder in the insurrection. 8 And the
multitude crying aloud began to desire *him to*
do as he had ever done unto them. 9 But Pilate
answered them, saying, Will ye that I release
unto you the King of the Jews? 10 For he knew
that the chief priests had delivered him for envy.
11 But the chief priests moved the people, that
he should rather release Barabbas unto them.
12 And Pilate answered and said again unto them,
What will ye then that I shall do *unto him* whom

Living Bible

15 Early in the morning the chief priests,
elders and teachers of religion—the entire
Supreme Court—met to discuss their next steps.
Their decision was to send Jesus under armed
guard to Pilate, the Roman governor.[a]
2 Pilate asked him, "Are you the King of the
Jews?"
"Yes," Jesus replied, "it is as you say."
3, 4 Then the chief priests accused him of
many crimes, and Pilate asked him, "Why don't
you say something? What about all these charges
against you?"
5 But Jesus said no more, much to Pilate's
amazement.
6 Now, it was Pilate's custom to release one
Jewish prisoner each year at Passover time—
any prisoner the people requested. 7 One of the
prisoners at that time was Barabbas, convicted
along with others for murder during an insurrection.
8 Now a mob began to crowd in toward
Pilate, asking him to release a prisoner as usual.
9 "How about giving you the 'King of Jews'?"
Pilate asked. "Is he the one you want released?"
10 (For he realized by now that this was a
frameup, backed by the chief priests because
they envied Jesus' popularity.)
11 But at this point the chief priests whipped
up the mob to demand the release of Barabbas
instead of Jesus.
12 "But if I release Barabbas," Pilate asked
them, "what shall I do with this man you call
your king?"

[*a*] Implied.

Today's English Version

Jesus before Pilate

15 Early in the morning the chief priests met
hurriedly with the elders, the teachers of
the Law, and the whole Council, and made their
plans. They put Jesus in chains, took him away,
and handed him over to Pilate. 2 Pilate questioned him, "Are you the king of the Jews?"
Jesus answered, "So you say."
3 The chief priests accused Jesus of many
things, 4 so Pilate questioned him again, "Aren't
you going to answer? See how many things they
accuse you of!"
5 Again Jesus refused to say a word, and
Pilate was filled with surprise.

Jesus sentenced to death

6 At every Passover Feast Pilate would set
free any prisoner the people asked for. 7 At that
time a man named Barabbas was in prison with
the rebels who had committed murder in the
riot. 8 When the crowd gathered and began to
ask Pilate for the usual favor, 9 he asked them,
"Do you want me to set free for you the king of
the Jews?" 10 He knew very well that the chief
priests had handed Jesus over to him because
they were jealous.
11 But the chief priests stirred up the crowd
to ask, instead, for Pilate to set Barabbas free
for them. 12 Pilate spoke again to the crowd,
"What, then, do you want me to do with the
one you call the king of the Jews?"

New International Version

Jesus before Pilate

15 Very early in the morning, the chief
priests, with the elders, the teachers of the
law and the whole Sanhedrin, reached a decision. They bound Jesus, led him away and
handed him over to Pilate.
2 "Are you the king of the Jews?" asked Pilate.
"Yes, it is as you say," Jesus replied.
3 The chief priests accused him of many
things. 4 So again Pilate asked him, "Aren't you
going to answer? See how many things they are
accusing you of."
5 But Jesus still made no reply, and Pilate
was amazed.
6 Now it was the custom at the Feast to release a prisoner whom the people requested. 7 A
man called Barabbas was in prison with the in-
surrectionists who had committed murder in the
uprising. 8 The crowd came up and asked Pilate
to do for them what he usually did.
9 "Do you want me to release to you the king
of the Jews?" asked Pilate, 10 knowing it was
out of envy that the chief priests had handed
Jesus over to him. 11 But the chief priests
stirred up the crowd to have Pilate release Barabbas instead.
12 "What shall I do, then, with the one you
call the king of the Jews?" Pilate asked them.

Phillips Modern English

15.1 Jesus before Pilate

The moment daylight came the chief priests called together a meeting of elders, scribes and the whole council. They bound Jesus and took him off and handed him over to Pilate. Pilate asked him straight out,

"Well, you—*are* you the king of the Jews?"

"You say that I am," he replied.

The chief priests brought many accusations. So Pilate questioned him again,

"Have you nothing to say? Listen to all their accusations!"

But Jesus made no further answer—to Pilate's astonishment.

Now it was Pilate's custom at festival-time to release a prisoner—anyone they asked for. There was in the prison at the time, with some other rioters who had committed murder in a recent revolt, a man called Barabbas. The crowd surged forward and began to demand that Pilate should do what he usually did for them. So he spoke to them,

"Do you want me to set free the king of the Jews for you?"

For he knew perfectly well that the chief priests had handed Jesus over to him through sheer malice. But the chief priests worked upon the crowd to get them to release Barabbas rather than Jesus. So Pilate addressed them once more,

"Then what am I to do with the man whom you call the king of the Jews?"

Revised Standard Version

15 And as soon as it was morning the chief
priests, with the elders and scribes, and
the whole council held a consultation; and they
bound Jesus and led him away and delivered
him to Pilate. 2And Pilate asked him, "Are you
the King of the Jews?" And he answered him,
"You have said so." 3And the chief priests accused him of many things. 4And Pilate again
asked him, "Have you no answer to make? See
how many charges they bring against you." 5 But
Jesus made no further answer, so that Pilate
wondered.
6 Now at the feast he used to release for them
one prisoner for whom they asked. 7And among
the rebels in prison, who had committed murder
in the insurrection, there was a man called
Barabbas. 8And the crowd came up and began
to ask Pilate to do as he was wont to do for
them. 9And he answered them, "Do you want
me to release for you the King of the Jews?"
10 For he perceived that it was out of envy that
the chief priests had delivered him up. 11 But
the chief priests stirred up the crowd to have
him release for them Barabbas instead. 12And
Pilate again said to them, "Then what shall I do
with the man whom you call the King of the

Jerusalem Bible

Jesus before Pilate

15 First thing in the morning, the chief priest
together with the elders and scribes, in
short the whole Sanhedrin, had their plan ready.
They had Jesus bound and took him away and
handed him over to Pilate.
2 Pilate questioned him, "Are you the king
of the Jews?" "It is you who say it," he answered. 3And the chief priests brought many
accusations against him. 4 Pilate questioned him
again, "Have you no reply at all? See how many
accusations they are bringing against you!" 5 But,
to Pilate's amazement, Jesus made no further
reply.
6 At festival time Pilate used to release a
prisoner for them, anyone they asked for. 7 Now
a man called Barabbas was then in prison with
the rioters who had committed murder during
the uprising. 8 When the crowd went up and began to ask Pilate the customary favor, 9 Pilate
answered them, "Do you want me to release for
you the king of the Jews?" 10 For he realized it
was out of jealousy that the chief priests had
handed Jesus over. 11 The chief priests, however,
had incited the crowd to demand that he should
release Barabbas for them instead. 12 Then Pilate
spoke again. "But in that case," he said to them,
"what am I to do with the 13 man you call king

New English Bible

15 As soon as morning came, the chief priests, having made their plan with the elders and lawyers in full council, put Jesus in chains; then they led him away and handed him over to Pilate. Pilate asked him, 'Are you the king of the Jews?' He replied, 'The words are yours.' [a] And the chief priests brought many charges against him. Pilate questioned him again: 'Have you nothing to say in your defence? You see how many charges they are bringing against you.' But, to Pilate's astonishment, Jesus made no further reply.

At the festival season the Governor used to release one prisoner at the people's request. As it happened, the man known as Barabbas was then in custody with the rebels who had committed murder in the rising. When the crowd appeared [b] asking for the usual favour, Pilate replied, 'Do you wish me to release for you the king of the Jews?' For he knew it was out of malice that they had brought Jesus before him. But the chief priests incited the crowd to ask him to release Barabbas rather than Jesus. Pilate spoke to them again: 'Then what shall I do with

[a] *Or* It is as you say. [b] *Some witnesses read* shouted.

King James Version

ye call the King of the Jews? 13And they cried out again, Crucify him. 14 Then Pilate said unto them, Why, what evil hath he done? And they cried out the more exceedingly, Crucify him.

15 And *so* Pilate, willing to content the people, released Barabbas unto them, and delivered Jesus, when he had scourged *him*, to be crucified. 16And the soldiers led him away into the hall, called Pretorium; and they call together the whole band. 17And they clothed him with purple, and platted a crown of thorns, and put it about his *head*, 18And began to salute him, Hail, King of the Jews! 19And they smote him on the head with a reed, and did spit upon him, and bowing *their* knees worshipped him. 20And when they had mocked him, they took off the purple from him, and put his own clothes on him, and led him out to crucify him. 21And they compel one Simon a Cyrenian, who passed by, coming out of the country, the father of

Living Bible

13 They shouted back, "Crucify him!"

14 "But why?" Pilate demanded. "What has he done wrong?" They only roared the louder, "Crucify him!"

15 Then Pilate, afraid of a riot and anxious to please the people, released Barabbas to them. And he ordered Jesus flogged with a leaded whip, and handed him over to be crucified.

16, 17 Then the Roman soldiers took him into the barracks of the palace, called out the entire palace guard, dressed him in a purple robe, and made a crown of long, sharp thorns and put it on his head. 18 Then they saluted, yelling, "Yea! King of the Jews!" 19And they beat him on the head with a cane, and spit on him and went down on their knees to "worship" him.

20 When they finally tired of their sport, they took off the purple robe and put his own clothes on him again, and led him away to be crucified.

21 Simon of Cyrene, who was coming in from the country just then, was pressed into service to carry Jesus' cross. (Simon is the father of Alexander and Rufus.)

Today's English Version

13 They shouted back, "Nail him to the cross!"

14 "But what crime has he committed?" Pilate asked.

They shouted all the louder, "Nail him to the cross!"

15 Pilate wanted to please the crowd, so he set Barabbas free for them. Then he had Jesus whipped and handed him over to be nailed to the cross.

The soldiers make fun of Jesus

16 The soldiers took Jesus inside the courtyard (that is, of the governor's palace) and called together the rest of the company. 17 They put a purple robe on Jesus, made a crown out of thorny branches, and put it on his head. 18 Then they began to salute him: "Long live the King of the Jews!" 19 They beat him over the head with a stick, spat on him, fell on their knees, and bowed down to him. 20 When they had finished making fun of him, they took off the purple robe and put his own clothes back on him. Then they led him out to nail him to the cross.

Jesus nailed to the cross

21 On the way they met a man named Simon, who was coming into the city from the country, and they forced him to carry Jesus' cross. (This was Simon from Cyrene, the father of Alex-

New International Version

13 "Crucify him!" they shouted.

14 "Why? What crime has he committed?" asked Pilate.

But they shouted all the louder, "Crucify him!"

15 Wanting to satisfy the crowd, Pilate released Barabbas to them. He had Jesus flogged, and handed him over to be crucified.

The soldiers mock Jesus

16 The soldiers led Jesus away into the palace (that is, the Praetorium) and called together the whole company of soldiers. 17 They put a purple robe on him, then wove a crown of thorns and set it on him. 18And they began to call out to him, "Hail, King of the Jews!" 19Again and again they struck him on the head with a staff and spit on him. Falling on their knees, they worshiped him. 20And when they had mocked him, they took off the purple robe and put his own clothes on him. Then they led him out to crucify him.

The crucifixion

21 A certain man from Cyrene, Simon, the father of Alexander and Rufus, was passing by on his way in from the country, and they forced

Phillips Modern English

They shouted back,
"Crucify him!"
But Pilate replied,
"Why, what crime has he committed?"
But their voices rose to a roar,
"Crucify him!"

And as Pilate wanted to satisfy the crowd, he set Barabbas free for them, and after having Jesus flogged handed him over to be crucified.

Then the soldiers marched him away inside the courtyard of the governor's residence and called their whole company together. They dressed Jesus in a purple robe, and twisting some thorn-twigs into a crown, they put it on his head. Then they began to salute him,

"Hail, your majesty—king of the Jews!"

They hit him on the head with a stick and spat at him, and then bowed low before him on bended knee. And when they had finished their fun with him, they took off the purple cloak and dressed him again in his own clothes. Then they led him outside to crucify him. They compelled Simon, a native of Cyrene in Africa (the father of Alexander and Rufus), who was on his way from the fields at the time, to carry Jesus' cross.

Revised Standard Version

Jews?" 13 And they cried out again, "Crucify
him." 14 And Pilate said to them, "Why, what
evil has he done?" But they shouted all the more,
"Crucify him." 15 So Pilate, wishing to satisfy the
crowd, released for them Barabbas; and having scourged Jesus, he delivered him to be crucified.
16 And the soldiers led him away inside the
palace (that is, the praetorium); and they called
together the whole battalion. 17 And they clothed
him in a purple cloak, and plaiting a crown of
thorns they put it on him. 18 And they began to
salute him, "Hail, King of the Jews!" 19 And
they struck his head with a reed, and spat upon
him, and they knelt down in homage to him.
20 And when they had mocked him, they stripped
him of the purple cloak, and put his own clothes
on him. And they led him out to crucify him.
21 And they compelled a passer-by, Simon of
Cyrene, who was coming in from the country,
the father of Alexander and Rufus, to carry his

Jerusalem Bible

of the Jews?" They shouted back, "Crucify him!"
14 "Why?" Pilate asked them. "What harm has
he done?" But they shouted all the louder,
"Crucify him!" 15 So Pilate, anxious to placate
the crowd, released Barabbas for them and, having ordered Jesus to be scourged, handed him
over to be crucified.

Jesus crowned with thorns

16 The soldiers led him away to the inner part
of the palace, that is, the Praetorium, and called
the whole cohort together. 17 They dressed him
up in purple, twisted some thorns into a crown
and put it on him. 18 And they began saluting
him, "Hail, king of the Jews!" 19 They struck
his head with a reed and spat on him; and they
went down on their knees to do him homage.
20 And when they had finished making fun of
him, they took off the purple and dressed him
in his own clothes.

The way of the cross

They led him out to crucify him. 21 They enlisted a passer-by, Simon of Cyrene, father of
Alexander and Rufus,[c] who was coming in from

[c] Alexander and Rufus were doubtless known to the Roman circle in which Mark wrote his gospel. Cf. Rm. 16:13.

New English Bible

the man you call king of the Jews?' They shouted back, 'Crucify him!' 'Why, what harm has he done?' Pilate asked; but they shouted all the louder, 'Crucify him!' So Pilate, in his desire to satisfy the mob, released Barabbas to them; and he had Jesus flogged and handed him over to be crucified.

Then the soldiers took him inside the courtyard (the Governor's headquarters[c]) and called together the whole company. They dressed him in purple, and plaiting a crown of thorns, placed it on his head. Then they began to salute him with, 'Hail, King of the Jews!' They beat him about the head with a cane and spat upon him, and then knelt and paid mock homage to him. When they had finished their mockery, they stripped him of the purple and dressed him in his own clothes.

Then they took him out to crucify him. A man called Simon, from Cyrene, the father of Alexander and Rufus, was passing by on his way in from the country, and they pressed him into service to carry his cross.

[c] *Greek* praetorium.

King James Version

Alexander and Rufus, to bear his cross. 22And
they bring him unto the place Golgotha, which
is, being interpreted, The place of a skull. 23And
they gave him to drink wine mingled with myrrh:
but he received *it* not. 24And when they had
crucified him, they parted his garments, casting
lots upon them, what every man should take.
25And it was the third hour, and they crucified
him. 26And the superscription of his accusation
was written over, THE KING OF THE JEWS.
27And with him they crucify two thieves; the
one on his right hand, and the other on his left.
28And the Scripture was fulfilled, which saith,
And he was numbered with the transgressors.
29And they that passed by railed on him, wagging
their heads, and saying, Ah, thou that destroyest
the temple, and buildest *it* in three days, 30 Save
thyself, and come down from the cross. 31 Likewise also the chief priests mocking said among
themselves with the scribes, He saved others;
himself he cannot save. 32 Let Christ the King
of Israel descend now from the cross, that we
may see and believe. And they that were cruci-

Living Bible

22 And they brought Jesus to a place called
Golgotha. (Golgotha means skull.) 23 Wine
drugged with bitter herbs was offered to him
there, but he refused it. 24And then they crucified
him—and threw dice for his clothes.

25 It was about nine o'clock in the morning
when the crucifixion took place.

26 A signboard was fastened to the cross
above his head, announcing his crime. It read,
"The King of the Jews."

27 Two robbers were also crucified that morning, their crosses on either side of his. 28 [b]And
so the Scripture was fulfilled that said, "He was
counted among evil men."

29, 30 The people jeered at him as they
walked by, and wagged their heads in mockery.
"Ha! Look at you now!" they yelled at him.
"Sure, you can destroy the Temple and rebuild
it in three days! If you're so wonderful, save
yourself and come down from the cross."

31 The chief priests and religious leaders were
also standing around joking about Jesus.

"He's quite clever at 'saving' others," they
said, "but he can't save himself!"

32 "Hey there, Messiah!" they yelled at him.
"You 'King of Israel'! Come on down from the
cross and we'll believe you!"

And even the two robbers dying with him,
cursed him.

[*b*] Verse 28 is omitted in some of the ancient manuscripts. The quotation is from Isaiah 53:12.

Today's English Version

ander and Rufus.) 22 They brought Jesus to a
place called Golgotha, which means "The Place
of the Skull." 23 There they tried to give him
wine mixed with a drug called myrrh, but Jesus
would not drink it. 24 So they nailed him to the
cross and divided his clothes among themselves,
throwing dice to see who would get which piece
of clothing. 25 It was nine o'clock in the morning when they nailed him to the cross. 26 The
notice of the accusation against him was written,
"The King of the Jews." 27 They also nailed two
bandits to crosses with Jesus, one on his right
and the other on his left. [28 In this way the
scripture came true which says, "He was included
with criminals."]

29 People passing by shook their heads and
hurled insults at Jesus: "Aha! You were going to
tear down the temple and build it up in three
days! 30 Now come down from the cross and save
yourself!"

31 In the same way the chief priests and the
teachers of the Law made fun of Jesus, saying to
each other, "He saved others, but he cannot save
himself! 32 Let us see the Messiah, the king of
Israel, come down from the cross now, and we
will believe in him!"

And the two who were crucified with Jesus insulted him also.

New International Version

him to carry the cross. 22 They brought Jesus
to the place called Golgotha (which means, The
Place of the Skull). 23 Then they offered him
wine mixed with myrrh, but he did not take it.
24And they crucified him. Dividing up his
clothes, they cast lots to see what each would
get.

25 It was the third hour when they crucified
him. 26 The written notice of the charge against
him read: THE KING OF THE JEWS. 27 They crucified two robbers with him, one on his right and
one on his left.[t] 29 Those who passed by hurled
insults at him, shaking their heads and saying,
"So! You who are going to destroy the temple
and build it in three days, 30 come down from
the cross and save yourself!"

31 In the same way the chief priests and the
teachers of the law mocked him among themselves. "He saved others," they said, "but he
can't save himself! 32 Let this Christ,[u] this King
of Israel, come down now from the cross, that
we may see and believe." Those crucified with
him also heaped insults on him.

[*t*] Some MSS add verse 28: ***and the scripture was fulfilled which says, "He was counted with the lawless ones."*** (Isaiah 53:12). [*u*] Or ***Messiah.***

Phillips Modern English

15.22 The crucifixion

They took him to a place called Golgotha (which means Skull Hill) and they offered him some drugged wine, but he would not take it. Then they crucified him, and shared out his garments, drawing lots to see what each of them would get. It was nine o'clock in the morning when they nailed him to the cross. Over his head the placard of his crime read, "THE KING OF THE JEWS." They also crucified two bandits at the same time, one on each side of him. And the passers-by jeered at him, shaking their heads in mockery, saying,

"Hi, you! You could destroy the Temple and build it up again in three days, why not come down from the cross and save yourself?"

The chief priests also made fun of him among themselves and the scribes, and said,

"He saved others, he cannot save himself. If only this Christ, the king of Israel, would come down now from the cross, we should see it and believe!"

And even the men who were crucified with him hurled abuse at him.

Revised Standard Version

cross. 22And they brought him to the place
called Golgotha (which means the place of a
skull). 23And they offered him wine mingled
with myrrh; but he did not take it. 24And they
crucified him, and divided his garments among
them, casting lots for them, to decide what each
should take. 25And it was the third hour, when
they crucified him. 26And the inscription of the
charge against him read, "The King of the
Jews." 27And with him they crucified two robbers, one on his right and one on his left.[g]
29And those who passed by derided him, wagging their heads, and saying, "Aha! You who
would destroy the temple and build it in three
days, 30 save yourself, and come down from the
cross!" 31 So also the chief priests mocked him
to one another with the scribes, saying, "He
saved others; he cannot save himself. 32 Let the
Christ, the King of Israel, come down now from
the cross, that we may see and believe." Those
who were crucified with him also reviled him.

[g] Other ancient authorities insert verse 28, *And the scripture was fulfilled which says, "He was reckoned with the transgressors."*

Jerusalem Bible

the country, to carry his cross. 22 They brought
Jesus to the place called Golgotha, which means
the place of the skull.

The crucifixion

23 They offered him wine mixed with myrrh,
but he refused it. 24 Then they crucified him, and
shared out his clothing, casting lots to decide
what each should get. 25 It was the third hour[d]
when they crucified him. 26 The inscription giving the charge against him read: "The King of
the Jews." 27And they crucified two robbers with
him, one on his right and one on his left.[e]

The crucified Christ is mocked

29 The passers-by jeered at him; they shook
their heads and said, "Aha! So you would destroy the Temple and rebuild it in three days!
30 Then save yourself: come down from the
cross!" 31 The chief priests and the scribes
mocked him among themselves in the same way.
"He saved others," they said, "he cannot save
himself. 32 Let the Christ, the king of Israel,
come down from the cross now, for us to see it
and believe." Even those who were crucified
with him taunted him.

[*d*] 9 A.M. [*e*] Add v. 28 "And the text of scripture was fulfilled that says: He was taken for a criminal (Is. 53:12). Cf. Lk. 22:37.

New English Bible

They brought him to the place called Golgotha, which means 'Place of a skull'. He was offered drugged wine, but he would not take it. Then they fastened him to the cross. They divided his clothes among them, casting lots to decide what each should have.

The hour of the crucifixion was nine in the morning, and the inscription giving the charge against him read, 'The king of the Jews.' Two bandits were crucified with him, one on his right and the other on his left.[a]

The passers-by hurled abuse at him: 'Aha!' they cried, wagging their heads, 'you would pull the temple down, would you, and build it in three days? Come down from the cross and save yourself!' So too the chief priests and lawyers jested with one another: 'He saved others,' they said, 'but he cannot save himself. Let the Messiah, the king of Israel, come down now from the cross. If we see that, we shall believe.' Even those who were crucified with him taunted him.

[*a*] *Some witnesses add* (28) Thus that text of Scripture came true which says, 'He was reckoned among criminals.'

King James Version

fied with him reviled him. 33And when the sixth hour was come, there was darkness over the whole land until the ninth hour. 34And at the ninth hour Jesus cried with a loud voice, saying, Eloi, Eloi, lama sabachthani? which is, being interpreted, My God, my God, why hast thou forsaken me? 35And some of them that stood by, when they heard *it*, said, Behold, he calleth Elias. 36And one ran and filled a sponge full of vinegar, and put *it* on a reed, and gave him to drink, saying, Let alone; let us see whether Elias will come to take him down. 37And Jesus cried with a loud voice, and gave up the ghost. 38And the vail of the temple was rent in twain from the top to the bottom.

39 And when the centurion, which stood over against him, saw that he so cried out, and gave up the ghost, he said, Truly this man was the Son of God. 40 There were also women looking on afar off: among whom was Mary Magdalene, and Mary the mother of James the less and of Joses, and Salome; 41 Who also, when he was in Galilee, followed him, and ministered unto him; and many other women which came up with him unto Jerusalem.

Living Bible

33 About noon, darkness fell across the entire land,[c] lasting until three o'clock that afternoon.

34 Then Jesus called out with a loud voice, "Eli, Eli, lama sabachthani?" [d] ("My God, my God, why have you deserted me?")

35 Some of the people standing there thought he was calling for the prophet Elijah. 36 So one man ran and got a sponge and filled it with sour wine and held it up to him on a stick.

"Let's see if Elijah will come and take him down!" he said.

37 Then Jesus uttered another loud cry, and dismissed his spirit.

38 And the curtain[e] in the Temple was split apart from top to bottom.

39 When the Roman officer standing beside his cross saw how he dismissed his spirit, he exclaimed, "Truly, this was the Son of God!"

40 Some women were there watching from a distance—Mary Magdalene, Mary (the mother of James the Younger and of Joses), Salome, and others. 41 They and many other Galilean women who were his followers had ministered to him when he was up in Galilee, and had come with him to Jerusalem.

[*c*] Or, "over the entire world." [*d*] He spoke here in Aramaic. The onlookers, who spoke Greek and Latin, misunderstood his first two words ("Eloi, Eloi") and thought he was calling for the prophet Elijah. [*e*] A heavy veil hung in front of the room in the Temple called "The Holy of Holies," a place reserved by God for himself; the veil separated him from sinful mankind. Now this veil was split from above, showing that Christ's death, for man's sin, had opened up access to the holy God.

Today's English Version

The death of Jesus

33 At noon the whole country was covered with darkness, which lasted for three hours. 34At three o'clock Jesus cried out with a loud shout, *"Eloi, Eloi, lema sabachthani?"* which means, "My God, my God, why did you abandon me?"

35 Some of the people who were there heard him and said, "Listen, he is calling for Elijah!" 36 One of them ran up with a sponge, soaked it in cheap wine, and put it on the end of a stick. Then he held it up to Jesus' lips and said, "Wait! Let us see if Elijah is coming to bring him down from the cross!"

37 With a loud cry Jesus died.

38 The curtain hanging in the temple was torn in two, from top to bottom. 39 The army officer, who was standing there in front of the cross, saw how Jesus had cried out and died. "This man was really the Son of God!" he said.

40 Some women were there, looking on from a distance. Among them were Mary Magdalene, Mary the mother of the younger James and of Joses, and Salome. 41 They had followed Jesus while he was in Galilee and helped him. Many other women were there also, who had come to Jerusalem with him.

New International Version

The death of Jesus

33 At the sixth hour darkness came over the whole land until the ninth hour. 34And at the ninth hour Jesus cried out in a loud voice, *"Eloi, Eloi, lama sabachthani?"*—which means, "My God, my God, why have you forsaken me?" [v]

35 When some of those standing near heard this, they said, "Listen, he's calling Elijah."

36 One man ran, filled a sponge with wine vinegar, put it on a stick, and offered it to Jesus to drink. "Leave him alone now. Let's see if Elijah comes to take him down," he said.

37 With a loud cry, Jesus breathed his last.

38 The curtain of the temple was torn in two from top to bottom. 39And when the centurion, who stood there in front of Jesus, heard his cry and [w] saw how he died, he said, "Surely this man was the Son[x] of God!"

40 Some women were watching from a distance. Among them were Mary Magdalene, Mary the mother of James the younger and of Joses, and Salome. 41 In Galilee these women had followed him and cared for his needs. Many other women who had come up with him to Jerusalem were also there.

[*v*] Psalm 22:1. [*w*] Some MSS omit *heard his cry and.* [*x*] Or *a son.*

Phillips Modern English

At midday darkness spread over the whole countryside and lasted until three o'clock in the afternoon, and at three o'clock Jesus cried out in a loud voice,

"My God, my God, why did you forsake me?"

Some of the bystanders heard these words which Jesus spoke in Aramaic (*Eloi, Eloi, lama sabachthani?*), and said,

"Listen, he's calling for Elijah!"

One man ran off and soaked a sponge in vinegar, put it on a stick, and held it up for Jesus to drink, calling out,

"Let him alone! Let's see if Elijah will come and take him down!"

But Jesus let out a great cry, and expired. The curtain of the Temple sanctuary was split in two from the top to the bottom. And when the centurion who stood in front of Jesus saw how he died, he said,

"This man was certainly a son of God!"

There were some women there looking on from a distance, among them Mary of Magdala, Mary the mother of the younger James and Joses, and Salome. These were the women who used to follow Jesus as he went about in Galilee and look after him. And there were many other women there who had come up to Jerusalem with him.

Revised Standard Version

33 And when the sixth hour had come, there was darkness over the whole land [h] until the ninth hour. 34 And at the ninth hour Jesus cried with a loud voice, "Eloi, Eloi, lama sabachthani?" which means, "My God, my God, why hast thou forsaken me?" 35 And some of the bystanders hearing it said, "Behold, he is calling Elijah." 36 And one ran and, filling a sponge full of vinegar, put it on a reed and gave it to him to drink, saying, "Wait, let us see whether Elijah will come to take him down." 37 And Jesus uttered a loud cry, and breathed his last. 38 And the curtain of the temple was torn in two, from top to bottom. 39 And when the centurion, who stood facing him, saw that he thus[i] breathed his last, he said, "Truly this man was the Son[x] of God!"

40 There were also women looking on from afar, among whom were Mary Magdalene, and Mary the mother of James the younger and of Joses, and Salome, 41 who, when he was in Galilee, followed him, and ministered to him; and also many other women who came up with him to Jerusalem.

[*h*] Or *earth*. [*i*] Other ancient authorities insert *cried out and*. [*x*] Or *a son*.

Jerusalem Bible

The death of Jesus

33 When the sixth hour came there was darkness over the whole land until the ninth hour. 34 And at the ninth hour Jesus cried out in a loud voice, "Eloi, Eloi, lama sabachthani?" which means, *"My God, my God, why have you deserted me?"* [f] 35 When some of those who stood by heard this, they said, "Listen, he is calling on Elijah." 36 Someone ran and soaked a sponge in vinegar and, putting it on a reed, gave it him to drink saying, "Wait and see if Elijah will come to take him down." 37 But Jesus gave a loud cry and breathed his last. 38 And the veil of the Temple was torn in two from top to bottom. 39 The centurion, who was standing in front of him, had seen how he had died, and he said, "In truth this man was a son of God."

The women on Calvary

40 There were some women watching from a distance. Among them were Mary of Magdala, Mary who was the mother of James the younger and Joset, and Salome. 41 These used to follow him and look after him when he was in Galilee. And there were many other women there who had come up to Jerusalem with him.

[*f*] Ps. 22:1.

New English Bible

At midday a darkness fell over the whole land, which lasted till three in the afternoon; and at three Jesus cried aloud, *'Eli, Eli, lema sabachthani?'*, which means, 'My God, my God, why hast thou forsaken me?' [b] Some of the bystanders on hearing this, said, 'Hark, he is calling Elijah.' A man ran and soaked a sponge in sour wine and held it to his lips on the end of a cane. 'Let us see', he said, 'if Elijah will come to take him down.' Then Jesus gave a loud cry and died. And the curtain of the temple was torn in two from top to bottom. And when the centurion who was standing opposite him saw how he died,[c] he said, 'Truly this man was a son of God.' [d]

A number of women were also present, watching from a distance. Among them were Mary of Magdala, Mary the mother of James the younger and of Joseph, and Salome, who had all followed him and waited on him when he was in Galilee, and there were several others who had come up to Jerusalem with him.

[*b*] *Some witnesses read* My God, my God, why hast thou shamed me? [*c*] *Some witnesses read* saw that he died with a cry. [*d*] *Or* the Son of God.

King James Version

42 And now when the even was come, because it was the preparation, that is, the day before the sabbath, 43 Joseph of Arimathea, an honourable counsellor, which also waited for the kingdom of God, came, and went in boldly unto Pilate, and craved the body of Jesus. 44 And Pilate marvelled if he were already dead: and calling *unto him* the centurion, he asked him whether he had been any while dead. 45 And when he knew *it* of the centurion, he gave the body to Joseph. 46 And he bought fine linen, and took him down, and wrapped him in the linen, and laid him in a sepulchre which was hewn out of a rock, and rolled a stone unto the door of the sepulchre. 47 And Mary Magdalene and Mary *the mother* of Joses beheld where he was laid.

16 And when the sabbath was past, Mary Magdalene, and Mary the *mother* of James, and Salome, had bought sweet spices, that they might come and anoint him. 2 And very early in the morning, the first *day* of the week, they came unto the sepulchre at the rising of the sun. 3 And they said among themselves, Who shall roll us away the stone from the door of the

Living Bible

42, 43 This all happened the day before the Sabbath. Late that afternoon Joseph from Arimathea, an honored member of the Jewish Supreme Court (who personally was eagerly expecting the arrival of God's Kingdom), gathered his courage and went to Pilate and asked for Jesus' body.

44 Pilate couldn't believe that Jesus was already dead so he called for the Roman officer in charge and asked him. 45 The officer confirmed the fact, and Pilate told Joseph he could have the body.

46 Joseph bought a long sheet of linen cloth and, taking Jesus' body down from the cross, wound it in the cloth and laid it in a rock-hewn tomb, and rolled a stone in front of the entrance.

47 (Mary Magdalene and Mary the mother of Joses were watching as Jesus was laid away.)

16 The next evening, when the Sabbath ended, Mary Magdalene and Salome and Mary the mother of James went out and purchased embalming spices.

Early the following morning, just at sunrise, they carried them out to the tomb. 3 On the way they were discussing how they could ever roll aside the huge stone from the entrance.

Today's English Version

The burial of Jesus

42, 43 It was getting on toward evening when Joseph of Arimathea arrived. He was a respected member of the Council, who looked for the coming of the Kingdom of God. It was Preparation day (that is, the day before the Sabbath); so Joseph went in bravely to the presence of Pilate and asked him for the body of Jesus. 44 Pilate was surprised to hear that Jesus was already dead. He called the army officer and asked him if Jesus had been dead a long time. 45 After hearing the officer's report, Pilate told Joseph he could have the body. 46 Joseph bought a linen sheet, took the body down, wrapped it in the sheet, and placed it in a grave which had been dug out of the rock. Then he rolled a large stone across the entrance to the grave. 47 Mary Magdalene and Mary the mother of Joses were watching, and saw where Jesus was placed.

The resurrection

16 After the Sabbath day was over, Mary Magdalene, Mary the mother of James, and Salome bought spices to go and anoint the body of Jesus. 2 Very early on Sunday morning, at sunrise, they went to the grave. 3, 4 On the way they said to one another, "Who will roll away for us the stone from the entrance to the grave?"

New International Version

The burial of Jesus

42 It was Preparation Day (that is, the day before the Sabbath). So as evening approached, 43 Joseph of Arimathea, a prominent member of the Council, who was himself waiting for the kingdom of God, went boldly to Pilate and asked for Jesus' body. 44 Pilate was surprised to hear that he was already dead. Summoning the centurion, he asked him if Jesus had already died. 45 When he learned from the centurion that it was so, he gave the body to Joseph. 46 So Joseph bought some linen cloth, took down the body, wrapped it in the linen, and placed it in a tomb cut out of rock. Then he rolled a stone against the entrance of the tomb. 47 Mary Magdalene and Mary the mother of Joses saw where he was laid.

The resurrection

16 When the Sabbath was over, Mary Magdalene, Mary the mother of James, and Salome bought spices so that they might go to anoint Jesus' body. 2 Very early on the first day of the week, just after sunrise, they were on their way to the tomb 3 and they asked each other, "Who will roll the stone away from the entrance of the tomb?"

Phillips Modern English

15.42 The body of Jesus is reverently laid in a tomb

When the evening came, because it was the day of preparation, that is the day before the Sabbath, Joseph from Arimathaea, a distinguished member of the council, who was himself prepared to accept the kingdom of God, went with great courage into Pilate's presence and asked for the body of Jesus. Pilate was surprised that he could be dead already and he sent for the centurion and asked whether he had been dead long. On hearing the centurion's report, he gave Joseph the body of Jesus. So Joseph brought a linen winding-sheet, took Jesus down and wrapped him in it, and then put him in a tomb which had been hewn out of the solid rock, rolling a stone over the entrance to it. Mary of Magdala and Mary the mother of Joses were looking on and saw where he was laid.

16.1 Early on the first Lord's day: the women are amazed

When the Sabbath was over, Mary of Magdala, Mary the mother of James, and Salome bought spices so that they could go and anoint him. And very early in the morning on the first day of the week, they came to the tomb, just as the sun was rising.

"Who is going to roll the stone back from the doorway of the tomb?" they asked each other.

Revised Standard Version

42 And when evening had come, since it was the day of Preparation, that is, the day before the sabbath, 43 Joseph of Arimathea, a respected member of the council, who was also himself looking for the kingdom of God, took courage and went to Pilate, and asked for the body of Jesus. 44 And Pilate wondered if he were already dead; and summoning the centurion, he asked him whether he was already dead.[j] 45 And when he learned from the centurion that he was dead, he granted the body to Joseph. 46 And he bought a linen shroud, and taking him down, wrapped him in the linen shroud, and laid him in a tomb which had been hewn out of the rock; and he rolled a stone against the door of the tomb. 47 Mary Magdalene and Mary the mother of Joses saw where he was laid.

16 And when the sabbath was past, Mary Magdalene, and Mary the mother of James, and Salome, bought spices, so that they might go and anoint him. 2 And very early on the first day of the week they went to the tomb when the sun had risen. 3 And they were saying to one another, "Who will roll away the stone for us

[j] Other ancient authorities read *whether he had been some time dead.*

Jerusalem Bible

The burial

42 It was now evening, and since it was Preparation Day (that is, the vigil of the sabbath), 43 there came Joseph of Arimathaea, a prominent member of the Council, who himself lived in the hope of seeing the kingdom of God, and he boldly went to Pilate and asked for the body of Jesus. 44 Pilate, astonished that he should have died so soon, summoned the centurion and inquired if he was already dead. 45 Having been assured of this by the centurion, he granted the corpse to Joseph 46 who bought a shroud, took Jesus down from the cross, wrapped him in the shroud and laid him in a tomb which had been hewn out of the rock. He then rolled a stone against the entrance to the tomb. 47 Mary of Magdala and Mary the mother of Joset were watching and took note of where he was laid.

The empty tomb. The angel's message

16 When the sabbath was over, Mary of Magdala, Mary the mother of James, and Salome, bought spices with which to go and anoint him. 2 And very early in the morning on the first day of the week they went to the tomb, just as the sun was rising.

3 They had been saying to one another, "Who will roll away the stone for us from the entrance

New English Bible

By this time evening had come; and as it was Preparation-day (that is, the day before the Sabbath), Joseph of Arimathaea, a respected member of the Council, a man who looked forward to the kingdom of God, bravely went in to Pilate and asked for the body of Jesus. Pilate was surprised to hear that he was already dead; so he sent for the centurion and asked him whether it was long since he died. And when he heard the centurion's report, he gave Joseph leave to take the dead body. So Joseph bought a linen sheet, took him down from the cross, and wrapped him in the sheet. Then he laid him in a tomb cut out of the rock, and rolled a stone against the entrance. And Mary of Magdala and Mary the mother of Joseph were watching and saw where he was laid.

16 When the Sabbath was over, Mary of Magdala, Mary the mother of James, and Salome bought[a] aromatic oils intending to go and anoint him; and very early on the Sunday morning, just after sunrise, they came to the tomb. They were wondering among themselves who would roll away the stone for them from

[a] *Some witnesses omit* When the Sabbath . . . Salome, *reading* And they went and bought . . .

King James Version

sepulchre? 4And when they looked, they saw that
the stone was rolled away: for it was very great.
5And entering into the sepulchre, they saw a
young man sitting on the right side, clothed in a
long white garment; and they were affrighted.
6And he saith unto them, Be not affrighted: ye
seek Jesus of Nazareth, which was crucified: he
is risen; he is not here: behold the place where
they laid him. 7 But go your way, tell his disciples and Peter that he goeth before you into
Galilee: there shall ye see him, as he said unto
you. 8And they went out quickly, and fled from
the sepulchre; for they trembled and were
amazed: neither said they any thing to any *man;*
for they were afraid.
9 Now when *Jesus* was risen early the first
day of the week, he appeared first to Mary
Magdalene, out of whom he had cast seven devils. 10*And* she went and told them that had been

Living Bible

4 But when they arrived they looked up and
saw that the stone—a *very* heavy one—was already moved away and the entrance was open!
5 So they entered the tomb—and there on the
right sat a young man clothed in white. The
women were startled, 6 but the angel said, "Don't
be so surprised. Aren't you looking for Jesus, the
Nazarene who was crucified? He isn't here! He
has come back to life! Look, that's where his
body was lying. 7 Now go and give this message
to his disciples including Peter:
" 'Jesus is going ahead of you to Galilee. You
will see him there, just as he told you before he
died!' "
8 The women fled from the tomb, trembling
and bewildered, too frightened to talk.
9 [a] It was early on Sunday morning when
Jesus came back to life, and the first person who
saw him was Mary Magdalene—the woman from
whom he had cast out seven demons. 10, 11 She

[*a*] Verses 9 through 20 are not found in the most ancient manuscripts, but may be considered an appendix giving additional facts.

Today's English Version

(It was a very large stone.) Then they looked up
and saw that the stone had already been rolled
back. 5 So they entered the grave, where they saw
a young man sitting at the right, wearing a white
robe—and they were filled with alarm.
6 "Don't be alarmed," he said. "I know you
are looking for Jesus of Nazareth, who was nailed
to the cross. He is not here—he has been raised!
Look, here is the place where they placed him.
7 Now go and give this message to his disciples,
including Peter: 'He is going to Galilee ahead of
you; there you will see him, just as he told you.' "
8 So they went out and ran from the grave,
because fear and terror were upon them. They
said nothing to anyone, because they were afraid.

AN OLD ENDING TO THE GOSPEL

Jesus appears to Mary Magdalene

[9 After Jesus rose from death, early on Sunday, he appeared first to Mary Magdalene, from
whom he had driven out seven demons. 10 She
went and told it to his companions. They were

New International Version

4 But when they looked up, they saw that the
stone, which was very large, had been rolled
away. 5As they entered the tomb, they saw a
young man dressed in a white robe sitting on
the right side, and they were alarmed.
6 "Don't be alarmed," he said. "You are looking for Jesus the Nazarene, who was crucified.
He has risen! He is not here. See the place where
they laid him. 7 But go, tell his disciples and
Peter, 'He is going ahead of you into Galilee.
There you will see him, just as he told you.' "
8 Trembling and bewildered, the women went
out and fled from the tomb. They said nothing
to anyone, because they were afraid.

[The most reliable early manuscripts omit Mark 16:9–20.]

The appearances and ascension of Jesus

9 When Jesus rose early on the first day of
the week, he appeared first to Mary Magdalene,
out of whom he had driven seven demons. 10 She
went and told those who had been with him and

Phillips Modern English

And then as they looked closer, they saw that the stone, which was a very large one, had been rolled back. So they went into the tomb and saw a young man in a white robe sitting on the right-hand side, and they were simply astonished. But he said to them,

"There is no need to be astonished. You are looking for Jesus of Nazareth who was crucified. He has risen; he is not here. Look, here is the place where they laid him. But now go and tell his disciples, and Peter, that he will be in Galilee before you. You will see him there just as he told you."

And they got out of the tomb and ran away from it. They were trembling with excitement. They did not dare to breathe a word to anyone.*

16.9 An ancient appendix

When Jesus rose early on that first day of the week, he appeared first of all to Mary of Magdala, from whom he had driven out seven evil spirits. And she went and reported this to his

**An alternative ending found in certain MSS. is on page 379.*

Revised Standard Version

from the door of the tomb?" 4And looking up,
they saw that the stone was rolled back—it was
very large. 5And entering the tomb, they saw a
young man sitting on the right side, dressed in a
white robe; and they were amazed. 6And he
said to them, "Do not be amazed; you seek
Jesus of Nazareth, who was crucified. He has
risen, he is not here; see the place where they
laid him. 7 But go, tell his disciples and Peter
that he is going before you to Galilee; there
you will see him, as he told you." 8And they
went out and fled from the tomb; for trembling
and astonishment had come upon them; and they
said nothing to any one, for they were afraid.

9 Now when he rose early on the first day of
the week, he appeared first to Mary Magdalene,
from whom he had cast out seven demons.
10 She went out and told those who had been

Jerusalem Bible

to the tomb?" 4 But when they looked they
could see that the stone—which was very big—
had already been rolled back. 5 On entering the
tomb they saw a young man in a white robe
seated on the right-hand side, and they were
struck with amazement. 6 But he said to them,
"There is no need for alarm. You are looking
for Jesus of Nazareth, who was crucified: he has
risen, he is not here. See, here is the place where
they laid him. 7 But you must go and tell his
disciples and Peter, 'He is going before you to
Galilee; it is there you will see him, just as he
told you.'" 8And the women came out and ran
away from the tomb because they were frightened out of their wits; and they said nothing to
a soul, for they were afraid . . .

Appearances of the risen Christ[g]

9 Having risen in the morning on the first day
of the week, he appeared first to Mary of Magdala from whom he had cast out seven devils.
10 She then went to those who had been his
companions, and who were mourning and in

[g] Many MSS omit vv, 9-20 and this ending to the gospel may not have been written by Mark, though it is old enough.

New English Bible

the entrance to the tomb, when they looked up and saw that the stone, huge as it was, had been rolled back already. They went into the tomb, where they saw a youth sitting on the right-hand side, wearing a white robe; and they were dumbfounded. But he said to them, 'Fear nothing; you are looking for Jesus of Nazareth, who was crucified. He has been raised again; he is not here; look, there is the place where they laid him. But go and give this message to his disciples and Peter: "He is going on before you into Galilee; there you will see him as he told you."' Then they went out and ran away from the tomb, beside themselves with terror. They said nothing to anybody, for they were afraid.[b]

And they delivered all these instructions briefly to Peter and his companions. Afterwards Jesus himself sent out by them from east to west the sacred and imperishable message of eternal salvation.[c]

When he had risen from the dead early on Sunday morning he appeared first to Mary of Magdala, from whom he had formerly cast out seven devils. She went and carried the news to

[b] At this point some of the most ancient witnesses bring the book to a close. [c] Some witnesses add this paragraph, which in one of them is the conclusion of the book.

King James Version

with him, as they mourned and wept. 11And
they, when they had heard that he was alive, and
had been seen of her, believed not.
12 After that he appeared in another form
unto two of them, as they walked, and went
into the country. 13And they went and told *it*
unto the residue: neither believed they them.
14 Afterward he appeared unto the eleven as
they sat at meat, and upbraided them with their
unbelief and hardness of heart, because they believed not them which had seen him after he was
risen. 15And he said unto them, Go ye into all
the world, and preach the gospel to every creature. 16 He that believeth and is baptized shall
be saved; but he that believeth not shall be
damned. 17And these signs shall follow them
that believe; In my name shall they cast out
devils; they shall speak with new tongues; 18 They
shall take up serpents; and if they drink any
deadly thing, it shall not hurt them; they shall
lay hands on the sick, and they shall recover.

Living Bible

found the disciples wet-eyed with grief and exclaimed that she had seen Jesus, and he was
alive! But they didn't believe her!
12 Later that day[b] he appeared to two who
were walking from Jerusalem into the country,
but they didn't recognize him at first because he
had changed his appearance. 13 When they finally realized who he was, they rushed back to
Jerusalem to tell the others, but no one believed
them.
14 Still later he appeared to the eleven disciples as they were eating together. He rebuked
them for their unbelief—their stubborn refusal
to believe those who had seen him alive from the
dead.
15 And then he told them, "You are to go
into all the world and preach the Good News to
everyone, everywhere. 16 Those who believe and
are baptized will be saved. But those who refuse
to believe will be condemned.
17 "And those who believe shall use my authority to cast out demons, and they shall speak
new languages.[c] 18 They will be able even to
handle snakes with safety, and if they drink anything poisonous, it won't hurt them; and they
will be able to place their hands on the sick and
heal them."

[*b*] Literally, "after these things." [*c*] Literally, "they will speak in new tongues." Some ancient manuscripts omit "new."

Today's English Version

mourning and crying; 11 and when they heard
her say that Jesus was alive and that she had
seen him, they did not believe her.

Jesus appears to two disciples

12 After this, Jesus appeared in a different
manner to two of them while they were on their
way to the country. 13 They returned and told it
to the others, but they would not believe it.

Jesus appears to the eleven

14 Last of all, Jesus appeared to the eleven
disciples as they were eating. He scolded them,
because they did not have faith and because they
were too stubborn to believe those who had seen
him alive. 15 He said to them, "Go to the whole
world and preach the gospel to all mankind.
16 Whoever believes and is baptized will be
saved; whoever does not believe will be condemned. 17 Believers will be given these signs of
power: they will drive out demons in my name;
they will speak in strange tongues; 18 if they pick
up snakes or drink any poison, they will not be
harmed; they will place their hands on the sick,
who will get well."

New International Version

who were mourning and weeping. 11 When they
heard that Jesus was alive and that she had seen
him, they did not believe it.
12 Afterward Jesus appeared in a different
form to two of them while they were walking in
the country. 13 These returned and reported it to
the rest; but they did not believe them either.
14 Later Jesus appeared to the Eleven as
they were eating; he rebuked them for their lack
of faith and their stubborn refusal to believe
those who had seen him after he had risen.
15 He said to them, "Go into all the world
and preach the good news to all creation.
16 Whoever believes and is baptized will be
saved, but whoever does not believe will be condemned. 17And these signs will accompany those
who believe: In my name they will drive out
demons; they will speak in new tongues; 18they
will pick up snakes with their hands; and when
they drink deadly poison, it will not hurt them
at all; they will place their hands on sick people, and they will get well."

Phillips Modern English

sorrowing and weeping followers. They heard her say that he was alive and that she had seen him, but they did not believe it.

Later, he appeared in a different form to two of them who were out walking, as they were on their way to the country. These two came back and told the others, but they did not believe them either. Still later he appeared to the eleven themselves as they were sitting at table and reproached them for their lack of faith and refusal to believe those who had seen him after he had risen. Then he said to them,

"You must go out to the whole world and proclaim the gospel to every creature. He who believes it and is baptised will be saved, but he who disbelieves it will be condemned. These signs will follow those who do believe: they will drive out evil spirits in my name; they will speak with new tongues; they will pick up snakes, and if they drink any poison it will do them no harm; they will lay their hands upon the sick and they will recover."

Revised Standard Version

with him, as they mourned and wept. 11 But
when they heard that he was alive and had been
seen by her, they would not believe it.
12 After this he appeared in another form to
two of them, as they were walking into the
country. 13 And they went back and told the rest,
but they did not believe them.
14 Afterward he appeared to the eleven themselves as they sat at table; and he upbraided
them for their unbelief and hardness of heart,
because they had not believed those who saw
him after he had risen. 15 And he said to them,
"Go into all the world and preach the gospel to
the whole creation. 16 He who believes and is
baptized will be saved; but he who does not believe will be condemned. 17 And these signs will
accompany those who believe: in my name they
will cast out demons; they will speak in new
tongues; 18 they will pick up serpents, and if
they drink any deadly thing, it will not hurt
them; they will lay their hands on the sick, and
they will recover."

Jerusalem Bible

tears, and told them. 11 But they did not believe
her when they heard her say that he was alive
and that she had seen him.
12 After this, he showed himself under another form to two of them as they were on their
way into the country. 13 These went back and
told the others, who did not believe them either.
14 Lastly, he showed himself to the Eleven
themselves while they were at table. He reproached them for their incredulity and obstinacy, because they had refused to believe those
who had seen him after he had risen. 15 And he
said to them, "Go out to the whole world; proclaim the Good News to all creation. 16 He who
believes and is baptized will be saved; he who
does not believe will be condemned. 17 These
are the signs that will be associated with believers: in my name they will cast out devils;
they will have the gift of tongues; 18 they will
pick up snakes in their hands, and be unharmed
should they drink deadly poison; they will lay
their hands on the sick, who will recover."

New English Bible

his mourning and sorrowful followers, but when they were told that he was alive and that she had seen him they did not believe it.

Later he appeared in a different guise to two of them as they were walking, on their way into the country. These also went and took the news to the others, but again no one believed them.

Afterwards while the Eleven were at table he appeared to them and reproached them for their incredulity and dullness, because they had not believed those who had seen him after he was raised from the dead. Then he said to them: 'Go forth to every part of the world, and proclaim the Good News to the whole creation. Those who believe it and receive baptism will find salvation; those who do not believe will be condemned. Faith will bring with it these miracles: believers will cast out devils in my name and speak in strange tongues; if they handle snakes or drink any deadly poison, they will come to no harm; and the sick on whom they lay their hands will recover.'

King James Version

19 So then, after the Lord had spoken unto them, he was received up into heaven, and sat on the right hand of God. 20And they went forth, and preached every where, the Lord working with *them,* and confirming the word with signs following. Amen.

Living Bible

19 When the Lord Jesus had finished talking with them, he was taken up into heaven and sat down at God's right hand.

20 And the disciples went everywhere preaching, and the Lord was with them and confirmed what they said by the miracles that followed their messages.

Today's English Version

Jesus is taken up to heaven

19 After the Lord Jesus had talked with them, he was taken up to heaven and sat at the right side of God. 20 The disciples went and preached everywhere, and the Lord worked with them and proved that their preaching was true by giving them the signs of power.]

ANOTHER OLD ENDING

[9 The women went to Peter and his friends and gave them a brief account of all they had been told. 10After this, Jesus himself sent out through his disciples, from the east to the west, the sacred and ever-living message of eternal salvation.]

New International Version

19 After the Lord Jesus had spoken to them, he was taken up into heaven and he sat at the right hand of God. 20 Then the disciples went out and preached everywhere, and the Lord worked with them and confirmed his word by the signs that accompanied it.

Phillips Modern English

16.19 Jesus, his mission accomplished, returns to Heaven

After these words to them, the Lord Jesus was taken up into Heaven and was enthroned at the right hand of God. They went out and preached everywhere. The Lord worked with them, confirming their message by the signs that followed.

** An alternative ending found in certain MSS. following verse 8.*

But they gave all these instructions briefly to Peter and his companions. Afterwards Jesus himself sent out through them, from east to west, the proclamation of the holy and incorruptible message of eternal salvation.

Revised Standard Version

19 So then the Lord Jesus, after he had spoken to them, was taken up into heaven, and sat down at the right hand of God. 20And they went forth and preached everywhere, while the Lord worked with them and confirmed the message by the signs that attended it. Amen.[k]

[k] Some of the most ancient authorities bring the book to a close at the end of verse 8. One authority concludes the book by adding after verse 8 the following: *But they reported briefly to Peter and those with him all that they had been told. And after this, Jesus himself sent out by means of them, from east to west, the sacred and imperishable proclamation of eternal salvation.* Other authorities include the preceding passage and continue with verses 9–20. In most authorities verses 9–20 follow immediately after verse 8; a few authorities insert additional material after verse 14.

Jerusalem Bible

19 And so the Lord Jesus, after he had spoken to them, was taken up into heaven: there at the right hand of God he took his place, 20 while they, going out, preached everywhere, the Lord working with them and confirming the word by the signs that accompanied it.

New English Bible

So after talking with them the Lord Jesus was taken up into heaven, and he took his seat at the right hand of God; but they went out to make their proclamation everywhere, and the Lord worked with them and confirmed their words by the miracles that followed.[d]

[d] *Some witnesses give verses 9-20 either instead of, or in addition to, the paragraph* And they delivered . . . eternal salvation (*here printed before verse 9*), *and so bring the book to a close. Others insert further additional matter.*

King James Version

THE GOSPEL ACCORDING TO SAINT LUKE

1 Forasmuch as many have taken in hand to set forth in order a declaration of those things which are most surely believed among us, 2 Even as they delivered them unto us, which from the beginning were eyewitnesses, and ministers of the word; 3 It seemed good to me also, having had perfect understanding of all things from the very first, to write unto thee in order, most excellent Theophilus, 4 That thou mightest know the certainty of those things, wherein thou hast been instructed.

Living Bible

LUKE

1 Dear Friend who loves God:[a]
1, 2 Several biographies of Christ have already been written using as their source material the reports circulating among us from the early disciples and other eyewitnesses. 3 However, it occurred to me that it would be well to recheck all these accounts from first to last and after thorough investigation to pass this summary on to you,[b] 4 to reassure you of the truth of all you were taught.

[a] From verse 3. Literally, "most excellent Theophilus." The name means "one who loves God." [b] Literally, "an account of the things accomplished among us."

Today's English Version

THE GOSPEL OF LUKE

Introduction

1 Dear Theophilus:
Many have done their best to write a report of the things that have taken place among us. 2 They wrote what we have been told by those who saw these things from the beginning and proclaimed the message. 3And so, your Excellency, because I have carefully studied all these matters from their beginning, I thought it good to write an orderly account for you. 4 I do this so that you will know the full truth of all those matters which you have been taught.

New International Version

LUKE

Introduction

1 Many have undertaken to draw up an account of the things that have been fulfilled[a] among us, 2 just as they were handed down to us by those who from the first were eyewitnesses and servants of the word. 3 Therefore, since I myself have carefully investigated everything from the beginning, it seemed good also to me to write an orderly account for you, most excellent Theophilus, 4 so that you may know the certainty of the things you have been taught.

[a] Or *surely believed.*

Phillips Modern English

THE GOSPEL OF LUKE

1.1 Prefatory note

Dear Theophilus,
Many people have already written an account of the events which have happened among us, basing their work on the evidence of those who, we know, were eye-witnesses as well as teachers of the message. I have therefore decided, since I have traced the course of these happenings carefully from the beginning, to set them down for you myself in their proper order, so that you may have reliable information about the matters in which you have already had instruction.

Revised Standard Version

THE GOSPEL ACCORDING TO LUKE

1 Inasmuch as many have undertaken to compile a narrative of the things which have been accomplished among us, 2 just as they were delivered to us by those who from the beginning were eyewitnesses and ministers of the word, 3 it seemed good to me also, having followed all things closely[a] for some time past, to write an orderly account for you, most excellent Theophilus, 4 that you may know the truth concerning the things of which you have been informed.

[a] Or *accurately*.

Jerusalem Bible

THE GOSPEL ACCORDING TO SAINT LUKE

Prologue

1 Seeing that many others have undertaken to draw up accounts of the events that have taken place among us, 2 exactly as these were handed down to us by those who from the outset were eyewitnesses and ministers of the word, 3 I in my turn, after carefully going over the whole story from the beginning, have decided to write an ordered account for you, Theophilus, 4 so that your Excellency may learn how well founded the teaching is that you have received.

New English Bible

THE GOSPEL ACCORDING TO LUKE

1 The author to Theophilus: Many writers have undertaken to draw up an account of the events that have happened among us, following the traditions handed down to us by the original eyewitnesses and servants of the Gospel. And so I in my turn, your Excellency, as one who has gone over the whole course of these events in detail, have decided to write a connected narrative for you, so as to give you authentic knowledge about the matters of which you have been informed.

King James Version

5 There was in the days of Herod, the king
of Judea, a certain priest named Zacharias, of
the course of Abia: and his wife *was* of the
daughters of Aaron, and her name *was* Elisabeth.
6And they were both righteous before God, walking in all the commandments and ordinances of
the Lord blameless. 7And they had no child,
because that Elisabeth was barren; and they both
were *now* well stricken in years. 8And it came
to pass, that, while he executed the priest's office
before God in the order of his course, 9Accord-
ing to the custom of the priest's office, his lot
was to burn incense when he went into the temple of the Lord. 10And the whole multitude of
the people were praying without at the time of
incense. 11And there appeared unto him an angel
of the Lord standing on the right side of the
altar of incense. 12And when Zacharias saw *him,*
he was troubled, and fear fell upon him. 13 But
the angel said unto him, Fear not, Zacharias:
for thy prayer is heard; and thy wife Elisabeth
shall bear thee a son, and thou shalt call his
name John. 14And thou shalt have joy and gladness; and many shall rejoice at his birth. 15 For

Living Bible

5 My story begins with a Jewish priest, Zacharias, who lived when Herod was king of Judea.
Zacharias was a member of the Abijah division
of the Temple service corps. (His wife Elizabeth
was, like himself, a member of the priest tribe of
the Jews, a descendant of Aaron.) 6 Zacharias
and Elizabeth were godly folk, careful to obey
all of God's laws in spirit as well as in letter.
7 But they had no children, for Elizabeth was
barren; and now they were both very old.
8, 9 One day as Zacharias was going about his
work in the Temple—for his division was on
duty that week—the honor fell to him by lot[c]
to enter the inner sanctuary and burn incense before the Lord. 10 Meanwhile, a great crowd stood
outside in the Temple court, praying as they
always did during that part of the service when
the incense was being burned.
11, 12 Zacharias was in the sanctuary when
suddenly an angel appeared, standing to the
right of the altar of incense! Zacharias was startled and terrified.
13 But the angel said, "Don't be afraid,
Zacharias! For I have come to tell you that God
has heard your prayer, and your wife Elizabeth
will bear you a son! And you are to name him
John. 14 You will both have great joy and gladness at his birth, and many will rejoice with you.
15 For he will be one of the Lord's great men.

[*c*] Probably by throwing dice or something similar —"drawing straws" would be a modern equivalent.

Today's English Version

The birth of John the Baptist announced

5 During the time when Herod was king of
the land of Israel, there was a priest named Zechariah, who belonged to the priestly order of Abijah. His wife's name was Elizabeth; she also
belonged to a priestly family. 6 They both lived
good lives in God's sight, and obeyed fully all
the Lord's commandments and rules. 7 They had
no children because Elizabeth could not have
any, and she and Zechariah were both very old.
8 One day Zechariah was doing his work as a
priest before God, taking his turn in the daily
service. 9According to the custom followed by
the priests, he was chosen by lot to burn the
incense on the altar. So he went into the temple
of the Lord, 10 while the crowd of people outside prayed during the hour of burning the incense. 11An angel of the Lord appeared to him,
standing at the right side of the altar where the
incense was burned. 12 When Zechariah saw him
he was troubled and felt afraid. 13 But the angel
said to him, "Don't be afraid, Zechariah! God
has heard your prayer, and your wife Elizabeth
will bear you a son. You are to name him John.
14 How glad and happy you will be, and how
happy many others will be when he is born! 15 He

New International Version

The birth of John the Baptist foretold

5 In the time of Herod, king of Judea, there
was a priest named Zechariah, who belonged to
the priestly division of Abijah; his wife Elizabeth was also a descendant of Aaron. 6 Both of
them were upright in the sight of God, observing
all the Lord's commandments and regulations
blamelessly. 7 But they had no children, because
Elizabeth was barren; and they were both well
along in years.
8 Once when Zechariah's division was on duty
and he was serving as priest before God, 9 he
was chosen by lot, according to the custom of
the priesthood, to go into the temple of the Lord
and burn incense. 10And when the time for the
burning of incense came, all the assembled worshipers were praying outside.
11 Then an angel of the Lord appeared to
him, standing at the right side of the altar of
incense. 12 When Zechariah saw him, he was
startled and was gripped with fear. 13 But the
angel said to him: "Do not be afraid, Zechariah;
your prayer has been heard. Your wife Elizabeth
will bear you a son, and you are to give him the
name John. 14 He will be a joy and delight to
you, and many will rejoice because of his birth,
15 for he will be great in the sight of the Lord.

Phillips Modern English

1.5 A vision comes to an old priest of God

The story begins in the days when Herod was king of Judaea with a priest called Zacharias (who belonged to the Abijah section of the priesthood), whose wife Elisabeth was, like him, a descendant of Aaron. They were both truly religious people, blamelessly observing all the Lord's commandments and requirements. They were childless through Elisabeth's infertility, and both of them were getting on in years. One day, while Zacharias was performing his priestly functions (it was the turn of his division to be on duty), it fell to him to go into the sanctuary and burn the incense. The crowded congregation outside was praying at the actual time of the incense-burning, when an angel of the Lord appeared on the right side of the incense-altar. When Zacharias saw him, he was terribly agitated and a sense of awe swept over him. But the angel spoke to him,

"Do not be afraid, Zacharias; your prayers have been heard. Elisabeth your wife will bear you a son, and you are to call him John. This will be joy and delight to you and many more will be glad because he is born. He will be one

Revised Standard Version

5 In the days of Herod, king of Judea, there was a priest name Zechariah,[b] of the division of Abijah; and he had a wife of the daughters of Aaron, and her name was Elizabeth. 6 And they were both righteous before God, walking in all the commandments and ordinances of the Lord blameless. 7 But they had no child, because Elizabeth was barren, and both were advanced in years.

8 Now while he was serving as priest before God when his division was on duty, 9 according to the custom of the priesthood, it fell to him by lot to enter the temple of the Lord and burn incense. 10 And the whole multitude of the people were praying outside at the hour of incense. 11 And there appeared to him an angel of the Lord standing on the right side of the altar of incense. 12 And Zechariah was troubled when he saw him, and fear fell upon him. 13 But the angel said to him, "Do not be afraid, Zechariah, for your prayer is heard, and your wife Elizabeth will bear you a son, and you shall call his name John.

14 And you will have joy and gladness,
and many will rejoice at his birth;
15 for he will be great before the Lord,

[b] Greek *Zacharias*.

Jerusalem Bible

I. The birth and hidden life of John the Baptist and of Jesus

The birth of John the Baptist foretold

5 In the days of King Herod of Judaea there lived a priest called Zechariah who belonged to the Abijah section of the priesthood, and he had a wife, Elizabeth by name, who was a descendant of Aaron. 6 Both were worthy in the sight of God, and scrupulously observed all the commandments and observances of the Lord. 7 But they were childless: Elizabeth was barren and they were both getting on in years.

8 Now it was the turn of Zechariah's section[a] to serve, and he was exercising his priestly office before God 9 when it fell to him by lot, as the ritual custom was, to enter the Lord's sanctuary and burn incense there.[b] 10 And at the hour of incense the whole congregation was outside, praying.

11 Then there appeared to him the angel of the Lord, standing on the right of the altar of incense. 12 The sight disturbed Zechariah and he was overcome with fear. 13 But the angel said to him, "Zechariah, do not be afraid, your prayer has been heard. Your wife Elizabeth is to bear you a son and you must name him John.[c] 14 He will be your joy and delight and many will rejoice at his birth, 15 for he will be

[a] The twenty-four families of the "sons of Aaron" were responsible in rotation for service in the Temple, and in each class or family the individual was chosen by lot. See 1 Ch. 24. [b] The priest tended the brazier on the altar of incense in front of the Most Holy Place. [c] The meaning of the name is "Yahweh is gracious."

New English Bible

The coming of Christ

In the days of Herod king of Judaea there was a priest named Zechariah, of the division of the priesthood called after Abijah. His wife also was of priestly descent; her name was Elizabeth. Both of them were upright and devout, blamelessly observing all the commandments and ordinances of the Lord. But they had no children, for Elizabeth was barren, and both were well on in years.

Once, when it was the turn of his division and he was there to take part in divine service, it fell to his lot, by priestly custom, to enter the sanctuary of the Lord and offer the incense; and the whole congregation was at prayer outside. It was the hour of the incense-offering. There appeared to him an angel of the Lord, standing on the right of the altar of incense. At this sight, Zechariah was startled, and fear overcame him. But the angel said to him, 'Do not be afraid, Zechariah; your prayer has been heard: your wife Elizabeth will bear you a son, and you shall name him John. Your heart will thrill with joy and many will be glad that he was born; for he

King James Version

he shall be great in the sight of the Lord, and shall drink neither wine nor strong drink; and he shall be filled with the Holy Ghost, even from his mother's womb. 16And many of the children of Israel shall he turn to the Lord their God. 17And he shall go before him in the spirit and power of Elias, to turn the hearts of the fathers to the children, and the disobedient to the wisdom of the just; to make ready a people prepared for the Lord. 18And Zacharias said unto the angel, Whereby shall I know this? for I am an old man, and my wife well stricken in years. 19And the angel answering said unto him, I am Gabriel, that stand in the presence of God; and am sent to speak unto thee, and to shew thee these glad tidings. 20And, behold, thou shalt be dumb, and not able to speak, until the day that these things shall be performed, because thou believest not my words, which shall be fulfilled in their season. 21And the people waited for Zacharias, and marvelled that he tarried so long in the temple. 22And when he came out, he could not speak unto them: and they perceived that he had seen a vision in the temple; for he beckoned unto them, and remained speechless. 23And it came to pass, that, as soon as the days of his ministration were accomplished, he departed to his own house. 24And after those days his wife Elisabeth conceived, and hid herself five months, saying, 25 Thus hath the Lord dealt with me in the days wherein he looked on *me*, to take away

Living Bible

He must never touch wine or hard liquor—and he will be filled with the Holy Spirit, even from before his birth! 16And he will persuade many a Jew to turn to the Lord his God. 17 He will be a man of rugged [d] spirit and power like Elijah, the prophet of old; and he will precede the coming of the Messiah, preparing the people for his arrival. He will soften adult hearts to become like little children's, and will change disobedient minds to the wisdom of faith." [e]

18 Zacharias said to the angel, "But this is impossible! I'm an old man now, and my wife is also well along in years."

19 Then the angel said, "I am Gabriel! I stand in the very presence of God. It was he who sent me to you with this good news! 20And now, because you haven't believed me, you are to be stricken silent, unable to speak until the child is born. For my words will certainly come true at the proper time."

21 Meanwhile the crowds outside were waiting for Zacharias to appear and wondered why he was taking so long. 22 When he finally came out, he couldn't speak to them, and they realized from his gestures that he must have seen a vision in the Temple. 23 He stayed on at the Temple for the remaining days of his Temple duties and then returned home. 24 Soon afterwards Elizabeth his wife became pregnant and went into seclusion for five months.

25 "How kind the Lord is," she exclaimed, "to take away my disgrace of having no children!"

[*d*] Implied. [*e*] Literally, "to turn the hearts of the fathers to the children, and the disobedient to the wisdom of the just."

Today's English Version

will be a great man in the Lord's sight. He must not drink any wine or strong drink. From his very birth he will be filled with the Holy Spirit. 16 He will bring back many of the people of Israel to the Lord their God. 17 He will go ahead of him, strong and mighty like the prophet Elijah. He will bring fathers and children together again; he will turn the disobedient people back to the way of thinking of the righteous; he will get the Lord's people ready for him."

18 Zechariah said to the angel, "How shall I know if this is so? I am an old man and my wife also is old."

19 "I am Gabriel," the angel answered. "I stand in the presence of God, who sent me to speak to you and tell you this good news. 20 But you have not believed my message, which will come true at the right time. Because you have not believed you will be unable to speak; you will remain silent until the day my promise to you comes true."

21 In the meantime the people were waiting for Zechariah, wondering why he was spending such a long time in the temple. 22 When he came out he could not speak to them, and so they knew that he had seen a vision in the temple. Unable to say a word, he made signs to them with his hands.

23 When his period of service in the temple was over, Zechariah went back home. 24 Some time later his wife Elizabeth became pregnant, and did not leave the house for five months. 25 "Now at last the Lord has helped me in this way," she said. "He has taken away my public disgrace!"

New International Version

He is never to take wine or other fermented drink, and he will be filled with the Holy Spirit even from birth.[b] 16 Many of the people of Israel will he bring back to the Lord their God. 17And he will go on before the Lord, in the spirit and power of Elijah, to turn the hearts of the fathers to their children and the disobedient to the wisdom of the righteous—to make ready a people prepared for the Lord."

18 Zechariah asked the angel, "How can I be sure of this? I am an old man and my wife is well along in years."

19 The angel answered, "I am Gabriel. I stand in the presence of God, and I have been sent to speak to you and to tell you this good news. 20And now you will be silent and not able to speak until the day this happens, because you did not believe my words, which will come true at their proper time."

21 Meanwhile, the people were waiting for Zechariah and wondering why he stayed so long in the temple. 22 When he came out, he could not speak to them. They realized he had seen a vision in the temple, for he kept making signs to them but remained unable to speak.

23 When his time of service was completed, he returned home. 24After this his wife Elizabeth became pregnant and for five months remained in seclusion. 25 "The Lord has done this for me," she said. "In these days he has shown his favor and taken away my disgrace among the people."

[*b*] Or *from his mother's womb.*

Phillips Modern English

of God's great men; he will touch neither wine nor strong drink and he will be filled with the Holy Spirit from the moment of his birth. He will turn many of Israel's children to the Lord their God. He will go out before God in the spirit and power of Elijah—to reconcile fathers and children, and bring back the disobedient to the wisdom of good men—and he will make a people fully ready for their Lord."

But Zacharias replied to the angel,

"How can I know that this is true? I am an old man myself and my wife is getting on in years. . ."

"I am Gabriel," the angel answered. "I stand in the presence of God, and I have been sent to speak to you and tell you this good news. Because you do not believe what I have said, you shall live in silence, and you shall be unable to speak a word until the day that it happens. But be sure that everything that I have told you will come true at the proper time."

Meanwhile, the people were waiting for Zacharias, wondering why he stayed so long in the sanctuary. But when he came out and was unable to speak a word to them—for although he kept making signs, not a sound came from his lips—they realised that he had seen a vision in the Temple. Later, when his days of duty were over, he went back home, and soon afterwards his wife Elisabeth became pregnant and kept herself secluded for five months.

"How good the Lord is to me," she would say, "now that he has taken away the shame that I have suffered."

Revised Standard Version

and he shall drink no wine nor strong drink,
and he will be filled with the Holy Spirit,
even from his mother's womb.
16 And he will turn many of the sons of Israel
to the Lord their God,
17 and he will go before him in the spirit and
power of Elijah,
to turn the hearts of the fathers to the children,
and the disobedient to the wisdom of the
just,
to make ready for the Lord a people prepared."

18 And Zechariah said to the angel, "How shall
I know this? For I am an old man, and my wife
is advanced in years." 19 And the angel answered
him, "I am Gabriel, who stand in the presence
of God; and I was sent to speak to you, and to
bring you this good news. 20 And behold, you
will be silent and unable to speak until the day
that these things come to pass, because you did
not believe my words, which will be fulfilled in
their time." 21 And the people were waiting for
Zechariah, and they wondered at his delay in
the temple. 22 And when he came out, he could
not speak to them, and they perceived that he
had seen a vision in the temple; and he made
signs to them and remained dumb. 23 And when
his time of service was ended, he went to his
home.

24 After these days his wife Elizabeth conceived, and for five months she hid herself, saying, 25 "Thus the Lord has done to me in the days when he looked on me, to take away my reproach among men."

Jerusalem Bible

great in the sight of the Lord; he must drink no
wine, no strong drink.[d] Even from his mother's
womb he will be filled with the Holy Spirit,
16 and he will bring back many of the sons of
Israel to the Lord their God. 17 With the spirit
and power of Elijah, he will go before him *to
turn the hearts of fathers toward their children*[e] and the disobedient back to the wisdom
that the virtuous have, preparing for the Lord a
people fit for him." 18 Zechariah said to the
angel, "*How can I be sure of this?* [f] I am an
old man and my wife is getting on in years."
19 The angel replied, "I am Gabriel who stand
in God's presence, and I have been sent to you
and bring you this good news. 20 Listen! Since
you have not believed my words, which will
come true at their appointed time, you will be
silenced and have no power of speech until this
has happened." 21 Meanwhile the people were
waiting for Zechariah and were surprised that
he stayed in the sanctuary so long. 22 When he
came out he could not speak to them, and they
realized that he had received a vision in the
sanctuary. But he could only make signs to them,
and remained dumb.

23 When his time of service came to an end
he returned home. 24 Some time later his wife
Elizabeth conceived, and for five months she
kept to herself. 25 "The Lord has done this for
me," she said, "now that it has pleased him to
take away the humiliation I suffered among
men."

[d] See Nb. 6:1, where this abstinence is required in anyone performing a vow to the Lord. [e] Ml. 3:23-24. [f] Zechariah asks for a sign in a way reminiscent of Abram, Gn. 15:8.

New English Bible

will be great in the eyes of the Lord. He shall never touch wine or strong drink. From his very birth he will be filled with the Holy Spirit; and he will bring back many Israelites to the Lord their God. He will go before him as forerunner,[a] possessed by the spirit and power of Elijah, to reconcile father and child, to convert the rebellious to the ways of the righteous, to prepare a people that shall be fit for the Lord.'

Zechariah said to the angel, 'How can I be sure of this? I am an old man and my wife is well on in years.'

The angel replied, 'I am Gabriel; I stand in attendance upon God, and I have been sent to speak to you and bring you this good news. But now listen: you will lose your power of speech, and remain silent until the day when these things happen to you, because you have not believed me, though at their proper time my words will be proved true.'

Meanwhile the people were waiting for Zechariah, surprised that he was staying so long inside. When he did come out he could not speak to them, and they realized that he had had a vision in the sanctuary. He stood there making signs to them, and remained dumb.

When his period of duty was completed Zechariah returned home. After this his wife Elizabeth conceived, and for five months she lived in seclusion, thinking, 'This is the Lord's doing; now at last he has deigned to take away my reproach among men.'

[a] *Or* In his sight he will go forth.

King James Version

my reproach among men. 26 And in the sixth
month the angel Gabriel was sent from God
unto a city of Galilee, named Nazareth, 27 To a
virgin espoused to a man whose name was
Joseph, of the house of David; and the virgin's
name *was* Mary. 28 And the angel came in unto
her, and said, Hail, *thou that art* highly favoured,
the Lord *is* with thee: blessed *art* thou among
women. 29 And when she saw *him*, she was
troubled at his saying, and cast in her mind
what manner of salutation this should be.
30 And the angel said unto her, Fear not, Mary:
for thou hast found favour with God. 31 And,
behold, thou shalt conceive in thy womb, and
bring forth a son, and shalt call his name
JESUS. 32 He shall be great, and shall be called
the Son of the Highest; and the Lord God shall
give unto him the throne of his father David:
33 And he shall reign over the house of Jacob
for ever; and of his kingdom there shall be no
end. 34 Then said Mary unto the angel, How
shall this be, seeing I know not a man? 35 And
the angel answered and said unto her, The Holy
Ghost shall come upon thee, and the power of
the Highest shall overshadow thee: therefore
also that holy thing which shall be born of thee
shall be called the Son of God. 36 And, behold,
thy cousin Elisabeth, she hath also conceived a
son in her old age; and this is the sixth month
with her, who was called barren. 37 For with
God nothing shall be impossible. 38 And Mary

Living Bible

26 The following month God sent the angel Gabriel to Nazareth, a village in Galilee, 27 to a virgin, Mary, engaged to be married to a man named Joseph, a descendant of King David.

28 Gabriel appeared to her and said, "Congratulations, favored lady! The Lord is with you!" [f]

29 Confused and disturbed, Mary tried to think what the angel could mean.

30 "Don't be frightened, Mary," the angel told her, "for God has decided to wonderfully bless you! 31 Very soon now, you will become pregnant and have a baby boy, and you are to name him 'Jesus.' 32 He shall be very great and shall be called the Son of God. And the Lord God shall give him the throne of his ancestor David. 33 And he shall reign over Israel forever; his Kingdom shall never end!"

34 Mary asked the angel, "But how can I have a baby? I am a virgin."

35 The angel replied, "The Holy Spirit shall come upon you, and the power of God shall overshadow you; so the baby born to you will be utterly holy—the Son of God. 36 Furthermore, six months ago your Aunt[g] Elizabeth—'the barren one,' they called her—became pregnant in her old age! 37 For every promise from God shall surely come true."

38 Mary said, "I am the Lord's servant, and

[f] Some ancient versions add, "Blessed are you among women," as in verse 42 which appears in all the manuscripts. [g] Literally, "relative."

Today's English Version

The birth of Jesus announced

26 In the sixth month of Elizabeth's pregnancy God sent the angel Gabriel to a town in Galilee named Nazareth. 27 He had a message for a girl promised in marriage to a man named Joseph, who was a descendant of King David. The girl's name was Mary. 28 The angel came to ner and said, "Peace be with you! The Lord is with you, and has greatly blessed you!"

29 Mary was deeply troubled by the angel's message, and she wondered what his words meant. 30 The angel said to her, "Don't be afraid, Mary, because God has been gracious to you. 31 You will become pregnant and give birth to a son, and you will name him Jesus. 32 He will be great and will be called the Son of the Most High God. The Lord God will make him a king, as his ancestor David was, 33 and he will be the king of the descendants of Jacob forever; his kingdom will never end!"

34 Mary said to the angel, "I am a virgin. How, then, can this be?"

35 The angel answered, "The Holy Spirit will come on you, and God's power will rest upon you. For this reason the holy child will be called the Son of God. 36 Remember your relative Elizabeth. It is said that she cannot have children; but she herself is now six months pregnant, even though she is very old. 37 For there is not a thing that God cannot do."

38 "I am the Lord's servant," said Mary; "may

New International Version

The birth of Jesus foretold

26 In the sixth month, God sent the angel Gabriel to Nazareth, a town in Galilee, 27 to a virgin pledged to be married to a man named Joseph, a descendant of David. The virgin's name was Mary. 28 The angel went to her and said, "Greetings, you who are highly favored! The Lord is with you."

29 Mary was greatly troubled at his words and wondered what kind of greeting this might be. 30 But the angel said to her, "Do not be afraid, Mary, you have found favor with God. 31 You will be with child and give birth to a son, and you are to give him the name Jesus. 32 He will be great and will be called the Son of the Most High. The Lord God will give him the throne of his father David, 33 and he will reign over the house of Jacob forever; his kingdom will never end."

34 "How can this be," Mary asked the angel, "since I am a virgin?"

35 The angel answered, "The Holy Spirit will come upon you, and the power of the Most High will overshadow you. So the holy one to be born will be called the Son of God. 36 Even Elizabeth your relative is going to have a child in her old age, and she who was said to be barren is in her sixth month. 37 For nothing is impossible with God."

38 "I am the Lord's servant," Mary answered.

Phillips Modern English

1.26 A vision comes to a young woman in Nazareth

Then, in the sixth month, the angel Gabriel was sent from God to a Galilean town, Nazareth by name, to a young woman who was engaged to a man called Joseph (a descendant of David). The girl's name was Mary. The angel entered her room and said,

"Greetings to you, Mary. O favoured one!—the Lord is with you!"

Mary was deeply perturbed at these words and wondered what such a greeting could possibly mean. But the angel said to her,

"Do not be afraid, Mary; God loves you dearly. You are going to be the mother of a son, and you will call him Jesus. He will be great and will be known as the Son of the Most High. The Lord God will give him the throne of his forefather, David, and he will be king over the people of Jacob for ever. His reign shall never end."

Then Mary spoke to the angel,

"How can this be," she said, "I am not married!"

But the angel made this reply to her:

"The Holy Spirit will come upon you, the power of the Most High will overshadow you. Your child will therefore be called holy—the Son of God. Your cousin Elisabeth has also conceived a son, old as she is. Indeed, this is the sixth month for her, a woman who was called barren. For no promise of God can fail to be fulfilled."

"I belong to the Lord, body and soul," re-

Revised Standard Version

26 In the sixth month the angel Gabriel was
sent from God to a city of Galilee named Nazareth, 27 to a virgin betrothed to a man whose
name was Joseph, of the house of David; and the
virgin's name was Mary. 28And he came to her
and said, "Hail, O favored one, the Lord is
with you!" [c] 29 But she was greatly troubled at
the saying, and considered in her mind what
sort of greeting this might be. 30And the angel
said to her, "Do not be afraid, Mary, for you
have found favor with God. 31And behold, you
will conceive in your womb and bear a son, and
you shall call his name Jesus.
32 He will be great, and will be called the
Son of the Most High;
and the Lord God will give to him the
throne of his father David,
33 and he will reign over the house of Jacob
for ever;
and of his kingdom there will be no end."
34And Mary said to the angel, "How shall this
be, since I have no husband?" 35And the angel
said to her,
"The Holy Spirit will come upon you,
and the power of the Most High will overshadow you;
therefore the child to be born[d] will be called
holy,
the Son of God.
36And behold, your kinswoman Elizabeth in her
old age has also conceived a son; and this is
the sixth month with her who was called barren.
37 For with God nothing will be impossible."
38And Mary said, "Behold, I am the handmaid

[c] Other ancient authorities add *"Blessed are you among women!"* [d] Other ancient authorities add *of you.*

Jerusalem Bible

The annunciation

26 In the sixth month the angel Gabriel was
sent by God to a town in Galilee called Nazareth, 27 to a virgin betrothed to a man named
Joseph, of the House of David; and the virgin's
name was Mary. 28 He went in and said to her,
"Rejoice, so highly favored! The Lord is with
you." 29 She was deeply disturbed by these
words and asked herself what this greeting could
mean, 30 but the angel said to her, "Mary, do
not be afraid; you have won God's favor. 31 Listen! You are to conceive and bear a son, and
you must name him Jesus. 32 He will be great
and will be called Son of the Most High. The
Lord God will give him the throne of his ancestor David; 33 he will rule over the House of
Jacob for ever and his reign will have no end."
34 Mary said to the angel, "But how can this
come about, since I am a virgin?" [g] 35 "The
Holy Spirit will come upon you," the angel answered, "and the power of the Most High will
cover you with its shadow. And so the child
will be holy and will be called Son of God.
36 Know this too: your kinswoman Elizabeth
has, in her old age, herself conceived a son, and
she whom people called barren is now in her
sixth month, 37 *for nothing is impossible to
God.*" [h] 38 "I am the handmaid of the Lord,"

[g] Literally "since I do not know man." [h] Gn. 8:14.

New English Bible

In the sixth month the angel Gabriel was sent from God to a town in Galilee called Nazareth, with a message for a girl betrothed to a man named Joseph, a descendant of David; the girl's name was Mary. The angel went in and said to her, 'Greetings, most favoured one! The Lord is with you.' But she was deeply troubled by what he said and wondered what this greeting might mean. Then the angel said to her, 'Do not be afraid, Mary, for God has been gracious to you; you shall conceive and bear a son, and you shall give him the name Jesus. He will be great; he will bear the title "Son of the Most High"; the Lord God will give him the throne of his ancestor David, and he will be king over Israel [a] for ever; his reign shall never end.' 'How can this be?' said Mary; 'I am still a virgin.' The angel answered, 'The Holy Spirit will come upon you, and the power of the Most High will overshadow you; and for that reason the holy child to be born will be called "Son of God".[b] Moreover your kinswoman Elizabeth has herself conceived a son in her old age; and she who is reputed barren is now in her sixth month, for God's promises can never fail.' [c] 'Here am I,' said Mary; 'I am the Lord's servant; as you have

[a] *Literally* the house of Jacob. [b] *Or* the child to be born will be called holy, "Son of God". [c] *Some witnesses read* for with God nothing will prove impossible.

King James Version

said, Behold the handmaid of the Lord; be it
unto me according to thy word. And the angel
departed from her. 39And Mary arose in those
days, and went into the hill country with haste,
into a city of Juda; 40And entered into the house
of Zacharias, and saluted Elisabeth. 41And it
came to pass, that, when Elisabeth heard the
salutation of Mary, the babe leaped in her
womb; and Elisabeth was filled with the Holy
Ghost: 42And she spake out with a loud voice,
and said, Blessed *art* thou among women, and
blessed *is* the fruit of thy womb. 43And whence
is this to me, that the mother of my Lord should
come to me? 44 For, lo, as soon as the voice of
thy salutation sounded in mine ears, the babe
leaped in my womb for joy. 45And blessed *is* she
that believed: for there shall be a performance
of those things which were told her from the
Lord. 46And Mary said, My soul doth magnify
the Lord, 47And my spirit hath rejoiced in God
my Saviour. 48 For he hath regarded the low
estate of his handmaiden: for, behold, from

Living Bible

I am willing to do whatever he wants. May
everything you said come true." And then the
angel disappeared.
39, 40 A few days later Mary hurried to the
highlands of Judea to the town where Zacharias
lived, to visit Elizabeth.
41 At the sound of Mary's greeting, Elizabeth's child leaped within her and she was filled
with the Holy Spirit.
42 "She gave a glad cry and exclaimed to
Mary, "You are favored by God above all other
women, and your child is destined for God's
mightiest praise. 43 What an honor this is, that
the mother of my Lord should visit me! 44 When
you came in and greeted me, the instant I heard
your voice, my baby moved in me for joy!
45 You believed that God would do what he
said; that is why he has given you this wonderful blessing."
46 Mary responded, "Oh, how I praise the
Lord. 47 How I rejoice in God my Savior! 48 For
he took notice of his lowly servant girl, and now

Today's English Version

it happen to me as you have said." And the angel
left her.

Mary visits Elizabeth

39 Soon afterward Mary got ready and hurried
off to the hill country, to a town in Judea. 40 She
went into Zechariah's house and greeted Elizabeth. 41 When Elizabeth heard Mary's greeting,
the baby moved within her. Elizabeth was filled
with the Holy Spirit, 42 and spoke in a loud
voice, "You are the most blessed of all women,
and blessed is the child you will bear! 43 Why
should this great thing happen to me, that my
Lord's mother comes to visit me? 44 For as soon
as I heard your greeting, the baby within me
jumped with gladness. 45 How happy are you to
believe that the Lord's message to you will come
true!"

Mary's song of praise

46 Mary said,

"My heart praises the Lord;
47 my soul is glad because of God my Savior,
48 because he has remembered me, his lowly
servant!

New International Version

"May it be to me as you have said." Then the
angel left her.

Mary visits Elizabeth

39 At that time Mary got ready and hurried
to a town in the hill country of Judah, 40 where
she entered Zechariah's home and greeted Elizabeth. 41 When Elizabeth heard Mary's greeting,
the baby leaped in her womb, and Elizabeth was
filled with the Holy Spirit. 42 In a loud voice she
exclaimed: "Blessed are you among women, and
blessed is the child you will bear! 43 But why am
I so favored, that the mother of my Lord should
come to me? 44As soon as the sound of your
greeting reached my ears, the baby in my womb
leaped for joy. 45 Blessed is she who has believed that what the Lord has said to her will be
accomplished!"

Mary's song

46 And Mary said:
"My soul praises the Lord
47 and my spirit rejoices in God my Savior,
48 for he has been mindful of the humble state
of his servant.

Phillips Modern English

plied Mary, "let it happen as you say." And at this the angel left her.

With little delay Mary got ready and hurried off to the hill-side town in Judaea where Zacharias and Elisabeth lived. She went into their house and greeted Elisabeth. When she heard Mary's greeting, the unborn child stirred inside her and she herself was filled with the Holy Spirit, and cried out,

*"Blessed are you among women,/and blessed is your child!/What an honour it is to have the mother of my Lord/come to see me!/As soon as your greeting reached my ears,/the child within me jumped for joy!/Oh, how happy is the woman who believes in God,/for his promises to her come true."/

Then Mary said,/"My heart is overflowing with praise of my Lord,/my soul is full of joy in God my Saviour./For he has deigned to notice me,

* This passage up to verse 55, and vv. 68–79, together with Ch. 2 vv. 29–32, were almost certainly known as hymns in the early Church and a likely verse form is indicated by oblique lines.

Revised Standard Version

of the Lord; let it be to me according to your
word." And the angel departed from her.
39 In those days Mary arose and went with
haste into the hill country, to a city of Judah,
40 and she entered the house of Zechariah and
greeted Elizabeth. 41 And when Elizabeth heard
the greeting of Mary, the babe leaped in her
womb; and Elizabeth was filled with the Holy
Spirit 42 and she exclaimed with a loud cry,
"Blessed are you among women, and blessed is
the fruit of your womb! 43 And why is this
granted me, that the mother of my Lord should
come to me? 44 For behold, when the voice of
your greeting came to my ears, the babe in my
womb leaped for joy. 45 And blessed is she who
believed that there would be[e] a fulfilment of
what was spoken to her from the Lord." 46 And
Mary said,

"My soul magnifies the Lord,
47 and my spirit rejoices in God my Savior,
48 for he has regarded the low estate of his
handmaiden.

[e] Or *believed, for there will be.*

Jerusalem Bible

said Mary, "let what you have said be done to me." And the angel left her.

The visitation

39 Mary set out at that time and went as
quickly as she could to a town in the hill country of Judah. 40 She went into Zechariah's house
and greeted Elizabeth. 41 Now as soon as Elizabeth heard Mary's greeting, the child leaped in
her womb and Elizabeth was filled with the
Holy Spirit. 42 She gave a loud cry and said,
"Of all women you are the most blessed, and
blessed is the fruit of your womb. 43 Why should
I be honored with a visit from the mother of
my Lord? 44 For the moment your greeting
reached my ears, the child in my womb leaped
for joy. 45 Yes, blessed is she who believed that
the promise made her by the Lord would be
fulfilled."

The Magnificat

46 And Mary[i] said:

"My soul proclaims the greatness of the Lord
47 and my spirit *exults in God my savior;*
48 because *he has looked upon his lowly handmaid.*

[i] Mary's canticle is reminiscent of Hannah's, 1 S. 2:1-10. Other quotations and allusions in the Magnificat are: 1 S. 1:11; Ps. 103:17; Ps. 111:9; Jb. 5:11 and 2:19; Ps. 98:3; Ps. 107:9; Is. 41:8-9.

New English Bible

spoken, so be it.' Then the angel left her.

About this time Mary set out and went straight to a town in the uplands of Judah. She went into Zechariah's house and greeted Elizabeth. And when Elizabeth heard Mary's greeting, the baby stirred in her womb. Then Elizabeth was filled with the Holy Spirit and cried aloud, 'God's blessing is on you above all women, and his blessing is on the fruit of your womb. Who am I, that the mother of my Lord should visit me? I tell you, when your greeting sounded in my ears, the baby in my womb leapt for joy. How happy is she who has had faith that the Lord's promise would be fulfilled!'

And Mary[d] said:

'Tell out, my soul, the greatness of the Lord,
rejoice, rejoice, my spirit, in God my saviour;
so tenderly has he looked upon his servant,
humble as she is.

[d] *So the majority of witnesses; some read* Elizabeth; *the original may have had no name.*

King James Version

henceforth all generations shall call me blessed.
49 For he that is mighty hath done to me great
things; and holy *is* his name. 50And his mercy *is*
on them that fear him from generation to generation. 51 He hath shewed strength with his arm;
he hath scattered the proud in the imagination
of their hearts. 52 He hath put down the mighty
from *their* seats, and exalted them of low degree.
53 He hath filled the hungry with good things;
and the rich he hath sent empty away. 54 He
hath holpen his servant Israel, in remembrance
of *his* mercy; 55As he spake to our fathers, to
Abraham, and to his seed for ever. 56And Mary
abode with her about three months, and returned
to her own house. 57 Now Elisabeth's full time
came that she should be delivered; and she
brought forth a son. 58And her neighbours and
her cousins heard how the Lord had shewed
great mercy upon her; and they rejoiced with

Living Bible

generation after generation forever shall call me
blest of God. 49 For he, the mighty Holy One,
has done great things to me. 50 His mercy goes
on from generation to generation, to all who
reverence him.
51 "How powerful is his mighty arm! How he
scatters the proud and haughty ones! 52 He has
torn princes from their thrones and exalted the
lowly. 53 He has satisfied the hungry hearts and
sent the rich away with empty hands. 54And
how he has helped his servant Israel! He has
not forgotten his promise to be merciful. 55 For
he promised our fathers—Abraham and his children—to be merciful to them forever."
56 Mary stayed with Elizabeth about three
months and then went back to her own home.
57 By now Elizabeth's waiting was over, for
the time had come for the baby to be born—
and it was a boy. 58 The word spread quickly to
her neighbors and relatives of how kind the Lord
had been to her, and everyone rejoiced.

Today's English Version

From now on all people will call me happy,
49 because of the great things the Mighty
God has done for me.
His name is holy;
50 he shows mercy to those who fear him,
from one generation to another.
51 He stretched out his mighty arm
and scattered the proud with all their
plans.
52 He brought down mighty kings from their
thrones,
and lifted up the lowly.
53 He filled the hungry with good things,
and sent the rich away with empty hands.
54 He kept the promise he made to our ancestors,
and came to the help of his servant Israel;
55 he remembered to show mercy to Abraham
and to all his descendants forever!"

56 Mary stayed about three months with Elizabeth, and then went back home.

The birth of John the Baptist

57 The time came for Elizabeth to have her
baby, and she gave birth to a son. 58 Her neighbors and relatives heard how wonderfully good
the Lord had been to her, and they all rejoiced
with her.

New International Version

From now on all generations will call me
blessed,
49 for the Mighty One has done great things
for me—
holy is his name.
50 His mercy extends to those who fear him,
from generation to generation.
51 He has performed mighty deeds with his
arm;
he has scattered those who are proud in
their inmost thoughts.
52 He has brought down rulers from their
thrones
but has lifted up the humble.
53 He has filled the hungry with good things
but has sent the rich away empty.
54 He has helped his servant Israel,
remembering to be merciful
55 to Abraham and his descendants forever,
even as he said to our fathers."
56 Mary stayed with Elizabeth for about three
months and then returned home.

The birth of John the Baptist

57 When it was time for Elizabeth to have
her baby, she gave birth to a son. 58 Her neighbors and relatives heard that the Lord had shown
her great mercy, and they shared her joy.

Phillips Modern English

his humble servant/and all generations to come/ will call me the happiest of women!/The One who can do all things/has done great things for me—/oh, holy is his Name!/Truly, his mercy rests on those who fear him/in every generation./He has shown the strength of his arm,/he has swept away the high and mighty./He has set kings down from their thrones/and lifted up the humble./He has satisfied the hungry with good things/and sent the rich away with empty hands./ Yes, he has helped Israel, his child:/he has remembered the mercy/that he promised to our forefathers,/to Abraham and his sons for evermore!"/

1.56 The old woman's son, John, is born

So Mary stayed with Elisabeth about three months, and then went back to her own home. Then came the time for Elisabeth's child to be born, and she gave birth to a son. Her neighbours and relations heard of the great mercy the Lord had shown her and shared her joy.

Revised Standard Version

For behold, henceforth all generations will call me blessed;
49 for he who is mighty has done great things for me,
and holy is his name.
50 And his mercy is on those who fear him from generation to generation.
51 He has shown strength with his arm,
he has scattered the proud in the imagination of their hearts,
52 he has put down the mighty from their thrones,
and exalted those of low degree;
53 he has filled the hungry with good things,
and the rich he has sent empty away.
54 He has helped his servant Israel,
in remembrance of his mercy,
55 as he spoke to our fathers,
to Abraham and to his posterity for ever."
56 And Mary remained with her about three
months, and returned to her home.
57 Now the time came for Elizabeth to be
delivered, and she gave birth to a son. 58 And
her neighbors and kinsfolk heard that the Lord
had shown great mercy to her, and they rejoiced

Jerusalem Bible

Yes, from this day forward all generations will call me blessed,
49 for the Almighty has done great things for me.
Holy is his name,
50 and *his mercy reaches from age to age for those who fear him.*
51 He has shown the power of his arm,
he has routed the proud of heart.
52 *He has pulled down princes* from their thrones *and exalted the lowly.*
53 *The hungry he has filled with good things,*
the rich sent empty away.
54 *He has come to the help of Israel his servant, mindful of his mercy*
55 —according to the promise he made to our ancestors—
of his mercy to Abraham and to his descendants for ever."

56 Mary stayed with Elizabeth about three months and then went back home.

The birth of John the Baptist and visit of the neighbors

57 Meanwhile the time came for Elizabeth to
have her child, and she gave birth to a son;
58 and when her neighbors and relations heard
that the Lord had shown her so great a kindness,
they shared her joy.

New English Bible

For, from this day forth,
all generations will count me blessed,
so wonderfully has he dealt with me,
the Lord, the Mighty One.

His name is Holy;
his mercy sure from generation to generation
toward those who fear him;
the deeds his own right arm has done
disclose his might:
the arrogant of heart and mind he has put to rout,
he has brought down monarchs from their thrones,
but the humble have been lifted high.
The hungry he has satisfied with good things,
the rich sent empty away.
He has ranged himself at the side of Israel his servant;
firm in his promise to our forefathers,
he has not forgotten to show mercy to Abraham
and his children's children, for ever.'

Mary stayed with her about three months and then returned home.

Now the time came for Elizabeth's child to be born, and she gave birth to a son. When her neighbours and relatives heard what great favour the Lord had shown her, they were as delighted

King James Version

her. 59And it came to pass, that on the eighth
day they came to circumcise the child; and they
called him Zacharias, after the name of his
father. 60And his mother answered and said,
Not *so;* but he shall be called John. 61And they
said unto her, There is none of thy kindred that
is called by this name. 62And they made signs to
his father, how he would have him called. 63And
he asked for a writing table, and wrote, saying,
His name is John. And they marvelled all. 64And
his mouth was opened immediately, and his
tongue *loosed,* and he spake, and praised God.
65And fear came on all that dwelt round about
them: and all these sayings were noised abroad
throughout all the hill country of Judea. 66And
all they that heard *them* laid *them* up in their
hearts, saying, What manner of child shall this
be! And the hand of the Lord was with him.
67And his father Zacharias was filled with the
Holy Ghost, and prophesied, saying, 68 Blessed
be the Lord God of Israel; for he hath visited
and redeemed his people, 69And hath raised up a
horn of salvation for us in the house of his
servant David; 70As he spake by the mouth of

Living Bible

59 When the baby was eight days old, all the
relatives and friends came for the circumcision
ceremony. They all assumed the baby's name
would be Zacharias, after his father.
60 But Elizabeth said, "No! He must be
named John!"
61 "What?" they exclaimed. "There is no one
in all your family by that name." 62 So they
asked the baby's father, talking to him by gestures.[h]
63 He motioned for a piece of paper and to
everyone's surprise wrote, "His name is *John!*"
64 Instantly Zacharias could speak again, and he
began praising God.
65 Wonder fell upon the whole neighborhood,
and the news of what had happened spread
through the Judean hills. 66And everyone who
heard about it thought long thoughts and asked,
"I wonder what this child will turn out to be?
For the hand of the Lord is surely upon him in
some special way."
67 Then his father Zacharias was filled with
the Holy Spirit and gave this prophecy:
68 "Praise the Lord, the God of Israel, for he
has come to visit his people and has redeemed
them. 69 He is sending us a Mighty Savior from
the royal line of his servant David, 70 just as he

[*h*] Zacharias was apparently stone deaf as well as speechless, and had not heard what his wife had said.

Today's English Version

59 When the baby was a week old they came
to circumcise him; they were going to name him
Zechariah, his father's name. 60 But his mother
said, "No! His name will be John."
61 They said to her, "But you don't have any
relative with that name!" 62 Then they made
signs to his father, asking him what name he
would like the boy to have.
63 Zechariah asked for a writing pad and
wrote, "His name is John." How surprised they
all were! 64At that moment Zechariah was able
to speak again, and he started praising God.
65 The neighbors were all filled with fear, and
the news about these things spread through all
the hill country of Judea. 66 Everyone who heard
of it thought about it and asked, "What is this
child going to be?" It was plain that the Lord's
power was with him.

Zechariah's prophecy

67 John's father Zechariah was filled with the
Holy Spirit, and he spoke God's message,

68 "Let us praise the Lord, the God of Israel!
He came to the help of his people and
set them free.
69 He provided a mighty Savior for us,
who is a descendant of his servant
David.
70 Long ago by means of his holy prophets

New International Version

59 On the eighth day they came to circumcise
the child, and they were going to name him after
his father Zechariah, 60 but his mother spoke up
and said, "No! He is to be called John."
61 They said to her, "There is no one among
your relatives who has that name."
62 Then they made signs to his father, to find
out what he would like to name the child. 63 He
asked for a writing tablet, and to everyone's
astonishment he wrote, "His name is John."
64 Immediately his mouth was opened and his
tongue was loosed, and he began to speak, praising God. 65 The neighbors were all filled with
awe, and throughout the hill country of Judea
people were talking about all these things.
66 Everyone who heard this wondered about it,
asking, "What then is this child going to be?"
For the Lord's hand was with him.

Zechariah's song

67 His father Zechariah was filled with the
Holy Spirit and prophesied:
68 "Praise the Lord, the God of Israel,
because he has come and has redeemed
his people.
69 He has raised up a horn[c] of salvation for
us
in the house of his servant David
70 (as he said through his holy prophets of

[*c*] *Horn* in the Old Testament symbolizes strength.

Phillips Modern English

When the eighth day came, they were going to circumcise the child and call him Zacharias, after his father, but his mother said,
"Oh, no! He must be called John."
"But none of your relations is called John," they replied. And they made signs to his father to see what name he wanted the child to have. He beckoned for a writing-tablet and wrote the words, "His name is John", which greatly surprised everybody. Then his power of speech suddenly came back, and his first words were to thank God. The neighbours were awe-struck at this, and all these incidents were reported everywhere in the hill-country of Judaea. People turned the whole matter over in their hearts, and said,
"What is this child's future going to be? For the Lord's blessing is plainly upon him."
Then Zacharias, his father, filled with the Holy Spirit and speaking like a prophet, said,
"Blessings on the Lord, the God of Israel,/because he has turned his face towards his people/ and has set them free!/And he has raised up for us a standard of salvation/in the house of his servant David./Long, long ago, through the

Revised Standard Version

with her. 59And on the eighth day they came to
circumcise the child; and they would have named
him Zechariah after his father, 60 but his mother
said, "Not so; he shall be called John." 61And
they said to her, "None of your kindred is called
by this name." 62And they made signs to his
father, inquiring what he would have him called.
63And he asked for a writing tablet, and wrote,
"His name is John." And they all marveled.
64And immediately his mouth was opened and
his tongue loosed, and he spoke, blessing God.
65And fear came on all their neighbors. And all
these things were talked about through all the
hill country of Judea; 66 and all who heard them
laid them up in their hearts, saying, "What then
will this child be?" For the hand of the Lord
was with him.
67 And his father Zechariah was filled with
the Holy Spirit, and prophesied, saying,
68 "Blessed be the Lord God of Israel,
for he has visited and redeemed his people,
69 and has raised up a horn of salvation for us
in the house of his servant David,
70 as he spoke by the mouth of his holy

Jerusalem Bible

The circumcision of John the Baptist

59 Now on the eighth day they came to circumcise the child; they were going to call [j] him
Zechariah after his father, 60 but his mother
spoke up. "No," she said, "he is to be called
John." 61 They said to her, "But no one in your
family has that name," 62 and made signs to his
father to find out what he wanted him called.
63 The father asked for a writing tablet and
wrote, "His name is John." And they were all
astonished. 64At that instant his power of speech
returned and he spoke and praised God. 65All
their neighbors were filled with awe and the
whole affair was talked about throughout the hill
country of Judaea. 66All those who heard of it
treasured it in their hearts. "What will this child
turn out to be?" they wondered. And indeed the
hand of the Lord was with him.

The Benedictus

67 His father Zechariah was filled with the
Holy Spirit and spoke this prophecy:

68 "*Blessed be the Lord, the God of Israel,*[k]
for he has visited his people, he has come to their rescue
69 and he has raised up for us a power for salvation
in the House of his servant David,
70 even as he proclaimed,

[j] The name was normally given at the time of circumcision. [k] Ps. 41:13.

New English Bible

as she was. Then on the eighth day they came to circumcise the child; and they were going to name him Zechariah after his father. But his mother spoke up and said, 'No! he is to be called John.' 'But', they said, 'there is nobody in your family who has that name.' They inquired of his father by signs what he would like him to be called. He asked for a writing-tablet and to the astonishment of all wrote down, 'His name is John.' Immediately his lips and tongue were freed and he began to speak, praising God. All the neighbours were struck with awe, and everywhere in the uplands of Judaea the whole story became common talk. All who heard it were deeply impressed and said, 'What will this child become?' For indeed the hand of the Lord was upon him.[a]
And Zechariah his father was filled with the Holy Spirit and uttered this prophecy:

'Praise to the God of Israel!
For he has turned to his people, saved them and set them free,
and has raised up a deliverer of victorious power
from the house of his servant David.

So he promised: age after age he proclaimed

[a] *Some witnesses read* 'What will this child become, for indeed the hand of the Lord is upon him?'

King James Version

his holy prophets, which have been since the
world began: 71 That we should be saved from
our enemies, and from the hand of all that hate
us; 72 To perform the mercy *promised* to our
fathers, and to remember his holy covenant;
73 The oath which he sware to our father Abraham, 74 That he would grant unto us, that we,
being delivered out of the hand of our enemies,
might serve him without fear, 75 In holiness and
righteousness before him, all the days of our
life. 76And thou, child, shalt be called the
prophet of the Highest: for thou shalt go before the face of the Lord to prepare his ways;
77 To give knowledge of salvation unto his people by the remission of their sins, 78 Through the
tender mercy of our God; whereby the dayspring from on high hath visited us, 79 To give
light to them that sit in darkness and *in* the
shadow of death, to guide our feet into the way
of peace. 80And the child grew, and waxed
strong in spirit, and was in the deserts till the
day of his shewing unto Israel.

Living Bible

promised through his holy prophets long ago—
71 someone to save us from our enemies, from
all who hate us.
72, 73 "He has been merciful to our ancestors,
yes, to Abraham himself, by remembering his
sacred promise to him, 74 and by granting us the
privilege of serving God fearlessly, freed from
our enemies, 75 and by making us holy and acceptable, ready to stand in his presence forever.
76 "And you, my little son, shall be called the
prophet of the glorious God, for you will prepare the way for the Messiah. 77 You will tell
his people how to find salvation through forgiveness of their sins. 78All this will be because the
mercy of our God is very tender, and heaven's
dawn is about to break upon us, 79 to give light
to those who sit in darkness and death's shadow,
and to guide us to the path of peace."
80 The little boy greatly loved God [i] and
when he grew up he lived out in the lonely
wilderness until he began his public ministry to
Israel.

[*i*] Literally, "became strong in spirit."

Today's English Version

he said this:
71 he promised to save us from our enemies,
and from the power of all those who hate us.
72 He said he would show mercy to our ancestors,
and remember his sacred covenant.
73, 74 He made a solemn promise to our ancestor Abraham,
and vowed that he would rescue us from our enemies,
and allow us to serve him without fear;
75 to be holy and righteous before him,
all the days of our life.

76 "You, my child, will be called a prophet of the Most High God.
You will go ahead of the Lord
to prepare his road for him;
77 to tell his people that they will be saved,
by having their sins forgiven.
78 Our God is merciful and tender.
He will cause the bright dawn of salvation to rise on us,
79 and shine from heaven on all those who live in the dark shadow of death,
to guide our steps into the path of peace."

80 The child grew and developed in body and
spirit. He lived in the desert until the day when
he would appear publicly to the people of Israel.

New International Version

long ago),
71 salvation from our enemies
and from the hand of all who hate us—
72 to show mercy to our fathers
and to remember his holy covenant,
73 the oath he swore to our father Abraham:
74 to rescue us from the hand of our enemies,
and to enable us to serve him without fear
75 in holiness and righteousness before him all our days.
76 And you, my child, will be called a prophet of the Most High;
for you will go on before the Lord to prepare the way for him,
77 to give his people the knowledge of salvation
through the forgiveness of their sins,
78 because of the tender mercy of our God,
by which the rising sun will come to us from heaven
79 to shine on those living in darkness
and in the shadow of death,
to guide our feet into the path of peace."
80 And the child grew and became strong in
spirit; and he lived in the desert until he appeared publicly to Israel.

Phillips Modern English

words of his holy prophets,/he promised to do this for us,/so that we should be safe from our enemies/and secure from all who hate us./So does he continue the mercy/he showed to our forefathers./So does he remember the holy agreement/he made with them/and the oath which he swore to our father Abraham,/to make us this gift:/that we should be saved/from the hands of our enemies,/and in his presence should serve him unafraid/in holiness and righteousness all our lives./

"And you, little child, will be called the prophet/of the Most High;/for you will go before the Lord/to prepare the way for his coming./It will be for you to give his people/knowledge of their salvation/through the forgiveness of their sins./Because the heart of our God/is full of mercy towards us,/the first light of Heaven shall come to visit us—/to shine on those who lie in darkness/and under the shadow of death,/and to guide our feet into the path of peace."/

The little child grew up and became strong in spirit. He lived in lonely places until the day came for him to show himself to Israel.

Revised Standard Version

prophets from of old,
71 that we should be saved from our enemies,
and from the hand of all who hate us;
72 to perform the mercy promised to our fathers,
and to remember his holy covenant,
73 the oath which he swore to our father Abraham, 74 to grant us
that we, being delivered from the hand of our enemies,
might serve him without fear,
75 in holiness and righteousness before him all the days of our life.
76 And you, child, will be called the prophet of the Most High;
for you will go before the Lord to prepare his ways,
77 to give knowledge of salvation to his people
in the forgiveness of their sins,
78 through the tender mercy of our God,
when the day shall dawn upon[f] us from on high
79 to give light to those who sit in darkness and in the shadow of death,
to guide our feet into the way of peace."
80 And the child grew and became strong in spirit, and he was in the wilderness till the day of his manifestation to Israel.

[f] Or *whereby the dayspring will visit.* Other ancient authorities read *since the dayspring has visited.*

Jerusalem Bible

by the mouth of his holy prophets from ancient times,
71 that he would save us from our enemies
and from the hands of all who hate us.
72 Thus he shows mercy to our ancestors,
thus *he remembers* his holy *covenant,*[l]
73 the oath he swore
to our father Abraham
74 that he would grant us, free from fear,
to be delivered from the hands of our enemies,
75 to serve him in holiness and virtue
in his presence, all our days.
76 And you, little child,
you shall be called Prophet of the Most High,
for you will go before the Lord
to prepare the way for him.
77 To give his people knowledge of salvation
through the forgiveness of their sins;
78 this by the tender mercy of our God
who from on high will bring the rising Sun to visit us,
79 to give light to *those who live*
in darkness and the shadow of death,[m]
and to guide our feet
into the way of peace."

The hidden life of John the Baptist

80 Meanwhile the child grew up and his spirit matured. And he lived out in the wilderness until the day he appeared openly to Israel.

[l] Lv. 26:42. [m] Is. 9:1.

New English Bible

by the lips of his holy prophets,
that he would deliver us from our enemies,
out of the hands of all who hate us;
that he would deal mercifully with our fathers,
calling to mind his solemn covenant.

Such was the oath he swore to our father Abraham,
to rescue us from enemy hands,
and grant us, free from fear, to worship him
with a holy worship, with uprightness of heart,
in his presence, our whole life long.

And you, my child, you shall be called Prophet of the Highest,
for you will be the Lord's forerunner, to prepare his way
and lead his people to salvation through knowledge of him,
by the forgiveness of their sins:
for in the tender compassion of our God
the morning sun from heaven will rise[b] upon us,
to shine on those who live in darkness, under the cloud of death,
and to guide our feet into the way of peace.'

As the child grew up he became strong in spirit; he lived out in the wilds until the day when he appeared publicly before Israel.

[b] *Some witnesses read* has risen.

King James Version

2 And it came to pass in those days, that there went out a decree from Cesar Augustus, that all the world should be taxed. 2 (*And* this taxing was first made when Cyrenius was governor of Syria.) 3 And all went to be taxed, every one into his own city. 4 And Joseph also went up from Galilee, out of the city of Nazareth, into Judea, unto the city of David, which is called Bethlehem, (because he was of the house and lineage of David,) 5 To be taxed with Mary his espoused wife, being great with child. 6 And so it was, that, while they were there, the days were accomplished that she should be delivered. 7 And she brought forth her firstborn son, and wrapped him in swaddling clothes, and laid him in a manger; because there was no room for them in the inn. 8 And there were in the same country shepherds abiding in the field, keeping watch over their flock by night. 9 And, lo, the angel of the Lord came upon them, and the glory of the Lord shone round about them; and they were sore afraid. 10 And the angel said unto them, Fear not: for, behold, I bring you good tidings of great joy, which shall be to all people. 11 For unto you is born this day in the city of David a Saviour, which is Christ the

Living Bible

2 About this time Caesar Augustus, the Roman Emperor, decreed that a census should be taken throughout the nation. 2 (This census was taken when Quirinius was governor of Syria.)

3 Everyone was required to return to his ancestral home for this registration. 4 And because Joseph was a member of the royal line, he had to go to Bethlehem in Judea, King David's ancient home—journeying there from the Galilean village of Nazareth. 5 He took with him Mary, his fiancée, who was obviously pregnant by this time.

6 And while they were there, the time came for her baby to be born; 7 and she gave birth to her first child, a son. She wrapped him in a blanket[a] and laid him in a manger, because there was no room for them in the village inn.

8 That night some shepherds were in the fields outside the village, guarding their flocks of sheep. 9 Suddenly an angel appeared among them, and the landscape shone bright with the glory of the Lord. They were badly frightened, 10 but the angel reassured them.

"Don't be afraid!" he said. "I bring you the most joyful news ever announced, and it is for everyone! 11 The Savior—yes, the Messiah, the Lord—has been born tonight in Bethlehem![b]

[*a*] Literally, "swaddling clothes." [*b*] Literally, "in the City of David."

Today's English Version

The birth of Jesus

2 At that time Emperor Augustus sent out an order for all the citizens of the Empire to register themselves for the census. 2 When this first census took place, Quirinius was the governor of Syria. 3 Everyone, then, went to register himself, each to his own town.

4 Joseph went from the town of Nazareth, in Galilee, to Judea, to the town named Bethlehem, where King David was born. Joseph went there because he was a descendant of David. 5 He went to register himself with Mary, who was promised in marriage to him. She was pregnant, 6 and while they were in Bethlehem, the time came for her to have her baby. 7 She gave birth to her first son, wrapped him in cloths and laid him in a manger—there was no room for them to stay in the inn.

The shepherds and the angels

8 There were some shepherds in that part of the country who were spending the night in the fields, taking care of their flocks. 9 An angel of the Lord appeared to them, and the glory of the Lord shone over them. They were terribly afraid, 10 but the angel said to them, "Don't be afraid! I am here with good news for you, which will bring great joy to all the people. 11 This very day in David's town your Savior was born—

New International Version

The birth of Jesus

2 In those days Caesar Augustus issued a decree that a census should be taken of the entire Roman world. 2 (This was the first census that took place while Quirinius was governor of Syria.) 3 And everyone went to his own town to register.

4 So Joseph also went up from the town of Nazareth in Galilee to Judea, to Bethlehem the town of David, because he belonged to the house and line of David. 5 He went there to register with Mary, who was pledged to be married to him and was expecting a child. 6 While they were there, the time came for the baby to be born, 7 and she gave birth to her firstborn, a son. She wrapped him in strips of cloth and placed him in a manger, because there was no room for them in the inn.

The shepherds and the angels

8 And there were shepherds living out in the fields nearby, keeping watch over their flocks at night. 9 An angel of the Lord appeared to them, and the glory of the Lord shone around them, and they were terrified. 10 But the angel said to them, "Do not be afraid. I bring you good news of great joy that will be for all the people. 11 Today in the town of David a Savior has been born to you; he is Christ[d] the Lord.

[*d*] Or *Messiah*. "The Christ" (Greek) and "the Messiah" (Hebrew) both mean "the Anointed One."

Phillips Modern English

2.1 The census brings Mary and Joseph to Bethlehem

At that time a proclamation was made by Caesar Augustus that all the inhabited world should be registered. This was the first census, undertaken while Cyrenius was governor of Syria; and everybody went to the town of his birth to be registered. Joseph went up from the town of Nazareth in Galilee to David's town, Bethlehem, in Judaea, because he was a direct descendant of David, to be registered with his future wife, Mary, who was pregnant. So it happened that it was while they were there in Bethlehem that she came to the end of her time. She gave birth to her first child, a son. And as there was no place for them inside the inn, she wrapped him up and laid him in a manger.

2.8 A vision comes to shepherds on the hill-side

There were some shepherds living in the same part of the country, keeping guard throughout the night over their flock in the open fields. Suddenly an angel of the Lord stood before them, the splendour of the Lord blazed around them, and they were terror-stricken. But the angel said to them,

"Do not be afraid! Listen, I bring you glorious news of great joy which is for all the people. This very day, in David's town, a Saviour has

Revised Standard Version

2 In those days a decree went out from
Caesar Augustus that all the world should
be enrolled. 2 This was the first enrollment, when
Quirinius was governor of Syria. 3 And all went
to be enrolled, each to his own city. 4 And Joseph also went up from Galilee, from the city
of Nazareth, to Judea, to the city of David,
which is called Bethlehem, because he was of
the house and lineage of David, 5 to be enrolled
with Mary, his betrothed, who was with child.
6 And while they were there, the time came for
her to be delivered. 7 And she gave birth to her
first-born son and wrapped him in swaddling
cloths, and laid him in a manger, because there
was no place for them in the inn.
8 And in that region there were shepherds out
in the field, keeping watch over their flock by
night. 9 And an angel of the Lord appeared to
them, and the glory of the Lord shone around
them, and they were filled with fear. 10 And the
angel said to them, "Be not afraid; for behold,
I bring you good news of a great joy which will
come to all the people; 11 for to you is born this
day in the city of David a Savior, who is Christ

Jerusalem Bible

The birth of Jesus and visit of the shepherds

2 Now at this time Caesar Augustus[n] issued
a decree for a census of the whole world to
be taken. 2 This census—the first[o]—took place
while Quirinius was governor of Syria, 3 and
everyone went to his own town to be registered.
4 So Joseph set out from the town of Nazareth
in Galilee and traveled up to Judaea, to the town
of David called Bethlehem, since he was of
David's House and line, 5 in order to be registered together with Mary, his betrothed, who
was with child. 6 While they were there the time
came for her to have her child, 7 and she gave
birth to a son, her first-born.[p] She wrapped him
in swaddling clothes, and laid him in a manger
because there was no room for them at the inn.
8 In the countryside close by there were shepherds who lived in the fields and took it in turns
to watch their flocks during the night. 9 The
angel of the Lord appeared to them and the
glory of the Lord shone around them. They were
terrified, 10 but the angel said, "Do not be afraid.
Listen, I bring you news of great joy, a joy to
be shared by the whole people. 11 Today in the
town of David a savior has been born to you;

[n] Emperor of Rome 30 B.C to 14 A.D. [o] About 8-6 B.C. [p] The term does not necessarily imply younger brothers.

New English Bible

2 In those days a decree was issued by the Emperor Augustus for a registration to be made throughout the Roman world. This was the first registration of its kind; it took place when Quirinius[a] was governor of Syria. For this purpose everyone made his way to his own town; and so Joseph went up to Judaea from the town of Nazareth in Galilee, to register at the city of David, called Bethlehem, because he was of the house of David by descent; and with him went Mary who was betrothed to him. She was expecting a child, and while they were there the time came for her baby to be born, and she gave birth to a son, her first-born. She wrapped him in his swaddling clothes, and laid him in a manger, because there was no room for them to lodge in the house.

Now in this same district there were shepherds out in the fields, keeping watch through the night over their flock, when suddenly there stood before them an angel of the Lord, and the splendour of the Lord shone round them. They were terror-stricken, but the angel said, 'Do not be afraid; I have good news for you: there is great joy coming to the whole people. Today in the city of David a deliverer has been born to you

[a] *Or* This was the first registration carried out while Quirinius . . .

King James Version

Lord. 12And this *shall be* a sign unto you; Ye
shall find the babe wrapped in swaddling clothes,
lying in a manger. 13And suddenly there was
with the angel a multitude of the heavenly host
praising God, and saying, 14 Glory to God in
the highest, and on earth peace, good will toward men. 15And it came to pass, as the angels
were gone away from them into heaven, the
shepherds said one to another, Let us now go
even unto Bethlehem, and see this thing which
is come to pass, which the Lord hath made
known unto us. 16And they came with haste, and
found Mary and Joseph, and the babe lying in a
manger. 17And when they had seen *it,* they made
known abroad the saying which was told them
concerning this child. 18And all they that heard
it wondered at those things which were told
them by the shepherds. 19 But Mary kept all
these things, and pondered *them* in her heart.
20And the shepherds returned, glorifying and
praising God for all the things that they had
heard and seen, as it was told unto them. 21And
when eight days were accomplished for the circumcising of the child, his name was called
JESUS, which was so named of the angel be-

Living Bible

12 How will you recognize him? You will find
a baby wrapped in a blanket,[c] lying in a manger!"

13 Suddenly, the angel was joined by a vast
host of others—the armies of heaven—praising
God:

14 "Glory to God in the highest heaven," they
sang,[d] "and peace on earth for all those pleasing
him."

15 When this great army of angels had returned again to heaven, the shepherds said to
each other, "Come on! Let's go to Bethlehem!
Let's see this wonderful thing that has happened,
which the Lord has told us about."

16 They ran to the village and found their
way to Mary and Joseph. And there was the
baby, lying in the manger. 17 The shepherds told
everyone what had happened and what the angel
had said to them about this child. 18All who
heard the shepherds' story expressed astonishment, 19 but Mary quietly treasured these things
in her heart and often thought about them.

20 Then the shepherds went back again to
their fields and flocks, praising God for the visit
of the angels, and because they had seen the
child, just as the angel had told them.

21 Eight days later, at the baby's circumcision
ceremony, he was named Jesus, the name given
him by the angel before he was even conceived.

[*c*] Literally, "swaddling clothes." [*d*] Literally, "said."

Today's English Version

Christ the Lord! 12 What will prove it to you is
this: you will find a baby wrapped in cloths and
lying in a manger."

13 Suddenly a great army of heaven's angels
appeared with the angel, singing praises to God,

14 "Glory to God in the highest heaven,
and peace on earth to those with whom
he is pleased!"

15 When the angels went away from them
back into heaven, the shepherds said to one another, "Let us go to Bethlehem and see this
thing that has happened, that the Lord has told
us."

16 So they hurried off and found Mary and
Joseph, and saw the baby lying in the manger.
17 When the shepherds saw him they told them
what the angel had said about this child. 18All
who heard it were filled with wonder at what
the shepherds told them. 19 Mary remembered
all these things and thought deeply about them.
20 The shepherds went back, singing praises to
God for all they had heard and seen; it had been
just as the angel had told them.

Jesus is named

21 A week later, when the time came for the
baby to be circumcised, he was named Jesus,
the name which the angel had given him before
he had been conceived.

New International Version

12 This will be a sign to you: You will find a
baby wrapped in strips of cloth and lying in a
manger."

13 Suddenly a great company of the heavenly
host appeared with the angel, praising God and
saying,

14 "Glory to God in the highest,
and on earth peace to men on whom his
favor rests."

15 When the angels had left them and gone
into heaven, the shepherds said to one another,
"Let's go to Bethlehem and see this thing that
has happened, which the Lord has told us
about."

16 So they hurried off and found Mary and
Joseph, and the baby, who was lying in the
manger. 17 When they had seen him, they
spread the word concerning what had been told
them about this child, 18 and all who heard it
were amazed at what the shepherds said to them.
19 But Mary treasured up all these things and
pondered them in her mind. 20 The shepherds
returned, glorifying and praising God for all
the things they had heard and seen, which were
just as they had been told.

Jesus presented in the temple

21 On the eighth day, when it was time to
circumcise him, he was named Jesus, the name
the angel had given him before he had been conceived.

Phillips Modern English

been born for you. He is Christ, the Lord. Let this prove it to you: you will find a baby, wrapped up and lying in a manger."

And in a flash there appeared with the angel a vast host of the armies of Heaven, praising God, saying,

"Glory to God in the highest Heaven! Peace upon earth among men of goodwill!"

When the angels left them and went back into Heaven, the shepherds said to each other,

"Now let us go straight to Bethlehem and see this thing which the Lord has made known to us."

So they went as fast as they could and they found Mary and Joseph—and the baby lying in the manger. And when they had seen this sight, they told everybody what had been said to them about the little child. And all those who heard them were amazed at what the shepherds said. But Mary treasured all these things and turned them over in her mind. The shepherds went back to work, glorifying and praising God for everything that they had heard and seen, which had happened just as they had been told.

2.21 Mary and Joseph bring their newly-born son to the Temple

At the end of the eight days, the time came for circumcising the child and he was called Jesus, the name given to him by the angel before his conception.

Revised Standard Version

the Lord. 12And this will be a sign for you: you
will find a babe wrapped in swaddling cloths and
lying in a manger." 13And suddenly there was
with the angel a multitude of the heavenly host
praising God and saying,
14 "Glory to God in the highest,
and on earth peace among men with whom
he is pleased!" [g]
15 When the angels went away from them
into heaven, the shepherds said to one another,
"Let us go over to Bethlehem and see this thing
that has happened, which the Lord has made
known to us." 16And they went with haste, and
found Mary and Joseph, and the babe lying in
a manger. 17And when they saw it they made
known the saying which had been told them
concerning this child; 18 and all who heard it
wondered at what the shepherds told them.
19 But Mary kept all these things, pondering
them in her heart. 20And the shepherds returned,
glorifying and praising God for all they had
heard and seen, as it had been told them.
21 And at the end of eight days, when he was
circumcised, he was called Jesus, the name given
by the angel before he was conceived in the
womb.

[g] Other ancient authorities read *peace, good will among men.*

Jerusalem Bible

he is Christ the Lord. 12And here is a sign for
you: you will find a baby wrapped in swaddling
clothes and lying in a manger." 13And suddenly
with the angel there was a great throng of the
heavenly host, praising God and singing:

14 "Glory to God in the highest heaven,
and peace to men who enjoy his favor."

15 Now when the angels had gone from them
into heaven, the shepherds said to one another,
"Let us go to Bethlehem and see this thing that
has happened which the Lord has made known
to us." 16 So they hurried away and found Mary
and Joseph, and the baby lying in the manger.
17 When they saw the child they repeated what
they had been told about him, 18 and everyone
who heard it was astonished at what the shepherds had to say. 19As for Mary, she treasured
all these things and pondered them in her heart.
20And the shepherds went back glorifying and
praising God for all they had heard and seen;
it was exactly as they had been told.

The circumcision of Jesus

21 When the eighth day came and the child
was to be circumcised, they gave him the name
Jesus, the name the angel had given him before
his conception.

New English Bible

—the Messiah, the Lord.[b] And this is your sign: you will find a baby lying wrapped in his swaddling clothes, in a manger.' All at once there was with the angel a great company of the heavenly host, singing the praises of God:

'Glory to God in highest heaven,
and on earth his peace for men on whom his favour rests.' [c]

After the angels had left them and gone into heaven the shepherds said to one another, 'Come, we must go straight to Bethlehem and see this thing that has happened, which the Lord has made known to us.' So they went with all speed and found their way to Mary and Joseph; and the baby was lying in the manger. When they saw him, they recounted what they had been told about this child; and all who heard were astonished at what the shepherds said. But Mary treasured up all these things and pondered over them. Meanwhile the shepherds returned glorifying and praising God for what they had heard and seen; it had all happened as they had been told.

Eight days later the time came to circumcise him, and he was given the name Jesus, the name given by the angel before he was conceived.

[b] *Some witnesses read* to you—the Lord's Messiah.
[c] *Some witnesses read* and on earth his peace, his favour towards men.

King James Version

fore he was conceived in the womb. 22And when
the days of her purification according to the law
of Moses were accomplished, they brought him
to Jerusalem, to present *him* to the Lord; 23 (As
it is written in the law of the Lord, Every male
that openeth the womb shall be called holy to
the Lord;) 24And to offer a sacrifice according
to that which is said in the law of the Lord, A
pair of turtledoves, or two young pigeons. 25And,
behold, there was a man in Jerusalem, whose
name *was* Simeon; and the same man *was* just
and devout, waiting for the consolation of
Israel: and the Holy Ghost was upon him.
26And it was revealed unto him by the Holy
Ghost, that he should not see death, before he
had seen the Lord's Christ. 27And he came by
the Spirit into the temple: and when the parents
brought in the child Jesus, to do for him after
the custom of the law, 28 Then took he him up
in his arms, and blessed God, and said, 29 Lord,
now lettest thou thy servant depart in peace, according to thy word: 30 For mine eyes have seen
thy salvation, 31 Which thou hast prepared be-

Living Bible

22 When the time came for Mary's purification offering at the Temple, as required by the
laws of Moses after the birth of a child, his
parents took him to Jerusalem to present him to
the Lord; 23 for in these laws God had said, "If
a woman's first child is a boy, he shall be dedicated to the Lord."
24 At that time Jesus' parents also offered
their sacrifice for purification—"either a pair of
turtledoves or two young pigeons" was the legal
requirement. 25 That day a man named Simeon,
a Jerusalem resident, was in the Temple. He was
a good man, very devout, filled with the Holy
Spirit and constantly expecting the Messiah[e] to
come soon. 26 For the Holy Spirit had revealed
to him that he would not die until he had seen
him—God's anointed King. 27 The Holy Spirit
had impelled him to go to the Temple that day;
and so, when Mary and Joseph arrived to present the baby Jesus to the Lord in obedience to
the law, 28 Simeon was there and took the child
in his arms, praising God.
29, 30, 31 "Lord," he said, "now I can die
content! For I have seen him as you promised
me I would. I have seen the Savior you have

[*e*] Literally, "the Consolation of Israel."

Today's English Version

Jesus is presented in the temple

22 The time came for Joseph and Mary to do
what the Law of Moses commanded and perform the ceremony of purification. So they took
the child to Jerusalem to present him to the
Lord, 23 as it is written in the law of the Lord,
"Every firstborn male shall be dedicated to the
Lord." 24 They also went to offer a sacrifice of
a pair of doves or two young pigeons, as required by the law of the Lord.
25 Now there was a man living in Jerusalem
whose name was Simeon. He was a good and
God-fearing man, and was waiting for Israel to
be saved. The Holy Spirit was with him, 26 and
he had been assured by the Holy Spirit that he
would not die before he had seen the Lord's
promised Messiah. 27 Led by the Spirit, Simeon
went into the temple. When the parents brought
the child Jesus into the temple to do for him
what the Law required, 28 Simeon took the child
in his arms, and gave thanks to God:

29 "Now, Lord, you have kept your promise,
and you may let your servant go in
peace.
30 With my own eyes I have seen your salvation,
31 which you have prepared in the presence of all peoples:

New International Version

22 When the time of their purification according to the Law of Moses had been completed,
Joseph and Mary took him to Jersualem to
present him to the Lord 23 (as it is written in
the Law of the Lord, "Every firstborn male is to
be consecrated to the Lord"[e]), 24 and to offer
a sacrifice in keeping with what is said in the
Law of the Lord: "A pair of doves or two young
pigeons."[f]
25 Now there was a man in Jerusalem called
Simeon, who was righteous and devout. He was
waiting for the consolation of Israel, and the
Holy Spirit was upon him. 26 It had been revealed to him by the Holy Spirit that he would
not die before he had seen the Lord's Christ.[g]
27 Moved by the Spirit, he went into the temple
courts. When the parents brought in the child
Jesus to do for him as the custom of the Law
required, 28 Simeon took him in his arms and
praised God, saying:
29 "Sovereign Lord, as you promised,
now dismiss your servant in peace.
30 For my eyes have seen your salvation,
31 which you have prepared in the sight of
all people,

[*e*] Exodus 13:2,12,15. [*f*] Lev. 12:8. [*g*] Or *Messiah.*

Phillips Modern English

When the "purification" time, stipulated by the Law of Moses, was completed, they brought Jesus to Jerusalem to present him to the Lord. This was to fulfil a requirement of the law of the Lord—

"Every male that openeth the womb shall be called holy to the Lord."

They also offered the sacrifice prescribed by the Law—

"A pair of turtle doves, or two young pigeons."

In Jerusalem there was at this time a man by the name of Simeon. He was an upright man, devoted to the service of God, living in expectation of the Restoration of Israel. His heart was open to the Holy Spirit, and it had been revealed to him that he would not die before he saw the Lord's Christ. He had been led by the Spirit to go into the Temple, and when Jesus' parents brought the child in to have done to him what the Law required, he took him up in his arms, blessed God and said—

"Now, Lord, you are dismissing your servant/ in peace, as you promised!/For with my own eyes I have seen your salvation/which you have

Revised Standard Version

22 And when the time came for their purification according to the law of Moses, they brought
him up to Jerusalem to present him to the Lord
23 (as it is written in the law of the Lord, "Every
male that opens the womb shall be called holy
to the Lord") 24 and to offer a sacrifice according to what is said in the law of the Lord, "a
pair of turtledoves, or two young pigeons."
25 Now there was a man in Jerusalem, whose
name was Simeon, and this man was righteous
and devout, looking for the consolation of Israel, and the Holy Spirit was upon him. 26And
it had been revealed to him by the Holy Spirit
that he should not see death before he had seen
the Lord's Christ. 27And inspired by the Spirit[h]
he came into the temple; and when the parents
brought in the child Jesus, to do for him according to the custom of the law, 28 he took him up
in his arms and blessed God and said,

29 "Lord, now lettest thou thy servant depart
in peace,
according to thy word;
30 for mine eyes have seen thy salvation
31 which thou hast prepared in the presence
of all peoples,

[*h*] Or *in the Spirit.*

Jerusalem Bible

Jesus is presented in the Temple

22 And when the day came for them to be
purified [q] as laid down by the Law of Moses,
they took him up to Jerusalem to present him to
the Lord—23 observing what stands written in
the Law of the Lord: *Every first-born male must
be consecrated to the Lord* [r]—24 also to offer in
sacrifice, in accordance with what is said in the
Law of the Lord, *a pair of turtledoves or two
young pigeons.*[s] 25 Now in Jerusalem there was
a man named Simeon. He was an upright and
devout man; he looked forward to Israel's comforting and the Holy Spirit rested on him. 26 It
had been revealed to him by the Holy Spirit that
he would not see death until he had set eyes on
the Christ of the Lord.[t] 27 Prompted by the
Spirit he came to the Temple; and when the
parents brought in the child Jesus to do for him
what the Law required, 28 he took him into his
arms and blessed God; and he said:

The Nunc Dimittis

29 "Now, Master, you can let your servant go
in peace,
just as you promised;
30 because my eyes have seen the salvation
31 which you have prepared for all the nations to see,

[*q*] The mother needed to be "purified"; the child had to be "redeemed." [*r*] Ex. 13:2. [*s*] The offering of the poor, Lv. 5:7. [*t*] "The anointed one of God."

New English Bible

Then, after their purification had been completed in accordance with the Law of Moses, they brought him up to Jerusalem to present him to the Lord (as prescribed in the law of the Lord: 'Every first-born male shall be deemed to belong to the Lord'), and also to make the offering as stated in the law: 'A pair of turtle doves or two young pigeons.'

There was at that time in Jerusalem a man called Simeon. This man was upright and devout, one who watched and waited for the restoration of Israel, and the Holy Spirit was upon him. It had been disclosed to him by the Holy Spirit that he would not see death until he had seen the Lord's Messiah. Guided by the Spirit he came into the temple; and when the parents brought in the child Jesus to do for him what was customary under the Law, he took him in his arms, praised God, and said:

'This day, Master, thou givest thy servant his
discharge in peace;
now thy promise is fulfilled.
For I have seen with my own eyes
the deliverance which thou hast made ready
in full view of all the nations:

King James Version

fore the face of all people; 32 A light to lighten
the Gentiles, and the glory of thy people Israel.
33 And Joseph and his mother marvelled at those
things which were spoken of him. 34 And Simeon
blessed them, and said unto Mary his mother,
Behold, this *child* is set for the fall and rising
again of many in Israel; and for a sign which
shall be spoken against; 35 (Yea, a sword shall
pierce through thy own soul also;) that the
thoughts of many hearts may be revealed. 36 And
there was one Anna, a prophetess, the daughter
of Phanuel, of the tribe of Aser: she was of a
great age, and had lived with a husband seven
years from her virginity; 37 And she *was* a widow
of about fourscore and four years, which departed not from the temple, but served *God*
with fastings and prayers night and day. 38 And
she coming in that instant gave thanks likewise
unto the Lord, and spake of him to all them

Living Bible

given to the world. 32 He is the Light that will
shine upon the nations, and he will be the glory
of your people Israel!"

33 Joseph and Mary just stood there, marveling at what was being said about Jesus.

34, 35 Simeon blessed them but then said to
Mary, "A sword shall pierce your soul, for this
child shall be rejected by many in Israel, and
this to their undoing. But he will be the greatest
joy of many others. And the deepest thoughts of
many hearts shall be revealed."

36, 37 Anna, a prophetess, was also there in
the Temple that day. She was the daughter of
Phanuel, of the Jewish tribe of Asher, and was
very old, for she had been a widow for eighty-
four years following seven years of marriage.
She never left the Temple but stayed there night
and day, worshiping God by praying and often
fasting.

38 She came along just as Simeon was talking
with Mary and Joseph, and she also began
thanking God and telling everyone in Jerusalem
who had been awaiting the coming of the Savior[f]
that the Messiah had finally arrived.

[*f*] Literally, "looking for the redemption of Jerusalem."

Today's English Version

32 A light to reveal your way to the Gentiles,
and bring glory to your people Israel."

33 The child's father and mother were amazed
at the things Simeon said about him. 34 Simeon
blessed them and said to Mary, his mother,
"This child is chosen by God for the destruction
and the salvation of many in Israel. He will be
a sign from God which many people will speak
against, 35 and so reveal their secret thoughts.
And sorrow, like a sharp sword, will break your
own heart."

36 There was a prophetess named Anna, daughter of Phanuel, of the tribe of Asher. She was
an old woman who had been married for seven
years, 37 and then had been a widow for eighty-
four years. She never left the temple; day and
night she worshiped God, fasting and praying.
38 That very same hour she arrived and gave
thanks to God, and spoke about the child to all
who were waiting for God to redeem Jerusalem.

New International Version

32 a light for revelation to the Gentiles
and for glory to your people Israel."

33 The child's father and mother marveled at
what was said about him. 34 Then Simeon
blessed them and said to Mary, his mother:
"This child is destined to cause the falling and
rising of many in Israel, and to be a sign that
will be spoken against, 35 so that the thoughts
of many hearts will be revealed. And a sword
will pierce your own soul too."

36 There was also a prophetess, Anna, the
daughter of Phanuel, of the tribe of Asher. She
was very old; she had lived with her husband
seven years after her marriage, 37 and then was
a widow until she was eighty-four. She never
left the temple but worshiped night and day,
fasting and praying. 38 Coming up to them at
that very moment, she gave thanks to God and
spoke about the child to all who were looking
forward to the redemption of Jerusalem.

Phillips Modern English

made ready for all peoples to see/—a light to show truth to the gentiles/and bring glory to your people Israel."/

The child's father and mother were still amazed at what was said about him, when Simeon gave them his blessing. He said to Mary, the child's mother,

"This child is destined to make many fall and many rise in Israel and to set up a standard which many will attack—for he will expose the secret thoughts of many hearts. And for you . . . your very soul will be pierced by a sword."

There was also present, Anna, the daughter of Phanuel of the tribe of Asher, who was a prophetess. She was a very old woman, having had seven years' married life and was now a widow of eighty-four. She spent her whole life in the Temple and worshipped God night and day with fastings and prayers. She came up at this very moment, praised God and spoke about Jesus to all those in Jerusalem who were expecting redemption.

Revised Standard Version

32 a light for revelation to the Gentiles,
and for glory to thy people Israel."
33 And his father and his mother marveled at
what was said about him; 34 and Simeon blessed
them and said to Mary his mother,
"Behold, this child is set for the fall and
rising of many in Israel,
and for a sign that is spoken against
35 (and a sword will pierce through your own
soul also),
that thoughts out of many hearts may be
revealed."
36 And there was a prophetess, Anna, the
daughter of Phanuel, of the tribe of Asher; she
was of a great age, having lived with her husband seven years from her virginity, 37 and as a
widow till she was eighty-four. She did not depart from the temple, worshiping with fasting
and prayer night and day. 38And coming up at
that very hour she gave thanks to God, and
spoke of him to all who were looking for the
redemption of Jerusalem.

Jerusalem Bible

32 a light to enlighten the pagans
and the glory of your people Israel."

The prophecy of Simeon

33 As the child's father and mother stood
there wondering at the things that were being
said about him, 34 Simeon blessed them and said
to Mary his mother, "You see this child: he is
destined for the fall and for the rising of many
in Israel, destined to be a sign that is rejected—
35 and a sword will pierce your own soul too
—so that the secret thoughts of many may be
laid bare."

The prophecy of Anna

36 There was a prophetess also, Anna the
daughter of Phanuel, of the tribe of Asher. She
was well on in years. Her days of girlhood over,
she had been married for seven years 37 before
becoming a widow. She was now eighty-four
years old and never left the Temple, serving
God night and day with fasting and prayer.
38 She came by just at that moment and began
to praise God; and she spoke of the child to all
who looked forward to the deliverance of Jerusalem.[u]

[u] I.e., Israel. Jerusalem is the holy city.

New English Bible

a light that will be a revelation to the heathen,
and glory to thy people Israel.'

The child's father and mother were full of wonder at what was being said about him. Simeon blessed them and said to Mary his mother, 'This child is destined to be a sign which men reject; and you too shall be pierced to the heart. Many in Israel will stand or fall[a] because of him, and thus the secret thoughts of many will be laid bare.'

There was also a prophetess, Anna the daughter of Phanuel, of the tribe of Asher. She was a very old woman, who had lived seven years with her husband after she was first married, and then alone as a widow to the age of eighty-four.[b] She never left the temple, but worshipped day and night, fasting and praying. Coming up at that very moment, she returned thanks to God; and she talked about the child to all who were looking for the liberation of Jerusalem.

[a] *Or* Many in Israel will fall and rise again . . .
[b] *Or* widow for another eighty-four years.

King James Version

that looked for redemption in Jerusalem. 39And
when they had performed all things according
to the law of the Lord, they returned into Galilee, to their own city Nazareth. 40And the child
grew, and waxed strong in spirit, filled with wisdom; and the grace of God was upon him.
41 Now his parents went to Jerusalem every year
at the feast of the passover. 42And when he was
twelve years old, they went up to Jerusalem
after the custom of the feast. 43And when they
had fulfilled the days, as they returned, the
child Jesus tarried behind in Jerusalem; and
Joseph and his mother knew not *of it.* 44 But
they, supposing him to have been in the company, went a day's journey; and they sought
him among *their* kinsfolk and acquaintance.
45And when they found him not, they turned
back again to Jerusalem, seeking him. 46And it
came to pass, that after three days they found
him in the temple, sitting in the midst of the
doctors, both hearing them, and asking them
questions. 47And all that heard him were astonished at his understanding and answers. 48And
when they saw him, they were amazed: and his
mother said unto him, Son, why hast thou thus
dealt with us? behold, thy father and I have
sought thee sorrowing. 49And he said unto them,
How is it that ye sought me? wist ye not that I

Living Bible

39 When Jesus' parents had fulfilled all the
requirements of the Law of God they returned
home to Nazareth in Galilee. 40 There the child
became a strong, robust lad, and was known for
wisdom beyond his years; and God poured out
his blessings on him.
41, 42 When Jesus was twelve years old he
accompanied his parents to Jerusalem for the
annual Passover Festival, which they attended
each year. 43After the celebration was over they
started home to Nazareth, but Jesus stayed behind in Jerusalem. His parents didn't miss him
the first day, 44 for they assumed he was with
friends among the other travelers. But when he
didn't show up that evening, they started to look
for him among their relatives and friends; 45 and
when they couldn't find him, they went back to
Jerusalem to search for him there.
46, 47 Three days later they finally discovered
him. He was in the Temple, sitting among the
teachers of Law, discussing deep questions with
them and amazing everyone with his understanding and answers.
48 His parents didn't know what to think.
"Son!" his mother said to him. "Why have you
done this to us? Your father and I have been
frantic, searching for you everywhere."
49 "But why did you need to search?" he

Today's English Version

The return to Nazareth

39 When they had finished doing all that was
required by the law of the Lord, they returned
to Galilee, to their home town of Nazareth.
40 The child grew and became strong; he was
full of wisdom, and God's blessings were with
him.

The boy Jesus in the temple

41 Every year the parents of Jesus went to
Jerusalem for the Feast of Passover. 42 When
Jesus was twelve years old, they went to the feast
as usual. 43 When the days of the feast were
over, they started back home, but the boy Jesus
stayed in Jerusalem. His parents did not know
this; 44 they thought that he was with the group,
so they traveled a whole day, and then started
looking for him among their relatives and friends.
45 They did not find him, so they went back to
Jerusalem looking for him. 46 On the third day
they found him in the temple, sitting with the
Jewish teachers, listening to them and asking
questions. 47All who heard him were amazed at
his intelligent answers. 48 His parents were
amazed when they saw him, and his mother said
to him, "Son, why have you done this to us?
Your father and I have been terribly worried
trying to find you."
49 He answered them, "Why did you have to

New International Version

39 When Joseph and Mary had done everything required by the Law of the Lord, they returned to Galilee to their own town of Nazareth.
40And the child grew and became strong; he
was filled with wisdom, and the grace of God
was upon him.

The boy Jesus at the temple

41 Every year his parents went to Jerusalem
for the Feast of the Passover. 42 When he was
twelve years old, they went up to the feast, according to the custom. 43After the feast was
over, while his parents were returning home, the
boy Jesus stayed behind in Jerusalem, but they
were unaware of it. 44 Thinking he was in their
company, they traveled on for a day. Then they
began looking for him among their relatives
and friends. 45 When they did not find him, they
went back to Jerusalem to look for him. 46After
three days they found him in the temple courts,
sitting among the teachers, listening to them
and asking them questions. 47 Everyone who
heard him was amazed at his understanding and
his answers. 48 When his parents saw him, they
were astonished. His mother said to him, "Son,
why have you treated us like this? Your father
and I have been anxiously searching for you."
49 "Why were you searching for me?" he

Phillips Modern English

When they had completed all the requirements of the Law of the Lord, they returned to Galilee, to their own town of Nazareth. The child grew up and became strong and full of wisdom. And God's blessing was upon him.

2.41 Twelve years later: the boy Jesus goes with his parents to Jerusalem

Every year at the Passover festival, Jesus' parents used to go to Jerusalem. When he was twelve years old they went up to the city as usual for the festival. When it was over they started back home, but the boy Jesus stayed behind in Jerusalem, without his parents' knowledge. They went a day's journey assuming that he was somewhere in their company, and then they began to look for him among their relations and acquaintances. They failed to find him, however, and turned back to the city, looking for him as they went. Three days later, they found him—in the Temple, sitting among the teachers, listening to them and asking them questions. All those who heard him were astonished at his powers of comprehension and at the answers that he gave. When Joseph and Mary saw him, they could hardly believe their eyes, and his mother said to him,

"Why have you treated us like this, my son? Here have your father and I been worried, looking for you everywhere!"

And Jesus replied,

"But why were you looking for me? Did you

Revised Standard Version

39 And when they had performed everything
according to the law of the Lord, they returned
into Galilee, to their own city, Nazareth. 40And
the child grew and became strong, filled with
wisdom; and the favor of God was upon him.
41 Now his parents went to Jerusalem every
year at the feast of the Passover. 42And when
he was twelve years old, they went up according to custom; 43 and when the feast was ended,
as they were returning, the boy Jesus stayed behind in Jerusalem. His parents did not know it,
44 but supposing him to be in the company they
went a day's journey, and they sought him among
their kinsfolk and acquaintances; 45 and when
they did not find him, they returned to Jerusalem, seeking him. 46After three days they found
him in the temple, sitting among the teachers,
listening to them and asking them questions;
47 and all who heard him were amazed at his
understanding and his answers. 48And when
they saw him they were astonished; and his
mother said to him, "Son, why have you treated
us so? Behold, your father and I have been looking for you anxiously." 49And he said to them,
"How is it that you sought me? Did you not

Jerusalem Bible

The hidden life of Jesus at Nazareth

39 When they had done everything the Law
of the Lord required, they went back to Galilee,
to their own town of Nazareth. 40 Meanwhile
the child grew to maturity, and he was filled
with wisdom; and God's favor was with him.

Jesus among the doctors of the Law

41 Every year his parents used to go to Jerusalem for the feast of the Passover. 42 When he
was twelve years old, they went up for the feast
as usual. 43 When they were on their way home
after the feast, the boy Jesus stayed behind in
Jerusalem without his parents knowing it.
44 They assumed he was with the caravan, and
it was only after a day's journey that they went
to look for him among their relations and
acquaintances. 45 When they failed to find him
they went back to Jerusalem looking for him
everywhere.
46 Three days later, they found him in the
Temple, sitting among the doctors, listening to
them, and asking them questions; 47 and all
those who heard him were astounded at his intelligence and his replies. 48 They were overcome when they saw him, and his mother said
to him, "My child, why have you done this to
us? See how worried your father and I have
been, looking for you." 49 "Why were you look-

New English Bible

When they had done everything prescribed in the law of the Lord, they returned to Galilee to their own town of Nazareth. The child grew big and strong and full of wisdom; and God's favour was upon him.

Now it was the practice of his parents to go to Jerusalem every year for the Passover festival; and when he was twelve, they made the pilgrimage as usual. When the festive season was over and they started for home, the boy Jesus stayed behind in Jerusalem. His parents did not know of this; but thinking that he was with the party they journeyed on for a whole day, and only then did they begin looking for him among their friends and relations. As they could not find him they returned to Jerusalem to look for him; and after three days they found him sitting in the temple surrounded by the teachers, listening to them and putting questions; and all who heard him were amazed at his intelligence and the answers he gave. His parents were astonished to see him there, and his mother said to him, 'My son, why have you treated us like this? Your father and I have been searching for you in great anxiety.' 'What made you search?' he said. 'Did

King James Version

must be about my Father's business? 50And they understood not the saying which he spake unto them. 51And he went down with them, and came to Nazareth, and was subject unto them: but his mother kept all these sayings in her heart. 52And Jesus increased in wisdom and stature, and in favour with God and man.

3 Now in the fifteenth year of the reign of Tiberius Cesar, Pontius Pilate being governor of Judea, and Herod being tetrarch of Galilee, and his bother Philip tetrarch of Iturea and of the region of Trachonitis, and Lysanias the tetrarch of Abilene, 2Annas and Caiaphas being

Living Bible

asked. "Didn't you realize that I would be here at the Temple, in my Father's House?" 50 But they didn't understand what he meant.

51 Then he returned to Nazareth with them and was obedient to them; and his mother stored away all these things in her heart. 52 So Jesus grew both tall and wise, and was loved by God and man.

3 In the fifteenth year of the reign of Emperor Tiberius Caesar, a message came from God to John (the son of Zacharias), as he was living out in the deserts. (Pilate was governor over Judea at that time; Herod, over Galilee; his brother Philip, over Iturea and Trachonitis; Lysanias, over Abilene; and Annas and Caiaphas

Today's English Version

look for me? Didn't you know that I had to be in my Father's house?" 50 But they did not understand what he said to them.

51 So Jesus went back with them to Nazareth, where he was obedient to them. His mother treasured all these things in her heart. 52And Jesus grew, both in body and in wisdom, gaining favor with God and men.

The preaching of John the Baptist

3 It was the fifteenth year of the rule of Emperor Tiberius; Pontius Pilate was governor of Judea, Herod was ruler of Galilee, and his brother Philip ruler of the territory of Iturea and Trachonitis; Lysanias was ruler of Abilene, 2 and Annas and Caiaphas were high priests. It

New International Version

asked. "Didn't you know I had to be in my Father's house?" 50 But they did not understand what he meant.

51 Then he went down to Nazareth with them and was obedient to them. But his mother treasured all these things in her heart. 52And Jesus grew in wisdom and stature, and in favor with God and men.

John the Baptist prepares the way

3 In the fifteenth year of the reign of Tiberius Caesar—when Pontius Pilate was governor of Judea, Herod tetrarch of Galilee, his brother Philip tetrarch of Iturea and Trachonitis, and Lysanias tetrarch of Abilene—2 and during the

Phillips Modern English

not know that I must be in my Father's house?"
But they did not understand his reply. Then he went home with them to Nazareth and was obedient to them. And his mother treasured all these things in her heart. And as Jesus continued to grow in body and mind, he grew also in the love of God and of those who knew him.

3.1 Several years later: John prepares the way of Christ

In the fifteenth year of the reign of the Emperor Tiberius (a year when Pontius Pilate was governor of Judaea, Herod tetrarch of Galilee, Philip, his brother, tetrarch of the territory of Ituraea and Trachonitis, and Lysanias tetrarch of Abilene, while Annas and Caiaphas were the

Revised Standard Version

know that I must be in my Father's house?"
50And they did not understand the saying which
he spoke to them. 51And he went down with
them and came to Nazareth, and was obedient
to them; and his mother kept all these things in
her heart.
52 And Jesus increased in wisdom and in
stature,[i] and in favor with God and man.

3 In the fifteenth year of the reign of Tiberius
Caesar, Pontius Pilate being governor of
Judea, and Herod being tetrarch of Galilee, and
his brother Philip tetrarch of the region of
Ituraea and Trachonitis, and Lysanias tetrarch
of Abilene, 2 in the high-priesthood of Annas

[*i*] Or *years*.

Jerusalem Bible

ing for me?" he replied. "Did you not know
that I must be busy with my Father's affairs?"
50 But they did not understand what he meant.

The hidden life at Nazareth resumed

51 He then went down with them and came
to Nazareth and lived under their authority. His
mother stored up all these things in her heart.
52And Jesus increased in wisdom, in stature, and
in favor with God and men.

II. Prelude to the public ministry of Jesus

The preaching of John the Baptist

3 In the fifteenth year of Tiberius Caesar's
reign,[v] when Pontius Pilate[w] was governor of
Judaea. Herod[x] tetrarch of Galilee, his brother
Philip[y] tetrarch of the lands of Ituraea and
Trachonitis, Lysanias tetrarch of Abilene, 2 dur-

[*v*] By Roman dating, the fifteenth year of Tiberius Caesar's reign was August 28 A.D. to August 29 A.Q.; by the Syrian method, it was September-October 27 A.D. to September-October 28 A.D. At that time Jesus was between thirty-three and thirty-six years old. The mistake in calculating "the Christian era" results from taking Lk. 3:23 as an exact statement. [*w*] Procurator of Judaea 26-36 A.D. [*x*] Herod Antipas, tetrarch of Galilee and Peraea 4 B.C. to 39 A.D. [*y*] Tetrarch from 4 B.C. to 34 A.D.

New English Bible

you not know that I was bound to be in my Father's house?' But they did not understand what he meant. Then he went back with them to Nazareth, and continued to be under their authority; his mother treasured up all these things in her heart. As Jesus grew up he advanced in wisdom and in favour with God and men.

3 In the fifteenth year of the Emperor Tiberius, when Pontius Pilate was governor of Judaea, when Herod was prince of Galilee, his brother Philip prince of Ituraea and Trachonitis, and Lysanias prince of Abilene, during the high-

King James Version

the high priests, the word of God came unto
John the son of Zacharias in the wilderness.
3And he came into all the country about Jordan,
preaching the baptism of repentance for the remission of sins; 4As it is written in the book of
the words of Esaias the prophet, saying, The
voice of one crying in the wilderness, Prepare ye
the way of the Lord, make his paths straight.
5 Every valley shall be filled, and every mountain
and hill shall be brought low; and the crooked
shall be made straight, and the rough ways *shall*
be made smooth; 6And all flesh shall see the
salvation of God. 7 Then said he to the multitude
that came forth to be baptized of him, O generation of vipers, who hath warned you to flee
from the wrath to come? 8 Bring forth therefore fruits worthy of repentance, and begin not
to say within yourselves, We have Abraham to
our father: for I say unto you, That God is able
of these stones to raise up children unto Abraham. 9And now also the axe is laid unto the root
of the trees: every tree therefore which bringeth
not forth good fruit is hewn down, and cast into
the fire. 10And the people asked him, saying,
What shall we do then? 11 He answereth and
saith unto them, He that hath two coats, let him
impart to him that hath none; and he that hath

Living Bible

were High Priests.) 3 Then John went from place
to place on both sides of the Jordan River,
preaching that people should be baptized to show
that they had turned to God and away from their
sins, in order to be forgiven.[a]
4 In the words of Isaiah the prophet, John
was "a voice shouting from the barren wilderness, 'Prepare a road for the Lord to travel on!
Widen the pathway before him! 5 Level the
mountains! Fill up the valleys! Straighten the
curves! Smooth out the ruts! 6And then all mankind shall see the Savior sent from God.' "
7 Here is a sample of John's preaching to the
crowds that came for baptism: "You brood of
snakes! You are trying to escape hell without
truly turning to God! That is why you want to
be baptized! 8 First go and prove by the way you
live that you really have repented. And don't
think you are safe because you are descendants
of Abraham. That isn't enough. God can produce
children of Abraham from these desert stones!
9 The axe of his judgment is poised over you,
ready to sever your roots and cut you down.
Yes, every tree that does not produce good fruit
will be chopped down and thrown into the fire."
10 The crowd replied, "What do you want us
to do?"
11 "If you have two coats," he replied, "give
one to the poor. If you have extra food, give it
away to those who are hungry."

[a] Or, "preaching the baptism of repentance for remission of sins."

Today's English Version

was at this time that the word of God came to
John, the son of Zechariah, in the desert. 3 So
John went throughout the whole territory of the
Jordan River. "Turn away from your sins and
be baptized," he preached, "and God will forgive your sins." 4As the prophet Isaiah had written in his book,

"Someone is shouting in the desert:
'Get the Lord's road ready for him;
make a straight path for him to travel!
5 All low places must be filled up,
all hills and mountains leveled off.
The winding roads must be made straight,
and the rough paths made smooth.
6 All mankind will see God's salvation!' "

7 Crowds of people came out to John to be
baptized by him. "You snakes!" he said to them.
"Who told you that you could escape from
God's wrath that is about to come? 8 Do the
things that will show that you have turned from
your sins. And don't start saying among yourselves, 'Abraham is our ancestor.' I tell you that
God can take these rocks and make descendants
for Abraham! 9 The ax is ready to cut down the
trees at the roots; every tree that does not bear
good fruit will be cut down and thrown in the
fire."
10 The people asked him, "What are we to
do, then?"
11 He answered, "Whoever has two shirts
must give one to the man who has none, and
whoever has food must share it."

New International Version

high-priesthood of Annas and Caiaphas, the
word of God came to John son of Zechariah in
the desert. 3 He went into all the country around
the Jordan, preaching a baptism of repentance
for the forgiveness of sins. 4As is written in the
book of the words of Isaiah the prophet:
"A voice of one calling in the desert,
'Prepare the way for the Lord,
make straight paths for him.
5 Every valley shall be filled in,
and every mountain and hill leveled off.
The crooked roads shall become straight,
and the rough ways smooth.
6 And all mankind shall see God's salvation.'[h] "
7 John said to the crowds coming out to be
baptized by him, "You brood of vipers! Who
warned you to flee from the coming wrath?
8 Produce fruit in keeping with repentance. And
do not begin to say to yourselves, 'We have
Abraham as our father.' For I tell you that out
of these stones God can raise up children for
Abraham. 9 The ax is already at the root of the
trees, and every tree that does not produce good
fruit will be cut down and thrown into the fire."
10 "What should we do then?" the crowd
asked.
11 John answered, "The man with two tunics
should share with him who has none, and the
one who has food should do the same."

[h] Isaiah 40:3-5.

Phillips Modern English

High Priests), the word of God came to John, the son of Zacharias, while he was in the desert. He went into the whole country round about the Jordan proclaiming baptism as a mark of a complete change of heart and of the forgiveness of sins, as the book of the prophet Isaiah says—

The voice of one crying in the wilderness,
Make ye ready the way of the Lord,
Make his paths straight.
Every valley shall be filled,
And every mountain and hill shall be brought low:
And the crooked shall become straight,
And the rough ways smooth:
And all flesh shall see the salvation of God.

So John used to say to the crowds who came out to be baptised by him,

"Who warned you, you serpent's brood, to escape from the wrath to come? See that your lives prove that your hearts are really changed! Don't start thinking that you can say to yourselves, 'We are Abraham's children', for I tell you that God could produce children of Abraham out of these stones! The axe already lies at the root of the tree, and the tree that fails to produce good fruit is cut down and thrown into the fire."

Then the crowds would ask him, "Then what shall we do?"

And his answer was, "The man who has two shirts must share with the man who has none, and the man who has food must do the same."

Revised Standard Version

and Caiaphas, the word of God came to John
the son of Zechariah in the wilderness; 3 and he
went into all the region about the Jordan, preaching a baptism of repentance for the forgiveness
of sins. 4 As it is written in the book of the words
of Isaiah the prophet,
"The voice of one crying in the wilderness:
Prepare the way of the Lord,
make his paths straight.
5 Every valley shall be filled,
and every mountain and hill shall be brought
low,
and the crooked shall be made straight,
and the rough ways shall be made smooth;
6 and all flesh shall see the salvation of God."
7 He said therefore to the multitudes that
came out to be baptized by him, "You brood of
vipers! Who warned you to flee from the wrath
to come? 8 Bear fruits that befit repentance, and
do not begin to say to yourselves, 'We have
Abraham as our father'; for I tell you, God is
able from these stones to raise up children to
Abraham. 9 Even now the axe is laid to the root
of the trees; every tree therefore that does not
bear good fruit is cut down and thrown into the
fire."
10 And the multitudes asked him, "What then
shall we do?" 11 And he answered them, "He
who has two coats, let him share with him who
has none; and he who has food, let him do like-

Jerusalem Bible

ing the pontificate of Annas and Caiaphas,[z] the
word of God came to John son of Zechariah, in
the wilderness. 3 He went through the whole Jordan district proclaiming a baptism of repentance
for the forgiveness of sins, 4 as it is written in
the book of the sayings of the prophet Isaiah:

A voice cries in the wilderness:
Prepare a way for the Lord,
make his paths straight.
5 *Every valley will be filled in,*
every mountain and hill be laid low,
winding ways will be straightened
and rough roads made smooth.
6 *And all mankind shall see the salvation of*
God.[a]

7 He said, therefore, to the crowds who came
to be baptized by him, "Brood of vipers, who
warned you to fly from the retribution that is
coming? 8 But if you are repentant, produce the
appropriate fruits, and do not think of telling
yourselves, 'We have Abraham for our father,'
because, I tell you, God can raise children for
Abraham from these stones. 9 Yes, even now the
ax is laid to the roots of the trees, so that any
tree which fails to produce good fruit will be
cut down and thrown on the fire."
10 When all the people asked him, "What
must we do, then?" 11 he answered, "If anyone
has two tunics he must share with the man who
has none, and the one with something to eat

[z] Caiaphas was high priest from 18 to 36 A.D. His father-in-law, Annas, is associated with him here and elsewhere; he had been high priest earlier and presumably still had great influence. [a] Is. 40:3-5.

New English Bible

priesthood of Annas and Caiaphas, the word of God came to John son of Zechariah in the wilderness. And he went all over the Jordan valley proclaiming a baptism in token of repentance for the forgiveness of sins, as it is written in the book of the prophecies of Isaiah:

'A voice crying aloud in the wilderness,
"Prepare a way for the Lord;
clear a straight path for him.
Every ravine shall be filled in,
and every mountain and hill levelled;
the corners shall be straightened,
and the rugged ways made smooth;
and all mankind shall see God's deliverance."'

Crowds of people came out to be baptized by him, and he said to them: 'You vipers' brood! Who warned you to escape from the coming retribution? Then prove your repentance by the fruit it bears; and do not begin saying to yourselves, "We have Abraham for our father." I tell you that God can make children for Abraham out of these stones here. Already the axe is laid to the roots of the trees; and every tree that fails to produce good fruit is cut down and thrown on the fire.'

The people asked him, 'Then what are we to do?' He replied, 'The man with two shirts must share with him who has none, and anyone who

King James Version

meat, let him do likewise. 12 Then came also
publicans to be baptized, and said unto him,
Master, what shall we do? 13And he said unto
them, Exact no more than that which is appointed you. 14And the soldiers likewise demanded of him, saying, And what shall we do?
And he said unto them, Do violence to no man,
neither accuse *any* falsely; and be content with
your wages. 15And as the people were in expectation, and all men mused in their hearts of
John, whether he were the Christ, or not;
16 John answered, saying unto *them* all, I indeed
baptize you with water; but one mightier than I
cometh, the latchet of whose shoes I am not
worthy to unloose: he shall baptize you with the
Holy Ghost and with fire: 17 Whose fan *is* in his
hand, and he will thoroughly purge his floor,
and will gather the wheat into his garner; but
the chaff he will burn with fire unquenchable.
18And many other things in his exhortation
preached he unto the people. 19 But Herod the
tetrarch, being reproved by him for Herodias
his brother Philip's wife, and for all the evils
which Herod had done, 20Added yet this above

Living Bible

12 Even tax collectors—notorious for their
corruption—came to be baptized and asked,
"How shall we prove to you that we have abandoned our sins?"
13 "By your honesty," he replied. "Make sure
you collect no more taxes than the Roman[b] government requires you to."
14 "And us," asked some soldiers, "what
about us?"
John replied, "Don't extort money by threats
and violence; don't accuse anyone of what you
know he didn't do; and be content with your
pay!"
15 Everyone was expecting the Messiah to
come soon, and eager to know whether or not
John was he. This was the question of the hour,
and was being discussed everywhere.
16 John answered the question by saying, "I
baptize only with water; but someone is coming
soon who has far higher authority than mine; in
fact, I am not even worthy of being his slave.[c]
He will baptize you with fire—with the Holy
Spirit. 17 He will separate chaff from grain, and
burn up the chaff with eternal fire and store
away the grain." 18 He used many such warnings as he announced the Good News to the
people.
19, 20 (But after John had publicly criticized
Herod, governor of Galilee, for marrying Herodias, his brother's wife, and for many other
wrongs he had done, Herod put John in prison,
thus adding this sin to all his many others.)

[*b*] Implied. [*c*] Literally, "of loosing (the sandal strap of) his shoe."

Today's English Version

12 Some tax collectors came to be baptized,
and they asked him, "Teacher, what are we to
do?"
13 "Don't collect more than is legal," he told
them.
14 Some soldiers also asked him, "What about
us? What are we to do?"
He said to them, "Don't take money from
anyone by force or accuse anyone falsely. Be
content with your pay."
15 People's hopes began to rise, and they began to wonder about John, thinking that perhaps
he might be the Messiah. 16 So John said to all
of them, "I baptize you with water, but one who
is much greater than I is coming. I am not good
enough even to untie his sandals. He will baptize
you with the Holy Spirit and fire. 17 He has his
winnowing shovel with him, to thresh out all the
grain and gather the wheat into his barn; but
he will burn the chaff in a fire that never goes
out."
18 In many different ways John urged the
people as he preached the Good News to them.
19 But John spoke against Governor Herod, because he had married Herodias, his brother's
wife, and had done many other evil things.
20 Then Herod did an even worse thing by
putting John in prison.

New International Version

12 Tax collectors also came to be baptized.
"Teacher," they asked, "what should we do?"
13 "Don't collect any more than you are required to," he told them.
14 Then some soldiers asked him, "And what
should we do?"
He replied, "Don't extort money and don't
accuse people falsely—be content with your
pay."
15 The people were waiting expectantly and
were all wondering in their hearts if John might
possibly be the Christ.[i] 16 John answered them
all, "I baptize you with[j] water. But one more
powerful than I will come, the thongs of whose
sandals I am not worthy to untie. He will baptize you with the Holy Spirit and fire. 17 His
winnowing fork is in his hand to clear his
threshing floor and to gather the wheat into his
barn, but he will burn up the chaff with unquenchable fire." 18And with many other words
John exhorted the people and preached the
good news to them.
19 But when John rebuked Herod the tetrarch
because of Herodias, his brother's wife, and all
the other evil things he had done, 20 Herod
added this to them all: He locked John up in
prison.

[*i*] Or *Messiah.* [*j*] Or *in.*

Phillips Modern English

Some of the tax-collectors also came to him to be baptised and they asked him,

"Master, what are we to do?"

"You must not demand more than you are entitled to," he replied.

And the soldiers asked him, "And what are we to do?"

"Don't bully people, don't bring false charges, and be content with your pay," he replied.

The people were in a great state of expectation and were all inwardly debating whether John could possibly be Christ. But John answered them all in these words,

"It is true that I baptise you with water, but the one who follows me is stronger than I am —indeed I am not fit to undo his shoe-laces—he will baptise you with the fire of the Holy Spirit. He will come all ready to separate the wheat from the chaff, and to clear the rubbish from his threshing-floor. The wheat he will gather into his barn and the chaff he will burn with a fire that cannot be put out."

These and many other things John said to the people as he exhorted them and announced the good news. But the tetrarch Herod, who had been condemned by John in the affair of Herodias, his brother's wife, as well as for the other evil things that he had done, crowned his misdeeds by putting John in prison.

Revised Standard Version

wise." 12 Tax collectors also came to be baptized, and said to him, "Teacher, what shall we do?" 13 And he said to them, "Collect no more than is appointed you." 14 Soldiers also asked him, "And we, what shall we do?" And he said to them, "Rob no one by violence or by false accusation, and be content with your wages."

15 As the people were in expectation, and all men questioned in their hearts concerning John, whether perhaps he were the Christ, 16 John answered them all, "I baptize you with water; but he who is mightier than I is coming, the thong of whose sandals I am not worthy to untie; he will baptize you with the Holy Spirit and with fire. 17 His winnowing fork is in his hand, to clear his threshing floor, and to gather the wheat into his granary, but the chaff he will burn with unquenchable fire."

18 So, with many other exhortations, he preached good news to the people. 19 But Herod the tetrarch, who had been reproved by him for Herodias, his brother's wife, and for all the evil things that Herod had done, 20 added this to them all, that he shut up John in prison.

Jerusalem Bible

must do the same." 12 There were tax collectors too who came for baptism, and these said to him, "Master, what must we do?" 13 He said to them, "Exact no more than your rate." 14 Some soldiers asked him in their turn, "What about us? What must we do?" He said to them, "No intimidation! No extortion! Be content with your pay!"

15 A feeling of expectancy had grown among the people, who were beginning to think that John might be the Christ, 16 so John declared before them all; "I baptize you with water, but someone is coming, someone who is more powerful than I am, and I am not fit to undo the strap of his sandals; he will baptize you with the Holy Spirit and fire. 17 His winnowing fan is in his hand to clear his threshing floor and to gather the wheat into his barn; but the chaff he will burn in a fire that will never go out." 18 As well as this, there were many other things he said to exhort the people and to announce the Good News to them.

John the Baptist imprisoned

19 But Herod the tetrarch, whom he criticized for his relations with his brother's wife Herodias and for all the other crimes Herod had committed, 20 added a further crime to all the rest by shutting John up in prison.

New English Bible

has food must do the same.' Among those who came to be baptized were tax-gatherers, and they said to him, 'Master, what are we to do?' He told them, 'Exact no more than the assessment.' Soldiers on service also asked him, 'And what of us?' To them he said, 'No bullying; no blackmail; make do with your pay!'

The people were on the tiptoe of expectation, all wondering about John, whether perhaps he was the Messiah, but he spoke out and said to them all: 'I baptize you with water; but there is one to come who is mightier than I. I am not fit to unfasten his shoes. He will baptize you with the Holy Spirit and with fire. His shovel is ready in his hand, to winnow his threshing-floor and gather the wheat into his granary; but he will burn the chaff on a fire that can never go out.'

In this and many other ways he made his appeal to the people and announced the good news. But Prince Herod, when he was rebuked by him over the affair of his brother's wife Herodias and for his other misdeeds, crowned them all by shutting John up in prison.

King James Version

all, that he shut up John in prison. 21 Now when
all the people were baptized, it came to pass,
that Jesus also being baptized, and praying, the
heaven was opened, 22And the Holy Ghost
descended in a bodily shape like a dove upon
him, and a voice came from heaven, which said,
Thou art my beloved Son; in thee I am well
pleased. 23And Jesus himself began to be about
thirty years of age, being (as was supposed) the
son of Joseph, which was *the son* of Heli,
24 Which was *the son* of Matthat, which was *the*
son of Levi, which was *the son* of Melchi, which
was *the son* of Janna, which was *the son* of
Joseph, 25 Which was *the son* of Mattathias,
which was *the son* of Amos, which was *the son*
of Naum, which was *the son* of Esli, which was
the son of Nagge, 26 Which was *the son* of
Maath, which was *the son* of Mattathias, which
was *the son* of Semei, which was *the son* of
Joseph, which was *the son* of Juda, 27 Which
was *the son* of Joanna, which was *the son* of
Rhesa, which was *the son* of Zorobabel, which
was *the son* of Salathiel, which was *the son* of
Neri, 28 Which was *the son* of Melchi, which
was *the son* of Addi, which was *the son* of
Cosam, which was *the son* of Elmodam, which

Living Bible

21 Then one day, after the crowds had been
baptized, Jesus himself was baptized; and as he
was praying, the heavens opened, 22 and the
Holy Spirit in the form of a dove settled upon
him, and a voice from heaven said, "You are my
much loved Son, yes, my delight."

23–38 Jesus was about thirty years old when
he began his public ministry.

Jesus was known as the son of Joseph.
Joseph's father was Heli;
Heli's father was Matthat;
Matthat's father was Levi;
Levi's father was Melchi;
Melchi's father was Jannai;
Jannai's father was Joseph;
Joseph's father was Mattathias;
Mattathias' father was Amos;
Amos' father was Nahum;
Nahum's father was Esli;
Esli's father was Naggai;
Naggai's father was Maath;
Maath's father was Mattathias;
Mattathias' father was Semein;
Semein's father was Josech;
Josech's father was Joda;
Joda's father was Joanan;
Joanan's father was Rhesa;
Rhesa's father was Zerubbabel;
Zerubbabel's father was Shealtiel;
Shealtiel's father was Neri;
Neri's father was Melchi;
Melchi's father was Addi;
Addi's father was Cosam;
Cosam's father was Elmadam;
Elmadam's father was Er;
Er's father was Joshua;

Today's English Version

The baptism of Jesus

21 After all the people had been baptized,
Jesus also was baptized. While he was praying,
heaven was opened, 22 and the Holy Spirit came
down upon him in bodily form, like a dove. And
a voice came from heaven, "You are my own
dear Son. I am well pleased with you."

The genealogy of Jesus

23 When Jesus began his work he was about
thirty years old; he was the son, so people
thought, of Joseph, who was the son of Heli,
24 the son of Matthat, the son of Levi, the son
of Melchi, the son of Jannai, the son of Joseph,
25 the son of Mattathias, the son of Amos, the
son of Nahum, the son of Esli, the son of
Naggai, 26 the son of Maath, the son of Mattathias, the son of Semein, the son of Josech, the
son of Joda, 27 the son of Joanan, the son of
Rhesa, the son of Zerubbabel, the son of Shealtiel, the son of Neri, 28 the son of Melchi, the
son of Addi, the son of Cosam, the son of

New International Version

The baptism and genealogy of Jesus

21 When all the people were being baptized,
Jesus was baptized too. And as he was praying,
heaven was opened 22 and the Holy Spirit descended on him in bodily form like a dove. And
a voice came from heaven: "You are my Son,
whom I love; with you I am well-pleased."

23 Now Jesus himself was about thirty years
old when he began his ministry. He was the son,
so it was thought, of Joseph,

the son of Heli, 24 the son of Matthat,
the son of Levi, the son of Melchi,
the son of Jannai, the son of Joseph,
25 the son of Mattathias, the son of Amos,
the son of Nahum, the son of Esli,
the son of Naggai, 26 the son of Maath,
the son of Mattathias, the son of Semein,
the son of Josech, the son of Joda,
27 the son of Joanan, the son of Rhesa,
the son of Zerubbabel, the son of Shealtiel,
the son of Neri, 28 the son of Melchi,
the son of Addi, the son of Cosam,
the son of Elmadam, the son of Er,

Phillips Modern English

3.21 Jesus is himself baptised.

When all the people had been baptised, and Jesus was praying after his own baptism, Heaven opened and the Holy Spirit came down upon him in the bodily form of a dove. Then there came a voice from Heaven, saying,

"You are my dearly-loved Son, in whom I am well pleased."

Jesus himself was about thirty years old at this time when he began his work.

3.23b The ancestry of Jesus traced to Adam

People assumed that Jesus was the son of Joseph, who was the son of Heli, who was the son of Matthat, who was the son of Levi, who was the son of Melchi, who was the son of Jannai, who was the son of Joseph, who was the son of Mattathias, who was the son of Amos, who was the son of Nahum, who was the son of Esli, who was the son of Naggai, who was the son of Maath, who was the son of Mattathias, who was the son of Semein, who was the son of Josech, who was the son of Joda, who was the son of Joanan, who was the son of Rhesa, who was the son of Zerubbabel, who was the son of Shealtiel, who was the son of Neri, who was the son of Melchi, who was the son of Addi, who was the son of Cosam, who was the

Revised Standard Version

21 Now when all the people were baptized,
and when Jesus also had been baptized and was
praying, the heaven was opened, 22 and the Holy
Spirit descended upon him in bodily form, as a
dove, and a voice came from heaven, "Thou art
my beloved Son;[j] with thee I am well pleased."[k]

23 Jesus, when he began his ministry, was
about thirty years of age, being the son (as was
supposed) of Joseph, the son of Heli, 24 the son
of Matthat, the son of Levi, the son of Melchi,
the son of Jannai, the son of Joseph, 25 the son
of Mattathias, the son of Amos, the son of
Nahum, the son of Esli, the son of Naggai,
26 the son of Maath, the son of Mattathias, the
son of Semein, the son of Josech, the son of
Joda, 27 the son of Joanan, the son of Rhesa, the
son of Zerubbabel, the son of Shealtiel,[l] the son
of Neri, 28 the son of Melchi, the son of Addi,
the son of Cosam, the son of Elmadam, the son

[j] Or *my Son, my* (or *the*) *Beloved.* [k] Other ancient authorities read *today I have begotten thee.* [l] Greek *Salathiel.*

Jerusalem Bible

Jesus is baptized

21 Now when all the people had been baptized and while Jesus after his own baptism was
at prayer, heaven opened 22 and the Holy Spirit
descended on him in bodily shape, like a dove.
And a voice came from heaven, "You are my
Son, the Beloved; my favor rests on you."

The ancestry of Jesus

23 When he started to teach, Jesus was about
thirty years old, being the son, 24 as it was
thought, of Joseph son of Heli, son of Matthat,
son of Levi, son of Melchi, son of Jannai, son
of Joseph, 25 son of Mattathias, son of Amos,
son of Nahum, son of Esli, son of Naggai,
26 son of Maath, son of Mattathias, son of
Semein, son of Josech, son of Joda, 27 son of
Joanan, son of Rhesa, son of Zerubbabel, son
of Shealtiel, son of Neri, 28 son of Melchi, son of
Addi, son of Cosam, son of Elmadam, son

New English Bible

During a general baptism of the people, when Jesus too had been baptized and was praying, heaven opened and the Holy Spirit descended on him in bodily form like a dove; and there came a voice from heaven, 'Thou art my Son, my Beloved;[a] on thee my favour rests.'[b]

When Jesus began his work he was about thirty years old, the son, as people thought, of Joseph, son of Heli, son of Matthat, son of Levi, son of Melchi, son of Jannai, son of Joseph, son of Mattathiah, son of Amos, son of Nahum, son of Esli, son of Naggai, son of Maath, son of Mattathiah, son of Semein, son of Josech, son of Joda, son of Johanan, son of Rhesa, son of Zerubbabel, son of Shealtiel, son of Neri, son of Melchi, son of Addi, son of Cosam, son of El-

[a] *Or* Thou art my only Son. [b] *Some witnesses read* My Son art thou; this day I have begotten thee.

King James Version

was *the son* of Er, 29 Which was *the son* of Jose,
which was *the son* of Eliezer, which was *the*
son of Jorim, which was *the son* of Matthat,
which was *the son* of Levi, 30 Which was *the*
son of Simeon, which was *the son* of Juda,
which was *the son* of Joseph, which was *the son*
of Jonan, which was *the son* of Eliakim,
31 Which was *the son* of Melea, which was *the*
son of Menan, which was *the son* of Mattatha,
which was *the son* of Nathan, which was *the*
son of David, 32 Which was *the son* of Jesse,
which was *the son* of Obed, which was *the son*
of Booz, which was *the son* of Salmon, which
was *the son* of Naasson, 33 Which was *the son*
of Aminadab, which was *the son* of Aram,
which was *the son* of Esrom, which was *the son*
of Phares, which was *the son* of Juda, 34 Which
was *the son* of Jacob, which was *the son* of
Isaac, which was *the son* of Abraham, which
was *the son* of Thara, which was *the son* of
Nachor, 35 Which was *the son* of Saruch, which
was *the son* of Ragau, which was *the son* of
Phalec, which was *the son* of Heber, which was
the son of Sala, 36 Which was *the son* of Cainan,

Living Bible

Joshua's father was Eliezer;
Eliezer's father was Jorim;
Jorim's father was Matthat;
Matthat's father was Levi;
Levi's father was Simeon;
Simeon's father was Judah;
Judah's father was Joseph;
Joseph's father was Jonam;
Jonam's father was Eliakim;
Eliakim's father was Melea;
Melea's father was Menna;
Menna's father was Mattatha;
Mattatha's father was Nathan;
Nathan's father was David;
David's father was Jesse;
Jesse's father was Obed;
Obed's father was Boaz;
Boaz' father was Salmon;[d]
Salmon's father was Nahshon;
Nahshon's father was Amminadab;
Amminadab's father was Admin;
Admin's father was Arni;
Arni's father was Hezron;
Hezron's father was Perez;
Perez' father was Judah;
Judah's father was Jacob;
Jacob's father was Isaac;
Isaac's father was Abraham;
Abraham's father was Terah;
Terah's father was Nahor;
Nahor's father was Serug;
Serug's father was Reu;
Reu's father was Peleg;
Peleg's father was Eber;
Eber's father was Shelah;
Shelah's father was Cainan;

[*d*] "Sala."

Today's English Version

Elmadam, the son of Er, 29 the son of Joshua,
the son of Eliezer, the son of Jorim, the son of
Matthat, the son of Levi, 30 the son of Simeon,
the son of Judah, the son of Joseph, the son of
Jonam, the son of Eliakim, 31 the son of Melea,
the son of Menna, the son of Mattatha, the son
of Nathan, the son of David, 32 the son of Jesse,
the son of Obed, the son of Boaz, the son of
Salmon, the son of Nahshon, 33 the son of Amminadab, the son of Admin, the son of Arni, the
son of Hezron, the son of Perez, the son of
Judah, 34 the son of Jacob, the son of Isaac, the
son of Abraham, the son of Terah, the son of
Nahor, 35 the son of Serug, the son of Reu, the
son of Peleg, the son of Eber, the son of Shelah,
36 the son of Cainan, the son of Arphaxad, the

New International Version

29 the son of Joshua, the son of Eliezer,
the son of Jorim, the son of Matthat,
the son of Levi, 30 the son of Simeon,
the son of Judah, the son of Joseph,
the son of Jonam, the son of Eliakim,
31 the son of Melea, the son of Menna,
the son of Mattatha, the son of Nathan,
the son of David, 32 the son of Jesse,
the son of Obed, the son of Boaz,
the son of Salmon,[k] the son of Nahshon,
33 the son of Amminadab, the son of Ram,[l]
the son of Hezron, the son of Perez,
the son of Judah, 34 the son of Jacob,
the son of Isaac, the son of Abraham,
the son of Terah, the son of Nahor,
35 the son of Serug, the son of Reu,
the son of Peleg, the son of Eber,
the son of Shelah, 36 the son of Cainan,

[*k*] Some early MSS read *Sala.* [*l*] Some MSS read *Amminadab, the son of Admin, the son of Arni;* other MSS vary widely.

Phillips Modern English

son of Elmadam, who was the son of Er, who was the son of Jesus, who was the son of Eliezer, who was the son of Jorim, who was the son of Matthat, who was the son of Levi, who was the son of Symeon, who was the son of Judas, who was the son of Joseph, who was the son of Jonam, who was the son of Eliakim, who was the son of Melea, who was the son of Menna, who was the son of Mattatha, who was the son of Nathan, who was the son of David, who was the son of Jesse, who was the son of Obed, who was the son of Boaz, who was the son of Salmon, who was the son of Nahshon, who was the son of Amminadab, who was the son of Arni, who was the son of Hezron, who was the son of Perez, who was the son of Judah, who was the son of Jacob, who was the son of Isaac, who was the son of Abraham, who was the son of Terah, who was the son of Nahor, who was the son of Serug, who was the son of Reu, who was the son of Peleg, who was the son of Eber, who was the son of Shelah, who was the son of

Revised Standard Version

of Er, 29 the son of Joshua, the son of Eliezer,
the son of Jorim, the son of Matthat, the son of
Levi, 30 the son of Simeon, the son of Judah,
the son of Joseph, the son of Jonam, the son of
Eliakim, 31 the son of Melea, the son of Menna,
the son of Mattatha, the son of Nathan, the son
of David, 32 the son of Jesse, the son of Obed,
the son of Boaz, the son of Sala, the son of
Nahshon, 33 the son of Amminadab, the son of
Admin, the son of Arni, the son of Hezron, the
son of Perez, the son of Judah, 34 the son of
Jacob, the son of Isaac, the son of Abraham, the
son of Terah, the son of Nahor, 35 the son of
Serug, the son of Reu, the son of Peleg, the son
of Eber, the son of Shelah, 36 the son of Cainan,

Jerusalem Bible

of Er, son of Joshua, 29 son of Joshua, son of
Eliezer, son of Jorim, son of Matthat, son of
Levi, 30 son of Symeon, son of Judah, son of
Joseph, son of Jonam, son of Eliakim, 31 son
of Melea, son of Menna, son of Mattatha, son of
Nathan, son of David, 32 son of Jesse, son of
Obed, son of Boaz, son of Sala, son of Nahshon,
33 son of Amminadab, son of Admin, son of
Arni, son of Hezron, son of Perez, son of
Judah, 34 son of Jacob, son of Isaac, son of
Abraham, son of Terah, son of Nahor, 35 son of
Serug, son of Reu, son of Peleg, son of Eber,
son of Shelah, 36 son of Cainan, son of

New English Bible

madam, son of Er, son of Joshua, son of Eliezer, son of Jorim, son of Matthat, son of Levi, son of Symeon, son of Judah, son of Joseph, son of Jonam, son of Eliakim, son of Melea, son of Menna, son of Mattatha, son of Nathan, son of David, son of Jesse, son of Obed, son of Boaz, son of Salmon, son of Nahshon, son of Amminadab,[c] son of Arni,[d] son of Hezron, son of Perez, son of Judah, son of Jacob, son of Isaac, son of Abraham, son of Terah, son of Nahor, son of Serug, son of Reu, son of Peleg, son of Eber, son of Shelah, son of Cainan, son of Arpachshad,

[c] *Some witnesses add* son of Admin. [d] *Some witnesses read* Aram; *Ruth 4. 19 & 1 Chronicles 2. 9 have* Ram.

King James Version

which was *the son* of Arphaxad, which was *the son* of Sem, which was *the son* of Noe, which was *the son* of Lamech, 37 Which was *the son* of Mathusala, which was *the son* of Enoch, which was *the son* of Jared, which was *the son* of Maleleel, which was *the son* of Cainan, 38 Which was *the son* of Enos, which was *the son* of Seth, which was *the son* of Adam, which was *the son* of God.

4 And Jesus being full of the Holy Ghost returned from Jordan, and was led by the Spirit into the wilderness, 2 Being forty days tempted of the devil. And in those days he did eat nothing: and when they were ended, he afterward hungered. 3 And the devil said unto him, If thou be the Son of God, command this stone that it be made bread. 4 And Jesus answered him, saying, It is written, That man shall not live by bread alone, but by every word of God. 5 And the devil, taking him up into a high mountain, shewed unto him all the kingdoms of the world in a moment of time. 6 And the devil said unto him, All this power will I give thee, and the glory of them: for that is delivered unto me; and to whomsoever I will, I give it. 7 If thou therefore wilt worship me, all shall be thine. 8 And Jesus answered and said unto him, Get

Living Bible

Cainan's father was Arphaxad;
Arphaxad's father was Shem;
Shem's father was Noah;
Noah's father was Lamech;
Lamech's father was Methuselah;
Methuselah's father was Enoch;
Enoch's father was Jared;
Jared's father was Mahalaleel;
Mahalaleel's father was Cainan;
Cainan's father was Enos;
Enos' father was Seth;
Seth's father was Adam;
Adam's father was God.

4 Then Jesus, full of the Holy Spirit, left the Jordan River, being urged by the Spirit out into the barren wastelands of Judea, where Satan tempted him for forty days. He ate nothing all that time, and was very hungry.

3 Satan said, "If you are God's Son, tell this stone to become a loaf of bread."

4 But Jesus replied, "It is written in the Scriptures, 'Other things in life are much more important than bread!' "[a]

5 Then Satan took him up and revealed to him all the kingdoms of the world in a moment of time; 6, 7 and the devil told him, "I will give you all these splendid kingdoms and their glory—for they are mine to give to anyone I wish—if you will only get down on your knees and worship me."

8 Jesus replied, "We must worship God, and

[*a*] Literally, "Man shall not live by bread alone." Deuteronomy 8:3.

Today's English Version

son of Shem, the son of Noah, the son of Lamech, 37 the son of Methuselah, the son of Enoch, the son of Jared, the son of Mahalaleel, the son of Cainan, 38 the son of Enos, the son of Seth, the son of Adam, the son of God.

The temptation of Jesus

4 Jesus returned from the Jordan full of the Holy Spirit, and was led by the Spirit into the desert, 2 where he was tempted by the Devil for forty days. In all that time he ate nothing, so that he was hungry when it was over.

3 The Devil said to him, "If you are God's Son, order this stone to turn into bread."

4 Jesus answered, "The scripture says, 'Man cannot live on bread alone.' "

5 Then the Devil took him up and showed him in a second all the kingdoms of the world. 6 "I will give you all this power, and all this wealth," the Devil told him. "It was all handed over to me and I can give it to anyone I choose. 7 All this will be yours, then, if you kneel down before me."

8 Jesus answered, "The scripture says, 'Wor-

New International Version

the son of Arphaxad, the son of Shem,
the son of Noah, the son of Lamech,
37 the son of Methuselah, the son of Enoch,
the son of Jared, the son of Mahalaleel,
the son of Cainan, 38 the son of Enos,
the son of Seth, the son of Adam,
the son of God.

The temptations of Jesus

4 Jesus, full of the Holy Spirit, returned from the Jordan and was led by the Spirit in the desert, 2 where for forty days he was tempted by the devil. He ate nothing during those days, and at the end of them he was hungry.

3 The devil said to him, "If you are the Son of God, tell this stone to become bread."

4 Jesus answered, "It is written: 'Man does not live on bread alone.'[m] "

5 The devil led him up to a high place and showed him in an instant all the kingdoms of the world. 6 And he said to him, "I will give you all their authority and splendor, for it has been given to me, and I can give it to anyone I want to. 7 So if you worship me, it will all be yours."

8 Jesus answered, "It is written: 'Worship the

[*m*] Deut. 8:3.

Phillips Modern English

Cainan, who was the son of Arphaxad, who was
the son of Shem, who was the son of Noah, who
was the son of Lamech, who was the son of
Methuselah, who was the son of Enoch, who
was the son of Jared, who was the son of Mahalaleel, who was the son of Cainan, who was
the son of Enos, who was the son of Seth, who
was the son of Adam, who was the son of God.

4.1 Jesus faces temptation

Jesus returned from the Jordan full of the
Holy Spirit and he was led by the Spirit to
spend forty days in the desert, where he was
tempted by the devil. He ate nothing during that
time and afterwards he felt very hungry.

"If you are the Son of God," the devil said to
him, "tell this stone to turn into a loaf."

Jesus answered,

"The scripture says, 'Man shall not live by
bread alone.' "

Then the devil took him up and showed him
all the kingdoms of mankind in a sudden vision,
and said to him,

"I will give you all this power and magnificence, for it belongs to me and I can give it
to anyone I please. It shall all be yours if you
will fall down and worship me."

To this Jesus replied,

Revised Standard Version

the son of Arphaxad, the son of Shem, the son
of Noah, the son of Lamech, 37 the son of
Methuselah, the son of Enoch, the son of Jared,
the son of Mahalaleel, the son of Cainan, 38 the
son of Enos, the son of Seth, the son of Adam,
the son of God.

4 And Jesus, full of the Holy Spirit, returned
from the Jordan, and was led by the Spirit
2 for forty days in the wilderness, tempted by
the devil. And he ate nothing in those days; and
when they were ended, he was hungry. 3 The
devil said to him, "If you are the Son of God,
command this stone to become bread." 4 And
Jesus answered him, "It is written, 'Man shall
not live by bread alone.' " 5 And the devil took
him up, and showed him all the kingdoms of
the world in a moment of time, 6 and said to
him, "To you I will give all this authority and
their glory; for it has been delivered to me, and
I give it to whom I will. 7 If you, then, will
worship me, it shall all be yours." 8 And Jesus
answered him, "It is written,

Jerusalem Bible

Arphaxad, son of Shem, son of Noah, son of
Lamech, 37 son of Methuselah, son of Enoch,
son of Jared, son of Mahalaleel, son of Cainan,
38 son of Enos, son of Seth, son of Adam, son
of God.

Temptation in the wilderness

4 Filled with the Holy Spirit, Jesus left the
Jordan and was led by the Spirit through
the wilderness, 2 being tempted there by the
devil for forty days. During that time he ate
nothing and at the end he was hungry. 3 Then
the devil said to him, "If you are the Son of
God, tell this stone to turn into a loaf." 4 But
Jesus replied, "Scripture says: *Man does not live
on bread alone.*" [b]
5 Then leading him to a height, the devil
showed him in a moment of time all the kingdoms of the world 6 and said to him, "I will
give you all this power and the glory of these
kingdoms, for it has been committed to me and
I give it to anyone I choose. 7 Worship me,
then, and it shall all be yours." 8 But Jesus
answered him, "Scripture says:

[b] Dt. 8:3.

New English Bible

son of Shem, son of Noah, son of Lamech, son
of Methuselah, son of Enoch, son of Jared, son
of Mahalaleel, son of Cainan, son of Enosh, son
of Seth, son of Adam, son of God.

4 Full of the Holy Spirit, Jesus returned from
the Jordan, and for forty days was led by the
Spirit up and down the wilderness and tempted
by the devil.

All that time he had nothing to eat, and at the
end of it he was famished. The devil said to him,
'If you are the Son of God, tell this stone to become bread.' Jesus answered, 'Scripture says,
"Man cannot live on bread alone." '

Next the devil led him up and showed him in
a flash all the kingdoms of the world. 'All this
dominion will I give to you,' he said, 'and the
glory that goes with it; for it has been put in my
hands and I can give it to anyone I choose. You
have only to do homage to me and it shall all be
yours.' Jesus answered him, 'Scripture says, "You

King James Version

thee behind me, Satan: for it is written, Thou
shalt worship the Lord thy God, and him only
shalt thou serve. 9And he brought him to Jerusalem, and set him on a pinnacle of the temple,
and said unto him, If thou be the Son of God,
cast thyself down from hence: 10 For it is written, He shall give his angels charge over thee,
to keep thee: 11And in *their* hands they shall
bear thee up, lest at any time thou dash thy
foot against a stone. 12And Jesus answering said
unto him, It is said, Thou shalt not tempt the
Lord thy God. 13And when the devil had ended
all the temptation, he departed from him for a
season.

Living Bible

him alone. So it is written in the Scriptures."

9, 10, 11 Then Satan took him to Jerusalem to a high roof of the Temple and said, "If you are the Son of God, jump off! For the Scriptures say that God will send his angels to guard you and to keep you from crashing to the pavement below!"

12 Jesus replied, "The Scriptures also say, 'Do not put the Lord your God to a foolish test.' "

13 When the devil had ended all the temptations, he left Jesus for a while and went away.

Today's English Version

ship the Lord your God and serve only him!' "

9 Then the Devil took him to Jerusalem and set him on the highest point of the temple, and said to him, "If you are God's Son, throw yourself down from here. 10 For the scripture says, 'God will order his angels to take good care of you.' 11 It also says, 'They will hold you up with their hands so that not even your feet will be hurt on the stones.' "

12 Jesus answered him, "The scripture says, 'You must not put the Lord your God to the test.' "

13 When the Devil finished tempting Jesus in every way, he left him for a while.

New International Version

Lord your God and serve him only.' [n] "

9 The devil led him to Jerusalem and had him stand on the highest point of the temple. "If you are the Son of God," he said, "throw yourself down from here. 10 For it is written:

'He will command his angels concerning you
to guard you carefully;
11 and they will lift you up in their hands,
so that you will not strike your foot
against a stone.' [o] "

12 Jesus answered, "It says: 'Do not put the Lord your God to the test.' [p] "

Jesus rejected at Nazareth

13 When the devil had finished all these temptations, he left him until an opportune time.

[*n*] Deut. 6:13. [*o*] Psalm 91:11,12. [*p*] Deut. 6:16.

Phillips Modern English

"It is written, 'Thou shalt worship the Lord thy God and him only shalt thou serve.' "

Then the devil took him to Jerusalem and set him on the highest pinnacle of the Temple.

"If you are the Son of God," he said, "throw yourself down from here, for the scripture says, 'He shall give his angels charge concerning thee, to guard thee', and 'On their hands they shall bear thee up, lest haply thou dash thy foot against a stone.' "

To which Jesus replied,

"It is also said, 'Thou shalt not tempt the Lord thy God.' "

And when he had exhausted every kind of temptation, the devil withdrew until his next opportunity.

Revised Standard Version

'You shall worship the Lord your God,
and him only shall you serve.' "
9 And he took him to Jerusalem, and set him on
the pinnacle of the temple, and said to him, "If
you are the Son of God, throw yourself down
from here; 10 for it is written,
'He will give his angels charge of you, to
guard you,'
11 and
'On their hands they will bear you up,
lest you strike your foot against a stone.' "
12 And Jesus answered him, "It is said, 'You shall
not tempt the Lord your God.' " 13 And when
the devil had ended every temptation, he departed from him until an opportune time.

Jerusalem Bible

You must worship the Lord your God,
and serve him alone." [c]

9 Then he led him to Jerusalem and made
him stand on the parapet of the Temple. "If
you are the Son of God," he said to him,
"throw yourself down from here, 10 for scripture
says:

He will put his angels in charge of you
to guard you,

and again:

11 *They will hold you up on their hands*
in case you hurt your foot against a
stone." [d]

12 But Jesus answered him, "It has been said:

You must not put the Lord your God to the test." [e]

13 Having exhausted all these ways of tempting
him, the devil left him, to return at the appointed time.

[c] Dt. 6:13. [d] Ps. 91:11-12. [e] Dt. 6:16.

New English Bible

shall do homage to the Lord your God and worship him alone." '

The devil took him to Jerusalem and set him on the parapet of the temple. 'If you are the Son of God,' he said, 'throw yourself down; for Scripture says, "He will give his angels orders to take care of you", and again, "They will support you in their arms for fear you should strike your foot against a stone." ' Jesus answered him, 'It has been said, "You are not to put the Lord your God to the test." '

So, having come to the end of all his temptations, the devil departed, biding his time.

King James Version

14 And Jesus returned in the power of the
Spirit into Galilee: and there went out a fame
of him through all the region round about.
15And he taught in their synagogues, being
glorified of all.
16 And he came to Nazareth, where he had
been brought up: and, as his custom was, he
went into the synagogue on the sabbath day, and
stood up for to read. 17And there was delivered
unto him the book of the prophet Esaias. And
when he had opened the book, he found the
place where it was written, 18 The Spirit of the
Lord *is* upon me, because he hath anointed me
to preach the gospel to the poor; he hath sent
me to heal the brokenhearted, to preach deliverance to the captives, and recovering of sight
to the blind, to set at liberty them that are
bruised, 19 To preach the acceptable year of the
Lord. 20And he closed the book, and he gave *it*
again to the minister, and sat down. And the
eyes of all them that were in the synagogue were
fastened on him. 21And he began to say unto
them, This day is this Scripture fulfilled in your

Living Bible

14 Then Jesus returned to Galilee, full of the
Holy Spirit's power. Soon he became well known
throughout all that region 15 for his sermons in
the synagogues; everyone praised him.
16 When he came to the village of Nazareth,
his boyhood home, he went as usual to the synagogue on Saturday, and stood up to read the
Scriptures. 17 The book of Isaiah the prophet
was handed to him, and he opened it to the
place where it says:
18, 19 "The Spirit of the Lord is upon me;
he has appointed me to preach Good News to
the poor; he has sent me to heal the brokenhearted and to announce that captives shall be
released and the blind shall see, that the downtrodden shall be freed from their oppressors,
and that God is ready to give blessings to all who
come to him." [b]
20 He closed the book and handed it back to
the attendant and sat down, while everyone in
the synagogue gazed at him intently. 21 Then he
added, "These Scriptures came true today!"

[*b*] Literally, "to proclaim the acceptable year of the Lord."

Today's English Version

Jesus begins his work in Galilee

14 Then Jesus returned to Galilee, and the
power of the Holy Spirit was with him. The
news about him spread throughout all that territory. 15 He taught in their synagogues and was
praised by all.

Jesus rejected at Nazareth

16 Then Jesus went to Nazareth, where he had
been brought up, and on the Sabbath day he
went as usual to the synagogue. He stood up to
read the Scriptures, 17 and was handed the book
of the prophet Isaiah. He unrolled the scroll and
found the place where it is written,

18 "The Spirit of the Lord is upon me,
because he has chosen me to preach the Good News to the poor.
He has sent me to proclaim liberty to the captives,
and recovery of sight to the blind;
to set free the oppressed,
19 and announce the year when the Lord will save his people."

20 Jesus rolled up the scroll, gave it back to
the attendant, and sat down. All the people in
the synagogue had their eyes fixed on him. 21 He
began speaking to them, "This passage of scripture has come true today, as you heard it being
read."

New International Version

14 Jesus returned to Galilee in the power of
the Spirit, and news about him spread through
the whole countryside. 15 He taught in their
synagogues, and everyone praised him.
16 He went to Nazareth, where he had been
brought up, and on the Sabbath day he went
into the synagogue, as was his custom. And he
stood up to read. 17 The scroll of the prophet
Isaiah was handed to him. Unrolling it, he found
the place where it is written:

18 "The Spirit of the Lord is on me;
therefore he has anointed me to preach good news to the poor.
He has sent me to proclaim freedom for the prisoners
and recovery of sight for the blind,
to release the oppressed,
19 to proclaim the year of the Lord's favor." [q]

20 Then he rolled up the scroll, gave it back
to the attendant and sat down. The eyes of
everyone in the synagogue were fastened on him,
21 and he said to them, "Today this scripture is
fulfilled in your hearing."

[*q*] Isaiah 61:1,2.

Phillips Modern English

4.14 Jesus begins his ministry in Galilee

And now Jesus returned to Galilee in the power of the Spirit, and news of him spread through all the surrounding district. He taught in their synagogues, to everyone's great admiration.

Then he came to Nazareth where he had been brought up and, according to his custom, went to the synagogue on the Sabbath day. He stood up to read the scriptures and the book of the prophet Isaiah was handed to him. He opened the book and found the place where these words are written—

The Spirit of the Lord is upon me,
Because he anointed me to preach good tidings to the poor:
He hath sent me to proclaim release to the captives,
And recovering of sight to the blind,
To set at liberty them that are bruised,
To proclaim the acceptable year of the Lord.

Then he shut the book, handed it back to the attendant and resumed his seat. Every eye in the synagogue was fixed upon him and he began to tell them, "This very day this scripture has been fulfilled, while you have been listening to it!"

Revised Standard Version

14 And Jesus returned in the power of the
Spirit into Galilee, and a report concerning him
went out through all the surrounding country.
15 And he taught in their synagogues, being glorified by all.
16 And he came to Nazareth, where he had
been brought up; and he went to the synagogue,
as his custom was, on the sabbath day. And he
stood up to read; 17 and there was given to him
the book of the prophet Isaiah. He opened the
book and found the place where it was written,
18 "The Spirit of the Lord is upon me,
because he has anointed me to preach good news to the poor.
He has sent me to proclaim release to the captives
and recovering of sight to the blind,
to set at liberty those who are oppressed,
19 to proclaim the acceptable year of the Lord."
20 And he closed the book, and gave it back to
the attendant, and sat down; and the eyes of all
in the synagogue were fixed on him. 21 And he
began to say to them, "Today this scripture

Jerusalem Bible

III. The Galilean ministry

Jesus begins to preach

14 Jesus, with the power of the Spirit in him,
returned to Galilee; and his reputation spread
throughout the countryside. 15 He taught in
their synagogues and everyone praised him.

Jesus at Nazareth

16 He came to Nazara, where he had been
brought up, and went into the synagogue on the
sabbath day as he usually did. He stood up to
read,[f] 17 and they handed him the scroll of the
prophet Isaiah. Unrolling the scroll he found the
place where it is written:

18 *The spirit of the Lord has been given to me,*
for he has anointed me.
He has sent me to bring the good news to the poor,
to proclaim liberty to captives
and to the blind new sight,
to set the downtrodden free,
19 *to proclaim the Lord's year of favor.*[g]

20 He then rolled up the scroll, gave it back to
the assistant and sat down. And all eyes in the
synagogue were fixed on him. 21 Then he began
to speak to them, "This text is being fulfilled to-

[*f*] Any adult man could be permitted by the president to read the scriptures. [*g*] Is. 61:1-2.

New English Bible

In Galilee: success and opposition

Then Jesus, armed with the power of the Spirit, returned to Galilee; and reports about him spread through the whole country-side. He taught in their synagogues and all men sang his praises.

So he came to Nazareth, where he had been brought up, and went to synagogue on the Sabbath day as he regularly did. He stood up to read the lesson and was handed the scroll of the prophet Isaiah. He opened the scroll and found the passage which says,

'The spirit of the Lord is upon me because he has anointed me;
he has sent me to announce good news to the poor,
to proclaim release for prisoners and recovery of sight for the blind;
to let the broken victims go free,
to proclaim the year of the Lord's favour.'

He rolled up the scroll, gave it back to the attendant, and sat down; and all eyes in the synagogue were fixed on him.

He began to speak: 'Today', he said, 'in your

King James Version

ears. 22 And all bare him witness, and wondered at the gracious words which proceeded out of his mouth. And they said, Is not this Joseph's son? 23 And he said unto them, Ye will surely say unto me this proverb, Physician, heal thyself: whatsoever we have heard done in Capernaum, do also here in thy country. 24 And he said, Verily I say unto you, No prophet is accepted in his own country. 25 But I tell you of a truth, many widows were in Israel in the days of Elias, when the heaven was shut up three years and six months, when great famine was throughout all the land; 26 But unto none of them was Elias sent, save unto Sarepta, *a city* of Sidon, unto a woman *that was* a widow. 27 And many lepers were in Israel in the time of Eliseus the prophet; and none of them was cleansed, saving Naaman the Syrian. 28 And all they in the synagogue, when they heard these things, were filled with wrath, 29 And rose up, and thrust him out of the city, and led him unto the brow of the hill whereon their city was built, that they might cast him down headlong. 30 But he, passing through the midst of them, went his way, 31 And came down to Capernaum, a city of Galilee, and taught them on the sabbath days. 32 And they were astonished at his doctrine: for his word was with power.

Living Bible

22 All who were there spoke well of him and were amazed by the beautiful words that fell from his lips. "How can this be?" they asked. "Isn't this Joseph's son?"

23 Then he said, "Probably you will quote me that proverb, 'Physician, heal yourself'—meaning, 'Why don't you do miracles here in your home town like those you did in Capernaum?' 24 But I solemnly declare to you that no prophet is accepted in his own home town! 25, 26 For example, remember how Elijah the prophet used a miracle to help the widow of Zarephath—a foreigner from the land of Sidon. There were many Jewish widows needing help in those days of famine, for there had been no rain for three and one-half years, and hunger stalked the land; yet Elijah was not sent to them. 27 Or think of the prophet Elisha, who healed Naaman, a Syrian, rather than the many Jewish lepers needing help."

28 These remarks stung them to fury; 29 and jumping up, they mobbed him and took him to the edge of the hill on which the city was built, to push him over the cliff. 30 But he walked away through the crowd and left them.

31 Then he returned to Capernaum, a city in Galilee, and preached there in the synagogue every Saturday. 32 Here, too, the people were amazed at the things he said. For he spoke as one who knew the truth, instead of merely quoting the opinions of others as his authority.

Today's English Version

22 They were all well impressed with him, and marveled at the beautiful words that he spoke. They said, "Isn't he the son of Joseph?"

23 He said to them, "I am sure that you will quote this proverb to me, 'Doctor, heal yourself.' You will also say to me, 'Do here in your own home town the same things we were told happened in Capernaum.' 24 I tell you this," Jesus added. "A prophet is never welcomed in his own home town. 25 Listen to me: it is true that there were many widows in Israel during the time of Elijah, when there was no rain for three and a half years and there was a great famine throughout the whole land. 26 Yet Elijah was not sent to a single one of them, but only to a widow of Zarephath, in the territory of Sidon. 27 And there were many lepers in Israel during the time of the prophet Elisha; yet not one of them was made clean, but only Naaman the Syrian."

28 All the people in the synagogue were filled with anger when they heard this. 29 They rose up, dragged Jesus out of town, and took him to the top of the hill on which their town was built, to throw him over the cliff. 30 But he walked through the middle of the crowd and went his way.

A man with an evil spirit

31 Then Jesus went to Capernaum, a town in Galilee, where he taught the people on the Sabbath. 32 They were all amazed at the way he

New International Version

22 All spoke well of him and were amazed at the gracious words that came from his lips. "Isn't this Joseph's son?" they asked.

23 Jesus said to them, "Surely you will quote this proverb to me: 'Physician, heal yourself! Do here in your home town what we have heard that you did in Capernaum.' "

24 "I tell you the truth," he continued, "no prophet is accepted in his home town. 25 I assure you that there were many widows in Israel in Elijah's time, when the sky was shut for three and a half years and there was a severe famine throughout the land. 26 Yet Elijah was not sent to any of them, but to a widow in Zarephath in the region of Sidon. 27 And there were many in Israel with leprosy[r] in the time of Elisha the prophet, yet not one of them was cleansed except Naaman the Syrian."

28 All the people in the synagogue were furious when they heard this. 29 They got up, drove him out of the town, and took him to the brow of the hill on which the town was built, in order to throw him down the cliff. 30 But he walked right through the crowd and went on his way.

Jesus drives out an evil spirit

31 Then he went down to Capernaum, a town in Galilee, and on the Sabbath began to teach the people. 32 They were amazed at his teaching, because his message had authority.

[*r*] The Greek word probably designated other related diseases also.

Phillips Modern English

Everybody heard what he said. They were amazed at the beautiful words that came from his lips, and they kept saying,

"Isn't this Joseph's son?"

So he said to them,

"I expect you will quote this proverb to me, 'Cure yourself, doctor!' Let us see you do in your own country all that we have heard that you did in Capernaum!" Then he added, "I assure you that no prophet is ever welcomed in his own country. I tell you the plain fact that in Elijah's time, when the heavens were shut up for three and a half years and there was a great famine through the whole country, there were many widows in Israel, but Elijah was not sent to any of them. But he *was* sent to Sarepta, to a widow in the country of Sidon. In the time of Elisha the prophet, there were many lepers in Israel, but not one of them was healed—only Naaman, the Syrian."

But when they heard this, everyone in the synagogue was furiously angry. They sprang to their feet and drove him right out of the town, taking him to the brow of the hill on which it was built, intending to hurl him down headlong. But he walked straight through the whole crowd and went on his way.

4.31 Jesus heals in Capernaum

Then he came down to Capernaum, a town in Galilee, and taught them on the Sabbath day. They were astonished at his teaching, for his words had the ring of authority.

Revised Standard Version

has been fulfilled in your hearing." 22And all
spoke well of him, and wondered at the gracious
words which proceeded out of his mouth; and
they said, "Is not this Joseph's son?" 23And he
said to them, "Doubtless you will quote to me
this proverb, 'Physician, heal yourself; what we
have heard you did at Capernaum, do here also
in your own country.'" 24And he said, "Truly,
I say to you, no prophet is acceptable in his own
country. 25 But in truth, I tell you, there were
many widows in Israel in the days of Elijah,
when the heaven was shut up three years and
six months, when there came a great famine over
all the land; 26 and Elijah was sent to none of
them but only to Zarephath, in the land of Sidon,
to a woman who was a widow. 27And there were
many lepers in Israel in the time of the prophet
Elisha; and none of them was cleansed, but only
Naaman the Syrian." 28 When they heard this,
all in the synagogue were filled with wrath.
29And they rose up and put him out of the city,
and led him to the brow of the hill on which
their city was built, that they might throw him
down headlong. 30 But passing through the
midst of them he went away.
31 And he went down to Capernaum, a city
of Galilee. And he was teaching them on the
sabbath; 32 and they were astonished at his

Jerusalem Bible

day even as you listen." 22And he won the approval of all, and they were astonished by the
gracious words that came from his lips.
They said, "This is Joseph's son, surely?"
23 But he replied, "No doubt you will quote me
the saying, 'Physician, heal yourself,' and tell
me, 'We have heard all that happened in Capernaum, do the same here in your own countryside.'" 24And he went on, "I tell you solemnly,
no prophet is ever accepted in his own country.
25 "There were many widows in Israel, I can
assure you, in Elijah's day, when heaven remained shut for three years and six months and
a great famine raged throughout the land, 26 but
Elijah was not sent to any of these: he was sent
to a widow at Zarephath, a Sidonian town.[h]
27And in the prophet Elisha's time there were
many lepers in Israel, but none of these was
cured, except the Syrian, Naaman."
28 When they heard this everyone in the
synagogue was enraged. 29 They sprang to their
feet and hustled him out of the town; and they
took him up to the brow of the hill their town
was built on, intending to throw him down the
cliff, 30 but he slipped through the crowd and
walked away.

Jesus teaches in Capernaum and cures a demoniac

31 He went down to Capernaum, a town in
Galilee, and taught them on the sabbath. 32And
his teaching made a deep impression on them
because he spoke with authority.

[*h*] 1 K. 17:9.

New English Bible

very hearing this text has come true.'[a] There was a general stir of admiration; they were surprised that words of such grace should fall from his lips. 'Is not this Joseph's son?' they asked. Then Jesus said, 'No doubt you will quote the proverb to me, "Physician, heal yourself!", and say, "We have heard of all your doings at Capernaum; do the same here in your own home town." I tell you this,' he went on: 'no prophet is recognized in his own country. There were many widows in Israel, you may be sure, in Elijah's time, when for three years and six months the skies never opened, and famine lay hard over the whole country; yet it was to none of those that Elijah was sent, but to a widow at Sarepta in the territory of Sidon. Again, in the time of the prophet Elisha there were many lepers in Israel, and not one of them was healed, but only Naaman, the Syrian.' At these words the whole congregation were infuriated. They leapt up, threw him out of the town, and took him to the brow of the hill on which it was built, meaning to hurl him over the edge. But he walked straight through them all, and went away.

Coming down to Capernaum, a town in Galilee, he taught the people on the Sabbath, and they were astounded at his teaching, for what

[*a*] *Or* 'Today', he said, 'this text which you have just heard has come true.'

King James Version

33 And in the synagogue there was a man, which had a spirit of an unclean devil, and cried out with a loud voice, 34 Saying, Let *us* alone; what have we to do with thee, *thou* Jesus of Nazareth? art thou come to destroy us? I know thee who thou art; the Holy One of God. 35And Jesus rebuked him, saying, Hold thy peace, and come out of him. And when the devil had thrown him in the midst, he came out of him, and hurt him not. 36And they were all amazed, and spake among themselves, saying, What a word *is* this! for with authority and power he commandeth the unclean spirits, and they come out. 37And the fame of him went out into every place of the country round about.

38 And he arose out of the synagogue, and entered into Simon's house. And Simon's wife's mother was taken with a great fever; and they besought him for her. 39And he stood over her, and rebuked the fever; and it left her: and immediately she arose and ministered unto them.

40 Now when the sun was setting, all they that had any sick with divers diseases brought them unto him; and he laid his hands on every one of them, and healed them. 41And devils also

Living Bible

33 Once as he was teaching in the synagogue, a man possessed by a demon began shouting at Jesus, 34 "Go away! We want nothing to do with you, Jesus from Nazareth. You have come to destroy us. I know who you are—the Holy Son of God."

35 Jesus cut him short. "Be silent!" he told the demon. "Come out!" The demon threw the man to the floor as the crowd watched, and then left him without hurting him further.

36 Amazed, the people asked, "What is in this man's words that even demons obey him?" 37 The story of what he had done spread like wildfire throughout the whole region.

38 After leaving the synagogue that day, he went to Simon's home where he found Simon's mother-in-law very sick with a high fever. "Please heal her," everyone begged.

39 Standing at her bedside he spoke to the fever, rebuking it, and immediately her temperature returned to normal and she got up and prepared a meal [c] for them!

40 As the sun went down that evening, all the villagers who had any sick people in their homes, no matter what their diseases were, brought them to Jesus; and the touch of his hands healed every one! 41 Some were possessed

[c] Literally, "ministered unto them."

Today's English Version

taught, because his words had authority. 33 There was a man in the synagogue who had the spirit of an evil demon in him; he screamed out in a loud voice, 34 "Ah! What do you want with us, Jesus of Nazareth? Are you here to destroy us? I know who you are: you are God's holy messenger!"

35 Jesus commanded the spirit, "Be quiet, and come out of the man!" The demon threw the man down in front of them and went out of him without doing him any harm.

36 They were all amazed, and said to one another, "What kind of words are these? With authority and power this man gives orders to the evil spirits, and they come out!" 37And the report about Jesus spread everywhere in that region.

Jesus heals many people

38 Jesus left the synagogue and went to Simon's home. Simon's mother-in-law was sick with a high fever, and they spoke to Jesus about her. 39 He went and stood at her bedside, and gave a command to the fever. The fever left her, and she got up at once and began to wait on them.

40 After sunset, all who had friends who were sick with various diseases brought them to Jesus; he placed his hands on every one of them and healed them all. 41 Demons, also, went out from

New International Version

33 In the synagogue there was a man possessed by a demon, an evil [s] spirit. He cried out at the top of his voice, 34 "Ha! What do you want with us, Jesus of Nazareth? Have you come to destroy us? I know who you are—the Holy One of God!"

35 "Be quiet!" Jesus said sternly. "Come out of him!" Then the demon threw the man down before them all and came out without injuring him.

36 All the people were amazed and said to each other, "What is this teaching? With authority and power he gives orders to evil [t] spirits and they come out!" 37And the news about him spread throughout the surrounding area.

Jesus heals many

38 Jesus left the synagogue and went to the home of Simon. Now Simon's mother-in-law was suffering from a high fever, and they asked Jesus to help her. 39 So he bent over her and rebuked the fever, and it left her. She got up at once and began to wait on them.

40 When the sun was setting, the people brought to Jesus all who had various kinds of sickness, and laying his hands on each one, he healed them. 41 Moreover, demons came out of

[s] Greek *unclean.* [t] Greek *unclean.*

Phillips Modern English

There was a man in the synagogue under the influence of some evil spirit and he yelled at the top of his voice, "Hi! What have you got to do with us, Jesus, you Nazarene—have you come to kill us? I know who you are all right, you're God's holy one!"

Jesus cut him short and spoke sharply,

"Be quiet! Get out of him!"

And after throwing the man down in front of them, the devil did come out of him without hurting him in the slightest. At this everybody present was amazed and they kept saying to each other,

"What sort of words are these? He speaks to these evil spirits with authority and power and out they go."

And his reputation spread over the whole surrounding district.

When Jesus got up and left the synagogue he went into Simon's house. Simon's mother-in-law was in the grip of a high fever, and they asked Jesus to help her. He stood over her as she lay in bed, brought the fever under control and it left her. At once she got up and began to see to their needs.

Then, as the sun was setting, all those who had friends suffering from every kind of disease brought them to Jesus and he laid his hands on each one of them separately and healed them. Evil spirits came out of many of these people,

Revised Standard Version

teaching, for his word was with authority. 33And in the synagogue there was a man who had the spirit of an unclean demon; and he cried out with a loud voice, 34 "Ah! [m] What have you to do with us, Jesus of Nazareth? Have you come to destroy us? I know who you are, the Holy One of God." 35 But Jesus rebuked him, saying, "Be silent, and come out of him!" And when the demon had thrown him down in the midst, he came out of him, having done him no harm. 36And they were all amazed and said to one another, "What is this word? For with authority and power he commands the unclean spirits, and they come out." 37And reports of him went out into every place in the surrounding region.

38 And he arose and left the synagogue, and entered Simon's house. Now Simon's mother-in-law was ill with a high fever, and they besought him for her. 39And he stood over her and rebuked the fever, and it left her; and immediately she rose and served them.

40 Now when the sun was setting, all those who had any that were sick with various diseases brought them to him; and he laid his hands on every one of them and healed them. 41And de-

[m] Or *Let us alone.*

Jerusalem Bible

33 In the synagogue there was a man who was possessed by the spirit of an unclean devil, and it shouted at the top of its voice, 34 "Ha! What do you want with us, Jesus of Nazareth? Have you come to destroy us? I know who you are: the Holy One of God." 35 But Jesus said sharply, "Be quiet! Come out of him!" And the devil, throwing the man down in front of everyone, went out of him without hurting him at all. 36Astonishment seized them and they were all saying to one another, "What teaching! He gives orders to unclean spirits with authority and power and they come out." 37And reports of him went all through the surrounding countryside.

Cure of Simon's mother-in-law

38 Leaving the synagogue he went to Simon's house. Now Simon's mother-in-law was suffering from a high fever and they asked him to do something for her. 39 Leaning over her he rebuked the fever and it left her. And she immediately got up and began to wait on them.

A number of cures

40 At sunset all those who had friends suffering from diseases of one kind or another brought them to him, and laying his hands on each he cured them. 41 Devils too came out of

New English Bible

he said had the note of authority. Now there was a man in the synagogue possessed by a devil, an unclean spirit. He shrieked at the top of his voice, 'What do you want with us, Jesus of Nazareth? Have you[a] come to destroy us? I know who you are—the Holy One of God.' Jesus rebuked him: 'Be silent', he said, 'and come out of him.' Then the devil, after throwing the man down in front of the people, left him without doing him any injury. Amazement fell on them all and they said to one another: 'What is there in this man's words? He gives orders to the unclean spirits with authority and power, and out they go.' So the news spread, and he was the talk of the whole district.

On leaving the synagogue he went to Simon's house. Simon's mother-in-law was in the grip of a high fever; and they asked him to help her. He came and stood over her and rebuked the fever. It left her, and she got up at once and waited on them.

At sunset all who had friends suffering from one disease or another brought them to him; and he laid his hands on them one by one and cured them. Devils also came out of many of them,

[a] *Or* You have.

King James Version

came out of many, crying out, and saying, Thou
art Christ the Son of God. And he rebuking
them suffered them not to speak: for they knew
that he was Christ. 42And when it was day, he
departed and went into a desert place: and the
people sought him, and came unto him, and
stayed him, that he should not depart from
them. 43And he said unto them, I must preach
the kingdom of God to other cities also: for
therefore am I sent. 44And he preached in the
synagogues of Galilee.

5 And it came to pass, that, as the people
pressed upon him to hear the word of God,
he stood by the lake of Gennesaret, 2And saw
two ships standing by the lake: but the fishermen were gone out of them, and were washing
their nets. 3And he entered into one of the ships,
which was Simon's, and prayed him that he
would thrust out a little from the land. And he
sat down, and taught the people out of the ship.
4 Now when he had left speaking, he said unto

Living Bible

by demons; and the demons came out at his
command, shouting, "You are the Son of God."
But because they knew he was the Christ, he
stopped them and told them to be silent.
42 Early the next morning he went out into
the desert. The crowds searched everywhere for
him and when they finally found him they
begged him not to leave them, but to stay at
Capernaum. 43 But he replied, "I must preach
the Good News of the Kingdom of God in
other places too, for that is why I was sent."
44 So he continued to travel around preaching in
synagogues throughout Judea.

5 One day as he was preaching on the shore
of Lake Gennesaret, great crowds pressed
in on him to listen to the Word of God. 2 He
noticed two empty boats standing at the water's
edge while the fishermen washed their nets.
3 Stepping into one of the boats, Jesus asked
Simon, its owner, to push out a little into the
water, so that he could sit in the boat and speak
to the crowds from there.
4 When he had finished speaking, he said to

Today's English Version

many people, screaming, "You are the Son of
God!"
Jesus commanded them and would not let
them speak, because they knew that he was the
Messiah.

Jesus preaches in the synagogues

42 At daybreak Jesus left the town and went
off to a lonely place. The people started looking
for him, and when they found him they tried to
keep him from leaving. 43 But he said to them,
"I must preach the Good News of the Kingdom
of God in other towns also, because that is what
God sent me to do."
44 So he preached in the synagogues all over
the country.

Jesus calls the first disciples

5 One time Jesus was standing on the shore
of Lake Gennesaret while the people pushed
their way up to him to listen to the word of
God. 2 He saw two boats pulled up on the beach;
the fishermen had left them and were washing
the nets. 3 Jesus got into one of the boats—it
belonged to Simon—and asked him to push off
a little from the shore. Jesus sat in the boat and
taught the crowd.
4 When he finished speaking, he said to Si-

New International Version

many people, shouting, "You are the Son of
God!" But he rebuked them and would not allow them to speak, because they knew he was
the Christ.[u]
42 At daybreak Jesus went out to a solitary
place. The people were looking for him and
when they came to where he was, they tried to
keep him from leaving them. 43 But he said, "I
must preach the good news of the kingdom of
God to the other towns also, because that is why
I was sent." 44And he kept on preaching in the
synagogues of Judea.[v]

The calling of the first disciples

5 One day as Jesus was standing by the Lake
of Gennesaret,[w] with the people crowding
around him and listening to the word of God,
2 he saw at the water's edge two boats, left there
by the fishermen, who were washing their nets.
3 He got into one of the boats, the one belonging to Simon, and asked him to put out a little
from shore. Then he sat down and taught the
people from the boat.
4 When he had finished speaking, he said to

[u] Or *Messiah.* [v] Or *the land of the Jews.* Some MSS read *Galilee.* [w] That is, the Sea of Galilee.

Phillips Modern English

shouting, "You are the Son of God!"
But he spoke sharply to them and would not allow them to say any more, for they knew perfectly well that he was Christ.

4.42 Jesus attempts to be alone—in vain

At daybreak, he went off to a deserted place, but the crowds tried to find him and when they did discover him, tried to prevent him from leaving them. But he told them, "I must tell the good news of the kingdom of God to other towns as well—that is my mission."
And he continued proclaiming his message in the synagogues of Judaea.

5.1 Simon, James and John become Jesus' followers

One day the people were crowding closely round Jesus to hear God's message, as he stood on the shore of Lake Gennesaret. Jesus noticed two boats drawn up on the beach, for the fishermen had left them there while they were cleaning their nets. He went aboard one of the boats, which belonged to Simon, and asked him to push out a little from the shore. Then he sat down and continued his teaching of the crowds from the boat.
When he had finished speaking, he said to

Revised Standard Version

mons also came out of many, crying, "You are
the Son of God!" But he rebuked them, and
would not allow them to speak, because they
knew that he was the Christ.
42 And when it was day he departed and went
into a lonely place. And the people sought him
and came to him, and would have kept him
from leaving them; 43 but he said to them, "I
must preach the good news of the kingdom of
God to the other cities also; for I was sent for
this purpose." 44 And he was preaching in the
synagogues of Judea.[n]

5 While the people pressed upon him to hear
the word of God, he was standing by the
lake of Gennesaret. 2 And he saw two boats by
the lake; but the fishermen had gone out of them
and were washing their nets. 3 Getting into one
of the boats, which was Simon's, he asked him
to put out a little from the land. And he sat
down and taught the people from the boat. 4 And

[n] Other ancient authorities read *Galilee*.

Jerusalem Bible

many people, howling, "You are the Son of God." But he rebuked them and would not allow them to speak because they knew that he was the Christ.

Jesus quietly leaves Capernaum and travels through Judaea

42 When daylight came he left the house and
made his way to a lonely place. The crowds
went to look for him, and when they had caught
up with him they wanted to prevent him leaving
them, 43 but he answered, "I must proclaim the
Good News of the kingdom of God to the other
towns too, because that is what I was sent to
do." 44 And he continued his preaching in the
synagogues of Judaea.

The first four disciples are called

5 Now he was standing one day by the Lake
of Gennesaret, with the crowd pressing
around him listening to the word of God,
2 when he caught sight of two boats close to the
bank. The fishermen had gone out of them and
were washing their nets. 3 He got into one of
the boats—it was Simon's—and asked him to
put out a little from the shore. Then he sat
down and taught the crowds from the boat.
4 When he had finished speaking he said to

New English Bible

shouting, 'You are the Son of God.' But he rebuked them and forbade them to speak, because they knew that he was the Messiah.
When day broke he went out and made his way to a lonely spot. But the people went in search of him, and when they came to where he was they pressed him not to leave them. But he said, 'I must give the good news of the kingdom of God to the other towns also, for that is what I was sent to do.' So he proclaimed the Gospel in the synagogues of Judaea.[b]

5 One day as he stood by the Lake of Gennesaret, and the people crowded upon him to listen to the word of God, he noticed two boats lying at the water's edge; the fishermen had come ashore and were washing their nets. He got into one of the boats, which belonged to Simon, and asked him to put out a little way from the shore; then he went on teaching the crowds from his seat in the boat. When he had finished

[b] *Or* the Jewish synagogues; *some witnesses read* the synagogues of Galilee.

King James Version

Simon, Launch out into the deep, and let down
your nets for a draught. 5And Simon answering
said unto him, Master, we have toiled all the
night, and have taken nothing: nevertheless at
thy word I will let down the net. 6And when
they had this done, they inclosed a great multitude of fishes: and their net brake. 7And they
beckoned unto *their* partners, which were in the
other ship, that they should come and help them.
And they came, and filled both the ships, so
that they began to sink. 8 When Simon Peter
saw *it*, he fell down at Jesus' knees, saying, Depart from me; for I am a sinful man, O Lord.
9 For he was astonished, and all that were with
him, at the draught of the fishes which they had
taken: 10And so *was* also James, and John, the
sons of Zebedee, which were partners with
Simon. And Jesus said unto Simon, Fear not;
from henceforth thou shalt catch men. 11And
when they had brought their ships to land, they
forsook all, and followed him.
12 And it came to pass, when he was in a
certain city, behold a man full of leprosy; who
seeing Jesus fell on *his* face, and besought him,
saying, Lord, if thou wilt, thou canst make me
clean. 13And he put forth *his* hand, and touched
him, saying, I will: be thou clean. And immedi-

Living Bible

Simon, "Now go out where it is deeper and let
down your nets and you will catch a lot of fish!"
5 "Sir," Simon replied, "we worked hard all
last night and didn't catch a thing. But if you
say so, we'll try again."
6 And this time their nets were so full that
they began to tear! 7A shout for help brought
their partners in the other boat and soon both
boats were filled with fish and on the verge of
sinking.
8 When Simon Peter realized what had happened, he fell to his knees before Jesus and said,
"Oh, sir, please leave us—I'm too much of a
sinner for you to have around." 9 For he was
awestruck by the size of their catch, as were the
others with him, 10 and his partners too—James
and John, the sons of Zebedee. Jesus replied,
"Don't be afraid! From now on you'll be fishing
for the souls of men!"
11 And as soon as they landed, they left
everything and went with him.
12 One day in a certain village he was visiting,
there was a man with an advanced case of leprosy. When he saw Jesus he fell to the ground
before him, face downward in the dust, begging
to be healed.
"Sir," he said, "if you only will, you can clear
me of every trace of my disease."
13 Jesus reached out and touched the man
and said, "Of course I will. Be healed." And the

Today's English Version

mon, "Push the boat out further to the deep
water, and you and your partners let your nets
down for a catch."
5 "Master," Simon answered, "we worked hard
all night long and caught nothing. But if you
say so, I will let down the nets." 6 They let the
nets down and caught such a large number of
fish that the nets were about to break. 7 So they
motioned to their partners in the other boat to
come and help them. They came and filled both
boats so full of fish that they were about to
sink. 8 When Simon Peter saw what had happened, he fell on his knees before Jesus and
said, "Go away from me, Lord! I am a sinful
man!"
9 He and the others with him were all
amazed at the large number of fish they had
caught. 10 The same was true of Simon's partners, James and John, the sons of Zebedee. Jesus
said to Simon, "Don't be afraid; from now on
you will be catching men."
11 They pulled the boats on the beach, left
everything, and followed Jesus.

Jesus makes a leper clean

12 Once Jesus was in a certain town where
there was a man who was covered with leprosy.
When he saw Jesus, he threw himself down and
begged him, "Sir, if you want to, you can make
me clean!"
13 Jesus reached out and touched him. "I do
want to," he answered. "Be clean!" At once the

New International Version

Simon, "Put out into deep water, and let down
the nets for a catch."
5 Simon answered, "Master, we've worked
hard all night and haven't caught anything. But
because you say so, I will let down the nets."
6 When they had done so, they caught such
a large number of fish that their nets began to
break. 7 So they signaled their partners in the
other boat to come and help them, and they
came and filled both boats so full that they
began to sink.
8 When Simon Peter saw this, he fell at
Jesus' knees and said, "Go away from me,
Lord; I am a sinful man!" 9 For he and all his
companions were astonished at the catch of fish
they had taken, 10 and so were James and John,
the sons of Zebedee, Simon's partners.
Then Jesus said to Simon, "Don't be afraid;
from now on you will catch men." 11 So they
pulled their boats up on shore, left everything
and followed him.

The man with leprosy

12 While Jesus was in one of the towns, a
man came along who was covered with leprosy.[x]
When he saw Jesus, he fell with his face to the
ground and begged him, "Lord, if you are willing, you can make me clean."
13 Jesus reached out his hand and touched
the man. "I am willing," he said. "Be clean!"
And immediately the leprosy left him.

[x] The Greek word probably designated other related diseases also.

Phillips Modern English

Simon, "Push out now into deep water and let down your nets for a catch."

Simon replied, "Master! We've worked all night and never caught a thing, but if you say so, I'll let the nets down."

And when they had done this, they caught an enormous shoal of fish—so big that the nets began to tear. So they signalled to their partners in the other boat to come and help them. They came and filled both the boats to sinking point. When Simon Peter saw this, he fell at Jesus' knees and said,

"Keep away from me, Lord, for I'm only a sinful man!"

For he and his companions (including Zebedee's sons, James and John, Simon's partners) were staggered at the haul of fish they had made. Jesus said to Simon, "Don't be afraid, Simon. From now on your catch will be *men*."

So they brought the boats ashore, left everything and followed him.

5.12 Jesus cures leprosy

While he was in one of the towns, Jesus came upon a man who was a mass of leprosy. When he saw Jesus, he prostrated himself before him and begged,

"If you want to Lord, you can make me clean."

Jesus stretched out his hand, placed it on the leper, saying,

"Certainly I want to. Be clean!"

Revised Standard Version

when he had ceased speaking, he said to Simon,
"Put out into the deep and let down your nets
for a catch." 5And Simon answered, "Master, we
toiled all night and took nothing! But at your
word I will let down the nets." 6And when they
had done this, they enclosed a great shoal of
fish; and as their nets were breaking, 7 they beckoned to their partners in the other boat to come
and help them. And they came and filled both
the boats, so that they began to sink. 8 But when
Simon Peter saw it, he fell down at Jesus' knees,
saying, "Depart from me, for I am a sinful man,
O Lord." 9 For he was astonished, and all that
were with him, at the catch of the fish which they
had taken; 10 and so also were James and John,
sons of Zebedee, who were partners with Simon.
And Jesus said to Simon, "Do not be afraid;
henceforth you will be catching men." 11And
when they had brought their boats to land, they
left everything and followed him.
12 While he was in one of the cities, there
came a man full of leprosy; and when he saw
Jesus, he fell on his face and besought him,
"Lord, if you will, you can make me clean."
13And he stretched out his hand, and touched
him, saying, "I will; be clean." And immediately

Jerusalem Bible

Simon, "Put out into deep water and pay out
your nets for a catch." 5 "Master," Simon replied, "we worked hard all night long and
caught nothing, but if you say so, I will pay out
the nets." 6And when they had done this they
netted such a huge number of fish that their nets
began to tear, 7 so they signaled to their companions in the other boat to come and help
them; when these came, they filled the two boats
to sinking point.
8 When Simon Peter saw this he fell at the
knees of Jesus saying, "Leave me, Lord; I am a
sinful man." 9 For he and all his companions
were completely overcome by the catch they had
made; 10 so also were James and John, sons of
Zebedee, who were Simon's partners. But Jesus
said to Simon, "Do not be afraid; from now on
it is men you will catch." 11 Then, bringing
their boats back to land, they left everything
and followed him.

Cure of a leper

12 Now Jesus was in one of the towns when
a man appeared, covered with leprosy. Seeing
Jesus he fell on his face and implored him.
"Sir," he said, "if you want to, you can cure
me." 13 Jesus stretched out his hand, touched
him and said, "Of course I want to! Be cured!"

New English Bible

speaking, he said to Simon, 'Put out into deep water and let down your nets for a catch.' Simon answered, 'Master, we were hard at work all night and caught nothing at all; but if you say so, I will let down the nets.' They did so and made a big haul of fish; and their nets began to split. So they signalled to their partners in the other boat to come and help them. This they did, and loaded both boats to the point of sinking. When Simon saw what had happened he fell at Jesus's knees and said, 'Go, Lord, leave me, sinner that I am!' For he and all his companions were amazed at the catch they had made; so too were his partners James and John, Zebedee's sons. 'Do not be afraid,' said Jesus to Simon; 'from now on you will be catching men.' As soon as they had brought the boats to land, they left everything and followed him.

He was once in a certain town where there happened to be a man covered with leprosy; seeing Jesus, he bowed to the ground and begged his help. 'Sir,' he said, 'if only you will, you can cleanse me.' Jesus stretched out his hand, touched him, and said, 'Indeed I will; be clean again.' The

King James Version

ately the leprosy departed from him. 14And he
charged him to tell no man: but go, and shew
thyself to the priest, and offer for thy cleansing,
according as Moses commanded, for a testimony
unto them. 15 But so much the more went there
a fame abroad of him: and great multitudes
came together to hear, and to be healed by him
of their infirmities.
16 And he withdrew himself into the wilderness, and prayed. 17And it came to pass on a
certain day, as he was teaching, that there were
Pharisees and doctors of the law sitting by,
which were come out of every town of Galilee,
and Judea, and Jerusalem: and the power of the
Lord was *present* to heal them.
18 And, behold, men brought in a bed a man
which was taken with a palsy: and they sought
means to bring him in, and to lay *him* before
him. 19And when they could not find by what
way they might bring him in because of the
multitude, they went upon the housetop, and let
him down through the tiling with *his* couch into
the midst before Jesus. 20And when he saw their
faith, he said unto him, Man, thy sins are forgiven thee. 21And the scribes and the Pharisees
began to reason, saying, Who is this which
speaketh blasphemies? Who can forgive sins, but
God alone? 22 But when Jesus perceived their

Living Bible

leprosy left him instantly! 14 Then Jesus instructed him to go at once without telling anyone what had happened and be examined by the
Jewish priest. "Offer the sacrifice Moses' law requires for lepers who are healed," he said. "This
will prove to everyone that you are well."
15 Now the report of his power spread even
faster and vast crowds came to hear him preach
and to be healed of their diseases. 16 But he
often withdrew to the wilderness for prayer.
17 One day while he was teaching, some Jewish religious leaders[a] and teachers of the Law
were sitting nearby. (It seemed that these men
showed up from every village in all Galilee and
Judea, as well as from Jerusalem.) And the
Lord's healing power was upon him.
18, 19 Then—look! Some men came carrying
a paralyzed man on a sleeping mat. They tried
to push through the crowd to Jesus but couldn't
reach him. So they went up on the roof above
him, took off some tiles and lowered the sick
man down into the crowd, still on his sleeping
mat, right in front of Jesus.
20 Seeing their faith, Jesus said to the man,
"My friend, your sins are forgiven!"
21 "Who does this fellow think he is?" the
Pharisees and teachers of the Law exclaimed
among themselves. "This is blasphemy! Who but
God can forgive sins?"
22 Jesus knew what they were thinking, and

[a] Literally, "Pharisees."

Today's English Version

leprosy left the man. 14 Jesus ordered him,
"Don't tell this to anyone, but go straight to
the priest and let him examine you; then offer
the sacrifice, as Moses ordered, to prove to everyone that you are now clean."
15 But the news about Jesus spread all the
more widely, and crowds of people came to hear
him and be healed from their diseases. 16 But he
would go away to lonely places, where he prayed.

Jesus heals a paralyzed man

17 One day when Jesus was teaching, some
Pharisees and teachers of the Law were sitting
there who had come from every town in Galilee
and Judea, and from Jerusalem. The power of
the Lord was present for Jesus to heal the sick.
18 Some men came carrying a paralyzed man on
a bed, and they tried to take him into the house
and lay him before Jesus. 19 Because of the
crowd, however, they could find no way to take
him in. So they carried him up on the roof,
made an opening in the tiles, and let him down
on his bed into the middle of the group in front
of Jesus. 20 When Jesus saw how much faith
they had, he said to the man, "Your sins are
forgiven you, my friend."
21 The teachers of the Law and the Pharisees
began to say to themselves, "Who is this man
who speaks against God in this way? No man
can forgive sins; God alone can!"
22 Jesus knew their thoughts and said to them,

New International Version

14 Then Jesus ordered him, "Don't tell anyone, but go, show yourself to the priest and offer
the sacrifices that Moses commanded for your
cleansing, as a testimony to them."
15 Yet the news about him spread all the
more, so that crowds of people came to hear
him and to be healed of their sicknesses. 16 But
Jesus often withdrew to lonely places and prayed.

Jesus heals a paralytic

17 One day as he was teaching, Pharisees and
teachers of the law, who had come from every
village of Galilee and from Judea and Jerusalem,
were sitting there. And the power of the Lord
was present for him to heal the sick. 18 Some
men came carrying a paralytic on a mat and
tried to take him into the house to lay him before Jesus. 19 When they could not find a way
to do this because of the crowd, they went up on
the roof and lowered him on his mat through the
tiles into the middle of the crowd, right in front
of Jesus.
20 When Jesus saw their faith, he said,
"Friend, your sins are forgiven."
21 The Pharisees and the teachers of the law
began thinking to themselves, "Who is this
fellow who speaks blasphemy? Who can forgive
sins but God alone?"
22 Jesus knew what they were thinking and

Phillips Modern English

Immediately the leprosy left him and Jesus warned him not to tell anybody, but to go and show himself to the priest and to make the offerings for his recovery which Moses prescribed, as evidence to the authorities.

Yet the news about him spread all the more, and enormous crowds collected to hear Jesus and to be healed of their complaints. But he slipped quietly away to deserted places for prayer.

5.17 Jesus cures a paralytic in soul and body

One day while Jesus was teaching, some Pharisees and experts in the Law were sitting near him. They had come out of every village in Galilee and Judaea as well as from Jerusalem. The Lord's power to heal people was with him. Soon some men arrived carrying a paralytic on a small bed and they kept trying to carry him in to put him down in front of Jesus. When they failed to find a way of getting him in because of the dense crowd, they went up on to the top of the house and let him down, bed and all, through the tiles, into the middle of the crowd in front of Jesus. When Jesus saw their faith, he said to the man,

"My friend, your sins are forgiven."

The scribes and the Pharisees began to argue about this, saying, "Who is this man who talks blasphemy? Who can forgive sins? Only God can do that."

Jesus realised what was going on in their

Revised Standard Version

the leprosy left him. 14And he charged him to tell no one; but "go and show yourself to the priest, and make an offering for your cleansing, as Moses commanded, for a proof to the people."[o] 15 But so much the more the report went abroad concerning him; and great multitudes gathered to hear and to be healed of their infirmities. 16 But he withdrew to the wilderness and prayed.

17 On one of those days, as he was teaching, there were Pharisees and teachers of the law sitting by, who had come from every village of Galilee and Judea and from Jerusalem; and the power of the Lord was with him to heal.[p] 18And behold, men were bringing on a bed a man who was paralyzed, and they sought to bring him in and lay him before Jesus;[q] 19 but finding no way to bring him in, because of the crowd, they went up on the roof and let him down with his bed through the tiles into the midst before Jesus. 20And when he saw their faith he said, "Man, your sins are forgiven you." 21And the scribes and the Pharisees began to question, saying, "Who is this that speaks blasphemies? Who can forgive sins but God only?" 22 When Jesus perceived their questionings, he answered

[*o*] Greek *to them.* [*p*] Other ancient authorities read *was present to heal them.* [*q*] Greek *him.*

Jerusalem Bible

And the leprosy left him at once. 14 He ordered him to tell no one, "But go and show yourself to the priest and make the offering for your healing as Moses prescribed it, as evidence for them."

15 His reputation continued to grow, and large crowds would gather to hear him and to have their sickness cured, 16 but he would always go off to some place where he could be alone and pray.

Cure of a paralytic

17 Now he was teaching one day, and among the audience there were Pharisees and doctors of the Law who had come from every village in Galilee, from Judaea and from Jerusalem. And the Power of the Lord was behind his works of
18 healing. Then some men appeared, carrying on a bed a paralyzed man whom they were trying to bring and lay down in front of him.
19 But as the crowd made it impossible to find a way of getting him in, they went up on to the flat roof and lowered him and his stretcher down through the tiles into the middle of the gathering, in front of Jesus. 20 Seeing their faith he said, "My friend, your sins are forgiven you."
21 The scribes and the Pharisees began to think this over. "Who is this man talking blasphemy? Who can forgive sins but God alone?" 22 But Jesus, aware of their thoughts, made them this

New English Bible

leprosy left him immediately. Jesus then ordered him not to tell anybody. 'But go,' he said, 'show yourself to the priest, and make the offering laid down by Moses for your cleansing; that will certify the cure.' But the talk about him spread all the more; great crowds gathered to hear him and to be cured of their ailments. And from time to time he would withdraw to lonely places for prayer.

One day he was teaching, and Pharisees and teachers of the law were sitting round. People had come from every village of Galilee and from Judaea and Jerusalem,[a] and the power of the Lord was with him to heal the sick. Some men appeared carrying a paralysed man on a bed. They tried to bring him in and set him down in front of Jesus, but finding no way to do so because of the crowd, they went up on to the roof and let him down through the tiling, bed and all, into the middle of the company in front of Jesus. When Jesus saw their faith, he said, 'Man, your sins are forgiven you.'

The lawyers and the Pharisees began saying to themselves, 'Who is this fellow with his blasphemous talk? Who but God alone can forgive sins?' But Jesus knew what they were thinking

[*a*] *Some witnesses read* and Pharisees and teachers of the law, who had come from every village of Galilee and from Judaea and Jerusalem, were sitting round.

King James Version

thoughts, he answering said unto them, What
reason ye in your hearts? 23 Whether is easier, to
say, Thy sins be forgiven thee; or to say, Rise
up and walk? 24 But that ye may know that the
Son of man hath power upon earth to forgive
sins, (he said unto the sick of the palsy,) I say
unto thee, Arise, and take up thy couch, and
go into thine house. 25 And immediately he rose
up before them, and took up that whereon he
lay, and departed to his own house, glorifying
God. 26 And they were all amazed, and they
glorified God, and were filled with fear, saying,
We have seen strange things to day.
27 And after these things he went forth, and
saw a publican, named Levi, sitting at the receipt
of custom: and he said unto him, Follow me.
28 And he left all, rose up, and followed him.
29 And Levi made him a great feast in his own
house: and there was a great company of publicans and of others that sat down with them.
30 But their scribes and Pharisees murmured
against his disciples, saying, Why do ye eat and
drink with publicans and sinners? 31 And Jesus
answering said unto them, They that are whole

Living Bible

he replied, "Why is it blasphemy? 23, 24 I, the
Messiah,[b] have the authority on earth to forgive sins. But talk is cheap—anybody could say
that. So I'll prove it to you by healing this man."
Then, turning to the paralyzed man, he commanded, "Pick up your stretcher and go on
home, for you are healed!"
25 And immediately, as everyone watched,
the man jumped to his feet, picked up his mat
and went home praising God! 26 Everyone present was gripped with awe and fear. And they
praised God, remarking over and over again,
"We have seen strange things today."
27 Later on as Jesus left the town he saw a
tax collector—with the usual reputation for
cheating—sitting at a tax collection booth. The
man's name was Levi. Jesus said to him, "Come
and be one of my disciples!" 28 So Levi left
everything, sprang up and went with him.
29 Soon Levi held a reception in his home
with Jesus as the guest of honor. Many of Levi's
fellow tax collectors and other guests were there.
30 But the Pharisees and teachers of the Law
complained bitterly to Jesus' disciples about his
eating with such notorious sinners.
31 Jesus answered them, "It is the sick who

[b] Literally, "the Son of Man."

Today's English Version

"Why do you think such things? 23 Is it easier
to say, 'Your sins are forgiven you,' or to say,
'Get up and walk'? 24 I will prove to you, then,
that the Son of Man has authority on earth to
forgive sins." So he said to the paralyzed man,
"I tell you, get up, pick up your bed, and go
home!"
25 At once the man got up before them all,
took the bed he had been lying on, and went
home, praising God. 26 They were all completely
amazed! Full of fear, they praised God, saying,
"What marvelous things we have seen today!"

Jesus calls Levi

27 After this, Jesus went out and saw a tax
collector named Levi, sitting in his office. Jesus
said to him, "Follow me." 28 Levi got up, left
everything, and followed him.
29 Then Levi had a big feast in his house for
Jesus, and there was a large number of tax collectors and other people at the table with them.
30 Some Pharisees and teachers of the Law who
belonged to their group complained to Jesus' disciples. "Why do you eat and drink with tax collectors and outcasts?" they asked.
31 Jesus answered them, "People who are well
do not need a doctor, but only those who are

New International Version

asked, "Why are you thinking these things in
your hearts? 23 Which is easier: to say, 'Your
sins are forgiven,' or to say, 'Get up and walk'?
24 But that you may know that the Son of
Man has authority on earth to forgive sins. . . ."
He said to the paralyzed man, "I tell you, get
up, take your mat and go home." 25 Immediately he stood up in front of them, took what he
had been lying on and went home praising God.
26 Everyone was amazed and gave praise to God.
They were filled with awe and said, "We have
seen remarkable things today."

The calling of Levi

27 After this, Jesus went out and saw a tax
collector by the name of Levi sitting at his tax
booth. "Follow me," Jesus said to him, 28 and
Levi got up, left everything and followed him.
29 Then Levi held a great banquet for Jesus
at his house, and a large crowd of tax collectors
and others were eating with them. 30 But the
Pharisees and the teachers of the law who belonged to their sect complained to his disciples,
"Why do you eat and drink with tax collectors
and 'sinners'?"
31 Jesus answered them, "It is not the healthy

Phillips Modern English

minds and spoke straight to them.
"Why must you argue like this in your minds? Which do you suppose is easier—to say, 'Your sins are forgiven' or to say, 'Get up and walk'? But to make you realise that the Son of Man has full authority on earth to forgive sins—I tell *you*," he said to the man who was paralysed, "get up, pick up your bed and go home!"
Instantly the man sprang to his feet before their eyes, picked up the bedding on which he used to lie, and went off home, praising God. Sheer amazement gripped every man present, and they praised God and said in awed voices, "We have seen incredible things today."

5.27 Jesus calls Levi to be his disciple

Later on, Jesus went out and looked straight at a tax-collector called Levi, as he sat in his office.
"Follow me," he said to him.
And he got to his feet, left everything behind and followed him.
Then Levi gave a big reception for Jesus in his own house, and there was a great crowd of tax-collectors and others at table with them. The Pharisees and their companions the scribes kept muttering indignantly about this to Jesus' disciples, saying,
"Why do you have your meals with tax-collectors and sinners?"
Jesus answered them,
"It is not the healthy who need the doctor,

Revised Standard Version

them, "Why do you question in your hearts?
23 Which is easier, to say, 'Your sins are forgiven
you,' or to say, 'Rise and walk'? 24 But that you
may know that the Son of man has authority on
earth to forgive sins"—he said to the man who
was paralyzed—"I say to you, rise, take up your
bed and go home." 25And immediately he rose
before them, and took up that on which he lay,
and went home, glorifying God. 26And amazement seized them all, and they glorified God and
were filled with awe, saying, "We have seen
strange things today."
27 After this he went out, and saw a tax collector, named Levi, sitting at the tax office; and
he said to him, "Follow me." 28And he left
everything, and rose and followed him.
29 And Levi made him a great feast in his
house; and there was a large company of tax
collectors and others sitting at table[r] with them.
30And the Pharisees and their scribes murmured
against his disciples, saying, "Why do you eat
and drink with tax collectors and sinners?"
31And Jesus answered them, "Those who are
well have no need of a physician, but those who

[r] Greek *reclining*.

Jerusalem Bible

reply, "What are these thoughts you have in
your hearts? 23 Which of these is easier: to say,
'Your sins are forgiven you' or to say, 'Get up
and walk'? 24 But to prove to you that the Son
of Man has authority on earth to forgive sins,"
—he said to the paralyzed man—"I order you:
get up, and pick up your stretcher and go
home." 25And immediately before their very
eyes he got up, picked up what he had been
lying on and went home praising God.
26 They were all astounded and praised God,
and were filled with awe, saying, "We have seen
strange things today."

The call of Levi

27 When he went out after this, he noticed a
tax collector, Levi by name, sitting by the customs house, and said to him, "Follow me."
28And leaving everything he got up and followed him.

Eating with sinners in Levi's house

29 In his honor Levi held a great reception
in his house and with them at table was a large
gathering of tax collectors and others. 30 The
Pharisees and their scribes complained to his
disciples and said, "Why do you eat and drink
with tax collectors and sinners?" 31 Jesus said
to them in reply, "It is not those who are well

New English Bible

and answered them: 'Why do you harbour thoughts like these? Is it easier to say, "Your sins are forgiven you", or to say, "Stand up and walk"? But to convince you that the Son of Man has the right on earth to forgive sins'—he turned to the paralysed man—'I say to you, stand up, take your bed, and go home.' And at once he rose to his feet before their eyes, took up the bed he had been lying on, and went home praising God. They were all lost in amazement and praised God; filled with awe they said, 'You would never believe the things we have seen today.'
Later, when he went out, he saw a tax-gatherer, Levi by name, at his seat in the custom-house, and said to him, 'Follow me'; and he rose to his feet, left everything behind, and followed him.
Afterwards Levi held a big reception in his house for Jesus; among the guests was a large party of tax-gatherers and others. The Pharisees and the lawyers of their sect complained to his disciples: 'Why do you eat and drink', they said, 'with tax-gatherers and sinners?' Jesus answered them: 'It is not the healthy that need a doctor,

King James Version

need not a physician; but they that are sick. 32 I
came not to call the righteous, but sinners to
repentance.
33 And they said unto him, Why do the disciples of John fast often, and make prayers, and
likewise *the disciples* of the Pharisees; but thine
eat and drink? 34 And he said unto them, Can ye
make the children of the bridechamber fast,
while the bridegroom is with them? 35 But the
days will come, when the bridegroom shall be
taken away from them, and then shall they fast
in those days.
36 And he spake also a parable unto them;
No man putteth a piece of a new garment upon
an old; if otherwise, then both the new maketh
a rent, and the piece that was *taken* out of the
new agreeth not with the old. 37 And no man
putteth new wine into old bottles; else the new
wine will burst the bottles, and be spilled, and
the bottles shall perish. 38 But new wine must
be put into new bottles; and both are preserved.
39 No man also having drunk old *wine* straightway desireth new; for he saith, The old is better.

Living Bible

need a doctor, not those in good health. 32 My
purpose is to invite sinners to turn from their
sins, not to spend my time with those who think
themselves already good enough."
33 Their next complaint was that Jesus' disciples were feasting instead of fasting. "John the
Baptist's disciples are constantly going without
food, and praying," they declared, "and so do
the disciples of the Pharisees. Why are yours
wining and dining?"
34 Jesus asked, "Do happy men fast? Do
wedding guests go hungry while celebrating with
the groom? 35 But the time will come when the
bridegroom will be killed;[c] then they won't want
to eat."
36 Then Jesus used this illustration: "No one
tears off a piece of a new garment to make a
patch for an old one. Not only will the new garment be ruined, but the old garment will look
worse with a new patch on it! 37 And no one
puts new wine into old wineskins, for the new
wine bursts the old skins, ruining the skins and
spilling the wine. 38 New wine must be put into
new wineskins. 39 But no one after drinking the
old wine seems to want the fresh and the new.
'The old ways are best,' they say."

[*c*] Literally, "taken away from them."

Today's English Version

sick. 32 I have not come to call the respectable
people to repent, but the outcasts."

The question about fasting

33 Some people said to Jesus, "The disciples
of John fast frequently and offer up prayers, and
the disciples of the Pharisees do the same; but
your disciples eat and drink."
34 Jesus answered, "Do you think you can
make the guests at a wedding party go without
food as long as the bridegroom is with them?
Of course not! 35 But the time will come when
the bridegroom will be taken away from them,
and they will go without food in those days."
36 Jesus told them this parable also, "No one
tears a piece off a new coat to patch up an old
coat. If he does, he will have torn the new coat,
and the piece of new cloth will not match the
old. 37 Nor does anyone pour new wine into
used wineskins. If he does, the new wine will
burst the skins, the wine will pour out, and the
skins will be ruined. 38 No! New wine should be
poured into fresh skins! 39 And no one wants
new wine after drinking old wine. 'The old is
better,' he says."

New International Version

who need a doctor, but the sick. 32 I have not
come to call the righteous, but sinners to repentance."

Jesus questioned about fasting

33 They said to him, "John's disciples often
fast and pray, and so do the disciples of the
Pharisees, but yours go on eating and drinking."
34 Jesus answered, "Can you make the guests
of the bridegroom fast while he is with them?
35 But the time will come when the bridegroom
will be taken from them; in those days they will
fast."
36 He told them this parable: "No one tears
a patch from a new garment and sews it on an
old one. If he does, he will have torn the new
garment, and the patch from the new will not
match the old. 37 And no one pours new wine
into old wineskins. If he does, the new wine will
burst the skins, the wine will run out and the
wineskins will be ruined. 38 No, new wine must
be poured into new wineskins. 39 And no one
after drinking old wine wants the new, for he
says, 'The old is better.' "

Phillips Modern English

but those who are ill. I did not come with an invitation for the 'righteous' but for the 'sinners' —to change their ways."

5.33 Jesus hints at who he is

Then people said to him,

"Why is it that John's disciples are always fasting and praying, just like the Pharisees' disciples, but yours both eat and drink?"

Jesus answered,

"Can you expect wedding-guests to fast while they have the bridegroom with them? The day will come when they will lose the bridegroom; that will be the time for them to fast!"

Then he gave them this illustration.

"Nobody tears a piece from a new coat to patch up an old one. If he does, he ruins the new one and the new piece does not match the old.

"Nobody puts new wine into old wineskins. If he does, the new wine will burst the skins—the wine will be spilt and the skins ruined. No, new wine must be put into new wineskins. Of course, nobody who has been drinking old wine will want the new at once. He is sure to say, 'The old is a good sound wine'."

Revised Standard Version

are sick; 32 I have not come to call the righteous,
but sinners to repentance."
33 And they said to him, "The disciples of
John fast often and offer prayers, and so do the
disciples of the Pharisees, but yours eat and
drink." 34 And Jesus said to them, "Can you
make wedding guests fast while the bridegroom
is with them? 35 The days will come, when the
bridegroom is taken away from them, and then
they will fast in those days." 36 He told them
a parable also: "No one tears a piece from a
new garment and puts it upon an old garment;
if he does, he will tear the new, and the piece
from the new will not match the old. 37 And no
one puts new wine into old wineskins; if he does,
the new wine will burst the skins and it will be
spilled, and the skins will be destroyed. 38 But
new wine must be put into fresh wineskins.
39 And no one after drinking old wine desires
new; for he says, 'The old is good.' "[s]

[s] Other ancient authorities read *better*.

Jerusalem Bible

who need the doctor, but the sick. 32 I have not
come to call the virtuous, but sinners to repentance."

Discussion on fasting

33 They then said to him, "John's disciples
are always fasting and saying prayers, and the
disciples of the Pharisees too, but yours go on
eating and drinking." 34 Jesus replied, "Surely
you cannot make the bridegroom's attendants
fast while the bridegroom is still with them?
35 But the time will come, the time for the
bridegroom to be taken away from them; that
will be the time when they will fast."
36 He also told them this parable, "No one
tears a piece from a new cloak to put it on an
old cloak; if he does, not only will he have
torn the new one, but the piece taken from the
new will not match the old.
37 "And nobody puts new wine into old
skins; if he does, the new wine will burst the
skins and then run out, and the skins will be
lost. 38 No; new wine must be put into fresh
skins. 39 And nobody who has been drinking old
wine wants new. 'The old is good,' he says."

New English Bible

but the sick; I have not come to invite virtuous people, but to call sinners to repentance.'

Then they said to him, 'John's disciples are much given to fasting and the practice of prayer, and so are the disciples of the Pharisees; but yours eat and drink.' Jesus replied, 'Can you make the bridegroom's friends fast while the bridegroom is with them? But a time will come: the bridegroom will be taken away from them, and that will be the time for them to fast.'

He told them this parable also: 'No one tears a piece from a new cloak to patch an old one; if he does, he will have made a hole in the new cloak, and the patch from the new will not match the old. Nor does anyone put new wine into old wine-skins; if he does, the new wine will burst the skins, the wine will be wasted, and the skins ruined. Fresh skins for new wine! And no one after drinking old wine wants new; for he says, "The old wine is good."'

King James Version

6 And it came to pass on the second sabbath
after the first, that he went through the corn
fields; and his disciples plucked the ears of corn,
and did eat, rubbing *them* in *their* hands. 2And
certain of the Pharisees said unto them, Why do
ye that which is not lawful to do on the sabbath
days? 3And Jesus answering them said, Have ye
not read so much as this, what David did, when
himself was a hungered, and they which were
with him; 4 How he went into the house of God,
and did take and eat the shewbread, and gave
also to them that were with him; which it is not
lawful to eat but for the priests alone? 5And he
said unto them, That the Son of man is Lord
also of the sabbath. 6And it came to pass also on
another sabbath, that he entered into the synagogue and taught: and there was a man whose
right hand was withered. 7And the scribes and
Pharisees watched him, whether he would heal
on the sabbath day; that they might find an accusation against him. 8 But he knew their
thoughts, and said to the man which had the
withered hand, Rise up, and stand forth in the
midst. And he arose and stood forth. 9 Then

Living Bible

6 One Sabbath as Jesus and his disciples
were walking through some grainfields, they
were breaking off the heads of wheat, rubbing
off the husks in their hands and eating the
grains.
2 But some Pharisees said, "That's illegal!
Your disciples are harvesting grain, and it's
against the Jewish law to work on the Sabbath."
3 Jesus replied, "Don't you read the Scriptures? Haven't you ever read what King David
did when he and his men were hungry? 4 He
went into the Temple and took the shewbread,
the special bread that was placed before the
Lord, and at it—illegal as this was—and shared
it with others." 5And Jesus added, "I [a] am master even of the Sabbath."
6 On another Sabbath he was in the synagogue teaching, and a man was present whose
right hand was deformed. 7 The teachers of the
Law and the Pharisees watched closely to see
whether he would heal the man that day, since it
was the Sabbath. For they were eager to find
some charge to bring against him.
8 How well he knew their thoughts! But he
said to the man with the deformed hand, "Come
and stand here where everyone can see." So he
did.
9 Then Jesus said to the Pharisees and teach-

[*a*] Literally, "the Son of Man."

Today's English Version

The question about the Sabbath

6 Jesus was walking through some wheat
fields on a Sabbath day. His disciples began
to pick the heads of wheat, rub them in their
hands, and eat the grain. 2 Some Pharisees said,
"Why are you doing what our Law says you
cannot do on the Sabbath?"
3 Jesus answered them, "Haven't you read
what David did when he and his men were hungry? 4 He went into the house of God, took the
bread offered to God, ate it, and gave it also to
his men. Yet it is against our Law for anyone
to eat it except the priests."
5 And Jesus concluded, "The Son of Man is
Lord of the Sabbath."

The man with a crippled hand

6 On another Sabbath Jesus went into a synagogue and taught. A man was there whose right
hand was crippled. 7 Some teachers of the Law
and Pharisees wanted some reason to accuse Jesus of doing wrong; so they watched him very
closely to see if he would cure on the Sabbath.
8 But Jesus knew their thoughts and said to the
man with the crippled hand, "Stand up and
come here to the front." The man got up and
stood there. 9 Then Jesus said to them, "I ask

New International Version

Lord of the Sabbath

6 One Sabbath Jesus was going through the
grainfields, and his disciples began to pick
some heads of grain, rub them in their hands
and eat the kernels. 2 Some of the Pharisees
asked, "Why are you doing what is unlawful on
the Sabbath?"
3 Jesus answered them, "Have you never read
what David did when he and his companions
were hungry? 4 He entered the house of God,
and taking the consecrated bread, he ate what
is lawful only for priests to eat. And he also
gave some to his companions." 5 Then Jesus said
to them, "The Son of Man is Lord of the Sabbath."
6 On another Sabbath he went into the synagogue and was teaching, and a man was there
whose right hand was shriveled. 7 The Pharisees
and the teachers of the law were looking for a
reason to accuse Jesus, so they watched him
closely to see if he would heal on the Sabbath.
8 But Jesus knew what they were thinking and
said to the man with the shriveled hand, "Get
up and stand in front of everyone." So he got
up and stood there.
9 Then Jesus said to them, "I ask you, which

Phillips Modern English

6.1 Jesus speaks of the Sabbath—

One Sabbath day, as Jesus happened to be passing through the cornfields, his disciples began picking the ears of corn, rubbing them in their hands, and eating them. Some of the Pharisees remarked,

"Why are you doing what the Law forbids men to do on the Sabbath day?"

Jesus answered them and said,

"Have you never read what David and his men did when they were hungry? He went into the house of God, took the presentation loaves, ate some bread himself and gave some to those with him, even though the Law does not permit anyone except the priests to eat it."

Then he added, "The Son of Man is master even of the Sabbath."

6.6 —and provokes violent antagonism

On another Sabbath day when he went into a synagogue to teach, there was a man there whose right hand was wasted away. The scribes and the Pharisees were watching Jesus closely to see whether he would heal on the Sabbath day, which would give them grounds for an accusation. But he knew what was going on in their minds, and said to the man with the wasted hand,

"Stand up and come forward."

And he got up and stood there. Then Jesus said to them,

Revised Standard Version

6 On a sabbath,[t] while he was going through the grainfields, his disciples plucked and ate some heads of grain, rubbing them in their hands. 2 But some of the Pharisees said, "Why are you doing what is not lawful to do on the sabbath?" 3 And Jesus answered, "Have you not read what David did when he was hungry, he and those who were with him: 4 how he entered the house of God, and took and ate the bread of the Presence, which it is not lawful for any but the priests to eat, and also gave it to those with him?" 5 And he said to them, "The Son of man is lord of the sabbath."

6 On another sabbath, when he entered the synagogue and taught, a man was there whose right hand was withered. 7 And the scribes and the Pharisees watched him, to see whether he would heal on the sabbath, so that they might find an accusation against him. 8 But he knew their thoughts, and he said to the man who had the withered hand, "Come and stand here." And he rose and stood there. 9 And Jesus said

[t] Other ancient authorities read *On the second first sabbath* (on the second sabbath after the first).

Jerusalem Bible

Picking corn on the sabbath

6 Now one sabbath he happened to be taking a walk through the cornfields, and his disciples were picking ears of corn, rubbing them in their hands and eating them. 2 Some of the Pharisees said, "Why are you doing something that is forbidden on the sabbath day?" 3 Jesus answered them, "So you have not read what David did when he and his followers were hungry—4 how he went into the house of God, took the loaves of offering and ate them and gave them to his followers, loaves which only the priests are allowed to eat?" 5 And he said to them, "The Son of Man is master of the sabbath."

Cure of the man with a withered hand

6 Now on another sabbath he went into the synagogue and began to teach, and a man was there whose right hand was withered. 7 The scribes and the Pharisees were watching him to see if he would cure a man on the sabbath, hoping to find something to use against him. 8 But he knew their thoughts; and he said to the man with the withered hand, "Stand up! Come out into the middle." And he came out and stood there. 9 Then Jesus said to them, "I put it

New English Bible

6 One Sabbath he was going through the cornfields, and his disciples were plucking the ears of corn, rubbing them in their hands, and eating them. Some of the Pharisees said, 'Why are you doing what is forbidden on the Sabbath?' Jesus answered, 'So you have not read what David did when he and his men were hungry? He went into the House of God and took the sacred bread to eat and gave it to his men, though priests alone are allowed to eat it, and no one else.' He also said, 'The Son of Man is sovereign even over the Sabbath.'

On another Sabbath he had gone to synagogue and was teaching. There happened to be a man in the congregation whose right arm was withered; and the lawyers and the Pharisees were on the watch to see whether Jesus would cure him on the Sabbath, so that they could find a charge to bring against him. But he knew what was in their minds and said to the man with the withered arm, 'Get up and stand out here.' So he got up and stood there. Then Jesus said to them,

King James Version

said Jesus unto them, I will ask you one thing;
Is it lawful on the sabbath days to do good, or
to do evil? to save life, or to destroy *it?* 10And
looking round about upon them all, he said unto
the man, Stretch forth thy hand. And he did so:
and his hand was restored whole as the other.
11And they were filled with madness; and communed one with another what they might do to
Jesus. 12And it came to pass in those days, that
he went out into a mountain to pray, and continued all night in prayer to God.
13 And when it was day, he called *unto him*
his disciples: and of them he chose twelve, whom
also he named apostles; 14 Simon, (whom he also
named Peter,) and Andrew his brother, James
and John, Philip and Bartholomew, 15 Matthew
and Thomas, James the *son* of Alpheus, and
Simon called Zelotes, 16And Judas *the brother*
of James, and Judas Iscariot, which also was
the traitor.
17 And he came down with them, and stood

Living Bible

ers of the Law, "I have a question for you. Is it
right to do good on the Sabbath day, or to do
harm? To save life, or to destroy it?"
10 He looked around at them one by one
and then said to the man, "Reach out your
hand." And as he did, it became completely normal again. 11At this, the enemies of Jesus were
wild with rage, and began to plot his murder.
12 One day soon afterwards he went out into
the mountains to pray, and prayed all night.
13At daybreak he called together his followers
and chose twelve of them to be the inner circle
of his disciples. (They were appointed as his
"apostles," or "missionaries.") 14, 15, 16 Here
are their names:

Simon (he also called him Peter),
Andrew (Simon's brother),
James,
John,
Philip,
Bartholomew,
Matthew,
Thomas,
James (the son of Alphaeus),
Simon (a member of the Zealots, a subversive political party),
Judas (son of James),
Judas Iscariot (who later betrayed him).

17,18 When they came down the slopes of

Today's English Version

you: What does our Law allow us to do on the
Sabbath? To help or to harm? To save a man's
life or destroy it?" 10 He looked around at them
all, then said to the man, "Stretch out your
hand." He did so, and his hand became well
again.
11 But they were filled with rage and began to
discuss among themselves what they could do to
Jesus.

Jesus chooses the twelve apostles

12 At that time Jesus went up a hill to pray,
and spent the whole night there praying to God.
13 When day came he called his disciples to him
and chose twelve of them, whom he named
apostles: 14 Simon (whom he also named Peter)
and his brother Andrew; James and John, Philip
and Bartholomew, 15 Matthew and Thomas,
James, the son of Alphaeus, and Simon (who
was called the Patriot), 16 Judas, the son of
James, and Judas Iscariot, who became the traitor.

Jesus teaches and heals

17 Coming down from the hill with them, Je-

New International Version

is lawful on the Sabbath: to do good or to do
evil, to save life or to destroy it?"
10 He looked around at them all, and then
said to the man, "Stretch out your hand." He
did so, and his hand was completely restored.
11 But they were furious and began to discuss
with one another what they might do to Jesus.

The twelve apostles

12 One of those days Jesus went out into the
hills to pray, and spent the night praying to
God. 13 When morning came, he called his disciples to him and chose twelve of them, whom
he also designated apostles: 14 Simon (whom he
named Peter), his brother Andrew, James, John,
Philip, Bartholomew, 15 Matthew, Thomas, James
son of Alphaeus, Simon who was called the
Zealot, 16 Judas son of James, and Judas Iscariot,
who became a traitor.

Blessings and woes

17 He went down with them and stood on a

Phillips Modern English

"I am going to ask you a question. Does the Law command us to do good on the Sabbath or do harm—to save life or destroy it?"

He looked round, meeting all their eyes, and said to the man,

"Now stretch out your hand."

He did so, and his hand was restored as sound as the other one. But they were filled with insane fury and kept discussing with each other what they could do to Jesus.

6.12 After a night of prayer Jesus selects the twelve

It was in those days that he went up the hillside to pray, and spent the whole night in prayer to God. When daylight came, he summoned his disciples to him and out of them he chose twelve whom he called apostles. They were—

Simon (whom he called Peter),
Andrew, his brother,
James,
John,
Philip,
Bartholomew,
Matthew,
Thomas,
James, the son of Alphaeus,
Simon, called the nationalist,
Judas, the son of James, and
Judas Iscariot, who later betrayed him.

Then he came down with them and stood on

Revised Standard Version

to them, "I ask you, is it lawful on the sabbath
to do good or to do harm, to save life or to
destroy it?" 10 And he looked around on them
all, and said to him, "Stretch out your hand."
And he did so, and his hand was restored. 11 But
they were filled with fury and discussed with one
another what they might do to Jesus.

12 In these days he went out to the mountain
to pray; and all night he continued in prayer to
God. 13 And when it was day, he called his disciples, and chose from them twelve, whom he
named apostles; 14 Simon, whom he named
Peter, and Andrew his brother, and James and
John, and Philip, and Bartholomew, 15 and Matthew, and Thomas, and James the son of Alphaeus, and Simon who was called the Zealot,
16 and Judas the son of James, and Judas Iscariot, who became a traitor.
17 And he came down with them and stood

Jerusalem Bible

to you: is it against the law on the sabbath to
do good, or to do evil; to save life, or to destroy
it?" 10 Then he looked around at them all and
said to the man, "Stretch out your hand." He
did so, and his hand was better. 11 But they were
furious, and began to discuss the best way of
dealing with Jesus.

The choice of the Twelve

12 Now it was about this time that he went
out into the hills to pray; and he spent the
whole night in prayer to God. 13 When day
came he summoned his disciples and picked out
twelve of them; he called them "apostles":
14 Simon whom he called Peter, and his brother
Andrew; James, John, Philip, Bartholomew,
15 Matthew, Thomas, James son of Alphaeus,
Simon called the Zealot, 16 Judas son of James,[i]
and Judas Iscariot who became a traitor.

The crowds follow Jesus

17 He then came down with them and stopped

[*i*] Or possibly "brother of James."

New English Bible

'I put the question to you: is it permitted to do good or to do evil on the Sabbath, to save life or to destroy it?' He looked round at them all and then said to the man, 'Stretch out your arm.' He did so, and his arm was restored. But they were beside themselves with anger, and began to discuss among themselves what they could do to Jesus.

During this time he went out one day into the hills to pray, and spent the night in prayer to God. When day broke he called his disciples to him, and from among them he chose twelve and named them Apostles: Simon, to whom he gave the name of Peter, and Andrew his brother, James and John, Philip and Bartholomew, Matthew and Thomas, James son of Alphaeus, and Simon who was called the Zealot, Judas son of James, and Judas Iscariot who turned traitor.

He came down the hill with them and took his

King James Version

in the plain, and the company of his disciples, and a great multitude of people out of all Judea and Jerusalem, and from the sea coast of Tyre and Sidon, which came to hear him, and to be healed of their diseases; 18 And they that were vexed with unclean spirits: and they were healed. 19 And the whole multitude sought to touch him: for there went virtue out of him, and healed *them* all.

20 And he lifted up his eyes on his disciples, and said, Blessed *be ye* poor: for yours is the kingdom of God. 21 Blessed *are ye* that hunger now: for ye shall be filled. Blessed *are ye* that weep now: for ye shall laugh. 22 Blessed are ye, when men shall hate you, and when they shall separate you *from their company,* and shall reproach *you,* and cast out your name as evil, for the Son of man's sake. 23 Rejoice ye in that day, and leap for joy: for, behold, your reward *is* great in heaven: for in the like manner did their fathers unto the prophets. 24 But woe unto

Living Bible

the mountain, they stood with Jesus on a large, level area, surrounded by many of his followers who, in turn, were surrounded by the crowds. For people from all over Judea and from Jerusalem and from as far north as the seacoasts of Tyre and Sidon had come to hear him or to be healed. And he cast out many demons. 19 Everyone was trying to touch him, for when they did healing power went out from him and they were cured.

20 Then he turned to his disciples and said, "What happiness there is for you who are poor, for the Kingdom of God is yours! 21 What happiness there is for you who are now hungry, for you are going to be satisfied! What happiness there is for you who weep, for the time will come when you shall laugh with joy! 22 What happiness it is when others hate you and exclude you and insult you and smear your name because you are mine! [b] 23 When that happens, rejoice! Yes, leap for joy! For you will have a great reward awaiting you in heaven. And you will be in good company—the ancient prophets were treated that way too!

24 "But, oh, the sorrows that await the rich.

[*b*] Literally, "on account of the Son of Man."

Today's English Version

sus stood on a level place with a large number of his disciples. A great crowd of people was there from all over Judea, and from Jerusalem, and from the coast cities of Tyre and Sidon; 18 they came to hear him and to be healed of their diseases. Those who were troubled by evil spirits also came and were healed. 19 All the people tried to touch him, for power was going out from him and healing them all.

Happiness and sorrow

20 Jesus looked at his disciples and said,

"Happy are you poor;
the Kingdom of God is yours!
21 "Happy are you who are hungry now;
you will be filled!
"Happy are you who weep now;
you will laugh!

22 "Happy are you when men hate you, and reject you, and insult you, and say that you are evil, because of the Son of Man! 23 Be glad when that happens, and dance for joy, because a great reward is kept for you in heaven. For their ancestors did the very same things to the prophets.

24 "But how terrible for you who are rich now;

New International Version

level place. A large crowd of his disciples was there and a great number of people from all over Judea, from Jerusalem, and from the seacoast of Tyre and Sidon, 18 who had come to hear him and to be healed of their diseases. Those troubled by evil [y] spirits were cured, 19 and the people all tried to touch him, because power was coming from him and healing them all.

20 Looking at his disciples, he said:
"Blessed are you who are poor,
for yours is the kingdom of God.
21 Blessed are you who hunger now,
for you will be satisfied.
Blessed are you who weep now,
for you will laugh.
22 Blessed are you when men hate you,
when they exclude you and insult you
and reject your name as evil,
because of the Son of Man.

23 "Rejoice in that day and leap for joy, because great is your reward in heaven. For that is how their fathers treated the prophets.

24 "But woe to you who are rich,

[*y*] Greek *unclean.*

Phillips Modern English

a level piece of ground, surrounded by a large crowd of his disciples and a great number of people from all parts of Judaea and Jerusalem and the coastal district of Tyre and Sidon, who had come to hear him and to be healed of their diseases. (And even those who were troubled with evil spirits were cured.) The whole crowd were trying to touch him with their hands, for power was going out from him and he healed them all.

6.20 Jesus declares who is happy and who is to be pitied, and defines a new attitude towards life

Then Jesus looked steadily at his disciples and said,

"How happy are you who own nothing, for the kingdom of God is yours!

"How happy are you who are hungry now, for you will be satisfied!

"How happy are you who weep now, for you are going to laugh!

"How happy you are when men hate you and turn you out of their company; when they slander you and reject all that you stand for because you are loyal to the Son of Man. Be glad when that happens and jump for joy—your reward in Heaven is magnificent. For that is exactly how their fathers treated the prophets.

"But how miserable for you who are rich, for

Revised Standard Version

on a level place, with a great crowd of his disciples and a great multitude of people from all Judea and Jerusalem and the seacoast of Tyre and Sidon, who came to hear him and to be
healed of their diseases; 18 and those who were
troubled with unclean spirits were cured. 19 And
all the crowd sought to touch him, for power came forth from him and healed them all.
20 And he lifted up his eyes on his disciples, and said:

"Blessed are you poor, for yours is the kingdom of God.
21 "Blessed are you that hunger now, for you shall be satisfied.

"Blessed are you that weep now, for you shall laugh.
22 "Blessed are you when men hate you, and when they exclude you and revile you, and cast out your name as evil, on account of the Son of
man! 23 Rejoice in that day, and leap for joy, for behold, your reward is great in heaven; for so their fathers did to the prophets.
24 "But woe to you that are rich, for you

Jerusalem Bible

at a piece of level ground where there was a large gathering of his disciples with a great crowd of people from all parts of Judaea and from Jerusalem and from the coastal region of
Tyre and Sidon 18 who had come to hear him and to be cured of their diseases. People tormented by unclean spirits were also cured,
19 and everyone in the crowd was trying to touch him because power came out of him that cured them all.

The inaugural discourse. The Beatitudes

20 Then fixing his eyes on his disciples he said:

"How happy are you who are poor: yours is the kingdom of God.
21 Happy you who are hungry now: you shall be satisfied.
Happy you who weep now: you shall laugh.

22 "Happy are you when people hate you, drive you out, abuse you, denounce your name as criminal, on account of the Son of Man.
23 Rejoice when that day comes and dance for joy, then your reward will be great in heaven. This was the way their ancestors treated the prophets.

The curses

24 "But alas for you who are rich: you are

New English Bible

stand on level ground. There was a large concourse of his disciples and great numbers of people from Jerusalem and Judaea and from the seaboard of Tyre and Sidon, who had come to listen to him, and to be cured of their diseases. Those who were troubled with unclean spirits were cured; and everyone in the crowd was trying to touch him, because power went out from him and cured them all.

Then turning to his disciples he began to speak:

'How blest are you who are in need; the kingdom of God is yours.

'How blest are you who now go hungry; your hunger shall be satisfied.

'How blest are you who weep now; you shall laugh.

'How blest you are when men hate you, when they outlaw you and insult you, and ban your very name as infamous, because of the Son of Man. On that day be glad and dance for joy; for assuredly you have a rich reward in heaven; in just the same way did their fathers treat the prophets.

'But alas for you who are rich; you have had

King James Version

you that are rich! for ye have received your
consolation. 25 Woe unto you that are full! for
ye shall hunger. Woe unto you that laugh now!
for ye shall mourn and weep. 26 Woe unto you,
when all men shall speak well of you! for so did
their fathers to the false prophets.
27 But I say unto you which hear, Love your
enemies, do good to them which hate you,
28 Bless them that curse you, and pray for them
which despitefully use you. 29 And unto him that
smiteth thee on the *one* cheek offer also the
other; and him that taketh away thy cloak forbid
not *to take thy* coat also. 30 Give to every man
that asketh of thee; and of him that taketh away
thy goods ask *them* not again. 31 And as ye
would that men should do to you, do ye also to
them likewise. 32 For if ye love them which love
you, what thank have ye? for sinners also love
those that love them. 33 And if ye do good to
them which do good to you, what thank have
ye? for sinners also do even the same. 34 And if
ye lend *to them* of whom ye hope to receive,
what thank have ye? for sinners also lend to
sinners, to receive as much again. 35 But love ye
your enemies, and do good, and lend, hoping for
nothing again; and your reward shall be great,

Living Bible

For they have their only happiness down here.
25 They are fat and prosperous now, but a time
of awful hunger is before them. Their careless
laughter now means sorrow then. 26 And what
sadness is ahead for those praised by the crowds
—for *false* prophets have *always* been praised.
27 "Listen, all of you. Love your *enemies.*
Do *good* to those who *hate* you. 28 Pray for the
happiness of those who *curse* you; implore God's
blessing on those who *hurt* you.
29 "If someone slaps you on one cheek, let
him slap the other too! If someone demands
your coat, give him your shirt besides. 30 Give
what you have to anyone who asks you for it;
and when things are taken away from you, don't
worry about getting them back. 31 Treat others
as you want them to treat you.
32 "Do you think you deserve credit for
merely loving those who love you? Even the
godless do that! 33 And if you do good only to
those who do you good—is that so wonderful?
Even sinners do that much! 34 And if you lend
money only to those who can repay you, what
good is that? Even the most wicked will lend to
their own kind for full return!
35 "Love your *enemies!* Do good to *them!*
Lend to *them!* And don't be concerned about
the fact that they won't repay. Then your reward from heaven will be very great, and you

Today's English Version

you have had your easy life!
25 "How terrible for you who are full now;
you will go hungry!
"How terrible for you who laugh now;
you will mourn and weep!

26 "How terrible when all men speak well of
you; because their ancestors said the very same
things to the false prophets."

Love for enemies

27 "But I tell you who hear me: Love your
enemies, do good to those who hate you, 28 bless
those who curse you, and pray for those who
mistreat you. 29 If anyone hits you on one cheek,
let him hit the other one too; if someone takes
your coat, let him have your shirt as well. 30 Give
to everyone who asks you for something, and
when someone takes what is yours, do not ask
for it back. 31 Do for others just what you want
them to do for you.
32 "If you love only the people who love you,
why should you receive a blessing? Even sinners
love those who love them! 33 And if you do good
only to those who do good to you, why should
you receive a blessing? Even sinners do that!
34 And if you lend only to those from whom you
hope to get it back, why should you receive a
blessing? Even sinners lend to sinners, to get
back the same amount! 35 No! Love your enemies and do good to them; lend and expect
nothing back. You will have a great reward, and

New International Version

for you have already received your comfort.
25 Woe to you who are well fed now,
for you will go hungry.
Woe to you who laugh now,
for you will mourn and weep.
26 Woe to you when all men speak well of
you,
for that is how their fathers treated the
false prophets.

Love for enemies

27 "But I tell you who hear me: Love your
enemies, do good to those who hate you, 28 bless
those who curse you, pray for those who mistreat you. 29 If someone strikes you on one
cheek, turn to him the other also. If someone
takes your cloak, do not stop him from taking
your tunic. 30 Give to everyone who asks you,
and if anyone takes what belongs to you, do not
demand it back. 31 Do to others as you would
have them do to you.
32 "If you love those who love you, what
credit is that to you? Even 'sinners' love those
who love them. 33 And if you do good to those
who are good to you, what credit is that to you?
Even 'sinners' do that. 34 And if you lend to those
from whom you expect repayment, what credit
is that to you? Even 'sinners' lend to 'sinners,'
expecting to be repaid in full. 35 But love your
enemies, do good to them, and lend to them
without expecting to get anything back. Then
your reward will be great, and you will be sons

Phillips Modern English

you have had all your comforts!

"How miserable for you who have all you want, for you are going to be hungry!

"How miserable for you who are laughing now, for you will know sorrow and tears!

"How miserable for you when everybody praises you, for that is exactly how their fathers treated the false prophets.

"But I say to all of you who will listen to me: love your enemies, do good to those who hate you, bless those who curse you, and pray for those who treat you spitefully.

"As for the man who hits you on one cheek, offer him the other one as well! And if a man is taking away your coat, do not stop him from taking your shirt as well. Give to everyone who asks you, and when a man has taken what belongs to you, don't demand it back.

"Treat men exactly as you would like them to treat you. If you love only those who love you, what credit is that to you? Even sinners love those who love them! And if you do good only to those who do good to you, what credit is that to you? Even sinners do that much. And if you lend only to those from whom you hope to get your money back, what credit is that to you? Even sinners lend to sinners and expect to get their money back. No, you are to love your *enemies* and do good and lend without hope of return. Your reward will be wonderful and you

Revised Standard Version

have received your consolation.
25 "Woe to you that are full now, for you
shall hunger.
"Woe to you that laugh now, for you shall mourn and weep.
26 "Woe to you, when all men speak well of
you, for so their fathers did to the false prophets.
27 "But I say to you that hear, Love your
enemies, do good to those who hate you, 28 bless
those who curse you, pray for those who abuse
you. 29 To him who strikes you on the cheek,
offer the other also; and from him who takes away your coat do not withhold even your shirt.
30 Give to every one who begs from you; and
of him who takes away your goods do not ask
them again. 31 And as you wish that men would
do to you, do so to them.
32 "If you love those who love you, what
credit is that to you? For even sinners love those
who love them. 33 And if you do good to those
who do good to you, what credit is that to you?
For even sinners do the same. 34 And if you
lend to those from whom you hope to receive, what credit is that to you? Even sinners lend to
sinners, to receive as much again. 35 But love
your enemies, and do good, and lend, expecting nothing in return;[v] and your reward will be

[v] Other ancient authorities read *despairing of no man*.

Jerusalem Bible

having your consolation now.
25 Alas for you who have your fill now: you shall go hungry.
Alas for you who laugh now: you shall mourn and weep.

26 "Alas for you when the world speaks well of you! This was the way their ancestors treated the false prophets.

Love of enemies

27 "But I say this to you who are listening:
Love your enemies, do good to those who hate
you, 28 bless those who curse you, pray for those
who treat you badly. 29 To the man who slaps
you on one cheek, present the other cheek too; to the man who takes your cloak from you, do
not refuse your tunic. 30 Give to everyone who
asks you, and do not ask for your property back
from the man who robs you. 31 Treat others as
you would like them to treat you. 32 If you love
those who love you, what thanks can you expect? Even sinners love those who love them.
33 And if you do good to those who do good to
you, what thanks can you expect? For even
sinners do that much. 34 And if you lend to
those from whom you hope to receive, what thanks can you expect? Even sinners lend to
sinners to get back the same amount. 35 Instead,
love your enemies and do good, and lend without any hope of return. You will have a great

New English Bible

your time of happiness.

'Alas for you who are well-fed now; you shall go hungry.

'Alas for you who laugh now; you shall mourn and weep.

'Alas for you when all speak well of you; just so did their fathers treat the false prophets.

'But to you who hear me I say:

'Love your enemies; do good to those who hate you; bless those who curse you; pray for those who treat you spitefully. When a man hits you on the cheek, offer him the other cheek too; when a man takes your coat, let him have your shirt as well. Give to everyone who asks you; when a man takes what is yours, do not demand it back. Treat others as you would like them to treat you.

'If you love only those who love you, what credit is that to you? Even sinners love those who love them. Again, if you do good only to those who do good to you, what credit is that to you? Even sinners do as much. And if you lend only where you expect to be repaid, what credit is that to you? Even sinners lend to each other to be repaid in full. But you must love your enemies and do good; and lend without expecting any return;[a] and you will have a rich reward:

[a] *Or* without ever giving up hope; *some witnesses read* without giving up hope of anyone.

King James Version

and ye shall be the children of the Highest: for
he is kind unto the unthankful and *to* the evil.
36 Be ye therefore merciful, as your Father also
is merciful. 37 Judge not, and ye shall not be
judged: condemn not, and ye shall not be condemned: forgive, and ye shall be forgiven:
38 Give, and it shall be given unto you; good
measure, pressed down, and shaken together,
and running over, shall men give into your
bosom. For with the same measure that ye mete
withal it shall be measured to you again.
39 And he spake a parable unto them; Can
the blind lead the blind? shall they not both fall
into the ditch? 40 The disciple is not above his
master: but every one that is perfect shall be as
his master. 41 And why beholdest thou the mote
that is in thy brother's eye, but perceivest not the
beam that is in thine own eye? 42 Either how
canst thou say to thy brother, Brother, let me
pull out the mote that is in thine eye, when thou
thyself beholdest not the beam that is in thine
own eye? Thou hypocrite, cast out first the beam
out of thine own eye, and then shalt thou see
clearly to pull out the mote that is in thy

Living Bible

will truly be acting as sons of God: for he is
kind to the *unthankful* and to those who are
very wicked.
36 "Try to show as much compassion as your
Father does. 37 Never criticize or condemn—or
it will all come back on you. Go easy on others;
then they will do the same for you.[c] 38 For if
you give, you will get! Your gift will return to
you in full and overflowing measure, pressed
down, shaken together to make room for more,
and running over. Whatever measure you use to
give—large or small—will be used to measure
what is given back to you."
39 Here are some of the story-illustrations Jesus used in his sermons: "What good is it for
one blind man to lead another? He will fall into
a ditch and pull the other down with him.
40 How can a student know more than his
teacher? But if he works hard, he may learn as
much.
41 "And why quibble about the speck in
someone else's eye—his little fault[d]—when a
board is in your own? 42 How can you think of
saying to him, 'Brother, let me help you get rid
of that speck in your eye,' when you can't see
past the board in yours? Hypocrite! First get rid
of the board, and then perhaps you can see well
enough to deal with his speck!

[c] Literally, "release, and you shall be released." [d] Implied.

Today's English Version

you will be sons of the Most High God. For he
is good to the ungrateful and the wicked. 36 Be
merciful, just as your Father is merciful."

Judging others

37 "Do not judge others, and God will not
judge you; do not condemn others, and God will
not condemn you; forgive others, and God will
forgive you. 38 Give to others, and God will give
to you: you will receive a full measure, a generous helping, poured into your hands—all that
you can hold. The measure you use for others is
the one God will use for you."
39 And Jesus told them this parable, "One
blind man cannot lead another one; if he does,
both will fall into a ditch. 40 No pupil is greater
than his teacher; but every pupil, when he has
completed his training, will be like his teacher.
41 "Why do you look at the speck in your
brother's eye, but pay no attention to the log in
your own eye? 42 How can you say to your
brother, 'Please, brother, let me take that speck
out of your eye,' yet not even see the log in your
own eye? You hypocrite! Take the log out of
your own eye first, and then you will be able
to see and take the speck out of your brother's
eye."

New International Version

of the Most High, because he is kind to the ungrateful and wicked. 36 Be merciful, just as your
Father is merciful.

Judging others

37 "Do not judge, and you will not be judged.
Do not condemn, and you will not be condemned. Forgive, and you will be forgiven.
38 Give, and it will be given to you. A good
measure, pressed down, shaken together and running over, will be poured into your lap. For
with the measure you use, it will be measured
to you."
39 He also told them this parable: "Can a
blind man lead a blind man? Will they not both
fall into a pit? 40 A student is not above his
teacher, but everyone who is fully trained will
be like his teacher.
41 "Why do you look at the speck of sawdust
in your brother's eye and pay no attention to
the plank in your own eye? 42 How can you say
to your brother, 'Brother, let me take the speck
out of your eye,' when you yourself fail to see
the plank in your own eye? You hypocrite, first
take the plank out of your eye, and then you
will see clearly to remove the speck from your
brother's eye.

Phillips Modern English

will be sons of the Most High. For he is kind to the ungrateful and the wicked!

"You must be merciful, as your Father is merciful. Don't judge other people and you will not be judged yourselves. Don't condemn and you will not be condemned. Forgive others and people will forgive you. Give and men will give to you—yes, good measure, pressed down, shaken together and running over will they pour into your lap. For whatever measure you use with other people, they will use in their dealings with you."

6.39 The need for thorough-going sincerity

Then he gave them an illustration—

"Can one blind man be guide to another blind man? Surely they will both fall into the ditch. A disciple is not above his teacher, but when he is fully trained he will be like his teacher.

"Why do you look at the speck of sawdust in your brother's eye and fail to notice the plank in your own? How can you say to your brother, 'Let me take the speck out of your eye' when you cannot see the plank in your own? You fraud, take the plank out of your own eye first and then you can see clearly to remove the speck out of your brother's eye.

Revised Standard Version

great, and you will be sons of the Most High; for
he is kind to the ungrateful and the selfish. 36 Be
merciful, even as your Father is merciful.
37 "Judge not, and you will not be judged;
condemn not, and you will not be condemned;
forgive, and you will be forgiven; 38 give, and it
will be given to you; good measure, pressed
down, shaken together, running over, will be
put into your lap. For the measure you give will
be the measure you get back."
39 He also told them a parable: "Can a blind
man lead a blind man? Will they not both fall
into a pit? 40 A disciple is not above his teacher,
but every one when he is fully taught will be
like his teacher. 41 Why do you see the speck
that is in your brother's eye, but do not notice
the log that is in your own eye? 42 Or how can
you say to your brother, 'Brother, let me take
out the speck that is in your eye,' when you
yourself do not see the log that is in your own
eye? You hypocrite, first take the log out of
your own eye, and then you will see clearly to
take out the speck that is in your brother's eye.

Jerusalem Bible

reward, and you will be sons of the Most High, for he himself is kind to the ungrateful and the wicked.

Compassion and generosity

36 "Be compassionate as your Father is compassionate. 37 Do not judge, and you will not be
judged yourselves; do not condemn, and you will
not be condemned yourselves; grant pardon, and
you will be pardoned. 38 Give, and there will be
gifts for you: a full measure, pressed down,
shaken together, and running over, will be
poured into your lap; because the amount you
measure out is the amount you will be given
back."

Integrity

39 He also told a parable to them, "Can one
blind man guide another? Surely both will fall
into a pit? 40 The disciple is not superior to
his teacher; the fully trained disciple will always
be like his teacher. 41 Why do you observe the
splinter in your brother's eye and never notice
the plank in your own? 42 How can you say to
your brother, 'Brother, let me take out the
splinter that is in your eye,' when you cannot
see the plank in your own? Hypocrite! Take the
plank out of your own eye first, and then you
will see clearly enough to take out the splinter
that is in your brother's eye.

New English Bible

you will be sons of the Most High, because he himself is kind to the ungrateful and wicked. Be compassionate as your Father is compassionate.

'Pass no judgement, and you will not be judged; do not condemn, and you will not be condemned; acquit, and you will be acquitted; give, and gifts will be given you. Good measure, pressed down, shaken together, and running over, will be poured into your lap; for whatever measure you deal out to others will be dealt to you in return.'

He also offered them a parable: 'Can one blind man be guide to another? Will they not both fall into the ditch? A pupil is not superior to his teacher; but everyone, when his training is complete, will reach his teacher's level.

'Why do you look at the speck of sawdust in your brother's eye, with never a thought for the great plank in your own? How can you say to your brother, "My dear brother, let me take the speck out of your eye", when you are blind to the plank in your own? You hypocrite! First take the plank out of your own eye, and then you will see clearly to take the speck out of your brother's.

King James Version

brother's eye. 43 For a good tree bringeth not
forth corrupt fruit; neither doth a corrupt tree
bring forth good fruit. 44 For every tree is known
by his own fruit. For of thorns men do not
gather figs, nor of a bramble bush gather they
grapes. 45 A good man out of the good treasure
of his heart bringeth forth that which is good;
and an evil man out of the evil treasure of his
heart bringeth forth that which is evil: for of
the abundance of the heart his mouth speaketh.
46 And why call ye me, Lord, Lord, and do
not the things which I say? 47 Whosoever cometh
to me, and heareth my sayings, and doeth them,
I will shew you to whom he is like: 48 He is like
a man which built a house, and digged deep, and
laid the foundation on a rock: and when the
flood arose, the stream beat vehemently upon
that house, and could not shake it; for it was
founded upon a rock. 49 But he that heareth,
and doeth not, is like a man that without a
foundation built a house upon the earth; against
which the stream did beat vehemently, and immediately it fell; and the ruin of that house was
great.

Living Bible

43 "A tree from good stock doesn't produce
scrub fruit nor do trees from poor stock produce
choice fruit. 44 A tree is identified by the kind of
fruit it produces. Figs never grow on thorns, or
grapes on bramble bushes. 45 A good man produces good deeds from a good heart. And an
evil man produces evil deeds from his hidden
wickedness. Whatever is in the heart overflows
into speech.
46 "So why do you call me 'Lord' when you
won't obey me? 47, 48 But all those who come
and listen and obey me are like a man who
builds a house on a strong foundation laid upon
the underlying rock. When the floodwaters rise
and break against the house, it stands firm, for
it is strongly built.
49 "But those who listen and don't obey are
like a man who builds a house without a foundation. When the floods sweep down against that
house, it crumbles into a heap of ruins."

Today's English Version

A tree and its fruit

43 "A healthy tree does not bear bad fruit, nor
does a poor tree bear good fruit. 44 Every tree is
known by the fruit it bears; you do not pick figs
from thorn bushes, or gather grapes from bramble bushes. 45 A good man brings good out of the
treasure of good things in his heart; a bad man
brings bad out of his treasure of bad things. For
a man's mouth speaks what his heart is full of."

The two house builders

46 "Why do you call me, 'Lord, Lord,' and
don't do what I tell you? 47 Everyone who comes
to me, and listens to my words, and obeys them
—I will show you what he is like. 48 He is like a
man who built a house: he dug deep and laid
the foundation on the rock. The river flooded
over and hit that house but could not shake it,
because it had been well built. 49 But the one
who hears my words and does not obey them is
like a man who built a house on the ground,
without laying a foundation; when the flood hit
that house it fell at once—what a terrible crash
that was!"

New International Version

A tree and its fruit

43 "No good tree bears bad fruit, nor does a
bad tree bear good fruit. 44 Each tree is recognized by its own fruit. People do not pick figs
from thornbushes, or grapes from briars. 45 The
good man brings good things out of the good
stored up in his heart, and the evil man brings
evil things out of the evil stored up in his heart.
For out of the overflow of his heart his mouth
speaks.

The wise and foolish builders

46 "Why do you call me, 'Lord, Lord,' and
do not do what I say? 47 I will show you what
he is like who comes to me and hears my words
and puts them into practice. 48 He is like a man
building a house, who dug down deep and laid
the foundation on rock. When a flood came,
the torrent struck that house but could not
shake it, because it was well built. 49 But the
one who hears my words and does not put them
into practice is like a man who built a house
on the ground without a foundation. The moment the torrent struck that house, it collapsed
and its destruction was complete."

Phillips Modern English

"It is impossible for a good tree to produce bad fruit—as impossible as it is for a bad tree to produce good fruit. Do not men know what a tree is by its fruit? You cannot pick figs from briars, or gather a bunch of grapes from a blackberry bush! A good man produces good things from the good stored up in his heart, and a bad man produces evil things from his own stores of evil. For a man's words express what overflows from his heart.

"And what is the point of calling me, 'Lord, Lord', without doing what I tell you to do? Let me show you what the man who comes to me, hears what I have to say, and puts it into practice, is really like. He is like a man building a house, who dug down to rock-bottom and laid the foundation of his house upon it. Then when the flood came and the flood-water swept down upon that house, it could not shift it because it was properly built. But the man who hears me and does not act upon what he hears is like a man who built his house upon soft earth without foundation. When the flood-water swept down upon it, it collapsed and the whole house crashed down in ruins."

Revised Standard Version

43 "For no good tree bears bad fruit, nor
again does a bad tree bear good fruit; 44 for
each tree is known by its own fruit. For figs are
not gathered from thorns, nor are grapes picked
from a bramble bush. 45 The good man out of
the good treasure of his heart produces good,
and the evil man out of his evil treasure produces evil; for out of the abundance of the
heart his mouth speaks.
46 "Why do you call me 'Lord, Lord,' and
not do what I tell you? 47 Every one who comes
to me and hears my words and does them, I will
show you what he is like: 48 he is like a man
building a house, who dug deep, and laid the
foundation upon rock; and when a flood arose,
the stream broke against that house, and could
not shake it, because it had been well built.[w]
49 But he who hears and does not do them is
like a man who built a house on the ground
without a foundation; against which the stream
broke, and immediately it fell, and the ruin of
that house was great."

[w] Other ancient authorities read *founded upon the rock.*

Jerusalem Bible

43 "There is no sound tree that produces
rotten fruit, nor again a rotten tree that produces sound fruit. 44 For every tree can be told
by its own fruit: people do not pick figs from
thorns, nor gathers grapes from brambles. 45 A
good man draws what is good from the store of
goodness in his heart; a bad man draws what is
bad from the store of badness. For a man's
words flow out of what fills his heart.

The true disciple

46 "Why do you call me, 'Lord, Lord' and
not do what I say?
47 "Everyone who comes to me and listens
to my words and acts on them—I will show you
what he is like. 48 He is like the man who
when he built his house dug, and dug deep, and
laid the foundations on rock; when the river
was in flood it bore down on that house but
could not shake it, it was so well built. 49 But
the one who listens and does nothing is like the
man who built his house on soil, with no foundations: as soon as the river bore down on it,
it collapsed; and what a ruin that house became!"

New English Bible

'There is no such thing as a good tree producing worthless fruit, nor yet a worthless tree producing good fruit. For each tree is known by its own fruit: you do not gather figs from thistles, and you do not pick grapes from brambles. A good man produces good from the store of good within himself; and an evil man from evil within produces evil. For the words that the mouth utters come from the overflowing of the heart.

'Why do you keep calling me "Lord, Lord"—and never do what I tell you? Everyone who comes to me and hears what I say, and acts upon it—I will show you what he is like. He is like a man who, in building his house, dug deep and laid the foundations on rock. When the flood came, the river burst upon that house, but could not shift it, because it had been soundly built. But he who hears and does not act is like a man who built his house on the soil without foundations. As soon as the river burst upon it, the house collapsed, and fell with a great crash.'

King James Version

7 Now when he had ended all his sayings in
the audience of the people, he entered into
Capernaum. 2And a certain centurion's servant,
who was dear unto him, was sick, and ready to
die. 3And when he heard of Jesus, he sent unto
him the elders of the Jews, beseeching him that
he would come and heal his servant. 4And when
they came to Jesus, they besought him instantly,
saying, That he was worthy for whom he should
do this: 5 For he loveth our nation, and he hath
built us a synagogue. 6 Then Jesus went with
them. And when he was now not far from the
house, the centurion sent friends to him, saying
unto him, Lord, trouble not thyself; for I am
not worthy that thou shouldest enter under my
roof: 7 Wherefore neither thought I myself
worthy to come unto thee: but say in a word,
and my servant shall be healed. 8 For I also am
a man set under authority, having under me
soldiers, and I say unto one, Go, and he goeth;
and to another, Come, and he cometh; and to
my servant, Do this, and he doeth *it*. 9 When
Jesus heard these things, he marvelled at him,
and turned him about, and said unto the people
that followed him, I say unto you, I have not
found so great faith, no, not in Israel. 10And
they that were sent, returning to the house,
found the servant whole that had been sick.

Living Bible

7 When Jesus had finished his sermon he
went back into the city of Capernaum.
2 Just at that time the highly prized slave of
a Roman[a] army captain was sick and near death.
3 When the captain heard about Jesus, he sent
some respected Jewish elders to ask him to come
and heal his slave. 4 So they began pleading
earnestly with Jesus to come with them and
help the man. They told him what a wonderful
person the captain was.
"If anyone deserves your help, it is he," they
said, 5 "for he loves the Jews and even paid personally to build us a synagogue!"
6, 7, 8 Jesus went with them; but just before
arriving at the house, the captain sent some
friends to say, "Sir, don't inconvenience yourself by coming to my home, for I am not worthy
of any such honor or even to come and meet
you. Just speak a word from where you are, and
my servant boy will be healed! I know, because
I am under the authority of my superior officers,
and I have authority over my men. I only need
to say 'Go!' and they go; or 'Come!' and they
come; and to my slave, 'Do this or that,' and he
does it. So just say, 'Be healed!' and my servant
will be well again!"
9 Jesus was amazed. Turning to the crowd he
said, "Never among all the Jews in Israel have I
met a man with faith like this."
10 And when the captain's friends returned to
his house, they found the slave completely
healed.

[a] Implied.

Today's English Version

Jesus heals a Roman officer's servant

7 When Jesus had finished saying all these
things to the people, he went to Capernaum.
2A Roman officer there had a servant who was
very dear to him; the man was sick and about to
die. 3 When the officer heard about Jesus, he
sent to him some Jewish elders to ask him to
come and heal his servant. 4 They came to Jesus
and begged him earnestly, "This man really deserves your help. 5 He loves our people and he
himself built a synagogue for us."
6 So Jesus went with them. He was not far
from the house when the officer sent friends to
tell him, "Sir, don't trouble yourself. I do not
deserve to have you come into my house, 7 neither do I consider myself worthy to come to you
in person. Just give the order and my servant will
get well. 8 I, too, am a man placed under the
authority of superior officers, and I have soldiers
under me. I order this one, 'Go!' and he goes; I
order that one, 'Come!' and he comes; and I
order my slave, 'Do this!' and he does it."
9 Jesus was surprised when he heard this; he
turned around and said to the crowd following
him, "I have never found such faith as this, I
tell you, not even in Israel!"
10 The messengers went back to the officer's
house and found his servant well.

New International Version

The faith of the centurion

7 When Jesus had finished saying all this in
the hearing of the people, he entered Capernaum. 2 There a centurion's servant, whom his
master valued highly, was sick and about to die.
3 The centurion heard of Jesus and sent some
elders of the Jews to him, asking him to come
and heal his servant. 4 When they came to Jesus,
they pleaded earnestly with him, "This man deserves to have you do this, 5 because he loves
our nation and has built our synagogue." 6 So
Jesus went with them.
He was not far from the house when the
centurion sent friends to say to him: "Lord,
don't trouble yourself, for I do not deserve to
have you come under my roof. 7 That is why
I did not even consider myself worthy to come
to you. But say the word, and my servant will
be healed. 8 For I myself am a man under authority, with soldiers under me. I tell this one,
'Go,' and he goes; and that one, 'Come,' and he
comes. I say to my servant, 'Do this,' and he
does it."
9 When Jesus heard this, he was amazed at
him, and turning to the crowd following him,
he said, "I tell you, I have not found such great
faith even in Israel." 10 Then the men who had
been sent returned to the house and found the
servant well.

Phillips Modern English

7.1 A Roman centurion's extraordinary faith in Jesus

When Jesus had finished these talks to the people, he came to Capernaum, where it happened that there was a man very seriously ill and in fact at the point of death. He was the slave of a centurion who thought very highly of him. When the centurion heard about Jesus, he sent some Jewish elders to him with the request that he would come and save his slave's life. When they came to Jesus, they urged him strongly to grant this request, saying that the centurion deserved to have this done for him. "He loves our nation and has built us a synagogue out of his own pocket," they said.

So Jesus went with them, but as he approached the house, the centurion sent some of his friends with the message,

"Don't trouble yourself, sir! I'm not important enough for you to come into my house—I didn't think I was fit to come to you in person. Just give the order, please, and my boy will recover. I am used to working under orders, and I have soldiers under me. I can say to one, 'Go', and he goes, or I can say to another, 'Come here', and he comes; or I can say to my slave, 'Do this job', and he does it."

These words amazed Jesus and he turned to the crowd who were following him and said,

"I have never found faith like this anywhere, even in Israel!"

Then those who had been sent by the centurion returned to the house and found the slave perfectly well.

Revised Standard Version

7 After he had ended all his sayings in the
hearing of the people he entered Capernaum.
2 Now a centurion had a slave who was dear[x]
to him, who was sick and at the point of death.
3 When he heard of Jesus, he sent to him elders
of the Jews, asking him to come and heal his
slave. 4 And when they came to Jesus, they besought him earnestly, saying, "He is worthy to
have you do this for him, 5 for he loves our
nation, and he built us our synagogue." 6 And
Jesus went with them. When he was not far
from the house, the centurion sent friends to
him, saying to him, "Lord, do not trouble yourself, for I am not worthy to have you come
under my roof; 7 therefore I did not presume to
come to you. But say the word, and let my
servant be healed. 8 For I am a man set under
authority, with soldiers under me: and I say to
one, 'Go,' and he goes; and to another, 'Come,'
and he comes; and to my slave, 'Do this,' and
he does it." 9 When Jesus heard this he marveled
at him, and turned and said to the multitude that
followed him, "I tell you, not even in Israel have
I found such faith." 10 And when those who had
been sent returned to the house, they found the
slave well.

[x] Or *valuable*.

Jerusalem Bible

Cure of the centurion's servant

7 When he had come to the end of all he
wanted the people to hear, he went into
Capernaum. 2 A centurion there had a servant, a
favorite of his, who was sick and near death.
3 Having heard about Jesus he sent some Jewish
elders to him to ask him to come and heal his
servant. 4 When they came to Jesus they pleaded
earnestly with him. "He deserves this of you,"
they said, 5 "because he is friendly toward our
people; in fact, he is the one who built the
synagogue." 6 So Jesus went with them, and was
not very far from the house when the centurion
sent word to him by some friends: "Sir," he
said, "do not put yourself to trouble; because
I am not worthy to have you under my roof;
7 and for this same reason I did not presume to
come to you myself; but give the word and let
my servant be cured. 8 For I am under authority
myself, and have soldiers under me; and I say to
one man: Go, and he goes; to another: Come
here, and he comes; to my servant: Do this, and
he does it." 9 When Jesus heard these words he
was astonished at him and, turning around, said
to the crowd following him, "I tell you, not even
in Israel have I found faith like this." 10 And
when the messengers got back to the house they
found the servant in perfect health.

New English Bible

7 When he had finished addressing the people, he went to Capernaum. A centurion there had a servant whom he valued highly; this servant was ill and near to death. Hearing about Jesus, he sent some Jewish elders with the request that he would come and save his servant's life. They approached Jesus and pressed their petition earnestly: 'He deserves this favour from you,' they said, 'for he is a friend of our nation and it is he who built us our synagogue.' Jesus went with them; but when he was not far from the house, the centurion sent friends with this message: 'Do not trouble further, sir; it is not for me to have you under my roof, and that is why I did not presume to approach you in person. But say the word and my servant will be cured. I know, for in my position I am myself under orders, with soldiers under me. I say to one, "Go", and he goes; to another, "Come here", and he comes; and to my servant, "Do this", and he does it.' When Jesus heard this, he admired the man, and, turning to the crowd that was following him, he said, 'I tell you, nowhere, even in Israel, have I found faith like this.' And the messengers returned to the house and found the servant in good health.

King James Version

11 And it came to pass the day after, that he
went into a city called Nain; and many of his
disciples went with him, and much people.
12 Now when he came nigh to the gate of the
city, behold, there was a dead man carried out,
the only son of his mother, and she was a
widow: and much people of the city was with
her. 13 And when the Lord saw her, he had compassion on her, and said unto her, Weep not.
14 And he came and touched the bier: and they
that bare *him* stood still. And he said, Young
man, I say unto thee, Arise. 15 And he that was
dead sat up, and began to speak. And he delivered him to his mother. 16 And there came a
fear on all: and they glorified God, saying, That
a great prophet is risen up among us: and, That
God hath visited his people. 17 And this rumour
of him went forth throughout all Judea, and
throughout all the region round about. 18 And
the disciples of John shewed him of all these
things.
19 And John calling *unto him* two of his disciples sent *them* to Jesus, saying, Art thou he
that should come? or look we for another?

Living Bible

11 Not long afterwards Jesus went with his
disciples to the village of Nain, with the usual
great crowd at his heels. 12 A funeral procession
was coming out as he approached the village
gate. The boy who had died was the only son
of his widowed mother, and many mourners
from the village were with her.
13 When the Lord saw her, his heart overflowed with sympathy. "Don't cry!" he said.
14 Then he walked over to the coffin and touched
it, and the bearers stopped. "Laddie," he said,
"come back to life again."
15 Then the boy sat up and began to talk to
those around him! And Jesus gave him back to
his mother.
16 A great fear swept the crowd, and they exclaimed with praises to God, "A mighty prophet
has risen among us," and, "We have seen the
hand of God at work today."
17 The report of what he did that day raced
from end to end of Judea and even out across
the borders.
18 The disciples of John the Baptist soon
heard of all that Jesus was doing. When they
told John about it, 19 he sent two of his disciples to Jesus to ask him, "Are you really the
Messiah?[b] Or shall we keep on looking for
him?"

[*b*] Literally, "the one who is coming."

Today's English Version

Jesus raises a widow's son

11 Soon afterward Jesus went to a town named
Nain; his disciples and a large crowd went with
him. 12 Just as he arrived at the gate of the town,
a funeral procession was coming out. The dead
man was the only son of a woman who was a
widow, and a large crowd from the city was
with her. 13 When the Lord saw her his heart
was filled with pity for her and he said to her,
"Don't cry." 14 Then he walked over and touched
the coffin, and the men carrying it stopped. Jesus said, "Young man! Get up, I tell you!"
15 The dead man sat up and began to talk, and
Jesus gave him back to his mother.
16 Everyone was filled with fear, and they
praised God, "A great prophet has appeared
among us!" and, "God has come to save his people!"
17 This news about Jesus went out through all
the country and the surrounding territory.

The messengers from John the Baptist

18 John's disciples told him about all these
things. He called two of them to him 19 and sent
them to the Lord to ask him, "Are you the one
John said was going to come, or should we expect someone else?"

New International Version

Jesus raises a widow's son

11 Soon afterward, Jesus went to a town
called Nain, and his disciples and a large crowd
went along with him. 12 As he approached the
town gate, a dead person was being carried out
—the only son of his mother, and she was a
widow. And a large crowd from the town was
with her. 13 When the Lord saw her, his heart
went out to her and he said, "Don't cry."
14 Then he went up and touched the coffin,
and those carrying it stood still. He said, "Young
man, I say to you, get up!" 15 The dead man
sat up and began to talk, and Jesus gave him
back to his mother.
16 They were all filled with awe and praised
God. "A great prophet has appeared among us,"
they said. "God has come to help his people."
17 This news about Jesus spread throughout Judea[z] and the surrounding country.

Jesus and John the Baptist

18 John's disciples told him about all these
things. Calling two of them, 19 he sent them to
the Lord to ask, "Are you the one who was to
come, or should we expect someone else?"

[z] Or *the land of the Jews*.

Phillips Modern English

7.11 Jesus brings a dead youth back to life

Not long afterwards, Jesus went into a town called Nain, accompanied by his disciples and a large crowd. As he approached the city gate, it happened that some people were carrying out a dead man, the only son of his widowed mother. The usual crowd of fellow-townsmen was with her. When the Lord saw her, his heart went out to her and he said,

"Don't cry."

Then he walked up and put his hand on the bier while the bearers stood still. Then he said, "Young man, get up!"

And the dead man sat up and began to talk, and Jesus handed him to his mother. Everybody present was awe-struck and they praised God, saying,

"A great prophet has arisen among us and God has turned his face towards his people."

And this report of him spread through the whole of Judaea and the surrounding countryside.

7.18 Jesus sends John a personal message

John's disciples reported all these happenings to him. Then he summoned two of them and sent them to the Lord with this message,

"Are you the one who is to come, or are we to look for someone else?"

Revised Standard Version

11 Soon afterward [y] he went to a city called Nain, and his disciples and a great crowd went with him. 12As he drew near to the gate of the city, behold, a man who had died was being carried out, the only son of his mother, and she was a widow; and a large crowd from the city was with her. 13And when the Lord saw her, he had compassion on her and said to her, "Do not weep." 14And he came and touched the bier, and the bearers stood still. And he said, "Young man, I say to you, arise." 15And the dead man sat up, and began to speak. And he gave him to his mother. 16 Fear seized them all; and they glorified God, saying, "A great prophet has arisen among us!" and "God has visited his people!" 17And this report concerning him spread through the whole of Judea and all the surrounding country.

18 The disciples of John told him of all these things. 19And John, calling to him two of his disciples, sent them to the Lord, saying, "Are you he who is to come, or shall we look for

[y] Other ancient authorities read *Next day*.

Jerusalem Bible

The son of the widow of Nain restored to life

11 Now soon afterward he went to a town called Nain, accompanied by his disciples and a great number of people. 12 When he was near the gate of the town it happened that a dead man was being carried out for burial, the only son of his mother, and she was a widow. And a considerable number of the townspeople were with her. 13 When the Lord [j] saw her he felt sorry for her. "Do not cry," he said. 14 Then he went up and put his hand on the bier and the bearers stood still, and he said, "Young man, I tell you to get up." 15And the dead man sat up and began to talk, and Jesus *gave him to his mother.*[k] 16 Everyone was filled with awe and praised God saying, "A great prophet has appeared among us; God has visited his people." 17And this opinion of him spread throughout Judaea and all over the countryside.

The Baptist's question. Jesus commends him

18 The disciples of John gave him all this news, and John, summoning two of his disciples, 19 sent them to the Lord to ask, "Are you the one who is to come, or must we wait for some-

[j] For the first time in the gospel narrative Jesus is given the title hitherto reserved for God. [k] 1 K. 17:23.

New English Bible

Afterwards[a] Jesus went to a town called Nain, accompanied by his disciples and a large crowd. As he approached the gate of the town he met a funeral. The dead man was the only son of his widowed mother; and many of the townspeople were there with her. When the Lord saw her his heart went out to her, and he said, 'Weep no more.' With that he stepped forward and laid his hand on the bier; and the bearers halted. Then he spoke: 'Young man, rise up!' The dead man sat up and began to speak; and Jesus gave him back to his mother. Deep awe fell upon them all, and they praised God. 'A great prophet has arisen among us', they said, and again, 'God has shown his care for his people.' The story of what he had done ran through all parts of Judaea and the whole neighbourhood.

John too was informed of all this by his disciples. Summoning two of their number he sent them to the Lord with this message: 'Are you the one who is to come, or are we to expect

[a] *Some witnesses read* On the next day.

King James Version

20 When the men were come unto him, they said, John Baptist hath sent us unto thee, saying, Art thou he that should come? or look we for another? 21 And in that same hour he cured many of *their* infirmities and plagues, and of evil spirits; and unto many *that were* blind he gave sight. 22 Then Jesus answering said unto them, Go your way, and tell John what things ye have seen and heard; how that the blind see, the lame walk, the lepers are cleansed, the deaf hear, the dead are raised, to the poor the gospel is preached. 23 And blessed is *he,* whosoever shall not be offended in me.

24 And when the messengers of John were departed, he began to speak unto the people concerning John, What went ye out into the wilderness for to see? A reed shaken with the wind? 25 But what went ye out for to see? A man clothed in soft raiment? Behold, they which are gorgeously apparelled, and live delicately, are in kings' courts. 26 But what went ye out for to see? A prophet? Yea, I say unto you, and much more than a prophet. 27 This is *he,* of whom it is written, Behold, I send my messenger before thy

Living Bible

20, 21, 22 The two disciples found Jesus while he was curing many sick people of their various diseases—healing the lame and the blind and casting out evil spirits. When they asked him John's question, this was his reply: "Go back to John and tell him all you have seen and heard here today: how those who were blind can see. The lame are walking without a limp. The lepers are completely healed. The deaf can hear again. The dead come back to life. And the poor are hearing the Good News. 23 And tell him, 'Blessed is the one who does not lose his faith in me.' "[c]

24 After they left, Jesus talked to the crowd about John. "Who is this man you went out into the Judean wilderness to see?" he asked. "Did you find him weak as grass, moved by every breath of wind? 25 Did you find him dressed in expensive clothes? No! Men who live in luxury are found in palaces, not out in the wilderness. 26 But did you find a prophet? Yes! And more than a prophet. 27 He is the one to whom the Scriptures refer when they say, 'Look! I am sending my messenger ahead of you, to prepare

[*c*] Literally, "Blessed is he who keeps from stumbling over me."

Today's English Version

20 When they came to Jesus they said, "John the Baptist sent us to ask, 'Are you the one he said was going to come, or should we expect someone else?' "

21 At that very time Jesus healed many people from their sicknesses, diseases, and evil spirits, and gave sight to many blind people. 22 He answered John's messengers, "Go back and tell John what you have seen and heard: the blind can see, the lame can walk, the lepers are made clean, the deaf can hear, the dead are raised to life, and the Good News is preached to the poor. 23 How happy is he who has no doubts about me!"

24 After John's messengers had left, Jesus began to speak about John to the crowds, "When you went out to John in the desert, what did you expect to see? A blade of grass bending in the wind? 25 What did you go out to see? A man dressed up in fancy clothes? Really, those who dress like that and live in luxury are found in palaces! 26 Tell me, what did you go out to see? A prophet? Yes, I tell you—you saw much more than a prophet. 27 For John is the one of whom the scripture says, 'Here is my messenger, says

New International Version

20 When the men came to Jesus, they said, "John the Baptist sent us to you to ask, 'Are you the one who was to come, or should we expect someone else?' "

21 At that very time Jesus cured many who had diseases, sicknesses and evil spirits, and gave sight to many who were blind. 22 So he replied to the messengers, "Go back and report to John what you have seen and heard: The blind receive sight, the lame walk, those who have leprosy[a] are cured, the deaf hear, the dead are raised, and the good news is preached to the poor. 23 Blessed is the man who does not fall away on account of me."

24 After John's messengers left, Jesus began to speak to the crowd about John: "What did you go out into the desert to see? A reed swayed by the wind? 25 If not, what did you go out to see? A man dressed in fine clothes? No, those who wear expensive clothes and indulge in luxury are in palaces. 26 But what did you go out to see? A prophet? Yes, I tell you, and more than a prophet. 27 This is the one about whom it is written:

'I will send my messenger ahead of you,

[*a*] The Greek word probably designated other related diseases also.

Phillips Modern English

When the men came to Jesus, they said,

"John the Baptist has sent us to you with this message, 'Are you the one who is to come, or are we to look for someone else?' "

At that very time Jesus was healing many people of their diseases and ailments and evil spirits, and he restored sight to many who were blind. Then he answered them,

"Go and tell John what you have seen and heard. The blind are recovering their sight, cripples are walking again, lepers being healed, the deaf hearing, dead men are being brought to life again, and the good news is being given to those in need. And happy is the man who never loses his faith in me."

7.24 Jesus emphasises the greatness of John—and the greater importance of the kingdom of God

When these messengers had gone back, Jesus began to talk to the crowd about John.

"What did you go out into the desert to look at? Was it a reed waving in the breeze? Well, *what* was it you went out to see? A man dressed in fine clothes? But the men who wear fine clothes live luxuriously in palaces. But what *did* you really go to see? A prophet? Yes, I tell you, a prophet and far more than a prophet! This is the man of whom the scripture says,

Behold, I send my messenger before thy face,

Revised Standard Version

another?" 20 And when the men had come to him, they said, "John the Baptist has sent us to you, saying, 'Are you he who is to come, or shall we look for another?' " 21 In that hour he cured many of diseases and plagues and evil spirits, and on many that were blind he bestowed sight. 22 And he answered them, "Go and tell John what you have seen and heard: the blind receive their sight, the lame walk, lepers are cleansed, and the deaf hear, the dead are raised up, the poor have good news preached to them. 23 And blessed is he who takes no offense at me."

24 When the messengers of John had gone, he began to speak to the crowds concerning John: "What did you go out into the wilderness to behold? A reed shaken by the wind? 25 What then did you go out to see? A man clothed in soft clothing? Behold, those who are gorgeously appareled and live in luxury are in kings' courts. 26 What then did you go out to see? A prophet? Yes, I tell you, and more than a prophet. 27 This is he of whom it is written,

'Behold, I send my messenger before thy face,

Jerusalem Bible

one else?" 20 When the men reached Jesus they said, "John the Baptist has sent us to you, to ask, 'Are you the one who is to come or have we to wait for someone else?' " 21 It was just then that he cured many people of diseases and afflictions and of evil spirits, and gave the gift of sight to many who were blind. 22 Then he gave the messengers their answer, "Go back and tell John what you have seen and heard: the blind see again, the lame walk, lepers are cleansed, and the deaf hear, the dead are raised to life, the Good News is proclaimed to the poor 23 and happy is the man who does not lose faith in me."

24 When John's messengers had gone he began to talk to the people about John, 25 "What did you go out into the wilderness to see? A reed swaying in the breeze? No? Then what did you go out to see? A man dressed in fine clothes? Oh no, those who go in for fine clothes and live luxuriously are to be found at court! 26 Then what did you go out to see? A prophet? Yes, I tell you, and much more than a prophet: 27 he is the one of whom scripture says:

See, I am going to send my messenger before you;

New English Bible

some other?' The messengers made their way to Jesus and said, 'John the Baptist has sent us to you: he asks, "Are you the one who is to come, or are we to expect some other?" ' There and then he cured many sufferers from diseases, plagues, and evil spirits; and on many blind people he bestowed sight. Then he gave them his answer: 'Go', he said, 'and tell John what you have seen and heard: how the blind recover their sight, the lame walk, the lepers are made clean, the deaf hear, the dead are raised to life, the poor are hearing the good news—and happy is the man who does not find me a stumbling-block.'

After John's messengers had left, Jesus began to speak about him to the crowds: 'What was the spectacle that drew you to the wilderness? A reed-bed swept by the wind? No? Then what did you go out to see? A man dressed in silks and satins? Surely you must look in palaces for grand clothes and luxury. But what did you go out to see? A prophet? Yes indeed, and far more than a prophet. He is the man of whom Scripture says,

"Here is my herald, whom I send on ahead of you,

King James Version

face, which shall prepare thy way before thee. 28 For I say unto you, Among those that are born of women there is not a greater prophet than John the Baptist: but he that is least in the kingdom of God is greater than he. 29 And all the people that heard *him,* and the publicans, justified God, being baptized with the baptism of John. 30 But the Pharisees and lawyers rejected the counsel of God against themselves, being not baptized of him.

31 And the Lord said, Whereunto then shall I liken the men of this generation? and to what are they like? 32 They are like unto children sitting in the marketplace, and calling one to another, and saying, We have piped unto you, and ye have not danced; we have mourned to you, and ye have not wept. 33 For John the Baptist came neither eating bread nor drinking wine; and ye say He hath a devil. 34 The Son of man is come eating and drinking; and ye say, Behold a gluttonous man, and a winebibber, a friend of publicans and sinners! 35 But wisdom is justified of all her children.

Living Bible

the way before you.' 28 In all humanity there is no one greater than John. And yet the least citizen of the Kingdom of God is greater than he."

29 And all who heard John preach—even the most wicked of them[d]—agreed that God's requirements were right, and they were baptized by him. 30 All, that is, except the Pharisees and teachers of Moses' Law. They rejected God's plan for them and refused John's baptism.

31 "What can I say about such men?" Jesus asked. "With what shall I compare them? 32 They are like a group of children who complain to their friends, 'You don't like it if we play "wedding" and you don't like it if we play "funeral"'![e] 33 For John the Baptist used to go without food and never took a drop of liquor all his life, and you said, 'He must be crazy!'[f] 34 But I eat my food and drink my wine, and you say, 'What a glutton Jesus is! And he drinks! And has the lowest sort of friends!'[g] 35 But I am sure you can always justify your inconsistencies."[h]

[*d*] Literally, "even the tax collectors"; i.e., the publicans. [*e*] Literally, "We played the flute for you and you didn't dance; we sang a dirge and you didn't weep." [*f*] Literally, "He has a demon." [*g*] Literally, "is a friend of tax gatherers and sinners." [*h*] Literally, "but wisdom is justified of all her children."

Today's English Version

God; I will send him ahead of you to open the way for you.' 28 I tell you," Jesus added, "John is greater than any man ever born; but he who is least in the Kingdom of God is greater than he."

29 All the people and the tax collectors heard him; they were the ones who had obeyed God's righteous demands and had been baptized by John. 30 But the Pharisees and the teachers of the Law rejected God's purpose for themselves, and refused to be baptized by John.

31 "Now, to what can I compare the people of this day? What are they like? 32 They are like children sitting in the market place. One group shouts to the other, 'We played wedding music for you, but you would not dance! We sang funeral songs, but you would not cry!' 33 John the Baptist came, and he fasted and drank no wine, and you said, 'He has a demon in him!' 34 The Son of Man came, and he ate and drank, and you said, 'Look at this man! He is a glutton and wine-drinker, a friend of tax collectors and outcasts!' 35 God's wisdom, however, is shown to be true by all who accept it."

New International Version

who will prepare your way before you.'[b]
28 I tell you, among those born of women there is no one greater than John; yet the one who is least in the kingdom of God is greater than he."

29 (All the people, even the tax collectors, when they heard Jesus' words, acknowledged that God's way was right, because they had been baptized by John. 30 But the Pharisees and experts in the law rejected God's purpose for themselves, because they had not been baptized by John.)

31 "To what, then, can I compare the people of this generation? What are they like? 32 They are like children sitting in the marketplace and calling out to each other:

'We played the flute for you, and you did not dance;
we sang a dirge, and you did not cry.'

33 For John the Baptist came neither eating bread nor drinking wine, and you say, 'He has a demon.' 34 The Son of Man came eating and drinking, and you say, 'Here is a glutton and a drunkard, a friend of tax collectors and "sinners."' 35 But wisdom is proved right by all her children."

[*b*] Mal. 3:1.

Phillips Modern English

Who shall prepare thy way before thee.

"Believe me, no one greater than John has ever been born, and yet a humble member of the kingdom of God is greater than he.

"All the people, yes, even the tax-collectors, when they heard John, acknowledged God and were baptised by his baptism. But the Pharisees and the experts in the Law frustrated God's purpose for them, for they refused John's baptism.

"What can I say that the men of this generation are like—what sort of men are they? They are like children sitting in the market-place and calling out to each other, 'We played at weddings for you, but you wouldn't dance, and we played at funerals for you, and you wouldn't cry!' For John the Baptist came in the strictest austerity and you say he is crazy. Then the Son of Man came, enjoying food and drink, and you say, 'Look, a drunkard and a glutton, a bosom-friend of the tax-collector and the outsider!' So wisdom is proved right by all her children!"

Revised Standard Version

who shall prepare thy way before thee.'
28 I tell you, among those born of women none
is greater than John; yet he who is least in the
kingdom of God is greater than he." 29 (When
they heard this all the people and the tax collectors justified God, having been baptized with the
baptism of John; 30 but the Pharisees and the
lawyers rejected the purpose of God for themselves, not having been baptized by him.)
31 "To what then shall I compare the men
of this generation, and what are they like?
32 They are like children sitting in the market
place and calling to one another,

'We piped to you, and you did not dance;
we wailed, and you did not weep.'

33 For John the Baptist has come eating no
bread and drinking no wine; and you say, 'He
has a demon.' 34 The Son of man has come eating and drinking; and you say, 'Behold, a glutton
and a drunkard, a friend of tax collectors and
sinners!' 35 Yet wisdom is justified by all her
children."

Jerusalem Bible

he will prepare the way before you.[l]

28 "I tell you, of all the children born of
women, there is no one greater than John; yet
the least in the kingdom of God is greater than
he is." 29 All the people who heard him, and the
tax collectors too, acknowledged God's plan by
accepting baptism from John; 30 but by refusing
baptism from him the Pharisees and the lawyers
had thwarted what God had in mind for them.

Jesus condemns his contemporaries

31 "What description, then, can I find for the
men of this generation? What are they like?
32 They are like children shouting to one another while they sit in the market place:

'We played the pipes for you,
and you wouldn't dance;
we sang dirges,
and you wouldn't cry.'

33 "For John the Baptist comes, not eating
bread, not drinking wine, and you say, 'He is
possessed.' 34 The Son of Man comes, eating
and drinking, and you say, 'Look, a glutton and
a drunkard, a friend of tax collectors and sinners.' 35 Yet Wisdom has been proved right by
all her children."

[l] Ml. 3:1.

New English Bible

and he will prepare your way before you."

I tell you, there is not a mother's son greater than John, and yet the least in the kingdom of God is greater than he.'

When they heard him, all the people, including the tax-gatherers, praised God, for they had accepted John's baptism; but the Pharisees and lawyers, who refused his baptism, had rejected[a] God's purpose for themselves.

'How can I describe the people of this generation? What are they like? They are like children sitting in the market-place and shouting at each other,

"We piped for you and you would not dance."
"We wept and wailed, and you would not
mourn."

For John the Baptist came neither eating bread nor drinking wine, and you say, "He is possessed." The Son of Man came eating and drinking, and you say, "Look at him! a glutton and a drinker, a friend of tax-gatherers and sinners!" And yet God's wisdom is proved right by all who are her children.'

[a] *Or* '. . . greater than he. And all the people, including the tax-gatherers, when they heard him, accepted John's baptism and acknowledged the righteous dealing of God; but the Pharisees and lawyers, by refusing his baptism, rejected . . .'

King James Version

36 And one of the Pharisees desired him that
he would eat with him. And he went into the
Pharisee's house, and sat down to meat. 37 And,
behold, a woman in the city, which was a sinner,
when she knew that *Jesus* sat at meat in the
Pharisee's house, brought an alabaster box of
ointment, 38 And stood at his feet behind *him*
weeping, and began to wash his feet with tears,
and did wipe *them* with the hairs of her head,
and kissed his feet, and anointed *them* with the
ointment. 39 Now when the Pharisee which had
bidden him saw *it,* he spake within himself, saying, This man, if he were a prophet, would have
known who and what manner of woman *this is*
that toucheth him; for she is a sinner. 40 And Jesus answering said unto him, Simon, I have
somewhat to say unto thee. And he saith, Master, say on. 41 There was a certain creditor which
had two debtors: the one owed five hundred
pence, and the other fifty. 42 And when they had
nothing to pay, he frankly forgave them both.
Tell me therefore, which of them will love him
most? 43 Simon answered and said, I suppose
that *he,* to whom he forgave most. And he said
unto him, Thou hast rightly judged. 44 And he
turned to the woman, and said unto Simon,
Seest thou this woman? I entered into thine
house, thou gavest me no water for my feet: but
she hath washed my feet with tears, and wiped
them with the hairs of her head. 45 Thou gavest

Living Bible

36 One of the Pharisees asked Jesus to come
to his home for lunch and Jesus accepted the
invitation. As they sat down to eat, 37 a woman
of the streets—a prostitute—heard he was there
and brought an exquisite flask filled with expensive perfume. 38 Going in, she knelt behind
him at his feet, weeping, with her tears falling
down upon his feet; and she wiped them off with
her hair and kissed them and poured the perfume on them.

39 When Jesus' host, a Pharisee, saw what was happening and who the woman was, he said to himself, "This proves that Jesus is no prophet, for if God had really sent him, he would know what kind of woman this one is!"

40 Then Jesus spoke up and answered his thoughts. "Simon," he said to the Pharisee, "I have something to say to you."

"All right, Teacher," Simon replied, "go ahead."

41 Then Jesus told him this story: "A man
loaned money to two people—$5,000 to one and
$500 to the other. 42 But neither of them could
pay him back, so he kindly forgave them both,
letting them keep the money! Which do you
suppose loved him most after that?"

43 "I suppose the one who had owed him the most," Simon answered.

"Correct," Jesus agreed.

44 Then he turned to the woman and said
to Simon, "Look! See this woman kneeling here!
When I entered your home, you didn't bother
to offer me water to wash the dust from my feet,
but she has washed them with her tears and
wiped them with her hair. 45 You refused me

Today's English Version

Jesus at the home of Simon the Pharisee

36 A Pharisee invited Jesus to have dinner
with him. Jesus went to his house and sat down
to eat. 37 There was a woman in that town who
lived a sinful life. She heard that Jesus was eating in the Pharisee's house, so she brought an
alabaster jar full of perfume 38 and stood behind Jesus, by his feet, crying and wetting his
feet with her tears. Then she dried his feet with
her hair, kissed them, and poured the perfume on
them. 39 When the Pharisee who had invited Jesus saw this, he said to himself, "If this man
really were a prophet, he would know who this
woman is who is touching him; he would know
what kind of sinful life she leads!"

40 Jesus spoke up and said to him, "Simon, I have something to tell you."

"Yes, Teacher," he said, "tell me."

41 "There were two men who owed money
to a moneylender," Jesus began; "one owed him
five hundred dollars and the other one fifty dollars. 42 Neither one could pay him back, so he
canceled the debts of both. Which one, then, will
love him more?"

43 "I suppose," answered Simon, "that it would be the one who was forgiven more."

"Your answer is correct," said Jesus. 44 Then
he turned to the woman and said to Simon, "Do
you see this woman? I came into your home, and
you gave me no water for my feet, but she has
washed my feet with her tears and dried them
with her hair. 45 You did not welcome me with

New International Version

Jesus anointed by a sinful woman

36 Now one of the Pharisees invited Jesus to
have dinner with him, so he went to the Pharisee's house and reclined at the table. 37 When a
woman who lived a sinful life in that town
learned that Jesus was eating at the Pharisee's
house, she brought an alabaster jar of perfume,
38 and as she stood behind him at his feet weeping, she began to wet his feet with her tears.
Then she wiped them with her hair, kissed them
and poured perfume on them.

39 When the Pharisee who had invited him saw this, he said to himself, "If this man were a prophet, he would know who is touching him and what kind of woman she is—that she is a sinner."

40 Jesus answered him, "Simon, I have something to tell you."

"Tell me, teacher," he said.

41 "Two men owed money to a certain money-
lender. One owed him five hundred denarii,[c] and
the other fifty. 42 Neither of them had the money
to pay him back, so he canceled the debts of
both. Now which of them will love him more?"

43 "Simon replied, "I suppose the one who had the bigger debt canceled."

"You have judged correctly," Jesus said.

44 Then he turned toward the woman and
said to Simon, "Do you see this woman? I came
into your house. You did not give me any water
for my feet, but she wet my feet with her tears
and wiped them with her hair. 45 You did not

[c] A denarius was a coin worth about a day's wage.

Phillips Modern English

7.36 Jesus contrasts unloving righteousness with loving penitence

Then one of the Pharisees asked Jesus to a meal with him. When Jesus came into the house, he took his place at the table and a woman, known in the town as a bad character, found out that Jesus was there and brought an alabaster flask of perfume and stood behind him crying, letting her tears fall on his feet and then drying them with her hair. Then she kissed them and anointed them with the perfume. When the Pharisee who had invited him saw this, he said to himself, "If this man were really a prophet, he would know who this woman is and what sort of a person is touching him. He would have realised that she is a bad woman." Then Jesus spoke to him,

"Simon, there is something I want to say to you."

"Very well, Master," he returned, "say it."

"Once upon a time, there were two men in debt to the same money-lender. One owed him fifty pounds and the other five. And since they were unable to pay, he generously cancelled both of their debts. Now, which one of them do you suppose will love him more?"

"Well," returned Simon, "I suppose it will be the one who has been more generously treated."

"Exactly," replied Jesus, and then turning to the woman, he said to Simon,

"You see this woman? I came into your house but you provided no water to wash my feet. But she has washed my feet with her tears and dried them with her hair. You gave me no kiss of

Revised Standard Version

36 One of the Pharisees asked him to eat with
him, and he went into the Pharisee's house, and
took his place at table. 37 And behold, a woman
of the city, who was a sinner, when she learned
that he was at table in the Pharisee's house,
brought an alabaster flask of ointment, 38 and
standing behind him at his feet, weeping, she began to wet his feet with her tears, and wiped
them with the hair of her head, and kissed his
feet, and anointed them with the ointment.
39 Now when the Pharisee who had invited him
saw it, he said to himself, "If this man were a
prophet, he would have known who and what
sort of woman this is who is touching him, for
she is a sinner." 40 And Jesus answering said
to him, "Simon, I have something to say to you."
And he answered, "What is it, Teacher?" 41 "A
certain creditor had two debtors; one owed five
hundred denarii, and the other fifty. 42 When
they could not pay, he forgave them both. Now
which of them will love him more?" 43 Simon
answered, "The one, I suppose, to whom he forgave more." And he said to him, "You have
judged rightly." 44 Then turning toward the
woman he said to Simon, "Do you see this
woman? I entered your house, you gave me no
water for my feet, but she has wet my feet with
her tears and wiped them with her hair. 45 You

Jerusalem Bible

The woman who was a sinner

36 One of the Pharisees invited him to a
meal. When he arrived at the Pharisee's house
and took his place at table, 37 a woman came
in, who had a bad name in the town. She had
heard he was dining with the Pharisee and had
brought with her an alabaster jar of ointment.
38 She waited behind him at his feet, weeping,
and her tears fell on his feet, and she wiped
them away with her hair; then she covered his
feet with kisses and anointed them with the
ointment.
39 When the Pharisee who had invited him
saw this, he said to himself, "If this man were
a prophet, he would know who this woman is
that is touching him and what a bad name she
has." 40 Then Jesus took him up and said, "Simon, I have something to say to you." "Speak,
Master," was the reply. 41 "There was once a
creditor who had two men in his debt; one owed
him five hundred denarii, the other fifty. 42 They
were unable to pay, so he pardoned them both.
Which of them will love him more?" 43 "The one
who was pardoned more, I suppose," answered
Simon. Jesus said, "You are right."
44 Then he turned to the woman. "Simon,"
he said, "you see this woman? I came into your
house, and you poured no water over my feet,
but she has poured out her tears over my feet
and wiped them away with her hair. 45 You gave

New English Bible

One of the Pharisees invited him to eat with him; he went to the Pharisee's house and took his place at table. A woman who was living an immoral life in the town had learned that Jesus was at table in the Pharisee's house and had brought oil of myrrh in a small flask. She took her place behind him, by his feet, weeping. His feet were wetted with her tears and she wiped them with her hair, kissing them and anointing them with the myrrh. When his host the Pharisee saw this he said to himself, 'If this fellow were a real prophet, he would know who this woman is that touches him, and what sort of woman she is, a sinner.' Jesus took him up and said, 'Simon, I have something to say to you.' 'Speak on, Master', said he. 'Two men were in debt to a money-lender: one owed him five hundred silver pieces, the other fifty. As neither had anything to pay with he let them both off. Now, which will love him most?' Simon replied, 'I should think the one that was let off most.' 'You are right', said Jesus. Then turning to the woman, he said to Simon, 'You see this woman? I came to your house: you provided no water for my feet; but this woman has made my feet wet with her tears and wiped them with her hair. You gave me no

King James Version

me no kiss: but this woman, since the time I came in, hath not ceased to kiss my feet. 46 My head with oil thou didst not anoint: but this woman hath anointed my feet with ointment. 47 Wherefore I say unto thee, Her sins, which are many, are forgiven; for she loved much: but to whom little is forgiven, *the same* loveth little. 48And he said unto her, Thy sins are forgiven. 49And they that sat at meat with him began to say within themselves, Who is this that forgiveth sins also? 50And he said to the woman, Thy faith hath saved thee; go in peace.

8 And it came to pass afterward, that he went throughout every city and village, preaching and shewing the glad tidings of the kingdom of God: and the twelve *were* with him, 2And certain women, which had been healed of evil spirits and infirmities, Mary called Magdalene, out of whom went seven devils, 3And Joanna the wife of Chuza Herod's steward, and Susanna, and many others, which ministered unto him of their substance.

Living Bible

the customary kiss of greeting, but she has kissed my feet again and again from the time I first came in. 46 You neglected the usual courtesy of olive oil to anoint my head, but she has covered my feet with rare perfume. 47 Therefore her sins—and they are many—are forgiven, for she loved me much; but one who is forgiven little, shows little love."

48 And he said to her, "Your sins are forgiven."

49 Then the men at the table said to themselves, "Who does this man think he is, going around forgiving sins?"

50 And Jesus said to the woman, "Your faith has saved you; go in peace."

8 Not long afterwards he began a tour of the cities and villages of Galilee[a] to announce the coming of the Kingdom of God, and took his twelve disciples with him. 2 Some women went along, from whom he had cast out demons or whom he had healed; among them were Mary Magdalene (Jesus had cast out seven demons from her), 3 Joanna, Chuza's wife (Chuza was King Herod's business manager and was in charge of his palace and domestic affairs), Susanna, and many others who were contributing from their private means to the support of Jesus and his disciples.

[*a*] Implied.

Today's English Version

a kiss, but she has not stopped kissing my feet since I came. 46 You provided no oil for my head, but she has covered my feet with perfume. 47 I tell you, then, the great love she has shown proves that her many sins have been forgiven. Whoever has been forgiven little, however, shows only a little love."

48 Then Jesus said to the woman, "Your sins are forgiven."

49 The others sitting at the table began to say to themselves, "Who is this, who even forgives sins?"

50 But Jesus said to the woman, "Your faith has saved you; go in peace."

Women who accompanied Jesus

8 Some time later Jesus traveled through towns and villages, preaching the Good News about the Kingdom of God. The twelve disciples went with him, 2 and so did some women who had been healed of evil spirits and diseases: Mary (who was called Magdalene), from whom seven demons had been driven out; 3 Joanna, the wife of Chuza who was an officer in Herod's court; and Susanna, and many other women who used their own resources to help Jesus and his disciples.

New International Version

give me a kiss, but this woman, from the time I entered, has not stopped kissing my feet. 46 You did not anoint my head with oil, but she has anointed my feet with perfume. 47 Therefore, I tell you, her many sins have been forgiven—for she loved much. But he loves little who has been forgiven little."

48 Then Jesus said to her, "Your sins are forgiven."

49 The other guests began to say among themselves, "Who is this who even forgives sins?"

50 Jesus said to the woman, "Your faith has saved you; go in peace."

The parable of the sower

8 After this, Jesus traveled about from one city and village to another, proclaiming the good news of the kingdom of God. The Twelve were with him, 2 and also some women who had been cured of evil spirits and diseases: Mary, called Magdalene, from whom seven demons had come out; 3 Joanna the wife of Chuza, the manager of Herod's household; Susanna; and many others. These women were helping to support them out of their own means.

Phillips Modern English

welcome, but she, from the moment I came in, has not stopped covering my feet with kisses. You gave me no oil for my head, but she has put perfume on my feet. That is why I tell you, Simon, that her sins, many as they are, are forgiven; for she has so much love. But the man who has little to be forgiven has only a little love to give."

Then he said to her,

"Your sins are forgiven."

And the men at table with him began to say to themselves,

"And who is this man, who even forgives sins?"

But Jesus said to the woman,

"It is your faith that has saved you. Go in peace."

Not long after this incident, Jesus went through every town and village preaching and telling the people the good news of the kingdom of God. He was accompanied by the twelve and some women who had been cured of evil spirits and illnesses—Mary, known as "the woman from Magdala" (who had once been possessed by seven evil spirits), Joanna the wife of Chuza, an agent of Herod, Susanna, and many others who used to look after Jesus' and his companions' comfort from their own resources.

Revised Standard Version

gave me no kiss, but from the time I came in
she has not ceased to kiss my feet. 46 You did
not anoint my head with oil, but she has
anointed my feet with ointment. 47 Therefore I
tell you, her sins, which are many, are forgiven,
for she loved much; but he who is forgiven little, loves little." 48 And he said to her, "Your
sins are forgiven." 49 Then those who were at
table with him began to say among themselves,
"Who is this, who even forgives sins?" 50 And
he said to the woman, "Your faith has saved
you; go in peace."

8 Soon afterward he went on through cities
and villages, preaching and bringing the
good news of the kingdom of God. And the
twelve were with him, 2 and also some women
who had been healed of evil spirits and infirmities: Mary, called Magdalene, from whom seven
demons had gone out, 3 and Joanna, the wife
of Chuza, Herod's steward, and Susanna, and
many others, who provided for them[z] out of
their means.

[z] Other ancient authorities read *him*.

Jerusalem Bible

me no kiss, but she has been covering my feet
with kisses ever since I came in. 46 You did not
anoint my head with oil, but she has anointed
my feet with ointment. 47 For this reason I tell
you that her sins, her many sins, must have been
forgiven her, or she would not have shown such
great love. It is the man who is forgiven little
who shows little love." 48 Then he said to her,
"Your sins are forgiven." 49 Those who were
with him at table began to say to themselves,
"Who is this man, that he even forgives sins?"
50 But he said to the woman, "Your faith has
saved you; go in peace."

The women accompanying Jesus

8 Now after this he made his way through
towns and villages preaching, and proclaim-
the Good News of the kingdom of God. With
him went the Twelve, 2 as well as certain women
who had been cured of evil spirits and ailments:
Mary surnamed the Magdalene, from whom
seven demons had gone out, 3 Joanna the wife of
Herod's steward Chuza, Susanna, and several
others who provided for them out of their own
resources.

New English Bible

kiss; but she has been kissing my feet ever since I came in. You did not anoint my head with oil; but she has anointed my feet with myrrh. And so, I tell you, her great love proves that her many sins have been forgiven; where little has been forgiven, little love is shown.' Then he said to her, 'Your sins are forgiven.' The other guests began to ask themselves, 'Who is this, that he can forgive sins?' But he said to the woman, 'Your faith has saved you; go in peace.'

8 After this he went journeying from town to town and village to village, proclaiming the good news of the kingdom of God. With him were the Twelve and a number of women who had been set free from evil spirits and infirmities: Mary, known as Mary of Magdala, from whom seven devils had come out, Joanna, the wife of Chuza a steward of Herod's, Susanna, and many others. These women provided for them out of their own resources.

King James Version

4 And when much people were gathered together, and were come to him out of every city,
he spake by a parable: 5 A sower went out to
sow his seed: and as he sowed, some fell by the
way side; and it was trodden down, and the
fowls of the air devoured it. 6 And some fell
upon a rock; and as soon as it was sprung up, it
withered away, because it lacked moisture. 7 And
some fell among thorns; and the thorns sprang
up with it, and choked it. 8 And other fell on
good ground, and sprang up, and bare fruit a
hundredfold. And when he had said these things,
he cried, He that hath ears to hear, let him
hear. 9 And his disciples asked him, saying, What
might this parable be? 10 And he said, Unto you
it is given to know the mysteries of the kingdom
of God: but to others in parables; that seeing
they might not see, and hearing they might not
understand. 11 Now the parable is this: The seed

Living Bible

4 One day he gave this illustration to a large
crowd that was gathering to hear him—while
many others were still on the way, coming from
other towns.

5 "A farmer went out to his field to sow grain.
As he scattered the seed on the ground, some of
it fell on a footpath and was trampled on; and
the birds came and ate it as it lay exposed.
6 Other seed fell on shallow soil with rock beneath. This seed began to grow, but soon withered and died for lack of moisture. 7 Other seed
landed in thistle patches, and the young grain
stalks were soon choked out. 8 Still other fell on
fertile soil; this seed grew and produced a crop
one hundred times as large as he had planted."
(As he was giving this illustration he said, "If
anyone has listening ears, use them now!")

9 His apostles asked him what the story
meant.

10 He replied, "God has granted you to know
the meaning of these parables, for they tell a
great deal about the Kingdom of God. But
these crowds hear the words and do not understand, just as the ancient prophets predicted.

11 "This is its meaning: The seed is God's

Today's English Version

The parable of the sower

4 People kept coming to Jesus from one town
after another; and when a great crowd gathered,
Jesus told this parable,

5 "A man went out to sow his seed. As he
scattered the seed in the field, some of it fell
along the path, where it was stepped on, and the
birds ate it up. 6 Some of it fell on rocky ground,
and when the plants sprouted they dried up, because the soil had no moisture. 7 Some of the
seed fell among thorns, which grew up with the
plants and choked them. 8 And some seeds fell in
good soil; the plants grew and bore grain, one
hundred grains each."

And Jesus concluded, "Listen, then, if you
have ears to hear with!"

The purpose of the parables

9 His disciples asked Jesus what this parable
meant. 10 Jesus answered, "The knowledge of the
secrets of the Kingdom of God has been given
to you; but to the rest it comes by means of
parables, so that they may look but not see, and
listen but not understand."

Jesus explains the parable of the sower

11 "This is what the parable means: the seed

New International Version

4 While a large crowd was gathering and
people were coming to Jesus from town after
town, he told this parable: 5 "A farmer went
out to sow his seed. As he was scattering the
seed, some fell along the path; it was trampled
on, and the birds of the air ate it up. 6 Some
fell on rock, and when it came up, the plants
withered because they had no moisture. 7 Other
seed fell among thorns, which grew up with it
and choked the plants. 8 Still other seed fell on
good soil. It came up and yielded a crop, a
hundred times more than was sown."

When he said this, he called out, "He who
has ears to hear, let him hear."

9 His disciples asked him what this parable
meant. 10 He said, "The knowledge of the secrets of the kingdom of God has been given to
you, but to others I speak in parables, so that,

'though seeing, they may not see;
though hearing, they may not understand.'[d]

11 "This is the meaning of the parable: The

[d] Isaiah 6:9.

Phillips Modern English

8.4 Jesus' parable of the mixed reception given to the truth

When a large crowd had collected and people were coming to him from one town after another, he spoke to them and gave them this parable:

"A sower went out to sow his seed, and while he was sowing, some of the seed fell by the roadside and was trodden down and the birds gobbled it up. Some fell on the rock, and when it sprouted it withered for lack of moisture. Some fell among thorn-bushes which grew up with the seeds and choked the life out of them. And some seed fell on good soil and grew and produced a crop—a hundred times what had been sown."

And when he had said this, he called out,

"Let the man who has ears to hear use them!"

Then his disciples asked him the meaning of the parable. To which Jesus replied,

"You have been given the privilege of understanding the secrets of the kingdom of God, but the others are given parables so that they may go through life with their eyes open and see nothing, and with their ears open, and understand nothing of what they hear.

"This is what the parable means. The seed is

Revised Standard Version

4 And when a great crowd came together and
people from town after town came to him, he
said in a parable: 5 "A sower went out to sow his
seed; and as he sowed, some fell along the path,
and was trodden under foot, and the birds of
the air devoured it. 6And some fell on the rock;
and as it grew up, it withered away, because it
had no moisture. 7And some fell among thorns;
and the thorns grew with it and choked it. 8And
some fell into good soil and grew, and yielded a
hundredfold." As he said this, he called out, "He
who has ears to hear, let him hear."
9 And when his disciples asked him what this
parable meant, 10 he said, "To you it has been
given to know the secrets of the kingdom of
God; but for others they are in parables, so that
seeing they may not see, and hearing they may
not understand. 11 Now the parable is this: The

Jerusalem Bible

Parable of the sower

4 With a large crowd gathering and people
from every town finding their way to him, he
used this parable:
5 "A sower went out to sow his seed. As he
sowed, some fell on the edge of the path and
was trampled on; and the birds of the air ate it
up. 6 Some seed fell on rock, and when it came
up it withered away, having no moisture. 7 Some
seed fell among thorns and the thorns grew with
it and choked it. 8And some seed fell into rich
soil and grew and produced its crop a hundredfold." Saying this he cried, "Listen, anyone who
has ears to hear!"

Why Jesus speaks in parables

9 His disciples asked him what this parable
might mean, 10 and he said, "The mysteries of
the kingdom of God are revealed to you; for the
rest there are only parables, so that

they may see but not perceive,
listen but not understand.[m]

The parable of the sower explained

11 "This, then, is what the parable means: the

[*m*] Is. 6:9.

New English Bible

People were now gathering in large numbers, and as they made their way to him from one town after another, he said in a parable: 'A sower went out to sow his seed. And as he sowed, some seed fell along the footpath, where it was trampled on, and the birds ate it up. Some seed fell on rock and, after coming up, withered for lack of moisture. Some seed fell in among thistles, and the thistles grew up with it and choked it. And some of the seed fell into good soil, and grew, and yielded a hundredfold.' As he said this he called out, 'If you have ears to hear, then hear.'

His disciples asked him what this parable meant, and he said, 'It has been granted to you to know the secrets of the kingdom of God: but the others have only parables, so that they may look but see nothing, hear but understand nothing.

'This is what the parable means. The seed is

King James Version

is the word of God. 12 Those by the way side are
they that hear; then cometh the devil, and
taketh away the word out of their hearts, lest
they should believe and be saved. 13 They on the
rock *are they*, which, when they hear, receive
the word with joy; and these have no root, which
for a while believe, and in time of temptation fall
away. 14And that which fell among thorns are
they, which, when they have heard, go forth,
and are choked with cares and riches and pleasures of *this* life, and bring no fruit to perfection.
15 But that on the good ground are they, which
in an honest and good heart, having heard the
word, keep *it*, and bring forth fruit with patience.
16 No man, when he hath lighted a candle,
covereth it with a vessel, or putteth *it* under a
bed; but setteth *it* on a candlestick, that they
which enter in may see the light. 17 For nothing
is secret, that shall not be made manifest;
neither *any thing* hid, that shall not be known
and come abroad. 18 Take heed therefore how
ye hear: for whosoever hath, to him shall be
given; and whosoever hath not, from him shall
be taken even that which he seemeth to have.

Living Bible

message to men. 12 The hard path where some
seed fell represents the hard hearts of those who
hear the words of God, but then the devil comes
and steals the words away and prevents people
from believing and being saved. 13 The stony
ground represents those who enjoy listening to
sermons, but somehow the message never really
gets through to them and doesn't take root and
grow. They know the message is true, and sort
of believe for awhile; but when the hot winds
of persecution blow, they lose interest. 14 The
seed among the thorns represents those who
listen and believe God's words but whose faith
afterwards is choked out by worry and riches
and the responsibilities and pleasures of life.
And so they are never able to help anyone else
to believe the Good News.
15 "But the good soil represents honest, good-
hearted people. They listen to God's words and
cling to them and steadily spread them to others
who also soon believe."
16 [Another time he asked,[b]] "Who ever heard
of someone lighting a lamp and then covering it
up to keep it from shining? No, lamps are
mounted in the open where they can be seen.
17 This illustrates the fact that someday everything [in men's hearts[b]] shall be brought to
light and made plain to all. 18 So be careful how
you listen; for whoever has, to him shall be
given more; and whoever does not have, even
what he thinks he has shall be taken away from
him."

[*b*] Implied. See Matthew 5:16.

Today's English Version

is the word of God. 12 The seed that fell along
the path stands for those who hear; but the
Devil comes and takes the message away from
their hearts to keep them from believing and being saved. 13 The seed that fell on rocky ground
stands for those who hear the message and receive it gladly. But it does not sink deep into
them; they believe only for a while, and fall away
when the time of testing comes. 14 The seed that
fell among thorns stands for those who hear; but
the worries and riches and pleasures of this life
crowd in and choke them, and their fruit never
ripens. 15 The seed that fell in good soil stands
for those who hear the message and retain it in
a good and obedient heart, and persist until they
bear fruit."

A lamp under a bowl

16 "No one lights a lamp and covers it with
a bowl or puts it under a bed. Instead, he puts
it on the lampstand, so that people will see the
light as they come in. 17 Whatever is hidden away
will be brought out into the open, and whatever
is covered up will be found and brought to light.
18 "Be careful, then, how you listen; because
whoever has something will be given more, but
whoever has nothing will have taken away from
him even the little he thinks he has."

New International Version

seed is the word of God. 12 Those along the path
are the ones who hear, and then the devil comes
and takes away the word from their hearts, so
that they cannot believe and be saved. 13 Those
on the rock are the ones who receive the word
with joy when they hear it, but they have no
root. They believe for a while, but in the time of
testing they fall away. 14 The seed that fell among
thorns stands for those who hear, but as they
go on their way they are choked by life's worries, riches and pleasures, and they do not mature. 15 But the seed on good soil stands for
those with a noble and good heart, who hear the
word, retain it, and by persevering produce a
crop.

A lamp on a stand

16 "No one lights a lamp and hides it in a
jar or puts it under a bed. Instead, he puts it
on a stand, so that those who come in can see
the light. 17 For there is nothing hidden that
will not be disclosed, and nothing concealed
that will not be known or brought out into the
open. 18 Therefore consider carefully how you
listen. Whoever has will be given more; whoever
does not have, even what he thinks he has will
be taken from him."

Phillips Modern English

the message of God. The seed sown by the roadside represents those who hear the message, and then the devil comes and takes it away from their hearts so that they cannot believe it and be saved. That sown on the rock represents those who accept the message with great delight when they hear it, but have no real root. They believe for a little while but when the time of temptation comes, they lose faith. And the seed sown among the thorns represents the people who hear the message and go on their way, and with the worries and riches and pleasures of living, the life is choked out of them, and in the end they produce nothing. But the seed sown on good soil means the men who hear the message and grasp it with a good and honest heart, and go on steadily producing a good crop.

8.16 Truth is not a secret to be hidden but a gift to be used

"Nobody lights a lamp and covers it with a basin or puts it under the bed. No, a man puts his lamp on a lamp-stand so that those who come in can see the light. For there is nothing hidden now which will not become perfectly plain and there are no secrets now which will not become as clear as daylight. So take care how you listen—more will be given to the man who has something already, but the man who has nothing will lose even what he thinks he has."

Revised Standard Version

seed is the word of God. 12 The ones along the
path are those who have heard; then the devil
comes and takes away the word from their
hearts, that they may not believe and be saved.
13 And the ones on the rock are those who, when
they hear the word, receive it with joy; but these
have no root, they believe for a while and in time
of temptation fall away. 14 And as for what fell
among the thorns, they are those who hear, but
as they go on their way they are choked by the
cares and riches and pleasures of life, and their
fruit does not mature. 15 And as for that in the
good soil, they are those who, hearing the word,
hold it fast in an honest and good heart, and
bring forth fruit with patience.
16 "No one after lighting a lamp covers it
with a vessel, or puts it under a bed, but puts it
on a stand, that those who enter may see the
light. 17 For nothing is hid that shall not be
made manifest, nor anything secret that shall
not be known and come to light. 18 Take heed
then how you hear; for to him who has will
more be given, and from him who has not, even
what he thinks that he has will be taken away."

Jerusalem Bible

seed is the word of God. 12 Those on the edge
of the path are people who have heard it, and
then the devil comes and carries away the word
from their hearts in case they should believe and
be saved. 13 Those on the rock are people who,
when they first hear it, welcome the word with
joy. But these have no root; they believe for a
while, and in time of trial they give up. 14 As for
the part that fell into thorns, this is people who
have heard, but as they go on their way they
are choked by the worries and riches and pleasures of life and do not reach maturity. 15 As for
the part in the rich soil, this is people with a
noble and generous heart who have heard the
word and take it to themselves and yield a harvest through their perseverance.

Parable of the lamp

16 "No one lights a lamp to cover it with a
bowl or to put it under a bed. No, he puts it
on a lampstand so that people may see the light
when they come in. 17 For nothing is hidden but
it will be made clear, nothing secret but it will be
known and brought to light. 18 So take care how
you hear; for anyone who has will be given
more; from anyone who has not, even what he
thinks he has will be taken away."

New English Bible

the word of God. Those along the footpath are the men who hear it, and then the devil comes and carries off the word from their hearts for fear they should believe and be saved. The seed sown on rock stands for those who receive the word with joy when they hear it, but have no root; they are believers for a while, but in the time of testing they desert. That which fell among thistles represents those who hear, but their further growth is choked by cares and wealth and the pleasures of life, and they bring nothing to maturity. But the seed in good soil represents those who bring a good and honest heart to the hearing of the word, hold it fast, and by their perseverance yield a harvest.

'Nobody lights a lamp and then covers it with a basin or puts it under the bed. On the contrary, he puts it on a lamp-stand so that those who come in may see the light. For there is nothing hidden that will not become public, nothing under cover that will not be made known and brought into the open.

'Take care, then, how you listen; for the man who has will be given more, and the man who has not will forfeit even what he thinks he has.'

King James Version

19 Then came to him *his* mother and his
brethren, and could not come at him for the
press. 20And it was told him *by certain* which
said, Thy mother and thy brethren stand without, desiring to see thee. 21And he answered and
said unto them, My mother and my brethren
are these which hear the word of God, and do it.
22 Now it came to pass on a certain day, that
he went into a ship with his disciples: and he
said unto them, Let us go over unto the other
side of the lake. And they launched forth. 23 But
as they sailed, he fell asleep: and there came
down a storm of wind on the lake; and they
were filled *with water,* and were in jeopardy.
24And they came to him, and awoke him, saying,
Master, Master, we perish. Then he arose, and
rebuked the wind and the raging of the water:
and they ceased, and there was a calm. 25And
he said unto them, Where is your faith? And
they being afraid wondered, saying one to another, What manner of man is this! for he commandeth even the winds and water, and they
obey him.

Living Bible

19 Once when his mother and brothers came
to see him, they couldn't get into the house
where he was teaching, because of the crowds.
20 When Jesus heard they were standing outside
and wanted to see him, 21 he remarked, "My
mother and my brothers are all those who hear
the message of God and obey it."
22 One day about that time, as he and his
disciples were out in a boat, he suggested that
they cross to the other side of the lake. 23 On
the way across he lay down for a nap, and while
he was sleeping the wind began to rise. A fierce
storm developed that threatened to swamp them,
and they were in real danger.
24 They rushed over and woke him up. "Master, Master, we are sinking!" they screamed.

So he spoke to the storm: "Quiet down," he
said, and the wind and waves subsided and all
was calm! 25 Then he asked them, "Where is
your faith?"

And they were filled with awe and fear of
him and said to one another, "Who is this man,
that even the winds and waves obey him?"

Today's English Version

Jesus' mother and brothers

19 Jesus' mother and brothers came to him,
but were unable to join him because of the
crowd. 20 Someone said to Jesus, "Your mother
and brothers are standing outside and want to
see you."
21 Jesus said to them all, "My mother and
brothers are those who hear the word of God
and obey it."

Jesus calms a storm

22 One day Jesus got into a boat with his
disciples and said to them, "Let us go across to
the other side of the lake." So they started out.
23As they were sailing, Jesus went to sleep. A
strong wind blew down on the lake, and the boat
began to fill with water, putting them all in great
danger. 24 The disciples came to Jesus and woke
him up, saying, "Master, Master! We are about
to die!"

Jesus got up and gave a command to the wind
and to the stormy water; they quieted down and
there was a great calm. 25 Then he said to the
disciples, "Where is your faith?"

But they were amazed and afraid, and said to
one another, "Who is this man? He gives orders
to the winds and waves, and they obey him!"

New International Version

Jesus' mother and brothers

19 Now Jesus' mother and brothers came to
see him, but they were not able to get near him
because of the crowd. 20 Someone told him,
"Your mother and brothers are standing outside,
wanting to see you."
21 He replied, "My mother and brothers are
those who hear God's word and put it into
practice."

Jesus calms the storm

22 One day Jesus said to his disciples, "Let's
go over to the other side of the lake." So they
got into a boat and set out. 23As they sailed, he
fell asleep. A squall came down on the lake, so
that the boat was being swamped, and they were
in great danger.
24 The disciples went and woke him, saying,
"Master, Master, we're going to drown!"

He got up and rebuked the wind and the
raging waters; the storm subsided, and all was
calm. 25 "Where is your faith?" he asked his
disciples.

In fear and amazement they asked one another, "Who is this? He commands even the
winds and the water, and they obey him."

Phillips Modern English

Then his mother and his brothers arrived to see him, but could not get near him because of the crowd. So a message was passed to him,

"Your mother and your brothers are standing outside wanting to see you."

To which he replied,

"My mother and my brothers? They are those who listen to God's message and obey it."

8.22 Jesus' mastery of wind and water

It happened on one of these days that he got into a boat with his disciples and said to them,

"Let us cross over to the other side of the lake."

So they set sail, and when they were under way he fell asleep. Then a squall of wind swept down upon the lake and they were in grave danger of being swamped. Coming forward, they woke him up, saying,

"Master, master, we're drowning!"

Then he got up and reprimanded the wind and the stormy waters, and they died down, and everything was still. Then he said to them,

"What has happened to your faith?"

But they were frightened and bewildered and kept saying to each other,

"Who ever can this be? He gives orders even to the winds and waters and they obey him."

Revised Standard Version

19 Then his mother and his brothers came to
him, but they could not reach him for the
crowd. 20 And he was told, "Your mother and
your brothers are standing outside, desiring to
see you." 21 But he said to them, "My mother
and my brothers are those who hear the word
of God and do it."
22 One day he got into a boat with his disciples, and he said to them, "Let us go across to
the other side of the lake." So they set out,
23 and as they sailed he fell asleep. And a storm
of wind came down on the lake, and they were
filling with water, and were in danger. 24 And
they went and woke him, saying, "Master, Master, we are perishing!" And he awoke and rebuked the wind and the raging waves; and they
ceased, and there was a calm. 25 He said to
them, "Where is your faith?" And they were
afraid, and they marveled, saying to one another,
"Who then is this, that he commands even wind
and water, and they obey him?"

Jerusalem Bible

The true kinsmen of Jesus

19 His mother and his brothers came looking
for him, but they could not get to him because
of the crowd. 20 He was told, "Your mother
and brothers are standing outside and want to
see you." 21 But he said in answer, "My mother
and my brothers are those who hear the word of
God and put it into practice."

The calming of the storm

22 One day, he got into a boat with his disciples and said to them, "Let us cross over to the
other side of the lake." So they put to sea, 23 and
as they sailed he fell asleep. When a squall came
down on the lake the boat started taking in water
and they found themselves in danger. 24 So they
went to rouse him saying, "Master! Master! We
are going down!" Then he woke up and rebuked
the wind and the rough water; and they subsided and it was calm again. 25 He said to them,
"Where is your faith?" They were awestruck and
astonished and said to one another, "Who can
this be, that gives orders even to winds and
waves and they obey him?"

New English Bible

His mother and his brothers arrived but could not get to him for the crowd. He was told, 'Your mother and brothers are standing outside, and they want to see you.' He replied, 'My mother and my brothers—they are those who hear the word of God and act upon it.'

One day he got into a boat with his disciples and said to them, 'Let us cross over to the other side of the lake.' So they put out; and as they sailed along he went to sleep. Then a heavy squall struck the lake; they began to ship water and were in grave danger. They went to him, and roused him, crying, 'Master, Master, we are sinking!' He awoke, and rebuked the wind and the turbulent waters. The storm subsided and all was calm. 'Where is your faith?' he asked. In fear and astonishment they said to one another, 'Who can this be? He gives his orders to wind and waves, and they obey him.'

King James Version

26 And they arrived at the country of the Gadarenes, which is over against Galilee. 27And when he went forth to land, there met him out of the city a certain man, which had devils long time, and ware no clothes, neither abode in *any* house, but in the tombs. 28 When he saw Jesus, he cried out, and fell down before him, and with a loud voice said, What have I to do with thee, Jesus, *thou* Son of God most high? I beseech thee, torment me not. 29 (For he had commanded the unclean spirit to come out of the man. For oftentimes it had caught him: and he was kept bound with chains and in fetters; and he brake the bands, and was driven of the devil into the wilderness.) 30And Jesus asked him, saying, What is thy name? And he said, Legion: because many devils were entered into him. 31And they besought him that he would not command them to go out into the deep. 32And there was there a herd of many swine feeding on the mountain: and they besought him that he would suffer them to enter into them. And he suffered them. 33 Then went the devils out of the man, and entered into the swine: and the herd ran violently down a steep place into the lake, and were choked. 34 When they that fed *them* saw what was done, they fled, and went and told *it* in the city and in the country. 35 Then they went out to see what was done; and came

Living Bible

26 So they arrived at the other side, in the Gerasene country across the lake from Galilee. 27As he was climbing out of the boat a man from the city of Gadara came to meet him, a man who had been demon-possessed for a long time. Homeless and naked, he lived in a cemetery among the tombs. 28As soon as he saw Jesus he shrieked and fell to the ground before him, screaming, "What do you want with me, Jesus, Son of God Most High? Please, I beg you, oh, don't torment me!"

29 For Jesus was already commanding the demon to leave him. This demon had often taken control of the man so that even when shackled with chains he simply broke them and rushed out into the desert, completely under the demon's power. 30 "What is your name?" Jesus asked the demon. "Legion," they replied—for the man was filled with thousands[c] of them! 31 They kept begging him not to order them into the Bottomless Pit.

32 A herd of pigs was feeding on the mountainside nearby, and the demons pled with him to let them enter into the pigs. And Jesus said they could. 33 So they left the man and went into the pigs, and immediately the whole herd rushed down the mountainside and fell over a cliff into the lake below, where they drowned. 34 The herdsmen rushed away to the nearby city, spreading the news as they ran.

35 Soon a crowd came out to see for them-

[*c*] Implied; a legion consisted of 6,000 troops. Whether the demons were speaking literally is, of course, unknown.

Today's English Version

Jesus heals a man with demons

26 They sailed on over to the territory of the Gergesenes, which is across the lake from Galilee. 27As Jesus stepped ashore, he was met by a man from the town who had demons in him. He had gone for a long time without clothes, and would not stay at home, but spent his time in the burial caves. 28 When he saw Jesus he gave a loud cry, fell down before him, and said in a loud voice, "Jesus, Son of the Most High God! What do you want with me? I beg you, don't punish me!" 29 He said this because Jesus had ordered the evil spirit to go out of him. Many times it had seized him, and even though he was kept a prisoner, his hands and feet tied with chains, he would break the chains and be driven by the demon out into the desert.

30 Jesus asked him, "What is your name?"

"My name is 'Mob,'" he answered—because many demons had gone into him. 31 The demons begged Jesus not to send them into the abyss.

32 A large herd of pigs was near by, feeding on the hillside. The demons begged Jesus to let them go into the pigs, and he let them. 33 So the demons went out of the man and into the pigs; the whole herd rushed down the side of the cliff into the lake and were drowned.

34 The men who were taking care of the pigs saw what happened, so they ran off and spread the news in the town and among the farms. 35 People went out to see what had happened.

New International Version

The healing of a demon-possessed man

26 They sailed to the region of the Gerasenes,[e] which is across the lake from Galilee. 27 When Jesus stepped ashore, he was met by a demon-possessed man from the town. For a long time this man had not worn clothes or lived in a house, but had lived in the tombs. 28 When he saw Jesus, he cried out and fell at his feet, shouting at the top of his voice, "What do you want with me, Jesus, Son of the Most High God? I beg you, don't torture me!" 29 For Jesus had commanded the evil[f] spirit to come out of the man. Many times it had seized him, and though he was chained hand and foot and kept under guard, he had broken his chains and had been driven by the demon into solitary places.

30 Jesus asked him, "What is your name?"

"Legion," he replied, because many demons had gone into him. 31And they begged him repeatedly not to order them to go into the Abyss.

32 A herd of many pigs was feeding there on the hillside. The demons begged Jesus to let them go into them, and he gave them permission. 33 When the demons came out of the man, they went into the pigs, and the herd rushed down the steep bank into the lake and was drowned.

34 When those tending the pigs saw what had happened, they ran off and reported this in the town and countryside, 35 and the people went

[*e*] Some MSS read *Gadarenes;* others read *Gergesenes.* [*f*] Greek *unclean.*

Phillips Modern English

8.26 *Jesus encounters and heals a dangerous lunatic*

They sailed on to the country of the Gergesenes which is on the opposite side of the lake to Galilee. And as Jesus disembarked, a man from the town who was possessed by evil spirits met him. He had worn no clothes for a long time and did not live inside a house, but among the tombs. When he saw Jesus, he let out a howl and fell down in front of him, yelling,

"What have you got to do with me, you Jesus, Son of the Most High God? Please, please, don't torment me."

For Jesus was commanding the evil spirit to come out of the man. Again and again the evil spirit had taken control of him, and though he was bound with chains and fetters and closely watched, he would snap his bonds and go off into the desert with the devil at his heels. Then Jesus asked him,

"What is your name?"

"Legion!" he replied. For many evil spirits had gone into him, and were now begging Jesus not to order them off to the bottomless pit. It happened that there was a large herd of pigs feeding on the hill-side, so they implored him to allow them to go into the pigs, and he let them go. And when the evil spirits came out of the man and went into the pigs, the whole herd stampeded down the cliff into the lake and was drowned. When the swineherds saw what had happened, they took to their heels, pouring out the story to the people in the town and countryside. These people came out to see what had

Revised Standard Version

26 Then they arrived at the country of the Gerasenes,[a] which is opposite Galilee. 27 And as he stepped out on land, there met him a man from the city who had demons; for a long time he had worn no clothes, and he lived not in a house but among the tombs. 28 When he saw Jesus, he cried out and fell down before him, and said with a loud voice, "What have you to do with me, Jesus, Son of the Most High God? I beseech you, do not torment me." 29 For he had commanded the unclean spirit to come out of the man. (For many a time it had seized him; he was kept under guard, and bound with chains and fetters, but he broke the bonds and was driven by the demon into the desert.) 30 Jesus then asked him, "What is your name?" And he said, "Legion"; for many demons had entered him. 31 And they begged him not to command them to depart into the abyss. 32 Now a large herd of swine was feeding there on the hillside; and they begged him to let them enter these. So he gave them leave. 33 Then the demons came out of the man and entered the swine, and the herd rushed down the steep bank into the lake and were drowned.

34 When the herdsmen saw what had happened, they fled, and told it in the city and in the country. 35 Then people went out to see

[a] Other ancient authorities read *Gadarenes,* others *Gergesenes.*

Jerusalem Bible

The Gerasene demoniac

26 They came to land in the country of the Gerasenes,[n] which is opposite Galilee. 27 He was stepping ashore when a man from the town who was possessed by devils came toward him; for a long time the man had worn no clothes, nor did he live in a house, but in the tombs.

28 Catching sight of Jesus he gave a shout, fell at his feet and cried out at the top of his voice, "What do you want with me, Jesus, son of the Most High God? I implore you, do not torture me." 29—For Jesus had been telling the unclean spirit to come out of the man. It was a devil that had seized on him a great many times, and then they used to secure him with chains and fetters to restrain him, but he would always break the fastenings, and the devil would drive him out into the wilds. 30 "What is your name?" Jesus asked. "Legion," he said—because many devils had gone into him. 31 And these pleaded with him not to order them to depart into the Abyss.[o]

32 Now there was a large herd of pigs feeding there on the mountain, and the devils pleaded with him to let them go into these. So he gave them leave. 33 The devils came out of the man and went into the pigs, and the herd charged down the cliff into the lake and were drowned.

34 When the swineherds saw what had happened they ran off and told their story in the town and in the country around about; 35 and the people went out to see what had happened.

[n] "Gadarenes" in some versions. [o] The underworld.

New English Bible

So they landed in the country of the Gergesenes,[a] which is opposite Galilee. As he stepped ashore he was met by a man from the town who was possessed by devils. For a long time he had neither worn clothes nor lived in a house, but stayed among the tombs. When he saw Jesus he cried out, and fell at his feet shouting, 'What do you want with me, Jesus, son of the Most High God? I implore you, do not torment me.'

For Jesus was already ordering the unclean spirit to come out of the man. Many a time it had seized him, and then, for safety's sake, they would secure him with chains and fetters; but each time he broke loose, and with the devil in charge made off to the solitary places.

Jesus asked him, 'What is your name?' 'Legion', he replied. This was because so many devils had taken possession of him. And they begged him not to banish them to the Abyss.

There happened to be a large herd of pigs nearby, feeding on the hill; and the spirits begged him to let them go into these pigs. He gave them leave; the devils came out of the man and went into the pigs, and the herd rushed over the edge into the lake and were drowned.

The men in charge of them saw what had happened, and, taking to their heels, they carried the news to the town and country-side; and the people came out to see for themselves. When

[a] *Some witnesses read* Gerasenes; *others read* Gadarenes.

King James Version

to Jesus, and found the man, out of whom the
devils were departed, sitting at the feet of Jesus,
clothed, and in his right mind: and they were
afraid. 36 They also which saw *it* told them by
what means he that was possessed of the devils
was healed.
37 Then the whole multitude of the country
of the Gadarenes round about besought him to
depart from them; for they were taken with
great fear: and he went up into the ship, and
returned back again. 38 Now the man, out of
whom the devils were departed, besought him
that he might be with him: but Jesus sent him
away, saying, 39 Return to thine own house, and
shew how great things God hath done unto
thee. And he went his way, and published
throughout the whole city how great things Jesus had done unto him. 40 And it came to pass,
that, when Jesus was returned, the people *gladly*
received him: for they were all waiting for him.
41 And, behold, there came a man named
Jairus, and he was a ruler of the synagogue; and
he fell down at Jesus' feet, and besought him
that he would come into his house: 42 For he
had one only daughter, about twelve years of
age, and she lay a dying. But as he went the
people thronged him.
43 And a woman having an issue of blood
twelve years, which had spent all her living upon
physicians, neither could be healed of any,
44 Came behind *him*, and touched the border of
his garment: and immediately her issue of blood
stanched. 45 And Jesus said, Who touched me?

Living Bible

selves what had happened and saw the man who
had been demon-possessed sitting quietly at
Jesus' feet, clothed and sane! And the whole
crowd was badly frightened. 36 Then those who
had seen it happen told how the demon-possessed
man had been healed. 37 And everyone begged
Jesus to go away and leave them alone (for a
deep wave of fear had swept over them). So he
returned to the boat and left, crossing back to
the other side of the lake.
38 The man who had been demon-possessed
begged to go too, but Jesus said no.
39 "Go back to your family," he told him,
"and tell them what a wonderful thing God has
done for you."
So he went all through the city telling everyone about Jesus' mighty miracle.
40 On the other side of the lake the crowds
received him with open arms, for they had been
waiting for him.
41 And now a man named Jairus, a leader of
a Jewish synagogue, came and fell down at Jesus'
feet and begged him to come home with him,
42 for his only child was dying, a little girl twelve
years old. Jesus went with him, pushing through
the crowds.
43, 44 As they went a woman who wanted to
be healed came up behind and touched him, for
she had been slowly bleeding for twelve years,
and could find no cure (though she had spent
everything she had on doctors[d]). But the instant
she touched the edge of his robe, the bleeding
stopped.
45 "Who touched me?" Jesus asked.

[*d*] This clause is not included in some of the ancient manuscripts.

Today's English Version

They came to Jesus and found the man from
whom the demons had gone out sitting at the
feet of Jesus, clothed, and in his right mind;
and they were all afraid. 36 Those who had seen
it told the people how the man had been cured.
37 Then all the people from the territory of the
Gergesenes asked Jesus to go away, because they
were terribly afraid. So Jesus got into the boat
and left. 38 The man from whom the demons had
gone out begged Jesus, "Let me go with you."
But Jesus sent him away, saying, 39 "Go back
home and tell what God has done for you."
The man went through the whole town telling
what Jesus had done for him.

Jairus' daughter and the woman who touched Jesus' cloak

40 When Jesus returned to the other side of
the lake the crowd welcomed him, because they
had all been waiting for him. 41 Then a man
named Jairus arrived, an official in the local synagogue. He threw himself down at Jesus' feet
and begged him to go to his home, 42 because
his only daughter, twelve years old, was dying.
As Jesus went along, the people were crowding him from every side. 43 A certain woman was
there who had suffered from severe bleeding for
twelve years; she had spent all she had on doctors, but no one had been able to cure her.
44 She came up in the crowd behind Jesus and
touched the edge of his cloak, and her bleeding
stopped at once. 45 Jesus asked, "Who touched
me?"

New International Version

out to see what had happened. When they came
to Jesus, they found the man from whom the
demons had gone out, sitting at Jesus' feet,
dressed and in his right mind; and they were
afraid. 36 Those who had seen it told the people
how the demon-possessed man had been cured.
37 Then all the people of the region of the
Gerasenes[e] asked Jesus to leave them, because
they were overcome with fear. So he got into
the boat and left.
38 The man from whom the demons had gone
out begged to go with him, but Jesus sent him
away, saying, 39 "Return home and tell how
much God has done for you." So the man went
away and told all over town how much Jesus
had done for him.

A dead girl and a sick woman

40 Now when Jesus returned, a crowd welcomed him, for they were all expecting him.
41 Just then a man named Jairus, a ruler of the
synagogue, came and fell at Jesus' feet, pleading
with him to come to his house 42 because his
only daughter, a girl of about twelve, was dying.
As Jesus was on his way, the crowds almost
crushed him. 43 And a woman was there who
had been subject to bleeding for twelve years,[g]
but no one could heal her. 44 She came up behind him and touched the edge of his cloak, and
immediately her bleeding stopped.
45 "Who touched me?" Jesus asked.

[*e*] Some MSS read *Gadarenes;* others read *Gergesenes.* [*g*] Many MSS add *and she had spent all she had on doctors.*

Phillips Modern English

happened, and approached Jesus. They found the man, whom the evil spirits had left, sitting down at Jesus' feet, properly clothed and quite sane. That frightened them. Those who had seen it told the others how the man with the evil spirits had been cured. And the whole crowd of people from the district surrounding the Gergesenes' country begged Jesus to go away from them, for they were thoroughly frightened. Then he re-embarked on the boat and turned back. The man who had had the evil spirits kept begging to go with Jesus, but he sent him away with the words,

"Go back home and tell them all that God has done for you."

So the man went away and told the story of what Jesus had done for him, all over the town.

On Jesus' return, the crowd welcomed him back, for they had all been looking for him.

8.41 Jesus heals in response to faith

Then up came Jairus (who was president of the synagogue), and fell at Jesus' feet, begging him to come into his house, for his daughter, an only child about twelve years old, was dying.

But as he went, the crowds nearly suffocated him. Among them was a woman, who had had a chronic haemorrhage for twelve years and who had derived no benefit from anybody's treatment. She came up behind Jesus and touched the edge of his cloak, and her haemorrhage stopped at once.

"Who was that who touched me?" said Jesus.

Revised Standard Version

what had happened, and they came to Jesus, and found the man from whom the demons had gone, sitting at the feet of Jesus, clothed and in his right mind; and they were afraid. 36 And those who had seen it told how he who had been possessed with demons was healed. 37 Then all the people of the surrounding country of the Gerasenes[a] asked him to depart from them; for they were seized with great fear; so he got into the boat and returned. 38 The man from whom the demons had gone begged that he might be with him; but he sent him away, saying, 39 "Return to your home, and declare how much God has done for you." And he went away, proclaiming throughout the whole city how much Jesus had done for him.

40 Now when Jesus returned, the crowd welcomed him, for they were all waiting for him. 41 And there came a man named Jairus, who was a ruler of the synagogue; and falling at Jesus' feet he besought him to come to his house, 42 for he had an only daughter, about twelve years of age, and she was dying.

As he went, the people pressed round him. 43 And a woman who had had a flow of blood for twelve years[b] and could not be healed by any one, 44 came up behind him, and touched the fringe of his garment; and immediately her flow of blood ceased. 45 And Jesus said, "Who was it that touched me?" When all denied it, Peter[c]

[a] Other ancient authorities read *Gadarenes,* others *Gergesenes.* [b] Other ancient authorities add *and had spent all her living upon physicians.* [c] Other ancient authorities add *and those who were with him.*

Jerusalem Bible

When they came to Jesus they found the man from whom the devils had gone out sitting at the feet of Jesus, clothed and in his full senses; and they were afraid. 36 Those who had witnessed it told them how the man who had been possessed came to be healed. 37 The entire population of the Gerasene territory was in a state of panic and asked Jesus to leave them. So he got into the boat and went back.

38 The man from whom the devils had gone out asked to be allowed to stay with him, but he sent him away. 39 "Go back home," he said, "and report all that God has done for you." So the man went off and spread throughout the town all that Jesus had done for him.

Cure of the woman with a hemorrhage. Jairus' daughter raised to life

40 On his return Jesus was welcomed by the crowd, for they were all there waiting for him. 41 And now there came a man named Jairus, who was an official of the synagogue. He fell at Jesus' feet and pleaded with him to come to his house, 42 because he had an only daughter about twelve years old, who was dying. And the crowds were almost stifling Jesus as he went.

43 Now there was a woman suffering from a hemorrhage for twelve years, whom no one had been able to cure. 44 She came up behind him and touched the fringe of his cloak; and the hemorrhage stopped at that instant. 45 Jesus said, "Who touched me?" When they all denied

New English Bible

they came to Jesus, and found the man from whom the devils had gone out sitting at his feet clothed and in his right mind, they were afraid. The spectators told them how the madman had been cured. Then the whole population of the Gergesene[a] district asked him to go, for they were in the grip of a great fear. So he got into the boat and returned. The man from whom the devils had gone out begged leave to go with him; but Jesus sent him away: 'Go back home,' he said, 'and tell them everything that God has done for you.' The man went all over the town spreading the news of what Jesus had done for him.

When Jesus returned, the people welcomed him, for they were all expecting him. Then a man appeared—Jairus was his name and he was president of the synagogue. Throwing himself down at Jesus's feet he begged him to come to his house, because he had an only daughter, about twelve years old, who was dying. And while Jesus was on his way he could hardly breathe for the crowds.

Among them was a woman who had suffered from haemorrhages for twelve years; and [b] nobody had been able to cure her. She came up from behind and touched the edge of [c] his cloak, and at once her haemorrhage stopped. Jesus said, 'Who was it that touched me?' All dis-

[a] *Some witnesses read* Gerasene; *others read* Gadarene. [b] *Some witnesses add* though she had spent all she had on doctors. [c] *Some witnesses omit* the edge of.

King James Version

When all denied, Peter and they that were with
him said, Master, the multitude throng thee and
press *thee,* and sayest thou, Who touched me?
46And Jesus said, Somebody hath touched me:
for I perceive that virtue is gone out of me.
47And when the woman saw that she was not
hid, she came trembling, and falling down before him, she declared unto him before all the
people for what cause she had touched him, and
how she was healed immediately. 48And he said
unto her, Daughter, be of good comfort: thy
faith hath made thee whole; go in peace.
49 While he yet spake, there cometh one from
the ruler of the synagogue's *house,* saying to
him, Thy daughter is dead; trouble not the
Master. 50 But when Jesus heard *it,* he answered him, saying, Fear not: believe only, and
she shall be made whole. 51And when he came
into the house, he suffered no man to go in, save
Peter, and James, and John, and the father and
the mother of the maiden. 52And all wept, and
bewailed her: but he said, Weep not; she is not
dead, but sleepeth. 53And they laughed him to
scorn, knowing that she was dead. 54And he put
them all out, and took her by the hand, and
called, saying, Maid, arise. 55And her spirit
came again, and she arose straightway: and he
commanded to give her meat. 56And her parents

Living Bible

Everyone denied it, and Peter said, "Master,
so many are crowding against you . . ."
46 But Jesus told him, "No, it was someone
who deliberately touched me, for I felt healing
power go out from me."
47 When the woman realized that Jesus knew,
she began to tremble and fell to her knees before him and told why she had touched him and
that now she was well.
48 "Daughter," he said to her, "your faith
has healed you. Go in peace."
49 While he was still speaking to her, a
messenger arrived from the Jairus' home with
the news that the little girl was dead. "She's
gone," he told her father; "there's no use troubling the Teacher now."
50 But when Jesus heard what had happened,
he said to the father, "Don't be afraid! Just
trust me, and she'll be all right."
51 When they arrived at the house Jesus
wouldn't let anyone into the room except Peter,
James, John, and the little girl's father and
mother. 52 The home was filled with mourning
people, but he said, "Stop the weeping! She isn't
dead; she is only asleep!" 53 This brought scoffing and laughter, for they all knew she was
dead.
54 Then he took her by the hand and called,
"Get up, little girl!" 55And at that moment her
life returned and she jumped up! "Give her
something to eat!" he said. 56 Her parents were

Today's English Version

Everyone denied it, and Peter said, "Master,
the people are all around you and crowding in
on you."
46 But Jesus said, "Someone touched me, for
I knew it when power went out of me." 47 The
woman saw that she had been found out, so she
came, trembling, and threw herself at Jesus' feet.
There, in front of everybody, she told him why
she had touched him and how she had been
healed at once. 48 Jesus said to her, "My daughter, your faith has made you well. Go in peace."
49 While Jesus was saying this, a messenger
came from the official's house. "Your daughter
has died," he told Jairus: "don't bother the
Teacher any longer."
50 But Jesus heard it and said to Jairus,
"Don't be afraid; only believe, and she will be
well."
51 When he arrived at the house he would not
let anyone go in with him except Peter, John,
and James, and the child's father and mother.
52 Everyone there was crying and mourning for
the child. Jesus said, "Don't cry; the child is
not dead—she is only sleeping!"
53 They all made fun of him, because they
knew that she was dead. 54 But Jesus took her by
the hand and called out, "Get up, child!" 55 Her
life returned and she got up at once; and Jesus
ordered them to give her something to eat. 56 Her

New International Version

When they all denied it, Peter said, "Master,
the people are crowding and pressing against
you."
46 But Jesus said, "Someone touched me; I
know that power has gone out from me."
47 Then the woman, seeing that she could not
go unnoticed, came trembling and fell at his
feet. In the presence of all the people, she told
why she had touched him and how she had
been instantly healed. 48 Then he said to her,
"Daughter, your faith has healed you. Go in
peace."
49 While Jesus was still speaking, someone
came from the house of Jairus, the synagogue
ruler. "Your daughter is dead," he said. "Don't
bother the teacher any more."
50 Hearing this, Jesus said to Jairus, "Don't
be afraid; just believe, and she will be healed."
51 When he arrived at the house of Jairus,
he did not let anyone go in with him except
Peter, John and James, and the child's father
and mother. 52 Meanwhile, all the people were
wailing and mourning for her. "Stop wailing,"
Jesus said. "She is not dead but asleep."
53 They laughed at him, knowing that she was
dead. 54 But he took her by the hand and said,
"My child, get up!" 55 Her spirit returned, and
at once she stood up. Then Jesus told them to
give her something to eat. 56 Her parents were

Phillips Modern English

And when everybody denied it, Peter remonstrated,

"Master, the crowds are all round you and are pressing you on all sides. . . ."

But Jesus said,

"Somebody touched me, for I felt that power went out from me."

When the woman realised that she had not escaped notice she came forward trembling, and fell at his feet and admitted before everybody why she had had to touch him, and how she had been instantly cured.

"Daughter," said Jesus, "it is your faith that has healed you—go in peace."

While he was still speaking, somebody came from the synagogue president's house to say,

"Your daughter is dead—there is no need to trouble the master any further."

But when Jesus heard this, he said to him,

"Now don't be afraid, go on believing and she will be all right."

Then when he came to the house, he would not allow anyone to go in with him except Peter, John and James, and the child's parents. All those already there were weeping and wailing over her, but he said,

"Stop crying! She is not dead, she is fast asleep."

This drew a scornful laugh from them, for they were quite certain that she had died. But he took the little girl's hand and called out to her,

"Get up, my child!"

And her spirit came back and she got to her feet at once, and Jesus told them to give her some food. Her parents were nearly out of their

Revised Standard Version

said, "Master, the multitudes surround you and
press upon you!" 46 But Jesus said, "Some one
touched me; for I perceive that power has gone
forth from me." 47 And when the woman saw
that she was not hidden, she came trembling,
and falling down before him declared in the presence of all the people why she had touched him,
and how she had been immediately healed.
48 And he said to her, "Daughter, your faith has
made you well; go in peace."
49 While he was still speaking, a man from
the ruler's house came and said, "Your daughter
is dead; do not trouble the Teacher any more."
50 But Jesus on hearing this answered him, "Do
not fear; only believe, and she shall be well."
51 And when he came to the house, he permitted
no one to enter with him, except Peter and John
and James, and the father and mother of the
child. 52 And all were weeping and bewailing her;
but he said, "Do not weep; for she is not dead
but sleeping." 53 And they laughed at him, knowing that she was dead. 54 But taking her by the
hand he called, saying, "Child, arise." 55 And her
spirit returned, and she got up at once; and he
directed that something should be given her to
eat. 56 And her parents were amazed; but he

Jerusalem Bible

that they had, Peter and his companions said,
"Master, it is the crowds around you, pushing."
46 But Jesus said, "Somebody touched me. I felt
that power had gone out from me." 47 Seeing
herself discovered, the woman came forward
trembling, and falling at his feet explained in
front of all the people why she had touched him
and how she had been cured at that very moment. 48 "My daughter," he said, "your faith has
restored you to health; go in peace."
49 While he was still speaking, someone arrived from the house of the synagogue official to
say, "Your daughter has died. Do not trouble the
Master any further." 50 But Jesus had heard this,
and he spoke to the man, "Do not be afraid, only
have faith and she will be safe." 51 When he
came to the house he allowed no one to go in
with him except Peter and John and James, and
the child's father and mother. 52 They were all
weeping and mourning for her, but Jesus said,
"Stop crying; she is not dead, but asleep." 53 But
they laughed at him, knowing she was dead.
54 But taking her by the hand he called to her,
"Child, get up." 55 And her spirit returned and
she got up at once. Then he told them to give
her something to eat. 56 Her parents were aston-

New English Bible

claimed it, and Peter and his companions said, 'Master, the crowds are hemming you in and pressing upon you!' But Jesus said, 'Someone did touch me, for I felt that power had gone out from me.' Then the woman, seeing that she was detected, came trembling and fell at his feet. Before all the people she explained why she had touched him and how she had been instantly cured. He said to her, 'My daughter, your faith has cured you. Go in peace.'

While he was still speaking, a man came from the president's house with the message, 'Your daughter is dead; trouble the Rabbi no further.' But Jesus heard, and interposed. 'Do not be afraid,' he said; 'only show faith and she will be well again.' On arrival at the house he allowed no one to go in with him except Peter, John, and James, and the child's father and mother. And all were weeping and lamenting for her. He said, 'Weep no more; she is not dead: she is asleep'; and they only laughed at him, well knowing that she was dead. But Jesus took hold of her hand and called her: 'Get up, my child.' Her spirit returned, she stood up immediately, and he told them to give her something to eat. Her parents were astounded; but he

King James Version

were astonished: but he charged them that they
should tell no man what was done.

9 Then he called his twelve disciples together,
and gave them power and authority over all
devils, and to cure diseases. 2And he sent them
to preach the kingdom of God, and to heal the
sick. 3And he said unto them, Take nothing for
your journey, neither staves, nor scrip, neither
bread, neither money; neither have two coats
apiece. 4And whatsoever house ye enter into,
there abide, and thence depart. 5And whosoever
will not receive you, when ye go out of that
city, shake off the very dust from your feet for
a testimony against them. 6And they departed,
and went through the towns, preaching the
gospel, and healing every where.
7 Now Herod the tetrarch heard of all that
was done by him: and he was perplexed, because that it was said of some, that John was
risen from the dead; 8And of some, that Elias
had appeared; and of others, that one of the old
prophets was risen again. 9And Herod said,

Living Bible

overcome with happiness, but Jesus insisted that
they not tell anyone the details of what had happened.

9 One day Jesus called together his twelve
apostles and gave them authority over all
demons—power to cast them out—and to heal
all diseases. 2 Then he sent them away to tell
everyone about the coming of the Kingdom of
God and to heal the sick.
3 "Don't even take along a walking stick," he
instructed them, "nor a beggar's bag, nor food,
nor money. Not even an extra coat. 4 Be a guest
in only one home at each village.
5 "If the people of a town won't listen to you
when you enter it, turn around and leave, demonstrating God's anger against it[a] by shaking its
dust from your feet as you go."
6 So they began their circuit of the villages,
preaching the Good News and healing the sick.
7 When reports of Jesus' miracles reached
Herod, the governor,[b] he was worried and puzzled, for some were saying, "This is John the
Baptist come back to life again"; 8 and others,
"It is Elijah or some other ancient prophet risen
from the dead." These rumors were circulating
all over the land.
9 "I beheaded John," Herod said, "so who is

[*a*] Literally, "as a testimony against them." [*b*] Literally, "Herod the Tetrarch."

Today's English Version

parents were astounded, but Jesus commanded
them not to tell anyone what had happened.

Jesus sends out the twelve disciples

9 Jesus called the twelve disciples together
and gave them power and authority to drive
out all demons and to cure diseases. 2 Then he
sent them out to preach the Kingdom of God
and to heal the sick. 3 He said to them, "Take
nothing with you for the trip: no walking stick,
no beggar's bag, no food, no money, not even an
extra shirt. 4 Wherever you are welcomed, stay
in the same house until you leave that town;
5 wherever people don't welcome you, leave that
town and shake the dust off your feet as a warning to them."
6 The disciples left and traveled through all
the villages, preaching the Good News and healing people everywhere.

Herod's confusion

7 Herod, the ruler of Galilee, heard about all
the things that were happening; he was very confused about it because some people were saying,
"John the Baptist has come back to life!"
8 Others said that Elijah had appeared, while
others said that one of the prophets of long ago
had come back to life. 9 Herod said, "I had

New International Version

astonished, but he ordered them not to tell anyone what had happened.

Jesus sends out the Twelve

9 When Jesus had called the Twelve together,
he gave them power and authority to drive
out all demons and to cure diseases, 2 and he
sent them out to preach the kingdom of God
and to heal the sick. 3 He told them: "Take
nothing for the journey—no staff, no bag, no
bread, no money, no extra tunic. 4 Whatever
house you enter, stay there until you leave that
town. 5 If people do not welcome you, shake
the dust off your feet when you leave their town,
as a testimony against them." 6 So they set out
and went from village to village, preaching the
gospel and healing people everywhere.
7 Now Herod the tetrarch heard about all
that was going on. And he was perplexed, because some were saying that John had been
raised from the dead, 8 others that Elijah had
appeared, and still others that one of the prophets of long ago had come back to life. 9 But

Phillips Modern English

minds with joy, but Jesus told them not to tell anyone what had happened.

9.1 Jesus commissions the twelve to preach and heal

Then he called the twelve together and gave them power and authority over all evil spirits and the ability to heal disease. He sent them out to preach the kingdom of God and to heal the sick, with these words,

"Take nothing for your journey—neither a stick nor a purse nor food nor money, nor even extra clothes! When you come to stay at a house, remain there until you go on your way again. And where they will not welcome you, leave that town, and shake the dust off your feet as a protest against them!"

So they set out, and went from village to village preaching the gospel and healing people everywhere.

9.7 Herod's uneasy conscience after his execution of John

All these things came to the ears of Herod the tetrarch and caused him acute anxiety, because some people were saying that John had risen from the dead, some maintaining that the prophet Elijah had appeared, and others that one of the old-time prophets had come back.

"I beheaded John," said Herod. "Who can

Revised Standard Version

charged them to tell no one what had happened.

9 And he called the twelve together and gave
them power and authority over all demons
and to cure diseases, 2 and he sent them out to
preach the kingdom of God and to heal. 3 And he
said to them, "Take nothing for your journey, no
staff, nor bag, nor bread, nor money; and do not
have two tunics. 4 And whatever house you enter,
stay there, and from there depart. 5 And wherever
they do not receive you, when you leave that
town shake off the dust from your feet as a testimony against them." 6 And they departed and
went through the villages, preaching the gospel
and healing everywhere.
7 Now Herod the tetrarch heard of all that
was done, and he was perplexed, because it was
said by some that John had been raised from the
dead, 8 by some that Elijah had appeared, and
by others that one of the old prophets had risen.
9 Herod said, "John I beheaded; but who is this

Jerusalem Bible

ished, but he ordered them not to tell anyone what had happened.

The mission of the Twelve

9 He called the Twelve together and gave
them power and authority over all devils and
to cure diseases, 2 and he sent them out to proclaim the kingdom of God and to heal. 3 He
said to them, "Take nothing for the journey;
neither staff, nor haversack, nor bread, nor
money; and let none of you take a spare tunic.
4 Whatever house you enter, stay there; and
when you leave, let it be from there. 5 As for
those who do not welcome you, when you leave
their town shake the dust from your feet as a
sign to them." 6 So they set out and went from
village to village proclaiming the Good News and
healing everywhere.

Herod and Jesus

7 Meanwhile Herod the tetrarch had heard
about all that was going on; and he was puzzled,
because some people were saying that John had
risen from the dead, 8 others that Elijah had re-
appeared, still others that one of the ancient
prophets had come back to life. 9 But Herod

New English Bible

forbade them to tell anyone what had happened.

9 He now called the Twelve together and gave them power and authority to overcome all the devils and to cure diseases, and sent them to proclaim the kingdom of God and to heal. 'Take nothing for the journey,' he told them, 'neither stick nor pack, neither bread nor money; nor are you each to have a second coat. When you are admitted to a house, stay there, and go on from there. As for those who will not receive you, when you leave their town shake the dust off your feet as a warning to them.' So they set out and travelled from village to village, and everywhere they told the good news and healed the sick.

Now Prince Herod heard of all that was happening, and did not know what to make of it: for some were saying that John had been raised from the dead, others that Elijah had appeared, others again that one of the old prophets had come back to life. Herod said, 'As for John, I

King James Version

John have I beheaded; but who is this, of whom I hear such things? And he desired to see him.

10 And the apostles, when they were returned, told him all that they had done. And he took them, and went aside privately into a desert place belonging to the city called Bethsaida. 11 And the people, when they knew *it*, followed him: and he received them, and spake unto them of the kingdom of God, and healed them that had need of healing. 12 And when the day began to wear away, then came the twelve, and said unto him, Send the multitude away, that they may go into the towns and country round about, and lodge, and get victuals: for we are here in a desert place. 13 But he said unto them, Give ye them to eat. And they said, We have no more but five loaves and two fishes; except we should go and buy meat for all this people. 14 For they were about five thousand men. And he said to

Living Bible

this man about whom I hear such strange stories?" And he tried to see him.

10 After the apostles returned to Jesus and reported what they had done, he slipped quietly away with them toward the city of Bethsaida. 11 But the crowds found out where he was going, and followed. And he welcomed them, teaching them again about the Kingdom of God and curing those who were ill.

12 Late in the afternoon all twelve of the disciples came and urged him to send the people away to the nearby villages and farms, to find food and lodging for the night. "For there is nothing to eat here in this deserted spot," they said.

13 But Jesus replied, "*You* feed them!"

"Why, we have only five loaves of bread and two fish among the lot of us," they protested; "or are you expecting us to go and buy enough for this whole mob?" 14 For there were about 5,000 men there!

"Just tell them to sit down on the ground in

Today's English Version

John's head cut off; but who is this man I hear these things about?" And he kept trying to see Jesus.

Jesus feeds the five thousand

10 The apostles came back and told Jesus everything they had done. He took them with him and they went off by themselves to a town named Bethsaida. 11 When the crowds heard about it they followed him. He welcomed them, spoke to them about the Kingdom of God, and healed those who needed it.

12 When the sun had begun to set, the twelve disciples came to him and said, "Send the people away so they can go to the villages and farms around here and find food and lodging, because this is a lonely place."

13 But Jesus said to them, "You yourselves give them something to eat."

They answered, "All we have is five loaves and two fish. Do you want us to go and buy food for this whole crowd?" 14 (There were about five thousand men there.)

Jesus said to his disciples, "Make the people

New International Version

Herod said, "I beheaded John. Who, then, is this I hear such things about?" And he tried to see him.

Jesus feeds the five thousand

10 When the apostles returned, they reported to Jesus what they had done. Then he took them with him and they withdrew by themselves to a town called Bethsaida, 11 but the crowds learned about it and followed him. He welcomed them and spoke to them about the kingdom of God, and healed those who needed healing.

12 Late in the afternoon the Twelve came to him and said, "Send the crowd away so they can go to the surrounding villages and countryside and find food and lodging, because we are in a remote place here."

13 He replied, "You give them something to eat."

They answered, "We have only five loaves of bread and two fish—unless we go and buy food for all this crowd." 14 (About five thousand men were there.)

But he said to his disciples, "Have them sit

Phillips Modern English

this be that I hear all these things about?"
And he tried to find a way of seeing Jesus.

9.10 The twelve return and tell their story

Then the apostles returned, and when they had made their report to Jesus of what they had done, he took them with him privately and retired into a town called Bethsaida.

9.11 Jesus welcomes the crowds, teaches, heals and feeds them

But the crowds observed this and followed him. And he welcomed them and talked to them about the kingdom of God, and cured those who were in need of healing. As the day drew to its close the twelve came to him and said,

"Please dismiss the crowd now so that they can go to the villages and farms round about and find some food and shelter, for we're quite in the wilds here."

"You give them something to eat!" returned Jesus.

"But we've nothing here," they replied, "except five loaves and two fish, unless you want us to go and buy food for all this crowd?" (There were approximately five thousand men there.)

Then Jesus said to the disciples,

Revised Standard Version

about whom I hear such things?" And he sought
to see him.
10 On their return the apostles told him what
they had done. And he took them and withdrew
apart to a city called Bethsaida. 11 When the
crowds learned it, they followed him; and he
welcomed them and spoke to them of the kingdom of God, and cured those who had need of
healing. 12 Now the day began to wear away;
and the twelve came and said to him, "Send
the crowd away, to go into the villages and country round about, to lodge and get provisions; for
we are here in a lonely place." 13 But he said
to them, "You give them something to eat."
They said, "We have no more than five loaves
and two fish—unless we are to go and buy food
for all these people." 14 For there were about
five thousand men. And he said to his disciples,

Jerusalem Bible

said, "John? I beheaded him. So who is this I hear such reports about?" And he was anxious to see him.

The return of the apostles. Miracle of the loaves

10 On their return the apostles gave him an
account of all they had done. Then he took
them with him and withdrew to a town called
Bethsaida where they could be by themselves.
11 But the crowds got to know and they went
after him. He made them welcome and talked
to them about the kingdom of God; and he
cured those who were in need of healing.
12 It was late afternoon when the Twelve
came to him and said, "Send the people away,
and they can go to the villages and farms around
about to find lodging and food; for we are in a
lonely place here." 13 He replied, "Give them
something to eat yourselves." But they said, "We
have no more than five loaves and two fish, unless we are to go ourselves and buy food for all
these people." 14 For there were about five
thousand men. But he said to his disciples, "Get

New English Bible

beheaded him myself; but who is this I hear such talk about?' And he was anxious to see him.

On their return the apostles told Jesus all they had done; and he took them with him and withdrew privately to a town called Bethsaida. But the crowds found out and followed him. He welcomed them, and spoke to them about the kingdom of God, and cured those who were in need of healing. When evening was drawing on, the Twelve came up to him and said, 'Send these people away; then they can go into the villages and farms round about to find food and lodging; for we are in a lonely place here.' 'Give them something to eat yourselves', he replied. But they said, 'All we have is five loaves and two fishes, nothing more—unless perhaps we ourselves are to go and buy provisions for all this company.' (There were about five thousand men.) He said to his disciples, 'Make them sit

King James Version

his disciples, Make them sit down by fifties in a
company. 15 And they did so, and made them all
sit down. 16 Then he took the five loaves and the
two fishes, and looking up to heaven, he blessed
them, and brake, and gave to the disciples to
set before the multitude. 17 And they did eat, and
were all filled: and there was taken up of fragments that remained to them twelve baskets.
18 And it came to pass, as he was alone praying, his disciples were with him; and he asked
them, saying, Whom say the people that I am?
19 They answering said, John the Baptist; but
some *say*, Elias; and others *say*, that one of the
old prophets is risen again. 20 He said unto
them, But whom say ye that I am? Peter answering said, The Christ of God. 21 And he

Living Bible

groups of about fifty each," Jesus replied. 15 So
they did.
16 Jesus took the five loaves and two fish and
looked up into the sky and gave thanks; then he
broke off pieces for his disciples to set before the
crowd. 17 And everyone ate and ate; still, twelve
basketfuls of scraps were picked up afterwards!
18 One day as he was alone, praying, with
his disciples nearby, he came over and asked
them, "Who are the people saying I am?"
19 "John the Baptist," they told him, "or perhaps Elijah or one of the other ancient prophets
risen from the dead."
20 Then he asked them, "Who do you think
I am?"
Peter replied, "The Messiah—the Christ of
God!"
21 He gave them strict orders not to speak

Today's English Version

sit down in groups of about fifty each."
15 The disciples did so and made them all sit
down. 16 Jesus took the five loaves and two fish,
looked up to heaven, thanked God for them,
broke them, and gave them to the disciples to distribute to the people. 17 They all ate and had
enough; and the disciples took up twelve baskets
of what the people left over.

Peter's declaration about Jesus

18 One time when Jesus was praying alone,
the disciples came to him. "Who do the crowds
say I am?" he asked them.
19 "Some say that you are John the Baptist,"
they answered. "Others say that you are Elijah,
while others say that one of the prophets of long
ago has come back to life."
20 "What about you?" he asked them. "Who
do you say I am?"
Peter answered, "You are God's Messiah."

Jesus speaks about his suffering and death

21 Then Jesus gave them strict orders not to

New International Version

down in groups of about fifty each." 15 The disciples did so, and everybody sat down. 16 Taking
the five loaves and the two fish and looking up
to heaven, he gave thanks and broke them. Then
he gave them to the disciples to set before the
people. 17 They all ate and were satisfied, and
the disciples picked up twelve basketfuls of
broken pieces that were left over.

Peter's confession of Christ

18 Once when Jesus was praying in private
and his disciples were with him, he asked them,
"Who do the crowds say I am?"
19 They replied, "Some say John the Baptist;
others say Elijah; and still others, that one of
the prophets of long ago has come back to life."
20 "But what about you?" he asked. "Who
do you say I am?"
Peter answered, "The Christ[h] of God."
21 Jesus strictly warned them not to tell this

[*h*] Or *Messiah*.

Phillips Modern English

"Get them to sit down in groups of about fifty."

This they did, making them all sit down. Then he took the five loaves and the two fish and looked up to Heaven, blessed them, broke them into pieces and passed them to his disciples to serve to the crowd. Everybody ate and was satisfied. Afterwards they collected twelve baskets full of broken pieces which were left over.

9.18 Jesus asks a question and receives Peter's momentous answer

Then came this incident. While Jesus was praying by himself, having only the disciples near him, he asked them this question:

"Who are the crowd saying that I am?"

"Some say that you are John the Baptist," they replied. "Others that you are Elijah, and others think that one of the old-time prophets has come back to life."

Then he said,

"And who do you say that I am?"

"God's Christ!" said Peter.

9.21 Jesus foretells his own suffering: the paradox of losing life to find it

But Jesus expressly told them not to say a

Revised Standard Version

"Make them sit down in companies, about fifty
each." 15And they did so, and made them all
sit down. 16And taking the five loaves and the
two fish he looked up to heaven, and blessed and
broke them, and gave them to the disciples to
set before the crowd. 17And all ate and were
satisfied. And they took up what was left over,
twelve baskets of broken pieces.
18 Now it happened that as he was praying
alone the disciples were with him; and he asked
them, "Who do the people say that I am?"
19And they answered, "John the Baptist; but
others say, Elijah; and others, that one of the
old prophets has risen." 20And he said to them,
"But who do you say that I am?" And Peter
answered, "The Christ of God." 21 But he

Jerusalem Bible

them to sit down in parties of about fifty."
15 They did so and made them all sit down.
16 Then he took the five loaves and the two fish,
raised his eyes to heaven, and said the blessing
over them; then he broke them and handed them
to his disciples to distribute among the crowd.
17 They all ate as much as they wanted, and
when the scraps remaining were collected they
filled twelve baskets.

Peter's profession of faith

18 Now one day when he was praying alone
in the presence of his disciples he put this question to them, "Who do the crowds say I am?"
19And they answered, "John the Baptist; others
Elijah; and others say one of the ancient prophets
come back to life." 20 "But you," he said, "who
do you say I am?" It was Peter who spoke up.
"The Christ of God," he said. 21 But he gave

New English Bible

down in groups of fifty or so.' They did so and got them all seated. Then, taking the five loaves and the two fishes, he looked up to heaven, said the blessing over them, broke them, and gave them to the disciples to distribute to the people. They all ate to their hearts' content; and when the scraps they left were picked up, they filled twelve great baskets.

One day when he was praying alone in the presence of his disciples, he asked them, 'Who do the people say I am?' They answered, 'Some say John the Baptist, others Elijah, others that one of the old prophets has come back to life.' 'And you,' he said, 'who do you say I am?' Peter answered, 'God's Messiah.' Then he gave them

King James Version

straitly charged them, and commanded *them* to
tell no man that thing; 22 Saying, The Son of
man must suffer many things, and be rejected of
the elders and chief priests and scribes, and be
slain, and be raised the third day.
23 And he said to *them* all, If any *man* will
come after me, let him deny himself, and take
up his cross daily, and follow me. 24 For whosoever will save his life shall lose it: but whosoever will lose his life for my sake, the same shall
save it. 25 For what is a man advantaged, if he
gain the whole world, and lose himself, or be
cast away? 26 For whosoever shall be ashamed
of me and of my words, of him shall the Son of
man be ashamed, when he shall come in his own
glory, and *in his* Father's, and of the holy angels.
27 But I tell you of a truth, there be some standing here, which shall not taste of death, till they
see the kingdom of God.

Living Bible

of this to anyone. 22 "For I, the Messiah,[c] must
suffer much," he said, "and be rejected by the
Jewish leaders—the elders, chief priests, and
teachers of the Law—and be killed; and three
days later I will come back to life again!"
23 Then he said to all, "Anyone who wants to
follow me must put aside his own desires and
conveniences and carry his cross with him every
day and *keep close to me!* 24 Whoever loses his
life for my sake will save it, but whoever insists
on keeping his life will lose it; 25 and what profit
is there in gaining the whole world when it
means forfeiting one's self?
26 "When I, the Messiah,[d] come in my glory
and in the glory of the Father and the holy
angels, I will be ashamed then of all who are
ashamed of me and of my words now. 27 But
this is the simple truth—some of you who are
standing here right now will not die until you
have seen the Kingdom of God."

[*c*] Literally, "the Son of Man." [*d*] Literally, "the Son of Man."

Today's English Version

tell this to anyone, 22 and added, "The Son of
Man must suffer much, and be rejected by the
elders, the chief priests, and the teachers of the
Law. He will be put to death, and be raised to
life on the third day."
23 And he said to all, "If anyone wants to
come with me, he must forget himself, take up
his cross every day, and follow me. 24 For whoever wants to save his own life will lose it; but
whoever loses his life for my sake will save it.
25 Will a man gain anything if he wins the whole
world but is himself lost or defeated? Of course
not! 26 If a man is ashamed of me and of my
teaching, then the Son of Man will be ashamed
of him when he comes in his glory and the glory
of the Father and of the holy angels. 27 Remember this! There are some here, I tell you, who
will not die until they have seen the Kingdom of
God."

New International Version

to anyone. 22 And he said, "The Son of Man
must suffer many things and be rejected by the
elders, chief priests and teachers of the law, and
he must be killed and on the third day be raised
to life."
23 Then he said to them all: "If anyone
would come after me, he must deny himself and
take up his cross daily and follow me. 24 For
whoever wants to save his life will lose it, but
whoever loses his life for me will save it. 25 What
good is it for a man to gain the whole world,
and yet lose or forfeit his very self? 26 If anyone is ashamed of me and my words, the Son
of Man will be ashamed of him when he comes
in his glory and in the glory of the Father and
of the holy angels. 27 I tell you the truth, some
who are standing here will not taste death before they see the kingdom of God."

Phillips Modern English

word to anybody, at the same time warning them of the inevitability of the Son of Man's great suffering, of his repudiation by the elders, chief priests and scribes, and of his death and of being raised to life again on the third day. Then he spoke to them all:

"If anyone wants to follow in my footsteps, he must give up all right to himself, carry his cross every day and keep close behind me. For the man who wants to save his life will lose it, but the man who loses his life for my sake will save it. For what is the use of a man gaining the whole world if he loses or forfeits his own soul? If anyone is ashamed of me and my words, the Son of Man will be ashamed of him, when he comes in his glory and the glory of the Father and the holy angels. I tell you the simple truth—there are men standing here today who will not taste death until they have seen the kingdom of God!"

Revised Standard Version

charged and commanded them to tell this to no
one, 22 saying, "The Son of man must suffer
many things, and be rejected by the elders and
chief priests and scribes, and be killed, and on
the third day be raised."
23 And he said to all, "If any man would
come after me, let him deny himself and take
up his cross daily and follow me. 24 For whoever
would save his life will lose it; and whoever loses
his life for my sake, he will save it. 25 For what
does it profit a man if he gains the whole world
and loses or forfeits himself? 26 For whoever is
ashamed of me and of my words, of him will
the Son of man be ashamed when he comes in
his glory and the glory of the Father and of
the holy angels. 27 But I tell you truly, there
are some standing here who will not taste death
before they see the kingdom of God."

Jerusalem Bible

them strict orders not to tell anyone anything about this.

First prophecy of the Passion

22 "The Son of Man," he said, "is destined to suffer grievously, to be rejected by the elders and chief priests and scribes and to be put to death, and to be raised up on the third day."

The condition of following Christ

23 Then to all he said, "If anyone wants to be
a follower of mine, let him renounce himself and
take up his cross every day and follow me. 24 For
anyone who wants to save his life will lose it;
but anyone who loses his life for my sake, that
man will save it. 25 What gain, then, is it for a
man to have won the whole world and to have
lost or ruined his very self? 26 For if anyone is
ashamed of me and of my words, of him the
Son of Man will be ashamed when he comes in
his own glory and in the glory of the Father and
the holy angels.

The kingdom will come soon

27 "I tell you truly, there are some standing here who will not taste death before they see the kingdom of God."

New English Bible

strict orders not to tell this to anyone. And he said, 'The Son of Man has to undergo great sufferings, and to be rejected by the elders, chief priests, and doctors of the law, to be put to death and to be raised again on the third day.'

And to all he said, 'If anyone wishes to be a follower of mine, he must leave self behind; day after day he must take up his cross, and come with me. Whoever cares for his own safety is lost; but if a man will let himself be lost for my sake, that man is safe. What will a man gain by winning the whole world, at the cost of his true self? For whoever is ashamed of me and mine,[a] the Son of Man will be ashamed of him, when he comes in his glory and the glory of the Father and the holy angels. And I tell you this: there are some of those standing here who will not taste death before they have seen the kingdom of God.'

[a] *Some witnesses read* me and my words.

King James Version

28 And it came to pass about an eight days
after these sayings, he took Peter and John and
James, and went up into a mountain to pray.
29And as he prayed, the fashion of his countenance was altered, and his raiment *was* white
and glistering. 30And, behold, there talked with
him two men, which were Moses and Elias:
31 Who appeared in glory, and spake of his
decease which he should accomplish at Jerusalem. 32 But Peter and they that were with him
were heavy with sleep: and when they were
awake, they saw his glory, and the two men that
stood with him. 33And it came to pass, as they
departed from him, Peter said unto Jesus, Master, it is good for us to be here: and let us make
three tabernacles; one for thee, and one for
Moses, and one for Elias: not knowing what he
said. 34 While he thus spake, there came a cloud,
and overshadowed them: and they feared as
they entered into the cloud. 35And there came a
voice out of the cloud, saying, This is my beloved Son: hear him. 36And when the voice
was past, Jesus was found alone. And they kept
it close, and told no man in those days any of
those things which they had seen.

Living Bible

28 Eight days later he took Peter, James, and
John with him into the hills to pray. 29And as
he was praying, his face began to shine,[e] and his
clothes became dazzling white and blazed with
light. 30 Then two men appeared and began
talking with him—Moses and Elijah! 31 They
were splendid in appearance, glorious to see; and
they were speaking of his death at Jerusalem, to
be carried out in accordance with God's plan.
32 Peter and the others had been very drowsy
and had fallen asleep. Now they woke up and
saw Jesus covered with brightness and glory, and
the two men standing with him. 33As Moses and
Elijah were starting to leave, Peter, all confused
and not even knowing what he was saying,
blurted out, "Master, this is wonderful! We'll put
up three shelters—one for you and one for
Moses and one for Elijah!"
34 But even as he was saying this, a bright[f]
cloud formed above them; and terror gripped
them as it covered them. 35And a voice from
the cloud said, "*This* is my Son, my Chosen One;
listen to *him*."
36 Then, as the voice died away, Jesus was
there alone with his disciples. They didn't tell
anyone what they had seen until long afterwards.

[e] Literally, "the appearance of his face changed."
[f] Implied.

Today's English Version

The transfiguration

28 About a week after he had said these
things, Jesus took Peter, John, and James with
him and went up a hill to pray. 29 While he was
praying, his face changed its appearance and
his clothes became dazzling white. 30 Suddenly
two men were there talking with him. They were
Moses and Elijah, 31 who appeared in heavenly
glory and talked with Jesus about how he would
soon fulfill God's purpose by dying in Jerusalem.
32 Peter and his companions were sound asleep,
but they awoke and saw Jesus' glory and the two
men who were standing with him. 33As the men
were leaving Jesus, Peter said to him, "Master,
it is a good thing that we are here. We will make
three tents, one for you, one for Moses, and one
for Elijah." (He really did not know what he
was saying.)
34 While he was still speaking, a cloud appeared and covered them with its shadow; and
the disciples were afraid as the cloud came over
them. 35A voice said from the cloud, "This is
my Son, whom I have chosen—listen to him!"
36 When the voice stopped, there was Jesus
all alone. The disciples kept quiet about all this,
and told no one at that time anything they had
seen.

New International Version

The transfiguration

28 About eight days after Jesus said this, he
took Peter, John and James with him and went
up onto a mountain to pray. 29As he was praying, the appearance of his face changed, and
his clothes became as bright as a flash of lightning. 30 Two men, Moses and Elijah, 31 appeared
in glorious splendor, talking with Jesus. They
spoke about his departure, which he was about
to bring to fulfillment at Jerusalem. 32 Peter and
his companions were very sleepy, but when they
became fully awake, they saw his glory and the
two men standing with him. 33As the men were
leaving Jesus, Peter said to him, "Master, it is
good for us to be here. Let us put up three
shelters[i]—one for you, one for Moses and one
for Elijah." (He did not know what he was
saying.)
34 While he was speaking, a cloud appeared
and enveloped them, and they were afraid as
they entered the cloud. 35A voice came from
the cloud, saying, "This is my Son whom I have
chosen; listen to him." 36 When the voice had
spoken, they found that Jesus was alone. The
disciples kept this to themselves, and told no
one at that time what they had seen.

[i] Or *sanctuaries.*

Phillips Modern English

9.28 Peter, John and James are allowed to see the glory of Jesus

About eight days after these sayings, Jesus took Peter, James and John and went off with them to the hill-side to pray. And then, while he was praying, the whole appearance of his face changed and his clothes became white and dazzling. Suddenly two men could be seen talking with Jesus. They were Moses and Elijah—revealed in heavenly splendour, and their talk was about the way he must take and the end he must fulfil in Jerusalem. But Peter and his companions had been overcome by sleep and it was as they struggled into wakefulness that they saw the glory of Jesus and the two men standing with him. Just as they were parting from him, Peter said to Jesus,

"Master, it is wonderful for us to be here! Let us put up three shelters—one for you, one for Moses and one for Elijah." But he did not know what he was saying. While he was still talking, a cloud overshadowed them and awe swept over them as it enveloped them. A voice came out of the cloud, saying,

"This is my Son, my chosen! Listen to him!"

But when the voice had spoken, they found no one there but Jesus. The disciples were reduced to silence, and in those days never breathed a word to anyone of what they had seen.

Revised Standard Version

28 Now about eight days after these sayings
he took with him Peter and John and James,
and went up on the mountain to pray. 29And
as he was praying, the appearance of his countenance was altered, and his raiment became
dazzling white. 30And behold, two men talked
with him, Moses and Elijah, 31 who appeared in
glory and spoke of his departure, which he was
to accomplish at Jerusalem. 32 Now Peter and
those who were with him were heavy with sleep,
and when they wakened they saw his glory and
the two men who stood with him. 33And as the
men were parting from him, Peter said to Jesus,
"Master, it is well that we are here; let us make
three booths, one for you and one for Moses
and one for Elijah"—not knowing what he said.
34As he said this, a cloud came and overshadowed them; and they were afraid as they
entered the cloud. 35And a voice came out of
the cloud, saying, "This is my Son, my Chosen;[d]
listen to him!" 36And when the voice had
spoken, Jesus was found alone. And they kept
silence and told no one in those days anything
of what they had seen.

[*d*] Other ancient authorities read *my Beloved*.

Jerusalem Bible

The transfiguration

28 Now about eight days after this had been
said, he took with him Peter and John and James
and went up the mountain to pray. 29 As he
prayed, the aspect of his face was changed and
his clothing became brilliant as lightning. 30 Suddenly there were two men there talking to him;
they were Moses and Elijah 31 appearing in
glory, and they were speaking of his passing
which he was to accomplish in 32 Jerusalem.
Peter and his companions were heavy with sleep,
but they kept awake and saw his glory and the
two men standing with him. 33As these were
leaving him, Peter said to Jesus, "Master, it is
wonderful for us to be here; so let us make three
tents, one for you, one for Moses and one for
Elijah."—He did not know what he was saying.
34As he spoke, a cloud came and covered them
with shadow; and when they went into the cloud
the disciples were afraid. 35And a voice came
from the cloud saying, "This is my Son, the
Chosen One. Listen to him." 36And after the
voice had spoken, Jesus was found alone. The
disciples kept silence and, at that time, told no
one what they had seen.

New English Bible

About eight days after this conversation he took Peter, John, and James with him and went up into the hills to pray. And while he was praying the appearance of his face changed and his clothes became dazzling white. Suddenly there were two men talking with him; these were Moses and Elijah, who appeared in glory and spoke of his departure, the destiny he was to fulfil in Jerusalem. Meanwhile Peter and his companions had been in a deep sleep; but when they awoke, they saw his glory and the two men who stood beside him. And as these were moving away from Jesus, Peter said to him, 'Master, how good it is that we are here! Shall we make three shelters, one for you, one for Moses, and one for Elijah?'; but he spoke without knowing what he was saying. The words were still on his lips, when there came a cloud which cast a shadow over them; they were afraid as they entered the cloud, and from it came a voice: 'This is my Son, my Chosen; listen to him.' When the voice had spoken, Jesus was seen to be alone. The disciples kept silence and at that time told nobody anything of what they had seen.

King James Version

37 And it came to pass, that on the next day, when they were come down from the hill, much people met him. 38And, behold, a man of the company cried out, saying, Master, I beseech thee, look upon my son; for he is mine only child. 39And, lo, a spirit taketh him, and he suddenly crieth out; and it teareth him that he foameth again, and bruising him, hardly departeth from him. 40And I besought thy disciples to cast him out; and they could not. 41And Jesus answering said, O faithless and perverse generation, how long shall I be with you, and suffer you? Bring thy son hither. 42And as he was yet a coming, the devil threw him down, and tare *him*. And Jesus rebuked the unclean spirit, and healed the child, and delivered him again to his father.

43 And they were all amazed at the mighty power of God. But while they wondered every one at all things which Jesus did, he said unto his disciples, 44 Let these sayings sink down into your ears: for the Son of man shall be delivered into the hands of men. 45 But they understood not this saying, and it was hid from

Living Bible

37 The next day as they descended from the hill, a huge crowd met him, 38 and a man in the crowd called out to him, "Teacher, this boy here is my only son, 39 and a demon keeps seizing him, making him scream; and it throws him into convulsions so that he foams at the mouth; it is always hitting him and hardly ever leaves him alone. 40 I begged your disciples to cast the demon out, but they couldn't."

41 "O you stubborn faithless people," Jesus said [to his disciples[f]], "how long should I put up with you? Bring him here."

42 As the boy was coming the demon knocked him to the ground and threw him into a violent convulsion. But Jesus ordered the demon to come out, and healed the boy and handed him over to his father.

43 Awe gripped the people as they saw this display of the power of God.

Meanwhile, as they were exclaiming over all the wonderful things he was doing, Jesus said to his disciples, 44 "Listen to me and remember what I say. I, the Messiah,[d] am going to be betrayed." 45 But the disciples didn't know what

[*f*] Implied. [*d*] Literally, "the Son of Man."

Today's English Version

Jesus heals a boy with an evil spirit

37 The next day they went down from the hill, and a large crowd met Jesus. 38A man shouted from the crowd, "Teacher! Look, I beg you, at my son—my only son! 39A spirit attacks him with a sudden shout and throws him into a fit, so that he foams at the mouth; it keeps on hurting him and will hardly let him go! 40 I begged your disciples to drive it out, but they couldn't."

41 Jesus answered, "How unbelieving and wrong you people are! How long must I stay with you? How long do I have to put up with you?" Then he said to the man, "Bring your son here."

42 As the boy was coming, the demon knocked him to the ground and threw him into a fit. Jesus gave a command to the evil spirit, healed the boy, and gave him back to his father. 43All the people were amazed at the mighty power of God.

Jesus speaks again about his death

The people were still marveling at everything Jesus was doing, when he said to his disciples, 44 "Don't forget what I am about to tell you! The Son of Man is going to be handed over to the power of men." 45 But they did not know

New International Version

The healing of a boy with an evil spirit

37 The next day, when they came down from the mountain, a large crowd met him. 38A man in the crowd called out, "Teacher, I beg you to look at my son, for he is my only child. 39A spirit seizes him and he suddenly screams; it throws him into convulsions so that he foams at the mouth. It scarcely ever leaves him and is destroying him. 40 I begged your disciples to drive it out, but they could not."

41 "O unbelieving and perverse generation," Jesus replied, "how long shall I stay with you and put up with you? Bring your son here."

42 Even while the boy was coming, the demon threw him to the ground in a convulsion. But Jesus rebuked the evil[j] spirit, healed the boy and gave him back to his father. 43And they were all amazed at the greatness of God.

While everyone was marveling at all that Jesus did, he said to his disciples, 44 "Listen carefully to what I am about to tell you: The Son of Man is going to be betrayed into the hands of men." 45 But they did not understand what

[*j*] Greek *unclean*.

Phillips Modern English

9.37 Jesus heals an epileptic boy

Then on the following day, as they came down the hill-side, a great crowd met him. Suddenly a man from the crowd shouted out,

"Master, please come and look at my son! He's my only child, and without any warning some spirit gets hold of him and he calls out suddenly. Then it convulses him until he foams at the mouth, and only after a fearful struggle does it go away and leave him bruised all over. I begged your disciples to get rid of it, but they couldn't."

"You really are an unbelieving and difficult people," replied Jesus. "How long must I be with you, how long must I put up with you? Bring him here to me."

But even while the boy was on his way, the spirit hurled him to the ground in a dreadful convulsion. Then Jesus reprimanded the evil spirit, healed the lad and handed him back to his father. And everybody present was amazed at this demonstration of the power of God.

9.43b The realism of Jesus in the midst of enthusiasm

And while everybody was full of wonder at all the things they saw him do, Jesus was saying to the disciples,

"Store up in your minds what I tell you nowadays, for the Son of Man is going to be handed over to the power of men."

But they made no sense of this saying—some-

Revised Standard Version

37 On the next day, when they had come
down from the mountain, a great crowd met
him. 38 And behold, a man from the crowd
cried, "Teacher, I beg you to look upon my son,
for he is my only child; 39 and behold, a spirit
seizes him, and he suddenly cries out; it convulses him till he foams, and shatters him, and
will hardly leave him. 40 And I begged your
disciples to cast it out, but they could not."
41 Jesus answered, "O faithless and perverse
generation, how long am I to be with you and
bear with you? Bring your son here." 42 While
he was coming, the demon tore him and convulsed him. But Jesus rebuked the unclean spirit, and healed the boy, and gave him back to his
father. 43 And all were astonished at the majesty
of God.

But while they were all marveling at everything
he did, he said to his disciples, 44 "Let these
words sink into your ears; for the Son of man
is to be delivered into the hands of men." 45 But
they did not understand this saying, and it was

Jerusalem Bible

The epileptic demoniac

37 Now on the following day when they were coming down from the mountain a large crowd
came to meet him. 38 Suddenly a man in the
crowd cried out, "Master," he said, "I implore you to look at my son: he is my only child.
39 All at once a spirit will take hold of him, and give a sudden cry and throw the boy into convulsions with foaming at the mouth; it is slow to leave him, but when it does it leaves the boy
worn out. 40 I begged your disciples to cast it
out, and they could not." 41 "Faithless and perverse generation!" Jesus said in reply. "How much longer must I be among you and put up
with you? Bring your son here." 42 The boy was
still moving toward Jesus when the devil threw him to the ground in convulsions. But Jesus rebuked the unclean spirit and cured the boy and
gave him back to his father, 43 and everyone was
awestruck by the greatness of God.

Second prophecy of the Passion

At a time when everyone was full of admiration for all he did, he said to his disciples,
44 "For your part, you must have these words constantly in your mind: The Son of Man is going to be handed over into the power of men."
45 But they did not understand him when he said

New English Bible

Next day when they came down from the hills he was met by a large crowd. All at once there was a shout from a man in the crowd: 'Master, look at my son, I implore you, my only child. From time to time a spirit seizes him, gives a sudden scream, and throws him into convulsions with foaming at the mouth, and it keeps on mauling him and will hardly let him go. I asked your disciples to cast it out, but they could not.' Jesus answered, 'What an unbelieving and perverse generation! How long shall I be with you and endure you all? Bring your son here.' But before the boy could reach him the devil dashed him to the ground and threw him into convulsions. Jesus rebuked the unclean spirit, cured the boy, and gave him back to his father. And they were all struck with awe at the majesty of God.

Amid the general wonder and admiration at all he was doing, Jesus said to his disciples, 'What I now say is for you: ponder my words. The Son of Man is to be given up into the power of men.' But they did not understand this saying;

King James Version

them, that they perceived it not: and they feared to ask him of that saying.
46 Then there arose a reasoning among them, which of them should be greatest. 47And Jesus, perceiving the thought of their heart, took a child, and set him by him, 48And said unto them, Whosoever shall receive this child in my name receiveth me; and whosoever shall receive me, receiveth him that sent me: for he that is least among you all, the same shall be great.
49 And John answered and said, Master, we saw one casting out devils in thy name; and we forbade him, because he followeth not with us.
50And Jesus said unto him, Forbid *him* not: for he that is not against us is for us.

Living Bible

he meant, for their minds had been sealed and they were afraid to ask him.
46 Now came an argument among them as to which of them would be greatest [in the coming Kingdom[f]]! 47 But Jesus knew their thoughts, so he stood a little child beside him 48 and said to them, "Anyone who takes care of a little child like this is caring for me! And whoever cares for me is caring for God who sent me. Your care for others is the measure of your greatness." 49 His disciple John came to him and said, "Master, we saw someone using your name to cast out demons. And we told him not to. After all, he isn't in our group."
50 But Jesus said, "You shouldn't have done that! For anyone who is not against you is for you."

[*f*] Implied.

Today's English Version

what this meant. It had been hidden from them so that they could not understand it, and they were afraid to ask him about the matter.

Who is the greatest?

46 An argument came up among the disciples as to which one of them was the greatest. 47 Jesus knew what they were thinking, so he took a child, stood him by his side, 48 and said to them, "Whoever in my name welcomes this child, welcomes me; and whoever welcomes me, also welcomes the one who sent me. For he who is least among you all is the greatest."

Who is not against you is for you

49 John spoke up, "Master, we saw a man driving out demons in your name, and we told him to stop, because he doesn't belong to our group."
50 "Do not try to stop him," Jesus said to him and to the other disciples, "because whoever is not against you is for you."

New International Version

this meant. It was hidden from them, so that they did not grasp it, and they were afraid to ask him about it.

Who will be the greatest?

46 An argument started among the disciples as to which of them would be the greatest. 47 Jesus, knowing their thoughts, took a little child and had him stand beside him. 48 Then he said to them, "Whoever welcomes this little child in my name welcomes me; and whoever welcomes me welcomes the one who sent me. For he who is least among you all—he is the greatest."
49 "Master," said John, "we saw a man driving out demons in your name and we tried to stop him, because he is not one of us."
50 "Do not stop him," Jesus said, "for whoever is not against you is for you."

Phillips Modern English

thing made it impossible for them to understand it, and they were afraid to ask him what he meant.

9.46 Jesus and "greatness"

• Then an argument arose among them as to who should be the greatest. But Jesus, knowing what they were arguing about, picked up a little child and stood him by his side. And then he said to them,

"Anyone who accepts a little child in my name is accepting me, and the man who accepts me is accepting the one who sent me. It is the humblest among you all who is really the greatest."

Then John broke in,

"Master, we saw a man driving out evil spirits in your name, but we stopped him, for he is not one of us who follow you."

But Jesus told him,

"You must not stop him. The man who is not against you is on your side."

Revised Standard Version

concealed from them, that they should not perceive it; and they were afraid to ask him about
this saying.
46 And an argument arose among them as to
which of them was the greatest. 47 But when
Jesus perceived the thought of their hearts, he
took a child and put him by his side, 48 and
said to them, "Whoever receives this child in
my name receives me, and whoever receives me
receives him who sent me; for he who is least
among you all is the one who is great."
49 John answered, "Master, we saw a man
casting out demons in your name, and we forbade him, because he does not follow with us."
50 But Jesus said to him, "Do not forbid him;
for he that is not against you is for you."

Jerusalem Bible

this; it was hidden from them so that they should not see the meaning of it, and they were afraid to ask him about what he had just said.

Who is the greatest?

46 An argument started between them about
which of them was the greatest. 47 Jesus knew
what thoughts were going through their minds,
and he took a little child and set him by his side,
48 and then said to them, "Anyone who welcomes
this little child in my name welcomes me; and
anyone who welcomes me welcomes the one who
sent me. For the least among you all, that is the
one who is great."

On using the name of Jesus

49 John spoke up. "Master," he said, "we
saw a man casting out devils in your name, and
because he is not with us we tried to stop him."
50 But Jesus said to him, "You must not stop
him: anyone who is not against you is for you."

New English Bible

it had been hidden from them, so that they should not[a] grasp its meaning, and they were afraid to ask him about it.

A dispute arose among them: which of them was the greatest? Jesus knew what was passing in their minds, so he took a child by the hand and stood him at his side, and said, 'Whoever receives this child in my name receives me; and whoever receives me receives the One who sent me. For the least among you all—he is the greatest.'

'Master,' said John, 'we saw a man driving out devils in your name, but as he is not one of us we tried to stop him.' Jesus said to him, 'Do not stop him, for he who is not against you is on your side.'

[a] *Or* it was so obscure to them that they could not . . .

King James Version

51 And it came to pass, when the time was come that he should be received up, he steadfastly set his face to go to Jerusalem, 52And sent messengers before his face: and they went, and entered into a village of the Samaritans, to make ready for him. 53And they did not receive him, because his face was as though he would go to Jerusalem. 54And when his disciples James and John saw *this,* they said, Lord, wilt thou that we command fire to come down from heaven, and consume them, even as Elias did? 55 But he turned, and rebuked them, and said, Ye know not what manner of spirit ye are of. 56 For the Son of man is not come to destroy men's lives, but to save *them.* And they went to another village.

57 And it came to pass, that, as they went in the way, a certain *man* said unto him, Lord, I will follow thee whithersoever thou goest. 58And Jesus said unto him, Foxes have holes, and birds of the air *have* nests; but the Son of man hath not where to lay *his* head. 59And he said unto another, Follow me. But he said, Lord, suffer me first to go and bury my father. 60 Jesus said unto him, Let the dead bury their dead: but go

Living Bible

51 As the time drew near for his return to heaven, he moved steadily onward towards Jerusalem with an iron will.

52 One day he sent messengers ahead to reserve rooms for them in a Samaritan village. 53 But they were turned away! The people of the village refused to have anything to do with them because they were headed for Jerusalem.[g]

54 When word came back of what had happened, James and John said to Jesus, "Master, shall we order fire down from heaven to burn them up?" 55 But Jesus turned and rebuked them,[h] 56 and they went on to another village.

57 As they were walking along someone said to Jesus, "I will always follow you no matter where you go."

58 But Jesus replied, "Remember, I don't even own a place to lay my head. Foxes have dens to live in, and birds have nests, but I, the Messiah,[i] have no earthly home at all."

59 Another time, when he invited a man to come with him and to be his disciple, the man agreed—but wanted to wait until his father's death.[j]

60 Jesus replied, "Let those without eternal life concern themselves with things like that.[k] Your duty is to come and preach the coming of

[g] A typical case of discrimination (cf. John 4:9). The Jews called the Samaritans "half-breeds," so the Samaritans naturally hated the Jews. [h] Later manuscripts add to verses 55 and 56, "And Jesus said, You don't realize what your hearts are like. For the Son of Man has not come to destroy men's lives, but to save them." [i] Literally, "the Son of Man." [j] Literally, "But he said, 'Lord, suffer me first to go and bury my father,' "—perhaps meaning that the man could, when his father died, collect the inheritance and have some security. [k] Or, "Let those who are spiritually dead care for their own dead."

Today's English Version

A Samaritan village refuses to receive Jesus

51 As the days drew near when Jesus would be taken up to heaven, he made up his mind and set out on his way to Jerusalem. 52 He sent messengers ahead of him, who left and went into a Samaritan village to get everything ready for him. 53 But the people there would not receive him, because it was plain that he was going to Jerusalem. 54 When the disciples James and John saw this, they said, "Lord, do you want us to call fire down from heaven and destroy them?"

55 Jesus turned and rebuked them; 56 and they went on to another village.

The would-be followers of Jesus

57 As they went on their way, a certain man said to Jesus, "I will follow you wherever you go."

58 Jesus said to him, "Foxes have holes, and birds have nests, but the Son of Man has no place to lie down and rest." 59 He said to another man, "Follow me."

But that man said, "Sir, first let me go back and bury my father."

60 Jesus answered, "Let the dead bury their own dead. You go and preach the Kingdom of

New International Version

Samaritan opposition

51 As the time approached for him to be taken up to heaven, Jesus resolutely set out for Jerusalem, 52 and he sent messengers on ahead. They went into a Samaritan village to get things ready for him, 53 but the people there did not welcome him, because he was heading for Jerusalem. 54 When the disciples James and John saw this, they asked, "Lord, do you want us to call fire down from heaven to destroy them[k]?" 55 But Jesus turned and rebuked them,[l] 56 and they went to another village.

The cost of following Jesus

57 As they were walking along the road, a man said to him, "I will follow you wherever you go."

58 Jesus replied, "Foxes have holes and birds of the air have nests, but the Son of Man has no place to lay his head."

59 He said to another man, "Follow me."

But the man replied, "Lord, first let me go and bury my father."

60 Jesus said to him, "Let the dead bury their own dead, but you go and proclaim the kingdom

[k] Some MSS add *even as Elijah did.* [l] Some MSS add *And he said, "You do not know what kind of spirit you are of, for the Son of Man did not come to destroy men's lives, but to save them."*

Phillips Modern English

9.51 He sets off for Jerusalem to meet inevitable death

Now as the days before he should be taken back into Heaven were running out, he set his face firmly towards Jerusalem, and sent messengers ahead of him. They set out and entered a Samaritan village to make preparations for him. But the people there refused to welcome him because he was obviously intending to go to Jerusalem. When the disciples James and John saw this, they said,

"Master, do you want us to call down fire from heaven and burn them all up?"

But Jesus turned and reproved them, and they all went on to another village.

As the little company made its way along the road, a man said to him,

"I'm going to follow you wherever you go."

And Jesus replied,

"Foxes have earths, birds have nests, but the Son of Man has nowhere to lay his head."

But he said to another man,

"Follow me."

And he replied,

"Let me go and bury my father first."

But Jesus told him,

"Leave the dead to bury their own dead. You must come away and preach the kingdom of

Revised Standard Version

51 When the days drew near for him to be
received up, he set his face to go to Jerusalem.
52And he sent messengers ahead of him, who
went and entered a village of the Samaritans,
to make ready for him; 53 but the people would
not receive him, because his face was set toward
Jerusalem. 54And when his disciples James and
John saw it, they said, "Lord, do you want us
to bid fire come down from heaven and consume them?"[e] 55 But he turned and rebuked
them.[f] 56And they went on to another village.
57 As they were going along the road, a man
said to him, "I will follow you wherever you go."
58And Jesus said to him, "Foxes have holes, and
birds of the air have nests; but the Son of man
has nowhere to lay his head." 59 To another he
said, "Follow me." But he said, "Lord, let me
first go and bury my father." 60 But he said to
him, "Leave the dead to bury their own dead;
but as for you, go and proclaim the kingdom of

[e] Other ancient authorities add *as Elijah did.*
[f] Other ancient authorities add *and he said, "You do not know what manner of spirit you are of; for the Son of man came not to destroy men's lives but to save them."*

Jerusalem Bible

IV. The journey to Jerusalem

A Samaritan village is inhospitable

51 Now as the time drew near for him to be
taken up to heaven, he resolutely took the road
for Jerusalem 52 and sent messengers ahead of
him. These set out, and they went into a Samaritan village to make preparations for him, 53 but
the people would not receive him because he
was making for Jerusalem.[p] 54 Seeing this, the
disciples James and John said, "Lord, do you
want us to call down fire from heaven to burn
them up?" 55 But he turned and rebuked them,
56 and they went off to another village.

Hardships of the apostolic calling

57 As they traveled along they met a man on
the road who said to him, "I will follow you
wherever you go." 58 Jesus answered, "Foxes
have holes and the birds of the air have nests,
but the Son of Man has nowhere to lay his
head."
59 Another to whom he said, "Follow me,"
replied, "Let me go and bury my father first."
60 But he answered, "Leave the dead to bury
their dead; your duty is to go and spread the

[p] The hatred of Samaritans for Jews would show itself particularly toward those who were on pilgrimage to Jerusalem.

New English Bible

Journeys and encounters

As the time approached when he was to be taken up to heaven, he set his face resolutely towards Jerusalem, and sent messengers ahead. They set out and went into a Samaritan village to make arrangements for him; but the villagers would not have him because he was making for Jerusalem. When the disciples James and John saw this they said, 'Lord, may we call down fire from heaven to burn them up[a]?' But he turned and rebuked them,[b] and they went on to another village.

As they were going along the road a man said to him, 'I will follow you wherever you go.' Jesus answered, 'Foxes have their holes, the birds their roosts; but the Son of Man has nowhere to lay his head.' To another he said, 'Follow me', but the man replied, 'Let me go and bury my father first.' Jesus said, 'Leave the dead to bury their dead; you must go and announce the

[a] *Some witnesses add* as Elijah did. [b] *Some witnesses insert* 'You do not know', he said, 'to what spirit you belong; (56) for the Son of Man did not come to destroy men's lives but to save them.'

King James Version

thou and preach the kingdom of God. 61And
another also said, Lord, I will follow thee: but
let me first go bid them farewell, which are at
home at my house. 62And Jesus said unto him,
No man, having put his hand to the plough, and
looking back, is fit for the kingdom of God.

10 After these things the Lord appointed
other seventy also, and sent them two and
two before his face into every city and place,
whither he himself would come. 2 Therefore said
he unto them, The harvest truly *is* great, but the
labourers *are* few: pray ye therefore the Lord
of the harvest, that he would send forth labourers into his harvest. 3 Go your ways: behold,
I send you forth as lambs among wolves.
4 Carry neither purse, nor scrip, nor shoes: and
salute no man by the way. 5And into whatsoever
house ye enter, first say, Peace *be* to this house.
6And if the son of peace be there, your peace
shall rest upon it: if not, it shall turn to you
again. 7And in the same house remain, eating
and drinking such things as they give: for the

Living Bible

the Kingdom of God to all the world."
61 Another said, "Yes, Lord, I will come, but
first let me ask permission of those at home." [l]
62 But Jesus told him, "Anyone who lets
himself be distracted from the work I plan for
him is not fit for the Kingdom of God."

10 The Lord now chose seventy other disciples and sent them on ahead in pairs to
all the towns and villages he planned to visit
later.
2 These were his instructions to them: "Plead
with the Lord of the harvest to send out more
laborers to help you, for the harvest is so plentiful and the workers so few. 3 Go now, and remember that I am sending you out as lambs
among wolves. 4 Don't take any money with
you, or a beggar's bag, or even an extra pair of
shoes. And don't waste time along the way.[a]
5 "Whenever you enter a home, give it your
blessing. 6 If it is worthy of the blessing, the
blessing will stand; if not, the blessing will return to you.
7 "When you enter a village, don't shift
around from home to home, but stay in one
place, eating and drinking without question
whatever is set before you. And don't hesitate

[*l*] Literally, "bid them farewell at home." [*a*] Literally, "Salute no one in the way."

Today's English Version

God."
61 Another man said, "I will follow you, sir;
but first let me go and say good-bye to my family."
62 Jesus said to him, "Anyone who starts to
plow and then keeps looking back is of no use
for the Kingdom of God."

Jesus sends out the seventy-two

10 After this the Lord chose another seventy-
two men and sent them out, two by two,
to go ahead of him to every town and place
where he himself was about to go. 2 He said to
them, "There is a large harvest, but few workers
to gather it in. Pray to the owner of the harvest
that he will send out workers to gather in his
harvest. 3 Go! I am sending you like lambs
among wolves. 4 Don't take a purse, or a beggar's bag, or shoes; don't stop to greet anyone
on the road. 5 Whenever you go into a house,
first say, 'Peace be with this house.' 6 If a peace-
loving man lives there, let your greeting of peace
remain on him; if not, take back your greeting of
peace. 7 Stay in that same house, eating and
drinking what they offer you, because a worker

New International Version

of God."
61 Still another said, "I will follow you, Lord;
but first let me go back and say good-by to my
family."
62 Jesus replied, "No one who puts his hand
to the plow and looks back is fit for service in
the kingdom of God."

Jesus sends out the seventy-two

10 After this the Lord appointed seventy-
two[m] others and sent them two by two
ahead of him to every town and place where he
was about to go. 2 He told them, "The harvest
is plentiful, but the workers are few. Ask the
Lord of the harvest, therefore, to send out workers into his harvest field. 3 Go! I am sending you
out like lambs among wolves. 4 Do not take a
purse or bag or sandals; and do not greet anyone on the road.
5 "When you enter a house, first say, 'Peace
to this house.' 6 If a man of peace is there, your
peace will rest on him; if not, it will return to
you. 7 Stay in that house, eating and drinking
whatever they give you, for the worker deserves

[*m*] Some MSS read *seventy*.

Phillips Modern English

God."

Another man said to him,

"I am going to follow you, Lord, but first let me bid farewell to my people at home."

But Jesus told him,

"Anyone who puts his hand to the plough and then looks behind him is useless for the kingdom of God."

10.1 Jesus now despatches thirty-five couples to preach and heal the sick

Later on the Lord commissioned seventy other disciples and sent them off in twos as advance-parties into every town and district where he intended to go himself.

"There is a great harvest," he told them, "but only a few are working in it—which means you must pray to the Lord of the harvest that he will send out more reapers to bring in his harvest.

"Now go on your way. I am sending you out like lambs among wolves. Don't carry a purse or a bag or a pair of shoes, and don't stop to greet anyone you meet on the road. When you go into a house, say first of all, 'Peace be to this household!' If there is a lover of peace there, he will accept your words of blessing, and if not, they will come back to you. Stay in the same house and eat and drink whatever they put be-

Revised Standard Version

God." 61 Another said, "I will follow you, Lord; but let me first say farewell to those at my home." 62 Jesus said to him, "No one who puts his hand to the plow and looks back is fit for the kingdom of God."

10 After this the Lord appointed seventy[g] others, and sent them on ahead of him, two by two, into every town and place where he himself was about to come. 2 And he said to them, "The harvest is plentiful, but the laborers are few; pray therefore the Lord of the harvest to send out laborers into his harvest. 3 Go your way; behold, I send you out as lambs in the midst of wolves. 4 Carry no purse, no bag, no sandals; and salute no one on the road. 5 Whatever house you enter, first say, 'Peace be to this house!' 6 And if a son of peace is there, your peace shall rest upon him; but if not, it shall return to you. 7 And remain in the same house, eating and drinking what they provide, for the

[g] Other ancient authorities read *seventy-two*.

Jerusalem Bible

news of the kingdom of God."

61 Another said, "I will follow you, sir, but first let me go and say good-by to my people at home." 62 Jesus said to him, "Once the hand is laid on the plow, no one who looks back is fit for the kingdom of God."

The mission of the seventy-two disciples

10 After this the Lord appointed seventy-two others and sent them out ahead of him, in pairs, to all the towns and places he himself was to visit. 2 He said to them, "The harvest is rich but the laborers are few, so ask the Lord of the harvest to send laborers to his harvest. 3 Start off now, but remember, I am sending you out like lambs among wolves. 4 Carry no purse, no haversack, no sandals. Salute no one on the road. 5 Whatever house you go into, let your first words be, 'Peace to this house!' 6 And if a man of peace lives there, your peace will go and rest on him; if not, it will come back to you. 7 Stay in the same house, taking what food and drink they have to offer, for the laborer deserves

New English Bible

kingdom of God.'

Yet another said, 'I will follow you, sir; but let me first say goodbye to my people at home.' To him Jesus said, 'No one who sets his hand to the plough and then keeps looking back[c] is fit for the kingdom of God.'

10 After this the Lord appointed a further seventy-two[d] and sent them on ahead in pairs to every town and place he was going to visit himself. He said to them: 'The crop is heavy, but labourers are scarce; you must therefore beg the owner to send labourers to harvest his crop. Be on your way. And look, I am sending you like lambs among wolves. Carry no purse or pack, and travel barefoot. Exchange no greetings on the road. When you go into a house, let your first words be, "Peace to this house." If there is a man of peace there, your peace will rest upon him; if not, it will return and rest upon you. Stay in that one house, sharing their food and drink; for the worker earns

[c] *Some witnesses read* No one who looks back as he sets hand to the plough . . . [d] *Some witnesses read* seventy.

King James Version

labourer is worthy of his hire. Go not from
house to house. 8And into whatsoever city ye
enter, and they receive you, eat such things as
are set before you: 9And heal the sick that are
therein, and say unto them, The kingdom of God
is come nigh unto you. 10 But into whatsoever
city ye enter, and they receive you not, go your
ways out into the streets of the same, and say,
11 Even the very dust of your city, which cleaveth
on us, we do wipe off against you: notwithstanding, be ye sure of this, that the kingdom of God
is come nigh unto you. 12 But I say unto you,
that it shall be more tolerable in that day for
Sodom, than for that city. 13 Woe unto thee,
Chorazin! woe unto thee, Bethsaida! for if the
mighty works had been done in Tyre and Sidon,
which have been done in you, they had a great
while ago repented, sitting in sackcloth and
ashes. 14 But it shall be more tolerable for Tyre
and Sidon at the judgment, than for you. 15And
thou, Capernaum, which art exalted to heaven,
shalt be thrust down to hell. 16 He that heareth
you heareth me; and he that despiseth you despiseth me; and he that despiseth me despiseth
him that sent me.

Living Bible

to accept hospitality, for the workman is worthy
of his wages!

8, 9 "If a town welcomes you, follow these
two rules:

(1) Eat whatever is set before you.
(2) Heal the sick; and as you heal them, say,
'The Kingdom of God is very near you
now.'

10 "But if a town refuses you, go out into its
streets and say, 11 'We wipe the dust of your
town from our feet as a public announcement
of your doom. Never forget how close you were
to the Kingdom of God!' 12 Even wicked Sodom
will be better off than such a city on the Judgment Day. 13 What horrors await you, you cities
of Chorazin and Bethsaida! For if the miracles
I did for you had been done in the cities of
Tyre and Sidon,[b] their people would have sat in
deep repentance long ago, clothed in sackcloth
and throwing ashes on their heads to show their
remorse. 14 Yes, Tyre and Sidon will receive less
punishment on the Judgment Day than you.
15And you people of Capernaum, what shall I
say about you? Will you be exalted to heaven?
No, you shall be brought down to hell."

16 Then he said to the disciples, "Those who
welcome you are welcoming me. And those who
reject you are rejecting me. And those who reject me are rejecting God who sent me."

[*b*] Cities destroyed by God in judgment for their wickedness. For a description of this event, see Ezekiel, chapters 26-28.

Today's English Version

should be given his pay. Don't move around from
one house to another. 8 Whenever you go into a
town and are made welcome, eat what is set before you, 9 heal the sick in that town, and say
to the people there, 'The Kingdom of God has
come near you.' 10 But whenever you go into a
town and are not welcomed there, go out in the
streets and say, 11 'Even the dust from your town
that sticks to our feet we wipe off against you;
but remember this, the Kingdom of God has
come near you!' 12 I tell you that on the Judgment Day God will show more mercy to Sodom
than to that town!"

The unbelieving towns

13 "How terrible it will be for you, Chorazin!
How terrible for you too, Bethsaida! If the miracles which were performed in you had been performed in Tyre and Sidon, long ago the people
there would have sat down, put on sackcloth,
and sprinkled ashes on themselves to show that
they had turned from their sins! 14 God will show
more mercy on the Judgment Day to Tyre and
Sidon than to you. 15And as for you, Capernaum!
You wanted to lift yourself up to heaven? You
will be thrown down to hell!"

16 Jesus said to his disciples, "Whoever listens
to you, listens to me; whoever rejects you, rejects
me; and whoever rejects me, rejects the one who
sent me."

New International Version

his wages. Do not move around from house to
house.

8 "When you enter a town and are welcomed,
eat what is set before you. 9 Heal the sick who
are there and tell them, 'The kingdom of God is
near you.' 10 But when you enter a town and
are not welcomed, go into its streets and say,
11 'Even the dust of your town that sticks to our
feet we wipe off against you. Yet be sure of this:
The kingdom of God is near.' 12 I tell you, it
will be more bearable on that day for Sodom
than for that town.

13 "Woe to you, Chorazin! Woe to you, Bethsaida! For if the miracles that were performed in
you had been performed in Tyre and Sidon, they
would have repented long ago, sitting in sackcloth and ashes. 14 But it will be more bearable
for Tyre and Sidon at the judgment than for
you. 15And you, Capernaum, will you be lifted
up to the skies? No, you will go down to the
depths.[n]

16 "He who listens to you listens to me; he
who rejects you rejects me; but he who rejects
me rejects him who sent me."

[*n*] Greek *Hades*.

Phillips Modern English

fore you—a workman deserves his wages. But don't move from one house to another.

"Whatever town you go into and the people welcome you, eat the meals they give you and heal the people who are ill there. Tell them, 'The kingdom of God is very near to you now.' But whenever you come into a town and they will not welcome you, you must go into the streets and say, 'We brush off even the dust of your town from our feet as a protest against you. But it is still true that the kingdom of God has arrived!' I assure you that it will be easier for Sodom in 'that day' than for that town.

"Alas for you, Chorazin, and alas for you, Bethsaida! For if Tyre and Sidon had seen the demonstrations of God's power that you have seen, they would have repented long ago and sat in sackcloth and ashes. It will be easier for Tyre and Sidon in the judgment than for you! As for you, Capernaum, do you think you will be exalted to the heavens? I tell you you will go hurtling down among the dead!"

Then he added to the seventy.

"Whoever listens to you is listening to me, and the man who rejects you rejects me too. And the man who rejects me rejects the One who sent me!"

Revised Standard Version

laborer deserves his wages; do not go from
house to house. 8 Whenever you enter a town
and they receive you, eat what is set before you;
9 heal the sick in it and say to them, 'The kingdom of God has come near to you.' 10 But whenever you enter a town and they do not receive
you, go into its streets and say, 11 'Even the
dust of your town that clings to our feet, we
wipe off against you; nevertheless know this,
that the kingdom of God has come near.' 12 I
tell you, it shall be more tolerable on that day
for Sodom than for that town.
13 "Woe to you, Chorazin! woe to you, Bethsaida! for if the mighty works done in you had
been done in Tyre and Sidon, they would have
repented long ago, sitting in sackcloth and ashes.
14 But it shall be more tolerable in the judgment
for Tyre and Sidon than for you. 15 And you,
Capernaum, will you be exalted to heaven? You
shall be brought down to Hades.
16 "He who hears you hears me, and he who
rejects you rejects me, and he who rejects me
rejects him who sent me."

Jerusalem Bible

his wages; do not move from house to house.
8 Whenever you go into a town where they
make you welcome, eat what is set before you.
9 Cure those in it who are sick, and say, 'The
kingdom of God is very near to you.' 10 But
whenever you enter a town and they do not
make you welcome, go out into the streets and
say, 11 'We wipe off the very dust of your town
that clings to our feet, and leave it with you. Yet
be sure of this: the kingdom of God is very
near.' 12 I tell you, on that day it will not go as
hard with Sodom as with that town.
13 "Alas for you, Chorazin! Alas for you,
Bethsaida! For if the miracles done in you had
been done in Tyre and Sidon, they would have
repented long ago, sitting in sackcloth and ashes.
14 And still, it will not go as hard with Tyre and
Sidon at the Judgment as with you. 15 And as for
you, Capernaum, did you want to be exalted high
as heaven? *You shall be thrown down to hell.*[q]
16 "Anyone who listens to you listens to me;
anyone who rejects you rejects me, and those
who reject me reject the one who sent me."

New English Bible

his pay. Do not move from house to house. When you come into a town and they make you welcome, eat the food provided for you; heal the sick there, and say, "The kingdom of God has come close to you." When you enter a town and they do not make you welcome, go out into its streets and say, "The very dust of your town that clings to our feet we wipe off to your shame. Only take note of this: the kingdom of God has come close." I tell you, it will be more bearable for Sodom on the great Day than for that town.

'Alas for you, Chorazin! Alas for you, Bethsaida! If the miracles that were performed in you had been performed in Tyre and Sidon, they would have repented long ago, sitting in sackcloth and ashes. But it will be more bearable for Tyre and Sidon at the Judgement than for you. And as for you, Capernaum, will you be exalted to the skies? No, brought down to the depths!

'Whoever listens to you listens to me; whoever rejects you rejects me. And whoever rejects me rejects the One who sent me.'

[q] See Is. 14:13,15.

King James Version

17 And the seventy returned again with joy,
saying, Lord, even the devils are subject unto us
through thy name. 18And he said unto them, I
beheld Satan as lightning fall from heaven. 19 Behold, I give unto you power to tread on serpents
and scorpions, and over all the power of the
enemy; and nothing shall by any means hurt
you. 20 Notwithstanding, in this rejoice not, that
the spirits are subject unto you; but rather rejoice, because your names are written in heaven.
21 In that hour Jesus rejoiced in spirit, and
said, I thank thee, O Father, Lord of heaven
and earth, that thou hast hid these things from
the wise and prudent, and hast revealed them
unto babes: even so, Father; for so it seemed
good in thy sight. 22All things are delivered to
me of my Father: and no man knoweth who the
Son is, but the Father; and who the Father is,
but the Son, and *he* to whom the Son will reveal
him.
23 And he turned him unto *his* disciples, and
said privately, Blessed *are* the eyes which see

Living Bible

17 When the seventy disciples returned, they
joyfully reported to him, "Even the demons obey
us when we use your name."
18 "Yes," he told them, "I saw Satan falling
from heaven as a flash of lightning! 19And I
have given you authority over all the power of
the Enemy, and to walk among serpents and
scorpions and to crush them. Nothing shall injure you! 20 However, the important thing is
not that demons obey you, but that your names
are registered as citizens of heaven."
21 Then he was filled with the joy of the Holy
Spirit and said, "I praise you, O Father, Lord of
heaven and earth, for hiding these things from
the intellectuals and worldly wise and for revealing them to those who are as trusting as little
children.[c] Yes, thank you, Father, for that is
the way you wanted it. 22 I am the Agent of my
Father in everything; and no one really knows
the Son except the Father, and no one really
knows the Father except the Son and those to
whom the Son chooses to reveal him."
23 Then, turning to the twelve disciples, he
said quietly, "How privileged you are to see what

[*c*] Literally, "babies."

Today's English Version

The return of the seventy-two

17 The seventy-two men came back in great
joy. "Lord," they said, "even the demons obeyed
us when we commanded them in your name!"
18 Jesus answered them, "I saw Satan fall like
lightning from heaven. 19 Listen! I have given
you authority, so that you can walk on snakes
and scorpions, and over all the power of the
Enemy, and nothing will hurt you. 20 But don't
be glad because the evil spirits obey you; rather
be glad because your names are written in
heaven."

Jesus rejoices

21 At that time Jesus was filled with joy by
the Holy Spirit, and said, "Father, Lord of
heaven and earth! I thank you because you have
shown to the unlearned what you have hidden
from the wise and learned. Yes, Father, this
was done by your own choice and pleasure.
22 "My Father has given me all things. No
one knows who the Son is except the Father,
and no one knows who the Father is except the
Son and those to whom the Son wants to reveal
him."
23 Then Jesus turned to the disciples and said
to them privately, "How fortunate you are, to see

New International Version

17 The seventy-two[o] returned with joy and
said, "Lord, even the demons submit to us in
your name."
18 He replied, "I saw Satan fall like lightning
from heaven. 19 I have given you authority to
trample on snakes and scorpions, and to overcome all the power of the enemy; nothing will
harm you. 20 However, do not rejoice that the
spirits submit to you, but rejoice that your
names are recorded in heaven."
21 At that time Jesus, full of joy through the
Holy Spirit, said, "I praise you, Father, Lord of
heaven and earth, because you have hidden these
things from the wise and learned, and revealed
them to little children. Yes, Father, for this was
your good pleasure.
22 "All things have been committed to me by
my Father. No one knows who the Son is except
the Father, and no one knows who the Father is
except the Son and those to whom the Son
chooses to reveal him."
23 Then he turned to his disciples and said
privately, "Blessed are the eyes that see what you

[*o*] Some MSS read *seventy*.

Phillips Modern English

10.17 Jesus tells the returned missioners not to be enthusiastic over mere power

Later the seventy came back full of joy.

"Lord," they said, "even evil spirits obey us when we use your name!"

"Yes," returned Jesus, "I was watching and saw Satan fall from heaven like a flash of lightning! It is true that I have given you the power to tread on snakes and scorpions and to overcome all the enemy's power—there is nothing at all that can do you any harm. Yet it is not your power over evil spirits which should give you such joy, but the fact that your names are written in Heaven."

10.21 Jesus prays aloud to his Father

At that moment Jesus' heart was filled with joy by the Holy Spirit, and he exclaimed,

"O Father, Lord of Heaven and earth, I thank you for hiding these things from the wise and the clever and for showing them to mere children! Yes, I thank you, Father, that this was your will." Then he went on,

"Everything has been put in my hands by my Father; and nobody knows who the Son is except the Father. Nobody knows who the Father is except the Son—and the man to whom the Son chooses to reveal him!"

Then he turned to his disciples and said to them quietly,

Revised Standard Version

17 The seventy[g] returned with joy, saying,
"Lord, even the demons are subject to us in your
name!" 18 And he said to them, "I saw Satan
fall like lightning from heaven. 19 Behold, I
have given you authority to tread upon serpents
and scorpions, and over all the power of the
enemy; and nothing shall hurt you. 20 Nevertheless do not rejoice in this, that the spirits are
subject to you; but rejoice that your names are
written in heaven."
21 In that same hour he rejoiced in the Holy
Spirit and said, "I thank thee, Father, Lord of
heaven and earth, that thou hast hidden these
things from the wise and understanding and
revealed them to babes; yea, Father, for such
was thy gracious will.[h] 22 All things have been
delivered to me by my Father; and no one knows
who the Son is except the Father, or who the
Father is except the Son and any one to whom
the Son chooses to reveal him."
23 Then turning to the disciples he said privately, "Blessed are the eyes which see what

[g] Other ancient authorities read *seventy-two*. [h] Or *so it was well-pleasing before thee.*

Jerusalem Bible

True cause for the apostles to rejoice

17 The seventy-two came back rejoicing.
"Lord," they said, "even the devils submit to us
when we use your name." 18 He said to them, "I
watched Satan fall like lightning from heaven.
19 Yes, I have given you power to tread underfoot serpents and scorpions and the whole
strength of the enemy; nothing shall ever hurt
you. 20 Yet do not rejoice that the Spirits submit to you; rejoice rather that your names are
written in heaven."

The Good News revealed to the simple. The Father and the Son

21 It was then that, filled with joy by the Holy
Spirit, he said, "I bless you, Father, Lord of
heaven and of earth, for hiding these things
from the learned and the clever and revealing
them to mere children. Yes, Father, for that is
what it pleased you to do. 22 Everything has been
entrusted to me by my Father; and no one knows
who the Son is except the Father, and who the
Father is except the Son and those to whom the
Son chooses to reveal him."

The privilege of the disciples

23 Then turning to his disciples he spoke to
them in private, "Happy the eyes that see what

New English Bible

The seventy-two[a] came back jubilant. 'In your name, Lord,' they said, 'even the devils submit to us.' He replied, 'I watched how Satan fell, like lightning, out of the sky. And now you see that I have given you the power to tread underfoot snakes and scorpions and all the forces of the enemy, and nothing will ever harm you.[b] Nevertheless, what you should rejoice over is not that the spirits submit to you, but that your names are enrolled in heaven.'

At that moment Jesus exulted in the Holy[c] Spirit and said, 'I thank thee, Father, Lord of heaven and earth, for hiding these things from the learned and wise, and revealing them to the simple. Yes, Father, such[d] was thy choice.' Then turning to his disciples he said,[e] 'Everything is entrusted to me by my Father; and no one knows who the Son is but the Father, or who the Father is but the Son, and those to whom the Son may choose to reveal him.'

Turning to his disciples in private he said,

[a] *Some witnesses read* seventy. [b] *Or* and he will have no way at all to harm you. [c] *Some witnesses omit* Holy. [d] *Or* Yes, I thank thee, Father, that such . . . [e] *Some witnesses omit* Then . . . he said.

King James Version

the things that ye see: 24 For I tell you, that
many prophets and kings have desired to see
those things which ye see, and have not seen
them; and to hear those things which ye hear,
and have not heard *them.*
25 And, behold, a certain lawyer stood up,
and tempted him, saying, Master, what shall I
do to inherit eternal life? 26 He said unto him,
What is written in the law? how readest thou?
27 And he answering said, Thou shalt love the
Lord thy God with all thy heart, and with all
thy soul, and with all thy strength, and with all
thy mind; and thy neighbour as thyself. 28 And
he said unto him, Thou hast answered right:
this do, and thou shalt live. 29 But he, willing to
justify himself, said unto Jesus, And who is my
neighbour? 30 And Jesus answering said, A certain *man* went down from Jerusalem to Jericho,
and fell among thieves, which stripped him of
his raiment, and wounded *him,* and departed,
leaving *him* half dead. 31 And by chance there
came down a certain priest that way; and when
he saw him, he passed by on the other side.
32 And likewise a Levite, when he was at the
place, came and looked *on him,* and passed by
on the other side. 33 But a certain Samaritan, as
he journeyed, came where he was; and when he

Living Bible

you have seen. 24 Many a prophet and king of
old has longed for these days, to see and hear
what you have seen and heard!"
25 One day an expert on Moses' laws came
to test Jesus' orthodoxy by asking him this question: "Teacher, what does a man need to do to
live forever in heaven?"
26 Jesus replied, "What does Moses' law say
about it?"
27 "It says," he replied, "that you must love
the Lord your God with all your heart, and with
all your soul, and with all your strength, and
with all your mind. And you must love your
neighbor just as much as you love yourself."
28 "Right!" Jesus told him. "*Do* this and
you shall live!"
29 The man wanted to justify (his lack of
love for some kinds of people),[d] so he asked,
"Which neighbors?"
30 Jesus replied with an illustration: "A Jew
going on a trip from Jerusalem to Jericho was
attacked by bandits. They stripped him of his
clothes and money and beat him up and left
him lying half dead beside the road.
31 "By chance a Jewish priest came along; and
when he saw the man lying there, he crossed to
the other side of the road and passed him by.
32 A Jewish Temple-assistant[e] walked over and
looked at him lying there, but then went on.
33 "But a despised Samaritan[f] came along,

[*d*] Literally, "wanting to justify himself." [*e*] Literally, "Levite." [*f*] Literally, "a Samaritan." All Samaritans were despised by Jews, and the feeling was mutual, due to historic reasons.

Today's English Version

the things you see! 24 Many prophets and kings,
I tell you, wanted to see what you see, but they
could not, and to hear what you hear, but they
did not."

The parable of the good Samaritan

25 A certain teacher of the Law came up and
tried to trap Jesus. "Teacher," he asked, "what
must I do to receive eternal life?"
26 Jesus answered him, "What do the Scriptures say? How do you interpret them?"
27 The man answered, " 'You must love the
Lord your God with all your heart, with all your
soul, with all your strength, and with all your
mind'; and, 'You must love your fellow-man as
yourself.' "
28 "Your answer is correct," replied Jesus;
"do this and you will live."
29 But the teacher of the Law wanted to put
himself in the right, so he asked Jesus, "Who is
my fellow-man?"
30 Jesus answered, "There was a man who
was going down from Jerusalem to Jericho, when
robbers attacked him, stripped him, and beat him
up, leaving him half dead. 31 It so happened that
a priest was going down that road; when he saw
the man he walked on by, on the other side. 32 In
the same way a Levite also came there, went
over and looked at the man, and then walked
on by, on the other side. 33 But a certain Samaritan who was traveling that way came upon him,

New International Version

see. 24 For I tell you that many prophets and
kings wanted to see what you see but did not
see it, and to hear what you hear but did not
hear it."

The parable of the good Samaritan

25 On one occasion an expert in the law stood
up to test Jesus. "Teacher," he asked, "what
must I do to inherit eternal life?"
26 "What is written in the Law?" he replied.
"How do you read it?"
27 He answered: " 'Love the Lord your God
with all your heart, with all your soul, with all
your strength and with all your mind'[p]; and,
'Love your neighbors as yourself.'[q] "
28 "You have answered correctly," Jesus replied. "Do this and you will live."
29 But he wanted to justify himself, so he
asked Jesus, "And who is my neighbor?"
30 In reply Jesus said: "A man was going
down from Jerusalem to Jericho, when he fell
into the hands of robbers. They stripped him of
his clothes, beat him and went away, leaving him
half dead. 31 A priest happened to be going down
the same road, and when he saw the man, he
passed by on the other side. 32 So too, a Levite,
when he came to the place and saw him, passed
by on the other side. 33 But a Samaritan, as he
traveled, came where the man was; and when he

[*p*] Deut. 6:5. [*q*] Lev. 19:18.

Phillips Modern English

"How fortunate you are to see what you are seeing! I tell you that many prophets and kings have wanted to see what you are seeing but they never saw it, and to hear what you are hearing but they never heard it."

10.25 Jesus shows the relevance of the Law to actual living

Once one of the experts in the Law stood up to test him and said,

"Master, what must I do to be sure of eternal life?"

"What does the Law say and what has your reading taught you?" said Jesus.

"The Law says, 'Thou shalt love the Lord thy God with all thy heart and with all thy soul and with all thy strength and with all thy mind—and thy neighbour as thyself'," he replied.

"Quite right," said Jesus. "Do that and you will live."

But the man, wanting to justify himself, continued,

"But who is my 'neighbour'?"

And Jesus gave him the following reply:

"A man was once on his way down from Jerusalem to Jericho. He fell into the hands of bandits who stripped off his clothes, beat him up, and left him half dead. It so happened that a priest was going down that road, and when he saw him, he passed by on the other side. A Levite also came on the scene and when he saw him, he too passed by on the other side. But then a Samaritan traveller came along to the

Revised Standard Version

you see! 24 For I tell you that many prophets
and kings desired to see what you see, and did
not see it, and to hear what you hear, and did
not hear it."
25 And behold, a lawyer stood up to put him
to the test, saying, "Teacher, what shall I do to
inherit eternal life?" 26 He said to him, "What is
written in the law? How do you read?" 27 And
he answered, "You shall love the Lord your God
with all your heart, and with all your soul, and
with all your strength, and with all your mind;
and your neighbor as yourself." 28 And he said
to him, "You have answered right; do this, and
you will live."
29 But he, desiring to justify himself, said to
Jesus, "And who is my neighbor?" 30 Jesus replied, "A man was going down from Jerusalem
to Jericho, and he fell among robbers, who
stripped him and beat him, and departed, leaving him half dead. 31 Now by chance a priest
was going down that road; and when he saw
him he passed by on the other side. 32 So likewise a Levite, when he came to the place and
saw him, passed by on the other side. 33 But a
Samaritan, as he journeyed, came to where he

Jerusalem Bible

you see, 24 for I tell you that many prophets and
kings wanted to see what you see, and never saw
it; to hear what you hear, and never heard it."

The great commandment

25 There was a lawyer who, to disconcert him,
stood up and said to him, "Master, what must
I do to inherit eternal life?" 26 He said to him,
"What is written in the Law? What do you read
there?" 27 He replied, *"You must love the Lord
your God with all your heart, with all your
soul, with all your strength,* and with all your
mind, *and your neighbor as yourself."* [r] 28 "You
have answered right," said Jesus, "do this and
life is yours."

Parable of the good Samaritan

29 But the man was anxious to justify himself
and said to Jesus, "And who is my neighbor?"
30 Jesus replied, "A man was once on his way
down from Jerusalem to Jericho and fell into
the hands of brigands; they took all he had, beat
him and then made off, leaving him half dead.
31 Now a priest happened to be traveling down
the same road, but when he saw the man, he
passed by on the other side. 32 In the same way
a Levite who came to the place saw him, and
passed by on the other side. 33 But a Samaritan
traveler who came upon him was moved with

[r] Dt. 6:5 and Lv. 19:18.

New English Bible

'Happy the eyes that see what you are seeing! I tell you, many prophets and kings wished to see what you now see, yet never saw it; to hear what you hear, yet never heard it.'

On one occasion a lawyer came forward to put this test question to him: 'Master, what must I do to inherit eternal life?' Jesus said, 'What is written in the Law? What is your reading of it?' He replied, 'Love the Lord your God with all your heart, with all your soul, with all your strength, and with all your mind; and your neighbour as yourself.' 'That is the right answer,' said Jesus; 'do that and you will live.'

But he wanted to vindicate himself, so he said to Jesus, 'And who is my neighbour?' Jesus replied, 'A man was on his way from Jerusalem down to Jericho when he fell in with robbers, who stripped him, beat him, and went off leaving him half dead. It so happened that a priest was going down by the same road; but when he saw him, he went past on the other side. So too a Levite came to the place, and when he saw him went past on the other side. But a Samaritan who was making the journey came upon him,

King James Version

saw him, he had compassion *on him,* 34And
went to *him,* and bound up his wounds, pouring
in oil and wine, and set him on his own beast,
and brought him to an inn, and took care of
him. 35And on the morrow when he departed,
he took out two pence, and gave *them* to the
host, and said unto him, Take care of him: and
whatsoever thou spendest more, when I come
again, I will repay thee. 36 Which now of these
three, thinkest thou, was neighbour unto him
that fell among the thieves? 37And he said, He
that shewed mercy on him. Then said Jesus unto
him, Go, and do thou likewise.
38 Now it came to pass, as they went, that
he entered into a certain village: and a certain
woman named Martha received him into her
house. 39And she had a sister called Mary, which
also sat at Jesus' feet, and heard his word. 40 But
Martha was cumbered about much serving, and
came to him, and said, Lord, dost thou not care
that my sister hath left me to serve alone? bid
her therefore that she help me. 41And Jesus answered and said unto her, Martha, Martha, thou
art careful and troubled about many things:
42 But one thing is needful; and Mary hath
chosen that good part, which shall not be taken
away from her.

Living Bible

and when he saw him, he felt deep pity. 34 Kneeling beside him the Samaritan soothed his wounds
with medicine and bandaged them. Then he put
the man on his donkey and walked along beside
him till they came to an inn, where he nursed
him through the night.[g] 35 The next day he
handed the innkeeper two twenty-dollar bills[h]
and told him to take care of the man. 'If his
bill runs higher than that,' he said, 'I'll pay the
difference the next time I am here.'
36 "Now which of these three would you say
was a neighbor to the bandits' victim?"
37 The man replied, "The one who showed
him some pity."
Then Jesus said, "Yes, now go and do the
same."
38 As Jesus and the disciples continued on
their way to Jerusalem[i] they came to a village
where a woman named Martha welcomed them
into her home. 39 Her sister Mary sat on the
floor, listening to Jesus as he talked.
40 But Martha was the jittery type, and was
worrying over the big dinner she was preparing.
She came to Jesus and said, "Sir, doesn't it
seem unfair to you that my sister just sits here
while I do all the work? Tell her to come and
help me."
41 But the Lord said to her, "Martha, dear
friend,[j] you are so upset over all these details!
42 There is really only one thing worth being
concerned about. Mary has discovered it—and
I won't take it away from her!"

[g] Literally, "took care of him." [h] Literally, "two denarii," each the equivalent of a modern day's wage. [i] Implied. [j] Literally, "Martha, Martha."

Today's English Version

and when he saw the man his heart was filled
with pity. 34 He went over to him, poured oil
and wine on his wounds and bandaged them;
then he put the man on his own animal and took
him to an inn, where he took care of him. 35 The
next day he took out two silver coins and gave
them to the innkeeper. 'Take care of him,' he
told the innkeeper, 'and when I come back this
way I will pay you back whatever you spend on
him.' "
36 And Jesus concluded, "In your opinion,
which one of these three acted like a fellow-man
toward the man attacked by the robbers?"
37 The teacher of the Law answered, "The
one who was kind to him."
Jesus replied, "You go, then, and do the same."

Jesus visits Martha and Mary

38 As Jesus and his disciples went on their
way, he came to a certain village where a woman
named Martha welcomed him in her home.
39 She had a sister named Mary, who sat down
at the feet of the Lord and listened to his teaching. 40 Martha was upset over all the work she
had to do; so she came and said, "Lord, don't
you care that my sister has left me to do all the
work by myself? Tell her to come and help me!"
41 The Lord answered her, "Martha, Martha!
You are worried and troubled over so many
things, 42 but just one is needed. Mary has chosen
the right thing, and it will not be taken away
from her."

New International Version

saw him, he took pity on him. 34 He went to
him and bandaged his wounds, pouring on oil
and wine. Then he put the man on his own
donkey, took him to an inn and took care of
him. 35 The next day he took out two silver
coins[r] and gave them to the innkeeper. 'Look
after him,' he said, 'and when I return, I will
reimburse you for any extra expense you may
have.'
36 "Which of these three do you think was a
neighbor to the man who fell into the hands of
robbers?"
37 The expert in the law replied, "The one
who had mercy on him."
Jesus told him, "Go and do likewise."

At the home of Martha and Mary

38 As Jesus and his disciples were on their
way, he came to a village where a woman named
Martha opened her home to him. 39 She had a
sister called Mary, who sat at the Lord's feet
listening to what he said. 40 But Martha was
distracted by all the preparations that had to
be made. She came to him and asked, "Lord,
don't you care that my sister has left me to do
the work by myself? Tell her to help me!"
41 "Martha, Martha," the Lord answered,
"you are worried and upset about many things,
42 but only one thing is needed.[s] Mary has
chosen what is better, and it will not be taken
away from her."

[r] Greek *two denarii.* [s] Or *but few things are needed—or only one.*

Phillips Modern English

place where the man was lying, and at the sight of him he was touched with pity. He went across to him and bandaged his wounds, pouring on oil and wine. Then he put him on his own mule, brought him to an inn and did what he could for him. Next day he took out two silver coins and gave them to the inn-keeper with the words, 'Look after him, will you? I will pay you back whatever more you spend, when I come through here on my return.' Which of these three seems to you to have been a neighbour to the bandits' victim?"

"The man who gave him practical sympathy," he replied.

"Then you go and give the same," returned Jesus.

10.38 Yet emphasises the need for quiet listening to his words

As they continued their journey, Jesus came to a village and a woman called Martha welcomed him to her house. She had a sister by the name of Mary who settled down at the Lord's feet and was listening to what he said. But Martha was very worried about her elaborate preparations and she burst in, saying,

"Lord, don't you mind that my sister has left me to do everything by myself? Tell her to come and help me!"

But the Lord answered her,

"Martha, my dear, you are worried and bothered about providing so many things. Only one thing is really needed. Mary has chosen the best part and it must not be taken away from her!"

Revised Standard Version

was; and when he saw him, he had compassion, 34 and went to him and bound up his wounds, pouring on oil and wine; then he set him on his own beast and brought him to an inn, and took care of him. 35 And the next day he took out two denarii[i] and gave them to the innkeeper, saying, 'Take care of him; and whatever more you spend, I will repay you when I come back.' 36 Which of these three, do you think, proved neighbor to the man who fell among the robbers?" 37 He said, "The one who showed mercy on him." And Jesus said to him, "Go and do likewise."

38 Now as they went on their way, he entered a village; and a woman named Martha received him into her house. 39 And she had a sister called Mary, who sat at the Lord's feet and listened to his teaching. 40 But Martha was distracted with much serving; and she went to him and said, "Lord, do you not care that my sister has left me to serve alone? Tell her then to help me." 41 But the Lord answered her, "Martha, Martha, you are anxious and troubled about many things; 42 one thing is needful.[j] Mary has chosen the good portion, which shall not be taken away from her."

[i] The denarius was a day's wage for a laborer.
[j] Other ancient authorities read *few things are needful, or only one.*

Jerusalem Bible

compassion when he saw him. 34 He went up and bandaged his wounds, pouring oil and wine on them. He then lifted him on to his own mount, carried him to the inn and looked after him. 35 Next day, he took out two denarii and handed them to the innkeeper. 'Look after him,' he said, 'and on my way back I will make good any extra expense you have.' 36 Which of these three, do you think, proved himself a neighbor to the man who fell into the brigands' hands?" 37 "The one who took pity on him," he replied. Jesus said to him, "Go and do the same yourself."

Martha and Mary

38 In the course of their journey he came to a village, and a woman named Martha welcomed him into her house. 39 She had a sister called Mary, who sat down at the Lord's feet and listened to him speaking. 40 Now Martha who was distracted with all the serving said, "Lord, do you not care that my sister is leaving me to do the serving all by myself? Please tell her to help me." 41 But the Lord answered: "Martha, Martha," he said, "you worry and fret about so many things, 42 and yet few are needed, indeed only one. It is Mary who has chosen the better part; it is not to be taken from her."

New English Bible

and when he saw him was moved to pity. He went up and bandaged his wounds, bathing them with oil and wine. Then he lifted him on to his own beast, brought him to an inn, and looked after him there. Next day he produced two silver pieces and gave them to the innkeeper, and said, "Look after him; and if you spend any more, I will repay you on my way back." Which of these three do you think was neighbour to the man who fell into the hands of the robbers?' He answered, 'The one who showed him kindness.' Jesus said, 'Go and do as he did.'

While they were on their way Jesus came to a village where a woman named Martha made him welcome in her home. She had a sister, Mary, who seated herself at the Lord's feet and stayed there listening to his words. Now Martha was distracted by her many tasks, so she came to him and said, 'Lord, do you not care that my sister has left me to get on with the work by myself? Tell her to come and lend a hand.' But the Lord answered, 'Martha, Martha, you are fretting and fussing about so many things; but one thing is necessary.[a] The part that Mary has chosen is best; and it shall not be taken away from her.'

[a] *Some witnesses read* but few things are necessary, or rather, one alone; *others omit* you are fretting . . . necessary.

King James Version

11 And it came to pass, that, as he was praying in a certain place, when he ceased, one
of his disciples said unto him, Lord, teach us to
pray, as John also taught his disciples. 2And he
said unto them, When ye pray, say, Our Father
which art in heaven, Hallowed be thy name.
Thy kingdom come. Thy will be done, as in
heaven, so in earth. 3 Give us day by day our
daily bread. 4And forgive us our sins; for we
also forgive every one that is indebted to us.
And lead us not into temptation; but deliver us
from evil. 5And he said unto them, Which of
you shall have a friend, and shall go unto him
at midnight, and say unto him, Friend, lend me
three loaves; 6 For a friend of mine in his journey is come to me, and I have nothing to set
before him? 7And he from within shall answer
and say, Trouble me not: the door is now shut,
and my children are with me in bed; I cannot
rise and give thee. 8 I say unto you, Though he
will not rise and give him, because he is his
friend, yet because of his importunity he will

Living Bible

11 Once when Jesus had been out praying,
one of his disciples came to him as he finished and said, "Lord, teach us a prayer to recite[a] just as John taught one to his disciples."
2 And this is the prayer he taught them:
"Father, may your name be honored for its
holiness; send your Kingdom soon. 3 Give us our
food day by day. 4And forgive our sins—for we
have forgiven those who sinned against us. And
don't allow us to be tempted."
5, 6 Then, teaching them more about prayer,[b]
he used this illustration: "Suppose you went to
a friend's house at midnight, wanting to borrow
three loaves of bread. You would shout up to
him, 'A friend of mine has just arrived for a visit
and I've nothing to give him to eat.' 7 He would
call down from his bedroom, 'Please don't ask
me to get up. The door is locked for the night
and we are all in bed. I just can't help you this
time.'
8 "But I'll tell you this—though he won't do
it as a friend, if you keep knocking long enough
he will get up and give you everything you

[a] Implied. [b] Some ancient manuscripts add at this point additional portions of the Lord's Prayer as recorded in Matthew 6:9-13.

Today's English Version

Jesus' teaching on prayer

11 One time Jesus was praying in a certain
place. When he finished, one of his disciples
said to him, "Lord, teach us to pray, just as John
taught his disciples."
2 Jesus said to them, "This is what you should
pray:

'Father:
May your holy name be honored;
may your Kingdom come.
3 Give us day by day the food we need.
4 Forgive us our sins,
because we forgive everyone who does us
wrong.
And do not bring us to hard testing.' "

5 And Jesus said to his disciples, "Suppose
one of you should go to a friend's house at midnight and tell him, 'Friend, let me borrow three
loaves of bread. 6A friend of mine who is on a
trip has just come to my house and I don't have
any food for him!' 7And suppose your friend
should answer from inside, 'Don't bother me!
The door is already locked, and my children and
I are in bed. I can't get up to give you anything.'
8 Well, what then? I tell you, even if he will not
get up and give you the bread because he is your
friend, yet he will get up and give you everything
you need because you are not ashamed to keep

New International Version

Jesus' teaching on prayer

11 One day Jesus was praying in a certain
place. When he finished, one of his disciples
said to him, "Lord, teach us to pray, just as
John taught his disciples."
2 He said to them, "When you pray, say:
'Father,[t]
hallowed be your name,
your kingdom come.[u]
3 Give us each day our daily bread.
4 Forgive us our sins,
for we also forgive everyone who sins
against us.[v]
And lead us not into temptation.' [w] "
5 Then he said to them, "Suppose one of you
has a friend, and he goes to him at midnight and
says, 'Friend, lend me three loaves of bread, 6 because a friend of mine on a journey has come to
me, and I have nothing to set before him.'
7 "Then the one inside answers, 'Don't bother
me. The door is already locked, and my children
are with me in bed. I can't get up and give you
anything.' 8 I tell you, though he will not get
up and give him the bread because he is his
friend, yet because of the man's persistence he
will get up and give him as much as he needs.

[b] *Some witnesses read* Our Father in heaven. [c] *One witness reads* thy kingdom come upon us; *some others have* thy Holy Spirit come upon us and cleanse us; *some insert* thy will be done, on earth as in heaven. [d] *Or* our bread for the morrow. [e] *Some witnesses add* but save us from the evil one (*or* from evil).

Phillips Modern English

11.1 Jesus gives a model prayer

One day it happened that Jesus was praying in a certain place, and after he had finished, one of his disciples said,

"Lord, teach us how to pray, as John used to teach his disciples."

"When you pray," returned Jesus, "you should say, 'Father, may your name be honoured—may your kingdom come. Give us the bread we need for each day, and forgive us our failures, for we forgive everyone who fails us; and keep us clear of temptation.' "

11.5 The willingness of the Father to answer prayer

Then he added,

"If any of you has a friend, and goes to him in the middle of the night and says, 'Lend me three loaves, my dear fellow, for a friend of mine has just arrived after a journey and I have no food to put in front of him'; and then he answers from inside the house, 'Don't bother me with your troubles. The front door is locked and my children and I have gone to bed. I simply cannot get up now and give you anything!' Yet, I tell you, that even if he won't get up and give him what he wants simply because he is his friend, yet if he persists, he will rouse

Revised Standard Version

11 He was praying in a certain place, and
when he ceased, one of his disciples said
to him, "Lord, teach us to pray, as John taught
his disciples." 2And he said to them, "When
you pray, say:
"Father, hallowed be thy name. Thy kingdom
come. 3 Give us each day our daily bread;[k] 4 and
forgive us our sins, for we ourselves forgive
every one who is indebted to us; and lead us not
into temptation."
5 And he said to them, "Which of you who
has a friend will go to him at midnight and say
to him, 'Friend, lend me three loaves; 6 for a
friend of mine has arrived on a journey, and I
have nothing to set before him'; 7 and he will
answer from within, 'Do not bother me; the
door is now shut, and my children are with me
in bed; I cannot get up and give you anything'?
8 I tell you, though he will not get up and give
him anything because he is his friend, yet because of his importunity he will rise and give

[k] Or *our bread for the morrow.*

Jerusalem Bible

The Lord's prayer

11 Now once he was in a certain place praying, and when he had finished one of his
disciples said, "Lord, teach us to pray, just as
John taught his disciples." 2 He said to them,
"Say this when you pray:

'Father, may your name be held holy,
Your kingdom come;
3 give us each day our daily bread,
and forgive us our sins,
4 for we ourselves forgive each one who is in
debt to us.
And do not put us to the test.' "

The importunate friend

5 He also said to them, "Suppose one of you
has a friend and goes to him in the middle of the
night to say, 'My friend, lend me three loaves, 6 because a friend of mine on his travels has just arrived at my house and I have nothing to offer him';
7 and the man answers from inside the house,
'Do not bother me. The door is bolted now, and
my children and I are in bed; I cannot get up
to give it you.' 8 I tell you, if the man does not
get up and give it him for friendship's sake, persistence will be enough to make him get up and
give his friend all he wants.

New English Bible

11 Once, in a certain place, Jesus was at prayer. When he ceased, one of his disciples said, 'Lord, teach us to pray, as John taught his disciples.' He answered, 'When you pray, say,

"Father,[b] thy name be hallowed;
thy kingdom come.[c]
Give us each day our daily bread.[d]
And forgive us our sins,
for we too forgive all who have done us wrong.
And do not bring us to the test." '[e]

Then he said to them, 'Suppose one of you has a friend who comes to him in the middle of the night and says, "My friend, lend me three loaves, for a friend of mine on a journey has turned up at my house, and I have nothing to offer him"; and he replies from inside, "Do not bother me. The door is shut for the night; my children and I have gone to bed; and I cannot get up and give you what you want." I tell you that even if he will not provide for him out of friendship, the very shamelessness of the request will make him get up and give him all he needs.

[t] Some MSS read *Our Father in heaven.* [u] Some MSS add *May your will be done on earth as it is in heaven.* [v] Greek *everyone who is indebted to us.* [w] Some MSS add *but deliver us from the evil one.*

King James Version

rise and give him as many as he needeth. 9And I say unto you, Ask, and it shall be given you; seek, and ye shall find; knock, and it shall be opened unto you. 10 For every one that asketh receiveth; and he that seeketh findeth; and to him that knocketh it shall be opened. 11 If a son shall ask bread of any of you that is a father, will he give him a stone? or if *he ask* a fish, will he for a fish give him a serpent? 12 Or if he shall ask an egg, will he offer him a scorpion? 13 If ye then, being evil, know how to give good gifts unto your children; how much more shall *your* heavenly Father give the Holy Spirit to them that ask him?

14 And he was casting out a devil, and it was dumb. And it came to pass, when the devil was gone out, the dumb spake; and the people wondered. 15 But some of them said, He casteth out devils through Beelzebub the chief of the devils. 16And others, tempting *him*, sought of him a sign from heaven. 17 But he, knowing their thoughts, said unto them, Every kingdom divided against itself is brought to desolation; and a house *divided* against a house falleth. 18 If Satan also be divided against himself, how shall his kingdom stand? because ye say that I cast out devils

Living Bible

want—just because of your persistence. 9And so it is with prayer—keep on asking and you will keep on getting; keep on looking and you will keep on finding; knock and the door will be opened. 10 Everyone who asks, receives; all who seek, find; and the door is opened to everyone who knocks.

11 "You men who are fathers—if your boy asks for bread, do you give him a stone? If he asks for fish, do you give him a snake? 12 If he asks for an egg, do you give him a scorpion? [Of course not! [c]]

13 "And if even sinful persons like yourselves give children what they need, don't you realize that your heavenly Father will do at least as much, and give the Holy Spirit to those who ask for him?"

14 Once, when Jesus cast out a demon from a man who couldn't speak, his voice returned to him. The crowd was excited and enthusiastic, 15 but some said, "No wonder he can cast them out. He gets his power from Satan,[d] the king of demons!" 16 Others asked for something to happen in the sky to prove his claim of being the Messiah.[e]

17 He knew the thoughts of each of them, so he said, "Any kingdom filled with civil war is doomed; so is a home filled with argument and strife. 18 Therefore, if what you say is true, that Satan is fighting against himself by empowering me to cast out his demons, how can his kingdom

[*c*] Implied. [*d*] Literally, "from Beelzebub." [*e*] Implied; literally, "Others, tempting, sought of him a sign from heaven."

Today's English Version

on asking. 9And so I say to you: Ask, and you will receive; seek, and you will find; knock, and the door will be opened to you. 10 For everyone who asks will receive, and he who seeks will find, and the door will be opened to him who knocks. 11 Would any of you who are fathers give your son a snake when he asks for fish? 12 Or would you give him a scorpion when he asks for an egg? 13As bad as you are, you know how to give good things to your children. How much more, then, the Father in heaven will give the Holy Spirit to those who ask him!"

Jesus and Beelzebul

14 Jesus was driving out a demon that could not talk; when the demon went out, the man began to talk. The crowds were amazed, 15 but some of the people said, "It is Beelzebul, the chief of the demons, who gives him the power to drive them out."

16 Others wanted to trap him, so they asked him to perform a miracle to show God's approval. 17 But Jesus knew their thoughts and said to them, "Any country that divides itself into groups that fight each other will not last very long; a family divided against itself falls apart. 18 So if Satan's kingdom has groups fighting each other, how can it last? You say that I drive out demons because Beelzebul gives me

New International Version

9 "So I say to you: Ask and it will be given to you; seek and you will find; knock and the door will be opened to you. 10 For everyone who asks receives; he who seeks finds; and to him who knocks, the door will be opened.

11 "Which of you fathers, if your son asks for a fish, will give him a snake instead? 12 Or if he asks for an egg, will give him a scorpion? 13 If you then, though you are evil, know how to give good gifts to your children, how much more will your Father in heaven give the Holy Spirit to those who ask him!"

Jesus and Beelzebub

14 Jesus was driving out a demon that was mute. When the demon left, the man who had been dumb spoke, and the crowd was amazed. 15 But some of them said, "By Beelzebub,[x] the prince of demons, he is driving out demons." 16 Others tested him by asking for a sign from heaven.

17 Jesus knew their thoughts and said to them: "Any kingdom divided against itself will be ruined, and a house divided against itself will fall. 18 If Satan is divided against himself, how can his kingdom stand? I say this because you claim that I drive out demons by Beelzebub.[x]

[*x*] Greek MSS *Beelzeboul* or *Beezeboul.*

Phillips Modern English

himself and give him everything he needs. And so I tell you, ask and it will be given you, search and you will find, knock and the door will be opened to you. The one who asks will always receive; the one who is searching will always find, and the door is opened to the man who knocks. Some of you are fathers, and if your son asks you for some fish, would you give him a snake instead, or if he asks you for an egg, would you make him a present of a scorpion? So, if you, for all your evil, know how to give good things to your children, how much more likely is it that your Heavenly Father will give the Holy Spirit to those who ask him!"

11.14 Jesus shows the absurdity of "his being in league with the devil"

Another time, Jesus was expelling an evil spirit which was preventing a man from speaking, and as soon as the evil spirit left him, the dumb man found his speech, to the amazement of the crowds.

But some of them said,

"He expels these spirits because he is in league with Beelzebub, the chief of the evil spirits."

Others among them, to test him, tried to get a sign from Heaven out of him. But he knew what they were thinking and told them,

"Any kingdom divided against itself is doomed and a disunited household will collapse. And if Satan disagrees with Satan, how does his kingdom continue?—for I know you are saying that

Revised Standard Version

him whatever he needs. 9And I tell you, Ask,
and it will be given you; seek, and you will find;
knock, and it will be opened to you. 10 For
every one who asks receives, and he who seeks
finds, and to him who knocks it will be opened.
11 What father among you, if his son asks for[l]
a fish, will instead of a fish give him a serpent;
12 or if he asks for an egg, will give him a
scorpion? 13 If you then, who are evil, know
how to give good gifts to your children, how
much more will the heavenly Father give the
Holy Spirit to those who ask him!"
14 Now he was casting out a demon that was
dumb; when the demon had gone out, the dumb
man spoke, and the people marveled. 15 But
some of them said, "He casts out demons by
Beelzebul, the prince of demons"; 16 while
others, to test him, sought from him a sign from
heaven. 17 But he, knowing their thoughts, said
to them, "Every kingdom divided against itself
is laid waste, and a divided household falls.
18And if Satan also is divided against himself,
how will his kingdom stand? For you say that

[l] Other ancient authorities insert *bread, will give him a stone; or if he asks for.*

Jerusalem Bible

Effective prayer

9 "So I say to you: Ask, and it will be given
to you; search, and you will find; knock, and the
door will be opened to you. 10 For the one who
asks always receives; the one who searches always finds; the one who knocks will always have
the door opened to him. 11 What father among
you would hand his son a stone when he asked
for bread? Or hand him a snake instead of a fish?
12 Or hand him a scorpion if he asked for an
egg? 13 If you then, who are evil, know how to
give your children what is good, how much
more will the heavenly Father give the Holy
Spirit to those who ask him!"

Jesus and Beelzebul

14 He was casting out a devil and it was
dumb; but when the devil had gone out the dumb
man spoke, and the people were amazed. 15 But
some of them said, "It is through Beelzebul, the
prince of devils, that he casts out devils." 16 Others asked him, as a test, for a sign from heaven;
17 but, knowing what they were thinking, he said
to them, "Every kingdom divided against itself
is heading for ruin, and a household divided
against itself collapses. 18 So too with Satan:
if he is divided against himself, how can his
kingdom stand?—Since you assert that it is

New English Bible

And so I say to you, ask, and you will receive; seek, and you will find; knock, and the door will be opened. For everyone who asks receives, he who seeks finds, and to him who knocks, the door will be opened.

'Is there a father among you who will offer his son[a] a snake when he asks for fish, or a scorpion when he asks for an egg? If you, then, bad as you are, know how to give your children what is good for them, how much more will the heavenly Father give the Holy Spirit[b] to those who ask him!'

He was driving out a devil which was dumb; and when the devil had come out, the dumb man began to speak. The people were astonished, but some of them said, 'It is by Beelzebub prince of devils that he drives the devils out.' Others, by way of a test, demanded of him a sign from heaven. But he knew what was in their minds, and said, 'Every kingdom divided against itself goes to ruin, and a divided household falls. Equally if Satan is divided against himself, how can his kingdom stand?—since, as you would

[a] *Some witnesses insert* a stone when he asks for bread, or . . . [b] *Some witnesses read* a good gift; *some others read* good things.

King James Version

through Beelzebub. 19 And if I by Beelzebub cast out devils, by whom do your sons cast *them* out? therefore shall they be your judges. 20 But if I with the finger of God cast out devils, no doubt the kingdom of God is come upon you. 21 When a strong man armed keepeth his palace, his goods are in peace: 22 But when a stronger than he shall come upon him, and overcome him, he taketh from him all his armour wherein he trusted, and divideth his spoils. 23 He that is not with me is against me; and he that gathereth not with me scattereth. 24 When the unclean spirit is gone out of a man, he walketh through dry places, seeking rest; and finding none, he saith, I will return unto my house whence I came out. 25 And when he cometh, he findeth *it* swept and garnished. 26 Then goeth he, and taketh *to him* seven other spirits more wicked than himself; and they enter in, and dwell there: and the last *state* of that man is worse than the first.

Living Bible

survive? 19 And if I am empowered by Satan, what about your own followers? For they cast out demons! Do you think this proves they are possessed by Satan? Ask *them* if you are right! 20 But if I am casting out demons because of power from God, it proves that the Kingdom of God has arrived.

21 "For when Satan,[f] strong and fully armed, guards his palace, it is safe—22 until someone stronger and better-armed attacks and overcomes him and strips him of his weapons and carries off his belongings.

23 "Anyone who is not for me is against me; if he isn't helping me, he is hurting my cause.

24 "When a demon is cast out of a man, it goes to the deserts, searching there for rest; but finding none, it returns to the person it left, 25 and finds that its former home is all swept and clean.[g] 26 Then it goes and gets seven other demons more evil than itself, and they all enter the man. And so the poor fellow is seven times[c] worse off than he was before."

[*f*] Literally, "the Strong." [*g*] But empty, since the person is neutral about Christ. [*c*] Implied.

Today's English Version

the power to do so. 19 If this is how I drive them out, how do your followers drive them out? Your own followers prove that you are wrong! 20 No, it is rather by means of God's power that I drive out demons, which proves that the Kingdom of God has already come to you.

21 "When a strong man, with all his weapons ready, guards his own house, all his belongings are safe. 22 But when a stronger man attacks him and defeats him, he carries away all the weapons the owner was depending on and divides up what he stole.

23 "Anyone who is not for me is really against me; anyone who does not help me gather is really scattering."

The return of the evil spirit

24 "When an evil spirit goes out of a man, it travels over dry country looking for a place to rest. If it can't find one, it says to itself, 'I will go back to my house which I left.' 25 So it goes back and finds the house clean and all fixed up. 26 Then it goes out and brings seven other spirits even worse than itself, and they come and live there. So that man is in worse shape, when it is all over, than he was at the beginning."

New International Version

19 Now if I drive out demons by Beelzebub,[x] by whom do your followers drive them out? So then, they will be your judges. 20 But if I drive out demons by the finger of God, then the kingdom of God has come to you.

21 "When a strong man, fully armed, guards his own house, his possessions are safe. 22 But when someone stronger attacks and overpowers him, he takes away the armor in which the man trusted and divides up the spoils.

23 "He who is not with me is against me, and he who does not gather with me, scatters.

24 "When an evil [y] spirit comes out of a man, it goes through arid places seeking rest and does not find it. Then it says, 'I will return to the house I left.' 25 When it arrives, it finds the house swept clean and put in order. 26 Then it goes and takes seven other spirits more wicked than itself, and they go in and live there. And the final condition of that man is worse than the first."

[*x*] Greek MSS *Beelzeboul* or *Beezeboul.* [*y*] Greek *unclean.*

Phillips Modern English

I expel evil spirits because I am in league with Beelzebub. But if I do expel devils because I am an ally of Beelzebub, who is your own sons' ally when they do the same thing? They can settle that question for you. But if it is by the finger of God that I am expelling evil spirits, then the kingdom of God has swept over you here and now.

"When a strong man armed to the teeth guards his own house, his property is secure. But when a stronger man comes and conquers him, he removes all the arms on which he pinned his faith and divides the spoil among his friends.

"Anyone who is not with me is against me, and the man who does not gather with me is really scattering.

11.24 The danger of a spiritual vacuum in a man's soul

"When the evil spirit comes out of a man, it wanders through waterless places looking for rest, and when it fails to find any, it says, 'I will go back to my house from which I came.' When it arrives, it finds it cleaned and all in order. Then it goes and collects seven other spirits more evil than itself to keep it company, and they all go in and make themselves at home. The last state of that man is worse than the first."

Revised Standard Version

I cast out demons by Beelzebul. 19And if I cast
out demons by Beelzebul, by whom do your sons
cast them out? Therefore they shall be your
judges. 20 But if it is by the finger of God that
I cast out demons, then the kingdom of God
has come upon you. 21 When a strong man, fully
armed, guards his own palace, his goods are in
peace; 22 but when one stronger than he assails
him and overcomes him, he takes away his
armor in which he trusted, and divides his spoil.
23 He who is not with me is against me, and he
who does not gather with me scatters.
24 "When the unclean spirit has gone out of
a man, he passes through waterless places seeking rest; and finding none he says, 'I will return
to my house from which I came.' 25And when he
comes he finds it swept and put in order. 26 Then
he goes and brings seven other spirits more evil
than himself, and they enter and dwell there;
and the last state of that man becomes worse
than the first."

Jerusalem Bible

through Beelzebul that I cast out devils. 19 Now
if it is through Beelzebul that I cast out devils,
through whom do your own experts cast them
out? Let them be your judges, then. 20 But if it
is through the finger of God that I cast out
devils, then know that the kingdom of God has
overtaken you. 21 So long as a strong man fully
armed guards his own palace, his goods are undisturbed; 22 but when someone stronger than
he is attacks and defeats him, the stronger man
takes away all the weapons he relied on and
shares out his spoil.

No compromise

23 "He who is not with me is against me; and he who does not gather with me scatters.

Return of the unclean spirit

24 "When an unclean spirit goes out of a man
it wanders through waterless country looking for
a place to rest, and not finding one it says, 'I will
go back to the home I came from.' 25 But on
arrival, finding it swept and tidied, 26 it then goes
off and brings seven other spirits more wicked
than itself, and they go in and set up house
there, so that the man ends up by being worse
than he was before."

New English Bible

have it, I drive out the devils by Beelzebub. If it is by Beelzebub that I cast out devils, by whom do your own people drive them out? If this is your argument, they themselves will refute you. But if it is by the finger of God that I drive out the devils, then be sure the kingdom of God has already come upon you.

'When a strong man fully armed is on guard over his castle his possessions are safe. But when someone stronger comes upon him and overpowers him, he carries off the arms and armour on which the man had relied and divides the plunder.

'He who is not with me is against me, and he who does not gather with me scatters.[c]

'When an unclean spirit comes out of a man it wanders over the deserts seeking a resting-place; and if it finds none, it says, "I will go back to the home I left." So it returns and finds the house[d] swept clean, and tidy. Off it goes and collects seven other spirits more wicked than itself, and they all come in and settle down; and in the end the man's plight is worse than before.'

[c] *Some witnesses add* me. [d] *Some witnesses insert* unoccupied.

King James Version

27 And it came to pass, as he spake these
things, a certain woman of the company lifted
up her voice, and said unto him, Blessed *is* the
womb that bare thee, and the paps which thou
hast sucked. 28 But he said, Yea, rather, blessed
are they that hear the word of God, and keep it.
29 And when the people were gathered thick
together, he began to say, This is an evil generation: they seek a sign; and there shall no sign
be given it, but the sign of Jonas the prophet.
30 For as Jonas was a sign unto the Ninevites,
so shall also the Son of man be to this generation. 31 The queen of the south shall rise up in
the judgment with the men of this generation,
and condemn them: for she came from the utmost parts of the earth to hear the wisdom of
Solomon; and, behold, a greater than Solomon
is here. 32 The men of Nineveh shall rise up in
the judgment with this generation, and shall condemn it: for they repented at the preaching of
Jonas; and, behold, a greater than Jonas *is* here.

Living Bible

27 As he was speaking, a woman in the
crowd called out, "God bless your mother—the
womb from which you came, and the breasts
that gave you suck!"
28 He replied, "Yes, but even more blessed
are all who hear the Word of God and put it
into practice."
29, 30 As the crowd pressed in upon him, he
preached them this sermon: "These are evil
times, with evil people. They keep asking for
some strange happening in the skies [to prove I
am the Messiah[c]], but the only proof I will give
them is a miracle like that of Jonah, whose experiences proved to the people of Nineveh that
God had sent him. My similar experience will
prove that God has sent me to these people.
31 "And at the Judgment Day the Queen of
Sheba[h] shall arise and point her finger at this
generation, condemning it, for she went on a
long, hard journey to listen to the wisdom of
Solomon; but one far greater than Solomon is
here [and few pay any attention[c]].
32 "The men of Nineveh, too, shall arise and
condemn this nation, for they repented at the
preaching of Jonah; and someone far greater
than Jonah is here [but this nation won't listen[c]].

[*c*] Implied. [*h*] Literally, "Queen of the South." See 1 Kings, chapter 10.

Today's English Version

True happiness

27 When Jesus had said this, a woman spoke
up from the crowd and said to him, "How happy
is the woman who bore you and nursed you!"
28 But Jesus answered, "Rather, how happy
are those who hear the word of God and obey
it!"

The demand for a miracle

29 As the people crowded around Jesus he
went on to say, "How evil are the people of this
day! They ask for a miracle, but none will be
given them except the miracle of Jonah. 30 In
the same way that the prophet Jonah was a sign
for the people of Nineveh, so the Son of Man
will be a sign for the people of this day. 31 On
the Judgment Day the Queen from the South will
stand up and accuse the people of today, because
she traveled halfway around the world to listen
to Solomon's wise teaching; and there is something here, I tell you, greater than Solomon.
32 On the Judgment Day the people of Nineveh
will stand up and accuse you, because they turned
from their sins when they heard Jonah preach;
and there is something here, I tell you, greater
than Jonah!"

New International Version

27 As Jesus was saying these things, a woman
in the crowd called out, "Blessed is the mother
who gave you birth and nursed you."
28 He replied, "Blessed rather are those who
hear the word of God and obey it."

The sign of Jonah

29 As the crowds increased, Jesus said, "This
is a wicked generation. It asks for a miraculous
sign, but none will be given it except the sign
of Jonah. 30 For as Jonah was a sign to the
Ninevites, so also will the Son of Man be to this
generation. 31 The Queen of the South will rise
at the judgment with the men of this generation
and condemn them, for she came from the ends
of the earth to listen to Solomon's wisdom, and
now one greater than Solomon is here. 32 The
men of Nineveh will stand up at the judgment
with this generation and condemn it, for they
repented at the preaching of Jonah, and now
one greater than Jonah is here.

Phillips Modern English

11.27 Jesus brings sentimentality down to earth

And while he was still saying this, a woman in the crowd called out and said,

"Oh, what a blessing for a woman to have brought you into the world and nursed you!"

But Jesus replied,

"Yes, but a far greater blessing is to hear the word of God and obey it."

11.29 His scathing judgment on his contemporary generation

Then as the people crowded closely around him, he continued,

"This is an evil generation! It looks for a sign and it will be given no sign except that of Jonah. Just as Jonah was a sign to the people of Nineveh, so will the Son of Man be a sign to this generation. When the judgment comes, the Queen of the South will rise up with the men of this generation and she will condemn them. For she came from the ends of the earth to listen to the wisdom of Solomon, and there is more than the wisdom of Solomon with you now. The men of Nineveh will stand up at the judgment with this generation and will condemn it. For they did repent when Jonah preached to them, and there is something more than Jonah's preaching with you now.

Revised Standard Version

27 As he said this, a woman in the crowd raised her voice and said to him, "Blessed is the womb that bore you, and the breasts that you sucked!" 28 But he said, "Blessed rather are those who hear the word of God and keep it!"

29 When the crowds were increasing, he began to say, "This generation is an evil generation; it seeks a sign, but no sign shall be given to it except the sign of Jonah. 30 For as Jonah became a sign to the men of Nineveh, so will the Son of man be to this generation. 31 The queen of the South will arise at the judgment with the men of this generation and condemn them; for she came from the ends of the earth to hear the wisdom of Solomon, and behold, something greater than Solomon is here. 32 The men of Nineveh will arise at the judgment with this generation and condemn it; for they repented at the preaching of Jonah, and behold, something greater than Jonah is here.

Jerusalem Bible

The truly happy

27 Now as he was speaking, a woman in the crowd raised her voice and said, "Happy the womb that bore you and the breasts you sucked!" 28 But he replied, "Still happier those who hear the word of God and keep it!"

The sign of Jonah

29 The crowds got even bigger and he addressed them, "This is a wicked generation; it is asking for a sign. The only sign it will be given is the sign of Jonah. 30 For just as Jonah became a sign to the Ninevites, so will the Son of Man be to this generation. 31 On Judgment day the Queen of the South will rise up with the men of this generation and condemn them, because she came from the ends of the earth to hear the wisdom of Solomon; and there is something greater than Solomon here. 32 On Judgment day the men of Nineveh will stand up with this generation and condemn it, because when Jonah preached they repented; and there is something greater than Jonah here.

New English Bible

While he was speaking thus, a woman in the crowd called out, 'Happy the womb that carried you and the breasts that suckled you!' He rejoined, 'No, happy are those who hear the word of God and keep it.'

With the crowds swarming round him he went on to say: 'This is a wicked generation. It demands a sign, and the only sign that will be given it is the sign of Jonah. For just as Jonah was a sign to the Ninevites, so will the Son of Man be to this generation. At the Judgement, when the men of this generation are on trial, the Queen of the South will appear against[a] them and ensure their condemnation, for she came from the ends of the earth to hear the wisdom of Solomon; and what is here is greater than Solomon. The men of Nineveh will appear at the Judgement when this generation is on trial, and ensure[b] its condemnation, for they repented at the preaching of Jonah; and what is here is greater than Jonah.

[a] Or will be raised to life together with . . . *[b] Or* At the Judgement the men of Nineveh will rise again together with this generation and will ensure . . .

King James Version

33 No man, when he hath lighted a candle, putteth *it* in a secret place, neither under a bushel,
but on a candlestick, that they which come in
may see the light. 34 The light of the body is
the eye: therefore when thine eye is single, thy
whole body also is full of light; but when *thine*
eye is evil, thy body also *is* full of darkness.
35 Take heed therefore, that the light which is
in thee be not darkness. 36 If thy whole body
therefore *be* full of light, having no part dark,
the whole shall be full of light, as when the
bright shining of a candle doth give thee light.
37 And as he spake, a certain Pharisee besought him to dine with him: and he went in,
and sat down to meat. 38 And when the Pharisee
saw *it*, he marvelled that he had not first washed
before dinner. 39 And the Lord said unto him,
Now do ye Pharisees make clean the outside of
the cup and the platter; but your inward part
is full of ravening and wickedness. 40 *Ye* fools,
did not he, that made that which is without,
make that which is within also? 41 But rather
give alms of such things as ye have; and, behold,
all things are clean unto you. 42 But woe unto
you, Pharisees! for ye tithe mint and rue and
all manner of herbs, and pass over judgment

Living Bible

33 "No one lights a lamp and hides it! Instead,
he puts it on a lampstand to give light to all who
enter the room. 34 Your eyes light up your inward being. A pure eye lets sunshine into your
soul. A lustful eye shuts out the light and
plunges you into darkness. 35 So watch out that
the sunshine isn't blotted out. 36 If you are filled
with light within, with no dark corners, then your
face will be radiant too, as though a floodlight
is beamed upon you."
37, 38 As he was speaking, one of the Pharisees asked him home for a meal. When Jesus arrived, he sat down to eat without first performing the ceremonial washing required by Jewish
custom. This greatly surprised his host.
39 Then Jesus said to him, "You Pharisees
wash the outside, but inside you are still dirty—
full of greed and wickedness! 40 Fools! Didn't
God make the inside as well as the outside?
41 Purity is best demonstrated by generosity.
42 "But woe to you Pharisees! For though
you are careful to tithe even the smallest part of
your income, you completely forget about justice
and the love of God. You should tithe, yes, but

Today's English Version

The light of the body

33 "No one lights a lamp and then hides it or
puts it under a bowl; instead, he puts it on the
lampstand, so that people may see the light as
they come in. 34 Your eyes are like a lamp for
the body. When your eyes are clear your whole
body is full of light; but when your eyes are bad
your whole body will be in darkness. 35 Be
careful, then, that the light in you is not darkness. 36 If, then, your whole body is full of light,
with no part of it in darkness, it will be bright
all over, as when a lamp shines on you with its
brightness."

Jesus accuses the Pharisees and the teachers of the Law

37 When Jesus finished speaking, a Pharisee
invited him to eat with him; so he went in and
sat down to eat. 38 The Pharisee was surprised
when he noticed that Jesus had not washed before eating. 39 So the Lord said to him, "Now,
then, you Pharisees clean the cup and plate on
the outside, but inside you are full of violence
and evil. 40 Fools! Did not God, who made the
outside, also make the inside? 41 But give what
is in your cups and plates to the poor, and everything will be clean for you.
42 "How terrible for you, Pharisees! You
give to God one tenth of the seasoning herbs,
such as mint and rue and all the other herbs, but
you neglect justice and love for God. These you

New International Version

The lamp of the body

33 "No one lights a lamp and puts it in a
place where it will be hidden, or under a bowl.
Instead he puts it on its stand, so that those
who come in may see the light. 34 Your eye is
the lamp of your body. When your eyes are
good, your whole body also is full of light. But
when they are bad, your body also is full of
darkness. 35 See to it, then, that the light within
you is not darkness. 36 Therefore, if your whole
body is full of light, and no part of it dark, it
will be completely lighted, as when the light of
a lamp shines on you."

Six woes

37 When Jesus had finished speaking, a Pharisee invited him to eat with him; so he went in
and reclined at the table. 38 But the Pharisee,
noticing that Jesus did not first wash before the
meal, was surprised.
39 Then the Lord said to him, "Now then,
you Pharisees clean the outside of the cup and
dish, but inside you are full of greed and wickedness. 40 You foolish people! Did not the one
who made the outside make the inside also?
41 But give what is inside to the poor, and everything will be clean for you.
42 "Woe to you Pharisees, because you give
God a tenth of your mint, rue and all other
kinds of garden herbs, but you neglect justice
and the love of God. You should have practiced

Phillips Modern English

11.33 The need for complete sincerity

"No one takes a lamp and puts it in a cupboard or under a bucket, but on a lamp-stand, so that those who come in can see the light. The lamp of your body is your eye. When your eye is sound, your whole body is full of light, but when your eye is evil, your whole body is full of darkness. So be very careful that your light never becomes darkness. For if your whole body is full of light, with no part of it in shadow, it will all be radiant—it will be like having a bright lamp to give you light."

While he was talking, a Pharisee invited him to dinner. So he went into his house and sat down at table. The Pharisee noticed with some surprise that he did not wash before the meal. But the Lord said to him,

"You Pharisees are fond of cleaning the outside of your cups and dishes, but inside yourselves you are full of greed and wickedness! Have you no sense? Don't you realise that the one who made the outside is the maker of the inside as well? If you would only make the inside clean by giving the contents to those in need, the outside becomes clean as a matter of course! But alas for you Pharisees, for you pay out your tithe of mint and rue and every little herb, and lose sight of the justice and the love of God. Yet these are the things you ought to have been

Revised Standard Version

33 "No one after lighting a lamp puts it in a cellar or under a bushel, but on a stand, that those who enter may see the light. 34 Your eye is the lamp of your body; when your eye is sound, your whole body is full of light; but when it is not sound, your body is full of darkness. 35 Therefore be careful lest the light in you be darkness. 36 If then your whole body is full of light, having no part dark, it will be wholly bright, as when a lamp with its rays gives you light."

37 While he was speaking, a Pharisee asked him to dine with him; so he went in and sat at table. 38 The Pharisee was astonished to see that he did not first wash before dinner. 39 And the Lord said to him, "Now you Pharisees cleanse the outside of the cup and of the dish, but inside you are full of extortion and wickedness. 40 You fools! Did not he who made the outside make the inside also? 41 But give for alms those things which are within; and behold, everything is clean for you.

42 "But woe to you Pharisees! for you tithe mint and rue and every herb, and neglect jus-

Jerusalem Bible

The parable of the lamp repeated

33 "No one lights a lamp and puts it in some hidden place or under a tub, but on the lampstand so that people may see the light when they come in. 34 The lamp of your body is your eye. When your eye is sound, your whole body too is filled with light; but when it is diseased your body too will be all darkness. 35 See to it then that the light inside you is not darkness. 36 If, therefore, your whole body is filled with light, and no trace of darkness, it will be light entirely, as when the lamp shines on you with its rays."

The Pharisees and the lawyers attacked

37 He had just finished speaking when a Pharisee invited him to dine at his house. He went in and sat down at the table. 38 The Pharisee saw this and was surprised that he had not first washed before the meal. 39 But the Lord said to him, "Oh, you Pharisees! You clean the outside of cup and plate, while inside yourselves you are filled with extortion and wickedness. 40 Fools! Did not he who made the outside make the inside too? 41 Instead, give alms from what you have and then indeed everything will be clean for you. 42 But alas for you Pharisees! You who pay your tithe of mint and rue and all sorts of garden herbs and overlook justice and

New English Bible

'No one lights a lamp and puts it in a cellar,[c] but rather on the lamp-stand so that those who enter may see the light. The lamp of your body is the eye. When your eyes are sound, you have light for your whole body; but when the eyes are bad, you are in darkness. See to it then that the light you have is not darkness. If you have light for your whole body with no trace of darkness, it will all be as bright as when a lamp flashes its rays upon you.'

When he had finished speaking, a Pharisee invited him to a meal. He came in and sat down. The Pharisee noticed with surprise that he had not begun by washing before the meal. But the Lord said to him, 'You Pharisees! You clean the outside of cup and plate; but inside you there is nothing but greed and wickedness. You fools! Did not he who made the outside make the inside too? But let what is in the cup[d] be given in charity, and all is clean.

'Alas for you Pharisees! You pay tithes of mint and rue and every garden-herb, but have no care for justice and the love of God. It is these

[c] *Some witnesses insert* or under the meal-tub.
[d] *Or* what you can afford.

King James Version

and the love of God: these ought ye to have
done, and not to leave the other undone. 43 Woe
unto you, Pharisees! for ye love the uppermost
seats in the synagogues, and greetings in the
markets. 44 Woe unto you, scribes and Pharisees,
hypocrites! for ye are as graves which appear
not, and the men that walk over *them* are not
aware *of them*.
45 Then answered one of the lawyers, and
said unto him, Master, thus saying thou re-
proachest us also. 46And he said, Woe unto you
also, *ye* lawyers! for ye lade men with burdens
grievous to be borne, and ye yourselves touch
not the burdens with one of your fingers. 47 Woe
unto you! for ye build the sepulchres of the
prophets, and your fathers killed them. 48 Truly
ye bear witness that ye allow the deeds of your
fathers: for they indeed killed them, and ye
build their sepulchres. 49 Therefore also said the
wisdom of God, I will send them prophets and
apostles, and *some* of them they shall slay and
persecute: 50 That the blood of all the prophets,
which was shed from the foundation of the world,
may be required of this generation; 51 From the
blood of Abel unto the blood of Zacharias,
which perished between the altar and the temple: verily I say unto you, It shall be required
of this generation. 52 Woe unto you, lawyers! for
ye have taken away the key of knowledge: ye

Living Bible

you should not leave these other things undone.
43 "Woe to you Pharisees! For how you love
the seats of honor in the synagogues and the
respectful greetings from everyone as you walk
through the markets! 44 Yes, awesome judgment
is awaiting you. For you are like hidden graves
in a field. Men go by you with no knowledge of
the corruption they are passing."
45 "Sir," said an expert in religious law who
was standing there, "you have insulted my profession, too, in what you just said."
46 "Yes," said Jesus, "the same horrors await
you! For you crush men beneath impossible religious demands—demands that you yourselves
would never think of trying to keep. 47 Woe to
you! For you are exactly like your ancestors who
killed the prophets long ago. 48 Murderers! You
agree with your fathers that what they did was
right—you would have done the same yourselves.
49 "This is what God says about you: 'I will
send prophets and apostles to you, and you will
kill some of them and chase away the others.'
50 "And you of this generation will be held
responsible for the murder of God's servants
from the founding of the world—51 from the
murder of Abel to the murder of Zechariah who
perished between the altar and the sanctuary.
Yes, it will surely be charged against you.
52 "Woe to you experts in religion! For you
hide the truth from the people. You won't ac-

Today's English Version

should practice, without neglecting the others.
43 "How terrible for you, Pharisees! You love
the reserved seats in the synagogues, and to be
greeted with respect in the market places. 44 How
terrible for you! You are like unmarked graves
which people walk on without knowing it."
45 One of the teachers of the Law said to him,
"Teacher, when you say this you insult us too!"
46 Jesus answered, "How terrible for you,
too, teachers of the Law! You put loads on
men's backs which are hard to carry, but you
yourselves will not stretch out a finger to help
them carry those loads. 47 How terrible for you!
You make fine tombs for the prophets—the very
prophets your ancestors murdered. 48 You yourselves admit, then, that you approve of what your
ancestors did; because they murdered the prophets, and you build their tombs. 49 For this reason the Wisdom of God said, 'I will send them
prophets and messengers; they will kill some of
them and persecute others.' 50 So the people of
this time will be punished for the murder of all
the prophets killed since the creation of the
world, 51 from the murder of Abel to the murder
of Zechariah, who was killed between the altar
and the holy place. Yes, I tell you, the people of
this time will be punished for them all!
52 "How terrible for you, teachers of the Law!
You have kept the key that opens the door to

New International Version

the latter without leaving the former undone.
43 "Woe to you Pharisees, because you love
the most important seats in the synagogues and
greetings in the marketplaces.
44 "Woe to you, because you are like unmarked graves, which men walk over without
knowing it."
45 One of the experts in the law answered
him, "Teacher, when you say these things, you
insult us also."
46 Jesus replied, "And you experts in the law,
woe to you, because you load people down with
burdens they can hardly carry, and you yourselves will not lift one finger to help them.
47 "Woe to you, because you build tombs for
the prophets, and it was your forefathers who
killed them. 48 So you testify that you approve
of what your forefathers did; they killed the
prophets, and you build their tombs. 49 Because
of this, God in his wisdom said, 'I will send
them prophets and apostles, some of whom they
will kill and others they will persecute.' 50 Therefore this generation will be held responsible for
the blood of all the prophets that has been shed
since the beginning of the world, 51 from the
blood of Abel to the blood of Zechariah, who
was killed between the altar and the sanctuary.
Yes, I tell you, this generation will be held responsible for it all.
52 "Woe to you experts in the law, because
you have taken away the key to knowledge. You

Phillips Modern English

concerned with—it need not mean leaving the lesser duties undone. Yes, alas for you Pharisees, who love the front seats in the synagogues and having men bow down to you in public! Alas for you, for you are like unmarked graves—men walk over your corruption without ever knowing it is there."

11.45 Jesus denounces the learned for obscuring the truth

Then one of the experts in the Law said to him,

"Master, when you say things like this, you are insulting us as well."

And he returned,

"Yes, and I do blame you experts in the Law! For you pile up back-breaking burdens for men to bear, but you yourselves will not raise a finger to lift them. Alas for you, for you build memorial tombs for the prophets—the very men whom your fathers murdered. You show clearly enough how you approve your fathers' actions. They did the killing and you put up the memorials. That is why the Wisdom of God has said, 'I will send them prophets and apostles; some they will kill and some they will persecute!' So that the blood of all the prophets shed from the foundation of the earth, from Abel to Zachariah who died between the altar and the sanctuary, shall be charged to this generation. Yes, I tell you this generation must answer for it all!

"Alas for you experts in the Law, for you have taken away the key of knowledge. You

Revised Standard Version

tice and the love of God; these you ought to
have done, without neglecting the others. 43 Woe
to you Pharisees! for you love the best seat in
the synagogues and salutations in the market
places. 44 Woe to you! for you are like graves
which are not seen, and men walk over them
without knowing it."
45 One of the lawyers answered him,
"Teacher, in saying this you reproach us also."
46 And he said, "Woe to you lawyers also! for
you load men with burdens hard to bear, and
you yourselves do not touch the burdens with
one of your fingers. 47 Woe to you! for you
build the tombs of the prophets whom your
fathers killed. 48 So you are witnesses and consent to the deeds of your fathers; for they killed
them, and you build their tombs. 49 Therefore
also the Wisdom of God said, 'I will send them
prophets and apostles, some of whom they will
kill and persecute,' 50 that the blood of all the
prophets, shed from the foundation of the world,
may be required of this generation, 51 from the
blood of Abel to the blood of Zechariah, who
perished between the altar and the sanctuary.
Yes, I tell you, it shall be required of this generation. 52 Woe to you lawyers! for you have
taken away the key of knowledge; you did not

Jerusalem Bible

the love of God! These you should have practiced, without leaving the others undone. 43 Alas
for you Pharisees who like taking the seats of
honor in the synagogues and being greeted obsequiously in the market squares! 44 Alas for you,
because you are like the unmarked tombs that
men walk on without knowing it! [s]
45 A lawyer then spoke up. "Master," he
said, "when you speak like this you insult us
too." 46 "Alas for you lawyers also," he replied,
"because you load on men burdens that are
unendurable, burdens that you yourselves do
not move a finger to lift.
47 "Alas for you who build the tombs of the
prophets, the men your ancestors killed! 48 In
this way you both witness what your ancestors
did and approve it; they did the killing, you do
the building.
49 "And that is why the Wisdom of God said,
'I will send them prophets and apostles; some
they will slaughter and persecute, 50 so that this
generation will have to answer for every prophet's blood that has been shed since the foundation of the world, 51 from the blood of Abel to
the blood of Zechariah, who was murdered between the altar and the sanctuary.' Yes, I tell
you, this generation will have to answer for it all.
52 "Alas for you lawyers who have taken
away the key of knowledge! You have not gone

[s] Thus contracting legal impurity, Nb. 19:16.

New English Bible

you should have practised, without neglecting the others.[e]

'Alas for you Pharisees! You love the seats of honour in synagogues, and salutations in the market-places.

'Alas, alas, you are like unmarked graves over which men may walk without knowing it.'

In reply to this one of the lawyers said, 'Master, when you say things like this you are insulting us too.' Jesus rejoined: 'Yes, you lawyers, it is no better with you! For you load men with intolerable burdens, and will not put a single finger to the load.

'Alas, you build the tombs of the prophets whom your fathers murdered, and so testify that you approve of the deeds your fathers did; they committed the murders and you provide the tombs.

'This is why the Wisdom of God said, "I will send them prophets and messengers; and some of these they will persecute and kill"; so that this generation will have to answer for the blood of all the prophets shed since the foundation of the world; from the blood of Abel to the blood of Zechariah who perished between the altar and the sanctuary. I tell you, this generation will have to answer for it all.

'Alas for you lawyers! You have taken away the key of knowledge. You did not go in your-

[e] *Some witnesses omit* It is . . . others.

King James Version

entered not in yourselves, and them that were
entering in ye hindered. 53 And as he said these
things unto them, the scribes and the Pharisees
began to urge *him* vehemently, and to provoke
him to speak of many things: 54 Laying wait for
him, and seeking to catch something out of his
mouth, that they might accuse him.

12 In the mean time, when there were gathered together an innumerable multitude of
people, insomuch that they trode one upon another, he began to say unto his disciples first of
all, Beware ye of the leaven of the Pharisees,
which is hypocrisy. 2 For there is nothing covered, that shall not be revealed; neither hid, that
shall not be known. 3 Therefore, whatsoever ye
have spoken in darkness shall be heard in the
light; and that which ye have spoken in the ear
in closets shall be proclaimed upon the housetops. 4 And I say unto you my friends, Be not
afraid of them that kill the body, and after that
have no more that they can do. 5 But I will
forewarn you whom ye shall fear: Fear him,
which after he hath killed hath power to cast

Living Bible

cept it for yourselves, and you prevent others
from having a chance to believe it."
53, 54 The Pharisees and legal experts were
furious; and from that time on they plied him
fiercely with a host of questions, trying to trap
him into saying something for which they could
have him arrested.

12 Meanwhile the crowds grew until thousands upon thousands were milling about
and crushing each other. He turned now to his
disciples and warned them, "More than anything else, beware of these Pharisees and the
way they pretend to be good when they aren't.
But such hypocrisy cannot be hidden forever.
2 It will become as evident as yeast in dough.
3 Whatever they[a] have said in the dark shall be
heard in the light, and what you have whispered
in the inner rooms shall be broadcast from the
housetops for all to hear!
4 "Dear friends, don't be afraid of these who
want to murder you. They can only kill the
body; they have no power over your souls.
5 But I'll tell you whom to fear—fear God who
has the power to kill and then cast into hell.

[a] Literally, "you."

Today's English Version

the house of knowledge; you yourselves will not
go in, and you stop those who are trying to go
in!"
53 When Jesus left that place the teachers of
the Law and the Pharisees began to criticize him
bitterly and ask him questions about many things,
54 trying to lay traps for him and catch him in
something wrong he might say.

A warning against hypocrisy

12 As thousands of people crowded together,
so that they were stepping on each other,
Jesus said first to his disciples, "Be on guard
against the yeast of the Pharisees—I mean their
hypocrisy. 2 Whatever is covered up will be uncovered, and every secret will be made known.
3 So then, whatever you have said in the dark
will be heard in broad daylight, and whatever
you have whispered in men's ears in a closed
room will be shouted from the housetops."

Whom to fear

4 "I tell you, my friends, do not be afraid of
those who kill the body but cannot afterward do
anything worse. 5 I will show you whom to fear:
fear God who, after killing, has the authority to
throw into hell. Yes, I tell you, be afraid of him!

New International Version

yourselves have not entered, and you have hindered those who were entering."
53 When Jesus left there, the Pharisees and
the teachers of the law began to oppose him
fiercely and to besiege him with questions,
54 waiting to catch him in something he might
say.

Warnings and encouragements

12 Meanwhile, when a crowd of many thousands had gathered, so that they were
trampling on one another, Jesus began to speak
first to his disciples, saying: "Be on your guard
against the yeast of the Pharisees, which is hypocrisy. 2 There is nothing concealed that will
not be disclosed, or hidden that will not be made
known. 3 What you have said in the dark will
be heard in the daylight, and what you have
whispered in the ear behind closed doors will be
proclaimed from the housetops.
4 "I tell you, my friends, do not be afraid of
those who kill the body and after that can do
no more. 5 But I will show you whom you should
fear: Fear him who, after the killing of the
body, has power to throw you into hell. Yes, I

Phillips Modern English

have never gone in yourselves and you have hindered everyone else who was at the door!"

And when he left that place, the scribes and the Pharisees began to nurture a bitter hatred against him, and tried to draw him out on a great many subjects, waiting to pounce on some incriminating remark.

Meanwhile, the crowds had gathered in thousands, so that they were actually treading on each other's toes, and Jesus, speaking primarily to his disciples, said,

"Be on your guard against yeast—I mean the yeast of the Pharisees, which is sheer pretence. For there is nothing covered up which is not going to be exposed, nor anything private which is not going to be made public. Whatever you may say in the dark will be heard in daylight, and whatever you whisper within four walls will be shouted from the house-tops.

12.4 Man need only fear God

"I tell you, as friends of mine, that you are not to be afraid of those who can kill the body, but afterwards cannot do anything more. I will show you the only one you need to fear—the one who, after he has killed, has the power to throw you into destruction! Yes, I tell you, it is

Revised Standard Version

enter yourselves, and you hindered those who were entering."

53 As he went away from there, the scribes and the Pharisees began to press him hard, and to provoke him to speak of many things, 54 lying in wait for him, to catch at something he might say.

12 In the meantime, when so many thousands of the multitude had gathered together that they trod upon one another, he began to say to his disciples first, "Beware of the leaven of the Pharisees, which is hypocrisy.
2 Nothing is covered up that will not be revealed, or hidden that will not be known.
3 Therefore whatever you have said in the dark shall be heard in the light, and what you have whispered in private rooms shall be proclaimed upon the housetops.

4 "I tell you, my friends, do not fear those who kill the body, and after that have no more that they can do. 5 But I will warn you whom to fear: fear him who, after he has killed, has power to cast into hell;[m] yes, I tell you, fear

[m] Greek *Gehenna*.

Jerusalem Bible

in yourselves, and have prevented others going in who wanted to."

53 When he left the house, the scribes and the Pharisees began a furious attack on him and tried to force answers from him on innumerable questions, 54 setting traps to catch him out in something he might say.

Open and fearless speech

12 Meanwhile the people had gathered in their thousands so that they were treading on one another. And he began to speak, first of all to his disciples. "Be on your guard against the yeast of the Pharisees—that is, their hypocrisy. 2 Everything that is now covered will be uncovered, and everything now hidden will be made clear. 3 For this reason, whatever you have said in the dark will be heard in the daylight, and what you have whispered in hidden places will be proclaimed on the housetops.

4 "To you my friends I say: Do not be afraid of those who kill the body and after that can do no more. 5 I will tell you whom to fear: fear him who, after he has killed, has the power to

New English Bible

selves, and those who were on their way in, you stopped.'

After he had left the house, the lawyers and Pharisees began to assail him fiercely and to ply him with a host of questions, laying snares to catch him with his own words.

12 Meanwhile, when a crowd of many thousands had gathered, packed so close that they were treading on one another, he began to speak first to his disciples: 'Beware of the leaven of the Pharisees; I mean their hypocrisy. There is nothing covered up that will not be uncovered, nothing hidden that will not be made known. You may take it, then, that everything you have said in the dark will be heard in broad daylight, and what you have whispered behind closed doors will be shouted from the house-tops.

'To you who are my friends I say: Do not fear those who kill the body and after that have nothing more they can do. I will warn you whom to fear: fear him who, after he has killed, has authority to cast into hell. Believe me, he is the one to fear.

King James Version

into hell; yea, I say unto you, Fear him. 6Are
not five sparrows sold for two farthings, and not
one of them is forgotten before God? 7 But even
the very hairs of your head are all numbered.
Fear not therefore: ye are of more value than
many sparrows. 8Also I say unto you, Whosoever shall confess me before men, him shall the
Son of man also confess before the angels of
God: 9 But he that denieth me before men shall
be denied before the angels of God. 10And whosoever shall speak a word against the Son of
man, it shall be forgiven him: but unto him that
blasphemeth against the Holy Ghost it shall not
be forgiven. 11And when they bring you unto the
synagogues, and *unto* magistrates, and powers,
take ye no thought how or what thing ye shall
answer, or what ye shall say: 12 For the Holy
Ghost shall teach you in the same hour what ye
ought to say.
13 And one of the company said unto him,
Master, speak to my brother, that he divide the
inheritance with me. 14And he said unto him,
Man, who made me a judge or a divider over
you? 15And he said unto them, Take heed, and

Living Bible

6 "What is the price of five sparrows? A
couple of pennies? Not much more than that.
Yet God does not forget a single one of them.
7And he knows the number of hairs on your
head! Never fear, you are far more valuable to
him than a whole flock of sparrows.
8 "And I assure you of this: I, the Messiah,[b]
will publicly honor you in the presence of God's
angels if you publicly acknowledge me here on
earth as your Friend. 9 But I will deny before
the angels those who deny me here among men.
10 (Yet those who speak against me[b] may be
forgiven—while those who speak against the
Holy Spirit shall never be forgiven.)
11 "And when you are brought to trial before
these Jewish rulers and authorities in the synagogues, don't be concerned about what to say
in your defense, 12 for the Holy Spirit will give
you the right words even as you are standing
there."
13 Then someone called from the crowd, "Sir,
please tell my brother to divide my father's estate
with me."
14 But Jesus replied, "Man, who made me a
judge over you to decide such things as that?
15 Beware! Don't always be wishing for what you

[b] Literally, "the Son of Man."

Today's English Version

6 "Aren't five sparrows sold for two pennies?
Yet not a single one of them is forgotten by God.
7 Even the hairs of your head have all been numbered. So do not be afraid; you are worth much
more than many sparrows!"

Confessing and denying Christ

8 "I tell you: whoever declares publicly that
he belongs to me, the Son of Man will do the
same for him before the angels of God; 9 but
whoever denies publicly that he belongs to me,
the Son of Man will also deny him before the
angels of God.
10 "Anyone who says a word against the Son
of Man can be forgiven; but the one who says
evil things against the Holy Spirit will not be
forgiven.
11 "When they bring you to be tried in the
synagogues, or before governors or rulers, do not
be worried about how you will defend yourself
or what you will say. 12 For the Holy Spirit will
teach you at that time what you should say."

The parable of the rich fool

13 A man in the crowd said to him, "Teacher,
tell my brother to divide with me the property
our father left us."
14 Jesus answered him, "Man, who gave me
the right to judge, or to divide the property between you two?" 15And he went on to say to

New International Version

tell you, fear him. 6Are not five sparrows sold
for two pennies? Yet not one of them is forgotten by God. 7 Indeed, the very hairs of your
head are all numbered. Don't be afraid; you are
worth more than many sparrows.
8 "I tell you, whoever acknowledges me before men, the Son of Man will also acknowledge
him before the angels of God. 9 But he who disowns me before men will be disowned before
the angels of God. 10And everyone who speaks
a word against the Son of Man will be forgiven,
but anyone who blasphemes against the Holy
Spirit will not be forgiven.
11 "When you are brought before synagogues,
rulers and authorities, do not worry about how
you will defend yourselves or what you will say,
12 for the Holy Spirit will teach you at that time
what you should say."

The parable of the rich fool

13 Someone in the crowd said to him,
"Teacher, tell my brother to divide the inheritance with me."
14 Jesus replied, "Man, who appointed me a
judge or an arbiter between you?" 15 Then he

Phillips Modern English

right to stand in awe of him. The market-price of five sparrows is two farthings, isn't it? Yet not one of them is forgotten in God's sight. Why, the very hairs of your heads are all numbered! Don't be afraid then; you are worth more than a great many sparrows! I tell you that every man who acknowledges me before men, I, the Son of Man, will acknowledge in the presence of the angels of God. But the man who disowns me before men will find himself disowned before the angels of God!

"Anyone who speaks against the Son of Man will be forgiven, but there is no forgiveness for the man who speaks evil against the Holy Spirit. And when they bring you before the synagogues and magistrates and authorities, don't worry as to what defence you are going to put up or what words you are going to use. For the Holy Spirit will tell you at the time what is the right thing for you to say."

12.13 Jesus gives a warning about the love of material security

Then someone out of the crowd said to him,

"Master, tell my brother to share his legacy with me."

But Jesus replied,

"My dear man, who appointed me a judge or arbitrator in your affairs?"

And then, turning to the disciples, he said to them,

Revised Standard Version

him! 6 Are not five sparrows sold for two pennies? And not one of them is forgotten before
God. 7 Why, even the hairs of your head are all
numbered. Fear not; you are of more value than
many sparrows.
8 "And I tell you, every one who acknowledges me before men, the Son of man also will
acknowledge before the angels of God; 9 but
he who denies me before men will be denied
before the angels of God. 10 And every one who
speaks a word against the Son of man will be
forgiven; but he who blasphemes against the
Holy Spirit will not be forgiven. 11 And when
they bring you before the synagogues and the
rulers and the authorities, do not be anxious how
or what you are to answer or what you are to
say; 12 for the Holy Spirit will teach you in that
very hour what you ought to say."
13 One of the multitude said to him,
"Teacher, bid my brother divide the inheritance
with me." 14 But he said to him, "Man, who
made me a judge or divider over you?" 15 And

Jerusalem Bible

cast into hell. Yes, I tell you, fear him. 6 Can
you not buy five sparrows for two pennies? And
yet not one is forgotten in God's sight. 7 Why,
every hair on your head has been counted. There
is no need to be afraid: you are worth more than
hundreds of sparrows.
8 "I tell you, if anyone openly declares himself
for me in the presence of men, the Son of Man
will declare himself for him in the presence of
God's angels. 9 But the man who disowns me
in the presence of men will be disowned in the
presence of God's angels.
10 "Everyone who says a word against the Son
of Man will be forgiven, but he who blasphemes
against the Holy Spirit will not be forgiven.
11 "When they take you before synagogues and
magistrates and authorities, do not worry about
how to defend yourselves or what to say, 12 because when the time comes, the Holy Spirit will
teach you what you must say."

On hoarding possessions

13 A man in the crowd said to him, "Master,
tell my brother to give me a share of our inheritance." 14 "My friend," he replied, "who
appointed me your judge, or the arbitrator of
your claims?" 15 Then he said to them, "Watch,

New English Bible

'Are not sparrows five for twopence? And yet not one of them is overlooked by God. More than that, even the hairs of your head have all been counted. Have no fear; you are worth more than any number of sparrows.

'I tell you this: everyone who acknowledges me before men, the Son of Man will acknowledge before the angels of God; but he who disowns me before men will be disowned before the angels of God.

'Anyone who speaks a word against the Son of Man will receive forgiveness; but for him who slanders the Holy Spirit there will be no forgiveness.

'When you are brought before synagogues and state authorities, do not begin worrying about how you will conduct your defence or what you will say. For when the time comes the Holy Spirit will instruct you what to say.'

A man in the crowd said to him, 'Master, tell my brother to divide the family property with me.' He replied, 'My good man, who set me over you to judge or arbitrate?'[a] Then he said

[a] *Some witnesses omit* or arbitrate.

King James Version

beware of covetousness: for a man's life consisteth not in the abundance of the things which he possesseth. 16 And he spake a parable unto them, saying, The ground of a certain rich man brought forth plentifully: 17 And he thought within himself, saying, What shall I do, because I have no room where to bestow my fruits? 18 And he said, This will I do: I will pull down my barns, and build greater; and there will I bestow all my fruits and my goods. 19 And I will say to my soul, Soul, thou hast much goods laid up for many years; take thine ease, eat, drink, *and* be merry. 20 But God said unto him, *Thou* fool, this night thy soul shall be required of thee: then whose shall those things be, which thou hast provided? 21 So *is* he that layeth up treasure for himself, and is not rich toward God.

22 And he said unto his disciples, Therefore I say unto you, Take no thought for your life, what ye shall eat; neither for the body, what ye shall put on. 23 The life is more than meat, and the body *is more* than raiment. 24 Consider the ravens: for they neither sow nor reap; which neither have storehouse nor barn; and God feedeth them: how much more are ye better than the fowls? 25 And which of you with taking thought can add to his stature one cubit? 26 If

Living Bible

don't have. For real life and real living are not related to how rich we are."

16 Then he gave an illustration: "A rich man had a fertile farm that produced fine crops. 17 In fact, his barns were full to overflowing—he couldn't get everything in. He thought about his problem, 18 and finally exclaimed, 'I know—I'll tear down my barns and build bigger ones! Then I'll have room enough. 19 And I'll sit back and say to myself, "Friend, you have enough stored away for years to come. Now take it easy! Wine, women, and song for you!"' [c]

20 "But God said to him, 'Fool! Tonight you die. Then who will get it all?'

21 "Yes, every man is a fool who gets rich on earth but not in heaven."

22 Then turning to his disciples he said, "Don't worry about whether you have enough food to eat or clothes to wear. 23 For life consists of far more than food and clothes. 24 Look at the ravens—they don't plant or harvest or have barns to store away their food, and yet they get along all right—for God feeds them. And you are far more valuable to him than any birds!

25 "And besides, what's the use of worrying? What good does it do? Will it add a single day to your life? Of course not! 26 And if worry can't

[c] Literally, "Eat, drink, and be merry."

Today's English Version

them all, "Watch out, and guard yourselves from all kinds of greed; because a man's true life is not made up of the things he owns, no matter how rich he may be."

16 Then Jesus told them this parable, "A rich man had land which bore good crops. 17 He began to think to himself, 'I don't have a place to keep all my crops. What can I do? 18 This is what I will do,' he told himself; 'I will tear my barns down and build bigger ones, where I will store the grain and all my other goods. 19 Then I will say to myself, Lucky man! You have all the good things you need for many years. Take life easy, eat, drink, and enjoy yourself!' 20 But God said to him, 'You fool! This very night you will have to give up your life; then who will get all these things you have kept for yourself?'"

21 And Jesus concluded, "This is how it is with those who pile up riches for themselves but are not rich in God's sight."

Trust in God

22 Then Jesus said to the disciples, "This is why I tell you: do not be worried about the food you need to stay alive, or about the clothes you need for your body. 23 Life is much more important than food, and body much more important than clothes. 24 Look at the crows: they don't plant seeds or gather a harvest; they don't have storage rooms or barns; God feeds them! You are worth so much more than birds! 25 Which one of you can live a few more years by worrying about it? 26 If you can't manage

New International Version

said to them, "Watch out! Be on your guard against all kinds of greed; a man's life does not consist in the abundance of his possessions."

16 And he told them this parable: "The ground of a certain rich man produced a good crop. 17 He thought to himself, 'What shall I do? I have no place to store my crops.'

18 "Then he said, 'This is what I'll do. I will tear down my barns and build bigger ones, and there I will store all my grain and my goods. 19 And I'll say to myself, "You have plenty of good things laid up for many years. Take life easy; eat, drink and be merry."'

20 "But God said to him, 'You fool! This very night your life will be demanded from you. Then who will get what you have prepared for yourself?'

21 "This is how it will be with anyone who stores things up for himself but is not rich toward God."

Do not worry

22 Then Jesus said to his disciples: "Therefore I tell you, do not worry about your life, what you will eat; or about your body, what you will wear. 23 Life is more than food, and the body more than clothes. 24 Consider the ravens: They do not sow or reap, they have no storeroom or barn; yet God feeds them. And how much more valuable you are than birds! 25 Who of you by worrying can add a single hour to his life? [z] 26 Since you cannot do this very little

[z] Or *single cubit to his height?*

Phillips Modern English

"Notice that, and be on your guard against covetousness in any shape or form. For a man's real life in no way depends upon the number of his possessions."

Then he gave them a parable in these words, "Once upon a time a rich man's farmland produced heavy crops. So he said to himself, 'What shall I do, for I have no room to store this harvest of mine?' Then he said, 'I know what I'll do. I'll pull down my barns and build bigger ones where I can store all my grain and my goods and I can say to my soul, Soul, you have plenty of good things stored up there for years to come. Relax! Eat, drink and have a good time!' But God said to him, 'You fool, this very night you will be asked for *your soul!* Then, who is going to possess all that you have prepared?' That is what happens to the man who hoards things for himself and is not rich in the eyes of God."

And then he added to the disciples,

"That is why I tell you, don't worry about life, wondering what you are going to eat, or what clothes your body will need. Life is much more important than food, and the body more important than clothes. Think of the ravens. They neither sow nor reap, and they have neither store nor barn, but God feeds them. And how much more valuable do you think you are than birds? Can any of you make himself even a few inches taller however much he worries about it? And if you can't manage a little thing like this,

Revised Standard Version

he said to them, "Take heed, and beware of all
covetousness; for a man's life does not consist
in the abundance of his possessions." 16And he
told them a parable, saying, "The land of a rich
man brought forth plentifully; 17 and he thought
to himself, 'What shall I do, for I have nowhere
to store my crops?' 18And he said, 'I will do
this: I will pull down my barns, and build larger
ones; and there I will store all my grain and my
goods. 19And I will say to my soul, Soul, you
have ample goods laid up for many years; take
your ease, eat, drink, be merry.' 20 But God said
to him, 'Fool! This night your soul is required
of you; and the things you have prepared, whose
will they be?' 21 So is he who lays up treasure
for himself, and is not rich toward God."
22 And he said to his disciples, "Therefore I
tell you, do not be anxious about your life, what
you shall eat, nor about your body, what you
shall put on. 23 For life is more than food, and
the body more than clothing. 24 Consider the ravens: they neither sow nor reap, they have
neither storehouse nor barn, and yet God feeds
them. Of how much more value are you than
the birds! 25And which of you by being anxious
can add a cubit to his span of life?[n] 26 If then

[n] Or *to his stature.*

Jerusalem Bible

and be on your guard against avarice of any
kind, for a man's life is not made secure by what
he owns, even when he has more than he needs."
16 Then he told them a parable: "There was
once a rich man who, having had a good harvest
from his hand, 17 thought to himself, 'What am
I to do? I have not enough room to store my
crops.' 18 Then he said, 'This is what I will do:
I will pull down my barns and build bigger ones,
and store all my grain and my goods in them,
19 and I will say to my soul: My soul, you have
plenty of good things laid by for many years to
come; take things easy, eat, drink, have a good
time.' 20 But God said to him, 'Fool! This very
night the demand will be made for your soul;
and this hoard of yours, whose will it be then?'
21 So it is when a man stores up treasure for
himself in place of making himself rich in the
sight of God."

Trust in Providence

22 Then he said to his disciples, "That is why
I am telling you not to worry about your life
and what you are to eat, nor about your body
and how you are to clothe it. 23 For life means
more than food, and the body more than clothing. 24 Think of the ravens. They do not sow or
reap; they have no storehouses and no barns; yet
God feeds them. And how much more are you
worth than the birds! 25 Can any of you, for all
his worrying, add a single cubit to his span of
life? 26 If the smallest things, therefore, are out-

New English Bible

to the people, 'Beware! Be on your guard against greed of every kind, for even when a man has more than enough, his wealth does not give him life.' And he told them this parable: 'There was a rich man whose land yielded heavy crops. He debated with himself: "What am I to do? I have not the space to store my produce. This is what I will do," said he: "I will pull down my storehouses and build them bigger. I will collect in them all my corn and other goods, and then say to myself, 'Man, you have plenty of good things laid by, enough for many years: take life easy, eat, drink, and enjoy yourself.' " But God said to him, "You fool, this very night you must surrender your life; you have made your money —who will get it now?" That is how it is with the man who amasses wealth for himself and remains a pauper in the sight of God.[b]

'Therefore', he said to his disciples, 'I bid you put away anxious thoughts about food to keep you alive and clothes to cover your body. Life is more than food, the body more than clothes. Think of the ravens: they neither sow nor reap; they have no storehouse or barn; yet God feeds them. You are worth far more than the birds! Is there a man among you who by anxious thought can add a foot to his height[c]? If, then,

[b] *Some witnesses omit* That . . . God; *others add at the end* When he said this he cried out, "If you have ears to hear, then hear." [c] *Or* a day to his life.

King James Version

ye then be not able to do that thing which is
least, why take ye thought for the rest? 27 Consider the lilies how they grow: they toil not,
they spin not; and yet I say unto you, that Solomon in all his glory was not arrayed like one of
these. 28 If then God so clothe the grass, which
is to day in the field, and to morrow is cast into
the oven; how much more *will he clothe* you,
O ye of little faith? 29 And seek not ye what ye
shall eat, or what ye shall drink, neither be ye of
doubtful mind. 30 For all these things do the
nations of the world seek after: and your Father
knoweth that ye have need of these things.
31 But rather seek ye the kingdom of God;
and all these things shall be added unto you.
32 Fear not, little flock; for it is your Father's
good pleasure to give you the kingdom. 33 Sell
that ye have, and give alms; provide yourselves
bags which wax not old, a treasure in the heavens that faileth not, where no thief approacheth,
neither moth corrupteth. 34 For where your treasure is, there will your heart be also. 35 Let your
loins be girded about, and *your* lights burning;

Living Bible

even do such little things as that, what's the use
of worrying over bigger things?
27 "Look at the lilies! They don't toil and
spin, and yet Solomon in all his glory was not
robed as well as they are. 28 And if God provides clothing for the flowers that are here today
and gone tomorrow, don't you suppose that he
will provide clothing for you, you doubters?
29 And don't worry about food—what to eat and
drink; don't worry at all that God will provide
it for you. 30 All mankind scratches for its daily
bread, but your heavenly Father knows your
needs. 31 He will always give you all you need
from day to day if you will make the Kingdom
of God your primary concern.
32 "So don't be afraid, little flock. For it
gives your Father great happiness to give you
the Kingdom. 33 Sell what you have and give to
those in need. This will fatten your purses in
heaven! And the purses of heaven have no rips
or holes in them. Your treasures there will never
disappear; no thief can steal them; no moth can
destroy them. 34 Wherever your treasure is, there
your heart and thoughts will also be.
35 "Be prepared—all dressed and ready—

Today's English Version

even such a small thing, why worry about the
other things? 27 Look how the wild flowers grow:
they don't work or make clothes for themselves.
But I tell you that not even Solomon, as rich as
he was, had clothes as beautiful as one of these
flowers. 28 It is God who clothes the wild grass—
grass that is here today, gone tomorrow, burned
up in the oven. Won't he be all the more sure to
clothe you? How little faith you have! 29 So
don't be all upset, always concerned about what
you will eat and drink. 30 (For the heathen of
this world are always concerned about all these
things.) Your Father knows that you need these
things. 31 Instead, be concerned with his Kingdom, and he will provide you with these things."

Riches in heaven

32 "Do not be afraid, little flock; because
your Father is pleased to give you the Kingdom.
33 Sell all your belongings and give the money
to the poor. Provide for yourselves purses that
don't wear out, and save your riches in heaven,
where they will never decrease, because no thief
can get to them, no moth can destroy them.
34 For your heart will always be where your
riches are."

Watchful servants

35 "Be ready for whatever comes, with your
clothes fastened tight at the waist and your lamps

New International Version

thing, why do you worry about the rest?
27 "Consider how the lilies grow. They do
not labor or spin. Yet I tell you, not even Solomon in all his splendor was dressed like one of
these. 28 If that is how God clothes the grass
of the field, which is here today and tomorrow
is thrown into the fire, how much more will he
clothe you, O you of little faith! 29 And do not
set your heart on what you will eat or drink; do
not worry about it. 30 For the pagan world runs
after all such things, and your Father knows
that you need them. 31 But seek his kingdom,
and these things will be given to you as well.
32 "Do not be afraid, little flock, for your
Father has been pleased to give you the kingdom. 33 Sell your possessions and give to the
poor. Provide purses for yourselves that will not
wear out, a treasure in heaven that will not be
exhausted, where no thief comes near and no
moth destroys. 34 For where your treasure is,
there your heart will be also.

Watchfulness

35 "Be dressed ready for service and keep your

Phillips Modern English

why do you worry about anything else? Think of the wild flowers, and how they neither work nor weave. Yet I tell you that Solomon in all his glory was never arrayed like one of these. If God so clothes the grass, which flowers in the field today and is burnt in the stove tomorrow, is he not much more likely to clothe you, you little-faiths? You must not set your heart on what you eat or drink, nor must you live in a state of anxiety. The whole heathen world is busy about getting food and drink, and your Father knows well enough that you need such things. No, set your heart on his kingdom, and your food and drink will come as a matter of course. Don't be afraid, you tiny flock! Your Father plans to give you the kingdom. Sell your possessions and give the money away to those in need. Get yourselves purses that never grow old, inexhaustible treasure in Heaven, where no thief can ever reach it, or moth destroy it. For wherever your treasure is, you may be certain that your heart will be there too!

12.35 Jesus' disciples must be on the alert

"You must be ready dressed and have your

Revised Standard Version

you are not able to do as small a thing as that, why are you anxious about the rest?
27 Consider the lilies, how they grow; they neither toil nor spin;[o] yet I tell you, even Solomon in all his glory was not arrayed like one of these.
28 But if God so clothes the grass which is alive in the field today and tomorrow is thrown into the oven, how much more will he clothe you, O men of little faith!
29 And do not seek what you are to eat and what you are to drink, nor be of anxious mind.
30 For all the nations of the world seek these things; and your Father knows that you need them.
31 Instead, seek his[p] kingdom, and these things shall be yours as well.

32 "Fear not, little flock, for it is your Father's good pleasure to give you the kingdom.
33 Sell your possessions, and give alms; provide yourselves with purses that do not grow old, with a treasure in the heavens that does not fail, where no thief approaches and no moth destroys.
34 For where your treasure is, there will your heart be also.

35 "Let your loins be girded and your lamps

[o] Other ancient authorities read *Consider the lilies; they neither spin nor weave.* [p] Other ancient authorities read *God's.*

Jerusalem Bible

side your control, why worry about the rest?
27 Think of the flowers; they never have to spin or weave; yet, I assure you, not even Solomon in all his regalia was robed like one of these.
28 Now if that is how God clothes the grass in the field which is there today and thrown into the furnace tomorrow, how much more will he look after you, you men of little faith!
29 But you, you must not set your hearts on things to eat and things to drink; nor must you worry.
30 It is the pagans of this world who set their hearts on all these things. Your Father well knows you need them.
31 No; set your hearts on his kingdom, and these other things will be given you as well.

32 "There is no need to be afraid, little flock, for it has pleased your Father to give you the kingdom.

On almsgiving

33 "Sell your possessions and give alms. Get yourselves purses that do not wear out, treasure that will not fail you, in heaven where no thief can reach it and no moth destroy it.
34 For where your treasure is, there will your heart be also.

On being ready for the Master's return

35 "See that you are dressed for action and

New English Bible

you cannot do even a very little thing, why are you anxious about the rest?

'Think of the lilies: they neither spin nor weave;[d] yet I tell you, even Solomon in all his splendour was not attired like one of these. But if that is how God clothes the grass, which is growing in the field today, and tomorrow is thrown on the stove, how much more will he clothe you! How little faith you have! And so you are not to set your mind on food and drink; you are not to worry. For all these are things for the heathen to run after; but you have a Father who knows that you need them. No, set your mind upon his kingdom, and all the rest will come to you as well.

'Have no fear, little flock; for your Father has chosen to give you the Kingdom. Sell your possessions and give in charity. Provide for yourselves purses that do not wear out, and never-failing treasure in heaven, where no thief can get near it, no moth destroy it. For where your treasure is, there will your heart be also.

'Be ready for action, with belts fastened and

[d] *Some witnesses read* they grow, they do not toil or spin.

King James Version

36And ye yourselves like unto men that wait for their lord, when he will return from the wedding; that, when he cometh and knocketh, they may open unto him immediately. 37 Blessed *are* those servants, whom the lord when he cometh shall find watching: verily I say unto you, that he shall gird himself, and make them to sit down to meat, and will come forth and serve them. 38And if he shall come in the second watch, or come in the third watch, and find *them* so, blessed are those servants. 39And this know, that if the goodman of the house had known what hour the thief would come, he would have watched, and not have suffered his house to be broken through. 40 Be ye therefore ready also: for the Son of man cometh at an hour when ye think not.

41 Then Peter said unto him, Lord, speakest thou this parable unto us, or even to all? 42And the Lord said, Who then is that faithful and wise steward, whom *his* lord shall make ruler over his household, to give *them their* portion of meat in due season? 43 Blessed *is* that servant, whom his lord when he cometh shall find so doing. 44 Of a truth I say unto you, that he will make him ruler over all that he hath. 45 But and if that servant say in his heart, My lord delayeth his coming; and shall begin to beat the menservants and maidens, and to eat and drink, and to be drunken; 46 The lord of that servant will

Living Bible

36 for your Lord's return from the wedding feast. Then you will be ready to open the door and let him in the moment he arrives and knocks. 37 There will be great joy for those who are ready and waiting for his return. He himself will seat them and put on a waiter's uniform and serve them as they sit and eat! 38 He may come at nine o'clock at night—or even at midnight. But whenever he comes there will be joy for his servants who are ready!

39 "Everyone would be ready for him if they knew the exact hour of his return—just as they would be ready for a thief if they knew when he was coming. 40 So be ready all the time. For I, the Messiah,[d] will come when least expected."

41 Peter asked, "Lord, are you talking just to us or to everyone?"

42, 43, 44 And the Lord replied, "I'm talking to any faithful, sensible man whose master gives him the responsibility of feeding the other servants. If his master returns and finds that he has done a good job, there will be a reward—his master will put him in charge of all he owns.

45 "But if the man begins to think, 'My Lord won't be back for a long time,' and begins to whip the men and women he is supposed to protect, and to spend his time at drinking parties and in drunkenness—46 well, his master will re-

[*d*] Literally, "the Son of Man."

Today's English Version

lit, 36 like servants who are waiting for their master to come back from a wedding feast. When he comes and knocks, they will open the door for him at once. 37 How happy are those servants whose master finds them awake and ready when he returns! I tell you, he will fasten his belt, have them sit down, and wait on them. 38 How happy are they if he finds them ready, even if he should come as late as midnight or even later! 39And remember this! If the man of the house knew the time when the thief would come, he would not let the thief break into his house. 40And you, too, be ready, because the Son of Man will come at an hour when you are not expecting him."

The faithful or the unfaithful servant

41 Peter said, "Lord, are you telling this parable to us, or do you mean it for everyone?"

42 The Lord answered, "Who, then, is the faithful and wise servant? He is the one whom his master will put in charge, to run the household and give the other servants their share of the food at the proper time. 43 How happy is that servant if his master finds him doing this when he comes home! 44 Indeed, I tell you, the master will put that servant in charge of all his property. 45 But if that servant says to himself, 'My master is taking a long time to come back,' and begins to beat the other servants, both the men and the women, and eats and drinks and gets drunk, 46 then the master will come back some day when

New International Version

lamps burning, 36 like men waiting for their master to return from a wedding banquet, so that when he comes and knocks they can immediately open the door for him. 37 It will be good for those servants whose master finds them watching when he comes. I tell you the truth, he will dress himself to serve, will have them recline at the table and will come and wait on them. 38 It will be good for those servants whose master finds them ready, even if he comes in the second or third watch of the night. 39 But understand this: If the owner of the house had known at what hour the thief was coming, he would not have let his house be broken into. 40 You also must be ready, because the Son of Man will come at an hour when you do not expect him."

41 Peter asked, "Lord, are you telling this parable to us, or to everyone?"

42 The Lord answered, "Who then is the faithful and wise manager, whom the master puts in charge of his servants to give them their food allowance at the proper time? 43 It will be good for that servant whom the master finds doing so when he returns. 44 I tell you the truth, he will put him in charge of all his possessions. 45 But suppose the servant says to himself, 'My master is taking a long time in coming,' and he then begins to beat the men and women servants and to eat and drink and get drunk. 46 The master of that servant will come on a day when

Phillips Modern English

lamps alight, like men who wait to welcome their lord and master on his return from the wedding-feast, so that when he comes and knocks at the door, they may open it for him at once. Happy are the servants whom their lord finds on the alert when he arrives. I assure you that he will then take off his outer clothes, make them sit down to dinner, and come and wait on them. And if he should come just after midnight or in the very early morning, and find them still on the alert, their happiness is assured. But be certain of this, that if the householder had known the time when the burglar would come, he would not have let his house be broken into. So you must be on the alert, for the Son of Man is coming at a time when you may not expect him."

Then Peter said to him,

"Lord, do you mean this parable for us or for everybody?"

But the Lord continued,

"Well, who will be the faithful, sensible steward whom his master will put in charge of his household to give them their supplies at the proper time? Happy is the servant if his master finds him so doing when he returns. I tell you he will promote him to look after all his property. But suppose the servant says to himself, 'My master takes his time about returning', and then begins to beat the men and women servants and to eat and drink and get drunk, that servant's master will return suddenly and unexpect-

Revised Standard Version

burning, 36 and be like men who are waiting for their master to come home from the marriage feast, so that they may open to him at once when he comes and knocks. 37 Blessed are those servants whom the master finds awake when he comes; truly, I say to you, he will gird himself and have them sit at table, and he will come and serve them. 38 If he comes in the second watch, or in the third, and finds them so, blessed are those servants! 39 But know this, that if the householder had known at what hour the thief was coming, he[q] would not have left his house to be broken into. 40 You also must be ready; for the Son of man is coming at an unexpected hour."

41 Peter said, "Lord, are you telling this parable for us or for all?" 42 And the Lord said, "Who then is the faithful and wise steward, whom his master will set over his household, to give them their portion of food at the proper time? 43 Blessed is that servant whom his master when he comes will find so doing. 44 Truly, I say to you, he will set him over all his possessions. 45 But if that servant says to himself, 'My master is delayed in coming,' and begins to beat the menservants and the maidservants, and to eat and drink and get drunk, 46 the master of that servant will come on a day when he does

[q] Other ancient authorities add *would have watched and*.

Jerusalem Bible

have your lamps lit. 36 Be like men waiting for their master to return from the wedding feast, ready to open the door as soon as he comes and knocks. 37 Happy those servants whom the master finds awake when he comes. I tell you solemnly, he will put on an apron, sit them down at table and wait on them. 38 It may be in the second watch he comes, or in the third, but happy those servants if he finds them ready. 39 You may be quite sure of this, that if the householder had known at what hour the burglar would come, he would not have let anyone break through the wall of his house. 40 You too must stand ready, because the Son of Man is coming at an hour you do not expect."

41 Peter said, "Lord, do you mean this parable for us, or for everyone?" 42 The Lord replied, "What sort of steward,[t] then, is faithful and wise enough for the master to place him over his household to give them their allowance of food at the proper time? 43 Happy that servant if his master's arrival finds him at this employment. 44 I tell you truly, he will place him over everything he owns. 45 But as for the servant who says to himself, 'My master is taking his time coming,' and sets about beating the menservants and the maids, and eating and drinking and getting drunk, 46 his master will come on a day he does not expect and at an

[t] I.e., a servant or employee with authority to act as his master's deputy in his absence.

New English Bible

lamps alight. Be like men who wait for their master's return from a wedding-party, ready to let him in the moment he arrives and knocks. Happy are those servants whom the master finds on the alert when he comes. I tell you this: he will fasten his belt, seat them at table, and come and wait on them. Even if it is the middle of the night or before dawn when he comes, happy they if he finds them alert. And remember, if the householder had known what time the burglar was coming he would not have let his house be broken into. Hold yourselves ready, then, because the Son of Man will come at the time you least expect him.'

Peter said, 'Lord, do you intend this parable specially for us or is it for everyone?' The Lord said, 'Well, who is the trusty and sensible man whom his master will appoint as his steward, to manage his servants and issue their rations at the proper time? Happy that servant who is found at his task when his master comes! I tell you this: he will be put in charge of all his master's property. But if that servant says to himself, "The master is a long time coming", and begins to bully the menservants and maids, and eat and drink and get drunk; then the master will arrive on a day that servant does

King James Version

come in a day when he looketh not for *him,* and at an hour when he is not aware, and will cut him in sunder, and will appoint him his portion with the unbelievers. 47 And that servant, which knew his lord's will, and prepared not *himself,* neither did according to his will, shall be beaten with many *stripes.* 48 But he that knew not, and did commit things worthy of stripes, shall be beaten with few *stripes.* For unto whomsoever much is given, of him shall be much required; and to whom men have committed much, of him they will ask the more.

49 I am come to send fire on the earth: and what will I, if it be already kindled? 50 But I have a baptism to be baptized with; and how am I straitened till it be accomplished! 51 Suppose ye that I am come to give peace on earth? I tell you, Nay; but rather division: 52 For from henceforth there shall be five in one house divided, three against two, and two against three. 53 The father shall be divided against the son, and the son against the father; the mother against the daughter, and the daughter against the mother; the mother in law against her daughter in law, and the daughter in law against her mother in law.

Living Bible

turn without notice and remove him from his position of trust and assign him to the place of the unfaithful. 47 He will be severely punished, for though he knew his duty he refused to do it.

48 "But anyone who is not aware that he is doing wrong will be punished only lightly. Much is required from those to whom much is given, for their responsibility is greater.

49 "I have come to bring fire to the earth, and, oh, that my task were completed! 50 There is a terrible baptism ahead of me, and how I am pent up until it is accomplished!

51 "Do you think I have come to give peace to the earth? *No!* Rather, strife and division! 52 From now on families will be split apart, three in favor of me, and two against—or perhaps the other way around. 53 A father will decide one way about me; his son, the other; mother and daughter will disagree; and the decision of an honored [e] mother-in-law will be spurned by her daughter-in-law."

[*e*] Implied by ancient custom.

Today's English Version

the servant does not expect him and at a time he does not know. The master will cut him to pieces, and make him share the fate of the disobedient.

47 "The servant who knows what his master wants him to do, but does not get himself ready and do what his master wants, will be punished with a heavy whipping; 48 but the servant who does not know what his master wants, and does something for which he deserves a whipping, will be punished with a light whipping. The man to whom much is given, of him much is required; the man to whom more is given, of him much more is required."

Jesus the cause of division

49 "I came to set the earth on fire; how I wish it were already kindled! 50 I have a baptism to receive; how distressed I am until it is over! 51 Do you suppose that I came to bring peace to the world? Not peace, I tell you, but division. 52 From now on a family of five will be divided, three against two, two against three. 53 Fathers will be against their sons, and sons against their fathers; mothers will be against their daughters, and daughters against their mothers; mothers-in-law will be against their daughters-in-law, and daughters-in-law against their mothers-in-law."

New International Version

he does not expect him and at an hour he is not aware of. He will cut him to pieces and assign him a place with the unbelievers.

47 "That servant who knows his master's will and does not get ready or does not do what his master wants will be beaten with many blows. 48 But the one who does not know and does things deserving punishment will be beaten with few blows. From everyone who has been given much, much will be demanded; and from the one who has been entrusted with much, much more will be asked.

Not peace but division

49 "I have come to bring fire on the earth, and how I wish it were already kindled! 50 But I have a baptism to undergo, and how distressed I am until it is completed! 51 Do you think I came to bring peace on earth? No, I tell you, but division. 52 From now on there will be five in one family divided against each other, three against two and two against three. 53 They will be divided, father against son and son against father, mother against daughter and daughter against mother, mother-in-law against daughter-in-law and daughter-in-law against mother-in-law."

Phillips Modern English

edly, and he will punish him severely and send him to share the penalty of the unfaithful. The slave who knows his master's plan but does not get ready or act upon it will be severely punished, but the servant who did not know the plan, though he has done wrong, will be let off lightly. Much will be expected from the one who has been given much, and the more a man is trusted, the more people will expect of him.

"It is fire that I have come to bring upon the earth—how I could wish it were already ablaze! There is a baptism that I must undergo and how strained I must be until it is all over!

12.51 Jesus declares that his coming is bound to bring division

"Do you think I have come to bring peace on the earth? No, I tell you, not peace, but division! For from now on, there will be five people divided against each other in one house, three against two, and two against three. It is going to be father against son, and son against father, mother against daughter, and daughter against mother; mother-in-law against her daughter-in-law, and daughter-in-law against mother-in-law!"

Revised Standard Version

not expect him and at an hour he does not know, and will punish[r] him, and put him with the unfaithful. 47 And that servant who knew his master's will, but did not make ready or act according to his will, shall receive a severe beating. 48 But he who did not know, and did what deserved a beating, shall receive a light beating. Every one to whom much is given, of him will much be required; and of him to whom men commit much they will demand the more.

49 "I came to cast fire upon the earth; and would that it were already kindled! 50 I have a baptism to be baptized with; and how I am constrained until it is accomplished! 51 Do you think that I have come to give peace on earth? No, I tell you, but rather division; 52 for henceforth in one house there will be five divided, three against two and two against three; 53 they will be divided, father against son and son against father, mother against daughter and daughter against her mother, mother-in-law against her daughter-in-law and daughter-in-law against her mother-in-law."

[r] Or *cut him in pieces.*

Jerusalem Bible

hour he does not know. The master will cut him off and send him to the same fate as the unfaithful.

47 "The servant who knows what his master wants, but has not even started to carry out those wishes, will receive very many strokes of the lash. 48 The one who did not know, but deserves to be beaten for what he has done, will receive fewer strokes. When a man has had a great deal given him, a great deal will be demanded of him; when a man has had a great deal given him on trust, even more will be expected of him.

Jesus and his Passion

49 "I have come to bring fire to the earth, and how I wish it were blazing already! 50 There is a baptism I must still receive, and how great is my distress till it is over!

Jesus the cause of dissension

51 "Do you suppose that I am here to bring peace on earth? No, I tell you, but rather division. 52 For from now on a household of five will be divided: three against two and two against three; 53 the father divided against the son, son against father, mother against daughter, daughter against mother, mother-in-law against daughter-in-law, daughter-in-law against mother-in-law."

New English Bible

not expect, at a time he does not know, and will cut him in pieces. Thus he will find his place among the faithless.

'The servant who knew his master's wishes, yet made no attempt to carry them out, will be flogged severely. But one who did not know them and earned a beating will be flogged less severely. Where a man has been given much, much will be expected of him; and the more a man has had entrusted to him the more he will be required to repay.

'I have come to set fire to the earth, and how I wish it were already kindled! I have a baptism to undergo, and what constraint I am under until the ordeal is over! Do you suppose I came to establish peace on earth? No indeed, I have come to bring division. For from now on, five members of a family will be divided, three against two and two against three; father against son and son against father, mother against daughter and daughter against mother, mother against son's wife and son's wife against her mother-in-law.'

King James Version

54 And he said also to the people, When ye see a cloud rise out of the west, straightway ye say, There cometh a shower; and so it is. 55And when *ye see* the south wind blow, ye say, There will be heat; and it cometh to pass. 56 *Ye* hypocrites, ye can discern the face of the sky and of the earth; but how is it that ye do not discern this time? 57 Yea, and why even of yourselves judge ye not what is right?

58 When thou goest with thine adversary to the magistrate, *as thou art* in the way, give diligence that thou mayest be delivered from him; lest he hale thee to the judge, and the judge deliver thee to the officer, and the officer cast thee into prison. 59 I tell thee, thou shalt not depart thence, till thou hast paid the very last mite.

13 There were present at that season some that told him of the Galileans, whose blood Pilate had mingled with their sacrifices. 2And Jesus answering said unto them, Suppose ye that

Living Bible

54 Then he turned to the crowd and said, "When you see clouds beginning to form in the west, you say, 'Here comes a shower.' And you are right.

55 "When the south wind blows you say, 'Today will be a scorcher.' And it is. 56 Hypocrites! You interpret the sky well enough, but you refuse to notice the warnings all around you about the crisis ahead. 57 Why do you refuse to see for yourselves what is right?

58 "If you meet your accuser on the way to court, try to settle the matter before it reaches the judge, lest he sentence you to jail; 59 for if that happens you won't be free again until the last penny is paid in full."

13 About this time he was informed that Pilate had butchered some Jews from Galilee as they were sacrificing at the Temple in Jerusalem.

2 "Do you think they were worse sinners than

Today's English Version

Understanding the time

54 Jesus said also to the people, "When you see a cloud coming up in the west, at once you say, 'It is going to rain,' and it does. 55And when you feel the south wind blowing, you say, 'It is going to get hot,' and it does. 56 Hypocrites! You can look at the earth and the sky and tell what it means; why, then, don't you know the meaning of this present time?"

Settle with your opponent

57 "Why do you not judge for yourselves the right thing to do? 58 If a man brings a lawsuit against you and takes you to court, do your best to settle the matter with him while you are on the way, so that he won't drag you before the judge, and the judge hand you over to the police, and the police put you in jail. 59 You will not come out of there, I tell you, until you pay the last penny of your fine."

Turn from your sins or die

13 At that time some people were there who told Jesus about the Galileans whom Pilate had killed while they were offering sacrifices to God. 2 Jesus answered them, "Because these

New International Version

Interpreting the times

54 He said to the crowd: "When you see a cloud rising in the west, immediately you say, 'It's going to rain,' and it does. 55And when the south wind blows, you say, 'It's going to be hot,' and it is. 56 Hypocrites! You know how to interpret the appearance of the earth and the sky. How is it that you don't know how to interpret this present time?

57 "Why don't you judge for yourselves what is right? 58As you are going with your adversary to the magistrate, try hard to be reconciled to him on the way, or he may drag you off to the judge, and the judge turn you over to the officer, and the officer throw you into prison. 59 I tell you, you will not get out until you have paid the last penny."

Repent or perish

13 Now there were some present at that time who told Jesus about the Galileans whose blood Pilate had mixed with their sacrifices. 2 Jesus answered, "Do you think that these Galileans

Phillips Modern English

12.54 Intelligence should be used not only about the weather but about the times in which men live

Then he said to the crowds,

"When you see a cloud rising in the west, you say at once that it is going to rain, and so it does. And when you feel the south wind blowing, you say that it is going to be hot, and so it is. You frauds! You know how to interpret the look of the earth and the sky. Why can't you interpret the meaning of the times in which you live?

"And why can't you decide for yourselves what is right? For instance, when you are going before the magistrate with your opponent, do your best to come to terms with him while you have the chance, or he may rush you off to the judge, and the judge hand you over to the police-officer, and the police-officer throw you into prison. I tell you you will never get out again until you have paid your last farthing."

13.1 Jesus is asked about the supposed significance of disasters

It was just at this moment that some people came up to tell him the story of the Galileans whose blood Pilate had mixed with that of their own sacrifices. Jesus made this reply to them:

"Are you thinking that these Galileans were

Revised Standard Version

54 He also said to the multitudes, "When
you see a cloud rising in the west, you say at
once, 'A shower is coming'; and so it happens.
55 And when you see the south wind blowing, you
say, 'There will be scorching heat'; and it happens. 56 You hypocrites! You know how to interpret the appearance of earth and sky; but why
do you not know how to interpret the present
time?
57 "And why do you not judge for yourselves
what is right? 58 As you go with your accuser before the magistrate, make an effort to settle with
him on the way, lest he drag you to the judge,
and the judge hand you over to the officer, and
the officer put you in prison. 59 I tell you, you
will never get out till you have paid the very
last copper."

13 There were some present at that very time who told him of the Galileans whose
blood Pilate had mingled with their sacrifices.
2 And he answered them, "Do you think that

Jerusalem Bible

On reading the signs of the times

54 He said again to the crowds, "When you
see a cloud looming up in the west you say at
once that rain is coming, and so it does. 55 And
when the wind is from the south you say it
will be hot, and it is. 56 Hypocrites! You know
how to interpret the face of the earth and the
sky. How is it you do not know how to interpret these times?
57 "Why not judge for yourselves what is
right? 58 For example: when you go to court
with your opponent, try to settle with him on
the way, or he may drag you before the judge
and the judge hand you over to the bailiff and
the bailiff have you thrown into prison. 59 I tell
you, you will not get out till you have paid the
very last penny."

Examples inviting repentance

13 It was just about this time that some people arrived and told him about the
Galileans whose blood Pilate had mingled with
that of their sacrifices.[u] 2 At this he said to

[u] The author expects this incident, and that mentioned in V. 4, to be known to his readers; no other evidence of them remains.

New English Bible

He also said to the people, 'When you see cloud banking up in the west, you say at once, "It is going to rain", and rain it does. And when the wind is from the south, you say, "There will be a heat-wave", and there is. What hypocrites you are! You know how to interpret the appearance of earth and sky; how is it you cannot interpret this fateful hour?

'And why can you not judge for yourselves what is the right course? When you are going with your opponent to court, make an effort to settle with him while you are still on the way; otherwise he may drag you before the judge, and the judge hand you over to the constable, and the constable put you in jail. I tell you, you will not come out till you have paid the last farthing.'

13 At that very time there were some people present who told him about the Galileans whose blood Pilate had mixed with their sacrifices. He answered them: 'Do you imagine that,

King James Version

these Galileans were sinners above all the Galileans, because they suffered such things? 3 I tell you, Nay: but, except ye repent, ye shall all likewise perish. 4 Or those eighteen, upon whom the tower in Siloam fell, and slew them, think ye that they were sinners above all men that dwelt in Jerusalem? 5 I tell you, Nay: but, except ye repent, ye shall all likewise perish.

6 He spake also this parable; A certain *man* had a fig tree planted in his vineyard; and he came and sought fruit thereon, and found none. 7 Then said he unto the dresser of his vineyard, Behold, these three years I come seeking fruit on this fig tree, and find none: cut it down; why cumbereth it the ground? 8And he answering said unto him, Lord, let it alone this year also, till I shall dig about it, and dung *it:* 9And if it bear fruit, *well:* and if not, *then* after that thou shalt cut it down.

Living Bible

other men from Galilee?" he asked. "Is that why they suffered? 3 Not at all! And don't you realize that you also will perish unless you leave your evil ways and turn to God?

4 "And what about the eighteen men who died when the Tower of Siloam fell on them? Were they the worst sinners in Jerusalem? 5 Not at all! And you, too, will perish unless you repent."

6 Then he used this illustration: "A man planted a fig tree in his garden and came again and again to see if he could find any fruit on it, but he was always disappointed. 7 Finally he told his gardener to cut it down. 'I've waited three years and there hasn't been a single fig!' he said. 'Why bother with it any longer? It's taking up space we can use for something else.'

8 " 'Give it one more chance,' the gardener answered. 'Leave it another year, and I'll give it special attention and plenty of fertilizer. 9 If we get figs next year, fine; if not, I'll cut it down.' "

Today's English Version

Galileans were killed in that way, do you think it proves that they were worse sinners than all the other Galileans? 3 No! I tell you that if you do not turn from your sins, you will all die as they did. 4 What about those eighteen in Siloam who were killed when the tower fell on them? Do you suppose this proves that they were worse than all the other people living in Jerusalem? 5 No! I tell you that if you do not turn from your sins, you will all die as they did."

The parable of the unfruitful fig tree

6 Then Jesus told them this parable, "A man had a fig tree growing in his vineyard. He went looking for figs on it but found none. 7 So he said to his gardener, 'Look, for three years I have been coming here looking for figs on this fig tree and I haven't found any. Cut it down! Why should it go on using up the soil?' 8 But the gardener answered, 'Leave it alone, sir, just this one year; I will dig a trench around it and fill it up with fertilizer. 9 Then if the tree bears figs next year, so much the better; if not, then you will have it cut down.' "

New International Version

were worse sinners than all the other Galileans because they suffered this way? 3 I tell you, no! But unless you repent, you too will all perish. 4 Or those eighteen who died when the tower in Siloam fell on them—do you think they were more guilty than all the others living in Jerusalem? 5 I tell you, no! But unless you repent, you too will all perish."

6 Then he told this parable: "A man had a fig tree, planted in his vineyard, and he went to look for fruit on it, but did not find any. 7 So he said to the man who took care of the vineyard, 'For three years now I've been coming to look for fruit on this fig tree and haven't found any. Cut it down! Why should it use up the soil?'

8 " 'Sir,' the man replied, 'leave it alone for one more year, and I'll dig around it and fertilize it. 9 If it bears fruit next year, fine! If not, then cut it down.' "

Phillips Modern English

worse sinners than any other men of Galilee because this happened to them? I assure you that is not so. You will all die just as miserable a death unless your hearts are changed! You remember those eighteen people who were killed at Siloam when the tower collapsed upon them? Are you imagining that they were worse offenders than any of the other people who lived in Jerusalem? I assure you they were not. You will all die as tragically unless your whole outlook is changed!"

13.6 And hints at God's patience with the Jewish nation

Then he gave them this parable:

"Once upon a time a man had a fig-tree growing in his garden, and when he came to look for the figs, he found none at all. So he said to his gardener, 'Look, I have come expecting fruit on this fig-tree for three years running and never found any. Better cut it down. Why should it use up valuable ground?' And the gardener replied, 'Master, don't touch it this year till I have had a chance to dig round it and give it a bit of manure. Then, if it bears after that, it will be all right. But if it doesn't, then you can cut it down.' "

Revised Standard Version

these Galileans were worse sinners than all the other Galileans, because they suffered thus? 3 I tell you, No; but unless you repent you will all likewise perish. 4 Or those eighteen upon whom the tower in Siloam fell and killed them, do you think that they were worse offenders than all the others who dwelt in Jerusalem? 5 I tell you, No; but unless you repent you will all likewise perish."

6 And he told this parable: "A man had a fig tree planted in his vineyard; and he came seeking fruit on it and found none. 7 And he said to the vinedresser, 'Lo, these three years I have come seeking fruit on this fig tree, and I find none. Cut it down; why should it use up the ground?' 8 And he answered him, 'Let it alone, sir, this year also, till I dig about it and put on manure. 9 And if it bears fruit next year, well and good; but if not, you can cut it down.' "

Jerusalem Bible

them, "Do you suppose these Galileans who suffered like that were greater sinners than any other Galileans? 3 They were not, I tell you. No; but unless you repent you will all perish as they did. 4 Or those eighteen on whom the tower at Siloam fell and killed them? Do you suppose that they were more guilty than all the other people living in Jerusalem? 5 They were not, I tell you. No; but unless you repent you will all perish as they did."

Parable of the barren fig tree

6 He told this parable: "A man had a fig tree planted in his vineyard, and he came looking for fruit on it but found none. 7 He said to the man who looked after the vineyard, 'Look here, for three years now I have been coming to look for fruit on this fig tree and finding none. Cut it down: why should it be taking up the ground?' 8 'Sir,' the man replied, 'leave it one more year and give me time to dig around it and manure it: 9 it may bear fruit next year; if not, then you can cut it down.' "

New English Bible

because these Galileans suffered this fate, they must have been greater sinners than anyone else in Galilee? I tell you they were not; but unless you repent, you will all of you come to the same end. Or the eighteen people who were killed when the tower fell on them at Siloam—do you imagine they were more guilty than all the other people living in Jerusalem? I tell you they were not; but unless you repent, you will all of you come to the same end.'

He told them this parable: 'A man had a fig-tree growing in his vineyard; and he came looking for fruit on it, but found none. So he said to the vine-dresser, "Look here! For the last three years I have come looking for fruit on this fig-tree without finding any. Cut it down. Why should it go on using up the soil?" But he replied, "Leave it, sir, this one year while I dig round it and manure it. And if it bears next season, well and good; if not, you shall have it down." '

King James Version

10 And he was teaching in one of the synagogues on the sabbath. 11 And, behold, there was
a woman which had a spirit of infirmity eighteen years, and was bowed together, and could
in no wise lift up *herself*. 12 And when Jesus saw
her, he called *her to him*, and said unto her,
Woman, thou art loosed from thine infirmity.
13 And he laid *his* hands on her: and immediately she was made straight, and glorified God.
14 And the ruler of the synagogue answered with
indignation, because that Jesus had healed on
the sabbath day, and said unto the people, There
are six days in which men ought to work: in
them therefore come and be healed, and not on
the sabbath day. 15 The Lord then answered
him, and said, *Thou* hypocrite, doth not each
one of you on the sabbath loose his ox or *his*
ass from the stall, and lead *him* away to watering? 16 And ought not this woman, being a
daughter of Abraham, whom Satan hath bound,
lo, these eighteen years, be loosed from this bond
on the sabbath day? 17 And when he had said
these things, all his adversaries were ashamed:
and all the people rejoiced for all the glorious
things that were done by him.
18 Then said he, Unto what is the kingdom
of God like? and whereunto shall I resemble it?

Living Bible

10 One Sabbath as he was teaching in a synagogue, 11 he saw a seriously handicapped woman
who had been bent double for eighteen years and
was unable to straighten herself.
12 Calling her over to him Jesus said,
"Woman, you are healed of your sickness!"
13 He touched her, and instantly she could stand
straight. How she praised and thanked God!
14 But the local Jewish leader in charge of
the synagogue was very angry about it because
Jesus had healed her on the Sabbath day. "There
are six days of the week to work," he shouted
to the crowd. "Those are the days to come for
healing, not on the Sabbath!"
15 But the Lord replied, "You hypocrite! You
work on the Sabbath! Don't you untie your cattle from their stalls on the Sabbath and lead
them out for water? 16 And is it wrong for me,
just because it is the Sabbath day, to free this
Jewish woman from the bondage in which Satan
has held her for eighteen years?"
17 This shamed his enemies. And all the people rejoiced at the wonderful things he did.
18 Now he began teaching them again about
the Kingdom of God: "What is the Kingdom

Today's English Version

Jesus heals a crippled woman on the Sabbath

10 One Sabbath day Jesus was teaching in a
synagogue. 11 A woman was there who had an
evil spirit in her that had kept her sick for eighteen years; she was bent over and could not
straighten up at all. 12 When Jesus saw her he
called out to her, "Woman, you are free from
your sickness!" 13 He placed his hands on her
and at once she straightened herself up and
praised God.
14 The official of the synagogue was angry
that Jesus had healed on the Sabbath; so he spoke
up and said to the people, "There are six days in
which we should work; so come during those
days and be healed, but not on the Sabbath!"
15 The Lord answered him by saying, "You
hypocrites! Any one of you would untie his ox
or his donkey from the stall and take it out to
give it water on the Sabbath. 16 Now here is
this descendant of Abraham whom Satan has
kept in bonds for eighteen years; should she not
be freed from her bonds on the Sabbath?"
17 His answer made all his enemies ashamed of
themselves, while all the people rejoiced over
every wonderful thing that he did.

The parable of the mustard seed

18 Jesus asked, "What is the Kingdom of God

New International Version

A crippled woman healed on the Sabbath

10 On a Sabbath Jesus was teaching in one
of the synagogues, 11 and a woman was there
who had been crippled by a spirit for eighteen
years. She was bent over and could not straighten
up at all. 12 When Jesus saw her, he called her
forward and said to her, "Woman, you are set
free from your infirmity." 13 Then he put his
hands on her, and immediately she straightened
up and praised God.
14 Indignant because Jesus had healed on the
Sabbath, the synagogue ruler said to the people,
"There are six days for work. So come and be
healed on those days, not on the Sabbath."
15 The Lord answered him, "You hypocrites!
Doesn't each of you on the Sabbath untie his ox
or donkey from the stall and lead it out to give
it water? 16 Then should not this woman, a
daughter of Abraham, whom Satan has kept
bound for eighteen long years, be set free on the
Sabbath day from what bound her?"
17 When he said this, all his opponents were
humiliated, but the people were delighted with
all the wonderful things he was doing.

The parables of the mustard seed and yeast

18 Then Jesus asked, "What is the kingdom

Phillips Modern English

13.10 Jesus reduces the sabbatarians to silence

It happened that he was teaching in one of the synagogues on the Sabbath day. In the congregation was a woman who for eighteen years had been ill from some psychological cause; she was bent double and was quite unable to straighten herself up. When Jesus noticed her, he called her and said,

"You are set free from your illness!"

And he put his hands upon her, and at once she stood upright and praised God. But the president of the synagogue, in his annoyance at Jesus' healing on the Sabbath, announced to the congregation,

"There are six days in which men may work. Come on one of them and be healed, and not on the Sabbath day!"

But the Lord answered him, saying,

"You hypocrites, every single one of you unties his ox or his donkey from the stall and leads him away to water on the Sabbath day! This woman, a daughter of Abraham, whom you all known Satan has kept bound for eighteen years—surely she should be released from such bonds on the Sabbath day!"

These words reduced his opponents to shame, but the crowd was thrilled at all the glorious things he did.

Then he went on,

"What is the kingdom of God like? What il-

Revised Standard Version

10 Now he was teaching in one of the synagogues on the sabbath. 11And there was a
woman who had had a spirit of infirmity for
eighteen years; she was bent over and could not
fully straighten herself. 12And when Jesus saw
her, he called her and said to her, "Woman, you
are freed from your infirmity." 13And he laid
his hands upon her, and immediately she was
made straight, and she praised God. 14 But the
ruler of the synagogue, indignant because Jesus
had healed on the sabbath, said to the people,
"There are six days on which work ought to be
done; come on those days and be healed, and
not on the sabbath day." 15 Then the Lord answered him, "You hypocrites! Does not each
of you on the sabbath untie his ox or his ass
from the manger, and lead it away to water it?
16And ought not this woman, a daughter of
Abraham whom Satan bound for eighteen years,
be loosed from this bond on the sabbath day?"
17As he said this, all his adversaries were put to
shame; and all the people rejoiced at all the
glorious things that were done by him.
18 He said therefore, "What is the kingdom
of God like? And to what shall I compare it?

Jerusalem Bible

Healing of the crippled woman on a sabbath

10 One sabbath day he was teaching in one
of the synagogues, 11 and a woman was there
who for eighteen years had been possessed by
a spirit that left her enfeebled; she was bent
double and quite unable to stand upright.
12 When Jesus saw her he called her over and
said, "Woman, you are rid of your infirmity,"
13 and he laid his hands on her. And at once
she straightened up, and she glorified God.
14 But the synagogue official was indignant
because Jesus had healed on the sabbath, and
he addressed the people present. "There are six
days," he said, "when work is to be done. Come
and be healed on one of those days and not on
the sabbath." 15 But the Lord answered him.
"Hypocrites!" he said. "Is there one of you
who does not untie his ox or his donkey from
the manger on the sabbath and take it out for
watering? 16And this woman, a daughter of
Abraham whom Satan has held bound these
eighteen years—was it not right to untie her
bonds on the sabbath day?" 17 When he said
this, all his adversaries were covered with confusion, and all the people were overjoyed at all
the wonders he worked.

Parable of the mustard seed

18 He went on to say, "What is the kingdom
of God like? What shall I compare it with?

New English Bible

One Sabbath he was teaching in a synagogue, and there was a woman there possessed by a spirit that had crippled her for eighteen years. She was bent double and quite unable to stand up straight. When Jesus saw her he called her and said, 'You are rid of your trouble.' Then he laid his hands on her, and at once she straightened up and began to praise God. But the president of the synagogue, indignant with Jesus for healing on the Sabbath, intervened and said to the congregation, 'There are six working-days: come and be cured on one of them, and not on the Sabbath.' The Lord gave him his answer: 'What hypocrites you are!' he said. 'Is there a single one of you who does not loose his ox or his donkey from the manger and take it out to water on the Sabbath? And here is this woman, a daughter of Abraham, who has been kept prisoner by Satan for eighteen long years: was it wrong for her to be freed from her bonds on the Sabbath?' At these words all his opponents were covered with confusion, while the mass of the people were delighted at all the wonderful things he was doing.

'What is the kingdom of God like?' he con-

King James Version

19 It is like a grain of mustard seed, which a
man took, and cast into his garden; and it grew,
and waxed a great tree; and the fowls of the
air lodged in the branches of it. 20 And again he
said, Whereunto shall I liken the kingdom of
God? 21 It is like leaven, which a woman took
and hid in three measures of meal, till the whole
was leavened. 22 And he went through the cities
and villages, teaching, and journeying toward
Jerusalem. 23 Then said one unto him, Lord, are
there few that be saved? And he said unto them,
24 Strive to enter in at the strait gate: for
many, I say unto you, will seek to enter in, and
shall not be able. 25 When once the master of
the house is risen up, and hath shut to the door,
and ye begin to stand without, and to knock at
the door, saying, Lord, Lord, open unto us; and
he shall answer and say unto you, I know you
not whence ye are: 26 Then shall ye begin to
say, We have eaten and drunk in thy presence,
and thou hast taught in our streets. 27 But he
shall say, I tell you, I know you not whence
ye are; depart from me, all *ye* workers of iniq-

Living Bible

like?" he asked. "How can I illustrate it? 19 It
is like a tiny mustard seed planted in a garden;
soon it grows into a tall bush, and the birds live
among its branches. 20, 21 It is like yeast kneaded
into dough, which works unseen until it has risen
high and light."
22 He went from city to city and village to
village, teaching as he went, always pressing onward toward Jerusalem.
23 Someone asked him, "Will only a few be
saved?"
And he replied, 24, 25 "The door to heaven is
narrow. Work hard to get in, for the truth is
that many will try to enter but when the head
of the house has locked the door, it will be too
late. Then if you stand outside knocking, and
pleading, 'Lord, open the door for us,' he will
reply, 'I do not know you.'
26 " 'But we ate with you, and you taught in
our streets,' you will say.
27 "And he will reply, 'I tell you, I don't
know you. You can't come in here, guilty as you
are. Go away.'

Today's English Version

like? What shall I compare it with? 19 It is like
a mustard seed, which a man took and planted
in his field; the plant grew and became a tree,
and the birds made their nests in its branches."

The parable of the yeast

20 Again Jesus asked, "What shall I compare
the Kingdom of God with? 21 It is like the yeast
which a woman takes and mixes in a bushel of
flour, until the whole batch of dough rises."

The narrow door

22 Jesus went through towns and villages,
teaching and making his way toward Jerusalem.
23 Someone asked him, "Sir, will just a few
people be saved?"
Jesus answered them, 24 "Do your best to go
in through the narrow door; because many people, I tell you, will try to go in but will not be
able. 25 The master of the house will get up and
close the door; then when you stand outside and
begin to knock on the door and say, 'Open the
door for us, sir!' he will answer you, 'I don't
know where you come from!' 26 Then you will
answer back, 'We ate and drank with you; you
taught in our town!' 27 He will say again, 'I
don't know where you come from. Get away

New International Version

of God like? What shall I compare it to? 19 It is
like a mustard seed, which a man took and
planted in his garden. It grew, became a tree,
and the birds of the air perched in its branches."
20 Again he asked, "What shall I compare the
kingdom of God to? 21 It is like yeast that a
woman took and mixed into a large amount[a] of
flour until it worked all through the dough."

The narrow door

22 Then Jesus went through the cities and villages, teaching as he made his way to Jerusalem.
23 Someone asked him, "Lord, are only a few
people going to be saved?"
He said to them, 24 "Make every effort to
enter through the narrow door, because many, I
tell you, will try to enter and will not be able
to. 25 Once the owner of the house gets up and
closes the door, you will stand outside knocking
and pleading, 'Sir, open the door for us.'
"But he will answer, 'I don't know you or
where you come from.'
26 "Then you will say, 'We ate and drank
with you, and you taught in our streets.'
27 "But he will reply, 'I don't know you or
where you come from. Away from me, all you
evildoers!'

[a] Greek *three satas* (about a bushel).

Phillips Modern English

lustration can I use to make it plain to you? It is like a grain of mustard-seed which a man took and dropped in his own garden. It grew and became a tree and the birds came and nested in its branches."

Then again he said,

"What can I say the kingdom of God is like? It is like the yeast which a woman took and covered up in three measures of flour until the whole had risen."

13.22 The kingdom is not entered by drifting but by decision

So he went on his way through towns and villages, teaching as he went and making his way towards Jerusalem. Someone asked him,

"Lord, are only a few men to be saved?"

And Jesus told them,

"You must try your hardest to get in through the narrow door, for many, I assure you, will try to do so and will not succeed. For once the master of the house has got up and shut the door, you will find yourselves standing outside and knocking at the door crying, 'Lord, please open the door for us.' He will reply to you, 'I don't know who you are or where you come from.' 'But', you will protest, 'we have had meals with you, and you taught in our streets!' Yet he will say to you, 'I tell you I do not know where you have come from. Be off, you are all

Revised Standard Version

19 It is like a grain of mustard seed which a man took and sowed in his garden; and it grew and became a tree, and the birds of the air made nests in its branches."

20 And again he said, "To what shall I compare the kingdom of God? 21 It is like leaven which a woman took and hid in three measures of flour, till it was all leavened."

22 He went on his way through towns and villages, teaching, and journeying toward Jerusalem. 23 And some one said to him, "Lord, will those who are saved be few?" And he said to them, 24 "Strive to enter by the narrow door; for many, I tell you, will seek to enter and will not be able. 25 When once the householder has risen up and shut the door, you will begin to stand outside and to knock at the door, saying, 'Lord, open to us.' He will answer you, 'I do not know where you come from.' 26 Then you will begin to say, 'We ate and drank in your presence, and you taught in our streets.' 27 But he will say, 'I tell you, I do not know where you come from; depart from me, all you work-

Jerusalem Bible

19 It is like a mustard seed which a man took and threw into his garden: it grew and became a tree, and the birds of the air sheltered in its branches."

Parable of the yeast

20 Another thing he said, "What shall I compare the kingdom of God with? 21 It is like the yeast a woman took and mixed in with three measures of flour till it was leavened all through."

The narrow door; rejection of the Jews, call of the Gentiles

22 Through towns and villages he went teaching, making his way to Jerusalem. 23 Someone said to him, "Sir, will there be only a few saved?" He said to them, 24 "Try your best to enter by the narrow door, because, I tell you, many will try to enter and will not succeed.

25 "Once the master of the house has got up and locked the door, you may find yourself knocking on the door, saying, 'Lord, open to us,' but he will answer, 'I do not know where you come from.' 26 Then you will find yourself saying, 'We once ate and drank in your company; you taught in our streets,' 27 but he will reply, I do not know where you come from. *Away from me, all you wicked men!'* [v]

[v] Ps. 6:8.

New English Bible

tinued. 'What shall I compare it with? It is like a mustard-seed which a man took and sowed in his garden; and it grew to be a tree and the birds came to roost among its branches.'

Again he said, 'The kingdom of God, what shall I compare it with? It is like yeast which a woman took and mixed with half a hundredweight of flour till it was all leavened.'

He continued his journey through towns and villages, teaching as he made his way towards Jerusalem. Someone asked him, 'Sir, are only a few to be saved?' His answer was: 'Struggle to get in through the narrow door; for I tell you that many will try to enter and not be able.

'When once the master of the house has got up and locked the door, you may stand outside and knock, and say, "Sir, let us in!", but he will only answer, "I do not know where you come from." Then you will begin to say, "We sat at table with you and you taught in our streets." But he will repeat, "I tell you, I do not know where you come from. Out of my sight,

King James Version

uity. 28 There shall be weeping and gnashing of
teeth, when ye shall see Abraham, and Isaac,
and Jacob, and all the prophets, in the kingdom
of God, and you *yourselves* thrust out. 29 And
they shall come from the east, and *from* the
west, and from the north, and *from* the south,
and shall sit down in the kingdom of God.
30 And, behold, there are last which shall be first;
and there are first which shall be last.
31 The same day there came certain of the
Pharisees, saying unto him, Get thee out, and
depart hence; for Herod will kill thee. 32 And
he said unto them, Go ye, and tell that fox, Behold, I cast out devils, and I do cures to day
and to morrow, and the third *day* I shall be perfected. 33 Nevertheless I must walk to day, and
to morrow, and the *day* following: for it cannot
be that a prophet perish out of Jerusalem. 34 O
Jerusalem, Jerusalem, which killest the prophets,
and stonest them that are sent unto thee; how
often would I have gathered thy children together, as a hen *doth gather* her brood under
her wings, and ye would not! 35 Behold, your
house is left unto you desolate: and verily I say

Living Bible

28 "And there will be great weeping and
gnashing of teeth as you stand outside and see
Abraham, Isaac, Jacob, and all the prophets
within the Kingdom of God—29 for people will
come from all over the world to take their
places there. 30 And note this: some who are
despised now will be greatly honored then; and
some who are highly thought of now will be
least important then."
31 A few minutes later some Pharisees said
to him, "Get out of here if you want to live, for
King Herod is after you!"
32 Jesus replied, "Go tell that fox that I will
keep on casting out demons and doing miracles
of healing today and tomorrow; and the third
day I will reach my destination. 33 Yes, today,
tomorrow, and the next day! For it wouldn't do
for a prophet of God to be killed except in Jerusalem!
34 "O Jerusalem, Jerusalem! The city that
murders the prophets. The city stones those sent
to help her. How often I have wanted to gather
your children together even as a hen protects
her brood under her wings, but you wouldn't let
me. 35 And now—now your house is left desolate.

Today's English Version

from me, all you evildoers!' 28 What crying and
gnashing of teeth there will be when you see
Abraham, Isaac, and Jacob and all the prophets
in the Kingdom of God, while you are thrown
out! 29 People will come from the east and the
west, from the north and the south, and sit at
the table in the Kingdom of God. 30 Then those
who are now last will be first, and those who are
now first will be last."

Jesus' love for Jerusalem

31 At that same time some Pharisees came to
Jesus and said to him, "You must get out of here
and go somewhere else, because Herod wants to
kill you."
32 Jesus answered them, "Go tell that fox: 'I
am driving out demons and performing cures
today and tomorrow, and on the third day I
shall finish my work.' 33 Yet I must be on my
way today, tomorrow, and the next day; it is not
right for a prophet to be killed anywhere except
in Jerusalem.
34 "Jerusalem, Jerusalem! You kill the prophets, you stone the messengers God has sent
you! How many times I wanted to put my arms
around all your people, just as a hen gathers her
chicks under her wings, but you would not let
me! 35 Now your home will be completely forsaken. You will not see me, I tell you, until the

New International Version

28 "There will be weeping and grinding of
teeth when you see Abraham, Isaac and Jacob
and all the prophets in the kingdom of God,
but you yourselves thrown out. 29 People will
come from east and west and north and south,
and will take their places at the feast in the
kingdom of God. 30 Indeed there are those who
are last who will be first, and first who will
be last."

Jesus' sorrow for Jerusalem

31 At that time some Pharisees came to Jesus
and said to him, "Leave this place and go somewhere else. Herod wants to kill you."
32 He replied, "Go tell that fox, 'I will drive
out demons and heal people today and tomorrow, and on the third day I will reach my goal.'
33 In any case, I must keep going today and
tomorrow and the next day—for surely no
prophet can die outside Jerusalem!
34 "O Jerusalem, Jerusalem, you who kill the
prophets and stone those sent to you, how often
I have longed to gather your children together,
as a hen gathers her chicks under her wings, but
you were not willing! 35 Look, your house is
left to you desolate. I tell you, you will not see

Phillips Modern English

scoundrels!' At that time there will be tears and bitter regret—to see Abraham and Isaac and Jacob and all the prophets inside the kingdom of God, and you yourselves banished outside! Yes, and people will come from the east and the west, and from the north and the south, and take their seats in the kingdom of God. There are some at the back now who will be in front then, and there are some in front now who will then be far behind."

13.31 The Pharisees warn Jesus of Herod; he replies

Just then some Pharisees arrived to tell him, "You must get right away from here, for Herod intends to kill you."

"Go and tell that fox," returned Jesus, "anyone can see that today and tomorrow I am expelling evil spirits and continuing my work of healing, and on the third day my work will be finished. But I must journey on today, tomorrow, and the next day, for it would never do for a prophet to meet his death outside Jerusalem!

"O Jerusalem, Jerusalem, you murder the prophets and stone the messengers that are sent to you! How often have I longed to gather your children round me like a bird gathering her brood together under her wings, but you would never have it. Now all you have left is your house. For I tell you that you will never see

Revised Standard Version

ers of iniquity!' 28 There you will weep and
gnash your teeth, when you see Abraham and
Isaac and Jacob and all the prophets in the
kingdom of God and you yourselves thrust out.
29 And men will come from east and west, and
from north and south, and sit at table in the
kingdom of God. 30 And behold, some are last
who will be first, and some are first who will be
last."
31 At that very hour some Pharisees came,
and said to him, "Get away from here, for
Herod wants to kill you." 32 And he said to
them, "Go and tell that fox, 'Behold, I cast out
demons and perform cures today and tomorrow,
and the third day I finish my course. 33 Nevertheless I must go on my way today and tomorrow and the day following; for it cannot be that
a prophet should perish away from Jerusalem.'
34 O Jerusalem, Jerusalem, killing the prophets
and stoning those who are sent to you! How
often would I have gathered your children together as a hen gathers her brood under her
wings, and you would not! 35 Behold, your house
is forsaken. And I tell you, you will not see me

Jerusalem Bible

28 "Then there will be weeping and grinding
of teeth, when you see Abraham and Isaac and
Jacob and all the prophets in the kingdom of
God, and yourselves turned outside. 29 And men
from east and west, from north and south, will
come to take their places at the feast in the
kingdom of God.
30 "Yes, there are those now last who will
be first, and those now first who will be last."

Herod the fox

31 Just at this time some Pharisees came up.
"Go away," they said. "Leave this place, because Herod means to kill you." 32 He replied,
"You may go and give that fox this message:
Learn that today and tomorrow I cast out devils
and on the third day[w] attain my end. 33 But
for today and tomorrow and the next day I must
go on, since it would not be right for a prophet
to die outside Jerusalem.

Jerusalem admonished

34 "Jerusalem, Jerusalem, you that kill the
prophets and stone those who are sent to you!
How often have I longed to gather your children, as a hen gathers her brood under her
wings, and you refused! 35 So be it! Your house
will be left to you. Yes, I promise you, you

[w] "after a short time."

New English Bible

all of you, you and your wicked ways!" There will be wailing and grinding of teeth there, when you see Abraham, Isaac, and Jacob, and all the prophets, in the kingdom of God, and yourselves thrown out. From east and west people will come, from north and south, for the feast in the kingdom of God. Yes, and some who are now last will be first, and some who are first will be last.'

At that time a number of Pharisees came to him and said, 'You should leave this place and go on your way; Herod is out to kill you.' He replied, 'Go and tell that fox, "Listen: today and tomorrow I shall be casting out devils and working cures; on the third day I reach my goal." However, I must be on my way today and tomorrow and the next day, because it is unthinkable for a prophet to meet his death anywhere but in Jerusalem.

'O Jerusalem, Jerusalem, the city that murders the prophets and stones the messengers sent to her! How often have I longed to gather your children, as a hen gathers her brood under her wings; but you would not let me. Look, look! there is your temple, forsaken by God. And I

King James Version

unto you, Ye shall not see me, until *the time* come when ye shall say, Blessed *is* he that cometh in the name of the Lord.

14 And it came to pass, as he went into the
house of one of the chief Pharisees to eat
bread on the sabbath day, that they watched
him. 2And, behold, there was a certain man before him which had the dropsy. 3And Jesus answering spake unto the lawyers and Pharisees,
saying, Is it lawful to heal on the sabbath day?
4And they held their peace. And he took *him*,
and healed him, and let him go; 5And answered
them, saying, Which of you shall have an ass or
an ox fallen into a pit, and will not straightway
pull him out on the sabbath day? 6And they
could not answer him again to these things.
7 And he put forth a parable to those which
were bidden, when he marked how they chose

Living Bible

And you will never again see me until you say, 'Welcome to him who comes in the name of the Lord.' "

14 One Sabbath as he was in the home of a member of the Jewish Council, the Pharisees were watching him like hawks to see if he would heal a man who was present who was suffering from dropsy.
3 Jesus said to the Pharisees and legal experts standing around, "Well, is it within the Law to heal a man on the Sabbath day, or not?"
4 And when they refused to answer, Jesus took the sick man by the hand and healed him and sent him away.
5 Then he turned to them: "Which of you doesn't work on the Sabbath?" he asked. "If your cow falls into a pit, don't you proceed at once to get it out?"
6 Again they had no answer.
7 When he noticed that all who came to the dinner were trying to sit near the head of the

Today's English Version

time comes when you say, 'God bless him who comes in the name of the Lord.' "

Jesus heals a sick man

14 One Sabbath day Jesus went to eat a meal at the home of one of the leading Pharisees; and people were watching Jesus closely. 2A man whose legs and arms were swollen came to Jesus, 3 and Jesus spoke up and asked the teachers of the Law and the Pharisees, "Does our Law allow healing on the Sabbath, or not?"
4 But they would not say a thing. Jesus took the man, healed him, and sent him away. 5 Then he said to them, "If any one of you had a son or an ox that happened to fall in a well on a Sabbath, would you not pull him out at once on the Sabbath itself?"
6 But they were not able to answer him about this.

Humility and hospitality

7 Jesus noticed how some of the guests were choosing the best places, so he told this parable

New International Version

me again until you say, 'Blessed is he who comes in the name of the Lord.' [b] "

Jesus at a Pharisee's house

14 One Sabbath, when Jesus went to eat in the house of a prominent Pharisee, he was being carefully watched. 2 There in front of him was a man suffering from dropsy. 3 Jesus asked the Pharisees and experts in the law, "Is it lawful to heal on the Sabbath or not?" 4 But they remained silent. So taking hold of the man, he healed him and sent him away.
5 Then he asked them, "If one of you has a son[c] or an ox that falls into a well on the Sabbath day, will you not immediately pull him out?" 6And they had nothing to say.
7 When he noticed how the guests picked the places of honor at the table, he told them this

[*b*] Psalm 118:26. [*c*] Some MSS read *donkey*.

Phillips Modern English

me again till the day when you cry, 'Blessed is he who comes in the name of the Lord!' "

14.1 Strict sabbatarianism is again rebuked

One Sabbath day he went into the house of one of the leading Pharisees for a meal, and they were watching him closely. Right in front of him was a man afflicted with dropsy. So Jesus spoke to the scribes and Pharisees and asked,

"Well, is it right to heal on the Sabbath day or not?"

But there was no reply. So Jesus took the man and healed him and let him go. Then he said to them,

"If a donkey or an ox belonging to one of you fell into a well, wouldn't you rescue it without the slightest hesitation even though it were the Sabbath?"

And this again left them quite unable to reply.

14.7 A lesson in humility

Then he gave a pointed word of advice to the guests when he noticed how they were choosing the best seats. He said to them,

Revised Standard Version

until you say, 'Blessed is he who comes in the name of the Lord!' "

14 One sabbath when he went to dine at
the house of a ruler who belonged to the
Pharisees, they were watching him. 2And behold, there was a man before him who had
dropsy. 3And Jesus spoke to the lawyers and
Pharisees, saying, "Is it lawful to heal on the
sabbath, or not?" 4 But they were silent. Then
he took him and healed him, and let him go.
5And he said to them, "Which of you, having a
son[s] or an ox that has fallen into a well, will
not immediately pull him out on a sabbath day?"
6And they could not reply to this.
7 Now he told a parable to those who were
invited, when he marked how they chose the

[s] Other ancient authorities read *an ass*.

Jerusalem Bible

shall not see me till the time comes when you say:

Blessings on him who comes in the name of the Lord!" [x]

Healing of a dropsical man on the sabbath

14 Now on a sabbath day he had gone for a
meal to the house of one of the leading
Pharisees; and they watched him closely. 2 There
in front of him was a man with dropsy, 3 and
Jesus addressed the lawyers and Pharisees. "Is
it against the law," he asked, "to cure a man
on the sabbath, or not?" 4 But they remained
silent, so he took the man and cured him and
sent him away. 5 Then he said to them, "Which
of you here, if his son falls into a well, or his
ox, will not pull him out on a sabbath day
without hesitation?" 6And to this they could
find no answer.

On choosing places at table

7 He then told the guests a parable, because
he had noticed how they picked the places of

[x] Ps. 118:26.

New English Bible

tell you, you shall never see me until the time comes when you say, "Blessings on him who comes in the name of the Lord!" '

14 One Sabbath he went to have a meal in the house of a leading Pharisee; and they were watching him closely. There, in front of him, was a man suffering from dropsy. Jesus asked the lawyers and the Pharisees: 'Is it permitted to cure people on the Sabbath or not?' They said nothing. So he took the man, cured him, and sent him away. Then he turned to them and said, 'If one of you has a donkey[a] or an ox and it falls into a well, will he hesitate to haul it up on the Sabbath day?' To this they could find no reply.

When he noticed how the guests were trying to secure the places of honour, he spoke to them

[a] *Some witnesses read* son.

King James Version

out the chief rooms; saying unto them, 8 When
thou art bidden of any *man* to a wedding, sit
not down in the highest room; lest a more honourable man than thou be bidden of him; 9And
he that bade thee and him come and say to thee,
Give this man place; and thou begin with shame
to take the lowest room. 10 But when thou art
bidden, go and sit down in the lowest room;
that when he that bade thee cometh, he may say
unto thee, Friend, go up higher: then shalt thou
have worship in the presence of them that sit at
meat with thee. 11 For whosoever exalteth himself shall be abased; and he that humbleth himself shall be exalted.

12 Then said he also to him that bade him,
When thou makest a dinner or a supper, call
not thy friends, nor thy brethren, neither thy
kinsmen, nor *thy* rich neighbours; lest they also
bid thee again, and a recompense be made thee.
13 But when thou makest a feast, call the poor,
the maimed, the lame, the blind: 14And thou
shalt be blessed; for they cannot recompense
thee: for thou shalt be recompensed at the resurrection of the just.

15 And when one of them that sat at meat
with him heard these things, he said unto him,

Living Bible

table, he gave them this advice: 8 "If you are
invited to a wedding feast, don't always head for
the best seat. For if someone more respected
than you shows up, 9 the host will bring him
over to where you are sitting and say, 'Let this
man sit here instead.' And you, embarrassed,
will have to take whatever seat is left at the
foot of the table!

10 "Do this instead—start at the foot; and
when your host sees you he will come and say,
'Friend, we have a better place than this for
you!' Thus you will be honored in front of all
the other guests. 11 For everyone who tries to
honor himself shall be humbled; and he who
humbles himself shall be honored." 12 Then he
turned to his host. "When you put on a dinner,"
he said, "don't invite friends, brothers, relatives,
and rich neighbors! For they will return the invitation. 13 Instead, invite the poor, the crippled,
the lame, and the blind. 14 Then at the resurrection of the godly, God will reward you for inviting those who can't repay you."

15 Hearing this, a man sitting at the table with
Jesus exclaimed, "What a privilege it would be

Today's English Version

to all of them, 8 "When someone invites you to
a wedding feast, do not sit down in the best
place. It could happen that someone more important than you had been invited, 9 and your
host, who invited both of you, would come and
say to you, 'Let him have this place.' Then you
would be ashamed and have to sit in the lowest
place. 10 Instead, when you are invited, go and
sit in the lowest place, so that your host will
come to you and say, 'Come on up, my friend,
to a better place.' This will bring you honor in
the presence of all the other guests. 11 Because
everyone who makes himself great will be humbled, and everyone who humbles himself will be
made great."

12 Then Jesus said to his host, "When you
give a lunch or a dinner, do not invite your
friends, or your brothers, or your relatives, or
your rich neighbors—because they will invite
you back and in this way you will be paid for
what you did. 13 When you give a feast, invite
the poor, the crippled, the lame, and the blind,
14 and you will be blessed; because they are not
able to pay you back. You will be paid by God
when the good people rise from death."

The parable of the great feast

15 One of the men sitting at the table heard
this and said to Jesus, "How happy are those

New International Version

parable: 8 "When someone invites you to a wedding feast, do not take the place of honor, for
a person more distinguished than you may have
been invited. 9 If so, the host who invited both
of you will come and say to you, 'Give this man
your seat.' Then, humiliated, you will have to
take the least important place. 10 But when you
are invited, take the lowest place, so that when
your host comes, he will say to you, 'Friend,
move up to a better place.' Then you will be
honored in the presence of all your fellow guests.
11 For everyone who exalts himself will be humbled, and he who humbles himself will be exalted."

12 Then Jesus said to his host, "When you
give a luncheon or dinner, do not invite your
friends, your brothers or relatives, or your rich
neighbors; if you do, they may invite you back
and so you will be repaid. 13 But when you give
a banquet, invite the poor, the crippled, the lame,
the blind, 14 and you will be blessed. Although
they cannot repay you, you will be repaid at
the resurrection of the righteous."

The parable of the great banquet

15 When one of those at the table with him
heard this, he said to Jesus, "Blessed is the man

Phillips Modern English

"When you are invited to a wedding reception, don't sit down in the best seat. It might happen that a more distinguished man than you has also been invited. Then your host might say, 'I am afraid you must give up your seat for this man.' And then, with considerable embarrassment, you will have to sit in the humblest place. No, when you are invited, go and take your seat in an inconspicuous place, so that when your host comes in he may say to you, 'Come on, my dear fellow, we have a much better seat than this for you.' That is the way to be important in the eyes of all your fellow-guests! For everyone who makes himself important will become insignificant, while the man who makes himself insignificant will find himself important."

Then, addressing his host, Jesus said,

"When you give a luncheon or a dinner party, don't invite your friends or your brothers or relations or wealthy neighbours, for the chances are they will invite you back, and you will be fully repaid. No, when you give a party, invite the poor, the crippled, the lame and the blind. That way lies real happiness for you. They have no means of repaying you, but you will be repaid when good men are rewarded—at the resurrection."

Then, one of the guests, hearing these remarks of Jesus, said,

Revised Standard Version

places of honor, saying to them, 8 "When you
are invited by any one to a marriage feast, do
not sit down in a place of honor, lest a more
eminent man than you be invited by him; 9 and
he who invited you both will come and say to
you, 'Give place to this man,' and then you will
begin with shame to take the lowest place. 10 But
when you are invited, go and sit in the lowest
place, so that when your host comes he may say
to you, 'Friend, go up higher'; then you will be
honored in the presence of all who sit at table
with you. 11 For every one who exalts himself
will be humbled, and he who humbles himself
will be exalted."

12 He said also to the man who had invited
him, "When you give a dinner or a banquet, do
not invite your friends or your brothers or your
kinsmen or rich neighbors, lest they also invite
you in return, and you be repaid. 13 But when
you give a feast, invite the poor, the maimed,
the lame, the blind, 14 and you will be blessed,
because they cannot repay you. You will be repaid at the resurrection of the just."

15 When one of those who sat at table with
him heard this, he said to him, "Blessed is he

Jerusalem Bible

honor. He said this, 8 "When someone invites
you to a wedding feast, do not take your seat
in the place of honor. A more distinguished
person than you may have been invited, 9 and
the person who invited you both may come and
say, 'Give up your place to this man.' And
then, to your embarrassment, you would have
to go and take the lowest place. 10 No; when
you are a guest, make your way to the lowest
place and sit there, so that, when your host
comes, he may say, 'My friend, move up higher.'
In that way, everyone with you at the table will
see you honored. 11 For everyone who exalts
himself will be humbled, and the man who humbles himself will be exalted."

On choosing guests to be invited

12 Then he said to his host, "When you give
a lunch or a dinner, do not ask your friends,
brothers, relations or rich neighbors, for fear
they repay your courtesy by inviting you in return. 13 No; when you have a party, invite the
poor, the crippled, the lame, the blind; 14 that
they cannot pay you back means that you are
fortunate, because repayment will be made to
you when the virtuous rise again."

The invited guests who made excuses

15 On hearing this, one of those gathered
around the table said to him, "Happy the man

New English Bible

in a parable: 'When you are asked by someone to a wedding-feast, do not sit down in the place of honour. It may be that some person more distinguished than yourself has been invited; and the host will come and say to you, "Give this man your seat." Then you will look foolish as you begin to take the lowest place. No, when you receive an invitation, go and sit down in the lowest place, so that when your host comes he will say, "Come up higher, my friend." Then all your fellow-guests will see the respect in which you are held. For everyone who exalts himself will be humbled; and whoever humbles himself will be exalted.'

Then he said to his host, 'When you are having a party for lunch or supper, do not invite your friends, your brothers or other relations, or your rich neighbours; they will only ask you back again and so you will be repaid. But when you give a party, ask the poor, the crippled, the lame, and the blind; and so find happiness. For they have no means of repaying you; but you will be repaid on the day when good men rise from the dead.'

One of the company, after hearing all this, said to him, 'Happy the man who shall sit at

King James Version

Blessed *is* he that shall eat bread in the kingdom
of God. 16 Then said he unto him, A certain
man made a great supper, and bade many:
17 And sent his servant at supper time to say to
them that were bidden, Come; for all things are
now ready. 18 And they all with one *consent* began to make excuse. The first said unto him, I
have bought a piece of ground, and I must needs
go and see it: I pray thee have me excused.
19 And another said, I have bought five yoke of
oxen, and I go to prove them: I pray thee have
me excused. 20 And another said, I have married
a wife, and therefore I cannot come. 21 So that
servant came, and shewed his lord these things.
Then the master of the house being angry said
to his servant, Go out quickly into the streets
and lanes of the city, and bring in hither the
poor, and the maimed, and the halt, and the
blind. 22 And the servant said, Lord, it is done as
thou hast commanded, and yet there is room.
23 And the lord said unto the servant, Go out
into the highways and hedges, and compel *them*
to come in, that my house may be filled. 24 For
I say unto you, That none of those men which
were bidden shall taste of my supper.
25 And there went great multitudes with him:

Living Bible

to get into the Kingdom of God!"
16 Jesus replied with this illustration: "A man
prepared a great feast and sent out many invitations. 17 When all was ready, he sent his servant
around to notify the guests that it was time for
them to arrive. 18 But they all began making
excuses. One said he had just bought a field and
wanted to inspect it, and asked to be excused.
19 Another said he had just bought five pair of
oxen and wanted to try them out. 20 Another had
just been married and for that reason couldn't
come.
21 "The servant returned and reported to his
master what they had said. His master was angry
and told him to go quickly into the streets and
alleys of the city and to invite the beggars,
crippled, lame, and blind. 22 But even then, there
was still room.
23 " 'Well, then,' said his master, 'go out
into the country lanes and out behind the hedges
and urge anyone you find to come, so that the
house will be full. 24 For none of those I invited first will get even the smallest taste of what
I had prepared for them.' "
25 Great crowds were following him. He
turned around and addressed them as follows:

Today's English Version

who will sit at the table in the Kingdom of God!"
16 Jesus said to him, "There was a man who
was giving a great feast, to which he invited many
people. 17 At the time for the feast he sent his
servant to tell his guests, 'Come, everything is
ready!' 18 But they all began, one after another,
to make excuses. The first one told the servant,
'I bought a field, and have to go and look at it;
please accept my apologies.' 19 Another one said,
'I bought five pairs of oxen and am on my way to
try them out; please accept my apologies.' 20 Another one said, 'I have just gotten married, and
for this reason I cannot come.' 21 The servant
went back and told all this to his master. The
master of the house was furious and said to his
servant, 'Hurry out to the streets and alleys of
the town, and bring back the poor, the crippled,
the blind, and the lame.' 22 Soon the servant
said, 'Your order has been carried out, sir, but
there is room for more.' 23 So the master said
to the servant, 'Go out to the country roads and
lanes, and make people come in, so that my
house will be full. 24 I tell you all that none of
those men who were invited will taste my dinner!' "

The cost of being a disciple

25 Great crowds of people were going along

New International Version

who will eat at the feast in the kingdom of
God."
16 Jesus replied: "A certain man was preparing a great banquet and invited many guests.
17 At the time of the banquet he sent his servant
to tell those who had been invited, 'Come, for
everything is now ready.'
18 "But they all alike began to make excuses.
The first said, 'I have just bought a field, and I
must go and see it. Please excuse me.'
19 "Another said, 'I have just bought five
yoke of oxen, and I'm on my way to try them
out. Please excuse me.'
20 "Still another said, 'I just got married, so
I can't come.'
21 "The servant came back and reported this
to his master. Then the owner of the house became angry and ordered his servant, 'Go out
quickly into the streets and alleys of the town
and bring in the poor, the crippled, the blind
and the lame.'
22 " 'Sir,' the servant said, 'what you ordered
has been done, but there is still room.'
23 "Then the master told his servant, 'Go out
to the roads and country lanes and make them
come in, so that my house will be full. 24 I tell
you, not one of those men who were invited will
get a taste of my banquet.' "

The cost of being a disciple

25 Large crowds were traveling with Jesus,

Phillips Modern English

"What happiness for a man to eat a meal in the kingdom of God!"

14.16 Men who are "too busy" for the kingdom of God

But Jesus said to him,

"Once upon a time, a man planned a big dinner party and invited a great many people. At dinner-time, he sent his servant out to tell those who were invited, 'Please come, everything is now ready.' But they all, as one man, began to make their excuses. The first one said to him, 'I have bought some land. I must go and look at it. Please excuse me.' Another one said, 'I have bought five yoke of oxen and am on my way to try them out. Please convey my apologies.' And another one said, 'I have just got married and I am sure you will understand I cannot come.' So the servant returned and reported all this to his master. The master of the house was extremely annoyed and said to his servant, 'Hurry out now into the streets and alleys of the town, and bring here the poor and crippled and blind and lame.' Then the servant said, 'I have done what you told me, sir, and there are still empty places.' Then the master replied, 'Now go out to the roads and hedgerows and make them come inside, so that my house may be full. For I tell you that not one of the men I invited shall have a taste of my dinner.' "

Now as Jesus proceeded on his journey, great crowds accompanied him, and he turned and spoke to them,

Revised Standard Version

who shall eat bread in the kingdom of God!"
16 But he said to him, "A man once gave a great
banquet, and invited many; 17 and at the time
for the banquet he sent his servant to say to
those who had been invited, 'Come; for all is
now ready.' 18 But they all alike began to make
excuses. The first said to him, 'I have bought
a field, and I must go out and see it; I pray you,
have me excused.' 19 And another said, 'I have
bought five yoke of oxen, and I go to examine
them; I pray you, have me excused.' 20 And another said, 'I have married a wife, and therefore
I cannot come.' 21 So the servant came and reported this to his master. Then the householder
in anger said to his servant, 'Go out quickly to
the streets and lanes of the city, and bring in
the poor and maimed and blind and lame.'
22 And the servant said, 'Sir, what you commanded has been done, and still there is room.'
23 And the master said to the servant, 'Go out to
the highways and hedges, and compel people to
come in, that my house may be filled. 24 For I
tell you,[a] none of those men who were invited
shall taste my banquet.' "
25 Now great multitudes accompanied him;

[a] The Greek word for *you* here is plural.

Jerusalem Bible

who will be at the feast in the kingdom of
God!" 16 But he said to him, "There was a man
who gave a great banquet, and he invited a
large number of people. 17 When the time for
the banquet came, he sent his servant to say to
those who had been invited, 'Come along:
everything is ready now.' 18 But all alike started
to make excuses. The first said, 'I have bought
a piece of land and must go and see it. Please
accept my apologies.' 19 Another said, 'I have
bought five yoke of oxen and am on my way
to try them out. Please accept my apologies.'
20 Yet another said, 'I have just got married
and so am unable to come.'
21 "The servant returned and reported this
to his master. Then the householder, in a rage,
said to his servant, 'Go out quickly into the
streets and alleys of the town and bring in here
the poor, the crippled, the blind and the lame.'
22 'Sir,' said the servant, 'your orders have been
carried out and there is still room.' 23 Then
the master said to his servant, 'Go to the open
roads and the hedgerows and force people to
come in to make sure my house is full; 24 because, I tell you, not one of those who were
invited shall have a taste of my banquet.' "

Renouncing all that one holds dear

25 Great crowds accompanied him on his

New English Bible

the feast in the kingdom of God!' Jesus answered, 'A man was giving a big dinner party and had sent out many invitations. At dinner-time he sent his servant with a message for his guests, "Please come, everything is now ready." They began one and all to excuse themselves. The first said, "I have bought a piece of land, and I must go and look over it; please accept my apologies." The second said, "I have bought five yoke of oxen, and I am on my way to try them out; please accept my apologies." The next said, "I have just got married and for that reason I cannot come." When the servant came back he reported this to his master. The master of the house was angry and said to him, "Go out quickly into the streets and alleys of the town, and bring me in the poor, the crippled, the blind, and the lame." The servant said, "Sir, your orders have been carried out and there is still room." The master replied, "Go out on to the highways and along the hedgerows and make them come in; I want my house to be full. I tell you that not one of those who were invited shall taste my banquet." '

Once when great crowds were accompanying

King James Version

and he turned, and said unto them, 26 If any *man* come to me, and hate not his father, and mother, and wife, and children, and brethren, and sisters, yea, and his own life also, he cannot be my disciple. 27 And whosoever doth not bear his cross, and come after me, cannot be my disciple. 28 For which of you, intending to build a tower, sitteth not down first, and counteth the cost, whether he have *sufficient* to finish *it?* 29 Lest haply, after he hath laid the foundation, and is not able to finish *it,* all that behold *it* begin to mock him, 30 Saying, This man began to build, and was not able to finish. 31 Or what king, going to make war against another king, sitteth not down first, and consulteth whether he be able with ten thousand to meet him that cometh against him with twenty thousand? 32 Or else, while the other is yet a great way off, he sendeth an ambassage, and desireth conditions of peace. 33 So likewise, whosoever he be of you that forsaketh not all that he hath, he cannot be my disciple.

34 Salt *is* good: but if the salt have lost his

Living Bible

26 "Anyone who wants to be my follower must love me far more than[a] he does his own father, mother, wife, children, brothers, or sisters—yes, more than his own life—otherwise he cannot be my disciple. 27 And no one can be my disciple who does not carry his own cross and follow me.

28 "But don't begin until you count the cost.[b] For who would begin construction of a building without first getting estimates and then checking to see if he has enough money to pay the bills? 29 Otherwise he might complete only the foundation before running out of funds. And then how everyone would laugh!

30 " 'See that fellow there?' they would mock. 'He started that building and ran out of money before it was finished!'

31 "Or what king would ever dream of going to war without first sitting down with his counselors and discussing whether his army of 10,000 is strong enough to defeat the 20,000 men who are marching against him?

32 "If the decision is negative, then while the enemy troops are still far away, he will send a truce team to discuss terms of peace. 33 So no one can become my disciple unless he first sits down and counts his blessings—and then renounces them all for me.

34 "What good is salt that has lost is salti-

[a] Literally, "If anyone comes to me and does not hate his father and mother. . . ." [b] Implied in verse 33.

Today's English Version

with Jesus. He turned and said to them, 26 "Whoever comes to me cannot be my disciple unless he hates his father and his mother, his wife and his children, his brothers and his sisters, and himself as well. 27 Whoever does not carry his own cross and come after me cannot be my disciple. 28 If one of you is planning to build a tower, he sits down first and figures out what it will cost, to see if he has enough money to finish the job. 29 If he doesn't, he will not be able to finish the tower after laying the foundation; and all who see what happened will make fun of him. 30 'This man began to build but can't finish the job!' they will say. 31 If a king goes out with ten thousand men to fight another king, who comes against him with twenty thousand men, he will sit down first and decide if he is strong enough to face that other king. 32 If he isn't, he will send messengers to meet the other king, while he is still a long way off, to ask for terms of peace. 33 In the same way," concluded Jesus, "none of you can be my disciple unless he gives up everything he has."

Worthless salt

34 "Salt is good, but if it loses its taste there

New International Version

and turning to them he said: 26 "If anyone comes to me and does not hate his father and mother, his wife and children, his brothers and sisters—yes, even his own life—he cannot be my disciple. 27 And anyone who does not carry his cross and follow me cannot be my disciple.

28 "Suppose one of you wants to build a tower. Will he not first sit down and estimate the cost to see if he has enough money to complete it? 29 For if he lays the foundation and is not able to finish it, everyone who sees it will ridicule him, 30 saying, 'This fellow began to build and was not able to finish.'

31 "Or suppose a king is about to go to war against another king. Will he not first sit down and consider whether he is able with ten thousand men to oppose the one coming against him with twenty thousand? 32 If he is not able, he will send a delegation while the other is still a long way off and will ask for terms of peace. 33 In the same way, any of you who does not give up everything he has cannot be my disciple.

34 "Salt is good, but if it loses its saltiness,

Phillips Modern English

"If anyone comes to me without 'hating' his father and mother and wife and children and brothers and sisters, and even his own life, he cannot be a disciple of mine. The man who will not take up his cross and follow in my footsteps cannot be my disciple.

"If any of you wanted to build a tower, wouldn't he first sit down and work out the cost of it, to see if he can afford to finish it? Otherwise, when he has laid the foundation and found himself unable to complete the building, everyone who sees it will begin to jeer at him, saying, 'This is the man who started to build a tower but couldn't finish it!' Or, suppose there is a king who is going to war with another king, doesn't he sit down first and consider whether he can engage the twenty thousand of the other king with his own ten thousand? And if he decides he can't, then, while the other king is still a long way off, he sends messengers to him to ask for conditions of peace. So it is with you; only the man who says goodbye to all his possessions can be my disciple.

"Salt is a very good thing, but if salt loses

Revised Standard Version

and he turned and said to them, 26 "If any one
comes to me and does not hate his own father
and mother and wife and children and brothers
and sisters, yes, and even his own life, he cannot be my disciple. 27 Whoever does not bear
his own cross and come after me, cannot be my
disciple. 28 For which of you, desiring to build
a tower, does not first sit down and count the
cost, whether he has enough to complete it?
29 Otherwise, when he has laid a foundation, and
is not able to finish, all who see it begin to mock
him, 30 saying, 'This man began to build, and
was not able to finish.' 31 Or what king, going
to encounter another king in war, will not sit
down first and take counsel whether he is able
with ten thousand to meet him who comes
against him with twenty thousand? 32 And if
not, while the other is yet a great way off, he
sends an embassy and asks terms of peace. 33 So
therefore, whoever of you does not renounce all
that he has cannot be my disciple.
34 "Salt is good; but if salt has lost its taste,

Jerusalem Bible

way and he turned and spoke to them. 26 "If
any man comes to me without hating[y] his father, mother, wife, children, brothers, sisters,
yes and his own life too, he cannot be my disciple. 27 Anyone who does not carry his cross
and come after me cannot be my disciple.

Renouncing possessions

28 "And indeed, which of you here, intending
to build a tower, would not first sit down and
work out the cost to see if he had enough to
complete it? 29 Otherwise, if he laid the foundation and then found himself unable to finish the
work, the onlookers would all start making fun
of him and saying, 30 'Here is a man who started
to build and was unable to finish.' 31 Or again,
what king marching to war against another king
would not first sit down and consider whether
with ten thousand men he could stand up to the
other who advanced against him with twenty
thousand? 32 If not, then while the other king
was still a long way off, he would send envoys
to sue for peace. 33 So in the same way, none
of you can be my disciple unless he gives up all
his possessions.

On loss of enthusiasm in a disciple

34 "Salt is a useful thing. But if the salt itself
loses its taste, how can it be seasoned again?

[y] Hebraism: an emphatic way of expressing a total detachment.

New English Bible

him, he turned to them and said: 'If anyone comes to me and does not hate his father and mother, wife and children, brothers and sisters, even his own life, he cannot be a disciple of mine. No one who does not carry his cross and come with me can be a disciple of mine. Would any of you think of building a tower without first sitting down and calculating the cost, to see whether he could afford to finish it? Otherwise, if he has laid its foundation and then is not able to complete it, all the onlookers will laugh at him. "There is the man", they will say, "who started to build and could not finish." Or what king will march to battle against another king, without first sitting down to consider whether with ten thousand men he can face an enemy coming to meet him with twenty thousand? If he cannot, then, long before the enemy approaches, he sends envoys, and asks for terms. So also none of you can be a disciple of mine without parting with all his possessions.

'Salt is a good thing; but if salt itself becomes

King James Version

savour, wherewith shall it be seasoned? 35 It is neither fit for the land, nor yet for the dunghill; *but* men cast it out. He that hath ears to hear, let him hear.

15 Then drew near unto him all the publicans and sinners for to hear him. 2 And the Pharisees and scribes murmured, saying, This man receiveth sinners, and eateth with them.

3 And he spake this parable unto them, saying, 4 What man of you, having a hundred sheep, if he lose one of them, doth not leave the ninety and nine in the wilderness, and go after that which is lost, until he find it? 5 And when he hath found *it,* he layeth *it* on his shoulders, rejoicing. 6 And when he cometh home, he calleth together *his* friends and neighbours, saying unto them, Rejoice with me; for I have found my sheep which was lost. 7 I say unto you, that likewise joy shall be in heaven over one sinner that repenteth, more than over ninety and nine just persons, which need no repentance.

Living Bible

ness?[c] 35 Flavorless salt is fit for nothing—not even for fertilizer. It is worthless and must be thrown out. Listen well, if you would understand my meaning."

15 Dishonest tax collectors and other notorious sinners often came to listen to Jesus' sermons; 2 but this caused complaints from the Jewish religious leaders and the experts on Jewish law because he was associating with such despicable people—even eating with them! 3, 4 So Jesus used this illustration: "If you had a hundred sheep and one of them strayed away and was lost in the wilderness, wouldn't you leave the ninety-nine others to go and search for the lost one until you found it? 5 And then you would joyfully carry it home on your shoulders. 6 When you arrived you would call together your friends and neighbors to rejoice with you because your lost sheep was found.

7 "Well, in the same way heaven will be happier over one lost sinner who returns to God than over ninety-nine others who haven't strayed away!

[c] Perhaps the reference is to impure salt; when wet, the salt dissolves and drains out, leaving a tasteless residue. Matthew 5:13.

Today's English Version

is no way to make it salty again. 35 It is no good for the soil or for the manure pile; it is thrown away. Listen, then, if you have ears!"

The lost sheep

15 One time many tax collectors and outcasts came to listen to Jesus. 2 The Pharisees and the teachers of the Law started grumbling, "This man welcomes outcasts and even eats with them!" 3 So Jesus told them this parable,

4 "Suppose one of you has a hundred sheep and loses one of them—what does he do? He leaves the other ninety-nine sheep in the pasture and goes looking for the one that got lost until he finds it. 5 When he finds it, he is so happy that he puts it on his shoulders, 6 and carries it back home. Then he calls his friends and neighbors together, and says to them, 'I am so happy I found my lost sheep. Let us celebrate!' 7 In the same way, I tell you, there will be more joy in heaven over one sinner who repents than over ninety-nine respectable people who do not need to repent."

New International Version

how can it be made salty again? 35 It is fit neither for the soil nor for the manure pile; it is thrown out.

"He who has ears to hear, let him hear."

The parable of the lost sheep

15 Now the tax collectors and "sinners" were all gathering around to hear him. 2 But the Pharisees and the teachers of the law muttered, "This man welcomes sinners and eats with them."

3 Then Jesus told them this parable: 4 "Suppose one of you has a hundred sheep and loses one of them. Does he not leave the ninety-nine in the open country and go after the lost sheep until he finds it? 5 And when he finds it, he joyfully puts it on his shoulders 6 and goes home. Then he calls his friends and neighbors together and says, 'Rejoice with me; I have found my lost sheep.' 7 I tell you that in the same way there is more rejoicing in heaven over one sinner who repents than over ninety-nine righteous persons who do not need to repent.

Phillips Modern English

its flavour, what can you use to restore it? It is no good for the ground and no good as manure. People just throw it away. Every man who has ears should use them!"

15.1 Jesus speaks of the love of God for "the lost"

Now all the tax-collectors and "outsiders" were crowding around to hear what he had to say. The Pharisees and the scribes complained of this, remarking,

"This man welcomes sinners and even eats his meals with them."

So Jesus spoke to them, using this parable:

"Wouldn't any man among you who owned a hundred sheep, and lost one of them, leave the ninety-nine to themselves in the open, and go after the one which is lost until he finds it? And when he has found it, he will lift it on to his shoulders with great joy, and as soon as he gets home, he will call his friends and neighbours together. 'Rejoice with me,' he will say, 'for I have found that sheep of mine which was lost.' I tell you that it is the same in Heaven—there is more joy over one sinner whose heart is changed than over ninety-nine righteous people who have no need for repentance.

Revised Standard Version

how shall its saltness be restored? 35 It is fit
neither for the land nor for the dunghill; men
throw it away. He who has ears to hear, let him
hear."

15 Now the tax collectors and sinners were
all drawing near to him. 2 And the Pharisees and the scribes murmured, saying, "This
man receives sinners and eats with them."
3 So he told them this parable: 4 "What man
of you, having a hundred sheep, if he has lost
one of them, does not leave the ninety-nine in
the wilderness, and go after the one which is
lost, until he finds it? 5 And when he has found
it, he lays it on his shoulders, rejoicing. 6 And
when he comes home, he calls together his
friends and his neighbors, saying to them, 'Rejoice with me, for I have found my sheep which
was lost.' 7 Just so, I tell you, there will be more
joy in heaven over one sinner who repents than
over ninety-nine righteous persons who need no
repentance.

Jerusalem Bible

35 It is good for neither soil nor manure heap.
People throw it out. Listen, anyone who has
ears to hear!"

The three parables of God's mercy

15 The tax collectors and the sinners, meanwhile, were all seeking his company to hear
what he had to say, 2 and the Pharisees and the
scribes complained. "This man," they said, "welcomes sinners and eats with them." 3 So he
spoke this parable to them:

The lost sheep

4 "What man among you with a hundred
sheep, losing one, would not leave the ninety-
nine in the wilderness and go after the missing
one till he found it? 5 And when he found it,
would he not joyfully take it on his shoulders
6 and then, when he got home, call together
his friends and neighbors? 'Rejoice with me,'
he would say, 'I have found my sheep that
was lost.' 7 In the same way, I tell you, there
will be more rejoicing in heaven over one repentant sinner than over ninety-nine virtuous
men who have no need of repentance.

New English Bible

tasteless, what will you use to season it? It is useless either on the land or on the dung-heap: it can only be thrown away. If you have ears to hear, then hear.'

15 Another time, the tax-gatherers and other bad characters were all crowding in to listen to him; and the Pharisees and the doctors of the law began grumbling among themselves: 'This fellow', they said, 'welcomes sinners and eats with them.' He answered them with this parable: 'If one of you has a hundred sheep and loses one of them, does he not leave the ninety-nine in the open pasture and go after the missing one until he has found it? How delighted he is then! He lifts it on to his shoulders, and home he goes to call his friends and neighbours together. "Rejoice with me!" he cries. "I have found my lost sheep." In the same way, I tell you, there will be greater joy in heaven over one sinner who repents than over ninety-nine righteous people who do not need to repent.

King James Version

8 Either what woman having ten pieces of
silver, if she lose one piece, doth not light a
candle, and sweep the house, and seek diligently
till she find *it?* 9 And when she hath found *it,*
she calleth *her* friends and *her* neighbours together, saying, Rejoice with me; for I have found
the piece which I had lost. 10 Likewise, I say
unto you, there is joy in the presence of the
angels of God over one sinner that repenteth.
11 And he said, A certain man had two sons:
12 And the younger of them said to *his* father,
Father, give me the portion of goods that falleth
to me. And he divided unto them *his* living.
13 And not many days after the younger son
gathered all together, and took his journey into
a far country, and there wasted his substance
with riotous living. 14 And when he had spent
all, there arose a mighty famine in that land;
and he began to be in want. 15 And he went and
joined himself to a citizen of that country; and he
sent him into his fields to feed swine. 16 And
he would fain have filled his belly with the husks
that the swine did eat: and no man gave unto
him. 17 And when he came to himself, he said,
How many hired servants of my father's have
bread enough and to spare, and I perish with
hunger! 18 I will arise and go to my father, and

Living Bible

8 "Or take another illustration: A woman has
ten valuable silver coins and loses one. Won't
she light a lamp and look in every corner of the
house and sweep every nook and cranny until
she finds it? 9 And then won't she call in her
friends and neighbors to rejoice with her? 10 In
the same way there is joy in the presence of the
angels of God when one sinner repents."
To further illustrate the point, he told them
this story: 11 "A man had two sons. 12 When
the younger told his father, 'I want my share of
your estate now, instead of waiting until you
die!' his father agreed to divide his wealth between his sons.
13 "A few days later this younger son packed
all his belongings and took a trip to a distant
land, and there wasted all his money on parties
and prostitutes. 14 About the time his money was
gone a great famine swept over the land, and he
began to starve. 15 He persuaded a local farmer
to hire him to feed his pigs. 16 The boy became
so hungry that even the pods he was feeding the
swine looked good to him. And no one gave him
anything.
17 "When he finally came to his senses, he
said to himself, 'At home even the hired men
have food enough and to spare, and here I am,
dying of hunger! 18 I will go home to my father

Today's English Version

The lost coin

8 "Or suppose a woman who has ten silver
coins loses one of them—what does she do? She
lights a lamp, sweeps her house, and looks carefully everywhere until she finds it. 9 When she
finds it, she calls her friends and neighbors together, and says to them, 'I am so happy I
found the coin I lost. Let us celebrate!' 10 In the
same way, I tell you, the angels of God rejoice
over one sinner who repents."

The lost son

11 Jesus went on to say, "There was a man
who had two sons. 12 The younger one said to
him, 'Father, give me now my share of the
property.' So the man divided the property between his two sons. 13 After a few days the
younger son sold his part of the property and
left home with the money. He went to a country
far away, where he wasted his money in reckless
living. 14 He spent everything he had. Then a
severe famine spread over that country, and he
was left without a thing. 15 So he went to work
for one of the citizens of that country, who sent
him out to his farm to take care of the pigs.
16 He wished he could fill himself with the bean
pods the pigs ate, but no one gave him anything
to eat. 17 At last he came to his senses and said,
'All my father's hired workers have more than
they can eat, and here I am, about to starve! 18 I
will get up and go to my father and say, "Father,

New International Version

The parable of the lost coin

8 "Or suppose a woman has ten silver coins[d]
and loses one. Does she not light a lamp, sweep
the house and search carefully until she finds it?
9 And when she finds it, she calls her friends and
neighbors together and says, 'Rejoice with me;
I have found my lost coin.' 10 In the same way,
I tell you, there is rejoicing in the presence of
the angels of God over one sinner who repents."

The parable of the lost son

11 Jesus continued: "There was a man who
had two sons. 12 The younger one said to his
father, 'Father, give me my share of the estate.'
So he divided his property between them.
13 "Not long after that, the younger son got
together all he had, set off for a distant country
and there squandered his wealth in wild living.
14 After he had spent everything, there was a
severe famine in that whole country, and he began to be in need. 15 So he went and hired himself out to a citizen of that country, who sent
him to his fields to feed pigs. 16 He longed to
fill his stomach with the pods that the pigs were
eating, but no one gave him anything.
17 "When he came to his senses, he said,
'How many of my father's hired men have food
to spare, and here I am starving to death! 18 I
will set out and go back to my father and say

[d] Greek *drachmas,* each worth about a day's wage.

Phillips Modern English

"Or if a woman who has ten silver coins should lose one, won't she take a lamp and sweep and search the house from top to bottom until she finds it? And when she has found it, she calls her friends and neighbours together. 'Rejoice with me,' she says, 'for I have found that coin I lost.' I tell you, it is the same in Heaven—there is rejoicing among the angels of God over one sinner whose heart is changed."

Then he continued,

"Once there was a man who had two sons. The younger one said to his father, 'Father, give me my share of the property that will come to me.' So he divided up his estate between the two of them. Before very long, the younger son collected all his belongings and went off to a distant land, where he squandered his wealth in the wildest extravagance. And when he had run through all his money, a terrible famine arose in that country, and he began to feel the pinch. Then he went and hired himself out to one of the citizens of that country who sent him out into the fields to feed the pigs. He got to the point of longing to stuff himself with the husks the pigs were eating, and not a soul gave him anything. Then he came to his senses and cried aloud, 'Why, dozens of my father's hired men have more food than they can eat and here am I dying of hunger! I will get up and go back to my father, and I will say

Revised Standard Version

8 "Or what woman, having ten silver coins,[t]
if she loses one coin, does not light a lamp and
sweep the house and seek diligently until she
finds it? 9And when she has found it, she calls
together her friends and neighbors, saying, 'Rejoice with me, for I have found the coin which
I had lost.' 10 Just so, I tell you, there is joy before the angels of God over one sinner who
repents."
11 And he said, "There was a man who had
two sons; 12 and the younger of them said to
his father, 'Father, give me the share of property
that falls to me.' And he divided his living between them. 13 Not many days later, the younger
son gathered all he had and took his journey
into a far country, and there he squandered his
property in loose living. 14And when he had
spent everything, a great famine arose in that
country, and he began to be in want. 15 So he
went and joined himself to one of the citizens
of that country, who sent him into his fields to
feed swine. 16And he would gladly have fed on[u]
the pods that the swine ate; and no one gave
him anything. 17 But when he came to himself
he said, 'How many of my father's hired servants
have bread enough and to spare, but I perish
here with hunger! 18 I will arise and go to my

[t] The drachma, rendered here by *silver coin*, was about a day's wage for a laborer. [u] Other ancient authorities read *filled his belly with*.

Jerusalem Bible

The lost drachma

8 "Or again, what woman with ten drachmas
would not, if she lost one, light a lamp and
sweep out the house and search thoroughly till
she found it? 9And then, when she had found
it, call together her friends and neighbors? 'Rejoice with me,' she would say, 'I have found the
drachma I lost.' 10 In the same way, I tell you,
there is rejoicing among the angels of God over
one repentant sinner."

The lost son (the "prodigal") and the dutiful son

11 He also said, "A man had two sons. 12 The
younger said to his father, 'Father, let me have
the share of the estate that would come to me.'
So the father divided the property between
them. 13A few days later, the younger son got
together everything he had and left for a distant
country where he squandered his money on a
life of debauchery.
14 "When he had spent it all, that country
experienced a severe famine, and now he began
to feel the pinch, 15 so he hired himself out to
one of the local inhabitants who put him on
his farm to feed the pigs. 16And he would willingly have filled his belly with the husks the
pigs were eating but no one offered him anything. 17 Then he came to his senses and said,
'How many of my father's paid servants have
more food than they want, and here am I dying
of hunger! 18 I will leave this place and go to

New English Bible

'Or again, if a woman has ten silver pieces and loses one of them, does she not light the lamp, sweep out the house, and look in every corner till she has found it? And when she has, she calls her friends and neighbours together, and says, "Rejoice with me! I have found the piece that I lost." In the same way, I tell you, there is joy among the angels of God over one sinner who repents.'

Again he said: 'There was once a man who had two sons; and the younger said to his father, "Father, give me my share of the property." So he divided his estate between them. A few days later the younger son turned the whole of his share into cash and left home for a distant country, where he squandered it in reckless living. He had spent it all, when a severe famine fell upon that country and he began to feel the pinch. So he went and attached himself to one of the local landowners, who sent him on to his farm to mind the pigs. He would have been glad to fill his belly with[a] the pods that the pigs were eating; and no one gave him anything. Then he came to his senses and said, "How many of my father's paid servants have more food than they can eat, and here am I, starving to death! I will set off and go to my father, and

[a] *Some witnesses read* to have his fill of . . .

King James Version

will say unto him, Father, I have sinned against heaven, and before thee, 19 And am no more worthy to be called thy son: make me as one of thy hired servants. 20 And he arose, and came to his father. But when he was yet a great way off, his father saw him, and had compassion, and ran, and fell on his neck, and kissed him. 21 And the son said unto him, Father, I have sinned against heaven, and in thy sight, and am no more worthy to be called thy son. 22 But the father said to his servants, Bring forth the best robe, and put *it* on him; and put a ring on his hand, and shoes on *his* feet: 23 And bring hither the fatted calf, and kill *it;* and let us eat, and be merry: 24 For this my son was dead, and is alive again; he was lost, and is found. And they began to be merry. 25 Now his elder son was in the field: and as he came and drew nigh to the house, he heard music and dancing. 26 And he called one of the servants, and asked what these things meant. 27 And he said unto him, Thy brother is come; and thy father hath killed the fatted calf, because he hath received him safe and sound. 28 And he was angry, and would not go in: therefore came his father out, and entreated him. 29 And he answering said to *his* father, Lo, these many years do I serve thee, neither transgressed I at any time thy commandment; and yet thou never gavest me a kid, that I might make merry with my friends: 30 But as soon as this thy son was come, which hath devoured thy living with harlots, thou hast killed

Living Bible

and say, "Father, I have sinned against both heaven and you, 19 and am no longer worthy of being called your son. Please take me on as a hired man." '

20 "So he returned home to his father. And while he was still a long distance away, his father saw him coming, and was filled with loving pity and ran and embraced him and kissed him.

21 "His son said to him, 'Father, I have sinned against heaven and you, and am not worthy of being called your son—'

22 "But his father said to the slaves, 'Quick! Bring the finest robe in the house and put it on him. And a jeweled ring for his finger; and shoes! 23 And kill the calf we have in the fattening pen. We must celebrate with a feast, 24 for this son of mine was dead and has returned to life. He was lost and is found.' So the party began.

25 "Meanwhile, the older son was in the fields working; when he returned home, he heard dance music coming from the house, 26 and he asked one of the servants what was going on.

27 " 'Your brother is back,' he was told, 'and your father has killed the calf we were fattening and has prepared a great feast to celebrate his coming home again unharmed.'

28 "The older brother was angry and wouldn't go in. His father came out and begged him, 29 but he replied, 'All these years I've worked hard for you and never once refused to do a single thing you told me to; and in all that time you never gave me even one young goat for a feast with my friends. 30 Yet when this son of yours comes back after spending your money on prostitutes, you celebrate by killing the finest calf we have on the place.'

Today's English Version

I have sinned against God and against you. 19 I am no longer fit to be called your son; treat me as one of your hired workers." ' 20 So he got up and started back to his father.

"He was still a long way from home when his father saw him; his heart was filled with pity and he ran, threw his arms around his son, and kissed him. 21 'Father,' the son said, 'I have sinned against God and against you. I am no longer fit to be called your son.' 22 But the father called his servants: 'Hurry!' he said. 'Bring the best robe and put it on him. Put a ring on his finger and shoes on his feet. 23 Then go get the prize calf and kill it, and let us celebrate with a feast! 24 Because this son of mine was dead, but now he is alive; he was lost, but now he has been found.' And so the feasting began.

25 "The older son, in the meantime, was out in the field. On his way back, when he came close to the house, he heard the music and dancing. 26 He called one of the servants and asked him, 'What's going on?' 27 'Your brother came back home,' the servant answered, 'and your father killed the prize calf, because he got him back safe and sound.' 28 The older brother was so angry that he would not go into the house; so his father came out and begged him to come in. 29 'Look,' he answered back to his father, 'all these years I have worked like a slave for you, and I never disobeyed your orders. What have you given me? Not even a goat for me to have a feast with my friends! 30 But this son of yours wasted all your property on prostitutes, and when he comes back home you kill the prize calf for

New International Version

to him: Father, I have sinned against heaven and against you. 19 I am no longer worthy to be called your son; make me like one of your hired men.' 20 So he got up and went to his father.

"But while he was still a long way off, his father saw him and was filled with compassion for him. He ran to his son, threw his arms around him and kissed him.

21 "The son said to him, 'Father, I have sinned against heaven and against you. I am no longer worthy to be called your son.' [e]

22 "But the father said to his servants, 'Quick! Bring the best robe and put it on him. Put a ring on his finger and sandals on his feet. 23 Bring the fattened calf and kill it. Let's have a feast and celebrate. 24 For this son of mine was dead and is alive again; he was lost and is found.' So they began to celebrate.

25 "Meanwhile, the older son was in the field. When he came near the house, he heard music and dancing. 26 So he called one of the servants and asked him what was going on. 27 'Your brother has come,' he replied, 'and your father has killed the fattened calf because he has him back safe and sound.'

28 "The older brother became angry and refused to go in. So his father went out and pleaded with him. 29 But he answered his father, 'Look! All these years I've been slaving for you and never disobeyed your orders. Yet you never gave me even a young goat so I could celebrate with my friends. 30 But when this son of yours who has squandered your property with prostitutes comes home, you kill the fattened calf for him!'

[*e*] Some early MSS add *Make me like one of your hired men.*

Phillips Modern English

to him, "Father, I have done wrong in the sight of Heaven and in your eyes. I don't deserve to be called your son any more. Please take me on as one of your hired men."' So he got up and went to his father. But while he was still some distance off, his father saw him and his heart went out to him, and he ran and fell on his neck and kissed him. But his son said, 'Father, I have done wrong in the sight of Heaven and in your eyes. I don't deserve to be called your son any more. . . .' 'Hurry!' called out his father to the servants, 'fetch the best clothes and put them on him! Put a ring on his finger and shoes on his feet, and get that fatted calf and kill it, and we will have a feast and a celebration! For this is my son—he was dead, and he's alive again. He was lost, and now he's found!' And they began to get the festivities going.

"But his elder son was out in the fields, and as he came near the house, he heard music and dancing. So he called one of the servants across to him and enquired what was the meaning of it all. 'Your brother has arrived, and your father has killed the fatted calf because he has got him home again safe and sound,' was the reply. But he was furious and refused to go inside the house. So his father came outside and pleaded with him. Then he burst out, 'Look, how many years have I slaved for you and never disobeyed a single order of yours, and yet you have never given me so much as a young goat so that I could give my friends a dinner? But when this son of yours arrives, who has spent all your money on prostitutes, for him you kill

Revised Standard Version

father, and I will say to him, "Father, I have
sinned against heaven and before you; 19 I am
no longer worthy to be called your son; treat
me as one of your hired servants."' 20 And he
arose and came to his father. But while he was
yet at a distance, his father saw him and had
compassion, and ran and embraced him and
kissed him. 21 And the son said to him, 'Father,
I have sinned against heaven and before you;
I am no longer worthy to be called your son.'[v]
22 But the father said to his servants, 'Bring
quickly the best robe, and put it on him; and put
a ring on his hand, and shoes on his feet; 23 and
bring the fatted calf and kill it, and let us eat
and make merry; 24 for this my son was dead,
and is alive again; he was lost, and is found.'
And they began to make merry.
25 "Now his elder son was in the field; and as
he came and drew near to the house, he heard
music and dancing. 26 And he called one of the
servants and asked what this meant. 27 And he
said to him, 'Your brother has come, and your
father has killed the fatted calf, because he has
received him safe and sound.' 28 But he was
angry and refused to go in. His father came out
and entreated him, 29 but he answered his father,
'Lo, these many years I have served you, and I
never disobeyed your command; yet you never
gave me a kid, that I might make merry with
my friends. 30 But when this son of yours came,
who has devoured your living with harlots, you

[v] Other ancient authorities add *treat me as one of your hired servants.*

Jerusalem Bible

my father and say: Father, I have sinned against
heaven and against you; 19 I no longer deserve
to be called your son; treat me as one of your
paid servants.' 20 So he left the place and went
back to his father.
"While he was still a long way off, his father
saw him and was moved with pity. He ran to
the boy, clasped him in his arms and kissed him
tenderly. 21 Then his son said, 'Father, I have
sinned against heaven and against you. I no
longer deserve to be called your son.' 22 But
the father said to his servants, 'Quick! Bring
out the best robe and put it on him; put a ring
on his finger and sandals on his feet. 23 Bring
the calf we have been fattening, and kill it; we
are going to have a feast, a celebration, 24 because this son of mine was dead and has come
back to life; he was lost and is found.' And
they began to celebrate.
25 "Now the elder son was out in the fields,
and on his way back, as he drew near the house,
he could hear music and dancing. 26 Calling one
of the servants he asked what it was all about.
27 'Your brother has come,' replied the servant,
'and your father has killed the calf we had
fattened because he has got him back safe and
sound.' 28 He was angry then and refused to go
in, and his father came out to plead with him;
29 but he answered his father, 'Look, all these
years I have slaved for you and never once disobeyed your orders, yet you never offered me
so much as a kid for me to celebrate with my
friends. 30 But, for this son of yours, when he
comes back after swallowing up your property
—he and his women—you kill the calf we had
been fattening.'

New English Bible

say to him, 'Father, I have sinned, against God and against you; I am no longer fit to be called your son; treat me as one of your paid servants.'" So he set out for his father's house. But while he was still a long way off his father saw him, and his heart went out to him. He ran to meet him, flung his arms round him, and kissed him. The son said, "Father, I have sinned, against God and against you; I am no longer fit to be called your son."[b] But the father said to his servants, "Quick! fetch a robe, my best one, and put it on him; put a ring on his finger and shoes on his feet. Bring the fatted calf and kill it, and let us have a feast to celebrate the day. For this son of mine was dead and has come back to life; he was lost and is found." And the festivities began.

'Now the elder son was out on the farm; and on his way back, as he approached the house, he heard music and dancing. He called one of the servants and asked what it meant. The servant told him, "Your brother has come home, and your father has killed the fatted calf because he has him back safe and sound." But he was angry and refused to go in. His father came out and pleaded with him; but he retorted, "You know how I have slaved for you all these years; I never once disobeyed your orders; and you never gave me so much as a kid, for a feast with my friends. But now that this son of yours turns up, after running through your money with his women, you kill the fatted calf for him."

[b] *Some witnesses add* treat me as one of your paid servants.

King James Version

for him the fatted calf. 31 And he said unto him,
Son, thou art ever with me, and all that I have
is thine. 32 It was meet that we should make
merry, and be glad: for this thy brother was
dead, and is alive again; and was lost, and is
found.

16 And he said also unto his disciples, There
was a certain rich man, which had a steward; and the same was accused unto him that he
had wasted his goods. 2 And he called him, and
said unto him, How is it that I hear this of thee?
give an account of thy stewardship; for thou
mayest be no longer steward. 3 Then the steward said within himself, What shall I do? for my
lord taketh away from me the stewardship: I
cannot dig; to beg I am ashamed. 4 I am resolved
what to do, that, when I am put out of the stewardship, they may receive me into their houses.
5 So he called every one of his lord's debtors
unto him, and said unto the first, How much
owest thou unto my lord? 6 And he said, A hundred measures of oil. And he said unto him,
Take thy bill, and sit down quickly, and write
fifty. 7 Then said he to another, And how much
owest thou? And he said, A hundred measures
of wheat. And he said unto him, Take thy bill,

Living Bible

31 " 'Look, dear son,' his father said to him,
'you and I are very close, and everything I have
is yours. 32 But it is right to celebrate. For he is
your brother; and he was dead and has come
back to life! He was lost and is found!' "

16 Jesus now told this story to his disciples:
"A rich man hired an accountant to handle
his affairs, but soon a rumor went around that
the accountant was thoroughly dishonest.
2 "So his employer called him in and said,
'What's this I hear about your stealing from
me? Get your report in order, for you are to be
dismissed.'
3 "The accountant thought to himself, 'Now
what? I'm through here, and I haven't the
strength to go out and dig ditches, and I'm too
proud to beg. 4 I know just the thing! And then
I'll have plenty of friends to take care of me
when I leave!'
5, 6 "So he invited each one who owed money
to his employer to come and discuss the situation. He asked the first one, 'How much do you
owe him?' 'My debt is 850 gallons of olive oil,'
the man replied. 'Yes, here is the contract you
signed,' the accountant told him. 'Tear it up
and write another one for half that much!'
7 " 'And how much do you owe him?' he
asked the next man. 'A thousand bushels of
wheat,' was the reply. 'Here,' the accountant

Today's English Version

him!' 31 'My son,' the father answered, 'you are
always here with me and everythng I have is
yours. 32 But we had to have a feast and be
happy, because your brother was dead, but now
he is alive; he was lost, but now he has been
found.' "

The shrewd manager

16 Jesus said to his disciples, "There was a
rich man who had a manager, and he was
told that the manager was wasting his master's
money. 2 He called him in and said, 'What is
this I hear about you? Turn in a complete account
of your handling of my property, because you
cannot be my manager any longer.' 3 'My master
is going to dismiss me from my job,' the man said
to himself. 'What shall I do? I am not strong
enough to dig ditches, and I am ashamed to beg.
4 Now I know what I will do! Then when my job
is gone I shall have friends who will welcome me
in their homes.' 5 So he called in all the people
who were in debt to his master. He said to the
first one, 'How much do you owe my master?'
6 'One hundred barrels of olive oil,' he answered.
'Here is your account,' the manager told him;
'sit down and write fifty.' 7 He said to another
one, 'And you—how much do you owe?' 'A thousand bushels of wheat,' he answered. 'Here is

New International Version

31 " 'My son,' the father said, 'you are always
with me, and everything I have is yours. 32 But
we had to celebrate and be glad, because this
brother of yours was dead and is alive again;
he was lost and is found.' "

The parable of the shrewd manager

16 Jesus told his disciples: "There was a
rich man whose manager was accused of
wasting his possessions. 2 So he called him in
and asked him, 'What is this I hear about you?
Give an account of your management, because
you cannot be manager any longer.'
3 "The manager said to himself, 'What shall
I do now? My master is taking away my job.
I'm not strong enough to dig, and I'm ashamed
to beg—4 I know what I'll do so that, when I
lose my job here, people will welcome me into
their houses.'
5 "So he called in each one of his master's
debtors. He asked the first, 'How much do you
owe my master?'
6 " 'Eight hundred gallons of olive oil,' he
replied.
"The manager told him, 'Take your bill, sit
down quickly, and make it four hundred.'
7 "Then he asked the second, 'And how much
do you owe?'
" 'A thousand bushels of wheat,' he replied.

Phillips Modern English

the fatted calf!' But the father replied, 'My dear son, you have been with me all the time and everything I have is yours. But we had to celebrate and show our joy. For this is your brother; he was dead—and he's alive. He was lost—and now he is found!' "

16.1 A clever rogue, and the right use of money

Then there is this story he told his disciples: "Once there was a rich man whose agent was reported to him to be mismanaging his property. So he summoned him and said, 'What's this that I hear about you? Give me an account of your stewardship—you're not fit to manage my household any longer.' At this the agent said to himself, 'What am I going to do now that my employer is taking away the management from me? I am not strong enough to dig and I can't sink to begging. Ah, I know what I'll do so that when I lose my position people will welcome me into their homes!' So he sent for each one of his master's debtors. 'How much do you owe my master?' he said to the first. 'A hundred barrels of oil,' he replied. 'Here,' replied the agent, 'take your bill, sit down, hurry up and write in fifty.' Then he said to another, 'And what's the size of your debt?' 'A thousand bushels of wheat,' he replied. 'Take your bill,'

Revised Standard Version

killed for him the fatted calf!' 31 And he said to him, 'Son, you are always with me, and all that is mine is yours. 32 It was fitting to make merry and be glad, for this your brother was dead, and is alive; he was lost, and is found.' "

16 He also said to the disciples, "There was a rich man who had a steward, and charges were brought to him that this man was wasting his goods. 2 And he called him and said to him, 'What is this that I hear about you? Turn in the account of your stewardship, for you can no longer be steward.' 3 And the steward said to himself, 'What shall I do, since my master is taking the stewardship away from me? I am not strong enough to dig, and I am ashamed to beg. 4 I have decided what to do, so that people may receive me into their houses when I am put out of the stewardship.' 5 So, summoning his master's debtors one by one, he said to the first, 'How much do you owe my master?' 6 He said, 'A hundred measures of oil.' And he said to him, 'Take your bill, and sit down quickly and write fifty.' 7 Then he said to another, 'And how much do you owe?' He said, 'A hundred measures of wheat.' He said to him, 'Take your bill,

Jerusalem Bible

31 "The father said, 'My son, you are with me always and all I have is yours. 32 But it was only right we should celebrate and rejoice, because your brother here was dead and has come to life; he was lost and is found.' "

The crafty steward

16 He also said to his disciples, "There was a rich man and he had a steward who was denounced to him for being wasteful with his property. 2 He called for the man and said, 'What is this I hear about you? Draw me up an account of your stewardship because you are not to be my steward any longer.' 3 Then the steward said to himself, 'Now that my master is taking the stewardship from me, what am I to do? Dig? I am not strong enough. Go begging? I should be too ashamed. 4 Ah, I know what I will do to make sure that when I am dismissed from office there will be some to welcome me into their homes.'

5 "Then he called his master's debtors one by one. To the first he said, 'How much do you owe my master?' 6 'One hundred measures of oil,' was the reply. The steward said, 'Here, take your bond; sit down straightaway and write fifty.' 7 To another he said, 'And you, sir, how much do you owe?' 'One hundred measures of wheat,' was the reply. The steward said, 'Here,

New English Bible

"My boy," said the father, "you are always with me, and everything I have is yours. How could we help celebrating this happy day? Your brother here was dead and has come back to life, was lost and is found." '

16 He said to his disciples, 'There was a rich man who had a steward, and he received complaints that this man was squandering the property. So he sent for him, and said, "What is this that I hear? Produce your accounts, for you cannot be manager here any longer." The steward said to himself, "What am I to do now that my employer is dismissing me? I am not strong enough to dig, and too proud to beg. I know what I must do, to make sure that, when I have to leave, there will be people to give me house and home." He summoned his master's debtors one by one. To the first he said, "How much do you owe my master?" He replied, "A thousand gallons of olive oil." He said, "Here is your account. Sit down and make it five hundred; and be quick about it." Then he said to another, "And you, how much do you owe?" He said, "A thousand bushels of wheat", and was

King James Version

and write fourscore. 8And the lord commended
the unjust steward, because he had done wisely:
for the children of this world are in their generation wiser than the children of light. 9And I say
unto you, Make to yourselves friends of the
mammon of unrighteousness; that, when ye fail,
they may receive you into everlasting habitations.
10 He that is faithful in that which is least is
faithful also in much: and he that is unjust in
the least is unjust also in much. 11 If therefore
ye have not been faithful in the unrighteous
mammon, who will commit to your trust the
true *riches?* 12And if ye have not been faithful
in that which is another man's, who shall give
you that which is your own?

13 No servant can serve two masters: for
either he will hate the one, and love the other;
or else he will hold to the one, and despise the
other. Ye cannot serve God and mammon. 14And
the Pharisees also, who were covetous, heard all
these things: and they derided him. 15And he
said unto them, Ye are they which justify your-

Living Bible

said, 'take your note and replace it with one for
only 800 bushels!'

8 "The rich man had to admire the rascal for
being so shrewd.[a] And it is true that the citizens
of this world are more clever [in dishonesty! [b]]
than the godly[c] are. 9 But shall I tell *you* to act
that way, to buy friendship through cheating?
Will this ensure your entry into an everlasting
home in heaven?[d] 10 *No!* [b] For unless you are
honest in small matters, you won't be in large
ones. If you cheat even a little, you won't be
honest with greater responsibilities. 11And if you
are untrustworthy about worldly wealth, who will
trust you with the true riches of heaven? 12And
if you are not faithful with other people's money,
why should you be entrusted with money of your
own?

13 "For neither you nor anyone else can
serve two masters. You will hate one and show
loyalty to the other, or else the other way around
—you will be enthusiastic about one and despise
the other. You cannot serve both God and
money."

14 The Pharisees, who dearly loved their
money, naturally scoffed at all this.

15 Then he said to them, "You wear a noble,
pious expression in public, but God knows your

[*a*] Or, "Do you think the rich man commended the scoundrel for being so shrewd?" [*b*] Implied. [*c*] Literally, "sons of the light." [*d*] Literally, and probably ironically, "Make to yourselves friends by means of the mammon of unrighteousness; that when it shall fail you, they may receive you into the eternal tabernacles!" Some commentators would interpret this to mean: "Use your money for good, so that it will be waiting to befriend you when you get to heaven." But this would imply the end justifies the means, an unbiblical idea.

Today's English Version

your account,' the manager told him; 'write eight
hundred.' 8 The master of this dishonest manager
praised him for doing such a shrewd thing; because the people of this world are much more
shrewd in handling their affairs than the people
who belong to the light."

9 And Jesus went on to say, "And so I tell
you: make friends for yourselves with worldly
wealth, so that when it gives out you will be welcomed in the eternal home. 10 Whoever is faithful in small matters will be faithful in large ones;
whoever is dishonest in small matters will be
dishonest in large ones. 11 If, then, you have
not been faithful in handling worldly wealth, how
can you be trusted with true wealth? 12And if
you have not been faithful with what belongs to
someone else, who will give you what belongs to
you?

13 "No servant can be the slave of two masters; he will hate one and love the other; he will
be loyal to one and despise the other. You cannot serve both God and money."

Some sayings of Jesus

14 The Pharisees heard all this, and they made
fun of Jesus, because they loved money. 15 Jesus
said to them, "You are the ones who make your-

New International Version

"He told him, 'Take your bill and make it
eight hundred.'

8 "The master commended the dishonest manager because he had acted shrewdly. For the people of this world are more shrewd in dealing
with their own kind than are the people of the
light. 9 I tell you, use worldly wealth to gain
friends for yourselves, so that when it is gone,
you will be welcomed into eternal dwellings.

10 "Whoever can be trusted with very little
can also be trusted with much, and whoever is
dishonest with very little will also be dishonest
with much. 11 So if you have not been trustworthy in handling worldly wealth, who will trust
you with true riches? 12And if you have not been
truthworthy with someone else's property, who
will give you property of your own?

13 "No servant can serve two masters. Either
he will hate the one and love the other, or he
will be devoted to the one and despise the other.
You cannot serve both God and Money."

14 The Pharisees, who loved money, heard all
this and were sneering at Jesus. 15 He said to
them, "You are the ones who justify yourselves

Phillips Modern English

said the agent, 'and write in eight hundred.' Now the master praised this rascally agent because he had been so careful for his own future. For the children of this world are considerably more shrewd in dealing with their contemporaries than the children of light. Now my advice to you is to use 'money', tainted as it is, to make yourselves friends, so that when it comes to an end, they may welcome you into the houses of eternity.

"The man who is faithful in the little things will be faithful in the big things, and the man who cheats in the little things will cheat in the big things too. So that if you are not fit to be trusted to deal with the wicked wealth of this world, who will trust you with the true riches? And if you are not trustworthy with someone else's property, who will give you property of your own? No servant can serve two masters. He is bound to hate one and love the other, or give his loyalty to one and despise the other. You cannot serve God and the power of money at the same time."

Now the Pharisees, who were very fond of money, heard all this with a sneer. But he said to them,

"You are the people who advertise your good-

Revised Standard Version

and write eighty.' 8 The master commended the
dishonest steward for his shrewdness; for the
sons of this world [w] are more shrewd in dealing
with their own generation than the sons of light.
9 And I tell you, make friends for yourselves by
means of unrighteous mammon,[a] so that when
it fails they may receive you into the eternal
habitations.
10 "He who is faithful in a very little is faithful also in much; and he who is dishonest in a
very little is dishonest also in much. 11 If then
you have not been faithful in the unrighteous
mammon,[a] who will entrust to you the true
riches? 12 And if you have not been faithful in
that which is another's, who will give you that
which is your own? 13 No servant can serve two
masters; for either he will hate the one and love
the other, or he will be devoted to the one and
despise the other. You cannot serve God and
mammon." [a]
14 The Pharisees, who were lovers of money,
heard all this, and they scoffed at him. 15 But
he said to them, "You are those who justify

[w] Greek *age*. [a] *Mammon* is a Semitic word for money or riches.

Jerusalem Bible

take your bond and write eighty.'
8 "The master praised the dishonest steward
for his astuteness.[z] For the children of this
world are more astute in dealing with their own
kind than are the children of light."

The right use of money

9 "And so I tell you this: use money, tainted
as it is, to win you friends, and thus make sure
that when it fails you, they will welcome you
into the tents of eternity. 10 The man who can
be trusted in little things can be trusted in great;
the man who is dishonest in little things will be
dishonest in great. 11 If then you cannot be
trusted with money, that tainted thing, who will
trust you with genuine riches? 12 And if you
cannot be trusted with what is not yours, who
will give you what is your very own?
13 "No servant can be the slave of two masters: he will either hate the first and love the
second, or treat the first with respect and the
second with scorn. You cannot be the slave
both of God and of money."

Against the Pharisees and their love of money

14 The Pharisees, who loved money, heard all
this and laughed at him. 15 He said to them,
"You are the very ones who pass yourselves off

[z] Not for his dishonesty.

New English Bible

told, "Take your account and make it eight hundred." And the master applauded the dishonest steward for acting so astutely. For the worldly are more astute than the other-worldly in dealing with their own kind.

'So I say to you, use your worldly wealth to win friends for yourselves, so that when money is a thing of the past you may be received into an eternal home.

'The man who can be trusted in little things can be trusted also in great; and the man who is dishonest in little things is dishonest also in great things. If, then, you have not proved trustworthy with the wealth of this world, who will trust you with the wealth that is real? And if you have proved untrustworthy with what belongs to another, who will give you what is your own?

'No servant can be the slave of two masters; for either he will hate the first and love the second, or he will be devoted to the first and think nothing of the second. You cannot serve God and Money.'

The Pharisees, who loved money, heard all this and scoffed at him. He said to them, 'You are the people who impress your fellowmen with

King James Version

selves before men; but God knoweth your hearts: for that which is highly esteemed among men is abomination in the sight of God. 16 The law and the prophets *were* until John: since that time the kingdom of God is preached, and every man presseth into it. 17 And it is easier for heaven and earth to pass, than one tittle of the law to fail. 18 Whosoever putteth away his wife, and marrieth another, committeth adultery: and whosoever marrieth her that is put away from *her* husband committeth adultery.

19 There was a certain rich man, which was clothed in purple and fine linen, and fared sump-

Living Bible

evil hearts. Your pretense brings you honor from the people, but it is an abomination in the sight of God. 16 Until John the Baptist began to preach, the laws of Moses and the messages of the prophets were your guides. But John introduced the Good News that the Kingdom of God would come soon. And now eager multitudes are pressing in. 17 But that doesn't mean that the Law has lost its force in even the smallest point. It is as strong and unshakable as heaven and earth.

18 "So anyone who divorces his wife and marries someone else commits adultery, and anyone who marries a divorced woman commits adultery."

19 "There was a certain rich man," Jesus said, "who was splendidly clothed and lived each day

Today's English Version

selves look right in men's sight, but God knows your hearts. For what men think is of great value is worth nothing in God's sight.

16 "The Law of Moses and the writings of the prophets were in effect up to the time of John the Baptist; since then the Good News about the Kingdom of God is being told, and everyone forces his way in. 17 But it is easier for heaven and earth to disappear than for the smallest detail of the Law to be done away with.

18 "Any man who divorces his wife and marries another woman commits adultery; and the man who marries a divorced woman commits adultery."

The rich man and Lazarus

19 "There was once a rich man who dressed in the most expensive clothes and lived in great

New International Version

in the eyes of men, but God knows your hearts. What is highly valued among men is detestable in God's sight.

16 "The Law and the Prophets were proclaimed until John. Since that time, the good news of the kingdom of God is being preached, and everyone is forcing his way into it. 17 It is easier for heaven and earth to disappear than for the least stroke of a pen to drop out of the Law.

18 "Anyone who divorces his wife and marries another woman commits adultery, and the man who marries a divorced woman commits adultery.

The rich man and Lazarus

19 "There was a rich man who was dressed in purple and fine linen and lived in luxury

Phillips Modern English

ness before men, but God knows your hearts. Remember, there are things men consider splendid which are detestable in the sight of God!

16.16 Jesus states that the kingdom of God has superseded "the Law and the Prophets"

"The Law and the Prophets were in force until John's day. From then on the good news of the kingdom of God has been proclaimed and everyone is trying to force his way into it.

"Yet it would be easier for Heaven and earth to disappear than for a single point of the Law to become a dead letter.

"Any man who divorces his wife and marries another woman commits adultery. And so does any man who marries the woman who was divorced from her husband.

16.19 Jesus shows the fearful consequence of social injustice

"There was once a rich man who used to dress in purple and fine linen and lead a life of

Revised Standard Version

yourselves before men, but God knows your hearts; for what is exalted among men is an abomination in the sight of God.

16 "The law and the prophets were until John; since then the good news of the kingdom of God is preached, and every one enters it violently. 17 But it is easier for heaven and earth to pass away, than for one dot of the law to become void.

18 "Every one who divorces his wife and marries another commits adultery, and he who marries a woman divorced from her husband commits adultery.

19 "There was a rich man, who was clothed in purple and fine linen and who feasted sumptu-

Jerusalem Bible

as virtuous in people's sight, but God knows your hearts. For what is thought highly of by men is loathsome in the sight of God.

The kingdom stormed

16 "Up to the time of John it was the Law and the Prophets; since then, the kingdom of God has been preached, and by violence everyone is getting in.

The Law remains

17 "It is easier for heaven and earth to disappear than for one little stroke to drop out of the Law.

Marriage indissoluble

18 "Everyone who divorces his wife and marries another is guilty of adultery, and the man who marries a woman divorced by her husband commits adultery.

The rich man and Lazarus

19 "There was a rich man who used to dress in purple and fine linen and feast magnificently

New English Bible

your righteousness; but God sees through you; for what sets itself up to be admired by men is detestable in the sight of God.

'Until John, it was the Law and the prophets: since then, there is the good news of the kingdom of God, and everyone forces his way in.

'It is easier for heaven and earth to come to an end than for one dot or stroke of the Law to lose its force.

'A man who divorces his wife and marries another commits adultery; and anyone who marries a woman divorced from her husband commits adultery.

'There was once a rich man, who dressed in purple and the finest linen, and feasted in great

King James Version

tuously every day: 20And there was a certain
beggar named Lazarus, which was laid at his
gate, full of sores, 21And desiring to be fed with
the crumbs which fell from the rich man's table:
moreover the dogs came and licked his sores.
22And it came to pass, that the beggar died, and
was carried by the angels into Abraham's bosom:
the rich man also died, and was buried; 23And
in hell he lifted up his eyes, being in torments,
and seeth Abraham afar off, and Lazarus in his
bosom. 24And he cried and said, Father Abraham, have mercy on me, and send Lazarus, that
he may dip the tip of his finger in water, and
cool my tongue; for I am tormented in this
flame. 25 But Abraham said, Son, remember that
thou in thy lifetime receivedst thy good things,
and likewise Lazarus evil things: but now he is
comforted, and thou art tormented. 26And beside
all this, between us and you there is a great gulf
fixed: so that they which would pass from hence
to you cannot; neither can they pass to us, that
would come from thence. 27 Then he said, I pray
thee therefore, father, that thou wouldest send
him to my father's house: 28 For I have five
brethren; that he may testify unto them, lest they
also come into this place of torment. 29Abraham
saith unto him, They have Moses and the prophets; let them hear them. 30And he said, Nay,
father Abraham: but if one went unto them

Living Bible

in mirth and luxury. 20 One day Lazarus, a diseased beggar, was laid at his door. 21As he lay
there longing for scraps from the rich man's table, the dogs would come and lick his open
sores. 22 Finally the beggar died and was carried
by the angels to be with Abraham in the place of
the righteous dead.[e] The rich man also died and
was buried, 23 and his soul went into hell.[f]
There, in torment, he saw Lazarus in the far
distance with Abraham.
24 " 'Father Abraham,' he shouted, 'have
some pity! Send Lazarus over here if only to dip
the tip of his finger in water and cool my tongue,
for I am in anguish in these flames.'
25 "But Abraham said to him, 'Son, remember that during your lifetime you had everything
you wanted, and Lazarus had nothing. So now
he is here being comforted and you are in anguish. 26And besides, there is a great chasm
separating us, and anyone wanting to come to
you from here is stopped at its edge; and no one
over there can cross to us.'
27 "Then the rich man said, 'O Father Abraham, then please send him to my father's home—
28 for I have five brothers—to warn them about
this place of torment lest they come here when
they die.'
29 "But Abraham said, 'The Scriptures have
warned them again and again. Your brothers
can read them any time they want to.'
30 "The rich man replied, 'No, Father Abraham, they won't bother to read them. But if
someone is sent to them from the dead, then
they will turn from their sins.'

[*e*] Literally, "into Abraham's bosom." [*f*] Literally, "into Hades."

Today's English Version

luxury every day. 20 There was also a poor man,
named Lazarus, full of sores, who used to be
brought to the rich man's door, 21 hoping to
fill himself with the bits of food that fell from
the rich man's table. Even the dogs would come
and lick his sores. 22 The poor man died and
was carried by the angels to Abraham's side, at
the feast in heaven; the rich man died and was
buried. 23 He was in great pain in Hades; and
he looked up and saw Abraham, far away, with
Lazarus at his side. 24 So he called out, 'Father
Abraham! Take pity on me, and send Lazarus
to dip his finger in some water and cool off my
tongue, because I am in great pain in this fire!'
25 But Abraham said, 'Remember, my son, that
in your lifetime you were given all the good
things, while Lazarus got all the bad things; but
now he is enjoying himself here, while you are
in pain. 26 Besides all that, there is a deep pit
lying between us, so that those who want to
cross over from here to you cannot do it, nor
can anyone cross over to us from where you are.'
27 The rich man said, 'Well, father, I beg you,
send Lazarus to my father's house, 28 where I
have five brothers; let him go and warn them
so that they, at least, will not come to this place
of pain.' 29Abraham said, 'Your brothers have
Moses and the prophets to warn them; let your
brothers listen to what they say.' 30 The rich man
answered, 'That is not enough, father Abraham!
But if someone were to rise from death and go
to them, then they would turn from their sins.'

New International Version

every day. 20At his gate was laid a beggar named
Lazarus, covered with sores 21 and longing to
eat what fell from the rich man's table. Even the
dogs came and licked his sores.
22 "The time came when the beggar died and
the angels carried him to Abraham's side. The
rich man also died and was buried. 23 In hell,[f]
where he was in torment, he looked up and saw
Abraham far away, with Lazarus by his side.
24 So he called to him, 'Father Abraham, have
pity on me and send Lazarus to dip the tip of his
finger in water and cool my tongue, because I
am in agony in this fire.'
25 "But Abraham replied, 'Son, remember
that in your lifetime you received your good
things, while Lazarus received bad things, but
now he is comforted here and you are in agony.
26And besides all this, between us and you a
great chasm has been fixed, so that those who
want to go from here to you cannot, nor can
anyone cross over from there to us.'
27 "He answered, 'Then I beg you, father,
send Lazarus to my father's house, 28 for I have
five brothers. Let him warn them, so that they
will not also come to this place of torment.'
29 "Abraham replied, 'They have Moses and
the Prophets; let them listen to them.'
30 " 'No, father Abraham,' he said, 'but if
someone from the dead goes to them, they will
repent.'

[*f*] Greek *Hades*.

Phillips Modern English

daily luxury. And there was a poor man called Lazarus who was put down at his gate. He was covered with sores. He used to long to be fed with the scraps from the rich man's table. Yes, and the dogs used to come and lick his sores. Well, it happened that the poor man died, and was carried by the angels into Abraham's bosom. The rich man also died and was buried. And from the place of the dead he looked up in torment and saw Abraham a long way away, and Lazarus in his arms. 'Father Abraham,' he cried out, 'please pity me! Send Lazarus to dip the tip of his finger in water and cool my tongue, for I am in agony in these flames.' But Abraham replied, 'Remember, my son, that you used to have the good things in your lifetime, just as Lazarus suffered the bad. Now he is being comforted here, while you are in agony. And besides this, a great chasm has been set between you and us, so that those who want to go to you from this side cannot do so, and people cannot come to us from your side.' At this he said, 'Then I beg you, father, to send him to my father's house for I have five brothers. He could warn them and prevent their coming to this place of torture.' But Abraham said, 'They have Moses and the Prophets: they can listen to them.' 'Ah no, father Abraham,' he said, 'if only someone were to go to them from the

Revised Standard Version

ously every day. 20 And at his gate lay a poor
man named Lazarus, full of sores, 21 who desired
to be fed with what fell from the rich man's
table; moreover the dogs came and licked his
sores. 22 The poor man died and was carried
by the angels to Abraham's bosom. The rich man
also died and was buried; 23 and in Hades, being
in torment, he lifted up his eyes, and saw Abraham far off and Lazarus in his bosom. 24 And
he called out, 'Father Abraham, have mercy
upon me, and send Lazarus to dip the end of
his finger in water and cool my tongue; for I
am in anguish in this flame.' 25 But Abraham
said, 'Son, remember that you in your lifetime
received your good things, and Lazarus in like
manner evil things; but now he is comforted
here, and you are in anguish. 26 And besides all
this, between us and you a great chasm has been
fixed, in order that those who would pass from
here to you may not be able, and none may
cross from there to us.' 27 And he said, 'Then I
beg you, father, to send him to my father's
house, 28 for I have five brothers, so that he
may warn them, lest they also come into this
place of torment.' 29 But Abraham said, 'They
have Moses and the prophets; let them hear
them.' 30 And he said, 'No, father Abraham; but
if some one goes to them from the dead, they

Jerusalem Bible

every day. 20 And at his gate there lay a poor
man called Lazarus, covered with sores, 21 who
longed to fill himself with the scraps that fell
from the rich man's table. Dogs even came and
licked his sores. 22 Now the poor man died and
was carried away by the angels to the bosom of
Abraham. The rich man also died and was
buried.
23 "In his torment in Hades he looked up
and saw Abraham a long way off with Lazarus
in his bosom. 24 So he cried out, 'Father Abraham, pity me and send Lazarus to dip the tip
of his finger in water and cool my tongue, for
I am in agony in these flames.' 25 'My son,'
Abraham replied, 'remember that during your
life good things came your way, just as bad
things came the way of Lazarus. Now he is being comforted here while you are in agony.
26 But that is not all: between us and you a
great gulf has been fixed, to stop anyone, if he
wanted to, crossing from our side to yours, and
to stop any crossing from your side to ours.'
27 "The rich man replied, 'Father, I beg you
then to send Lazarus to my father's house, 28 since
I have five brothers, to give them warning so
that they do not come to this place of torment
too.' 29 'They have Moses and the prophets,'
said Abraham, 'let them listen to them.' 30 'Ah
no, father Abraham,' said the rich man, 'but if
someone comes to them from the dead, they

New English Bible

magnificence every day. At his gate, covered with sores, lay a poor man named Lazarus, who would have been glad to satisfy his hunger with the scraps from the rich man's table. Even the dogs used to come and lick his sores. One day the poor man died and was carried away by the angels to be with Abraham. The rich man also died and was buried, and in Hades, where he was in torment, he looked up; and there, far away, was Abraham with Lazarus close beside him. "Abraham, my father," he called out, "take pity on me! Send Lazarus to dip the tip of his finger in water, to cool my tongue, for I am in agony in this fire." But Abraham said, "Remember, my child, that all the good things fell to you while you were alive, and all the bad to Lazarus; now he has his consolation here and it is you who are in agony. But that is not all: there is a great chasm fixed between us; no one from our side who wants to reach you can cross it, and none may pass from your side to us." "Then, father," he replied, "will you send him to my father's house, where I have five brothers, to warn them, so that they too may not come to this place of torment?" But Abraham said, "They have Moses and the prophets; let them listen to them." "No, father Abraham," he replied, "but if someone from the dead visits them,

King James Version

from the dead, they will repent. 31And he said
unto him, If they hear not Moses and the prophets, neither will they be persuaded, though one
rose from the dead.

17 Then said he unto the disciples, It is impossible but that offences will come: but
woe *unto him*, through whom they come! 2 It
were better for him that a millstone were hanged
about his neck, and he cast into the sea, than
that he should offend one of these little ones.
3 Take heed to yourselves: If thy brother trespass against thee, rebuke him; and if he repent,
forgive him. 4And if he trespass against thee
seven times in a day, and seven times in a day
turn again to thee, saying, I repent; thou shalt
forgive him. 5And the apostles said unto the
Lord, Increase our faith. 6And the Lord said,
If ye had faith as a grain of mustard seed, ye

Living Bible

31 "But Abraham said, 'If they won't listen
to Moses and the prophets, they won't listen
even though someone rises from the dead.' " [g]

17 "There will always be temptations to sin,"
Jesus said one day to his disciples, "but
woe to the man who does the tempting. 2, 3 If
he were thrown into the sea with a huge rock
tied to his neck, he would be far better off than
facing the punishment in store for those who
harm these little children's souls. I am warning
you!
"Rebuke your brother if he sins, and forgive
him if he is sorry. 4 Even if he wrongs you seven
times a day and each time turns again and asks
forgiveness, forgive him."
5 One day the apostles said to the Lord, "We
need more faith; tell us how to get it."
6 "If your faith were only the size of a mustard seed," Jesus answered, "it would be large

[g] Even Christ's resurrection failed to convince the Pharisees, to whom he gave this illustration.

Today's English Version

31 But Abraham said, 'If they will not listen to
Moses and the prophets, they will not be convinced even if someone were to rise from
death.' "

Sin

17 Jesus said to his disciples, "Things that
make people fall into sin are bound to happen; but how terrible for the one who makes
them happen! 2 It would be better for him if a
large millstone were tied around his neck and
he were thrown into the sea, than for him to
cause one of these little ones to sin. 3 Be on your
guard!
"If your brother sins, rebuke him, and if he
repents, forgive him. 4 If he sins against you
seven times in one day, and each time he comes
to you saying, 'I repent,' you must forgive him."

Faith

5 The apostles said to the Lord, "Make our
faith greater."
6 The Lord answered, "If you had faith as
big as a mustard seed, you could say to this

New International Version

31 "He said to him, 'If they do not listen to
Moses and the Prophets, they will not be convinced even if someone rises from the dead.' "

Sin, faith, duty

17 Jesus said to his disciples: "Things that
cause people to sin are bound to come, but
woe to that person through whom they come.
2 It would be better for him to be thrown into
the sea with a millstone tied around his neck
than for him to cause one of these little ones to
sin. 3 So watch yourselves.
"If your brother sins, rebuke him, and if he
repents, forgive him. 4 If he sins against you
seven times in a day, and seven times comes
back to you and says, 'I repent,' forgive him."
5 The apostles said to the Lord, "Increase
our faith!"
6 He replied, "If you have faith as small as
a mustard seed, you can say to this mulberry

Phillips Modern English

dead, they would change completely.' But Abraham told him, 'If they will not listen to Moses and the Prophets, they would not be convinced even if somebody were to rise from the dead.' "

17.1 Jesus warns his disciples about spoiling the spirit of the new kingdom

Then Jesus said to his disciples,

"It is inevitable that there should be pitfalls, but alas for the man who is responsible for them! It would be better for that man to have a mill-stone hung round his neck and be thrown into the sea, than that he should trip up one of these little ones. So be careful how you live. If your brother offends you, take him to task about it, and if he is sorry, forgive him. Yes, if he wrongs you seven times in one day and turns to you and says, 'I am sorry' seven times, you must forgive him."

And the apostles said to the Lord,

"Give us more faith."

And he replied,

"If your faith were as big as a grain of mustard-seed, you could say to this mulberry

Revised Standard Version

will repent.' 31 He said to him, 'If they do not
hear Moses and the prophets, neither will they be convinced if some one should rise from the dead.' "

17 And he said to his disciples, "Temptations
to sin[x] are sure to come; but woe to him
by whom they come! 2 It would be better for
him if a millstone were hung round his neck and he were cast into the sea, than that he should cause one of these little ones to sin.[y]
3 Take heed to yourselves; if your brother sins,
rebuke him, and if he repents, forgive him; 4 and
if he sins against you seven times in the day, and turns to you seven times, and says, 'I repent,' you must forgive him."
5 The apostles said to the Lord, "Increase
our faith!" 6And the Lord said, "If you had
faith as a grain of mustard seed, you could say

[x] Greek *stumbling blocks.* [y] Greek *stumble.*

Jerusalem Bible

will repent.' 31 Then Abraham said to him, 'If
they will not listen either to Moses or to the prophets, they will not be convinced even if someone should rise from the dead.' "

On leading others astray

17 He said to his disciples, "Obstacles are
sure to come, but alas for the one who
provides them! 2 It would be better for him to
be thrown into the sea with a millstone put around his neck than that he should lead astray a single one of these little ones. 3 Watch yourselves!

Brotherly correction

"If your brother does something wrong, reprove him and, if he is sorry, forgive him.
4And if he wrongs you seven times a day and seven times comes back to you and says, 'I am sorry,' you must forgive him."

The power of faith

5 The apostles said to the Lord, "Increase
our faith." 6 The Lord replied, "Were your faith
the size of a mustard seed you could say to this

New English Bible

they will repent." Abraham answered, "If they do not listen to Moses and the prophets they will pay no heed even if someone should rise from the dead." '

17 He said to his disciples, 'Causes of stumbling are bound to arise; but woe betide the man through whom they come. It would be better for him to be thrown into the sea with a millstone round his neck than to cause one of these little ones to stumble. Keep watch on yourselves.

'If your brother wrongs you, reprove him; and if he repents, forgive him. Even if he wrongs you seven times in a day and comes back to you seven times saying, "I am sorry", you are to forgive him.'

The apostles said to the Lord, 'Increase our faith'; and the Lord replied, 'If you had faith no bigger even than a mustard-seed, you could

King James Version

might say unto this sycamine tree, Be thou plucked up by the root, and be thou planted in the sea; and it should obey you. 7 But which of you, having a servant ploughing or feeding cattle, will say unto him by and by, when he is come from the field, Go and sit down to meat? 8And will not rather say unto him, Make ready wherewith I may sup, and gird thyself, and serve me, till I have eaten and drunken; and afterward thou shalt eat and drink? 9 Doth he thank that servant because he did the things that were commanded him? I trow not. 10 So likewise ye, when ye shall have done all those things which are commanded you, say, We are unprofitable servants: we have done that which was our duty to do.

11 And it came to pass, as he went to Jerusalem, that he passed through the midst of Samaria and Galilee. 12And as he entered into a certain village, there met him ten men that were lepers, which stood afar off: 13And they lifted up *their* voices, and said, Jesus, Master, have mercy on us. 14And when he saw *them,* he said unto them, Go shew yourselves unto the priests.

Living Bible

enough to uproot that mulberry tree over there and send it hurtling into the sea! Your command would bring immediate results! 7, 8, 9 When a servant comes in from plowing or taking care of sheep, he doesn't just sit down and eat, but first prepares his master's meal and serves him his supper before he eats his own. And he is not even thanked, for he is merely doing what he is supposed to do. 10 Just so, if you merely obey me, you should not consider yourselves worthy of praise. For you have simply done your duty!"

11 As they continued onward toward Jerusalem, they reached the border between Galilee and Samaria, 12 and as they entered a village there, ten lepers stood at a distance, 13 crying out, "Jesus, sir, have mercy on us!"

14 He looked at them and said, "Go to the Jewish priest and show him that you are healed!"

Today's English Version

mulberry tree, 'Pull yourself up by the roots and plant yourself in the sea!' and it would obey you."

A servant's duty

7 "Suppose one of you has a servant who is plowing or looking after the sheep. When he comes in from the field, do you say to him, 'Hurry along and eat your meal'? 8 Of course not! Instead, you say to him, 'Get my supper ready, then put on your apron and wait on me while I eat and drink; after that you may eat and drink.' 9 The servant does not deserve thanks for obeying orders, does he? 10 It is the same with you; when you have done all you have been told to do, say, 'We are ordinary servants; we have only done our duty.' "

Jesus makes ten lepers clean

11 As Jesus made his way to Jerusalem he went between Samaria and Galilee. 12 He was going into a village when he was met by ten lepers. They stood at a distance 13 and shouted, "Jesus! Master! Have pity on us!"

14 Jesus saw them and said to them, "Go and let the priests examine you."

New International Version

tree, 'Be uprooted and planted in the sea,' and it will obey you.

7 "Suppose one of you had a servant plowing or looking after the sheep. Would he say to the servant when he comes in from the field, 'Come along now and sit down to eat'? 8 Would he not rather say, 'Prepare my supper, get yourself ready and wait on me while I eat and drink; after that you may eat and drink'? 9 Would he thank the servant because he did what he was told to do? 10 So you also, when you have done everything you were told to do, should say, 'We are unworthy servants; we have only done our duty.' "

Ten healed of leprosy

11 Now on his way to Jerusalem, Jesus traveled along the border between Samaria and Galilee. 12As he was going into a village, ten men who had leprosy[g] met him. They stood at a distance 13 and called out in a loud voice, "Jesus, Master, have pity on us!"

14 When he saw them, he said, "Go, show

[g] The Greek word probably designated other related diseases also.

Phillips Modern English

tree, 'Pull yourself up by the roots and plant yourself in the sea', and it would obey you!

17.7 Work in the kingdom must be taken as a matter of course

"If any of you has a servant ploughing or looking after the sheep, are you likely to say to him when he comes in from the fields, 'Come straight in and sit down to your meal'? Aren't you more likely to say, 'Get my supper ready: change your coat, and wait on me while I eat and drink: and then, when I've finished, you can have your meal'? Do you feel grateful to your servant for doing what you tell him? I don't think so. It is the same with yourselves—when you have done everything that you are told to do, you can say, 'We are not much good as servants; we have only done what we ought to do.'"

17.11 Jesus heals ten men of leprosy: only one shows his gratitude

In the course of his journey to Jerusalem, Jesus crossed the boundary between Samaria and Galilee, and as he was approaching a village. ten lepers met him. They kept their distance but shouted out,

"Jesus, Master, have pity on us!"

When Jesus saw them, he said,

"Go and show yourselves to the priests."

Revised Standard Version

to this sycamine tree, 'Be rooted up, and be planted in the sea,' and it would obey you.
7 "Will any one of you, who has a servant plowing or keeping sheep, say to him when he has come in from the field, 'Come at once and sit down at table'? 8 Will he not rather say to him, 'Prepare supper for me, and gird yourself and serve me, till I eat and drink; and afterward you shall eat and drink'? 9 Does he thank the servant because he did what was commanded? 10 So you also, when you have done all that is commanded you, say, 'We are unworthy servants; we have only done what was our duty.'"
11 On the way to Jerusalem he was passing along between Samaria and Galilee. 12 And as he entered a village, he was met by ten lepers, who stood at a distance 13 and lifted up their voices and said, "Jesus, Master, have mercy on us." 14 When he saw them he said to them, "Go and show yourselves to the priests." And

Jerusalem Bible

mulberry tree, 'Be uprooted and planted in the sea,' and it would obey you.

Humble service

7 "Which of you, with a servant plowing or minding sheep, would say to him when he returned from the fields, 'Come and have your meal immediately?' 8 Would he not be more likely to say, 'Get my supper laid; make yourself tidy and wait on me while I eat and drink. You can eat and drink yourself afterward?' 9 Must he be grateful to the servant for doing what he was told? 10 So with you: when you have done all you have been told to do, say, 'We are merely servants: we have done no more than our duty.'"

The ten lepers

11 Now on the way to Jerusalem he traveled along the border between Samaria and Galilee.[a]
12 As he entered one of the villages, ten lepers came to meet him. They stood some way off
13 and called to him, "Jesus! Master! Take pity on us." 14 When he saw them he said, "Go and show yourselves to the priests." Now as they

[a] Making for the Jordan valley and Jericho; from there he goes up to Jerusalem.

New English Bible

say to this mulberry tree, "Be rooted up and replanted in the sea"; and it would at once obey you.

'Suppose one of you has a servant ploughing or minding sheep. When he comes back from the fields, will the master say, "Come along at once and sit down"? Will he not rather say, "Prepare my supper, fasten your belt, and then wait on me while I have my meal; you can have yours afterwards"? Is he grateful to the servant for carrying out his orders? So with you: when you have carried out all your orders, you should say, "We are servants and deserve no credit; we have only done our duty."'

In the course of his journey to Jerusalem he was travelling through the borderlands of Samaria and Galilee. As he was entering a village he was met by ten men with leprosy. They stood some way off and called out to him, 'Jesus, Master, take pity on us.' When he saw them he said, 'Go and show yourselves to the priests'; and

King James Version

And it came to pass, that, as they went, they were cleansed. 15And one of them, when he saw that he was healed, turned back, and with a loud voice glorified God, 16And fell down on *his* face at his feet, giving him thanks: and he was a Samaritan. 17And Jesus answering said, Were there not ten cleansed? but where *are* the nine? 18 There are not found that returned to give glory to God, save this stranger. 19And he said unto him, Arise, go thy way: thy faith hath made thee whole.

20 And when he was demanded of the Pharisees, when the kingdom of God should come, he answered them and said, The kingdom of God cometh not with observation: 21 Neither shall they say, Lo here! or, lo there! for, behold, the kingdom of God is within you. 22And he said unto the disciples, The days will come, when ye shall desire to see one of the days of the Son of man, and ye shall not see *it*. 23And they shall say to you, See here; or, see there: go not after

Living Bible

And as they were going, their leprosy disappeared.

15 One of them came back to Jesus, shouting, "Glory to God, I'm healed!" 16 He fell flat on the ground in front of Jesus, face downward in the dust, thanking him for what he had done. This man was a despised[a] Samaritan.

17 Jesus asked, "Didn't I heal ten men? Where are the nine? 18 Does only this foreigner return to give glory to God?"

19 And Jesus said to the man, "Stand up and go; your faith has made you well."

20 One day the Pharisees asked Jesus, "When will the Kingdom of God begin?" Jesus replied, "The Kingdom of God isn't ushered in with visible signs. 21 You won't be able to say, 'It has begun here in this place or there in that part of the country.' For the Kingdom of God is within you."[b]

22 Later he talked again about this with his disciples. "The time is coming when you will long for me[c] to be with you even for a single day, but I won't be here," he said. 23 "Reports will reach you that I have returned and that I am in this

[*a*] Implied. Samaritans were despised by Jews as being only "half-breed" Hebrews. [*b*] Or, "among you." [*c*] Or, "long for the Son of Man."

Today's English Version

On the way they were made clean. 15 One of them, when he saw that he was healed, came back, praising God in a loud voice. 16 He threw himself to the ground at Jesus' feet, thanking him. The man was a Samaritan. 17 Jesus spoke up, "There were ten men made clean; where are the other nine? 18 Why is this foreigner the only one who came back to give thanks to God?" 19And Jesus said to him, "Get up and go; your faith has made you well."

The coming of the Kingdom

20 Some Pharisees asked Jesus when the Kingdom of God would come. His answer was, "The Kingdom of God does not come in such a way as to be seen. 21 No one will say, 'Look, here it is!' or, 'There it is!'; because the Kingdom of God is within you."

22 Then he said to the disciples, "The time will come when you will wish you could see one of the days of the Son of Man, but you will not see it. 23 There will be those who will say to you, 'Look, over there!' or, 'Look, over here!'

New International Version

yourselves to the priests." And as they went, they were cleansed.

15 One of them, when he saw he was healed, came back, praising God in a loud voice. 16 He threw himself at Jesus' feet and thanked him—and he was a Samaritan.

17 Jesus asked, "Were not all ten cleansed? Where are the other nine? 18 Was no one found to return and give praise to God except this foreigner?" 19 Then he said to him, "Rise and go; your faith has made you well."

The coming of the kingdom of God

20 Once, having been asked by the Pharisees when the kingdom of God would come, Jesus replied, "The kingdom of God does not come visibly, 21 nor will people say, 'Here it is,' or 'There it is,' because the kingdom of God is within you.[h]"

22 Then he said to his disciples, "The time is coming when you will long to see one of the days of the Son of Man, but you will not see it. 23 Men will tell you, 'There he is!' or 'Here he

[*h*] Or *is among you.*

Phillips Modern English

And it happened that as they went on their way they were cured. One of their number, when he saw that he was healed, turned round and praised God at the top of his voice, and then fell on his face before Jesus and thanked him. This man was a Samaritan. And at this Jesus remarked,

"Weren't there ten men cured? Where are the other nine? Is nobody going to turn and praise God, except this stranger?"

And he said to the man,

"Stand up now, and go on your way. It is your faith that has made you well."

17.20 Jesus tells the Pharisees that the kingdom is here and now

Later, he was asked by the Pharisees when the kingdom of God was coming, and he gave them this reply:

"The kingdom of God never comes by looking for signs of it. Men cannot say, 'Look, here it is', or 'there it is', for the kingdom of God is inside you."

17.22 Jesus tells his disciples about the future

Then he said to the disciples,

"The time will come when you will long to see again a single day of the Son of Man, but you will not see it. People will say to you, 'Look,

Revised Standard Version

as they went they were cleansed. 15 Then one
of them, when he saw that he was healed, turned
back, praising God with a loud voice; 16 and he
fell on his face at Jesus' feet, giving him thanks.
Now he was a Samaritan. 17 Then said Jesus,
"Were not ten cleansed? Where are the nine?
18 Was no one found to return and give praise to
God except this foreigner?" 19 And he said to
him, "Rise and go your way; your faith has
made you well."
20 Being asked by the Pharisees when the
kingdom of God was coming, he answered them,
"The kingdom of God is not coming with signs
to be observed; 21 nor will they say, 'Lo, here
it is!' or 'There!' for behold, the kingdom of
God is in the midst of you." [z]
22 And he said to the disciples, "The days
are coming when you will desire to see one of
the days of the Son of man, and you will not
see it. 23 And they will say to you, 'Lo, there!' or

[z] Or *within you.*

Jerusalem Bible

were going away they were cleansed. 15 Finding
himself cured, one of them turned back praising
God at the top of his voice 16 and threw himself at the feet of Jesus and thanked him. The
man was a Samaritan. 17 This made Jesus say,
"Were not all ten made clean? The other nine,
where are they? 18 It seems that no one has
come back to give praise to God, except this
foreigner." 19 And he said to the man, "Stand
up and go on your way. Your faith has saved
you."

The coming of the kingdom of God

20 Asked by the Pharisees when the kingdom
of God was to come, he gave them this answer,
"The coming of the kingdom of God does not
admit of observation 21 and there will be no
one to say, 'Look here! Look there!' For, you
must know, the kingdom of God is among you."

The day of the Son of Man

22 He said to the disciples, "A time will come
when you will long to see one of the days of
the Son of Man and will not see it. 23 They
will say to you, 'Look there!' or, 'Look here!'

New English Bible

while they were on their way, they were made clean. One of them, finding himself cured, turned back praising God aloud. He threw himself down at Jesus's feet and thanked him. And he was a Samaritan. At this Jesus said: 'Were not all ten cleansed? The other nine, where are they? Could none be found to come back and give praise to God except this foreigner?' And he said to the man, 'Stand up and go on your way; your faith has cured you.'

The Pharisees asked him, 'When will the kingdom of God come?' He said, 'You cannot tell by observation when the kingdom of God comes. There will be no saying, "Look, here it is!" or "there it is!"; for in fact the kingdom of God is among you.' [a]

He said to the disciples, 'The time will come when you will long to see one of the days of the Son of Man, but you will not see it. They will say to you, "Look! There!" and "Look!

[a] *Or* for in fact the kingdom of God is within you, *or* for in fact the kingdom of God is within your grasp, *or* for suddenly the kingdom of God will be among you.

King James Version

them, nor follow *them.* 24 For as the lightning,
that lighteneth out of the one *part* under heaven,
shineth unto the other *part* under heaven; so
shall also the Son of man be in his day. 25 But
first must he suffer many things, and be rejected
of this generation. 26 And as it was in the days
of Noe, so shall it be also in the days of the
Son of man. 27 They did eat, they drank, they
married wives, they were given in marriage, until
the day that Noe entered into the ark, and the
flood came, and destroyed them all. 28 Likewise
also as it was in the days of Lot; they did eat,
they drank, they bought, they sold, they planted,
they builded; 29 But the same day that Lot went
out of Sodom it rained fire and brimstone from
heaven, and destroyed *them* all. 30 Even thus
shall it be in the day when the Son of man is
revealed. 31 In that day, he which shall be upon
the housetop, and his stuff in the house, let him
not come down to take it away: and he that is
in the field, let him likewise not return back.
32 Remember Lot's wife. 33 Whosoever shall seek
to save his life shall lose it; and whosoever shall
lose his life shall preserve it. 34 I tell you, in
that night there shall be two *men* in one bed;
the one shall be taken, and the other shall be
left. 35 Two *women* shall be grinding together;
the one shall be taken, and the other left. 36 Two
men shall be in the field; the one shall be taken,

Living Bible

place or that; don't believe it or go out to look
for me. 24 For when I return, you will know it
beyond all doubt. It will be as evident as the
lightning that flashes across the skies. 25 But first
I must suffer terribly and be rejected by this
whole nation.

26 "[When I return[d]] the word will be [as indifferent to the things of God [d]] as the people
were in Noah's day. 27 They ate and drank and
married—everything just as usual right up to the
day when Noah went into the ark and the flood
came and destroyed them all.

28 "And the world will be as it was in the
days of Lot: people went about their daily business—eating and drinking, buying and selling,
farming and building—29 until the morning Lot
left Sodom. Then fire and brimstone rained down
from heaven and destroyed them all. 30 Yes, it
will be 'business as usual' right up to the hour
of my return.[e]

31 "Those away from home that day must
not return to pack; those in the fields must not
return to town—32 remember what happened to
Lot's wife! 33 Whoever clings to his life shall
lose it, and whoever loses his life shall save it.
34 That night two men will be asleep in the same
room, and one will be taken away, the other left.
35, 36 Two women will be working together at
household tasks; one will be taken, the other left;
and so it will be with men working side by side
in the fields."

[*d*] Implied. [*e*] Or, "the hour I am revealed."

Today's English Version

But don't go out looking for it. 24 As the lightning
flashes across the sky and lights it up from one
side to the other, so will the Son of Man be in
his day. 25 But first he must suffer much and be
rejected by the people of this day. 26 As it was in
the time of Noah, so shall it be in the days of
the Son of Man. 27 Everybody kept on eating
and drinking, men and women married, up to the
very day Noah went into the ark and the Flood
came and killed them all. 28 It will be as it was
in the time of Lot. Everybody kept on eating and
drinking, buying and selling, planting and building. 29 On the day Lot left Sodom, fire and sulfur
rained down from heaven and killed them all.
30 That is how it will be on the day the Son of
Man is revealed.

31 "The man who is on the roof of his house
on that day must not go down into the house to
get his belongings that are there; in the same way,
the man who is out in the field must not go back
to the house. 32 Remember Lot's wife! 33 Whoever tries to save his own life will lose it; whoever loses his life will save it. 34 On that night,
I tell you, there will be two men sleeping in one
bed: one will be taken away, the other left behind. 35 Two women will be grinding meal together: one will be taken away, the other left
behind. [36 Two men will be in the field: one
will be taken away, the other left behind.]"

New International Version

is!' Do not go running off after them. 24 For the
Son of Man in his day[i] will be like the lightning,
which flashes and lights up the sky from one end
to the other. 25 But first he must suffer many
things and be rejected by this generation.

26 "Just as it was in the days of Noah, so also
will it be in the days of the Son of Man. 27 People were eating, drinking, marrying and being
given in marriage up to the day Noah entered
the ark. Then the flood came and destroyed them
all.

28 "It was the same in the days of Lot. People
were eating, drinking, buying, selling, planting
and building. 29 But the day Lot left Sodom, fire
and sulfur rained down from heaven and destroyed them all.

30 "It will be just like this on the day the
Son of Man is revealed. 31 On that day no one
who is on the roof of his house, with his goods
inside, should go down to get them. Likewise,
no one in the field should go back for anything.
32 Remember Lot's wife! 33 Whoever tries to
keep his life will lose it, and whoever loses his
life will preserve it. 34 I tell you, on that night
two people will be in one bed; one will be taken
and the other left. 35 Two women will be grinding grain together; one will be taken and the
other left." [j]

[*i*] Some MSS omit *in his day.* [*j*] Some MSS add verse 36: *Two men will be in the field; one will be taken and the other left.*

Phillips Modern English

there it is', or 'Look, here it is.' Stay where you are and don't follow them! For the day of the Son of Man will be like lightning flashing from one end of the sky to the other. But before that happens, he must go through much suffering and be utterly rejected by this generation. In the time of the coming of the Son of Man, life will be as it was in the days of Noah. People ate and drank, married and were given in marriage, right up to the day when Noah entered the ark—and then came the flood and destroyed them all. It will be just the same as it was in the days of Lot. People ate and drank, bought and sold, planted and built, but on the day that Lot left Sodom, it rained fire and brimstone from heaven, and destroyed them all. That is how it will be on the day when the Son of Man is revealed. When that day comes, the man who is on the roof of his house, with his goods inside it, must not come down to get them. And the man out in the fields must not turn back for anything. Remember what happened to Lot's wife. Whoever tries to keep his life safe will lose it, and the man who is prepared to lose his life will preserve it. I tell you, that night there will be two men in one bed; one man will be taken and the other will be left. Two women will be turning the grinding-mill together; one will be taken and the other left."

Revised Standard Version

'Lo, here!' Do not go, do not follow them. 24 For as the lightning flashes and lights up the sky from one side to the other, so will the Son of man be in his day.[a] 25 But first he must suffer many things and be rejected by this generation. 26 As it was in the days of Noah, so will it be in the days of the Son of man. 27 They ate, they drank, they married, they were given in marriage, until the day when Noah entered the ark, and the flood came and destroyed them all. 28 Likewise as it was in the days of Lot—they ate, they drank, they bought, they sold, they planted, they built, 29 but on the day when Lot went out from Sodom fire and sulphur rained from heaven and destroyed them all—30 so will it be on the day when the Son of man is revealed. 31 On that day, let him who is on the housetop, with his goods in the house, not come down to take them away; and likewise let him who is in the field not turn back. 32 Remember Lot's wife. 33 Whoever seeks to gain his life will lose it, but whoever loses his life will preserve it. 34 I tell you, in that night there will be two in one bed; one will be taken and the other left. 35 There will be two women grinding together; one will be taken and the

[a] Other ancient authorities omit *in his day*.

Jerusalem Bible

Make no move; do not set off in pursuit; 24 for as the lightning flashing from one part of heaven lights up the other, so will be the Son of Man when his day comes. 25 But first he must suffer grievously and be rejected by this generation.

26 "As it was in Noah's day, so will it also be in the days of the Son of Man. 27 People were eating and drinking, marrying wives and husbands, right up to the day Noah went into the ark, and the Flood came and destroyed them all. 28 It will be the same as it was in Lot's day: people were eating and drinking, buying and selling, planting and building, 29 but the day Lot left Sodom, God rained fire and brimstone from heaven and it destroyed them all. 30 It will be the same when the day comes for the Son of Man to be revealed.

31 "When that day comes, anyone on the housetop, with his possessions in the house, must not come down to collect them, nor must anyone in the fields turn back either. 32 Remember Lot's wife. 33 Anyone who tries to preserve his life will lose it; and anyone who loses it will keep it safe. 34 I tell you, on that night two will be in one bed: one will be taken, the other left; 35 two women will be grinding corn together:

New English Bible

Here!" Do not go running off in pursuit. For like the lightning-flash that lights up the earth from end to end, will the Son of Man be when his day comes. But first he must endure much suffering and be repudiated by this generation.

'As things were in Noah's days, so will they be in the days of the Son of Man. They ate and drank and married, until the day that Noah went into the ark and the flood came and made an end of them all. As things were in Lot's days, also: they ate and drank; they bought and sold; they planted and built; but the day that Lot went out from Sodom, it rained fire and sulphur from the sky and made an end of them all—it will be like that on the day when the Son of Man is revealed.

'On that day the man who is on the roof and his belongings in the house must not come down to pick them up; he, too, who is in the fields must not go back. Remember Lot's wife. Whoever seeks to save his life will lose it; and whoever loses it will save it, and live.

'I tell you, on that night there will be two men in one bed: one will be taken, the other left. There will be two women together grinding

King James Version

and the other left. 37And they answered and said unto him, Where, Lord? And he said unto them, Wheresoever the body *is*, thither will the eagles be gathered together.

18 And he spake a parable unto them *to this end*, that men ought always to pray, and not to faint; 2 Saying, There was in a city a judge, which feared not God, neither regarded man: 3And there was a widow in that city; and she came unto him, saying, Avenge me of mine adversary. 4And he would not for a while: but afterward he said within himself, Though I fear not God, nor regard man; 5 Yet because this widow troubleth me, I will avenge her, lest by her continual coming she weary me. 6And the Lord said, Hear what the unjust judge saith. 7And shall not God avenge his own elect, which cry day and night unto him, though he bear long with them? 8 I tell you that he will avenge them speedily. Nevertheless, when the Son of man cometh, shall he find faith on the earth?

Living Bible

37 "Lord, where will they be taken?" the disciples asked.

Jesus replied, "Where the body is, the vultures gather!" [f]

18 One day Jesus told his disciples a story to illustrate their need for constant prayer and to show them that they must keep praying until the answer comes.

2 "There was a city judge," he said, "a very godless man who had great contempt for everyone. 3A widow of that city came to him frequently to appeal for justice against a man who had harmed her. 4, 5 The judge ignored her for a while, but eventually she got on his nerves.

"'I fear neither God nor man,' he said to himself, 'but this woman bothers me. I'm going to see that she gets justice, for she is wearing me out with her constant coming!'"

6 Then the Lord said, "If even an evil judge can be worn down like that, 7 don't you think that God will surely give justice to his people who plead with him day and night? 8 Yes! He will answer them quickly! But the question is: When I, the Messiah,[a] return, how many will I find who have faith [and are praying[b]]?"

[*f*] This may mean that God's people will be taken out to the execution grounds and their bodies left to the vultures. [*a*] Literally, "the Son of Man." [*b*] Implied.

Today's English Version

37 The disciples asked him, "Where, Lord?"

Jesus answered, "Where there is a dead body the vultures will gather."

The parable of the widow and the judge

18 Then Jesus told them this parable, to teach them that they should always pray and never become discouraged. 2 "There was a judge in a certain town who neither feared God nor respected men. 3And there was a widow in that same town who kept coming to him and pleading for her rights: 'Help me against my opponent!' 4 For a long time the judge was not willing, but at last he said to himself, 'Even though I don't fear God or respect men, 5 yet because of all the trouble this widow is giving me I will see to it that she gets her rights; or else she will keep on coming and finally wear me out!'"

6 And the Lord continued, "Listen to what that corrupt judge said. 7 Now, will God not judge in favor of his own people who cry to him for help day and night? Will he be slow to help them? 8 I tell you, he will judge in their favor, and do it quickly. But will the Son of Man find faith on earth when he comes?"

New International Version

37 "Where, Lord?" they asked.

He replied, "Where there is a dead body, there the vultures will gather."

The parable of the persistent widow

18 Then Jesus told his disciples a parable to show them that they should always pray and not give up. 2 He said: "In a certain town there was a judge who neither feared God nor cared about men. 3And there was a widow in that town who kept coming to him with the plea, 'Grant me justice against my adversary.'

4 "For some time he refused. But finally he said to himself, 'Even though I don't fear God or care about men, 5 yet because this widow keeps bothering me, I will see that she gets justice, so that she won't eventually wear me out with her coming!'"

6 And the Lord said, "Listen to what the unjust judge says. 7And will not God bring about justice for his chosen ones, who cry out to him day and night? Will he keep putting them off? 8 I tell you, he will see that they get justice, and quickly. However, when the Son of Man comes, will he find faith on the earth?"

Phillips Modern English

"But where, Lord?" they asked him.

"Wherever there is a dead body, there the vultures will flock," he replied.

18.1 *Jesus urges his disciples to persist in prayer*

Then he gave them an illustration to show that they must always pray and never lose heart. "Once upon a time," he said, "there was a magistrate in a town who had neither fear of God nor respect for his fellow-men. There was a widow in the town who kept coming to him, saying, 'Please protect me from the man who is trying to ruin me.' And for a long time he refused. But later he said to himself, 'Although I don't fear God and have no respect for men, yet this woman is such a nuisance that I shall give judgment in her favour, or else her continual visits will be the death of me!' "

Then the Lord said,

"Notice how this dishonest magistrate behaved. Do you suppose God, patient as he is, will not see justice done for his chosen, who appeal to him day and night? I assure you he will not delay in seeing justice done. Yet, when the Son of Man comes, will he find men on earth who believe in him?"

Revised Standard Version

other left." [b] 37And they said to him, "Where, Lord?" He said to them, "Where the body is, there the eagles[c] will be gathered together."

18 And he told them a parable, to the effect
that they ought always to pray and not lose
heart. 2 He said, "In a certain city there was a
judge who neither feared God nor regarded man;
3 and there was a widow in that city who kept
coming to him and saying, 'Vindicate me against
my adversary.' 4 For a while he refused; but
afterward he said to himself, 'Though I neither
fear God nor regard man, 5 yet because this
widow bothers me, I will vindicate her, or she
will wear me out by her continual coming.' "
6And the Lord said, "Hear what the unrighteous
judge says. 7And will not God vindicate his
elect, who cry to him day and night? Will he
delay long over them? 8 I tell you, he will vindicate them speedily. Nevertheless, when the Son of man comes, will he find faith on earth?"

[b] Other ancient authorities add verse 36, *"Two men will be in the field; one will be taken and the other left."* [c] Or *vultures*.

Jerusalem Bible

one will be taken, the other left." [b] 37 The disciples interrupted. "Where, Lord?" they asked. He said, "Where the body is, there too will the vultures gather."

The unscrupulous judge and the importunate widow

18 Then he told them a parable about the
need to pray continually and never lose
heart. 2 "There was a judge in a certain town,"
he said, "who had neither fear of God nor respect for man. 3 In the same town there was
a widow who kept on coming to him and saying, 'I want justice from you against my enemy!' 4 For a long time he refused, but at last
he said to himself, 'Maybe I have neither fear of
God nor respect for man, 5 but since she keeps
pestering me I must give this widow her just rights, or she will persist in coming and worry me to death.' "
6 And the Lord said, "You notice what the
unjust judge has to say? 7 Now will not God
see justice done to his chosen who cry to him
day and night even when he delays to help
them? 8 I promise you, he will see justice done
to them, and done speedily. But when the Son of Man comes, will he find any faith on earth?"

[b] Add v. 36 "There will be two men in the fields; one will be taken, the other left," cf. Mt. 24:40.

New English Bible

corn: one will be taken, the other left.' [a] When they heard this they asked, 'Where, Lord?' He said, 'Where the corpse is, there the vultures will gather.'

18 He spoke to them in a parable to show that they should keep on praying and never lose heart: 'There was once a judge who cared nothing for God or man, and in the same town there was a widow who constantly came before him demanding justice against her opponent. For a long time he refused; but in the end he said to himself, "True, I care nothing for God or man; but this widow is so great a nuisance that I will see her righted before she wears me out with her persistence." ' The Lord said, 'You hear what the unjust judge says; and will not God vindicate his chosen, who cry out to him day and night, while he listens patiently to them[b]? I tell you, he will vindicate them soon enough. But when the Son of Man comes, will he find faith on earth?'

[a] *Some witnesses add* (36) two men in the fields: one will be taken, the other left. [b] *Or* delays to help them.

King James Version

9And he spake this parable unto certain which
trusted in themselves that they were righteous,
and despised others: 10 Two men went up into
the temple to pray; the one a Pharisee, and the
other a publican. 11 The Pharisee stood and
prayed thus with himself, God, I thank thee, that
I am not as other men *are,* extortioners, unjust,
adulterers, or even as this publican. 12 I fast
twice in the week, I give tithes of all that I
possess. 13And the publican, standing afar off,
would not lift up so much as *his* eyes unto
heaven, but smote upon his breast, saying, God
be merciful to me a sinner. 14 I tell you, this
man went down to his house justified *rather* than
the other: for every one that exalteth himself
shall be abased; and he that humbleth himself
shall be exalted. 15And they brought unto him
also infants, that he would touch them: but
when *his* disciples saw *it,* they rebuked them.
16 But Jesus called them *unto him,* and said,
Suffer little children to come unto me, and forbid them not: for of such is the kingdom of

Living Bible

9 Then he told this story to some who boasted
of their virtue and scorned everyone else:
10 "Two men went to the Temple to pray.
One was a proud, self-righteous Pharisee, and
the other a cheating tax collector. 11 The proud
Pharisee 'prayed' this prayer: 'Thank God, I am
not a sinner like everyone else, especially like
that tax collector over there! For I never cheat,
I don't commit adultery, 12 I go without food
twice a week, and I give to God a tenth of everything I earn.'
13 "But the corrupt tax collector stood at a
distance and dared not even lift his eyes to
heaven as he prayed, but beat upon his chest in
sorrow, exclaiming, 'God, be merciful to me, a
sinner.' 14 I tell you, this sinner, not the Pharisee,
returned home forgiven! For the proud shall be
humbled, but the humble shall be honored."
15 One day some mothers brought their babies to him to touch and bless. But the disciples
told them to go away.
16, 17 Then Jesus called the children over to
him and said to the disciples, "Let the little children come to me! Never send them away! For
the Kingdom of God belongs to men who have

Today's English Version

The parable of the Pharisee and the tax collector

9 Jesus also told this parable to people who
were sure of their own goodness and despised
everybody else. 10 "Two men went up to the
temple to pray; one was a Pharisee, the other a
tax collector. 11 The Pharisee stood apart by
himself and prayed, 'I thank you, God, that I
am not greedy, dishonest, or immoral, like everybody else; I thank you that I am not like that tax
collector. 12 I fast two days every week, and I
give you one tenth of all my income.' 13 But the
tax collector stood at a distance and would not
even raise his face to heaven, but beat on his
breast and said, 'God, have pity on me, a sinner!' 14 I tell you," said Jesus, "this man, and
not the other, was in the right with God when
he went home. Because everyone who makes
himself great will be humbled, and everyone who
humbles himself will be made great."

Jesus blesses little children

15 Some people brought their babies to Jesus
to have him place his hands on them. But the
disciples saw them and scolded them for doing
so. 16 But Jesus called the children to him, and
said, "Let the children come to me, and do not
stop them, because the Kingdom of God belongs

New International Version

The parable of the Pharisee and the tax collector

9 To some who were confident of their own
righteousness and looked down on everybody
else, Jesus told this parable: 10 "Two men went
up to the temple to pray, one a Pharisee and the
other a tax collector. 11 The Pharisee stood up
and prayed about himself: 'God, I thank you
that I am not like all other men—robbers, evildoers, adulterers—or even like this tax collector. 12 I fast twice a week and give a tenth of
all my income.'
13 "But the tax collector stood at a distance.
He would not even look up to heaven, but beat
his breast and said, 'God, have mercy on me, a
sinner.'
14 "I tell you that this man, rather than the
other, went home justified before God. For
everyone who exalts himself will be humbled,
and he who humbles himself will be exalted."

The little children and Jesus

15 People were also bringing babies to Jesus
to have him touch them. When the disciples saw
this, they rebuked them. 16 But Jesus called the
children to him and said, "Let the little children
come to me, and do not hinder them, for the

Phillips Modern English

18.9 Jesus tells a story against the self-righteous

Then he gave this illustration to certain people who were confident of their own goodness and looked down on others:

"Two men went up to the Temple to pray, one was a Pharisee, the other was a tax-collector. The Pharisee stood and prayed like this with himself, 'O God, I do thank thee that I am not like the rest of mankind, greedy, dishonest, impure, or even like that tax-collector over there. I fast twice every week; I give away a tenth-part of all my income.' But the tax-collector stood in a distant corner, scarcely daring to look up to Heaven, and with a gesture of despair, said, 'God, have mercy on a sinner like me.' I assure you that he was the man who went home justified in God's sight, rather than the other one. For everyone who sets himself up as somebody will become a nobody, and the man who makes himself nobody will become somebody."

18.15 Jesus welcomes babies

Then people began to bring babies to him so that he could put his hands on them. But when the disciples noticed it, they frowned on them. But Jesus called them to him, and said,

"You must let little children come to me, and you must never prevent their coming. The kingdom of God belongs to little children like

Revised Standard Version

9 He also told this parable to some who
trusted in themselves that they were righteous
and despised others: 10 "Two men went up into
the temple to pray, one a Pharisee and the other
a tax collector. 11 The Pharisee stood and prayed
thus with himself, 'God, I thank thee that I am
not like other men, extortioners, unjust, adulterers, or even like this tax collector. 12 I fast
twice a week, I give tithes of all that I get.'
13 But the tax collector, standing far off, would
not even lift up his eyes to heaven, but beat his
breast, saying, 'God, be merciful to me a sinner!' 14 I tell you, this man went down to his
house justified rather than the other; for every
one who exalts himself will be humbled, but he
who humbles himself will be exalted."
15 Now they were bringing even infants to
him that he might touch them; and when the
disciples saw it, they rebuked them. 16 But Jesus
called them to him, saying, "Let the children
come to me, and do not hinder them; for to

Jerusalem Bible

The Pharisee and the publican

9 He spoke the following parable to some
people who prided themselves on being virtuous
and despised everyone else, 10 "Two men went
up to the Temple to pray, one a Pharisee, the
other a tax collector. 11 The Pharisee stood
there and said this prayer to himself, 'I thank
you, God, that I am not grasping, unjust, adulterous like the rest of mankind, and particularly
that I am not like this tax collector here. 12 I
fast twice a week; I pay tithes on all I get.'
13 The tax collector stood some distance away,
not daring even to raise his eyes to heaven; but
he beat his breast and said, 'God, be merciful
to me, a sinner.' 14 This man, I tell you, went
home again at rights with God; the other did
not. For everyone who exalts himself will be
humbled, but the man who humbles himself will
be exalted."

Jesus and the children

15 People even brought little children to him,
for him to touch them; but when the disciples
saw this they turned them away. 16 But Jesus
called the children to him and said, "Let the
little children come to me, and do not stop
them; for it is to such as these that the king-

New English Bible

And here is another parable that he told. It was aimed at those who were sure of their own goodness and looked down on everyone else. 'Two men went up to the temple to pray, one a Pharisee and the other a tax-gatherer. The Pharisee stood up and prayed thus:[c] "I thank thee, O God, that I am not like the rest of men, greedy, dishonest, adulterous; or, for that matter, like this tax-gatherer. I fast twice a week; I pay tithes on all that I get." But the other kept his distance and would not even raise his eyes to heaven, but beat upon his breast, saying, "O God, have mercy on me, sinner that I am." It was this man, I tell you, and not the other, who went home acquitted of his sins. For everyone who exalts himself will be humbled; and whoever humbles himself will be exalted.'

They even brought babies for him to touch. When the disciples saw them they rebuked them, but Jesus called for the children and said, 'Let the little ones come to me; do not try to stop them; for the kingdom of God belongs to such

[c] Some witnesses read stood up by himself and played thus; *others read* stood up and prayed thus privately.

King James Version

God. 17 Verily I say unto you, Whosoever shall
not receive the kingdom of God as a little child
shall in no wise enter therein. 18 And a certain
ruler asked him, saying, Good Master, what
shall I do to inherit eternal life? 19 And Jesus
said unto him, Why callest thou me good? none
is good, save one, *that is,* God. 20 Thou knowest
the commandments, Do not commit adultery, Do
not kill, Do not steal, Do not bear false witness,
Honour thy father and thy mother. 21 And he
said, All these have I kept from my youth up.
22 Now when Jesus heard these things, he said
unto him, Yet lackest thou one thing: sell all
that thou hast, and distribute unto the poor, and
thou shalt have treasure in heaven: and come,
follow me. 23 And when he heard this, he was
very sorrowful: for he was very rich. 24 And
when Jesus saw that he was very sorrowful, he
said, How hardly shall they that have riches
enter into the kingdom of God! 25 For it is easier
for a camel to go through a needle's eye, than
for a rich man to enter into the kingdom of God.

Living Bible

hearts as trusting as these little children's. And anyone who doesn't have their kind of faith will never get within the Kingdom's gates."

18 Once a Jewish religious leader asked him this question: "Good sir, what shall I do to get to heaven?"

19 "Do you realize what you are saying when you call me 'good'?" Jesus asked him. "Only God is truly good, and no one else.

20 "But as to your question, you know what the ten commandments say—don't commit adultery, don't murder, don't steal, don't lie, honor your parents, and so on."
21 The man replied,
"I've obeyed every one of these laws since I was a small child."

22 "There is still one thing you lack," Jesus said. "Sell all you have and give the money to the poor—it will become treasure for you in heaven—and come, follow me."

23 But when the man heard this he went sadly away, for he was very rich.

24 Jesus watched him go and then said to his disciples, "How hard it is for the rich to enter the Kingdom of God!
25 It is easier for a camel to go through the eye of a needle than for a rich man to enter the Kingdom of God."

Today's English Version

to such as these.
17 Remember this! Whoever does not receive the Kingdom of God like a child will never enter it."

The rich man

18 A Jewish leader asked Jesus, "Good Teacher, what must I do to receive eternal life?"

19 "Why do you call me good?" Jesus asked him. "No one is good except God alone.
20 You know the commandments: 'Do not commit adultery; do not murder; do not steal; do not lie; honor your father and mother.' "

21 The man replied, "Ever since I was young I have obeyed all these commandments."

22 When Jesus heard this, he said to him, "You still need to do one thing. Sell all you have and give the money to the poor, and you will have riches in heaven; then come and follow me."
23 But when the man heard this he became very sad, because he was very rich.

24 Jesus saw that he was sad and said, "How hard it is for rich people to enter the Kingdom of God!
25 It is much harder for a rich man to enter the Kingdom of God than for a camel to go through the eye of a needle."

New International Version

kingdom of God belongs to such as these.
17 I tell you the truth, anyone who will not receive the kingdom of God like a little child will never enter it."

The rich ruler

18 A certain ruler asked him, "Good teacher, what must I do to inherit eternal life?"

19 "Why do you call me good?" Jesus answered. "No one is good—except God alone.
20 You know the commandments: 'Do not commit adultery, do not murder, do not steal, do not give false testimony, honor your father and mother.'[k]"

21 "All these I have kept since I was a boy," he said.

22 When Jesus heard this, he said to him, "You still lack one thing. Sell everything you have and give to the poor, and you will have treasure in heaven. Then come, follow me."

23 When he heard this, he became very sad, because he was a man of great wealth.
24 Jesus looked at him and said, "How hard it is for the rich to enter the kingdom of God!
25 Indeed, it is easier for a camel to go through the eye of a needle than for a rich man to enter the kingdom of God."

[*k*] Exodus 20:12-16; Deut. 5:16-20.

Phillips Modern English

these. I tell you, the man who will not accept the kingdom of God like a little child will never get into it at all."

18.18 Jesus and riches

Then one of the Jewish rulers put this question to him,

"Master, I know that you are good; tell me, please, what must I do to be sure of eternal life?"

"I wonder why you call me good?" returned Jesus. "No one is good—only the one God. You know the commandments—

"Thou shalt not commit adultery.
"Thou shalt not commit murder.
"Thou shalt not steal.
"Thou shalt not bear false witness.
"Honour thy father and thy mother."

"All these," he replied, "I have carefully kept since I was quite young."

And when Jesus heard that, he said to him,

"There is still one thing you have missed. Sell everything you possess and give the money away to the poor, and you will have riches in Heaven. Then come and follow me."

But when he heard this, he was greatly distressed for he was very rich.

And when Jesus saw how his face fell, he remarked,

"How difficult it is for those who have great possessions to enter the kingdom of God! A camel could squeeze through the eye of a needle more easily than a rich man could get into the kingdom of God."

Revised Standard Version

such belongs the kingdom of God. 17 Truly, I
say to you, whoever does not receive the kingdom of God like a child shall not enter it."
18 And a ruler asked him, "Good Teacher,
what shall I do to inherit eternal life?" 19 And
Jesus said to him, "Why do you call me good?
No one is good but God alone. 20 You know
the commandments: 'Do not commit adultery, Do not kill, Do not steal, Do not bear false
witness, Honor your father and mother.'" 21 And
he said, "All these I have observed from my youth." 22 And when Jesus heard it, he said to him, "One thing you still lack. Sell all that you have and distribute to the poor, and you will have treasure in heaven; and come, follow me."
23 But when he heard this he became sad, for he
was very rich. 24 Jesus looking at him said, "How hard it is for those who have riches to enter the
kingdom of God! 25 For it is easier for a camel to go through the eye of a needle than for a rich man to enter the kingdom of God."

Jerusalem Bible

dom of God belongs. 17 I tell you solemnly,
anyone who does not welcome the kingdom of God like a little child will never enter it."

The rich aristocrat

18 A member of one of the leading families
put this question to him, "Good Master, what
have I to do to inherit eternal life?" 19 Jesus
said to him, "Why do you call me good? No
one is good but God alone. 20 You know the
commandments: *You must not commit adultery; You must not kill; You must not steal; You must not bring false witness; Honor your father and mother.*" 21 He replied, "I have kept
all these from my earliest days till now." 22 And
when Jesus heard this he said, "There is still one thing you lack. Sell all that you own and distribute the money to the poor, and you will have treasure in heaven; then come, follow me."
23 But when he heard this he was filled with
sadness, for he was very rich.

The danger of riches

24 Jesus looked at him and said, "How hard it is for those who have riches to make their
way into the kingdom of God! 25 Yes, it is
easier for a camel to pass through the eye of a needle than for a rich man to enter the kingdom

New English Bible

as these. I tell you that whoever does not accept the kingdom of God like a child will never enter it.'

A man of the ruling class put this question to him: 'Good Master, what must I do to win eternal life?' Jesus said to him, 'Why do you call me good? No one is good except God alone. You know the commandments: "Do not commit adultery; do not murder; do not steal; do not give false evidence; honour your father and mother."' The man answered, 'I have kept all these since I was a boy.' On hearing this Jesus said, 'There is still one thing lacking: sell everything you have and distribute to the poor, and you will have riches in heaven; and come, follow me.' At these words his heart sank; for he was a very rich man. When Jesus saw it he said, 'How hard it is for the wealthy to enter the kingdom of God! It is easier for a camel to go through the eye of a needle than for a rich man

King James Version

26And they that heard *it* said, Who then can be saved? 27And he said, The things which are impossible with men are possible with God. 28 Then Peter said, Lo, we have left all, and followed thee. 29And he said unto them, Verily I say unto you, There is no man that hath left house, or parents, or brethren, or wife, or children, for the kingdom of God's sake, 30 Who shall not receive manifold more in this present time, and in the world to come life everlasting.

31 Then he took *unto him* the twelve, and said unto them, Behold, we go up to Jerusalem, and all things that are written by the prophets concerning the Son of man shall be accomplished. 32 For he shall be delivered unto the Gentiles, and shall be mocked, and spitefully entreated, and spitted on: 33And they shall scourge *him,* and put him to death; and the third day he shall rise again. 34And they understood none of these things: and this saying was hid from them, neither knew they the things which were spoken.

Living Bible

26 Those who heard him say this exclaimed, "If it is that hard, how can *anyone* be saved?"

27 He replied, "God can do what men can't!"

28 And Peter said, "We have left our homes and followed you."

29 "Yes," Jesus replied, "and everyone who has done as you have, leaving home, wife, brothers, parents, or children for the sake of the Kingdom of God, 30 will be repaid many times over now, as well as receiving eternal life in the world to come."

31 Gathering the Twelve around him he told them, "As you know, we are going to Jerusalem. And when we get there, all the predictions of the ancient prophets concerning me will come true. 32 I will be handed over to the Gentiles to be mocked and treated shamefully and spat upon, 33 and lashed and killed. And the third day I will rise again."

34 But they didn't understand a thing he said. He seemed to be talking in riddles.

Today's English Version

26 The people who heard him asked, "Who, then, can be saved?"

27 Jesus answered, "What is impossible for men is possible for God."

28 Then Peter said, "Look! We have left our homes to follow you."

29 "Yes," Jesus said to them, "and I tell you this: anyone who leaves home or wife or brothers or parents or children for the sake of the Kingdom of God 30 will receive much more in this present age, and eternal life in the age to come."

Jesus speaks a third time about his death

31 Jesus took the twelve disciples aside and said to them, "Listen! We are going to Jerusalem where everything the prophets wrote about the Son of Man will come true. 32 He will be handed over to the Gentiles, who will make fun of him, insult him, and spit on him. 33 They will whip him and kill him, but on the third day he will rise to life."

34 The disciples did not understand any of these things; the meaning of the words was hidden from them, and they did not know what Jesus was talking about.

New International Version

26 Those who heard this asked, "Who then can be saved?"

27 Jesus replied, "What is impossible with men is possible with God."

28 Peter said to him, "We have left all we had to follow you!"

29 "I tell you the truth," Jesus said to them, "no one who has left home or wife or brothers or parents or children for the sake of the kingdom of God 30 will fail to receive many times as much in this age and, in the age to come, eternal life."

Jesus again predicts his death

31 Jesus took the Twelve aside and told them, "We are going up to Jerusalem, and everything that is written by the prophets about the Son of Man will be fulfilled. 32 He will be handed over to the Gentiles. They will mock him, insult him, spit on him, flog him and kill him. 33 On the third day he will rise again."

34 The disciples did not understand any of this. Its meaning was hidden from them, and they did not know what he was talking about.

Phillips Modern English

Those who heard Jesus say this, exclaimed, "Then who can possibly be saved?"
Jesus replied,
"What men find impossible is possible with God."
"Well," rejoined Peter, "we have left all that we ever had and followed you."
And Jesus told them,
"Believe me, nobody has left his home or wife, or brothers or parents or children for the sake of the kingdom of God, without receiving very much more in this present life—and eternal life in the world to come."

18.31 Jesus foretells his death and resurrection

Then Jesus took the twelve on one side and spoke to them,
"Listen to me. We are now going up to Jerusalem and everything that has been written by the prophets about the Son of Man will come true. For he will be handed over to the heathen, and he is going to be jeered at and insulted and spat upon, and then they will flog him and kill him. But he will rise again on the third day."
But they did not understand any of this. His words were quite obscure to them and they had no idea of what he meant.

Revised Standard Version

26 Those who heard it said, "Then who can be
saved?" 27 But he said, "What is impossible
with men is possible with God." 28 And Peter
said, "Lo, we have left our homes and followed
you." 29 And he said to them, "Truly, I say to
you, there is no man who has left house or wife
or brothers or parents or children, for the sake
of the kingdom of God, 30 who will not receive
manifold more in this time, and in the age to
come eternal life."
31 And taking the twelve, he said to them,
"Behold, we are going up to Jerusalem, and
everything that is written of the Son of man by
the prophets will be accomplished. 32 For he will
be delivered to the Gentiles, and will be mocked
and shamefully treated and spit upon; 33 they
will scourge him and kill him, and on the third
day he will rise." 34 But they understood none
of these things; this saying was hid from them,
and they did not grasp what was said.

Jerusalem Bible

of God." 26 "In that case," said the listeners,
"who can be saved?" 27 "Things that are impossible for men," he replied, "are possible for
God."

The reward of renunciation

28 Then Peter said, "What about us? We left
all we had to follow you." 29 He said to them,
"I tell you solemnly, there is no one who has
left house, wife, brothers, parents or children
for the sake of the kingdom of God 30 who
will not be given repayment many times over
in this present time and, in the world to come,
eternal life."

Third prophecy of the Passion

31 Then taking the Twelve aside he said to
them, "Now we are going up to Jerusalem, and
everything that is written by the prophets about
the Son of Man is to come true. 32 For he will
be handed over to the pagans and will be
mocked, maltreated and spat on, 33 and when
they have scourged him they will put him to
death; and on the third day he will rise again."
34 But they could make nothing of this; what
he said was quite obscure to them, they had no
idea what it meant.

New English Bible

to enter the kingdom of God.' Those who heard asked, 'Then who can be saved?' He answered, 'What is impossible for men is possible for God.'
Peter said, 'We here have left our belongings to become your followers.' Jesus said, 'I tell you this: there is no one who has given up home, or wife, brothers, parents, or children, for the sake of the kingdom of God, who will not be repaid many times over in this age, and in the age to come have eternal life.'

Challenge to Jerusalem

He took the Twelve aside and said, 'We are now going up to Jerusalem; and all that was written by the prophets will come true for the Son of Man. He will be handed over to the foreign power. He will be mocked, maltreated, and spat upon. They will flog him and kill him. And on the third day he will rise again.' But they understood nothing of all this; they did not grasp what he was talking about; its meaning was concealed from them.

King James Version

35 And it came to pass, that as he was come nigh unto Jericho, a certain blind man sat by the way side begging: 36And hearing the multitude pass by, he asked what it meant. 37And they told him, that Jesus of Nazareth passeth by. 38And he cried, saying, Jesus, *thou* Son of David, have mercy on me. 39And they which went before rebuked him, that he should hold his peace: but he cried so much the more, *Thou* Son of David, have mercy on me. 40And Jesus stood, and commanded him to be brought unto him: and when he was come near, he asked him, 41 Saying, What wilt thou that I shall do unto thee? And he said, Lord, that I may receive my sight. 42And Jesus said unto him, Receive thy sight: thy faith hath saved thee. 43And immediately he received his sight, and followed him, glorifying God: and all the people, when they saw *it*, gave praise unto God.

19 And *Jesus* entered and passed through Jericho. 2And, behold, *there was* a man named Zaccheus, which was the chief among the publicans, and he was rich. 3And he sought to see Jesus who he was; and could not for the

Living Bible

35 As they approached Jericho, a blind man was sitting beside the road, begging from travelers. 36 When he heard the noise of a crowd going past, he asked what was happening. 37 He was told that Jesus from Nazareth was going by, 38 so he began shouting, "Jesus, Son of David, have mercy on me!"

39 The crowds ahead of Jesus tried to hush the man, but he only yelled the louder, "Son of David, have mercy on me!"

40 When Jesus arrived at the spot, he stopped. "Bring the blind man over here," he said. 41 Then Jesus asked the man, "What do you want?"

"Lord," he pleaded, "I want to see!"

42 And Jesus said, "All right, begin seeing! Your faith has healed you."

43 And instantly the man could see, and followed Jesus, praising God. And all who saw it happen praised God too.

19 As Jesus was passing through Jericho, a man named Zacchaeus, one of the most influential Jews in the Roman tax-collecting business (and, of course, a very rich man), 3 tried to get a look at Jesus, but he was too short to

Today's English Version

Jesus heals a blind beggar

35 Jesus was coming near Jericho, and a certain blind man was sitting by the road, begging. 36 When he heard the crowd passing by he asked, "What is this?"

37 "Jesus of Nazareth is passing by," they told him.

38 He cried out, "Jesus! Son of David! Have mercy on me!"

39 The people in front scolded him and told him to be quiet. But he shouted even more loudly, "Son of David! Have mercy on me!"

40 So Jesus stopped and ordered that the blind man be brought to him. When he came near, Jesus asked him, 41 "What do you want me to do for you?"

"Sir," he answered, "I want to see again."

42 Then Jesus said to him, "See! Your faith has made you well."

43 At once he was able to see, and he followed Jesus, giving thanks to God. When the crowd saw it, they all praised God.

Jesus and Zacchaeus

19 Jesus went on into Jericho and was passing through. 2 There was a chief tax collector there, named Zacchaeus, who was rich. 3 He was trying to see who Jesus was, but he was a little man and could not see Jesus because of the

New International Version

A blind beggar receives his sight

35 As Jesus approached Jericho, a blind man was sitting by the roadside begging. 36 When he heard the crowd going by, he asked what was happening. 37 They told him, "Jesus of Nazareth is passing by."

38 He called out, "Jesus, Son of David, have mercy on me!"

39 Those who led the way rebuked him and told him to be quiet, but he shouted all the more, "Son of David, have mercy on me!"

40 Jesus stopped and ordered the man to be brought to him. When he came near, Jesus asked him, 41 "What do you want me to do for you?"

"Lord, I want to see," he replied.

42 Jesus said to him, "Receive your sight; your faith has healed you." 43 Immediately he received his sight and followed Jesus, praising God. When all the people saw it, they also praised God.

Zacchaeus the tax collector

19 Jesus entered Jericho and was passing through. 2A man was there by the name of Zacchaeus; he was a chief tax collector and was wealthy. 3 He wanted to see who Jesus was, but being a short man he could not, because of

Phillips Modern English

18.35 On the way to Jericho he heals a blind beggar

Then, as he was approaching Jericho, it happened that there was a blind man sitting by the roadside, begging. He heard the crowd passing and enquired what it was all about. And they told him, "Jesus the man from Nazareth is going past you." So he shouted out,

"Jesus, Son of David, have pity on me!"

Those who were in front tried to hush his cries. But that made him call out all the more,

"Son of David, have pity on me!"

So Jesus stood quite still and ordered the man to be brought to him. And when he was quite close, he said to him,

"What do you want me to do for you?"

"Lord, make me see again," he cried.

"You can see again! Your faith has cured you," returned Jesus.

And his sight was restored at once, and he followed Jesus, praising God. All the people who saw it thanked God too.

19.1 The chief tax-collector is converted to faith in Jesus

Then he went into Jericho and was making his way through it. And here we find a wealthy man called Zacchaeus, a chief collector of taxes, wanting to see what sort of person Jesus was. But the crowd prevented him from doing so,

Revised Standard Version

35 As he drew near to Jericho, a blind man was sitting by the roadside begging; 36 and hearing a multitude going by, he inquired what this meant. 37 They told him, "Jesus of Nazareth is passing by." 38 And he cried, "Jesus, Son of David, have mercy on me!" 39 And those who were in front rebuked him, telling him to be silent; but he cried out all the more, "Son of David, have mercy on me!" 40 And Jesus stopped, and commanded him to be brought to him; and when he came near, he asked him, 41 "What do you want me to do for you?" He said, "Lord, let me receive my sight." 42 And Jesus said to him, "Receive your sight; your faith has made you well." 43 And immediately he received his sight and followed him, glorifying God; and all the people, when they saw it, gave praise to God.

19 He entered Jericho and was passing through. 2 And there was a man named Zacchaeus; he was a chief tax collector, and rich. 3 And he sought to see who Jesus was, but could not, on account of the crowd, because he

Jerusalem Bible

Entering Jericho: the blind man

35 Now as he drew near to Jericho there was a blind man sitting at the side of the road begging. 36 When he heard the crowd going past he asked what it was all about, 37 and they told him that Jesus the Nazarene was passing by. 38 So he called out, "Jesus, Son of David, have pity on me." 39 The people in front scolded him and told him to keep quiet, but he shouted all the louder, "Son of David, have pity on me." 40 Jesus stopped and ordered them to bring the man to him, and when he came up, asked him, 41 "What do you want me to do for you?" "Sir," he replied, "let me see again." 42 Jesus said to him, "Receive your sight. Your faith has saved you." 43 And instantly his sight returned and he followed him praising God, and all the people who saw it gave praise to God for what had happened.

Zacchaeus

19 He entered Jericho and was going through the town 2 when a man whose name was Zacchaeus made his appearance; he was one of the senior tax collectors and a wealthy man. 3 He was anxious to see what kind of man Jesus was, but he was too short and could not see

New English Bible

As he approached Jericho a blind man sat at the roadside begging. Hearing a crowd going past, he asked what was happening. They told him, 'Jesus of Nazareth is passing by.' Then he shouted out, 'Jesus, Son of David, have pity on me.' The people in front told him to hold his tongue; but he called out all the more, 'Son of David, have pity on me.' Jesus stopped and ordered the man to be brought to him. When he came up he asked him, 'What do you want me to do for you?' 'Sir, I want my sight back', he answered. Jesus said to him, 'Have back your sight; your faith has cured you.' He recovered his sight instantly; and he followed Jesus, praising God. And all the people gave praise to God for what they had seen.

19 Entering Jericho he made his way through the city. There was a man there named Zacchaeus; he was superintendent of taxes and very rich. He was eager to see what Jesus looked like; but, being a little man, he could not see

King James Version

press, because he was little of stature. 4And he ran before, and climbed up into a sycamore tree to see him; for he was to pass that *way*. 5And when Jesus came to the place, he looked up, and saw him, and said unto him, Zaccheus, make haste, and come down; for to day I must abide at thy house. 6And he made haste, and came down, and received him joyfully. 7And when they saw *it*, they all murmured, saying, That he was gone to be guest with a man that is a sinner. 8And Zaccheus stood, and said unto the Lord; Behold, Lord, the half of my goods I give to the poor; and if I have taken any thing from any man by false accusation, I restore *him* fourfold. 9And Jesus said unto him, This day is salvation come to this house, forasmuch as he also is a son of Abraham. 10 For the Son of man is come to seek and to save that which was lost. 11And as they heard these things, he added and spake a parable, because he was nigh to Jerusalem, and because they thought that the kingdom of God should immediately appear. 12 He said therefore, A certain nobleman went into a far country to receive for himself a kingdom,

Living Bible

see over the crowds. 4 So he ran ahead and climbed into a sycamore tree beside the road, to watch from there.

5 When Jesus came by he looked up at Zacchaeus and called him by name! "Zacchaeus!" he said. "Quick! Come down! For I am going to be a guest in your home today!"

6 Zacchaeus hurriedly climbed down and took Jesus to his house in great excitement and joy.

7 But the crowds were displeased. "He has gone to be the guest of a notorious sinner," they grumbled.

8 Meanwhile, Zacchaeus stood before the Lord and said, "Sir, from now on I will give half my wealth to the poor, and if I find I have overcharged anyone on his taxes, I will penalize myself by giving him back four times as much!"

9, 10 Jesus told him, "This shows[a] that salvation has come to this home today. This man was one of the lost sons of Abraham, and I, the Messiah,[b] have come to search for and to save such souls as his."

11 And because Jesus was nearing Jerusalem, he told a story to correct the impression that the Kingdom of God would begin right away.

12 "A nobleman living in a certain province was called away to the distant capital of the empire to be crowned king of his province.

[*a*] Implied. [*b*] Literally, "the Son of Man."

Today's English Version

crowd. 4 So he ran ahead of the crowd and climbed a sycamore tree to see Jesus, who would be going that way. 5 When Jesus came to that place, he looked up and said to Zacchaeus, "Hurry down, Zacchaeus, because I must stay in your house today."

6 Zacchaeus hurried down and welcomed him with great joy. 7All the people who saw it started grumbling, "This man has gone as a guest to the home of a sinner!"

8 Zacchaeus stood up and said to the Lord, "Listen, sir! I will give half my belongings to the poor; and if I have cheated anyone, I will pay him back four times as much."

9 Jesus said to him, "Salvation has come to this house today; this man, also, is a descendant of Abraham. 10 For the Son of Man came to seek and to save the lost."

The parable of the gold coins

11 While the people were listening to this, Jesus continued and told them a parable. He was now almost at Jerusalem, and they supposed that the Kingdom of God was just about to appear. 12 So he said, "There was a nobleman who went to a country far away to be made king and then

New International Version

the crowd. 4 So he ran ahead and climbed a sycamore-fig tree to see him, since Jesus was coming that way.

5 When Jesus reached the spot, he looked up and said to him, "Zacchaeus, come down immediately. I must stay at your house today." 6 So he came down at once and welcomed him gladly.

7 All the people saw this and began to mutter, "He has gone to be the guest of a sinner."

8 But Zacchaeus stood up and said to the Lord, "Look, Lord! Here and now I give half of my possessions to the poor, and if I have cheated anybody out of anything, I will pay back four times the amount."

9 Jesus said to him, "Today salvation has come to this house, because this man, too, is a son of Abraham. 10 For the Son of Man came to seek and to save what was lost."

The parable of the ten minas

11 While they were listening to this, he went on to tell them a parable, because he was near Jerusalem and the people thought that the kingdom of God was going to appear at once. 12 He said: "A man of noble birth went to a distant country to have himself appointed king and then

Phillips Modern English

for he was very short. So he ran ahead and climbed up into a sycamore tree to get a view of Jesus as he was heading that way. When Jesus reached the spot, he looked up and said to him,

"Zacchaeus, hurry up and come down. I must be your guest today."

So Zacchaeus hurriedly climbed down and gladly welcomed him. But the bystanders muttered their disapproval, saying,

"Now he has gone to stay with a real sinner."

But Zacchaeus himself stood and said to the Lord,

"Look, sir, I will give half my property to the poor. And if I have swindled anybody out of anything I will pay him back four times as much."

Jesus said to him,

"Salvation has come to this house today! Zacchaeus is a descendant of Abraham, and it was the lost that the Son of Man came to seek—and to save."

19.11 Life requires courage, and is hard on those who dare not use their gifts

Then as the crowd still listened attentively, Jesus went on to give them this parable. For the fact that he was nearing Jerusalem made them imagine that the kingdom of God was on the point of appearing.

"Once upon a time a man of good family went abroad to accept a kingdom and then re-

Revised Standard Version

was small of stature. 4 So he ran on ahead and
climbed up into a sycamore tree to see him, for
he was to pass that way. 5 And when Jesus came
to the place, he looked up and said to him,
"Zacchaeus, make haste and come down; for I
must stay at your house today." 6 So he made
haste and came down, and received him joyfully. 7 And when they saw it they all murmured, "He has gone in to be the guest of a
man who is a sinner." 8 And Zacchaeus stood
and said to the Lord, "Behold, Lord, the half of
my goods I give to the poor; and if I have defrauded any one of anything, I restore it fourfold." 9 And Jesus said to him, "Today salvation
has come to this house, since he also is a son of
Abraham. 10 For the Son of man came to seek
and to save the lost."
11 As they heard these things, he proceeded to
tell a parable, because he was near to Jerusalem,
and because they supposed that the kingdom of
God was to appear immediately. 12 He said
therefore, "A nobleman went into a far country

Jerusalem Bible

him for the crowd; 4 so he ran ahead and
climbed a sycamore tree to catch a glimpse of
Jesus who was to pass that way. 5 When Jesus
reached the spot he looked up and spoke to him:
"Zacchaeus, come down. Hurry, because I must
stay at your house today." 6 And he hurried
down and welcomed him joyfully. 7 They all
complained when they saw what was happening. "He has gone to stay at a sinner's house,"
they said. 8 But Zacchaeus stood his ground and
said to the Lord, "Look, sir, I am going to give
half my property to the poor, and if I have
cheated anybody I will pay him back four times
the amount."[c] 9 And Jesus said to him, "Today
salvation has come to this house, because this
man too is a son of Abraham[d]; 10 for the Son
of Man has come to seek out and save what was
lost."

Parable of the pounds

11 While the people were listening to this he
went on to tell a parable, because he was near
Jerusalem and they imagined that the kingdom
of God was going to show itself then and there.
12 Accordingly he said, "A man of noble birth
went to a distant country to be appointed king

[c] I.e., at the highest rate known to Jewish law (Ex. 21:37) or the rate imposed by Roman law on convicted thieves. [d] Although he belongs to a profession generally ranked with pagans.

New English Bible

him for the crowd. So he ran on ahead and climbed a sycomore-tree in order to see him, for he was to pass that way. When Jesus came to the place, he looked up and said, 'Zacchaeus, be quick and come down; I must come and stay with you today.' He climbed down as fast as he could and welcomed him gladly. At this there was a general murmur of disapproval. 'He has gone in', they said, 'to be the guest of a sinner.' But Zacchaeus stood there and said to the Lord, 'Here and now, sir, I give half my possessions to charity; and if I have cheated anyone, I am ready to repay him four times over.' Jesus said to him, 'Salvation has come to this house today! —for this man too is a son of Abraham, and the Son of Man has come to seek and save what is lost.'

While they were listening to this, he went on to tell them a parable, because he was now close to Jerusalem and they thought the reign of God might dawn at any moment. He said, 'A man of noble birth went on a long journey abroad, to

King James Version

and to return. 13And he called his ten servants, and delivered them ten pounds, and said unto them, Occupy till I come. 14 But his citizens hated him, and sent a message after him, saying, We will not have this *man* to reign over us. 15And it came to pass, that when he was returned, having received the kingdom, then he commanded these servants to be called unto him, to whom he had given the money, that he might know how much every man had gained by trading. 16 Then came the first, saying, Lord, thy pound hath gained ten pounds. 17And he said unto him, Well, thou good servant: because thou hast been faithful in a very little, have thou authority over ten cities. 18And the second came, saying, Lord, thy pound hath gained five pounds. 19And he said likewise to him, Be thou also over five cities. 20And another came, saying, Lord, behold, *here is* thy pound, which I have kept laid up in a napkin: 21 For I feared thee, because thou art an austere man: thou takest up that thou layedst not down, and reapest that thou didst not sow. 22And he saith unto him, Out of thine own mouth will I judge thee, *thou* wicked servant. Thou knewest that I was an austere man, taking up that I laid not down, and reaping that I did not sow: 23 Wherefore then gavest not thou my money into the bank, that at my coming I might have required mine own with usury? 24And he said unto them that stood by, Take from him the pound, and give *it*

Living Bible

13 Before he left he called together ten assistants and gave them each $2,000 to invest while he was gone. 14 But some of his people hated him and sent him their declaration of independence, stating that they had rebelled and would not acknowledge him as their king.

15 "Upon his return he called in the men to whom he had given the money, to find out what they had done with it, and what their profits were.

16 "The first man reported a tremendous gain—ten times as much as the original amount!

17 " 'Fine!' the king exclaimed. 'You are a good man. You have been faithful with the little I entrusted to you, and as your reward, you shall be governor of ten cities.'

18 "The next man also reported a splendid gain—five times the original amount.

19 " 'All right!' his master said. 'You can be governor over five cities.'

20 "But the third man brought back only the money he had started with. 'I've kept it safe,' he said, 21 'because I was afraid [you would demand my profits[a]], for you are a hard man to deal with, taking what isn't yours and even confiscating the crops that others plant.' 22 'You vile and wicked slave,' the king roared. 'Hard, am I? That's exactly how I'll be toward you! If you knew so much about me and how tough I am, 23 then why didn't you deposit the money in the bank so that I could at least get some interest on it?'

24 "Then turning to the others standing by he ordered, 'Take the money away from him and give it to the man who earned the most.'

[*a*] Implied.

Today's English Version

come back home. 13 Before he left, he called his ten servants and gave them each a gold coin and told them, 'See what you can earn with this while I am gone.' 14 Now, his countrymen hated him, and so they sent messengers after him to say, 'We don't want this man to be our king.'

15 "The nobleman was made king and came back. At once he ordered his servants, to whom he had given the money, to appear before him in order to find out how much they had earned. 16 The first one came and said, 'Sir, I have earned ten gold coins with the one you gave me.' 17 'Well done,' he said; 'you are a good servant! Since you were faithful in small matters, I will put you in charge of ten cities.' 18 The second servant came and said, 'Sir, I have earned five gold coins with the one you gave me.' 19 To this one he said, 'You will be in charge of five cities.' 20Another servant came and said, 'Sir, here is your gold coin; I kept it hidden in a handkerchief. 21 I was afraid of you, because you are a hard man. You take what is not yours, and reap what you did not plant.' 22 He said to him, 'You bad servant! I will use your own words to condemn you! You know that I am a hard man, taking what is not mine and reaping what I have not planted. 23 Well, then, why didn't you put my money in the bank? Then I would have received it back with interest when I returned.' 24 Then he said to those who were standing there, 'Take the gold coin away from him and give it to the

New International Version

to return. 13 So he called ten of his servants and gave them ten minas.[l] 'Put this money to work,' he said, 'until I come back.'

14 "But his subjects hated him and sent a delegation after him to say, 'We don't want this man to be our king.'

15 "He was made king, however, and returned home. Then he sent for the servants to whom he had given the money, in order to find out what they had gained with it.

16 "The first one came and said, 'Sir, your mina has earned ten more.'

17 " 'Well done, my good servant!' his master replied. 'Because you have been trustworthy in a very small matter, take charge of ten cities.'

18 "The second came and said, 'Sir, your mina has earned five more.'

19 "His master answered, 'You take charge of five cities.'

20 "Then another servant came and said, 'Sir, here is your mina; I have kept it laid away in a piece of cloth. 21 I was afraid of you, because you are a hard man. You take out what you did not put in and reap what you did not sow.'

22 "His master replied, 'I will judge you by your own words, you wicked servant! You knew, did you, that I am a hard man, taking out what I did not put in, and reaping what I did not sow? 23 Why then didn't you put my money on deposit, so that when I came back, I could have collected it with interest?'

24 "Then he said to those standing by, 'Take his mina away from him and give it to the one who has ten minas.'

[*l*] A mina was about three months' wages.

Phillips Modern English

turn. He summoned ten of his servants and gave them a pound each, with the words, 'Use this money to trade with until I come back.' But the citizens detested him and they sent a delegation after him, to say, 'We will not have this man to be our king.' Then later, when he had received his kingdom, he returned and gave orders for the servants to whom he had given the money to be called to him, so that he could find out what profit they had made. The first came into his presence, and said, 'Sire, your pound has made ten pounds more.' 'Splendid, my good fellow,' he said, 'since you have proved trustworthy over this small amount, I am going to put you in charge of ten towns.' The second came in and said, 'Sire, your pound has made five pounds.' And he said to him, 'Good, you're appointed governor of five towns.' When the last came, he said, 'Sire, here is your pound, which I have been keeping wrapped up in a handkerchief. I have been scared—I know you're a hard man, getting something for nothing and reaping where you never sowed.' To which he replied, 'You scoundrel, your own words condemn you! You knew perfectly well, did you, that I am a hard man who gets something for nothing and reaps where he never sowed? Then why didn't you put my money into the bank, and then when I returned I could have had it back with interest?' Then he said to those who were standing by, 'Take away his pound and give it to the fellow who has ten.'

Revised Standard Version

to receive a kingdom and then return. 13 Calling ten of his servants, he gave them ten pounds,[e] and said to them, 'Trade with these till I come.' 14 But his citizens hated him and sent an embassy after him, saying, 'We do not want this man to reign over us.' 15 When he returned, having received the kingdom, he commanded these servants, to whom he had given the money, to be called to him, that he might know what they had gained by trading. 16 The first came before him, saying, 'Lord, your pound has made ten pounds more.' 17 And he said to him, 'Well done, good servant! Because you have been faithful in a very little, you shall have authority over ten cities.' 18 And the second came, saying, 'Lord, your pound has made five pounds.' 19 And he said to him, 'And you are to be over five cities.' 20 Then another came, saying, 'Lord, here is your pound, which I kept laid away in a napkin; 21 for I was afraid of you, because you are a severe man; you take up what you did not lay down, and reap what you did not sow.' 22 He said to him, 'I will condemn you out of your own mouth, you wicked servant! You knew that I was a severe man, taking up what I did not lay down and reaping what I did not sow? 23 Why then did you not put my money into the bank, and at my coming I should have collected it with interest?' 24 And he said to those who stood by, 'Take the pound from him, and

[e] The mina, rendered here by *pound,* was about three months' wages for a laborer.

Jerusalem Bible

and afterward return.[e] 13 He summoned ten of his servants and gave them ten pounds. 'Do business with these,' he told them, 'until I get back.' 14 But his compatriots detested him and sent a delegation to follow him with this message, 'We do not want this man to be our king.'

15 "Now on his return, having received his appointment as king, he sent for those servants to whom he had given the money, to find out what profit each had made. 16 The first came in and said, 'Sir, your one pound has brought in ten.' 17 'Well done, my good servant!' he replied. 'Since you have proved yourself faithful in a very small thing, you shall have the government of ten cities.' 18 Then came the second and said, 'Sir, your one pound has made five.' 19 To this one also he said, 'And you shall be in charge of five cities.' 20 Next came the other and said, 'Sir, here is your pound. I put it away safely in a piece of linen 21 because I was afraid of you; for you are an exacting man: you pick up what you have not put down and reap what you have not sown.' 22 'You wicked servant!' he said. 'Out of your own mouth I condemn you. So you knew I was an exacting man, picking up what I have not put down and reaping what I have not sown? 23 Then why did you not put my money in the bank? On my return I could have drawn it out with interest.' 24 And he said to those standing by, 'Take the pound from him and give it to

[e] Probably alluding to the journey of Archelaus to Rome in 4 B.C. to have the will of Herod the Great confirmed in his favor. A deputation of Jews followed him there to contest his claim.

New English Bible

be appointed king and then return. But first he called ten of his servants and gave them a pound each, saying, "Trade with this while I am away." His fellow-citizens hated him, and they sent a delegation on his heels to say, "We do not want this man as our king." However, back he came as king, and sent for the servants to whom he had given the money, to see what profit each had made. The first came and said, "Your pound, sir, has made ten more." "Well done," he replied; "you are a good servant. You have shown yourself trustworthy in a very small matter, and you shall have charge of ten cities." The second came and said, "Your pound, sir, has made five more"; and he also was told, "You too, take charge of five cities." The third came and said, "Here is your pound, sir; I kept it put away in a handkerchief. I was afraid of you, because you are a hard man: you draw out what you never put in and reap what you did not sow." "You rascal!" he replied; "I will judge you by your own words. You knew, did you, that I am a hard man, that I draw out what I never put in, and reap what I did not sow? Then why did you not put my money on deposit, and I could have claimed it with interest when I came back?" Turning to his attendants he said, "Take the pound from him and give it to the man with

King James Version

to him that hath ten pounds. 25 (And they said
unto him, Lord, he hath ten pounds.) 26 For I
say unto you, That unto every one which hath
shall be given; and from him that hath not,
even that he hath shall be taken away from him.
27 But those mine enemies, which would not
that I should reign over them, bring hither, and
slay *them* before me.

28 And when he had thus spoken, he went before, ascending up to Jerusalem. 29 And it came
to pass, when he was come nigh to Bethphage
and Bethany, at the mount called *the mount* of
Olives, he sent two of his disciples, 30 Saying, Go
ye into the village over against *you;* in the
which at your entering ye shall find a colt tied,
whereon yet never man sat: loose him, and bring
him hither. 31 And if any man ask you, Why do
ye loose *him?* thus shall ye say unto him, Because the Lord hath need of him. 32 And they
that were sent went their way, and found even
as he had said unto them. 33 And as they were
loosing the colt, the owners thereof said unto
them, Why loose ye the colt? 34 And they said,
The Lord hath need of him. 35 And they brought
him to Jesus: and they cast their garments upon
the colt, and they set Jesus thereon. 36 And as
he went, they spread their clothes in the way.
37 And when he was come nigh, even now at the
descent of the mount of Olives, the whole multitude of the disciples began to rejoice and praise

Living Bible

25 " 'But, sir,' they said, 'he has enough already!'

26 " 'Yes,' the king replied, 'but it is always
true that those who have, get more, and those
who have little, soon lose even that. 27 And now
about these enemies of mine who revolted—
bring them in and execute them before me.' "

28 After telling this story, Jesus went on towards Jerusalem, walking along ahead of his
disciples. 29 As they came to the towns of Bethphage and Bethany, on the Mount of Olives, he
sent two disciples ahead, 30 with instructions to
go to the next village, and as they entered they
were to look for a donkey tied beside the road.
It would be a colt, not yet broken for riding.

"Untie him," Jesus said, "and bring him here.
31 And if anyone asks you what you are doing,
just say, 'The Lord needs him.' "

32 They found the colt as Jesus said, 33 and
sure enough, as they were untying it, the owners
demanded an explanation.

"What are you doing?" they asked. "Why are
you untying our colt?"

34 And the disciples simply replied, "The
Lord needs him!" 35 So they brought the colt to
Jesus and threw some of their clothing across its
back for Jesus to sit on.

36, 37 Then the crowds spread out their robes
along the road ahead of him, and as they
reached the place where the road started down
from the Mount of Olives, the whole procession

Today's English Version

servant who has ten coins.' 25 They said to him,
'Sir, he already has ten coins!' 26 'I tell you,' he
replied, 'that to every one who has, even more
will be given; but the one who does not have,
even the little that he has will be taken away
from him. 27 Now, as for these enemies of mine
who did not want me to be their king: bring
them here and kill them before me!' "

The triumphant entry into Jerusalem

28 Jesus said this and then went on to Jerusalem ahead of them. 29 As he came near Bethphage and Bethany, at the Mount of Olives, he
sent two disciples ahead 30 with these instructions,
"Go to the village there ahead of you; as you
go in you will find a colt tied up that has never
been ridden. Untie it and bring it here. 31 If
someone asks you, 'Why are you untying it?' tell
him, 'The Master needs it.' "

32 They went on their way and found everything just as Jesus had told them. 33 As they were
untying the colt, its owners said to them, "Why
are you untying it?"

34 "The Master needs it," they answered,
35 and took the colt to Jesus. Then they threw
their cloaks over the animal and helped Jesus
get on. 36 As he rode on, they spread their
cloaks on the road.

37 When he came near Jerusalem, at the place
where the road went down the Mount of Olives,
the large crowd of his disciples began to thank

New International Version

25 " 'Sir,' they said, 'he already has ten!'

26 "He replied, 'I tell you that to everyone
who has, more will be given, but as for the one
who has nothing, even what he has will be taken
away. 27 But those enemies of mine who did not
want me to be king over them—bring them here
and kill them in front of me.' "

The triumphal entry

28 After Jesus had said this, he went on ahead,
going up to Jerusalem. 29 As he approached
Bethphage and Bethany at the hill called the
Mount of Olives, he sent two of his disciples,
saying to them: 30 "Go to the village ahead of
you, and as you enter it, you will find a colt
tied there, which no one has ever ridden. Untie
it and bring it here. 31 If anyone asks you, 'Why
are you untying it?' tell him, 'The Lord needs
it.' "

32 Those who were sent went and found it
just as he had told them. 33 As they were untying the colt, its owners asked them, "Why are
you untying the colt?"

34 They replied, "The Lord needs it."

35 They brought it to Jesus, threw their cloaks
on the colt and put Jesus on it. 36 As he went
along, people spread their cloaks on the road.

37 When he came near the place where the
road goes down the Mount of Olives, the whole
crowd of disciples began joyfully to praise God

Phillips Modern English

" 'But, sire, he has ten pounds already,' they said to him. 'Yes,' he replied, 'and I tell you that the man who has something will get more given to him. But as for the man who has nothing, even his "nothing" will be taken away. And as for these enemies of mine who objected to my being their king, bring them here and execute them in my presence.' "

After these words, Jesus walked on ahead of them on his way up to Jerusalem.

19.29 Jesus arranges his own entrance into Jerusalem

Then as he was approaching Bethphage and Bethany, near the hill called the Mount of Olives, he sent off two of his disciples, telling them,

"Go into the village just ahead of you, and there you will find a colt tied, on which no one has ever yet ridden. Untie it and bring it here. And if anybody asks you, 'Why are you untying it?' just say, 'The Lord needs it.' "

So the messengers went off and found things just as he had told them. In fact, as they were untying the colt, the owners did say, "Why are you untying it?" and they replied, "The Lord needs it." So they brought it to Jesus and, throwing their cloaks upon the colt, mounted Jesus on its back. Then as he rode along, people spread out their coats in the roadway. And as he approached the city, where the road slopes down from the Mount of Olives, the whole crowd of his disciples joyfully shouted praises

Revised Standard Version

give it to him who has the ten pounds.' 25 (And
they said to him, 'Lord, he has ten pounds!')
26 'I tell you, that to every one who has will
more be given; but from him who has not, even
what he has will be taken away. 27 But as for
these enemies of mine, who did not want me to
reign over them, bring them here and slay them
before me.' "
28 And when he had said this, he went on
ahead, going up to Jerusalem. 29 When he drew
near to Bethphage and Bethany, at the mount
that is called Olivet, he sent two of the disciples,
30 saying, "Go into the village opposite, where
on entering you will find a colt tied, on which no
one has ever yet sat; untie it and bring it here.
31 If any one asks you, 'Why are you untying
it?' you shall say this, 'The Lord has need of
it.' " 32 So those who were sent went away and
found it as he had told them. 33 And as they
were untying the colt, its owners said to them,
"Why are you untying the colt?" 34 And they
said, "The Lord has need of it." 35 And they
brought it to Jesus, and throwing their garments
on the colt they set Jesus upon it. 36 And as he
rode along, they spread their garments on the
road. 37 As he was now drawing near, at the descent of the Mount of Olives, the whole multitude of the disciples began to rejoice and praise

Jerusalem Bible

the man who has ten pounds.' 25 And they said
to him, 'But, sir, he has ten pounds . . .' 26 'I
tell you, to everyone who has will be given
more; but from the man who has not, even what
he has will be taken away.
27 'But as for my enemies who did not want
me for their king, bring them here and execute
them in my presence.' "

V. The Jerusalem ministry

The Messiah enters Jerusalem

28 When he had said this he went on ahead,
going up to Jerusalem. 29 Now when he was
near Bethphage and Bethany, close by the
Mount of Olives as it is called, he sent two of
the disciples, telling them, 30 "Go off to the village opposite, and as you enter it you will find
a tethered colt that no one has yet ridden. Untie it and bring it here. 31 If anyone asks you,
'Why are you untying it?' you are to say this,
'The Master needs it.' " 32 The messengers went
off and found everything just as he had told
them. 33 As they were untying the colt, its owner
said, "Why are you untying that colt?" 34 and
they answered, "The Master needs it."
35 So they took the colt to Jesus, and throwing their garments over its back they helped
Jesus onto it. 36 As he moved off, people spread
their cloaks in the road, 37 and now, as he was
approaching the downward slope of the Mount
of Olives, the whole group of disciples joyfully

New English Bible

ten." "But, sir," they replied, "he has ten already." "I tell you," he went on, "the man who has will always be given more; but the man who has not will forfeit even what he has. But as for those enemies of mine who did not want me for their king, bring them here and slaughter them in my presence." '

With that Jesus went forward and began the ascent to Jerusalem. As he approached Bethphage and Bethany at the hill called Olivet, he sent two of the disciples with these instructions: 'Go to the village opposite; as you enter it you will find tethered there a colt which no one has yet ridden. Untie it and bring it here. If anyone asks why you are untying it, say, "Our Master needs it." ' The two went on their errand and found it as he had told them; and while they were untying the colt, its owners asked, 'Why are you untying that colt?' They answered, 'Our Master needs it.' So they brought the colt to Jesus.

Then they threw their cloaks on the colt, for Jesus to mount, and they carpeted the road with them as he went on his way. And now, as he approached the descent from the Mount of Olives, the whole company of his disciples in

King James Version

God with a loud voice for all the mighty works
that they had seen; 38 Saying, Blessed *be* the
King that cometh in the name of the Lord:
peace in heaven, and glory in the highest. 39And
some of the Pharisees from among the multitude
said unto him, Master, rebuke thy disciples.
40And he answered and said unto them, I tell
you that, if these should hold their peace, the
stones would immediately cry out.
41 And when he was come near, he beheld
the city, and wept over it, 42 Saying, If thou
hadst known, even thou, at least in this thy day,
the things *which belong* unto thy peace! but now
they are hid from thine eyes. 43 For the days
shall come upon thee, that thine enemies shall
cast a trench about thee, and compass thee
round, and keep thee in on every side, 44And
shall lay thee even with the ground, and thy
children within thee; and they shall not leave
in thee one stone upon another; because thou

Living Bible

began to shout and sing as they walked along,
praising God for all the wonderful miracles Jesus had done.
38 "God has given us a King!" they exulted.
"Long live the King! Let all heaven rejoice!
Glory to God in the highest heavens!"
39 But some of the Pharisees among the
crowd said, "Sir, rebuke your followers for saying things like that!"
40 He replied, "If they keep quiet, the stones
along the road will burst into cheers!"
41 But as they came closer to Jerusalem and
he saw the city ahead, he began to cry. 42 "Eternal peace was within your reach and you turned
it down," he wept, "and now it is too late.
43 Your enemies will pile up earth against your
walls and encircle you and close in on you,
44 and crush you to the ground, and your children within you; your enemies will not leave one
stone upon another—for you have rejected the
opportunity God offered you."

Today's English Version

God and praise him in loud voices for all the
great things that they had seen: 38 "God bless
the king who comes in the name of the Lord!
Peace in heaven, and glory to God!"
39 Then some of the Pharisees spoke up from
the crowd to Jesus. "Teacher," they said, "command your disciples to be quiet!"
40 Jesus answered, "If they keep quiet, I tell
you, the stones themselves will shout."

Jesus weeps over Jerusalem

41 He came closer to the city and when he
saw it he wept over it, 42 saying, "If you only
knew today what is needed for peace! But now
you cannot see it! 43 The days will come upon
you when your enemies will surround you with
barricades, blockade you, and close in on you
from every side. 44 They will completely destroy
you and the people within your walls; not a single
stone will they leave in its place, because you did
not recognize the time when God came to save
you!"

New International Version

in loud voices for all the miracles they had seen:
38 "Blessed is the king who comes in the name
of the Lord! [m]
Peace in heaven and glory in the highest!"
39 Some of the Pharisees in the crowd said to
Jesus, "Teacher, rebuke your disciples!"
40 "I tell you," he replied, "if they keep quiet,
the stones will cry out."
41 As he approached Jerusalem and saw the
city, he wept over it 42 and said, "If you, even
you, had only known on this day what would
bring you peace—but now it is hidden from your
eyes. 43 The days will come upon you when your
enemies will build an embankment against you
and encircle you and hem you in on every side.
44 They will dash you to the ground, you and
the children within your walls. They will not
leave one stone on another, because you did not
recognize the time of God's coming to you."

[*m*] Psalm 118:26.

Phillips Modern English

to God for all the marvellous things that they had seen done.

"God bless the king who comes in the name of the Lord!" they cried. "There is peace in Heaven and glory on high!"

There were some Pharisees in the crowd who said to Jesus,

"Master, restrain your disciples!"

To which he replied,

"I tell you that if they kept quiet, the very stones in the road would burst out cheering!"

19.41 The sight of the city moves him to tears

And as he came still nearer to the city, he caught sight of it and wept over it, saying,

"Ah, if you only knew, even at this eleventh hour, on what your peace depends—but you cannot see it. The time is coming when your enemies will encircle you with ramparts, surrounding you and hemming you in on every side. And they will hurl you and all your children to the ground—yes, they will not leave you one stone standing upon another—all because you did not recognise when God Himself was visiting you!"

Revised Standard Version

God with a loud voice for all the mighty works
that they had seen, 38 saying, "Blessed is the
King who comes in the name of the Lord! Peace
in heaven and glory in the highest!" 39 And some
of the Pharisees in the multitude said to him,
"Teacher, rebuke your disciples." 40 He answered, "I tell you, if these were silent, the very stones would cry out."

41 And when he drew near and saw the city
he wept over it, 42 saying, "Would that even today you knew the things that make for peace!
But now they are hid from your eyes. 43 For the
days shall come upon you, when your enemies
will cast up a bank about you and surround
you, and hem you in on every side, 44 and dash
you to the ground, you and your children within
you, and they will not leave one stone upon
another in you; because you did not know the
time of your visitation."

Jerusalem Bible

began to praise God at the top of their voices
for all the miracles they had seen. 38 They cried
out:

"Blessings on the King who comes,
in the name of the Lord!
Peace in heaven
and glory in the highest heavens!"

Jesus defends his disciples for acclaiming him

39 Some Pharisees in the crowd said to him,
"Master, check your disciples," 40 but he answered, "I tell you, if these keep silence the stones will cry out."

Lament for Jerusalem

41 As he drew near and came in sight of the
city he shed tears over it 42 and said, "If you
in your turn had only understood on this day
the message of peace! But, alas, it is hidden
from your eyes! 43 Yes, a time is coming when
your enemies will raise fortifications all around
you, when they will encircle you and hem you
in on every side; 44 they will dash you and the
children inside your walls to the ground; they
will leave not one stone standing on another
within you—and all because you did not recognize your opportunity when God offered it!"

New English Bible

their joy began to sing aloud the praises of God for all the great things they had seen:

'Blessings on him who comes as king in the name of the Lord!
Peace in heaven, glory in highest heaven!'

Some Pharisees who were in the crowd said to him, 'Master, reprimand your disciples.' He answered, 'I tell you, if my disciples keep silence the stones will shout aloud.'

When he came in sight of the city, he wept over it and said, 'If only you had known, on this great day, the way that leads to peace! But no; it is hidden from your sight. For a time will come upon you, when your enemies will set up siege-works against you; they will encircle you and hem you in at every point; they will bring you to the ground, you and your children within your walls, and not leave you one stone standing on another, because you did not recognize God's moment when it came.'

King James Version

knewest not the time of thy visitation. 45And he went into the temple, and began to cast out them that sold therein, and them that bought; 46 Saying unto them, It is written, My house is the house of prayer; but ye have made it a den of thieves. 47And he taught daily in the temple. But the chief priests and the scribes and the chief of the people sought to destroy him, 48And could not find what they might do: for all the people were very attentive to hear him.

20 And it came to pass, *that* on one of those days, as he taught the people in the temple, and preached the gospel, the chief priests and the scribes came upon *him* with the elders, 2And spake unto him, saying, Tell us, by what authority doest thou these things? or who is he that gave thee this authority? 3And he answered and said unto them, I will also ask you one thing; and answer me: 4 The baptism of John,

Living Bible

45 Then he entered the Temple and began to drive out the merchants from their stalls, 46 saying to them, "The Scriptures declare, 'My Temple is a place of prayer; but you have turned it into a den of thieves.'"

47 After that he taught daily in the Temple, but the chief priests and other religious leaders and the business community[c] were trying to find some way to get rid of him. 48 But they could think of nothing, for he was a hero to the people—they hung on every word he said.

20 On one of those days when he was teaching and preaching the Good News in the Temple, he was confronted by the chief priests and other religious leaders and councilmen. 2 They demanded to know by what authority he had driven out the merchants from the Temple.

3 "I'll ask you a question before I answer," he replied. 4 "Was John sent by God, or was he

[c] Literally, "the leading men among the people."

Today's English Version

Jesus goes to the temple

45 Jesus went into the temple and began to drive out the merchants, 46 saying to them, "It is written in the Scriptures that God said, 'My house will be called a house of prayer.' But you have turned it into a hideout for thieves!"

47 Jesus taught in the temple every day. The chief priests, the teachers of the Law, and the leaders of the people wanted to kill him, 48 but they could not find how to do it, because all the people kept listening to him, not wanting to miss a single word.

The question about Jesus' authority

20 One day, when Jesus was in the temple teaching the people and preaching the Good News, the chief priests and the teachers of the Law, together with the elders, came 2 and said to him, "Tell us, what right do you have to do these things? Who gave you the right to do them?"

3 Jesus answered them, "Now let me ask you a question. Tell me, 4 did John's right to baptize

New International Version

Jesus at the temple

45 Then he entered the temple area and began driving out those who were selling. 46 "It is written," he said to them, "'My house will be a house of prayer'[n]; but you have made it 'a den of robbers.'[o]"

47 Every day he was teaching at the temple. But the chief priests, the teachers of the law and the leaders among the people were trying to kill him. 48 Yet they could not find any way to do it, because all the people hung on his words.

The authority of Jesus questioned

20 One day as he was teaching the people in the temple courts and preaching the gospel, the chief priests and the teachers of the law, together with the elders, came up to him. 2 "Tell us by what authority you are doing these things," they said. "Who gave you this authority?"

3 He replied, "I will also ask you a question. Tell me, 4 John's baptism—was it from heaven,

[n] Isaiah 56:7. [o] Jer. 7:11.

Phillips Modern English

Then he went into the Temple, and began to throw out the traders there.

"It is written," he told them, "'My house shall be a house of prayer', but you have turned it into a thieves' kitchen!"

19.47 Jesus teaches daily in the Temple

Then day after day he was teaching inside the Temple. The chief priests, the scribes and the national leaders were all the time looking for an opportunity to destroy him, but they could not find any way to do it since all the people hung upon his words.

Then one day as he was teaching the people in the Temple, and preaching the gospel to them, the chief priests, the scribes and elders confronted him in a body and asked him this direct question,

"Tell us by whose authority you act as you do—who gave you such authority?"

"I have a question for you, too," replied Jesus. "John's baptism, now—tell me, did it come

Revised Standard Version

45 And he entered the temple and began to drive out those who sold, 46 saying to them, "It is written, 'My house shall be a house of prayer'; but you have made it a den of robbers."

47 And he was teaching daily in the temple. The chief priests and the scribes and the principal men of the people sought to destroy him; 48 but they did not find anything they could do, for all the people hung upon his words.

20 One day, as he was teaching the people in the temple and preaching the gospel, the chief priests and the scribes with the elders came up 2 and said to him, "Tell us by what authority you do these things, or who it is that gave you this authority." 3 He answered them, "I also will ask you a question; now tell me, 4 Was the bap-

Jerusalem Bible

The expulsion of the dealers from the Temple

45 Then he went into the Temple and began driving out those who were selling. 46 "According to scripture," he said, *"my house will be a house of prayer.*[f] But you have turned it into *a robbers' den."*[g]

Jesus teaches in the Temple

47 He taught in the Temple every day. The chief priests and the scribes, with the support of the leading citizens, tried to do away with him, 48 but they did not see how they could carry this out because the people as a whole hung on his words.

The Jews question the authority of Jesus

20 Now one day while he was teaching the people in the Temple and proclaiming the Good News, the chief priests and the scribes came up, together with the elders, 2 and spoke to him. "Tell us," they said, "what authority have you for acting like this? Or who is it that gave you this authority?" 3 "And I," replied Jesus, "will ask you a question. Tell me: 4 John's

[f] Is. 56:7. [g] Jr. 7:11.

New English Bible

Then he went into the temple and began driving out the traders, with these words: 'Scripture says, "My house shall be a house of prayer"; but you have made it a robbers' cave.'

Day by day he taught in the temple. And the chief priests and lawyers were bent on making an end of him, with the support of the leading citizens, but found they were helpless, because the people all hung upon his words.

20 One day, as he was teaching the people in the temple and telling them the good news, the priests and lawyers, and the elders with them, came upon him and accosted him. 'Tell us', they said, 'by what authority you are acting like this; who gave you this authority?' He answered them, 'I have a question to ask you too: tell me, was

King James Version

was it from heaven, or of men? 5And they reasoned with themselves, saying, If we shall say,
From heaven; he will say, Why then believed ye
him not? 6 But and if ye say, Of men; all the
people will stone us: for they be persuaded that
John was a prophet. 7And they answered, that
they could not tell whence *it was.* 8And Jesus
said unto them, Neither tell I you by what
authority I do these things. 9 Then began he to
speak to the people this parable; A certain man
planted a vineyard, and let it forth to husbandmen, and went into a far country for a long
time. 10And at the season he sent a servant to
the husbandmen, that they should give him of
the fruit of the vineyard: but the husbandmen
beat him, and sent *him* away empty. 11And again
he sent another servant: and they beat him also,
and entreated *him* shamefully, and sent *him*
away empty. 12And again he sent a third: and
they wounded him also, and cast *him* out.
13 Then said the lord of the vineyard, What shall
I do? I will send my beloved son: it may be they
will reverence *him* when they see him. 14 But
when the husbandmen saw him, they reasoned
among themselves, saying, This is the heir: come,

Living Bible

merely acting under his own authority?"
5 They talked it over among themselves. "If
we say his message was from heaven, then we
are trapped because he will ask, 'Then why
didn't you believe him?' 6 But if we say John
was not sent from God, the people will mob us,
for they are convinced that he was a prophet."
7 Finally they replied, "We don't know!"
8 And Jesus responded, "Then I won't answer your question either."
9 Now he turned to the people again and told
them this story: "A man planted a vineyard and
rented it out to some farmers, and went away to
a distant land to live for several years. 10 When
harvest time came, he sent one of his men to
the farm to collect his share of the crops. But
the tenants beat him up and sent him back
empty-handed. 11 Then he sent another, but the
same thing happened; he was beaten up and insulted and sent away without collecting. 12A
third man was sent and the same thing happened.
He, too, was wounded and chased away.
13 " 'What shall I do?' the owner asked himself. 'I know! I'll send my cherished son. Surely
they will show respect for him.'
14 "But when the tenants saw his son, they
said, 'This is our chance! This fellow will inherit
all the land when his father dies. Come on. Let's

Today's English Version

come from God or from men?"
5 They started to argue among themselves,
"What shall we say? If we say, 'From God,' he
will say, 'Why, then, did you not believe John?'
6 But if we say, 'From men,' this whole crowd
here will stone us, because they are convinced
that John was a prophet." 7 So they answered,
"We don't know where it came from."
8 And Jesus said to them, "Neither will I tell
you, then, by what right I do these things."

The parable of the tenants in the vineyard

9 Then Jesus told the people this parable, "A
man planted a vineyard, rented it out to tenants,
and then left home for a long time. 10 When the
time came for harvesting the grapes, he sent a
slave to the tenants to receive from them his
share of the harvest. But the tenants beat the
slave and sent him back without a thing. 11 So
he sent another slave; but the tenants beat him
also, treated him shamefully, and sent him back
without a thing. 12 Then he sent a third slave; the
tenants hurt him, too, and threw him out. 13 Then
the owner of the vineyard said, 'What shall I do?
I will send my own dear son; surely they will
respect him!' 14 But when the tenants saw him
they said to one another, 'This is the owner's
son. Let us kill him, and his property will be

New International Version

or from men?"
5 They discussed it among themselves and
said, "If we say, 'From heaven,' he will ask,
'Why didn't you believe him?' 6 But if we say,
'From men,' all the people will stone us, because
they are persuaded that John was a prophet."
7 So they answered, "We don't know where it
was from."
8 Jesus said, "Neither will I tell you by what
authority I am doing these things."

The parable of the tenants

9 He went on to tell the people this parable:
"A man planted a vineyard, rented it to some
farmers and went away for a long time. 10At
harvest time he sent a servant to the tenants so
they would give him some of the fruit of the
vineyard. But the tenants beat him and sent him
away empty-handed. 11 He sent another servant,
but that one also they beat and treated shamefully and sent away empty-handed. 12 He sent
still a third, and they wounded him and threw
him out.
13 "Then the owner of the vineyard said,
'What shall I do? I will send my son, whom I
love; perhaps they will respect him.'
14 "But when the tenants saw him, they
talked the matter over. 'This is the heir,' they

Phillips Modern English

from Heaven or was it purely human?"

At this they began arguing with each other, saying,

"If we say, 'from Heaven,' he will say to us, 'Then why didn't you believe in him?' but if we say it was purely human, this mob will stone us to death, for they are convinced that John was a prophet." So they replied that they did not know where it came from.

"Then," returned Jesus, "neither will I tell you by what authority I do what I am doing."

20.9 He tells the people a pointed story

Then he turned to the people and told them this parable:

"There was once a man who planted a vineyard, let it out to farm-workers, and went abroad for some time. Then, when the season arrived, he sent a servant to the farm-workers so that they could give him his share of the crop. But the farm-workers beat him up and sent him back empty-handed. So he sent another servant, and they beat him up as well, manhandling him disgracefully, and sent him back empty-handed. Then he sent a third servant, but after wounding him severely they threw him out. Then the owner of the vineyard said, 'What shall I do now? I will send them my son who is so dear to me. Perhaps they will respect him.' But when the farm-workers saw him, they talked the matter over with each other and said, 'This man is the heir—come on, let's kill him,

Revised Standard Version

tism of John from heaven or from men?" 5And
they discussed it with one another, saying, "If we
say, 'From heaven,' he will say, 'Why did you
not believe him?' 6 But if we say, 'From men,'
all the people will stone us; for they are convinced that John was a prophet." 7 So they answered that they did not know whence it was.
8And Jesus said to them, "Neither will I tell
you by what authority I do these things."
9 And he began to tell the people this parable: "A man planted a vineyard, and let it out
to tenants, and went into another country for a
long while. 10 When the time came, he sent a
servant to the tenants, that they should give him
some of the fruit of the vineyard; but the tenants beat him, and sent him away empty-handed.
11And he sent another servant; him also they
beat and treated shamefully, and sent him away
empty-handed. 12And he sent yet a third; this
one they wounded and cast out. 13 Then the
owner of the vineyard said, 'What shall I do? I
will send my beloved son; it may be they will
respect him.' 14 But when the tenants saw him,
they said to themselves, 'This is the heir; let us

Jerusalem Bible

baptism: did it come from heaven, or from
man?" 5And they argued it out this way among
themselves, "If we say from heaven, he will
say, 'Why did you refuse to believe him?'; 6 and
if we say from man, the people will all stone us,
for they are convinced that John was a prophet."
7 So their reply was that they did not know
where it came from. 8And Jesus said to them,
"Nor will I tell you my authority for acting like
this."

Parable of the wicked husbandmen

9 And he went on to tell the people this
parable: "A man planted a vineyard and leased
it to tenants, and went abroad for a long while.
10 When the time came, he sent a servant to the
tenants to get his share of the produce of the
vineyard from them. But the tenants thrashed
him, and sent him away empty-handed. 11 But
he persevered and sent a second servant; they
thrashed him too and treated him shamefully
and sent him away empty-handed. 12 He still
persevered and sent a third; they wounded this
one also, and threw him out. 13 Then the owner
of the vineyard said, 'What am I to do? I will
send them my dear son. Perhaps they will respect him.' 14 But when the tenants saw him
they put their heads together. 'This is the heir,'

New English Bible

the baptism of John from God or from men?' This set them arguing among themselves: 'If we say, "from God", he will say, "Why did you not believe him?" And if we say, "from men", the people will all stone us, for they are convinced that John was a prophet.' So they replied that they could not tell. And Jesus said to them, 'Then neither will I tell you by what authority I act.'

He went on to tell the people this parable: 'A man planted a vineyard, let it out to vine-growers, and went abroad for a long time. When the season came, he sent a servant to the tenants to collect from them his share of the produce; but the tenants thrashed him and sent him away empty-handed. He tried again and sent a second servant; but he also was thrashed, outrageously treated, and sent away empty-handed. He tried once more with a third; this one too they wounded and flung out. Then the owner of the vineyard said, "What am I to do? I will send my own dear son;[a] perhaps they will respect him." But when the tenants saw him they talked it over together. "This is the heir," they said;

[a] *Or* my only son.

King James Version

let us kill him, that the inheritance may be ours.
15 So they cast him out of the vineyard, and
killed *him*. What therefore shall the lord of the
vineyard do unto them? 16 He shall come and
destroy these husbandmen, and shall give the
vineyard to others. And when they heard *it*,
they said, God forbid. 17 And he beheld them,
and said, What is this then that is written, The
stone which the builders rejected, the same is become the head of the corner? 18 Whosoever shall
fall upon that stone shall be broken; but on
whomsoever it shall fall, it will grind him to
powder.
19 And the chief priests and the scribes the
same hour sought to lay hands on him; and they
feared the people: for they perceived that he
had spoken this parable against them. 20 And
they watched *him*, and sent forth spies, which
should feign themselves just men, that they
might take hold of his words, that so they might
deliver him unto the power and authority of the
governor. 21 And they asked him, saying, Master,
we know that thou sayest and teachest rightly,
neither acceptest thou the person *of any*, but
teachest the way of God truly: 22 Is it lawful for

Living Bible

kill him, and then it will be ours.' 15 So they
dragged him out of the vineyard and killed him.
"What do you think the owner will do? 16 I'll
tell you—he will come and kill them and rent
the vineyard to others."
"But they would never do a thing like that,"
his listeners protested.
17 Jesus looked at them and said, "Then what
does the Scripture mean where it says, 'The
Stone rejected by the builders was made the cornerstone'?" 18 And he added, "Whoever stumbles
over that Stone shall be broken; and those on
whom it falls will be crushed to dust."
19 When the chief priests and religious leaders
heard about this story he had told, they wanted
him arrested immediately, for they realized that
he was talking about them. They were the
wicked tenants in his illustration. But they were
afraid that if they themselves arrested him there
would be a riot. So they tried to get him to say
something that could be reported to the Roman
governor as reason for arrest by him.
20 Watching their opportunity, they sent secret agents pretending to be honest men. 21 They
said to Jesus, "Sir, we know what an honest
teacher you are. You always tell the truth and
don't budge an inch in the face of what others
think, but teach the ways of God. 22 Now tell

Today's English Version

ours!' 15 So they threw him out of the vineyard
and killed him.
"What, then, will the owner of the vineyard do
to the tenants?" Jesus asked. 16 "He will come
and kill those men, and turn over the vineyard
to other tenants."
When the people heard this they said, "Surely
not!"
17 Jesus looked at them and asked, "What,
then, does this scripture mean?

'The very stone which the builders rejected
turned out to be the most important stone.'

18 Everyone who falls on that stone will be cut
to pieces; and if the stone falls on someone, it
will crush him to dust."

The question about paying taxes

19 The teachers of the Law and the chief
priests tried to arrest Jesus on the spot, because
they knew that he had told this parable against
them; but they were afraid of the people. 20 So
they watched for the right time. They bribed
some men to pretend they were sincere, and sent
them to trap Jesus with questions, so they could
hand him over to the authority and power of the
Governor. 21 These spies said to Jesus, "Teacher,
we know that what you say and teach is right.
We know that you pay no attention to a man's
status, but teach the truth about God's will for
man. 22 Tell us, is it against our Law for us to

New International Version

said. 'Let's kill him, and the inheritance will be
ours.' 15 So they threw him out of the vineyard and killed him.
"What then will the owner of the vineyard do
to them? 16 He will come and kill those tenants
and give the vineyard to others."
When the people heard this, they said, "May
this never be!"
17 Jesus looked directly at them and asked,
"Then what is the meaning of that which is
written:
'The stone the builders rejected
has become the capstone' [p] ?
18 Everyone who falls on that stone will be
broken to pieces, but he on whom it falls will be
crushed."
19 The teachers of the law and the chief
priests looked for a way to arrest him immediately, because they knew he had spoken this
parable against them. But they were afraid of the
people.

Paying taxes to Caesar

20 Keeping a close watch on him, they sent
spies, who pretended to be honest. They hoped
to catch Jesus in something he said so that they
might hand him over to the power and authority of the governor. 21 So the spies questioned
him: "Teacher, we know that you speak and
teach what is right, and that you do not show
partiality but teach the way of God in accordance with the truth. 22 Is it right for us to pay

[p] Psalm 118:22.

Phillips Modern English

and the property will be ours!' And they threw him out of the vineyard and killed him. What then do you suppose the owner will do to them? He will come and destroy the men who were working his property, and hand it over to others."

When they heard this, they said,
"God forbid!"

But he looked them straight in the eyes and said,
"Then what is the meaning of this scripture—

The stone which the builders rejected,
The same was made the head of the corner?

The man who falls on that stone will be broken, and the man on whom it falls will be crushed to powder."

20.19 The authorities resort to trickery

The scribes and chief priests longed to get their hands on him at that moment, but they were afraid of the people. They knew well enough that his parable referred to them. They watched him, however, and sent some spies into the crowd, pretending that they were honest men, to fasten on something that he might say which could be used to hand him over to the authority and power of the governor.

These men asked him,
"Master, we know that what you say and teach is right, and that you teach the way of God truly without fear or favour. Now, is it

Revised Standard Version

kill him, that the inheritance may be ours.'
15And they cast him out of the vineyard and
killed him. What then will the owner of the vineyard do to them? 16 He will come and destroy
those tenants, and give the vineyard to others."
When they heard this, they said, "God forbid!"
17 But he looked at them and said, "What then
is this that is written:

'The very stone which the builders rejected
has become the head of the corner'?

18 Every one who falls on that stone will be
broken to pieces; but when it falls on any one it
will crush him."
19 The scribes and the chief priests tried to
lay hands on him at that very hour, but they
feared the people; for they perceived that he
had told this parable against them. 20 So they
watched him, and sent spies, who pretended to
be sincere, that they might take hold of what
he said, so as to deliver him up to the authority
and jurisdiction of the governor. 21 They asked
him, "Teacher, we know that you speak and
teach rightly, and show no partiality, but truly
teach the way of God. 22 Is it lawful for us to

Jerusalem Bible

they said, 'let us kill him so that the inheritance
will be ours.' 15 So they threw him out of the
vineyard and killed him.
"Now what will the owner of the vineyard do
to them? 16 He will come and make an end of
these tenants and give the vineyard to others."
Hearing this they said, "God forbid!" 17 But he
looked hard at them and said, "Then what does
this text in the scriptures mean:

It was the stone rejected by the builders
that became the keystone? [h]

18Anyone who falls on that stone will be dashed
to pieces; anyone it falls on will be crushed."
19 But for their fear of the people, the scribes
and the chief priests would have liked to lay
hands on him that very moment, because they
realized that this parable was aimed at them.

On tribute to Caesar

20 So they waited their opportunity and sent
agents to pose as men devoted to the Law,
and to fasten on something he might say and
so enable them to hand him over to the jurisdiction and authority of the governor. 21 They
put to him this question, "Master, we know
that you say and teach what is right; you favor
no one, but teach the way of God in all honesty. 22 Is it permissible for us to pay taxes

[h] Ps. 118:22.

New English Bible

"let us kill him so that the property may come to us." So they flung him out of the vineyard and killed him. What then will the owner of the vineyard do to them? He will come and put these tenants to death and let the vineyard to others.'

When they heard this, they said, 'God forbid!' But he looked straight at them and said, 'Then what does this text of Scripture mean: "The stone which the builders rejected has become the main corner-stone"? Any man who falls on that stone will be dashed to pieces; and if it falls on a man he will be crushed by it.'

The lawyers and chief priests wanted to lay hands on him there and then, for they saw that this parable was aimed at them; but they were afraid of the people. So they watched their opportunity and sent secret agents in the guise of honest men, to seize upon some word of his as a pretext for handing him over to the authority and jurisdiction of the Governor. They put a question to him: 'Master,' they said, 'we know that what you speak and teach is sound; you pay deference to no one, but teach in all honesty the way of life that God requires. Are we or are

King James Version

us to give tribute unto Cesar, or no? 23 But he
perceived their craftiness, and said unto them,
Why tempt ye me? 24 Shew me a penny. Whose
image and superscription hath it? They answered
and said, Cesar's. 25And he said unto them,
Render therefore unto Cesar the things which
be Cesar's, and unto God the things which be
God's. 26And they could not take hold of his
words before the people: and they marvelled at
his answer, and held their peace.
27 Then came to *him* certain of the Sadducees, which deny that there is any resurrection; and they asked him, 28 Saying, Master,
Moses wrote unto us, If any man's brother die,
having a wife, and he die without children, that
his brother should take his wife, and raise up
seed unto his brother. 29 There were therefore
seven brethren: and the first took a wife, and
died without children. 30And the second took her
to wife, and he died childless. 31And the third
took her; and in like manner the seven also: and
they left no children, and died. 32 Last of all the
woman died also. 33 Therefore in the resurrection whose wife of them is she? for seven had
her to wife. 34And Jesus answering said unto
them, The children of this world marry, and are
given in marriage: 35 But they which shall be
accounted worthy to obtain that world, and the

Living Bible

us—is it right to pay taxes to the Roman government or not?"
23 He saw through their trickery and said,
24 "Show me a coin. Whose portrait is this on
it? And whose name?"
They replied, "Caesar's—the Roman emperor's."
25 He said, "Then give the emperor all that
is his—and give to God all that is his!"
26 Thus their attempt to outwit him before
the people failed; and marveling at his answer,
they were silent.
27 Then some Sadducees—men who believed
that death is the end of existence, that there is
no resurrection—28 came to Jesus with this:
"The laws of Moses state that if a man dies
without children, the man's brother shall marry
the widow and their children will legally belong
to the dead man, to carry on his name. 29 We
know of a family of seven brothers. The oldest
married and then died without any children.
30 His brother married the widow and he, too,
died. Still no children. 31And so it went, one
after the other, until each of the seven had married her and died, leaving no children. 32 Finally
the woman died also. 33 Now here is our question: Whose wife will she be in the resurrection?
For all of them were married to her!"
34, 35 Jesus replied, "Marriage is for people
here on earth, but when those who are counted
worthy of being raised from the dead get to

Today's English Version

pay taxes to the Roman Emperor, or not?"
23 But Jesus saw through their trick and said
to them, 24 "Show me a silver coin. Whose face
and name are these on it?"
"The Emperor's," they answered.
25 So Jesus said, "Well, then, pay to the Emperor what belongs to him, and pay to God what
belongs to God."
26 They could not catch him in a thing there
before the people, so they kept quiet, amazed at
his answer.

The question about rising from death

27 Some Sadducees came to Jesus. (They are
the ones who say that people will not rise from
death.) They asked him, 28 "Teacher, Moses
wrote this law for us: 'If a man dies and leaves
a wife, but no children, that man's brother must
marry the widow so they can have children for
the dead man.' 29 Once there were seven brothers; the oldest got married, and died without having children. 30 Then the second one married the
woman, 31 and then the third. The same thing
happened to all seven—they died without having
children. 32 Last of all, the woman died. 33 Now,
on the day when the dead rise to life, whose wife
will she be? All seven of them had married her."
34 Jesus answered them, "The men and women
of this age marry, 35 but the men and women
who are worthy to rise from death and live in

New International Version

taxes to Caesar or not?"
23 He saw through their duplicity and said
to them, 24 "Show me a denarius. Whose portrait and inscription are on it?"
25 "Caesar's," they replied.
He said to them, "Then give to Caesar what
is Caesar's, and to God what is God's."
26 They were unable to trap him in what he
had said there in public. And astonished by his
answer, they became silent.

The resurrection and marriage

27 Some of the Sadducees, who say there is
no resurrection, came to Jesus with a question.
28 "Teacher," they said, "Moses wrote for us
that if a man's brother dies and leaves a wife
but no children, the man must marry the widow
and have children for his brother. 29 Now there
were seven brothers. The first one married a
woman and died childless. 30 The second 31 and
then the third married her, and in the same way
the seven died, leaving no children. 32 Finally,
the woman died too. 33 Now then, at the resurrection whose wife will she be, since the seven
were married to her?"
34 Jesus replied, "The people of this age
marry and are given in marriage. 35 But those
who are considered worthy of taking part in

Phillips Modern English

right for us to pay taxes to Caesar or not?"

But Jesus saw through their cunning and said to them,

"Show me one of the coins. Whose face is this, and whose name is in the inscription?"

"Caesar's," they said.

"Then give to Caesar," he replied, "what belongs to Caesar, and to God what belongs to God."

So his reply gave them no sort of handle that they could use against him publicly. And in fact they were so taken aback by his answer that they had nothing more to say.

20.27 *Jesus exposes the ignorance of the Sadducees*

Then up came some of the Sadducees (who deny that there is any resurrection) and they asked him,

"Master, Moses told us in the scripture, 'If a man's brother should die leaving a wife but no children, he should marry the widow and raise up a family for his brother.' Now, there were once seven brothers. The first married and died childless, and the second and the third married the woman, and in fact all the seven married her and died without leaving any children. Lastly, the woman herself died. Now in this 'resurrection' whose wife is she of these seven men, for she was wife to all of them?"

"People in this world," Jesus replied, "marry and are given in marriage. But those who are considered worthy of reaching that world, which

Revised Standard Version

give tribute to Caesar, or not?" 23 But he perceived their craftiness, and said to them,
24 "Show me a coin.[f] Whose likeness and inscription has it?" They said, "Caesar's." 25 He
said to them, "Then render to Caesar the things
that are Caesar's, and to God the things that
are God's." 26 And they were not able in the
presence of the people to catch him by what he
said; but marveling at his answer they were
silent.

27 There came to him some Sadducees, those
who say that there is no resurrection, 28 and
they asked him a question, saying, "Teacher,
Moses wrote for us that if a man's brother dies,
having a wife but no children, the man[g] must
take the wife and raise up children for his
brother. 29 Now there were seven brothers; the
first took a wife, and died without children; 30 and
the second 31 and the third took her, and likewise all seven left no children and died. 32 Afterward the woman also died. 33 In the resurrection,
therefore, whose wife will the woman be? For
the seven had her as wife."

34 And Jesus said to them, "The sons of this
age marry and are given in marriage; 35 but
those who are accounted worthy to attain to that

[f] Greek *denarius*. [g] Greek *his brother*.

Jerusalem Bible

to Caesar or not?" 23 But he was aware of
their cunning and said, 24 "Show me a denarius.
Whose head and name are on it?" "Caesar's,"
they said. 25 "Well then," he said to them,
"give back to Caesar what belongs to Caesar—
and to God what belongs to God."

26 As a result, they were unable to find fault
with anything he had to say in public; his answer took them by surprise and they were
silenced.

The resurrection of the dead

27 Some Sadducees—those who say that there
is no resurrection—approached him and they
put this question to him, 28 "Master, we have
it from Moses in writing, that if a man's married brother dies childless, the man must marry
the widow to raise up children for his brother.
29 Well then, there were seven brothers. The
first, having married a wife, died childless. 30 The
second 31 and then the third married the widow.
And the same with all seven, they died leaving
no children. 32 Finally the woman herself died.
33 Now, at the resurrection, to which of them
will she be wife since she had been married to
all seven?"

34 Jesus replied, "The children of this world
take wives and husbands, 35 but those who are
judged worthy of a place in the other world

New English Bible

we not permitted to pay taxes to the Roman Emperor?' He saw through their trick and said, 'Show me a silver piece. Whose head does it bear, and whose inscription?' 'Caesar's', they replied. 'Very well then,' he said, 'pay Caesar what is due to Caesar, and pay God what is due to God.' Thus their attempt to catch him out in public failed, and, astonished by his reply, they fell silent.

Then some Sadducees came forward. They are the people who deny that there is a resurrection. Their question was this: 'Master, Moses laid it down for us that if there are brothers, and one dies leaving a wife but no child, then the next should marry the widow and carry on his brother's family. Now, there were seven brothers: the first took a wife and died childless; then the second married her, then the third. In this way the seven of them died leaving no children. Afterwards the woman also died. At the resurrection whose wife is she to be, since all seven had married her?' Jesus said to them, 'The men and women of this world marry; but those who have been judged worthy of a place in the

King James Version

resurrection from the dead, neither marry, nor
are given in marriage: 36 Neither can they die
any more: for they are equal unto the angels;
and are the children of God, being the children
of the resurrection. 37 Now that the dead are
raised, even Moses shewed at the bush, when
he calleth the Lord the God of Abraham, and
the God of Isaac, and the God of Jacob. 38 For
he is not a God of the dead, but of the living:
for all live unto him.
39 Then certain of the scribes answering said,
Master, thou hast well said. 40And after that
they durst not ask him any *question at all*. 41 And
he said unto them, How say they that Christ is
David's son? 42And David himself saith in the
book of Psalms, The LORD said unto my Lord,
Sit thou on my right hand, 43 Till I make thine
enemies thy footstool. 44 David therefore calleth
him Lord, how is he then his son?

Living Bible

heaven, they do not marry. 36And they never
die again; in these respects they are like angels,
and are sons of God, for they are raised up in
new life from the dead.
37, 38 "But as to your real question—whether
or not there is a resurrection—why, even the
writings of Moses himself prove this. For when
he describes how God appeared to him in the
burning bush, he speaks of God as 'the God of
Abraham, the God of Isaac, and the God of
Jacob.' To say that the Lord *is*[a] some person's
God means that person is *alive*, not dead! So
from God's point of view, all men are living."
39 "Well said, sir!" remarked some of the experts in the Jewish law who were standing there.
40And that ended their questions, for they dared
ask no more!
41 Then he presented *them* with a question.
"Why is it," he asked, "that Christ, the Messiah, is said to be a descendant of King David?
42, 43 For David himself wrote in the book of
Psalms: 'God said to my Lord, the Messiah,
"Sit at my right hand until I place your enemies
beneath your feet."' 44 How can the Messiah be
both David's son and David's God at the same
time?"

[*a*] Otherwise the statement would be, "He *had been* that person's God."

Today's English Version

the age to come do not marry. 36 They are like
angels and cannot die. They are the sons of God,
because they have risen from death. 37And Moses
clearly proves that the dead are raised to life. In
the passage about the burning bush he speaks of
the Lord as 'the God of Abraham, the God of
Isaac, and the God of Jacob.' 38 This means that
he is the God of the living, not of the dead, because all are alive to him."
39 Some of the teachers of the Law spoke up,
"A good answer, Teacher!" 40 For they did not
dare ask him any more questions.

The question about the Messiah

41 Jesus said to them, "How can it be said
that the Messiah will be the descendant of David?
42 Because David himself says in the book of
Psalms,

'The Lord said to my Lord:
Sit here at my right side,
43 until I put your enemies as a footstool under your feet.'

44 David, then, called him 'Lord.' How can the
Messiah be David's descendant?"

New International Version

that age and in the resurrection from the dead
will neither marry nor be given in marriage,
36 and they can no longer die; for they are like
the angels. They are God's children, since they
are children of the resurrection. 37 But in the
account of the bush, even Moses showed that
the dead rise, for he calls the Lord 'the God of
Abraham, and the God of Isaac, and the God of
Jacob.'[q] 38 He is not the God of the dead, but
of the living, for to him all are alive."
39 Some of the teachers of the law responded,
"Well said, teacher!" 40And no one dared to ask
him any more questions.

Whose son is the Christ?

41 Then Jesus said to them, "How is it that
they say the Christ[r] is the Son of David? 42 David himself declares in the Book of Psalms:
'The Lord said to my Lord:
Sit at my right hand,
43 until I make your enemies your footstool.'[s]
44 David calls him 'Lord.' How then can he be
his son?"

[*q*] Exodus 3:6. [*r*] Or *Messiah*. [*s*] Psalm 110:1.

Phillips Modern English

means rising from the dead, neither marry nor are they given in marriage. They cannot die any more but live like the angels; for being children of the resurrection, they are the sons of God. But that the dead are raised, even Moses showed to be true in the story of the bush, when he calls the Lord the God of Abraham, the God of Isaac and the God of Jacob. For God is not God of the dead, but of the living. For all men are alive to him."

To this some of the scribes replied,

"Master, that was a good answer."

And indeed nobody had the courage to ask him any more questions. But Jesus went on to say,

"How can they say that Christ is David's *son?* For David himself says in the book of psalms—

The Lord said unto my *Lord.*
Sit thou on my right hand,
Till I make thine enemies the footstool of thy
feet.

David is plainly calling him 'Lord'. How then can he be his *son?*"

Revised Standard Version

age and to the resurrection from the dead neither
marry nor are given in marriage, 36 for they
cannot die any more, because they are equal to
angels and are sons of God, being sons of the
resurrection. 37 But that the dead are raised,
even Moses showed, in the passage about the
bush, where he calls the Lord the God of
Abraham and the God of Isaac and the God of
Jacob. 38 Now he is not God of the dead, but
of the living; for all live to him." 39 And some
of the scribes answered, "Teacher, you have
spoken well." 40 For they no longer dared to
ask him any question.
41 But he said to them, "How can they say
that the Christ is David's son? 42 For David
himself says in the Book of Psalms,
'The Lord said to my Lord,
Sit at my right hand,
43 till I make thy enemies a stool for thy feet.'
44 David thus calls him Lord; so how is he his
son?"

Jerusalem Bible

and in the resurrection from the dead do not
marry 36 because they can no longer die, for
they are the same as the angels, and being children of the resurrection they are sons of God.
37 And Moses himself implies that the dead rise
again, in the passage about the bush where he
calls the Lord *the God of Abraham, the God
of Isaac and the God of Jacob.*[i] 38 Now he is
God, not of the dead, but of the living; for to
him all men are in fact alive."
39 Some scribes[j] then spoke up. "Well put,
Master," they said 40 —because they would not
dare to ask him any more questions.

Christ, not only son but also Lord of David

41 He then said to them, "How can people
maintain that the Christ is son of David?
42 Why, David himself says in the Book of
Psalms:
The Lord said to my Lord:
Sit at my right hand
43 *and I will make your enemies*
a footstool for you.[k]
44 David here calls him Lord; how then can he
be his son?"

[i] Ex. 3:6. [j] Most scribes were Pharisees and believed in the resurrection of the dead. [k] Ps. 110:1.

New English Bible

other world and of the resurrection from the dead, do not marry, for they are not subject to death any longer. They are like angels; they are sons of God, because they share in the resurrection. That the dead are raised to life again is shown by Moses himself in the story of the burning bush, when he calls the Lord, "the God of Abraham, Isaac, and Jacob". God is not God of the dead but of the living; for him all are[a] alive.'

At this some of the lawyers said, 'Well spoken, Master.' For there was no further question that they ventured to put to him.

He said to them, 'How can they say that the Messiah is son of David? For David himself says in the Book of Psalms: "The Lord said to my Lord, 'Sit at my right hand until I make your enemies your footstool.'" Thus David calls him "Lord"; how then can he be David's son?'

[a] *Or* they are all.

King James Version

45 Then in the audience of all the people he said unto his disciples, 46 Beware of the scribes, which desire to walk in long robes, and love greetings in the markets, and the highest seats in the synagogues, and the chief rooms at feasts; 47 Which devour widows' houses, and for a shew make long prayers: the same shall receive greater damnation.

21 And he looked up, and saw the rich men casting their gifts into the treasury. 2 And he saw also a certain poor widow casting in thither two mites. 3 And he said, Of a truth I say unto you, that this poor widow hath cast in more than they all: 4 For all these have of their abundance cast in unto the offerings of God: but she of her penury hath cast in all the living that she had.

Living Bible

45 Then, with the crowds listening, he turned to his disciples and said, 46 "Beware of these experts in religion, for they love to parade in dignified robes and to be bowed to by the people as they walk along the street. And how they love the seats of honor in the synagogues and at religious festivals! 47 But even while they are praying long prayers with great outward piety, they are planning schemes to cheat widows out of their property. Therefore God's heaviest sentence awaits these men."

21 As he stood in the Temple, he was watching the rich tossing their gifts into the collection box. 2 Then a poor widow came by and dropped in two small copper coins.

3 "Really," he remarked, "this poor widow has given more than all the rest of them combined. 4 For they have given a little of what they didn't need, but she, poor as she is has given everything she has."

Today's English Version

Jesus warns against the teachers of the Law

45 As all the people listened to him, Jesus said to his disciples, 46 "Watch out for the teachers of the Law, who like to walk around in their long robes, and love to be greeted with respect in the market place; who choose the reserved seats in the synagogues and the best places at feasts; 47 who take advantage of widows and rob them of their homes, and then make a show of saying long prayers! Their punishment will be all the worse!"

The widow's offering

21 Jesus looked around and saw rich men dropping their gifts in the temple treasury, 2 and he also saw a very poor widow dropping in two little copper coins. 3 He said, "I tell you that this poor widow put in more than all the others. 4 For the others offered their gifts from what they had to spare of their riches; but she, poor as she is, gave all she had to live on."

New International Version

45 While all the people were listening, Jesus said to his disciples, 46 "Beware of the teachers of the law. They like to walk around in flowing robes and love to be greeted in the marketplaces and have the most important seats in the synagogues and the places of honor at banquets. 47 They devour widows' houses and for a show make lengthy prayers. Such men will be punished most severely."

The widow's offering

21 As he looked up, Jesus saw the rich putting their gifts into the temple treasury. 2 He also saw a poor widow put in two very small copper coins. 3 "I tell you the truth," he said, "this poor widow has put in more than all the others. 4 All these people gave their gifts out of their wealth; but she out of her poverty put in all she had to live on."

Phillips Modern English

20.45 Jesus warns his disciples against religious pretentiousness

Then while everybody was listening, Jesus remarked to his disciples,

"Be on your guard against the scribes, who enjoy walking round in long robes and love having men bow to them in public, getting front seats in the synagogue, and the best places at dinner parties—while all the time they are battening on widows' property and covering it up with long prayers. These men are only heading for deeper damnation."

Then he looked up and saw the rich people dropping their gifts into the treasury, and he noticed a poor widow drop in two coppers, and he commented,

"I assure you that this poor widow has put in more than all of them, for they have all put in what they can easily spare, but she in her poverty has given away her whole living."

Revised Standard Version

45 And in the hearing of all the people he
said to his disciples, 46 "Beware of the scribes,
who like to go about in long robes, and love
salutations in the market places and the best
seats in the synagogues and the places of honor
at feasts, 47 who devour widows' houses and for
a pretense make long prayers. They will receive the greater condemnation."

21 He looked up and saw the rich putting
their gifts into the treasury; 2 and he saw
a poor widow put in two copper coins. 3 And he
said, "Truly I tell you, this poor widow has put
in more than all of them; 4 for they all contributed out of their abundance, but she out of
her poverty put in all the living that she had."

Jerusalem Bible

The scribes condemned by Jesus

45 While all the people were listening he
said to the disciples, 46 "Beware of the scribes
who like to walk about in long robes and love
to be greeted obsequiously in the market squares,
to take the front seats in the synagogues and
the places of honor at banquets, 47 who swallow the property of widows, while making a
show of lengthy prayers. The more severe will
be the sentence they receive."

The widow's mite

21 As he looked up he saw rich people
putting their offerings into the treasury;
2 then he happened to notice a poverty-stricken
widow putting in two small coins, 3 and he said,
"I tell you truly, this poor widow has put in
more than any of them; 4 for these have all
contributed money they had over, but she from
the little she had has put in all she had to live
on."

New English Bible

In the hearing of all the people Jesus said to his disciples: 'Beware of the doctors of the law who love to walk up and down in long robes, and have a great liking for respectful greetings in the street, the chief seats in our synagogues, and places of honour at feasts. These are the men who eat up the property of widows, while they say long prayers for appearance' sake; and they will receive the severest sentence.'

21 He looked up and saw the rich people
dropping their gifts into the chest of the
temple treasury; and he noticed a poor widow putting in two tiny coins. 'I tell you this,' he said: 'this poor widow has given more than any of them; for those others who have given had more than enough, but she, with less than enough, has given all she had to live on.'

King James Version

5 And as some spake of the temple, how it
was adorned with goodly stones and gifts, he
said, 6 *As for* these things which ye behold, the
days will come, in the which there shall not be
left one stone upon another, that shall not be
thrown down. 7 And they asked him, saying,
Master, but when shall these things be? and
what sign *will there be* when these things shall
come to pass? 8 And he said, Take heed that ye
be not deceived: for many shall come in my
name, saying, I am *Christ;* and the time draweth
near: go ye not therefore after them. 9 But when
ye shall hear of wars and commotions, be not
terrified: for these things must first come to
pass; but the end *is* not by and by. 10 Then said
he unto them, Nation shall rise against nation,
and kingdom against kingdom: 11 And great
earthquakes shall be in divers places, and famines, and pestilences; and fearful sights and
great signs shall there be from heaven. 12 But
before all these, they shall lay their hands on

Living Bible

5 Some of his disciples began talking about
the beautiful stonework of the Temple and the
memorial decorations on the walls.
6 But Jesus said, "The time is coming when
all these things you are admiring will be knocked
down, and not one stone will be left on top of
another; all will become one vast heap of rubble."
7 "Master!" they exclaimed. "When? And will
there be any warning ahead of time?"
8 He replied, "Don't let anyone mislead you.
For many will come announcing themselves as
the Messiah,[a] and saying, 'The time has come.'
But don't believe them! 9 And when you hear of
wars and insurrections beginning, don't panic.
True, wars must come, but the end won't follow
immediately—10 for nation shall rise against
nation and kingdom against kingdom, 11 and
there will be great earthquakes, and famines in
many lands, and epidemics, and terrifying things
happening in the heavens.
12 "But before all this occurs, there will be a
time of special persecution, and you will be

[a] Literally, "will come in my name."

Today's English Version

Jesus speaks of the destruction of the temple

5 Some of them were talking about the temple,
how beautiful it looked with its fine stones and
the gifts offered to God. Jesus said, 6 "All this
you see—the time will come when not a single
stone here will be left in its place; every one will
be thrown down."

Troubles and persecutions

7 "Teacher," they asked, "when will this be?
And what will happen to show that the time has
come for it to take place?"
8 Jesus said, "Watch out; don't be fooled. Because many men will come in my name saying,
'I am he!' and, 'The time has come!' But don't
follow them. 9 Don't be afraid when you hear of
wars and revolutions; such things must happen
first, but they do not mean that the end is near."
10 He went on to say, "Countries will fight
each other, kingdoms will attack one another.
11 There will be terrible earthquakes, famines,
and plagues everywhere; there will be awful
things and great signs from the sky. 12 Before all
these things take place, however, you will be ar-

New International Version

Signs of the end of the age

5 Some of his disciples were remarking about
how the temple was adorned with beautiful
stones and with gifts dedicated to God. But Jesus said, 6 "As for what you see here, the time
will come when not one stone will be left on
another; every one of them will be thrown
down."
7 "Teacher," they asked, "when will these
things happen? And what will be the sign that
they are about to take place?"
8 He replied: "Watch out that you are not
deceived. For many will come in my name,
claiming, 'I am he,' and, 'The time is near.' Do
not follow them. 9 When you hear of wars and
revolutions, do not be frightened. These things
must happen first, but the end will not come
right away."
10 Then he said to them: "Nation will rise
against nation, and kingdom against kingdom.
11 There will be great earthquakes, famines and
pestilences in various places, and fearful events
and great signs from heaven.
12 "But before all this, they will lay hands on
you and persecute you. They will deliver you to

Phillips Modern English

21.5 Jesus foretells the destruction of the Temple

Then when some of them were talking about the Temple and pointing out the beauty of its lovely stonework and the various ornaments that people had given, he said,

"Yes, you can gaze on all this today, but the time is coming when not a single stone will be left upon another without being thrown down."

So they asked him,

"Master, when will this happen, and what sign will there be that these things are going to take place?"

"Be careful that you are not deceived," he replied. "There will be many coming in my name, saying 'I am he' and 'The time is very near now.' Never follow men like that. And when you hear about wars and disturbances, don't be alarmed. These things must indeed happen first, but the end will not come immediately."

21.10 And prophesies world-wide suffering

Then he continued,

"Nation will rise up against nation, and kingdom against kingdom; there will be great earthquakes and famines and plagues in this place or that. There will be dreadful sights, and great signs from heaven. But before all this happens, men will arrest you and persecute you, handing

Revised Standard Version

5 And as some spoke of the temple, how it
was adorned with noble stones and offerings, he
said, 6 "As for these things which you see, the
days will come when there shall not be left here
one stone upon another that will not be thrown
down." 7 And they asked him, "Teacher, when
will this be, and what will be the sign when this
is about to take place?" 8 And he said, "Take
heed that you are not led astray; for many will
come in my name, saying, 'I am he!' and, 'The
time is at hand!' Do not go after them. 9 And
when you hear of wars and tumults, do not be
terrified; for this must first take place, but the
end will not be at once."
10 Then he said to them, "Nation will rise
against nation, and kingdom against kingdom;
11 there will be great earthquakes, and in various
places famines and pestilences; and there will be
terrors and great signs from heaven. 12 But before all this they will lay their hands on you

Jerusalem Bible

Discourse on the destruction of Jerusalem[l]: Introduction

5 When some were talking about the Temple,
remarking how it was adorned with fine stonework and votive offerings, he said, 6 "All these
things you are staring at now—the time will
come when not a single stone will be left on
another: everything will be destroyed." 7 And
they put to him this question: "Master," they
said, "when will this happen, then, and what
sign will there be that this is about to take
place?"

The warning signs

8 "Take care not to be deceived," he said,
"because many will come using my name and
saying, 'I am he,' and, 'The time is near at
hand.' Refuse to join them. 9 And when you
hear of wars and revolutions, do not be frightened, for this is something that must happen
but the end is not so soon." 10 Then he said
to them, "Nation will fight against nation, and
kingdom against kingdom. 11 There will be great
earthquakes and plagues and famines here and
there; there will be fearful sights and great signs
from heaven.
12 "But before all this happens, men will
seize you and persecute you; they will hand

[l] This passage on the End Time also includes some elements of a prophecy of the destruction of Jerusalem.

New English Bible

Some people were talking about the temple and the fine stones and votive offerings with which it was adorned. He said, 'These things which you are gazing at—the time will come when not one stone of them will be left upon another; all will be thrown down.' 'Master,' they asked, 'when will it all come about? What will be the sign when it is due to happen?'

He said, 'Take care that you are not misled. For many will come claiming my name and saying, "I am he", and, "The Day is upon us." Do not follow them. And when you hear of wars and insurrections, do not fall into a panic. These things are bound to happen first; but the end does not follow immediately.' Then he added, 'Nation will make war upon nation, kingdom upon kingdom; there will be great earthquakes, and famines and plagues in many places; in the sky terrors and great portents.

'But before all this happens they will set upon you and persecute you. You will be brought be-

King James Version

you, and persecute *you,* delivering *you* up to the synagogues, and into prisons, being brought before kings and rulers for my name's sake. 13 And it shall turn to you for a testimony. 14 Settle *it* therefore in your hearts, not to meditate before what ye shall answer: 15 For I will give you a mouth and wisdom, which all your adversaries shall not be able to gainsay nor resist. 16 And ye shall be betrayed both by parents, and brethren, and kinsfolks, and friends; and *some* of you shall they cause to be put to death. 17 And ye shall be hated of all *men* for my name's sake. 18 But there shall not a hair of your head perish. 19 In your patience possess ye your souls. 20 And when ye shall see Jerusalem compassed with armies, then know that the desolation thereof is nigh. 21 Then let them which are in Judea flee to the mountains; and let them which are in the midst of it depart out; and let not them that are in the countries enter thereinto. 22 For these be the days of vengeance, that all things which are written may be fulfilled. 23 But woe unto them that are with child, and to them that give suck, in those days! for there shall be great distress in the land, and wrath upon this people. 24 And

Living Bible

dragged into synagogues and prisons and before kings and governors for my name's sake. 13 But as a result, the Messiah will be widely known and honored.[b] 14 Therefore, don't be concerned about how to answer the charges against you, 15 for I will give you the right words and such logic that none of your opponents will be able to reply! 16 Even those closest to you—your parents, brothers, relatives, and friends will betray you and have you arrested; and some of you will be killed. 17 And everyone will hate you because you are mine and are called by my name. 18 But not a hair of your head will perish! 19 For if you stand firm, you will win your souls.

20 "But when you see Jerusalem surrounded by armies, then you will know that the time of its destruction has arrived. 21 Then let the people of Judea flee to the hills. Let those in Jerusalem try to escape, and those outside the city must not attempt to return. 22 For those will be days of God's judgment,[c] and the words of the ancient Scriptures written by the prophets will be abundantly fulfilled. 23 Woe to expectant mothers in those days, and those with tiny babies. For there will be great distress upon this nation[d] and wrath upon this people. 24 They will be brutally killed

[*b*] Literally, "It shall turn out unto you for a testimony." [*c*] Literally, "days of vengeance." [*d*] Literally, "upon the land," or, "upon the earth."

Today's English Version

rested and persecuted; you will be handed over to trial in synagogues and be put in prison; you will be brought before kings and rulers for my sake. 13 This will be your chance to tell the Good News. 14 Make up your minds ahead of time not to worry about how you will defend yourselves; 15 because I will give you such words and wisdom that none of your enemies will be able to resist or deny what you say. 16 You will be handed over by your parents, your brothers, your relatives, and your friends; they will put some of you to death. 17 Everyone will hate you because of me. 18 But not a single hair from your heads will be lost. 19 Stand firm, because this is how you will save yourselves."

Jesus speaks of the destruction of Jerusalem

20 "When you see Jerusalem surrounded by armies, then you will know that soon she will be destroyed. 21 Then those who are in Judea must run away to the hills; those who are in the city must leave, and those who are out in the country must not go into the city. 22 For these are 'The Days of Punishment,' to make come true all that the Scriptures say. 23 How terrible it will be in those days for women who are pregnant, and for mothers with little babies! Terrible distress will come upon this land, and God's wrath will be against this people. 24 Some will be killed by the

New International Version

synagogues and prisons, and you will be brought before kings and governors, and all on account of my name. 13 This will result in your being witnesses to them. 14 But make up your mind not to worry beforehand how you will defend yourselves. 15 For I will give you words and wisdom that none of your adversaries will be able to resist or contradict. 16 You will be betrayed by parents, brothers, relatives and friends, and they will put some of you to death. 17 All men will hate you because of me. 18 But not a hair of your head will perish. 19 By standing firm you will save yourselves.

20 "When you see Jerusalem surrounded by armies, you will know that its desolation is near. 21 Then let those who are in Judea flee to the mountains, let those in the city get out, and let those in the country not enter the city. 22 For this is the time of punishment in fulfillment of all that has been written. 23 How dreadful it will be in those days for pregnant women and nursing mothers! There will be great distress in the land and wrath against this people. 24 They

Phillips Modern English

you over to synagogue or prison, or bringing you before kings and governors, for my name's sake. This will be your chance to witness for me. So make up your minds not to think out your defence beforehand. I will give you such eloquence and wisdom that none of your opponents will be able to resist or contradict it. But you will be betrayed, even by parents and brothers and kinsfolk and friends, and there will be some of you who will be killed and you will be hated everywhere for my name's sake. Yet, not a hair of your head will perish. Hold on, and you will win your souls!

"But when you see Jerusalem surrounded by armed forces, then you will know that the time of her devastation has arrived. Then is the time for those who are in Judaea to fly to the hills. And those who are in the city itself must get out of it, and those who are already in the country must not try to get into the city. For these are the days of vengeance, when all that the scriptures have said will come true. Alas for those who are pregnant and those who have babies at the breast in those days! For there will be bitter misery in the land and great anger against this people. They will die by the sword.

Revised Standard Version

and persecute you, delivering you up to the
synagogues and prisons, and you will be brought
before kings and governors for my name's sake.
13 This will be a time for you to bear testimony.
14 Settle it therefore in your minds, not to meditate beforehand how to answer; 15 for I will give
you a mouth and wisdom, which none of your
adversaries will be able to withstand or contradict. 16 You will be delivered up even by parents
and brothers and kinsmen and friends, and some
of you they will put to death; 17 you will be
hated by all for my name's sake. 18 But not a
hair of your head will perish. 19 By your endurance you will gain your lives.

20 "But when you see Jerusalem surrounded
by armies, then know that its desolation has
come near. 21 Then let those who are in Judea
flee to the mountains, and let those who are inside the city depart, and let not those who are
out in the country enter it; 22 for these are days
of vengeance, to fulfil all that is written. 23 Alas
for those who are with child and for those who
give suck in those days! For great distress shall
be upon the earth and wrath upon this people;
24 they will fall by the edge of the sword, and

Jerusalem Bible

you over to the synagogues and to imprisonment, and bring you before kings and governors
because of my name 13 —and that will be your
opportunity to bear witness. 14 Keep this carefully in mind: you are not to prepare your defense, 15 because I myself shall give you an
eloquence and a wisdom that none of your
opponents will be able to resist or contradict.
16 You will be betrayed even by parents and
brothers, relations and friends; and some of
you will be put to death. 17 You will be hated
by all men on account of my name, 18 but not
a hair of your head will be lost. 19 Your endurance will win you your lives.

The siege

20 "When you see Jerusalem surrounded by
armies, you must realize that she will soon be
laid desolate. 21 Then those in Judaea must escape to the mountains, those inside the city
must leave it, and those in country districts must
not take refuge in it. 22 For this is the time of
vengeance when all that scripture says[m] must
be fulfilled. 23 Alas for those with child, or with
babies at the breast, when those days come!

The disaster and the age of the pagans

"For great misery will descend on the land
and wrath on this people. 24 They will fall by

New English Bible

fore synagogues and put in prison; you will be haled before kings and governors for your allegiance to me. This will be your opportunity to testify; so make up your minds not to prepare your defence beforehand, because I myself will give you power of utterance and a wisdom which no opponent will be able to resist or refute. Even your parents and brothers, your relations and friends, will betray you. Some of you will be put to death; and all will hate you for your allegiance to me. But not a hair of your head shall be lost. By standing firm you will win true life for yourselves.

'But when you see Jerusalem encircled by armies, then you may be sure that her destruction is near. Then those who are in Judaea must take to the hills; those who are in the city itself must leave it, and those who are out in the country must not enter; because this is the time of retribution, when all that stands written is to be fulfilled. Alas for women who are with child in those days, or have children at the breast! For there will be great distress in the land and a terrible judgement upon this people. They will fall

[m] Possibly alluding to Dn. 9:27.

King James Version

they shall fall by the edge of the sword, and shall
be led away captive into all nations: and Jerusalem shall be trodden down of the Gentiles,
until the times of the Gentiles be fulfilled.
25 And there shall be signs in the sun, and
in the moon, and in the stars; and upon the earth
distress of nations, with perplexity; the sea and
the waves roaring; 26 Men's hearts failing them
for fear, and for looking after those things
which are coming on the earth: for the powers
of heaven shall be shaken. 27 And then shall they
see the Son of man coming in a cloud with
power and great glory. 28 And when these things
begin to come to pass, then look up, and lift up
your heads; for your redemption draweth nigh.
29 And he spake to them a parable; Behold the
fig tree, and all the trees; 30 When they now shoot
forth, ye see and know of your own selves that
summer is now nigh at hand. 31 So likewise ye,
when ye see these things come to pass, know ye
that the kingdom of God is nigh at hand.
32 Verily I say unto you, This generation shall
not pass away, till all be fulfilled. 33 Heaven and
earth shall pass away; but my words shall not
pass away.

Living Bible

by enemy weapons, or sent away as exiles and
captives to all the nations of the world; and
Jerusalem shall be conquered and trampled down
by the Gentiles until the period of Gentile triumph ends in God's good time.
25 "Then there will be strange events in the
skies—warnings, evil omens and portents in the
sun, moon and stars; and down here on earth
the nations will be in turmoil, perplexed by the
roaring seas and strange tides. 26 The courage
of many people will falter because of the fearful
fate they see coming upon the earth, for the
stability of the very heavens will be broken up.
27 Then the peoples of the earth shall see me,[e]
the Messiah, coming in a cloud with power and
great glory. 28 So when all these things begin to
happen, stand straight and look up! For your
salvation is near."
29 Then he gave them this illustration: "Notice the fig tree, or any other tree. 30 When the
leaves come out, you know without being told
that summer is near. 31 In the same way, when
you see the events taking place that I've described you can be just as sure that the Kingdom
of God is near.
32 "I solemnly declare to you that when these
things happen, the end of this age[f] has come.
33 And though all heaven and earth shall pass
away, yet my words remain forever true.

[e] Literally, "the Son of Man." [f] Or, "this generation."

Today's English Version

sword, and others taken as prisoners to all countries; and the heathen will trample over Jerusalem
until their time is up."

The coming of the Son of Man

25 "There will be signs in the sun, the moon,
and the stars. On earth, whole countries will be
in despair, afraid of the roar of the sea and the
raging tides. 26 Men will faint from fear as they
wait for what is coming over the whole earth; for
the powers in space will be driven from their
courses. 27 Then the Son of Man will appear,
coming in a cloud with great power and glory.
28 When these things begin to happen, stand up
and raise your heads, because your salvation is
near."

The lesson of the fig tree

29 Then Jesus told them this parable, "Remember the fig tree and all the other trees.
30 When you see their leaves beginning to appear
you know that summer is near. 31 In the same
way, when you see these things happening, you
will know that the Kingdom of God is about to
come.
32 "Remember this! All these things will take
place before the people now living have all died.
33 Heaven and earth will pass away; my words
will never pass away."

New International Version

will fall by the sword and will be taken as prisoners to all the nations. Jerusalem will be
trampled on by the Gentiles until the times of
the Gentiles are fulfilled.
25 "There will be signs in the sun, moon and
stars. On the earth, nations will be in anguish
and perplexity at the roaring and tossing of the
sea. 26 Men will faint from terror, apprehensive
of what is coming on the world, for the heavenly bodies will be shaken. 27 At that time they
will see the Son of Man coming in a cloud with
power and great glory. 28 When these things begin to take place, stand up and lift up your
heads, because your redemption is drawing
near."
29 He told them this parable: "Look at the
fig tree and all the trees. 30 When they sprout
leaves, you can see for yourselves and know that
summer is near. 31 Even so, when you see these
things happening, you know that the kingdom of
God is near.
32 "I tell you the truth, this generation[t] will
certainly not pass away until all these things
have happened. 33 Heaven and earth will pass
away, but my words will never pass away.

[t] Or *race*.

Phillips Modern English

They will be taken off as prisoners into all nations. Jerusalem will be trampled under foot by the heathens until the heathen's day is over. There will be signs in the sun and moon and stars, and on the earth there will be dismay among the nations and bewilderment at the roar of the surging sea. Men's courage will fail completely as they realise what is threatening the world, for the very powers of heaven will be shaken. Then men will see the Son of Man coming in a cloud with great power and splendour! But when these things begin to happen, stand up, hold your heads high, for you will soon be free."

21.29 Vigilance is essential

Then he gave them a parable.

"Look at a fig-tree, or indeed any tree, when it begins to burst its buds, and you realise without anybody telling you that summer is nearly here. So, when you see these things happening, you can be equally sure that the kingdom of God has nearly come. Believe me, this generation will not disappear until all this has taken place. Heaven and earth will pass away, but my words will never pass away.

Revised Standard Version

be led captive among all nations; and Jerusalem will be trodden down by the Gentiles, until the times of the Gentiles are fulfilled.
25 "And there will be signs in sun and moon and stars, and upon the earth distress of nations in perplexity at the roaring of the sea and the waves, 26 men fainting with fear and with foreboding of what is coming on the world; for the powers of the heavens will be shaken. 27And then they will see the Son of man coming in a cloud with power and great glory. 28 Now when these things begin to take place, look up and raise your heads, because your redemption is drawing near."
29 And he told them a parable: "Look at the fig tree, and all the trees; 30 as soon as they come out in leaf, you see for yourselves and know that the summer is already near. 31 So also, when you see these things taking place, you know that the kingdom of God is near. 32 Truly, I say to you, this generation will not pass away till all has taken place. 33 Heaven and earth will pass away, but my words will not pass away.

Jerusalem Bible

the edge of the sword and be led captive to every pagan country; and Jerusalem will be trampled down by the pagans until the age of the pagans is completely over.

Cosmic disasters and the coming of the Son of Man

25 "There will be signs in the sun and moon and stars; on earth nations in agony, bewildered by the clamor of the ocean and its waves; 26 men dying of fear as they await what menaces the world, for the powers of heaven will be shaken. 27And then they will see the Son of Man coming in a cloud with power and great glory. 28 When these things begin to take place, stand erect, hold your heads high, because your liberation[n] is near at hand."

The time of this coming

29 And he told them a parable, "Think of the fig tree and indeed every tree. 30As soon as you see them bud, you know that summer is now near. 31 So with you when you see these things happening: know that the kingdom of God is near. 32 I tell you solemnly, before this generation has passed away all will have taken place. 33 Heaven and earth will pass away, but my words will never pass away.

[n] Or "redemption."

New English Bible

at the sword's point; they will be carried captive into all countries; and Jerusalem will be trampled down by foreigners until their day has run its course.

'Portents will appear in sun, moon, and stars. On earth nations will stand helpless, not knowing which way to turn from the roar and surge of the sea; men will faint with terror at the thought of all that is coming upon the world; for the celestial powers will be shaken. And then they will see the Son of Man coming on a cloud with great power and glory. When all this begins to happen, stand upright and hold your heads high, because your liberation is near.'

He told them this parable: 'Look at the fig-tree, or any other tree. As soon as it buds, you can see for yourselves that summer is near. In the same way, when you see all this happening, you may know that the kingdom of God is near.

'I tell you this: the present generation will live to see it all. Heaven and earth will pass away; my words will never pass away.

King James Version

34 And take heed to yourselves, lest at any time your hearts be overcharged with surfeiting, and drunkenness, and cares of this life, and *so* that day come upon you unawares. 35 For as a snare shall it come on all them that dwell on the face of the whole earth. 36 Watch ye therefore, and pray always, that ye may be accounted worthy to escape all these things that shall come to pass, and to stand before the Son of man. 37 And in the daytime he was teaching in the temple; and at night he went out, and abode in the mount that is called *the mount* of Olives. 38 And all the people came early in the morning to him in the temple, for to hear him.

22 Now the feast of unleavened bread drew nigh, which is called the passover. 2 And the chief priests and scribes sought how they

Living Bible

34, 35 "Watch out! Don't let my sudden coming catch you unawares; don't let me find you living in careless ease, carousing and drinking, and occupied with the problems of this life, like all the rest of the world. 36 Keep a constant watch. And pray that if possible you may arrive in my presence without having to experience these horrors." [g]

37, 38 Every day Jesus went to the Temple to teach, and the crowds began gathering early in the morning to hear him. And each evening he returned to spend the night on the Mount of Olives.

22 And now the Passover celebration was drawing near—the Jewish festival when only bread made without yeast was used. 2 The chief priests and other religious leaders were ac-

[g] Or, "Pray for strength to pass safely through these coming horrors."

Today's English Version

The need to watch

34 "Watch yourselves! Don't let yourselves become occupied with too much feasting and strong drink, and the worries of this life, or that Day may come on you suddenly. 35 For it will come like a trap upon all men over the whole earth. 36 Be on watch and pray always that you will have the strength to go safely through all these things that will happen, and to stand before the Son of Man."

37 Jesus spent those days teaching in the temple, and when evening came he would go out and spend the night on the Mount of Olives. 38 All the people would go to the temple early in the morning to listen to him.

The plot against Jesus

22 The time was near for the Feast of Unleavened Bread, which is called the Passover. 2 The chief priests and the teachers of the

New International Version

34 "Be careful, or your hearts will be weighed down with dissipation, drunkenness and the anxieties of life, and that day will close on you unexpectedly like a trap. 35 For it will come upon all those who live on the face of the whole earth. 36 Be always on the watch, and pray that you may be able to escape all that is about to happen, and that you may be able to stand before the Son of Man."

37 Each day Jesus was teaching at the temple, and each evening he went out to spend the night on the hill called the Mount of Olives, 38 and all the people came early in the morning to hear him at the temple.

Judas agrees to betray Jesus

22 Now the Feast of Unleavened Bread, called the Passover, was approaching, 2 and the chief priests and the teachers of the

Phillips Modern English

"Be on your guard—see to it that your minds are never clouded by dissipation or drunkenness or the worries of this life, or else that day may catch you like the springing of a trap—for it will come upon every inhabitant of the whole earth.

"You must be vigilant at all times, praying that you may be strong enough to come safely through all that is going to happen, and stand in the presence of the Son of Man."

And every day he went on teaching in the Temple, and every evening he went off and spent the night on the hill which is called the Mount of Olives. And all the people used to come early in the morning to listen to him in the Temple.

22.1 *Judas Iscariot becomes the tool of the authorities*

Now as the feast of unleavened bread, called the Passover, was approaching, fear of the people made the chief priests and scribes try des-

Revised Standard Version

34 "But take heed to yourselves lest your
hearts be weighed down with dissipation and
drunkenness and cares of this life, and that day
come upon you suddenly like a snare; 35 for it
will come upon all who dwell upon the face of
the whole earth. 36 But watch at all times, praying that you may have strength to escape all
these things that will take place, and to stand
before the Son of man."
37 And every day he was teaching in the temple, but at night he went out and lodged on the
mount called Olivet. 38 And early in the morning
all the people came to him in the temple to hear
him.

22 Now the feast of Unleavened Bread drew
near, which is called the Passover. 2 And
the chief priests and the scribes were seeking

Jerusalem Bible

Be on the alert

34 "Watch yourselves, or your hearts will be
coarsened with debauchery and drunkenness and
the cares of life, and that day will be sprung
on you suddenly, 35 like a trap. For it will come
down on every living man on the face of the
earth. 36 Stay awake, praying at all times for
the strength to survive all that is going to happen, and to stand with confidence before the
Son of Man."

The last days of Jesus

37 In the daytime he would be in the Temple teaching, but would spend the night on the
hill called the Mount of Olives. 38 And from
early morning the people would gather around
him in the Temple to listen to him.

VI. The Passion

The conspiracy against Jesus: Judas betrays him

22 The feast of Unleavened Bread, called
the Passover, was now drawing near, 2 and
the chief priests and the scribes were looking

New English Bible

'Keep a watch on yourselves; do not let your minds be dulled by dissipation and drunkenness and worldly cares so that the great Day closes upon you suddenly like a trap; for that day will come on all men, wherever they are, the whole world over. Be on the alert, praying at all times for strength to pass safely through all these imminent troubles and to stand in the presence of the Son of Man.'

His days were given to teaching in the temple; and then he would leave the city and spend the night on the hill called Olivet. And in the early morning the people flocked to listen to him in the temple.[a]

The final conflict

22 Now the festival of Unleavened Bread, known as Passover, was approaching, and the chief priests and the doctors of the law were

[a] *Some witnesses here insert the pasage printed on pages 705 and 709.*

King James Version

might kill him; for they feared the people.
3 Then entered Satan into Judas surnamed
Iscariot, being of the number of the twelve. 4And
he went his way, and communed with the chief
priests and captains, how he might betray him
unto them. 5And they were glad, and covenanted
to give him money. 6And he promised, and
sought opportunity to betray him unto them in
the absence of the multitude.
7 Then came the day of unleavened bread,
when the passover must be killed. 8And he sent
Peter and John, saying, Go and prepare us the
passover, that we may eat. 9And they said unto
him, Where wilt thou that we prepare? 10And he
said unto them, Behold, when ye are entered
into the city, there shall a man meet you, bearing a pitcher of water; follow him into the house
where he entereth in. 11And ye shall say unto
the goodman of the house, The Master saith
unto thee, Where is the guestchamber, where I
shall eat the passover with my disciples? 12And

Living Bible

tively plotting Jesus' murder, trying to find a
way to kill him without starting a riot—a possibility they greatly feared.
3 Then Satan entered into Judas Iscariot, who
was one of the twelve disciples, 4 and he went
over to the chief priests and captains of the Temple guards to discuss the best way to betray Jesus to them. 5 They were, of course, delighted to
know that he was ready to help them and promised him a reward. 6 So he began to look for an
opportunity for them to arrest Jesus quietly when
the crowds weren't around.
7 Now the day of the Passover celebration arrived, when the Passover lamb was killed and
eaten with the unleavened bread. 8 Jesus sent
Peter and John ahead to find a place to prepare
their Passover meal.
9 "Where do you want us to go?" they asked.
10 And he replied, "As soon as you enter
Jerusalem,[a] you will see a man walking along
carrying a pitcher of water. Follow him into the
house he enters, 11 and say to the man who lives
there, 'Our Teacher says for you to show us the
guest room where he can eat the Passover meal
with his disciples.' 12 He will take you upstairs

[a] Literally, "the city."

Today's English Version

Law were trying to find some way of killing Jesus; because they were afraid of the people.

Judas agrees to betray Jesus

3 Then Satan went into Judas, called Iscariot,
who was one of the twelve disciples. 4 So Judas
went off and spoke with the chief priests and the
officers of the temple guard about how he could
hand Jesus over to them. 5 They were pleased
and offered to pay him money. 6 Judas agreed
to it and started looking for a good chance to
betray Jesus to them without the people knowing
about it.

Jesus prepares to eat the Passover meal

7 The day came during the Feast of Unleavened Bread when the lambs for the Passover
meal had to be killed. 8 Jesus sent Peter and
John with these instructions, "Go and get our
Passover meal ready for us to eat."
9 "Where do you want us to get it ready?"
they asked him.
10 He said, "Listen! As you go into the city a
man carrying a jar of water will meet you. Follow him into the house that he enters, 11 and
say to the owner of the house: 'The Teacher
says to you, Where is the room where my disciples and I will eat the Passover meal?' 12 He

New International Version

law were looking for some way to get rid of
Jesus, for they were afraid of the people. 3 Then
Satan entered Judas, called Iscariot, one of the
Twelve. 4And Judas went to the chief priests and
the officers of the temple guard and discussed
with them how he might betray Jesus. 5 They
were delighted and agreed to give him money.
6 He consented, and watched for an opportunity to hand Jesus over to them when no crowd
was present.

The Last Supper

7 Then came the day of Unleavened Bread
on which the Passover lamb had to be sacrificed. 8 Jesus sent Peter and John, saying, "Go
and make preparations for us to eat the Passover."
9 "Where do you want us to prepare for it?"
they asked.
10 He replied, "As you enter the city, a man
carrying a jar of water will meet you. Follow
him to the house that he enters, 11 and say to
the owner of the house, 'The Teacher asks:
Where is the guest room, where I may eat the
Passover with my disciples?' 12 He will show

Phillips Modern English

perately to find a way of getting rid of Jesus. Then Satan entered into the mind of Judas Iscariot, who was one of the twelve. He went and discussed with the chief priests and officers a method of getting Jesus into their hands. They were delighted and arranged to pay him cash for it. He agreed, and began to look for a suitable opportunity for betrayal when there was no crowd present.

22.7 Jesus makes arrangements for his last Passover with his disciples

Then the day of unleavened bread arrived, on which the Passover lamb had to be sacrificed, and Jesus sent off Peter and John with the words, "Go and make all the preparations for us to eat the Passover."

"Where would you like us to do this?" they asked.

And he replied,

"Listen, just as you're going into the city a man carrying a jug of water will meet you. Follow him to the house he is making for. Then say to the owner of the house, 'The master has this message for you—which is the room where my disciples and I may eat the Passover?' And

Revised Standard Version

how to put him to death; for they feared the
people.
3 Then Satan entered into Judas called Iscariot,
who was of the number of the twelve; 4 he went
away and conferred with the chief priests and
officers how he might betray him to them. 5And
they were glad, and engaged to give him money.
6 So he agreed, and sought an opportunity to betray him to them in the absence of the multitude.
7 Then came the day of Unleavened Bread,
on which the passover lamb had to be sacrificed.
8 So Jesus[h] sent Peter and John, saying, "Go
and prepare the passover for us, that we may eat
it." 9 They said to him, "Where will you have us
prepare it?" 10 He said to them, "Behold, when
you have entered the city, a man carrying a jar
of water will meet you; follow him into the
house which he enters, 11 and tell the householder, 'The Teacher says to you, Where is the
guest room, where I am to eat the passover with
my disciples?' 12And he will show you a large

[*h*] Greek *he*.

Jerusalem Bible

for some way of doing away with him, because
they mistrusted the people.
3 Then Satan entered into Judas, surnamed
Iscariot, who was numbered among the Twelve.
4 He went to the chief priests and the officers of
the guard[o] to discuss a scheme for handing
Jesus over to them. 5 They were delighted and
agreed to give him money. 6 He accepted, and
looked for an opportunity to betray him to them
without the people knowing.

Preparation for the Passover supper

7 The day of Unleavened Bread came around,
the day on which the passover had to be sacrificed, 8 and he sent Peter and John, saying, "Go
and make the preparations for us to eat the
passover." 9 "Where do you want us to prepare
it?" they asked. 10 "Listen," he said, "as you go
into the city you will meet a man carrying a
pitcher of water. Follow him into the house he
enters 11 and tell the owner of the house, 'The
Master has this to say to you: Where is the
dining room in which I can eat the passover with
my disciples?' 12 The man will show you a large

[*o*] The Temple police, chosen from among the Levites.

New English Bible

trying to devise some means of doing away with him; for they were afraid of the people.

Then Satan entered into Judas Iscariot, who was one of the Twelve; and Judas went to the chief priests and officers of the temple police to discuss ways and means of putting Jesus into their power. They were greatly pleased and undertook to pay him a sum of money. He agreed, and began to look out for an opportunity to betray him to them without collecting a crowd.

Then came the day of Unleavened Bread, on which the Passover victim had to be slaughtered, and Jesus sent Peter and John with these instructions: 'Go and prepare for our Passover supper.' 'Where would you like us to make the preparations?' they asked. He replied, 'As soon as you set foot in the city a man will meet you carrying a jar of water. Follow him into the house that he enters and give this message to the householder: "The Master says, 'Where is the room in which I may eat the Passover with my disciples?' " He will show you a large room up-

King James Version

he shall shew you a large upper room furnished:
there make ready. 13 And they went, and found
as he had said unto them: and they made ready
the passover. 14 And when the hour was come,
he sat down, and the twelve apostles with him.
15 And he said unto them, With desire I have
desired to eat this passover with you before I
suffer: 16 For I say unto you, I will not any more
eat thereof, until it be fulfilled in the kingdom
of God. 17 And he took the cup, and gave thanks,
and said, Take this, and divide *it* among yourselves: 18 For I say unto you, I will not drink
of the fruit of the vine, until the kingdom of
God shall come.
19 And he took bread, and gave thanks, and
brake *it,* and gave unto them, saying, This is my
body which is given for you: this do in remembrance of me. 20 Likewise also the cup after
supper, saying, This cup *is* the new testament in
my blood, which is shed for you.

Living Bible

to a large room all ready for us. That is the
place. Go ahead and prepare the meal there."
13 They went off to the city and found
everything just as Jesus had said, and prepared
the Passover supper.
14 Then Jesus and the others arrived, and at
the proper time all sat down together at the
table; 15 and he said, "I have looked forward to
this hour with deep longing, anxious to eat this
Passover meal with you before my suffering
begins. 16 For I tell you now that I won't eat it
again until what it represents has occurred in the
Kingdom of God."
17 Then he took a glass of wine, and when
he had given thanks for it, he said, "Take this
and share it among yourselves. 18 For I will not
drink wine again until the Kingdom of God has
come."
19 Then he took a loaf of bread; and when
he had thanked God for it, he broke it apart
and gave it to them, saying, "This is my body,
given for you. Eat it in remembrance of me."
20 After supper he gave them another glass
of wine, saying, "This wine is the token of God's
new agreement to save you—an agreement sealed
with the blood I shall pour out to purchase back

Today's English Version

will show you a large furnished room upstairs,
where you will get everything ready."
13 They went off and found everything just as
Jesus had told them, and prepared the Passover
meal.

The Lord's supper

14 When the hour came, Jesus took his place
at the table with the apostles. 15 He said to them,
"I have wanted so much to eat this Passover
meal with you before I suffer! 16 For I tell you,
I will never eat it until it is given its full meaning in the Kingdom of God."
17 Then Jesus took the cup, gave thanks to
God, and said, "Take this and share it among
yourselves; 18 for I tell you that I will not drink
this wine from now on until the Kingdom of
God comes."
19 Then he took the bread, gave thanks to
God, broke it, and gave it to them, saying, "This
is my body [which is given for you. Do this in
memory of me." 20 In the same way he gave
them the cup, after the supper, saying, "This cup
is God's new covenant sealed with my blood
which is poured out for you.]

New International Version

you a large upper room, all furnished. Make
preparations there."
13 They left and found things just as Jesus
had told them. So they prepared the Passover.
14 When the hour came, Jesus and his apostles reclined at the table. 15 And he said to them,
"I have eagerly desired to eat this Passover with
you before I suffer. 16 For I tell you, I will not
eat it again until it finds fulfillment in the kingdom of God."
17 After taking the cup, he gave thanks and
said, "Take this and divide it among you. 18 For
I tell you I will not drink again from the fruit
of the vine until the kingdom of God comes."
19 And he took some bread, gave thanks and
broke it, and gave it to them, saying, "This is
my body given for you; do this in remembrance
of me."
20 In the same way, after the supper he took
the cup, saying, "This cup is the new covenant

Phillips Modern English

he will take you upstairs and show you a large room furnished for our needs. Make all the preparations there."

So they went off and found everything exactly as he had told them it would be, and they made the Passover preparations.

Then, when the time came, he took his seat at table with the apostles, and spoke to them,

"With all my heart I have longed to eat this Passover with you before the time comes for me to suffer. Believe me, I shall not eat the Passover again until all that it means is fulfilled in the kingdom of God."

Then taking a cup from them, he thanked God and said,

"Take this and share it amongst yourselves, for I tell you that from this moment I shall drink no more wine until the kingdom of God comes."

22.19 The mysterious words which were remembered later

Then he took a loaf and after thanking God he broke it and gave it to them, with these words,

"This is my body which is given for you: do this in remembrance of me."

So too, he gave them a cup after supper with the words,

"This cup is the new agreement made in my

Revised Standard Version

upper room furnished; there make ready." 13And
they went, and found it as he had told them; and
they prepared the passover.
14 And when the hour came, he sat at table,
and the apostles with him. 15And he said to
them, "I have earnestly desired to eat this passover with you before I suffer; 16 for I tell you
I shall not eat it[i] until it is fulfilled in the kingdom of God." 17And he took a cup, and when
he had given thanks he said, "Take this, and
divide it among yourselves; 18 for I tell you that
from now on I shall not drink of the fruit of the
vine until the kingdom of God comes." 19And
he took bread, and when he had given thanks
he broke it and gave it to them, saying, "This
is my body which is given for you. Do this in
remembrance of me." 20And likewise the cup
after supper, saying, "This cup which is poured
out for you is the new covenant in my blood.[j]

[i] Other ancient authorities read *never eat it again*.
[j] Other authorities omit, in whole or in part, verses 19b-20 (*which is given . . . in my blood*).

Jerusalem Bible

upper room furnished with couches. Make the
preparations there." 13 They set off and found
everything as he had told them, and prepared
the passover.

The supper

14 When the hour came he took his place at
table, and the apostles with him. 15And he said
to them, "I have longed to eat this passover with
you before I suffer; 16 because, I tell you, I shall
not eat it again until it is fulfilled in the kingdom
of God."
17 Then, taking a cup,[p] he gave thanks and
said, "Take this and share it among you, 18 because from now on, I tell you, I shall not drink
wine until the kingdom of God comes."

The institution of the Eucharist

19 Then he took some bread and when he had
given thanks, broke it and gave it to them, saying, "This is my body which will be given for
you; do this as a memorial of me." 20 He did the
same with the cup after supper, and said, "This
cup is the new covenant in my blood which will
be poured out for you.

[p] Luke distinguishes the Passover and the cup of vv. 15-18 from the bread and the cup of vv. 19-20.

New English Bible

stairs all set out: make the preparations there.' They went and found everything as he had said. So they prepared for Passover.

When the time came he took his place at table, and the apostles with him; and he said to them, 'How I have longed [a] to eat this Passover with you before my death! For I tell you, never again shall I [b] eat it until the time when it finds its fulfilment in the kingdom of God.'

Then he took a cup, and after giving thanks he said, 'Take this and share it among yourselves; for I tell you, from this moment I shall drink from the fruit of the vine no more until the time when the kingdom of God comes.' And he took bread, gave thanks, and broke it; and he gave it to them, with the words: 'This is my body.' [c]

[a] *Or* said to them, 'I longed . . .' [b] *Some witnesses read* For I tell you, I shall not . . . [c] *Some witnesses add, in whole or in part, and with various arrangements, the following:* 'which is given for you; do this as a memorial of me.' (20) In the same way he took the cup after supper, and said, 'This cup, poured out for you, is the new covenant sealed by my blood.'

King James Version

21 But, behold, the hand of him that betrayeth me *is* with me on the table. 22And truly the
Son of man goeth, as it was determined: but woe
unto that man by whom he is betrayed! 23And
they began to inquire among themselves, which
of them it was that should do this thing.
24 And there was also a strife among them,
which of them should be accounted the greatest.
25And he said unto them, The kings of the
Gentiles exercise lordship over them; and they
that exercise authority upon them are called
benefactors. 26 But ye *shall* not *be* so: but he
that is greatest among you, let him be as the
younger; and he that is chief, as he that doth
serve. 27 For whether *is* greater, he that sitteth
at meat, or he that serveth? *is* not he that sitteth
at meat? but I am among you as he that serveth.
28 Ye are they which have continued with me in
my temptations. 29And I appoint unto you a
kingdom, as my Father hath appointed unto me;
30 That ye may eat and drink at my table in my
kingdom, and sit on thrones judging the twelve
tribes of Israel.

Living Bible

your souls.[b] 21 But here at this table, sitting
among us as a friend, is the man who will betray me. 22 I [c] must die. It is part of God's plan.
But, oh, the horror awaiting that man who betrays me."
23 Then the disciples wondered among themselves which of them would ever do such a thing.
24 And they began to argue among themselves
as to who would have the highest rank [in the
coming Kingdom[d]].
25 Jesus told them, "In this world the kings
and great men order their slaves around, and the
slaves have no choice but to like it! [e] 26 But
among you, the one who serves you best will be
your leader. 27 Out in the world the master sits
at the table and is served by his servants. But
not here! For I am your servant. 28 Nevertheless,
because you have stood true to me in these terrible days,[f] 29 and because my Father has
granted me a Kingdom, I, here and now, grant
you the right 30 to eat and drink at my table in
that Kingdom; and you will sit on thrones judging the twelve tribes of Israel.

[*b*] Literally, "This cup is the new covenant in my blood, poured out for you." [*c*] Literally, "the Son of Man." [*d*] Implied. [*e*] Literally, "they (the kings and great men) are called 'benefactors.'" [*f*] Literally, "you have continued with me in my temptation."

Today's English Version

21 "But, look! The one who betrays me is here
at the table with me! 22 Because the Son of
Man will die as God has decided it; but how
terrible for that man who betrays him!"
23 Then they began to ask among themselves
which one of them it could be who was going to
do this.

The argument about greatness

24 An argument came up among the disciples
as to which one of them should be thought of as
the greatest. 25 Jesus said to them, "The kings
of this world have power over their people, and
the rulers are called 'Friends of the People.'
26 But this is not the way it is with you; rather,
the greatest one among you must be like the
youngest, and the leader must be like the servant.
27 Who is greater, the one who sits down to eat
or the one who serves him? The one who sits
down, of course. But I am among you as one
who serves.
28 "You have stayed with me all through my
trials; 29 and just as my Father has given me
the right to rule, so I will make the same agreement with you. 30 You will eat and drink at my
table in my Kingdom, and you will sit on thrones
to judge the twelve tribes of Israel."

New International Version

in my blood, which is poured out for you. 21 But
the hand of him who is going to betray me is
with mine on the table. 22 The Son of Man will
go as it has been decreed, but woe to that man
who betrays him." 23 They began to question
among themselves which of them it might be
who would do this.
24 Also a dispute arose among them as to
which of them was considered to be greatest.
25 Jesus said to them, "The kings of the Gentiles lord it over them; and those who exercise
authority over them are given the title Benefactor. 26 But you are not to be like that. Instead, the greatest among you should be like
the youngest, and the one who rules like the one
who serves. 27 For who is greater, the one who
is at the table or the one who serves? Is it not
the one who is at the table? But I am among
you as one who serves. 28 You are those who
have stood by me in my trials. 29And I confer
on you a kingdom, just as my Father conferred
one on me, 30 so that you may eat and drink at
my table in my kingdom and sit on thrones,
judging the twelve tribes of Israel.

Phillips Modern English

own blood which is shed for you. Yet the hand of the man who is betraying me lies with mine on this table. The Son of Man goes on his appointed way: yet alas for the man by whom he is betrayed!"

22.23 Jesus again teaches humility

And at this they began to debate among themselves as to which of them would do this thing.

And then a dispute arose among them as to who should be considered the most important.

But Jesus said to them,

"Among the heathen it is their kings who lord it over them, and their rulers are given the title of 'benefactors'. But it must not be so with you! Your greatest man must become like a junior and your leader must be a servant. Who is the greater, the man who sits down to dinner or the man who serves him? Obviously, the man who sits down to dinner—yet I am among you as your servant. But you are the men who have stood by me in all that I have gone through, and as surely as my Father has given me my kingdom, so I give you the right to eat and drink at my table in that kingdom. Yes, you will sit on thrones and judge the twelve tribes of Israel!

Revised Standard Version

21 But behold the hand of him who betrays me
is with me on the table. 22 For the Son of man
goes as it has been determined; but woe to that
man by whom he is betrayed!" 23 And they began to question one another, which of them it
was that would do this.
24 A dispute also arose among them, which
of them was to be regarded as the greatest.
25 And he said to them, "The kings of the Gentiles exercise lordship over them; and those in
authority over them are called benefactors.
26 But not so with you; rather let the greatest
among you become as the youngest, and the
leader as one who serves. 27 For which is the
greater, one who sits at table, or one who serves?
Is it not the one who sits at table? But I am
among you as one who serves.
28 "You are those who have continued with
me in my trials; 29 and I assign to you, as my
Father assigned to me, a kingdom, 30 that you
may eat and drink at my table in my kingdom,
and sit on thrones judging the twelve tribes of
Israel.

Jerusalem Bible

The treachery of Judas foretold

21 "And yet, here with me on the table is the
hand of the man who betrays me. 22 The Son
of Man does indeed go to his fate even as it
has been decreed, but alas for that man by whom
he is betrayed!" 23 And they began to ask one
another which of them it could be who was to
do this thing.

Who is the greatest?

24 A dispute arose also between them about
which should be reckoned the greatest, 25 but he
said to them, "Among pagans it is the kings who
lord it over them, and those who have authority
over them are given the title Benefactor. 26 This
must not happen with you. No; the greatest
among you must behave as if he were the youngest, the leader as if he were the one who serves.
27 For who is the greater: the one at table or
the one who serves? The one at table, surely? Yet
here am I among you as one who serves!

The reward promised to the apostles

28 "You are the men who have stood by me
faithfully in my trials; 29 and now I confer a
kingdom on you, just as my Father conferred
one on me: 30 you will eat and drink at my
table in my kingdom, and you will sit on thrones
to judge the twelve tribes of Israel.

New English Bible

'But mark this—my betrayer is here, his hand with mine on the table. For the Son of Man is going his appointed way; but alas for that man by whom he is betrayed!' At this they began to ask among themselves which of them it could possibly be who was to do this thing.

Then a jealous dispute broke out: who among them should rank highest? But he said, 'In the world, kings lord it over their subjects; and those in authority are called their country's "Benefactors". Not so with you: on the contrary, the highest among you must bear himself like the youngest, the chief of you like a servant. For who is greater—the one who sits at table or the servant who waits on him? Surely the one who sits at table. Yet here am I among you like a servant.

'You are the men who have stood firmly by me in my times of trial; and now I vest in you the kingship which my Father vested in me; you shall eat and drink at my table in my kingdom and sit[a] on thrones as judges of the twelve tribes of Israel.

[a] *Or* trial; and as my Father gave me the right to reign, so I give you the right to eat and to drink . . . and to sit . . .

King James Version

31 And the Lord said, Simon, Simon, behold,
Satan hath desired *to have* you, that he may sift
you as wheat: 32 But I have prayed for thee,
that thy faith fail not: and when thou art converted, strengthen thy brethren. 33 And he said
unto him, Lord, I am ready to go with thee,
both into prison, and to death. 34 And he said, I
tell thee, Peter, the cock shall not crow this
day, before that thou shalt thrice deny that thou
knowest me. 35 And he said unto them, When I
sent you without purse, and scrip, and shoes,
lacked ye any thing? And they said, Nothing.
36 Then said he unto them, But now, he that
hath a purse, let him take *it,* and likewise *his*
scrip: and he that hath no sword, let him sell his
garment, and buy one. 37 For I say unto you,
that this that is written must yet be accomplished in me, And he was reckoned among the
transgressors: for the things concerning me have

Living Bible

31 "Simon, Simon, Satan has asked to have
you, to sift you like wheat, 32 but I have pleaded
in prayer for you that your faith should not
completely fail.[g] So when you have repented and
turned to me again, strengthen and build up the
faith of your brothers."
33 Simon said, "Lord, I am ready to go to
jail with you, and even to die with you."
34 But Jesus said, "Peter, let me tell you
something. Between now and tomorrow morning when the rooster crows, you will deny me
three times, declaring that you don't even know
me."
35 Then Jesus asked them, "When I sent you
out to preach the Good News and you were
without money, duffle bag, or extra clothing,
how did you get along?"
"Fine," they replied.
36 "But now," he said, "take a duffle bag if
you have one, and your money. And if you don't
have a sword, better sell your clothes and buy
one! 37 For the time has come for this prophecy
about me to come true: 'He will be condemned
as a criminal!' Yes, everything written about me
by the prophets will come true."

[g] Literally, "fail not."

Today's English Version

Jesus predicts Peter's denial

31 "Simon, Simon! Listen! Satan has received
permission to test all of you, as a farmer separates the wheat from the chaff. 32 But I have
prayed for you, Simon, that your faith will not
fail. And when you turn back to me, you must
strengthen your brothers."
33 Peter answered, "Lord, I am ready to go
to prison with you and to die with you!"
34 "I tell you, Peter," Jesus answered, "the
rooster will not crow today until you have said
three times that you do not know me."

Purse, bag, and sword

35 Then Jesus said to them, "When I sent you
out that time without purse, bag, or shoes, did
you lack anything?"
"Not a thing," they answered.
36 "But now," Jesus said, "whoever has a
purse or a bag must take it; and whoever does
not have a sword must sell his coat and buy one.
37 For I tell you this: the scripture that says,
'He was included with criminals,' must come
true about me. Because that which was written
about me is coming true."

New International Version

31 "Simon, Simon, Satan has asked to sift
you all as wheat. 32 But I have prayed for you,
Simon, that your faith may not fail. And when
you have returned to me, strengthen your brothers."
33 But he replied, "Lord, I am ready to go
with you to prison and to death."
34 Jesus answered, "I tell you, Peter, before
the rooster crows today, you will deny three
times that you know me."
35 Then Jesus asked them, "When I sent you
without purse, bag or sandals, did you lack anything?"
"Nothing," they answered.
36 He said to them, "But now if you have a
purse, take it, and also a bag; and if you don't
have a sword, sell your cloak and buy one. 37 It
is written: 'And he was numbered with the transgressors'[u]; and I tell you that this must be fulfilled in me. Yes, what is written about me is
reaching its fulfillment."

[u] Isaiah 53:12.

Phillips Modern English

22.31 The personal warning to Simon

"Oh, Simon, Simon, do you know that Satan has asked to have you all to sift like wheat?—but I have prayed for you that you may not lose your faith. Yes, when you have turned back to me, you must strengthen these brothers of yours."

Peter said to him,

"Lord, I am ready to go to prison, or even to die with you!"

"I tell you, Peter," returned Jesus, "before the cock crows today you will deny three times that you know me!"

22.35 Jesus tells his disciples that the crisis has arrived

Then he continued to them all,

"That time when I sent you out without any purse or wallet or shoes—did you find you needed anything?"

"No, not a thing," they replied.

"But now," Jesus continued, "if you have a purse or wallet, take it with you, and if you have no sword, sell your coat and buy one! For I tell you that this scripture must be fulfilled in me—

And he was reckoned with transgressors.

So comes the end of what they wrote about me."

Revised Standard Version

31 "Simon, Simon, behold, Satan demanded
to have you,[k] that he might sift you[k] like wheat,
32 but I have prayed for you that your faith may
not fail; and when you have turned again,
strengthen your brethren." 33 And he said to him,
"Lord, I am ready to go with you to prison
and to death." 34 He said, "I tell you, Peter, the
cock will not crow this day, until you three
times deny that you know me."
35 And he said to them, "When I sent you
out with no purse or bag or sandals, did you
lack anything?" They said, "Nothing." 36 He
said to them, "But now, let him who has a purse
take it, and likewise a bag. And let him who has
no sword sell his mantle and buy one. 37 For I
tell you that this scripture must be fulfilled in
me, 'And he was reckoned with transgressors';
for what is written about me has its fulfilment."

[k] The Greek word for *you* here is plural; in verse 32 it is singular.

Jerusalem Bible

Peter's denial and repentance foretold

31 "Simon, Simon! Satan, you must know, has
got his wish to sift you all like wheat; 32 but I
have prayed for you, Simon, that your faith may
not fail, and once you have recovered, you in
your turn must strengthen your brothers."
33 "Lord," he answered, "I would be ready to go
to prison with you, and to death." 34 Jesus replied,
"I tell you, Peter, by the time the cock
crows today you will have denied three times
that you know me."

A time of crisis

35 He said to them, "When I sent you out
without purse or haversack or sandals, were you
short of anything?" 36 "No," they said. He said
to them, "But now if you have a purse, take it;
if you have a haversack, do the same; if you
have no sword, sell your cloak and buy one,
37 because I tell you these words of scripture
have to be fulfilled in me: *He let himself be
taken for a criminal.*[q] Yes, what scripture says
about me is even now reaching its fulfillment."

[q] Is. 53:12.

New English Bible

'Simon, Simon, take heed: Satan has been given leave to sift all of you like wheat; but for you I have prayed that your faith may not fail; and when you have come to yourself, you must lend strength to your brothers.' 'Lord,' he replied, 'I am ready to go with you to prison and death.' Jesus said, 'I tell you, Peter, the cock will not crow tonight until you have three times over denied that you know me.'

He said to them, 'When I sent you out barefoot without purse or pack, were you ever short of anything?' 'No,' they answered. 'It is different now,' he said; 'whoever has a purse had better take it with him, and his pack too; and if he has no sword, let him sell his cloak to buy one. For Scripture says, "And he was counted among the outlaws", and these words, I tell you, must find fulfilment in me; indeed, all that is written of me

King James Version

an end. 38And they said, Lord, behold, here *are*
two swords. And he said unto them, It is enough.
39 And he came out, and went, as he was
wont, to the mount of Olives; and his disciples
also followed him. 40And when he was at the
place, he said unto them, Pray that ye enter not
into temptation. 41And he was withdrawn from
them about a stone's cast, and kneeled down,
and prayed, 42 Saying, Father, if thou be willing,
remove this cup from me: nevertheless, not my
will, but thine, be done. 43And there appeared
an angel unto him from heaven, strengthening
him. 44And being in an agony he prayed more
earnestly: and his sweat was as it were great
drops of blood falling down to the ground.
45And when he rose up from prayer, and was
come to his disciples, he found them sleeping
for sorrow, 46And said unto them, Why sleep
ye? rise and pray, lest ye enter into temptation.
47 And while he yet spake, behold a multitude, and he that was called Judas, one of the
twelve, went before them, and drew near unto

Living Bible

38 "Master," they replied, "we have two
swords among us."
"Enough!" he said.
39 Then, accompanied by the disciples, he left
the upstairs room and went as usual to the
Mount of Olives. 40 There he told them, "Pray
God that you will not be overcome[h] by temptation."
41, 42 He walked away, perhaps a stone's
throw, and knelt down and prayed this prayer:
"Father, if you are willing, please take away this
cup of horror from me. But I want your will, not
mine." 43 Then an angel from heaven appeared
and strengthened him, 44 for he was in such
agony of spirit that he broke into a sweat of
blood, with great drops falling to the ground as
he prayed more and more earnestly. 45At last
he stood up again and returned to the disciples
—only to find them asleep, exhausted from grief.
46 "Asleep!" he said. "Get up! Pray God that
you will not fall when you are tempted."
47 But even as he said this, a mob approached, led by Judas, one of his twelve disciples. Judas walked over to Jesus and kissed him
on the cheek in friendly greeting.[i]

[h] Literally, "that you enter not into temptation."
[i] Literally, "approached Jesus to kiss him." This is still the traditional greeting among men in eastern lands.

Today's English Version

38 The disciples said, "Look! Here are two
swords, Lord!"
"That is enough!" he answered.

Jesus prays on the Mount of Olives

39 Jesus left the city and went, as he usually
did, to the Mount of Olives; and the disciples
went with him. 40 When he came to the place he
said to them, "Pray that you will not fall into
temptation."
41 Then he went off from them, about the distance of a stone's throw, and knelt down and
prayed. 42 "Father," he said, "if you will, take
this cup away from me. Not my will, however,
but your will be done." [43An angel from heaven
appeared to him and strengthened him. 44 In
great anguish he prayed even more fervently; his
sweat was like drops of blood, falling to the
ground.]
45 Rising from his prayer, he went back to
the disciples and found them asleep, worn out
by their grief. 46And he said to them, "Why are
you sleeping? Get up, and pray that you will not
fall into temptation."

The arrest of Jesus

47 Jesus was still speaking when a crowd
arrived. Judas, one of the twelve disciples, was
leading them, and he came up to Jesus to kiss

New International Version

38 The disciples said, "See, Lord, here are
two swords."
"That is enough," he replied.

Jesus prays on the Mount of Olives

39 Jesus went out as usual to the Mount of
Olives, and his disciples followed him. 40 On
reaching the place, he said to them, "Pray so
that you will not fall into temptation." 41 He
withdrew about a stone's throw beyond them,
knelt down and prayed, 42 "Father, if you are
willing, take this cup from me; yet not my will,
but yours be done." 43An angel from heaven
appeared to him and strengthened him. 44And
being in anguish, he prayed more earnestly, and
his sweat was like drops of blood falling to the
ground.[v]
45 When he rose from prayer and went back
to the disciples, he found them asleep, exhausted
from sorrow. 46 "Why are you sleeping?" he
asked them. "Get up and pray so that you will
not fall into temptation."

Jesus arrested

47 While he was still speaking a crowd came
up, and the man who was called Judas, one of
the Twelve, was leading them. He approached

[v] Some early MSS omit verses 43 and 44.

Phillips Modern English

Then the disciples said,
"Lord, look, here are two swords."
And Jesus returned,
"That is enough."

Then he went out of the city and up on to the Mount of Olives, as he had often done before, with the disciples following him. And when he reached his usual place, he said to them,

"Pray that you may not have to face temptation!"

Then he went off by himself, about a stone's throw away, and falling on his knees, prayed in these words—

"Father, if you are willing, take this cup away from me—but it is not my will, but yours, that must be done."

Then he got to his feet from his prayer and walking back to the disciples, he found them sleeping through sheer grief.

"Why are you sleeping?" he said to them. "You must get up and go on praying that you may not have to face temptation."

22.47 The mob arrives and Judas betrays

While he was still speaking a crowd of people suddenly appeared led by the man called Judas, one of the twelve. He stepped up to Jesus to kiss him.

Revised Standard Version

38 And they said, "Look, Lord, here are two
swords." And he said to them, "It is enough."
39 And he came out, and went, as was his
custom, to the Mount of Olives; and the disciples followed him. 40 And when he came to the
place he said to them, "Pray that you may not
enter into temptation." 41 And he withdrew from
them about a stone's throw, and knelt down and
prayed, 42 "Father, if thou art willing, remove
this cup from me; nevertheless not my will, but
thine, be done." [l] 45 And when he rose from
prayer, he came to the disciples and found them
sleeping for sorrow, 46 and he said to them,
"Why do you sleep? Rise and pray that you may
not enter into temptation."
47 While he was still speaking, there came a
crowd, and the man called Judas, one of the
twelve, was leading them. He drew near to Jesus

[l] Other ancient authorities add verses 43 and 44: 43 *And there appeared to him an angel from heaven, strengthening him.* 44 *And being in an agony he prayed more earnestly; and his sweat became like great drops of blood falling down upon the ground.*

Jerusalem Bible

38 "Lord," they said, "there are two swords here
now." He said to them, "That is enough!"

The Mount of Olives

39 He then left to make his way as usual to
the Mount of Olives, with the disciples following. 40 When they reached the place he said to
them, "Pray not to be put to the test."
41 Then he withdrew from them, about a
stone's throw away, and knelt down and prayed.
42 "Father," he said, "if you are willing, take this
cup away from me. Nevertheless, let your will
be done, not mine." 43 Then an angel appeared
to him, coming from heaven to give him strength.
44 In his anguish he prayed even more earnestly,
and his sweat fell to the ground like great drops
of blood.
45 When he rose from prayer he went to the
disciples and found them sleeping for sheer grief.
46 "Why are you asleep?" he said to them. "Get
up and pray not to be put to the test."

The arrest

47 He was still speaking when a number of
men appeared, and at the head of them the
man called Judas, one of the Twelve, who went

New English Bible

is being fulfilled.' 'Look, Lord,' they said, 'we have two swords here.' 'Enough, enough!' he replied.

Then he went out and made his way as usual to the Mount of Olives, accompanied by the disciples. When he reached the place he said to them, 'Pray that you may be spared the hour of testing.' He himself withdrew from them about a stone's throw, knelt down, and began to pray: 'Father, if it be thy will, take this cup away from me. Yet not my will but thine be done.'

And now there appeared to him an angel from heaven bringing him strength, and in anguish of spirit he prayed the more urgently; and his sweat was like clots of blood falling to the ground.[a]

When he rose from prayer and came to the disciples he found them asleep, worn out by grief. 'Why are you sleeping?' he said. 'Rise and pray that you may be spared the test.'

While he was still speaking a crowd appeared with the man called Judas, one of the Twelve, at

[a] *Some witnesses omit* And now . . . ground.

King James Version

Jesus to kiss him. 48 But Jesus said unto him,
Judas, betrayest thou the Son of man with a
kiss? 49 When they which were about him saw
what would follow, they said unto him, Lord,
shall we smite with the sword?
50 And one of them smote the servant of the
high priest, and cut off his right ear. 51And Jesus answered and said, Suffer ye thus far. And
he touched his ear, and healed him. 52 Then
Jesus said unto the chief priests, and captains of
the temple, and the elders, which were come to
him, Be ye come out, as against a thief, with
swords and staves? 53 When I was daily with you
in the temple, ye stretched forth no hands against
me: but this is your hour, and the power of
darkness.
54 Then took they him, and led *him,* and
brought him into the high priest's house. And
Peter followed afar off. 55And when they had
kindled a fire in the midst of the hall, and were
set down together, Peter sat down among them.
56 But a certain maid beheld him as he sat by
the fire, and earnestly looked upon him, and
said, This man was also with him. 57And he
denied him, saying, Woman, I know him not.
58And after a little while another saw him, and
said, Thou art also of them. And Peter said,

Living Bible

48 But Jesus said, "Judas, how can you do
this—betray the Messiah with a kiss?"
49 When the other disciples saw what was
about to happen, they exclaimed, "Master, shall
we fight? We brought along the swords!" 50And
one of them slashed at the High Priest's servant,
and cut off his right ear.
51 But Jesus said, "Don't resist any more."
And he touched the place where the man's ear
had been and restored it. 52 Then Jesus addressed
the chief priests and captains of the Temple
guards and the religious leaders who headed the
mob. "Am I a robber," he asked, "that you
have come armed with swords and clubs to get
me? 53 Why didn't you arrest me in the Temple? I was there every day. But this is your moment—the time when Satan's power reigns supreme."
54 So they seized him and led him to the
High Priest's residence, and Peter followed at a
distance. 55 The soldiers lit a fire in the courtyard and sat around it for warmth, and Peter
joined them there.
56 A servant girl noticed him in the firelight
and began staring at him. Finally she spoke:
"This man was with Jesus!"
57 Peter denied it. "Woman," he said, "I
don't even know the man!"
58 After a while someone else looked at him
and said, "You must be one of them!"

Today's English Version

him. 48 But Jesus said, "Is it with a kiss, Judas,
that you betray the Son of Man?"
49 When the disciples who were with Jesus saw
what was going to happen, they said, "Shall we
strike with our swords, Lord?" 50And one of
them struck the High Priest's slave and cut off
his right ear.
51 But Jesus said, "Enough of this!" He
touched the man's ear and healed him.
52 Then Jesus said to the chief priests and
the officers of the temple guard and the elders
who had come there to get him, "Did you have
to come with swords and clubs, as though I were
an outlaw? 53 I was with you in the temple every
day, and you did not try to arrest me. But this
is your hour to act, when the power of darkness
rules."

Peter denies Jesus

54 They arrested Jesus and took him away
into the house of the High Priest; and Peter followed from a distance. 55A fire had been lit in
the center of the courtyard, and Peter joined
those who were sitting around it. 56 When one
of the servant girls saw him sitting there at the
fire, she looked straight at him and said, "This
man too was with him!"
57 But Peter denied it, "Woman, I don't even
know him!"
58 After a little while, a man noticed him and
said, "You are one of them, too!"

New International Version

Jesus to kiss him, 48 but Jesus asked him, "Judas,
are you betraying the Son of Man with a kiss?"
49 When Jesus' followers saw what was going
to happen, they said, "Lord, should we strike
with our swords?" 50And one of them struck
the servant of the high priest, cutting off his
right ear.
51 But Jesus answered, "No more of this!"
And he touched the man's ear and healed him.
52 Then Jesus said to the chief priests, the
officers of the temple guard, and the elders, who
had come for him, "Am I leading a rebellion,
that you have come with swords and clubs?
53 Every day I was with you in the temple
courts, and you did not lay a hand on me. But
this is your hour—when darkness reigns."

Peter disowns Jesus

54 Then seizing him, they led him away and
took him into the house of the high priest. Peter
followed at a distance. 55 But when they had
kindled a fire in the midde of the courtyard and
had sat down together, Peter sat down with
them. 56A servant girl saw him seated there in
the firelight. She looked closely at him and said,
"This man was with him."
57 But he denied it. "Girl, I don't know him,"
he said.
58 A little later someone else saw him and
said, "You also are one of them."

Phillips Modern English

"Judas, would you betray the Son of Man with a kiss?" said Jesus to him.

And the disciples, seeing what was going to happen cried,

"Lord, shall we use our swords?"

And one of them did slash at the High Priest's servant, cutting off his right ear. But Jesus retorted,

"That is enough!"

And he touched his ear and healed him. Then he spoke to the chief priests, Temple officers and elders who were there to arrest him,

"So you have come out with your swords and staves as if I were a bandit. Day after day I was with you in the Temple and you never laid a finger on me—but this is your hour and the power of darkness is yours!"

22.54 Jesus is arrested: Peter follows but denies his master three times

Then they arrested him and marched him off to the High Priest's house. Peter followed at a distance, and sat down among some people who had lighted a fire in the middle of the courtyard and were sitting round it. A maid-servant saw him sitting there in the firelight, peered into his face and said,

"This man was with him too."

But he denied it and said,

"I don't know him, girl!"

A few minutes later someone else noticed Peter, and said,

Revised Standard Version

to kiss him; 48 but Jesus said to him, "Judas, would you betray the Son of man with a kiss?" 49 And when those who were about him saw what would follow, they said, "Lord, shall we strike with the sword?" 50 And one of them struck the slave of the high priest and cut off his right ear. 51 But Jesus said, "No more of this!" And he touched his ear and healed him. 52 Then Jesus said to the chief priests and officers of the temple and elders, who had come out against him, "Have you come out as against a robber, with swords and clubs? 53 When I was with you day after day in the temple, you did not lay hands on me. But this is your hour, and the power of darkness."

54 Then they seized him and led him away, bringing him into the high priest's house. Peter followed at a distance; 55 and when they had kindled a fire in the middle of the courtyard and sat down together, Peter sat among them. 56 Then a maid, seeing him as he sat in the light and gazing at him, said, "This man also was with him." 57 But he denied it, saying, "Woman, I do not know him." 58 And a little later some one else saw him and said, "You

Jerusalem Bible

up to Jesus to kiss him. 48 Jesus said, "Judas, are you betraying the Son of Man with a kiss?" 49 His followers, seeing what was happening, said, "Lord, shall we use our swords?" 50 And one of them struck out at the high priest's servant and cut off his right ear. 51 But at this Jesus spoke. "Leave off!" he said. "That will do!" And touching the man's ear he healed him.

52 Then Jesus spoke to the chief priests and captains of the Temple guard and elders who had come for him. "Am I a brigand," he said, "that you had to set out with swords and clubs? 53 When I was among you in the Temple day after day you never moved to lay hands on me. But this is your hour; this is the reign of darkness."

Peter's denials

54 They seized him then and led him away, and they took him to the high priest's house. Peter followed at a distance. 55 They had lit a fire in the middle of the courtyard and Peter sat down among them, 56 and as he was sitting there by the blaze a servant girl saw him, peered at him, and said, "This person was with him too." 57 But he denied it. "Woman," he said, "I do not know him." 58 Shortly afterward someone else saw him and said, "You are another of them."

New English Bible

their head. He came up to Jesus to kiss him; but Jesus said, 'Judas, would you betray the Son of Man with a kiss?'

When his followers saw what was coming, they said, 'Lord, shall we use our swords?' And one of them struck at the High Priest's servant, cutting off his right ear. But Jesus answered, 'Let them have their way.' Then he touched the man's ear and healed him.[b]

Turning to the chief priests, the officers of the temple police, and the elders, who had come to seize him, he said, 'Do you take me for a bandit, that you have come out with swords and cudgels to arrest me? Day after day, when I was in the temple with you, you kept your hands off me. But this is your moment—the hour when darkness reigns.'

Then they arrested him and led him away. They brought him to the High Priest's house, and Peter followed at a distance. They lit a fire in the middle of the courtyard and sat round it, and Peter sat among them. A serving-maid who saw him sitting in the firelight stared at him and said, 'This man was with him too.' But he denied it: 'Woman,' he said, 'I do not know him.' A little later someone else noticed him and said, 'You also are one of them.' But Peter said to

[b] *Or* 'Let me do as much as this', and touching the man's ear, he healed him.

King James Version

Man, I am not. 59And about the space of one
hour after another confidently affirmed, saying,
Of a truth this *fellow* also was with him; for he
is a Galilean. 60And Peter said, Man, I know
not what thou sayest. And immediately, while he
yet spake, the cock crew. 61And the Lord turned,
and looked upon Peter. And Peter remembered
the word of the Lord, how he had said unto
him, Before the cock crow, thou shalt deny me
thrice. 62And Peter went out, and wept bitterly.
63 And the men that held Jesus mocked him,
and smote *him*. 64And when they had blindfolded him, they struck him on the face, and
asked him, saying, Prophesy, who is it that smote
thee? 65And many other things blasphemously
spake they against him.

66 And as soon as it was day, the elders of
the people and the chief priests and the scribes
came together, and led him into their council,
saying, 67Art thou the Christ? tell us. And he
said unto them, If I tell you, ye will not believe: 68And if I also ask *you*, ye will not answer me, nor let *me* go. 69 Hereafter shall the

Living Bible

"No sir, I am not!" Peter replied.
59 About an hour later someone else flatly
stated, "I know this fellow is one of Jesus' disciples, for both are from Galilee."
60 But Peter said, "Man, I don't know what
you are talking about." And as he said the
words, a rooster crowed.
61 At that moment Jesus turned and looked
at Peter. Then Peter remembered what he had
said—"Before the rooster crows tomorrow morning, you will deny me three times." 62And Peter
walked out of the courtyard, crying bitterly.
63, 64 Now the guards in charge of Jesus began mocking him. They blindfolded him and hit
him with their fists and asked, "Who hit you that
time, prophet?" 65And they threw all sorts of
other insults at him.
66 Early the next morning at daybreak the
Jewish Supreme Court assembled, including the
chief priests and all the top religious authorities
of the nation. Jesus was led before this Council,
67, 68 and instructed to state whether or not he
claimed to be the Messiah.
But he replied, "If I tell you, you won't believe me or let me present my case. 69 But the

Today's English Version

But Peter answered, "Man, I am not!"
59 And about an hour later another man insisted strongly, "There isn't any doubt that this
man was with him, because he also is a Galilean!"
60 But Peter answered, "Man, I don't know
what you are talking about!"
At once, while he was still speaking, a rooster
crowed. 61 The Lord turned around and looked
straight at Peter, and Peter remembered the
Lord's words, how he had said, "Before the
rooster crows today, you will say three times that
you do not know me." 62 Peter went out and
wept bitterly.

Jesus mocked and beaten

63 The men who were guarding Jesus made
fun of him and beat him. 64 They blindfolded
him and asked him, "Who hit you? Guess!"
65And they said many other insulting things to
him.

Jesus before the Council

66 When day came, the elders of the Jews, the
chief priests, and the teachers of the Law met
together, and Jesus was brought to their Council. 67 "Tell us," they said, "are you the Messiah?"
He answered, "If I tell you, you will not believe me, 68 and if I ask you a question you will
not answer. 69 But from now on the Son of Man

New International Version

"Man, I am not!" Peter replied.
59 About an hour later another asserted,
"Certainly this fellow was with him, for he is a
Galilean."
60 Peter replied, "Man, I don't know what
you're talking about!" Just as he was speaking,
the rooster crowed. 61 The Lord turned and
looked straight at Peter. Then Peter remembered the word the Lord had spoken to him:
"Before the rooster crows today, you will disown
me three times." 62And he went outside and
wept bitterly.

The soldiers mock Jesus

63 The men who were guarding Jesus began
mocking and beating him. 64 They blindfolded
him and demanded, "Prophesy! Who hit you?"
65And they said many other insulting things to
him.

Jesus before Pilate and Herod

66 At daybreak the council of the elders of
the people, both the chief priests and teachers
of the law, met together, and Jesus was led before them. 67 "If you are the Christ,[w] " they
said, "tell us."
Jesus answered, "If I tell you, you will not
believe me, 68 and if I asked you, you would not
answer. 69 But from now on, the Son of Man

[w] Or *Messiah*.

Phillips Modern English

"You're one of these men too."
But Peter said,
"Man, I am not!"
Then about an hour later someone else insisted,
"I am convinced this fellow was with him. Why, he is a Galilean!"
"Man," returned Peter, "I don't know what you're talking about."
And immediately, while he was still speaking, the cock crew. The Lord turned his head and looked straight at Peter, and into his mind flashed the words that the Lord had said to him . . . "You will disown me three times before the cock crows today." And he went outside and wept bitterly.
Then the men who held Jesus made a great game of knocking him about. And they blindfolded him and asked him,
"Now, prophet, guess who hit you that time!"
And that was only the beginning of the way they insulted him.

22.66 In the early morning Jesus is formally interrogated

Then when daylight came, the assembly of the elders of the people, which included both chief priests and scribes, met and marched him off to their own council. There they asked him,
"If you really are Christ, tell us!"
"If I tell you, you will never believe me, and if I ask you a question, you will not answer me. But from now on the Son of Man will take his

Revised Standard Version

also are one of them." But Peter said, "Man, I am not." 59And after an interval of about an hour still another insisted, saying, "Certainly this man also was with him; for he is a Galilean." 60 But Peter said, "Man, I do not know what you are saying." And immediately, while he was still speaking, the cock crowed. 61And the Lord turned and looked at Peter. And Peter remembered the word of the Lord, how he had said to him, "Before the cock crows today, you will deny me three times." 62And he went out and wept bitterly.

63 Now the men who were holding Jesus mocked him and beat him; 64 they also blindfolded him and asked him, "Prophesy! Who is it that struck you?" 65And they spoke many other words against him, reviling him.

66 When day came, the assembly of the elders of the people gathered together, both chief priests and scribes; and they led him away to their council, and they said, 67 "If you are the Christ, tell us." But he said to them, "If I tell you, you will not believe; 68 and if I ask you, you will not answer. 69 But from now on

Jerusalem Bible

But Peter replied, "I am not, my friend." 59About an hour later another man insisted, saying, "This fellow was certainly with him. Why, he is a Galilean." 60 "My friend," said Peter, "I do not know what you are talking about." At that instant, while he was still speaking, the cock crew, 61 and the Lord turned and looked straight at Peter, and Peter remembered what the Lord had said to him, "Before the cock crows today, you will have disowned me three times." 62And he went outside and wept bitterly.

Jesus mocked by the guards

63 Meanwhile the men who guarded Jesus were mocking and beating him. 64 They blindfolded him and questioned him. "Play the prophet," they said. "Who hit you then?" 65And they continued heaping insults on him.

Jesus before the Sanhedrin

66 When day broke there was a meeting of the elders of the people, attended by the chief priests and scribes. He was brought before their council, 67 and they said to him, "If you are the Christ, tell us." "If I tell you," he replied, "you will not believe me, 68 and if I question you, you will not answer. 69 But from now on, the Son

New English Bible

him, 'No, I am not.' About an hour passed and another spoke more strongly still: 'Of course this fellow was with him. He must have been; he is a Galilean.' But Peter said, 'Man, I do not know what you are talking about.' At that moment, while he was still speaking, a cock crew; and the Lord turned and looked at Peter. And Peter remembered the Lord's words, 'Tonight before the cock crows you will disown me three times.' [c]

The men who were guarding Jesus mocked at him. They beat him, they blindfolded him, and they kept asking him, 'Now, prophet, who hit you? Tell us that.' And so they went on heaping insults upon him.

When day broke, the elders of the nation, chief priests, and doctors of the law assembled, and he was brought before their Council. 'Tell us,' they said, 'are you the Messiah?' 'If I tell you,' he replied, 'you will not believe me; and if I ask questions, you will not answer. But from

[c] *Some witnesses add* (62) He went outside, and wept bitterly, *as in Matthew 26.75.*

King James Version

Son of man sit on the right hand of the power
of God. 70 Then said they all, Art thou then the
Son of God? And he said unto them, Ye say
that I am. 71 And they said, What need we any
further witness? for we ourselves have heard of
his own mouth.

23 And the whole multitude of them arose,
and led him unto Pilate. 2 And they began
to accuse him, saying, We found this *fellow*
perverting the nation, and forbidding to give
tribute to Cesar, saying that he himself is Christ
a king. 3 And Pilate asked him, saying, Art thou
the King of the Jews? And he answered him and
said, Thou sayest *it*. 4 Then said Pilate to the
chief priests and *to* the people, I find no fault
in this man. 5 And they were the more fierce,
saying, He stirreth up the people, teaching
throughout all Jewry, beginning from Galilee to
this place. 6 When Pilate heard of Galilee, he
asked whether the man were a Galilean. 7 And

Living Bible

time is soon coming when I, the Messiah,[j] shall
be enthroned beside Almighty God."
70 They all shouted, "Then you claim you are
the Son of God?"
And he replied, "Yes, I am."
71 "What need do we have for other witnesses?" they shouted. "For we ourselves have
heard him say it."

23 Then the entire Council took Jesus over
to Pilate, the governor.[a] 2 They began at
once accusing him: "This fellow has been leading
our people to ruin by telling them not to pay
their taxes to the Roman government and by
claiming he is our Messiah—a King."
3 So Pilate asked him, "Are you their Messiah—their King?"[b]
"Yes," Jesus replied, "it is as you say."
4 Then Pilate turned to the chief priests and
to the mob and said, "So? That isn't a crime!"
5 Then they became desperate. "But he is
causing riots against the government everywhere
he goes, all over Judea, from Galilee to Jerusalem!"
6 "Is he then a Galilean?" Pilate asked.
7 When they told him yes, Pilate said to take

[j] Literally, "the Son of Man." [a] Implied. [b] Literally, "Are you the King of the Jews?"

Today's English Version

will be seated at the right side of the Almighty
God."
70 They all said, "Are you, then, the Son of
God?"
He answered them, "You say that I am."
71 And they said, "We don't need any witnesses! We ourselves have heard his very own
words!"

Jesus before Pilate

23 The whole group rose up and took Jesus
before Pilate, 2 where they began to accuse him, "We caught this man misleading our
people, telling them not to pay taxes to the Emperor and claiming that he himself is Christ, a
king."
3 Pilate asked him, "Are you the king of the
Jews?"
"You say it," answered Jesus.
4 Then Pilate said to the chief priests and the
crowds, "I find no reason to condemn this man."
5 But they insisted even more strongly, "He is
starting a riot among the people all through
Judea with his teaching. He began in Galilee,
and now has come here."

Jesus before Herod

6 When Pilate heard this he asked, "Is this
man a Galilean?" 7 When he learned that Jesus

New International Version

will be seated at the right hand of the mighty
God."
70 They all asked, "Are you then the Son of
God?"
He replied, "You are right in saying I am."
71 Then they said, "Why do we need any
more testimony? We have heard it from his own
lips."

23 Then the whole assembly rose and led
him off to Pilate. 2 And they began to accuse him, saying, "We have found this man
subverting our nation. He opposes payment of
taxes to Caesar and claims to be Christ,[w] a
king."
3 So Pilate asked Jesus, "Are you the king of
the Jews?"
"Yes, it is as you say," Jesus replied.
4 Then Pilate announced to the chief priests
and the crowd, "I find no basis for a charge
against this man."
5 But they insisted, "He stirs up the people
all over Judea[x] by his teaching. He started in
Galilee and has come all the way here."
6 On hearing this, Pilate asked if the man
was a Galilean. 7 When he learned that Jesus

[w] Or *Messiah*. [x] Or *the land of the Jews*.

Phillips Modern English

seat at the right hand of almighty God."

Then they all said,

"So you are the Son of God then?"

"You are right; I am," Jesus told them.

Then they said,

"Why do we need to call any more witnesses, for we ourselves have heard this thing from his own lips?"

23.1 Jesus is taken before Pilate and Herod

Then they rose up in a body and took him off to Pilate, and began their accusation in these words,

"Here is this man whom we have found corrupting our people, and telling them that it is wrong to pay taxes to Caesar, claiming that he himself is Christ, a king."

But Pilate addressed his question to Jesus,

"Are you the king of the Jews?"

"That is what you say," he replied.

Then Pilate spoke to the chief priests and the crowd,

"I find nothing criminal about this man."

But they pressed their charge, saying,

"He's a trouble-maker among the people. He teaches through the whole of Judaea, all the way from Galilee to this place."

When Pilate heard this, he enquired whether the man were a Galilean, and when he discov-

Revised Standard Version

the Son of man shall be seated at the right hand
of the power of God." 70And they all said,
"Are you the Son of God, then?" And he said
to them, "You say that I am." 71And they said,
"What further testimony do we need? We have
heard it ourselves from his own lips."

23 Then the whole company of them arose,
and brought him before Pilate. 2And they
began to accuse him, saying, "We found this
man perverting our nation, and forbidding us
to give tribute to Caesar, and saying that he
himself is Christ a king." 3And Pilate asked
him, "Are you the King of the Jews?" And he
answered him, "You have said so." 4And Pilate
said to the chief priests and the multitudes, "I
find no crime in this man." 5But they were
urgent, saying, "He stirs up the people, teaching
throughout all Judea, from Galilee even to this
place."

6 When Pilate heard this, he asked whether
the man was a Galilean. 7And when he learned

Jerusalem Bible

of Man will be *seated at the right hand* of the
Power *of God*."[r] 70 Then they all said, "So you
are the Son of God then?" He answered, "It is
you who say I am." 71 "What need of witnesses
have we now?" they said. "We have heard it
for ourselves from his own lips."

23 The whole assembly then rose, and they
brought him before Pilate.

Jesus before Pilate

2 They began their accusation by saying, "We
found this man inciting our people to revolt, opposing payment of the tribute to Caesar, and
claiming to be Christ, a king." 3 Pilate put to
him this question, "Are you the king of the
Jews?" "It is you who say it," he replied. 4 Pilate
then said to the chief priests and the crowd, "I
find no case against this man." 5 But they persisted, "He is inflaming the people with his teaching all over Judaea; it has come all the way from
Galilee, where he started, down to here."
6 When Pilate heard this, he asked if the man
were a Galilean; 7 and finding that he came un-

[r] Ps. 110:1.

New English Bible

now on, the Son of Man will be seated at the
right hand of Almighty God.'[a] 'You are the Son
of God, then?' they all said, and he replied, 'It is
you who say I am.'[b] They said, 'Need we call
further witnesses? We have heard it ourselves
from his own lips.'

23 With that the whole assembly rose, and
they brought him before Pilate. They
opened the case against him by saying, 'We
found this man subverting our nation, opposing
the payment of taxes to Caesar, and claiming to
be Messiah, a king.'[c] Pilate asked him, 'Are you
the king of the Jews?' He replied, 'The words are
yours.'[d] Pilate then said to the chief priests and
the crowd, 'I find no case for this man to answer.' But they insisted: 'His teaching is causing
disaffection among the people all through Judaea. It started from Galilee and has spread as
far as this city.'

When Pilate heard this, he asked if the man
was a Galilean, and on learning that he belonged

[a] *Literally* of the Power of God. [b] *Or* You are right, for I am. [c] *Or* to be an anointed king. [d] *Or* It is as you say.

King James Version

as soon as he knew that he belonged unto
Herod's jurisdiction, he sent him to Herod, who
himself also was at Jerusalem at that time.
8 And when Herod saw Jesus, he was exceeding glad: for he was desirous to see him of
a long *season,* because he had heard many things
of him; and he hoped to have seen some miracle
done by him. 9 Then he questioned with him in
many words; but he answered him nothing.
10 And the chief priests and scribes stood and
vehemently accused him. 11 And Herod with his
men of war set him at nought, and mocked *him,*
and arrayed him in a gorgeous robe, and sent
him again to Pilate.
12 And the same day Pilate and Herod were
made friends together; for before they were at
enmity between themselves.
13 And Pilate, when he had called together
the chief priests and the rulers and the people,
14 Said unto them, Ye have brought this man
unto me, as one that perverteth the people; and,
behold, I, having examined *him* before you, have
found no fault in this man touching those things
whereof ye accuse him: 15 No, nor yet Herod:
for I sent you to him; and, lo, nothing worthy of
death is done unto him. 16 I will therefore

Living Bible

him to King Herod, for Galilee was under
Herod's jurisdiction; and Herod happened to be
in Jerusalem at the time. 8 Herod was delighted
at the opportunity to see Jesus, for he had heard
a lot about him and had been hoping to see
him perform a miracle.
9 He asked Jesus question after question, but
there was no reply. 10 Meanwhile, the chief
priests and the other religious leaders stood there
shouting their accusations.
11 Now Herod and his soldiers began mocking and ridiculing Jesus; and putting a kingly
robe on him, they sent him back to Pilate.
12 That day Herod and Pilate—enemies before—
became fast friends.
13 Then Pilate called together the chief priests
and other Jewish leaders, along with the people,
14 and announced his verdict:
"You brought this man to me, accusing him
of leading a revolt against the Roman government.[c] I have examined him thoroughly on this
point and find him innocent. 15 Herod came to
the same conclusion and sent him back to us—
nothing this man has done calls for the death
penalty. 16 I will therefore have him scourged

[c] Literally, "as one who perverts the people."

Today's English Version

was from the region ruled by Herod, he sent
him to Herod, who was also in Jerusalem at that
time. 8 Herod was very pleased when he saw Jesus, because he had heard about him and had
been wanting to see him for a long time. He was
hoping to see Jesus perform some miracle. 9 So
Herod asked Jesus many questions, but Jesus
did not answer a word. 10 The chief priests and
the teachers of the Law stepped forward and
made strong accusations against Jesus. 11 Herod
and his soldiers made fun of Jesus and treated
him with contempt. They put a fine robe on him
and sent him back to Pilate. 12 On that very day
Herod and Pilate became friends; they had been
enemies before this.

Jesus sentenced to death

13 Pilate called together the chief priests, the
leaders, and the people, 14 and said to them,
"You brought this man to me and said that he
was misleading the people. Now, I have examined him here in your presence, and I have not
found him guilty of any of the crimes you accuse him of. 15 Nor did Herod find him guilty,
because he sent him back to us. There is nothing
this man has done to deserve death. 16 I will

New International Version

was under Herod's jurisdiction, he sent him to
Herod, who was also in Jerusalem at that time.
8 When Herod saw Jesus, he was greatly
pleased, because for a long time he had been
wanting to see him. From what he had heard
about him, he hoped to see him perform some
miracle. 9 He plied him with many questions,
but Jesus gave him no answer. 10 The chief
priests and the teachers of the law were standing there, vehemently accusing him. 11 Then
Herod and his soldiers ridiculed and mocked
him. Dressing him in an elegant robe, they sent
him back to Pilate. 12 That day Herod and Pilate became friends—before this they had been
enemies.
13 Pilate called together the chief priests, the
rulers and the people, 14 and said to them, "You
brought me this man as one who was inciting
the people to rebellion. I have examined him in
your presence and have found no basis for your
charges against him. 15 Neither has Herod, for
he sent him back to us; as you can see, he has
done nothing to deserve death. 16 Therefore, I

Phillips Modern English

ered that he came under Herod's jurisdiction, he passed him on to Herod who happened to be in Jerusalem at that time. When Herod saw Jesus, he was delighted, for he had been wanting to see him for a long time. He had heard a lot about Jesus and was hoping to see him perform a miracle. He questioned him thoroughly, but Jesus gave him absolutely no reply, though the chief priests and scribes stood there making the most violent accusations. So Herod joined his own soldiers in scoffing and jeering at Jesus. Finally, they dressed him up in a gorgeous cloak, and sent him back to Pilate. On that day Herod and Pilate became firm friends, though previously they had been at daggers drawn.

23.13 Pilate declares Jesus' innocence

Then Pilate summoned the chief priests, the officials and the people and addressed them in these words,

"You have brought this man to me as a mischief-maker among the people, and I want you all to realise that, after examining him in your presence, I have found nothing criminal about him, in spite of all your accusations. And neither has Herod, for he has sent him back to us. Obviously, then, he has done nothing to deserve the death penalty. I propose, therefore.

Revised Standard Version

that he belonged to Herod's jurisdiction, he sent
him over to Herod, who was himself in Jerusalem at that time. 8 When Herod saw Jesus, he
was very glad, for he had long desired to see
him, because he had heard about him, and he
was hoping to see some sign done by him. 9 So
he questioned him at some length; but he made
no answer. 10 The chief priests and the scribes
stood by, vehemently accusing him. 11 And
Herod with his soldiers treated him with contempt and mocked him; then, arraying him in
gorgeous apparel, he sent him back to Pilate.
12 And Herod and Pilate became friends with
each other that very day, for before this they
had been at enmity with each other.
13 Pilate then called together the chief priests
and the rulers and the people, 14 and said to
them, "You brought me this man as one who
was perverting the people; and after examining
him before you, behold, I did not find this man
guilty of any of your charges against him; 15 neither did Herod, for he sent him back to us.
Behold, nothing deserving death has been done
by him; 16 I will therefore chastise him and

Jerusalem Bible

der Herod's jurisdiction he passed him over to Herod who was also in Jerusalem at that time.

Jesus before Herod

8 Herod was delighted to see Jesus; he had
heard about him and had been wanting for a
long time to set eyes on him; moreover, he was
hoping to see some miracle worked by him. 9 So
he questioned him at some length; but without
getting any reply. 10 Meanwhile the chief priests
and the scribes were there, violently pressing
their accusations. 11 Then Herod, together with
his guards, treated him with contempt and made
fun of him; he put a rich cloak[s] on him and
sent him back to Pilate. 12 And though Herod
and Pilate had been enemies before, they were
reconciled that same day.

Jesus before Pilate again

13 Pilate then summoned the chief priests and
the leading men and the people. 14 "You brought
this man before me," he said, "as a political agitator. Now I have gone into the matter myself
in your presence and found no case against the
man in respect of all the charges you bring
against him. 15 Nor has Herod either, since he
has sent him back to us. As you can see, the
man has done nothing that deserves death, 16 so

[s] Ceremonial dress of a prince.

New English Bible

to Herod's jurisdiction he remitted the case to him, for Herod was also in Jerusalem at that time. When Herod saw Jesus he was greatly pleased; having heard about him, he had long been wanting to see him, and had been hoping to see some miracle performed by him. He questioned him at some length without getting any reply; but the chief priests and lawyers appeared and pressed the case against him vigorously. Then Herod and his troops treated him with contempt and ridicule, and sent him back to Pilate dressed in a gorgeous robe. That same day Herod and Pilate became friends; till then there had been a standing feud between them.

Pilate now called together the chief priests, councillors, and people, and said to them, 'You brought this man before me on a charge of subversion. But, as you see, I have myself examined him in your presence and found nothing in him to support your charges. No more did Herod, for he has referred him back to us. Clearly he has done nothing to deserve death. I therefore pro-

King James Version

chastise him, and release *him.* 17 (For of necessity he must release one unto them at the
feast.) 18And they cried out all at once, saying,
Away with this *man,* and release unto us Barabbas: 19 (Who for a certain sedition made in
the city, and for murder, was cast into prison.)
20 Pilate therefore, willing to release Jesus, spake
again to them. 21 But they cried, saying, Crucify
him, crucify him. 22And he said unto them the
third time, Why, what evil hath he done? I have
found no cause of death in him: I will therefore
chastise him, and let *him* go. 23And they were
instant with loud voices, requiring that he might
be crucified: and the voices of them and of the
chief priests prevailed. 24And Pilate gave sentence that it should be as they required. 25And
he released unto them him that for sedition and
murder was cast into prison, whom they had
desired; but he delivered Jesus to their will.
26And as they led him away, they laid hold upon
one Simon, a Cyrenian, coming out of the country, and on him they laid the cross, that he might
bear *it* after Jesus.
27 And there followed him a great company
of people, and of women, which also bewailed
and lamented him. 28 But Jesus turning unto

Living Bible

with leaded thongs, and release him."
17,[d] 18 But now a mighty roar rose from the
crowd as with one voice they shouted, "Kill him,
and release Barabbas to us!" 19 (Barabbas was
in prison for starting an insurrection in Jerusalem against the government, and for murder.)
20 Pilate argued with them, for he wanted to release Jesus. 21 But they shouted, "Crucify him!
Crucify him!"
22 Once more, for the third time, he demanded, "Why? What crime has he committed?
I have found no reason to sentence him to death.
I will therefore scourge him and let him go."
23 But they shouted louder and louder for Jesus'
death, and their voices prevailed.
24 So Pilate sentenced Jesus to die as they
demanded. 25And he released Barabbas, the man
in prison for insurrection and murder, at their
request. But he delivered Jesus over to them to
do with as they would.
26 As the crowd led Jesus away to his death,
Simon of Cyrene, who was just coming into
Jerusalem from the country, was forced to follow, carrying Jesus' cross. 27 Great crowds
trailed along behind, and many grief-stricken
women.
28 But Jesus turned and said to them,

[d] Some ancient authorities add verse 17, "For it was necessary for him to release unto them at the feast one (prisoner)."

Today's English Version

have him whipped, then, and let him go."
[17 At each Passover Feast Pilate had to set
free one prisoner for them.] 18 The whole crowd
cried out, "Kill him! Set Barabbas free for us!"
19 (Barabbas had been put in prison for a riot
that had taken place in the city, and for murder.)
20 Pilate wanted to set Jesus free, so he called
out to the crowd again. 21 But they shouted back,
"To the cross with him! To the cross!"
22 Pilate said to them the third time, "But
what crime has he committed? I cannot find anything he has done to deserve death! I will have
him whipped and set him free."
23 But they kept on shouting at the top of
their voices that Jesus should be nailed to the
cross; and finally their shouting won. 24 So Pilate
passed the sentence on Jesus that they were asking for. 25 He set free the man they wanted, the
one who had been put in prison for riot and
murder, and turned Jesus over to them to do as
they wished.

Jesus nailed to the cross

26 They took Jesus away. As they went, they
met a man named Simon, from Cyrene, who was
coming into the city from the country. They
seized him, put the cross on him, and made him
carry it behind Jesus.
27 A large crowd of people followed him;
among them were some women who were weeping and wailing for him. 28 Jesus turned to them

New International Version

will punish him and then release him." [y]
18 With one voice they cried out, "Away with
this man! Release Barabbas to us!" 19 (Barabbas
had been thrown into prison for an insurrection
in the city, and for murder.)
20 Wanting to release Jesus, Pilate appealed
to them again. 21 But they kept shouting, "Crucify him! Crucify him!"
22 For the third time he spoke to them:
"Why? What crime has this man committed? I
have found in him no grounds for the death
penalty. Therefore, I will have him punished
and then release him."
23 But with loud shouts they insistently demanded that he be crucified, and their shouts
prevailed. 24 So Pilate decided to grant their
demand. 25 He released the man who had been
thrown into prison for insurrection and murder,
the one they asked for, and surrendered Jesus
to their will.

The crucifixion

26 As they led him away, they seized Simon
from Cyrene, who was on his way in from the
country, and put the cross on him and made
him carry it behind Jesus. 27A large number of
people followed him, including women who
mourned and wailed for him. 28 Jesus turned

[y] Some MSS add verse 17: *Now he was obliged to release one man to them at the feast.*

Phillips Modern English

to teach him a sharp lesson and let him go."
But they all yelled as one man,
"Take this man away! We want Barabbas set free!"
(Barabbas was a man who had been put in prison for causing a riot in the city and for murder.) But Pilate wanted to set Jesus free and he called out to them again, but they shouted back at him,
"Crucify, crucify him!"
Then he spoke to them, for the third time,
"What is his crime, then? I have found nothing in him that deserves execution; I am going to teach him his lesson and let him go."
But they shouted him down, yelling their demand that he should be crucified.
Their shouting won the day, and Pilate gave the decision that their request should be granted. He released the man for whom they asked, the man who had been imprisoned for rioting and murder, and surrendered Jesus to their demands.
And as they were marching him away, they caught hold of Simon, a native of Cyrene in Africa, who was on his way home from the fields, and put the cross on his back for him to carry behind Jesus.

23.27 On the way to the cross

A huge crowd of people followed him, including women who wrung their hands and wept for him. But Jesus turned to them and said,

Revised Standard Version

release him." [m]
18 But they all cried out together, "Away with this man, and release to us Barabbas"—
19 a man who had been thrown into prison for an insurrection started in the city, and for murder.
20 Pilate addressed them once more, desiring to release Jesus;
21 but they shouted out, "Crucify, crucify him!"
22 A third time he said to them, "Why, what evil has he done? I have found in him no crime deserving death; I will therefore chastise him and release him."
23 But they were urgent, demanding with loud cries that he should be crucified. And their voices prevailed.
24 So Pilate gave sentence that their demand should be granted.
25 He released the man who had been thrown into prison for insurrection and murder, whom they asked for; but Jesus he delivered up to their will.
26 And as they led him away, they seized one Simon of Cyrene, who was coming in from the country, and laid on him the cross, to carry it behind Jesus.
27 And there followed him a great multitude of the people, and of women who bewailed and lamented him.
28 But Jesus turned-

[m] Here, or after verse 19, other ancient authorities add verse 17, *Now he was obliged to release one man to them at the festival.*

Jerusalem Bible

I shall have him flogged and then let him go." [t]
18 But as one man they howled, "Away with him! Give us Barabbas!"
19 (This man had been thrown into prison for causing a riot in the city and for murder.)
20 Pilate was anxious to see Jesus free and addressed them again,
21 but they shouted back, "Crucify him! Crucify him!"
22 And for the third time he spoke to them, "Why? What harm has this man done? I have found no case against him that deserves death, so I shall have him punished and then let him go."
23 But they kept on shouting at the top of their voices, demanding that he should be crucified. And their shouts were growing louder.
24 Pilate then gave his verdict: their demand was to be granted.
25 He released the man they asked for, who had been imprisoned for rioting and murder, and handed Jesus over to them to deal with as they pleased.

The way to Calvary

26 As they were leading him away they seized on a man, Simon from Cyrene, who was coming in from the country, and made him shoulder the cross and carry it behind Jesus.
27 Large numbers of people followed him, and of women too,[u] who mourned and lamented for him.
28 But Jesus turned to them and said, "Daughters of

[t] V. 17 "He was under obligation to release one man for them every feast day" seems to be an explanatory gloss, cf. Mt. 27:15. [u] The Talmud records that noblewomen of Jerusalem used to give soothing drinks to condemned criminals.

New English Bible

pose to let him off with a flogging.' But[a] there was a general outcry, 'Away with him! Give us Barabbas.' (This man had been put in prison for a rising that had taken place in the city, and for murder.) Pilate addressed them again, in his desire to release Jesus, but they shouted back, 'Crucify him, crucify him!' For the third time he spoke to them: 'Why, what wrong has he done? I have not found him guilty of any capital offence. I will therefore let him off with a flogging.' But they insisted on their demand, shouting that Jesus should be crucified. Their shouts prevailed and Pilate decided that they should have their way. He released the man they asked for, the man who had been put in prison for insurrection and murder, and gave Jesus up to their will.

As they led him away to execution they seized upon a man called Simon, from Cyrene, on his way in from the country, put the cross on his back, and made him walk behind Jesus carrying it.
Great numbers of people followed, many women among them, who mourned and lamented over him. Jesus turned to them and said, 'Daugh-

[a] *Some witnesses read* (17) At festival time he was obliged to release one person for them; (18) and now . . .

King James Version

them said, Daughters of Jerusalem, weep not
for me, but weep for yourselves, and for your
children. 29 For, behold, the days are coming, in
the which they shall say, Blessed *are* the barren,
and the wombs that never bare, and the paps
which never gave suck. 30 Then shall they begin
to say to the mountains, Fall on us; and to the
hills, Cover us. 31 For if they do these things in
a green tree, what shall be done in the dry?
32And there were also two others, malefactors,
led with him to be put to death. 33And when
they were come to the place, which is called
Calvary, there they crucified him, and the malefactors, one on the right hand, and the other on
the left.
34 Then said Jesus, Father, forgive them; for
they know not what they do. And they parted his
raiment, and cast lots. 35And the people stood
beholding. And the rulers also with them derided *him*, saying, He saved others; let him save
himself, if he be Christ, the chosen of God.
36And the soldiers also mocked him, coming to
him, and offering him vinegar, 37And saying, If
thou be the King of the Jews, save thyself. 38And
a superscription also was written over him in
letters of Greek, and Latin, and Hebrew, THIS
IS THE KING OF THE JEWS.

Living Bible

"Daughters of Jerusalem, don't weep for me, but
for yourselves and for your children. 29 For the
days are coming when the women who have no
children will be counted fortunate indeed.
30 Mankind will beg the mountains to fall on
them and crush them, and the hills to bury
them. 31 For if such things as this are done to
me, the Living Tree, what will they do to you?" [e]
32, 33 Two others, criminals, were led out to
be executed with him at a place called "The
Skull." There all three were crucified—Jesus on
the center cross, and the two criminals on either
side.
34 "Father, forgive these people," Jesus said,
"for they don't know what they are doing."
And the soldiers gambled for his clothing,
throwing dice for each piece. 35 The crowd
watched. And the Jewish leaders laughed and
scoffed. "He was so good at helping others,"
they said, "let's see him save himself if he is
really God's Chosen One, the Messiah."
36 The soldiers mocked him, too, by offering
him a drink—of sour wine. 37And they called
to him, "If you are the King of the Jews, save
yourself!"
38 A signboard was nailed to the cross above
him with these words: "This is the King of the
Jews."

[*e*] Literally, "For if they do this when the tree is green, what will happen when it is dry?"

Today's English Version

and said, "Women of Jerusalem! Don't cry for
me, but for yourselves and your children. 29 For
the days are coming when people will say, 'How
lucky are the women who never had children,
who never bore babies, who never nursed them!'
30 That will be the time when people will say to
the mountains, 'Fall on us!' and to the hills,
'Hide us!' 31 For if such things as these are done
when the wood is green, what will it be like
when it is dry?"
32 They took two others also, both of them
criminals, to be put to death with Jesus. 33 When
they came to the place called "The Skull," they
nailed Jesus to the cross there, and the two criminals, one on his right and one on his left. 34 Jesus said, "Forgive them, Father! They don't
know what they are doing."
They divided his clothes among themselves by
throwing dice. 35 The people stood there watching, while the Jewish leaders made fun of him,
"He saved others; let him save himself, if he is
the Messiah whom God has chosen!"
36 The soldiers also made fun of him; they
came up to him and offered him cheap wine,
37 and said, "Save yourself, if you are the king
of the Jews!"
38 These words were written above him:
"This is the King of the Jews."

New International Version

and said to them, "Daughters of Jerusalem, do
not weep for me; weep for yourselves and for
your children. 29 For the time will come when
you will say, 'Blessed are the barren women, the
wombs that never bore and the breasts that
never nursed!' 30 Then,
'they will say to the mountains: Fall on us;
and to the hills: Cover us.' [z]
31 For if men do these things when the tree is
green, what will happen when it is dry?"
32 Two other men, both criminals, were also
led out with him to be executed. 33 When they
came to the place called The Skull, there they
crucified him, along with the criminals—one on
his right, the other on his left. 34 Jesus said,
"Father, forgive them, for they do not know
what they are doing." [a] And they divided up his
clothes by casting lots.
35 The people stood watching, and the rulers
even sneered at him. They said, "He saved
others; let him save himself if he is the Christ[b]
of God, the Chosen One."
36 The soldiers also came up and mocked
him. They offered him wine vinegar 37 and said,
"If you are the king of the Jews, save yourself."
38 There was a written notice above him,
which read: THIS IS THE KING OF THE JEWS.

[*z*] Hosea 10:8. [*a*] Some early MSS omit verse 34a.
[*b*] Or *Messiah*.

Phillips Modern English

"Women of Jerusalem, do not shed your tears for me, but for yourselves and for your children! For the days are coming when men will say, 'Lucky are the women who are childless—the bodies which have never borne, and the breasts which have never given nourishment.' Then men will begin to say to the mountains, 'Fall upon us!' and will say to the hills, 'Cover us up!' For if this is what men do when the wood is green, what will they do when it is seasoned?"

23.32 Jesus is crucified with two criminals

Two criminals were also led out with him for execution, and when they came to the place called The Skull, they crucified him with the criminals, one on either side of him. But Jesus himself was saying,

"Father, forgive them; they do not know what they are doing."

Then they shared out his clothes by casting lots.

The people stood and stared while their rulers continued to scoff, saying, "He saved other people, let's see him save himself, if he is really God's Christ—his chosen!"

The soldiers also mocked him by coming up and presenting sour wine to him, saying,

"If you are the king of the Jews, why not save yourself?" For there was a placard over his head which read,

THIS IS THE KING OF THE JEWS.

Revised Standard Version

ing to them said, "Daughters of Jerusalem, do
not weep for me, but weep for yourselves and
for your children. 29 For behold, the days are
coming when they will say, 'Blessed are the
barren, and the wombs that never bore, and the
breasts that never gave suck!' 30 Then they will
begin to say to the mountains, 'Fall on us'; and
to the hills, 'Cover us.' 31 For if they do this
when the wood is green, what will happen when
it is dry?"
32 Two others also, who were criminals, were
led away to be put to death with him. 33 And
when they came to the place which is called
The Skull, there they crucified him, and the
criminals, one on the right and one on the left.
34 And Jesus said, "Father, forgive them; for
they know not what they do." [n] And they cast
lots to divide his garments. 35 And the people
stood by, watching; but the rulers scoffed at
him, saying, "He saved others; let him save
himself, if he is the Christ of God, his Chosen
One!" 36 The soldiers also mocked him, coming up and offering him vinegar, 37 and saying,
"If you are the King of the Jews, save yourself!" 38 There was also an inscription over
him,[o] "This is the King of the Jews."

[n] Other ancient authorities omit the sentence *And Jesus . . . what they do.* [o] Other ancient authorities add *in letters of Greek and Latin and Hebrew.*

Jerusalem Bible

Jerusalem, do not weep for me; weep rather for
yourselves and for your children. 29 For the days
will surely come when people will say, 'Happy
are those who are barren, the wombs that have
never borne, the breasts that have never suckled!'
30 Then they will begin to *say to the mountains,
'Fall on us!'; to the hill, 'Cover us!'* [v] 31 'For if
men use the green wood like this, what will happen when it is dry?' " 32 Now with him they were
also leading out two other criminals to be executed.

The crucifixion

33 When they reached the place called The Skull, they crucified him there and the two criminals also, one on the right, the other on the left.
34 Jesus said, "Father, forgive them; they do not know what they are doing." Then they cast lots to share out his clothing.

The crucified Christ is mocked

35 The people stayed there watching him. As for the leaders, they jeered at him. "He saved others," they said, "let him save himself if he is the Christ of God, the Chosen One." 36 The
soldiers mocked him too, and when they approached to offer him vinegar 37 they said, "If you are the king of the Jews, save yourself."
38 Above him there was an inscription: "This is the King of the Jews."

[v] Ho. 10:8.

New English Bible

ters of Jerusalem, do not weep for me; no, weep for yourselves and your children. For the days are surely coming when they will say, "Happy are the barren, the wombs that never bore a child, the breasts that never fed one." Then they will start saying to the mountains, "Fall on us", and to the hills, "Cover us." For if these things are done when the wood is green, what will happen when it is dry?"

There were two others with him, criminals who were being led away to execution; and when they reached the place called The Skull, they crucified him there, and the criminals with him, one on his right and the other on his left. Jesus said, 'Father, forgive them; they do not know what they are doing.' [b]

They divided his clothes among them by casting lots. The people stood looking on, and their rulers jeered at him: 'He saved others: now let him save himself, if this is God's Messiah, his Chosen.' The soldiers joined in the mockery and came forward offering him their sour wine. 'If you are the king of the Jews,' they said, 'save yourself.' There was an inscription above his head which ran: 'This is the king of the Jews.'

[b] *Some witnesses omit* Jesus said, 'Father . . . doing.'

King James Version

39 And one of the malefactors which were
hanged railed on him, saying, If thou be Christ,
save thyself and us. 40 But the other answering
rebuked him, saying, Dost not thou fear God,
seeing thou art in the same condemnation?
41 And we indeed justly; for we receive the due
reward of our deeds: but this man hath done
nothing amiss. 42 And he said unto Jesus, Lord,
remember me when thou comest into thy kingdom. 43 And Jesus said unto him, Verily I say
unto thee, To day shalt thou be with me in paradise. 44 And it was about the sixth hour, and
there was a darkness over all the earth until the
ninth hour. 45 And the sun was darkened, and
the vail of the temple was rent in the midst.
46 And when Jesus had cried with a loud
voice, he said, Father, into thy hands I commend my spirit: and having said thus, he gave
up the ghost. 47 Now when the centurion saw
what was done, he glorified God, saying, Certainly this was a righteous man. 48 And all the
people that came together to that sight, beholding the things which were done, smote their

Living Bible

39 One of the criminals hanging beside him
scoffed, "So you're the Messiah, are you? Prove
it by saving yourself—and us, too, while you're
at it!"
40, 41 But the other criminal protested.
"Don't you even fear God when you are dying?
We deserve to die for our evil deeds, but this
man hasn't done one thing wrong." 42 Then he
said, "Jesus, remember me when you come into
your Kingdom."
43 And Jesus replied, "Today you will be with
me in Paradise. This is a solemn promise."
44 By now it was noon, and darkness fell
across the whole land[f] for three hours, until
three o'clock. 45 The light from the sun was
gone—and suddenly[g] the thick veil hanging in
the Temple split apart.
46 Then Jesus shouted, "Father, I commit my
spirit to you," and with those words he died.[h]
47 When the captain of the Roman military
unit handling the executions saw what had happened, he was stricken with awe before God and
said, "Surely this man was innocent."[i]
48 And when the crowd that came to see the
crucifixion saw that Jesus was dead, they went

[f] Or, "the whole world." [g] Implied. [h] Literally, "yielded up the spirit." [i] Literally, "righteous."

Today's English Version

39 One of the criminals hanging there hurled
insults at him, "Aren't you the Messiah? Save
yourself and us!"
40 The other one, however, rebuked him, saying, "Don't you fear God? We are all under the
same sentence. 41 Ours, however, is only right,
because we are getting what we deserve for what
we did; but he has done no wrong." 42 And he
said to Jesus, "Remember me, Jesus, when you
come as King!"
43 Jesus said to him, "I tell you this: today
you will be in Paradise with me."

The death of Jesus

44 It was about twelve o'clock when the sun
stopped shining and darkness covered the whole
country until three o'clock; 45 and the curtain
hanging in the temple was torn in two. 46 Jesus
cried out in a loud voice, "Father! In your hands
I place my spirit!" He said this and died.
47 The army officer saw what had happened,
and he praised God, saying, "Certainly he was a
good man!"
48 When the people who had gathered there
to watch the spectacle saw what happened, they

New International Version

39 One of the criminals who hung there
hurled insults at him: "Aren't you the Christ[c]?
Save yourself and us!"
40 But the other criminal rebuked him. "Don't
you fear God," he said, "since you are under
the same sentence? 41 We are punished justly,
for we are getting what our deeds deserve. But
this man has done nothing wrong."
42 Then he said, "Jesus, remember me when
you come into your kingdom."
43 Jesus answered him, "I tell you the truth,
today you will be with me in paradise."

Jesus' death

44 It was now about the sixth hour, and darkness came over the whole land until the ninth
hour, 45 for the sun stopped shining. And the
curtain of the temple was torn in two. 46 Jesus
called out with a loud voice, "Father, into your
hands I commit my spirit." When he had said
this, he breathed his last.
47 The centurion, seeing what had happened,
praised God and said, "Surely this was a righteous man." 48 When all the people who had
gathered to witness this sight saw what took
place, they beat their breasts and went away.

[c] Or *Messiah*.

Phillips Modern English

One of the criminals hanging there covered him with abuse, and said,

"Aren't you Christ? Why don't you save yourself—and us?"

But the other one checked him with the words,

"Aren't you afraid of God even when you're getting the same punishment as he is? And it's fair enough for us, for we've only got what we deserve, but this man never did anything wrong."

Then he said,

"Jesus, remember me when you come into your kingdom."

And Jesus answered,

"I tell you truly, this very day you will be with me in paradise."

23.44 The darkness, and the death of Jesus

It was now about midday, but darkness came over the whole countryside until three in the afternoon, for the sun's light was eclipsed. The veil in the Temple sanctuary was split in two. Then Jesus gave a great cry and said,

"Father, I commend my spirit into your hands."

And with these words, he expired.

When the centurion saw what had happened, he exclaimed reverently,

"That was indeed a good man!"

And the whole crowd who had collected for the spectacle, when they saw what had hap-

Revised Standard Version

39 One of the criminals who were hanged
railed at him, saying, "Are you not the Christ?
Save yourself and us!" 40 But the other rebuked him, saying, "Do you not fear God, since
you are under the same sentence of condemnation? 41 And we indeed justly; for we are receiving the due reward of our deeds; but this
man has done nothing wrong." 42 And he said,
"Jesus, remember me when you come into[p] your
kingdom." 43 And he said to him, "Truly, I say
to you, today you will be with me in Paradise."
44 It was now about the sixth hour, and
there was darkness over the whole land[q] until
the ninth hour, 45 while the sun's light failed;[r]
and the curtain of the temple was torn in two.
46 Then Jesus, crying with a loud voice, said,
"Father, into thy hands I commit my spirit!"
And having said this he breathed his last. 47 Now
when the centurion saw what had taken place,
he praised God, and said, "Certainly this man
was innocent!" 48 And all the multitudes who
assembled to see the sight, when they saw what
had taken place, returned home beating their

[*p*] Other ancient authorities read *in*. [*q*] Or *earth*. [*r*] Or *the sun was eclipsed*. Other ancient authorities read *the sun was darkened*.

Jerusalem Bible

The good thief

39 One of the criminals hanging there abused
him. "Are you not the Christ?" he said. "Save
yourself and us as well." 40 But the other spoke
up and rebuked him. "Have you no fear of God
at all?" he said. "You got the same sentence as
he did, 41 but in our case we deserved it: we
are paying for what we did. But this man has
done nothing wrong. 42 Jesus," he said, "remember me when you come into your kingdom." 43 "Indeed, I promise you," he replied,
"today you will be with me in paradise."

The death of Jesus

44 It was now about the sixth hour and, with
the sun eclipsed, a darkness came over the whole
land until the ninth hour. 45 The veil of the Temple was torn right down the middle; 46 and when
Jesus had cried out in a loud voice, he said,
"Father, *into your hands I commit my spirit.*"[w]
With these words he breathed his last.

After the death

47 When the centurion saw what had taken
place, he gave praise to God and said, "This was
a great and good man." 48 And when all the
people who had gathered for the spectacle saw
what had happened, they went home beating
their breasts.

[*w*] Ps. 31:5.

New English Bible

One of the criminals who hung there with him taunted him: 'Are not you the Messiah? Save yourself, and us.' But the other rebuked him: 'Have you no fear of God? You are under the same sentence as he. For us it is plain justice; we are paying the price for our misdeeds; but this man has done nothing wrong.' And he said, 'Jesus, remember me when you come to your throne.'[a] He answered, 'I tell you this: today you shall be with me in Paradise.'

By now it was about midday and a darkness fell over the whole land, which lasted until three in the afternoon; the sun's light failed. And the curtain of the temple was torn in two. Then Jesus gave a loud cry and said, 'Father, into thy hands I commit my spirit'; and with these words he died. The centurion saw it all, and gave praise to God. 'Beyond all doubt', he said, 'this man was innocent.'

The crowd who had assembled for the spectacle, when they saw what had happened, went home beating their breasts.

[*a*] *Some witnesses read* come in royal power.

King James Version

breasts, and returned. 49And all his acquaintance, and the women that followed him from
Galilee, stood afar off, beholding these things.
50 And, behold, *there was* a man named
Joseph, a counsellor; *and he was* a good man,
and a just: 51 (The same had not consented to
the counsel and deed of them:) *he was* of
Arimathea, a city of the Jews; who also himself
waited for the kingdom of God. 52 This *man*
went unto Pilate, and begged the body of Jesus.
53And he took it down, and wrapped it in linen,
and laid it in a sepulchre that was hewn in stone,
wherein never man before was laid. 54And that
day was the preparation, and the sabbath drew
on. 55And the women also, which came with him
from Galilee, followed after, and beheld the
sepulchre, and how his body was laid. 56And
they returned, and prepared spices and ointments; and rested the sabbath day according to
the commandment.

Living Bible

home in deep sorrow. 49 Meanwhile, Jesus'
friends, including the women who had followed
him down from Galilee, stood in the distance
watching.
50, 51, 52 Then a man named Joseph, a member of the Jewish Supreme Court, from the city
of Arimathea in Judea, went to Pilate and asked
for the body of Jesus. He was a godly man who
had been expecting the Messiah's coming and
had not agreed with the decision and actions of
the other Jewish leaders. 53 So he took down
Jesus' body and wrapped it in a long linen cloth
and laid it in a new, unused tomb hewn into the
rock [at the side of a hill [g]]. 54 This was done
late on Friday afternoon, the day of preparation for the Sabbath.
55 As the body was taken away, the women
from Galilee followed and saw it carried into
the tomb. 56 Then they went home and prepared spices and ointments to embalm him; but
by the time they were finished it was the Sabbath,
so they rested all that day as required by the
Jewish law.

[g] Implied.

Today's English Version

all went back home, beating their breasts. 49All
those who knew Jesus personally, including the
women who had followed him from Galilee,
stood off at a distance to see these things.

The burial of Jesus

50, 51 There was a man named Joseph, from
the Jewish town of Arimathea. He was a good
and honorable man, and waited for the coming
of the Kingdom of God. Although a member
of the Council, he had not agreed with their decision and action. 52 He went into the presence
of Pilate and asked for the body of Jesus.
53 Then he took the body down, wrapped it in a
linen sheet, and placed it in a grave which had
been dug out of the rock—a grave which had
never been used. 54 It was Friday, and the Sabbath was about to begin.
55 The women who had followed Jesus from
Galilee went with Joseph and saw the grave and
how Jesus' body was placed in it. 56 Then they
went back home and prepared the spices and
ointments for his body.

On the Sabbath they rested, as the Law commanded.

New International Version

49 But all those who knew him, including the
women who had followed him from Galilee,
stood at a distance, watching these things.

Jesus' burial

50 Now there was a man named Joseph, a
member of the Council, a good and upright
man, 51 who had not consented to their decision
and action. He came from the Judean town
of Arimathea and he was waiting for the kingdom of God. 52 Going to Pilate, he asked for
Jesus' body. 53 Then he took it down, wrapped
it in linen cloth and placed it in a tomb cut in
the rock, one in which no one had yet been laid.
54 It was Preparation Day, and the Sabbath
was about to begin.
55 The women who had come with Jesus from
Galilee followed Joseph and saw the tomb and
how his body was laid in it. 56 Then they went
home and prepared spices and perfumes. But
they rested on the Sabbath in obedience to the
commandment.

Phillips Modern English

pened, went home in deep distress. And all those who had known him, as well as the women who had followed him from Galilee, remained standing at a distance and saw these things happen.

23.50 Joseph from Arimathaea lays the body of Jesus in a tomb

Now there was a man called Joseph, a member of the Jewish council. He was a good and just man, and had neither agreed with their plan nor voted for their decision. He came from the Jewish city of Arimathaea and was awaiting the kingdom of God. He went to Pilate and asked for Jesus' body. He took it down and wrapped it in linen and placed it in a rock-hewn tomb which had not been used before.

It was now the day of the preparation and the Sabbath was beginning to dawn, so the women who had accompanied Jesus from Galilee followed Joseph, noted the tomb and the position of the body, and then went home to prepare spices and perfumes. On the Sabbath they rested, in obedience to the commandment.

Revised Standard Version

breasts. 49 And all his acquaintances and the
women who had followed him from Galilee
stood at a distance and saw these things.
50 Now there was a man named Joseph from
the Jewish town of Arimathea. He was a member of the council, a good and righteous man,
51 who had not consented to their purpose and
deed, and he was looking for the kingdom of
God. 52 This man went to Pilate and asked for
the body of Jesus. 53 Then he took it down and
wrapped it in a linen shroud, and laid him in a
rock-hewn tomb, where no one had ever yet
been laid. 54 It was the day of Preparation, and
the sabbath was beginning.[s] 55 The women who
had come with him from Galilee followed, and
saw the tomb, and how his body was laid;
56 then they returned, and prepared spices and
ointments.

On the sabbath they rested according to the commandment.

[s] Greek *was dawning*.

Jerusalem Bible

49 All his friends stood at a distance; so also did the women who had accompanied him from Galilee, and they saw all this happen.

The burial

50 Then a member of the council arrived, an
upright and virtuous man named Joseph. 51 He
had not consented to what the others had
planned and carried out. He came from Arimathaea, a Jewish town, and he lived in the hope
of seeing the kingdom of God. 52 This man went
to Pilate and asked for the body of Jesus. 53 He
then took it down, wrapped it in a shroud and
put him in a tomb which was hewn in stone in
which no one had yet been laid. 54 It was
Preparation Day and the sabbath was imminent.

55 Meanwhile the women who had come from Galilee with Jesus were following behind. They took note of the tomb and of the position of the body.

56 Then they returned and prepared spices and ointments. And on the sabbath day they rested, as the Law required.

New English Bible

His friends had all been standing at a distance; the women who had accompanied him from Galilee stood with them and watched it all.

Now there was a man called Joseph, a member of the Council, a good, upright man, who had dissented from their policy and the action they had taken. He came from the Judaean town of Arimathaea, and he was one who looked forward to the kingdom of God. This man now approached Pilate and asked for the body of Jesus. Taking it down from the cross, he wrapped it in a linen sheet, and laid it in a tomb cut out of the rock, in which no one had been laid before. It was Friday, and the Sabbath was about to begin.

The women who had accompanied him from Galilee followed; they took note of the tomb and observed how his body was laid. Then they went home and prepared spices and perfumes; and on the Sabbath they rested in obedience to the commandment.

King James Version

24 Now upon the first *day* of the week, very early in the morning, they came unto the sepulchre, bringing the spices which they had prepared, and certain *others* with them. 2 And they found the stone rolled away from the sepulchre. 3 And they entered in, and found not the body of the Lord Jesus. 4 And it came to pass, as they were much perplexed thereabout, behold, two men stood by them in shining garments: 5 And as they were afraid, and bowed down *their* faces to the earth, they said unto them, Why seek ye the living among the dead? 6 He is not here, but is risen: remember how he spake unto you when he was yet in Galilee, 7 Saying, The Son of man must be delivered into the hands of sinful men, and be crucified, and the third day rise again. 8 And they remembered his words, 9 And returned from the sepulchre, and told all these things unto the eleven, and to all the rest. 10 It was Mary Magdalene, and Joanna, and Mary *the mother* of James, and other *women that were* with them, which told these things unto the apostles. 11 And their words seemed to them as idle tales, and they be-

Living Bible

24 But very early on Sunday morning they took the ointments to the tomb—2 and found that the huge stone covering the entrance had been rolled aside. 3 So they went in—but the Lord Jesus' body was gone.

4 They stood there puzzled, trying to think what could have happened to it. Suddenly two men appeared before them, clothed in shining robes so bright their eyes were dazzled. 5 The women were terrified and bowed low before them.

Then the men asked, "Why are you looking in a tomb for someone who is alive? 6, 7 He isn't here! He has come back to life again! Don't you remember what he told you back in Galilee—that the Messiah[a] must be betrayed into the power of evil men and be crucified and that he would rise again the third day?"

8 Then they remembered, 9 and rushed back to Jerusalem[b] to tell his eleven disciples—and everyone else—what had happened. 10 (The women who went to the tomb were Mary Magdalene and Joanna and Mary the mother of James, and several others.) 11 But the story sounded like a fairy tale to the men—they didn't believe it.

[*a*] Literally, "the Son of Man." [*b*] Literally, "returned from the tomb."

Today's English Version

The resurrection

24 Very early on Sunday morning the women went to the grave carrying the spices they had prepared. 2 They found the stone rolled away from the entrance to the grave, 3 so they went in; but they did not find the body of the Lord Jesus. 4 They stood there puzzled about this, when suddenly two men in bright shining clothes stood by them. 5 Full of fear, the women bowed down to the ground, as the men said to them, "Why are you looking among the dead for one who is alive? 6 He is not here; he has been raised. Remember what he said to you while he was in Galilee: 7 'The Son of Man must be handed over to sinful men, be nailed to the cross, and rise to life on the third day.' "

8 Then the women remembered his words, 9 returned from the grave, and told all these things to the eleven disciples and all the rest. 10 The women were Mary Magdalene, Joanna, and Mary the mother of James; they and the other women with them told these things to the apostles. 11 But the apostles thought that what the women said was nonsense, and did not be-

New International Version

The resurrection

24 On the first day of the week, very early in the morning, the women took the spices they had prepared and went to the tomb. 2 They found the stone rolled away from the tomb, 3 but when they entered, they did not find the body of the Lord Jesus. 4 While they were wondering about this, suddenly two men in clothes that gleamed like lightning stood beside them. 5 In their fright the women bowed down with their faces to the ground, but the men said to them, "Why do you look for the living among the dead? 6 He is not here; he has risen! Remember how he told you, while he was still with you in Galilee: 7 'The Son of Man must be delivered into the hands of sinful men, be crucified and on the third day be raised again.' " 8 Then they remembered his words.

9 When they came back from the tomb, they told all these things to the Eleven and to all the others. 10 It was Mary Magdalene, Joanna, Mary the mother of James, and the others with them who told this to the apostles. 11 But they did not believe the women, because their words seemed

Phillips Modern English

24.1 The first day of the week: the empty tomb

But at the first signs of dawn on the first day of the week, they went to the tomb, taking with them the aromatic spices they had prepared. They discovered that the stone had been rolled away from the tomb, but on going inside, the body of the Lord Jesus was not to be found. While they were still puzzling over this, two men suddenly stood at their elbow, dressed in dazzling light. The women were terribly frightened, and turned their eyes away and looked at the ground. But the two men spoke to them,

"Why do you look for the living among the dead? He is not here: he has been raised! Remember what he said to you, while he was still in Galilee—that the Son of Man must be betrayed into the hands of sinful men, and must be crucified, and must rise again on the third day."

Then they did remember what he had said, and they turned their backs on the tomb and went and told all this to the eleven and the others who were with them.

It was Mary of Magdala, Joanna, Mary, the mother of James, and their companions who made this report to the apostles. But it struck them as sheer imagination, and they did not be-

Revised Standard Version

24 But on the first day of the week, at early dawn, they went to the tomb, taking the spices which they had prepared. 2 And they found the stone rolled away from the tomb, 3 but when they went in they did not find the body.[t] 4 While they were perplexed about this, behold, two men stood by them in dazzling apparel; 5 and as they were frightened and bowed their faces to the ground, the men said to them, "Why do you seek the living among the dead?[u] 6 Remember how he told you, while he was still in Galilee, 7 that the Son of man must be delivered into the hands of sinful men, and be crucified, and on the third day rise." 8 And they remembered his words, 9 and returning from the tomb they told all this to the eleven and to all the rest. 10 Now it was Mary Magdalene and Joanna and Mary the mother of James and the other women with them who told this to the apostles; 11 but these words seemed to them an idle tale, and they did not believe them.[v]

[t] Other ancient authorities add *of the Lord Jesus.* [u] Other ancient authorities add *He is not here, but has risen.* [v] Other ancient authorities add verse 12, *But Peter rose and ran to the tomb; stooping and looking in, he saw the linen cloths by themselves; and he went home wondering at what had happened.*

Jerusalem Bible

VII. After the resurrection

The empty tomb. The angel's message

24 On the first day of the week, at the first sign of dawn, they went to the tomb with the spices they had prepared. 2 They found that the stone had been rolled away from the tomb, 3 but on entering discovered that the body of the Lord Jesus was not there. 4 As they stood there not knowing what to think, two men in brilliant clothes suddenly appeared at their side. 5 Terrified, the women lowered their eyes. But the two men said to them, "Why look among the dead for someone who is alive? 6 He is not here; he has risen. Remember what he told you when he was still in Galilee: 7 that the Son of Man had to be handed over into the power of sinful men and be crucified, and rise again on the third day." 8 And they remembered his words.

The apostles refuse to believe the women

9 When the women returned from the tomb they told all this to the Eleven and to all the others. 10 The women were Mary of Magdala, Joanna, and Mary the mother of James. The other women with them also told the apostles, 11 but this story of theirs seemed pure nonsense, and they did not believe them.

New English Bible

24 But on the Sunday morning very early they came to the tomb bringing the spices they had prepared. Finding that the stone had been rolled away from the tomb, they went inside; but the body was not to be found. While they stood utterly at a loss, all of a sudden two men in dazzling garments were at their side. They were terrified, and stood with eyes cast down, but the men said, 'Why search among the dead for one who lives?[a] Remember what he told you while he was still in Galilee, about the Son of Man: how he must be given up into the power of sinful men and be crucified, and must rise again on the third day.' Then they recalled his words and, returning from the tomb, they reported all this to the Eleven and all the others.

The women were Mary of Magdala, Joanna, and Mary the mother[b] of James, and they, with the other women, told the apostles. But the story appeared to them to be nonsense, and they would not believe them.[c]

[a] *Some witnesses insert* He is not here: he has been raised. [b] *Or* wife, *or* daughter. [c] *Some witnesses add* (12) Peter, however, got up and ran to the tomb, and, peering in, saw the wrappings and nothing more; and he went home amazed at what had happened.

King James Version

lieved them not. 12 Then arose Peter, and ran
unto the sepulchre; and stooping down, he beheld the linen clothes laid by themselves, and
departed, wondering in himself at that which
was come to pass.
13 And, behold, two of them went that same
day to a village called Emmaus, which was from
Jerusalem *about* threescore furlongs. 14 And they
talked together of all these things which had
happened. 15 And it came to pass, that, while
they communed *together* and reasoned, Jesus
himself drew near, and went with them. 16 But
their eyes were holden that they should not
know him. 17 And he said unto them, What manner of communications *are* these that ye have
one to another, as ye walk, and are sad? 18 And
the one of them, whose name was Cleopas, answering said unto him, Art thou only a stranger
in Jerusalem, and hast not known the things
which are come to pass there in these days?
19 And he said unto them, What things? And
they said unto him, Concerning Jesus of Nazareth, which was a prophet mighty in deed and
word before God and all the people: 20 And how
the chief priests and our rulers delivered him to
be condemned to death, and have crucified him.
21 But we trusted that it had been he which
should have redeemed Israel: and beside all
this, to day is the third day since these things
were done. 22 Yea, and certain women also of

Living Bible

12 However, Peter ran to the tomb to look.
Stooping, he peered in and saw the empty linen
wrappings; and then he went back home again,
wondering what had happened.
13 That same day, Sunday, two of Jesus' followers were walking to the village of Emmaus,
seven miles out of Jerusalem. 14 As they walked
along they were talking of Jesus' death, 15 when
suddenly Jesus himself came along and joined
them and began walking beside them. 16 But they
didn't recognize him, for God kept them from it.
17 "You seem to be in a deep discussion about
something," he said. "What are you so concerned about?" They stopped short, sadness written across their faces. 18 And one of them, Cleopas replied, "You must be the only person in
Jerusalem who hasn't heard about the terrible
things that happened there last week." [c]
19 "What things?" Jesus asked.
"The things that happened to Jesus, the Man
from Nazareth," they said. "He was a Prophet
who did incredible miracles and was a mighty
Teacher, highly regarded by both God and man.
20 But the chief priests and our religious leaders
arrested him and handed him over to the Roman
government to be condemned to death, and they
crucified him. 21 We had thought he was the
glorious Messiah and that he had come to rescue
Israel.
"And now, besides all this—which happened
three days ago—22, 23 some women from our

[*c*] Literally, "in these days."

Today's English Version

lieve them. 12 But Peter got up and ran to the
grave; he bent down and saw the grave cloths
and nothing else. Then he went back home wondering at what had happened.

The walk to Emmaus

13 On that same day two of them were going
to a village named Emmaus, about seven miles
from Jerusalem, 14 and they were talking to each
other about all the things that had happened.
15 As they talked and discussed, Jesus himself
drew near and walked along with them; 16 they
saw him, but somehow did not recognize him.
17 Jesus said to them, "What are you talking
about, back and forth, as you walk along?"
They stood still, with sad faces. 18 One of
them, named Cleopas, asked him, "Are you the
only man living in Jerusalem who does not know
what has been happening there these last few
days?"
19 "What things?" he asked.
"The things that happened to Jesus of Nazareth," they answered. "This man was a prophet,
and was considered by God and by all the people
to be mighty in words and deeds. 20 Our chief
priests and rulers handed him over to be sentenced to death, and he was nailed to the cross.
21 And we had hoped that he would be the one
who was going to redeem Israel! Besides all
that, this is now the third day since it happened.
22 Some of the women of our group surprised

New International Version

to them like nonsense. 12 Peter, however, got up
and ran to the tomb. Stooping down, he saw
the strips of linen lying by themselves, and he
went away, wondering to himself what had happened.

On the road to Emmaus

13 Now that same day two of them were going to a village called Emmaus, about seven
miles from Jerusalem. 14 They were talking with
each other about everything that had happened.
15 As they talked and discussed these things with
each other, Jesus himself came up and walked
along with them; 16 but they were kept from
recognizing him.
17 He asked them, "What are you discussing
together as you walk along?"
They stood still, their faces downcast. 18 One
of them, named Cleopas, asked him, "Are you
the only one living in Jerusalem who doesn't
know what things have happened there in these
days?"
19 "What things?" he asked.
"About Jesus of Nazareth," they replied. "He
was a prophet, powerful in word and deed before God and all the people. 20 The chief priests
and our rulers handed him over to be sentenced
to death, and they crucified him; 21 but we had
hoped that he was the one who was going to
redeem Israel. And what is more, it is the third
day since all this took place. 22 In addition,

Phillips Modern English

lieve the women. Only Peter got up and ran to the tomb. He stooped down and saw nothing but the linen clothes lying there, and he went home wondering at what had happened.

24.13 The walk to Emmaus

Then on the same day we find two of them going off to Emmaus, a village about seven miles from Jerusalem. As they went they were deep in conversation about everything that had happened. While they were absorbed in their serious talk and discussion, Jesus himself approached and walked along with them, but something prevented them from recognising him. Then he spoke to them,

"What is all this discussion that you are having on your walk?"

They stopped, their faces drawn with misery, and the one called Cleopas replied,

"You must be the only visitor to Jerusalem who hasn't heard all the things that have happened there recently!"

"What things?" asked Jesus.

"Oh, all about Jesus, from Nazareth. There was a man—a prophet strong in what he did and what he said, in God's eyes as well as the people's. Haven't you heard how our chief priests and rulers handed him over for execution, and had him crucified? But we were hoping he was the one who was to come and set Israel free. . . .

"Yes, and as if that were not enough, it's three days since all this happened; and some of

Revised Standard Version

13 That very day two of them were going to
a village named Emmaus, about seven miles[w]
from Jerusalem, 14 and talking with each other
about all these things that had happened.
15 While they were talking and discussing together, Jesus himself drew near and went with
them. 16 But their eyes were kept from recognizing him. 17 And he said to them, "What is
this conversation which you are holding with
each other as you walk?" And they stood still,
looking sad. 18 Then one of them, named Cleopas, answered him, "Are you the only visitor
to Jerusalem who does not know the things
that have happened there in these days?" 19 And
he said to them, "What things?" And they said
to him, "Concerning Jesus of Nazareth, who
was a prophet mighty in deed and word before
God and all the people, 20 and how our chief
priests and rulers delivered him up to be condemned to death, and crucified him. 21 But we
had hoped that he was the one to redeem Israel.
Yes, and besides all this, it is now the third day
since this happened. 22 Moreover, some women

[w] Greek *sixty stadia;* some ancient authorities read *a hundred and sixty stadia.*

Jerusalem Bible

Peter at the tomb

12 Peter, however, went running to the tomb.
He bent down and saw the binding cloths but
nothing else; he then went back home, amazed
at what had happened.

The road to Emmaus

13 That very same day, two of them were on
their way to a village called Emmaus, seven
miles[x] from Jerusalem, 14 and they were talking
together about all that had happened. 15 Now
as they talked this over, Jesus himself came up
and walked by their side; 16 but something prevented them from recognizing him. 17 He said
to them, "What matters are you discussing as you
walk along?" They stopped short, their faces
downcast.
18 Then one of them, called Cleopas, answered him, "You must be the only person staying in Jerusalem who does not know the things
that have been happening there these last few
days." 19 "What things?" he asked. "All about
Jesus of Nazareth," they answered, "who proved
he was a great prophet by the things he said and
did in the sight of God and of the whole people;
20 and how our chief priests and our leaders
handed him over to be sentenced to death, and
had him crucified. 21 Our own hope had been
that he would be the one to set Israel free. And
this is not all: two whole days have gone by
since it all happened; 22 and some women from

[x] The identity of the village is disputed.

New English Bible

That same day two of them were on their way to a village called Emmaus, which lay about seven miles from Jerusalem, and they were talking together about all these happenings. As they talked and discussed it with one another, Jesus himself came up and walked along with them; but something kept them from seeing who it was. He asked them, 'What is it you are debating as you walk?' They halted, their faces full of gloom, and one, called Cleopas, answered, 'Are you the only person staying in Jerusalem not to know[d] what has happened there in the last few days?' 'What do you mean?' he said. 'All this about Jesus of Nazareth,' they replied, 'a prophet powerful in speech and action before God and the whole people: how our chief priests and rulers handed him over to be sentenced to death, and crucified him. But we had been hoping that he was the man to liberate Israel. What is more, this is the third day since it happened, and now some women of our company have

[d] *Or* Have you been staying by yourself in Jerusalem, that you do not know . . .

King James Version

our company made us astonished, which were
early at the sepulchre; 23And when they found
not his body, they came, saying, that they had
also seen a vision of angels, which said that he
was alive. 24And certain of them which were
with us went to the sepulchre, and found *it* even
so as the women had said: but him they saw not.
25 Then he said unto them, O fools, and slow of
heart to believe all that the prophets have
spoken: 26 Ought not Christ to have suffered
these things, and to enter into his glory? 27And
beginning at Moses and all the prophets, he expounded unto them in all the Scriptures the
things concerning himself. 28And they drew nigh
unto the village, whither they went: and he
made as though he would have gone further.
29 But they constrained him, saying, Abide with
us; for it is toward evening, and the day is far
spent. And he went in to tarry with them. 30And
it came to pass, as he sat at meat with them, he
took bread, and blessed *it*, and brake, and gave
to them. 31And their eyes were opened, and
they knew him; and he vanished out of their
sight. 32And they said one to another, Did not
our heart burn within us, while he talked with us
by the way, and while he opened to us the
Scriptures? 33And they rose up the same hour,
and returned to Jerusalem, and found the eleven

Living Bible

group of his followers were at his tomb early
this morning and came back with an amazing
report that his body was missing, and that they
had seen some angels there who told them Jesus
is alive! 24 Some of our men ran out to see, and
sure enough, Jesus' body was gone, just as the
women had said."
25 Then Jesus said to them, "You are such
foolish, foolish people! You find it so hard to
believe all that the prophets wrote in the Scriptures! 26 Wasn't it clearly predicted by the
prophets that the Messiah would have to suffer
all these things before entering his time of
glory?"
27 Then Jesus quoted them passage after passage from the writings of the prophets, beginning with the book of Genesis and going right
on through the Scriptures, explaining what the
passages meant and what they said about himself.
28 By this time they were nearing Emmaus
and the end of their journey. Jesus would have
gone on, 29 but they begged him to stay the
night with them, as it was getting late. So he
went home with them. 30As they sat down to
eat, he asked God's blessing on the food and
then took a small loaf of bread and broke it
and was passing it over to them, 31 when suddenly—it was as though their eyes were opened
—they recognized him! And at that moment he
disappeared!
32 They began telling each other how their
hearts had felt strangely warm as he talked with
them and explained the Scriptures during the
walk down the road. 33, 34 Within the hour they
were on their way back to Jerusalem, where the

Today's English Version

us; they went at dawn to the grave, 23 but could
not find his body. They came back saying they
had seen a vision of angels who told them that
he is alive. 24 Some of our group went to the
grave and found it exactly as the women had
said; but they did not see him."
25 Then Jesus said to them, "How foolish you
are, how slow you are to believe everything the
prophets said! 26 Was it not necessary for the
Messiah to suffer these things and enter his
glory?" 27And Jesus explained to them what was
said about him in all the Scriptures, beginning
with the books of Moses and the writings of all
the prophets.
28 They came near the village to which they
were going, and Jesus acted as if he were going
farther; 29 but they held him back, saying, "Stay
with us; the day is almost over and it is getting
dark." So he went in to stay with them. 30 He
sat at table with them, took the bread, and said
the blessing; then he broke the bread and gave
it to them. 31 Their eyes were opened and they
recognized him; but he disappeared from their
sight. 32 They said to each other, "Wasn't it like
a fire burning in us when he talked to us on the
road and explained the Scriptures to us?"
33 They got up at once and went back to
Jerusalem, where they found the eleven disciples

New International Version

some of our women amazed us. They went to
the tomb early this morning 23 but didn't find
his body. They came and told us that they had
seen a vision of angels, who said he was alive.
24 Then some of our companions went to the
tomb and found it just as the women had said,
but him they did not see."
25 He said to them, "How foolish you are,
and how slow of heart that you do not believe
all that the prophets have spoken! 26 Did not
the Christ[d] have to suffer these things and then
enter his glory?" 27And beginning with Moses
and all the Prophets, he explained to them what
was said in all the Scriptures concerning himself.
28 As they approached the village to which
they were going, Jesus acted as if he were going
farther. 29 But they urged him strongly, "Stay
with us, for it is nearly evening; the day is almost over." So he went in to stay with them.
30 When he was at the table with them, he
took bread, gave thanks, broke it and began to
give it to them. 31 Then their eyes were opened
and they recognized him, and he disappeared
from their sight. 32 They asked each other,
"Were not our hearts burning within us while
he talked with us on the road and opened the
Scriptures to us?"
33 They got up and returned at once to Jerusalem. There they found the Eleven and those

[d] Or *Messiah.*

Phillips Modern English

our womenfolk have disturbed us profoundly. For they went to the tomb at dawn, and then when they couldn't find his body they said that they had had a vision of angels who said that he was alive. Some of our people went straight off to the tomb and found things just as the women had described them—but they didn't see *him!*"

Then he himself spoke to them,

"Oh, how foolish you are, how slow to believe in all that the prophets have said! Was it not inevitable that Christ should suffer like that and so find his glory?"

Then, beginning with Moses and all the prophets, he explained to them everything in the scriptures that referred to himself.

They were by now approaching the village to which they were going. He gave the impression that he meant to go on further, but they stopped him with the words,

"Do stay with us. It is nearly evening and the day will soon be over."

So he went indoors to stay with them. Then it happened! While he was sitting at table with them he took the loaf, gave thanks, broke it and passed it to them. Their eyes opened wide and they knew him! But he vanished from their sight. Then they said to each other,

"Weren't our hearts glowing while he was with us on the road when he made the scriptures plain to us?"

And they got to their feet without delay and turned back to Jerusalem. There they found the

Revised Standard Version

of our company amazed us. They were at the
tomb early in the morning 23 and did not find
his body; and they came back saying that they
had even seen a vision of angels, who said that
he was alive. 24 Some of those who were with
us went to the tomb, and found it just as the
women had said; but him they did not see."
25 And he said to them, "O foolish men, and
slow of heart to believe all that the prophets
have spoken! 26 Was it not necessary that the
Christ should suffer these things and enter into
his glory?" 27 And beginning with Moses and
all the prophets, he interpreted to them in all
the scriptures the things concerning himself.
28 So they drew near to the village to which
they were going. He appeared to be going further, 29 but they constrained him, saying, "Stay
with us, for it is toward evening and the day is
now far spent." So he went in to stay with
them. 30 When he was at table with them, he
took the bread and blessed, and broke it, and
gave it to them. 31 And their eyes were opened
and they recognized him; and he vanished out of
their sight. 32 They said to each other, "Did not
our hearts burn within us[c] while he talked to us
on the road, while he opened to us the scriptures?" 33 And they rose that same hour and returned to Jerusalem; and they found the eleven

[c] Other ancient authorities omit *within us*.

Jerusalem Bible

our group have astounded us: they went to the
tomb in the early morning, 23 and when they
did not find the body, they came back to tell
us they had seen a vision of angels who declared
he was alive. 24 Some of our friends went to the
tomb and found everything exactly as the women
had reported, but of him they saw nothing."
25 Then he said to them, "You foolish men!
So slow to believe the full message of the prophets! 26 Was it not ordained that the Christ should
suffer and so enter into his glory?" 27 Then,
starting with Moses and going through all the
prophets, he explained to them the passages
throughout the scriptures that were about himself.
28 When they drew near to the village to
which they were going, he made as if to go on;
29 but they pressed him to stay with them. "It
is nearly evening," they said, "and the day is
almost over." So he went in to stay with them.
30 Now while he was with them at table, he took
the bread and said the blessing; then he broke it
and handed it to them. 31 And their eyes were
opened and they recognized him; but he had
vanished from their sight. 32 Then they said to
each other, "Did not our hearts burn within us
as he talked to us on the road and explained
the scriptures to us?"
33 They set out that instant and returned to
Jerusalem. There they found the Eleven assem-

New English Bible

astounded us: they went early to the tomb, but failed to find his body, and returned with a story that they had seen a vision of angels who told them he was alive. So some of our people went to the tomb and found things just as the women had said; but him they did not see.'

'How dull you are!' he answered. 'How slow to believe all that the prophets said! Was the Messiah not bound to suffer thus before entering upon his glory?' Then he began with Moses and all the prophets, and explained to them the passages which referred to himself in every part of the scriptures.

By this time they had reached the village to which they were going, and he made as if to continue his journey, but they pressed him: 'Stay with us, for evening draws on, and the day is almost over.' So he went in to stay with them. And when he had sat down with them at table, he took bread and said the blessing; he broke the bread, and offered it to them. Then their eyes were opened, and they recognized him; and he vanished from their sight. They said to one another, 'Did we not feel our hearts on fire as he talked with us on the road and explained the scriptures to us?'

Without a moment's delay they set out and returned to Jerusalem. There they found that the

King James Version

gathered together, and them that were with
them, 34 Saying, The Lord is risen indeed, and
hath appeared to Simon. 35And they told what
things *were done* in the way, and how he was
known of them in breaking of bread.
36 And as they thus spake, Jesus himself
stood in the midst of them, and saith unto them,
Peace *be* unto you. 37 But they were terrified
and affrighted, and supposed that they had seen
a spirit. 38And he said unto them, Why are ye
troubled? and why do thoughts arise in your
hearts? 39 Behold my hands and my feet, that it
is I myself: handle me, and see; for a spirit hath
not flesh and bones, as ye see me have. 40And
when he had thus spoken, he shewed them *his*
hands and *his* feet. 41And while they yet believed
not for joy, and wondered, he said unto them,
Have ye here any meat? 42And they gave him a
piece of a broiled fish, and of a honeycomb.
43And he took *it*, and did eat before them. 44And
he said unto them, These *are* the words which I
spake unto you, while I was yet with you, that
all things must be fulfilled, which were written
in the law of Moses, and *in* the prophets, and *in*

Living Bible

eleven disciples and the other followers of Jesus
greeted them with these words, "The Lord has
really risen! He appeared to Peter!"
35 Then the two from Emmaus told their
story of how Jesus had appeared to them as they
were walking along the road and how they had
recognized him as he was breaking the bread.
36And just as they were telling about it, Jesus
himself was suddenly standing there among them,
and greeted them. 37 But the whole group was
terribly frightened, thinking they were seeing a
ghost!
38 "Why are you frightened?" he asked. "Why
do you doubt that it is really I? 39 Look at my
hands! Look at my feet! You can see that it is I,
myself! Touch me and make sure that I am not
a ghost! For ghosts don't have bodies, as you see
that I do!" 40As he spoke, he held out his hands
for them to see [the marks of the nails[d]], and
showed them [the wounds in[d]] his feet.
41 Still they stood there undecided, filled with
joy and doubt.
Then he asked them, "Do you have anything
here to eat?"
42 They gave him a piece of broiled fish,
43 and he ate it as they watched!
44 Then he said, "When I was with you before, don't you remember my telling you that
everything written about me by Moses and the
prophets and in the Psalms must all come true?"

[*d*] Implied.

Today's English Version

gathered together with the others 34 and saying,
"The Lord is risen indeed! He has appeared to
Simon!"
35 The two then explained to them what had
happened on the road, and how they had recognized the Lord when he broke the bread.

Jesus appears to his disciples

36 While they were telling them this, suddenly
the Lord himself stood among them and said to
them, "Peace be with you."
37 Full of fear and terror, they thought that
they were seeing a ghost. 38 But he said to them,
"Why are you troubled? Why are these doubts
coming up in your minds? 39 Look at my hands
and my feet and see that it is I, myself. Feel me,
and you will see, because a ghost doesn't have
flesh and bones, as you can see I have."
40 He said this and showed them his hands
and his feet. 41 They still could not believe, they
were so full of joy and wonder; so he asked
them, "Do you have anything to eat here?"
42 They gave him a piece of cooked fish,
43 which he took and ate before them.
44 Then he said to them, "These are the very
things I told you while I was still with you:
everything written about me in the Law of
Moses, the writings of the prophets, and the
Psalms had to come true."

New International Version

with them, assembled together 34 and saying, "It
is true! The Lord has risen and has appeared to
Simon." 35 Then the two told what had happened on the way, and how Jesus was recognized
by them when he broke the bread.

Jesus appears to the disciples

36 While they were still talking about this,
Jesus himself stood among them and said to
them, "Peace be with you."
37 They were startled and frightened, thinking they saw a ghost. 38 He said to them, "Why
are you troubled, and why do doubts rise in
your minds? 39 Look at my hands and my feet.
It is I myself! Touch me and see; a ghost does
not have flesh and bones, as you see I have."
40 When he had said this, he showed them
his hands and feet. 41And while they still did not
believe it because of joy and amazement, he
asked them, "Do you have anything here to
eat?" 42 They gave him a piece of broiled fish,
43 and he took it and ate it in their presence.
44 He said to them, "This is what I told you
while I was still with you: Everything must be
fulfilled that is written about me in the Law of
Moses, the Prophets and the Psalms."

Phillips Modern English

eleven and their friends all together, full of the news—

"The Lord is really risen—he has appeared to Simon now!"

Then they told the story of their walk, and how they recognised him when he broke the loaf.

24.36 Jesus suddenly appears to the disciples

And while they were still talking about these things, Jesus himself stood among them and said,

"Peace be with you all!"

But they shrank back in terror for they thought they were seeing a ghost.

"Why are you so worried?" said Jesus, "and why do doubts arise in your minds? Look at my hands and my feet—it is really I myself! Feel me and see; ghosts have no flesh or bones as you can see that I have."

But while they still could not believe it through sheer joy and were quite bewildered, Jesus said to them,

"Have you anything here to eat?"

They gave him a piece of broiled fish, which he took and ate before their eyes. Then he said,

"Here and now are fulfilled the words that I told you when I was with you: that everything written about me in the Law of Moses and in the prophets and psalms must come true."

Revised Standard Version

gathered together and those who were with them,
34 who said, "The Lord has risen indeed, and
has appeared to Simon!" 35 Then they told what
had happened on the road, and how he was
known to them in the breaking of the bread.
36 As they were saying this, Jesus himself
stood among them.[x] 37 But they were startled
and frightened, and supposed that they saw a
spirit. 38 And he said to them, "Why are you
troubled, and why do questionings rise in your
hearts? 39 See my hands and my feet, that it is
I myself; handle me, and see; for a spirit has
not flesh and bones as you see that I have."[y]
41 And while they still disbelieved for joy, and
wondered, he said to them, "Have you anything
here to eat?" 42 They gave him a piece of broiled
fish, 43 and he took it and ate before them.
44 Then he said to them, "These are my
words which I spoke to you, while I was still
with you, that everything written about me in
the law of Moses and the prophets and the

[x] Other ancient authorities add *and said to them, "Peace to you!"* [y] Other ancient authorities add verse 40, *And when he had said this, he showed them his hands and his feet.*

Jerusalem Bible

bled together with their companions, 34 who
said to them, "Yes, it is true. The Lord has risen
and has appeared to Simon." 35 Then they told
their story of what had happened on the road
and how they had recognized him at the breaking of bread.

Jesus appears to the apostles

36 They were still talking about all this when
he himself stood among them and said to them,
"Peace be with you!" 37 In a state of alarm and
fright, they thought they were seeing a ghost.
38 But he said, "Why are you so agitated, and
why are these doubts rising in your hearts?
39 Look at my hands and feet; yes, it is I indeed.
Touch me and see for yourselves; a ghost has
no flesh and bones as you can see I have."
40 And as he said this he showed them his hands
and feet. 41 Their joy was so great that they still
could not believe it, and they stood there dumfounded; so he said to them, "Have you anything here to eat?" 42 And they offered him a piece
of grilled fish, 43 which he took and ate before
their eyes.

Last instructions to the apostles

44 Then he told them, "This is what I meant
when I said, while I was still with you, that
everything written about me in the Law of
Moses, in the Prophets and in the Psalms, has

New English Bible

Eleven and the rest of the company had assembled, and were saying, 'It is true: the Lord has risen; he has appeared to Simon.' Then they gave their account of the events of their journey and told how he had been recognized by them at the breaking of the bread.

As they were talking about all this, there he was, standing among them.[a] Startled and terrified, they thought they were seeing a ghost. But he said, 'Why are you so perturbed? Why do questionings arise in your minds? Look at my hands and feet. It is I myself. Touch me and see; no ghost has flesh and bones as you can see that I have.'[b] They were still unconvinced, still wondering, for it seemed too good to be true. So he asked them, 'Have you anything here to eat?' They offered him a piece of fish they had cooked, which he took and ate before their eyes.

And he said to them, 'This is what I meant by saying, while I was still with you, that everything written about me in the Law of Moses and in the prophets and psalms was bound to be ful-

[a] *Some witnesses insert* And he said to them, 'Peace be with you!' [b] *Some witnesses insert* (40) After saying this he showed them his hands and feet.

King James Version

the psalms, concerning me. 45 Then opened he
their understanding, that they might understand
the Scriptures, 46And said unto them, Thus it is
written, and thus it behoved Christ to suffer,
and to rise from the dead the third day: 47And
that repentance and remission of sins should be
preached in his name among all nations, beginning at Jerusalem. 48And ye are witnesses of
these things.
49 And, behold, I send the promise of my
Father upon you: but tarry ye in the city of
Jerusalem, until ye be endued with power from
on high.
50 And he led them out as far as to Bethany,
and he lifted up his hands, and blessed them.
51And it came to pass, while he blessed them, he
was parted from them, and carried up into
heaven. 52And they worshipped him, and returned to Jerusalem with great joy: 53And were
continually in the temple, praising and blessing
God. Amen.

Living Bible

45 Then he opened their minds to understand at
last these many Scriptures! 46And he said, "Yes,
it was written long ago that the Messiah must
suffer and die and rise again from the dead on
the third day; 47 and that this message of salvation should be taken from Jerusalem to all the
nations: *There is forgiveness of sins for all who
turn to me.* 48 You have seen these prophecies
come true.
49 "And now I will send the Holy Spirit[e]
upon you, just as my Father promised. Don't
begin telling others[f] yet—stay here in the city
until the Holy Spirit comes and fills you with
power from heaven."
50 Then Jesus led them out along the road[g]
to Bethany, and lifting his hands to heaven, he
blessed them, 51 and then began rising into the
sky, and went on to heaven. 52And they worshiped him, and returned to Jerusalem filled
with mighty joy, 53 and were continually in the
Temple, praising God.

[*e*] Implied. Literally, "the promise of my Father." [*f*] Literally, "but wait here in the city until. . . ." The paraphrase relates this to verse 47. [*g*] Implied. Bethany was a mile or so away, across the valley on the Mount of Olives.

Today's English Version

45 Then he opened their minds to understand
the Scriptures, 46 and said to them, "This is
what is written: that the Messiah must suffer,
and rise from death on the third day, 47 and
that in his name the message about repentance
and the forgiveness of sins must be preached to
all nations, beginning in Jerusalem. 48 You are
witnesses of these things. 49And I myself will
send upon you what my Father has promised.
But you must wait in the city until the power
from above comes down upon you."

Jesus is taken up to heaven

50 Then he led them out of the city as far as
Bethany, where he raised his hands and blessed
them. 51As he was blessing them, he departed
from them and was taken up into heaven.
52 They worshiped him and went back into Jerusalem, filled with great joy, 53 and spent all their
time in the temple giving thanks to God.

New International Version

45 Then he opened their minds so they could
understand the Scriptures. 46 He told them, "This
is what is written: The Christ[e] will suffer and
rise from the dead on the third day, 47 and repentance and forgiveness of sins will be preached
in his name to all nations, beginning at Jerusalem. 48 You are witnesses of these things. 49 I
am going to send you what my Father has promised; but stay in the city until you have been
clothed with power from on high."

The ascension

50 When he had led them out to the vicinity
of Bethany, he lifted up his hands and blessed
them. 51 While he was blessing them, he left
them and was taken up into heaven. 52 Then
they worshiped him and returned to Jerusalem
with great joy. 53And they stayed continually at
the temple, praising God.

[*e*] Or *Messiah*.

Phillips Modern English

Then he opened their minds so that they could understand the scriptures, and added,

"That is how it was written, and that is why it was inevitable that Christ should suffer, and rise from the dead on the third day. So must the change of heart which leads to the forgiveness of sins be proclaimed in his name to all nations, beginning at Jerusalem.

24.48 Jesus commissions them with the new message

"You are eye-witnesses of these things. Now I hand over to you the promise of my Father. Stay in the city, then, until you are clothed with power from on high."

Then he led them outside as far as Bethany, where he blessed them with uplifted hands. While he was in the act of blessing them he was parted from them and was carried up to Heaven. They worshipped him, and turned back to Jerusalem with great joy, and spent their days in the Temple, praising God.

Revised Standard Version

psalms must be fulfilled." 45 Then he opened
their minds to understand the scriptures, 46 and
said to them, "Thus it is written, that the Christ
should suffer and on the third day rise from the
dead, 47 and that repentance and forgiveness of
sins should be preached in his name to all nations,[z] beginning from Jerusalem. 48 You are
witnesses of these things. 49 And behold, I send
the promise of my Father upon you; but stay
in the city, until you are clothed with power
from on high."
50 Then he led them out as far as Bethany,
and lifting up his hands he blessed them.
51 While he blessed them, he parted from them,
and was carried up into heaven.[a] 52 And they[b]
returned to Jerusalem with great joy, 53 and
were continually in the temple blessing God.

[z] *Or nations. Beginning from Jerusalem you are witnesses.* [a] Other ancient authorities omit *and was carried up into heaven.* [b] Other ancient authorities add *worshiped him, and.*

Jerusalem Bible

to be fulfilled." 45 He then opened their minds
to understand the scriptures, 46 and he said to
them, "So you see how it is written that the
Christ would suffer and on the third day rise
from the dead, 47 and that, in his name, repentance for the forgiveness of sins would be
preached to all the nations, beginning from
Jerusalem. 48 You are witnesses to this.
49 "And now I am sending down to you what
the Father has promised. Stay in the city then,
until you are clothed with the power from on
high."

The ascension

50 Then he took them out as far as the outskirts of Bethany, and lifting up his hands he
blessed them. 51 Now as he blessed them, he
withdrew from them and was carried up to
heaven. 52 They worshiped him and then went
back to Jerusalem full of joy; 53 and they were
continually in the Temple praising God.

New English Bible

filled.' Then he opened their minds to understand the scriptures. 'This', he said, 'is what is written: that the Messiah is to suffer death and to rise from the dead on the third day, and that in his name repentance bringing the forgiveness of sins is to be proclaimed to all nations. Begin from Jerusalem; it is you who are the witnesses to it all. And mark this: I am sending upon you my Father's promised gift; so stay here in this city until you are armed with the power from above.'

Then he led them out as far as Bethany, and blessed them with uplifted hands; and in the act of blessing he parted from them.[c] And they[d] returned to Jerusalem with great joy, and spent all their time in the temple praising God.

[c] *Some witnesses add* and was carried up into heaven. [d] *Some witnesses insert* worshipped him and . . .

King James Version

THE GOSPEL ACCORDING TO SAINT JOHN

1 In the beginning was the Word, and the Word was with God, and the Word was God. 2 The same was in the beginning with God. 3 All things were made by him; and without him was not any thing made that was made. 4 In him was life; and the life was the light of men. 5 And the light shineth in darkness; and the darkness comprehended it not.

Living Bible

JOHN

1 Before anything else existed,[a] there was Christ,[b] with God. He has always[a] been alive and is himself God. 3 He created everything there is—nothing exists that he didn't make. 4 Eternal life is in him, and this life gives light to all mankind. 5 His life is the light that shines through the darkness—and the darkness can never extinguish it.

[a] Literally, "In the beginning." [b] Literally, "the Word," meaning Christ, the wisdom and power of God and the first cause of all things; God's personal expression of himself to men.

Today's English Version

THE GOSPEL OF JOHN

The Word of life

1 Before the world was created, the Word already existed; he was with God, and he was the same as God. 2 From the very beginning, the Word was with God. 3 Through him God made all things; not one thing in all creation was made without him. 4 The Word was the source of life, and this life brought light to men. 5 The light shines in the darkness, and the darkness has never put it out.

New International Version

JOHN

The Word became flesh

1 In the beginning was the Word, and the Word was with God, and the Word was God. 2 He was with God in the beginning.

3 Through him all things were made; without him nothing was made that has been made. 4 In him was life, and that life was the light of men. 5 The light shines in the darkness, but the darkness has not understood [a] it.

[a] Or *overpowered.*

Phillips Modern English

THE GOSPEL OF JOHN

1.1 *Prologue*

At the beginning God expressed himself. That personal expression, that word, was with God, and was God, and he existed with God from the beginning. All creation took place through him, and none took place without him. In him appeared life and this life was the light of mankind. The light still shines in the darkness and the darkness has never put it out.

Revised Standard Version

THE GOSPEL ACCORDING TO JOHN

1 In the beginning was the Word, and the
Word was with God, and the Word was
God. 2 He was in the beginning with God; 3 all
things were made through him, and without him
was not anything made that was made. 4 In him
was life,[a] and the life was the light of men.
5 The light shines in the darkness, and the darkness has not overcome it.

[a] Or *was not anything made. That which has been made was life in him.*

Jerusalem Bible

THE GOSPEL ACCORDING TO SAINT JOHN

Prologue

1 In the beginning was the Word:
the Word was with God
and the Word was God.
2 He was with God in the beginning.
3 Through him all things came to be,
not one thing had its being but through him.
4 All that came to be had life in him
and that life was the light of men,
5 a light that shines in the dark,
a light that darkness could not overpower.[a]

[a] Or "grasp," in the sense of "enclose" or "understand."

New English Bible

THE GOSPEL ACCORDING TO JOHN

The coming of Christ

1 When all things began, the Word already was.[a] The Word dwelt with God, and what God was, the Word was. The Word, then, was with God at the beginning, and through him all things came to be; no single thing was created without him. All that came to be was alive with his life,[b] and that life was the light of men. The light shines on in the dark, and the darkness has never mastered it.

[a] *Or* The Word was at the creation. [b] *Or* no single created thing came into being without him. There was life in him . . .

King James Version

6 There was a man sent from God, whose name *was* John. 7 The same came for a witness, to bear witness of the Light, that all *men* through him might believe. 8 He was not that Light, but *was sent* to bear witness of that Light. 9 *That* was the true Light, which lighteth every man that cometh into the world. 10 He was in the world, and the world was made by him, and the world knew him not. 11 He came unto his own, and his own received him not. 12 But as many as received him, to them gave he power to become the sons of God, *even* to them that believe on his name: 13 Which were born, not of blood, nor of the will of the flesh, nor of the will of man, but of God. 14 And the Word was made flesh, and dwelt among us, (and we beheld his glory, the glory as of the only begotten of the Father,) full of grace and truth.

15 John bare witness of him, and cried, saying, This was he of whom I spake, He that cometh after me is preferred before me; for he

Living Bible

6, 7 God sent John the Baptist as a witness to the fact that Jesus Christ is the true Light. 8 John himself was not the Light; he was only a witness to identify it. 9 Later on, the one who is the true Light arrived to shine on everyone coming into the world.

10 But although he made the world, the world didn't recognize him when he came. 11, 12 Even in his own land and among his own people, the Jews, he was not accepted. Only a few would welcome and receive him. But to all who received him, he gave the right to become children of God. All they needed to do was to trust him to save them.[c] 13 All those who believe this are reborn!—not a physical rebirth[d] resulting from human passion or plan—but from the will of God.

14 And Christ[b] became a human being and lived here on earth among us and was full of loving forgiveness[e] and truth. And some of us have seen his glory[f]—the glory of the only Son of the heavenly Father! [g]

15 John pointed him out to the people, telling the crowds, "This is the one I was talking about when I said, 'Someone is coming who is greater by far than I am—for he existed long before I

[c] Literally, "to believe on his name." [d] Literally, "not of blood." [b] Literally, "the Word," meaning Christ, the wisdom and power of God and the first cause of all things; God's personal expression of himself to men. [e] Literally, "grace." [f] See Matthew 17:2 [g] Or, "his unique Son."

Today's English Version

6 God sent his messenger, a man named John, 7 who came to tell people about the light. He came to tell them, so that all should hear the message and believe. 8 He himself was not the light; he came to tell about the light. 9 This was the real light, the light that comes into the world and shines on all men.

10 The Word, then, was in the world. God made the world through him, yet the world did not know him. 11 He came to his own country, but his own people did not receive him. 12 Some, however, did receive him and believed in him; so he gave them the right to become God's children. 13 They did not become God's children by natural means, by being born as the children of a human father; God himself was their Father.

14 The Word became a human being and lived among us. We saw his glory, full of grace and truth. This was the glory which he received as the Father's only Son.

15 John told about him. He cried out, "This is the one I was talking about when I said, 'He comes after me, but he is greater than I am, because he existed before I was born.' "

New International Version

6 There came a man who was sent from God; his name was John. 7 He came as a witness to testify concerning that light, so that through him all men might believe. 8 He himself was not the light; he came only as a witness to the light. 9 The true light that gives light to every man was coming into the world.[b]

10 He was in the world, and though the world was made through him, the world did not recognize him. 11 He came to that which was his own, but his own did not receive him. 12 Yet to all who received him, to those who believed in his name, he gave the right to become children of God—13 children born not of natural descent,[c] nor of human decision or a husband's will, but born of God.

14 The Word became flesh and lived for a while among us. We have seen his glory, the glory of the one and only [Son] [d], who came from the Father, full of grace and truth.

15 John testifies concerning him. He cries out, saying, "This was he of whom I said, 'He who comes after me has surpassed me because

[b] Or *This was the true light that gives light to every man who comes into the world.* [c] Greek *of bloods.* [d] Or *the Only Begotten.*

Phillips Modern English

1.6 The gospel's beginning on earth

A man called John was sent by God as a witness to the light, so that all who heard his testimony might believe in the light. This man was not himself the light: he was sent simply as a witness to that light.

That was the true light, which shines upon every man, which was now coming into the world. He came into the world—the world he had created—and the world failed to recognise him. He came into his own world, and his own people would not accept him. Yet wherever men did accept him he gave them the power to become sons of God. These were the men who truly believed in him, and their birth depended not on natural descent nor on any physical impulse or plan of man, but on God.

So the word of God became a human being and lived among us. We saw his glory (the glory like that of a father's only son), full of grace and truth. And it was about him that John stood up and testified, exclaiming: "Here is the one I was speaking about when I said that although he would come after me he would always be in front of me; for he existed before I was born!"

Revised Standard Version

6 There was a man sent from God, whose
name was John. 7 He came for testimony, to
bear witness to the light, that all might believe
through him. 8 He was not the light, but came
to bear witness to the light.
9 The true light that enlightens every man
was coming into the world. 10 He was in the
world, and the world was made through him, yet
the world knew him not. 11 He came to his
own home, and his own people received him
not. 12 But to all who received him, who believed in his name, he gave power to become
children of God; 13 who were born, not of blood
nor of the will of the flesh nor of the will of
man, but of God.
14 And the Word became flesh and dwelt
among us, full of grace and truth; we have beheld his glory, glory as of the only Son from
the Father. 15 (John bore witness to him, and
cried, "This was he of whom I said, 'He who
comes after me ranks before me, for he was

Jerusalem Bible

6 A man came, sent by God.
His name was John.
7 He came as a witness,
as a witness to speak for the light,
so that everyone might believe through him.
8 He was not the light,
only a witness to speak for the light.

9 The Word was the true light
that enlightens all men;
and he was coming into the world.
10 He was in the world
that had its being through him,
and the world did not know him.
11 He came to his own domain
and his own people did not accept him.
12 But to all who did accept him
he gave power to become children of God,
to all who believe in the name of him
13 who was born not out of human stock
or urge of the flesh
or will of man
but of God himself.
14 The Word was made flesh,
he lived among us,[b]
and we saw his glory,
the glory that is his as the only Son of the Father,
full of grace and truth.

15 John appears as his witness. He proclaims:
"This is the one of whom I said:
He who comes after me
ranks before me
because he existed before me."

[b] "pitched his tent among us."

New English Bible

There appeared a man named John, sent from God; he came as a witness to testify to the light, that all might become believers through him. He was not himself the light; he came to bear witness to the light. The real light which enlightens every man was even then coming into the world.[c]

He was in the world;[d] but the world, though it owed its being to him, did not recognize him. He entered his own realm, and his own would not receive him. But to all who did receive him, to those who have yielded him their allegiance, he gave the right to become children of God, not born of any human stock, or by the fleshly desire of a human father, but the offspring of God himself. So the Word became flesh; he came to dwell among us, and we saw his glory, such glory as befits the Father's only Son, full of grace and truth.

Here is John's testimony to him: he cried aloud, 'This is the man I meant when I said, "He comes after me, but takes rank before me"; for before I was born, he already was.'

[c] *Or* The light was in being, light absolute, enlightening every man born into the world. [d] *Or* The Word, then, was in the world.

King James Version

was before me. 16And of his fulness have all we received, and grace for grace. 17 For the law was given by Moses, *but* grace and truth came by Jesus Christ. 18 No man hath seen God at any time; the only begotten Son, which is in the bosom of the Father, he hath declared *him*.

19 And this is the record of John, when the Jews sent priests and Levites from Jerusalem to ask him, Who art thou? 20And he confessed, and denied not; but confessed, I am not the Christ. 21And they asked him, What then? Art thou Elias? And he saith, I am not. Art thou that Prophet? And he answered, No. 22 Then said they unto him, Who art thou? that we may give an answer to them that sent us. What sayest

Living Bible

did!' " 16 We have all benefited from the rich blessings he brought to us—blessing upon blessing heaped upon us! 17 For Moses gave us only the Law with its rigid demands and merciless justice, while Jesus Christ brought us loving forgiveness as well. 18 No one has ever actually seen God, but, of course, his only Son has, for he is the companion of the Father and has told us all about him.

19 The Jewish leaders[h] sent priests and assistant priests from Jerusalem to ask John whether he claimed to be the Messiah.

20 He denied it flatly. "I am not the Christ," he said.

21 "Well then, who are you?" they asked. "Are you Elijah?"

"No," he replied.

"Are you the Prophet?" [i]

"No."

22 "Then who are you? Tell us, so we can give an answer to those who sent us. What do you have to say for yourself?"

[*h*] Literally, "the Jews." [*i*] See Deuteronomy 18:15.

Today's English Version

16 Out of the fulness of his grace he has blessed us all, giving us one blessing after another. 17 God gave the Law through Moses; but grace and truth came through Jesus Christ. 18 No one has ever seen God. The only One, who is the same as God and is at the Father's side, he has made him known.

John the Baptist's message

19 The Jewish authorities in Jerusalem sent priests and Levites to John, to ask him, "Who are you?"

20 John did not refuse to answer, but spoke out openly and clearly. This is what he said, "I am not the Messiah."

21 "Who are you, then?" they asked. "Are you Elijah?"

"No, I am not," John answered.

"Are you the Prophet?" they asked.

"No," he replied.

22 "Tell us who you are," they said. "We have to take an answer back to those who sent us. What do you say about yourself?"

New International Version

he was before me.' " 16 From the fullness of his grace we have all received one blessing after another. 17 For the law was given through Moses; grace and truth came through Jesus Christ. 18 No man has ever seen God, but God the only[e] [Son],[f] who is at the Father's side, has made him known.

John the Baptist denies being the Christ

19 Now this was John's testimony when the Jews of Jerusalem sent priests and Levites to ask him who he was. 20 He did not fail to confess, but confessed freely, "I am not the Christ.[g] "

21 They asked him, "Then who are you? Are you Elijah?"

He said, "I am not."

"Are you the Prophet?"

He answered, "No."

22 Finally they said, "Who are you? Give us an answer to take back to those who sent us. What do you say about yourself?"

[*e*] Or *but God the only begotten*. [*f*] Some MSS read *but the only Son* (or *but the only begotten Son*). [*g*] Or *Messiah*. "The Christ" (Greek) and "the Messiah" (Hebrew) both mean "the Anointed One."

Phillips Modern English

Indeed, every one of us has shared in his riches—there is a grace in our lives because of his grace. For while the Law was given by Moses, grace and truth came through Jesus Christ. It is true that no one has ever seen God at any time. Yet the divine and only Son, who lives in the closest intimacy with the Father, has made him known.

1.19 John's witness

This then is the testimony of John, when the Jews sent priests and Levites from Jerusalem to ask him who he was. He admitted with complete candour, "I am not Christ."

So they asked him, "Who are you then? Are you Elijah?"

"No, I am not," he replied.

"Are you the Prophet?"

"No," he replied.

"Well then," they asked again, "who are you? We want to give an answer to those who sent us. What would you call yourself?"

Revised Standard Version

before me.' ") 16And from his fulness have we
all received, grace upon grace. 17 For the law
was given through Moses; grace and truth came
through Jesus Christ. 18 No one has ever seen
God; the only Son,[b] who is in the bosom of the
Father, he has made him known.

19 And this is the testimony of John, when
the Jews sent priests and Levites from Jerusalem to ask him, "Who are you?" 20 He confessed, he did not deny, but confessed, "I am
not the Christ." 21And they asked him, "What
then? Are you Elijah?" He said, "I am not."
"Are you the prophet?" And he answered, "No."
22 They said to him then, "Who are you? Let us
have an answer for those who sent us. What do

[b] Other ancient authorities read *God*.

Jerusalem Bible

16 Indeed, from his fullness we have, all of us, received—
yes, grace in return for grace,
17 since, though the Law was given through Moses,
grace and truth have come through Jesus Christ.
18 No one has ever seen God;
it is the only Son, who is nearest to the Father's heart,
who has made him known.

I. The first Passover

A. The opening week

The witness of John

19 This is how John appeared as a witness.
When the Jews[c] sent priests and Levites from
Jerusalem to ask him, "Who are you?" 20 he
not only declared, but he declared quite openly,
"I am not the Christ." 21 "Well then," they
asked, "are you Elijah?"[d] "I am not," he said.
"Are you the Prophet?"[e] He answered, "No."
22 So they said to him, "Who are you? We must
take back an answer to those who sent us. What

[c] In Jn. this usually indicates the Jewish religious authorities who were hostile to Jesus; but occasionally the Jews as a whole. [d] Whose return was expected, Ml. 3:23-24. [e] The Prophet greater than Moses who was expected as Messiah, on an interpretation of Dt. 18:15.

New English Bible

Out of his full store we have all received grace upon grace; for while the Law was given through Moses, grace and truth came through Jesus Christ. No one has ever seen God; but God's only Son, he who is nearest to the Father's heart, he has made him known.[e]

This is the testimony which John gave when the Jews of Jerusalem sent a deputation of priests and Levites to ask him who he was. He confessed without reserve and avowed, 'I am not the Messiah.' 'What then? Are you Elijah?' 'No', he replied. 'Are you the prophet we await?' He answered 'No.' 'Then who are you?' they asked. 'We must give an answer to those who sent us.

[e] *Some witnesses read* but the only one, the one nearest to the Father's heart, has made him known; *others read* but the only one, himself God, the nearest to the Father's heart, has made him known.

King James Version

thou of thyself? 23 He said, I *am* the voice of
one crying in the wilderness, Make straight the
way of the Lord, as said the prophet Esaias.
24 And they which were sent were of the Pharisees. 25 And they asked him, and said unto him,
Why baptizest thou then, if thou be not that
Christ, nor Elias, neither that Prophet? 26 John
answered them, saying, I baptize with water:
but there standeth one among you, whom ye
know not; 27 He it is, who coming after me is
preferred before me, whose shoe's latchet I am
not worthy to unloose. 28 These things were done
in Bethabara beyond Jordan, where John was
baptizing.
29 The next day John seeth Jesus coming unto
him, and saith, Behold the Lamb of God, which
taketh away the sin of the world! 30 This is he of
whom I said, After me cometh a man which is
preferred before me; for he was before me.
31 And I knew him not: but that he should be
made manifest to Israel, therefore am I come
baptizing with water. 32 And John bare record,
saying, I saw the Spirit descending from heaven
like a dove, and it abode upon him. 33 And I
knew him not: but he that sent me to baptize

Living Bible

23 He replied, "I am a voice from the barren
wilderness, shouting as Isaiah prophesied, 'Get
ready for the coming of the Lord!' "
24, 25 Then those who were sent by the
Pharisees asked him, "If you aren't the Messiah
or Elijah or the Prophet, what right do you have
to baptize?"
26 John told them, "I merely baptize with[j]
water, but right here in the crowd is someone
you have never met, 27 who will soon begin his
ministry among you, and I am not even fit to
be his slave."
28 This incident took place at Bethany, a village on the other side of the Jordan River where
John was baptizing.
29 The next day John saw Jesus coming toward him and said, "Look! There is the Lamb
of God who takes away the world's sin! 30 He
is the one I was talking about when I said, 'Soon
a man far greater than I am is coming, who
existed long before me!' 31 I didn't know he
was the one, but I am here baptizing with[j] water
in order to point him out to the nation of Israel."
32 Then John told about seeing the Holy
Spirit in the form of a dove descending from
heaven and resting upon Jesus.
33 "I didn't know he was the one," John said
again, "but at the time God sent me to baptize

[j] Or, "in."

Today's English Version

23 John answered, "This is what I am:

'The voice of one who shouts in the desert:
Make a straight path for the Lord to
travel!' "

(This is what the prophet Isaiah had said.)
24 The messengers had been sent by the Pharisees. 25 They asked John, "If you are not the
Messiah, nor Elijah, nor the Prophet, why do
you baptize?"
26 John answered, "I baptize with water;
among you stands the one you do not know.
27 He is coming after me, but I am not good
enough even to untie his sandals."
28 All this happened in Bethany, on the east
side of the Jordan River, where John was baptizing.

The Lamb of God

29 The next day John saw Jesus coming to
him, and said, "Here is the Lamb of God, who
takes away the sin of the world! 30 This is the
one I was talking about when I said, 'A man
is coming after me, but he is greater than I am,
because he existed before I was born.' 31 I did
not know who he would be, but I came baptizing with water in order to make him known
to Israel."
32 This is the testimony that John gave: "I
saw the Spirit come down like a dove from
heaven and stay on him. 33 I still did not know
him, but God, who sent me to baptize with water,

New International Version

23 John replied in the words of Isaiah the
prophet, "I am the voice of one calling in the
desert, 'Make straight the way for the Lord.' "[h]
24 Now some Pharisees who had been sent
25 questioned him, "Why then do you baptize if
you are not the Christ,[g] nor Elijah, nor the
Prophet?"
26 "I baptize with[i] water," John replied, "but
among you stands one you do not know. 27 He
is the one who comes after me, the thongs of
whose sandals I am not worthy to untie."
28 This all happened at Bethany on the other
side of the Jordan, where John was baptizing.

Jesus the Lamb of God

29 The next day John saw Jesus coming toward him and said, "Look, the Lamb of God,
who takes away the sin of the world! 30 This is
the one I meant when I said, 'A man who comes
after me has surpassed me because he was before me.' 31 I myself did not know him, but the
reason I came baptizing with[j] water was that he
might be revealed to Israel."
32 Then John gave this testimony: "I saw the
Spirit come down from heaven as a dove and
remain on him. 33 I would not have known him,
except that the one who sent me to baptize with[j]

[h] Isaiah 40:3. [g] Or *Messiah*. "The Christ" (Greek) and "the Messiah" (Hebrew) both mean "the Anointed One." [i] Or *in*. [j] Or *in*.

Phillips Modern English

"I am a voice shouting in the desert, 'Make straight the way of the Lord!' as Isaiah the prophet said."

Now some of the Pharisees had been sent to John, and they questioned him, "What is the reason, then, for your baptising people if you are not Christ and not Elijah and not the Prophet?"

To which John returned, "I do baptise—with water. But somewhere among you stands a man you do not know. He comes after me, it is true, but I am not fit to undo his shoes!" (All this happened in Bethany on the far side of the Jordan where the baptisms of John took place.)

On the following day, John saw Jesus coming towards him and said, "Look, there is the lamb of God who takes away the sin of the world! This is the man I meant when I said 'A man comes after me who is always in front of me, for he existed before I was born!' It is true I have not known him, yet it was to make him known to Israel that I came and baptised with water."

Then John gave this testimony, "I have seen the Spirit come down like a dove from Heaven and rest upon him. Indeed I did not recognise him, but he who sent me to baptise with water

Revised Standard Version

you say about yourself?" 23 He said, "I am the voice of one crying in the wilderness, 'Make straight the way of the Lord,' as the prophet Isaiah said."

24 Now they had been sent from the Pharisees. 25 They asked him, "Then why are you baptizing, if you are neither the Christ, nor Elijah, nor the prophet?" 26 John answered them, "I baptize with water; but among you stands one whom you do not know, 27 even he who comes after me, the thong of whose sandal I am not worthy to untie." 28 This took place in Bethany beyond the Jordan, where John was baptizing.

29 The next day he saw Jesus coming toward him, and said, "Behold, the Lamb of God, who takes away the sin of the world! 30 This is he of whom I said, 'After me comes a man who ranks before me, for he was before me.' 31 I myself did not know him; but for this I came baptizing with water, that he might be revealed to Israel." 32 And John bore witness, "I saw the Spirit descend as a dove from heaven, and it remained on him. 33 I myself did not know him; but he who sent me to baptize with water said

Jerusalem Bible

have you to say about yourself?" 23 So John said, "I am, as Isaiah prophesied:

a voice that cries in the wilderness:
Make a straight way for the Lord." [f]

24 Now these men had been sent by the Pharisees, 25 and they put this further question to him, "Why are you baptizing if you are not the Christ, and not Elijah, and not the prophet?" 26 John replied, "I baptize with water; but there stands among you—unknown to you—27 the one who is coming after me; and I am not fit to undo his sandal strap." 28 This happened at Bethany, on the far side of the Jordan, where John was baptizing.

29 The next day, seeing Jesus coming toward him, John said, "Look, there is the Lamb of God that takes away the sin of the world. 30 This is the one I spoke of when I said: A man is coming after me who ranks before me because he existed before me. 31 I did not know him myself, and yet it was to reveal him to Israel that I came baptizing with water." 32 John also declared, "I saw the Spirit coming down on him from heaven like a dove and resting on him. 33 I did not know him myself, but he who sent me to baptize with water had said to me,

[f] Is. 40:3.

New English Bible

What account do you give of yourself?' He answered in the words of the prophet Isaiah: 'I am a voice crying aloud in the wilderness, "Make the Lord's highway straight."'

Some Pharisees who were in the deputation asked him, 'If you are not the Messiah, nor Elijah, nor the prophet, why then are you baptizing?' 'I baptize in water,' John replied, 'but among you, though you do not know him, stands the one who is to come after me. I am not good enough to unfasten his shoes.' This took place at Bethany beyond Jordan, where John was baptizing.

The next day he saw Jesus coming towards him. 'Look,' he said, 'there is the Lamb of God; it is he who takes away the sin of the world. This is he of whom I spoke when I said, "After me a man is coming who takes rank before me"; for before I was born, he already was. I myself did not know who he was; but the very reason why I came, baptizing in water, was that he might be revealed to Israel.'

John testified further: 'I saw the Spirit coming down from heaven like a dove and resting upon him. I did not know him, but he who sent me to baptize in water had told me, "When you see

King James Version

with water, the same said unto me, Upon whom
thou shalt see the Spirit descending, and remaining on him, the same is he which baptizeth
with the Holy Ghost. 34And I saw, and bare
record that this is the Son of God.
35 Again the next day after, John stood, and
two of his disciples; 36And looking upon Jesus
as he walked, he saith, Behold the Lamb of
God! 37And the two disciples heard him speak,
and they followed Jesus. 38 Then Jesus turned,
and saw them following, and saith unto them,
What seek ye? They said unto him, Rabbi,
(which is to say, being interpreted, Master,)
where dwellest thou? 39 He saith unto them,
Come and see. They came and saw where he
dwelt, and abode with him that day: for it was
about the tenth hour. 40 One of the two which
heard John *speak,* and followed him, was Andrew, Simon Peter's brother. 41 He first findeth
his own brother Simon, and saith unto him, We
have found the Messias, which is, being interpreted, the Christ. 42And he brought him to
Jesus. And when Jesus beheld him, he said, Thou
art Simon the son of Jona: thou shalt be called
Cephas, which is by interpretation, A stone.

Living Bible

he told me, 'When you see the Holy Spirit descending and resting upon someone—he is the
one you are looking for. He is the one who baptizes with[j] the Holy Spirit.' 34 I saw it happen to
this man, and I therefore testify that he is the
Son of God."
35 The following day as John was standing
with two of his disciples, 36 Jesus walked by.
John looked at him intently and then declared,
"See! There is the Lamb of God!"
37 Then John's two disciples turned and followed Jesus.
38 Jesus looked around and saw them following. "What do you want?" he asked them.
"Sir," they replied, "where do you live?"
39 "Come and see," he said. So they went
with him to the place where he was staying and
were with him from about four o'clock that
afternoon until the evening. 40 (One of these
men was Andrew, Simon Peter's brother.)
41 Andrew then went to find his brother Peter
and told him, "We have found the Messiah!"
42And he brought Peter to meet Jesus.
Jesus looked intently at Peter for a moment
and then said, "You are Simon, John's son—
but you shall be called Peter, the rock!"

[*j*] Or, "in."

Today's English Version

said to me, 'You will see the Spirit come down
and stay on a man; he is the one who baptizes
with the Holy Spirit.' 34 I have seen it," said
John, "and I tell you that he is the Son of God."

The first disciples of Jesus

35 The next day John was there again with
two of his disciples, 36 when he saw Jesus walking by. "Here is the Lamb of God!" he said.
37 The two disciples heard him say this and
went with Jesus. 38 Jesus turned, saw them following him, and asked, "What are you looking
for?"
They answered, "Where do you live, Rabbi?"
(This word, translated, means "Teacher.")
39 "Come and see," he answered. So they
went with him and saw where he lived, and spent
the rest of that day with him. (It was about four
o'clock in the afternoon.)
40 One of the two who heard John, and went
with Jesus, was Andrew, Simon Peter's brother.
41At once Andrew found his brother Simon and
told him, "We have found the Messiah." (This
word means "Christ.") 42 Then he took Simon
to Jesus.
Jesus looked at him and said, "You are Simon,
the son of John. Your name will be Cephas."
(This is the same as Peter, and means "Rock.")

New International Version

water told me, 'The man on whom you see the
Spirit come down and remain is he who will
baptize with the Holy Spirit.' 34 I have seen and
I testify that this is the Son of God."

Jesus' first disciples

35 The next day John was there again with
two of his disciples. 36 When he saw Jesus passing by, he said, "Look, the Lamb of God!"
37 When the two disciples heard him say
this, they followed Jesus. 38 Turning around,
Jesus saw them following and asked, "What do
you want?"
They said, "Rabbi" (which means, Teacher),
"where are you staying?"
39 "Come," he replied, "and you will see."
So they went and saw where he was staying,
and spent that day with him. It was about the
tenth hour.
40 Andrew, Simon Peter's brother, was one of
the two who heard what John had said and who
had followed Jesus. 41 The first thing Andrew
did was to find his brother Simon and tell him,
"We have found the Messiah" (that is, the
Christ).
42 Then he brought Simon to Jesus, who
looked at him and said, "You are Simon, the
son of John. You will be called Cephas" (which,
when translated, is Peter[k]).

[*k*] Both *Cephas* (Aramaic) and *Peter* (Greek) mean *rock*.

Phillips Modern English

told me this: 'The one on whom you will see the Spirit coming down and resting is the man who baptises with the Holy Spirit!' Now I have seen this and I declare before you all that he is the Son of God!"

1.35 Men begin to follow Jesus

On the following day John was again standing with two of his disciples. He looked straight at Jesus as he walked along and said, "There is the lamb of God!" The two disciples heard what he said and followed Jesus. Then Jesus turned round and when he saw them following him, spoke to them. "What do you want?" he said.

"Rabbi, where are you staying?" they replied.

"Come and see," returned Jesus.

So they went and saw where he was staying and remained with him the rest of that day. (It was then about four o'clock in the afternoon.) One of the two men who had heard what John said and had followed Jesus was Andrew, Simon Peter's brother. He went straight off and found his own brother, Simon, and told him, "We have found the Messiah!" (meaning Christ). And he brought him to Jesus.

Jesus looked steadily at him and said, "You are Simon, the son of John. From now on your name is Cephas"—(that is, Peter, meaning "a rock").

Revised Standard Version

to me, 'He on whom you see the Spirit descend and remain, this is he who baptizes with the Holy Spirit.' 34 And I have seen and have borne witness that this is the Son of God."

35 The next day again John was standing with two of his disciples; 36 and he looked at Jesus as he walked, and said, "Behold, the Lamb of God!" 37 The two disciples heard him say this, and they followed Jesus. 38 Jesus turned, and saw them following, and said to them, "What do you seek?" And they said to him, "Rabbi" (which means Teacher), "where are you staying?" 39 He said to them, "Come and see." They came and saw where he was staying; and they stayed with him that day, for it was about the tenth hour. 40 One of the two who heard John speak, and followed him, was Andrew, Simon Peter's brother. 41 He first found his brother Simon, and said to him, "We have found the Messiah" (which means Christ). 42 He brought him to Jesus. Jesus looked at him, and said, "So you are Simon the son of John? You shall be called Cephas" (which means Peter[c]).

[c] From the word for *rock* in Aramaic and Greek, respectively.

Jerusalem Bible

'The man on whom you see the Spirit come down and rest is the one who is going to baptize with the Holy Spirit.' 34 Yes, I have seen and I am the witness that he is the Chosen One of God."

The first disciples

35 On the following day as John stood there again with two of his disciples, 36 Jesus passed, and John stared hard at him and said, "Look, there is the lamb of God." 37 Hearing this, the two disciples followed Jesus. 38 Jesus turned around, saw them following and said, "What do you want?" They answered, "Rabbi,"—which means Teacher—"where do you live?" 39 "Come and see," he replied; so they went and saw where he lived, and stayed with him the rest of that day. It was about the tenth hour.[g]

40 One of these two who became followers of Jesus after hearing what John had said was Andrew, the brother of Simon Peter. 41 Early next morning, Andrew met his brother and said to him, "We have found the Messiah"—which means the Christ—42 and he took Simon to Jesus. Jesus looked hard at him and said, "You are Simon son of John; you are to be called Cephas"—meaning Rock.

[g] 4 P.M.

New English Bible

the Spirit coming down upon someone and resting upon him, you will know that this is he who is to baptize in Holy Spirit." I saw it myself, and I have borne witness. This is God's Chosen One.'[a]

The next day again John was standing with two of his disciples when Jesus passed by. John looked towards him and said, 'There is the Lamb of God.' The two disciples heard him say this, and followed Jesus. When he turned and saw them following him, he asked, 'What are you looking for?' They said, 'Rabbi' (which means a teacher), 'where are you staying?' 'Come and see', he replied. So they went and saw where he was staying, and spent the rest of the day with him. It was then about four in the afternoon.

One of the two who followed Jesus after hearing what John said was Andrew, Simon Peter's brother. The first thing he did was to find[b] his brother Simon. He said to him, 'We have found the Messiah' (which is the Hebrew for 'Christ'). He brought Simon to Jesus, who looked at him and said, 'You are Simon son of John. You shall be called Cephas' (that is, Peter, the Rock).

[a] *Some witnesses read* This is the Son of God.
[b] *Some witnesses read* In the morning he found . . .

King James Version

43 The day following Jesus would go forth into Galilee, and findeth Philip, and saith unto him, Follow me. 44 Now Philip was of Bethsaida, the city of Andrew and Peter. 45 Philip findeth Nathanael, and saith unto him, We have found him, of whom Moses in the law, and the prophets, did write, Jesus of Nazareth, the son of Joseph. 46And Nathanael said unto him, Can there any good thing come out of Nazareth? Philip saith unto him, Come and see. 47 Jesus saw Nathanael coming to him, and saith of him, Behold an Israelite indeed, in whom is no guile! 48 Nathanael saith unto him, Whence knowest thou me? Jesus answered and said unto him, Before that Philip called thee, when thou wast under the fig tree, I saw thee. 49 Nathanael answered and saith unto him, Rabbi, thou art the Son of God; thou art the King of Israel. 50 Jesus answered and said unto him, Because I said unto thee, I saw thee under the fig tree, believest thou? thou shalt see greater things than these. 51And he saith unto him, Verily, verily, I say unto you, Hereafter ye shall see heaven open, and the angels of God ascending and descending upon the Son of man.

Living Bible

43 The next day Jesus decided to go to Galilee. He found Philip and told him, "Come with me." 44 (Philip was from Bethsaida, Andrew and Peter's home town.)

45 Philip now went off to look for Nathanael and told him, "We have found the Messiah!—the very person Moses and the prophets told about! His name is Jesus, the son of Joseph from Nazareth!"

46 "Nazareth!" exclaimed Nathanael. "Can anything good come from there?"

"Just come and see for yourself," Philip declared.

47 As they approached, Jesus said, "Here comes an honest man—a true son of Israel."

48 "How do you know what I am like?" Nathanael demanded.

And Jesus replied, "I could see you under the fig tree before Philip found you."

49 Nathanael replied, "Sir, you are the Son of God—the King of Israel!"

50 Jesus asked him, "Do you believe all this just because I told you I had seen you under the fig tree? You will see greater proofs than this. 51 You will even see heaven open and the angels of God coming back and forth to me, the Messiah." [k]

[k] Literally, "the Son of Man."

Today's English Version

Jesus calls Philip and Nathanael

43 The next day Jesus decided to go to Galilee. He found Philip and said to him, "Come with me!" 44 (Philip was from Bethsaida, the town where Andrew and Peter lived.) 45 Philip found Nathanael and told him, "We have found the one of whom Moses wrote in the book of the Law, and of whom the prophets also wrote. He is Jesus, the son of Joseph, from Nazareth."

46 "Can anything good come from Nazareth?" Nathanael asked.

"Come and see," answered Philip.

47 When Jesus saw Nathanael coming to him, he said about him, "Here is a real Israelite; there is nothing false in him!"

48 Nathanael asked him, "How do you know me?"

Jesus answered, "I saw you when you were under the fig tree, before Philip called you."

49 "Teacher," answered Nathanael, "you are the Son of God! You are the King of Israel!"

50 Jesus said, "Do you believe just because I told you I saw you when you were under the fig tree? You will see much greater things than this!" 51And he said to them, "I tell you the truth: you will see heaven open and God's angels going up and coming down on the Son of Man."

New International Version

Jesus calls Philip and Nathanael

43 The next day Jesus decided to leave for Galilee. Finding Philip, he said to him, "Follow me."

44 Philip, like Andrew and Peter, was from the town of Bethsaida. 45 Philip found Nathanael and told him, "We have found the one Moses wrote about in the Law, and about whom the prophets also wrote—Jesus of Nazareth, the son of Joseph."

46 "Nazareth! Can anything good come from there?" Nathanael asked.

"Come and see," said Philip.

47 When Jesus saw Nathanael approaching, he said of him, "Here is a true Israelite, in whom there is nothing false."

48 "How do you know me?" Nathanael asked.

Jesus answered, "I saw you while you were still under the fig tree before Philip called you."

49 Then Nathanael declared, "Rabbi, you are the Son of God; you are the King of Israel."

50 Jesus said, "You believe[l] because I told you I saw you under the fig tree. You shall see greater things than that." 51 He then added, "I tell you the truth, you shall all see heaven open, and the angels of God ascending and descending on the Son of Man."

[l] Or *Do you believe. . . ?*

Phillips Modern English

The following day Jesus decided to go into Galilee. He found Philip and said to him, "Follow me!" Philip was a man from Bethsaida, the town that Andrew and Peter came from. Now Philip found Nathanael and told him, "We have discovered the man whom Moses wrote about in the Law and about whom the Prophets wrote too. He is Jesus, the son of Joseph and comes from Nazareth."

"Can anything good come out of Nazareth?" retorted Nathanael.

"You come and see," replied Philip.

Jesus saw Nathanael coming towards him and remarked, "Now here is a true man of Israel; there is no deceit in him!"

"How can you know me?" returned Nathanael.

"When you were underneath that fig-tree," replied Jesus, "before Philip called you, I saw you."

At which Nathanael exclaimed, "Rabbi, you are the Son of God, you are the king of Israel!"

"Do you believe in me," replied Jesus, "because I said I had seen you underneath that fig-tree? You are going to see greater things than that! Believe me," he added, "I tell you all that you will see Heaven wide open and God's angels ascending and descending upon the Son of Man!"

Revised Standard Version

43 The next day Jesus decided to go to Galilee. And he found Philip and said to him, "Follow me." 44 Now Philip was from Bethsaida, the city of Andrew and Peter. 45 Philip found Nathanael, and said to him, "We have found him of whom Moses in the law and also the prophets wrote, Jesus of Nazareth, the son of Joseph." 46 Nathanael said to him, "Can anything good come out of Nazareth?" Philip said to him, "Come and see." 47 Jesus saw Nathanael coming to him, and said of him, "Behold, an Israelite indeed, in whom is no guile!" 48 Nathanael said to him, "How do you know me?" Jesus answered him, "Before Philip called you, when you were under the fig tree, I saw you." 49 Nathanael answered him, "Rabbi, you are the Son of God! You are the King of Israel!" 50 Jesus answered him, "Because I said to you, I saw you under the fig tree, do you believe? You shall see greater things than these." 51 And he said to him, "Truly, truly, I say to you, you will see heaven opened, and the angels of God ascending and descending upon the Son of man."

Jerusalem Bible

43 The next day, after Jesus had decided to leave for Galilee, he met Philip and said, "Follow me." 44 Philip came from the same town, Bethsaida, as Andrew and Peter. 45 Philip found Nathanael [h] and said to him, "We have found the one Moses wrote about in the Law, the one about whom the prophets wrote: he is Jesus son of Joseph, from Nazareth." 46 "From Nazareth?" said Nathanael. "Can anything good come from that place?" "Come and see," replied Philip. 47 When Jesus saw Nathanael coming he said of him, "There is an Israelite who deserves the name, incapable of deceit." 48 "How do you know me?" said Nathanael. "Before Philip came to call you," said Jesus, "I saw you under the fig tree." 49 Nathanael answered, "Rabbi, you are the Son of God, you are the King of Israel." 50 Jesus replied, "You believe that just because I said: I saw you under the fig tree. You will see greater things than that." 51 And then he added, "I tell you most solemnly, you will see heaven laid open and, above the Son of Man, the angels of God ascending and descending."

[h] Probably the Bartholomew of the other gospels.

New English Bible

The next day Jesus decided to leave for Galilee. He met Philip, who, like Andrew and Peter, came from Bethsaida, and said to him, 'Follow me.' Philip went to find Nathanael, and told him, 'We have met the man spoken of by Moses in the Law, and by the prophets: it is Jesus son of Joseph, from Nazareth.' 'Nazareth!' Nathanael exclaimed; 'can anything good come from Nazareth?' Philip said, 'Come and see.' When Jesus saw Nathanael coming, he said, 'Here is an Israelite worthy of the name; there is nothing false in him.' Nathanael asked him, 'How do you come to know me?' Jesus replied, 'I saw you under the fig-tree before Philip spoke to you.' 'Rabbi,' said Nathanael, 'you are the Son of God; you are king of Israel.' Jesus answered, 'Is this the ground of your faith, that I told you I saw you under the fig-tree? You shall see greater things than that.' Then he added, 'In truth, in very truth I tell you all, you shall see heaven wide open, and God's angels ascending and descending upon the Son of Man.'

King James Version

2 And the third day there was a marriage in Cana of Galilee; and the mother of Jesus was there: 2 And both Jesus was called, and his disciples, to the marriage. 3 And when they wanted wine, the mother of Jesus saith unto him, They have no wine. 4 Jesus saith unto her, Woman, what have I to do with thee? mine hour is not yet come. 5 His mother saith unto the servants, Whatsoever he saith unto you, do *it*. 6 And there were set there six waterpots of stone, after the manner of the purifying of the Jews, containing two or three firkins apiece. 7 Jesus saith unto them, Fill the waterpots with water. And they filled them up to the brim. 8 And he saith unto them, Draw out now, and bear unto the governor of the feast. And they bare *it*. 9 When the ruler of the feast had tasted the water that was made wine, and knew not whence it was, (but the servants which drew the water knew,) the governor of the feast called the bridegroom, 10 And saith unto him, Every man at the beginning doth set forth good wine; and when men have well drunk, then that which is worse: *but* thou hast kept the good wine until now. 11 This beginning of miracles did Jesus in Cana of Galilee, and manifested forth his glory; and his disciples believed on him.

Living Bible

2 Two days later Jesus' mother was a guest at a wedding in the village of Cana in Galilee, 2 and Jesus and his disciples were invited too. 3 The wine supply ran out during the festivities, and Jesus' mother came to him with the problem.

4 "I can't help you now," he said.[a] "It isn't yet my time for miracles."

5 But his mother told the servants, "Do whatever he tells you to."

6 Six stone waterpots were standing there; they were used for Jewish ceremonial purposes and held perhaps twenty to thirty gallons each. 7, 8 Then Jesus told the servants to fill them to the brim with water. When this was done he said, "Dip some out and take it to the master of ceremonies."

9 When the master of ceremonies tasted the water that was now wine, not knowing where it had come from (though, of course, the servants did), he called the bridegroom over.

10 "This is wonderful stuff!" he said. "You're different from most. Usually a host uses the best wine first, and afterwards, when everyone is full and doesn't care, then he brings out the less expensive brands. But you have kept the best for the last!"

11 This miracle at Cana in Galilee was Jesus' first public demonstration of his heaven-sent power. And his disciples believed that he really was the Messiah.[b]

[a] Literally, "Woman, what have I to do with you?"
[b] Literally, "His disciples believed on him."

Today's English Version

The wedding at Cana

2 Two days later there was a wedding in the town of Cana, in Galilee. Jesus' mother was there, 2 and Jesus and his disciples had also been invited to the wedding. 3 When all the wine had been drunk, Jesus' mother said to him, "They are out of wine."

4 "You must not tell me what to do, woman," Jesus replied. "My time has not yet come."

5 Jesus' mother then told the servants, "Do whatever he tells you."

6 The Jews have religious rules about washing, and for this purpose six stone water jars were there, each one large enough to hold between twenty and thirty gallons. 7 Jesus said to the servants, "Fill these jars with water." They filled them to the brim, 8 and then he told them, "Now draw some water out and take it to the man in charge of the feast." They took it to him, 9 and he tasted the water, which had turned into wine. He did not know where this wine had come from (but the servants who had drawn out the water knew); so he called the bridegroom 10 and said to him, "Everyone else serves the best wine first, and after the guests have drunk a lot he serves the ordinary wine. But you have kept the best wine until now!"

11 Jesus performed this first of his mighty works in Cana of Galilee; there he revealed his glory, and his disciples believed in him.

New International Version

Jesus changes water to wine

2 On the third day a wedding took place at Cana in Galilee. Jesus' mother was there, 2 and Jesus and his disciples had also been invited to the wedding. 3 When the wine was gone, Jesus' mother said to him, "They have no more wine."

4 "Why do you involve me[m] ?" Jesus replied, "My time has not yet come."

5 His mother said to the servants, "Do whatever he tells you."

6 Nearby stood six stone water jars, the kind used by the Jews for ceremonial washing, each holding from twenty to thirty gallons.

7 Jesus said to the servants, "Fill the jars with water"; so they filled them to the brim.

8 Then he told them, "Now draw some out and take it to the master of the banquet."

They did so, 9 and the master of the banquet tasted the water that had been turned into wine. He did not realize where it had come from, though the servants who had drawn the water knew. Then he called the bridegroom aside 10 and said, "Everyone brings out the choice wine first and then the cheaper wine after the guests have had too much to drink; but you have saved the best till now."

11 This, the first of his miraculous signs, Jesus performed in Cana of Galilee. He thus revealed his glory, and his disciples put their faith in him.

[m] Greek *involve me, woman* (a polite form of address).

Phillips Modern English

2.1 *The Son of God and a village wedding*

Two days later there was a wedding in the Galilean village of Cana. Jesus' mother was there and he and his disciples were invited to the festivities. The supply of wine gave out, and Jesus' mother told him, "They have no more wine."

"Is that your concern, or mine, Mother?" replied Jesus. "My time has not come yet."

So his mother said to the servants, "Do whatever he tells you."

In the room were six stone water-jars (actually for the Jewish ceremonial cleansing), each holding about twenty gallons. Jesus said to them, "Fill the jars with water", and they filled them to the brim. Then he said to them, "Now draw some out and take it to the master of ceremonies", and they did so. When this man tasted the water, which had now become wine, without knowing where it came from (although the servants who had drawn the water knew), he called out to the bridegroom and said to him,"Everybody I know puts his good wine on first and then when men have had plenty to drink, he brings out the poor stuff. But you have kept back your good wine till now!" Jesus gave this, the first of his signs, at Cana in Galilee. So he showed his glory and his disciples believed in him.

Revised Standard Version

2 On the third day there was a marriage at Cana in Galilee, and the mother of Jesus was there; 2 Jesus also was invited to the marriage, with his disciples. 3 When the wine gave out, the mother of Jesus said to him, "They have no wine." 4 And Jesus said to her, "O woman, what have you to do with me? My hour has not yet come." 5 His mother said to the servants, "Do whatever he tells you." 6 Now six stone jars were standing there, for the Jewish rites of purification, each holding twenty or thirty gallons. 7 Jesus said to them, "Fill the jars with water." And they filled them up to the brim. 8 He said to them, "Now draw some out, and take it to the steward of the feast." So they took it. 9 When the steward of the feast tasted the water now become wine, and did not know where it came from (though the servants who had drawn the water knew), the steward of the feast called the bridegroom 10 and said to him, "Every man serves the good wine first; and when men have drunk freely, then the poor wine; but you have kept the good wine until now." 11 This, the first of his signs, Jesus did at Cana in Galilee, and manifested his glory; and his disciples believed in him.

Jerusalem Bible

The wedding at Cana

2 Three days later there was a wedding at Cana in Galilee. The mother of Jesus was there, 2 and Jesus and his disciples had also been invited. 3 When they ran out of wine, since the wine provided for the wedding was all finished, the mother of Jesus said to him, "They have no wine." 4 Jesus said, "Woman, why turn to me? My hour has not come yet." 5 His mother said to the servants, *"Do whatever he tells you."*[i] 6 There were six stone water jars standing there, meant for the ablutions that are customary among the Jews: each could hold twenty or thirty gallons. 7 Jesus said to the servants, "Fill the jars with water," and they filled them to the brim. 8 "Draw some out now," he told them, "and take it to the steward." 9 They did this; the steward tasted the water, and it had turned into wine. Having no idea where it came from—only the servants who had drawn the water knew—the steward called the bridegroom 10 and said, "People generally serve the best wine first, and keep the cheaper sort till the guests have had plenty to drink; but you have kept the best wine till now."

11 This was the first of the signs given by Jesus: it was given at Cana in Galilee. He let his glory be seen, and his disciples believed in

[i] Gn. 41:55.

New English Bible

Christ the giver of life

2 On the third day there was a wedding at Cana-in-Galilee. The mother of Jesus was there, and Jesus and his disciples were guests also. The wine gave out, so Jesus's mother said to him, 'They have no wine left.' He answered, 'Your concern, mother, is not mine. My hour has not yet come.' His mother said to the servants, 'Do whatever he tells you.' There were six stone water-jars standing near, of the kind used for Jewish rites of purification; each held from twenty to thirty gallons. Jesus said to the servants, 'Fill the jars with water', and they filled them to the brim. 'Now draw some off', he ordered, 'and take it to the steward of the feast'; and they did so. The steward tasted the water now turned into wine, not knowing its source; though the servants who had drawn the water knew. He hailed the bridegroom and said, 'Everyone serves the best wine first, and waits until the guests have drunk freely before serving the poorer sort; but you have kept the best wine till now.'

This deed at Cana-in-Galilee is the first of the signs by which Jesus revealed his glory and led his disciples to believe in him.

King James Version

12 After this he went down to Capernaum,
he, and his mother, and his brethren, and his
disciples; and they continued there not many
days.
13 And the Jews' passover was at hand, and
Jesus went up to Jerusalem, 14And found in the
temple those that sold oxen and sheep and
doves, and the changers of money sitting: 15And
when he had made a scourge of small cords, he
drove them all out of the temple, and the sheep,
and the oxen; and poured out the changers'
money, and overthrew the tables; 16And said
unto them that sold doves, Take these things
hence; make not my Father's house a house of
merchandise. 17And his disciples remembered
that it was written, The zeal of thine house hath
eaten me up.
18 Then answered the Jews and said unto him,
What sign shewest thou unto us, seeing that thou
doest these things? 19 Jesus answered and said
unto them, Destroy this temple, and in three
days I will raise it up. 20 Then said the Jews,
Forty and six years was this temple in building,
and wilt thou rear it up in three days? 21 But he
spake of the temple of his body. 22 When therefore he was risen from the dead, his disciples remembered that he had said this unto them; and
they believed the Scripture, and the word which
Jesus had said.

Living Bible

12 After the wedding he left for Capernaum
for a few days with his mother, brothers, and
disciples.
13 Then it was time for the annual Jewish
Passover celebration, and Jesus went to Jerusalem.
14 In the Temple area he saw merchants selling cattle, sheep, and doves for sacrifices, and
money changers behind their counters. 15 Jesus
made a whip from some ropes and chased them
all out, and drove out the sheep and oxen, scattering the money changers' coins over the floor
and turning over their tables! 16 Then, going
over to the men selling doves, he told them, "Get
these things out of here. Don't turn my Father's
House into a market!"
17 Then his disciples remembered this prophecy from the Scriptures: "Concern for God's
House will be my undoing."
18 "What right have you to order them out?"
the Jewish leaders[c] demanded. "If you have this
authority from God, show us a miracle to prove
it."
19 "All right," Jesus replied, "this is the miracle I will do for you: Destroy this sanctuary and
in three days I will raise it up!"
20 "What!" they exclaimed. "It took forty-six
years to build this Temple, and you can do it in
three days?" 21 But by "this sanctuary" he meant
his body. 22After he came back to life again,
the disciples remembered his saying this and realized that what he had quoted from the Scriptures really did refer to him, and had all come
true!

[c] Literally, "the Jews."

Today's English Version

12 After this, Jesus and his mother, brothers,
and disciples went to Capernaum, and stayed
there a few days.

Jesus goes to the temple

13 It was almost time for the Jewish Feast of
Passover, so Jesus went to Jerusalem. 14 In the
temple he found men selling cattle, sheep, and
pigeons, and also the moneychangers sitting at
their tables. 15 He made a whip from cords and
drove the animals out of the temple, both the
sheep and the cattle; he overturned the tables of
the moneychangers and scattered their coins;
16 and he ordered the men who sold the pigeons,
"Take them out of here! Do not make my father's house a market place!" 17 His disciples
remembered that the scripture says, "My devotion to your house, God, burns in me like a fire."
18 The Jewish authorities came back at him
with a question, "What miracle can you perform
to show us that you have the right to do this?"
19 Jesus answered, "Tear down this house of
God and in three days I will build it again."
20 "You are going to build it again in three
days?" they asked him. "It has taken forty-six
years to build this temple!"
21 But the temple Jesus spoke of was his body.
22 So when he was raised from death, his disciples remembered that he said this; and they believed the scripture and what Jesus had said.

New International Version

Jesus clears the temple

12 After this he went down to Capernaum
with his mother and brothers and his disciples.
Here they stayed for a few days.
13 When it was almost time for the Jewish
Passover, Jesus went up to Jerusalem. 14 In the
temple court he found men selling cattle, sheep
and doves, and others sitting at tables exchanging money. 15 So he made a whip out of cords,
and drove all from the temple area, both sheep
and cattle; he scattered the coins of the money-
changers and overturned their tables. 16 To
those who sold doves, he said, "Get these out
of here! How dare you turn my Father's house
into a market!"
17 His disciples remembered that it is written:
"Zeal for your house will consume me." [n]
18 Then the Jews demanded of him, "What
miraculous sign can you show us to prove your
authority to do all this?"
19 Jesus answered them, "Destroy this temple, and I will raise it again in three days."
20 The Jews replied, "It has taken forty-six
years to build this temple, and you are going
to raise it in three days?" 21 But the temple he
had spoken of was his body. 22After he was
raised from the dead, his disciples recalled what
he had said. Then they believed the Scripture
and the words that Jesus had spoken.

[n] Psalm 69:9.

Phillips Modern English

2.12 Jesus in the Temple

After this incident, Jesus, accompanied by his mother, his brothers and his disciples, went down to Capernaum and stayed there a few days. The Jewish Passover was approaching and Jesus made the journey up to Jerusalem. In the Temple-precincts he discovered cattle and sheep dealers and dove-sellers, as well as money-changers sitting at their tables. So he made a whip out of cords and drove the whole lot of them, sheep and cattle as well, out of the Temple. He sent the coins of the money-changers flying and turned their tables upside down. Then he said to the dove-sellers, "Take those things out of here. Don't you dare turn my Father's house into a market!" His disciples remembered the scripture—

The zeal of thine house shall eat me up.

As a result of this, the Jews said to him, "What sign can you give us to justify what you are doing?"

"Destroy this Temple," Jesus retorted, "and I will rebuild it in three days!"

To which the Jews replied, "This Temple took forty-six years to build, and are you going to rebuild it in three days?"

He was, in fact, speaking about the temple of his own body, and when he was raised from the dead the disciples remembered what he had said to them and that made them believe both the scripture and the words that Jesus had spoken.

Revised Standard Version

12 After this he went down to Capernaum,
with his mother and his brothers and his disciples;
and there they stayed for a few days.
13 The Passover of the Jews was at hand, and
Jesus went up to Jerusalem. 14 In the temple he
found those who were selling oxen and sheep
and pigeons, and the money-changers at their
business. 15And making a whip of cords, he
drove them all, with the sheep and oxen, out of
the temple; and he poured out the coins of the
money-changers and overturned their tables.
16And he told those who sold the pigeons, "Take
these things away; you shall not make my Father's
house a house of trade." 17 His disciples
remembered that it was written, "Zeal for thy
house will consume me." 18 The Jews then said
to him, "What sign have you to show us for
doing this?" 19 Jesus answered them, "Destroy
this temple, and in three days I will raise it up."
20 The Jews then said, "It has taken forty-six
years to build this temple, and will you raise it
up in three days?" 21 But he spoke of the temple
of his body. 22 When therefore he was raised
from the dead, his disciples remembered that
he had said this; and they believed the scripture
and the word which Jesus had spoken.

Jerusalem Bible

him. 12After this he went down to Capernaum
with his mother and the brothers, but they
stayed there only a few days.

B. The Passover

The cleansing of the Temple

13 Just before the Jewish Passover Jesus went
up to Jerusalem, 14 and in the Temple he found
people selling cattle and sheep and pigeons, and
the money-changers sitting at their counters
there. 15 Making a whip out of some cord, he
drove them all out of the Temple, cattle and
sheep as well, scattered the money-changers'
coins, knocked their tables over 16 and said to
the pigeon sellers, "Take all this out of here and
stop turning my Father's house into a market."
17 Then his disciples remembered the words of
scripture: *Zeal for your house will devour me.*[j]
18 The Jews intervened and said, "What sign
can you show us to justify what you have
done?" 19 Jesus answered, "Destroy this sanctuary,
and in three days I will raise it up." 20 The
Jews replied, "It has taken forty-six years to
build this sanctuary[k]: are you going to raise it
up in three days?" 21 But he was speaking of the
sanctuary that was his body, 22 and when Jesus
rose from the dead, his disciples remembered
that he had said this, and they believed the
scripture and the words he had said.

[*j*] Ps. 69:9. [*k*] Reconstruction work on the Temple began in 19 B.C. This is therefore the Passover of A.D. 28.

New English Bible

After this he went down to Capernaum in company with his mother, his brothers, and his disciples, but they did not stay there long. As it was near the time of the Jewish Passover, Jesus went up to Jerusalem. There he found in the temple the dealers in cattle, sheep, and pigeons, and the money-changers seated at their tables. Jesus made a whip of cords and drove them out of the temple, sheep, cattle, and all. He upset the tables of the money-changers, scattering their coins. Then he turned on the dealers in pigeons: 'Take them out,' he said; 'you must not turn my Father's house into a market.' His disciples recalled the words of Scripture, 'Zeal for thy house will destroy me.' The Jews challenged Jesus: 'What sign', they asked, 'can you show as authority for your action?' 'Destroy this temple,' Jesus replied, 'and in three days I will raise it again.' They said, 'It has taken forty-six years to build this temple. Are you going to raise it again in three days?' But the temple he was speaking of was his body. After his resurrection his disciples recalled what he had said, and they believed the Scripture and the words that Jesus had spoken.

King James Version

23 Now when he was in Jerusalem at the passover, in the feast *day*, many believed in his name, when they saw the miracles which he did. 24 But Jesus did not commit himself unto them, because he knew all *men*, 25And needed not that any should testify of man: for he knew what was in man.

3 There was a man of the Pharisees, named Nicodemus, a ruler of the Jews: 2 The same came to Jesus by night, and said unto him, Rabbi, we know that thou art a teacher come from God: for no man can do these miracles that thou doest, except God be with him. 3 Jesus answered and said unto him, Verily, verily, I say unto thee, Except a man be born again, he cannot see the kingdom of God. 4 Nicodemus saith unto him, How can a man be born when he is old? can he enter the second time into his mother's womb, and be born? 5 Jesus answered, Verily, verily, I say unto thee, Except a man be born of water and *of* the Spirit, he cannot enter

Living Bible

23 Because of the miracles he did in Jerusalem at the Passover celebration, many people were convinced that he was indeed the Messiah. 24, 25 But Jesus didn't trust them, for he knew mankind to the core. No one needed to tell him how changeable human nature is!

3 After dark one night a Jewish religious leader named Nicodemus, a member of the sect of the Pharisees, came for an interview with Jesus. "Sir," he said, "we all know that God has sent you to teach us. Your miracles are proof enough of this."

3 Jesus replied, "With all the earnestness I possess I tell you this: Unless you are born again, you can never get into the Kingdom of God."

4 "Born again!" exclaimed Nicodemus. "What do you mean? How can an old man go back into his mother's womb and be born again?"

5 Jesus replied, "What I am telling you so earnestly is this: Unless one is born of water[a] and the Spirit, he cannot enter the Kingdom of

[*a*] Or, "Physical birth is not enough. You must also be born spiritually. . . ." This alternate paraphrase interprets "born of water" as meaning the normal process observed during every human birth. Some think this means water baptism.

Today's English Version

Jesus knows all men

23 While Jesus was in Jerusalem during the Passover Feast, many believed in him as they saw the mighty works he did. 24 But Jesus did not trust himself to them, because he knew all men well. 25 There was no need for anyone to tell him about men, because he knew what was in their hearts.

Jesus and Nicodemus

3 There was a man named Nicodemus, a leader of the Jews, who belonged to the party of the Pharisees. 2 One night he went to Jesus and said to him, "We know, Rabbi, that you are a teacher sent by God. No one could do the mighty works you are doing unless God were with him."

3 Jesus answered, "I tell you the truth: no one can see the Kingdom of God unless he is born again."

4 "How can a grown man be born again?" Nicodemus asked. "He certainly cannot enter his mother's womb and be born a second time!"

5 "I tell you the truth," replied Jesus, "that no one can enter the Kingdom of God unless he

New International Version

23 Now while he was in Jerusalem at the Passover Feast, many people saw the miraculous signs he was doing and trusted in his name.[o] 24 But Jesus would not trust himself to them, for he knew all men. 25 He did not need man's testimony about man, for he knew what was in a man.

Jesus teaches Nicodemus

3 Now there was a man of the Pharisees named Nicodemus, a member of the Jewish ruling council. 2 He came to Jesus at night and said, "Rabbi, we know you are a teacher who has come from God. For no one could perform the miraculous signs you are doing if God were not with him."

3 In reply Jesus declared, "I tell you the truth, unless a man is born again,[p] he cannot see the kingdom of God."

4 "But," said Nicodemus, "how can a man be born when he is old? Surely he cannot enter a second time into his mother's womb to be born!"

5 Jesus answered, "I tell you the truth, unless a man is born of water and the Spirit, he

[*o*] Or *and put their trust in him*. [*p*] Or *born from above*.

Phillips Modern English

While he was in Jerusalem at Passover-time, during the festivities many believed in him as they saw the signs that he gave. But Jesus, on his side, did not trust himself to them—for he knew them all. He did not need anyone to tell him what people were like: he understood human nature.

3.1 Jesus and a religious leader

One night Nicodemus, a leading Jew and a Pharisee, came to see Jesus.

"Rabbi," he began, "we realise that you are a teacher who has come from God. For no one could show the signs that you show unless God were with him."

"Believe me," returned Jesus, "when I assure you that a man cannot see the kingdom of God without being born again."

"And how can a man who has grown old possibly be born?" replied Nicodemus. "Surely he cannot go into his mother's womb a second time to be born?"

"I do assure you," said Jesus, "that unless a man is born from water and from spirit he can-

Revised Standard Version

23 Now when he was in Jerusalem at the Passover feast, many believed in his name when they saw the signs which he did; 24 but Jesus did not trust himself to them, 25 because he knew all men and needed no one to bear witness of man; for he himself knew what was in man.

3 Now there was a man of the Pharisees, named Nicodemus, a ruler of the Jews. 2 This man came to Jesus[d] by night and said to him, "Rabbi, we know that you are a teacher come from God; for no one can do these signs that you do, unless God is with him." 3 Jesus answered him, "Truly, truly, I say to you, unless one is born anew,[e] he cannot see the kingdom of God." 4 Nicodemus said to him, "How can a man be born when he is old? Can he enter a second time into his mother's womb and be born?" 5 Jesus answered, "Truly, truly, I say to you, unless one is born of water and the Spirit,

[d] Greek *him.* [e] Or *from above.*

Jerusalem Bible

23 During his stay in Jerusalem for the Passover many believed in his name when they saw the signs that he gave, 24 but Jesus knew them all and did not trust himself to them; 25 he never needed evidence about any man; he could tell what a man had in him.

C. The mystery of the Spirit revealed to a master in Israel

The conversation with Nicodemus

3 There was one of the Pharisees called Nicodemus, a leading Jew, 2 who came to Jesus by night and said, "Rabbi, we know that you are a teacher who comes from God; for no one could perform the signs that you do unless God were with him." 3 Jesus answered:

"I tell you most solemnly,
unless a man is born from above,
he cannot see the kingdom of God."

4 Nicodemus said, "How can a grown man be born? Can he go back into his mother's womb and be born again?" 5 Jesus replied:

"I tell you most solemnly,
unless a man is born through water and the Spirit,
he cannot enter the kingdom of God:

New English Bible

While he was in Jerusalem for Passover many gave their allegiance to him when they saw the signs that he performed. But Jesus for his part would not trust himself to them. He knew men so well, all of them, that he needed no evidence from others about a man, for he himself could tell what was in a man.

3 There was one of the Pharisees named Nicodemus, a member of the Jewish Council, who came to Jesus by night. 'Rabbi,' he said, 'we know that you are a teacher sent by God; no one could perform these signs of yours unless God were with him.' Jesus answered, 'In truth, in very truth I tell you, unless a man has been born over again he cannot see the kingdom of God.' 'But how is it possible', said Nicodemus, 'for a man to be born when he is old? Can he enter his mother's womb a second time and be born?' Jesus answered, 'In truth I tell you, no one can enter the kingdom of God without be-

King James Version

into the kingdom of God. 6 That which is born
of the flesh is flesh; and that which is born of
the Spirit is spirit. 7 Marvel not that I said unto
thee, Ye must be born again. 8 The wind bloweth
where it listeth, and thou hearest the sound
thereof, but canst not tell whence it cometh, and
whither it goeth: so is every one that is born of
the Spirit. 9 Nicodemus answered and said unto
him, How can these things be? 10 Jesus answered and said unto him, Art thou a master of
Israel, and knowest not these things? 11 Verily,
verily, I say unto thee, We speak that we do
know, and testify that we have seen; and ye receive not our witness. 12 If I have told you
earthly things, and ye believe not, how shall ye
believe, if I tell you *of* heavenly things? 13And
no man hath ascended up to heaven, but he that
came down from heaven, *even* the Son of man
which is in heaven.
14 And as Moses lifted up the serpent in the
wilderness, even so must the Son of man be
lifted up: 15 That whosoever believeth in him
should not perish, but have eternal life.
16 For God so loved the world, that he gave
his only begotten Son, that whosoever believeth
in him should not perish, but have everlasting

Living Bible

God. 6 Men can only reproduce human life, but
the Holy Spirit gives new life from heaven; 7 so
don't be surprised at my statement that you must
be born again! 8 Just as you can hear the wind
but can't tell where it comes from or where it
will go next, so it is with the Spirit. We do not
know on whom he will next bestow this life from
heaven."
9 "What do you mean?" Nicodemus asked.
10, 11 Jesus replied, "You, a respected Jewish
teacher, and yet you don't understand these
things? I am telling you what I know and have
seen—and yet you won't believe me. 12 But if
you don't even believe me when I tell you about
such things as these that happen here among
men, how can you possibly believe if I tell you
what is going on in heaven? 13 For only I, the
Messiah,[b] have come to earth and will return to
heaven again. 14And as Moses in the wilderness
lifted up the bronze image of a serpent on a pole,
even so I must be lifted up upon a pole, 15 so
that anyone who believes in me will have eternal
life. 16 For God loved the world so much that
he gave his only[c] Son so that anyone who believes in him shall not perish but have eternal

[*b*] Literally, "the Son of Man." [*c*] Or, "the unique Son of God."

Today's English Version

is born of water and the Spirit. 6A man is born
physically of human parents, but he is born
spiritually of the Spirit. 7 Do not be surprised
because I tell you, 'You must all be born again.'
8 The wind blows wherever it wishes; you hear
the sound it makes, but you do not know where
it comes from or where it is going. It is the same
way with everyone who is born of the Spirit."
9 "How can this be?" asked Nicodemus.
10 Jesus answered, "You are a great teacher
of Israel, and you don't know this? 11 I tell you
the truth: we speak of what we know, and tell
what we have seen, yet none of you is willing to
accept our message. 12 You do not believe me
when I tell you about the things of this world;
how will you ever believe me, then, when I tell
you about the things of heaven? 13And no one
has ever gone up to heaven except the Son of
Man, who came down from heaven."
14 As Moses lifted up the bronze snake on
a pole in the desert, in the same way the Son of
Man must be lifted up, 15 so that everyone who
believes in him may have eternal life. 16 For God
loved the world so much that he gave his only
Son, so that everyone who believes in him may

New International Version

cannot enter the kingdom of God. 6 Flesh gives
birth to flesh, but the Spirit[q] gives birth to spirit.
7 You should not be surprised at my saying,
'You[r] must be born again.'[p] 8 The wind blows
wherever it pleases. You may hear its sound, but
you cannot tell where it comes from or where it
is going. So it is with everyone born of the
Spirit."
9 "How can this be?" Nicodemus asked.
10 "You are a teacher of Israel," said Jesus,
"and do you not understand these things? 11 I
tell you the truth, we speak of what we know,
and we testify to what we have seen, but still
you people do not accept our testimony. 12 I
have spoken to you of earthly things and you
do not believe; how then will you believe if I
speak of heavenly things? 13 No one has ever
gone into heaven except the one who came from
heaven—the Son of Man. 14 Just as Moses lifted
up the snake in the desert, so the Son of Man
must be lifted up, 15 that everyone who believes
in him may have eternal life.[s]
16 "For God so loved the world that he gave
his one and only Son,[t] that whoever believes in

[*q*] Or *but spirit.* [*r*] The Greek is plural. [*p*] Or *born from above.* [*s*] Or *believes may have eternal life in him.* [*t*] Or *his only begotten Son.*

Phillips Modern English

not enter the kingdom of God. Flesh gives birth to flesh and spirit gives birth to spirit: you must not be surprised that I told you that all of you must be born again. The wind blows where it likes, you can hear the sound of it but you have no idea where it comes from or where it goes. Nor can you tell how a man is born by the wind of the Spirit."

"How on earth can things like this happen?" replied Nicodemus.

"So you are the teacher of Israel," said Jesus, "and you do not understand such things? I assure you that we are talking about what we know and we are witnessing to what we have observed, yet you will not accept our evidence. Yet if I have spoken to you about things which happen on this earth and you will not believe me, what chance is there that you will believe me if I tell you about what happens in Heaven? No one has ever been up to Heaven except the Son of Man who came down from Heaven. The Son of Man must be lifted above the heads of men —as Moses lifted up that serpent in the desert— so that any man who believes in him may have eternal life. For God loved the world so much that he gave his only Son, so that everyone who believes in him should not be lost, but should

Revised Standard Version

he cannot enter the kingdom of God. 6 That
which is born of the flesh is flesh, and that which
is born of the Spirit is spirit.[f] 7 Do not marvel
that I said to you, 'You must be born anew.'[e]
8 The wind[f] blows where it wills, and you hear
the sound of it, but you do not know whence
it comes or whither it goes; so it is with every
one who is born of the Spirit." 9 Nicodemus
said to him, "How can this be?" 10 Jesus answered him, "Are you a teacher of Israel, and
yet you do not understand this? 11 Truly, truly,
I say to you, we speak of what we know, and
bear witness to what we have seen; but you do
not receive our testimony. 12 If I have told you
earthly things and you do not believe, how can
you believe if I tell you heavenly things? 13 No
one has ascended into heaven but he who descended from heaven, the Son of man.[g] 14 And
as Moses lifted up the serpent in the wilderness, so must the Son of man be lifted up,
15 that whoever believes in him may have eternal life."[h]

16 For God so loved the world that he gave
his only Son, that whoever believes in him

[f] The same Greek word means both *wind* and *spirit*. [g] Other ancient authorities add *who is in heaven*. [h] Some interpreters hold that the quotation continues through verse 21.

Jerusalem Bible

6 what is born of the flesh is flesh;
what is born of the Spirit is spirit.
7 Do not be surprised when I say:
You must be born from above.
8 The wind blows wherever it pleases;
you hear its sound,
but you cannot tell where it comes from or where it is going.
That is how it is with all who are born of the Spirit."

9 "How can that be possible?" asked Nicodemus. 10 "You, a teacher in Israel, and you do not know these things!" replied Jesus.

11 "I tell you most solemnly,
we speak only about what we know
and witness only to what we have seen
and yet you people reject our evidence.
12 If you do not believe me
when I speak about things in this world,
how are you going to believe me
when I speak to you about heavenly things?
13 No one has gone up to heaven
except the one who came down from heaven,
the Son of Man who is in heaven;
and the Son of Man must be lifted up
14 as Moses lifted up the serpent in the desert,
15 so that everyone who believes may have eternal life in him.
16 Yes, God loved the world so much that he gave his only Son,
so that everyone who believes in him may

New English Bible

ing born from water and spirit. Flesh can give birth only to flesh; it is spirit that gives birth to spirit. You ought not to be astonished, then, when I tell you that you must be born over again. The wind[a] blows where it wills; you hear the sound of it, but you do not know where it comes from, or where it is going. So with everyone who is born from spirit[a].'

Nicodemus replied, 'How is this possible?' 'What!' said Jesus. 'Is this famous teacher of Israel ignorant of such things? In very truth I tell you, we speak of what we know, and testify to what we have seen, and yet you all reject our testimony. If you disbelieve me when I talk to you about things on earth, how are you to believe if I should talk about the things of heaven?

'No one ever went up into heaven except the one who came down from heaven, the Son of Man whose home is in heaven.[b] This Son of Man must be lifted up as the serpent was lifted up by Moses in the wilderness, so that everyone who has faith in him may in him possess eternal life.

'God loved the world so much that he gave his only Son, that everyone who has faith in him

[a] wind *and* spirit *are translations of the same Greek word, which has both meanings.* [b] *Some witnesses omit* whose home is in heaven.

King James Version

life. 17 For God sent not his Son into the world to condemn the world; but that the world through him might be saved.

18 He that believeth on him is not condemned: but he that believeth not is condemned already, because he hath not believed in the name of the only begotten Son of God. 19 And this is the condemnation, that light is come into the world, and men loved darkness rather than light, because their deeds were evil. 20 For every one that doeth evil hateth the light, neither cometh to the light, lest his deeds should be reproved. 21 But he that doeth truth cometh to the light, that his deeds may be made manifest, that they are wrought in God.

22 After these things came Jesus and his disciples into the land of Judea; and there he tarried with them, and baptized.

Living Bible

life. 17 God did not send his Son into the world to condemn it, but to save it.

18 "There is no eternal doom awaiting those who trust him to save them. But those who don't trust him have already been tried and condemned for not believing in the only[c] Son of God. 19 Their sentence is based on this fact: that the Light from heaven came into the world, but they loved the darkness more than the Light, for their deeds were evil. 20 They hated the heavenly Light because they wanted to sin in the darkness. They stayed away from that Light for fear their sins would be exposed and they would be punished. 21 But those doing right come gladly to the Light to let everyone see that they are doing what God wants them to."

22 Afterwards Jesus and his disciples left Jerusalem and stayed for a while in Judea and baptized there.

[c] Or, "the unique Son of God."

Today's English Version

not die but have eternal life. 17 For God did not send his Son into the world to be its Judge, but to be its Savior.

18 Whoever believes in the Son is not judged; whoever does not believe has already been judged, because he has not believed in God's only Son. 19 This is how the judgment works: the light has come into the world, but men love the darkness rather than the light, because they do evil things. 20 Anyone who does evil things hates the light and will not come to the light, because he does not want his evil deeds to be shown up. 21 But whoever does what is true comes to the light, in order that the light may show that he did his works in obedience to God.

Jesus and John

22 After this, Jesus and his disciples went to the province of Judea. He spent some time with

New International Version

him shall not perish but have everlasting life. 17 For God did not send his Son into the world to condemn the world, but to save the world through him. 18 Whoever believes in him is not condemned, but whoever does not believe stands condemned already because he has not believed in the name of God's one and only Son.[u] 19 This is the verdict: Light has come into the world, but men loved darkness instead of light because their deeds were evil. 20 Everyone who does evil hates the light, and will not come into the light for fear that his deeds will be exposed. 21 But whoever lives by the truth comes into the light, so that it may be seen plainly that what he has done has been done through God."[v]

John the Baptist's testimony about Jesus

22 After this, Jesus and his disciples went out into the Judean countryside, where he spent

[u] Or *God's only begotten Son.* [v] Some interpreters end the quotation after verse 15.

Phillips Modern English

have eternal life. God has not sent his Son into the world to pass sentence upon it, but to save it—through him. Any man who believes in him is not judged at all. It is the one who will not believe who stands already condemned, because he will not believe in the character of God's only Son. This *is* the judgment—that light has entered the world and men have preferred darkness to light because their deeds were evil. Everybody who does wrong hates the light and keeps away from it, for fear his deeds may be exposed. But everybody who is living by the truth will come to the light to make it plain that all he has done has been done through God."

3.22 Jesus and John again

After this Jesus went into the country of Judaea with his disciples and stayed there with them while the work of baptism was being car-

Revised Standard Version

should not perish but have eternal life. 17 For
God sent the Son into the world, not to condemn the world, but that the world might be
saved through him. 18 He who believes in him
is not condemned; he who does not believe is condemned already, because he has not believed in the name of the only Son of God. 19And
this is the judgment, that the light has come into the world, and men loved darkness rather than light, because their deeds were evil. 20 For every
one who does evil hates the light, and does not come to the light, lest his deeds should be exposed. 21 But he who does what is true comes
to the light, that it may be clearly seen that his deeds have been wrought in God.

22 After this Jesus and his disciples went
into the land of Judea; there he remained with

Jerusalem Bible

not be lost but may have eternal life.
17 For God sent his Son into the world
not to condemn the world,
but so that through him the world might be saved.
18 No one who believes in him will be condemned;
but whoever refuses to believe is condemned already,
because he has refused to believe
in the name of God's only Son.
19 On these grounds is sentence pronounced:
that though the light has come into the world
men have shown they prefer
darkness to the light
because their deeds were evil.
20 And indeed, everybody who does wrong
hates the light and avoids it,
for fear his actions should be exposed;
21 but the man who lives by the truth
comes out into the light,
so that it may be plainly seen that what he does is done in God."

II. Journeys in Samaria and Galilee

John bears witness for the last time

22 After this, Jesus went with his disciples
into the Judaean countryside and stayed with

New English Bible

may not die but have eternal life. It was not to judge the world that God sent his Son into the world, but that through him the world might be saved.

'The man who puts his faith in him does not come under judgement; but the unbeliever has already been judged in that he has not given his allegiance to God's only Son. Here lies the test: the light has come into the world, but men preferred darkness to light because their deeds were evil. Bad men all hate the light and avoid it, for fear their practices should be shown up. The honest man comes to the light so that it may be clearly seen that God is in all he does.'

After this, Jesus went into Judaea with his disciples, stayed there with them, and baptized.

King James Version

23 And John also was baptizing in Enon near to Salim, because there was much water there: and they came, and were baptized. 24 For John was not yet cast into prison.

25 Then there arose a question between *some* of John's disciples and the Jews about purifying. 26 And they came unto John, and said unto him, Rabbi, he that was with thee beyond Jordan, to whom thou barest witness, behold, the same baptizeth, and all *men* come to him. 27 John answered and said, A man can receive nothing, except it be given him from heaven. 28 Ye yourselves bear me witness, that I said, I am not the Christ, but that I am sent before him. 29 He that hath the bride is the bridegroom: but the friend of the bridegroom, which standeth and heareth him, rejoiceth greatly because of the bridegroom's voice: this my joy therefore is fulfilled. 30 He must increase, but I *must* decrease. 31 He that cometh from above is above all: he that is of the earth is earthly, and speaketh of the earth: he that cometh from heaven is

Living Bible

23, 24 At this time John the Baptist was not yet in prison. He was baptizing at Aenon, near Salim, because there was plenty of water there. 25 One day someone began an argument with John's disciples, telling them that Jesus' baptism was best.[d] 26 So they came to John and said, "Master, the man you met on the other side of the Jordan River—the one you said was the Messiah—he is baptizing too, and everybody is going over there instead of coming here to us."

27 John replied, "God in heaven appoints each man's work. 28 My work is to prepare the way for that man so that everyone will go to him. You yourselves know how plainly I told you that I am not the Messiah. I am here to prepare the way for him—that is all. 29 The crowds will naturally go to the main attraction[e] —the bride will go where the bridegroom is! A bridegroom's friends rejoice with him. I am the Bridegroom's friend, and I am filled with joy at his success. 30 He must become greater and greater, and I must become less and less.

31 "He has come from heaven and is greater than anyone else. I am of the earth, and my un-

[*d*] Literally, "about purification." [*e*] Implied.

Today's English Version

them there, and baptized. 23 John also was baptizing in Aenon, not far from Salim, because there was plenty of water there. People were going to him and he was baptizing them. 24 (John had not yet been put in prison.)

25 Some of John's disciples began arguing with a Jew about the matter of religious washing. 26 So they went to John and told him, "Teacher, you remember the man who was with you on the other side of the Jordan, the one you spoke about? Well, he is baptizing now, and everyone is going to him!"

27 John answered, "No one can have anything unless God gives it to him. 28 You yourselves are my witnesses that I said, 'I am not the Messiah, but I have been sent ahead of him.' 29 The bridegroom is the one to whom the bride belongs; the bridegroom's friend stands by and listens, and he is glad when he hears the bridegroom's voice. This is how my own happiness is made complete. 30 He must become more important, while I become less important."

He who comes from heaven

31 He who comes from above is greater than all; he who is from the earth belongs to the earth and speaks about earthly matters. He who

New International Version

some time with them, and baptized. 23 Now John also was baptizing at Aenon near Salim, because there was plenty of water, and people were constantly coming to be baptized. 24 (This was before John was put in prison.) 25 An argument developed between some of John's disciples and a certain Jew over the matter of ceremonial washing. 26 They came to John and said to him, "Rabbi, that man who was with you on the other side of the Jordan—the one about whom you testified—well, he is baptizing, and everyone is going to him."

27 To this John replied, "A man can receive only what is given him from heaven. 28 You yourselves can testify that I said, 'I am not the Christ[w] but am sent ahead of him.' 29 The bride belongs to the bridegroom. The friend who attends the bridegroom waits and listens for him, and is full of joy when he hears the bridegroom's voice. That joy is mine, and it is now complete. 30 He must become greater; I must become less important.

31 "The one who comes from above is above all; the one who is from the earth belongs to the earth, and speaks as one from the earth.

[*w*] Or *Messiah*.

Phillips Modern English

ried on. John, too, was in Aenon near Salim, baptising people because there was plenty of water in that district and they were continually coming to him for baptism. (John, of course, had not yet been put in prison.)

This led to a question arising between John's disciples and one of the Jews about the whole matter of being cleansed. They approached John and said to him, "Rabbi, look, the man who was with you on the other side of the Jordan, the one you testified to, is now baptising and everybody is coming to him!"

"A man can receive nothing at all," replied John, "unless it is given him from Heaven. You yourselves can witness that I said, 'I am not Christ but I have been sent as his forerunner.' It is the bridegroom who possesses the bride, yet the bridegroom's friend who merely stands and listens to him can be overjoyed to hear the bridegroom's voice. That is why my happiness is now complete. He must grow greater and greater and I less and less.

"The one who comes from above is naturally above everybody. The one who arises from the earth belongs to the earth and speaks from the

Revised Standard Version

them and baptized. 23 John also was baptizing at Aenon near Salim, because there was much water there; and people came and were baptized. 24 For John had not yet been put in prison.

25 Now a discussion arose between John's disciples and a Jew over purifying. 26 And they came to John, and said to him, "Rabbi, he who was with you beyond the Jordan, to whom you bore witness, here he is, baptizing, and all are going to him." 27 John answered, "No one can receive anything except what is given him from heaven. 28 You yourselves bear me witness, that I said, I am not the Christ, but I have been sent before him. 29 He who has the bride is the bridegroom; the friend of the bridegroom, who stands and hears him, rejoices greatly at the bridegroom's voice; therefore this joy of mine is now full. 30 He must increase, but I must decrease." [i]

31 He who comes from above is above all; he who is of the earth belongs to the earth, and of the earth he speaks; he who comes from

[i] Some interpreters hold that the quotation continues through verse 36.

Jerusalem Bible

them there and baptized. 23 At the same time John was baptizing at Aenon[l] near Salim, where there was plenty of water, and people were going there to be baptized. 24 This was before John had been put in prison.

25 Now some of John's disciples had opened a discussion with a Jew about purification, 26 so they went to John and said, "Rabbi, the man who was with you on the far side of the Jordan, the man to whom you bore witness, is baptizing now; and everyone is going to him." 27 John replied:

"A man can lay claim
only to what is given him from heaven.

28 "You yourselves can bear me out: I said: I myself am not the Christ; I am the one who has been sent in front of him.

29 "The bride is only for the bridegroom;
and yet the bridegroom's friend,
who stands there and listens,
is glad when he hears the bridegroom's voice.
This same joy I feel, and now it is complete.
30 He must grow greater,
I must grow smaller.
31 He who comes from above
is above all others;
he who is born of the earth
is earthly himself and speaks in an earthly way.

[l] A tradition locates Aenon ("Springs") in the Jordan valley seven miles from Scythopolis.

New English Bible

John too was baptizing at Aenon, near to Salim, because water was plentiful in that region; and people were constantly coming for baptism. This was before John's imprisonment.

Some of John's disciples had fallen into a dispute with Jews about purification; so they came to him and said, 'Rabbi, there was a man with you on the other side of the Jordan, to whom you bore your witness. Here he is, baptizing, and crowds are flocking to him.' John's answer was: 'A man can have only what God gives him. You yourselves can testify that I said, "I am not the Messiah; I have been sent as his forerunner." It is the bridegroom to whom the bride belongs. The bridegroom's friend, who stands by and listens to him, is overjoyed at hearing the bridegroom's voice. This joy, this perfect joy, is now mine. As he grows greater, I must grow less.'

He who comes from above is above all others; he who is from the earth belongs to the earth and uses earthly speech. He who comes from

King James Version

above all. 32 And what he hath seen and heard,
that he testifieth; and no man receiveth his testimony. 33 He that hath received his testimony
hath set to his seal that God is true. 34 For he
whom God hath sent speaketh the words of
God: for God giveth not the Spirit by measure
unto him. 35 The Father loveth the Son, and
hath given all things into his hand. 36 He that believeth on the son hath everlasting life: and he
that believeth not the Son shall not see life; but
the wrath of God abideth on him.

4 When therefore the Lord knew how the
Pharisees had heard that Jesus made and
baptized more disciples than John, 2 (Though
Jesus himself baptized not, but his disciples,)
3 He left Judea, and departed again into Galilee.
4 And he must needs go through Samaria. 5 Then
cometh he to a city of Samaria, which is called
Sychar, near to the parcel of ground that Jacob
gave to his son Joseph. 6 Now Jacob's well was
there. Jesus therefore, being wearied with *his*
journey, sat thus on the well: *and* it was about
the sixth hour. 7 There cometh a woman of

Living Bible

derstanding is limited to the things of earth.
32 He tells what he has seen and heard, but how
few believe what he tells them! 33, 34 Those who
believe him discover that God is a fountain of
truth. For this one—sent by God—speaks God's
words, for God's Spirit is upon him without
measure or limit. 35 The Father loves this man
because he is his Son, and God has given him
everything there is. 36 And all who trust him—
God's Son—to save them have eternal life; those
who don't believe and obey him shall never see
heaven, but the wrath of God remains upon
them."

4 When the Lord knew that the Pharisees
had heard about the greater crowds coming
to him than to John to be baptized and to become his disciples—(though Jesus himself didn't
baptize them, but his disciples did)—3 he left
Judea and returned to the province of Galilee.
4 He had to go through Samaria on the way,
5, 6 and around noon as he approached the village of Sychar, he came to Jacob's Well, located
on the parcel of ground Jacob gave to his son
Joseph. Jesus was tired from the long walk in the
hot sun and sat wearily beside the well.
7 Soon a Samaritan woman came to draw wa-

Today's English Version

comes from heaven is above all. 32 He tells what
he has seen and heard, but no one accepts his
message. 33 Whoever accepts his message proves
by this that God is true. 34 The one whom God
has sent speaks God's words, because God gives
him the fulness of his Spirit. 35 The Father loves
his Son and has put everything in his power.
36 Whoever believes in the Son has eternal life;
whoever disobeys the Son will never have life,
but God's wrath will remain on him forever.

Jesus and the woman of Samaria

4 The Pharisees heard that Jesus was winning
and baptizing more disciples than John.
2 (Actually, Jesus himself did not baptize anyone; only his disciples did.) 3 When Jesus heard
what was being said, he left Judea and went back
to Galilee; 4 on his way there he had to go
through Samaria.
5 He came to a town in Samaria named
Sychar, which was not far from the field that
Jacob had given to his son Joseph. 6 Jacob's
well was there, and Jesus, tired out by the trip,
sat down by the well. It was about noon.
7 A Samaritan woman came to draw some

New International Version

The one who comes from heaven is above all.
32 He testifies to what he has seen and heard,
but no one accepts his testimony. 33 The man
who has accepted it has certified that God is
truthful. 34 For the one whom God has sent
speaks the words of God; to him God gives the
Spirit without limit. 35 The Father loves the
Son and has placed everything in his hands.
36 Whoever puts his faith in the Son has eternal
life, but whoever rejects the Son will not see that
life, for God's wrath remains on him."

Jesus talks with a Samaritan woman

4 The Pharisees heard that Jesus was gaining and baptizing more disciples than John,
2 although in fact it was not Jesus who baptized,
but his disciples. 3 When the Lord learned of
this, he left Judea and went back once more to
Galilee.
4 Now he had to go through Samaria. 5 So he
came to a town in Samaria called Sychar, near
the plot of ground Jacob had given to his son
Joseph. 6 Jacob's well was there, and Jesus, tired
as he was from the journey, sat down by the
well. It was about the sixth hour.
7 When a Samaritan woman came to draw

Phillips Modern English

earth. The one who comes from Heaven is above all others and he bears witness to what he has seen and heard—yet no one is accepting his testimony. Yet if a man does accept it, he is acknowledging the fact that God is true. For the one whom God sent speaks the authentic words of God—and there can be no measuring of the Spirit given to *him!* The Father loves the Son and has put everything under his control. The man who believes in the Son has eternal life. The man who refuses to believe in the Son will not see life; he lives under the anger of God."

4.1 Jesus meets a Samaritan woman

Now, when Jesus learned that the Pharisees had heard that he was making and baptising more disciples than John—although, in fact, it was not Jesus who did the baptising but his disciples—he left Judaea and went off again to Galilee, which meant his passing through Samaria. There he came to a Samaritan town called Sychar, which is near the plot of land that Jacob gave to his son, Joseph, and "Jacob's Spring" was there. Jesus, tired with the journey, sat down beside it, just as he was. The time was about midday. Presently, a Samaritan woman arrived

Revised Standard Version

heaven is above all. 32 He bears witness to what
he has seen and heard, yet no one receives his
testimony; 33 he who receives his testimony sets
his seal to this, that God is true. 34 For he
whom God has sent utters the words of God,
for it is not by measure that he gives the Spirit;
35 the Father loves the Son, and has given all
things into his hand. 36 He who believes in the
Son has eternal life; he who does not obey the
Son shall not see life, but the wrath of God
rests upon him.

4 Now when the Lord knew that the Pharisees had heard that Jesus was making and
baptizing more disciples than John 2 (although
Jesus himself did not baptize, but only his disciples), 3 he left Judea and departed again to
Galilee. 4 He had to pass through Samaria. 5 So
he came to a city of Samaria, called Sychar,
near the field that Jacob gave to his son Joseph.
6 Jacob's well was there, and so Jesus, wearied
as he was with his journey, sat down beside the
well. It was about the sixth hour.
7 There came a woman of Samaria to draw

Jerusalem Bible

He who comes from heaven
32 bears witness to the things he has seen and heard,
even if his testimony is not accepted;
33 though all who do accept his testimony
are attesting the truthfulness of God,
34 since he whom God has sent
speaks God's own words:
God gives him the Spirit without reserve.
35 The Father loves the Son
and has entrusted everything to him.
36 Anyone who believes in the Son has eternal life,
but anyone who refuses to believe in the Son will never see life:
the anger of God stays on him."

The savior of the world revealed to the Samaritans

4 When Jesus heard that the Pharisees had found out that he was making and baptizing
more disciples than John—2 though in fact it
was his disciples who baptized, not Jesus himself—3 he left Judaea and went back to Galilee.
4 This meant that he had to cross Samaria.
5 On the way he came to the Samaritan town
called Sychar,[m] near the land that Jacob gave to
his son Joseph. 6 Jacob's well is there and Jesus,
tired by the journey, sat straight down by the
well. It was about the sixth hour.[n] 7 When a

[m] Either Schechem (Aramaic: Sichara), or Askar at the foot of Mount Ebal. "Jacob's Well" is not mentioned in Gn. [n] Noon.

New English Bible

heaven[a] bears witness to what he has seen and heard, yet no one accepts his witness. To accept his witness is to attest that God speaks the truth; for he whom God sent utters the words of God, so measureless is God's gift of the Spirit. The Father loves the Son and has entrusted him with all authority. He who puts his faith in the Son has hold of eternal life, but he who disobeys the Son shall not see that life; God's wrath rests upon him.

4 A report now reached the Pharisees: 'Jesus is winning and baptizing more disciples than John'; although, in fact, it was only the disciples who were baptizing and not Jesus himself. When Jesus learned this, he left Judaea and set out once more for Galilee. He had to pass through Samaria, and on his way came to a Samaritan town called Sychar, near the plot of ground which Jacob gave to his son Joseph and the spring called Jacob's well. It was about noon, and Jesus, tired after his journey, sat down by the well.

The disciples had gone away to the town to buy food. Meanwhile a Samaritan woman came

[a] *Some witnesses insert* is above all and . . .

King James Version

Samaria to draw water: Jesus saith unto her, Give me to drink. 8 (For his disciples were gone away unto the city to buy meat.) 9 Then saith the woman of Samaria unto him, How is it that thou, being a Jew, askest drink of me, which am a woman of Samaria? for the Jews have no dealings with the Samaritans. 10 Jesus answered and said unto her, If thou knewest the gift of God, and who it is that saith to thee, Give me to drink; thou wouldest have asked of him, and he would have given thee living water. 11 The woman saith unto him, Sir, thou hast nothing to draw with, and the well is deep: from whence then hast thou that living water? 12 Art thou greater than our father Jacob, which gave us the well, and drank thereof himself, and his children, and his cattle? 13 Jesus answered and said unto her, Whosoever drinketh of this water shall thirst again: 14 But whosoever drinketh of the water that I shall give him shall never thirst; but the water that I shall give him shall be in him a well of water springing up into everlasting life. 15 The woman saith unto him, Sir, give me this water, that I thirst not, neither come hither to draw. 16 Jesus saith unto her, Go, call thy husband, and come hither. 17 The woman answered and said, I have no husband. Jesus

Living Bible

ter, and Jesus asked her for a drink. 8 He was alone at the time as his disciples had gone into the village to buy some food. 9 The woman was surprised that a Jew would ask a "despised Samaritan" for anything—usually they wouldn't even speak to them!—and she remarked about this to Jesus.

10 He replied, "If you only knew what a wonderful gift God has for you, and who I am, you would ask me for some *living* water!"

11 "But you don't have a rope or a bucket," she said, "and this is a very deep well! Where would you get this living water? 12 And besides, are you greater than our ancestor Jacob? How can you offer better water than this which he and his sons and cattle enjoyed?"

13 Jesus replied that people soon became thirsty again after drinking this water. 14 "But the water I give them," he said, "becomes a perpetual spring within them, watering them forever with eternal life."

15 "Please, sir," the woman said, "give me some of that water! Then I'll never be thirsty again and won't have to make this long trip out here every day."

16 "Go and get your husband," Jesus told her.

17, 18 "But I'm not married," the woman replied.

Today's English Version

water, and Jesus said to her, "Give me a drink of water." 8 (His disciples had gone into town to buy food.)

9 The woman answered, "You are a Jew and I am a Samaritan—how can you ask me for a drink?" (Jews will not use the same dishes that Samaritans use.)

10 Jesus answered, "If you only knew what God gives, and who it is that is asking you for a drink, you would ask him and he would give you living water."

11 "Sir," the woman said, "you don't have a bucket and the well is deep. Where would you get living water? 12 Our ancestor Jacob gave us this well; he, his sons, and his flocks all drank from it. You don't claim to be greater than Jacob, do you?"

13 Jesus answered, "Whoever drinks this water will get thirsty again; 14 but whoever drinks the water that I will give him will never be thirsty again. The water that I will give him will become in him a spring which will provide him with living water, and give him eternal life."

15 "Sir," the woman said, "give me this water! Then I will never be thirsty again, nor will I have to come here and draw water."

16 "Go call your husband," Jesus told her, "and come back here."

17 "I don't have a husband," the woman said.

Jesus replied, "You are right when you say

New International Version

water, Jesus said to her, "Will you give me a drink?" 8 (His disciples had gone into the town to buy food.)

9 The Samaritan woman said to him, "You are a Jew and I am a Samaritan woman. How can you ask me for a drink?" (For Jews do not associate with Samaritans.[x])

10 Jesus answered her, "If you knew the gift of God and who it is that asks you for a drink, you would have asked him and he would have given you living water."

11 "Sir," the woman said, "you have nothing to draw with and the well is deep. Where can you get this living water? 12 Are you greater than our father Jacob, who gave us the well and drank from it himself, as did also his sons and his flocks and herds?"

13 Jesus answered, "Everyone who drinks this water will be thirsty again, 14 but whoever drinks the water I give him will never thirst. Indeed, the water I give him will become in him a spring of water welling up to everlasting life."

15 The woman said to him, "Sir, give me this water so that I won't get thirsty and have to keep coming here to draw water."

16 He told her, "Go, call your husband and come back."

17 "I have no husband," she replied.

[x] Or *do not use dishes Samaritans have used.*

Phillips Modern English

to draw some water.

"Please give me a drink," Jesus said to her, for his disciples had gone away to the town to buy food. The Samaritan woman said to him, "How can you, a Jew, ask for a drink from me, a woman of Samaria?" (For Jews have no dealings with Samaritans.)

"If you knew what God can give," Jesus replied, "and if you knew who it is that said to you, 'Give me a drink', you would have asked him, and he would have given you living water!"

"Sir," said the woman, "you have no bucket and this well is deep—where can you get your living water? Are you a greater man than our ancestor, Jacob, who gave us this well, and drank here himself with his family, and his cattle?"

Jesus said to her, "Everyone who drinks this water will be thirsty again. But whoever drinks the water I will give him will never be thirsty again. For my gift will become a spring in the man himself, welling up into eternal life."

The woman said, "Sir, give me this water, so that I may stop being thirsty—and not have to make this journey to draw water any more!"

"Go and call your husband and then come back here," said Jesus to her.

"I haven't got a husband!" the woman answered.

Revised Standard Version

water. Jesus said to her, "Give me a drink." 8 For his disciples had gone away into the city to buy food. 9 The Samaritan woman said to him, "How is it that you, a Jew, ask a drink of me, a woman of Samaria?" For Jews have no dealings with Samaritans. 10 Jesus answered her, "If you knew the gift of God, and who it is that is saying to you, 'Give me a drink,' you would have asked him, and he would have given you living water." 11 The woman said to him, "Sir, you have nothing to draw with, and the well is deep; where do you get that living water? 12 Are you greater than our father Jacob, who gave us the well, and drank from it himself, and his sons, and his cattle?" 13 Jesus said to her, "Every one who drinks of this water will thirst again, 14 but whoever drinks of the water that I shall give him will never thirst; the water that I shall give him will become in him a spring of water welling up to eternal life." 15 The woman said to him, "Sir, give me this water, that I may not thirst, nor come here to draw."

16 Jesus said to her, "Go, call your husband, and come here." 17 The woman answered him, "I have no husband." Jesus said to her, "You

Jerusalem Bible

Samaritan woman came to draw water, Jesus said to her, "Give me a drink." 8 His disciples had gone into the town to buy food. 9 The Samaritan woman said to him, "What? You are a Jew and you ask me, a Samaritan, for a drink?"—Jews, in fact, do not associate with Samaritans. 10 Jesus replied:

"If you only knew what God is offering
and who it is that is saying to you:
Give me a drink,
you would have been the one to ask,
and he would have given you living water."

11 "You have no bucket, sir," she answered, "and the well is deep: how could you get this living water? 12 Are you a greater man than our father Jacob who gave us this well and drank from it himself with his sons and his cattle?" 13 Jesus replied:

"Whoever drinks this water
will get thirsty again;
14 but anyone who drinks the water that I shall give
will never be thirsty again:
the water that I shall give
will turn into a spring inside him, welling up to eternal life."

15 "Sir," said the woman, "give me some of that water, so that I may never get thirsty and never have to come here again to draw water." 16 "Go and call your husband," said Jesus to her, "and come back here." 17 The woman answered, "I have no husband." He said to her,

New English Bible

to draw water. Jesus said to her, 'Give me a drink.' The Samaritan woman said, 'What! You, a Jew, ask a drink of me, a Samaritan woman?' (Jews and Samaritans, it should be noted, do not use vessels in common.[b]) Jesus answered her, 'If only you knew what God gives, and who it is that is asking you for a drink, you would have asked him and he would have given you living water.' 'Sir,' the woman said, 'you have no bucket and this well is deep. How can you give me "living water"? Are you a greater man than Jacob our ancestor, who gave us the well, and drank from it himself, he and his sons, and his cattle too?' Jesus said, 'Everyone who drinks this water will be thirsty again, but whoever drinks the water that I shall give him will never suffer thirst any more. The water that I shall give him will be an inner spring always welling up for eternal life.' 'Sir,' said the woman, 'give me that water, and then I shall not be thirsty, nor have to come all this way to draw.'

Jesus replied, 'Go home, call your husband and come back.' She answered, 'I have no husband.' 'You are right', said Jesus, 'in saying that

[b] *Or* Jews, it should be noted, are not on familiar terms with Samaritans; *some witnesses omit these words.*

King James Version

said unto her, Thou hast well said, I have no
husband: 18 For thou hast had five husbands;
and he whom thou now hast is not thy husband: in that saidst thou truly. 19 The woman
saith unto him, Sir, I perceive that thou art a
prophet. 20 Our fathers worshipped in this mountain; and ye say, that in Jerusalem is the place
where men ought to worship. 21 Jesus saith unto
her, Woman, believe me, the hour cometh, when
ye shall neither in this mountain, nor yet at
Jerusalem, worship the Father. 22 Ye worship
ye know not what: we know what we worship;
for salvation is of the Jews. 23 But the hour
cometh, and now is, when the true worshippers
shall worship the Father in spirit and in truth:
for the Father seeketh such to worship him.
24 God *is* a Spirit: and they that worship him
must worship *him* in spirit and in truth. 25 The
woman saith unto him, I know that Messias
cometh, which is called Christ: when he is come,
he will tell us all things. 26 Jesus saith unto her,
I that speak unto thee am *he*.
27 And upon this came his disciples, and
marvelled that he talked with the woman: yet no
man said, What seekest thou? or, Why talkest
thou with her? 28 The woman then left her

Living Bible

"All too true!" Jesus said. "For you have had five husbands, and you aren't even married to the man you're living with now."

19 "Sir," the woman said, "you must be a prophet. 20 But say, tell me, why is it that you Jews insist that Jerusalem is the only place of worship, while we Samaritans claim it is here [at Mount Gerazim[a]], where our ancestors worshiped?"

21–24 Jesus replied, "The time is coming, ma'am, when we will no longer be concerned about whether to worship the Father here or in Jerusalem. For it's not *where* we worship that counts, but *how* we worship—is our worship spiritual and real? Do we have the Holy Spirit's help? For God is Spirit, and we must have his help to worship as we should. The Father wants this kind of worship from us. But you Samaritans know so little about him, worshiping blindly, while we Jews know all about him, for salvation comes to the world through the Jews."

25 The woman said, "Well, at least I know that the Messiah will come—the one they call Christ—and when he does, he will explain everything to us."

26 Then Jesus told her, "I am the Messiah!"

27 Just then his disciples arrived. They were surprised to find him talking to a woman, but none of them asked him why, or what they had been discussing.

28, 29 Then the woman left her waterpot be-

[*a*] Implied.

Today's English Version

you don't have a husband. 18 You have been married to five men, and the man you live with now is not really your husband. You have told me the truth."

19 "I see you are a prophet, sir," the woman said. 20 "My Samaritan ancestors worshiped God on this mountain, but you Jews say that Jerusalem is the place where we should worship God."

21 Jesus said to her, "Believe me, woman, the time will come when men will not worship the Father either on this mountain or in Jerusalem. 22 You Samaritans do not really know whom you worship; we Jews know whom we worship, because salvation comes from the Jews. 23 But the time is coming, and is already here, when the real worshipers will worship the Father in spirit and in truth. These are the worshipers the Father wants to worship him. 24 God is Spirit, and those who worship him must worship in spirit and in truth."

25 The woman said to him, "I know that the Messiah, called Christ, will come. When he comes he will tell us everything."

26 Jesus answered, "I am he, I who am talking with you."

27 At that moment Jesus' disciples returned; and they were greatly surprised to find him talking with a woman. But none of them said to her, "What do you want?" or asked him, "Why are you talking with her?"

28 Then the woman left her water jar, went

New International Version

Jesus said to her, "You are right when you say you have no husband. 18 The fact is, you have had five husbands, and the man you now have is not your husband. What you have just said is quite true."

19 "Sir," the woman said, "I can see that you are a prophet. 20 Our fathers worshiped on this mountain, but you Jews claim that the place where we must worship is in Jerusalem."

21 Jesus declared, "Believe me, woman, a time is coming when you will worship the Father neither on this mountain nor in Jerusalem. 22 You Samaritans worship what you do not know; we worship what we do know, for salvation is from the Jews. 23 Yet a time is coming and has now come when the true worshipers will worship the Father in spirit and truth, for they are the kind of worshipers the Father seeks. 24 God is spirit, and his worshipers must worship in spirit and in truth."

25 The woman said, "I know that Messiah" (called Christ) "is coming. When he comes, he will explain everything to us."

26 Then Jesus declared, "I who speak to you am he."

The disciples rejoin Jesus

27 Just then his disciples returned and were surprised to find him talking with a woman. But no one asked, "What do you want?" or "Why are you talking with her?"

28 Then, leaving her water jar, the woman

Phillips Modern English

"You are quite right in saying, 'I haven't got a husband'," replied Jesus, "for you have had five husbands and the man you have now is not your husband at all. Yes, you spoke the truth when you said that."

"Sir," said the woman again, "I can see that you are a prophet! Now our ancestors worshipped on this hill-side, but you Jews say that Jerusalem is the place where men ought to worship——"

"Believe me," returned Jesus, "the time is coming when worshipping the Father will not be a matter of 'on this hill-side' or 'in Jerusalem'. Nowadays you are worshipping what you do not know. We Jews are worshipping what we know, for the salvation of mankind is to come from our race. Yet the time is coming, yes, and has already come, when true worshippers will worship the Father in spirit and in reality. Indeed, the Father looks for men who will worship him like that. God is Spirit, and those who worship him can only worship in spirit and in reality."

"Of course I know that Messiah is coming," returned the woman, "you know, the one who is called Christ. When he comes he will make everything plain to us."

"I am Christ speaking to you now," said Jesus.

At this point his disciples arrived, and were very surprised to find him talking to a woman, but none of them asked, "What do you want with her?" or "Why are you talking to her?" So the woman left her water-pot behind and went

Revised Standard Version

are right in saying, 'I have no husband'; 18 for
you have had five husbands, and he whom you
now have is not your husband; this you said
truly." 19 The woman said to him, "Sir, I perceive that you are a prophet. 20 Our fathers
worshiped on this mountain; and you say that
in Jerusalem is the place where men ought to
worship." 21 Jesus said to her, "Woman, believe me, the hour is coming when neither on
this mountain nor in Jerusalem will you worship the Father. 22 You worship what you do
not know; we worship what we know, for salvation is from the Jews. 23 But the hour is
coming, and now is, when the true worshipers
will worship the Father in spirit and truth, for
such the Father seeks to worship him. 24 God
is spirit, and those who worship him must worship in spirit and truth." 25 The woman said to
him, "I know that Messiah is coming (he who
is called Christ); when he comes, he will show
us all things." 26 Jesus said to her, "I who speak
to you am he."

27 Just then his disciples came. They marveled that he was talking with a woman, but
none said, "What do you wish?" or, "Why are
you talking with her?" 28 So the woman left her

Jerusalem Bible

"You are right to say, 'I have no husband';
18 for although you have had five, the one you
have now is not your husband. You spoke the
truth there." 19 "I see you are a prophet, sir,"
said the woman. 20 "Our fathers worshiped on
this mountain,[o] while you say that Jerusalem is
the place where one ought to worship." 21 Jesus
said:

"Believe me, woman, the hour is coming
when you will worship the Father
neither on this mountain nor in Jerusalem.
22 You worship what you do not know;
we worship what we do know;
for salvation comes from the Jews.
23 But the hour will come—in fact it is here
already—
when true worshipers will worship the
Father in spirit and truth:
that is the kind of worshiper
the Father wants.
24 God is spirit,
and those who worship
must worship in spirit and truth."

25 The woman said to him, "I know that
Messiah—that is, Christ—is coming; and when
he comes he will tell us everything." 26 "I who
am speaking to you," said Jesus, "I am he."

27 At this point his disciples returned, and
were surprised to find him speaking to a woman,
though none of them asked, "What do you want
from her?" or, "Why are you talking to her?"
28 The woman put down her water jar and hur-

[o] Gerizim, the mountain on which the Samaritans built a rival to the Jerusalem Temple; it was destroyed by Hyrcanus, 129 B.C.

New English Bible

you have no husband, for, although you have had five husbands, the man with whom you are now living is not your husband; you told me the truth there.' 'Sir,' she replied, 'I can see that you are a prophet. Our fathers worshipped on this mountain, but you Jews say that the temple where God should be worshipped is in Jerusalem.' 'Believe me,' said Jesus, 'the time is coming when you will worship the Father neither on this mountain, nor in Jerusalem. You Samaritans worship without knowing what you worship, while we worship what we know. It is from the Jews that salvation comes. But the time approaches, indeed it is already here, when those who are real worshippers will worship the Father in spirit and in truth. Such are the worshippers whom the Father wants. God is spirit, and those who worship him must worship in spirit and in truth.' The woman answered, 'I know that Messiah' (that is Christ) 'is coming. When he comes he will tell us everything.' Jesus said, 'I am he, I who am speaking to you now.'

At that moment his disciples returned, and were astonished to find him talking with a woman; but none of them said, 'What do you want?' or, 'Why are you talking with her?' The woman put down her water-jar and went away

King James Version

waterpot, and went her way into the city, and saith to the men, 29 Come, see a man, which told me all things that ever I did: is not this the Christ? 30 Then they went out of the city, and came unto him.

31 In the mean while his disciples prayed him, saying, Master, eat. 32 But he said unto them, I have meat to eat that ye know not of. 33 Therefore said the disciples one to another, Hath any man brought him *aught* to eat? 34 Jesus saith unto them, My meat is to do the will of him that sent me, and to finish his work. 35 Say not ye, There are yet four months, and *then* cometh harvest? behold, I say unto you, Lift up your eyes, and look on the fields; for they are white already to harvest. 36 And he that reapeth receiveth wages, and gathereth fruit unto life eternal: that both he that soweth and he that reapeth may rejoice together. 37 And herein is that saying true, One soweth, and another reapeth. 38 I sent you to reap that whereon ye bestowed no labour: other men laboured, and ye are entered into their labours.

39 And many of the Samaritans of that city believed on him for the saying of the woman, which testified, He told me all that ever I did.

Living Bible

side the well and went back to the village and told everyone, "Come and meet a man who told me everything I ever did! Can this be the Messiah?" 30 So the people came streaming from the village to see him.

31 Meanwhile, the disciples were urging Jesus to eat. 32 "No," he said, "I have some food you don't know about."

33 "Who brought it to him?" the disciples asked each other.

34 Then Jesus explained: "My nourishment comes from doing the will of God who sent me, and from finishing his work. 35 Do you think the work of harvesting will not begin until the summer ends four months from now? Look around you! Vast fields of human souls are ripening all around us, and are ready now for reaping. 36 The reapers will be paid good wages and will be gathering eternal souls into the granaries of heaven! What joys await the sower and the reaper, both together! 37 For it is true that one sows and someone else reaps. 38 I sent you to reap where you didn't sow; others did the work, and you received the harvest."

39 Many from the Samaritan village believed he was the Messiah because of the woman's report: "He told me everything I ever did!"

Today's English Version

back to town, and said to the people there, 29 "Come and see the man who told me everything I have ever done. Could he be the Messiah?" 30 So they left the town and went to Jesus.

31 In the meantime the disciples were begging Jesus, "Teacher, have something to eat!"

32 But he answered, "I have food to eat that you know nothing about."

33 So the disciples started asking among themselves, "Could somebody have brought him food?"

34 "My food," Jesus said to them, "is to obey the will of him who sent me and finish the work he gave me to do. 35 You have a saying, 'Four more months and then the harvest.' I tell you, take a good look at the fields; the crops are now ripe and ready to be harvested! 36 The man who reaps the harvest is being paid and gathers the crops for eternal life; so that the man who plants and the man who reaps will be glad together. 37 The saying is true, 'One man plants, another man reaps.' 38 I have sent you to reap a harvest in a field where you did not work; others worked there, and you profit from their work."

39 Many of the Samaritans in that town believed in Jesus because the woman had said, "He

New International Version

went back to the town and said to the people, 29 "Come, see a man who told me everything I ever did. Could this be the Christ[y]?" 30 They came out of the town and made their way toward him.

31 Meanwhile his disciples urged him, "Rabbi, eat something."

32 But he said to them, "I have food to eat that you know nothing about."

33 Then his disciples said to each other, "Could someone have brought him food?"

34 "My food," said Jesus, "is to do the will of him who sent me and to finish his work. 35 Do you not say, 'Four months more and then the harvest'? I tell you, open your eyes and look at the fields! They are ripe for harvest. 36 Even now the reaper draws his wages, even now he harvests the crop for eternal life, so that the sower and the reaper may be glad together. 37 Thus the saying 'One sows and another reaps' is true. 38 I sent you to reap what you have not worked for. Others have done the hard work, and you have reaped the benefits of their labor."

Many Samaritans believe

39 Many of the Samaritans from that town believed in him because of the woman's testi-

[y] Or *Messiah*.

Phillips Modern English

into the town and began to say to the people, "Come out and see the man who told me everything I've ever done! Can this be 'Christ'?" So they left the town and started to come to Jesus.

Meanwhile the disciples were begging him, "Master, do eat something."

To which Jesus replied, "I have food to eat that you know nothing about."

This, of course, made the disciples ask each other, "Do you think anyone has brought him any food?"

Jesus said to them, "My food is doing the will of him who sent me and finishing the work he has given me. Don't you say, 'Four months more and then comes the harvest'? But I tell you to open your eyes and look at the fields—they are gleaming white, all ready for the harvest! The reaper is already being rewarded and getting in a harvest for eternal life, so that both sower and reaper may be glad together. For in this harvest the old saying comes true, 'One man sows and another reaps.' I have sent you to reap a harvest for which you never laboured; other men have worked hard and you have reaped the result of their labours."

Many of the Samaritans who came out of that town believed in him through the woman's testimony—"He told me everything I've ever done."

Revised Standard Version

water jar, and went away into the city, and said
to the people, 29 "Come, see a man who told
me all that I ever did. Can this be the Christ?"
30 They went out of the city and were coming
to him.

31 Meanwhile the disciples besought him, saying, "Rabbi, eat." 32 But he said to them, "I
have food to eat of which you do not know."
33 So the disciples said to one another, "Has
any one brought him food?" 34 Jesus said to
them, "My food is to do the will of him who
sent me, and to accomplish his work. 35 Do you
not say, 'There are yet four months, then comes
the harvest'? I tell you, lift up your eyes, and
see how the fields are already white for harvest. 36 He who reaps receives wages, and gathers fruit for eternal life, so that sower and
reaper may rejoice together. 37 For here the
saying holds true, 'One sows and another reaps.'
38 I sent you to reap that for which you did not
labor; others have labored, and you have entered into their labor."

39 Many Samaritans from that city believed
in him because of the woman's testimony, "He

Jerusalem Bible

ried back to the town to tell the people,
29 "Come and see a man who has told me everything I ever did; I wonder if he is the Christ?"
30 This brought people out of the town and
they started walking toward him.

31 Meanwhile, the disciples were urging him,
"Rabbi, do have something to eat"; 32 but he
said, "I have food to eat that you do not know
about." 33 So the disciples asked one another,
"Has someone been bringing him food?" 34 But
Jesus said:

"My food
is to do the will of the one who sent me,
and to complete his work.
35 Have you not got a saying:
Four months and then the harvest?
Well, I tell you:
Look around you, look at the fields;
already they are white, ready for harvest!
Already 36 the reaper is being paid his wages,
already he is bringing in the grain for eternal life,
and thus sower and reaper rejoice together.
37 For here the proverb holds good:
one sows, another reaps;
38 I sent you to reap
a harvest you had not worked for.
Others worked for it;
and you have come into the rewards of their trouble."

39 Many Samaritans of that town had believed in him on the strength of the woman's
testimony when she said, "He told me all I have

New English Bible

to the town, where she said to the people, 'Come and see a man who has told me everything I ever did. Could this be the Messiah?' They came out of the town and made their way towards him.

Meanwhile the disciples were urging him, 'Rabbi, have something to eat.' But he said, 'I have food to eat of which you know nothing.' At this the disciples said to one another, 'Can someone have brought him food?' But Jesus said, 'It is meat and drink for me to do the will of him who sent me until I have finished his work.

'Do you not say, "Four months more and then comes harvest"? But look, I tell you, look round on the fields; they are already white, ripe for harvest. The reaper is drawing his pay and gathering a crop for eternal life, so that sower and reaper may rejoice together. That is how the saying comes true: "One sows, and another reaps." I sent you to reap a crop for which you have not toiled. Others toiled and you have come in for the harvest of their toil.'

Many Samaritans of that town came to believe in him because of the woman's testimony:

King James Version

40 So when the Samaritans were come unto him,
they besought him that he would tarry with
them: and he abode there two days. 41 And many
more believed because of his own word; 42 And
said unto the woman, Now we believe, not because of thy saying: for we have heard *him* ourselves, and know that this is indeed the Christ,
the Saviour of the world.
43 Now after two days he departed thence,
and went into Galilee. 44 For Jesus himself testified, that a prophet hath no honour in his own
country. 45 Then when he was come into Galilee,
the Galileans received him, having seen all the
things that he did at Jerusalem at the feast: for
they also went unto the feast. 46 So Jesus came
again into Cana of Galilee, where he made the
water wine. And there was a certain nobleman,
whose son was sick at Capernaum. 47 When he
heard that Jesus was come out of Judea into
Galilee, he went unto him, and besought him
that he would come down, and heal his son: for
he was at the point of death. 48 Then said Jesus
unto him, Except ye see signs and wonders, ye
will not believe. 49 The nobleman saith unto him,
Sir, come down ere my child die. 50 Jesus saith
unto him, Go thy way; thy son liveth. And the
man believed the word that Jesus had spoken

Living Bible

40, 41 When they came out to see him at the
well, they begged him to stay at their village;
and he did, for two days, long enough for many
of them to believe in him after hearing him.
42 Then they said to the woman, "Now we believe because we have heard him ourselves, not
just because of what you told us. He is indeed
the Savior of the world."
43, 44 At the end of the two days' stay he
went on into Galilee. Jesus used to say, "A
prophet is honored everywhere except in his own
country!" 45 But the Galileans welcomed him
with open arms, for they had been in Jerusalem
at the Passover celebration and had seen some
of his miracles.[b]
46, 47 In the course of his journey through
Galilee he arrived at the town of Cana, where
he had turned the water into wine. While he was
there, a man in the city of Capernaum, a government official, whose son was very sick, heard
that Jesus had come from Judea and was traveling in Galilee. This man went over to Cana,
found Jesus, and begged him to come to Capernaum with him and heal his son, who was now
at death's door.
48 Jesus asked, "Won't any of you believe in
me unless I do more and more miracles?"
49 The official pled, "Sir, please come now
before my child dies."
50 Then Jesus told him, "Go back home.
Your son is healed!" And the man believed Jesus

[*b*] See John 2:23.

Today's English Version

told me everything I have ever done." 40 So
when the Samaritans came to him they begged
him to stay with them; and Jesus stayed there
two days.
41 Many more believed because of his message, 42 and they told the woman, "We believe
now, not because of what you said, but because
we ourselves have heard him, and we know that
he is really the Savior of the world."

Jesus heals an official's son

43 After spending two days there, Jesus left
and went to Galilee. 44 For Jesus himself had
said, "A prophet is not respected in his own
country." 45 When he arrived in Galilee the
people there welcomed him, because they had
gone to the Passover Feast in Jerusalem and had
seen everything that he had done during the
feast.
46 So Jesus went back to Cana of Galilee,
where he had turned the water into wine. There
was a government official there whose son in
Capernaum was sick. 47 When he heard that
Jesus had come from Judea to Galilee, he went
to him and asked him to go to Capernaum and
heal his son, who was about to die. 48 Jesus said
to him, "None of you will ever believe unless you
see great and wonderful works."
49 "Sir," replied the official, "come with me
before my child dies."
50 Jesus said to him, "Go, your son will live!"

New International Version

mony, "He told me everything I ever did." 40 So
when the Samaritans came to him, they urged
him to stay with them, and he stayed two days.
41 And because of his words many more became
believers.
42 They said to the woman, "We no longer
believe just because of what you said; now we
have heard for ourselves, and we know that
this man really is the Savior of the world."

Jesus heals the official's son

43 After the two days he left for Galilee.
44 (Now Jesus himself had pointed out that a
prophet has no honor in his own country.)
45 When he arrived in Galilee, the Galileans
welcomed him. They had seen all that he had
done in Jerusalem at the Passover Feast, for
they also had been there.
46 Once more he visited Cana in Galilee,
where he had turned the water into wine. And
there was a certain royal official whose son lay
sick at Capernaum. 47 When this man heard
that Jesus had arrived in Galilee from Judea, he
went to him and begged him to come and heal
his son, who was close to death.
48 "Unless you people see miraculous signs
and wonders," Jesus told him, "you will never
believe."
49 The royal official said, "Sir, come down
before my child dies."
50 Jesus replied, "You may go. Your son will
live."
The man took Jesus at his word and departed.

Phillips Modern English

And when they arrived they begged him to stay with them. He did stay there two days and far more believed in him because of what he himself said. As they told the woman, "We don't believe any longer now because of what you said. We have heard him with our own ears. We know now that this really is the Saviour of the World!"

4.43 Jesus, in Cana again, heals in response to faith

After the two days were over, Jesus left and went away to Galilee. (For Jesus himself testified that a prophet enjoys no honour in his own country.) And on his arrival the people received him with open arms. For they had seen all that he had done in Jerusalem during the festival, since they had themselves been present. So Jesus came again to Cana in Galilee, the place where he had made the water into wine. At Capernaum there was an official whose son was very ill. When he heard that Jesus had left Judaea and had arrived in Galilee, he went off to see him and begged him to come down and heal his son, who was by this time at the point of death.

Jesus said to him, "Will you never believe unless you see signs and wonders?"

"Sir," returned the official, "please come down before my boy dies!"

"You can go home," returned Jesus, "your son is alive."

And the man believed what Jesus had said to him and went on his way.

Revised Standard Version

told me all that I ever did." 40 So when the
Samaritans came to him, they asked him to stay
with them; and he stayed there two days. 41 And
many more believed because of his word.
42 They said to the woman, "It is no longer because of your words that we believe, for we
have heard for ourselves, and we know that this
is indeed the Savior of the world."
43 After the two days he departed to Galilee. 44 For Jesus himself testified that a prophet
has no honor in his own country. 45 So when
he came to Galilee, the Galileans welcomed him,
having seen all that he had done in Jerusalem
at the feast, for they too had gone to the feast.
46 So he came agan to Cana in Galilee,
where he had made the water wine. And at
Capernaum there was an official whose son was
ill. 47 When he heard that Jesus had come from
Judea to Galilee, he went and begged him to
come down and heal his son, for he was at the
point of death. 48 Jesus therefore said to him,
"Unless you see signs and wonders you will not
believe." 49 The official said to him, "Sir, come
down before my child dies." 50 Jesus said to
him, "Go; your son will live." The man believed the word that Jesus spoke to him and

Jerusalem Bible

ever done," 40 so, when the Samaritans came
up to him, they begged him to stay with them.
He stayed for two days, and 41 when he spoke
to them many more came to believe; 42 and they
said to the woman, "Now we no longer believe
because of what you told us; we have heard him
ourselves and we know that he really is the
savior of the world."

The cure of the nobleman's son

43 When the two days were over Jesus left
for Galilee. 44 He himself had declared that
there is no respect for a prophet in his own
country, 45 but on his arrival the Galileans received him well, having seen all that he had
done at Jerusalem during the festival which they
too had attended.
46 He went again to Cana in Galilee, where
he had changed the water into wine. Now there
was a court official there whose son was ill at
Capernaum 47 and, hearing that Jesus had arrived in Galilee from Judaea, he went and asked
him to come and cure his son as he was at the
point of death. 48 Jesus said, "So you will not
believe unless you see signs and portents!"
49 "Sir," answered the official, "come down before my child dies." 50 "Go home," said Jesus,
"your son will live." The man believed what

New English Bible

'He told me everything I ever did.' So when these Samaritans had come to him they pressed him to stay with them; and he stayed there two days. Many more became believers because of what they heard from his own lips. They told the woman, 'It is no longer because of what you said that we believe, for we have heard him ourselves; and we know that this is in truth the Saviour of the world.'

When the two days were over he set out for Galilee; for Jesus himself declared that a prophet is without honour in his own country. On his arrival in Galilee the Galileans gave him a welcome, because they had seen all that he did at the festival in Jerusalem; they had been at the festival themselves.

Once again he visited Cana-in-Galilee, where he had turned the water into wine. An officer in the royal service was there, whose son was lying ill at Capernaum. When he heard that Jesus had come from Judaea into Galilee, he came to him and begged him to go down and cure his son, who was at the point of death. Jesus said to him, 'Will none of you ever believe without seeing signs and portents?' The officer pleaded with him, 'Sir, come down before my boy dies.' Then Jesus said, 'Return home; your son will live.' The man believed what Jesus said and started for

King James Version

unto him, and he went his way. 51And as he
was now going down, his servants met him, and
told *him,* saying, Thy son liveth. 52 Then inquired
he of them the hour when he began to amend.
And they said unto him, Yesterday at the seventh
hour the fever left him. 53 So the father knew
that *it was* at the same hour, in the which Jesus
said unto him, Thy son liveth: and himself believed, and his whole house. 54 This *is* again
the second miracle *that* Jesus did, when he was
come out of Judea into Galilee.

5 After this there was a feast of the Jews;
and Jesus went up to Jerusalem. 2 Now there
is at Jerusalem by the sheep *market* a pool,
which is called in the Hebrew tongue Bethesda,
having five porches. 3 In these lay a great multitude of impotent folk, of blind, halt, withered,
waiting for the moving of the water. 4 For an
angel went down at a certain season into the
pool, and troubled the water: whosoever then
first after the troubling of the water stepped in
was made whole of whatsoever disease he had.
5And a certain man was there, which had an

Living Bible

and started home. 51 While he was on his way,
some of his servants met him with the news that
all was well—his son had recovered. 52 He asked
them when the lad had began to feel better, and
they replied, "Yesterday afternoon at about one
o'clock his fever suddenly disappeared!" 53 Then
the father realized it was the same moment that
Jesus had told him, "Your son is healed." And
the officer and his entire household believed that
Jesus was the Messiah.
54 This was Jesus' second miracle in Galilee
after coming from Judea.

5 Afterwards Jesus returned to Jerusalem for
one of the Jewish religious holidays. 2 Inside
the city, near the Sheep Gate, was Bethesda
Pool, with five covered platforms or porches
surrounding it. 3 Crowds of sick folks—lame,
blind, or with paralyzed limbs—lay on the platforms (waiting for a certain movement of the
water, 4 for an angel of the Lord came from
time to time and disturbed the water, and the
first person to step down into it afterwards was
healed).[a]
5 One of the men lying there had been sick

[*a*] Many of the ancient manuscripts omit the material within the parentheses.

Today's English Version

The man believed Jesus' words and went. 51 On
his way home his servants met him with the
news, "Your boy is going to live!"
52 He asked them what time it was when his
son got better, and they said, "It was one o'clock
yesterday afternoon when the fever left him."
53 The father remembered, then, that it was at
that very hour when Jesus had told him, "Your
son will live." So he and all his family believed.
54 This was the second mighty work that Jesus
did after coming from Judea to Galilee.

The healing at the pool

5 After this, there was a Jewish religious
feast, and Jesus went to Jerusalem. 2 There
is in Jerusalem, by the Sheep Gate, a pool with
five porches; in the Hebrew language it is called
Bethzatha. 3A large crowd of sick people were
lying on the porches—the blind, the lame, and
the paralyzed. [They were waiting for the water
to move, 4 because every now and then an angel
of the Lord went down into the pool and stirred
up the water. The first sick person to go into the
pool after the water was stirred up was healed
from whatever disease he had.] 5A man was

New International Version

51 While he was still on the way, his servants
met him with the news that his boy was
living. 52 When he inquired as to the time when
his son had gotten better, they said to him, "The
fever left him yesterday at the seventh hour."
53 Then the father realized that this was the
exact time at which Jesus had said to him, "Your
son will live." So he and all his household believed.
54 This was the second miraculous sign that
Jesus performed, having come from Judea to
Galilee.

The healing at the pool

5 Some time later, Jesus went up to Jerusalem for a feast of the Jews. 2 Now there
is in Jerusalem near the Sheep Gate a pool,
which in Aramaic is called Bethesda[z] and which
is surrounded by five covered colonnades. 3 Here
a great number of disabled people used to lie
—the blind, the lame, the paralyzed.[a] 5 One who

[z] Some early MSS read *Bethzatha;* others *Bethsaida.* [*a*] Some MSS add—*and they waited for the moving of the waters.* Some less important MSS also add verse 4: *From time to time an angel of the Lord would come down and stir up the waters. The first one into the pool after each such disturbance would be cured of whatever disease he had.*

Phillips Modern English

On the journey back his servants met him with the report: "Your son is alive and well." So he asked them at what time he had begun to recover, and they replied: "The fever left him yesterday at one o'clock in the afternoon." Then the father knew that this must have happend at the very moment when Jesus had said to him, "Your son is alive." And he and his whole household believed in Jesus. This, then, was the second sign that Jesus gave on his return from Judaea to Galilee.

5.1 Jesus heals in Jerusalem

Some time later came one of the Jewish feast-days and Jesus went up to Jerusalem. There is in Jerusalem near the sheep-pens a pool surrounded by five arches, which has the Hebrew name of Bethzatha. Under these arches a great many sick people were in the habit of lying; some of them were blind, some lame, and some had withered limbs. (They used to wait there for the "moving of the water", for at certain times an angel used to come down into the pool and disturb the water, and then the first person who stepped into the water after the disturbance would be healed of whatever he was suffering from.) One particular man had been there ill

Revised Standard Version

went his way. 51 As he was going down, his servants met him and told him that his son was living. 52 So he asked them the hour when he began to mend, and they said to him, "Yesterday at the seventh hour the fever left him." 53 The father knew that was the hour when Jesus had said to him, "Your son will live"; and he himself believed, and all his household. 54 This was now the second sign that Jesus did when he had come from Judea to Galilee.

5 After this there was a feast of the Jews, and Jesus went up to Jerusalem.
2 Now there is in Jerusalem by the Sheep Gate a pool, in Hebrew called Bethzatha,[j] which has five porticoes. 3 In these lay a multitude of invalids, blind, lame, paralyzed.[k] 5 One

[j] Other ancient authorities read *Bethesda,* others *Bethsaida.* [k] Other ancient authorities insert, wholly or in part, *waiting for the moving of the water;* [4] *for an angel of the Lord went down at certain seasons into the pool, and troubled the water; whoever stepped in first after the troubling of the water was healed of whatever disease he had.*

Jerusalem Bible

Jesus had said and started on his way; 51 and while he was still on the journey back his servants met him with the news that his boy was alive. 52 He asked them when the boy had begun to recover. "The fever left him yesterday," they said, "at the seventh hour." 53 The father realized that this was exactly the time when Jesus had said, "Your son will live"; and he and all his household believed.

54 This was the second sign given by Jesus, on his return from Judaea to Galilee.

III. The second feast at Jerusalem

The cure of a sick man at the Pool of Bethzatha

5 Some time after this there was a Jewish festival, and Jesus went up to Jerusalem.
2 Now at the Sheep Pool in Jerusalem there is a building, called Bethzatha in Hebrew, consisting of five porticoes; 3 and under these were crowds of sick people—blind, lame, paralyzed—waiting for the water to move; 4 for at intervals the angel of the Lord came down into the pool, and the water was disturbed, and the first person to enter the water after this disturbance was cured of any ailment he suffered from. 5 One man

New English Bible

home. When he was on his way down his servants met him with the news, 'Your boy is going to live.' So he asked them what time it was when he began to recover. They said, 'Yesterday at one in the afternoon the fever left him.' The father noted that this was the exact time when Jesus had said to him, 'Your son will live', and he and all his household became believers.

This was now the second sign which Jesus performed after coming down from Judaea into Galilee.

5 Later on Jesus went up to Jerusalem for one of the Jewish festivals.[a] Now at the Sheep-Pool in Jerusalem there is a place with five colonnades. Its name in the language of the Jews is Bethesda. In these colonnades there lay a crowd of sick people, blind, lame, and paralysed.[b] Among them was a man who had been crip-

[a] *Some witnesses read* for the Jewish festival. [b] *Some witnesses add* waiting for the disturbance of the water; *some further insert* (4) for from time to time an angel came down into the pool and stirred up the water. The first to plunge in after this disturbance recovered from whatever disease had afflicted him.

King James Version

infirmity thirty and eight years. 6 When Jesus
saw him lie, and knew that he had been now a
long time *in that case,* he saith unto him, Wilt
thou be made whole? 7 The impotent man answered him, Sir, I have no man, when the water
is troubled, to put me into the pool: but while
I am coming, another steppeth down before me.
8 Jesus saith unto him, Rise, take up thy bed,
and walk. 9 And immediately the man was made
whole, and took up his bed, and walked: and
on the same day was the sabbath.
10 The Jews therefore said unto him that was
cured, It is the sabbath day: it is not lawful for
thee to carry *thy* bed. 11 He answered them, He
that made me whole, the same said unto me,
Take up thy bed, and walk. 12 Then asked they
him, What man is that which said unto thee,
Take up thy bed, and walk? 13 And he that was
healed wist not who it was: for Jesus had conveyed himself away, a multitude being in *that*
place. 14 Afterward Jesus findeth him in the temple, and said unto him, Behold, thou art made
whole: sin no more, lest a worse thing come
unto thee. 15 The man departed, and told the
Jews that it was Jesus, which had made him
whole. 16 And therefore did the Jews persecute
Jesus, and sought to slay him, because he had
done these things on the sabbath day.
17 But Jesus answered them, My Father work-

Living Bible

for thirty-eight years. 6 When Jesus saw him and
knew how long he had been ill, he asked him,
"Would you like to get well?"
7 "I can't," the sick man said, "for I have no
one to help me into the pool at the movement
of the water. While I am trying to get there,
someone else always gets in ahead of me."
8 Jesus told him, "Stand up, roll up your
sleeping mat and go on home!"
9 Instantly, the man was healed! He rolled up
the mat and began walking!
But it was on the Sabbath when this miracle
was done. 10 So the Jewish leaders objected.
They said to the man who was cured, "You
can't work on the Sabbath! It's illegal to carry
that sleeping mat!"
11 "The man who healed me told me to,"
was his reply.
12 "Who said such a thing as that?" they demanded.
13 The man didn't know, and Jesus had disappeared into the crowd. 14 But afterwards Jesus
found him in the Temple and told him, "Now
you are well; don't sin as you did before,[b] or
something even worse may happen to you."
15 Then the man went to find the Jewish leaders and told them it was Jesus who had healed
him.
16 So they began harassing Jesus as a Sabbath breaker. 17 But Jesus replied, "My Father
constantly does good,[c] and I'm following his
example."

[*b*] Implied. Literally, "sin no more." [*c*] Implied. Literally, "My Father works even until now, and I work."

Today's English Version

there who had been sick for thirty-eight years.
6 Jesus saw him lying there, and he knew that the
man had been sick for such a long time; so he
said to him, "Do you want to get well?"
7 The sick man answered, "Sir, I don't have
anyone here to put me in the pool when the
water is stirred up; while I am trying to get in,
somebody else gets there first."
8 Jesus said to him, "Get up, pick up your
mat, and walk." 9 Immediately the man got well;
he picked up his mat, and walked.
The day this happened was a Sabbath, 10 so
the Jewish authorities told the man who had been
healed, "This is a Sabbath, and it is against our
Law for you to carry your mat."
11 He answered, "The man who made me
well told me, 'Pick up your mat and walk.' "
12 They asked him, "Who is this man who
told you to pick up your mat and walk?"
13 But the man who had been healed did not
know who he was, because there was a crowd
in that place and Jesus had slipped out.
14 Afterward, Jesus found him in the temple and said, "Look, you are well now. Quit your
sins, or something worse may happen to you."
15 Then the man left and told the Jewish authorities that it was Jesus who had healed him.
16 For this reason they began to persecute Jesus, because he had done this healing on a Sabbath. 17 Jesus answered them, "My Father works
always, and I too must work."

New International Version

was there had been an invalid for thirty-eight
years. 6 When Jesus saw him lying there and
learned that he had been in this condition for a
long time, he asked him, "Do you want to get
well?"
7 "Sir," the invalid replied, "I have no one
to help me into the pool when the water is
stirred. While I am trying to get in, someone
else goes down ahead of me."
8 Then Jesus said to him, "Get up! Pick up
your mat and walk." 9 At once the man was
cured; he picked up his mat and walked.
The day on which this took place was a Sabbath, 10 and so the Jews said to the man who
had been healed, "It is the Sabbath; the law forbids you to carry your mat."
11 But he replied, "The man who made me
well said to me, 'Pick up your mat and walk.' "
12 So they asked him, "Who is this fellow
who told you to pick it up and walk?"
13 The man who was healed had no idea who
it was, for Jesus had slipped away in the crowd.
14 Later Jesus found him at the temple and
said to him, "See, you are well again. Stop sinning or something worse may happen to you."
15 The man went away and told the Jews that it
was Jesus who had made him well.

Life through the Son

16 So, because Jesus was doing these things
on the Sabbath, the Jews persecuted him. 17 Jesus said to them, "My Father is always at his
work to this very day, and I, too, am working."

Phillips Modern English

for thirty-eight years. When Jesus saw him lying there on his back—knowing that he had been like that for a long time, he said to him, "Do you want to get well again?"

"Sir," replied the sick man, "I haven't got anybody to put me into the pool when the water is all stirred up. While I'm trying to get there somebody else gets down into it first."

"Get up," said Jesus, "pick up your bed and walk!"

At once the man recovered, picked up his bed and began to walk.

This happened on a Sabbath day, which made the Jews keep on telling the man who had been healed, "It's the Sabbath; it is not right for you to carry your bed."

"The man who made me well," he replied, "was the one who told me, 'Pick up your bed and walk.' "

Then they asked him, "And who is the man who told you to do that?"

But the one who had been healed had no idea who it was, for Jesus had slipped away in the dense crowd. Later Jesus found him in the Temple and said to him, "Look: you are a fit man now. Do not sin again or something worse might happen to you!"

Then the man went off and informed the Jews that the one who had made him well was Jesus. It was because Jesus did such things on the Sabbath day that the Jews persecuted him. But Jesus' answer to them was this, "My Father is still at work and therefore I work as well."

Revised Standard Version

man was there, who had been ill for thirty-
eight years. 6 When Jesus saw him and knew
that he had been lying there a long time, he
said to him, "Do you want to be healed?"
7 The sick man answered him, "Sir, I have no
man to put me into the pool when the water
is troubled, and while I am going another steps
down before me." 8 Jesus said to him, "Rise,
take up your pallet, and walk." 9 And at once
the man was healed, and he took up his pallet
and walked.
Now that day was the sabbath. 10 So the
Jews said to the man who was cured, "It is the
sabbath, it is not lawful for you to carry your
pallet." 11 But he answered them, "The man
who healed me said to me, 'Take up your pallet,
and walk.' " 12 They asked him, "Who is the
man who said to you, 'Take up your pallet, and
walk'?" 13 Now the man who had been healed
did not know who it was, for Jesus had withdrawn, as there was a crowd in the place. 14 Afterward, Jesus found him in the temple, and
said to him, "See, you are well! Sin no more,
that nothing worse befall you." 15 The man
went away and told the Jews that it was Jesus
who had healed him. 16 And this was why the
Jews persecuted Jesus, because he did this on
the sabbath. 17 But Jesus answered them, "My
Father is working still, and I am working."

Jerusalem Bible

there had an illness which had lasted thirty-eight
years, 6 and when Jesus saw him lying there and
knew he had been in this condition for a long
time, he said, "Do you want to be well again?"
7 "Sir," replied the sick man, "I have no one to
put me into the pool when the water is disturbed; and while I am still on the way, someone else gets there before me." 8 Jesus said,
"Get up, pick up your sleeping mat and walk."
9 The man was cured at once, and he picked up
his mat and walked away.
Now that day happened to be the sabbath,
10 so the Jews said to the man who had been
cured, "It is the sabbath; you are not allowed
to carry your sleeping mat." 11 He replied, "But
the man who cured me told me, 'Pick up your
mat and walk.' " 12 They asked, "Who is the
man who said to you, 'Pick up your mat and
walk'?" 13 The man had no idea who it was,
since Jesus had disappeared into the crowd that
filled the place. 14 After a while Jesus met him
in the Temple and said, "Now you are well
again, be sure not to sin any more, or something worse may happen to you." 15 The man
went back and told the Jews that it was Jesus
who had cured him. 16 It was because he did
things like this on the sabbath that the Jews
began to persecute Jesus. 17 His answer to them
was, "My Father goes on working, and so do I."

New English Bible

pled for thirty-eight years. When Jesus saw him lying there and was aware that he had been ill a long time, he asked him, 'Do you want to recover?' 'Sir,' he replied, 'I have no one to put me in the pool when the water is disturbed, but while I am moving, someone else is in the pool before me.' Jesus answered, 'Rise to your feet, take up your bed and walk.' The man recovered instantly, took up his stretcher, and began to walk.

That day was a Sabbath. So the Jews said to the man who had been cured, 'It is the Sabbath. You are not allowed to carry your bed on the Sabbath.' He answered, 'The man who cured me said, "Take up your bed and walk." ' They asked him, 'Who is the man who told you to take up your bed and walk?' But the cripple who had been cured did not know; for the place was crowded and Jesus had slipped away. A little later Jesus found him in the temple and said to him, 'Now that you are well again, leave your sinful ways, or you may suffer something worse.' The man went away and told the Jews that it was Jesus who had cured him.

It was works of this kind done on the Sabbath that stirred the Jews to persecute Jesus. He defended himself by saying, 'My Father has never yet ceased his work, and I am working too.'

King James Version

eth hitherto, and I work. 18 Therefore the Jews
sought the more to kill him, because he not only
had broken the sabbath, but said also that God
was his Father, making himself equal with God.
19 Then answered Jesus and said unto them,
Verily, verily, I say unto you, The Son can do
nothing of himself, but what he seeth the Father
do: for what things soever he doeth, these also
doeth the Son likewise. 20 For the Father loveth
the Son, and sheweth him all things that himself
doeth: and he will shew him greater works than
these, that ye may marvel. 21 For as the Father
raiseth up the dead, and quickeneth *them;* even
so the Son quickeneth whom he will. 22 For the
Father judgeth no man, but hath committed all
judgment unto the Son: 23 That all *men* should
honour the Son, even as they honour the Father.
He that honoureth not the Son honoureth not
the Father which hath sent him. 24 Verily, verily,
I say unto you, He that heareth my word, and
believeth on him that sent me, hath everlasting
life, and shall not come into condemnation; but
is passed from death unto life. 25 Verily, verily,
I say unto you, The hour is coming, and now is,

Living Bible

18 Then the Jewish leaders were all the more
eager to kill him because in addition to disobeying their Sabbath laws, he had spoken of God as
his Father, thereby making himself equal with
God.

19 Jesus replied, "The Son can do nothing by
himself. He does only what he sees the Father
doing, and in the same way. 20 For the Father
loves the Son, and tells him everything he is doing; and the Son will do far more awesome
miracles than this man's healing. 21 He will even
raise from the dead anyone he wants to, just as
the Father does. 22 And the Father leaves all
judgment of sin to his Son, 23 so that everyone
will honor the Son, just as they honor the Father. But if you refuse to honor God's Son,
whom he sent to you, then you are certainly not
honoring the Father.

24 "I say emphatically that anyone who listens
to my message and believes in God who sent me
has eternal life, and will never be damned for
his sins, but has already passed out of death into
life. 25 And I solemnly declare that the time is
coming, in fact, it is here, when the dead shall

Today's English Version

18 This saying made the Jewish authorities all
the more determined to kill him; not only had
he broken the Sabbath law, but he had said
that God was his own Father, and in this way
had made himself equal with God.

The authority of the Son

19 So Jesus answered them, "I tell you the
truth: the Son does nothing on his own; he does
only what he sees his Father doing. What the
Father does, the Son also does. 20 For the Father
loves the Son and shows him all that he himself
is doing. He will show him even greater things
than this to do, and you will all be amazed.
21 Even as the Father raises the dead and gives
them life, in the same way the Son gives life to
those he wants to. 22 Nor does the Father himself judge anyone. He has given his Son the full
right to judge, 23 so that all will honor the Son
in the same way as they honor the Father. Whoever does not honor the Son does not honor the
Father who sent him.

24 "I tell you the truth: whoever hears my
words, and believes in him who sent me, has
eternal life. He will not be judged, but has already passed from death to life. 25 I tell you the
truth: the time is coming—the time has already
come—when the dead will hear the voice of the

New International Version

18 For this reason the Jews tried all the harder
to kill him; not only was he breaking the Sabbath, but he was even calling God his own
Father, making himself equal with God. 19 Jesus gave them this answer: "I tell you the truth,
the Son can do nothing by himself; he can do
only what he sees his Father doing, because
whatever the Father does the Son also does.
20 For the Father loves the Son and shows him
all he does. Yes, to your amazement he will show
him even greater things than these. 21 For just
as the Father raises the dead and gives them life,
even so the Son gives life to whom he is pleased
to give it. 22 Moreover, the Father judges no
one, but has entrusted all judgment to the Son,
23 that all may honor the Son just as they honor
the Father. He who does not honor the Son does
not honor the Father who sent him.

24 "I tell you the truth, whoever hears my
word and believes him who sent me has eternal
life and will not be condemned; he has crossed
over from death to life. 25 I tell you the truth, a
time is coming and has now come when the

Phillips Modern English

This remark made the Jews all the more determined to kill him, because not only did he break the Sabbath but he referred to God as his own Father, so putting himself on equal terms with God.

5.19 *Jesus makes his tremendous claim*

Jesus therefore said to them, "I solemnly assure you that the Son can do nothing of his own accord, but only what he sees the Father doing. For whatever the Father does the Son does the same. For the Father loves the Son and shows him everything that he does himself. Yes, and he will show him even greater things than these to fill you with wonder. For just as the Father raises the dead and makes them live, so does the Son give life to any man he chooses. The Father is no man's judge: he has put judgment entirely into the Son's hands, so that all men may honour the Son equally with the Father. The man who does not honour the Son does not honour the Father who sent him. I solemnly assure you that the man who hears what I have to say and believes in the one who has sent me has eternal life. He does not have to face judgment; he has already passed from death into life. Yes, I assure you that a time is coming, in fact has already come, when the dead will hear the voice

Revised Standard Version

18 This was why the Jews sought all the more
to kill him, because he not only broke the sabbath
but also called God his own Father, making
himself equal with God.
19 Jesus said to them, "Truly, truly, I say
to you, the Son can do nothing of his own accord,
but only what he sees the Father doing;
for whatever he does, that the Son does likewise.
20 For the Father loves the Son, and shows him
all that he himself is doing; and greater works
than these will he show him, that you may marvel.
21 For as the Father raises the dead and
gives them life, so also the Son gives life to
whom he will. 22 The Father judges no one, but
has given all judgment to the Son, 23 that all
may honor the Son, even as they honor the
Father. He who does not honor the Son does
not honor the Father who sent him. 24 Truly,
truly, I say to you, he who hears my word and
believes him who sent me, has eternal life; he
does not come into judgment, but has passed
from death to life.
25 "Truly, truly, I say to you, the hour is
coming, and now is, when the dead will hear

Jerusalem Bible

18 But that only made the Jews even more intent on killing him, because, not content with breaking the sabbath, he spoke of God as his own Father, and so made himself God's equal.
19 To this accusation Jesus replied:

"I tell you most solemnly,
the Son can do nothing by himself;
he can do only what he sees the Father doing:
and whatever the Father does the Son does too.
20 For the Father loves the Son
and shows him everything he does himself,
and he will show him even greater things than these,
works that will astonish you.
21 Thus, as the Father raises the dead and gives them life,
so the Son gives life to anyone he chooses;
22 for the Father judges no one;
he has entrusted all judgment to the Son,
23 so that all may honor the Son
as they honor the Father.
Whoever refuses honor to the Son
refuses honor to the Father who sent him.
24 I tell you most solemnly,
whoever listens to my words,
and believes in the one who sent me,
has eternal life;
without being brought to judgment
he has passed from death to life.
25 I tell you most solemnly,
the hour will come—in fact it is here already—
when the dead will hear the voice of the

New English Bible

This made the Jews still more determined to kill him, because he was not only breaking the Sabbath, but, by calling God his own Father, he claimed equality with God.

To this charge Jesus replied, 'In truth, in very truth I tell you, the Son can do nothing by himself; he does only what he sees the Father doing: what the Father does, the Son does. For the Father loves the Son and shows him all his works, and will show greater yet, to fill you with wonder. As the Father raises the dead and gives them life, so the Son gives life to men, as he determines. And again, the Father does not judge anyone, but has given full jurisdiction to the Son; it is his will that all should pay the same honour to the Son as to the Father. To deny honour to the Son is to deny it to the Father who sent him.

'In very truth, anyone who gives heed to what I say and puts his trust in him who sent me has hold of eternal life, and does not come up for judgement, but has already passed from death to life. In truth, in very truth I tell you, a time is coming, indeed it is already here, when the

King James Version

when the dead shall hear the voice of the Son of God: and they that hear shall live. 26 For as the Father hath life in himself; so hath he given to the Son to have life in himself; 27 And hath given him authority to execute judgment also, because he is the Son of man. 28 Marvel not at this: for the hour is coming, in the which all that are in the graves shall hear his voice, 29 And shall come forth; they that have done good, unto the resurrection of life; and they that have done evil, unto the resurrection of damnation. 30 I can of mine own self do nothing: as I hear, I judge: and my judgment is just; because I seek not mine own will, but the will of the Father which hath sent me. 31 If I bear witness of myself, my witness is not true.

32 There is another that beareth witness of me; and I know that the witness which he witnesseth of me is true. 33 Ye sent unto John, and he bare witness unto the truth. 34 But I receive not testimony from man: but these things I say, that ye might be saved. 35 He was a burning and a shining light: and ye were willing for a season to rejoice in his light.

36 But I have greater witness than *that* of John: for the works which the Father hath given me to finish, the same works that I do, bear

Living Bible

hear my voice—the voice of the Son of God—and those who listen shall live. 26 The Father has life in himself, and has granted his Son to have life in himself, 27 and to judge the sins of all mankind because he is the Son of Man. 28 Don't be so surprised! Indeed the time is coming when all the dead in their graves shall hear the voice of God's Son, 29 and shall rise again—those who have done good, to eternal life; and those who have continued in evil, to judgment.

30 "But I pass no judgment without consulting the Father. I judge as I am told. And my judgment is absolutely fair and just, for it is according to the will of God who sent me and is not merely my own.

31 "When I make claims about myself they aren't believed, 32, 33 but someone else, yes, John the Baptist,[d] is making these claims for me too. You have gone out to listen to his preaching, and I can assure you that all he says about me is true! 34 But the truest witness I have is not from a man, though I have reminded you about John's witness so that you will believe in me and be saved. 35 John shone brightly for a while, and you benefited and rejoiced, 36 but I have a greater witness than John. I refer to the miracles I do; these have been assigned me by the Father, and they prove that the Father has sent

[*d*] Implied. However, most commentators believe the reference is to the witness of his Father. See verse 37.

Today's English Version

Son of God, and those who hear it will live. 26 Even as the Father is himself the source of life, in the same way he has made his Son to be the source of life. 27 And he has given the Son the right to judge, because he is the Son of Man. 28 Do not be surprised at this; the time is coming when all the dead in the graves will hear his voice, 29 and they will come out of their graves: those who have done good will rise and live, and those who have done evil will rise and be condemned."

Witnesses to Jesus

30 "I can do nothing on my own; I judge only as God tells me, so my judgment is right, because I am not trying to do what I want, but only what he who sent me wants.

31 "If I testify on my own behalf, what I say is not to be accepted as real proof. 32 But there is someone else who testifies on my behalf, and I know that what he says about me is true. 33 You sent your messengers to John, and he spoke on behalf of the truth. 34 It is not that I must have a man's witness; I say this only in order that you may be saved. 35 John was like a lamp, burning and shining, and you were willing for a while to enjoy his light. 36 But I have a witness on my behalf even greater than the witness that John gave: the works that I do, the works my Father gave me to do, these speak on

New International Version

dead will hear the voice of the Son of God and those who hear will live. 26 For as the Father has life in himself, so he has granted the Son to have life in himself. 27 And he has given him authority to judge because he is the Son of Man.

28 "Do not be amazed at this, for a time is coming when all who are in their graves will hear his voice 29 and come out—those who have done good will rise to live, and those who have done evil will rise to be condemned. 30 By myself I can do nothing; I judge only as I hear, and my judgment is just, for I seek not to please myself but him who sent me.

Testimonies about Jesus

31 "If I testify about myself, my testimony is not valid. 32 There is another who testifies in my favor, and I know that his testimony about me is valid.

33 "You have sent to John and he has testified to the truth. 34 Not that I accept human testimony; but I mention it that you may be saved. 35 John was a lamp that burned and gave light, and you chose for a time to enjoy his light.

36 "I have testimony weightier than that of John. For the very work that the Father has given me to finish, and which I am doing, testi-

Phillips Modern English

of the Son of God and those who have heard it will live! For just as the Father has life in himself, so by the Father's gift, the Son also has life in himself. And he has given him authority to judge because he is Son of Man. No, do not be surprised—the time is coming when all those who are dead and buried will hear his voice and out they will come—those who have done right will rise again to life, but those who have done wrong will rise to face judgment!

"By myself I can do nothing. As I hear from God, I judge, and my judgment is true because I do not live to please myself but to do the will of the Father who sent me. You may say that I am bearing witness about myself, that therefore what I say about myself has no value, but I would remind you that there is one who witnesses about me and I know that his witness about me is absolutely true. You sent to John, and he testified to the truth. Not that it is man's testimony that I need—I only tell you this to help you to be saved. John certainly was a lamp that burned and shone, and for a time you were willing to enjoy the light that he gave. But I have a higher testimony than John's. The work that the Father gave me to complete, yes, these very actions which I do are my witness that the

Revised Standard Version

the voice of the Son of God, and those who
hear will live. 26 For as the Father has life in
himself, so he has granted the Son also to have
life in himself, 27 and has given him authority
to execute judgment, because he is the Son of
man. 28 Do not marvel at this; for the hour is
coming when all who are in the tombs will hear
his voice 29 and come forth, those who have
done good, to the resurrection of life, and those
who have done evil, to the resurrection of judgment.
30 "I can do nothing on my own authority;
as I hear, I judge; and my judgment is just, because I seek not my own will but the will of
him who sent me. 31 If I bear witness to myself, my testimony is not true; 32 there is another who bears witness to me, and I know that
the testimony which he bears to me is true.
33 You sent to John, and he has borne witness
to the truth. 34 Not that the testimony which I
receive is from man; but I say this that you may
be saved. 35 He was a burning and shining lamp,
and you were willing to rejoice for a while in
his light. 36 But the testimony which I have is
greater than that of John; for the works which
the Father has granted me to accomplish, these
very works which I am doing, bear me witness

Jerusalem Bible

Son of God,
and all who hear it will live.
26 For the Father, who is the source of life,
has made the Son the source of life;
27 and, because he is the Son of Man,
has appointed him supreme judge.
28 Do not be surprised at this,
for the hour is coming
when the dead will leave their graves
at the sound of his voice:
29 those who did good
will rise again to life;
and those who did evil, to condemnation.
30 I can do nothing by myself;
I can only judge as I am told to judge,
and my judging is just,
because my aim is to do not my own will,
but the will of him who sent me.

31 "Were I to testify on my own behalf,
my testimony would not be valid;
32 but there is another witness who can speak
on my behalf,
and I know that his testimony is valid.
33 You sent messengers to John,
and he gave his testimony to the truth:
34 not that I depend on human testimony;
no, it is for your salvation that I speak of
this.
35 John was a lamp alight and shining
and for a time you were content to enjoy
the light that he gave.
36 But my testimony is greater than John's:
the works my Father has given me to
carry out,
these same works of mine

New English Bible

dead shall hear the voice of the Son of God, and all who hear shall come to life. For as the Father has life-giving power in himself, so has the Son, by the Father's gift.

'As Son of Man, he has also been given the right to pass judgement. Do not wonder at this, because the time is coming when all who are in the grave shall hear his voice and come out: those who have done right will rise to life; those who have done wrong will rise to hear their doom. I cannot act by myself; I judge as I am bidden, and my sentence is just, because my aim is not my own will, but the will of him who sent me.

'If I testify on my own behalf, that testimony does not hold good. There is another who bears witness for me, and I know that his testimony holds. Your messengers have been to John; you have his testimony to the truth. Not that I rely on human testimony, but I remind you of it for your own salvation. John was a lamp, burning brightly, and for a time you were ready to exult in his light. But I rely on a testimony higher than John's. There is enough to testify that the Father has sent me, in the works my Father gave me to do and to finish—the very works I have in

King James Version

witness of me, that the Father hath sent me.
37 And the Father himself, which hath sent me,
hath borne witness of me. Ye have neither heard
his voice at any time, nor seen his shape. 38 And
ye have not his word abiding in you: for whom
he hath sent, him ye believe not.
39 Search the Scriptures; for in them ye think
ye have eternal life: and they are they which
testify of me. 40 And ye will not come to me,
that ye might have life. 41 I receive not honour
from men. 42 But I know you, that ye have not
the love of God in you. 43 I am come in my
Father's name, and ye receive me not: if another
shall come in his own name, him ye will receive.
44 How can ye believe, which receive honour one
of another, and seek not the honour that *cometh*
from God only? 45 Do not think that I will
accuse you to the Father: there is *one* that ac-
cuseth you, *even* Moses, in whom ye trust. 46 For
had ye believed Moses, ye would have believed
me: for he wrote of me. 47 But if ye believe not
his writings, how shall ye believe my words?

Living Bible

me. 37 And the Father himself has also testified
about me, though not appearing to you personally, or speaking to you directly. 38 But you are
not listening to him, for you refuse to believe
me—the one sent to you with God's message.
39 "You search the Scriptures, for you believe they give you eternal life. And the Scriptures point to me! 40 Yet you won't come to me
so that I can give you this life eternal!
41, 42 "Your approval or disapproval means
nothing to me, for as I know so well, you don't
have God's love within you. 43 I know, because
I have come to you representing my Father and
you refuse to welcome me, though you readily
enough receive those who aren't sent from him,
but represent only themselves! 44 No wonder
you can't believe! For you gladly honor each
other, but you don't care about the honor that
comes from the only God!
45 "Yet it is not I who will accuse you of
this to the Father—Moses will! Moses, on whose
laws you set your hopes of heaven. 46 For you
have refused to believe Moses. He wrote about
me, but you refuse to believe him, so you refuse
to believe in me. 47 And since you don't believe
what he wrote, no wonder you don't believe me
either."

Today's English Version

my behalf and show that the Father has sent
me. 37 And the Father, who sent me, also testifies
on my behalf. You have never heard his voice, or
seen his face, 38 and you do not keep his message in your hearts, because you do not believe in the one whom he sent. 39 You study the
Scriptures because you think that in them you
will find eternal life. And they themselves speak
about me! 40 Yet you are not willing to come to
me in order to have life.
41 "I am not looking for praise from men.
42 But I know you; I know that you have no
love for God in your hearts. 43 I have come
with my Father's authority, but you have not
received me; when someone comes with his own
authority, you will receive him. 44 You like to
have praise from one another, but you do not
try to win praise from the only God; how, then,
can you believe? 45 Do not think, however, that
I will accuse you to my Father. Moses is the one
who will accuse you—Moses, in whom you have
hoped. 46 If you had really believed Moses, you
would have believed me, because he wrote about
me. 47 But since you do not believe what he
wrote, how can you believe what I say?"

New International Version

fies that the Father has sent me. 37 And the
Father who sent me has himself testified concerning me. You have never heard his voice nor seen
his form, 38 nor does his word dwell in you, for
you do not believe the one he sent. 39 You diligently study[b] the Scriptures because you think
that by them you possess eternal life. These are
the Scriptures that testify about me, 40 yet you
refuse to come to me to have life.
41 "I do not accept praise from men, 42 but
I know you. I know that you do not have God's
love in your hearts. 43 I have come in my Father's name, and you do not accept me; but if
someone else comes in his own name, you will
accept him. 44 How can you believe if you accept praise from one another, yet make no effort
to obtain the praise that comes from the only
God?[c]
45 "But do not think I will accuse you before the Father. Your accuser is Moses, on
whom your hopes are set. 46 If you believed
Moses, you would believe me, for he wrote
about me. 47 But since you do not believe what
he wrote, how are you going to believe what I
say?"

[*b*] Or ***Study diligently*** (the imperative). [*c*] Some early MSS read *the Only One*.

Phillips Modern English

Father has sent me. This is how the Father who has sent me has given his own personal testimony to me.

"Now you have never at any time heard what he says or seen what he is like. Nor do you really allow his word to find a home in your hearts, for you refuse to believe the man whom he has sent. You pore over the scriptures for you imagine that you will find eternal life in them. All the time they give their testimony to me, but you are not willing to come to me to have real life! I do not need the praise of men, but I can tell that you have none of the love of God in your hearts. I have come in the name of my Father and you will not accept me. Yet if another man comes simply in his own name, you will accept him. How on earth can you believe while you are for ever looking for each other's approval and not for the glory that comes from the one God? There is no need for you to think that I have come to accuse you before the Father. You already have an accuser—Moses, in whom you put all your confidence! For if you really believed Moses, you would be bound to believe me; for it was about me that he wrote. But if you do not believe what he wrote, how can you believe what I say?"

Revised Standard Version

that the father has sent me. 37And the Father
who sent me has himself borne witness to me.
His voice you have never heard, his form you
have never seen; 38 and you do not have his
word abiding in you, for you do not believe him
whom he has sent. 39 You search the scriptures, because you think that in them you have
eternal life; and it is they that bear witness to
me; 40 yet you refuse to come to me that you
may have life. 41 I do not receive glory from
men. 42 But I know that you have not the love
of God within you. 43 I have come in my Father's name, and you do not receive me; if
another comes in his own name, him you will
receive. 44 How can you believe, who receive
glory from one another and do not seek the
glory that comes from the only God? 45 Do not
think that I shall accuse you to the Father; it
is Moses who accuses you, on whom you set
your hope. 46 If you believed Moses, you would
believe me, for he wrote of me. 47 But if you
do not believe his writings, how will you believe my words?"

Jerusalem Bible

testify that the Father has sent me.
37 Besides, the Father who sent me
bears witness to me himself.
You have never heard his voice,
you have never seen his shape,
38 and his word finds no home in you
because you do not believe
in the one he has sent.

39 "You study the scriptures,
believing that in them you have eternal life;
now these same scriptures testify to me,
40 and yet you refuse to come to me for life!
41 As for human approval, this means nothing to me.
42 Besides, I know you too well:
you have no love of God in you.
43 I have come in the name of my Father
and you refuse to accept me;
if someone else comes in his own name
you will accept him.

44 How can you believe,
since you look to one another for approval
and are not concerned
with the approval that comes from the one God?
45 Do not imagine that I am going to accuse you before the Father:
you place your hopes on Moses,
and Moses will be your accuser.
46 If you really believed him
you would believe me too,
since it was I that he was writing about;
47 but if you refuse to believe what he wrote,
how can you believe what I say?"

New English Bible

hand. This testimony to me was given by the Father who sent me, although you never heard his voice, or saw his form. But his word has found no home in you, for you do not believe the one whom he sent. You study the scriptures diligently, supposing that in having them you have eternal life; yet, although their testimony points to me, you refuse to come to me for that life.

'I do not look to men for honour. But with you it is different, as I know well, for you have no love for God in you. I have come accredited by my Father, and you have no welcome for me; if another comes self-accredited you will welcome him. How can you have faith so long as you receive honour from one another, and care nothing for the honour that comes from him who alone is God? Do not imagine that I shall be your accuser at the Father's tribunal. Your accuser is Moses, the very Moses on whom you have set your hope. If you believed Moses you would believe what I tell you, for it was about me that he wrote. But if you do not believe what he wrote, how are you to believe what I say?'

King James Version

6 After these things Jesus went over the sea
of Galilee, which is *the sea* of Tiberias. 2And
a great multitude followed him, because they
saw his miracles which he did on them that were
diseased. 3And Jesus went up into a mountain,
and there he sat with his disciples. 4And the
passover, a feast of the Jews, was nigh.
5 When Jesus then lifted up *his* eyes, and saw
a great company come unto him, he saith unto
Philip, Whence shall we buy bread, that these
may eat? 6And this he said to prove him: for he
himself knew what he would do. 7 Philip answered him, Two hundred pennyworth of bread
is not sufficient for them, that every one of them
may take a little. 8 One of his disciples, Andrew,
Simon Peter's brother, saith unto him, 9 There is
a lad here, which hath five barley loaves, and
two small fishes: but what are they among so
many? 10And Jesus said, Make the men sit down.
Now there was much grass in the place. So the
men sat down, in number about five thousand.
11And Jesus took the loaves; and when he had
given thanks, he distributed to the disciples, and
the disciples to them that were set down; and
likewise of the fishes as much as they would.

Living Bible

6 After this, Jesus crossed over the Sea of
Galilee, also known as the Sea of Tiberias.
2–5And a huge crowd, many of them pilgrims
on their way to Jerusalem for the annual Passover celebration,[a] were following him wherever
he went, to watch him heal the sick. So when
Jesus went up into the hills and sat down with
his disciples around him, he soon saw a great
multitude of people climbing the hill, looking
for him.
Turning to Philip he asked, "Philip, where
can we buy bread to feed all these people?"
6 (He was testing Philip, for he already knew
what he was going to do.)
7 Philip replied, "It would take a fortune[b] to
begin to do it!"
8, 9 Then Andrew, Simon Peter's brother,
spoke up. "There's a youngster here with five
barley loaves and a couple of fish! But what
good is that with all this mob?"
10 "Tell everyone to sit down," Jesus ordered.
And all of them—the approximate count of the
men only was 5,000—sat down on the grassy
slopes. 11 Then Jesus took the loaves and gave
thanks to God and passed them out to the people. Afterwards he did the same with the fish.
And everyone ate until full!

[*a*] Literally, "Now the Passover, the feast of the Jews, was at hand." [*b*] Literally, 200 denarii, a denarius being a full day's wage.

Today's English Version

Jesus feeds the five thousand

6 After this, Jesus went back across Lake
Galilee (or, Lake Tiberias). 2A large crowd
followed him, because they had seen his mighty
works in healing the sick. 3 Jesus went up a hill
and sat down with his disciples. 4 The Passover
Feast of the Jews was near. 5 Jesus looked around
and saw that a large crowd was coming to him,
so he said to Philip, "Where can we buy enough
food to feed all these people?" 6 (He said this
to test Philip; actually he already knew what he
would do.)
7 Philip answered, "For everyone to have
even a little, it would take more than two hundred dollars' worth of bread."
8 Another one of his disciples, Andrew, Simon Peter's brother, said, 9 "There is a boy here
who has five loaves of barley bread and two fish.
But what good are they for all these people?"
10 "Make the people sit down," Jesus told
them. (There was a lot of grass there.) So all the
people sat down; there were about five thousand
men. 11 Jesus took the bread, gave thanks to
God, and distributed it to the people who were
sitting there. He did the same with the fish, and

New International Version

Jesus feeds the five thousand

6 Some time after this, Jesus crossed to the
far shore of the Sea of Galilee (that is, the
Sea of Tiberias), 2 and a great crowd of people
followed him because they saw the miraculous
signs he had performed on the sick. 3 Then Jesus went up on the hillside and sat down with
his disciples. 4 The Jewish Passover Feast was
near.
5 When Jesus looked up and saw a great
crowd coming toward him, he said to Philip,
"Where shall we buy bread for these people to
eat?" 6 He asked this only to test him, for he
already had in mind what he was going to do.
7 Philip answered him, "Eight months' wages[d]
would not buy enough bread for each one to
have a bite!"
8 Another of his disciples, Andrew, Simon Peter's brother, spoke up, 9 "Here is a boy with
five small barley loaves and two small fish, but
how far will they go among so many?"
10 Jesus said, "Have the people sit down."
There was plenty of grass in that place, and the
men sat down, above five thousand of them.
11 Jesus then took the loaves, gave thanks, and
distributed to those who were seated as much as
they wanted. He did the same with the fish.

[*d*] Greek *200 denarii.*

Phillips Modern English

6.1 Jesus shows his power over material things

After this, Jesus crossed the Lake of Galilee (or Tiberias), and a great crowd followed him because they had seen the signs which he gave in his dealings with the sick. But Jesus went up the hill-side and sat down there with his disciples. The Passover, the Jewish festival, was near. So Jesus, raising his eyes and seeing a great crowd on their way towards him, said to Philip, "Where can we buy food for these people to eat?" (He said this to test Philip, for he himself knew what he was going to do.)

"Twenty pounds' worth of bread would not be enough for them," Philip replied, "even if they had only a little each."

Then Andrew, Simon Peter's brother, another disciple, put in, "There is a boy here who has five barley loaves and a couple of fish, but what's the good of that for such a crowd?"

Then Jesus said, "Get the people to sit down."

There was plenty of grass there, and the men, some five thousand of them, sat down. Then Jesus took the loaves, gave thanks for them and distributed them to the people sitting on the grass, and he distributed the fish in the same

Revised Standard Version

6 After this Jesus went to the other side of
the Sea of Galilee, which is the Sea of
Tiberias. 2And a multitude followed him, because they saw the signs which he did on those
who were diseased. 3 Jesus went up on the mountain, and there sat down with his disciples.
4 Now the Passover, the feast of the Jews, was
at hand. 5 Lifting up his eyes, then, and seeing
that a multitude was coming to him, Jesus said
to Philip, "How are we to buy bread, so that
these people may eat?" 6 This he said to test
him, for he himself knew what he would do.
7 Philip answered him, "Two hundred denarii[l]
would not buy enough bread for each of them to
get a little." 8 One of his disciples, Andrew, Simon
Peter's brother, said to him, 9 "There is a lad
here who has five barley loaves and two fish; but
what are they among so many?" 10 Jesus said,
"Make the people sit down." Now there was
much grass in the place; so the men sat down,
in number about five thousand. 11 Jesus then
took the loaves, and when he had given thanks,
he distributed them to those who were seated;

[l] The denarius was a day's wage for a laborer.

Jerusalem Bible

IV. Another Passover, the bread of life

The miracle of the loaves

6 Some time after this, Jesus went off to the
other side of the Sea of Galilee—or of
Tiberias—2 and a large crowd followed him,
impressed by the signs he gave by curing the
sick. 3 Jesus climbed the hillside, and sat down
there with his disciples. 4 It was shortly before
the Jewish feast of Passover.
5 Looking up, Jesus saw the crowds approaching and said to Philip, "Where can we
buy some bread for these people to eat?" 6 He
only said this to test Philip; he himself knew
exactly what he was going to do. 7 Philip answered, "Two hundred denarii would only buy
enough to give them a small piece each." 8 One
of his disciples, Andrew, Simon Peter's brother,
said, 9 "There is a small boy here with five
barley loaves and two fish; but what is that between so many?" 10 Jesus said to them, "Make
the people sit down." There was plenty of grass
there, and as many as five thousand men sat
down. 11 Then Jesus took the loaves, gave
thanks, and gave them out to all who were sitting ready; he then did the same with the fish,

New English Bible

6 Some time later Jesus withdrew to the farther shore of the Sea of Galilee (or Tiberias), and a large crowd of people followed who had seen the signs he performed in healing the sick. Then Jesus went up the hill-side and sat down with his disciples. It was near the time of Passover, the great Jewish festival. Raising his eyes and seeing a large crowd coming towards him, Jesus said to Philip, 'Where are we to buy bread to feed these people?' This he said to test him; Jesus himself knew what he meant to do. Philip replied, 'Twenty pounds[a] would not buy enough bread for every one of them to have a little.' One of his disciples, Andrew, the brother of Simon Peter, said to him, 'There is a boy here who has five barley loaves and two fishes; but what is that among so many?' Jesus said, 'Make the people sit down.' There was plenty of grass there, so the men sat down, about five thousand of them. Then Jesus took the loaves, gave thanks, and distributed them to the people as they sat there. He did the same with the fishes, and they

[a] *Literally* 200 denarii.

King James Version

12 When they were filled, he said unto his disciples, Gather up the fragments that remain, that nothing be lost. 13 Therefore they gathered *them* together, and filled twelve baskets with the fragments of the five barley loaves, which remained over and above unto them that had eaten. 14 Then those men, when they had seen the miracle that Jesus did, said, This is of a truth that Prophet that should come into the world.

15 When Jesus therefore perceived that they would come and take him by force, to make him a king, he departed again into a mountain himself alone. 16 And when even was *now* come, his disciples went down unto the sea, 17 And entered into a ship, and went over the sea toward Capernaum. And it was now dark, and Jesus was not come to them. 18 And the sea arose by reason of a great wind that blew. 19 So when they had rowed about five and twenty or thirty furlongs, they see Jesus walking on the sea, and drawing nigh unto the ship: and they were afraid. 20 But he saith unto them, It is I; be not afraid. 21 Then they willingly received him into the ship: and immediately the ship was at the land whither they went.

22 The day following, when the people, which stood on the other side of the sea, saw that

Living Bible

12 "Now gather the scraps," Jesus told his disciples, "so that nothing is wasted." 13 And twelve baskets were filled with the leftovers!

14 When the people realized what a great miracle had happened, they exclaimed, "Surely, he is the Prophet we have been expecting!"

15 Jesus saw that they were ready to take him by force and make him their king, so he went higher into the mountains alone.

16 That evening his disciples went down to the shore to wait for him. 17 But as darkness fell and Jesus still hadn't come back, they got into the boat and headed out across the lake toward Capernaum. 18, 19 But soon a gale swept down upon them as they rowed, and the sea grew very rough. They were three or four miles out when suddenly they saw Jesus walking toward the boat! They were terrified, 20 but he called out to them and told them not to be afraid. 21 Then they were willing to let him in, and immediately the boat was where they were going! [c]

22, 23 The next morning, back across the lake, crowds began gathering on the shore [wait-

[c] Literally, "and straightway the boat was at the land. . . ."

Today's English Version

they all had as much as they wanted. 12 When they were all full, he said to his disciples, "Pick up the pieces left over; let us not waste a bit." 13 So they took them all up, and filled twelve baskets with the pieces left over from the five barley loaves which the people had eaten.

14 The people there, seeing this mighty work that Jesus had done, said, "Surely this is the Prophet who was to come to the world!" 15 Jesus knew that they were about to come and get him, to make him king by force; so he went off again to the hills by himself.

Jesus walks on the water

16 When evening came, his disciples went down to the lake, 17 got into the boat, and went back across the lake toward Capernaum. Night came on, and Jesus still had not come to them. 18 By now a strong wind was blowing and stirring up the water. 19 The disciples had rowed about three or four miles when they saw Jesus walking on the water, coming near the boat, and they were terrified. 20 "Don't be afraid," Jesus told them, "it is I!" 21 They were willing to take him into the boat; and immediately the boat reached land at the place they were heading for.

The people seek Jesus

22 Next day the crowd which had stayed on the other side of the lake saw that only one boat

New International Version

12 When they had all had enough to eat, he said to his disciples, "Gather the pieces that are left over. Let nothing be wasted." 13 So they gathered them and filled twelve baskets with the pieces of the five barley loaves left over by those who had eaten.

14 After the people saw the miraculous sign that Jesus did, they began to say, "Surely this is the Prophet who is to come into the world." 15 Jesus, knowing that they intended to come and make him king by force, withdrew again into the hills by himself.

Jesus walks on the water

16 When evening came, his disciples went down to the lake, 17 where they got into a boat and set off across the lake for Capernaum. By now it was dark, and Jesus had not yet joined them. 18 A strong wind was blowing and the waters grew rough. 19 When they had rowed three or four miles, they saw Jesus approaching the boat, walking on the water; and they were terrified. 20 But he said to them, "It is I; don't be afraid." 21 Then they were willing to take him into the boat, and immediately the boat reached the shore where they were heading.

22 The next day the crowd that had stayed on the opposite shore of the lake realized that only

Phillips Modern English

way, giving them as much as they wanted. When they had eaten enough, Jesus said to his disciples, "Collect the pieces that are left over so that nothing is wasted."

So they did as he suggested and filled twelve baskets with the broken pieces of the five barley loaves, which were left over after the people had eaten. When the men saw this sign of Jesus' power, they kept saying, "This is surely the Prophet who was to come into the world!"

Then Jesus, realising that they were going to carry him off and make him their king by force, retired once more to the hill-side quite alone.

In the evening, his disciples went down to the lake, embarked on the boat and made their way across the lake to Capernaum. Darkness had already fallen and Jesus had not yet returned to them. A strong wind sprang up and the water grew very rough. When they had rowed about three or four miles, they saw Jesus walking on the water and coming towards the boat, and they were terrified. But he spoke to them, "Don't be afraid: it is I myself."

So they gladly took him aboard, and at once the boat reached the shore they were making for.

6.22 Jesus teaches about the true bread

The following day, the crowd, who had remained on the other side of the lake, noticed

Revised Standard Version

so also the fish, as much as they wanted. 12 And
when they had eaten their fill, he told his disciples, "Gather up the fragments left over, that
nothing may be lost." 13 So they gathered them
up and filled twelve baskets with fragments from the five barley loaves, left by those who had
eaten. 14 When the people saw the sign which
he had done, they said, "This is indeed the prophet who is to come into the world!"
15 Perceiving then that they were about to come and take him by force to make him king, Jesus withdrew again to the mountan by himself.
16 When evening came, his disciples went
down to the sea, 17 got into a boat, and started
across the sea to Capernaum. It was now dark, and Jesus had not yet come to them. 18 The sea
rose because a strong wind was blowing. 19 When
they had rowed about three or four miles,[m] they saw Jesus walking on the sea and drawing near to the boat. They were frightened, 20 but he
said to them, "It is I; do not be afraid." 21 Then
they were glad to take him into the boat, and immediately the boat was at the land to which they were going.
22 On the next day the people who remained on the other side of the sea saw that there had

[m] Greek *twenty-five or thirty stadia.*

Jerusalem Bible

giving out as much as was wanted. 12 When
they had eaten enough he said to the disciples, "Pick up the pieces left over, so that nothing
gets wasted." 13 So they picked them up, and filled twelve hampers with scraps left over from
the meal of five barley loaves. 14 The people,
seeing this sign that he had given, said, "This really is the prophet who is to come into the
world." 15 Jesus, who could see they were about to come and take him by force and make him king, escaped back to the hills by himself.

Jesus walks on the waters

16 That evening the disciples went down to
the shore of the lake and 17 got into a boat to
make for Capernaum on the other side of the lake. It was getting dark by now and Jesus had
still not rejoined them. 18 The wind was strong,
and the sea was getting rough. 19 They had
rowed three or four miles when they saw Jesus walking on the lake and coming toward the
boat. This frightened them, 20 but he said, "It
is I. Do not be afraid." 21 They were for taking
him into the boat, but in no time it reached the shore at the place they were making for.

The discourse in the synagogue at Capernaum

22 Next day, the crowd that had stayed on the other side saw that only one boat had been

New English Bible

had as much as they wanted. When everyone had had enough, he said to his disciples, 'Collect the pieces left over, so that nothing may be lost.' This they did, and filled twelve baskets with the pieces left uneaten of the five barley loaves.

When the people saw the sign Jesus had performed, the word went round, 'Surely this must be the prophet that was to come into the world.' Jesus, aware that they meant to come and seize him to proclaim him king, withdrew again to the hills by himself.

At nightfall his disciples went down to the sea, got into their boat, and pushed off to cross the water to Capernaum. Darkness had already fallen, and Jesus had not yet joined them. By now a strong wind was blowing and the sea grew rough. When they had rowed about three or four miles they saw Jesus walking on the sea and approaching the boat. They were terrified, but he called out, 'It is I; do not be afraid.' Then they were ready to take him aboard, and immediately the boat reached the land they were making for.

Next morning the crowd was standing on the opposite shore. They had seen only one boat

King James Version

there was none other boat there, save that one whereinto his disciples were entered, and that Jesus went not with his disciples into the boat, but *that* his disciples were gone away alone;
23 Howbeit there came other boats from Tiberias nigh unto the place where they did eat bread, after that the Lord had given thanks:
24 When the people therefore saw that Jesus was not there, neither his disciples, they also took shipping, and came to Capernaum, seeking for Jesus.
25 And when they had found him on the other side of the sea, they said unto him, Rabbi, when camest thou hither?
26 Jesus answered them and said, Verily, verily, I say unto you, Ye seek me, not because ye saw the miracles, but because ye did eat of the loaves, and were filled.
27 Labour not for the meat which perisheth, but for that meat which endureth unto everlasting life, which the Son of man shall give unto you: for him hath God the Father sealed.
28 Then said they unto him, What shall we do, that we might work the works of God?
29 Jesus answered and said unto them, This is the work of God, that ye believe on him whom he hath sent.
30 They said therefore unto him, What sign shewest thou then, that we may see, and believe thee? what dost thou work?
31 Our fathers did eat manna in the desert; as it is written, He gave them bread from heaven to eat.
32 Then Jesus said unto them,

Living Bible

ing to see Jesus[d]]. For they knew that he and his disciples had come over together and that the disciples had gone off in their boat, leaving him behind. Several small boats from Tiberias were nearby,
24 so when the people saw that Jesus wasn't there, nor his disciples, they got into the boats and went across to Capernaum to look for him.

25 When they arrived and found him, they said, "Sir, how did you get here?"
26 Jesus replied, "The truth of the matter is that you want to be with me because I fed you, not because you believe in me.
27 But you shouldn't be so concerned about perishable things like food. No, spend your energy seeking the eternal life that I, the Messiah,[e] can give you. For God the Father has sent me for this very purpose."

28 They replied, "What should we do to satisfy God?"

29 Jesus told them, "This is the will of God, that you believe in the one he has sent."

30, 31 They replied, "You must show us more miracles if you want us to believe you are the Messiah. Give us free bread every day, like our fathers had while they journeyed through the wilderness! As the Scriptures say, 'Moses gave them bread from heaven.' "

32 Jesus said, "Moses didn't give it to them.

[*d*] Implied. [*e*] Literally, "the Son of Man."

Today's English Version

was left there. They knew that Jesus had not gone in the boat with his disciples, but that they had left without him.
23 Other boats, from Tiberias, came to shore near the place where the crowd had eaten the bread, after the Lord had given thanks.
24 When the crowd saw that Jesus was not there, nor his disciples, they got into boats and went to Capernaum, looking for him.

Jesus the bread of life

25 When the people found Jesus on the other side of the lake they said to him, "Teacher, when did you get here?"

26 Jesus answered, "I tell you the truth: you are looking for me because you ate the bread and had all you wanted, not because you understood my works of power.
27 Do not work for food that spoils; instead, work for the food that lasts for eternal life. This food the Son of Man will give you, because God, the Father, has put his mark of approval on him."

28 So they asked him, "What can we do in order to do God's works?"

29 Jesus answered, "This is the work God wants you to do: believe in the one he sent."

30 They replied, "What sign of power will you perform so that we may see it and believe you? What will you do?
31 Our ancestors ate manna in the desert, just as the scripture says, 'He gave them bread from heaven to eat.' "

32 "I tell you the truth," Jesus said. "What

New International Version

one boat had been there, and that Jesus had not entered it with his disciples, but that they had gone away alone.
23 Then some boats from Tiberias landed near the place where the people had eaten the bread after the Lord had given thanks.
24 Once the crowd realized that neither Jesus nor his disciples were there, they got into the boats and went to Capernaum in search of Jesus.

Jesus the bread of life

25 When they found him on the other side of the lake, they asked him, "Rabbi, when did you get here?"

26 Jesus answered, "I tell you the truth, you are looking for me, not because you saw miraculous signs but because you ate the loaves and had your fill.
27 Do not work for food that spoils, but for food that endures to eternal life, which the Son of Man will give you. On him God the Father has placed his seal of approval."

28 Then they asked him, "What must we do to do the work of God?"

29 Jesus answered, "The work of God is this: to believe in the one whom he has sent."

30 So they asked him, "What miraculous sign then will you give that we may see it and believe you? What will you do?
31 Our forefathers ate the manna in the desert; as it is written: 'He gave them bread from heaven to eat.'[e] "

32 Jesus said to them, "I tell you the truth,

[*e*] Exodus 16:4; Psalm 78:24.

Phillips Modern English

that only the one boat had been there, and that Jesus had not embarked on it with his disciples, but that they had in fact gone off by themselves. Some other small boats from Tiberias had landed near the place where they had eaten the food and the Lord had given thanks. When the crowd realised that neither Jesus nor the disciples were there any longer, they themselves went aboard the boats and went off to Capernaum to look for Jesus. When they had found him on the other side of the lake, they said to him, "Rabbi, when did you come here?"

"Believe me," replied Jesus, "when I tell you that you are looking for me now not because you saw my signs but because you ate that food and had all you wanted. You should not work for the food which does not last but for the food which lasts on into eternal life. This is the food the Son of Man will give you, and he is the one who bears the stamp of God the Father."

This made them ask him, "What must we do to carry out the work of God?"

"The work of God for you," replied Jesus, "is to believe in the one whom he has sent to you."

Then they asked him, "Then what sign can you give us that will make us believe in you? What work are you doing? Our forefathers ate manna in the desert just as the scripture says,

He gave them bread out of Heaven to eat."

To which Jesus replied, "That is true indeed,

Revised Standard Version

been only one boat there, and that Jesus had
not entered the boat with his disciples, but that
his disciples had gone away alone. 23 However,
boats from Tiberias came near the place where
they ate the bread after the Lord had given
thanks. 24 So when the people saw that Jesus was
not there, nor his disciples, they themselves got
into the boats and went to Capernaum, seeking
Jesus.
25 When they found him on the other side of
the sea, they said to him, "Rabbi, when did you
come here?" 26 Jesus answered them, "Truly,
truly, I say to you, you seek me, not because
you saw signs, but because you ate your fill of
the loaves. 27 Do not labor for the food which
perishes, but for the food which endures to
eternal life, which the Son of man will give to
you; for on him has God the Father set his seal."
28 Then they said to him, "What must we do, to
be doing the works of God?" 29 Jesus answered
them, "This is the work of God, that you believe
in him whom he has sent." 30 So they said to
him, "Then what sign do you do, that we may
see, and believe you? What work do you perform? 31 Our fathers ate the manna in the wilderness; as it is written, 'He gave them bread
from heaven to eat.' " 32 Jesus then said to them,

Jerusalem Bible

there, and that Jesus had not got into the boat
with his disciples, but that the disciples had set
off by themselves. 23 Other boats, however, had
put in from Tiberias, near the place where the
bread had been eaten. 24 When the people saw
that neither Jesus nor his disciples were there,
they got into those boats and crossed to Capernaum to look for Jesus. 25 When they found
him on the other side, they said to him, "Rabbi,
when did you come here?" 26 Jesus answered:

"I tell you most solemnly,
you are not looking for me
because you have seen the signs
but because you had all the bread you wanted to eat.
27 Do not work for food that cannot last,
but work for food that endures to eternal life,
the kind of food the Son of Man is offering you,
for on him the Father, God himself, has set his seal."

28 Then they said to him, "What must we do
if we are to do the works that God wants?"
29 Jesus gave them this answer, "This is working
for God: you must believe in the one he has
sent." 30 So they said, "What sign will you give
to show us that we should believe in you? What
work will you do? 31 Our fathers had manna to
eat in the desert; as scripture says: *He gave them bread from heaven to eat.*" [p]
32 Jesus answered:

[*p*] Ex. 16:4f.

New English Bible

there, and Jesus, they knew, had not embarked with his disciples, who had gone away without him. Boats from Tiberias, however, came ashore[a] near the place where the people had eaten the bread over which the Lord gave thanks.[b] When the people saw that neither Jesus nor his disciples were any longer there, they themselves went aboard these boats and made for Capernaum in search of Jesus. They found him on the other side. 'Rabbi,' they said, 'when did you come here?' Jesus replied, 'In very truth I know that you have not come looking for me because you saw signs, but because you ate the bread and your hunger was satisfied. You must work, not for this perishable food, but for the food that lasts, the food of eternal life.

'This food the Son of Man will give you, for he it is upon whom God the Father has set the seal of his authority.' 'Then what must we do', they asked him, 'if we are to work as God would have us work?' Jesus replied, 'This is the work that God requires: believe in the one whom he has sent.'

They said, 'What sign can you give us to see, so that we may believe you? What is the work you do? Our ancestors had manna to eat in the desert; as Scripture says, "He gave them bread from heaven to eat." ' Jesus answered, 'I tell you

[*a*] *Some witnesses read* Other boats from Tiberias came ashore . . . [*b*] *Some witnesses omit* over which . . . thanks.

King James Version

Verily, verily, I say unto you, Moses gave you
not that bread from heaven; but my Father
giveth you the true bread from heaven. 33 For
the bread of God is he which cometh down from
heaven, and giveth life unto the world. 34 Then
said they unto him, Lord, evermore give us this
bread. 35And Jesus said unto them, I am the
bread of life: he that cometh to me shall never
hunger; and he that believeth on me shall never
thirst. 36 But I said unto you, That ye also have
seen me, and believe not. 37All that the Father
giveth me shall come to me; and him that
cometh to me I will in no wise cast out. 38 For
I came down from heaven, not to do mine own
will, but the will of him that sent me. 39And
this is the Father's will which hath sent me, that
of all which he hath given me I should lose
nothing, but should raise it up again at the last
day. 40And this is the will of him that sent me,
that every one which seeth the Son, and believeth
on him, may have everlasting life: and I will raise

Living Bible

My Father did.[d] And now he offers you true
Bread from heaven. 33 The true Bread is a Person—the one sent by God from heaven, and he
gives life to the world."
34 "Sir," they said, "give us that bread every
day of our lives!"
35 Jesus replied, "I am the Bread of Life.
No one coming to me will ever be hungry again.
Those believing in me will never thirst. 36 But
the trouble is, as I have told you before, you
haven't believed even though you have seen me.
37 But some will come to me—those the Father
has given me—and I will never, never reject
them. 38 For I have come here from heaven to
do the will of God who sent me, not to have
my own way. 39And this is the will of God, that
I should not lose even one of all those he has
given me, but that I should raise them to eternal life at the Last Day. 40 For it is my Father's
will that everyone who sees his Son and believes
on him should have eternal life—that I should
raise him at the Last Day."

[d] Implied.

Today's English Version

Moses gave you was not the bread from heaven;
it is my Father who gives you the real bread from
heaven. 33 For the bread that God gives is he
who comes down from heaven and gives life to
the world."
34 "Sir," they asked him, "give us this bread
always."
35 "I am the bread of life," Jesus told them.
"He who comes to me will never be hungry; he
who believes in me will never be thirsty. 36 Now,
I told you that you have seen me but will not
believe. 37 Everyone whom my Father gives me
will come to me. I will never turn away anyone
who comes to me, 38 because I have come down
from heaven to do the will of him who sent me,
not my own will. 39 He who sent me wants me
to do this: that I should not lose any of all those
he has given me, but that I should raise them all
to life on the last day. 40 For what my Father
wants is this: that all who see the Son and believe in him should have eternal life; and I will
raise them to life on the last day."

New International Version

it is not Moses who has given you the bread
from heaven, but it is my Father who gives you
the true bread from heaven. 33 For the bread of
God is he who comes down from heaven and
gives life to the world."
34 "Sir," they said, "from now on give us this
bread."
35 Then Jesus declared, "I am the bread of
life. He who comes to me will never go hungry,
and he who believes in me will never be thirsty.
36 But as I told you, you have seen me and still
you do not believe. 37All that the Father gives
me will come to me, and whoever comes to me
I will never drive away. 38 For I have come
down from heaven not to do my will but to do
the will of him who sent me. 39And this is the
will of him who sent me, that I shall lose none
of all that he has given me, but raise them up
at the last day. 40 For my Father's will is that
everyone who looks to the Son and believes in
him shall have eternal life, and I will raise him
up at the last day."

Phillips Modern English

but what matters is not that Moses *gave you* bread from Heaven but that my Father is *giving you* the true bread from Heaven. For the bread of God which comes down from Heaven gives life to the world."

This made them say to him, "Lord, please give us this bread, now and always!"

Then Jesus said to them, "I myself am the bread of life. The man who comes to me will never be hungry and the man who believes in me will never be thirsty. Yet I have told you that you have seen me and do not believe. Everything that my Father gives me will come to me and I will never refuse anyone who comes to me. For I have come down from Heaven, not to do what I want, but to do the will of him who sent me. The will of him who sent me is that I should not lose anything of what he has given me, but should raise it up when the last day comes. And this is the will of the One who sent me, that everyone who sees the Son and trusts him should have eternal life, and I will raise him up when the last day comes."

Revised Standard Version

"Truly, truly, I say to you, it was not Moses who
gave you the bread from heaven; my Father
gives you the true bread from heaven. 33 For
the bread of God is that which comes down from
heaven, and gives life to the world." 34 They said
to him, "Lord, give us this bread always."
35 Jesus said to them, "I am the bread of life;
he who comes to me shall not hunger, and he
who believes in me shall never thirst. 36 But I
said to you that you have seen me and yet do not
believe. 37 All that the Father gives me will come
to me; and him who comes to me I will not cast
out. 38 For I have come down from heaven, not
to do my own will, but the will of him who sent
me; 39 and this is the will of him who sent me,
that I should lose nothing of all that he has
given me, but raise it up at the last day. 40 For
this is the will of my Father, that every one who
sees the Son and believes in him should have
eternal life; and I will raise him up at the last
day."

Jerusalem Bible

"I tell you most solemnly,
it was not Moses who gave you bread from heaven,
it is my Father who gives you the bread from heaven,
the true bread;
33 for the bread of God
is that which comes down from heaven
and gives life to the world."

34 "Sir," they said, "give us that bread always." 35 Jesus answered:

"I am the bread of life.
He who comes to me will never be hungry;
he who believes in me will never thirst.
36 But, as I have told you,
you can see me and still you do not believe.
37 All that the Father gives me will come to me,
and whoever comes to me
I shall not turn him away;
38 because I have come from heaven,
not to do my own will,
but to do the will of the one who sent me.
39 Now the will of him who sent me
is that I should lose nothing
of all that he has given to me,
and that I should raise it up on the last day.
40 Yes, it is my Father's will
that whoever sees the Son and believes in him
shall have eternal life,
and that I shall raise him up on the last day."

New English Bible

this: the truth is, not that Moses gave you the bread from heaven, but that my Father gives you the real bread from heaven. The bread that God gives comes down[c] from heaven and brings life to the world.' They said to him, 'Sir, give us this bread now and always.' Jesus said to them, 'I am the bread of life. Whoever comes to me shall never be hungry, and whoever believes in me shall never be thirsty. But you, as I said, do not believe although you have seen.[d] All that the Father gives me will come to me, and the man who comes to me I will never turn away. I have come down from heaven, not to do my own will, but the will of him who sent me. It is his will that I should not lose even one of all that he has given me, but raise them all up on the last day. For it is my Father's will that everyone who looks upon the Son and puts his faith in him shall possess eternal life; and I will raise him up on the last day.'

[c] *Or* is he who comes down . . . [d] *Some witnesses add* me.

King James Version

him up at the last day. 41 The Jews then murmured at him, because he said, I am the bread
which came down from heaven. 42 And they said,
Is not this Jesus, the son of Joseph, whose father
and mother we know? how is it then that he
saith, I came down from heaven? 43 Jesus therefore answered and said unto them, Murmur not
among yourselves. 44 No man can come to me,
except the Father which hath sent me draw him:
and I will raise him up at the last day. 45 It is
written in the prophets, And they shall be all
taught of God. Every man therefore that hath
heard, and hath learned of the Father, cometh
unto me. 46 Not that any man hath seen the
Father, save he which is of God, he hath seen
the Father. 47 Verily, verily, I say unto you, He
that believeth on me hath everlasting life. 48 I am
that bread of life. 49 Your fathers did eat manna
in the wilderness, and are dead. 50 This is the
bread which cometh down from heaven, that a
man may eat thereof, and not die. 51 I am the
living bread which came down from heaven: if
any man eat of this bread, he shall live for ever:
and the bread that I will give is my flesh, which

Living Bible

41 Then the Jews began to murmur against
him because he claimed to be the bread from
heaven.
42 "What?" they exclaimed. "Why, he is
merely Jesus the son of Joseph, whose father
and mother we know. What is this he is saying,
that he came down from heaven?"
43 But Jesus replied, "Don't murmur among
yourselves about my saying that. 44 For no one
can come to me unless the Father who sent me
draws him to me, and at the Last Day I will
cause all such to rise again from the dead. 45 As
it is written in the Scriptures, 'They shall all be
taught of God.' Those the Father speaks to, who
learn the truth from him, will be attracted to me.
46 (Not that anyone actually sees the Father, for
only I have seen him.)
47 "How earnestly I tell you this—anyone
who believes in me already has eternal life!
48–51 Yes, I am the Bread of Life! When your
fathers in the wilderness ate bread from the
skies, they all died. But the Bread from heaven
gives eternal life to everyone who eats it. I am
that Living Bread that came down out of heaven.
Anyone eating this Bread shall live forever; this
Bread is my flesh given to redeem humanity."

Today's English Version

41 The Jews started grumbling about him, because he said, "I am the bread that came down
from heaven." 42 So they said, "This man is
Jesus the son of Joseph, isn't he? We know his
father and mother. How, then, does he now say
he came down from heaven?"
43 Jesus answered, "Stop grumbling among
yourselves. 44 No one can come to me unless the
Father who sent me draws him to me; and I
will raise him to life on the last day. 45 The
prophets wrote, 'All men will be taught by God.'
Everyone who hears the Father and learns from
him comes to me. 46 This does not mean that
anyone has seen the Father; he who is from God
is the only one who has seen the Father. 47 I tell
you the truth: he who believes has eternal life.
48 I am the bread of life. 49 Your ancestors ate
the manna in the desert, but they died. 50 But
the bread that comes down from heaven is such
that whoever eats it will not die. 51 I am the
living bread that came down from heaven. If
anyone eats this bread he will live forever. The
bread that I will give him is my flesh, which I
give so that the world may live."

New International Version

41 At this the Jews began to murmur against
him because he said, "I am the bread that came
down from heaven." 42 They said, "Is this not
Jesus, the son of Joseph, whose father and
mother we know? How can he now say, 'I came
down from heaven'?"
43 "Stop murmuring among yourselves," Jesus answered. 44 "No one can come to me unless
the Father who sent me draws him, and I will
raise him up at the last day. 45 It is written in
the Prophets: 'They will all be taught by God.' [f]
Everyone who listens to the Father and learns
from him comes to me. 46 No one has seen the
Father except the one who is from God; only he
has seen the Father. 47 I tell you the truth, he
who believes has everlasting life. 48 I am the
bread of life. 49 Your forefathers ate the manna
in the desert, yet they died. 50 But here is the
bread that comes down from heaven, which a
man may eat and not die. 51 I am the living
bread that came down from heaven. If a man
eats of this bread, he will live forever. This
bread is my flesh, which I will give for the life
of the world."

[f] Isaiah 54:13.

Phillips Modern English

At this, the Jews began grumbling at him because he said, "I am the bread which came down from Heaven", remarking "Is not this Jesus, the son of Joseph, whose parents we know? How can he now say that 'I have come down from Heaven'?"

So Jesus answered them, "Do not grumble among yourselves. Nobody comes to me unless he is drawn to me by the Father who sent me, and I will raise him up when the last day comes. In the Prophets it is written—

'And they shall all be taught of God,'

and this means that everybody who has heard the Father's voice and learned from him will come to me. Not that anyone has ever seen the Father except the one who comes from God—he alone has seen the Father. I solemnly assure you that the man who trusts in him has eternal life already. I myself am the bread of life. Your forefathers ate manna in the desert, *and they died*. This is bread that comes down from Heaven, so that a man may eat it and never die. I myself am the living bread which came down from Heaven, and if anyone eats this bread he will live for ever. The bread which I will give is my own body and I shall give it for the life of the world."

Revised Standard Version

41 The Jews then murmured at him, because
he said, "I am the bread which came down from
heaven." 42 They said, "Is not this Jesus, the son
of Joseph, whose father and mother we know?
How does he now say, 'I have come down from
heaven'?" 43 Jesus answered them, "Do not murmur among yourselves. 44 No one can come to
me unless the Father who sent me draws him;
and I will raise him up at the last day. 45 It is
written in the prophets, 'And they shall all be
taught by God.' Every one who has heard and
learned from the Father comes to me. 46 Not
that any one has seen the Father except him
who is from God; he has seen the Father.
47 Truly, truly, I say to you, he who believes has
eternal life. 48 I am the bread of life. 49 Your
fathers ate the manna in the wilderness, and they
died. 50 This is the bread which comes down
from heaven, that a man may eat of it and not
die. 51 I am the living bread which came down
from heaven; if any one eats of this bread, he
will live for ever; and the bread which I shall
give for the life of the world is my flesh."

Jerusalem Bible

41 Meanwhile the Jews were complaining to
each other about him, because he had said, "I
am the bread that came down from heaven."
42 "Surely this is Jesus son of Joseph," they said.
"We know his father and mother. How can he
now say, 'I have come down from heaven'?"
43 Jesus said in reply, "Stop complaining to each
other.

44 "No one can come to me
unless he is drawn by the Father who sent me,
and I will raise him up at the last day.
45 It is written in the prophets:
They will all be taught by God,[q]
and to hear the teaching of the Father,
and learn from it,
is to come to me.
46 Not that anybody has seen the Father,
except the one who comes from God:
he has seen the Father.
47 I tell you most solemnly,
everybody who believes has eternal life.
48 I am the bread of life.
49 Your fathers ate the manna in the desert
and they are dead;
50 but this is the bread that comes down from heaven,
so that a man may eat it and not die.
51 I am the living bread which has come down from heaven.
Anyone who eats this bread will live for ever;
and the bread that I shall give
is my flesh, for the life of the world."

[q] Is. 54:13.

New English Bible

At this the Jews began to murmur disapprovingly because he said, 'I am the bread which came down from heaven.' They said, 'Surely this is Jesus son of Joseph; we know his father and mother. How can he now say, "I have come down from heaven"?' Jesus answered, 'Stop murmuring among yourselves. No man can come to me unless he is drawn by the Father who sent me; and I will raise him up on the last day. It is written in the prophets: "And they shall all be taught by God." Everyone who has listened to the Father and learned from him comes to me.

'I do not mean that anyone has seen the Father. He who has come from God has seen the Father, and he alone. In truth, in very truth I tell you, the believer possesses eternal life. I am the bread of life. Your forefathers ate the manna in the desert and they are dead. I am speaking of the bread that comes down from heaven, which a man may eat, and never die. I am that living bread which has come down from heaven; if anyone eats this bread he shall live for ever. Moreover, the bread which I will give is my own flesh; I give it for the life of the world.'

King James Version

I will give for the life of the world. 52 The Jews
therefore strove among themselves, saying, How
can this man give us *his* flesh to eat? 53 Then
Jesus said unto them, Verily, verily, I say unto
you, Except ye eat the flesh of the Son of man,
and drink his blood, ye have no life in you.
54 Whoso eateth my flesh, and drinketh my
blood, hath eternal life; and I will raise him up
at the last day. 55 For my flesh is meat indeed,
and my blood is drink indeed. 56 He that eateth
my flesh, and drinketh my blood, dwelleth in
me, and I in him. 57 As the living Father hath
sent me, and I live by the Father; so he that
eateth me, even he shall live by me. 58 This is
that bread which came down from heaven: not
as your fathers did eat manna, and are dead: he
that eateth of this bread shall live for ever.
59 These things said he in the synagogue, as he
taught in Capernaum. 60 Many therefore of his
disciples, when they had heard *this,* said, This is
a hard saying; who can hear it? 61 When Jesus
knew in himself that his disciples murmured at
it, he said unto them, Doth this offend you?
62 *What* and if ye shall see the Son of man as-

Living Bible

52 Then the Jews began arguing with each
other about what he meant. "How can this man
give us his flesh to eat?" they asked.
53 So Jesus said it again, "With all the earnestness I possess I tell you this: Unless you eat
the flesh of the Messiah[f] and drink his blood,
you cannot have eternal life within you. 54 But
anyone who does eat my flesh and drink my
blood has eternal life, and I will raise him at
the Last Day. 55 For my flesh is the true food,
and my blood is the true drink. 56 Everyone who
eats my flesh and drinks my blood is in me, and
I in him. 57 I live by the power of the living
Father who sent me, and in the same way those
who partake of me shall live because of me!
58 I am the true Bread from heaven; and anyone who eats this Bread shall live forever, and
not die as your fathers did—though they ate
bread from heaven." 59 (He preached this sermon in the synagogue in Capernaum.)
60 Even his disciples said, "This is very hard
to understand. Who can tell what he means?"
61 Jesus knew within himself that his disciples
were complaining and said to them, "Does *this*
offend you? 62 Then what will you think if you
see me, the Messiah,[g] return to heaven again?

[*f*] Implied. Literally, "Son of Man." [*g*] Literally, "the Son of Man."

Today's English Version

52 This started an angry argument among the
Jews. "How can this man give us his flesh to
eat?" they asked.
53 Jesus said to them, "I tell you the truth: if
you do not eat the flesh of the Son of Man and
drink his blood you will not have life in yourselves. 54 Whoever eats my flesh and drinks my
blood has eternal life, and I will raise him to
life on the last day. 55 For my flesh is the real
food, my blood is the real drink. 56 Whoever eats
my flesh and drinks my blood lives in me and I
live in him. 57 The living Father sent me, and because of him I live also. In the same way, whoever eats me will live because of me. 58 This,
then, is the bread that came down from heaven;
it is not like the bread that your ancestors ate,
but then died. The one who eats this bread will
live forever."
59 Jesus said this as he taught in the synagogue in Capernaum.

The words of eternal life

60 Many of his disciples heard this and said,
"This teaching is too hard. Who can listen to
this?"
61 Without being told, Jesus knew that his
disciples were grumbling about this; so he said to
them, "Does this make you want to give up?
62 Suppose, then, that you should see the Son of
Man go back up to the place where he was be-

New International Version

52 Then the Jews began to argue sharply
among themselves, "How can this man give us
his flesh to eat?"
53 Jesus said to them, "I tell you the truth,
unless you eat the flesh of the Son of Man and
drink his blood, you have no life in you. 54 Whoever eats my flesh and drinks my blood has
eternal life, and I will raise him up at the last
day. 55 For my flesh is real food and my blood
is real drink. 56 Whoever eats my flesh and
drinks my blood remains in me, and I in him.
57 Just as the living Father sent me and I live
because of the Father, so the one who feeds on
me will live because of me. 58 This is the bread
that came down from heaven. Our forefathers
ate [manna] and died, but he who feeds on this
bread will live forever." 59 He said this while
teaching in the synagogue in Capernaum.

Many disciples desert Jesus

60 On hearing it, many of his disciples said,
"This is a hard teaching. Who can accept it?"
61 Aware that his disciples were grumbling
about this, Jesus said to them, "Does this offend
you? 62 What if you see the Son of Man ascend

Phillips Modern English

This led to a fierce argument among the Jews, some of them saying, "How can this man give us his body to eat?"

So Jesus said to them, "Unless you do eat the body of the Son of Man and drink his blood, I assure you that you are not really living at all. The man who eats my flesh and drinks my blood has eternal life and I will raise him up when the last day comes. For my body is real food and my blood is real drink. The man who eats my body and drinks my blood shares my life and I share his. Just as the living Father sent me and I am alive because of the Father, so the man who lives on me will live because of me. *This* is the bread which came down from Heaven! It is not like the manna which your forefathers used to eat, *and died.* The man who eats this bread will live for ever."

Jesus said all these things while teaching in the synagogue at Capernaum. Many of his disciples heard him say these things, and commented, "This is hard teaching indeed; who could accept that?"

Then Jesus, knowing intuitively that his disciples were complaining about what he had just said, went on, "Is this too much for you? Then what would happen if you were to see the Son of Man going up to the place where he was be-

Revised Standard Version

52 The Jews then disputed among themselves,
saying, "How can this man give us his flesh to
eat?" 53 So Jesus said to them, "Truly, truly, I
say to you, unless you eat the flesh of the Son
of man and drink his blood, you have no life
in you; 54 he who eats my flesh and drinks my
blood has eternal life, and I will raise him up
at the last day. 55 For my flesh is food indeed,
and my blood is drink indeed. 56 He who eats
my flesh and drinks my blood abides in me, and
I in him. 57 As the living Father sent me, and I
live because of the Father, so he who eats me
will live because of me. 58 This is the bread
which came down from heaven, not such as the
fathers ate and died; he who eats this bread will
live for ever." 59 This he said in the synagogue,
as he taught at Capernaum.

60 Many of his disciples, when they heard it,
said, "This is a hard saying; who can listen to
it?" 61 But Jesus, knowing in himself that his
disciples murmured at it, said to them, "Do you
take offense at this? 62 Then what if you were
to see the Son of man ascending where he was

Jerusalem Bible

52 Then the Jews started arguing with one another: "How can this man give us his flesh to
eat?" they said. 53 Jesus replied:

"I tell you most solemnly,
if you do not eat the flesh of the Son of Man
and drink his blood,
you will not have life in you.
54 Anyone who does eat my flesh and drink my blood
has eternal life,
and I shall raise him up on the last day.
55 For my flesh is real food
and my blood is real drink.
56 He who eats my flesh and drinks my blood lives in me
and I live in him.
57 As I, who am sent by the living Father,
myself draw life from the Father,
so whoever eats me will draw life from me.
58 This is the bread come down from heaven;
not like the bread our ancestors ate:
they are dead,
but anyone who eats this bread will live for ever."

59 He taught this doctrine at Capernaum, in
the synagogue. 60 After hearing it, many of his
followers said, "This is intolerable language. How
could anyone accept it?" 61 Jesus was aware that
his followers were complaining about it and
said, "Does this upset you? 62 What if you
should see the Son of Man ascend to where he
was before?

New English Bible

This led to a fierce dispute among the Jews. 'How can this man give us his flesh to eat?' they said. Jesus replied, 'In truth, in very truth I tell you, unless you eat the flesh of the Son of Man and drink his blood you can have no life in you. Whoever eats my flesh and drinks my blood possesses eternal life, and I will raise him up on the last day. My flesh is real food; my blood is real drink. Whoever eats my flesh and drinks my blood dwells continually in me and I dwell in him. As the living Father sent me, and I live because of the Father, so he who eats me shall live because of me. This is the bread which came down from heaven; and it is not like the bread which our fathers ate: they are dead, but whoever eats this bread shall live for ever.'

This was spoken in synagogue when Jesus was teaching in Capernaum. Many of his disciples on hearing it exclaimed, 'This is more than we can stomach! Why listen to such talk?' Jesus was aware that his disciples were murmuring about it and asked them, 'Does this shock you? What if you see the Son of Man ascending to

King James Version

cend up where he was before? 63 It is the Spirit
that quickeneth; the flesh profiteth nothing: the
words that I speak unto you, *they* are spirit, and
they are life. 64 But there are some of you that
believe not. For Jesus knew from the beginning
who they were that believed not, and who should
betray him. 65 And he said, Therefore said I unto
you, that no man can come unto me, except it
were given unto him of my Father.
66 From that *time* many of his disciples went
back, and walked no more with him. 67 Then
said Jesus unto the twelve, Will ye also go away?
68 Then Simon Peter answered him, Lord, to
whom shall we go? thou hast the words of eternal life. 69 And we believe and are sure that thou
art that Christ, the Son of the living God. 70 Jesus answered them, Have not I chosen you
twelve, and one of you is a devil? 71 He spake
of Judas Iscariot *the son* of Simon: for he it was
that should betray him, being one of the twelve.

Living Bible

63 Only the Holy Spirit gives eternal life.[h] Those
born only once, with physical birth,[i] will never
receive this gift. But now I have told you how
to get this true spiritual life. 64 But some of you
don't believe me." (For Jesus knew from the
beginning who didn't believe and knew the one
who would betray him.)
65 And he remarked, "That is what I meant
when I said that no one can come to me unless
the Father attracts him to me."
66 At this point many of his disciples turned
away and deserted him.
67 Then Jesus turned to the Twelve and asked,
"Are you going too?"
68 Simon Peter replied, "Master, to whom
shall we go? You alone have the words that
give eternal life, 69 and we believe them and
know you are the holy Son of God."
70 Then Jesus said, "I chose the twelve of
you, and one is a devil." 71 He was speaking of
Judas, son of Simon Iscariot, one of the Twelve,
who would betray him.

[*h*] Literally, "It is the Spirit who quickens." [*i*] See
John 1:13. Literally, "the flesh profits nothing."

Today's English Version

fore? 63 What gives life is God's Spirit; man's
power is of no use at all. The words I have
spoken to you are Spirit and life. 64 Yet some
of you do not believe." (Jesus knew from the
very beginning who were the ones that would
not believe, and which one would betray him.)
65 And he added, "This is the very reason I told
you that no one can come to me unless the
Father makes it possible for him to do so."
66 Because of this, many of his followers
turned back and would not go with him any
more. 67 So Jesus said to the twelve disciples,
"And you—would you like to leave also?"
68 Simon Peter answered him, "Lord, to
whom would we go? You have the words that
give eternal life. 69 And now we believe and know
that you are the Holy One from God."
70 Jesus answered them, "Did I not choose
the twelve of you? Yet one of you is a devil!"
71 He was talking about Judas, the son of Simon
Iscariot. For Judas, even though he was one of
the twelve disciples, was going to betray him.

New International Version

to where he was before! 63 The Spirit gives life;
the flesh counts for nothing. The words I have
spoken to you are spirit[g] and they are life. 64 Yet
there are some of you who do not believe." For
Jesus had known from the beginning which of
them did not believe and who would betray him.
65 He went on to say, "This is why I told you
that no one can come to me unless the Father
has enabled him."
66 From this time many of his disciples turned
back and no longer followed him.
67 "Do you want to leave too?" Jesus asked
the Twelve.
68 Simon Peter answered him, "Lord, to
whom shall we go? You have the words of
eternal life. 69 We believe and know that you
are the Holy One of God."
70 Then Jesus replied, "Have I not chosen
you, the Twelve? Yet one of you is a devil!"
71 (He meant Judas, the son of Simon Iscariot,
who, though one of the Twelve, was later to
betray him.)

[*g*] Or *Spirit*.

Phillips Modern English

fore? It is the Spirit which gives life. The flesh will not help you. The things which I have told you are spiritual and are life. But some of you do not believe me."

For Jesus knew from the beginning which of his followers did not trust him and who was the man who would betray him. Then he added, "This is why I said to you, 'No one can come to me unless my Father puts it into his heart to come.' "

As a consequence of this, many of his disciples withdrew and no longer followed him. So Jesus said to the twelve, "And are you too wanting to go away?"

"Lord," answered Simon Peter, "who else should we go to? Your words have the ring of eternal life! And we believe and are convinced that you are the Holy One of God."

Jesus replied, "Did I not choose you twelve —and one of you has the devil in his heart?"

He was speaking of Judas, the son of Simon Iscariot, one of the twelve, who was planning to betray him.

Revised Standard Version

before? 63 It is the spirit that gives life, the flesh
is of no avail; the words that I have spoken to
you are spirit and life. 64 But there are some of
you that do not believe." For Jesus knew from
the first who those were that did not believe, and
who it was that would betray him. 65 And he
said, "This is why I told you that no one can
come to me unless it is granted him by the
Father."
66 After this many of his disciples drew back
and no longer went about with him. 67 Jesus
said to the twelve, "Do you also wish to go
away?" 68 Simon Peter answered him, "Lord, to
whom shall we go? You have the words of
eternal life; 69 and we have believed, and have
come to know, that you are the Holy One of
God." 70 Jesus answered them, "Did I not
choose you, the twelve, and one of you is a
devil?" 71 He spoke of Judas the son of Simon
Iscariot, for he, one of the twelve, was to betray
him.

Jerusalem Bible

63 "It is the spirit that gives life,
the flesh has nothing to offer.
The words I have spoken to you are spirit
and they are life.

64 "But there are some of you who do not
believe." For Jesus knew from the outset those
who did not believe, and who it was that would
betray him. 65 He went on, "This is why I told
you that no one could come to me unless the
Father allows him." 66 After this, many of his
disciples left him and stopped going with him.

Peter's profession of faith

67 Then Jesus said to the Twelve, "What
about you, do you want to go away too?"
68 Simon Peter answered, "Lord, who shall we
go to? You have the message of eternal life,
69 and we believe; we know that you are the
Holy One of God." 70 Jesus replied, "Have I
not chosen you, you Twelve? Yet one of you is
a devil." 71 He meant Judas son of Simon Iscariot,
since this was the man, one of the
Twelve, who was going to betray him.

New English Bible

the place where he was before? The spirit alone gives life; the flesh is of no avail; the words which I have spoken to you are both spirit and life. And yet there are some of you who have no faith.' For Jesus knew all along who were without faith and who was to betray him. So he said, 'This is why I told you that no one can come to me unless it has been granted to him by the Father.'

From that time on, many of his disciples withdrew and no longer went about with him. So Jesus asked the Twelve, 'Do you also want to leave me?' Simon Peter answered him, 'Lord, to whom shall we go? Your words are words of eternal life. We have faith, and we know that you are the Holy One of God.' Jesus answered, 'Have I not chosen you, all twelve? Yet one of you is a devil.' He meant Judas, son of Simon Iscariot. He it was who would betray him, and he was one of the Twelve.

King James Version

7 After these things Jesus walked in Galilee: for he would not walk in Jewry, because the Jews sought to kill him. 2 Now the Jews' feast of tabernacles was at hand. 3 His brethren therefore said unto him, Depart hence, and go into Judea, that thy disciples also may see the works that thou doest. 4 For *there is* no man *that* doeth any thing in secret, and he himself seeketh to be known openly. If thou do these things, shew thyself to the world. 5 For neither did his brethren believe in him. 6 Then Jesus said unto them, My time is not yet come: but your time is always ready. 7 The world cannot hate you; but me it hateth, because I testify of it, that the works thereof are evil. 8 Go ye up unto this feast: I go not up yet unto this feast; for my time is not yet full come. 9 When he had said these words unto them, he abode *still* in Galilee.

10 But when his brethren were gone up, then went he also up unto the feast, not openly, but as it were in secret. 11 Then the Jews sought him at the feast, and said, Where is he? 12And there

Living Bible

7 After this, Jesus went to Galilee, going from village to village, for he wanted to stay out of Judea where the Jewish leaders were plotting his death. 2 But soon it was time for the Tabernacle Ceremonies, one of the annual Jewish holidays, 3 and Jesus' brothers urged him to go to Judea for the celebration.

"Go where more people can see your miracles!" they scoffed. 4 "You can't be famous when you hide like this! If you're so great, prove it to the world!" 5 For even his brothers didn't believe in him.

6 Jesus replied, "It is not the right time for me to go now. But you can go anytime and it will make no difference, 7 for the world can't hate you; but it does hate me, because I accuse it of sin and evil. 8 You go on, and I'll come later[a] when it is the right time." 9 So he remained in Galilee.

10 But after his brothers had left for the celebration, then he went too, though secretly, staying out of the public eye. 11 The Jewish leaders tried to find him at the celebration and kept asking if anyone had seen him. 12 There was a lot

[*a*] Literally, "I go not up (yet) unto this feast." The word "yet" is included in the text of many ancient manuscripts.

Today's English Version

Jesus and his brothers

7 After this, Jesus traveled in Galilee; he did not want to travel in Judea, because the Jewish authorities there were wanting to kill him. 2 The Jewish Feast of Tabernacles was near, 3 so Jesus' brothers said to him, "Leave this place and go to Judea, so that your disciples will see the works you are doing. 4 No one hides what he is doing if he wants to be well known. Since you are doing these things, let the whole world know about you!" 5 (Not even his brothers believed in him.)

6 Jesus said to them, "The right time for me has not yet come. Any time is right for you. 7 The world cannot hate you, but it hates me, because I keep telling it that its ways are bad. 8 You go on to the feast. I am not going to this feast, because the right time has not come for me." 9 He said this, and then stayed on in Galilee.

Jesus at the feast of tabernacles

10 After his brothers went to the feast, Jesus also went; however, he did not go openly, but went secretly. 11 The Jewish authorities were looking for him at the feast. "Where is he?" they asked.

12 There was much whispering about him in

New International Version

Jesus goes to the Feast of Tabernacles

7 After this, Jesus went around in Galilee, purposely staying away from Judea because the Jews there were waiting to take his life. 2 But when the Jewish Feast of Tabernacles was near, 3 Jesus' brothers said to him, "You ought to leave here and go to Judea, so that your disciples may see the miracles you do. 4 No one who wants to become a public figure acts in secret. Since you are doing these things, show yourself to the world." 5 For even his own brothers did not believe in him.

6 Therefore Jesus told them, "The right time for me has not yet come; for you any time is right. 7 The world cannot hate you, but it hates me because I testify that what it does is evil. 8 You go to the Feast. I am not yet[h] going up to this Feast, because for me the right time has not yet come." 9 Having said this, he stayed in Galilee.

10 However, after his brothers had left for the Feast, he went also, not publicly, but in secret. 11 Now at the Feast the Jews were watching for him and asking, "Where is that man?"

12 Among the crowds there was widespread

[*h*] Some early MSS omit *yet*.

Phillips Modern English

7.1 *Jesus delays his arrival at the festival*

After this, Jesus moved about in Galilee but decided not to do so in Judaea since the Jews were planning to take his life. As the Jewish festival, "The feast of the tabernacles", was approaching, his brothers said to him, "You ought to leave here and go to Judaea so that your disciples can see what you are doing, for nobody works in secret if he wants to be known publicly. If you are doing things like this, let the world see what you are doing." For not even his brothers had any faith in him. Jesus replied by saying, "It is not yet the right time for me, but any time is right for you. It is impossible for you to arouse the world's hatred, but I provoke hatred because I show the world how evil its deeds really are. No, you go up to the festival; I shall not go up now, for it is not yet time for me to go." And after these words he remained where he was in Galilee.

Later, after his brothers had gone to the festival, he went up himself, not openly but as though he did not want to be seen. Consequently, the Jews kept looking for him at the festival and asking "Where is that man?" And there was an

Revised Standard Version

7 After this Jesus went about in Galilee; he
would not go about in Judea, because the
Jews[n] sought to kill him. 2 Now the Jews' feast
of Tabernacles was at hand. 3 So his brothers
said to him, "Leave here and go to Judea, that
your disciples may see the works you are doing.
4 For no man works in secret if he seeks to be
known openly. If you do these things, show
yourself to the world." 5 For even his brothers
did not believe in him. 6 Jesus said to them, "My
time has not yet come, but your time is always
here. 7 The world cannot hate you, but it hates
me because I testify of it that its works are evil.
8 Go to the feast yourselves; I am not [o] going up
to this feast, for my time has not yet fully come."
9 So saying, he remained in Galilee.
10 But after his brothers had gone up to the
feast, then he also went up, not publicly but in
private. 11 The Jews were looking for him at the
feast, and saying, "Where is he?" 12 And there

[n] Or *Judeans*. [o] Other ancient authorities add *yet*.

Jerusalem Bible

V. The feast of Tabernacles

Jesus goes up to Jerusalem for the feast and teaches there

7 After this Jesus stayed in Galilee; he could
not stay in Judaea, because the Jews were
out to kill him.
2 As the Jewish feast of Tabernacles drew
near, 3 his brothers[r] said to him, "Why not
leave this place and go to Judaea, and let your
disciples[s] see the works you are doing; 4 if a
man wants to be known he does not do things
in secret; since you are doing all this, you should
let the whole world see." 5 Not even his brothers,
in fact, had faith in him. 6 Jesus answered,
"The right time for me has not come yet, but
any time is the right time for you. 7 The world
cannot hate you, but it does hate me, because
I give evidence that its ways are evil. 8 Go up
to the festival yourselves: I am not going to
this festival, because for me the time is not ripe
yet." 9 Having said that, he stayed behind in
Galilee.
10 However, after his brothers had left for
the festival, he went up as well, but quite privately,
without drawing attention to himself. 11 At
the festival the Jews were on the lookout for
him: "Where is he?" they said. 12 People stood

[r] In the wide sense, as in Mt. 12:46: relations of his own generation. [s] Those in Jerusalem and Judaea.

New English Bible

The great controversy

7 Afterwards Jesus went about in Galilee. He wished to avoid Judaea because the Jews were looking for a chance to kill him. As the Jewish Feast of Tabernacles was close at hand, his brothers said to him, 'You should leave this district and go into Judaea, so that your disciples there may see the great things you are doing. Surely no one can hope to be in the public eye if he works in seclusion. If you really are doing such things as these, show yourself to the world.' For even his brothers had no faith in him. Jesus said to them, 'The right time for me has not yet come, but any time is right for you. The world cannot hate you; but it hates me for exposing the wickedness of its ways. Go to the festival yourselves. I am not[a] going up to this festival because the right time for me has not yet come.' With this answer he stayed behind in Galilee.

Later, when his brothers had gone to the festival, he went up himself, not publicly, but almost in secret. The Jews were looking for him at the festival and asking, 'Where is he?', and

[a] *Some witnesses read* not yet.

King James Version

was much murmuring among the people concerning him: for some said, He is a good man:
others said, Nay; but he deceiveth the people.
13 Howbeit no man spake openly of him for fear
of the Jews.
14 Now about the midst of the feast Jesus
went up into the temple, and taught. 15 And the
Jews marvelled, saying, How knoweth this man
letters, having never learned? 16 Jesus answered
them, and said, My doctrine is not mine, but his
that sent me. 17 If any man will do his will, he
shall know of the doctrine, whether it be of God,
or *whether* I speak of myself. 18 He that speaketh of himself seeketh his own glory: but he
that seeketh his glory that sent him, the same is
true, and no unrighteousness is in him. 19 Did
not Moses give you the law, and *yet* none of
you keepeth the law? Why go ye about to kill
me? 20 The people answered and said, Thou hast
a devil: who goeth about to kill thee? 21 Jesus
answered and said unto them, I have done one
work, and ye all marvel. 22 Moses therefore gave
unto you circumcision; (not because it is of Moses, but of the fathers;) and ye on the sabbath
day circumcise a man. 23 If a man on the sabbath day receive circumcision, that the law of
Moses should not be broken; are ye angry at

Living Bible

of discussion about him among the crowds. Some
said, "He's a wonderful man," while others said,
"No, he's duping the public." 13 But no one had
the courage to speak out for him in public for
fear of reprisals from the Jewish leaders.
14 Then, midway through the festival, Jesus
went up to the Temple and preached openly.
15 The Jewish leaders were surprised when they
heard him. "How can he know so much when
he's never been to our schools?" they asked.
16 So Jesus told them, "I'm not teaching you
my own thoughts, but those of God who sent me.
17 If any of you really determines to do God's
will, then you will certainly know whether my
teaching is from God or is merely my own.
18 Anyone presenting his own ideas is looking for
praise for himself, but anyone seeking to honor
the one who sent him is a good and true person.
19 None of *you* obeys the laws of Moses! So
why pick on *me* for breaking them? Why kill *me*
for this?"
20 The crowd replied, "You're out of your
mind! Who's trying to kill you?"
21, 22, 23 Jesus replied, "I worked on the
Sabbath by healing a man, and you were surprised. But you work on the Sabbath, too, whenever you obey Moses' law of circumcision (actually, however, this tradition of circumcision is
older than the Mosaic law); for if the correct
time for circumcising your children falls on the
Sabbath, you go ahead and do it, as you should.

Today's English Version

the crowd. "He is a good man," some people
said. "No," others said, "he fools the people."
13 But no one talked about him openly, because they were afraid of the Jewish authorities.
14 The feast was nearly half over when Jesus
went to the temple and began teaching. 15 The
Jewish authorities, greatly surprised, said, "How
does this man know so much when he has never
been to school?"
16 Jesus answered, "What I teach is not my
teaching, but comes from God, who sent me.
17 Whoever is willing to do what God wants will
know whether what I teach comes from God or
whether I speak on my own authority. 18 A person
who speaks on his own is trying to gain glory for
himself. He who wants glory for the one who sent
him, however, is honest and there is nothing false
in him. 19 Moses gave you the Law, did he not?
But not one of you obeys the Law. Why are you
trying to kill me?"
20 The crowd answered, "You have a demon
in you! Who is trying to kill you?"
21 Jesus answered, "I did one great work and
you were all surprised. 22 Because Moses ordered you to circumcise your sons (although it
was not Moses but your ancestors who started
it), you will circumcise a boy on the Sabbath.
23 If a boy is circumcised on the Sabbath so
that Moses' Law will not be broken, why are you

New International Version

whispering about him. Some said, "He is a good
man."
Others replied, "No, he deceives the people."
13 But no one would say anything publicly
about him for fear of the Jews.

Jesus teaches at the Feast

14 Not until halfway through the Feast did
Jesus go up to the temple court and begin to
teach. 15 The Jews were amazed and asked,
"How did this man get such learning without
having studied?"
16 Jesus answered, "My teaching is not my
own. It comes from him who sent me. 17 If a
man chooses to do God's will, he will find out
whether my teaching comes from God or
whether I speak on my own. 18 He who speaks
on his own does so to gain honor for himself,
but he who works for the honor of the one who
sent him is a man of truth; there is nothing false
about him. 19 Has not Moses given you the law?
Yet not one of you keeps the law. Why are you
trying to kill me?"
20 "You are demon-possessed," the crowd answered. "Who is trying to kill you?"
21 Jesus said to them, "I did one miracle, and
you are all astonished. 22 Yet, because Moses
gave you circumcision (though actually it did
not come from Moses, but from the patriarchs),
you circumcise a child on the Sabbath. 23 Now
if a child can be circumcised on the Sabbath so
that the law of Moses may not be broken, why

Phillips Modern English

undercurrent of discussion about him among the crowds. Some would say, "He is a good man", others maintained that he was not, but that he was "misleading the people". Nobody, however spoke openly about him for fear of the Jews.

7.14 *Jesus openly declares his authority*

But in the middle of the festival, Jesus went up to the Temple and began teaching. The Jews were amazed and remarked, "How does this man know all this—he has never been taught?"

Jesus replied to them, "My teaching is not really mine but comes from the One who sent me. If anyone wants to do God's will, he will know whether my teaching is from God or whether I merely speak on my own authority. A man who speaks on his own authority has an eye for his own reputation. But the man who is considering the glory of God who sent him is a true man. There can be no dishonesty about him.

"Did not Moses give you the Law? Yet not one of you keeps the Law. Why are you trying to kill me?"

The crowd answered, "You must be mad! Who is trying to kill you?"

Jesus answered them, "I have done one thing and you are all amazed at it. Moses gave you circumcision (not that it came from Moses originally but from your forefathers), and you circumcise a man even on the Sabbath. If a man receives the cutting of circumcision on the Sabbath to avoid breaking the Law of Moses, why

Revised Standard Version

was much muttering about him among the people. While some said, "He is a good man," others said, "No, he is leading the people astray."
13 Yet for fear of the Jews no one spoke openly
of him.
14 About the middle of the feast Jesus went
up into the temple and taught. 15 The Jews marveled at it, saying, "How is it that this man has
learning,[p] when he has never studied?" 16 So
Jesus answered them, "My teaching is not mine,
but his who sent me; 17 if any man's will is to
do his will, he shall know whether the teaching
is from God or whether I am speaking on my
own authority. 18 He who speaks on his own authority seeks his own glory; but he who seeks the
glory of him who sent him is true, and in him
there is no falsehood. 19 Did not Moses give you
the law? Yet none of you keeps the law. Why do
you seek to kill me?" 20 The people answered,
"You have a demon! Who is seeking to kill
you?" 21 Jesus answered them, "I did one deed,
and you all marvel at it. 22 Moses gave you circumcision (not that it is from Moses, but from
the fathers), and you circumcise a man upon
the sabbath. 23 If on the sabbath a man receives
circumcision, so that the law of Moses may not

[p] Or *this man knows his letters.*

Jerusalem Bible

in groups whispering[t] about him. Some said, "He is a good man"; others, "No, he is leading the
people astray." 13 Yet no one spoke about him
openly, for fear of the Jews.
14 When the festival was half over, Jesus went
to the Temple and began to teach. 15 The Jews
were astonished and said, "How did he learn to
read? He has not been taught." 16 Jesus answered them:

"My teaching is not from myself:
it comes from the one who sent me;
17 and if anyone is prepared to do his will,
he will know whether my teaching is from God
or whether my doctrine is my own.
18 When a man's doctrine is his own
he is hoping to get honor for himself;
but when he is working for the honor of one who sent him,
then he is sincere
and by no means an impostor.
19 Did not Moses give you the Law?
And yet not one of you keeps the Law!

"Why do you want to kill me?" 20 The crowd
replied, "You are mad! Who wants to kill you?"
21 Jesus answered, "One work I did, and you are
all surprised by it. 22 Moses ordered you to practice circumcision—not that it began with him, it
goes back to the patriarchs—and you circumcise
on the sabbath. 23 Now if a man can be circumcised on the sabbath so that the Law of Moses

[t] Or "In the crowds there was whispering about him."

New English Bible

there was much whispering about him in the crowds. 'He is a good man', said some. 'No,' said others, 'he is leading the people astray.' However, no one talked about him openly, for fear of the Jews.

When the festival was already half over, Jesus went up to the temple and began to teach. The Jews were astonished: 'How is it', they said, 'that this untrained man has such learning?' Jesus replied, 'The teaching that I give is not my own; it is the teaching of him who sent me. Whoever has the will to do the will of God shall know whether my teaching comes from him or is merely my own. Anyone whose teaching is merely his own, aims at honour for himself. But if a man aims at the honour of him who sent him he is sincere, and there is nothing false in him.

'Did not Moses give you the Law? Yet you all break it. Why are you trying to kill me?' The crowd answered, 'You are possessed! Who wants to kill you?' Jesus replied, 'Once only have I done work on the Sabbath, and you are all taken aback. But consider: Moses gave you the law of circumcision (not that it originated with Moses but with the patriarchs) and you circumcise on the Sabbath. Well then, if a child is circumcised on the Sabbath to avoid breaking the Law of Moses, why are you indignant with

King James Version

me, because I have made a man every whit whole on the sabbath day? 24 Judge not according to the appearance, but judge righteous judgment. 25 Then said some of them of Jerusalem, Is not this he, whom they seek to kill? 26 But, lo, he speaketh boldly, and they say nothing unto him. Do the rulers know indeed that this is the very Christ? 27 Howbeit we know this man whence he is: but when Christ cometh, no man knoweth whence he is. 28 Then cried Jesus in the temple as he taught, saying, Ye both know me, and ye know whence I am: and I am not come of myself, but he that sent me is true, whom ye know not. 29 But I know him; for I am from him, and he hath sent me. 30 Then they sought

Living Bible

So why should I be condemned for making a man completely well on the Sabbath? 24 Think this through and you will see that I am right."

25 Some of the people who lived there in Jerusalem said among themselves, "Isn't this the man they are trying to kill? 26 But here he is preaching in public, and they say nothing to him. Can it be that our leaders have learned, after all, that he really is the Messiah? 27 But how could he be? For we know where this man was born; when Christ comes, he will just appear and no one will know where he comes from."

28 So Jesus, in a sermon in the Temple, called out, "Yes, you know me and where I was born and raised, but I am the representative of one you don't know, and he is Truth. 29 I know him because I was with him, and he sent me to you."

30 Then the Jewish leaders sought to arrest

Today's English Version

angry with me because I made a man completely well on the Sabbath? 24 Stop judging by external standards, and judge by true standards."

Is he the Messiah?

25 Some of the people of Jerusalem said, "Isn't this the man they are trying to kill? 26 Look! He is talking in public, and nobody says anything against him! Can it be that the authorities really know that he is the Messiah? 27 But when the Messiah comes, no one will know where he is from. And we all know where this man comes from."

28 As Jesus taught in the temple he said in a loud voice, "Do you really know me, and know where I am from? But I have not come on my own. He who sent me, however, is true. You do not know him, 29 but I know him, because I come from him and he sent me."

30 Then they tried to arrest him, but no one

New International Version

are you angry with me for healing the whole man on the Sabbath? 24 Stop judging by mere appearances, and make a right judgment."

Is Jesus the Christ?

25 At that point some of the people of Jerusalem began to ask, "Isn't this the man they are trying to kill? 26 Here he is, speaking publicly, and they are not saying a word to him. Have the authorities really concluded that he is the Christ[i]? 27 But we know where this man is from; when the Christ[i] comes, no one will know where he is from."

28 Then Jesus, still teaching in the temple court, cried out, "Yes, you know me, and you know where I am from. I am not here on my own, but he who sent me is true. You do not know him, 29 but I know him because I am from him and he sent me."

30 At this they tried to seize him, but no one

[*i*] Or *Messiah*.

Phillips Modern English

should you be angry with me because I have made a man's body perfectly whole on the Sabbath? You must not judge by the appearance of things but by the reality!"

Some of the people of Jerusalem, hearing him talk like this, were saying, "Isn't this the man whom they are trying to kill? Yet here he is, talking quite openly and they haven't a word to say to him. Surely our rulers haven't decided that this really is Christ! But then, we know this man and where he comes from—when Christ comes, no one will know where he comes from."

7.28 Jesus makes more unique claims

Then Jesus, in the middle of his teaching, called out in the Temple, "So you know me and know where I have come from? But I have not come of my own accord; I am sent by One who is true and you do not know him! I do know him, because I come from him and he has sent me here."

Then they attempted to arrest him, but actually

Revised Standard Version

be broken, are you angry with me because on the
sabbath I made a man's whole body well? 24 Do
not judge by appearances, but judge with right
judgment."
25 Some of the people of Jerusalem therefore
said, "Is not this the man whom they seek to
kill? 26 And here he is, speaking openly, and they
say nothing to him! Can it be that the authorities
really know that this is the Christ? 27 Yet we
know where this man comes from; and when
the Christ appears, no one will know where he
comes from." 28 So Jesus proclaimed, as he taught
in the temple, "You know me, and you know
where I come from? But I have not come of my
own accord; he who sent me is true, and him
you do not know. 29 I know him, for I come
from him, and he sent me." 30 So they sought to

Jerusalem Bible

is not broken, why are you angry with me for
making a man whole and complete on a sabbath? 24 Do not keep judging according to appearances; let your judgment be according to
what is right."

The people discuss the origin of the Messiah

25 Meanwhile some of the people of Jerusalem were saying, "Isn't this the man they want
to kill? 26 And here he is, speaking freely, and
they have nothing to say to him! Can it be true
the authorities have made up their minds that
he is the Christ? 27 Yet we all know where he
comes from, but when the Christ appears no one
will know where he comes from." [u]
28 Then, as Jesus taught in the Temple, he
cried out:

"Yes, you know me and you know where I
came from.
Yet I have not come of myself:
no, there is one who sent me and I really
come from him,
and you do not know him,
29 but I know him
because I have come from him
and it was he who sent me."

30 They would have arrested him then, but

[u] Although the prophecy that the Messiah would be born in Bethlehem was well known, it was commonly believed that he would appear suddenly from some secret place.

New English Bible

me for giving health on the Sabbath to the whole of a man's body? Do not judge superficially, but be just in your judgements.'

At this some of the people of Jerusalem began to say, 'Is not this the man they want to put to death? And here he is, speaking openly, and they have not a word to say to him. Can it be that our rulers have actually decided that this is the Messiah? And yet we know where this man comes from, but when the Messiah appears no one is to know where he comes from.' Thereupon Jesus cried aloud as he taught in the temple, 'No doubt you know me; no doubt you know where I come from.[a] Yet I have not come of my own accord. I was sent by the One who truly is, and him you do not know. I know him because I come from him and he it is who sent me.' At this they tried to seize him, but no one

[a] *Or* Do you know me? And do you know where I come from?

King James Version

to take him: but no man laid hands on him, because his hour was not yet come. 31And many of the people believed on him, and said, When Christ cometh, will he do more miracles than these which this *man* hath done?

32 The Pharisees heard that the people murmured such things concerning him; and the Pharisees and the chief priests sent officers to take him. 33 Then said Jesus unto them, Yet a little while am I with you, and *then* I go unto him that sent me. 34 Ye shall seek me, and shall not find *me:* and where I am, *thither* ye cannot come. 35 Then said the Jews among themselves, Whither will he go, that we shall not find him? will he go unto the dispersed among the Gentiles, and teach the Gentiles? 36 What *manner of* saying is this that he said, Ye shall seek me, and shall not find *me:* and where I am, *thither* ye

Living Bible

him; but no hand was laid on him, for God's time had not yet come.

31 Many among the crowds at the Temple believed on him. "After all," they said, "what miracles do you expect the Messiah to do that this man hasn't done?"

32 When the Pharisees heard that the crowds were in this mood, they and the chief priests sent officers to arrest Jesus. 33 But Jesus told them, "[Not yet![b]] I am to be here a little longer. Then I shall return to the one who sent me. 34 You will search for me but not find me. And you won't be able to come where I am!"

35 The Jewish leaders were puzzled by this statement. "Where is he planning to go?" they asked. "Maybe he is thinking of leaving the country and going as a missionary among the Jews in other lands, or maybe even to the Gentiles! 36 What does he mean about our looking for him and not being able to find him, and, 'You won't be able to come where I am'?"

[*b*] Implied.

Today's English Version

laid a hand on him, because his hour had not yet come. 31 But many in the crowd believed in him, and said, "When the Messiah comes, will he do more mighty works than this man has done?"

Guards are sent to arrest Jesus

32 The Pharisees heard the crowd whispering these things about him, so they and the chief priests sent some guards to arrest Jesus. 33 Jesus said, "I shall be with you a little while longer, and then I shall go away to him who sent me. 34 You will look for me, but you will not find me, because where I shall be you cannot go."

35 The Jewish authorities said among themselves, "Where is he about to go so that we shall not find him? Will he go to the Greek cities where the Jews live, and teach the Greeks? 36 He says, 'You will look for me but you will not find me,' and, 'You cannot go where I shall be.' What does he mean?"

New International Version

laid a hand on him, because his time had not yet come. 31 Still, many in the crowd put their faith in him. They said, "When the Christ[i] comes, will he do more miraculous signs than this man?"

32 The Pharisees heard the crowd whispering such things about him. Then the chief priests and the Pharisees sent temple guards to arrest him.

33 Jesus said, "I am with you for only a short time, and then I go to the one who sent me. 34 You will look for me, but you will not find me; and where I am, you cannot come."

35 The Jews said to one another, "Where does this man intend to go that we cannot find him? Will he go where our people live scattered among the Greeks, and teach the Greeks? 36 What did he mean when he said, 'You will look for me, but you will not find me,' and 'Where I am, you cannot come'?"

[*i*] Or *Messiah*.

Phillips Modern English

no one laid a finger on him because the right moment had not yet come. Yet many of the crowd believed in him and kept on saying, "When Christ comes, is he going to show greater signs than this man?"

The Pharisees heard the crowd whispering these things about him, and they and the chief priests sent officers to arrest him. Then Jesus said, "I shall be with you only a little while longer and then I am going to him who sent me. You will look for me then but you will never find me. You cannot come where I shall be."

This made the Jews say to each other, "Where is he going to go so that we cannot find him? Surely he's not going to our refugees among the Greeks to teach Greeks? What does he mean when he says, 'You will look for me and you will never find me' and 'You cannot come where I shall be'?"

Revised Standard Version

arrest him; but no one laid hands on him, because his hour had not yet come. 31 Yet many
of the people believed in him; they said, "When
the Christ appears, will he do more signs than
this man has done?"
32 The Pharisees heard the crowd thus muttering about him, and the chief priests and
Pharisees sent officers to arrest him. 33 Jesus
then said, "I shall be with you a little longer, and
then I go to him who sent me; 34 you will seek
me and you will not find me; where I am you
cannot come." 35 The Jews said to one another,
"Where does this man intend to go that we shall
not find him? Does he intend to go to the Dispersion among the Greeks and teach the Greeks?
36 What does he mean by saying, 'You will seek
me and you will not find me,' and, 'Where I am
you cannot come'?"

Jerusalem Bible

because his time had not yet come no one laid a hand on him.

Jesus foretells his approaching departure

31 There were many people in the crowds, however, who believed in him; they were saying, "When the Christ comes, will he give more signs than this man?" 32 Hearing that rumors like this about him were spreading among the people, the Pharisees sent the Temple police to arrest him.

33 Then Jesus said:

"I shall remain with you for only a short
time now;
then I shall go back to the one who sent me.
34 You will look for me and will not find me:
where I am
you cannot come."

35 The Jews then said to one another, "Where
is he going that we shan't be able to find him?
Is he going abroad to the people who are dispersed among the Greeks and will he teach the
Greeks? 36 What does he mean when he says:

'You will look for me and will not find me:
where I am,
you cannot come'?"

New English Bible

laid a hand on him because his appointed hour had not yet come. Yet among the people many believed in him. 'When the Messiah comes,' they said, 'is it likely that he will perform more signs than this man?'

The Pharisees overheard these mutterings of the people about him, so the chief priests and the Pharisees sent temple police to arrest him. Then Jesus said, 'For a little longer I shall be with you; then I am going away to him who sent me. You will look for me, but you will not find me. Where I am, you cannot come.' So the Jews said to one another, 'Where does he intend to go, that we should not be able to find him? Will he go to the Dispersion among the Greeks, and teach the Greeks? What did he mean by saying, "You will look for me, but you will not find me. Where I am, you cannot come"?' [b]

[*b*] *Some witnesses here insert the passage printed on pages 705 and 709.*

King James Version

cannot come? 37 In the last day, that great *day*
of the feast, Jesus stood and cried, saying, If
any man thirst, let him come unto me, and drink.
38 He that believeth on me, as the Scripture
hath said, out of his belly shall flow rivers of
living water. 39 (But this spake he of the Spirit,
which they that believe on him should receive:
for the Holy Ghost was not yet *given;* because
that Jesus was not yet glorified.)
40 Many of the people therefore, when they
heard this saying, said, Of a truth this is the
Prophet. 41 Others said, This is the Christ. But
some said, Shall Christ come out of Galilee?
42 Hath not the Scripture said, That Christ
cometh of the seed of David, and out of the
town of Bethlehem, where David was? 43 So
there was a division among the people because
of him. 44 And some of them would have taken
him; but no man laid hands on him.
45 Then came the officers to the chief priests

Living Bible

37 On the last day, the climax of the holidays, Jesus shouted to the crowds, "If anyone is
thirsty, let him come to me and drink. 38 For the
Scriptures declare that rivers of living water shall
flow from the inmost being of anyone who believes in me." 39 (He was speaking of the Holy
Spirit, who would be given to everyone believing
in him; but the Spirit had not yet been given,
because Jesus had not yet returned to his glory
in heaven.)
40 When the crowds heard him say this, some
of them declared, "This man surely is the
prophet who will come just before the Messiah."
41, 42 Others said, "He *is* the Messiah." Still
others, "But he *can't* be! Will the Messiah come
from *Galilee?* For the Scriptures clearly state
that the Messiah will be born of the royal line
of David, in *Bethlehem,* the village where David
was born." 43 So the crowd was divided about
him. 44 And some wanted him arrested, but no
one touched him.
45 The Temple police who had been sent to

Today's English Version

Streams of living water

37 The last day of the feast was the most important. On that day Jesus stood up and said
in a loud voice, "Whoever is thirsty should come
to me and drink. 38 As the scripture says, 'Whoever believes in me, streams of living water will
pour out from his heart.'" 39 Jesus said this
about the Spirit, which those who believed in
him were going to receive. At that time the
Spirit had not yet been given, because Jesus had
not been raised to glory.

Division among the people

40 Many of the people in the crowd heard him
say this and said, "This man is really the
Prophet!"
41 Others said, "He is the Messiah!"
But others said, "The Messiah will not come
from Galilee! 42 The scripture says that the
Messiah will be a descendant of David, and will
be born in Bethlehem, the town where David
lived." 43 So there was a division in the crowd
because of him. 44 Some wanted to arrest him,
but no one laid a hand on him.

The unbelief of the Jewish authorities

45 The guards went back to the chief priests

New International Version

37 On the last and greatest day of the Feast,
Jesus stood and said in a loud voice, "If a
man is thirsty, let him come to me and drink.
38 Whoever believes in me,[j] as the Scripture has
said, streams of living water will flow from
within him." 39 By this he meant the Spirit,
whom those who believed in him were later to
receive. Up to that time the Spirit had not been
given, since Jesus had not yet been glorified.
40 On hearing his words, some of the people
said, "Surely this man is the Prophet."
41 Others said, "He is the Christ.[k]"
Still others asked, "How can the Christ[k]
come from Galilee? 42 Does not the Scripture
say that the Christ[k] will come from David's family[l] and from Bethlehem, the town where David
lived?" 43 Thus the people were divided because
of Jesus. 44 Some wanted to seize him, but no
one laid a hand on him.

Unbelief of the Jewish leaders

45 Finally the temple guards went back to

[j] Or *If a man is thirsty,*
let him come to me.
And let him drink,
who believes in me.
[k] Or *Messiah.* [l] Greek *seed.*

Phillips Modern English

Then, on the last day, the climax of the festival, Jesus stood up and cried out, "If any man is thirsty, he may come to me and drink! The man who believes in me, as the scripture said, will have rivers of living water flowing from his inmost heart." (Here he was speaking about the Spirit which those who believe in him would receive. The Spirit had not yet been given because Jesus had not yet been glorified.) When they heard these words, some of the people were saying, "This really is the Prophet." Others said, "This is Christ!" But some said, "And does Christ come from Galilee? Don't the scriptures say that Christ will be descended from David, and will come from Bethlehem, the village where David lived?"

So the people were in two minds about him—some of them wanted to arrest him, but no one laid hands on him.

Then the officers returned to the Pharisees and

Revised Standard Version

37 On the last day of the feast, the great day,
Jesus stood up and proclaimed, "If any one
thirst, let him come to me and drink. 38 He who
believes in me, as[q] the scripture has said, 'Out
of his heart shall flow rivers of living water.'"
39 Now this he said about the Spirit, which those
who believed in him were to receive; for as yet
the Spirit had not been given, because Jesus was
not yet glorified.
40 When they heard these words, some of the
people said, "This is really the prophet." 41 Others said, "This is the Christ." But some said, "Is
the Christ to come from Galilee? 42 Has not the
scripture said that the Christ is descended from
David, and comes from Bethlehem, the village
where David was?" 43 So there was a division
among the people over him. 44 Some of them
wanted to arrest him, but no one laid hands on
him.
45 The officers then went back to the chief

[q] Or *let him come to me, and let him who believes in me drink. As.*

Jerusalem Bible

The promise of living water

37 On the last day and greatest day of the
festival, Jesus stood there and cried out:

"If any man is thirsty, let him come to me!
Let the man come and drink 38 who believes
in me!"

As scripture says: From his breast shall flow fountains of living water.[v]

39 He was speaking of the Spirit which those who believed in him were to receive; for there was no Spirit as yet because Jesus had not yet been glorified.

Fresh discussions on the origin of the Messiah

40 Several people who had been listening said,
"Surely he must be the prophet," 41 and some
said, "He is the Christ," but others said, "Would
the Christ be from Galilee? 42 Does not scripture say that the Christ must be descended from
David and come from the town of Bethlehem?"
43 So the people could not agree about him.
44 Some would have liked to arrest him, but no
one actually laid hands on him.
45 The police went back to the chief priests

[v] Life-giving water for Zion was a theme of the readings from scripture on the feast of Tabernacles (Zc. 14:8, Ezk. 47:1f); the liturgy included prayers for rain and the commemoration of the miracle of Moses and the water, Ex. 17.

New English Bible

On the last and greatest day of the festival Jesus stood and cried aloud, 'If anyone is thirsty let him come to me; whoever believes in me, let him drink.' As Scripture says, 'Streams of living water shall flow out from within him.'[c] He was speaking of the Spirit which believers in him would receive later; for the Spirit had not yet been given, because Jesus had not yet been glorified.

On hearing this some of the people said, 'This must certainly be the expected prophet.' Others said, 'This is the Messiah.' Others again, 'Surely the Messiah is not to come from Galilee? Does not Scripture say that the Messiah is to be of the family of David, from David's village of Bethlehem?' Thus he caused a split among the people. Some were for seizing him, but no one laid hands on him.

The temple police came back to the chief

[c] *Or* 'If any man is thirsty let him come to me and drink. He who believes in me, as Scripture says, streams of living water shall flow out from within him.'

King James Version

and Pharisees; and they said unto them, Why have ye not brought him? 46 The officers answered, Never man spake like this man. 47 Then answered them the Pharisees, Are ye also deceived? 48 Have any of the rulers or of the Pharisees believed on him? 49 But this people who knoweth not the law are cursed. 50 Nicodemus saith unto them, (he that came to Jesus by night, being one of them,) 51 Doth our law judge *any* man, before it hear him, and know what he doeth? 52 They answered and said unto him, Art thou also of Galilee? Search, and look: for out of Galilee ariseth no prophet.

53 And every man went unto his own house.

8 Jesus went unto the mount of Olives. 2 And early in the morning he came again into the temple, and all the people came unto him; and

Living Bible

arrest him returned to the chief priests and Pharisees. "Why didn't you bring him in?" they demanded.

46 "He says such wonderful things!" they mumbled. "We've never heard anything like it."

47 "So you also have been led astray?" the Pharisees mocked. 48 "Is there a single one of us Jewish rulers or Pharisees who believes he is the Messiah? 49 These stupid crowds do, yes; but what do they know about it? A curse upon them anyway!" [c]

50 Then Nicodemus spoke up. (Remember him? He was the Jewish leader who came secretely to interview Jesus.) 51 "Is it legal to convict a man before he is even tried?" he asked.

52 They replied, "Are you a wretched Galilean too? Search the Scriptures and see for yourself—no prophets will come from Galilee!" 53 [d] Then the meeting broke up and everybody went home.

8 Jesus returned to the Mount of Olives, 2 but early the next morning he was back again at the Temple. A crowd soon gathered, and he sat

[*c*] Literally, "This multitude is accursed." [*d*] Most ancient manuscripts omit John 7:53-8:11.

Today's English Version

and Pharisees, who asked them, "Why did you not bring him?"

46 The guards answered, "Nobody has ever talked the way this man does!"

47 "Did he fool you, too?" the Pharisees asked them. 48 "Have you ever known one of the authorities or one Pharisee to believe in him? 49 This crowd does not know the Law of Moses, so they are under God's curse!"

50 Nicodemus was one of them; he was the one who had gone to see Jesus before. He said to them, 51 "According to our Law we cannot condemn a man before hearing him and finding out what he has done."

52 "Well," they answered, "are you also from Galilee? Study the Scriptures and you will learn that no prophet ever comes from Galilee."

The woman caught in adultery

8 [Then everyone went home, but Jesus went to the Mount of Olives. 2 Early the next morning he went back to the temple. The whole crowd gathered around him, and he sat down and

New International Version

the chief priests and Pharisees, who asked them, "Why didn't you bring him in?"

46 "No one ever spoke the way this man does," the guards declared.

47 "You mean he has deceived you also?" the Pharisees retorted. 48 "Has any of the rulers or of the Pharisees put his trust in him? 49 No! But this mob that knows nothing of the law—there is a curse on them."

50 Nicodemus, who had gone to Jesus earlier and who was one of their own number, asked, 51 "Does our law condemn a man without first hearing him to find out what he is doing?"

52 They replied, "Are you from Galilee, too? Look into it, and you will find that a prophet[m] does not come out of Galilee."

[The most reliable early manuscripts omit John 7:53–8:11.]

53 Then they all left, each to his own home.

The woman caught in adultery

8 But Jesus went to the Mount of Olives. 2 At dawn he appeared again in the temple court, where all the people gathered around him, and

[*m*] Or *the Prophet.*

Phillips Modern English

chief priests, who said to them, "Why haven't you brought him?"

"No man ever spoke as this man speaks!" they replied.

"Has he pulled the wool over your eyes, too?" retorted the Pharisees. "Have any of the authorities or any of the Pharisees believed in him? But this crowd, who know nothing about the Law, is damned anyway!"

One of their number, Nicodemus (the one who had previously been to see Jesus), said to them, "But surely our Law does not judge the accused without first hearing what he has to say, and finding out what he has done?"

"Are you a Galilean, too?" they retorted. "Look where you will—you won't find that any prophet comes out of Galilee!"

So they broke up their meeting and went home, while Jesus went off to the Mount of Olives.

8.1 *Jesus deflates the rigorists*

Early next morning he returned to the Temple and the entire crowd came to him. So he sat

Revised Standard Version

priests and Pharisees, who said to them, "Why
did you not bring him?" 46 The officers answered,
"No man ever spoke like this man!" 47 The
Pharisees answered them, "Are you led astray,
you also? 48 Have any of the authorities or of
the Pharisees believed in him? 49 But this crowd,
who do not know the law, are accursed." 50 Nicodemus, who had gone to him before, and who
was one of them, said to them, 51 "Does our law
judge a man without first giving him a hearing
and learning what he does?" 52 They replied,
"Are you from Galilee too? Search and you will
see that no prophet is to rise from Galilee."

8 53 They went each to his own house, 1 but
Jesus went to the Mount of Olives. 2 Early
in the morning he came again to the temple; all
the people came to him, and he sat down and

Jerusalem Bible

and Pharisees who said to them, "Why haven't
you brought him?" 46 The police replied, "There
has never been anybody who has spoken like
him." 47 "So," the Pharisees answered, "you have
been led astray as well? 48 Have any of the authorities believed in him? Any of the Pharisees?
49 This rabble knows nothing about the Law—
they are damned." 50 One of them, Nicodemus
—the same man who had come to Jesus earlier—
said to them, 51 "But surely the Law does not
allow us to pass judgment on a man without
giving him a hearing and discovering what he is
about?" 52 To this they answered, "Are you a
Galilean too? Go into the matter, and see for
yourself: prophets do not come out of Galilee."

The adulterous woman[w]

53 They all went home,

8 and Jesus went to the Mount of Olives.
2 At daybreak he appeared in the Temple
again; and as all the people came to him, he sat
down and began to teach them.

[w] The author of this passage is not John; the oldest MSS do not include it or place it elsewhere. The style is that of the Synoptics.

New English Bible

priests and Pharisees, who asked, 'Why have you not brought him?' 'No man', they answered, 'ever spoke as this man speaks.' The Pharisees retorted, 'Have you too been misled? Is there a single one of our rulers who has believed in him, or of the Pharisees? As for this rabble, which cares nothing for the Law, a curse is on them.' Then one of their number, Nicodemus (the man who had once visited Jesus), intervened. 'Does our law', he asked them, 'permit us to pass judgement on a man unless we have first given him a hearing and learned the facts?' 'Are you a Galilean too?' they retorted. 'Study the scriptures and you will find that prophets do not come from Galilee.' [d]

*An incident in the temple**

8 *And they went each to his home, and Jesus to the Mount of Olives. At daybreak he appeared again in the temple, and all the people gathered round him. He had taken his seat and*

** This passage, which in the most widely received editions of the New Testament is printed in the text of John, 7. 53-8. 11, has no fixed place in our witnesses. Some of them do not contain it at all. Some place it after Luke 21. 38, others after John 7. 36, or 7. 52, or 21. 24.*

[d] *Some witnesses here insert the passage 7.53 – 8.11, which is printed on pages 705 and 709.*

King James Version

he sat down, and taught them. 3And the scribes
and Pharisees brought unto him a woman taken
in adultery; and when they had set her in the
midst, 4 They say unto him, Master, this woman
was taken in adultery, in the very act. 5 Now
Moses in the law commanded us, that such
should be stoned: but what sayest thou? 6 This
they said, tempting him, that they might have to
accuse him. But Jesus stooped down, and with
his finger wrote on the ground, *as though he*
heard them not. 7 So when they continued asking
him, he lifted up himself, and said unto them,
He that is without sin among you, let him first
cast a stone at her. 8And again he stooped down,
and wrote on the ground. 9And they which heard
it, being convicted by *their own* conscience, went
out one by one, beginning at the eldest, *even*
unto the last: and Jesus was left alone, and the
woman standing in the midst. 10 When Jesus had
lifted up himself, and saw none but the woman,
he said unto her, Woman, where are those thine
accusers? hath no man condemned thee? 11 She
said, No man, Lord. And Jesus said unto her,
Neither do I condemn thee: go, and sin no more.
12 Then spake Jesus again unto them, saying,
I am the light of the world: he that followeth

Living Bible

down and talked to them. 3As he was speaking,
the Jewish leaders and Pharisees brought a
woman caught in adultery and placed her out
in front of the staring crowd.
4 "Teacher," they said to Jesus, "this woman
was caught in the very act of adultery. 5 Moses'
law says to kill her. What about it?"
6 They were trying to trap him into saying
something they could use against him, but Jesus
stooped down and wrote in the dust with his
finger. 7 They kept demanding an answer, so he
stood up again and said, "All right, hurl the
stones at her until she dies. But only he who
never sinned may throw the first!"
8 Then he stooped down again and wrote
some more in the dust. 9And the Jewish leaders
slipped away one by one, beginning with the eldest, until only Jesus was left in front of the
crowd with the woman.
10 Then Jesus stood up again and said to her,
"Where are your accusers? Didn't even one of
them condemn you?"
11 "No, sir," she said.
And Jesus said, "Neither do I. Go and sin no
more."
12 Later, in one of his talks, Jesus said to the
people, "I am the Light of the world. So if you

Today's English Version

began to teach them. 3 The teachers of the Law
and the Pharisees brought in a woman who had
been caught committing adultery, and made her
stand before them all. 4 "Teacher," they said to
Jesus, "this woman was caught in the very act
of committing adultery. 5 In our Law Moses gave
a commandment that such a woman must be
stoned to death. Now, what do you say?" 6 They
said this to trap him, so they could accuse him.
But Jesus bent over and wrote on the ground
with his finger. 7As they stood there asking him
questions, he straightened up and said to them,
"Whichever one of you has committed no sin
may throw the first stone at her." 8 Then he bent
over again and wrote on the ground. 9 When
they heard this they all left, one by one, the
older ones first. Jesus was left alone, with the
woman still standing there. 10 He straightened
up and said to her, "Where are they, woman? Is
there no one left to condemn you?"
11 "No one, sir," she answered.
"Well, then," Jesus said, "I do not condemn
you either. Go, but do not sin again."]

Jesus the light of the world

12 Jesus spoke to them again, "I am the light
of the world. Whoever follows me will have the

New International Version

he sat down to teach them. 3 The teachers of
the law and the Pharisees brought in a woman
caught in adultery. They made her stand before
the group and 4 said to Jesus, "Teacher, this
woman was caught in the act of adultery. 5 In
the Law Moses commanded us to stone such
women. Now what do you say?" 6 They were
using this question as a trap, in order to have a
basis for accusing him.
But Jesus bent down and started to write on
the ground with his finger. 7 When they kept on
questioning him, he straightened up and said to
them, "If any one of you is without sin, let him
begin stoning her." 8Again he stooped down and
wrote on the ground.
9 At this, those who heard began to go away
one at a time, the older ones first, until only Jesus was left, with the woman still standing there.
10 Jesus straightened up and asked her, "Woman,
where are they? Has no one condemned you?"
11 "No one, sir," she said.
"Then neither do I condemn you," Jesus declared. "Go now and leave your life of sin."

The validity of Jesus' testimony

12 When Jesus spoke again to the people, he
said, "I am the light of the world. Whoever fol-

Phillips Modern English

down and began to teach them. But the scribes and Pharisees brought in to him a woman who had been caught in adultery. They made her stand in front, and then said to him, "Now, master, this woman has been caught in adultery, in the very act. According to the Law, Moses commanded us to stone such women to death. Now, what do you say about it?"

They said this to test him, so that they might have some good grounds for an accusation. But Jesus stooped down and began to write with his finger in the dust on the ground. But as they persisted in their questioning, he straightened himself up and said to them, "Let the one among you who has never sinned throw the first stone at her." Then he stooped down again and continued writing with his finger on the ground. And when they heard what he said, they were convicted by their own consciences and went out, one by one, beginning with the eldest.

Jesus was left alone, with the woman still standing where they had put her. So he stood up and said to her, "Where are they all—did no one condemn you?"

And she said, "No one, sir."

"Neither do I condemn you," said Jesus to her. "Go away now and do not sin again."

8.12 *Jesus' bold claims—about himself—and his Father*

Later, Jesus spoke to the people again and said, "I am the light of the world. The man who

Revised Standard Version

taught them. 3 The scribes and the Pharisees brought a woman who had been caught in adultery, and placing her in the midst 4 they said to him, "Teacher, this woman has been caught in the act of adultery. 5 Now in the law Moses commanded us to stone such. What do you say about her?" 6 This they said to test him, that they might have some charge to bring against him. Jesus bent down and wrote with his finger on the ground. 7 And as they continued to ask him, he stood up and said to them, "Let him who is without sin among you be the first to throw a stone at her." 8 And once more he bent down and wrote with his finger on the ground. 9 But when they heard it, they went away, one by one, beginning with the eldest, and Jesus was left alone with the woman standing before him. 10 Jesus looked up and said to her, "Woman, where are they? Has no one condemned you?" 11 She said, "No one, Lord." And Jesus said, "Neither do I condemn you; go, and do not sin again." [r]

12 Again Jesus spoke to them, saying, "I am the light of the world; he who follows me will

[*r*] The most ancient authorities omit 7.53–8.11; other authorities add the passage here or after 7.36 or after 21.25 or after Luke 21.38, with variations of text.

Jerusalem Bible

3 The scribes and Pharisees brought a woman along who had been caught committing adultery; and making her stand there in full view of everybody, 4 they said to Jesus, "Master, this woman was caught in the very act of committing adultery, 5 and Moses has ordered us in the Law to condemn women like this to death by stoning. What have you to say?" 6 They asked him this as a test, looking for something to use against him. But Jesus bent down and started writing on the ground with his finger. 7 As they persisted with their question, he looked up and said, "If there is one of you who has not sinned, let him be the first to throw a stone at her." 8 Then he bent down and wrote on the ground again. 9 When they heard this they went away one by one, beginning with the eldest, until Jesus was left alone with the woman, who remained standing there. 10 He looked up and said, "Woman, where are they? Has no one condemned you?" 11 "No one, sir," she replied. "Neither do I condemn you," said Jesus, "go away and don't sin any more."

Jesus, the light of the world

12 When Jesus spoke to the people again, he said:

"I am the light of the world;

New English Bible

was engaged in teaching them when the doctors of the law and the Pharisees brought in a woman caught committing adultery. Making her stand out in the middle they said to him, 'Master, this woman was caught in the very act of adultery. In the Law Moses has laid down that such women are to be stoned. What do you say about it?' They put the question as a test, hoping to frame a charge against him. Jesus bent down and wrote with his finger on the ground. When they continued to press their question he sat up straight and said, 'That one of you who is faultless shall throw the first stone.' Then once again he bent down and wrote on the ground. When they heard what he said, one by one they went away,[a] *the eldest first; and Jesus was left alone, with the woman still standing there. Jesus again sat up and*[b] *said to the woman, 'Where are they? Has no one condemned you?' She answered, 'No one, sir.' Jesus said, 'Nor do I condemn you. You may go; do not sin again.'*

Once again Jesus addressed the people: 'I am the light of the world. No follower of

[*a*] *Some witnesses insert* convicted by their conscience. [*b*] *Some witnesses insert* seeing no one but the woman.

King James Version

me shall not walk in darkness, but shall have
the light of life. 13 The Pharisees therefore said
unto him, Thou bearest record of thyself; thy
record is not true. 14 Jesus answered and said
unto them, Though I bear record of myself, *yet*
my record is true: for I know whence I came,
and whither I go; but ye cannot tell whence I
come, and whither I go. 15 Ye judge after the
flesh; I judge no man. 16 And yet if I judge, my
judgment is true: for I am not alone, but I and
the Father that sent me. 17 It is also written in
your law, that the testimony of two men is true.
18 I am one that bear witness of myself, and
the Father that sent me beareth witness of me.
19 Then said they unto him, Where is thy Father?

Living Bible

follow me, you won't be stumbling through the
darkness, for living light will flood your path."

13 The Pharisees replied, "You are boasting—
and lying!"

14 Jesus told them, "These claims are true
even though I make them concerning myself. For
I know where I came from and where I am going, but you don't know this about me. 15 You
pass judgment on me without knowing the facts.
I am not judging you now; 16 but if I were, it
would be an absolutely correct judgment in every
respect, for I have with me the Father who sent
me. 17 Your laws say that if two men agree on
something that has happened, their witness is
accepted as fact. 18 Well, I am one witness, and
my Father who sent me is the other."

19 "Where is your father?" they asked.

Today's English Version

light of life and will never walk in the darkness."

13 The Pharisees said to him, "Now you are
testifying on your own behalf; what you say
proves nothing."

14 "No," Jesus answered, "even if I do testify on my own behalf, what I say is true, because I know where I came from and where I
am going. You do not know where I came from
or where I am going. 15 You make judgments in
a purely human way; I pass judgment on no
one. 16 But if I were to pass judgment, my judging would be true, because I am not alone in
this; the Father who sent me is with me. 17 It
is written in your Law that when two witnesses
agree, what they say is true. 18 I testify on my
own behalf, and the Father who sent me also
testifies on my behalf."

19 "Where is your father?" they asked him.

New International Version

lows me will never walk in darkness, but will
have the light of life."

13 The Pharisees challenged him, "Here you
are, appearing as your own witness; your testimony is not valid."

14 Jesus answered, "Even if I testify on my
own behalf, my testimony is valid, for I know
where I came from and where I am going. But
you have no idea where I come from or where
I am going. 15 You judge by human standards;
I pass judgment on no one. 16 But if I do judge,
my decisions are right, because I am not alone.
I stand with the Father who sent me. 17 In your
own Law it is written that the testimony of two
men is valid. 18 I am one who testifies for myself; my other witness is the one who sent me—
the Father."

19 Then they asked him, "Where is your father?"

Phillips Modern English

follows me will never walk in the dark but will live his life in the light."

This made the Pharisees say to him, "You are testifying to yourself—your evidence is not valid."

Jesus answered. "Even if I am testifying to myself, my evidence is valid, for I know where I have come from and I know where I am going. But as for you, you have no idea where I come from or where I am going. You are judging by human standards, but I am not judging anyone. Yet if I should judge, my decision would be just, for I am not alone—the Father who sent me is with me. In your Law, it is stated that the witness of two persons is valid. I am one testifying to myself and the second witness to me is the Father who sent me."

"And where is this father of yours?" they asked.

Revised Standard Version

not walk in darkness, but will have the light of
life." 13 The Pharisees then said to him, "You
are bearing witness to yourself; your testimony
is not true." 14 Jesus answered, "Even if I do
bear witness to myself, my testimony is true, for
I know whence I have come and whither I am
going, but you do not know whence I come or
whither I am going. 15 You judge according to
the flesh, I judge no one. 16 Yet even if I do
judge, my judgment is true, for it is not I alone
that judge, but I and he[s] who sent me. 17 In your
law it is written that the testimony of two men
is true; 18 I bear witness to myself, and the
Father who sent me bears witness to me."
19 They said to him therefore, "Where is your

[s] Other ancient authorities read *the Father*.

Jerusalem Bible

anyone who follows me will not be walking
in the dark;
he will have the light of life."

A discussion on the testimony of Jesus to himself

13 At this the Pharisees said to him, "You are testifying on your own behalf; your testimony is not valid." 14 Jesus replied:

"It is true that I am testifying on my own behalf,
but my testimony is still valid,
because I know
where I came from and where I am going;
but you do not know
where I come from or where I am going.
15 You judge by human standards;
I judge no one,
16 but if I judge,
my judgment will be sound,
because I am not alone:
the one who sent me is with me;
17 and in your Law it is written
that the testimony of two witnesses is valid.
18 I may be testifying on my own behalf,
but the Father who sent me is my witness too."

19 They asked him, "Where is your Father?" Jesus answered:

New English Bible

mine shall wander in the dark; he shall have the light of life.' The Pharisees said to him, 'You are witness in your own cause; your testimony is not valid.' Jesus replied, 'My testimony is valid, even though I do bear witness about myself; because I know where I come from, and where I am going. You do not know either where I come from or where I am going. You judge by worldly standards. I pass judgement on no man, but if I do judge, my judgement is valid because it is not I alone who judge, but I and he who sent me. In your own law it is written that the testimony of two witnesses is valid. Here am I, a witness in my own cause, and my other witness is the Father who sent me.' They asked, 'Where

King James Version

Jesus answered, Ye neither know me, nor my
Father: if ye had known me, ye should have
known my Father also. 20 These words spake
Jesus in the treasury, as he taught in the temple:
and no man laid hands on him; for his hour was
not yet come. 21 Then said Jesus again unto
them, I go my way, and ye shall seek me, and
shall die in your sins: whither I go, ye cannot
come. 22 Then said the Jews, Will he kill himself? because he saith, Whither I go, ye cannot
come. 23 And he said unto them, Ye are from
beneath; I am from above: ye are of this world;
I am not of this world. 24 I said therefore unto
you, that ye shall die in your sins: for if ye believe not that I am *he,* ye shall die in your sins.
25 Then said they unto him, Who art thou? And

Living Bible

Jesus answered, "You don't know who I am, so you don't know who my Father is. If you knew me, then you would know him too."

20 Jesus made these statements while in the section of the Temple known as the Treasury. But he was not arrested, for his time had not yet run out.

21 Later he said to them again, "I am going away; and you will search for me, and die in your sins. And you cannot come where I am going."

22 The Jews asked, "Is he planning suicide? What does he mean, 'You cannot come where I am going'?"

23 Then he said to them, "You are from below; I am from above. You are of this world; I
am not. 24 That is why I said that you will die
in your sins; for unless you believe that I am
the Messiah, the Son of God, you will die in
your sins."

25 "Tell us who you are," they demanded.

Today's English Version

"You know neither me nor my Father," Jesus answered. "If you knew me you would know my Father also."

20 Jesus said all this as he taught in the temple, in the room where the offering boxes were placed. And no one arrested him, because his hour had not come.

You cannot go where I am going

21 Jesus said to them again, "I will go away; you will look for me, but you will die in your sins. You cannot go where I am going."

22 So the Jewish authorities said, "He says, 'You cannot go where I am going.' Does this mean that he will kill himself?"

23 Jesus answered, "You come from here below, but I come from above. You come from
this world, but I do not come from this world.
24 That is why I told you that you will die in
your sins. And you will die in your sins if you
do not believe that 'I Am Who I Am'."

25 "Who are you?" they asked him.

New International Version

"You do not know me or my Father," Jesus
replied. "If you knew me, you would know my
Father also." 20 He spoke these words while
teaching in the temple area near the place where
the offerings were put. Yet no one seized him,
because his time had not yet come.

21 Once more Jesus said to them, "I am going away, and you will look for me, and you will die in your sin. Where I go, you cannot come."

22 This made the Jews ask, "Will he kill himself? Is that why he says, 'Where I go, you cannot come'?"

23 But he continued, "You are from below; I
am from above. You are of this world; I am not
of this world. 24 I told you that you would die
in your sins; if you do not believe that I am
[the one I claim to be],[n] you will indeed die in
your sins."

25 "Who are you, anyway?" they asked.

[*n*] Or *I am he.*

Phillips Modern English

"You do not know my Father," returned Jesus, "any more than you know me: if you had known me, you would have known him also."

Jesus made these statements while he was teaching in the Temple treasury. Yet no one arrested him, for his time had not yet come.

Later, Jesus spoke to them again and said, "I am going away and you will try to find me, but you will die in your sins. You cannot come where I am going."

This made the Jews say, "Is he going to kill himself, then? Is *that* why he says, 'You cannot come where I am going'?"

"The difference between us," Jesus said to them, "is that you come from below and I am from above. You belong to this world but I do not. That is why I told you you will die in your sins. For unless you believe that I am who I am, you will die in your sins."

Then they said, *"Who are you?"*

Revised Standard Version

Father?" Jesus answered, "You know neither me nor my Father; if you knew me, you would know my Father also." 20 These words he spoke in the treasury, as he taught in the temple; but no one arrested him, because his hour had not yet come.
21 Again he said to them, "I go away, and you will seek me and die in your sin; where I am going, you cannot come." 22 Then said the Jews, "Will he kill himself, since he says, 'Where I am going, you cannot come'?" 23 He said to them, "You are from below, I am from above; you are of this world, I am not of this world.
24 I told you that you would die in your sins, for you will die in your sins unless you believe that I am he." 25 They said to him, "Who are you?"

Jerusalem Bible

"You do not know me, nor do you know my Father;
if you did know me, you would know my Father as well."

20 He spoke these words in the Treasury, while teaching in the Temple. No one arrested him, because his time had not yet come.

The unbelieving Jews warned

21 Again he said to them:

"I am going away; you will look for me
and you will die in your sin.
Where I am going, you cannot come."

22 The Jews said to one another, "Will he kill himself? Is that what he means by saying, 'Where I am going, you cannot come'?" 23 Jesus went on:

"You are from below;
I am from above.
You are of this world;
I am not of this world.
24 I have told you already: You will die in your sins.
Yes, if you do not believe that I am He,
you will die in your sins."

25 So they said to him, "Who are you?" Jesus answered:

New English Bible

is your father?' Jesus replied, 'You know neither me nor my Father; if you knew me you would know my Father as well.'

These words were spoken by Jesus in the treasury as he taught in the temple. Yet no one arrested him, because his hour had not yet come.

Again he said to them, 'I am going away. You will look for me, but you will die in your sin; where I am going you cannot come.' The Jews then said, 'Perhaps he will kill himself: is that what he means when he says, "Where I am going you cannot come"?' So Jesus continued, 'You belong to this world below, I to the world above. Your home is in this world, mine is not. That is why I told you that you would die in your sins. If you do not believe that I am what I am, you will die in your sins.' They asked him,

King James Version

Jesus saith unto them, Even *the same* that I said unto you from the beginning. 26 I have many things to say and to judge of you: but he that sent me is true; and I speak to the world those things which I have heard of him. 27 They understood not that he spake to them of the Father. 28 Then said Jesus unto them, When ye have lifted up the Son of man, then shall ye know that I am *he,* and *that* I do nothing of myself; but as my Father hath taught me, I speak these things. 29And he that sent me is with me: the Father hath not left me alone; for I do always those things that please him. 30As he spake these words, many believed on him. 31 Then said Jesus to those Jews which believed on him, If ye continue in my word, *then* are ye my disciples indeed; 32And ye shall know the truth, and the truth shall make you free.

33 They answered him, We be Abraham's seed, and were never in bondage to any man: how

Living Bible

He replied, "I am the one I have always claimed to be. 26 I could condemn you for much and teach you much, but I won't, for I say only what I am told to by the one who sent me; and he is Truth." 27 But they still didn't understand that he was talking to them about God.[a]

28 So Jesus said, "When you have killed the Messiah,[b] then you will realize that I am he and that I have not been telling you my own ideas, but have spoken what the Father taught me. 29And he who sent me is with me—he has not deserted me—for I always do those things that are pleasing to him."

30, 31 Then many of the Jewish leaders who heard him say these things began believing him to be the Messiah.

Jesus said to them, "You are truly my disciples if you live as I tell you to, 32 and you will know the truth, and the truth will set you free."

33 "But we are descendants of Abraham," they said, "and have never been slaves to any

[a] Literally, "the Father." [b] Literally, "when you have lifted up the Son of Man."

Today's English Version

Jesus answered, "What I have told you from the very beginning. 26 There are many things I have to say and judge about you. The one who sent me, however, is true, and I tell the world only what I have heard from him."

27 They did not understand that he was talking to them about the Father. 28 So Jesus said to them, "When you lift up the Son of Man you will know that 'I Am Who I Am'; then you will know that I do nothing on my own, but say only what the Father has taught me. 29And he who sent me is with me; he has not left me alone, because I always do what pleases him."

30 Many who heard Jesus say these things believed in him.

Free men and slaves

31 So Jesus said to the Jews who believed in him, "If you obey my teaching you are really my disciples; 32 you will know the truth, and the truth will make you free."

33 "We are the descendants of Abraham," they answered, "and we have never been any-

New International Version

"Just what I have been claiming all along," Jesus replied. 26 "I have much to say in judgment of you. But he who sent me is reliable, and what I have heard from him I tell the world."

27 They did not understand that he was telling them about his Father. 28 So Jesus said, "When you have lifted up the Son of Man, then you will know who I am[o] and that I do nothing on my own but speak just what the Father has taught me. 29 The one who sent me is with me; he has not left me alone, for I always do what pleases him." 30 Even as he spoke, many put their faith in him.

The children of Abraham

31 To the Jews who had believed him, Jesus said, "If you hold to my teaching, you are really my disciples. 32 Then you will know the truth, and the truth will set you free."

33 They answered him, "We are Abraham's descendants[p] and have never been slaves of any-

[o] Or *know that I am he.* [p] Greek *seed.*

Phillips Modern English

"I am what I have told you I was from the beginning," replied Jesus. "There is much in you that I could speak about and condemn. But he who sent me is true and I am only speaking to this world what I myself have heard from him."

They did not realise that he was talking to them about the Father. So Jesus resumed, "When you have lifted up the Son of Man, then you will realise that I am who I say I am, and that I do nothing on my own authority but speak simply as my Father has taught me. The one who sent me is with me now: the Father has never left me alone for I always do what pleases him." And even while he said these words, many people believed in him.

8.31 Jesus speaks of personal freedom

So Jesus said to the Jews who believed in him, "If you are faithful to what I have said, you are truly my disciples. And you will know the truth and the truth will set you free!"

"But we are decendants of Abraham," they replied, "and we have never in our lives been

Revised Standard Version

Jesus said to them, "Even what I have told you
from the beginning.[t] 26 I have much to say
about you and much to judge; but he who sent
me is true, and I declare to the world what I
have heard from him." 27 They did not understand that he spoke to them of the Father. 28 So
Jesus said, "When you have lifted up the Son
of man, then you will know that I am he, and
that I do nothing on my own authority but speak
thus as the Father taught me. 29 And he who
sent me is with me; he has not left me alone, for
I always do what is pleasing to him." 30 As he
spoke thus, many believed in him.
31 Jesus then said to the Jews who had believed in him, "If you continue in my word, you
are truly my disciples, 32 and you will know the
truth, and the truth will make you free." 33 They
answered him, "We are descendants of Abraham,
and have never been in bondage to any one.

[t] Or *Why do I talk to you at all?*

Jerusalem Bible

"What I have told you from the outset.
26 About you I have much to say
and much to condemn;
but the one who sent me is truthful,
and what I have learned from him
I declare to the world."

27 They failed to understand that he was talking to them about the Father. 28 So Jesus said:

"When you have lifted up the Son of Man,
then you will know that I am He
and that I do nothing of myself:
what the Father has taught me
is what I preach;
29 he who sent me is with me,
and has not left me to myself,
for I always do what pleases him."

30 As he was saying this, many came to believe in him.

Jesus and Abraham

31 To the Jews who believed in him Jesus said:

"If you make my word your home
you will indeed be my disciples,
32 you will learn the truth
and the truth shall make you free."

33 They answered, "We are descended from Abraham and we have never been the slaves of

New English Bible

'Who are you?' Jesus answered, 'Why should I speak to you at all?[a] I have much to say about you—and in judgement. But he who sent me speaks the truth, and what I heard from him I report to the world.'

They did not understand that he was speaking to them about the Father. So Jesus said to them, 'When you have lifted up the Son of Man you will know that I am what I am. I do nothing on my own authority, but in all that I say, I have been taught by my Father. He who sent me is present with me, and has not left me alone; for I always do what is acceptable to him.' As he said this, many put their faith in him.

Turning to the Jews who had believed him, Jesus said, 'If you dwell within the revelation I have brought, you are indeed my disciples; you shall know the truth, and the truth will set you free.' They replied, 'We are Abraham's descendants; we have never been in slavery to any man.

[a] *Or* What I have told you all along.

King James Version

sayest thou, Ye shall be made free? 34 Jesus answered them, Verily, verily, I say unto you, Whosoever committeth sin is the servant of sin. 35 And the servant abideth not in the house for ever: *but* the Son abideth ever. 36 If the Son therefore shall make you free, ye shall be free indeed. 37 I know that ye are Abraham's seed; but ye seek to kill me, because my word hath no place in you. 38 I speak that which I have seen with my Father: and ye do that which ye have seen with your father. 39 They answered and said unto him, Abraham is our father. Jesus saith unto them, If ye were Abraham's children, ye would do the works of Abraham. 40 But now ye seek to kill me, a man that hath told you the truth, which I have heard of God: this did not Abraham. 41 Ye do the deeds of your father. Then said they to him, We be not born of fornication; we have one Father, *even* God. 42 Jesus said unto

Living Bible

man on earth! What do you mean, 'set free'?"

34 Jesus replied, "You are slaves of sin, every one of you. 35 And slaves don't have rights, but the Son has every right there is! 36 So if the Son sets you free, you will indeed be free— 37 (Yes, I realize that you are descendants of Abraham!) And yet some of you are trying to kill me because my message does not find a home within your hearts. 38 I am telling you what I saw when I was with my Father. But you are following the advice of *your* father."

39 "Our father is Abraham," they declared.

"No!" Jesus replied, "for if he were, you would follow his good example. 40 But instead you are trying to kill me—and all because I told you the truth I heard from God. Abraham wouldn't do a thing like that! 41 No, you are obeying your *real* father when you act that way."

They replied, "We were not born out of wedlock—our true Father is God himself."

42 Jesus told them, "If that were so, then you

Today's English Version

body's slaves. What do you mean, then, by saying, 'You will be free'?"

34 Jesus said to them, "I tell you the truth: everyone who sins is a slave of sin. 35 A slave does not belong to the family always, but a son belongs there forever. 36 If the Son makes you free, then you will be really free. 37 I know you are Abraham's descendants. Yet you are trying to kill me, because you will not accept my teaching. 38 I talk about what my Father has shown me, but you do what your father has told you."

39 They answered him, "Our father is Abraham."

"If you really were Abraham's children," Jesus replied, "you would do the same works that he did. 40 All I have ever done is to tell you the truth I heard from God. Yet you are trying to kill me. Abraham did nothing like this! 41 You are doing what your father did."

"God himself is the only Father we have," they answered. "We are his true sons."

42 Jesus said to them, "If God really were

New International Version

one. How can you say that we shall be set free?"

34 Jesus replied, "I tell you the truth, everyone who sins is a slave to sin. 35 Now a slave has no permanent place in the family, but a son belongs to it forever. 36 So if the Son sets you free, you will be free indeed. 37 I know you are Abraham's descendants.[p] Yet you are ready to kill me, because you have no room for my word. 38 I am telling you what I have seen in the Father's presence, and you do what you have heard from your father."[q]

39 "Abraham is our father," they answered.

"If you were Abraham's children," said Jesus, "then you would do the things Abraham did.[r] 40 As it is, you are determined to kill me, a man who has told you the truth that I heard from God. Abraham did not do such things. 41 You are doing the things your own father does."

"We are not illegitimate children," they protested. "The only Father we have is God himself."

The children of the devil

42 Jesus said to them, "If God were your Fa-

[p] Greek *seed.* [q] Or *presence. Therefore do what you have heard from the Father.* [r] Some early MSS read *then do the things Abraham did.*

Phillips Modern English

any man's slaves. How can you say to us, 'You will be set free'?"

Jesus returned, "Believe me when I tell you that every man who commits sin is a slave. For a slave is no permanent part of a household, but a son is. If the Son, then, sets you free, you are really free! I know that you are descended from Abraham, but some of you are looking for a way to kill me because you can't bear my words. I am telling you what I have seen in the presence of my Father, and you are doing what you have seen in the presence of your father."

"Our father is Abraham!" they retorted.

"If you were the children of Abraham, you would do the sort of things Abraham did. But in fact you are looking for a way to kill me, simply because I am a man who has told you the truth that I have heard from God. Abraham would never have done that. No, you are doing your father's work."

"We are not illegitimate!" they retorted. "We have one Father—God."

"If God were really your Father," replied

Revised Standard Version

How is it that you say, 'You will be made free'?"
34 Jesus answered them, "Truly, truly, I say
to you, every one who commits sin is a slave to
sin. 35 The slave does not continue in the house
for ever; the son continues for ever. 36 So if the
Son makes you free, you will be free indeed.
37 I know that you are descendants of Abraham;
yet you seek to kill me, because my word finds
no place in you. 38 I speak of what I have seen
with my Father, and you do what you have
heard from your father."
39 They answered him, "Abraham is our father." Jesus said to them, "If you were Abraham's children, you would do what Abraham
did, 40 but now you seek to kill me, a man who
has told you the truth which I heard from God;
this is not what Abraham did. 41 You do what
your father did." They said to him, "We were
not born of fornication; we have one Father,
even God." 42 Jesus said to them, "If God were

Jerusalem Bible

anyone, what do you mean, 'You will be made
free'?" 34 Jesus replied:

"I tell you most solemnly,
everyone who commits sin is a slave.
35 Now the slave's place in the house is not assured,
but the son's place is assured.
36 So if the Son makes you free,
you will be free indeed.
37 I know that you are descended from Abraham;
but in spite of that you want to kill me
because nothing I say has penetrated into you.
38 What I, for my part, speak of
is what I have seen with my Father;
but you, you put into action
the lessons learned from your father."

39 They repeated, "Our father is Abraham."
Jesus said to them:

"If you were Abraham's children,
you would do as Abraham did.
40 As it is, you want to kill me
when I tell you the truth
as I have learned it from God;
that is not what Abraham did.
41 What you are doing is what your father does."

"We were not born of prostitution,"[x] they
went on, "we have one father: God." 42 Jesus
answered:

[x] By "prostitution" the prophets often mean religious infidelity, cf. Ho. 1:2.

New English Bible

What do you mean by saying, "You will become free men"?' 'In very truth I tell you', said Jesus, 'that everyone who commits sin is a slave. The slave has no permanent standing in the household, but the son belongs to it for ever. If then the Son sets you free, you will indeed be free.

'I know that you are descended from Abraham, but you are bent on killing me because my teaching makes no headway with you. I am revealing in words what I saw in my Father's presence; and you are revealing in action what you learned from your father.' They retorted, 'Abraham is our father.' 'If you were Abraham's children', Jesus replied, 'you would do as Abraham did.[b] As it is, you are bent on killing me, a man who told you the truth, as I heard it from God. That is not how Abraham acted. You are doing your own father's work.'

They said, 'We are not base-born; God is our father, and God alone.' Jesus said, 'If God were

[b] *Some witnesses read* 'If you are Abraham's children', Jesus replied, 'do as Abraham did.'

King James Version

them, If God were your Father, ye would love me: for I proceeded forth and came from God; neither came I of myself, but he sent me. 43 Why do ye not understand my speech? *even* because ye cannot hear my word. 44 Ye are of *your* father the devil, and the lusts of your father ye will do: he was a murderer from the beginning, and abode not in the truth, because there is no truth in him. When he speaketh a lie, he speaketh of his own: for he is a liar, and the father of it. 45And because I tell *you* the truth, ye believe me not. 46 Which of you convinceth me of sin? And if I say the truth, why do ye not believe me? 47 He that is of God heareth God's words: ye therefore hear *them* not, because ye are not of God. 48 Then answered the Jews, and said unto him, Say we not well that thou art a Samaritan, and hast a devil? 49 Jesus answered, I

Living Bible

would love me, for I have come to you from God. I am not here on my own, but he sent me. 43 Why can't you understand what I am saying? It is because you are prevented from doing so! 44 For you are the children of your father the devil and you love to do the evil things he does. He was a murderer from the beginning and a hater of truth—there is not an iota of truth in him. When he lies, it is perfectly normal; for he is the father of liars. 45And so when I tell the truth, you just naturally don't believe it!

46 "Which of you can truthfully accuse me of one single sin? [No one! [c]] And since I am telling you the truth, why don't you believe me? 47Anyone whose Father is God listens gladly to the words of God. Since you don't, it proves you aren't his children."

48 "You Samaritan! Foreigner! Devil!" the Jewish leaders snarled. "Didn't we say all along you were possessed by a demon?"

49 "No," Jesus said, "I have no demon in me.

[*c*] Implied.

Today's English Version

your father, you would love me, because I came from God and now I am here. I did not come on my own, but he sent me. 43 Why do you not understand what I say? It is because you cannot bear to listen to my message. 44 You are the children of your father, the Devil, and you want to follow your father's desires. From the very beginning he was a murderer. He has never been on the side of truth, because there is no truth in him. When he tells a lie he is only doing what is natural to him, because he is a liar and the father of all lies. 45 I tell the truth, and that is why you do not believe me. 46 Which one of you can prove that I am guilty of sin? If I tell the truth, then why do you not believe me? 47 He who comes from God listens to God's words. You, however, are not from God, and this is why you will not listen."

Jesus and Abraham

48 The Jews replied to Jesus, "Were we not right in saying that you are a Samaritan and have a demon in you?"

49 "I have no demon," Jesus answered. "I

New International Version

ther, you would love me, for I came from God and now am here. I have not come on my own; but he sent me. 43 Why is my language not clear to you? Because you are unable to hear what I say. 44 You belong to your father, the devil, and you want to carry out your father's desire. He was a murderer from the beginning, not holding to the truth, for there is no truth in him. When he lies, he speaks his native language, for he is a liar and the father of lies. 45 Yet because I tell the truth, you do not believe me! 46 Can any of you prove me guilty of sin? If I am telling the truth, why don't you believe me? 47 He who belongs to God hears what God says. The reason you do not hear is that you do not belong to God."

The claims of Jesus about himself

48 The Jews answered him, "Aren't we right in saying that you are a Samaritan and demon-possessed?"

49 "I am not possessed by a demon," said

Phillips Modern English

Jesus, "you would have loved me. For I came from God; and I am here. I did not come of my own accord—he sent me, and I am here. Why do you not understand my words? It is because you cannot hear what I am really saying. Your father is the devil, and what you are wanting to do is what your father longs to do. He always was a murderer, and has never dealt with the truth, since the truth will have nothing to do with him. Whenever he tells a lie, he speaks in character, for he is a liar and the father of lies. And it is because I speak the truth that you will not believe me. Which of you can prove me guilty of sin? If I am speaking the truth, why is it that you do not believe me? The man who is born of God can hear the words of God and the reason why you cannot hear the words of God is simply this, that you are not the sons of God."

"How right we are," retorted the Jews, "in calling you a Samaritan, and mad at that!"

"No," replied Jesus, "I am not mad. I am

Revised Standard Version

your Father, you would love me, for I proceeded and came forth from God; I came not
of my own accord, but he sent me. 43 Why do
you not understand what I say? It is because you
cannot bear to hear my word. 44 You are of
your father the devil, and your will is to do
your father's desires. He was a murderer from
the beginning, and has nothing to do with the
truth, because there is no truth in him. When
he lies, he speaks according to his own nature,
for he is a liar and the father of lies. 45 But,
because I tell the truth, you do not believe me.
46 Which of you convicts me of sin? If I tell the
truth, why do you not believe me? 47 He who is
of God hears the words of God; the reason why
you do not hear them is that you are not of
God."

48 The Jews answered him, "Are we not right
in saying that you are a Samaritan and have a
demon?" 49 Jesus answered, "I have not a de-

Jerusalem Bible

"If God were your father, you would love me,
since I have come here from God; yes, I have come from him;
not that I came because I chose,
no, I was sent, and by him.
43 Do you know why you cannot take in what I say?
It is because you are unable to understand my language.
44 The devil is your father,
and you prefer to do
what your father wants.
He was a murderer from the start;
he was never grounded in the truth;
there is no truth in him at all:
when he lies
he is drawing on his own store,
because he is a liar, and the father of lies.
45 But as for me, I speak the truth
and for that very reason,
you do not believe me.
46 Can one of you convict me of sin?
If I speak the truth, why do you not believe me?
47 A child of God
listens to the words of God;
if you refuse to listen,
it is because you are not God's children."

48 The Jews replied, "Are we not right in saying that you are a Samaritan and possessed by a devil?" Jesus answered:

49 "I am not possessed;
no, I honor my Father,

New English Bible

your father, you would love me, for God is the source of my being, and from him I come. I have not come of my own accord; he sent me. Why do you not understand my language? It is because my revelation is beyond your grasp.

'Your father is the devil and you choose to carry out your father's desires. He was a murderer from the beginning, and is not rooted in the truth; there is no truth in him. When he tells a lie he is speaking his own language, for he is a liar and the father of lies. But I speak the truth and therefore you do not believe me. Which of you can prove me in the wrong? [c] If what I say is true, why do you not believe me? He who has God for his father listens to the words of God. You are not God's children; that is why you do not listen.'

The Jews answered, 'Are we not right in saying that you are a Samaritan, and that you are possessed?' 'I am not possessed,' said Jesus;

[c] *Or* Which of you convicts me of sin?

King James Version

have not a devil; but I honour my Father, and
ye do dishonour me. 50And I seek not mine own
glory: there is one that seeketh and judgeth.
51 Verily, verily, I say unto you, If a man keep
my saying, he shall never see death. 52 Then
said the Jews unto him, Now we know that
thou hast a devil. Abraham is dead, and the
prophets; and thou sayest, If a man keep my
saying, he shall never taste of death. 53Art thou
greater than our father Abraham, which is dead?
and the prophets are dead: whom makest thou
thyself? 54 Jesus answered, If I honour myself,
my honour is nothing: it is my Father that honoureth me; of whom ye say, that he is your God:
55 Yet ye have not known him; but I know him:
and if I should say, I know him not, I shall be
a liar like unto you: but I know him, and keep
his saying. 56 Your father Abraham rejoiced to
see my day: and he saw *it*, and was glad. 57 Then
said the Jews unto him, Thou art not yet fifty
years old, and hast thou seen Abraham? 58 Jesus

Living Bible

For I honor my Father—and you dishonor me.
50And though I have no wish to make myself
great, God wants this for me and judges [those
who reject me[d]]. 51 With all the earnestness I
have I tell you this—no one who obeys me shall
ever die!"
52 The leaders of the Jews said, "Now we
know you are possessed by a demon. Even Abraham and the mightiest prophets died, and yet you
say that obeying you will keep a man from dying!
53 So you are greater than our father Abraham,
who died? And greater than the prophets, who
died? Who do you think you are?" 54 Then Jesus
told them this: "If I am merely boasting about
myself, it doesn't count. But it is my Father—
and you claim him as your God—who is saying
these glorious things about me. 55 But you do
not even know him. I do. If I said otherwise, I
would be as great a liar as you! But it is true—
I know him and fully obey him. 56 Your father
Abraham rejoiced to see my day. He knew I was
coming and was glad."
57 *The Jewish leaders:* "You aren't even fifty
years old—sure, you've seen Abraham!"
58 *Jesus:* "The absolute truth is that I was

[*d*] Implied. Literally, "There is one who seeks and judges."

Today's English Version

honor my Father, but you dishonor me. 50 I am
not seeking honor for myself. There is one who
is seeking it and who judges in my favor. 51 I
tell you the truth: whoever obeys my message
will never die."
52 The Jews said to him, "Now we know for
sure that you have a demon! Abraham died, and
the prophets died, yet you say, 'Whoever obeys
my message will never die.' 53 Our father Abraham died; you do not claim to be greater than
Abraham, do you? And the prophets also died.
Who do you think you are?"
54 Jesus answered, "If I were to honor myself, my own honor would be worth nothing.
The one who honors me is my Father—the very
one you say is your God. 55 You have never
known him, but I know him. If I were to say
that I do not know him, I would be a liar, like
you. But I do know him, and I obey his word.
56 Your father Abraham rejoiced that he was to
see my day; he saw it and was glad."
57 The Jews said to him, "You are not even
fifty years old—and you have seen Abraham?"
58 "I tell you the truth," Jesus replied. "Be-

New International Version

Jesus, "but I honor my Father and you dishonor
me. 50 I am not seeking glory for myself; but
there is one who seeks it, and he is the judge.
51 I tell you the truth, if a man keeps my word,
he will never see death."
52 At this the Jews exclaimed, "Now we know
that you are demon-possessed! Abraham died
and so did the prophets, yet you say that if a
man keeps your word, he will never taste death.
53Are you greater than our father Abraham?
He died, and so did the prophets. Who do you
think you are?"
54 Jesus replied, "If I glorify myself, my glory
means nothing. My Father, whom you claim as
your God, is the one who glorifies me. 55 Though
you do not know him, I know him. If I said I
did not, I would be a liar like you, but I do
know him and keep his word. 56 Your father
Abraham rejoiced at the thought of seeing my
day; he saw it and was glad."
57 "You are not yet fifty years old," the Jews
said to him, "and you have seen Abraham!"
58 "I tell you the truth," Jesus answered, "be-

Phillips Modern English

honouring my Father and you are dishonouring me. But I am not concerned with my own glory: there is one whose concern it is, and he is the true judge. Believe me when I assure you that if anybody accepts my words, he will never see death at all."

"Now we know that you're mad," replied the Jews. "Why, Abraham died and the prophets, too, and yet you say, 'If a man accepts my words, he will never experience death!' Are you greater than our father, Abraham? He died, and so did the prophets—who are you making yourself out to be?"

"If I were to glorify myself," returned Jesus, "such glory would be worthless. But it is my Father who glorifies me, the very one whom you say is your God—though you have never known him. But I know him, and if I said I did not know him, I should be as much a liar as you are! But I do know him and I am faithful to what he says. As for your Father, Abraham, his great joy was that he would see my coming. Now he has seen it and he is overjoyed."

"Look," said the Jews to him, "you are not fifty yet—and have you seen Abraham?"

"I tell you in solemn truth," returned Jesus,

Revised Standard Version

mon; but I honor my Father, and you dishonor
me. 50 Yet I do not seek my own glory; there is
One who seeks it and he will be the judge.
51 Truly, truly, I say to you, if any one keeps
my word, he will never see death." 52 The Jews
said to him, "Now we know that you have a
demon. Abraham died, as did the prophets; and
you say, 'If any one keeps my word, he will
never taste death.' 53 Are you greater than our
father Abraham, who died? And the prophets
died! Who do you claim to be?" 54 Jesus answered, "If I glorify myself, my glory is nothing;
it is my Father who glorifies me, of whom you
say that he is your God. 55 But you have not
known him; I know him. If I said, I do not know
him, I should be a liar like you; but I do know
him and I keep his word. 56 Your father Abraham rejoiced that he was to see my day; he saw
it and was glad." 57 The Jews then said to him,
"You are not yet fifty years old, and have you seen
Abraham?"[u] 58 Jesus said to them, "Truly, truly,

[u] Other ancient authorities read *has Abraham seen you?*

Jerusalem Bible

but you want to dishonor me.
50 Not that I care for my own glory,
there is someone who takes care of that
and is the judge of it.
51 I tell you most solemnly,
whoever keeps my word
will never see death."

52 The Jews said, "Now we know for certain that you are possessed. Abraham is dead, and the prophets are dead, and yet you say, 'Whoever keeps my word will never know the taste of death.' 53 Are you greater than our father Abraham, who is dead? The prophets are dead too. Who are you claiming to be?" 54 Jesus answered:

"If I were to seek my own glory
that would be no glory at all;
my glory is conferred by the Father,
by the one of whom you say, 'He is our God,'
55 although you do not know him.
But I know him,
and if I were to say: I do not know him,
I should be a liar, as you are liars yourselves.
But I do know him, and I faithfully keep his word.
56 Your father Abraham rejoiced
to think that he would see my Day;
he saw it and was glad."

57 The Jews then said, "You are not fifty yet, and you have seen Abraham!" 58 Jesus replied:

New English Bible

'I am honouring my Father, but you dishonour me. I do not care about my own glory; there is one who does care, and he is judge. In very truth I tell you, if anyone obeys my teaching he shall never know what it is to die.'

The Jews said, 'Now we are certain that you are possessed. Abraham is dead; the prophets are dead; and yet you say, "If anyone obeys my teaching he shall not know what it is to die." Are you greater than our father Abraham, who is dead? The prophets are dead too. What do you claim to be?'

Jesus replied, 'If I glorify myself, that glory of mine is worthless. It is the Father who glorifies me, he of whom you say, "He is our God", though you do not know him. But I know him; if I said that I did not know him I should be a liar like you. But in truth I know him and obey his word.

'Your father Abraham was overjoyed to see my day; he saw it and was glad.' The Jews protested, 'You are not yet fifty years old. How can you have seen Abraham?'[a] Jesus said, 'In

[a] *Some witnesses read* How can Abraham have seen you?

King James Version

said unto them, Verily, verily, I say unto you,
Before Abraham was, I am. 59 Then took they
up stones to cast at him: but Jesus hid himself,
and went out of the temple, going through the
midst of them, and so passed by.

9 And as *Jesus* passed by, he saw a man which
was blind from *his* birth. 2 And his disciples
asked him, saying, Master, who did sin, this
man, or his parents, that he was born blind?
3 Jesus answered, Neither hath this man sinned,
nor his parents: but that the works of God
should be made manifest in him. 4 I must work
the works of him that sent me, while it is day:
the night cometh, when no man can work. 5 As
long as I am in the world, I am the light of the
world. 6 When he had thus spoken, he spat on
the ground, and made clay of the spittle, and
he anointed the eyes of the blind man with the
clay, 7 And said unto him, Go, wash in the pool
of Siloam, (which is by interpretation, Sent.) He

Living Bible

in existence before Abraham was ever born!"
59 At that point the Jewish leaders picked up
stones to kill him. But Jesus was hidden from
them, and walked past them and left the Temple.

9 As he was walking along, he saw a man
blind from birth.
2 "Master," his disciples asked him, "why was
this man born blind? Was it a result of his own
sins or those of his parents?"
3 "Neither," Jesus answered. "But to demonstrate the power of God. 4 All of us must quickly
carry out the tasks assigned us by the one who
sent me, for there is little time left before the
night falls and all work comes to an end. 5 But
while I am still here in the world, I give it my
light."
6 Then he spat on the ground and made mud
from the spittle and smoothed the mud over the
blind man's eyes, 7 and told him, "Go and wash
in the Pool of Siloam" (the word "Siloam"
means "Sent"). So the man went where he was

Today's English Version

fore Abraham was born, 'I Am'."
59 They picked up stones to throw at him;
but Jesus hid himself and left the temple.

Jesus heals a man born blind

9 As Jesus walked along he saw a man who
had been born blind. 2 His disciples asked
him, "Teacher, whose sin was it that caused him
to be born blind? His own or his parents' sin?"
3 Jesus answered, "His blindness has nothing
to do with his sins or his parents' sins. He is
blind so that God's power might be seen at work
in him. 4 We must keep on doing the works of
him who sent me, as long as it is day; the night
is coming, when no one can work. 5 While I am
in the world I am the light for the world."
6 After he said this, Jesus spat on the ground
and made some mud with the spittle; he rubbed
the mud on the man's eyes, 7 and told him, "Go
wash your face in the Pool of Siloam." (This
name means "Sent.") So the man went, washed

New International Version

fore Abraham was born, I am!" 59 At this, they
picked up stones to stone him, but Jesus hid
himself, slipping away from the temple grounds.

Jesus heals a man born blind

9 As he went along, he saw a man blind from
birth. 2 His disciples asked him, "Rabbi, who
sinned, this man or his parents, that he was born
blind?"
3 "Neither this man nor his parents sinned,"
said Jesus, "but this happened so that the work
of God might be displayed in his life. 4 As long
as it is day, we must do the work of him who
sent me. Night is coming, when no one can
work. 5 While I am in the world, I am the light
of the world."
6 Having said this, he spit on the ground,
made some mud with the saliva, and put it on
the man's eyes. 7 "Go," he told him, "wash in
the pool of Siloam" (this word means Sent). So

Phillips Modern English

"before there was an Abraham, I AM!"
At this, they picked up stones to hurl at him, but Jesus was nowhere to be seen; and he made his way out of the Temple.

9.1 Jesus and blindness, physical and spiritual

Later, as Jesus walked along he saw a man who had been blind from birth.
"Rabbi, whose sin caused this man's blindness," asked the disciples, "his own or his parents'?"
"He was not born blind because of his own sin or that of his parents," returned Jesus, "but to show the power of God at work in him. We must carry on the work of him who sent me while the daylight lasts. Night is coming, when no one can work. I am the world's light as long as I am in it."
Having said this, he spat on the ground and made a sort of clay with the saliva. This he applied to the man's eyes and said, "Go and wash in the pool of Siloam." (Siloam means "one who has been sent".) So the man went off and

Revised Standard Version

I say to you, before Abraham was, I am." 59 So
they took up stones to throw at him; but Jesus
hid himself, and went out of the temple.

9 As he passed by, he saw a man blind from
his birth. 2 And his disciples asked him,
"Rabbi, who sinned, this man or his parents, that
he was born blind?" 3 Jesus answered, "It was
not that this man sinned, or his parents, but that
the works of God might be made manifest in
him. 4 We must work the works of him who sent
me, while it is day; night comes, when no one
can work. 5 As long as I am in the world, I am
the light of the world." 6 As he said this, he spat
on the ground and made clay of the spittle and
anointed the man's eyes with the clay, 7 saying
to him, "Go, wash in the pool of Siloam"
(which means Sent). So he went and washed

Jerusalem Bible

"I tell you most solemnly,
before Abraham ever was,
I Am."

59 At this they picked up stones to throw at him[y]; but Jesus hid himself and left the Temple.

The cure of the man born blind

9 As he went along, he saw a man who had been blind from birth. 2 His disciples asked him, "Rabbi, who sinned, this man or his parents, for him to have been born blind?" 3 "Neither he nor his parents sinned," Jesus answered, "he was born blind so that the works of God might be displayed in him.

4 "As long as the day lasts
I must carry out the work of the one who sent me;
the night will soon be here when no one can work.
5 As long as I am in the world
I am the light of the world."

6 Having said this, he spat on the ground, made a paste with the spittle, put this over the eyes of the blind man, 7 and said to him, "Go and wash in the Pool of Siloam[z] (a name that means "sent"). So the blind man went off and

[y] Stoning was the penalty for blasphemy. Cf. 10:33.
[z] Water from this pool was drawn during the feast of Tabernacles to symbolize the waters of blessing.

New English Bible

very truth I tell you, before Abraham was born, I am.'
They picked up stones to throw at him, but Jesus was not to be seen; and he left the temple.[b]

9 As he went on his way Jesus saw a man blind from his birth. His disciples put the question, 'Rabbi, who sinned, this man or his parents? Why was he born blind?' 'It is not that this man or his parents sinned,' Jesus answered; 'he was born blind so that God's power might be displayed in curing him. While daylight lasts we[c] must carry on the work of him who sent me; night comes, when no one can work. While I am in the world I am the light of the world.'
With these words he spat on the ground and made a paste with the spittle; he spread it on the man's eyes, and said to him, 'Go and wash in the pool of Siloam.' (The name means 'sent'.) The man went away and washed, and when he

[b] *Or the division may be made after the words* was not to be seen; *the paragraph following would then begin* Then Jesus left the temple, and as he went . . . [c] *Some witnesses read* I.

King James Version

went his way therefore, and washed, and came
seeing.
8 The neighbours therefore, and they which
before had seen him that he was blind, said, Is
not this he that sat and begged? 9 Some said,
This is he: others *said*, He is like him: *but* he
said, I am *he*. 10 Therefore said they unto him,
How were thine eyes opened? 11 He answered
and said, A man that is called Jesus made clay,
and anointed mine eyes, and said unto me, Go
to the pool of Siloam, and wash: and I went
and washed, and I received sight. 12 Then said
they unto him, Where is he? He said, I know not.
13 They brought to the Pharisees him that
aforetime was blind. 14 And it was the sabbath
day when Jesus made the clay, and opened his
eyes. 15 Then again the Pharisees also asked him
how he had received his sight. He said unto
them, He put clay upon mine eyes, and I washed,
and do see. 16 Therefore said some of the Pharisees, This man is not of God, because he keepeth
not the sabbath day. Others said, How can a
man that is a sinner do such miracles? And
there was a division among them. 17 They say
unto the blind man again, What sayest thou of

Living Bible

sent and washed and came back seeing!
8 His neighbors and others who knew him as
a blind beggar asked each other, "Is this the
same fellow—that beggar?"
9 Some said yes, and some said no. "It can't
be the same man," they thought, "but he surely
looks like him!"
And the beggar said, "I *am* the same man!"
10 Then they asked him how in the world he
could see. What had happened?
11 And he told them, "A man they call Jesus
made mud and smoothed it over my eyes and
told me to go to the Pool of Siloam and wash
off the mud. I did, and I can see!"
12 "Where is he now?" they asked.
"I don't know," he replied.
13 Then they took the man to the Pharisees.
14 Now as it happened, this all occurred on a
Sabbath.[a] 15 Then the Pharisees asked him all
about it. So he told them how Jesus had
smoothed the mud over his eyes, and when it
was washed away, he could see!
16 Some of them said, "Then this fellow Jesus
is not from God, because he is working on the
Sabbath."
Others said, "But how could an ordinary sinner do such miracles?" So there was a deep division of opinion among them.
17 Then the Pharisees turned on the man who
had been blind and demanded, "This man who

[*a*] i.e., on Saturday, the weekly Jewish holy day when all work was forbidden.

Today's English Version

his face, and came back seeing.
8 His neighbors, then, and the people who
had seen him begging before this, asked, "Isn't
this the man who used to sit and beg?"
9 Some said, "He is the one," but others
said, "No he isn't, he just looks like him."
So the man himself said, "I am the man."
10 "How were your eyes opened?" they asked
him.
11 He answered, "The man named Jesus made
some mud, rubbed it on my eyes, and told me,
'Go to Siloam and wash your face.' So I went,
and as soon as I washed I could see."
12 "Where is he?" they asked.
"I do not know," he answered.

The Pharisees investigate the healing

13 Then they took the man who had been
blind to the Pharisees. 14 The day that Jesus
made the mud and opened the man's eyes was
a Sabbath. 15 The Pharisees, then, asked the
man again how he had received his sight. He
told them, "He put some mud on my eyes, I
washed my face, and now I can see."
16 Some of the Pharisees said, "The man who
did this cannot be from God, because he does
not obey the Sabbath law."
Others, however, said, "How could a man who
is a sinner do such mighty works as these?" And
there was a division among them.
17 So the Pharisees asked the man once more,
"You say he opened your eyes—well, what do

New International Version

the man went and washed, and came home
seeing.
8 His neighbors and those who had formerly
seen him begging asked, "Isn't this the same
man who used to sit and beg?" 9 Some claimed
that he was.
Others said, "No, he only looks like him."
But he himself insisted, "I am the man."
10 "How then were your eyes opened?" they
demanded.
11 He replied, "The man they call Jesus made
some mud and put it on my eyes. He told me to
go to Siloam and wash. So I went and washed,
and then I could see."
12 "Where is this man?" they asked him.
"I don't know," he said.

The Pharisees investigate the healing

13 They brought to the Pharisees the man
who had been blind. 14 Now the day on which
Jesus had made the mud and opened the man's
eyes was a Sabbath. 15 Therefore the Pharisees
also asked him how he had received his sight.
"He put mud on my eyes," the man replied,
"and I washed, and now I see."
16 Some of the Pharisees said, "This man is
not from God, for he does not keep the Sabbath."
But others asked, "How can a sinner do such
miraculous signs?" So they were divided.
17 Finally they turned again to the blind man,
"What have you to say about him? It was your

Phillips Modern English

washed and came back with his sight restored.

His neighbours and the people who had often seen him before as a beggar remarked, "Isn't this the man who used to sit and beg?"

"Yes, that's the one," said some.

Others said, "No, but he's very like him."

But he himself said, "I'm the man all right!"

"Then how was your blindness cured?" they asked.

"The man called Jesus made some clay and smeared it on my eyes," he replied, "and then he said, 'Go to Siloam and wash.' So off I went and washed—and that's how I got my sight!"

"Where is he now?" they asked.

"I don't know," he returned.

So they brought the man who had been blind before the Pharisees. (It should be noted that Jesus made the clay and restored his sight on a Sabbath day.) The Pharisees asked the question all over again as to how he had become able to see.

"He put clay on my eyes; I washed it off; now I can see—that's all," he replied.

Some of the Pharisees commented, "This man cannot be from God since he does not observe the Sabbath."

"But how can a sinner give such wonderful signs as these?" others demurred. And they were in two minds about him. Finally, they asked the blind man again, "And what do *you* say about

Revised Standard Version

and came back seeing. 8 The neighbors and
those who had seen him before as a beggar,
said, "Is not this the man who used to sit
and beg?" 9 Some said, "It is he"; others
said, "No, but he is like him." He said, "I am
the man." 10 They said to him, "Then how were
your eyes opened?" 11 He answered, "The man
called Jesus made clay and anointed my eyes
and said to me, 'Go to Siloam and wash'; so I
went and washed and received my sight." 12 They
said to him, "Where is he?" He said, "I do not
know."
13 They brought to the Pharisees the man
who had formerly been blind. 14 Now it was a
sabbath day when Jesus made the clay and
opened his eyes. 15 The Pharisees again asked
him how he had received his sight. And he said
to them, "He put clay on my eyes, and I washed,
and I see." 16 Some of the Pharisees said, "This
man is not from God, for he does not keep the
sabbath." But others said, "How can a man who
is a sinner do such signs?" There was a division
among them. 17 So they again said to the blind
man, "What do you say about him, since he has

Jerusalem Bible

washed himself, and came away with his sight restored.
8 His neighbors and people who earlier had
seen him begging said, "Isn't this the man who
used to sit and beg?" 9 Some said, "Yes, it is
the same one." Others said, "No, he only looks
like him." The man himself said, "I am the
man." 10 So they said to him, "Then how do
your eyes come to be open?" 11 "The man called
Jesus" he answered, "made a paste, daubed my
eyes with it and said to me, 'Go and wash at
Siloam'; so I went, and when I washed I could
see." 12 They asked, "Where is he?" "I don't
know," he answered.
13 They brought the man who had been blind
to the Pharisees. 14 It had been a sabbath day
when Jesus made the paste and opened the
man's eyes, 15 so when the Pharisees asked him
how he had come to see, he said, "He put a
paste on my eyes, and I washed, and I can see."
16 Then some of the Pharisees said, "This man
cannot be from God: he does not keep the
sabbath." Others said, "How could a sinner
produce signs like this?" And there was disagreement among them. 17 So they spoke to the
blind man again, "What have you to say about

New English Bible

returned he could see.

His neighbours and those who were accustomed to see him begging said, 'Is not this the man who used to sit and beg?' Others said, 'Yes, this is the man.' Others again said, 'No, but it is someone like him.' The man himself said, 'I am the man.' They asked him, 'How were your eyes opened?' He replied, 'The man called Jesus made a paste and smeared my eyes with it, and told me to go to Siloam and wash. I went and washed, and gained my sight.' 'Where is he?' they asked. He answered, 'I do not know.'

The man who had been blind was brought before the Pharisees. As it was a Sabbath day when Jesus made the paste and opened his eyes, the Pharisees now asked him by what means he had gained his sight. The man told them, 'He spread a paste on my eyes; then I washed, and now I can see.' Some of the Pharisees said, 'This fellow is no man of God; he does not keep the Sabbath.' Others said, 'How could such signs come from a sinful man?' So they took different sides. Then they continued to question him: 'What have you to say about him? It was your eyes he

King James Version

him, that he hath opened thine eyes? He said,
He is a prophet. 18 But the Jews did not believe
concerning him, that he had been blind, and
received his sight, until they called the parents
of him that had received his sight. 19 And they
asked them, saying, Is this your son, who ye say
was born blind? how then doth he now see?
20 His parents answered them and said, We know
that this is our son, and that he was born blind:
21 But by what means he now seeth, we know
not; or who hath opened his eyes, we know not:
he is of age; ask him: he shall speak for himself. 22 These *words* spake his parents, because
they feared the Jews: for the Jews had agreed
already, that if any man did confess that he was
Christ, he should be put out of the synagogue.
23 Therefore said his parents, He is of age; ask
him. 24 Then again called they the man that was
blind, and said unto him, Give God the praise:
we know that this man is a sinner. 25 He answered and said, Whether he be a sinner *or no,*
I know not: one thing I know, that, whereas I
was blind, now I see. 26 Then said they to him
again, What did he to thee? how opened he
thine eyes? 27 He answered them, I have told
you already, and ye did not hear: wherefore
would ye hear *it* again? will ye also be his disciples? 28 Then they reviled him, and said, Thou
art his disciple; but we are Moses' disciples.
29 We know that God spake unto Moses: *as for*

Living Bible

opened your eyes—who do you say he is?"
"I think he must be a prophet sent from God,"
the man replied.
18 The Jewish leaders wouldn't believe he had
been blind, until they called in his parents 19 and
asked them, "Is this your son? Was he born
blind? If so, how can he see?"
20 His parents replied, "We know this is our
son and that he was born blind, 21 but we don't
know what happened to make him see, or who
did it. He is old enough to speak for himself.
Ask him."
22, 23 They said this in fear of the Jewish
leaders who had announced that anyone saying
Jesus was the Messiah would be excommunicated.
24 So for the second time they called in the
man who had been blind and told him, "Give
the glory to God, not to Jesus, for we know
Jesus is an evil person."
25 "I don't know whether he is good or bad,"
the man replied, "but I know this: *I was blind,*
and now I see!"
26 "But what did he do?" they asked. "How
did he heal you?"
27 "Look!" the man exclaimed. "I told you
once; didn't you listen? Why do you want to
hear it again? Do you want to become his
disciples too?"
28 Then they cursed him and said, "You are
his disciple, but we are disciples of Moses. 29 We

Today's English Version

you say about him?"
"He is a prophet," he answered.
18 The Jewish authorities, however, were not
willing to believe that he had been blind and
could now see, until they called the man's parents 19 and asked them, "Is this your son? You
say that he was born blind; well, how is it that
he can see now?"
20 His parents answered, "We know that he
is our son, and we know that he was born blind.
21 But we do not know how it is that he is now
able to see, nor do we know who opened his
eyes. Ask him; he is old enough, and he can
answer for himself!" 22 His parents said this because they were afraid of the Jewish authorities,
who had already agreed that anyone who professed that Jesus was the Messiah would be put
out of the synagogue. 23 That is why his parents
said, "He is old enough; ask him!"
24 A second time they called back the man
who had been born blind and said to him,
"Promise before God that you will tell the
truth! We know that this man is a sinner."
25 "I do not know if he is a sinner or not,"
the man replied. "One thing I do know: I was
blind, and now I see."
26 "What did he do to you?" they asked.
"How did he open your eyes?"
27 "I have already told you," he answered,
"and you would not listen. Why do you want to
hear it again? Maybe you, too, would like to be
his disciples?"
28 They insulted him and said, "You are that
fellow's disciple; we are Moses' disciples. 29 We

New International Version

eyes he opened."
The man replied, "He is a prophet."
18 The Jews still did not believe that he had
been blind and had received his sight until they
sent for the man's parents. 19 "Is this your son?"
they asked. "Is this the one you say was born
blind? How is it that now he can see?"
20 "We know he is our son," the parents answered, "and we know he was born blind. 21 But
how he can see now, or who opened his eyes,
we don't know. Ask him. He is of age; he will
speak for himself." 22 His parents said this because they were afraid of the Jews, for already
the Jews had decided that anyone who acknowledged that Jesus was the Christ[s] would be put
out of the synagogue. 23 That was why his
parents said, "He is of age; ask him."
24 A second time they summoned the man
who had been blind. "Give glory to God,"[t] they
said. "We know this man is a sinner."
25 He replied, "Whether he is a sinner or not,
I don't know. One thing I do know. I was blind
but now I see!"
26 Then they asked him, "What did he do to
you? How did he open your eyes?"
27 He answered, "I have told you already and
you did not listen. Why do you want to hear it
again? Do you want to become his disciples,
too?"
28 Then they hurled insults at him and said,
"You are this fellow's disciple! We are disciples
of Moses! 29 We know that God spoke to Moses,

[*s*] Or *Messiah*. [*t*] A solemn charge to tell the truth (see Joshua 7:19).

Phillips Modern English

him? You're the one whose sight was restored."

"I believe he is a prophet," he replied.

The Jews did not really believe that the man had been blind and then had become able to see, until they had summoned his parents and asked them, "Is this your son who you say was born blind? How does it happen that he can now see?"

"We know that this is our son, and we know that he was born blind," returned his parents, "but how he can see now, or who made him able to see, we have no idea. Why don't you ask him? He is a grown-up man; he can speak for himself."

His parents said this because they were afraid of the Jews who had already agreed that anybody who admitted that the man was Christ should be excommunicated. It was this which made his parents say, "Ask him, he is a grown-up man."

So, once again they summoned the man who had been born blind and said to him, "You should give God the glory for what has happened to you. We know that this man is a sinner."

"Whether he is a sinner or not, I couldn't tell, but one thing I am sure of," the man replied, "I used to be blind, now I can see!"

"But what did he *do* to you—how did he make you see?" they continued.

"I've told you before," he replied. "Weren't you listening? Why do you want to hear it all over again? Are you wanting to be his disciples too?"

At this, they turned on him furiously.

"You're the one who is his disciple! We are disciples of Moses. We know that God spoke to

Revised Standard Version

opened your eyes?" He said, "He is a prophet."
18 The Jews did not believe that he had been
blind and had received his sight, until they
called the parents of the man who had received
his sight, 19 and asked them, "Is this your son,
who you say was born blind? How then does he
now see?" 20 His parents answered, "We know
that this is our son, and that he was born blind;
21 but how he now sees we do not know, nor
do we know who opened his eyes. Ask him; he
is of age, he will speak for himself." 22 His
parents said this because they feared the Jews,
for the Jews had already agreed that if any one
should confess him to be Christ, he was to be
put out of the synagogue. 23 Therefore his parents said, "He is of age, ask him."
24 So for the second time they called the man
who had been blind, and said to him, "Give God
the praise; we know that this man is a sinner."
25 He answered, "Whether he is a sinner, I do
not know; one thing I know, that though I was
blind, now I see." 26 They said to him, "What did
he do to you? How did he open your eyes?"
27 He answered them, "I have told you already,
and you would not listen. Why do you want to
hear it again? Do you too want to become his
disciples?" 28And they reviled him, saying, "You
are his disciple, but we are disciples of Moses.
29 We know that God has spoken to Moses,

Jerusalem Bible

him yourself, now that he has opened your
eyes?" "He is a prophet," replied the man.
18 However, the Jews would not believe that
the man had been blind and had gained his
sight, without first sending for his parents and
19 asking them, "Is this man really your son who
you say was born blind? If so, how is it that he
is now able to see?" 20 His parents answered,
"We know he is our son and we know he was
born blind, 21 but we don't know how it is that
he can see now, or who opened his eyes. He is
old enough: let him speak for himself." 22 His
parents spoke like this out of fear of the Jews,
who had already agreed to expel from the synagogue anyone who should acknowledge Jesus as
the Christ. 23 This was why his parents said, "He
is old enough; ask him."
24 So the Jews again sent for the man and
said to him, "Give glory to God! [a] For our part,
we know that this man is a sinner." 25 The man
answered, "I don't know if he is a sinner; I only
know that I was blind and now I can see."
26 They said to him, "What did he do to you?
How did he open your eyes?" 27 He replied,
"I have told you once and you wouldn't listen.
Why do you want to hear it all again? Do you
want to become his disciples too?" 28At this
they hurled abuse at him: "You can be his
disciple," they said, "we are disciples of Moses:
29 we know that God spoke to Moses, but as for

[a] I.e., putting the man on oath.

New English Bible

opened.' He answered, 'He is a prophet.'

The Jews would not believe that the man had been blind and had gained his sight, until they had summoned his parents and questioned them: 'Is this man your son? Do you say that he was born blind? How is it that he can see now?' The parents replied, 'We know that he is our son, and that he was born blind. But how it is that he can now see, or who opened his eyes, we do not know. Ask him; he is of age; he will speak for himself.' His parents gave this answer because they were afraid of the Jews; for the Jewish authorities had already agreed that anyone who acknowledged Jesus as Messiah should be banned from the synagogue. That is why the parents said, 'He is of age; ask him.'

So for the second time they summoned the man who had been blind, and said, 'Speak the truth before God. We know that this fellow is a sinner.' 'Whether or not he is a sinner, I do not know,' the man replied. 'All I know is this: once I was blind, now I can see.' 'What did he do to you?' they asked. 'How did he open your eyes?' 'I have told you already,' he retorted, 'but you took no notice. Why do you want to hear it again? Do you also want to become his disciples?' Then they became abusive. 'You are that man's disciple,' they said, 'but we are disciples of Moses. We know that God spoke to Moses,

King James Version

this *fellow*, we know not from whence he is. 30 The man answered and said unto them, Why herein is a marvellous thing, that ye know not from whence he is, and *yet* he hath opened mine eyes. 31 Now we know that God heareth not sinners: but if any man be a worshipper of God, and doeth his will, him he heareth. 32 Since the world began was it not heard that any man opened the eyes of one that was born blind. 33 If this man were not of God, he could do nothing. 34 They answered and said unto him, Thou wast altogether born in sins, and dost thou teach us? And they cast him out. 35 Jesus heard that they had cast him out; and when he had found him, he said unto him, Dost thou believe on the Son of God? 36 He answered and said, Who is he, Lord, that I might believe on him? 37 And Jesus said unto him, Thou hast both seen him, and it is he that talketh with thee. 38 And he said, Lord, I believe. And he worshipped him.

39 And Jesus said, For judgment I am come into this world, that they which see not might see; and that they which see might be made blind. 40 And *some* of the Pharisees which were with him heard these words, and said unto him,

Living Bible

know God has spoken to Moses, but as for this fellow, we don't know anything about him."

30 "Why, that's very strange!" the man replied. "He can heal blind men, and yet you don't know anything about him! 31 Well, God doesn't listen to evil men, but he has open ears to those who worship him and do his will. 32 Since the world began there has never been anyone who could open the eyes of someone born blind. 33 If this man were not from God, he couldn't do it."

34 "You illegitimate bastard,[b] you!" they shouted. "Are you trying to teach *us?*" And they threw him out.

35 When Jesus heard what had happened, he found the man and said, "Do you believe in the Messiah?"[c]

36 The man answered, "Who is he, sir, for I want to."

37 "You have seen him," Jesus said, "and he is speaking to you!"

38 "Yes, Lord," the man said, "I believe!" And he worshiped Jesus.

39 Then Jesus told him, "I have come into the world to give sight to those who are spiritually blind and to show those who think they see that they are blind."

40 The Pharisees who were standing there asked, "Are you saying we are blind?"

[*b*] Literally, "You were altogether born in sin."
[*c*] Literally, "the Son of Man."

Today's English Version

know that God spoke to Moses; as for that fellow, we do not even know where he comes from!"

30 The man answered, "What a strange thing this is! You do not know where he comes from, but he opened my eyes! 31 We know that God does not listen to sinners; he does listen to people who respect him and do what he wants them to do. 32 Since the beginning of the world it has never been heard of that someone opened the eyes of a man born blind; 33 unless this man came from God, he would not be able to do a thing."

34 They answered back, "You were born and raised in sin—and you are trying to teach us?" And they threw him out of the synagogue.

Spiritual blindness

35 Jesus heard that they had thrown him out. He found him and said, "Do you believe in the Son of Man?"

36 The man answered, "Tell me who he is, sir, so I can believe in him!"

37 Jesus said to him, "You have already seen him, and he is the one who is talking with you now."

38 "I believe, Lord!" the man said, and knelt down before Jesus.

39 Jesus said, "I came to this world to judge, so that the blind should see, and those who see should become blind."

40 Some Pharisees, who were there with him, heard him say this and asked him, "You don't mean that we are blind, too?"

New International Version

but as for this fellow, we don't even know where he comes from."

30 The man answered, "Now that is remarkable! You don't know where he comes from, yet he opened my eyes. 31 We know that God does not listen to sinners. He listens to the godly man who does his will. 32 Nobody has ever heard of opening the eyes of a man born blind. 33 If this man were not from God, he could do nothing."

34 To this they replied, "You were steeped in sin at birth; how dare you lecture us!" And they threw him out.

Spiritual blindness

35 Jesus heard that they had thrown him out, and when he found him, he said, "Do you believe in the Son of Man?"

36 "Who is he, sir?" the man asked. "Tell me so that I may believe in him."

37 Jesus said, "You have now seen him; in fact, he is the one speaking with you."

38 Then the man said, "Lord, I believe," and he worshiped him.

39 Jesus said, "For judgment I have come into this world, so that the blind will see and those who see will turn out to be blind."

40 Some Pharisees who were with him heard him say this and asked, "What? Are we blind too?"

Phillips Modern English

Moses, but as for this man, we don't even know where he came from."

"Now here's the extraordinary thing," he retorted, "you don't know where he came from and yet he gave me the gift of sight. Everybody knows that God does not listen to sinners. It is the man who has a proper respect for God and does what he wants him to do—he's the one God listens to. Why, since the world began, nobody's ever heard of a man who was born blind being given his sight. If this man did not come from God, he couldn't do anything!"

"You misbegotten wretch!" they flung back at him. "Are you trying to teach *us?*" And they threw him out.

Jesus heard that they had expelled him and when he had found him, he said, "Do you believe in the Son of Man?"

"And who is he, sir?" the man replied. "Tell me, so that I can believe in him."

"You have seen him," replied Jesus. "It is the one who is talking to you now."

"Lord, I do believe," he said, and worshipped him.

Then Jesus said, "My coming into this world is itself a judgment—those who cannot see have their eyes opened and those who think they can see become blind."

Some of the Pharisees near him overheard this and said, "So we're blind, too, are we?"

Revised Standard Version

but as for this man, we do not know where
he comes from." 30 The man answered, "Why,
this is a marvel! You do not know where he
comes from, and yet he opened my eyes. 31 We
know that God does not listen to sinners, but
if any one is a worshiper of God and does his
will, God listens to him. 32 Never since the
world began has it been heard that any one
opened the eyes of a man born blind. 33 If
this man were not from God, he could do nothing." 34 They answered him, "You were born
in utter sin, and would you teach us?" And
they cast him out.
35 Jesus heard that they had cast him out,
and having found him he said, "Do you believe
in the Son of man?" [v] 36 He answered, "And
who is he, sir, that I may believe in him?"
37 Jesus said to him, "You have seen him, and
it is he who speaks to you." 38 He said, "Lord,
I believe"; and he worshiped him. 39 Jesus said,
"For judgment I came into this world, that those
who do not see may see, and that those who see
may become blind." 40 Some of the Pharisees
near him heard this, and they said to him, "Are

[v] Other ancient authorities read *the Son of God.*

Jerusalem Bible

this man, we don't know where he comes from."
30 The man replied, "Now here is an astonishing
thing! He has opened my eyes, and you don't
know where he comes from! 31 We know that
God doesn't listen to sinners, but God does
listen to men who are devout and do his will.
32 Ever since the world began it is unheard of
for anyone to open the eyes of a man who was
born blind; 33 if this man were not from God,
he couldn't do a thing." 34 "Are you trying to
teach us," they replied, "and you a sinner
through and through, since you were born!"
And they drove him away.
35 Jesus heard they had driven him away, and
when he found him he said to him, "Do you
believe in the Son of Man?" 36 "Sir," the man
replied, "tell me who he is so that I may believe
in him." 37 Jesus said, "You are looking at him;
he is speaking to you." 38 The man said, "Lord,
I believe," and worshiped him.
39 Jesus said:

"It is for judgment
that I have come into this world,
so that those without sight may see
and those with sight turn blind."

40 Hearing this, some Pharisees who were present said to him, "We are not blind, surely?"

New English Bible

but as for this fellow, we do not know where he comes from.'

The man replied, 'What an extraordinary thing! Here is a man who has opened my eyes, yet you do not know where he comes from! It is common knowledge that God does not listen to sinners; he listens to anyone who is devout and obeys his will. To open the eyes of a man born blind—it is unheard of since time began. If that man had not come from God he could have done nothing.' 'Who are you to give us lessons,' they retorted, 'born and bred in sin as you are?' Then they expelled him from the synagogue.

Jesus heard that they had expelled him. When he found him he asked, 'Have you faith in the Son of Man[a]?' The man answered, 'Tell me who he is, sir, that I should put my faith in him.' 'You have seen him,' said Jesus; 'indeed, it is he who is speaking to you.' 'Lord, I believe', he said, and bowed before him.

Jesus said, 'It is for judgement that I have come into this world—to give sight to the sightless and to make blind those who see.' Some Pharisees in his company asked, 'Do you mean

[a] *Some witnesses read* Son of God.

King James Version

Are we blind also? 41 Jesus said unto them, If ye were blind, ye should have no sin: but now ye say, We see; therefore your sin remaineth.

10 Verily, verily, I say unto you, He that entereth not by the door into the sheepfold, but climbeth up some other way, the same is a thief and a robber. 2 But he that entereth in by the door is the shepherd of the sheep. 3 To him the porter openeth; and the sheep hear his voice: and he calleth his own sheep by name, and leadeth them out. 4 And when he putteth forth his own sheep, he goeth before them, and the sheep follow him: for they know his voice. 5 And a stranger will they not follow, but will flee from him; for they know not the voice of strangers. 6 This parable spake Jesus unto them; but they understood not what things they were which he spake unto them. 7 Then said Jesus unto them again, Verily, verily, I say unto you, I am the door of the sheep. 8 All that ever came before me are thieves and robbers: but the sheep did not hear them. 9 I am the door: by me if

Living Bible

41 "If you were blind, you wouldn't be guilty," Jesus replied. "But your guilt remains because you claim to know what you are doing.

10 "Anyone refusing to walk through the gate into a sheepfold, who sneaks over the wall, must surely be a thief! 2 For a shepherd comes through the gate. 3 The gatekeeper opens the gate for him, and the sheep hear his voice and come to him; and he calls his own sheep by name and leads them out. 4 He walks ahead of them; and they follow him, for they recognize his voice. 5 They won't follow a stranger but will run from him, for they don't recognize his voice."

6 Those who heard Jesus use this illustration didn't understand what he meant, 7 so he explained it to them.

"I am the Gate for the sheep," he said. 8 "All others who came before me were thieves and robbers. But the true sheep did not listen to them. 9 Yes, I am the Gate. Those who come

Today's English Version

41 Jesus answered, "If you were blind, then you would not be guilty; but since you say, 'We can see,' this means that you are still guilty."

The parable of the sheepfold

10 "I tell you the truth: the man who does not enter the sheepfold by the door, but climbs in some other way, is a thief and a robber. 2 The man who goes in by the door is the shepherd of the sheep. 3 The gatekeeper opens the gate for him; the sheep hear his voice as he calls his own sheep by name, and he leads them out. 4 When he has brought them out, he goes ahead of them, and the sheep follow him, because they know his voice. 5 They will not follow someone else; instead, they will run away from him, because they do not know his voice."

6 Jesus told them this parable, but they did not understand what he was telling them.

Jesus the good shepherd

7 So Jesus said again, "I tell you the truth: I am the door for the sheep. 8 All others who came before me are thieves and robbers; but the sheep did not listen to them. 9 I am the door. Whoever

New International Version

41 Jesus said, "If you were blind, you would not be guilty of sin; but now that you claim you can see, your guilt remains.

The shepherd and his flock

10 "I tell you the truth, the man who does not enter the sheep pen by the gate, but climbs in by some other way, is a thief and a robber. 2 The man who enters by the gate is the shepherd of his sheep. 3 The watchman opens the gate for him, and the sheep listen to his voice. He calls his own sheep by name and leads them out. 4 When he has brought out all his own, he goes on ahead of them, and his sheep follow him because they know his voice. 5 But they will never follow a stranger; in fact, they will run away from him because they do not recognize a stranger's voice." 6 Jesus used this figure of speech, but they did not understand what he was telling them.

7 Therefore Jesus said again, "I tell you the truth, I am the gate for the sheep. 8 All who ever came before me were thieves and robbers, but the sheep did not listen to them. 9 I am the

Phillips Modern English

"If you were blind," returned Jesus, "nobody could blame you, but, as you insist 'We can see', your guilt remains."

10.1 Jesus declares himself the true shepherd of men

Then Jesus said, "Believe me when I tell you that anyone who does not enter the sheepfold through the door, but climbs in by some other way, is a thief and a rogue. It is the shepherd of the flock who goes in by the door. It is to him the door-keeper opens the door and it is his voice that the sheep recognise. He calls his own sheep by name and leads them out of the fold, and when he has brought all his own flock outside, he goes in front of them himself, and the sheep follow him because they know his voice. They will never follow a stranger—indeed, they will run away from him, for they do not recognise strange voices."

Jesus gave them this illustration but they did not grasp the point of what he was saying to them. So Jesus said to them once more, "I do assure you that I myself am the door for the sheep. All who have gone before me are like thieves and rogues, but the sheep did not listen to them. I am the door. If a man goes in

Revised Standard Version

we also blind?" 41 Jesus said to them, "If you
were blind, you would have no guilt; but now
that you say, 'We see,' your guilt remains.

10 "Truly, truly, I say to you, he who does
not enter the sheepfold by the door but
climbs in by another way, that man is a thief
and a robber; 2 but he who enters by the door
is the shepherd of the sheep. 3 To him the gatekeeper opens; the sheep hear his voice, and he
calls his own sheep by name and leads them out.
4 When he has brought out all his own, he goes
before them, and the sheep follow him, for they
know his voice. 5 A stranger they will not follow, but they will flee from him, for they do
not know the voice of strangers." 6 This figure
Jesus used with them, but they did not understand what he was saying to them.
7 So Jesus again said to them, "Truly, truly,
I say to you, I am the door of the sheep. 8 All
who came before me are thieves and robbers;
but the sheep did not heed them. 9 I am the

Jerusalem Bible

41 Jesus replied:

"Blind? If you were,
you would not be guilty,
but since you say, 'We see,'
your guilt remains.

The good shepherd

10 "I tell you most solemnly, anyone who
does not enter the sheepfold through the
gate, but gets in some other way is a thief and
a brigand. 2 The one who enters through the
gate is the shepherd of the flock; 3 the gatekeeper lets him in, the sheep hear his voice, one
by one he calls his own sheep and leads them
out. 4 When he has brought out his flock, he
goes ahead of them, and the sheep follow because they know his voice. 5 They never follow
a stranger but run away from him: they do not
recognize the voice of strangers."
6 Jesus told them[b] this parable but they failed
to understand what he meant by telling it to
them.
7 So Jesus spoke to them again:

"I tell you most solemnly,
I am the gate of the sheepfold.
8 All others who have come
are thieves and brigands;
but the sheep took no notice of them.
9 I am the gate.

[b] The Pharisees.

New English Bible

that we are blind?' 'If you were blind,' said Jesus, 'you would not be guilty, but because you say "We see", your guilt remains.

10 'In truth I tell you, in very truth, the man who does not enter the sheepfold by the door, but climbs in some other way, is nothing but a thief or a robber. The man who enters by the door is the shepherd in charge of the sheep. The door-keeper admits him, and the sheep hear his voice; he calls his own sheep by name, and leads them out. When he has brought them all out, he goes ahead and the sheep follow, because they know his voice. They will not follow a stranger; they will run away from him, because they do not recognize the voice of strangers.'

This was a parable that Jesus told them, but they did not understand what he meant by it.

So Jesus spoke again: 'In truth, in very truth I tell you, I am the door of the sheepfold. The sheep paid no heed to any who came before me, for these were all thieves and robbers. I am the

King James Version

any man enter in, he shall be saved, and shall go in and out, and find pasture. 10 The thief cometh not, but for to steal, and to kill, and to destroy: I am come that they might have life, and that they might have *it* more abundantly. 11 I am the good shepherd: the good shepherd giveth his life for the sheep. 12 But he that is a hireling, and not the shepherd, whose own the sheep are not, seeth the wolf coming, and leaveth the sheep, and fleeth; and the wolf catcheth them, and scattereth the sheep. 13 The hireling fleeth, because he is a hireling, and careth not for the sheep. 14 I am the good shepherd, and know my *sheep,* and am known of mine. 15 As the Father knoweth me, even so know I the Father: and I lay down my life for the sheep. 16 And other sheep I have, which are not of this fold: them also I must bring, and they shall hear my voice; and there shall be one fold, *and* one shepherd. 17 Therefore doth my Father love me, because I lay down my life, that I might take it again. 18 No man taketh it from me, but I lay it down of myself. I have power to lay it

Living Bible

in by way of the Gate will be saved and will go in and out and find green pastures. 10 The thief's purpose is to steal, kill and destroy. My purpose is to give life in all its fullness.

11 "I am the Good Shepherd. The Good Shepherd lays down his life for the sheep. 12 A hired man will run when he sees a wolf coming and will leave the sheep, for they aren't his and he isn't their shepherd. And so the wolf leaps on them and scatters the flock. 13 The hired man runs because he is hired and has no real concern for the sheep.

14 "I am the Good Shepherd and know my own sheep, and they know me, 15 just as my Father knows me and I know the Father; and I lay down my life for the sheep. 16 I have other sheep, too, in another fold. I must bring them also, and they will heed my voice; and there will be one flock with one Shepherd.

17 "The Father loves me because I lay down my life that I may have it back again. 18 No one can kill me without my consent—I lay down my

Today's English Version

comes in by me will be saved; he will come in and go out, and find pasture. 10 The thief comes only in order to steal, kill, and destroy. I have come in order that they might have life, life in all its fulness.

11 "I am the good shepherd. The good shepherd is willing to die for the sheep. 12 The hired man, who is not a shepherd and does not own the sheep, leaves them and runs away when he sees a wolf coming; so the wolf snatches the sheep and scatters them. 13 The hired man runs away because he is only a hired man and does not care for the sheep. 14, 15 I am the good shepherd. As the Father knows me and I know the Father, in the same way I know my sheep and they know me. And I am willing to die for them. 16 There are other sheep that belong to me that are not in this sheepfold. I must bring them, too; they will listen to my voice, and they will become one flock with one shepherd.

17 "The Father loves me because I am willing to give up my life, in order that I may receive it back again. 18 No one takes my life away from me. I give it up of my own free will. I have the

New International Version

gate; whoever enters through me will be saved.[u] He will come in and go out, and find pasture. 10 The thief comes only to steal and kill and destroy; I have come that they may have life, and have it to the full.

11 "I am the good shepherd. The good shepherd lays down his life for the sheep. 12 The hired hand is not the shepherd who owns the sheep. So when he sees the wolf coming, he abandons the sheep and runs away. Then the wolf attacks the flock and scatters it. 13 The man runs away because he is a hired hand and cares nothing for the sheep.

14 "I am the good shepherd; I know my sheep and my sheep know me—15 just as the Father knows me and I know the Father—and I lay down my life for the sheep. 16 I have other sheep that are not of this flock. I must bring them also. They too will listen to my voice, and there shall be one flock and one shepherd. 17 The reason my Father loves me is that I lay down my life—only to take it up again. 18 No one takes it from me, but I lay it down of my own accord.

[u] Or *kept safe.*

Phillips Modern English

through me, he will be safe and sound; he can come in and out and find his food. The thief comes only to steal, to kill and to destroy, but I have come to bring them life in its fullness. I am the good shepherd. The good shepherd gives his life for the sake of his sheep. But the hired man, who is not the shepherd, and does not own the sheep, will see the wolf coming, desert the sheep and run away. And the wolf will attack the flock and send them flying. The hired man runs away because he is only a hired man and has no interest in the sheep. I am the good shepherd, and I know those that are mine and my sheep know me, just as the Father knows me and I know the Father. And I give my life for the sake of the sheep.

"And I have other sheep who do not belong to this fold. I must lead these also, and they will hear my voice. So there will be one flock and one shepherd. This is the reason why the Father loves me—that I lay down my life so that I may take it up again! No one is taking it from me, but I lay it down of my own free

Revised Standard Version

door; if any one enters by me, he will be saved,
and will go in and out and find pasture. 10 The
thief comes only to steal and kill and destroy;
I came that they may have life, and have it
abundantly. 11 I am the good shepherd. The
good shepherd lays down his life for the sheep.
12 He who is a hireling and not a shepherd,
whose own the sheep are not, sees the wolf coming and leaves the sheep and flees; and the wolf
snatches them and scatters them. 13 He flees
because he is a hireling and cares nothing for
the sheep. 14 I am the good shepherd; I know
my own and my own know me, 15 as the Father
knows me and I know the Father; and I lay
down my life for the sheep. 16 And I have other
sheep, that are not of this fold; I must bring
them also, and they will heed my voice. So
there shall be one flock, one shepherd. 17 For
this reason the Father loves me, because I lay
down my life, that I may take it again. 18 No
one takes it from me, but I lay it down of my

Jerusalem Bible

Anyone who enters through me will be safe:
he will go freely in and out
and be sure of finding pasture.
10 The thief comes
only to steal and kill and destroy.
I have come
so that they may have life
and have it to the full.
11 I am the good shepherd:
the good shepherd is one who lays down his
life for his sheep.
12 The hired man, since he is not the shepherd
and the sheep do not belong to him,
abandons the sheep and runs away
as soon as he sees a wolf coming,
and then the wolf attacks and scatters the
sheep;
13 this is because he is only a hired man
and has no concern for the sheep.
14 I am the good shepherd;
I know my own
and my own know me,
15 just as the Father knows me
and I know the Father;
and I lay down my life for my sheep.
16 And there are other sheep I have
that are not of this fold,
and these I have to lead as well.
They too will listen to my voice,
and there will be only one flock,
and one shepherd.
17 The Father loves me,
because I lay down my life
in order to take it up again.
18 No one takes it from me;
I lay it down of my own free will,

New English Bible

door; anyone who comes into the fold through me shall be safe. He shall go in and out and shall find pasturage.

'The thief comes only to steal, to kill, to destroy; I have come that men may have life, and may have it in all its fullness. I am the good shepherd; the good shepherd lays down his life for the sheep. The hireling, when he sees the wolf coming, abandons the sheep and runs away, because he is no shepherd and the sheep are not his. Then the wolf harries the flock and scatters the sheep. The man runs away because he is a hireling and cares nothing for the sheep.

'I am the good shepherd; I know my own sheep and my sheep know me—as the Father knows me and I know the Father—and I lay down my life for the sheep. But there are other sheep of mine, not belonging to this fold, whom I must bring in; and they too will listen to my voice. There will then be one flock, one shepherd. The Father loves me because I lay down my life, to receive it back again. No one has robbed me of it; I am laying it down of my own free will.

King James Version

down, and I have power to take it again. This commandment have I received of my Father.
19 There was a division therefore again among the Jews for these sayings. 20And many of them said, He hath a devil, and is mad; why hear ye him? 21 Others said, These are not the words of him that hath a devil. Can a devil open the eyes of the blind?
22 And it was at Jerusalem the feast of the dedication, and it was winter. 23And Jesus walked in the temple in Solomon's porch. 24 Then came the Jews round about him, and said unto him, How long dost thou make us to doubt? If thou be the Christ, tell us plainly. 25 Jesus answered them, I told you, and ye believed not: the works that I do in my Father's name, they bear witness of me. 26But ye believe not, because ye are not of my sheep, as I said unto you. 27 My sheep hear my voice, and I know them, and

Living Bible

life voluntarily. For I have the right and power to lay it down when I want to and also the right and power to take it again. For the Father has given me this right."
19 When he said these things, the Jewish leaders were again divided in their opinions about him. 20 Some of them said, "He has a demon or else is crazy. Why listen to a man like that?"
21 Others said, "This doesn't sound to us like a man possessed by a demon! Can a demon open the eyes of blind men?"
22, 23 It was winter,[a] and Jesus was in Jerusalem at the time of the Dedication Celebration. He was at the Temple, walking through the section known as Solomon's Hall. 24 The Jewish leaders surrounded him and asked, "How long are you going to keep us in suspense? If you are the Messiah, tell us plainly."
25 "I have already told you,[b] and you don't believe me," Jesus replied. "The proof is in the miracles I do in the name of my Father. 26 But you don't believe me because you are not part of my flock. 27 My sheep recognize my voice,

[*a*] December 25 was the usual date for this celebration of the cleansing of the Temple. [*b*] Chapter 5:19; 8:36,56,58, etc.

Today's English Version

right to give it, and I have the right to take it back. This is what my Father has commanded me to do."
19 Again there was a division among the Jews because of these words. 20 Many of them were saying, "He has a demon! He is crazy! Why do you listen to him?"
21 But others were saying, "A man with a demon could not talk like this! How could a demon open the eyes of blind men?"

Jesus rejected by the Jews

22 The time came to celebrate the Feast of Dedication in Jerusalem; it was winter. 23 Jesus was walking in Solomon's Porch in the temple, 24 when the Jews gathered around him and said, "How long are you going to keep us in suspense? Tell us the plain truth: are you the Messiah?"
25 Jesus answered, "I have already told you, but you would not believe me. The works I do by my Father's authority speak on my behalf; 26 but you will not believe because you are not my sheep. 27 My sheep listen to my voice; I know

New International Version

I have authority to lay it down and authority to take it up again. This command I received from my Father."
19 At these words the Jews were again divided. 20 Many of them said, "He is demon-possessed and raving mad. Why listen to him?"
21 But others said, "These are not the sayings of a man possessed by a demon. How can a demon open the eyes of the blind?"

The unbelief of the Jews

22 Then came the Feast of Dedication[v] at Jerusalem. It was winter, 23 and Jesus was in the temple area walking in Solomon's Colonnade. 24 The Jews gathered around him, saying, "How long will you keep us in suspense? If you are the Christ,[w] tell us plainly."
25 Jesus answered, "I did tell you, but you do not believe. The miracles I do in my Father's name speak for me, 26 but you do not believe because you do not belong to my flock. 27 My sheep listen to my voice; I know them, and they

[*v*] That is, Hanukkah. [*w*] Or *Messiah*.

Phillips Modern English

will. I have the power to lay it down and I have the power to take it up again. This is the command that I have received from my Father."

10.19 Jesus plainly declares who he is

Once again, the Jews were in two minds about him because of these words, many of them remarking, "The devil's in him and he's insane. Why do you listen to him?"

But others were saying, "This is not the sort of thing a devil-possessed man would say! Can a devil make a blind man see?"

Then came the dedication festival at Jerusalem. It was wintertime and Jesus was walking about inside the Temple in Solomon's cloisters. So the Jews closed in on him and said, "How much longer are you going to keep us in suspense? If you really are Christ, tell us so straight out!"

"I have told you," replied Jesus, "and you do not believe it. What I have done in my Father's name is sufficient to prove my claim, but you do not believe because you are not my sheep. My sheep recognise my voice and I know who they

Revised Standard Version

own accord. I have power to lay it down, and
I have power to take it again; this charge I have
received from my Father."
19 There was again a division among the
Jews because of these words. 20 Many of them
said, "He has a demon, and he is mad; why
listen to him?" 21 Others said, "These are not
the sayings of one who has a demon. Can a
demon open the eyes of the blind?"
22 It was the feast of the Dedication at Jerusalem;
23 it was winter, and Jesus was walking
in the temple, in the portico of Solomon. 24 So
the Jews gathered round him and said to him,
"How long will you keep us in suspense? If you
are the Christ, tell us plainly." 25 Jesus answered
them, "I told you, and you do not believe. The
works that I do in my Father's name, they bear
witness to me; 26 but you do not believe, because
you do not belong to my sheep. 27 My sheep
hear my voice, and I know them, and they follow

Jerusalem Bible

and as it is in my power to lay it down,
so it is in my power to take it up again;
and this is the command I have been given
by my Father."

19 These words caused disagreement among
the Jews. 20 Many said, "He is possessed, he is
raving; why bother to listen to him?" 21 Others
said, "These are not the words of a man possessed
by a devil: could a devil open the eyes of
the blind?"

VI. The feast of Dedication

Jesus claims to be the Son of God

22 It was the time when the feast of Dedication
was being celebrated in Jerusalem. It was
winter, 23 and Jesus was in the Temple walking
up and down in the Portico of Solomon. 24 The
Jews gathered around him and said, "How much
longer are you going to keep us in suspense? If
you are the Christ, tell us plainly." 25 Jesus replied:

"I have told you, but you do not believe.
The works I do in my Father's name are my witness;
26 but you do not believe,
because you are no sheep of mine.
27 The sheep that belong to me listen to my voice;

New English Bible

I have the right to lay it down, and I have the right to receive it back again; this charge I have received from my Father.'

These words once again caused a split among the Jews. Many of them said, 'He is possessed, he is raving. Why listen to him?' Others said, 'No one possessed by an evil spirit could speak like this. Could an evil spirit open blind men's eyes?'

It was winter, and the festival of the Dedication was being held in Jerusalem. Jesus was walking in the temple precincts, in Solomon's Portico. The Jews gathered round him and asked: 'How long must you keep us in suspense? If you are the Messiah say so plainly.' 'I have told you,' said Jesus, 'but you do not believe. My deeds done in my Father's name are my credentials, but because you are not sheep of my flock you do not believe. My own sheep listen to my voice; I know them and they fol-

King James Version

they follow me: 28 And I give unto them eternal
life; and they shall never perish, neither shall
any *man* pluck them out of my hand. 29 My
Father, which gave *them* me, is greater than all;
and no *man* is able to pluck *them* out of my
Father's hand. 30 I and *my* Father are one.
31 Then the Jews took up stones again to stone
him. 32 Jesus answered them, Many good works
have I shewed you from my Father; for which
of those works do ye stone me? 33 The Jews
answered him, saying, For a good work we stone
thee not; but for blasphemy; and because that
thou, being a man, makest thyself God. 34 Jesus
answered them, Is it not written in your law, I
said, Ye are gods? 35 If he called them gods,
unto whom the word of God came, and the
Scripture cannot be broken; 36 Say ye of him,
whom the Father hath sanctified, and sent into
the world, Thou blasphemest; because I said, I
am the Son of God? 37 If I do not the works
of my Father, believe me not. 38 But if I do,
though ye believe not me, believe the works;
that ye may know, and believe, that the Father

Living Bible

and I know them, and they follow me. 28 I give
them eternal life and they shall never perish. No
one shall snatch them away from me, 29 for my
Father has given them to me, and he is more
powerful than anyone else, so no one can kidnap
them from me. 30 I and the Father are one."

31 Then again the Jewish leaders picked up
stones to kill him.

32 Jesus said, "At God's direction I have
done many a miracle to help the people. For
which one are you killing me?"

33 They replied, "Not for any good work, but
for blasphemy; you, a mere man, have declared
yourself to be God."

34, 35, 36 "In your own Law it says that men
are gods!" he replied. "So if the Scripture, which
cannot be untrue, speaks of those as gods to
whom the message of God came, do you call
it blasphemy when the one sanctified and sent
into the world by the Father says, 'I am the Son
of God'? 37 Don't believe me unless I do miracles of God. 38 But if I do, believe them even
if you don't believe me. Then you will become

Today's English Version

them, and they follow me. 28 I give them eternal
life, and they shall never die; and no one can
snatch them away from me. 29 What my Father
has given me is greater than all, and no one can
snatch them away from the Father's care. 30 The
Father and I are one."

31 Then the Jews once more picked up stones
to throw at him. 32 Jesus said to them, "I have
done many good works before you which the
Father gave me to do; for which one of these do
you want to stone me?"

33 The Jews answered back, "We do not want
to stone you because of any good works, but because of the way in which you insult God! You
are only a man, but you are trying to make yourself God!"

34 Jesus answered, "It is written in your own
Law that God said, 'You are gods.' 35 We know
that what the scripture says is true forever; and
God called them gods, those people to whom his
message was given. 36 As for me, the Father
chose me and sent me into the world. How,
then, can you say that I insult God because I
said that I am the Son of God? 37 Do not believe me, then, if I am not doing my Father's
works. 38 But if I do them, even though you do
not believe me, you should at least believe my
works, in order that you may know once and for

New International Version

follow me. 28 I give them eternal life, and they
shall never perish; no one can snatch them out
of my hand. 29 My Father, who has given them
to me, is greater than all [x]; no one can snatch
them out of my Father's hand. 30 I and the
Father are one."

31 Again the Jews picked up stones to stone
him, 32 but Jesus said to them, "I have shown
you many great miracles from the Father. For
which of these do you stone me?"

33 "We are not stoning you for any of these,"
replied the Jews, "but for blasphemy, because
you, a mere man, claim to be God."

34 Jesus answered them, "Is it not written in
your Law, 'I have said you are gods' [y]? 35 If he
called them 'gods,' to whom the word of God
came—and the Scripture cannot be broken—
36 what about the one whom the Father set
apart as his very own and sent into the world?
Why then do you accuse me of blasphemy because I said, 'I am God's Son'? 37 Do not believe me unless I do what my Father does.
38 But if I do it, even though you do not believe
me, believe the evidence of the miracles, that
you may learn and understand that the Father is

[x] Many early MSS read ***What my Father has given me is greater than all.*** [y] Psalm 82:6.

Phillips Modern English

are. They follow me and I give them eternal life. They will never die and no one can snatch them out of my hand. My Father, who has given them to me, is greater than all. And no one can snatch anything out of the Father's hand. I and the Father are One."

Again the Jews reached for stones to stone him to death, but Jesus answered them, "I have shown you many good things from the Father —for which of these do you intend to stone me?"

"We're not going to stone you for any good things," replied the Jews, "but for blasphemy: because you, who are only a man, are making yourself out to be God."

"Is it not written in your own Law," replied Jesus, " 'I have said ye are gods'? And if he called those men 'gods' to whom the word of God came (and the Scripture cannot be broken), can you say to the one whom the Father has consecrated and sent into the world, 'You are blaspheming' because I said, 'I am the Son of God'? If I fail to do what my Father does, then do not believe me. But if I do, even though you have no faith in me personally, then believe in the things that I do. Then you may come to know

Revised Standard Version

me; 28 and I give them eternal life, and they
shall never perish, and no one shall snatch them
out of my hand. 29 My Father, who has given
them to me,[w] is greater than all, and no one is
able to snatch them out of the Father's hand.
30 I and the Father are one."
31 The Jews took up stones again to stone
him. 32 Jesus answered them, "I have shown you
many good works from the Father; for which of
these do you stone me?" 33 The Jews answered
him, "It is not for a good work that we stone
you but for blasphemy; because you, being a
man, make yourself God." 34 Jesus answered
them, "Is it not written in your law, 'I said, you
are gods'? 35 If he called them gods to whom
the word of God came (and scripture cannot be
broken), 36 do you say of him whom the
Father consecrated and sent into the world, 'You
are blaspheming,' because I said, 'I am the Son
of God'? 37 If I am not doing the works of
my Father, then do not believe me; 38 but if I
do them, even though you do not believe me,
believe the works, that you may know and un-

[w] Other ancient authorities read *What my Father has given to me*.

Jerusalem Bible

I know them and they follow me.
28 I give them eternal life;
they will never be lost
and no one will ever steal them from me.
29 The Father who gave them to me is greater
than anyone,
and no one can steal from the Father.
30 The Father and I are one."

31 The Jews fetched stones to stone him,
32 so Jesus said to them, "I have done many
good works for you to see, works from my
Father; for which of these are you stoning me?"
33 The Jews answered him, "We are not stoning
you for doing a good work but for blasphemy:
you are only a man and you claim to be God."
34 Jesus answered:

"Is it not written in your Law:
I said, you are gods? [c]

35 So the Law uses the word gods
of those to whom the word of God was
addressed,
and scripture cannot be rejected.
36 Yet you say to someone the Father has consecrated and sent into the world,
'You are blaspheming,'
because he says, 'I am the Son of God.'
37 If I am not doing my Father's work,
there is no need to believe me;
38 but if I am doing it,
then even if you refuse to believe in me,
at least believe in the work I do;
then you will know for sure

[c] Ps. 82:6.

New English Bible

low me. I give them eternal life and they shall never perish; no one shall snatch them from my care. My Father who has given them to me is greater than all, and no one can snatch them[a] out of the Father's care. My Father and I are one.'

Once again the Jews picked up stones to stone him. At this Jesus said to them, 'I have set before you many good deeds, done by my Father's power; for which of these would you stone me?' The Jews replied, 'We are not going to stone you for any good deed, but for your blasphemy. You, a mere man, claim to be a god.'[b] Jesus answered, 'Is it not written in your own Law, "I said: You are gods"? Those are called gods to whom the word of God was delivered—and Scripture cannot be set aside. Then why do you charge me with blasphemy because I, consecrated and sent into the world by the Father, said, "I am God's son"?

'If I am not acting as my Father would, do not believe me. But if I am, accept the evidence of my deeds, even if you do not believe me, so that you may recognize and know that the

[a] *Some witnesses read* My Father is greater than all, and that which he has given me no one can snatch . . . ; *others read* That which my Father has given me is greater than all, and no one can snatch it . . . [b] *Or* claim to be God.

King James Version

is in me, and I in him. 39 Therefore they sought
again to take him; but he escaped out of their
hand, 40And went away again beyond Jordan
into the place where John at first baptized; and
there he abode. 41And many resorted unto him,
and said, John did no miracle: but all things
that John spake of this man were true. 42And
many believed on him there.

11 Now a certain *man* was sick, *named* Lazarus, of Bethany, the town of Mary and
her sister Martha. 2 (It was *that* Mary which
anointed the Lord with ointment, and wiped his
feet with her hair, whose brother Lazarus was
sick.) 3 Therefore his sisters sent unto him, saying, Lord, behold, he whom thou lovest is sick.
4 When Jesus heard *that,* he said, This sickness
is not unto death, but for the glory of God, that
the Son of God might be glorified thereby.
5 Now Jesus loved Martha, and her sister, and

Living Bible

convinced that the Father is in me, and I in the
Father."
39 Once again they started to arrest him. But
he walked away and left them, 40 and went beyond the Jordan River to stay near the place
where John was first baptizing. 41And many
followed him.
"John didn't do miracles," they remarked to
one another, "but all his predictions concerning
this man have come true." 42And many came
to the decision that he was the Messiah.[c]

11 Do you remember Mary, who poured the
costly perfume on Jesus' feet and wiped
them with her hair?[a] Well, her brother Lazarus,
who lived in Bethany with Mary and her sister
Martha, was sick. 3 So the two sisters sent a
message to Jesus telling him, "Sir, your good
friend is very, very sick."
4 But when Jesus heard about it he said, "The
purpose of his illness is not death, but for the
glory of God. I, the Son of God, will receive
glory from this situation."
5 Although Jesus was very fond of Martha,

[*c*] Literally, "Many believed on him there." [*a*] See John 12:3.

Today's English Version

all that the Father is in me, and I am in the
Father."
39 Once more they tried to arrest him, but he
slipped out of their hands.
40 Jesus went back again across the Jordan
River to the place where John had been baptizing, and stayed there. 41 Many people came
to him. "John did no mighty works," they said,
"but everything he said about this man was
true." 42And many people there believed in him.

The death of Lazarus

11 A man named Lazarus, who lived in Bethany, became sick. Bethany was the town
where Mary and her sister Martha lived. 2 (This
Mary was the one who poured the perfume on
the Lord's feet and wiped them with her hair; it
was her brother Lazarus who was sick.) 3 The
sisters sent Jesus a message, "Lord, your dear
friend is sick."
4 When Jesus heard it he said, "The final result of this sickness will not be the death of
Lazarus; this has happened to bring glory to
God, and will be the means by which the Son of
God will receive glory."
5 Jesus loved Martha and her sister, and Laz-

New International Version

in me, and I in the Father." 39Again they tried
to seize him, but he escaped their grasp.
40 Then Jesus went back across the Jordan to
the place where John had been baptizing in the
early days. Here he stayed 41 and many people
came to him. They said, "Though John never
performed a miraculous sign, all that John said
about this man was true." 42And in that place
many believed in Jesus.

The death of Lazarus

11 Now a man named Lazarus was sick. He
was from Bethany, the village of Mary and
her sister Martha. 2 This Mary, whose brother
Lazarus now lay sick, was the same one who
poured perfume on the Lord and wiped his feet
with her hair. 3 So the sisters sent word to Jesus, "Lord, the one you love is sick."
4 When he heard this, Jesus said, "This sickness will not end in death. No, it is for God's
glory so that God's Son may be glorified through
it." 5 Jesus loved Martha and her sister and

Phillips Modern English

and realise that the Father is in me and I am in the Father."

And again they tried to arrest him, but he moved out of their reach.

Then Jesus went off again across the Jordan to the place where John had first baptised and there he stayed. A great many people came to him, and said, "John never gave us any sign but all that he said about this man was true."

And in that place many believed in him.

11.1 Jesus shows his power over death

Now there was a man by the name of Lazarus who became seriously ill. He lived in Bethany, the village where Mary and her sister Martha lived. (Lazarus was the brother of the Mary who poured perfume upon the Lord and wiped his feet with her hair.) So the sisters sent word to Jesus: "Lord, your friend is very ill."

When Jesus received the message, he said, "This illness will not end in death; it will bring glory to God—for it will show the glory of the Son of God."

Now Jesus loved Martha and her sister and

Revised Standard Version

derstand that the Father is in me and I am in
the Father." 39Again they tried to arrest him,
but he escaped from their hands.
40 He went away again across the Jordan to
the place where John at first baptized, and there
he remained. 41And many came to him; and
they said, "John did no sign, but everything that
John said about this man was true." 42And many
believed in him there.

11 Now a certain man was ill, Lazarus of
Bethany, the village of Mary and her sister
Martha. 2 It was Mary who anointed the Lord
with ointment and wiped his feet with her hair,
whose brother Lazarus was ill. 3 So the sisters
sent to him, saying, "Lord, he whom you love
is ill." 4 But when Jesus heard it he said, "This
illness is not unto death; it is for the glory of
God, so that the Son of God may be glorified
by means of it."
5 Now Jesus loved Martha and her sister and

Jerusalem Bible

that the Father is in me and I am in the Father."

39 They wanted to arrest him then, but he
eluded them.

Jesus withdraws to the other side of the Jordan

40 He went back again to the far side of the
Jordan to stay in the district where John had
once been baptizing. 41 Many people who came
to him there said, "John gave no signs, but all
he said about this man was true"; 42 and many
of them believed in him.

The resurrection of Lazarus

11 There was a man named Lazarus who
lived in the village of Bethany with the
two sisters, Mary and Martha, and he was ill.—
2 It was the same Mary, the sister of the sick
man Lazarus, who anointed the Lord with ointment and wiped his feet with her hair. 3 The
sisters sent this message to Jesus, "Lord, the
man you love is ill." 4 On receiving the message,
Jesus said, "The sickness will end not in death
but in God's glory, and through it the Son of
God will be glorified."
5 Jesus loved Martha and her sister and

New English Bible

Father is in me, and I in the Father.'

This provoked them to one more attempt to seize him. But he escaped from their clutches.

Victory over death

Jesus withdrew again across the Jordan, to the place where John had been baptizing earlier. There he stayed, while crowds came to him. They said, 'John gave us no miraculous sign, but all that he said about this man was true.' Many came to believe in him there.

11 There was a man named Lazarus who had fallen ill. His home was at Bethany, the village of Mary and her sister Martha. (This Mary, whose brother Lazarus had fallen ill, was the woman who anointed the Lord with ointment and wiped his feet with her hair.) The sisters sent a message to him: 'Sir, you should know that your friend lies ill.' When Jesus heard this he said, 'This illness will not end in death; it has come for the glory of God, to bring glory to the Son of God.' And therefore, though he

King James Version

Lazarus. 6 When he had heard therefore that he
was sick, he abode two days still in the same
place where he was. 7 Then after that saith he to
his disciples, Let us go into Judea again. 8 *His*
disciples say unto him, Master, the Jews of late
sought to stone thee; and goest thou thither
again? 9 Jesus answered, Are there not twelve
hours in the day? If any man walk in the day, he
stumbleth not, because he seeth the light of this
world. 10 But if a man walk in the night, he
stumbleth, because there is no light in him.
11 These things said he: and after that he saith
unto them, Our friend Lazarus sleepeth; but I
go, that I may awake him out of sleep. 12 Then
said his disciples, Lord, if he sleep, he shall do
well. 13 Howbeit Jesus spake of his death: but
they thought that he had spoken of taking of rest
in sleep. 14 Then said Jesus unto them plainly,
Lazarus is dead. 15 And I am glad for your sakes
that I was not there, to the intent ye may believe; nevertheless let us go unto him. 16 Then
said Thomas, which is called Didymus, unto his
fellow disciples, Let us also go, that we may die
with him. 17 Then when Jesus came, he found
that he had *lain* in the grave four days already.
18 Now Bethany was nigh unto Jerusalem, about
fifteen furlongs off: 19 And many of the Jews
came to Martha and Mary, to comfort them

Living Bible

Mary, and Lazarus, 6 he stayed where he was
for the next two days and made no move to go
to them. 7 Finally, after the two days, he said
to his disciples, "Let's go to Judea."
8 But his disciples objected. "Master," they
said, "only a few days ago the Jewish leaders in
Judea were trying to kill you. Are you going
there again?"
9 Jesus replied, "There are twelve hours of
daylight every day, and during every hour of it a
man can walk safely and not stumble. 10 Only
at night is there danger of a wrong step, because
of the dark." 11 Then he said, "Our friend
Lazarus has gone to sleep, but now I will go and
waken him!"
12, 13 The disciples, thinking Jesus meant
Lazarus was having a good night's rest, said,
"That means he is getting better!" But Jesus
meant Lazarus had died.
14 Then he told them plainly, "Lazarus is
dead. 15 And for your sake, I am glad I wasn't
there, for this will give you another opportunity
to believe in me. Come, let's go to him."
16 Thomas, nicknamed "The Twin," said to
his fellow disciples, "Let's go too—and die with
him."
17 When they arrived at Bethany, they were
told that Lazarus had already been in his tomb
for four days. 18 Bethany was only a couple of
miles down the road from Jerusalem, 19 and
many of the Jewish leaders had come to pay
their respects and to console Martha and Mary

Today's English Version

arus. 6 When he received the news that Lazarus
was sick, he stayed where he was for two more
days. 7 Then he said to the disciples, "Let us go
back to Judea."
8 "Teacher," the disciples answered, "just a
short time ago the Jews wanted to stone you;
and you plan to go back there?"
9 Jesus said, "A day has twelve hours, has it
not? So if a man walks in broad daylight he does
not stumble, because he sees the light of this
world. 10 But if he walks during the night he
stumbles, because there is no light in him." 11 Jesus said this, and then added, "Our friend Lazarus has fallen asleep, but I will go wake him
up."
12 The disciples answered, "If he is asleep,
Lord, he will get well."
13 But Jesus meant that Lazarus had died;
they thought he meant natural sleep. 14 So Jesus
told them plainly, "Lazarus is dead; 15 but for
your sake I am glad that I was not with him, so
you will believe. Let us go to him."
16 Thomas (called the Twin) said to his fellow disciples, "Let us all go along with the
Teacher, so that we may die with him!"

Jesus the resurrection and the life

17 When Jesus arrived, he found that Lazarus
had been buried four days before. 18 Bethany
was less than two miles from Jerusalem, 19 and
many Jews had come to see Martha and Mary
to comfort them about their brother's death.

New International Version

Lazarus. 6 Yet when he heard that Lazarus was
sick, he stayed where he was two more days.
7 Then he said to his disciples, "Let us go
back to Judea."
8 "But Rabbi," they said, "a short while ago
the Jews tried to stone you, and yet you are
going back there?"
9 Jesus answered, "Are there not twelve hours
of daylight? A man who walks by day will not
stumble, for he sees by this world's light. 10 It is
when he walks by night that he stumbles, for
he has no light."
11 After he had said this, he went on to tell
them, "Our friend Lazarus has fallen asleep; but
I am going there to wake him up."
12 His disciples replied, "Lord, if he sleeps,
he will get better." 13 Jesus had been speaking
of his death, but his disciples thought he meant
natural sleep.
14 So then he told them plainly, "Lazarus is
dead, 15 yet for your sake so that you may believe, I am glad I was not there. But let us go
to him."
16 Then Thomas, called Didymus, said to the
rest of the disciples, "Let us also go, that we
may die with him."

Jesus comforts the sisters

17 On his arrival, Jesus found that Lazarus
had already been in the tomb for four days.
18 Bethany was less than two miles from Jerusalem, 19 and many Jews had come to Martha and
Mary to comfort them in the loss of their

Phillips Modern English

Lazarus. So when he heard of Lazarus' illness he stayed where he was two days longer. Only then did he say to the disciples, "Let us go back into Judaea."

"Rabbi!" returned the disciples, "only a few days ago, the Jews were trying to stone you to death—are you going there again?"

"There are twelve hours of daylight every day, are there not?" replied Jesus. "If a man walks in the daytime, he does not stumble, for he has the daylight to see by. But if he walks at night he stumbles, because he has no light to see by."

Jesus spoke these words; then after a pause he said to them, "Our friend Lazarus has fallen asleep, but I am going to wake him up."

At this, his disciples said, "Lord, if he has fallen asleep, he will be all right."

Actually Jesus had spoken about his death, but they thought that he was speaking about falling into natural sleep. This made Jesus tell them quite plainly, "Lazarus has died, and I am glad that I was not there—for your sakes, that you may learn to believe. And now, let us go to him."

Thomas (known as the Twin) then said to his fellow-disciples, "Come on, then, let us all go and die with him!"

When Jesus arrived, he found that Lazarus had already been in the grave four days. Now Bethany is quite near Jerusalem, rather less than two miles away, and many of the Jews had come out to see Martha and Mary to offer them

Revised Standard Version

Lazarus. 6 So when he heard that he was ill, he
stayed two days longer in the place where he
was. 7 Then after this he said to the disciples,
"Let us go into Judea again." 8 The disciples
said to him, "Rabbi, the Jews were but now seeking to stone you, and are you going there again?"
9 Jesus answered, "Are there not twelve hours
in the day? If any one walks in the day, he does
not stumble, because he sees the light of this
world. 10 But if any one walks in the night, he
stumbles, because the light is not in him."
11 Thus he spoke, and then he said to them,
"Our friend Lazarus has fallen asleep, but I go
to awake him out of sleep." 12 The disciples
said to him, "Lord, if he has fallen asleep, he
will recover." 13 Now Jesus had spoken of his
death, but they thought that he meant taking
rest in sleep. 14 Then Jesus told them plainly,
"Lazarus is dead; 15 and for your sake I am
glad that I was not there, so that you may believe. But let us go to him." 16 Thomas, called
the Twin, said to his fellow disciples, "Let us
also go, that we may die with him."
17 Now when Jesus came, he found that
Lazarus[x] had already been in the tomb four days.
18 Bethany was near Jerusalem, about two miles[y]
off, 19 and many of the Jews had come to
Martha and Mary to console them concerning

[x] Greek *he*. [y] Greek *fifteen stadia*.

Jerusalem Bible

Lazarus, 6 yet when he heard that Lazarus was
ill he stayed where he was for two more days
7 before saying to the disciples, "Let us go to
Judaea." 8 The disciples said, "Rabbi, it is not
long since the Jews wanted to stone you; are
you going back again?" 9 Jesus replied:

"Are there not twelve hours in the day?
A man can walk in the daytime without stumbling
because he has the light of this world to see by;
10 but if he walks at night he stumbles,
because there is no light to guide him."

11 He said that and then added, "Our friend
Lazarus is resting, I am going to wake him."
12 The disciples said to him, "Lord, if he is able
to rest he is sure to get better." 13 The phrase
Jesus used referred to the death of Lazarus, but
they thought that by "rest" he meant "sleep," so
14 Jesus put it plainly, "Lazarus is dead; 15 and
for your sake I am glad I was not there because
now you will believe. But let us go to him."
16 Then Thomas—known as the Twin—said to
the other disciples, "Let us go too, and die with
him."
17 On arriving, Jesus found that Lazarus had
been in the tomb for four days already. 18 Bethany is only about two miles from Jerusalem,
19 and many Jews had come to Martha and
Mary to sympathize with them over their

New English Bible

loved Martha and her sister and Lazarus, after hearing of his illness Jesus waited for two days in the place where he was.

After this, he said to his disciples, 'Let us go back to Judaea.' 'Rabbi,' his disciples said, 'it is not long since the Jews there were wanting to stone you. Are you going there again?' Jesus replied, 'Are there not twelve hours of daylight? Anyone can walk in day-time without stumbling, because he sees the light of this world. But if he walks after nightfall he stumbles, because the light fails him.'

After saying this he added, 'Our friend Lazarus has fallen asleep, but I shall go and wake him.' The disciples said, 'Master, if he has fallen asleep he will recover.' Jesus, however, had been speaking of his death, but they thought that he meant natural sleep. Then Jesus spoke out plainly: 'Lazarus is dead. I am glad not to have been there; it will be for your good and for the good of your faith. But let us go to him.' Thomas, called 'the Twin', said to his fellow-disciples, 'Let us also go, that we may die with him.'

On his arrival Jesus found that Lazarus had already been four days in the tomb. Bethany was just under two miles from Jerusalem, and many of the people had come from the city to Martha and Mary to condole with them on their broth-

King James Version

concerning their brother. 20 Then Martha, as
soon as she heard that Jesus was coming, went
and met him: but Mary sat *still* in the house.
21 Then said Martha unto Jesus, Lord, if thou
hadst been here, my brother had not died. 22 But
I know, that even now, whatsoever thou wilt ask
of God, God will give *it* thee. 23 Jesus saith unto
her, Thy brother shall rise again. 24 Martha saith
unto him, I know that he shall rise again in the
resurrection at the last day. 25 Jesus said unto
her, I am the resurrection, and the life: he that
believeth in me, though he were dead, yet shall
he live: 26 And whosoever liveth and believeth in
me shall never die. Believest thou this? 27 She
saith unto him, Yea, Lord: I believe that thou
art the Christ, the Son of God, which should
come into the world. 28 And when she had so
said, she went her way, and called Mary her
sister secretly, saying, The Master is come, and
calleth for thee. 29 As soon as she heard *that,* she
arose quickly, and came unto him. 30 Now Jesus
was not yet come into the town, but was in that
place where Martha met him. 31 The Jews then
which were with her in the house, and comforted her, when they saw Mary, that she rose
up hastily and went out, followed her, saying,
She goeth unto the grave to weep there. 32 Then
when Mary was come where Jesus was, and saw
him, she fell down at his feet, saying unto him,

Living Bible

on their loss. 20 When Martha got word that
Jesus was coming, she went to meet him. But
Mary stayed at home.
21 Martha said to Jesus, "Sir, if you had
been here, my brother wouldn't have died. 22 And
even now it's not too late, for I know that God
will bring my brother back to life again, if you
will only ask him to."
23 Jesus told her, "Your brother will come
back to life again."
24 "Yes," Martha said, "when everyone else
does, on Resurrection Day."
25 Jesus told her, "I am the one who raises
the dead and gives them life again. Anyone who
believes in me, even though he dies like anyone
else, shall live again. 26 He is given eternal life
for believing in me and shall never perish. Do
you believe this, Martha?"
27 "Yes, Master," she told him. "I believe
you are the Messiah, the Son of God, the one
we have so long awaited."
28 Then she left him and returned to Mary
and calling her aside from the mourners, told
her, "He is here and wants to see you." 29 So
Mary went to him at once.
30 Now Jesus had stayed outside the village,
at the place where Martha met him. 31 When
the Jewish leaders who were at the house trying
to console Mary saw her leave so hastily, they
assumed she was going to Lazarus' tomb to
weep; so they followed her.
32 When Mary arrived where Jesus was, she
fell down at his feet, saying, "Sir, if you had

Today's English Version

20 When Martha heard that Jesus was coming,
she went out to meet him; but Mary stayed at
home. 21 Martha said to Jesus, "If you had been
here, Lord, my brother would not have died!
22 But I know that even now God will give you
whatever you ask of him."
23 "Your brother will rise to life," Jesus told
her.
24 "I know," she replied, "that he will rise to
life on the last day."
25 Jesus said to her, "I am the resurrection
and the life. Whoever believes in me will live,
even though he dies; 26 and whoever lives and
believes in me will never die. Do you believe
this?"
27 "Yes, Lord!" she answered. "I do believe
that you are the Messiah, the Son of God, who
was to come into the world."

Jesus weeps

28 After Martha said this she went back and
called her sister Mary privately. "The Teacher is
here," she told her, "and is asking for you."
29 When Mary heard this she got up and hurried out to meet him. 30 (Jesus had not arrived
in the village yet, but was still in the place where
Martha had met him.) 31 The Jews who were
in the house with Mary comforting her followed
her when they saw her get up and hurry out.
They thought that she was going to the grave, to
weep there.
32 When Mary arrived where Jesus was and
saw him, she fell at his feet. "Lord," she said,

New International Version

brother. 20 When Martha heard that Jesus was
coming, she went out to meet him, but Mary
stayed at home.
21 "Lord," Martha said to Jesus, "if you had
been here, my brother would not have died.
22 But I know that even now God will give you
whatever you ask."
23 Jesus said to her, "Your brother will rise
again."
24 Martha answered, "I know he will rise
again in the resurrection at the last day."
25 Jesus said to her, "I am the resurrection
and the life. He who believes in me will live,
even though he dies; 26 and whoever lives and
believes in me will never die. Do you believe
this?"
27 "Yes, Lord," she told him, "I believe that
you are the Christ,[z] the Son of God, who was
to come into the world."
28 And after she had said this, she went back
and called her sister Mary aside. "The Teacher
is here," she said, "and is asking for you."
29 When Mary heard this, she got up quickly
and went to him. 30 Now Jesus had not yet
entered the village, but was still at the place
where Martha had met him. 31 When the Jews
who had been with Mary in the house, comforting her, noticed how quickly she got up and
went out, they followed her, supposing she was
going to the tomb to mourn there.
32 When Mary reached the place where Jesus
was and saw him, she fell at his feet and said,

[z] Or *Messiah.*

Phillips Modern English

sympathy over their brother's death. When Martha heard that Jesus was on his way, she went out and met him, while Mary stayed in the house.

"If only you had been here, Lord," said Martha, "my brother would never have died. And I know that, even now, God will give you whatever you ask from him."

"Your brother will rise again," Jesus replied to her.

"I know," said Martha, "that he will rise again in the resurrection on the last day."

"I myself am the resurrection and the life," Jesus told her.

"The man who believes in me will live even though he dies, and anyone who is alive and believes in me will never die at all. Can you believe that?"

"Yes, Lord," replied Martha. "I do believe that you are Christ, the Son of God, the one who was to come into the world." Saying this she went away and called Mary her sister, whispering, "The master's here and is asking for you." When Mary heard this she sprang to her feet and went to him. Now Jesus had not yet arrived at the village itself, but was still where Martha had met him. So when the Jews who had been comforting Mary in the house saw her get up quickly and go out, they followed her, imagining that she was going to the grave to weep there.

When Mary met Jesus, she looked at him, and then fell down at his feet. "If only you had been

Revised Standard Version

their brother. 20 When Martha heard that Jesus was coming, she went and met him, while Mary sat in the house. 21 Martha said to Jesus, "Lord, if you had been here, my brother would not have died. 22 And even now I know that whatever you ask from God, God will give you." 23 Jesus said to her, "Your brother will rise again." 24 Martha said to him, "I know that he will rise again in the resurrection at the last day." 25 Jesus said to her, "I am the resurrection and the life;[z] he who believes in me, though he die, yet shall he live, 26 and whoever lives and believes in me shall never die. Do you believe this?" 27 She said to him, "Yes, Lord; I believe that you are the Christ, the Son of God, he who is coming into the world."

28 When she had said this, she went and called her sister Mary, saying quietly, "The Teacher is here and is calling for you." 29 And when she heard it, she rose quickly and went to him. 30 Now Jesus had not yet come to the village, but was still in the place where Martha had met him. 31 When the Jews who were with her in the house, consoling her, saw Mary rise quickly and go out, they followed her, supposing that she was going to the tomb to weep there. 32 Then Mary, when she came where Jesus was and saw him, fell at his feet, saying to him,

[z] Other ancient authorities omit *and the life*.

Jerusalem Bible

brother. 20 When Martha heard that Jesus had come she went to meet him. Mary remained sitting in the house. 21 Martha said to Jesus, "If you had been here, my brother would not have died, 22 but I know that, even now, whatever you ask of God, he will grant you." 23 "Your brother," said Jesus to her, "will rise again." 24 Martha said, "I know he will rise again at the resurrection on the last day." 25 Jesus said:

"I am the resurrection.
If anyone believes in me, even though he dies he will live,
26 and whoever lives and believes in me will never die.
Do you believe this?"

27 "Yes, Lord," she said, "I believe that you are the Christ, the Son of God, the one who was to come into this world."

28 When she had said this, she went and called her sister Mary, saying in a low voice, "The Master is here and wants to see you." 29 Hearing this, Mary got up quickly and went to him. 30 Jesus had not yet come into the village; he was still at the place where Martha had met him. 31 When the Jews who were in the house sympathizing with Mary saw her get up so quickly and go out, they followed her, thinking that she was going to the tomb to weep there.

32 Mary went to Jesus, and as soon as she saw him she threw herself at his feet, saying,

New English Bible

er's death. As soon as she heard that Jesus was on his way, Martha went to meet him, while Mary stayed at home.

Martha said to Jesus, 'If you had been here, sir, my brother would not have died. Even now I know that whatever you ask of God, God will grant you.' Jesus said, 'Your brother will rise again.' 'I know that he will rise again', said Martha, 'at the resurrection on the last day.' Jesus said, 'I am the resurrection and I am life.[a] If a man has faith in me, even though he die, he shall come to life; and no one who is alive and has faith shall ever die. Do you believe this?' 'Lord, I do,' she answered; 'I now believe that you are the Messiah, the Son of God who was to come into the world.'

With these words she went to call her sister Mary, and taking her aside, she said, 'The Master is here; he is asking for you.' When Mary heard this she rose up quickly and went to him. Jesus had not yet reached the village, but was still at the place where Martha had met him. The Jews who were in the house condoling with Mary, when they saw her start up and leave the house, went after her, for they supposed that she was going to the tomb to weep there.

So Mary came to the place where Jesus was. As soon as she caught sight of him she fell at his feet and said, 'O sir, if you had only been

[a] *Some witnesses omit* and I am life.

King James Version

Lord, if thou hadst been here, my brother had
not died. 33 When Jesus therefore saw her weeping, and the Jews also weeping which came with
her, he groaned in the spirit, and was troubled,
34 And said, Where have ye laid him? They say
unto him, Lord, come and see. 35 Jesus wept.
36 Then said the Jews, Behold how he loved him!
37 And some of them said, Could not this man,
which opened the eyes of the blind, have caused
that even this man should not have died? 38 Jesus therefore again groaning in himself cometh
to the grave. It was a cave, and a stone lay upon
it. 39 Jesus said, Take ye away the stone. Martha,
the sister of him that was dead, saith unto him,
Lord, by this time he stinketh: for he hath been
dead four days. 40 Jesus saith unto her, Said I
not unto thee, that, if thou wouldest believe, thou
shouldest see the glory of God? 41 Then they
took away the stone *from the place* where the
dead was laid. And Jesus lifted up *his* eyes, and
said, Father, I thank thee that thou hast heard
me. 42 And I knew that thou hearest me always:
but because of the people which stand by I said
it, that they may believe that thou hast sent me.
43 And when he thus had spoken, he cried with a
loud voice, Lazarus, come forth. 44 And he that
was dead came forth, bound hand and foot with

Living Bible

been here, my brother would still be alive."

33 When Jesus saw her weeping and the Jewish leaders wailing with her, he was moved with
indignation and deeply troubled. 34 "Where is
he buried?" he asked them.

They told him, "Come and see." 35 Tears
came to Jesus' eyes.

36 "They were close friends," the Jewish leaders said. "See how much he loved him."

37, 38 But some said, "This fellow healed a
blind man—why couldn't he keep Lazarus from
dying?" And again Jesus was moved with deep
anger. Then they came to the tomb. It was a
cave with a heavy stone rolled across its door.

39 "Roll the stone aside," Jesus told them.

But Martha, the dead man's sister, said, "By
now the smell will be terrible, for he has been
dead four days."

40 "But didn't I tell you that you will see a
wonderful miracle from God if you believe?"
Jesus asked her.

41 So they rolled the stone aside. Then Jesus
looked up to heaven and said, "Father, thank
you for hearing me. 42 (You always hear me,
of course, but I said it because of all these people standing here, so that they will believe you
sent me.)" 43 Then he shouted, "Lazarus, come
out!"

44 And Lazarus came—bound up in the grave-
cloth, his face muffled in a head swath. Jesus

Today's English Version

"if you had been here, my brother would not
have died!"

33 Jesus saw her weeping, and the Jews who
had come with her weeping also; his heart was
touched, and he was deeply moved. 34 "Where
have you buried him?" he asked them.

"Come and see, Lord," they answered.

35 Jesus wept. 36 So the Jews said, "See how
much he loved him!"

37 But some of them said, "He opened the
blind man's eyes, didn't he? Could he not have
kept Lazarus from dying?"

Lazarus brought to life

38 Deeply moved once more, Jesus went to
the tomb, which was a cave with a stone placed
at the entrance. 39 "Take the stone way!" Jesus
ordered.

Martha, the dead man's sister, answered,
"There will be a bad smell, Lord. He has been
buried four days!"

40 Jesus said to her, "Didn't I tell you that
you would see God's glory if you believed?"
41 They took the stone away. Jesus looked up
and said, "I thank you, Father, that you listen to
me. 42 I know that you always listen to me, but
I say this because of the people here, so they
will believe that you sent me." 43 After he had
said this he called out in a loud voice, "Lazarus,
come out!" 44 The dead man came out, his hands
and feet wrapped in grave cloths, and a cloth

New International Version

"Lord, if you had been here, my brother would
not have died."

33 When Jesus saw her weeping, and the Jews
who had come along with her also weeping, he
was deeply moved and troubled. 34 Where have
you laid him?" he asked.

"Come and see, Lord," they replied.

35 Jesus wept.

36 Then the Jews said, "See how he loved
him!"

37 But some of them said, "Could not he who
opened the eyes of the blind man have kept
this man from dying?"

Jesus raises Lazarus from the dead

38 Jesus, once more deeply moved, came to
the tomb. It was a cave with a stone laid across
the entrance. 39 "Take away the stone," he said.

"But, Lord," said Martha, the sister of the
dead man, "by this time there is a bad odor,
for he has been there four days."

40 Then Jesus said, "Did I not tell you that
if you believed, you would see the glory of
God?"

41 So they took away the stone. Then Jesus
looked up and said, "Father, I thank you that
you have heard me. 42 I knew that you always
hear me, but I said this for the benefit of the
people standing here, that they may believe that
you sent me."

43 When he had said this, Jesus called in a
loud voice, "Lazarus, come out!" 44 The dead
man came out, his hands and feet wrapped with

Phillips Modern English

here, Lord," she said, "my brother would never have died."

When Jesus saw Mary weep and noticed the tears of the Jews who came with her, he was deeply moved and visibly distressed.

"Where have you laid him?" he asked.

"Lord, come and see," they replied, and at this Jesus himself wept.

"Look how much he loved him!" remarked the Jews, though some of them asked, "Could he not have kept this man from dying if he could open that blind man's eyes?"

Jesus was again deeply moved, and went on to the grave. It was a cave, and a stone lay in front of it.

"Take away the stone," said Jesus.

"But Lord," said Martha, the dead man's sister, "he has been dead four days. By this time he will be decaying. . . ."

"Did I not tell you," replied Jesus, "that if you believed, you would see the wonder of what God can do?"

Then they took the stone away and Jesus raised his eyes and said, "Father, I thank you that you have heard me. I know that you always hear me, but I have said this for the sake of these people standing here so that they may believe that you have sent me."

And when he had said this, he called out in a loud voice, "Lazarus, come out!"

And the dead man came out, his hands and feet bound with grave-clothes and his face muf-

Revised Standard Version

"Lord, if you had been here, my brother would
not have died." 33 When Jesus saw her weeping,
and the Jews who came with her also weeping,
he was deeply moved in spirit and troubled;
34 and he said, "Where have you laid him?"
They said to him, "Lord, come and see." 35 Jesus
wept. 36 So the Jews said, "See how he loved
him!" 37 But some of them said, "Could not he
who opened the eyes of the blind man have
kept this man from dying?"
38 Then Jesus, deeply moved again, came to
the tomb; it was a cave, and a stone lay upon
it. 39 Jesus said, "Take away the stone." Martha,
the sister of the dead man, said to him, "Lord,
by this time there will be an odor, for he has
been dead four days." 40 Jesus said to her, "Did
I not tell you that if you would believe you
would see the glory of God?" 41 So they took
away the stone. And Jesus lifted up his eyes and
said, "Father, I thank thee that thou hast heard
me. 42 I knew that thou hearest me always, but
I have said this on account of the people standing by, that they may believe that thou didst
send me." 43 When he had said this, he cried
with a loud voice, "Lazarus, come out." 44 The
dead man came out, his hands and feet bound

Jerusalem Bible

"Lord, if you had been here, my brother would
not have died." At the sight of her tears, and
those of the Jews who followed her, Jesus said
in great distress, with a sigh that came straight
from the heart, 34 "Where have you put him?"
They said, "Lord, come and see." 35 Jesus wept;
36 and the Jews said, "See how much he loved
him!" 37 But there were some who remarked,
"He opened the eyes of the blind man, could he
not have prevented this man's death?" 38 Still
sighing, Jesus reached the tomb: it was a cave
with a stone to close the opening. 39 Jesus said,
"Take the stone away." Martha said to him,
"Lord, by now he will smell; this is the fourth
day." 40 Jesus replied, "Have I not told you
that if you believe you will see the glory of
God?" 41 So they took away the stone. Then
Jesus lifted up his eyes and said:

> "Father, I thank you for hearing my prayer.
> 42 I knew indeed that you always hear me,
> but I speak
> for the sake of all these who stand around me,
> so that they may believe it was you who sent me."

43 When he had said this, he cried in a loud
voice, "Lazarus, here! Come out!" 44 The dead
man came out, his feet and hands bound with

New English Bible

here my brother would not have died.' When Jesus saw her weeping and the Jews her companions weeping, he sighed heavily and was deeply moved. 'Where have you laid him?' he asked. They replied, 'Come and see, sir.' Jesus wept. The Jews said, 'How dearly he must have loved him!' But some of them said, 'Could not this man, who opened the blind man's eyes, have done something to keep Lazarus from dying?'

Jesus again sighed deeply; then he went over to the tomb. It was a cave, with a stone placed against it. Jesus said, 'Take away the stone.' Martha, the dead man's sister, said to him, 'Sir, by now there will be a stench; he has been there four days.' Jesus said, 'Did I not tell you that if you have faith you will see the glory of God?' So they removed the stone.

Then Jesus looked upwards and said, 'Father, I thank thee; thou hast heard me. I knew already that thou always hearest me, but I spoke for the sake of the people standing round, that they might believe that thou didst send me.'

Then he raised his voice in a great cry: 'Lazarus, come forth.' The dead man came out, his hands and feet swathed in linen bands, his

King James Version

graveclothes; and his face was bound about with a napkin. Jesus saith unto them, Loose him, and let him go. 45 Then many of the Jews which came to Mary, and had seen the things which Jesus did, believed on him. 46 But some of them went their ways to the Pharisees, and told them what things Jesus had done.

47 Then gathered the chief priests and the Pharisees a council, and said, What do we? for this man doeth many miracles. 48 If we let him thus alone, all *men* will believe on him; and the Romans shall come and take away both our place and nation. 49 And one of them, *named* Caiaphas, being the high priest that same year, said unto them, Ye know nothing at all, 50 Nor consider that it is expedient for us, that one man should die for the people, and that the whole nation perish not. 51 And this spake he not of himself: but being high priest that year, he prophesied that Jesus should die for that nation; 52 And not for that nation only, but that also he should gather together in one the children of God that were scattered abroad. 53 Then from that day forth they took counsel together for to put him to death. 54 Jesus therefore walked no more openly among the Jews; but went thence

Living Bible

told them, "Unwrap him and let him go!"

45 And so at last many of the Jewish leaders who were with Mary and saw it happen, finally believed on him. 46 But some went away to the Pharisees and reported it to them.

47 Then the chief priests and Pharisees convened a council to discuss the situation.

"What are we going to do?" they asked each other. "For this man certainly does miracles. 48 If we let him alone the whole nation will follow him—and then the Roman army will come and kill us and take over the Jewish government."

49 And one of them, Caiaphas, who was High Priest that year, said, "You stupid idiots—50 let this one man die for the people—why should the whole nation perish?"

51 This prophecy that Jesus should die for the entire nation came from Caiaphas in his position as High Priest—he didn't think of it by himself, but was inspired to say it. 52 It was a prediction that Jesus' death would not be for Israel only, but for all the children of God scattered around the world. 53 So from that time on the Jewish leaders began plotting Jesus' death.

54 Jesus now stopped his public ministry and left Jerusalem; he went to the edge of the desert,

Today's English Version

around his face. "Untie him," Jesus told them, "and let him go."

The plot against Jesus

45 Many of the Jews who had come to visit Mary saw what Jesus did, and believed in him. 46 But some of them returned to the Pharisees and told them what Jesus had done. 47 So the Pharisees and the chief priests met with the Council and said, "What shall we do? All the mighty works this man is doing! 48 If we let him go on in this way everyone will believe in him, and the Roman authorities will take action and destroy the temple and our whole nation!"

49 One of them, named Caiaphas, who was High Priest that year, said, "You do not know a thing! 50 Don't you realize that it is better for you to have one man die for the people, instead of the whole nation being destroyed?" 51 Actually, he did not say this of his own accord; rather, as he was High Priest that year, he was prophesying that Jesus was going to die for the Jewish people, 52 and not only for them, but also to bring together into one body all the scattered children of God.

53 From that day on the Jewish authorities made plans to kill Jesus. 54 So Jesus did not travel openly in Judea, but left and went to a

New International Version

strips of linen, and a cloth around his face.

Jesus said to them, "Take off the grave clothes and let him go."

The plot to kill Jesus

45 Therefore many of the Jews who had come to visit Mary, and had seen what Jesus did, put their faith in him. 46 But some of them went to the Pharisees and told them what Jesus had done. 47 Then the chief priests and the Pharisees called a meeting of the Sanhedrin.

"What are we accomplishing?" they asked. "Here is this man performing many miraculous signs. 48 If we let him go on like this, everyone will put his trust in him, and then the Romans will come and take away both our place[a] and our nation."

49 Then one of them, named Caiaphas, who was high priest that year, spoke up, "You know nothing at all! 50 You do not realize that it is better for you that one man die for the people than that the whole nation perish."

51 He did not say this on his own, but as high priest that year he prophesied that Jesus would die for the Jewish nation, 52 and not only for that nation but also for the scattered children of God, to bring them together and make them one. 53 So from that day on they plotted to take his life.

54 Therefore Jesus no longer moved about publicly among the Jews. Instead he withdrew

[a] Or *temple*.

Phillips Modern English

fled with a handkerchief.

"Now unbind him," Jesus told them, "and let him go home."

11.45 Jesus' miracle leads to deadly hostility

After this many of the Jews who had accompanied Mary and observed what Jesus did, believed in him. But some of them went off to the Pharisees and told them what Jesus had done. Consequently, the chief priests and Pharisees summoned the council and said, "What can we do? This man obviously shows many remarkable signs. If we let him go on doing this sort of thing we shall have everybody believing in him. Then we shall have the Romans coming and that will be the end of our holy place and our very existence as a nation!"

But one of them, Caiaphas, who was High Priest that year, addressed the meeting: "You plainly don't understand what is involved here. You do not realise that it would be a good thing for us if one man should die for the sake of the people—instead of the whole nation being destroyed." (He did not make this remark on his own initiative but, since he was High Priest that year, he was in fact inspired to say that Jesus was going to die for the nation's sake —and in fact not for that nation only, but to bring together into one family all the children of God scattered through out the world.) From that day then, they planned to kill him. As a consequence Jesus made no further public ap-

Revised Standard Version

with bandages, and his face wrapped with a cloth. Jesus said to them, "Unbind him, and let him go."

45 Many of the Jews therefore, who had come with Mary and had seen what he did, believed in him; 46 but some of them went to the Pharisees and told them what Jesus had done. 47 So the chief priests and the Pharisees gathered the council, and said, "What are we to do? For this man performs many signs. 48 If we let him go on thus, every one will believe in him, and the Romans will come and destroy both our holy place[a] and our nation." 49 But one of them, Caiaphas, who was high priest that year, said to them, "You know nothing at all; 50 you do not understand that it is expedient for you that one man should die for the people, and that the whole nation should not perish." 51 He did not say this of his own accord, but being high priest that year he prophesied that Jesus should die for the nation, 52 and not for the nation only, but to gather into one the children of God who are scattered abroad. 53 So from that day on they took counsel how to put him to death.

54 Jesus therefore no longer went about openly among the Jews, but went from there to

[a] Greek *our place*.

Jerusalem Bible

bands of stuff and a cloth around his face. Jesus said to them, "Unbind him, let him go free."

The Jewish leaders decide on the death of Jesus

45 Many of the Jews who had come to visit Mary and had seen what he did believed in him, 46 but some of them went to tell the Pharisees what Jesus had done. 47 Then the chief priests and Pharisees called a meeting. "Here is this man working all these signs," they said, "and what action are we taking? 48 If we let him go on in this way everybody will believe in him, and the Romans will come and destroy the Holy Place and our nation." 49 One of them, Caiaphas, the high priest that year, said, "You don't seem to have grasped the situation at all; 50 you fail to see that it is better for one man to die for the people, than for the whole nation to be destroyed." 51 He did not speak in his own person, it was as high priest that he made this prophecy that Jesus was to die for the nation— 52 and not for the nation only, but to gather together in unity the scattered children of God. 53 From that day they were determined to kill him. 54 So Jesus no longer went about openly among the Jews, but left the district for a town

New English Bible

face wrapped in a cloth. Jesus said, 'Loose him; let him go.'

Now many of the Jews who had come to visit Mary and had seen what Jesus did, put their faith in him. But some of them went off to the Pharisees and reported what he had done.

Thereupon the chief priests and the Pharisees convened a meeting of the Council. 'What action are we taking?' they said. 'This man is performing many signs. If we leave him alone like this the whole populace will believe in him. Then the Romans will come and sweep away our temple and our nation.' But one of them, Caiaphas, who was High Priest that year, said, 'You know nothing whatever; you do not use your judgement; it is more to your interest that one man should die for the people, than that the whole nation should be destroyed.' He did not say this of his own accord, but as the High Priest in office that year, he was prophesying that Jesus would die for the nation—would die not for the nation alone but to gather together the scattered children of God. So from that day on they plotted his death.

Accordingly Jesus no longer went about publicly in Judaea, but left that region for the coun-

King James Version

unto a country near to the wilderness, into a city called Ephraim, and there continued with his disciples.
55 And the Jews' passover was nigh at hand: and many went out of the country up to Jerusalem before the passover, to purify themselves.
56 Then sought they for Jesus, and spake among themselves, as they stood in the temple, What think ye, that he will not come to the feast?
57 Now both the chief priests and the Pharisees had given a commandment, that, if any man knew where he were, he should shew *it,* that they might take him.

12 Then Jesus six days before the passover came to Bethany, where Lazarus was which had been dead, whom he raised from the dead.
2 There they made him a supper; and Martha served: but Lazarus was one of them that sat at the table with him. 3 Then took Mary a pound of ointment of spikenard, very costly, and

Living Bible

to the village of Ephraim, and stayed there with his disciples.
55 The Passover, a Jewish holy day, was near, and many country people arrived in Jerusalem several days early so that they could go through the cleansing ceremony before the Passover began. 56 They wanted to see Jesus, and as they gossiped in the Temple, they asked each other, "What do you think? Will he come for the Passover?" 57 Meanwhile the chief priests and Pharisees had publicly announced that anyone seeing Jesus must report him immediately so that they could arrest him.

12 Six days before the Passover ceremonies began, Jesus arrived in Bethany where Lazarus was—the man he had brought back to life.
2 A banquet was prepared in Jesus' honor. Martha served, and Lazarus sat at the table with him. 3 Then Mary took a jar of costly perfume made from essence of nard, and anointed Jesus'

Today's English Version

place near the desert, to a town named Ephraim, where he stayed with the disciples.
55 The Jewish Feast of Passover was near, and many people went up from the country to Jerusalem, to perform the ceremony of purification before the feast. 56 They were looking for Jesus, and as they gathered in the temple they asked one another, "What do you think? Surely he will not come to the feast, will he?" 57 The chief priests and the Pharisees had given orders that if anyone knew where Jesus was he must report it, so they could arrest him.

Jesus anointed at Bethany

12 Six days before the Passover, Jesus went to Bethany, where Lazarus lived, the man Jesus had raised from death. 2 They prepared a dinner for him there, and Martha helped serve it, while Lazarus sat at the table with Jesus.
3 Then Mary took a whole pint of a very expensive perfume made of pure nard, poured it

New International Version

to a region near the desert, to a village called Ephraim, where he stayed with his disciples.
55 When it was almost time for the Jewish Passover, many went up from the country to Jerusalem for their ceremonial cleansing before the Passover. 56 They kept looking for Jesus, and as they stood in the temple area they asked one another, "What do you think? Isn't he coming to the Feast at all?" 57 But the chief priests and Pharisees had given orders that if anyone found out where Jesus was, he should report it so that they might arrest him.

Jesus anointed at Bethany

12 Six days before the Passover, Jesus arrived at Bethany, where Lazarus lived, whom Jesus had raised from the dead. 2 Here a dinner was given in Jesus' honor. Martha served, while Lazarus was among those reclining at the table with him. 3 Then Mary took about a pint of pure nard, an expensive perfume; she poured

Phillips Modern English

pearance among the Jews but went away to the countryside on the edge of the desert, and stayed with his disciples in a town called Ephraim. The Jewish Passover was approaching and many people went up from the country to Jerusalem before the actual Passover, to go through a ceremonial cleansing. They were looking for Jesus there and kept saying to one another as they stood in the Temple, "What do you think? Surely he won't come to the festival?"

It should be understood that the chief priests and the Pharisees had issued an order that anyone who knew of Jesus' whereabouts should tell them, so that they could arrest him.

12.1 An act of love as the end approaches

Six days before the Passover, Jesus came to Bethany, the village of Lazarus whom he had raised from the dead. They gave a supper for him there, and Martha waited on the party while Lazarus took his place at table with Jesus. Then Mary took a whole pound of very expensive perfume, pure nard, and anointed Jesus'

Revised Standard Version

the country near the wilderness, to a town called Ephraim; and there he stayed with the disciples.
55 Now the Passover of the Jews was at hand, and many went up from the country to Jerusalem before the Passover, to purify themselves.
56 They were looking for Jesus and saying to one another as they stood in the temple, "What do you think? That he will not come to the feast?" 57 Now the chief priests and the Pharisees had given orders that if any one knew where he was, he should let them know, so that they might arrest him.

12 Six days before the Passover, Jesus came to Bethany, where Lazarus was, whom Jesus had raised from the dead. 2 There they made him a supper; Martha served, and Lazarus was one of those at table with him. 3 Mary took a pound of costly ointment of pure nard and

Jerusalem Bible

called Ephraim, in the country bordering on the desert, and stayed there with his disciples.

VII. The last Passover

A. Before the Passion

The Passover draws near

55 The Jewish Passover drew near, and many of the country people who had gone up to Jerusalem to purify themselves 56 looked out for Jesus, saying to one another as they stood about in the Temple, "What do you think? Will he come to the festival or not?" 57 The chief priests and Pharisees had by now given their orders: anyone who knew where he was must inform them so that they could arrest him.

The anointing at Bethany

12 Six days before the Passover, Jesus went to Bethany, where Lazarus was, whom he had raised from the dead. 2 They gave a dinner for him there; Martha waited on them and Lazarus was among those at table. 3 Mary brought in a pound of very costly ointment, pure

New English Bible

try bordering on the desert, and came to a town called Ephraim, where he stayed with his disciples.

The Jewish Passover was now at hand, and many people went up from the country to Jerusalem to purify themselves before the festival. They looked out for Jesus, and as they stood in the temple they asked one another, 'What do you think? Perhaps he is not coming to the festival.' Now the chief priests and the Pharisees had given orders that anyone who knew where he was should give information, so that they might arrest him.

12 Six days before the Passover festival Jesus came to Bethany, where Lazarus lived whom he had raised from the dead. There a supper was given in his honour, at which Martha served, and Lazarus sat among the guests with Jesus. Then Mary brought a pound of very costly perfume, pure oil of nard, and anointed

King James Version

anointed the feet of Jesus, and wiped his feet
with her hair: and the house was filled with the
odour of the ointment. 4 Then saith one of his
disciples, Judas Iscariot, Simon's *son,* which
should betray him, 5 Why was not this ointment
sold for three hundred pence, and given to the
poor? 6 This he said, not that he cared for the
poor; but because he was a thief, and had the
bag, and bare what was put therein. 7 Then said
Jesus, Let her alone: against the day of my
burying hath she kept this. 8 For the poor always
ye have with you; but me ye have not always.
9 Much people of the Jews therefore knew that
he was there: and they came not for Jesus' sake
only, but that they might see Lazarus also, whom
he had raised from the dead.
10 But the chief priests consulted that they
might put Lazarus also to death; 11 Because that
by reason of him many of the Jews went away,
and believed on Jesus.
12 On the next day much people that were
come to the feast, when they heard that Jesus
was coming to Jerusalem, 13 Took branches of
palm trees, and went forth to meet him, and
cried, Hosanna: blessed *is* the King of Israel

Living Bible

feet with it and wiped them with her hair. And
the house was filled with fragrance.
4 But Judas Iscariot, one of his disciples—
the one who would betray him—said, 5 "That
perfume was worth a fortune. It should have
been sold and the money given to the poor."
6 Not that he cared for the poor, but he was in
charge of the disciples' funds and often dipped
into them for his own use!
7 Jesus replied, "Let her alone. She did it in
preparation for my burial. 8 You can always help
the poor, but I won't be with you very long."
9 When the ordinary people of Jerusalem
heard of his arrival, they flocked to see him and
also to see Lazarus—the man who had come
back to life again. 10 Then the chief priests decided to kill Lazarus too, 11 for it was because
of him that many of the Jewish leaders had deserted and believed in Jesus as their Messiah.
12 The next day, the news that Jesus was on
the way to Jerusalem swept through the city, and
a huge crowd of Passover visitors 13 took palm
branches and went down the road to meet him,
shouting, "The Savior! God bless the King of

Today's English Version

on Jesus' feet, and wiped them with her hair.
The sweet smell of the perfume filled the whole
house. 4 One of Jesus' disciples, Judas Iscariot—
the one who was going to betray him—said,
5 "Why wasn't this perfume sold for three hundred dollars and the money given to the poor?"
6 He said this, not because he cared for the
poor, but because he was a thief; he carried the
money bag and would help himself from it.
7 But Jesus said, "Leave her alone! Let her
keep what she has for the day of my burial.
8 You will always have poor people with you,
but I will not be with you always."

The plot against Lazarus

9 A large crowd of the Jews heard that Jesus
was in Bethany, so they went there; they went,
not only because of Jesus, but also to see Lazarus, whom Jesus had raised from death. 10 So
the chief priests made plans to kill Lazarus too;
11 because on his account many Jews were leaving their leaders and believing in Jesus.

The triumphant entry into Jerusalem

12 The next day the large crowd that had
come to the Passover Feast heard that Jesus was
coming to Jerusalem. 13 So they took branches
of palm trees and went out to meet him, shouting, "Praise God! God bless him who comes in

New International Version

it on Jesus' feet and wiped his feet with her
hair. And the house was filled with the fragrance
of the perfume.
4 But one of his disciples, Judas Iscariot, who
was later to betray him, objected, 5 "Why wasn't
this perfume sold and the money given to the
poor? It was worth a year's wages.[b]" 6 He did
not say this because he cared about the poor
but because he was a thief; as keeper of the
money bag, he used to help himself to what was
put into it.
7 "Leave her alone," Jesus replied. "It was
meant that she should save this perfume for the
day of my burial. 8 You will always have the
poor among you, but you will not always have
me."
9 Meanwhile a large crowd of Jews found out
that Jesus was there and came, not only because
of him but also to see Lazarus, whom he had
raised from the dead. 10 So the chief priests
made plans to kill Lazarus as well, 11 for on account of him many of the Jews were going over
to Jesus and putting their faith in him.

The triumphal entry

12 The next day the great crowd that had
come for the Feast heard that Jesus was on his
way to Jerusalem. 13 They took palm branches
and went out to meet him, shouting,
"Hosanna! [c]

[*b*] Greek *300 denarii.* [*c*] A Hebrew expression meaning "Save!" which became an exclamation of praise.

Phillips Modern English

feet and then wiped them with her hair. The entire house was filled with the fragrance of the perfume. But one of his disciples, Judas Iscariot (the man who was going to betray Jesus), burst out, "Why on earth wasn't this perfume sold? It's worth thirty pounds, which could have been given to the poor!"

He said this, not because he cared about the poor, but because he was dishonest, and when he was in charge of the purse used to help himself from the contents.

But Jesus replied to this outburst. "Let her alone, she has saved this for the day of my burial. You have the poor with you always—you will not always have me!"

The large crowd of Jews discovered that he was there and came to the scene—not only because of Jesus but to catch sight of Lazarus, the man whom he had raised from the dead. Then the chief priests planned to kill Lazarus as well, because he was the reason for many of the Jews' going away and putting their faith in Jesus.

12.12 Jesus experiences a temporary triumph

The next day, the great crowd who had come to the festival heard that Jesus was coming into Jerusalem, and went out to meet him with palm branches in their hands, shouting, "God save

Revised Standard Version

anointed the feet of Jesus and wiped his feet
with her hair; and the house was filled with the
fragrance of the ointment. 4 But Judas Iscariot,
one of his disciples (he who was to betray him),
said, 5 "Why was this ointment not sold for three
hundred denarii[b] and given to the poor?" 6 This
he said, not that he cared for the poor but because he was a thief, and as he had the money
box he used to take what was put into it. 7 Jesus
said, "Let her alone, let her keep it for the day
of my burial. 8 The poor you always have with
you, but you do not always have me."
9 When the great crowd of the Jews learned
that he was there, they came, not only on account of Jesus but also to see Lazarus, whom he
had raised from the dead. 10 So the chief priests
planned to put Lazarus also to death, 11 because
on account of him many of the Jews were going
away and believing in Jesus.
12 The next day a great crowd who had
come to the feast heard that Jesus was coming
to Jerusalem. 13 So they took branches of palm
trees and went out to meet him, crying, "Hosanna! Blessed is he who comes in the name of

[b] The denarius was a day's wage for a laborer.

Jerusalem Bible

nard, and with it anointed the feet of Jesus,
wiping them with her hair; the house was full
of the scent of the ointment. 4 Then Judas Iscariot—one of his disciples, the man who was
to betray him—said, 5 "Why wasn't this ointment sold for three hundred denarii, and the
money given to the poor?" 6 He said this, not because he cared about the poor, but because he
was a thief; he was in charge of the common
fund and used to help himself to the contributions. 7 So Jesus said, "Leave her alone; she had
to keep this scent for the day of my burial.
8 You have the poor with you always, you will
not always have me."
9 Meanwhile a large number of Jews heard
that he was there and came not only on account
of Jesus but also to see Lazarus whom he had
raised from the dead. 10 Then the chief priests
decided to kill Lazarus as well, 11 since it was
on his account that many of the Jews were
leaving them and believing in Jesus.

The Messiah enters Jerusalem

12 The next day the crowds who had come
up for the festival heard that Jesus was on his
way to Jerusalem. 13 They took branches of
palm and went out to meet him, shouting,
"Hosanna! Blessings on the King of Israel, *who*

New English Bible

the feet of Jesus and wiped them with her hair, till the house was filled with the fragrance. At this, Judas Iscariot, a disciple of his—the one who was to betray him—said, 'Why was this perfume not sold for thirty pounds[a] and given to the poor?' He said this, not out of any care for the poor, but because he was a thief; he used to pilfer the money put into the common purse, which was in his charge. 'Leave her alone', said Jesus. 'Let her keep it till the day when she prepares for my burial; for you have the poor among you always, but you will not always have me.' [b]

A great number of the Jews heard that he was there, and came not only to see Jesus but also Lazarus whom he had raised from the dead. The chief priests then resolved to do away with Lazarus as well, since on his account many Jews were going over to Jesus and putting their faith in him.

The next day the great body of pilgrims who had come to the festival, hearing that Jesus was on the way to Jerusalem, took palm branches and went out to meet him, shouting, 'Hosanna!

[a] *Literally* for 300 denarii. [b] *Some witnesses omit* for you have . . . have me.

King James Version

that cometh in the name of the Lord. 14And
Jesus, when he had found a young ass, sat
thereon; as it is written, 15 Fear not, daughter of
Sion: behold, thy King cometh, sitting on an
ass's colt. 16 These things understood not his disciples at the first: but when Jesus was glorified,
then remembered they that these things were
written of him, and *that* they had done these
things unto him. 17 The people therefore that
was with him when he called Lazarus out of his
grave, and raised him from the dead, bare
record. 18 For this cause the people also met him,
for that they heard that he had done this
miracle. 19 The Pharisees therefore said among
themselves, Perceive ye how ye prevail nothing?
behold, the world is gone after him.
20 And there were certain Greeks among
them that came up to worship at the feast:
21 The same came therefore to Philip, which
was of Bethsaida of Galilee, and desired him,
saying, Sir, we would see Jesus. 22 Philip cometh
and telleth Andrew: and again Andrew and
Philip tell Jesus.
23 And Jesus answered them, saying, The
hour is come, that the Son of man should be

Living Bible

Israel! Hail to God's Ambassador!"
14 Jesus rode along on a young donkey, fulfilling the prophecy that said: 15 "Don't be
afraid of your King, people of Israel, for he will
come to you meekly, sitting on a donkey's colt!"
16 (His disciples didn't realize at the time
that this was a fulfillment of prophecy; but after
Jesus returned to his glory in heaven, then they
noticed how many prophecies of Scripture had
come true before their eyes.)
17 And those in the crowd who had seen Jesus call Lazarus back to life were telling all
about it. 18 That was the main reason why so
many went out to meet him—because they had
heard about this mighty miracle.
19 Then the Pharisees said to each other,
"We've lost. Look—the whole world has gone
after him!"
20 Some Greeks who had come to Jerusalem
to attend the Passover 21 paid a visit to Philip,[a]
who was from Bethsaida, and said, "Sir, we
want to meet Jesus." 22 Philip told Andrew
about it, and they went together to ask Jesus.
23, 24 Jesus replied that the time had come

[a] Philip's name was Greek, though he was a Jew.

Today's English Version

the name of the Lord! God bless the King of
Israel!"
14 Jesus found a donkey and sat on it, just as
the scripture says,

15 "Do not be afraid, city of Zion!
Here comes your king,
riding on a young donkey."

16 His disciples did not understand this at the
time; but when Jesus had been raised to glory
they remembered that the scripture said this
about him, and that they had done this for him.
17 The crowd that had been with Jesus when
he called Lazarus out of the grave and raised
him from death had reported what had happened. 18 That was why the crowd met him—
because they heard that he had done this mighty
work. 19 The Pharisees then said to each other,
"You see, we are not succeeding at all! Look, the
whole world is following him!"

Some Greeks seek Jesus

20 Some Greeks were among those who went
to Jerusalem to worship during the feast. 21 They
came to Philip (he was from Bethsaida, in Galilee) and said, "Sir, we want to see Jesus."
22 Philip went and told Andrew, and the two
of them went and told Jesus. 23 Jesus answered
them, "The hour has now come for the Son of

New International Version

Blessed is he who comes in the name of the
Lord! [d]
Blessed is the King of Israel!"
14 Jesus found a young donkey and sat upon
it, as Scripture says,
15 "Do not be afraid, O Zion;
see, your king is coming,
seated on a donkey's colt." [e]
16 At first his disciples did not understand
all this. Only after Jesus was glorified did they
realize that these things had been written about
him and that they had done these things to him.
17 Now the crowd that was with him had
continued to spread the word that he had called
Lazarus from the tomb, raising him from the
dead.[f] 18 Many people, because they had heard
that he had given this miraculous sign, went out
to meet him. 19 So the Pharisees said to one
another, "See, this is getting us nowhere. Look
how the whole world has gone after him!"

Jesus predicts his death

20 Now there were some Greeks among those
who went up to worship at the Feast. 21 They
came to Philip, who was from Bethsaida in
Galilee, with a request. "Sir," they said, "we
would like to see Jesus." 22 Philip went to tell
Andrew; Andrew and Philip in turn told Jesus.
23 Jesus replied, "The hour has come for the

[d] Psalm 118:25,26. [e] Zech. 9:9. [f] Or *Now the crowd that had been with him when he called Lazarus from the tomb and raised him from the dead were telling everyone.*

Phillips Modern English

him! God bless the man who comes in the name of the Lord, God bless the king of Israel!"

For Jesus had found a young donkey and was seated upon it, just as the scripture foretold—

> Fear not, daughter of Zion: behold, thy king cometh, sitting on an ass's colt.

(The disciples did not realise the significance of what was happening at the time, but when Jesus was glorified, then they recollected that these things had been written about him and that they had carried them out for him.)

The people who had been with him, when he had summoned Lazarus from the grave and raised him from the dead, were continually talking about it. This accounts for the crowd who went out to meet him, for they had heard that he had given this sign. Seeing all this, the Pharisees remarked to one another, "You see?—There's nothing one can do! The whole world is running after him."

Among those who had come up to worship at the festival were some Greeks. They approached Philip (whose home town was Bethsaida in Galilee) with the request, "Sir, we want to see Jesus."

Philip went and told Andrew, and Andrew went with Philip and told Jesus.

Jesus told them, "The time has come for the

Revised Standard Version

the Lord, even the King of Israel!" 14 And Jesus
found a young ass and sat upon it; as it is
written,
15 "Fear not, daughter of Zion;
behold, your king is coming,
sitting on an ass's colt!"
16 His disciples did not understand this at first;
but when Jesus was glorified, then they remembered that this had been written of him and
had been done to him. 17 The crowd that had
been with him when he called Lazarus out of
the tomb and raised him from the dead bore
witness. 18 The reason why the crowd went to
meet him was that they heard he had done this
sign. 19 The Pharisees then said to one another,
"You see that you can do nothing; look, the
world has gone after him."
20 Now among those who went up to worship at the feast were some Greeks. 21 So these
came to Philip, who was from Bethsaida in Galilee, and said to him, "Sir, we wish to see Jesus."
22 Philip went and told Andrew; Andrew went
with Philip and they told Jesus. 23 And Jesus answered them, "The hour has come for the Son

Jerusalem Bible

comes in the name of the Lord." [d] 14 Jesus found
a young donkey and mounted it—as scripture
says: 15 *Do not be afraid, daughter of Zion; see,
your king is coming, mounted on the colt of a
donkey.* [e] 16 At the time his disciples did not
understand this, but later, after Jesus had been
glorified, they remembered that this had been
written about him and that this was in fact how
they had received him. 17 All who had been with
him when he called Lazarus out of the tomb
and raised him from the dead were telling how
they had witnessed it; 18 it was because of this,
too, that the crowd came out to meet him: they
had heard that he had given this sign. 19 Then
the Pharisees said to one another, "You see,
there is nothing you can do; look, the whole
world is running after him!"

Jesus foretells his death and subsequent glorification

20 Among those who went up to worship at
the festival were some Greeks.[f] 21 These approached Philip, who came from Bethsaida in
Galilee, and put this request to him, "Sir, we
should like to see Jesus." 22 Philip went to tell
Andrew, and Andrew and Philip together went
to tell Jesus.
23 Jesus replied to them:

> "Now the hour has come
> for the Son of Man to be glorified.

[d] Ps. 118:26. [e] Zc. 9:9f. [f] The "God-fearing men" of Ac. 10:2: converts who observed certain specific Mosaic observances.

New English Bible

Blessings on him who comes in the name of the Lord! God bless the king of Israel!' Jesus found a donkey and mounted it, in accordance with the text of Scripture: 'Fear no more, daughter of Zion; see, your king is coming, mounted on an ass's colt.'

At the time his disciples did not understand this, but after Jesus had been glorified they remembered that this had been written about him, and that this had happened to him. The people who were present when he called Lazarus out of the tomb and raised him from the dead told what they had seen and heard. That is why the crowd went to meet him; they had heard of this sign that he had performed. The Pharisees said to one another, 'You see you are doing no good at all; why, all the world has gone after him!'

Among those who went up to worship at the festival were some Greeks. They came to Philip, who was from Bethsaida in Galilee, and said to him, 'Sir, we should like to see Jesus.' So Philip went and told Andrew, and the two of them went to tell Jesus. Then Jesus replied: 'The hour

King James Version

glorified. 24 Verily, verily, I say unto you, Except a corn of wheat fall into the ground and
die, it abideth alone: but if it die, it bringeth
forth much fruit. 25 He that loveth his life shall
lose it; and he that hateth his life in this world
shall keep it unto life eternal. 26 If any man
serve me, let him follow me; and where I am,
there shall also my servant be: if any man serve
me, him will *my* Father honour. 27 Now is my
soul troubled; and what shall I say? Father, save
me from this hour: but for this cause came I
unto this hour. 28 Father, glorify thy name. Then
came there a voice from heaven, *saying,* I have
both glorified *it,* and will glorify *it* again. 29 The
people therefore that stood by, and heard *it,*
said that it thundered: others said, An angel
spake to him. 30 Jesus answered and said, This
voice came not because of me, but for your
sakes. 31 Now is the judgment of this world:
now shall the prince of this world be cast out.
32 And I, if I be lifted up from the earth, will

Living Bible

for him to return to his glory in heaven, and
that "I must fall and die like a kernel of wheat
that falls into the furrows of the earth. Unless I
die I will be alone—a single seed. But my death
will produce many new wheat kernels—a plentiful harvest of new lives. 25 If you love your life
down here—you will lose it. If you despise your
life down here—you will exchange it for eternal
glory.

26 "If these Greeks[b] want to be my disciples,
tell them to come and follow me, for my servants
must be where I am. And if they follow me, the
Father will honor them. 27 Now my soul is
deeply troubled. Shall I pray, 'Father, save me
from what lies ahead'? But that is the very reason why I came! 28 Father, bring glory and
honor to your name."

Then a voice spoke from heaven saying, "I
have already done this, and I will do it again."
29 When the crowd heard the voice, some of
them thought it was thunder, while others declared an angel had spoken to him.

30 Then Jesus told them, "The voice was for
your benefit, not mine. 31 The time of judgment
for the world has come—and the time when
Satan,[c] the prince of this world, shall be cast
out. 32 And when I am lifted up [on the cross[d]],

[*b*] Literally, "if any man." [*c*] Literally, "prince of this world." See 2 Corinthians 4:4, and Ephesians 2:2 and 6:12. [*d*] Implied.

Today's English Version

Man to be given great glory. 24 I tell you the
truth: a grain of wheat remains no more than a
single grain unless it is dropped into the ground
and dies. If it does die, then it produces many
grains. 25 Whoever loves his own life will lose
it; whoever hates his own life in this world will
keep it for life eternal. 26 Whoever wants to
serve me must follow me, so that my servant
will be with me where I am. My Father will
honor him who serves me."

Jesus speaks about his death

27 "Now my heart is troubled—and what shall
I say? Shall I say, 'Father, do not let this hour
come upon me'? But that is why I came, to go
through this hour of suffering. 28 Father, bring
glory to your name!"

Then a voice spoke from heaven, "I have
brought glory to it, and I will do so again."

29 The crowd standing there heard the voice
and said, "It thundered!"

Others said, "An angel spoke to him!"

30 But Jesus said to them, "It was not for my
sake that this voice spoke, but for yours. 31 Now
is the time for the world to be judged; now the
ruler of this world will be overthrown. 32 When
I am lifted up from the earth, I will draw all

New International Version

Son of Man to be glorified. 24 I tell you the
truth, unless a kernel of wheat falls to the
ground and dies, it remains only a single seed.
But if it dies, it produces many seeds. 25 The
man who loves his life will lose it, while the
man who hates his life in this world will keep it
for eternal life. 26 Whoever serves me must follow me; and where I am, my servant also will
be. My Father will honor the one who serves
me.

27 "Now my heart is troubled, and what shall
I say? 'Father, save me from this hour'? No, it
was for this very reason I came to this hour.
28 Father, glorify your name!"

Then a voice came from heaven, "I have glorified it, and will glorify it again." 29 The crowd
that was there and heard it said it had thundered; others said an angel had spoken to him.

30 Jesus said, "This voice was for your benefit, not mine. 31 Now is the time for judgment
on this world; now the prince of this world will
be driven out. 32 But I, when I am lifted up
from the earth, will draw all men to myself."

Phillips Modern English

Son of Man to be glorified. I tell you truly that unless a grain of wheat falls into the earth and dies, it remains a single grain of wheat; but if it dies, it brings a good harvest. The man who loves his own life will lose it, and the man who hates his life in this world will preserve it for eternal life. If a man wants to enter my service, he must follow my way; and where I am, my servant will also be. And my Father will honour every man who enters my service.

"Now comes my hour of heart-break, and what can I say, 'Father, save me from this hour'? No, it was for this very purpose that I came to this hour. 'Father, honour your own name!'"

At this there came a voice from Heaven, "I have honoured it and I will honour it again!"

When the crowd of bystanders heard this, they said it thundered, but some of them said, "An angel spoke to him."

Then Jesus said, "That voice came for your sake, not for mine. Now is the time for the judgment of this world to begin, and now will the spirit that rules this world be driven out. As for me, if I am lifted up from the earth, I will

Revised Standard Version

of man to be glorified. 24 Truly, truly, I say to
you, unless a grain of wheat falls into the earth
and dies, it remains alone; but if it dies, it bears
much fruit. 25 He who loves his life loses it,
and he who hates his life in this world will keep
it for eternal life. 26 If any one serves me, he
must follow me; and where I am, there shall my
servant be also; if any one serves me, the Father
will honor him.
27 "Now is my soul troubled. And what shall
I say? 'Father, save me from this hour'? No, for
this purpose I have come to this hour. 28 Father,
glorify thy name." Then a voice came from
heaven, "I have glorified it, and I will glorify it
again." 29 The crowd standing by heard it and
said that it had thundered. Others said, "An
angel has spoken to him." 30 Jesus answered,
"This voice has come for your sake, not for
mine. 31 Now is the judgment of this world, now
shall the ruler of this world be cast out; 32 and
I, when I am lifted up from the earth, will

Jerusalem Bible

24 I tell you, most solemnly,
unless a wheat grain falls on the ground and dies,
it remains only a single grain;
but if it dies,
it yields a rich harvest.
25 Anyone who loves his life loses it;
anyone who hates his life in this world
will keep it for the eternal life.
26 If a man serves me, he must follow me,
wherever I am, my servant will be there too.
If anyone serves me, my Father will honor him.
27 Now my soul is troubled.
What shall I say:
Father, save me from this hour?
But it was for this very reason that I have come to this hour.
28 Father, glorify your name!"

A voice came from heaven, "I have glorified
it, and I will glorify it again."
29 People standing by, who heard this, said
it was a clap of thunder; others said, "It was an
angel speaking to him." 30 Jesus answered, "It
was not for my sake that this voice came, but
for yours.

31 "Now sentence is being passed on this world;
now the prince of this world is to be overthrown.[g]
32 And when I am lifted up from the earth,
I shall draw all men to myself."

[g] Satan.

New English Bible

has come for the Son of Man to be glorified. In truth, in very truth I tell you, a grain of wheat remains a solitary grain unless it falls into the ground and dies; but if it dies, it bears a rich harvest. The man who loves himself is lost, but he who hates himself in this world will be kept safe for eternal life. If anyone serves me, he must follow me; where I am, my servant will be. Whoever serves me will be honoured by my Father.

'Now my soul is in turmoil, and what am I to say? Father, save me from this hour.[a] No, it was for this that I came to this hour. Father, glorify thy name.' A voice sounded from heaven: 'I have glorified it, and I will glorify it again.' The crowd standing by said it was thunder, while others said, 'An angel has spoken to him.' Jesus replied, 'This voice spoke for your sake, not mine. Now is the hour of judgement for this world; now shall the Prince of this world be driven out. And I shall draw all men to myself,

[a] *Or* . . . turmoil. Shall I say, "Father, save me from this hour"?

King James Version

draw all *men* unto me. 33 This he said, signifying what death he should die. 34 The people answered him, We have heard out of the law that Christ abideth for ever: and how sayest thou, The Son of man must be lifted up? who is this Son of man? 35 Then Jesus said unto them, Yet a little while is the light with you. Walk while ye have the light, lest darkness come upon you: for he that walketh in darkness knoweth not whither he goeth. 36 While ye have light, believe in the light, that ye may be the children of light. These things spake Jesus, and departed, and did hide himself from them.

37 But though he had done so many miracles before them, yet they believed not on him: 38 That the saying of Esaias the prophet might be fulfilled, which he spake, Lord, who hath believed our report? and to whom hath the arm of the Lord been revealed? 39 Therefore they could not believe, because that Esaias said again, 40 He hath blinded their eyes, and hardened their heart; that they should not see with *their* eyes, nor understand with *their* heart, and be con-

Living Bible

I will draw everyone to me." 33 He said this to indicate how he was going to die.

34 "Die?" asked the crowd. "We understood that the Messiah would live forever and never die. Why are you saying he will die? What Messiah are you talking about?"

35 Jesus replied, "My light will shine out for you just a little while longer. Walk in it while you can, and go where you want to go before the darkness falls, for then it will be too late for you to find your way. 36 Make use of the Light while there is still time; then you will become light bearers."[e] After saying these things, Jesus went away and was hidden from them.

37 But despite all the miracles he had done, most of the people would not believe he was the Messiah. 38 This is exactly what Isaiah the prophet had predicted: "Lord, who will believe us? Who will accept God's mighty miracles as proof?"[f] 39 But they couldn't believe, for as Isaiah also said: 40 "God[g] has blinded their eyes and hardened their hearts so that they can neither see nor understand nor turn to me to

[e] Literally, "sons of light." [f] Literally, "To whom has the arm of the Lord been revealed?" Isaiah 53:1. [g] Literally, "He." The Greek here is a very free rendering, or paraphrase, of Isaiah 6:10.

Today's English Version

men to me." 33 (In saying this he indicated the kind of death he was going to suffer.)

34 The crowd answered back, "Our Law tells us that the Messiah will live forever. How, then, can you say that the Son of Man must be lifted up? Who is this Son of Man?"

35 Jesus answered, "The light will be among you a little longer. Continue on your way while you have the light, so the darkness will not come upon you; because the one who walks in the dark does not know where he is going. 36 Believe in the light, then, while you have it, so that you will be the people of the light."

The unbelief of the Jews

After Jesus said this he went off and hid himself from them. 37 Even though he had done all these mighty works before their very eyes they did not believe in him, 38 so that what the prophet Isaiah had said might come true,

"Lord, who believed the message we told?
To whom did the Lord show his power?"

39 For this reason they were not able to believe, because Isaiah also said,

40 "God has blinded their eyes,
and closed their minds,
so that their eyes would not see,
and their minds would not understand,
and they would not turn to me, says God,
for me to heal them."

New International Version

33 He said this to show the kind of death he was going to die.

34 The crowd spoke up, "We have heard from the Law that the Christ[g] will remain forever, so how can you say, 'The Son of Man must be lifted up?' Who is this 'Son of Man'?"

35 Then Jesus told them, "You are going to have the light just a little while longer. Walk while you have the light, before darkness overtakes you. The man who walks in the dark does not know where he is going. 36 Put your trust in the light while you have it, so that you may become sons of light." When he had finished speaking, Jesus left and hid himself from them.

The Jews continue in their unbelief

37 Even after Jesus had done all these miraculous signs in their presence, they still would not believe in him. 38 This was to fulfill the word of Isaiah the prophet:

"Lord, who has believed our message,
and to whom has the arm of the Lord been revealed?"[h]

39 For this reason they could not believe, because, as Isaiah says elsewhere:

40 "He has blinded their eyes
and deadened their hearts,
so they can neither see with their eyes,
nor understand with their hearts,
nor turn—and I would heal them."[i]

[g] Or *Messiah*. [h] Isaiah 53:1. [i] Isaiah 6:10.

Phillips Modern English

draw all men to myself." (He said this to show the kind of death he was going to die.)

Then the crowd said, "We have heard from the Law that Christ lives for ever. How can you say that the Son of Man must be 'lifted up'? Who is this Son of Man?"

At this, Jesus said to them, "You have the light with you only a little while longer. Go on while the light is good, before the darkness comes down upon you. For the man who walks in the dark has no idea where he is going. You must believe in the light while you have the light, that you may become the sons of light."

Jesus said all these things, and then went away, out of their sight. But though he had given so many signs, yet they did not believe in him, so that the prophecy of Isaiah was fulfilled, when he said,

Lord, who hath believed our report?
And to whom hath the arm of the Lord been revealed?

Thus, they could not believe, for Isaiah said again—

He hath blinded their eyes, and he hardened their heart:
Lest they should see with their eyes, and perceive with their heart,
And should turn,
And I should heal them.

Revised Standard Version

draw all men to myself." 33 He said this to show
by what death he was to die. 34 The crowd answered him, "We have heard from the law that
the Christ remains for ever. How can you say
that the Son of man must be lifted up? Who is
this Son of man?" 35 Jesus said to them, "The
light is with you for a little longer. Walk while
you have the light, lest the darkness overtake
you; he who walks in the darkness does not
know where he goes. 36 While you have the
light, believe in the light, that you may become
sons of light."

When Jesus had said this, he departed and
hid himself from them. 37 Though he had done
so many signs before them, yet they did not
believe in him; 38 it was that the word spoken
by the prophet Isaiah might be fulfilled:

"Lord, who has believed our report,
and to whom has the arm of the Lord been revealed?"

39 Therefore they could not believe. For Isaiah
again said,

40 "He has blinded their eyes and hardened their heart,
lest they should see with their eyes and perceive with their heart,
and turn for me to heal them."

Jerusalem Bible

33 By these words he indicated the kind of
death he would die. 34 The crowd answered, "The
Law has taught us that the Christ will remain
for ever. How can you say, 'The Son of Man
must be lifted up'? Who is this Son of Man?"
35 Jesus then said:

"The light will be with you only a little longer now.
Walk while you have the light,
or the dark will overtake you;
he who walks in the dark does not know where he is going.
36 While you still have the light,
believe in the light
and you will become sons of light."

Having said this, Jesus left them and kept himself hidden.

Conclusion: the unbelief of the Jews

37 Though they had been present when he
gave so many signs, they did not believe in him;
38 this was to fulfill the words of the prophet
Isaiah: *Lord, who could believe what we have heard said, and to whom has the power of the Lord been revealed?* [h] 39 Indeed, they were unable to believe because, as Isaiah says again:
40 *He has blinded their eyes, he has hardened their heart, for fear they should see with their eyes and understand with their heart, and turn to me for healing.* [i]

[*h*] Is. 53:1. [*i*] Is. 6:9f.

New English Bible

when I am lifted up from the earth.' This he said to indicate the kind of death he was to die.

The people answered, 'Our Law teaches us that the Messiah continues for ever. What do you mean by saying that the Son of Man must be lifted up? What Son of Man is this?' Jesus answered them: 'The light is among you still, but not for long. Go on your way while you have the light, so that darkness may not overtake you. He who journeys in the dark does not know where he is going. While you have the light, trust to the light, so that you may become men of light.' After these words Jesus went away from them into hiding.

In spite of the many signs which Jesus had performed in their presence they would not believe in him, for the prophet Isaiah's utterance had to be fulfilled: 'Lord, who has believed what we reported, and to whom has the Lord's power been revealed?' So it was that they could not believe, for there is another saying of Isaiah's: 'He has blinded their eyes and dulled their minds, lest they should see with their eyes, and perceive with their minds, and turn to me to heal

King James Version

verted, and I should heal them. 41 These things
said Esaias, when he saw his glory, and spake of
him.
42 Nevertheless among the chief rulers also
many believed on him; but because of the Pharisees they did not confess *him,* lest they should
be put out of the synagogue: 43 For they loved
the praise of men more than the praise of God.
44 Jesus cried and said, He that believeth on
me, believeth not on me, but on him that sent
me. 45And he that seeth me seeth him that sent
me. 46 I am come a light into the world, that
whosoever believeth on me should not abide in
darkness. 47And if any man hear my words, and
believe not, I judge him not: for I came not to
judge the world, but to save the world. 48 He
that rejecteth me, and receiveth not my words,
hath one that judgeth him: the word that I have
spoken, the same shall judge him in the last day.
49 For I have not spoken of myself; but the
Father which sent me, he gave me a commandment, what I should say, and what I should

Living Bible

heal them." 41 Isaiah was referring to Jesus when
he made this prediction, for he had seen a vision
of the Messiah's glory.
42 However, even many of the Jewish leaders
believed him to be the Messiah but wouldn't
admit it to anyone because of their fear that the
Pharisees would excommunicate them from the
synagogue; 43 for they loved the praise of men
more than the praise of God.
44 Jesus shouted to the crowds, "If you trust
me, you are really trusting God. 45 For when
you see me, you are seeing the one who sent me.
46 I have come as a Light to shine in this dark
world, so that all who put their trust in me will
no longer wander in the darkness. 47 If anyone
hears me and doesn't obey me, I am not his
judge—for I have come to save the world and
not to judge it. 48 But all who reject me and my
message will be judged at the Day of Judgment
by the truths I have spoken. 49 For these are not
my own ideas, but I have told you what the

Today's English Version

41 Isaiah said this because he saw Jesus' glory,
and spoke about him.
42 Even then, many Jewish authorities believed
in Jesus; but because of the Pharisees they did
not talk about it openly, so as not to be put
out of the synagogue. 43 They loved the approval of men rather than the approval of God.

Judgment by Jesus' word

44 Jesus said in a loud voice, "Whoever believes in me, believes not only in me but also in
him who sent me. 45 Whoever sees me, also sees
him who sent me. 46 I have come into the world
as light, that everyone who believes in me should
not remain in the darkness. 47 Whoever hears
my message and does not obey it, I will not
judge him. I came, not to judge the world, but
to save it. 48 Whoever rejects me and does not
accept my message, has one who will judge him.
The word I have spoken will be his judge on the
last day! 49 Yes, because I have not spoken on
my own, but the Father who sent me has com-

New International Version

41 Isaiah said this because he saw Jesus' glory,
and spoke about him.
42 Yet at the same time many even among
the leaders believed in him. But because of the
Pharisees they would not confess their faith for
fear they would be put out of the synagogue;
43 for they loved praise from men more than
praise from God.
44 Then Jesus cried out, "When a man believes in me, he does not believe in me only,
but in the one who sent me. 45 When he looks
at me, he sees the one who sent me. 46 I have
come into the world as a light, so that no one
who believes in me should stay in darkness.
47 "As for the person who hears my words
but does not keep them, I do not judge him. For
I did not come to judge the world, but to save
it. 48 There is a judge for the one who rejects
me and does not accept my words; that very
word which I spoke will condemn him at the
last day. 49 For I did not speak of my own accord, but the Father who sent me commanded

Phillips Modern English

Isaiah said these things because he saw the glory of Christ, and spoke about him. Nevertheless, many even of the authorities did believe in him. But they would not admit it for fear of the Pharisees, in case they should be excommunicated. They were more concerned to have the approval of men than to have the approval of God.

But later, Jesus cried aloud, "Every man who believes in me, is believing in the one who sent me rather than in me; and every man who sees me is seeing the one who sent me. I have come into the world as light, so that no one who believes in me need remain in the dark. Yet, if anyone hears my sayings and does not keep them, I do not judge him—for I did not come to judge the world but to save it. Every man who rejects me and will not accept my sayings has a judge—on the last day, the very words that I have spoken will be his judge. For I have not spoken on my own authority: the Father who sent me has commanded me what

Revised Standard Version

41 Isaiah said this because he saw his glory and
spoke of him. 42 Nevertheless many even of the
authorities believed in him, but for fear of the
Pharisees they did not confess it, lest they should
be put out of the synagogue: 43 for they loved
the praise of men more than the praise of God.
44 And Jesus cried out and said, "He who believes in me, believes not in me but in him who
sent me. 45And he who sees me sees him who
sent me. 46 I have come as light into the world,
that whoever believes in me may not remain in
darkness. 47 If any one hears my sayings and
does not keep them, I do not judge him; for I
did not come to judge the world but to save the
world. 48 He who rejects me and does not receive my sayings has a judge; the word that I
have spoken will be his judge on the last day.
49 For I have not spoken on my own authority;
the Father who sent me has himself given me
commandment what to say and what to speak.

Jerusalem Bible

41 Isaiah said this when he saw his glory,[j] and his words referred to Jesus.

42 And yet there were many who did believe in him, even among the leading men, but they did not admit it, through fear of the Pharisees and fear of being expelled from the synagogue:
43 they put honor from men before the honor that comes from God.

44 Jesus declared publicly:

"Whoever believes in me
believes not in me
but in the one who sent me,
45 and whoever sees me,
sees the one who sent me.
46 I, the light, have come into the world,
so that whoever believes in me
need not stay in the dark any more.
47 If anyone hears my words and does not keep them faithfully,
it is not I who shall condemn him,
since I have come not to condemn the world,
but to save the world:
48 he who rejects me and refuses my words
has his judge already:
the word itself that I have spoken
will be his judge on the last day.
49 For what I have spoken does not come from myself;
no, what I was to say, what I had to speak,
was commanded by the Father who sent me,

[j] Isaiah's vision in the Temple, Is. 6:4, interpreted as a prophetic vision of Christ's glory.

New English Bible

them.' Isaiah said this because[a] he saw his glory and spoke about him.

For all that, even among those in authority a number believed in him, but would not acknowledge him on account of the Pharisees, for fear of being banned from the synagogue. For they valued their reputation with men rather than the honour which comes from God.

So Jesus cried aloud: 'When a man believes in me, he believes in him who sent me rather than in me; seeing me, he sees him who sent me. I have come into the world as light, so that no one who has faith in me should remain in darkness. But if anyone hears my words and pays no regard to them, I am not his judge; I have not come to judge the world, but to save the world. There is a judge for the man who rejects me and does not accept my words; the word that I spoke will be his judge on the last day. I do not speak on my own authority, but the Father who sent me has himself commanded me what to say and how to

[a] *Some witnesses read* when.

King James Version

speak. 50And I know that his commandment is life everlasting: whatsoever I speak therefore, even as the Father said unto me, so I speak.

13 Now before the feast of the passover, when Jesus knew that his hour was come that he should depart out of this world unto the Father, having loved his own which were in the world, he loved them unto the end. 2And supper being ended, the devil having now put into the heart of Judas Iscariot, Simon's *son*, to betray him; 3 Jesus knowing that the Father had given all things into his hands, and that he was come from God, and went to God; 4 He riseth from supper, and laid aside his garments; and took a towel, and girded himself. 5After that he poureth water into a basin, and began to wash the disciples' feet, and to wipe *them* with the towel wherewith he was girded. 6 Then cometh he to Simon Peter: and Peter saith unto him, Lord, dost thou wash my feet? 7 Jesus answered and said unto him, What I do thou knowest not now; but thou shalt know hereafter. 8 Peter saith unto him, Thou shalt never wash my feet. Jesus an-

Living Bible

Father said to tell you. 50And I know his instructions lead to eternal life; so whatever he tells me to say, I say!"

13 Jesus knew on the evening of Passover Day that it would be his last night on earth before returning to his Father. During supper the devil had already suggested to Judas Iscariot, Simon's son, that this was the night to carry out his plan to betray Jesus. Jesus knew that the Father had given him everything and that he had come from God and would return to God. And how he loved his disciples! 4 So he got up from the supper table, took off his robe, wrapped a towel around his loins,[a] 5 poured water into a basin, and began to wash the disciples' feet and to wipe them with the towel he had around him.

6 When he came to Simon Peter, Peter said to him, "Master, you shouldn't be washing our feet like this!"

7 Jesus replied, "You don't understand now why I am doing it; some day you will."

8 "No," Peter protested, "you shall never wash my feet!"

"But if I don't, you can't be my partner," Je-

[a] As the lowliest of slaves would dress.

Today's English Version

manded me what I must say and speak. 50And I know that his command brings eternal life. What I say, then, is what the Father has told me to say."

Jesus washes his disciples' feet

13 It was now the day before the Feast of Passover. Jesus knew that his hour had come for him to leave this world and go to the Father. He had always loved those who were his own in the world, and he loved them to the very end.

2 Jesus and his disciples were at supper. The Devil had already decided that Judas, the son of Simon Iscariot, would betray Jesus. 3 Jesus knew that the Father had given him complete power; he knew that he had come from God and was going to God. 4 So Jesus rose from the table, took off his outer garment, and tied a towel around his waist. 5 Then he poured some water into a washbasin and began to wash the disciples' feet and dry them with the towel around his waist. 6 He came to Simon Peter, who said to him, "Are you going to wash my feet, Lord?"

7 Jesus answered him, "You do not know now what I am doing, but you will know later."

8 Peter declared, "You will never, at any time, wash my feet!"

"If I do not wash your feet," Jesus answered,

New International Version

me what to say and how to say it. 50 I know that his command leads to eternal life. So whatever I say is just what the Father has told me to say."

Jesus washes his disciples' feet

13 It was just before the Passover Feast. Jesus knew that the time had come for him to leave this world and go to the Father. Having loved his own who were in the world, he now showed them the full extent of his love.

2 The evening meal was being served, and the devil had already prompted Judas Iscariot, son of Simon, to betray Jesus. 3 Jesus knew that the Father had put all things under his power, and that he had come from God and was returning to God, 4 so he got up from the meal, took off his outer clothing, and wrapped a towel around his waist. 5After that, he poured water into a basin and began to wash his disciples' feet, drying them with the towel that was wrapped around him.

6 He came to Simon Peter, who said to him, "Lord, are you going to wash my feet?"

7 Jesus replied, "You do not realize now what I am doing, but later you will understand."

8 "No," said Peter, "you shall never wash my feet."

Jesus answered, "Unless I wash you, you have

Phillips Modern English

to say and how to speak. And I know that what he commands means eternal life. All that I say I speak only in accordance with what the Father has told me."

13.1 Jesus teaches his disciples humility

Before the festival of the Passover began, Jesus realised that the time had come for him to leave this world and return to the Father. He had loved those who were his own in this world and he loved them to the end. By supper-time, the devil had already put the thought of betraying Jesus into the mind of Judas Iscariot, Simon's son. Jesus, with the full knowledge that the Father had put everything into his hands and that he had come from God and was going to God, rose from the supper-table, took off his outer clothes, picked up a towel and fastened it round his waist. Then he poured water into a basin and began to wash the disciples' feet and to dry them with the towel around his waist.

So he came to Simon Peter, who said to him, "Lord, are you going to wash my feet?"

"You do not realise now what I am doing," replied Jesus, "but later on you will understand."

Then Peter said to him, "You must never wash my feet!"

"Unless you let me wash you, Peter," replied

Revised Standard Version

50 And I know that his commandment is eternal
life. What I say, therefore, I say as the Father
has bidden me."

13 Now before the feast of the Passover,
when Jesus knew that his hour had come
to depart out of this world to the Father, having loved his own who were in the world, he
loved them to the end. 2 And during supper,
when the devil had already put it into the heart
of Judas Iscariot, Simon's son, to betray him,
3 Jesus, knowing that the Father had given all
things into his hands, and that he had come from
God and was going to God, 4 rose from supper,
laid aside his garments, and girded himself with
a towel. 5 Then he poured water into a basin,
and began to wash the disciples' feet, and to
wipe them with the towel with which he was
girded. 6 He came to Simon Peter; and Peter
said to him, "Lord, do you wash my feet?"
7 Jesus answered him, "What I am doing you
do not know now, but afterward you will understand." 8 Peter said to him, "You shall never
wash my feet." Jesus answered him, "If I do

Jerusalem Bible

50 and I know that his commands mean eternal life.
And therefore what the Father has told me
is what I speak."

B. The Last Supper

Jesus washes his disciples' feet

13 It was before the festival of the Passover, and Jesus knew that the hour had
come for him to pass from this world to the
Father. He had always loved those who were
his in the world, but now he showed how perfect his love was.
2 They were at supper, and the devil had already put it into the mind of Judas Iscariot son
of Simon, to betray him. 3 Jesus knew that the
Father had put everything into his hands, and
that he had come from God and was returning
to God, 4 and he got up from table, removed
his outer garment and, taking a towel, wrapped
it around his waist; 5 he then poured water into
a basin and began to wash the disciples' feet[k]
and to wipe them with the towel he was wearing.
6 He came to Simon Peter, who said to him,
"Lord, are you going to wash my feet?" 7 Jesus
answered, "At the moment you do not know
what I am doing, but later you will understand."
8 "Never!" said Peter. "You shall never wash
my feet." Jesus replied, "If I do not wash you,

[k] The dress and the duty are those of a slave.

New English Bible

speak. I know that his commands are eternal life. What the Father has said to me, therefore —that is what I speak.'

Farewell discourses

13 It was before the Passover festival. Jesus knew that his hour had come and he must leave this world and go to the Father. He had always loved his own who were in the world, and now he was to show the full extent of his love.

The devil had already put it into the mind of Judas son of Simon Iscariot to betray him. During supper, Jesus, well aware that the Father had entrusted everything to him, and that he had come from God and was going back to God, rose from table, laid aside his garments, and taking a towel, tied it round him. Then he poured water into a basin, and began to wash his disciples' feet and to wipe them with the towel.

When it was Simon Peter's turn, Peter said to him, 'You, Lord, washing my feet?' Jesus replied, 'You do not understand now what I am doing, but one day you will.' Peter said, 'I will never let you wash my feet.' 'If I do not wash

King James Version

swered him, If I wash thee not, thou hast no part
with me. 9 Simon Peter saith unto him, Lord,
not my feet only, but also *my* hands and *my*
head. 10 Jesus saith to him, He that is washed
needeth not save to wash *his* feet, but is clean
every whit: and ye are clean, but not all. 11 For
he knew who should betray him; therefore said
he, Ye are not all clean. 12 So after he had
washed their feet, and had taken his garments,
and was set down again, he said unto them,
Know ye what I have done to you? 13 Ye call
me Master and Lord: and ye say well; for *so* I
am. 14 If I then, *your* Lord and Master, have
washed your feet; ye also ought to wash one
another's feet. 15 For I have given you an example, that ye should do as I have done to you.
16 Verily, verily, I say unto you, The servant is
not greater than his lord; neither he that is sent
greater than he that sent him. 17 If ye know
these things, happy are ye if ye do them.
18 I speak not of you all: I know whom I
have chosen: but that the Scripture may be fulfilled, He that eateth bread with me hath lifted
up his heel against me. 19 Now I tell you before

Living Bible

sus replied.
9 Simon Peter exclaimed, "Then wash my
hands and head as well—not just my feet!"
10 Jesus replied, "One who has bathed all
over needs only to have his feet washed to be
entirely clean. Now you are clean—but that isn't
true of everyone here." 11 For Jesus knew who
would betray him. That is what he meant when
he said, "Not all of you are clean."
12 After washing their feet he put on his robe
again and sat down and asked, "Do you understand what I was doing? 13 You call me 'Master'
and 'Lord,' and you do well to say it, for it is
true. 14 And since I, the Lord and Teacher, have
washed your feet, you ought to wash each other's
feet. 15 I have given you an example to follow:
do as I have done to you. 16 How true it is that
a servant is not greater than his master. Nor is
the messenger more important than the one who
sends him. 17 You know these things—now do
them! That is the path of blessing.
18 "I am not saying these things to all of you;
I know so well each one of you I chose. The
Scripture declares, 'One who eats supper with
me will betray me,' and this will soon come true.
19 I tell you this now so that when it happens,

Today's English Version

"you will no longer be my disciple."
9 Simon Peter answered, "Lord, do not wash
only my feet, then! Wash my hands and head,
too!"
10 Jesus said, "Whoever has taken a bath is
completely clean and does not have to wash
himself, except for his feet. All of you are clean
—all except one." 11 (Jesus already knew who
was going to betray him; that is why he said,
"All of you, except one, are clean.")
12 After he had washed their feet, Jesus put
his outer garment back on and returned to his
place at the table. "Do you understand what I
have just done to you?" he asked. 13 "You call
me Teacher and Lord, and it is right that you
do so, because I am. 14 I am your Lord and
Teacher, and I have just washed your feet. You,
then, should wash each other's feet. 15 I have
set an example for you, so that you will do just
what I have done for you. 16 I tell you the
truth: no slave is greater than his master; no
messenger is greater than the one who sent him.
17 Now you know this truth; how happy you
will be if you put it into practice!
18 "I am not talking about all of you; I know
those I have chosen. But the scripture must come
true that says, 'The man who ate my food turned
against me.' 19 I tell you this now before it hap-

New International Version

no part with me."
9 "Then, Lord," Simon Peter replied, "not
just my feet but my hands and my head as
well!"
10 Jesus answered, "A person who has had a
bath needs only to wash his feet; his whole body
is clean. And you are clean, though not every
one of you." 11 For he knew who was going to
betray him, and that was why he said not every
one was clean.
12 When he had finished washing their feet, he
put on his clothes and returned to his place.
"Do you understand what I have done for you?"
he asked them. 13 "You call me 'Teacher' and
'Lord,' and rightly so, for that is what I am.
14 Now that I, your Lord and Teacher, have
washed your feet, you also should wash one another's feet. 15 I have set you an example that
you should do as I have done for you. 16 I tell
you the truth, no servant is greater than his
master, nor is a messenger greater than the one
who sent him. 17 Once you know these things,
you will be blessed if you do them.

Jesus predicts his betrayal

18 "I am not referring to all of you; I know
those I have chosen. But this is to fulfill the
scripture: 'He who shares my bread has lifted
up his heel against me.' [j]
19 "I am telling you now before it happens,

[*j*] Psalm 41:9.

Phillips Modern English

Jesus, "you cannot be my true partner."

"Then Lord," returned Simon Peter, "please—not just my feet but my hands and my face as well!"

"The man who has bathed," returned Jesus, "only needs to wash his feet to be clean all over. And you are clean—though not all of you."

(For Jesus knew his betrayer and that is why he said, "though not all of you".)

When Jesus had washed their feet and put on his clothes, he sat down again and spoke to them, "Do you realise what I have just done to you? You call me 'teacher' and 'Lord' and you are quite right, for I am your teacher and your Lord. But if I, your teacher and Lord, have washed your feet, you must be ready to wash one another's feet. I have given you this as an example so that you may do as I have done. Believe me, the servant is not greater than his master and the messenger is not greater than the man who sent him. Once you have realised these things, you will find your happiness in doing them.

13.18 Jesus foretells his betrayal

"I am not speaking about all of you—I know the men I have chosen. But let this scripture be fulfilled—

He that eateth my bread lifted up his heel
against me.

From now onwards, I shall tell you about things

Revised Standard Version

not wash you, you have no part in me." 9 Simon
Peter said to him, "Lord, not my feet only but
also my hands and my head!" 10 Jesus said to
him, "He who has bathed does not need to wash,
except for his feet,[c] but he is clean all over; and
you[x] are clean, but not every one of you." 11 For
he knew who was to betray him; that was why
he said, "You are not all clean."
12 When he had washed their feet, and taken
his garments, and resumed his place, he said to
them, "Do you know what I have done to you?
13 You call me Teacher and Lord; and you are
right, for so I am. 14 If I then, your Lord and
Teacher, have washed your feet, you also ought
to wash one another's feet. 15 For I have given
you an example, that you also should do as I
have done to you. 16 Truly, truly, I say to you, a
servant[d] is not greater than his master; nor is
he who is sent greater than he who sent him.
17 If you know these things, blessed are you if
you do them. 18 I am not speaking of you all;
I know whom I have chosen; it is that the scripture may be fulfilled, 'He who ate my bread has
lifted his heel against me.' 19 I tell you this now,

[c] Other ancient authorities omit *except for his feet.* [x] The Greek word for *you* here is plural [d] Or *slave.*

Jerusalem Bible

you can have nothing in common with me."
9 "Then, Lord," said Simon Peter, "not only my
feet, but my hands and my head as well!" 10 Jesus said, "No one who has taken a bath needs
washing, he is clean all over. You too are clean,
though not all of you are." 11 He knew who
was going to betray him, that was why he said,
"though not all of you are."
12 When he had washed their feet and put on
his clothes again he went back to the table. "Do
you understand," he said, "what I have done to
you? 13 You call me Master and Lord, and
rightly; so I am. 14 If I, then, the Lord and
Master, have washed your feet, you should wash
each other's feet. 15 I have given you an example so that you may copy what I have done
to you.

16 "I tell you most solemnly,
no servant is greater than his master,
no messenger is greater than the man who
sent him.

17 "Now that you know this, happiness will
be yours if you behave accordingly. 18 I am not
speaking about all of you: I know the ones I
have chosen; but what scripture says must be
fulfilled: *Someone who shares my table rebels
against me.*[l]

19 "I tell you this now, before it happens,

[l] Ps. 41:9.

New English Bible

you,' Jesus replied, 'you are not in fellowship with me.' 'Then, Lord,' said Simon Peter, 'not my feet only; wash my hands and head as well!'

Jesus said, 'A man who has bathed needs no further washing;[a] he is altogether clean; and you are clean, though not every one of you.' He added the words 'not every one of you' because he knew who was going to betray him.

After washing their feet and taking his garments again, he sat down. 'Do you understand what I have done for you?' he asked. 'You call me "Master" and "Lord", and rightly so, for that is what I am. Then if I, your Lord and Master, have washed your feet, you also ought to wash one another's feet. I have set you an example: you are to do as I have done for you. In very truth I tell you, a servant is not greater than his master, nor a messenger than the one who sent him. If you know this, happy are you if you act upon it.

'I am not speaking about all of you; I know whom I have chosen. But there is a text of Scripture to be fulfilled: "He who eats bread with me has turned against me."[b] I tell you this now,

[a] *Some witnesses read* needs only to wash his feet. [b] *Literally* has lifted his heel against me.

King James Version

it come, that, when it is come to pass, ye may believe that I am *he.* 20 Verily, verily, I say unto you, He that receiveth whomsoever I send receiveth me; and he that receiveth me receiveth him that sent me. 21 When Jesus had thus said, he was troubled in spirit, and testified, and said, Verily, verily, I say unto you, that one of you shall betray me. 22 Then the disciples looked one on another, doubting of whom he spake. 23 Now there was leaning on Jesus' bosom one of his disciples, whom Jesus loved. 24 Simon Peter therefore beckoned to him, that he should ask who it should be of whom he spake. 25 He then lying on Jesus' breast saith unto him, Lord, who is it? 26 Jesus answered, He it is, to whom I shall give a sop, when I have dipped *it.* And when he had dipped the sop, he gave *it* to Judas Iscariot, *the son* of Simon. 27 And after the sop Satan entered into him. Then said Jesus unto him, That thou doest, do quickly. 28 Now no man at the table knew for what intent he spake this unto him. 29 For some *of them* thought, because Judas had the bag, that Jesus had said unto him, Buy *those things* that we have need of against the feast; or, that he should give something to the poor. 30 He then, having received the sop, went immediately out; and it was night.

Living Bible

you will believe on me.

20 "Truly, anyone welcoming my messenger is welcoming me. And to welcome me is to welcome the Father who sent me."

21 Now Jesus was in great anguish of spirit and exclaimed, "Yes, it is true—one of you will betray me." 22 The disciples looked at each other, wondering whom he could mean. 23 Since I [b] was sitting next[c] to Jesus at the table, being his closest friend, 24 Simon Peter motioned to me to ask him who it was who would do this terrible deed.

25 So I turned [d] and asked him, "Lord, who is it?"

26 He told me, "It is the one I honor by giving the bread dipped in the sauce." [e]

And when he had dipped it, he gave it to Judas, son of Simon Iscariot.

27 As soon as Judas had eaten it, Satan entered into him. Then Jesus told him, "Hurry—do it now."

28 None of the others at the table knew what Jesus meant. 29 Some thought that since Judas was their treasurer, Jesus was telling him to go and pay for the food or to give some money to the poor. 30 Judas left at once, going out into the night.

[*b*] Literally, "There was one at the table." All commentators believe him to be John, the writer of this book. [*c*] Literally, "reclining on Jesus' bosom." The custom of the period was to recline around the table, leaning on the left elbow. John, next to Jesus, was at his side. [*d*] Literally, "leaning back against Jesus' chest," to whisper his inquiry. [*e*] Literally, "He it is for whom I shall dip the sop and give it him." The honored guest was thus singled out in the custom of that time.

Today's English Version

pens, so that when it does happen you will believe that 'I Am Who I Am'. 20 I tell you the truth: whoever receives anyone I send, receives me also; and whoever receives me, receives him who sent me."

Jesus predicts his betrayal

21 After Jesus said this, he was deeply troubled, and declared openly, "I tell you the truth: one of you is going to betray me."

22 The disciples looked at one another, completely puzzled about whom he meant. 23 One of the disciples, whom Jesus loved, was sitting next to Jesus. 24 Simon Peter motioned to him and said, "Ask him who it is that he is talking about."

25 So that disciple moved closer to Jesus' side and asked, "Who is it, Lord?"

26 Jesus answered, "I will dip the bread in the sauce and give it to him; he is the man." So he took a piece of bread, dipped it, and gave it to Judas, the son of Simon Iscariot. 27 As soon as Judas took the bread, Satan went into him. Jesus said to him, "Hurry and do what you must!" 28 None of those at the table understood why Jesus said this to him. 29 Since Judas was in charge of the money bag, some of the disciples thought that Jesus had told him to go and buy what they needed for the feast, or else that he had told him to give something to the poor.

30 Judas accepted the bread and went out at once. It was night.

New International Version

so that when it does happen you will believe that I am He. 20 I tell you the truth, whoever accepts anyone I send accepts me; and whoever accepts me accepts the one who sent me."

21 After he had said this, Jesus was deeply troubled and testified, "I tell you the truth, one of you is going to betray me."

22 His disciples stared at one another, at a loss to know which of them he meant. 23 One of them, the disciple whom Jesus loved, was reclining next to him. 24 Simon Peter motioned to this disciple and said, "Ask him which one he means."

25 Leaning back against Jesus, he asked him, "Lord, who is it?"

26 Jesus answered, "It is the one to whom I will give this piece of bread when I have dipped it in the dish." Then, dipping the piece of bread, he gave it to Judas Iscariot, son of Simon. 27 As soon as Judas took the bread, Satan entered into him.

"What you are about to do, do quickly," Jesus told him, 28 but no one at the meal understood why Jesus said this to him. 29 Since Judas had charge of the money, some thought Jesus was telling him to buy what was needed for the Feast, or to give something to the poor. 30 As soon as Judas had taken the bread, he went out. And it was night.

Phillips Modern English

before they happen, so that when they do happen, you may believe that I am the one I claim to be. I tell you truly that anyone who accepts my messenger will be accepting me, and anyone who accepts me will be accepting the One who sent me."

After Jesus had said this, he was clearly in anguish of soul, and he added, solemnly

"I tell you plainly, one of you is going to betray me."

At this the disciples stared at each other, completely mystified as to whom he could mean. And it happened that one of them, whom Jesus loved, was sitting very close to him. So Simon Peter nodded to this man and said, "Tell us who he means."

He simply leaned forward on Jesus' shoulder, and asked, "Lord, who is it?"

And Jesus answered, "It is the one I am going to give this piece of bread to, after I have dipped it in the dish."

Then he took a piece of bread, dipped it in the dish and gave it to Simon's son, Judas Iscariot. After he had taken the piece of bread, Satan entered his heart. Then Jesus said to him, "Be quick about your business!"

No one else at table knew what he meant in telling him this. Indeed, some of them thought that, since Judas had charge of the purse, Jesus was telling him to buy what they needed for the festival, or that he should give something to the poor. So Judas took the piece of bread and went out quickly—into the night.

Revised Standard Version

before it takes place, that when it does take place
you may believe that I am he. 20 Truly, truly, I
say to you, he who receives any one whom I
send receives me; and he who receives me receives him who sent me."
21 When Jesus had thus spoken, he was
troubled in spirit, and testified, "Truly, truly, I
say to you, one of you will betray me." 22 The
disciples looked at one another, uncertain of
whom he spoke. 23 One of his disciples, whom
Jesus loved, was lying close to the breast of
Jesus; 24 so Simon Peter beckoned to him and
said, "Tell us who it is of whom he speaks."
25 So lying thus, close to the breast of Jesus,
he said to him, "Lord, who is it?" 26 Jesus answered, "It is he to whom I shall give this morsel
when I have dipped it." So when he had dipped
the morsel, he gave it to Judas, the son of Simon
Iscariot. 27 Then after the morsel, Satan entered into him. Jesus said to him, "What you are
going to do, do quickly." 28 Now no one at the
table knew why he said this to him. 29 Some
thought that, because Judas had the money box,
Jesus was telling him, "Buy what we need for
the feast"; or, that he should give something to
the poor. 30 So, after receiving the morsel, he
immediately went out; and it was night.

Jerusalem Bible

so that when it does happen
you may believe that I am He.
20 I tell you most solemnly,
whoever welcomes the one I send welcomes me,
and whoever welcomes me welcomes the one who sent me."

The treachery of Judas foretold

21 Having said this, Jesus was troubled in
spirit and declared, "I tell you most solemnly,
one of you will betray me." 22 The disciples
looked at one another, wondering which he
meant. 23 The disciple Jesus loved was reclining
next to Jesus; 24 Simon Peter signed to him and
said, "Ask who it is he means," 25 so leaning
back on Jesus' breast he said, "Who is it, Lord?"
26 "It is the one," replied Jesus, "to whom I
give the piece of bread that I shall dip in the
dish." He dipped the piece of bread and gave it
to Judas son of Simon Iscariot. 27 At that instant, after Judas had taken the bread, Satan
entered him. Jesus then said, "What you are going to do, do quickly." 28 None of the others at
table understood the reason he said this. 29 Since
Judas had charge of the common fund, some of
them thought Jesus was telling him, "Buy what
we need for the festival," or telling him to give
something to the poor. 30 As soon as Judas had
taken the piece of bread he went out. Night had
fallen.

New English Bible

before the event, so that when it happens you may believe that I am what I am. In very truth I tell you, he who receives any messenger of mine receives me; receiving me, he receives the One who sent me.'

After saying this, Jesus exclaimed in deep agitation of spirit, 'In truth, in very truth I tell you, one of you is going to betray me.' The disciples looked at one another in bewilderment: whom could he be speaking of? One of them, the disciple he loved, was reclining close beside Jesus. So Simon Peter nodded to him and said, 'Ask who it is he means.' That disciple, as he reclined, leaned back close to Jesus and asked, 'Lord, who is it?' Jesus replied, 'It is the man to whom I give this piece of bread when I have dipped it in the dish.' Then, after dipping it in the dish, he took it out and gave it to Judas son of Simon Iscariot. As soon as Judas had received it Satan entered him. Jesus said to him, 'Do quickly what you have to do.' No one at the table understood what he meant by this. Some supposed that, as Judas was in charge of the common purse, Jesus was telling him to buy what was needed for the festival, or to make some gift to the poor. As soon as Judas had received the bread he went out. It was night.

King James Version

31 Therefore, when he was gone out, Jesus
said, Now is the Son of man glorified, and God
is glorified in him. 32 If God be glorified in him,
God shall also glorify him in himself, and shall
straightway glorify him. 33 Little children, yet a
little while I am with you. Ye shall seek me;
and as I said unto the Jews, Whither I go, ye
cannot come; so now I say to you. 34 A new
commandment I give unto you, That ye love one
another; as I have loved you, that ye also love
one another. 35 By this shall all *men* know that
ye are my disciples, if ye have love one to another.

36 Simon Peter said unto him, Lord, whither
goest thou? Jesus answered him, Whither I go,
thou canst not follow me now; but thou shalt
follow me afterwards. 37 Peter said unto him,
Lord, why cannot I follow thee now? I will lay
down my life for thy sake. 38 Jesus answered
him, Wilt thou lay down thy life for my sake?
Verily, verily, I say unto thee, The cock shall
not crow, till thou hast denied me thrice.

Living Bible

31 As soon as Judas left the room, Jesus said,
"My time has come; the glory of God will soon
surround me—and God shall receive great praise
because of all that happens to me. 32 And God
shall give me his own glory, and this so very
soon. 33 Dear, dear children, how brief are these
moments before I must go away and leave you!
Then, though you search for me, you cannot
come to me—just as I told the Jewish leaders.

34 "And so I am giving a new commandment
to you now—love each other just as much as I
love you. 35 Your strong love for each other will
prove to the world that you are my disciples."

36 Simon Peter said, "Master, where are you
going?"

And Jesus replied, "You can't go with me now;
but you will follow me later."

37 "But why can't I come now?" he asked,
"for I am ready to die for you."

38 Jesus answered, "Die for me? No—three
times before the cock crows tomorrow morning,
you will deny that you even know me!

Today's English Version

The new commandment

31 After Judas had left, Jesus said, "Now the
Son of Man's glory is revealed; now God's glory
is revealed through him. 32 And if God's glory is
revealed through him, then God will reveal the
glory of the Son of Man in himself, and he will
do so at once. 33 My children, I shall not be
with you very much longer. You will look for
me; but I tell you now what I told the Jews,
'You cannot go where I am going.' 34 A new
commandment I give you: love one another. As
I have loved you, so you must love one another.
35 If you have love for one another, then all
will know that you are my disciples."

Jesus predicts Peter's denial

36 "Where are you going, Lord?" Simon Peter
asked him.

"You cannot follow me now where I am going," answered Jesus; "but later you will follow
me."

37 "Lord, why can't I follow you now?" asked
Peter. "I am ready to die for you!"

38 Jesus answered, "Are you really ready to
die for me? I tell you the truth: before the
rooster crows you will say three times that you
do not know me."

New International Version

Jesus predicts Peter's denial

31 When he was gone, Jesus said, "Now is
the Son of Man glorified and God is glorified in
him. 32 If God is glorified in him,[k] then God
will glorify the Son in himself, and will glorify
him at once.

33 "My children, I will be with you only a
little longer. You will look for me, and just as
I told the Jews, so I tell you now: Where I am
going, you cannot come.

34 "A new commandment I give you: Love
one another. As I have loved you, so you must
love one another. 35 All men will know that you
are my disciples if you love one another."

36 Simon Peter asked him, "Lord, where are
you going?"

Jesus replied, "Where I am going, you cannot
follow now, but you will follow later."

37 Peter asked, "Lord, why can't I follow
you now? I will lay down my life for you."

38 Then Jesus answered, "Will you really lay
down your life for me? I tell you the truth, be-
for the rooster crows, you will disown me three
times!

[k] Many early MSS omit *If God is glorified in him.*

Phillips Modern English

When he had gone, Jesus spoke, "Now comes the glory of the Son of Man, and the glory of God in him! If God is glorified through him then God will glorify the Son of Man—and that without delay. Oh, my children, I am with you such a short time! You will look for me and I have to tell you as I told the Jews, 'Where I am going, you cannot follow.' Now I am giving you a new command—love one another. Just as I have loved you, so you must love one another. This is how all men will know that you are my disciples, because you have such love for one another."

Simon Peter said to him, "Lord, where are you going?"

"I am going," replied Jesus, "where you cannot follow me now, though you will follow me later."

"Lord, why can't I follow you now?" said Peter. "I would lay down my life for you!"

"Would you lay down your life for me?" replied Jesus. "Believe me, you will disown me three times before the cock crows!"

Revised Standard Version

31 When he had gone out, Jesus said, "Now
is the Son of man glorified, and in him God is
glorified; 32 if God is glorified in him, God will
also glorify him in himself, and glorify him at
once. 33 Little children, yet a little while I am
with you. You will seek me; and as I said to the
Jews so now I say to you, 'Where I am going
you cannot come.' 34 A new commandment I
give to you, that you love one another; even as
I have loved you, that you also love one another.
35 By this all men will know that you are my
disciples, if you have love for one another."
36 Simon Peter said to him, "Lord, where are
you going?" Jesus answered, "Where I am going
you cannot follow me now; but you shall
follow afterward." 37 Peter said to him, "Lord,
why cannot I follow you now? I will lay down my
life for you." 38 Jesus answered, "Will you lay
down your life for me? Truly, truly, I say to you,
the cock will not crow, till you have denied me
three times.

Jerusalem Bible

31 When he had gone Jesus said:

"Now has the Son of Man been glorified,
and in him God has been glorified.
32 If God has been glorified in him,
God will in turn glorify him in himself,[m]
and will glorify him very soon.

Farewell discourses

33 "My little children,
I shall not be with you much longer.
You will look for me,
and, as I told the Jews,
where I am going,
you cannot come.
34 I give you a new commandment:
love one another;
just as I have loved you,
you also must love one another.
35 By this love you have for one another,
everyone will know that you are my disciples."

36 Simon Peter said, "Lord, where are you
going?" Jesus replied, "Where I am going you
cannot follow me now; you will follow me later."
37 Peter said to him, "Why can't I follow you
now? I will lay down my life for you." 38 "Lay
down your life for me?" answered Jesus. "I tell
you most solemnly, before the cock crows you
will have disowned me three times.

[*m*] I.e., the Father will take the Son of Man to himself in glory.

New English Bible

When he had gone out Jesus said, 'Now the Son of Man is glorified, and in him God is glorified. If God is glorified in him,[c] God will also glorify him in himself; and he will glorify him now. My children, for a little longer I am with you; then you will look for me, and, as I told the Jews, I tell you now, where I am going you cannot come. I give you a new commandment: love one another; as I have loved you, so you are to love one another. If there is this love among you, then all will know that you are my disciples.'

Simon Peter said to him, 'Lord, where are you going?' Jesus replied, 'Where I am going you cannot follow me now, but one day you will.' Peter said, 'Lord, why cannot I follow you now? I will lay down my life for you.' Jesus answered, 'Will you indeed lay down your life for me? I tell you in very truth, before the cock crows you will have denied me three times.

[*c*] *Some witnesses omit* If God . . . in him.

King James Version

14 Let not your heart be troubled: ye believe in God, believe also in me. 2 In my
Father's house are many mansions: if *it were*
not *so,* I would have told you. I go to prepare a
place for you. 3 And if I go and prepare a place
for you, I will come again, and receive you unto
myself; that where I am, *there* ye may be also.
4 And whither I go ye know, and the way ye
know. 5 Thomas saith unto him, Lord, we know
not whither thou goest; and how can we know
the way? 6 Jesus saith unto him, I am the way,
the truth, and the life: no man cometh unto the
Father, but by me. 7 If ye had known me, ye
should have known my Father also: and from
henceforth ye know him, and have seen him.
8 Philip saith unto him, Lord, shew us the
Father, and it sufficeth us. 9 Jesus saith unto him,
Have I been so long time with you, and yet hast
thou not known me, Philip? he that hath seen
me hath seen the Father; and how sayest thou
then, Shew us the Father? 10 Believest thou not
that I am in the Father, and the Father in me?

Living Bible

14 "Let not your heart be troubled. You are
trusting God, now trust in me. 2, 3 There
are many homes up there where my Father lives,
and I am going to prepare them for your coming. When everything is ready, then I will come
and get you, so that you can always be with me
where I am. If this weren't so, I would tell you
plainly. 4 And you know where I am going and
how to get there."
5 "No, we don't," Thomas said. "We haven't
any idea where you are going, so how can we
know the way?"
6 Jesus told him, "I am the Way—yes, and the
Truth and the Life. No one can get to the Father
except by means of me. 7 If you had known who
I am, then you would have known why my
Father is. From now on you know him—and
have seen him!"
8 Philip said, "Sir, show us the Father and
we will be satisfied."
9 Jesus replied, "Don't you even yet know
who I am, Philip, even after all this time I have
been with you? Anyone who has seen me has
seen the Father! So why are you asking to see
him? 10 Don't you believe that I am the Father
and the Father is in me? The words I say are

Today's English Version

Jesus the way to the Father

14 "Do not be worried and upset," Jesus told
them. "Believe in God, and believe also in
me. 2 There are many rooms in my Father's
house, and I am going to prepare a place for
you. I would not tell you this if it were not so.
3 And after I go and prepare a place for you, I
will come back and take you to myself, so that
you will be where I am. 4 You know how to get
to the place where I am going."
5 Thomas said to him, "Lord, we do not
know where you are going; how can we know
the way to get there?"
6 Jesus answered him, "I am the way, the
truth, and the life; no one goes to the Father
except by me. 7 Now that you have known me,"
he said to them, "you will know my Father also;
and from now on you do know him, and you
have seen him."
8 Philip said to him, "Lord, show us the Father; that is all we need."
9 Jesus answered, "For a long time I have
been with you all; yet you do not know me,
Philip? Whoever has seen me has seen the Father. Why, then, do you say, 'Show us the Father'? 10 Do you not believe, Philip, that I am
in the Father and the Father is in me? The

New International Version

Jesus comforts his disciples

14 "Do not let your hearts be troubled. Trust
in God [l]; trust also in me. 2 There are
many rooms in my Father's house; otherwise,
I would have told you. I am going there to prepare a place for you. 3 And if I go and prepare
a place for you, I will come back and take you
to be with me that you also may be where I
am. 4 You know the way to the place where I
am going."

Jesus the way to the Father

5 Thomas said to him, "Lord, we don't know
where you are going, so how can we know the
way?"
6 Jesus answered, "I am the way—and the
truth and the life. No one comes to the Father
except through me. 7 If you really knew me, you
would know[m] my Father as well. From now on,
you do know him and have seen him."
8 Philip said, "Lord, show us the Father and
that will be enough for us."
9 Jesus answered, "Don't you know me, Philip,
even after I have been among you such a long
time? Anyone who has seen me has seen the Father. How can you say, 'Show us the Father'?
10 Don't you believe that I am in the Father,
and that the Father is in me? The words I say

[*l*] Or *You trust in God.* [*m*] Some early MSS read *If you really have known me, you will know.*

Phillips Modern English

14.1 Jesus reveals spiritual truths

"You must not let yourselves be distressed—you must hold on to your faith in God and to your faith in me. There are many rooms in my Father's House. If there were not, should I have told you that I am going away to prepare a place for you? It is true that I am going away to prepare a place for you, but it is just as true that I am coming again to welcome you into my own home, so that you may be where I am. You know where I am going and you know the way I am going to take."

"Lord," Thomas remonstrated, "we do not know where you're going, and how can we know what way you're going to take?"

"I myself am the way," replied Jesus, "and the truth and the life. No one approaches the Father except through me. If you had known who I am, you would have known my Father. From now on, you do know him and you have seen him."

14.8 Jesus explains his relationship with the Father

Then Philip said to him, "Show us the Father, Lord, and we shall be satisfied."

"Have I been so long with you," returned Jesus, "without your really knowing me, Philip? The man who has seen me has seen the Father. How can you say, 'Show us the Father'? Do you not believe that I am in the Father and the

Revised Standard Version

14 "Let not your hearts be troubled; believe[e]
in God, believe also in me. 2 In my Father's
house are many rooms; if it were not so, would
I have told you that I go to prepare a place for
you? 3 And when I go and prepare a place for
you, I will come again and will take you to myself, that where I am you may be also. 4 And
you know the way where I am going."[f]
5 Thomas said to him, "Lord, we do not know
where you are going; how can we know the
way?" 6 Jesus said to him, "I am the way, and
the truth, and the life; no one comes to the
Father, but by me. 7 If you had known me, you
would have known my Father also; henceforth
you know him and have seen him."
8 Philip said to him, "Lord, show us the
Father, and we shall be satisfied." 9 Jesus said
to him, "Have I been with you so long, and yet
you do not know me, Philip? He who has seen
me has seen the Father; how can you say, 'Show
us the Father'? 10 Do you not believe that I am
in the Father and the Father in me? The words

[e] Or *you believe.* [f] Other ancient authorities read *where I am going you know, and the way you know.*

Jerusalem Bible

14 "Do not let your hearts be troubled.
Trust in God still, and trust in me.
2 There are many rooms in my Father's house;
if there were not, I should have told you.
I am going now to prepare a place for you,
3 and after I have gone and prepared you a place,
I shall return to take you with me;
so that where I am
you may be too.
4 You know the way to the place where I am going."

5 Thomas said, "Lord, we do not know where you are going, so how can we know the way?"
6 Jesus said:

"I am the Way, the Truth and the Life.
No one can come to the Father except through me.
7 If you know me, you know my Father too.
From this moment you know him and have seen him."

8 Philip said, "Lord, let us see the Father and
then we shall be satisfied." 9 "Have I been with
you all this time, Philip," said Jesus to him,
"and you still do not know me?

"To have seen me is to have seen the Father,
so how can you say, 'Let us see the Father'?
10 Do you not believe
that I am in the Father and the Father is in me?

New English Bible

14 'Set your troubled hearts at rest. Trust in God always; trust also in me. There are many dwelling-places in my Father's house; if it were not so I should have told you; for I am going there on purpose to prepare a place for you.[a] And if I go and prepare a place for you, I shall come again and receive you to myself, so that where I am you may be also; and my way there is known to you.'[b] Thomas said, 'Lord, we do not know where you are going, so how can we know the way?' Jesus replied, 'I am the way; I am the truth and I am life; no one comes to the Father except by me.

'If you knew me you would know my Father too.[c] From now on you do know him; you have seen him.' Philip said to him, 'Lord, show us the Father and we ask no more.' Jesus answered, 'Have I been all this time with you, Philip, and you still do not know me? Anyone who has seen me has seen the Father. Then how can you say, "Show us the Father"? Do you not believe that I am in the Father, and the Father in me? I am

[a] *Or* if it were not so, should I have told you that I am going to prepare a place for you? [b] *Some witnesses read* also. You know where I am going and you know the way. [c] *Some witnesses read* If you know me you will know my Father too.

King James Version

the words that I speak unto you I speak not of
myself: but the Father that dwelleth in me, he
doeth the works. 11 Believe me that I *am* in the
Father, and the Father in me: or else believe
me for the very works' sake. 12 Verily, verily, I
say unto you, He that believeth on me, the
works that I do shall he do also; and greater
works than these shall he do; because I go unto
my Father. 13 And whatsoever ye shall ask in
my name, that will I do, that the Father may be
glorified in the Son. 14 If ye shall ask any thing
in my name, I will do *it*.
15 If ye love me, keep my commandments.
16 And I will pray the Father, and he shall give
you another Comforter, that he may abide with
you for ever; 17 *Even* the Spirit of truth; whom
the world cannot receive, because it seeth him
not, neither knoweth him: but ye know him; for
he dwelleth with you, and shall be in you. 18 I
will not leave you comfortless: I will come to
you. 19 Yet a little while, and the world seeth me
no more; but ye see me: because I live, ye shall

Living Bible

not my own but are from my Father who lives
in me. And he does his work through me. 11 Just
believe it—that I am in the Father and the
Father is in me. Or else believe it because of the
mighty miracles you have seen me do.
12, 13 "In solemn truth I tell you, anyone believing in me shall do the same miracles I have
done, and even greater ones, because I am going to be with the Father. You can ask him for
anything, using my name, and I will do it, for
this will bring praise to the Father because of
what I, the Son, will do for you. 14 Yes, ask
anything, using my name, and I will do it!
15, 16 "If you love me, obey me; and I will
ask the Father and he will give you another
Comforter, and he will never leave you. 17 He
is the Holy Spirit, the Spirit who leads into all
truth. The world at large cannot receive him, for
it isn't looking for him and doesn't recognize
him. But you do, for he lives with you now and
some day shall be in you. 18 No, I will not
abandon you or leave you as orphans in the
storm—I will come to you. 19 In just a little
while I will be gone from the world, but I will
still be present with you. For I will live again—

Today's English Version

words that I have spoken to you," Jesus said to
his disciples, "do not come from me. The Father,
who remains in me, does his own works. 11 Believe me that I am in the Father and the Father
is in me. If not, believe because of these works.
12 I tell you the truth: whoever believes in me
will do the works I do—yes, he will do even
greater ones, because I am going to the Father.
13 And I will do whatever you ask for in my
name, so that the Father's glory will be shown
through the Son. 14 If you ask me for anything
in my name, I will do it."

The promise of the Holy Spirit

15 "If you love me, you will obey my commandments. 16 I will ask the Father, and he
will give you another Helper, the Spirit of truth,
to stay with you forever. 17 The world cannot
receive him, because it cannot see him or know
him. But you know him, because he remains
with you and lives in you.
18 "I will not leave you alone; I will come
back to you. 19 In a little while the world will
see me no more, but you will see me; and be-

New International Version

to you are not just my own. Rather, it is the
Father, living in me, who is doing his work.
11 Believe me when I say that I am in the Father and the Father is in me; or at least believe
on the evidence of the miracles themselves. 12 I
tell you the truth, anyone who has faith in me
will do what I have been doing. He will do
even greater things than these, because I am
going to the Father. 13 And I will do whatever
you ask in my name, so that the Son may bring
glory to the Father. 14 You may ask me for
anything in my name, and I will do it. 15 If you
love me, you will do what I command.

Jesus promises the Holy Spirit

16 "I will ask the Father, and he will give
you another Counselor, 17 the Spirit of truth, to
be with you forever. The world cannot accept
this Counselor, because it neither sees him nor
knows him. But you know him, for he lives with
you and will be in you. 18 I will not leave you
as orphans; I will come to you. 19 Before long,
the world will not see me any more, but you will

Phillips Modern English

Father is in me? The very words I say to you are not my own. It is the Father who lives in me who carries out his work through me. You must believe me when I say that I am in the Father and the Father is in me. But if you cannot, then believe me because of what you have seen me do. I assure you that the man who believes in me will do the same things that I have done, yes, and he will do even greater things than these, for I am going away to the Father. Whatever you ask the Father in my name, I will do—that the Son may bring glory to the Father. And if you ask me anything in my name, I will grant it.

14.15 Jesus promises the Spirit

"If you really love me, you will keep the commandments I have given you and I shall ask the Father to give you Someone else to stand by you, to be with you always. I mean the Spirit of truth, whom the world cannot accept, for it can neither see nor recognise that Spirit. But you recognise him, for he is with you now and is in your hearts. I am not going to leave you alone in the world—I am coming to you. In a very little while, the world will see me no more but you will see me, because I am really

Revised Standard Version

that I say to you I do not speak on my own authority; but the Father who dwells in me does his
works. 11 Believe me that I am in the Father and
the Father in me; or else believe me for the sake
of the works themselves.
12 "Truly, truly, I say to you, he who believes
in me will also do the works that I do; and
greater works than these will he do, because I
go to the Father. 13 Whatever you ask in my
name, I will do it, that the Father may be glorified in the Son; 14 if you ask[g] anything in my
name, I will do it.
15 "If you love me, you will keep my commandments. 16 And I will pray the Father, and
he will give you another Counselor, to be with
you for ever, 17 even the Spirit of truth, whom
the world cannot receive, because it neither sees
him nor knows him; you know him, for he
dwells with you, and will be in you.
18 "I will not leave you desolate; I will come
to you. 19 Yet a little while, and the world will
see me no more, but you will see me; because

[g] Other ancient authorities add *me*.

Jerusalem Bible

The words I say to you I do not speak as from myself:
it is the Father, living in me, who is doing this work.
11 You must believe me when I say
that I am in the Father and the Father is in me;
believe it on the evidence of this work, if for no other reason.
12 I tell you most solemnly,
whoever believes in me
will perform the same works as I do myself,
he will perform even greater works,
because I am going to the Father.
13 Whatever you ask for in my name I will do,
so that the Father may be glorified in the Son.
14 If you ask for anything in my name,
I will do it.
15 If you love me you will keep my commandments.
16 I shall ask the Father,
and he will give you another Advocate[n]
to be with you for ever,
17 that Spirit of truth
whom the world can never receive
since it neither sees nor knows him;
but you know him,
because he is with you, he is in you.
18 I will not leave you orphans;
I will come back to you.
19 In a short time the world will no longer see me;
but you will see me,

[n] Greek *parakletos:* advocate or counselor or protector.

New English Bible

not myself the source of the words I speak to you: it is the Father who dwells in me doing his own work. Believe me when I say that I am in the Father and the Father in me; or else accept the evidence of the deeds themselves. In truth, in very truth I tell you, he who has faith in me will do what I am doing; and he will do greater things still because I am going to the Father. Indeed anything you ask in my name I will do, so that the Father may be glorified in the Son. If you ask[d] anything in my name I will do it.

'If you love me you will obey my commands; and I will ask the Father, and he will give you another to be your Advocate, who will be with you for ever—the Spirit of truth. The world cannot receive him, because the world neither sees nor knows him; but you know him, because he dwells with you and is[a] in you. I will not leave you bereft; I am coming back to you. In a little while the world will see me no longer, but you

[d] *Some witnesses insert* me. [a] *Some witnesses read* shall be.

King James Version

live also. 20 At that day ye shall know that I *am*
in my Father, and ye in me, and I in you. 21 He
that hath my commandments, and keepeth them,
he it is that loveth me: and he that loveth me
shall be loved of my Father, and I will love
him, and will manifest myself to him. 22 Judas
saith unto him, not Iscariot, Lord, how is it that
thou wilt manifest thyself unto us, and not unto
the world? 23 Jesus answered and said unto him,
If a man love me, he will keep my words: and
my Father will love him, and we will come unto
him, and make our abode with him. 24 He that
loveth me not keepeth not my sayings: and the
word which ye hear is not mine, but the Father's
which sent me. 25 These things have I spoken
unto you, being *yet* present with you. 26 But the
Comforter, *which is* the Holy Ghost, whom the
Father will send in my name, he shall teach you
all things, and bring all things to your remembrance, whatsoever I have said unto you.
27 Peace I leave with you, my peace I give unto
you: not as the world giveth, give I unto you.

Living Bible

and you will too. 20 When I come back to life
again, you will know that I am in my Father,
and you in me, and I in you. 21 The one who
obeys me is the one who loves me; and because
he loves me, my Father will love him; and I
will too, and I will reveal myself to him."

22 Judas (not Judas Iscariot, but his other
disciple with that name) said to him, "Sir, why
are you going to reveal yourself only to us disciples and not to the world at large?"

23 Jesus replied, "Because I will only reveal
myself to those who love me and obey me. The
Father will love them too, and we will come to
them and live with them. 24Anyone who doesn't
obey me doesn't love me. And remember, I am
not making up this answer to your question! It
is the answer given by the Father who sent me.
25 I am telling you these things now while I am
still with you. 26 But when the Father sends the
Comforter[a] instead of me[b]—and by the Comforter I mean the Holy Spirit—he will teach you
much, as well as remind you of everything I
myself have told you.

27 "I am leaving you with a gift—peace of
mind and heart! And the peace I give isn't fragile

[*a*] Or, "Helper." [*b*] Literally, "in my name."

Today's English Version

cause I live, you also will live. 20 When that day
comes, you will know that I am in my Father,
and that you are in me, just as I am in you.

21 "Whoever accepts my commandments and
obeys them, he is the one who loves me. My
Father will love him who loves me; I too will
love him and reveal myself to him."

22 Judas (not Judas Iscariot) said, "Lord,
how can it be that you will reveal yourself to us
and not to the world?"

23 Jesus answered him, "Whoever loves me
will obey my message. My Father will love him,
and my Father and I will come to him and
live with him. 24 Whoever does not love me does
not obey my words. The message you have
heard is not mine, but comes from the Father,
who sent me.

25 "I have told you this while I am still with
you. 26 The Helper, the Holy Spirit whom the
Father will send in my name, will teach you
everything, and make you remember all that I
have told you.

27 "Peace I leave with you; my own peace I
give you. I do not give it to you as the world

New International Version

see me. Because I live, you also will live. 20 On
that day you will realize that I am in my Father,
and you are in me, and I am in you. 21 Whoever has my commands and obeys them, he is
the one who loves me. He who loves me will be
loved by my Father, and I too will love him
and show myself to him."

22 Then Judas (not Judas Iscariot) said, "But,
Lord, why do you intend to show yourself to us
and not to the world?"

23 Jesus replied, "If anyone loves me, he will
obey my teaching. My Father will love him, and
we will come to him and make our home with
him. 24 He who does not love me will not obey
my teaching. These words you hear are not my
own; they belong to the Father who sent me.

25 "All this I have spoken while still with
you. 26 But the Counselor, the Holy Spirit,
whom the Father will send in my name, will
teach you all things and will remind you of
everything I have said to you. 27 Peace I leave
with you; my peace I give you. I do not give

Phillips Modern English

alive and you will be alive too. When that day comes, you will realise that I am in my Father, that you are in me, and I am in you.

"Every man who knows my commandments and obeys them is the man who really loves me, and every man who really loves me will himself be loved by my Father, and I too will love him and make myself known to him."

Then Judas (not Iscariot) said, "Lord, how is it that you are going to make yourself known to us but not to the world?"

And to this Jesus replied, "When a man loves me, he follows my teaching. Then my Father will love him, and he will come to that man and make our home within him. The man who does not really love me will not follow my teaching. Indeed, what you are hearing from me now is not really my saying, but comes from the Father who sent me.

"I have said all this while I am still with you. But the one who is coming to stand by you, the Holy Spirit whom the Father will send in my name, will be your teacher and will bring to your minds all that I have said to you.

"I leave behind with you—peace; I give you my own peace and my gift is nothing like the

Revised Standard Version

I live, you will live also. 20 In that day you will
know that I am in my Father, and you in me,
and I in you. 21 He who has my commandments
and keeps them, he it is who loves me; and he
who loves me will be loved by my Father, and
I will love him and manifest myself to him."
22 Judas (not Iscariot) said to him, "Lord, how
is it that you will manifest yourself to us, and not
to the world?" 23 Jesus answered him, "If a man
loves me, he will keep my word, and my Father
will love him, and we will come to him and make
our home with him. 24 He who does not love
me does not keep my words; and the word which
you hear is not mine but the Father's who sent
me.
25 "These things I have spoken to you, while
I am still with you. 26 But the Counselor, the
Holy Spirit, whom the Father will send in my
name, he will teach you all things, and bring to
your remembrance all that I have said to you.
27 Peace I leave with you; my peace I give to
you; not as the world gives do I give to you.

Jerusalem Bible

because I live and you will live.
20 On that day
you will understand that I am in my Father
and you in me and I in you.
21 Anybody who receives my commandments
and keeps them
will be one who loves me;
and anybody who loves me will be loved by
my Father,
and I shall love him and show myself to
him."

22 Judas[o]—this was not Judas Iscariot—said
to him, "Lord, what is all this about? Do you
intend to show yourself to us and not to the
world?" 23 Jesus replied:

"If anyone loves me he will keep my word,
and my Father will love him,
and we shall come to him
and make our home with him.
24 Those who do not love me do not keep my
words.
And my word is not my own:
it is the word of the one who sent me.
25 I have said these things to you
while still with you;
26 but the Advocate, the Holy Spirit,
whom the Father will send in my name,
will teach you everything
and remind you of all I have said to you.
27 Peace[p] I bequeath to you,
my own peace I give you,
a peace the world cannot give, this is my

[o] "Judas, brother of James" in Lk. 6:16 and Ac. 1:13; the Thaddaeus of Mt. 10:3 and Mk. 3:18.
[p] The customary Jewish farewell.

New English Bible

will see me; because I live, you too will live; then you will know that I am in my Father, and you in me and I in you. The man who has received my commands and obeys them—he it is who loves me; and he who loves me will be loved by my Father; and I will love him and disclose myself to him.'

Judas asked him—the other Judas, not Iscariot—'Lord, what can have happened, that you mean to disclose yourself to us alone and not to the world?' Jesus replied, 'Anyone who loves me will heed what I say; then my Father will love him, and we will come to him and make our dwelling with him; but he who does not love me does not heed what I say. And the word you hear is not mine: it is the word of the Father who sent me. I have told you all this while I am still here with you; but your Advocate, the Holy Spirit whom the Father will send in my name, will teach you everything, and will call to mind all that I have told you.

'Peace is my parting gift to you, my own peace, such as the world cannot give. Set your

King James Version

Let not your heart be troubled, neither let it be afraid. 28 Ye have heard how I said unto you, I go away, and come *again* unto you. If ye loved me, ye would rejoice, because I said, I go unto the Father: for my Father is greater than I. 29 And now I have told you before it come to pass, that, when it is come to pass, ye might believe. 30 Hereafter I will not talk much with you: for the prince of this world cometh, and hath nothing in me. 31 But that the world may know that I love the Father; and as the Father gave me commandment, even so I do. Arise, let us go hence.

15 I am the true vine, and my Father is the husbandman. 2 Every branch in me that beareth not fruit he taketh away: and every *branch* that beareth fruit, he purgeth it, that it may bring forth more fruit. 3 Now ye are clean through the word which I have spoken unto you. 4 Abide in me, and I in you. As the branch

Living Bible

like the peace the world gives. So don't be troubled or afraid.[c] 28 Remember what I told you—I am going away, but I will come back to you again. If you really love me, you will be very happy for me, for now I can go to the Father, who is greater than I am. 29 I have told you these things before they happen so that when they do, you will believe [in me[c]].

30 "I don't have much more time to talk to you, for the evil prince of this world approaches. He has no power over me, 31 but I will freely do what the Father requires of me so that the world will know that I love the Father. Come, let's be going.

15 "I am the true Vine, and my Father is the Gardener. 2 He lops off every branch that doesn't produce. And he prunes those branches that bear fruit for even larger crops. 3 He has already tended you by pruning you back for greater strength and usefulness by means of the commands I gave you. 4 Take care to live in me,

[c] Implied.

Today's English Version

does. Do not be worried and upset; do not be afraid. 28 You heard me say to you, 'I am leaving, but I will come back to you.' If you loved me, you would be glad that I am going to the Father, because he is greater than I. 29 I have told you this now, before it all happens, so that when it does happen you will believe. 30 I cannot talk with you much longer, because the ruler of this world is coming. He has no power over me, 31 but the world must know that I love the Father; that is why I do everything as he commands me.

"Come, let us go from this place."

Jesus the real vine

15 "I am the real vine, and my Father is the gardener. 2 He breaks off every branch in me that does not bear fruit, and prunes every branch that does bear fruit, so that it will be clean and bear more fruit. 3 You have been made clean already by the message I have spoken to you. 4 Remain united to me, and I

New International Version

to you as the world gives. Do not let your hearts be troubled and do not be afraid.

28 "You heard me say, 'I am going away and I am coming back to you.' If you loved me, you would be glad that I am going to the Father, for the Father is greater than I. 29 I have told you now before it happens, so that when it does happen you will believe. 30 I will not speak with you much longer, for the prince of this world is coming. He has no effect on me, 31 but the world must learn that I love the Father and that I do exactly what my Father has commanded me. Come now; let us leave.

The vine and the branches

15 "I am the true vine and my Father is the gardener. 2 He cuts off every branch in me that bears no fruit, while every branch that does bear fruit he trims clean so that it will be even more fruitful. 3 You are already clean because of the word I have spoken to you. 4 Remain in

Phillips Modern English

peace of this world. You must not be distressed and you must not be daunted. You have heard me say, 'I am going away and I am coming back to you.' If you really loved me, you would be glad because I am going to my Father, for the Father is greater than I. And I have told you of it now, before it happens, so that when it does happen, your faith in me will not be shaken. I shall not be able to talk much longer to you, for the spirit that rules this world is coming very close. He has no hold over me, but I go on my way to show the world that I love the Father and do what he sent me to do. . . . Get up now! Let us leave this place.

15.1 Jesus teaches union with himself

"I am the real vine, my Father is the vinedresser. He removes any of my branches which is not bearing fruit and he prunes every branch that does bear fruit to increase its yield. Now, you have already been pruned by my words. You must go on growing in me and I will

Revised Standard Version

Let not your hearts be troubled, neither let them
be afraid. 28 You heard me say to you, 'I go
away, and I will come to you.' If you loved me,
you would have rejoiced, because I go to the
Father; for the Father is greater than I. 29 And
now I have told you before it takes place, so
that when it does take place, you may believe.
30 I will no longer talk much with you, for the
ruler of this world is coming. He has no power
over me; 31 but I do as the Father has commanded me, so that the world may know that
I love the Father. Rise, let us go hence.

15 "I am the true vine, and my Father is
the vinedresser. 2 Every branch of mine
that bears no fruit, he takes away, and every
branch that does bear fruit he prunes, that it
may bear more fruit. 3 You are already made
clean by the word which I have spoken to you.
4 Abide in me, and I in you. As the branch

Jerusalem Bible

gift to you.
Do not let your hearts be troubled or afraid.
28 You heard me say:
I am going away, and shall return.
If you loved me you would have been glad
to know that I am going to the Father,
for the Father is greater than I.
29 I have told you this now before it happens,
so that when it does happen you may believe.
30 I shall not talk with you any longer,
because the prince of this world is on his way.
He has no power over me,
31 but the world must be brought to know that
I love the Father
and that I am doing exactly what the Father told me.
Come now, let us go.

The true vine

15 "I am the true vine,
and my Father is the vinedresser.
2 Every branch in me that bears no fruit
he cuts away,
and every branch that does bear fruit he prunes
to make it bear even more.
3 You are pruned already,
by means of the word that I have spoken to you.
4 Make your home in me, as I make mine in you.

New English Bible

troubled hearts at rest, and banish your fears. You heard me say, "I am going away, and coming back to you." If you loved me you would have been glad to hear that I was going to the Father; for the Father is greater than I. I have told you now, beforehand, so that when it happens you may have faith.

'I shall not talk much longer with you, for the Prince of this world approaches. He has no rights over me; but the world must be shown that I love the Father, and do exactly as he commands; so up, let us go forward! [b]

15 'I am the real vine, and my Father is the gardener. Every barren branch of mine he cuts away; and every fruiting branch he cleans, to make it more fruitful still. You have already been cleansed by the word that I spoke to you. Dwell in me, as I in you. No branch can bear

[b] *Or* for the Prince of this world is coming, though he has nothing in common with me. But he is coming so that the world may recognize that I love the Father, and do exactly as he commands. Up, and let us go forward to meet him!

King James Version

cannot bear fruit of itself, except it abide in the
vine; no more can ye, except ye abide in me.
5 I am the vine, ye *are* the branches. He that
abideth in me, and I in him, the same bringeth
forth much fruit; for without me ye can do
nothing. 6 If a man abide not in me, he is cast
forth as a branch, and is withered; and men
gather them, and cast *them* into the fire, and
they are burned. 7 If ye abide in me, and my
words abide in you, ye shall ask what ye will,
and it shall be done unto you. 8 Herein is my
Father glorified, that ye bear much fruit; so shall
ye be my disciples. 9 As the Father hath loved
me, so have I loved you: continue ye in my
love. 10 If ye keep my commandments, ye shall
abide in my love; even as I have kept my
Father's commandments, and abide in his love.
11 These things have I spoken unto you, that
my joy might remain in you, and *that* your joy
might be full. 12 This is my commandment, That
ye love one another, as I have loved you.

Living Bible

and let me live in you. For a branch can't produce fruit when severed from the vine. Nor can
you be fruitful apart from me.
5 "Yes, I am the Vine; you are the branches.
Whoever lives in me and I in him shall produce
a large crop of fruit. For apart from me you
can't do a thing. 6 If anyone separates from me,
he is thrown away like a useless branch, withers,
and is gathered into a pile with all the others
and burned. 7 But if you stay in me and obey
my commands, you may ask any request you
like, and it will be granted! 8 My true disciples
produce bountiful harvests. This brings great
glory to my Father.
9 "I have loved you even as the Father has
loved me. Live within my love. 10 When you
obey me you are living in my love, just as I
obey my Father and live in his love. 11 I have
told you this so that you will be filled with my
joy. Yes, your cup of joy will overflow! 12 I demand that you love each other as much as I

Today's English Version

will remain united to you. A branch cannot
bear fruit by itself; it can do so only if it remains in the vine. In the same way you cannot
bear fruit unless you remain in me.
5 "I am the vine, you are the branches. Whoever remains in me, and I in him, will bear
much fruit; for you can do nothing without me.
6 Whoever does not remain in me is thrown out,
like a branch, and dries up; such branches are
gathered up and thrown into the fire, where
they are burned. 7 If you remain in me, and my
words remain in you, then you will ask for anything you wish, and you shall have it. 8 This is
how my Father's glory is shown: by your bearing
much fruit; and in this way you become my disciples. 9 I love you just as the Father loves me;
remain in my love. 10 If you obey my commands,
you will remain in my love, just as I have obeyed
my Father's commands and remain in his love.
11 "I have told you this so that my joy may
be in you, and that your joy may be complete.
12 My commandment is this: love one another,

New International Version

me, and I will remain in you. No branch can
bear fruit by itself; it must remain in the vine.
Neither can you bear fruit unless you remain in
me.
5 "I am the vine; you are the branches. If a
man remains in me and I in him, he will bear
much fruit; apart from me you can do nothing.
6 If anyone does not remain in me, he is like a
branch that is thrown away and withers; such
branches are picked up, thrown into the fire and
burned. 7 If you remain in me and my words
remain in you, ask whatever you wish, and it
will be given you. 8 This is to my Father's glory,
that you bear much fruit, showing yourselves
to be my disciples.
9 "As the Father has loved me, so have I
loved you. Now remain in my love. 10 If you
obey my commands, you will remain in my love,
just as I have obeyed my Father's commands
and remain in his love. 11 I have told you this
so that my joy may be in you and that your
joy may be complete. 12 My command is this:

Phillips Modern English

grow in you. For just as the branch cannot bear any fruit unless it shares the life of the vine, so you can produce nothing unless you go on growing in me. I am the vine itself, you are the branches. It is the man who shares my life and whose life I share who proves fruitful. For apart from me you can do nothing at all. The man who does not share my life is like a branch that is broken off and withers away. He becomes just like the dry sticks that men collect and use for firewood. But if you live your life in me, and my words live in your hearts, you can ask for whatever you like and it will come true for you. This is how my Father will be glorified—in your becoming fruitful and being my disciples.

"I have loved you just as the Father has loved me. You must go on living in my love. If you keep my commandments you will live in my love just as I have kept my Father's commandments and live in his love. I have told you this so that you can share my joy, and that your joy may be complete. This is my commandment: that you

Revised Standard Version

cannot bear fruit by itself, unless it abides in
the vine, neither can you, unless you abide in
me. 5 I am the vine, you are the branches. He
who abides in me, and I in him, he it is that
bears much fruit, for apart from me you can
do nothing. 6 If a man does not abide in me, he
is cast forth as a branch and withers; and the
branches are gathered, thrown into the fire and
burned. 7 If you abide in me, and my words
abide in you, ask whatever you will, and it shall
be done for you. 8 By this my Father is glorified,
that you bear much fruit, and so prove to be
my disciples. 9 As the Father has loved me, so
have I loved you; abide in my love. 10 If you
keep my commandments, you will abide in my
love, just as I have kept my Father's commandments and abide in his love. 11 These things I
have spoken to you, that my joy may be in you,
and that your joy may be full.
12 "This is my commandment, that you love

Jerusalem Bible

As a branch cannot bear fruit all by itself,
but must remain part of the vine,
neither can you unless you remain in me.
5 I am the vine,
you are the branches.
Whoever remains in me, with me in him,
bears fruit in plenty;
for cut off from me you can do nothing.
6 Anyone who does not remain in me
is like a branch that has been thrown away
—he withers;
these branches are collected and thrown on the fire,
and they are burned.
7 If you remain in me
and my words remain in you,
you may ask what you will
and you shall get it.
8 It is to the glory of my Father that you should bear much fruit,
and then you will be my disciples.
9 As the Father has loved me,
so I have loved you.
Remain in my love.
10 If you keep my commandments
you will remain in my love,
just as I have kept my Father's commandments
and remain in his love.
11 I have told you this
so that my own joy may be in you
and your joy be complete.
12 This is my commandment:
love one another,
as I have loved you.

New English Bible

fruit by itself, but only if it remains united with the vine; no more can you bear fruit, unless you remain united with me.

'I am the vine, and you the branches. He who dwells in me, as I dwell in him, bears much fruit; for apart from me you can do nothing. He who does not dwell in me is thrown away like a withered branch. The withered branches are heaped together, thrown on the fire, and burnt. 'If you dwell in me, and my words dwell in you, ask what you will, and you shall have it. This is my Father's glory, that you may bear fruit in plenty and so be my disciples.[c] As the Father has loved me, so I have loved you. Dwell in my love. If you heed my commands, you will dwell in my love, as I have heeded my Father's commands and dwell in his love.

'I have spoken thus to you, so that my joy may be in you, and your joy complete.[a] This is my commandment: love one another, as I have

[c] *Some witnesses read* that you may bear fruit in plenty. Thus you will be my disciples. [a] *Or* so that I may have joy in you and your joy may be complete.

King James Version

13 Greater love hath no man than this, that a
man lay down his life for his friends. 14 Ye are
my friends, if ye do whatsoever I command you.
15 Henceforth I call you not servants; for the
servant knoweth not what his lord doeth: but I
have called you friends; for all things that I
have heard of my Father I have made known
unto you. 16 Ye have not chosen me, but I have
chosen you, and ordained you, that ye should
go and bring forth fruit, and *that* your fruit
should remain; that whatsoever ye shall ask of
the Father in my name, he may give it you.
17 These things I command you, that ye love one
another. 18 If the world hate you, ye know that
it hated me before *it hated* you. 19 If ye were
of the world, the world would love his own; but
because ye are not of the world, but I have
chosen you out of the world, therefore the world
hateth you. 20 Remember the word that I said
unto you, The servant is not greater than his
lord. If they have persecuted me, they will also

Living Bible

love you. 13 And here is how to measure it—the
greatest love is shown when a person lays down
his life for his friends; 14 and you are my friends
if you obey me. 15 I no longer call you slaves,
for a master doesn't confide in his slaves; now
you are my friends, proved by the fact that I
have told you everything the Father told me.
16 "You didn't choose me! I chose you! I
appointed you to go and produce lovely fruit
always, so that no matter what you ask for from
the Father, using my name, he will give it to you.
17 I demand that you love each other, 18 for you
get enough hate from the world! But then, it
hated me before it hated you. 19 The world
would love you if you belonged to it; but you
don't—for I chose you to come out of the world,
and so it hates you. 20 Do you remember what
I told you? 'A slave isn't greater than his master!' So since they persecuted me, naturally they

Today's English Version

just as I love you. 13 The greatest love a man
can have for his friends is to give his life for
them. 14 And you are my friends, if you do what
I command you. 15 I do not call you servants
any longer, because a servant does not know
what his master is doing. Instead, I call you
friends, because I have told you everything I
heard from my Father. 16 You did not choose
me; I chose you, and appointed you to go and
bear much fruit, the kind of fruit that endures.
And so the Father will give you whatever you
ask of him in my name. 17 This, then, is what I
command you: love one another."

The world's hatred

18 "If the world hates you, you must remember that it has hated me first. 19 If you belonged to the world, then the world would love
you as its own. But I chose you from this world,
and you do not belong to it; this is why the
world hates you. 20 Remember what I told you:
'No slave is greater than his master.' If they
persecuted me, they will persecute you too; if

New International Version

Love each other as I have loved you. 13 No one
has greater love than the one who lays down
his life for his friends. 14 You are my friends if
you do what I command. 15 I no longer call
you servants, because a servant does not know
his master's business. Instead, I have called you
friends, for everything that I learned from my
Father I have made known to you. 16 You did
not choose me, but I chose you to go and bear
fruit—fruit that will last. Then the Father will
give you whatever you ask in my name. 17 This
is my command: Love each other.

The world hates the disciples

18 "If the world hates you, keep in mind
that it hated me first. 19 If you belonged to the
world, it would love you as its own. As it is,
you do not belong to the world, but I have
chosen you out of the world. That is why the
world hates you. 20 Remember the words I spoke
to you: 'No servant is greater than his master.'[n]
If they persecuted me, they will persecute you

[*n*] John 13:16.

Phillips Modern English

love each other as I have loved you. There is no greater love than this—that a man should lay down his life for his friends. You are my friends if you do what I tell you to do. I shall not call you servants any longer, for a servant does not share his master's confidence. No, I call you friends, now, because I have told you everything that I have heard from the Father.

"It is not that you have chosen me; but it is I who have chosen you. I have appointed you to go and bear fruit that will be lasting; so that whatever you ask the Father in my name, he will give it to you.

15.17 Jesus speaks of the world's hatred

"This I command you, love one another! If the world hates you, you know that it hated me first. If you belonged to the world, the world would love its own. But because you do not belong to the world and I have chosen you out of it, the world will hate you. Do you remember what I said to you, 'The servant is not greater than his master'? If they have persecuted me, they will

Revised Standard Version

one another as I have loved you. 13 Greater love
has no man than this, that a man lay down his
life for his friends. 14 You are my friends if you
do what I command you. 15 No longer do I call
you servants,[h] for the servant[i] does not know
what his master is doing; but I have called you
friends, for all that I have heard from my Father
I have made known to you. 16 You did not
choose me, but I chose you and appointed you
that you should go and bear fruit and that your
fruit should abide; so that whatever you ask the
Father in my name, he may give it to you.
17 This I command you, to love one another.
18 "If the world hates you, know that it has
hated me before it hated you. 19 If you were of
the world, the world would love its own; but
because you are not of the world, but I chose
you out of the world, therefore the world hates
you. 20 Remember the word that I said to you,
'A servant[i] is not greater than his master.' If
they persecuted me, they will persecute you; if

[h] Or *slaves.* [i] Or *slave.*

Jerusalem Bible

13 A man can have no greater love
than to lay down his life for his friends.
14 You are my friends,
if you do what I command you.
15 I shall not call you servants any more,
because a servant does not know
his master's business;
I call you friends,
because I have made known to you
everything I have learned from my Father.
16 You did not choose me,
no, I chose you;
and I commissioned you
to go out and to bear fruit,
fruit that will last;
and then the Father will give you
anything you ask him in my name.
17 What I command you
is to love one another.

The hostile world

18 "If the world hates you,
remember that it hated me before you.
19 If you belonged to the world,
the world would love you as its own;
but because you do not belong to the world,
because my choice withdrew you from the world,
therefore the world hates you.
20 Remember the words I said to you:
A servant is not greater than his master.
If they persecuted me,

New English Bible

loved you. There is no greater love than this, that a man should lay down his life for his friends. You are my friends, if you do what I command you. I call you servants no longer; a servant does not know what his master is about. I have called you friends, because I have disclosed to you everything that I heard from my Father. You did not choose me: I chose you. I appointed you to go on and bear fruit, fruit that shall last; so that the Father may give you all that you ask in my name. This is my commandment to you: love one another.

'If the world hates you, it hated me first, as you know well.[b] If you belonged to the world, the world would love its own; but because you do not belong to the world, because I have chosen you out of the world, for that reason the world hates you. Remember what I said: "A servant is not greater than his master." As they persecuted me, they will persecute you; they will

[b] *Or* bear in mind that it hated me first.

King James Version

persecute you; if they have kept my saying, they will keep yours also. 21 But all these things will they do unto you for my name's sake, because they know not him that sent me. 22 If I had not come and spoken unto them, they had not had sin: but now they have no cloak for their sin. 23 He that hateth me hateth my Father also. 24 If I had not done among them the works which none other man did, they had not had sin: but now have they both seen and hated both me and my Father. 25 But *this cometh to pass,* that the word might be fulfilled that is written in their law, They hated me without a cause. 26 But when the Comforter is come, whom I will send unto you from the Father, *even* the Spirit of truth, which proceedeth from the Father, he shall testify of me: 27 And ye also shall bear witness, because ye have been with me from the beginning.

Living Bible

will persecute you. And if they had listened to me, they would listen to you! 21 The people of the world will persecute you because you belong to me, for they don't know God who sent me.

22 "They would not be guilty if I had not come and spoken to them. But now they have no excuse for their sin. 23 Anyone hating me is also hating my Father. 24 If I hadn't done such mighty miracles among them they would not be counted guilty. But as it is, they saw these miracles and yet they hated both of us—me and my Father. 25 This has fulfilled what the prophets said concerning the Messiah, 'They hated me without reason.'

26 "But I will send you the Comforter—the Holy Spirit, the source of all truth. He will come to you from the Father and will tell you all about me. 27 And you also must tell everyone about me, because you have been with me from the beginning.

Today's English Version

they obeyed my message, they will obey yours too. 21 But they will do all this to you because you are mine; for they do not know him who sent me. 22 They would not have been guilty of sin if I had not come and spoken to them; as it is, they no longer have any excuse for their sin. 23 Whoever hates me hates my Father also. 24 They would not have been guilty of sin if I had not done the works among them that no one else ever did; as it is, they have seen what I did and they hate both me and my Father. 25 This must be, however, so that what is written in their Law may come true, 'They hated me for no reason at all.'

26 "The Helper will come—the Spirit of truth, who comes from the Father. I will send him to you from the Father, and he will speak about me. 27 And you, too, will speak about me, because you have been with me from the very beginning.

New International Version

also. If they obeyed my teaching, they will obey yours also. 21 They will treat you this way because of my name, for they do not know the one who sent me. 22 If I had not come and spoken to them, they would not be guilty of sin. Now, however, they have no excuse for their sin. 23 He who hates me hates my Father as well. 24 If I had not done among them what no one else did, they would not be guilty of sin. But now they have seen these miracles, and yet they have hated both me and my Father. 25 But this is to fulfill what is written in their Law: 'They hated me without reason.' "

26 "When the Counselor comes, whom I will send to you from the Father, the Spirit of truth who goes out from the Father, he will testify about me; 27 but you also must testify, for you have been with me from the beginning.

[*o*] Psalm 35:19; 69:4.

Phillips Modern English

persecute you as well, but if they have followed my teaching, they will also follow yours. They will do all these things to you as my disciples because they do not know the One who sent me. If I had not come and spoken to them, they would not have been guilty of sin, but now they have no excuse for their sin. The man who hates me, hates my Father as well. If I had not done among them things that no other man has ever done, they would not have been guilty of sin, but as it is they have seen and they have hated both me and my Father. Yet this only fulfils what is written in their Law—

They hated me without a cause.

But when the Helper comes, that is, the Spirit of truth, who comes from the Father and whom I myself will send to you from the Father, he will speak plainly about me. And you yourselves will also speak plainly about me for you have been with me from the first.

Revised Standard Version

they kept my word, they will keep yours also.
21 But all this they will do to you on my account, because they do not know him who sent
me. 22 If I had not come and spoken to them,
they would not have sin; but now they have no
excuse for their sin. 23 He who hates me hates
my Father also. 24 If I had not done among
them the works which no one else did, they
would not have sin; but now they have seen and
hated both me and my Father. 25 It is to fulfil
the word that is written in their law, 'They hated
me without a cause.' 26 But when the Counselor
comes, whom I shall send to you from the
Father, even the Spirit of truth, who proceeds
from the Father, he will bear witness to me;
27 and you also are witnesses, because you have
been with me from the beginning.

Jerusalem Bible

they will persecute you too;
if they kept my word,
they will keep yours as well.
21 But it will be on my account that they will do all this,
because they do not know the one who sent me.
22 If I had not come,
if I had not spoken to them,
they would have been blameless;
but as it is they have no excuse for their sin.
23 Anyone who hates me hates my Father.
24 If I had not performed such works among them
as no one else has ever done,
they would be blameless;
but as it is, they have seen all this,
and still they hate both me and my Father.
25 But all this was only to fulfill the words written in their Law:
They hated me for no reason.[q]
26 When the Advocate comes,
whom I shall send to you from the Father,
the Spirit of truth who issues from the Father,
he will be my witness.
27 And you too will be witnesses,
because you have been with me from the outset.

[q] Ps. 35:19.

New English Bible

follow your teaching as little as they have followed mine. It is on my account that they will treat you thus, because they do not know the One who sent me.

'If I had not come and spoken to them, they would not be guilty of sin; but now they have no excuse for their sin: he who hates me, hates my Father. If I had not worked among them and accomplished what no other man has done, they would not be guilty of sin; but now they have both seen and hated both me and my Father.[c] However, this text in their Law had to come true:[d] "They hated me without reason."

'But when your Advocate has come, whom I will send you from the Father—the Spirit of truth that issues from the Father—he will bear witness to me. And you also are my witnesses, because you have been with me from the first.

[c] *Or* but now they have indeed seen my work and yet have hated both me and my Father. [d] *Or* let this text in their Law come true.

King James Version

16 These things have I spoken unto you, that
ye should not be offended. 2 They shall put
you out of the synagogues: yea, the time
cometh, that whosoever killeth you will think
that he doeth God service. 3 And these things
will they do unto you, because they have not
known the Father, nor me. 4 But these things
have I told you, that when the time shall come,
ye may remember that I told you of them. And
these things I said not unto you at the beginning, because I was with you. 5 But now I go
my way to him that sent me; and none of you
asketh me, Whither goest thou? 6 But because I
have said these things unto you, sorrow hath
filled your heart. 7 Nevertheless I tell you the
truth; It is expedient for you that I go away: for
if I go not away, the Comforter will not come
unto you; but if I depart, I will send him unto
you. 8 And when he is come, he will reprove the

Living Bible

16 "I have told you these things so that you
won't be staggered [by all that lies ahead.[a]]
2 For you will be excommunicated from the synagogues, and indeed the time is coming when
those who kill you will think they are doing God
a service. 3 This is because they have never
known the Father or me. 4 Yes, I'm telling you
these things now so that when they happen you
will remember I warned you. I didn't tell you
earlier because I was going to be with you for
a while longer.
5 "But now I am going away to the one who
sent me; and none of you seems interested in the
purpose of my going; none wonders why.[b]
6 Instead you are only filled with sorrow. 7 But
the fact of the matter is that it is best for you
that I go away, for if I don't, the Comforter
won't come. If I do, he will—for I will send him
to you.
8 "And when he has come he will convince

[a] Implied. [b] Literally, "none of you is asking me whither I am going." The question had been asked before (John 13:36, 14:5), but apparently not in this deeper sense.

Today's English Version

16 "I have told you this so that you will not
fall away. 2 They will put you out of their
synagogues. And the time will come when anyone who kills you will think that by doing this
he is serving God. 3 They will do these things
to you because they have not known either the
Father or me. 4 But I have told you this, so
that when the time comes for them to do these
things, you will remember that I told you."

The work of the Holy Spirit

"I did not tell you these things at the beginning, because I was with you. 5 But now I am
going to him who sent me; yet none of you asks
me, 'Where are you going?' 6 And now that I
have told you, sadness has filled your hearts.
7 But I tell you the truth: it is better for you
that I go away, because if I do not go, the
Helper will not come to you. But if I do go
away, then I will send him to you. 8 And when

New International Version

16 "All this I have told you so that you will
not go astray. 2 They will put you out of
the synagogue; in fact, a time is coming when
anyone who kills you will think he is offering a
service to God. 3 They will do such things because they have not known the Father or me.
4 I have told you this, so that when the time
comes you will remember that I warned you. I
did not tell you this at first because I was with
you.

The work of the Holy Spirit

5 "Now I am going to him who sent me, yet
none of you even asks me, 'Where are you going?' 6 Because I have said these things, you are
filled with grief. 7 But I tell you the truth: It is
for your good that I am going away. Unless I
go away, the Counselor will not come to you;
but if I go, I will send him to you. 8 When he

Phillips Modern English

16.1 Jesus speaks of the future without his bodily presence

"I have told you this now so that your faith in me may not be shaken. They will excommunicate you from their synagogues. Yes, the time is coming when a man who kills you will think he is thereby serving God! They will act like this because they have never had any true knowledge of the Father or of me, but I have told you all this so that when the time comes for such things to happen you may remember that I told you about them. I have not spoken like this to you before, because I have been with you; but now the time has come for me to go away to the One who sent me. None of you asks me, 'Where are you going?' That is because you are so distressed at what I have told you. Yet I am telling you the simple truth when I assure you that it is a good thing for you that I should go away. For if I did not go away, the divine Helper would not come to you. But if I go, then I will send him to you. When he comes, he will con-

Revised Standard Version

16 "I have said all this to you to keep you
from falling away. 2 They will put you out
of the synagogues; indeed, the hour is coming
when whoever kills you will think he is offering
service to God. 3 And they will do this because
they have not known the Father, nor me. 4 But
I have said these things to you, that when their
hour comes you may remember that I told you
of them.
"I did not say these things to you from the
beginning, because I was with you. 5 But now
I am going to him who sent me; yet none of you
asks me, 'Where are you going?' 6 But because
I have said these things to you, sorrow has filled
your hearts. 7 Nevertheless I tell you the truth:
it is to your advantage that I go away, for if I
do not go away, the Counselor will not come
to you; but if I go, I will send him to you. 8 And

Jerusalem Bible

16 "I have told you all this
so that your faith may not be shaken.
2 They will expel you from the synagogues,
and indeed the hour is coming
when anyone who kills you will think he is doing a holy duty for God.
3 They will do these things
because they have never known either the Father or myself.
4 But I have told you all this,
so that when the time for it comes
you may remember that I told you.

The coming of the Advocate

"I did not tell you this from the outset,
because I was with you;
5 but now I am going to the one who sent me.
Not one of you has asked, 'Where are you going?'
6 Yet you are sad at heart because I have told you this.
7 Still, I must tell you the truth:
it is for your own good that I am going
because unless I go,
the Advocate will not come to you;
but if I do go,
I will send him to you.
8 And when he comes,

New English Bible

16 'I have told you all this to guard you against the breakdown of your faith. They will ban you from the synagogue; indeed, the time is coming when anyone who kills you will suppose that he is performing a religious duty. They will do these things because they do not know either the Father or me. I have told you all this so that when the time comes for it to happen you may remember my warning. I did not tell you this at first, because then I was with you; but now I am going away to him who sent me. None of you asks me "Where are you going?" Yet you are plunged into grief because of what I have told you. Nevertheless I tell you the truth: it is for your good that I am leaving you. If I do not go, your Advocate will not come, whereas if I go, I will send him to you. When he comes, he will confute the world, and

King James Version

world of sin, and of righteousness, and of judgment: 9 Of sin, because they believe not on me;
10 Of righteousness, because I go to my Father,
and ye see me no more; 11 Of judgment, because
the prince of this world is judged. 12 I have yet
many things to say unto you, but ye cannot bear
them now. 13 Howbeit when he, the Spirit of
truth, is come, he will guide you into all truth:
for he shall not speak of himself; but whatsoever he shall hear *that* shall he speak: and he
will shew you things to come. 14 He shall glorify
me: for he shall receive of mine, and shall shew
it unto you. 15 All things that the Father hath are
mine: therefore said I, that he shall take of
mine, and shall shew *it* unto you. 16 A little
while, and ye shall not see me: and again, a little
while, and ye shall see me, because I go to the

Living Bible

the world of its sin, and of the availability of
God's goodness, and of deliverance from judgment.[c] 9 The world's sin is unbelief in me;
10 there is righteousness available because I go
to the Father and you shall see me no more;
11 there is deliverance from judgment because
the prince of this world has already been judged.
12 "Oh, there is so much more I want to tell
you, but you can't understand it now. 13 When
the Holy Spirit, who is truth, comes, he shall
guide you into all truth, for he will not be presenting his own ideas, but will be passing on to
you what he has heard. He will tell you about
the future. 14 He shall praise me and bring me
great honor by showing you my glory. 15 All the
Father's glory is mine; this is what I mean when
I say that he will show you my glory. 16 In just
a little while I will be gone, and you will see me
no more; but just a little while after that, and
you will see me again!"

[c] Literally, "he will convict the world of sin and righteousness and judgment."

Today's English Version

he comes he will prove to the people of the
world that they are wrong about sin, and about
what is right, and about God's judgment. 9 They
are wrong about sin, because they do not believe in me; 10 about what is right, because I
am going to the Father and you will not see
me any more; 11 about judgment, because the
ruler of this world has already been judged.
12 "I have much more to tell you, but now it
would be too much for you to bear. 13 But when
the Spirit of truth comes, he will lead you into
all the truth. He will not speak on his own, but
he will speak of what he hears and tell you of
things to come. 14 He will give me glory, because he will take what I have to say and tell
it to you. 15 All that my Father has is mine;
that is why I said that the Spirit will take what
I give him and tell it to you."

Sadness and gladness

16 "In a little while you will not see me any
more; and then a little while later you will see
me."

New International Version

comes, he will prove the world wrong about sin
and righteousness and judgment: 9 about sin,
because men do not believe in me; 10 about
righteousness, because I am going to the Father,
where you can see me no longer; 11 and about
judgment, because the prince of this world now
stands condemned.
12 "I have much more to say to you, more
than you can now bear. 13 But when he, the
Spirit of truth, comes, he will guide you into all
truth. He will not speak on his own; he will
speak only what he hears, and he will tell you
what is yet to come. 14 He will bring glory to
me by taking from what is mine and making it
known to you. 15 All that belongs to the Father
is mine. That is why I said the Spirit will take
from what is mine and make it known to you.
16 "In a little while you will see me no more,
and then after a little while you will see me."

Phillips Modern English

vince the world of the meaning of sin, of true goodness and of judgment. He will expose their sin because they do not believe in me; he will reveal true goodness for I am going away to the Father and you will see me no longer; and he will show them the meaning of judgment, for the spirit which rules this world will have been judged.

"I have much more to tell you but you cannot bear it now. Yet when that one I have spoken to you about comes—the Spirit of truth—he will guide you into everything that is true. For he will not be speaking of his own accord but exactly as he hears, and he will inform you about what is to come. He will bring glory to me for he will draw on my truth and reveal it to you. Whatever the Father possesses is also mine; that is why I tell you that he will draw on my truth and will show it to you.

16.16 The disciples are puzzled: Jesus explains

"In a little while you will not see me any longer, and again, in a little while you will see me."

Revised Standard Version

when he comes, he will convince[x] the world concerning sin and righteousness and judgment:
9 concerning sin, because they do not believe in
me; 10 concerning righteousness, because I go to
the Father, and you will see me no more; 11 concerning judgment, because the ruler of this world
is judged.
12 "I have yet many things to say to you, but
you cannot bear them now. 13 When the Spirit
of truth comes, he will guide you into all the
truth; for he will not speak on his own authority,
but whatever he hears he will speak, and he will
declare to you the things that are to come. 14 He
will glorify me, for he will take what is mine and
declare it to you. 15 All that the Father has is
mine; therefore I said that he will take what is
mine and declare it to you.
16 "A little while, and you will see me no
more; again a little while, and you will see me."

[x] Or *convict.*

Jerusalem Bible

he will show the world how wrong it was,
about sin,
and about who was in the right,
and about judgment:
9 about sin:
proved by their refusal to believe in me;
10 about who was in the right:
proved by my going to the Father
and your seeing me no more;
11 about judgment:
proved by the prince of this world being
already condemned.
12 I still have many things to say to you
but they would be too much for you now.
13 But when the Spirit of truth comes
he will lead you to the complete truth,
since he will not be speaking as from himself
but will say only what he has learned;
and he will tell you of the things to come.
14 He will glorify me,
since all he tells you
will be taken from what is mine.
15 Everything the Father has is mine;
that is why I said:
All he tells you
will be taken from what is mine.

Jesus to return very soon

16 "In a short time you will no longer see me,
and then a short time later you will see me
again."

New English Bible

show where wrong and right and judgement lie. He will convict them of wrong, by their refusal to believe in me; he will convince them that right is on my side, by showing that I go to the Father when I pass from your sight; and he will convince them of divine judgement, by showing that the Prince of this world stands condemned.

"There is still much that I could say to you, but the burden would be too great for you now. However, when he comes who is the Spirit of truth, he will guide you into all the truth; for he will not speak on his own authority, but will tell only what he hears; and he will make known to you the things that are coming. He will glorify me, for everything that he makes known to you he will draw from what is mine. All that the Father has is mine, and that is why I said, "Everything that he makes known to you he will draw from what is mine."

'A little while, and you see me no more; again

King James Version

Father. 17 Then said *some* of his disciples among
themselves, What is this that he saith unto us, A
little while, and ye shall not see me: and again,
a little while, and ye shall see me: and, Because
I go to the Father? 18 They said therefore, What
is this that he saith, A little while? we cannot
tell what he saith. 19 Now Jesus knew that they
were desirous to ask him, and said unto them,
Do ye inquire among yourselves of that I said,
A little while, and ye shall not see me: and
again, a little while, and ye shall see me?
20 Verily, verily, I say unto you, That ye shall
weep and lament, but the world shall rejoice: and
ye shall be sorrowful, but your sorrow shall be
turned into joy. 21 A woman when she is in
travail hath sorrow, because her hour is come:
but as soon as she is delivered of the child, she
remembereth no more the anguish, for joy that a
man is born into the world. 22 And ye now therefore have sorrow: but I will see you again, and
your heart shall rejoice, and your joy no man
taketh from you. 23 And in that day ye shall ask
me nothing. Verily, verily, I say unto you, Whatsoever ye shall ask the Father in my name, he
will give *it* you. 24 Hitherto have ye asked nothing in my name: ask, and ye shall receive, that
your joy may be full. 25 These things have I

Living Bible

17, 18 "Whatever is he saying?" some of his
disciples asked. "What is this about 'going to the
Father'? We don't know what he means."
19 Jesus realized they wanted to ask him so he
said, "Are you asking yourselves what I mean?
20 The world will greatly rejoice over what is
going to happen to me, and you will weep. But
your weeping shall suddenly be turned to wonderful joy [when you see me again[d]]. 21 It will
be the same joy as that of a woman in labor
when her child is born—her anguish gives place
to rapturous joy and the pain is forgotten. 22 You
have sorrow now, but I will see you again and
then you will rejoice; and no one can rob you of
that joy. 23 At that time you won't need to ask
me for anything, for you can go directly to the
Father and ask him, and he will give you what
you ask for because you use my name. 24 You
haven't tried this before, [but begin now[d]]. Ask,
using my name, and you will receive, and your
cup of joy will overflow.
25 "I have spoken of these matters very

[*d*] Implied.

Today's English Version

17 Some of his disciples said to the others,
"What does this mean? He tells us, 'In a little
while you will not see me, and then a little while
later you will see me'; and he also says, 'It is
because I am going to the Father.' 18 What does
this 'a little while' mean?" they asked. "We do
not know what he is talking about!"
19 Jesus knew that they wanted to ask him,
so he said to them, "I said, 'In a little while
you will not see me, and then a little while later
you will see me.' Is this what you are asking
about among yourselves? 20 I tell you the truth:
you will cry and weep, but the world will be
glad; you will be sad, but your sadness will turn
into gladness. 21 When a woman is about to give
birth to a child she is sad, because her hour of
suffering has come; but when the child is born
she forgets her suffering, because she is happy
that a baby has been born into the world.
22 That is the way it is with you: now you are
sad, but I will see you again, and your hearts
will be filled with gladness, the kind of gladness
that no one can take away from you.
23 "When that day comes you will not ask
me for anything. I tell you the truth: the Father will give you whatever you ask of him in
my name. 24 Until now you have not asked for
anything in my name; ask and you will receive,
so that your happiness may be complete."

Victory over the world

25 "I have told you these things by means of

New International Version

The disciples' grief will turn to joy

17 Some of his disciples said to one another,
"What does he mean by saying, 'In a little while
you will see me no more,' and 'Then after a
little while you will see me,' and 'Because I am
going to the Father'?" 18 They kept asking,
"What does he mean by 'a little while'? We don't
understand what he is saying."
19 Jesus saw that they wanted to ask him
about this, so he said to them, "Are you asking
one another what I meant when I said, 'In a little while you will see me no more,' and 'Then
after a little while you will see me'? 20 I tell
you the truth, you will weep and mourn while
the world rejoices. You will grieve, but your
grief will turn to joy. 21 A woman giving birth
to a child has pain because her time has come;
but when her baby is born she forgets the anguish because of her joy that a child is born into
the world. 22 So with you: Now is your time of
grief, but I will see you again and you will rejoice, and no one will take away your joy. 23 In
that day you will no longer ask me anything. I
tell you the truth, my Father will give you
whatever you ask in my name. 24 Until now you
have not asked for anything in my name. Ask
and you will receive, and your joy will be complete.
25 "Though I have been speaking figuratively,

Phillips Modern English

At this some of his disciples remarked to each other, "What is this that he tells us now, 'A little while and you will not see me, and again, in a little while you will see me' and 'for I am going away to the Father'? What is this 'little while' that he talks about?" they were saying. "We simply do not know what he means!"

Jesus knew that they wanted to ask him what he meant, so he said to them, "Are you trying to find out from each other what I meant when I said, 'In a little while you will not see me, and again, in a little while you will see me'? I tell you truly that you are going to be both sad and sorry while the world is glad. Yes, you will be deeply distressed, but your grief will turn into joy. When a woman gives birth to a child, she knows grievous pain when her time comes. Yet as soon as she has given birth to the child, she no longer remembers her agony for joy that a man has been born into the world. Now you are going through pain, but I shall see you again and your hearts will thrill with joy—the joy that no one can take away from you—and on that day you will not ask me any questions.

"I assure you that whatever you ask the Father he will give you in my name. Up to now you have asked nothing in my name; ask, and you will receive, that your joy may be overflowing.

16.25 Jesus speaks further of the future

"I have been speaking to you in parables—but

Revised Standard Version

17 Some of his disciples said to one another,
"What is this that he says to us, 'A little while,
and you will not see me, and again a little while,
and you will see me'; and, 'because I go to the
Father'?" 18 They said, "What does he mean
by 'a little while'? We do not know what he
means." 19 Jesus knew that they wanted to ask
him; so he said to them, "Is this what you are
asking yourselves, what I meant by saying, 'A
little while, and you will not see me, and again
a little while, and you will see me'? 20 Truly,
truly, I say to you, you will weep and lament,
but the world will rejoice; you will be sorrowful,
but your sorrow will turn into joy. 21 When a
woman is in travail she has sorrow, because her
hour has come; but when she is delivered of the
child, she no longer remembers the anguish, for
joy that a child [j] is born into the world. 22 So
you have sorrow now, but I will see you again
and your hearts will rejoice, and no one will
take your joy from you. 23 In that day you will
ask nothing of me. Truly, truly, I say to you,
if you ask anything of the Father, he will give
it to you in my name. 24 Hitherto you have
asked nothing in my name; ask, and you will
receive, that your joy may be full.
25 "I have said this to you in figures; the hour

[j] Greek *a human being.*

Jerusalem Bible

17 Then some of his disciples said to one another, "What does he mean, 'In a short time
you will no longer see me, and then a short time
later you will see me again' and, 'I am going to
the Father'? 18 What is this 'short time'? We
don't know what he means." 19 Jesus knew that
they wanted to question him, so he said, "You
are asking one another what I meant by saying:
In a short time you will no longer see me, and
then a short time later you will see me again.

20 "I tell you most solemnly,
you will be weeping and wailing
while the world will rejoice;
you will be sorrowful,
but your sorrow will turn to joy.
21 A woman in childbirth suffers,
because her time has come;
but when she has given birth to the child
she forgets the suffering
in her joy that a man has been born into
the world.
22 So it is with you: you are sad now,
but I shall see you again, and your hearts
will be full of joy,
and that joy no one shall take from you.
23 When that day comes,
you will not ask me any questions.
I tell you most solemnly,
anything you ask for from the Father
he will grant in my name.
24 Until now you have not asked for anything in my name.
Ask and you will receive,
and so your joy will be complete.
25 I have been telling you all this in metaphors,

New English Bible

a little while, and you will see me.' Some of his disciples said to one another, 'What does he mean by this: "A little while, and you will not see me, and again a little while, and you will see me", and by this: "Because I am going to my Father"?' So they asked, 'What is this "little while" that he speaks of? We do not know what he means.'

Jesus knew that they were wanting to question him, and said, 'Are you discussing what I said: "A little while, and you will not see me, and again a little while, and you will see me"? In very truth I tell you, you will weep and mourn, but the world will be glad. But though you will be plunged in grief, your grief will be turned to joy. A woman in labour is in pain because her time has come; but when the child is born she forgets the anguish in her joy that a man has been born into the world. So it is with you: for the moment you are sad at heart; but I shall see you again, and then you will be joyful, and no one shall rob you of your joy. When that day comes you will ask nothing of me. In very truth I tell you, if you ask the Father for anything in my name, he will give it you.[a] So far you have asked nothing in my name. Ask and you will receive, that your joy may be complete.

'Till now I have been using figures of speech;

[a] *Some witnesses read* if you ask the Father for anything, he will give it you in my name.

King James Version

spoken unto you in proverbs: but the time
cometh, when I shall no more speak unto you in
proverbs, but I shall shew you plainly of the
Father. 26 At that day ye shall ask in my name:
and I say not unto you, that I will pray the
Father for you: 27 For the Father himself
loveth you, because ye have loved me, and have
believed that I came out from God. 28 I came
forth from the Father, and am come into the
world: again, I leave the world, and go to the
Father. 29 His disciples said unto him, Lo, now
speakest thou plainly, and speakest no proverb.
30 Now are we sure that thou knowest all things,
and needest not that any man should ask thee:
by this we believe that thou camest forth from
God. 31 Jesus answered them, Do ye now believe? 32 Behold, the hour cometh, yea, is now
come, that ye shall be scattered, every man to
his own, and shall leave me alone: and yet I
am not alone, because the Father is with me.
33 These things I have spoken unto you, that in

Living Bible

guardedly, but the time will come when this will
not be necessary and I will tell you plainly all
about the Father. 26 Then you will present your
petitions over my signature! [e] And I won't need
to ask the Father to grant you these requests,
27 for the Father himself loves you dearly because you love me and believe that I came from
the Father. 28 Yes, I came from the Father into
the world and will leave the world and return
to the Father."

29 "At last you are speaking plainly," his disciples said, "and not in riddles. 30 Now we understand that you know everything and don't
need anyone to tell you anything.[f] From this we
believe that you came from God."

31 "Do you finally believe this?" Jesus asked.
32 "But the time is coming—in fact, it is here—
when you will be scattered, each one returning
to his own home, leaving me alone. Yet I will
not be alone, for the Father is with me. 33 I have

[e] Literally, "you shall ask *in my name*." The above paraphrase is the modern equivalent of this idea, otherwise obscure. [f] Literally, "and need not that anyone should ask you," i.e., discuss what is true.

Today's English Version

parables. But the time will come when I will use
parables no more, but I will speak to you in
plain words about the Father. 26 When that day
comes you will ask him in my name; and I do
not say that I will ask him on your behalf, 27 because the Father himself loves you. He loves
you because you love me and have believed that
I came from God. 28 I did come from the Father and I came into the world; and now I am
leaving the world and going to the Father."

29 Then his disciples said to him, "Look, you
are speaking very plainly now, without using
parables. 30 We know now that you know everything; you do not need someone to ask you
questions. This makes us believe that you came
from God."

31 Jesus answered them, "Do you believe
now? 32 The time is coming, and is already
here, when all of you will be scattered, each one
to his own home, and I will be left all alone.
But I am not really alone, because the Father
is with me. 33 I have told you this so that you

New International Version

a time is coming when I will no longer use this
kind of language but will tell you plainly about
my Father. 26 In that day you will ask in my
name. I am not saying that I will ask the Father
on your behalf. 27 No, the Father himself loves
you because you have loved me and have believed that I came from God. 28 I came from the
Father and entered the world; now I am leaving
the world and going back to the Father."

29 Then Jesus' disciples said, "Now you are
speaking clearly and without figures of speech.
30 Now we can see that you know all things and
that you do not even need to have anyone ask
you questions. This makes us believe that you
came from God."

31 "You believe at last!" [p] Jesus answered.
32 "But a time is coming, and has come, when
you will be scattered, each to his own home.
You will leave me all alone. Yet I am not alone,
for my Father is with me.

33 "I have told you these things, so that in

[p] Or *"Do you now believe?"*

Phillips Modern English

the time is coming to give up parables and tell you plainly about the Father. When that day comes, you will make your requests to him in my name, for I need make no promise to plead to the Father for you, for the Father himself loves you, because you have loved me and have believed that I came from God. Yes, I did come from the Father and I came into the world. Now I leave the world behind and return to the Father."

"Now you are speaking plainly," cried the disciples, "and are not using parables. Now we know that everything is known to you—no more questions are needed. This makes us sure that you did come from God."

"So you believe in me now?" replied Jesus. "The time is coming, indeed, it has already come, when you will be scattered, every one of you going home and leaving me alone. Yet I am not really alone, for the Father is with me. I have told you all this so that you may find

Revised Standard Version

is coming when I shall no longer speak to you
in figures but tell you plainly of the Father.
26 In that day you will ask in my name; and
I do not say to you that I shall pray the Father
for you; 27 for the Father himself loves you, because you have loved me and have believed that
I came from the Father. 28 I came from the
Father and have come into the world; again, I
am leaving the world and going to the Father."
29 His disciples said, "Ah, now you are speaking plainly, not in any figure! 30 Now we know
that you know all things, and need none to question you; by this we believe that you came from
God." 31 Jesus answered them, "Do you now
believe? 32 The hour is coming, indeed it has
come, when you will be scattered, every man
to his home, and will leave me alone; yet I am
not alone, for the Father is with me. 33 I have

Jerusalem Bible

the hour is coming
when I shall no longer speak to you in metaphors;
but tell you about the Father in plain words.
26 When that day comes
you will ask in my name;
and I do not say that I shall pray to the Father for you,
27 because the Father himself loves you
for loving me
and believing that I came from God.
28 I came from the Father and have come into the world
and now I leave the world to go to the Father."

29 His disciples said, "Now you are speaking
plainly and not using metaphors! 30 Now we see
that you know everything, and do not have to
wait for questions to be put into words; because
of this we believe that you came from God."
31 Jesus answered them:

"Do you believe at last?
32 Listen; the time will come—in fact it has come already—
when you will be scattered, each going his own way
and leaving me alone.
And yet I am not alone,
because the Father is with me.
33 I have told you all this

New English Bible

a time is coming when I shall no longer use figures, but tell you of the Father in plain words. When that day comes you will make your request in my name, and I do not say that I shall pray to the Father for you, for the Father loves you himself, because you have loved me and believed that I came from God. I came from the Father and have come into the world. Now I am leaving the world again and going to the Father.' His disciples said, 'Why, this is plain speaking; this is no figure of speech. We are certain now that you know everything, and do not need to be questioned; because of this we believe that you have come from God.'

Jesus answered, 'Do you now believe? Look,[a] the hour is coming, has indeed already come, when you are all to be scattered, each to his home, leaving me alone. Yet I am not alone, because the Father is with me. I have told you

[a] *Or* At the moment you believe; but look . . .

King James Version

me ye might have peace. In the world ye shall
have tribulation: but be of good cheer; I have
overcome the world.

17 These words spake Jesus, and lifted up his
eyes to heaven, and said, Father, the hour
is come; glorify thy Son, that thy Son also may
glorify thee: 2As thou hast given him power
over all flesh, that he should give eternal life to
as many as thou hast given him. 3And this is life
eternal, that they might know thee the only true
God, and Jesus Christ, whom thou hast sent.
4 I have glorified thee on the earth: I have
finished the work which thou gavest me to do.
5And now, O Father, glorify thou me with thine
own self with the glory which I had with thee
before the world was. 6 I have manifested thy
name unto the men which thou gavest me out of
the world: thine they were, and thou gavest them

Living Bible

told you all this so that you will have peace of
heart and mind. Here on earth you will have
many trials and sorrows; but cheer up, for I have
overcome the world."

17 When Jesus had finished saying all these
things he looked up to heaven and said,
"Father, the time has come. Reveal the glory of
your Son so that he can give the glory back to
you. 2 For you have given him authority over
every man and woman in all the earth. He gives
eternal life to each one you have given him.
3And this is the way to have eternal life—by
knowing you, the only true God, and Jesus
Christ, the one you sent to earth! 4 I brought
glory to you here on earth by doing everything
you told me to. 5And now, Father, reveal my
glory as I stand in your presence, the glory we
shared before the world began.
6 "I have told these men all about you. They
were in the world, but then you gave them to
me. Actually, they were always yours, and you
gave them to me; and they have obeyed you.

Today's English Version

will have peace by being united to me. The
world will make you suffer. But be brave! I have
defeated the world!"

Jesus prays for his disciples

17 After Jesus finished saying this, he looked
up to heaven and said, "Father, the hour
has come. Give glory to your Son, that the Son
may give glory to you. 2 For you gave him authority over all men, so that he might give eternal life to all those you gave him. 3And this is
eternal life: for men to know you, the only true
God, and to know Jesus Christ, whom you sent.
4 I showed your glory on earth; I finished the
work you gave me to do. 5 Father! Give me
glory in your presence now, the same glory I
had with you before the world was made.
6 "I have made you known to the men you
gave me out of the world. They belonged to
you, and you gave them to me. They have

New International Version

me you may have peace. In this world you will
have trouble. But take heart! I have overcome
the world."

Jesus prays for himself

17 After Jesus said this, he looked toward
heaven and prayed: "Father, the time has
come. Glorify your Son, that your Son may
glorify you. 2 For you granted him authority
over all men that he might give eternal life to
all those you have given to him. 3 Now this is
eternal life: that they may know you, the only
true God, and Jesus Christ, whom you have
sent. 4 I have brought you glory on earth by
completing the work you gave me to do. 5And
now, Father, glorify me in your presence with
the glory I had with you before the world
began.

Jesus prays for his disciples

6 "I have revealed you to those whom you
gave me out of the world. They were yours; you
gave them to me and they have obeyed your

Phillips Modern English

your peace in me. You will find trouble in the world—but, never lose heart, I have conquered the world!"

17.1 Jesus' prayer for his disciples—present and future

When Jesus had said these words, he raised his eyes to Heaven and said, "Father, the hour has come. Glorify your Son now so that he may bring glory to you, for you have given him authority over all men to give eternal life to all that you have given to him. And this is eternal life, to know you, the only true God, and him whom you have sent—Jesus Christ.

"I have brought you honour upon earth, I have completed the task which you gave me to do. Now, Father, honour me in your own presence with the glory that I knew with you before the world was made. I have shown your self to the men whom you gave me from the world. They were your men and you gave them to me,

Revised Standard Version

said this to you, that in me you may have peace. In the world you have tribulation; but be of good cheer, I have overcome the world."

17 When Jesus had spoken these words, he
lifted up his eyes to heaven and said,
"Father, the hour has come; glorify thy Son that
the Son may glorify thee, 2 since thou hast given
him power over all flesh, to give eternal life to
all whom thou hast given him. 3 And this is
eternal life, that they know thee the only true
God, and Jesus Christ whom thou hast sent. 4 I
glorified thee on earth, having accomplished the
work which thou gavest me to do; 5 and now,
Father, glorify thou me in thy own presence with
the glory which I had with thee before the world
was made.
6 "I have manifested thy name to the men
whom thou gavest me out of the world; thine
they were, and thou gavest them to me, and they

Jerusalem Bible

so that you may find peace in me.
In the world you will have trouble,
but be brave:
I have conquered the world."

The priestly prayer of Christ

17 After saying this, Jesus raised his eyes to heaven and said:

"Father, the hour has come:
glorify your Son
so that your Son may glorify you;
2 and, through the power over all mankind[r]
that you have given him,
let him give eternal life to all those you have entrusted to him.
3 And eternal life is this:
to know you,
the only true God,
and Jesus Christ whom you have sent.
4 I have glorified you on earth
and finished the work
that you gave me to do.
5 Now, Father, it is time for you to glorify me
with that glory I had with you
before ever the world was.
6 I have made your name known
to the men you took from the world to give me.
They were yours and you gave them to me,

[r] Literally, "all flesh."

New English Bible

all this so that in me you may find peace. In the world you will have trouble. But courage! The victory is mine; I have conquered the world.'

17 After these words Jesus looked up to heaven and said:

'Father, the hour has come. Glorify thy Son, that the Son may glorify thee. For thou hast made him sovereign over all mankind, to give eternal life to all whom thou hast given him. This is eternal life: to know thee who alone art truly God, and Jesus Christ whom thou hast sent.

'I have glorified thee on earth by completing the work which thou gavest me to do; and now, Father, glorify me in thy own presence with the glory which I had with thee before the world began.

'I have made thy name known to the men whom thou didst give me out of the world. They were thine, thou gavest them to me, and they

King James Version

me; and they have kept thy word. 7 Now they
have known that all things whatsoever thou hast
given me are of thee. 8 For I have given unto
them the words which thou gavest me; and they
have received *them*, and have known surely that
I came out from thee, and they have believed
that thou didst send me. 9 I pray for them: I
pray not for the world, but for them which thou
hast given me; for they are thine. 10 And all mine
are thine, and thine are mine; and I am glorified
in them. 11 And now I am no more in the world,
but these are in the world, and I come to thee.
Holy Father, keep through thine own name
those whom thou hast given me, that they may
be one, as we *are*. 12 While I was with them in
the world, I kept them in thy name: those that
thou gavest me I have kept, and none of them is
lost, but the son of perdition; that the Scripture
might be fulfilled. 13 And now come I to thee;
and these things I speak in the world, that they

Living Bible

7 Now they know that everything I have is a
gift from you, 8 for I have passed on to them
the commands you gave me; and they accepted
them and know of a certainty that I came down
to earth from you, and they believe you sent me.
9 "My plea is not for the world but for those
you have given me because they belong to you.
10 And all of them, since they are mine, belong
to you; and you have given them back to me
with everything else of yours, and so *they are
my glory!* 11 Now I am leaving the world, and
leaving them behind, and coming to you. Holy
Father, keep them in your own care—all those
you have given me—so that they will be united
just as we are, with none missing. 12 During my
time here I have kept safe within your family[a]
all of these you gave me. I guarded them so that
not one perished, except the son of hell, as the
Scriptures foretold.
13 "And now I am coming to you. I have told
them many things while I was with them so that

[*a*] Literally, "kept in your name those whom you have given me."

Today's English Version

obeyed your word, 7 and now they know that
everything you gave me comes from you. 8 I
gave them the message that you gave me, and
they received it; they know that it is true that I
came from you, and they believe that you sent
me.
9 "I pray for them. I do not pray for the
world, but for the men you gave me, because
they belong to you. 10 All I have is yours, and
all you have is mine; and my glory is shown
through them. 11 And now I am coming to you;
I am no longer in the world, but they are in the
world. Holy Father! Keep them safe by the
power of your name, the name you gave me, so
they may be one just as you and I are one.
12 While I was with them I kept them safe by
the power of your name, the name you gave
me. I protected them, and not one of them was
lost, except the man who was bound to be lost
—that the scripture might come true. 13 And
now I am coming to you, and I say these things
in the world so that they might have my joy

New International Version

word. 7 Now they know that everything you
have given me comes from you. 8 For I gave
them the words you gave me and they accepted
them. They knew with certainty that I came from
you, and they believed that you sent me. 9 I pray
for them. I am not praying for the world, but
for those you have given me, for they are yours.
10 All I have is yours, and all you have is mine.
And glory has come to me through them. 11 I
will remain in the world no longer, but they are
still in the world, and I am coming to you. Holy
Father, protect them by the power of your name
—the name you gave me—so that they may be
one as we are one. 12 While I was with them, I
protected them and kept them safe by that name
you gave me. None has been lost except the
child of hell so that Scripture would be fulfilled.
13 "I am coming to you now, but I say these
things while I am still in the world, so that they
may have the full measure of my joy within

Phillips Modern English

and they have accepted your word. Now they realise that all that you have given me comes from you—and that every message which you gave me I have given them. They have accepted it all and have come to know in their hearts that I did come from you—they are convinced that you sent me.

"I am praying to you for them: I am not praying for the world but for the men whom you gave me, for they are yours—everything that is mine is yours and yours mine—and they have done me honour. Now I am no longer in the world, but they are in the world and I am returning to you. Holy Father, keep the men you gave me by your power that they may be one, as we are one. As long as I was with them, I kept them by the power that you gave me; I guarded them, and not one of them has been lost, except the son of destruction—that the scripture might come true.

"And now I come to you and I say these things in the world that these men may find my

Revised Standard Version

have kept thy word. 7 Now they know that everything that thou hast given me is from thee; 8 for
I have given them the words which thou gavest me,
and they have received them and know in truth
that I came from thee; and they have believed
that thou didst send me. 9 I am praying for
them; I am not praying for the world but for
those whom thou hast given me, for they are
thine; 10 all mine are thine, and thine are mine,
and I am glorified in them. 11 And now I am
no more in the world, but they are in the world,
and I am coming to thee. Holy Father, keep
them in thy name, which thou hast given me,
that they may be one, even as we are one.
12 While I was with them, I kept them in thy
name, which thou hast given me; I have guarded
them, and none of them is lost but the son of
perdition, that the scripture might be fulfilled.
13 But now I am coming to thee; and these
things I speak in the world, that they may have

Jerusalem Bible

and they have kept your word.
7 Now at last they know
that all you have given me comes indeed from you;
8 for I have given them
the teaching you gave to me,
and they have truly accepted this, that I came from you,
and have believed that it was you who sent me.
9 I pray for them;
I am not praying for the world
but for those you have given me,
because they belong to you:
10 all I have is yours
and all you have is mine,
and in them I am glorified.
11 I am not in the world any longer,
but they are in the world,
and I am coming to you.
Holy Father,
keep those you have given me true to your name,
so that they may be one like us.
12 While I was with them,
I kept those you had given me true to your name.
I have watched over them and not one is lost
except the one who chose to be lost,[s]
and this was to fulfill the scriptures.
13 But now I am coming to you
and while still in the world I say these things
to share my joy with them to the full.

[s] Literally, "the son of perdition."

New English Bible

have obeyed thy command. Now they know that all thy gifts have come to me from thee; for I have taught them all that I learned from thee, and they have received it: they know with certainty that I came from thee; they have had faith to believe that thou didst send me.

'I pray for them; I am not praying for the world but for those whom thou hast given me, because they belong to thee. All that is mine is thine, and what is thine is mine; and through them has my glory shone.

'I am to stay no longer in the world, but they are still in the world, and I am on my way to thee. Holy Father, protect by the power of thy name those whom thou hast given me,[b] that they may be one, as we are one. When I was with them, I protected by the power of thy name those whom thou hast given me,[c] and kept them safe. Not one of them is lost except the man who must be lost, for Scripture has to be fulfilled.

'And now I am coming to thee; but while I am still in the world I speak these words, so that they may have my joy within them in full

[b] *Or* keep in loyalty to thee those whom thou hast given me; *some witnesses read* protect them by the power of thy name which thou hast given me. [c] *Or* kept in loyalty to thee those whom thou hast given me; *some witnesses read* protected them by the power of thy name which thou hast given me.

King James Version

might have my joy fulfilled in themselves. 14 I
have given them thy word; and the world hath
hated them, because they are not of the world,
even as I am not of the world. 15 I pray not that
thou shouldest take them out of the world, but
that thou shouldest keep them from the evil.
16 They are not of the world, even as I am not
of the world. 17 Sanctify them through thy truth:
thy word is truth. 18 As thou hast sent me into
the world, even so have I also sent them into
the world. 19 And for their sakes I sanctify myself, that they also might be sanctified through
the truth. 20 Neither pray I for these alone, but
for them also which shall believe on me through
their word; 21 That they all may be one; as thou,
Father, *art* in me, and I in thee, that they also
may be one in us: that the world may believe
that thou hast sent me. 22 And the glory which
thou gavest me I have given them; that they may
be one, even as we are one: 23 I in them, and
thou in me, that they may be made perfect in
one; and that the world may know that thou
hast sent me, and hast loved them, as thou hast
loved me. 24 Father, I will that they also, whom
thou hast given me, be with me where I am; that
they may behold my glory, which thou hast given

Living Bible

they would be filled with my joy. 14 I have given
them your commands. And the world hates them
because they don't fit in with it, just as I don't.
15 I'm not asking you to take them out of the
world, but to keep them safe from Satan's power.
16 They are not part of this world any more than
I am. 17 Make them pure and holy through
teaching them your words of truth. 18 As you sent
me into the world, I am sending them into the
world, 19 and I consecrate myself to meet their
need for growth in truth and holiness.

20 "I am not praying for these alone but also
for the future believers who will come to me because of the testimony of these. 21 My prayer
for all of them is that they will be of one heart
and mind, just as you and I are, Father—that
just as you are in me and I am in you, so they
will be in us, and the world will believe you sent
me.

22 "I have given them the glory you gave me
—the glorious unity of being one, as we are—
23 I in them and you in me, all being perfected
into one—so that the world will know you sent
me and will understand that you love them as
much as you love me. 24 Father, I want them
with me—these you've given me—so that they
can see my glory. You gave me the glory because

Today's English Version

in their hearts, in all its fulness. 14 I gave them
your message and the world hated them, because they do not belong to the world, just as
I do not belong to the world. 15 I do not ask
you to take them out of the world, but I do
ask you to keep them safe from the Evil One.
16 Just as I do not belong to the world, they
do not belong to the world. 17 Dedicate them to
yourself, by means of the truth; your word is
truth. 18 I sent them into the world just as you
sent me into the world. 19 And for their sake I
dedicate myself to you, in order that they, too,
may be truly dedicated to you.

20 "I do not pray only for them, but also for
those who believe in me because of their message. 21 I pray that they may all be one. Father!
May they be in us, just as you are in me and I
am in you. May they be one, so that the world
will believe that you sent me. 22 I gave them the
same glory you gave me, so that they may be
one, just as you and I are one: 23 I in them
and you in me, so that they may be completely
one, in order that the world may know that you
sent me and that you love them as you love me.

24 "Father! You have given them to me, and
I want them to be with me where I am, so that
they may see my glory, the glory you gave me;

New International Version

them. 14 I have given them your word and the
world has hated them, for they are not of the
world any more than I am of the world. 15 My
prayer is not that you take them out of the
world but that you protect them from the evil
one. 16 They are not of the world, even as I
am not of it. 17 Sanctify[q] them by the truth;
your word is truth. 18 As you sent me into the
world, I have sent them into the world. 19 For
them I sanctify[q] myself, that they too may be
truly sanctified.[q]

Jesus prays for all believers

20 "My prayer is not for them alone. I pray
also for those who will believe in me through
their message, 21 that all of them may be one,
Father, just as you are in me and I am in you.
May they also be in us so that the world may
believe that you have sent me. 22 I have given
them the glory that you gave me, that they may
be one as we are one: 23 I in them and you in
me. May they be brought to complete unity to
let the world know that you sent me and have
loved them even as you have loved me.

24 "Father, I want those you have given me
to be with me where I am, and to see my glory,

[q] Greek *hagiazo* (*set apart for sacred use* or *make holy*).

Phillips Modern English

joy completed in themselves. I have given them your word, and the world has hated them, for they are no more sons of the world than I am. I am not praying that you will take them out of the world but that you will keep them from the evil one. They are no more the sons of the world than I am—make them holy by the truth; for your word is the truth. I have sent them to the world just as you sent me to the world and I consecrated myself for their sakes that they may be made holy by the truth.

"I am not praying only for these men but for all those who will believe in me through their message, that they may all be one. Just as you, Father, live in me and I live in you, I am asking that they may live in us, and that the world may believe that you did send me. I have given them the honour that you gave me, that they may be one, as we are one—I in them and you in me, that they may grow complete into one, so that the world may realise that you sent me and have loved them as you loved me. Father, I want those whom you have given me to be with me where I am; I want them to see that glory which you

Revised Standard Version

my joy fulfilled in themselves. 14 I have given
them thy word; and the world has hated them
because they are not of the world, even as I
am not of the world. 15 I do not pray that thou
shouldst take them out of the world, but that
thou shouldst keep them from the evil one.[k]
16 They are not of the world, even as I am not
of the world. 17 Sanctify them in the truth; thy
word is truth. 18 As thou didst send me into the
world, so I have sent them into the world.
19 And for their sake I consecrate myself, that
they also may be consecrated in truth.
20 "I do not pray for these only, but also for
those who believe in me through their word,
21 that they may all be one; even as thou, Father,
art in me, and I in thee, that they also may be in
us, so that the world may believe that thou hast
sent me. 22 The glory which thou hast given me I
have given to them, that they may be one even
as we are one, 23 I in them and thou in me, that
they may become perfectly one, so that the world
may know that thou hast sent me and hast
loved them even as thou hast loved me. 24 Father, I desire that they also, whom thou hast
given me, may be with me where I am, to behold my glory which thou hast given me in thy

[k] Or *from evil.*

Jerusalem Bible

14 I passed your word on to them,
and the world hated them,
because they belong to the world
no more than I belong to the world.
15 I am not asking you to remove them from
the world,
but to protect them from the evil one.
16 They do not belong to the world
any more than I belong to the world.
17 Consecrate them in the truth;
your word is truth.
18 As you sent me into the world,
I have sent them into the world,
19 and for their sake I consecrate myself
so that they too may be consecrated in
truth.
20 I pray not only for these,
but for those also
who through their words will believe in me.
21 May they all be one.
Father, may they be one in us,
as you are in me and I am in you,
so that the world may believe it was you
who sent me.
22 I have given them the glory you gave to me,
that they may be one as we are one.
23 With me in them and you in me,
may they be so completely one
that the world will realize that it was you
who sent me
and that I have loved them as much as you
loved me.
24 Father,
I want those you have given me
to be with me where I am,
so that they may always see the glory

New English Bible

measure. I have delivered thy word to them, and the world hates them because they are strangers in the world, as I am. I pray thee, not to take them out of the world, but to keep them from the evil one. They are strangers in the world, as I am. Consecrate them by the truth;[d] thy word is truth. As thou hast sent me into the world, I have sent them into the world, and for their sake I now consecrate myself, that they too may be consecrated by the truth.[a]

'But it is not for these alone that I pray, but for those also who through their words put their faith in me; may they all be one: as thou, Father, art in me, and I in thee, so also may they be in us, that the world may believe that thou didst send me. The glory which thou gavest me I have given to them, that they may be one, as we are one; I in them and thou in me, may they be perfectly one. Then the world will learn that thou didst send me, that thou didst love them as thou didst me.

'Father, I desire that these men, who are thy gift to me, may be with me where I am, so that they may look upon my glory, which thou hast

[d] *Or* in truth. [a] *Or* in truth.

King James Version

me: for thou lovedst me before the foundation of the world. 25 O righteous Father, the world hath not known thee: but I have known thee, and these have known that thou hast sent me. 26 And I have declared unto them thy name, and will declare *it;* that the love wherewith thou hast loved me may be in them, and I in them.

18 When Jesus had spoken these words, he went forth with his disciples over the brook Cedron, where was a garden, into the which he entered, and his disciples. 2 And Judas also, which betrayed him, knew the place: for Jesus ofttimes resorted thither with his disciples. 3 Judas then, having received a band *of men* and officers from the chief priests and Pharisees, cometh thither with lanterns and torches and weapons. 4 Jesus therefore, knowing all things that should come upon him, went forth, and

Living Bible

you loved me before the world began!

25 "O righteous Father, the world doesn't know you, but I do; and these disciples know you sent me. 26 And I have revealed you to them, and will keep on revealing you so that the mighty love you have for me may be in them, and I in them."

18 After saying these things Jesus crossed the Kidron ravine with his disciples and entered a grove of olive trees. 2 Judas, the betrayer, knew this place, for Jesus had gone there many times with his disciples.

3 The chief priests and Pharisees had given Judas a squad of soldiers and police to accompany him. Now with blazing torches, lanterns, and weapons they arrived at the olive grove.

4, 5 Jesus fully realized all that was going to happen to him. Stepping forward to meet them he asked, "Whom are looking for?"

Today's English Version

because you loved me before the world was made. 25 Righteous Father! The world does not know you, but I know you, and these know that you sent me. 26 I made you known to them and I will continue to do so, in order that the love you have for me may be in them, and I also may be in them."

The arrest of Jesus

18 After Jesus had said this prayer he left with his disciples and went across the brook Kidron. There was a garden in that place, and Jesus and his disciples went in. 2 Judas, the traitor, knew where it was, because many times Jesus had met there with his disciples. 3 So Judas went to the garden, taking with him a group of soldiers and some temple guards sent by the chief priests and the Pharisees; they were armed, and carried lanterns and torches. 4 Jesus knew everything that was going to happen to him; so he stepped forward and said to them, "Who is it you are looking for?"

New International Version

the glory you have given me because you loved me before the creation of the world.

25 "Righteous Father, though the world does not know you, I know you, and they know that you have sent me. 26 I have revealed you[r] to them, and will continue to make you known in order that the love you have for me may be theirs and that I myself may be in them."

Jesus arrested

18 When he had finished praying, Jesus left with his disciples and crossed the Kidron Valley. On the other side there was an olive grove, and he and his disciples went into it.

2 Now Judas, who betrayed him, knew the place, because Jesus had often met there with his disciples. 3 So Judas came to the grove, guiding a detachment of soldiers and some officials from the chief priests and Pharisees. They were carrying torches, lanterns and weapons.

4 Jesus, knowing all that was going to happen to him, went out and asked them, "Who is it you want?"

[r] Or *have made your name known.*

Phillips Modern English

have made mine—for you loved me before the world began. Father of all goodness the world has not known you, but I have known you and these men now know that you have sent me. I have made your self known to them and I will continue to do so that the love which you have had for me may be in their hearts—and that I may be there also."

18.1 Jesus is arrested in the garden

When Jesus had spoken these words, he went out with his disciples across the Cedron valley to a place where there was a garden, and they went into it together. Judas who betrayed him knew the place, for Jesus often met his disciples there. So Judas fetched the guard and the officers which the chief priests and Pharisees had provided for him, and came to the place with torches and lanterns and weapons. Jesus, fully realising all that was going to happen to him, went forward and said to them, "Who are you looking for?"

Revised Standard Version

love for me before the foundation of the world.
25 O righteous Father, the world has not known
thee, but I have known thee; and these know
that thou hast sent me. 26 I made known to
them thy name, and I will make it known, that
the love with which thou hast loved me may be
in them, and I in them."

18 When Jesus had spoken these words, he
went forth with his disciples across the
Kidron valley, where there was a garden, which
he and his disciples entered. 2 Now Judas, who
betrayed him, also knew the place; for Jesus
often met there with his disciples. 3 So Judas,
procuring a band of soldiers and some officers
from the chief priests and the Pharisees, went
there with lanterns and torches and weapons.
4 Then Jesus, knowing all that was to befall him,
came forward and said to them, "Whom do you

Jerusalem Bible

you have given me
because you loved me
before the foundation of the world.
25 Father, Righteous One,
the world has not known you,
but I have known you,
and these have known
that you have sent me.
26 I have made your name known to them
and will continue to make it known,
so that the love with which you loved me
may be in them,
and so that I may be in them."

C. The Passion

The arrest of Jesus

18 After he had said all this Jesus left with
his disciples and crossed the Kedron valley. There was a garden there, and he went into
it with his disciples. 2 Judas the traitor knew the
place well, since Jesus had often met his disciples there, 3 and he brought the cohort[t] to this
place together with a detachment of guards sent
by the chief priests and the Pharisees, all with
lanterns and torches and weapons. 4 Knowing
everything that was going to happen to him, Jesus then came forward and said, "Who are you

[t] A detachment from the Roman garrison in Jerusalem.

New English Bible

given me because thou didst love me before the world began. O righteous Father, although the world does not know thee, I know thee, and these men know that thou didst send me. I made thy name known to them, and will make it known, so that the love thou hadst for me may be in them, and I may be in them.'

The final conflict

18 After these words, Jesus went out with his disciples, and crossed the Kedron ravine. There was a garden there, and he and his disciples went into it. The place was known to Judas, his betrayer, because Jesus had often met there with his disciples. So Judas took a detachment of soldiers, and police provided by the chief priests and the Pharisees, equipped with lanterns, torches, and weapons, and made his way to the garden. Jesus, knowing all that was coming upon him, went out to them and asked,

King James Version

said unto them, Whom seek ye? 5 They answered him, Jesus of Nazareth. Jesus saith unto them, I am *he*. And Judas also, which betrayed him, stood with them. 6 As soon then as he had said unto them, I am *he*, they went backward, and fell to the ground. 7 Then asked he them again, Whom seek ye? And they said, Jesus of Nazareth. 8 Jesus answered, I have told you that I am *he:* if therefore ye seek me, let these go their way: 9 That the saying might be fulfilled, which he spake, Of them which thou gavest me have I lost none. 10 Then Simon Peter having a sword drew it, and smote the high priest's servant, and cut off his right ear. The servant's name was Malchus. 11 Then said Jesus unto Peter, Put up thy sword into the sheath: the cup which my Father hath given me, shall I not drink it? 12 Then the band and the captain and officers of the Jews took Jesus, and bound him, 13 And led him away to Annas first; for he was father in law to Caiaphas, which was the high priest that same year. 14 Now Caiaphas was he, which gave counsel to the Jews, that it was expedient that one man should die for the people.

Living Bible

"Jesus of Nazareth," they replied.

"I am he," Jesus said. 6 And as he said it, they all fell backwards to the ground!

7 Once more he asked them, "Whom are you searching for?"

And again they replied, "Jesus of Nazareth."

8 "I told you I am he," Jesus said; "and since I am the one you are after, let these others go." 9 He did this to carry out the prophecy he had just made, "I have not lost a single one of those you gave me . . . ."

10 Then Simon Peter drew a sword and slashed off the right ear of Malchus, the High Priest's servant.

11 But Jesus said to Peter, "Put your sword away. Shall I not drink from the cup the Father has given me?"

12 So the Jewish police, with the soldiers and their lieutenant, arrested Jesus and tied him. 13 First they took him to Annas, the father-in-law of Caiaphas, the High Priest that year. 14 Caiaphas was the one who told the other Jewish leaders, "Better that one should die for

Today's English Version

5 "Jesus of Nazareth," they answered.

"I am he," he said.

Judas, the traitor, was standing there with them. 6 When Jesus said to them, "I am he," they moved back and fell to the ground. 7 Jesus asked them again, "Who is it you are looking for?"

"Jesus of Nazareth," they said.

8 "I have already told you that I am he," Jesus said. "If, then, you are looking for me, let these others go." 9 (He said this so that what he had said might come true, "Father, I have not lost even one of those you gave me.")

10 Simon Peter had a sword; he drew it and struck the High Priest's slave, cutting off his right ear. The name of the slave was Malchus. 11 Jesus said to Peter, "Put your sword back in its place! Do you think that I will not drink the cup of suffering my Father has given me?"

Jesus before Annas

12 The group of soldiers with their commanding officer and the Jewish guards arrested Jesus, tied him up, 13 and took him first to Annas. He was the father-in-law of Caiaphas, who was High Priest that year. 14 It was Caiaphas who had advised the Jews that it was better that one man die for all the people.

New International Version

5 "Jesus of Nazareth," they replied.

"I am he," Jesus said. (And Judas the traitor was standing there with them.) 6 When Jesus said, "I am he," they drew back and fell to the ground.

7 Again he asked them, "Who is it you want?" And they said, "Jesus of Nazareth."

8 "I told you that I am he," Jesus answered. "If you are looking for me, then let these men go." 9 This happened so that the words he had spoken would be fulfilled: "I have not lost one of those you gave me." [s]

10 Then Simon Peter, who had a sword, drew it and struck the high priest's servant, cutting off his right ear. (The servant's name was Malchus.)

11 Jesus commanded Peter, "Put your sword away! Shall I not drink the cup the Father has given me?"

Jesus taken to Annas

12 Then the detachment of soldiers with its commander and the Jewish officials arrested Jesus. They bound him 13 and brought him first to Annas, who was the father-in-law of Caiaphas, the high priest that year. 14 Caiaphas was the one who had advised the Jews that it would be good if one man died for the people.

[s] John 6:39.

Phillips Modern English

"Jesus of Nazareth," they answered.

"I am the man," said Jesus. (Judas who was betraying him was standing there with the others.)

When he said to them, "I am the man", they retreated and fell to the ground. So Jesus asked them again, "Who are you looking for?"

And again they said, "Jesus of Nazareth."

"I have told you that I am the man," replied Jesus. "If I am the man you are looking for, let these others go." (Thus fulfilling his previous words, "I have not lost one of those whom you gave me.")

At this, Simon Peter, who had a sword, drew it and slashed at the High Priest's servant, cutting off his right ear. (The servant's name was Malchus.) But Jesus said to Peter, "Put your sword back into its sheath. Am I not to drink the cup the Father has given me?"

18.12 Peter follows Jesus, only to deny him

Then the guard, with their captain and the Jewish Officers, took hold of Jesus and tied his hands together, and led him off first to Annas, for he was father-in-law to Caiaphas, who was High Priest that year. Caiaphas was the man who advised the Jews, "that it would be a good thing that one man should die for the sake of

Revised Standard Version

seek?" 5 They answered him, "Jesus of Nazareth." Jesus said to them, "I am he." Judas, who
betrayed him, was standing with them. 6 When
he said to them, "I am he," they drew back and
fell to the ground. 7 Again he asked them,
"Whom do you seek?" And they said, "Jesus
of Nazareth." 8 Jesus answered, "I told you that
I am he; so, if you seek me, let these men go."
9 This was to fulfil the word which he had
spoken, "Of those whom thou gavest me I lost
not one." 10 Then Simon Peter, having a sword,
drew it and struck the high priest's slave and cut
off his right ear. The slave's name was Malchus.
11 Jesus said to Peter, "Put your sword into its
sheath; shall I not drink the cup which the
Father has given me?"

12 So the band of soldiers and their captain
and the officers of the Jews seized Jesus and
bound him. 13 First they led him to Annas; for
he was the father-in-law of Caiaphas, who was
high priest that year. 14 It was Caiaphas who had
given counsel to the Jews that it was expedient
that one man should die for the people.

Jerusalem Bible

looking for?" 5 They answered, "Jesus the Nazarene." He said, "I am he." Now Judas the
traitor was standing among them. 6 When Jesus
said, "I am he," they moved back and fell to the
ground. 7 He asked them a second time, "Who
are you looking for?" They said, "Jesus the Nazarene." 8 "I have told you that I am he," replied Jesus. "If I am the one you are looking
for, let these others go." 9 This was to fulfill the
words he had spoken, "Not one of those you
gave me have I lost."

10 Simon Peter, who carried a sword, drew it
and wounded the high priest's servant, cutting
off his right ear. The servant's name was Malchus. 11 Jesus said to Peter, "Put your sword
back in its scabbard; am I not to drink the cup
that the Father has given me?"

Jesus before Annas and Caiaphas. Peter disowns him

12 The cohort and its captain and the Jewish
guards seized Jesus and bound him. 13 They took
him first to Annas, because Annas was the father-
in-law of Caiaphas, who was high priest that
year. 14 It was Caiaphas who had suggested to
the Jews, "It is better for one man to die for
the people."

New English Bible

'Who is it you want?' 'Jesus of Nazareth', they answered. Jesus said, 'I am he.' And there stood Judas the traitor with them. When he said, 'I am he', they drew back and fell to the ground. Again Jesus asked, 'Who is it you want?' 'Jesus of Nazareth', they answered. Then Jesus said, 'I have told you that I am he. If I am the man you want, let these others go.' (This was to make good his words, 'I have not lost one of those whom thou gavest me.') Thereupon Simon Peter drew the sword he was wearing and struck at the High Priest's servant, cutting off his right ear. (The servant's name was Malchus.) Jesus said to Peter, 'Sheathe your sword. This is the cup the Father has given me; shall I not drink it?'

The troops with their commander, and the Jewish police, now arrested Jesus and secured him. They took him first to Annas.[b] Annas was father-in-law of Caiaphas, the High Priest for that year[b]—the same Caiaphas who had advised the Jews that it would be to their interest if one

[b] *See note on verse 24.*

King James Version

15 And Simon Peter followed Jesus, and *so*
did another disciple: that disciple was known
unto the high priest, and went in with Jesus into
the palace of the high priest. 16 But Peter stood
at the door without. Then went out that other
disciple, which was known unto the high priest,
and spake unto her that kept the door, and
brought in Peter. 17 Then saith the damsel that
kept the door unto Peter, Art not thou also *one*
of this man's disciples? He saith, I am not.
18 And the servants and officers stood there, who
had made a fire of coals, for it was cold; and
they warmed themselves: and Peter stood with
them, and warmed himself.

19 The high priest then asked Jesus of his disciples, and of his doctrine. 20 Jesus answered
him, I spake openly to the world; I ever taught
in the synagogue, and in the temple, whither
the Jews always resort; and in secret have I said
nothing. 21 Why askest thou me? ask them which
heard me, what I have said unto them: behold,
they know what I said. 22 And when he had thus
spoken, one of the officers which stood by struck
Jesus with the palm of his hand, saying, Answerest thou the high priest so? 23 Jesus answered
him, If I have spoken evil, bear witness of the

Living Bible

all." 15 Simon Peter followed along behind, as
did another of the disciples who was acquainted
with the High Priest. So that other disciple was
permitted into the courtyard along with Jesus,
16 while Peter stood outside the gate. Then the
other disciple spoke to the girl watching at the
gate, and she let Peter in. 17 The girl asked Peter,
"Aren't you one of Jesus' disciples?"

"No," he said, "I am not!"

18 The police and the household servants were
standing around a fire they had made, for it was
cold. And Peter stood there with them, warming himself.

19 Inside, the High Priest began asking Jesus
about his followers and what he had been teaching them.

20 Jesus replied, "What I teach is widely
known, for I have preached regularly in the
synagogue and Temple; I have been heard by
all the Jewish leaders and teach nothing in
private that I have not said in public. 21 Why are
you asking me this question? Ask those who
heard me. You have some of them here. They
know what I said."

22 One of the soldiers standing there struck
Jesus with his fist. "Is that the way to answer
the High Priest?" he demanded.

23 "If I lied, prove it," Jesus replied. "Should

Today's English Version

Peter denies Jesus

15 Simon Peter and another disciple followed
Jesus. That other disciple was well known to
the High Priest, so he went with Jesus into the
courtyard of the High Priest's house. 16 Peter
stayed outside by the gate. The other disciple,
who was well known to the High Priest, went
back out, spoke to the girl at the gate and
brought Peter inside. 17 The girl at the gate said
to Peter, "Aren't you one of the disciples of
that man?"

"No, I am not," answered Peter.

18 It was cold, so the servants and guards
had built a charcoal fire and were standing
around it, warming themselves. Peter went over
and stood with them, warming himself.

The High Priest questions Jesus

19 The High Priest questioned Jesus about his
disciples and about his teaching. 20 Jesus answered, "I have always spoken publicly to everyone; all my teaching was done in the synagogues
and in the temple, where all the Jews come together. I have never said anything in secret.
21 Why, then, do you question me? Question the
people who heard me. Ask them what I told
them—they know what I said."

22 When Jesus said this, one of the guards
there slapped him and said, "How dare you talk
like this to the High Priest!"

23 Jesus answered him, "If I have said something wrong, tell everyone here what it was. But

New International Version

Peter's first denial

15 Simon Peter and another disciple were following Jesus. Because this disciple was known
to the high priest, he went with Jesus into the
high priest's courtyard, 16 but Peter had to wait
outside at the door. The other disciple, who was
known to the high priest, came back, spoke to
the girl on duty there, and brought Peter in.

17 "Surely you are not another of this man's
disciples?" the girl at the door asked Peter.

He replied, "I am not."

18 It was cold, and the servants and officials
stood around a fire they had made to keep warm.
Peter also was standing with them, warming
himself.

The high priest questions Jesus

19 Meanwhile, the high priest questioned Jesus about his disciples and his teaching.

20 "I have spoken openly to the world," Jesus
replied. "I always taught in synagogues or at the
temple, where all the Jews come together. I said
nothing in secret. 21 Why question me? Ask
those who heard me. Surely they know what I
said."

22 When Jesus had said this, one of the officials nearby struck him in the face. "Is that any
way to answer the high priest?" he demanded.

23 "If I said something wrong," Jesus replied,

Phillips Modern English

the people". Behind Jesus followed Simon Peter, and one other disciple who was known personally to the High Priest. He went in with Jesus into the High Priest's courtyard, but Peter was left standing at the door outside. So this other disciple, who was acquainted with the High Priest, went out and spoke to the doorkeeper, and brought Peter inside. The young woman at the door remarked to Peter, "Are you one of this man's disciples, too?"

"No, I am not," retorted Peter.

In the courtyard, the servants and officers stood around a charcoal fire which they had made, for it was cold. They were warming themselves, and Peter stood there with them, keeping himself warm.

Meanwhile the High Priest interrogated Jesus about his disciples and about his own teaching. "I have always spoken quite openly to the world," replied Jesus. "I have always taught in the synagogue or in the Temple-precincts where all Jews meet together, and I have said nothing in secret. Why do you question me? Why not question those who have heard me about what I said to them? Obviously they are the ones who know what I actually said."

As he said this, one of those present, an officer, slapped Jesus with his open hand, remarking, "Is that the way for you to answer the High Priest?"

"If I have said anything wrong," Jesus said to him, "you must give evidence about it, but if

Revised Standard Version

15 Simon Peter followed Jesus, and so did
another disciple. As this disciple was known to
the high priest, he entered the court of the high
priest along with Jesus, 16 while Peter stood
outside at the door. So the other disciple, who
was known to the high priest, went out and
spoke to the maid who kept the door, and
brought Peter in. 17 The maid who kept the door
said to Peter, "Are not you also one of this
man's disciples?" He said, "I am not." 18 Now
the servants[l] and officers had made a charcoal
fire, because it was cold, and they were standing and warming themselves; Peter also was with
them, standing and warming himself.
19 The high priest then questioned Jesus
about his disciples and his teaching. 20 Jesus
answered him, "I have spoken openly to the
world; I have always taught in synagogues and
in the temple, where all Jews come together; I
have said nothing secretly. 21 Why do you ask me?
Ask those who have heard me, what I said to
them; they know what I said." 22 When he had
said this, one of the officers standing by struck
Jesus with his hand, saying, "Is that how you
answer the high priest?" 23 Jesus answered him,
"If I have spoken wrongly, bear witness to the

[l] Or *slaves.*

Jerusalem Bible

15 Simon Peter, with another disciple, followed Jesus. This disciple, who was known to
the high priest, went with Jesus into the high
priest's palace, 16 but Peter stayed outside the
door. So the other disciple, the one known to
the high priest, went out, spoke to the woman
who was keeping the door and brought Peter in.
17 The maid on duty at the door said to Peter,
"Aren't you another of that man's disciples?" He
answered, "I am not." 18 Now it was cold, and
the servants and guards had lit a charcoal fire
and were standing there warming themselves; so
Peter stood there too, warming himself with the
others.
19 The high priest questioned Jesus about his
disciples and his teaching. 20 Jesus answered, "I
have spoken openly for all the world to hear;
I have always taught in the synagogue and in the
Temple where all the Jews meet together: I have
said nothing in secret. 21 But why ask me? Ask
my hearers what I taught: they know what I
said." 22 At these words, one of the guards standing by gave Jesus a slap in the face, saying, "Is
that the way to answer the high priest?" 23 Jesus
replied, "If there is something wrong in what I

New English Bible

man died for the whole people. Jesus was followed by Simon Peter and another disciple. This disciple, who was acquainted with the High Priest, went with Jesus into the High Priest's courtyard, but Peter halted at the door outside. So the other disciple, the High Priest's acquaintance, went out again and spoke to the woman at the door, and brought Peter in. The maid on duty at the door said to Peter, 'Are you another of this man's disciples?' 'I am not', he said. The servants and the police had made a charcoal fire, because it was cold, and were standing round it warming themselves. And Peter too was standing with them, sharing the warmth.

The High Priest questioned Jesus about his disciples and about what he taught. Jesus replied, 'I have spoken openly to all the world; I have always taught in synagogue and in the temple, where all Jews congregate; I have said nothing in secret. Why question me? Ask my hearers what I told them; they know what I said.' When he said this, one of the police who was standing next to him struck him on the face, exclaiming, 'Is that the way to answer the High Priest?' Jesus replied, 'If I spoke amiss, state

King James Version

evil: but if well, why smitest thou me? 24 Now
Annas had sent him bound unto Caiaphas the
high priest. 25 And Simon Peter stood and
warmed himself. They said therefore unto him,
Art not thou also *one* of his disciples? He denied *it*, and said, I am not. 26 One of the servants of the high priest, being *his* kinsman whose
ear Peter cut off, saith, Did not I see thee in the
garden with him? 27 Peter then denied again;
and immediately the cock crew.
28 Then led they Jesus from Caiaphas unto
the hall of judgment: and it was early; and they
themselves went not into the judgment hall, lest
they should be defiled; but that they might eat
the passover. 29 Pilate then went out unto them,
and said, What accusation bring ye against this
man? 30 They answered and said unto him, If he
were not a malefactor, we would not have delivered him up unto thee. 31 Then said Pilate
unto them, Take ye him, and judge him according to your law. The Jews therefore said

Living Bible

you hit a man for telling the truth?"

24 Then Annas sent Jesus, bound, to Caiaphas the High Priest.

25 Meanwhile, as Simon Peter was standing by the fire, he was asked again, "Aren't you one of his disciples?"

"Of course not," he replied.

26 But one of the household slaves of the High Priest—a relative of the man whose ear Peter had cut off—asked, "Didn't I see you out there in the olive grove with Jesus?"

27 Again Peter denied it. And immediately a rooster crowed.

28 Jesus' trial before Caiaphas ended in the early hours of the morning. Next he was taken to the palace of the Roman governor. His accusers wouldn't go in themselves for that would "defile"[a] them, they said, and they wouldn't be allowed to eat the Passover lamb. 29 So Pilate, the governor, went out to them and asked, "What is your charge against this man? What are you accusing him of doing?"

30 "We wouldn't have arrested him if he weren't a criminal!" they retorted.

31 "Then take him away and judge him yourselves by your own laws," Pilate told them.

[a] By Jewish law, entering the house of a Gentile was a serious offense.

Today's English Version

if I am right in what I have said, why do you hit me?"

24 So Annas sent him, still tied up, to Caiaphas the High Priest.

Peter denies Jesus again

25 Peter was still standing there keeping himself warm. So the others said to him, "Aren't you one of the disciples of that man?"

But Peter denied it. "No, I am not," he said.

26 One of the High Priest's slaves, a relative of the man whose ear Peter had cut off, spoke up. "Didn't I see you with him in the garden?" he asked.

27 Again Peter said "No"—and at once a rooster crowed.

Jesus before Pilate

28 They took Jesus from Caiaphas' house to the governor's palace. It was early in the morning. The Jews did not go inside the palace because they wanted to keep themselves ritually clean, in order to be able to eat the Passover meal. 29 So Pilate went outside to them and asked, "What do you accuse this man of?"

30 Their answer was, "We would not have brought him to you if he had not committed a crime."

31 Pilate said to them, "You yourselves take him and try him according to your own law."

New International Version

"speak up about it. But if I spoke the truth, why did you hit me?" 24 Then Annas sent him, still bound, to Caiaphas, the high priest.[t]

Peter's second and third denials

25 As Simon Peter stood warming himself, he was asked, "Surely you are not another of his disciples?"

He denied it, saying, "I am not."

26 One of the high priest's servants, a relative of the man whose ear Peter had cut off, challenged him, "Didn't I see you with him in the olive grove?" 27 Again Peter denied it, and at that moment a rooster began to crow.

Jesus before Pilate

28 Then the Jews led Jesus from Caiaphas to the palace of the Roman governor. By now it was early morning, and to avoid ceremonial uncleanness the Jews did not enter the palace; they wanted to be able to eat the Passover. 29 So Pilate came out to them and asked, "What charges are you bringing against this man?"

30 "If he were not a criminal," they replied, "we would not have handed him over to you."

31 Pilate said, "Take him yourselves and judge him by your own law."

[t] Or (*Now Annas had sent him, still bound, to Caiaphas the high priest.*)

Phillips Modern English

what I said was true, why do you strike me?"
Then Annas sent him, with his hands still tied, to the High Priest Caiaphas.

18.25 Peter's denial

In the meantime Simon Peter was still standing, keeping himself warm. Some of them said to him, "Surely you too are one of his disciples, aren't you?"
And he denied it and said, "No I am not."
Then one of the High Priest's servants, a relation of the man whose ear Peter had cut off, remarked, "Didn't I see you in the garden with him?"
And again Peter denied it. And immediately the cock crew.

18.28 Jesus is taken before the Roman authority

Then they led Jesus from Caiaphas' presence into the palace. It was now early morning and the Jews themselves did not go into the palace, for fear that they would be contaminated and would not be able to eat the Passover. So Pilate walked out to them and said, "What is the charge that you are bringing against this man?"
"If he were not an evil-doer, we should not have handed him over to you," they replied.
To which Pilate retorted, "Then take him yourselves and judge him according to your law."

Revised Standard Version

wrong; but if I have spoken rightly, why do
you strike me?" 24Annas then sent him bound
to Caiaphas the high priest.
25 Now Simon Peter was standing and warming himself. They said to him, "Are not you also
one of his disciples?" He denied it and said, "I
am not." 26 One of the servants[l] of the high
priest, a kinsman of the man whose ear Peter had cut off, asked, "Did I not see you in the garden with him?" 27 Peter again denied it; and
at once the cock crowed.
28 Then they led Jesus from the house of Caiaphas to the praetorium. It was early. They themselves did not enter the praetorium, so that they might not be defiled, but might eat the passover. 29 So Pilate went out to them and said, "What accusation do you bring against this
man?" 30 They answered him, "If this man were not an evildoer, we would not have handed him
over." 31 Pilate said to them, "Take him yourselves and judge him by your own law." The

[l] Or *slaves.*

Jerusalem Bible

said, point it out; but if there is no offense in it, why do you strike me?" 24 Then Annas sent
him, still bound, to Caiaphas the high priest.
25 As Simon Peter stood there warming himself, someone said to him, "Aren't you another of his disciples?" He denied it saying, "I am
not." 26 One of the high priest's servants, a relation of the man whose ear Peter had cut off, said, "Didn't I see you in the garden with him?"
27Again Peter denied it; and at once a cock crew.

Jesus before Pilate

28 They then led Jesus from the house of Caiaphas to the Praetorium.[u] It was now morning. They did not go into the Praetorium themselves or they would be defiled[v] and unable to eat the passover. 29 So Pilate came outside to
them and said, "What charge do you bring against this man?" They replied, 30 "If he were
not a criminal, we should not be handing him
over to you." 31 Pilate said, "Take him yourselves, and try him by your own Law." The Jews

[u] The judicial court of the Roman procurator.
[v] By entering the house of a pagan. Cf. Lk. 7:6.

New English Bible

it in evidence; if I spoke well, why strike me?'
So Annas sent him bound to Caiaphas the High Priest.[a]
Meanwhile Simon Peter stood warming himself. The others asked, 'Are you another of his disciples?' But he denied it: 'I am not', he said. One of the High Priest's servants, a relation of the man whose ear Peter had cut off, insisted, 'Did I not see you with him in the garden?' Peter denied again; and just then a cock crew.

From Caiaphas Jesus was led into the Governor's headquarters. It was now early morning, and the Jews themselves stayed outside the headquarters to avoid defilement, so that they could eat the Passover meal.[b] So Pilate went out to them and asked, 'What charge do you bring against this man?' 'If he were not a criminal,' they replied, 'we should not have brought him before you.' Pilate said, 'Take him away and try him by your own law.' The Jews

[a] *Some witnesses give this verse after* first to Annas *in verse 13; others at the end of verse 13.*
[b] *Or* could share in the offerings of the Passover season.

King James Version

unto him, It is not lawful for us to put any man
to death: 32 That the saying of Jesus might be
fulfilled, which he spake, signifying what death
he should die. 33 Then Pilate entered into the
judgment hall again, and called Jesus, and said
unto him, Art thou the King of the Jews? 34 Jesus answered him, Sayest thou this thing of thyself, or did others tell it thee of me? 35 Pilate
answered, Am I a Jew? Thine own nation and
the chief priests have delivered thee unto me:
what hast thou done? 36 Jesus answered, My
kingdom is not of this world: if my kingdom
were of this world, then would my servants fight,
that I should not be delivered to the Jews: but
now is my kingdom not from hence. 37 Pilate
therefore said unto him, Art thou a king then?
Jesus answered, Thou sayest that I am a king.
To this end was I born, and for this cause came
I into the world, that I should bear witness unto
the truth. Every one that is of the truth heareth
my voice. 38 Pilate saith unto him, What is
truth? And when he had said this, he went out
again unto the Jews, and saith unto them, I find
in him no fault *at all*. 39 But ye have a custom,
that I should release unto you one at the passover: will ye therefore that I release unto you

Living Bible

"But we want him crucified," they demanded, "and your approval is required." [b] 32 This fulfilled Jesus' prediction concerning the method of his execution.[c]

33 Then Pilate went back into the palace and called for Jesus to be brought to him. "Are you the King of the Jews?" he asked him.

34 " 'King' as *you* use the word or as the *Jews* use it?" Jesus asked.[d]

35 "Am I a Jew?" Pilate retorted. "Your own people and their chief priests brought you here. Why? What have you done?"

36 Then Jesus answered, "I am not an earthly king. If I were, my followers would have fought when I was arrested by the Jewish leaders. But my Kingdom is not of the world."

37 Pilate replied, "But you are a king then?"

"Yes," Jesus said, "I was born for that purpose. And I came to bring truth to the world. All who love the truth are my followers."

38 "What is truth?" Pilate exclaimed. Then he went out again to the people and told them, "He is not guilty of any crime. 39 But you have a custom of asking me to release someone from prison each year at Passover. So if you want me to, I'll release the 'King of the Jews.' "

[*b*] Literally, "It is not lawful for us to put any man to death." [*c*] This prophecy is recorded in Matthew 20:19, which indicates his death by crucifixion, a practice under Roman law. [*d*] A paraphrase of this verse—that goes beyond the limits of this book's paraphrasing—would be, "Do you mean their King, or their Messiah?" If Pilate was asking as the Roman governor, he would be inquiring whether Jesus was setting up a rebel government. But the Jews were using the word "King" to mean their religious ruler, the Messiah. Literally this verse reads, "Are you saying this of yourself, or did someone else say it about me?"

Today's English Version

The Jews replied, "We are not allowed to put anyone to death." 32 (This happened to make come true what Jesus had said when he indicated the kind of death he would die.)

33 Pilate went back into the palace and called Jesus. "Are you the king of the Jews?" he asked him.

34 Jesus answered, "Does this question come from you or have others told you about me?"

35 Pilate replied, "Do you think I am a Jew? It was your own people and their chief priests who handed you over to me. What have you done?"

36 Jesus said, "My kingdom does not belong to this world; if my kingdom belonged to this world, my followers would fight to keep me from being handed over to the Jews. No, my kingdom does not belong here!"

37 So Pilate asked him, "Are you a king, then?"

Jesus answered, "You say that I am a king. I was born and came into the world for this one purpose, to speak about the truth. Whoever belongs to the truth listens to me."

38 "And what is truth?" Pilate asked.

Jesus sentenced to death

Then Pilate went back outside to the Jews and said to them, "I cannot find any reason to condemn him. 39 But according to the custom you have, I always set free a prisoner for you during the Passover. Do you want me to set the king of the Jews free for you?"

New International Version

"But we have no right to execute anyone," the Jews objected. 32 This happened so that the words Jesus had spoken indicating the kind of death he was going to die would be fulfilled.

33 Pilate then went back inside the palace, summoned Jesus, and asked him, "Are you the king of the Jews?"

34 "Is that your own idea," Jesus asked, "or did others talk to you about me?"

35 "Do you think I am a Jew?" Pilate replied. "It was your people and your chief priests who handed you over to me. What is it you have done?"

36 Jesus said, "My kingdom is not of this world. If it were, my servants would fight to prevent my arrest by the Jews. But now my kingdom is from another place."

37 "You are a king, then!" said Pilate.

Jesus answered, "You are right in saying I am a king. In fact, for this reason I was born, and for this I came into the world, to testify to the truth. Everyone on the side of truth listens to me."

38 "What is truth?" Pilate asked. With this he went out again to the Jews and said, "I find no basis for a charge against him. 39 But it is your custom for me to release to you one prisoner at the time of the Passover. Do you want me to release 'the king of the Jews'?"

Phillips Modern English

"We are not allowed to put a man to death," replied the Jews (thus fulfilling Christ's prophecy of the method of his own death).

So Pilate went back into the palace and called Jesus to him. "Are you the king of the Jews?" he asked.

"Are you asking this of your own accord," replied Jesus, "or have other people spoken to you about me?"

"Do you think *I* am a Jew?" replied Pilate. "It's your people and your chief priests who handed you over to me. What have you done, anyway?"

"My kingdom is not founded in this world—if it were, my servants would have fought to prevent my being handed over to the Jews. But in fact my kingdom is not founded on all this!"

"So you are a king, are you?" returned Pilate.

"You say that I am a king," Jesus replied; "the reason for my birth and the reason for my coming into the world is to witness to the truth. Every man who loves truth recognises my voice."

To which Pilate retorted, "What is 'truth'?" and went straight out again to the Jews and said:

"I find nothing criminal about him at all. But I have an arrangement with you to set one prisoner free at Passover time. Do you wish me then to set free for you the 'king of the Jews'?"

Revised Standard Version

Jews said to him, "It is not lawful for us to put any man to death." 32 This was to fulfil the word which Jesus had spoken to show by what death he was to die.

33 Pilate entered the praetorium again and called Jesus, and said to him, "Are you the King of the Jews?" 34 Jesus answered, "Do you say this of your own accord, or did others say it to you about me?" 35 Pilate answered, "Am I a Jew? Your own nation and the chief priests have handed you over to me; what have you done?" 36 Jesus answered, "My kingship is not of this world; if my kingship were of this world, my servants would fight, that I might not be handed over to the Jews; but my kingship is not from the world." 37 Pilate said to him, "So you are a king?" Jesus answered, "You say that I am a king. For this I was born, and for this I have come into the world, to bear witness to the truth. Every one who is of the truth hears my voice." 38 Pilate said to him, "What is truth?"

After he had said this, he went out to the Jews again, and told them, "I find no crime in him. 39 But you have a custom that I should release one man for you at the Passover; will you have me release for you the King of the Jews?"

Jerusalem Bible

answered, "We are not allowed to put a man to death." 32 This was to fulfill the words Jesus had spoken indicating the way he was going to die.

33 So Pilate went back into the Praetorium and called Jesus to him, "Are you the king of the Jews?" he asked. 34 Jesus replied, "Do you ask this of your own accord, or have others spoken to you about me?" 35 Pilate answered, "Am I a Jew? It is your own people and the chief priests who have handed you over to me: what have you done?" 36 Jesus replied, "Mine is not a kingdom of this world; if my kingdom were of this world, my men would have fought to prevent my being surrendered to the Jews. But my kingdom is not of this kind." 37 "So you are a king then?" said Pilate. "It is you who say it," answered Jesus. "Yes, I am a king. I was born for this, I came into the world for this: to bear witness to the truth; and all who are on the side of truth listen to my voice." 38 "Truth?" said Pilate, "What is that?"; and with that he went out again to the Jews and said, "I find no case against him. 39 But according to a custom of yours I should release one prisoner at the Passover; would you like me, then, to release the

New English Bible

answered, 'We are not allowed to put any man to death.' Thus they ensured the fulfilment of the words by which Jesus had indicated the manner of his death.

Pilate then went back into his headquarters and summoned Jesus. 'Are you the king of the Jews?' he asked.[c] Jesus said, 'Is that your own idea, or have others suggested it to you?' 'What! am I a Jew?' said Pilate. 'Your own nation and their chief priests have brought you before me. What have you done?' Jesus replied, 'My kingdom does not belong to this world. If it did, my followers would be fighting to save me from arrest by the Jews. My kingly authority comes from elsewhere.' 'You are a king, then?' said Pilate. Jesus answered, ' "King" is your word. My task is to bear witness to the truth. For this was I born; for this I came into the world, and all who are not deaf to truth listen to my voice.' Pilate said, 'What is truth?', and with those words went out again to the Jews. 'For my part,' he said, 'I find no case against him. But you have a custom that I release one prisoner for you at Passover. Would you like

[c] *Or* 'You are king of the Jews, I take it,' he said.

King James Version

the King of the Jews? 40 Then cried they all again, saying, Not this man, but Barabbas. Now Barabbas was a robber.

19 Then Pilate therefore took Jesus, and scourged *him*. 2 And the soldiers platted a crown of thorns, and put *it* on his head, and they put on him a purple robe, 3 And said, Hail, King of the Jews! and they smote him with their hands. 4 Pilate therefore went forth again, and saith unto them, Behold, I bring him forth to you, that ye may know that I find no fault in him. 5 Then came Jesus forth, wearing the crown of thorns, and the purple robe. And *Pilate* saith unto them, Behold the man! 6 When the chief priests therefore and officers saw him, they cried out, saying, Crucify *him*, crucify *him*. Pilate saith unto them, Take ye him, and crucify *him:* for I find no fault in him. 7 The Jews answered him, We have a law, and by our law he ought to die, because he made himself the Son of God.

8 When Pilate therefore heard that saying, he was the more afraid; 9 And went again into the judgment hall, and saith unto Jesus, Whence art thou? But Jesus gave him no answer. 10 Then saith Pilate unto him, Speakest thou not unto me? knowest thou not that I have power to

Living Bible

40 But they screamed back, "No! Not this man, but Barabbas!" Barabbas was a robber.

19 Then Pilate laid open Jesus' back with a leaded whip, 2 and the soldiers made a crown of thorns and placed it on his head and robed him in royal purple. 3 "Hail, 'King of the Jews!' " they mocked, and struck him with their fists.

4 Pilate went outside again and said to the Jews, "I am going to bring him out to you now, but understand clearly that I find him *not guilty*."

5 Then Jesus came out wearing the crown of thorns and the purple robe. And Pilate said, "Behold the man!"

6 At sight of him the chief priests and Jewish officials began yelling, "Crucify! Crucify!"

"*You* crucify him," Pilate said. "I find him *not guilty*."

7 They replied "By our laws he ought to die because he called himself the Son of God."

8 When Pilate heard this, he was more frightened than ever. 9 He took Jesus back into the palace again and asked him, "Where are you from?" but Jesus gave no answer.

10 "You won't talk to me?" Pilate demanded. "Don't you realize that I have the power to

Today's English Version

40 They answered him with a shout, "No, not him! We want Barabbas!" (Barabbas was a bandit.)

19 Then Pilate took Jesus and had him whipped. 2 The soldiers made a crown of thorny branches and put it on his head; they put a purple robe on him, 3 and came to him and said, "Long live the King of the Jews!" And they went up and slapped him.

4 Pilate went back out once more and said to the crowd, "Look, I will bring him out here to you, to let you see that I cannot find any reason to condemn him." 5 So Jesus went outside, wearing the crown of thorns and the purple robe. Pilate said to them, "Look! Here is the man!"

6 When the chief priests and the guards saw him they shouted, "Nail him to the cross! Nail him to the cross!"

Pilate said to them, "You take him, then, and nail him to the cross. I find no reason to condemn him."

7 The Jews answered back, "We have a law that says he ought to die, because he claimed to be the Son of God."

8 When Pilate heard them say this, he was even more afraid. 9 He went back into the palace and asked Jesus, "Where do you come from?"

But Jesus did not answer. 10 Pilate said to him, "You will not speak to me? Remember, I have the authority to set you free, and also to

New International Version

40 They shouted back, "No, not him! Give us Barabbas!" Now Barabbas had taken part in a rebellion.

Jesus sentenced to be crucified

19 Then Pilate took Jesus and had him flogged. 2 The soldiers twisted together a crown of thorns and put it on his head. They clothed him in a purple robe 3 and went up to him again and again, saying, "Hail, O king of the Jews!" And they struck him in the face.

4 Once more Pilate came out and said to the Jews, "Look, I am bringing him out to you to let you know that I find no basis for a charge against him." 5 When Jesus came out wearing the crown of thorns and the purple robe, Pilate said to them, "Here is the man!"

6 As soon as the chief priests and their officials saw him, they shouted, "Crucify! Crucify!"

But Pilate answered, "You take him and crucify him. As for me, I find no basis for a charge against him."

7 The Jews insisted, "We have a law, and according to that law he must die, because he claimed to be the Son of God."

8 When Pilate heard this, he was even more afraid, 9 and he went back inside the palace. "Where do you come from?" he asked Jesus, but Jesus gave him no answer. 10 "Do you refuse to speak to me?" Pilate said. "Don't you realize I have power either to free you or to crucify you?"

Phillips Modern English

At this, they shouted at the top of their voices, "No, not this man, but Barabbas!"
Barabbas was a bandit.

19.1 Pilate's vain efforts to save Jesus

Then Pilate took Jesus and had him flogged, and the soldiers twisted thorn-twigs into a crown and put it on his head, threw a purple robe around him and kept coming into his presence, saying, "Hail, king of the Jews!" And then they slapped him with their open hands.

Then Pilate went outside again and said to them, "Look, I bring him out before you here, to show that I find nothing criminal about him at all."

And at this Jesus came outside too, wearing the thorn crown and the purple robe.

"Look," said Pilate, "here's the man!"

The sight of him made the chief priests and Jewish officers shout at the top of their voices, "Crucify! Crucify!"

"You take him and crucify him," retorted Pilate. "He's no criminal as far as I can see!"

The Jews answered him, "We have a Law, and according to that Law, he must die, for he made himself out to be Son of God!"

When Pilate heard them say this, he became much more uneasy, and returned to the palace and again spoke to Jesus, "Where *do* you come from?"

But Jesus gave him no reply. So Pilate said to him, "Won't you speak to me? Don't you realise that I have the power to set you free,

Revised Standard Version

40 They cried out again, "Not this man, but
Barabbas!" Now Barabbas was a robber.

19 Then Pilate took Jesus and scourged
him. 2 And the soldiers plaited a crown of
thorns, and put it on his head, and arrayed him
in a purple robe; 3 they came up to him, saying, "Hail, King of the Jews!" and struck him
with their hands. 4 Pilate went out again, and
said to them, "See, I am bringing him out to
you, that you may know that I find no crime in
him." 5 So Jesus came out, wearing the crown
of thorns and the purple robe. Pilate said to
them, "Behold the man!" 6 When the chief
priests and the officers saw him, they cried out,
"Crucify him, crucify him!" Pilate said to them,
"Take him yourselves and crucify him, for I find
no crime in him." 7 The Jews answered him,
"We have a law, and by that law he ought to
die, because he has made himself the Son of
God." 8 When Pilate heard these words, he was
the more afraid; 9 he entered the praetorium
again and said to Jesus, "Where are you from?"
But Jesus gave no answer. 10 Pilate therefore
said to him, "You will not speak to me? Do you
not know that I have power to release you, and

Jerusalem Bible

king of the Jews?" 40 At this they shouted: "Not
this man," they said, "but Barabbas." Barabbas
was a brigand.

19 Pilate then had Jesus taken away and
scourged; 2 and after this, the soldiers
twisted some thorns into a crown and put it on
his head, and dressed him in a purple robe.
3 They kept coming up to him and saying, "Hail,
king of the Jews!"; and they slapped him in the
face.
4 Pilate came outside again and said to them,
"Look, I am going to bring him out to you to
let you see that I find no case." 5 Jesus then
came out wearing the crown of thorns and the
purple robe. Pilate said, "Here is the man."
6 When they saw him the chief priests and the
guards shouted, "Crucify him! Crucify him!" Pilate said, "Take him yourselves and crucify him:
I can find no case against him." 7 "We have a
Law," the Jews replied, "and according to that
Law he ought to die, because he has claimed to
be the Son of God."
8 When Pilate heard them say this his fears
increased. 9 Re-entering the Praetorium, he said
to Jesus, "Where do you come from?" But Jesus
made no answer. 10 Pilate then said to him,
"Are you refusing to speak to me? Surely you
know I have power to release you and I have

New English Bible

me to release the king of the Jews?' Again the clamour rose: 'Not him; we want Barabbas!' (Barabbas was a bandit.)

19 Pilate now took Jesus and had him flogged; and the soldiers plaited a crown of thorns and placed it on his head, and robed him in a purple cloak. Then time after time they came up to him, crying, 'Hail, King of the Jews!', and struck him on the face.

Once more Pilate came out and said to the Jews, 'Here he is; I am bringing him out to let you know that I find no case against him'; and Jesus came out, wearing the crown of thorns and the purple cloak. 'Behold the Man!' said Pilate. The chief priests and their henchmen saw him and shouted, 'Crucify! crucify!' 'Take him and crucify him yourselves,' said Pilate; 'for my part I find no case against him.' The Jews answered, 'We have a law; and by that law he ought to die, because he has claimed to be Son of God.'

When Pilate heard that, he was more afraid than ever, and going back into his headquarters he asked Jesus, 'Where have you come from?' But Jesus gave him no answer. 'Do you refuse to speak to me?' said Pilate. 'Surely you know that I have authority to release you, and I have

King James Version

crucify thee, and have power to release thee?
11 Jesus answered, Thou couldest have no power
at all against me, except it were given thee from
above: therefore he that delivered me unto thee
hath the greater sin. 12And from thenceforth
Pilate sought to release him: but the Jews cried
out, saying, If thou let this man go, thou art not
Cesar's friend: whosoever maketh himself a king
speaketh against Cesar.
13 When Pilate therefore heard that saying,
he brought Jesus forth, and sat down in the
judgment seat in a place that is called the Pavement, but in the Hebrew, Gabbatha. 14And it
was the preparation of the passover, and about
the sixth hour: and he saith unto the Jews, Behold your King! 15 But they cried out, Away
with *him,* away with *him,* crucify him. Pilate
saith unto them, Shall I crucify your King?
The chief priests answered, We have no king but
Cesar. 16 Then delivered he him therefore unto
them to be crucified. And they took Jesus, and
led *him* away. 17And he bearing his cross went
forth into a place called *the place* of a skull,

Living Bible

release you or to crucify you?"
11 Then Jesus said, "You would have no
power at all over me unless it were given to you
from above. So those[a] who brought me to you
have the greater sin."
12 Then Pilate tried to release him, but the
Jewish leaders told him, "If you release this man,
you are no friend of Caesar's. Anyone who declares himself a king is a rebel against Caesar."
13 At these words Pilate brought Jesus out to
them again and sat down at the judgment bench
on the stone-paved platform.[b] 14 It was now
about noon of the day before Passover.

And Pilate said to the Jews, "Here is your
king!"

15 "Away with him," they yelled. "Away with
him—crucify him!"

"What? Crucify your king?" Pilate asked.

"We have no king but Caesar," the chief
priests shouted back.

16 Then Pilate gave Jesus to them to be crucified.

17 So they had him at last, and he was taken
out of the city, carrying his cross to the place

[a] Literally, "he." [b] Literally, "the judgment seat in a place that is called The Pavement, but in Hebrew, Gabbatha."

Today's English Version

have you nailed to the cross."

11 Jesus answered, "You have authority over
me only because it was given to you by God. So
the man who handed me over to you is guilty of
a worse sin."

12 When Pilate heard this he tried to find a
way to set Jesus free. But the Jews shouted back,
"If you set him free that means you are not the
Emperor's friend! Anyone who claims to be a
king is the Emperor's enemy!"

13 When Pilate heard these words, he took
Jesus outside and sat down on the judge's seat
in the place called "The Stone Pavement." (In
Hebrew the name is "Gabbatha.") 14 It was then
almost noon of the day before the Passover.
Pilate said to the Jews, "Here is your king!"

15 They shouted back, "Kill him! Kill him!
Nail him to the cross!"

Pilate asked them, "Do you want me to nail
your king to the cross?"

The chief priests answered, "The only king
we have is the Emperor!"

16 Then Pilate handed Jesus over to them to
be nailed to the cross.

Jesus nailed to the cross

So they took charge of Jesus. 17 He went out,
carrying his cross, and came to "The Place of

New International Version

11 Jesus answered, "You have no power over
me that was not given to you from above. Therefore the one who handed me over to you is
guilty of a greater sin."

12 From then on, Pilate tried to set Jesus free,
but the Jews kept shouting, "If you let this man
go, you are no friend of Caesar. Anyone who
claims to be a king opposes Caesar."

13 When Pilate heard this, he brought Jesus
out and sat down on the judge's seat at a place
known as The Stone Pavement (which in Aramaic is Gabbatha). 14 It was the day of Preparation of Passover Week, about the sixth hour.

"Here is your king," Pilate said to the Jews.

15 But they shouted, "Take him away! Take
him away! Crucify him!"

"Shall I crucify your king?" Pilate asked.

"We have no king but Caesar," the chief
priests answered.

16 Finally Pilate handed him over to them to
be crucified.

The crucifixion

So the soldiers took charge of Jesus. 17 Carrying his own cross, he went out to The Place of

Phillips Modern English

and I have the power to have you crucified?"
"You have no power at all against me," replied Jesus, "except what was given to you from above. And for that reason the one who handed me over to you is even more guilty than you are."
From that moment, Pilate tried hard to set him free but the Jews were yelling, "If you set this man free, you are no friend of Caesar! Anyone who makes himself out to be a king is anti-Caesar!"
When Pilate heard this, he led Jesus outside and sat down upon the Judgment-seat in the place called the Pavement (in Hebrew, Gabbatha). It was the preparation day of the Passover and it was now about midday. Pilate now said to the Jews, "Look, here's your king!"
At which they yelled, "Take him away, take him away, crucify him!"
"Am I to crucify your king?" Pilate asked them.
"Caesar is our king and no one else," replied the chief priests. And at this Pilate handed Jesus over to them for crucifixion.

19.17 The crucifixion

So they took Jesus and he went out carrying the cross himself, to a place called Skull Hill (in

Revised Standard Version

power to crucify you?" 11 Jesus answered him,
"You would have no power over me unless it
had been given you from above; therefore he
who delivered me to you has the greater sin."
12 Upon this Pilate sought to release him,
but the Jews cried out, "If you release this man,
you are not Caesar's friend; every one who
makes himself a king sets himself against Caesar." 13 When Pilate heard these words, he
brought Jesus out and sat down on the judgment seat at a place called The Pavement, and
in Hebrew, Gabbatha. 14 Now it was the day of
Preparation of the Passover; it was about the
sixth hour. He said to the Jews, "Behold your
King!" 15 They cried out, "Away with him,
away with him, crucify him!" Pilate said to
them, "Shall I crucify your King?" The chief
priests answered, "We have no king but Caesar." 16 Then he handed him over to them to be
crucified.
17 So they took Jesus, and he went out, bearing his own cross, to the place called the place

Jerusalem Bible

power to crucify you?" 11 "You would have no
power over me," replied Jesus, "if it had not
been given you from above; that is why the one
who handed me over to you has the greater
guilt."

Jesus is condemned to death

12 From that moment Pilate was anxious to
set him free, but the Jews shouted, "If you set
him free you are no friend of Caesar's; anyone
who makes himself king is defying Caesar."
13 Hearing these words, Pilate had Jesus brought
out, and seated himself on the chair of judgment
at a place called the Pavement, in Hebrew Gabbatha. 14 It was Passover Preparation Day, about
the sixth hour.[w] "Here is your king," said Pilate
to the Jews. 15 "Take him away, take him away!"
they said. "Crucify him!" "Do you want me to
crucify your king?" said Pilate. The chief priests
answered, "We have no king except Caesar."
16 So in the end Pilate handed him over to them
to be crucified.

The crucifixion

They then took charge of Jesus, 17 and carrying his own cross he went out of the city to

[w] On Preparation Day, the Passover supper was made ready for eating after sunset. The sixth hour is midday, by which time all leaven had to be removed from the house; during the feast only unleavened bread was eaten.

New English Bible

authority to crucify you?' 'You would have no authority at all over me', Jesus replied, 'if it had not been granted you from above; and therefore the deeper guilt lies with the man who handed me over to you.'

From that moment Pilate tried hard to release him; but the Jews kept shouting, 'If you let this man go, you are no friend to Caesar; any man who claims to be a king is defying Caesar.' When Pilate heard what they were saying, he brought Jesus out and took his seat on the tribunal at the place known as 'The Pavement' ('Gabbatha' in the language of the Jews). It was the eve of Passover,[a] about noon. Pilate said to the Jews, 'Here is your king.' They shouted, 'Away with him! Away with him! Crucify him!' 'Crucify your king?' said Pilate. 'We have no king but Caesar', the Jews replied. Then at last, to satisfy them, he handed Jesus over to be crucified.

Jesus was now taken in charge and, carrying his own cross, went out to the Place of the

[a] *Or* It was Friday in Passover.

King James Version

which is called in the Hebrew Golgotha:
18 Where they crucified him, and two others with
him, on either side one, and Jesus in the midst.
19 And Pilate wrote a title, and put *it* on the
cross. And the writing was, JESUS OF NAZA-
RETH THE KING OF THE JEWS. 20 This title
then read many of the Jews; for the place where
Jesus was crucified was nigh to the city: and it
was written in Hebrew, *and* Greek, *and* Latin.
21 Then said the chief priests of the Jews to
Pilate, Write not, The King of the Jews; but
that he said, I am King of the Jews. 22 Pilate
answered, What I have written I have written.
23 Then the soldiers, when they had crucified
Jesus, took his garments, and made four parts,
to every soldier a part; and also *his* coat: now
the coat was without seam, woven from the top
throughout. 24 They said therefore among themselves, Let us not rend it, but cast lots for it,
whose it shall be: that the Scripture might be fulfilled, which saith, They parted my raiment
among them, and for my vesture they did cast

Living Bible

known as "The Skull," in Hebrew, "Golgotha."
18 There they crucified him and two others with
him, one on either side, with Jesus between them.
19 And Pilate posted a sign over him reading,
"Jesus of Nazareth, the King of the Jews."
20 The place where Jesus was crucified was near
the city; and the signboard was written in Hebrew, Latin, and Greek, so that many people
read it.
21 Then the chief priests said to Pilate,
"Change it from 'The King of the Jews' to '*He
said,* I am King of the Jews.' "
22 Pilate replied, "What I have written, I have
written. It stays exactly as it is."
23, 24 When the soldiers had crucified Jesus,
they put his garments into four piles, one for
each of them. But they said, "Let's not tear up
his robe," for it was seamless. "Let's throw dice
to see who gets it." This fulfilled the Scripture
that says,

"They divided my clothes among them, and
cast lots for my robe." [c]

[*c*] Psalm 22:18.

Today's English Version

the Skull," as it is called. (In Hebrew it is called
"Golgotha.") 18 There they nailed him to the
cross; they also nailed two other men to crosses,
one on each side, with Jesus between them. 19 Pilate wrote a notice and had it put on the cross.
"Jesus of Nazareth, the King of the Jews," is
what he wrote. 20 Many Jews read this, because
the place where Jesus was nailed to the cross
was not far from the city. The notice was written in Hebrew, Latin, and Greek. 21 The Jewish
chief priests said to Pilate, "Do not write 'The
King of the Jews,' but rather, 'This man said, I
am the King of the Jews.' "
22 Pilate answered, "What I have written stays
written."
23 After the soldiers had nailed Jesus to the
cross, they took his clothes and divided them
into four parts, one part for each soldier. They
also took the robe, which was made of one piece
of woven cloth, without any seams in it. 24 The
soldiers said to each other, "Let us not tear it;
let us throw dice to see who will get it." This
happened to make the scripture come true,

"They divided my clothes among themselves,
and gambled for my robe."

New International Version

the Skull (which in Aramaic is called Golgotha).
18 Here they crucified him, and with him two
others—one on either side and Jesus in the middle.
19 Pilate had a notice prepared and fastened
to the cross. It read, JESUS OF NAZARETH, THE
KING OF THE JEWS. 20 Many of the Jews read
this sign, for the place where Jesus was crucified
was near the city, and the sign was written in
Aramaic, Latin and Greek. 21 The chief priests
of the Jews protested to Pilate, "Do not write
'The King of the Jews,' but that this man
claimed to be king of the Jews."
22 Pilate answered, "What I have written, I
have written."
23 When the soldiers crucified Jesus, they
took his clothes, dividing them into four shares,
one for each of them, with the undergarment
remaining. This garment was seamless, woven
in one piece from top to bottom.
24 "Let's not tear it," they said to one another. "Let's decide by lot who will get it."
This happened that the scripture might be fulfilled which said,

"They divided my garments among themselves
and cast lots for my clothing." [u]

[*u*] Psalm 22:18.

Phillips Modern English

Hebrew, Golgotha). There they crucified him, and two others, one on either side of him with Jesus in the middle. Pilate had a placard written out and put on the cross, reading, JESUS OF NAZARETH, THE KING OF THE JEWS. This placard was read by many of the Jews because the place where Jesus was crucified was quite near Jerusalem, and it was written in Hebrew as well as in Latin and Greek. So the chief priests said to Pilate, "You should not write 'The King of the Jews', but 'This man said, I am King of the Jews.' "

To which Pilate retorted, "What I have written, I have written."

When the soldiers had crucified Jesus, they divided his clothes between them, taking a quarter-share each. There remained his tunic, which was seamless—woven in one piece from the top to the bottom. So they said to each other, "Don't let us tear it; let's draw lots and see who gets it."

This happened to fulfil the scripture which says—

They parted my garments among them,
And upon my vesture did they cast lots.

Revised Standard Version

of a skull, which is called in Hebrew Golgotha.
18 There they crucified him, and with him two
others, one on either side, and Jesus between
them. 19 Pilate also wrote a title and put it on
the cross; it read, "Jesus of Nazareth, the King
of the Jews." 20 Many of the Jews read this
title, for the place where Jesus was crucified was
near the city; and it was written in Hebrew, in
Latin, and in Greek. 21 The chief priests of the
Jews then said to Pilate, "Do not write, 'The
King of the Jews,' but, 'This man said, I am
King of the Jews.' " 22 Pilate answered, "What
I have written I have written."
23 When the soldiers had crucified Jesus they
took his garments and made four parts, one for
each soldier; also his tunic. But the tunic was
without seam, woven from top to bottom; 24 so
they said to one another, "Let us not tear it,
but cast lots for it to see whose it shall be."
This was to fulfil the scripture,

"They parted my garments among them,
and for my clothing they cast lots."

Jerusalem Bible

the place of the skull or, as it was called in
Hebrew, Golgotha, 18 where they crucified him
with two others, one on either side with Jesus in
the middle. 19 Pilate wrote out a notice and had
it fixed to the cross; it ran: "Jesus the Nazarene,
King of the Jews." 20 The notice was read by
many of the Jews, because the place where Jesus
was crucified was not far from the city, and the
writing was in Hebrew, Latin and Greek. 21 So
the Jewish chief priests said to Pilate, "You
should not write 'King of the Jews,' but 'This
man said: I am King of the Jews.' " 22 Pilate
answered, "What I have written, I have written."

Christ's garments divided

23 When the soldiers had finished crucifying
Jesus they took his clothing and divided it into
four shares, one for each soldier. His undergarment was seamless, woven in one piece from
neck to hem; 24 so they said to one another,
"Instead of tearing it, let's throw dice to decide
who is to have it." In this way the words of
scripture were fulfilled:

They shared out my clothing among them.
They cast lots for my clothes.[x]

[x] Ps. 22:18.

New English Bible

Skull, as it is called (or, in the Jews' language, 'Golgotha'), where they crucified him, and with him two others, one on the right, one on the left, and Jesus between them.

And Pilate wrote an inscription to be fastened to the cross; it read, 'Jesus of Nazareth King of the Jews.' This inscription was read by many Jews, because the place where Jesus was crucified was not far from the city, and the inscription was in Hebrew, Latin, and Greek. Then the Jewish chief priests said to Pilate, 'You should not write "King of the Jews"; write, "He claimed to be king of the Jews." ' Pilate replied, 'What I have written, I have written.'

The soldiers, having crucified Jesus, took possession of his clothes, and divided them into four parts, one for each soldier, leaving out the tunic. The tunic was seamless, woven in one piece throughout; so they said to one another, 'We must not tear this; let us toss for it'; and thus the text of Scripture came true: 'They shared my garments among them, and cast lots for my clothing.'

King James Version

lots. These things therefore the soldiers did.
25 Now there stood by the cross of Jesus his
mother, and his mother's sister, Mary the *wife*
of Cleophas, and Mary Magdalene. 26 When Jesus therefore saw his mother, and the disciple
standing by, whom he loved, he saith unto his
mother, Woman, behold thy son! 27 Then saith
he to the disciple, Behold thy mother! And from
that hour that disciple took her unto his own
home.
28 After this, Jesus knowing that all things
were now accomplished, that the Scripture might
be fulfilled, saith, I thirst. 29 Now there was set
a vessel full of vinegar: and they filled a sponge
with vinegar, and put *it* upon hyssop, and put
it to his mouth. 30 When Jesus therefore had received the vinegar, he said, It is finished: and
he bowed his head, and gave up the ghost. 31 The
Jews therefore, because it was the preparation,
that the bodies should not remain upon the cross
on the sabbath day, (for that sabbath day was a
high day,) besought Pilate that their legs might
be broken, and *that* they might be taken away.

Living Bible

25 So that is what they did.
Standing near the cross were Jesus' mother,
Mary, his aunt, the wife of Cleopas, and Mary
Magdalene. 26 When Jesus saw his mother standing there beside me, his close friend,[d] he said to
her, "He is your son."
27 And to me[e] he said, "She is your mother!"
And from then on I took her into my home.
28 Jesus knew that everything was now finished, and to fulfill the Scriptures said, "I'm
thirsty." 29 A jar of sour wine was sitting there,
so a sponge was soaked in it and put on a hyssop
branch and held up to his lips.
30 When Jesus had tasted[f] it, he said, "It is
finished," and bowed his head and dismissed his
spirit.
31 The Jewish leaders didn't want the victims
hanging there the next day, which was the Sabbath (and a very special Sabbath at that, for it
was the Passover), so they asked Pilate to order
the legs of the men broken to hasten death; then

[d] Literally, "standing by the disciple whom he loved." [e] Literally, "to the disciple." [f] Literally, "had received."

Today's English Version

So the soldiers did this.
25 Standing close to Jesus' cross were his
mother, his mother's sister, Mary the wife of
Clopas, and Mary Magdalene. 26 Jesus saw his
mother and the disciple he loved standing there;
so he said to his mother, "Woman, here is your
son."
27 Then he said to the disciple, "Here is your
mother." From that time the disciple took her
to live in his home.

The death of Jesus

28 Jesus knew that by now everything had
been completed; and in order to make the scripture come true he said, "I am thirsty."
29 A bowl was there, full of cheap wine; they
soaked a sponge in the wine, put it on a branch
of hyssop, and lifted it up to his lips. 30 Jesus
took the wine and said, "It is finished!"
Then he bowed his head and died.

Jesus' side pierced

31 Then the Jews asked Pilate to allow them
to break the legs of the men who had been put
to death, and take them down from the crosses.
They did this because it was Friday, and they
did not want the bodies to stay on the crosses
on the Sabbath day, since the coming Sabbath

New International Version

So this is what the soldiers did.
25 Near the cross of Jesus stood his mother,
his mother's sister, Mary the wife of Clopas, and
Mary of Magdala. 26 When Jesus saw his mother
there, and the disciple whom he loved standing
nearby, he said to his mother, "Here is[v] your
son," 27 and to the disciple, "Here is your
mother." From that time on, this disciple took
her into his home.

The death of Jesus

28 Later, knowing that all was now completed, and so that the scripture would be fulfilled, Jesus said, "I am thirsty." 29 A jar of wine
vinegar was there, so they soaked a sponge in it,
put the sponge on a stalk of the hyssop plant,
and lifted it to Jesus' lips. 30 When he had received the drink, Jesus said, "It is finished."
With that, he bowed his head and gave up his
life.
31 Now it was the day of Preparation, and
the next day was to be a special Sabbath. Because the Jews did not want the bodies left on
the crosses during the Sabbath, they asked Pilate to have the legs broken and the bodies

[v] Greek *"Woman, here is . . ."* (a polite form of address).

Phillips Modern English

19.25 Jesus provides for his mother from the cross

While the soldiers were doing this, Jesus' mother was standing near his cross with her sister, and with them Mary, the wife of Clopas, and Mary of Magdala. Jesus saw his mother and the disciple whom he loved standing by her side, and said to her, "Mother, there is your son!" And then he said to the disciple, "And there is your mother!"

And from that time the disciple took Mary into his own home.

After this, Jesus realising that everything was now completed, said (fulfilling the saying of scripture), "I am thirsty."

There was a bowl of sour wine standing there. So they soaked a sponge in the wine, put it on a spear, and pushed it up towards his mouth. When Jesus had taken it, he cried, "It is finished!" his head fell forward, and he breathed his last breath.

19.31 The body of Jesus is removed

As it was the day of preparation for the Passover, the Jews wanted to avoid the bodies being left on the crosses over the Sabbath (for that was a particularly important Sabbath), and they requested Pilate to have the men's legs broken

Revised Standard Version

25 So the soldiers did this. But standing by
the cross of Jesus were his mother, and his
mother's sister, Mary the wife of Clopas, and
Mary Magdalene. 26 When Jesus saw his mother,
and the disciple whom he loved standing near,
he said to his mother, "Woman, behold, your
son!" 27 Then he said to the disciple, "Behold,
your mother!" And from that hour the disciple
took her to his own home.
28 After this Jesus, knowing that all was
now finished, said (to fulfil the scripture), "I
thirst." 29 A bowl full of vinegar stood there;
so they put a sponge full of the vinegar on hyssop and held it to his mouth. 30 When Jesus
had received the vinegar, he said, "It is finished";
and he bowed his head and gave up his spirit.
31 Since it was the day of Preparation, in
order to prevent the bodies from remaining on
the cross on the sabbath (for that sabbath was
a high day), the Jews asked Pilate that their legs
might be broken, and that they might be taken

Jerusalem Bible

This is exactly what the soldiers did.

Jesus and his mother

25 Near the cross of Jesus stood his mother
and his mother's sister, Mary the wife of Clopas,
and Mary of Magdala. 26 Seeing his mother and
the disciple he loved standing near her, Jesus
said to his mother, "Woman, this is your son."
27 Then to the disciple he said, "This is your
mother." And from that moment the disciple
made a place for her in his home.

The death of Jesus

28 After this, Jesus knew that everything had
now been completed, and to fulfill the scripture
perfectly he said:

"I am thirsty." [y]

29 A jar full of vinegar stood there, so putting
a sponge soaked in the vinegar on a hyssop stick
they held it up to his mouth. 30 After Jesus had
taken the vinegar he said, "It is accomplished";
and bowing his head he gave up his spirit.

The pierced Christ

31 It was Preparation Day, and to prevent the
bodies remaining on the cross during the sabbath—since that sabbath was a day of special
solemnity—the Jews asked Pilate to have the

[y] Ps. 22:15.

New English Bible

That is what the soldiers did. But meanwhile near the cross where Jesus hung stood his mother, with her sister, Mary wife of Clopas, and Mary of Magdala. Jesus saw his mother, with the disciple whom he loved standing beside her. He said to her, 'Mother, there is your son'; and to the disciple, 'There is your mother'; and from that moment the disciple took her into his home.

After that, Jesus, aware that all had now come to its appointed end, said in fulfilment of Scripture, 'I thirst.' A jar stood there full of sour wine; so they soaked a sponge with the wine, fixed it on a javelin,[a] and held it up to his lips. Having received the wine, he said, 'It is accomplished!' He bowed his head and gave up his spirit.[b]

Because it was the eve of Passover,[c] the Jews were anxious that the bodies should not remain on the cross for the coming Sabbath, since that Sabbath was a day of great solemnity; so they requested Pilate to have the legs broken

[a] *So one witness; the others read* on marjoram. [b] *Or* breathed out his life. [c] *Or* Because it was Friday in Passover . . .

King James Version

32 Then came the soldiers, and brake the legs of
the first, and of the other which was crucified
with him. 33 But when they came to Jesus, and
saw that he was dead already, they brake not his
legs: 34 But one of the soldiers with a spear
pierced his side, and forthwith came there out
blood and water. 35 And he that saw *it* bare
record, and his record is true; and he knoweth
that he saith true, that ye might believe. 36 For
these things were done, that the Scripture should
be fulfilled, A bone of him shall not be broken.
37 And again another Scripture saith, They shall
look on him whom they pierced.
38 And after this Joseph of Arimathea, being
a disciple of Jesus, but secretly for fear of the
Jews, besought Pilate that he might take away
the body of Jesus: and Pilate gave *him* leave. He
came therefore, and took the body of Jesus.
39 And there came also Nicodemus, (which at the
first came to Jesus by night,) and brought a mix-

Living Bible

their bodies could be taken down. 32 So the
soldiers came and broke the legs of the two men
crucified with Jesus; 33 but when they came to
him, they saw that he was dead already, so they
didn't break his. 34 However, one of the soldiers
pierced his side with a spear, and blood and
water flowed out. 35 I saw all this myself and
have given an accurate report so that you also
can believe.[g] 36, 37 The soldiers did this in fulfillment of the Scripture that says, "Not one of
his bones shall be broken," and, "They shall look
on him whom they pierced."
38 Afterwards Joseph of Arimathea, who had
been a secret disciple of Jesus for fear of the
Jewish leaders, boldly asked Pilate for permission to take Jesus' body down; and Pilate told
him to go ahead. So he came and took it away.
39 Nicodemus, the man who had come to Jesus at night,[h] came too, bringing a hundred

[g] Literally, "And he who has seen has borne witness, and his witness is true; and he knows what he says is true, that you also may believe." [h] See chapter 3.

Today's English Version

was especially holy. 32 So the soldiers went and
broke the legs of the first man and then of the
other man who had been put to death with Jesus. 33 But when they came to Jesus they saw
that he was already dead, so they did not break
his legs. 34 One of the soldiers, however, plunged
his spear into Jesus' side, and at once blood
and water poured out. 35 (The one who saw this
happen has spoken of it, so that you also may
believe. What he said is true, and he knows that
he speaks the truth.) 36 This was done to make
the scripture come true, "Not one of his bones
will be broken." 37 And there is another scripture that says, "People will look at him whom
they pierced."

The burial of Jesus

38 After this, Joseph, who was from the town
of Arimathea, asked Pilate if he could take Jesus' body. (Joseph was a follower of Jesus, but
in secret, because he was afraid of the Jewish
authorities.) Pilate told him he could have the
body, so Joseph went and took it away. 39 Nicodemus, who at first had gone to see Jesus at
night, went with Joseph, taking with him about

New International Version

taken down. 32 The soldiers therefore came and
broke the legs of the first man who had been
crucified with Jesus, and then those of the other.
33 But when they came to Jesus and found that
he was already dead, they did not break his legs.
34 Instead, one of the soldiers pierced Jesus'
side with a spear, bringing a sudden flow of
blood and water. 35 The man who saw it has
given testimony, and his testimony is true. He
knows that he tells the truth, and he testifies so
that you also may have faith. 36 These things
happened so that the scripture would be fulfilled: "Not one of his bones will be broken,"[w]
37 and, as another scripture says, "They will look
on the one they have pierced."[x]

The burial of Jesus

38 Later, Joseph of Arimathea asked Pilate
for the body of Jesus. Now Joseph was a disciple of Jesus, but secretly because he feared the
Jews. With Pilate's permission, he came and
took the body. 39 He was accompanied by Nicodemus, the man who earlier had visited Jesus at
night. Nicodemus brought a mixture of myrrh

[w] Exodus 12:46; Num. 9:12; Psalm 34:20. [x] Zech. 12:10.

Phillips Modern English

and the bodies removed. So the soldiers went and broke the legs of the first man and of the other who was crucified with Jesus. But when they came to him, they saw that he was dead already and they did not break his legs. But one of the soldiers pierced his side with a spear, and at once there was an outrush of blood and water. And the man who saw this is our witness: his evidence is true. He is certain that he is speaking the truth, so that you may believe as well. For this happened to fulfil the scripture,

A bone of him shall not be broken.

And again another scripture says—

They shall look on him whom they pierced.

After it was all over, Joseph (who came from Arimathaea and was a disciple of Jesus, though secretly for fear of the Jews) requested Pilate that he might take away Jesus' body, and Pilate gave him permission. So he came and took his body down. Nicodemus also, the man who had come to him at the beginning by night, arrived

Revised Standard Version

away. 32 So the soldiers came and broke the
legs of the first, and of the other who had been
crucified with him; 33 but when they came to
Jesus and saw that he was already dead, they
did not break his legs. 34 But one of the soldiers pierced his side with a spear, and at once
there came out blood and water. 35 He who saw
it has borne witness—his testimony is true, and
he knows that he tells the truth—that you also
may believe. 36 For these things took place that
the scripture might be fulfilled, "Not a bone of
him shall be broken." 37 And again another
scripture says, "They shall look on him whom
they have pierced."
38 After this Joseph of Arimathea, who was
a disciple of Jesus, but secretly, for fear of the
Jews, asked Pilate that he might take away the
body of Jesus, and Pilate gave him leave. So he
came and took away his body. 39 Nicodemus
also, who had at first come to him by night,

Jerusalem Bible

legs broken[z] and the bodies taken away. 32 Consequently the soldiers came and broke the legs
of the first man who had been crucified with him
and then of the other. 33 When they came to
Jesus, they found he was already dead, and so
instead of breaking his legs 34 one of the soldiers
pierced his side with a lance; and immediately
there came out blood and water. 35 This is the
evidence of one who saw it—trustworthy evidence, and he knows he speaks the truth—and
he gives it so that you may believe as well.
36 Because all this happened to fulfill the words
of scripture:

Not one bone of his will be broken,[a]

37 and again, in another place scripture says:

They will look on the one whom they have pierced.[b]

The burial

38 After this, Joseph of Arimathaea, who was
a disciple of Jesus—though a secret one because
he was afraid of the Jews—asked Pilate to let
him remove the body of Jesus. Pilate gave permission, so they came and took it away. 39 Nicodemus came as well—the same one who had
first come to Jesus at nighttime—and he brought

[z] To hasten death. [a] Two texts are here combined: Ps. 34:20 and Ex. 12:46. The allusion is both to God protecting the good man, and to the ritual for preparing the Passover lamb. [b] Zc. 12:10.

New English Bible

and the bodies taken down. The soldiers accordingly came to the first of his fellow-victims and to the second, and broke their legs; but when they came to Jesus, they found that he was already dead, so they did not break his legs. But one of the soldiers stabbed his side with a lance, and at once there was a flow of blood and water. This is vouched for by an eyewitness, whose evidence is to be trusted. He knows that he speaks the truth, so that you too may believe; for this happened in fulfilment of the text of Scripture: 'No bone of his shall be broken.' And another text says, 'They shall look on him whom they pierced.'

After that, Pilate was approached by Joseph of Arimathaea, a disciple of Jesus, but a secret disciple for fear of the Jews, who[a] asked to be allowed to remove the body of Jesus. Pilate gave the permission; so Joseph came and took the body away. He was joined by Nicodemus (the man who had first visited Jesus by night), who

[a] *Or* of Arimathaea. He was a disciple of Jesus, but had gone into hiding for fear of the Jews. He now . . .

King James Version

ture of myrrh and aloes, about a hundred pound *weight.* 40 Then took they the body of Jesus, and wound it in linen clothes with the spices, as the manner of the Jews is to bury. 41 Now in the place where he was crucified there was a garden; and in the garden a new sepulchre, wherein was never man yet laid. 42 There laid they Jesus therefore because of the Jews' preparation *day;* for the sepulchre was nigh at hand.

20 The first *day* of the week cometh Mary Magdalene early, when it was yet dark, unto the sepulchre, and seeth the stone taken away from the sepulchre. 2 Then she runneth, and cometh to Simon Peter, and to the other disciple, whom Jesus loved, and saith unto them, They have taken away the Lord out of the sepulchre, and we know not where they have laid him. 3 Peter therefore went forth, and that other disciple, and came to the sepulchre. 4 So they ran both together: and the other disciple did outrun Peter, and came first to the sepulchre. 5 And he stooping down, *and looking in,* saw the linen clothes lying; yet went he not in. 6 Then cometh Simon Peter following him, and went into the sepulchre, and seeth the linen clothes

Living Bible

pounds of embalming ointment made from myrrh and aloes. 40 Together they wrapped Jesus' body in a long linen cloth saturated with the spices, as is the Jewish custom of burial. 41 The place of crucifixion was near a grove of trees,[i] where there was a new tomb, never used before. 42 And so, because of the need for haste before the Sabbath, and because the tomb was close at hand, they laid him there.

20 Early Sunday[a] morning, while it was still dark, Mary Magdalene came to the tomb and found that the stone was rolled aside from the entrance.

2 She ran and found Simon Peter and me[b] and said, "They have taken the Lord's body out of the tomb, and I don't know where they have put him!"

3, 4 We[c] ran to the tomb to see; I[d] outran Peter and got there first, 5 and stooped and looked in and saw the linen cloth lying there, but I didn't go in. 6 Then Simon Peter arrived and went on inside. He also noticed the cloth

[*i*] Literally "a garden." [*a*] Literally, "on the first day of the week." [*b*] Literally, "the other disciple whom Jesus loved." [*c*] Literally, "Peter and the other disciple." [*d*] Literally, "the other disciple also, who came first."

Today's English Version

one hundred pounds of spices, a mixture of myrrh and aloes. 40 The two men took Jesus' body and wrapped it in linen cloths with the spices; for this is how the Jews prepare a body for burial. 41 There was a garden in the place where Jesus had been put to death, and in it there was a new tomb where no one had ever been buried. 42 Since it was the day before the Jewish Sabbath, and because the tomb was close by, they placed Jesus there.

The empty tomb

20 Early on Sunday morning, while it was still dark, Mary Magdalene went to the tomb and saw that the stone had been taken away from the entrance. 2 She ran and went to Simon Peter and the other disciple, whom Jesus loved, and told them, "They have taken the Lord from the tomb and we don't know where they have put him!"

3 Then Peter and the other disciple left and went to the tomb. 4 The two of them were running, but the other disciple ran faster than Peter and reached the tomb first. 5 He bent over and saw the linen cloths, but he did not go in. 6 Behind him came Simon Peter, and he went straight into the tomb. He saw the linen cloths lying there

New International Version

and aloes, about seventy-five pounds. 40 Taking Jesus' body, the two of them wrapped it, with the spices, in strips of linen. This was in accordance with Jewish burial customs. 41 At the place where Jesus was crucified, there was a garden, and in the garden a new tomb, in which no one had ever been laid. 42 Because it was the Jewish day of Preparation and since the tomb was nearby, they laid Jesus there.

The empty tomb

20 Early on the first day of the week, while it was still dark, Mary of Magdala went to the tomb and saw that the stone had been removed from the entrance. 2 So she came running to Simon Peter and the other disciple, the one Jesus loved, and said, "They have taken the Lord out of the tomb, and we don't know where they have put him!"

3 So Peter and the other disciple started for the tomb. 4 Both were running, but the other disciple outran Peter, and reached the tomb first. 5 He bent over and looked in at the strips of linen lying there but did not go in. 6 Then Simon Peter, who was behind him, arrived and went into the tomb. He saw the strips of linen

Phillips Modern English

bringing a mixture of myrrh and aloes, weighing about a hundred pounds. So they took his body and wound it round with linen strips with the spices, according to the Jewish custom of preparing a body for burial. In the place where he was crucified, there was a garden containing a new tomb in which nobody had yet been laid. Because it was the preparation day and because the tomb was conveniently near, they laid Jesus in this tomb.

20.1 The first day of the week: the risen Lord

But on the first day of the week, Mary of Magdala arrived at the tomb, very early in the morning, while it was still dark, and noticed that the stone had been taken away from the tomb. At this she ran, found Simon Peter and the other disciple whom Jesus loved, and told them, "They have taken the Lord out of the tomb and we don't know where they have laid him."

Peter and the other disciple set off at once for the tomb, the two of them running together. The other disciple ran faster than Peter and was the first to arrive at the tomb. He stooped and looked inside and saw the linen cloths lying there but did not go in himself. Hard on his heels came Simon Peter and went straight into the tomb. He noticed that the linen cloths were

Revised Standard Version

came bringing a mixture of myrrh and aloes,
about a hundred pounds' weight. 40 They took
the body of Jesus, and bound it in linen cloths
with the spices, as is the burial custom of the
Jews. 41 Now in the place where he was crucified there was a garden, and in the garden a
new tomb where no one had ever been laid.
42 So because of the Jewish day of Preparation,
as the tomb was close at hand, they laid Jesus
there.

20 Now on the first day of the week Mary
Magdalene came to the tomb early, while
it was still dark, and saw that the stone had
been taken away from the tomb. 2 So she ran,
and went to Simon Peter and the other disciple, the one whom Jesus loved, and said to them,
"They have taken the Lord out of the tomb,
and we do not know where they have laid him."
3 Peter then came out with the other disciple,
and they went toward the tomb. 4 They both
ran, but the other disciple outran Peter and
reached the tomb first; 5 and stooping to look
in, he saw the linen cloths lying there, but he
did not go in. 6 Then Simon Peter came, following him, and went into the tomb; he saw

Jerusalem Bible

a mixture of myrrh and aloes, weighing about a
hundred pounds. 40 They took the body of Jesus
and wrapped it with the spices in linen cloths,
following the Jewish burial custom. 41 At the
place where he had been crucified there was a
garden, and in this garden a new tomb in which
no one had yet been buried. 42 Since it was the
Jewish Day of Preparation and the tomb was
near at hand, they laid Jesus there.

VIII. The day of Christ's resurrection

The empty tomb

20 It was very early on the first day of the
week and still dark, when Mary of Magdala came to the tomb. She saw that the stone
had been moved away from the tomb 2 and came
running to Simon Peter and the other disciple,
the one Jesus loved. "They have taken the Lord
out of the tomb," she said, "and we don't know
where they have put him."
3 So Peter set out with the other disciple to
go to the tomb. 4 They ran together, but the
other disciple, running faster than Peter, reached
the tomb first; 5 he bent down and saw the linen
cloths lying on the ground, but did not go in.
6 Simon Peter who was following now came
up, went right into the tomb, saw the linen

New English Bible

brought with him a mixture of myrrh and aloes, more than half a hundredweight. They took the body of Jesus and wrapped it, with the spices, in strips of linen cloth according to Jewish burial-customs. Now at the place where he had been crucified there was a garden, and in the garden a new tomb, not yet used for burial. There, because the tomb was near at hand and it was the eve of the Jewish Sabbath, they laid Jesus.

20 Early on the Sunday morning, while it was still dark, Mary of Magdala came to the tomb. She saw that the stone had been moved away from the entrance, and ran to Simon Peter and the other disciple, the one whom Jesus loved. 'They have taken the Lord out of his tomb,' she cried, 'and we do not know where they have laid him.' So Peter and the other set out and made their way to the tomb. They were running side by side, but the other disciple outran Peter and reached the tomb first. He peered in and saw the linen wrappings lying there, but did not enter. Then Simon Peter came up, following him, and he went into the tomb. He saw

King James Version

lie, 7And the napkin, that was about his head, not lying with the linen clothes, but wrapped together in a place by itself. 8 Then went in also that other disciple, which came first to the sepulchre, and he saw, and believed. 9 For as yet they knew not the Scripture, that he must rise again from the dead. 10 Then the disciples went away again unto their own home.

11 But Mary stood without at the sepulchre weeping: and as she wept, she stooped down, *and looked* into the sepulchre, 12And seeth two angels in white sitting, the one at the head, and the other at the feet, where the body of Jesus had lain. 13And they say unto her, Woman, why weepest thou? She saith unto them, Because they have taken away my Lord, and I know not where they have laid him. 14And when she had thus said, she turned herself back, and saw Jesus standing, and knew not that it was Jesus. 15 Jesus saith unto her, Woman, why weepest thou? whom seekest thou? She, supposing him to be the gardener, saith unto him, Sir, if thou have borne him hence, tell me where thou hast laid him, and I will take him away. 16 Jesus saith unto her, Mary. She turned herself, and saith unto him, Rabboni: which is to say, Master. 17 Jesus saith unto her, Touch me not; for I am not yet ascended to my Father: but go to my brethren,

Living Bible

lying there, 7 while the swath that had covered Jesus' head was rolled up in a bundle and was lying at the side. 8 Then I went in too, and saw, and believed [that he had risen[e]]—9 for until then we hadn't realized that the Scriptures said he would come to life again!

10 We[f] went on home, 11 and by that time Mary had returned to the tomb[e] and was standing outside crying. And as she wept, she stooped and looked in 12 and saw two white-robed angels sitting at the head and foot of the place where the body of Jesus had been lying.

13 "Why are you crying?" the angels asked her.

"Because they have taken away my Lord," she replied, "and I don't know where they have put him."

14 She glanced over her shoulder and saw someone standing behind her. It was Jesus, but she didn't recognize him!

15 "Why are you crying?" he asked her. "Whom are you looking for?"

She thought he was the gardener. "Sir," she said, "if you have taken him away, tell me where you have put him, and I will go and get him."

16 "Mary!" Jesus said. She turned toward him. "Master!" she exclaimed.

17 "Don't touch me," he cautioned, "for I haven't yet ascended to the Father. But go find

[e] Implied. [f] Literally, "the disciples."

Today's English Version

7 and the cloth which had been around Jesus' head. It was not lying with the linen cloths but was rolled up by itself. 8 Then the other disciple, who had reached the tomb first, also went in; he saw and believed. 9 (They still did not understand the scripture which said that he must rise from death.) 10 Then the disciples went back home.

Jesus appears to Mary Magdalene

11 Mary stood crying outside the tomb. Still crying, she bent over and looked in the tomb, 12 and saw two angels there, dressed in white, sitting where the body of Jesus had been, one at the head, the other at the feet. 13 "Woman, why are you crying?" they asked her.

She answered, "They have taken my Lord away, and I do not know where they have put him!"

14 When she had said this, she turned around and saw Jesus standing there; but she did not know that it was Jesus. 15 "Woman, why are you crying?" Jesus asked her. "Who is it that you are looking for?"

She thought he was the gardener, so she said to him, "If you took him away, sir, tell me where you have put him, and I will go and get him."

16 Jesus said to her, "Mary!"

She turned toward him and said in Hebrew, "Rabboni!" (This means "Teacher.")

17 "Do not hold on to me," Jesus told her, "because I have not yet gone back up to the

New International Version

lying there, 7 as well as the burial cloth that had been around Jesus' head. The cloth was folded up by itself, separate from the linen. 8 Finally the other disciple, who had reached the tomb first, also went inside. He saw and believed. 9 (They still did not understand from Scripture that Jesus had to rise from the dead.)

Jesus appears to Mary of Magdala

10 Then the disciples went back to their homes, 11 but Mary stood outside the tomb crying. As she wept, she bent over to look into the tomb 12 and saw two angels in white, seated where Jesus' body had been, one at the head and the other at the foot.

13 They asked her, "Woman, why are you crying?"

"They have taken my Lord away," she said, "and I don't know where they have put him." 14At this, she turned around and saw Jesus standing there, but she did not realize that it was Jesus.

15 "Woman," he said, "why are you crying? Who is it you are looking for?"

Thinking he was the gardener, she said, "Sir, if you have carried him away, tell me where you have put him, and I will get him."

16 Jesus said to her, "Mary."

She turned toward him and cried out in Aramaic, "Rabboni!" (which means Teacher).

17 Jesus said, "Do not hold on to me, for I have not yet returned to the Father. Go instead

Phillips Modern English

lying there, and that the handkerchief, which had been round Jesus' head, was not lying with the linen cloths but was rolled up by itself, a little way apart. Then the other disciple, who was the first to arrive at the tomb, came inside as well, saw what had happened and believed. (They did not yet understand the scripture which said that he must rise from the dead.) So the disciples went back again to their homes.

But Mary stood just outside the tomb, and she was crying. And as she cried, she looked into the tomb and saw two angels in white who sat, one at the head and the other at the foot of the place where the body of Jesus had lain.

The angels spoke to her, "Why are you crying?" they asked.

"Because they have taken away my Lord, and I don't know where they have laid him!" she said.

With these words she turned and noticed Jesus standing there, without realising that it was Jesus.

"Why are you crying?" said Jesus to her. "Who are you looking for?"

She, supposing that he was the gardener, said, "Oh, sir, if you have carried him away, please tell me where you have laid him and I will take him away."

Jesus said to her, "Mary!"

At this she turned right round and said to him, in Hebrew, "Master!"

"No!" said Jesus, "do not hold me now. I have not yet gone up to the Father. Go and

Revised Standard Version

the linen cloths lying, 7 and the napkin, which
had been on his head, not lying with the linen
cloths but rolled up in a place by itself. 8 Then
the other disciple, who reached the tomb first,
also went in, and he saw and believed; 9 for as
yet they did not know the scripture, that he
must rise from the dead. 10 Then the disciples went back to their homes.
11 But Mary stood weeping outside the tomb,
and as she wept she stooped to look into the
tomb; 12 and she saw two angels in white, sitting where the body of Jesus had lain, one at
the head and one at the feet. 13 They said to
her, "Woman, why are you weeping?" She said
to them, "Because they have taken away my
Lord, and I do not know where they have laid
him." 14 Saying this, she turned round and saw
Jesus standing, but she did not know that it
was Jesus. 15 Jesus said to her, "Woman, why
are you weeping? Whom do you seek?" Supposing him to be the gardener, she said to him,
"Sir, if you have carried him away, tell me
where you have laid him, and I will take him
away." 16 Jesus said to her, "Mary." She turned
and said to him in Hebrew, "Rabboni!" (which
means Teacher). 17 Jesus said to her, "Do not
hold me, for I have not yet ascended to the
Father; but go to my brethren and say to them,

Jerusalem Bible

cloths on the ground, 7 and also the cloth that
had been over his head; this was not with the
linen cloths but rolled up in a place by itself.
8 Then the other disciple who had reached the
tomb first also went in; he saw and he believed.
9 Till this moment they had failed to understand
the teaching of scripture, that he must rise from
the dead. 10 The disciples then went home again.

The appearance to Mary of Magdala

11 Meanwhile Mary stayed outside near the
tomb, weeping. Then, still weeping, she stooped
to look inside, 12 and saw two angels in white
sitting where the body of Jesus had been, one at
the head, the other at the feet. 13 They said,
"Woman, why are you weeping?" "They have
taken my Lord away," she replied, "and I don't
know where they have put him." 14 As she said
this she turned around and saw Jesus standing
there, though she did not recognize him. 15 Jesus
said, "Woman, why are you weeping? Who are
you looking for?" Supposing him to be the gardener, she said, "Sir, if you have taken him
away, tell me where you have put him, and I
will go and remove him." 16 Jesus said, "Mary!"
She knew him then and said to him in Hebrew,
"Rabbuni!"—which means Master. 17 Jesus said
to her, "Do not cling to me, because I have not
yet ascended to the Father. But go and find the

New English Bible

the linen wrappings lying, and the napkin which had been over his head, not lying with the wrappings but rolled together in a place by itself. Then the disciple who had reached the tomb first went in too, and he saw and believed; until then they had not understood the scriptures, which showed that he must rise from the dead.

So the disciples went home again; but Mary stood at the tomb outside, weeping. As she wept, she peered into the tomb; and she saw two angels in white sitting there, one at the head, and one at the feet, where the body of Jesus had lain. They said to her, 'Why are you weeping?' She answered, 'They have taken my Lord away, and I do not know where they have laid him.' With these words she turned round and saw Jesus standing there, but did not recognize him. Jesus said to her, 'Why are you weeping? Who is it you are looking for?' Thinking it was the gardener, she said, 'If it is you, sir, who removed him, tell me where you have laid him, and I will take him away.' Jesus said, 'Mary!' She turned to him and said, 'Rabbuni!' (which is Hebrew for 'My Master'). Jesus said, 'Do not cling to me,[b] for I have not yet ascended to the Father. But go to my brothers, and tell

[b] *Or* Touch me no more.

King James Version

and say unto them, I ascend unto my Father, and
your Father; and *to* my God, and your God.
18 Mary Magdalene came and told the disciples
that she had seen the Lord, and *that* he had
spoken these things unto her.
19 Then the same day at evening, being the
first *day* of the week, when the doors were shut
where the disciples were assembled for fear of
the Jews, came Jesus and stood in the midst, and
saith unto them, Peace *be* unto you. 20 And
when he had so said, he shewed unto them *his*
hands and his side. Then were the disciples glad,
when they saw the Lord. 21 Then said Jesus to
them again, Peace *be* unto you: as *my* Father
hath sent me, even so send I you. 22 And when
he had said this, he breathed on *them,* and saith
unto them, Receive ye the Holy Ghost: 23 Whosesoever sins ye remit, they are remitted unto
them; *and* whosesoever *sins* ye retain, they are
retained.
24 But Thomas, one of the twelve, called
Didymus, was not with them when Jesus came.
25 The other disciples therefore said unto him,
We have seen the Lord. But he said unto them,

Living Bible

my brothers and tell them that I ascend to my
Father and your Father, my God and your God."
18 Mary Magdalene found the disciples and
told them, "I have seen the Lord!" Then she
gave them his message.
19 That evening the disciples were meeting
behind locked doors, in fear of the Jewish leaders, when suddenly Jesus was standing there
among them! After greeting them, 20 he showed
them his hands and side. And how wonderful was
their joy as they saw their Lord!
21 He spoke to them again and said, "As the
Father has sent me, even so I am sending you."
22 Then he breathed on them and told them, "Receive the Holy Spirit. 23 If you forgive anyone's
sins, they are forgiven. If you refuse to forgive
them, they are unforgiven."
24 One of the disciples, Thomas, "The Twin,"
was not there at the time with the others.
25 When they kept telling him, "We have seen
the Lord," he replied, "I won't believe it unless

Today's English Version

Father. But go to my brothers and tell them for
me, 'I go back up to him who is my Father and
your Father, my God and your God.' "
18 So Mary Magdalene went and told the
disciples that she had seen the Lord, and that he
had told her this.

Jesus appears to his disciples

19 It was late that Sunday evening, and the
disciples were gathered together behind locked
doors, because they were afraid of the Jewish
authorities. Then Jesus came and stood among
them. "Peace be with you," he said. 20 After saying this, he showed them his hands and his side.
The disciples were filled with joy at seeing the
Lord. 21 Then Jesus said to them again, "Peace
be with you. As the Father sent me, so I send
you." 22 He said this, and then he breathed on
them and said, "Receive the Holy Spirit. 23 If
you forgive men's sins, they are forgiven; if you
do not forgive them, they are not forgiven."

Jesus and Thomas

24 One of the twelve disciples, Thomas (called
the Twin), was not with them when Jesus came.
25 So the other disciples told him, "We saw the
Lord!"
Thomas said to them, "If I do not see the scars

New International Version

to my brothers and tell them, 'I am returning to
my Father and your Father, to my God and
your God.' " 18 Mary of Magdala went to the
disciples with the news that she had seen the
Lord and that he had told her this.

Jesus appears to his disciples

19 On the evening of that first day of the
week, when the disciples were together, with the
doors locked for fear of the Jews, Jesus came
and stood among them and said, "Peace be with
you!" 20 After he said this, he showed them his
hands and side. The disciples were overjoyed
when they saw the Lord.
21 Again Jesus said, "Peace be with you! As
the Father has sent me, I am sending you."
22 And with that he breathed on them and said,
"Receive the Holy Spirit. 23 If you forgive anyone his sins, they are forgiven; if you do not forgive them, they are not forgiven."

Jesus appears to Thomas

24 Now Thomas (called Didymus), one of
the Twelve, was not with the disciples when Jesus came. 25 When the other disciples told him
that they had seen the Lord, he declared, "Un-

Phillips Modern English

tell my brothers that I am going up to my Father and your Father, to my God and your God."

And Mary of Magdala went off to the disciples, with the news, "I have seen the Lord!", and she told them what he had said to her.

In the evening of that first day of the week, the disciples had met together with the doors locked for fear of the Jews. Jesus came and stood right in the middle of them and said, "Peace be with you!"

Then he showed them his hands and his side, and when they saw the Lord the disciples were overjoyed.

Jesus said to them again, "Yes, peace be with you! Just as the Father sent me, so I am now going to send you."

And then he breathed upon them and said, "Receive the Holy Spirit. If you forgive any men's sins, they are forgiven, and if you hold them unforgiven, they are unforgiven."

20.24 The risen Jesus and Thomas

But one of the twelve, Thomas (called the Twin), was not with them when Jesus came. The other disciples kept on telling him, "We have seen the Lord," but he replied, "Unless I see in

Revised Standard Version

I am ascending to my Father and your Father, to my God and your God." 18 Mary Magdalene went and said to the disciples, "I have
seen the Lord"; and she told them that he had
said these things to her.
19 On the evening of that day, the first day
of the week, the doors being shut where the
disciples were, for fear of the Jews, Jesus came
and stood among them and said to them, "Peace
be with you." 20 When he had said this, he
showed them his hands and his side. Then the
disciples were glad when they saw the Lord.
21 Jesus said to them again, "Peace be with you.
As the Father has sent me, even so I send you."
22And when he had said this, he breathed on
them, and said to them, "Receive the Holy
Spirit. 23 If you forgive the sins of any, they
are forgiven; if you retain the sins of any, they
are retained."
24 Now Thomas, one of the twelve, called
the Twin, was not with them when Jesus came.
25 So the other disciples told him, "We have
seen the Lord." But he said to them, "Unless I

Jerusalem Bible

brothers, and tell them: I am ascending to my
Father and your Father, to my God and your
God." 18 So Mary of Magdala went and told
the disciples that she had seen the Lord and that
he had said these things to her.

Appearances to the disciples

19 In the evening of that same day, the first
day of the week, the doors were closed in the
room where the disciples were, for fear of the
Jews. Jesus came and stood among them. He
said to them, "Peace be with you," 20 and
showed them his hands and his side. The disciples were filled with joy when they saw the
Lord, 21 and he said to them again, "Peace be
with you.

"As the Father sent me,
so am I sending you."

22After saying this he breathed on them and
said:

"Receive the Holy Spirit.
23 For those whose sins you forgive,
they are forgiven;
for those whose sins you retain,
they are retained."

24 Thomas, called the Twin, who was one of
the Twelve, was not with them when Jesus came.
25 When the disciples said, "We have seen the
Lord," he answered, "Unless I see the holes that

New English Bible

them that I am now ascending[c] to my Father and your Father, my God and your God.' Mary of Magdala went to the disciples with her news: 'I have seen the Lord!' she said, and gave them his message.

Late that Sunday evening, when the disciples were together behind locked doors, for fear of the Jews, Jesus came and stood among them. 'Peace be with you!' he said, and then showed them his hands and his side. So when the disciples saw the Lord, they were filled with joy. Jesus repeated, 'Peace be with you!', and said, 'As the Father sent me, so I send you.' Then he breathed on them, saying, 'Receive the Holy Spirit! If you forgive any man's sins, they stand forgiven; if you pronounce them unforgiven, unforgiven they remain.'

One of the Twelve, Thomas, that is 'the Twin', was not with the rest when Jesus came. So the disciples told him, 'We have seen the Lord.' He said, 'Unless I see the mark of the nails on his

[c] *Or* I am going to ascend . . .

King James Version

Except I shall see in his hands the print of the nails, and put my finger into the print of the nails, and thrust my hand into his side, I will not believe.

26 And after eight days again his disciples were within, and Thomas with them: *then* came Jesus, the doors being shut, and stood in the midst, and said, Peace *be* unto you. 27 Then saith he to Thomas, Reach hither thy finger, and behold my hands; and reach hither thy hand, and thrust *it* into my side; and be not faithless, but believing. 28 And Thomas answered and said unto him, My Lord and my God. 29 Jesus saith unto him, Thomas, because thou hast seen me, thou hast believed: blessed *are* they that have not seen, and *yet* have believed.

30 And many other signs truly did Jesus in the presence of his disciples, which are not written in this book: 31 But these are written, that ye might believe that Jesus is the Christ, the Son of God; and that believing ye might have life through his name.

Living Bible

I see the nail wounds in his hands—and put my fingers into them—and place my hand into his side."

26 Eight days later the disciples were together again, and this time Thomas was with them. The doors were locked; but suddenly, as before, Jesus was standing among them and greeting them.

27 Then he said to Thomas, "Put your finger into my hands. Put your hand into my side. Don't be faithless any longer. Believe!"

28 "My Lord and my God!" Thomas said.

29 Then Jesus told him, "You believe because you have seen me. But blessed are those who haven't seen me and believe anyway."

30, 31 Jesus' disciples saw him do many other miracles besides the ones told about in this book, but these are recorded so that you will believe that he is the Messiah, the Son of God, and that believing in him you will have life.

Today's English Version

of the nails in his hands, and put my finger on those scars, and my hand in his side, I will not believe."

26 A week later the disciples were together indoors again, and Thomas was with them. The doors were locked, but Jesus came and stood among them and said, "Peace be with you." 27 Then he said to Thomas, "Put your finger here, and look at my hands; then stretch out your hand and put it in my side. Stop your doubting, and believe!"

28 Thomas answered him, "My Lord and my God!"

29 Jesus said to him, "Do you believe because you see me? How happy are those who believe without seeing me!"

The purpose of this book

30 Jesus did many other mighty works in his disciples' presence which are not written down in this book. 31 These have been written that you may believe that Jesus is the Messiah, the Son of God, and that through this faith you may have life in his name.

New International Version

less I see the nail marks in his hands and put my finger where the nails were, and put my hand into his side, I will not believe it."

26 A week later his disciples were in the house again, and Thomas was with them. Though the doors were locked, Jesus came and stood among them, and said, "Peace be with you!" 27 Then he said to Thomas, "Put your finger here; see my hands. Reach out your hand and put it into my side. Stop doubting and believe."

28 Thomas said to him, "My Lord and my God!"

29 Then Jesus told him, "Because you have seen me, you have believed; blessed are those who have not seen and yet have believed."

30 Jesus did many other miraculous signs in the presence of his disciples, which are not recorded in this book. 31 But these are written that you may believe[y] that Jesus is the Christ, the Son of God, and that by believing you may have life in his name.

[y] Or *that you may continue to believe . . .*

Phillips Modern English

his own hands the mark of the nails, and put my finger where the nails were, and put my hand into his side, I will never believe!"

Just over a week later, the disciples were indoors again and Thomas was with them. The doors were locked, but Jesus came and stood in the middle of them and said, "Peace be with you!"

Then he said to Thomas, "Put your finger here—look, here are my hands. Take your hand and put it in my side. You must not doubt, but believe."

"My Lord and my God!" cried Thomas.

"Is it because you have seen me that you believe?" Jesus said to him. "Happy are those who have never seen me and yet have believed!"

Jesus gave a great many other signs in the presence of his disciples which are not recorded in this book. But these have been written so that you may believe that Jesus is Christ, the Son of God, and that in that faith you may have life through his name.

Revised Standard Version

see in his hands the print of the nails, and place
my finger in the mark of the nails, and place
my hand in his side, I will not believe."
26 Eight days later, his disciples were again
in the house, and Thomas was with them. The
doors were shut, but Jesus came and stood
among them, and said, "Peace be with you."
27 Then he said to Thomas, "Put your finger
here, and see my hands; and put out your
hand, and place it in my side; do not be faithless, but believing." 28 Thomas answered him,
"My Lord and my God!" 29 Jesus said to him,
"Have you believed because you have seen me?
Blessed are those who have not seen and yet
believe."

30 Now Jesus did many other signs in the
presence of the disciples, which are not written
in this book; 31 but these are written that you
may believe that Jesus is the Christ, the Son
of God, and that believing you may have life
in his name.

Jerusalem Bible

the nails made in his hands and can put my
finger into the holes they made, and unless I can
put my hand into his side, I refuse to believe."
26 Eight days later the disciples were in the
house again and Thomas was with them. The
doors were closed, but Jesus came in and stood
among them. "Peace be with you," he said.
27 Then he spoke to Thomas, "Put your finger
here; look, here are my hands. Give me your
hand; put it into my side. Doubt no longer but
believe." 28 Thomas replied, "My Lord and my
God!" 29 Jesus said to him:

"You believe because you can see me.
Happy are those who have not seen and yet
believe."

Conclusion

30 There were many other signs that Jesus
worked and the disciples saw, but they are not
recorded in this book. 31 These are recorded so
that you may believe that Jesus is the Christ, the
son of God, and that believing this you may
have life through his name.

New English Bible

hands, unless I put my finger into the place where the nails were, and my hand into his side, I will not believe it.'

A week later his disciples were again in the room, and Thomas was with them. Although the doors were locked, Jesus came and stood among them, saying, 'Peace be with you!' Then he said to Thomas, 'Reach your finger here; see my hands. Reach your hand here and put it into my side. Be unbelieving no longer, but believe.' Thomas said, 'My Lord and my God!' Jesus said, 'Because you have seen me you have found faith. Happy are they who never saw me and yet have found faith.'

There were indeed many other signs that Jesus performed in the presence of his disciples, which are not recorded in this book. Those here written have been recorded in order that you may hold the faith[a] that Jesus is the Christ, the Son of God, and that through this faith you may possess life by his name.

[a] *Some witnesses read* that you may come to believe . . .

King James Version

21 After these things Jesus shewed himself
again to the disciples at the sea of Tiberias; and on this wise shewed he *himself.* 2 There
were together Simon Peter, and Thomas called
Didymus, and Nathanael of Cana in Galilee,
and the *sons* of Zebedee, and two other of his
disciples. 3 Simon Peter saith unto them, I go a
fishing. They say unto him, We also go with
thee. They went forth, and entered into a ship
immediately; and that night they caught nothing.
4 But when the morning was now come, Jesus
stood on the shore; but the disciples knew not
that it was Jesus. 5 Then Jesus saith unto them,
Children, have ye any meat? They answered him,
No. 6 And he said unto them, Cast the net on
the right side of the ship, and ye shall find. They
cast therefore, and now they were not able to
draw it for the multitude of fishes. 7 Therefore
that disciple whom Jesus loved saith unto Peter,
It is the Lord. Now when Simon Peter heard
that it was the Lord, he girt *his* fisher's coat
unto him, (for he was naked,) and did cast himself into the sea. 8 And the other disciples came
in a little ship, (for they were not far from
land, but as it were two hundred cubits,) dragging the net with fishes. 9 As soon then as they
were come to land, they saw a fire of coals

Living Bible

21 Later Jesus appeared again to the disciples
beside the Lake of Galilee. This is how it
happened:
2 A group of us were there—Simon Peter,
Thomas, "The Twin," Nathanael from Cana in
Galilee, my brother James and I [a] and two other
disciples.
3 Simon Peter said, "I'm going fishing."
"We'll come too," we all said. We did, but
caught nothing all night. 4 At dawn we saw a
man standing on the beach but couldn't see who
he was.
5 He called, "Any fish, boys?" [b]
"No," we replied.
6 Then he said, "Throw out your net on the
right-hand side of the boat, and you'll get
plenty of them!" So we did, and couldn't draw
in the net because of the weight of the fish, there
were so many!
7 Then I [c] said to Peter, "It is the Lord!" At
that, Simon Peter put on his tunic (for he was
stripped to the waist) and jumped into the
water [and swam ashore[d]]. 8 The rest of us
stayed in the boat and pulled the loaded net to
the beach, about 300 feet away. 9 When we got
there, we saw that a fire was kindled and fish
were frying over it, and there was bread.

[*a*] Literally, "the sons of Zebedee." [*b*] Literally, "children." [*c*] Literally, "that disciple therefore whom Jesus loved." [*d*] Implied.

Today's English Version

Jesus appears to seven disciples

21 After this, Jesus showed himself once
more to his disciples at Lake Tiberias.
This is how he did it. 2 Simon Peter, Thomas
(called the Twin), Nathanael (the one from
Cana in Galilee), the sons of Zebedee, and two
other disciples of Jesus were all together. 3 Simon
Peter said to the others, "I am going fishing."
"We will come with you," they told him. So
they went and got into the boat; but all that
night they did not catch a thing. 4 As the sun was
rising, Jesus stood at the water's edge, but the
disciples did not know that it was Jesus. 5 Then
he said to them, "Young men, haven't you caught
anything?"
"Not a thing," they answered.
6 He said to them, "Throw your net out on
the right side of the boat, and you will find
some." So they threw the net out, and could not
pull it back in, because they had caught so many
fish.
7 The disciple whom Jesus loved said to
Peter, "It is the Lord!" When Simon Peter
heard that it was the Lord, he wrapped his
outer garment around him (for he had taken
his clothes off) and jumped into the water. 8 The
other disciples came to shore in the boat, pulling
the net full of fish. They were not very far from
land, about a hundred yards away. 9 When they
stepped ashore they saw a charcoal fire there

New International Version

Jesus and the miraculous catch of fish

21 Afterward Jesus appeared again to his
disciples by the Sea of Tiberias. It happened this way: 2 Simon Peter, Thomas (called
Didymus), Nathanael from Cana in Galilee, the
sons of Zebedee, and two other disciples were
together. 3 "I'm going out to fish," Simon Peter
told them, and they said, "We'll go with you."
So they went out and got into the boat, but
that night they caught nothing.
4 Early in the morning, Jesus stood on the
shore, but the disciples did not realize that it was
Jesus.
5 He called out to them, "Friends, haven't
you caught any fish?"
"No," they answered.
6 He said, "Throw your net on the right side
of the boat and you will find some." When they
did, they were unable to haul the net in because
of the large number of fish.
7 Then the disciple whom Jesus loved said to
Peter, "It is the Lord!" As soon as Simon Peter
heard him say, "It is the Lord," he wrapped
his outer garment around him (for he had taken
it off) and jumped into the water. 8 The other
disciples followed in the boat, towing the net
full of fish, for they were not far from shore,
about a hundred yards. 9 When they landed,
they saw a fire of burning coals there with fish
on it, and some bread.

Phillips Modern English

21.1 The risen Jesus and Peter

Later on, Jesus showed himself again to his disciples on the shore of Lake Tiberias, and he did it in this way. Simon Peter, Thomas (called the Twin), Nathanael from Cana of Galilee, the sons of Zebedee and two other disciples were together, when Simon Peter said,

"I'm going fishing."

"All right," they replied, "we'll go with you."

So they went out and got into the boat and during the night caught nothing at all. But just as dawn began to break, Jesus stood there on the beach, although the disciples had no idea that it was Jesus.

"Have you caught anything, lads?" Jesus called out to them.

"No," they replied.

"Throw the net on the right side of the boat," said Jesus, "and you'll have a catch."

So they threw out the net and found that they were now not strong enough to pull it in because it was so full of fish! At this, the disciple that Jesus loved said to Peter, "It is the Lord!"

Hearing this, Peter slipped on his clothes, for he had been naked, and plunged into the sea. The other disciples followed in the boat, for they were only about a hundred yards from the shore, dragging in the net full of fish. When they had landed, they saw that a charcoal fire was burning, with a fish placed on it, and some bread.

Revised Standard Version

21 After this Jesus revealed himself again to the disciples by the Sea of Tiberias; and he revealed himself in this way. 2 Simon Peter, Thomas called the Twin, Nathanael of Cana in Galilee, the sons of Zebedee, and two others of his disciples were together. 3 Simon Peter said to them, "I am going fishing." They said to him, "We will go with you." They went out and got into the boat; but that night they caught nothing.

4 Just as day was breaking, Jesus stood on the beach; yet the disciples did not know that it was Jesus. 5 Jesus said to them, "Children, have you any fish?" They answered him, "No." 6 He said to them, "Cast the net on the right side of the boat, and you will find some." So they cast it, and now they were not able to haul it in, for the quantity of fish. 7 That disciple whom Jesus loved said to Peter, "It is the Lord!" When Simon Peter heard that it was the Lord, he put on his clothes, for he was stripped for work, and sprang into the sea. 8 But the other disciples came in the boat, dragging the net full of fish, for they were not far from the land, but about a hundred yards[m] off.

9 When they got out on land, they saw a charcoal fire there, with fish lying on it, and

[m] Greek *two hundred cubits.*

Jerusalem Bible

Appendix[c]

The appearance on the shore of Tiberias

21 Later on, Jesus showed himself again to the disciples. It was by the Sea of Tiberias, and it happened like this: 2 Simon Peter, Thomas called the Twin, Nathanael from Cana in Galilee, the sons of Zebedee and two more of his disciples were together. 3 Simon Peter said, "I'm going fishing." They replied, "We'll come with you." They went out and got into the boat but caught nothing that night.

4 It was light by now and there stood Jesus on the shore, though the disciples did not realize that it was Jesus. 5 Jesus called out, "Have you caught anything, friends?" And when they answered, "No," 6 he said, "Throw the net out to starboard and you'll find something." So they dropped the net, and there were so many fish that they could not haul it in. 7 The disciple Jesus loved said to Peter, "It is the Lord." At these words "It is the Lord," Simon Peter, who had practically nothing on, wrapped his cloak around him and jumped into the water. 8 The other disciples came on in the boat, towing the net and the fish; they were only about a hundred yards from land.

9 As soon as they came ashore they saw that there was some bread there, and a charcoal fire

[c] Added either by the evangelist or by a disciple of his.

New English Bible

21 Some time later, Jesus showed himself to his disciples once again, by the Sea of Tiberias; and in this way. Simon Peter and Thomas 'the Twin' were together with Nathanael of Cana-in-Galilee. The sons of Zebedee and two other disciples were also there. Simon Peter said, 'I am going out fishing.' 'We will go with you', said the others. So they started and got into the boat. But that night they caught nothing.

Morning came, and there stood Jesus on the beach, but the disciples did not know that it was Jesus. He called out to them, 'Friends, have you caught anything?' They answered 'No.' He said, 'Shoot the net to starboard, and you will make a catch.' They did so, and found they could not haul the net aboard, there were so many fish in it. Then the disciple whom Jesus loved said to Peter, 'It is the Lord!' When Simon Peter heard that, he wrapped his coat about him (for he had stripped) and plunged into the sea. The rest of them came on in the boat, towing the net full of fish; for they were not far from land, only about a hundred yards.

When they came ashore, they saw a charcoal fire there, with fish laid on it, and some bread.

King James Version

there, and fish laid thereon, and bread. 10 Jesus
saith unto them, Bring of the fish which ye have
now caught. 11 Simon Peter went up, and drew
the net to land full of great fishes, a hundred
and fifty and three: and for all there were so
many, yet was not the net broken. 12 Jesus saith
unto them, Come *and* dine. And none of the
disciples durst ask him, Who art thou? knowing
that it was the Lord. 13 Jesus then cometh, and
taketh bread, and giveth them, and fish likewise.
14 This is now the third time that Jesus shewed
himself to his disciples, after that he was risen
from the dead.
15 So when they had dined, Jesus saith to
Simon Peter, Simon, *son* of Jonas, lovest thou
me more than these? He saith unto him, Yea,
Lord; thou knowest that I love thee. He saith
unto him, Feed my lambs. 16 He saith to him
again the second time, Simon, *son* of Jonas,
lovest thou me? He saith unto him, Yea, Lord;
thou knowest that I love thee. He saith unto him,
Feed my sheep. 17 He saith unto him the third
time, Simon, *son* of Jonas, lovest thou me?
Peter was grieved because he said unto him the
third time, Lovest thou me? And he said unto
him, Lord, thou knowest all things; thou know-

Living Bible

10 "Bring some of the fish you've just caught,"
Jesus said. 11 So Simon Peter went out and
dragged the net ashore. By his count there were
153 large fish; and yet the net hadn't torn.
12 "Now come and have some breakfast!"
Jesus said; and none of us dared ask him if he
really was the Lord, for we were quite sure of it.
13 Then Jesus went around serving us the bread
and fish.
14 This was the third time Jesus had appeared
to us since his return from the dead.
15 After breakfast Jesus said to Simon Peter,
"Simon, son of John, do you love me more than
these others?" [e]
"Yes," Peter replied, "You know I am your
friend."
"Then feed my lambs," Jesus told him.
16 Jesus repeated the question: "Simon, son
of John, do you *really* love me?"
"Yes, Lord," Peter said, "you know I am your
friend."
"Then take care of my sheep," Jesus said.
17 Once more he asked him, "Simon, son of
John, are you even my friend?"
Peter was grieved at the way Jesus asked the
question this third time. "Lord, you know my

[*e*] Literally, "more than these." See Mark 14:29.

Today's English Version

with fish on it, and some bread. 10 Then Jesus
said to them, "Bring some of the fish you have
just caught."
11 Simon Peter went aboard and dragged the
net ashore, full of big fish, a hundred and fifty-
three in all; even though there were so many,
still the net did not tear. 12 Jesus said to them,
"Come and eat." None of the disciples dared
ask him, "Who are you?" because they knew it
was the Lord. 13 So Jesus went over, took the
bread, and gave it to them; he did the same with
the fish.
14 This, then, was the third time Jesus showed
himself to the disciples after he was raised from
death.

Jesus and Peter

15 After they had eaten, Jesus said to Simon
Peter, "Simon, son of John, do you love me more
than these?"
"Yes, Lord," he answered, "you know that I
love you."
Jesus said to him, "Take care of my lambs."
16 A second time Jesus said to him, "Simon, son
of John, do you love me?"
"Yes, Lord," he answered, "you know that I
love you."
Jesus said to him, "Take care of my sheep."
17 A third time Jesus said, "Simon, son of John,
do you love me?"
Peter became sad because Jesus asked him the
third time, "Do you love me?" and said to him,
"Lord, you know everything; you know that I
love you!"

New International Version

10 Jesus said to them, "Bring some of the
fish you have just caught."
11 Simon Peter climbed aboard and dragged
the net ashore. It was full of large fish, 153, but
even with so many the net was not torn. 12 Jesus said to them, "Come and have breakfast."
None of the disciples dared ask him, "Who are
you?" They knew it was the Lord. 13 Jesus came,
took the bread and gave it to them, and did the
same with the fish. 14 This was now the third
time Jesus appeared to his disciples after he was
raised from the dead.

Jesus reinstates Peter

15 When they had finished eating, Jesus said
to Simon Peter, "Simon son of John, do you
truly love me more than these?"
"Yes, Lord," he said, "you know that I love
you."
Jesus said, "Feed my lambs."
16 Again Jesus said, "Simon son of John, do
you truly love me?"
He answered, "Yes, Lord, you know that I
love you."
Jesus said, "Take care of my sheep."
17 The third time he said to him, "Simon son
of John, do you love me?"
Peter was hurt because Jesus asked him the
third time, "Do you love me?" He said, "Lord,
you know all things; you know that I love you."

Phillips Modern English

Jesus said to them, "Bring me some of the fish you've just caught."

So Simon Peter got into the boat and hauled the net ashore full of large fish, one hundred and fifty-three altogether. But in spite of the large number the net was not torn.

Then Jesus said to them, "Come and have your breakfast."

None of the disciples dared to ask him who he was; they knew it was the Lord.

Jesus went and took the bread and gave it to them and gave them all fish as well. This was now the third time that Jesus showed himself to his disciples after his resurrection from the dead.

When they had finished breakfast Jesus said to Simon Peter, "Simon, son of John, do you love me more than these others?"

"Yes, Lord," he replied, "you know that I am your friend."

"Then feed my lambs," returned Jesus. Then he said for the second time.

"Simon, son of John, do you love me?"

"Yes, Lord," returned Peter. "You know that I am your friend."

"Then care for my sheep," replied Jesus. Then for the third time, Jesus spoke to him and said, "Simon, son of John, *are* you my friend?"

Peter was deeply hurt because Jesus' third question to him was "Are you my friend?", and he said, "Lord, you know everything. You know

Revised Standard Version

bread. 10 Jesus said to them, "Bring some of
the fish that you have just caught." 11 So Simon
Peter went aboard and hauled the net ashore,
full of large fish, a hundred and fifty-three of
them; and although there were so many, the net
was not torn. 12 Jesus said to them, "Come and
have breakfast." Now none of the disciples
dared ask him, "Who are you?" They knew it
was the Lord. 13 Jesus came and took the bread
and gave it to them, and so with the fish. 14 This
was now the third time that Jesus was revealed
to the disciples after he was raised from the
dead.

15 When they had finished breakfast, Jesus
said to Simon Peter, "Simon, son of John, do
you love me more than these?" He said to him,
"Yes, Lord; you know that I love you." He
said to him, "Feed my lambs." 16A second time
he said to him, "Simon, son of John, do you
love me?" He said to him, "Yes, Lord; you
know that I love you." He said to him, "Tend
my sheep." 17 He said to him the third time,
"Simon, son of John, do you love me?" Peter
was grieved because he said to him the third
time, "Do you love me?" And he said to him,
"Lord, you know everything; you know that I

Jerusalem Bible

with fish cooking on it. 10 Jesus said, "Bring
some of the fish you have just caught." 11 Simon
Peter went aboard and dragged the net to the
shore, full of big fish, one hundred and fifty-
three of them; and in spite of there being so
many the net was not broken. 12 Jesus said to
them, "Come and have breakfast." None of the
disciples was bold enough to ask, "Who are
you?"; they knew quite well it was the Lord.
13 Jesus then stepped forward, took the bread
and gave it to them, and the same with the fish.
14 This was the third time that Jesus showed
himself to the disciples after rising from the
dead.

15 After the meal Jesus said to Simon Peter,
"Simon son of John, do you love me more than
these others do?" He answered, "Yes Lord, you
know I love you." Jesus said to him, "Feed my
lambs." 16A second time he said to him, "Simon
son of John, do you love me?" He replied, "Yes,
Lord, you know I love you." Jesus said to him,
"Look after my sheep." 17 Then he said to him
a third time, "Simon son of John, do you love
me?" Peter was upset that he asked him the
third time, "Do you love me?" and said, "Lord,
you know everything; you know I love you."

New English Bible

Jesus said, 'Bring some of your catch.' Simon Peter went aboard and dragged the net to land, full of big fish, a hundred and fifty-three of them; and yet, many as they were, the net was not torn. Jesus said, 'Come and have breakfast.' None of the disciples dared to ask 'Who are you?' They knew it was the Lord. Jesus now came up, took the bread, and gave it to them, and the fish in the same way.

This makes the third time that Jesus appeared to his disciples after his resurrection from the dead.

After breakfast, Jesus said to Simon Peter, 'Simon son of John, do you love me more than all else[a]?' 'Yes, Lord,' he answered, 'you know that I love you.' [b] 'Then feed my lambs', he said. A second time he asked, 'Simon son of John, do you love me?' 'Yes, Lord, you know I love you.' [b] 'Then tend my sheep.' A third time he said, 'Simon son of John, do you love me[c]?' Peter was hurt that he asked him a third time, 'Do you love me?' [d] 'Lord,' he said, 'you know

[*a*] *Or* more than they do. [*b*] *Or* that I am your friend. [*c*] *Or* are you my friend. [*d*] *Or* that at the third asking he should have said, 'Are you my friend?'

King James Version

est that I love thee. Jesus saith unto him, Feed my sheep. 18 Verily, verily, I say unto thee, When thou wast young, thou girdedst thyself, and walkedst whither thou wouldest: but when thou shalt be old, thou shalt stretch forth thy hands, and another shall gird thee, and carry *thee* whither thou wouldest not. 19 This spake he, signifying by what death he should glorify God. And when he had spoken this, he saith unto him, Follow me. 20 Then Peter, turning about, seeth the disciple whom Jesus loved following; which also leaned on his breast at supper, and said, Lord, which is he that betrayeth thee? 21 Peter seeing him saith to Jesus, Lord, and what *shall* this man *do?* 22 Jesus saith unto him, If I will that he tarry till I come, what *is that* to thee? follow thou me. 23 Then went this saying abroad among the brethren, that that disciple should not die: yet Jesus said not unto him, He shall not die; but, If I will that he tarry till I come, what

Living Bible

heart;[f] you know I am," he said.

Jesus said, "Then feed my little sheep. 18 When you were young, you were able to do as you liked and go wherever you wanted to; but when you are old, you will stretch out your hands and others will direct you and take you where you don't want to go." 19 Jesus said this to let him know what kind of death he would die to glorify God. Then Jesus told him, "Follow me."

20 Peter turned around and saw the disciple Jesus loved following, the one who had leaned around at supper that time to ask Jesus, "Master, which of us will betray you?" 21 Peter asked Jesus, "What about him, Lord? What sort of death will he die?"[g]

22 Jesus replied, "If I want him to live[h] until I return, what is that to you? *You* follow me."

23 So the rumor spread among the brotherhood that that disciple wouldn't die! But that isn't what Jesus said at all! He only said, "If I want him to live[h] until I come, what is that to you?"

[*f*] Literally, "all things." [*g*] Implied. Literally, "and this man, what?" [*h*] Literally, "tarry."

Today's English Version

Jesus said to him, "Take care of my sheep. 18 I tell you the truth: when you were young you used to fasten your belt and go anywhere you wanted to; but when you are old you will stretch out your hands and someone else will tie them and take you where you don't want to go." 19 (In saying this Jesus was indicating the way in which Peter would die and bring glory to God.) Then Jesus said to him, "Follow me!"

Jesus and the other disciple

20 Peter turned around and saw behind him that other disciple, whom Jesus loved—the one who had leaned close to Jesus at the meal and asked, "Lord, who is going to betray you?" 21 When Peter saw him, he said to Jesus, "Lord, what about this man?"

22 Jesus answered him, "If I want him to live until I come, what is that to you? Follow me!"

23 So a report spread among the followers of Jesus that this disciple would not die. But Jesus did not say that he would not die; he said, "If I want him to live until I come, what is that to you?"

New International Version

Jesus said, "Feed my sheep. 18 I tell you the truth, when you were younger you dressed yourself and went where you wanted; but when you are old you will stretch out your hands, and someone else will dress you and lead you where you do not want to go." 19 Jesus said this to indicate the kind of death by which Peter would glorify God. Then he said to him, "Follow me!"

20 Peter turned and saw that the disciple whom Jesus loved was following them. (This was the one who had leaned back against Jesus at the supper and had said, "Lord, who is going to betray you?") 21 When Peter saw him, he asked, "Lord, what about him?"

22 Jesus answered, "If I want him to remain alive until I return, what is that to you? You must follow me." 23 Because of this, the rumor spread among the brothers that this disciple would not die. But Jesus did not say that he would not die; he only said, "If I want him to remain alive until I return, what is that to you?"

Phillips Modern English

that I am your friend!"
"Then feed my sheep," Jesus said to him. "I tell you truly, Peter, that when you were younger, you used to dress yourself and go where you liked, but when you are an old man, you are going to stretch our your hands and someone else will dress you and take you where you do not want to go."
(He said this to show the kind of death by which Peter was going to honour God.)
Then Jesus said to him, "You must follow me."
Then Peter turned round and noticed the disciple whom Jesus loved following behind them. (He was the one who had his head on Jesus' shoulder at supper and had asked, "Lord, who is the one who is going to betray you?") So he said, "Yes, Lord, but what about him?"
"If it is my wish," returned Jesus, "for him to stay until I come, is that your business, Peter? You must follow me."
This gave rise to the saying among the brothers that this disciple would not die. Yet, of course, Jesus did not say, "He will not die", but simply, "If it is my wish for him to stay until I come, is that your business?"

Revised Standard Version

love you." Jesus said to him, "Feed my sheep.
18 Truly, truly, I say to you, when you were
young, you girded yourself and walked where
you would; but when you are old, you will
stretch out your hands, and another will gird
you and carry you where you do not wish to
go." 19 (This he said to show by what death he
was to glorify God.) And after this he said to
him, "Follow me."
20 Peter turned and saw following them the
disciple whom Jesus loved, who had lain close
to his breast at the supper and had said, "Lord,
who is it that is going to betray you?" 21 When
Peter saw him, he said to Jesus, "Lord, what
about this man?" 22 Jesus said to him, "If it is
my will that he remain until I come, what is
that to you? Follow me!" 23 The saying spread
abroad among the brethren that this disciple
was not to die; yet Jesus did not say to him
that he was not to die, but, "If it is my will
that he remain until I come, what is that to
you?"

Jerusalem Bible

Jesus said to him, "Feed my sheep.

18 "I tell you most solemnly,
when you were young
you put on your own belt
and walked where you liked;
but when you grow old
you will stretch out your hands,
and somebody else will put a belt around you
and take you where you would rather not go."

19 In these words he indicated the kind of death
by which Peter would give glory to God. After
this he said, "Follow me."
20 Peter turned and saw the disciple Jesus
loved following them—the one who had leaned
on his breast at the supper and had said to him,
"Lord, who is it that will betray you?" 21 Seeing
him, Peter said to Jesus, "What about him,
Lord?" 22 Jesus answered, "If I want him to
stay behind till I come, what does it matter to
you? You are to follow me." 23 The rumor then
went out among the brothers that this disciple
would not die. Yet Jesus had not said to Peter,
"He will not die," but, "If I want him to stay
behind till I come."

New English Bible

everything; you know I love you.' [b] Jesus said, 'Feed my sheep.
'And further, I tell you this in very truth: when you were young you fastened your belt about you and walked where you chose; but when you are old you will stretch out your arms, and a stranger will bind you fast, and carry you where you have no wish to go.' He said this to indicate the manner of death by which Peter was to glorify God. Then he added, 'Follow me.'
Peter looked round, and saw the disciple whom Jesus loved following—the one who at supper had leaned back close to him to ask the question, 'Lord, who is it that will betray you?' When he caught sight of him, Peter asked, 'Lord, what will happen to him?' Jesus said, 'If it should be my will that he wait until I come, what is it to you? Follow me.'
That saying of Jesus became current in the brotherhood, and was taken to mean that that disciple would not die. But in fact Jesus did not say that he would not die; he only said, 'If it should be my will that he wait until I come, what is it to you?'

[b] *Or* that I am your friend.

King James Version

is that to thee? 24 This is the disciple which testifieth of these things, and wrote these things: and we know that his testimony is true. 25 And there are also many other things which Jesus did, the which, if they should be written every one, I suppose that even the world itself could not contain the books that should be written. Amen.

Living Bible

24 *I am that disciple!* I saw these events and have recorded them here. And we all know that my account of these things is accurate.

25 And I suppose that if all the other events in Jesus' life were written, the whole world could hardly contain the books!

Today's English Version

24 He is the disciple who spoke of these things, the one who also write them down; and we know that what he said is true.

Conclusion

25 Now, there are many other things that Jesus did. If they were all written down one by one, I suppose that the whole world could not hold the books that would be written.

New International Version

24 This is the disciple who testifies to these things and who wrote them down. We know that his testimony is true.

25 Jesus did many other things as well. If every one of them were written down, I suppose that even the whole world would not have room for the books that would be written.

Phillips Modern English

21.24 All the above was written by an eye-witness

Now it is this same disciple who is hereby giving his testimony to these things and has written them down. We know that his witness is reliable. Of course, there are many other things which Jesus did, and I suppose that if each one were written down in detail, there would not be room in the whole world for all the books that would have to be written.

Revised Standard Version

24 This is the disciple who is bearing witness to these things, and who has written these things; and we know that his testimony is true.
25 But there are also many other things which Jesus did; were every one of them to be written, I suppose that the world itself could not contain the books that would be written.

Jerusalem Bible

Conclusion

24 This disciple is the one who vouches for these things and has written them down, and we know that his testimony is true.
25 There were many other things that Jesus did; if all were written down, the world itself, I suppose, would not hold all the books that would have to be written.

New English Bible

It is this same disciple who attests what has here been written. It is in fact he who wrote it, and we know that his testimony is true.[e]

There is much else that Jesus did. If it were all to be recorded in detail, I suppose the whole world could not hold the books that would be written.

[e] *Some witnesses here insert the passage printed on pages 705 and 709.*

King James Version

THE ACTS OF THE APOSTLES

1 The former treatise have I made, O Theophilus, of all that Jesus began both to do and teach, 2 Until the day in which he was taken up, after that he through the Holy Ghost had given commandments unto the apostles whom he had chosen: 3 To whom also he shewed himself alive after his passion by many infallible proofs, being seen of them forty days, and speaking of the things pertaining to the kingdom of

Living Bible

ACTS

1 Dear friend who loves God:
In my first letter[a] I told you about Jesus' life and teachings and how he returned to heaven after giving his chosen apostles further instructions from the Holy Spirit. 3 During the forty days after his crucifixion he appeared to the apostles from time to time, actually alive, and proved to them in many ways that it was really he himself they were seeing. And on these occasions he talked to them about the Kingdom of God.

[a] i.e., the book of Luke; see footnote chapter 1, verse 1.

Today's English Version

THE ACTS OF THE APOSTLES

1 Dear Theophilus:
In my first book I wrote about all the things that Jesus did and taught, from the time he began his work 2 until the day he was taken up to heaven. Before he was taken up he gave instructions by the power of the Holy Spirit to the men he had chosen as his apostles. 3 For forty days after his death he showed himself to them many times, in ways that proved beyond doubt that he was alive; he was seen by them, and talked with them about the Kingdom of

New International Version

ACTS

Jesus taken up into heaven

1 In my former book, Theophilus, I wrote about all that Jesus began to do and to teach 2 until the day he was taken up to heaven, after giving instructions through the Holy Spirit to the apostles he had chosen. 3After his suffering, he showed himself to these men and gave many convincing proofs that he was alive. He appeared to them over a period of forty days and

Phillips Modern English

THE ACTS OF THE APOSTLES

1.1 Introduction

My dear Theophilus,
In my first book I gave you some account of all that Jesus began to do and teach until the time of his ascension. Before he ascended he gave his instructions, through the Holy Spirit, to the messengers of his choice. For after his suffering he showed himself alive to them in many convincing ways, and appeared to them repeatedly over a period of forty days talking with them about the affairs of the kingdom of God.

Revised Standard Version

THE ACTS OF THE APOSTLES

1 In the first book, O Theophilus, I have dealt with all that Jesus began to do and
teach, 2 until the day when he was taken up,
after he had given commandment through the
Holy Spirit to the apostles whom he had chosen.
3 To them he presented himself alive after his
passion by many proofs, appearing to them during forty days, and speaking of the kingdom of

Jerusalem Bible

THE ACTS OF THE APOSTLES

Prologue

1 In my earlier work,[a] Theophilus, I dealt with everything Jesus had done and taught
from the beginning 2 until the day he gave his
instructions to the apostles he had chosen through the Holy Spirit, and was taken up to
heaven. 3 He had shown himself alive to them
after his Passion by many demonstrations: for forty days he had continued to appear to them

[a] The gospel according to Luke.

New English Bible

ACTS OF THE APOSTLES

The beginnings of the church

1 In the first part of my work, Theophilus, I wrote of all that Jesus did and taught from the beginning until the day when, after giving instructions through the Holy Spirit to the apostles whom he had chosen, he was taken up to heaven. He showed himself to these men after his death, and gave ample proof that he was alive: over a period of forty days he appeared to them and taught them about the kingdom of

King James Version

God: 4And, being assembled together with *them,*
commanded them that they should not depart
from Jerusalem, but wait for the promise of the
Father, which, *saith he,* ye have heard of me.
5 For John truly baptized with water; but ye
shall be baptized with the Holy Ghost not many
days hence. 6 When they therefore were come
together, they asked of him, saying, Lord, wilt
thou at this time restore again the kingdom to
Israel? 7And he said unto them, It is not for you
to know the times or the seasons, which the
Father hath put in his own power. 8 But ye shall
receive power, after that the Holy Ghost is come
upon you: and ye shall be witnesses unto me
both in Jerusalem, and in all Judea, and in
Samaria, and unto the uttermost part of the
earth. 9And when he had spoken these things,
while they beheld, he was taken up; and a cloud
received him out of their sight. 10And while they
looked steadfastly toward heaven as he went up,
behold, two men stood by them in white apparel;
11 Which also said, Ye men of Galilee, why
stand ye gazing up into heaven? this same Jesus,
which is taken up from you into heaven, shall
so come in like manner as ye have seen him go

Living Bible

4 In one of these meetings he told them not
to leave Jerusalem until the Holy Spirit came
upon them in fulfillment of the Father's promise, a matter he had previously discussed with
them.

5 "John baptized you with[b] water," he reminded them, "but you shall be baptized with[b]
the Holy Spirit in just a few days."

6 And another time when he appeared to
them, they asked him, "Lord, are you going to
free Israel [from Rome[c]] now and restore us as
an independent nation?"

7 "The Father sets those dates," he replied,
"and they are not for you to know. 8 But when
the Holy Spirit has come upon you, you will
receive power to testify about me with great effect, to the people in Jerusalem, throughout
Judea, in Samaria, and to the ends of the earth,
about my death and resurrection."

9 It was not long afterwards that he rose into
the sky and disappeared into a cloud, leaving
them staring after him. 10As they were straining
their eyes for another glimpse, suddenly two
white-robed men were standing there among
them, 11 and said, "Men of Galilee, why are you
standing here staring at the sky? Jesus has gone
away to heaven, and some day, just as he went,
he will return!"

[*b*] Or, "in." [*c*] Implied.

Today's English Version

God. 4And when they came together, he gave
them this order, "Do not leave Jerusalem, but
wait for the gift my Father promised, that I told
you about. 5 John baptized with water, but in a
few days you will be baptized with the Holy
Spirit."

Jesus is taken up to heaven

6 When the apostles met together with Jesus
they asked him, "Lord, will you at this time give
the Kingdom back to Israel?"

7 Jesus said to them, "The times and occasions
are set by my Father's own authority, and it is
not for you to know when they will be. 8 But you
will be filled with power when the Holy Spirit
comes on you, and you will be witnesses for me
in Jerusalem, in all of Judea and Samaria, and
to the ends of the earth." 9After saying this, he
was taken up to heaven as they watched him; and
a cloud hid him from their sight.

10 They still had their eyes fixed on the sky
as he went away, when two men dressed in white
suddenly stood beside them. 11 "Men of Galilee,"
they said, "why do you stand there looking up
at the sky? This Jesus, who was taken up from
you into heaven, will come back in the same way
that you saw him go to heaven."

New International Version

spoke about the kingdom of God. 4 On one
occasion, while he was eating with them, he gave
them this command: "Do not leave Jerusalem,
but wait for the gift my Father promised, which
you have heard me speak about. 5 For John
baptized with water, but in a few days you will
be baptized with the Holy Spirit."

6 So when they met together, they asked him,
"Lord, are you at this time going to restore the
kingdom to Israel?"

7 He said to them: "It is not for you to know
the times or dates the Father has set by his own
authority. 8 But you will receive power when the
Holy Spirit comes on you; and you will be my
witnesses in Jerusalem, and in all Judea and
Samaria, and to the ends of the earth."

9 After he said this, he was taken up before
their very eyes, and a cloud hid him from their
sight.

10 They were looking intently up into the sky
as he was going, when suddenly two men dressed
in white stood beside them. 11 "Men of Galilee,"
they said, "why do you stand here looking into
the sky? This same Jesus, who has been taken
from you into heaven, will come back in the
same way you have seen him go into heaven."

Phillips Modern English

1.4 Jesus' parting words before his ascension

On one occasion, while he was eating a meal with them, he emphasised that they were not to leave Jerusalem, but to wait for the Father's promise.

"You have already heard me speak about this," he said, "for John used to baptise with water, but before many days are passed you will be baptised with the Holy Spirit."

This naturally brought them all together, and they asked him,

"Lord, is this the time when you are going to restore the kingdom to Israel?"

To this he replied,

"You cannot know times and dates which have been fixed by the Father's sole authority. But you are to be given power when the Holy Spirit has come to you. You will be witnesses to me, not only in Jerusalem, not only throughout Judaea, not only in Samaria, but to the very ends of the earth."

When he had said these words he was lifted up before their eyes till a cloud hid him from their sight. While they were still gazing up into the sky as he went, suddenly two men dressed in white stood beside them and said,

"Men of Galilee, why are you standing here looking up into the sky? This very Jesus who has been taken up from you into Heaven will come back in just the same way as you have seen him go."

Revised Standard Version

God. 4And while staying[a] with them he charged
them not to depart from Jerusalem, but to wait
for the promise of the Father, which, he said,
"you heard from me, 5 for John baptized with
water, but before many days you shall be baptized with the Holy Spirit."
6 So when they had come together, they
asked him, "Lord, will you at this time restore
the kingdom to Israel?" 7 He said to them, "It
is not for you to know times or seasons which
the Father has fixed by his own authority. 8 But
you shall receive power when the Holy Spirit
has come upon you; and you shall be my witnesses in Jerusalem and in all Judea and Samaria
and to the end of the earth." 9And when he had
said this, as they were looking on, he was lifted
up, and a cloud took him out of their sight.
10And while they were gazing into heaven as
he went, behold, two men stood by them in
white robes, 11 and said, "Men of Galilee, why
do you stand looking into heaven? This Jesus,
who was taken up from you into heaven, will
come in the same way as you saw him go into
heaven."

[a] Or *eating*.

Jerusalem Bible

and tell them about the kingdom of God. 4 When
he had been at table with them, he had told
them not to leave Jerusalem, but to wait there
for what the Father had promised. "It is," he
had said, "what you have heard me speak about:
5 John baptized with water but you, not many
days from now, will be baptized with the Holy
Spirit."

The ascension

6 Now having met together,[b] they asked him,
"Lord, has the time come? Are you going to restore the kingdom to Israel?" 7 He replied, "It is
not for you to know times or dates that the
Father has decided by his own authority, 8 but
you will receive power when the Holy Spirit
comes on you, and then you will be my witnesses
not only in Jerusalem but throughout Judaea and
Samaria, and indeed to the ends of the earth."
9 As he said this he was lifted up while they
looked on, and a cloud took him from their
sight. 10 They were still staring into the sky
when suddenly two men in white were standing
near them 11 and they said, "Why are you men
from Galilee standing here looking into the
sky? Jesus who has been taken up from you into
heaven, this same Jesus will come back in the
same way as you have seen him go there."

[b] This verse takes up the narrative broken off in Lk. 24:49.

New English Bible

God. While he was in their company he told them not to leave Jerusalem. 'You must wait', he said, 'for the promise made by my Father, about which you have heard me speak: John, as you know, baptized with water, but you will be baptized with the Holy Spirit, and within the next few days.'

So, when they were all together, they asked him, 'Lord, is this the time when you are to establish once again the sovereignty of Israel?' He answered, 'It is not for you to know about dates or times, which the Father has set within his own control. But you will receive power when the Holy Spirit comes upon you; and you will bear witness for me in Jerusalem, and all over Judaea and Samaria, and away to the ends of the earth.'

When he had said this, as they watched, he was lifted up, and a cloud removed him from their sight. As he was going, and as they were gazing intently into the sky, all at once there stood beside them two men in white who said, 'Men of Galilee, why stand there looking up into the sky? This Jesus, who has been taken away from you up to heaven, will come in the same way as you have seen him go.'

King James Version

into heaven. 12 Then returned they unto Jerusalem from the mount called Olivet, which is from Jerusalem a sabbath day's journey. 13 And when they were come in, they went up into an upper room, where abode both Peter, and James, and John, and Andrew, Philip, and Thomas, Bartholomew, and Matthew, James *the son* of Alpheus, and Simon Zelotes, and Judas *the brother* of James. 14 These all continued with one accord in prayer and supplication, with the women, and Mary the mother of Jesus, and with his brethren.

15 And in those days Peter stood up in the midst of the disciples, and said, (the number of names together were about a hundred and twenty,) 16 Men *and* brethren, this Scripture must needs have been fulfilled, which the Holy Ghost by the mouth of David spake before concerning Judas, which was guide to them that took Jesus. 17 For he was numbered with us,

Living Bible

12 They were at the Mount of Olives when this happened, so now they walked the half mile back to Jerusalem 13 and held a prayer meeting in an upstairs room of the house where they were staying.

14 Here is the list of those who were present at the meeting:

Peter,
John, James,
Andrew,
Philip, Thomas,
Bartholomew,
Matthew,
James (son of Alphaeus),
Simon (also called "The Zealot"),
Judas (son of James),
And the brothers of Jesus.
Several women, including Jesus' mother, were also there.

15 This prayer meeting went on for several days. During this time, on a day when about 120 people were present, Peter stood up and addressed them as follows:

16 "Brothers, it was necessary for the Scriptures to come true concerning Judas, who betrayed Jesus by guiding the mob to him, for this was predicted long ago by the Holy Spirit, speaking through King David. 17 Judas was one of us, chosen to be an apostle just as we were.

Today's English Version

Judas' successor

12 Then the apostles went back to Jerusalem from the Mount of Olives, which is about half a mile away from the city. 13 They entered Jerusalem and went up to the room where they were staying: Peter, John, James and Andrew, Philip and Thomas, Bartholomew and Matthew, James, the son of Alphaeus, Simon the Patriot, and Judas, the son of James. 14 They gathered frequently to pray as a group, together with the women, and with Mary the mother of Jesus, and his brothers.

15 A few days later there was a meeting of the believers, about one hundred and twenty in all, and Peter stood up to speak. 16 "My brothers," he said, "the scripture had to come true in which the Holy Spirit, speaking through David, predicted about Judas, who was the guide of those who arrested Jesus. 17 Judas was a member of our group, because he had been chosen to have a part in our work."

New International Version

Matthias chosen to replace Judas

12 Then they returned to Jerusalem from the hill called the Mount of Olives, a Sabbath day's walk[a] from the city. 13 When they arrived, they went upstairs to the room where they were staying. Those present were Peter, John, James and Andrew; Philip and Thomas, Bartholomew and Matthew; James son of Alphaeus and Simon the Zealot, and Judas son of James. 14 They all joined together constantly in prayer, along with the women and Mary the mother of Jesus, and his brothers.

15 In those days Peter stood up among the believers (a group numbering about one hundred and twenty) 16 and said, "Brothers, the Scripture had to be fulfilled which the Holy Spirit spoke long ago through the mouth of David concerning Judas, who served as guide for those who arrested Jesus—17 he was one of our number and shared in this ministry."

[a] That is, about half a mile.

Phillips Modern English

At this they returned to Jerusalem from the Mount of Olives which is near the city, only a sabbath day's journey away. On entering Jerusalem they went straight to the upstairs room where they had been staying. There were Peter, John, James, Andrew, Philip, Thomas, Bartholomew, Matthew, James the son of Alphaeus, Simon the Nationalist, and Judas the son of James. By common consent all these men, together with the women who had followed Jesus, Mary his mother, as well as his brothers, devoted themselves to prayer.

1.15 Judas' place is filled

It was during this period that Peter stood up among the brothers—there were about a hundred and twenty present at the time—and said, "My brothers, the prophecy of scripture given through the Holy Spirit by the lips of David concerning Judas was bound to come true. He was the man who acted as guide to those who arrested Jesus, though he was one of our number and he had a share in this ministry of ours."

Revised Standard Version

12 Then they returned to Jerusalem from the mount called Olivet, which is near Jerusalem, a sabbath day's journey away; 13 and when they had entered, they went up to the upper room, where they were staying, Peter and John and James and Andrew, Philip and Thomas, Bartholomew and Matthew, James the son of Alphaeus and Simon the Zealot and Judas the son of James. 14 All these with one accord devoted themselves to prayer, together with the women and Mary the mother of Jesus, and with his brothers.

15 In those days Peter stood up among the brethren (the company of persons was in all about a hundred and twenty), and said, 16 "Brethren, the scripture had to be fulfilled, which the Holy Spirit spoke beforehand by the mouth of David, concerning Judas who was guide to those who arrested Jesus. 17 For he was numbered among us, and was alloted his share in

Jerusalem Bible

I. The Jerusalem church

The group of apostles

12 So from the Mount of Olives, as it is called, they went back to Jerusalem, a short distance away, no more than a sabbath walk; 13 and when they reached the city they went to the upper room where they were staying; there were Peter and John, James and Andrew, Philip and Thomas, Bartholomew and Matthew, James son of Alphaeus and Simon the Zealot, and Jude son of James.[c] 14 All these joined in continuous prayer, together with several women, including Mary the mother of Jesus, and with his brothers.[d]

The election of Matthias

15 One day Peter stood up to speak to the brothers[e]—there were about a hundred and twenty persons in the congregation: 16 "Brothers, the passage of scripture had to be fulfilled in which the Holy Spirit, speaking through David, foretells the fate of Judas, who offered himself as a guide to the men who arrested Jesus—17 after having been one of our number

[c] "Son" (of Alphaeus, of James) is not in the Greek. This Jude is not the Jude "brother" of Jesus, Mt. 13:55 and Mk. 6:3, and brother of James (Jude 1). Nor is it likely that "James of Alphaeus" was James brother of the Lord. [d] Cousins, as in the gospels. [e] The term for Christians, usually the laity as distinct from apostles and elders.

New English Bible

Then they returned to Jerusalem from the hill called Olivet, which is near Jerusalem, no farther than a Sabbath day's journey. Entering the city they went to the room upstairs where they were lodging: Peter and John and James and Andrew, Philip and Thomas, Bartholomew and Matthew, James son of Alphaeus and Simon the Zealot, and Judas son of James. All these were constantly at prayer together, and with them a group of women, including Mary the mother of Jesus, and his brothers.

It was during this time that Peter stood up before the assembled brotherhood, about one hundred and twenty in all, and said: 'My friends, the prophecy in Scripture was bound to come true, which the Holy Spirit, through the mouth of David, uttered about Judas who acted as guide to those who arrested Jesus. For he was one of our number and had his place in this

King James Version

and had obtained part of this ministry. 18 Now this man purchased a field with the reward of iniquity; and falling headlong, he burst asunder in the midst, and all his bowels gushed out. 19 And it was known unto all the dwellers at Jerusalem; insomuch as that field is called, in their proper tongue, Aceldama, that is to say, The field of blood. 20 For it is written in the book of Psalms, Let his habitation be desolate, and let no man dwell therein: and, His bishoprick let another take. 21 Wherefore of these men which have companied with us all the time that the Lord Jesus went in and out among us, 22 Beginning from the baptism of John, unto that same day that he was taken up from us, must one be ordained to be a witness with us of his resurrection. 23 And they appointed two, Joseph called Barsabas, who was surnamed Justus, and Matthias. 24 And they prayed, and said, Thou, Lord, which knowest the hearts of all *men*, shew whether of these two thou hast chosen, 25 That he may take part of this ministry and apostleship, from which Judas by transgression fell, that he might go to his own place. 26 And they gave forth their lots; and the lot fell upon Matthias; and he was numbered with the eleven apostles.

Living Bible

18 He bought a field with the money he received for his treachery and falling headlong there, he burst open, spilling out his bowels. 19 The news of his death spread rapidly among all the people of Jerusalem, and they named the place 'The Field of Blood.' 20 King David's prediction of this appears in the Book of Psalms, where he says, 'Let his home become desolate with no one living in it.' [d] And again, 'Let his work be given to someone else to do.' [e]

21, 22 "So now we must choose someone else to take Judas' place and to join us as witnesses of Jesus' resurrection. Let us select someone who has been with us constantly from our first association with the Lord—from the time he was baptized by John until the day he was taken from us into heaven."

23 The assembly nominated two men: Joseph Justus (also called Barsabbas) and Matthias. 24, 25 Then they all prayed for the right man to be chosen. "O Lord," they said, "you know every heart; show us which of these men you have chosen as an apostle to replace Judas the traitor, who has gone on to his proper place."

26 Then they drew straws,[f] and in this manner Matthias was chosen and became an apostle with the other eleven.

[*d*] Psalm 69:25. [*e*] Psalm 109:8. [*f*] Literally, "cast lots," or, "threw dice."

Today's English Version

18 (With the money that Judas got for his evil act he bought a field, where he fell to his death; he burst open and all his insides spilled out. 19 All the people living in Jerusalem heard about it, and so in their own language they call that field Akeldama, which means "Field of Blood.")

20 "For it is written in the book of Psalms,

'May his house become empty,
let no one live in it.'

It is also written,

'May someone else take his place of service.'

21, 22 "So then, someone must join us as a witness to the resurrection of the Lord Jesus. He must be one of those who were in our group during the whole time that the Lord Jesus traveled about with us, beginning from the time John preached his baptism until the day Jesus was taken up from us to heaven."

23 So they proposed two men: Joseph, who was called Barsabbas (he was also called Justus), and Matthias. 24 Then they prayed, "Lord, you know the hearts of all men. And so, Lord, show us which one of these two you have chosen 25 to take this place of service as an apostle which Judas left to go to the place where he belongs." 26 Then they drew lots to choose between the two names. The name chosen was that of Matthias, and he was added to the group of the eleven apostles.

New International Version

18 (With the reward he got for his wickedness, Judas bought a field; there he fell headlong, his body burst open and all his intestines spilled out. 19 Everyone in Jerusalem heard about this, so they called that field in their language Akeldama, that is, Field of Blood.)

20 "For," said Peter, "it is written in the book of Psalms,

'May his place be deserted;
let there be no one to dwell in it,' [b]

and,

'May another take his place of leadership.' [c]

21 Therefore it is necessary to choose one of the men who have been with us the whole time the Lord Jesus went in and out among us, 22 beginning from John's baptism to the time when Jesus was taken up from us. For one of these must become a witness with us of his resurrection."

23 So they proposed two men: Joseph called Barsabbas (also known as Justus) and Matthias. 24 Then they prayed, "Lord, you know everyone's heart. Show us which of these two you have chosen 25 to take over this apostolic ministry, which Judas left to go where he belongs." 26 Then they drew lots, and the lot fell to Matthias; so he was added to the eleven apostles.

[*b*] Psalm 69:25. [*c*] Psalm 109:8.

Phillips Modern English

(This man had bought a piece of land with the price of his treachery, but his body swelled up and ruptured, so that his intestines poured out. This fact became well known to all the residents of Jerusalem so that the piece of land came to be called in their language Akeldama, which means Field of Blood.) "Now it is written in the book of psalms of such a man:

Let his habitation be made desolate,
And let no man dwell therein:

and

His office let another take.

"It becomes necessary then that whoever joins us must be someone who has been in our company during the whole time that the Lord Jesus lived his life with us, from the beginning when John baptised him until the day when he was taken up from us. This man must be an eyewitness with us to the resurrection of Jesus."

Two men were put forward, Joseph called Barsabas who was also called Justus, and Matthias. Then they prayed,

"Thou Lord, who knowest the hearts of all men, show us which of these two thou hast chosen to accept the ministry of an apostle which Judas forfeited to go where he belonged."

Then they drew lots for these men, and the lot fell to Matthias, and thereafter he was considered equally an apostle with the eleven.

Revised Standard Version

this ministry. 18 (Now this man bought a field with the reward of his wickedness; and falling headlong[b] he burst open in the middle and all his bowels gushed out. 19 And it became known to all the inhabitants of Jerusalem, so that the field was called in their language Akeldama, that is, Field of Blood.) 20 For it is written in the book of Psalms,

'Let his habitation become desolate,
and let there be no one to live in it';

and

'His office let another take.'

21 So one of the men who have accompanied us during all the time that the Lord Jesus went in and out among us, 22 beginning from the baptism of John until the day when he was taken up from us—one of these men must become with us a witness to his resurrection." 23 And they put forward two, Joseph called Barsabbas, who was surnamed Justus, and Matthias. 24 And they prayed and said, "Lord, who knowest the hearts of all men, show which one of these two thou hast chosen 25 to take the place in this ministry and apostleship from which Judas turned aside, to go to his own place." 26 And they cast lots for them, and the lot fell on Matthias; and he was enrolled with the eleven apostles.

[b] Or *swelling up*.

Jerusalem Bible

and actually sharing this ministry of ours. 18 As you know, he bought a field with the money he was paid for his crime. He fell headlong and burst open, and all his entrails poured out. 19 Everybody in Jerusalem heard about it and the field came to be called the Bloody Acre, in their language Hakeldama. 20 Now in the Book of Psalms it says:

Let his camp be reduced to ruin,
Let there be no one to live in it.[f]

And again:

Let someone else take his office.[g]

21 "We must therefore choose someone who has been with us the whole time that the Lord Jesus was traveling around with us, 22 someone who was with us right from the time when John was baptizing until the day when he was taken up from us—and he can act with us as a witness to his resurrection."

23 Having nominated two candidates, Joseph known as Barsabbas, whose surname was Justus, and Matthias, 24 they prayed, "Lord, you can read everyone's heart; show us therefore which of these two you have chosen 25 to take over this ministry and apostolate which Judas abandoned to go to his proper place." 26 They then drew lots for them, and as the lot fell to Matthias, he was listed as one of the twelve apostles.

[f] Ps. 69:25. [g] Ps. 109:8.

New English Bible

ministry.' (This Judas, be it noted, after buying a plot of land with the price of his villainy, fell forward on the ground, and burst open, so that his entrails poured out. This became known to everyone in Jerusalem, and they named the property in their own language Akeldama, which means 'Blood Acre'.) 'The text I have in mind', Peter continued, 'is in the Book of Psalms: "Let his homestead fall desolate; let there be none to inhabit it"; and again, "Let another take over his charge." Therefore one of those who bore us company all the while we had the Lord Jesus with us, coming and going, from John's ministry of baptism until the day when he was taken up from us—one of those must now join us as a witness to his resurrection.'

Two names were put forward: Joseph, who was known as Barsabbas, and bore the added name of Justus; and Matthias. Then they prayed and said, 'Thou, Lord, who knowest the hearts of all men, declare which of these two thou hast chosen to receive this office of ministry and apostleship which Judas abandoned to go where he belonged.' They drew lots and the lot fell on Matthias, who was then assigned a place among the twelve apostles.[a]

[a] *Some witnesses read* was then appointed a colleague of the eleven apostles.

King James Version

2 And when the day of Pentecost was fully come, they were all with one accord in one place. 2And suddenly there came a sound from heaven as of a rushing mighty wind, and it filled all the house where they were sitting. 3And there appeared unto them cloven tongues like as of fire, and it sat upon each of them. 4And they were all filled with the Holy Ghost, and began to speak with other tongues, as the Spirit gave them utterance. 5And there were dwelling at Jerusalem Jews, devout men, out of every nation under heaven. 6 Now when this was noised abroad, the multitude came together, and were confounded, because that every man heard them speak in his own language. 7And they were all amazed and marvelled, saying one to another, Behold, are not all these which speak Galileans? 8And how hear we every man in our own tongue, wherein we were born? 9 Parthians, and Medes, and Elamites, and the dwellers in Mesopotamia, and in Judea, and Cappadocia, in Pontus, and Asia, 10 Phrygia, and Pamphylia, in Egypt, and in the parts of Libya about Cyrene, and strangers of Rome, Jews and proselytes, 11 Cretes and

Living Bible

2 Seven weeks had gone by since Jesus' death and resurrection, and the Day of Pentecost had now arrived.[a] As the believers met together that day, 2 suddenly there was a sound like the roaring of a mighty windstorm in the skies above them and it filled the house where they were meeting. 3 Then, what looked like flames or tongues of fire appeared and settled on their heads. 4And everyone present was filled with the Holy Spirit and began speaking in languages they didn't know,[b] for the Holy Spirit gave them this ability.

5 Many godly Jews were in Jerusalem that day for the religious celebrations, having arrived from many nations. 6And when they heard the roaring in the sky above the house, crowds came running to see what it was all about, and were stunned to hear their own languages being spoken by the disciples.

7 "How can this be?" they exclaimed. "For these men are all from Galilee, 8 and yet we hear them speaking all the native languages of the lands where we were born! 9 Here we are—Parthians, Medes, Elamites, men from Mesopotamia, Judea, Cappadocia, Pontus, Ausia,[c] 10 Phrygia, Pamphylia, Egypt, the Cyrene language areas of Libya, visitors from Rome—both Jews and Jewish converts—11 Cretans, and

[*a*] This annual celebration came fifty days after the Passover ceremonies, when Christ was crucified. See Leviticus 23:16. [*b*] Literally, "in other tongues." [*c*] Literally, "Asia," a province of what is now Turkey.

Today's English Version

The coming of the Holy Spirit

2 When the day of Pentecost arrived, all the believers were gathered together in one place. 2 Suddenly there was a noise from the sky which sounded like a strong wind blowing, and it filled the whole house where they were sitting. 3 Then they saw what looked like tongues of fire spreading out; and each person there was touched by a tongue. 4 They were all filled with the Holy Spirit and began to talk in other languages, as the Spirit enabled them to speak.

5 There were Jews living in Jerusalem, religious men who had come from every country in the world. 6 When they heard this noise, a large crowd gathered. They were all excited, because each one of them heard the believers talking in his own language. 7 In amazement and wonder they exclaimed, "These men who are talking like this—they are all Galileans! 8 How is it, then, that all of us hear them speaking in our own native language? 9 We are from Parthia, Media, and Elam; from Mesopotamia, Judea, and Cappadocia; from Pontus and Asia, 10 from Phrygia and Pamphylia, from Egypt and the regions of Libya near Cyrene; some of us are from Rome, 11 both Jews and Gentiles con-

New International Version

The Holy Spirit comes at Pentecost

2 When the day of Pentecost came, they were all together in one place. 2 Suddenly a sound like the blowing of a violent wind came from heaven and filled the whole house where they were sitting. 3 They saw what seemed to be tongues of fire that separated and came to rest on each of them. 4All of them were filled with the Holy Spirit and began to speak in other tongues[d] as the Spirit enabled them.

5 Now there were staying in Jerusalem God-fearing Jews from every nation of the world. 6 When they heard this sound, a crowd came together in bewilderment, because each one heard them speaking in his own language. 7 Utterly amazed, they asked: "Are not all these men who are speaking Galileans? 8 Then how is it that each of us hears them in his own native language? 9 Parthians, Medes and Elamites; residents of Mesopotamia, Judea and Cappadocia, Pontus and Asia, 10 Phrygia and Pamphylia, Egypt and the parts of Libya near Cyrene; visitors from Rome 11 (both Jews and converts to

[*d*] Or *languages.*

Phillips Modern English

2.1 *The first Pentecost for the young Church*

Then when the actual day of Pentecost came
they were all assembled together. Suddenly there
was a sound from heaven like the rushing of a
violent wind, and it filled the whole house where
they were seated. Before their eyes appeared
tongues like flames, which separated off and settled upon each one of them. They were all filled
with the Holy Spirit and began to speak in different languages as the Spirit gave them power
to proclaim the message.

2.5 *The Church's first impact on devout Jews*

Now there were living in Jerusalem Jews of
deep faith from every nation of the world. When
they heard this sound a crowd quickly collected
and were completely bewildered because each
one of them heard these men speaking in his
own language. They were absolutely amazed and
said in their astonishment,
"Listen, surely all these speakers are Galileans?
Then how does it happen that every single one of
us can hear the particular language he has
known from a child? There are Parthians, Medes
and Elamites; there are men whose homes are
in Mesopotamia, in Judaea and Cappadocia,
Pontus, Asia, Phrygia, Pamphylia, Egypt, and
the parts of Libya near Cyrene, as well as visitors from Rome! There are Jews and proselytes,

Revised Standard Version

2 When the day of Pentecost had come, they
were all together in one place. 2 And suddenly a sound came from heaven like the rush
of a mighty wind, and it filled all the house
where they were sitting. 3 And there appeared
to them tongues as of fire, distributed and resting on each one of them. 4 And they were all
filled with the Holy Spirit and began to speak
in other tongues, as the Spirit gave them utterance.
5 Now there were dwelling in Jerusalem Jews,
devout men from every nation under heaven.
6 And at this sound the multitude came together,
and they were bewildered, because each one
heard them speaking in his own language. 7 And
they were amazed and wondered, saying, "Are
not all these who are speaking Galileans? 8 And
how is it that we hear, each of us in his own
native language? 9 Parthians and Medes and
Elamites and residents of Mesopotamia, Judea
and Cappadocia, Pontus and Asia, 10 Phrygia
and Pamphylia, Egypt and the parts of Libya
belonging to Cyrene, and visitors from Rome,
both Jews and proselytes, 11 Cretans and Ara-

Jerusalem Bible

Pentecost

2 When Pentecost day came around, they had
all met in one room, 2 when suddenly they
heard what sounded like a powerful wind from
heaven, the noise of which filled the entire house
in which they were sitting; 3 and something appeared to them that seemed like tongues of fire;
these separated and came to rest on the head of
each of them. 4 They were all filled with the
Holy Spirit, and began to speak foreign languages as the Spirit gave them the gift of
speech.
5 Now there were devout men living in Jerusalem from every nation under heaven, 6 and at
this sound they all assembled, each one bewildered to hear these men speaking his own
language. 7 They were amazed and astonished.
"Surely," they said, "all these men speaking are
Galileans? 8 How does it happen that each of
us hears them in his own native language?
9 Parthians, Medes and Elamites; people from
Mesopotamia, Judaea and Cappadocia, Pontus
and Asia, 10 Phrygia and Pamphylia, Egypt and
the parts of Libya around Cyrene; as well as
visitors from Rome—11 Jews and proselytes[h]

[h] Converts from paganism.

New English Bible

2 While the day of Pentecost was running its
course they were all together in one place,
when suddenly there came from the sky a noise
like that of a strong driving wind, which filled
the whole house where they were sitting. And
there appeared to them tongues like flames of
fire, dispersed among them and resting on each
one. And they were all filled with the Holy Spirit
and began to talk in other tongues, as the
Spirit gave them power of utterance.
Now there were living in Jerusalem devout
Jews[b] drawn from every nation under heaven;
and at this sound the crowd gathered, all bewildered because each one heard his own language spoken. They were amazed and in their
astonishment exclaimed, 'Why, they are all Galileans, are they not, these men who are speaking?
How is it then that we hear them, each of us in
his own native language? Parthians, Medes,
Elamites; inhabitants of Mesopotamia, of Judaea
and Cappadocia, of Pontus and Asia, of Phrygia
and Pamphylia, of Egypt and the districts of
Libya around Cyrene; visitors from Rome, both
Jews and proselytes, Cretans and Arabs, we hear

[b] *Some witnesses read* devout men.

King James Version

Arabians, we do hear them speak in our tongues
the wonderful works of God. 12 And they were
all amazed, and were in doubt, saying one to
another, What meaneth this? 13 Others mocking
said, These men are full of new wine.
14 But Peter, standing up with the eleven,
lifted up his voice, and said unto them, Ye men
of Judea, and all *ye* that dwell at Jerusalem, be
this known unto you, and hearken to my words:
15 For these are not drunken, as ye suppose,
seeing it is *but* the third hour of the day. 16 But
this is that which was spoken by the prophet
Joel; 17 And it shall come to pass in the last days,
saith God, I will pour out of my Spirit upon all
flesh: and your sons and your daughters shall
prophesy, and your young men shall see visions,
and your old men shall dream dreams: 18 And
on my servants and on my handmaidens I will
pour out in those days of my Spirit; and they

Living Bible

Arabians. And we all hear these men telling in
our own languages about the mighty miracles of
God!"
12 They stood there amazed and perplexed.
"What can this mean?" they asked each other.
13 But others in the crowd were mocking.
"They're drunk, that's all!" they said.
14 Then Peter stepped forward with the eleven
apostles, and shouted to the crowd, "Listen, all
of you, visitors and residents of Jerusalem alike!
15 Some of you are saying these men are drunk!
It isn't true! It's much too early for that! People
don't get drunk by 9 A.M.! 16 No! What you see
this morning was predicted centuries ago by the
prophet Joel—17 'In the last days,' God said,
'I will pour out my Holy Spirit upon all mankind, and your sons and daughters shall prophesy, and your young men shall see visions, and
your old men dream dreams. 18 Yes, the Holy
Spirit shall come upon all my servants, men and

Today's English Version

verted to Judaism; and some of us are from
Crete and Arabia—yet all of us hear them speaking in our own languages of the great things that
God has done!" 12 Amazed and confused they
all kept asking each other, "What does this
mean?"
13 But others made fun of the believers, saying, "These men are drunk!"

Peter's message

14 Then Peter stood up with the other eleven
apostles, and in a loud voice began to speak to
the crowd, "Fellow Jews, and all of you who
live in Jerusalem, listen to me and let me tell you
what this means. 15 These men are not drunk, as
you suppose; it is only nine o'clock in the morning. 16 Rather, this is what the prophet Joel spoke
about,

17 'This is what I will do in the last days, God
says:
I will pour out my Spirit upon all men.
Your sons and your daughters will prophesy;
your young men will see visions,
and your old men will dream dreams.
18 Yes, even on my slaves, both men and
women,
I will pour out my Spirit in those days,

New International Version

Judaism); Cretans and Arabs—we hear them declaring the wonders of God in our own
tongues[d]!" 12 Amazed and perplexed, they asked
one another, "What does this mean?"
13 Some, however, made fun of them and
said, "They have had too much wine.[e]"

Peter addresses the crowd

14 Then Peter stood up with the Eleven,
raised his voice and addressed the crowd: "Fellow Jews and all of you who are in Jerusalem,
let me explain this to you; listen carefully to
what I say. 15 These men are not drunk, as you
suppose. It's only nine in the morning! 16 No,
this is what was spoken by the prophet Joel:
17 'In the last days, God says,
I will pour out my Spirit on all people.
Your sons and daughters will prophesy,
your young men will see visions,
and your old men will dream dreams.
18 Even on my servants, both men and
women,
I will pour out my Spirit in those days,

[d] Or *languages*. [e] Or *sweet wine*.

Phillips Modern English

men from Crete and men from Arabia, yet we can all hear these men speaking of the glorious works of God in our native language."

Everyone was utterly amazed and did not know what to make of it. Indeed they kept saying to each other,

"What on earth can this mean?"

But there were others who laughed mockingly and said,

"These fellows have drunk too much sweet wine!"

2.14 Peter explains the fulfilment of God's promise

Then Peter, with the eleven standing by him, raised his voice and addressed them:

"Fellow-Jews, and all who are living now in Jerusalem, listen carefully to what I say while I explain to you what has happened! These men are not drunk as you suppose—it is only nine o'clock in the morning of this great feast day. No, this is something which was predicted by the prophet Joel:

And it shall be in the last days, saith God,
I will pour forth of my Spirit upon all flesh:
And your sons and your daughters shall prophesy,
And your young men shall see visions,
And your old men shall dream dreams:
Yea and on my servants and on my handmaidens in those days
Will I pour forth of my Spirit; and they shall prophesy.

Revised Standard Version

bians, we hear them telling in our own tongues
the mighty works of God." 12And all were
amazed and perplexed, saying to one another,
"What does this mean?" 13 But others mocking
said, "They are filled with new wine."
14 But Peter, standing with the eleven, lifted
up his voice and addressed them, "Men of Judea and all who dwell in Jerusalem, let this be
known to you, and give ear to my words. 15 For
these men are not drunk, as you suppose, since
it is only the third hour of the day; 16 but this
is what was spoken by the prophet Joel:
17 'And in the last days it shall be, God declares,
that I will pour out my Spirit upon all flesh,
and your sons and your daughters shall prophesy,
and your young men shall see visions,
and your old men shall dream dreams;
18 yea, and on my menservants and my maidservants in those days
I will pour out my Spirit; and they shall prophesy.

Jerusalem Bible

alike—Cretans and Arabs; we hear them preaching in our own language about the marvels of
God." 12 Everyone was amazed and unable to
explain it; they asked one another what it all
meant. 13 Some, however, laughed it off. "They
have been drinking too much new wine," they
said.

Peter's address to the crowd

14 Then Peter stood up with the Eleven and addressed them in a loud voice:
"Men of Judaea, and all you who live in
Jerusalem, make no mistake about this, but
listen carefully to what I say. 15 These men are
not drunk, as you imagine; why, it is only the
third hour of the day.[i] 16 On the contrary, this
is what the prophet[j] spoke of:

17 In the days to come—it is the Lord who speaks—
I will pour out my spirit on all mankind.
Their sons and daughters shall prophesy,
your young men shall see visions,
your old men shall dream dreams.
18 Even on my slaves, men and women,
in those days, I will pour out my spirit.

[i] About 9 A.M. [j] Joel. See Jl. 3:1-5.

New English Bible

them telling in our own tongues the great things God has done.' And they were all amazed and perplexed, saying to one another, 'What can this mean?' Others said contemptuously, 'They have been drinking!'

But Peter stood up with the Eleven, raised his voice, and addressed them: 'Fellow Jews, and all you who live in Jerusalem, mark this and give me a hearing. These men are not drunk, as you imagine; for it is only nine in the morning. No, this is what the prophet spoke of: "God says, 'This will happen in the last days: I will pour out upon everyone a portion of my spirit; and your sons and daughters shall prophesy; your young men shall see visions, and your old men shall dream dreams. Yes, I will endue even my slaves, both men and women, with a portion of

King James Version

shall prophesy: 19And I will shew wonders in
heaven above, and signs in the earth beneath;
blood, and fire, and vapour of smoke: 20 The
sun shall be turned into darkness, and the moon
into blood, before that great and notable day of
the Lord come: 21And it shall come to pass,
that whosoever shall call on the name of the
Lord shall be saved. 22 Ye men of Israel, hear
these words; Jesus of Nazareth, a man approved
of God among you by miracles and wonders and
signs, which God did by him in the midst of you,
as ye yourselves also know: 23 Him, being delivered by the determinate counsel and foreknowledge of God, ye have taken, and by wicked
hands have crucified and slain: 24 Whom God
hath raised up, having loosed the pains of death:
because it was not possible that he should be
holden of it. 25 For David speaketh concerning
him, I foresaw the Lord always before my face;
for he is on my right hand, that I should not be
moved: 26 Therefore did my heart rejoice, and
my tongue was glad; moreover also my flesh
shall rest in hope: 27 Because thou wilt not leave
my soul in hell, neither wilt thou suffer thine
Holy One to see corruption. 28 Thou hast made
known to me the ways of life; thou shalt make

Living Bible

women alike, and they shall prophesy. 19And I
will cause strange demonstrations in the heavens
and on the earth—blood and fire and clouds of
smoke; 20 the sun shall turn black and the moon
blood-red before that awesome Day of the Lord
arrives. 21 But anyone who asks for mercy from
the Lord shall have it and shall be saved.'
22 "O men of Israel, listen! God publicly endorsed Jesus of Nazareth by doing tremendous
miracles through him, as you well know. 23 But
God, following his prearranged plan, let you use
the Roman[d] government to nail him to the cross
and murder him. 24 Then God released him
from the horrors of death and brought him back
to life again, for death could not keep this man
within its grip.
25 "King David quoted Jesus as saying:
'I know the Lord is always with me. He is
helping me. God's mighty power supports me.
26 'No wonder my heart is filled with joy
and my tongue shouts his praises! For I know
all will be well with me in death—
27 'You will not leave my soul in hell or
let the body of your Holy Son decay.
28 'You will give me back my life, and give

[*d*] Literally, "men without the Law." See Romans 2:12.

Today's English Version

and they will prophesy.
19 I will perform miracles in the sky above,
and marvels on the earth below.
There will be blood, fire, and thick smoke,
20 the sun will become dark,
and the moon red as blood,
before the great and glorious Day of the
Lord arrives.
21 And then, whoever calls on the name of
the Lord will be saved.'

22 "Listen to these words, men of Israel! Jesus
of Nazareth was a man whose divine mission was
clearly shown to you by the miracles, wonders,
and signs which God did through him; you yourselves know this, for it took place here among
you. 23 God, in his own will and knowledge, had
already decided that Jesus would be handed over
to you; and you killed him, by letting sinful men
nail him to the cross. 24 But God raised him from
the dead; he set him free from the pains of death,
because it was impossible that death should hold
him prisoner. 25 For David said about him,

'I saw the Lord before me at all times;
he is by my right side, so that I will not
be troubled.
26 Because of this my heart is glad
and my words are full of joy;
and I, mortal though I am,
will rest assured in hope,
27 because you will not abandon my soul in
the world of the dead;
you will not allow your devoted servant
to suffer decay.
28 You have shown me the paths that lead to
life,

New International Version

and they will prophesy.
19 And I will show wonders in the heaven
above
and signs on the earth below,
blood and fire and billows of smoke.
20 The sun will be turned to darkness
and the moon become as blood
before the coming of the great and glorious day of the Lord.
21 And everyone who calls on the name of
the Lord will be saved.'[f]
22 "Men of Israel, listen to this: Jesus of
Nazareth was a man accredited by God to you
by miracles, wonders and signs, which God did
among you through him, as you yourselves
know. 23 This man was handed over to you by
God's set purpose and foreknowledge; and you,
with the help of wicked men, put him to death
by nailing him to the cross. 24 But God raised
him from the dead, freeing him from the agony
of death, because it was impossible for death to
keep its hold on him. 25 David said about him:
'I saw the Lord always before me.
Because he is at my right hand, I will not
be shaken.
26 Therefore my heart is glad and my tongue
rejoices;
my body also will live in hope,
27 because you will not abandon me to the
grave,
nor will you let your Holy One undergo
decay.
28 You have made known to me the paths of
life;

[*f*] Joel 2:28-32.

Phillips Modern English

And I will shew wonders in the heaven above,
And signs on the earth beneath;
Blood, and fire, and vapour of smoke:
The sun shall be turned into darkness,
And the moon into blood,
Before the day of the Lord come,
That great and notable day:
And it shall be, that whosoever shall call on the name of the Lord shall be saved.

"Men of Israel, I beg you to listen to my words. Jesus of Nazareth was a man proved to you by God himself through the works of power, the miracles and the signs which God showed through him here amongst you—as you very well know. This man, who was put into your power by the predetermined plan and foreknowledge of God, you nailed up and murdered, and you used for your purpose men without the Law! But God would not allow the bitter pains of death to hold him. He raised him to life again—and indeed there was nothing by which death could hold such a man. When David speaks about him he says,

I beheld the Lord always before my face;
For he is on my right hand, that I should not be moved:
Therefore my heart was glad, and my tongue rejoiced;
Moreover my flesh also shall dwell in hope:
Because thou wilt not leave my soul in Hades,
Neither wilt thou give thy holy one to see corruption.
Thou madest known unto me the ways of life;

Revised Standard Version

19 And I will show wonders in the heaven above
and signs on the earth beneath,
blood, and fire, and vapor of smoke;
20 the sun shall be turned into darkness and the moon into blood,
before the day of the Lord comes,
the great and manifest day.
21 And it shall be that whoever calls on the name of the Lord shall be saved.'
22 "Men of Israel, hear these words: Jesus of
Nazareth, a man attested to you by God with
mighty works and wonders and signs which
God did through him in your midst, as you yourselves know—23 this Jesus, delivered up according to the definite plan and foreknowledge of
God, you crucified and killed by the hands of
lawless men. 24 But God raised him up, having
loosed the pangs of death, because it was not
possible for him to be held by it. 25 For David
says concerning him,
'I saw the Lord always before me,
for he is at my right hand that I may not be shaken;
26 therefore my heart was glad, and my tongue rejoiced;
moreover my flesh will dwell in hope.
27 For thou wilt not abandon my soul to Hades,
nor let thy Holy One see corruption.
28 Thou hast made known to me the ways of life;

Jerusalem Bible

19 I will display portents in heaven *above*
and *signs* on earth *below*.
20 The sun will be turned into darkness
and the moon into blood
before the great Day of the Lord dawns.
21 All who call on the name of the Lord will be saved.
22 "Men of Israel, listen to what I am going
to say: Jesus the Nazarene was a man commended to you by God by the miracles and
portents and signs that God worked through
him when he was among you, as you all know.
23 This man, who was put into your power by
the deliberate intention and foreknowledge of
God, you took and had crucified by men outside
the Law.[k] You killed him, 24 but God raised him
to life, freeing him from the pangs of Hades;
for it was impossible for him to be held in its
power since, 25 as David says of him:

I saw the Lord before me always,
for with him at my right hand nothing can shake me.
26 *So my heart was glad*
and my tongue cried out with joy;
my body, too, will rest in the hope
27 *that you will not abandon my soul to Hades*
nor allow your holy one to experience corruption.
28 *You have made known the way of life to me,*

[k] The Romans.

New English Bible

my spirit, and they shall prophesy. And I will show portents in the sky above, and signs on the earth below—blood and fire and drifting smoke. The sun shall be turned to darkness, and the moon to blood, before that great, resplendent day, the day of the Lord, shall come. And then, everyone who invokes the name of the Lord shall be saved.'"

'Men of Israel, listen to me: I speak of Jesus of Nazareth, a man singled out by God and made known to you through miracles, portents, and signs, which God worked among you through him, as you well know. When he had been given up to you, by the deliberate will and plan of God, you used heathen men to crucify and kill him. But God raised him to life again, setting him free from the pangs of death, because it could not be that death should keep him in its grip.

'For David says of him:

"I foresaw that the presence of the Lord would be with me always,
for he is at my right hand so that I may not be shaken;
therefore my heart was glad and my tongue spoke my joy;
moreover, my flesh shall dwell in hope,
for thou wilt not abandon my soul to death,
nor let thy loyal servant suffer corruption.
Thou hast shown me the ways of life,

King James Version

me full of joy with thy countenance. 29 Men
and brethren, let me freely speak unto you of
the patriarch David, that he is both dead and
buried, and his sepulchre is with us unto this
day. 30 Therefore being a prophet, and knowing
that God had sworn with an oath to him, that
of the fruit of his loins, according to the flesh,
he would raise up Christ to sit on his throne;
31 He, seeing this before, spake of the resurrection of Christ, that his soul was not left in hell,
neither his flesh did see corruption. 32 This Jesus
hath God raised up, whereof we all are witnesses.
33 Therefore being by the right hand of God exalted, and having received of the Father the
promise of the Holy Ghost, he hath shed forth
this, which ye now see and hear. 34 For David
is not ascended into the heavens: but he saith
himself, The LORD said unto my Lord, Sit thou
on my right hand, 35 Until I make thy foes thy
footstool. 36 Therefore let all the house of Israel
know assuredly, that God hath made that same
Jesus, whom ye have crucified, both Lord and
Christ.

Living Bible

me wonderful joy in your presence.'
29 "Dear brothers, think! David wasn't referring to himself when he spoke these words I
have quoted,[e] for he died and was buried, and
his tomb is still here among us. 30 But he was a
prophet, and knew God had promised with an
unbreakable oath that one of David's own descendants would [be the Messiah and [e]] sit on
David's throne. 31 David was looking far into
the future and predicting the Messiah's resurrection, and saying that the Messiah's soul would
not be left in hell and his body would not decay.
32 He was speaking of Jesus, and we all are
witnesses that Jesus rose from the dead.
33 "And now he sits on the throne of highest
honor in heaven, next to God. And just as
promised, the Father gave him the authority to
send the Holy Spirit—with the results you are
seeing and hearing today.
34 "[No, David was not speaking of himself
in these words of his I have quoted [e]], for he
never ascended into the skies. Moreover, he
further stated, 'God spoke to my Lord, the Messiah, and said to him, Sit here in honor beside
me 35 until I bring your enemies into complete
subjection.'
36 "Therefore I clearly state to everyone in
Israel that God has made this Jesus you crucified to be the Lord, the Messiah!"

[*e*] Implied in verse 31.

Today's English Version

and by your presence you will fill me
with joy.'

29 "Brothers: I must speak to you quite
plainly about our patriarch David. He died and
was buried, and his grave is here with us to this
very day. 30 He was a prophet, and he knew
God's promise to him: God made a vow that he
would make one of David's descendants a king,
just as David was. 31 David saw what God was
going to do, and so he spoke about the resurrection of the Messiah when he said,

'He was not abandoned in the world of the
dead;
his flesh did not decay.'

32 God has raised this very Jesus from the dead,
and we are all witnesses to this fact. 33 He has
been raised to the right side of God and received from him the Holy Spirit, as his Father
had promised; and what you now see and hear
is his gift that he has poured out on us. 34 For
David himself did not go up into heaven; rather
he said,

'The Lord said to my Lord:
Sit here at my right side,
35 until I put your enemies as a footstool under your feet.'

36 "All the people of Israel, then, are to know
for sure that it is this Jesus, whom you nailed to
the cross, that God has made Lord and Messiah!"

New International Version

you will fill me with joy in your presence.' [g]
29 "Brothers, I can tell you confidently that
the patriarch David died and was buried, and
his tomb is here to this day. 30 But he was a
prophet and knew that God had promised with
an oath that he would place one of his descendants on his throne. 31 Seeing what was ahead,
he spoke of the resurrection of the Christ,[h] that
he was not abandoned to the grave, nor did his
body undergo decay. 32 God has raised this
Jesus to life, and we are all witnesses of the fact.
33 Exalted to the right hand of God, he has received from the Father the promised Holy
Spirit, and has poured out what you now see
and hear. 34 For David did not ascend to heaven,
and yet he said,

'The Lord said to my Lord:
Sit at my right hand
35 until I make your enemies your footstool.' [i]

36 "Therefore, let all Israel be assured of this:
God has made this Jesus whom you crucified
both Lord and Christ.[h] "

[*g*] Psalm 16:8-11. [*h*] Or *Messiah*. "The Christ" (Greek) and "the Messiah" (Hebrew) both mean "the Anointed One." [*i*] Psalm 110:1.

Phillips Modern English

Thou shalt make me full of gladness with thy countenance.

"Men and brother-Jews, I can surely speak freely to you about the patriarch David. There is no doubt that he died and was buried, and his grave is here among us to this day. But while he was alive he was a prophet. He knew that God had given him a most solemn promise that he would place one of his descendants upon his throne. He foresaw the resurrection of Christ, and it is this of which he is speaking. Christ did not 'leave his soul in Hades' and his body 'did not see corruption'. This man Jesus God raised up—a fact of which all of us are eye-witnesses! He has been raised to the right hand of God; he has received from the Father and poured out upon us the promised Holy Spirit—*that* is what you now see and hear! David never ascended to Heaven, but he certainly said,

The Lord said unto my *Lord,*
Sit thou on my right hand,
Till I make thine enemies the footstool of thy feet.

"Now therefore the whole nation of Israel must know beyond the shadow of a doubt that this Jesus, whom you crucified, God has declared to be both Lord and Christ."

Revised Standard Version

thou wilt make me full of gladness with thy presence.'
29 "Brethren, I may say to you confidently
of the patriarch David that he both died and
was buried, and his tomb is with us to this day.
30 Being therefore a prophet, and knowing that
God had sworn with an oath to him that he
would set one of his descendants upon his
throne, 31 he foresaw and spoke of the resurrection of the Christ, that he was not abandoned
to Hades, nor did his flesh see corruption. 32 This
Jesus God raised up, and of that we all are
witnesses. 33 Being therefore exalted at the right
hand of God, and having received from the Father the promise of the Holy Spirit, he has
poured out this which you see and hear. 34 For
David did not ascend into the heavens; but he
himself says,
'The Lord said to my Lord, Sit at my right hand,
35 till I make thy enemies a stool for thy feet.'
36 Let all the house of Israel therefore know
assuredly that God has made him both Lord
and Christ, this Jesus whom you crucified."

Jerusalem Bible

you will fill me with gladness through your presence.[l]

29 "Brothers, no one can deny that the patriarch David himself is dead and buried: his tomb
is still with us. 30 But since he was a prophet,
and knew that God *had sworn him* an oath *to make one of his descendants succeed him on the*
throne,[m] 31 what he foresaw and spoke about
was the resurrection of the Christ: he is the one
who was *not abandoned to Hades,* and whose
body did not *experience corruption.* 32 God
raised this man Jesus to life, and all of us are
witnesses to that. 33 Now raised to the heights
by God's right hand, he has received from the
Father the Holy Spirit, who was promised, and
what you see and hear is the outpouring of that
Spirit. 34 For David himself never went up to
heaven; and yet these words are his:

The Lord said to my Lord:
Sit at my right hand
35 *until I make your enemies*
a footstool for you.[n]

36 "For this reason the whole House of Israel can be certain that God has made this Jesus whom you crucified both Lord and Christ."

[*l*] Ps. 16:8-11; quoted according to the LXX. [*m*] 2 S. 7:12 and Ps. 132:11. [*n*] Ps. 110:1.

New English Bible

thou wilt fill me with gladness by thy presence."

'Let me tell you plainly, my friends, that the patriarch David died and was buried, and his tomb is here to this very day. It is clear therefore that he spoke as a prophet, who knew that God had sworn to him that one of his own direct descendants should sit on his throne; and when he said he was not abandoned to death, and his flesh never suffered corruption, he spoke with foreknowledge of the resurrection of the Messiah. The Jesus we speak of has been raised by God, as we can all bear witness. Exalted thus with[a] God's right hand, he received the Holy Spirit from the Father, as was promised, and all that you now see and hear flows from him. For it was not David who went up to heaven; his own words are: "The Lord said to my Lord, 'Sit at my right hand until I make your enemies your footstool.'" Let all Israel then accept as certain that God has made this Jesus, whom you crucified, both Lord and Messiah.'

[*a*] *Or* at.

King James Version

37 Now when they heard *this,* they were pricked in their heart, and said unto Peter and to the rest of the apostles, Men *and* brethren, what shall we do? 38 Then Peter said unto them, Repent, and be baptized every one of you in the name of Jesus Christ for the remission of sins, and ye shall receive the gift of the Holy Ghost. 39 For the promise is unto you, and to your children, and to all that are afar off, *even* as many as the Lord our God shall call. 40 And with many other words did he testify and exhort, saying, Save yourselves from this untoward generation.

41 Then they that gladly received his word were baptized: and the same day there were added *unto them* about three thousand souls. 42 And they continued steadfastly in the apostles' doctrine and fellowship, and in breaking of bread, and in prayers. 43 And fear came upon every soul: and many wonders and signs were done by the apostles. 44 And all that believed were together, and had all things common; 45 And sold their possessions and goods, and parted

Living Bible

37 These words of Peter's moved them deeply, and they said to him and to the other apostles, "Brothers, what should we do?"

38 And Peter replied, "Each one of you must turn from sin, return to God, and be baptized in the name of Jesus Christ for the forgiveness of your sins; then you also shall receive this gift, the Holy Spirit. 39 For Christ promised him to each one of you who has been called by the Lord our God, and to your children and even to those in distant lands!"

40 Then Peter preached a long sermon, telling about Jesus and strongly urging all his listeners to save themselves from the evils of their nation. 41 And those who believed Peter were baptized —about 3,000 in all! 42 They joined with the other believers in regular attendance at the apostles' teaching sessions and at the Communion services[f] and prayer meetings. 43 A deep sense of awe was on them all, and the apostles did many miracles.

44 And all the believers met together constantly and shared everything with each other, 45 selling their possessions and dividing with

[*f*] Literally, "the breaking of bread," i.e., "the Lord's Supper."

Today's English Version

37 When the people heard this, they were deeply troubled, and said to Peter and the other apostles, "What shall we do, brothers?"

38 Peter said to them, "Turn away from your sins, each one of you, and be baptized in the name of Jesus Christ, so that your sins will be forgiven; and you will receive God's gift, the Holy Spirit. 39 For God's promise was made to you and your children, and to all who are far away—all whom the Lord our God calls to himself."

40 Peter made his appeal to them and with many other words he urged them, saying, "Save yourselves from the punishment coming to this wicked people!" 41 Many of them believed his message and were baptized; about three thousand people were added to the group that day. 42 They spent their time in learning from the apostles, taking part in the fellowship, and sharing in the fellowship meals and the prayers.

Life among the believers

43 Many miracles and wonders were done through the apostles, and this caused everyone to be filled with awe. 44 All the believers continued together in close fellowship and shared their belongings with one another. 45 They would sell their property and possessions and distribute the money among all, according to what each

New International Version

37 When the people heard this, they were cut to the heart and said to Peter and the other apostles, "Brothers, what shall we do?"

38 Peter replied: "Repent and be baptized, every one of you, in the name of Jesus Christ so that your sins may be forgiven. And you will receive the gift of the Holy Spirit. 39 The promise is for you and your children and for all who are far off—for all whom the Lord our God will call."

40 With many other words he warned them; and he pleaded with them, "Save yourselves from this corrupt generation." 41 Those who accepted his message were baptized, and about three thousand were added to their number that day.

The fellowship of the believers

42 They devoted themselves to the apostles' teaching and to the fellowship, to the breaking of bread and to prayer. 43 Everyone was filled with awe, and many wonders and miracles were done by the apostles. 44 All the believers were together and had everything in common. 45 Selling their possessions and goods, they gave to anyone

Phillips Modern English

2.37 The reaction to Peter's speech

When they heard this they were cut to the quick, and they cried to Peter and the other apostles,

"Men and fellow-Jews, what shall we do now?"

Peter told them,

"You must repent and every one of you must be baptised in the name of Jesus Christ, so that you may have your sins forgiven and receive the gift of the Holy Spirit. For this great promise is for you and your children—yes, and for all who are far away, for as many as the Lord our God shall call to himself!"

Peter said much more than this as he gave his testimony and implored them, saying,

"Save yourselves from this perverse generation!"

2.41 The first large-scale conversion

Then those who welcomed this message were baptised, and on that day alone about three thousand souls were added to the number of disciples. They continued steadily learning the teaching of the apostles, and joined in their fellowship, in the breaking of bread, and in prayer.

Everyone felt a deep sense of awe, while many miracles and signs took place through the apostles. All the believers joined together and shared everything in common; they sold their possessions and goods and divided the proceeds among the fellowship according to individual need.

Revised Standard Version

37 Now when they heard this they were cut to the heart, and said to Peter and the rest of the apostles, "Brethren, what shall we do?"
38 And Peter said to them, "Repent, and be baptized every one of you in the name of Jesus Christ for the forgiveness of your sins; and you shall receive the gift of the Holy Spirit. 39 For the promise is to you and to your children and to all that are far off, every one whom the Lord our God calls to him." 40 And he testified with many other words and exhorted them, saying, "Save yourselves from this crooked generation."
41 So those who received his word were baptized, and there were added that day about three thousand souls. 42 And they devoted themselves to the apostles' teaching and fellowship, to the breaking of bread and the prayers.
43 And fear came upon every soul; and many wonders and signs were done through the apostles. 44 And all who believed were together and had all things in common; 45 and they sold their possessions and goods and distributed them

Jerusalem Bible

The first conversions

37 Hearing this, they were cut to the heart and said to Peter and the apostles, "What must we do, brothers?" 38 "You must repent," Peter answered, "and every one of you must be baptized in the name of Jesus Christ for the forgiveness of your sins, and you will receive the gift of the Holy Spirit. 39 The promise that was made is for you and your children, and for all *those who are far away, for all those whom the Lord* our God *will call to himself.*" [o] 40 He spoke to them for a long time using many arguments, and he urged them, "Save yourselves from this perverse generation." 41 They were convinced by his arguments, and they accepted what he said and were baptized. That very day about three thousand were added to their number.

The early Christian community

42 These remained faithful to the teaching of the apostles, to the brotherhood, to the breaking of bread and to the prayers.

43 The many miracles and signs worked through the apostles made a deep impression on everyone.

44 The faithful all lived together and owned everything in common; 45 they sold their goods and possessions and shared out the proceeds among themselves according to what each one needed.

[o] Is. 57:19.

New English Bible

When they heard this they were cut to the heart, and said to Peter and the apostles,[b] 'Friends, what are we to do?' 'Repent,' said Peter, 'repent and be baptized, every one of you, in the name of Jesus the Messiah for the forgiveness of your sins; and you will receive the gift of the Holy Spirit. For the promise is to you, and to your children, and to all who are far away, everyone whom the Lord our God may call.'

In these and many other words he pressed his case and pleaded with them: 'Save yourselves', he said, 'from this crooked age.' Then those who accepted his word were baptized, and some three thousand were added to their number that day.

They met constantly to hear the apostles teach, and to share the common life, to break bread, and to pray. A sense of awe was everywhere, and many marvels and signs were brought about through the apostles. All whose faith had drawn them together held everything in common:[c] they would sell their property and possessions and make a general distribution as the need of each

[b] *Some witnesses read* the rest of the apostles. [c] *Or* All who had become believers held everything together in common.

King James Version

them to all *men*, as every man had need. 46And they, continuing daily with one accord in the temple, and breaking bread from house to house, did eat their meat with gladness and singleness of heart, 47 Praising God, and having favour with all the people. And the Lord added to the church daily such as should be saved.

3 Now Peter and John went up together into the temple at the hour of prayer, *being* the ninth *hour*. 2And a certain man lame from his mother's womb was carried, whom they laid daily at the gate of the temple which is called Beautiful, to ask alms of them that entered into the temple; 3 Who, seeing Peter and John about to go into the temple, asked an alms. 4And Peter, fastening his eyes upon him with John, said, Look on us. 5And he gave heed unto them, expecting to receive something of them. 6 Then Peter said, Silver and gold have I none; but such as I have give I thee: In the name of Jesus Christ of Nazareth rise up and walk. 7And he took him by the right hand, and lifted *him* up: and immediately his feet and ankle bones received strength. 8And he leaping up stood, and walked, and entered with them into the temple, walking and leaping, and praising God. 9And all the peo-

Living Bible

those in need. 46 They worshiped together regularly at the Temple each day, met in small groups in the homes for Communion, and shared their meals with great joy and thankfulness, 47 praising God. The whole city was favorable to them, and each day God added to them all who were being saved.

3 Peter and John went to the Temple one afternoon to take part in the three o'clock daily prayer meeting. 2As they approached the Temple, they saw a man lame from birth carried along the street and laid beside the Temple gate—the one called The Beautiful Gate—as was his custom every day. 3As Peter and John were passing by, he asked them for some money.

4 They looked at him intently, and then Peter said, "Look here!"

5 The lame man looked at them eagerly, expecting a gift.

6 But Peter said, "We don't have any money for you! But I'll give you something else! I command you in the name of Jesus Christ of Nazareth, *walk!*"

7, 8 Then Peter took the lame man by the hand and pulled him to his feet. And as he did, the man's feet and ankle-bones were healed and strengthened so that he came up with a leap, stood there a moment and began walking! Then, walking, leaping, and praising God, he went into the Temple with them.

9 When the people inside saw him walking

Today's English Version

one needed. 46 Every day they continued to meet as a group in the temple, and they had their meals together in their homes, eating the food with glad and humble hearts, 47 praising God, and enjoying the good will of all the people. And every day the Lord added to their group those who were being saved.

The lame man healed

3 One day Peter and John went to the temple at three o'clock in the afternoon, the hour for prayers. 2 There, at the "Beautiful Gate," as it was called, was a man who had been lame all his life. Every day he was carried to this gate to beg for money from the people who were going into the temple. 3 When he saw Peter and John going in, he begged them to give him something. 4 They looked straight at him and Peter said, "Look at us!" 5 So he looked at them, expecting to get something from them. 6 Peter said to him, "I have no money at all, but I will give you what I have: in the name of Jesus Christ of Nazareth I order you to walk!" 7 Then he took him by his right hand and helped him up. At once the man's feet and ankles became strong; 8 he jumped up, stood on his feet, and started walking around. Then he went into the temple with them, walking and jumping and praising God. 9 The whole crowd saw him walking and

New International Version

as he had need. 46 Every day they continued to meet together in the temple courts. They broke bread in their homes and ate together with glad and sincere hearts, 47 praising God and enjoying the favor of all the people. And the Lord added to their number daily those who were being saved.

Peter heals the crippled beggar

3 One day Peter and John were going up to the temple at the time of prayer—at three in the afternoon. 2 Now a man crippled from birth was being carried to the temple gate called Beautiful, where he was put every day to beg from those going into the temple courts. 3 When he saw Peter and John about to enter, he asked them for money. 4 Peter looked straight at him, as did John. Then Peter said, "Look at us!" 5 So the man gave them his attention, expecting to get something from them.

6 Then Peter said, "I have no silver or gold, but what I have I give you. In the name of Jesus Christ of Nazareth, walk." 7 Taking him by the right hand, he helped him up, and instantly the man's feet and ankles became strong. 8 He jumped to his feet and began to walk. Then he went with them into the temple courts, walking and jumping, and praising God. 9 When all the people saw him walking and praising God,

Phillips Modern English

Day after day they met by common consent in the Temple; they broke bread together in their homes, sharing meals with simple joy. They praised God continually and all the people respected them. Every day the Lord increased the number of those who were finding salvation.

3.1 A public miracle and its explanation

One afternoon Peter and John were on their way to the Temple for the three o'clock hour of prayer. A man who had been lame from birth was being carried along in the crowd, for it was the daily practice to put him down at what was known as the Beautiful Gate of the Temple, so that he could beg from the people as they went in. As this man saw Peter and John just about to enter he asked them to give him something. Peter looked intently at the man and so did John. Then Peter said,

"Look straight at us!"

The man looked at them expectantly, hoping for a gift from them.

"I have neither silver nor gold," said Peter, "but what I have I will certainly give you. In the name of Jesus Christ of Nazareth, *walk!*"

Then he grasped him by the right hand and lifted him up. At once his feet and ankle bones were strengthened, and he sprang to his feet, stood, and then walked. Then he went with them into the Temple, where he walked about, leaping and thanking God. Everyone noticed him

Revised Standard Version

to all, as any had need. 46And day by day, attending the temple together and breaking bread
in their homes, they partook of food with glad
and generous hearts, 47 praising God and having favor with all the people. And the Lord
added to their number day by day those who
were being saved.

3 Now Peter and John were going up to the
temple at the hour of prayer, the ninth hour.
2And a man lame from birth was being carried,
whom they laid daily at that gate of the temple
which is called Beautiful to ask alms of those
who entered the temple. 3 Seeing Peter and John
about to go into the temple, he asked for alms.
4And Peter directed his gaze at him, with John,
and said, "Look at us." 5And he fixed his attention upon them, expecting to receive something from them. 6 But Peter said, "I have no
silver and gold, but I give you what I have; in
the name of Jesus Christ of Nazareth, walk."
7And he took him by the right hand and raised
him up; and immediately his feet and ankles
were made strong. 8And leaping up he stood
and walked and entered the temple with them,
walking and leaping and praising God. 9And all
the people saw him walking and praising God,

Jerusalem Bible

46 They went as a body to the Temple every
day but met in their houses for the breaking of
bread; they shared their food gladly and generously; 47 they praised God and were looked
up to by everyone. Day by day the Lord added
to their community those destined to be saved.

The cure of a lame man

3 Once, when Peter and John were going up
to the Temple for the prayers at the ninth
hour,[p] 2 it happened that there was a man being carried past. He was a cripple from birth;
and they used to put him down every day near
the Temple entrance called the Beautiful Gate
so that he could beg from the people going in.
3 When this man saw Peter and John on their
way into the Temple he begged from them.
4 Both Peter and John looked straight at him
and said, "Look at us." 5 He turned to them expectantly, hoping to get something from them,
6 but Peter said, "I have neither silver nor gold,
but I will give you what I have: in the name of
Jesus Christ the Nazarene, walk!" 7 Peter then
took him by the hand and helped him to stand
up. Instantly his feet and ankles became firm,
8 he jumped up, stood, and began to walk, and
he went with them into the Temple, walking and
jumping and praising God. 9 Everyone could see

[p] The time of evening sacrifice.

New English Bible

required. With one mind they kept up their daily attendance at the temple, and, breaking bread in private houses, shared their meals with unaffected joy, as they praised God and enjoyed the favour of the whole people. And day by day the Lord added to their number those whom he was saving.

3 One day at three in the afternoon, the hour of prayer, Peter and John were on their way up to the temple. Now a man who had been a cripple from birth used to be carried there and laid every day by the gate of the temple called 'Beautiful Gate', to beg from people as they went in. When he saw Peter and John on their way into the temple he asked for charity. But Peter fixed his eyes on him, as John did also, and said, 'Look at us.' Expecting a gift from them, the man was all attention. And Peter said, 'I have no silver or gold; but what I have I give you: in the name of Jesus Christ of Nazareth, walk.' Then he grasped him by the right hand and pulled him up; and at once his feet and ankles grew strong; he sprang up, stood on his feet, and started to walk. He entered the temple with them, leaping and praising God as he went. Everyone saw him walking and praising God,

King James Version

ple saw him walking and praising God: 10And
they knew that it was he which sat for alms at
the Beautiful gate of the temple: and they were
filled with wonder and amazement at that which
had happened unto him. 11And as the lame man
which was healed held Peter and John, all the
people ran together unto them in the porch that
is called Solomon's, greatly wondering.
12 And when Peter saw *it,* he answered unto
the people, Ye men of Israel, why marvel ye at
this? or why look ye so earnestly on us, as
though by our own power or holiness we had
made this man to walk? 13 The God of Abraham, and of Isaac, and of Jacob, the God of our
fathers, hath glorified his Son Jesus; whom ye
delivered up, and denied him in the presence of
Pilate, when he was determined to let *him* go.
14 But ye denied the Holy One and the Just, and
desired a murderer to be granted unto you;
15And killed the Prince of life, whom God hath
raised from the dead; whereof we are witnesses.
16And his name, through faith in his name, hath
made this man strong, whom ye see and know:
yea, the faith which is by him hath given him
this perfect soundness in the presence of you all.
17And now, brethren, I wot that through igno-

Living Bible

and heard him praising God, 10 and realized he
was the lame beggar they had seen so often at
The Beautiful Gate, they were inexpressibly surprised! 11 They all rushed out to Solomon's
Hall, where he was holding tightly to Peter and
John! Everyone stood there awed by the wonderful thing that had happened.
12 Peter saw his opportunity and addressed
the crowd. "Men of Israel," he said, "what is
so surprising about this? And why look at us
as though we by our own power and godliness
had made this man walk? 13 For it is the God
of Abraham, Isaac, Jacob and of all our ancestors who has brought glory to his servant
Jesus by doing this. I refer to the Jesus whom
you rejected before Pilate, despite Pilate's determination to release him. 14 You didn't want
him freed—this holy, righteous one. Instead you
demanded the release of a murderer. 15And you
killed the Author of Life; but God brought him
back to life again. And John and I are witnesses
of this fact, for after you killed him we saw him
alive!
16 "Jesus' name has healed this man—and
you know how lame he was before. Faith in
Jesus' name—faith given us from God—has
caused this perfect healing.
17 "Dear brothers, I realize that what you
did to Jesus was done in ignorance; and the

Today's English Version

praising God; 10 and when they recognized him
as the beggar who sat at the temple's "Beautiful
Gate," they were all filled with surprise and
amazement at what had happened to him.

Peter's message in the temple

11 As the man held on to Peter and John, all
the people were amazed and ran to them in
"Solomon's Porch," as it was called. 12 When
Peter saw the people, he said to them, "Men of
Israel, why are you surprised at this, and why
do you stare at us? Do you think that it was by
means of our own power or godliness that we
made this man walk? 13 The God of Abraham,
Isaac, and Jacob, the God of our ancestors, has
given divine glory to his Servant Jesus. You
handed him over to the authorities, and you rejected him in Pilate's presence, even after Pilate
had decided to set him free. 14 He was holy and
good, but you rejected him and instead you asked
Pilate to do you the favor of turning loose a
murderer. 15And so you killed the one who leads
men to life. But God raised him from the dead—
and we are witnesses to this. 16 It was the power
of his name that gave strength to this lame man.
What you see and know was done by faith in
his name; it was faith in Jesus that made him
well like this before you all.
17 "And now, my brothers. I know that what
you and your leaders did to Jesus was done be-

New International Version

10 they recognized him as the same man who
used to sit begging at the temple gate called
Beautiful, and they were filled with wonder and
amazement at what had happened to him.

Peter speaks to the onlookers

11 While the beggar held on to Peter and
John, all the people were astonished and came
running to them in the place called Solomon's
Colonnade. 12 When Peter saw this, he said to
them: "Men of Israel, why does this surprise
you? Why do you stare at us as if by our own
power or godliness we had made this man
walk? 13 The God of Abraham, Isaac and Jacob,
the God of our fathers, has glorified his servant
Jesus. You handed him over to be killed, and
you disowned him before Pilate, though he had
decided to let him go. 14 You disowned the
Holy and Righteous One and asked that a murderer be released to you. 15 You killed the author
of life, but God raised him from the dead. We
are witnesses of this. 16 By faith in the name of
Jesus, this man whom you see and know was
made strong. It is Jesus' name and the faith that
comes through him that has given this complete
healing to him, as you can all see.
17 "Now, brothers, I know that you acted in

Phillips Modern English

as he walked and praised God and recognised him as the beggar who used to sit at the Beautiful Gate, and they were all overcome with wonder and sheer astonishment at what had happened to him. Then while the man himself still clung to Peter and John all the people in their excitement ran together and crowded round them in what is called Solomon's Porch. When Peter saw this he spoke to the crowd.

"Men of Israel, why are you so surprised at this, and why are you staring at us as though we had made this man walk through some power or piety of our own? It is the God of Abraham and Isaac and Jacob, the God of our fathers, who has done this thing to honour his servant Jesus—the man whom you betrayed and denied in the presence of Pilate, even when he had decided to let him go. But you disowned the holy and righteous one, and begged to be granted instead a man who was a murderer! You killed the pioneer of Life, but God raised him from the dead—a fact of which we are eye-witnesses. It is the name of this same Jesus, it is faith in that name, which has cured this man whom you see and recognise. Yes, it was faith in Christ which gave this man perfect health and strength in full view of you all.

3.17 Peter explains ancient prophecy

"Now of course I know, my brothers, that you had no idea of what you were doing any more

Revised Standard Version

10 and recognized him as the one who sat for alms at the Beautiful Gate of the temple; and they were filled with wonder and amazement at what had happened to him.

11 While he clung to Peter and John, all the people ran together to them in the portico called Solomon's, astounded. 12 And when Peter saw it he addressed the people, "Men of Israel, why do you wonder at this, or why do you stare at us, as though by our own power or piety we had made him walk? 13 The God of Abraham and of Isaac and of Jacob, the God of our fathers, glorified his servant[c] Jesus, whom you delivered up and denied in the presence of Pilate, when he had decided to release him. 14 But you denied the Holy and Righteous One, and asked for a murderer to be granted to you, 15 and killed the Author of life, whom God raised from the dead. To this we are witnesses. 16 And his name, by faith in his name, has made this man strong whom you see and know; and the faith which is through Jesus[d] has given the man this perfect health in the presence of you all.

17 "And now, brethren, I know that you acted

[c] Or *child.* [d] Greek *him.*

Jerusalem Bible

him walking and praising God, 10 and they recognized him as the man who used to sit begging at the Beautiful Gate of the Temple. They were all astonished and unable to explain what had happened to him.

Peter's address to the people

11 Everyone came running toward them in great excitement, to the Portico of Solomon, as it is called, where the man was still clinging to Peter and John. 12 When Peter saw the people he addressed them, "Why are you so surprised at this? Why are you staring at us as though we had made this man walk by our own power or holiness? 13 You are Israelites, and it is *the God of Abraham, Isaac and Jacob, the God of our ancestors, who has glorified his servant*[q] Jesus, the same Jesus you handed over and then disowned in the presence of Pilate after Pilate had decided to release him. 14 It was you who accused the Holy One, the Just One, you who demanded the reprieve of a murderer 15 while you killed the prince of life. God, however, raised him from the dead, and to that fact we are the witnesses; 16 and it is the name of Jesus which, through our faith in it, has brought back the strength of this man whom you see here and who is well known to you. It is faith in that name that has restored this man to health, as you can all see.

17 "Now I know, brothers, that neither you nor your leaders had any idea what you were

[q] Ex. 3:6,15 and Is. 52:13.

New English Bible

and when they recognized him as the man who used to sit begging at Beautiful Gate, they were filled with wonder and amazement at what had happened to him.

And as he was clutching Peter and John all the people came running in astonishment towards them in Solomon's Portico, as it is called. Peter saw them coming and met them with these words: 'Men of Israel, why be surprised at this? Why stare at us as if we had made this man walk by some power or godliness of our own? The God of Abraham, Isaac, and Jacob, the God of our fathers, has given the highest honour to his servant Jesus, whom you committed for trial and repudiated in Pilate's court—repudiated the one who was holy and righteous when Pilate had decided to release him. You begged as a favour the release of a murderer, and killed him who has led the way to life. But God raised him from the dead; of that we are witnesses. And the name of Jesus, by awakening faith, has strengthened this man, whom you see and know, and this faith has made him completely well, as you can all see for yourselves.

'And now, my friends, I know quite well that you acted in ignorance, and so did your rulers;

King James Version

rance ye did *it,* as *did* also your rulers. 18 But those things, which God before had shewed by the mouth of all his prophets, that Christ should suffer, he hath so fulfilled.

19 Repent ye therefore, and be converted, that your sins may be blotted out, when the times of refreshing shall come from the presence of the Lord; 20 And he shall send Jesus Christ, which before was preached unto you: 21 Whom the heaven must receive until the times of restitution of all things, which God hath spoken by the mouth of all his holy prophets since the world began. 22 For Moses truly said unto the fathers, A Prophet shall the Lord your God raise up unto you of your brethren, like unto me; him shall ye hear in all things whatsoever he shall say unto you. 23 And it shall come to pass, *that* every soul, which will not hear that Prophet, shall be destroyed from among the people. 24 Yea, and all the prophets from Samuel and those that follow after, as many as have spoken, have likewise foretold of these days. 25 Ye are the children of the prophets, and of the covenant which God made with our fathers, saying unto Abraham, And in thy seed shall all the kindreds of the earth be blessed. 26 Unto you first God, having raised up his Son Jesus, sent him to bless you, in turning away every one of you from his iniquities.

Living Bible

same can be said of your leaders. 18 But God was fulfilling the prophecies that the Messiah must suffer all these things. 19 Now change your mind and attitude to God and turn to him so he can cleanse away your sins and send you wonderful times of refreshment from the presence of the Lord 20 and send Jesus your Messiah back to you again. 21, 22 For he must remain in heaven until the final recovery of all things from sin, as prophesied from ancient times. Moses, for instance, said long ago, 'The Lord God will raise up a Prophet among you, who will resemble me! [a] Listen carefully to everything he tells you. 23 Anyone who will not listen to him shall be utterly destroyed.' [b]

24 "Samuel and every prophet since have all spoken about what is going on today. 25 You are the children of those prophets; and you are included in God's promise to your ancestors to bless the entire world through the Jewish race—that is the promise God gave to Abraham. 26 And as soon as God had brought his servant to life again, he sent him first of all to you men of Israel, to bless you by turning you back from your sins."

[*a*] Literally, "like unto me." [*b*] Literally, "destroyed among the people."

Today's English Version

cause of your ignorance. 18 God long ago announced by means of all the prophets that his Messiah had to suffer; and he made it come true in this way. 19 Repent, then, and turn to God, so that he will wipe away your sins, 20 so that times of spiritual strength may come from the Lord's presence, and that he may send Jesus, who is the Messiah he has already chosen for you. 21 He must remain in heaven until the time comes for all things to be made new, as God announced by means of his holy prophets of long ago. 22 For Moses said, 'The Lord your God will send you a prophet, just as he sent me, who will be of your own people. You must listen to everything that he tells you. 23 Anyone who does not listen to what that prophet says will be separated from God's people and destroyed.' 24 And the prophets, including Samuel and those who came after him, all of them who had a message, also announced these present days. 25 The promises of God through his prophets are for you, and you share in the covenant which God made with your ancestors. As he said to Abraham, 'Through your descendants I will bless all the people on earth.' 26 And so God chose and sent his Servant to you first, to bless you by making all of you turn away from your wicked ways."

New International Version

ignorance, as did your leaders. 18 But this is how God fulfilled what he had foretold through all the prophets, saying that his Christ[j] would suffer. 19 Repent, then, and turn to God, so that your sins may be wiped out, 20 that times of refreshing may come from the Lord, and that he may send the Christ,[j] who has been appointed for you—even Jesus. 21 He must remain in heaven until the time comes for God to restore everything, as he promised long ago through his holy prophets. 22 For Moses said, 'The Lord your God will raise up for you a prophet like me from among your own people; you must listen to everything he tells you. 23 Anyone who does not listen to him will be completely cut off from among his people.' [k]

24 "Indeed, all the prophets from Samuel on, as many as have spoken, have foretold these days. 25 And you are heirs of the prophets and of the covenant God made with your fathers. He said to Abraham, 'Through your offspring all peoples on earth will be blessed.' [l] 26 When God raised up his servant, he sent him first to you to bless you by turning each of you from his wicked ways."

[*j*] Or *Messiah.* [*k*] Deut. 18:15,18,19. [*l*] Gen. 22:18; 26:4.

Phillips Modern English

than your leaders had. But God had foretold through all his prophets that his Christ must suffer and this was how his words came true. Now you must repent and turn to God so that your sins may be wiped out, that your souls may know the times of refreshment which come from the presence of the Lord. Then he will send you your long-heralded Christ, that is Jesus. Heaven must receive him until that universal restoration of which God spoke in ancient times through all his holy prophets. For Moses said,

> A prophet shall the Lord God raise up unto you from among your brethren, like unto me; to him shall ye hearken in all things whatsoever he shall speak unto you. And it shall be that every soul, which shall not hearken to that prophet, shall be utterly destroyed from among the people.

Indeed, all the prophets who have spoken from Samuel onwards have foretold these days. You are the sons of the prophets and heirs of the agreement which God made with your fathers when he said to Abraham, 'Through your children shall all the families of the earth be blessed.' It was to you first that God sent his servant after he had raised him up, to bring you great blessing by turning every one of you away from his evil ways."

Revised Standard Version

in ignorance, as did also your rulers. 18 But what God foretold by the mouth of all the prophets, that his Christ should suffer, he thus fulfilled. 19 Repent therefore, and turn again, that your sins may be blotted out, that times of refreshing may come from the presence of the Lord, 20 and that he may send the Christ appointed for you, Jesus, 21 whom heaven must receive until the time for establishing all that God spoke by the mouth of his holy prophets from of old. 22 Moses said, 'The Lord God will raise up for you a prophet from your brethren as he raised me up. You shall listen to him in whatever he tells you. 23 And it shall be that every soul that does not listen to that prophet shall be destroyed from the people.' 24 And all the prophets who have spoken, from Samuel and those who came afterwards, also proclaimed these days. 25 You are the sons of the prophets and of the covenant which God gave to your fathers, saying to Abraham, 'And in your posterity shall all the families of the earth be blessed.' 26 God, having raised up his servant,[c] sent him to you first, to bless you in turning every one of you from your wickedness."

[c] Or *child*.

Jerusalem Bible

really doing; 18 this was the way God carried out what he had foretold, when he said through all his prophets that his Christ would suffer. 19 Now you must repent and turn to God, so that your sins may be wiped out, 20 and so that the Lord may send the time of comfort. Then he will send you the Christ he has predestined, that is Jesus, 21 whom heaven must keep till the universal restoration comes which God proclaimed, speaking through his holy prophets. 22 Moses, for example, said: *The Lord God will raise up a prophet like myself for you, from among your own brothers; you must listen to whatever he tells you.* 23 *The man who does not listen to that prophet is to be cut off from the people.*[r] 24 In fact, all the prophets that have ever spoken, from Samuel onward, have predicted these days.

25 "You are the heirs of the prophets, the heirs of the covenant God made with our ancestors when he told Abraham: *in your offspring all the families of the earth will be blessed.*[s] 26 It was for you in the first place that God raised up his servant and sent him to bless you by turning every one of you from your wicked ways."

[r] Dt. 18:18,19. [s] Gn. 12:3.

New English Bible

but this is how God fulfilled what he had foretold in the utterances of all the prophets: that his Messiah should suffer. Repent then and turn to God, so that your sins may be wiped out. Then the Lord may grant you a time of recovery and send you the Messiah he has already appointed, that is, Jesus. He must be received into heaven until the time of universal restoration comes, of which God spoke by his holy prophets.[a] Moses said, "The Lord God will raise up a prophet for you from among yourselves as he raised me;[b] you shall listen to everything he says to you, and anyone who refuses to listen to that prophet must be extirpated from Israel." And so said all the prophets, from Samuel onwards; with one voice they all predicted this present time.

'You are the heirs of the prophets; you are within the covenant which God made with your fathers, when he said to Abraham, "And in your offspring all the families on earth shall find blessing." When God raised up his Servant, he sent him to you first, to bring you blessing by turning every one of you from your wicked ways.'

[a] *Some witnesses add* from the beginning of the world. [b] *Or* like me.

King James Version

4 And as they spake unto the people, the
priests, and the captain of the temple, and the
Sadducees, came upon them, 2 Being grieved that
they taught the people, and preached through
Jesus the resurrection from the dead. 3 And they
laid hands on them, and put *them* in hold unto
the next day: for it was now eventide. 4 Howbeit
many of them which heard the word believed;
and the number of the men was about five thousand.
5 And it came to pass on the morrow that
their rulers, and elders, and scribes, 6 And Annas
the high priest, and Caiaphas, and John, and
Alexander, and as many as were of the kindred
of the high priest, were gathered together at Jerusalem. 7 And when they had set them in the
midst, they asked, By what power, or by what
name, have ye done this? 8 Then Peter, filled
with the Holy Ghost, said unto them, Ye rulers
of the people, and elders of Israel, 9 If we this
day be examined of the good deed done to the
impotent man, by what means he is made whole;
10 Be it known unto you all, and to all the peo-

Living Bible

4 While they were talking to the people, the
chief priests, the captain of the Temple police, and some of the Sadducees[a] came over to
them, 2 very disturbed that Peter and John were
claiming that Jesus had risen from the dead.
3 They arrested them and since it was already
evening, jailed them overnight. 4 But many of the
people who heard their message believed it, so
that the number of believers now reached a new
high of about 5,000 men!
5 The next day it happened that the Council
of all the Jewish leaders was in session in Jerusalem—6 Annas the High Priest was there, and
Caiaphas, John, Alexander, and others of the
High Priest's relatives. 7 So the two disciples
were brought in before them.
"By what power, or by whose authority have
you done this?" the Council demanded.
8 Then Peter, filled with the Holy Spirit, said
to them, "Honorable leaders and elders of our
nation, 9 if you mean the good deed done to
the cripple, and how he was healed, 10 let me
clearly state to you and to all the people of
Israel that it was done in the name and power

[a] The Sadducees were members of a Jewish religious sect that denied the resurrection of the dead.

Today's English Version

Peter and John before the Council

4 Peter and John were still speaking to the
people when the priests, the officer in charge
of the temple guards, and the Sadducees came
to them. 2 They were annoyed because the two
apostles were teaching the people that Jesus had
risen from death, which proved that the dead
will rise to life. 3 So they arrested them and put
them in jail until the next day, since it was already late. 4 But many who heard the message
believed; and the number of men came to about
five thousand.
5 The next day the Jewish leaders, the elders,
and the teachers of the Law gathered in Jerusalem. 6 They met with the High Priest Annas, and
Caiaphas, and John, and Alexander, and the
others who belonged to the High Priest's family.
7 They made the apostles stand before them
and asked them, "How did you do this? What
power do you have, or whose name did you use?"
8 Peter, full of the Holy Spirit, answered them,
"Leaders of the people and elders: 9 if we are
being questioned today about the good deed
done to the lame man and how he was made well,
10 then you should all know, and all the people
of Israel should know, that this man stands here
before you completely well by the power of the

New International Version

Peter and John before the Sanhedrin

4 The priests and the captain of the temple
guard and the Sadducees came up to Peter
and John while they were speaking to the people.
2 They were greatly disturbed because the apostles were teaching the people and proclaiming
in Jesus the resurrection of the dead. 3 They
seized Peter and John, and because it was evening, they put them in jail until the next day.
4 But many who heard the message believed, and
the number of men grew to about five thousand.
5 The next day the rulers, elders and teachers
of the law met in Jerusalem. 6 Annas the high
priest was there, and so were Caiaphas, John,
Alexander and the other men of the high
priest's family. 7 They had Peter and John
brought before them and began to question
them: "By what power or what name did you
do this?"
8 Then Peter, filled with the Holy Spirit, said
to them: "Rulers and elders of the people! 9 If
we are being called to account today for an act
of kindness shown to a cripple and are asked
how he was healed, 10 then know this, you and
everyone else in Israel: It is by the name of

Phillips Modern English

4.1 The first clash with Jewish authorities

While they were still talking to the people the priests, the captain of the Temple guard and the Sadducees moved towards them, thoroughly incensed that they should be teaching the people and should assure them that the resurrection of the dead had been proved through the rising of Jesus. So they arrested them and, since it was now evening, kept them in custody until the next day. Nevertheless, many of those who had heard what they said believed, and the number of men alone rose to about five thousand.

4.5 Peter's boldness at formal questioning

Next day the leading members of the council, the elders and scribes, met in Jerusalem with Annas the High Priest, Caiaphas, John, Alexander, and the whole of the High Priest's family. They had the apostles brought in to stand before them and they asked them formally,

"By what power and in whose name have you done this thing?"

At this Peter, filled with the Holy Spirit, spoke to them,

"Leaders of the people and elders, if we are being called in question today over the matter of a kindness done to a helpless man and as to how he was healed, it is high time that all of you and the whole people of Israel knew that it was

Revised Standard Version

4 And as they were speaking to the people,
the priests and the captain of the temple and
the Sadducees came upon them, 2 annoyed because they were teaching the people and proclaiming in Jesus the resurrection from the dead.
3 And they arrested them and put them in custody until the morrow, for it was already evening. 4 But many of those who heard the word
believed; and the number of the men came to
about five thousand.
5 On the morrow their rulers and elders and
scribes were gathered together in Jerusalem,
6 with Annas the high priest and Caiaphas and
John and Alexander, and all who were of the
high-priestly family. 7 And when they had set
them in the midst, they inquired, "By what
power or by what name did you do this?" 8 Then
Peter, filled with the Holy Spirit, said to them,
"Rulers of the people and elders, 9 if we are
being examined today concerning a good deed
done to a cripple, by what means this man has
been healed, 10 be it known to you all, and to
all the people of Israel, that by the name of

Jerusalem Bible

Peter and John before the Sanhedrin

4 While they were still talking to the people
the priests came up to them, accompanied by
the captain of the Temple and the Sadducees.[t]
2 They were extremely annoyed at their teaching the people the doctrine of the resurrection
from the dead by proclaiming the resurrection of
Jesus. 3 They arrested them, but as it was already late, they held them till the next day.
4 But many of those who had listened to their
message became believers, the total number of
whom had now risen to something like five
thousand.
5 The next day the rulers, elders and scribes[u]
had a meeting in Jerusalem 6 with Annas the
high priest, Caiaphas, Jonathan, Alexander and
all the members of the high-priestly families.
7 They made the prisoners stand in the middle
and began to interrogate them, "By what power,
and by whose name have you men done this?"
8 Then Peter, filled with the Holy Spirit, addressed them, "Rulers of the people, and elders!
9 If you are questioning us today about an act of
kindness to a cripple, and asking us how he was
healed, 10 then I am glad to tell you all, and
would indeed be glad to tell the whole people

[t] The Sadducees (see note on Mt. 3:7) are always represented as denying the doctrine of the resurrection, e.g., Ac. 23. [u] I.e., the Sanhedrin, explained for the non-Jewish reader.

New English Bible

4 They were still addressing the people when the chief[a] priests came upon them, together with the Controller of the Temple and the Sadducees, exasperated at their teaching the people and proclaiming the resurrection from the dead —the resurrection of Jesus. They were arrested and put in prison for the night, as it was already evening. But many of those who had heard the message became believers. The number of men now reached about five thousand.

Next day the Jewish rulers, elders, and doctors of the law met in Jerusalem. There were present Annas the High Priest, Caiaphas, Jonathan,[b] Alexander, and all who were of the high-priestly family. They brought the apostles before the court and began the examination. 'By what power', they asked, 'or by what name have such men as you done this?' Then Peter, filled with the Holy Spirit, answered, 'Rulers of the people and elders, if the question put to us today is about help given to a sick man, and we are asked by what means he was cured, here is the answer, for all of you and for all the people of Israel: it

[a] *Some witnesses omit* chief. [b] *Some witnesses read* John.

King James Version

ple of Israel, that by the name of Jesus Christ
of Nazareth, whom ye crucified, whom God
raised from the dead, *even* by him doth this
man stand here before you whole. 11 This is the
stone which was set at nought of you builders,
which is become the head of the corner. 12 Neither is there salvation in any other: for there is
none other name under heaven given among
men, whereby we must be saved.

13 Now when they saw the boldness of Peter
and John, and perceived that they were unlearned and ignorant men, they marvelled; and
they took knowledge of them, that they had been
with Jesus. 14 And beholding the man which was
healed standing with them, they could say nothing against it. 15 But when they had commanded
them to go aside out of the council, they conferred among themselves, 16 Saying, What shall
we do to these men? for that indeed a notable
miracle hath been done by them *is* manifest to
all them that dwell in Jerusalem; and we cannot
deny *it*. 17 But that it spread no further among
the people, let us straitly threaten them, that
they speak henceforth to no man in this name.
18 And they called them, and commanded them
not to speak at all nor teach in the name of

Living Bible

of Jesus from Nazareth, the Messiah, the man
you crucified—but God raised back to life again.
It is by his authority that this man stands here
healed! 11 For Jesus the Messiah is (the one referred to in the Scriptures when they speak of)
a 'stone discarded by the builders which became
the capstone of the arch.' [b] 12 There is salvation
in no one else! Under all heaven there is no
other name for men to call upon to save them."

13 When the Council saw the boldness of
Peter and John, and could see that they were
obviously uneducated non-professionals, they
were amazed and realized what being with Jesus
had done for them! 14 And the Council could
hardly discredit the healing when the man they
had healed was standing right there beside them!
15 So they sent them out of the Council chamber
and conferred among themselves.

16 "What shall we do with these men?" they
asked each other. "We can't deny that they have
done a tremendous miracle, and everybody in
Jerusalem knows about it. 17 But perhaps we
can stop them from spreading their propaganda.
We'll tell them that if they do it again we'll
really throw the book at them." 18 So they called
them back in, and told them never again to

[b] Implied. Literally, "became the head of the corner."

Today's English Version

name of Jesus Christ of Nazareth—whom you
crucified and God raised from death. 11 Jesus is
the one of whom the scripture says,

'The stone that you the builders despised
turned out to be the most important stone.'

12 Salvation is to be found through him alone; for
there is no one else in all the world, whose name
God has given to men, by whom we can be
saved."

13 The members of the Council were amazed
to see how bold Peter and John were, and to
learn that they were ordinary men of no education. They realized then that they had been companions of Jesus. 14 But there was nothing that
they could say, because they saw the man who
had been made well standing there with Peter and
John. 15 So they told them to leave the Council
room, and started discussing among themselves.
16 "What shall we do with these men?" they
asked. "Everyone living in Jerusalem knows that
this extraordinary miracle has been performed by
them, and we cannot deny it. 17 But to keep this
matter from spreading any further among the
people, let us warn these men never again to
speak to anyone in the name of Jesus."

18 So they called them back in and told them
that under no condition were they to speak or to

New International Version

Jesus Christ of Nazareth, whom you crucified
but whom God raised from the dead, that this
man stands before you completely healed. 11 He
is

'the stone you builders rejected,
which has become the capstone.' [m]

12 Salvation is found in no one else; for there
is no other name under heaven given to men by
which we must be saved."

13 When they saw the courage of Peter and
John and realized that they were unschooled,
ordinary men, they were astonished and they
took note that these men had been with Jesus.
14 But since they could see the man who had
been healed standing there with them, there was
nothing they could say. 15 So they ordered them
to withdraw from the Sanhedrin and then conferred together. 16 "What are we going to do
with these men?" they asked. "Everybody living in Jerusalem knows they have done an outstanding miracle, and we cannot deny it. 17 But
to stop this thing from spreading any further
among the people, we must warn these men to
speak no longer to anyone in this name."

18 Then they called them in again and commanded them not to speak or teach at all in the

[m] Psalm 118:22.

Phillips Modern English

done in the name of Jesus Christ of Nazareth! He is the one whom you crucified but whom God raised from the dead, and it is by his power that this man at our side stands in your presence perfectly well. He is the 'stone which you builders rejected, which has now become the head of the corner'. In no one else can salvation be found. For in all the world no other name has been given to men but this, and it is by this name that we must be saved!"

4.13 The embarrassment of the authorities

When they saw the complete assurance of Peter and John, who were in their view uneducated and untrained men, they were staggered, recognising them as men who had been with Jesus. Yet since they could see the man who had been cured standing beside them, they could find no effective reply. All they could do was to order them out of the Sanhedrin and hold a conference among themselves.

"What are we going to do with these men?" they said to each other. "It is evident to everyone living in Jerusalem that an extraordinary miracle has taken place through them, and that is something we cannot deny. Nevertheless, to prevent such a thing spreading further among the people, let us warn them that if they say anything more to anyone in this name it will be at their peril."

So they called them in and ordered them bluntly not to speak or teach a single further

Revised Standard Version

Jesus Christ of Nazareth, whom you crucified,
whom God raised from the dead, by him this
man is standing before you well. 11 This is the
stone which was rejected by you builders, but
which has become the head of the corner. 12 And
there is salvation in no one else, for there is no
other name under heaven given among men by
which we must be saved."

13 Now when they saw the boldness of Peter
and John, and perceived that they were uneducated, common men, they wondered; and they
recognized that they had been with Jesus. 14 But
seeing the man that had been healed standing
beside them, they had nothing to say in opposition. 15 But when they had commanded them
to go aside out of the council, they conferred
with one another, 16 saying, "What shall we do
with these men? For that a notable sign has
been performed through them is manifest to all
the inhabitants of Jerusalem, and we cannot
deny it. 17 But in order that it may spread no
further among the people, let us warn them to
speak no more to any one in this name." 18 So
they called them and charged them not to speak

Jerusalem Bible

of Israel, that it was by the name of Jesus Christ the Nazarene, the one you crucified, whom God raised from the dead, by this name and by no other that this man is able to stand up perfectly
healthy, here in your presence, today. 11 This is
the stone rejected by you *the builders, but which*
has proved to be the keystone.[v] 12 For of all the
names in the world given to men, this is the only one by which we can be saved."

13 They were astonished at the assurance shown by Peter and John, considering they were uneducated laymen; and they recognized them
as associates of Jesus; 14 but when they saw the
man who had been cured standing by their side,
they could find no answer. 15 So they ordered
them to stand outside while the Sanhedrin had
a private discussion. 16 "What are we going to
do with these men?" they asked. "It is obvious to everybody in Jerusalem that a miracle has been worked through them in public, and we
cannot deny it. 17 But to stop the whole thing
spreading any further among the people, let us caution them never to speak to anyone in this name again."

18 So they called them in and gave them a
warning on no account to make statements or

[v] Ps. 18:22.

New English Bible

was by the name of Jesus Christ of Nazareth, whom you crucified, whom God raised from the dead; it is by his name[c] that this man stands here before you fit and well. This Jesus is the stone rejected by the builders which has become the keystone—and you are the builders. There is no salvation in anyone else at all,[d] for there is no other name under heaven granted to men, by which we may receive salvation.'

Now as they observed the boldness of Peter and John, and noted that they were untrained laymen, they began to wonder, then recognized them as former companions of Jesus. And when they saw the man who had been cured standing with them, they had nothing to say in reply. So they ordered them to leave the court, and then discussed the matter among themselves. 'What are we to do with these men?' they said; 'for it is common knowledge in Jerusalem that a notable miracle has come about through them; and we cannot deny it. But to stop this from spreading further among the people, we had better caution them never again to speak to anyone in this name.' They then called them in and ordered them to refrain from all public speaking and

[c] *Some witnesses insert* and no other. [d] Some *witnesses omit* There is no . . . at all.

King James Version

Jesus. 19 But Peter and John answered and said
unto them, Whether it be right in the sight of
God to hearken unto you more than unto God,
judge ye. 20 For we cannot but speak the things
which we have seen and heard. 21 So when they
had further threatened them, they let them go,
finding nothing how they might punish them, because of the people: for all *men* glorified God
for that which was done. 22 For the man was
above forty years old, on whom this miracle of
healing was shewed.
23 And being let go, they went to their own
company, and reported all that the chief priests
and elders had said unto them. 24 And when they
heard that, they lifted up their voice to God
with one accord, and said, Lord, thou *art* God,
which hast made heaven, and earth, and the sea,
and all that in them is; 25 Who by the mouth of
thy servant David hast said, Why did the heathen
rage, and the people imagine vain things? 26 The
kings of the earth stood up, and the rulers were
gathered together against the Lord, and against

Living Bible

speak about Jesus.
19 But Peter and John replied, "You decide
whether God wants us to obey you instead of
him! 20 We cannot stop telling about the wonderful things we saw Jesus do and heard him
say."
21 The Council then threatened them further,
and finally let them go because they didn't know
how to punish them without starting a riot. For
everyone was praising God for this wonderful
miracle—22 the healing of a man who had been
lame for forty years.
23 As soon as they were freed, Peter and John
found the other disciples and told them what the
Council had said.
24 Then all the believers united in this prayer:
"O Lord, Creator of heaven and earth and
of the sea and everything in them—25, 26 you
spoke long ago by the Holy Spirit through our
ancestor King David, your servant, saying, 'Why
do the heathen rage against the Lord, and the
foolish nations plan their little plots against
Almighty God? The kings of the earth unite to
fight against him, and against the anointed Son
of God!'

Today's English Version

teach in the name of Jesus. 19 But Peter and John
answered them, "You yourselves judge which is
right in God's sight, to obey you or to obey God.
20 For we cannot stop speaking of what we ourselves have seen and heard." 21 The Council
warned them even more strongly, and then set
them free. They could find no reason for punishing them, because the people were all praising
God for what had happened. 22 The man on
whom this miracle of healing had been performed
was over forty years old.

The believers pray for boldness

23 As soon as they were set free, Peter and
John returned to their group and told them what
the chief priests and the elders had said. 24 When
they heard it, they all joined together in prayer
to God: "Master and Creator of heaven, earth,
and sea, and all that is in them! 25 By means of
the Holy Spirit you spoke through our ancestor
David, your servant, when he said,

'Why were the Gentiles furious;
why did the peoples plot in vain?
26 The kings of the earth prepared themselves,
and the rulers met together
against the Lord and his Messiah.'

New International Version

name of Jesus. 19 But Peter and John replied,
"Judge for yourselves whether it is right in
God's sight to obey you rather than God. 20 For
we cannot help speaking about what we have
seen and heard."
21 After further threats they let them go.
They could not decide how to punish them, because all the people were praising God for what
had happened. 22 For the man who was miraculously healed was over forty years old.

The believers' prayer

23 On their release, Peter and John went
back to their own people and reported all that
the chief priests and elders had said to them.
24 When they heard this, they raised their voices
together in prayer to God. "Sovereign Lord,"
they said, "you made the heaven and the earth
and the sea, and everything in them. 25 You
spoke by the Holy Spirit through the mouth of
your servant, our father David:

'Why do the nations rage,
and the people plot in vain?
26 The kings of the earth take their stand,
and the rulers gather together
against the Lord
and against his Anointed One.[n]' [o]

[n] That is, Christ or Messiah. [o] Psalm 2:1,2.

Phillips Modern English

word to anyone in the name of Jesus. But Peter and John gave them this reply:

"Whether it is right in the eyes of God for us to listen to what you say rather than to what he says, you must decide; for we cannot help speaking about what we have actually seen and heard!"

After further threats they let them go. They could not think of any way of punishing them because of the attitude of the people. Everybody was thanking God for what had happened—that this miracle of healing had taken place in a man who was more than forty years old.

4.23 The united prayer of the young Church—

After their release the apostles went back to their friends and reported to them what the chief priests and elders had said to them. When they heard it they raised their voices to God in united prayer and said,

"Almighty Lord, thou art the one who hast made the heaven and the earth, the sea and all that is in them. It was thou who didst speak by the Holy Spirit through the lips of our forefather David thy servant in the words:

Why did the gentiles rage,
And the peoples imagine vain things?
The kings of the earth set themselves in array,
And the rulers were gathered together,
Against the Lord, and against his anointed:

Revised Standard Version

or teach at all in the name of Jesus. 19 But
Peter and John answered them, "Whether it is right in the sight of God to listen to you rather than to God, you must judge; 20 for we cannot
but speak of what we have seen and heard."
21 And when they had further threatened them,
they let them go, finding no way to punish them, because of the people; for all men praised
God for what had happened. 22 For the man on
whom this sign of healing was performed was more than forty years old.
23 When they were released they went to their friends and reported what the chief priests
and the elders had said to them. 24 And when
they heard it, they lifted their voices together to God and said, "Sovereign Lord, who didst make the heaven and the earth and the sea and everything in them,
25 who by the mouth of our
father David, thy servant,[c] didst say by the Holy Spirit,

'Why did the Gentiles rage,
and the peoples imagine vain things?
26 The kings of the earth set themselves in array,
and the rulers were gathered together,
against the Lord and against his Anointed'—[e]

[c] Or *child.* [e] Or *Christ.*

Jerusalem Bible

to teach in the name of Jesus. 19 But Peter and
John retorted, "You must judge whether in God's eyes it is right to listen to you and not
to God. 20 We cannot promise to stop proclaiming what we have seen and heard."
21 The
court repeated the warnings and then released them; they could not think of any way to punish them, since all the people were giving glory to
God for what had happened. 22 The man who
had been miraculously cured was over forty years old.

The apostles' prayer under persecution

23 As soon as they were released they went to the community and told them everything the chief priests and elders had said to them.
24 When they heard it they lifted up their voice to God all together. "Master," they prayed, "it is you who made heaven and earth and sea, and
everything in them; 25 you it is who said through the Holy Spirit and speaking through our ancestor David, your servant:

Why this arrogance among the nations,
these futile plots among the peoples?
26 *Kings on earth setting out to war,*
princes making an alliance,
against the Lord and against his Anointed.[w]

[w] Ps. 2:1-2.

New English Bible

teaching in the name of Jesus.

But Peter and John said to them in reply: 'Is it right in God's eyes for us to obey you rather than God? Judge for yourselves. We cannot possibly give up speaking of things we have seen and heard.'

The court repeated the caution and discharged them. They could not see how they were to punish them, because the people were all giving glory to God for what had happened. The man upon whom this miracle of healing had been performed was over forty years old.

As soon as they were discharged they went back to their friends and told them everything that the chief priests and elders had said. When they heard it, they raised their voices as one man and called upon God:

'Sovereign Lord, maker of heaven and earth and sea and of everything in them, who by the Holy Spirit,[a] through the mouth of David thy servant, didst say,

"Why did the Gentiles rage and the peoples lay their plots in vain?
The kings of the earth took their stand and the rulers made common cause
against the Lord and against his Messiah."

[a] *Some witnesses omit* by the Holy Spirit.

King James Version

his Christ. 27 For of a truth against thy holy child Jesus, whom thou hast anointed, both Herod, and Pontius Pilate, with the Gentiles, and the people of Israel, were gathered together, 28 For to do whatsoever thy hand and thy counsel determined before to be done. 29 And now, Lord, behold their threatenings: and grant unto thy servants, that with all boldness they may speak thy word, 30 By stretching forth thine hand to heal; and that signs and wonders may be done by the name of thy holy child Jesus.

31 And when they had prayed, the place was shaken where they were assembled together; and they were all filled with the Holy Ghost, and they spake the word of God with boldness. 32 And the multitude of them that believed were of one heart and of one soul: neither said any *of them* that aught of the things which he possessed was his own; but they had all things common. 33 And with great power gave the apostles witness of the resurrection of the Lord Jesus: and great grace was upon them all. 34 Neither was there any among them that lacked: for as many as were possessors of lands or houses sold them, and brought the prices of the things that were sold, 35 And laid *them* down at the apostles' feet: and distribution was made unto every man

Living Bible

27 "That is what is happening here in this city today! For Herod the king, and Pontius Pilate the governor, and all the Romans—as well as the people of Israel—are united against Jesus, your anointed Son, your holy servant. 28 They won't stop at anything that you in your wise power will let them do. 29 And now, O Lord, hear their threats, and grant to your servants great boldness in their preaching, 30 and send your healing power, and may miracles and wonders be done by the name of your holy servant Jesus."

31 After this prayer, the building where they were meeting shook and they were all filled with the Holy Spirit and boldly preached God's message.

32 All the believers were of one heart and mind, and no one felt that what he owned was his own; everyone was sharing. 33 And the apostles preached powerful sermons about the resurrection of the Lord Jesus, and there was warm fellowship[c] among all the believers, 34, 35 and no poverty—for all who owned land or houses sold them and brought the money to the apostles to give to others in need.

[c] Literally, "great grace was upon them all."

Today's English Version

27 For indeed Herod and Pontius Pilate met together in this city with the Gentiles and the people of Israel against Jesus, your holy Servant, whom you made Messiah. 28 They gathered to do everything that you, by your power and will, had already decided would take place. 29 And now, Lord, take notice of the threats they made and allow us, your servants, to speak your message with all boldness. 30 Stretch out your hand to heal, and grant that wonders and miracles may be performed through the name of your holy Servant Jesus."

31 When they finished praying, the place where they were meeting was shaken. They were all filled with the Holy Spirit and began to speak God's message with boldness.

All things together

32 The group of believers was one in mind and heart. No one said that any of his belongings was his own, but they all shared with one another everything they had. 33 With great power the apostles gave witness of the resurrection of the Lord Jesus, and God poured rich blessings on them all. 34 There was no one in the group who was in need. Those who owned fields or houses would sell them, bring the money received from the sale 35 and turn it over to the apostles; and the money was distributed to each one according to his need.

New International Version

27 Indeed Herod and Pontius Pilate met together with the Gentiles and the people of Israel in this city to conspire against your holy servant Jesus, whom you anointed. 28 They did what your power and will had decided beforehand should happen. 29 Now, Lord, consider their threats and enable your servants to speak your word with great boldness. 30 Stretch out your hand to heal and perform miraculous signs and wonders through the name of your holy servant Jesus."

31 After they prayed, the place where they were meeting was shaken. And they were all filled with the Holy Spirit and spoke the word of God boldly.

The believers share their possessions

32 All the believers were one in heart and mind. No one claimed that any of his possessions was his own, but they shared everything they had. 33 With great power the apostles continued to testify to the resurrection of the Lord Jesus, and much grace was with them all. 34 There were no needy persons among them. For from time to time those who owned lands or houses sold them, brought the money from the sales 35 and put it at the apostles' feet, and it was distributed to anyone as he had need.

Phillips Modern English

For indeed in this city the rulers have joined together against thy holy servant, Jesus, thine anointed—yes, Herod and Pontius Pilate, the gentiles and the peoples of Israel have gathered together to carry out what thine hand and will had planned to happen. And now, O Lord, observe their threats and give thy servants courage to speak thy word fearlessly, while thou dost stretch out thine hand to heal, and cause signs and wonders to be performed in the name of thy holy servant Jesus."

When they had prayed their meeting-place was shaken; they were all filled with the Holy Spirit and spoke the Word of God fearlessly.

4.32 —and their close fellowship

Among the large number who had become believers there was complete agreement of heart and soul. Not one of them claimed any of his possessions as his own but everything was common property. The apostles continued to give their witness to the resurrection of the Lord Jesus with great force, and a wonderful spirit of generosity pervaded the whole fellowship. Indeed, there was not a single person in need among them. For those who owned land or property would sell them and bring the proceeds of the sales and place them at the apostles' feet. They would distribute to each one if he were in need.

Revised Standard Version

27 for truly in this city there were gathered
together against thy holy servant[c] Jesus, whom
thou didst anoint, both Herod and Pontius Pilate, with the Gentiles and the peoples of Israel,
28 to do whatever thy hand and thy plan had
predestined to take place. 29 And now, Lord,
look upon their threats, and grant to thy servants[f] to speak thy word with all boldness,
30 while thou stretchest out thy hand to heal,
and signs and wonders are performed through
the name of thy holy servant[c] Jesus." 31 And
when they had prayed, the place in which they
were gathered together was shaken; and they
were all filled with the Holy Spirit and spoke
the word of God with boldness.

32 Now the company of those who believed
were of one heart and soul, and no one said that
any of the things which he possessed was his
own, but they had everything in common. 33 And
with great power the apostles gave their testimony to the resurrection of the Lord Jesus, and
great grace was upon them all. 34 There was not
a needy person among them, for as many as were
possessors of lands or houses sold them, and
brought the proceeds of what was sold 35 and
laid it at the apostles' feet; and distribution was

[c] Or *child.* [f] Or *slaves.*

Jerusalem Bible

27 "This is what has come true: in this very
city Herod and Pontius Pilate *made an alliance*
with the pagan *nations* and the *peoples* of Israel, against your holy servant Jesus whom you
anointed,[x] 28 but only to bring about the very
thing that you in your strength and your wisdom
had predetermined should happen. 29 And now,
Lord, take note of their threats and help your
servants to proclaim your message with all boldness, 30 by stretching out your hand to heal and
to work miracles and marvels through the name
of your holy servant Jesus." 31 As they prayed,
the house where they were assembled rocked;
they were all filled with the Holy Spirit and
began to proclaim the word of God boldly.

The early Christian community

32 The whole group of believers was united, heart and soul; no one claimed for his own use anything that he had, as everything they owned was held in common.

33 The apostles continued to testify to the resurrection of the Lord Jesus with great power, and they were all given great respect.

34 None of their members was ever in want, as all those who owned land or houses would sell them, and bring the money from them,
35 to present it to the apostles; it was then distributed to any members who might be in need.

[x] I.e., made the Christ, the anointed Messiah.

New English Bible

They did indeed make common cause in this very city against thy holy servant Jesus whom thou didst anoint as Messiah. Herod and Pontius Pilate conspired with the Gentiles and peoples of Israel to do all the things which, under thy hand and by thy decree, were foreordained. And now, O Lord, mark their threats, and enable thy servants to speak thy word with all boldness. Stretch out thy hand to heal and cause signs and wonders to be done through the name of thy holy servant Jesus.'

When they had ended their prayer, the building where they were assembled rocked, and all were filled with the Holy Spirit and spoke the word of God with boldness.

The whole body of believers was united in heart and soul. Not a man of them claimed any of his possessions as his own, but everything was held in common, while the apostles bore witness with great power to the resurrection of the Lord Jesus. They were all held in high esteem; for they had never a needy person among them, because all who had property in land or houses sold it, brought the proceeds of the sale, and laid the money at the feet of the apostles; it was then distributed to any who stood in need.

King James Version

according as he had need. 36And Joses, who by
the apostles was surnamed Barnabas, (which is,
being interpreted, The son of consolation,) a
Levite, *and* of the country of Cyprus, 37 Having
land, sold *it*, and brought the money, and laid *it*
at the apostles' feet.

5 But a certain man named Ananias, with Sapphira his wife, sold a possession, 2And kept
back *part* of the price, his wife also being privy
to it, and brought a certain part, and laid *it* at
the apostles' feet. 3 But Peter said, Ananias, why
hath Satan filled thine heart to lie to the Holy
Ghost, and to keep back *part* of the price of the
land? 4 While it remained, was it not thine own?
and after it was sold, was it not in thine own
power? why hast thou conceived this thing in
thine heart? thou hast not lied unto men, but
unto God. 5And Ananias hearing these words
fell down, and gave up the ghost: and great fear
came on all them that heard these things. 6And
the young men arose, wound him up, and carried
him out, and buried *him*. 7And it was about the
space of three hours after, when his wife, not
knowing what was done, came in. 8And Peter
answered unto her, Tell me whether ye sold the

Living Bible

36 For instance, there was Joseph (the one
the apostles nicknamed "Barny the Preacher"!
He was of the tribe of Levi, from the island of
Cyprus). 37 He was one of those who sold a
field he owned and brought the money to the
apostles for distribution to those in need.

5 But there was a man named Ananias (with
his wife Sapphira) who sold some property,
2 and brought only part of the money, claiming
it was the full price. (His wife had agreed to
this deception.)

3 But Peter said, "Ananias, Satan has filled
your heart. When you claimed this was the full
price, you were lying to the Holy Spirit. 4 The
property was yours to sell or not, as you wished.
And after selling it, it was yours to decide how
much to give. How could you do a thing like
this? You weren't lying to us, but to God."

5 As soon as Ananias heard these words, he
fell to the floor, dead! Everyone was terrified,
6 and the younger men covered him with a sheet
and took him out and buried him.

7 About three hours later his wife came in,
not knowing what had happened. 8 Peter asked
her, "Did you people sell your land for such

Today's English Version

36 And so it was that Joseph, a Levite born
in Cyprus, whom the apostles called Barnabas
(which means "One who Encourages"), 37 sold
a field he owned, brought the money, and turned
it over to the apostles.

Ananias and Sapphira

5 But there was a man named Ananias, whose
wife was named Sapphira. He sold some
property that belonged to them, 2 but kept part
of the money for himself, as his wife knew, and
turned the rest over to the apostles. 3 Peter said
to him, "Ananias, why did you let Satan take
control of your heart and make you lie to the
Holy Spirit by keeping part of the money you
received for the property? 4 Before you sold the
property it belonged to you, and after you sold
it the money was yours. Why, then, did you decide in your heart that you would do such a
thing? You have not lied to men—you have lied
to God!" 5As soon as Ananias heard this he fell
down dead; and all who heard about it were
filled with fear. 6 The young men came in,
wrapped up his body, took him out, and buried
him.

7 About three hours later his wife came in, but
she did not know what had happened. 8 Peter said
to her, "Tell me, was this the full amount you

New International Version

36 Joseph, a Levite from Cyprus, whom the
apostles called Barnabas (which means, Son of
Encouragement), 37 sold a field he owned and
brought the money and put it at the apostles'
feet.

Ananias and Sapphira

5 Now a man named Ananias, together with
his wife Sapphira, also sold a piece of property. 2 With his wife's full knowledge he kept
back part of the money for himself, but brought
the rest and put it at the apostles' feet.

3 Then Peter said, "Ananias, how is it that
Satan has so filled your heart that you have lied
to the Holy Spirit and have kept for yourself
some of the money you received for the land?
4 Didn't it belong to you before it was sold? And
after it was sold, wasn't the money at your disposal? What made you think of doing such a
thing? You have not lied to man but to God."

5 When Ananias heard this, he fell down and
died. And great fear seized all who heard what
had happened. 6 Then the young men came forward, wrapped up his body, and carried him out
and buried him.

7 About three hours later his wife came in,
not knowing what had happened. 8 Peter asked
her, "Tell me, is this the price you and Ananias

Phillips Modern English

4.36 Generosity and covetousness

It was at this time that Barnabas (the name, meaning son of comfort, given by the apostles to Joseph, a Levite from Cyprus) sold his farm and put the proceeds at the apostles' disposal.

But there was a man named Ananias who, with his wife Sapphira, had sold a piece of property, but with her full knowledge, reserved part of the price for himself. He brought the remainder to put at the apostles' disposal. But Peter said to him,

"Ananias, why has Satan so filled your mind that you could cheat the Holy Spirit and keep back for yourself part of the price of the land? Before the land was sold it was yours, and after the sale the disposal of the price you received was entirely in your hands, wasn't it? Then whatever made you think of such a thing as this? You have not lied to men, but to God!"

As soon as Ananias heard these words he collapsed and died. All who were within earshot were awe-struck at this incident. The young men got to their feet and after wrapping up his body carried him out and buried him.

About three hours later it happened that his wife came in not knowing what had taken place. Peter spoke directly to her,

"Tell me, did you sell your land for so much?"

Revised Standard Version

made to each as any had need. 36 Thus Joseph who was surnamed by the apostles Barnabas (which means, Son of encouragement), a Levite, a native of Cyprus, 37 sold a field which belonged to him, and brought the money and laid it at the apostles' feet.

5 But a man named Ananias with his wife Sapphira, sold a piece of property, 2 and with his wife's knowledge he kept back some of the proceeds, and brought only a part and laid it at the apostles' feet. 3 But Peter said, "Ananias, why has Satan filled your heart to lie to the Holy Spirit and to keep back part of the proceeds of the land? 4 While it remained unsold, did it not remain your own? And after it was sold, was it not at your disposal? How is it that you have contrived this deed in your heart? You have not lied to men but to God." 5 When Ananias heard these words, he fell down and died. And great fear came upon all who heard of it. 6 The young men rose and wrapped him up and carried him out and buried him.

7 After an interval of about three hours his wife came in, not knowing what had happened. 8 And Peter said to her, "Tell me whether you

Jerusalem Bible

The generosity of Barnabas

36 There was a Levite of Cypriot origin called Joseph whom the apostles surnamed Barnabas (which means "son of encouragement"). 37 He owned a piece of land and he sold it and brought the money, and presented it to the apostles.

The fraud of Ananias and Sapphira

5 There was another man, however, called Ananias. He and his wife, Sapphira, agreed to sell a property; 2 but with his wife's connivance he kept back part of the proceeds, and brought the rest and presented it to the apostles. 3 "Ananias," Peter said, "how can Satan have so possessed you that you should lie to the Holy Spirit and keep back part of the money from the land? 4 While you still owned the land, wasn't it yours to keep, and after you had sold it wasn't the money yours to do with as you liked? What put this scheme into your mind? It is not to men that you have lied, but to God." 5 When he heard this Ananias fell down dead. This made a profound impression on everyone present. 6 The younger men got up, wrapped the body in a sheet, carried it out and buried it.

7 About three hours later his wife came in, not knowing what had taken place. 8 Peter challenged her, "Tell me, was this the price you

New English Bible

For instance, Joseph, surnamed by the apostles Barnabas (which means 'Son of Exhortation'), a Levite, by birth a Cypriot, owned an estate, which he sold; he brought the money, and laid it at the apostles' feet.

5 But there was another man, called Ananias, with his wife Sapphira, who sold a property. With the full knowledge of his wife he kept back part of the purchase-money, and part he brought and laid at the apostles' feet. But Peter said, 'Ananias, how was it that Satan so possessed your mind that you lied to the Holy Spirit, and kept back part of the price of the land? While it remained, did it not remain yours? When it was turned into money, was it not still at your own disposal? What made you think of doing this thing? You have lied not to men but to God.' When Ananias heard these words he dropped dead; and all the others who heard were awe-struck. The younger men rose and covered his body, then carried him out and buried him.

About three hours passed, and then his wife came in, unaware of what had happened. Peter turned to her and said, 'Tell me, were you paid

King James Version

land for so much? And she said, Yea, for so
much. 9 Then Peter said unto her, How is it that
ye have agreed together to tempt the Spirit of
the Lord? behold, the feet of them which have
buried thy husband *are* at the door, and shall
carry thee out. 10 Then fell she down straightway
at his feet, and yielded up the ghost: and the
young men came in, and found her dead, and,
carrying *her* forth, buried *her* by her husband.
11 And great fear came upon all the church, and
upon as many as heard these things.
12 And by the hands of the apostles were
many signs and wonders wrought among the people; (and they were all with one accord in Solomon's porch. 13 And of the rest durst no man
join himself to them: but the people magnified
them. 14 And believers were the more added to
the Lord, multitudes both of men and women;)

Living Bible

and such a price?"
"Yes," she replied, "we did."
9 And Peter said, "How could you and your
husband even think of doing a thing like this—
conspiring together to test the Spirit of God's
ability to know what is going on? [a] Just outside
that door are the young men who buried your
husband, and they will carry you out too."
10 Instantly she fell to the floor, dead, and
the young men came in and, seeing that she was
dead, carried her out and buried her beside her
husband. 11 Terror gripped the entire church and
all others who heard what had happened.
12 Meanwhile, the apostles were meeting regularly at the Temple in the area known as Solomon's Hall, and they did many remarkable
miracles among the people. 13 The other believers didn't dare join them, though, but all
had the highest regard for them. 14 And more
and more believers were added to the Lord,

[a] Literally, "to try the Spirit of the Lord."

Today's English Version

and your husband received for your property?"
"Yes," she answered, "the full amount."
9 So Peter said to her, "Why did you and your
husband decide to put the Lord's Spirit to the
test? The men who buried your husband are at
the door right now, and they will carry you out
too!" 10 At once she fell down at his feet and died.
The young men came in and saw that she was
dead, so they carried her out and buried her beside her husband. 11 The whole church and all
the others who heard of this were filled with
great fear.

Miracles and wonders

12 Many miracles and wonders were being performed among the people by the apostles. All the
believers met together in a group in Solomon's
Porch. 13 Nobody outside the group dared join
them, even though the people spoke highly of
them. 14 But more and more people were added
to the group—a crowd of men and women who

New International Version

got for the land?"
"Yes," she said, "that is the price."
9 Peter said to her, "How could you agree to
test the Spirit of the Lord? Look! The feet of
the men who buried your husband are at the
door, and they will carry you out also."
10 At that moment she fell down at his feet
and died. Then the young men came in and, finding her dead, carried her out and buried her beside her husband. 11 Great fear seized the whole
church and all who heard about these events.

The apostles heal many

12 The apostles performed many miraculous
signs and wonders among the people. And all
the believers used to meet together in Solomon's
Colonnade. 13 No one else dared join them, even
though they were highly regarded by the people.
14 Nevertheless, more and more men and women
believed in the Lord and were added to their

Phillips Modern English

"Yes," she replied, "that was it."

Then Peter said to her,

"How could you two have agreed to put the Spirit of the Lord to such a test? Listen, you can hear the footsteps of the men who have just buried your husband coming back through the door, and they will carry you out as well!"

Immediately she collapsed at Peter's feet and died. When the young men came into the room they found her a dead woman, and they carried her out and buried her by the side of her husband. At this happening a deep sense of awe swept over the whole Church and indeed over all those who heard about it.

5.12b The young Church takes its stand in the Temple—

By common consent they all used to meet now in Solomon's Porch. But as far as the others were concerned no one dared to associate with them, even though their general popularity was very great. Yet more and more believers in the Lord joined them, both men and women in really large numbers.

Revised Standard Version

sold the land for so much." And she said, "Yes,
for so much." 9 But Peter said to her, "How is
it that you have agreed together to tempt the
Spirit of the Lord? Hark, the feet of those that
have buried your husband are at the door, and
they will carry you out." 10 Immediately she fell
down at his feet and died. When the young men
came in they found her dead, and they carried
her out and buried her beside her husband.
11 And great fear came upon the whole church,
and upon all who heard of these things.

12 Now many signs and wonders were done
among the people by the hands of the apostles.
And they were all together in Solomon's Portico.
13 None of the rest dared join them, but the
people held them in high honor. 14 And more
than ever believers were added to the Lord, mul-

Jerusalem Bible

sold the land for?" "Yes," she said, "that was
the price." 9 Peter then said, "So you and your
husband have agreed to put the Spirit of the
Lord to the test! What made you do it? You hear
those footsteps? They have just been to bury
your husband; they will carry you out, too."
10 Instantly she dropped dead at his feet. When
the young men came in they found she was dead,
and they carried her out and buried her by the
side of her husband. 11 This made a profound
impression on the whole Church and on all who
heard it.

The general situation

12b They all used to meet by common consent in the Portico of Solomon. 13 No one else
ever dared to join them, but the people were loud
in their praise 14 and the numbers of men and
women who came to believe in the Lord in-

New English Bible

such and such a price for the land?' 'Yes,' she said, 'that was the price.' Then Peter said, 'Why did you both conspire to put the Spirit of the Lord to the test? Hark! there at the door are the footsteps of those who buried your husband; and they will carry you away.' And suddenly she dropped dead at his feet. When the young men came in, they found her dead; and they carried her out and buried her beside her husband. And a great awe fell upon the whole church, and upon all who heard of these events; and many remarkable and wonderful things took place among the people at the hands of the apostles.

They used to meet by common consent in Solomon's Portico, no one from outside their number venturing to join with them. But people in general spoke highly of them,[a] and more than that, numbers of men and women were added to

[a] *Or* . . . Portico. Although others did not venture to join them, the common people spoke highly of them.

King James Version

15 Insomuch that they brought forth the sick into the streets, and laid *them* on beds and couches, that at the least the shadow of Peter passing by might overshadow some of them. 16 There came also a multitude *out* of the cities round about unto Jerusalem, bringing sick folks, and them which were vexed with unclean spirits: and they were healed every one.

17 Then the high priest rose up, and all they that were with him, (which is the sect of the Sadducees,) and were filled with indignation, 18 And laid their hands on the apostles, and put them in the common prison. 19 But the angel of the Lord by night opened the prison doors, and brought them forth, and said, 20 Go, stand and speak in the temple to the people all the words of this life. 21 And when they heard *that*, they entered into the temple early in the morning, and taught. But the high priest came, and they that were with him, and called the council together, and all the senate of the children of Israel, and sent to the prison to have them

Living Bible

crowds both of men and women. 15 Sick people were brought out into the streets on beds and mats so that at least Peter's shadow would fall across some of them as he went by! 16 And crowds came in from the Jerusalem suburbs, bringing their sick folk and those possessed by demons; and every one of them was healed.

17 The High Priest and his relatives and friends among the Sadducees reacted with violent jealousy 18 and arrested the apostles, and put them in the public jail.

19 But an angel of the Lord came at night, opened the gates of the jail and brought them out. Then he told them, 20 "Go over to the Temple and preach about this Life!"

21 They arrived at the Temple about daybreak, and immediately began preaching! Later that morning[b] the High Priest and his courtiers arrived at the Temple, and, convening the Jewish Council and the entire Senate, they sent for the

[*b*] Implied.

Today's English Version

believed in the Lord. 15 As a result of what the apostles were doing, the sick people were carried out in the streets and placed on beds and mats so that, when Peter walked by, at least his shadow might fall on some of them. 16 And crowds of people came in from the towns around Jerusalem, bringing their sick and those who had evil spirits in them; and they were all healed.

The apostles persecuted

17 Then the High Priest and all his companions, members of the local party of the Sadducees, became extremely jealous of the apostles; so they decided to take action. 18 They arrested the apostles and placed them in the public jail. 19 But that night an angel of the Lord opened the prison gates, led the apostles out, and said to them, 20 "Go and stand in the temple, and tell the people all about this new life." 21 The apostles obeyed, and at dawn they entered the temple and started teaching.

The High Priest and his companions called together all the Jewish elders for a full meeting of the Council; then they sent orders to the prison

New International Version

number. 15 As a result, people brought the sick into the streets and laid them on beds and mats so that at least Peter's shadow might fall on some of them as he passed by. 16 Crowds gathered also from the towns around Jerusalem, bringing their sick and those tormented by evil[p] spirits, and all of them were healed.

The apostles persecuted

17 Then the high priest and all his associates, who were members of the party of the Sadducees, were filled with jealousy. 18 They arrested the apostles and put them in the public jail. 19 But during the night an angel of the Lord opened the doors of the jail and brought them out. 20 "Go, stand in the temple courts," he said, "and tell the people the full message of this new life."

21 At daybreak they entered the temple courts, as they had been told, and began to teach the people.

When the high priest and his associates arrived, they called together the Sanhedrin—the full assembly of the elders of Israel—and sent

[*p*] Greek *unclean.*

Phillips Modern English

5.15 —and miraculous power radiates from it

* Many signs and wonders were now being shown among the people through the apostles' ministry. In consequence people would bring out their sick into the streets and lay them down on beds or stretchers, so that as Peter came by at least his shadow might fall upon some of them. In addition a large crowd collected from the cities round about Jerusalem, bringing with them their sick and all those who were suffering from evil spirits. And they were all cured.

5.17 Furious opposition reduced to impotence

All this roused the High Priest and his allies the Sadducean party of the day, and in a fury of jealousy they had the apostles arrested and put into the common jail. But during the night an angel of the Lord opened the prison doors and led them out, saying,

"Go and stand and speak in the Temple. Tell the people all about this new life!"

After receiving these instructions they entered the Temple about daybreak, and began to teach. When the High Priest arrived he and his supporters summoned the Sanhedrin and indeed the whole senate of the people of Israel. Then he sent to the jail to have the apostles brought

* Transposing the first part of v. 12 to the beginning of v. 15, which makes better sense.

Revised Standard Version

titudes both of men and women, 15 so that they
even carried out the sick into the streets, and
laid them on beds and pallets, that as Peter came
by at least his shadow might fall on some of
them. 16 The people also gathered from the
towns around Jerusalem, bringing the sick and
those afflicted with unclean spirits, and they were
all healed.
17 But the high priest rose up and all who
were with him, that is, the party of the Sadducees, and filled with jealousy 18 they arrested
the apostles and put them in the common prison.
19 But at night an angel of the Lord opened the
prison doors and brought them out and said,
20 "Go and stand in the temple and speak to the
people all the words of this Life." 21 And when
they heard this, they entered the temple at daybreak and taught.
Now the high priest came and those who were with him and called together the council and all the senate of Israel, and sent to the prison to

Jerusalem Bible

creased steadily. 12[a] So many signs and wonders
were worked among the people at the hands of
the apostles 15 that the sick were even taken
out into the streets and laid on beds and sleeping
mats in the hope that at least the shadow of
Peter might fall across some of them as he went
past. 16 People even came crowding in from the
towns around about Jerusalem, bringing with
them their sick and those tormented by unclean
spirits, and all of them were cured.

The apostles' arrest and miraculous deliverance

17 Then the high priest intervened with all his
supporters from the party of the Sadducees.
Prompted by jealousy, 18 they arrested the apostles and had them put in the common jail.
19 But at night the angel of the Lord opened
the prison gates and said as he led them out,
20 "Go and stand in the Temple, and tell the
people all about this new Life." 21 They did as
they were told; they went into the Temple at
dawn and began to preach.

A summons to appear before the Sanhedrin

When the high priest arrived, he and his supporters convened the Sanhedrin—this was the full Senate of Israel—and sent to the jail for

New English Bible

their ranks as believers in the Lord.[b] In the end the sick were actually carried out into the streets and laid there on beds and stretchers, so that even the shadow of Peter might fall on one or another as he passed by; and the people from the towns round Jerusalem flocked in, bringing those who were ill or harassed by unclean spirits, and all of them were cured.

Then the High Priest and his colleagues, the Sadducean party as it then was, were goaded into action by jealousy. They proceeded to arrest the apostles, and put them in official custody. But an angel of the Lord opened the prison doors during the night, brought them out, and said, 'Go, take your place in the temple and speak to the people, and tell them about this new life and all it means.' Accordingly they entered the temple at daybreak and went on with their teaching.

When the High Priest arrived with his colleagues they summoned the 'Sanhedrin', that is, the full senate of the Israelite nation, and sent

[b] *Or* and an ever-increasing number of believers, both men and women, were added to the Lord.

King James Version

brought. 22 But when the officers came, and
found them not in the prison, they returned, and
told, 23 Saying, The prison truly found we shut
with all safety, and the keepers standing without
before the doors: but when we had opened, we
found no man within. 24 Now when the high
priest and the captain of the temple and the
chief priests heard these things, they doubted
of them whereunto this would grow. 25 Then
came one and told them, saying, Behold, the
men whom ye put in prison are standing in the
temple, and teaching the people. 26 Then went
the captain with the officers, and brought them
without violence: for they feared the people, lest
they should have been stoned. 27 And when they
had brought them, they set *them* before the
council: and the high priest asked them, 28 Saying, Did not we straitly command you that ye
should not teach in this name? and, behold, ye
have filled Jerusalem with your doctrine, and
intend to bring this man's blood upon us.
29 Then Peter and the *other* apostles answered
and said, We ought to obey God rather than
men. 30 The God of our fathers raised up Jesus,

Living Bible

apostles to be brought for trial. 22 But when
the police arrived at the jail, the men weren't
there, so they returned to the Council and reported, 23 "The jail doors were locked, and the
guards were standing outside, but when we
opened the gates, no one was there!"
24 When the police captain[c] and the chief
priests heard this, they were frantic, wondering
what would happen next and where all this
would end! 25 Then someone arrived with the
news that the men they had jailed were out in
the Temple, preaching to the people!
26, 27 The police captain went with his officers and arrested them (without violence, for
they were afraid the people would kill them if
they roughed up the disciples) and brought them
in before the Council.
28 "Didn't we tell you never again to preach
about this Jesus?" the High Priest demanded.
"And instead you have filled all Jerusalem with
your teaching and intend to bring the blame
for this man's death on us!"
29 But Peter and the apostles replied, "We
must obey God rather than men. 30 The God
of our ancestors brought Jesus back to life again

[c] Literally, "the captain of the Temple."

Today's English Version

to have the apostles brought before them. 22 But
when the officials arrived, they did not find the
apostles in prison; so they returned to the Council and reported, 23 "When we arrived at the jail
we found it locked up tight and all the guards on
watch at the gates; but when we opened the gates
we did not find anyone inside!" 24 When the officer in charge of the temple guards and the chief
priests heard this, they wondered what had happened to the apostles. 25 Then a man came in
who said to them, "Listen! The men you put in
prison are standing in the temple teaching the
people!" 26 So the officer went off with his men
and brought the apostles back. They did not use
force, however, because they were afraid that
the people might stone them.
27 They brought the apostles in and made
them stand before the Council, and the High
Priest questioned them. 28 "We gave you strict
orders not to teach in the name of this man," he
said; "but see what you have done! You have
spread your teaching all over Jerusalem, and you
want to make us responsible for his death!"
29 Peter and the other apostles answered back,
"We must obey God, not men. 30 The God of
our fathers raised Jesus from death, after you

New International Version

to the jail for the apostles. 22 But on arriving
at the jail, the officers did not find them there.
So they went back and reported, 23 "We found
the jail securely locked, with the guards standing at the doors; but when we opened them, we
found no one inside." 24 On hearing this report,
the captain of the temple guard and the chief
priests were puzzled, wondering what would
come of this.
25 Then someone came and said, "Look! The
men you put in jail are standing in the temple
courts teaching the people." 26 At that, the captain went with his officers and brought the
apostles. They did not use force, because they
feared that the people would stone them.
27 Having brought the apostles, they made
them appear before the Sanhedrin to be questioned by the high priest. 28 "We gave you strict
orders not to teach in this name," he said. "Yet
you have filled Jerusalem with your teaching and
are determined to make us guilty of this man's
blood."
29 Peter and the other apostles replied: "We
must obey God rather than men! 30 The God of
our fathers raised Jesus from the dead—whom

Phillips Modern English

in. But when the officers arrived at the prison they could not find them there. They came back and reported,

"We found the prison securely locked and the guard standing on duty at the doors, but when we opened up we found no one inside."

When the captain of the Temple guard and the chief priests heard this report they were completely mystified at the apostles' disappearance and wondered what else could happen. However, someone arrived and reported to them,

"Why, the men you put in jail are standing in the Temple teaching the people!"

Then the captain went out with his men and fetched them. They dared not use any violence however, for the people might have stoned them. So they brought them in and made them stand before the Sanhedrin. The High Priest called for an explanation.

"We gave you the strictest possible orders," he said to them, "not to give any teaching in this name. And look what has happened—you have filled Jerusalem with your teaching, and what is more you are determined to fasten the guilt of that man's death upon us!"

5.29 The apostles speak the unpalatable truth

Then Peter and the apostles answered him,

"It is our duty to obey the orders of God rather than the orders of men. It was the God of our fathers who raised up Jesus, whom you

Revised Standard Version

have them brought. 22 But when the officers
came, they did not find them in the prison, and
they returned and reported, 23 "We found the
prison securely locked and the sentries standing
at the doors, but when we opened it we found
no one inside." 24 Now when the captain of the
temple and the chief priests heard these words,
they were much perplexed about them, wondering what this would come to. 25 And some one
came and told them, "The men whom you put
in prison are standing in the temple and teaching the people." 26 Then the captain with the
officers went and brought them, but without violence, for they were afraid of being stoned by
the people.
27 And when they had brought them, they
set them before the council. And the high priest
questioned them, 28 saying, "We strictly charged
you not to teach in this name, yet here you have
filled Jerusalem with your teaching and you intend to bring this man's blood upon us." 29 But
Peter and the apostles answered, "We must obey
God rather than men. 30 The God of our fathers raised Jesus whom you killed by hanging

Jerusalem Bible

them to be brought. 22 But when the officials
arrived at the prison they found they were not
inside, so they went back and reported, 23 "We
found the jail securely locked and the warders
on duty at the gates, but when we unlocked the
door we found no one inside." 24 When the
captain of the Temple and the chief priests heard
this news they wondered what this could mean.
25 Then a man arrived with fresh news. "At this
very moment," he said, "the men you imprisoned
are in the Temple. They are standing there
preaching to the people." 26 The captain went
with his men and fetched them. They were
afraid to use force in case the people stoned
them.
27 When they had brought them in to face
the Sanhedrin, the high priest demanded an explanation. 28 "We gave you a formal warning,"
he said, "not to preach in this name, and what
have you done? You have filled Jerusalem with
your teaching, and seem determined to fix the
guilt of this man's death on us." 29 In reply
Peter and the apostles said, "Obedience to God
comes before obedience to men; 30 it was the
God of our ancestors who raised up Jesus, but it

New English Bible

to the jail to fetch the prisoners. But the police who went to the prison failed to find them there, so they returned and reported, 'We found the jail securely locked at every point, with the warders at their posts by the doors, but when we opened them we found no one inside.' When they heard this, the Controller of the Temple and the chief priests were wondering what could have become of them,[a] and then a man arrived with the report, 'Look! the men you put in prison are there in the temple teaching the people.' At that the Controller went off with the police and fetched them, but without using force for fear of being stoned by the people.

So they brought them and stood them before the Council; and the High Priest began his examination. 'We expressly ordered you', he said, 'to desist from teaching in that name; and what has happened? You have filled Jerusalem with your teaching, and you are trying to make us responsible for that man's death.' Peter replied for himself and the apostles: 'We must obey God rather than men. The God of our fathers raised up Jesus whom you had done to death[b]

[a] *Or* wondering about them, what this could possibly mean. [b] *Or* . . . Jesus, and you did him to death . . .

King James Version

whom ye slew and hanged on a tree. 31 Him
hath God exalted with his right hand *to be* a
Prince and a Saviour, for to give repentance to
Israel, and forgiveness of sins. 32And we are his
witnesses of these things; and *so is* also the Holy
Ghost, whom God hath given to them that obey
him.
33 When they heard *that,* they were cut *to
the heart,* and took counsel to slay them. 34 Then
stood there up one in the council, a Pharisee,
named Gamaliel, a doctor of the law, had in
reputation among all the people, and commanded
to put the apostles forth a little space; 35And
said unto them, Ye men of Israel, take heed to
yourselves what ye intend to do as touching these
men. 36 For before these days rose up Theudas,
boasting himself to be somebody; to whom a
number of men, about four hundred, joined
themselves: who was slain; and all, as many as
obeyed him, were scattered, and brought to
nought. 37After this man rose up Judas of Galilee in the days of the taxing, and drew away
much people after him: he also perished; and
all, *even* as many as obeyed him, were dispersed.
38And now I say unto you, Refrain from these
men, and let them alone: for if this counsel or
this work be of men, it will come to nought:
39 But if it be of God, ye cannot overthrow it;

Living Bible

after you had killed him by hanging him on a
cross. 31 Then, with mighty power, God exalted
him to be a Prince and Savior, so that the people of Israel would have an opportunity for
repentance, and for their sins to be forgiven.
32And we are witnesses of these things, and so
is the Holy Spirit, who is given by God to all
who obey him."
33 At this, the Council was furious, and decided to kill them. 34 But one of their members,
a Pharisee named Gamaliel (an expert on religious law and very popular with the people),
stood up and requested that the apostles be sent
outside the Council chamber while he talked.
35 Then he addressed his colleagues as follows:
"Men of Israel, take care what you are planning to do to these men! 36 Some time ago there
was that fellow Theudas, who pretended to be
someone great. About 400 others joined him, but
he was killed, and his followers were harmlessly
dispersed.
37 "After him, at the time of the taxation,
there was Judas of Galilee. He drew away some
people as disciples, but he also died, and his
followers scattered.
38 "And so my advice is, leave these men
alone. If what they teach and do is merely on
their own, it will soon be overthrown. 39 But if

Today's English Version

had killed him by nailing him to a cross. 31 God
raised him to his right side as Leader and Savior,
to give to the people of Israel the opportunity to
repent and have their sins forgiven. 32 We are
witnesses to these things—we and the Holy Spirit,
who is God's gift to those who obey him."
33 When the members of the Council heard
this they were so furious that they decided to
have the apostles put to death. 34 But one of
them, a Pharisee named Gamaliel, a teacher of
the Law who was highly respected by all the
people, stood up in the Council. He ordered
the apostles to be taken out, 35 and then said to
the Council, "Men of Israel, be careful what you
are about to do to these men. 36 Some time ago
Theudas appeared, claiming that he was somebody great; and about four hundred men joined
him. But he was killed, all his followers were
scattered, and his movement died out. 37After
this, Judas the Galilean appeared during the time
of the census; he also drew a crowd after him,
but he also was killed and all his followers were
scattered. 38And so in this case now, I tell you,
do not take any action against these men. Leave
them alone, because if this plan and work of
theirs is a man-made thing, it will disappear;
39 but if it comes from God you cannot possibly

New International Version

you had killed by hanging him on a tree. 31 God
exalted him to his own right hand as Prince and
Savior that he might give repentance and forgiveness of sins to Israel. 32 We are witnesses of
these things, and so is the Holy Spirit, whom
God has given to those who obey him."
33 When they heard this, they were furious
and wanted to put them to death. 34 But a
Pharisee named Gamaliel, a teacher of the law,
who was honored by all the people, stood up in
the Sanhedrin and ordered that the men be put
outside for a little while. 35 Then he addressed
them: "Men of Israel, consider carefully what
you intend to do to these men. 36 Some time
ago Theudas appeared, claiming to be somebody, and about four hundred men rallied to
him. He was killed, all his followers were dispersed, and it all came to nothing. 37After him,
Judas the Galilean appeared in the days of the
census and led a band of people in revolt. He
too was killed, and all his followers were scattered. 38 Therefore, in the present case I advise
you: Leave these men alone! Let them go! For
if their purpose or activity is of human origin, it
will fail. 39 But if it is from God, you will not

Phillips Modern English

murdered by hanging him on a cross of wood. God has raised this man to his own right hand as prince and saviour, to bring repentance and the forgiveness of sins to Israel. What is more, we are witnesses to these matters, and so is the Holy Spirit given by God to those who obey his commands."

5.33 Calm counsel temporarily prevails

When the members of the council heard these words they were stung to fury and wanted to kill them. But one man stood up in the assembly, a Pharisee by the name of Gamaliel, a teacher of the Law who was held in great respect by the people, and gave orders for the apostles to be taken outside for a few minutes. Then he addressed the assembly:

"Men of Israel, be very careful of what action you intend to take against these men! Remember that some time ago a man called Theudas made himself conspicuous by claiming to be someone or other, and he had a following of four hundred men. He was killed, all his followers were dispersed, and the movement came to nothing. Then later, in the days of the census, that man Judas from Galilee appeared and enticed many of the people to follow him. But he too died and his whole following melted away. My advice to you now therefore is to let these men alone; leave them to themselves. For if this teaching or movement is merely human it will collapse of its own accord. But if it should

Revised Standard Version

him on a tree. 31 God exalted him at his right
hand as Leader and Savior, to give repentance
to Israel and forgiveness of sins. 32 And we are
witnesses to these things, and so is the Holy
Spirit whom God has given to those who obey
him."

33 When they heard this they were enraged
and wanted to kill them. 34 But a Pharisee in
the council named Gamaliel, a teacher of the
law, held in honor by all the people, stood up
and ordered the men to be put outside for a
while. 35 And he said to them, "Men of Israel,
take care what you do with these men. 36 For
before these days Theudas arose, giving himself
out to be somebody, and a number of men,
about four hundred, joined him; but he was
slain and all who followed him were dispersed
and came to nothing. 37 After him Judas the
Galilean arose in the days of the census and
drew away some of the people after him; he also
perished, and all who followed him were scattered.
38 So in the present case I tell you, keep
away from these men and let them alone; for
if this plan or this undertaking is of men, it will
fail; 39 but if it is of God, you will not be able

Jerusalem Bible

was you who had him executed by hanging on a
tree.[y] 31 By his own right hand God has now
raised him up to be leader and savior, to give
repentance and forgiveness of sins through him
to Israel. 32 We are witnesses to all this, we
and the Holy Spirit whom God has given to
those who obey him." 33 This so infuriated them
that they wanted to put them to death.

Gamaliel's intervention

34 One member of the Sanhedrin, however, a
Pharisee called Gamaliel, who was a doctor of
the Law and respected by the whole people,[z]
stood up and asked to have the men taken outside
for a time. 35 Then he addressed the Sanhedrin,
"Men of Israel, be careful how you
deal with these people. 36 There was Theudas
who became notorious not so long ago. He
claimed to be someone important, and he even
collected about four hundred followers; but
when he was killed, all his followers scattered
and that was the end of them. 37 And then there
was Judas the Galilean, at the time of the census,
who attracted crowds of supporters; but he
got killed too, and all his followers dispersed.
38 What I suggest, therefore, is that you leave
these men alone and let them go. If this enterprise,
this movement of theirs, is of human
origin it will break up of its own accord; 39 but

[y] The phrase recalls Dt. 21:23. [z] Gamaliel I, a Pharisee of the school of Hillel; he was Paul's teacher.

New English Bible

by hanging him on a gibbet. He it is whom God has exalted with his own right hand [c] as leader and saviour, to grant Israel repentance and forgiveness of sins. And we are witnesses to all this, and so is the Holy Spirit given by God to those who are obedient to him.'

This touched them on the raw, and they wanted to put them to death. But a member of the Council rose to his feet, a Pharisee called Gamaliel, a teacher of the law held in high regard by all the people. He moved that the men be put outside for a while. Then he said, 'Men of Israel, be cautious in deciding what to do with these men. Some time ago Theudas came forward, claiming to be somebody, and a number of men, about four hundred, joined him. But he was killed and his whole following was broken up and disappeared. After him came Judas the Galilean at the time of the census; he induced some people to revolt under his leadership, but he too perished and his whole following was scattered. And so now: keep clear of these men, I tell you; leave them alone. For if this idea of theirs or its execution is of human origin, it will collapse; but if it is from God, you will

[c] *Or* at his right hand.

King James Version

lest haply ye be found even to fight against God.
40And to him they agreed: and when they had
called the apostles, and beaten *them,* they commanded that they should not speak in the name
of Jesus, and let them go.
41 And they departed from the presence of
the council, rejoicing that they were counted
worthy to suffer shame for his name. 42And daily
in the temple, and in every house, they ceased
not to teach and preach Jesus Christ.

6 And in those days, when the number of the
disciples was multiplied, there arose a murmuring of the Grecians against the Hebrews, because their widows were neglected in the daily
ministration. 2 Then the twelve called the multitude of the disciples *unto them,* and said, It is
not reason that we should leave the word of
God, and serve tables. 3 Wherefore, brethren,
look ye out among you seven men of honest re-

Living Bible

it is of God, you will not be able to stop them,
lest you find yourselves fighting even against
God."
40 The Council accepted his advice, called
in the apostles, had them beaten, and then told
them never again to speak in the name of Jesus,
and finally let them go. 41 They left the Council
chamber rejoicing that God had counted them
worthy to suffer dishonor for his name. 42And
every day, in the Temple and in their home Bible
classes, they continued to teach and preach that
Jesus is the Messiah.

6 But with the believers multiplying rapidly,
there were rumblings of discontent. Those
who spoke only Greek complained that their
widows were being discriminated against, that
they were not being given as much food, in the
daily distribution, as the widows who spoke
Hebrew. 2 So the Twelve called a meeting of all
the believers.
"We should spend our time preaching, not
administering a feeding program," they said.
3 "Now look around among yourselves, dear
brothers, and select seven men, wise and full of

Today's English Version

defeat them. You could find yourselves fighting
against God!"
The Council followed Gamaliel's advice.
40 They called the apostles in, had them whipped,
and ordered them never again to speak in the
name of Jesus; and then they set them free.
41 The apostles left the Council, full of joy that
God had considered them worthy to suffer disgrace for the name of Jesus. 42And every day in
the temple and in people's homes they continued
to teach and preach the Good News about Jesus
the Messiah.

The seven helpers

6 Some time later, as the number of disciples
kept growing, there was a quarrel between
the Greek-speaking Jews and the native Jews.
The Greek-speaking Jews said that their widows
were being neglected in the daily distribution of
funds. 2 So the twelve apostles called the whole
group of disciples together and said, "It is not
right for us to neglect the preaching of God's
word in order to handle finances. 3 So then,
brothers, choose seven men among you who are

New International Version

be able to stop these men; you will only find
yourselves fighting against God."
40 His speech persuaded them. They called
the apostles in and had them flogged. Then they
ordered them not to speak in the name of Jesus,
and let them go.
41 The apostles left the Sanhedrin, rejoicing
because they had been counted worthy of suffering disgrace for the Name. 42 Day after day,
in the temple courts and from house to house,
they never stopped teaching and proclaiming
the good news that Jesus is the Christ.[q]

The choosing of the seven

6 In those days when the number of disciples
was increasing, the Grecian Jews among
them complained against those of the Aramaic-
speaking community because their widows were
being overlooked in the daily distribution of
food. 2 So the Twelve gathered all the disciples
together and said: "It would not be right for us
to neglect the ministry of the word of God in
order to wait on tables. 3 Brothers, choose seven
men from among you who are known to be full

[q] Or *Messiah.*

Phillips Modern English

be from God you cannot defeat them, and you might actually find yourselves to be fighting against God!"

They accepted his advice and called in the apostles. They had them beaten and after commanding them not to speak in the name of Jesus they let them go. So the apostles went out from the presence of the Sanhedrin full of joy that they had been considered worthy to bear humiliation for the sake of the name. Then day after day in the Temple and in people's houses they continued to teach unceasingly and to proclaim the good news of Jesus Christ.

6.1 The first deacons are chosen

About this time, when the number of disciples was continually increasing, the Greeks complained that in the daily distribution of food the Hebrew widows were being given preferential treatment. The twelve summoned the whole body of the disciples together, and said,

"It is not right that we should have to neglect preaching the Word of God in order to look after the accounts. You, our brothers, must look round and pick out from your number seven

Revised Standard Version

to overthrow them. You might even be found opposing God!"
40 So they took his advice, and when they had
called in the apostles, they beat them and
charged them not to speak in the name of Jesus,
and let them go. 41 Then they left the presence
of the council, rejoicing that they were counted
worthy to suffer dishonor for the name. 42 And
every day in the temple and at home they did
not cease teaching and preaching Jesus as the
Christ.

6 Now in these days when the disciples were
increasing in number, the Hellenists murmured against the Hebrews because their widows
were neglected in the daily distribution. 2 And
the twelve summoned the body of the disciples
and said, "It is not right that we should give up
preaching the word of God to serve tables.
3 Therefore, brethren, pick out from among you
seven men of good repute, full of the Spirit and

Jerusalem Bible

if it does in fact come from God you will not only be unable to destroy them, but you might find yourselves fighting against God."
His advice was accepted; 40 and they had the
apostles called in, gave orders for them to be flogged, warned them not to speak in the name
of Jesus and released them. 41 And so they left
the presence of the Sanhedrin glad to have had the honor of suffering humiliation for the sake of the name.
42 They preached every day both in the Temple and in private houses, and their proclamation of the Good News of Christ Jesus was never interrupted.

II. The earliest missions

The institution of the Seven

6 About this time, when the number of disciples was increasing, the Hellenists made a complaint against the Hebrews[a]: in the daily distribution their own widows were being overlooked. 2 So the Twelve called a full meeting of the disciples and addressed them, "It would not be right for us to neglect the word of God so
as to give out food; 3 you, brothers, must select
from among yourselves seven men of good rep-

[a] "Hellenists": Jews from outside Palestine; they had their own synagogues in Jerusalem, where the scriptures were read in Greek. The "Hebrews" were Palestinian Jews and in their synagogues scriptures were read in Hebrew.

New English Bible

never be able to put them down, and you risk finding yourselves at war with God.'

They took his advice. They sent for the apostles and had them flogged; then they ordered them to give up speaking in the name of Jesus, and discharged them. So the apostles went out from the Council rejoicing that they had been found worthy to suffer indignity for the sake of the Name. And every day they went steadily on with their teaching in the temple and in private houses, telling the good news of Jesus the Messiah.[a]

The church moves outwards

6 During this period, when disciples were growing in number, there was disagreement between those of them who spoke Greek[b] and those who spoke the language of the Jews.[c] The former party complained that their widows were being overlooked in the daily distribution. So the Twelve called the whole body of disciples together and said, 'It would be a grave mistake for us to neglect the word of God in order to wait at table. Therefore, friends, look out seven men of good reputation from your number, men

[a] *Or* the good news that the Messiah was Jesus. [b] *Literally* the Hellenists. [c] *Literally* the Hebrews.

King James Version

port, full of the Holy Ghost and wisdom, whom we may appoint over this business. 4 But we will give ourselves continually to prayer, and to the ministry of the word.

5 And the saying pleased the whole multitude: and they chose Stephen, a man full of faith and of the Holy Ghost, and Philip, and Prochorus, and Nicanor, and Timon, and Parmenas, and Nicolas a proselyte of Antioch; 6 Whom they set before the apostles: and when they had prayed, they laid *their* hands on them. 7 And the word of God increased; and the number of the disciples multiplied in Jerusalem greatly; and a great company of the priests were obedient to the faith. 8 And Stephen, full of faith and power, did great wonders and miracles among the people.

9 Then there arose certain of the synagogue, which is called *the synagogue* of the Libertines, and Cyrenians, and Alexandrians, and of them of Cilicia and of Asia, disputing with Stephen. 10 And they were not able to resist the wisdom and the spirit by which he spake. 11 Then they suborned men, which said, We have heard him speak blasphemous words against Moses, and

Living Bible

the Holy Spirit, who are well thought of by everyone; and we will put them in charge of this business. 4 Then we can spend our time in prayer, preaching, and teaching."

5 This sounded reasonable to the whole assembly, and they elected the following:

Stephen (a man unusually full of faith and the Holy Spirit),
Philip,
Prochorus,
Nicanor,
Timon,
Parmenas,
Nicolaus of Antioch (a Gentile convert to the Jewish faith, who had become a Christian).

6 These seven were presented to the apostles, who prayed for them and laid their hands on them in blessing.

7 God's message was preached in ever-widening circles, and the number of disciples increased vastly in Jerusalem; and many of the Jewish priests were converted too. 8 Stephen, the man so full of faith and the Holy Spirit's power,[a] did spectacular miracles among the people.

9 But one day some of the men from the Jewish cult of "The Freedmen" started an argument with him, and they were soon joined by Jews from Cyrene, Alexandria in Egypt, and the Turkish provinces of Cilicia, and Ausia. 10 But none of them were able to stand against Stephen's wisdom and spirit.

11 So they brought in some men to lie about him, claiming they had heard Stephen curse Moses, and even God.

[a] Literally, "full of grace and power." See verse 5.

Today's English Version

known to be full of the Holy Spirit and wisdom, and we will put them in charge of this matter. 4 We ourselves, then, will give our full time to prayers and the work of preaching."

5 The whole group was pleased with the apostles' proposal; so they chose Stephen, a man full of faith and the Holy Spirit, and Philip, Prochorus, Nicanor, Timon, Parmenas, and Nicolaus, a Gentile from Antioch who had been converted to Judaism. 6 The group presented them to the apostles, who prayed and placed their hands on them.

7 And so the word of God continued to spread. The number of disciples in Jerusalem grew larger and larger, and a great number of priests accepted the faith.

The arrest of Stephen

8 Stephen, a man richly blessed by God and full of power, performed great miracles and wonders among the people. 9 But some men opposed him; they were members of the synagogue of the Free Men (as it was called), which had Jews from Cyrenia and Alexandria. They and other Jews from Cilicia and Asia started arguing with Stephen. 10 But the Spirit gave Stephen such wisdom that when he spoke they could not resist him. 11 So they bribed some men to say, "We heard him speaking against Moses and against

New International Version

of the Spirit and wisdom. We will turn this responsibility over to them 4 and will give our attention to prayer and the ministry of the word."

5 This proposal pleased the whole group. They chose Stephen, a man full of faith and of the Holy Spirit; also Philip, Prochorus, Nicanor, Timon, Parmenas, and Nicolas from Antioch, a convert to Judaism. 6 They presented these men to the apostles, who prayed and laid their hands on them.

7 So the word of God spread. The number of disciples in Jerusalem increased rapidly, and a large number of priests became obedient to the faith.

Stephen seized

8 Now Stephen, a man full of God's grace and power, did great wonders and miraculous signs among the people. 9 Opposition arose, however, from members of the Synagogue of the Freedmen (as it was called)—Jews of Cyrene and Alexandria as well as the provinces of Cilicia and Asia. These men began to argue with Stephen, 10 but they could not stand up against his wisdom or the Spirit by which he spoke.

11 Then they secretly persuaded some men to say, "We have heard Stephen speak words of blasphemy against Moses and against God."

Phillips Modern English

men of good reputation who are both practical and spiritually-minded and we will put them in charge of this matter. Then we shall devote ourselves whole-heartedly to prayer and the ministry of the Word."

This suggestion met with unanimous approval and they chose Stephen a man full of faith and the Holy Spirit, Philip, Prochorus, Nicanor, Timon, Parmenas, and Nicolas of Antioch who had previously been a convert to the Jewish faith. They brought these men before the apostles, and they, after prayer, laid their hands upon them.

So the Word of God gained more and more ground. The number of disciples in Jerusalem greatly increased, while a considerable proportion of the priesthood accepted the faith.

6.8 *The attack on the new deacon, Stephen*

Stephen, full of grace and spiritual power, continued to perform miracles and remarkable signs among the people. However, members of a Jewish synagogue known as that of the Freed Men, together with some from the synagogues of Cyrene and Alexandria, as well as some men from Cilicia and Asia, tried debating with Stephen, but found themselves quite unable to stand up against either his practical wisdom or the spiritual force with which he spoke. In the end they bribed men to allege, "We have heard this man making blasphemous statements against

Revised Standard Version

of wisdom, whom we may appoint to this duty.
4 But we will devote ourselves to prayer and to
the ministry of the word." 5 And what they said
pleased the whole multitude, and they chose
Stephen, a man full of faith and of the Holy
Spirit, and Philip, and Prochorus, and Nicanor,
and Timon, and Parmenas, and Nicolaus, a
proselyte of Antioch. 6 These they set before the
apostles, and they prayed and laid their hands
upon them.
7 And the word of God increased; and the
number of the disciples multiplied greatly in
Jerusalem, and a great many of the priests were
obedient to the faith.
8 And Stephen, full of grace and power, did
great wonders and signs among the people.
9 Then some of those who belonged to the synagogue of the Freedmen (as it was called), and
of the Cyrenians, and of the Alexandrians, and
of those from Cilicia and Asia, arose and disputed with Stephen. 10 But they could not withstand the wisdom and the Spirit with which he
spoke. 11 Then they secretly instigated men,
who said, "We have heard him speak blasphe-

Jerusalem Bible

utation, filled with the Spirit and with wisdom;
we will hand over this duty to them, 4 and continue to devote ourselves to prayer and to the
service of the word." 5 The whole assembly approved of this proposal and elected Stephen, a
man full of faith and of the Holy Spirit, together with Philip, Prochorus, Nicanor, Timon,
Parmenas, and Nicolaus of Antioch, a convert
to Judaism. 6 They presented these to the
apostles, who prayed and laid their hands on
them.[b]
7 The word of the Lord continued to spread:
the number of disciples in Jerusalem was greatly
increased, and a large group of priests made
their submission to the faith.

Stephen's arrest

8 Stephen was filled with grace and power and
began to work miracles and great signs among
the people. 9 But then certain people came forward to debate with Stephen, some from Cyrene
and Alexandria who were members of the synagogue called the Synagogue of Freedmen,[c] and
others from Cilicia and Asia. 10 They found
they could not get the better of him because of
his wisdom, and because it was the Spirit that
prompted what he said. 11 So they procured
some men to say, "We heard him using blasphemous language against Moses and against

[*b*] "and they prayed and laid their hands on them"; probably meaning the apostles, handing over their duties as in v. 3. [*c*] Probably the descendants of Jews carried off to Rome, 63 B.C. and sold as slaves but later released.

New English Bible

full of the Spirit and of wisdom, and we will appoint them to deal with these matters, while we devote ourselves to prayer and to the ministry of the Word.' This proposal proved acceptable to the whole body. They elected Stephen, a man full of faith and of the Holy Spirit, Philip, Prochorus, Nicanor, Timon, Parmenas, and Nicolas of Antioch, a former convert to Judaism. These they presented to the apostles, who prayed and laid their hands on them.

The word of God now spread more and more widely; the number of disciples in Jerusalem went on increasing rapidly, and very many of the priests adhered to the Faith.

Stephen, who was full of grace and power, began to work great miracles and signs among the people. But some members of the synagogue called the Synagogue of Freedmen, comprising Cyrenians and Alexandrians and people from Cilicia and Asia, came forward and argued with Stephen, but could not hold their own against the inspired wisdom with which he spoke. They then put up men who alleged that they had heard him make blasphemous statements against

King James Version

against God. 12 And they stirred up the people,
and the elders, and the scribes, and came upon
him, and caught him, and brought *him* to the
council, 13 And set up false witnesses, which said,
This man ceaseth not to speak blasphemous
words against this holy place, and the law:
14 For we have heard him say, that this Jesus
of Nazareth shall destroy this place, and shall
change the customs which Moses delivered us.
15 And all that sat in the council, looking steadfastly on him, saw his face as it had been the
face of an angel.

7 Then said the high priest, Are these things
so? 2 And he said, Men, brethren, and fathers,
hearken; The God of glory appeared unto our
father Abraham, when he was in Mesopotamia,
before he dwelt in Charran, 3 And said unto him,
Get thee out of thy country, and from thy kindred, and come into the land which I shall shew
thee. 4 Then came he out of the land of the
Chaldeans, and dwelt in Charran: and from
thence, when his father was dead, he removed
him into this land, wherein ye now dwell. 5 And
he gave him none inheritance in it, no, not *so
much as* to set his foot on: yet he promised that

Living Bible

12 This accusation roused the crowds to fury
against Stephen, and the Jewish leaders[b] arrested
him and brought him before the Council. 13 The
lying witnesses testified again that Stephen was
constantly speaking against the Temple and
against the laws of Moses.
14 They declared, "We have heard him say
that this fellow Jesus of Nazareth will destroy
the Temple, and throw out all of Moses' laws."
15 At this point everyone in the Council chamber
saw Stephen's face become as radiant as an
angel's!

7 Then the High Priest asked him, "Are
these accusations true?"
2 This was Stephen's lengthy reply: "The
glorious God appeared to our ancestor Abraham in Iraq[a] before he moved to Syria,[b] 3 and
told him to leave his native land, to say good-
bye to his relatives and to start out for a country
that God would direct him to. 4 So he left the
land of the Chaldeans and lived in Haran, in
Syria, until his father died. Then God brought
him here to the land of Israel, 5 but gave him
no property of his own, not one little tract of
land.

[*b*] Literally, "the elders and the Scribes." [*7a*] Literally, "Mesopotamia." [*b*] Literally, "Haran," a city in the area we now know as Syria.

Today's English Version

God!" 12 In this way they stirred up the people,
the elders, and the teachers of the Law. They
came to Stephen, seized him, and took him before the Council. 13 Then they brought in some
men to tell lies about him. "This man," they
said, "is always talking against our sacred temple and the Law of Moses. 14 We heard him say
that this Jesus of Nazareth will tear down the
temple and change all the customs which have
come down to us from Moses!" 15 All those sitting
in the Council fixed their eyes on Stephen and
saw that his face looked like the face of an
angel.

Stephen's speech

7 The High Priest asked Stephen, "Is this
really so?"
2 Stephen answered, "Brothers and fathers!
Listen to me! The God of glory appeared to
our ancestor Abraham while he was living in
Mesopotamia, before he had gone to live in
Haran, 3 and said to him, 'Leave your family
and country and go to the land that I will show
you.' 4 And so he left the land of Chaldea and
went to live in Haran. After Abraham's father
died, God made him move to this country, where
you now live. 5 God did not then give Abraham
any part of it as his own, not even a square foot

New International Version

12 So they stirred up the people and the elders
and the teachers of the law. They seized Stephen
and brought him before the Sanhedrin. 13 They
produced false witnesses, who testified, "This fellow never stops speaking against the holy place
and against the law. 14 For we have heard him
say that this Jesus of Nazareth will destroy this
place and change the customs Moses handed
down to us."
15 All who were sitting in the Sanhedrin
looked intently at Stephen, and they saw that
his face was like the face of an angel.

Stephen's speech to the Sanhedrin

7 Then the high priest asked him, "Are these
charges true?"
2 To this he replied: "Brothers and fathers,
listen to me! The God of glory appeared to our
father Abraham while he was still in Mesopotamia, before he lived in Haran. 3 'Leave your
country and your people,' God said, 'and go to
the land I will show you.' [r]
4 "So he left Chaldea and settled in Haran.
After the death of his father, God sent him to
this land where you are now living. 5 He gave
him no inheritance here, not even a foot of

[*r*] Gen. 12:1.

Phillips Modern English

Moses and against God." At the same time they worked upon the feelings of the people, the elders and the scribes. Then they suddenly confronted Stephen, seized him and took him before the Sanhedrin. There they brought forward false witnesses to say, "This man's speeches are one long attack against this holy place and the Law. We have heard him say that Jesus of Nazareth will destroy this place and change the customs which Moses handed down to us." All who sat there in the Sanhedrin looked intently at Stephen, and as they looked his face appeared to them like the face of an angel.

7.1 *Stephen makes his defence from Israel's history:*

i. THE TIME OF ABRAHAM

Then the High Priest said,
"Is this statement true?"
And Stephen answered,
"My brothers and my fathers, listen to me. Our glorious God appeared to our forefather Abraham while he was in Mesopotamia before he ever came to live in Charran, and said to him, 'Get thee out of thy land and from thy kindred, and come into a land which I shall shew thee.' That was how he came to leave the land of the Chaldeans and settle in Charran. And it was from there after his father's death that God moved him into this very land where you are living today. Yet God gave him no part of it as an inheritance, not a foot that he could call his

Revised Standard Version

mous words against Moses and God." 12 And they stirred up the people and the elders and the scribes, and they came upon him and seized him and brought him before the council, 13 and set up false witnesses who said, "This man never ceases to speak words against this holy place and the law; 14 for we have heard him say that this Jesus of Nazareth will destroy this place, and will change the customs which Moses delivered to us." 15 And gazing at him, all who sat in the council saw that his face was like the face of an angel.

7 And the high priest said, "Is this so?" 2 And Stephen said:
"Brethren and fathers, hear me. The God of glory appeared to our father Abraham, when he was in Mesopotamia, before he lived in Haran, 3 and said to him, 'Depart from your land and from your kindred and go into the land which I will show you.' 4 Then he departed from the land of the Chaldeans, and lived in Haran. And after his father died, God removed him from there into this land in which you are now living; 5 yet he gave him no inheritance in it, not even a foot's length, but promised to give it to him in

Jerusalem Bible

God." 12 Having in this way turned the people against him as well as the elders and scribes, they took Stephen by surprise, and arrested him and brought him before the Sanhedrin. 13 There they put up false witnesses to say, "This man is always making speeches against this Holy Place and the Law. 14 We have heard him say that Jesus the Nazarene is going to destroy this Place and alter the traditions that Moses handed down to us." 15 The members of the Sanhedrin all looked intently at Stephen, and his face appeared to them like the face of an angel.

Stephen's speech

7 The high priest asked, "Is this true?" 2 He replied, "My brothers, my fathers, listen to what I have to say. The God of glory appeared to our ancestor Abraham, while he was in Mesopotamia before settling in Haran, 3 *and said to him, 'Leave your country and your family and go to the land I will show you.'* [d] 4 So he left Chaldaea and settled in Haran; and after his father died God made him leave Haran and come to this land where you are living today. 5 God did not give him a single square foot of this land

[d] Gn. 12:1.

New English Bible

Moses and against God. They stirred up the people and the elders and doctors of the law, set upon him and seized him, and brought him before the Council. They produced false witnesses who said, 'This man is for ever saying things against this holy place and against the Law. For we have heard him say that Jesus of Nazareth will destroy this place and alter the customs handed down to us by Moses.' And all who were sitting in the Council fixed their eyes on him, and his face appeared to them like the face of an angel.

7 Then the High Priest asked, 'Is this so?' And he said, 'My brothers, fathers of this nation, listen to me. The God of glory appeared to Abraham our ancestor while he was in Mesopotamia, before he had settled in Harran, and said: "Leave your country and your kinsfolk and come away to a land that I will show you." Thereupon he left the land of the Chaldaeans and settled in Harran. From there, after his father's death, God led him to migrate to this land where you now live. He gave him nothing in it to call his own, not one yard; but promised

King James Version

he would give it to him for a possession, and to
his seed after him, when *as yet* he had no child.
6 And God spake on this wise, That his seed
should sojourn in a strange land; and that they
should bring them into bondage, and entreat
them evil four hundred years. 7 And the nation
to whom they shall be in bondage will I judge,
said God: and after that shall they come forth,
and serve me in this place. 8 And he gave him
the covenant of circumcision: and so *Abraham*
begat Isaac, and circumcised him the eighth day;
and Isaac *begat* Jacob; and Jacob *begat* the
twelve patriarchs. 9 And the patriarchs, moved
with envy, sold Joseph into Egypt: but God was
with him, 10 And delivered him out of all his
afflictions, and gave him favour and wisdom in
the sight of Pharaoh king of Egypt; and he made
him governor over Egypt and all his house.
11 Now there came a dearth over all the land of
Egypt and Chanaan, and great affliction: and
our fathers found no sustenance. 12 But when
Jacob heard that there was corn in Egypt, he
sent out our fathers first. 13 And at the second
time Joseph was made known to his brethren;
and Joseph's kindred was made known unto
Pharaoh. 14 Then sent Joseph, and called his

Living Bible

"However, God promised that eventually the
whole country would belong to him and his descendants—though as yet he had no children!
6 But God also told him that these descendants
of his would leave the land and live in a foreign
country and there become slaves for 400 years.
7 'But I will punish the nation that enslaves
them,' God told him, 'and afterwards my people
will return to this land of Israel and worship me
here.'

8 "God also gave Abraham the ceremony of
circumcision at that time, as evidence of the
covenant between God and the people of Abraham. And so Isaac, Abraham's son, was circumcised when he was eight days old. Isaac became
the father of Jacob, and Jacob was the father of
the twelve patriarchs of the Jewish nation.
9 These men were very jealous of Joseph and
sold him to be a slave in Egypt. But God was
with him, 10 and delivered him out of all of his
anguish, and gave him favor before Pharaoh,
king of Egypt. God also gave Joseph unusual
wisdom, so that Pharaoh appointed him governor over all Egypt, as well as putting him in
charge of all the affairs of the palace.

11 "But a famine developed in Egypt and
Canaan and there was great misery for our ancestors. When their food was gone, 12 Jacob
heard that there was still grain in Egypt, so he
sent his sons[c] to buy some. 13 The second time
they went, Joseph revealed his identity to his
brothers, and they were introduced to Pharaoh.
14 Then Joseph sent for his father Jacob and all

[*c*] Literally, "our fathers."

Today's English Version

of ground; but God promised that he would give
it to him, and that it would belong to him and
his descendants after him. At the time God made
this promise Abraham had no children. 6 This is
what God said to him, 'Your descendants will
live in a foreign country, where they will be slaves
and will be badly treated for four hundred years.
7 But I will pass judgment on the pople that they
will serve,' God said, 'and afterward they will
come out of that country and will worship me in
this place.' 8 Then God gave to Abraham the
ceremony of circumcision as a sign of the covenant. So Abraham circumcised Isaac a week after
he was born; Isaac circumcised Jacob, and Jacob
circumcised the twelve patriarchs.

9 "The patriarchs were jealous of Joseph, and
sold him to be a slave in Egypt. But God was
with him, 10 and brought him safely through all
his troubles. When Joseph appeared before
Pharaoh, the king of Egypt, God gave him a
pleasing manner and wisdom. Pharaoh made
Joseph governor over the country and the royal
household. 11 Then there was a famine in all of
Egypt and Canaan, which caused much suffering.
Our ancestors could not find any food. 12 So
when Jacob heard that there was grain in Egypt,
he sent his sons, our ancestors, on their first visit
there. 13 On the second visit Joseph made himself known to his brothers, and Pharaoh came
to know about Joseph's family. 14 So Joseph sent

New International Version

ground. But God promised him that he and his
descendants after him would possess the land,
even though at that time Abraham had no child.
6 God spoke to him in this way: 'Your descendants will be strangers in a foreign country, and
they will be enslaved and mistreated four hundred years. 7 I will punish the nation that makes
them slaves,' God said, 'and afterward they
will come out of that country and worship me
in this place.'[s] 8 Then he gave Abraham the
covenant of circumcision. And Abraham became
the father of Isaac and circumcised him eight
days after his birth. Later Isaac became the father of Jacob, and Jacob became the father of
the twelve patriarchs.

9 "Because the patriarchs were jealous of Joseph, they sold him as a slave into Egypt. But
God was with him 10 and rescued him from all
his troubles. He gave Joseph wisdom and enabled him to gain the good will of Pharaoh, king
of Egypt; so he made him ruler over Egypt and
all his palace.

11 "Then a famine struck all Egypt and Canaan, bringing great suffering, and our fathers
could not find food. 12 When Jacob heard that
there was grain in Egypt, he sent our fathers on
their first visit. 13 On their second visit, Joseph
told his brothers who he was, and Pharaoh
learned about Joseph's family. 14 After this, Jo-

[*s*] Gen. 15:13,14.

Phillips Modern English

own, and yet promised that it should eventually belong to him and his descendants—even though at the time he had no descendant at all. And this is the way in which God spoke to him: he told him that his descendants should live as strangers in a foreign land where they would become slaves and be ill-treated for four hundred years, 'And the nation to which they shall be in bondage will I judge, said God: and after that shall they come forth, and serve me in this place.'

"Further, he gave him the agreement of circumcision, so that when Abraham became the father of Isaac he circumcised him on the eighth day.

7.8b *Stephen's defence:*

ii. THE PATRIARCHS

"Isaac became the father of Jacob, and Jacob the father of the twelve patriarchs. Then the patriarchs in their jealousy of Joseph sold him as a slave into Egypt. But God was with him and saved him from all his troubles and gave him favour and wisdom in the eyes of Pharaoh the king of Egypt. Pharaoh made him governor of Egypt and put him in charge of his own entire household.

"Then came the famine over all the land of Egypt and Canaan which caused great suffering, and our forefathers could find no food. But when Jacob heard that there was grain in Egypt he sent our forefathers out of their own country for the first time. It was on their second visit that Joseph was recognised by his brothers, and his ancestry became plain to Pharaoh. Then

Revised Standard Version

possession and to his posterity after him, though
he had no child. 6And God spoke to this effect,
that his posterity would be aliens in a land belonging to others, who would enslave them and
ill-treat them four hundred years. 7 'But I will
judge the nation which they serve,' said God,
'and after that they shall come out and worship
me in this place.' 8And he gave him the covenant
of circumcision. And so Abraham became the
father of Isaac, and circumcised him on the
eighth day; and Isaac became the father of
Jacob, and Jacob of the twelve patriarchs.
9 "And the patriarchs, jealous of Joseph, sold
him into Egypt; but God was with him, 10 and
rescued him out of all his afflictions, and gave
him favor and wisdom before Pharaoh, king of
Egypt, who made him governor over Egypt and
over all his household. 11 Now there came a
famine throughout all Egypt and Canaan, and
great affliction, and our fathers could find no
food. 12 But when Jacob heard that there was
grain in Egypt, he sent forth our fathers the first
time. 13And at the second visit Joseph made
himself known to his brothers, and Joseph's
family became known to Pharaoh. 14And Jo-

Jerusalem Bible

to call his own, yet he promised to *give it to*
him and after him to his descendants, childless[e]
though he was. 6 The actual words God used
when he spoke to him are that *his descendants*
would be exiles in a foreign land, where they
would be slaves and oppressed for four hundred
years. 7 *'But I will pass judgment on the nation*
that enslaves them,' God said, *'and after this*
they will leave and worship me in this place.'[f]
8 Then he made the covenant of circumcision:
so when his son Isaac was born he circumcised
him on the eighth day. Isaac did the same for
Jacob, and Jacob for the twelve patriarchs.
9 "The patriarchs were *jealous of Joseph and*
sold him into slavery in Egypt.[g] But *God was*
with him,[h] 10 and rescued him from all his miseries by making him wise enough to attract the
attention of Pharaoh king of Egypt, who *made*
him governor of Egypt[i] and put him in charge
of the royal household. 11 *Then a famine came*
that caused much suffering *throughout Egypt*
and Canaan, and our ancestors could find
nothing to eat. 12 When Jacob *heard that there*
was grain for sale in Egypt, he sent our ancestors
there on a first visit, 13 but it was on the second
that *Joseph made himself known to his brothers,*
and told Pharaoh about his family. 14 Joseph

[*e*] Gn. 15:2. [*f*] Gn. 15:2,13,14; Ex. 3:12. [*g*] Gn. 37. [*h*] Gn. 39. [*i*] Gn. 41. Other direct quotations and allusions in this paragraph are from Gn. 42-50.

New English Bible

to give it in possession to him and his descendants after him, though he was then childless. God spoke in these terms: "Abraham's descendants shall live as aliens in a foreign land, held in slavery and oppression for four hundred years. And I will pass judgement", said God, "on the nation whose slaves they are; and after that they shall come out free, and worship me in this place." He then gave him the covenant of circumcision, and so, after Isaac was born, he circumcised him on the eighth day; and Isaac begot Jacob, and Jacob the twelve patriarchs.

'The patriarchs out of jealousy sold Joseph into slavery in Egypt, but God was with him and rescued him from all his troubles. He also gave him a presence and powers of mind which so commended him to Pharaoh king of Egypt, that he appointed him chief administrator for Egypt and the whole of the royal household.

'But famine struck all Egypt and Canaan, and caused great hardship; and our ancestors could find nothing to eat. But Jacob heard that there was food in Egypt and sent our fathers there. This was their first visit. On the second visit Joseph was recognized by his brothers, and his family connections were disclosed to Pharaoh. So Joseph sent an invitation to his

King James Version

father Jacob to *him*, and all his kindred, threescore and fifteen souls. 15 So Jacob went down into Egypt, and died, he, and our fathers, 16 And were carried over into Sychem, and laid in the sepulchre that Abraham bought for a sum of money of the sons of Emmor, *the father* of Sychem. 17 But when the time of the promise drew nigh, which God had sworn to Abraham, the people grew and multiplied in Egypt, 18 Till another king arose, which knew not Joseph. 19 The same dealt subtilely with our kindred, and evil entreated our fathers, so that they cast out their young children, to the end they might not live. 20 In which time Moses was born, and was exceeding fair, and nourished up in his father's house three months: 21 And when he was cast out, Pharaoh's daughter took him up, and nourished him for her own son. 22 And Moses was learned in all the wisdom of the Egyptians,

Living Bible

his brothers' families to come to Egypt, seventy-five persons in all. 15 So Jacob came to Egypt, where he died, and all his sons. 16 All of them were taken to Shechem and buried in the tomb Abraham bought from the sons of Hamor, Shechem's father.

17, 18 "As the time drew near when God would fulfill his promise to Abraham to free his descendants from slavery, the Jewish people greatly multiplied in Egypt; but then a king was crowned who had no respect for Joseph's memory. 19 This king plotted against our race, forcing parents to abandon their children in the fields.

20 "About that time Moses was born—a child of divine beauty. His parents hid him at home for three months, 21 and when at last they could no longer keep him hidden, and had to abandon him, Pharaoh's daughter found him and adopted him as her own son, 22 and taught him all the wisdom of the Egyptians, and he became a mighty prince and orator.

Today's English Version

a message to his father Jacob, telling him and the whole family to come to Egypt; there were seventy-five people in all. 15 Then Jacob went down to Egypt, where he and our ancestors died. 16 Their bodies were moved to Shechem, where they were buried in the grave which Abraham had bought from the tribe of Hamor for a sum of money.

17 "When the time drew near for God to keep the promise he had made to Abraham, the number of our people in Egypt had grown much larger. 18 At last a different king, who had not known Joseph, began to rule in Egypt. 19 He tricked our people and was cruel to our ancestors, forcing them to put their babies out of their homes, so that they would die. 20 It was at this time that Moses was born, a very beautiful child. He was brought up at home for three months, 21 and when he was put out of his home the daughter of Pharaoh adopted him and brought him up as her own son. 22 He was taught all the wisdom of the Egyptians, and became a great man in words and deeds.

New International Version

seph sent for his father Jacob and his whole family, seventy-five in all. 15 Then Jacob went down to Egypt, where he and our fathers died. 16 Their bodies were brought back to Shechem and placed in the tomb that Abraham had bought from the sons of Hamor at Shechem for a certain sum of money.

17 "As the time drew near for God to fulfill his promise to Abraham, the number of our people in Egypt greatly increased. 18 Then another king, who knew nothing about Joseph, became ruler of Egypt. 19 He dealt treacherously with our people and oppressed our ancestors by forcing them to throw out their newborn babies so that they would die.

20 "At that time Moses was born, and he was no ordinary child.[t] For three months he was cared for in his father's house. 21 When he was placed outside, Pharaoh's daughter took him and brought him up as her own son. 22 Moses was educated in all the wisdom of the Egyptians and was powerful in speech and action.

[t] Or *was fair in the sight of God.*

Phillips Modern English

Joseph sent and invited to come and live with him his father and all his kinsmen, seventy-five people in all. So Jacob came down to Egypt and both he and our fathers ended their days there. After their death they were carried back into Sychem and laid in the tomb which Abraham had bought with silver from the sons of Hemmor in Sychem.

"But as the time drew near for the fulfilment of the promise which God had made to Abraham, our people grew and became more and more numerous in Egypt. But at last another king came to the Egyptian throne who knew nothing of Joseph. This man cleverly victimised our race. He treated our forefathers with cunning cruelty, forcing them to expose their infant children so that they should not survive.

7.20 Stephen's defence:

iii. GOD'S PROVIDENCE AND MOSES

"It was at this very time that Moses was born. He was a child of divine beauty, and for three months he was brought up in his father's house, and then when the time came for him to be abandoned Pharaoh's daughter adopted him and brought him up as her own son. So Moses was trained in all the wisdom of the Egyptians, and became not only an excellent speaker but a man of action as well.

[j] Old Testament quotations from here to v. 35 are from Ex. 1-3.

Revised Standard Version

seph sent and called to him Jacob his father and
all his kindred, seventy-five souls; 15 and Jacob
went down into Egypt. And he died, himself and
our fathers, 16 and they were carried back to
Shechem and laid in the tomb that Abraham
had bought for a sum of silver from the sons of
Hamor in Shechem.
17 "But as the time of the promise drew near,
which God had granted to Abraham, the people
grew and multiplied in Egypt 18 till there arose
over Egypt another king who had not known
Joseph. 19 He dealt craftily with our race and
forced our fathers to expose their infants, that
they might not be kept alive. 20 At this time
Moses was born, and was beautiful before God.
And he was brought up for three months in his
father's house; 21 and when he was exposed,
Pharaoh's daughter adopted him and brought
him up as her own son. 22 And Moses was instructed in all the wisdom of the Egyptians, and
he was mighty in his words and deeds.

Jerusalem Bible

then sent for his father Jacob and his whole
family, a total of *seventy-five people.* 15 Jacob
went down into Egypt and after he and our ancestors had died there, 16 their bodies were
brought back to Shechem and buried in the tomb
that Abraham had bought and paid for from the
sons of Hamor, the father of Shechem.
17 "As the time drew near for God to fulfill
the promise he had solemnly made to Abraham,
our nation in Egypt *grew larger and larger,*
18 *until a new king came to power in Egypt who*
new nothing of[j] Joseph. 19 *He exploited* our
race, and ill-treated our ancestors, forcing them
to expose their babies to prevent their surviving. 20 It was at this period that Moses was
born, *a fine child* and favored by God. He was
looked after for three months in his father's
house, 21 and after he had been exposed,
Pharaoh's daughter adopted him and *brought*
him up as her own son. 22 So Moses was taught
all the wisdom of the Egyptians and became a
man with power both in his speech and his
actions.

New English Bible

father Jacob and all his relatives, seventy-five persons altogether; and Jacob went down into Egypt. There he ended his days, as also our forefathers did. Their remains were later removed to Shechem and buried in the tomb which Abraham had bought and paid for from the clan of Emmor at Shechem.

'Now as the time approached for God to fulfil the promise he had made to Abraham, our nation in Egypt grew and increased in numbers. At length another king, who knew nothing of Joseph, ascended the throne of Egypt. He made a crafty attack on our race, and cruelly forced our ancestors to expose their children so that they should not survive. At this time Moses was born. He was a fine child, and pleasing to God. For three months he was nursed in his father's house, and when he was exposed, Pharaoh's daughter herself adopted him and brought him up as her own son. So Moses was trained in all the wisdom of the Egyptians, a powerful speaker and a man of action.

King James Version

and was mighty in words and in deeds. 23And when he was full forty years old, it came into his heart to visit his brethren the children of Israel. 24And seeing one *of them* suffer wrong, he defended *him*, and avenged him that was oppressed, and smote the Egyptian: 25 For he supposed his brethren would have understood how that God by his hand would deliver them; but they understood not. 26And the next day he shewed himself unto them as they strove, and would have set them at one again, saying, Sirs, ye are brethren; why do ye wrong one to another? 27 But he that did his neighbour wrong thrust him away, saying, Who made thee a ruler and a judge over us? 28 Wilt thou kill me, as thou didst the Egyptian yesterday? 29 Then fled Moses at this saying, and was a stranger in the land of Madian, where he begat two sons. 30And when forty years were expired, there appeared to him in the wilderness of mount Sina an angel of the Lord in a flame of fire in a bush. 31 When Moses saw *it*, he wondered at the sight: and as he drew near to behold *it*, the voice of the Lord came unto him, 32 *Saying*, I *am* the God of thy fathers, the God of Abraham, and the God of

Living Bible

23 "One day as he was nearing his fortieth birthday, it came into his mind to visit his brothers, the people of Israel. 24 During this visit he saw an Egyptian mistreating a man of Israel. So Moses killed the Egyptian. 25 Moses supposed his brothers would realize that God had sent him to help them, but they didn't.

26 "The next day he visited them again and saw two men of Israel fighting. He tried to be a peacemaker. 'Gentlemen,' he said, 'you are brothers and shouldn't be fighting like this! It is wrong!'

27 "But the man in the wrong told Moses to mind his own business. 'Who made *you* a ruler and judge over us?' he asked. 28 'Are you going to kill me as you killed that Egyptian yesterday?'

29 "At this, Moses fled the country, and lived in the land of Midian, where his two sons were born.

30 "Forty years later, in the desert near Mount Sinai, an Angel appeared to him in a flame of fire in a bush. 31 Moses saw it and wondered what it was, and as he ran to see, the voice of the Lord called out to him, 32 'I am the God of your ancestors—of Abraham, Isaac and Jacob.'

Today's English Version

23 "When Moses was forty years old he decided to visit his fellow Israelites. 24 He saw one of them being mistreated by an Egyptian; so he went to his help and took revenge on the Egyptian by killing him. 25 (He thought that his own people would understand that God was going to use him to set them free; but they did not understand.) 26 The next day he saw two Israelites fighting, and he tried to make peace between them. 'Listen, men,' he said, 'you are brothers; why do you mistreat each other?' 27 But the one who was mistreating the other pushed Moses aside. 'Who made you ruler and judge over us?' he asked. 28 'Do you want to kill me, just as you killed that Egyptian yesterday?' 29 When Moses heard this he fled from Egypt and started living in the land of Midian. There he had two sons.

30 "After forty years had passed, an angel appeared to Moses in the flames of a burning bush in the desert near Mount Sinai. 31 Moses was amazed by what he saw, and went near the bush to look at it closely. But he heard the Lord's voice: 32 'I am the God of your ancestors, the God of Abraham, Isaac, and Jacob.'

New International Version

23 "When Moses was forty years old, he decided to visit his fellow Israelites. 24 He saw one of them being mistreated by an Egyptian, so he went to his defense and avenged him by killing the Egyptian. 25 Moses thought that his own people would realize that God was using him to rescue them, but they did not. 26 The next day Moses came upon two Israelites who were fighting. He tried to reconcile them by saying, 'Men, you are brothers; why do you want to hurt each other?'

27 "But the man who was mistreating the other pushed Moses aside and said, 'Who made you ruler and judge over us? 28 Do you want to kill me as you killed the Egyptian yesterday?' [u] 29 When Moses heard this, he fled to Midian, where he settled as a foreigner and had two sons.

30 "After forty years had passed, an angel appeared to Moses in the flames of a burning bush in the desert near Mount Sinai. 31 When he saw this, he was amazed at the sight. As he went over to look more closely, he heard the Lord's voice: 32 'I am the God of your fathers,

[u] Exodus 2:14.

Phillips Modern English

7.23 Moses' first abortive attempt at rescue

"Now when he was forty years old the thought came into his mind that he should go and look into the condition of his own brothers, the sons of Israel. He saw one of them being unjustly treated, went to the rescue and avenged the man who had been ill-treated by striking down the Egyptian. He fully imagined that his brothers would understand that God was using him to rescue them. But they did not understand. Indeed, on the very next day he came upon two of them who were quarrelling and urged them to make peace, saying, 'Men, you are brothers. What good can come from your injuring each other?' But the man who was wronging his neighbour pushed Moses aside, saying, 'Who made you a ruler and judge over us? Do you want to kill me as you killed that Egyptian yesterday?' At that retort Moses fled and lived as an exile in the land of Midian, where he became the father of two sons.

7.30 Moses hears the voice of God

"It was forty years later in the desert of Mount Sinai that an angel appeared to him in the flames of a burning bush, and the sight filled Moses with wonder. As he approached to look at it more closely the voice of the Lord spoke to him, saying, 'I am the God of thy fathers, the God of Abraham, and the God of Isaac, and the God

Revised Standard Version

23 "When he was forty years old, it came into
his heart to visit his brethren, the sons of Israel.
24And seeing one of them being wronged, he
defended the oppressed man and avenged him by
striking the Egyptian. 25 He supposed that his
brethren understood that God was giving them
deliverance by his hand, but they did not understand. 26And on the following day he appeared
to them as they were quarreling and would have
reconciled them, saying, 'Men, you are brethren,
why do you wrong each other?' 27 But the man
who was wronging his neighbor thrust him aside,
saying, 'Who made you a ruler and a judge over
us? 28 Do you want to kill me as you killed the
Egyptian yesterday?' 29At this retort Moses fled,
and became an exile in the land of Midian,
where he became the father of two sons.
30 "Now when forty years had passed, an
angel appeared to him in the wilderness of
Mount Sinai, in a flame of fire in a bush.
31 When Moses saw it he wondered at the sight;
and as he drew near to look, the voice of the
Lord came, 32 'I am the God of your fathers,
the God of Abraham and of Isaac and of Jacob.'

Jerusalem Bible

23 "At the age of forty he decided to visit
his countrymen, the sons of Israel. 24 When he
saw one of them being ill-treated he went to his
defense and rescued the man by *killing the*
Egyptian. 25 He thought his brothers realized
that through him God would liberate them, but
they did not. 26 The next day, when he came
across some of them fighting, he tried to reconcile them. 'Friends,' he said, 'you are brothers;
why are you hurting each other?' 27 But *the*
man who was attacking his fellow countryman
pushed him aside. *'And who appointed you,'*
he said, *'to be our leader and judge? 28 Do you*
intend to kill me as you killed the Egyptian
yesterday?' 29 Moses fled when he heard this[k]
and *he went to stay in the land of Midian,*
where he became the father of two sons.
30 "Forty years later, *in the wilderness* near
Mount Sinai, *an angel appeared to him in the*
flames of a bush that was on fire. 31 Moses was
amazed by what he saw. *As he went nearer to*
look at it the voice of the Lord was heard,
32 *'I am the God of your ancestors, the God*

[k] In Ex. 2:15 Moses runs away because he is afraid of Pharaoh.

New English Bible

'He was approaching the age of forty, when it occurred to him to look into the conditions of his fellow-countrymen the Israelites. He saw one of them being ill-treated, so he went to his aid, and avenged the victim by striking down the Egyptian. He thought his fellow-countrymen would understand that God was offering them deliverance through him, but they did not understand. The next day he came upon two of them fighting, and tried to bring them to make up their quarrel. "My men," he said, "you are brothers; why are you ill-treating one another?" But the man who was at fault pushed him away. "Who set you up as a ruler and judge over us?" he said. "Are you going to kill me as you killed the Egyptian yesterday?" At this Moses fled the country and settled in Midianite territory. There two sons were born to him.

'After forty years had passed, an angel appeared to him in the flame of a burning bush in the desert near Mount Sinai. Moses was amazed at the sight. But as he approached to look closely, the voice of the Lord was heard: "I am the God of your fathers, the God of Abraham, Isaac, and

King James Version

Isaac, and the God of Jacob. Then Moses trembled, and durst not behold. 33 Then said the Lord to him, Put off thy shoes from thy feet: for the place where thou standest is holy ground. 34 I have seen, I have seen the affliction of my people which is in Egypt, and I have heard their groaning, and am come down to deliver them. And now come, I will send thee into Egypt. 35 This Moses whom they refused, saying, Who made thee a ruler and a judge? the same did God send *to be* a ruler and a deliverer by the hand of the angel which appeared to him in the bush. 36 He brought them out, after that he had shewed wonders and signs in the land of Egypt, and in the Red sea, and in the wilderness forty years.

37 This is that Moses, which said unto the children of Israel, A Prophet shall the Lord your God raise up unto you of your brethren, like unto me; him shall ye hear. 38 This is he, that was in the church in the wilderness with the angel which spake to him in the mount Sina, and *with* our fathers: who received the lively oracles to give unto us: 39 To whom our fathers would not obey, but thrust *him* from them, and in their hearts turned back again into Egypt, 40 Saying unto Aaron, Make us gods to go before us: for *as for* this Moses, which brought us out of the land of Egypt, we wot not what is become of him. 41 And they made a calf in those days, and offered sacrifice unto the idol, and rejoiced in the works of their own hands.

Living Bible

Moses shook with terror and dared not look.

33 "And the Lord said to him, 'Take off your shoes, for you are standing on holy ground. 34 I have seen the anguish of my people in Egypt and have heard their cries. I have come down to deliver them. Come, I will send you to Egypt.' 35 And so God sent back the same man his people had previously rejected by demanding, 'Who made *you* a ruler and judge over us?' Moses was sent to be their ruler and savior. 36 And by means of many remarkable miracles he led them out of Egypt and through the Red Sea, and back and forth through the wilderness for forty years.

37 "Moses himself told the people of Israel, 'God will raise up a Prophet much like me[d] from among your brothers.' 38 How true this proved to be, for in the wilderness, Moses was the go-between—the mediator between the people of Israel and the Angel who gave them the Law of God—the Living Word—on Mount Sinai.

39 "But our fathers rejected Moses and wanted to return to Egypt. 40 They told Aaron, 'Make idols for us, so that we will have gods to lead us back; for we don't know what has become of this Moses, who brought us out of Egypt.' 41 So they made a calf-idol and sacrificed to it, and rejoiced in this thing they had made.

[*d*] Literally, "like unto me."

Today's English Version

Moses trembled with fear and dared not look. 33 The Lord said to him, 'Take your sandals off, for the place where you are standing is holy ground. 34 I have looked and seen the cruel suffering of my people in Egypt. I have heard their groans, and I have come down to save them. Come now, I will send you to Egypt.'

35 "Moses is the one who was rejected by the people of Israel. 'Who made you ruler and judge over us?' they asked. He is the one whom God sent as ruler and savior, with the help of the angel who appeared to him in the burning bush. 36 He led the people out of Egypt, performing miracles and wonders in Egypt and the Red Sea, and in the desert for forty years. 37 Moses is the one who said to the people of Israel, 'God will send you a prophet, just as he sent me, who will be of your own people.' 38 He is the one who was with the people of Israel assembled in the desert; he was there with our ancestors and with the angel who spoke to him on Mount Sinai; he received God's living messages to pass on to us.

39 "But our ancestors refused to obey him; they pushed him aside and wished that they could go back to Egypt. 40 So they said to Aaron, 'Make us some gods who will go in front of us. We do not know what has happened to that Moses who brought us out of Egypt.' 41 It was then that they made an idol in the shape of a calf, offered sacrifice to it, and had a feast to

New International Version

the God of Abraham, Isaac and Jacob.' [v] Moses trembled with fear and did not dare to look.

33 "Then the Lord said to him, 'Take off your sandals; the place where you are standing is holy ground. 34 I have indeed seen the oppression of my people in Egypt. I have heard their groaning and have come down to set them free. Now come, I will send you back to Egypt.' [w]

35 "This is the same Moses whom they had rejected with the words, 'Who made you ruler and judge?' He was sent to be their ruler and deliverer by God himself, through the angel who appeared to him in the bush. 36 He led them out of Egypt and did wonders and miraculous signs in Egypt, at the Red Sea[x] and for forty years in the desert. 37 This is that Moses who told the Israelites, 'God will send you a prophet like me from your own people.' [y] 38 He was in the congregation in the desert, with our fathers and with the angel who spoke to him on Mount Sinai; and he received living words to pass on to us.

39 "But our fathers refused to obey him. Instead, they rejected him and in their hearts turned back to Egypt. 40 They told Aaron, 'Make some gods who will lead the way for us. As for this fellow Moses who led us out of Egypt—we don't know what has happened to him!' [z] 41 That was the time they made an idol in the form of a calf. They brought sacrifices to it and held a celebration in honor of what their

[*v*] Exodus 3:6. [*w*] Exodus 3:5,7,8,10. [*x*] That is, Sea of Reeds. [*y*] Deut. 18:15. [*z*] Exodus 32:1.

Phillips Modern English

of Jacob.' Then Moses trembled and was afraid to look any more. But the Lord spoke to him and said, 'Loose the shoes from thy feet: for the place whereon thou standest is holy ground. I have surely seen the affliction of my people which is in Egypt, and have heard their groaning, and I am come down to deliver them: and now come, I will send thee into Egypt.'

7.35 But Israel rejects Moses

"So this same Moses whom they had rejected in the words, 'Who appointed you a ruler and judge?' God sent to be both ruler and deliverer with the help of the angel who had appeared to him in the bush. This is the man who showed wonders and signs in Egypt and in the Red Sea, the man who led them out of Egypt and was their leader in the desert for forty years. He was Moses, the man who said to the sons of Israel, 'A prophet shall God raise up unto you from among your brethren, like unto me.' In that assembly in the desert this was the man who was the mediator between the angel who spoke to him on Mount Sinai and our fathers. This was the man who received words, living words, which were to be given to us; and this was the man to whom our forefathers turned a deaf ear! They disregarded him, and in their hearts hankered after Egypt. They said to Aaron, 'Make us gods to go before us. For as for this Moses who led us out of Egypt, we do not know what has become of him.' In those days they even made a calf, and offered sacrifices to their idol. They re-

Revised Standard Version

And Moses trembled and did not dare to look.
33 And the Lord said to him, 'Take off the shoes
from your feet, for the place where you are
standing is holy ground. 34 I have surely seen
the ill-treatment of my people that are in Egypt
and heard their groaning, and I have come down
to deliver them. And now come, I will send you
to Egypt.'
35 "This Moses whom they refused, saying,
'Who made you a ruler and a judge?' God sent
as both ruler and deliverer by the hand of the
angel that appeared to him in the bush. 36 He
led them out, having performed wonders and
signs in Egypt and at the Red Sea, and in the
wilderness for forty years. 37 This is the Moses
who said to the Israelites, 'God will raise up for
you a prophet from your brethren as he raised
me up.' 38 This is he who was in the congregation in the wilderness with the angel who spoke
to him at Mount Sinai, and with our fathers; and
he received living oracles to give to us. 39 Our
fathers refused to obey him, but thrust him aside,
and in their hearts they turned to Egypt, 40 saying to Aaron, 'Make for us gods to go before us;
as for this Moses who led us out from the land
of Egypt, we do not know what has become of
him.' 41 And they made a calf in those days, and
offered a sacrifice to the idol and rejoiced in the

Jerusalem Bible

of Abraham, Isaac and Jacob.' Moses trembled
and *did not dare to look any more.* 33 The Lord
said to him, *'Take off your shoes; the place
where you are standing is holy ground.* 34 *I have
seen the way my people are ill-treated in Egypt,
I have heard their groans, and I have come
down to liberate them. So come here and let
me send you into Egypt.'*
35 "It was the same Moses that they had disowned when they said, *'Who appointed you to
be our leader and judge?'* who was now sent to
be both leader and redeemer through the angel
who had appeared to him in the bush. 36 It was
Moses who, after performing *miracles and signs
in Egypt,* led them out across the Red Sea and
through the wilderness for forty years.[l] 37 It
was Moses who told the sons of Israel, *'God
will raise up a prophet like myself for you from
among your own brothers.'*[m] 38 When they held
the assembly in the wilderness it was only
through Moses that our ancestors could communicate with the angel who had spoken to
him on Mount Sinai; it was he who was entrusted with words of life to hand on to us.
39 This is the man that our ancestors refused
to listen to: they pushed him aside, *turned back
to Egypt* in their thoughts, 40 *and said to Aaron,
'Make some gods to be our leaders; we do not
understand what has come over this Moses who
led us out of Egypt.'*[n] 41 It was then that *they
made a bull calf and offered sacrifice* to the
idol. They were perfectly happy with something

[l] Nb. 14:33. [m] Dt. 18:15,18. [n] Ex. 32:1,23 and 32:4,6.

New English Bible

Jacob." Moses was terrified and dared not look. Then the Lord said to him, "Take off your shoes; the place where you are standing is holy ground. I have indeed seen how my people are oppressed in Egypt and have heard their groans; and I have come down to rescue them. Up, then; let me send you to Egypt."

'This Moses, whom they had rejected with the words, "Who made you ruler and judge?"—this very man was commissioned as ruler and liberator by God himself, speaking through the angel who appeared to him in the bush. It was Moses who led them out, working miracles and signs in Egypt, at the Red Sea, and for forty years in the desert. It was he again who said to the Israelites, "God will raise up a prophet for you from among yourselves as he raised me."[a] He it was who, when they were assembled there in the desert, conversed with the angel who spoke to him on Mount Sinai, and with our forefathers; he received the living utterances of God, to pass on to us.

'But our forefathers would not accept his leadership. They thrust him aside. They wished themselves back in Egypt, and said to Aaron, "Make us gods to go before us. As for that Moses, who brought us out of Egypt, we do not know what has become of him." That was when they made the bull-calf, and offered sacrifice to the idol, and held a feast in honour of the thing

[a] *Or* like me.

King James Version

42 Then God turned, and gave them up to worship the host of heaven; as it is written in the
book of the prophets, O ye house of Israel, have
ye offered to me slain beasts and sacrifices *by the
space of* forty years in the wilderness? 43 Yea,
ye took up the tabernacle of Moloch, and the
star of your god Remphan, figures which ye
made to worship them: and I will carry you
away beyond Babylon. 44 Our fathers had the
tabernacle of witness in the wilderness, as he had
appointed, speaking unto Moses, that he should
make it according to the fashion that he had
seen. 45 Which also our fathers that came after
brought in with Jesus into the possession of the
Gentiles, whom God drave out before the face
of our fathers, unto the days of David; 46 Who
found favour before God, and desired to find
a tabernacle for the God of Jacob. 47 But Solomon built him a house. 48 Howbeit the Most
High dwelleth not in temples made with hands;
as saith the prophet, 49 Heaven *is* my throne,

Living Bible

42 "Then God turned away from them and
gave them up, and let them serve the sun, moon
and stars as their gods! In the book of Amos'
prophecies the Lord God asks, 'Was it to me you
were sacrificing during those forty years in the
desert, Israel? 43 No, your real interest was in
your heathen gods—Sakkuth, and the star god
Kaiway, and in all the images you made. So I
will send you into captivity far away beyond
Babylon.'

44 "Our ancestors carried along with them a
portable Temple, or Tabernacle, through the
wilderness. In it they kept the stone tablets with
the Ten Commandments written on them. This
building was constructed in exact accordance
with the plan shown to Moses by the Angel.
45 Years later, when Joshua led the battles
against the Gentile nations, this Tabernacle was
taken with them into their new territory, and
used until the time of King David.

46 "God blessed David greatly, and David
asked for the privilege of building a permanent
Temple for the God of Jacob. 47 But it was
Solomon who actually built it. 48, 49 However,
God doesn't live in temples made by human
hands. 'The heaven is my throne,' says the Lord

Today's English Version

celebrate what they themselves had made. 42 But
God turned away from them, and gave them over
to worship the stars of heaven, as it is written in
the book of the prophets,

'People of Israel! It was not to me
that you slaughtered and sacrificed animals
for forty years in the desert.
43 It was the tent of the god Moloch that you
carried,
and the image of the star of your god
Rephan;
they were idols that you had made to
worship.
And so I will send you away beyond Babylon.'

44 "Our ancestors had the tent of God's presence with them in the desert. It had been made
as God had told Moses to make it, according to
the pattern that Moses had been shown. 45 Later
on, our ancestors who received the tent from
their fathers carried it with them when they went
with Joshua and took over the land from the nations that God drove out before them. And it
stayed there until the time of David. 46 He won
God's favor, and asked God to allow him to
provide a house for the God of Jacob. 47 But it
was Solomon who built him a house.

48 "But the Most High God does not live in
houses built by men; as the prophet says,

49 'Heaven is my throne, says the Lord,

New International Version

hands had made. 42 But God turned away and
gave them over to the worship of the heavenly
bodies. This agrees with what is written in the
book of the prophets:

'Did you bring me sacrifices and offerings
forty years in the desert, O Israel?
43 No, you have lifted up the shrine of Moloch
and the star of your god Rephan,
the idols you made to worship.
Therefore, I will send you into exile'[a] beyond Babylon.

44 "Our ancestors had the tabernacle of testimony with them in the desert. It had been made
as God directed Moses, according to the pattern
he had seen. 45 Having received the tabernacle,
our fathers under Joshua brought it with them
when they took the land from the nations God
drove out before them. It remained in the land
until the time of David, 46 who enjoyed God's
favor and asked that he might provide a dwelling place for the God of Jacob.[b] 47 But it was
Solomon who built the house for him.

48 "However, the Most High does not live
in houses made by men. As the prophet says:
49 'Heaven is my throne,

[*a*] Amos 5:25-27. [*b*] Some early MSS read *house of Jacob*.

Phillips Modern English

joiced in the work of their own hands. So God turned away from them and left them to worship the Host of Heaven, as it is written in the book of the prophets,

Did ye offer unto me slain beasts and sacrifices
Forty years in the wilderness, O house of Israel?
And ye took up the tabernacle of Moloch,
And the star of the god Rephan,
The figures which ye made to worship them:
And I will carry you away beyond Babylon.

7.44 *God's privileges to Israel*

"There in the desert our forefather possessed the Tabernacle of witness made according to the pattern which Moses saw when God instructed him to build it. This Tabernacle was handed down to our forefathers, and they brought it here when the gentiles were defeated under Joshua, for God drove them out as our ancestors advanced. Here it stayed until the time of David. David won the approval of God and prayed that he might find a habitation for the God of Jacob, even though it was not he but Solomon who actually built a house for him. Yet of course the Most High does not live in man-made houses. As the prophet says,

The heaven is my throne,

Revised Standard Version

works of their hands. 42 But God turned and
gave them over to worship the host of heaven, as
it is written in the book of the prophets:
'Did you offer to me slain beasts and sacrifices,
forty years in the wilderness, O house of Israel?
43 And you took up the tent of Moloch,
and the star of the god Rephan,
the figures which you made to worship;
and I will remove you beyond Babylon.'
44 "Our fathers had the tent of witness in the
wilderness, even as he who spoke to Moses directed him to make it, according to the pattern
that he had seen. 45 Our fathers in turn brought
it in with Joshua when they dispossessed the nations which God thrust out before our fathers.
So it was until the days of David, 46 who found
favor in the sight of God and asked leave to find
a habitation for the God of Jacob. 47 But it was
Solomon who built a house for him. 48 Yet the
Most High does not dwell in houses made with
hands; as the prophet says,
49 'Heaven is my throne,

Jerusalem Bible

they had made for themselves. 42 God turned
away from them and abandoned them to the
worship of the army of heaven,[o] as scripture
says in the book of the prophets:

Did you bring me victims and sacrifices in the wilderness
for all those forty years, you House of Israel?
43 *No, you carried the tent of Moloch on your shoulders*
and the star of the god Rephan,
those idols that you had made to adore.
So now I will exile you even further than Babylon.[p]

44 "While they were in the desert our ancestors possessed the Tent of Testimony that
had been constructed according to the instructions God gave Moses, telling him to *make an
exact copy of the pattern*[q] he had been shown.
45 It was handed down from one ancestor of
ours to another until Joshua brought it into the
country we had conquered from the nations
which were driven out by God as we advanced.
Here it stayed until the time of David. 46 He
won God's favor and asked permission *to have
a temple built for* the House of *Jacob*, 47 though
it was *Solomon* who actually *built God's house*[r]
for him. 48 Even so the Most High does not
live in a house that human hands have built:
for as the prophet says:

49 *With heaven my throne*

[o] The stars and planets. [p] Am. 5:25-27 (LXX). [q] Ex. 25:40. [r] 1 K. 6:2.

New English Bible

their hands had made. But God turned away from them and gave them over to the worship of the host of heaven, as it stands written in the book of the prophets: "Did you bring me victims and offerings those forty years in the desert, you house of Israel? No, you carried aloft the shrine of Moloch and the star of the god Rephan, the images which you had made for your adoration. I will banish you beyond Babylon."

'Our forefathers had the Tent of the Testimony in the desert, as God commanded when he told Moses to make it after the pattern which he had seen. Our fathers of the next generation, with Joshua, brought it with them when they dispossessed the nations whom God drove out before them, and there it was until the time of David. David found favour with God and asked to be allowed to provide a dwelling-place for the God of Jacob;[b] but it was Solomon who built him a house. However, the Most High does not live in houses made by men: as the prophet says, "Heaven is my throne and earth my footstool.

[b] *Some witnesses read* for the house of Jacob.

King James Version

and earth *is* my footstool: what house will ye build me? saith the Lord: or what *is* the place of my rest? 50 Hath not my hand made all these things?

51 Ye stiffnecked and uncircumcised in heart and ears, ye do always resist the Holy Ghost: as your fathers *did,* so *do* ye. 52 Which of the prophets have not your fathers persecuted? and they have slain them which shewed before of the coming of the Just One; of whom ye have been now the betrayers and murderers: 53 Who have received the law by the disposition of angels, and have not kept *it.*

54 When they heard these things, they were cut to the heart, and they gnashed on him with *their* teeth. 55 But he, being full of the Holy Ghost, looked up steadfastly into heaven, and saw the glory of God, and Jesus standing on the right hand of God, 56 And said, Behold, I see

Living Bible

through his prophets, 'and earth is my footstool. What kind of home could you build?' asks the Lord. 'Would I stay in it? 50 Didn't I make both heaven and earth?'

51 "You stiff-necked heathen! Must you forever resist the Holy Spirit? But your fathers did, and so do you! 52 Name one prophet your ancestors didn't persecute! They even killed the ones who predicted the coming of the Righteous One—the Messiah whom you betrayed and murdered. 53 Yes, and you deliberately destroyed God's Laws, though you received them from the hands of angels." [e]

54 The Jewish leaders were stung to fury by Stephen's accusation, and ground their teeth in rage. 55 But Stephen, full of the Holy Spirit, gazed steadily upward into heaven and saw the glory of God and Jesus standing at God's right hand. 56 And he told them, "Look, I see the

[*e*] Literally, "the Law as it was ordained by angels."

Today's English Version

and earth is my footstool.
What kind of house would you build for me?
Where is the place for me to rest?
50 Did not I myself make all these things?'

51 "How stubborn you are! How heathen your hearts, how deaf you are to God's message! You are just like your ancestors: you too have always resisted the Holy Spirit! 52 Was there any prophet that your ancestors did not persecute? They killed God's messengers, who long ago announced the coming of his righteous Servant. And now you have betrayed and murdered him. 53 You are the ones who received God's law, that was handed down by angels—yet you have not obeyed it!"

The stoning of Stephen

54 As the members of the Council listened to Stephen they became furious and ground their teeth at him in anger. 55 But Stephen, full of the Holy Spirit, looked up to heaven and saw God's glory, and Jesus standing at the right side of God. 56 "Look!" he said. "I see heaven opened

New International Version

and the earth is my footstool.
What kind of house will you make for me?
says the Lord.
Or where will my resting place be?
50 Has not my hand made all these things?' [c]

51 "You stubborn people, with uncircumcised hearts and ears! You are just like your fathers: You always resist the Holy Spirit! 52 Was there ever a prophet your fathers did not persecute? They even killed those who predicted the coming of the Righteous One. And now you have betrayed and murdered him—53 you who have received the law that was put into effect through angels but have not obeyed it."

The stoning of Stephen

54 When they heard this, they were furious and ground their teeth at him. 55 But Stephen, filled with the Holy Spirit, looked up to heaven and saw the glory of God, and Jesus standing at the right hand of God. 56 "Look," he said, "I

[*c*] Isaiah 66:1,2.

Phillips Modern English

And the earth the footstool of my feet:
What manner of house will ye build me? saith the Lord:
Or what is the place of my rest?
Did not my hand make all these things?

7.51 Yet Israel is blind and disobedient

"You obstinate people, heathen in your thinking, heathen in the way you are listening to me now! It is always the same—you never fail to resist the Holy Spirit! Just as your fathers did so are you doing now. Can you name a single prophet whom your fathers did not persecute? They killed the men who foretold the coming of the just one, and now in our own day you have become his betrayers and his murderers. You are the men who have received the Law of God by the hand of angels, and you are the men who have failed to keep it!"

7.54 The truth arouses murderous fury

These words stung them to fury and they ground their teeth at him in rage. Stephen, filled through all his being with the Holy Spirit, looked steadily up into Heaven. He saw the glory of God, and Jesus himself standing at his right hand.
"Look!" he exclaimed, "the heavens are

Revised Standard Version

and earth my footstool.
What house will you build for me, says the Lord,
or what is the place of my rest?
50 Did not my hand make all these things?'
51 "You stiff-necked people, uncircumcised
in heart and ears, you always resist the Holy
Spirit. As your fathers did, so do you. 52 Which
of the prophets did not your fathers persecute?
And they killed those who announced beforehand the coming of the Righteous One, whom
you have now betrayed and murdered, 53 you
who received the law as delivered by angels and
did not keep it."
54 Now when they heard these things they
were enraged, and they ground their teeth against
him. 55 But he, full of the Holy Spirit, gazed into
heaven and saw the glory of God, and Jesus
standing at the right hand of God; 56 and he
said, "Behold, I see the heavens opened, and the

Jerusalem Bible

and earth my footstool,
what house could you build me,
what place could you make for my rest?
50 *Was not all this made by hand?* [s]

51 "You stubborn people, with your pagan
hearts and pagan ears. You are always resisting
the Holy Spirit, just as your ancestors used to
do. 52 Can you name a single prophet your
ancestors never persecuted? In the past they
killed those who foretold the coming of the Just
One, and now you have become his betrayers,
his murderers. 53 You who had the Law brought
to you by angels are the very ones who have not
kept it."
54 They were infuriated when they heard this,
and ground their teeth at him.

The stoning of Stephen. Saul as persecutor

55 But Stephen, filled with the Holy Spirit,
gazed into heaven and saw the glory of God,
and Jesus standing at God's right hand. 56 "I
can see heaven thrown open," he said, "and the

[s] Is. 66:1-2.

New English Bible

What kind of house will you build for me, says the Lord; where is my resting-place? Are not all these things of my own making?"
'How stubborn you are, heathen still at heart and deaf to the truth! You always fight against the Holy Spirit. Like fathers, like sons. Was there ever a prophet whom your fathers did not persecute? They killed those who foretold the coming of the Righteous One; and now you have betrayed him and murdered him, you who received the Law as God's angels gave it to you, and yet have not kept it.'
This touched them on the raw and they ground their teeth with fury. But Stephen, filled with the Holy Spirit, and gazing intently up to heaven, saw the glory of God, and Jesus standing at God's right hand. 'Look,' he said, 'there is a rift

King James Version

the heavens opened, and the Son of man standing on the right hand of God. 57 Then they cried out with a loud voice, and stopped their ears, and ran upon him with one accord, 58And cast *him* out of the city, and stoned *him:* and the witnesses laid down their clothes at a young man's feet, whose name was Saul. 59And they stoned Stephen, calling upon *God,* and saying, Lord Jesus, receive my spirit. 60And he kneeled down, and cried with a loud voice, Lord, lay not this sin to their charge. And when he had said this, he fell asleep.

8 And Saul was consenting unto his death. And at that time there was a great persecution against the church which was at Jerusalem; and they were all scattered abroad throughout the regions of Judea and Samaria, except the apostles. 2And devout men carried Stephen *to his burial,* and made great lamentation over him.

Living Bible

heavens opened and Jesus the Messiah[f] standing beside God, at his right hand!"

57 Then they mobbed him, putting their hands over their ears, and drowning out his voice with their shouts, 58 and dragged him out of the city to stone him. The official witnesses—the executioners—took off their coats and laid them at the feet of a young man named Paul.[g]

59 And as the murderous stones came hurtling at him, Stephen prayed, "Lord Jesus, receive my spirit." 60And he fell to his knees shouting, "Lord, don't charge them with this sin!" and with that, he died.

8 Paul was in complete agreement with the killing of Stephen. And a great wave of persecution of the believers began that day, sweeping over the church in Jerusalem, and everyone except the apostles fled into Judea and Samaria. 2 (But some godly Jews[a] came and with

[f] Literally, "the Son of Man." [g] Paul is also known as Saul. [a] Literally, "devout men." It is not clear whether these were Christians who braved the persecution, or whether they were godly and sympathetic Jews.

Today's English Version

and the Son of Man standing at the right side of God!"

57 With a loud cry they covered their ears with their hands. Then they all rushed together at him at once, 58 threw him out of the city and stoned him. The witnesses left their cloaks in charge of a young man named Saul. 59 They kept on stoning Stephen as he called on the Lord, "Lord Jesus, receive my spirit!" 60 He knelt down and cried out in a loud voice, "Lord! Do not remember this sin against them!" He said this and died.

8 And Saul approved of his murder.

Saul persecutes the church

That very day the church in Jerusalem began to suffer cruel persecution. All the believers, except the apostles, were scattered throughout the provinces of Judea and Samaria. 2 Some devout men buried Stephen, mourning for him with loud cries.

New International Version

see heaven open and the Son of Man standing at the right hand of God."

57 At this they covered their ears and, yelling at the top of their voices, they all rushed at him, 58 dragged him out of the city and began to stone him. Meanwhile, the witnesses laid their clothes at the feet of a young man named Saul.

59 While they were stoning him, Stephen prayed, "Lord Jesus, receive my spirit." 60 Then he fell on his knees and cried out, "Lord, do not hold this sin against them." When he had said this, he fell asleep.

8 And Saul was there, giving approval to his death.

The church persecuted and scattered

On that day a great persecution broke out against the church at Jerusalem, and all except the apostles were scattered throughout Judea and Samaria. 2 Godly men buried Stephen and

Phillips Modern English

opened and I can see the Son of Man standing at God's right hand!"

At this they put their fingers in their ears. Yelling with fury, as one man they made a rush at him and hustled him out of the city and stoned him. The witnesses* of the execution flung their clothes at the feet of a young man by the name of Saul.

So they stoned Stephen while he called upon God, and said,

"Lord Jesus, receive my spirit!"

Then, on his knees, he cried in ringing tones,

"Lord, forgive them for this sin."

And with these words he fell into the sleep of death, while Saul gave silent assent to his execution.

8.1b Widespread persecution follows Stephen's death

On that very day a great storm of persecution burst upon the Church in Jerusalem. All except the apostles were scattered over the countryside of Judaea and Samaria. While reverent men buried Stephen and mourned deeply over him,

* In Jewish Law the "witnesses" were also the executioners.

Revised Standard Version

Son of man standing at the right hand of God."
57 But they cried out with a loud voice and
stopped their ears and rushed together upon
him. 58 Then they cast him out of the city and
stoned him; and the witnesses laid down their
garments at the feet of a young man named
Saul. 59 And as they were stoning Stephen, he
prayed, "Lord Jesus, receive my spirit." 60 And
he knelt down and cried with a loud voice,
"Lord, do not hold this sin against them." And
when he had said this, he

8 fell asleep. 1 And Saul was consenting to his
death.

And on that day a great persecution arose
against the church in Jerusalem; and they were
all scattered throughout the region of Judea
and Samaria, except the apostles. 2 Devout men
buried Stephen, and made great lamentation

Jerusalem Bible

Son of Man standing at the right hand of God."
57 At this all the members of the council shouted
out and stopped their ears with their hands;
then they all rushed at him, 58 sent him out of
the city and stoned him. The witnesses[t] put
down their clothes at the feet of a young man
called Saul. 59 As they were stoning him, Stephen
said in invocation, "Lord Jesus, receive my
spirit." 60 Then he knelt down and said aloud,
"Lord, do not hold this sin against them"; and
with these words he fell asleep.

8 Saul entirely approved of the killing.
That day a bitter persecution started against
the church in Jerusalem and everyone[u] except
the apostles fled to the country districts of
Judaea and Samaria.
2 There were some devout people, however,
who buried Stephen and made great mourning
for him.

[t] By the Law, the accusers had to begin the execution of the sentence. [u] The persecution seems to have been directed principally against the Hellenists.

New English Bible

in the sky; I can see the Son of Man standing at God's right hand!' At this they gave a great shout and stopped their ears. Then they made one rush at him and, flinging him out of the city, set about stoning him. The witnesses laid their coats at the feet of a young man named Saul. So they stoned Stephen, and as they did so, he called out, 'Lord Jesus, receive my spirit.' Then he fell on his knees and cried aloud, 'Lord, do not hold this sin against them', and with that he died.

8 And Saul was among those who approved of his murder.

This was the beginning of a time of violent persecution for the church in Jerusalem; and all except the apostles were scattered over the country districts of Judaea and Samaria. Stephen was given burial by certain devout men, who made

King James Version

3As for Saul, he made havock of the church,
entering into every house, and haling men and
women committed *them* to prison. 4 Therefore
they that were scattered abroad went every where
preaching the word. 5 Then Philip went down
to the city of Samaria, and preached Christ unto
them. 6And the people with one accord gave
heed unto those things which Philip spake, hearing and seeing the miracles which he did. 7 For
unclean spirits, crying with loud voice, came
out of many that were possessed *with them:* and
many taken with palsies, and that were lame,
were healed. 8And there was great joy in that
city. 9 But there was a certain man, called Simon,
which beforetime in the same city used sorcery,
and bewitched the people of Samaria, giving out
that himself was some great one: 10 To whom
they all gave heed, from the least to the greatest,
saying, This man is the great power of God.
11And to him they had regard, because that of
long time he had bewitched them with sorceries.
12 But when they believed Philip preaching the

Living Bible

great sorrow buried Stephen.) 3 Paul was like a
wild man, going everywhere to devastate the believers, even entering private homes and dragging
out men and women alike and jailing them.
4 But the believers[b] who had fled Jerusalem
went everywhere preaching the Good News
about Jesus! 5 Philip, for instance, went to the
city of Samaria and told the people there about
Christ. 6 Crowds listened intently to what he had
to say because of the miracles he did. 7 Many
evil spirits were cast out, screaming as they left
their victims, and many who were paralyzed or
lame were healed, 8 so there was much joy in
that city!
9, 10, 11 A man named Simon had formerly
been a sorcerer there for many years; he was a
very influential, proud man because of the
amazing things he could do—in fact, the Samaritan people often spoke of him as the Messiah.[c]
12 But now they believed Philip's message that

[*b*] Literally, "the church." [*c*] Literally, "this man is that Power of God which is called great."

Today's English Version

3 But Saul tried to destroy the church; going
from house to house, he dragged out the believers, both men and women, and threw them
into jail.

The gospel preached in Samaria

4 The believers who were scattered went everywhere, preaching the message. 5 Philip went to
the city of Samaria and preached the Messiah to
the people there. 6 The crowds paid close attention to what Philip said. They all listened to him
and saw the miracles that he performed. 7 Evil
spirits came out with a loud cry from many people; many paralyzed and lame people were also
healed. 8 So there was great joy in Samaria.
9 In that city lived a man named Simon, who
for some time had astounded the Samaritans with
his magic. He claimed that he was someone great,
10 and everyone in the city, from all classes of
society, paid close attention to him. "He is that
power of God known as 'The Great Power,'"
they said. 11 He had astounded them with his
magic for such a long time that they paid close
attention to him. 12 But when they believed

New International Version

mourned deeply for him. 3 But Saul began to
destroy the church. Going from house to house,
he dragged off men and women and put them in
prison.

Philip in Samaria

4 Those who had been scattered preached the
word wherever they went. 5 Philip went down to
a city in Samaria and proclaimed the Christ[d]
there. 6 When the crowds heard Philip and saw
the miraculous signs he did, they all paid close
attention to what he said. 7 With shrieks, evil[e]
spirits came out of many, and many paralytics
and cripples were healed. 8 So there was great
joy in that city.

Simon the sorcerer

9 Now for some time a man named Simon
had practiced sorcery in the city and amazed all
the people of Samaria. He boasted that he was
someone great, 10 and all the people, both high
and low, gave him their attention and exclaimed,
"This man is the divine power known as the
Great Power." 11 They followed him because he
had amazed them for a long time with his magic.
12 But when they believed Philip as he preached

[*d*] Or *Messiah*. [*e*] Greek *unclean*.

Phillips Modern English

Saul harassed the Church bitterly. He would go from house to house, drag out both men and women and have them committed to prison. Those who were dispersed went throughout the country, preaching the good news of the message as they went. Philip went down to the city of Samaria and preached Christ to the people there. His words met with a ready and sympathetic response from the large crowds who listened to him and saw the miracles which he performed. With loud cries evil spirits came out of those who had been possessed by them; and many paralysed and lame people were cured. There was great rejoicing in that city.

8.9 A magician believes in Christ

But there was a man named Simon in the city who had been practising magic for some time and mystifying the people of Samaria. He pretended that he was somebody great and everyone from the lowest to the highest was fascinated by him. Indeed, they used to say, "This man must be that great power of God." They paid him great attention because he had been astounding them for a long time by his magical practices. But when they had come to believe

Revised Standard Version

over him. 3 But Saul was ravaging the church,
and entering house after house, he dragged off
men and women and committed them to prison.
4 Now those who were scattered went about
preaching the word. 5 Philip went down to a
city of Samaria, and proclaimed to them the
Christ. 6And the multitudes with one accord
gave heed to what was said by Philip, when they
heard him and saw the signs which he did. 7 For
unclean spirits came out of many who were
possessed, crying with a loud voice; and many
who were paralyzed or lame were healed. 8 So
there was much joy in that city.
9 But there was a man named Simon who had
previously practiced magic in the city and
amazed the nation of Samaria, saying that he
himself was somebody great. 10 They all gave
heed to him, from the least to the greatest, saying, "This man is that power of God which is
called Great." 11And they gave heed to him,
because for a long time he had amazed them
with his magic. 12 But when they believed Philip

Jerusalem Bible

3 Saul then worked for the total destruction
of the Church; he went from house to house
arresting both men and women and sending
them to prison.

Philip in Samaria

4 Those who had escaped went from place to
place preaching the Good News. 5 One of them
was Philip who went to a Samaritan town and
proclaimed the Christ to them. 6 The people
united in welcoming the message Philip preached,
either because they had heard of the miracles
he worked or because they saw them for themselves. 7 There were, for example, unclean spirits
that came shrieking out of many who were possessed, and several paralytics and cripples were
cured. 8As a result there was great rejoicing in
that town.

Simon the magician

9 Now a man called Simon had already practiced magic arts in the town and astounded the
Samaritan people. He had given it out that he
was someone momentous, 10 and everyone believed what he said; eminent citizens and ordinary people alike had declared, "He is the
divine power that is called Great." 11 They had
only been won over to him because of the long
time he had spent working on them with his
magic. 12 But when they believed Philip's preach-

New English Bible

a great lamentation for him. Saul, meanwhile, was harrying the church; he entered house after house, seizing men and women, and sending them to prison.

As for those who had been scattered, they went through the country preaching the Word. Philip came down to a city in Samaria and began proclaiming the Messiah to them. The crowds, to a man, listened eagerly to what Philip said, when they heard him and saw the miracles that he performed. For in many cases of possession the unclean spirits came out with a loud cry; and many paralysed and crippled folk were cured; and there was great joy in that city.

A man named Simon had been in the city for some time, and had swept the Samaritans off their feet with his magical arts, claiming to be someone great. All of them, high and low, listened eagerly to him. 'This man', they said, 'is that power of God which is called "The Great Power".' They listened because they had for so long been carried away by his magic. But when

King James Version

things concerning the kingdom of God, and the
name of Jesus Christ, they were baptized, both
men and women. 13 Then Simon himself believed
also: and when he was baptized, he continued
with Philip, and wondered, beholding the miracles and signs which were done. 14 Now when
the apostles which were at Jerusalem heard that
Samaria had received the word of God, they
sent unto them Peter and John: 15 Who, when
they were come down, prayed for them, that
they might receive the Holy Ghost: 16 (For as
yet he was fallen upon none of them: only they
were baptized in the name of the Lord Jesus.)
17 Then laid they *their* hands on them, and they
received the Holy Ghost. 18 And when Simon
saw that through laying on of the apostles' hands
the Holy Ghost was given, he offered them
money, 19 Saying, Give me also this power, that
on whomsoever I lay hands, he may receive the

Living Bible

Jesus was the Messiah, and his words concerning the Kingdom of God; and many men and
women were baptized. 13 Then Simon himself believed and was baptized and began following Philip wherever he went, and was amazed
by the miracles he did.
14 When the apostles back in Jerusalem heard
that the people of Samaria had accepted God's
message, they sent down Peter and John. 15 As
soon as they arrived, they began praying for
these new Christians to receive the Holy Spirit,
16 for as yet he had not come upon any of them.
For they had only been baptized in the name of
the Lord Jesus. 17 Then Peter and John laid their
hands upon these believers, and they received the
Holy Spirit.
18 When Simon saw this—that the Holy
Spirit was given when the apostles placed their
hands upon people's heads—he offered money
to buy this power.
19 "Let me have this power too," he exclaimed, "so that when I lay my hands on people, they will receive the Holy Spirit!"

Today's English Version

Philip's message about the Good News of the
Kingdom of God and the name of Jesus Christ,
they were baptized, both men and women. 13 Simon himself also believed; and after being baptized he stayed close to Philip, and was astounded
when he saw the great wonders and miracles that
were being performed.
14 The apostles in Jerusalem heard that the
people of Samaria had received the word of God;
so they sent Peter and John to them. 15 When
they arrived, they prayed for the believers that
they might receive the Holy Spirit. 16 For the
Holy Spirit had not yet come down on any of
them; they had only been baptized in the name
of the Lord Jesus. 17 Then Peter and John placed
their hands on them, and they received the Holy
Spirit.
18 Simon saw that the Spirit had been given
to them when the apostles placed their hands on
them. So he offered money to Peter and John,
19 and said, "Give this power to me too, so that
anyone I place my hands on will receive the Holy
Spirit."

New International Version

the good news of the kingdom of God and the
name of Jesus Christ, they were baptized, both
men and women. 13 Simon himself believed and
was baptized. And he followed Philip everywhere, astonished by the great signs and miracles
he saw.
14 When the apostles in Jerusalem heard that
Samaria had accepted the word of God, they
sent Peter and John to them. 15 When they arrived, they prayed for them that they might receive the Holy Spirit, 16 because the Holy Spirit
had not yet come upon any of them; they had
simply been baptized into[f] the name of the Lord
Jesus. 17 Then Peter and John placed their hands
on them, and they received the Holy Spirit.
18 When Simon saw that the Spirit was given
at the laying on of the apostles' hands, he offered
them money and said, 19 "Give me also this
ability so that everyone on whom I lay my hands
may receive the Holy Spirit."

[f] Or *in*.

Phillips Modern English

Philip as he proclaimed to them the good news of the kingdom of God and of the name of Jesus Christ, men and women alike were baptised. Even Simon himself became a believer and after his baptism attached himself closely to Philip. As he saw the signs and remarkable demonstrations of power which took place, he lived in a state of constant wonder.

8.14 *God confirms Samaria's acceptance of the gospel*

When the apostles in Jerusalem heard that Samaria had accepted the Word of God, they sent Peter and John down to them. When these two had arrived they prayed for the Samaritans that they might receive the Holy Spirit for as yet he had not fallen upon any of them. They were living simply as those who had been baptised in the name of the Lord Jesus. So then and there they laid their hands on them and they received the Holy Spirit.

8.18 *Simon's monstrous suggestion is sternly rebuked*

When Simon saw that the Spirit was given through the apostles' laying their hands upon people he offered them money with the words,

"Give me this power too, so that if I were to put my hands on anyone he would receive the Holy Spirit."

Revised Standard Version

as he preached good news about the kingdom of God and the name of Jesus Christ, they were baptized, both men and women. 13 Even Simon himself believed, and after being baptized he continued with Philip. And seeing signs and great miracles performed, he was amazed.
14 Now when the apostles at Jerusalem heard that Samaria had received the word of God, they sent to them Peter and John, 15 who came down and prayed for them that they might receive the Holy Spirit; 16 for it had not yet fallen on any of them, but they had only been baptized in the name of the Lord Jesus. 17 Then they laid their hands on them and they received the Holy Spirit. 18 Now when Simon saw that the Spirit was given through the laying on of the apostles' hands, he offered them money, 19 saying, "Give me also this power, that any one on whom I lay

Jerusalem Bible

ing of the Good News about the kingdom of God and the name of Jesus Christ, they were baptized, both men and women, 13 and even Simon himself became a believer. After his baptism Simon, who went around constantly with Philip, was astonished when he saw the wonders and great miracles that took place.
14 When the apostles in Jerusalem heard that Samaria had accepted the word of God, they sent Peter and John to them, 15 and they went down there, and prayed for the Samaritans to receive the Holy Spirit, 16 for as yet he had not come down on any of them: they had only been baptized in the name of the Lord Jesus. 17 Then they laid hands on them, and they received the Holy Spirit.
18 When Simon saw that the Spirit was given through the imposition of hands by the apostles, he offered them some money. 19 "Give me the same power," he said, "so that anyone I lay my

New English Bible

they came to believe Philip with his good news about the kingdom of God and the name of Jesus Christ, they were baptized, men and women alike. Even Simon himself believed, and was baptized, and thereupon was constantly in Philip's company. He was carried away when he saw the powerful signs and miracles that were taking place.

The apostles in Jerusalem now heard that Samaria had accepted the word of God. They sent off Peter and John, who went down there and prayed for the converts, asking that they might receive the Holy Spirit. For until then the Spirit had not come upon any of them. They had been baptized into the name of the Lord Jesus, that and nothing more. So Peter and John laid their hands on them and they received the Holy Spirit.

When Simon saw that the Spirit was bestowed through the laying on of the apostles' hands, he offered them money and said, 'Give me the same power too, so that when I lay my hands on any-

King James Version

Holy Ghost. 20 But Peter said unto him, Thy money perish with thee, because thou hast thought that the gift of God may be purchased with money. 21 Thou hast neither part nor lot in this matter: for thy heart is not right in the sight of God. 22 Repent therefore of this thy wickedness, and pray God, if perhaps the thought of thine heart may be forgiven thee. 23 For I perceive that thou art in the gall of bitterness, and *in* the bond of iniquity. 24 Then answered Simon, and said, Pray ye to the Lord for me, that none of these things which ye have spoken come upon me. 25And they, when they had testified and preached the word of the Lord, returned to Jerusalem, and preached the gospel in many villages of the Samaritans. 26And the angel of the Lord spake unto Philip, saying, Arise, and go toward the south, unto the way that goeth down from Jerusalem unto Gaza, which is desert. 27And he arose and went: and, behold, a man of Ethiopia, a eunuch of great authority under Candace queen of the Ethiopians, who had the charge of all her treasure, and had come to Jerusalem for to worship, 28 Was returning, and sitting in his chariot read Esaias the prophet.

Living Bible

20 But Peter replied, "Your money perish with you for thinking God's gift can be bought! 21 You can have no part in this, for your heart is not right before God. 22 Turn from this great wickedness and pray. Perhaps God will yet forgive your evil thoughts—23 for I can see that there is jealousy[d] and sin in your heart."

24 "Pray for me," Simon exclaimed, "that these terrible things won't happen to me."

25 After testifying and preaching in Samaria, Peter and John returned to Jerusalem, stopping at several Samaritan villages along the way to preach the Good News to them too.

26 But as for Philip, an angel of the Lord said to him, "Go over to the road that runs from Jerusalem through the Gaza Desert, arriving around noon." 27 So he did, and who should be coming down the road but the Treasurer of Ethiopia, a eunuch of great authority under Candace the queen. He had gone to Jerusalem to worship at the Temple, 28 and was now returning in his chariot, reading aloud from the book of the prophet Isaiah.

[*d*] Literally, "the gall of bitterness."

Today's English Version

20 But Peter answered him, "May you and your money go to hell, for thinking that you can buy God's gift with money! 21 You have no part or share in our work, because your heart is not right in God's sight. 22 Repent, then, from this evil plan of yours, and pray to the Lord that he will forgive you for thinking such a thing as this. 23 For I see that you are full of bitter envy, and are a prisoner of sin."

24 Simon said to Peter and John, "Please pray to the Lord for me, so that none of these things you said will happen to me."

25 After they had given their testimony and spoken the Lord's message, Peter and John went back to Jerusalem. On their way they preached the Good News in many villages of Samaria.

Philip and the Ethiopian official

26 An angel of the Lord spoke to Philip, "Get yourself ready and go south to the road that goes from Jerusalem to Gaza." (This road is no longer used.) 27, 28 So Philip got ready and went. Now an Ethiopian eunuch was on his way home. This man was an important official in charge of the treasury of the Queen, or Candace, of Ethiopia. He had been to Jerusalem to worship God, and was going back in his carriage. As he rode along he was reading from the book of the prophet

New International Version

20 Peter answered: "May your money perish with you, because you thought you could buy the gift of God with money! 21 You have no part or share in this ministry, because your heart is not right before God. 22 Repent of this wickedness and pray to the Lord. Perhaps he will forgive you for having such a thought in your heart. 23 For I see that you are full of bitterness and captive to sin."

24 Then Simon answered, "Pray to the Lord for me so that nothing you have said may happen to me."

25 When they had testified and proclaimed the word of the Lord, Peter and John returned to Jerusalem, preaching the gospel in many Samaritan villages.

Philip and the Ethiopian

26 Now an angel of the Lord said to Philip, "Go south to the road—the desert road—that goes down from Jerusalem to Gaza." 27 So he started out, and on his way he met an Ethiopian eunuch, an important official in charge of all the treasury of Candace, queen of the Ethiopians. This man had gone to Jerusalem to worship, 28 and on his way home was sitting in his chariot reading the book of Isaiah the prophet.

Phillips Modern English

But Peter said to him,
"To hell with you and your money! * How dare you think you could buy the gift of God for money! You can have no share or part in this matter, for your heart is not honest before God. All you can do now is to repent of this wickedness of yours and pray earnestly to the Lord that if possible the evil intention of your heart may be forgiven. For I can see inside you, and I see a man bitter with jealousy and bound with his own sin!"
To this Simon answered,
"Please pray to the Lord for me that none of these things that you have spoken about may come upon me!"
When Peter and John had given their clear witness and spoken the Word of the Lord, they returned to Jerusalem, preaching the goods news to many Samaritan villages as they went.

8.26 Philip is given an unique opportunity

But an angel of the Lord said to Philip,
"Get up and go south down the road which runs from Jerusalem to Gaza, out in the desert."
Philip arose and began his journey. At the same time an Ethiopian eunuch, a minister and in fact the treasurer to Candace, queen of the Ethiopians, was on his way home after going to Jerusalem to worship. He was sitting in his

* This is really what the Greek says. It is a pity that modern English usage obscures the literal meaning.

Revised Standard Version

my hands may receive the Holy Spirit." 20 But
Peter said to him, "Your silver perish with you,
because you thought you could obtain the gift
of God with money! 21 You have neither part
nor lot in this matter, for your heart is not right
before God. 22 Repent therefore of this wickedness of yours, and pray to the Lord that, if possible, the intent of your heart may be forgiven
you. 23 For I see that you are in the gall of bitterness and in the bond of iniquity." 24 And Simon answered, "Pray for me to the Lord, that
nothing of what you have said may come upon
me."
25 Now when they had testified and spoken
the word of the Lord, they returned to Jerusalem, preaching the gospel to many villages of the
Samaritans.
26 But an angel of the Lord said to Philip,
"Rise and go toward the south[g] to the road that
goes down from Jerusalem to Gaza." This is a
desert road. 27 And he rose and went. And behold, an Ethiopian, a eunuch, a minister of the
Candace, queen of the Ethiopians, in charge of
all her treasure, had come to Jerusalem to worship 28 and was returning; seated in his chariot,

[g] Or *at noon*.

Jerusalem Bible

hands on will receive the Holy Spirit." 20 Peter
answered, "May your silver be lost forever, and
you with it, for thinking that money could buy
what God has given for nothing! 21 You have no
share, no rights, in this: God can see how your
heart is warped. 22 Repent of this wickedness
of yours, and pray to the Lord; you may still
be forgiven for thinking as you did; 23 it is plain
to me that you are trapped in the bitterness of
gall and the chains of sin." 24 "Pray to the Lord
for me yourselves," Simon replied, "so that none
of the things you have spoken about may happen to me."
25 Having given their testimony and proclaimed the word of the Lord, they went back
to Jerusalem, preaching the Good News to a
number of Samaritan villages.

Philip baptizes a eunuch

26 The angel of the Lord spoke to Philip
saying, "Be ready to set out at noon along the
road that goes from Jerusalem down to Gaza,
the desert road." 27 So he set off on his journey. Now it happened that an Ethiopian had
been on pilgrimage to Jerusalem; he was a eunuch and an officer at the court of the kandake,
or queen, of Ethiopia, and was in fact her chief
treasurer. 28 He was now on his way home; and
as he sat in his chariot he was reading the

New English Bible

one, he will receive the Holy Spirit.' Peter replied, 'Your money go with you to damnation, because you thought God's gift was for sale! You have no part nor lot in this, for you are dishonest with God. Repent of this wickedness and pray the Lord to forgive you for imagining such a thing. I can see that you are doomed to taste the bitter fruit and wear the fetters of sin.' [a] Simon answered, 'Pray to the Lord for me yourselves and ask that none of the things you have spoken of may fall upon me.'

So, after giving their testimony and speaking the word of the Lord, they took the road back to Jerusalem, bringing the good news to many Samaritan villages on the way.

Then the angel of the Lord said to Philip, 'Start out and go south to the road that leads down from Jerusalem to Gaza.' (This is the desert road.) So he set out and was on his way when he caught sight of an Ethiopian. This man was a eunuch, a high official of the Kandake, or Queen, of Ethiopia, in charge of all her treasure. He had been to Jerusalem on a pilgrimage and was now on his way home, sitting in his carriage

[a] *Literally* you are for gall of bitterness and a fetter of unrighteousness.

King James Version

29 Then the Spirit said unto Philip, Go near, and
join thyself to this chariot. 30 And Philip ran
thither to *him*, and heard him read the prophet
Esaias, and said, Understandest thou what thou
readest? 31 And he said, How can I, except some
man should guide me? And he desired Philip
that he would come up and sit with him. 32 The
place of the Scripture which he read was this,
He was led as a sheep to the slaughter; and like
a lamb dumb before his shearer, so opened he
not his mouth: 33 In his humiliation his judgment was taken away: and who shall declare
his generation? for his life is taken from the
earth. 34 And the eunuch answered Philip, and
said, I pray thee, of whom speaketh the prophet
this? of himself, or of some other man? 35 Then
Philip opened his mouth, and began at the same
Scripture, and preached unto him Jesus. 36 And
as they went on *their* way, they came unto a
certain water: and the eunuch said, See, *here is*
water; what doth hinder me to be baptized?
37 And Philip said, If thou believest with all thine
heart, thou mayest. And he answered and said, I
believe that Jesus Christ is the Son of God.

Living Bible

29 The Holy Spirit said to Philip, "Go over
and walk along beside the chariot."
30 Philip ran over and heard what he was
reading and asked, "Do you understand it?"
31 "Of course not!" the man replied. "How
can I when there is no one to instruct me?" And
he begged Philip to come up into the chariot
and sit with him.
32 The passage of Scripture he had been
reading from was this:
"He was led as a sheep to the slaughter, and
as a lamb is silent before the shearers, so he
opened not his mouth; 33 in his humiliation,
justice was denied him; and who can express
the wickedness of the people of his generation? [e] For his life is taken from the earth."
34 The eunuch asked Philip, "Was Isaiah talking about himself or someone else?"
35 So Philip began with this same Scripture
and then used many others to tell him about
Jesus.
36 As they rode along, they came to a small
body of water, and the eunuch said, "Look!
Water! Why can't I be baptized?"
37 [f] "You can," Philip answered, "if you believe with all your heart."
And the eunuch replied, "I believe that Jesus
Christ is the Son of God."

[*e*] Implied. Literally, "Who can declare his generation." Alternatively, "Who will be able to speak of his posterity? For . . ." [*f*] Many ancient manuscripts omit verse 37 wholly or in part.

Today's English Version

Isaiah. 29 The Holy Spirit said to Philip, "Go
over and stay close to that carriage." 30 Philip
ran over and heard him reading from the book
of the prophet Isaiah; so he asked him, "Do
you understand what you are reading?"
31 "How can I understand," the official replied, "unless someone explains it to me?" And
he invited Philip to climb up and sit in the carriage with him. 32 The passage of scripture which
he was reading was this,

"He was like a sheep that is taken to be
slaughtered;
he was like a lamb that makes no sound
when its wool is cut off;
he did not say a word.
33 He was humiliated, and justice was denied
him.
No one will be able to tell about his descendants,
because his life on earth has come to an
end."

34 The official said to Philip, "Tell me, of
whom is the prophet saying this? Of himself or
of someone else?" 35 Philip began to speak; starting from this very passage of scripture, he told
him the Good News about Jesus. 36 As they
traveled down the road they came to a place
where there was some water, and the official said,
"Here is some water. What is to keep me from
being baptized?"
[37 Philip said to him, "You may be baptized
if you believe with all your heart."
"I do," he answered; "I believe that Jesus
Christ is the Son of God."]

New International Version

29 The Spirit told Philip, "Go to that chariot and
stay near it."
30 Then Philip ran up to the chariot and
heard the man reading Isaiah the prophet. "Do
you understand what you are reading?" Philip
asked.
31 "How can I," he said, "unless someone explains it to me?" So he invited Philip to come
up and sit with him.
32 The eunuch was reading this passage of
Scripture:
"He was led like a sheep to the slaughter,
and as a lamb before the shearer is silent,
so he did not open his mouth.
33 In his humiliation he was deprived of justice.
Who can speak of his descendants?
For his life was taken from the earth." [g]
34 The eunuch asked Philip, "Tell me, please,
who is the prophet talking about, himself or
someone else?" 35 Then Philip began with that
very passage of Scripture and told him the good
news about Jesus.
36 As they traveled along the road, they came
to some water and the eunuch said, "Look, here

[*g*] Isaiah 53:7,8.

Phillips Modern English

carriage reading the prophet Isaiah. The Spirit said to Philip,

"Approach this carriage, and keep close to it."

Then as Philip ran forward he heard the man reading the prophet Isaiah, and he said,

"Do you understand what you are reading?"

And he replied,

"How can I unless I have someone to guide me?"

And he invited Philip to get up and sit by his side. The passage of scripture he was reading was this:

He was led as a sheep to the slaughter;
And as a lamb before his shearer is dumb,
So he openeth not his mouth:
In his humiliation his judgment was taken away:
His generation who shall declare?
For his life is taken from the earth.

The eunuch turned to Philip and said,

"Tell me, I beg you, about whom is the prophet saying this—is he speaking about himself or about someone else?"

Then Philip began, and using this scripture as a starting point, he told him the good news about Jesus. As they proceeded along the road they came to some water, and the eunuch said,

"Look, here is some water; is there any reason why I should not be baptised?"

Revised Standard Version

he was reading the prophet Isaiah. 29And the
Spirit said to Philip, "Go up and join this
chariot." 30 So Philip ran to him, and heard him
reading Isaiah the prophet, and asked, "Do you
understand what you are reading?" 31And he
said, "How can I, unless some one guides me?"
And he invited Philip to come up and sit with
him. 32 Now the passage of the scripture which
he was reading was this:
"As a sheep led to the slaughter
or a lamb before its shearer is dumb,
so he opens not his mouth.
33 In his humiliation justice was denied him.
Who can describe his generation?
For his life is taken up from the earth."
34And the eunuch said to Philip, "About whom,
pray, does the prophet say this, about himself
or about some one else?" 35 Then Philip opened
his mouth, and beginning with this scripture he
told him the good news of Jesus. 36And as they
went along the road they came to some water,
and the eunuch said, "See, here is water! What

Jerusalem Bible

prophet Isaiah. 29 The Spirit said to Philip, "Go
up and meet that chariot." 30 When Philip ran
up, he heard him reading Isaiah the prophet and
asked, "Do you understand what you are reading?" 31 "How can I," he replied, "unless I have
someone to guide me?" So he invited Philip to
get in and sit by his side. 32 Now the passage
of scripture he was reading was this:

Like a sheep that is led to the slaughter-house,
like a lamb that is dumb in front of its shearers,
like these he never opens his mouth.
33 *He has been humiliated and has no one to defend him.*
Who will ever talk about his descendants,
since his life on earth has been cut short! [v]

34 The eunuch turned to Philip and said,
"Tell me, is the prophet referring to himself or
someone else?" 35 Starting, therefore, with this
text of scripture Philip proceeded to explain
the Good News of Jesus to him.
36 Further along the road they came to some
water, and the eunuch said, "Look, there is
some water here; is there anything to stop me

[v] Is. 53:7-8, quoted from the LXX version.

New English Bible

and reading aloud the prophet Isaiah. The Spirit said to Philip, 'Go and join the carriage.' When Philip ran up he heard him reading the prophet Isaiah and said, 'Do you understand what you are reading?' He said, 'How can I understand unless someone will give me the clue?' So he asked Philip to get in and sit beside him.

The passage he was reading was this: 'He was led like a sheep to be slaughtered; and like a lamb that is dumb before the shearer, he does not open his mouth. He has been humiliated and has no redress. Who will be able to speak of his posterity? For he is cut off from the world of living men.'

'Now', said the eunuch to Philip, 'tell me, please, who it is that the prophet is speaking about here: himself or someone else?' Then Philip began. Starting from this passage, he told him the good news of Jesus. As they were going along the road, they came to some water. 'Look,' said the eunuch, 'here is water: what is there to

King James Version

38And he commanded the chariot to stand still: and they went down both into the water, both Philip and the eunuch; and he baptized him. 39And when they were come up out of the water, the Spirit of the Lord caught away Philip, that the eunuch saw him no more: and he went on his way rejoicing. 40 But Philip was found at Azotus: and passing through he preached in all the cities, till he came to Cesarea.

9 And Saul, yet breathing out threatenings and slaughter against the disciples of the Lord, went unto the high priest, 2And desired of him letters to Damascus to the synagogues, that if he found any of this way, whether they were men or women, he might bring them bound unto Jerusalem. 3And as he journeyed, he came near Damascus: and suddenly there shined round about him a light from heaven: 4And he fell to the earth, and heard a voice saying unto him, Saul, Saul, why persecutest thou me? 5And he said, Who art thou, Lord? And the Lord said, I am Jesus whom thou persecutest: *it is* hard for thee to kick against the pricks. 6And he trembling and astonished said, Lord, what wilt thou have me to do? And the Lord *said* unto him, Arise, and go into the city, and it shall be told

Living Bible

38 He stopped the chariot, and they went down into the water and Philip baptized him. 39And when they came up out of the water, the Spirit of the Lord caught away Philip, and the eunuch never saw him again, but went on his way rejoicing. 40 Meanwhile, Philip found himself at Azotus! He preached the Good News there and in every city along the way, as he traveled to Caesarea.

9 But Paul, threatening with every breath and eager to destroy every Christian, went to the High Priest in Jerusalem. 2 He requested a letter addressed to synagogues in Damascus, requiring their cooperation in the persecution of any believers he found there, both men and women, so that he could bring them in chains to Jerusalem.

3 As he was nearing Damascus on this mission, suddenly a brilliant light from heaven spotted down upon him! 4 He fell to the ground and heard a voice saying to him, "Paul! Paul! Why are you persecuting me?"

5 "Who is speaking, sir?" Paul asked.

And the voice replied, "I am Jesus, the one you are persecuting! 6 Now get up and go into the city and await my further instructions."

Today's English Version

38 The official ordered the carriage to stop; and both of them, Philip and the official, went down into the water, and Philip baptized him. 39 When they came up out of the water the Spirit of the Lord took Philip away. The official did not see him again, but continued on his way, full of joy. 40 Philip found himself in Ashdod; and he went through all the towns preaching the Good News, until he arrived at Caesarea.

The conversion of Saul

9 In the meantime Saul kept up his violent threats of murder against the disciples of the Lord. He went to the High Priest 2 and asked for letters of introduction to the Jewish synagogues in Damascus, so that if he should find any followers of the Way of the Lord there, he would be able to arrest them, both men and women, and take them back to Jerusalem.

3 On his way to Damascus, as he came near the city, suddenly a light from the sky flashed around him. 4 He fell to the ground and heard a voice saying to him, "Saul, Saul! Why do you persecute me?"

5 "Who are you, Lord?" he asked.

"I am Jesus, whom you persecute," the voice said. 6 "But get up and go into the city, where you will be told what you must do."

New International Version

is water. Why shouldn't I be baptized?" [h] 38And he ordered the chariot to stop. Then both Philip and the eunuch went down into the water and Philip baptized him. 39 When they came up out of the water, the Spirit of the Lord suddenly took Philip away, and the eunuch did not see him again, but went on his way rejoicing. 40 Philip, however, appeared at Azotus and traveled about, preaching the gospel in all the towns until he reached Caesarea.

Saul's conversion

9 Meanwhile, Saul was still breathing out murderous threats against the Lord's disciples. He went to the high priest 2 and asked him for letters to the synagogues in Damascus, so that if he found any there who belonged to the Way, whether men or women, he might take them as prisoners to Jerusalem. 3As he neared Damascus on his journey, suddenly a light from heaven flashed around him. 4 He fell to the ground and heard a voice say to him, "Saul, Saul, why do you persecute me?"

5 "Who are you, Lord?" Saul asked.

"I am Jesus whom you are persecuting," he replied. 6 "Now get up and go into the city, and you will be told what you must do."

[*h*] Some MSS add verse 37: *Philip said, "If you believe with all your heart, you may." The official answered, "I believe that Jesus Christ is the Son of God."*

Phillips Modern English

And he gave orders for the carriage to stop. Then both of them went down to the water and Philip baptised the eunuch. When they came up out of the water the Spirit of the Lord took Philip away suddenly and the eunuch saw no more of him, but proceeded on his journey with a heart full of joy. Philip found himself at Azotus and as he passed through the countryside he went on telling the good news in all the cities until he came to Caesarea.

9.1 The crisis for Saul

But Saul, still breathing murderous threats against the disciples of the Lord, went to the High Priest requesting him for letters of authority to the synagogues in Damascus, so that if he should find there any followers of the Way, whether men or women, he could bring them back to Jerusalem as prisoners.

But on his journey, as he neared Damascus, a light from the sky suddenly blazed around him, and he fell to the ground. Then he heard a voice speaking to him,

"Saul, Saul, why are you persecuting me?"

"Who are you, Lord?" he asked.

"I am Jesus whom you are persecuting," was the reply. "But now stand up and go into the city and there you will be told what you must do."

Revised Standard Version

is to prevent my being baptized?"[h] 38And he
commanded the chariot to stop, and they both
went down into the water, Philip and the
eunuch, and he baptized him. 39And when they
came up out of the water, the Spirit of the Lord
caught up Philip; and the eunuch saw him no
more, and went on his way rejoicing. 40 But
Philip was found at Azotus, and passing on he
preached the gospel to all the towns till he came
to Caesarea.

9 But Saul, still breathing threats and murder
against the disciples of the Lord, went to
the high priest 2 and asked him for letters to
the synagogues at Damascus, so that if he found
any belonging to the Way, men or women, he
might bring them bound to Jerusalem. 3 Now as
he journeyed he approached Damascus, and suddenly a light from heaven flashed about him.
4And he fell to the ground and heard a voice
saying to him, "Saul, Saul, why do you persecute me?" 5And he said, "Who are you, Lord?"
And he said, "I am Jesus, whom you are persecuting; 6 but rise and enter the city, and you will

[h] Other ancient authorities add all or most of verse 37, *And Philip said, "If you believe with all your heart, you may." And he replied, "I believe that Jesus Christ is the Son of God."*

Jerusalem Bible

being baptized?[w] 38 He ordered the chariot to
stop, then Philip and the eunuch both went
down into the water and Philip baptized him.
39 But after they had come up out of the water
again Philip was taken away by the Spirit of
the Lord, and the eunuch never saw him again
but went on his way rejoicing. 40 Philip found
that he had reached Azotus and continued his
journey proclaiming the Good News in every
town as far as Caesarea.

The conversion of Saul

9 Meanwhile Saul was still breathing threats
to slaughter the Lord's disciples. He had
gone to the high priest 2 and asked for letters
addressed to the synagogues in Damascus, that
would authorize him to arrest and take to Jerusalem any followers of the Way, men or women,
that he could find.

3 Suddenly, while he was traveling to Damascus and just before he reached the city,
there came a light from heaven all around him.
4 He fell to the ground, and then he heard a
voice saying, "Saul, Saul, why are you persecuting me?" 5 "Who are you, Lord?" he asked,
and the voice answered, "I am Jesus, and you
are persecuting me. 6 Get up now and go into
the city, and you will be told what you have to

[w] At the time when verse numbers were introduced, there was a gloss, numbered v. 37, at this point.

New English Bible

prevent my being baptized?';[a] and he ordered the carriage to stop. Then they both went down into the water, Philip and the eunuch; and he baptized him. When they came up out of the water the Spirit snatched Philip away, and the eunuch saw no more of him, but went happily on his way. Philip appeared at Azotus, and toured the country, preaching in all the towns till he reached Caesarea.

9 Meanwhile Saul was still breathing murderous threats against the disciples of the Lord. He went to the High Priest and applied for letters to the synagogues at Damascus authorizing him to arrest anyone he found, men or women, who followed the new way, and bring them to Jerusalem. While he was still on the road and nearing Damascus, suddenly a light flashed from the sky all around him. He fell to the ground and heard a voice saying, 'Saul, Saul, why do you persecute me?' 'Tell me, Lord,' he said, 'who you are.' The voice answered, 'I am Jesus, whom you are persecuting. But get up and go into the city, and you will be told what you have

[a] *Some witnesses insert* (37) Philip said, 'If you whole-heartedly believe, it is permitted.' He replied, 'I believe that Jesus Christ is the Son of God.'

King James Version

thee what thou must do. 7And the men which
journeyed with him stood speechless, hearing a
voice, but seeing no man. 8And Saul arose from
the earth; and when his eyes were opened, he
saw no man: but they led him by the hand, and
brought *him* into Damascus. 9And he was three
days without sight, and neither did eat nor
drink.
10 And there was a certain disciple at Damascus, named Ananias; and to him said the
Lord in a vision, Ananias. And he said, Behold,
I *am here,* Lord. 11And the Lord *said* unto him,
Arise, and go into the street which is called
Straight, and inquire in the house of Judas for
one called Saul, of Tarsus: for, behold, he
prayeth, 12And hath seen in a vision a man
named Ananias coming in, and putting *his* hand
on him, that he might receive his sight. 13 Then
Ananias answered, Lord, I have heard by many
of this man, how much evil he hath done to thy
saints at Jerusalem: 14And here he hath authority from the chief priests to bind all that call on
thy name. 15 But the Lord said unto him, Go
thy way: for he is a chosen vessel unto me, to
bear my name before the Gentiles, and kings,

Living Bible

7 The men with Paul stood speechless with
surprise, for they heard the sound of someone's
voice but saw no one! 8, 9As Paul picked himself up off the ground, he found that he was
blind. He had to be led into Damascus and was
there three days, blind, going without food and
water all that time.
10 Now there was in Damascus a believer
named Ananias. The Lord spoke to him in a
vision, calling, "Ananias!"
"Yes, Lord!" he replied.
11 And the Lord said, "Go over to Straight
Street and find the house of a man named Judas
and ask there for Paul of Tarsus. He is praying
to me right now, for 12 I have shown him a
vision of a man named Ananias coming in and
laying his hands on him so that he can see
again!"
13 "But Lord," exclaimed Ananias, "I have
heard about the terrible things this man has
done to the believers in Jerusalem! 14And we
hear that he has arrest warrants with him from
the chief priests, authorizing him to arrest every
believer in Damascus!"
15 But the Lord said, "Go and do what I say.
For Paul is my chosen instrument to take my
message to the nations and before kings, as well

Today's English Version

7 The men who were traveling with Saul had
stopped, not saying a word; they heard the voice
but could not see anyone. 8 Saul got up from the
ground and opened his eyes, but could not see a
thing. So they took him by the hand and led him
into Damascus. 9 For three days he was not able
to see, and during that time he did not eat or
drink anything.
10 There was a disciple in Damascus named
Ananias. He had a vision, in which the Lord said
to him, "Ananias!"
"Here I am, Lord," he answered.
11 The Lord said to him, "Get ready and go
to Straight Street, and at the house of Judas ask
for a man from Tarsus named Saul. He is praying, 12 and in a vision he saw a man named
Ananias come in and place his hands on him so
that he might see again."
13 Ananias answered, "Lord, many people
have told me about this man, about all the terrible things he has done to your people in Jerusalem. 14And he has come to Damascus with
authority from the chief priests to arrest all who
call on your name."
15 The Lord said to him, "Go, because I have
chosen him to serve me, to make my name known
to Gentiles and kings, and to the people of Is-

New International Version

7 The men traveling with Saul stood there
speechless; they heard the sound but did not
see anyone. 8 Saul got up from the ground, but
when he opened his eyes he could see nothing.
So they led him by the hand into Damascus.
9 For three days he was blind, and did not eat
or drink anything.
10 In Damascus there was a disciple named
Ananias. The Lord called to him in a vision,
"Ananias!"
"Yes, Lord," he answered.
11 The Lord told him, "Go to the house of
Judas on Straight Street and ask for a man
from Tarsus named Saul, for he is praying. 12 In
a vision he has seen a man named Ananias come
and place his hands on him to restore his sight."
13 "Lord," Ananias answered, "I have heard
many reports about this man and all the harm
he has done to your saints in Jerusalem. 14And
he has come here with authority from the chief
priests to arrest all who call on your name."
15 But the Lord said to Ananias, "Go! This
man is my chosen instrument to carry my name
before the Gentiles and their kings and before

Phillips Modern English

His companions on the journey stood there speechless, for they had heard the voice but could see no one. Saul got up from the ground, but when he opened his eyes he could see nothing. So they took him by the hand and led him into Damascus. There he remained sightless for three days, and during that time he had nothing either to eat or drink.

9.10 God's preparation for the converted Saul

Now in Damascus there was a disciple by the name of Ananias. The Lord spoke to this man in a dream, calling him by his name.

"I am here, Lord," he replied.

Then the Lord said to him,

"Get up and go down to the street called Straight and enquire at the house of Judas for a man named Saul from Tarsus. At this moment he is praying and he sees in his mind's eye a man by the name of Ananias coming into the house, and placing his hands upon him to restore his sight."

But Ananias replied,

"Lord, I have heard on all hands about this man and how much harm he has done to your holy people in Jerusalem! Why even now he holds powers from the chief priests to arrest all who call upon your name."

But the Lord said to him,

"Go on your way, for this man is my chosen instrument to bear my name before the gentiles and their kings, as well as to the sons of Israel.

Revised Standard Version

be told what you are to do." 7 The men who were traveling with him stood speechless, hearing the voice but seeing no one. 8 Saul arose from the ground; and when his eyes were opened, he could see nothing; so they led him by the hand and brought him into Damascus. 9 And for three days he was without sight, and neither ate nor drank.

10 Now there was a disciple at Damascus named Ananias. The Lord said to him in a vision, "Ananias." And he said, "Here I am, Lord." 11 And the Lord said to him, "Rise and go to the street called Straight, and inquire in the house of Judas for a man of Tarsus named Saul; for behold, he is praying, 12 and he has seen a man named Ananias come in and lay his hands on him so that he might regain his sight." 13 But Ananias answered, "Lord, I have heard from many about this man, how much evil he has done to thy saints at Jerusalem; 14 and here he has authority from the chief priests to bind all who call upon thy name." 15 But the Lord said to him, "Go, for he is a chosen instrument of mine to carry my name before the Gentiles and

Jerusalem Bible

do." 7 The men traveling with Saul stood there speechless, for though they heard the voice they could see no one. 8 Saul got up from the ground, but even with his eyes wide open he could see nothing at all, and they had to lead him into Damascus by the hand. 9 For three days he was without his sight, and took neither food nor drink.

10 A disciple called Ananias who lived in Damascus had a vision in which he heard the Lord say to him, "Ananias!" When he replied, "Here I am, Lord," 11 the Lord said, "You must go to Straight Street and ask at the house of Judas for someone called Saul, who comes from Tarsus. At this moment he is praying, 12 having had a vision of a man called Ananias coming in and laying hands on him to give him back his sight."

13 When he heard that, Ananias said, "Lord, several people have told me about this man and all the harm he has been doing to your saints in Jerusalem. 14 He has only come here because he holds a warrant from the chief priests to arrest everybody who invokes your name." 15 The Lord replied, "You must go all the same, because this man is my chosen instrument to bring my name before pagans and pagan kings and

New English Bible

to do.' Meanwhile the men who were travelling with him stood speechless; they heard the voice but could see no one. Saul got up from the ground, but when he opened his eyes he could not see; so they led him by the hand and brought him into Damascus. He was blind for three days, and took no food or drink.

There was a disciple in Damascus named Ananias. He had a vision in which he heard the voice of the Lord: 'Ananias!' 'Here I am, Lord', he answered. The Lord said to him, 'Go at once to Straight Street, to the house of Judas, and ask for a man from Tarsus named Saul. You will find him at prayer; he has had a vision of a man named Ananias coming in and laying his hands on him to restore his sight.' Ananias answered, 'Lord, I have often heard about this man and all the harm he has done to thy people in Jerusalem. And he is here with authority from the chief priests to arrest all who invoke thy name.' But the Lord said to him, 'You must go, for this man is my chosen instrument to bring my name before the nations and their kings, and

King James Version

and the children of Israel: 16 For I will shew him
how great things he must suffer for my name's
sake. 17And Ananias went his way, and entered
into the house; and putting his hands on him
said, Brother Saul, the Lord, *even* Jesus, that
appeared unto thee in the way as thou camest,
hath sent me, that thou mightest receive thy
sight, and be filled with the Holy Ghost. 18And
immediately there fell from his eyes as it had
been scales: and he received sight forthwith, and
arose, and was baptized. 19And when he had received meat, he was strengthened. Then was Saul
certain days with the disciples which were at
Damascus. 20And straightway he preached Christ
in the synagogues, that he is the Son of God.
21 But all that heard *him* were amazed, and said;
Is not this he that destroyed them which called
on this name in Jerusalem, and came hither for
that intent, that he might bring them bound unto
the chief priests? 22 But Saul increased the more
in strength, and confounded the Jews which
dwelt at Damascus, proving that this is very
Christ.

Living Bible

as to the people of Israel. 16And I will show
him how much he must suffer for me."
17 So Ananias went over and found Paul and
laid his hands on him and said, "Brother Paul,
the Lord Jesus, who appeared to you on the
road, has sent me so that you may be filled with
the Holy Spirit and get your sight back."
18 Instantly (it was as though scales fell from
his eyes) Paul could see, and was immediately
baptized. 19 Then he ate and was strengthened.
He stayed with the believers in Damascus for a
few days 20 and went at once to the synagogue
to tell everyone there the Good News about Jesus—that he is indeed the Son of God!
21 All who heard him were amazed. "Isn't
this the same man who persecuted Jesus' followers so bitterly in Jerusalem?" they asked.
"And we understand that he came here to arrest
them all and take them in chains to the chief
priests."
22 Paul became more and more fervent in his
preaching, and the Damascus Jews couldn't withstand his proofs that Jesus was indeed the Christ.

Today's English Version

rael. 16And I myself will show him all that he
must suffer for my sake."
17 So Ananias went, entered the house, and
placed his hands on Saul. "Brother Saul," he
said, "the Lord has sent me—Jesus himself, who
appeared to you on the road as you were coming
here. He sent me so that you might see again and
be filled with the Holy Spirit." 18At once something like fish scales fell from Saul's eyes and he
was able to see again. He stood up and was baptized; 19 and after he had eaten, his strength
came back.

Saul preaches in Damascus

Saul stayed for a few days with the disciples
in Damascus. 20 He went straight to the synagogues and began to preach about Jesus. "He is
the Son of God," he said.
21 All who heard him were amazed, and
asked, "Isn't this the man who in Jerusalem was
killing those who call on this name? And didn't
he come here for the very purpose of arresting
them and taking them back to the chief priests?"
22 But Saul's preaching became even more
powerful, and his proofs that Jesus was the Messiah were so convincing that the Jews who lived
in Damascus could not answer him.

New International Version

the people of Israel. 16 I will show him how
much he must suffer for my name."
17 Then Ananias went to the house and entered it. Placing his hands on Saul, he said,
"Brother Saul, the Lord—Jesus, who appeared
to you on the road as you were coming here—
has sent me so that you may see again and be
filled with the Holy Spirit." 18 Immediately,
something like scales fell from Saul's eyes, and
he could see again. He got up and was baptized,
19 and after taking some food, he regained his
strength.

Saul in Damascus and Jerusalem

Saul spent several days with the disciples in
Damascus. 20At once he began to preach in
the synagogues that Jesus is the Son of God.
21All those who heard him were astonished and
asked, "Isn't he the man who raised havoc in
Jerusalem among those who call on this name?
And hasn't he come here to take them as prisoners to the chief priests?" 22 Yet Saul grew
more and more powerful and baffled the Jews
living in Damascus by proving that Jesus is the
Christ.[i]

[*i*] Or *Messiah*.

Phillips Modern English

Indeed, I myself will show him how much he must suffer for the sake of my name."

Then Ananias set out and went to the house, and there he laid his hands upon Saul, and said, "Saul, brother, the Lord has sent me—Jesus who appeared to you on your journey here—so that you may recover your sight, and be filled with the Holy Spirit."

Immediately something like scales fell from Saul's eyes, and he could see again. He got to his feet and was baptised. Then he took some food and regained his strength.

9.19b Saul's conversion astounds the disciples

Saul stayed with the disciples in Damascus for some time. Without delay he began to proclaim Jesus in the synagogues declaring that he is the Son of God. All his hearers were amazed and kept saying,

"Isn't this the man who so bitterly persecuted those who called on the name in Jerusalem, and came down here with the sole object of taking back all such people as prisoners before the chief priests?"

But Saul went on from strength to strength, reducing to confusion the Jews who lived at Damascus by proving beyond doubt that this man is Christ.

Revised Standard Version

kings and the sons of Israel; 16 for I will show
him how much he must suffer for the sake of
my name." 17 So Ananias departed and entered
the house. And laying his hands on him he said,
"Brother Saul, the Lord Jesus who appeared to
you on the road by which you came, has sent
me that you may regain your sight and be
filled with the Holy Spirit." 18 And immediately
something like scales fell from his eyes and he
regained his sight. Then he rose and was baptized, 19 and took food and was strengthened.
For several days he was with the disciples at
Damascus. 20 And in the synagogues immediately
he proclaimed Jesus, saying, "He is the Son of
God." 21 And all who heard him were amazed,
and said, "Is not this the man who made havoc
in Jerusalem of those who called on this name?
And he has come here for this purpose, to
bring them bound before the chief priests."
22 But Saul increased all the more in strength,
and confounded the Jews who lived in Damascus
by proving that Jesus was the Christ.

Jerusalem Bible

before the people of Israel; 16 I myself will
show him how much he himself must suffer for
my name." 17 Then Ananias went. He entered
the house, and at once laid his hands on Saul
and said, "Brother Saul, I have been sent by
the Lord Jesus who appeared to you on your
way here so that you may recover your sight
and be filled with the Holy Spirit." 18 Immediately it was as though scales fell away from
Saul's eyes and he could see again. So he was
baptized there and then, 19 and after taking
some food he regained his strength.

Saul's preaching at Damascus

After he had spent only a few days with the
disciples in Damascus, 20 he began preaching
in the synagogues, "Jesus is the Son of God."
21 All his hearers were amazed. "Surely," they
said, "this is the man who organized the attack
in Jerusalem against the people who invoke this
name, and who came here for the sole purpose
of arresting them to have them tried by the chief
priests?" 22 Saul's power increased steadily, and
he was able to throw the Jewish colony at Damascus into complete confusion by the way
he demonstrated that Jesus was the Christ.

New English Bible

before the people of Israel. I myself will show him all that he must go through for my name's sake.'

So Ananias went. He entered the house, laid his hands on him and said, 'Saul, my brother, the Lord Jesus, who appeared to you on your way here, has sent me to you so that you may recover your sight, and be filled with the Holy Spirit.' And immediately it seemed that scales fell from his eyes, and he regained his sight. Thereupon he was baptized, and afterwards he took food and his strength returned.

He stayed some time with the disciples in Damascus. Soon he was proclaiming Jesus publicly in the synagogues: 'This', he said, 'is the Son of God.' All who heard were astounded. 'Is not this the man', they said, 'who was in Jerusalem trying to destroy those who invoke this name? Did he not come here for the sole purpose of arresting them and taking them to the chief priests?' But Saul grew more and more forceful, and silenced the Jews of Damascus with his cogent proofs that Jesus was the Messiah.

King James Version

23 And after that many days were fulfilled,
the Jews took counsel to kill him: 24 But their
laying wait was known of Saul. And they
watched the gates day and night to kill him.
25 Then the disciples took him by night, and let
him down by the wall in a basket. 26And when
Saul was come to Jerusalem he assayed to join
himself to the disciples: but they were all afraid
of him, and believed not that he was a disciple.
27 But Barnabas took him, and brought *him* to
the apostles, and declared unto them how he
had seen the Lord in the way, and that he had
spoken to him, and how he had preached boldly
at Damascus in the name of Jesus. 28And he was
with them coming in and going out at Jerusalem.
29And he spake boldly in the name of the Lord
Jesus, and disputed against the Grecians: but
they went about to slay him. 30 *Which* when the
brethren knew, they brought him down to

Living Bible

23 After a while the Jewish leaders determined to kill him. 24 But Paul was told about
their plans, that they were watching the gates
of the city day and night prepared to murder
him. 25 So during the night some of his converts
let him down in a basket through an opening in
the city wall!

26 Upon arrival in Jerusalem he tried to meet
with the believers, but they were all afraid of
him. They thought he was faking! 27 Then Barnabas brought him to the apostles and told them
how Paul had seen the Lord on the way to
Damascus, what the Lord had said to him, and
all about his powerful preaching in the name
of Jesus. 28 Then they accepted him, and after
that he was constantly with the believers 29 and
preached boldly in the name of the Lord. But
then some Greek-speaking Jews with whom he
had argued plotted to murder him. 30 However,
when the other believers heard about his danger,
they took him to Caesarea and then sent him to
his home[a] in Tarsus.

[a] Implied.

Today's English Version

23 After many days had gone by, the Jews
gathered and made plans to kill Saul; 24 but he
was told of what they planned to do. Day and
night they watched the city gates in order to kill
him. 25 But one night Saul's followers took him
and let him down through an opening in the
wall, lowering him in a basket.

Saul in Jerusalem

26 Saul went to Jerusalem and tried to join
the disciples. They would not believe, however,
that he was a disciple, and they were all afraid
of him. 27 Then Barnabas came to his help and
took him to the apostles. He explained to them
how Saul had seen the Lord on the road, and
that the Lord had spoken to him. He also told
them how boldly Saul had preached in the name
of Jesus in Damascus. 28And so Saul stayed
with them and went all over Jerusalem, preaching boldly in the name of the Lord. 29 He also
talked and disputed with the Greek-speaking
Jews, but they tried to kill him. 30 When the
brothers found out about this, they took Saul
down to Caesarea and sent him away to Tarsus.

New International Version

23 After many days had gone by, the Jews
conspired to kill him, 24 but Saul learned of
their plan. Day and night they kept close watch
on the city gates in order to kill him. 25 But his
followers took him by night and lowered him in
a basket through an opening in the wall.

26 When he came to Jerusalem, he tried to
join the disciples, but they were all afraid of
him, not believing that he really was a disciple.
27 But Barnabas took him and brought him to
the apostles. He told them how Saul on his journey had seen the Lord and that the Lord had
spoken to him, and how in Damascus he had
preached fearlessly in the name of Jesus. 28 So
Saul stayed with them and moved about freely
in Jerusalem, speaking boldly in the name of the
Lord. 29 He talked and debated with the Grecian
Jews, but they tried to kill him. 30 When the
brothers learned of this, they took him down to
Caesarea and sent him off to Tarsus.

Phillips Modern English

9.23 The long revenge on the "renegade" begins

After some time the Jews made a plot to kill Saul, but news of this came to his ears. Although in their murderous scheme the Jews watched the gates day and night for him, his disciples took him one night and let him down through an opening in the wall by lowering him in a basket.

9.26 At Jerusalem Saul is suspect: Barnabas conciliates

When Saul reached Jerusalem he tried to join the disciples. But they were all afraid of him, finding it impossible to believe that he was a disciple. Barnabas, however, took him by the hand and introduced him to the apostles, and explained to them how he had seen the Lord on his journey, and how the Lord had spoken to him. He further explained how Saul had spoken in Damascus with the utmost boldness in the name of Jesus. After that Saul joined with them in all their activities in Jerusalem, preaching fearlessly in the name of the Lord. He used to talk and argue with the Greek-speaking Jews, but they made several attempts on his life. When the brothers realised this they took him down to Caesarea and sent him off to Tarsus.

Revised Standard Version

23 When many days had passed, the Jews plotted to kill him, 24 but their plot became known to Saul. They were watching the gates day and night, to kill him; 25 but his disciples took him by night and let him down over the wall, lowering him in a basket.

26 And when he had come to Jerusalem he attempted to join the disciples; and they were all afraid of him, for they did not believe that he was a disciple. 27 But Barnabas took him, and brought him to the apostles, and declared to them how on the road he had seen the Lord, who spoke to him, and how at Damascus he had preached boldly in the name of Jesus. 28 So he went in and out among them at Jerusalem, 29 preaching boldly in the name of the Lord. And he spoke and disputed against the Hellenists; but they were seeking to kill him. 30 And when the brethren knew it, they brought him down to Caesarea, and sent him off to Tarsus.

Jerusalem Bible

23 Some time passed,[x] and the Jews worked out a plot to kill him, 24 but news of it reached Saul. To make sure of killing him they kept watch on the gates day and night, 25 but when it was dark the disciples took him and let him down from the top of the wall, lowering him in a basket.

Saul's visit to Jerusalem

26 When he got to Jerusalem he tried to join the disciples, but they were all afraid of him: they could not believe he was really a disciple. 27 Barnabas, however, took charge of him, introduced him to the apostles, and explained how the Lord had appeared to Saul and spoken to him on his journey, and how he had preached boldly at Damascus in the name of Jesus. 28 Saul now started to go around with them in Jerusalem, preaching fearlessly in the name of the Lord. 29 But after he had spoken to the Hellenists, and argued with them, they became determined to kill him. 30 When the brothers knew, they took him to Caesarea, and sent him off from there to Tarsus.

[x] Three years, according to Ga. 1:17-18.

New English Bible

As the days mounted up, the Jews hatched a plot against his life; but their plans became known to Saul. They kept watch on the city gates day and night so that they might murder him; but his converts took him one night and let him down by the wall, lowering him in a basket.

When he reached Jerusalem he tried to join the body of disciples there; but they were all afraid of him, because they did not believe that he was really a convert. Barnabas, however, took him by the hand and introduced him to the apostles. He described to them how Saul had seen the Lord on his journey, and heard his voice, and how he had spoken out boldly in the name of Jesus at Damascus. Saul now stayed with them, moving about freely in Jerusalem. He spoke out boldly and openly in the name of the Lord, talking and debating with the Greek-speaking Jews.[a] But they planned to murder him, and when the brethren learned of this they escorted him to Caesarea and saw him off to Tarsus.

[a] *Literally* the Hellenists.

King James Version

Cesarea, and sent him forth to Tarsus. 31 Then had the churches rest throughout all Judea and Galilee and Samaria, and were edified; and walking in the fear of the Lord, and in the comfort of the Holy Ghost, were multiplied.

32 And it came to pass, as Peter passed throughout all *quarters,* he came down also to the saints which dwelt at Lydda. 33 And there he found a certain man named Eneas, which had kept his bed eight years, and was sick of the palsy. 34 And Peter said unto him, Eneas, Jesus Christ maketh thee whole: arise, and make thy bed. And he arose immediately. 35 And all that dwelt at Lydda and Saron saw him, and turned to the Lord.

36 Now there was at Joppa a certain disciple named Tabitha, which by interpretation is called Dorcas: this woman was full of good works and almsdeeds which she did. 37 And it came to pass in those days, that she was sick, and died: whom when they had washed, they laid *her* in an upper chamber. 38 And forasmuch as Lydda was nigh to Joppa, and the disciples had heard that Peter

Living Bible

31 Meanwhile, the church had peace throughout Judea, Galilee and Samaria, and grew in strength and numbers. The believers learned how to walk in the fear of the Lord and in the comfort of the Holy Spirit.

32 Peter traveled from place to place to visit them,[a] and in his travels came to the believers in the town of Lydda. 33 There he met a man named Aeneas, paralyzed and bedridden for eight years.

34 Peter said to him, "Aeneas! Jesus Christ has healed you! Get up and make your bed." And he was healed instantly. 35 Then the whole population of Lydda and Sharon turned to the Lord when they saw Aeneas walking around.

36 In the city of Joppa there was a woman named Dorcas ("Gazelle"), a believer who was always doing kind things for others, especially for the poor. 37 About this time she became ill and died. Her friends prepared her for burial and laid her in an upstairs room. 38 But when they learned that Peter was nearby at Lydda,

[*a*] Implied.

Today's English Version

31 And so it was that the church throughout all of Judea, Galilee, and Samaria had a time of peace. It was built up and grew in numbers through the help of the Holy Spirit, as it lived in reverence for the Lord.

Peter in Lydda and Joppa

32 Peter traveled everywhere, and one time he went to visit God's people who lived in Lydda. 33 There he met a man named Aeneas, who was paralyzed and had not been able to get out of bed for eight years. 34 "Aeneas," Peter said to him, "Jesus Christ makes you well. Get up and make your bed." At once Aeneas got up. 35 All the people living in Lydda and Sharon saw him, and they turned to the Lord.

36 In Joppa there was a woman named Tabitha, who was a believer. (Her name in Greek is Dorcas, meaning a deer.) She spent all her time doing good and helping the poor. 37 At that time she got sick and died. Her body was washed and laid in a room upstairs. 38 Joppa was not very far from Lydda, and when the disciples in

New International Version

31 Then the church throughout Judea, Galilee and Samaria enjoyed a time of peace. It was strengthened; and encouraged by the Holy Spirit, it grew in numbers, living in the fear of the Lord.

Aeneas and Dorcas

32 As Peter traveled about the country, he went to visit the saints in Lydda. 33 There he found a man named Aeneas, a paralytic who had been bedridden for eight years. 34 "Aeneas," Peter said to him, "Jesus Christ heals you. Get up and arrange your things." Immediately Aeneas got up. 35 All those who lived in Lydda and Sharon saw him and turned to the Lord.

36 In Joppa there was a disciple named Tabitha (which, when translated, is Dorcas[j]), who was always doing good and helping the poor. 37 About that time she became sick and died, and her body was washed and placed in an upstairs room. 38 Lydda was near Joppa; so when the disciples heard that Peter was in Lydda,

[*j*] Both *Tabitha* (Aramaic) and *Dorcas* (Greek) mean *gazelle*.

Phillips Modern English

9.31 A time of peace

The whole Church throughout Judaea, Galilee and Samaria now enjoyed a period of peace. It became established and as it went forward in reverence for the Lord and in the strengthening presence of the Holy Spirit, continued to grow in numbers.

9.32 Peter heals at Lydda

Now it happened that Peter, in the course of travelling about among them all, came down to God's people living at Lydda. There he found a man called Æneas who had been bed-ridden for eight years through paralysis. Peter said to him, "Æneas, Jesus Christ heals you! Get up and make your bed."

He got to his feet at once. And all those who lived in Lydda and Sharon saw him and turned to the Lord.

9.36 And again at Joppa

Then there was a woman in Joppa, a disciple called Tabitha, whose name in Greek was Dorcas (meaning Gazelle). She was a woman whose whole life was full of good and kindly actions, but in those days she became seriously ill and died. So when they had washed her body they laid her in a room upstairs. Now Lydda is quite near Joppa, and when the disciples heard that

Revised Standard Version

31 So the church throughout all Judea and
Galilee and Samaria had peace and was built
up; and walking in the fear of the Lord and in
the comfort of the Holy Spirit it was multiplied.

32 Now as Peter went here and there among
them all, he came down also to the saints that
lived at Lydda. 33 There he found a man named
Aeneas, who had been bedridden for eight years
and was paralyzed. 34 And Peter said to him,
"Aeneas, Jesus Christ heals you; rise and make
your bed." And immediately he rose. 35 And all
the residents of Lydda and Sharon saw him, and
they turned to the Lord.
36 Now there was at Joppa a disciple named
Tabitha, which means Dorcas.[x] She was full of
good works and acts of charity. 37 In those days
she fell sick and died; and when they had washed
her, they laid her in an upper room. 38 Since
Lydda was near Joppa, the disciples, hearing

[x] The name Tabitha in Aramaic and the name Dorcas in Greek mean *gazelle*.

Jerusalem Bible

A lull

31 The churches throughout Judaea, Galilee
and Samaria were now left in peace, building
themselves up, living in the fear of the Lord,
and filled with the consolation of the Holy
Spirit.

Peter cures a paralytic at Lydda

32 Peter visited one place after another and
eventually came to the saints living down in
Lydda. 33 There he found a man called Aeneas,
a paralytic who had been bedridden for eight
years. 34 Peter said to him, "Aeneas, Jesus Christ
cures you: get up and fold up your sleeping
mat." Aeneas got up immediately; 35 everybody
who lived in Lydda and Sharon saw him, and
they were all converted to the Lord.

Peter raises a woman to life at Jaffa

36 At Jaffa there was a woman disciple called
Tabitha, or Dorcas in Greek,[y] who never tired
of doing good or giving in charity. 37 But the
time came when she got ill and died, and they
washed her and laid her out in a room upstairs.
38 Lydda is not far from Jaffa, so when the

[y] I.e., "Gazelle."

New English Bible

Meanwhile the church, throughout Judaea, Galilee, and Samaria, was left in peace to build up its strength. In the fear of the Lord, upheld by the Holy Spirit, it held on its way and grew in numbers.

Peter was making a general tour, in the course of which he went down to visit God's people at Lydda. There he found a man named Aeneas who had been bed-ridden with paralysis for eight years. Peter said to him, 'Aeneas, Jesus Christ cures you; get up and make your bed', and immediately he stood up. All who lived in Lydda and Sharon saw him; and they turned to the Lord.

In Joppa there was a disciple named Tabitha (in Greek, Dorcas, meaning a gazelle), who filled her days with acts of kindness and charity. At that time she fell ill and died; and they washed her body and laid it in a room upstairs. As Lydda was near Joppa, the disciples, who had

King James Version

was there, they sent unto him two men, desiring *him* that he would not delay to come to them.
39 Then Peter arose and went with them. When he was come, they brought him into the upper chamber: and all the widows stood by him weeping, and shewing the coats and garments which Dorcas made, while she was with them.
40 But Peter put them all forth, and kneeled down, and prayed; and turning *him* to the body said, Tabitha, arise. And she opened her eyes: and when she saw Peter, she sat up.
41 And he gave her *his* hand, and lifted her up; and when he had called the saints and widows, he presented her alive.
42 And it was known throughout all Joppa; and many believed in the Lord.
43 And it came to pass, that he tarried many days in Joppa with one Simon a tanner.

10 There was a certain man in Cesarea called Cornelius, a centurion of the band called the Italian *band,*
2 *A* devout *man,* and one that feared God with all his house, which gave much alms to the people, and prayed to God always.
3 He saw in a vision evidently, about the ninth hour of the day, an angel of God coming in to

Living Bible

they sent two men to beg him to return with them to Joppa.
39 This he did; as soon as he arrived, they took him upstairs where Dorcas lay. The room was filled with weeping widows who were showing one another the coats and other garments Dorcas had made for them.
40 But Peter asked them all to leave the room; then he knelt and prayed. Turning to the body he said, "Get up, Dorcas," [b] and she opened her eyes! And when she saw Peter, she sat up!
41 He gave her his hand and helped her up and called in the believers and widows, presenting her to them.

42 The news raced through the town, and many believed in the Lord.
43 And Peter stayed a long time in Joppa, living with Simon, the tanner.

10 In Caesarea there lived a Roman army officer, Cornelius, a captain of an Italian regiment.
2 He was a godly man, deeply reverent, as was his entire household. He gave generously to charity and was a man of prayer.
3 While wide awake one afternoon he had a vision—it was about three o'clock—and in this vision he saw an angel of God coming toward him.

[b] Literally, "Tabitha," her name in Hebrew.

Today's English Version

Joppa heard that Peter was in Lydda, they sent two men to him with the message, "Please hurry and come to us."
39 So Peter got ready and went with them. When he arrived he was taken to the room upstairs. All the widows crowded around him, crying and showing him the shirts and coats that Dorcas had made while she was alive.
40 Peter put them all out of the room, and knelt down and prayed; then he turned to the body and said, "Tabitha, get up!" She opened her eyes, and when she saw Peter she sat up.
41 Peter reached over and helped her get up. Then he called the believers and the widows, and presented her alive to them.
42 The news about this spread all over Joppa, and many people believed in the Lord.
43 Peter stayed on in Joppa for many days with a leatherworker named Simon.

Peter and Cornelius

10 There was a man in Caesarea named Cornelius, a captain in the Roman army regiment called "The Italian Regiment."
2 He was a religious man; he and his whole family worshiped God. He did much to help the Jewish poor people, and was constantly praying to God.
3 It was about three o'clock one afternoon when he had a vision, in which he clearly saw an angel of God

New International Version

they sent two men to him and urged him, "Please come at once!"

39 Peter went with them, and when he arrived he was taken upstairs to the room. All the widows stood around him, crying and showing him the robes and other clothing that Dorcas had made while she was still with them.

40 Peter sent them all out of the room; then he got down on his knees and prayed. Turning toward the dead woman, he said, "Tabitha, get up." She opened her eyes, and seeing Peter she sat up.
41 He took her by the hand and helped her to her feet. Then he called the believers and the widows and presented her to them alive.
42 This became known all over Joppa, and many people believed in the Lord.
43 Peter stayed in Joppa for some time with a tanner named Simon.

Cornelius calls for Peter

10 At Caesarea there was a man named Cornelius, a centurion in what was known as the Italian Regiment.
2 He and all his family were devout and God-fearing; he gave generously to those in need and prayed to God regularly.
3 One day at about three in the afternoon he had a vision. He distinctly saw an angel of

Phillips Modern English

Peter was in Lydda, they sent two men to him and begged him,

"Please come to us without delay."

Peter got up and went back with them, and when he arrived in Joppa they took him to the room upstairs. All the widows stood around him with tears in their eyes, holding out for him to see the dresses and cloaks which Dorcas used to make for them while she was with them. But Peter put them all outside the room and knelt down and prayed. Then he turned to the body and said,

"Tabitha, get up!"

She opened her eyes, and as soon as she saw Peter she sat up. He took her by the hand, helped her to her feet, and then called out to the believers and widows and presented her to them alive. This became known throughout the whole of Joppa and many believed in the Lord. Peter himself remained there for some time, staying with a tanner called Simon.

10.1 God speaks to a good-living gentile

There was a man in Caesarea by the name of Cornelius, a centurion in what was called the Italian regiment. He was a deeply religious man who reverenced God, as did all his household. He made many charitable gifts to the people and was a man of regular prayer. About three o'clock one afternoon he saw perfectly clearly in a vision an angel of God coming into his room, approaching him, and saying,

Revised Standard Version

that Peter was there, sent two men to him en-
treating him, "Please come to us without delay."
39 So Peter rose and went with them. And when
he had come, they took him to the upper room.
All the widows stood beside him weeping, and
showing tunics and other garments which Dorcas
made while she was with them. 40 But Peter put
them all outside and knelt down and prayed;
then turning to the body he said, "Tabitha, rise."
And she opened her eyes, and when she saw
Peter she sat up. 41 And he gave her his hand and
lifted her up. Then calling the saints and widows
he presented her alive. 42 And it became known
throughout all Joppa, and many believed in the
Lord. 43 And he stayed in Joppa for many days
with one Simon, a tanner.

10 At Caesarea there was a man named Cornelius, a centurion of what was known as
the Italian Cohort, 2 a devout man who feared
God with all his household, gave alms liberally
to the people, and prayed constantly to God.
3 About the ninth hour of the day he saw clearly
in a vision an angel of God coming in and say-

Jerusalem Bible

disciples heard that Peter was there, they sent
two men with an urgent message for him, "Come
and visit us as soon as possible."
39 Peter went back with them straightaway,
and on his arrival they took him to the upstairs
room, where all the widows stood around him
in tears, showing him tunics and other clothes
Dorcas had made when she was with them.
40 Peter sent them all out of the room and
knelt down and prayed. Then he turned to the
dead woman and said, "Tabitha, stand up." She
opened her eyes, looked at Peter and sat up.
41 Peter helped her to her feet, then he called
in the saints and widows and showed them she
was alive. 42 The whole of Jaffa heard about
it and many believed in the Lord.
43 Peter stayed on some time in Jaffa, lodging with a leather tanner called Simon.

Peter visits a Roman centurion

10 One of the centurions of the Italica cohort stationed in Caesarea was called Cornelius. 2 He and the whole of his household
were devout and God-fearing, and he gave generously to Jewish causes and prayed constantly
to God.
3 One day at about the ninth hour he had a
vision in which he distinctly saw the angel of
God come into his house and call out to him,

New English Bible

heard that Peter was there, sent two men to him with the urgent request, 'Please come over to us without delay.' Peter thereupon went off with them. When he arrived they took him upstairs to the room, where all the widows came and stood round him in tears, showing him the shirts and coats that Dorcas used to make while she was with them. Peter sent them all outside, and knelt down and prayed. Then, turning towards the body, he said, 'Get up, Tabitha.' She opened her eyes, saw Peter, and sat up. He gave her his hand and helped her to her feet. Then he called the members of the congregation and the widows and showed her to them alive. The news spread all over Joppa, and many came to believe in the Lord. Peter stayed on in Joppa for some time with one Simon, a tanner.

10 At Caesarea there was a man named Cornelius, a centurion in the Italian Cohort, as it was called. He was a religious man, and he and his whole family joined in the worship of God. He gave generously to help the Jewish people, and was regular in his prayers to God. One day about three in the afternoon he had a vision in which he clearly saw an angel of God,

King James Version

him, and saying unto him, Cornelius. 4And when
he looked on him, he was afraid, and said, What
is it, Lord? And he said unto him, Thy prayers
and thine alms are come up for a memorial before God. 5And now send men to Joppa, and
call for *one* Simon, whose surname is Peter:
6 He lodgeth with one Simon a tanner, whose
house is by the sea side: he shall tell thee what
thou oughtest to do. 7And when the angel which
spake unto Cornelius was departed, he called
two of his household servants, and a devout
soldier of them that waited on him continually;
8And when he had declared all *these* things unto
them, he sent them to Joppa.
9 On the morrow, as they went on their journey, and drew nigh unto the city, Peter went up
upon the housetop to pray about the sixth hour:
10And he became very hungry, and would have
eaten: but while they made ready, he fell into a
trance, 11And saw heaven opened, and a certain
vessel descending unto him, as it had been a
great sheet knit at the four corners, and let down
to the earth: 12 Wherein were all manner of
fourfooted beasts of the earth, and wild beasts,
and creeping things, and fowls of the air. 13And
there came a voice to him, Rise, Peter; kill, and
eat. 14 But Peter said, Not so, Lord; for I have
never eaten any thing that is common or unclean. 15And the voice *spake* unto him again the
second time, What God hath cleansed, *that* call

Living Bible

"Cornelius!" the angel said.
4 Cornelius stared at him in terror. "What do
you want, sir?" he asked the angel.
And the angel replied, "Your prayers and
charities have not gone unnoticed by God!
5, 6 Now send some men to Joppa to find a man
named Simon Peter, who is staying with Simon,
the tanner, down by the shore, and ask him to
come and visit you."
7 As soon as the angel was gone, Cornelius
called two of his household servants and a
godly soldier, one of his personal bodyguard,
8 and told them what had happened and sent
them off to Joppa.
9, 10 The next day, as they were nearing the
city, Peter went up on the flat roof of his house
to pray. It was noon and he was hungry, but
while lunch was being prepared, he fell into a
trance. 11 He saw the sky open, and a great
canvas[a] sheet, suspended by its four corners,
settle to the ground. 12 In the sheet were all
sorts of animals, snakes and birds [forbidden to
the Jews for food [b]].
13 Then a voice said to him, "Go kill and eat
any of them you wish."
14 "Never, Lord," Peter declared, "I have
never in all my life eaten such creatures, for
they are forbidden by our Jewish laws."
15 The voice spoke again, "Don't contradict
God! If he says something is kosher, then it is."

[*a*] Implied. [*b*] Implied; see Leviticus 11 for the forbidden list.

Today's English Version

come in and say to him, "Cornelius!"
4 He stared at the angel in fear and said,
"What is it, sir?"
The angel answered, "God has accepted your
prayers and works of charity, and has remembered you. 5And now send some men to Joppa
to call for a certain man whose full name is Simon Peter. 6 He is a guest in the home of a
leatherworker named Simon, who lives by the
sea." 7 Then the angel who was speaking to him
went away, and Cornelius called two of his house
servants and a soldier, a religious man who was
one of his personal attendants. 8 He told them
what had happened and sent them off to Joppa.
9 The next day, as they were on their way and
coming near Joppa, Peter went up on the roof
of the house about noon in order to pray. 10 He
became hungry, and wanted to eat; while the
food was being prepared he had a vision. 11 He
saw heaven opened and something coming down
that looked like a large sheet being lowered by
its four corners to the earth. 12 In it were all
kinds of animals, reptiles, and wild birds. 13A
voice said to him, "Get up, Peter; kill and eat!"
14 But Peter said, "Certainly not, Lord! I have
never eaten anything considered defiled or unclean."
15 The voice spoke to him again, "Do not
consider anything unclean that God has declared

New International Version

God, who came to him and said, "Cornelius!"
4 Cornelius stared at him in fear. "What is it,
Lord?" he asked.
The angel answered, "Your prayers and gifts
to the poor have come up as a remembrance
before God. 5 Now send men to Joppa to bring
back a man named Simon who is called Peter.
6 He is staying with Simon the tanner, whose
house is by the sea."
7 When the angel who spoke to him had gone,
Cornelius called two of his servants and one of
his military aides who was a devout man. 8 He
told them everything that had happened and
sent them to Joppa.

Peter's vision

9 About noon the following day as they were
approaching the city, Peter went up on the roof
to pray. 10 He became hungry and wanted
something to eat, and while the meal was being
prepared, he fell into a trance. 11 He saw heaven
opened and something like a large sheet being
let down to earth by its four corners. 12 It contained all kinds of four-footed animals, as well
as reptiles of the earth and birds of the air.
13 Then a voice told him, "Get up, Peter. Kill
and eat."
14 "Surely not, Lord!" Peter replied. "I have
never eaten anything impure or unclean."
15 The voice spoke to him a second time, "Do
not call anything impure that God has made
clean."

Phillips Modern English

"Cornelius!"

He stared at the angel in terror, and said, "What is it, Lord?"

The angel replied,

"Your prayers and your deeds of charity have gone up to Heaven and are remembered before God. Now send men to Joppa for a man called Simon, who is also known as Peter. He is staying as a guest with another Simon, a tanner, whose house is down by the sea."

When the angel who had spoken to him had gone, Cornelius called out for two of his house-servants and a devout soldier, who was one of his personal attendants. He told them the whole story and then sent them off to Joppa.

10.9 Peter's startling vision

Next day, while these men were still on their journey and approaching the city, Peter went up about midday on to the flat roof of the house to pray. He became very hungry and longed for something to eat. But while the meal was being prepared he fell into a trance and saw the heavens open and something like a great sheet descending upon the earth, let down by its four corners. In it were all kinds of animals, reptiles and birds. Then came a voice which said to him,

"Get up, Peter, kill and eat!"

But Peter said,

"Never, Lord! For not once in all my life have I ever eaten anything common or unclean."

Then the voice spoke to him a second time,

"You must not call what God has cleansed common."

Revised Standard Version

ing to him, "Cornelius." 4 And he stared at him
in terror, and said, "What is it, Lord?" And he
said to him, "Your prayers and your alms have
ascended as a memorial before God. 5 And now
send men to Joppa, and bring one Simon who
is called Peter; 6 he is lodging with Simon, a
tanner, whose house is by the seaside." 7 When
the angel who spoke to him had departed, he
called two of his servants and a devout soldier
from among those that waited on him, 8 and
having related everything to them, he sent them
to Joppa.
9 The next day, as they were on their journey
and coming near the city, Peter went up on the
housetop to pray, about the sixth hour. 10 And
he became hungry and desired something to eat;
but while they were preparing it, he fell into a
trance 11 and saw the heaven opened, and something
descending, like a great sheet, let down by
four corners upon the earth. 12 In it were all
kinds of animals and reptiles and birds of the air.
13 And there came a voice to him, "Rise, Peter;
kill and eat." 14 But Peter said, "No, Lord; for
I have never eaten anything that is common or
unclean." 15 And the voice came to him again a
second time, "What God has cleansed, you must

Jerusalem Bible

"Cornelius!" 4 He stared at the vision in terror
and exclaimed, "What is it, Lord?" "Your offering
of prayers and alms," the angel answered,
"has been accepted by God. 5 Now you must
send someone to Jaffa and fetch a man called
Simon, known as Peter, 6 who is lodging with
Simon the tanner whose house is by the sea."
7 When the angel who said this had gone, Cornelius
called two of the slaves and a devout
soldier of his staff, 8 told them what had happened,
and sent them off to Jaffa.
9 Next day, while they were still on their
journey and had only a short distance to go
before reaching Jaffa, Peter went to the housetop
at about the sixth hour to pray. 10 He felt
hungry and was looking forward to his meal,
but before it was ready he fell into a trance
11 and saw heaven thrown open and something
like a big sheet being let down to earth by its
four corners; 12 it contained every possible sort
of animal and bird, walking, crawling or flying
ones. 13 A voice then said to him, "Now, Peter;
kill and eat!" 14 But Peter answered, "Certainly
not, Lord; I have never yet eaten anything
profane or unclean." 15 Again, a second
time, the voice spoke to him, "What God has
made clean, you have no right to call profane."

New English Bible

who came into his room and said, 'Cornelius!' He stared at him in terror. 'What is it, my lord?' he asked. The angel said, 'Your prayers and acts of charity have gone up to heaven to speak for you before God. And now send to Joppa for a man named Simon, also called Peter: he is lodging with another Simon, a tanner, whose house is by the sea.' So when the angel who was speaking to him had gone, he summoned two of his servants and a military orderly who was a religious man, told them the whole story, and sent them to Joppa.

Next day, while they were still on their way and approaching the city, about noon Peter went up on the roof to pray. He grew hungry and wanted something to eat. While they were getting it ready, he fell into a trance. He saw a rift in the sky, and a thing coming down that looked like a great sheet of sail-cloth. It was slung by the four corners, and was being lowered to the ground. In it he saw creatures of every kind, whatever walks or crawls or flies. Then there was a voice which said to him, 'Up, Peter, kill and eat.' But Peter said, 'No, Lord, no: I have never eaten anything profane or unclean.' The voice came again a second time: 'It is not for you to

King James Version

not thou common. 16 This was done thrice: and the vessel was received up again into heaven. 17 Now while Peter doubted in himself what this vision which he had seen should mean, behold, the men which were sent from Cornelius had made inquiry for Simon's house, and stood before the gate, 18 And called, and asked whether Simon, which was surnamed Peter, were lodged there.

19 While Peter thought on the vision, the Spirit said unto him, Behold, three men seek thee. 20 Arise therefore, and get thee down, and go with them, doubting nothing: for I have sent them. 21 Then Peter went down to the men which were sent unto him from Cornelius; and said, Behold, I am he whom ye seek: what *is* the cause wherefore ye are come? 22 And they said, Cornelius the centurion, a just man, and one that feareth God, and of good report among all the nation of the Jews, was warned from God by a holy angel to send for thee into his house, and to hear words of thee. 23 Then called he them in, and lodged *them*. And on the morrow

Living Bible

16 The same vision was repeated three times. Then the sheet was pulled up again to heaven. 17 Peter was very perplexed. What could the vision mean? What was he supposed to do?

Just then the men sent by Cornelius had found the house and were standing outside at the gate, 18 inquiring whether this was the place where Simon Peter lived!

19 Meanwhile, as Peter was puzzling over the vision, the Holy Spirit said to him, "Three men have come to see you. 20 Go down and meet them and go with them. All is well, I have sent them."

21 So Peter went down. "I'm the man you're looking for," he said. "Now what is it you want?"

22 Then they told him about Cornelius the Roman officer, a good and godly man, well thought of by the Jews, and how an angel had instructed him to send for Peter to come and tell him what God wanted him to do.

23 So Peter invited them in and lodged them

Today's English Version

clean." 16 This happened three times; and then the thing was taken back up into heaven.

17 Peter was wondering about the meaning of this vision that he had seen. In the meantime the men sent by Cornelius had learned where Simon's house was, and were now standing in front of the gate. 18 They called out and asked, "Is there a guest here by the name of Simon Peter?"

19 Peter was still trying to understand what the vision meant, when the Spirit said, "Listen! Three men are here looking for you. 20 So get yourself ready and go down, and do not hesitate to go with them, because I have sent them." 21 So Peter went down and said to the men, "I am the man you are looking for. Why have you come?"

22 "Captain Cornelius sent us," they answered. "He is a good man who worships God and is highly respected by all the Jewish people. He was told by one of God's angels to invite you to his house, so that he could hear what you have to say." 23 Peter invited the men in and had them spend the night there.

New International Version

16 This happened three times, and immediately the sheet was taken back to heaven.

17 While Peter was wondering about the meaning of the vision, the men sent by Cornelius found out where Simon's house was and stopped at the gate. 18 They called out asking if Simon who was known as Peter was staying there.

19 While Peter was still thinking about the vision, the Spirit said to him, "Simon, three[k] men are looking for you. 20 So get up and go downstairs. Do not hesitate to go with them, for I have sent them."

21 Peter went down and said to the men, "I'm the one you're looking for. Why have you come?"

22 The men replied, "We have come from Cornelius the centurion. He is a righteous and God-fearing man, who is respected by all the Jewish people. A holy angel told him to have you come to his house so that he could hear what you have to say." 23 Then Peter invited the men into the house to be his guests.

[k] One early MS reads *two;* other MSS omit the number.

Phillips Modern English

This happened three times, and then the thing was gone, taken back into heaven.

10.17 *The meaning of the vision becomes apparent*

While Peter was still puzzling about the meaning of the vision which he had just seen, the men sent by Cornelius had arrived asking for the house of Simon. They were in fact standing at the very doorway calling out to enquire if Simon, surnamed Peter, were lodging there. Peter was still thinking deeply about the vision when the Spirit said to him,

"There are some men here looking for you. Get up and go downstairs. Go with them without any misgiving, for I myself have sent them."

So Peter went down to the men and said,

"I am the man you are looking for; what brings you here?"

They replied,

"Cornelius the centurion, a good-living and God-fearing man, whose character can be vouched for by the whole Jewish people, was commanded by a holy angel to send for you to come to his house, and to listen to your message."

Then Peter invited them in and entertained them.

Revised Standard Version

not call common." 16 This happened three times,
and the thing was taken up at once to heaven.
17 Now while Peter was inwardly perplexed as to what the vision which he had seen might mean, behold, the men that were sent by Cornelius, having made inquiry for Simon's house,
stood before the gate 18 and called out to ask whether Simon who was called Peter was lodging
there. 19 And while Peter was pondering the vision, the Spirit said to him, "Behold, three men
are looking for you. 20 Rise and go down, and accompany them without hesitation; for I have
sent them." 21 And Peter went down to the men and said, "I am the one you are looking for;
what is the reason for your coming?" 22 And they said, "Cornelius, a centurion, an upright and God-fearing man, who is well spoken of by the whole Jewish nation, was directed by a holy angel to send for you to come to his house, and
to hear what you have to say." 23 So he called them in to be his guests.

Jerusalem Bible

16 This was repeated three times, and then suddenly the container was drawn up to heaven again.
17 Peter was still worrying over the meaning of the vision he had seen, when the men sent by Cornelius arrived. They had asked where Simon's house was and they were now standing
at the door, 18 calling out to know if the Simon
known as Peter was lodging there. 19 Peter's
mind was still on the vision and the Spirit had to tell him, "Some men have come to see you.
20 Hurry down, and do not hesitate about going back with them; it was I who told them to
come." 21 Peter went down and said to them, "I am the man you are looking for; why have
you come?" 22 They said, "The centurion Cornelius, who is an upright and God-fearing man, highly regarded by the entire Jewish people, was directed by a holy angel to send for you and bring you to his house and to listen to what you
have to say." 23 So Peter asked them in and gave them lodging.

New English Bible

call profane what God counts clean.' This happened three times; and then the thing was taken up again into the sky.

While Peter was still puzzling over the meaning of the vision he had seen, the messengers of Cornelius had been asking the way to Simon's house, and now arrived at the entrance. They called out and asked if Simon Peter was lodging there. But Peter was thinking over the vision, when the Spirit said to him, 'Some[a] men are here looking for you; make haste and go downstairs. You may go with them without any misgiving, for it was I who sent them.' Peter came down to the men and said, 'You are looking for me? Here I am. What brings you here?' 'We are from the centurion Cornelius,' they replied, 'a good and religious man, acknowledged as such by the whole Jewish nation. He was directed by a holy angel to send for you to his house and to listen to what you have to say.' So Peter asked them in and gave them a night's lodging. Next

[a] *One witness reads* Two; *others read* Three.

King James Version

Peter went away with them, and certain brethren
from Joppa accompanied him. 24And the morrow after they entered into Cesarea. And Cornelius waited for them, and had called together his
kinsmen and near friends. 25And as Peter was
coming in, Cornelius met him, and fell down at
his feet, and worshipped *him*. 26 But Peter took
him up, saying, Stand up; I myself also am a
man. 27And as he talked with him, he went in,
and found many that were come together. 28And
he said unto them, Ye know how that it is an
unlawful thing for a man that is a Jew to keep
company, or come unto one of another nation;
but God hath shewed me that I should not call
any man common or unclean. 29 Therefore came
I *unto you* without gainsaying, as soon as I was
sent for: I ask therefore for what intent ye have
sent for me? 30And Cornelius said, Four days
ago I was fasting until this hour; and at the
ninth hour I prayed in my house, and, behold, a
man stood before me in bright clothing, 31And
said, Cornelius, thy prayer is heard, and thine
alms are had in remembrance in the sight of
God. 32 Send therefore to Joppa, and call hither
Simon, whose surname is Peter; he is lodged in
the house of *one* Simon a tanner by the sea side:
who, when he cometh, shall speak unto thee.
33 Immediately therefore I sent to thee; and
thou hast well done that thou art come. Now

Living Bible

overnight. The next day he went with them, accompanied by some other believers from Joppa.
24 They arrived in Caesarea the following day,
and Cornelius was waiting for him, and had
called together his relatives and close friends to
meet Peter. 25As Peter entered his home, Cornelius fell to the floor before him in worship.
26 But Peter said, "Stand up! I'm not a god!"
27 So he got up and they talked together for
a while and then went in where the others were
assembled.
28 Peter told them, "You know it is against
the Jewish laws for me to come into a Gentile
home like this. But God has shown me in a
vision that I should never think of anyone as
inferior. 29 So I came as soon as I was sent for.
Now tell me what you want."
30 Cornelius replied, "Four days ago I was
praying as usual at this time of the afternoon,
when suddenly a man was standing before me
clothed in a radiant robe! 31 He told me, 'Cornelius, your prayers are heard and your charities
have been noticed by God! 32 Now send some
men to Joppa and summon Simon Peter, who is
staying in the home of Simon, a tanner, down by
the shore.' 33 So I sent for you at once, and you
have done well to come so soon. Now here we

Today's English Version

The next day he got ready and went with them;
and some of the brothers from Joppa went along
with him. 24 The following day he arrived in
Caesarea, where Cornelius was waiting for him,
together with relatives and close friends that he
had invited. 25As Peter was about to go in, Cornelius met him, fell at his feet, and bowed down
before him. 26 But Peter made him rise. "Stand
up," he said, "because I myself am only a man."
27 Peter kept on talking to Cornelius as he went
into the house, where he found many people
gathered. 28 He said to them, "You yourselves
know very well that a Jew is not allowed by his
religion to visit or associate with a Gentile. But
God has shown me that I must not consider any
man unclean or defiled. 29And so when you sent
for me I came without any objection. I ask you,
then, why did you send for me?"
30 Cornelius said, "It was about this time
three days ago that I was praying in my house
at three o'clock in the afternoon. Suddenly a
man dressed in shining clothes stood in front of
me 31 and said: 'Cornelius! God has heard your
prayer, and has remembered your works of charity. 32 Send someone to Joppa to call for a man
whose full name is Simon Peter. He is a guest in
the home of Simon the leatherworker, who lives
by the sea.' 33And so I sent for you at once, and
you have been good enough to come. Now we

New International Version

Peter at Cornelius' house

The next day Peter started out with them, and
some of the brothers from Joppa went along.
24 The following day he arrived in Caesarea.
Cornelius was expecting them and had called
together his relatives and close friends. 25As
Peter entered the house, Cornelius met him and
fell at his feet in reverence. 26 But Peter made
him get up. "Stand up," he said, "I am only a
man myself."
27 Talking with him, Peter went inside and
found a large gathering of people. 28 He said to
them: "You are well aware that it is against our
law for a Jew to associate with a Gentile or visit
him. But God has shown me that I should not
call any man impure or unclean. 29 So when I
was sent for, I came without raising any objection. May I ask why you sent for me?"
30 Cornelius answered: "Four days ago I was
in my house praying at this hour, at three in the
afternoon. Suddenly a man in shining clothes
stood before me 31 and said, 'Cornelius, God has
heard your prayer and remembered your gifts to
the poor. 32 Send to Joppa for Simon who is
called Peter. He is a guest in the home of Simon
the tanner, who lives by the sea.' 33 So I sent for
you immediately, and it was good of you to

Phillips Modern English

10.23b Peter, obeying the Spirit, disobeys Jewish law

On the next day he got up and set out with them, accompanied by some of the brothers from Joppa, arriving at Caesarea on the day after that. Cornelius was expecting them and had invited together his relations and intimate friends. As Peter entered the house Cornelius met him by falling at his feet and worshipping him. But Peter raised him with the words,

"Stand up, I am a human being too!"

Then Peter went right into the house in deep conversation with Cornelius and found that a large number of people had assembled. Then he spoke to them,

"You all know that it is forbidden for a man who is a Jew to associate with, or even visit, a man of another nation. But God has shown me plainly that no man must be called 'common' or 'unclean'. That is why I came here when I was sent for without raising any objection. Now I want to know what made you send for me."

Then Cornelius replied,

"Four days ago, about this time, I was observing the afternoon hour of prayer in my house, when suddenly a man in shining clothes stood before me and said, 'Cornelius, your prayer has been heard and your charitable deeds have been remembered before God. Now you must send to Joppa and invite here a man called Simon whose surname is Peter. He is staying in the house of a tanner by the name of Simon, down by the sea.' So I sent to you without delay and you have been most kind in com-

Revised Standard Version

The next day he rose and went off with them,
and some of the brethren from Joppa accompanied him. 24 And on the following day they entered Caesarea. Cornelius was expecting them
and had called together his kinsmen and close
friends. 25 When Peter entered, Cornelius met
him and fell down at his feet and worshiped
him. 26 But Peter lifted him up, saying, "Stand
up; I too am a man." 27 And as he talked with
him, he went in and found many persons gathered; 28 and he said to them, "You yourselves
know how unlawful it is for a Jew to associate
with or to visit any one of another nation; but
God has shown me that I should not call any
man common or unclean. 29 So when I was sent
for, I came without objection. I ask then why
you sent for me."
30 And Cornelius said, "Four days ago, about
this hour, I was keeping the ninth hour of prayer
in my house; and behold, a man stood before
me in bright apparel, 31 saying, 'Cornelius, your
prayer has been heard and your alms have been
remembered before God. 32 Send therefore to
Joppa and ask for Simon who is called Peter; he
is lodging in the house of Simon, a tanner, by
the seaside.' 33 So I sent to you at once, and you
have been kind enough to come. Now therefore

Jerusalem Bible

Next day, he was ready to go off with them,
accompanied by some of the brothers from
Jaffa. 24 They reached Caesarea the following
day, and Cornelius was waiting for them. He
had asked his relations and close friends to be
there, 25 and as Peter reached the house Cornelius went out to meet him, knelt at his feet
and prostrated himself. 26 But Peter helped him
up. "Stand up," he said, "I am only a man
after all!" 27 Talking together they went in to
meet all the people assembled there, 28 and
Peter said to them, "You know it is forbidden
for Jews to mix with people of another race and
visit them, but God has made it clear to me
that I must not call anyone profane or unclean.
29 That is why I made no objection to coming
when I was sent for; but I should like to know
exactly why you sent for me." 30 Cornelius replied, "Three days ago I was praying in my
house at the ninth hour, when I suddenly saw
a man in front of me in shining robes. 31 He
said, 'Cornelius, your prayer has been heard
and your alms have been accepted as a sacrifice
in the sight of God; 32 so now you must send
to Jaffa and fetch Simon known as Peter who
is lodging in the house of Simon the tanner, by
the sea.' 33 So I sent for you at once, and you
have been kind enough to come. Here we all

New English Bible

day he set out with them, accompanied by some members of the congregation at Joppa.

The day after that, he arrived at Caesarea. Cornelius was expecting them and had called together his relatives and close friends. When Peter arrived, Cornelius came to meet him, and bowed to the ground in deep reverence. But Peter raised him to his feet and said, 'Stand up; I am a man like anyone else.' Still talking with him he went in and found a large gathering. He said to them, 'I need not tell you that a Jew is forbidden by his religion to visit or associate with a man of another race; yet God has shown me clearly that I must not call any man profane or unclean. That is why I came here without demur when you sent for me. May I ask what was your reason for sending?'

Cornelius said, 'Four days ago, just about this time, I was in the house here saying the afternoon prayers, when suddenly a man in shining robes stood before me. He said: "Cornelius, your prayer has been heard and your acts of charity remembered before God. Send to Joppa, then, to Simon Peter, and ask him to come. He is lodging in the house of Simon the tanner, by the sea." So I sent to you there and then; it was kind of you to come. And now we are all met

King James Version

therefore are we all here present before God, to
hear all things that are commanded thee of God.
34 Then Peter opened *his* mouth, and said, Of
a truth I perceive that God is no respecter of
persons: 35 But in every nation he that feareth
him, and worketh righteousness, is accepted with
him. 36 The word which *God* sent unto the children of Israel, preaching peace by Jesus Christ:
(he is Lord of all:) 37 That word, *I say,* ye
know, which was published throughout all
Judea, and began from Galilee, after the baptism
which John preached; 38 How God anointed
Jesus of Nazareth with the Holy Ghost and with
power: who went about doing good, and healing
all that were oppressed of the devil; for God
was with him. 39 And we are witnesses of all
things which he did both in the land of the Jews,
and in Jerusalem; whom they slew and hanged
on a tree: 40 Him God raised up the third day,
and shewed him openly; 41 Not to all the people,
but unto witnesses chosen before of God, *even*
to us, who did eat and drink with him after he
rose from the dead. 42 And he commanded us to
preach unto the people, and to testify that it is

Living Bible

are, waiting before the Lord, anxious to hear
what he has told you to tell us!"
34 Then Peter replied, "I see very clearly that
the Jews are not God's only favorites! 35 In
every nation he has those who worship him and
do good deeds and are acceptable to him.
36, 37 I'm sure you have heard about the Good
News for the people of Israel—that there is
peace with God through Jesus, the Messiah, who
is Lord of all creation. This message has spread
all through Judea, beginning with John the Baptist in Galilee. 38 And you no doubt know that
Jesus of Nazareth was anointed by God with the
Holy Spirit and with power, and he went around
doing good and healing all who were possessed
by demons, for God was with him.
39 "And we apostles are witnesses of all he
did throughout Israel and in Jerusalem, where
he was murdered on a cross. 40, 41 But God
brought him back to life again three days later
and showed him to certain witnesses God had
selected beforehand—not to the general public,
but to us who ate and drank with him after he
rose from the dead. 42 And he sent us to preach

Today's English Version

are all here in the presence of God, waiting to
hear anything that the Lord has ordered you to
say."

Peter's speech

34 Peter began to speak: "I now realize that
it is true that God treats all men on the same
basis. 35 Whoever fears him and does what is
right is acceptable to him, no matter what race he
belongs to. 36 You know the message he sent to
the people of Israel, proclaiming the Good News
of peace through Jesus Christ, who is Lord of all
men. 37 You know of the great event that took
place throughout all the land of Israel, beginning
in Galilee, after the baptism that John preached.
38 You know about Jesus of Nazareth, how God
poured out on him the Holy Spirit and power. He
went everywhere, doing good and healing all who
were under the power of the Devil, because God
was with him. 39 We are witnesses of all that he
did in the country of the Jews and in Jerusalem.
They put him to death by nailing him to the
cross. 40 But God raised him from death on the
third day, and caused him to appear, 41 not to
all the people, but only to us who are the witnesses that God had already chosen. We ate and
drank with him after he rose from death. 42 And
he commanded us to preach the gospel to the

New International Version

come. Now we are all here in the presence of
God to listen to everything the Lord has commanded you to tell us."
34 Then Peter began to speak: "I now realize how true it is that God does not show
favoritism 35 but accepts men from every nation who fear him and do what is right. 36 This
is the message God sent to the people of Israel,
telling the good news of peace through Jesus
Christ, who is Lord of all. 37 You know what
has happened throughout Judea, beginning in
Galilee after the baptism that John preached—
38 how God anointed Jesus of Nazareth with
the Holy Spirit and power, and how he went
around doing good and healing all who were
under the power of the devil, because God was
with him.
39 "We are witnesses of everything he did
in the country of the Jews and in Jerusalem.
They killed him by hanging him on a tree, 40 but
God raised him from the dead on the third day
and caused him to be seen. 41 He was not seen
by all the people, but by witnesses whom God
had already chosen—by us who ate and drank
with him after he rose from the dead. 42 He
commanded us to preach to the people and to

Phillips Modern English

ing. Now we are all here in the presence of God to listen to everything that the Lord has commanded you to say."

10.34 Peter's momentous discovery

Then Peter began to speak,

"In solemn truth I can see now that God does not discriminate between people, but that in every nation the man who reverences him and does what is right is acceptable to him! He has sent his message to the sons of Israel by giving us the good news of peace through Jesus Christ—he is Lord of all. You must know the story of Jesus of Nazareth—why, it has spread through the whole of Judaea, beginning from Galilee after the baptism that John proclaimed. You must have heard how God anointed him with the power of the Holy Spirit, of how he went about doing good and healing all who suffered under the devil's power—because God was with him. Now we are eye-witnesses of everything that he did, both in the Judaean country and in Jerusalem itself, and they murdered him by hanging him on a cross. But on the third day God raised that same Jesus and let him be clearly seen, not indeed by the whole people, but by witnesses whom God had previously chosen. We are those witnesses, we who ate and drank with him after he had risen from the dead! Moreover, we are the men whom he

Revised Standard Version

we are all here present in the sight of God, to hear all that you have been commanded by the Lord."

34 And Peter opened his mouth and said: "Truly I perceive that God shows no partiality, 35 but in every nation any one who fears him and does what is right is acceptable to him. 36 You know the word which he sent to Israel, preaching good news of peace by Jesus Christ (he is Lord of all), 37 the word which was proclaimed throughout all Judea, beginning from Galilee after the baptism which John preached: 38 how God anointed Jesus of Nazareth with the Holy Spirit and with power; how he went about doing good and healing all that were oppressed by the devil, for God was with him. 39 And we are witnesses to all that he did both in the country of the Jews and in Jerusalem. They put him to death by hanging him on a tree; 40 but God raised him on the third day and made him manifest; 41 not to all the people but to us who were chosen by God as witnesses, who ate and drank with him after he rose from the dead. 42 And he commanded us to preach to the people, and

Jerusalem Bible

are, assembled in front of you to hear what message God has given you for us."

Peter's address in the house of Cornelius

34 Then Peter addressed them: "The truth I have now come to realize," he said, "is that God does not have favorites, 35 but that anybody of any nationality who fears God and does what is right is acceptable to him.

36 "It is true, God sent his word to the people of Israel, and it was to them that *the good news of peace was brought*[z] by Jesus Christ—but Jesus Christ is Lord of all men. 37 You must have heard about the recent happenings in Judaea; about Jesus of Nazareth and how he began in Galilee, after John had been preaching baptism. 38 *God had anointed him with the Holy Spirit*[a] and with power, and because God was with him, Jesus went about doing good and curing all who had fallen into the power of the devil. 39 Now I, and those with me, can witness to everything he did throughout the countryside of Judaea and in Jerusalem itself: and also to the fact that they killed him by hanging him on a tree, 40 yet three days afterward God raised him to life and allowed him to be seen, 41 not by the whole people but only by certain witnesses God had chosen beforehand. Now we are those witnesses—we have eaten and drunk with him after his resurrection from the dead—42 and he has ordered us to proclaim this to his

[z] Is. 52:7. [a] Is. 61:1.

New English Bible

here before God, to hear all that the Lord has ordered you to say.'

Peter began: 'I now see how true it is that God has no favourites, but that in every nation the man who is godfearing and does what is right is acceptable to him. He sent his word to the Israelites and gave the good news of peace through Jesus Christ, who is Lord of all. I need not tell you what happened lately all over the land of the Jews, starting from Galilee after the baptism proclaimed by John. You know about Jesus of Nazareth, how God anointed him with the Holy Spirit and with power. He went about doing good and healing all who were oppressed by the devil, for God was with him. And we can bear witness to all that he did in the Jewish country-side and in Jerusalem. He was put to death by hanging on a gibbet; but God raised him to life on the third day, and allowed him to appear, not to the whole people, but to witnesses whom God had chosen in advance—to us, who ate and drank with him after he rose from the dead. He commanded us to proclaim him to the

King James Version

he which was ordained of God *to be* the Judge of quick and dead. 43 To him give all the prophets witness, that through his name whosoever believeth in him shall receive remission of sins.

44 While Peter yet spake these words, the Holy Ghost fell on all them which heard the word. 45And they of the circumcision which believed were astonished, as many as came with Peter, because that on the Gentiles also was poured out the gift of the Holy Ghost. 46 For they heard them speak with tongues, and magnify God. Then answered Peter, 47 Can any man forbid water, that these should not be baptized, which have received the Holy Ghost as well as we? 48And he commanded them to be baptized in the name of the Lord. Then prayed they him to tarry certain days.

Living Bible

the Good News everywhere and to testify that Jesus is ordained of God to be the Judge of all —living and dead. 43And all the prophets have written about him, saying that everyone who believes in him will have their sins forgiven through his name."

44 Even as Peter was saying these things, the Holy Spirit fell upon all those listening! 45 The Jews who came with Peter were amazed that the gift of the Holy Spirit would be given to Gentiles too! 46, 47 But there could be no doubt about it,[c] for they heard them speaking in tongues and praising God.

Peter asked, "Can anyone object to my baptizing them, now that they have received the Holy Spirit just as we did?" 48 So he did, baptizing them in the name of Jesus, the Messiah. Afterwards Cornelius begged him to stay with them for several days.

[*c*] Implied.

Today's English Version

people, and to testify that he is the one whom God has appointed judge of the living and the dead. 43All the prophets spoke about him, saying that everyone who believes in him will have his sins forgiven through the power of his name."

The Gentiles receive the Holy Spirit

44 While Peter was still speaking, the Holy Spirit came down on all those who were listening to the message. 45 The Jewish believers who had come from Joppa with Peter were amazed that God had poured out his gift of the Holy Spirit on the Gentiles also. 46 For they heard them speaking in strange tongues and praising God's greatness. Peter spoke up, 47 "These people have received the Holy Spirit, just as we also did. Can anyone, then, stop them from being baptized with water?" 48 So he ordered them to be baptized in the name of Jesus Christ. Then they asked him to stay with them for a few days.

New International Version

testify that he is the one whom God appointed as judge of the living and the dead. 43All the prophets testify about him that everyone who believes in him receives forgiveness of sins through his name."

44 While Peter was still speaking these words, the Holy Spirit came on all who heard the message. 45 The circumcised believers who had come with Peter were astonished that the gift of the Holy Spirit had been poured out even on the Gentiles. 46 For they heard them speaking in tongues[l] and praising God.

Then Peter said, 47 "Can anyone keep these people from being baptized with water? They have received the Holy Spirit just as we have." 48 So he ordered that they be baptized in the name of Jesus Christ. Then they asked Peter to stay with them for a few days.

[*l*] Or *other languages.*

Phillips Modern English

commanded to preach to the people and solemnly witness to the fact that he is the one appointed by God to be the judge of both the living and the dead. It is to him that all the prophets bear witness, so that every man who believes in him may receive forgiveness of sins through his name."

10.44 The Holy Spirit confirms Peter's action

While Peter was still speaking these words the Holy Spirit fell upon all who were listening to his message. The Jewish believers who had come with Peter were absolutely amazed that the gift of the Holy Spirit was being poured out even upon gentiles; for they heard them speaking in foreign tongues and glorifying God.

Then Peter exclaimed,

"Could anyone refuse water or object to these men being baptised—men who have received the Holy Spirit just as we did ourselves?"

And he gave orders for them to be baptised in the name of Jesus Christ. Afterwards they asked him to stay with them for some days.

Revised Standard Version

to testify that he is the one ordained by God
to be judge of the living and the dead. 43 To
him all the prophets bear witness that every
one who believes in him receives forgiveness of
sins through his name."
44 While Peter was still saying this, the Holy
Spirit fell on all who heard the word. 45 And the
believers from among the circumcised who came
with Peter were amazed, because the gift of the
Holy Spirit had been poured out even on the
Gentiles. 46 For they heard them speaking in
tongues and extolling God. Then Peter declared,
47 "Can any one forbid water for baptizing these
people who have received the Holy Spirit just
as we have?" 48 And he commanded them to be
baptized in the name of Jesus Christ. Then they
asked him to remain for some days.

Jerusalem Bible

people and to tell them that God has appointed
him to judge everyone, alive or dead. 43 It is to
him that all the prophets bear this witness: that
all who believe in Jesus will have their sins forgiven through his name."

Baptism of the first pagans

44 While Peter was still speaking the Holy
Spirit came down on all the listeners. 45 Jewish
believers who had accompanied Peter were all
astonished that the gift of the Holy Spirit should
be poured out on the pagans too, 46 since they
could hear them speaking strange languages and
proclaiming the greatness of God. Peter himself then said, 47 "Could anyone refuse the water of baptism to these people, now they have
received the Holy Spirit just as much as we
have?" 48 He then gave orders for them to be
baptized in the name of Jesus Christ. Afterward
they begged him to stay on for some days.

New English Bible

people, and affirm that he is the one who has been designated by God as judge of the living and the dead. It is to him that all the prophets testify, declaring that everyone who trusts in him receives forgiveness of sins through his name.'

Peter was still speaking when the Holy Spirit came upon all who were listening to the message. The believers who had come with Peter, men of Jewish birth, were astonished that the gift of the Holy Spirit should have been poured out even on Gentiles. For they could hear them speaking in tongues of ecstasy and acclaiming the greatness of God. Then Peter spoke: 'Is anyone prepared to withhold the water for baptism from these persons, who have received the Holy Spirit just as we did ourselves?' Then he ordered them to be baptized in the name of Jesus Christ. After that they asked him to stay on with them for a time.

King James Version

11 And the apostles and brethren that were in Judea heard that the Gentiles had also received the word of God. 2 And when Peter was come up to Jerusalem, they that were of the circumcision contended with him, 3 Saying, Thou wentest in to men uncircumcised, and didst eat with them. 4 But Peter rehearsed *the matter* from the beginning, and expounded *it* by order unto them, saying, 5 I was in the city of Joppa praying: and in a trance I saw a vision, A certain vessel descend, as it had been a great sheet, let down from heaven by four corners; and it came even to me: 6 Upon the which when I had fastened mine eyes, I considered, and saw fourfooted beasts of the earth, and wild beasts, and creeping things, and fowls of the air. 7 And I heard a voice saying unto me, Arise, Peter; slay and eat. 8 But I said, Not so, Lord: for nothing common or unclean hath at any time entered into my mouth. 9 But the voice answered me again from heaven, What God hath cleansed, *that* call not thou common. 10 And this was done three times: and all were drawn up again into heaven. 11 And, behold, immediately there were three men already come unto the house where I was, sent from Cesarea unto me. 12 And the Spirit bade me go with them, nothing doubting. Moreover these six brethren accompanied me,

Living Bible

11 Soon the news reached the apostles and other brothers in Judea that Gentiles also were being converted! 2 But when Peter arrived back in Jerusalem, the Jewish believers argued with him.

3 "You fellowshiped with Gentiles and even ate with them," they accused.

4 Then Peter told them the whole story. 5 "One day in Joppa," he said, "while I was praying, I saw a vision—a huge sheet, let down by its four corners from the sky. 6 Inside the sheet were all sorts of animals, reptiles and birds [which we are not to eat[a]]. 7 And I heard a voice say, 'Kill and eat whatever you wish.'

8 " 'Never, Lord,' I replied. 'For I have never yet eaten anything forbidden by our Jewish laws!'

9 "But the voice came again, 'Don't say it isn't right when God declares it is!'

10 "This happened *three times* before the sheet and all it contained disappeared into heaven. 11 Just then three men who had come to take me with them to Caesarea arrived at the house where I was staying! 12 The Holy Spirit told me to go with them and not to worry about their being Gentiles! These six brothers here accompanied me, and we soon arrived at the home of

[*a*] Implied.

Today's English Version

Peter's report to the church at Jerusalem

11 The apostles and the brothers throughout all of Judea heard that the Gentiles also had received the word of God. 2 When Peter went up to Jerusalem, those who were in favor of circumcising Gentiles criticized him, 3 "You were a guest in the home of uncircumcised Gentiles, and you even ate with them!" 4 So Peter gave them a full account of what had happened, from the very beginning:

5 "I was praying in the city of Joppa, and I had a vision. I saw something coming down that looked like a large sheet being lowered by its four corners from heaven, and it stopped next to me. 6 I looked closely inside and saw animals, beasts, reptiles, and wild birds. 7 Then I heard a voice saying to me, 'Get up, Peter; kill and eat!' 8 But I said, 'Certainly not, Lord! No defiled or unclean food has ever entered my mouth.' 9 The voice spoke again from heaven, 'Do not consider anything unclean that God has declared clean.' 10 This happened three times, and finally the whole thing was drawn back up into heaven. 11 At that very moment three men who had been sent to me from Caesarea arrived at the house where I was staying. 12 The Spirit told me to go with them without hesitation. These six brothers from Joppa also went with me to Caesarea,

New International Version

Peter explains his actions

11 The apostles and the brothers throughout Judea heard that the Gentiles also had received the word of God. 2 So when Peter went up to Jerusalem, the circumcised believers criticized him 3 and said, "You went into the house of uncircumcised men and ate with them."

4 Peter began and explained everything to them precisely as it had happened: 5 "I was in the city of Joppa praying, and in a trance I saw a vision. I saw something like a large sheet being let down from heaven by its four corners, and it came down to where I was. 6 I looked into it and saw four-footed animals of the earth, wild beasts, reptiles, and birds of the air. 7 Then I heard a voice telling me, 'Get up, Peter. Kill and eat.'

8 "I replied, 'Surely not, Lord! Nothing impure or unclean has ever entered my mouth.'

9 "The voice spoke from heaven a second time, 'Do not call anything impure that God has made clean.' 10 This happened three times, and then it was all pulled up to heaven again.

11 "Right then three men who had been sent to me from Caesarea stopped at the house where I was staying. 12 The Spirit told me to have no hesitation about going with them. These six brothers also went with me, and we entered the

Phillips Modern English

11.1 The Church's disquiet at Peter's action

Now the apostles and the brothers who were in Judaea heard that the gentiles also had received God's message. So when Peter next visited Jerusalem the circumcision-party were full of criticism, saying to him, "You actually went in and shared a meal with uncircumcised men!"

11.4 Peter's explanation

But Peter began to explain how the situation had actually arisen.

"I was in the city of Joppa praying," he said, "and while completely unconscious of my surroundings I saw a vision—something like a great sheet coming down towards me, let down from heaven by its four corners. It came right down to me and when I looked at it closely I saw animals and wild beasts, reptiles and birds. Then I heard a voice say to me, 'Get up, Peter, kill and eat.' But I said, 'Never, Lord, for nothing common or unclean has ever passed my lips.' But the voice from Heaven spoke a second time and said, 'You must not call what God has cleansed common.' This happened three times, and then the whole thing was drawn up again into heaven. The extraordinary thing is that at that very moment three men arrived at the house where we were staying, sent to me personally from Caesarea. The Spirit told me to go with these men without any misgiving. And these six of our brothers accompanied me and we went into the

Revised Standard Version

11 Now the apostles and the brethren who
were in Judea heard that the Gentiles also
had received the word of God. 2 So when Peter
went up to Jerusalem, the circumcision party
criticized him, 3 saying, "Why did you go to uncircumcised men and eat with them?" 4 But
Peter began and explained to them in order: 5 "I
was in the city of Joppa praying; and in a trance
I saw a vision, something descending, like a
great sheet, let down from heaven by four corners; and it came down to me. 6 Looking at it
closely I observed animals and beasts of prey
and reptiles and birds of the air. 7 And I heard a
voice saying to me, 'Rise, Peter; kill and eat.'
8 But I said, 'No, Lord; for nothing common or
unclean has ever entered my mouth.' 9 But the
voice answered a second time from heaven,
'What God has cleansed you must not call common.' 10 This happened three times, and all was
drawn up again into heaven. 11 At that very moment three men arrived at the house in which we
were, sent to me from Caesarea. 12 And the Spirit
told me to go with them, making no distinction.
These six brethren also accompanied me, and

Jerusalem Bible

Jerusalem: Peter justifies his conduct

11 The apostles and the brothers in Judaea
heard that the pagans too had accepted
the word of God, 2 and when Peter came up to
Jerusalem the Jews criticized him 3 and said,
"So you have been visiting the uncircumcised
and eating with them, have you?" 4 Peter in reply gave them the details point by point: 5 "One
day, when I was in the town of Jaffa," he began, "I fell into a trance as I was praying and
had a vision of something like a big sheet being
let down from heaven by its four corners. This
sheet reached the ground quite close to me. 6 I
watched it intently and saw all sorts of animals
and wild beasts—everything possible that could
walk, crawl or fly. 7 Then I heard a voice that
said to me, 'Now, Peter; kill and eat!' 8 But I
answered: Certainly not, Lord; nothing profane
or unclean has ever crossed my lips. 9 And a
second time the voice spoke from heaven, 'What
God has made clean, you have no right to call
profane.' 10 This was repeated three times, before the whole of it was drawn up to heaven
again.
11 "Just at that moment, three men stopped
outside the house where we were staying; they
had been sent from Caesarea to fetch me, 12 and
the Spirit told me to have no hesitation about
going back with them. The six brothers here
came with me as well, and we entered the man's

New English Bible

11 News came to the apostles and the members of the church in Judaea that Gentiles too had accepted the word of God; and when Peter came up to Jerusalem those who were of Jewish birth raised the question with him. 'You have been visiting men who are uncircumcised,' they said, 'and sitting at table with them!' Peter began by laying before them the facts as they had happened.

'I was in the city of Joppa', he said, 'at prayer; and while in a trance I had a vision: a thing was coming down that looked like a great sheet of sail-cloth, slung by the four corners and lowered from the sky till it reached me. I looked intently to make out what was in it and I saw four-footed creatures of the earth, wild beasts, and things that crawl or fly. Then I heard a voice saying to me, "Up, Peter, kill and eat." But I said, "No, Lord, no: nothing profane or unclean has ever entered my mouth." A voice from heaven answered a second time, "It is not for you to call profane what God counts clean." This happened three times, and then they were all drawn up again into the sky. At that moment three men, who had been sent to me from Caesarea, arrived at the house where I was[a] staying; and the Spirit told me to go with them.[b] My six companions here came with me and we went into

[*a*] *Some witnesses read* we were. [*b*] *Some witnesses add* making no distinctions; *others add* without any misgiving, *as in 10. 20.*

King James Version

and we entered into the man's house: 13And he shewed us how he had seen an angel in his house, which stood and said unto him, Send men to Joppa, and call for Simon, whose surname is Peter; 14 Who shall tell thee words, whereby thou and all thy house shall be saved. 15And as I began to speak, the Holy Ghost fell on them, as on us at the beginning. 16 Then remembered I the word of the Lord, how that he said, John indeed baptized with water; but ye shall be baptized with the Holy Ghost. 17 Forasmuch then as God gave them the like gift as *he did* unto us, who believed on the Lord Jesus Christ, what was I, that I could withstand God? 18 When they heard these things, they held their peace, and glorified God, saying, Then hath God also to the Gentiles granted repentance unto life.

19 Now they which were scattered abroad upon the persecution that arose about Stephen travelled as far as Phenice, and Cyprus, and Antioch, preaching the word to none but unto

Living Bible

the man who had sent the messengers. 13 He told us how an angel had appeared to him and told him to send messengers to Joppa to find Simon Peter! 14 'He will tell you how you and all your household can be saved!' the angel had told him.

15 "Well, I began telling them the Good News, but just as I was getting started with my sermon, the Holy Spirit fell on them, just as he fell on us at the beginning! 16 Then I thought of the Lord's words when he said, 'Yes, John baptized with[b] water, but you shall be baptized with[b] the Holy Spirit.' 17And since it was *God* who gave these Gentiles the same gift he gave us when we believed on the Lord Jesus Christ, who was I to argue?"

18 When the others heard this, all their objections were answered and they began praising God! "Yes," they said, "God has given to the Gentiles, too, the privilege of turning to him and receiving eternal life!"

19 Meanwhile, the believers who fled from Jerusalem during the persecution after Stephen's death traveled as far as Phoenicia, Cyprus, and Antioch, scattering the Good News, but only to

[*b*] Or, "in."

Today's English Version

and we all went into the house of Cornelius. 13 He told us how he had seen an angel standing in his house who said to him, 'Send someone to Joppa to call for a man whose full name is Simon Peter. 14 He will speak words to you by which you and all your family will be saved.' 15And when I began to speak, the Holy Spirit came down on them just as on us at the beginning. 16 Then I remembered what the Lord had said, 'John baptized with water, but you will be baptized with the Holy Spirit.' 17 It is clear that God gave those Gentiles the same gift that he gave us when we believed in the Lord Jesus Christ; who was I, then, to try to stop God!"

18 When they heard this, they stopped their criticism and praised God, saying, "Then God has given to the Gentiles also the opportunity to repent and live!"

The church at Antioch

19 The believers were scattered by the persecution which took place when Stephen was killed. Some of them went as far as Phoenicia and Cyprus and Antioch, telling the message to Jews

New International Version

man's house. 13 He told us how he had seen an angel appear in his house and say, 'Send to Joppa for Simon who is called Peter. 14 He will bring you a message through which you and all your household will be saved.'

15 "Just as I was starting to speak, the Holy Spirit came on them as he had come on us at the beginning. 16 Then I remembered what the Lord had said, 'John baptized with water, but you will be baptized with the Holy Spirit.' 17 So if God gave them the same gift as he gave us when we believed in the Lord Jesus Christ, who was I to think that I could oppose God!"

18 When they heard this, they had no further objections and praised God, saying, "So then, God has even granted the Gentiles repentance unto life."

The church in Antioch

19 Now those who had been scattered by the persecution in connection with Stephen traveled as far as Phoenicia, Cyprus and Antioch, telling

Phillips Modern English

man's house. He told us how he had seen the angel standing in his house, saying, 'Send to Joppa and bring Simon, surnamed Peter. He will give you a message which will save both you and your whole household.' While I was beginning to tell them this message the Holy Spirit fell upon them just as on us at the beginning. There came into my mind the words of our Lord when he said, 'John indeed baptised with water, but you will be baptised with the Holy Spirit.' If then God gave to them exactly the same gift as he gave to us when we believed on the Lord Jesus Christ, who was I to try to hinder the working of God?"

11.18 The flexibility of the young Church

When they heard this they had no further objection to raise. And they praised God, saying,

"Then obviously God has given to the gentiles also the gift of repentance which leads to life."

11.19 Persecution has spread the gospel

Now those who had been dispersed by the persecution which arose over Stephen travelled as far as Phoenicia, Cyprus and Antioch, giving the message as they went to Jews only.

Revised Standard Version

we entered the man's house. 13 And he told us how he had seen the angel standing in his house and saying, 'Send to Joppa and bring Simon called Peter; 14 he will declare to you a message by which you will be saved, you and all your household.' 15 As I began to speak, the Holy Spirit fell on them just as on us at the beginning. 16 And I remembered the word of the Lord, how he said, 'John baptized with water, but you shall be baptized with the Holy Spirit.' 17 If then God gave the same gift to them as he gave to us when we believed in the Lord Jesus Christ, who was I that I could withstand God?" 18 When they heard this they were silenced. And they glorified God, saying, "Then to the Gentiles also God has granted repentance unto life."

19 Now those who were scattered because of the persecution that arose over Stephen traveled as far as Phoenicia and Cyprus and Antioch,

Jerusalem Bible

house. 13 He told us he had seen an angel standing in his house who said, 'Send to Jaffa and fetch Simon known as Peter; 14 he has a message for you that will save you and your entire household.'

15 "I had scarcely begun to speak when the Holy Spirit came down on them in the same way as it came on us at the beginning, 16 and I remembered that the Lord had said, 'John baptized with water, but you will be baptized with the Holy Spirit.' 17 I realized then that God was giving them the identical thing he gave to us when we believed in the Lord Jesus Christ; and who was I to stand in God's way?"

18 This account satisfied them, and they gave glory to God. "God," they said, "can evidently grant even the pagans the repentance that leads to life."

Foundation of the church of Antioch

19 Those who had escaped during the persecution that happened because of Stephen traveled as far as Phoenicia and Cyprus and Antioch,[b] but they usually proclaimed the message

[*b*] Antioch on the Orontes, capital of Syria.

New English Bible

the man's house. He told us how he had seen an angel standing in his house who said, "Send to Joppa for Simon also called Peter. He will speak words that will bring salvation to you and all your household." Hardly had I begun speaking, when the Holy Spirit came upon them, just as upon us at the beginning. Then I recalled what the Lord had said: "John baptized with water, but you will be baptized with the Holy Spirit." God gave them no less a gift than he gave us when we put our trust in the Lord Jesus Christ; then how could I possibly stand in God's way?'

When they heard this their doubts were silenced. They gave praise to God and said, 'This means that God has granted life-giving repentance to the Gentiles also.'

Meanwhile those who had been scattered after the persecution that arose over Stephen made their way to Phoenicia, Cyprus, and Antioch, bringing the message to Jews only and to no

King James Version

the Jews only. 20And some of them were men
of Cyprus and Cyrene, which, when they were
come to Antioch, spake unto the Grecians,
preaching the Lord Jesus. 21And the hand of the
Lord was with them: and a great number believed, and turned unto the Lord.
22 Then tidings of these things came unto the
ears of the church which was in Jerusalem: and
they sent forth Barnabas, that he should go as
far as Antioch. 23 Who, when he came, and had
seen the grace of God, was glad, and exhorted
them all, that with purpose of heart they would
cleave unto the Lord. 24 For he was a good man,
and full of the Holy Ghost and of faith: and
much people was added unto the Lord. 25 Then
departed Barnabas to Tarsus, for to seek Saul:
26And when he had found him, he brought him
unto Antioch. And it came to pass, that a whole
year they assembled themselves with the church,
and taught much people. And the disciples were
called Christians first in Antioch.
27 And in these days came prophets from
Jerusalem unto Antioch. 28And there stood up
one of them named Agabus, and signified by

Living Bible

Jews. 20 However, some of the believers who
went to Antioch from Cyprus and Cyrene also
gave their message about the Lord Jesus to some
Greeks. 21And the Lord honored this effort so
that large numbers of these Gentiles became believers.
22 When the church at Jerusalem heard what
had happened, they sent Barnabas to Antioch to
help the new converts. 23 When he arrived and
saw the wonderful things God was doing, he was
filled with excitement and joy, and encouraged
the believers to stay close to the Lord, whatever
the cost. 24 Barnabas was a kindly person, full
of the Holy Spirit and strong in faith. As a result large numbers of people were added to the
Lord.
25 Then Barnabas went on to Tarsus to hunt
for Paul. 26 When he found him, he brought
him back to Antioch; and both of them stayed
there for a full year, teaching the many new
converts. (It was there at Antioch that the believers were first called "Christians.")
27 During this time some prophets came down
from Jerusalem to Antioch, 28 and one of them,
named Agabus, stood up in one of the meetings

Today's English Version

only. 20 But some of the believers, men from
Cyprus and Cyrene, went to Antioch and proclaimed the message to Gentiles also, telling
them the Good News about the Lord Jesus.
21 The Lord's power was with them, and a great
number of people believed and turned to the
Lord.
22 The news about this reached the church in
Jerusalem, so they sent Barnabas to Antioch.
23 When he arrived and saw how God had
blessed the people, he was glad and urged them
all to be faithful and true to the Lord with all
their hearts. 24 Barnabas was a good man, full
of the Holy Spirit and faith. Many people were
brought to the Lord.
25 Then Barnabas went to Tarsus to look for
Saul. 26 When he found him, he brought him to
Antioch. For a whole year the two met with the
people of the church and taught a large group.
It was at Antioch that the disciples were first
called Christians.
27 About that time some prophets went down
from Jerusalem to Antioch. 28 One of them,
named Agabus, stood up and by the power of

New International Version

the message only to Jews. 20 Some of them,
however, men from Cyprus and Cyrene, went
to Antioch and began to speak to Greeks also,
telling them the good news about the Lord Jesus. 21 The Lord's hand was with them, and a
great number of people believed and turned to
the Lord.
22 News of this reached the ears of the
church at Jerusalem, and they sent Barnabas to
Antioch. 23 When he arrived and saw the evidence of the grace of God, he was glad and
encouraged them all to remain true to the Lord
with all their hearts. 24 He was a good man, full
of the Holy Spirit and faith, and a great number
of people were brought to the Lord.
25 Then Barnabas went to Tarsus to look for
Saul, 26 and when he found him, he brought
him to Antioch. So for a whole year Barnabas
and Saul met with the church and taught great
numbers of people. The disciples were first
called Christians at Antioch.
27 During this time some prophets came down
from Jerusalem to Antioch. 28 One of them,
named Agabus, stood up and through the Spirit

Phillips Modern English

However, among their number were natives of Cyprus and Cyrene, and these men, on their arrival at Antioch, proclaimed their message to the Greeks as well, telling them the good news of the Lord Jesus. The hand of the Lord was with them, and a great number believed and turned to the Lord. News of these things came to the ears of the Church in Jerusalem and they sent Barnabas to Antioch. When he arrived and saw this working of God's grace, he was delighted. He urged them all to be resolute in their faithfulness to the Lord, for he was a good man, full of the Holy Spirit and of faith. So it happened that a considerable number of people became followers of the Lord.

11.25 Believers are called "Christians" for the first time

Then Barnabas went to Tarsus to find Saul. When he found him he brought him to Antioch. Then for a whole year they met together with the Church and taught a large crowd. It was in Antioch that the disciples were first given the name of "Christians".

11.27 The young Church and famine relief

During this period some prophets came down from Jerusalem to Antioch. One of them by the name of Agabus stood up and foretold by the

Revised Standard Version

speaking the word to none except Jews. 20 But
there were some of them, men of Cyprus and
Cyrene, who on coming to Antioch spoke to the
Greeks[i] also, preaching the Lord Jesus. 21 And
the hand of the Lord was with them, and a
great number that believed turned to the Lord.
22 News of this came to the ears of the church
in Jerusalem, and they sent Barnabas to Antioch.
23 When he came and saw the grace of God,
he was glad; and he exhorted them all to remain
faithful to the Lord with steadfast purpose; 24 for
he was a good man, full of the Holy Spirit and
of faith. And a large company was added to the
Lord. 25 So Barnabas went to Tarsus to look for
Saul; 26 and when he had found him, he brought
him to Antioch. For a whole year they met with[j]
the church, and taught a large company of people; and in Antioch the disciples were for the
first time called Christians.
27 Now in these days prophets came down
from Jerusalem to Antioch. 28 And one of them
named Agabus stood up and foretold by the

[*i*] Other ancient authorities read *Hellenists*. [*j*] Or *were guests of*.

Jerusalem Bible

only to Jews. 20 Some of them, however, who
came from Cyprus and Cyrene, went to Antioch
where they started preaching to the Greeks,
proclaiming the Good News of the Lord Jesus
to them as well. 21 The Lord helped them, and
a great number believed and were converted to
the Lord.
22 The church in Jerusalem heard about this
and they sent Barnabas to Antioch. 23 There he
could see for himself that God had given grace,
and this pleased him, and he urged them all to
remain faithful to the Lord with heartfelt devotion; 24 for he was a good man, filled with the
Holy Spirit and with faith. And a large number
of people were won over to the Lord.
25 Barnabas then left for Tarsus to look for
Saul, 26 and when he found him he brought him
to Antioch. As things turned out they were to
live together in that church a whole year, instructing a large number of people. It was at
Antioch that the disciples were first called
"Christians."

Barnabas and Saul sent as deputies to Jerusalem

27 While they were there some prophets[c]
came down to Antioch from Jerusalem, 28 and
one of them whose name was Agabus, seized by

[*c*] Christian prophets, inspired speakers, generally ranked second to the apostles in the lists of the persons "gifted by the Spirit."

New English Bible

others. But there were some natives of Cyprus and Cyrene among them, and these, when they arrived at Antioch, began to speak to Gentiles as well, telling them the good news of the Lord Jesus. The power of the Lord was with them, and a great many became believers, and turned to the Lord.

The news reached the ears of the church in Jerusalem; and they sent Barnabas to Antioch. When he arrived and saw the divine grace at work, he rejoiced, and encouraged them all to hold fast to the Lord with resolute hearts; for he was a good man, full of the Holy Spirit and of faith. And large numbers were won over to the Lord.

He then went off to Tarsus to look for Saul; and when he had found him, he brought him to Antioch. For a whole year the two of them lived in fellowship with the congregation there, and gave instruction to large numbers. It was in Antioch that the disciples first got the name of Christians.

During this period some prophets came down from Jerusalem to Antioch. One of them, Agabus by name, was inspired to stand up and predict

King James Version

the Spirit that there should be great dearth throughout all the world: which came to pass in the days of Claudius Cesar. 29 Then the disciples, every man according to his ability, determined to send relief unto the brethren which dwelt in Judea: 30 Which also they did, and sent it to the elders by the hands of Barnabas and Saul.

12 Now about that time Herod the king stretched forth *his* hands to vex certain of the church. 2 And he killed James the brother of John with the sword. 3 And because he saw it pleased the Jews, he proceeded further to take Peter also. (Then were the days of unleavened bread.) 4 And when he had apprehended him, he put *him* in prison, and delivered *him* to four quaternions of soldiers to keep him; intending after Easter to bring him forth to the people. 5 Peter therefore was kept in prison: but prayer was made without ceasing of the church unto God for him. 6 And when Herod would have brought him forth, the same night Peter was sleeping between two soldiers, bound with two

Living Bible

to predict by the Spirit that a great famine was coming upon the land of Israel.[c] (This was fulfilled during the reign of Claudius.) 29 So the believers decided to send relief to the Christians in Judea, each giving as much as he could. 30 This they did, consigning their gifts to Barnabas and Paul to take to the elders of the church in Jerusalem.

12 About that time King Herod moved against some of the believers, 2 and killed the apostle[a] James (John's brother). 3 When Herod saw how much this pleased the Jewish leaders, he arrested Peter during the Passover celebration 4 and imprisoned him, placing him under the guard of sixteen soldiers. Herod's intention was to deliver Peter to the Jews for execution after the Passover. 5 But earnest prayer was going up to God from the Church for his safety all the time he was in prison.

6 The night before he was to be executed, he was asleep, double-chained between two soldiers

[*c*] Literally, "upon the earth." [*a*] Implied.

Today's English Version

the Spirit predicted that a great famine was about to come over all the earth. (It came when Claudius was Emperor.) 29 The disciples decided that each of them would send as much as he could to help their brothers who lived in Judea. 30 They did this, then, and sent the money to the church elders by Barnabas and Saul.

More persecution

12 About this time King Herod began to persecute some members of the church. 2 He had James, the brother of John, put to death by the sword. 3 When he saw that this pleased the Jews, he went ahead and had Peter arrested. (This happened during the time of the Feast of Unleavened Bread.) 4 After his arrest Peter was put in jail, where he was handed over to be guarded by four groups of four soldiers each. Herod planned to put him on trial in public after Passover. 5 So Peter was kept in jail, but the people of the church were praying earnestly to God for him.

Peter set free from prison

6 The night before Herod was going to bring him out to the people, Peter was sleeping between two guards. He was tied with two chains,

New International Version

predicted that a severe famine would spread over the entire Roman world. (This happened during the reign of Claudius.) 29 The disciples, each according to his ability, decided to provide help for the brothers living in Judea. 30 This they did, sending their gift to the elders by Barnabas and Saul.

Peter's miraculous escape from prison

12 It was about this time that King Herod arrested some who belonged to the church, intending to persecute them. 2 He had James, the brother of John, put to death with the sword. 3 When he saw that this pleased the Jews, he proceeded to seize Peter also. This happened during the Feast of Unleavened Bread. 4 After arresting him, he put him in prison, handing him over to be guarded by four squads of four soldiers each. Herod intended to bring him out for public trial after the Passover.

5 So Peter was kept in prison, but the church was earnestly praying to God for him.

6 The night before Herod was to bring him to trial, Peter was sleeping between two soldiers, bound with two chains, and sentries stood

Phillips Modern English

Spirit that there was to be a great famine throughout the world. (This actually happened in the days of Claudius.) The disciples determined to send relief to the brothers in Judaea, each contributing as he was able. This they did, sending their contribution to the elders there personally through Barnabas and Saul.

12.1 Herod kills James and imprisons Peter

It was at this time that King Herod made a violent attack on some of the Church members. James, John's brother, he executed with the sword, and when he found this action pleased the Jews he went on to arrest Peter as well. It was during the days of unleavened bread that he actually made the arrest. He put Peter in prison with no less than four squads of soldiers to guard him, intending to bring him out to the people after the Passover. So Peter was closely guarded in the prison, while the Church prayed to God earnestly on his behalf.

12.6 Peter's miraculous rescue

On the very night that Herod was planning to bring him out, Peter was asleep between two soldiers, secured by double chains, while guards

Revised Standard Version

Spirit that there would be a great famine over
all the world; and this took place in the days of
Claudius. 29And the disciples determined, every
one according to his ability, to send relief to the
brethren who lived in Judea; 30 and they did so,
sending it to the elders by the hand of Barnabas
and Saul.

12 About that time Herod the king laid violent hands upon some who belonged to
the church. 2 He killed James, the brother of
John with the sword; 3 and when he saw that
it pleased the Jews, he proceeded to arrest Peter
also. This was during the days of Unleavened
Bread. 4And when he had seized him, he put
him in prison, and delivered him to four squads
of soldiers to guard him, intending after the
Passover to bring him out to the people. 5 So
Peter was kept in prison; but earnest prayer for
him was made to God by the church.
6 The very night when Herod was about to
bring him out, Peter was sleeping between two
soldiers, bound with two chains, and sentries

Jerusalem Bible

the Spirit, stood up and predicted that a famine
would spread over the whole empire. This in
fact happened before the reign of Claudius came
to an end.[d] 29 The disciples decided to send relief, each to contribute what he could afford, to
the brothers living in Judaea. 30 They did this
and delivered their contributions to the elders
in the care of Barnabas and Saul.

Peter's arrest and miraculous deliverance[e]

12 It was about this time that King Herod started persecuting certain members of the
Church. 2 He beheaded James the brother of
John, 3 and when he saw that this pleased the
Jews he decided to arrest Peter as well. 4 This
was during the days of Unleavened Bread, and
he put Peter in prison, assigning four squads of
four soldiers each to guard him in turns. Herod
meant to try Peter in public after the end of
Passover week. 5All the time Peter was under
guard the Church prayed to God for him un-
remittingly.
6 On the night before Herod was to try him,
Peter was sleeping between two soldiers, fastened
with double chains, while guards kept watch at

[d] Claudius reigned until A.D. 54. [e] Herod Agrippa I was king of Judaea and Samaria, A.D. 41-44. This episode, though fitted in the book between 11:30 and 12:52, must have taken place before Barnabas and Saul visited Jerusalem.

New English Bible

a severe and world-wide famine, which in fact occurred in the reign of Claudius. So the disciples agreed to make a contribution, each according to his means, for the relief of their fellow-Christians in Judaea. This they did, and sent it off to the elders, in the charge of Barnabas and Saul.

12 It was about this time that King Herod attacked certain members of the church. He beheaded James, the brother of John, and then, when he saw that the Jews approved, proceeded to arrest Peter also. This happened during the festival of Unleavened Bread. Having secured him, he put him in prison under a military guard, four squads of four men each, meaning to produce him in public after Passover. So Peter was kept in prison under constant watch, while the church kept praying fervently for him to God.

On the very night before Herod had planned to bring him forward, Peter was asleep between two soldiers, secured by two chains, while out-

King James Version

chains: and the keepers before the door kept the prison. 7And, behold, the angel of the Lord came upon *him,* and a light shined in the prison: and he smote Peter on the side, and raised him up, saying, Arise up quickly. And his chains fell off from *his* hands. 8And the angel said unto him, Gird thyself, and bind on thy sandals: and so he did. And he saith unto him, Cast thy garment about thee, and follow me. 9And he went out, and followed him; and wist not that it was true which was done by the angel; but thought he saw a vision. 10 When they were past the first and the second ward, they came unto the iron gate that leadeth unto the city; which opened to them of his own accord: and they went out, and passed on through one street; and forthwith the angel departed from him 11And when Peter was come to himself, he said, Now I know of a surety, that the Lord hath sent his angel, and hath delivered me out of the hand of Herod, and *from* all the expectation of the people of the Jews. 12And when he had considered *the thing,* he came to the house of Mary the mother of John, whose surname was Mark; where many were gathered together praying. 13And as Peter knocked at the door of the gate, a damsel came to hearken, named Rhoda. 14And when she knew Peter's voice, she opened not the gate for gladness, but ran in, and told how Peter stood before the gate. 15And they said unto her, Thou art mad. But she constantly affirmed that it was even so. Then said they, It is his angel. 16 But Peter continued knocking: and when they had opened *the door,* and saw him, they were

Living Bible

with others standing guard before the prison gate, 7 when suddenly there was a light in the cell and an angel of the Lord stood beside Peter! The angel slapped him on the side to awaken him and said, "Quick! Get up!" And the chains fell off his wrists! 8 Then the angel told him, "Get dressed and put on your shoes." And he did. "Now put on your coat and follow me!" the angel ordered.

9 So Peter left the cell, following the angel. But all the time he thought it was a dream or vision, and didn't believe it was really happening. 10 They passed the first and second cell blocks and came to the iron gate to the street, and this opened to them of its own accord! So they passed through and walked along together for a block, and then the angel left him.

11 Peter finally realized what had happened! "It's really true!" he said to himself. "The Lord has sent his angel and saved me from Herod and from what the Jews were hoping to do to me!" 12After a little thought he went to the home of Mary, mother of John Mark, where many were gathered for a prayer meeting.

13 He knocked at the door in the gate, and a girl named Rhoda came to open it. 14 When she recognized Peter's voice, she was so overjoyed that she ran back inside to tell everyone that Peter was standing outside in the street. 15 They didn't believe her. "You're out of your mind," they said. When she insisted they decided, "It must be his angel. [They must have killed him.[b]]"

16 Meanwhile Peter continued knocking. When they finally went out and opened the door, their

[*b*] Implied.

Today's English Version

and there were guards on duty at the prison gate. 7 Suddenly an angel of the Lord stood there, and a light shone in the cell. The angel shook Peter by the shoulder, woke him up, and said, "Hurry! Get up!" At once the chains fell off Peter's hands. 8 Then the angel said, "Tighten your belt and tie on your sandals." Peter did so, and the angel said, "Put your cloak around you and come with me." 9 Peter followed him out of the prison. He did not know, however, if what the angel was doing was real; he thought he was seeing a vision. 10 They passed by the first guard station, and then the second, and came at last to the iron gate that opens into the city. The gate opened for them by itself, and they went out. They walked down a street, and suddenly the angel left Peter.

11 Then Peter realized what had happened to him, and said, "Now I know that it is really true! The Lord sent his angel, and he rescued me from Herod's power and from all the things the Jewish people expected to do."

12 Aware of his situation, he went to the home of Mary, the mother of John Mark. Many people had gathered there and were praying. 13 Peter knocked at the outside door, and a servant girl named Rhoda came to answer it. 14 She recognized Peter's voice and was so happy that she ran back in without opening the door, and announced that Peter was standing outside. 15 "You are crazy!" they told her. But she insisted that it was true. So they answered, "It is his angel."

16 Meanwhile, Peter kept on knocking. They opened the door at last and when they saw him

New International Version

guard at the entrance. 7 Suddenly an angel of the Lord appeared and a light shone in the cell. He struck Peter on the side and woke him up. "Quick, get up!" he said, and the chains fell off Peter's wrists.

8 Then the angel said to him, "Put on your clothes and sandals." And Peter did so. "Wrap your cloak around you and follow me," the angel told him. 9 Peter followed him out of the prison, but he had no idea that what the angel was doing was really happening; he thought he was seeing a vision. 10 They passed the first and second guards and came to the iron gate leading to the city. It opened for them by itself, and they went through it. When they had walked the length of one street, suddenly the angel left him.

11 Then Peter came to himself and said, "Now I know without a doubt that the Lord sent his angel and rescued me from Herod's clutches and from everything the Jewish people were anticipating."

12 When this had dawned on him, he went to the house of Mary the mother of John, also called Mark, where many people had gathered and were praying. 13 Peter knocked at the outer entrance, and a servant girl named Rhoda came to answer the door. 14 When she recognized Peter's voice, she was so overjoyed she ran back without opening it and exclaimed, "Peter is at the door!"

15 "You're out of your mind," they told her. When she kept insisting that it was so, they said, "It must be his angel."

16 But Peter kept on knocking, and when they opened the door and saw him, they were aston-

Phillips Modern English

maintained a strict watch at the doorway of the prison. Suddenly an angel of the Lord appeared, and light shone in the cell. He tapped Peter on the side and woke him up, saying, "Get up quickly." His chains fell away from his hands and the angel said to him, "Fasten your belt and put on your sandals." And he did so. Then the angel continued, "Wrap your cloak round you and follow me." So Peter followed him out, not knowing whether what the angel was doing were real—indeed he felt he must be seeing a vision. They passed right through the first and second guard-points and came to the iron gate that led out into the city. This opened for them of its own accord, and they went out and had passed along one street when the angel suddenly vanished from Peter's sight. Then Peter came to himself and said, "Now I know for certain that the Lord has sent his angel to rescue me from the power of Herod and from all that the Jewish people were expecting." As the truth broke upon him he went to the house of Mary, the mother of John surnamed Mark, where many were gathered together in prayer. As he knocked at the outer door a young maid called Rhoda came to answer it, but on recognising Peter's voice failed to open the door from sheer joy. Instead she ran inside and reported that Peter was standing outside. At this they said to her,

"You must be mad!"

But she insisted that it was true. Then they said,

"Then it is his angel."

But Peter continued to stand there knocking on the door, and when they opened it they saw

Revised Standard Version

before the door were guarding the prison; 7 and
behold, an angel of the Lord appeared, and a
light shone in the cell; and he struck Peter on
the side and woke him, saying, "Get up quickly."
And the chains fell off his hands. 8 And the angel
said to him, "Dress yourself and put on your
sandals." And he did so. And he said to him,
"Wrap your mantle around you and follow me."
9 And he went out and followed him; he did not
know that what was done by the angel was real,
but thought he was seeing a vision. 10 When they
had passed the first and the second guard, they
came to the iron gate leading into the city. It
opened to them of its own accord, and they
went out and passed on through one street; and
immediately the angel left him. 11 And Peter
came to himself, and said, "Now I am sure that
the Lord has sent his angel and rescued me from
the hand of Herod and from all that the Jewish
people were expecting."

12 When he realized this, he went to the house
of Mary, the mother of John whose other name
was Mark, where many were gathered together
and were praying. 13 And when he knocked at the
door of the gateway, a maid named Rhoda came
to answer. 14 Recognizing Peter's voice, in her
joy she did not open the gate but ran in and
told that Peter was standing at the gate. 15 They
said to her, "You are mad." But she insisted
that it was so. They said, "It is his angel!" 16 But
Peter continued knocking; and when they

Jerusalem Bible

the main entrance to the prison. 7 Then suddenly
the angel of the Lord stood there, and the cell
was filled with light. He tapped Peter on the
side and woke him. "Get up!" he said, "Hurry!"
—and the chains fell from his hands. 8 The
angel then said, "Put on your belt and sandals."
After he had done this, the angel next said,
"Wrap your cloak around you and follow me."
9 Peter followed him, but had no idea that what
the angel did was all happening in reality; he
thought he was seeing a vision. 10 They passed
through two guard posts one after the other,
and reached the iron gate leading to the city.
This opened of its own accord; they went
through it and had walked the whole length of
one street when suddenly the angel left him.
11 It was only then that Peter came to himself.
"Now I know it is all true," he said. "The
Lord really did send his angel and has saved
me from Herod and from all that the Jewish
people were so certain would happen to me."

12 As soon as he realized this he went straight
to the house of Mary the mother of John Mark,[f]
where a number of people had assembled and
were praying. 13 He knocked at the outside door
and a servant called Rhoda came to answer it.
14 She recognized Peter's voice and was so
overcome with joy that, instead of opening the
door, she ran inside with the news that Peter
was standing at the main entrance. 15 They said
to her, "You are out of your mind," but she
insisted that it was true. Then they said, "It
must be his angel!" 16 Peter, meanwhile, was
still knocking, so they opened the door and were

[f] Mark is mentioned in ch. 12, 13 and 15: also in Col. 4 and Phm. 24 and 2 Tim. 4. Tradition names him as author of the second gospel.

New English Bible

side the doors sentries kept guard over the prison. All at once an angel of the Lord stood there, and the cell was ablaze with light. He tapped Peter on the shoulder and woke him. 'Quick! Get up', he said, and the chains fell away from his wrists. The angel then said to him, 'Do up your belt and put your sandals on.' He did so. 'Now wrap your cloak round you and follow me.' He followed him out, with no idea that the angel's intervention was real: he thought it was just a vision. But they passed the first guard-post, then the second, and reached the iron gate leading out into the city, which opened for them of its own accord. And so they came out and walked the length of one street; and the angel left him.

Then Peter came to himself. 'Now I know it is true,' he said; 'the Lord has sent his angel and rescued me from Herod's clutches and from all that the Jewish people were expecting.' When he realized how things stood, he made for the house of Mary, the mother of John Mark, where a large company was at prayer. He knocked at the outer door and a maid called Rhoda came to answer it. She recognized Peter's voice and was so overjoyed that instead of opening the door she ran in and announced that Peter was standing outside. 'You are crazy', they told her; but she insisted that it was so. Then they said, 'It must be his guardian angel.'

Meanwhile Peter went on knocking, and when they opened the door and saw him, they were

King James Version

astonished. 17 But he, beckoning unto them with
the hand to hold their peace, declared unto them
how the Lord had brought him out of the prison.
And he said, Go shew these things unto James,
and to the brethren. And he departed, and went
into another place. 18 Now as soon as it was
day, there was no small stir among the soldiers,
what was become of Peter. 19 And when Herod
had sought for him, and found him not, he examined the keepers, and commanded that *they*
should be put to death. And he went down from
Judea to Cesarea, and *there* abode.
20 And Herod was highly displeased with
them of Tyre and Sidon: but they came with one
accord to him, and, having made Blastus the
king's chamberlain their friend, desired peace;
because their country was nourished by the
king's *country*. 21 And upon a set day Herod, arrayed in royal apparel, sat upon his throne, and
made an oration unto them. 22 And the people
gave a shout, *saying, It is* the voice of a god,
and not of a man. 23 And immediately the angel
of the Lord smote him, because he gave not

Living Bible

surprise knew no bounds. 17 He motioned for
them to quiet down and told them what had
happened and how the Lord had brought him
out of jail. "Tell James and the others what happened," he said—and left for safer quarters.
18 At dawn, the jail was in great commotion.
What had happened to Peter? 19 When Herod
sent for him and found that he wasn't there, he
had the sixteen guards arrested, court-martialed
and sentenced to death.[b] Afterwards he left to
live in Caesarea for a while.
20 While he was in Caesarea, a delegation
from Tyre and Sidon arrived to see him. He was
highly displeased with the people of those two
cities, but the delegates made friends with Blastus, the royal secretary, and asked for peace,
for their cities were economically dependent upon
trade with Herod's country. 21 An appointment
with Herod was granted, and when the day arrived he put on his royal robes, sat on his throne
and made a speech to them. 22 At its conclusion
the people gave him a great ovation, shouting,
"It is the voice of a god and not of a man!"
23 Instantly, an angel of the Lord struck
Herod with a sickness so that he was filled with
maggots and died—because he accepted the peo-

[b] Implied.

Today's English Version

they were amazed. 17 He motioned with his hand
for them to be quiet, and explained to them how
the Lord had brought him out of prison. "Tell
this to James and the rest of the brothers," he
said; then he left and went somewhere else.
18 When morning came, there was a tremendous confusion among the guards; what had
happened to Peter? 19 Herod gave orders to
search for him, but they could not find him. So
he had the guards questioned and ordered them
to be put to death.
After this Herod went down from Judea and
spent some time in Caesarea.

The death of Herod

20 Herod was very angry with the people of
Tyre and Sidon; so they went in a group to see
Herod. First they won Blastus over to their
side; he was in charge of the palace. Then they
went to Herod and asked him for peace, because
their country got its food supplies from the king's
country.
21 On a chosen day Herod put on his royal
robes, sat on his throne, and made a speech to
the people. 22 "It isn't a man speaking, but a
god!" they shouted. 23 At once the angel of the
Lord struck Herod down, because he did not

New International Version

ished. 17 Peter motioned for them to be quiet
and described how the Lord had brought him
out of prison. "Tell James and the brothers
about this," he said, and then he left for another
place.
18 In the morning, there was a great commotion among the soldiers. "What could have
happened to Peter?" they asked. 19 After Herod
had a thorough search made for him and did
not find him, he cross-examined the guards and
ordered that they be executed.

Herod's death

Then Herod went from Judea to Caesarea and
stayed there a while. 20 He had been quarreling
with the people of Tyre and Sidon; they now
joined together and sought an audience with
him. Having secured the support of Blastus, a
trusted personal servant of the king, they asked
for peace, because they depended on the king's
country for their food supply.
21 On the appointed day Herod, wearing his
royal robes, sat on his throne and delivered a
public address to the people. 22 They shouted,
"This is the voice of a god, not of a man."
23 Immediately, because Herod did not give
praise to God, an angel of the Lord struck him

Phillips Modern English

him and were simply amazed. Peter, however, made a gesture to them to stop talking while he explained to them how the Lord had brought him out of prison. Then he said,

"Go and tell James and the other brothers what has happened."

After this he left the house and went on to another place.

12.18 Peter's escape infuriates Herod

But when morning came there was a great commotion among the soldiers as to what could have happened to Peter. When Herod had had a search put out for him without success, he cross-examined the guards and then ordered their execution. Then he left Judaea and went down to Caesarea and stayed there.

12.20 But Herod dies a terrible death

Now Herod was very angry with the people of Tyre and Sidon. They approached him in a body and after winning over Blastus the king's chamberlain, they begged him for peace, for their country's food supply was dependent on the king's lands. So on an appointed day Herod put on his royal robes, took his seat on the public throne and made a speech to them. At this the people kept shouting. "This is a god speaking, not a mere man!" Immediately an angel of the Lord struck him down because he did not give

Revised Standard Version

opened, they saw him and were amazed. 17 But
motioning to them with his hand to be silent, he
described to them how the Lord had brought
him out of the prison. And he said, "Tell this to
James and to the brethren." Then he departed
and went to another place.
18 Now when day came, there was no small
stir among the soldiers over what had become of
Peter. 19 And when Herod had sought for him
and could not find him, he examined the sentries
and ordered that they should be put to death.
Then he went down from Judea to Caesarea, and
remained there.
20 Now Herod was angry with the people of
Tyre and Sidon; and they came to him in a body,
and having persuaded Blastus, the king's chamberlain, they asked for peace, because their
country depended on the king's country for food.
21 On an appointed day Herod put on his royal
robes, took his seat upon the throne, and made
an oration to them. 22 And the people shouted,
"The voice of a god, and not of man!" 23 Immediately an angel of the Lord smote him, be-

Jerusalem Bible

amazed to see that it really was Peter himself.
17 With a gesture of his hand he stopped them
talking, and described to them how the Lord
had led him out of prison. He added, "Tell
James and the brothers." Then he left and went
to another place.
18 When daylight came there was a great
commotion among the soldiers, who could not
imagine what had become of Peter. 19 Herod
put out an unsuccessful search for him; he had
the guards questioned, and before leaving Judaea
to take up residence in Caesarea he gave orders
for their execution.

The death of the persecutor

20 Now Herod was on bad terms with the
Tyrians and Sidonians. However, they sent a
joint deputation which managed to enlist the
support of Blastus, the king's chamberlain, and
through him negotiated a treaty, since their
country depended for its food supply on King
Herod's territory. 21 A day was fixed, and Herod,
wearing his robes of state and enthroned on a
dais, made a speech to them. 22 The people acclaimed him with, "It is a god speaking, not a
man!", 23 and at that moment the angel of the
Lord struck him down, because he had not given

New English Bible

astounded. With a movement of the hand he signed to them to keep quiet, and told them how the Lord had brought him out of prison. 'Report this to James and the members of the church', he said. Then he left the house and went off elsewhere.

When morning came, there was consternation among the soldiers: what could have become of Peter? Herod made close search, but failed to find him, so he interrogated the guards and ordered their execution.

Afterwards he left Judaea to reside for a time at Caesarea. He had for some time been furiously angry with the people of Tyre and Sidon, who now by common agreement presented themselves at his court. There they won over Blastus the royal chamberlain, and sued for peace, because their country drew its supplies from the king's territory. So, on an appointed day, attired in his royal robes and seated on the rostrum, Herod harangued them; and the populace shouted back, 'It is a god speaking, not a man!' Instantly an angel of the Lord struck him down, because he had usurped the honour due to God;

King James Version

God the glory: and he was eaten of worms, and
gave up the ghost.
24 But the word of God grew and multiplied.
25And Barnabas and Saul returned from Jerusalem, when they had fulfilled *their* ministry,
and took with them John, whose surname was
Mark.

13 Now there were in the church that was at
Antioch certain prophets and teachers; as
Barnabas, and Simeon that was called Niger, and
Lucius of Cyrene, and Manaen, which had been
brought up with Herod the tetrarch, and Saul.
2As they ministered to the Lord, and fasted, the
Holy Ghost said, Separate me Barnabas and
Saul for the work whereunto I have called them.
3And when they had fasted and prayed, and

Living Bible

ple's worship instead of giving the glory to God.
24 God's Good News was spreading rapidly
and there were many new believers.
25 Barnabas and Paul now visited Jerusalem
and, as soon as they had finished their business,
returned to Antioch,[b] taking John Mark with
them.

13 Among the prophets and teachers of the
church at Antioch were Barnabas and
Symeon (also called "The Black Man"), Lucius
(from Cyrene), Manaen (the foster-brother of
King Herod), and Paul. 2 One day as these men
were worshiping and fasting the Holy Spirit said,
"Dedicate Barnabas and Paul for a special job I
have for them." 3 So after more fasting and

[*b*] Implied.

Today's English Version

give honor to God. He was eaten by worms and
died.
24 The word of God continued to spread and
grow.
25 Barnabas and Saul finished their mission
and returned from Jerusalem, taking John Mark
with them.

Barnabas and Saul chosen and sent

13 In the church at Antioch there were some
prophets and teachers: Barnabas, Simeon
(called the Black), Lucius (from Cyrene),
Manaen (who had been brought up with Governor Herod), and Saul. 2 While they were serving the Lord and fasting, the Holy Spirit said
to them, "Set apart for me Barnabas and Saul,
to do the work to which I have called them."
3 They fasted and prayed, placed their hands

New International Version

down, and he was eaten by worms and died.
24 But the word of God continued to increase and spread.
25 When Barnabas and Saul had finished
their mission, they returned from Jerusalem,[m]
taking with them John, also called Mark.

Barnabas and Saul sent off

13 In the church at Antioch there were
prophets and teachers: Barnabas, Simeon
called Niger, Lucius of Cyrene, Manaen (who
had been brought up with Herod the tetrarch)
and Saul. 2 While they were worshiping the Lord
and fasting, the Holy Spirit said, "Set apart for
me Barnabas and Saul for the work to which I
have called them." 3 So after they had fasted

[*m*] Some MSS read *to Jerusalem.*

Phillips Modern English

God the glory. And he was eaten by worms and died.

12.24 The message continues to spread

But the Word of the Lord continued to gain ground and increase its influence. Barnabas and Saul returned from Jerusalem when they had completed their mission there, bringing with them to Antioch John whose surname was Mark.

13.1 Saul and Barnabas are called to a special task

Now there were in the church at Antioch both prophets and teachers—Barnabas, Simeon surnamed Niger, Lucius the Cyrenian, Manaen the foster-brother of the governor Herod, and Saul. While they were worshipping the Lord and fasting, the Holy Spirit spoke to them, saying,

"Set Barnabas and Saul apart for me for a task to which I have called them."

At this, after further fasting and prayer, they

Revised Standard Version

cause he did not give God the glory; and he was eaten by worms and died.

24 But the word of God grew and multiplied.

25 And Barnabas and Saul returned from[k] Jerusalem when they had fulfilled their mission, bringing with them John whose other name was Mark.

13 Now in the church at Antioch there were prophets, and teachers, Barnabas, Simeon who was called Niger, Lucius of Cyrene, Manaen a member of the court of Herod the tetrarch, and Saul. 2 While they were worshiping the Lord and fasting, the Holy Spirit said, "Set apart for me Barnabas and Saul for the work to which I have called them." 3 Then after fasting and

[k] Other ancient authorities read *to*.

Jerusalem Bible

the glory to God. He was eaten away with worms and died.

Barnabas and Saul return to Antioch

24 The word of God continued to spread and to gain followers. 25 Barnabas and Saul completed their task and came back from Jerusalem, bringing John Mark with them.

III. The mission of Barnabas and Paul

The Council of Jerusalem

The mission sent out

13 In the church at Antioch the following were prophets and teachers: Barnabas, Simeon called Niger, and Lucius of Cyrene, Manaen, who had been brought up with Herod the tetrarch, and Saul. 2 One day while they were offering worship to the Lord and keeping a fast, the Holy Spirit said, "I want Barnabas and Saul set apart for the work to which I have called them." 3 So it was that after fasting

New English Bible

he was eaten up with worms and died.

Meanwhile the word of God continued to grow and spread.

Barnabas and Saul, their task fulfilled, returned from Jerusalem,[a] taking John Mark with them.

The church breaks barriers

13 There were at Antioch, in the congregation there, certain prophets and teachers: Barnabas, Simeon called Niger, Lucius of Cyrene, Manaen, who had been at the court of Prince Herod, and Saul. While they were keeping a fast

[a] *Some witnesses read* their task fulfilled, returned to Jerusalem; *or, as it might be rendered,* their task at Jerusalem fulfilled, returned.

King James Version

laid *their* hands on them, they sent *them* away.
4 So they, being sent forth by the Holy Ghost,
departed unto Seleucia; and from thence they
sailed to Cyprus. 5And when they were at
Salamis, they preached the word of God in the
synagogues of the Jews: and they had also John
to *their* minister. 6And when they had gone
through the isle unto Paphos, they found a certain sorcerer, a false prophet, a Jew, whose name
was Bar-jesus: 7 Which was with the deputy of
the country, Sergius Paulus, a prudent man;
who called for Barnabas and Saul, and desired
to hear the word of God. 8 But Elymas the
sorcerer (for so is his name by interpretation)
withstood them, seeking to turn away the deputy
from the faith. 9 Then Saul, (who also *is called*
Paul,) filled with the Holy Ghost, set his eyes on
him, 10And said, O full of all subtilty and all
mischief, *thou* child of the devil, *thou* enemy of
all righteousness, wilt thou not cease to pervert
the right ways of the Lord? 11And now, behold,
the hand of the Lord *is* upon thee, and thou
shalt be blind, not seeing the sun for a season.
And immediately there fell on him a mist and
a darkness; and he went about seeking some to
lead him by the hand. 12 Then the deputy, when
he saw what was done, believed, being astonished

Living Bible

prayer, the men laid their hands on them—and
sent them on their way.
4 Directed by the Holy Spirit they went to
Seleucia and then sailed for Cyprus. 5 There, in
the town of Salamis, they went to the Jewish
synagogue and preached. (John Mark went with
them as their assistant.)
6, 7 Afterwards they preached from town to
town across the entire island until finally they
reached Paphos where they met a Jewish sorcerer, a fake prophet named Bar-Jesus. He had
attached himself to the governor, Sergius Paulus,
a man of considerable insight and understanding.
The governor invited Barnabas and Paul to visit
him, for he wanted to hear their message from
God. 8 But the sorcerer, Elymas (his name in
Greek), interfered and urged the governor to
pay no attention to what Paul and Barnabas
said, trying to keep him from trusting the Lord.
9 Then Paul, filled with the Holy Spirit, glared
angrily at the sorcerer and said, 10 "You son of
the devil, full of every sort of trickery and villainy, enemy of all that is good, will you never
end your opposition to the Lord? 11And now
God has laid his hand of punishment upon you,
and you will be stricken awhile with blindness."
Instantly mist and darkness fell upon him, and
he began wandering around begging for someone
to take his hand and lead him. 12 When the
governor saw what happened he believed and

Today's English Version

on them, and sent them off.

In Cyprus

4 Barnabas and Saul, then, having been sent
by the Holy Spirit, went down to Seleucia and
sailed from there to the island of Cyprus. 5 When
they arrived at Salamis, they preached the word
of God in the Jewish synagogues. They had John
Mark with them to help in the work.
6 They went all the way across the island to
Paphos, where they met a certain magician
named Bar-Jesus, a Jew who claimed to be a
prophet. 7 He was a friend of the Governor of
the island, Sergius Paulus, who was an intelligent man. The Governor called Barnabas and
Saul before him because he wanted to hear the
word of God. 8 But they were opposed by the
magician Elymas (this is his name in Greek); he
tried to turn the Governor away from the faith.
9 Then Saul—also known as Paul—was filled
with the Holy Spirit; he looked straight at the
magician 10 and said, "You son of the Devil!
You are the enemy of everything that is good;
you are full of all kinds of evil tricks, and you
always keep trying to turn the Lord's truths into
lies! 11 The Lord's hand will come down on you
now; you will be blind, and will not see the light
of day for a time."
At once Elymas felt a black mist cover his
eyes, and he walked around trying to find someone to lead him by the hand. 12 The Governor
believed when he saw what had happened; he

New International Version

and prayed, they placed their hands on them and
sent them off.

On Cyprus

4 The two of them, sent on their way by the
Holy Spirit, went down to Seleucia and sailed
from there to Cyprus. 5 When they arrived at
Salamis, they proclaimed the word of God in
the Jewish synagogues. John was with them as
their helper.
6 They traveled through the whole island until they came to Paphos. There they met a Jewish sorcerer and false prophet named Bar-Jesus,
7 who was an attendant of the proconsul, Sergius
Paulus. The proconsul, an intelligent man, sent
for Barnabas and Saul because he wanted to
hear the word of God. 8 But Elymas the sorcerer
(for that is what his name means) opposed them
and tried to turn the proconsul from the faith.
9 Then Saul, who was also called Paul, filled
with the Holy Spirit, looked straight at Elymas
and said, 10 "You are a child of the devil and
an enemy of everything that is right! You are
full of all kinds of deceit and trickery. Will you
never stop perverting the right ways of the Lord?
11 Now the hand of the Lord is against you. You
are going to be blind, and for a time you will be
unable to see the light of the sun."
Immediately mist and darkness came over him,
and he groped about, seeking someone to lead
him by the hand. 12 When the proconsul saw

Phillips Modern English

laid their hands on them and set them free for this work. So these two, sent out at the Holy Spirit's command, went down to Seleucia and from there they sailed off to Cyprus. On their arrival at Salamis they began to proclaim God's message in the Jewish synagogues, having John as their assistant. As they made their way through the island as far as Paphos they came across a man named Bar-Jesus, a Jew who was both a false prophet and a magician. This man was attached to Sergius Paulus, the proconsul, who was himself a man of intelligence. He had sent for Barnabas and Saul as he was anxious to hear God's message. But Elymas the magician (for that is the translation of his name) opposed them, doing his best to dissuade the proconsul from accepting the faith. Then Saul (who is also called Paul), filled with the Holy Spirit, eyed him closely and said,

"You son of the devil, you enemy of all true goodness, you monster of trickery and evil, is it not high time you gave up trying to pervert the truth of the Lord? Now listen, the Lord himself will touch you, for some time you will not see the light of the sun—you will be blind!"

Immediately a mist and then an utter blackness came over his eyes, and he went round trying to find someone to lead him by the hand. When the proconsul saw what had happened he

Revised Standard Version

praying they laid their hands on them and sent
them off.
4 So, being sent out by the Holy Spirit, they
went down to Seleucia; and from there they
sailed to Cyprus. 5 When they arrived at Salamis,
they proclaimed the word of God in the synagogues of the Jews. And they had John to assist
them. 6 When they had gone through the whole
island as far as Paphos, they came upon a certain
magician, a Jewish false prophet, named Bar-
Jesus. 7 He was with the proconsul, Sergius
Paulus, a man of intelligence, who summoned
Barnabas and Saul and sought to hear the word
of God. 8 But Elymas the magician (for that is
the meaning of his name) withstood them, seeking to turn away the proconsul from the faith.
9 But Saul, who is also called Paul, filled with the
Holy Spirit, looked intently at him 10 and said,
"You son of the devil, you enemy of all righteousness, full of all deceit and villainy, will you
not stop making crooked the straight paths of
the Lord? 11 And now, behold, the hand of the
Lord is upon you, and you shall be blind and
unable to see the sun for a time." Immediately
mist and darkness fell upon him and he went
about seeking people to lead him by the hand.
12 Then the proconsul believed, when he saw

Jerusalem Bible

and prayer they laid their hands on them and sent them off.

Cyprus: the magician Elymas

4 So these two, sent on their mission by the
Holy Spirit, went down to Seleucia and from
there sailed to Cyprus. 5 They landed at Salamis
and proclaimed the word of God in the synagogues of the Jews; John acted as their assistant.
6 They traveled the whole length of the island, and at Paphos they came in contact with
a Jewish magician called Barjesus. 7 This false
prophet was one of the attendants of the proconsul Sergius Paulus who was an extremely
intelligent man. The proconsul summoned Barnabas and Saul and asked to hear the word of
God, 8 but Elymas Magos—as he was called
in Greek—tried to stop them so as to prevent
the proconsul's conversion to the faith. 9 Then
Saul, whose other name is Paul, looked him
full in the face 10 and said, "You utter fraud,
you impostor, you son of the devil, you enemy
of all true religion, why don't you stop twisting
the straightforward ways of the Lord? 11 Now
watch how the hand of the Lord will strike
you: you will be blind, and for a time you will
not see the sun." That instant, everything went
misty and dark for him, and he groped about
to find someone to lead him by the hand. 12 The
proconsul, who had watched everything, became

New English Bible

and offering worship to the Lord, the Holy Spirit said, 'Set Barnabas and Saul apart for me, to do the work to which I have called them.' Then, after further fasting and prayer, they laid their hands on them and let them go.

So these two, sent out on their mission by the Holy Spirit, came down to Seleucia, and from there sailed to Cyprus. Arriving at Salamis, they declared the word of God in the Jewish synagogues. They had John with them as their assistant. They went through the whole island as far as Paphos, and there they came upon a sorcerer, a Jew who posed as a prophet, Bar-Jesus by name. He was in the retinue of the Governor, Sergius Paulus, an intelligent man, who had sent for Barnabas and Saul and wanted to hear the word of God. This Elymas the sorcerer (so his name may be translated) opposed them, trying to turn the Governor away from the Faith. But Saul, also known as Paul, filled with the Holy Spirit, fixed his eyes on him and said, 'You swindler, you rascal, son of the devil and enemy of all goodness, will you never stop falsifying the straight ways of the Lord? Look now, the hand of the Lord strikes: you shall be blind, and for a time you shall not see the sunlight.' Instantly mist and darkness came over him and he groped about for someone to lead him by the hand. When the Governor saw what had happened he became a believer, deeply

King James Version

at the doctrine of the Lord. 13 Now when Paul
and his company loosed from Paphos, they came
to Perga in Pamphylia: and John departing from
them returned to Jerusalem.
14 But when they departed from Perga, they
came to Antioch in Pisidia, and went into the
synagogue on the sabbath day, and sat down.
15And after the reading of the law and the
prophets, the rulers of the synagogue sent unto
them, saying, *Ye* men *and* brethren, if ye have
any word of exhortation for the people, say on.
16 Then Paul stood up, and beckoning with *his*
hand said, Men of Israel, and ye that fear God,
give audience. 17 The God of this people of
Israel chose our fathers, and exalted the people
when they dwelt as strangers in the land of
Egypt, and with a high arm brought he them out
of it. 18And about the time of forty years suffered he their manners in the wilderness. 19And
when he had destroyed seven nations in the land
of Chanaan, he divided their land to them by lot.

Living Bible

was astonished at the power of God's message.
13 Now Paul and those with him left Paphos
by ship for Turkey,[a] landing at the port town of
Perga. There John deserted [b] them and returned
to Jerusalem. 14 But Barnabas and Paul went
on to Antioch, a city in the province of Pisidia.
On the Sabbath they went into the synagogue
for the services. 15After the usual readings from
the Books of Moses and from the Prophets, those
in charge of the service sent them this message:
"Brothers, if you have any word of instruction
for us come and give it!"
16 So Paul stood, waved a greeting to them[c]
and began. "Men of Israel," he said, "and all
others here who reverence God, [let me begin
my remarks with a bit of history[d]].
17 "The God of this nation Israel chose our
ancestors and honored them in Egypt by glori-
ously leading them out of their slavery. 18And
he nursed them through forty years of wandering around in the wilderness. 19, 20 Then he destroyed seven nations in Canaan, and gave Israel

[*a*] Literally, "Pamphylia." [*b*] Literally, "departed from them." See chapter 15, verse 38. [*c*] Literally, "beckoning with the hand." [*d*] Implied.

Today's English Version

was greatly amazed at the teaching about the
Lord.

In Antioch of Pisidia

13 Paul and his companions sailed from
Paphos and came to Perga, in Pamphylia; but
John Mark left them there and went back to
Jerusalem. 14 They went on from Perga and came
to Antioch of Pisidia; and on the Sabbath day
they went into the synagogue and sat down.
15After the reading from the Law of Moses and
the writings of the prophets, the officials of the
synagogue sent them a message: "Brothers, we
want you to speak to the people if you have a
message of encouragement for them." 16 Paul
stood up, motioned with his hand, and began to
speak:
"Fellow Israelites and all Gentiles here who
worship God: hear me! 17 The God of this people of Israel chose our ancestors, and made the
people a great nation during the time they lived
as foreigners in the land of Egypt. God brought
them out of Egypt by his great power, 18 and
for forty years he endured them in the desert.
19 He destroyed seven nations in the land of
Canaan and made his people the owners of the

New International Version

what had happened, he believed, for he was
amazed at the teaching about the Lord.

In Pisidian Antioch

13 From Paphos, Paul and his companions
sailed to Perga in Pamphylia, where John left
them to return to Jerusalem. 14 From Perga they
went on to Pisidian Antioch. On the Sabbath
they entered the synagogue and sat down.
15After the reading from the Law and the
Prophets, the synagogue rulers sent word to
them, saying, "Brothers, if you have a message
of encouragement for the people, please speak."
16 Standing up, Paul motioned with his hand
and said: "Men of Israel and you Gentiles who
worship God, listen to me! 17 The God of the
people of Israel chose our fathers and made the
people prosper during their stay in Egypt. With
mighty power he led them out of that country
18 and endured their conduct[n] forty years in the
desert. 19 He overthrew seven nations in Canaan
and gave their land to his people as their in-

[*n*] Some MSS read ***and cared for them.***

Phillips Modern English

believed, for he was shaken to the core at the Lord's teaching.

13.13 Saul (now Paul) comes to Antioch in Pisidia

Then Paul and his companions set sail from Paphos and went to Perga in Pamphylia. There John left them and turned back to Jerusalem, but they continued their journey through Perga and arrived at Antioch in Pisidia. They went to the synagogue on the Sabbath day and took their seats. After the reading of the Law and Prophets, the leaders of the synagogue sent to them with a message,

"Men and brothers, if you have any message of encouragement for the people, by all means speak."

13.16 Paul shows the Jews where their history leads

So Paul stood up, and motioning with his hand, began:

"Men of Israel and all of you who fear God, listen to me. The God of this people Israel chose our fathers and made them into a great people while they were exiles in the land of Egypt. Then he lifted up his arm and led them out of that land. Yes, and he sustained them for some forty years in the desert. He destroyed seven nations in the land of Canaan before he gave them that

Revised Standard Version

what had occurred, for he was astonished at the teaching of the Lord.
13 Now Paul and his company set sail from
Paphos, and came to Perga in Pamphylia. And
John left them and returned to Jerusalem; 14 but
they passed on from Perga and came to Antioch
of Pisidia. And on the sabbath day they went
into the synagogue and sat down. 15After the
reading of the law and the prophets, the rulers
of the synagogue sent to them, saying, "Brethren,
if you have any word of exhortation for the
people, say it." 16 So Paul stood up, and motioning with his hand said:
"Men of Israel, and you that fear God, listen.
17 The God of this people Israel chose our fathers and made the people great during their
stay in the land of Egypt, and with uplifted arm
he led them out of it. 18And for about forty
years he bore with[m] them in the wilderness.
19And when he had destroyed seven nations in
the land of Canaan, he gave them their land as

[*m*] Other ancient authorities read *cared for* (Deut 1.31).

Jerusalem Bible

a believer, being astonished by what he had learned about the Lord.

They arrive at Antioch in Pisidia

13 Paul and his friends went by sea from
Paphos to Perga in Pamphylia where John left
them to go back to Jerusalem. 14 The others
carried on from Perga till they reached Antioch
in Pisidia. Here they went to synagogue on the
sabbath and took their seats. 15After the lessons from the Law and the Prophets had been
read, the presidents of the synagogue sent them
a message: "Brothers, if you would like to address some words of encouragement to the congregation, please do so." 16 Paul stood up, held
up a hand for silence and began to speak:

Paul's preaching before the Jews

"Men of Israel, and fearers of God, listen!
17 The God of our nation Israel chose our ancestors, and made our people great when they
were living as foreigners in Egypt; then by divine power he led them out, 18 and for about
forty years *took care of them in the wilderness.*
19 *When he had destroyed seven nations in Canaan, he put them in possession*[g] of their land

[*g*] Dt. 1:31; 7:1.

New English Bible

impressed by what he learned about the Lord.

Leaving Paphos, Paul and his companions went by sea to Perga in Pamphylia; John, however, left them and returned to Jerusalem. From Perga they continued their journey as far as Pisidian Antioch. On the Sabbath they went to synagogue and took their seats; and after the readings from the Law and the prophets, the officials of the synagogue sent this message to them: 'Friends, if you have anything to say to the people by way of exhortation, let us hear it.' Paul rose, made a gesture with his hand, and began:

'Men of Israel and you who worship our God, listen to me! The God of this people of Israel chose our fathers. When they were still living as aliens in Egypt he made them into a nation and brought them out of that country with arm outstretched. For some forty years he bore with their conduct[a] in the desert. Then in the Canaanite country he overthrew seven nations, whose lands he gave them to be their heritage for some

[*a*] *Some witnesses read* he sustained them.

King James Version

20And after that he gave *unto them* judges about
the space of four hundred and fifty years, until
Samuel the prophet. 21And afterward they desired a king: and God gave unto them Saul the
son of Cis, a man of the tribe of Benjamin, by
the space of forty years. 22And when he had removed him, he raised up unto them David to be
their king; to whom also he gave testimony, and
said, I have found David the *son* of Jesse, a man
after mine own heart, which shall fulfil all my
will. 23 Of this man's seed hath God, according
to *his* promise, raised unto Israel a Saviour, Jesus: 24 When John had first preached before his
coming the baptism of repentance to all the people of Israel. 25And as John fulfilled his course,
he said, Whom think ye that I am? I am not *he.*
But, behold, there cometh one after me, whose
shoes of *his* feet I am not worthy to loose.
26 Men *and* brethren, children of the stock of
Abraham, and whosoever among you feareth
God, to you is the word of this salvation sent.
27 For they that dwell at Jerusalem, and their
rulers, because they knew him not, nor yet the
voices of the prophets which are read every
sabbath day, they have fulfilled *them* in condemning *him.* 28And though they found no cause
of death *in him,* yet desired they Pilate that he
should be slain. 29And when they had fulfilled

Living Bible

their land as an inheritance. Judges ruled for
about 450 years, and were followed by Samuel
the prophet.
21 "Then the people begged for a king, and
God gave them Saul (son of Kish), a man of
the tribe of Benjamin, who reigned for forty
years. 22 But God removed him and replaced
him with David as king, a man about whom God
said, 'David (son of Jesse) is a man after my
own heart, for he will obey me.' 23And it is one
of King David's descendants, Jesus, who is God's
promised Savior of Israel!
24 "But before he came, John the Baptist
preached the need for everyone in Israel to turn
from sin to God. 25As John was finishing his
work he asked, 'Do you think I am the Messiah?
No! But he is coming soon—and in comparison
with him, I am utterly worthless.'
26 "Brothers—you sons of Abraham, and also
all of you Gentiles here who reverence God—
this salvation is for all of us! 27 The Jews in
Jerusalem and their leaders fulfilled prophecy
by killing Jesus; for they didn't recognize him,
or realize that he is the one the prophets had
written about, though they heard the prophets'
words read every Sabbath. 28 They found no just
cause to execute him, but asked Pilate to have
him killed anyway. 29 When they had fulfilled all

Today's English Version

land 20 for about four hundred and fifty years.
"After this he gave them judges, until the
time of the prophet Samuel. 21And when they
asked for a king, God gave them Saul, the son
of Kish, from the tribe of Benjamin, to be their
king for forty years. 22After removing him, God
made David their king. This is what God said
about him, 'I have found that David, the son of
Jesse, is the kind of man I like, a man who will
do all I want him to do.' 23 It was Jesus, a
descendant of David, that God made the Savior
of the people of Israel, as he had promised.
24 Before Jesus began his work, John preached
to all the people of Israel that they should turn
from their sins and be baptized. 25And as John
was about to finish his mission, he said to the
people, 'Who do you think I am? I am not the
one you are waiting for. But look! He is coming after me, and I am not good enough to take
his sandals off his feet.'
26 "My brothers, descendants of Abraham,
and all Gentiles here who worship God: it is to
us that this message of salvation has been sent!
27 For the people who live in Jerusalem, and
their leaders, did not know that he is the Savior,
nor did they understand the words of the prophets that are read every Sabbath day. Yet they
made the prophets' words come true by condemning Jesus. 28And even though they could
find no reason to pass the death sentence on him,
they asked Pilate to have him put to death.
29And after they had done everything that the

New International Version

heritance. 20All this took about 450 years.
"After this, God gave them judges until the
time of Samuel the prophet. 21 Then the people
asked for a king, and he gave them Saul son
of Kish, of the tribe of Benjamin, who ruled
forty years. 22After removing Saul, he made
David their king. He testified concerning him:
'I have found David son of Jesse, a man after
my own heart; he will do everything I want him
to do.' 23 From this man's descendants God has
brought to Israel the Savior Jesus, as he promised. 24 Before the coming of Jesus, John
preached repentance and baptism to all the people of Israel. 25As John was completing his
work, he said: 'Who do you think I am? I am
not that one. No, but he is coming after me,
whose sandals I am not worthy to untie.'
26 "Brothers, children of Abraham, and you
God-fearing Gentiles, it is to us that this message
of salvation has been sent. 27 The people of
Jerusalem and their rulers did not recognize
Jesus, yet in condemning him they fulfilled the
words of the prophets that are read every Sabbath. 28 Though they found no proper ground
for a death sentence, they asked Pilate to have
him executed. 29 When they had carried out all

Phillips Modern English

land as their inheritance for some four hundred and fifty years. After that he gave them judges until the time of the prophet Samuel. Then when they begged for a king God gave them Saul the son of Kish, a man of the tribe of Benjamin, to be their king for forty years. After he had deposed him he raised David to the throne, a man of whom God himself bore testimony in the words, 'I have found David, the son of Jesse, a man after my own heart, who shall do all my will.' From the descendants of this man, according to his promise, God has brought Jesus to Israel to be their saviour. John came before him to prepare his way, preaching the baptism of repentance for all the people of Israel. Indeed, as John reached the end of his time he said these words: 'What do you think I am? I am not he. But know this, someone comes after me whose shoelace I am not fit to untie!'

13.26 Now the message is urgent and contemporary

"Men and brothers, sons of the race of Abraham, and all among you who fear God, it is to us that this message of salvation has now been sent! For the people of Jerusalem and their rulers refused to recognise him or to understand the voice of the prophets which are read every Sabbath day—even though in condemning him they fulfilled these very prophecies! For though they found no cause for putting him to death, they begged Pilate to have him executed. And when they had completed everything that was

Revised Standard Version

an inheritance, for about four hundred and fifty
years. 20 And after that he gave them judges until
Samuel the prophet. 21 Then they asked for a
king; and God gave them Saul the son of Kish,
a man of the tribe of Benjamin, for forty years.
22 And when he had removed him, he raised up
David to be their king; of whom he testified
and said, 'I have found in David the son of
Jesse a man after my heart, who will do all my
will.' 23 Of this man's posterity God has brought
to Israel a Savior, Jesus, as he promised. 24 Before his coming John had preached a baptism of
repentance to all the people of Israel. 25 And as
John was finishing his course, he said, 'What do
you suppose that I am? I am not he. No, but
after me one is coming, the sandals of whose feet
I am not worthy to untie.'
26 "Brethren, sons of the family of Abraham,
and those among you that fear God, to us has
been sent the message of this salvation. 27 For
those who live in Jerusalem and their rulers,
because they did not recognize him nor understand the utterances of the prophets which are
read every sabbath, fulfilled these by condemning him. 28 Though they could charge him with
nothing deserving death, yet they asked Pilate to
have him killed. 29 And when they had fulfilled

Jerusalem Bible

20 for about four hundred and fifty years. After
this he gave them judges, down to the prophet
Samuel. 21 Then they demanded a king, and
God gave them Saul son of Kish, a man of the
tribe of Benjamin. 22 After forty years, he deposed him and made David their king, of whom
he approved in these words, *'I have selected Da-*
vid son of Jesse, a man after my own heart, who
will carry out my whole purpose.' [h] 23 To keep
his promise, God has raised up for Israel one of
David's descendants, Jesus, as Savior, 24 whose
coming was heralded by John when he proclaimed a baptism of repentance for the whole
people of Israel. 25 Before John ended his career he said, 'I am not the one you imagine me
to be; that one is coming after me and I am not
fit to undo his sandal.'
26 "My brothers, sons of Abraham's race, and
all you who fear God, this message of salvation
is meant for you. 27 What the people of Jerusalem and their rulers did, though they did not
realize it, was in fact to fulfill the prophecies
read on every sabbath. 28 Though they found
nothing to justify his death, they condemned
him and asked Pilate to have him executed.
29 When they had carried out everything that

[*h*] 1 S. 13:14.

New English Bible

four hundred and fifty years, and afterwards appointed judges for them until the time of the prophet Samuel.

'Then they asked for a king and God gave them Saul the son of Kish, a man of the tribe of Benjamin, who reigned for forty years. Then he removed him and set up David as their king, giving him his approval in these words: "I have found David son of Jesse to be a man after my own heart, who will carry out all my purposes." This is the man from whose posterity God, as he promised, has brought Israel a saviour, Jesus. John made ready for his coming by proclaiming baptism as a token of repentance to the whole people of Israel. And when John was nearing the end of his course, he said, "I am not what you think I am. No, after me comes one whose shoes I am not fit to unfasten."

'My brothers, you who come of the stock of Abraham, and others among you who revere our God, we are the people to whom the message of this salvation has been sent. The people of Jerusalem and their rulers did not recognize him, or understand the words of the prophets which are read Sabbath by Sabbath; indeed they fulfilled them by condemning him. Though they failed to find grounds for the sentence of death, they asked Pilate to have him executed. And when they had carried out all that the scrip-

King James Version

all that was written of him, they took *him* down
from the tree, and laid *him* in a sepulchre.
30 But God raised him from the dead: 31 And he
was seen many days of them which came up
with him from Galilee to Jerusalem, who are his
witnesses unto the people. 32 And we declare
unto you glad tidings, how that the promise
which was made unto the fathers, 33 God hath
fulfilled the same unto us their children, in that
he hath raised up Jesus again; as it is also written in the second psalm, Thou art my Son, this
day have I begotten thee. 34 And as concerning
that he raised him up from the dead, *now* no
more to return to corruption, he said on this
wise, I will give you the sure mercies of David.
35 Wherefore he saith also in another *psalm,*
Thou shalt not suffer thine Holy One to see corruption. 36 For David, after he had served his
own generation by the will of God, fell on sleep,
and was laid unto his fathers, and saw corruption: 37 But he, whom God raised again, saw no
corruption.
38 Be it known unto you therefore, men *and*
brethren, that through this man is preached unto
you the forgiveness of sins: 39 And by him all
that believe are justified from all things, from
which ye could not be justified by the law of
Moses. 40 Beware therefore, lest that come upon

Living Bible

the prophecies concerning his death, he was taken
from the cross and placed in a tomb.
30 "But God brought him back to life again!
31 And he was seen many times during the next
few days by the men who had accompanied him
to Jerusalem from Galilee—these men have constantly testified to this in public witness.
32, 33 "And now Barnabas and I are here to
bring you this Good News—that God's promise
to our ancestors has come true in our own time,
in that God brought Jesus back to life again.
This is what the second Psalm is talking about
when it says concerning Jesus, 'Today I have
honored you as my son.'[e]
34 "For God had promised to bring him back
to life again, no more to die. This is stated in
the Scripture that says, 'I will do for you the
wonderful thing I promised David.' 35 In another
Psalm he explained more fully, saying, 'God will
not let his Holy One decay.' 36 This was not a
reference to David, for after David had served
his generation according to the will of God, he
died and was buried, and his body decayed.
37 [No, it was a reference to another[f]]—someone God brought back to life, whose body was
not touched at all by the ravages of death.[g]
38 "Brothers! Listen! In this man Jesus, there
is forgiveness for your sins! 39 Everyone who
trusts in him is freed from all guilt and declared
righteous—something the Jewish law could never
do. 40 Oh, be careful! Don't let the prophets'

[*e*] Literally, "This day have I begotten you." [*f*] Implied. [*g*] Literally, "saw no corruption."

Today's English Version

Scriptures say about him, they took him down
from the cross and placed him in a grave. 30 But
God raised him from the dead, 31 and for many
days he appeared to those who had traveled with
him from Galilee to Jerusalem. They are now witnesses for him to the people of Israel. 32, 33 And
we are here to bring the Good News to you:
what God promised our ancestors he would do,
he has now done for us, who are their descendants, by raising Jesus to life. As it is written in
the second Psalm,

'You are my Son;
today I have become your Father.'

34 And this is what God said about raising him
from the dead, never again to return to decay,

'I will give you the sacred and sure blessings
that I promised to David.'

35 As indeed he says in another passage,

'You will not allow your devoted servant to
suffer decay.'

36 For David served God's purposes in his own
time; and then he died, was buried beside his
ancestors, and suffered decay. 37 But the one
whom God raised from the dead did not suffer
decay. 38, 39 All of you, my brothers, are to know
for sure that it is through Jesus that the message
about forgiveness of sins is preached to you; you
are to know that everyone who believes in him
is set free from all the sins from which the Law
of Moses could not set you free. 40 Take care,

New International Version

that was written about him, they took him down
from the tree and laid him in a tomb. 30 But God
raised him from the dead, 31 and for many days
he was seen by those who had traveled with him
from Galilee to Jerusalem. They are now his
witnesses to our people.
32 "We tell you the good news: What God
promised our fathers 33 he has fulfilled for us,
their children, by raising Jesus from the dead.
As it is written in the second Psalm:
'You are my Son;
today I have become your Father.[o]'[p]
34 The fact that God raised him from the dead,
never to decay, is stated in these words:
'I will give you the holy and sure blessings
promised to David.'[q]
35 So it is stated elsewhere:
'You will not let your Holy One undergo decay.'[r]
36 "For when David had served God's purpose in his own generation, he fell asleep; he
was buried with his ancestors and his body decayed. 37 But the one whom God raised from
the dead did not undergo decay. 38, 39 Therefore, my brothers, I want you to know that
through Jesus the forgiveness of sins is proclaimed to you. Through him everyone who believes is justified from everything from which
you could not be justified by the law of Moses.
40 Take care that what the prophets have said

[*o*] Or *have begotten you.* [*p*] Psalm 2:7. [*q*] Isaiah 55:3. [*r*] Psalm 16:10.

Phillips Modern English

written about him, they took him down from the cross and laid him in a tomb. But God raised him from the dead. For many days he was seen by those who had come up from Galilee to Jerusalem with him, and these men are now his witnesses to the people. And as for us we tell you the good news that the promise made to our forefathers has come true—that, in raising up Jesus, God has fulfilled it for us their children. This is endorsed in the second psalm: 'Thou art my son, this day have I begotten thee.' And as for the fact of God's raising him from the dead, never to return to corruption, he has spoken in these words: 'I will give you the sure mercies of David.' And then going further he says in another psalm, 'Thou shalt not suffer thine holy one to see corruption'. For David, remember, after he had served God's purpose in his own generation fell asleep and was laid with his ancestors. He did in fact 'see corruption', but this man whom God raised never saw corruption! It is therefore imperative, men and brothers, that every one of you should realise that forgiveness of sins is now proclaimed to you through this man. And through faith in him a man is absolved from all those things from which the Law of Moses could never set him free. Take care

Revised Standard Version

all that was written of him, they took him down
from the tree, and laid him in a tomb. 30 But
God raised him from the dead; 31 and for many
days he appeared to those who came up with
him from Galilee to Jerusalem, who are now his
witnesses to the people. 32 And we bring you the
good news that what God promised to the fathers,
33 this he has fulfilled to us their children by
raising Jesus; as also it is written in the second
psalm,

'Thou art my Son,
today I have begotten thee.'

34 And as for the fact that he raised him from
the dead, no more to return to corruption, he
spoke in this way,

'I will give you the holy and sure blessings of
David.'

35 Therefore he says also in another psalm,

'Thou wilt not let thy Holy One see corruption.'

36 For David, after he had served the counsel
of God in his own generation, fell asleep, and
was laid with his fathers, and saw corruption;
37 but he whom God raised up saw no corruption.
38 Let it be known to you therefore, brethren,
that through this man forgiveness of sins is
proclaimed to you, 39 and by him every one that
believes is freed from everything from which you
could not be freed by the law of Moses. 40 Be-

Jerusalem Bible

scripture foretells about him they took him
down from the tree and buried him in a tomb.
30 But God raised him from the dead, 31 and
for many days he appeared to those who had
accompanied him from Galilee to Jerusalem:
and it is these same companions of his who are
now his witnesses before our people.

32 "We have come here to tell you the Good
News. It was to our ancestors that God made
the promise but 33 it is to us, their children, that
he has fulfilled it, by raising Jesus from the dead.
As scripture says in the first psalm: *You are my
son: today I have become your father.* 34 The
fact that God raised him from the dead, never
to return to corruption, is no more than what
he had declared: *To you I shall give the sure
and holy things promised to David.*[i] 35 This
is explained by another text: *You will not allow
your holy one to experience corruption.*[j] 36 Now
when David in his own time had served God's
purposes he died; he was buried with his ancestors
and has certainly *experienced corruption.*
37 The one whom God has raised up, however,
has not *experienced corruption.*

38 "My brothers, I want you to realize that
it is through him that forgiveness of your sins
is proclaimed. Through him justification from
all sins which the Law of Moses was unable
to justify 39 is offered to every believer.

40 "So be careful—or what the prophets say

[i] Is. 55:3. [j] Ps. 16:9.

New English Bible

tures said about him, they took him down from the gibbet and laid him in a tomb. But God raised him from the dead; and there was a period of many days during which he appeared to those who had come up with him from Galilee to Jerusalem.

They are now his witnesses before our nation; and we are here to give you the good news that God, who made the promise to the fathers, has fulfilled it for the children[a] by raising Jesus from the dead, as indeed it stands written, in the second[b] Psalm: "You are my son; this day I have begotten you." Again, that he raised him from the dead, never again to revert to corruption, he declares in these words: "I will give you the blessings promised to David, holy and sure." This is borne out by another passage: "Thou wilt not let thy loyal servant suffer corruption." As for David, when he had served the purpose of God in his own generation, he died, and was gathered to his fathers, and suffered corruption; but the one whom God raised up did not suffer corruption; and you must understand, my brothers, that it is through him that forgiveness of sins is now being proclaimed to you. It is through him that everyone who has faith is acquitted of everything for which there was no acquittal under the Law of Moses. Beware, then, lest you

[a] *Some witnesses read* our children; *others read* us their children. [b] *Some witnesses read* first.

King James Version

you, which is spoken of in the prophets; 41 Behold, ye despisers, and wonder, and perish: for I
work a work in your days, a work which ye shall
in no wise believe, though a man declare it unto
you. 42 And when the Jews were gone out of the
synagogue, the Gentiles besought that these
words might be preached to them the next sabbath. 43 Now when the congregation was broken
up, many of the Jews and religious proselytes
followed Paul and Barnabas; who, speaking to
them, persuaded them to continue in the grace
of God.
44 And the next sabbath day came almost the
whole city together to hear the word of God.
45 But when the Jews saw the multitudes, they
were filled with envy, and spake against those
things which were spoken by Paul, contradicting
and blaspheming. 46 Then Paul and Barnabas
waxed bold, and said, It was necessary that the
word of God should first have been spoken to
you: but seeing ye put it from you, and judge
yourselves unworthy of everlasting life, lo, we

Living Bible

words apply to you. For they said, 41 'Look and
perish, you despisers [of the truth[f]], for I am
doing something in your day—something that
you won't believe when you hear it announced.' "
42 As the people left the synagogue that day,
they asked Paul to return and speak to them
again the next week. 43 And many Jews and godly
Gentiles who worshiped at the synagogue followed Paul and Barnabas down the street as the
two men urged them to accept the mercies God
was offering. 44 The following week almost the
entire city turned out to hear them preach the
Word of God.
45 But when the Jewish leaders[h] saw the
crowds, they were jealous, and cursed [i] and argued against whatever Paul said.
46 Then Paul and Barnabas spoke out boldly
and declared, "It was necessary that this Good
News from God should be given first to you
Jews. But since you have rejected it, and shown
yourselves unworthy of eternal life—well, we

[f] Implied. [h] Literally, "the Jews." [i] Or, "blasphemed."

Today's English Version

then, so that what the prophets said may not
happen to you,

41 'Look, you scoffers! Wonder and die!
For the work that I am doing in your own day
is something that you will not believe,
even when someone explains it to you!' "

42 As Paul and Barnabas were leaving the
synagogue, the people invited them to come back
the next Sabbath and tell them more about these
things. 43 After the people had left the meeting,
Paul and Barnabas were followed by many Jews
and many Gentiles converted to Judaism. The
apostles spoke to them and encouraged them to
keep on living in the grace of God.
44 The next Sabbath day nearly everyone in
the town came to hear the word of the Lord.
45 When the Jews saw the crowds, they were
filled with jealousy; they spoke against what
Paul was saying and insulted him. 46 But Paul
and Barnabas spoke out even more boldly, "It
was necessary that the word of God should be
spoken first to you. But since you reject it, and
do not consider yourselves worthy of eternal life,

New International Version

does not happen to you:
41 'Look, you scoffers,
wonder and perish,
because I am going to do something in your days
that you would never believe,
even if someone told you.' [s] "
42 As Paul and Barnabas were leaving the
synagogue, the people invited them to speak
further about these things on the next Sabbath.
43 When the congregation was dismissed, many
of the Jews and devout converts to Judaism followed Paul and Barnabas, who talked with them
and urged them to continue in the grace of God.
44 On the next Sabbath almost the whole city
gathered to hear the word of the Lord. 45 When
the Jews saw the crowds, they were filled with
jealousy and talked abusively against what Paul
was saying.
46 Then Paul and Barnabas answered them
boldly: "We had to speak the word of God to
you first. Since you reject it and do not consider
yourselves worthy of eternal life, we now turn to

[s] Hab. 1:5.

Phillips Modern English

then that this saying of the prophets should never apply to you:

Behold, ye despisers, and wonder, and perish;
For I work a work in your days,
A work which ye shall in no wise believe, if one declare it unto you."

13.42 Paul succeeds in arousing deep interest—

As they were going out the people kept on asking them to say all this again on the following Sabbath. After the meeting of the synagogue broke up many of the Jews and devout proselytes followed Paul and Barnabas who spoke personally to them and urged them to put their trust in the grace of God.

13.44 —but a week later he meets bitter opposition

On the next Sabbath almost the entire population of the city assembled to hear the message of the Lord, but when the Jews saw the crowds they were filled with jealousy and contradicted what Paul was saying, covering him with abuse. At this Paul and Barnabas did not mince their words but said,

"We felt it our duty to speak the message of God to you first, but since you spurn it and evidently do not think yourselves fit for eternal life,

Revised Standard Version

ware, therefore, lest there come upon you what is said in the prophets:
41 'Behold, you scoffers, and wonder, and perish;
for I do a deed in your days,
a deed you will never believe, if one declares it to you.' "
42 As they went out, the people begged that these things might be told them the next sabbath.
43 And when the meeting of the synagogue broke up, many Jews and devout converts to Judaism followed Paul and Barnabas, who spoke to them and urged them to continue in the grace of God.
44 The next sabbath almost the whole city gathered together to hear the word of God.
45 But when the Jews saw the multitudes, they were filled with jealousy, and contradicted what was spoken by Paul, and reviled him.
46 And Paul and Barnabas spoke out boldly, saying, "It was necessary that the word of God should be spoken first to you. Since you thrust it from you, and judge yourselves unworthy of eternal

Jerusalem Bible

will happen to you.

41 *Cast your eyes around you, mockers;*
be amazed, and perish!
For I am doing something in your own days
that you would not believe if you were to be told of it." [k]

42 As they left they were asked to preach on the same theme the following sabbath.
43 When the meeting broke up many Jews and devout converts joined Paul and Barnabas, and in their talks with them Paul and Barnabas urged them to remain faithful to the grace God had given them.

Paul and Barnabas preach to the pagans

44 The next sabbath almost the whole town assembled to hear the word of God.
45 When they saw the crowds, the Jews, prompted by jealousy, used blasphemies and contradicted everything Paul said.
46 Then Paul and Barnabas spoke out boldly. "We had to proclaim the word of God to you first, but since you have rejected it, since you do not think yourselves worthy of eternal life, we must turn to the pa-

[k] Hab. 1:5.

New English Bible

bring down upon yourselves the doom proclaimed by the prophets: "See this, you scoffers, wonder, and begone; for I am doing a deed in your days, a deed which you will never believe when you are told of it." '

As they were leaving the synagogue they were asked to come again and speak on these subjects next Sabbath; and after the congregation had dispersed, many Jews and gentile worshippers went along with Paul and Barnabas, who spoke to them and urged them to hold fast to the grace of God.

On the following Sabbath almost the whole city gathered to hear the word of God. When the Jews saw the crowds, they were filled with jealous resentment, and contradicted what Paul said, with violent abuse. But Paul and Barnabas were outspoken in their reply. 'It was necessary', they said, 'that the word of God should be declared to you first. But since you reject it and thus condemn yourselves as unworthy of

King James Version

turn to the Gentiles. 47 For so hath the Lord
commanded us, *saying,* I have set thee to be a
light of the Gentiles, that thou shouldest be for
salvation unto the ends of the earth. 48 And when
the Gentiles heard this, they were glad, and
glorified the word of the Lord: and as many as
were ordained to eternal life believed. 49 And the
word of the Lord was published throughout all
the region. 50 But the Jews stirred up the devout
and honourable women, and the chief men of the
city, and raised persecution against Paul and
Barnabas, and expelled them out of their coasts.
51 But they shook off the dust of their feet
against them, and came unto Iconium. 52 And
the disciples were filled with joy, and with the
Holy Ghost.

14 And it came to pass in Iconium, that they
went both together into the synagogue of
the Jews, and so spake, that a great multitude
both of the Jews and also of the Greeks believed. 2 But the unbelieving Jews stirred up the
Gentiles, and made their minds evil affected
against the brethren. 3 Long time therefore abode

Living Bible

will offer it to Gentiles. 47 For this is as the Lord
commanded when he said, 'I have made you a
light to the Gentiles, to lead them from the
farthest corners of the earth to my salvation.' "
48 When the Gentiles heard this, they were
very glad and rejoiced in Paul's message; and as
many as wanted [j] eternal life, believed. 49 So
God's message spread all through that region.
50 Then the Jewish leaders stirred up both the
godly women and the civic leaders of the city
and incited a mob against Paul and Barnabas,
and ran them out of town. 51 But they shook
off the dust of their feet against the town and
went on to the city of Iconium. 52 And their converts[k] were filled with joy and with the Holy
Spirit.

14 At Iconium, Paul and Barnabas went together to the synagogue and preached with
such power that many—both Jews and Gentiles
—believed.
2 But the Jews who spurned God's message
stirred up distrust among the Gentiles against
Paul and Barnabas, saying all sorts of evil things
about them. 3 Nevertheless, they stayed there a

[j] Or, "were disposed to," or, "ordained to." [k] Literally, "the disciples."

Today's English Version

we will leave you and go to the Gentiles. 47 For
this is the commandment that the Lord has given
us,

'I have set you to be a light for the Gentiles,
to be the way of salvation for the whole
world.' "

48 When the Gentiles heard this they were
glad and praised the Lord's message; and those
who had been chosen for eternal life became believers.
49 The word of the Lord spread everywhere
in that region. 50 But the Jews stirred up the
leading men of the city and the Gentile women
of high social standing who worshiped God. They
started a persecution against Paul and Barnabas,
and threw them out of their region. 51 The apostles shook the dust off their feet against them
and went on to Iconium. 52 The disciples in
Antioch were full of joy and the Holy Spirit.

In Iconium

14 The same thing happened in Iconium:
Paul and Barnabas went to the Jewish synagogue and spoke in such a way that a great
number of Jews and Gentiles became believers.
2 But the Jews who would not believe stirred up
the Gentiles and turned their feelings against the
brothers. 3 The apostles stayed there for a long

New International Version

the Gentiles. 47 For this is what the Lord has
commanded us:

'I have made you a light for the Gentiles,
that you may bring salvation to the ends of
the earth.' [t] "

48 When the Gentiles heard this, they were
glad and honored the word of the Lord; and all
who were appointed for eternal life believed.
49 The word of the Lord spread through the
whole region. 50 But the Jews incited the God-
fearing women of high standing and the leading
men of the city. They stirred up persecution
against Paul and Barnabas, and expelled them
from their region. 51 So they shook the dust
from their feet in protest against them and went
to Iconium. 52 And the disciples were filled with
joy and with the Holy Spirit.

In Iconium

14 At Iconium Paul and Barnabas went as
usual into the Jewish synagogue. There
they spoke so effectively that a great number of
Jews and Gentiles believed. 2 But the Jews who
refused to believe stirred up the Gentiles and
poisoned their minds against the brothers. 3 Paul

[t] Isaiah 49:6.

Phillips Modern English

watch us now as we turn to the gentiles! Indeed the Lord has commanded us to do so in the words:

I have set thee for a light of the gentiles,
That thou shouldest be for salvation unto the uttermost part of the earth."

When the gentiles heard this they were delighted and thanked God for his message. All those who were destined for eternal life believed, and the Word of the Lord spread over the whole country. But the Jews worked upon the feelings of devout and reputable women and of the leading citizens, and succeeded in starting a persecution against Paul and Barnabas, and expelled them from the district. But they on their part simply shook off the dust from their feet in protest and went on to Iconium. And the disciples continued to be full of joy and the Holy Spirit.

14.1 Jewish behaviour repeats itself

Much the same thing happened at Iconium. On their arrival they went to the Jewish synagogue and spoke with such conviction that a very large number of both Jews and Greeks believed. But the unbelieving Jews stirred up the feelings of the gentiles and poisoned their minds against the brothers. So they remained there for

Revised Standard Version

life, behold, we turn to the Gentiles. 47 For so the Lord has commanded us, saying,
'I have set you to be a light for the Gentiles,
that you may bring salvation to the uttermost parts of the earth.' "
48 And when the Gentiles heard this, they were glad and glorified the word of God; and as many as were ordained to eternal life believed. 49 And the word of the Lord spread throughout all the region. 50 But the Jews incited the devout women of high standing and the leading men of the city, and stirred up persecution against Paul and Barnabas, and drove them out of their district. 51 But they shook off the dust from their feet against them, and went to Iconium. 52 And the disciples were filled with joy and with the Holy Spirit.

14 Now at Iconium they entered together into the Jewish synagogue, and so spoke that a great company believed, both of Jews and of Greeks. 2 But the unbelieving Jews stirred up the Gentiles and poisoned their minds against the brethren. 3 So they remained for a long time,

Jerusalem Bible

gans. 47 For this is what the Lord commanded us to do when he said:

I have made you a light for the nations,
so that my salvation may reach the ends of the earth." [l]

48 It made the pagans very happy to hear this and they thanked the Lord for his message; all who were destined for eternal life became believers. 49 Thus the word of the Lord spread through the whole countryside.

50 But the Jews worked upon some of the devout women of the upper classes and the leading men of the city and persuaded them to turn against Paul and Barnabas and expel them from their territory. 51 So they shook the dust from their feet in defiance and went off to Iconium; 52 but the disciples were filled with joy and the Holy Spirit.

Iconium evangelized

14 At Iconium they went to the Jewish synagogue, as they had at Antioch, and they spoke so effectively that a great many Jews and Greeks became believers.

2 Some of the Jews, however, refused to believe, and they poisoned the minds of the pagans against the brothers.[m]

3 Accordingly Paul and Barnabas stayed on

[*l*] Is. 49:6, quoted freely from the LXX. [*m*] This sentence is a parenthesis. V.3 continues from v.1.

New English Bible

eternal life, we now turn to the Gentiles. For these are our instructions from the Lord: "I have appointed you to be a light for the Gentiles, and a means of salvation to earth's farthest bounds." ' When the Gentiles heard this, they were overjoyed and thankfully acclaimed the word of the Lord, and those who were marked out for eternal life became believers. So the word of the Lord spread far and wide through the region. But the Jews stirred up feeling among the women of standing who were worshippers, and among the leading men of the city; a persecution was started against Paul and Barnabas, and they were expelled from the district. So they shook the dust off their feet in protest against them and went to Iconium. And the converts were filled with joy and with the Holy Spirit.

14 At Iconium similarly they went[a] into the Jewish synagogue and spoke to such purpose that a large body both of Jews and Gentiles became believers. But the unconverted Jews stirred up the Gentiles and poisoned their minds against the Christians. For some time Paul and

[*a*] *Or* At Iconium they went together . . .

King James Version

they speaking boldly in the Lord, which gave
testimony unto the word of his grace, and
granted signs and wonders to be done by their
hands. 4 But the multitude of the city was divided: and part held with the Jews, and part
with the apostles. 5 And when there was an as-
sault made both of the Gentiles, and also of the
Jews with their rulers, to use *them* despitefully,
and to stone them, 6 They were ware of *it*, and
fled unto Lystra and Derbe, cities of Lycaonia,
and unto the region that lieth round about:
7 And there they preached the gospel.
8 And there sat a certain man at Lystra, impotent in his feet, being a cripple from his
mother's womb, who never had walked: 9 The
same heard Paul speak: who steadfastly beholding him, and perceiving that he had faith
to be healed, 10 Said with a loud voice, Stand
upright on thy feet. And he leaped and walked.
11 And when the people saw what Paul had
done, they lifted up their voices, saying in the
speech of Lycaonia, The gods are come down
to us in the likeness of men. 12 And they called
Barnabas, Jupiter; and Paul, Mercurius, because he was the chief speaker. 13 Then the
priest of Jupiter, which was before their city,
brought oxen and garlands unto the gates, and

Living Bible

long time, preaching boldly, and the Lord proved
their message was from him by giving them
power to do great miracles. 4 But the people of
the city were divided in their opinion about
them. Some agreed with the Jewish leaders, and
some backed the apostles.
5, 6 When Paul and Barnabas learned of a
plot to incite a mob of Gentiles, Jews, and Jewish leaders to attack and stone them, they fled
for their lives, going to the cities of Lycaonia,
Lystra, Derbe, and the surrounding area, 7 and
preaching the Good News there.
8 While they were at Lystra, they came upon
a man with crippled feet who had been that way
from birth, so he had never walked. 9 He was
listening as Paul preached, and Paul noticed him
and realized he had faith to be healed. 10 So
Paul called to him, "Stand up!" and the man
leaped to his feet and started walking!
11 When the listening crowd saw what Paul
had done, they shouted (in their local dialect, of
course), "These men are gods in human bodies!"
12 They decided that Barnabas was the Greek
god Jupiter, and that Paul, because he was the
chief speaker, was Mercury! 13 The local priest
of the Temple of Jupiter, located on the outskirts of the city, brought them cartloads of

Today's English Version

time. They spoke boldly about the Lord, who
proved that their message about his grace was
true by giving them the power to perform miracles and wonders. 4 The crowd in the city was
divided: some were for the Jews, others for the
apostles.
5 Then the Gentiles and the Jews, together
with their leaders, decided to mistreat the apostles and stone them. 6 When the apostles learned
about it they fled to Lystra and Derbe, cities
in Lycaonia, and to the surrounding territory.
7 There they preached the Good News.

In Lystra and Derbe

8 There was a man living in Lystra whose feet
were crippled; he had been lame from birth and
had never been able to walk. 9 Sitting there, he
listened to Paul's words. Paul saw that he believed and could be healed, so he looked straight
at him 10 and said in a loud voice, "Stand up
straight on your feet!" The man jumped up and
started walking around. 11 When the crowds saw
what Paul had done, they started to shout in
their own Lycaonian language, "The gods have
become like men and have come down to us!"
12 They gave Barnabas the name Zeus, and Paul
the name Hermes, because he was the one who
did the speaking. 13 The priest of the god Zeus,
whose temple stood just outside the town,

New International Version

and Barnabas spent considerable time there,
speaking boldly for the Lord, who confirmed
the message of his grace by enabling them to do
miraculous signs and wonders. 4 The people of
the city were divided; some sided with the Jews,
others with the apostles. 5 There was a plot afoot
among the Gentiles and Jews, together with their
leaders, to mistreat them and stone them. 6 But
they found out about it and fled to the Lycaonian
cities of Lystra and Derbe and to the surrounding country, 7 where they continued to preach
the good news.

In Lystra and Derbe

8 In Lystra there sat a man crippled in his
feet, who was lame from birth and had never
walked. 9 He listened to Paul as he was speaking. Paul looked directly at him, saw that he
had faith to be healed 10 and called out, "Stand
up on your feet!" At that, the man jumped up
and began to walk.
11 When the crowd saw what Paul had done,
they shouted in the Lycaonian language, "The
gods have come down to us in human form!"
12 Barnabas they called Zeus, and Paul they
called Hermes because he was the chief speaker.
13 The priest of Zeus, whose temple was just
outside the city, brought bulls and wreaths to

Phillips Modern English

a long time and spoke fearlessly about the Lord, who made it plain that they were proclaiming the Word of his grace, by allowing them to perform signs and miracles. But the great mass of the people of the city were divided, some taking the side of the Jews, and some that of the apostles. But when a hostile movement arose from both gentiles and Jews in collaboration with the authorities to insult and stone them, they got to know about it, fled to the Lycaonian cities of Lystra and Derbe, and the surrounding countryside—and from there they continued to proclaim the gospel.

14.8 A miracle in a completely pagan city

Now it happened at Lystra that a man was sitting who had no power in his feet. He had in fact been lame from birth and had never been able to walk. He was listening to Paul as he spoke, and Paul, looking him straight in the eye and seeing that he had the faith to be made well, said in a loud voice,

"Stand straight up on your feet!"

And he sprang to his feet and began to walk about. When the crowd saw what Paul had done they shouted in the Lycaonian language,

"The gods have come down to us in human form!"

They began to call Barnabas Zeus, and Paul Hermes, since he was the chief speaker. What is more, the high priest of Zeus whose temple was at the gateway of the city, brought garlanded

Revised Standard Version

speaking boldly for the Lord, who bore witness to the word of his grace, granting signs and wonders to be done by their hands. 4 But the people of the city were divided; some sided with the Jews, and some with the apostles. 5 When an attempt was made by both Gentiles and Jews, with their rulers, to molest them and to stone them, 6 they learned of it and fled to Lystra and Derbe, cities of Lycaonia, and to the surrounding country; 7 and there they preached the gospel.

8 Now at Lystra there was a man sitting, who could not use his feet; he was a cripple from birth, who had never walked. 9 He listened to Paul speaking; and Paul, looking intently at him and seeing that he had faith to be made well, 10 said in a loud voice, "Stand upright on your feet." And he sprang up and walked. 11 And when the crowds saw what Paul had done, they lifted up their voices, saying in Lycaonian, "The gods have come down to us in the likeness of men!" 12 Barnabas they called Zeus, and Paul, because he was the chief speaker, they called Hermes. 13 And the priest of Zeus, whose temple was in front of the city, brought oxen and

Jerusalem Bible

for some time, preaching fearlessly for the Lord; and the Lord supported all they said about his gift of grace, allowing signs and wonders to be performed by them.

4 The people in the city were divided, some supported the Jews, others the apostles, 5 but eventually with the connivance of the authorities a move was made by pagans as well as Jews to make attacks on them and to stone them. 6 When the apostles came to hear of this, they went off for safety to Lycaonia where, in the towns of Lystra and Derbe and in the surrounding country, 7 they preached the Good News.

Healing of a cripple

8 A man sat there[n] who had never walked in his life, because his feet were crippled from birth; 9 and as he listened to Paul preaching, he managed to catch his eye. Seeing that the man had the faith to be cured, 10 Paul said in a loud voice, "Get to your feet—stand up," and the cripple jumped up and began to walk.

11 When the crowd saw what Paul had done they shouted in the language of Lycaonia, "These people are gods who have come down to us disguised as men." 12 They addressed Barnabas as Zeus, and since Paul was the principal speaker they called him Hermes.[o] 13 The priests of Zeus-outside-the-Gate, proposing that all the people

[n] In Lystra. [o] Mercury, the messenger or herald of the gods.

New English Bible

Barnabas stayed on and spoke boldly and openly in reliance on the Lord; and he confirmed the message of his grace by causing signs and miracles to be worked at their hands. The mass of the townspeople were divided, some siding with the Jews, others with the apostles. But when a move was made by Gentiles and Jews together, with the connivance of the city authorities, to maltreat them and stone them, they got wind of it and made their escape to the Lycaonian cities of Lystra and Derbe and the surrounding country, where they continued to spread the good news.

At Lystra sat a crippled man, lame from birth, who had never walked in his life. This man listened while Paul was speaking. Paul fixed his eyes on him and saw that he had the faith to be cured, so he said to him in a loud voice, 'Stand up straight on your feet'; and he sprang up and started to walk. When the crowds saw what Paul had done, they shouted, in their native Lycaonian, 'The gods have come down to us in human form.' And they called Barnabas Jupiter, and Paul they called Mercury, because he was the spokesman. And the priest of Jupiter, whose temple was just outside the city, brought oxen

King James Version

would have done sacrifice with the people.
14 *Which* when the apostles, Barnabas and
Paul, heard *of*, they rent their clothes, and ran
in among the people, crying out, 15 And saying,
Sirs, why do ye these things? We also are men
of like passions with you, and preach unto you
that ye should turn from these vanities unto the
living God, which made heaven, and earth, and
the sea, and all things that are therein: 16 Who
in times past suffered all nations to walk in
their own ways. 17 Nevertheless he left not himself without witness, in that he did good, and
gave us rain from heaven, and fruitful seasons,
filling our hearts with food and gladness. 18 And
with these sayings scarce restrained they the
people, that they had not done sacrifice unto
them.
19 And there came thither *certain* Jews from
Antioch and Iconium, who persuaded the people, and, having stoned Paul, drew *him* out of
the city, supposing he had been dead. 20 Howbeit, as the disciples stood round about him, he
rose up, and came into the city: and the next
day he departed with Barnabas to Derbe. 21 And
when they had preached the gospel to that city,
and had taught many, they returned again to

Living Bible

flowers and prepared to sacrifice oxen to them at
the city gates before the crowds.
14 But when Barnabas and Paul saw what
was happening they ripped at their clothing in
dismay and ran out among the people, shouting,
15 "Men! What are you doing? We are merely
human beings like yourselves! We have come to
bring you the Good News that you are invited to
turn from the worship of these foolish things and
to pray instead to the living God who made
heaven and earth and sea and everything in
them. 16 In bygone days he permitted the nations
to go their own ways, 17 but he never left himself without witness; there were always his reminders—the kind things he did such as sending
you rain and good crops and giving you food
and gladness."
18 But even so, Paul and Barnabas could
scarcely restrain the people from sacrificing to
them!
19 Yet only a few days later, some Jews arrived from Antioch and Iconium and turned
the crowds into a murderous mob that stoned
Paul and dragged him out of the city, apparently
dead. 20 But as the believers stood around him,
he got up and went back into the city!
The next day he left with Barnabas for Derbe.
21 After preaching the Good News there and
making many disciples, they returned again to

Today's English Version

brought bulls and flowers to the gate. He and
the crowds wanted to offer sacrifice to the apostles.
14 When Barnabas and Paul heard what they
were about to do, they tore their clothes and ran
into the middle of the crowd, shouting, 15 "Why
are you doing this, men? We are just men, human beings like you! We are here to announce
the Good News, to turn you away from these
worthless things to the living God, who made
heaven, earth, sea, and all that is in them. 16 In
the past he allowed all peoples to go their own
way. 17 But he has always given proof of himself by the good things he does: he gives you
rain from heaven and crops at the right times;
he gives you food and fills your hearts with
happiness." 18 Even with these words the apostles could hardly keep the crowds from offering
a sacrifice to them.
19 Some Jews came from Antioch of Pisidia
and from Iconium; they won the crowds to their
side, stoned Paul and dragged him out of town,
thinking that he was dead. 20 But when the believers gathered around him, he got up and went
back into the town. The next day he and Barnabas went to Derbe.

The return to Antioch in Syria

21 Paul and Barnabas preached the Good
News in Derbe, and won many disciples. Then
they went back to Lystra, then to Iconium, and

New International Version

the city gates because he and the crowd wanted
to offer sacrifices to them.
14 But when the apostles Barnabas and Paul
heard of this, they tore their clothes and rushed
into the crowd, shouting: 15 "Men, why are you
doing this? We too are only men, human like
you. We are bringing you good news, telling you
to turn from these worthless things to the living
God, who made heaven and earth and sea and
everything in them. 16 In the past, he let all nations go their own way. 17 Yet he has not left
himself without testimony: He has shown kindness by giving you rain from heaven and crops
in their seasons; he provides you with plenty of
food and fills your hearts with joy." 18 Even
with these words, they had difficulty keeping the
crowd from sacrificing to them.
19 Then some Jews came from Antioch and
Iconium and won the crowd over. They stoned
Paul and dragged him outside the city, thinking
he was dead. 20 But after the disciples had
gathered around him, he got up and went back
into the city. The next day he and Barnabas left
for Derbe.

The return to Antioch in Syria

21 They preached the good news in that city
and won a large number of disciples. Then they
returned to Lystra, Iconium and Antioch,

Phillips Modern English

oxen to the gates and wanted to offer sacrifice with the people. But when the apostles, Barnabas and Paul, heard of their intention they tore their clothes and rushed into the crowd, crying at the top of their voices,

"Men, why are you doing these things? We are only human beings with feelings just like yours! We are here to tell you good news—that you should turn from these meaningless things to the living God! He is the one who made heaven and earth, the sea and all that is in them. In generations gone by he allowed all nations to go on in their own ways—not that he left men without evidence of himself. For he has shown kindnesses to you; he has sent you rain from heaven and fruitful seasons, giving you food and happiness to your hearts' content."

Yet even with these words they only just succeeded in restraining the crowd from making sacrifices to them.

14.19 Paul is dogged by his Jewish enemies

Then some Jews arrived from Antioch and Iconium and after turning the minds of the people against Paul they stoned him and dragged him out of the city thinking he was dead. But while the disciples were gathered in a circle round him, Paul got up and walked back to the city. And the next day he went out with Barnabas to Derbe, and when they had preached the gospel to that city and made many disciples, they turned back to Lystra, then to Iconium and on

Revised Standard Version

garlands to the gates and wanted to offer sacrifice with the people. 14 But when the apostles Barnabas and Paul heard of it, they tore their garments and rushed out among the multitude, crying, 15 "Men, why are you doing this? We also are men, of like nature with you, and bring you good news, that you should turn from these vain things to a living God who made the heaven and the earth and the sea and all that is in them. 16 In past generations he allowed all the nations to walk in their own ways; 17 yet he did not leave himself without witness, for he did good and gave you from heaven rains and fruitful seasons, satisfying your hearts with food and gladness." 18 With these words they scarcely restrained the people from offering sacrifice to them.

19 But Jews came there from Antioch and Iconium; and having persuaded the people, they stoned Paul and dragged him out of the city, supposing that he was dead. 20 But when the disciples gathered about him, he rose up and entered the city; and on the next day he went on with Barnabas to Derbe. 21 When they had preached the gospel to that city and had made many disciples, they returned to Lystra and to

Jerusalem Bible

should offer sacrifice with them, brought garlanded oxen to the gates. 14 When the apostles Barnabas and Paul heard what was happening they tore their clothes,[p] and rushed into the crowd, shouting, 15 "Friends, what do you think you are doing? We are only human beings like you. We have come with good news to make you turn from these empty idols to the living God who made heaven and earth and the sea and all that these hold. 16 In the past he allowed each nation to go its own way; 17 but even then he did not leave you without evidence of himself in the good things he does for you: he sends you rain from heaven, he makes your crops grow when they should, he gives you food and makes you happy." 18 Even this speech, however, was scarcely enough to stop the crowd offering them sacrifice.

The mission is disrupted

19 Then some Jews arrived from Antioch and Iconium, and turned the people against the apostles. They stoned Paul and dragged him outside the town, thinking he was dead. 20 The disciples came crowding around him but, as they did so, he stood up and went back to the town. The next day he and Barnabas went off to Derbe.

21 Having preached the Good News in that town and made a considerable number of disciples, they went back through Lystra and Iconium

[p] Conventional sign of despair.

New English Bible

and garlands to the gates, and he and all the people were about to offer sacrifice.

But when the apostles Barnabas and Paul heard of it, they tore their clothes and rushed into the crowd shouting, 'Men, what is this that you are doing? We are only human beings, no less mortal than you. The good news we bring tells you to turn from these follies to the living God, who made heaven and earth and sea and everything in them. In past ages he allowed all nations to go their own way; and yet he has not left you without some clue to his nature, in the kindness he shows: he sends you rain from heaven and crops in their seasons, and gives you food and good cheer in plenty.'

With these words they barely managed to prevent the crowd from offering sacrifice to them.

Then Jews from Antioch and Iconium came on the scene and won over the crowds. They stoned Paul, and dragged him out of the city, thinking him dead. The converts formed a ring round him, and he got to his feet and went into the city. Next day he left with Barnabas for Derbe.

After bringing the good news to that town, where they gained many converts, they returned to Lystra, then to Iconium, and then to Antioch,

King James Version

Lystra, and *to* Iconium, and Antioch, 22 Confirming the souls of the disciples, *and* exhorting them to continue in the faith, and that we must through much tribulation enter into the kingdom of God. 23 And when they had ordained them elders in every church, and had prayed with fasting, they commended them to the Lord, on whom they believed. 24 And after they had passed throughout Pisidia, they came to Pamphylia. 25 And when they had preached the word in Perga, they went down into Attalia: 26 And thence sailed to Antioch, from whence they had been recommended to the grace of God for the work which they fulfilled. 27 And when they were come, and had gathered the church together, they rehearsed all that God had done with them, and how he had opened the door of faith unto the Gentiles. 28 And there they abode long time with the disciples.

15 And certain men which came down from Judea taught the brethren, *and said,* Except ye be circumcised after the manner of Moses, ye cannot be saved. 2 When therefore Paul and Barnabas had no small dissension and disputation with them, they determined that Paul and Barnabas, and certain other of them, should go up to Jerusalem unto the apostles

Living Bible

Lystra, Iconium and Antioch, 22 where they helped the believers to grow in love for God and each other. They encouraged them to continue in the faith in spite of all the persecution, reminding them that they must enter into the Kingdom of God through many tribulations. 23 Paul and Barnabas also appointed elders in every church and prayed for them with fasting, turning them over to the care of the Lord in whom they trusted.

24 Then they traveled back through Pisidia to Pamphylia, 25 preached again in Perga, and went on to Attalia.

26 Finally they returned by ship to Antioch, where their journey had begun, and where they had been committed to God for the work now completed.

27 Upon arrival they called together the believers and reported on their trip, telling how God had opened the door of faith to the Gentiles too. 28 And they stayed there with the believers at Antioch for a long while.

15 While Paul and Barnabas were at Antioch, some men from Judea arrived and began to teach the believers that unless they adhered to the ancient Jewish custom of circumcision, they could not be saved. 2 Paul and Barnabas argued and discussed this with them at length, and finally the believers sent them to Jerusalem, accompanied by some local men, to talk to the apostles and elders there about this

Today's English Version

then to Antioch of Pisidia. 22 They strengthened the believers and encouraged them to remain true to the faith. "We must pass through many troubles to enter the Kingdom of God," they taught. 23 In each church they appointed elders for them; and with prayers and fasting they commended them to the Lord, in whom they had put their trust.

24 After going through the territory of Pisidia, they came to Pamphylia. 25 They preached the message in Perga and then went down to Attalia, 26 and from there they sailed back to Antioch, the place where they had been commended to the care of God's grace for the work they had now completed.

27 When they arrived in Antioch they gathered the people of the church together and told them of all that God had done with them, and how he had opened the way for the Gentiles to believe. 28 They stayed a long time there with the believers.

The meeting at Jerusalem

15 Some men came from Judea to Antioch and started teaching the brothers, "You cannot be saved unless you are circumcised as the Law of Moses requires." 2 Paul and Barnabas had a fierce argument and dispute with them about this; so it was decided that Paul and Barnabas and some of the others in Antioch should go to Jerusalem and see the apostles and elders about this matter.

New International Version

22 strengthening the disciples and encouraging them to remain true to the faith. "We must go through many hardships to enter the kingdom of God," they said. 23 Paul and Barnabas appointed elders[u] for them in each church and, with prayer and fasting, committed them to the Lord in whom they had put their trust. 24 After going through Pisidia, they came into Pamphylia, 25 and when they had preached the word in Perga, they went down to Attalia.

26 From Attalia they sailed back to Antioch, where they had been committed to the grace of God for the work they had now completed. 27 On arriving there, they gathered the church together and reported all that God had done through them and how he had opened the door of faith to the Gentiles. 28 And they stayed there a long time with the disciples.

The council at Jerusalem

15 Some men came down from Judea to Antioch and were teaching the brothers: "Unless you are circumcised according to the custom taught by Moses, you cannot be saved." 2 This brought Paul and Barnabas into sharp dispute and debate with them. So Paul and Barnabas were appointed, along with some other believers, to go up to Jerusalem to see the apos-

[u] Or ***Barnabas ordained elders;*** or ***Barnabas had elders elected.***

Phillips Modern English

to Antioch. They put fresh heart into the disciples, urging them to stand firm in the faith, and reminding them that it is "through many tribulations" that we must enter into the kingdom of God. They appointed elders for them in each church, and with prayer and fasting commended these men to the Lord in whom they had believed. They then crossed Pisidia and arrived in Pamphylia. They proclaimed their message in Perga and then went down to Attalia. From there they sailed back to Antioch (in Syria) where they had first been commended to the grace of God for the task which they had now completed. When they arrived there they called the church together and reported to them how greatly God had worked with them and how he had opened the door of faith to the gentiles. And here at Antioch they spent a considerable time with the disciples.

15.1 The opposition from reactionaries

Then some men came down from Judaea and began to teach the brothers, saying, "unless you are circumcised according to the custom of Moses you cannot be saved". Paul and Barnabas sharply disagreed with them and there was a good deal of argument. Finally it was settled that Paul and Barnabas should go up to Jerusalem with some of their own people to confer with the apostles and elders about the whole question.

Revised Standard Version

Iconium and to Antioch,
22 strengthening the souls of the disciples, exhorting them to continue in the faith, and saying that through many tribulations we must enter the kingdom of God.
23 And when they had appointed elders for them in every church, with prayer and fasting, they committed them to the Lord in whom they believed.
24 Then they passed through Pisidia, and came to Pamphylia.
25 And when they had spoken the word in Perga, they went down to Attalia;
26 and from there they sailed to Antioch, where they had been commended to the grace of God for the work which they had fulfilled.
27 And when they arrived, they gathered the church together and declared all that God had done with them, and how he had opened a door of faith to the Gentiles.
28 And they remained no little time with the disciples.

15 But some men came down from Judea and were teaching the brethren, "Unless you are circumcised according to the custom of Moses, you cannot be saved."
2 And when Paul and Barnabas had no small dissension and debate with them, Paul and Barnabas and some of the others were appointed to go up to Jerusalem to the apostles and the elders about this ques-

Jerusalem Bible

to Antioch.
22 They put fresh heart into the disciples, encouraging them to persevere in the faith. "We all have to experience many hardships," they said, "before we enter the kingdom of God."
23 In each of these churches they appointed elders, and with prayer and fasting they commended them to the Lord in whom they had come to believe.
24 They passed through Pisidia and reached Pamphylia.
25 Then after proclaiming the word at Perga they went down to Attalia
26 and from there sailed for Antioch, where they had originally been commended to the grace of God for the work they had now completed.
27 On their arrival they assembled the church and gave an account of all that God had done with them, and how he had opened the door of faith to the pagans.
28 They stayed there with the disciples for some time.

Controversy at Antioch

15 Then some men came down from Judaea[q] and taught the brothers, "Unless you have yourselves circumcised in the tradition of Moses you cannot be saved."
2 This led to disagreement, and after Paul and Barnabas had had a long argument with these men it was arranged that Paul and Barnabas and others of the church should go up to Jerusalem and discuss the problem with the apostles and elders.

[q] In the allusion to this incident in Galatians, they are said to have come "from James," Ga. 2:12.

New English Bible

heartening the converts and encouraging them to be true to their religion. They warned them that to enter the kingdom of God we must pass through many hardships. They also appointed elders for them in each congregation, and with prayer and fasting committed them to the Lord in whom they had put their faith.

Then they passed through Pisidia and came into Pamphylia. When they had given the message at Perga, they went down to Attalia, and from there set sail for Antioch, where they had originally been commended to the grace of God for the task which they had now completed. When they arrived and had called the congregation together, they reported all that God had done through them, and how he had thrown open the gates of faith to the Gentiles. And they stayed for some time with the disciples there.

15 Now certain persons who had come down from Judaea began to teach the brotherhood that those who were not circumcised in accordance with Mosaic practice could not be saved. That brought them into fierce dissension and controversy with Paul and Barnabas. And so it was arranged that these two and some others from Antioch should go up to Jerusalem to see the apostles and elders about this question.

King James Version

and elders about this question. 3 And being brought on their way by the church, they passed through Phenice and Samaria, declaring the conversion of the Gentiles: and they caused great joy unto all the brethren. 4 And when they were come to Jerusalem, they were received of the church, and *of* the apostles and elders, and they declared all things that God had done with them. 5 But there rose up certain of the sect of the Pharisees which believed, saying, That it was needful to circumcise them, and to command *them* to keep the law of Moses.

6 And the apostles and elders came together for to consider of this matter. 7 And when there had been much disputing, Peter rose up, and said unto them, Men *and* brethren, ye know how that a good while ago God made choice among us, that the Gentiles by my mouth should hear the word of the gospel, and believe. 8 And God, which knoweth the hearts, bare them witness, giving them the Holy Ghost, even as *he did* unto us; 9 And put no difference between us and them, purifying their hearts by faith. 10 Now therefore why tempt ye God, to put a

Living Bible

question. 3 After the entire congregation had escorted them out of the city the delegates went on to Jerusalem, stopping along the way in the cities of Phoenicia and Samaria to visit the believers, telling them—much to everyone's joy—that the Gentiles, too, were being converted.

4 Arriving in Jerusalem, they met with the church leaders—all the apostles and elders were present—and Paul and Barnabas reported on what God had been doing through their ministry. 5 But then some of the men who had been Pharisees before their conversion stood to their feet and declared that all Gentile converts must be circumcised and required to follow all the Jewish customs and ceremonies. 6 So the apostles and church elders set a further meeting to decide this question.

7 At the meeting, after long discussion, Peter stood and addressed them as follows: "Brothers, you all know that God chose me from among you long ago to preach the Good News to the Gentiles, so that they also could believe. 8 God, who knows men's hearts, confirmed the fact that he accepts Gentiles by giving them the Holy Spirit, just as he gave him to us. 9 He made no distinction between them and us, for he cleansed their lives through faith, just as he did ours. 10 And now are you going to correct God by

Today's English Version

3 They were sent on their way by the church, and as they went through Phoenicia and Samaria they reported how the Gentiles had turned to God; this news brought great joy to all the brothers. 4 When they arrived in Jerusalem, they were welcomed by the church, the apostles, and the elders, to whom they told all that God had done with them. 5 But some of the believers who belonged to the party of the Pharisees stood up and said, "They have to be circumcised and told to obey the Law of Moses."

6 The apostles and the elders met together to consider this question. 7 After a long debate Peter stood up and said, "My brothers, you know that a long time ago God chose me from among you to preach the message of Good News to the Gentiles, so that they could hear and believe. 8 And God, who knows the hearts of men, showed his approval of the Gentiles by giving the Holy Spirit to them, just as he had to us. 9 He made no difference between us and them; he purified their hearts because they believed. 10 So then, why do you want to put God to the

New International Version

tles and elders about this question. 3 The church sent them on their way, and as they traveled through Phoenicia and Samaria, they told how the Gentiles had been converted. This news made all the brothers very glad. 4 When they came to Jerusalem, they were welcomed by the church and the apostles and elders, to whom they reported everything God had done through them.

5 Then some of the believers who belonged to the party of the Pharisees stood up and said, "The Gentiles must be circumcised and required to obey the law of Moses."

6 The apostles and elders met to consider this question. 7 After much discussion, Peter got up and addressed them: "Brothers, you know that some time ago God made a choice among you that the Gentiles might hear from my lips the message of the gospel and believe. 8 God, who knows the heart, showed that he accepted them by giving the Holy Spirit to them, just as he did to us. 9 He made no distinction between us and them, for he purified their hearts by faith. 10 Now then, why do you try to test God by put-

Phillips Modern English

The church sent them off on their journey and as they went through Phoenicia and Samaria they told the story of the conversion of the gentiles, and all the brothers were overjoyed to hear about it. On their arrival at Jerusalem they were welcomed by the Church, by the apostles and elders, and they reported how greatly God had worked with them. But some members of the Pharisees' party who had become believers stood up and declared that it was essential that these men be circumised and told to observe the Law of Moses.

15.6 Peter declares that God is doing something new

The apostles and elders met to consider this matter. After an exhaustive debate Peter stood up and addressed them in these words:

"Men and brothers, you know that from our earliest days together God chose me as the one from whose lips the gentiles should hear the message of the gospel and should believe it. Moreover, God who knows men's inmost thoughts has plainly shown that this is so, for he gave the Holy Spirit to the gentiles exactly as he did to us. He made no distinction between us and them, once he had cleansed their hearts by faith. Why then must you now strain the pa-

Revised Standard Version

tion. 3 So, being sent on their way by the
church, they passed through both Phoenicia and
Samaria, reporting the conversation of the Gentiles, and they gave great joy to all the brethren.
4 When they came to Jerusalem, they were welcomed by the church and the apostles and the
elders, and they declared all that God had done
with them. 5 But some believers who belonged
to the party of the Pharisees rose up, and said,
"It is necessary to circumcise them, and to
charge them to keep the law of Moses."
6 The apostles and the elders were gathered
together to consider this matter. 7 And after
there had been much debate, Peter rose and
said to them, "Brethren, you know that in the
early days God made choice among you, that by
my mouth the Gentiles should hear the word of
the gospel and believe. 8 And God who knows
the heart bore witness to them, giving them the
Holy Spirit just as he did to us; 9 and he made
no distinction between us and them, but cleansed
their hearts by faith. 10 Now therefore why do

Jerusalem Bible

3 All the members of the church saw them
off, and as they passed through Phoenicia and
Samaria they told how the pagans had been
converted, and this news was received with the
greatest satisfaction by the brothers. 4 When
they arrived in Jerusalem they were welcomed
by the church and by the apostles and elders,
and gave an account of all that God had done
with them.

Controversy at Jerusalem

5 But certain members of the Pharisees' party
who had become believers objected, insisting that
the pagans should be circumcised and instructed
to keep the Law of Moses. 6 The apostles and
elders met to look into the matter, 7 and after
the discussion had gone on a long time, Peter
stood up and addressed them.

Peter's speech

"My brothers," he said, "you know perfectly
well that in the early days God made his choice
among you: the pagans were to learn the Good
News from me and so become believers. 8 In
fact God, who can read everyone's heart, showed
his approval of them by giving the Holy Spirit
to them just as he had to us. 9 God made no distinction between them and us, since he purified
their hearts by faith. 10 It would only provoke

New English Bible

They were sent on their way by the congregation, and travelled through Phoenicia and Samaria, telling the full story of the conversion of the Gentiles. The news caused great rejoicing among all the Christians there.

When they reached Jerusalem they were welcomed by the church and the apostles and elders, and reported all that God had done through them. Then some of the Pharisaic party who had become believers came forward and said, 'They must be circumcised and told to keep the Law of Moses.'

The apostles and elders held a meeting to look into this matter; and, after a long debate, Peter rose and addressed them. 'My friends,' he said, 'in the early days, as you yourselves know, God made his choice among you and ordained that from my lips the Gentiles should hear and believe the message of the Gospel. And God, who can read men's minds, showed his approval of them by giving the Holy Spirit to them, as he did to us. He made no difference between them and us; for he purified their hearts by faith. Then why do you now provoke God by laying

King James Version

yoke upon the neck of the disciples, which
neither our fathers nor we were able to bear?
11 But we believe that through the grace of the
Lord Jesus Christ we shall be saved, even as
they.
12 Then all the multitude kept silence, and
gave audience to Barnabas and Paul, declaring
what miracles and wonders God had wrought
among the Gentiles by them.
13 And after they had held their peace, James
answered, saying, Men *and* brethren, hearken
unto me: 14 Simeon hath declared how God at
the first did visit the Gentiles, to take out of
them a people for his name. 15 And to this agree
the words of the prophets; as it is written,
16 After this I will return, and will build again
the tabernacle of David, which is fallen down;
and I will build again the ruins thereof, and I
will set it up: 17 That the residue of men might
seek after the Lord, and all the Gentiles, upon
whom my name is called, saith the Lord, who
doeth all these things. 18 Known unto God are
all his works from the beginning of the world.

Living Bible

burdening the Gentiles with a yoke that neither
we nor our fathers were able to bear? 11 Don't
you believe that all are saved the same way, by
the free gift of the Lord Jesus?"
12 There was no further discussion, and everyone now listened as Barnabas and Paul told
about the miracles God had done through them
among the Gentiles.
13 When they had finished, James took the
floor. "Brothers," he said, "listen to me. 14 Peter
has told you about the time God first visited the
Gentiles to take from them a people to bring
honor to his name. 15 And this fact of Gentile
conversion agrees with what the prophets predicted. For instance, listen to this passage from
the prophet Amos[a]:
16 'Afterwards' [says the Lord[a]], 'I will return and renew the broken contract with
David,[b] 17 so that Gentiles, too, will find the
Lord—all those marked with my name.'
18 That is what the Lord says, who reveals his
plans made from the beginning.

[*a*] Implied. See Amos 9:11-12. [*b*] Literally, "rebuild the tabernacle of David which is fallen."

Today's English Version

test now by laying a load on the backs of the
believers which neither our ancestors nor we ourselves were able to carry? 11 No! We believe and
are saved by the grace of the Lord Jesus, just as
they are."
12 The whole group was silent as they heard
Barnabas and Paul report all the wonders and
miracles that God had done through them among
the Gentiles. 13 When they finished speaking,
James spoke up, "Listen to me, brothers! 14 Simon has just explained how God first showed
his care for the Gentiles by taking from among
them a people to be all his own. 15 The words
of the prophets agree completely with this. As
the scripture says,

16 'After this I will return, says the Lord,
and I will raise David's fallen house.
I will restore its ruins,
and build it up again.
17 And so all other people will seek the Lord,
all the Gentiles whom I have called to
be my own.
18 So says the Lord, who made this known
long ago.'

New International Version

ting on the necks of the disciples a yoke that
neither we nor our fathers have been able to
bear? 11 No! We believe it is through the grace
of our Lord Jesus that we are saved, just as they
are."
12 The whole assembly became silent as they
listened to Barnabas and Paul telling about the
miraculous signs and wonders God had done
among the Gentiles through them. 13 When they
finished, James spoke up: "Brothers, listen to
me. 14 Simon[v] has described to us how God at
first showed his concern by taking from the
Gentiles a people for himself. 15 The words of
the prophets are in agreement with this, as it is
written:
16 'After this I will return
and rebuild the fallen house of David.
Its ruins I will rebuild,
and I will restore it,
17 that the rest of mankind may seek the
Lord,
and all the Gentiles who bear my name,
says the Lord, who does these things' [w]
18 that have been known for ages.[x]

[*v*] Greek *Simeon.* [*w*] Amos 9:11,12. [*x*] Some MSS read *things'—18known to the Lord for ages is his work.*

Phillips Modern English

tience of God by trying to put on the shoulders of these disciples a burden which neither our fathers nor we are able to bear? Surely the fact is that it is by the grace of the Lord Jesus that we are saved through faith, just as they are!"

These words produced absolute silence, and they listened to Barnabas and Paul while they gave a detailed account of the signs and wonders which God had worked through them among the gentiles.

15.13 James expresses the feeling of the meeting

Silence again followed their words and then James made this reply:

"Men and brothers, listen to me. Symeon has shown how in the first place God decided to choose a people from among the nations who should bear his name. This is in full agreement with what the prophets wrote, as in this scripture:

After these things I will return,
And I will build again the tabernacle of David,
which is fallen;
And I will build again the ruins thereof,
And I will set it up:
That the residue of men may seek after the Lord,
And all the gentiles, upon whom my name is called,
Saith the Lord who maketh these things known from the beginning of the world.

Revised Standard Version

you make trial of God by putting a yoke upon
the neck of the disciples which neither our fathers nor we have been able to bear? 11 But we
believe that we shall be saved through the grace
of the Lord Jesus, just as they will."
12 And all the assembly kept silence; and they
listened to Barnabas and Paul as they related
what signs and wonders God had done through
them among the Gentiles. 13After they finished
speaking, James replied, "Brethren, listen to me.
14 Simeon has related how God first visited the
Gentiles, to take out of them a people for his
name. 15And with this the words of the prophets
agree, as it is written,
16 'After this I will return,
and I will rebuild the dwelling of David,
which has fallen;
I will rebuild its ruins,
and I will set it up,
17 that the rest of men may seek the Lord,
and all the Gentiles who are called by my name,
18 says the Lord, who has made these things
known from of old.'

Jerusalem Bible

God's anger now, surely, if you imposed on the
disciples the very burden that neither we nor
our ancestors were strong enough to support?
11 Remember, we believe that we are saved in
the same way as they are: through the grace of
the Lord Jesus."
12 This silenced the entire assembly, and they
listened to Barnabas and Paul describing all the
signs and wonders God had worked through
them among the pagans.

James' speech

13 When they had finished it was James who
spoke. "My brothers," he said, "listen to me.
14 Simeon[r] has described how God first arranged
to enlist a people for his name out of the pagans.
15 This is entirely in harmony with the words
of the prophets, since the scriptures say:

16 *After that I shall return*
and rebuild the fallen House of David;
I shall rebuild it from its ruins
and restore it.
17 *Then the rest of mankind,*
all the pagans who are consecrated to my name,
will look for the Lord,
says the Lord who made this 18 *known so long ago.*[s]

[r] Semitic form of Simon Peter's name. [s] Am. 9:11,12, quoted according to the LXX.

New English Bible

on the shoulders of these converts a yoke which neither we nor our fathers were able to bear? No, we believe that it is by the grace of the Lord Jesus that we are saved, and so are they.'

At that the whole company fell silent and listened to Barnabas and Paul as they told of all the signs and miracles that God had worked among the Gentiles through them.

When they had finished speaking, James summed up: 'My friends,' he said, 'listen to me. Simeon has told how it first happened that God took notice of the Gentiles, to choose from among them a people to bear his name; and this agrees with the words of the prophets, as Scripture has it:

"Thereafter I will return and rebuild the fallen house of David;
even from its ruins I will rebuild it, and set it up again,
that they may seek the Lord—all the rest of mankind,
and the Gentiles, whom I have claimed for my own.
Thus says the Lord, whose work it is,
made known long ago."

King James Version

19 Wherefore my sentence is, that we trouble
not them, which from among the Gentiles are
turned to God: 20 But that we write unto them,
that they abstain from pollutions of idols, and
from fornication, and *from* things strangled,
and *from* blood. 21 For Moses of old time hath
in every city them that preach him, being read
in the synagogues every sabbath day. 22 Then
pleased it the apostles and elders, with the whole
church, to send chosen men of their own company to Antioch with Paul and Barnabas;
namely, Judas surnamed Barsabas, and Silas,
chief men among the brethren: 23 And they
wrote *letters* by them after this manner; The
apostles and elders and brethren *send* greeting
unto the brethren which are of the Gentiles in
Antioch and Syria and Cilicia: 24 Forasmuch as
we have heard, that certain which went out
from us have troubled you with words, subverting your souls, saying, *Ye must* be circumcised, and keep the law; to whom we gave no
such commandment: 25 It seemed good unto us,
being assembled with one accord, to send chosen
men unto you with our beloved Barnabas and
Paul, 26 Men that have hazarded their lives for

Living Bible

19 "And so my judgment is that we should
not insist that the Gentiles who turn to God
must obey our Jewish laws, 20 except that we
should write to them to refrain from eating meat
sacrificed to idols, from all fornication, and also
from eating unbled meat of strangled animals.
21 For these things have been preached against
in Jewish synagogues in every city on every Sabbath for many generations."

22 Then the apostles and elders and the whole
congregation voted to send delegates to Antioch
with Paul and Barnabas, to report on this decision. The men chosen were two of the church
leaders—Judas (also called Barsabbas) and
Silas.

23 This is the letter they took along with
them:

"*From:* The apostles, elders and brothers at
Jerusalem.

"*To:* The Gentile brothers in Antioch, Syria
and Cilicia. Greetings!

24 "We understand that some believers from
here have upset you and questioned your salvation,[c] but they had no such instructions from us.
25 So it seemed wise to us, having unanimously
agreed on our decision, to send to you these two
official representatives, along with our beloved
Barnabas and Paul. 26 These men—Judas and
Silas, who have risked their lives for the sake of

[*c*] Literally, "subverted your souls."

Today's English Version

19 "It is my opinion," James went on, "that
we should not trouble the Gentiles who are turning to God. 20 Instead, we should write a letter
telling them not to eat any food that is unclean
because it has been offered to idols; to keep themselves from immorality; not to eat any animal
that has been strangled, or any blood. 21 For the
Law of Moses has been read for a very long
time in the synagogues every Sabbath, and his
words are preached in every town."

The letter to the Gentile believers

22 Then the apostles and the elders, together
with the whole church, decided to choose some
men from the group and send them to Antioch
with Paul and Barnabas. They chose Judas, called
Barsabbas, and Silas, two men who were highly
respected by the brothers. 23 They sent the following letter by them:

"We, the apostles and the elders, your brothers, send greetings to all brothers of Gentile
birth who live in Antioch, Syria, and Cilicia.
24 We have heard that some men of our group
went out and troubled and upset you by what
they said; they had not, however, received any
instructions from us to do this. 25 And so we
have met together and have all agreed to choose
some messengers and send them to you. They
will go with our dear friends Barnabas and Paul,
26 who have risked their lives in the service of

New International Version

19 "It is my judgment, therefore, that we
should not make it difficult for the Gentiles who
are turning to God. 20 Instead we should write
to them, telling them to abstain from food polluted by idols, from sexual immorality, from
the meat of strangled animals and from blood.
21 For Moses has been preached in every city
from the earliest times and is read in the synagogues on every Sabbath."

The council's letter to Gentile believers

22 Then the apostles and elders, with the
whole church, decided to choose some of their
own men and send them to Antioch with Paul
and Barnabas. They chose Judas, called Barsabbas, and Silas, two men who were leaders among
the brothers. 23 With them they sent the following letter:

The apostles and elders, your brothers,

To the Gentile believers in Antioch, Syria
and Cilicia:

Greetings.

24 We have heard that some went out from
us without our authorization and disturbed
you, troubling your minds by what they said.
25 So we all agreed to choose some men and
send them to you with our dear friends
Barnabas and Paul—26 men who have risked
their lives for the name of our Lord Jesus

Phillips Modern English

"I am firmly of the opinion that we should not put any additional obstacles before any gentiles who are turning towards God. Instead, I think we should write to them telling them to avoid anything polluted by idols, sexual immorality, eating the meat of strangled animals, or tasting blood. For after all, for many generations now Moses has had his preachers in every city and has been read aloud in the synagogues every Sabbath day."

15.22 The Church's deputation: the message to gentile Christians

Then the apostles, the elders and the whole Church agreed to choose representatives and send them to Antioch with Paul and Barnabas. Their names were Judas, surnamed Barsabas, and Silas, both leading men of the brotherhood. They carried with them a letter bearing this message: "The apostles and elders who are your brothers send their greetings to the brothers who are gentiles in Antioch, Syria and Cilicia. Since we have heard that some of our number have caused you deep distress and have unsettled your minds by giving you a message which certainly did not originate from us, we are unanimously agreed to send you chosen representatives with our well-loved Barnabas and Paul—men who have risked their lives for the name of our Lord

Revised Standard Version

19 Therefore my judgment is that we should not
trouble those of the Gentiles who turn to God,
20 but should write to them to abstain from the
pollutions of idols and from unchastity and
from what is strangled[n] and from blood. 21 For
from early generations Moses has had in every
city those who preach him, for he is read every
sabbath in the synagogues."
22 Then it seemed good to the apostles and
the elders, with the whole church, to choose men
from among them and send them to Antioch
with Paul and Barnabas. They sent Judas called
Barsabbas, and Silas, leading men among the
brethren, 23 with the following letter: "The
brethren, both the apostles and the elders, to the
brethren who are of the Gentiles in Antioch and
Syria and Cilicia, greeting. 24 Since we have
heard that some persons from us have troubled
you with words, unsettling your minds, although
we gave them no instructions, 25 it has seemed
good to us, having come to one accord, to
choose men and send them to you with our
beloved Barnabas and Paul, 26 men who have
risked their lives for the sake of our Lord Jesus

[n] Other early authorities omit *and from what is strangled.*

Jerusalem Bible

19 "I rule, then, that instead of making things
more difficult for pagans who turn to God, 20 we
send them a letter telling them merely to abstain
from anything polluted by idols,[t] from fornication,[u] from the meat of strangled animals and
from blood. 21 For Moses has always had his
preachers in every town, and is read aloud in
the synagogues every sabbath."

The apostolic letter

22 Then the apostles and elders decided to
choose delegates to send to Antioch with Paul
and Barnabas; the whole church concurred with
this. They chose Judas known as Barsabbas and
Silas,[v] both leading men in the brotherhood,
23 and gave them this letter to take with them:
"The apostles and elders, your brothers, send
greetings to the brothers of pagan birth in Antioch, Syria and Cilicia. 24 We hear that some
of our members have disturbed you with their
demands and have unsettled your minds. They
acted without any authority from us, 25 and so
we have decided unanimously to elect delegates
and to send them to you with Barnabas and
Paul, men we highly respect 26 who have dedicated their lives to the name of our Lord Jesus

[t] I.e., which has been offered in sacrifice to false gods. [u] Perhaps all the irregular marriages listed in Lv. 18. [v] Silas, also mentioned in Ac. 18; 1 Th., 2 Th., 2 Co., 1 P.

New English Bible

'My judgement therefore is that we should impose no irksome restrictions on those of the Gentiles who are turning to God, but instruct them by letter to abstain from things polluted by contact with idols, from fornication, from anything that has been strangled, and from blood.[a] Moses, after all, has never lacked spokesmen in every town for generations past; he is read in the synagogues Sabbath by Sabbath.'

Then the apostles and elders, with the agreement of the whole church, resolved to choose representatives and send them to Antioch with Paul and Barnabas. They chose two leading men in the community, Judas Barsabbas and Silas, and gave them this letter to deliver:

'We, the apostles and elders, send greetings as brothers to our brothers of gentile origin in Antioch, Syria, and Cilicia. Forasmuch as we have heard that some of our number, without any instructions from us, have[b] disturbed you with their talk and unsettled your minds, we have resolved unanimously to send to you our chosen representatives with our well-beloved Barnabas and Paul, who have devoted themselves

[a] *Some witnesses omit* from fornication; *others omit* from anything that has been strangled; *some add* (*after* blood) and to refrain from doing to others what they would not like done to themselves. [b] *Some witnesses read* have gone out and . . .

King James Version

the name of our Lord Jesus Christ. 27 We have sent therefore Judas and Silas, who shall also tell *you* the same things by mouth. 28 For it seemed good to the Holy Ghost, and to us, to lay upon you no greater burden than these necessary things; 29 That ye abstain from meats offered to idols, and from blood, and from things strangled, and from fornication: from which if ye keep yourselves, ye shall do well. Fare ye well. 30 So when they were dismissed, they came to Antioch: and when they had gathered the multitude together, they delivered the epistle: 31 *Which* when they had read, they rejoiced for the consolation. 32 And Judas and Silas, being prophets also themselves, exhorted the brethren with many words, and confirmed *them*. 33 And after they had tarried *there* a space, they were let go in peace from the brethren unto the apostles. 34 Notwithstanding it pleased Silas to abide there still. 35 Paul also and Barnabas continued in Antioch, teaching and preaching the word of the Lord, with many others also.

Living Bible

our Lord Jesus Christ—will confirm orally what we have decided concerning your question.

27, 28, 29 "For it seemed good to the Holy Spirit and to us to lay no greater burden of Jewish laws on you than to abstain from eating food offered to idols and from unbled meat of strangled animals,[d] and, of course, from fornication. If you do this, it is enough. Farewell."

30 The four messengers went at once to Antioch, where they called a general meeting of the Christians and gave them the letter. 31 And there was great joy throughout the church that day as they read it.

32 Then Judas and Silas, both being gifted speakers,[e] preached long sermons to the believers, strengthening their faith. 33 They stayed several days,[f] and then Judas and Silas returned to Jerusalem taking greetings and appreciation to those who had sent them. 34, 35 Paul and Barnabas stayed on at Antioch to assist several others who were preaching and teaching there.

[d] Literally, "and from blood." [e] Or "prophets." [f] Literally, "spent some time."

Today's English Version

our Lord Jesus Christ. 27 We send you, then, Judas and Silas, who will tell you in person the same things we are writing. 28 The Holy Spirit and we have agreed not to put any other burden on you besides these necessary rules: 29 eat no food that has been offered to idols; eat no blood; eat no animal that has been strangled; and keep yourselves from immorality. You will do well if you keep yourselves from doing these things. Good-bye."

30 The messengers were sent off and went to Antioch, where they gathered the whole group of believers and gave them the letter. 31 When the people read the letter, they were filled with joy by the message of encouragement. 32 Judas and Silas, who were themselves prophets, spoke a long time with the brothers, giving them courage and strength. 33 After spending some time there, they were sent off in peace by the brothers, and went back to those who had sent them. [34 But Silas decided to stay there.]

35 Paul and Barnabas spent some time in Antioch. Together with many others, they taught and preached the word of the Lord.

New International Version

Christ. 27 Therefore we are sending Judas and Silas to confirm by word of mouth what we are writing. 28 It seemed good to the Holy Spirit and to us not to burden you with anything beyond the following requirements: 29 You are to abstain from food offered to idols, from blood, from the meat of strangled animals and from sexual immorality. You will do well to avoid these things.

Farewell.

30 The men were sent off and went down to Antioch, where they gathered the church together and delivered the letter. 31 The people read it and were glad for its encouraging message. 32 Judas and Silas, who themselves were prophets, said much to encourage and strengthen the brothers. 33 After spending some time there, they were sent off by the brothers with the blessing of peace to return to those who had sent them.[y] 35 But Paul and Barnabas remained in Antioch, where they and many others taught and preached the word of the Lord.

[y] Some MSS add verse 34: ***but Silas decided to remain there.***

Phillips Modern English

Jesus Christ. So we have sent you Judas and Silas who will give you the same message personally by word of mouth. For it has seemed right to the Holy Spirit and to us to lay no further burden upon you except what is absolutely essential, namely, that you avoid what has been sacrificed to idols, tasting blood, eating the meat of what has been strangled and sexual immorality. Keep yourselves clear of these things and you will make good progress. Farewell."

15.30 The message is received with delight

So this party, sent off by the Church, went down to Antioch and after gathering the congregation together, they handed over the letter to them. And they, when they read it, were delighted with the encouragement it gave them. Judas and Silas were themselves both inspired preachers and greatly encouraged and strengthened the brothers by many talks to them. Then, after spending some time there, the brothers sent them back in peace to those who had commissioned them. Paul and Barnabas however stayed on in Antioch teaching and preaching the gospel of the Word of the Lord in company with many others.

Revised Standard Version

Christ. 27 We have therefore sent Judas and Silas, who themselves will tell you the same things by word of mouth. 28 For it has seemed good to the Holy Spirit and to us to lay upon you no greater burden than these necessary things: 29 that you abstain from what has been sacrificed to idols and from blood and from what is strangled[n] and from unchastity. If you keep yourselves from these, you will do well. Farewell."

30 So when they were sent off, they went down to Antioch; and having gathered the congregation together, they delivered the letter. 31 And when they read it, they rejoiced at the exhortation. 32 And Judas and Silas, who were themselves prophets, exhorted the brethren with many words and strengthened them. 33 And after they had spent some time, they were sent off in peace by the brethren to those who had sent them.[o] 35 But Paul and Barnabas remained in Antioch, teaching and preaching the word of the Lord, with many others also.

[n] Other early authorities omit *and from what is strangled.* [o] Other ancient authorities insert verse 34, *But it seemed good to Silas to remain there.*

Jerusalem Bible

Christ. 27 Accordingly we are sending you Judas and Silas, who will confirm by word of mouth what we have written in this letter. 28 It has been decided by the Holy Spirit and by ourselves not to saddle you with any burden beyond these essentials: 29 you are to abstain from food sacrificed to idols, from blood, from the meat of strangled animals and from fornication. Avoid these, and you will do what is right. Farewell."

The delegates at Antioch

30 The party left and went down to Antioch, where they summoned the whole community and delivered the letter. 31 The community read it and were delighted with the encouragement it gave them. 32 Judas and Silas, being themselves prophets, spoke for a long time, encouraging and strengthening the brothers. 33 These two spent some time there, and then the brothers wished them peace and they went back to those who had sent them.[w] 35 Paul and Barnabas, however, stayed on in Antioch, and there with many others they taught and proclaimed the Good News, the word of the Lord.

[w] Western Text adds v. 34 "But Silas decided to stay there." Several MSS further add "Jude set out by himself."

New English Bible

to the cause of our Lord Jesus Christ. We are therefore sending Judas and Silas, who will themselves confirm this by word of mouth. It is the decision of the Holy Spirit, and our decision, to lay no further burden upon you beyond these essentials: you are to abstain from meat that has been offered to idols, from blood, from anything that has been strangled,[a] and from fornication.[b] If you keep yourselves free from these things you will be doing right. Farewell.'

So they were sent off on their journey and travelled down to Antioch, where they called the congregation together, and delivered the letter. When it was read, they all rejoiced at the encouragement it brought. Judas and Silas, who were prophets themselves, said much to encourage and strengthen the members, and, after spending some time there, were dismissed with the good wishes of the brethren, to return to those who had sent them.[c] But Paul and Barnabas stayed on at Antioch, and there, along with many others, they taught and preached the word of the Lord.

[a] *Some witnesses omit* from anything that has been strangled. [b] *Some witnesses omit* and from fornication; *and some add* and refrain from doing to others what you would not like done to yourselves. [c] *Some witnesses add* (34) But Silas decided to remain there.

King James Version

36 And some days after, Paul said unto Barnabas, Let us go again and visit our brethren in every city where we have preached the word of the Lord, *and see* how they do. 37And Barnabas determined to take with them John, whose surname was Mark. 38 But Paul thought not good to take him with them, who departed from them from Pamphylia, and went not with them to the work. 39And the contention was so sharp between them, that they departed asunder one from the other: and so Barnabas took Mark, and sailed unto Cyprus; 40And Paul chose Silas, and departed, being recommended by the brethren unto the grace of God. 41And he went through Syria and Cilicia, confirming the churches.

16 Then came he to Derbe and Lystra: and, behold, a certain disciple was there, named Timotheus, the son of a certain woman, which was a Jewess, and believed; but his father *was* a Greek: 2 Which was well reported of by the

Living Bible

36 Several days later Paul suggested to Barnabas that they return again to Turkey, and visit each city where they had preached before,[g] to see how the new converts were getting along. 37 Barnabas agreed, and wanted to take along John Mark. 38 But Paul didn't like that idea at all, since John had deserted them in Pamphylia. 39 Their disagreement over this was so sharp that they separated. Barnabas took Mark with him and sailed for Cyprus, 40, 41 while Paul chose Silas and, with the blessing of the believers, left for Syria and Cilicia, to encourage the churches there.

16 Paul and Silas went first to Derbe and then on to Lystra where they met Timothy, a believer whose mother was a Christian Jewess but his father a Greek. 2 Timothy was well

[g] Implied. Literally, "return now and visit every city wherein we proclaimed the word of the Lord."

Today's English Version

Paul and Barnabas separate

36 Some time later Paul said to Barnabas, "Let us go back and visit our brothers in every city where we preached the word of the Lord, and find out how they are getting along." 37 Barnabas wanted to take John Mark with them, 38 but Paul did not think it was right to take him, because he had not stayed with them to the end of their mission, but had turned back and left them in Pamphylia. 39 They had a sharp argument between them, and separated from each other. Barnabas took Mark and sailed off for Cyprus, 40 while Paul chose Silas and left, commended by the brothers to the care of the Lord's grace. 41 He went through Syria and Cilicia, strengthening the churches.

Timothy goes with Paul and Silas

16 Paul traveled on to Derbe and Lystra. A believer named Timothy lived there; his mother, also a believer, was Jewish, but his father was Greek. 2All the brothers in Lystra and

New International Version

Disagreement between Paul and Barnabas

36 Some time later Paul said to Barnabas, "Let us go back and visit the brothers in all the towns where we preached the word of the Lord and see how they are doing." 37 Barnabas wanted to take John, also called Mark, with them, 38 but Paul did not think it wise to take him, because he had deserted them in Pamphylia and had not continued with them in the work. 39 They had such a sharp disagreement that they parted company. Barnabas took Mark and sailed for Cyprus, 40 but Paul chose Silas and left, commended by the brothers to the grace of the Lord. 41 He went through Syria and Cilicia, strengthening the churches.

Timothy joins Paul and Silas

16 He came to Derbe and then to Lystra, where a disciple named Timothy lived, whose mother was a Jewess and a believer, but whose father was a Greek. 2 The brothers at

Phillips Modern English

15.36 Paul and Barnabas flatly disagree, but the work prospers

Some days later Paul spoke to Barnabas, "Now let us go back and visit the brothers in every city where we have proclaimed the Word of the Lord to see how they are."

Barnabas wanted to take John, surnamed Mark, as their companion. But Paul strongly disapproved of taking with them a man who had deserted them in Pamphylia and was not prepared to go on with them in their work. There was a sharp clash of opinion, so much so that they went their separate ways, Barnabas taking Mark and sailing to Cyprus, while Paul chose Silas and set out on his journey, commended to the grace of the Lord by the brothers as he did so. He travelled through Syria and Cilicia and strengthened the churches.

16.1 Paul chooses Timothy as companion

He went to Derbe and on to Lystra. At Lystra there was a disciple by the name of Timothy whose mother was a Jewish Christian, though his father was a Greek. Timothy was held in high

Revised Standard Version

36 And after some days Paul said to Barnabas, "Come, let us return and visit the brethren
in every city where we proclaimed the word of
the Lord, and see how they are." 37 And Barnabas wanted to take with them John called Mark.
38 But Paul thought best not to take with them
one who had withdrawn from them in Pamphylia, and had not gone with them to the work.
39 And there arose a sharp contention, so that
they separated from each other; Barnabas took
Mark with him and sailed away to Cyprus, 40 but
Paul chose Silas and departed, being commended
by the brethren to the grace of the Lord. 41 And
he went through Syria and Cilicia, strengthening
the churches.

16 And he came also to Derbe and to Lystra.
A disciple was there, named Timothy, the
son of a Jewish woman who was a believer; but
his father was a Greek. 2 He was well spoken of

Jerusalem Bible

IV. Paul's missions

Paul separates from Barnabas and recruits Silas

36 On a later occasion Paul said to Barnabas,
"Let us go back and visit all the towns where
we preached the word of the Lord, so that we
can see how the brothers are doing." 37 Barnabas
suggested taking John Mark, 38 but Paul was not
in favor of taking along the very man who had
deserted them in Pamphylia and had refused to
share in their work.
39 After a violent quarrel they parted company, and Barnabas sailed off with Mark to
Cyprus. 40 Before Paul left, he chose Silas to
accompany him and was commended by the
brothers to the grace of God.

Lycaonia: Paul recruits Timothy

41 He traveled through Syria and Cilicia, con-
solidating the churches.

16 From there he went to Derbe, and then
on to Lystra. Here there was a disciple
called Timothy, whose mother was a Jewess who
had become a believer; but his father was a
Greek. 2 The brothers at Lystra and Iconium

New English Bible

Paul leads the advance

After a while Paul said to Barnabas, 'Ought we not to go back now to see how our brothers are faring in the various towns where we proclaimed the word of the Lord?' Barnabas wanted to take John Mark with them; but Paul judged that the man who had deserted them in Pamphylia and had not gone on to share in their work was not the man to take with them now. The dispute was so sharp that they parted company. Barnabas took Mark with him and sailed for Cyprus, while Paul chose Silas. He started on his journey, commended by the brothers to the grace of the Lord, and travelled through Syria and Cilicia bringing new strength to the congregations.

16 He went on to Derbe and to Lystra, and
there he found a disciple named Timothy,
the son of a Jewish Christian mother and a Gentile father. He was well spoken of by the Chris-

King James Version

brethren that were at Lystra and Iconium. 3 Him
would Paul have to go forth with him; and took
and circumcised him because of the Jews which
were in those quarters: for they knew all that
his father was a Greek. 4And as they went
through the cities, they delivered them the
decrees for to keep, that were ordained of the
apostles and elders which were at Jerusalem.
5And so were the churches established in the
faith, and increased in number daily. 6 Now
when they had gone throughout Phrygia and the
region of Galatia, and were forbidden of the
Holy Ghost to preach the word in Asia, 7After
they were come to Mysia, they assayed to go
into Bithynia: but the Spirit suffered them not.
8And they passing by Mysia came down to
Troas. 9And a vision appeared to Paul in the
night; There stood a man of Macedonia, and
prayed him, saying, Come over into Macedonia,
and help us. 10And after he had seen the vision,
immediately we endeavoured to go into Macedonia, assuredly gathering that the Lord had
called us for to preach the gospel unto them.

Living Bible

thought of by the brothers in Lystra and Iconium, 3 so Paul asked him to join them on their
journey. In deference to the Jews of the area,
he circumcised Timothy before they left, for
everyone knew that his father was a Greek [and
hadn't permitted this before[a]]. 4 Then they went
from city to city, making known the decision
concerning the Gentiles, as decided by the apostles and elders in Jerusalem. 5 So the church
grew daily in faith and numbers.

6 Next they traveled through Phrygia and
Galatia, because the Holy Spirit had told them
not to go into the Turkish province of Ausia at
that time. 7 Then going along the borders of
Mysia they headed north for the province of
Bithynia, but again the Spirit of Jesus said no.
8 So instead they went on through Mysia province to the city of Troas.

9 That night[b] Paul had a vision. In his dream
he saw a man over in Macedonia, Greece, pleading with him, "Come over here and help us."
10 Well, that settled it. We[c] would go to Macedonia, for we could only conclude that God was
sending us to preach the Good News there.

[a] Implied. [b] Literally, "in the night." [c] Luke, the writer of this book, now joined Paul and accompanied him on his journey.

Today's English Version

Iconium spoke well of Timothy. 3 Paul wanted
to take Timothy along with him, so he circumcised him. He did so because all the Jews who
lived in those places knew that Timothy's father
was Greek. 4As they went through the towns
they delivered to the believers the rules decided
upon by the apostles and elders in Jerusalem, and
told them to obey these rules. 5 So the churches
were made stronger in the faith and grew in numbers every day.

In Troas: Paul's vision

6 They traveled through the region of Phrygia
and Galatia, because the Holy Spirit did not let
them preach the message in the province of
Asia. 7 When they reached the border of Mysia,
they tried to go into the province of Bithynia, but
the Spirit of Jesus did not allow them. 8 So they
traveled right on through Mysia and went down
to Troas. 9 Paul had a vision that night in which
he saw a man of Macedonia standing and begging him, "Come over to Macedonia and help
us!" 10As soon as Paul had this vision, we got
ready to leave for Macedonia, because we decided that God had called us to preach the
Good News to the people there.

New International Version

Lystra and Iconium spoke well of him. 3 Paul
wanted to take him along on the journey, so he
circumcised him because of the Jews who lived
in that area, for they all knew that his father
was a Greek. 4As they traveled from town to
town, they delivered the decisions reached by
the apostles and elders in Jerusalem for the people to obey. 5 So the churches were strengthened in the faith and grew daily in numbers.

Paul's vision of the Macedonian

6 Paul and his companions traveled throughout the region of Phrygia and Galatia, having
been kept by the Holy Spirit from preaching the
word in the province of Asia. 7 When they came
to the border of Mysia, they tried to enter Bithynia, but the Spirit of Jesus would not allow them
to. 8 So they passed by Mysia and went down to
Troas. 9 During the night Paul had a vision of
a man of Macedonia standing and begging him,
"Come over to Macedonia and help us." 10After
Paul had seen the vision, we got ready at once
to leave for Macedonia, concluding that God had
called us to preach the gospel to them.

Phillips Modern English

regard by the brothers at Lystra and Iconium, and Paul wanted to take him on as his companion. Everybody knew that his father was a Greek, and Paul therefore had him circumcised because of the attitude of the Jews in these places. As they went on their way through the cities they passed on to them for their observance the decisions which had been reached by the apostles and elders in Jerusalem. Consequently the churches grew stronger in the faith and their numbers increased daily.

16.6 Paul and Silas find their journey divinely directed

They made their way through Phrygia and the Galatia district, since the Holy Spirit prevented them from speaking God's message in the province of Asia. When they approached Mysia they tried to enter Bithynia, but again the Spirit of Jesus would not allow them. So they passed by Mysia and came down to Troas. One night Paul had a vision of a Macedonian man standing and appealing to him in the words: "Come over to Macedonia and help us!" As soon as Paul had seen this vision we made every effort to get on to Macedonia, convinced that God had called us to give them the good news.

Revised Standard Version

by the brethren at Lystra and Iconium. 3 Paul
wanted Timothy to accompany him; and he took
him and circumcised him because of the Jews
that were in those places, for they all knew that
his father was a Greek. 4 As they went on their
way through the cities, they delivered to them for
observance the decisions which had been reached
by the apostles and elders who were at Jerusalem. 5 So the churches were strengthened in the
faith, and they increased in numbers daily.
6 And they went through the region of Phrygia
and Galatia, having been forbidden by the Holy
Spirit to speak the word in Asia. 7 And when they
had come opposite Mysia, they attempted to go
into Bithynia, but the Spirit of Jesus did not
allow them; 8 so, passing by Mysia, they went
down to Troas. 9 And a vision appeared to Paul
in the night: a man of Macedonia was standing
beseeching him and saying, "Come over to Macedonia and help us." 10 And when he had seen
the vision, immediately we sought to go on into
Macedonia, concluding that God had called us
to preach the gospel to them.

Jerusalem Bible

spoke well of Timothy, 3 and Paul, who wanted
to have him as a traveling companion, had him
circumcised. This was on account of the Jews
in the locality where everyone knew his father
was a Greek.
4 As they visited one town after another, they
passed on the decisions reached by the apostles
and elders in Jerusalem, with instructions to
respect them.
5 So the churches grew strong in the faith, as
well as growing daily in numbers.

The crossing into Asia Minor

6 They traveled through Phrygia and the Galatian country, having been told by the Holy
Spirit not to preach the word in Asia. 7 When
they reached the frontier of Mysia they thought
to cross it into Bithynia, but as the Spirit of
Jesus would not allow them, 8 they went through
Mysia and came down to Troas.
9 One night Paul had a vision: a Macedonian
appeared and appealed to him in these words,
"Come across to Macedonia and help us."
10 Once he had seen this vision we lost no time
in arranging a passage to Macedonia, convinced
that God had called us to bring them the Good
News.

New English Bible

tians at Lystra and Iconium, and Paul wanted to have him in his company when he left the place. So he took him and circumcised him, out of consideration for the Jews who lived in those parts; for they all knew that his father was a Gentile. As they made their way from town to town they handed on the decisions taken by the apostles and elders in Jerusalem and enjoined their observance. And so, day by day, the congregations grew stronger in faith and increased in numbers.

They travelled through the Phrygian and Galatian region,[d] because they were prevented by the Holy Spirit from delivering the message in the province of Asia; and when they approached the Mysian border they tried to enter Bithynia; but the Spirit of Jesus would not allow them, so they skirted[a] Mysia and reached the coast at Troas. During the night a vision came to Paul: a Macedonian stood there appealing to him and saying, 'Come across to Macedonia and help us.' After he had seen this vision we at once set about getting a passage to Macedonia, concluding that God had called us to bring them the good news.

[d] *Or* through Phrygia and the Galatian region.
[a] *Possibly* traversed.

King James Version

11 Therefore loosing from Troas, we came with
a straight course to Samothracia, and the next
day to Neapolis; 12And from thence to Philippi,
which is the chief city of that part of Macedonia, *and* a colony: and we were in that city
abiding certain days. 13And on the sabbath we
went out of the city by a river side, where prayer
was wont to be made; and we sat down, and
spake unto the women which resorted *thither*.
14 And a certain woman named Lydia, a
seller of purple, of the city of Thyatira, which
worshipped God, heard *us*: whose heart the
Lord opened, that she attended unto the things
which were spoken of Paul. 15And when she
was baptized, and her household, she besought
us, saying, If ye have judged me to be faithful
to the Lord, come into my house, and abide
there. And she constrained us.
16 And it came to pass, as we went to prayer,
a certain damsel possessed with a spirit of
divination met us, which brought her masters
much gain by soothsaying: 17 The same followed
Paul and us, and cried, saying, These men are
the servants of the most high God, which shew

Living Bible

11 We went aboard a boat at Troas, and sailed
straight across to Samothrace, and the next day
on to Neapolis, 12 and finally reached Philippi, a
Roman[d] colony just inside the Macedonian border, and stayed there several days.
13 On the Sabbath, we went a little way outside the city to a river bank where we understood
some people met for prayer; and we taught the
Scriptures to some women who came. 14 One of
them was Lydia, a saleswoman from Thyatira, a
merchant of purple cloth. She was already a
worshiper of God and, as she listened to us, the
Lord opened her heart and she accepted all that
Paul was saying. 15 She was baptized along with
all her household and asked us to be her guests.
"If you agree that I am faithful to the Lord,"
she said, "come and stay at my home." And she
urged us until we did.
16 One day as we were going down to the
place of prayer beside the river, we met a demon-possessed slave girl who was a fortune-
teller, and earned much money for her masters.
17 She followed along behind us shouting, "These
men are servants of God and they have come to
tell you how to have your sins forgiven."

[d] Implied.

Today's English Version

In Philippi: the conversion of Lydia

11 We left by ship from Troas and sailed
straight across to Samothrace, and the next day
to Neapolis. 12 From there we went inland to
Philippi, a city of the first district of Macedonia;
it is also a Roman colony. We spent several days
in that city. 13 On the Sabbath day we went out
of the city to the riverside, where we thought
there would be a Jewish place for prayer. We
sat down and talked to the women who gathered
there. 14 One of those who heard us was Lydia,
from Thyatira, who was a dealer in purple
goods. She was a woman who worshiped God,
and the Lord opened her mind to pay attention
to what Paul was saying. 15 She and the people
of her house were baptized. Then she invited us,
"Come and stay in my house, if you have decided
that I am a true believer in the Lord." And she
persuaded us to go.

In prison at Philippi

16 One day as we were going to the place of
prayer, we were met by a slave girl who had an
evil spirit in her that made her predict the future. She earned much money for her owners
by telling fortunes. 17 She followed Paul and us,
shouting, "These men are servants of the Most
High God! They announce to you how you can

New International Version

Lydia's conversion in Philippi

11 From Troas we put out to sea and sailed
straight for Samothrace, and the next day on to
Neapolis. 12 From there we traveled to Philippi,
a Roman colony and the leading city of that
district of Macedonia. And we stayed there
several days.
13 On the Sabbath we went outside the city
gate to the river, where we expected to find a
place of prayer. We sat down and began to
speak to the women who had gathered there.
14 One of those listening was a woman named
Lydia, a dealer in purple cloth from the city of
Thyatira, who was a worshiper of God. The
Lord opened her heart to respond to Paul's
message. 15 When she and the members of her
household were baptized, she invited us to her
home. "If you consider me a believer in the
Lord," she said, "come and stay at my house."
And she persuaded us.

Paul and Silas in prison

16 Once when we were going to the place of
prayer, we were met by a slave girl who had a
spirit by which she predicted the future. She
earned a lot of money for her owners by fortune-
telling. 17 This girl followed Paul and the rest
of us, shouting, "These men are servants of the
Most High God, who are telling you the way to

Phillips Modern English

16.11 The gospel comes to Europe: a business-woman is converted

So we set sail from Troas and ran a straight course to Samothrace, and on the following day to Neapolis. From there we went to Philippi, a Roman garrison-town and the chief city in that part of Macedonia. We spent some days in Philippi and on the Sabbath day we went out of the city gate to the riverside, where we supposed there was a place for prayer. There we sat down and spoke to the women who had assembled. One of our hearers was a woman named Lydia. (She came from Thyatira and was a dealer in purple-dyed cloth.) She was already a believer in God, who had opened her heart to accept Paul's words. When she and her household had been baptised, she appealed to us, saying,

"If you are satisfied that I am a true believer in the Lord, then come down to my house and stay there."

And she insisted on our doing so.

16.16 Conflict with evil spirits and evil men

One day while we were going to the place of prayer we met a young girl who had a spirit of clairvoyance and brought her owners a good deal of profit by foretelling the future. She would follow Paul and the rest of us, crying out, "These men are servants of the Most High God, and

Revised Standard Version

11 Setting sail therefore from Troas, we made a direct voyage to Samothrace, and the following day to Neapolis, 12 and from there to Philippi, which is the leading city of the district[x] of Macedonia, and a Roman colony. We remained in this city some days; 13 and on the sabbath day we went outside the gate to the riverside, where we supposed there was a place of prayer; and we sat down and spoke to the women who had come together. 14 One who heard us was a woman named Lydia, from the city of Thyatira, a seller of purple goods, who was a worshiper of God. The Lord opened her heart to give heed to what was said by Paul. 15 And when she was baptized, with her household, she besought us, saying, "If you have judged me to be faithful to the Lord, come to my house and stay." And she prevailed upon us.

16 As we were going to the place of prayer, we were met by a slave girl who had a spirit of divination and brought her owners much gain by soothsaying. 17 She followed Paul and us, crying, "These men are servants of the Most High God, who proclaim to you the way of salvation."

[x] The Greek text is uncertain.

Jerusalem Bible

Arrival at Philippi

11 Sailing from Troas we made a straight run for Samothrace; the next day for Neapolis, 12 and from there for Philippi, a Roman colony and the principal city of that particular district of Macedonia. After a few days in this city 13 we went along the river outside the gates as it was the sabbath and this was a customary place for prayer.[x] We sat down and preached to the women who had come to the meeting. 14 One of these women was called Lydia, a devout woman from the town of Thyatira who was in the purple-dye trade. She listened to us, and the Lord opened her heart to accept what Paul was saying. 15 After she and her household had been baptized she sent us an invitation: "If you really think me a true believer in the Lord," she said, "come and stay with us"; and she would take no refusal.

Imprisonment of Paul and Silas

16 One day as we were going to prayer, we met a slave girl who was a soothsayer and made a lot of money for her masters by telling fortunes. 17 This girl started following Paul and the rest of us and shouting, "Here are the servants of the Most High God; they have come to

[x] There was no synagogue in this Latin city; the Jews met by the river for ritual ablutions.

New English Bible

So we sailed from Troas and made a straight run to Samothrace, the next day to Neapolis, and from there to Philippi, a city of the first rank in that district of Macedonia, and a Roman colony. Here we stayed for some days, and on the Sabbath day we went outside the city gate by the river-side, where we thought there would be a place of prayer,[b] and sat down and talked to the women who had gathered there. One of them named Lydia, a dealer in purple fabric from the city of Thyatira, who was a worshipper of God, was listening, and the Lord opened her heart to respond to what Paul said. She was baptized, and her household with her, and then she said to us, 'If you have judged me to be a believer in the Lord, I beg you to come and stay in my house.' And she insisted on our going.

Once, when we were on our way to the place of prayer, we met a slave-girl who was possessed by an oracular spirit and brought large profits to her owners by telling fortunes. She followed Paul and the rest of us, shouting, 'These men are servants of the Supreme God, and are declaring

[b] Some witnesses read where there was a recognized place of prayer.

King James Version

unto us the way of salvation. 18 And this did
she many days. But Paul, being grieved, turned
and said to the spirit, I command thee in the
name of Jesus Christ to come out of her. And
he came out the same hour.
19 And when her masters saw that the hope
of their gains was gone, they caught Paul and
Silas, and drew *them* into the marketplace unto
the rulers, 20 And brought them to the magistrates, saying, These men, being Jews, do exceedingly trouble our city, 21 And teach customs,
which are not lawful for us to receive, neither
to observe, being Romans. 22 And the multitude
rose up together against them; and the magistrates rent off their clothes, and commanded to
beat *them*. 23 And when they had laid many
stripes upon them, they cast *them* into prison,
charging the jailer to keep them safely: 24 Who,
having received such a charge, thrust them into
the inner prison, and made their feet fast in
the stocks.
25 And at midnight Paul and Silas prayed,
and sang praises unto God: and the prisoners
heard them. 26 And suddenly there was a great
earthquake, so that the foundations of the
prison were shaken: and immediately all the
doors were opened, and every one's bands were

Living Bible

18 This went on day after day until Paul, in
great distress, turned and spoke to the demon
within her. "I command you in the name of Jesus Christ to come out of her," he said. And
instantly it left her.
19 Her masters' hopes of wealth were now
shattered; they grabbed Paul and Silas and
dragged them before the judges at the market-
place.
20, 21 "These Jews are corrupting our city,"
they shouted. "They are teaching the people to
do things that are against the Roman laws."
22 A mob was quickly formed against Paul
and Silas, and the judges ordered them stripped
and beaten with wooden whips. 23 Again and
again the rods slashed down across their bared
backs; and afterwards they were thrown into
prison. The jailer was threatened with death if
they escaped,[d] 24 so he took no chances, but put
them into the inner dungeon and clamped their
feet into the stocks.
25 Around midnight, as Paul and Silas were
praying and singing hymns to the Lord—and
the other prisoners were listening—26 suddenly
there was a great earthquake; the prison was
shaken to its foundations, all the doors flew open
—and the chains of every prisoner fell off!

[*d*] Implied.

Today's English Version

be saved!" 18 She did this for many days, until
Paul became so upset that he turned around and
said to the spirit, "In the name of Jesus Christ
I order you to come out of her!" The spirit
went out of her that very moment. 19 When her
owners realized that their chance of making
money was gone, they grabbed Paul and Silas
and dragged them to the authorities in the public square. 20 They brought them before the
Roman officials and said, "These men are Jews,
and they are causing trouble in our city. 21 They
are teaching customs that are against our law;
we are Romans and cannot accept or practice
them." 22 The crowd joined the attack against
them; the officials tore the clothes off Paul and
Silas, and ordered them to be whipped. 23 After
a severe beating they were thrown into jail, and
the jailer was ordered to lock them up tight.
24 Upon receiving this order, the jailer threw
them into the inner cell and fastened their feet
between heavy blocks of wood.
25 About midnight Paul and Silas were praying and singing hymns to God, and the other
prisoners were listening to them. 26 Suddenly
there was a violent earthquake, which shook
the prison to its foundations. At once all the
doors opened, and the chains fell off all the

New International Version

be saved." 18 She kept this up for many days.
Finally Paul became so troubled that he turned
around and said to the spirit, "In the name of
Jesus Christ I command you to come out of
her!" At that moment the spirit left her.
19 When the owners of the slave girl realized
that their hope of making money was gone, they
seized Paul and Silas and dragged them into the
marketplace to face the authorities. 20 They
brought them before the magistrates and said,
"These men are Jews, and are throwing our city
into an uproar 21 by advocating customs unlawful for us Romans to accept or practice."
22 The crowd joined in the attack against
Paul and Silas, and the magistrates ordered them
to be stripped and beaten. 23 After they had been
severely flogged, they were thrown into prison,
and the jailer was commanded to guard them
carefully. 24 Upon receiving such orders, he put
them in the inner cell and fastened their feet in
the stocks.
25 About midnight Paul and Silas were praying and singing hymns to God, and the other
prisoners were listening to them. 26 Suddenly
there was such a violent earthquake that the
foundations of the prison were shaken. At once
all the prison doors flew open, and everybody's

Phillips Modern English

they are telling you the way of salvation." She continued this behaviour for many days, and then Paul, in a burst of irritation, turned round and spoke to the spirit in her.

"I command you in the name of Jesus Christ to come out of her!"

And it came out immediately. But when the girl's owners saw that their hope of making money out of her had disappeared, they seized Paul and Silas and dragged them before the authorities in the market-square. There they brought them before the magistrates, and said, "These men are Jews and are causing a great disturbance in our city. They are proclaiming customs which it is illegal for us as Roman citizens to accept or practise."

At this the crowd joined in the attack, and the magistrates had them stripped and ordered them to be beaten with rods. Then, after giving them a severe beating, they threw them into prison, instructing the jailer to keep them safe. On receiving such strict orders, he hustled them into the inner jail and fastened their feet securely in the stocks.

16.25 The midnight deliverance: the jailer becomes a Christian

But about midnight Paul and Silas were praying and singing hymns to God while the other prisoners were listening to them. Suddenly there was a great earthquake, big enough to shake the foundations of the prison. Immediately all the doors flew open and everyone's chains were un-

Revised Standard Version

18 And this she did for many days. But Paul was
annoyed, and turned and said to the spirit, "I
charge you in the name of Jesus Christ to come
out of her." And it came out that very hour.
19 But when her owners saw that their hope
of gain was gone, they seized Paul and Silas and
dragged them into the market place before the
rulers; 20 and when they had brought them to
the magistrates they said, "These men are Jews
and they are disturbing our city. 21 They advocate customs which it is not lawful for us Romans to accept or practice." 22 The crowd joined
in attacking them; and the magistrates tore the
garments off them and gave orders to beat them
with rods. 23 And when they had inflicted many
blows upon them, they threw them into prison,
charging the jailer to keep them safely. 24 Having
received this charge, he put them into the inner
prison and fastened their feet in the stocks.
25 But about midnight Paul and Silas were
praying and singing hymns to God, and the
prisoners were listening to them, 26 and suddenly
there was a great earthquake, so that the foundations of the prison were shaken; and immediately
all the doors were opened and every one's fetters

Jerusalem Bible

tell you how to be saved!" 18 She did this every
day afterward until Paul lost his temper one
day and turned around and said to the spirit, "I
order you in the name of Jesus Christ to leave
that woman." The spirit went out of her then
and there.
19 When her masters saw that there was no
hope of making any more money out of her, they
seized Paul and Silas and dragged them to the
law courts in the market place 20 where they
charged them before the magistrates and said,
"These people are causing a disturbance in our
city. They are Jews 21 and are advocating practices which it is unlawful for us as Romans to
accept or follow." [y] 22 The crowd joined in and
showed its hostility to them, so the magistrates
had them stripped and ordered them to be
flogged. 23 They were given many lashes and
then thrown into prison, and the jailer was told
to keep a close watch on them. 24 So, following
his instructions, he threw them into the inner
prison and fastened their feet in the stocks.

The miraculous deliverance of Paul and Silas

25 Late that night Paul and Silas were praying and singing God's praises, while the other
prisoners listened. 26 Suddenly there was an
earthquake that shook the prison to its foundations. All the doors flew open and the chains

[y] The Jews had no right to proselytize Romans.

New English Bible

to you a way of salvation.' She did this day after day, until Paul could bear it no longer. Rounding on the spirit he said, 'I command you in the name of Jesus Christ to come out of her', and it went out there and then.

When the girl's owners saw that their hope of gain had gone, they seized Paul and Silas and dragged them to the city authorities in the main square; and bringing them before the magistrates, they said, 'These men are causing a disturbance in our city; they are Jews; they are advocating customs which it is illegal for us Romans to adopt and follow.' The mob joined in the attack; and the magistrates tore off the prisoners' clothes and ordered them to be flogged. After giving them a severe beating they flung them into prison and ordered the jailer to keep them under close guard. In view of these orders, he put them in the inner prison and secured their feet in the stocks.

About midnight Paul and Silas, at their prayers, were singing praises to God, and the other prisoners were listening, when suddenly there was such a violent earthquake that the foundations of the jail were shaken; all the doors burst open and all the prisoners found their fetters

King James Version

loosed. 27And the keeper of the prison awaking
out of his sleep, and seeing the prison doors
open, he drew out his sword, and would have
killed himself, supposing that the prisoners had
been fled. 28 But Paul cried with a loud voice,
saying, Do thyself no harm: for we are all
here. 29 Then he called for a light, and sprang
in, and came trembling, and fell down before
Paul and Silas, 30And brought them out, and
said, Sirs, what must I do to be saved? 31And
they said, Believe on the Lord Jesus Christ, and
thou shalt be saved, and thy house. 32And they
spake unto him the word of the Lord, and to all
that were in his house. 33And he took them the
same hour of the night, and washed *their*
stripes; and was baptized, he and all his,
straightway. 34And when he had brought them
into his house, he set meat before them, and
rejoiced, believing in God with all his house.
35And when it was day, the magistrates sent the
serjeants, saying, Let those men go. 36And the
keeper of the prison told this saying to Paul,
The magistrates have sent to let you go: now
therefore depart, and go in peace. 37 But Paul
said unto them, They have beaten us openly uncondemned, being Romans, and have cast *us*

Living Bible

27 The jailer wakened to see the prison doors
wide open, and assuming the prisoners had escaped, he drew his sword to kill himself.
28 But Paul yelled to him, "Don't do it! We
are all here!"
29 Trembling with fear, the jailer called for
lights and ran to the dungeon and fell down before Paul and Silas. 30 He brought them out and
begged them, "Sirs, what must I do to be
saved?"
31 They replied, "Believe on the Lord Jesus
and you will be saved, and your entire household."
32 Then they told him and all his household
the Good News from the Lord. 33 That same
hour he washed their stripes and he and all his
family were baptized. 34 Then he brought them
up into his house and set a meal before them.
How he and his household rejoiced because all
were now believers! 35 The next morning the
judges sent police officers over to tell the jailer,
"Let those men go!" 36 So the jailer told Paul
they were free to leave.
37 But Paul replied, "Oh, no they don't! They
have publicly beaten us without trial and jailed

Today's English Version

prisoners. 27 The jailer woke up, and when he
saw the prison doors open he thought that all
the prisoners had escaped; so he pulled out his
sword and was about to kill himself. 28 But Paul
shouted at the top of his voice, "Don't harm
yourself! We are all here!"
29 The jailer called for a light, rushed in, and
fell trembling at the feet of Paul and Silas.
30 Then he led them out and asked, "What must
I do, sirs, to be saved?"
31 "Believe in the Lord Jesus," they said,
"and you will be saved—you and your family."
32 Then they preached the word of the Lord to
him and to all the others in his house. 33At that
very hour of the night the jailer took them and
washed off their wounds; and he and all his
family were baptized at once. 34 He took Paul
and Silas up into his house and gave them some
food to eat. He and his family were filled with
joy, because he now believed in God.
35 The next morning the Roman authorities
sent police officers with the order, "Let those
men go."
36 So the jailer told it to Paul, "The officials
have sent an order for you and Silas to be released. You may leave, then, and go in peace."
37 But Paul said to the police officers, "We
were not found guilty of any crime, yet they

New International Version

chains came loose. 27 The jailer woke up, and
when he saw the prison doors open, he drew his
sword and was about to kill himself because he
thought the prisoners had escaped. 28 But Paul
shouted, "Don't harm yourself! We are all here!"
29 The jailer called for lights, rushed in and
fell trembling before Paul and Silas. 30 He then
brought them out and asked, "Men, what must
I do to be saved?"
31 They replied, "Believe in the Lord Jesus,
and you will be saved—you and your household." 32 Then they spoke the word of the Lord
to him and to all the others in his house. 33At
that hour of the night the jailer took them and
washed their wounds; then immediately he and
all his family were baptized. 34 The jailer brought
them into his house and set a meal before them,
and the whole family was filled with joy, because they had come to believe in God.
35 When it was daylight, the magistrates sent
their officers to the jailer with the order: "Release those men." 36 The jailer told Paul, "The
magistrates have ordered that you and Silas be
released. Now you can leave. Go in peace."
37 But Paul said to the officers: "They beat
us publicly without a trial, even though we are

Phillips Modern English

fastened. When the jailer woke and saw that the doors of the prison had been opened he drew his sword and was on the point of killing himself, for he imagined that all the prisoners had escaped. But Paul called out to him at the top of his voice,

"Don't hurt yourself—we are all here!"

Then the jailer called for lights, rushed in, and trembling all over, fell at the feet of Paul and Silas. He led them outside, and said,

"Sirs, what must I do to be saved?"

And they replied,

"Believe in the Lórd Jesus and then you will be saved, you and your household."

Then they told him and all the members of his household the message of the Lord. There and then in the middle of the night he took them aside and washed their wounds and he himself and all his family were baptised without delay. Then he took them into his house and offered them food, he and his whole household overjoyed at finding faith in God.

16.35 Paul, in a strong position, makes the authorities apologise

When morning came, the magistrates sent their constables with the message, "Let those men go." The jailer reported this message to Paul, saying,

"The magistrates have sent to have you released. So now you can leave this place and go on your way in peace."

But Paul said to the constables,

"They beat us publicly without any kind of

Revised Standard Version

were unfastened. 27 When the jailer woke and
saw that the prison doors were open, he drew his
sword and was about to kill himself, supposing
that the prisoners had escaped. 28 But Paul
cried with a loud voice, "Do not harm yourself,
for we are all here." 29 And he called for lights
and rushed in, and trembling with fear he fell
down before Paul and Silas, 30 and brought
them out and said, "Men, what must I do to be
saved?" 31 And they said, "Believe in the Lord
Jesus, and you will be saved, you and your
household." 32 And they spoke the word of the
Lord to him and to all that were in his house.
33 And he took them the same hour of the night,
and washed their wounds, and he was baptized
at once, with all his family. 34 Then he brought
them up into his house, and set food before
them; and he rejoiced with all his household that
he had believed in God.

35 But when it was day, the magistrates sent
the police, saying, "Let those men go." 36 And
the jailer reported the words to Paul, saying,
"The magistrates have sent to let you go; now
therefore come out and go in peace." 37 But
Paul said to them, "They have beaten us publicly,
uncondemned, men who are Roman citizens, and

Jerusalem Bible

fell from all the prisoners. 27 When the jailer
woke and saw the doors wide open he drew his
sword and was about to commit suicide, presuming that the prisoners had escaped. 28 But
Paul shouted at the top of his voice, "Don't do
yourself any harm; we are all here."

29 The jailer called for lights, then rushed in,
threw himself trembling at the feet of Paul and
Silas, 30 and escorted them out, saying, "Sirs,
what must I do to be saved?" 31 They told him,
"Become a believer in the Lord Jesus, and you
will be saved, and your household too." 32 Then
they preached the word of the Lord to him and
to all his family. 33 Late as it was, he took them
to wash their wounds, and was baptized then
and there with all his household. 34 Afterward
he took them home and gave them a meal, and
the whole family celebrated their conversion to
belief in God.

35 When it was daylight the magistrates sent
the officers with the order: "Release those men."
36 The jailer reported the message to Paul, "The
magistrates have sent an order for your release;
you can go now and be on your way."
37 "What!" Paul replied, "They flog Roman
citizens in public and without trial and throw

New English Bible

unfastened. The jailer woke up to see the prison doors wide open, and assuming that the prisoners had escaped, drew his sword intending to kill himself. But Paul shouted, 'Do yourself no harm; we are all here.' The jailer called for lights, rushed in and threw himself down before Paul and Silas, trembling with fear. He then escorted them out and said, 'Masters, what must I do to be saved?' They said, 'Put your trust in the Lord Jesus, and you will be saved, you and your household.' Then they spoke the word of the Lord[a] to him and to everyone in his house. At that late hour of the night he took them and washed their wounds; and immediately afterwards he and his whole family were baptized. He brought them into his house, set out a meal, and rejoiced with his whole household in his new-found faith in God.

When daylight came the magistrates sent their officers with instructions to release the men. The jailer reported the message to Paul: 'The magistrates have sent word that you are to be released. So now you may go free, and blessings on your journey.'[b] But Paul said to the officers: 'They gave us a public flogging, though we are Roman

[a] *Some witnesses read* of God. [b] *Some witnesses read* . . . free and take your journey.

King James Version

into prison; and now do they thrust us out
privily? nay verily; but let them come themselves and fetch us out. 38And the serjeants
told these words unto the magistrates: and they
feared, when they heard that they were Romans.
39And they came and besought them, and
brought *them* out, and desired *them* to depart
out of the city. 40And they went out of the
prison, and entered into *the house of* Lydia:
and when they had seen the brethren, they comforted them, and departed.

17 Now when they had passed through Amphipolis and Apollonia, they came to Thessalonica, where was a synagogue of the Jews:
2And Paul, as his manner was, went in unto
them, and three sabbath days reasoned with
them out of the Scriptures, 3 Opening and alleging, that Christ must needs have suffered, and
risen again from the dead; and that this Jesus,
whom I preach unto you, is Christ. 4And some
of them believed, and consorted with Paul and
Silas; and of the devout Greeks a great multitude, and of the chief women not a few.
5 But the Jews which believed not, moved
with envy, took unto them certain lewd fellows
of the baser sort, and gathered a company, and

Living Bible

us—and we are Roman citizens! So now they
want us to leave secretly? Never! Let them come
themselves and release us!"
38 The police officers reported to the judges,
who feared for their lives when they heard Paul
and Silas were Roman citizens. 39 So they came
to the jail and begged them to go, and brought
them out and pled with them to leave the city.
40 Paul and Silas then returned to the home of
Lydia where they met with the believers and
preached to them once more before leaving town.

17 Now they traveled through the cities of
Amphipolis and Apollonia and came to Thessalonica, where there was a Jewish synagogue.
2As was Paul's custom, he went there to preach,
and for three Sabbaths in a row he opened the
Scriptures to the people, 3 explaining the prophecies about the sufferings of the Messiah and his
coming back to life, and proving that Jesus is
the Messiah. 4 Some who listened were persuaded and became converts—including a large
number of godly Greek men, and also many
important women of the city.[a]
5 But the Jewish leaders were jealous and
incited some worthless fellows from the streets
to form a mob and start a riot. They attacked

[a] Some manuscripts read, "many of the wives of the leading men."

Today's English Version

whipped us in public—and we are Roman citizens! Then they threw us in prison. And now
they want to send us away secretly? Not at all!
The Roman officials themselves must come here
and let us out."
38 The police officers reported these words to
the Roman officials; and when they heard that
Paul and Silas were Roman citizens, they were
afraid. 39 So they went and apologized to them;
then they led them out of the prison and asked
them to leave the city. 40 Paul and Silas left the
prison and went to Lydia's house. There they
met the brothers, spoke words of encouragement to them, and left.

In Thessalonica

17 They traveled on through Amphipolis and
Apollonia, and came to Thessalonica, where
there was a Jewish synagogue. 2According to his
usual habit, Paul went to the synagogue. There
during three Sabbath days he argued with the
people from the Scriptures, 3 explaining them
and proving from them that the Messiah had to
suffer, and rise from death. "This Jesus whom
I announce to you," Paul said, "is the Messiah."
4 Some of them were convinced and joined Paul
and Silas; so did a large group of Greeks who
worshiped God, and many of the leading women.
5 But the Jews were jealous and gathered
some of the worthless loafers from the streets
and formed a mob. They set the whole city in

New International Version

Roman citizens, and threw us into prison. And
now do they want to get rid of us quietly? No!
Let them come themselves and escort us out."
38 The officers reported this to the magistrates, and when they heard that Paul and Silas
were Roman citizens, they were alarmed. 39 They
came to appease them and escorted them from
the prison, requesting them to leave the city.
40After Paul and Silas came out of the prison,
they went to Lydia's house, where they met with
the brothers and encouraged them. Then they
left.

In Thessalonica

17 When they had passed through Amphipolis and Apollonia, they came to Thessalonica, where there was a Jewish synagogue. 2As
his custom was, Paul went into the synagogue,
and on three Sabbath days he reasoned with
them from the Scriptures, 3 explaining and
proving that the Christ[z] had to suffer and rise
from the dead. "This Jesus I am proclaiming to
you is the Christ,[z]" he said. 4 Some of the Jews
were persuaded and joined Paul and Silas, as did
a large number of God-fearing Greeks and not
a few prominent women.
5 But the Jews were jealous; so they rounded
up some bad characters from the marketplace,
formed a mob and started a riot in the city.

[z] Or *Messiah.*

Phillips Modern English

trial; they threw us into prison despite the fact
that we are Roman citizens. And now do they
want to get rid of us in this underhand way?
Oh no, let them come and take us out themselves!"
The constables reported these words to the
magistrates, who were thoroughly alarmed when
they heard that they were Romans. So they
came in person and apologised to them, and after
taking them outside the prison, requested them
to leave the city. But on leaving the prison Paul
and Silas went to Lydia's house, and when they
had seen the brothers and given them fresh
courage, they took their leave.

17.1 Bitter opposition at Thessalonica—

Next they journeyed through Amphipolis and
Apollonia and arrived at Thessalonica. Here
there was a synagogue of the Jews which Paul
entered, following his usual custom. On three
Sabbath days he argued with them from the
scriptures, explaining and quoting passages to
prove the necessity for the death of Christ and
his rising again from the dead. "This Jesus whom
I am proclaiming to you," he concluded, "is
God's Christ!" Some of them were convinced
and sided with Paul and Silas, and they were
joined by a great many believing Greeks and a
considerable number of influential women. But
the Jews, in a fury of jealousy, got hold of some
of the unprincipled loungers of the market-place
to incite a mob together and set the city in an

Revised Standard Version

have thrown us into prison; and do they now
cast us out secretly? No! let them come themselves and take us out." 38 The police reported
these words to the magistrates, and they were
afraid when they heard that they were Roman
citizens; 39 so they came and apologized to them.
And they took them out and asked them to leave
the city. 40 So they went out of the prison, and
visited Lydia; and when they had seen the brethren, they exhorted them and departed.

17 Now when they had passed through Amphipolis and Apollonia, they came to Thessalonica, where there was a synagogue of the
Jews. 2 And Paul went in, as was his custom, and
for three weeks[p] he argued with them from the
scriptures, 3 explaining and proving that it was
necessary for the Christ to suffer and to rise
from the dead, and saying, "This Jesus, whom I
proclaim to you, is the Christ." 4 And some of
them were persuaded, and joined Paul and Silas;
as did a great many of the devout Greeks and
not a few of the leading women. 5 But the Jews
were jealous, and taking some wicked fellows of
the rabble, they gathered a crowd, set the city

[p] Or *sabbaths*.

Jerusalem Bible

us into prison, and then think they can push us
out on the quiet! Oh no! They must come and
escort us out themselves."
38 The officers reported this to the magistrates,
who were horrified to hear the men were Roman
citizens. 39 They came and begged them to leave
the town. 40 From the prison they went to
Lydia's house where they saw all the brothers
and gave them some encouragement; then they
left.

Thessalonika: difficulties with the Jews

17 Passing through Amphipolis and Apollonia, they eventually reached Thessalonika,
where there was a Jewish synagogue. 2 Paul as
usual introduced himself and for three consecu-
tive sabbaths developed the arguments from
scripture for them, 3 explaining and proving how
it was ordained that the Christ should suffer and
rise from the dead. "And the Christ," he said,
"is this Jesus who I am proclaiming to you."
4 Some of them were convinced and joined
Paul and Silas, and so did a great many God-
fearing people and Greeks, as well as a number
of rich women.
5 The Jews, full of resentment, enlisted the
help of a gang from the market place, stirred
up a crowd, and soon had the whole city in an

New English Bible

citizens and have not been found guilty; they
threw us into prison, and are they now to
smuggle us out privately? No indeed! Let them
come in person and escort us out.' The officers
reported his words. The magistrates were
alarmed to hear that they were Roman citizens,
and came and apologized to them. Then they
escorted them out and requested them to go
away from the city. On leaving the prison, they
went to Lydia's house, where they met their
fellow-Christians, and spoke words of encouragement to them; then they departed.

17 They now travelled by way of Amphipolis and Apollonia and came to Thessalonica, where there was a Jewish synagogue.
Following his usual practice Paul went to their
meetings; and for the next three Sabbaths he
argued with them, quoting texts of Scripture
which he expounded and applied to show that
the Messiah had to suffer and rise from the
dead. 'And this Jesus,' he said, 'whom I am proclaiming to you, is the Messiah.' Some of them
were convinced and joined Paul and Silas; so
did a great number of godfearing Gentiles and a
good many influential women.[a]
But the Jews in their jealousy recruited some
low fellows from the dregs of the populace,
roused the rabble, and had the city in an uproar.

[a] *Some witnesses read* a good many wives of leading men.

King James Version

set all the city on an uproar, and assaulted the house of Jason, and sought to bring them out to the people. 6And when they found them not, they drew Jason and certain brethren unto the rulers of the city, crying, These that have turned the world upside down are come hither also; 7 Whom Jason hath received: and these all do contrary to the decrees of Cesar, saying that there is another king, *one* Jesus. 8And they troubled the people and the rulers of the city, when they heard these things. 9And when they had taken security of Jason, and of the others, they let them go.

10 And the brethren immediately sent away Paul and Silas by night unto Berea: who coming *thither* went into the synagogue of the Jews. 11 These were more noble than those in Thessalonica, in that they received the word with all readiness of mind, and searched the Scriptures daily, whether those things were so. 12 Therefore many of them believed; also of honourable women which were Greeks, and of men, not a few. 13 But when the Jews of Thessalonica had knowledge that the word of God was preached of Paul at Berea, they came thither also, and stirred up the people. 14And then immediately the brethren sent away Paul to go as it were to the sea: but Silas and Timotheus abode there

Living Bible

the home of Jason, planning to take Paul and Silas to the City Council for punishment.

6 Not finding them there, they dragged out Jason and some of the other believers, and took them before the Council instead. "Paul and Silas have turned the rest of the world upside down, and now they are here disturbing our city," they shouted, 7 "and Jason has let them into his home. They are all guilty of treason, for they claim another king, Jesus, instead of Caesar."

8, 9 The people of the city, as well as the judges, were concerned at these reports and let them go only after they had posted bail.

10 That night the Christians hurried Paul and Silas to Beroea, and, as usual,[b] they went to the synagogue to preach. 11 But the people of Beroea were more open minded than those in Thessalonica, and gladly listened to the message. They searched the Scriptures day by day to check up on Paul and Silas' statements to see if they were really so. 12As a result, many of them believed, including several prominent Greek women and many men also.

13 But when the Jews in Thessalonica learned that Paul was preaching in Beroea, they went over and stirred up trouble. 14 The believers acted at once, sending Paul on to the coast, while Silas and Timothy remained behind.

[b] Implied.

Today's English Version

an uproar, and attacked the home of Jason, trying to find Paul and Silas and bring them out to the people. 6 But when they did not find them, they dragged Jason and some other brothers to the city authorities and shouted, "These men have caused trouble everywhere! Now they have come to our city, 7 and Jason has kept them in his house. They are all breaking the laws of the Emperor, saying that there is another king, by the name of Jesus." 8 With these words they threw the crowd and the city authorities in an uproar. 9 The authorities made Jason and the others pay the required amount of money to be released, and then let them go.

In Berea

10 As soon as night came, the brothers sent Paul and Silas to Berea. When they arrived, they went to the Jewish synagogue. 11 The people there were more openminded than the people in Thessalonica. They listened to the message with great eagerness, and every day they studied the Scriptures to see if what Paul said was really true. 12 Many of them believed; and many Greek women of high social standing and many Greek men also believed. 13 But when the Jews in Thessalonica heard that Paul had preached the word of God in Berea also, they came there and started exciting and stirring up the mobs. 14At once the brothers sent Paul away to the coast; but both Silas and Timothy stayed in Berea.

New International Version

They rushed to Jason's house in search of Paul and Silas in order to bring them out to the crowd.[a] 6 But when they did not find them, they dragged Jason and some other brothers before the city officials, shouting: "These men who have caused trouble all over the world have now come here, 7 and Jason has welcomed them into his house. They are all defying Caesar's decrees, saying that there is another king, one called Jesus." 8 When they heard this, the crowd and the city officials were thrown into turmoil. 9 Then they made Jason and the others post bond and let them go.

In Berea

10 As soon as it was night, the brothers sent Paul and Silas away to Berea. On arriving there, they went to the Jewish synagogue. 11 Now the Bereans were of more noble character than the Thessalonians, for they received the message with great eagerness and examined the Scriptures every day to see if what Paul said was true. 12 Many of the Jews believed, as did also a number of prominent Greek women and many Greek men.

13 When the Jews in Thessalonica learned that Paul was preaching the word of God at Berea, they went there too, agitating the crowds and stirring them up. 14 The brothers immediately sent Paul to the coast, but Silas and Timothy

[a] Or *assembly of the people.*

Phillips Modern English

uproar. Then they attacked Jason's house in an attempt to bring Paul and Silas out before the people. When they could not find them they hustled Jason and some of the brothers before the civic authorities, shouting, "These are the men who have turned the world upside down and have now come here, and Jason has taken them into his house. What is more, all these men act against the decrees of Caesar, saying that there is another king called Jesus!" By these words the Jews succeeded in alarming both the people and the authorities, and they only released Jason and the others after binding them over to keep the peace.

17.10 —followed by encouragement at Berœa

Without delay the brothers despatched Paul and Silas off to Berœa that night. On their arrival there they went to the Jewish synagogue. The Jews proved more sympathetic than those in Thessalonica, for they accepted the message most eagerly and studied the scriptures every day to see if what they were now being told were true. As a result many of them became believers, and so did a number of Greek women of social standing and quite a number of men. But when the Jews at Thessalonica found out that God's message had been proclaimed by Paul at Berœa as well, they came there too to stir up trouble and spread alarm among the crowds. The brothers at Berœa then sent Paul off at once to make his way to the sea-coast, but Silas and Timothy

Revised Standard Version

in an uproar, and attacked the house of Jason,
seeking to bring them out to the people. 6And
when they could not find them, they dragged
Jason and some of the brethren before the city
authorities, crying, "These men who have turned
the world upside down have come here also,
7 and Jason has received them; and they are all
acting against the decrees of Caesar, saying that
there is another king, Jesus." 8And the people
and the city authorities were disturbed when
they heard this. 9And when they had taken security from Jason and the rest, they let them go.
10 The brethren immediately sent Paul and
Silas away by night to Beroea; and when they
arrived they went into the Jewish synagogue.
11 Now these Jews were more noble than those
in Thessalonica, for they received the word with
all eagerness, examining the scriptures daily to
see if these things were so. 12 Many of them
therefore believed, with not a few Greek women
of high standing as well as men. 13 But when
the Jews of Thessalonica learned that the word
of God was proclaimed by Paul at Beroea also,
they came there too, stirring up and inciting
the crowds. 14 Then the brethren immediately
sent Paul off on his way to the sea, but Silas

Jerusalem Bible

uproar. They made for Jason's house, hoping to
find them there and drag them off to the People's Assembly; 6 however, they only found
Jason and some of the brothers, and these they
dragged before the city council, shouting, "The
people who have been turning the whole world
upside down have come here now; 7 they have
been staying at Jason's. They have broken every
one of Caesar's edicts by claiming that there
is another emperor, Jesus." 8 This accusation
alarmed the citizens and the city councilors 9 and
they made Jason and the rest give security before
setting them free.

Fresh difficulties at Beroea

10 When it was dark the brothers immediately
sent Paul and Silas away to Beroea, where they
visited the Jewish synagogue as soon as they
arrived. 11 Here the Jews were more open-minded than those in Thessalonika, and they welcomed the word very readily; every day they
studied the scriptures to check whether it was
true. 12 Many Jews became believers, and so did
many Greek women from the upper classes and
a number of the men.
13 When the Jews of Thessalonika heard that
the word of God was being preached by Paul in
Beroea as well, they went there to make trouble
and stir up the people. 14 So the brothers arranged for Paul to go immediately as far as the

New English Bible

They mobbed Jason's house, with the intention of bringing Paul and Silas before the town assembly. Failing to find them, they dragged Jason himself and some members of the congregation before the magistrates, shouting, 'The men who have made trouble all over the world have now come here; and Jason has harboured them. They all flout the Emperor's laws, and assert that there is a rival king, Jesus.' These words caused a great commotion in the mob, which affected the magistrates also. They bound over Jason and the others, and let them go.

As soon as darkness fell, the members of the congregation sent Paul and Silas off to Beroea. On arrival. they made their way to the synagogue. The Jews here were more civil than those at Thessalonica: they received the message with great eagerness, studying the scriptures every day to see whether it was as they said. Many of them therefore became believers, and so did a fair number of Gentiles, women of standing as well as men. But when the Thessalonian Jews learned that the word of God had now been proclaimed by Paul in Beroea, they came on there to stir up trouble and rouse the rabble. Thereupon the members of the congregation sent Paul off at once to go down to the coast, while Silas and Timothy both stayed behind.

King James Version

still. 15 And they that conducted Paul brought
him unto Athens: and receiving a commandment unto Silas and Timotheus for to come to
him with all speed, they departed.
16 Now while Paul waited for them at Athens,
his spirit was stirred in him, when he saw the
city wholly given to idolatry. 17 Therefore disputed he in the synagogue with the Jews, and
with the devout persons, and in the market daily
with them that met with him. 18 Then certain
philosophers of the Epicureans, and of the
Stoics, encountered him. And some said, What
will this babbler say? other some, He seemeth to
be a setter forth of strange gods: because he
preached unto them Jesus, and the resurrection.
19 And they took him, and brought him unto
Areopagus, saying, May we know what this new
doctrine, whereof thou speakest, *is?* 20 For thou
bringest certain strange things to our ears: we
would know therefore what these things mean.
21 (For all the Athenians, and strangers which
were there, spent their time in nothing else, but
either to tell or to hear some new thing.)

Living Bible

15 Those accompanying Paul went on with him
to Athens, and then returned to Beroea with a
message for Silas and Timothy to hurry and join
him.
16 While Paul was waiting for them in Athens,
he was deeply troubled by all the idols he saw
everywhere throughout the city. 17 He went to
the synagogue for discussions with the Jews
and the devout Gentiles, and spoke daily in the
public square to all who happened to be there.
18 He also had an encounter with some of
the Epicurean and Stoic philosophers. Their
reaction, when he told them about Jesus and his
resurrection, was, "He's a dreamer," or, "He's
pushing some foreign religion."
19 But they invited him to the forum at Mars
Hill. "Come and tell us more about this new
religion," they said, 20 "for you are saying some
rather startling things and we want to hear
more." 21 (I should explain that all the Athenians as well as the foreigners in Athens seemed
to spend all their time discussing the latest new
ideas!)

Today's English Version

15 The men who were taking Paul went with him
as far as Athens. Then they went back to Berea
with instructions from Paul that Silas and Timothy join him as soon as possible.

In Athens

16 While Paul was waiting in Athens for Silas
and Timothy, he was greatly upset when he
noticed how full of idols the city was. 17 So he
argued in the synagogue with the Jews and the
Gentiles who worshiped God, and in the public
square every day with the people who happened
to come by. 18 Certain Epicurean and Stoic
teachers also debated with him. Some said,
"What is this ignorant show-off trying to say?"
Others said, "He seems to be talking about
foreign gods." They said this because Paul was
preaching about Jesus and the resurrection. 19 So
they took Paul, brought him before the meeting
of the Areopagus, and said, "We would like to
know this new teaching that you are talking
about. 20 Some of the things we hear you say
sound strange to us, and we would like to
know what they mean." 21 (For all the citizens
of Athens and the foreigners who lived there
liked to spend all their time telling and hearing
the latest new thing.)

New International Version

stayed at Berea. 15 The men who accompanied
Paul brought him to Athens and then left with
instructions for Silas and Timothy to join him
as soon as possible.

In Athens

16 While Paul was waiting for them in Athens,
he was greatly distressed to see that the city
was full of idols. 17 So he reasoned in the synagogue with the Jews and the God-fearing Greeks,
as well as in the marketplace day by day with
those who happened to be there. 18 A group of
Epicurean and Stoic philosophers began to dispute with him. Some of them asked, "What is
this babbler trying to say?" Others remarked,
"He seems to be advocating foreign gods." They
said this because Paul was preaching about Jesus and the resurrection. 19 Then they took him
and brought him to a meeting of the Areopagus,
where they said to him, "May we know what
this new teaching is that you are presenting?
20 You are bringing some strange ideas to our
ears, and we want to know what they mean."
21 (All the Athenians and the foreigners who
lived there spent their time doing nothing but
talking about and listening to the latest ideas.)

Phillips Modern English

remained there. The men who escorted Paul took him as far as Athens and returned with instructions for Silas and Timothy to rejoin Paul as soon as possible.

17.16 Paul is irritated by the idols of Athens

Paul had some days to wait at Athens for Silas and Timothy to arrive, and while he was there his soul was exasperated at the sight of a city so completely idolatrous. He felt compelled to discuss the matter with the Jews in the synagogue as well as with God-fearing gentiles, and he even argued daily in the open market-place with the passers-by. While he was speaking there some Epicurean and Stoic philosophers came across him, and some of them remarked,

"What is this cock-sparrow trying to say?"

Others said,

"He seems to be trying to proclaim some more gods to us, and foreign ones at that!"

For Paul was actually proclaiming "Jesus" and "the resurrection". So they got hold of him and conducted him to their council, the Areopagus. There they asked him,

"May we know what this new teaching of yours really is? You talk of matters which sound strange to our ears, and we should like to know what they mean." (For all the Athenians, and even foreign visitors to Athens, had an obsession for any novelty and would spend their whole time talking about or listening to anything new.)

Revised Standard Version

and Timothy remained there. 15 Those who conducted Paul brought him as far as Athens; and receiving a command for Silas and Timothy to come to him as soon as possible, they departed.

16 Now while Paul was waiting for them at Athens, his spirit was provoked within him as he saw that the city was full of idols. 17 So he argued in the synagogue with the Jews and the devout persons, and in the market place every day with those who chanced to be there. 18 Some also of the Epicurean and Stoic philosophers met him. And some said, "What would this babbler say?" Others said, "He seems to be a preacher of foreign divinities"—because he preached Jesus and the resurrection. 19 And they took hold of him and brought him to the Areopagus, saying, "May we know what this new teaching is which you present? 20 For you bring some strange things to our ears; we wish to know therefore what these things mean." 21 Now all the Athenians and the foreigners who lived there spent their time in nothing except telling or hearing something new.

Jerusalem Bible

coast, leaving Silas and Timothy behind. 15 Paul's escort took him as far as Athens, and went back with instructions for Silas and Timothy to rejoin Paul as soon as they could.

Paul in Athens

16 Paul waited for them in Athens and there his whole soul was revolted at the sight of a city given over to idolatry. 17 In the synagogue he held debates with the Jews and the God-fearing, but in the market place he had debates every day with anyone who would face him. 18 Even a few Epicurean and Stoic philosophers argued with him. Some said, "Does this parrot know what he's talking about?" And, because he was preaching about Jesus and the resurrection, others said, "He sounds like a propagandist for some outlandish gods." [z]

19 They invited him to accompany them to the Council of the Areopagus, where they said to him, "How much of this new teaching you were speaking about are we allowed to know? 20 Some of the things you said seemed startling to us and we would like to find out what they mean." 21 The one amusement the Athenians and the foreigners living there seem to have, apart from discussing the latest ideas, is listening to lectures about them.

[z] They assumed that *Anastasis* ("Resurrection") was the name of a goddess.

New English Bible

Paul's escort brought him as far as Athens, and came away with instructions for Silas and Timothy to rejoin him with all speed.

Now while Paul was waiting for them at Athens he was exasperated to see how the city was full of idols. So he argued in the synagogue with the Jews and gentile worshippers, and also in the city square every day with casual passers-by. And some of the Epicurean and Stoic philosophers joined issue with him. Some said, 'What can this charlatan be trying to say?'; others, 'He would appear to be a propagandist for foreign deities'—this because he was preaching about Jesus and Resurrection. So they took him and brought him before the Court of Areopagus[b] and said, 'May we know what this new doctrine is that you propound? You are introducing ideas that sound strange to us, and we should like to know what they mean.' (Now the Athenians in general and the foreigners there had no time for anything but talking or hearing about the latest novelty.)

[*b*] *Or* brought him to Mars' Hill.

King James Version

22 Then Paul stood in the midst of Mars' hill,
and said, *Ye* men of Athens, I perceive that in
all things ye are too superstitious. 23 For as I
passed by, and beheld your devotions, I found
an altar with this inscription, TO THE UN-
KNOWN GOD. Whom therefore ye ignorantly
worship, him declare I unto you. 24 God that
made the world and all things therein, seeing
that he is Lord of heaven and earth, dwelleth
not in temples made with hands; 25 Neither is
worshipped with men's hands, as though he
needed any thing, seeing he giveth to all life,
and breath, and all things; 26And hath made of
one blood all nations of men for to dwell on all
the face of the earth, and hath determined the
times before appointed, and the bounds of their
habitation; 27 That they should seek the Lord,
if haply they might feel after him, and find him,
though he be not far from every one of us:
28 For in him we live, and move, and have our
being; as certain also of your own poets have

Living Bible

22 So Paul, standing before them at the Mars
Hill forum, addressed them as follows:
"Men of Athens, I notice that you are very
religious, 23 for as I was walking I saw your
many altars, and one of them had this inscription on it—'To the Unknown God.' You have
been worshiping him without knowing who he
is, and now I wish to tell you about him.
24 "He made the world and everything in it,
and since he is Lord of heaven and earth, he
doesn't live in man-made temples; 25 and human
hands can't minister to his needs—for he has
no needs! He himself gives life and breath to
everything, and satisfies every need there is.
26 He created all the people of the world from
one man, Adam,[c] and scattered the nations
across the face of the earth. He decided beforehand which should rise and fall, and when. He
determined their boundaries.
27 "His purpose in all of this is that they
should seek after God, and perhaps feel their
way toward him and find him—though he is not
far from any one of us. 28 For in him we live
and move and are! As one of your own poets

[c] Implied.

Today's English Version

22 Paul stood up in front of the meeting of
the Areopagus and said, "Men of Athens! I see
that in every way you are very religious. 23 For
as I walked through your city and looked at the
places where you worship, I found also an altar
on which is written, 'To an Unknown God.'
That which you worship, then, even though you
do not know it, is what I now proclaim to you.
24 God, who made the world and everything in
it, is Lord of heaven and earth, and does not
live in temples made by men. 25 Nor does he
need anything that men can supply by working
for him, since it is he himself who gives life
and breath and everything else to all men.
26 From the one man he created all races of
men, and made them live over the whole earth.
He himself fixed beforehand the exact times and
the limits of the places where they would live.
27 He did this so that they would look for him,
and perhaps find him as they felt around for
him. Yet God is actually not far from any one
of us; 28 as someone has said,

'In him we live and move and exist.'

It is as some of your poets have said,

New International Version

22 Paul then stood up in the meeting of the
Areopagus and said: "Men of Athens! I see that
in every way you are very religious. 23 For as I
walked around and observed your objects of
worship, I even found an altar with this inscription: TO AN UNKNOWN GOD. Now what you worship as something unknown I am going to proclaim to you.
24 "The God who made the world and everything in it is the Lord of heaven and earth and
does not live in temples built by hands. 25And
he is not served by human hands, as if he needed
anything, because he himself gives all men life
and breath and everything else. 26 From one
man he made every nation of men, that they
should inhabit the whole earth; and he determined the times set for them and the exact
places where they should live. 27 God did this
so that men would seek him and perhaps reach
out for him and find him, though he is not far
from each one of us. 28 'For in him we live and
move and have our being.' As some of your own

Phillips Modern English

17.22 Paul's speech to the "gentlemen of Athens"

So Paul got to his feet in the middle of their council, and began,

"Gentlemen of Athens, my own eyes tell me that you are in all respects an extremely religious people. For as I walked through your city looking at your shrines, I even found one altar on which were inscribed the words, TO GOD THE UNKNOWN. It is this God whom you are worshipping in ignorance that I am here to proclaim to you! God who made the world and all that is in it, being Lord of both Heaven and earth, does not live in man-made temples, nor is he ministered to by human hands, as though he had need of anything—seeing that he is the one who gives to all men life and breath and everything else. From one ancestor he has created every race of men to live over the face of the whole earth. He has determined the times of their existence and the limits of their habitation, so that they might search for God, in the hope that they might feel for him and find him—yes, even though he is not far from any one of us. Indeed, it is in him that we live and move and have our being. Some of your own poets have

Revised Standard Version

22 So Paul, standing in the middle of the
Areopagus, said: "Men of Athens, I perceive
that in every way you are very religious. 23 For
as I passed along, and observed the objects of
your worship, I found also an altar with this
inscription, 'To an unknown god.' What therefore you worship as unknown, this I proclaim
to you. 24 The God who made the world and
everything in it, being Lord of heaven and earth,
does not live in shrines made by man, 25 nor is
he served by human hands, as though he needed
anything, since he himself gives to all men life
and breath and everything. 26 And he made from
one every nation of men to live on all the face
of the earth, having determined allotted periods
and the boundaries of their habitation, 27 that
they should seek God, in the hope that they
might feel after him and find him. Yet he is not
far from each one of us, 28 for

'In him we live and move and have our being';
as even some of your poets have said,

Jerusalem Bible

22 So Paul stood before the whole Council of the Areopagus and made this speech:

Paul's speech before the Council of the Areopagus

"Men of Athens, I have seen for myself how
extremely scrupulous you are in all religious
matters, 23 because I noticed, as I strolled
around admiring your sacred monuments, that
you had an altar inscribed: To An Unknown
God. Well, the God whom I proclaim is in fact
the one whom you already worship without
knowing it.

24 "Since the God who made the world and
everything in it is himself Lord of heaven and
earth, he does not make his home in shrines
made by human hands. 25 Nor is he dependent
on anything that human hands can do for him,
since he can never be in need of anything; on
the contrary, it is he who gives everything—
including life and breath—to everyone. 26 From
one single stock he not only created the whole
human race so that they could occupy the entire
earth, but he decreed how long each nation
should flourish and what the boundaries of its
territory should be. 27 And he did this so that
all nations might seek the deity and, by feeling
their way toward him, succeed in finding him.
Yet in fact he is not far from any of us, 28 since
it is in him that we live, and move, and exist,[a]
as indeed some of your own writers have said:

[a] Expression suggested by the poet Epimenides.

New English Bible

Then Paul stood up before the Court of Areopagus[a] and said: 'Men of Athens, I see that in everything that concerns religion you are uncommonly scrupulous. For as I was going round looking at the objects of your worship, I noticed among other things an altar bearing the inscription "To an Unknown God". What you worship but do not know—this is what I now proclaim.

'The God who created the world and everything in it, and who is Lord of heaven and earth, does not live in shrines made by men. It is not because he lacks anything that he accepts service at men's hands, for he is himself the universal giver of life and breath and all else. He created every race of men of one stock, to inhabit the whole earth's surface. He fixed the epochs of their history[b] and the limits of their territory. They were to seek God, and, it might be, touch and find him; though indeed he is not far from each one of us, for in him we live and move, in him we exist; as some of your own poets[c] have

[a] *Or* in the middle of Mars' Hill. [b] *Or* fixed the ordered seasons . . . [c] *Some witnesses read* some among you.

King James Version

said, For we are also his offspring. 29 Forasmuch then as we are the offspring of God, we ought not to think that the Godhead is like unto gold, or silver, or stone, graven by art and man's device. 30 And the times of this ignorance God winked at; but now commandeth all men every where to repent: 31 Because he hath appointed a day, in the which he will judge the world in righteousness by *that* man whom he hath ordained; *whereof* he hath given assurance unto all *men*, in that he hath raised him from the dead.

32 And when they heard of the resurrection of the dead, some mocked: and others said, We will hear thee again of this *matter*. 33 So Paul departed from among them. 34 Howbeit certain men clave unto him, and believed: among the which *was* Dionysius the Areopagite, and a woman named Damaris, and others with them.

18 After these things Paul departed from Athens, and came to Corinth; 2 And found a certain Jew named Aquila, born in Pontus, lately come from Italy, with his wife Priscilla, (because that Claudius had commanded all Jews to depart from Rome,) and came unto them.

Living Bible

says it, 'We are the sons of God.' 29 If this is true, we shouldn't think of God as an idol made by men from gold or silver or chipped from stone. 30 God tolerated man's past ignorance about these things, but now he commands everyone to put away idols and worship only him. 31 For he has set a day for justly judging the world by the man he has appointed, and has pointed him out by bringing him back to life again."

32 When they heard Paul speak of the resurrection of a person who had been dead, some laughed, but others said, "We want to hear more about this later." 33 That ended Paul's discussion with them, 34 but a few joined him and became believers. Among them was Dionysius, a member of the City Council, and a woman named Damaris, and others.

18 Then Paul left Athens and went to Corinth. 2, 3 There he became acquainted with a Jew named Aquila, born in Pontus, who had recently arrived from Italy with his wife, Priscilla. They had been expelled from Italy as a result of Claudius Caesar's order to deport all

Today's English Version

'We too are his children.'

29 Since we are God's children, we should not suppose that his nature is anything like an image of gold or silver or stone, shaped by the art and skill of man. 30 God has overlooked the times when men did not know, but now he commands all men everywhere to turn away from their evil ways. 31 For he has fixed a day in which he will judge the whole world with justice, by means of a man he has chosen. He has given proof of this to everyone by raising that man from death!"

32 When they heard Paul speak about a raising from death, some of them made fun of him, but others said, "We want to hear you speak about this again." 33 And so Paul left the meeting. 34 Some men joined him and believed; among them was Dionysius, a member of the Areopagus, a woman named Damaris, and some others.

In Corinth

18 After this, Paul left Athens and went on to Corinth. 2 There he met a Jew named Aquila, born in Pontus, who had just come from Italy with his wife Priscilla, because Emperor Claudius had ordered all the Jews to leave Rome.

New International Version

poets have said, 'We are his children.'

29 "Therefore since we are God's children, we should not think that the divine being is like gold or silver or stone—an image made by man's design and skill. 30 In the past God overlooked such ignorance, but now he commands all people everywhere to repent. 31 For he has set a day when he will judge the world with justice by the man he has appointed. He has given proof of this to all men by raising him from the dead."

32 When they heard about the resurrection of the dead, some of them sneered, but others said, "We want to hear you again on this subject." 33 At that, Paul left the Council. 34 A few men became followers of Paul and believed. Among them was Dionysius, a member of the Areopagus, also a woman named Damaris, and a number of others.

In Corinth

18 After this, Paul left Athens and went to Corinth. 2 There he met a Jew named Aquila, a native of Pontus, who had recently come from Italy with his wife Priscilla, because Claudius had ordered all the Jews to leave Rome.

Phillips Modern English

endorsed this in the words, 'For we are indeed his children'. If then we are the children of God, we ought not to think of him in terms of gold or silver or stone, designed by human art and imagination. Now while it is true that God has overlooked the days of ignorance he now commands all men everywhere to repent. For he has fixed a day on which he will judge the whole world in justice by the standard of a man whom he has appointed. That this is so he has guaranteed to all men by raising this man from the dead."

But when his audience heard Paul talk about the resurrection from the dead some of them jeered, but others said,

"We should like to hear you speak again on this subject."

So with this mixed reception Paul retired from their assembly. Yet some did in fact join him and accept the faith, including Dionysius a member of the Areopagus, a woman by the name of Damaris, and some others as well.

18.1 At Corinth Paul is yet again rejected by the Jews

Before long Paul left Athens and went on to Corinth where he found a Jew called Aquila, a native of Pontus. This man had recently come from Italy with his wife Priscilla, because Claudius had issued a decree that all Jews should

Revised Standard Version

'For we are indeed his offspring.'
29 Being then God's offspring, we ought not to
think that the Deity is like gold, or silver, or
stone, a representation by the art and imagination of man. 30 The times of ignorance God
overlooked, but now he commands all men
everywhere to repent, 31 because he has fixed a
day on which he will judge the world in righteousness by a man whom he has appointed, and
of this he has given assurance to all men by
raising him from the dead."
32 Now when they heard of the resurrection
of the dead, some mocked; but others said,
"We will hear you again about this." 33 So Paul
went out from among them. 34 But some men
joined him and believed, among them Dionysius
the Areopagite and a woman named Damaris
and others with them.

18 After this he left Athens and went to
Corinth. 2 And he found a Jew named
Aquila, a native of Pontus, lately come from
Italy with his wife Priscilla, because Claudius
had commanded all the Jews to leave Rome.

Jerusalem Bible

'We are all his children.' [b]
29 "Since we are the children of God, we have
no excuse for thinking that the deity looks like
anything in gold, silver or stone that has been
carved and designed by a man.
30 "God overlooked that sort of thing when
men were ignorant, but now he is telling everyone everywhere that they must repent, 31 because
he has fixed a day when the whole world will
be judged, and judged in righteousness, and he
has appointed a man to be the judge. And God
has publicly proved this by raising this man
from the dead."
32 At this mention of rising from the dead,
some of them burst out laughing; others said,
"We would like to hear you talk about this
again." 33 After that Paul left them, 34 but there
were some who attached themselves to him and
became believers, among them Dionysius the
Areopagite and a woman called Damaris, and
others besides.

Foundation of the church of Corinth

18 After this Paul left Athens and went to
Corinth, 2 where he met a Jew called
Aquila whose family came from Pontus. He and
his wife Priscilla[c] had recently left Italy because
an edict of Claudius had expelled all the Jews

[b] From the *Phainomena* of Aratus. [c] Also called Prisca, Rm. 16:3; 1 Co. 16:19; 2 Tm. 4:19.

New English Bible

said, "We are also his offspring." As God's offspring, then, we ought not to suppose that the deity is like an image in gold or silver or stone, shaped by human craftsmanship and design. As for the times of ignorance, God has overlooked them; but now he commands mankind, all men everywhere, to repent, because he has fixed the day on which he will have the world judged, and justly judged, by a man of his choosing; of this he has given assurance to all by raising him from the dead.'

When they heard about the raising of the dead, some scoffed; and others said, 'We will hear you on this subject some other time.' And so Paul left the assembly. However, some men joined him and became believers, including Dionysius, a member of the Court of Areopagus; also a woman named Damaris, and others besides.

18 After this he left Athens and went to Corinth. There he fell in with a Jew named Aquila, a native of Pontus, and his wife Priscilla; he had recently arrived from Italy because Claudius had issued an edict that all Jews should

King James Version

3And because he was of the same craft, he abode
with them, and wrought: (for by their occupation they were tentmakers.) 4And he reasoned
in the synagogue every sabbath, and persuaded
the Jews and the Greeks. 5And when Silas and
Timotheus were come from Macedonia, Paul
was pressed in the spirit, and testified to the
Jews *that* Jesus *was* Christ. 6And when they opposed themselves, and blasphemed, he shook *his*
raiment, and said unto them, Your blood *be*
upon your own heads; I *am* clean: from henceforth I will go unto the Gentiles.
7 And he departed thence, and entered into
a certain *man's* house, named Justus, *one* that
worshipped God, whose house joined hard to the
synagogue. 8And Crispus, the chief ruler of the
synagogue, believed on the Lord with all his
house; and many of the Corinthians hearing believed, and were baptized. 9 Then spake the
Lord to Paul in the night by a vision, Be not
afraid, but speak, and hold not thy peace:
10 For I am with thee, and no man shall set on
thee to hurt thee: for I have much people in
this city. 11And he continued *there* a year and
six months, teaching the word of God among
them.

Living Bible

Jews from Rome. Paul lived and worked with
them, for they were tentmakers just as he was.
4 Each Sabbath found Paul at the synagogue,
trying to convince the Jews and Greeks alike.
5And after the arrival of Silas and Timothy
from Macedonia, Paul spent his full time preaching and testifying to the Jews that Jesus is the
Messiah. 6 But when the Jews opposed him and
blasphemed, hurling abuse at Jesus, Paul shook
off the dust from his robe and said, "Your blood
be upon your own heads—I am innocent—from
now on I will preach to the Gentiles."
7 After that he stayed with Titus Justus, a
Gentile[a] who worshiped God and lived next
door to the synagogue. 8 However, Crispus, the
leader of the synagogue, and all his household
believed in the Lord and were baptized—as were
many others in Corinth.
9 One night the Lord spoke to Paul in a vision
and told him, "Don't be afraid! Speak out!
Don't quit! 10 For I am with you and no one
can harm you. Many people here in this city belong to me." 11 So Paul stayed there the next
year and a half, teaching the truths of God.

[*a*] Implied.

Today's English Version

Paul went to see them, 3 and stayed and worked
with them, because he earned his living by making tents, just as they did. 4 He argued in the
synagogue every Sabbath, trying to convince
both Jews and Greeks.
5 When Silas and Timothy arrived from Macedonia, Paul gave his whole time to preaching
the message, testifying to the Jews that Jesus is
the Messiah. 6 When they opposed him and said
evil things about him, he protested by shaking
the dust from his clothes and saying to them,
"If you are lost, you yourselves must take the
blame for it! I am not responsible. From now
on I will go to the Gentiles." 7 So he left them
and went to live in the house of a Gentile named
Titius Justus, who worshiped God; his house
was next to the synagogue. 8 Crispus, the leader
of the synagogue, believed in the Lord, he and
all his family; and many other people in Corinth
heard the message, believed, and were baptized.
9 One night Paul had a vision, in which the
Lord said to him, "Do not be afraid, but keep
on speaking and do not give up, 10 because I
am with you. No one will be able to harm you,
because many in this city are my people." 11 So
Paul stayed there for a year and a half, teaching
the people the word of God.

New International Version

Paul went to see them, 3 and because he was a
tentmaker as they were, he stayed and worked
with them. 4 Every Sabbath he reasoned in the
synagogue, trying to persuade Jews and Greeks.
5 When Silas and Timothy came from Macedonia, Paul devoted himself exclusively to preaching, testifying to the Jews that Jesus was the
Christ.[b] 6 But when the Jews opposed Paul and
became abusive, he shook out his clothes in
protest and said to them, "Your blood be on
your own heads! I am clear of my responsibility.
From now on I will go to the Gentiles."
7 Then Paul left the synagogue and went next
door to the house of Titius Justus, a worshiper
of God. 8 Crispus, the synagogue ruler, and his
entire household believed in the Lord; and many
of the Corinthians who heard him believed and
were baptized.
9 One night the Lord spoke to Paul in a
vision: "Do not be afraid; keep on speaking, do
not be silent. 10 For I am with you, and no one
is going to attack and harm you, because I have
many people in this city." 11 So Paul stayed for
a year and a half, teaching them the word of
God.

[*b*] Or *Messiah.*

Phillips Modern English

leave Rome. He went to see them in their house and because they practised the same trade as himself he stayed with them. They all worked together, for their trade was tent-making. Every Sabbath Paul used to speak in the synagogue trying to persuade both Jews and Greeks. By the time Silas and Timothy arrived from Macedonia Paul was completely absorbed in preaching the message, showing the Jews as clearly as he could that Jesus is Christ. However, when they turned against him and abused him he shook his garments at them, and said,

"Your blood be on your own heads! From now on I go with a perfectly clear conscience to the gentiles."

Then he left them and went to the house of a man called Titius Justus, a man who reverenced God and whose house was next door to the synagogue. Crispus, the president of the synagogue, became a believer in the Lord, with all his household, and many of the Corinthians who heard the message believed and were baptised. Then one night the Lord spoke to Paul in a vision,

"Do not be afraid, but go on speaking and let no one silence you, for I myself am with you and no man shall lift a finger to harm you. There are many in this city who belong to me."

So Paul settled down there for eighteen months and taught them God's message.

Revised Standard Version

And he went to see them; 3 and because he
was of the same trade he stayed with them, and
they worked, for by trade they were tentmakers. 4 And he argued in the synagogue every
sabbath, and persuaded Jews and Greeks.
5 When Silas and Timothy arrived from
Macedonia, Paul was occupied with preaching,
testifying to the Jews that the Christ was Jesus.
6 And when they opposed and reviled him, he
shook out his garments and said to them, "Your
blood be upon your heads! I am innocent. From
now on I will go to the Gentiles." 7 And he left
there and went to the house of a man named
Titius[q] Justus, a worshiper of God; his house
was next door to the synagogue. 8 Crispus, the
ruler of the synagogue, believed in the Lord,
together with all his household; and many of
the Corinthians hearing Paul believed and were
baptized. 9 And the Lord said to Paul one night
in a vision, "Do not be afraid, but speak and
do not be silent; 10 for I am with you, and no
man shall attack you to harm you; for I have
many people in this city." 11 And he stayed a
year and six months, teaching the word of God
among them.

[q] Other early authorities read *Titus*.

Jerusalem Bible

from Rome.[d] Paul went to visit them, 3 and when
he found they were tentmakers, of the same trade
as himself, he lodged with them, and they worked
together. 4 Every sabbath he used to hold debates
in the synagogues, trying to convert Jews as well
as Greeks.
5 After Silas and Timothy had arrived from
Macedonia, Paul devoted all his time to preaching, declaring to the Jews that Jesus was the
Christ. 6 When they turned against him and
started to insult him, he took his cloak and
shook it out in front of them, saying, "Your
blood be on your own heads; from now on I can
go to the pagans with a clear conscience." 7 Then
he left the synagogue and moved to the house
next door that belonged to a worshiper of God
called Justus. 8 Crispus, president of the synagogue, and his whole household, all became believers in the Lord. A great many Corinthians
who had heard him became believers and were
baptized. 9 One night the Lord spoke to Paul
in a vision, "Do not be afraid to speak out, nor
allow yourself to be silenced: 10 I am with you.
I have so many people on my side in this city
that no one will even attempt to hurt you."
11 So Paul stayed there preaching the word of
God among them for eighteen months.

[d] This edict was issued in 49 or 50.

New English Bible

leave Rome. Paul approached them and, because he was of the same trade, he made his home with them, and they carried on business together; they were tent-makers. He also held discussions in the synagogue Sabbath by Sabbath, trying to convince both Jews and Gentiles.

Then Silas and Timothy came down from Macedonia, and Paul devoted himself entirely to preaching, affirming before the Jews that the Messiah was Jesus. But when they opposed him and resorted to abuse, he shook out the skirts of his cloak and said to them, 'Your blood be on your own heads! My conscience is clear; now I shall go to the Gentiles.' With that he left, and went to the house of a worshipper of God named Titius Justus, who lived next door to the synagogue. Crispus, who held office in the synagogue, now became a believer in the Lord, with all his household; and a number of Corinthians listened and believed, and were baptized. One night in a vision the Lord said to Paul, 'Have no fear: go on with your preaching and do not be silenced, for I am with you and no one shall attempt to do you harm;[a] and there are many in this city who are my people.' So he settled down for eighteen months, teaching the word of God among them.

[a] *Or* and you will not be harmed by anyone's attacks.

King James Version

12 And when Gallio was the deputy of Achaia, the Jews made insurrection with one accord against Paul, and brought him to the judgment seat, 13 Saying, This *fellow* persuadeth men to worship God contrary to the law. 14And when Paul was now about to open *his* mouth, Gallio said unto the Jews, If it were a matter of wrong or wicked lewdness, O *ye* Jews, reason would that I should bear with you: 15 But if it be a question of words and names, and *of* your law, look ye *to it;* for I will be no judge of such *matters.* 16And he drave them from the judgment seat. 17 Then all the Greeks took Sosthenes, the chief ruler of the synagogue, and beat *him* before the judgment seat. And Gallio cared for none of those things.

18 And Paul *after this* tarried *there* yet a good while, and then took his leave of the brethren, and sailed thence into Syria, and with him Priscilla and Aquila; having shorn *his* head in Cenchrea: for he had a vow. 19And he came to Ephesus, and left them there: but he himself entered into the synagogue, and reasoned with

Living Bible

12 But when Gallio became governor of Achaia, the Jews rose in concerted action against Paul and brought him before the governor for judgment. 13 They accused Paul of "persuading men to worship God in ways that are contrary to Roman law." 14 But just as Paul started to make his defense, Gallio turned to his accusers and said, "Listen, you Jews, if this were a case involving some crime, I would be obliged to listen to you, 15 but since it is merely a bunch of questions of semantics and personalities and your silly Jewish laws, you take care of it. I'm not interested and I'm not touching it." 16And he drove them out of the courtroom.

17 Then the mob[a] grabbed Sosthenes, the new leader of the synagogue, and beat him outside the courtroom. But Gallio couldn't have cared less.

18 Paul stayed in the city several days after that and then said good-bye to the Christians and sailed for the coast of Syria, taking Priscilla and Aquila with him. At Cenchreae, Paul had his head shaved according to Jewish custom, for he had taken a vow.[b] 19Arriving at the port of Ephesus, he left us aboard ship while he went over to the synagogue for a discussion with the

[*a*] Implied. [*b*] Probably a vow to offer a sacrifice in Jerusalem in thanksgiving for answered prayer. The head was shaved thirty days before such gifts and sacrifices were given to God at the Temple.

Today's English Version

12 When Gallio was made the Roman governor of Greece, the Jews got together, seized Paul and took him into court. 13 "This man," they said, "is trying to persuade people to worship God in a way that is against the law!"

14 Paul was about to speak, when Gallio said to the Jews, "If this were a matter of some wrong or evil crime that has been committed, it would be reasonable for me to be patient with you Jews. 15 But since it is an argument about words and names and your own law, you yourselves must settle it. I will not be the judge of such things!" 16And he drove them out of the court. 17 They all grabbed Sosthenes, the leader of the synagogue, and beat him in front of the court. But that did not bother Gallio a bit.

The return to Antioch

18 Paul stayed on in Corinth with the brothers for many days, then left them and sailed off with Priscilla and Aquila for Syria. Before sailing he made a vow in Cenchreae and had his head shaved. 19 They arrived in Ephesus, where Paul left Priscilla and Aquila. He went into the

New International Version

12 While Gallio was proconsul of Achaia, the Jews made a united attack on Paul and brought him into court. 13 "This man," they charged, "is persuading the people to worship God in ways contrary to the law."

14 Just as Paul was about to speak, Gallio said to the Jews, "If you Jews were making a complaint about some misdemeanor or serious crime, it would be reasonable for me to listen to you. 15 But since it involves questions about words and names and your own law—settle the matter yourselves. I will not be a judge of such things." 16 So he had them ejected from the court. 17 Then they all turned on Sosthenes, the synagogue ruler, and beat him in front of the court. But Gallio showed no concern whatever.

Priscilla, Aquila and Apollos

18 Paul stayed on in Corinth for some time. Then he left the brothers and sailed for Syria, accompanied by Priscilla and Aquila. Before he sailed, he had his hair cut off at Cenchrea because of a vow he had taken. 19 They arrived at Ephesus, where Paul left Priscilla and Aquila. He himself went into the synagogue and rea-

Phillips Modern English

18.12 Paul's enemies fail to impress the governor

Then, while Gallio was proconsul of Achaia, the Jews banded together to attack Paul, and took him to court, saying,

"This man is perverting men's minds to make them worship God in a way that is contrary to the Law."

Paul was all ready to speak, but before he could utter a word Gallio said to the Jews,

"Listen, Jews! If this were a matter of some crime or wrongdoing I might reasonably be expected to put up with you. But if it is a question which concerns words and names and your own Law, you must attend to it yourselves. I flatly refuse to be judge in these matters."

And he had them ejected from the court. Then they all seized Sosthenes, the president of the synagogue, and beat him in front of the court-house. But Gallio remained completely unconcerned.

18.18 Paul returns, and reports to Jerusalem and Antioch

Paul stayed for some time after this incident and then took leave of the brothers and sailed for Syria, taking Priscilla and Aquila with him. At Cenchrea he had his hair cut short, for he had taken a solemn vow. They all arrived at Ephesus and there Paul left Aquila and Priscilla, but he himself went into the synagogue and debated

Revised Standard Version

12 But when Gallio was proconsul of Achaia,
the Jews made a united attack upon Paul and
brought him before the tribunal, 13 saying, "This
man is persuading men to worship God contrary
to the law." 14 But when Paul was about to open
his mouth, Gallio said to the Jews, "If it were
a matter of wrongdoing or vicious crime, I
should have reason to bear with you, O Jews;
15 but since it is a matter of questions about
words and names and your own law, see to it
yourselves; I refuse to be a judge of these
things." 16 And he drove them from the tribunal.
17 And they all seized Sosthenes, the ruler of the
synagogue, and beat him in front of the tribunal. But Gallio paid no attention to this.
18 After this Paul stayed many days longer,
and then took leave of the brethren and sailed
for Syria, and with him Priscilla and Aquila.
At Cenchreae he cut his hair, for he had a vow.
19 And they came to Ephesus, and he left them
there; but he himself went into the synagogue

Jerusalem Bible

The Jews take Paul to court

12 But while Gallio was proconsul of Achaia,[e]
the Jews made a concerted attack on Paul and
brought him before the tribunal. 13 "We accuse
this man," they said, "of persuading people to
worship God in a way that breaks the Law."
14 Before Paul could open his mouth, Gallio
said to the Jews, "Listen, you Jews. If this were
a misdemeanor or a crime, I would not hesitate
to attend to you; 15 but if it is only quibbles
about words and names, and about your own
Law, then you must deal with it yourselves—I
have no intention of making legal decisions about
things like that." 16 Then he sent them out of
the court, 17 and at once they all turned on
Sosthenes, the synagogue president, and beat
him in front of the courthouse. Gallio refused to
take any notice at all.

Return to Antioch and departure for the third journey

18 After staying on for some time, Paul took
leave of the brothers and sailed for Syria,[f] accompanied by Priscilla and Aquila. At Cenchreae
he had his hair cut off, because of a vow he had
made.
19 When they reached Ephesus, he left them,
but first he went alone to the synagogue to de-

[e] In 52, according to an inscription from Delphi.
[f] To Antioch.

New English Bible

But when Gallio was proconsul of Achaia, the Jews set upon Paul in a body and brought him into court. 'This man', they said, 'is inducing people to worship God in ways that are against the law.' Paul was just about to speak when Gallio said to them, 'If it had been a question of crime or grave misdemeanour, I should, of course, have given you Jews a patient hearing, but if it is some bickering about words and names and your Jewish law, you may see to it yourselves; I have no mind to be a judge of these matters.' And he had them ejected from the court. Then there was a general attack on Sosthenes, who held office in the synagogue, and they gave him a beating in full view of the bench. But all this left Gallio quite unconcerned.

Paul stayed on for some time, and then took leave of the brotherhood and set sail for Syria, accompanied by Priscilla and Aquila. At Cenchreae he had his hair cut off, because he was under a vow. When they reached Ephesus he parted from them and went himself into the synagogue, where he held a discussion with the

King James Version

the Jews. 20 When they desired *him* to tarry longer time with them, he consented not; 21 But bade them farewell, saying, I must by all means keep this feast that cometh in Jerusalem: but I will return again unto you, if God will. And he sailed from Ephesus. 22 And when he had landed at Cesarea, and gone up, and saluted the church, he went down to Antioch. 23 And after he had spent some time *there,* he departed, and went over *all* the country of Galatia and Phrygia in order, strengthening all the disciples.

24 And a certain Jew named Apollos, born at Alexandria, an eloquent man, *and* mighty in the Scriptures, came to Ephesus. 25 This man was instructed in the way of the Lord; and being fervent in the spirit, he spake and taught diligently the things of the Lord, knowing only the baptism of John. 26 And he began to speak boldly in the synagogue: whom when Aquila and Priscilla had heard, they took him unto *them,* and expounded unto him the way of God more perfectly. 27 And when he was disposed to pass into Achaia, the brethren wrote, exhorting the disciples to receive him: who, when he was come, helped them much which had believed

Living Bible

Jews. 20 They asked him to stay for a few days, but he felt that he had no time to lose.[c]

21 "I must by all means be at Jerusalem for the holiday,"[d] he said. But he promised to return to Ephesus later if God permitted; and so he set sail again.

22 The next stop was at the port of Caesarea from where he visited the church [at Jerusalem[e]] and then sailed on to Antioch. 23 After spending some time there, he left for Turkey again, going through Galatia and Phrygia visiting all the believers, encouraging them and helping them grow in the Lord.

24 As it happened, a Jew named Apollos, a wonderful Bible teacher and preacher, had just arrived in Ephesus from Alexandria in Egypt. 25, 26 While he was in Egypt, someone had told him about John the Baptist and what John had said about Jesus, but that is all he knew. He had never heard the rest of the story! So he was preaching boldly and enthusiastically in the synagogue, "The Messiah is coming! Get ready to receive him!" Priscilla and Aquila were there and heard him—and it was a powerful sermon. Afterwards they met with him and explained what had happened to Jesus since the time of John, and all that it meant![f]

27 Apollos had been thinking about going to Greece, and the believers encouraged him in this. They wrote to their fellow-believers there, telling them to welcome him. And upon his arrival in Greece, he was greatly used of God to

[c] Possibly in order to arrive in Jerusalem within the prescribed thirty days. [d] Literally, "feast." This entire sentence is omitted in many of the ancient manuscripts. [e] Implied. [f] Literally, "explained to him the way of God more accurately."

Today's English Version

synagogue and argued with the Jews. 20 They asked him to stay with them a long time, but he would not consent. 21 Instead, he told them as he left, "If it is the will of God, I will come back to you." And so he sailed from Ephesus.

22 When he arrived at Caesarea he went to Jerusalem and greeted the church, and then went to Antioch. 23 After spending some time there he left. He went through the region of Galatia and Phrygia, strengthening all the believers.

Apollos in Ephesus and Corinth

24 A certain Jew named Apollos, born in Alexandria, came to Ephesus. He was an eloquent speaker and had a thorough knowledge of the Scriptures. 25 He had been instructed in the Way of the Lord, and with great enthusiasm spoke and taught correctly the facts about Jesus. However, he knew only the baptism of John. 26 He began to speak boldly in the synagogue. When Priscilla and Aquila heard him, they took him home with them and explained to him more correctly the Way of God. 27 Apollos decided to go to Greece, so the believers in Ephesus helped him by writing to their brothers in Greece, urging them to welcome him there. When he arrived, he was a great help to those who through God's grace had become believers.

New International Version

soned with the Jews. 20 When they asked him to spend more time with them, he declined. 21 But as he left, he promised, "I will come back if it is God's will." Then he set sail from Ephesus.

22 When he landed at Caesarea, he went up and greeted the church and then went down to Antioch. 23 After spending some time in Antioch, Paul set out from there and traveled from place to place throughout the region of Galatia and Phrygia, strengthening all the disciples.

24 Meanwhile a Jew named Apollos, a native of Alexandria, came to Ephesus. He was a learned man, with a thorough knowledge of the Scriptures. 25 He had been instructed in the way of the Lord, and he spoke with great fervor and taught about Jesus accurately, knowing only the baptism of John. 26 He began to speak boldly in the synagogue. When Priscilla and Aquila heard him, they invited him to their home and explained to him the way of God more adequately.

27 When Apollos wanted to go to Achaia, the brothers encouraged him and wrote to the disciples there to welcome him. On arriving, he was a great help to those who by grace had be-

Phillips Modern English

with the Jews. When they asked him to stay longer he refused, bidding them farewell with the words, "If it is God's will I will come back to you again." Then he set sail from Ephesus and went down to Caesarea. Here he disembarked and after paying his respects to the Church in Jerusalem, he went down to Antioch. He spent some time there before he left and proceeded to visit systematically throughout Galatia and Phrygia, putting new heart into all the disciples as he went.

18.24 Apollos speaks powerfully at Ephesus and Corinth

Now a Jew called Apollos, a native of Alexandria and a gifted speaker, well-versed in the scriptures, arrived at Ephesus. He had been instructed in the way of the Lord, and he spoke with burning zeal, teaching the facts about Jesus faithfully even though he only knew the baptism of John. This man began to speak with great boldness in the synagogue. But when Priscilla and Aquila heard him they took him aside and explained the Way of God to him more accurately. Then as he wanted to cross into Achaia, the brothers gave him every encouragement and wrote a letter to the disciples there, asking them to make him welcome. On his arrival he proved a source of great strength to those who had be-

Revised Standard Version

and argued with the Jews. 20 When they asked him to stay for a longer period, he declined; 21 but on taking leave of them he said, "I will return to you if God wills," and he set sail from Ephesus.

22 When he had landed at Caesarea, he went up and greeted the church, and then went down to Antioch. 23 After spending some time there he departed and went from place to place through the region of Galatia and Phrygia, strengthening all the disciples.

24 Now a Jew named Apollos, a native of Alexandria, came to Ephesus. He was an eloquent man, well versed in the scriptures. 25 He had been instructed in the way of the Lord; and being fervent in spirit, he spoke and taught accurately the things concerning Jesus, though he knew only the baptism of John. 26 He began to speak boldly in the synagogue; but when Priscilla and Aquila heard him, they took him and expounded to him the way of God more accurately. 27 And when he wished to cross to Achaia, the brethren encouraged him, and wrote to the disciples to receive him. When he arrived, he greatly helped those who through grace had be-

Jerusalem Bible

bate with the Jews. 20 They asked him to stay longer but he declined, 21 though when he left he said, "I will come back another time, God willing." Then he sailed from Ephesus.

22 He landed at Caesarea, and went up to greet the church. Then he came down to Antioch 23 where he spent a short time before continuing his journey through the Galatian country and then through Phrygia, encouraging all the followers.

Apollos

24 An Alexandrian Jew named Apollos now arrived in Ephesus. He was an eloquent man, with a sound knowledge of the scriptures, and yet, 25 though he had been given instruction in the Way of the Lord had preached with great spiritual earnestness and was accurate in all the details he taught about Jesus, he had only experienced the baptism of John. 26 When Priscilla and Aquila heard him speak boldly in the synagogue, they took an interest in him and gave him further instruction about the Way.

27 When Apollos thought of crossing over to Achaia, the brothers encouraged him and wrote asking the disciples to welcome him. When he arrived there he was able by God's grace to

New English Bible

Jews. He was asked to stay longer, but declined and set out from Ephesus, saying, as he took leave of them, 'I shall come back to you if it is God's will.' On landing at Caesarea, he went up and paid his respects to the church, and then went down to Antioch. After spending some time there, he set out again and made a journey through the Galatian country and on through Phrygia, bringing new strength to all the converts.

Now there arrived at Ephesus a Jew named Apollos, an Alexandrian by birth, an eloquent man,[a] powerful in his use of the scriptures. He had been instructed in the way of the Lord and was full of spiritual fervour; and in his discourses he taught accurately the facts about Jesus,[b] though he knew only John's baptism. He now began to speak boldly in the synagogue, where Priscilla and Aquila heard him; they took him in hand and expounded the new way[c] to him in greater detail. Finding that he wished to go across to Achaia, the brotherhood gave him their support, and wrote to the congregation there to make him welcome. From the time of his arrival, he was very helpful to those who had

[a] *Or* a learned man. [b] *Some witnesses read* about the Lord. [c] *Some witnesses read* the way of God.

King James Version

through grace: 28 For he mightily convinced the
Jews, *and that* publicly, shewing by the Scriptures that Jesus was Christ.

19 And it came to pass, that, while Apollos
was at Corinth, Paul having passed through
the upper coasts came to Ephesus; and finding
certain disciples, 2 He said unto them, Have ye
received the Holy Ghost since ye believed? And
they said unto him, We have not so much as
heard whether there be any Holy Ghost. 3 And
he said unto them, Unto what then were ye
baptized? And they said, Unto John's baptism.
4 Then said Paul, John verily baptized with the
baptism of repentance, saying unto the people,
that they should believe on him which should
come after him, that is, on Christ Jesus. 5 When
they heard *this,* they were baptized in the name
of the Lord Jesus. 6 And when Paul had laid *his*
hands upon them, the Holy Ghost came on
them; and they spake with tongues, and prophesied. 7 And all the men were about twelve. 8 And

Living Bible

strengthen the church, 28 for he powerfully refuted all the Jewish arguments in public debate,
showing by the Scriptures that Jesus is indeed
the Messiah.

19 While Apollos was in Corinth, Paul traveled through Turkey and arrived in Ephesus, where he found several disciples. 2 "Did you
receive the Holy Spirit when you believed?" he
asked them.

"No," they replied, "we don't know what you
mean. What is the Holy Spirit?"

3 "Then what beliefs did you acknowledge at
your baptism?" he asked.

And they replied, "What John the Baptist
taught."

4 Then Paul pointed out to them that John's
baptism was to demonstrate a desire to turn
from sin to God and that those receiving his
baptism must then go on to believe in Jesus, the
one John said would come later.

5 As soon as they heard this, they were baptized in[a] the name of the Lord Jesus. 6 Then,
when Paul laid his hands upon their heads, the
Holy Spirit came on them, and they spoke in
other languages and prophesied. 7 The men involved were about twelve in number.

[*a*] Or, "into."

Today's English Version

28 For with his strong arguments he defeated
the Jews in public debates, proving from the
Scriptures that Jesus is the Messiah.

Paul in Ephesus

19 While Apollos was in Corinth, Paul traveled through the interior of the province
and arrived in Ephesus. There he found some
disciples, 2 and asked them, "Did you receive
the Holy Spirit when you believed?"

"We have not even heard that there is a
Holy Spirit," they answered.

3 "Well, then, what kind of baptism did you
receive?" Paul asked.

"The baptism of John," they answered.

4 Paul said, "The baptism of John was for
those who turned from their sins; and he told
the people of Israel to believe in the one who
was coming after him—that is, in Jesus."

5 When they heard this, they were baptized
in the name of the Lord Jesus. 6 Paul placed
his hands on them, and the Holy Spirit came
upon them; they spoke in strange tongues and
also proclaimed God's message. 7 They were
about twelve men in all.

New International Version

lieved. 28 For he vigorously refuted the Jews in
public debate, proving from the Scriptures that
Jesus was the Christ.[c]

Paul in Ephesus

19 While Apollos was at Corinth, Paul took
the road through the interior and arrived
at Ephesus. There he found some disciples 2 and
asked them, "Did you receive the Holy Spirit
when you believed?"

They answered, "No, we have not even heard
that there is a Holy Spirit."

3 So Paul asked, "Then what baptism did you
receive?"

"John's baptism," they replied.

4 Paul said, "John's baptism was a baptism
of repentance. He told the people to believe in
the one coming after him, that is, in Jesus."
5 On hearing this, they were baptized into[d] the
name of the Lord Jesus. 6 When Paul placed his
hands on them, the Holy Spirit came on them,
and they spoke in tongues[e] and prophesied.
7 There were about twelve men in all.

[*c*] Or *Messiah.* [*d*] Or *in.* [*e*] Or *other languages.*

Phillips Modern English

lieved through grace, for by his powerful arguments he publicly refuted the Jews, quoting from the scriptures to prove that Jesus is Christ.

19.1 Ephesus has its own Pentecost

While Apollos was in Corinth Paul journeyed through the upper parts of the country and arrived at Ephesus. There he discovered some disciples, and he asked them,

"Did you receive the Holy Spirit when you believed?"

"No," they replied, "we have never even heard that there is a Holy Spirit."

"Well then, how were you baptised?" asked Paul.

"We were baptised with John's baptism," they replied.

"John's baptism was a baptism to show a change of heart," Paul explained, "but he always told the people that they must believe in the one who should come after him, that is, in Jesus."

When these men heard this they were baptised in the name of the Lord Jesus, and then, when Paul had laid his hands on them, the Holy Spirit came upon them and they began to speak with tongues and the inspiration of prophets. (There were about twelve of them in all.)

Revised Standard Version

lieved, 28 for he powerfully confuted the Jews in public, showing by the scriptures that the Christ was Jesus.

19 While Apollos was at Corinth, Paul passed through the upper country and came to Ephesus. There he found some disciples. 2 And he said to them, "Did you receive the Holy Spirit when you believed?" And they said, "No, we have never even heard that there is a Holy Spirit." 3 And he said, "Into what then were you baptized?" They said, "Into John's baptism." 4 And Paul said, "John baptized with the baptism of repentance, telling the people to believe in the one who was to come after him, that is, Jesus." 5 On hearing this, they were baptized in the name of the Lord Jesus. 6 And when Paul had laid his hands upon them, the Holy Spirit came on them; and they spoke with tongues and prophesied. 7 There were about twelve of them in all.

Jerusalem Bible

help the believers considerably 28 by the energetic way he refuted the Jews in public and demonstrated from the scriptures that Jesus was the Christ.

The disciples of John at Ephesus

19 While Apollos was in Corinth, Paul made his way overland as far as Ephesus, where he found a number of disciples. 2 When he asked, "Did you receive the Holy Spirit when you became believers?" they answered, "No, we were never even told there was such a thing as a Holy Spirit." 3 "Then how were you baptized?" he asked. "With John's baptism," they replied. 4 "John's baptism," said Paul, "was a baptism of repentance; but he insisted that the people should believe in the one who was to come after him—in other words Jesus." 5 When they heard this, they were baptized in the name of the Lord Jesus, 6 and the moment Paul had laid hands on them the Holy Spirit came down on them, and they began to speak with tongues and to prophesy. 7 There were about twelve of these men.

New English Bible

by God's grace become believers; for he strenuously confuted the Jews, demonstrating publicly from the scriptures that the Messiah is Jesus.

19 While Apollos was at Corinth, Paul travelled through the inland regions till he came to Ephesus. There he found a number of converts, to whom he said, 'Did you receive the Holy Spirit when you became believers?' 'No,' they replied, 'we have not even heard that there is a Holy Spirit.' He said, 'Then what baptism were you given?' 'John's baptism', they answered. Paul then said, 'The baptism that John gave was a baptism in token of repentance, and he told the people to put their trust in one who was to come after him, that is, in Jesus.' On hearing this they were baptized into the name of the Lord Jesus; and when Paul had laid his hands on them, the Holy Spirit came upon them and they spoke in tongues of ecstasy and prophesied. Altogether they were about a dozen men.

King James Version

he went into the synagogue, and spake boldly
for the space of three months, disputing and
persuading the things concerning the kingdom of
God. 9 But when divers were hardened, and believed not, but spake evil of that way before
the multitude, he departed from them, and separated the disciples, disputing daily in the school
of one Tyrannus. 10And this continued by the
space of two years; so that all they which dwelt
in Asia heard the word of the Lord Jesus, both
Jews and Greeks. 11And God wrought special
miracles by the hands of Paul: 12 So that from
his body were brought unto the sick handkerchiefs or aprons, and the diseases departed from
them, and the evil spirits went out of them.

13 Then certain of the vagabond Jews, exorcists, took upon them to call over them which
had evil spirits the name of the Lord Jesus,
saying, We adjure you by Jesus whom Paul
preacheth. 14And there were seven sons of *one*
Sceva, a Jew, *and* chief of the priests, which
did so. 15And the evil spirit answered and said,

Living Bible

8 Then Paul went to the synagogue and
preached boldly each Sabbath day[b] for three
months, telling what[c] he believed and why, and
persuading many to believe in Jesus. 9 But some
rejected his message and publicly spoke against
Christ, so he left, refusing to preach to them
again. Pulling out the believers, he began a
separate meeting at the lecture hall of Tyrannus
and preached there daily. 10 This went on for
the next two years, so that everyone in the
Turkish province of Ausia—both Jews and
Greeks—heard the Lord's message. 11And God
gave Paul the power to do unusual miracles,
12 so that even when his handkerchiefs or parts
of his clothing were placed upon sick people,
they were healed, and any demons within them
came out.

13 A team of itinerant Jews who were traveling from town to town casting out demons
planned to experiment by using the name of the
Lord Jesus. The incantation they decided on
was this: "I adjure you by Jesus, whom Paul
preaches, to come out!" 14 Seven sons of Sceva,
a Jewish priest, were doing this. 15 But when

[*b*] Implied. [*c*] Literally, "concerning the Kingdom of God."

Today's English Version

8 Paul went into the synagogue, and for three
months spoke boldly with the people, arguing
with them and trying to convince them about
the Kingdom of God. 9 But some of them were
stubborn and would not believe, and said evil
things about the Way of the Lord before the
whole group. So Paul left them and took the
disciples with him; and every day he held discussions in the lecture hall of Tyrannus. 10 This
went on for two years, so that all the people
who lived in the province of Asia, both Jews
and Gentiles, heard the word of the Lord.

The sons of Sceva

11 God was performing unusual miracles
through Paul. 12 Even handkerchiefs and aprons
he had used were taken to the sick, and their
diseases were driven away and the evil spirits
would go out of them. 13 Some Jews who traveled around and drove out evil spirits also tried
to use the name of the Lord Jesus to do this.
They said to the evil spirits, "I command you
in the name of Jesus, whom Paul preaches."
14 There were seven sons of a Jewish High
Priest named Sceva who were doing this.
15 But the evil spirit said to them, "I know

New International Version

8 Paul entered the synagogue and spoke boldly
there for three months, arguing persuasively
about the kingdom of God. 9 But some of them
became obstinate; they refused to believe and
publicly maligned the Way. So Paul left them.
He took the disciples with him and had discussions daily in the lecture hall of Tyrannus.
10 This went on for two years, so that all the
Jews and Greeks who lived in the province of
Asia heard the word of the Lord.

11 God did extraordinary miracles through
Paul. 12 Handkerchiefs and aprons that had
touched him were taken to the sick, and their
illnesses were cured and the evil spirits left them.
13 Some Jews who went around driving out
evil spirits tried to invoke the name of the Lord
Jesus over those who were demon-possessed.
They would say, "In the name of Jesus whom
Paul preaches, I command you to come out."
14 Seven sons of Sceva, a Jewish chief priest,
were doing this. 15 The evil spirit answered

Phillips Modern English

19.8 Paul's two-year ministry at Ephesus

Then Paul made his way into the synagogue there and for three months he spoke with the utmost confidence, using both argument and persuasion as he talked of the kingdom of God. But when some of them hardened in their attitude towards the message and refused to believe it, and, what is more, spoke offensively about the Way in public, Paul left them, and withdrew his disciples, and held daily discussions in the lecture-hall of Tyrannus. He continued this practice for two years, so that all who lived in the province of Asia, both Greeks and Jews, could hear the Lord's message. God gave most unusual demonstrations of power through Paul's hands, so much so that people took to the sick any towels or handkerchiefs which had been in contact with his body, and they were cured of their diseases and their evil spirits left them.

19.13 The violence of evil and the power of the "name"

But there were some itinerant Jewish exorcists who attempted to invoke the name of the Lord Jesus when dealing with those who had evil spirits. They would say, "I command you in the name of Jesus whom Paul preaches." Seven brothers, sons of a chief priest called Sceva, were engaged in this practice on one occasion, when the evil spirit answered, "Jesus I know,

Revised Standard Version

8 And he entered the synagogue and for
three months spoke boldly, arguing and pleading about the kingdom of God; 9 but when
some were stubborn and disbelieved, speaking
evil of the Way before the congregation, he
withdrew from them, taking the disciples with
him, and argued daily in the hall of Tyrannus.[r]
10 This continued for two years, so that all the
residents of Asia heard the word of the Lord,
both Jews and Greeks.
11 And God did extraordinary miracles by
the hands of Paul, 12 so that handkerchiefs or
aprons were carried away from his body to the
sick, and diseases left them and the evil spirits
came out of them. 13 Then some of the itinerant
Jewish exorcists undertook to pronounce the
name of the Lord Jesus over those who had evil
spirits, saying, "I adjure you by the Jesus whom
Paul preaches." 14 Seven sons of a Jewish high
priest named Sceva were doing this. 15 But the

[r] Other ancient authorities add *from the fifth hour to the tenth.*

Jerusalem Bible

Foundation of the church of Ephesus

8 He began by going to the synagogue, where
he spoke out boldly and argued persuasively
about the kingdom of God. He did this for
three months, 9 till the attitude of some of the
congregation hardened into unbelief. As soon as
they began attacking the Way in front of the others, he broke with them and took his disciples
apart to hold daily discussions in the lecture
room of Tyrannus. 10 This went on for two years,
with the result that people from all over Asia,[g]
both Jews and Greeks, were able to hear the
word of the Lord.

The Jewish exorcists

11 So remarkable were the miracles worked
by God at Paul's hands 12 that handkerchiefs
or aprons which had touched him were taken
to the sick, and they were cured of their illnesses,
and the evil spirits came out of them.
13 But some itinerant Jewish exorcists tried
pronouncing the name of the Lord Jesus over
people who were possessed by evil spirits; they
used to say, "I command you by the Jesus whose
spokesman is Paul." 14 Among those who did this
were seven sons of Sceva, a Jewish chief priest.
15 The evil spirit replied, "Jesus I recognize, and

[g] I.e., the region around Ephesus, including the seven towns of Rv. 1:11.

New English Bible

During the next three months he attended the synagogue and, using argument and persuasion, spoke boldly and freely about the kingdom of God. But when some proved obdurate and would not believe, speaking evil of the new way before the whole congregation, he left them, withdrew his converts, and continued to hold discussions daily in the lecture-hall of Tyrannus. This went on for two years, with the result that the whole population of the province of Asia, both Jews and Gentiles, heard the word of the Lord. And through Paul God worked singular miracles: when handkerchiefs and scarves which had been in contact with his skin were carried to the sick, they were rid of their diseases and the evil spirits came out of them.

But some strolling Jewish exorcists tried their hand at using the name of the Lord Jesus on those possessed by evil spirits; they would say, 'I adjure you by Jesus whom Paul proclaims.' There were seven sons of Sceva, a Jewish chief priest, who were using this method, when the

King James Version

Jesus I know, and Paul I know; but who are ye?
16 And the man in whom the evil spirit was
leaped on them, and overcame them, and prevailed against them, so that they fled out of
that house naked and wounded. 17 And this was
known to all the Jews and Greeks also dwelling
at Ephesus; and fear fell on them all, and the
name of the Lord Jesus was magnified. 18 And
many that believed came, and confessed, and
shewed their deeds. 19 Many of them also which
used curious arts brought their books together,
and burned them before all *men:* and they
counted the price of them, and found *it* fifty
thousand *pieces* of silver. 20 So mightily grew
the word of God and prevailed.
21 After these things were ended, Paul purposed in the spirit, when he had passed through
Macedonia and Achaia, to go to Jerusalem, saying, After I have been there, I must also see
Rome. 22 So he sent into Macedonia two of
them that ministered unto him, Timotheus and
Erastus; but he himself stayed in Asia for a

Living Bible

they tried it on a man possessed by a demon,
the demon replied, "I know Jesus and I know
Paul, but who are you?" 16 And he leaped on two
of them and beat them up, so that they fled out
of his house naked and badly injured.
17 The story of what happened spread quickly
all through Ephesus, to Jews and Greeks alike;
and a solemn fear descended on the city, and
the name of the Lord Jesus was greatly honored.
18, 19 Many of the believers who had been practicing black magic confessed their deeds and
brought their incantation books and charms and
burned them at a public bonfire. (Someone estimated the value of the books at $10,000.[d])
20 This indicates how deeply the whole area was
stirred by God's message.
21 Afterwards, Paul felt impelled by the Holy
Spirit[e] to go across to Greece before returning
to Jerusalem. "And after that," he said, "I must
go on to Rome!" 22 He sent his two assistants,
Timothy and Erastus, on ahead to Greece while
he stayed awhile longer in Turkey.

[*d*] Approximately £3,500. [*e*] Literally, "purposed in the spirit."

Today's English Version

Jesus and I know about Paul; but you—who
are you?"
16 The man who had the evil spirit in him
attacked them with such violence that he defeated them. They all ran away from his house,
wounded and with their clothes torn off. 17 All
the Jews and Gentiles who lived in Ephesus
heard about this; they were all filled with fear,
and the name of the Lord Jesus was given
greater honor. 18 Many of the believers came,
publicly admitting and revealing what they had
done. 19 Many of those who had practiced magic
brought their books together and burned them
in the presence of everyone. They added up the
price of the books and the total came to fifty
thousand dollars. 20 In this powerful way the
word of the Lord kept spreading and growing
stronger.

The riot in Ephesus

21 After these things had happened, Paul
made up his mind to travel through Macedonia
and Greece and go on to Jerusalem. "After I
go there," he said, "I must also see Rome."
22 So he sent Timothy and Erastus, two of his
helpers, to Macedonia, while he spent more time
in the province of Asia.

New International Version

them, "Jesus I know and Paul I know, but who
are you?" 16 Then the man who had the evil
spirit jumped on them and overpowered them
all. He gave them such a beating that they ran
out of the house naked and bleeding.
17 When this became known to the Jews and
Greeks living in Ephesus, they were all seized
with fear, and the name of the Lord Jesus was
held in high honor. 18 Many of those who believed now came and openly confessed their evil
deeds. 19 A number who had practiced sorcery
brought their scrolls together and burned them
publicly. When they calculated the value of the
scrolls, the total came to fifty thousand drachmas.[f] 20 In this way the word of the Lord spread
widely and grew in power.
21 After all this had happened, Paul decided
to go to Jerusalem, passing through Macedonia
and Achaia. "After I have been there," he said,
"I must visit Rome also." 22 He sent two of his
helpers, Timothy and Erastus, to Macedonia,
while he stayed in the province of Asia a little
longer.

[*f*] A drachma was about a day's wage.

Phillips Modern English

and I know about Paul, but who are you?" And the man in whom the evil sprit was living sprang at them and overpowered them all with such violence that they rushed out of that house wounded, with their clothes torn off their backs. This incident became known to all the Jews and Greeks who were living in Ephesus, and a great sense of awe came over them all, while the name of the Lord Jesus became even more respected. Many of those who had professed their faith began openly to admit their former practices. A number of those who had previously practised magic collected their books and burned them publicly. (They estimated the value of these books and found it to be no less than five thousand pounds.) In this way the Word of the Lord continued to grow in influence and power.

19.21 Paul speaks of his plans

After these events Paul was led by the Spirit to plan a journey to Jerusalem, going by way of Macedonia and Achaia, remarking,

"After I have been there I must see Rome as well."

Then he despatched to Macedonia two of his assistants, Timothy and Erastus, while he himself stayed for a while in Asia.

Revised Standard Version

evil spirit answered them, "Jesus I know, and Paul I know; but who are you?" 16 And the man in whom the evil spirit was leaped on them, mastered all of them, and overpowered them, so that they fled out of that house naked and wounded. 17 And this became known to all residents of Ephesus, both Jews and Greeks; and fear fell upon them all; and the name of the Lord Jesus was extolled. 18 Many also of those who were now believers came, confessing and divulging their practices. 19 And a number of those who practiced magic arts brought their books together and burned them in the sight of all; and they counted the value of them and found it came to fifty thousand pieces of silver. 20 So the word of the Lord grew and prevailed mightily.

21 Now after these events Paul resolved in the Spirit to pass through Macedonia and Achaia and go to Jerusalem, saying, "After I have been there, I must also see Rome." 22 And having sent into Macedonia two of his helpers, Timothy and Erastus, he himself stayed in Asia for a while.

Jerusalem Bible

I know who Paul is, but who are you?" 16 and the man with the evil spirit hurled himself at them and overpowered first one and then another, and handled them so violently that they fled from that house naked and badly mauled. 17 Everybody in Ephesus, both Jews and Greeks, heard about this episode; they were all greatly impressed, and the name of the Lord Jesus came to be held in great honor.

18 Some believers, too, came forward to admit in detail how they had used spells 19 and a number of them who had practiced magic collected their books and made a bonfire of them in public. The value of these was calculated to be fifty thousand silver pieces.

20 In this impressive way the word of the Lord spread more and more widely and successfully.

V. A prisoner for Christ

Paul's plans

21 When all this was over Paul made up his mind to go back to Jerusalem through Macedonia and Achaia. "After I have been there," he said, "I must go on to see Rome as well." 22 So he sent two of his helpers, Timothy and Erastus, ahead of him to Macedonia, while he remained for a time in Asia.

New English Bible

evil spirit answered back and said, 'Jesus I acknowledge, and I know about Paul, but who are you?' And the man with the evil spirit flew at them, overpowered them all, and handled them with such violence that they ran out of the house stripped and battered. This became known to everybody in Ephesus, whether Jew or Gentile; they were all awestruck, and the name of the Lord Jesus gained in honour. Moreover many of those who had become believers came and openly confessed that they had been using magical spells. And a good many of those who formerly practised magic collected their books and burnt them publicly. The total value was reckoned up and it came to fifty thousand pieces of silver. In such ways the word of the Lord showed its power, spreading more and more widely and effectively.

When things had reached this stage, Paul made up his mind [a] to visit Macedonia and Achaia and then go on to Jerusalem; and he said, 'After I have been there, I must see Rome also.' So he sent two of his assistants, Timothy and Erastus, to Macedonia, while he himself stayed some time longer in the province of Asia.

[a] *Or* Paul, led by the Spirit, resolved . . .

King James Version

season. 23 And the same time there arose no small stir about that way. 24 For a certain *man* named Demetrius, a silversmith, which made silver shrines for Diana, brought no small gain unto the craftsmen; 25 Whom he called together with the workmen of like occupation, and said, Sirs, ye know that by this craft we have our wealth. 26 Moreover ye see and hear, that not alone at Ephesus, but almost throughout all Asia, this Paul hath persuaded and turned away much people, saying that they be no gods, which are made with hands: 27 So that not only this our craft is in danger to be set at nought; but also that the temple of the great goddess Diana should be despised, and her magnificence should be destroyed, whom all Asia and the world worshippeth. 28 And when they heard *these sayings*, they were full of wrath, and cried out, saying, Great *is* Diana of the Ephesians. 29 And the whole city was filled with confusion: and having caught Gaius and Aristarchus, men of Macedonia, Paul's companions in travel, they rushed with one accord into the theatre. 30 And when Paul would have entered in unto the people, the disciples suffered him not. 31 And certain of the chief of Asia, which were his friends, sent unto him, desiring *him* that he would not adventure

Living Bible

23 But about that time, a big blowup developed in Ephesus concerning the Christians. 24 It began with Demetrius, a silversmith who employed many craftsmen to manufacture silver shrines of the Greek goddess Diana. 25 He called a meeting of his men, together with others employed in related trades, and addressed them as follows:

"Gentlemen, this business is our income. 26 As you know so well from what you've seen and heard, this man Paul has persuaded many, many people that handmade gods aren't gods at all. As a result, our sales volume is going down! And this trend is evident not only here in Ephesus, but throughout the entire province! 27 Of course, I am not only talking about the business aspects of this situation and our loss of income, but also of the possibility that the temple of the great goddess Diana will lose its influence, and that Diana—this magnificent goddess worshiped not only throughout this part of Turkey but all around the world—will be forgotten!"

28 At this their anger boiled and they began shouting, "Great is Diana of the Ephesians!"

29 A crowd began to gather and soon the city was filled with confusion. Everyone rushed to the amphitheater, dragging along Gaius and Aristarchus, Paul's traveling companions, for trial. 30 Paul wanted to go in, but the disciples wouldn't let him. 31 Some of the Roman officers of the province, friends of Paul, also sent a message to him, begging him not to risk his life by entering.

Today's English Version

23 It was at this time that there was serious trouble in Ephesus because of the Way of the Lord. 24 A certain silversmith named Demetrius made silver models of the temple of the goddess Artemis, and his business brought a great deal of profit to the workers. 25 So he called them all together, with others whose work was like theirs, and said to them, "Men, you know that our prosperity comes from this work. 26 You can see and hear for yourselves what this fellow Paul is doing. He says that gods made by men are not gods at all, and has succeeded in convincing many people, both here in Ephesus and in nearly the whole province of Asia. 27 There is the danger, then, that this business of ours will get a bad name. Not only that, there is also the danger that the temple of the great goddess Artemis will come to mean nothing, and that her greatness will be destroyed—the goddess worshiped by everyone in Asia and in all the world!"

28 As the crowd heard these words they became furious, and started shouting, "Great is Artemis of Ephesus!" 29 The uproar spread throughout the whole city. The mob grabbed Gaius and Aristarchus, two Macedonians who were traveling with Paul, and rushed with them to the theater. 30 Paul himself wanted to go before the crowd, but the believers would not let him. 31 Some of the provincial authorities, who were his friends, also sent him a message begging him not to show himself in the theater.

New International Version

The riot in Ephesus

23 About that time there arose a great disturbance about the Way. 24 A silversmith named Demetrius, who made silver shrines of Artemis, brought in no little business for the craftsmen. 25 He called them together, along with the workmen in related trades, and said: "Men, you know we receive a good income from this business. 26 And you see and hear how this fellow Paul has convinced and led astray large numbers of people here in Ephesus and in practically the whole province of Asia. He says that man-made gods are no gods at all. 27 There is danger not only that our trade will lose its good name, but also that the temple of the great goddess Artemis will be discredited, and the goddess herself, who is worshiped throughout the province of Asia and the world, will be robbed of her divine majesty."

28 When they heard this, they were furious and began shouting: "Great is Artemis of the Ephesians!" 29 Soon the whole city was in an uproar. The people seized Gaius and Aristarchus, Paul's traveling companions from Macedonia, and rushed as one man into the theater. 30 Paul wanted to appear before the crowd, but the disciples would not let him. 31 Even some of the officials of the province, friends of Paul, sent him a message begging him not to venture into the theater.

Phillips Modern English

19.23 The silversmiths' riot at Ephesus

Now it happened about this time that a great commotion arose concerning the Way. A man by the name of Demetrius, a silversmith who made silver shrines of Artemis, provided considerable business for his craftsmen. He gathered these men together with workers in similar trades, and spoke to them,

"Men," he said, "you all realise how our prosperity depends on this particular work. If you use your eyes and ears you also know that not only in Ephesus but practically throughout Asia this man Paul has succeeded in changing the minds of a great number of people by telling them that gods made by human hands are not gods at all. Now the danger is not only that this craft of ours might fall into disrepute, but also that the temple of the great goddess Artemis herself might come to be lightly regarded. There is a further danger, that her actual majesty might be degraded, she whom the whole of Asia, and indeed the whole world, worships!"

When they heard this they were furiously angry, and shouted,

"Great is Artemis of the Ephesians!"

Soon the whole city was in an uproar, and on a common impulse the people rushed into the theatre dragging with them Gaius and Aristarchus, two Macedonians who were Paul's travelling companions. Paul himself wanted to go in among the crowd, but the disciples would not allow him. Moreover, some high-ranking officials who were Paul's friends sent to him begging

Revised Standard Version

23 About that time there arose no little stir
concerning the Way. 24 For a man named
Demetrius, a silversmith, who made silver shrines
of Artemis, brought no little business to the
craftsmen. 25 These he gathered together, with
the workmen of like occupation, and said,
"Men, you know that from this business we
have our wealth. 26 And you see and hear that
not only at Ephesus but almost throughout all
Asia this Paul has persuaded and turned away
a considerable company of people, saying that
gods made with hands are not gods. 27 And
there is danger not only that this trade of ours
may come into disrepute but also that the temple of the great goddess Artemis may count for
nothing, and that she may even be deposed
from her magnificence, she whom all Asia and
the world worship."
28 When they heard this they were enraged,
and cried out, "Great is Artemis of the Ephesians!" 29 So the city was filled with the confusion; and they rushed together into the theater, dragging with them Gaius and Aristarchus,
Macedonians who were Paul's companions in
travel. 30 Paul wished to go in among the crowd,
but the disciples would not let him; 31 some of
the Asiarchs also, who were friends of his, sent
to him and begged him not to venture into the

Jerusalem Bible

Ephesus: the silversmiths' riot

23 It was during this time that a rather serious
disturbance broke out in connection with the
Way. 24 A silversmith called Demetrius, who
employed a large number of craftsmen making
silver shrines of Diana, 25 called a general meeting of his own men with others in the same
trade. "As you men know," he said, "it is on
this industry that we depend for our prosperity.
26 Now you must have seen and heard how, not
just in Ephesus but nearly everywhere in Asia,
this man Paul has persuaded and converted a
great number of people with his argument that
gods made by hand are not gods at all. 27 This
threatens not only to discredit our trade, but
also to reduce the sanctuary of the great goddess Diana to unimportance. It could end up by
taking away all the prestige of a goddess venerated all over Asia, yes, and everywhere in the
civilized world." 28 This speech roused them to
fury, and they started to shout, "Great is Diana
of the Ephesians!" 29 The whole town was in an
uproar and the mob rushed to the theater dragging along two of Paul's Macedonian traveling
companions, Gaius and Aristarchus. 30 Paul
wanted to make an appeal to the people, but the
disciples refused to let him; 31 in fact, some of
the Asiarchs,[h] who were friends of his, sent
messages imploring him not to take the risk of
going into the theater.

[h] Local leaders of the official state worship.

New English Bible

Now about that time, the Christian movement gave rise to a serious disturbance. There was a man named Demetrius, a silversmith who made silver shrines of Diana and provided a great deal of employment for the craftsmen. He called a meeting of these men and the workers in allied trades, and addressed them. 'Men,' he said, 'you know that our high standard of living depends on this industry. And you see and hear how this fellow Paul with his propaganda has perverted crowds of people, not only at Ephesus but also in practically the whole of the province of Asia. He is telling them that gods made by human hands are not gods at all. There is danger for us here; it is not only that our line of business will be discredited, but also that the sanctuary of the great goddess Diana will cease to command respect; and then it will not be long before she who is worshipped by all Asia and the civilized world is brought down from her divine pre-eminence.'

When they heard this they were roused to fury and shouted, 'Great is Diana of the Ephesians!' The whole city was in confusion; they seized Paul's travelling-companions, the Macedonians Gaius and Aristarchus, and made a concerted rush with them into the theatre. Paul wanted to appear before the assembly but the other Christians would not let him. Even some of the dignitaries of the province, who were friendly towards him, sent and urged him

King James Version

himself into the theatre. 32 Some therefore cried
one thing, and some another: for the assembly
was confused; and the more part knew not
wherefore they were come together. 33 And they
drew Alexander out of the multitude, the Jews
putting him forward. And Alexander beckoned
with the hand, and would have made his defence
unto the people. 34 But when they knew that he
was a Jew, all with one voice about the space
of two hours cried out, Great *is* Diana of the
Ephesians. 35 And when the townclerk had ap-
peased the people, he said, *Ye* men of Ephesus,
what man is there that knoweth not how that
the city of the Ephesians is a worshipper of the
great goddess Diana, and of the *image* which
fell down from Jupiter? 36 Seeing then that these
things cannot be spoken against, ye ought to be
quiet, and to do nothing rashly. 37 For ye have
brought hither these men, which are neither robbers of churches, nor yet blasphemers of your
goddess. 38 Wherefore if Demetrius, and the
craftsmen which are with him, have a matter
against any man, the law is open, and there are
deputies: let them implead one another. 39 But
if ye inquire any thing concerning other matters,
it shall be determined in a lawful assembly.
40 For we are in danger to be called in question
for this day's uproar, there being no cause
whereby we may give an account of this con-

Living Bible

32 Inside, the people were all shouting, some
one thing and some another—everything was in
confusion. In fact, most of them didn't even
know why they were there.
33 Alexander was spotted among the crowd
by some of the Jews and dragged forward. He
motioned for silence and tried to speak. 34 But
when the crowd realized he was a Jew, they
started shouting again and kept it up for two
hours: "Great is Diana of the Ephesians! Great
is Diana of the Ephesians!"
35 At last the mayor was able to quiet them
down enough to speak. "Men of Ephesus," he
said, "everyone knows that Ephesus is the center[f] of the religion of the great Diana, whose
image fell down to us from heaven. 36 Since
this is an indisputable fact, you shouldn't be
disturbed no matter what is said, and should do
nothing rash. 37 Yet you have brought these
men here who have stolen nothing from her
temple and have not defamed her. 38 If Demetrius and the craftsmen have a case against
them, the courts are currently in session and the
judges can take the case at once. Let them go
through legal channels. 39 And if there are complaints about other matters, they can be settled
at the regular City Council meetings; 40 for we
are in danger of being called to account by the
Roman government for today's riot, since there
is no cause for it. And if Rome demands an

[f] Literally, "is the temple-keeper."

Today's English Version

32 Meanwhile, the whole meeting was in an uproar: some people were shouting one thing,
others were shouting something else, because
most of them did not even know why they had
come together. 33 Some of the people concluded that Alexander was responsible, since the
Jews made him go up to the front. Then Alexander motioned with his hand and tried to make
a speech of defense before the people. 34 But
when they recognized that he was a Jew, they
all shouted together the same thing for two
hours, "Great is Artemis of Ephesus!"
35 At last the city clerk was able to calm the
crowd. "Men of Ephesus!" he said. "Everyone
knows that the city of Ephesus is the keeper of
the temple of the great Artemis and of the
sacred stone that fell down from heaven. 36 Nobody can deny these things. So then, you must
calm down and not do anything reckless. 37 You
have brought these men here, even though they
have not robbed temples or said evil things about
our goddess. 38 If Demetrius and his workers
have an accusation against someone, there are
the regular days for court and there are the authorities; they can accuse each other there.
39 But if there is something more that you want,
it will have to be settled in the legal meeting
of citizens. 40 For there is the danger that we
will be accused of a riot in what has happened
today. There is no excuse for all this uproar,
and we would not be able to give a good reason

New International Version

32 The assembly was in confusion: Some were
shouting one thing, some another. Most of the
people did not even know why they were there.
33 The Jews pushed Alexander to the front, and
some of the crowd shouted instructions to him.
He motioned for silence in order to make a
defense before the people. 34 But when they
realized he was a Jew, they all shouted in unison
for about two hours: "Great is Artemis of the
Ephesians!"
35 The city clerk quieted the crowd and said:
"Men of Ephesus, doesn't all the world know
that the city of Ephesus is the guardian of the
temple of the great Artemis and of her image,
which fell from heaven? 36 Therefore, since these
facts are undeniable, you ought to be quiet and
not do anything rash. 37 You have brought these
men here, though they have neither robbed temples nor blasphemed our goddess. 38 If, then,
Demetrius and his fellow craftsmen have a grievance against anybody, the courts are open and
there are proconsuls. They can press charges.
39 If there is anything further you want to bring
up, it must be settled in a legal assembly. 40 As
it is, we are in danger of being charged with
rioting because of today's events. In that case
we would not be able to account for this com-

Phillips Modern English

him not to risk himself in the theatre. Meanwhile some were shouting one thing and some another, and the whole assembly was at sixes and sevens for most of them had no idea why they had come together at all. A man called Alexander whom the Jews put forward was pushed as spokesman into the forefront of the crowd, and there, after making a gesture with his hand, he tried to make a speech of defence to the people. But as soon as they realised that he was a Jew they shouted as one man for about two hours, "Great is Artemis of the Ephesians!"

19.35 Public authority intervenes

But when the town clerk had finally quietened the crowd, he said,

"Gentlemen of Ephesus, who in the world could be ignorant of the fact that our city of Ephesus is temple-guardian of the great Artemis and of the image which fell from the sky? These are undeniable facts and it is your plain duty to remain calm and do nothing which you might afterwards regret. For you have brought these men forward, though they are neither plunderers of the temple, nor have they uttered any blasphemy against our goddess. If Demetrius and his fellow-craftsmen have a charge to bring against anyone, well, the courts are open and there are proconsuls; let them take legal action. But if you require anything beyond that then it must be resolved in the regular assembly. For all of us are in danger of being charged with rioting over today's events particularly as we

Revised Standard Version

theater. 32 Now some cried one thing, some
another; for the assembly was in confusion,
and most of them did not know why they had
come together. 33 Some of the crowd prompted
Alexander, whom the Jews had put forward.
And Alexander motioned with his hand, wishing
to make a defense to the people. 34 But when
they recognized that he was a Jew, for about
two hours they all with one voice cried out,
"Great is Artemis of the Ephesians!" 35And
when the town clerk had quieted the crowd, he
said, "Men of Ephesus, what man is there who
does not know that the city of the Ephesians
is temple keeper of the great Artemis, and of the
sacred stone that fell from the sky? [s] 36 Seeing
then that these things cannot be contradicted,
you ought to be quiet and do nothing rash.
37 For you have brought these men here who
are neither sacrilegious nor blasphemers of our
goddess. 38 If therefore Demetrius and the craftsmen with him have a complaint against one,
the courts are open, and there are proconsuls;
let them bring charges against one another.
39 But if you seek anything further,[t] it shall be
settled in the regular assembly. 40 For we are
in danger of being charged with rioting today,
there being no cause that we can give to justify

[s] The meaning of the Greek is uncertain. [t] Other ancient authorities read *about other matters*.

Jerusalem Bible

32 By now everybody was shouting different
things till the assembly itself had no idea what
was going on; most of them did not even know
why they had been summoned. 33 The Jews
pushed Alexander to the front, and when some
of the crowd shouted encouragement he raised
his hand for silence in the hope of being able
to explain things to the people. 34 When they
realized he was a Jew, they all started shouting
in unison, "Great is Diana of the Ephesians!"
and they kept this up for two hours. 35 When
the town clerk eventually succeeded in calming
the crowd, he said, "Citizens of Ephesus! Is there
anybody alive who does not know that the city
of the Ephesians is the guardian of the temple
of great Diana and of her statue that fell from
heaven? 36 Nobody can contradict this and there
is no need for you to get excited or do anything
rash. 37 These men you have brought here are
not guilty of any sacrilege or blasphemy against
our goddess. 38 If Demetrius and the craftsmen
he has with him want to complain about anyone, there are the assizes and the proconsuls;
let them take the case to court. 39And if you
want to ask any more questions you must raise
them in the regular assembly. 40 We could easily
be charged with rioting for today's happenings:
there was no ground for it all, and we can give

New English Bible

not to venture into the theatre. Meanwhile some were shouting one thing, some another; for the assembly was in confusion and most of them did not know what they had all come for. But some of the crowd explained the trouble to Alexander, whom the Jews had pushed to the front, and he, motioning for silence, attempted to make a defence before the assembly. But when they recognized that he was a Jew, a single cry arose from them all: for about two hours they kept on shouting, 'Great is Diana of the Ephesians!'

The town clerk, however, quieted the crowd. 'Men of Ephesus,' he said, 'all the world knows that our city of Ephesus is temple-warden of the great Diana and of that symbol of her which fell from heaven. Since these facts are beyond dispute, your proper course is to keep quiet and do nothing rash. These men whom you have brought here as culprits have committed no sacrilege and uttered no blasphemy against our goddess. If therefore Demetrius and his craftsmen have a case against anyone, assizes are held and there are such people as proconsuls; let the parties bring their charges and countercharges. If, on the other hand, you have some further question to raise, it will be dealt with in the statutory assembly. We certainly run the risk of being charged with riot for this day's work. There is no justification for it, and if the issue is raised we shall be unable to give any explana-

King James Version

course. 41And when he had thus spoken, he dismissed the assembly.

20 And after the uproar was ceased, Paul
called unto *him* the disciples, and embraced
them, and departed for to go into Macedonia.
2And when he had gone over those parts, and
had given them much exhortation, he came into
Greece, 3And *there* abode three months. And
when the Jews laid wait for him, as he was about
to sail into Syria, he purposed to return through
Macedonia. 4And there accompanied him into
Asia Sopater of Berea; and of the Thessalonians,
Aristarchus and Secundus; and Gaius of Derbe,
and Timotheus; and of Asia, Tychicus and
Trophimus. 5 These going before tarried for us
at Troas. 6And we sailed away from Philippi
after the days of unleavened bread, and came
unto them to Troas in five days; where we abode

Living Bible

explanation, I won't know what to say."
41 Then he dismissed them, and they dispersed.

20 When it was all over, Paul sent for the
disciples, preached a farewell message to
them, said good-bye and left for Greece,
2 preaching to the believers along the way, in
all the cities he passed through. 3 He was in
Greece three months and was preparing to sail
for Syria when he discovered a plot by the Jews
against his life, so he decided to go north to
Macedonia first.
4 Several men were traveling with him, going
as far as Turkey;[a] they were Sopater of Beroea,
the son of Pyrrhus; Aristarchus and Secundus,
from Thessalonica; Gaius, from Derbe; and Timothy; and Tychicus and Trophimus, who were
returning to their homes in Turkey, 5 and had
gone on ahead and were waiting for us at Troas.
6As soon as the Passover ceremonies ended, we
boarded ship at Philippi in northern Greece and
five days later arrived in Troas, Turkey, where
we stayed a week.

[a] Literally, "Asia."

Today's English Version

for it." 41After saying this, he dismissed the
meeting.

To Macedonia and Greece

20 After the uproar died down, Paul called
together the believers, and with words of
encouragement said good-bye to them. Then he
left and went on to Macedonia. 2 He went
through those regions and encouraged the people with many messages. Then he came to
Greece, 3 where he stayed three months. He was
getting ready to go to Syria when he discovered
that the Jews were plotting against him; so he
decided to go back through Macedonia. 4 Sopater, the son of Pyrrhus, from Berea, went with
him; so did Aristarchus and Secundus, from
Thessalonica; Gaius, from Derbe; Timothy; and
Tychicus and Trophimus, from the province of
Asia. 5 They went ahead and waited for us in
Troas. 6 We sailed from Philippi after the Feast
of Unleavened Bread, and five days later joined
them in Troas, where we spent a week.

New International Version

motion, since there is no reason for it." 41After
he had said this, he dismissed the assembly.

Through Macedonia and Greece

20 When the uproar had ended, Paul sent
for the disciples and, after encouraging
them, said good-by and set out for Macedonia.
2 He traveled through that area, speaking many
words of encouragement to the people, and finally arrived in Greece, 3 where he stayed three
months. Because the Jews made a plot against
him just as he was about to sail for Syria, he
decided to go back through Macedonia. 4 He
was accompanied by Sopater son of Pyrrhus
from Berea, Aristarchus and Secundus from
Thessalonica, Gaius from Derbe, Timothy also,
and from the province of Asia Tychicus and
Trophimus. 5 These men went on ahead and
waited for us at Troas. 6 But we sailed from
Philippi after the Feast of Unleavened Bread,
and five days later joined the others at Troas,
where we stayed seven days.

Phillips Modern English

have no real excuse to offer for this commotion." And with these words he dismissed the assembly.

20.1 Paul departs on his second journey to Europe

After this disturbance had died down, Paul sent for the disciples and after speaking encouragingly said good-bye to them, and set out on his journey to Macedonia. As he made his journey through these districts he spoke many heartening words to the people and then went on to Greece, where he stayed for three months. Then when he was on the point of setting sail for Syria the Jews made a further plot against him and he decided to make his way back through Macedonia. His companions on the journey were Sopater a Berœan, the son of Pyrrhus, two Thessalonians, Aristarchus and Secundus, Gaius from Derbe, Timothy, and two Asians, Tychicus and Trophimus. This party proceeded to Troas to await us there, while we sailed from Philippi after the days of unleavened bread, and joined them five days later at Troas, where we spent a week.

Revised Standard Version

this commotion." 41 And when he had said this,
he dismissed the assembly.

20 After the uproar ceased, Paul sent for
the disciples and having exhorted them
took leave of them and departed for Macedonia.
2 When he had gone through these parts and
had given them much encouragement, he came
to Greece. 3 There he spent three months, and
when a plot was made against him by the Jews
as he was about to set sail for Syria, he determined to return through Macedonia. 4 Sopater of Beroea, the son of Pyrrhus, accompanied
him; and of the Thessalonians, Aristarchus and
Secundus; and Gaius of Derbe, and Timothy;
and the Asians, Tychicus and Trophimus.
5 These went on and were waiting for us at
Troas, 6 but we sailed away from Philippi after
the days of Unleavened Bread, and in five days
we came to them at Troas, where we stayed for
seven days.

Jerusalem Bible

no reason for this gathering." 41 When he had
finished this speech he dismissed the assembly.

Paul leaves Ephesus

20 When the disturbance was over, Paul sent
for the disciples and, after speaking words
of encouragement to them, said good by and set
out for Macedonia. 2 On his way through those
areas he said many words of encouragement to
them and then made his way into Greece, 3 where
he spent three months. He was leaving by ship
for Syria[i] when a plot organized against him
by the Jews made him decide to go back by way
of Macedonia. 4 He was accompanied by Sopater, son of Pyrrhus, who came from Beroea;
Aristarchus and Secundus who came from Thessalonika; Gaius from Doberus, and Timothy, as
well as Tychicus and Trophimus who were from
Asia. 5 They all went on to Troas where they
waited for us. 6 We ourselves left Philippi by
ship after the days of Unleavened Bread and
met them five days later at Troas, where we
stopped for a week.

[i] Taking to Jerusalem the proceeds of the collection, Rm. 15:25.

New English Bible

tion of this uproar.' With that he dismissed the assembly.

20 When the disturbance had ceased, Paul sent for the disciples and, after encouraging them, said good-bye and set out on his journey to Macedonia. He travelled through those parts of the country, often speaking words of encouragement to the Christians there, and so came into Greece. When he had spent three months there and was on the point of embarking for Syria, a plot was laid against him by the Jews, so he decided to return by way of Macedonia. He was accompanied by Sopater son of Pyrrhus, from Beroea, the Thessalonians Aristarchus and Secundus, Gaius the Doberian[a] and Timothy, and the Asians Tychicus and Trophimus. These went ahead and waited for us at Troas; we ourselves set sail from Philippi after the Passover season,[b] and in five days reached them at Troas, where we spent a week.

[a] *Some witnesses read* the Derbaean. [b] *Literally* after the days of Unleavened Bread.

King James Version

seven days. 7And upon the first *day* of the week,
when the disciples came together to break bread,
Paul preached unto them, ready to depart on
the morrow; and continued his speech until midnight. 8And there were many lights in the upper
chamber, where they were gathered together.
9And there sat in a window a certain young man
named Eutychus, being fallen into a deep sleep:
and as Paul was long preaching, he sunk down
with sleep, and fell down from the third loft,
and was taken up dead. 10And Paul went down,
and fell on him, and embracing *him* said, Trouble not yourselves; for his life is in him. 11 When
he therefore was come up again, and had broken
bread, and eaten, and talked a long while, even
till break of day, so he departed. 12And they
brought the young man alive, and were not a
little comforted.

13 And we went before to ship, and sailed
unto Assos, there intending to take in Paul: for
so had he appointed, minding himself to go
afoot. 14And when he met with us at Assos, we
took him in, and came to Mitylene. 15And we
sailed thence, and came the next *day* over

Living Bible

7 On Sunday,[b] we gathered for a communion
service, with Paul preaching. And since he was
leaving the next day, he talked until midnight!
8 The upstairs room where we met was lighted
with many flickering lamps; 9 and as Paul spoke
on and on, a young man named Eutychus,
sitting on the window sill, went fast asleep
and fell three stories to his death below.
10, 11, 12 Paul went down and took him into his
arms. "Don't worry," he said, "he's all right!"
And he was! What a wave of awesome joy swept
through the crowd! They all went back upstairs
and ate the Lord's Supper together; then Paul
preached another long sermon—so it was dawn
when he finally left them!

13 Paul was going by land to Assos, and we
went on ahead by ship. 14 He joined us there
and we sailed together to Mitylene; 15 the next
day we passed Chios; the next, we touched at

[*b*] Or, "on Saturday night." Literally, "the first day of the week," by Jewish reckoning, from sundown to sundown.

Today's English Version

Paul's last visit in Troas

7 On Saturday evening we gathered together
for the fellowship meal. Paul spoke to the people, and kept on speaking until midnight, since
he was going to leave the next day. 8 There were
many lamps in the upstairs room where we were
meeting. 9A young man named Eutychus was
sitting in the window; and as Paul kept on
talking, Eutychus got sleepier and sleepier, until
he finally went sound asleep and fell from the
third story to the ground. They picked him up,
and he was dead. 10 But Paul went down and
threw himself on him and hugged him. "Don't
worry," he said, "he is still alive!" 11 Then he
went back upstairs, broke bread, and ate. After
talking with them for a long time until sunrise,
Paul left. 12 They took the young man home
alive, and were greatly comforted.

From Troas to Miletus

13 We went on ahead to the ship and sailed
off to Assos, where we were going to take Paul
aboard. He had told us to do this, because he
was going there by land. 14 When he met us in
Assos, we took him aboard and went on to
Mitylene. 15 We sailed from there and arrived
off Chios the next day. A day later we came to

New International Version

Eutychus raised from the dead at Troas

7 On the first day of the week we came together to break bread. Paul preached to the people and, because he intended to leave the next
day, kept on talking until midnight. 8 There were
many lamps in the upstairs room where we were
meeting. 9 Seated in a window was a young man
named Eutychus, who was sinking into a deep
sleep as Paul talked on and on. When he was
sound asleep, he fell to the ground from the
third story and was picked up dead. 10 Paul
went down, threw himself on the young man and
put his arms around him. "Don't be alarmed,"
he said. "He's alive!" 11 Then he went upstairs
again and broke bread and ate. After talking
until daylight, he left. 12 The people took the
young man home alive and were greatly comforted.

Paul's farewell to the Ephesian elders

13 We went on ahead to the ship and sailed
for Assos, where we were going to take Paul
aboard. He had made this arrangement because
he was going there on foot. 14 When he met us
at Assos, we took him aboard and went on to
Mitylene. 15 The next day we set sail from there
and arrived off Chios. The day after that we

Phillips Modern English

20.7 *Paul's enthusiasm leads to an accident*

On the Saturday, when we were assembled for the breaking of bread, Paul, since he intended to leave on the following day, began to speak to them and prolonged his address until midnight. There were a great many lamps burning in the upper room where we met, and a young man called Eytychus who was sitting on the window-sill grew more and more sleepy as Paul's address became longer and longer. Finally, completely overcome by sleep, he fell to the ground from the third storey and was picked up as dead. But Paul went down, flung himself beside him and holding him gently in his arms, said,

"Don't be alarmed; he is still alive."

Then he went upstairs again and, when he had broken bread and eaten, continued a long earnest talk with them until daybreak, and so finally departed. As for the boy, they took him home alive, feeling immeasurably relieved.

20.13 We sail to Miletus

Meanwhile we had gone aboard the ship and sailed on ahead for Assos, intending to pick up Paul there, for that was the arrangement he had made, since he himself had planned to go overland. When he met us on our arrival at Assos we took him aboard and went on to Mitylene. We sailed from there and arrived off the coast of Chios the next day. On the day following we

Revised Standard Version

7 On the first day of the week, when we were gathered together to break bread, Paul talked with them, intending to depart on the morrow; and he prolonged his speech until midnight.
8 There were many lights in the upper chamber
where we were gathered. 9 And a young man
named Eutychus was sitting in the window. He sank into a deep sleep as Paul talked still longer; and being overcome by sleep, he fell down from
the third story and was taken up dead. 10 But
Paul went down and bent over him, and embracing him said, "Do not be alarmed, for his
life is in him." 11 And when Paul had gone up
and had broken bread and eaten, he conversed with them a long while, until daybreak, and so
departed. 12 And they took the lad away alive,
and were not a little comforted.
13 But going ahead to the ship, we set sail for Assos, intending to take Paul aboard there; for so he had arranged, intending himself to go
by land. 14 And when he met us at Assos, we
took him on board and came to Mitylene. 15 And
sailing from there we came the following day

Jerusalem Bible

Troas: Paul raises a dead man to life

7 On the first day of the week[j] we met to break bread. Paul was due to leave the next day, and he preached a sermon that went on till the
middle of the night. 8 A number of lamps were
lit in the upstairs room where we were assembled,
9 and as Paul went on and on, a young man called Eutychus who was sitting on the window sill grew drowsy and was overcome by sleep and fell to the ground three floors below. He was
picked up dead. 10 Paul went down and stooped
to clasp the boy to him. "There is no need to worry," he said, "there is still life in him."
11 Then he went back upstairs where he broke bread and ate and carried on talking till he left
at daybreak. 12 They took the boy away alive,
and were greatly encouraged.

From Troas to Miletus

13 We were now to go on ahead by sea, so we set sail for Assos, where we were to take Paul on board; this was what he had arranged,
for he wanted to go by road. 14 When he rejoined us at Assos we took him aboard and went
on to Mitylene. 15 The next day we sailed from
there and arrived opposite Chios. The second

[j] The day was reckoned in the Jewish fashion; the Lord's day began on the evening of Saturday and it was then that this meeting was held.

New English Bible

On the Saturday night, in our assembly for the breaking of bread, Paul, who was to leave next day, addressed them, and went on speaking until midnight. Now there were many lamps in the upper room where we were assembled; and a youth named Eutychus, who was sitting on the window-ledge, grew more and more sleepy as Paul went on talking. At last he was completely overcome by sleep, fell from the third storey to the ground, and was picked up for dead. Paul went down, threw himself upon him, seizing him in his arms, and said to them, 'Stop this commotion; there is still life in him.' He then went upstairs, broke bread and ate, and after much conversation, which lasted until dawn, he departed. And they took the boy away alive and were immensely comforted.

We went ahead to the ship and sailed for Assos, where we were to take Paul aboard. He had made this arrangement, as he was going to travel by road. When he met us at Assos, we took him aboard and went on to Mitylene. Next day we sailed from there and arrived opposite Chios, and on the second day we made Samos.

King James Version

against Chios; and the next *day* we arrived at Samos, and tarried at Trogyllium; and the next *day* we came to Miletus. 16 For Paul had determined to sail by Ephesus, because he would not spend the time in Asia: for he hasted, if it were possible for him, to be at Jerusalem the day of Pentecost.

17 And from Miletus he sent to Ephesus, and called the elders of the church. 18 And when they were come to him, he said unto them, Ye know, from the first day that I came into Asia, after what manner I have been with you at all seasons, 19 Serving the Lord with all humility of mind, and with many tears, and temptations, which befell me by the lying in wait of the Jews: 20 *And* how I kept back nothing that was profitable *unto you,* but have shewed you, and have taught you publicly, and from house to house, 21 Testifying both to the Jews, and also to the Greeks, repentance toward God, and faith toward our Lord Jesus Christ. 22 And now, behold, I go bound in the spirit unto Jerusalem, not knowing the things that shall befall me there: 23 Save that the Holy Ghost witnesseth in every city, saying that bonds and afflictions abide me. 24 But none of these things move me, neither count I my life dear unto myself, so that I might finish my course with joy, and the ministry, which I have received of the Lord Jesus, to

Living Bible

Samos; and a day later we arrived at Miletus.

16 Paul had decided against stopping at Ephesus this time, as he was hurrying to get to Jerusalem, if possible, for the celebration of Pentecost. 17 But when we landed at Miletus, he sent a message to the elders of the church at Ephesus asking them to come down to the boat to meet him.

18 When they arrived he told them, "You men know that from the day I set foot in Turkey until now 19 I have done the Lord's work humbly—yes, and with tears—and have faced grave danger from the plots of the Jews against my life. 20 Yet I never shrank from telling you the truth, either publicly or in your homes. 21 I have had one message for Jews and Gentiles alike—the necessity of turning from sin to God through faith in our Lord Jesus Christ.

22 And now I am going to Jerusalem, drawn there irresistibly by the Holy Spirit,[c] not knowing what awaits me, 23 except that the Holy Spirit has told me in city after city that jail and suffering lie ahead. 24 But life is worth nothing unless I use it for doing the work assigned me by the Lord Jesus—the work of telling others the Good News about God's mighty kindness and love.

[c] Or, "by an inner compulsion."

Today's English Version

Samos, and the following day we reached Miletus. 16 Paul had decided to sail on by Ephesus, so as not to lose any time in the province of Asia. He was in a hurry to arrive in Jerusalem, if at all possible, by the day of Pentecost.

Paul's farewell speech to the elders of Ephesus

17 Paul sent a message from Miletus to Ephesus, asking the elders of the church to meet him. 18 When they arrived, he said to them, "You know how I spent the whole time I was with you, from the first day I arrived in the province of Asia. 19 With all humility and many tears I did my work as the Lord's servant, through the hard times that came to me because of the plots of the Jews. 20 You know that I did not hold back anything that would be of help to you as I preached and taught you in public and in your homes. 21 To Jews and Gentiles alike I gave solemn warning that they should turn from their sins to God, and believe in our Lord Jesus. 22 And now, in obedience to the Holy Spirit, I am going to Jerusalem, not knowing what will happen to me there. 23 I only know that in every city the Holy Spirit has warned me that prison and troubles wait for me. 24 But I reckon my own life to be worth nothing to me, in order that I may complete my mission and finish the work that the Lord Jesus gave me to do, which is to declare the Good News of the grace of God.

New International Version

crossed over to Samos, and on the following day arrived at Miletus. 16 Paul had decided to sail past Ephesus to avoid spending time in the province of Asia, for he was in a hurry to reach Jerusalem, if possible, by the day of Pentecost.

17 From Miletus, Paul sent to Ephesus for the elders of the church. 18 When they arrived, he said to them: "You know how I lived the whole time I was with you, from the first day I came into the province of Asia. 19 I served the Lord with great humility and with tears, although I was severely tested by the plots of the Jews. 20 You know that I have not hesitated to preach anything that would be helpful to you but have taught you publicly and from house to house. 21 I have declared to both Jews and Greeks that they must turn to God in repentance and have faith in our Lord Jesus.

22 "And now, compelled by the Spirit, I am going to Jerusalem, not knowing what will happen to me there. 23 I only know that in every city the Holy Spirit warns me that prison and hardships are facing me. 24 However, I consider my life worth nothing to me, if only I may finish the race and complete the task the Lord Jesus has given me—the task of testifying to the gospel of God's grace.

Phillips Modern English

crossed to Samos, and the day after that we reached Miletus. For Paul had decided to sail past Ephesus with the idea of spending as little time as possible in the province of Asia. He hoped, if it should prove possible, to reach Jerusalem in time for the day of Pentecost.

20.17 Paul's moving farewell message to the elders of Ephesus

At Miletus he sent to Ephesus to summon the elders of the church. On their arrival he addressed them in these words:

"I am sure you know how I have lived among you ever since I first set foot in Asia. You know how I have served the Lord most humbly and what tears I have shed and what trials have come to me through the plots of the Jews. You know I have never shrunk from telling you anything that was for your good, nor from teaching you in public or in your own homes. On the contrary I have most emphatically urged upon both Jews and Greeks repentance towards God and faith in our Lord Jesus. And now here I am, compelled by the Spirit to go to Jerusalem. I do not know what may happen to me there, except that the Holy Spirit warns me that imprisonment and persecution await me in every city that I visit. But I do not consider my own life important or valuable to me, so long as I can finish my course and complete the ministry which the Lord Jesus has given me in declaring the good

Revised Standard Version

opposite Chios; the next day we touched at
Samos; and [u] the day after that we came to
Miletus. 16 For Paul had decided to sail past
Ephesus, so that he might not have to spend
time in Asia; for he was hastening to be at
Jerusalem, if possible, on the day of Pentecost.
17 And from Miletus he sent to Ephesus and
called to him the elders of the church. 18 And
when they came to him, he said to them:
"You yourselves know how I lived among
you all the time from the first day that I set
foot in Asia, 19 serving the Lord with all humility and with tears and with trials which befell me through the plots of the Jews; 20 how
I did not shrink from declaring to you anything
that was profitable, and teaching you in public
and from house to house, 21 testifying both to
Jews and to Greeks of repentance to God and
of faith in our Lord Jesus Christ. 22 And now,
behold, I am going to Jerusalem, bound in the
Spirit, not knowing what shall befall me there;
23 except that the Holy Spirit testifies to me in
every city that imprisonment and afflictions
await me. 24 But I do not account my life of
any value nor as precious to myself, if only I
may accomplish my course and the ministry
which I received from the Lord Jesus, to testify

[u] Other ancient authorities add *after remaining at Trogyllium.*

Jerusalem Bible

day we touched at Samos and, after stopping at
Trogyllium, made Miletus the next day. 16 Paul
had decided to pass wide of Ephesus so as to
avoid spending time in Asia, since he was anxious
to be in Jerusalem, if possible, for the day of
Pentecost.

Farewell to the elders of Ephesus

17 From Miletus he sent for the elders of the
church of Ephesus. 18 When they arrived he addressed these words to them:
"You know what my way of life has been ever
since the first day I set foot among you in Asia,
19 how I have served the Lord in all humility,
with all the sorrows and trials that came to me
through the plots of the Jews. 20 I have not
hesitated to do anything that would be helpful
to you; I have preached to you, and instructed
you both in public and in your homes, 21 urging
both Jews and Greeks to turn to God and to
believe in our Lord Jesus.
22 "And now you see me a prisoner already
in spirit; I am on my way to Jerusalem, but
have no idea what will happen to me there,
23 except that the Holy Spirit, in town after
town, has made it clear enough that imprisonment and persecution await me. 24 But life to
me is not a thing to waste words on, provided
that when I finish my race I have carried out
the mission the Lord Jesus gave me—and that
was to bear witness to the Good News of God's
grace.

New English Bible

On the following day[a] we reached Miletus. For Paul had decided to pass by Ephesus and so avoid having to spend time in the province of Asia; he was eager to be in Jerusalem, if he possibly could, on the day of Pentecost. He did, however, send from Miletus to Ephesus and summon the elders of the congregation; and when they joined him, he spoke as follows:

'You know how, from the day that I first set foot in the province of Asia, for the whole time that I was with you, I served the Lord in all humility amid the sorrows and trials that came upon me through the machinations of the Jews. You know that I kept back nothing that was for your good: I delivered the message to you; I taught you, in public and in your homes; with Jews and Gentiles alike I insisted on repentance before God and trust in our Lord Jesus. And now, as you see, I am on my way to Jerusalem, under the constraint of the Spirit.[b] Of what will befall me there I know nothing, except that in city after city the Holy Spirit assures me that imprisonment and hardships await me. For myself, I set no store by life; I only want to finish the race, and complete the task which the Lord Jesus assigned to me, of bearing my testimony to the gospel of God's grace.

[a] *Some witnesses read* . . . Samos, and, after stopping at Trogyllium, on the following day . . .
[b] *Or* under an inner compulsion.

King James Version

testify the gospel of the grace of God. 25And
now, behold, I know that ye all among whom I
have gone preaching the kingdom of God, shall
see my face no more. 26 Wherefore I take you
to record this day, that I *am* pure from the
blood of all *men*. 27 For I have not shunned to
declare unto you all the counsel of God.
28 Take heed therefore unto yourselves, and
to all the flock, over the which the Holy Ghost
hath made you overseers, to feed the church of
God, which he hath purchased with his own
blood. 29 For I know this, that after my departing shall grievous wolves enter in among you,
not sparing the flock. 30 Also of your own selves
shall men arise, speaking perverse things, to
draw away disciples after them. 31 Therefore
watch, and remember, that by the space of three
years I ceased not to warn every one night and
day with tears. 32And now, brethren, I commend
you to God, and to the word of his grace, which
is able to build you up, and to give you an inheritance among all them which are sanctified.
33 I have coveted no man's silver, or gold, or
apparel. 34 Yea, ye yourselves know, that these
hands have ministered unto my necessities, and
to them that were with me. 35 I have shewed
you all things, how that so labouring ye ought
to support the weak, and to remember the words
of the Lord Jesus, how he said, It is more
blessed to give than to receive.
36 And when he had thus spoken, he kneeled
down, and prayed with them all. 37And they all
wept sore, and fell on Paul's neck, and kissed
him, 38 Sorrowing most of all for the words

Living Bible

25 "And now I know that none of you among
whom I went about teaching the Kingdom will
ever see me again. 26 Let me say plainly that no
man's blood can be laid at my door, 27 for I
didn't shrink from declaring all God's message
to you.
28 "And now beware! Be sure that you feed
and shepherd God's flock—his church, purchased
with his blood—for the Holy Spirit is holding
you responsible as overseers. 29 I know full well
that after I leave you, false teachers, like vicious
wolves, will appear among you, not sparing the
flock. 30 Some of you yourselves will distort the
truth in order to draw a following. 31 Watch
out! Remember the three years I was with you
—my constant watchcare over you night and
day and my many tears for you.
32 "And now I entrust you to God and his
care and to his wonderful words which are able
to build your faith and give you all the inheritance of those who are set apart for himself.
33 "I have never been hungry for money or
fine clothing—34 you know that these hands of
mine worked to pay my own way and even to
supply the needs of those who were with me.
35And I was a constant example to you in helping the poor; for I remembered the words of
the Lord Jesus, 'It is more blessed to give than
to receive.' "
36 When he had finished speaking, he knelt
and prayed with them, 37 and they wept aloud
as they embraced him in farewell, 38 sorrowing

Today's English Version

25 "I have gone about among all of you,
preaching the Kingdom of God. And now I
know that none of you will ever see me again.
26 So I solemnly declare to you this very day:
if any of you should be lost, I am not responsible. 27 For I have not held back from announcing to you the whole purpose of God.
28 Keep watch over yourselves and over all the
flock which the Holy Spirit has placed in your
care. Be shepherds of the church of God, which
he made his own through the death of his own
Son. 29 I know that after I leave, fierce wolves
will come among you, and they will not spare
the flock. 30 The time will come when some
men from your own group will tell lies to lead
the believers away after them. 31 Watch, then,
and remember that with many tears, day and
night, I taught every one of you for three years.
32 "And now I place you in the care of God
and the message of his grace. He is able to build
you up and give you the blessings he keeps for
all his people. 33 I have not coveted anyone's
silver or gold or clothing. 34 You yourselves
know that with these hands of mine I have
worked and provided everything that my companions and I have needed. 35 I have shown you
in all things that by working hard in this way
we must help the weak, remembering the words
that the Lord Jesus himself said, 'There is more
happiness in giving than in receiving.' "
36 When Paul finished, he knelt down with
them all and prayed. 37 They were all crying as
they hugged him and kissed him good-bye.
38 They were especially sad at the words he had

New International Version

25 "Now I know that none of you among
whom I have gone about preaching the kingdom
will ever see me again. 26 Therefore, I declare
to you today that I am innocent of the blood
of all men. 27 For I have not hesitated to proclaim to you the whole will of God. 28 Guard
yourselves and all the flock of which the Holy
Spirit has made you overseers.[g] Be shepherds of
the church of God,[h] which he bought with his
own blood. 29 I know that after I leave, savage
wolves will come in among you and will not
spare the flock. 30 Even from your own number
men will arise and distort the truth in order to
draw away disciples after them. 31 So be on your
guard! Remember that for three years I never
stopped warning each of you night and day with
tears.
32 "Now I commit you to God and to the
word of his grace, which can build you up and
give you an inheritance among all those who
are sanctified. 33 I have not coveted anyone's
silver or gold or clothing. 34 You yourselves
know that these hands of mine have supplied
my own needs and the needs of my companions.
35 In everything I did, I showed you that by this
kind of hard work we must help the weak, remembering the words of the Lord Jesus: 'It is
more blessed to give than to receive.' "
36 When he had said this, he knelt down with
all of them and prayed. 37 They all wept as they
embraced him and kissed him. 38 What grieved

[g] Or *bishops*. [h] Some MSS read *of the Lord*.

Phillips Modern English

news of the grace of God. Now I know well enough that not one of you among whom I have moved as I preached the kingdom of God will ever see my face again. That is why I must tell you solemnly today that my conscience is clear as far as any of you is concerned, for I have never shrunk from declaring to you the whole purpose of God. Now be on your guard for yourselves and for every flock of which the Holy Spirit has made you guardians—you are to be shepherds to the Church of God, which he won at the cost of his own blood. I know that after my departure savage wolves will come in among you without mercy for the flock. Yes, and even from among you men will arise speaking perversions of the truth, trying to draw away the disciples and make them followers of themselves. This is why I tell you to keep on the alert, remembering that for three years I never failed night and day to warn every one of you, even with tears in my eyes. Now I commend you to God and to the message of his grace which can build you up and give you your inheritance among all those who are consecrated to him. I have never coveted anybody's gold or silver or clothing. You know well enough that these hands of mine have provided for my own needs and for those of my companions. In everything I have shown you that by such hard work we must help the weak and must remember the words of the Lord Jesus when he said, 'To give is happier than to receive'."

With these words he knelt down with them all and prayed. All of them were in tears, and throwing their arms round Paul's neck they kissed him affectionately. What saddened them

Revised Standard Version

to the gospel of the grace of God. 25And now,
behold, I know that all you among whom I have
gone preaching the kingdom will see my face no
more. 26 Therefore I testify to you this day that
I am innocent of the blood of all of you, 27 for
I did not shrink from declaring to you the whole
counsel of God. 28 Take heed to yourselves and
to all the flock, in which the Holy Spirit has
made you overseers, to care for the church of
God [v] which he obtained with the blood of his
own Son.[w] 29 I know that after my departure
fierce wolves will come in among you, not sparing the flock; 30 and from among your own
selves will arise men speaking perverse things,
to draw away the disciples after them. 31 Therefore be alert, remembering that for three years
I did not cease night or day to admonish every
one with tears. 32And now I commend you to
God and to the word of his grace, which is able
to build you up and to give you the inheritance
among all those who are sanctified. 33 I coveted
no one's silver or gold or apparel. 34 You yourselves know that these hands ministered to my
necessities, and to those who were with me. 35 In
all things I have shown you that by so toiling
one must help the weak, remembering the words
of the Lord Jesus, how he said, 'It is more
blessed to give than to receive.'"
36 And when he had spoken thus, he knelt
down and prayed with them all. 37And they all
wept and embraced Paul and kissed him, 38 sor-

[v] Other ancient authorities read *of the Lord*. [w] Greek *with the blood of his Own* or *with his own blood*.

Jerusalem Bible

25 "I now feel sure that none of you among
whom I have gone about proclaiming the kingdom will ever see my face again. 26And so here
and now I swear that my conscience is clear as
far as all of you are concerned, 27 for I have
without faltering put before you the whole of
God's purpose.
28 "Be on your guard for yourselves and for
all the flock of which the Holy Spirit has made
you the overseers, to feed the Church of God
which he bought with his own blood. 29 I know
quite well that when I have gone fierce wolves
will invade you and will have no mercy on the
flock. 30 Even from your own ranks there will
be men coming forward with a travesty of the
truth on their lips to induce the disciples to
follow them. 31 So be on your guard, remembering how night and day for three years I never
failed to keep you right, shedding tears over
each one of you. 32And now I commend you to
God, and to the word of his grace that has
power to build you up and to give you your inheritance among all the sanctified.
33 "I have never asked anyone for money or
clothes; 34 you know for yourselves that the
work I did earned enough to meet my needs and
those of my companions. 35 I did this to show
you that this is how we must exert ourselves to
support the weak, remembering the words of the
Lord Jesus, who himself said, 'There is more
happiness in giving than in receiving.'"
36 When he had finished speaking he knelt
down with them all and prayed. 37 By now they
were all in tears; they put their arms around
Paul's neck and kissed him; 38 what saddened

New English Bible

'One word more: I have gone about among you proclaiming the Kingdom, but now I know that none of you will see my face again. That being so, I here and now declare that no man's fate can be laid at my door; for I have kept back nothing; I have disclosed to you the whole purpose of God. Keep watch over yourselves and over all the flock of which the Holy Spirit has given you charge, as shepherds of the church of the Lord,[c] which he won for himself by his own blood.[d] I know that when I am gone, savage wolves will come in among you and will not spare the flock. Even from your own body there will be men coming forward who will distort the truth to induce the disciples to break away and follow them. So be on the alert; remember how for three years, night and day, I never ceased to counsel each of you, and how I wept over you.

'And now I commend you to God and to his gracious word, which has power to build you up and give you your heritage among all who are dedicated to him. I have not wanted anyone's money or clothes for myself; you all know that these hands of mine earned enough for the needs of myself and my companions. I showed you that it is our duty to help the weak in this way, by hard work, and that we should keep in mind the words of the Lord Jesus, who himself said, "Happiness lies more in giving than in receiving."'

As he finished speaking, he knelt down with them all and prayed. Then there were loud cries of sorrow from them all, as they folded Paul in their arms and kissed him. What distressed them

[c] *Some witnesses read* of God. [d] *Or, according to some witnesses,* by the blood of his Own.

King James Version

which he spake, that they should see his face no more. And they accompanied him unto the ship.

21 And it came to pass, that after we were gotten from them, and had launched, we came with a straight course unto Coos, and the *day* following unto Rhodes, and from thence unto Patara: 2And finding a ship sailing over unto Phenicia, we went aboard, and set forth. 3 Now when we had discovered Cyprus, we left it on the left hand, and sailed into Syria, and landed at Tyre: for there the ship was to unlade her burden. 4And finding disciples, we tarried there seven days: who said to Paul through the Spirit, that he should not go up to Jerusalem. 5And when we had accomplished those days, we departed and went our way; and they all brought us on our way, with wives and children, till *we were* out of the city: and we kneeled down on the shore, and prayed. 6And when we had taken our leave one of another, we took ship; and they returned home again. 7And when we had finished *our* course from Tyre, we came to Ptolemais, and saluted the brethren, and abode with them one day. 8And the next *day* we that were of Paul's company departed, and came unto Cesarea; and we entered into the house of Philip the evangelist, which was *one* of the seven; and abode with him. 9And the same man had four daughters, virgins, which did prophesy.

Living Bible

most of all because he said that he would never see them again. Then they accompanied him down to the ship.

21 After parting from the Ephesian elders, we sailed straight to Cos. The next day we reached Rhodes and then went to Patara. 2 There we boarded a ship sailing for the Syrian province of Phoenicia. 3 We sighted the island of Cyprus, passed it on our left and landed at the harbor of Tyre, in Syria, where the ship unloaded. 4 We went ashore, found the local believers and stayed with them a week. These disciples warned Paul —the Holy Spirit prophesying through them— not to go on to Jerusalem. 5At the end of the week when we returned to the ship, the entire congregation including wives and children walked down to the beach with us where we prayed and said our farewells. 6 Then we went aboard and they returned home.

7 The next stop after leaving Tyre was Ptolemais where we greeted the believers, but stayed only one day. 8 Then we went on to Caesarea and stayed at the home of Philip the Evangelist, one of the first seven deacons.[a] 9 He had four unmarried [b] daughters who had the gift of prophecy.

[*a*] See Acts 6:5, 8:1-13. [*b*] Literally, "virgins."

Today's English Version

said that they would never see him again. And so they went with him to the ship.

Paul goes to Jerusalem

21 We said good-bye to them and left. After sailing straight across, we came to Cos; the next day we reached Rhodes, and from there we went on to Patara. 2 There we found a ship that was going to Phoenicia; so we went aboard and sailed away. 3 We came to where we could see Cyprus, and sailed south of it on to Syria. We went ashore at Tyre, where the ship was going to unload its cargo. 4 We found some believers there, and stayed with them a week. By the power of the Spirit they told Paul not to go to Jerusalem. 5 But when our time with them was over, we left and went on our way. All of them, with their wives and children, went with us out of the city. We all knelt down on the beach and prayed. 6 Then we said good-bye to one another, and we went on board the ship while they went back home.

7 We continued our voyage, sailing from Tyre to Ptolemais, where we greeted the brothers and stayed with them for a day. 8 On the following day we left and arrived in Caesarea. There we went to the house of the evangelist Philip, and stayed with him. He was one of the seven men who had been chosen in Jerusalem. 9 He had four unmarried daughters who proclaimed God's

New International Version

them most was his statement that they would never see his face again. Then they accompanied him to the ship.

On to Jerusalem

21 After we had torn ourselves away from them, we put out to sea and sailed straight to Cos. The next day we went to Rhodes and from there to Patara. 2 We found a ship crossing over to Phoenicia, went on board and set sail. 3After sighting Cyprus and passing to the south of it, we sailed on to Syria. We landed at Tyre, where our ship was to unload its cargo. 4 Finding the disciples there, we stayed with them seven days. Through the Spirit they urged Paul not to go on to Jerusalem. 5 But when our time was up, we left and continued on our way. All the disciples and their wives and children accompanied us out of the city, and there on the beach we knelt to pray. 6After saying good-by to each other, we went aboard the ship, and they returned home.

7 We continued our voyage from Tyre and landed at Ptolemais, where we greeted the brothers and stayed with them for a day. 8 Leaving the next day, we reached Caesarea and stayed at the house of Philip the evangelist, one of the Seven. 9 He had four unmarried daughters who had the gift of prophecy.

Phillips Modern English

most of all was his saying that they would never see his face again. And they went with him down to the ship.

21.1 The brothers of Tyre warn Paul not to go to Jerusalem

When we had finally said farewell to them we set sail, running a straight course to Cos, and the next day we went to Rhodes and from there to Patara. Here we found a ship bound for Phoenicia, and we went aboard her and set sail. After sighting Cyprus and leaving it on our left we sailed to Syria and put in at Tyre, since that was where the ship was to discharge her cargo. We sought out the disciples there and stayed with them for a week. They felt led by the Spirit again and again to warn Paul not to go up to Jerusalem. But when our time was up we left them and continued our journey. They all came out to see us off, bringing their wives and children with them, accompanying us till we were outside the city. Then kneeling down on the beach we prayed and said good-bye to each other. Then we went aboard the ship, while the disciples went back home. We sailed away from Tyre and arrived at Ptolemais. We greeted the brothers there and stayed with them for just one day. On the following day we left and came to Caesarea and there we went to stay at the house of Philip the evangelist, one of the seven deacons. He had four unmarried daughters, all of whom

Revised Standard Version

rowing most of all because of the word he had spoken, that they should see his face no more. And they brought him to the ship.

21 And when we had parted from them and
set sail, we came by a straight course to
Cos, and the next day to Rhodes, and from
there to Patara.[x] 2And having found a ship
crossing to Phoenicia, we went aboard, and set
sail. 3 When we had come in sight of Cyprus,
leaving it on the left we sailed to Syria, and
landed at Tyre; for there the ship was to unload
its cargo. 4And having sought out the disciples,
we stayed there for seven days. Through the
Spirit they told Paul not to go on to Jerusalem.
5And when our days there were ended, we departed and went on our journey; and they all,
with wives and children, brought us on our way
till we were outside the city; and kneeling down
on the beach we prayed and bade one another
farewell. 6 Then we went on board the ship, and
they returned home.
7 When we had finished the voyage from
Tyre, we arrived at Ptolemais; and we greeted
the brethren and stayed with them for one day.
8 On the morrow we departed and came to
Caesarea; and we entered the house of Philip
the evangelist, who was one of the seven, and
stayed with them. 9And he had four unmarried

[x] Other ancient authorities add *and Myra*.

Jerusalem Bible

them most was his saying they would never see his face again. Then they escorted him to the ship.

The journey to Jerusalem

21 When we had at last torn ourselves away
from them and put to sea, we set a straight
course and arrived at Cos; the next day we
reached Rhodes, and from there went on to
Patara. 2 Here we found a ship bound for Phoenicia, so we went on board and sailed in her.
3After sighting Cyprus and leaving it to port, we
sailed to Syria and put in at Tyre, since the ship
was to unload her cargo there. 4 We sought out
the disciples and stayed there a week. Speaking
in the Spirit, they kept telling Paul not to go on
to Jerusalem, 5 but when our time was up we
set off. Together with the women and children
they all escorted us on our way till we were out
of the town. When we reached the beach, we
knelt down and prayed; 6 then, after saying
good-by to each other, we went aboard and they
returned home.
7 The end of our voyage from Tyre came
when we landed at Ptolemais, where we greeted
the brothers and stayed one day with them.
8 The next day we left and came to Caesarea.
Here we called on Philip the evangelist, one of
the Seven, and stayed with him. 9 He had four

New English Bible

most was his saying that they would never see his face again. So they escorted him to his ship.

21 When we had parted from them and set sail, we made a straight run and came to Cos; next day to Rhodes, and thence to Patara.[a] There we found a ship bound for Phoenicia, so we went aboard and sailed in her. We came in sight of Cyprus, and leaving it to port, we continued our voyage to Syria, and put in at Tyre, for there the ship was to unload her cargo. We went and found the disciples and stayed there a week; and they, warned by the Spirit, urged Paul to abandon his visit to Jerusalem. But when our time ashore was ended, we left and continued our journey; and they and their wives and children all escorted us out of the city. We knelt down on the beach and prayed, then bade each other good-bye; we went aboard, and they returned home.

We made the passage from Tyre and reached Ptolemais, where we greeted the brotherhood and spent one day with them. Next day we left and came to Caesarea. We went to the home of Philip the evangelist, who was one of the Seven, and stayed with him. He had four unmarried daughters, who possessed the gift of prophecy.

[a] *Some witnesses add* and Myra.

King James Version

10And as we tarried *there* many days, there
came down from Judea a certain prophet, named
Agabus. 11And when he was come unto us, he
took Paul's girdle, and bound his own hands
and feet, and said, Thus saith the Holy Ghost,
So shall the Jews at Jerusalem bind the man
that owneth this girdle, and shall deliver *him*
into the hands of the Gentiles. 12And when we
heard these things, both we, and they of that
place, besought him not to go up to Jerusalem.
13 Then Paul answered, What mean ye to weep
and to break mine heart? for I am ready not to
be bound only, but also to die at Jerusalem for
the name of the Lord Jesus. 14And when he
would not be persuaded, we ceased, saying, The
will of the Lord be done. 15And after those days
we took up our carriages, and went up to Jerusalem. 16 There went with us also *certain* of the
disciples of Cesarea, and brought with them one
Mnason of Cyprus, an old disciple, with whom

Living Bible

10 During our stay of several days, a man
named Agabus, who also had the gift of prophecy, arrived from Judea 11 and visited us. He
took Paul's belt, bound his own feet and hands
with it and said, "The Holy Spirit declares, 'So
shall the owner of this belt be bound by the
Jews in Jerusalem and turned over to the Romans.' " 12 Hearing this, all of us—the local
believers and his traveling companions—begged
Paul not to go on to Jerusalem.

13 But he said, "Why all this weeping? You
are breaking my heart! For I am ready not only
to be jailed at Jerusalem, but also to die for the
sake of the Lord Jesus." 14 When it was clear
that he wouldn't be dissuaded, we gave up and
said, "The will of the Lord be done."

15 So shortly afterwards, we packed our things
and left for Jerusalem. 16 Some disciples from
Caesarea accompanied us, and on arrival we
were guests at the home of Mnason, originally

Today's English Version

message. 10 We had been there for several days
when a prophet named Agabus arrived from
Judea. 11 He came to us, took Paul's belt, tied
up his own feet and hands with it, and said,
"This is what the Holy Spirit says: The owner
of this belt will be tied up in this way by the
Jews in Jerusalem, and they will hand him over
to the Gentiles."

12 When we heard this, we and the others
there begged Paul not to go to Jerusalem. 13 But
he answered, "What are you doing, crying like
this and breaking my heart? I am ready not only
to be tied up in Jerusalem but even to die there
for the sake of the Lord Jesus."

14 We could not convince him, so we gave
up and said, "May the Lord's will be done."

15 After spending some time there, we got
our things ready and left for Jerusalem. 16 Some
of the disciples from Caesarea also went with
us, and took us to the house of the man we
were going to stay with—Mnason, from Cyprus,
who had been a believer since the early days.

New International Version

10 After we had been there a number of days,
a prophet named Agabus came down from Judea. 11 Coming over to us, he took Paul's belt,
tied his own hands and feet with it and said,
"The Holy Spirit says, 'In this way the Jews of
Jerusalem will bind the owner of this belt and
will hand him over to the Gentiles.' "

12 When we heard this, we and the people
there pleaded with Paul not to go up to Jerusalem. 13 Then Paul answered, "Why are you weeping and breaking my heart? I am ready not
only to be bound, but also to die in Jerusalem
for the name of the Lord Jesus." 14 When he
would not be dissuaded, we gave up and said,
"The Lord's will be done."

15 After this, we got ready and went up to
Jerusalem. 16 Some of the disciples from Caesarea accompanied us and brought us to the home
of Mnason, where we were to stay. He was a
man from Cyprus and one of the early disciples.

Phillips Modern English

spoke by the Spirit of God. During our stay there of several days a prophet by the name of Agabus came down from Judaea. When he came to see us he took Paul's girdle and used it to tie his own hands and feet together, saying, "The Holy Spirit says this: the man to whom this girdle belongs will be bound like this by the Jews in Jerusalem and handed over to the gentiles!"

21.12 We all warn Paul, but he is immovable

When we heard him say this, we and the people there begged Paul not to go up to Jerusalem. Then Paul answered us,

"What do you mean by unnerving me with all your tears? I am perfectly prepared not only to be bound but to die in Jerusalem for the sake of the name of the Lord Jesus."

Since he could not be dissuaded all we could do was to say, "May the Lord's will be done," and no more.

21.15 Paul is warmly welcomed at first

After this we made our preparations and went up to Jerusalem. Some of the disciples from Caesarea accompanied us and they took us to Mnason, a native of Cyprus and one of the earliest disciples, with whom we were going to stay.

Revised Standard Version

daughters, who prophesied. 10 While we were
staying for some days, a prophet named Agabus
came down from Judea. 11 And coming to us
he took Paul's girdle and bound his own feet
and hands, and said, "Thus says the Holy Spirit,
'So shall the Jews at Jerusalem bind the man
who owns this girdle and deliver him into the
hands of the Gentiles.' " 12 When we heard this,
we and the people there begged him not to go
up to Jerusalem. 13 Then Paul answered, "What
are you doing, weeping and breaking my heart?
For I am ready not only to be imprisoned but
even to die at Jerusalem for the name of the
Lord Jesus." 14 And when he would not be persuaded, we ceased and said, "The will of the
Lord be done."

15 After these days we made ready and went
up to Jerusalem. 16 And some of the disciples
from Caesarea went with us, bringing us to the
house of Mnason of Cyprus, an early disciple,
with whom we should lodge.

Jerusalem Bible

virgin daughters who were prophets. 10 When
we had been there several days a prophet called
Agabus arrived from Judaea 11 to see us. He
took Paul's girdle, and tied up his own feet and
hands, and said, "This is what the Holy Spirit
says, 'The man this girdle belongs to will be
bound like this by the Jews in Jerusalem, and
handed over to the pagans.' " 12 When we heard
this, we and everybody there implored Paul not
to go on to Jerusalem. 13 To this he replied,
"What are you trying to do—weaken my resolution by your tears? For my part, I am ready not
only to be tied up but even to die in Jerusalem
for the name of the Lord Jesus." 14 And so, as he
would not be persuaded, we gave up the attempt,
saying, "The Lord's will be done."

Paul's arrival in Jerusalem

15 After this we packed and went on up to
Jerusalem. 16 Some of the disciples from Caesarea accompanied us and took us to the house
of a Cypriot with whom we were to lodge; he
was called Mnason and had been one of the
earliest disciples.

New English Bible

When we had been there several days, a prophet named Agabus arrived from Judaea. He came to us, took Paul's belt, bound his own feet and hands with it, and said, 'These are the words of the Holy Spirit: Thus will the Jews in Jerusalem bind the man to whom this belt belongs, and hand him over to the Gentiles.' When we heard this, we and the local people begged and implored Paul to abandon his visit to Jerusalem. Then Paul gave his answer: 'Why all these tears? Why are you trying to weaken my resolution? For my part I am ready not merely to be bound but even to die at Jerusalem for the name of the Lord Jesus.' So, as he would not be persuaded, we gave up and said, 'The Lord's will be done.'

At the end of our stay we packed our baggage and took the road up to Jerusalem. Some of the disciples from Caesarea came along with us, bringing a certain Mnason of Cyprus, a Christian from the early days, with whom we were to

King James Version

we should lodge. 17And when we were come to Jerusalem, the brethren received us gladly. 18And the *day* following Paul went in with us unto James; and all the elders were present. 19And when he had saluted them, he declared particularly what things God had wrought among the Gentiles by his ministry. 20And when they heard *it*, they glorified the Lord, and said unto him, Thou seest, brother, how many thousands of Jews there are which believe; and they are all zealous of the law: 21And they are informed of thee, that thou teachest all the Jews which are among the Gentiles to forsake Moses, saying that they ought not to circumcise *their* children, neither to walk after the customs. 22 What is it therefore? the multitude must needs come together: for they will hear that thou art come. 23 Do therefore this that we say to thee: We have four men which have a vow on them; 24 Them take, and purify thyself with them, and be at charges with them, that they may shave *their* heads: and all may know that those things, whereof they were informed concerning thee, are nothing; but *that* thou thyself also walkest orderly, and keepest the law. 25As touching the Gentiles which believe, we have written *and* concluded that they observe no such thing, save only that they keep themselves from *things* offered to idols, and from blood, and from stran-

Living Bible

from Cyprus, one of the early believers; 17 and all the believers at Jerusalem welcomed us cordially.

18 The second day Paul took us with him to meet with James and the elders of the Jerusalem church. 19After greetings were exchanged, Paul recounted the many things God had accomplished among the Gentiles through his work.

20 They praised God but then said, "You know, dear brother, how many thousands of Jews have also believed, and they are all very insistent that Jewish believers must continue to follow the Jewish traditions and customs.[c] 21 Our Jewish Christians here at Jerusalem have been told that you are against the laws of Moses, against our Jewish customs, and that you forbid the circumcision of their children. 22 Now what can be done? For they will certainly hear that you have come.

23 "We suggest this: We have four men here who are preparing to shave their heads and take some vows. 24 Go with them to the Temple and have your head shaved too—and pay for theirs to be shaved.

"Then everyone will know that you approve of this custom for the Hebrew Christians and that you yourself obey the Jewish laws and are in line with our thinking in these matters.

25 "As for the Gentile Christians, we aren't asking them to follow these Jewish customs at all—except for the ones we wrote to them about: not to eat food offered to idols, not to eat unbled meat from strangled animals, and not to commit fornication."

[c] Literally, "they are all zealous for the law."

Today's English Version

Paul visits James

17 When we arrived in Jerusalem the brothers welcomed us warmly. 18 The next day Paul went with us to see James; and all the church elders were present. 19 Paul greeted them and gave a complete report of everything that God had done among the Gentiles through his work. 20After hearing him, they all praised God. Then they said to Paul, "You can see how it is, brother. There are thousands of Jews who have become believers, and they are all very devoted to the Law. 21 They have been told about you that you have been teaching all the Jews who live in Gentile countries to abandon the Law of Moses, telling them not to circumcise their children or follow the Jewish customs. 22 They are sure to hear that you have arrived. What should be done, then? 23 Do what we tell you. There are four men here who have taken a vow. 24 Go along with them and join them in the ceremony of purification and pay their expenses; then they will be able to shave their heads. In this way everyone will know that there is no truth in any of the things that they have been told about you, but that you yourself live in accordance with the Law of Moses. 25 But as to the Gentiles who have become believers, we have sent them a letter telling them we decided that they must not eat any food that has been offered to idols, or any blood, or any animal that has been strangled, and that they must keep themselves from immorality."

New International Version

Paul's arrival at Jerusalem

17 When we arrived at Jerusalem, the brothers received us warmly. 18 The next day Paul and the rest of us went to see James, and all the elders were present. 19 Paul greeted them and reported in detail what God had done among the Gentiles through his ministry.

20 When they heard this, they praised God. Then they said to Paul: "You see, brother, how many thousands of Jews have believed, and all of them are zealous for the law. 21 They have been informed that you teach all the Jews who live among the Gentiles to turn away from Moses, telling them not to circumcise their children or live according to our customs. 22 What shall we do? They will certainly hear that you have come, 23 so do what we tell you. There are four men with us who have made a vow. 24 Take these men, join in their purification rites and pay their expenses, so that they can have their heads shaved. Then everybody will know there is no truth in these reports about you, but that you yourself are living in obedience to the law. 25As for the Gentile believers, we have written to them our decision that they should abstain from food offered to idols, from blood, from the meat of strangled animals and from sexual immorality."

Phillips Modern English

On our arrival at Jerusalem the brothers gave us a very warm welcome. On the following day Paul went with us to visit James, and all the elders were present. When he had greeted them he gave them a detailed account of all that God had done among the gentiles through his ministry, and they, on hearing this account, glorified God. Then they said to him,

"You know, brother, how many thousands there are among the Jews who have become believers, and that every one of these is a staunch upholder of the Law. They have been informed about you—that you teach all Jews who live among the gentiles to disregard the Law of Moses, and tell them not to circumcise their children nor observe the old customs. What will happen now, for they are bound to hear that you have arrived? Now why not follow this suggestion of ours? We have four men here under a vow. Suppose you join them and be purified with them, pay their expenses so that they may have their hair cut short, and then everyone will know there is no truth in the stories about you, but that you yourself observe the Law. As for those gentiles who have believed, we have sent them a letter with our decision that they should abstain from what has been offered to idols, from blood and from what has been strangled, and from sexual immorality."

Revised Standard Version

17 When we had come to Jerusalem, the
brethren received us gladly. 18 On the following
day Paul went in with us to James; and all the
elders were present. 19 After greeting them, he
related one by one the things that God had
done among the Gentiles through his ministry.
20 And when they heard it, they glorified God.
And they said to him, "You see, brother, how
many thousands there are among the Jews of
those who have believed; they are all zealous
for the law, 21 and they have been told about
you that you teach all the Jews who are among
the Gentiles to forsake Moses, telling them not
to circumcise their children or observe the customs. 22 What then is to be done? They will
certainly hear that you have come. 23 Do therefore what we tell you. We have four men who
are under a vow; 24 take these men and purify
yourself along with them and pay their expenses, so that they may shave their heads.
Thus all will know that there is nothing in what
they have been told about you but that you
yourself live in observance of the law. 25 But as
for the Gentiles who have believed, we have
sent a letter with our judgment that they should
abstain from what has been sacrificed to idols
and from blood and from what is strangled[y]

[y] Other early authorities omit *and from what is strangled*.

Jerusalem Bible

17 On our arrival in Jerusalem the brothers
gave us a very warm welcome. 18 The next day
Paul went with us to visit James, and all the
elders were present. 19 After greeting them he
gave a detailed account of all that God had done
among the pagans through his ministry. 20 They
gave glory to God when they heard this. "But
you see, brother," they said, "how thousands of
Jews have now become believers, all of them
staunch upholders of the Law, and 21 they have
heard that you instruct all Jews living among
the pagans to break away from Moses, authorizing them not to circumcise their children or
to follow the customary practices. 22 What is
to be done? Inevitably there will be a meeting
of the whole body, since they are bound to hear
that you have come. 23 So do as we suggest. We
have four men here who are under a vow; 24 take
these men along and be purified with them and
pay all the expenses connected with the shaving
of their heads.[k] This will let everyone know
there is no truth in the reports they have heard
about you and that you still regularly observe
the Law. 25 The pagans who have become believers, as we wrote when we told them our decisions, must abstain from things sacrificed to
idols, from blood, from the meat of strangled
animals and from fornication."

[k] For the duration of a Nazirite vow, the hair was not to be cut. Discharge from the vow, on fulfillment, had to be celebrated with expensive sacrifices.

New English Bible

lodge. So we reached Jerusalem, where the brotherhood welcomed us gladly.

Next day Paul paid a visit to James; we were with him, and all the elders attended. He greeted them, and then described in detail all that God had done among the Gentiles through his ministry. When they heard this, they gave praise to God. Then they said to Paul: 'You see, brother, how many thousands of converts we have among the Jews, all of them staunch upholders of the Law. Now they have been given certain information about you: it is said that you teach all the Jews in the gentile world to turn their backs on Moses, telling them to give up circumcising their children and following our way of life. What is the position, then? They are sure to hear that you have arrived. You must therefore do as we tell you. We have four men here who are under a vow; take them with you and go through the ritual of purification with them, paying their expenses, after which they may shave their heads. Then everyone will know that there is nothing in the stories they were told about you, but that you are a practising Jew and keep the Law yourself. As for the gentile converts, we sent them our decision that they must abstain from meat that has been offered to idols, from blood, from anything that has been

King James Version

gled, and from fornication. 26 Then Paul took the men, and the next day purifying himself with them entered into the temple, to signify the accomplishment of the days of purification, until that an offering should be offered for every one of them. 27 And when the seven days were almost ended, the Jews which were of Asia, when they saw him in the temple, stirred up all the people, and laid hands on him, 28 Crying out, Men of Israel, help: This is the man, that teacheth all *men* every where against the people, and the law, and this place: and further brought Greeks also into the temple, and hath polluted this holy place. 29 (For they had seen before with him in the city Trophimus an Ephesian, whom they supposed that Paul had brought into the temple.) 30 And all the city was moved, and the people ran together: and they took Paul, and drew him out of the temple: and forthwith the doors were shut. 31 And as they went about to kill him, tidings came unto the chief captain of the band, that all Jerusalem was in an uproar: 32 Who immediately took soldiers and centurions, and ran down unto them: and when they saw the chief captain and the soldiers, they left

Living Bible

26, 27 So Paul agreed to their request and the next day went with the men to the Temple for the ceremony, thus publicizing his vow to offer a sacrifice seven[d] days later with the others.

The seven days were almost ended when some Jews from Turkey saw him in the Temple and roused a mob against him. They grabbed him, 28 yelling, "Men of Israel! Help! Help! This is the man who preaches against our people and tells everybody to disobey the Jewish laws. He even talks against the Temple and defies it by bringing Gentiles in!" 29 (For down in the city earlier that day, they had seen him with Trophimus, a Gentile[e] from Ephesus in Turkey, and assumed that Paul had taken him into the Temple.)

30 The whole population of the city was electrified by these accusations and a great riot followed. Paul was dragged out of the Temple, and immediately the gates were closed behind him. 31 As they were killing him, word reached the commander of the Roman garrison that all Jerusalem was in an uproar. 32 He quickly ordered out his soldiers and officers and ran down among the crowd. When the mob saw the troops

[d] Literally, "the days of purification." [e] Implied.

Today's English Version

26 So Paul took the men and the next day performed the ceremony of purification with them. Then he went into the temple and gave notice of how many days it would be until the end of the period of purification, when the sacrifice for each one of them would be offered.

Paul arrested in the temple

27 When the seven days were about to come to an end, some Jews from the province of Asia saw Paul in the temple. They stirred up the whole crowd and grabbed Paul. 28 "Men of Israel!" they shouted. "Help! This is the man who goes everywhere teaching everyone against the people of Israel, the Law of Moses, and this temple. And now he has even brought some Gentiles into the temple and defiled this holy place!" 29 (They said this because they had seen Trophimus from Ephesus with Paul in the city, and they thought that Paul had taken him into the temple.)

30 Confusion spread through the whole city, and the people all ran together, grabbed Paul, and dragged him out of the temple. At once the temple doors were closed. 31 The mob was trying to kill Paul when a report was sent up to the commander of the Roman troops that all of Jerusalem was rioting. 32 At once the commander took some officers and soldiers and rushed down to the crowd. When the people saw him with

New International Version

26 The next day Paul took the men and purified himself along with them. Then he went to the temple to give notice of the date when the days of purification would end and the offering would be made for each of them.

Paul arrested

27 When the seven days were nearly over, some Jews from the province of Asia saw Paul at the temple. They stirred up the whole crowd and seized him, 28 shouting, "Men of Israel, help us! This is the man who teaches all men everywhere against our people and our law and this place. And besides, he has brought Greeks into the temple area and defiled this holy place." 29 (They had previously seen Trophimus the Ephesian in the city with Paul and assumed that Paul had brought him into the temple area.)
30 The whole city was aroused, and the people came running from all directions. Seizing Paul, they dragged him from the temple, and immediately the gates were shut. 31 While they were trying to kill him, news reached the commander of the Roman troops that the whole city of Jerusalem was in an uproar. 32 He at once took some officers and soldiers and ran down to the crowd. When the rioters saw the commander and his soldiers, they stopped beating Paul.

Phillips Modern English

21.26 But his enemies attempt to murder him

So Paul joined the four men and on the following day, after being purified with them, went into the Temple to give notice of the time when the period of purification would be finished and an offering would be made on behalf of each one of them. The seven days were almost over when the Jews from the province of Asia caught sight of Paul in the Temple. They stirred up the whole crowd and seized him, shouting, "Men of Israel, help! This is the man who is teaching everybody everywhere to despise our people, our Law and this place. Why, he has even brought Greeks into the Temple and he has defiled this holy place!" For they had previously seen Trophimus the Ephesian with Paul in the city and they had concluded that Paul had brought him into the Temple. The whole city was stirred by this speech and a mob collected who seized Paul and dragged him outside the Temple, and the doors were slammed behind him.

21.31 Paul is rescued by Roman soldiers

They were trying to kill him when a report reached the ears of the colonel of the regiment that the whole of Jerusalem was in an uproar. Without a moment's delay he took soldiers and centurions and ran down to them. When they saw the colonel and the soldiers they stopped

Revised Standard Version

and from unchastity." 26 Then Paul took the
men, and the next day he purified himself with
them and went into the temple, to give notice
when the days of purification would be fulfilled
and the offering presented for every one of them.
27 When the seven days were almost completed, the Jews from Asia, who had seen him
in the temple, stirred up all the crowd, and laid
hands on him, 28 crying out, "Men of Israel,
help! This is the man who is teaching men everywhere against the people and the law and this
place; moreover he also brought Greeks into
the temple, and he has defiled this holy place."
29 For they had previously seen Trophimus the
Ephesian with him in the city, and they supposed
that Paul had brought him into the temple.
30 Then all the city was aroused, and the people ran together; they seized Paul and dragged
him out of the temple, and at once the gates
were shut. 31 And as they were trying to kill
him, word came to the tribune of the cohort
that all Jerusalem was in confusion. 32 He at
once took soldiers and centurions, and ran down
to them; and when they saw the tribune and the

Jerusalem Bible

26 So the next day Paul took the men along and was purified with them, and he visited the Temple to give notice of the time when the period of purification would be over and the offering would have to be presented on behalf of each of them.

Paul's arrest

27 The seven days were nearly over when
some Jews from Asia caught sight of him in the
Temple and stirred up the crowd and seized him,
28 shouting, "Men of Israel, help! This is the
man who preaches to everyone everywhere
against our people, against the Law and against
this place. Now he has profaned this Holy Place
by bringing Greeks into the Temple." 29 They
had, in fact, previously seen Trophimus the
Ephesian in the city with him, and thought that
Paul had brought him into the Temple.
30 This roused the whole city; people came
running from all sides; they seized Paul and
dragged him out of the Temple, and the gates
were closed behind them. 31 They would have
killed him if a report had not reached the tribune of the cohort[l] that there was rioting all over
Jerusalem. 32 He immediately called out soldiers
and centurions, and charged down on the crowd,
who stopped beating Paul when they saw the

[l] Commanding officer of the Roman garrison.

New English Bible

strangled,[a] and from fornication.' So Paul took the four men, and next day, after going through the ritual of purification with them, he went into the temple to give notice of the date when the period of purification would end and the offering be made for each one of them.

From Jerusalem to Rome

But just before the seven days were up, the Jews from the province of Asia saw him in the temple. They stirred up the whole crowd, and seized him, shouting, 'Men of Israel, help, help! This is the fellow who spreads his doctrine all over the world, attacking our people, our law, and this sanctuary. On top of all this he has brought Gentiles into the temple and profaned this holy place.' For they had previously seen Trophimus the Ephesian with him in the city, and assumed that Paul had brought him into the temple.

The whole city was in a turmoil, and people came running from all directions. They seized Paul and dragged him out of the temple; and at once the doors were shut. While they were clamouring for his death, a report reached the officer commanding the cohort, that all Jerusalem was in an uproar. He immediately took a force of soldiers with their centurions and came down on the rioters at the double. As soon as they saw the commandant and his troops, they

[a] *Some witnesses omit* from anything that has been strangled.

King James Version

beating of Paul. 33 Then the chief captain came near, and took him, and commanded *him* to be bound with two chains; and demanded who he was, and what he had done. 34And some cried one thing, some another, among the multitude: and when he could not know the certainty for the tumult, he commanded him to be carried into the castle. 35And when he came upon the stairs, so it was, that he was borne of the soldiers for the violence of the people. 36 For the multitude of the people followed after, crying, Away with him. 37And as Paul was to be led into the castle, he said unto the chief captain, May I speak unto thee? Who said, Canst thou speak Greek? 38Art not thou that Egyptian, which before these days madest an uproar, and leddest out into the wilderness four thousand men that were murderers? 39 But Paul said, I am a man *which am* a Jew of Tarsus, *a city* in Cilicia, a citizen of no mean city: and, I beseech thee, suffer me to speak unto the people. 40And when he had given him license, Paul stood on the stairs, and beckoned with the hand unto the people. And when there was made a great silence, he spake unto *them* in the Hebrew tongue, saying,

Living Bible

coming, they quit beating Paul. 33 The commander arrested him and ordered him bound with double chains. Then he asked the crowd who he was and what he had done. 34 Some shouted one thing and some another. When he couldn't find out anything in all the uproar and confusion, he ordered Paul to be taken to the armory.[f] 35As they reached the stairs, the mob grew so violent that the soldiers lifted Paul to their shoulders to protect him, 36 and the crowd surged behind shouting, "Away with him, away with him!"

37, 38 As Paul was about to be taken inside, he said to the commander, "May I have a word with you?"

"Do you know Greek?" the commander asked, surprised. "Aren't you that Egyptian who led a rebellion a few years ago[g] and took 4,000 members of the Assassins with him into the desert?"

39 "No," Paul replied, "I am a Jew from Tarsus in Cilicia which is no small town. I request permission to talk to these people."

40 The commander agreed, so Paul stood on the stairs and motioned to the people to be quiet; soon a deep silence enveloped the crowd, and he addressed them in Hebrew as follows:

[f] Literally, "castle," or "fort." [g] Literally, "before these days."

Today's English Version

the soldiers, they stopped beating Paul. 33 The commander went over to Paul, arrested him, and ordered him to be tied up with two chains. Then he asked, "Who is this man, and what has he done?" 34 Some in the crowd shouted one thing, others something else. There was such confusion that the commander could not find out exactly what had happened; so he ordered his men to take Paul up into the fort. 35 They got with him to the steps, and then the soldiers had to carry him because the mob was so wild. 36 They were all coming after him and screaming, "Kill him!"

Paul defends himself

37 As they were about to take Paul into the fort, he spoke to the commander, "May I say something to you?"

"Do you speak Greek?" the commander asked. 38 "Then you are not that Egyptian fellow who some time ago started a revolution and led four thousand armed terrorists out into the desert?"

39 Paul answered, "I am a Jew, born in Tarsus of Cilicia, a citizen of an important city. Please, let me speak to the people."

40 The commander gave him permission, so Paul stood on the steps and motioned with his hand to the people. When they were quiet, Paul spoke to them in Hebrew,

New International Version

33 The commander came up and arrested him and ordered him to be bound with two chains. Then he asked who he was and what he had done. 34 Some in the crowd shouted one thing and some another, and since the commander could not get at the truth because of the uproar, he ordered that Paul be taken into the barracks. 35 When Paul reached the steps, the violence of the mob was so great he had to be carried by the soldiers. 36 The crowd that followed kept shouting, "Away with him!"

Paul speaks to the crowd

37 As the soldiers were about to take Paul into the barracks, he asked the commander, "May I say something to you?"

"Do you speak Greek?" he replied. 38 "Aren't you the Egyptian who started a revolt and led four thousand terrorists out into the desert some time ago?"

39 Paul answered, "I am a Jew, from Tarsus in Cilicia, a citizen of no ordinary city. Please let me speak to the people."

40 Having received the commander's permission, Paul stood on the steps and motioned to the crowd. When they were all silent, he said to

Phillips Modern English

beating Paul. The colonel came up to Paul and arrested him and ordered him to be shackled with two chains. Then he enquired who the man was and what he had been doing. Some of the crowd shouted one thing and some another, and since he could not be certain of the facts because of the shouting that was going on, the colonel ordered him to be brought to the barracks. When Paul got to the steps he was actually carried by the soldiers because of the violence of the mob. For the mass of the people followed, shouting, "Kill him!" Just as they were going to take him into the barracks Paul asked the colonel,

"May I say something to you?"

"So you know Greek, do you?" the colonel replied. "Aren't you that Egyptian who not long ago raised a riot and led those four thousand assassins into the desert?"

"I am a Jew," replied Paul. "I am a man of Tarsus in Cilicia, a citizen of that not insignificant city. I ask you to let me speak to the people."

21.40 Paul attempts to defend himself

On being given permission Paul stood on the steps and made a gesture with his hand to the people. There was a deep hush as he began to speak to them in Hebrew.

Revised Standard Version

soldiers, they stopped beating Paul. 33 Then the
tribune came up and arrested him, and ordered
him to be bound with two chains. He inquired
who he was and what he had done. 34 Some in
the crowd shouted one thing, some another; and
as he could not learn the facts because of the
uproar, he ordered him to be brought into the
barracks. 35 And when he came to the steps, he
was actually carried by the soldiers because of
the violence of the crowd; 36 for the mob of
the people followed, crying, "Away with him!"
37 As Paul was about to be brought into the
barracks, he said to the tribune, "May I say
something to you?" And he said, "Do you know
Greek? 38 Are you not the Egyptian, then, who
recently stirred up a revolt and led the four
thousand men of the Assassins out into the wilderness?" 39 Paul replied, "I am a Jew, from
Tarsus in Cilicia, a citizen of no mean city; I
beg you, let me speak to the people." 40 And
when he had given him leave, Paul, standing on
the steps, motioned with his hand to the people;
and when there was a great hush, he spoke to
them in the Hebrew language, saying:

Jerusalem Bible

tribune and the soldiers. 33 When the tribune
came up he arrested Paul, had him bound with
two chains and inquired who he was and what
he had done. 34 People in the crowd called out
different things, and since the noise made it
impossible for him to get any positive information, the tribune ordered Paul to be taken into
the fortress. 35 When Paul reached the steps,
the crowd became so violent that he had to be
carried by the soldiers; 36 and indeed the whole
mob was after them, shouting, "Kill him!"
37 Just as Paul was being taken into the fortress, he asked the tribune if he could have a
word with him. The tribune said, "You speak
Greek, then? 38 So you are not the Egyptian
who started the recent revolt and led those four
thousand cutthroats[m] out into the desert?"
39 "I?" said Paul. "I am a Jew and a citizen of
the well-known city of Tarsus in Cilicia. Please
give me permission to speak to the people."
40 The man gave his consent and Paul, standing
at the top of the steps, gestured to the people
with his hand. When all was quiet again he spoke
to them in Hebrew.[n]

[m] Nationalist extremists. [n] I.e., Aramaic.

New English Bible

stopped beating Paul. The commandant stepped forward, arrested him, and ordered him to be shackled with two chains; he then asked who the man was and what he had been doing. Some in the crowd shouted one thing, some another. As he could not get at the truth because of the hubbub, he ordered him to be taken into barracks. When Paul reached the steps, he had to be carried by the soldiers because of the violence of the mob. For the whole crowd were at their heels yelling, 'Kill him!'

Just before Paul was taken into the barracks he said to the commandant, 'May I have a word with you?' The commandant said, 'So you speak Greek, do you? Then you are not the Egyptian who started a revolt some time ago and led a force of four thousand terrorists out into the wilds?' Paul replied, 'I am a Jew, a Tarsian from Cilicia, a citizen of no mean city. I ask your permission to speak to the people.' When permission had been given, Paul stood on the steps and with a gesture called for the attention of the people. As soon as quiet was restored, he addressed them in the Jewish language:

King James Version

22 Men, brethren, and fathers, hear ye my defence *which I make* now unto you. 2 (And when they heard that he spake in the Hebrew tongue to them, they kept the more silence: and he saith,) 3 I am verily a man *which am* a Jew, born in Tarsus, *a city* in Cilicia, yet brought up in this city at the feet of Gamaliel, *and* taught according to the perfect manner of the law of the fathers, and was zealous toward God, as ye all are this day. 4 And I persecuted this way unto the death, binding and delivering into prisons both men and women. 5 As also the high priest doth bear me witness, and all the estate of the elders: from whom also I received letters unto the brethren, and went to Damascus, to bring them which were there bound unto Jerusalem, for to be punished. 6 And it came to pass, that, as I made my journey, and was come nigh unto Damascus about noon, suddenly there shone from heaven a great light round about me. 7 And I fell unto the ground, and heard a voice saying unto me, Saul, Saul, why persecutest thou me? 8 And I answered, Who art thou, Lord? And he said unto me, I am Jesus of Nazareth, whom thou persecutest. 9 And they that were with me saw indeed the light, and were afraid; but they heard not the voice of him that spake to me. 10 And I said,

Living Bible

22 "Brothers and fathers, listen to me as I offer my defense." 2 (When they heard him speaking in Hebrew, the silence was even greater.) 3 "I am a Jew," he said, "born in Tarsus, a city in Cilicia, but educated here in Jerusalem under Gamaliel, at whose feet I learned to follow our Jewish laws and customs very carefully. I became very anxious to honor God in everything I did, just as you have tried to do today. 4 And I persecuted the Christians, hounding them to death, binding and delivering both men and women to prison. 5 The High Priest or any member of the Council can testify that this is so. For I asked them for letters to the Jewish leaders in Damascus, with instructions to let me bring any Christians I found to Jerusalem in chains to be punished.

6 "As I was on the road, nearing Damascus, suddenly about noon a very bright light from heaven shone around me. 7 And I fell to the ground and heard a voice saying to me, 'Saul, Saul, why are you persecuting me?'

8 " 'Who is it speaking to me, sir?' I asked. And he replied, 'I am Jesus of Nazareth, the one you are persecuting.' 9 The men with me saw the light but didn't understand what was said.

10 "And I said, 'What shall I do, Lord?'

Today's English Version

22 "Men, brothers and fathers, listen to me as I make my defense before you!" 2 When they heard him speaking to them in Hebrew, they were even quieter; and Paul went on,

3 "I am a Jew, born in Tarsus of Cilicia, but brought up here in Jerusalem as a student of Gamaliel. I received strict instruction in the Law of our ancestors, and was just as dedicated to God as all of you here today are. 4 I persecuted to the death the people who followed this Way. I arrested men and women and threw them into prison. 5 The High Priest and the whole Council can prove that I am telling the truth. I received from them letters written to the Jewish brothers in Damascus, so I went there to arrest these people and bring them back in chains to Jerusalem to be punished."

Paul tells of his conversion

6 "As I was traveling and coming near Damascus, about midday a bright light from the sky flashed suddenly around me. 7 I fell to the ground and heard a voice saying to me, 'Saul, Saul! Why do you persecute me?' 8 'Who are you, Lord?' I asked. 'I am Jesus of Nazareth, whom you persecute,' he said to me. 9 The men with me saw the light but did not hear the voice of the one who was speaking to me. 10 I asked,

New International Version

22 them in Aramaic: 1 "Brothers and fathers, listen now to my defense."

2 When they heard him speak to them in Aramaic, they became very quiet.

Then Paul said: 3 "I am a Jew, born in Tarsus of Cilicia, but brought up in this city. Under Gamaliel I was thoroughly trained in the law of our fathers and was just as zealous for God as any of you are today. 4 I persecuted the followers of this Way to their death, arresting both men and women and throwing them into prison, 5 as also the high priest and all the council can testify. I even obtained letters from them to their brothers in Damascus, and went there to bring these people as prisoners to Jerusalem to be punished.

6 "About noon as I came near Damascus, suddenly a bright light from heaven flashed around me. 7 I fell to the ground and heard a voice say to me, 'Saul! Saul! Why do you persecute me?'

8 " 'Who are you, Lord?' I asked.

" 'I am Jesus of Nazareth, whom you are persecuting,' he replied. 9 My companions saw the light, but they did not understand the voice of him who was speaking to me.

10 " 'What shall I do, Lord?' I asked.

Phillips Modern English

"My brothers and my fathers, listen to what I have to say in my own defense."

As soon as they heard him addressing them in Hebrew the silence became intense.

"I myself am a Jew," Paul went on. "I was born in Tarsus in Cilicia, but I was brought up here in this city, I received my training at the feet of Gamaliel, and I was schooled in the strictest observance of our fathers' Law. I was as much on fire with zeal for God as you all are today. I am also the man who persecuted this Way to the death, arresting both men and women and throwing them into prison, as the High Priest and the whole council can readily testify. Indeed, it was after receiving letters from them to their brothers in Damascus that I set out for that city, intending to arrest any followers of the Way I could find there and bring them back to Jerusalem as prisoners for punishment. Then this happened to me. As I was on my journey and getting near to Damascus, about midday a great light from the sky suddenly blazed around me. I fell to the ground, and I heard a voice saying to me, 'Saul, Saul, why are you persecuting me?' I replied, 'Who are you, Lord?' He said to me, 'I am Jesus of Nazareth whom you are persecuting.' My companions naturally saw the light, but they did not hear the voice of the one who was talking to me. 'What

Revised Standard Version

22 "Brethren and fathers, hear the defense
which I now make before you."
2 And when they heard that he addressed
them in the Hebrew language, they were the
more quiet. And he said:
3 "I am a Jew, born at Tarsus in Cilicia, but
brought up in this city at the feet of Gamaliel,
educated according to the strict manner of the
law of our fathers, being zealous for God as
you all are this day. 4 I persecuted this Way to
the death, binding and delivering to prison both
men and women, 5 as the high priest and the
whole council of elders bear me witness. From
them I received letters to the brethren, and I
journeyed to Damascus to take those also who
were there and bring them in bonds to Jerusalem to be punished.
6 "As I made my journey and drew near to
Damascus, about noon a great light from heaven
suddenly shone about me. 7 And I fell to the
ground and heard a voice saying to me, 'Saul,
Saul, why do you persecute me?' 8 And I answered, 'Who are you, Lord?' And he said to
me, 'I am Jesus of Nazareth whom you are
persecuting.' 9 Now those who were with me
saw the light but did not hear the voice of the
one who was speaking to me. 10 And I said,

Jerusalem Bible

Paul's address to the Jews of Jerusalem

22 "My brothers, my fathers, listen to what
I have to say to you in my defense."
2 When they realized he was speaking in Hebrew,
the silence was even greater than before. 3 "I am
a Jew," Paul said, "and was born at Tarsus in
Cilicia. I was brought up here in this city. I
studied under Gamaliel and was taught the exact
observance of the Law of our ancestors. In fact,
I was as full of duty toward God as you are today. 4 I even persecuted this Way to the death,
and sent women as well as men to prison in
chains 5 as the high priest and the whole councils of elders can testify, since they even sent
me with letters to their brothers in Damascus.
When I set off it was with the intention of bringing prisoners back from there to Jerusalem for
punishment.
6 "I was on that journey and nearly at Damascus when about midday a bright light from
heaven suddenly shone around me. 7 I fell to
the ground and heard a voice saying, 'Saul,
Saul, why are you persecuting me?' 8 I answered:
Who are you, Lord? and he said to me, 'I am
Jesus the Nazarene and you are persecuting me.'
9 The people with me saw the light but did not
hear his voice as he spoke to me. 10 I said:

New English Bible

22 'Brothers and fathers, give me a hearing while I make my defence before you.' When they heard him speaking to them in their own language, they listened the more quietly. 'I am a true-born Jew,' he said, 'a native of Tarsus in Cilicia. I was brought up in this city, and as a pupil of Gamaliel I was thoroughly trained in every point of our ancestral law. I have always been ardent in God's service, as you all are today. And so I began to persecute this movement to the death, arresting its followers, men and women alike, and putting them in chains. For this I have as witnesses the High Priest and the whole Council of Elders. I was given letters from them to our fellow-Jews at Damascus, and had started out to bring the Christians there to Jerusalem as prisoners for punishment; and this is what happened. I was on the road and nearing Damascus, when suddenly about midday a great light flashed from the sky all around me, and I fell to the ground. Then I heard a voice saying to me, "Saul, Saul, why do you persecute me?" I answered, "Tell me, Lord, who you are." "I am Jesus of Nazareth," he said, "whom you are persecuting." My companions saw the light, but did not hear the voice that spoke to me. "What shall I do, Lord?"

King James Version

What shall I do, Lord? And the Lord said unto
me, Arise, and go into Damascus; and there it
shall be told thee of all things which are appointed for thee to do. 11And when I could not
see for the glory of that light, being led by the
hand of them that were with me, I came into
Damascus. 12And one Ananias, a devout man
according to the law, having a good report of
all the Jews which dwelt *there,* 13 Came unto
me, and stood, and said unto me, Brother Saul,
receive thy sight. And the same hour I looked
up upon him. 14And he said, The God of our
fathers hath chosen thee, that thou shouldest
know his will, and see that Just One, and
shouldest hear the voice of his mouth. 15 For
thou shalt be his witness unto all men of what
thou hast seen and heard. 16And now why tar-
riest thou? arise, and be baptized, and wash
away thy sins, calling on the name of the Lord.
17And it came to pass, that, when I was come
again to Jerusalem, even while I prayed in the
temple, I was in a trance; 18And saw him saying unto me, Make haste, and get thee quickly
out of Jerusalem: for they will not receive thy
testimony concerning me. 19And I said, Lord,
they know that I imprisoned and beat in every
synagogue them that believed on thee: 20And
when the blood of thy martyr Stephen was shed,
I also was standing by, and consenting unto his
death, and kept the raiment of them that slew

Living Bible

"And the Lord told me, 'Get up and go into
Damascus, and there you will be told what
awaits you in the years ahead.'
11 "I was blinded by the intense light, and
had to be led into Damascus by my companions.
12 There a man named Ananias, as godly a man
as you could find for obeying the law, and well
thought of by all the Jews of Damascus, 13 came
to me, and standing beside me said, 'Brother
Saul, receive your sight!' And that very hour I
could see him!
14 "Then he told me, 'The God of our fathers
has chosen you to know his will and to see the
Messiah[a] and hear him speak. 15 You are to take
his message everywhere, telling what you have
seen and heard. 16And now, why delay? Go and
be baptized, and be cleansed from your sins,
calling on the name of the Lord.'
17, 18 "One day after my return to Jerusalem,
while I was praying in the Temple, I fell into a
trance and saw a vision of God saying to me,
'Hurry! Leave Jerusalem, for the people here
won't believe you when you give them my message.'
19 " 'But Lord,' I argued, 'they certainly know
that I imprisoned and beat those in every synagogue who believed on you. 20And when your
witness Stephen was killed, I was standing there
agreeing—keeping the coats they laid aside as
they stoned him.'

[a] Literally, "Righteous One."

Today's English Version

'What shall I do, Lord?' and the Lord said to
me, 'Get up and go into Damascus, and there
you will be told everything that God has determined for you to do.' 11 I was blind because
of the bright light, and so my companions took
me by the hand and led me into Damascus.
12 "There was a man named Ananias, a religious man who obeyed our Law and was
highly respected by all the Jews living in Damascus. 13 He came to me, stood by me and
said, 'Brother Saul, see again!' At that very moment I saw again and looked at him. 14 He said,
'The God of our ancestors has chosen you to
know his will, to see his righteous Servant, and
hear him speaking with his own voice. 15 For
you will be a witness for him to tell all men
what you have seen and heard. 16And now, why
wait any longer? Get up and be baptized and
have your sins washed away by calling on his
name.' "

Paul's call to preach to the Gentiles

17 "I went back to Jerusalem, and while I
was praying in the temple I had a vision, 18 in
which I saw the Lord as he said to me, 'Hurry
and leave Jerusalem quickly, because the people
here will not accept your witness about me.'
19 'Lord,' I answered, 'they know very well that
I went to the synagogues and arrested and beat
those who believe in you. 20And when your
witness Stephen was put to death, I myself was
there, approving of his murder and taking care

New International Version

" 'Get up,' the Lord said, 'and go into Damascus. There you will be told all that you have
been assigned to do.' 11 My companions led me
by the hand into Damascus, because the brilliance of the light had blinded me.
12 "A man named Ananias came to see me.
He was a devout observer of the law and highly
respected by all the Jews living there. 13 He
stood beside me and said, 'Brother Saul, receive
your sight!' And at that very moment I was able
to see him.
14 "Then he said: 'The God of our fathers
has chosen you to know his will and to see the
Righteous One and to hear words from his
mouth. 15 You will be his witness to all men
of what you have seen and heard. 16And now
what are you waiting for? Get up, be baptized
and wash your sins away, calling on his name.'
17 "When I returned to Jerusalem and was
praying at the temple, I fell into a trance 18 and
saw the Lord speaking. 'Quick!' he said to me.
'Leave Jerusalem immediately, because they will
not accept your testimony about me.'
19 " 'Lord,' I replied, 'these men know that
I went from one synagogue to another to imprison and beat those who believe in you. 20And
when the blood of your martyr Stephen was
shed, I stood there giving my approval and
guarding the clothes of those who were killing
him.'

Phillips Modern English

am I to do, Lord?' I asked. And the Lord told me, 'Get up and go on to Damascus and there you will be told of all that has been determined for you to do.' I was blinded by the brightness of that light and my companions had to take me by the hand and so I came to Damascus. There, there was a man called Ananias, a reverent observer of the Law and a man highly respected by all the Jews who lived there. He came to visit me and as he stood by my side said, 'Saul, brother, you may see again!' At once I regained my sight and looked at him. 'The God of our fathers,' he went on, 'has chosen you to know his will, to see the Righteous One, to hear words from his own lips, for you will be his witness before all men of what you have seen and heard. And now what are you waiting for? Get up and be baptised! Be clean from your sins as you call on his name.'

22.17 Paul claims that God sent him to the gentiles

"Then it happened that after my return to Jerusalem, while I was at prayer in the Temple, I fell into a trance and saw Jesus, and he said to me, 'Make haste and leave Jerusalem at once, for they will not accept your testimony about me.' And I said, 'Lord, they know how I have been through the synagogues imprisoning and beating all those who believe in you. They know also that when the blood of your martyr Stephen was shed I stood by, giving my approval—why, I was even in charge of the outer garments of

Revised Standard Version

'What shall I do, Lord?' And the Lord said to
me, 'Rise, and go into Damascus, and there you
will be told all that is appointed for you to do.'
11 And when I could not see because of the
brightness of that light, I was led by the hand
by those who were with me, and came into
Damascus.
12 "And one Ananias, a devout man according
to the law, well spoken of by all the Jews
who lived there, 13 came to me, and standing
by me said to me, 'Brother Saul, receive your
sight.' And in that very hour I received my
sight and saw him. 14 And he said, 'The God of
our fathers appointed you to know his will, to
see the Just One and to hear a voice from his
mouth; 15 for you will be a witness for him to
all men of what you have seen and heard. 16 And
now why do you wait? Rise and be baptized, and
wash away your sins, calling on his name.'
17 "When I had returned to Jerusalem and
was praying in the temple, I fell into a trance
18 and saw him saying to me, 'Make haste and
get quickly out of Jerusalem, because they will
not accept your testimony about me.' 19 And I
said, 'Lord, they themselves know that in every
synagogue I imprisoned and beat those who believed
in thee. 20 And when the blood of Stephen
thy witness was shed, I also was standing by
and approving, and keeping the garments of

Jerusalem Bible

What am I to do, Lord? The Lord answered,
'Stand up and go into Damascus, and there you
will be told what you have been appointed to
do.' 11 The light had been so dazzling that I
was blind and my companions had to take me
by the hand; and so I came to Damascus.
12 "Someone called Ananias, a devout follower
of the Law and highly thought of by all
the Jews living there, 13 came to see me; he
stood beside me and said, 'Brother Saul, receive
your sight.' Instantly my sight came back
and I was able to see him. 14 Then he said, 'The
God of our ancestors has chosen you to know
his will, to see the Just One and hear his own
voice speaking, 15 because you are to be his
witness before all mankind, testifying to what
you have seen and heard. 16 And now why delay?
It is time you were baptized and had your
sins washed away while invoking his name.'
17 "Once, after I had got back to Jerusalem,
when I was praying in the Temple, I fell into
a trance 18 and then I saw him. 'Hurry,' he said,
'leave Jerusalem at once; they will not accept
the testimony you are giving about me.' 19 Lord,
I answered, it is because they know that I used to
go from synagogue to synagogue, imprisoning
and flogging those who believed in you; 20 and
that when the blood of your witness[o] Stephen
was being shed, I was standing by in full agreement
with his murderers, and minding their

[*o*] Martyr: the word had not yet acquired its restricted meaning.

New English Bible

I said, and the Lord replied, "Get up and continue your journey to Damascus; there you will be told of all the tasks that are laid upon you." As I had been blinded by the brilliance of that light, my companions led me by the hand, and so I came to Damascus.

'There, a man called Ananias, a devout observer of the Law and well spoken of by all the Jews of that place, came and stood beside me and said, "Saul, my brother, recover your sight." Instantly I recovered my sight and saw him. He went on: "The God of our fathers appointed you to know his will and to see the Righteous One and to hear his very voice, because you are to be his witness before the world, and testify to what you have seen and heard. And now why delay? Be baptized at once, with invocation of his name, and wash away your sins."

'After my return to Jerusalem, I was praying in the temple when I fell into a trance and saw him there, speaking to me. "Make haste", he said, "and leave Jerusalem without delay, for they will not accept your testimony about me." "Lord," I said, "they know that I imprisoned those who believe in thee, and flogged them in every synagogue; and when the blood of Stephen thy witness was shed I stood by, approving, and I looked after the clothes of those who killed

King James Version

him. 21And he said unto me, Depart: for I will
send thee far hence unto the Gentiles. 22And
they gave him audience unto this word, and
then lifted up their voices, and said, Away with
such a *fellow* from the earth: for it is not fit
that he should live. 23And as they cried out, and
cast off *their* clothes, and threw dust into the
air, 24 The chief captain commanded him to be
brought into the castle, and bade that he should
be examined by scourging; that he might know
wherefore they cried so against him. 25And as
they bound him with thongs, Paul said unto the
centurion that stood by, Is it lawful for you to
scourge a man that is a Roman, and uncondemned? 26 When the centurion heard *that,* he
went and told the chief captain, saying, Take
heed what thou doest; for this man is a Roman.
27 Then the chief captain came, and said unto
him, Tell me, art thou a Roman? He said, Yea.
28And the chief captain answered, With a great
sum obtained I this freedom. And Paul said,
But I was *free* born. 29 Then straightway they
departed from him which should have examined

Living Bible

21 "But God said to me, 'Leave Jerusalem,
for I will send you far away to the *Gentiles!'* "
22 The crowd listened until Paul came to that
word, then with one voice they shouted, "Away
with such a fellow! Kill him! He isn't fit to live!"
23 They yelled and threw their coats in the air
and tossed up handfuls of dust.
24 So the commander brought him inside
and ordered him lashed with whips to make him
confess his crime. He wanted to find out why the
crowd had become so furious!
25 As they tied Paul down to lash him, Paul
said to an officer standing there, "Is it legal for
you to whip a Roman citizen who hasn't even
been tried?"
26 The officer went to the commander and
asked, "What are you doing? This man is a
Roman citizen!"
27 So the commander went over and asked
Paul, "Tell me, are you a Roman citizen?"
"Yes, I certainly am."
28 "I am too," the commander muttered,
"and it cost me plenty!"
"But I am a citizen by birth!"
29 The soldiers standing ready to lash him,
quickly disappeared when they heard Paul was a

Today's English Version

of the cloaks of his murderers.' 21 'Go,' the Lord
said to me, 'because I will send you far away
to the Gentiles.' "
22 The people listened to Paul until he said
this; but then they started shouting at the top
of their voices, "Away with him! Kill him! He's
not fit to live!" 23 They were screaming, waving
their clothes, and throwing dust up in the air.
24 The Roman commander ordered his men to
take Paul into the fort, and told them to whip
him to find out why the Jews were screaming
like this against him. 25 But when they had tied
him up to be whipped, Paul said to the officer
standing there, "Is it lawful for you to whip a
Roman citizen who hasn't even been tried for
any crime?"
26 When the officer heard this, he went to the
commander and asked him, "What are you doing? That man is a Roman citizen!"
27 So the commander went to Paul and asked
him, "Tell me, are you a Roman citizen?"
"Yes," answered Paul.
28 The commander said, "I became one by
paying a large amount of money."
"But I am one by birth," Paul answered.
29 At once the men who were going to question Paul drew back from him; and the com-

New International Version

21 "Then the Lord said to me, 'Go; I will
send you far away to the Gentiles.' "

Paul the Roman citizen

22 The crowd listened to Paul until he said
this. Then they raised their voices and shouted,
"Rid the earth of him! He's not fit to live!"
23 As they were shouting and throwing off
their cloaks and flinging dust into the air, 24 the
commander ordered Paul to be taken into the
barracks. He directed that he be flogged and
questioned in order to find out why the people
were shouting at him like this. 25As they
stretched him out to flog him, Paul said to the
centurion standing there, "Is it legal for you to
flog a Roman citizen who hasn't even been
found guilty?"
26 When the centurion heard this, he went to
the commander and reported it. "What are you
going to do?" he asked. "This man is a Roman
citizen."
27 The commander went to Paul and asked,
"Tell me, are you a Roman citizen?"
"Yes, I am," he answered.
28 Then the commander said, "I had to pay
a big price for my citizenship."
"But I was born a citizen," Paul replied.
29 Those who were about to question him
withdrew immediately. The commander himself

Phillips Modern English

those who killed him.' But he said to me, 'Go, for I will send you far away to the gentiles'."

22.22 The consequence of Paul's speech

They had listened to him until he said this, but now they raised a great shout,

"Away with him, rid the earth of such a man! He is not fit to live!"

As they were yelling and flapping their clothes and hurling dust into the air, the colonel gave orders to bring Paul into the barracks and directed that he should be examined by scourging, so that he might discover the reason for such an uproar against him. But when they had strapped him up, Paul spoke to the centurion standing by,

"Is it legal for you to flog a man who is a Roman citizen, and untried at that?"

On hearing this the centurion went in to the colonel and reported to him, saying,

"Do you realise what you were about to do? This man is a Roman citizen!"

Then the colonel himself came up to Paul, and said,

"Tell me, are you a Roman citizen?"

And he said,

"Yes."

Whereupon the colonel replied,

"It cost me a good deal to get my citizenship."

"Ah," replied Paul, "but I was born a citizen."

Then those who had been about to examine him left hurriedly, while even the colonel him-

Revised Standard Version

those who killed him.' 21And he said to me, 'Depart; for I will send you far away to the Gentiles.' "

22 Up to this word they listened to him; then they lifted up their voices and said, "Away with such a fellow from the earth! For he ought not to live." 23And as they cried out and waved their garments and threw dust into the air, 24 the tribune commanded him to be brought into the barracks, and ordered him to be examined by scourging, to find out why they shouted thus against him. 25 But when they had tied him up with the thongs, Paul said to the centurion who was standing by, "Is it lawful for you to scourge a man who is a Roman citizen, and uncondemned?" 26 When the centurion heard that, he went to the tribune and said to him, "What are you about to do? For this man is a Roman citizen." 27 So the tribune came and said to him, "Tell me, are you a Roman citizen?" And he said, "Yes." 28 The tribune answered, "I bought this citizenship for a large sum." Paul said, "But I was born a citizen." 29 So those who were about to examine him withdrew from him in-

Jerusalem Bible

clothes. 21 Then he said to me, 'Go! I am sending you out to the pagans far away.' "

Paul the Roman citizen

22 So far they had listened to him, but at these words they began to shout, "Rid the earth of the man! He is not fit to live!" 23 They were yelling, waving their cloaks and throwing dust into the air, 24 and so the tribune had him brought into the fortress and ordered him to be examined under the lash, to find out the reason for the outcry against him. 25 But when they had strapped him down Paul said to the centurion on duty, "Is it legal for you to flog a man who is a Roman citizen and has not been brought to trial?" 26 When he heard this the centurion went and told the tribune; "Do you realize what you are doing?" he said. "This man is a Roman citizen." 27 So the tribune came and asked him, "Tell me, are you a Roman citizen?" "I am," Paul said. 28 The tribune replied, "It cost me a large sum to acquire this citizenship." "But I was born to it," said Paul. 29 Then those who were about to examine him hurriedly with-

New English Bible

him." But he said to me, "Go, for I am sending you far away to the Gentiles." '

Up to this point they had given him a hearing; but now they began shouting, 'Down with him! A scoundrel like that is better dead!' And as they were yelling and waving their cloaks and flinging dust in the air, the commandant ordered him to be brought into the barracks and gave instructions to examine him by flogging, and find out what reason there was for such an outcry against him. But when they tied him up for the lash,[a] Paul said to the centurion who was standing there, 'Can you legally flog a man who is a Roman citizen, and moreover has not been found guilty?' When the centurion heard this, he went and reported it to the commandant. 'What do you mean to do?' he said. 'This man is a Roman citizen.' The commandant came to Paul. 'Tell me, are you a Roman citizen?' he asked. 'Yes', said he. The commandant rejoined, 'It cost me a large sum to acquire this citizenship.' Paul said, 'But it was mine by birth.' Then those who were about to examine him withdrew hastily, and

[a] *Or* tied him up with thongs.

King James Version

him: and the chief captain also was afraid, after
he knew that he was a Roman, and because
he had bound him. 30 On the morrow, because he
would have known the certainty wherefore he
was accused of the Jews, he loosed him from
his bands, and commanded the chief priests and
all their council to appear, and brought Paul
down, and set him before them.

23 And Paul, earnestly beholding the council, said, Men *and* brethren, I have lived in
all good conscience before God until this day.
2 And the high priest Ananias commanded them
that stood by him to smite him on the mouth.
3 Then said Paul unto him, God shall smite thee,
thou whited wall: for sittest thou to judge me
after the law, and commandest me to be smitten
contrary to the law? 4 And they that stood by
said, Revilest thou God's high priest? 5 Then

Living Bible

Roman citizen, and the commander was frightened because he had ordered him bound and whipped.

30 The next day the commander freed him from his chains and ordered the chief priests into session with the Jewish Council. He had Paul brought in before them to try to find out what the trouble was all about.

23 Gazing intently at the Council, Paul began:

"Brothers, I have always lived before God in all good conscience!"

2 Instantly Ananias the High Priest commanded those close to Paul to slap him on the mouth.

3 Paul said to him, "God shall slap you, you whitewashed pigpen.[a] What kind of judge are you to break the law yourself by ordering me struck like that?"

4 Those standing near Paul said to him, "Is that the way to talk to God's High Priest?"

5 "I didn't realize he was the High Priest,

[a] Literally, "you whitewashed wall."

Today's English Version

mander was afraid when he realized that Paul was a Roman citizen, and that he had put him in chains.

Paul before the Council

30 The commander wanted to find out for sure what the Jews were accusing Paul of; so the next day he had Paul's chains taken off and ordered the chief priests and the whole Council to meet. Then he took Paul, and made him stand before them.

23 Paul looked straight at the Council and said, "My brothers! My conscience is perfectly clear about my whole life before God, to this very day." 2 The High Priest Ananias ordered those who were standing close to Paul to strike him on the mouth. 3 Paul said to him, "God will certainly strike you—you whitewashed wall! You sit there to judge me according to the Law, yet you break the Law by ordering them to strike me!"

4 The men close to Paul said to him, "You are insulting God's High Priest!"

5 Paul answered, "I did not know, my broth-

New International Version

was alarmed when he realized that he had put Paul, a Roman citizen, in chains.

Before the Sanhedrin

30 The next day, since the commander wanted to find out exactly why Paul was being accused by the Jews, he released him and ordered the chief priests and all the Sanhedrin to assemble. Then he brought Paul and had him stand before them.

23 Paul looked straight at the Sanhedrin and said, "My brothers, I have fulfilled my duty to God in all good conscience to this day." 2 At this the high priest Ananias ordered those standing near Paul to strike him on the mouth. 3 Then Paul said to him, "God will strike you, you white-washed wall! You sit there to judge me according to the law, yet you yourself violate the law by commanding that I be struck!"

4 Those who were standing near Paul said, "You dare to insult God's high priest?"

5 Paul replied, "Brothers, I did not realize

Phillips Modern English

self was alarmed at discovering that Paul was a Roman and that he had had him bound.

22.30 Roman fair-mindedness

Next day the colonel, determined to get to the bottom of Paul's accusation by the Jews, released him and ordered the assembly of the chief priests and the whole Sanhedrin. Then he took Paul down and placed him in front of them.

23.1 Paul again attempts defence

Paul looked steadily at the Sanhedrin and spoke to them,

"Men and brothers, I have lived my life with a perfectly clear conscience before God up to the present day——" Then Ananias the High Priest ordered those who were standing near to strike him on the mouth. At this Paul said to him,

"God will strike you, you white-washed wall! How dare you sit there judging me by the Law and give orders for me to be struck, which is clean contrary to the Law?"

Those who stood by said,

"Do you mean to insult God's High Priest?"

But Paul said,

Revised Standard Version

stantly; and the tribune also was afraid, for he realized that Paul was a Roman citizen and that he had bound him.

30 But on the morrow, desiring to know the real reason why the Jews accused him, he unbound him, and commanded the chief priests and all the council to meet, and he brought Paul down and set him before them.

23 And Paul, looking intently at the council, said, "Brethren, I have lived before God in all good conscience up to this day."
2And the high priest Ananias commanded those who stood by him to strike him on the mouth.
3 Then Paul said to him, "God shall strike you, you whitewashed wall! Are you sitting to judge me according to the law, and yet contrary to the law you order me to be struck?" 4 Those who stood by said, "Would you revile God's high priest?" 5And Paul said, "I did not know,

Jerusalem Bible

drew, and the tribune himself was alarmed when he realized that he had put a Roman citizen in chains.

His appearance before the Sanhedrin

30 The next day, since he wanted to know what precise charge the Jews were bringing, he freed Paul and gave orders for a meeting of the chief priests and the entire Sanhedrin; then he brought Paul down and stood him in front of them.

23 Paul looked steadily at the Sanhedrin and began to speak, "My brothers, to this day I have conducted myself before God with a perfectly clear conscience." 2At this the high priest Ananias ordered his attendants to strike him on the mouth. 3 Then Paul said to him, "God will surely strike you, you whitewashed wall! How can you sit there to judge me according to the Law, and then break the Law by ordering a man to strike me?" 4 The attendants said, "It is God's high priest you are insulting!" 5 Paul answered,

New English Bible

the commandant himself was alarmed when he realized that Paul was a Roman citizen and that he had put him in irons.

The following day, wishing to be quite sure what charge the Jews were bringing against Paul, he released him and ordered the chief priests and the entire Council to assemble. He then took Paul down and stood him before them.

23 Paul fixed his eyes on the Council and said, 'My brothers, I have lived all my life, and still live today, with a perfectly clear conscience before God.' At this the High Priest Ananias ordered his attendants to strike him on the mouth. Paul retorted, 'God will strike you, you whitewashed wall! You sit there to judge me in accordance with the Law; and then in defiance of the Law you order me to be struck!' The attendants said, 'Would you insult God's High Priest?' 'My brothers,' said Paul, 'I had

King James Version

said Paul, I wist not, brethren, that he was the high priest: for it is written, Thou shalt not speak evil of the ruler of thy people. 6 But when Paul perceived that the one part were Sadducees, and the other Pharisees, he cried out in the council, Men *and* brethren, I am a Pharisee, the son of a Pharisee: of the hope and resurrection of the dead I am called in question. 7And when he had so said, there arose a dissension between the Pharisees and the Sadducees: and the multitude was divided. 8 For the Sadducees say that there is no resurrection, neither angel, nor spirit: but the Pharisees confess both. 9And there arose a great cry: and the scribes *that were* of the Pharisees' part arose, and strove, saying, We find no evil in this man: but if a spirit or an angel hath spoken to him, let us not fight against God. 10And when there arose a great dissension, the chief captain, fearing lest Paul should have been pulled in pieces of them, commanded the soldiers to go down, and to take him by force from among them, and

Living Bible

brothers," Paul replied, "for the Scriptures say, 'Never speak evil of any of your rulers.' "

6 Then Paul thought of something! Part of the Council were Sadducees, and part were Pharisees! So he shouted, "Brothers, I am a Pharisee, as were all my ancestors! And I am being tried here today because I believe in the resurrection of the dead!"

7 This divided the Council right down the middle—the Pharisees against the Sadducees—8 for the Sadducees say there is no resurrection or angels or even eternal spirit within us,[b] but the Pharisees believe in all of these.

9 So a great clamor arose. Some of the Jewish leaders[c] jumped up to argue that Paul was all right. "We see nothing wrong with him," they shouted. "Perhaps a spirit or angel spoke to him [there on the Damascus road [d]]."

10 The shouting grew louder and louder, and the men were tugging at Paul from both sides, pulling him this way and that. Finally the commander, fearing they would tear him apart, ordered his soldiers to take him away from them by force and bring him back to the armory.

[*b*] Literally, "nor spirit." [*c*] Literally, "scribes." [*d*] Implied.

Today's English Version

ers, that he was the High Priest. The scripture says, 'You must not speak evil of the ruler of your people.' "

6 When Paul saw that some of the group were Sadducees and that others were Pharisees, he called out in the Council, "My brothers! I am a Pharisee, the son of Pharisees. I am on trial here because I hope that the dead will rise to life!"

7 As soon as he said this, the Pharisees and Sadducees started to quarrel, and the group was divided. 8 (For the Sadducees say that people will not rise from death, and that there are no angels or spirits; but the Pharisees believe in all three.) 9 The shouting became louder, and some of the teachers of the Law who belonged to the party of the Pharisees stood up and protested strongly, "We cannot find a thing wrong with this man! Perhaps a spirit or an angel really did speak to him!"

10 The argument became so violent that the commander was afraid that Paul would be torn to pieces by them. So he ordered his soldiers to go down into the group and get Paul away from them, and take him into the fort.

New International Version

that he was the high priest; for it is written: 'Do not speak evil about the ruler of your people.' [i] "

6 Then Paul, knowing that some of them were Sadducees and the others Pharisees, called out in the Sanhedrin, "My brothers, I am a Pharisee, the son of a Pharisee. I stand on trial because of my hope in the resurrection of the dead." 7 When he said this, a dispute broke out between the Pharisees and the Sadducees, and the assembly was divided. 8 (The Sadducees say that there is no resurrection, and that there are neither angels nor spirits, but the Pharisees acknowledge them all.)

9 There was a great uproar, and some of the teachers of the law who were Pharisees stood up and argued vigorously. "We find nothing wrong with this man," they said. "What if a spirit or an angel has spoken to him?" 10 The dispute became so violent that the commander was afraid Paul would be torn to pieces by them. He ordered the troops to go down and take him away from them by force and bring him into the barracks.

[*i*] Exodus 22:28.

Phillips Modern English

"My brothers, I did not know that he was the High Priest, for it is written:

Thou shalt not speak evil of a ruler of thy people."

23.6 Paul seizes his opportunity

Then Paul, realising that part of the council were Sadducees and the other part Pharisees, raised his voice and said to them,

"I am a Pharisee, the son of Pharisees. It is for my hope in the resurrection of the dead that I am on trial!"

At these words an immediate tension arose between the Pharisees and the Sadducees, and the meeting was divided. For the Sadducees claim that there is no resurrection and that there is neither angel nor spirit, while the Pharisees believe in all three. A great uproar ensued and some of the scribes of the Pharisees' party jumped to their feet and protested violently.

"We find nothing wrong with this man! Suppose some angel or spirit has really spoken to him?"

As the tension mounted the colonel began to fear that Paul would be torn to pieces between them. He therefore ordered his soldiers to come down and rescue him from them and bring him back to the barracks.

Revised Standard Version

brethren, that he was the high priest; for it is written, 'You shall not speak evil of a ruler of your people.' "
6 But when Paul perceived that one part were Sadducees and the other Pharisees, he cried out in the council, "Brethren, I am a Pharisee, a son of Pharisees; with respect to the hope and the resurrection of the dead I am on trial." 7And
when he had said this, a dissension arose between the Pharisees and the Sadducees; and the assembly was divided. 8 For the Sadducees say that there is no resurrection, nor angel, nor spirit; but the Pharisees acknowledge them all.
9 Then a great clamor arose; and some of the scribes of the Pharisees' party stood up and contended, "We find nothing wrong in this man. What if a spirit or an angel spoke to him?"
10And when the dissension became violent, the tribune, afraid that Paul would be torn in pieces by them, commanded the soldiers to go down and take him by force from among them and bring him into the barracks.

Jerusalem Bible

"Brothers, I did not realize it was the high priest, for scripture says: *You must not curse a ruler of your people.*" [p]
6 Now Paul was well aware that one section was made up of Sadducees and the other of Pharisees, so he called out in the Sanhedrin, "Brothers, I am a Pharisee and the son of Pharisees. It is for our hope in the resurrection of the
dead that I am on trial." 7As soon as he said this a dispute broke out between the Pharisees and Sadducees, and the assembly was split between the two parties. 8 For the Sadducees say there is neither resurrection, nor angel, nor spirit,
while the Pharisees accept all three. 9 The shouting grew louder, and some of the scribes from the Pharisees' party stood up and protested strongly, "We find nothing wrong with this man. Suppose a spirit has spoken to him, or an angel?"
10 Feeling was running high, and the tribune, afraid that they would tear Paul to pieces, ordered his troops to go down and haul him out and bring him into the fortress.

[p] Ex. 22:27.

New English Bible

no idea that he was High Priest; Scripture, I know, says: "You must not abuse the ruler of your people." '

Now Paul was well aware that one section of them were Sadducees and the other Pharisees, so he called out in the Council, 'My brothers, I am a Pharisee, a Pharisee born and bred; and the true issue in this trial is our hope of the resurrection of the dead.' At these words the Pharisees and Sadducees fell out among themselves, and the assembly was divided. (The Sadducees deny that there is any resurrection, or angel, or spirit, but the Pharisees accept them.) So a great uproar broke out; and some of the doctors of the law belonging to the Pharisaic party openly took sides and declared, 'We can find no fault with this man; perhaps an angel or spirit has spoken to him.' The dissension was mounting, and the commandant was afraid that Paul would be torn in pieces, so he ordered the troops to go down, pull him out of the crowd, and bring him into the barracks.

King James Version

to bring *him* into the castle. 11 And the night following the Lord stood by him, and said, Be of good cheer, Paul: for as thou hast testified of me in Jerusalem, so must thou bear witness also at Rome. 12 And when it was day, certain of the Jews banded together, and bound themselves under a curse, saying that they would neither eat nor drink till they had killed Paul. 13 And they were more than forty which had made this conspiracy. 14 And they came to the chief priests and elders, and said, We have bound ourselves under a great curse, that we will eat nothing until we have slain Paul. 15 Now therefore ye with the council signify to the chief captain that he bring him down unto you to morrow, as though ye would inquire something more perfectly concerning him: and we, or ever he come near, are ready to kill him. 16 And when Paul's sister's son heard of their lying in wait, he went and entered into the castle, and told Paul. 17 Then Paul called one of the centurions

Living Bible

11 That night the Lord stood beside Paul and said, "Don't worry, Paul; just as you have told the people about me here in Jerusalem, so you must also in Rome."

12, 13 The next morning some forty or more of the Jews got together and bound themselves by a curse neither to eat nor drink until they had killed Paul! 14 Then they went to the chief priests and elders and told them what they had done. 15 "Ask the commander to bring Paul back to the Council again," they requested. "Pretend you want to ask a few more questions. We will kill him on the way."

16 But Paul's nephew got wind of their plan and came to the armory and told Paul.

17 Paul called one of the officers and said,

Today's English Version

11 The following night the Lord stood by Paul and said, "Courage! You have given your witness to me here in Jerusalem, and you must do the same in Rome also."

The plot against Paul's life

12 The next morning some Jews met together and made a plan. They took a vow that they would not eat or drink anything until they had killed Paul. 13 There were more than forty of them who planned this together. 14 Then they went to the chief priests and elders and said, "We have taken a solemn vow together not to eat a thing until we kill Paul. 15 Now then, you and the Council send word to the Roman commander to bring Paul down to you, pretending that you want to get more accurate information about him. But we will be ready to kill him before he ever gets here."

16 But the son of Paul's sister heard of the plot; so he went and entered the fort and told it to Paul. 17 Then Paul called one of the officers

New International Version

11 The following night the Lord stood near Paul and said, "Take courage! As you have testified about me in Jerusalem, so you must also testify in Rome."

The plot to kill Paul

12 The next morning the Jews formed a conspiracy and bound themselves with an oath not to eat or drink until they had killed Paul. 13 More than forty men were involved in this plot. 14 They went to the chief priests and elders and said, "We have taken a solemn oath not to eat anything until we have killed Paul. 15 Now then, you and the Sanhedrin petition the commander to bring him before you on the pretext of wanting more accurate information about his case. We are ready to kill him before he gets here."

16 But when the son of Paul's sister heard of this plot, he went into the barracks and told Paul.

17 Then Paul called one of the centurions and

Phillips Modern English

23.11 God's direct encouragement to Paul

That night the Lord stood by Paul, and said, "Take heart!—for as you have witnessed boldly for me in Jerusalem so you must give your witness for me in Rome."

23.12 Paul's acute danger

Early in the morning the Jews formed a conspiracy and bound themselves by a solemn oath that they would neither eat nor drink until they had killed Paul. Over forty of them were involved in this plot, and they approached the chief priests and elders, and said,

"We have bound ourselves by a solemn oath to let nothing pass our lips until we have killed Paul. Now you and the council must make it plain to the colonel that you want him to bring Paul down to you, suggesting that you want to examine his case more closely. We shall be standing by ready to kill him before he gets here."

23.16 Leakage of information leads to Paul's protection

However, Paul's nephew got wind of this plot and he came and found his way into the barracks and told Paul about it. Paul called one of the centurions and said,

Revised Standard Version

11 The following night the Lord stood by
him and said, "Take courage, for as you have
testified about me at Jerusalem, so you must
bear witness also at Rome."
12 When it was day, the Jews made a plot
and bound themselves by an oath neither to eat
nor drink till they had killed Paul. 13 There
were more than forty who made this conspiracy.
14 And they went to the chief priests and elders,
and said, "We have strictly bound ourselves by
an oath to taste no food till we have killed
Paul. 15 You therefore, along with the council,
give notice now to the tribune to bring him
down to you, as though you were going to determine his case more exactly. And we are ready
to kill him before he comes near."
16 Now the son of Paul's sister heard of their
ambush; so he went and entered the barracks
and told Paul. 17 And Paul called one of the

Jerusalem Bible

11 Next night, the Lord appeared to him and
said, "Courage! You have borne witness for me
in Jerusalem, now you must do the same in
Rome."

The conspiracy of the Jews against Paul

12 When it was day, the Jews held a secret
meeting at which they made a vow not to eat or
drink until they had killed Paul. 13 There were
more than forty who took part in this conspiracy,
14 and they went to the chief priests and elders,
and told them, "We have made a solemn vow
to let nothing pass our lips until we have killed
Paul. 15 Now it is up to you and the Sanhedrin
together to apply to the tribune to bring him
down to you, as though you meant to examine
his case more closely; we, on our side, are prepared to dispose of him before he reaches you."
16 But the son of Paul's sister heard of the
ambush they were laying and made his way into
the fortress and told Paul, 17 who called one of

New English Bible

The following night the Lord appeared to him and said, 'Keep up your courage; you have affirmed the truth about me in Jerusalem, and you must do the same in Rome.'

When day broke, the Jews banded together and took an oath not to eat or drink until they had killed Paul. There were more than forty in this conspiracy. They came to the chief priests and elders and said, 'We have bound ourselves by a solemn oath not to taste food until we have killed Paul. It is now for you, acting with the Council, to apply to the commandant to bring him down to you, on the pretext of a closer investigation of his case; and we have arranged to do away with him before he arrives.'

But the son of Paul's sister heard of the ambush; he went to the barracks, obtained entry, and reported it to Paul. Paul called one of the

King James Version

unto *him,* and said, Bring this young man unto the chief captain: for he hath a certain thing to tell him. 18 So he took him, and brought *him* to the chief captain, and said, Paul the prisoner called me unto *him,* and prayed me to bring this young man unto thee, who hath something to say unto thee. 19 Then the chief captain took him by the hand, and went *with him* aside privately, and asked *him,* What is that thou hast to tell me? 20And he said, The Jews have agreed to desire thee that thou wouldest bring down Paul to morrow into the council, as though they would inquire somewhat of him more perfectly. 21 But do not thou yield unto them: for there lie in wait for him of them more than forty men, which have bound themselves with an oath, that they will neither eat nor drink till they have killed him: and now are they ready, looking for a promise from thee. 22 So the chief captain *then* let the young man depart, and charged *him, See thou* tell no man that thou hast shewed these things to me. 23And he called unto *him* two centurions, saying, Make ready two hundred soldiers to go to Cesarea, and horsemen threescore and ten, and spearmen two hundred, at the third hour of the night; 24And provide *them* beasts, that they may set Paul on, and bring

Living Bible

"Take this boy to the commander. He has something important to tell him."

18 So the officer did, explaining, "Paul, the prisoner, called me over and asked me to bring this young man to you to tell you something."

19 The commander took the boy by the hand, and leading him aside asked, "What is it you want to tell me, lad?"

20 "Tomorrow," he told him, "the Jews are going to ask you to bring Paul before the Council again, pretending they want to get some more information. 21 But don't do it! There are more than forty men hiding along the road ready to jump him and kill him. They have bound themselves under a curse to neither eat nor drink till he is dead. They are out there now, expecting you to agree to their request."

22 "Don't let a soul know you told me this," the commander warned the boy as he left. 23, 24 Then the commander called two of his officers and ordered, "Get 200 soldiers ready to leave for Caesarea at nine o'clock tonight! Take 200 spearmen and 70 mounted cavalry. Give Paul a horse to ride and get him safely to Governor Felix."

Today's English Version

and said to him, "Take this young man to the commander; he has something to tell him." 18 The officer took him, led him to the commander and said, "The prisoner Paul called me and asked me to bring this young man to you, because he has something to say to you."

19 The commander took him by the hand, led him off by himself, and asked him, "What do you have to tell me?"

20 He said, "The Jewish authorities have agreed to ask you tomorrow to take Paul down to the Council, pretending that the Council wants to get more accurate information about him. 21 But don't listen to them, because there are more than forty men who will be hiding and waiting for him. They have taken a vow not to eat or drink until they kill him. They are now ready to do it, and are waiting for your decision."

22 The commander said, "Don't tell anyone that you have reported this to me." And he sent the young man away.

Paul sent to Governor Felix

23 Then the commander called two of his officers and said, "Get two hundred soldiers ready to go to Caesarea, together with seventy horsemen and two hundred spearmen, and be ready to leave by nine o'clock tonight. 24 Provide some horses for Paul to ride, and get him safely

New International Version

said, "Take this young man to the commander; he has something to tell him." 18 So he took him to the commander.

The centurion said, "The prisoner Paul sent for me and asked me to bring this young man to you because he has something to tell you."

19 The commander took the young man by the hand, drew him aside and asked, "What is it you want to tell me?"

20 He said: "The Jews have agreed to ask you to bring Paul before the Sanhedrin tomorrow on the pretext of wanting more accurate information about him. 21 Don't give in to them, because more than forty of them are waiting in ambush for him. They have taken an oath not to eat or drink until they have killed him. They are ready now, waiting for your consent to their request."

22 The commander dismissed the young man and cautioned him, "Don't tell anyone that you have reported this to me."

Paul transferred to Caesarea

23 Then he called two of his centurions and ordered them, "Get ready a detachment of two hundred soldiers, seventy horsemen and two hundred spearmen to go to Caesarea tonight at the third hour.[j] 24 Provide mounts for Paul so that he may be taken safely to Governor Felix."

[j] That is, *about 9:00 P.M.*

Phillips Modern English

"Take this young man to the colonel for he has something to report to him."

So the centurion took him and brought him into the colonel's presence, and said,

"The prisoner Paul called for me and requested that this young man should be brought to you as he has something to tell you."

The colonel took his hand, and drew him aside (where they could not be overheard), and asked,

"What have you got to report to me?"

And he replied,

"The Jews have agreed to ask you to bring Paul down to the Sanhedrin tomorrow as though they were going to enquire more carefully into his case. But I beg you not to let them persuade you. For more than forty of them are waiting for him—they have sworn a solemn oath that they will neither eat nor drink until they have killed him. They are all ready at this moment—all they want is for you to give the order."

At this the colonel dismissed the young man with the caution,

"Don't let anyone know that you have given me this information."

Then he summoned two of his centurions, and said,

"Get two hundred men ready to proceed to Caesarea, with seventy horsemen and two hundred spearmen, by nine o'clock tonight. Mounts must also be provided to carry Paul safely to Felix the governor."

Revised Standard Version

centurions and said, "Take this young man to
the tribune; for he has something to tell him."
18 So he took him and brought him to the
tribune and said, "Paul the prisoner called me
and asked me to bring this young man to you,
as he has something to say to you." 19 The
tribune took him by the hand, and going aside
asked him privately, "What is it that you have to
tell me?" 20 And he said, "The Jews have agreed
to ask you to bring Paul down to the council
tomorrow, as though they were going to inquire
somewhat more closely about him. 21 But do not
yield to them; for more than forty of their men
lie in ambush for him, having bound themselves
by an oath neither to eat nor drink till they
have killed him; and now they are ready, waiting
for the promise from you." 22 So the tribune
dismissed the young man, charging him, "Tell
no one that you have informed me of this."
23 Then he called two of the centurions and
said, "At the third hour of the night get ready
two hundred soldiers with seventy horsemen and
two hundred spearmen to go as far as Caesarea.
24 Also provide mounts for Paul to ride, and

Jerusalem Bible

the centurions and said, "Take this young man
to the tribune; he has something to tell him."
18 So the man took him to the tribune, and reported, "The prisoner Paul summoned me and
requested me to bring this young man to you;
he has something to tell you." 19 Then the
tribune took him by the hand and drew him
aside and asked, "What is it you have to tell
me?" 20 He replied, "The Jews have made a
plan to ask you to take Paul down to the Sanhedrin tomorrow, as though they meant to inquire more closely into his case. 21 Do not let
them persuade you. There are more than forty
of them lying in wait for him, and they have
vowed not to eat or drink until they have got rid
of him. They are ready now and only waiting
for your order to be given." 22 The tribune let
the young man go with this caution, "Tell no
one that you have given me this information."

Paul transferred to Caesarea

23 Then he summoned two of the centurions
and said, "Get two hundred soldiers ready to
leave for Caesarea by the third hour of the
night with seventy cavalry and two hundred
auxiliaries; 24 provide horses for Paul, and deliver him unharmed to Felix the governor." [q]

[q] Antoninus Felix, procurator of Judaea from 52 to 59 or 60.

New English Bible

centurions and said, 'Take this young man to the commandant; he has something to report.' The centurion took him and brought him to the commandant. 'The prisoner Paul', he said, 'sent for me and asked me to bring this young man to you; he has something to tell you.' The commandant took him by the arm, drew him aside, and asked him, 'What is it you have to report?' He said, 'The Jews have made a plan among themselves and will request you to bring Paul down to the Council tomorrow, on the pretext of obtaining more precise information about him. Do not listen to them; for a party more than forty strong are lying in wait for him. They have sworn not to eat or drink until they have done away with him; they are now ready, and wait only for your consent.' So the commandant dismissed the young man, with orders not to let anyone know that he had given him this information.

Then he called a couple of his centurions and issued these orders: 'Get ready two hundred infantry to proceed to Caesarea, together with seventy cavalrymen and two hundred light-armed troops;[a] parade three hours after sunset. Provide also mounts for Paul so that he may ride through under safe escort to Felix the

[a] *Or* two hundred spearmen (*the meaning of the Greek word is uncertain*).

King James Version

him safe unto Felix the governor. 25 And he wrote a letter after this manner: 26 Claudius Lysias unto the most excellent governor Felix *sendeth* greeting. 27 This man was taken of the Jews, and should have been killed of them: then came I with an army, and rescued him, having understood that he was a Roman. 28 And when I would have known the cause wherefore they accused him, I brought him forth into their council: 29 Whom I perceived to be accused of questions of their law, but to have nothing laid to his charge worthy of death or of bonds. 30 And when it was told me how that the Jews laid wait for the man, I sent straightway to thee, and gave commandment to his accusers also to say before thee what *they had* against him. Farewell. 31 Then the soldiers, as it was commanded them, took Paul, and brought *him* by night to Antipatris. 32 On the morrow they left the horsemen to go with him, and returned to the castle: 33 Who, when they came to Cesarea, and delivered the epistle to the governor, presented

Living Bible

25 Then he wrote this letter to the governor:
26 "*From:* Claudius Lysias
"*To:* His Excellency, Governor Felix.
"Greetings!

27 "This man was seized by the Jews and they were killing him when I sent the soldiers to rescue him, for I learned that he was a Roman citizen. 28 Then I took him to their Council to try to find out what he had done. 29 I soon discovered it was something about their Jewish beliefs, certainly nothing worthy of imprisonment or death. 30 But when I was informed of a plot to kill him, I decided to send him on to you and will tell his accusers to bring their charges before you."

31 So that night, as ordered, the soldiers took Paul to Antipatris. 32 They returned to the armory the next morning, leaving him with the cavalry to take him on to Caesarea.

33 When they arrived in Caesarea, they pre-

Today's English Version

through to Governor Felix." 25 Then the commander wrote a letter that went like this:

26 "Claudius Lysias to his Excellency, the Governor Felix: Greetings. 27 The Jews seized this man and were about to kill him. I learned that he is a Roman citizen, so I went with my soldiers and rescued him. 28 I wanted to know what they were accusing him of, so I took him down to their Council. 29 I found out that he had not done a thing for which he deserved to die or be put in prison; the accusation against him had to do with questions about their own law. 30 And when I was informed that some Jews were making a plot against him, I decided to send him to you. I told his accusers to make their charges against him before you."

31 The soldiers carried out their orders. They got Paul and took him that night as far as Antipatris. 32 The next day the foot soldiers returned to the fort and left the horsemen to go on with him. 33 They took him to Caesarea, delivered the letter to the Governor, and turned

New International Version

25 He wrote a letter as follows:

26 Claudius Lysias,

To His Excellency, Governor Felix:

Greetings.

27 This man was seized by the Jews and they were about to kill him, but I came with my troops and rescued him, for I had learned that he is a Roman citizen. 28 I wanted to know why they were accusing him, so I brought him to their Sanhedrin. 29 I found that the accusation had to do with questions about their law, but there was no charge against him that deserved death or imprisonment. 30 When I was informed of a plot to be carried out against the man, I sent him to you at once. I also ordered his accusers to present to you their case against him.

31 So the soldiers, carrying out their orders, took Paul with them during the night and brought him as far as Antipatris. 32 The next day they let the cavalry go on with him, while they returned to the barracks. 33 When the cavalry arrived in Caesarea, they delivered the letter to the governor and handed Paul over to him.

Phillips Modern English

23.25 The Roman view of Paul's position

He further wrote a letter to Felix in these terms:

"Claudius Lysias sends greeting to his excellency the governor Felix.

"This man had been seized by the Jews and was on the point of being murdered by them when I arrived with my troops and rescued him, since I had discovered that he was a Roman citizen. Wishing to find out what the accusation was that they were making against him, I had him brought down to their Sanhedrin. There I discovered he was being accused over questions of their laws, and that there was no charge against him which deserved either death or imprisonment. Now, however, that I have received private information of a plot against his life, I have sent him to you without delay. At the same time I have notified his accusers that they must make their charges against him in your presence."

23.31 Paul is taken into protective custody

The soldiers, acting on their orders, took Paul and, moving by night, brought him down to Antipatris. Next day they returned to the barracks, leaving the horsemen to accompany him further. They went into Caesarea and after delivering the letter to the governor, they handed

Revised Standard Version

bring him safely to Felix the governor." 25And
he wrote a letter to this effect:
26 "Claudius Lysias to his Excellency the governor Felix, greeting. 27 This man was seized by
the Jews, and was about to be killed by them, when I came upon them with the soldiers and rescued him, having learned that he was a Roman citizen. 28And desiring to know the charge on which they accused him, I brought him down
to their council. 29 I found that he was accused about questions of their law, but charged with nothing deserving death or imprisonment. 30And
when it was disclosed to me that there would be a plot against the man, I sent him to you at once, ordering his accusers also to state before you what they have against him."
31 So the soldiers, according to their instructions, took Paul and brought him by night to
Antipatris. 32And on the morrow they returned to the barracks, leaving the horsemen to go on
with him. 33 When they came to Caesarea and delivered the letter to the governor, they pre-

Jerusalem Bible

25 He also wrote a letter in these terms:
26 "Claudius Lysias to his Excellency the governor Felix, greetings. 27 This man had been
seized by the Jews and would have been murdered by them but I came on the scene with my troops and got him away, having discovered that he was a Roman citizen. 28 Wanting to find
out what charge they were making against him, I brought him before their Sanhedrin. 29 I found
that the accusation concerned disputed points of their Law, but that there was no charge deserving death or imprisonment. 30 My information is that there is a conspiracy against the man, so I hasten to send him to you, and have notified his accusers that they must state their case against him in your presence."
31 The soldiers carried out their orders; they took Paul and escorted him by night to Antipatris. 32 Next day they left the mounted escort to go on with him and returned to the
fortress. 33 On arriving at Caesarea the escort delivered the letter to the governor and handed

New English Bible

Governor.' And he wrote a letter to this effect: 'Claudius Lysias to His Excellency the Governor Felix. Your Excellency: This man was seized by the Jews and was on the point of being murdered when I intervened with the troops and removed him, because I discovered that he was a Roman citizen. As I wished to ascertain the charge on which they were accusing him, I took him down to their Council. I found that the accusation had to do with controversial matters in their law, but there was no charge against him meriting death or imprisonment. However, I have now been informed of an attempt to be made on the man's life, so I am sending him to you at once, and have also instructed his accusers to state their case against him before you.' [b]

Acting on their orders, the infantry took Paul and brought him by night to Antipatris. Next day they returned to their barracks, leaving the cavalry to escort him the rest of the way. The cavalry entered Caesarea, delivered the letter to the Governor, and handed Paul over to him.

[b] *Some witnesses read* '. . . before you. Farewell.'

King James Version

Paul also before him. 34 And when the governor had read *the letter,* he asked of what province he was. And when he understood that *he was* of Cilicia; 35 I will hear thee, said he, when thine accusers are also come. And he commanded him to be kept in Herod's judgment hall.

24 And after five days Ananias the high priest descended with the elders, and *with* a certain orator *named* Tertullus, who informed the governor against Paul. 2 And when he was called forth, Tertullus began to accuse *him,* saying, Seeing that by thee we enjoy great quietness, and that very worthy deeds are done unto this nation by thy providence, 3 We accept *it* always, and in all places, most noble Felix, with all thankfulness. 4 Notwithstanding, that I be not further tedious unto thee, I pray thee that thou wouldest hear us of thy clemency a few words. 5 For we have found this man *a* pestilent *fellow,* and a mover of sedition among all the Jews throughout the world, and a ringleader of the sect of the Nazarenes: 6 Who also hath gone about to profane the temple: whom we took,

Living Bible

sented Paul and the letter to the governor. 34 He read it and then asked Paul where he was from.

"Cilicia," Paul answered.

35 "I will hear your case fully when your accusers arrive," the governor told him, and ordered him kept in the prison at King Herod's palace.

24 Five days later Ananias the High Priest arrived with some of the Jewish leaders[a] and the lawyer[b] Tertullus, to make their accusations against Paul. 2 When Tertullus was called forward, he laid charges against Paul in the following address to the governor:

"Your Excellency, you have given quietness and peace to us Jews and have greatly reduced the discrimination against us. 3 And for this we are very, very grateful to you. 4 But lest I bore you, kindly give me your attention for only a moment as I briefly outline our case against this man. 5 For we have found him to be a troublemaker, a man who is constantly inciting the Jews throughout the entire world to riots and rebellions against the Roman government. He is a ringleader of the sect known as the Nazarenes. 6 Moreover, he was trying to defile the Temple

[a] Literally, "elders." [b] Literally, "orator."

Today's English Version

Paul over to him. 34 The Governor read the letter and asked Paul what province he was from. When he found out that he was from Cilicia, 35 he said, "I will hear you when your accusers arrive." Then he gave orders that Paul be kept under guard in Herod's palace.

Paul accused by the Jews

24 Five days later the Hight Priest Ananias went to Caesarea with some elders and a lawyer named Tertullus. They appeared before Governor Felix and made their charges against Paul. 2 Tertullus was called and began to accuse Paul as follows:

"Your Excellency! Your wise leadership has brought us a long period of peace, and many necessary reforms are being made for the good of our country. 3 We welcome this everywhere at all times, and we are deeply grateful to you. 4 I do not want to take up too much of your time, however, so I beg you to be kind and listen to our brief account. 5 We found this man to be a dangerous nuisance; he starts riots among the Jews all over the world, and is a leader of the party of the Nazarenes. 6 He also tried to defile the temple, and we arrested him.

New International Version

34 The governor read the letter and asked what province he was from. Learning that he was from Cilicia, 35 he said, "I will hear your case when your accusers get here." Then he ordered that Paul be kept under guard in Herod's palace.

The trial before Felix

24 Five days later the high priest Ananias went down to Caesarea with some of the elders and a lawyer named Tertullus, and they brought their charges against Paul before the governor. 2 When Paul was called in, Tertullus presented his case before Felix: "We have enjoyed a long period of peace under you, and your foresight has brought about reforms in this nation. 3 Everywhere and in every way, most excellent Felix, we acknowledge this with profound gratitude. 4 But in order not to weary you further, I would request that you be kind enough to hear us briefly.

5 "We have found this man to be a troublemaker, stirring up riots among the Jews all over the world. He is a ringleader of the Nazarene sect 6 and even tried to desecrate the temple; so

Phillips Modern English

Paul over to him. When the governor had read the letter he asked Paul what province he came from, and on learning that he came from Cilicia, he said,

"I will hear your case as soon as your accusers arrive."

Then he ordered him to be kept under guard in Herod's palace.

24.1 The "professional" puts the case against Paul

Five days later Ananias the High Priest came down himself with some of the elders and a barrister by the name of Tertullus. They presented their case against Paul before the governor, and when Paul had been summoned, Tertullus began the prosecution in these words:

"We owe it to you personally, your excellency, that we enjoy lasting peace, and we know that it is due to your foresight that the nation enjoys improved conditions of living. At all times, and indeed everywhere, we acknowledge these things with the deepest gratitude. However—for I must not detain you too long—I beg you to give us a brief hearing with your customary kindness. The simple fact is that we have found this man a pestilential disturber of the peace among the Jews all over the world. He is a ringleader of the Nazarene sect, and he was on the point of desecrating the Temple when we over-

Revised Standard Version

sented Paul also before him. 34 On reading the
letter, he asked to what province he belonged.
When he learned that he was from Cilicia 35 he
said, "I will hear you when your accusers arrive." And he commanded him to be guarded in Herod's praetorium.

24 And after five days the high priest Ananias came down with some elders and a spokesman, one Tertullus. They laid before the governor their case against Paul;
2 and when he was called, Tertullus began to accuse him, saying:
"Since through you we enjoy much peace, and since by your provision, most excellent Felix, reforms are introduced on behalf of this
nation, 3 in every way and everywhere we accept
this with all gratitude. 4 But, to detain you no
further, I beg you in your kindness to hear us
briefly. 5 For we have found this man a pestilent fellow, an agitator among all the Jews throughout the world, and a ringleader of the sect of
the Nazarenes. 6 He even tried to profane the

Jerusalem Bible

Paul over to him. 34 The governor read the letter and asked him what province he came from.
Learning that he was from Cilicia he said, 35 "I
will hear your case as soon as your accusers are here too." Then he ordered him to be held in Herod's praetorium.

The case before Felix

24 Five days later the high priest Ananias came down with some of the elders and an advocate named Tertullus, and they laid information against Paul before the governor.
2 Paul was called, and Tertullus opened for the prosecution, "Your Excellency, Felix, the unbroken peace we enjoy and the reforms this nation owes to your foresight
3 are matters we accept, always and everywhere, with all gratitude.
4 I do not want to take up too much of your time, but I beg you to give us a brief hearing.
5 The plain truth is that we find this man a perfect pest; he stirs up trouble among Jews the world over, and is a ringleader of the Nazarene sect.
6 He has even attempted to profane

New English Bible

He read the letter, asked him what province he was from, and learned that he was from Cilicia. 'I will hear your case', he said, 'when your accusers arrive.' He then ordered him to be held in custody at his headquarters in Herod's palace.

24 Five days later the High Priest Ananias came down, accompanied by some of the elders and an advocate named Tertullus, and they laid an information against Paul before the Governor. When the prisoner was called, Tertullus opened the case.

'Your Excellency,' he said, 'we owe it to you that we enjoy unbroken peace. It is due to your provident care that, in all kinds of ways and in all sorts of places, improvements are being made for the good of this province. We welcome this, sir, most gratefully. And now, not to take up too much of your time, I crave your indulgence for a brief statement of our case. We have found this man to be a perfect pest, a fomenter of discord among the Jews all over the world, a ringleader of the sect of the Nazarenes. He even made an attempt to profane the temple;

King James Version

and would have judged according to our law. 7 But the chief captain Lysias came *upon us,* and with great violence took *him* away out of our hands, 8 Commanding his accusers to come unto thee: by examining of whom thyself mayest take knowledge of all these things, whereof we accuse him. 9 And the Jews also assented, saying that these things were so. 10 Then Paul, after that the governor had beckoned unto him to speak, answered, Forasmuch as I know that thou hast been of many years a judge unto this nation, I do the more cheerfully answer for myself: 11 Because that thou mayest understand, that there are yet but twelve days since I went up to Jerusalem for to worship. 12 And they neither found me in the temple disputing with any man, neither raising up the people, neither in the synagogues, nor in the city: 13 Neither can they prove the things whereof they now accuse me. 14 But this I confess unto thee, that after the way which they call heresy, so worship I the God of my fathers, believing all things which are written in the law and in the prophets: 15 And have hope toward God, which they themselves also allow, that there shall be a resurrection of the dead, both of the just and unjust. 16 And herein do I exercise myself, to have al-

Living Bible

when we arrested him.

"We would have given him what he justly deserves, 7 but Lysias, the commander of the garrison, came and took him violently away from us, 8 demanding that he be tried by Roman law. You can find out the truth of our accusations by examining him yourself."

9 Then all the other Jews chimed in, declaring that everything Tertullus said was true.

10 Now it was Paul's turn. The governor motioned for him to rise and speak.

Paul began: "I know, sir, that you have been a judge of Jewish affairs for many years, and this gives me confidence as I make my defense. 11 You can quickly discover that it was no more than twelve days ago that I arrived in Jerusalem to worship at the Temple, 12 and you will discover that I have never incited a riot in any synagogue or on the streets of any city; 13 and these men certainly cannot prove the things they accuse me of doing.

14 "But one thing I do confess, that I believe in the way of salvation, which they refer to as a sect; I follow that system of serving the God of our ancestors; I firmly believe in the Jewish law and everything written in the books of prophecy; 15 and I believe, just as these men do, that there will be a resurrection of both the righteous and ungodly. 16 Because of this I try

Today's English Version

[We planned to judge him according to our own Law, 7 but the commander Lysias came in and with great violence took him from us. 8 Then Lysias gave orders that his accusers should come before you.] If you question this man, you yourself will be able to learn from him all the things that we are accusing him of." 9 The Jews joined in the accusation and said that all this was true.

Paul's defense before Felix

10 The Governor then motioned to Paul to speak, and Paul said,

"I know that you have been a judge over this nation for many years, and so I am happy to defend myself before you. 11 As you can find out for yourself, it was no more than twelve days ago that I went up to Jerusalem to worship. 12 The Jews did not find me arguing with anyone in the temple, nor did they find me stirring up the people, either in the synagogues or anywhere else in the city. 13 Nor can they give you proof of the accusations they now bring against me. 14 I do admit this to you: I worship the God of our ancestors by following that Way which they say is false. But I also believe in all the things written in the Law of Moses and the books of the prophets. 15 I have the same hope in God that these themselves hold, that all men, both the good and the bad, will rise from death. 16 And so I do my best always to have a clear

New International Version

we seized him.[k] 8 By examining him yourself you will be able to learn the truth about all these charges we are bringing against him."

9 The Jews joined in the accusation, asserting that these things were true.

10 When the governor motioned for him to speak, Paul replied: "I know that for a number of years you have been a judge over this nation; so I gladly make my defense. 11 You can easily verify that no more than twelve days ago I went up to Jerusalem to worship. 12 My accusers did not find me arguing with anyone at the temple, or stirring up a crowd in the synagogues or anywhere else in the city. 13 And they cannot prove to you the charges they are now making against me. 14 However, I admit that I worship the God of our fathers, as a follower of the Way, which they call a sect. I believe everything that agrees with the Law and that is written in the Prophets, 15 and I have the same hope in God as these men, that there will be a resurrection of both the righteous and the wicked. 16 So I strive al-

[k] Some MSS add *and wanted to judge him according to our law. 7 But the commander, Lysias, came and with the use of much force snatched him from our hands 8 and ordered his accusers to come before you.*

Phillips Modern English

came him. But you yourself will soon discover from the man himself all the facts about which we are accusing him."

24.9 Paul is given the chance to defend himself

The Jews joined in, asserting that these were the facts. Then Paul, at a nod from the governor, made his reply:

"I am well aware that you have been governor of this nation for many years, and I can therefore make my defence with every confidence. You can easily verify the fact that it is not more than twelve days ago that I went up to worship at Jerusalem. I was never found either arguing with anyone in the temple or gathering a crowd, either in the synagogues or anywhere in the city. These men are quite unable to prove the charges they are now making against me. I will freely admit to you, however, that I do worship the God of our fathers according to the Way which they call a sect, although in fact I believe in the scriptural authority of both the Law and the Prophets. I have the same hope in God which they themselves hold, that there is to be a resurrection of both good men and bad. With this hope before me I also do my utmost

Revised Standard Version

temple, but we seized him.[z] 8 By examining him yourself you will be able to learn from him about everything of which we accuse him."

9 The Jews also joined in the charge, affirming that all this was so.

10 And when the governor had motioned to him to speak, Paul replied:

"Realizing that for many years you have been judge over this nation, I cheerfully make my defense. 11 As you may ascertain, it is not more than twelve days since I went up to worship at Jerusalem; 12 and they did not find me disputing with any one or stirring up a crowd, either in the temple or in the synagogues, or in the city. 13 Neither can they prove to you what they now bring up against me. 14 But this I admit to you, that according to the Way, which they call a sect, I worship the God of our fathers, believing everything laid down by the law or written in the prophets, 15 having a hope in God which these themselves accept, that there will be a resurrection of both the just and the unjust. 16 So I always take pains to have a

[z] Other ancient authorities add *and we would have judged him according to our law. 7 But the chief captain Lysias came and with great violence took him out of our hands, 8 commanding his accusers to come before you.*

Jerusalem Bible

the Temple. We placed him under arrest, intending to judge him according to our Law, 7 but the tribune Lysias intervened and took him out of our hands by force, 8 ordering his accusers to appear before you; if you ask him[r] you can find out for yourself the truth of all our accusations against this man." 9 The Jews supported him, asserting that these were the facts.

10 When the governor motioned him to speak, Paul answered:

Paul's speech before the Roman governor

"I know that you have administered justice over this nation for many years, and I can therefore speak with confidence in my defense. 11 As you can verify for yourself, it is no more than twelve days since I went up to Jerusalem on pilgrimage, 12 and it is not true that they ever found me arguing with anyone or stirring up the mob, either in the Temple, in the synagogues, or about the town; 13 neither can they prove any of the accusations they are making against me now.

14 "What I do admit to you is this: it is according to the Way which they describe as a sect that I worship the God of my ancestors, retaining my belief in all points of the Law and in what is written in the prophets; 15 and I hold the same hope in God as they do that there will be a resurrection of good men and bad men alike. 16 In these things, I, as much as

[r] Lysias.

New English Bible

and then we arrested him.[a] If you will examine him yourself you can ascertain from him the truth of all the charges we bring.' The Jews supported the attack, alleging that the facts were as he stated.

Then the Governor motioned to Paul to speak, and he began his reply: 'Knowing as I do that for many years you have administered justice in this province, I make my defence with confidence. You can ascertain the facts for yourself. It is not more than twelve days since I went up to Jerusalem on a pilgrimage. They did not find me arguing with anyone, or collecting a crowd, either in the temple or in the synagogues or up and down the city; and they cannot make good the charges they bring against me. But this much I will admit: I am a follower of the new way (the "sect" they speak of), and it is in that manner that I worship the God of our fathers; for I believe all that is written in the Law and the prophets, and in reliance on God I hold the hope, which my accusers too accept, that there is to be a resurrection of good and wicked alike. Accordingly I, no less than they, train myself

[a] *Some witnesses insert* It was our intention to try him under our law; (7) but Lysias the commandant intervened and took him by force out of our hands, (8) ordering his accusers to come before you.

King James Version

ways a conscience void of offence toward God, and *toward* men. 17 Now after many years I came to bring alms to my nation, and offerings. 18 Whereupon certain Jews from Asia found me purified in the temple, neither with multitude, nor with tumult. 19 Who ought to have been here before thee, and object, if they had aught against me. 20 Or else let these same *here* say, if they have found any evil doing in me, while I stood before the council, 21 Except it be for this one voice, that I cried standing among them, Touching the resurrection of the dead I am called in question by you this day. 22 And when Felix heard these things, having more perfect knowledge of *that* way, he deferred them, and said, When Lysias the chief captain shall come down, I will know the uttermost of your matter. 23 And he commanded a centurion to keep Paul, and to let *him* have liberty, and that he should forbid none of his acquaintance to

Living Bible

with all my strength to always maintain a clear conscience before God and man.

17 "After several years away, I returned to Jerusalem with money to aid the Jews, and to offer a sacrifice to God. 18 My accusers saw me in the Temple as I was presenting my thank offering.[c] I had shaved my head as their laws required, and there was no crowd around me, and no rioting! But some Jews from Turkey were there 19 (who ought to be here if they have anything against me)—20 but look! Ask these men right here what wrongdoing their Council found in me, 21 except that I said one thing I shouldn't[d] when I shouted out, 'I am here before the Council to defend myself for believing that the dead will rise again!' "

22 Felix, who knew Christians didn't go around starting riots,[e] told the Jews to wait for the arrival of Lysias, the garrison commander, and then he would decide the case. 23 He ordered Paul to prison but instructed the guards to treat him gently and not to forbid any of his friends from visiting him or bringing him gifts to make his stay more comfortable.

[*c*] Implied. [*d*] Literally, "except it be for this one voice." [*e*] Literally, "having more accurate knowledge."

Today's English Version

conscience before God and men.

17 "After being away from Jerusalem for several years, I went there to take some money to my own people and to offer sacrifices. 18 It was while I was doing this that they found me in the temple, after I had completed the ceremony of purification. There was no crowd with me, and no disorder. 19 But some Jews from the province of Asia were there; they themselves ought to come before you and make their accusations, if they have anything against me. 20 Or let these men here tell what crime they found me guilty of when I stood before the Council—21 except for the one thing I called out when I stood before them: 'I am being judged by you today for believing that the dead will rise to life.' "

22 Then Felix, who was well informed about the Way, brought the hearing to a close. "I will decide your case," he told them, "when the commander Lysias arrives." 23 He ordered the officer in charge of Paul to keep him under guard, but to give him some freedom and allow his friends to provide for his needs.

New International Version

ways to keep my conscience clear before God and man.

17 "After an absence of several years, I came to Jerusalem to bring my people gifts for the poor and to present offerings. 18 I was ceremonially clean when they found me in the temple courts doing this. There was no crowd with me, nor was I involved in any disturbance. 19 But there are some Jews from the province of Asia, who ought to be here before you and bring charges if they have anything against me. 20 Or these who are here should state what crime they found in me, when I stood before the Sanhedrin —21 unless it was this one thing I shouted as I stood in their presence: 'It is concerning the resurrection of the dead that I am on trial before you today.' "

22 Then Felix, who was well acquainted with the Way, adjourned the proceedings. "When Lysias the commander comes," he said, "I will decide your case." 23 He ordered the centurion to keep Paul under guard but to give him some freedom and permit his friends to take care of his needs.

Phillips Modern English

to live my whole life with a clear conscience before God and man.

24.17 Paul has nothing to hide

"It was after several years' absence from Jerusalem that I came back to make charitable gifts to my own nation and to make my offerings. It was in the middle of these duties that they found me, a man purified in the Temple. There was no mob and there was no disturbance until these Jews from Asia came, who should in my opinion have come before you and made their accusation, if they had anything against me. Or else, let these men themselves speak out now and say what crime they found me guilty of when I stood before the Sanhedrin—unless it was that one sentence that I shouted as I stood among them. All I said was this, 'It is about the resurrection of the dead that I am on trial before you this day'."

24.22 Felix defers decision

Then Felix, who was better acquainted with the Way than most people, adjourned the case and said,

"As soon as Colonel Lysias arrives I will give you my decision."

Then he gave orders to the centurion to keep Paul in custody, but to grant him reasonable liberty and allow any of his personal friends to look after his needs.

Revised Standard Version

clear conscience toward God and toward men.
17 Now after some years I came to bring to my
nation alms and offerings. 18 As I was doing
this, they found me purified in the temple, without any crowd or tumult. But some Jews from
Asia—19 they ought to be here before you and
to make an accusation, if they have anything
against me. 20 Or else let these men themselves
say what wrongdoing they found when I stood
before the council, 21 except this one thing which
I cried out while standing among them, 'With
respect to the resurrection of the dead I am on
trial before you this day.'"

22 But Felix, having a rather accurate knowledge of the Way, put them off, saying, "When
Lysias the tribune comes down, I will decide
your case." 23 Then he gave orders to the centurion that he should be kept in custody but
should have some liberty, and that none of his
friends should be prevented from attending to
his needs.

Jerusalem Bible

they, do my best to keep a clear conscience at
all times before God and man.
17 "After several years I came to bring alms
to my nation and to make offerings; 18 it was in
connection with these that they found me in
the Temple; I had been purified, and there was
no crowd involved, and no disturbance. 19 But
some Jews from Asia . . . —these are the ones
who should have appeared before you and accused me of whatever they had against me. 20 At
least let those who are present say what crime
they found me guilty of when I stood before the
Sanhedrin, 21 unless it were to do with this single
outburst, when I stood up among them and
called out: It is about the resurrection of the
dead that I am on trial before you today."

Paul's captivity at Caesarea

22 At this Felix, who knew more about the
Way than most people, adjourned the case, saying, "When Lysias the tribune has come down
I will go into your case." 23 He then gave orders
to the centurion that Paul should be kept under
arrest but free from restriction, and that none
of his own people should be prevented from
seeing to his needs.

New English Bible

to keep at all times a clear conscience before God and man.

'After an absence of several years I came to bring charitable gifts to my nation and to offer sacrifices. They found me in the temple ritually purified and engaged in this service. I had no crowd with me, and there was no disturbance. But some Jews from the province of Asia were there, and if they had any charge against me it is they who ought to have been in court to state it. Failing that, it is for these persons here present to say what crime they discovered when I was brought before the Council, apart from this one open assertion which I made as I stood there: "The true issue in my trial before you today is the resurrection of the dead." '

Then Felix, who happened to be well informed about the Christian movement, adjourned the hearing. 'When Lysias the commanding officer comes down', he said, 'I will go into your case.' He gave orders to the centurion to keep Paul under open arrest and not to prevent any of his friends from making themselves useful to him.

King James Version

minister or come unto him. 24And after certain days, when Felix came with his wife Drusilla, which was a Jewess, he sent for Paul, and heard him concerning the faith in Christ. 25And as he reasoned of righteousness, temperance, and judgment to come, Felix trembled, and answered, Go thy way for this time; when I have a convenient season, I will call for thee. 26 He hoped also that money should have been given him of Paul, that he might loose him: wherefore he sent for him the oftener, and communed with him. 27 But after two years Porcius Festus came into Felix' room: and Felix, willing to shew the Jews a pleasure, left Paul bound.

25 Now when Festus was come into the province, after three days he ascended from Cesarea to Jerusalem. 2 Then the high priest and the chief of the Jews informed him against Paul, and besought him, 3And desired favour against him, that he would send for him to Jerusalem, laying wait in the way to kill him. 4 But Festus

Living Bible

24 A few days later Felix came with Drusilla, his legal [f] wife, a Jewess. Sending for Paul, they listened as he told them about faith in Christ Jesus. 25And as he reasoned with them about righteousness and self-control and the judgment to come, Felix was terrified.

"Go away for now," he replied, "and when I have a more convenient time, I'll call for you again."

26 He also hoped that Paul would bribe him, so he sent for him from time to time and talked with him. 27 Two years went by in this way; then Felix was succeeded by Porcius Festus. And because Felix wanted to gain favor with the Jews, he left Paul in chains.

25 Three days after Festus arrived in Caesarea to take over his new responsibilities, he left for Jerusalem, 2 where the chief priests and other Jewish leaders got hold of him and gave him their story about Paul. 3 They begged him to bring Paul to Jerusalem at once. (Their plan was to waylay and kill him.) 4 But Festus

[f] Literally, "his own wife."

Today's English Version

Paul before Felix and Drusilla

24 After some days Felix came with his wife Drusilla, who was Jewish. He sent for Paul and listened to him as he talked about faith in Christ Jesus. 25 But as Paul went on discussing about goodness, self-control, and the coming Day of Judgment, Felix was afraid and said, "You may leave now. I will call you again when I get the chance." 26At the same time he was hoping that Paul would give him some money; and for this reason he would call for him often and talk with him.

27 After two years had passed, Porcius Festus took the place of Felix as Governor. Felix wanted to gain favor with the Jews, so he left Paul in prison.

Paul appeals to the Emperor

25 Three days after Festus arrived in the province, he went from Caesarea to Jerusalem. 2 There the chief priests and the Jewish leaders brought their charges against Paul. They begged Festus 3 to do them the favor of having Paul come to Jerusalem, because they had made a plot to kill him on the way. 4 Festus answered,

New International Version

24 Several days later Felix arrived with his wife Drusilla, who was a Jewess. He sent for Paul and listened to him as he spoke about faith in Christ Jesus. 25As Paul discoursed on righteousness, self-control and the judgment to come, Felix was afraid and said, "That's enough for now! You may leave. When I find it convenient, I will send for you." 26At the same time he was hoping that Paul would offer him a bribe, so he sent for him frequently and talked with him.

27 When two years had passed, Felix was succeeded by Porcius Festus, but because Felix wanted to grant a favor to the Jews, he left Paul in prison.

The trial before Festus

25 Three days after arriving in the province, Festus went up from Caesarea to Jerusalem, 2 where the chief priests and Jewish leaders appeared before him and presented the charges against Paul. 3 They urgently requested Festus, as a favor to them, to have Paul transferred to Jerusalem, for they were preparing an ambush to kill him along the way. 4 Festus answered,

Phillips Modern English

24.24 Felix plays for safety—and hopes for personal gain

Some days later Felix arrived with his wife Drusilla, herself a Jewess, and sent for Paul, and heard what he had to say about faith in Christ Jesus. But while Paul was talking about goodness, self-control and the judgment that is to come, Felix became alarmed, and said,

"You may go for the present. When I find a convenient moment I will send for you again."

At the same time he nursed a secret hope that Paul would pay him money—which is why Paul was frequently summoned to come and talk with him. However, when two full years had passed, Felix was succeeded by Porcius Festus and, as he wanted to remain in favour with the Jews, he left Paul still a prisoner.

25.1 Felix's successor begins his duties with vigour—

Three days after Festus had taken over his province he went up from Caesarea to Jerusalem. The chief priests and leaders of the Jews informed him of the case against Paul and begged him as a special favour to have Paul sent to Jerusalem. They themselves had already made a plot to kill him on the way. But Festus replied

Revised Standard Version

24 After some days Felix came with his wife Drusilla, who was a Jewess; and he sent for Paul and heard him speak upon faith in Christ Jesus. 25 And as he argued about justice and self-control and future judgment, Felix was alarmed and said, "Go away for the present; when I have an opportunity I will summon you." 26 At the same time he hoped that money would be given him by Paul. So he sent for him often and conversed with him. 27 But when two years had elapsed, Felix was succeeded by Porcius Festus; and desiring to do the Jews a favor, Felix left Paul in prison.

25 Now when Festus had come into his province, after three days he went up to Jerusalem from Caesarea. 2 And the chief priests and the principal men of the Jews informed him against Paul; and they urged him, 3 asking as a favor to have the man sent to Jerusalem, planning an ambush to kill him on the way. 4 Festus replied that Paul was being kept at

Jerusalem Bible

24 Some days later Felix came with his wife Drusilla who was a Jewess.[s] He sent for Paul and gave him a hearing on the subject of faith in Christ Jesus. 25 But when he began to treat of righteousness, self-control and the coming Judgment, Felix took fright and said, "You may go for the present; I will send for you when I find it convenient." 26 At the same time he had hopes of receiving money from Paul, and for this reason he sent for him frequently and had talks with him.

27 When the two years[t] came to an end, Felix was succeeded by Porcius Festus and, being anxious to gain favor with the Jews, Felix left Paul in custody.

Paul appeals to Caesar

25 Three days after his arrival in the province, Festus went up to Jerusalem from Caesarea. 2 The chief priests and leaders of the Jews informed him of the case against Paul, urgently 3 asking him to support them rather than Paul, and to have him transferred to Jerusalem. They were, in fact, preparing an ambush to murder him on the way. 4 But Festus replied

[s] Youngest daughter of Herod Agrippa. [t] The maximum length of protective custody; Felix was breaking the law by continuing to detain Paul.

New English Bible

Some days later Felix came with his wife Drusilla, who was a Jewess, and sending for Paul he let him talk to him about faith in Christ Jesus. But when the discourse turned to questions of morals, self-control, and the coming judgement, Felix became alarmed and exclaimed, 'That will do for the present; when I find it convenient I will send for you again.' At the same time he had hopes of a bribe from Paul; and for this reason he sent for him very often and talked with him. When two years had passed, Felix was succeeded by Porcius Festus. Wishing to curry favour with the Jews, Felix left Paul in custody.

25 Three days after taking up his appointment Festus went up from Caesarea to Jerusalem, where the chief priests and the Jewish leaders brought before him the case against Paul. They asked Festus to favour them against him, and pressed for him to be brought up to Jerusalem, for they were planning an ambush to kill him on the way. Festus, however, replied, 'Paul

King James Version

answered, that Paul should be kept at Cesarea, and that he himself would depart shortly *thither*. 5 Let them therefore, said he, which among you are able, go down with *me*, and accuse this man, if there be any wickedness in him. 6 And when he had tarried among them more than ten days, he went down unto Cesarea; and the next day sitting on the judgment seat commanded Paul to be brought. 7 And when he was come, the Jews which came down from Jerusalem stood round about, and laid many and grievous complaints against Paul, which they could not prove. 8 While he answered for himself, Neither against the law of the Jews, neither against the temple, nor yet against Cesar, have I offended any thing at all. 9 But Festus, willing to do the Jews a pleasure, answered Paul, and said, Wilt thou go up to Jerusalem, and there be judged of these things before me? 10 Then said Paul, I stand at Cesar's judgment seat, where I ought to be judged: to the Jews have I done no wrong, as thou very well knowest. 11 For if I be an offender, or have committed any thing worthy of

Living Bible

replied that since Paul was at Caesarea and he himself was returning there soon, 5 those with authority in this affair should return with him for the trial.

6 Eight or ten days later he returned to Caesarea and the following day opened Paul's trial.

7 On Paul's arrival in court the Jews from Jerusalem gathered around, hurling many serious accusations which they couldn't prove. 8 Paul denied the charges: "I am not guilty," he said. "I have not opposed the Jewish laws or desecrated the Temple or rebelled against the Roman government."

9 Then Festus, anxious to please the Jews, asked him, "Are you willing to go to Jerusalem and stand trial before me?"

10, 11 But Paul replied, "No! I demand my privilege of a hearing before the Emperor himself. You know very well I am not guilty. If I have done something worthy of death, I don't

Today's English Version

"Paul is being kept a prisoner in Caesarea, and I myself will be going back there soon. 5 Let your leaders go to Caesarea with me and accuse the man, if he has done anything wrong."

6 Festus spent another eight or ten days with them, and then went to Caesarea. On the next day he sat down in the judgment court, and ordered Paul to be brought in. 7 When Paul arrived, the Jews who had come from Jerusalem stood around him and started making many serious charges against him, which they were not able to prove. 8 But Paul defended himself, "I have done nothing wrong against the Law of the Jews, or the temple, or the Roman Emperor."

9 Festus wanted to gain favor with the Jews, so he asked Paul, "Would you be willing to go to Jerusalem and be tried on these charges before me there?"

10 Paul said, "I am standing before the Emperor's own judgment court, where I should be tried. I have done no wrong to the Jews, as you yourself well know. 11 If I have broken the law and done something for which I deserve the

New International Version

"Paul is being held at Caesarea, and I myself am going there soon. 5 Let some of your leaders come with me and press charges against the man there, if he has done anything wrong."

6 After spending eight or ten days with them, he went down to Caesarea, and the next day he convened the court and ordered that Paul be brought before him. 7 When Paul appeared, the Jews who had come down from Jerusalem stood around him, bringing many serious charges against him, which they could not prove.

8 Then Paul made his defense: "I have done nothing wrong against the law of the Jews or against the temple or against Caesar."

9 Festus, wishing to do the Jews a favor, said to Paul, "Are you willing to go up to Jerusalem and stand trial before me there on these charges?"

10 Paul answered: "I am now standing before Caesar's court, where I ought to be tried. I have not done any wrong to the Jews, as you yourself know very well. 11 If, however, I am guilty of doing anything deserving death, I do not refuse

Phillips Modern English

that Paul was in custody in Caesarea, and that he himself was going there shortly.

"What you must do," he told them, "is to provide some competent men of your own to go down with me and if there is anything wrong with the man they can present their charges against him."

Festus spent not more than eight or ten days among them at Jerusalem and then went down to Caesarea. On the day after his arrival he took his seat on the bench and ordered Paul to be brought in. As soon as he arrived the Jews from Jerusalem stood up on all sides of him, bringing forward many serious accusations which they were quite unable to substantiate. Paul, in his defence, maintained,

"I have committed no offence in any way against the Jewish Law, or against the Temple or against Caesar."

25.9 —but is afraid of antagonising the Jews

But Festus, wishing to show goodwill to the Jews, spoke directly to Paul,

"Are you prepared to go up to Jerusalem and stand your trial over these matters in my presence there?"

But Paul replied,

"I am now standing in Caesar's court and that is where I should be judged. I have done the Jews no harm, as you very well know. It comes to this: if I were a criminal and had committed some crime which deserved the death penalty,

Revised Standard Version

Caesarea, and that he himself intended to go
there shortly. 5 "So," said he, "let the men of
authority among you go down with me, and if
there is anything wrong about the man, let them
accuse him."
6 When he had stayed among them not more
than eight or ten days, he went down to
Caesarea; and the next day he took his seat on
the tribunal and ordered Paul to be brought.
7 And when he had come, the Jews who had
gone down from Jerusalem stood about him,
bringing against him many serious charges which
they could not prove. 8 Paul said in his defense,
"Neither against the law of the Jews, nor against
the temple, nor against Caesar have I offended
at all." 9 But Festus, wishing to do the Jews a
favor, said to Paul, "Do you wish to go up to
Jerusalem, and there be tried on these charges
before me?" 10 But Paul said, "I am standing
before Caesar's tribunal, where I ought to be
tried; to the Jews I have done no wrong, as you
know very well. 11 If then I am a wrongdoer,
and have committed anything for which I de-

Jerusalem Bible

that Paul would remain in custody in Caesarea,
and that he would be going back there shortly
himself. 5 "Let your authorities come down with
me," he said, "and if there is anything wrong
about the man, they can bring a charge against
him."
6 After staying with them for eight or ten days
at the most, he went down to Caesarea and the
next day he took his seat on the tribunal and
had Paul brought in. 7 As soon as Paul appeared,
the Jews who had come down from Jerusalem
surrounded him, making many serious accusations which they were unable to substantiate.
8 Paul's defense was this, "I have committed
no offense whatever against either Jewish law,
or the Temple, or Caesar." 9 Festus was anxious
to gain favor with the Jews, so he said to Paul,
"Are you willing to go up to Jerusalem and be
tried on these charges before me there?" 10 But
Paul replied, "I am standing before the tribunal
of Caesar and this is where I should be tried. I
have done the Jews no wrong, as you very well
know. 11 If I am guilty of committing any capi-

New English Bible

is in safe custody at Caesarea, and I shall be leaving Jerusalem shortly myself; so let your leading men come down with me, and if there is anything wrong, let them prosecute him.'

After spending eight or ten days at most in Jerusalem, he went down to Caesarea, and next day he took his seat in court and ordered Paul to be brought up. When he appeared, the Jews who had come down from Jerusalem stood round bringing many grave charges, which they were unable to prove. Paul's plea was: 'I have committed no offence, either against the Jewish law, or against the temple, or against the Emperor.' Festus, anxious to ingratiate himself with the Jews, turned to Paul and asked, 'Are you willing to go up to Jerusalem and stand trial on these charges before me there?' But Paul said, 'I am now standing before the Emperor's tribunal, and that is where I must be tried. Against the Jews I have committed no offence, as you very well know. If I am guilty of any

King James Version

death, I refuse not to die: but if there be none
of these things whereof these accuse me, no man
may deliver me unto them. I appeal unto Cesar.
12 Then Festus, when he had conferred with
the council, answered, Hast thou appealed unto
Cesar? unto Cesar shalt thou go. 13 And after
certain days king Agrippa and Bernice came
unto Cesarea to salute Festus. 14 And when they
had been there many days, Festus declared
Paul's cause unto the king, saying, There is a
certain man left in bonds by Felix: 15 About
whom, when I was at Jerusalem, the chief priests
and the elders of the Jews informed *me*, desiring
to have judgment against him. 16 To whom I
answered, It is not the manner of the Romans
to deliver any man to die, before that he which
is accused have the accusers face to face, and
have license to answer for himself concerning
the crime laid against him. 17 Therefore, when
they were come hither, without any delay on the
morrow I sat on the judgment seat, and commanded the man to be brought forth. 18 Against
whom when the accusers stood up, they brought
none accusation of such things as I supposed:
19 But had certain questions against him of their
own superstition, and of one Jesus, which was

Living Bible

refuse to die! But if I am innocent, neither you
nor anyone else has a right to turn me over to
these men to kill me. *I appeal to Caesar*."
12 Festus conferred with his advisors and
then replied, "Very well! You have appealed to
Caesar, and to Caesar you shall go!"
13 A few days later King Agrippa arrived
with Bernice[a] for a visit with Festus. 14 During
their stay of several days Festus discussed Paul's
case with the king. "There is a prisoner here,"
he told him, "whose case was left for me by
Felix. 15 When I was in Jerusalem, the chief
priests and other Jewish leaders gave me their
side of the story and asked me to have him
killed. 16 Of course I quickly pointed out to
them that Roman law does not convict a man
before he is tried. He is given an opportunity to
defend himself face to face with his accusers.
17 "When they came here for the trial, I
called the case the very next day and ordered
Paul brought in. 18 But the accusations made
against him weren't at all what I supposed they
would be. 19 It was something about their religion, and about someone called Jesus who died,

[a] She was his sister.

Today's English Version

death penalty, I do not ask to escape it. But if
there is no truth in the charges they bring
against me, no one can hand me over to them.
I appeal to the Emperor."
12 Then Festus, after conferring with his advisers, answered, "You have appealed to the Emperor, so to the Emperor you will go."

Paul before Agrippa and Bernice

13 Some time later King Agrippa and Bernice
came to Caesarea to pay a visit of welcome to
Festus. 14 After they had been there several days,
Festus explained Paul's situation to the king,
"There is a man here who was left a prisoner by
Felix; 15 and when I went to Jerusalem, the
Jewish chief priests and elders brought charges
against him and asked me to condemn him.
16 But I told them that the Romans are not in
the habit of handing over any man accused of a
crime before he has met his accusers face to
face, and has the chance of defending himself
against the accusation. 17 When they came here,
then, I lost no time, but on the very next day I
sat in the judgment court and ordered the man
to be brought in. 18 His opponents stood up, but
they did not accuse him of any of the evil crimes
that I thought they would. 19 All they had were
some arguments with him about their own religion and about a man named Jesus, who has

New International Version

to die. But if the charges brought against me
by these Jews are not true, no one has the right
to hand me over to them. I appeal to Caesar!"
12 After Festus had conferred with his council, he declared: "You have appealed to Caesar.
To Caesar you will go!"

Festus consults King Agrippa

13 A few days later King Agrippa and Bernice
arrived at Caesarea to pay their respects to
Festus. 14 Since they were spending many days
there, Festus discussed Paul's case with the king.
He said: "There is a man here whom Felix left
as a prisoner. 15 When I went to Jerusalem, the
chief priests and elders of the Jews brought
charges against him and asked that he be condemned.
16 "I told them that it is not the Roman
custom to hand over any man before he has
faced his accusers and has had an opportunity
to defend himself against their charges. 17 When
they came here with me, I did not delay the
case, but convened the court the next day and
ordered the man to be brought in. 18 When his
accusers got up to speak, they did not charge
him with any of the crimes I had expected. 19 Instead, they had some points of dispute with him
about their own religion and about a dead man

Phillips Modern English

I do not object to dying. But as in fact there is no truth in the accusations these men have made, no one can use me as a gift to the Jews—*I appeal to Caesar!*"

Then Festus, after a conference with his advisers, replied,

"You have appealed to Caesar—then to Caesar you shall go!"

25.13 Festus outlines Paul's case to Agrippa

Some days later King Agrippa and Bernice arrived at Caesarea on a state visit to Festus. They prolonged their stay for some days, and this gave Festus an opportunity of laying Paul's case before the king.

"I have a man here," he said, "who was left a prisoner by Felix. When I was in Jerusalem the chief priests and Jewish elders made allegations against him and demanded his conviction. I told them that the Romans were not in the habit of giving anybody up to please anyone, until the accused had had the chance of facing his accusers personally and been given the opportunity of defending himself on the charges made against him. Since these Jews came back here with me, I wasted no time but on the very next day I took my seat on the bench and ordered the man to be brought in. But when his accusers got up to speak they did not charge him with any such crimes as I had anticipated. Their differences with him were about their own religion and concerning a certain Jesus who had died, but

Revised Standard Version

serve to die, I do not seek to escape death; but if there is nothing in their charges against me, no one can give me up to them. I appeal to Caesar." 12 Then Festus, when he had conferred with his council, answered, "You have appealed to Caesar; to Caesar you shall go."

13 Now when some days had passed, Agrippa the king and Bernice arrived at Caesarea to welcome Festus. 14 And as they stayed there many days, Festus laid Paul's case before the king, saying, "There is a man left prisoner by Felix; 15 and when I was at Jerusalem, the chief priests and the elders of the Jews gave information about him, asking for sentence against him. 16 I answered them that it was not the custom of the Romans to give up any one before the accused met the accusers face to face, and had opportunity to make his defense concerning the charge laid against him. 17 When therefore they came together here, I made no delay, but on the next day took my seat on the tribunal and ordered the man to be brought in. 18 When the accusers stood up, they brought no charge in his case of such evils as I supposed; 19 but they had certain points of dispute with him about their own superstition and about one Jesus, who was dead, but whom Paul asserted to be alive.

Jerusalem Bible

tal crime, I do not ask to be spared the death penalty. But if there is no substance in the accusations these persons bring against me, no one has a right to surrender me to them. I appeal to Caesar." 12 Then Festus conferred with his advisers and replied, "You have appealed to Caesar; to Caesar you shall go."

Paul appears before King Agrippa

13 Some days later King Agrippa and Bernice[u] arrived in Caesarea and paid their respects to Festus. 14 Their visit lasted several days, and Festus put Paul's case before the king. "There is a man here," he said, "whom Felix left behind in custody, 15 and while I was in Jerusalem the chief priests and elders of the Jews laid information against him, demanding his condemnation. 16 But I told them that Romans are not in the habit of surrendering any man, until the accused confronts his accusers and is given an opporunity to defend himself against the charge. 17 So they came here with me, and I wasted no time but took my seat on the tribunal the very next day and had the man brought in. 18 When confronted with him, his accusers did not charge him with any of the crimes I had expected; 19 but they had some argument or other with him about their own religion and about a dead man called

[u] Agrippa, Bernice and Drusilla (24:24) were children of Herod Agrippa I

New English Bible

capital crime, I do not ask to escape the death penalty; but if there is no substance in the charges which these men bring against me, it is not open to anyone to hand me over as a sop to them. I appeal to Caesar!' Then Festus, after conferring with his advisers, replied, 'You have appealed to Caesar: to Caesar you shall go.'

After an interval of some days King Agrippa and Bernice arrived at Caesarea on a courtesy visit to Festus. They spent several days there, and during this time Festus laid Paul's case before the king. 'We have a man', he said, 'left in custody by Felix; and when I was in Jerusalem the chief priests and elders of the Jews laid an information against him, demanding his condemnation. I answered them, "It is not Roman practice to hand over any accused man before he is confronted with his accusers and given an opportunity of answering the charge." So when they had come here with me I lost no time; the very next day I took my seat in court and ordered the man to be brought up. But when his accusers rose to speak, they brought none of the charges I was expecting; they merely had certain points of disagreement with him about their peculiar religion, and about someone called Jesus, a dead man whom Paul alleged to be

King James Version

dead, whom Paul affirmed to be alive. 20And because I doubted of such manner of questions, I asked *him* whether he would go to Jerusalem, and there be judged of these matters. 21 But when Paul had appealed to be reserved unto the hearing of Augustus, I commanded him to be kept till I might send him to Cesar. 22 Then Agrippa said unto Festus, I would also hear the man myself. To morrow, said he, thou shalt hear him. 23And on the morrow, when Agrippa was come, and Bernice, with great pomp, and was entered into the place of hearing, with the chief captains, and principal men of the city, at Festus' commandment Paul was brought forth. 24And Festus said, King Agrippa, and all men which are here present with us, ye see this man, about whom all the multitude of the Jews have dealt with me, both at Jerusalem, and *also* here, crying that he ought not to live any longer. 25 But when I found that he had committed nothing worthy of death, and that he himself hath appealed to Augustus, I have determined to send him. 26 Of whom I have no certain thing to write unto my lord. Wherefore I have brought him forth before you, and specially before thee, O king Agrippa, that, after examination had, I

Living Bible

but Paul insists is alive! 20 I was perplexed as to how to decide a case of this kind and asked him whether he would be willing to stand trial on these charges in Jerusalem. 21 But Paul appealed to Caesar! So I ordered him back to jail until I could arrange to get him to the Emperor."

22 "I'd like to hear the man myself," Agrippa said.

And Festus replied, "You shall—tomorrow!"

23 So the next day, after the king and Bernice had arrived at the courtroom with great pomp, accompanied by military officers and prominent men of the city, Festus ordered Paul brought in.

24 Then Festus addressed the audience: "King Agrippa and all present," he said, "this is the man whose death is demanded both by the local Jews and by those in Jerusalem! 25 But in my opinion he has done nothing worthy of death. However, he appealed his case to Caesar, and I have no alternative but to send him. 26 But what shall I write the Emperor? For there is no real charge against him! So I have brought him before you all, and especially you, King Agrippa,

Today's English Version

died; but Paul claims that he is alive. 20 I was undecided about how I could get information on these matters, so I asked Paul if he would be willing to go to Jerusalem and be tried there on these charges. 21 But Paul appealed; he asked to be kept under guard and let the Emperor decide his case. So I gave orders for him to be kept under guard until I could send him to the Emperor."

22 Agrippa said to Festus, "I would like to hear this man myself."

"You will hear him tomorrow," Festus answered.

23 The next day Agrippa and Bernice came with great pomp and ceremony, and entered the audience hall with the military chiefs and the leading men of the city. Festus gave the order and Paul was brought in. 24 Festus said, "King Agrippa, and all who are here with us: You see this man against whom all the Jewish people, both here and in Jerusalem, have brought complaints to me. They scream that he should not live any longer. 25 But I could not find that he had done anything for which he deserved the death sentence. And since he himself made an appeal to the Emperor, I have decided to send him. 26 But I do not have anything definite about him to write to the Emperor. So I have brought him here before you—and especially before you, King Agrippa!—so that, after investi-

New International Version

named Jesus who Paul claimed was alive. 20 I was at a loss how to investigate such matters; so I asked if he would be willing to go to Jerusalem and stand trial there on these charges. 21 When Paul made his appeal to be held over for the Emperor's decision, I ordered him held until I could send him to Caesar."

22 Then Agrippa said to Festus, "I would like to hear this man myself."

He replied, "Tomorrow you will hear him."

Paul before Agrippa

23 The next day Agrippa and Bernice came with great pomp and entered the audience room with the high ranking officers and the leading men of the city. At the command of Festus, Paul was brought in. 24 Festus said: "King Agrippa, and all who are present with us, you see this man! The whole Jewish community has petitioned me about him in Jerusalem and here in Caesarea, shouting that he ought not to live any longer. 25 I found he had done nothing deserving of death, but because he made his appeal to the Emperor I decided to send him to Rome. 26 But I have nothing definite to write to His Majesty about him. Therefore I have brought him before all of you, and especially before you, King Agrippa, so that as a result of

Phillips Modern English

whom Paul claimed to be still alive. I did not feel qualified to investigate such matters and so I asked the man if he were willing to go to Jerusalem and stand his trial over these matters there. But when Paul appealed to be kept in custody for the decision of the Emperor himself, I ordered him to be detained until such time as I could send him to Caesar."

Then Agrippa said to Festus,

"I have been wanting to hear this man myself."

"Then you shall hear him tomorrow," replied Festus.

25.23 Festus formally explains the difficulty of Paul's case

When the next day came, Agrippa and Bernice proceeded to the audience chamber with great pomp and ceremony, with an escort of military officers and prominent townsmen. Festus ordered Paul to be brought in and then he spoke:

"King Agrippa and all of you who are present, you see here the man about whom the whole Jewish people both at Jerusalem and in this city have petitioned me. They din it into my ears that he ought not to live any longer, but I for my part discovered nothing that he has done which deserves the death penalty. And since he has appealed to Caesar, I have decided to send him to Rome. But I have nothing specific to write to the emperor about him, and I have therefore brought him forward before you all, and especially before you, King Agrippa, so that from your ex-

Revised Standard Version

20 Being at a loss how to investigate these questions, I asked whether he wished to go to Jerusalem and be tried there regarding them. 21 But when Paul had appealed to be kept in custody for the decision of the emperor, I commanded him to be held until I could send him to Caesar." 22And Agrippa said to Festus, "I should like to hear the man myself." "Tomorrow," said he, "you shall hear him."

23 So on the morrow Agrippa and Bernice came with great pomp, and they entered the audience hall with the military tribunes and the prominent men of the city. Then by command of Festus Paul was brought in. 24And Festus said, "King Agrippa and all who are present with us, you see this man about whom the whole Jewish people petitioned me, both at Jerusalem and here, shouting that he ought not to live any longer. 25 But I found that he had done nothing deserving death; and as he himself appealed to the emperor, I decided to send him. 26 But I have nothing definite to write to my lord about him. Therefore I have brought him before you, and, especially before you, King

Jerusalem Bible

Jesus whom Paul alleged to be alive. 20 Not feeling qualified to deal with questions of this sort, I asked him if he would be willing to go to Jerusalem to be tried there on this issue. 21 But Paul put in an appeal for his case to be reserved for the judgment of the august emperor, so I ordered him to be remanded until I could send him to Caesar." 22Agrippa said to Festus, "I should like to hear the man myself." "Tomorrow," he answered, "you shall hear him."

23 So the next day Agrippa and Bernice arrived in great state and entered the audience chamber attended by the tribunes and the city notables; and Festus ordered Paul to be brought in. 24 Then Festus said, "King Agrippa, and all here present with us, you see before you the man about whom the whole Jewish community has petitioned me, both in Jerusalem and here, loudly protesting that he ought not to be allowed to remain alive. 25 For my own part I am satisfied that he has committed no capital crime, but when he himself appealed to the august emperor I decided to send him. 26 But I have nothing definite that I can write to his Imperial Majesty about him; that is why I have produced him before you all, and before you in particular, King Agrippa, so that after the

New English Bible

alive. Finding myself out of my depth in such discussions, I asked if he was willing to go to Jerusalem and stand his trial there on these issues. But Paul appealed to be remanded in custody for His Imperial Majesty's decision, and I ordered him to be detained until I could send him to the Emperor.' Agrippa said to Festus, 'I should rather like to hear the man myself.' 'Tomorrow', he answered, 'you shall hear him.'

So next day Agrippa and Bernice came in full state and entered the audience-chamber accompanied by high-ranking officers and prominent citizens; and on the orders of Festus Paul was brought up. Then Festus said, 'King Agrippa, and all you gentlemen here present with us, you see this man: the whole body of the Jews approached me both in Jerusalem and here, loudly insisting that he had no right to remain alive. But it was clear to me that he had committed no capital crime, and when he himself appealed to His Imperial Majesty, I decided to send him. But I have nothing definite about him to put in writing for our Sovereign. Accordingly I have brought him up before you all and particularly before you, King Agrippa, so that as a result of

King James Version

might have somewhat to write. 27 For it seemeth to me unreasonable to send a prisoner, and not withal to signify the crimes *laid* against him.

26 Then Agrippa said unto Paul, Thou art permitted to speak for thyself. Then Paul stretched forth the hand, and answered for himself: 2 I think myself happy, king Agrippa, because I shall answer for myself this day before thee touching all the things whereof I am accused of the Jews: 3 Especially *because I know* thee to be expert in all customs and questions which are among the Jews: wherefore I beseech thee to hear me patiently. 4 My manner of life from my youth, which was at the first among mine own nation at Jerusalem, know all the Jews; 5 Which knew me from the beginning, if they would testify, that after the most straitest sect of our religion I lived a Pharisee. 6 And now I stand and am judged for the hope of the promise made of God unto our fathers: 7 Unto which

Living Bible

to examine him and then tell me what to write. 27 For it doesn't seem reasonable to send a prisoner to the Emperor without any charges against him!"

26 Then Agrippa said to Paul, "Go ahead. Tell us your story."

So Paul, with many gestures,[a] presented his defense:

2 "I am fortunate, King Agrippa," he began, "to be able to present my answer before you, 3 for I know you are an expert on Jewish laws and customs. Now please listen patiently!

4 "As the Jews are well aware, I was given a thorough Jewish training from my earliest childhood in Tarsus[b] and later at Jerusalem, and I lived accordingly. 5 If they would admit it, they know that I have always been the strictest of Pharisees when it comes to obedience to Jewish laws and customs. 6 But the real reason behind their accusations is something else—it is because I am looking forward to the fulfillment of God's promise made to our ancestors. 7 The

[a] Literally, "stretched forth his hand." [b] Literally, "my own nation."

Today's English Version

gating his case, I may have something to write. 27 For it seems unreasonable to me to send a prisoner without clearly indicating the charges against him."

Paul defends himself before Agrippa

26 Agrippa said to Paul, "You have permission to speak on your own behalf." Paul stretched out his hand and defended himself as follows:

2 "King Agrippa! I consider myself fortunate that today I am to defend myself before you from all the things the Jews accuse me of. 3 This is especially true because you know so well all the Jewish customs and questions. I ask you, then, to listen to me with patience.

4 "All the Jews know how I have lived ever since I was young. They know from the beginning how I have spent my whole life in my own country and in Jerusalem. 5 They have always known, if they are willing to testify, that from the very first I have lived as a member of the strictest party of our religion, the Pharisees. 6 And now I stand here to be tried because I hope in the promise that God made to our ancestors—7 the very promise that all twelve tribes

New International Version

this investigation I may have something to write. 27 For I think it is unreasonable to send on a prisoner without specifying the charges against him."

26 Then Agrippa said to Paul, "You have permission to speak for yourself."

So Paul motioned with his hand and began his defense: 2 "King Agrippa, I consider myself fortunate to stand before you today as I make my defense against all the accusations of the Jews, 3 and especially so because you are well acquainted with all the Jewish customs and controversies. Therefore, I beg you to listen to me patiently.

4 "The Jews all know the way I have lived ever since I was a child, from the beginning of my life in my own country, and also in Jerusalem. 5 They have known me for a long time and can testify, if they are willing, that according to the strictest sect of our religion, I lived as a Pharisee. 6 And now it is because of my hope in what God has promised our fathers that I am on trial today. 7 This is the promise our twelve

Phillips Modern English

amination of him there may emerge some charge which I may put in writing. For it seems senseless to me to send a prisoner before the emperor without indicating the charges against him."

Then Agrippa said to Paul,
"You have our permission to speak for yourself."

26.1b Paul repeats his story on a state occasion

So Paul, with a gesture of the hand, began his defence:
"King Agrippa, in answering all the charges that the Jews have made against me, I must say how fortunate I consider myself to be in making my defence before you personally today. For I know that you are thoroughly familiar with all the customs and disputes that exist among the Jews. I therefore ask you to listen to me patiently.
"The fact that I lived from my youth upwards among my own people in Jerusalem is well known to all Jews. They have known all the time, and could witness to the fact if they wished, that I lived as a Pharisee according to the strictest sect of our religion. Even today I stand here on trial because of a hope that I hold in a promise that God made to our forefathers—a promise

Revised Standard Version

Agrippa, that, after we have examined him, I
may have something to write. 27 For it seems to
me unreasonable, in sending a prisoner, not to
indicate the charges against him."

26 Agrippa said to Paul, "You have permission to speak for yourself." Then Paul
stretched out his hand and made his defense:
2 "I think myself fortunate that it is before
you, King Agrippa, I am to make my defense
today against all the accusations of the Jews,
3 because you are especially familiar with all
customs and controversies of the Jews; therefore I beg you to listen to me patiently.
4 "My manner of life from my youth, spent
from the beginning among my own nation and
at Jerusalem, is known by all the Jews. 5 They
have known for a long time, if they are willing
to testify, that according to the strictest party of
our religion I have lived as a Pharisee. 6 And
now I stand here on trial for hope in the promise
made by God to our fathers, 7 to which our

Jerusalem Bible

examination I may have something to write.
27 It seems to me pointless to send a prisoner
without indicating the charges against him."

26 Then Agrippa said to Paul, "You have
leave to speak on your own behalf." And
Paul held up his hand and began his defense:

Paul's speech before King Agrippa

2 "I consider myself fortunate, King Agrippa,
in that it is before you I am to answer today
all the charges made against me by the Jews,
3 the more so because you are an expert in
matters of custom and controversy among the
Jews. So I beg you to listen to me patiently.
4 "My manner of life from my youth, a life
spent from the beginning among my own people and in Jerusalem, is common knowledge
among the Jews. 5 They have known me for a
long time and could testify, if they would, that
I followed the strictest party in our religion
and lived as a Pharisee. 6 And now it is for my
hope in the promise made by God to our ancestors that I am on trial, 7 the promise that

New English Bible

this preliminary inquiry I may have something to report. There is no sense, it seems to me, in sending on a prisoner without indicating the charges against him.'

26 Agrippa said to Paul, 'You have our permission to speak for yourself.' Then Paul stretched out his hand and began his defence:
'I consider myself fortunate, King Agrippa, that it is before you that I am to make my defence today upon all the charges brought against me by the Jews, particularly as you are expert in all Jewish matters, both our customs and our disputes. And therefore I beg you to give me a patient hearing.
'My life from my youth up, the life I led from the beginning among my people and in Jerusalem, is familiar to all Jews. Indeed they have known me long enough and could testify, if they only would, that I belonged to the strictest group in our religion: I lived as a Pharisee. And it is for a hope kindled by God's promise to our forefathers that I stand in the dock today. Our

King James Version

promise our twelve tribes, instantly serving *God* day and night, hope to come. For which hope's sake, king Agrippa, I am accused of the Jews. 8 Why should it be thought a thing incredible with you, that God should raise the dead? 9 I verily thought with myself, that I ought to do many things contrary to the name of Jesus of Nazareth. 10 Which thing I also did in Jerusalem: and many of the saints did I shut up in prison, having received authority from the chief priests; and when they were put to death, I gave my voice against *them*. 11 And I punished them oft in every synagogue, and compelled *them* to blaspheme; and being exceedingly mad against them, I persecuted *them* even unto strange cities. 12 Whereupon as I went to Damascus with authority and commission from the chief priests, 13 At midday, O king, I saw in the way a light from heaven, above the brightness of the sun, shining round about me and them which journeyed with me. 14 And when we were all fallen to the earth, I heard a voice speaking unto me, and saying in the Hebrew tongue, Saul, Saul, why persecutest thou me? *it is* hard for thee to kick against the pricks. 15 And I said, Who art thou, Lord? And he said, I am Jesus whom thou persecutest. 16 But rise, and stand upon thy feet: for I have appeared unto thee for this purpose, to make thee a minister and a witness both of these things which thou hast seen, and of those things in the which I will appear unto thee;

Living Bible

twelve tribes of Israel strive night and day to attain this same hope I have! Yet, O King, for me it is a crime, they say! 8 But is it a crime to believe in the resurrection of the dead? Does it seem incredible to you that God can bring men back to life again?

9 "I used to believe that I ought to do many horrible things to the followers[c] of Jesus of Nazareth. 10 I imprisoned many of the saints in Jerusalem, as authorized by the High Priests; and when they were condemned to death, I cast my vote against them. 11 I used torture to try to make Christians everywhere curse Christ. I was so violently opposed to them that I even hounded them in distant cities in foreign lands.

12 "I was on such a mission to Damascus, armed with the authority and commission of the chief priests, 13 when one day about noon, sir, a light from heaven brighter than the sun shone down on me and my companions. 14 We all fell down, and I heard a voice speaking to me in Hebrew, 'Saul, Saul, why are you persecuting me? You are only hurting yourself.'[d]

15 " 'Who are you, sir?' I asked.

"And the Lord replied, 'I am Jesus, the one you are persecuting. 16 Now stand up! For I have appeared to you to appoint you as my servant and my witness. You are to tell the world about this experience and about the many other occasions when I shall appear to you.

[*c*] Literally, "the name." [*d*] Literally, "It is hard for you to kick against the oxgoad!"

Today's English Version

of our people hope to receive, as they worship God day and night. And it is because of this hope, your Majesty, that I am being accused by the Jews! 8 Why do you Jews find it impossible to believe that God raises the dead?

9 "I myself thought that I should do everything I could against the name of Jesus of Nazareth. 10 That is what I did in Jerusalem. I received authority from the chief priests and put many of God's people in prison; and when they were sentenced to death, I also voted for it. 11 Many times I had them punished in all the synagogues, and tried to make them deny their faith. I was so furious with them that I even went to foreign cities to persecute them."

Paul tells of his conversion

12 "It was for this purpose that I went to Damascus with the authority and orders from the chief priests. 13 It was on the road at midday, your Majesty, that I saw a light much brighter than the sun shining from the sky around me and the men traveling with me. 14 All of us fell to the ground, and I heard a voice say to me in the Hebrew language, 'Saul, Saul! Why are you persecuting me? You hurt yourself by hitting back, like an ox kicking against its owner's stick.' 15 'Who are you, Lord?' I asked. And the Lord said: 'I am Jesus, whom you persecute. 16 But get up and stand on your feet. I have appeared to you to appoint you as my servant; you are to tell others what you have seen of me today, and what I will show

New International Version

tribes are hoping to see fulfilled as they earnestly serve God day and night. Your Majesty, it is because of this hope that the Jews are accusing me. 8 Why should any of you consider it incredible that God raises the dead?

9 "I too was convinced that I ought to do all that was possible to oppose the name of Jesus of Nazareth. 10 And that is just what I did in Jerusalem. On the authority of the chief priests I put many of the saints in prison, and when they were put to death, I cast my vote against them. 11 Many a time I went from one synagogue to another to have them punished, and I tried to force them to blaspheme. In my obsession against them, I even went to foreign cities to persecute them.

12 "On one of these journeys I was going to Damascus with the authority and commission of the chief priests. 13 About noon, Your Majesty, as I was on the road, I saw a light from heaven, brighter than the sun, blazing around me and my companions. 14 We all fell to the ground, and I heard a voice saying to me in Aramaic,[l] 'Saul, Saul, why do you persecute me? It is hard for you to kick against the goads.'

15 "Then I asked, 'Who are you, Lord?'

" 'I am Jesus, whom you are persecuting,' the Lord replied. 16 'Now get up and stand on your feet. I have appeared to you to appoint you as a servant and as a witness of what you have

[*l*] Or *Hebrew*.

Phillips Modern English

for which our twelve tribes serve God zealously day and night, hoping to see it fulfilled. It is about this hope, your majesty, that I am being accused by Jews! Why does it seem incredible to you all that God should raise the dead? I once thought it my duty to oppose with the utmost vigour the name of Jesus of Nazareth. Yes, that is what I did in Jerusalem, and I had many of God's people imprisoned on the authority of the chief priests, and when they were condemned to death I gave my vote against them. Many and many a time in all the synagogues I had them punished and I used to try and force them to deny their Lord. I was mad with fury against them, and I hounded them even to distant cities. Once, your majesty, on my way to Damascus on this business, armed with the full authority and commission of the chief priests, at midday I saw a light from the sky, far brighter than the sun, blazing about me and my fellow-travellers. We all fell to the ground and I heard a voice saying to me in Hebrew, 'Saul, Saul, why are you persecuting me? It is hard for you to kick against your own conscience.' 'Who are you, Lord?' I said. And the Lord said to me, 'I am Jesus whom you are persecuting. Now get up and stand on your feet for I have shown myself to you for a reason—you are chosen to be my servant and a witness of what you have seen of me today, and of visions of me which you will

Revised Standard Version

twelve tribes hope to attain, as they earnestly
worship night and day. And for this hope I am
accused by Jews, O king! 8 Why is it thought
incredible by any of you that God raises the
dead?
9 "I myself was convinced that I ought to do
many things in opposing the name of Jesus of
Nazareth. 10 And I did so in Jerusalem; I not
only shut up many of the saints in prison, by
authority from the chief priests, but when they
were put to death I cast my vote against them.
11 And I punished them often in all the synagogues and tried to make them blaspheme; and
in raging fury against them, I persecuted them
even to foreign cities.
12 "Thus I journeyed to Damascus with the
authority and commission of the chief priests.
13 At midday, O king, I saw on the way a light
from heaven, brighter than the sun, shining
round me and those who journeyed with me.
14 And when we had all fallen to the ground, I
heard a voice saying to me in the Hebrew language, 'Saul, Saul, why do you persecute me? It
hurts you to kick against the goads.' 15 And I
said, 'Who are you, Lord?' And the Lord said,
'I am Jesus whom you are persecuting. 16 But
rise and stand upon your feet; for I have appeared to you for this purpose, to appoint you
to serve and bear witness to the things in which
you have seen me and to those in which I will

Jerusalem Bible

our twelve tribes, constant in worship night and
day, hope to attain. For that hope, Sire, I am
actually put on trial by Jews! 8 Why does it
seem incredible to you that God should raise
the dead?
9 "As for me, I once thought it was my
duty to use every means to oppose the name
of Jesus the Nazarene. 10 This I did in Jerusalem; I myself threw many of the saints into
prison, acting on authority from the chief priests,
and when they were sentenced to death I cast
my vote against them. 11 I often went around
the synagogues inflicting penalties, trying in this
way to force them to renounce their faith; my
fury against them was so extreme that I even
pursued them into foreign cities.
12 "On one such expedition I was going to
Damascus, armed with full powers and a commission from the chief priests, 13 and at midday as I was on my way, your Majesty, I saw
a light brighter than the sun come down from
heaven. It shone brilliantly around me and my
fellow travelers. 14 We all fell to the ground,
and I heard a voice saying to me in Hebrew,
"Saul, Saul, why are you persecuting me? It is
hard for you, kicking like this against the
goad." [v] 15 Then I said: Who are you, Lord?
And the Lord answered, 'I am Jesus, and you
are persecuting me. 16 But get up and stand on
your feet, for I have appeared to you for this
reason: to appoint you as my servant and as
witness of this vision in which you have seen
me, and of others in which I shall appear to

[v] Greek proverbial expression for useless resistance.

New English Bible

twelve tribes hope to see the fulfilment of that promise, worshipping with intense devotion day and night; and for this very hope I am impeached, and impeached by Jews, Your Majesty. Why is it considered incredible among you that God should raise dead men to life?

'I myself once thought it my duty to work actively against the name of Jesus of Nazareth; and I did so in Jerusalem. It was I who imprisoned many of God's people by authority obtained from the chief priests; and when they were condemned to death, my vote was cast against them. In all the synagogues I tried by repeated punishment to make them renounce their faith; indeed my fury rose to such a pitch that I extended my persecution to foreign cities.

'On one such occasion I was travelling to Damascus with authority and commission from the chief priests; and as I was on my way, Your Majesty, in the middle of the day I saw a light from the sky, more brilliant than the sun, shining all around me and my travelling-companions. We all fell to the ground, and then I heard a voice saying to me in the Jewish language, "Saul, Saul, why do you persecute me? It is hard for you, this kicking against the goad." I said, "Tell me, Lord, who you are"; and the Lord replied, "I am Jesus, whom you are persecuting. But now, rise to your feet and stand upright. I have appeared to you for a purpose: to appoint you my servant and witness, to testify both to what you have seen and to what you shall yet see of

King James Version

17 Delivering thee from the people, and *from* the Gentiles, unto whom now I send thee, 18 To open their eyes, *and* to turn *them* from darkness to light, and *from* the power of Satan unto God, that they may receive forgiveness of sins, and inheritance among them which are sanctified by faith that is in me. 19 Whereupon, O king Agrippa, I was not disobedient unto the heavenly vision: 20 But shewed first unto them of Damascus, and at Jerusalem, and throughout all the coasts of Judea, and *then* to the Gentiles, that they should repent and turn to God, and do works meet for repentance. 21 For these causes the Jews caught me in the temple, and went about to kill *me*. 22 Having therefore obtained help of God, I continue unto this day, witnessing both to small and great, saying none other things than those which the prophets and Moses did say should come: 23 That Christ should suffer, *and* that he should be the first that should rise from the dead, and should shew light unto the people, and to the Gentiles. 24 And as he thus spake for himself, Festus said with a loud voice, Paul, thou art beside thyself; much learning doth make thee mad. 25 But he said, I am not mad, most noble Festus; but speak forth the words of truth and soberness. 26 For the king knoweth of these things, before whom also I speak freely: for I am persuaded

Living Bible

17 And I will protect you from both your own people and the Gentiles. Yes, I am going to send you to the Gentiles 18 to open their eyes to their true condition so that they may repent and live in the light of God instead of in Satan's darkness, so that they may receive forgiveness for their sins and God's inheritance along with all people everywhere whose sins are cleansed away, who are set apart by faith in me.'

19 "And so, O King Agrippa, I was not disobedient to that vision from heaven! 20 I preached first to those in Damascus, then in Jerusalem and through Judea, and also to the Gentiles that all must forsake their sins and turn to God—and prove their repentance by doing good deeds. 21 The Jews arrested me in the Temple for preaching this, and tried to kill me, 22 but God protected me so that I am still alive today to tell these facts to everyone, both great and small. I teach nothing except what the prophets and Moses said—23 that the Messiah would suffer, and be the First to rise from the dead, to bring light to Jews and Gentiles alike."

24 Suddenly Festus shouted, "Paul, you are insane. Your long studying has broken your mind!"

25 But Paul replied, "I am not insane, Most Excellent Festus. I speak words of sober truth. 26 And King Agrippa knows about these things. I speak frankly for I am sure these events are

Today's English Version

you in the future. 17 I will save you from the people of Israel and from the Gentiles, to whom I will send you. 18 You are to open their eyes and turn them from the darkness to the light, and from the power of Satan to God, so that through their faith in me they will have their sins forgiven and receive their place among God's chosen people.' "

Paul tells of his work

19 "And so, King Agrippa, I did not disobey the vision I had from heaven. 20 First in Damascus and in Jerusalem, and then in the whole country of the Jews and among the Gentiles, I preached that they must repent of their sins and turn to God, and do the things that would show they had repented. 21 It was for this reason that the Jews seized me while I was in the temple, and tried to kill me. 22 But to this very day I have been helped by God, and so I stand here giving my witness to all, to the small and great alike. What I say is the very same thing the prophets and Moses said was going to happen: 23 that the Messiah must suffer and be the first one to rise from death, to announce the light of salvation to the Jews and to the Gentiles."

24 As Paul defended himself in this way, Festus shouted at him, "You are mad, Paul! Your great learning is driving you mad!"

25 Paul answered, "I am not mad, your Excellency! The words I speak are true and sober. 26 King Agrippa! I can speak to you with all boldness, because you know about these things.

New International Version

seen of me and what I will show you. 17 I will rescue you from your own people and from the Gentiles. I am sending you 18 to open their eyes and turn them from darkness to light, and from the power of Satan to God, so that they may receive forgiveness of sins and a place among those who are sanctified by faith in me.'

19 "So then, King Agrippa, I was not disobedient to the vision from heaven. 20 First to those in Damascus, then to those in Jerusalem and in all Judea, and to the Gentiles also, I preached that they should repent and turn to God and prove their repentance by their deeds. 21 That is why the Jews seized me in the temple courts and tried to kill me. 22 But I have had God's help to this very day, and so I stand here and testify to small and great alike. I am saying nothing beyond what the prophets and Moses said would happen—23 that the Christ[m] would suffer and, as the first to rise from the dead, would proclaim light to his own people and to the Gentiles."

24 At this point Festus interrupted Paul's defense. "You are out of your mind, Paul!" he shouted. "Your great learning is driving you insane."

25 "I am not insane, most excellent Festus," Paul replied. "What I am saying is true and reasonable. 26 The king is familiar with these things, and I can speak freely to him. I am

[m] Or *Messiah*.

Phillips Modern English

see. I will rescue you both from your own people and from the gentiles to whom I now send you. I send you to open their eyes, to turn them from darkness to light, from the power of Satan to God, so that they may know forgiveness of their sins and take their place with all those who are made holy by their faith in me.'

"After that, King Agrippa, I could not disobey the heavenly vision. But first in Damascus and then in Jerusalem, through the whole of Judaea, and to the gentiles, I preached that men should repent and turn to God and live lives to prove their change of heart. This is why the Jews seized me in the Temple and tried to murder me. To this day I have received help from God himself, and I stand here as a witness to high and low, adding nothing to what the prophets and Moses foretold should take place, that is, that Christ should suffer, that he should be the first to rise from the dead, and so proclaim the message of light both to our people and to the gentiles!"

26.24 Festus concludes that Paul's enthusiasm is insanity

While he was thus defending himself Festus burst out,

"You are raving, Paul! All your learning has driven you mad!"

But Paul replied,

"I am not mad, your excellency. I speak nothing but the sober truth. The king knows of these matters, and I can speak freely before him. I

Revised Standard Version

appear to you, 17 delivering you from the people
and from the Gentiles—to whom I send you
18 to open their eyes, that they may turn from
darkness to light and from the power of Satan
to God, that they may receive forgiveness of
sins and a place among those who are sanctified
by faith in me.'
19 "Wherefore, O King Agrippa, I was not
disobedient to the heavenly vision, 20 but declared first to those at Damascus, then at Jerusalem and throughout all the country of Judea,
and also to the Gentiles, that they should repent and turn to God and perform deeds worthy
of their repentance. 21 For this reason the Jews
seized me in the temple and tried to kill me.
22 To this day I have had the help that comes
from God, and so I stand here testifying both
to small and great, saying nothing but what the
prophets and Moses said would come to pass:
23 that the Christ must suffer, and that, by being
the first to rise from the dead, he would proclaim light both to the people and to the Gentiles."
24 And as he thus made his defense, Festus
said with a loud voice, "Paul, you are mad;
your great learning is turning you mad." 25 But
Paul said, "I am not mad, most excellent Festus,
but I am speaking the sober truth. 26 For the
king knows about these things, and to him I

Jerusalem Bible

you. 17 *I shall deliver you* from the people and
from the pagans, to whom I am sending you
18 *to open their eyes,* so that they may turn
from darkness to light,[w] from the dominion of
Satan to God, and receive, through faith in me,
forgiveness of their sins and a share in the inheritance of the sanctified.'
19 "After that, King Agrippa, I could not disobey the heavenly vision. 20 On the contrary I
started preaching first to the people of Damascus, then to those of Jerusalem and all the
countryside of Judaea, and also to the pagans,
urging them to repent and turn to God, proving
their change of heart by their deeds. 21 This
was why the Jews laid hands on me in the Temple and tried to do away with me. 22 But I was
blessed with God's help, and so I have stood
firm to this day, testifying to great and small
alike, saying nothing more than what the prophets and Moses himself said would happen:
23 that the Christ was to suffer and that, as the
first to rise from the dead, he was to proclaim
that light now shone for our people and for the
pagans too."

His hearers' reactions

24 He had reached this point in his defense
when Festus shouted out, "Paul, you are out of
your mind; all that learning of yours is driving
you mad." 25 "Festus, your Excellency," answered Paul, "I am not mad: I am speaking
nothing but the sober truth. 26 The king understands these matters, and to him I now speak

[w] Quotations from Jr. 1; Is. 42; Is. 9.

New English Bible

me. I will rescue you from this people and from the Gentiles to whom I am sending you. I send you to open their eyes and turn them from darkness to light, from the dominion of Satan to God, so that, by trust in me, they may obtain forgiveness of sins, and a place with those whom God has made his own."

'And so, King Agrippa, I did not disobey the heavenly vision. I turned first to the inhabitants of Damascus, and then to Jerusalem and all the country of Judaea, and to the Gentiles, and sounded the call to repent and turn to God, and to prove their repentance by deeds. That is why the Jews seized me in the temple and tried to do away with me. But I had God's help, and so to this very day I stand and testify to great and small alike. I assert nothing beyond what was foretold by the prophets and by Moses: that the Messiah must suffer, and that he, the first to rise from the dead, would announce the dawn to Israel and to the Gentiles.'

While Paul was thus making his defence, Festus shouted at the top of his voice, 'Paul, you are raving; too much study is driving you mad.' 'I am not mad, Your Excellency,' said Paul; 'what I am saying is sober truth. The king is well versed in these matters, and to him I can

King James Version

that none of these things are hidden from him;
for this thing was not done in a corner. 27 King
Agrippa, believest thou the prophets? I know
that thou believest. 28 Then Agrippa said unto
Paul, Almost thou persuadest me to be a Christian. 29 And Paul said, I would to God, that not
only thou, but also all that hear me this day,
were both almost, and altogether such as I am,
except these bonds. 30 And when he had thus
spoken, the king rose up, and the governor, and
Bernice, and they that sat with them: 31 And
when they were gone aside, they talked between
themselves, saying, This man doeth nothing worthy of death or of bonds. 32 Then said Agrippa
unto Festus, This man might have been set at
liberty, if he had not appealed unto Cesar.

27 And when it was determined that we
should sail into Italy, they delivered Paul
and certain other prisoners unto *one* named

Living Bible

all familiar to him, for they were not done in a
corner! 27 King Agrippa, do you believe the
prophets? But I know you do—"
28 Agrippa interrupted him. "With trivial
proofs like these,[e] you expect me to become a
Christian?"
29 And Paul replied, "Would to God that
whether my arguments are trivial or strong, both
you and everyone here in this audience might
become the same as I am, except for these
chains."
30 Then the king, the governor, Bernice, and
all the others stood and left. 31 As they talked it
over afterwards they agreed, "This man hasn't
done anything worthy of death or imprisonment."
32 And Agrippa said to Festus, "He could
be set free if he hadn't appealed to Caesar!"

27 Arrangements were finally made to start
us on our way to Rome by ship; so Paul
and several other prisoners were placed in the

[*e*] Literally, "with little (persuasion)."

Today's English Version

I am sure that you have taken notice of every
one of them, for this thing has not happened
hidden away in a corner. 27 King Agrippa, do
you believe the prophets? I know that you do!"
28 Agrippa said to Paul, "In this short time
do you think you will make me a Christian?"
29 "Whether a short time or a long time,"
Paul answered, "my prayer to God is that you
and all the rest of you who are listening to me
today might become what I am—except, of
course, for these chains!"
30 Then the King, the Governor, Bernice, and
all the others got up, 31 and after leaving they
said to each other, "This man has not done
anything for which he should die or be put in
prison." 32 And Agrippa said to Festus, "This
man could have been released if he had not appealed to the Emperor."

Paul sails for Rome

27 When it was decided that we should sail
to Italy, they handed Paul and some other
prisoners over to Julius, an officer in the Roman

New International Version

convinced that none of this has escaped his notice, because it was not done in a corner. 27 King
Agrippa, do you believe the prophets? I know
you do."
28 Then Agrippa said to Paul, "Do you think
that in such a short time you can persuade me
to be a Christian?"
29 Paul replied, "Short time or long—I pray
God that not only you but all who are listening
to me today may become what I am, except for
these chains."
30 The king rose, and with him the governor
and Bernice and those sitting with them. 31 They
left the room, and while talking with one another, they said, "This man is not doing anything
that deserves death or imprisonment."
32 Agrippa said to Festus, "This man could
have been set free, if he had not appealed to
Caesar."

Paul sails for Rome

27 When it was decided that we would sail
for Italy, Paul and some other prisoners
were handed over to a centurion named Julius,

Phillips Modern English

cannot believe that any of these matters has escaped his notice, for it has been no hole-and-corner business. King Agrippa, do you believe the prophets? But I know that you believe them."

"Much more of this, Paul," returned Agrippa, "and you will be making me a Christian!"

"Ah," returned Paul, "whether it means 'much more' or only a little, I would to God that both you and all who can hear me this day might become as I am—but without these chains!"

26.30 The Roman officials consider Paul innocent

Then the king rose to his feet and so did the governor and Bernice and those sitting with them, and when they had retired from the assembly they discussed the matter among themselves and agreed, "This man is doing nothing to deserve either death or imprisonment."

Agrippa said to Festus,

"This man might easily have been discharged if he had not appealed to Caesar."

27.1 The last journey begins

As soon as it was decided that we should sail to Italy, Paul and some other prisoners were put under the charge of a centurion named Julius,

Revised Standard Version

speak freely; for I am persuaded that none of these things has escaped his notice, for this was not done in a corner. 27 King Agrippa, do you believe the prophets? I know that you believe."
28 And Agrippa said to Paul, "In a short time you think to make me a Christian!" 29 And Paul said, "Whether short or long, I would to God that not only you but also all who hear me this day might become such as I am—except for these chains."

30 Then the king rose, and the governor and Bernice and those who were sitting with them;
31 and when they had withdrawn, they said to one another, "This man is doing nothing to deserve death or imprisonment." 32 And Agrippa said to Festus, "This man could have been set free if he had not appealed to Caesar."

27 And when it was decided that we should sail for Italy, they delivered Paul and some other prisoners to a centurion of the Augustan

Jerusalem Bible

with assurance, confident that nothing of all this is lost on him; after all, these things were not done in a corner. 27 King Agrippa, do you believe in the prophets? I know you do." 28 At this Agrippa said to Paul, "A little more, and your arguments would make a Christian of me."
29 "Little or more," Paul replied, "I wish before God that not only you but all who have heard me today would come to be as I am—except for these chains."

30 At this the king rose to his feet, with the governor and Bernice and those who sat there with them. 31 When they had retired they talked together and agreed, "This man is doing nothing that deserves death or imprisonment." 32 And Agrippa remarked to Festus, "The man could have been set free if he had not appealed to Caesar."

The departure for Rome

27 When it had been decided that we should sail for Italy, Paul and some other prisoners were handed over to a centurion called

New English Bible

speak freely. I do not believe that he can be unaware of any of these facts, for this has been no hole-and-corner business. King Agrippa, do you believe the prophets? I know you do.' Agrippa said to Paul, 'You think it will not take much to win me over and make a Christian of me.' 'Much or little,' said Paul, 'I wish to God that not only you, but all those also who are listening to me today, might become what I am, apart from these chains.'

With that the king rose, and with him the Governor, Bernice, and the rest of the company, and after they had withdrawn they talked it over. 'This man', they said, 'is doing nothing that deserves death or imprisonment.' Agrippa said to Festus, 'The fellow could have been discharged, if he had not appealed to the Emperor.'

27 When it was decided that we should sail for Italy, Paul and some other prisoners were handed over to a centurion named Julius,

King James Version

Julius, a centurion of Augustus' band. 2And entering into a ship of Adramyttium, we launched, meaning to sail by the coasts of Asia; *one* Aristarchus, a Macedonian of Thessalonica, being with us. 3And the next *day* we touched at Sidon. And Julius courteously entreated Paul, and gave *him* liberty to go unto his friends to refresh himself. 4And when we had launched from thence, we sailed under Cyprus, because the winds were contrary. 5And when we had sailed over the sea of Cilicia and Pamphylia, we came to Myra, *a city* of Lycia. 6And there the centurion found a ship of Alexandria sailing into Italy; and he put us therein. 7And when we had sailed slowly many days, and scarce were come over against Cnidus, the wind not suffering us, we sailed under Crete, over against Salmone; 8And, hardly passing it, came unto a place which is called the Fair Havens; nigh whereunto was the city *of* Lasea. 9 Now when much time was spent, and when sailing was now dangerous, because the fast was now already past, Paul admonished *them,* 10And said unto them, Sirs, I perceive

Living Bible

custody of an officer named Julius, a member of the imperial guard. 2 We left on a boat[a] which was scheduled to make several stops along the Turkish coast.[b] I should add that Aristarchus,[c] a Greek from Thessalonica, was with us.

3 The next day when we docked at Sidon, Julius was very kind to Paul and let him go ashore to visit with friends and receive their hospitality. 4 Putting to sea from there, we encountered headwinds that made it difficult to keep the ship on course, so we sailed north of Cyprus between the island and the mainland,[d] 5 and passed along the coast of the provinces of Cilicia and Pamphylia, landing at Myra, in the province of Lycia. 6 There our officer found an Egyptian ship from Alexandria, bound for Italy, and put us aboard.

7, 8 We had several days of rough sailing, and finally neared Cnidus;[e] but the winds had become too strong, so we ran across to Crete, passing the port of Salmone. Beating into the wind with great difficulty and moving slowly along the southern coast, we arrived at Fair Havens, near the city of Lasea. 9 There we stayed for several days. The weather was becoming dangerous for long voyages by then, because it was late in the year,[f] and Paul spoke to the ship's officers about it.

10 "Sirs," he said, "I believe there is trouble

[*a*] Literally, "a ship of Adramyttium." [*b*] Literally, "the coast of Asia." [*c*] See Acts 19:29, 20:4, Philemon 24. [*d*] Implied. Literally, "we sailed under the lee of Cyprus." Narratives from that period interpret this as meaning what is indicated in the paraphrase above. [*e*] Cnidus was a port on the southeast coast of Turkey. [*f*] Literally, "because the Fast was now already gone by." It came at about the time of the autumn equinox.

Today's English Version

army regiment called "The Emperor's Regiment." 2 We went aboard a ship from Adramyttium, which was ready to leave for the seaports of the province of Asia, and sailed away. Aristarchus, a Macedonian from Thessalonica, was with us. 3 The next day we arrived at Sidon. Julius was kind to Paul and allowed him to go and see his friends, to be given what he needed. 4 We went on from there, and because the winds were blowing against us we sailed on the sheltered side of the island of Cyprus. 5 We crossed over the sea off Cilicia and Pamphylia, and came to Myra, in Lycia. 6 There the officer found a ship from Alexandria that was going to sail for Italy, so he put us aboard.

7 We sailed slowly for several days, and with great difficulty finally arrived off the town of Cnidus. The wind would not let us go any farther in that direction, so we sailed down the sheltered side of the island of Crete, passing by Cape Salmone. 8 We kept close to the coast, and with great difficulty came to a place called Safe Harbors, not far from the town of Lasea.

9 We spent a long time there, until it became dangerous to continue the voyage, because by now the day of Atonement was already past. So Paul gave them this advice, 10 "Men, I see that

New International Version

who belonged to the Imperial Regiment. 2 We boarded a ship from Adramyttium about to sail for ports along the coast of the province of Asia, and we put out to sea. Aristarchus, a Macedonian from Thessalonica, was with us.

3 The next day we landed at Sidon; and Julius, in kindness to Paul, allowed him to go to his friends so they might provide for his needs. 4 From there we put out to sea again and passed to the lee of Cyprus because the winds were against us. 5 When we had sailed across the open sea off the coast of Cilicia and Pamphylia, we landed at Myra in Lycia. 6 There the centurion found an Alexandrian ship sailing for Italy and put us on board. 7 We made slow headway for many days and had difficulty arriving off Cnidus. When the wind did not allow us to hold our course, we sailed to the lee of Crete, opposite Salmone. 8 We moved along the coast with difficulty and came to a place called Fair Havens, near the town of Lasea.

9 Much time had been lost, and sailing had already become dangerous because by now it was after the Fast.[n] So Paul warned them, 10 "Men, I can see that our voyage is going to

[*n*] That is, the Day of Atonement (Yom Kippur).

Phillips Modern English

of the emperor's own regiment. We embarked on a ship hailing from Adramyttium, bound for the Asian ports, and set sail. Among our company was Aristarchus, a Macedonian from Thessalonica. On the following day we put in at Sidon, where Julius treated Paul most considerately by allowing him to visit his friends and accept their hospitality. From Sidon we put to sea again and sailed to leeward of Cyprus, since the winds were against us. Then, when we had crossed the gulf that lies off the coasts of Cilicia and Pamphylia, we arrived at Myra in Lycia. There the centurion found an Alexandrian ship bound for Italy and put us aboard her. For several days we beat slowly up to windward and only just succeeded in arriving off Cnidus. Then, since the wind was still blowing against us, we sailed under the lee of Crete, and rounded Cape Salmone. Coasting along with difficulty we came to a place called Fair Havens, near which is the city of Lasea. We had by now lost a great deal of time and sailing had already become dangerous as it was so late in the year. (The time of the autumn Fast was over.)

27.9b Paul's warning is disregarded

So Paul warned them, and said,

"Men, I can see that this voyage is likely to

Revised Standard Version

Cohort, named Julius. 2And embarking in a ship
of Adramyttium, which was about to sail to the
ports along the coast of Asia, we put to sea,
accompanied by Aristarchus, a Macedonian from
Thessalonica. 3 The next day we put in at Sidon;
and Julius treated Paul kindly, and gave him
leave to go to his friends and be cared for. 4And
putting to sea from there we sailed under the
lee of Cyprus, because the winds were against
us. 5And when we had sailed across the sea
which is off Cilicia and Pamphylia, we came to
Myra in Lycia. 6 There the centurion found a
ship of Alexandria sailing for Italy, and put us
on board. 7 We sailed slowly for a number of
days, and arrived with difficulty off Cnidus, and
as the wind did not allow us to go on, we sailed
under the lee of Crete off Salmone. 8 Coasting
along it with difficulty, we came to a place
called Fair Havens, near which was the city of
Lasea.
9 As much time had been lost, and the voyage
was already dangerous because the fast had already gone by, Paul advised them, 10 saying,

Jerusalem Bible

Julius, of the Augustan cohort. 2 We boarded a
vessel from Adramyttium bound for ports on the
Asiatic coast, and put to sea; we had Aristarchus
with us, a Macedonian of Thessalonika. 3 Next
day we put in at Sidon, and Julius was considerate enough to allow Paul to go to his friends
to be looked after.
4 From there we put to sea again, but as the
winds were against us we sailed under the lee
of Cyprus, 5 then across the open sea off Cilicia
and Pamphylia, taking a fortnight to reach
Myra in Lycia. 6 There the centurion found an
Alexandrian ship leaving for Italy and put us
aboard.
7 For some days we made little headway, and
we had difficulty in making Cnidus. The wind
would not allow us to touch there, so we sailed
under the lee of Crete off Cape Salmone 8 and
struggled along the coast until we came to a
place called Fair Havens, near the town of
Lasea.

Storm and shipwreck

9 A great deal of time had been lost, and
navigation was already hazardous since it was
now well after the time of the Fast,[x] so Paul
gave them this warning, 10 "Friends, I can see

[x] "the Fast," the feast of Atonement, was kept about the time of the autumn equinox; winter was coming on.

New English Bible

of the Augustan Cohort. We embarked in a ship of Adramyttium, bound for ports in the province of Asia, and put out to sea. In our party was Aristarchus, a Macedonian from Thessalonica. Next day we landed at Sidon; and Julius very considerately allowed Paul to go to his friends to be cared for. Leaving Sidon we sailed under the lee of Cyprus because of the head-winds, then across the open sea off the coast of Cilicia and Pamphylia, and so reached Myra in Lycia.

There the centurion found an Alexandrian vessel bound for Italy and put us aboard. For a good many days we made little headway, and we were hard put to it to reach Cnidus. Then, as the wind continued against us, off Salmone we began to sail under the lee of Crete, and, hugging the coast, struggled on to a place called Fair Havens, not far from the town of Lasea.

By now much time had been lost, the Fast was already over, and it was risky to go on with the voyage. Paul therefore gave them this advice: 'I can see, gentlemen,' he said, 'that this voyage

King James Version

that this voyage will be with hurt and much
damage, not only of the lading and ship, but also
of our lives. 11 Nevertheless the centurion believed the master and the owner of the ship,
more than those things which were spoken by
Paul. 12And because the haven was not com-
modious to winter in, the more part advised to
depart thence also, if by any means they might
attain to Phenice, *and there* to winter; *which is*
a haven of Crete, and lieth toward the south-
west and northwest. 13And when the south wind
blew softly, supposing that they had obtained
their purpose, loosing *thence*, they sailed close
by Crete. 14 But not long after there arose
against it a tempestuous wind, called Euroclyd-
don. 15And when the ship was caught, and
could not bear up into the wind, we let *her*
drive. 16And running under a certain island
which is called Clauda, we had much work to
come by the boat: 17 Which when they had
taken up, they used helps, undergirding the
ship; and, fearing lest they should fall into the
quicksands, strake sail, and so were driven.
18And we being exceedingly tossed with a tempest, the next *day* they lightened the ship;
19And the third *day* we cast out with our own

Living Bible

ahead if we go on—perhaps shipwreck, loss of
cargo, injuries, and death." 11 But the officers in
charge of the prisoners listened more to the
ship's captain and the owner than to Paul. 12And
since Fair Havens was an exposed[g] harbor—a
poor place to spend the winter—most of the
crew advised trying to go further up the coast to
Phoenix, in order to winter there; Phoenix was
a good harbor with only a northwest and south-
west exposure.

13 Just then a light wind began blowing from
the south, and it looked like a perfect day for
the trip; so they pulled up anchor and sailed
along close to shore.

14, 15 But shortly afterwards, the weather
changed abruptly and a heavy wind of typhoon
strength (a "northeaster," they called it) caught
the ship and blew it out to sea. They tried at
first to face back to shore but couldn't, so they
gave up and let the ship run before the gale.

16 We finally sailed behind a small island
named Clauda, where with great difficulty we
hoisted aboard the lifeboat that was being towed
behind us, 17 and then banded the ship with
ropes to strengthen the hull. The sailors were
afraid of being driven across to the quicksands
of the African coast,[h] so they lowered the top-
sails and were thus driven before the wind.

18 The next day as the seas grew higher, the
crew began throwing the cargo overboard. 19 The

[g] Implied. [h] Literally, "fearing lest they should be cast upon the Syrtis."

Today's English Version

our voyage from here on will be dangerous;
there will be great damage to the cargo and to
the ship, and loss of life as well." 11 But the
army officer was convinced by what the captain
and the owner of the ship said, and not by what
Paul said. 12 The harbor was not a good one to
spend the winter in; so most of the men were
in favor of putting out to sea and trying to
reach Phoenix, if possible. It is a harbor in
Crete that faces southwest and northwest, and
they could spend the winter there.

The storm at sea

13 A soft wind from the south began to blow,
and the men thought that they could carry out
their plan; so they pulled up the anchor and
sailed as close as possible along the coast of
Crete. 14 But soon a very strong wind—the one
called "Northeaster"—blew down from the island. 15 It hit the ship, and since it was impossible to keep the ship headed into the wind,
we gave up trying and let it be carried along
by the wind. 16 We got some shelter when we
passed to the south of the little island of Cauda.
There, with some difficulty, we managed to make
the ship's boat secure. 17 They pulled it aboard,
and then fastened some ropes tight around the
ship. They were afraid that they might run into
the sandbanks off the coast of Libya; so they
lowered the sail and let the ship be carried by
the wind. 18 The violent storm continued, so on
the next day they began to throw the ship's
cargo overboard, 19 and on the following day

New International Version

be disastrous and bring great loss to ship and
cargo, and to our own lives also." 11 But the
centurion, instead of listening to what Paul said,
followed the advice of the pilot and of the owner
of the ship. 12 Since the harbor was unsuitable
to winter in, the majority decided that we should
sail on, hoping to reach Phoenix and winter
there. This was a harbor in Crete, facing both
southwest and northwest.

The storm

13 When a gentle south wind began to blow,
they thought they had obtained what they
wanted; so they weighed anchor and sailed along
the shore of Crete. 14 Before very long, a wind
of hurricane force, called the "Northeaster,"
swept down from the island. 15 The ship was
caught by the storm and could not head into
the wind; so we gave way to it and were driven
along. 16As we passed to the lee of a small island called Cauda, we were hardly able to make
the lifeboat secure. 17 When the men had hoisted
it aboard, they tied ropes around the ship itself
to hold it together. Fearing that they would run
aground on the sandbars of Syrtis, they lowered
the sea anchor and let the ship be driven along.
18 We took such a violent battering from the
storm that the next day they began to throw the
cargo overboard. 19 On the third day, they threw

Phillips Modern English

result in damage and considerable loss—not only to ship and cargo, but even of our own lives as well."

But Julius paid more attention to the helmsman and the captain than to Paul's words of warning. Moreover, since the harbour is unsuitable for a ship to winter in, the majority were in favour of setting sail again in the hope of reaching Phoenix and wintering there. Phoenix is a harbour in Crete, facing south-west and north-west. So, when a moderate breeze sprang up, thinking they had obtained just what they wanted, they weighed anchor, and coasted along, hugging the shores of Crete. But before long a terrific gale, which they called a north-easter, swept down upon us. The ship was caught by it and since she could not be brought up into the wind we had to let her fall off and run before it. Then, running under the lee of a small island called Clauda, we managed with some difficulty to secure the ship's boat. After hoisting it aboard they used cables to undergird the ship. To add to the difficulties they were afraid all the time of difting on to the Syrtis banks, so they shortened sail and let her drift. The next day, as we were still at the mercy of the violent storm, they began to throw cargo overboard. On the third day

Revised Standard Version

"Sirs, I perceive that the voyage will be with
injury and much loss, not only of the cargo and
the ship, but also of our lives." 11 But the centurion paid more attention to the captain and
to the owner of the ship than to what Paul said.
12And because the harbor was not suitable to
winter in, the majority advised to put to sea
from there, on the chance that somehow they
could reach Phoenix, a harbor of Crete, looking
northeast and southeast,[a] and winter there.
13 And when the south wind blew gently, supposing that they had obtained their purpose, they
weighed anchor and sailed along Crete, close inshore. 14 But soon a tempestuous wind, called the
northeaster, struck down from the land; 15 and
when the ship was caught and could not face the
wind, we gave way to it and were driven. 16And
running under the lee of a small island called
Cauda,[b] we managed with difficulty to secure the
boat; 17 after hoisting it up, they took measures[c]
to undergird the ship; then, fearing that they
should run on the Syrtis, they lowered the gear,
and so were driven. 18As we were violently
storm-tossed, they began next day to throw the
cargo overboard; 19 and the third day they cast

[*a*] Or *southwest and northwest.* [*b*] Other ancient authorities read *Clauda.* [*c*] Greek *helps.*

Jerusalem Bible

this voyage will be dangerous and that we run
the risk of losing not only the cargo and the
ship but also our lives as well." 11 But the centurion took more notice of the captain and the
ship's owner than of what Paul was saying;
12 and since the harbor was unsuitable for wintering, the majority were for putting out from
there in the hope of wintering at Phoenix—a
harbor in Crete, facing southwest and northwest.
13 A southerly breeze sprang up and, thinking their objective as good as reached, they
weighed anchor and began to sail past Crete,
close inshore. 14 But it was not long before a
hurricane, the "northeaster" as they call it, burst
on them from across the island. 15 The ship
was caught and could not be turned head on
to the wind, so we had to give way to it and let
ourselves be driven. 16 We ran under the lee of
a small island called Cauda and managed with
some difficulty to bring the ship's boat under
control. 17 They hoisted it aboard and with the
help of tackle bound cables around the ship;
then, afraid of running aground on the Syrtis
banks, they floated out the sea anchor and so
let themselves drift. 18As we were making very
heavy weather of it, the next day they began
to jettison the cargo, 19 and the third day they

New English Bible

will be disastrous: it will mean grave loss, loss not only of ship and cargo but also of life.' But the centurion paid more attention to the captain and to the owner of the ship than to what Paul said; and as the harbour was unsuitable for wintering, the majority were in favour of putting out to sea, hoping, if they could get so far, to winter at Phoenix, a Cretan harbour exposed south-west and north-west. So when a southerly breeze sprang up, they thought that their purpose was as good as achieved, and, weighing anchor, they sailed along the coast of Crete hugging the land. But before very long a fierce wind, the 'North-easter' as they call it, tore down from the landward side. It caught the ship and, as it was impossible to keep head to wind, we had to give way and run before it. We ran under the lee of a small island called Cauda, and with a struggle managed to get the ship's boat under control. When they had hoisted it aboard, they made use of tackle and undergirded the ship. Then, because they were afraid of running on to the shallows of Syrtis, they lowered the mainsail and let her drive. Next day, as we were making very heavy weather, they began to lighten the ship; and on the third day they

King James Version

hands the tackling of the ship. 20And when
neither sun nor stars in many days appeared,
and no small tempest lay on *us,* all hope that we
should be saved was then taken away. 21 But
after long abstinence, Paul stood forth in the
midst of them, and said, Sirs, ye should have
hearkened unto me, and not have loosed from
Crete, and to have gained this harm and loss.
22And now I exhort you to be of good cheer:
for there shall be no loss of *any man's* life
among you, but of the ship. 23 For there stood
by me this night the angel of God, whose I
am, and whom I serve, 24 Saying, Fear not,
Paul; thou must be brought before Cesar: and,
lo, God hath given thee all them that sail with
thee. 25 Wherefore, sirs, be of good cheer: for I
believe God, that it shall be even as it was told
me. 26 Howbeit we must be cast upon a certain
island. 27 But when the fourteenth night was
come, as we were driven up and down in Adria,
about midnight the shipmen deemed that they
drew near to some country; 28And sounded,

Living Bible

following day they threw out the tackle and
anything else they could lay their hands on.
20 The terrible storm raged unabated many days,[i]
until at last all hope was gone.
21 No one had eaten for a long time, but
finally Paul called the crew together and said,
"Men, you should have listened to me in the
first place and not left Fair Havens—you would
have avoided all this injury and loss! 22 But
cheer up! Not one of us will lose our lives, even
though the ship will go down.
23 "For last night an angel of the God to
whom I belong and whom I serve stood beside
me, 24 and said, 'Don't be afraid, Paul—for you
will surely stand trial before Caesar! What's
more, God has granted your request and will
save the lives of all those sailing with you.' 25 So
take courage! For I believe God! It will be just
as he said! 26 But we will be shipwrecked on an
island."
27 About midnight on the fourteenth night
of the storm, as we were being driven to and
fro on the Adriatic Sea, the sailors suspected
land was near. 28 They sounded, and found 120

[*i*] Literally, "neither sun nor stars shone upon us."

Today's English Version

they threw the ship's equipment overboard with
their own hands. 20 For many days we could not
see the sun or the stars, and the wind kept on
blowing very hard. We finally gave up all hope
of being saved.
21 After the men had gone a long time without food, Paul stood before them and said,
"Men, you should have listened to me and not
have sailed from Crete; then we would have
avoided all this damage and loss. 22 But now I
beg you, take courage! Not one of you will lose
his life; only the ship will be lost. 23 For last
night an angel of the God to whom I belong
and whom I worship came to me 24 and said,
'Don't be afraid, Paul! You must stand before
the Emperor; and God, in his goodness, has given
you the lives of all those who are sailing with
you.' 25And so, men, take courage! For I trust
in God that it will be just as I was told. 26 But
we will be driven ashore on some island."
27 It was the fourteenth night, and we were
being driven by the storm on the Mediterranean.
About midnight the sailors suspected that we
were getting close to land. 28 So they dropped

New International Version

the ship's tackle overboard with their own hands.
20 When neither sun nor stars appeared for many
days and the storm continued raging, we finally
gave up all hope of being saved.
21 After the men had gone a long time without food, Paul stood up before them and said:
"Men, you should have taken my advice not to
sail from Crete; then you would have spared
yourselves this damage and loss. 22 But now I
urge you to keep up your courage, because not
one of you will be lost; only the ship will be
destroyed. 23 Last night an angel of the God
whose I am and whom I serve stood beside me
24 and said, 'Do not be afraid, Paul. You must
stand trial before Caesar; and God has graciously
given you the lives of all who sail with you.'
25 So keep up your courage, men, for I have
faith in God that it will happen just as he told
me. 26 Nevertheless, we must run aground on
some island."

The shipwreck

27 On the fourteenth night we were still being driven across the Adriatic Sea, when about
midnight the sailors sensed they were approaching land. 28 They took soundings and found

Phillips Modern English

with their own hands they threw the ship's tackle over the side. Then, when for many days there was no glimpse of sun or stars and we were still in the grip of the gale, all hope of our being saved was given up.

27.21 Paul's practical courage and faith

Nobody had eaten for some time, when Paul came forward among the men and said,

"Men, you should have listened to me and not have set sail from Crete and suffered this damage and loss. However, now I beg you to keep up your spirits for no one's life is going to be lost, though we shall lose the ship. I know this because last night, the angel of God to whom I belong, and whom I serve, stood by me and said, 'Have no fear, Paul! You must stand before Caesar, and God has granted you the lives of those who are sailing with you.' Take courage then, men, for I believe God, and I am certain that everything will happen exactly as I have been told. But we shall have to run the ship ashore on some island."

27.27 At last we near land

On the fourteenth night of the storm, as we were drifting in the Adriatic, about midnight the sailors sensed that we were nearing land. Indeed, when they sounded they found twenty

Revised Standard Version

out with their own hands the tackle of the ship.
20 And when neither sun nor stars appeared for
many a day, and no small tempest lay on us, all
hope of our being saved was at last abandoned.
21 As they had been long without food, Paul
then came forward among them and said, "Men,
you should have listened to me, and should not
have set sail from Crete and incurred this injury and loss. 22 I now bid you take heart; for
there will be no loss of life among you, but only
of the ship. 23 For this very night there stood by
me an angel of the God to whom I belong and
whom I worship, 24 and he said, 'Do not be
afraid, Paul; you must stand before Caesar; and
lo, God has granted you all those who sail with
you.' 25 So take heart, men, for I have faith in
God that it will be exactly as I have been told.
26 But we shall have to run on some island."
27 When the fourteenth night had come, as
we were drifting across the sea of Adria, about
midnight the sailors suspected that they were
nearing land. 28 So they sounded and found

Jerusalem Bible

threw the ship's gear overboard with their own
hands. 20 For a number of days both the sun
and the stars were invisible and the storm raged
unabated until at last we gave up all hope of
surviving.
21 Then, when they had been without food
for a long time, Paul stood up among the men.
"Friends," he said, "if you had listened to me
and not put out from Crete, you would have
spared yourselves all this damage and loss.
22 But now I ask you not to give way to despair.
There will be no loss of life at all, only of the
ship. 23 Last night there was standing beside
me an angel of the God to whom I belong and
whom I serve, 24 and he said, 'Do not be
afraid, Paul. You are destined to appear before
Caesar, and for this reason God grants you the
safety of all who are sailing with you.' 25 So
take courage, friends; I trust in God that things
will turn out just as I was told; 26 but we are
to be stranded on some island."
27 On the fourteenth night we were being
driven one way and another in the Adriatic,[y]
when about midnight the crew sensed that land
of some sort was near. 28 They took soundings

[y] The term includes the seas between Greece, Italy and Africa.

New English Bible

jettisoned the ship's gear with their own hands. For days on end there was no sign of either sun or stars, a great storm was raging, and our last hopes of coming through alive began to fade.

When they had gone for a long time without food, Paul stood up among them and said, 'You should have taken my advice, gentlemen, not to sail from Crete; then you would have avoided this damage and loss. But now I urge you not to lose heart; not a single life will be lost, only the ship. For last night there stood by me an angel of the God whose I am and whom I worship. "Do not be afraid, Paul," he said; "it is ordained that you shall appear before the Emperor; and, be assured, God has granted you the lives of all who are sailing with you." So keep up your courage: I trust in God that it will turn out as I have been told; though we have to be cast ashore on some island.'

The fourteenth night came and we were still drifting in the Sea of Adria. In the middle of the night the sailors felt that land was getting nearer. They sounded and found twenty fathoms.

King James Version

and found *it* twenty fathoms: and when they had gone a little further, they sounded again, and found *it* fifteen fathoms. 29 Then fearing lest we should have fallen upon rocks, they cast four anchors out of the stern, and wished for the day. 30 And as the shipmen were about to flee out of the ship, when they had let down the boat into the sea, under colour as though they would have cast anchors out of the foreship, 31 Paul said to the centurion and to the soldiers, Except these abide in the ship, ye cannot be saved. 32 Then the soldiers cut off the ropes of the boat, and let her fall off. 33 And while the day was coming on, Paul besought *them* all to take meat, saying, This day is the fourteenth day that ye have tarried and continued fasting, having taken nothing. 34 Wherefore I pray you to take *some* meat; for this is for your health: for there shall not a hair fall from the head of any of you. 35 And when he had thus spoken, he took bread, and gave thanks to God in presence of them all; and when he had broken *it*, he began to eat. 36 Then were they all of good cheer, and they also took *some* meat. 37 And we were in all in the ship two hundred threescore and sixteen souls. 38 And when they had eaten enough, they lightened the ship, and cast out the wheat into the sea.

Living Bible

feet of water below them. A little later they sounded again, and found only ninety feet. 29 At this rate they knew they would soon be driven ashore; and fearing rocks along the coast, they threw out four anchors from the stern and prayed for daylight.

30 Some of the sailors planned to abandon the ship, and lowered the emergency boat as though they were going to put out anchors from the prow. 31 But Paul said to the soldiers and commanding officer, "You will all die unless everyone stays aboard." 32 So the soldiers cut the ropes and let the boat fall off.

33 As the darkness gave way to the early morning light, Paul begged everyone to eat. "You haven't touched food for two weeks," he said. 34 "Please eat something now for your own good! For not a hair of your heads shall perish!"

35 Then he took some hardtack and gave thanks to God before them all, and broke off a piece and ate it. 36 Suddenly everyone felt better and began eating, 37 all two hundred seventy-six of us—for that is the number we had aboard. 38 After eating, the crew lightened the ship further by throwing all the wheat overboard.

Today's English Version

a line with a weight tied to it and found that the water was one hundred and twenty feet deep; a little later they did the same and found that it was ninety feet deep. 29 They were afraid that our ship would go on the rocks, so they lowered four anchors from the back of the ship and prayed for daylight. 30 The sailors tried to escape from the ship; they lowered the boat into the water and pretended that they were going to put out some anchors from the front of the ship. 31 But Paul said to the army officer and soldiers, "If these sailors don't stay on board, you cannot be saved." 32 So the soldiers cut the ropes that held the boat and let it go.

33 Day was about to come, and Paul begged them all to eat some food, "You have been waiting for fourteen days now, and all this time you have not eaten a thing. 34 I beg you, then, eat some food; you need it in order to survive. Not even a hair of your heads will be lost." 35 After saying this, Paul took some bread, gave thanks to God before them all, broke it, and began to eat. 36 They took courage, and every one of them also ate some food. 37 There was a total of two hundred and seventy-six of us on board. 38 After everyone had eaten enough, they lightened the ship by throwing the wheat into the sea.

New International Version

that the water was one hundred and twenty feet deep. A short time later they took soundings again and found it was ninety feet deep. 29 Fearing that we would be dashed against the rocks, they dropped four anchors from the stern and prayed for daylight. 30 In an attempt to escape from the ship, the sailors let the lifeboat down into the sea, pretending they were going to lower some anchors from the bow. 31 Then Paul said to the centurion and the soldiers, "Unless these men stay with the ship, you cannot be saved." 32 So the soldiers cut the ropes that held the lifeboat and let it fall away.

33 Just before dawn Paul urged them all to eat. "For the last fourteen days," he said, "you have been in constant suspense and have gone without food—you haven't eaten anything. 34 Now I urge you to take some food. You need it to survive. Not one of you will lose a single hair from his head." 35 After he said this, he took some bread and gave thanks to God in front of them all. Then he broke it and began to eat. 36 They were all encouraged and ate some food themselves. 37 Altogether there were 276 of us on board. 38 When they had eaten as much as they wanted, they lightened the ship by throwing the grain into the sea.

Phillips Modern English

fathoms, and then after sailing on only a little way they sounded again and found fifteen. So, for fear that we might be hurled on the rocks, they threw out four anchors from the stern and prayed for daylight. The sailors wanted to desert the ship and they got as far as letting a boat down into the sea, pretending that they were going to run out anchors from the bows. But Paul said to the centurion and the soldiers,

"Unless these men stay aboard the ship there is no hope of your being saved."

At this the soldiers cut the ropes of the boat and let her fall away.

27.33 Paul's sturdy commonsense

Then while everyone waited for the day to break Paul urged them to take some food, saying,

"For fourteen days now you've had no food—you haven't had a bite while you've been on watch. Now take some food, I beg of you—you need it for your survival. I assure you that not a hair of anyone's head will be lost."

When he had said this he took some bread and, after thanking God before them all, he broke it and began to eat. This raised everybody's spirits and they began to take food themselves. There were about two hundred and seventy-six of us all told aboard that ship. When they had eaten enough they lightened the ship by throwing the grain into the sea.

Revised Standard Version

twenty fathoms; a little farther on they sounded
again and found fifteen fathoms. 29And fearing
that we might run on the rocks, they let out
four anchors from the stern, and prayed for day
to come. 30And as the sailors were seeking to
escape from the ship, and had lowered the boat
into the sea, under pretense of laying out anchors from the bow, 31 Paul said to the centurion and the soldiers, "Unless these men stay
in the ship, you cannot be saved." 32 Then the
soldiers cut away the ropes of the boat, and let
it go.
33 As day was about to dawn, Paul urged
them all to take some food, saying, "Today is the
fourteenth day that you have continued in suspense and without food, having taken nothing.
34 Therefore I urge you to take some food; it
will give you strength, since not a hair is to
perish from the head of any of you." 35And
when he had said this, he took bread, and giving thanks to God in the presence of all he broke
it and began to eat. 36 Then they all were encouraged and ate some food themselves. 37 (We
were in all two hundred and seventy-six[d] persons in the ship.) 38And when they had eaten
enough, they lightened the ship, throwing out the
wheat into the sea.

[*d*] Other ancient authorities read *seventy-six* or *about seventy-six*.

Jerusalem Bible

and found twenty fathoms; after a short interval
they sounded again and found fifteen fathoms.
29 Then, afraid that we might run aground somewhere on a reef, they dropped four anchors
from the stern and prayed for daylight. 30 When
some of the crew tried to escape from the ship
and lowered the ship's boat into the sea as
though to lay out anchors from the bows,
31 Paul said to the centurion and his men,
"Unless those men stay on board you cannot
hope to be saved." 32 So the soldiers cut the
boat's ropes and let it drop away.
33 Just before daybreak Paul urged them all
to have something to eat. "For fourteen days,"
he said, "you have been in suspense, going hungry and eating nothing. 34 Let me persuade you
to have something to eat; your safety is not in
doubt. Not a hair of your heads will be lost."
35 With these words he took some bread, gave
thanks to God in front of them all, broke it and
began to eat. 36 Then they all plucked up courage and took something to eat themselves.
37 We were in all two hundred and seventy-six
souls on board that ship. 38 When they had
eaten what they wanted they lightened the ship
by throwing the corn overboard into the sea.

New English Bible

Sounding again after a short interval they found fifteen fathoms; and fearing that we might be cast ashore on a rugged coast they dropped four anchors from the stern and prayed for daylight to come. The sailors tried to abandon ship; they had already lowered the ship's boat, pretending they were going to lay out anchors from the bows, when Paul said to the centurion and the soldiers, 'Unless these men stay on board you can none of you come off safely.' So the soldiers cut the ropes of the boat and let her drop away.

Shortly before daybreak Paul urged them all to take some food. 'For the last fourteen days', he said, 'you have lived in suspense and gone hungry; you have eaten nothing whatever. So I beg you to have something to eat; your lives depend on it. Remember, not a hair of your heads will be lost.' With these words, he took bread, gave thanks to God in front of them all, broke it, and began eating. Then they all plucked up courage, and took food themselves. There were on board two hundred and seventy-six of us in all. When they had eaten as much as they wanted they lightened the ship by dumping the corn in the sea.

King James Version

39And when it was day, they knew not the land: but they discovered a certain creek with a shore, into the which they were minded, if it were possible, to thrust in the ship. 40And when they had taken up the anchors, they committed *themselves* unto the sea, and loosed the rudder bands, and hoised up the mainsail to the wind, and made toward shore. 41And falling into a place where two seas met, they ran the ship aground; and the forepart stuck fast, and remained unmoveable, but the hinder part was broken with the violence of the waves. 42And the soldiers' counsel was to kill the prisoners, lest any of them should swim out, and escape. 43 But the centurion, willing to save Paul, kept them from *their* purpose; and commanded that they which could swim should cast *themselves* first *into the sea,* and get to land: 44And the rest, some on boards, and some on *broken pieces* of the ship. And so it came to pass, that they escaped all safe to land.

28 And when they were escaped, then they knew that the island was called Melita. 2And the barbarous people shewed us no little kindness: for they kindled a fire, and received us every one, because of the present rain, and

Living Bible

39 When it was day, they didn't recognize the coastline, but noticed a bay with a beach and wondered whether they could get between the rocks and be driven up onto the beach. 40 They finally decided to try. Cutting off the anchors and leaving them in the sea, they lowered the rudders, raised the foresail and headed ashore. 41 But the ship hit a sandbar[j] and ran aground. The bow of the ship stuck fast, while the stern was exposed to the violence of the waves and began to break apart.

42 The soldiers advised their commanding officer to let them kill the prisoners lest any of them swim ashore and escape. 43 But Julius[k] wanted to spare Paul, so he told them no. Then he ordered all who could swim to jump overboard and make for land, 44 and the rest to try for it on planks and debris from the broken ship. So everyone escaped safely ashore!

28 We soon learned that we were on the island of Malta. The people of the island were very kind to us, building a bonfire on the beach to welcome and warm us in the rain and cold.

[j] Literally, "a place where two seas meet." [k] Implied.

Today's English Version

The shipwreck

39 When day came, the sailors did not recognize the coast, but they noticed a bay with a beach and decided that, if possible, they would run the ship aground there. 40 So they cut off the anchors and let them sink in the sea, and at the same time they untied the ropes that held the steering oars. Then they raised the sail at the front of the ship so that the wind would blow the ship forward, and headed for shore. 41 But the ship hit a sandbank and went aground; the front part of the ship got stuck and could not move, while the back part was being broken to pieces by the violence of the waves.

42 The soldiers made a plan to kill all the prisoners, so that none of them would swim ashore and escape. 43 But the army officer wanted to save Paul, so he stopped them from doing this. Instead, he ordered all the men who could swim to jump overboard first and swim ashore; 44 the rest were to follow, holding on to the planks or to some broken pieces of the ship. And this was how we all got safely ashore.

In Malta

28 When we were safely ashore, we learned that the island was called Malta. 2 The natives there were very friendly to us. It had started to rain and was cold, so they built a fire

New International Version

39 When daylight came, they did not recognize the land, but they saw a bay with a sandy beach, where they decided to run the ship aground if they could. 40 Cutting loose the anchors, they left them in the sea and at the same time untied the ropes that held the rudders. Then they hoisted the foresail to the wind and made for the beach. 41 But the ship struck a sandbar and ran aground. The bow stuck fast and would not move, and the stern was broken to pieces by the pounding of the surf.

42 The soldiers planned to kill the prisoners to prevent any of them from swimming away and escaping. 43 But the centurion wanted to spare Paul's life and kept them from carrying out their plan. He ordered those who could swim to jump overboard first and get to land. 44 The rest were to get there on planks or on pieces of the ship. In this way everyone reached land in safety.

Ashore on Malta

28 Once safely on shore, we found out that the island was called Malta. 2 The islanders showed us unusual kindness. They built a fire and welcomed us all because it was raining

Phillips Modern English

27.39 Land at last—but we lose the ship

When daylight came no one recognised the land. But they made out a bay with a sandy shore where they planned to beach the ship if they could. So they cut away the anchors and left them in the sea, and at the same time unlashed the ropes which held the steering-oars. Then they hoisted the foresail to catch the wind and made for the beach. But they struck a shoal and the ship ran aground. The bow stuck fast, while the stern began to break up under the pounding of the waves. The soldiers' plan had been to kill the prisoners in case any of them should try to swim to shore and escape. But the centurion, in his desire to save Paul, put a stop to this, and gave orders that all those who could swim should jump overboard first and get to land, while the rest should follow, some on planks and others in the wreckage of the ship. So it came true that everyone reached the shore in safety.

28.1 A small incident establishes Paul's reputation

After our escape we discovered that the island was called Melita. The natives treated us with exceptional kindness. Because of the driving rain and cold they lit a fire and made us all welcome.

Revised Standard Version

39 Now when it was day, they did not recognize the land, but they noticed a bay with a
beach, on which they planned if possible to
bring the ship ashore. 40 So they cast off the
anchors and left them in the sea, at the same
time loosening the ropes that tied the rudders;
then hoisting the foresail to the wind they made
for the beach. 41 But striking a shoal [e] they ran
the vessel aground; the bow stuck and remained
immovable, and the stern was broken up by the
surf. 42 The soldiers' plan was to kill the prisoners, lest any should swim away and escape;
43 but the centurion, wishing to save Paul, kept
them from carrying out their purpose. He ordered those who could swim to throw themselves overboard first and make for the land,
44 and the rest on planks or on pieces of the
ship. And so it was that all escaped to land.

28 After we had escaped, we then learned
that the island was called Malta. 2 And
the natives showed us unusual kindness, for they
kindled a fire and welcomed us all, because it

[e] Greek *place of two seas.*

Jerusalem Bible

39 When day came they did not recognize the
land, but they could make out a kind of bay
with a beach; they planned to run the ship
aground on this if they could. 40 They slipped
the anchors and left them to the sea, and at the
same time loosened the lashings of the rudders;
then, hoisting the foresail to the wind, they
headed for the beach. 41 But the cross-currents
carried them into a shoal and the vessel ran
aground. The bows were wedged in and stuck
fast, while the stern began to break up with
the pounding of the waves.
42 The soldiers planned to kill the prisoners
for fear that any should swim off and escape.
43 But the centurion was determined to bring
Paul safely through, and would not let them do
what they intended. He gave orders that those
who could swim should jump overboard first
and so get ashore, 44 and the rest follow either
on planks or on pieces of wreckage. In this way
all came safe and sound to land.

Waiting in Malta

28 Once we had come safely through, we
discovered that the island was called Malta.
2 The inhabitants treated us with unusual kindness. They made us all welcome, and they lit a
huge fire because it had started to rain and the

New English Bible

When day broke they could not recognize the land, but they noticed a bay with a sandy beach, on which they planned, if possible, to run the ship ashore. So they slipped the anchors and let them go; at the same time they loosened the lashings of the steering-paddles, set the foresail to the wind, and let her drive to the beach. But they found themselves caught between cross-currents and ran the ship aground, so that the bow stuck fast and remained immovable, while the stern was being pounded to pieces by the breakers. The soldiers thought they had better kill the prisoners for fear that any should swim away and escape; but the centurion wanted to bring Paul safely through and prevented them from carrying out their plan. He gave orders that those who could swim should jump overboard first and get to land; the rest were to follow, some on planks, some on parts of the ship. And thus it was that all came safely to land.

28 Once we had made our way to safety we identified the island as Malta. The rough islanders treated us with uncommon kindness: because it was cold and had started to rain, they lit

King James Version

because of the cold. 3And when Paul had gathered a bundle of sticks, and laid *them* on the fire, there came a viper out of the heat, and fastened on his hand. 4And when the barbarians saw the *venomous* beast hang on his hand, they said among themselves, No doubt this man is a murderer, whom, though he hath escaped the sea, yet vengeance suffereth not to live. 5And he shook off the beast into the fire, and felt no harm. 6 Howbeit they looked when he should have swollen, or fallen down dead suddenly: but after they had looked a great while, and saw no harm come to him, they changed their minds, and said that he was a god. 7 In the same quarters were possessions of the chief man of the island, whose name was Publius; who received us, and lodged us three days courteously. 8And it came to pass, that the father of Publius lay sick of a fever and of a bloody flux: to whom Paul entered in, and prayed, and laid his hands on him, and healed him. 9 So when this was done, others also, which had diseases in the island, came, and were healed: 10 Who also honoured us with many honours; and when we departed, they laded *us* with such things as were

Living Bible

3 As Paul gathered an armful of sticks to lay on the fire, a poisonous snake, driven out by the heat, fastened itself onto his hand! 4 The people of the island saw it hanging there and said to each other, "A murderer, no doubt! Though he escaped the sea, justice will not permit him to live!"

5 But Paul shook off the snake into the fire and was unharmed. 6 The people waited for him to begin swelling or suddenly fall dead; but when they had waited a long time and no harm came to him, they changed their minds and decided he was a god.

7 Near the shore where we landed was an estate belonging to Publius, the governor of the island. He welcomed us courteously and fed us for three days. 8As it happened, Publius' father was ill with fever and dysentery. Paul went in and prayed for him, and laying his hands on him, healed him! 9 Then all the other sick people in the island came and were cured. 10As a result we were showered with gifts,[a] and when the time came to sail, people put on board all sorts of things we would need for the trip.

[a] Literally, "honors."

Today's English Version

and made us all welcome. 3 Paul gathered up a bundle of sticks and was putting them on the fire when a snake came out, on account of the heat, and fastened itself to his hand. 4 The natives saw the snake hanging on Paul's hand and said to one another, "This man must be a murderer, but Fate will not let him live, even though he escaped from the sea." 5 But Paul shook the snake off into the fire without being harmed at all. 6 They were waiting for him to swell up or suddenly fall down dead. But after waiting for a long time and not seeing anything unusual happening to him, they changed their minds and said, "He is a god!"

7 Not far from that place were some fields that belonged to Publius, the chief of the island. He welcomed us kindly and for three days we were his guests. 8 Publius' father was in bed, sick with fever and dysentery. Paul went into his room, prayed, placed his hands on him, and healed him. 9 When this happened, all the other sick people on the island came and were healed. 10 They gave us many gifts, and when we sailed they put on board what we needed for the voyage.

New International Version

and cold. 3 Paul gathered a pile of brushwood and, as he put it on the fire, a viper, driven out by the heat, fastened itself on his hand. 4 When the islanders saw the snake hanging from his hand, they said to each other, "This man must be a murderer; for though he escaped from the sea, Justice has not allowed him to live." 5 But Paul shook the snake off into the fire and suffered no ill effects. 6 The people expected him to swell up or suddenly fall over dead, but after waiting a long time and seeing nothing unusual happen to him, they changed their minds and said he was a god.

7 There was an estate nearby that belonged to Publius, the chief official of the island. He welcomed us to his home and for three days entertained us hospitably. 8 His father was sick in bed, suffering from fever and dysentery. Paul went in to see him and, after prayer, placed his hands on him and healed him. 9 When this had happened, the rest of the sick on the island came and were cured. 10 They honored us in many ways and when we were ready to sail, they furnished us with the supplies we needed.

Phillips Modern English

Then when Paul had collected a large bundle of sticks and was about to put it on the fire, a viper driven out by the heat fastened itself on his hand. When the natives saw the creature hanging from his hand they said to each other, "This man is obviously a murderer. He has escaped from the sea but justice will not let him live." But Paul shook off the viper into the fire without suffering any ill effect. Naturally they expected him to swell up or suddenly fall down dead, but after waiting a long time and seeing nothing out of the ordinary happen to him, they changed their minds and kept saying that he was a god.

28.7 Paul's acts of healing: the islanders' gratitude

In that part of the island were estates belonging to the governor, whose name was Publius. This man welcomed us and entertained us most kindly for three days. Now it happened that Publius' father was lying ill with attacks of fever and dysentery. Paul visited him and after prayer laid his hands on him and healed him. After that all the other sick people on the island came forward and were cured. Consequently they honoured us with many presents, and when the time came for us to sail they provided us with everything we needed.

Revised Standard Version

had begun to rain and was cold. 3 Paul had gathered a bundle of sticks and put them on the fire, when a viper came out because of the heat and fastened on his hand. 4 When the natives saw the creature hanging from his hand, they said to one another, "No doubt this man is a murderer. Though he has escaped from the sea, justice has not allowed him to live." 5 He, however, shook off the creature into the fire and suffered no harm. 6 They waited, expecting him to swell up or suddenly fall down dead; but when they had waited a long time and saw no misfortune come to him, they changed their minds and said that he was a god.

7 Now in the neighborhood of that place were lands belonging to the chief man of the island, named Publius, who received us and entertained us hospitably for three days. 8 It happened that the father of Publius lay sick with fever and dysentery; and Paul visited him and prayed, and putting his hands on him healed him. 9 And when this had taken place, the rest of the people on the island who had diseases also came and were cured. 10 They presented many gifts to us;[f] and when we sailed, they put on board whatever we needed.

[f] Or *honored us with many honors.*

Jerusalem Bible

weather was cold. 3 Paul had collected a bundle of sticks and was putting them on the fire when a viper brought out by the heat attached itself to his hand. 4 When the natives saw the creature hanging from his hand they said to one another, "That man must be a murderer; he may have escaped the sea, but divine vengeance would not let him live." 5 However, he shook the creature off into the fire and came to no harm, 6 although they were expecting him at any moment to swell up or drop dead on the spot. After they had waited a long time without seeing anything out of the ordinary happen to him, they changed their minds and began to say he was a god.

7 In that neighborhood there were estates belonging to the prefect of the island, whose name was Publius. He received us and entertained us hospitably for three days. 8 It so happened that Publius' father was in bed, suffering from feverish attacks and dysentery. Paul went in to see him, and after a prayer he laid his hands on the man and healed him. 9 When this happened, the other sick people on the island came as well and were cured; 10 they honored us with many marks of respect, and when we sailed they put on board the provisions we needed.

New English Bible

a bonfire and made us all welcome. Paul had got together an armful of sticks and put them on the fire, when a viper, driven out by the heat, fastened on his hand. The islanders, seeing the snake hanging on to his hand, said to one another, 'The man must be a murderer; he may have escaped from the sea, but divine justice has not let him live.' Paul, however, shook off the snake into the fire and was none the worse. They still expected that any moment he would swell up or drop down dead, but after waiting a long time without seeing anything extraordinary happen to him, they changed their minds and now said, 'He is a god.'

In the neighbourhood of that place there were lands belonging to the chief magistrate of the island, whose name was Publius. He took us in and entertained us hospitably for three days. It so happened that this man's father was in bed suffering from recurrent bouts of fever and dysentery. Paul visited him and, after prayer, laid his hands upon him and healed him; whereupon the other sick people on the island came also and were cured. They honoured us with many marks of respect, and when we were leaving they put on board provision for our needs.

King James Version

necessary. 11And after three months we departed in a ship of Alexandria, which had wintered in the isle, whose sign was Castor and Pollux. 12And landing at Syracuse, we tarried *there* three days. 13And from thence we fetched a compass, and came to Rhegium: and after one day the south wind blew, and we came the next day to Puteoli: 14 Where we found brethren, and were desired to tarry with them seven days: and so we went toward Rome. 15And from thence, when the brethren heard of us, they came to meet us as far as Appii Forum, and the Three Taverns; whom when Paul saw, he thanked God, and took courage. 16And when we came to Rome, the centurion delivered the prisoners to the captain of the guard: but Paul was suffered to dwell by himself with a soldier that kept him. 17And it came to pass, that after three days Paul called the chief of the Jews together: and when they were come together, he

Living Bible

11 It was three months after the shipwreck before we set sail again, and this time it was in *The Twin Brothers* of Alexandria, a ship that had wintered at the island. 12 Our first stop was Syracuse, where we stayed three days. 13 From there we circled around to Rhegium; a day later a south wind began blowing, so the following day we arrived at Puteoli, 14 where we found some believers! They begged us to stay with them seven days. Then we went on to Rome.

15 The brothers in Rome had heard we were coming and came to meet us at the Forum[b] on the Appian Way. Others joined us at The Three Taverns.[c] When Paul saw them, he thanked God and took courage.

16 When we arrived in Rome, Paul was permitted to live wherever he wanted to, though guarded by a soldier. 17 Three days after his arrival, he called together the local Jewish leaders and spoke to them as follows:

[*b*] About forty-three miles from Rome. [*c*] About thirty-five miles from Rome.

Today's English Version

From Malta to Rome

11 After three months we sailed away on a ship from Alexandria, called "The Twin Gods," which had spent the winter in the island. 12 We arrived in the city of Syracuse and stayed there for three days. 13 From there we sailed on and arrived in the city of Rhegium. The next day a wind began to blow from the south, and in two days we came to the town of Puteoli. 14 We found some believers there who asked us to stay with them a week. And so we came to Rome. 15 The brothers in Rome heard about us and came as far as Market of Appius and Three Inns to meet us. When Paul saw them, he thanked God and took courage.

In Rome

16 When we arrived in Rome, Paul was allowed to live by himself with a soldier guarding him.

17 After three days Paul called the local Jewish leaders to a meeting. When they gathered, he

New International Version

Arrival at Rome

11 After three months we put out to sea in a ship that had wintered in the island. It was an Alexandrian ship with the figurehead of the twin gods Castor and Pollux. 12 We put in at Syracuse and stayed there three days. 13 From there we set sail and arrived at Rhegium. The next day the south wind came up, and on the following day we reached Puteoli. 14 There we found some brothers who invited us to spend a week with them. And so we went to Rome. 15 The brothers there had heard that we were coming, and they traveled as far as the Forum of Appius and the Three Taverns to meet us. At the sight of these men Paul thanked God and was encouraged. 16 When we got to Rome, Paul was allowed to live by himself, with a soldier to guard him.

Paul preaches at Rome under guard

17 Three days later he called together the leaders of the Jews. When they had assembled,

Phillips Modern English

28.11 Spring returns and we resume our journey

It was no less than three months later that we set sail in an Alexandrian ship which had wintered in the island, a ship that had the heavenly twins as her figurehead. We put in at Syracuse and stayed there three days, and from there we tacked round to Rhegium. A day later the south wind sprang up and we sailed to Puteoli, reaching it in only two days. There we found some of the brothers and they begged us to stay a week with them, and so we came to Rome.

28.15 A Christian welcome awaits us in the capital

The brothers there had heard about us and came out from the city to meet us, as far as the Market of Appius and the Three Taverns. When Paul saw them he thanked God and his spirits rose. When we reached Rome Paul was given permission to live alone with the soldier who was guarding him.

28.17 Paul explains himself frankly to the Jews in Rome

Three days later Paul invited the leading Jews to meet him, and when they arrived he spoke to them,

Revised Standard Version

11 After three months we set sail in a ship which had wintered in the island, a ship of Alexandria, with the Twin Brothers as figurehead.
12 Putting in at Syracuse, we stayed there for three days. 13 And from there we made a circuit and arrived at Rhegium; and after one day a south wind sprang up, and on the second day we came to Puteoli. 14 There we found brethren, and were invited to stay with them for seven days. And so we came to Rome. 15 And the brethren there, when they heard of us, came as far as the Forum of Appius and Three Taverns to meet us. On seeing them Paul thanked God and took courage. 16 And when we came into Rome, Paul was allowed to stay by himself, with the soldier that guarded him.
17 After three days he called together the local leaders of the Jews; and when they had

Jerusalem Bible

From Malta to Rome

11 At the end of three months we set sail in a ship that had wintered in the island; she came from Alexandria and her figurehead was the Twins. 12 We put in at Syracuse and spent three days there; 13 from there we followed the coast up to Rhegium. After one day there a south wind sprang up and on the second day we made Puteoli,[z] 14 where we found some brothers and were much rewarded by staying a week with them. And so we came to Rome.
15 When the brothers there heard of our arrival they came to meet us, as far as the Forum of Appius and the Three Taverns. When Paul saw them he thanked God and took courage.
16 On our arrival in Rome Paul was allowed to stay in lodgings of his own with the soldier who guarded him.

Paul makes contact with the Roman Jews

17 After three days he called together the leading Jews. When they had assembled, he said

[z] Pozzuoli, on the Gulf of Naples.

New English Bible

Three months had passed when we set sail in a ship which had wintered in the island; she was the *Castor and Pollux* of Alexandria. We put in at Syracuse and spent three days there; then we sailed round and arrived at Rhegium. After one day a south wind sprang up and we reached Puteoli in two days. There we found fellow-Christians and were invited to stay a week with them. And so to Rome. The Christians there had had news of us and came out to meet us as far as Appii Forum and Tres Tabernae, and when Paul saw them, he gave thanks to God and took courage.

When we entered Rome Paul was allowed to lodge by himself with a soldier in charge of him. Three days later he called together the local Jewish leaders; and when they were assembled,

King James Version

said unto them, Men *and* brethren, though I
have committed nothing against the people, or
customs of our fathers, yet was I delivered
prisoner from Jerusalem into the hands of the
Romans: 18 Who, when they had examined me,
would have let *me* go, because there was no
cause of death in me. 19 But when the Jews
spake against *it,* I was constrained to appeal
unto Cesar; not that I had aught to accuse my
nation of. 20 For this cause therefore have I
called for you, to see *you,* and to speak with
you: because that for the hope of Israel I am
bound with this chain. 21 And they said unto him,
We neither received letters out of Judea concerning thee, neither any of the brethren that
came shewed or spake any harm of thee. 22 But
we desire to hear of thee what thou thinkest: for
as concerning this sect, we know that every
where it is spoken against. 23 And when they had
appointed him a day, there came many to him
into *his* lodging; to whom he expounded and
testified the kingdom of God, persuading them
concerning Jesus, both out of the law of Moses,
and *out of* the prophets, from morning till
evening. 24 And some believed the things which
were spoken, and some believed not. 25 And

Living Bible

"Brothers, I was arrested by the Jews in Jerusalem and handed over to the Roman government for prosecution, even though I had harmed
no one nor violated the customs of our ancestors.
18 The Romans gave me a trial and wanted to
release me, for they found no cause for the
death sentence demanded by the Jewish leaders.
19 But when the Jews protested the decision, I
felt it necessary, with no malice against them,
to appeal to Caesar. 20 I asked you to come
here today so we could get acquainted and I
could tell you that it is because I believe the
Messiah[d] has come that I am bound with this
chain."

21 They replied, "We have heard nothing
against you! We have had no letters from Judea
or reports from those arriving from Jerusalem.[e]
22 But we want to hear what you believe, for
the only thing we know about these Christians
is that they are denounced everywhere!"

23 So a time was set and on that day large
numbers came to his house. He told them about
the Kingdom of God and taught them about
Jesus from the Scriptures—from the five books
of Moses and the books of prophecy. He began
lecturing in the morning and went on into the
evening!

24 Some believed, and some didn't. 25 But

[*d*] Literally, "the hope of Israel." But perhaps he is referring here, as in his other defenses, to his belief in the resurrection of the dead. [*e*] Implied.

Today's English Version

said to them, "My brothers! Even though I did
nothing against our people or the customs that we
received from our ancestors, I was made a prisoner in Jerusalem and handed over to the Romans.
18 They questioned me and wanted to release me,
because they found that I had done nothing for
which I deserved to die. 19 But when the Jews
opposed this, I was forced to appeal to the Emperor, even though I had no accusation to make
against my own people. 20 That is why I asked to
see you and talk with you; because I have this
chain on me for the sake of him for whom the
people of Israel hope."

21 They said to him, "We have not received
any letters from Judea about you, nor have any
of our brothers come from there with any news,
or to say anything bad about you. 22 But we
would like to hear your ideas, because we know
that everywhere people speak against this party
that you belong to."

23 So they set a date with Paul, and a larger
number of them came that day to where Paul was
staying. From morning till night he explained and
gave them his message about the Kingdom of
God. He tried to convince them about Jesus by
quoting from the Law of Moses and the writings
of the prophets. 24 Some of them were convinced
by his words, but others would not believe. 25 So

New International Version

Paul said to them: "My brothers, although I
have done nothing against our people or against
the customs of our ancestors, I was arrested in
Jerusalem and handed over to the Romans.
18 They examined me and wanted to release me,
because I was not guilty of any crime deserving
death. 19 But when the Jews objected, I was
compelled to appeal to Caesar—not that I had
any charge to bring against my own people.
20 For this reason I have asked to see you and
talk with you. It is because of the hope of Israel
that I am bound with this chain."

21 They replied, "We have not received any
letters from Judea concerning you, and none of
the brothers who had come from there has reported or said anything bad about you. 22 But
we want to hear what your views are, for we
know that people everywhere are talking against
this sect."

23 They arranged to meet Paul on a certain
day, and came in even larger numbers to the
place where he was staying. From morning till
evening he explained and declared to them the
kingdom of God and tried to convince them
about Jesus from the Law of Moses and from
the Prophets. 24 Some were convinced by what
he said, but others would not believe. 25 They

Phillips Modern English

"Men and brothers, although I have done nothing against our people or the customs of our forefathers, I was handed over to the Romans as a prisoner in Jerusalem. They examined me and were prepared to release me, since they found me guilty of nothing deserving the death penalty. But the attacks of the Jews there forced me to appeal to Caesar—not that I had any charge to make against my own nation. But it is because of this accusation of the Jews that I have asked to see you and talk matters over with you. In actual fact it is on account of the hope of Israel that I am here in chains."

But they replied,

"We have received no letters about you from Judaea, nor have any of the brothers who have arrived here said anything, officially or unofficially, against you. We want to hear you state your views, although as far as this sect is concerned we do know that serious objections have been raised to it everywhere."

28.23 Paul's earnest and prolonged effort to win his own people for Christ

When they had arranged a day for him they came to his lodging in great numbers. From morning till evening he explained the kingdom of God to them, giving his personal testimony, trying to persuade them about Jesus from the Law of Moses and the Prophets. As a result several of them were won over by his words, but others would not believe. When they could not reach

Revised Standard Version

gathered, he said to them, "Brethren, though I had done nothing against the people or the customs of our fathers, yet I was delivered prisoner from Jerusalem into the hands of the Romans. 18 When they had examined me, they wished to set me at liberty, because there was no reason for the death penalty in my case. 19 But when the Jews objected, I was compelled to appeal to Caesar—though I had no charge to bring against my nation. 20 For this reason therefore I have asked to see you and speak with you, since it is because of the hope of Israel that I am bound with this chain." 21 And they said to him, "We have received no letters from Judea about you, and none of the brethren coming here has reported or spoken any evil about you. 22 But we desire to hear from you what your views are; for with regard to this sect we know that everywhere it is spoken against."

23 When they had appointed a day for him, they came to him at his lodging in great numbers. And he expounded the matter to them from morning till evening, testifying to the kingdom of God and trying to convince them about Jesus both from the law of Moses and from the prophets. 24 And some were convinced by what he said, while others disbelieved. 25 So,

Jerusalem Bible

to them, "Brothers, although I have done nothing against our people or the customs of our ancestors, I was arrested in Jerusalem and handed over to the Romans. 18 They examined me and would have set me free, since they found me guilty of nothing involving the death penalty; 19 but the Jews lodged an objection, and I was forced to appeal to Caesar, not that I had any accusation to make against my own nation. 20 That is why I have asked to see you and talk to you, for it is on account of the hope of Israel that I wear this chain."

21 They answered, "We have received no letters from Judaea about you, nor has any countryman of yours arrived here with any report or story of anything to your discredit. 22 We think it would be as well to hear your own account of your position; all we know about this sect is that opinion everywhere condemns it."

Paul's declaration to the Roman Jews

23 So they arranged a day with him and a large number of them visited him at his lodgings. He put his case to them, testifying to the kingdom of God and trying to persuade them about Jesus, arguing from the Law of Moses and the prophets. This went on from early morning until evening, 24 and some were convinced by what he said, while the rest were skeptical. 25 So they disagreed among themselves

New English Bible

he said to them: 'My brothers, I, who never did anything against our people or the customs of our forefathers, am here as a prisoner; I was handed over to the Romans at Jerusalem. They examined me and would have liked to release me because there was no capital charge against me; but the Jews objected, and I had no option but to appeal to the Emperor; not that I had any accusation to bring against my own people. That is why I have asked to see you and talk to you, because it is for the sake of the hope of Israel that I am in chains, as you see.' They replied, 'We have had no communication from Judaea, nor has any countryman of ours arrived with any report or gossip to your discredit. We should like to hear from you what your views are; all we know about this sect is that no one has a good word to say for it.'

So they fixed a day, and came in large numbers as his guests. He dealt at length with the whole matter; he spoke urgently of the kingdom of God and sought to convince them about Jesus by appealing to the Law of Moses and the prophets. This went on from dawn to dusk. Some were won over by his arguments; others remained sceptical. Without reaching any agree-

King James Version

when they agreed not among themselves, they departed, after that Paul had spoken one word, Well spake the Holy Ghost by Esaias the prophet unto our fathers,
26 Saying, Go unto this people, and say, Hearing ye shall hear, and shall not understand; and seeing ye shall see, and not perceive:
27 For the heart of this people is waxed gross, and their ears are dull of hearing, and their eyes have they closed; lest they should see with *their* eyes, and hear with *their* ears, and understand with *their* heart, and should be converted, and I should heal them.
28 Be it known therefore unto you, that the salvation of God is sent unto the Gentiles, and *that* they will hear it.
29 And when he had said these words, the Jews departed, and had great reasoning among themselves.
30 And Paul dwelt two whole years in his own hired house, and received all that came in unto him,
31 Preaching the kingdom of God, and teaching those things which concern the Lord Jesus Christ, with all confidence, no man forbidding him.

Living Bible

after they had argued back and forth among themselves, they left with this final word from Paul ringing in their ears: "The Holy Spirit was right when he said through Isaiah the prophet,
26 " 'Say to the Jews, "You will hear and see but not understand,
27 for your hearts are too fat and your ears don't listen and you have closed your eyes against understanding, for you don't want to see and hear and understand and turn to me to heal you." ' [f]
28, 29 [g] So I want you to realize that this salvation from God is available to the Gentiles too, and they will accept it."
30 Paul lived for the next two years in his rented house[h] and welcomed all who visited him,
31 telling them with all boldness about the Kingdom of God and about the Lord Jesus Christ; and no one tried to stop him.

[*f*] Isaiah 6:9,10. [*g*] Some of the ancient manuscripts add, "And when he had said these words, the Jews departed, having much dissenting among themselves." [*h*] Or, "at his own expense."

Today's English Version

they left, disagreeing among themselves, after Paul had said this one thing, "How well the Holy Spirit spoke through the prophet Isaiah to your ancestors!
26 For he said,

'Go and say to this people:
You will listen and listen, but not understand;
you will look and look, but not see.
27 Because this people's minds are dull,
they have stopped up their ears,
and have closed their eyes.
Otherwise, their eyes would see,
their ears would hear,
their minds would understand,
and they would turn to me, says God,
and I would heal them.' "

28 And Paul concluded, "You are to know, then, that God's message of salvation has been sent to the Gentiles. They will listen!"
[29 After Paul said this, the Jews left, arguing violently among themselves.]
30 For two years Paul lived there in a place he rented for himself, and welcomed all who came to see him.
31 He preached about the kingdom of God and taught about the Lord Jesus Christ, speaking with all boldness and freedom.

New International Version

disagreed among themselves and began to leave, after Paul had made this final statement: "The Holy Spirit spoke the truth to your ancestors when he said through Isaiah the prophet:
26 'Go to this people and say,
You will be ever hearing but never understanding;
you will be ever seeing but never perceiving.
27 For this people's heart has become calloused;
they hardly hear with their ears,
and they have closed their eyes.
Otherwise they might see with their eyes,
hear with their ears,
understand with their hearts
and turn and I would heal them.' [o]
28 "Therefore I want you to know that God's salvation has been sent to the Gentiles, and they will listen!" [p]
30 For two whole years Paul stayed there in his own rented house and welcomed all who came to see him.
31 Boldly and without hindrance he preached the kingdom of God and taught about the Lord Jesus Christ.

[*o*] Isaiah 6:9,10. [*p*] Some MSS add verse 29: *After he said this, the Jews left, arguing vigorously among themselves.*

Phillips Modern English

any agreement among themselves and began to go away, Paul added as a parting shot, "How rightly did the Holy Spirit speak to your forefathers through the prophet Isaiah when he said,

Go thou unto this people, and say,
By hearing ye shall hear, and shall in no wise understand;
And seeing ye shall see, and shall in no wise perceive:
For this people's heart is waxed gross,
And their ears are dull of hearing,
And their eyes they have closed;
Lest haply they should perceive with their eyes,
And hear with their ears,
And understand with their heart,
And should turn again,
And I should heal them.

"Let it be plainly understood then that this salvation of our God has been sent to the gentiles, and they at least will listen to it!"

28.30 The last glimpse of Paul . . .

So Paul stayed for two full years in his own rented apartment welcoming all who came to see him. He proclaimed to them all the kingdom of God and gave them the teaching of the Lord Jesus Christ with the utmost freedom and without hindrance from anyone.

Revised Standard Version

as they disagreed among themselves, they departed, after Paul had made one statement: "The Holy Spirit was right in saying to your fathers through Isaiah the prophet:
26 'Go to this people, and say,
You shall indeed hear but never understand,
and you shall indeed see but never perceive.
27 For this people's heart has grown dull,
and their ears are heavy of hearing,
and their eyes they have closed;
lest they should perceive with their eyes,
and hear with their ears,
and understand with their heart,
and turn for me to heal them.'
28 Let it be known to you then that this salvation of God has been sent to the Gentiles; they will listen." [g]
30 And he lived there two whole years at his own expense,[h] and welcomed all who came to him, 31 preaching the kingdom of God and teaching about the Lord Jesus Christ quite openly and unhindered.

[g] Other ancient authorities add verse 29, *And when he had said these words, the Jews departed, holding much dispute among themselves.* [h] Or *in his own hired dwelling.*

Jerusalem Bible

and, as they went away, Paul had one last thing to say to them, "How aptly the Holy Spirit spoke when he told your ancestors through the prophet Isaiah:

26 *Go to this nation and say:*
You will hear and hear again but not understand,
see and see again, but not perceive.
27 *For the heart of this nation has grown coarse,*
their ears are dull of hearing and they have shut their eyes,
for fear they should see with their eyes,
hear with their ears,
understand with their heart,
and be converted
and be healed by me.[a]

28 "Understand, then, that this salvation of God has been sent to the pagans; they will listen to it." [b]

Epilogue

30 Paul spent the whole of the two years[c] in his own rented lodging. He welcomed all who came to visit him, 31 proclaiming the kingdom of God and teaching the truth about the Lord Jesus Christ with complete freedom and without hindrance from anyone.

[a] Is. 6:9-10. [b] The Western Text adds v. 29. "And when he had said this, the Jews left, arguing hotly between themselves." [c] See note on 24:27.

New English Bible

ment among themselves they began to disperse, but not before Paul had said one thing more: 'How well the Holy Spirit spoke to your fathers through the prophet Isaiah when he said, "Go to this people and say: You may hear and hear, but you will never understand; you may look and look, but you will never see. For this people's mind has become gross; their ears are dulled, and their eyes are closed. Otherwise, their eyes might see, their ears hear, and their mind understand, and then they might turn again, and I would heal them." Therefore take notice that this salvation of God has been sent to the Gentiles; the Gentiles will listen.' [a]

He stayed there two full years at his own expense, with a welcome for all who came to him, proclaiming the kingdom of God and teaching the facts about the Lord Jesus Christ quite openly and without hindrance.

[a] *Some witnesses add* (29) After he had spoken, the Jews went away, arguing vigorously among themselves.

King James Version

THE EPISTLE OF PAUL THE APOSTLE TO THE ROMANS

1 Paul, a servant of Jesus Christ, called *to be* an apostle, separated unto the gospel of God, 2 (Which he had promised afore by his prophets in the holy Scriptures,) 3 Concerning his Son Jesus Christ our Lord, which was made of the seed of David according to the flesh; 4 And declared *to be* the Son of God with power, according to the Spirit of holiness, by the resurrection from the dead: 5 By whom we have received grace and apostleship, for obedience to the faith among all nations, for his name: 6 Among whom are ye also the called of Jesus

Living Bible

ROMANS

1 Dear friends in Rome: 1 This letter is from Paul, Jesus Christ's slave, chosen to be a missionary, and sent out to preach God's Good News. 2 This Good News was promised long ago by God's prophets in the Old Testament. 3 It is the Good News about his Son, Jesus Christ our Lord, who came as a human baby, born into King David's royal family line; 4 and by being raised from the dead he was proved to be the mighty Son of God, with the holy nature of God himself.

5 And now, through Christ, all the kindness of God has been poured out upon us undeserving sinners; and now he is sending us out around the world to tell all people everywhere the great things God has done for them, so that they, too, will believe and obey him.

6, 7 And you, dear friends in Rome, are among those he dearly loves; you, too, are in-

Today's English Version

PAUL'S LETTER TO THE ROMANS

1 From Paul, a servant of Christ Jesus, and an apostle chosen and called by God to preach his Good News.

2 The Good News was promised long ago by God through his prophets, and written in the Holy Scriptures. 3 It is about his Son, our Lord Jesus Christ: as to his humanity, he was born a descendant of David; 4 as to his divine holiness, he was shown with great power to be the Son of God by being raised from death. 5 Through him God gave me the privilege of being an apostle, for the sake of Christ, in order to lead people of all nations to believe and obey. 6 This also includes you who are in Rome, whom God has called to belong to Jesus Christ.

New International Version

ROMANS

1 Paul, a servant of Christ Jesus, called to be an apostle and set apart for the gospel of God —2 the gospel he promised beforehand through his prophets in the Holy Scriptures 3 regarding his Son, who as to his human nature was a descendant of David, 4 and who through the Spirit of holiness[a] was declared with power to be the Son of God by his resurrection from the dead: Jesus Christ our Lord. 5 Through him and for his name's sake, we received grace and apostleship to call people from among all the Gentiles to the obedience that comes from faith. 6 And you also are among those who are called to belong to Jesus Christ.

[a] Or *and who as to his spirit of holiness.*

Phillips Modern English

THE LETTER TO THE CHRISTIANS AT ROME

This letter comes to you from Paul, a servant of Christ Jesus, called as a messenger, and appointed for the service of that gospel of God which was long ago promised by the prophets in the holy scriptures.

The gospel is centred in God's Son, a descendant of David by human genealogy and patently marked out as the Son of God by the power of that Spirit of holiness which raised him to life again from the dead. He is our Lord, Jesus Christ, from whom we received grace and our commission in his name to forward obedience to the faith in all nations. And of this great number you are also called to belong to him.

Revised Standard Version

THE LETTER OF PAUL TO THE ROMANS

1 Paul, a servant[a] of Jesus Christ, called to be
an apostle, set apart for the gospel of God
2 which he promised beforehand through his
prophets in the holy scriptures, 3 the gospel concerning his Son, who was descended from David
according to the flesh 4 and designated Son of
God in power according to the Spirit of holiness
by his resurrection from the dead, Jesus Christ
our Lord, 5 through whom we have received
grace and apostleship to bring about the obedience of faith for the sake of his name among all
the nations, 6 including yourselves who are called
to belong to Jesus Christ;

[a] Or *slave*.

Jerusalem Bible

THE LETTER OF PAUL TO THE CHURCH IN ROME
ROMANS

Address

1 From Paul, a servant of Christ Jesus who
has been called to be an apostle, and specially chosen to preach the Good News that
God 2 promised long ago through his prophets
in the scriptures.
3 This news is about the Son of God who,
according to the human nature he took, was a
descendant of David: 4 it is about Jesus Christ
our Lord who, in the order of the spirit, the
spirit of holiness that was in him, was proclaimed Son of God in all his power through
his resurrection from the dead. 5 Through him
we received grace and our apostolic mission to
preach the obedience of faith to all pagan nations in honor of his name. 6 You are one of
these nations, and by his call belong to Jesus

New English Bible

THE LETTER OF PAUL TO THE ROMANS

The Gospel according to Paul

1 From Paul, servant of Christ Jesus, apostle by God's call, set apart for the service of the Gospel.

This gospel God announced beforehand in sacred scriptures through his prophets. It is about his Son: on the human level he was born of David's stock, but on the level of the spirit—the Holy Spirit—he was declared Son of God by a mighty act in that he rose from the dead:[a] it is about Jesus Christ our Lord. Through him I received the privilege of a commission in his name to lead to faith and obedience men in all nations, yourselves among them, you who have heard the call and belong to Jesus Christ.

[a] *Or* declared Son of God with full powers from the time when he rose from the dead.

King James Version

Christ: 7 To all that be in Rome, beloved of God, called *to be* saints: Grace to you, and peace, from God our Father and the Lord Jesus Christ. 8 First, I thank my God through Jesus Christ for you all, that your faith is spoken of throughout the whole world. 9 For God is my witness, whom I serve with my spirit in the gospel of his Son, that without ceasing I make mention of you always in my prayers; 10 Making request, if by any means now at length I might have a prosperous journey by the will of God to come unto you. 11 For I long to see you, that I may impart unto you some spiritual gift, to the end ye may be established; 12 That is, that I may be comforted together with you by the mutual faith both of you and me. 13 Now I would not have you ignorant, brethren, that oftentimes I purposed to come unto you, (but was let hitherto,) that I might have some fruit among you also, even as among other Gentiles. 14 I am debtor both to the Greeks, and to the Barbarians; both to the wise, and to the unwise. 15 So, as much as in me is, I am ready to preach the gospel to you that are

Living Bible

vited by Jesus Christ to be God's very own—yes, his holy people. May all God's mercies and peace be yours from God our Father and from Jesus Christ our Lord.

8 Let me say first of all that wherever I go I hear you being talked about! For your faith in God is becoming known around the world. How I thank God through Jesus Christ for this good report, and for each one of you. 9 God knows how often I pray for you. Day and night I bring you and your needs in prayer to the one I serve with all my might, telling others the Good News about his Son.

10 And one of the things I keep on praying for is the opportunity, God willing,[a] to come at last to see you and, if possible, that I will have a safe trip.[b] 11, 12 For I long to visit you so that I can impart to you the faith[c] that will help your church grow strong in the Lord. Then, too, I need your help, for I want not only to share my faith with you but to be encouraged by yours: Each of us will be a blessing to the other.

13 I want you to know, dear brothers, that I planned to come many times before (but was prevented) so that I could work among you and see good results, just as I have among the other Gentile churches.[d] 14 For I owe a great debt to you and to everyone else, both to civilized people and uncivilized alike; yes, to the educated and uneducated alike. 15 So, to the fullest extent of my ability, I am ready to come also to you in Rome to preach God's Good News.

[*a*] Literally, "in the will of God." [*b*] Or, "that I will finally succeed in coming." [*c*] Literally, "some spiritual gift . . . that is, . . . faith." [*d*] Literally, "among the Gentiles."

Today's English Version

7 And so I write to all of you in Rome whom God loves and has called to be his own people:

May God our Father and the Lord Jesus Christ give you grace and peace.

Prayer of thanksgiving

8 First, I thank my God, through Jesus Christ, for all of you; because the whole world is hearing of your faith. 9 God can prove that what I say is true—the God whom I serve with all my heart by preaching the Good News about his Son. God knows that I always remember you 10 every time I pray. I ask that God, in his good will, may at last make it possible for me to visit you now. 11 For I want very much to see you in order to share a spiritual blessing with you, to make you strong. 12 What I mean is that both you and I will be helped at the same time, you by my faith and I by your faith.

13 You must remember this, my brothers: many times I have planned to visit you, but something has always kept me from doing so. I want to win converts among you, too, as I have among other Gentiles. 14 For I have an obligation to all peoples, to the civilized and to the savage, to the educated and to the ignorant. 15 So then, I am eager to preach the Good News to you also who live in Rome.

New International Version

7 To all in Rome who are loved by God and called to be saints:

Grace and peace to you from God our Father and from the Lord Jesus Christ.

Paul's longing to visit Rome

8 First, I thank my God through Jesus Christ for all of you, because your faith is being reported all over the world. 9 God, whom I serve with my whole heart in preaching the gospel of his Son, is my witness how constantly I remember you 10 in my prayers at all times; and I pray that now at last by God's will the way may be opened for me to come to you.

11 I long to see you so that I may impart to you some spiritual gift to make you strong—12 that is, that you and I may be mutually encouraged by each other's faith. 13 I do not want you to be unaware, brothers, that I planned many times to come to you (but have been prevented from doing so until now) in order that I might have a harvest among you, just as I have had among the other Gentiles.

14 I am obligated both to Greeks and non-Greeks, both to the wise and the foolish. 15 That is why I am so eager to preach the gospel also to you who are at Rome.

Phillips Modern English

To you all in Rome then, loved of God and called to be Christ's men and women, grace and peace from God our Father and from the Lord Jesus Christ.

1.8 A personal message

I must begin by telling you how I thank God through Jesus Christ for you all, since the news of your faith has become known everywhere. Before God, whom I serve with my spirit in the gospel of his Son, I assure you that you are always in my prayers. I am constantly asking him that he will somehow make it possible for me now, at long last, to come to see you. I am longing to see you: I want to bring you some spiritual gift to deepen your faith; and that will mean that I shall be encouraged by you, each of us cheered by the other's faith.

Then I should like you to know, my brothers, that I have long intended to come to you (but something has always prevented me), for I should like to see some results among you, as I have among other gentiles. I feel myself under a sort of universal obligation, I owe something to all men, from cultured Greek to ignorant savage. That is why I want, as far as my ability will carry me, to preach the gospel to you who

Revised Standard Version

7 To all God's beloved in Rome, who are
called to be saints:
Grace to you and peace from God our Father
and the Lord Jesus Christ.

8 First, I thank my God through Jesus Christ
for all of you, because your faith is proclaimed
in all the world. 9 For God is my witness, whom
I serve with my spirit in the gospel of his Son,
that without ceasing I mention you always in
my prayers, 10 asking that somehow by God's
will I may now at last succeed in coming to you.
11 For I long to see you, that I may impart to
you some spiritual gift to strengthen you, 12 that
is, that we may be mutually encouraged by each
other's faith, both yours and mine. 13 I want
you to know, brethren, that I have often intended to come to you (but thus far have been
prevented), in order that I may reap some harvest among you as well as among the rest of the
Gentiles. 14 I am under obligation both to
Greeks and to barbarians, both to the wise and
to the foolish: 15 so I am eager to preach the
gospel to you also who are in Rome.

Jerusalem Bible

Christ. 7 To you all, then, who are God's beloved in Rome, called to be saints, may God our
Father and the Lord Jesus Christ send grace
and peace.

Thanksgiving and prayer

8 First I thank my God through Jesus Christ
for all of you and for the way in which your
faith is spoken of all over the world. 9 The God
I worship spiritually by preaching the Good
News of his Son knows that I never fail to
mention you in my prayers, 10 and to ask to be
allowed at long last the opportunity to visit
you, if he so wills. 11 For I am longing to see
you either to strengthen you by sharing a spiritual gift with you, 12 or what is better, to find
encouragement among you from our common
faith. 13 I want you to know, brothers, that I
have often planned to visit you—though until
now I have always been prevented—in the hope
that I might work as fruitfully among you as I
have done among the other pagans. 14 I owe a
duty to Greeks[a] just as much as to barbarians,
to be educated just as much as to the uneducated, 15 and it is this that makes me want to
bring the Good News to you too in Rome.

[a] When contrasted with "barbarians" (as here), "Greeks" means the inhabitants of the Hellenic world, including the Romans; when contrasted with "Jews," it means the pagans in general.

New English Bible

I send greetings to all of you in Rome whom God loves and has called to be his dedicated people. Grace and peace to you from God our Father and the Lord Jesus Christ.

Let me begin by thanking my God, through Jesus Christ, for you all, because all over the world they are telling the story of your faith. God is my witness, the God to whom I offer the humble service of my spirit by preaching the gospel of his Son: God knows how continually I make mention of you in my prayers, and am always asking that by his will I may, somehow or other, succeed at long last in coming to visit you. For I long to see you; I want to bring you some spiritual gift to make you strong; or rather, I want to be among you to be myself encouraged by your faith as well as you by mine.

But I should like you to know,[b] my brothers, that I have often planned to come, though so far without success, in the hope of achieving something among you, as I have in other parts of the world. I am under obligation to Greek and non-Greek, to learned and simple; hence my eagerness to declare the Gospel to you in Rome

[b] *Some witnesses read* I believe you know.

King James Version

at Rome also. 16 For I am not ashamed of the gospel of Christ: for it is the power of God unto salvation to every one that believeth; to the Jew first, and also to the Greek. 17 For therein is the righteousness of God revealed from faith to faith: as it is written, The just shall live by faith. 18 For the wrath of God is revealed from heaven against all ungodliness and unrighteousness of men, who hold the truth in unrighteousness; 19 Because that which may be known of God is manifest in them; for God hath shewed *it* unto them. 20 For the invisible things of him from the creation of the world are clearly seen, being understood by the things that are made, *even* his eternal power and Godhead; so that they are without excuse: 21 Because that, when they knew God, they glorified *him* not as God, neither were thankful; but became vain in their imaginations, and their foolish

Living Bible

16 For I am not ashamed of this Good News about Christ. It is God's powerful method of bringing all who believe it to heaven. This message was preached first to the Jews alone, but now everyone is invited to come to God in this same way. 17 This Good News tells us that God makes us ready for heaven—makes us right in God's sight—when we put our faith and trust in Christ to save us. This is accomplished from start to finish by faith.[e] As the Scripture says it, "The man who finds life will find it through trusting God."[f]

18 But God shows his anger from heaven against all sinful, evil men who push away the truth from them. 19 For the truth about God is known to them instinctively[g]; God has put this knowledge in their hearts. 20 Since earliest times men have seen the earth and sky and all God made, and have known of his existence and great eternal power. So they will have no excuse [when they stand before God at Judgment Day[h]].

21 Yes, they knew about him all right, but they wouldn't admit it or worship him or even thank him for all his daily care. And after awhile they began to think up silly ideas of what God was like and what he wanted them to do. The result was that their foolish minds became

[e] Literally: "(this) righteousness of God is *revealed* from faith to faith." [f] Habakkuk 2:4. [g] Literally, "is manifest in them." [h] Implied. Or, "They have no excuse for saying there is no God."

Today's English Version

The power of the gospel

16 I have complete confidence in the gospel; it is God's power to save all who believe, first the Jews and also the Gentiles. 17 For the gospel reveals how God puts men right with himself: it is through faith, from beginning to end. As the scripture says, "He who is put right with God through faith shall live."

The guilt of mankind

18 God's wrath is revealed coming down from heaven upon all the sin and evil of men whose evil ways prevent the truth from being known. 19 God punishes them, because what men can know about God is plain to them. God himself made it plain to them. 20 Ever since God created the world, his invisible qualities, both his eternal power and his divine nature, have been clearly seen. Men can perceive them in the things that God has made. So they have no excuse at all! 21 They know God, but they do not give him the honor that belongs to him, nor do they thank him. Instead, their thoughts have become complete nonsense and their empty minds are

New International Version

16 I am not ashamed of the gospel, because it is the power of God for the salvation of everyone who believes: first for the Jew, then for the Gentile. 17 For in the gospel a righteousness from God is revealed, a righteousness that is by faith from first to last, just as it is written: "The righteous will live by faith."[b]

God's wrath against mankind

18 The wrath of God is being revealed from heaven against all the godlessness and wickedness of men who suppress the truth by their wickedness, 19 since what may be known about God is plain to them, because God has made it plain to them. 20 For since the creation of the world God's invisible qualities—his eternal power and divine nature—have been clearly seen, being understood from what has been made, so that men are without excuse.

21 For although they knew God, they neither glorified him as God nor gave thanks to him, but their thinking became futile and their foolish

[b] Hab. 2:4.

Phillips Modern English

live in Rome as well. For I am not ashamed of the gospel. I see it as the very power of God working for the salvation of everyone who believes it, for the Jew first but also for the Greek. I see in it God's plan for making men right in his sight, a process begun and continued by their faith. For, as the scripture says:

The righteous shall live by faith.

1.18 The righteousness of God and the sin of man

Now the holy anger of God is disclosed from Heaven against the godlessness and evil of those men who render truth dumb and impotent by their wickedness. It is not that they do not know the truth about God; indeed he has made it quite plain to them. For since the beginning of the world the invisible attributes of God, e.g. his eternal power and deity, have been plainly discernible through things which he has made and which are commonly seen and known, thus leaving these men without a rag of excuse. They knew all the time that there is a God, yet they refused to acknowledge him as such, or to thank him for what he is or does. Thus they became fatuous in their argumentations, and plunged

Revised Standard Version

16 For I am not ashamed of the gospel: it is
the power of God for salvation to every one who
has faith, to the Jew first and also to the Greek.
17 For in it the righteousness of God is revealed
through faith for faith; as it is written, "He who
through faith is righteous shall live." [b]

18 For the wrath of God is revealed from
heaven against all ungodliness and wickedness of
men who by their wickedness suppress the truth.
19 For what can be known about God is plain
to them, because God has shown it to them.
20 Ever since the creation of the world his invisible nature, namely, his eternal power and
deity, has been clearly perceived in the things
that have been made. So they are without excuse;
21 for although they knew God they did not
honor him as God or give thanks to him, but
they became futile in their thinking and their

[b] Or *The righteous shall live by faith.*

Jerusalem Bible

Salvation by faith

I. Justification

The theme stated

16 For I am not ashamed of the Good News:
it is the power of God saving all who have faith
—Jews first, but Greeks as well—17 since this is
what reveals the justice of God to us: it shows
how faith leads to faith, or as scripture says:
The upright man finds life through faith.[b]

A. God's anger against pagan and Jew

God's anger against the pagans

18 The anger of God is being revealed from
heaven against all the impiety and depravity of
men who keep truth imprisoned in their wickedness. 19 For what can be known about God is
perfectly plain to them since God himself has
made it plain. 20 Ever since God created the
world his everlasting power and deity—however
invisible—have been there for the mind to see in
the things he has made. That is why such people
are without excuse: 21 they knew God and yet
refused to honor him as God or to thank him;
instead, they made nonsense out of logic and

[b] Hab. 2:4.

New English Bible

as well as to others. For I am not ashamed of the Gospel. It is the saving power of God for everyone who has faith—the Jew first, but the Greek also—because here is revealed God's way of righting wrong, a way that starts from faith and ends in faith;[c] as Scripture says, 'he shall gain life who is justified through faith'.

For we see divine retribution revealed from heaven and falling upon all the godless wickedness of men. In their wickedness they are stifling the truth. For all that may be known of God by men lies plain before their eyes; indeed God himself has disclosed it to them. His invisible attributes, that is to say his everlasting power and deity, have been visible, ever since the world began, to the eye of reason, in the things he has made. There is therefore no possible defence for their conduct; knowing God, they have refused to honour him as God, or to render him thanks. Hence all their thinking has ended in futility, and their misguided minds are

[c] *Or* . . . wrong. It is based on faith and addressed to faith.

King James Version

heart was darkened. 22 Professing themselves to
be wise, they became fools, 23 And changed the
glory of the uncorruptible God into an image
made like to corruptible man, and to birds, and
fourfooted beasts, and creeping things. 24 Wherefore God also gave them up to uncleanness,
through the lusts of their own hearts, to dishonour their own bodies between themselves:
25 Who changed the truth of God into a lie, and
worshipped and served the creature more than
the Creator, who is blessed for ever. Amen.
26 For this cause God gave them up unto vile
affections: for even their women did change the
natural use into that which is against nature:
27 And likewise also the men, leaving the natural use of the woman, burned in their lust one
toward another; men with men working that
which is unseemly, and receiving in themselves
that recompense of their error which was meet.
28 And even as they did not like to retain God
in *their* knowledge, God gave them over to a
reprobate mind, to do those things which are not
convenient; 29 Being filled with all unrighteousness, fornication, wickedness, covetousness, maliciousness; full of envy, murder, debate, deceit,
malignity; whisperers, 30 Backbiters, haters of
God, despiteful, proud, boasters, inventors of

Living Bible

dark and confused. 22 Claiming themselves to
be wise without God, they became utter fools
instead. 23 And then, instead of worshiping the
glorious, ever-living God, they took wood and
stone and made idols for themselves, carving
them to look like mere birds and animals and
snakes and puny[i] men.
24 So God let them go ahead into every sort
of sex sin, and do whatever they wanted to—
yes, vile and sinful things with each other's
bodies. 25 Instead of believing what they knew
was the truth about God, they deliberately chose
to believe lies. So they prayed to the things God
made, but wouldn't obey the blessed God who
made these things.
26 That is why God let go of them and let
them do all these evil things, so that even their
women turned against God's natural plan for
them and indulged in sex sin with each other.
27 And the men, instead of having a normal sex
relationship with women, burned with lust for
each other, men doing shameful things with other
men and, as a result, getting paid within their
own souls with the penalty they so richly deserved.
28 So it was that when they gave God up and
would not even acknowledge him, God gave
them up to doing everything their evil minds
could think of. 29 Their lives became full of
every kind of wickedness and sin, of greed and
hate, envy, murder, fighting, lying, bitterness, and
gossip. 30 They were backbiters, haters of God,
insolent, proud braggarts, always thinking of

[*i*] Literally, "mortal."

Today's English Version

filled with darkness. 22 They say they are wise,
but they are fools; 23 instead of worshiping the
immortal God, they worship images made to
look like mortal man or birds or animals or
reptiles.
24 Because men are such fools, God has given
them over to do the filthy things their hearts desire, and they do shameful things with each
other. 25 They exchange the truth about God
for a lie; they worship and serve what God has
created instead of the Creator himself, who is
to be praised forever! Amen.
26 Because men do this, God has given them
over to shameful passions. Even the women pervert the natural use of their sex by unnatural
acts. 27 In the same way the men give up
natural sexual relations with women and burn
with passion for each other. Men do shameful
things with each other, and as a result they
themselves are punished as they deserve for their
wrongdoing.
28 Because men refuse to keep in mind the
true knowledge about God, he has given them
over to corrupted minds, so that they do the
things that they should not. 29 They are filled
with all kinds of wickedness, evil, greed, and
vice; they are full of jealousy, murder, fighting,
deceit, and malice. They gossip, 30 and speak
evil of one another; they are hateful to God, in-

New International Version

hearts were darkened. 22 Although they claimed
to be wise, they became fools 23 and exchanged
the glory of the immortal God for images made
to look like mortal man and birds and animals
and reptiles.
24 Therefore God gave them over in the sinful desires of their hearts to sexual impurity
for the degrading of their bodies with one another. 25 They exchanged the truth of God for
a lie, and worshiped and served created things
rather than the Creator—who is forever praised.
Amen.
26 Because of this, God gave them over to
shameful lusts. Even their women exchanged
natural relations for unnatural ones. 27 In the
same way the men also abandoned natural relations with women and were inflamed with lust
for one another. Men committed indecent acts
with other men, and received in themselves the
due penalty for their perversion.
28 Furthermore, since they did not think it
worthwhile to retain the knowledge of God, he
gave them over to a depraved mind, to do what
ought not to be done. 29 They have become
filled with every kind of wickedness, evil, greed
and depravity. They are full of envy, murder,
strife, deceit and malice. They are gossips,
30 slanderers, God-haters, insolent, arrogant and

Phillips Modern English

their silly minds still further into the dark. Behind a façade of "wisdom" they became just fools, fools who would exchange the glory of the immortal God for an image of a mortal man, or of creatures that run or fly or crawl. They gave up God: and therefore God gave them up—to be the playthings of their own foul desires in dishonouring their own bodies.

1.25 The fearful consequence of deliberate atheism

These men deliberately forfeited the truth of God and accepted a lie, paying homage and giving service to the creature instead of the Creator, who alone is worthy to be worshipped for ever and ever, amen. God therefore handed them over to disgraceful passions. Their women exchanged the normal practices of sexual intercourse for something which is abnormal and unnatural. Similarly the men, turning from natural intercourse with women, were swept into lustful passions for one another. Men with men performed these shameful horrors, receiving in their own personalities the consequences of their perversity.

Moreover, since they considered themselves too high and mighty to acknowledge God, he allowed them to become the slaves of their degenerate minds, and to perform unmentionable deeds. They became filled with wickedness, rottenness, greed and malice; their minds became steeped in envy, murder, quarrelsomeness, deceitfulness and spite. They became whisperers-behind-doors, stabbers-in-the-back, God-haters; they overflowed

Revised Standard Version

senseless minds were darkened. 22 Claiming to
be wise, they became fools, 23 and exchanged
the glory of the immortal God for images resembling mortal man or birds or animals or reptiles.
24 Therefore God gave them up in the lusts of their hearts to impurity, to the dishonoring of
their bodies among themselves, 25 because they
exchanged the truth about God for a lie and worshiped and served the creature rather than the Creator, who is blessed for ever! Amen.
26 For this reason God gave them up to dishonorable passions. Their women exchanged
natural relations for unnatural, 27 and the men
likewise gave up natural relations with women and were consumed with passion for one another, men committing shameless acts with men and receiving in their own persons the due penalty for their error.
28 And since they did not see fit to acknowledge God, God gave them up to a base mind
and to improper conduct. 29 They were filled
with all manner of wickedness, evil, covetousness, malice. Full of envy, murder, strife, deceit,
malignity, they are gossips, 30 slanderers, haters
of God, insolent, haughty, boastful, inventors of

Jerusalem Bible

their empty minds were darkened. 22 The more
they called themselves philosophers, the more
stupid they grew, 23 until *they exchanged the glory*[c] of the immortal God for a worthless imitation, *for the image* of mortal man, of birds, of quadrupeds and reptiles. 24 That is why God
left them to their filthy enjoyments and the practices with which they dishonor their own bodies,
25 since they have given up divine truth for a lie and have worshiped and served creatures instead of the creator, who is blessed for ever. Amen!
26 That is why God has abandoned them to degrading passions: why their women have turned from natural intercourse to unnatural practices
27 and why their menfolk have given up natural intercourse to be consumed with passion for each other, men doing shameless things with men and getting an appropriate reward for their perversion.
28 In other words, since they refused to see it was rational to acknowledge God, God has left them to their own irrational ideas and to their monstrous behavior.
29And so they are steeped in all sorts of depravity, rottenness, greed and malice, and addicted to envy, murder, wrangling, treachery and spite.
30 Libelers, slanderers, enemies of God, rude, arrogant and

[c] Ps. 106:20.

New English Bible

plunged in darkness. They boast of their wisdom, but they have made fools of themselves, exchanging the splendour of immortal God for an image shaped like mortal man, even for images like birds, beasts, and creeping things.

For this reason God has given them up to the vileness of their own desires, and the consequent degradation of their bodies, because they have bartered away the true God for a false one,[a] and have offered reverence and worship to created things instead of to the Creator, who is blessed for ever; amen.

In consequence, I say, God has given them up to shameful passions. Their women have exchanged natural intercourse for unnatural, and their men in turn, giving up natural relations with women, burn with lust for one another; males behave indecently with males, and are paid in their own persons the fitting wage of such perversion.

Thus, because they have not seen fit to acknowledge God, he has given them up to their own depraved reason. This leads them to break all rules of conduct. They are filled with every kind of injustice, mischief, rapacity, and malice; they are one mass of envy, murder, rivalry, treachery, and malevolence; whisperers and scandal-mongers, hateful to God, insolent, arrogant,

[a] *Or* the truth of God for the lie.

King James Version

evil things, disobedient to parents, 31 Without understanding, covenant-breakers, without natural affection, implacable, unmerciful: 32 Who, knowing the judgment of God, that they which commit such things are worthy of death, not only do the same, but have pleasure in them that do them.

2 Therefore thou art inexcusable, O man, whosoever thou art that judgest: for wherein thou judgest another, thou condemnest thyself; for thou that judgest doest the same things. 2 But we are sure that the judgment of God is according to truth against them which commit such things. 3 And thinkest thou this, O man, that judgest them which do such things, and doest the same, that thou shalt escape the judgment of God? 4 Or despisest thou the riches of his goodness and forbearance and long suffering; not knowing that the goodness of God leadeth thee to repentance? 5 But, after thy hardness and impenitent heart, treasurest up unto thyself wrath against the day of wrath and

Living Bible

new ways of sinning and continually being disobedient to their parents. 31 They tried to misunderstand,[j] broke their promises, and were heartless—without pity. 32 They were fully aware of God's death penalty for these crimes, yet they went right ahead and did them anyway, and encouraged others to do them, too.

2 "Well," you may be saying, "what terrible people you have been talking about!" But wait a minute! You are just as bad. When you say they are wicked and should be punished, you are talking about yourselves, for you do these very same things. 2 And we know that God, in justice, will punish anyone who does such things as these. 3 Do you think that God will judge and condemn others for doing them and overlook you when you do them, too? 4 Don't you realize how patient he is being with you? Or don't you care? Can't you see that he has been waiting all this time without punishing you, to give you time to turn from your sin? His kindness is meant to lead you to repentance.

5 But no, you won't listen; and so you are saving up terrible punishment for yourselves because of your stubbornness in refusing to turn

[j] Or, "were confused fools."

Today's English Version

solent, proud, and boastful; they think of more ways to do evil; they disobey their parents; 31 they are immoral; they do not keep their promises, and they show no kindness or pity to others. 32 They know that God's law says that people who live in this way deserve death. Yet, not only do they continue to do these very things, but they also approve of others who do them.

God's judgment

2 Do you, my friend, pass judgment on others? You have no excuse at all, whoever you are. For when you judge others, but do the same things that they do, you condemn yourself. 2 We know that God is right when he judges the people who do such things as these. 3 But you, my friend, do these very things yourself for which you pass judgment on others! Do you think you will escape God's judgment? 4 Or perhaps you despise his great kindness, tolerance, and patience. Surely you know that God is kind because he is trying to lead you to repent. 5 But you have a hard and stubborn heart. So then, you are making your own punishment even

New International Version

boastful; they invent ways of doing evil; they disobey their parents; 31 they are senseless, faithless, heartless, ruthless. 32 Although they know God's righteous decree that those who do such things deserve death, they not only continue to do these very things, but also approve of those who practice them.

God's righteous judgment

2 You, therefore, have no excuse, you who pass judgment on someone else, for at whatever point you judge the other, you are condemning yourself, because you who pass judgment do the same things. 2 Now we know that God's judgment against those who do such things is based on truth. 3 So when you, a mere man, pass judgment on them and yet do the same things, do you think you will escape God's judgment? 4 Or do you show contempt for the riches of his kindness, tolerance and patience, not realizing that God's kindness should lead you to repentance?

5 But because of your stubbornness and your unrepentant heart, you are storing up wrath

Phillips Modern English

with insolent pride and boastfulness, and their minds teemed with diabolical invention. They scoffed at duty to parents, they mocked at conscience, recognised no obligations of honour, lost all natural affection, and had no use for mercy. More than this—being well aware of God's pronouncement that all who do these things deserve to die, they not only continued their own practices, but did not hesitate to give their thorough approval to others who did the same.

2.1 Yet we cannot judge them, for we also are sinners: God is the only judge

Now if you feel inclined to set yourself up as a judge of those who sin, let me assure you, whoever you are, that you are in no position to do so. For at whatever point you condemn others you automatically condemn yourself, since you, the judge, commit the same sins. God's judgment, we know, is utterly impartial in its action against such evil-doers. What makes you think that you, who so readily judge the sins of others, can consider yourself beyond the judgment of God? Are you, perhaps, misinterpreting God's generosity and patient mercy towards you as weakness on his part? Don't you realise that God's kindness is meant to lead you to repentance? Or are you by your obstinate refusal to repent simply storing up for yourself an experience of the wrath of

Revised Standard Version

evil, disobedient to parents, 31 foolish, faithless,
heartless, ruthless. 32 Though they know God's
decree that those who do such things deserve to
die, they not only do them but approve those
who practice them.

2 Therefore you have no excuse, O man,
whoever you are, when you judge another;
for in passing judgment upon him you condemn
yourself, because you, the judge, are doing the
very same things. 2 We know that the judgment
of God rightly falls upon those who do such
things. 3 Do you suppose, O man, that when you
judge those who do such things and yet do them
yourself, you will escape the judgment of God?
4 Or do you presume upon the riches of his kindness and forbearance and patience? Do you not
know that God's kindness is meant to lead you
to repentance? 5 But by your hard and impenitent heart you are storing up wrath for yourself

Jerusalem Bible

boastful, enterprising in sin, rebellious to parents, 31 without brains, honor, love or pity.
32 They know what God's verdict is: that those
who behave like this deserve to die—and yet
they do it; and what is worse, encourage others
to do the same.

The Jews are not exempt from God's anger

2 So no matter who you are, if you pass
judgment you have no excuse. In judging
others you condemn yourself, since you behave
no differently from those you judge. 2 We know
that God condemns that sort of behavior impartially: 3 and when you judge those who behave like this while you are doing exactly the
same, do you think you will escape God's judgment? 4 Or are you abusing his abundant goodness, patience and toleration, not realizing that
this goodness of God is meant to lead you to
repentance? 5 Your stubborn refusal to repent is
only adding to the anger God will have toward

New English Bible

and boastful; they invent new kinds of mischief, they show no loyalty to parents, no conscience, no fidelity to their plighted word; they are without natural affection and without pity. They know well enough the just decree of God, that those who behave like this deserve to die, and yet they do it; not only so, they actually applaud such practices.

2 You therefore have no defence—you who sit in judgement, whoever you may be—for in judging your fellow-man you condemn yourself, since you, the judge, are equally guilty. It is admitted that God's judgement is rightly passed upon all who commit such crimes as these; and do you imagine—you who pass judgement on the guilty while committing the same crimes yourself—do you imagine that you, any more than they, will escape the judgement of God? Or do you think lightly of his wealth of kindness, of tolerance, and of patience, without recognizing that God's kindness is meant to lead you to a change of heart? In the rigid obstinacy of your heart you are laying up for yourself a

King James Version

revelation of the righteous judgment of God;
6 Who will render to every man according to his
deeds: 7 To them who by patient continuance
in well doing seek for glory and honour and immortality, eternal life: 8 But unto them that are
contentious, and do not obey the truth, but
obey unrighteousness, indignation and wrath,
9 Tribulation and anguish, upon every soul of
man that doeth evil; of the Jew first, and also
of the Gentile; 10 But glory, honour, and peace,
to every man that worketh good; to the Jew
first, and also to the Gentile: 11 For there is no
respect of persons with God. 12 For as many as
have sinned without law shall also perish without law; and as many as have sinned in the law
shall be judged by the law; 13 (For not the
hearers of the law *are* just before God, but the
doers of the law shall be justified. 14 For when
the Gentiles, which have not the law, do by
nature the things contained in the law, these,
having not the law, are a law unto themselves:
15 Which shew the work of the law written in
their hearts, their conscience also bearing witness, and *their* thoughts the mean while ac-

Living Bible

from your sin; for there is going to come a day
of wrath when God will be the just Judge of all
the world. 6 He will give each one whatever his
deeds deserve. 7 He will give eternal life to those
who patiently do the will of God,[a] seeking for
the unseen[b] glory and honor and eternal life
that he offers.[b] 8 But he will terribly punish
those who fight against the truth of God and
walk in evil ways—God's anger will be poured
out upon them. 9 There will be sorrow and suffering for Jews and Gentiles alike who keep on
sinning. 10 But there will be glory and honor and
peace from God for all who obey him,[c] whether
they are Jews or Gentiles. 11 For God treats
everyone the same.

12–15 He will punish sin wherever it is found.
He will punish the heathen when they sin, even
though they never had God's written laws, for
down in their hearts they know right from
wrong. God's laws are written within them; their
own conscience accuses them, or sometimes excuses them. And God will punish the Jews for
sinning because they have his written laws but
don't obey them. They know what is right but
don't do it. After all, salvation is not given to
those who know what to do, unless they do it.

[a] Literally, "who patiently do good." [b] Implied.
[c] Literally, "all who do good."

Today's English Version

greater on the Day when God's wrath and right
judgments will be revealed. 6 For God will reward
every person according to what he has done.
7 Some men keep on doing good, and seek glory,
honor, and immortal life; to them God will give
eternal life. 8 Other men are selfish and reject
what is right, to follow what is wrong; on them
God will pour his wrath and anger. 9 There will
be suffering and pain for all men who do what
is evil, for the Jews first and also for the Gentiles.
10 But God will give glory, honor, and peace to
all who do what is good, to the Jews first, and
also to the Gentiles. 11 For God judges everyone
by the same standard.

12 The Gentiles do not have the Law of
Moses; they sin and are lost apart from the Law.
The Jews have the Law; they sin and are judged
by the Law. 13 For it is not by hearing the Law
that men are put right with God, but by doing
what the Law commands. 14 The Gentiles do not
have the Law; but whenever of their own free
will they do what the Law commands, they are
a law to themselves, even though they do not
have the Law. 15 Their conduct shows that what
the Law commands is written in their hearts.
Their consciences also show that this is true, since
their thoughts sometimes accuse them and some-

New International Version

against yourself for the day of God's wrath,
when his righteous judgment will be revealed.
6 God "will give to each person according to
what he has done." [c] 7 To those who by persistence in doing good seek glory, honor and immortality, he will give eternal life. 8 But for
those who are self-seeking and who reject the
truth and follow evil, there will be wrath and
anger. 9 There will be trouble and distress for
every human being who does evil: first for the
Jew, then for the Gentile; 10 but glory, honor
and peace for everyone who does good: first
for the Jew, then for the Gentile. 11 For God
does not show favoritism.

12 All who sin apart from the law will also
perish apart from the law, and all who sin under
the law will be judged by the law. 13 For it is
not those who hear the law who are righteous
in God's sight, but it is those who obey the law
who will be declared righteous. 14 (Indeed, when
Gentiles, who do not have the law, do by nature
things required by the law, they are a law for
themselves, even though they do not have the
law, 15 since they show that the requirements
of the law are written on their hearts, their consciences also bearing witness, and their thoughts

[c] Psalm 62:12; Prov. 24:12.

Phillips Modern English

God in the day of his anger when he shows his hand in righteous judgment?

He will "render to every man according to his works", and that means eternal life to those who, in patiently doing good, aim at the unseen glory and honour of the eternal world. It also means anger and wrath for those who rebel against God's plan of life, and refuse to obey his rules, and who, in so doing, make themselves the very servants of evil. Yes, it means bitter pain and agony for every human soul who works on the side of evil, for the Jew first and then the Greek. But there is glory and honour and peace for every worker on the side of good, for the Jew first and also for the Greek. For there is no preferential treatment with God.

2.12 God's judgment is absolutely just

All who have sinned without knowledge of the Law will die without reference to the Law; and all who have sinned knowing the Law shall be judged according to the Law. It is not familiarity with the Law that justifies a man in the sight of God, but obedience to it.

When the gentiles, who have no knowledge of the Law, act in accordance with it by the light of nature, they show that they have a law in themselves, for they demonstrate the effect of a law operating in their own hearts. Their own consciences endorse the existence of such a law, for there is something which condemns or excuses their actions.

Revised Standard Version

on the day of wrath when God's righteous judgment will be revealed. 6 For he will render to
every man according to his works: 7 to those
who by patience in well-doing seek for glory and
honor and immortality, he will give eternal life;
8 but for those who are factious and do not obey
the truth, but obey wickedness, there will be
wrath and fury. 9 There will be tribulation and
distress for every human being who does evil, the
Jew first and also the Greek, 10 but glory and
honor and peace for every one who does good,
the Jew first and also the Greek. 11 For God
shows no partiality.
12 All who have sinned without the law will
also perish without the law, and all who have
sinned under the law will be judged by the law.
13 For it is not the hearers of the law who are
righteous before God, but the doers of the law
who will be justified. 14 When Gentiles who have
not the law do by nature what the law requires,
they are a law to themselves, even thoug' they
do not have the law. 15 They show that what the
law requires is written on their hearts, while their
conscience also bears witness and their conflicting thoughts accuse or perhaps excuse them

Jerusalem Bible

you on that day of anger when his just judgments will be made known. 6 *He will repay each
one as his works deserve.*[d] 7 For those who
sought renown and honor and immortality by
always doing good there will be eternal life;
8 for the unsubmissive who refused to take truth
for their guide and took depravity instead, there
will be anger and fury. 9 Pain and suffering will
come to every human being who employs himself in evil—Jews first, but Greeks as well;
10 renown, honor and peace will come to everyone who does good—Jews first, but Greeks as
well. 11 God has no favorites.

The Law will not save them

12 Sinners who were not subject to the Law
will perish all the same, without that Law; sinners who were under the Law will have that
Law to judge them. 13 It is not listening to the
Law but keeping it that will make people holy
in the sight of God. 14 For instance, pagans who
never heard of the Law but are led by reason
to do what the Law commands, may not actually "possess" the Law, but they can be said to
"be" the Law. 15 They can point to the substance of the Law engraved on their hearts—
they can call a witness, that is, their own conscience—they have accusation and defense, that

[d] Ps. 6:12.

New English Bible

store of retribution for the day of retribution, when God's just judgement will be revealed, and he will pay every man for what he has done. To those who pursue glory, honour, and immortality by steady persistence in well-doing, he will give eternal life; but for those who are governed by selfish ambition, who refuse obedience to the truth and take the wrong for their guide, there will be the fury of retribution. There will be trouble and distress for every human being who is an evil-doer, for the Jew first and for the Greek also; and for every well-doer there will be glory, honour, and peace, for the Jew first and also for the Greek.

For God has no favourites: those who have sinned outside the pale of the Law of Moses will perish outside its pale, and all who have sinned under that law will be judged by the law. It is not by hearing the law, but by doing it, that men will be justified before God. When Gentiles who do not possess the law carry out its precepts by the light of nature, then, although they have no law, they are their own law, for they display the effect of the law inscribed on their hearts. Their conscience is called as witness, and their own thoughts argue the case on either side, against

King James Version

cusing or else excusing one another;) 16 In the
day when God shall judge the secrets of men by
Jesus Christ according to my gospel. 17 Behold,
thou art called a Jew, and restest in the law,
and makest thy boast of God, 18And knowest
his will, and approvest the things that are more
excellent, being instructed out of the law; 19And
art confident that thou thyself art a guide of the
blind, a light of them which are in darkness,
20An instructor of the foolish, a teacher of
babes, which hast the form of knowledge and of
the truth in the law. 21 Thou therefore which
teachest another, teachest thou not thyself? thou
that preachest a man should not steal, dost thou
steal? 22 Thou that sayest a man should not
commit adultery, dost thou commit adultery?
thou that abhorrest idols, dost thou commit
sacrilege? 23 Thou that makest thy boast of the
law, through breaking the law dishonourest thou
God? 24 For the name of God is blasphemed
among the Gentiles through you, as it is written.

Living Bible

16 The day will surely come when at God's command Jesus Christ will judge the secret lives of everyone, their inmost thoughts and motives; this is all part of God's great plan which I proclaim.

17 You Jews think all is well between yourselves and God because he gave his laws to
you;[d] you brag that you are his special friends.
18 Yes, you know what he wants; you know
right from wrong and favor the right because
you have been taught his laws from earliest
youth. 19 You are so sure of the way to God
that you could point it out to a blind man. You
think of yourselves as beacon lights, directing
men who are lost in darkness to God. 20 You
think that you can guide the simple and teach
even children the affairs of God, for you really
know his laws, which are full of all knowledge
and truth.

21 Yes, you teach others—then why don't
you teach yourselves? You tell others not to
steal—do *you* steal? 22 You say it is wrong to
commit adultery—do *you* do it? You say, "Don't
pray to idols," and then make money your god
instead.[e]

23 You are so proud of knowing God's laws,
but you dishonor him by breaking them. 24 No
wonder the Scriptures say that the world speaks
evil of God because of you.

[*d*] Or, "you rely upon the law for your salvation."
[*e*] Literally, "do you rob temples?"

Today's English Version

times defend them. 16And so, according to the
Good News I preach, this is how it will be on
that Day when God, through Jesus Christ, will
judge the secret thoughts of men.

The Jews and the Law

17 What about you? You call yourself a Jew;
you depend on the Law and boast about God;
18 you know what God wants you to do, and you
have learned from the Law to choose what is
right; 19 you are sure that you are a guide for
the blind, a light for those who are in darkness,
20 an instructor for the foolish, and a teacher
for the young. You are certain that in the Law
you have the full content of knowledge and of
truth. 21 You teach others—why don't you teach
yourself? You preach, "Do not steal"—but do
you yourself steal? 22 You say, "Do not commit
adultery"—but do you commit adultery? You
detest idols—but do you rob temples? 23 You
boast about having God's law—but do you
bring shame on God by breaking his law? 24 The
scripture says, "Because of you Jews, the Gentiles speak evil of God's name."

New International Version

now accusing, now even defending them.) 16 This
will take place on the day when God will judge
men's secrets through Jesus Christ, as my gospel
declares.

The Jews and the law

17 Now you, if you call yourself a Jew; if
you rely on the law and brag about your relationship to God; 18 if you know his will and
approve of what is superior because you are instructed by the law; 19 if you are convinced that
you are a guide for the blind, a light for those
who are in the dark, 20 an instructor of the
foolish, a teacher of infants, because you have in
the law the embodiment of knowledge and truth
—21 you, then, who teach others, do you not
teach yourself? You who preach against stealing,
do you steal? 22 You who say that people should
not commit adultery, do you commit adultery?
You who abhor idols, do you rob temples?
23 You who brag about the law, do you dishonor God by breaking the law? 24As it is written: "God's name is blasphemed among the Gentiles because of you." [d]

[*d*] Isaiah 52:5; Ezek. 36:22.

Phillips Modern English

We may be sure that all this will be taken into account in the day of true judgment, when God will judge men's secret lives by Christ Jesus, as my gospel plainly states.

2.17 You Jews are privileged—do you live up to your privileges?

Now you, my reader, who bear the name of Jew, take your stand upon the Law, and are, so to speak, proud of your God. You know his plan, and are able through your knowledge of the Law truly to appreciate moral values. You can, therefore, confidently look upon yourself as a guide to those who do not know the way, and as a light to those who are groping in the dark. You can instruct those who have no spiritual wisdom: you can teach those who, spiritually speaking, are only just out of the cradle. You have in the Law a certain grasp of the basis of true knowledge. But, prepared as you are to instruct others, do you ever teach yourself anything? You preach against stealing, for example, but are you sure of your own honesty? You denounce the practice of adultery, but are you sure of your own purity? You loathe idolatry, but how honest are you towards the property of heathen temples? Everyone knows how proud you are of the Law, but that means a proportionate dishonour to God when men know that you break it! Don't you know that the very name of God is cursed among the gentiles because of the behaviour of Jews? There is a verse of scripture to that effect.

Revised Standard Version

16 on that day when, according to my gospel, God judges the secrets of men by Christ Jesus.

17 But if you call yourself a Jew and rely upon the law and boast of your relation to God 18 and know his will and approve what is excellent, because you are instructed in the law, 19 and if you are sure that you are a guide to the blind, a light to those who are in darkness, 20 a corrector of the foolish, a teacher of children, having in the law the embodiment of knowledge and truth—21 you then who teach others, will you not teach yourself? While you preach against stealing, do you steal? 22 You who say that one must not commit adultery, do you commit adultery? You who abhor idols, do you rob temples? 23 You who boast in the law, do you dishonor God by breaking the law? 24 For, as it is written, "The name of God is blasphemed among the Gentiles because of you."

Jerusalem Bible

is, their own inner mental dialogue.[e] 16 . . . on the day when, according to the Good News I preach, God, through Jesus Christ, judges the secrets of mankind.

17 If you call yourself a Jew, if you really trust in the Law and are proud of your God, 18 if you know God's will through the Law and can tell what is right, 19 if you are convinced you can guide the blind and be a beacon to those in the dark, 20 if you can teach the ignorant and instruct the unlearned because your Law embodies all knowledge and truth, 21 then why not teach yourself as well as the others? You preach against stealing, yet you steal; 22 you forbid adultery, yet you commit adultery; you despise idols, yet you rob their temples. 23 By boasting about the Law and then disobeying it, you bring God into contempt. 24 As scripture says: *It is your fault that the name of God is blasphemed among the pagans.*

[e] This verse follows on from v. 13.

New English Bible

them or even for them, on the day when God judges the secrets of human hearts through Christ Jesus. So my gospel declares.

But as for you—you may bear the name of Jew; you rely upon the law and are proud of your God; you know his will; instructed by the law, you know right from wrong; you are confident that you are the one to guide the blind, to enlighten the benighted, to train the stupid, and to teach the immature, because in the law you see the very shape of knowledge and truth. You, then, who teach your fellow-man, do you fail to teach yourself? You proclaim, 'Do not steal'; but are you yourself a thief? You say, 'Do not commit adultery'; but are you an adulterer? You abominate false gods; but do you rob their shrines? While you take pride in the law, you dishonour God by breaking it. For, as Scripture says, 'Because of you the name of God is dishonoured among the Gentiles.'

King James Version

25 For circumcision verily profiteth, if thou keep the law: but if thou be a breaker of the law, thy circumcision is made uncircumcision. 26 Therefore, if the uncircumcision keep the righteousness of the law, shall not his uncircumcision be counted for circumcision? 27 And shall not uncircumcision which is by nature, if it fulfil the law, judge thee, who by the letter and circumcision dost transgress the law? 28 For he is not a Jew, which is one outwardly; neither *is that* circumcision, which is outward in the flesh: 29 But he *is* a Jew, which is one inwardly; and circumcision *is that* of the heart, in the spirit, *and* not in the letter; whose praise *is* not of men, but of God.

3 What advantage then hath the Jew? or what profit *is there* of circumcision? 2 Much every way: chiefly, because that unto them were com-

Living Bible

25 Being a Jew is worth something if you obey God's laws; but if you don't, then you are no better off than the heathen. 26 And if the heathen obey God's laws, won't God give them all the rights and honors he planned to give the Jews? 27 In fact, those heathen will be much better off [f] than you Jews who know so much about God and have his promises but don't obey his laws.

28 For you are not real Jews just because you were born of Jewish parents or because you have gone through the Jewish initiation ceremony of circumcision. 29 No, a real Jew is anyone whose heart is right with God. For God is not looking for those who cut their bodies in actual body circumcision, but he is looking for those with changed hearts and minds. Whoever has that kind of change in his life will get his praise from God, even if not from you.

3 Then what's the use of being a Jew? Are there any special benefits for them from God? Is there any value in the Jewish circumcision ceremony? 2 Yes, being a Jew has many advantages.

[f] Literally, "will condemn" you.

Today's English Version

25 If you obey the Law, your circumcision is of value; but if you disobey the Law, you might as well never have been circumcised. 26 If the Gentile, who is not circumcised, obeys the commands of the Law, will not God regard him as though he were circumcised? 27 And so you Jews will be condemned by the Gentiles, because you break the Law, even though you have it written down and are circumcised, while they obey the Law, even though they are not physically circumcised. 28 After all, who is a real Jew, truly circumcised? Not the man who is a Jew on the outside, whose circumcision is a physical thing. 29 Rather, the real Jew is the man who is a Jew on the inside, that is, whose heart has been circumcised, which is the work of God's Spirit, not of the written Law. This man receives his praise from God, not from men.

3 Do the Jews have any advantage over the Gentiles, then? Or is there any value in being circumcised? 2 Much, indeed, in every way!

New International Version

25 Circumcision has value if you observe the law, but if you break the law, you have become as though you had not been circumcised. 26 If those who are not circumcised keep the law's requirements, will they not be regarded as though they were circumcised? 27 The one who is not circumcised physically and yet obeys the law will condemn you who, even though you have the[e] written code and circumcision, are a lawbreaker.

28 A man is not a Jew if he is only one outwardly, nor is circumcision merely outward and physical. 29 No, a man is a Jew if he is one inwardly; and circumcision is circumcision of the heart, by the Spirit, not by the written code. Such a man's praise is not from men, but from God.

God's faithfulness

3 What advantage, then, is there in being a Jew, or what value is there in circumcision? 2 Much in every way! First of all, they have

[e] Or *who by means of a.*

Phillips Modern English

2.25 Being a true "Jew" is an inward not an outward matter

That most intimate sign of belonging to God that we call circumcision does indeed mean something if you keep the Law. But if you flout the Law you are to all intents and purposes uncircumcising yourself! Conversely, if an uncircumcised man keep the Law's commandments, does he not thereby "circumcise" himself? Moreover, is it not plain to you that those who are physically uncircumcised, and yet keep the Law, are a continual judgment upon you who, for all your circumcision and knowledge of the Law, break it?

I have come to the conclusion that a true Jew is not the man who is merely a Jew outwardly, and real circumcision is not just a matter of the body. The true Jew is one who belongs to God in heart, a man whose circumcision is not just an outward physical affair but is a God-made sign upon the heart and soul, and results not in the approval of man, but in the approval of God.

3.1 Jews are privileged, but even they have failed

Is there any advantage then in being a Jew? Does circumcision mean anything? Yes, of course, a great deal in every way. You have only

Revised Standard Version

25 Circumcision indeed is of value if you obey the law; but if you break the law, your circumcision becomes uncircumcision. 26 So, if a man who is uncircumcised keeps the precepts of the law, will not his uncircumcision be regarded as circumcision? 27 Then those who are physically uncircumcised but keep the law will condemn you who have the written code and circumcision but break the law. 28 For he is not a real Jew who is one outwardly, nor is true circumcision something external and physical. 29 He is a Jew who is one inwardly, and real circumcision is a matter of the heart, spiritual and not literal. His praise is not from men but from God.

3 Then what advantage has the Jew? Or what is the value of circumcision? 2 Much in every way. To begin with, the Jews are entrusted with

Jerusalem Bible

Circumcision will not save them

25 It is a good thing to be circumcised if you keep the Law; but if you break the Law, you might as well have stayed uncircumcised. 26 If a man who is not circumcised obeys the commandments of the Law, surely that makes up for not being circumcised? 27 More than that, the man who keeps the Law, even though he has not been physically circumcised, is a living condemnation of the way you disobey the Law in spite of being circumcised and having it all written down. 28 To be a Jew is not just to look like a Jew, and circumcision is more than a physical operation. 29 The real Jew is the one who is inwardly a Jew, and the real circumcision is in the heart—something not of the letter but of the spirit. A Jew like that may not be praised by man, but he will be praised by God.

God's promises will not save them

3 Well then, is a Jew any better off? Is there any advantage in being circumcised? 2 A great advantage in every way. First, the Jews are

New English Bible

Circumcision has value, provided you keep the law; but if you break the law, then your circumcision is as if it had never been. Equally, if an uncircumcised man keeps the precepts of the law, will he not count as circumcised? He may be uncircumcised in his natural state, but by fulfilling the law he will pass judgement on you who break it, for all your written code and your circumcision. The true Jew is not he who is such in externals, neither is the true circumcision the external mark in the flesh. The true Jew is he who is such inwardly, and the true circumcision is of the heart, directed not by written precepts but by the Spirit; such a man receives his commendation not from men but from God.

3 Then what advantage has the Jew? What is the value of circumcision? Great, in every way. In the first place, the Jews were entrusted

King James Version

mitted the oracles of God. 3 For what if some
did not believe? shall their unbelief make the
faith of God without effect? 4 God forbid: yea,
let God be true, but every man a liar; as it is
written, That thou mightest be justified in thy
sayings, and mightest overcome when thou art
judged. 5 But if our unrighteousness commend
the righteousness of God, what shall we say? *Is*
God unrighteous who taketh vengeance? (I
speak as a man) 6 God forbid: for then how
shall God judge the world? 7 For if the truth
of God hath more abounded through my lie
unto his glory; why yet am I also judged as a
sinner? 8 And not *rather,* (as we be slanderously reported, and as some affirm that we say,)
Let us do evil, that good may come? whose damnation is just. 9 What then? are we better *than
they?* No, in no wise: for we have before proved
both Jews and Gentiles, that they are all under
sin; 10 As it is written, There is none righteous,
no, not one: 11 There is none that understandeth, there is none that seeketh after God.
12 They are all gone out of the way, they are

Living Bible

First of all, God trusted them with his laws
[so that they could know and do his will[a]].
3 True, some of them were unfaithful, but just
because they broke their promises to God, does
that mean God will break his promises? 4 Of
course not! Though everyone else in the world
is a liar, God is not. Do you remember what the
book of Psalms says about this?[b] That God's
words will always prove true and right, no matter who questions them.
5 "But," some say, "our breaking faith with
God is good, our sins serve a good purpose, for
people will notice how good God is when they
see how bad we are. Is it fair, then, for him to
punish us when our sins are helping him?" (That
is the way some people talk.) 6 God forbid!
Then what kind of God would he be, to overlook sin? How could he ever condemn anyone?
7 For he could not judge and condemn me as a
sinner if my dishonesty brought him glory by
pointing up his honesty in contrast to my lies.
8 If you follow through with that idea you come
to this: the worse we are, the better God likes
it! But the damnation of those who say such
things is just. Yet some claim that this is what
I preach!
9 Well, then, are we Jews *better* than others?
No, not at all, for we have already shown that
all men alike are sinners, whether Jews or Gentiles. 10 As the Scriptures say,
"No one is good—no one in all the world is
innocent."[c]
11 No one has ever really followed God's
paths, or even truly wanted to.
12 Every one has turned away; all have gone

[*a*] Implied. [*b*] Psalm 51:4. [*c*] Psalm 14:3.

Today's English Version

In the first place, God trusted his message to the
Jews. 3 What if some of them were not faithful?
Does it mean that for this reason God will not be
faithful? 4 Certainly not! God must be true, even
though every man is a liar. As the scripture says,

"You must be shown to be right when you
speak;
you must win your case when you are being
tried."

5 But what if our doing wrong serves to show
up more clearly God's doing right? What can we
say? That God does wrong when he punishes us?
(I speak here as men do.) 6 By no means! If
God is not just, how can he judge the world?
7 But what if my untruth serves God's glory by
making his truth stand out more clearly? Why
should I still be condemned as a sinner? 8 Why
not say, then, "Let us do evil that good may
come"? Some people, indeed, have insulted me
by accusing me of saying this very thing! They
will be condemned, as they should be.

No man is righteous

9 Well then, are we Jews in any better condition than the Gentiles? Not at all! I have already shown that Jews and Gentiles alike are all
under the power of sin. 10 As the Scriptures say:

"There is no one who is righteous,
11 no one who understands,
or who seeks for God.
12 All men have turned away from God;
they have all gone wrong;

New International Version

been entrusted with the very words of God.
3 What if some did not have faith? Will their
lack of faith nullify God's faithfulness? 4 Not
at all! Let God be true, and every man a liar.
As it is written:
"So that you may be proved right in your
words
and prevail in your judging."[f]
5 But if our unrighteousness brings out God's
righteousness more clearly, what shall we say?
That God is unjust in bringing his wrath on us?
(I am using a human argument.) 6 Certainly
not! If that were so, how could God judge the
world? 7 Someone might argue, "If my falsehood enhances God's truthfulness and so increases his glory, why am I still condemned as
a sinner?" 8 Why not say—as we are being
slanderously reported and as some claim that we
say—"Let us do evil that good may result"?
Their condemnation is deserved.

No one is righteous

9 What shall we conclude then? Are we any
better[g]? Not at all! We have already made the
charge that Jews and Gentiles alike are all under
sin. 10 As it is written:
"There is no one righteous, not even one;
11 there is no one who understands,
no one who searches for God.
12 All have turned away
and together become worthless.

[*f*] Psalm 51:4. [*g*] Or *worse.*

Phillips Modern English

to think of one thing to begin with—it was the Jews to whom God's messages were entrusted. Some of them were undoubtedly faithless, but what then? Can you imagine that their faithlessness could disturb the faithfulness of God? Of course not! God must be true, even if every living man be proved a liar. Remember the scripture?

That thou mightest be justified in thy words,
And mightest prevail when thou comest into
judgment.

But if our wickedness advertises the goodness of God, do we feel that God is being unfair to punish us in return? (I'm using a human tit-for-tat argument.) Not a bit of it! How then could God judge the world? It is like saying that if my lying throws into sharp relief the truth of God and increases his glory, then why should he still judge me a sinner? Why not do evil that good may come? As a matter of fact, I am reported as urging this very thing, by some slanderously and others quite seriously! But, of course, such an argument is quite properly condemned.

Are we Jews then a march ahead of other men? By no means. For I have shown above that all men from Jews to Greeks are under the condemnation of sin. The scriptures endorse this fact plainly enough.

There is none righteous, no, not one.
There is none that understandeth,
There is none that seeketh after God;
They have all turned aside, they are together
become unprofitable;

Revised Standard Version

the oracles of God. 3 What if some were unfaithful? Does their faithlessness nullify the faithfulness of God? 4 By no means! Let God be
true though every man be false, as it is written,
"That thou mayest be justified in thy words,
and prevail when thou art judged."
5 But if our wickedness serves to show the justice of God, what shall we say? That God is
unjust to inflict wrath on us? (I speak in a
human way.) 6 By no means! For then how
could God judge the world? 7 But if through my
falsehood God's truthfulness abounds to his
glory, why am I still being condemned as a
sinner? 8And why not do evil that good may
come?—as some people slanderously charge us
with saying. Their condemnation is just.
9 What then? Are we Jews any better off? [c]
No, not at all; for I [d] have already charged that
all men, both Jews and Greeks, are under the
power of sin, 10 as it is written:
"None is righteous, no, not one;
11 no one understands, no one seeks for God.
12 All have turned aside, together they have
gone wrong;

[c] Or *at any disadvantage?* [d] Greek *we*.

Jerusalem Bible

the people to whom God's message was entrusted. 3 What if some of them were unfaithful? Will their lack of fidelity cancel God's
fidelity? 4 That would be absurd. God will always be true even though *everyone* proves to be
false[f], so scripture says: *In all you say your
justice shows, and when you are judged you win
your case.*[g] 5 But if our lack of holiness makes
God demonstrate his integrity, how can we say
God is unjust when—to use a human analogy—
he gets angry with us in return? 6 That would
be absurd, it would mean God could never
judge the world. 7 You might as well say that
since my untruthfulness makes God demonstrate
his truthfulness and thus gives him glory, I
should not be judged to be a sinner at all.
8 That would be the same as saying: Do evil as
a means to good. Some slanderers have accused
us of teaching this, but they are justly condemned.

All are guilty

9 Well: are we any better off? Not at all: as
we said before, Jews and Greeks are all under
sin's dominion. 10As scripture says:

There is not a good man left, no, not one:
11 *there is not one who understands,*
not one who looks for God.
12 *All have turned aside, tainted all alike;*

[f] Ps. 116:11. [g] Ps. 51:4 (LXX).

New English Bible

with the oracles of God. What if some of them were unfaithful? Will their faithlessness cancel the faithfulness of God? Certainly not! God must be true though every man living were a liar; for we read in Scripture, 'When thou speakest thou shalt be vindicated, and win the verdict when thou art on trial.'

Another question: if our injustice serves to bring out God's justice, what are we to say? Is it unjust of God (I speak of him in human terms) to bring retribution upon us? Certainly not! If God were unjust, how could he judge the world?

Again, if the truth of God brings him all the greater honour because of my falsehood, why should I any longer be condemned as a sinner? Why not indeed 'do evil that good may come', as some libellously report me as saying? To condemn such men as these is surely no injustice.

What then? Are we Jews any better off? [a] No, not at all! [b] For we have already drawn up the accusation that Jews and Greeks alike are all under the power of sin. This has scriptural warrant:

'There is no just man, not one;
no one who understands, no one who seeks God.
All have swerved aside, all alike have become
debased;

[a] *Or* Are we Jews any worse off? [b] *Or* Not in all respects.

King James Version

together become unprofitable; there is none that
doeth good, no, not one. 13 Their throat *is* an
open sepulchre; with their tongues they have
used deceit; the poison of asps *is* under their
lips: 14 Whose mouth *is* full of cursing and bitterness: 15 Their feet *are* swift to shed blood:
16 Destruction and misery *are* in their ways:
17 And the way of peace have they not known:
18 There is no fear of God before their eyes.
19 Now we know that what things soever the law
saith, it saith to them who are under the law:
that every mouth may be stopped, and all the
world may become guilty before God. 20 Therefore by the deeds of the law there shall no flesh
be justified in his sight: for by the law *is* the
knowledge of sin. 21 But now the righteousness
of God without the law is manifested, being witnessed by the law and the prophets; 22 Even the
righteousness of God *which is* by faith of Jesus

Living Bible

wrong. No one anywhere has kept on doing what is right; not one.

13 Their talk is foul and filthy like the stench from an open grave.[d] Their tongues are loaded with lies. Everything they say has in it the sting and poison of deadly snakes.

14 Their mouths are full of cursing and bitterness.

15 They are quick to kill, hating anyone who disagrees with them.[e]

16 Wherever they go they leave misery and
trouble behind them, 17 and they have never
known what it is to feel secure or enjoy God's
blessing.

18 They care nothing about God nor what he thinks of them.

19 So the judgment of God lies very heavily upon the Jews, for they are responsible to keep God's laws instead of doing all these evil things; not one of them has any excuse; in fact, all the world stands hushed and guilty before Almighty God.

20 Now do you see it? No one can ever be made right in God's sight by doing what the law commands. For the more we know of God's laws, the clearer it becomes that we aren't obeying them; his laws serve only to make us see that we are sinners.

21, 22 But now God has shown us a different way to heaven[f]—not by "being good enough" and trying to keep his laws, but by a new way (though not new, really, for the Scriptures told about it long ago). Now God says he will accept and acquit us—declare us "not guilty"—if

[d] Literally, "Their throat is an open grave." Perhaps the meaning is "Their speech injures others." [e] Implied. [f] Implied. Literally, "A righteousness of God has been manifested."

Today's English Version

no one does what is good, not even one.
13 Their mouths are like an open grave;
wicked lies roll off their tongues,
and deadly words, like snake's poison,
from their lips;
14 their mouths are full of bitter curses.
15 They are quick to hurt and kill;
16 they leave ruin and misery wherever
they go.
17 They have not known the path of peace,
18 nor have they learned to fear God."

19 Now we know that everything in the Law
applies to those who live under the Law, in
order to stop all human excuses and bring the
whole world under God's judgment. 20 Because
no man is put right in God's sight by doing what
the Law requires; what the Law does is to make
man know that he has sinned.

How God puts men right

21 But now God's way of putting men right
with himself has been revealed, and it has nothing to do with law. The Law and the prophets
gave their witness to it: 22 God puts men right
through their faith in Jesus Christ. God does this

New International Version

There is no one who does good,
not even one."[h]
13 "Their throats are open graves;
their tongues practice deceit."[i]
"The poison of vipers is on their lips."[j]
14 "Their mouths are full of cursing and
bitterness."[k]
15 "Their feet are swift to shed blood;
16 ruin and misery mark their paths,
17 and the way of peace they do not know."[l]
18 "There is no fear of God before their
eyes."[m]

19 Now we know that whatever the law says,
it says to those who are under the law, so that
every mouth may be silenced and the whole
world held accountable to God. 20 Therefore no
one will be declared righteous in his sight by
observing the law; rather, through the law we
become conscious of sin.

Righteousness through faith

21 But now a righteousness from God, apart
from law, has been made known, to which the
Law and the Prophets testify. 22 This righteousness from God comes through faith in Jesus

[h] Psalm 14:1-3; 53:1-3; Eccles. 7:20. [i] Psalm 5:9. [j] Psalm 140:3. [k] Psalm 10:7. [l] Isaiah 59:7,8. [m] Psalm 36:1.

Phillips Modern English

There is none that doeth good, no, not so much as one:
Their throat is an open sepulchre;
With their tongues they have used deceit;
The poison of asps is under their lips:
Whose mouth is full of cursing and bitterness:
Their feet are swift to shed blood;
Destruction and misery are in their ways:
And the way of peace have they not known;
There is no fear of God before their eyes.

We know what the message of the Law is, to those who live under it—that every excuse may die on the lips of him who makes it and no living man can be beyond the judgment of God. No man can justify himself before God by a perfect performance of the Law's demands—indeed it is the straight-edge of the Law that shows us how crooked we are.

3.21 God's new plan—righteousness by faith, not through the Law

But now we are seeing the righteousness of God declared quite apart from the Law (though amply testified to by both Law and Prophets)—it is a right relationship given to, and operating

Revised Standard Version

no one does good, not even one."
13 "Their throat is an open grave,
they use their tongues to deceive."
"The venom of asps is under their lips."
14 "Their mouth is full of curses and bitterness."
15 "Their feet are swift to shed blood,
16 in their paths are ruin and misery,
17 and the way of peace they do not know."
18 "There is no fear of God before their eyes."
19 Now we know that whatever the law says it
speaks to those who are under the law, so that
every mouth may be stopped, and the whole
world may be held accountable to God. 20 For
no human being will be justified in his sight by
works of the law, since through the law comes
knowledge of sin.
21 But now the righteousness of God has
been manifested apart from law, although the
law and the prophets bear witness to it, 22 the
righteousness of God through faith in Jesus

Jerusalem Bible

there is not one good man left, not a single one.
13 *Their throats are yawning graves;*
their tongues are full of deceit.
Vipers' venom is on their lips,
14 *bitter curses fill their mouths.*
15 *Their feet are swift when blood is to be shed,*
16 *wherever they go there is havoc and ruin.*
17 *They know nothing of the way of peace,*
18 *there is no fear of God before their eyes.*[h]

19 Now all this that the Law says is said, as
we know, for the benefit of those who are subject to the Law, but it is meant to silence everyone and to lay the whole world open to God's
judgment; 20 and this is because *no one can be*
justified in the sight of [i] God by keeping the
Law: all that law does is to tell us what is
sinful.

B. Faith and the justice of God

The revelation of God's justice

21 God's justice that was made known
through the Law and the Prophets has now been
revealed outside the Law, 22 since it is the same
justice of God that comes through faith to

[h] Quotations from Ps. 14, Ps. 5, Ps. 140, Ps. 10, Is. 59, Ps. 36. [i] Ps. 143:2.

New English Bible

there is no one to show kindness; no, not one.

Their throat is an open grave,
they use their tongues for treachery,
adders' venom is on their lips,
and their mouth is full of bitter curses.

Their feet hasten to shed blood,
ruin and misery lie along their paths,
they are strangers to the high-road of peace,
and reverence for God does not enter their thoughts.'

Now all the words of the law are addressed, as we know, to those who are within the pale of the law, so that no one may have anything to say in self-defence, but the whole world may be exposed to the judgement of God. For (again from Scripture) 'no human being can be justified in the sight of God' for having kept the law: law brings only the consciousness of sin.

But now, quite independently of law, God's justice has been brought to light. The Law and the prophets both bear witness to it: it is God's way of righting wrong, effective through faith in

King James Version

Christ unto all and upon all them that believe; for there is no difference: 23 For all have sinned, and come short of the glory of God; 24 Being justified freely by his grace through the redemption that is in Christ Jesus: 25 Whom God hath set forth *to be* a propitiation through faith in his blood, to declare his righteousness for the remission of sins that are past, through the forbearance of God; 26 To declare, *I say,* at this time his righteousness: that he might be just, and the justifier of him which believeth in Jesus. 27 Where *is* boasting then? It is excluded. By what law? of works? Nay; but by the law of faith. 28 Therefore we conclude that a man is justified by faith without the deeds of the law. 29 *Is he* the God of the Jews only? *is he* not also of the Gentiles? Yes, of the Gentiles also: 30 Seeing *it is* one God, which shall justify the circumcision by faith, and uncircumcision

Living Bible

we trust Jesus Christ to take away our sins. And we all can be saved in this same way, by coming to Christ, no matter who we are or what we have been like. 23 Yes, all have sinned; all fall short of God's glorious ideal; 24 yet now God declares us "not guilty" of offending him if we trust in Jesus Christ, who in his kindness freely takes away our sins.

25 For God sent Christ Jesus to take the punishment for our sins and to end all God's anger against us. He used Christ's blood and our faith as the means of saving us from his wrath.[g] In this way he was being entirely fair, even though he did not punish those who sinned in former times. For he was looking forward to the time when Christ would come and take away those sins. 26 And now in these days also he can receive sinners in this same way, because Jesus took away their sins.

But isn't this unfair for God to let criminals go free, and say that they are innocent? No, for he does it on the basis of their trust in Jesus who took away their sins.

27 Then what can we boast about doing, to earn our salvation? Nothing at all. Why? Because our acquittal is not based on our good deeds; it is based on what Christ has done and our faith in him. 28 So it is that we are saved[h] by faith in Christ and not by the good things we do.

29 And does God save only the Jews in this way? No, the Gentiles, too, may come to him in this same manner. 30 God treats us all the same; all, whether Jews or Gentiles, are acquit-

[g] Literally, "to be a propitiation." [h] Literally, "justified."

Today's English Version

to all who believe in Christ, because there is no difference at all: 23 all men have sinned and are far away from God's saving presence. 24 But by the free gift of God's grace they are all put right with him through Christ Jesus, who sets them free. 25 God offered him so that by his death he should become the means by which men's sins are forgiven, through their faith in him. God did this in order to demonstrate his righteousness. In the past, he was patient and overlooked men's sins; 26 but now in the present time he deals with men's sins, to demonstrate his righteousness. In this way God shows that he himself is righteous and that he puts right everyone who believes in Jesus.

27 What, then, can we boast about? Nothing! And what is the reason for this? Is it that we obey the Law? No, but that we believe. 28 For we conclude that a man is put right with God only through faith, and not by doing what the Law commands. 29 Or is God only the God of the Jews? Is he not the God of the Gentiles also? Of course he is. 30 God is one, and he will put the Jews right with himself on the basis of their faith, and the Gentiles right through their faith.

New International Version

Christ to all who believe. There is no difference, 23 for all have sinned and fall short of the glory of God, 24 and are justified freely by his grace through the redemption that came by Christ Jesus. 25 God presented him as a sacrifice of atonement, through faith in his blood. He did this to demonstrate his justice, because in his forbearance he had left the sins committed beforehand unpunished—26 he did it to demonstrate his justice at the present time, so as to be just and the one who justifies the man who has faith in Jesus.

27 Where, then, is boasting? It is excluded. On what principle? On that of observing the law? No, but on that of faith. 28 For we maintain that a man is justified by faith apart from observing the law. 29 Is God the God of Jews only? Is he not the God of Gentiles too? Yes, of Gentiles too, 30 since there is only one God, who will justify the circumcised by faith and

Phillips Modern English

in, all who have faith in Jesus Christ. For there is no distinction to be made anywhere: everyone has sinned, everyone falls short of the beauty of God's plan. A man who has faith is now freely acquitted in the eyes of God by his generous dealing in the redemptive act of Christ Jesus. God has appointed him as the means of propitiation, a propitiation accomplished by the shedding of his blood, to be received and made effective in ourselves by faith. God has done this to demonstrate his righteousness both by the wiping out of the sins of the past (the time when he withheld his hand), and by showing in the present time that he is a just God and that he justifies every man who has faith in Jesus.

3.27 Faith, not pride of achievement

What happens now to human pride of achievement? There is no more room for it. Why, because failure to keep the Law has killed it? Not at all, but because the whole matter is now on a different plane—believing instead of achieving. We see now that a man is justified before God by the fact of his faith in God's appointed Saviour and not by what he has managed to achieve under the Law.

Do you think that God is only God for the Jews and not for the gentiles? Certainly not! God is God of the gentiles as well. The one God is ready to justify the circumcised by faith and the uncircumcised by faith also.

Revised Standard Version

Christ for all who believe. For there is no distinction; 23 since all have sinned and fall short
of the glory of God, 24 they are justified by
his grace as a gift, through the redemption which
is in Christ Jesus, 25 whom God put forward as
an expiation by his blood, to be received by
faith. This was to show God's righteousness, because in his divine forbearance he had passed
over former sins; 26 it was to prove at the present time that he himself is righteous and that
he justifies him who has faith in Jesus.
27 Then what becomes of our boasting? It
is excluded. On what principle? On the principle
of works? No, but on the principle of faith.
28 For we hold that a man is justified by faith
apart from works of law. 29 Or is God the God
of Jews only? Is he not the God of Gentiles
also? Yes, of Gentiles also, 30 since God is one;
and he will justify the circumcised on the ground
of their faith and the uncircumcised through

Jerusalem Bible

everyone, Jew and pagan alike, who believes in
Jesus Christ. 23 Both Jew and pagan sinned and
forfeited God's glory, 24 and both are justified
through the free gift of his grace by being redeemed in Christ Jesus 25 who was appointed by
God to sacrifice his life so as to win reconciliation through faith. In this way God makes his
justice known; first, for the past, when sins went
unpunished because he held his hand, 26 then,
for the present age, by showing positively that
he is just, and that he justifies everyone who believes in Jesus.

What faith does

27 So what becomes of our boasts? There is
no room for them. What sort of law excludes
them? The sort of law that tells us what to do?
On the contrary, it is the law of faith, 28 since,
as we see it, a man is justified by faith and not
by doing something the Law tells him to do.
29 Is God the God of Jews alone and not of
the pagans too? Of the pagans too, most certainly, 30 since there is only one God, and he is
the one who will justify the circumcised because
of their faith and justify the uncircumcised

New English Bible

Christ for all who have such faith—all, without distinction. For all alike have sinned, and are deprived of the divine splendour, and all are justified by God's free grace alone, through his act of liberation in the person of Christ Jesus. For God designed him to be the means of expiating sin by his sacrificial death, effective through faith. God meant by this to demonstrate his justice, because in his forbearance he had overlooked the sins of the past—to demonstrate his justice now in the present, showing that he is himself just and also justifies any man who puts his faith in Jesus.

What room then is left for human pride? It is excluded. And on what principle? The keeping of the law would not exclude it, but faith does. For our argument is that a man is justified by faith quite apart from success in keeping the law.

Do you suppose God is the God of the Jews alone? Is he not the God of Gentiles also? Certainly, of Gentiles also, if it be true that God is one. And he will therefore justify both the circumcised in virtue of their faith, and the uncir-

King James Version

through faith. 31 Do we then make void the law
through faith? God forbid: yea, we establish the
law.

4 What shall we say then that Abraham our
father, as pertaining to the flesh, hath found?
2 For if Abraham were justified by works, he
hath *whereof* to glory; but not before God. 3 For
what saith the Scripture? Abraham believed
God, and it was counted unto him for righteousness. 4 Now to him that worketh is the reward not reckoned of grace, but of debt. 5 But
to him that worketh not, but believeth on him
that justifieth the ungodly, his faith is counted
for righteousness. 6 Even as David also describeth the blessedness of the man, unto whom
God imputeth righteousness without works,
7 *Saying,* Blessed *are* they whose iniquities are
forgiven, and whose sins are covered. 8 Blessed
is the man to whom the Lord will not impute

Living Bible

ted if they have faith. 31 Well then, if we are
saved by faith, does this mean that we no longer
need obey God's laws? Just the opposite! In fact,
only when we trust Jesus can we truly obey him.

4 Abraham was, humanly speaking, the
founder of our Jewish nation. What were his
experiences concerning this question of being
saved by faith? Was it because of his good deeds
that God accepted him? If so, then he would
have something to boast about. But from God's
point of view Abraham had no basis at all for
pride. 3 For the Scriptures tell us Abraham *believed God,* and that is why God canceled his
sins and declared him "not guilty."

4, 5 But didn't he earn his right to heaven by
all the good things he did? No, for being saved
is a gift; if a person could earn it by being good,
then it wouldn't be free—but it is! It is *given* to
those who do *not* work for it. For God declares
sinners to be good in his sight if they have faith
in Christ to save them from God's wrath.[a]

6 King David spoke of this, describing the happiness of an undeserving sinner who is declared "not
guilty"[b] by God. 7 "Blessed, and to be envied," he
said, "are those whose sins are forgiven and put out
of sight. 8 Yes, what joy there is for anyone whose
sins are no longer counted against him by the
Lord."[c]

[*a*] Literally, "faith is reckoned for righteousness."
[*b*] Literally, "righteous." [*c*] Psalm 32:1-2.

Today's English Version

31 Does this mean that we do away with the
Law by this faith? No, not at all; instead, we
uphold the Law.

The example of Abraham

4 What shall we say, then, of Abraham, our
racial ancestor? What was his experience?
2 If he was put right with God by the things he
did, he would have something to boast about.
But he cannot boast before God. 3 The scripture says, "Abraham believed God, and because
of his faith God accepted him as righteous."
4 A man who works is paid; his wages are not
regarded as a gift, but as something that he has
earned. 5 But the man who has faith, not works,
who believes in the God who declares the guilty
to be innocent, it is his faith that God takes into
account in order to put him right with himself.
6 This is what David meant when he spoke of
the happiness of the man whom God accepts as
righteous, apart from any works:

7 "Happy are those whose wrongs God has
forgiven,
whose sins he has covered over!
8 Happy is the man whose sins the Lord will
not keep account of!"

New International Version

the uncircumcised through that same faith. 31 Do
we, then, nullify the law by this faith? Not at
all! Rather, we uphold the law.

Abraham justified by faith

4 What then shall we say that Abraham, our
forefather, discovered in this matter? 2 If, in
fact, Abraham was justified by works, he had
something to boast about—but not before God.
3 What does the Scripture say? "Abraham believed God, and it was credited to him as righteousness."[n]

4 Now when a man works, his wages are not
credited to him as a gift, but as an obligation.
5 However, to the man who does not work but
trusts God who justifies the wicked, his faith is
credited as righteousness. 6 David says the same
thing when he speaks of the blessedness of the
man to whom God credits righteousness apart
from works:

7 "Blessed are they whose offenses have been
forgiven
and whose sins have been covered.
8 Blessed is the man whose sin the Lord will
never count against him."[o]

[*n*] Gen. 15:6. [*o*] Psalm 32:1,2.

Phillips Modern English

Are we then undermining the Law by this insistence on faith? Not a bit of it! We put the Law in its proper place.

4.1 Let us go back and consider our father Abraham

Now how does all this affect the position of our human ancestor Abraham? Well, if justification were by achievement he could quite fairly be proud of what he achieved—but not, I am sure, proud before God. For what does the scripture say about him?

And Abraham believed God, and it was reckoned unto him for righteousness.

Now if a man *works* his wages are not counted as a gift but as a fair reward. But if a man, irrespective of his work, has faith in him who justifies the sinful, then that man's *faith* is counted as righteousness. This is the happy state of the man whom God accounts righteous, apart from his achievements, as David expresses it:

Blessed are they whose iniquities are forgiven
And whose sins are covered.
Blessed is the man to whom the Lord will not reckon sin.

Revised Standard Version

their faith. 31 Do we then overthrow the law by
this faith? By no means! On the contrary, we
uphold the law.

4 What then shall we say about[e] Abraham,
our forefather according to the flesh? 2 For
if Abraham was justified by works, he has something to boast about, but not before God. 3 For
what does the scripture say? "Abraham believed
God, and it was reckoned to him as righteousness." 4 Now to one who works, his wages are
not reckoned as a gift but as his due. 5 And to
one who does not work but trusts him who justifies the ungodly, his faith is reckoned as righteousness. 6 So also David pronounces a blessing
upon the man to whom God reckons righteousness apart from works:
7 "Blessed are those whose iniquities are forgiven, and whose sins are covered;
8 blessed is the man against whom the Lord will not reckon his sin."

[e] Other ancient authorities read *was gained by*.

Jerusalem Bible

through their faith. 31 Do we mean that faith
makes the Law pointless? Not at all: we are
giving the Law its true value.

C. The example of Abraham

Abraham justified by faith

4 Apply this to Abraham, the ancestor from
whom we are all descended. 2 If Abraham
was justified as a reward for doing something,
he would really have had something to boast
about, though not in God's sight 3 because
scripture says: *Abraham put his faith in God,
and this faith was considered as justifying him.*[j]
4 If a man has work to show, his wages are not
considered as a favor but as his due; 5 but when
a man has nothing to show except faith in the
one who justifies sinners, then his faith is considered as justifying him. 6 And David says the
same: a man is happy if God considers him
righteous, irrespective of good deeds:

7 *Happy those whose crimes are forgiven, whose sins are blotted out;*
8 *happy the man whom the Lord considers sinless.*[k]

[j] Gn. 15:6. [k] Ps. 32:1-2.

New English Bible

cumcised through their faith. Does this mean that we are using faith to undermine law? By no means: we are placing law itself on a firmer footing.

4 What, then, are we to say about Abraham, our ancestor in the natural line? If Abraham was justified by anything he had done, then he has a ground for pride. But he has no such ground before God; for what does Scripture say? 'Abraham put his faith in God, and that faith was counted to him as righteousness.' Now if a man does a piece of work, his wages are not 'counted' as a favour; they are paid as debt. But if without any work to his credit he simply puts his faith in him who acquits the guilty, then his faith is indeed 'counted as righteousness'. In the same sense David speaks of the happiness of the man whom God 'counts' as just, apart from any specific acts of justice: 'Happy are they', he says, 'whose lawless deeds are forgiven, whose sins are buried away; happy is the man whose

King James Version

sin. 9 *Cometh* this blessedness then upon the circumcision *only,* or upon the uncircumcision
also? for we say that faith was reckoned to
Abraham for righteousness. 10 How was it then
reckoned? when he was in circumcision, or in
uncircumcision? Not in circumcision, but in uncircumcision. 11 And he received the sign of circumcision, a seal of the righteousness of the
faith which *he had yet* being uncircumcised:
that he might be the father of all them that believe, though they be not circumcised; that
righteousness might be imputed unto them also:
12 And the father of circumcision to them who
are not of the circumcision only, but who also
walk in the steps of that faith of our father
Abraham, which *he had* being *yet* uncircumcised. 13 For the promise, that he should be the
heir of the world, *was* not to Abraham, or to
his seed, through the law, but through the
righteousness of faith. 14 For if they which are
of the law *be* heirs, faith is made void, and the

Living Bible

9 Now then, the question: Is this blessing
given only to those who have faith in Christ
but also keep the Jewish laws, or is the blessing
also given to those who do not keep the Jewish
rules, but only trust in Christ? Well, what about
Abraham? We say that he received these blessings through his faith. Was it by faith alone? Or
because he also kept the Jewish rules?
10 For the answer to that question, answer
this one: *When* did God give this blessing to
Abraham? It was *before he became a Jew*—before he went through the Jewish initiation ceremony of circumcision.
11 It wasn't until later on, *after* God had
promised to bless him *because of his faith,* that
he was circumcised. The circumcision ceremony
was a sign that Abraham already had faith and
that God had already accepted him and declared
him just and good in his sight—before the ceremony took place. So Abraham is the spiritual
father of those who believe and are saved without obeying Jewish laws. We see, then, that those
who do not keep these rules are justified by God
through faith. 12 And Abraham is also the spiritual father of those Jews who have been circumcised. They can see from his example that it is
not this ceremony that saves them, for Abraham
found favor with God by faith alone, *before he
was circumcised.*
13 It is clear, then, that God's promise to
give the whole earth to Abraham and his descendants was not because Abraham obeyed
God's laws but because he trusted God to keep
his promise. 14 So if you still claim that God's
blessings go to those who are "good enough,"

Today's English Version

9 Does this happiness that David spoke of belong only to those who are circumcised? No.
It belongs also to those who are not circumcised.
For we have quoted the scripture, "Abraham
believed God, and because of his faith God
accepted him as righteous." 10 When did this
take place? Was it before or after Abraham was
circumcised? Before, not after. 11 He was circumcised later, and his circumcision was a sign
to prove that because of Abraham's faith God
had accepted him as righteous before he had been
circumcised. And so Abraham is the spiritual
father of all who believe in God and are accepted
as righteous by him, even though they are not
circumcised. 12 He is also the father of those
who are circumcised, not just because they are
circumcised, but because they live the same life
of faith that our father Abraham lived before he
was circumcised.

God's promise received through faith

13 God promised Abraham and his descendants that the world would belong to him. This
promise was made, not because Abraham obeyed
the Law, but because he believed and was accepted as righteous by God. 14 For if what God
promises is to be given to those who obey the

New International Version

9 Is this blessedness only for the circumcised,
or also for the uncircumcised? We have been
saying that Abraham's faith was credited to him
as righteousness. 10 Under what circumstances
was it credited? Was it after he was circumcised,
or before? It was not after, but before! 11 And
he received circumcision as a sign and seal of
the righteousness that he had by faith while he
was still uncircumcised. So then, he is the father
of all who believe but have not been circumcised,
in order that righteousness might be credited to
them. 12 And he is also the father of the circumcised who not only are circumcised but who also
walk in the footsteps of the faith that our father
Abraham had before he was circumcised.
13 It was not through law that Abraham and
his offspring received the promise that he would
be heir of the world, but through the righteousness that comes by faith. 14 For if those who
live by law are heirs, faith has no value and

Phillips Modern English

4.9 It is a matter of faith, not circumcision

Now the question arises: is this happiness for the circumcised only, or for the uncircumcised as well?

Note this carefully. We began by saying that Abraham's faith was counted unto him for righteousness. When this happened, was he a circumcised man? He was not, he was still uncircumcised. It was *afterwards* that the sign of circumcision was given to him, as a seal upon that righteousness which God was accounting to him *as yet an uncircumcised man!* God's purpose here was that Abraham might be the spiritual father of all who since that time, despite their uncircumcision, show the faith that is counted as righteousness, and that he might be the circumcised father of all those who are not only circumcised, but are living by the same sort of faith which he himself had before he was circumcised.

4.13 The promise, from the beginning, was made to faith

The ancient promise made to Abraham and his descendants, that they should eventually possess the world, was given not because of any achievements made through obedience to the Law, but because of the righteousness which had its root in faith. For if, after all, they who pin their faith to keeping the Law were to in-

Revised Standard Version

9 Is this blessing pronounced only upon the circumcised, or also upon the uncircumcised? We say that faith was reckoned to Abraham as righteousness. 10 How then was it reckoned to him? Was it before or after he had been circumcised? It was not after, but before he was circumcised. 11 He received circumcision as a sign or seal of the righteousness which he had by faith while he was still uncircumcised. The purpose was to make him the father of all who believe without being circumcised and who thus have righteousness reckoned to them, 12 and likewise the father of the circumcised who are not merely circumcised but also follow the example of the faith which our father Abraham had before he was circumcised.

13 The promise to Abraham and his descendants, that they should inherit the world, did not come through the law but through the righteousness of faith. 14 If it is the adherents of the law who are to be the heirs, faith is null and the

Jerusalem Bible

Justified before circumcision

9 Is this happiness meant only for the circumcised, or is it meant for others as well? Think of Abraham again: *his faith,* we say, *was considered as justifying him,* 10 but when was this done? When he was already circumcised or before he had been circumcised? It was before he had been circumcised, not after; 11 and when he was *circumcised* later it was only *as a sign* and guarantee that the faith he had before his circumcision justified him. In this way Abraham became the ancestor of all uncircumcised believers, so that they too might be considered righteous; 12 and ancestor, also, of those who though circumcised do not rely on that fact alone, but follow our ancestor Abraham along the path of faith he trod before he had been circumcised.

Not justified by obedience to the Law

13 The promise of inheriting the world was not made to Abraham and his descendants on account of any law but on account of the righteousness which consists in faith. 14 If the world is only to be inherited by those who sub-

New English Bible

sins the Lord does not count against him.' Is this happiness confined to the circumcised, or is it for the uncircumcised also? Consider: we say, 'Abraham's faith was counted as righteousness'; in what circumstances was it so counted? Was he circumcised at the time, or not? He was not yet circumcised, but uncircumcised; and he later received the symbolic rite of circumcision as the hall-mark of the righteousness which faith had given him when he was still uncircumcised. Consequently, he is the father of all who have faith when uncircumcised, so that righteousness is 'counted' to them; and at the same time he is the father of such of the circumcised as do not rely upon their circumcision alone, but also walk in the footprints of the faith which our father Abraham had while he was yet uncircumcised.

For it was not through law that Abraham, or his posterity, was given the promise that the world should be his inheritance, but through the righteousness that came from faith. For if those who hold by the law, and they alone, are heirs,

King James Version

promise made of none effect: 15 Because the law worketh wrath: for where no law is, *there is* no transgression. 16 Therefore *it is* of faith, that *it might be* by grace; to the end the promise might be sure to all the seed; not to that only which is of the law, but to that also which is of the faith of Abraham; who is the father of us all, 17 (As it is written, I have made thee a father of many nations,) before him whom he believed, *even* God, who quickeneth the dead, and calleth those things which be not as though they were: 18 Who against hope believed in hope, that he might become the father of many nations, according to that which was spoken, So shall thy seed be. 19 And being not weak in faith, he considered not his own body now dead, when he was about a hundred years old, neither yet the deadness of Sarah's womb: 20 He staggered not at the promise of God through unbelief; but was

Living Bible

then you are saying that God's promises to those who have faith are meaningless, and faith is foolish. 15 But the fact of the matter is this: when we try to gain God's blessing and salvation by keeping his laws we always end up under his anger, for we always fail to keep them. The only way we can keep from breaking laws is not to have any to break!

16 So God's blessings are given to us by faith, as a free gift; we are certain to get them whether or not we follow Jewish customs if we have faith like Abraham's, for Abraham is the father of us all when it comes to these matters of faith. 17 That is what the Scriptures mean when they say that God made Abraham the father of many nations. God will accept all people in every nation who trust God as Abraham did. And this promise is from God himself, who makes the dead live again and speaks of future events with as much certainty as though they were already past.

18 So, when God told Abraham that he would give him a son who would have many descendants and become a great nation, Abraham believed God even though such a promise just couldn't come to pass! 19 And because his faith was strong, he didn't worry about the fact that he was too old to be a father, at the age of one hundred, and that Sarah his wife, at ninety,[d] was also much too old to have a baby.

20 But Abraham never doubted. He believed

[*d*] Genesis 17:17.

Today's English Version

Law, then man's faith means nothing and God's promise is worthless. 15 The Law brings God's wrath; but where there is no law, there is no disobeying of the law.

16 The promise was based on faith, then, in order that the promise should be guaranteed as God's free gift to all of Abraham's descendants—not just those who obey the Law, but also those who believe as Abraham did. For Abraham is the spiritual father of us all; 17 as the scripture says, "I have made you father of many nations." So the promise is good in the sight of God, in whom Abraham believed—the God who brings the dead to life and whose command brings into being what did not exist. 18 Abraham believed and hoped, when there was no hope, and so became "the father of many nations." Just as the scripture says, "Your descendants will be this many." 19 He was almost one hundred years old; but his faith did not weaken when he thought of his body, which was already practically dead, or of the fact that Sarah could not have children. 20 His faith did not leave him, and he did not

New International Version

the promise is worthless, 15 because law brings wrath. And where there is no law there is no transgression.

16 Therefore, the promise comes by faith, so that it may be by grace and may be guaranteed to all Abraham's offspring—not only to those who are of the law but also to those who are of the faith of Abraham. He is the father of us all. 17 As it is written: "I have made you a father of many nations." [p] He is our father in the sight of God, in whom he believed—the God who gives life to the dead and calls things that are not as though they were.

18 Against all hope, Abraham in hope believed and so became the father of many nations, just as it had been said to him, "So shall your offspring be." [q] 19 Without weakening in his faith, he faced the fact that his body was as good as dead—since he was about a hundred years old—and that Sarah's womb was also dead. 20 Yet he did not waver through unbelief regarding the

[*p*] Gen. 17:5. [*q*] Gen. 15:5.

Phillips Modern English

herit God's world, it would make faith meaningless and destroy the whole point of the promise. For the Law can produce no promise, only the threat of wrath to come. And, indeed, if there were no Law the question of sin would not arise.

The whole thing, then, is a matter of faith on man's part and generosity on God's. He gives the security of his own promise to all men who can be called "children of Abraham", i.e. both those who have lived in faith by the Law, and those who have exhibited a faith like that of Abraham. To whichever group we belong, Abraham is in a real sense our father, as the scripture says:

A father of many nations have I made thee.

This promise was valid because of his faith in God himself, who can make the dead live, and summon those who are in existence as though they were not yet born.

4.18 Abraham was a shining example of faith

Abraham, when hope was dead within him, went on hoping in faith, believing that he would become "the father of many nations". He relied on the word of God which definitely referred to "thy seed". With undaunted faith he looked at the facts—his own impotence (he was practically a hundred years old at the time) and his wife Sarah's apparent barrenness. Yet he refused to allow any distrust of a definite

Revised Standard Version

promise is void. 15 For the law brings wrath, but where there is no law there is no transgression.

16 That is why it depends on faith, in order that the promise may rest on grace and be guaranteed to all his descendants—not only to the adherents of the law but also to those who share the faith of Abraham, for he is the father of us all, 17 as it is written, "I have made you the father of many nations"—in the presence of the God in whom he believed, who gives life to the dead and calls into existence the things that do not exist. 18 In hope he believed against hope, that he should become the father of many nations; as he had been told, "So shall your descendants be." 19 He did not weaken in faith when he considered his own body, which was as good as dead because he was about a hundred years old, or when he considered the barrenness of Sarah's womb. 20 No distrust made him

Jerusalem Bible

mit to the Law, then faith is pointless and the promise worth nothing. 15 Law involves the possibility of punishment for breaking the law—only where there is no law can that be avoided. 16 That is why what fulfills the promise depends on faith, so that it may be a free gift and be available to all of Abraham's descendants, not only those who belong to the Law but also those who belong to the faith of Abraham who is the father of all of us. 17As scripture says: *I have made you the ancestor of many nations*[l]—Abraham is our father in the eyes of God, in whom he put his faith, and who brings the dead to life and calls into being what does not exist.

Abraham's faith, a model of Christian faith

18 Though it seemed Abraham's hope could not be fulfilled, he hoped and he believed, and through doing so he did become *the father of many nations* exactly as he had been promised: *Your descendants will be as many as the stars.*[m] 19 Even the thought that his body was past fatherhood—he was about a hundred years old—and Sarah too old to become a mother, did not shake his belief. 20 Since God had promised it,

[*l*] Gn. 17:5 (the same chapter to which allusion is made in v. 11, above). [*m*] Gn. 15:5.

New English Bible

then faith is empty and the promise goes for nothing, because law can bring only retribution; but where there is no law there can be no breach of law. The promise was made on the ground of faith, in order that it might be a matter of sheer grace, and that it might be valid for all Abraham's posterity, not only for those who hold by the law, but for those also who have the faith of Abraham. For he is the father of us all, as Scripture says: 'I have appointed you to be father of many nations.' This promise, then, was valid before God, the God in whom he put his faith, the God who makes the dead live and summons things that are not yet in existence as if they already were. When hope seemed hopeless, his faith was such that he became 'father of many nations', in agreement with the words which had been spoken to him: 'Thus shall your descendants be.' Without any weakening of faith he contemplated his own body, as good as dead (for he was about a hundred years old), and the deadness of Sarah's womb, and never doubted God's promise in unbelief, but, strong

King James Version

strong in faith, giving glory to God; 21And being fully persuaded, that what he had promised, he was able also to perform. 22And therefore it was imputed to him for righteousness. 23 Now it was not written for his sake alone, that it was imputed to him; 24 But for us also, to whom it shall be imputed, if we believe on him that raised up Jesus our Lord from the dead; 25 Who was delivered for our offences, and was raised again for our justification.

5 Therefore being justified by faith, we have peace with God through our Lord Jesus Christ: 2 By whom also we have access by faith into this grace wherein we stand, and rejoice in hope of the glory of God. 3And not only *so,* but we glory in tribulations also; knowing that tribulation worketh patience; 4And patience, ex-

Living Bible

God, for his faith and trust grew ever stronger, and he praised God for this blessing even before it happened. 21 He was completely sure that God was well able to do anything he promised. 22And because of Abraham's faith God forgave his sins and declared him "not guilty."

23 Now this wonderful statement—that he was accepted and approved through his faith—wasn't just for Abraham's benefit. 24 It was for us, too, assuring us that God will accept us in the same way he accepted Abraham—when we believe the promises of God who brought back Jesus our Lord from the dead. 25 He died for our sins and rose again to make us right with God, filling us with God's goodness.[e]

5 So now, since we have been made right in God's sight by faith in his promises, we can have real peace with him because of what Jesus Christ our Lord has done for us. 2 For because of our faith, he has brought us into this place of highest privilege where we now stand, and we confidently and joyfully look forward to actually becoming all that God has had in mind for us to be.

3 We can rejoice, too, when we run into problems and trials for we know that they are good for us—they help us learn to be patient. 4And patience develops strength of character in us and helps us trust God more each time we use it until finally our hope and faith are strong

[e] Literally, "raised for our justification."

Today's English Version

doubt God's promise; his faith filled him with power, and he gave praise to God. 21 He was absolutely sure that God would be able to do what he had promised. 22 That is why Abraham, through faith, "was accepted as righteous by God." 23 The words "he was accepted as righteous" were not written for him alone. 24 They were written also for us who are to be accepted as righteous, who believe in him who raised Jesus our Lord from death. 25 He was given over to die because of our sins, and was raised to life to put us right with God.

Right with God

5 Now that we have been put right with God through faith, we have peace with God through our Lord Jesus Christ. 2 He has brought us, by faith, into this experience of God's grace, in which we now live. We rejoice, then, in the hope we have of sharing God's glory! 3And we also rejoice in our troubles, because we know that trouble produces endurance, 4 endurance brings God's approval, and his approval creates

New International Version

promise of God, but was strengthened in his faith and gave glory to God, 21 being fully persuaded that God had power to do what he had promised. 22 This is why "it was credited to him as righteousness."[r] 23 The words "it was credited to him" were written not for him alone, 24 but also for us, to whom God will credit righteousness—for us who believe in him who raised Jesus our Lord from the dead. 25 He was delivered over to death for our sins and was raised to life for our justification.

Peace and joy

5 Therefore, since we have been justified through faith, we[s] have peace with God through our Lord Jesus Christ, 2 through whom we have gained access by faith into this grace in which we now stand. And we[s] rejoice in the hope of the glory of God. 3 Not only so, but we[s] also rejoice in our sufferings, because we know that suffering produces perseverance; 4 per-

[r] Gen. 15:6. [s] Or *let us.*

Phillips Modern English

pronouncement of God to make him waver. He drew strength from his faith, and, while giving the glory to God, remained absolutely convinced that God was able to implement his own promise. This was the "faith" which was counted unto him for righteousness.

Now this counting of faith for righteousness was not recorded simply for Abraham's credit, but as a divine principle which should apply to us as well. Faith is to be reckoned as righteousness to us also, who believe in him who raised from the dead Jesus our Lord, who was delivered to death for our sins and raised again to secure our justification.

5.1 Faith means the certainty of God's love, now and hereafter

Since then it is by faith that we are justified, let us grasp the fact that we *have* peace with God through our Lord Jesus Christ. Through him we have confidently entered into this new relationship of grace, and here we take our stand, in happy certainty of the glorious things he has for us in the future.

This doesn't mean, of course, that we have only a hope of future joys—we can be full of joy here and now even in our trials and troubles. These very things will give us patient endurance; this in turn will develop a mature character, and a character of this sort produces a steady hope, a hope that will never disappoint

Revised Standard Version

waver concerning the promise of God, but he grew strong in his faith as he gave glory to God, 21 fully convinced that God was able to do what he had promised. 22 That is why his faith was "reckoned to him as righteousness." 23 But the words, "it was reckoned to him," were written not for his sake alone, 24 but for ours also. It will be reckoned to us who believe in him that raised from the dead Jesus our Lord, 25 who was put to death for our trespasses and raised for our justification.

5 Therefore, since we are justified by faith, we[f] have peace with God through our Lord Jesus Christ. 2 Through him we have obtained access[g] to this grace in which we stand, and we[h] rejoice in our hope of sharing the glory of God. 3 More than that, we[h] rejoice in our sufferings, knowing that suffering produces endurance, 4 and endurance produces character, and character

[*f*] Other ancient authorities read *let us.* [*g*] Other ancient authorities add *by faith.* [*h*] Or *let us.*

Jerusalem Bible

Abraham refused either to deny it or even to doubt it, but drew strength from faith and gave glory to God, 21 convinced that God had power to do what he had promised. 22 This is the faith that was *"considered as justifying him."* 23 Scripture however does not refer only to him but to us as well when it says that his faith was thus "considered"; 24 our faith too will be "considered" if we believe in him who raised Jesus our Lord from the dead, 25 Jesus who was *put to death for our sins*[n] and raised to life to justify us.

II. Salvation

Faith guarantees salvation

5 So far then we have seen that, through our Lord Jesus Christ, by faith we are judged righteous and at peace with God, 2 since it is by faith and through Jesus that we have entered this state of grace in which we can boast about looking forward to God's glory. 3 But that is not all we can boast about; we can boast about our sufferings. These sufferings bring patience, as we know, 4 and patience brings perseverance, and

[*n*] Is. 53:5,6.

New English Bible

in faith, gave honour to God, in the firm conviction of his power to do what he had promised. And that is why Abraham's faith was 'counted to him as righteousness'.

Those words were written, not for Abraham's sake alone, but for our sake too: it is to be 'counted' in the same way to us who have faith in the God who raised Jesus our Lord from the dead; for he was given up to death for our misdeeds, and raised to life to justify us.[a]

5 Therefore, now that we have been justified through faith, let us continue at peace[b] with God through our Lord Jesus Christ, through whom we have been allowed to enter the sphere of God's grace, where we now stand. Let us exult[c] in the hope of the divine splendour that is to be ours. More than this: let us even exult[d] in our present sufferings, because we know that suffering trains us to endure, and endurance brings proof that we have stood the test, and this

[*a*] *Or* raised to life because we were now justified. [*b*] *Some witnesses read* we are at peace. [*c*] *Or* We exult. [*d*] *Or* we even exult.

King James Version

perience; and experience, hope: 5 And hope
maketh not ashamed; because the love of God is
shed abroad in our hearts by the Holy Ghost
which is given unto us. 6 For when we were yet
without strength, in due time Christ died for
the ungodly. 7 For scarcely for a righteous man
will one die: yet peradventure for a good man
some would even dare to die. 8 But God commendeth his love toward us, in that, while we
were yet sinners, Christ died for us. 9 Much more
then, being now justified by his blood, we shall be
saved from wrath through him. 10 For if, when
we were enemies, we were reconciled to God by
the death of his Son; much more, being reconciled, we shall be saved by his life. 11 And not
only *so,* but we also joy in God through our
Lord Jesus Christ, by whom we have now received the atonement. 12 Wherefore, as by one
man sin entered into the world, and death by
sin; and so death passed upon all men, for that
all have sinned: 13 (For until the law sin was

Living Bible

and steady. 5 Then, when that happens, we are
able to hold our heads high no matter what happens and know that all is well, for we know how
dearly God loves us, and we feel this warm
love everywhere within us because God has
given us the Holy Spirit to fill our hearts with
his love.

6 When we were utterly helpless with no way
of escape, Christ came at just the right time and
died for us sinners who had no use for him.
7 Even if we were good, we really wouldn't expect anyone to die for us, though, of course,
that might be barely possible. 8 But God showed
his great love for us by sending Christ to die
for us while we were still sinners. 9 And since
by his blood he did all this for us sinners, how
much more will he do for us now that he has
declared us not guilty? Now he will save us
from all of God's wrath to come. 10 And since,
when we were his enemies, we were brought
back to God by the death of his Son, what
blessings he must have for us now that we are
his friends, and he is living within us!

11 Now we rejoice in our wonderful new relationship with God—all because of what our
Lord Jesus Christ has done in dying for our
sins—making us friends of God.

12 When Adam sinned, sin entered the entire human race. His sin spread death throughout all the world, so everything began to grow
old and die,[a] for all sinned. 13 [We know that it

[*a*] Literally, "Sin entered into the world, and death through sin."

Today's English Version

hope. 5 This hope does not disappoint us, because God has poured out his love into our hearts
by means of the Holy Spirit, who is God's gift to
us.

6 For when we were still helpless, Christ died
for the wicked, at the time that God chose. 7 It is
a difficult thing for someone to die for a righteous
person. It may be that someone might dare to die
for a good person. 8 But God has shown us how
much he loves us; it was while we were still sinners that Christ died for us! 9 By his death we
are now put right with God; how much more,
then, will we be saved by him from God's wrath.
10 We were God's enemies, but he made us his
friends through the death of his Son. Now that
we are God's friends, how much more will we be
saved by Christ's life! 11 But that is not all; we
rejoice in God through our Lord Jesus Christ,
who has now made us God's friends.

Adam and Christ

12 Sin came into the world through one man,
and his sin brought death with it. As a result, death
spread to the whole human race, because all men
sinned. 13 There was sin in the world before the

New International Version

severance, character; and character, hope. 5 And
hope does not disappoint us, because God has
poured out his love into our hearts by the Holy
Spirit, whom he has given us.

6 You see, at just the right time, when we
were still powerless, Christ died for the ungodly.
7 Very rarely will anyone die for a righteous
man, though for a good man someone might
possibly dare to die. 8 But God demonstrates
his own love for us in this: While we were still
sinners, Christ died for us.

9 Since we have now been justified by his
blood, how much more shall we be saved from
God's wrath through him! 10 For if, when we
were God's enemies, we were reconciled to him
through the death of his Son, how much more,
having been reconciled, shall we be saved
through his life! 11 Not only is this so, but we
also rejoice in God through our Lord Jesus
Christ, through whom we have now received
reconciliation.

Death through Adam, life through Christ

12 Therefore, just as sin entered the world
through one man, and death through sin, and in
this way death came to all men, because all
sinned—13 for before the law was given, sin was

Phillips Modern English

us. Already we have the love of God flooding through our hearts by the Holy Spirit given to us. And we can see that it was at the very time that we were powerless to help ourselves that Christ died for sinful men. In human experience it is a rare thing for one man to give his life for another, even if the latter be a good man, though there have been a few who have had the courage to do it. Yet the proof of God's amazing love is this: that it was while we were sinners that Christ died for us. Moreover, if he did that for us while we were sinners, now that we are men justified by the shedding of his blood, what reason have we to fear the wrath of God? If, while we were his enemies, Christ reconciled us to God by dying for us, surely now that we are reconciled we may be perfectly certain of our salvation through his living in us. Nor, I am sure, is this a matter of bare salvation—we may hold our heads high in the light of God's love because of the reconciliation which Christ has made.

5.12 A brief résumé—the consequence of sin and the gift of God

This, then, is what has happened. Sin made its entry into the world through one man, and through sin, death. The entail of sin and death passed on to the whole human race, and no one could break it for no one was himself free from sin.

Sin, you see, was in the world long before the

Revised Standard Version

produces hope, 5 and hope does not disappoint us, because God's love has been poured into our hearts through the Holy Spirit which has been given to us.

6 While we were still weak, at the right time Christ died for the ungodly. 7 Why, one will hardly die for a righteous man—though perhaps for a good man one will dare even to die. 8 But God shows his love for us in that while we were yet sinners Christ died for us. 9 Since, therefore, we are now justified by his blood, much more shall we be saved by him from the wrath of God. 10 For if while we were enemies we were reconciled to God by the death of his Son, much more, now that we are reconciled, shall we be saved by his life. 11 Not only so, but we also rejoice in God through our Lord Jesus Christ, through whom we have now received our reconciliation.

12 Therefore as sin came into the world through one man and death through sin, and so death spread to all men because all men sinned —13 sin indeed was in the world before the law

Jerusalem Bible

perseverance brings hope, 5 and this hope is not deceptive, because the love of God has been poured into our hearts by the Holy Spirit which has been given us. 6 We were still helpless when at his appointed moment Christ died for sinful men. 7 It is not easy to die even for a good man —though of course for someone really worthy, a man might be prepared to die—8 but what proves that God loves us is that Christ died for us while we were still sinners. 9 Having died to make us righteous, is it likely that he would now fail to save us from God's anger? 10 When we were reconciled to God by the death of his Son, we were still enemies; now that we have been reconciled, surely we may count on being saved by the life of his Son? 11 Not merely because we have been reconciled but because we are filled with joyful trust in God, through our Lord Jesus Christ, through whom we have already gained our reconciliation.

A. Deliverance from sin and death and law

Adam and Jesus Christ

12 Well then, sin *entered the world* through one man, and through sin death, and thus death has spread through the whole human race because everyone has sinned. 13 Sin existed in the

New English Bible

proof is the ground of hope. Such a hope is no mockery, because God's love has flooded our inmost heart through the Holy Spirit he has given us.

For at the very time when we were still powerless, then Christ died for the wicked. Even for a just man one of us would hardly die, though perhaps for a good man one might actually brave death; but Christ died for us while we were yet sinners, and that is God's own proof of his love towards us. And so, since we have now been justified by Christ's sacrificial death, we shall all the more certainly be saved through him from final retribution. For if, when we were God's enemies, we were reconciled to him through the death of his Son, how much more, now that we are reconciled, shall we be saved by his life! But that is not all: we also exult in God through our Lord Jesus, through whom we have now been granted reconciliation.

Mark what follows. It was through one man that sin entered the world, and through sin death, and thus death pervaded the whole human race, inasmuch as all men have sinned. For sin was

King James Version

in the world: but sin is not imputed when there is no law. 14 Nevertheless death reigned from Adam to Moses, even over them that had not sinned after the similitude of Adam's transgression, who is the figure of him that was to come. 15 But not as the offence, so also *is* the free gift: for if through the offence of one many be dead, much more the grace of God, and the gift by grace, *which is* by one man, Jesus Christ, hath abounded unto many. 16 And not as *it was* by one that sinned, *so is* the gift: for the judgment *was* by one to condemnation, but the free gift *is* of many offences unto justification. 17 For if by one man's offence death reigned by one; much more they which receive abundance of grace and of the gift of righteousness shall reign in life by one, Jesus Christ.) 18 Therefore, as by the offence of one *judgment came* upon all men to condemnation; even so by the righteousness of one *the free gift came* upon all men unto justification of life. 19 For as by one man's disobedience many were made sinners, so by the obedience of one shall many be made right-

Living Bible

was Adam's sin that caused this[b]] because although, of course, people were sinning from the time of Adam until Moses, God did not in those days judge them guilty of death for breaking his laws—because he had not yet given his laws to them, nor told them what he wanted them to do. 14 So when their bodies died it was not for their own sins[b] since they themselves had never disobeyed God's special law against eating the forbidden fruit, as Adam had.

What a contrast between Adam and Christ who was yet to come! 15 And what a difference between man's sin and God's forgiveness!

For this one man, Adam, brought death to many through his *sin.* But this one man, Jesus Christ, brought forgiveness to many through God's *mercy.* 16 Adam's *one* sin brought the penalty of death to many, while Christ freely takes away *many* sins and gives glorious life instead. 17 The sin of this one man, Adam, caused *death to be king over all,* but all who will take God's gift of forgiveness and acquittal are *kings of life*[c] because of this one man, Jesus Christ. 18 Yes, Adam's *sin* brought *punishment* to all, but Christ's *righteousness* makes men *right with God,* so that they can live. 19 Adam caused many to be sinners because he *disobeyed* God, and Christ caused many to be made acceptable to God because he *obeyed.*

[*b*] Implied. [*c*] Literally, "reign in life."

Today's English Version

Law was given; but where there is no law, no account is kept of sins. 14 But from the time of Adam to the time of Moses death ruled over all men, even over those who did not sin as Adam did by disobeying God's command.

Adam was a figure of the one who was to come. 15 But the two are not the same, because God's free gift is not like Adam's sin. It is true that many men died because of the sin of that one man. But God's grace is much greater, and so is his free gift to so many men through the grace of the one man, Jesus Christ. 16 And there is a difference between God's gift and the sin of one man. After the one sin came the judgment of "Guilty"; but after so many sins comes the undeserved gift of "Not guilty!" 17 It is true that through the sin of one man death began to rule, because of that one man. But how much greater is the result of what was done by the one man, Jesus Christ! All who receive God's abundant grace and the free gift of his righteousness will rule in life through Christ.

18 So then, as the one sin condemned all men, in the same way the one righteous act sets all men free and gives them life. 19 And just as many men were made sinners as the result of the disobedience of one man, in the same way many will be put right with God as the result of the obedience of the one man.

New International Version

in the world. But sin is not taken into account when there is no law. 14 Nevertheless, death reigned from the time of Adam to the time of Moses, even over those who did not sin by breaking a command, as did Adam, who was a pattern of the one to come.

15 But the gift is not like the trespass. For if the many died by the trespass of the one man, how much more did God's grace and the gift that came by the grace of the one man, Jesus Christ, overflow to the many! 16 Again, the gift of God is not like the result of the one man's sin: The judgment followed one sin and brought condemnation, but the gift followed many trespasses and brought justification. 17 For if, by the trespass of the one man, death reigned through that one man, how much more will those who receive God's abundant provision of grace and of the gift of righteousness reign in life through the one man, Jesus Christ.

18 Consequently, just as the result of one trespass was condemnation for all men, so also the result of one act of righteousness was justification that brings life for all men. 19 For just as through the disobedience of the one man the many were made sinners, so also through the obedience of the one man the many will be made righteous.

Phillips Modern English

Law, though I suppose, technically speaking, it was not "sin" where there was no law to define it. Nevertheless death, the complement of sin, held sway over mankind from Adam to Moses, even over those whose sin was quite unlike Adam's.

Adam, the first man, foreshadows in some degree the man who has to come. But the gift of God through Christ is a very different matter from the "account rendered" through the sin of Adam. For while as a result of one man's sin death by natural consequence became the common lot of men, it was by the generosity of God, the free giving of the grace of the one man Jesus Christ, that the love of God overflowed for the benefit of all men.

Nor is the effect of God's gift the same as the effect of that one man's sin. For in the one case one man's sin brought its inevitable judgment, and the result was condemnation. But, in the other, countless men's sins are met with the free gift of grace, and the result is justification before God.

For if one man's offence meant that men should be slaves to death all their lives, it is a far greater thing that through another man, Jesus Christ, men by their acceptance of his more than sufficient grace and righteousness, should live their lives victoriously.

We see, then, that as one act of sin exposed the whole race of men to God's judgment and condemnation, so one act of perfect righteousness presents all men freely acquitted in the sight of God. One man's disobedience placed all men under the threat of condemnation, but one man's obedience has the power to present all men righteous before God.

Revised Standard Version

was given, but sin is not counted where there is
no law. 14 Yet death reigned from Adam to
Moses, even over those whose sins were not
like the transgression of Adam, who was a type
of the one who was to come.
15 But the free gift is not like the trespass.
For if many died through one man's trespass,
much more have the grace of God and the free
gift in the grace of that one man Jesus Christ
abounded for many. 16 And the free gift is not
like the effect of that one man's sin. For the
judgment following one trespass brought condemnation,
but the free gift following many
trespasses brings justification. 17 If, because of
one man's trespass, death reigned through that
one man, much more will those who receive
the abundance of grace and the free gift of
righteousness reign in life through the one man
Jesus Christ.
18 Then as one man's trespass led to condemnation
for all men, so one man's act of
righteousness leads to acquittal and life for all
men. 19 For as by one man's disobedience many
were made sinners, so by one man's obedience

Jerusalem Bible

world long before the Law was given. There
was no law and so no one could be accused of
the sin of "lawbreaking," 14 yet death reigned
over all from Adam to Moses, even though their
sin, unlike that of Adam, was not a matter of
breaking a law.
Adam prefigured the One to come, 15 but the
gift itself considerably outweighed the fall. If it
is certain that through one man's fall so many
died, it is even more certain that divine grace,
coming through the one man, Jesus Christ, came
to so many as an abundant free gift. 16 The results
of the gift also outweigh the results of one
man's sin: for after one single fall came judgment
with a verdict of condemnation, now after
many falls comes grace with its verdict of acquittal.
17 If it is certain that death reigned over
everyone as the consequence of one man's fall,
it is even more certain that one man, Jesus
Christ, will cause everyone to reign in life who
receives the free gift that he does not deserve,
of being made righteous. 18 Again, as one man's
fall brought condemnation on everyone, so the
good act of one man brings everyone life and
makes them justified. 19 As by one man's disobedience
many were made sinners, so by one
man's obedience many will be made righteous.

New English Bible

already in the world before there was law, though in the absence of law no reckoning is kept of sin. But death held sway from Adam to Moses, even over those who had not sinned as Adam did, by disobeying a direct command—and Adam foreshadows the Man who was to come.

But God's act of grace is out of all proportion to Adam's wrongdoing. For if the wrongdoing of that one man brought death upon so many, its effect is vastly exceeded by the grace of God and the gift that came to so many by the grace of the one man, Jesus Christ. And again, the gift of God is not to be compared in its effect with that one man's sin; for the judicial action, following upon the one offence, issued in a verdict of condemnation, but the act of grace, following upon so many misdeeds, issued in a verdict of acquittal. For if by the wrongdoing of that one man death established its reign, through a single sinner, much more shall those who receive in far greater measure God's grace, and his gift of righteousness, live and reign through the one man, Jesus Christ.

It follows, then, that as the issue of one misdeed was condemnation for all men, so the issue of one just act is acquittal and life for all men. For as through the disobedience of the one man the many were made sinners, so through the obedience of the one man the many will be made righteous.

King James Version

eous. 20 Moreover the law entered, that the offence might abound. But where sin abounded, grace did much more abound: 21 That as sin hath reigned unto death, even so might grace reign through righteousness unto eternal life by Jesus Christ our Lord.

6 What shall we say then? Shall we continue in sin, that grace may abound? 2 God forbid. How shall we, that are dead to sin, live any longer therein? 3 Know ye not, that so many of us as were baptized into Jesus Christ were baptized into his death? 4 Therefore we are buried with him by baptism into death: that like as Christ was raised up from the dead by the glory of the Father, even so we also should walk in newness of life. 5 For if we have been planted together in the likeness of his death, we shall be also *in the likeness* of *his* resurrection:

Living Bible

20 The Ten Commandments were given so that all could see the extent of their failure to obey God's laws. But the more we see our sinfulness, the more we see God's abounding grace forgiving us. 21 Before, sin ruled over all men and brought them to death, but now God's kindness rules instead, giving us right standing with God and resulting in eternal life through Jesus Christ our Lord.

6 Well then, shall we keep on sinning so that God can keep on showing us more and more kindness and forgiveness?

2, 3 Of course not! Should we keep on sinning when we don't have to? For sin's power over us was broken when we became Christians and were baptized to become a part of Jesus Christ; through his death the power of your sinful nature was shattered. 4 Your old sin-loving nature was buried with him by baptism when he died, and when God the Father, with glorious power, brought him back to life again, you were given his wonderful new life to enjoy.

5 For you have become a part of him, and so you died with him, so to speak, when he died[a], and now you share his new life, and shall

[a] Literally, "united with him in the likeness of his death."

Today's English Version

20 Law was introduced in order to increase wrongdoing; but where sin increased, God's grace increased much more. 21 So then, just as sin ruled by means of death, so also God's grace rules by means of righteousness, leading us to eternal life through Jesus Christ our Lord.

Dead to sin but alive in Christ

6 What shall we say, then? That we should continue to live in sin so that God's grace will increase? 2 Certainly not! We have died to sin—how then can we go on living in it? 3 For surely you know this: when we were baptized into union with Christ Jesus, we were baptized into union with his death. 4 By our baptism, then, we were buried with him and shared his death, in order that, just as Christ was raised from death by the glorious power of the Father, so also we might live a new life.

5 For if we became one with him in dying as he did, in the same way we shall be one with

New International Version

20 The law was added so that the trespass might increase. But where sin increased, grace increased all the more, 21 so that, just as sin reigned in death, so also grace might reign through righteousness to bring eternal life through Jesus Christ our Lord.

Dead to sin, alive in Christ

6 What shall we say, then? Shall we go on sinning so that grace may increase? 2 By no means! We died to sin; how can we live in it any longer? 3 Or don't you know that all of us who were baptized into Christ Jesus were baptized into his death? 4 We were therefore buried with him through baptism into death in order that, just as Christ was raised from the dead through the glory of the Father, we too may live a new life.

5 If we have been united with him in his death, we will certainly also be united with him

Phillips Modern English

5.20 Grace is a bigger thing than the Law

Now we find that the Law keeps slipping into the picture to point the vast extent of sin. Yet, though sin is shown to be wide and deep, thank God his grace is wider and deeper still! The whole outlook changes—sin used to be the master of men and in the end handed them over to death; now grace is the ruling factor, with its purpose making men right with God and its end the bringing of them to eternal life through Jesus Christ our Lord.

6.1 Righteousness by faith, in practice

Now what is our response to be? Shall we sin to our heart's content and see how far we can exploit the grace of God? What a terrible thought! We, who have died to sin—how could we live in sin a moment longer? Have you forgotten that all of us who were baptised into Jesus Christ were, by that very action, sharing in his death? We were dead and buried with him in baptism, so that just as he was raised from the dead by that splendid revelation of the Father's power so we too might rise to life on a new plane altogether. If we have, as it were, shared his death, we shall also share in his resur-

Revised Standard Version

many will be made righteous. 20 Law came in,
to increase the trespass; but where sin increased,
grace abounded all the more, 21 so that, as sin
reigned in death, grace also might reign through
righteousness to eternal life through Jesus Christ
our Lord.

6 What shall we say then? Are we to continue in sin that grace may abound? 2 By no
means! How can we who died to sin still live
in it? 3 Do you not know that all of us who
have been baptized into Christ Jesus were baptized into his death? 4 We were buried therefore with him by baptism into death, so that as
Christ was raised from the dead by the glory
of the Father, we too might walk in newness of
life.
5 For if we have been united with him in a
death like his, we shall certainly be united with

Jerusalem Bible

20 When law came, it was to multiply the opportunities of falling, but however great the
number of sins committed, grace was even
greater; 21 and so, just as sin reigned wherever
there was death, so grace will reign to bring
eternal life thanks to the righteousness that
comes through Jesus Christ our Lord.

Baptism

6 Does it follow that we should remain in
sin so as to let grace have greater scope?
2 Of course not. We are dead to sin, so how
can we continue to live in it? 3 You have been
taught that when we were baptized in Christ
Jesus we were baptized in his death; 4 in other
words, when we were baptized we went into the
tomb with him and joined him in death, so that
as Christ was raised from the dead by the Father's glory, we too might live a new life.
5 If in union with Christ we have imitated his
death, we shall also imitate him in his resurrec-

New English Bible

Law intruded into this process to multiply law-breaking. But where sin was thus multiplied, grace immeasurably exceeded it, in order that, as sin established its reign by way of death, so God's grace might establish its reign in righteousness, and issue in eternal life through Jesus Christ our Lord.

6 What are we to say, then? Shall we persist in sin, so that there may be all the more grace? No, no! We died to sin: how can we live in it any longer? Have you forgotten that when we were baptized into union with Christ Jesus we were baptized into his death? By baptism we were buried with him, and lay dead, in order that, as Christ was raised from the dead in the splendour of the Father, so also we might set our feet upon the new path of life.

For if we have become incorporate with him in a death like his, we shall also be one with him

King James Version

6 Knowing this, that our old man is crucified with *him*, that the body of sin might be destroyed, that henceforth we should not serve sin. 7 For he that is dead is freed from sin. 8 Now if we be dead with Christ, we believe that we shall also live with him: 9 Knowing that Christ being raised from the dead dieth no more; death hath no more dominion over him. 10 For in that he died, he died unto sin once: but in that he liveth, he liveth unto God. 11 Likewise reckon ye also yourselves to be dead indeed unto sin, but alive unto God through Jesus Christ our Lord. 12 Let not sin therefore reign in your mortal body, that ye should obey it in the lusts thereof. 13 Neither yield ye your members *as* instruments of unrighteousness unto sin: but yield yourselves unto God, as those that are alive from the dead, and your members *as* instruments of righteousness unto God. 14 For sin shall not have dominion over you: for ye are not under the law, but under grace. 15 What then? shall we sin, because we are not under the law, but

Living Bible

rise as he did. 6 Your old evil desires were nailed to the cross with him; that part of you that loves to sin was crushed and fatally wounded, so that your sin-loving body is no longer under sin's control, no longer needs to be a slave to sin; 7 for when you are deadened to sin you are freed from all its allure and its power over you. 8 And since your old sin-loving nature "died" with Christ, we know that you will share his new life. 9 Christ rose from the dead and will never die again. Death no longer has any power over him. 10 He died once for all to end sin's power, but now he lives forever in unbroken fellowship with God. 11 So look upon your old sin nature as dead and unresponsive to sin, and instead be alive to God, alert to him, through Jesus Christ our Lord.

12 Do not let sin control your puny body any longer; do not give in to its sinful desires. 13 Do not let any part of your bodies become tools of wickedness, to be used for sinning; but give yourselves completely to God—every part of you—for you are back from death and you want to be tools in the hands of God, to be used for his good purposes. 14 Sin need[b] never again be your master, for now you are no longer tied to the law where sin enslaves you, but you are free under God's favor and mercy.

15 Does this mean that now we can go ahead and sin and not worry about it? (For our salvation does not depend on keeping the law, but on receiving God's grace!) Of course not!

[*b*] Literally, "Sin will never again be your master."

Today's English Version

him by being raised to life as he was. 6 And we know this: our old being has been put to death with Christ on his cross, in order that the power of the sinful self might be destroyed, so that we should no longer be the slaves of sin. 7 For when a person dies he is set free from the power of sin. 8 If we have died with Christ, we believe that we will also live with him. 9 For we know that Christ has been raised from death and will never die again—death has no more power over him. 10 The death he died was death to sin, once and for all; and the life he now lives is life to God. 11 In the same way you are to think of yourselves as dead to sin but alive to God in union with Christ Jesus.

12 Sin must no longer rule in your mortal bodies, so that you obey the desires of your natural self. 13 Nor must you surrender any part of yourselves to sin, to be used for wicked purposes. Instead, give yourselves to God, as men who have been brought from death to life, and surrender your whole being to him to be used for righteous purposes. 14 Sin must not rule over you; you do not live under law but under God's grace.

Slaves of righteousness

15 What, then? Shall we sin, because we are not under law but under God's grace? By no

New International Version

in his resurrection. 6 For we know that our old self was crucified with him so that the body of sin might be rendered powerless, that we should no longer be slaves to sin— 7 because anyone who has died has been freed from sin.

8 Now if we died with Christ, we believe that we will also live with him. 9 For we know that since Christ was raised from the dead, he cannot die again; death no longer has mastery over him. 10 The death he died, he died to sin once for all; but the life he lives, he lives to God.

11 In the same way, count yourselves dead to sin but alive to God in Christ Jesus. 12 Therefore, do not let sin reign in your mortal body so that you obey its evil desires. 13 Do not offer the parts of your body to sin, as instruments of wickedness, but rather offer yourselves to God, as those who have returned from death to life; and offer the parts of your body to him as instruments of righteousness. 14 For sin shall not be your master, because you are not under law, but under grace.

Slaves to righteousness

15 What then? Shall we sin because we are not under law but under grace? By no means!

Phillips Modern English

rection. Let us never forget that our old selves died with him on the cross that the tyranny of sin over us might be broken—for a dead man can safely be said to be free from the power of sin. And if we were dead men with Christ we can believe that we shall also be men alive with him. We can be sure that the risen Christ never dies again—death's power to master him is finished. He died, because of sin, once: he lives for God for ever. In the same way look upon yourselves as dead to the appeal and power of sin but alive to God through Christ Jesus our Lord.

Do not, then, allow sin to establish any power over your mortal bodies in making you give way to its lusts. Nor hand over your bodily parts to be, as it were, weapons of evil for the devil's purposes. But, like men rescued from certain death, put yourselves in God's hands as weapons of good for his own purposes. For sin can never be your master—you are no longer living under the Law, but under grace.

6.15 The new service completely ousts the old

Now, what shall we do? Shall we go on sinning because we have no Law to condemn us any more, but are living under grace? Never!

Revised Standard Version

him in a resurrection like his. 6 We know that
our old self was crucified with him so that the
sinful body might be destroyed, and we might
no longer be enslaved to sin. 7 For he who has
died is freed from sin. 8 But if we have died
with Christ, we believe that we shall also live
with him. 9 For we know that Christ being raised
from the dead will never die again; death no
longer has dominion over him. 10 The death he
died he died to sin, once for all, but the life he
lives he lives to God. 11 So you also must consider yourselves dead to sin and alive to God
in Christ Jesus.
12 Let not sin therefore reign in your mortal
bodies, to make you obey their passions. 13 Do
not yield your members to sin as instruments of
wickedness, but yield yourselves to God as men
who have been brought from death to life, and
your members to God as instruments of righteousness. 14 For sin will have no dominion over
you, since you are not under law but under
grace.
15 What then? Are we to sin because we are
not under law but under grace? By no means!

Jerusalem Bible

tion. 6 We must realize that our former selves
have been crucified with him to destroy this sinful body and to free us from the slavery of sin.
7 When a man dies, of course, he has finished
with sin.
8 But we believe that having died with Christ
we shall return to life with him: 9 Christ, as we
know, having been raised from the dead will
never die again. Death has no power over him
any more. 10 When he died, he died, once for
all, to sin, so his life now is life with God;
11 and in that way, you too must consider yourselves to be dead to sin but alive for God in
Christ Jesus.

Holiness, not sin, to be the master

12 That is why you must not let sin reign in
your mortal bodies or command your obedience
to bodily passions, 13 why you must not let any
part of your body turn into an unholy weapon
fighting on the side of sin; you should, instead,
offer yourselves to God, and consider yourselves
dead men brought back to life; you should make
every part of your body into a weapon fighting
on the side of God; 14 and then sin will no
longer dominate your life, since you are living
by grace and not by law.

The Christian is freed from the slavery of sin

15 Does the fact that we are living by grace
and not by law mean that we are free to sin?

New English Bible

in a resurrection like his. We know that the man we once were has been crucified with Christ, for the destruction of the sinful self, so that we may no longer be the slaves of sin, since a dead man is no longer answerable for his sin. But if we thus died with Christ, we believe that we shall also come to life with him. We know that Christ, once raised from the dead, is never to die again: he is no longer under the dominion of death. For in dying as he died, he died to sin, once for all, and in living as he lives, he lives to God. In the same way you must regard yourselves as dead to sin and alive to God, in union with Christ Jesus.

So sin must no longer reign in your mortal body, exacting obedience to the body's desires. You must no longer put its several parts at sin's disposal, as implements for doing wrong. No: put yourselves at the disposal of God, as dead men raised to life; yield your bodies to him as implements for doing right; for sin shall no longer be your master, because you are no longer under law, but under the grace of God.

What then? Are we to sin, because we are not

King James Version

under grace? God forbid. 16 Know ye not, that
to whom ye yield yourselves servants to obey, his
servants ye are to whom ye obey; whether of
sin unto death, or of obedience unto righteousness? 17 But God be thanked, that ye were the
servants of sin, but ye have obeyed from the
heart that form of doctrine which was delivered
you. 18 Being then made free from sin, ye became the servants of righteousness. 19 I speak
after the manner of men because of the infirmity
of your flesh: for as ye have yielded your members servants to uncleanness and to iniquity unto
iniquity; even so now yield your members servants to righteousness unto holiness. 20 For when
ye were the servants of sin, ye were free from
righteousness. 21 What fruit had ye then in those
things whereof ye are now ashamed? for the end
of those things *is* death. 22 But now being made
free from sin, and become servants to God, ye
have your fruit unto holiness, and the end everlasting life. 23 For the wages of sin *is* death; but
the gift of God *is* eternal life through Jesus
Christ our Lord.

7 Know ye not, brethren, (for I speak to
them that know the law,) how that the law
hath dominion over a man as long as he liveth?

Living Bible

16 Don't you realize that you can choose
your own master? You can choose sin (with
death) or else obedience (with acquittal). The
one to whom you offer yourself—he will take
you and be your master and you will be his
slave. 17 Thank God that though you once chose
to be slaves of sin, now you have obeyed with
all your heart the teaching to which God has
committed you. 18 And now you are free from
your old master, sin; and you have become
slaves to your new master, righteousness.
19 I speak this way, using the illustration of
slaves and masters, because it is easy to understand: just as you used to be slaves to all kinds
of sin, so now you must let yourselves be slaves
to all that is right and holy.
20 In those days when you were slaves of
sin you didn't bother much with goodness.
21 And what was the result? Evidently not good,
since you are ashamed now even to think about
those things you used to do, for all of them end
in eternal doom. 22 But now you are free from
the power of sin and are slaves of God, and
his benefits to you include holiness and everlasting life. 23 For the wages of sin is death,
but the free gift of God is eternal life through
Jesus Christ our Lord.

7 Don't you understand yet, dear Jewish[a]
brothers in Christ, that when a person dies
the law no longer holds him in its power?

[*a*] Implied. Literally, "men who know (the) law."

Today's English Version

means! 16 Surely you know that when you surrender yourselves as slaves to obey someone,
you are in fact the slaves of the master you obey
—either of sin, which results in death, or of obedience, which results in being put right with
God. 17 But thanks be to God! For at one time
you were slaves to sin; but then you obeyed with
all your heart the truths found in the teaching
you received. 18 You were set free from sin and
became the slaves of righteousness. 19 I use ordinary words because of the weakness of your
natural selves. At one time you surrendered
yourselves entirely as slaves to impurity and wickedness, for wicked purposes. In the same way
you must now surrender yourselves entirely as
slaves of righteousness, for holy purposes.
20 When you were the slaves of sin, you
were free from righteousness. 21 What did you
gain from doing the things that you are ashamed
of now? The result of those things is death!
22 But now you have been set free from sin and
are the slaves of God; your gain is a life fully
dedicated to him, and the result is eternal life.
23 For sin pays its wage—death; but God's free
gift is eternal life in union with Christ Jesus our
Lord.

An illustration from marriage

7 Certainly you understand what I am about
to say, my brothers, because all of you know
about law. The law rules over a man only as

New International Version

16 Don't you know that when you offer yourselves to someone to obey him as slaves, you are
slaves to the one whom you obey—whether you
are slaves to sin, which leads to death, or to
obedience, which leads to righteousness? 17 But
thanks be to God that, though you used to be
slaves to sin, you wholeheartedly obeyed the
form of teaching to which you were committed.
18 You have been set free from sin and have
become slaves to righteousness.
19 I put this in human terms because you are
weak in your natural selves. Just as you used to
offer the parts of your body in slavery to impurity and to ever-increasing wickedness, so now
offer them in slavery to righteousness and holiness. 20 When you were slaves to sin, you were
free from the control of righteousness. 21 What
benefit did you reap at that time from the things
you are now ashamed of? Those things result in
death! 22 But now that you have been set free
from sin and have become slaves to God, the
benefit you reap leads to holiness, and the result
is eternal life. 23 For the wages of sin is death,
but the gift of God is eternal life through
Christ Jesus our Lord.

An illustration from marriage

7 Do you not know, brothers—for I am
speaking to men who know the law—that
the law has authority over a man only as long

Phillips Modern English

Just think what it would mean. You *belong* to the power which you choose to obey, whether you choose sin, whose reward is death, or God, obedience to whom means the reward of righteousness. Thank God that you, who were at one time the servants of sin, honestly responded to the impact of Christ's teaching when you came under its influence. Then, released from the service of sin, you entered the service of righteousness. (I use an everyday illustration because human nature grasps truth more readily that way.) In the past you voluntarily gave your bodies to the service of vice and wickedness—for the purposes of evil. So, now, give yourselves to the service of righteousness—for the purpose of becoming truly good. For when you were employed by sin you owed no duty to righteousness. Yet what sort of a harvest did you reap from those things that today you blush to remember? In the long run those things mean one thing only—death.

But now that you are freed from sin and employed by God, you owe no duty to sin, and you reap the fruit of being made righteous, while at the end of the road there is life for evermore.

Sin *pays* its servants: the wage is death. But God *gives* to those who serve him: his free gift is eternal life through Jesus Christ our Lord.

7.1 How to be free from the Law

You know very well, my brothers (for I am speaking to those well acquainted with the subject), that the Law can only exercise authority

Revised Standard Version

16 Do you not know that if you yield yourselves to any one as obedient slaves, you are
slaves of the one whom you obey, either of sin,
which leads to death, or of obedience, which
leads to righteousness? 17 But thanks be to God,
that you who were once slaves of sin have become obedient from the heart to the standard
of teaching to which you were committed,
18 and, having been set free from sin, have become slaves of righteousness. 19 I am speaking
in human terms, because of your natural limitations. For just as you once yielded your members to impurity and to greater and greater
iniquity, so now yield your members to righteousness for sanctification.
20 When you were slaves of sin, you were
free in regard to righteousness. 21 But then what
return did you get from the things of which you
are now ashamed? The end of those things is
death. 22 But now that you have been set free
from sin and have become slaves of God, the
return you get is sanctification and its end,
eternal life. 23 For the wages of sin is death,
but the free gift of God is eternal life in Christ
Jesus our Lord.

7 Do you not know, brethren—for I am
speaking to those who know the law—that
the law is binding on a person only during his

Jerusalem Bible

Of course not. 16 You know that if you agree
to serve and obey a master you become his
slaves. You cannot be slaves of sin that leads to
death and at the same time slaves of obedience
that leads to righteousness. 17 You were once
slaves of sin, but thank God you submitted without reservation to the creed you were taught.
18 You may have been freed from the slavery
of sin, but only to become "slaves" of righteousness. 19 If I may use human terms to help your
natural weakness: as once you put your bodies
at the service of vice and immorality, so now
you must put them at the service of righteousness for your sanctification.

The reward of sin and the reward of holiness

20 When you were slaves of sin, you felt no
obligation to righteousness, 21 and what did you
get from this? Nothing but experiences that now
make you blush, since that sort of behavior ends
in death. 22 Now, however, you have been set
free from sin, you have been made slaves of
God, and you get a reward leading to your
sanctification and ending in eternal life. 23 For
the wage paid by sin is death; the present given
by God is eternal life in Christ Jesus our Lord.

The Christian is not bound by the Law

7 Brothers, those of you who have studied
law will know that laws affect a person only

New English Bible

under law but under grace? Of course not. You know well enough that if you put yourselves at the disposal of a master, to obey him, you are slaves of the master whom you obey; and this is true whether you serve sin, with death as its result; or obedience, with righteousness as its result. But God be thanked, you, who once were slaves of sin, have yielded whole-hearted obedience to the pattern of teaching to which you were made subject,[a] and, emancipated from sin, have become slaves of righteousness (to use words that suit your human weakness)—I mean, as you once yielded your bodies to the service of impurity and lawlessness, making for moral anarchy, so now you must yield them to the service of righteousness, making for a holy life.

When you were slaves of sin, you were free from the control of righteousness; and what was the gain? Nothing but what now makes you ashamed, for the end of that is death. But now, freed from the commands of sin, and bound to the service of God, your gains are such as make for holiness, and the end is eternal life. For sin pays a wage, and the wage is death, but God gives freely, and his gift is eternal life, in union with Christ Jesus our Lord.

7 You cannot be unaware, my friends—I am
speaking to those who have some knowledge
of law—that a person is subject to the law so

[a] *Or* which was handed on to you.

King James Version

2 For the woman which hath a husband is bound
by the law to *her* husband so long as he liveth;
but if the husband be dead, she is loosed from
the law of *her* husband. 3 So then if, while *her*
husband liveth, she be married to another man,
she shall be called an adulteress: but if her
husband be dead, she is free from that law; so
that she is no adulteress, though she be married
to another man. 4 Wherefore, my brethren, ye
also are become dead to the law by the body of
Christ; that ye should be married to another,
even to him who is raised from the dead, that
we should bring forth fruit unto God. 5 For
when we were in the flesh, the motions of sins,
which were by the law, did work in our members to bring forth fruit unto death. 6 But now
we are delivered from the law, that being dead
wherein we were held; that we should serve in
newness of spirit, and not *in* the oldness of the
letter. 7 What shall we say then? *Is* the law sin?
God forbid. Nay, I had not known sin, but by
the law: for I had not known lust, except the

Living Bible

2 Let me illustrate: when a woman marries,
the law binds her to her husband as long as he
is alive. But if he dies, she is no longer bound
to him; the laws of marriage no longer apply to
her. 3 Then she can marry someone else if she
wants to. That would be wrong while he was
alive, but it is perfectly all right after he dies.
4 Your "husband," your master, used to be
the Jewish law; but you "died," as it were, with
Christ on the cross; and since you are "dead,"
you are no longer "married to the law," and it
has no more control over you. Then you came
back to life again when Christ did, and are a
new person. And now you are "married," so to
speak, to the one who rose from the dead, so
that you can produce good fruit, that is, good
deeds for God. 5 When your old nature was still
active, sinful desires were at work within you,
making you want to do whatever God said not
to, and producing sinful deeds, the rotting fruit
of death. 6 But now you need no longer worry
about the Jewish laws and customs[b] because you
"died" while in their captivity, and now you can
really serve God; not in the old way, mechani-
cally obeying a set of rules, but in the new way,
[with all of your hearts and minds[c]]
7 Well then, am I suggesting that these laws
of God are evil? Of course not! No, the law is
not sinful but it was the law that showed me my
sin. I would never have known the sin in my
heart—the evil desires that are hidden there—if
the law had not said, "You must not have evil

[*b*] Literally, "Now we are delivered from the law."
[*c*] Implied.

Today's English Version

long as he lives. 2A married woman, for example, is bound by the law to her husband as long
as he lives; but if he dies, then she is free from
the law that bound her to him. 3 So then, if she
lives with another man while her husband is
alive, she will be called an adulteress; but if her
husband dies, she is legally a free woman, and
does not commit adultery if she marries another
man. 4 That is the way it is with you, my brothers. You also have died, as far as the Law is
concerned, because you are part of the body of
Christ; and now you belong to him who was
raised from death in order that we might be
useful in the service of God. 5 For when we
lived according to our human nature, the sinful
desires stirred up by the Law were at work in
our bodies, and we were useful in the service of
death. 6 Now, however, we are free from the
Law, because we died to that which once held
us prisoners. No longer do we serve in the old
way of a written law, but in the new way of the
Spirit.

Law and sin

7 What shall we say, then? That the Law itself is sinful? Of course not! But it was the
Law that made me know what sin is. I would
not have known what it is to covet if the Law

New International Version

as he lives? 2 For example, by law a married
woman is bound to her husband as long as
he is alive, but if her husband dies, she is released from the law of marriage. 3 So then, if
she marries another man while her husband is
still alive, she is called an adulteress. But if her
husband dies, she is released from that law and
is not an adulteress, even though she marries
another man.
4 So, my brothers, you also died to the law
through the body of Christ, that you might belong to another, to him who was raised from the
dead, in order that we might bear fruit to God.
5 For when we were controlled by our sinful nature, the sinful passions aroused by the law were
at work in our bodies, so that we bore fruit for
death. 6 But now, by dying to what once bound
us, we have been released from the law so that
we serve in the new way of the Spirit, and not in
the old way of the written code.

Struggling with sin

7 What shall we say, then? Is the law sin? Far
from it! Indeed I would not have known what
sin was except through the law. For I would
not have known what it was to covet if the law

Phillips Modern English

over a man so long as he is alive. A married woman, for example, is bound by law to her husband so long as he is alive. But if he dies, then his legal claim over her disappears. This means that, if she should give herself to another man while her husband is alive, she incurs the stigma of adultery. But if, after her husband's death, she does exactly the same thing, no one could call her an adulteress, for the legal hold over her has been dissolved by her husband's death.

So, my brothers, the death of Christ on the cross has made you "dead" to the claims of the Law, and you are free to give yourselves in marriage, so to speak, to another, the one who was raised from the dead, that we may be productive for God.

While we were "in the flesh" the Law stimulated our sinful passions and so worked in our nature that we became productive—for death! But now that we stand clear of the Law, the claims which existed are dissolved by our "death", and we are free to serve God not in the old obedience to the letter of the Law, but in a new way, in the Spirit.

7.7 Sin and the Law

It now beings to look as if sin and the Law were the same thing—can this be a fact? Of course it cannot. But it must be admitted that I should never have had sin brought home to me but for the Law. For example, I should never have felt guilty of the sin of coveting if I had not heard the Law saying "Thou shalt not

Revised Standard Version

life? 2 Thus a married woman is bound by law
to her husband as long as he lives; but if her
husband dies she is discharged from the law
concerning the husband. 3 Accordingly, she will
be called an adulteress if she lives with another
man while her husband is alive. But if her husband dies she is free from that law, and if she
marries another man she is not an adulteress.
4 Likewise, my brethren, you have died to
the law through the body of Christ, so that you
may belong to another, to him who has been
raised from the dead in order that we may bear
fruit for God. 5 While we were living in the
flesh, our sinful passions, aroused by the law,
were at work in our members to bear fruit for
death. 6 But now we are discharged from the
law, dead to that which held us captive, so that
we serve not under the old written code but in
the new life of the Spirit.
7 What then shall we say? That the law is
sin? By no means! Yet, if it had not been for
the law, I should not have known sin. I should
not have known what it is to covet if the law

Jerusalem Bible

during his lifetime. 2 A married woman, for instance, has legal obligations to her husband
while he is alive, but all these obligations come
to an end if the husband dies. 3 So if she gives
herself to another man while her husband is still
alive, she is legally an adulteress; but after her
husband is dead her legal obligations come to
an end, and she can marry someone else without
becoming an adulteress. 4 That is why you, my
brothers, who through the body of Christ are
now dead to the Law, can now give yourselves
to another husband, to him who rose from the
dead to make us productive for God. 5 Before
our conversion[o] our sinful passions, quite un-
subdued by the Law, fertilized our bodies to
make them give birth to death. 6 But now we
are rid of the Law, freed by death from our imprisonment, free to serve in the new spiritual
way and not the old way of a written law.

The function of the Law

7 Does it follow that the Law itself is sin? Of
course not. What I mean is that I should not
have known what sin was except for the Law. I
should not for instance have known what it
means to covet if the Law had not said *You*

[o] "While we were in the flesh."

New English Bible

long as he is alive, and no longer. For example, a married woman is by law bound to her husband while he lives; but if her husband dies, she is discharged from the obligations of the marriage-law. If, therefore, in her husband's lifetime she consorts with another man, she will incur the charge of adultery; but if her husband dies she is free of the law, and she does not commit adultery by consorting with another man. So you, my friends, have died to the law by becoming identified with the body of Christ, and accordingly you have found another husband in him who rose from the dead, so that we may bear fruit for God. While we lived on the level of our lower nature, the sinful passions evoked by the law worked in our bodies, to bear fruit for death. But now, having died to that which held us bound, we are discharged from the law, to serve God in a new way, the way of the spirit, in contrast to the old way, the way of a written code.

What follows? Is the law identical with sin? Of course not. But except through law I should never have become acquainted with sin. For example, I should never have known what it was to covet, if the law had not said, 'Thou shalt

King James Version

law had said, Thou shalt not covet. 8 But sin, taking occasion by the commandment, wrought in me all manner of concupiscence. For without the law sin *was* dead. 9 For I was alive without the law once: but when the commandment came, sin revived, and I died. 10 And the commandment, which *was ordained* to life, I found *to be* unto death. 11 For sin, taking occasion by the commandment, deceived me, and by it slew *me*. 12 Wherefore the law *is* holy, and the commandment holy, and just, and good. 13 Was then that which is good made death unto me? God forbid. But sin, that it might appear sin, working death in me by that which is good; that sin by the commandment might become exceeding sinful. 14 For we know that the law is spiritual: but I am carnal, sold under sin. 15 For that which I do, I allow not: for what I would, that do I not; but what I hate, that do I. 16 If then I do that which I would not, I consent unto the law that *it is* good. 17 Now then it is no more I that do it, but sin that dwelleth in me.

Living Bible

desires in your heart." 8 But sin used this law against evil desires by reminding me that such desires are wrong and arousing all kinds of forbidden desires within me! Only if there were no laws to break would there be no sinning.

9 That is why I felt fine so long as I did not understand what the law really demanded. But when I learned the truth, I realized that I had broken the law and was a sinner, doomed to die. 10 So as far as I was concerned, the good law which was supposed to show me the way of life resulted instead in my being given the death penalty. 11 Sin fooled me by taking the good laws of God and using them to make me guilty of death. 12 But still, you see, the law itself was wholly right and good.

13 But how can that be? Didn't the law cause my doom? How then can it be good? No, it was sin, devilish stuff that it is, that used what was good to bring about my condemnation. So you can see how cunning and deadly and damnable it is. For it uses God's good laws for its own evil purposes. 14 The law is good, then, and the trouble is not there but with *me*, because I am sold into slavery with Sin as my owner.

15 I don't understand myself at all, for I really want to do what is right, but I can't. I do what I don't want to—what I hate. 16 I know perfectly well that what I am doing is wrong, and my bad conscience proves that I agree with these laws I am breaking. 17 But I can't help myself, because I'm no longer doing it. It is sin

Today's English Version

had not said, "Do not covet." 8 Sin found its chance to stir up all kinds of covetousness in me by working through the commandment. For sin is a dead thing apart from law. 9 I myself was once alive apart from law; but when the commandment came, sin sprang to life, 10 and I died. And the commandment which was meant to bring life, in my case brought death. 11 Sin found its chance and deceived me by working through the commandment; by means of the commandment sin killed me.

12 So then, the Law itself is holy, and the commandment is holy, right, and good. 13 Does this mean that what is good brought about my death? By no means! It was sin that did it; by using what is good, sin brought death to me in order that its true nature as sin might be revealed. And so, by means of the commandment, sin is shown to be even more terribly sinful.

The conflict in man

14 We know that the Law is spiritual; but I am mortal man, sold as a slave to sin. 15 I do not understand what I do; for I don't do what I would like to do, but instead I do what I hate. 16 When I do what I don't want to do, this shows that I agree that the Law is right. 17 So I am not really the one who does this thing; rather

New International Version

had not said, "Do not covet." [t] 8 But sin, seizing the opportunity afforded by the commandment, produced in me every kind of covetous desire. For apart from law, sin is dead. 9 Once I was alive apart from law; but when the commandment came, sin sprang to life 10 and I died. I found that the very commandment that was intended to bring life actually brought death. 11 For sin, seizing the opportunity afforded by the commandment, deceived me, and through the commandment put me to death. 12 So then, the law is holy, and the commandment is holy, righteous and good.

13 Did that which is good, then, become death to me? By no means! But in order that sin might be recognized as sin, it produced death in me through what was good, so that through the commandment sin might become utterly sinful.

14 We know that the law is spiritual; but I am unspiritual, sold as a slave to sin. 15 I do not know what I am doing. For what I want to do I do not do, but what I hate I do. 16 And if I do what I do not want to do, I agree that the law is good. 17 As it is, it is no longer I myself who

[t] Exodus 20:17; Deut. 5:21.

Phillips Modern English

covet". But the sin in me, finding in the commandment an opportunity to express itself, stimulated all my desires. For sin, in the absence of the Law, has no life of its own. As long, then as I was without the Law I was alive. But when the commandment arrived, sin sprang to life and I "died". The commandment, which was meant to be a direction to life, I found was a sentence to death. The commandment gave sin its opportunity, and without my realising what it was doing, it "killed" me.

7.12 The Law is itself good

It can scarcely be doubted that the Law itself is holy, and the commandment is holy, fair and good. Can it be that something that is intrinsically good could mean death to me? No, what happened was this. Sin, at the touch of the Law, was forced to show itself as sin, and *that* meant death for me. The contact of the Law showed the utterly sinful nature of sin.

7.14 But it cannot make men good

For we know that the Law itself is concerned with the spiritual—it is I who am carnal, and have sold my soul to sin. My own behaviour baffles me. For I find myself doing what I really loathe but not doing what I really want to do. Yet surely if I do things that I really don't want to do, I am admitting that I really agree that the Law is good. But it cannot be said that "I" am doing them at all—it must be sin that has

Revised Standard Version

had not said, "You shall not covet." 8 But sin, finding opportunity in the commandment, wrought in me all kinds of covetousness. Apart from the law sin lies dead. 9 I was once alive apart from the law, but when the commandment came, sin revived and I died; 10 the very commandment which promised life proved to be death to me. 11 For sin, finding opportunity in the commandment, deceived me and by it killed me. 12 So the law is holy, and the commandment is holy and just and good.

13 Did that which is good, then, bring death to me? By no means! It was sin, working death in me through what is good, in order that sin might be shown to be sin, and through the commandment might become sinful beyond measure. 14 We know that the law is spiritual; but I am carnal, sold under sin. 15 I do not understand my own actions. For I do not do what I want, but I do the very thing I hate. 16 Now if I do what I do not want, I agree that the law is good. 17 So then it is no longer I that do it,

Jerusalem Bible

shall not covet. 8 But it was this commandment that sin took advantage of to produce all kinds of covetousness in me, for when there is no Law, sin is dead.

9 Once, when there was no Law, I [p] was alive; but when the commandment came, sin came to life 10 and I died: the commandment was meant to lead me to life but it turned out to mean death for me, 11 because sin took advantage of the commandment to mislead me, and so sin, through that commandment, killed me.

12 The Law is sacred, and what it commands is sacred, just and good. 13 Does that mean that something good killed me? Of course not. But sin, to show itself in its true colors, used that good thing to kill me; and thus sin, thanks to the commandment, was able to exercise all its sinful power.

The inward struggle

14 The Law, of course, as we all know, is spiritual; but I am unspiritual; I have been sold as a slave to sin. 15 I cannot understand my own behavior. I fail to carry out the things I want to do, and I find myself doing the very things I hate. 16 When I act against my own will, that means I have a self that acknowledges that the Law is good, 17 and so the thing behaving in that

[*p*] Rhetorical figure; Paul speaks in the person of mankind.

New English Bible

not covet.' Through that commandment sin found its opportunity, and produced in me all kinds of wrong desires. In the absence of law, sin is a dead thing. There was a time when, in the absence of law, I was fully alive; but when the commandment came, sin sprang to life and I died. The commandment which should have led to life proved in my experience to lead to death, because sin found its opportunity in the commandment, seduced me, and through the commandment killed me.

Therefore the law is in itself holy, and the commandment is holy and just and good. Are we to say then that this good thing was the death of me? By no means. It was sin that killed me, and thereby sin exposed its true character: it used a good thing to bring about my death, and so, through the commandment, sin became more sinful than ever.

We know that the law is spiritual; but I am not: I am unspiritual, the purchased slave of sin. I do not even acknowledge my own actions as mine, for what I do is not what I want to do, but what I detest. But if what I do is against my will, it means that I agree with the law and hold it to be admirable. But as things are, it is no longer I who perform the action, but sin that

King James Version

18 For I know that in me (that is, in my flesh,) dwelleth no good thing: for to will is present with me; but *how* to perform that which is good I find not. 19 For the good that I would, I do not: but the evil which I would not, that I do. 20 Now if I do that I would not, it is no more I that do it, but sin that dwelleth in me. 21 I find then a law, that, when I would do good, evil is present with me. 22 For I delight in the law of God after the inward man: 23 But I see another law in my members, warring against the law of my mind, and bringing me into captivity to the law of sin which is in my members. 24 O wretched man that I am! who shall deliver me from the body of this death? 25 I thank God through Jesus Christ our Lord. So then with the mind I myself serve the law of God; but with the flesh the law of sin.

8 *There is* therefore now no condemnation to them which are in Christ Jesus, who walk not after the flesh, but after the Spirit. 2 For the law of the Spirit of life in Christ Jesus hath

Living Bible

inside me that is stronger than I am that makes me do these evil things.

18 I know I am rotten through and through so far as my old sinful nature is concerned. No matter which way I turn I can't make myself do right. I want to but I can't. 19 When I want to do good, I don't; and when I try not to do wrong, I do it anyway. 20 Now if I am doing what I don't want to, it is plain where the trouble is: sin still has me in its evil grasp.

21 It seems to be a fact of life that when I want to do what is right, I inevitably do what is wrong. 22 I love to do God's will so far as my new nature is concerned; 23, 24, 25 but there is something else deep within me, in my lower nature, that is at war with my mind and wins the fight and makes me a slave to the sin that is still within me. In my mind I want to be God's willing servant but instead I find myself still enslaved to sin.

So you see how it is: my new life tells me to do right, but the old nature that is still inside me loves to sin. Oh, what a terrible predicament I'm in! Who will free me from my slavery to this deadly lower nature? Thank God! It has been done[d] by Jesus Christ our Lord. He has set me free.

8 So there is now no condemnation awaiting those who belong to Christ Jesus. 2 For the power of the life-giving Spirit—and this power

[*d*] Or, "It will be done." Literally, "I thank God through Jesus Christ our Lord."

Today's English Version

it is the sin that lives in me. 18 I know that good does not live in me—that is, in my human nature. For even though the desire to do good is in me, I am not able to do it. 19 I don't do the good I want to do; instead, I do the evil that I do not want to do. 20 If I do what I don't want to do, this means that no longer am I the one who does it; instead, it is the sin that lives in me.

21 So I find that this law is at work: when I want to do what is good, what is evil is the only choice I have. 22 My inner being delights in the law of God. 23 But I see a different law at work in my body—a law that fights against the law that my mind approves of. It makes me a prisoner to the law of sin which is at work in my body. 24 What an unhappy man I am! Who will rescue me from this body that is taking me to death? 25 Thanks be to God, through our Lord Jesus Christ!

This, then, is my condition: by myself I can serve God's law only with my mind, while my human nature serves the law of sin.

Life in the Spirit

8 There is no condemnation now for those who live in union with Christ Jesus. 2 For the law of the Spirit, which brings us life in

New International Version

do it, but it is sin living in me. 18 I know that nothing good lives in me, that is, in my sinful nature. For I have the desire to do what is good, but I cannot carry it out. 19 For what I do is not the good I want to do; no, the evil I do not want to do—this I keep on doing. 20 Now if I do what I do not want to do, it is no longer I who do it, but it is sin living in me that does it.

21 So I find this law at work: When I want to do good, evil is right there with me. 22 For in my inner being I delight in God's law; 23 but I see another law at work in the members of my body, waging war against the law of my mind and making me a prisoner of the law of sin at work within my members. 24 What a wretched man I am! Who will rescue me from this body of death? 25 Thanks be to God—through Jesus Christ our Lord!

So then, I myself in my mind am a slave to God's law, but in my sinful nature a slave to the law of sin.

Life through the Spirit

8 Therefore, there is now no condemnation for those who are in Christ Jesus,[u] 2 because through Christ Jesus the law of the Spirit of life

[*u*] Some later MSS add *who do not live according to their sinful nature but according to the Spirit.*

Phillips Modern English

made its home in my nature. And, indeed, I know from experience that the carnal side of my being can scarcely be called the home of good! I often find that I have the will to do good, but not the power. That is, I don't accomplish the good I set out to do, and the evil I don't really want to do I find I am always doing. Yet if I do things that I don't really want to do then it is not, I repeat, "I" who do them, but the sin which has made its home within me. My experience of the Law is that when I want to do good, only evil is within my reach. For I am in hearty agreement with God's Law so far as my inner self is concerned. But then I find another law in my bodily members, which is in continual conflict with the Law which my mind approves, and makes me a prisoner to the law of sin which is inherent in my mortal body. For left to myself, I serve the Law of God with my mind, but in my unspiritual nature I serve the law of sin. It is an agonising situation, and who can set me free from the prison of this mortal body? I thank God there is a way out through Jesus Christ our Lord.

8.1 The way out—new life in Christ

The truth is that no condemnation now hangs over the head of those who are "in" Christ Jesus. For the new spiritual principle of life "in"

Revised Standard Version

but sin which dwells within me. 18 For I know
that nothing good dwells within me, that is, in
my flesh. I can will what is right, but I cannot
do it. 19 For I do not do the good I want, but
the evil I do not want is what I do. 20 Now if
I do what I do not want, it is no longer I that
do it, but sin which dwells within me.
21 So I find it to be a law that when I want
to do right, evil lies close at hand. 22 For I
delight in the law of God, in my inmost self,
23 but I see in my members another law at war
with the law of my mind and making me captive to the law of sin which dwells in my members.
24 Wretched man that I am! Who will deliver me from this body of death? 25 Thanks be
to God through Jesus Christ our Lord! So then,
I of myself serve the law of God with my mind,
but with my flesh I serve the law of sin.

8 There is therefore now no condemnation for those who are in Christ Jesus. 2 For the
law of the Spirit of life in Christ Jesus has set

Jerusalem Bible

way is not my self but sin living in me. 18 The
fact is, I know of nothing good living in me—living, that is, in my unspiritual self—for though
the will to do what is good is in me, the performance is not, 19 with the result that instead
of doing the good things I want to do, I carry
out the sinful things I do not want. 20 When I
act against my will, then, it is not my true self
doing it, but sin which lives in me.
21 In fact, this seems to be the rule, that
every single time I want to do good it is something evil that comes to hand.. 22 In my inmost
self I dearly love God's Law, but 23 I can see
that my body follows a different law that battles
against the law which my reason dictates. This is
what makes me a prisoner of that law of sin
which lives inside my body.
24 What a wretched man I am! Who will rescue me from this body doomed to death?
25 Thanks be to God through Jesus Christ our
Lord!
In short, it is I who with my reason serve the Law of God, and no less I who serve in my unspiritual self the law of sin.

B. The Christian's spiritual life

The life of the spirit

8 The reason, therefore, why those who are in Christ Jesus are not condemned, 2 is that
the law of the spirit of life in Christ Jesus has

New English Bible

lodges in me. For I know that nothing good lodges in me—in my unspiritual nature, I mean —for though the will to do good is there, the deed is not. The good which I want to do, I fail to do; but what I do is the wrong which is against my will; and if what I do is against my will, clearly it is no longer I who am the agent, but sin that has its lodging in me.

I discover this principle, then: that when I want to do the right, only the wrong is within my reach. In my inmost self I delight in the law of God, but I perceive that there is in my bodily members a different law, fighting against the law that my reason approves and making me a prisoner under the law[a] that is in my members, the law of sin. Miserable creature that I am, who is there to rescue me out of this body doomed to death[b]? God alone, through Jesus Christ our Lord! Thanks be to God! In a word then, I myself, subject to God's law as a rational being, am yet,[c] in my unspiritual nature, a slave to the law of sin.

8 The conclusion of the matter is this: there is no condemnation for those who are united with Christ Jesus, because in Christ Jesus the life-giving law of the Spirit has set you free from

[a] *Or* by means of the law. [b] *Or* out of the body doomed to this death. [c] *Or* Thus, left to myself, while subject . . . rational being, I am yet . . .

King James Version

made me free from the law of sin and death.
3 For what the law could not do, in that it was weak through the flesh, God sending his own Son in the likeness of sinful flesh, and for sin, condemned sin in the flesh:
4 That the righteousness of the law might be fulfilled in us, who walk not after the flesh, but after the Spirit.
5 For they that are after the flesh do mind the things of the flesh; but they that are after the Spirit, the things of the Spirit.
6 For to be carnally minded *is* death; but to be spiritually minded *is* life and peace.
7 Because the carnal mind *is* enmity against God: for it is not subject to the law of God, neither indeed can be.
8 So then they that are in the flesh cannot please God.
9 But ye are not in the flesh, but in the Spirit, if so be that the Spirit of God dwell in you. Now if any man have not the Spirit of Christ, he is none of his.
10 And if Christ *be* in you, the body *is* dead because of sin; but the Spirit *is* life because of righteousness.
11 But if the Spirit of him that raised up Jesus from the

Living Bible

is mine through Christ Jesus—has freed me from the vicious circle of sin and death.
3 We aren't saved from sin's grasp by knowing the commandments of God, because we can't and don't keep them, but God put into effect a different plan to save us. He sent his own Son in a human body like ours—except that ours are sinful—and destroyed sin's control over us by giving himself as a sacrifice for our sins.
4 So now we can obey God's laws if we follow after the Holy Spirit and no longer obey the old evil nature within us.

5 Those who let themselves be controlled by their lower natures live only to please themselves, but those who follow after the Holy Spirit find themselves doing those things that please God.
6 Following after the Holy Spirit leads to life and peace, but following after the old nature leads to death,
7 because the old sinful nature within us is against God. It never did obey God's laws and it never will.
8 That's why those who are still under the control of their old sinful selves, bent on following their old evil desires, can never please God.

9 But you are not like that. You are controlled by your new nature if you have the Spirit of God living in you. (And remember that if anyone doesn't have the Spirit of Christ living in him, he is not a Christian at all.)
10 Yet, even though Christ lives within you, your body will die because of sin; but your spirit will live, for Christ has pardoned it.[a]
11 And if the Spirit of God, who raised up Jesus from the dead, lives

[a] Or possibly, "but the Holy Spirit who lives in you will give you life, for he has already given you righteousness." Literally, "but the spirit is life because of righteousness."

Today's English Version

union with Christ Jesus, has set me free from the law of sin and death.
3 What the Law could not do, because human nature was weak, God did. He condemned sin in human nature by sending his own Son, who came with a nature like man's sinful nature to do away with sin.
4 God did this so that the righteous demands of the Law might be fully satisfied in us who live according to the Spirit, not according to human nature.
5 Those who live as their human nature tells them to, have their minds controlled by what human nature wants. Those who live as the Spirit tells them to, have their minds controlled by what the Spirit wants.
6 To have your mind controlled by human nature results in death; to have your mind controlled by the Spirit results in life and peace.
7 And so a man becomes an enemy of God when his mind is controlled by human nature; for he does not obey God's law, and in fact he cannot obey it.
8 Those who obey their human nature cannot please God.

9 But you do not live as your human nature tells you to; you live as the Spirit tells you to—if, in fact, God's Spirit lives in you. Whoever does not have the Spirit of Christ does not belong to him.
10 But if Christ lives in you, although your bodies are going to die because of sin, yet the Spirit is life for you because you have been put right with God.
11 If the Spirit of God, who raised Jesus from death, lives in

New International Version

set me free from the law of sin and death.
3 For what the law was powerless to do in that it was weakened by our sinful nature, God did by sending his own Son in the likeness of sinful man to be a sin offering.[v] And so he condemned sin in sinful man,
4 in order that the righteous requirements of the law might be fully met in us, who do not live according to our sinful nature but according to the Spirit.

5 Those who live according to their sinful nature have their minds set on what that nature desires; but those who live in accordance with the Spirit have their minds set on what the Spirit desires.
6 The mind of sinful man is death, but the mind controlled by the Spirit is life and peace,
7 because the sinful mind is hostile to God. It does not submit to God's law, nor can it do so.
8 Those controlled by their sinful nature cannot please God.

9 You, however, are controlled not by your sinful nature but by the Spirit, if the Spirit of God lives in you. And if anyone does not have the Spirit of Christ, he does not belong to Christ.
10 But if Christ is in you, your body is dead because of sin, yet your spirit is alive because of righteousness.
11 And if the Spirit of him who raised Jesus from the dead is living in you, he

[v] Or *man, for sin.*

Phillips Modern English

Christ Jesus lifts me out of the old vicious circle of sin and death.

The Law never succeeded in producing righteousness—the failure was always the weakness of human nature. But God has met this by sending his own Son to live in sinful human nature like ours. And, while Christ was dealing with sin, God condemned that sinful nature. Therefore we are able to meet the Law's requirements, for we are living no longer by the dictates of our sinful nature, but in obedience to the promptings of the Spirit. The carnal man sees no further than carnal things. But the spiritual man is concerned with the things of the spirit. The former attitude means, bluntly, death: the latter means life and inward peace. And this is only to be expected, for the carnal attitude is inevitably opposed to the purpose of God, and neither can nor will follow his Law. Men who hold this attitude cannot possibly please God.

8.9 *What the presence of Christ within means*

But you are not carnal but spiritual if the Spirit of God finds a home within you. You cannot, indeed, be a Christian at all unless you have something of his Spirit in you. Now if Christ does live within you his presence means that your sinful nature is dead, but your spirit becomes alive because of the righteousness he brings with him. Once the Spirit of him who raised Christ Jesus from the dead lives within

Revised Standard Version

me free from the law of sin and death. 3 For
God has done what the law, weakened by the
flesh, could not do: sending his own Son in the
likeness of sinful flesh and for sin,[i] he condemned sin in the flesh, 4 in order that the just
requirement of the law might be fulfilled in us,
who walk not according to the flesh but according to the Spirit. 5 For those who live according to the flesh set their minds on the things of
the flesh, but those who live according to the
Spirit set their minds on the things of the Spirit.
6 To set the mind on the flesh is death, but to
set the mind on the Spirit is life and peace.
7 For the mind that is set on the flesh is hostile
to God; it does not submit to God's law, indeed
it cannot; 8 and those who are in the flesh cannot please God.
9 But you are not in the flesh, you are in the
Spirit, if in fact the Spirit of God dwells in you.
Any one who does not have the Spirit of Christ
does not belong to him. 10 But if Christ is in
you, although your bodies are dead because of
sin, your spirits are alive because of righteousness. 11 If the Spirit of him who raised Jesus
from the dead dwells in you, he who raised

[i] Or *and as a sin offering.*

Jerusalem Bible

set you free from the law of sin and death.
3 God has done what the Law, because of our
unspiritual nature,[q] was unable to do. God dealt
with sin by sending his own Son in a body as
physical as any sinful body, and in that body
God condemned sin. 4 He did this in order that
the Law's just demands might be satisfied in us,
who behave not as our unspiritual nature but as
the spirit dictates.
5 The unspiritual are interested only in what
is unspiritual, but the spiritual are interested in
spiritual things. 6 It is death to limit oneself to
what is unspiritual; life and peace can only come
with concern for the spiritual. 7 That is because
to limit oneself to what is unspiritual is to be
at enmity with God: such a limitation never
could and never does submit to God's law. 8 People who are interested only in unspiritual things
can never be pleasing to God. 9 Your interests,
however, are not in the unspiritual, but in the
spiritual, since the Spirit of God has made his
home in you. In fact, unless you possessed the
Spirit of Christ you would not belong to him.
10 Though your body may be dead it is because
of sin, but if Christ is in you then your spirit is
life itself because you have been justified; 11 and
if the Spirit of him who raised Jesus from the

[q] "flesh."

New English Bible

the law of sin and death. What the law could never do, because our lower nature robbed it of all potency, God has done: by sending his own Son in a form like that of our own sinful nature, and as a sacrifice for sin,[d] he has passed judgement against sin within that very nature, so that the commandment of the law may find fulfilment in us, whose conduct, no longer under the control of our lower nature, is directed by the Spirit.

Those who live on the level of our lower nature have their outlook formed by it, and that spells death; but those who live on the level of the spirit have the spiritual outlook, and that is life and peace. For the outlook of the lower nature is enmity with God; it is not subject to the law of God; indeed it cannot be: those who live on such a level cannot possibly please God.

But that is not how you live. You are on the spiritual level, if only God's Spirit dwells within you; and if a man does not possess the Spirit of Christ, he is no Christian. But if Christ is dwelling within you, then although the body is a dead thing because you sinned, yet the spirit is life itself because you have been justified.[e] Moreover, if the Spirit of him who raised Jesus from

[d] *Or* and to deal with sin. [e] *Or* so that you may live rightly.

King James Version

dead dwell in you, he that raised up Christ from
the dead shall also quicken your mortal bodies
by his Spirit that dwelleth in you. 12 Therefore,
brethren, we are debtors, not to the flesh, to live
after the flesh. 13 For if ye live after the flesh,
ye shall die: but if ye through the Spirit do
mortify the deeds of the body, ye shall live.
14 For as many as are led by the Spirit of God,
they are the sons of God. 15 For ye have not received the spirit of bondage again to fear; but ye
have received the Spirit of adoption, whereby
we cry, Abba, Father. 16 The Spirit itself beareth
witness with our spirit, that we are the children
of God: 17 And if children, then heirs; heirs of
God, and joint heirs with Christ; if so be that we
suffer with *him,* that we may be also glorified
together. 18 For I reckon that the sufferings of
this present time *are* not worthy *to be com-*

Living Bible

in you, he will make your dying bodies live again
after you die, by means of this same Holy Spirit
living within you.
12 So, dear brothers, you have no obligations
whatever to your old sinful nature to do what it
begs you to do. 13 For if you keep on following
it you are lost and will perish, but if through the
power of the Holy Spirit you crush it and its
evil deeds, you shall live. 14 For all who are led
by the Spirit of God are sons of God.
15 And so we should not be like cringing,
fearful slaves, but we should behave like God's
very own children, adopted into the bosom of
his family, and calling to him, "Father, Father."
16 For his Holy Spirit speaks to us deep in our
hearts, and tells us that we really are God's
children. 17 And since we are his children, we
shall share his treasures—for all God gives to
his Son Jesus is now ours too. But if we are to
share his glory, we must also share his suffering.
18 Yet what we suffer now is nothing com-

Today's English Version

you, then he who raised Christ from death will
also give life to your mortal bodies by the presence of his Spirit in you.
12 So then, my brothers, we have an obligation, but not to live as our human nature wants
us to. 13 For if you live according to your human nature, you are going to die; but if, by the
Spirit, you kill your sinful actions, you will live.
14 Those who are led by God's Spirit are God's
sons. 15 For the Spirit that God has given you
does not make you a slave and cause you to be
afraid; instead, the Spirit makes you God's sons,
and by the Spirit's power we cry to God, "Father! my Father!" 16 God's Spirit joins himself
to our spirits to declare that we are God's children. 17 Since we are his children, we will possess the blessings he keeps for his people, and
we will also possess with Christ what God has
kept for him; for if we share Christ's suffering,
we will also share his glory.

The future glory

18 I consider that what we suffer at this present time cannot be compared at all with the glory

New International Version

who raised Christ from the dead will also give
life to your mortal bodies through his Spirit, who
lives in you.
12 Therefore, brothers, we have an obligation
—but it is not to our sinful nature, to live according to it. 13 For if you live according to the
sinful nature, you will die; but if by the Spirit
you put to death the misdeeds of the body, you
will live.
14 Those who are led by the Spirit of God are
sons of God. 15 For you did not receive a spirit
that makes you a slave again to fear, but you
received the Spirit who makes you sons. And
by him we cry, "*Abba,*[w] Father." 16 The Spirit
himself testifies with our spirit that we are God's
children. 17 Now if we are children, then we are
heirs—heirs of God and co-heirs with Christ, if
indeed we share in his sufferings in order that
we may also share in his glory.

Future glory

18 I consider that our present sufferings are
not worth comparing with the glory that will

[w] Aramaic for *Father.*

Phillips Modern English

you he will, by that same Spirit, bring to your whole being, yes even your mortal bodies, new strength and vitality. For he now lives in you.

So then, my brothers, you can see that we owe no duty to our sensual nature, or to live life on the level of the instincts. Indeed that way of living leads to certain spiritual death. But if on the other hand you cut the nerve of your instinctive actions by obeying the Spirit, you will live.

8.14 Christ is within—follow the lead of his Spirit

All who follow the leading of God's Spirit are God's own sons. Nor are you meant to relapse into the old slavish attitude of fear—you have been adopted into the very family circle of God and you can say with a full heart, "Father, my Father". The Spirit himself endorses our inward conviction that we really are the children of God. Think what that means. If we are his children then we are God's heirs, and all that Christ inherits will belong to all of us as well! Yes, if we share in his sufferings we shall certainly share in his glory.

8.18 Present distress is temporary and negligible

In my opinion whatever we may have to go through now is less than nothing compared with

Revised Standard Version

Christ Jesus from the dead will give life to your
mortal bodies also through his Spirit which
dwells in you.
12 So then, brethren, we are debtors, not to
the flesh, to live according to the flesh—13 for
if you live according to the flesh you will die,
but if by the Spirit you put to death the deeds
of the body you will live. 14 For all who are
led by the Spirit of God are sons of God. 15 For
you did not receive the spirit of slavery to fall
back into fear, but you have received the spirit
of sonship. When we cry, "Abba! Father!" 16 it
is the Spirit himself bearing witness with our
spirit that we are children of God, 17 and if
children, then heirs, heirs of God and fellow
heirs with Christ, provided we suffer with him
in order that we may also be glorified with him.
18 I consider that the sufferings of this present time are not worth comparing with the glory

Jerusalem Bible

dead is living in you, then he who raised Jesus
from the dead will give life to your own mortal
bodies through his Spirit living in you.
12 So then, my brothers, there is no necessity
for us to obey our unspiritual selves or to live
unspiritual lives. 13 If you do live in that way,
you are doomed to die; but if by the Spirit you
put an end to the misdeeds of the body you will
live.

Children of God

14 Everyone moved by the Spirit is a son of
God. 15 The spirit you received is not the spirit
of slaves bringing fear into your lives again; it
is the spirit of sons, and it makes us cry out,
"Abba, Father!"[r] 16 The Spirit himself and our
spirit bear united witness that we are children of
God. 17 And if we are children we are heirs as
well: heirs of God and coheirs with Christ,
sharing his sufferings so as to share his glory.

Glory as our destiny

18 I think that what we suffer in this life can never be compared to the glory, as yet unre-

[r] The prayer of Christ in Gethsemane.

New English Bible

the dead dwells within you, then the God who raised Christ Jesus from the dead will also give new life to your mortal bodies through his indwelling Spirit.

It follows, my friends, that our lower nature has no claim upon us; we are not obliged to live on that level. If you do so, you must die. But if by the Spirit you put to death all the base pursuits of the body, then you will live.

For all who are moved by the Spirit of God are sons of God. The Spirit you have received is not a spirit of slavery leading you back into a life of fear, but a Spirit that makes us sons, enabling us to cry 'Abba! Father!' In that cry the Spirit of God joins with our spirit in testifying that we are God's children; and if children, then heirs. We are God's heirs and Christ's fellow-heirs, if we share his sufferings now in order to share his splendour hereafter.

For I reckon that the sufferings we now endure bear no comparison with the splendour, as

King James Version

pared with the glory which shall be revealed in
us. 19 For the earnest expectation of the creature
waiteth for the manifestation of the sons of God.
20 For the creature was made subject to vanity,
not willingly, but by reason of him who hath
subjected *the same* in hope; 21 Because the
creature itself also shall be delivered from the
bondage of corruption into the glorious liberty
of the children of God. 22 For we know that the
whole creation groaneth and travaileth in pain
together until now. 23 And not only *they*, but
ourselves also, which have the firstfruits of the
Spirit, even we ourselves groan within ourselves,
waiting for the adoption, *to wit*, the redemption
of our body. 24 For we are saved by hope: but
hope that is seen is not hope: for what a man
seeth, why doth he yet hope for? 25 But if we
hope for that we see not, *then* do we with patience wait for *it*. 26 Likewise the Spirit also
helpeth our infirmities: for we know not what
we should pray for as we ought: but the Spirit
itself maketh intercession for us with groanings
which cannot be uttered. 27 And he that search-

Living Bible

pared to the glory he will give us later. 19 For
all creation is waiting patiently and hopefully
for that future day when God will resurrect his
children.[b] 20, 21 For on that day thorns and
thistles, sin, death, and decay[c]—the things that
overcame the world against its will at God's
command—will all disappear, and the world
around us will share in the glorious freedom
from sin which God's children enjoy.

22 For we know that even the things of nature, like animals and plants, suffer in sickness
and death as they await this great event.[d] 23 And
even we Christians, although we have the Holy
Spirit within us as a foretaste of future glory,
also groan to be released from pain and suffering. We, too, wait anxiously for that day when
God will give us our full rights as his children,
including the new bodies he has promised us—
bodies that will never be sick again and will
never die.

24 We are saved by trusting. And trusting
means looking forward to getting something we
don't yet have—for a man who already has
something doesn't need to hope and trust that
he will get it. 25 But if we must keep trusting
God for something that hasn't happened yet, it
teaches us to wait patiently and confidently.

26 And in the same way—by our faith[e]—the
Holy Spirit helps us with our daily problems and
in our praying. For we don't even know what
we should pray for, nor how to pray as we
should; but the Holy Spirit prays for us with
such feeling that it cannot be expressed in words.
27 And the Father who knows all hearts knows,

[*b*] Literally, "waiting for the revelation of the sons of God." [*c*] Implied. [*d*] Literally, "The whole creation has been groaning in travail together until now." [*e*] Implied. Literally, "in like manner."

Today's English Version

that is going to be revealed to us. 19 All of creation waits with eager longing for God to reveal
his sons. 20 For creation was condemned to become worthless, not of its own will, but because
God willed it to be so. Yet there was this hope,
21 that creation itself would one day be set free
from its slavery to decay, and share the glorious
freedom of the children of God. 22 For we know
that up to the present time all of creation groans
with pain like the pain of childbirth. 23 But not
just creation alone; we who have the Spirit as
the first of God's gifts, we also groan within
ourselves as we wait for God to make us his
sons and set our whole being free. 24 For it was
by hope that we were saved; but if we see what
we hope for, then it is not really hope. For who
hopes for something that he sees? 25 But if we
hope for what we do not see, we wait for it with
patience.

26 In the same way the Spirit also comes to
help us, weak that we are. For we do not know
how we ought to pray; the Spirit himself pleads
with God for us, in groans that words cannot
express. 27 And God, who sees into the hearts of

New International Version

be revealed in us. 19 The creation waits in eager
expectation for the sons of God to be revealed.
20 For the creation was subjected to frustration,
not by its own choice, but by the will of the one
who subjected it, in hope 21 that the creation itself will be liberated from its bondage to decay
and brought into the glorious freedom of the
children of God.

22 We know that the whole creation has been
groaning as in the pains of childbirth right up to
the present time. 23 Not only so, but we ourselves, who have the firstfruits of the Spirit,
groan inwardly as we wait eagerly for our
adoption as sons, the redemption of our bodies.
24 For in this hope we were saved. But hope
that is seen is no hope at all. Who hopes for
what he already has? 25 But if we hope for what
we do not yet have, we wait for it patiently.

26 In the same way, the Spirit helps us in our
weakness. We do not know how we ought to
pray, but the Spirit himself intercedes for us with
groans that words cannot express. 27 And he who

Phillips Modern English

the magnificent future God has in store for us. The whole creation is on tiptoe to see the wonderful sight of the sons of God coming into their own. The world of creation cannot as yet see reality, not because it chooses to be blind, but because in God's purpose it has been so limited—yet it has been given hope. And the hope is that in the end the whole of created life will be rescued from the tyranny of change and decay, and have its share in that magnificent liberty which can only belong to the children of God!

It is plain to anyone with eyes to see that at the present time all created life groans in a sort of universal travail. And it is plain, too, that we who have a foretaste of the Spirit are in a state of painful tension, while we wait for that redemption of our bodies which will mean that we have realised our full sonship in him. We were saved by this hope, and let us remember that hope always means waiting for something that we do not yet see. For whoever hopes when he can *see?* But if we hope for something we cannot see, then we must settle down to wait for it in patience.

8.26 *This is not mere theory—the Spirit helps us to find it true*

The Spirit also helps us in our present limitations. For example, we do not know how to pray worthily, but his Spirit within us is actually praying for us in those agonising longings which cannot find words. He who knows the heart's

Revised Standard Version

that is to be revealed to us. 19 For the creation
waits with eager longing for the revealing of the
sons of God; 20 for the creation was subjected
to futility, not of its own will but by the will of
him who subjected it in hope; 21 because the
creation itself will be set free from its bondage
to decay and obtain the glorious liberty of the
children of God. 22 We know that the whole
creation has been groaning in travail together
until now; 23 and not only the creation, but we
ourselves, who have the first fruits of the Spirit,
groan inwardly as we wait for adoption as sons,
the redemption of our bodies. 24 For in this hope
we were saved. Now hope that is seen is not
hope. For who hopes for what he sees? 25 But
if we hope for what we do not see, we wait for
it with patience.

26 Likewise the Spirit helps us in our weakness; for we do not know how to pray as we
ought, but the Spirit himself intercedes for us
with sighs too deep for words. 27 And he who

Jerusalem Bible

vealed, which is waiting for us. 19 The whole
creation is eagerly waiting for God to reveal his
sons. 20 It was not for any fault on the part of
creation that it was made unable to attain its
purpose, it was made so by God; but creation
still retains the hope 21 of being freed, like us,
from its slavery to decadence, to enjoy the same
freedom and glory as the children of God.
22 From the beginning till now the entire creation, as we know, has been groaning in one
great act of giving birth; 23 and not only creation, but all of us who possess the first fruits
of the Spirit, we too groan inwardly as we wait
for our bodies to be set free. 24 For we must be
content to hope that we shall be saved—our
salvation is not in sight, we should not have to
be hoping for it if it were—25 but, as I say, we
must hope to be saved since we are not saved
yet—it is something we must wait for with patience.

26 The Spirit too comes to help us in our weakness. For when we cannot choose words in order to pray properly, the Spirit himself expresses our plea in a way that could never be
put into words, 27 and God who knows every-

New English Bible

yet unrevealed, which is in store for us. For the created universe waits with eager expectation for God's sons to be revealed. It was made the victim of frustration, not by its own choice, but because of him who made it so;[a] yet always there was hope, because[b] the universe itself is to be freed from the shackles of mortality and enter upon the liberty and splendour of the children of God. Up to the present, we know, the whole created universe groans in all its parts as if in the pangs of childbirth. Not only so, but even we, to whom the Spirit is given as firstfruits of the harvest to come, are groaning inwardly while we wait for God to make us his sons and [c] set our whole body free. For we have been saved, though only in hope. Now to see is no longer to hope: why should a man endure and wait[d] for what he already sees? But if we hope for something we do not yet see, then, in waiting for it, we show our endurance.

In the same way the Spirit comes to the aid of our weakness. We do not even know how we ought to pray,[e] but through our inarticulate groans the Spirit himself is pleading for us, and God who searches our inmost being knows what

[a] *Or* because God subjected it. [b] *Or* with the hope that . . . [c] *Some witnesses omit* make us his sons and. [d] *Some witnesses read* why should a man hope . . . [e] *Or* what it is right to pray for.

King James Version

eth the hearts knoweth what *is* the mind of the
Spirit, because he maketh intercession for the
saints according to *the will of* God. 28And we
know that all things work together for good to
them that love God, to them who are the called
according to *his* purpose. 29 For whom he did
foreknow, he also did predestinate *to be* conformed to the image of his Son, that he might
be the firstborn among many brethren. 30 Moreover, whom he did predestinate, them he also
called: and whom he called, them he also justified: and whom he justified, them he also glorified. 31 What shall we then say to these things?
If God *be* for us, who *can be* against us? 32 He
that spared not his own Son, but delivered him
up for us all, how shall he not with him also
freely give us all things? 33 Who shall lay any
thing to the charge of God's elect? *It is* God that
justifieth. 34 Who *is* he that condemneth? *It is*
Christ that died, yea rather, that is risen again,
who is even at the right hand of God, who also
maketh intercession for us. 35 Who shall separate us from the love of Christ? *shall* tribulation, or distress, or persecution, or famine, or
nakedness, or peril, or sword? 36As it is written,

Living Bible

of course, what the Spirit is saying as he pleads
for us in harmony with God's own will. 28And
we know that all that happens to us is working
for our good if we love God and are fitting into
his plans.
29 For from the very beginning God decided
that those who came to him—and all along he
knew who would—should become like his Son,
so that his Son would be the First, with many
brothers. 30And having chosen us, he called us
to come to him; and when we came, he declared
us "not guilty," filled us with Christ's goodness,
gave us right standing with himself, and promised us his glory.
31 What can we ever say to such wonderful
things as these? If God is on our side, who can
ever be against us? 32 Since he did not spare
even his own Son for us but gave him up for us
all, won't he also surely give us everything else?
33 Who dares accuse us whom God has
chosen for his own? Will God? No! He is the
one who has forgiven us and given us right
standing with himself.
34 Who then will condemn us? Will Christ?
No! For he is the one who died for us and
came back to life again for us and is sitting at
the place of highest honor next to God, pleading for us there in heaven.
35 Who then can ever keep Christ's love from
us? When we have trouble or calamity, when we
are hunted down or destroyed, is it because he
doesn't love us anymore? And if we are hungry,
or penniless, or in danger, or threatened with
death, has God deserted us?
36 No, for the Scriptures tell us that for his

Today's English Version

men, knows what the thought of the Spirit is;
because the Spirit pleads with God on behalf
of his people and in accordance with his will.
28 We know that in all things God works for
good with those who love him, those whom he
has called according to his purpose. 29 Those
whom God had already chosen he had also set
apart to become like his Son, so that the Son
would be the first among many brothers. 30And
so God called those that he had set apart; and
those that he called he also put right with himself; and with those that he put right with himself he also shared his glory.

God's love in Christ Jesus

31 Faced with all this, what can we say? If
God is for us, who can be against us? 32 He did
not even keep back his own Son, but offered
him for us all! He gave us his Son—will he not
also freely give us all things? 33 Who will accuse
God's chosen people? God himself declares them
not guilty! 34 Can anyone, then, condemn them?
Christ Jesus is the one who died, or rather, who
was raised to life and is at the right side of God.
He pleads with God for us! 35 Who, then, can
separate us from the love of Christ? Can trouble
do it, or hardship, or persecution, or hunger, or
poverty, or danger, or death? 36As the scripture
says,

New International Version

searches our hearts knows the mind of the Spirit,
because the Spirit intercedes for the saints in
accordance with God's will.

More than conquerors

28 And we know that in all things God works
for the good of those who love him,[x] who have
been called according to his purpose. 29 For
those God foreknew he also predestined to be
conformed to the likeness of his Son, that he
might be the firstborn among many brothers.
30And those he predestined, he also called; those
he called, he also justified; those he justified, he
also glorified.
31 What, then, shall we say in response to
this? If God is for us, who can be against us?
32 He who did not spare his own Son, but gave
him up for us all—how will he not also, along
with him, graciously give us all things? 33 Who
will bring any charge against those whom God
has chosen? It is God who justifies. 34 Who is
he that condemns? Christ Jesus, who died—
more than that, who was raised to life—is at
the right hand of God and is also interceding for
us. 35 Who shall separate us from the love of
Christ? Shall trouble or hardship or persecution
or famine or nakedness or danger or sword?
36As it is written:

[x] Some MSS read *And we know that all things work together for good to those who love God.*

Phillips Modern English

secrets understands the Spirit's intention as he prays according to God's will for those who love him.

Moreover we know that to those who love God, who are called according to his plan, everything that happens fits into a pattern for good. For God, in his foreknowledge, chose them to bear the family likeness of his Son, that he might be the eldest of a family of many brothers. He chose them long ago; when the time came he called them, he made them righteous in his sight, and then lifted them to the splendour of life as his own sons.

8.31 We hold, in Christ, an impregnable position

In face of all this, what is there left to say? If God is for us, who can be against us? He who did not grudge his own Son but gave him up for us all—can we not trust such a God to give us, with him, everything else that we can need?

Who would dare to accuse us, whom God has chosen? God himself has declared us free from sin. Who is in a position to condemn? Only Christ Jesus, and Christ died for us, Christ also rose for us, Christ reigns in power for us, Christ prays for us!

Who can separate us from the love of Christ? Can trouble, pain or persecution? Can lack of clothes and food, danger to life and limb, the threat of force of arms? Indeed some of us know the truth of that ancient text:

Revised Standard Version

searches the hearts of men knows what is the mind of the Spirit, because[j] the Spirit intercedes for the saints according to the will of God.
28 We know that in everything God works for good [k] with those who love him,[l] who are called according to his purpose. 29 For those whom he foreknew he also predestined to be conformed to the image of his Son, in order that he might be the first-born among many brethren. 30 And those whom he predestined he also called; and those whom he called he also justified; and those whom he justified he also glorified.
31 What then shall we say to this? If God is for us, who is against us? 32 He who did not spare his own Son but gave him up for us all, will he not also give us all things with him?
33 Who shall bring any charge against God's elect? It is God who justifies; 34 who is to condemn? Is it Christ Jesus, who died, yes, who was raised from the dead, who is at the right hand of God, who indeed intercedes for us? [m]
35 Who shall separate us from the love of Christ? Shall tribulation, or distress, or persecution, or famine, or nakedness, or peril, or sword? 36 As it is written,

[j] Or *that*. [k] Other ancient authorities read *in everything he works for good*. [l] Greek *God*. [m] Or *It is Christ Jesus . . . for us*.

Jerusalem Bible

thing in our hearts knows perfectly well what he means, and that the pleas of the saints expressed by the Spirit are according to the mind of God.

God has called us to share his glory

28 We know that by turning everything to their good God co-operates with all those who love him, with all those that he has called according to his purpose. 29 They are the ones he chose specially long ago and intended to become true images of his Son, so that his Son might be the eldest of many brothers. 30 He called those he intended for this; those he called he justified, and with those he justified he shared his glory.

A hymn to God's love

31 After saying this, what can we add? With God on our side who can be against us? 32 Since God did not spare his own Son, but gave him up to benefit us all, we may be certain, after such a gift, that he will not refuse anything he can give. 33 Could anyone accuse those that God has chosen? When God acquits, 34 could anyone condemn? Could Christ Jesus? No! He not only died for us—he rose from the dead, and there at God's right hand he stands and pleads for us.
35 Nothing therefore can come between us and the love of Christ, even if we are troubled or worried, or being persecuted, or lacking food or clothes, or being threatened or even attacked.
36 As scripture promised: *For your sake we are*

New English Bible

the Spirit means, because he pleads for God's people in God's own way; and in everything, as we know, he co-operates for good with those who love God [f] and are called according to his purpose. For God knew his own before ever they were, and also ordained that they should be shaped to the likeness of his Son, that he might be the eldest among a large family of brothers; and it is these, so fore-ordained, whom he has also called. And those whom he called he has justified, and to those whom he justified he has also given his splendour.

With all this in mind, what are we to say? If God is on our side, who is against us? He did not spare his own Son, but gave him up for us all; and with this gift how can he fail to lavish upon us all he has to give? Who will be the accuser of God's chosen ones? It is God who pronounces acquittal; then who can condemn? It is Christ—Christ who died, and, more than that, was raised from the dead—who is at God's right hand, and indeed pleads our cause.[a] Then what can separate us from the love of Christ? Can affliction or hardship? Can persecution, hunger, nakedness, peril, or the sword? 'We are being done to death for thy sake all day

[f] *Or* and, as we know, all things work together for good for those who love God; *some witnesses read* and we know God himself co-operates for good with those who love God. [a] *Or* Who will be the accuser of God's chosen ones? Will it be God himself? No, he it is who pronounces acquittal. Who will be the judge to condemn? Will it be Christ—he who died, and, more than that, . . . right hand? No, he it is who pleads our cause.

King James Version

For thy sake we are killed all the day long; we
are accounted as sheep for the slaughter. 37 Nay,
in all these things we are more than conquerors
through him that loved us. 38 For I am persuaded, that neither death, nor life, nor angels,
nor principalities, nor powers, nor things present, nor things to come, 39 Nor height, nor
depth, nor any other creature, shall be able to
separate us from the love of God, which is in
Christ Jesus our Lord.

9 I say the truth in Christ, I lie not, my conscience also bearing me witness in the Holy
Ghost, 2 That I have great heaviness and continual sorrow in my heart. 3 For I could wish
that myself were accursed from Christ for my
brethren, my kinsmen according to the flesh:
4 Who are Israelites; to whom *pertaineth* the
adoption, and the glory, and the covenants, and
the giving of the law, and the service *of God,*
and the promises; 5 Whose *are* the fathers, and
of whom as concerning the flesh Christ *came,*

Living Bible

sake we must be ready to face death at every
moment of the day—we are like sheep awaiting
slaughter; 37 but despite all this, overwhelming
victory is ours through Christ who loved us
enough to die for us. 38 For I am convinced that
nothing can ever separate us from his love.
Death can't, and life can't. The angels won't,
and all the powers of hell itself cannot keep
God's love away. Our fears for today, our worries about tomorrow, 39 or where we are—high
above the sky, or in the deepest ocean—nothing
will ever be able to separate us from the love of
God demonstrated by our Lord Jesus Christ
when he died for us.

9 Oh, Israel, my people! Oh, my Jewish brothers! How I long for you to come to Christ.
My heart is heavy within me and I grieve bitterly day and night because of you. Christ
knows and the Holy Spirit knows that it is no
mere pretense when I say that I would be willing
to be forever damned if that would save you.
4 God has given you so much, but still you will
not listen to him. He took you as his own special, chosen people and led you along with a
bright cloud of glory and told you how very
much he wanted to bless you. He gave you his
rules for daily life so you would know what he
wanted you to do. He let you worship him, and
gave you mighty promises. 5 Great men of God
were your fathers, and Christ himself was one of

Today's English Version

"For your sake we are in danger of death the
whole day long;
we are treated like sheep that are going to
be slaughtered."

37 No, in all these things we have complete
victory through him who loved us! 38 For I am
certain that nothing can separate us from his
love: neither death nor life; neither angels nor
other heavenly rulers or powers; neither the present nor the future; 39 neither the world above
nor the world below—there is nothing in all creation that will ever be able to separate us from
the love of God which is ours through Christ
Jesus our Lord.

God and his chosen people

9 What I say is true; I belong to Christ and
I do not lie. My conscience, ruled by the
Holy Spirit, also assures me that I am not lying.
2 How great is my sorrow, how endless the pain
in my heart for my people, my own flesh and
blood! 3 For their sake I could wish that I myself were under God's curse and separated from
Christ. 4 They are God's chosen people; he made
them his sons and shared his glory with them;
he made his covenants with them and gave them
the Law; they have the true worship; they have
received God's promises; 5 they are descended
from the patriarchs, and Christ, as a human be-

New International Version

"For your sake we face death all the day long;
we are considered as sheep to be slaughtered." [y]

37 No, in all these things we are more than conquerors through him who loved us. 38 For I am
convinced that neither death nor life, neither
angels nor demons, neither the present nor the
future, nor any powers, 39 neither height nor
depth, nor anything else in all creation, will be
able to separate us from the love of God that is
in Christ Jesus our Lord.

God's sovereign choice

9 I speak the truth in Christ—I am not lying,
my conscience confirms it in the Holy Spirit
—2 I have great sorrow and unceasing anguish
in my heart. 3 For I could wish that I myself
were cursed and cut off from Christ for the sake
of my brothers, those of my own race, 4 the people of Israel. Theirs is the adoption as sons;
theirs the divine glory, the covenants, the receiving of the law, the temple worship and the promises. 5 Theirs are the patriarchs, and from them
is traced the human ancestry of Christ, who is

[y] Psalm 44:22.

Phillips Modern English

For thy sake we are killed all the day long;
We were accounted as sheep for the slaughter.

No, in all these things we win an overwhelming victory through him who has proved his love for us.

I have become absolutely convinced that neither death nor life, neither messenger of Heaven nor monarch of earth, neither what happens today nor what may happen tomorrow, neither a power from on high nor a power from below, nor anything else in God's whole world has any power to separate us from the love of God in Christ Jesus our Lord!

9.1 The fly in the ointment—the infidelity of my own race

Before Christ and my own conscience in the Holy Spirit I assure you that I am speaking the plain truth when I say that there is something that makes me feel very depressed, like a pain that never leaves me. It is the condition of my brothers and fellow-Israelites, and I have actually reached the pitch of wishing myself cut off from Christ if it meant that they could be won for God.

Just think what the Israelites have had given to them. The privilege of being adopted as sons of God, the experience of the glory of God, the agreements made with God, the gift of the Law, true ways of worship, God's own promises—all these are theirs. The patriarchs are theirs, and so too, as far as human descent goes, is Christ

Revised Standard Version

"For thy sake we are being killed all the day long;
we are regarded as sheep to be slaughtered."

37 No, in all these things we are more than conquerors through him who loved us. 38 For I am sure that neither death, nor life, nor angels, nor principalities, nor things present, nor things to come, nor powers, 39 nor height, nor depth, nor anything else in all creation, will be able to separate us from the love of God in Christ Jesus our Lord.

9 I am speaking the truth in Christ, I am not lying; my conscience bears me witness in the Holy Spirit, 2 that I have great sorrow and unceasing anguish in my heart. 3 For I could wish that I myself were accursed and cut off from Christ for the sake of my brethren, my kinsmen by race. 4 They are Israelites, and to them belong the sonship, the glory, the covenants, the giving of the law, the worship, and the promises; 5 to them belong the patriarchs, and of their race, according to the flesh, is the

Jerusalem Bible

being massacred daily and reckoned as sheep for the slaughter.[s] 37 These are the trials through which we triumph, by the power of him who loved us.

38 For I am certain of this: neither death nor life, no angel, no prince, nothing that exists, nothing still to come, not any power, 39 or height or depth,[t] nor any created thing, can ever come between us and the love of God made visible in Christ Jesus our Lord.

C. The place of Israel

The privileges of Israel

9 What I want to say now is no pretense; I say it in union with Christ—it is the truth—my conscience in union with the Holy Spirit assures me of it too. 2 What I want to say is this: my sorrow is so great, my mental anguish so endless, 3 I would willingly be condemned[u] and be cut off from Christ if it could help my brothers of Israel, my own flesh and blood. 4 They were adopted as sons, they were given the glory and the covenants; the Law and the ritual were drawn up for them, and the promises were made to them. 5 They are descended from the patriarchs and from their flesh and blood came

[s] Ps. 44:11. [t] "powers," "heights" and "depths" are probably cosmic forces hostile to mankind. [u] *Anathema*, cursed and excommunicated.

New English Bible

long,' as Scripture says; 'we have been treated like sheep for slaughter'—and yet, in spite of all, overwhelming victory is ours through him who loved us. For I am convinced that there is nothing in death or life, in the realm of spirits or superhuman powers, in the world as it is or the world as it shall be, in the forces of the universe, in heights or depths—nothing in all creation that can separate us from the love of God in Christ Jesus our Lord.

The purpose of God in history

9 I am speaking the truth as a Christian, and my own conscience, enlightened by the Holy Spirit, assures me it is no lie: in my heart there is great grief and unceasing sorrow. For I could even pray to be outcast from Christ myself for the sake of my brothers, my natural kinsfolk. They are Israelites: they were made God's sons; theirs is the splendour of the divine presence, theirs the covenants, the law, the temple worship, and the promises. Theirs are the patriarchs, and from them, in natural descent, sprang the Mes-

King James Version

who is over all, God blessed for ever. Amen.
6 Not as though the word of God hath taken
none effect. For they *are* not all Israel, which
are of Israel: 7 Neither, because they are the
seed of Abraham, *are they* all children: but, In
Isaac shall thy seed be called. 8 That is, They
which are the children of the flesh, these *are* not
the children of God: but the children of the
promise are counted for the seed. 9 For this *is*
the word of promise, At this time will I come,
and Sarah shall have a son. 10 And not only
this; but when Rebecca also had conceived by
one, *even* by our father Isaac, 11 (For *the children* being not yet born, neither having done any
good or evil, that the purpose of God according to election might stand, not of works, but
of him that calleth;) 12 It was said unto her,
The elder shall serve the younger. 13 As it is
written, Jacob have I loved, but Esau have I

Living Bible

you, a Jew so far as his human nature is concerned, he who now rules over all things. Praise God forever!

6 Well then, has God failed to fulfill his promises to the Jews? No! [For these promises are
only to those who are truly Jews.[a]] And not
everyone born into a Jewish family is truly a
Jew! 7 Just the fact that they come from Abraham doesn't make them truly Abraham's children. For the Scriptures say that the promises
apply only to Abraham's son Isaac and Isaac's
descendants, though Abraham had other children too. 8 This means that not all of Abraham's
children are children of God, but only those
who believe the promise of salvation which he
made to Abraham.

9 For God had promised, "Next year I will
give you and Sarah a son." 10–13 And years later,
when this son, Isaac, was grown up and married, and Rebecca his wife was about to bear him twin children, God told her that Esau, the child born first, would be a servant to Jacob, his twin brother. In the words of the Scripture, "I chose to bless Jacob, but not Esau." And God said this before the children were even born, before they had done anything either good or bad. This proves that God was doing what he had decided from the beginning; it was not because of what the children did but because of what God wanted and chose.

[a] Implied.

Today's English Version

ing, belongs to their race. May God, who rules over all, be praised forever! Amen.

6 I am not saying that the promise of God
has failed; because not all the people of Israel
are the chosen people of God. 7 Neither are all
Abraham's descendants the children of God.
God said to Abraham, "The descendants of Isaac
will be counted as yours." 8 This means that the
children born in the natural way are not the
children of God; instead, the children born as a
result of God's promise are regarded as the true
descendants. 9 For God's promise was made in
these words: "At the right time I will come back
and Sarah will have a son."

10 And this is not all. For Rebecca's two
sons had the same father, our ancestor Isaac.
11, 12 But in order that the choice of one son
might be completely the result of God's own
purpose, God said to her, "The older will serve
the younger." He said this before they were
born, before they had done anything either good
or bad; so God's choice was based on his call,
and not on anything they did. 13 As the scripture says, "I loved Jacob, but I hated Esau."

New International Version

God over all, forever praised! [z] Amen.

6 It is not as though God's word had failed.
For not all who are descended from Israel are
Israel. 7 Nor because they are his descendants
are they all Abraham's children. On the contrary, "Through Isaac shall your offspring
come." [a] 8 In other words, it is not the natural
children who are God's children, but it is the
children of the promise who are regarded as
Abraham's offspring. 9 For this was how the
promise was stated: "At the appointed time I
will return, and Sarah shall have a son." [b]

10 Not only that, but Rebecca's children had
one and the same father, our ancestor Isaac.
11 Yet, before the twins were born or had done
anything good or bad—in order that God's purpose in election might stand: 12 not by works
but by him who calls—she was told, "The older
will serve the younger." [c] 13 Just as it is written:
"Jacob I loved, but Esau I hated." [d]

[z] Or *Christ, who is over all. God be forever praised!* Or *Christ. God who is over all be forever praised!* [a] Gen. 21:12. [b] Gen. 18:10,14. [c] Gen. 25:23. [d] Mal. 1:2,3.

Phillips Modern English

himself, Christ who is over all. May God be blessed for ever. Amen.

9.6 *God's purpose is not utterly defeated by this infidelity*

Now this does not mean that God's word to Israel has failed. For you cannot count all "Israelites" as the true Israel of God. Nor can all Abraham's descendants be considered truly children of Abraham. The promise was that "in Isaac shall thy children be called". That means that it is not the natural descendants who are children of God, but that the children of the promise are to be considered truly Abraham's children. For this was the promise: "About this time I will come and Sarah shall have a son." And then, again, a word of promise came to Rebecca, at the time when she was pregnant with two children by the one man, Isaac our forefather. It came before the children were born or had done anything good or bad, plainly showing that God's act of choice has nothing to do with achievements, but is entirely a matter of his will. She was told:

The elder shall serve the younger.

And we get a later endorsement of this in the words:

Jacob I loved, but Esau I hated.

Revised Standard Version

Christ. God who is over all be blessed for ever.[n]
Amen.
6 But it is not as though the word of God
had failed. For not all who are descended from
Israel belong to Israel, 7 and not all are children
of Abraham because they are his descendants;
but "Through Isaac shall your descendants be
named." 8 This means that it is not the children of the flesh who are the children of God,
but the children of the promise are reckoned as
descendants. 9 For this is what the promise said,
"About this time I will return and Sarah shall
have a son." 10 And not only so, but also when
Rebecca had conceived children by one man,
our forefather Isaac, 11 though they were not
yet born and had done nothing either good or
bad, in order that God's purpose of election
might continue, not because of works but because of his call, 12 she was told, "The elder
will serve the younger." 13 As it is written, "Jacob I loved, but Esau I hated."

[n] Or *Christ, who is God over all, blessed for ever.*

Jerusalem Bible

Christ who is above all, God for ever blessed!
Amen.

God has kept his promise

6 Does this mean that God has failed to keep
his promise? Of course not. Not all those who
descend from Israel are Israel; 7 not all the
descendants of Abraham are his true children.
Remember: *It is through Isaac that your name
will be carried on*,[v] 8 which means that it is not
physical descent that decided who are the children of God; it is only the children of the
promise who will count as the true descendants.
9 The actual words in which the promise was
made were: *I shall visit you* at such and such a
time, *and Sarah will have a son*.[w] 10 Even more
to the point is what was said to Rebecca when
she was pregnant by our ancestor Isaac, 11 but
before her twin children were born and before
either had done good or evil. In order to stress
that God's choice is free, 12 since it depends on
the one who calls, not on human merit, Rebecca
was told: *the elder shall serve the younger*,[x]
13 or as scripture says elsewhere: *I showed my
love for Jacob and my hatred for Esau*.[y]

[v] Gn. 21:12. [w] Gn. 18:10. [x] Gn. 25:23. [y] Ml. 1:2-3.

New English Bible

siah.[q] May God, supreme above all, be blessed for ever![r] Amen.

It is impossible that the word of God should have proved false. For not all descendants of Israel are truly Israel, nor, because they are Abraham's offspring, are they all his true children;[s] but, in the words of Scripture, 'Through the line of Isaac your descendants shall be traced.'[t] That is to say, it is not those born in the course of nature who are children of God; it is the children born through God's promise who are reckoned as Abraham's descendants. For the promise runs: 'At the time fixed I will come, and Sarah shall have a son.'

But that is not all, for Rebekah's children had one and the same father, our ancestor Isaac; and yet, in order that God's selective purpose might stand, based not upon men's deeds but upon the call of God, she was told, even before they were born, when they had as yet done nothing, good or ill, 'The elder shall be servant to the younger'; and that accords with the text of Scripture, 'Jacob I loved and Esau I hated.'

[q] *Greek* Christ. [r] *Or* sprang the Messiah, supreme above all, God blessed for ever; *or* sprang the Messiah, who is supreme above all. Blessed be God for ever! [s] *Or* all children of God. [t] *Or* God's call shall be for your descendants in the line of Isaac.

King James Version

hated. 14 What shall we say then? *Is there* unrighteousness with God? God forbid. 15 For he
saith to Moses, I will have mercy on whom I
will have mercy, and I will have compassion on
whom I will have compassion. 16 So then *it is*
not of him that willeth, nor of him that runneth,
but of God that sheweth mercy. 17 For the
Scripture saith unto Pharaoh, Even for this
same purpose have I raised thee up, that I might
shew my power in thee, and that my name might
be declared throughout all the earth. 18 Therefore hath he mercy on whom he will *have
mercy*, and whom he will he hardeneth. 19 Thou
wilt say then unto me, Why doth he yet find
fault? For who hath resisted his will? 20 Nay
but, O man, who art thou that repliest against
God? Shall the thing formed say to him that
formed *it,* Why hast thou made me thus?
21 Hath not the potter power over the clay, of
the same lump to make one vessel unto honour,
and another unto dishonour? 22 *What* if God,
willing to shew *his* wrath, and to make his power

Living Bible

14 Was God being unfair? Of course not.
15 For God had said to Moses, "If I want to
be kind to someone, I will. And I will take pity
on anyone I want to." 16 And so God's blessings
are not given just because someone decides to
have them or works hard to get them. They are
given because God takes pity on those he wants
to.

17 Pharaoh, king of Egypt, was an example
of this fact. For God told him he had given
him the kingdom of Egypt for the very purpose
of displaying the awesome power of God against
him: so that all the world would hear about
God's glorious name.[b] 18 So you see, God is
kind to some just because he wants to be, and he
makes some refuse to listen. 19 Well then, why
does God blame them for not listening? Haven't
they done what he made them do?

20 No, don't say that. Who are you to criticize God? Should the thing made say to the one
who made it, "Why have you made me like
this?" 21 When a man makes a jar out of clay,
doesn't he have a right to use the same lump of
clay to make one jar beautiful, to be used for
holding flowers, and another to throw garbage
into? 22 Does not God have a perfect right to
show his fury and power against those who are

[*b*] Literally, "that my name might be published abroad in all the earth."

Today's English Version

14 What shall we say, then? That God is unjust? Not at all. 15 For he said to Moses, "I will
have mercy on whom I wish, I will take pity on
whom I wish." 16 So then, it does not depend on
what man wants or does, but only on God's
mercy. 17 For the scripture says to Pharaoh, "I
made you king for this very purpose, to use you
to show my power, and to make my name known
in all the world." 18 So then, God has mercy on
whom he wishes, and he makes stubborn whom
he wishes.

God's wrath and mercy

19 One of you, then, will say to me, "If this
is so, how can God find fault with a man? Who
can resist God's will?" 20 But who are you, my
friend, to talk back to God? A clay pot does not
ask the man who made it, "Why did you make
me like this?" 21 After all, the man who makes
the pots has the right to use the clay as he
wishes, and to make two pots from the same
lump of clay, one for special occasions, and the
other for ordinary use.

22 And the same is true of what God has
done. He wanted to show his wrath and to make
his power known. So he was very patient in en-

New International Version

14 What then shall we say? Is God unjust?
Not at all! 15 For he says to Moses,

"I will have mercy on whom I have mercy,
and I will have compassion on whom I
have compassion."[e]

16 It does not, therefore, depend on man's desire
or effort, but on God's mercy. 17 For the Scripture says to Pharaoh: "I raised you up for this
very purpose, that I might display my power in
you and that my name might be proclaimed in
all the earth."[f] 18 Therefore God has mercy on
whom he wants to have mercy, and he hardens
whom he wants to harden.

19 One of you will say to me: "Then why does
God still blame us? For who resists his will?"
20 But who are you, O man, to talk back to
God? "Shall what is formed say to him who
formed it, 'Why did you make me like this?' "[g]
21 Does not the potter have the right to make
out of the same lump of clay some pottery for
noble purposes and some for common use?

22 What if God, choosing to show his wrath
and make his power known, bore with great pa-

[*e*] Exodus 33:19. [*f*] Exodus 9:16. [*g*] Isaiah 29:16; 45:9.

Phillips Modern English

9.14 *We must not jump to conclusions about God*

Now do we conclude that God is unjust? Never! For God says long ago to Moses:

I will have mercy on whom I have mercy, and
I will have compassion on whom I have
compassion.

It is obviously not a question of human will or human effort, but of divine mercy. The scripture says to Pharaoh:

For this very purpose did I raise thee up, that
I might show in thee my power, and that
my name might be published abroad in all
the earth.

It seems plain, then, that God chooses on whom he will have mercy, and whom he will harden in their sin.

I can almost hear your retort: "If this is so, and God's will is irresistible, why does God blame men for what they do?" But the question really is this: "Who are you, a man, to make any such reply to God?" When a craftsman makes anything he doesn't expect it to turn round and say, "Why did you make me like this?" The potter, for instance, has complete control over the clay, making with one part of the lump a lovely vase, and with another a pipe for sewage. May it not be that God, though he must sooner or later expose his wrath against sin and show his controlling hand, has yet most

Revised Standard Version

14 What shall we say then? Is there injustice
on God's part? By no means! 15 For he says to
Moses, "I will have mercy on whom I have
mercy, and I will have compassion on whom I
have compassion." 16 So it depends not upon
man's will or exertion, but upon God's mercy.
17 For the scripture says to Pharaoh, "I have
raised you up for the very purpose of showing
my power in you, so that my name may be proclaimed in all the earth." 18 So then he has
mercy upon whomever he wills, and he hardens
the heart of whomever he wills.
19 You will say to me then, "Why does he
still find fault? For who can resist his will?"
20 But who are you, a man, to answer back to
God? Will what is molded say to its molder,
"Why have you made me thus?" 21 Has the
potter no right over the clay, to make out of
the same lump one vessel for beauty and another for menial use? 22 What if God, desiring
to show his wrath and to make known his

Jerusalem Bible

God is not unjust

14 Does it follow that God is unjust? Of
course not. 15 Take what God said to Moses:
*I have mercy on whom I will, and I show pity
to whom I please.*[z] 16 In other words, the only
thing that counts is not what human beings
want or try to do, but the mercy of God. 17 For
in scripture he says to Pharaoh: *It was for this
I raised you up, to use you as a means of showing my power and to make my name known
throughout the world.*[a] 18 In other words, when
God wants to show mercy he does, and when
he wants to harden someone's heart he does so.
19 You will ask me, "In that case, how can
God ever blame anyone, since no one can oppose his will?" 20 But what right have you, a
human being, to cross-examine God? *The pot
has no right to say to the potter: Why did you
make me this shape?*[b] 21 Surely a potter can do
what he likes with the clay? It is surely for him
to decide whether he will use a particular lump
of clay to make a special pot or an ordinary
one?
22 Or else imagine that although God is
ready to show his anger and display his power,
yet he patiently puts up with the people who

[z] Ex. 33:19. [a] Ex. 9:16. [b] Is. 29:16.

New English Bible

What shall we say to that? Is God to be charged with injustice? By no means. For he says to Moses, 'Where I show mercy, I will show mercy, and where I pity, I will pity.' Thus it does not depend on man's will or effort, but on God's mercy. For Scripture says to Pharaoh, 'I have raised you up for this very purpose, to exhibit my power in my dealings with you, and to spread my fame over all the world.' Thus he not only shows mercy as he chooses, but also makes men stubborn as he chooses.

You will say, 'Then why does God blame a man? For who can resist his will?' Who are you, sir, to answer God back? Can the pot speak to the potter and say, 'Why did you make me like this?'? Surely the potter can do what he likes with the clay. Is he not free to make out of the same lump two vessels, one to be treasured, the other for common use?

But what if God, desiring to exhibit[c] his retribution at work and to make his power known,

[c] *Or* although he had the will to exhibit . . .

King James Version

known, endured with much longsuffering the vessels of wrath fitted to destruction: 23And that he might make known the riches of his glory on the vessels of mercy, which he had afore prepared unto glory, 24 Even us, whom he hath called, not of the Jews only, but also of the Gentiles? 25As he saith also in Osee, I will call them my people, which were not my people; and her beloved, which was not beloved. 26And it shall come to pass, *that* in the place where it was said unto them, Ye *are* not my people; there shall they be called the children of the living God. 27 Esaias also crieth concerning Israel, Though the number of the children of Israel be as the sand of the sea, a remnant shall be saved: 28 For he will finish the work, and cut *it* short in righteousness: because a short work will the Lord make upon the earth. 29And as Esaias said before, Except the Lord of Sabaoth had left us a seed, we had been as Sodoma, and been made like unto Gomorrah.

Living Bible

fit only for destruction, those he has been patient with for all this time? 23, 24And he has a right to take others such as ourselves, who have been made for pouring the riches of his glory into, whether we are Jews or Gentiles, and to be kind to us so that everyone can see how very great his glory is.

25 Remember what the prophecy of Hosea says? There God says that he will find other children for himself (who are not from his Jewish family) and will love them, though no one had ever loved them before. 26And the heathen, of whom it once was said, "You are not my people," shall be called "sons of the Living God." [c]

27 Isaiah the prophet cried out concerning the Jews that though there would be millions[d] of them, only a small number would ever be saved. 28 "For the Lord will execute his sentence upon the earth, quickly ending his dealings, justly cutting them short." [e]

29 And Isaiah says in another place that except for God's mercy all the Jews would be destroyed—all of them—just as everyone in the cities of Sodom and Gomorrah perished.[f]

[*c*] Hosea 2:23. [*d*] Literally, "as the sand of the sea," i.e., numberless. [*e*] Isaiah 10:22; 28:22. [*f*] Isaiah 1:9.

Today's English Version

during those who were the objects of his wrath, who were ready to be destroyed. 23And he wanted also to reveal his rich glory, which was poured out on us who are the objects of his mercy, those of us whom he has prepared to receive his glory. 24 For we are the ones whom he called, not only from among the Jews but also from among the Gentiles. 25 This is what he says in the book of Hosea,

"The people who were not mine,
I will call 'My People.'
The nation that I did not love,
I will call 'My Beloved.'
26 And in the very place where they were told, 'You are not my people,'
there they will be called the sons of the living God."

27And Isaiah exclaims about Israel, "Even if the people of Israel are as many as the grains of sand by the sea, yet only a few of them will be saved; 28 for the Lord will quickly settle his full account with all the world." 29 It is as Isaiah had said before, "If the Lord Almighty had not left us some descendants, we would have become like Sodom, we would have been like Gomorrah."

New International Version

tience the objects of his wrath—prepared for destruction? 23 What if he did this to make the riches of his glory known to the objects of his mercy, whom he prepared in advance for glory—24 even us, whom he also called, not only from the Jews but also from the Gentiles? 25As he says in Hosea:

"I will call them 'my people' who are not my people;
and I will call her 'my loved one' who is not my loved one," [h]

26 and,

"It will happen that in the very place where it was said to them,
'You are not my people,'
they will be called 'sons of the living God.'" [i]

27 Isaiah cries out concerning Israel: "Though the number of the Israelites should be like the sand by the sea, only the remnant will be saved. 28 For the Lord will carry out his sentence on earth with speed and finality." [j] 29 It is just as Isaiah said previously:

"Unless the Lord All-powerful had left us descendants,
we would have become like Sodom,
and we would have been like Gomorrah." [k]

[*h*] Hosea 2:23. [*i*] Hosea 1:10. [*j*] Isaiah 10:22,23. [*k*] Isaiah 1:9.

Phillips Modern English

patiently endured the presence in his world of things that cry out to be destroyed? Can we not see, in this, his purpose in demonstrating the boundless resources of his glory upon those whom he considers fit to receive his mercy, and whom he long ago planned to raise to glorious life? And by these chosen people I mean you and me, whom he has called out from both Jews and gentiles. He says in Hosea:

I will call that my people, which was not my people;
And her beloved, which was not beloved.
And it shall be, that in the place where it was said unto them, Ye are not my people,
There shall they be called sons of the living God.

And Isaiah, speaking about Israel, proclaims:

If the number of the children of Israel be as the sand of the sea, it is the remnant that shall be saved:
For the Lord will execute his word upon the earth, finishing it and cutting it short.

And previously, Isaiah said:

Except the Lord of Sabaoth had left us a seed,
We had become as Sodom and had been made like unto Gomorrah.

Revised Standard Version

power, has endured with much patience the vessels of wrath made for destruction,
23 in order to make known the riches of his glory for the vessels of mercy, which he has prepared beforehand for glory,
24 even us whom he has called, not from the Jews only but also from the Gentiles?
25 As indeed he says in Hosea,
"Those who were not my people
I will call 'my people,'
and her who was not beloved
I will call 'my beloved.'"
26 "And in the very place where it was said to them, 'You are not my people,'
they will be called 'sons of the living God.'"
27 And Isaiah cries out concerning Israel: "Though the number of the sons of Israel be as the sand of the sea, only a remnant of them will be saved;
28 for the Lord will execute his sentence upon the earth with rigor and dispatch."
29 And as Isaiah predicted,
"If the Lord of hosts had not left us children,
we would have fared like Sodom and been made like Gomorrah."

Jerusalem Bible

make him angry, however much they deserve to be destroyed.
23 He puts up with them for the sake of those other people, to whom he wants to be merciful, to whom he wants to reveal the richness of his glory, people he had prepared for this glory long ago.
24 Well, we are those people; whether we were Jews or pagans we are the ones he has called.

All has been foretold in the Old Testament

25 That is exactly what God says in Hosea: *I shall say to a people that was not mine, "You are my people," and to a nation I never loved, "I love you."*
26 *Instead of being told, "You are no people of mine," they will now be called the sons of the living God.*[c]
27 Referring to Israel Isaiah had this to say: *Though Israel should have as many descendants as there are grains of sand on the seashore, only a remnant will be saved,*
28 *for without hesitation or delay the Lord will execute his sentence on the earth.*[d]
29 As Isaiah foretold: *Had the Lord of hosts not left us some descendants we should now be like Sodom, we should be like Gomorrah.*[e]

[c] Ho. 2:25 and 2:1. [d] Is. 10:22-23. [e] Is. 1:9.

New English Bible

tolerated very patiently those vessels which were objects of retribution due for destruction, and did so in order to make known the full wealth of his splendour upon vessels which were objects of mercy, and which from the first had been prepared for this splendour?

Such vessels are we, whom he has called from among Gentiles as well as Jews, as it says in the Book of Hosea: 'Those who were not my people I will call My People, and the unloved nation I will call my Beloved. For in the very place where they were told "you are no people of mine", they shall be called Sons of the living God.' But Isaiah makes this proclamation about Israel: 'Though the Israelites be countless as the sands of the sea, only a remnant shall be saved; for the Lord's sentence on the land will be summary and final'; as also he said previously, 'If the Lord of Hosts had not left us the mere germ of a nation, we should have become like Sodom, and no better than Gomorrah.'

King James Version

30 What shall we say then? That the Gentiles, which followed not after righteousness, have attained to righteousness, even the righteousness which is of faith. 31 But Israel, which followed after the law of righteousness, hath not attained to the law of righteousness. 32 Wherefore? Because *they sought it* not by faith, but as it were by the works of the law. For they stumbled at that stumblingstone; 33 As it is written, Behold, I lay in Sion a stumblingstone and rock of offence: and whosoever believeth on him shall not be ashamed.

10 Brethren, my heart's desire and prayer to God for Israel is, that they might be saved. 2 For I bear them record that they have a zeal of God, but not according to knowledge. 3 For they, being ignorant of God's righteousness, and going about to establish their own righteousness, have not submitted themselves unto the righteousness of God. 4 For Christ *is* the end of the law for righteousness to every one that be-

Living Bible

30 Well then, what shall we say about these things? Just this, that God has given the Gentiles the opportunity to be acquitted by faith, even though they had not been really seeking God. 31 But the Jews, who tried so hard to get right with God by keeping his laws, never succeeded. 32 Why not? Because they were trying to be saved by keeping the law and being good instead of by depending on faith. They have stumbled over the great stumbling stone. 33 God warned them of this in the Scriptures when he said, "I have put a Rock in the path of the Jews, and many will stumble over him (Jesus). Those who believe in him will never be disappointed." [g]

10 Dear brothers, the longing of my heart and my prayers is that the Jewish people might be saved. 2 I know what enthusiasm they have for the honor of God, but it is misdirected zeal. 3 For they don't understand that Christ has died to make them right with God. Instead they are trying to make themselves good enough to gain God's favor by keeping the Jewish laws and customs, but that is not God's way of salvation. 4 They don't understand that Christ gives to those who trust in him everything they are trying to get by keeping his laws. He ends all of that.

[g] Isaiah 28:16.

Today's English Version

Israel and the gospel

30 What shall we say, then? This: that the Gentiles, who were not trying to put themselves right with God, were put right with him through faith; 31 while the chosen people, who were seeking a law that would put them right with God, did not find it. 32 And why not? Because what they did was not based on faith but on works. They stumbled over the "stumbling stone" 33 that the scripture speaks of:

"Look, I place in Zion a stone
 that will make people stumble,
 a rock that will make them fall.
But whoever believes in him will not be disappointed."

10 My brothers, how I wish with all my heart that my own people might be saved! How I pray to God for them! 2 I can be a witness for them that they are deeply devoted to God. But their devotion is not based on true knowledge. 3 They have not known the way in which God puts men right with himself, and have tried to set up their own way; and so they did not submit themselves to God's way of putting men right. 4 For Christ has brought the Law to an end, so that everyone who believes is put right with God.

New International Version

Israel's unbelief

30 What then shall we say? That the Gentiles, who did not pursue righteousness, have obtained it, a righteousness that is by faith; 31 but Israel, who pursued a law of righteousness, has not attained it. 32 Why not? Because they pursued it not by faith but as if it were by works. They stumbled over the "stumbling stone." 33 As it is written:

"See, I lay in Zion a stone that causes men to stumble
 and a rock that makes them fall,
and the one who trusts in him will never be put to shame." [l]

10 Brothers, my heart's desire and prayer to God for the Israelites is that they may be saved. 2 For I can testify about them that they are zealous for God, but their zeal is not based on knowledge. 3 Since they disregarded the righteousness that comes from God and sought to establish their own, they did not submit to God's righteousness. 4 Christ is the end of the law so that there may be righteousness for everyone who believes.

[l] Isaiah 8:14; 28:16.

Phillips Modern English

9.30 At present the gentiles have gone further than the Jews

Now, what do we conclude? That the gentiles who never seriously pursued righteousness, have attained righteousness, righteousness-by-faith. But Israel, earnestly following the Law of righteousness, failed to reach their goal. And why? Because their minds were fixed on what they achieved instead of on what they believed. They tripped over that very stone the scripture mentions:

Behold, I lay in Zion a stone of stumbling
and a rock of offence:
And he that believeth on him shall not be put
to shame.

10.1 How Israel has missed the way

My brothers, from the bottom of my heart I long and pray to God that Israel may be saved! I know from experience what a passion for God they have, but alas, it is not a passion based on knowledge. They do not know God's righteousness, and all the time they are trying to prove their own righteousness they have the wrong attitude to receive his. For Christ means the end of the struggle for righteousness-by-the-Law for everyone who believes in him.

Revised Standard Version

30 What shall we say, then? That Gentiles
who did not pursue righteousness have attained
it, that is, righteousness through faith; 31 but
that Israel who pursued the righteousness which
is based on law did not succeed in fulfilling that
law. 32 Why? Because they did not pursue it
through faith, but as if it were based on works.
They have stumbled over the stumbling stone,
33 as it is written,

"Behold, I am laying in Zion a stone that will
make men stumble,
a rock that will make them fall;
and he who believes in him will not be put
to shame."

10 Brethren, my heart's desire and prayer to
God for them is that they may be saved.
2 I bear them witness that they have a zeal for
God, but it is not enlightened. 3 For, being ignorant of the righteousness that comes from
God, and seeking to establish their own, they
did not submit to God's righteousness. 4 For
Christ is the end of the law, that every one who
has faith may be justified.

Jerusalem Bible

30 From this it follows that the pagans who
were not looking for righteousness found it all
the same, a righteousness that comes of faith,
31 while Israel, looking for a righteousness derived from law failed to do what that law required. 32 Why did they fail? Because they relied
on good deeds instead of trusting in faith. In
other words, they *stumbled over the stumbling*
stone[f] 33 mentioned in scripture: *See how I lay*
in Zion a stone to stumble over, a rock to trip
men up—only those who believe in him will
have no cause for shame.[g]

Israel fails to see that it is God who makes us holy

10 Brothers, I have the very warmest love
for the Jews, and I pray to God for them
to be saved. 2 I can swear to their fervor for
God, but their zeal is misguided. 3 Failing to
recognize the righteousness that comes from God,
they try to promote their own idea of it, instead of submitting to the righteousness of God.
4 But now the Law has come to an end with
Christ, and everyone who has faith may be justified.

[f] Is. 8:14. [g] Is. 28:16.

New English Bible

Then what are we to say? That Gentiles, who made no effort after righteousness, nevertheless achieved it, a righteousness based on faith; whereas Israel made great efforts after a law of righteousness, but never attained to it. Why was this? Because their efforts were not based on faith, but (as they supposed) on deeds. They fell over the 'stone' mentioned in Scripture: 'Here I lay in Zion a stone to trip over, a rock to stumble against; but he who has faith in him will not be put to shame.'

10 Brothers, my deepest desire and my prayer to God is for their salvation. To their zeal for God I can testify; but it is an ill-informed zeal. For they ignore God's way of righteousness, and try to set up their own, and therefore they have not submitted themselves to God's righteousness. For Christ ends the law and brings righteousness for everyone who has faith.[a]

[a] *Or* Christ is the end of the law as a way to righteousness for everyone who has faith.

King James Version

lieveth. 5 For Moses describeth the righteousness which is of the law, That the man which
doeth those things shall live by them. 6 But the
righteousness which is of faith speaketh on this
wise, Say not in thine heart, Who shall ascend
into heaven? (that is, to bring Christ down *from
above:*) 7 Or, Who shall descend into the deep?
(that is, to bring up Christ again from the
dead.) 8 But what saith it? The word is nigh
thee, *even* in thy mouth, and in thy heart: that
is, the word of faith, which we preach; 9 That if
thou shalt confess with thy mouth the Lord Jesus, and shalt believe in thine heart that God
hath raised him from the dead, thou shalt be
saved. 10 For with the heart man believeth unto
righteousness; and with the mouth confession is
made unto salvation. 11 For the Scripture saith,
Whosoever believeth on him shall not be
ashamed. 12 For there is no difference between
the Jew and the Greek: for the same Lord over
all is rich unto all that call upon him. 13 For
whosoever shall call upon the name of the Lord
shall be saved. 14 How then shall they call on
him in whom they have not believed? and how
shall they believe in him of whom they have not
heard? and how shall they hear without a
preacher? 15 And how shall they preach, except

Living Bible

5 For Moses wrote that if a person could be
perfectly good and hold out against temptation
all his life and never sin once, only then could
he be pardoned and saved. 6 But the salvation
that comes through faith says, "You don't need
to search the heavens to find Christ and bring
him down to help you," and, 7 "You don't need
to go among the dead to bring Christ back to
life again."

8 For salvation that comes from trusting
Christ—which is what we preach—is already
within easy reach of each of us; in fact, it is as
near as our own hearts and mouths. 9 For if you
tell others with your own mouth that Jesus
Christ is your Lord, and believe in your own
heart that God has raised him from the dead,
you will be saved. 10 For it is by believing in his
heart that a man becomes right with God; and
with his mouth he tells others of his faith, confirming his salvation.[a] 11 For the Scriptures tell
us that no one who believes in Christ will ever
be disappointed. 12 Jew and Gentile are the same
in this respect: they all have the same Lord who
generously gives his riches to all those who ask
him for them. 13 Anyone who calls upon the
name of the Lord will be saved.

14 But how shall they ask him to save them
unless they believe in him? And how can they
believe in him if they have never heard about
him? And how can they hear about him unless
someone tells them? 15 And how will anyone go

[a] Literally, "Confession is made unto salvation."

Today's English Version

Salvation is for all

5 This is what Moses wrote about being put
right with God by obeying the Law: "Whoever
does what the Law commands will live by it."
6 But this is what is said about being put right
with God through faith: "Do not say to yourself, Who will go up into heaven?" (that is, to
bring Christ down). 7 "Do not say either, Who
will go down into the world below?" (that is,
to bring Christ up from the dead). 8 What it
says is this: "God's message is near you, on your
lips and in your heart"—that is, the message of
faith that we preach. 9 If you declare with your
lips, "Jesus is Lord," and believe in your heart
that God raised him from the dead, you will be
saved. 10 For we believe in our hearts and are
put right with God; we declare with our lips and
are saved. 11 The scripture says, "Whoever believes in him will not be disappointed." 12 This
includes everyone, because there is no difference
between Jews and Gentiles; God is the same
Lord of all, and richly blesses all who call to
him. 13 As the scripture says, "Everyone who
calls on the name of the Lord will be saved."

14 But how can they call to him, if they have
not believed? And how can they believe, if they
have not heard the message? And how can they
hear, if the message is not proclaimed? 15 And
how can the message be proclaimed, if the mes-

New International Version

5 Moses describes in this way the righteousness that is by the law: "The man who does these
things will live by them." [m] 6 But the righteousness that is by faith says: "Do not say in your
heart, 'Who will ascend into heaven?' [n]" (that
is, to bring Christ down), 7 or " 'Who will descend into the deep?' [o]" (that is, to bring Christ
up from the dead). 8 But what does it say?

"The word is near you;
it is in your mouth and in your heart" [p];

that is, the word of faith we are proclaiming:
9 That if you confess with your mouth, "Jesus is
Lord," and believe in your heart that God raised
him from the dead, you will be saved. 10 For it
is with your heart that you believe and are justified, and it is with your mouth that you confess
and are saved. 11 As the Scripture says, "He who
believes in him will not be put to shame." [q]
12 For there is no difference between Jew and
Gentile—the same Lord is Lord of all and
richly blesses all who call on him, 13 for, "Everyone who calls on the name of the Lord will be
saved." [r]

14 How, then, can they call on the one they
have not believed in? And how can they believe
in the one of whom they have not heard? And
how can they hear without someone preaching
to them? 15 And how can they preach unless

[m] Lev. 18:5. [n] Deut. 30:12. [o] Deut. 30:13.
[p] Deut. 30:14. [q] Isaiah 28:16. [r] Joel 2:32.

Phillips Modern English

Moses writes of righteousness-by-the-Law when he says that the man who perfectly obeys the Law shall find life in it. But righteousness-by-faith speaks like this:

"You need not say in your heart, 'Who could go up to Heaven to bring Christ down to us, or who could descend into the depths to bring him up from the dead?' No, the word is very near you, *on your own lips* and in *your own heart!*" It is this word, which is the burden of our preaching, and it says, in effect, "If you openly admit by your own lips that Jesus is the Lord, and if you believe in *your own heart* that God raised him from the dead, you will be saved." For it is believing *in the heart* that makes a man righteous before God, and it is stating his belief by *his own lips* that confirms his salvation. And the scripture says: "Whosoever believes in him shall not be disappointed." And that "whosoever" means anyone, without distinction between Jew or Greek. For all have the same Lord, whose boundless resources are sufficient for all who turn to him in faith. For:

Whosoever shall call upon the name of the Lord shall be saved.

10.14 Can we offer the excuse of ignorance on Israel's behalf?

Now how can they call on one in whom they have never believed? How can they believe in one of whom they have never heard? And how can they hear unless someone proclaims him? And who will go to tell them unless he is sent?

Revised Standard Version

5 Moses writes that the man who practices the righteousness which is based on the law shall live by it. 6 But the righteousness based on faith says, Do not say in your heart, "Who will ascend into heaven?" (that is, to bring Christ down) 7 or "Who will descend into the abyss?" (that is, to bring Christ up from the dead). 8 But what does it say? The word is near you, on your lips and in your heart (that is, the word of faith which we preach); 9 because, if you confess with your lips that Jesus is Lord and believe in your heart that God raised him from the dead, you will be saved. 10 For man believes with his heart and so is justified, and he confesses with his lips and so is saved. 11 The scripture says, "No one who believes in him will be put to shame." 12 For there is no distinction between Jew and Greek; the same Lord is Lord of all and bestows his riches upon all who call upon him. 13 For, "every one who calls upon the name of the Lord will be saved."

14 But how are men to call upon him in whom they have not believed? And how are they to believe in him of whom they have never heard? And how are they to hear without a preacher? 15 And how can men preach unless

Jerusalem Bible

The testimony of Moses

5 When Moses refers to being justified by the Law, he writes: *those who keep the Law will draw life from it.*[h] 6 But the righteousness that comes from faith says this: Do not tell yourself you have to bring Christ down—as in the text: *Who will go up to heaven?* [i] 7 or that you have to bring Christ back from the dead—as in the text: *Who will go down to the underworld?* 8 On the positive side it says: *The word,* that is the faith we proclaim, *is very near to you, it is on your lips and in your heart.* 9 If your lips confess that Jesus is Lord and if you believe in your heart that God raised him from the dead, then you will be saved. 10 By believing from the heart you are made righteous; by confessing with your lips you are saved. 11 When scripture says: *those who believe in him will have no cause for shame,*[j] 12 it makes no distinction between Jew and Greek: all belong to the same Lord who is rich enough, however many ask his help, 13 *for everyone who calls on the name of the Lord will be saved.*[k]

Israel has no excuse

14 But they will not ask his help unless they believe in him, and they will not believe in him unless they have heard of him, and they will not hear of him unless they get a preacher, 15 and they will never have a preacher unless one is

[*h*] Lv. 18:5. [*i*] This quotation, and the two following, are a free rendering of Dt. 30:12-14. [*j*] Is. 28:16. [*k*] Jl. 3:5.

New English Bible

Of legal righteousness Moses writes, 'The man who does this shall gain life by it.' But the righteousness that comes by faith says, 'Do not say to yourself, "Who can go up to heaven?"' (that is to bring Christ down), 'or, "Who can go down to the abyss?"' (to bring Christ up from the dead). But what does it say? 'The word is near you: it is upon your lips and in your heart.' This means the word of faith which we proclaim. If on your lips is the confession, 'Jesus is Lord', and in your heart the faith that God raised him from the dead, then you will find salvation. For the faith that leads to righteousness is in the heart, and the confession that leads to salvation is upon the lips.

Scripture says, 'Everyone who has faith in him will be saved from shame'—everyone: there is no distinction between Jew and Greek, because the same Lord is Lord of all, and is rich enough for the need of all who invoke him. For everyone, as it says again—'everyone who invokes the name of the Lord will be saved'. How could they invoke one in whom they had no faith? And how could they have faith in one they had never heard of? And how hear without someone to spread the news? And how could anyone spread the news without a commission

King James Version

they be sent? as it is written, How beautiful are
the feet of them that preach the gospel of peace,
and bring glad tidings of good things! 16 But
they have not all obeyed the gospel. For Esaias
saith, Lord, who hath believed our report? 17 So
then faith *cometh* by hearing, and hearing by
the word of God. 18 But I say, Have they not
heard? Yes verily, their sound went into all the
earth, and their words unto the ends of the
world. 19 But I say, Did not Israel know? First
Moses saith, I will provoke you to jealousy by
them that are no people, *and* by a foolish nation I will anger you. 20 But Esaias is very bold,
and saith, I was found of them that sought me
not; I was made manifest unto them that asked
not after me. 21 But to Israel he saith, All day

Living Bible

and tell them unless someone sends him? That
is what the Scriptures are talking about when
they say, "How beautiful are the feet of those
who preach the Gospel of peace with God and
bring glad tidings of good things." [b] In other
words, how welcome are those who come preaching God's Good News!
16 But not everyone who hears the Good News
has welcomed it, for Isaiah the prophet said,
"Lord, who has believed me when I told them?" [c]
17 Yet faith comes from listening to this Good
News—the Good News about Christ.
18 But what about the Jews? Have they heard
God's Word? Yes, for it has gone wherever they
are; the Good News has been told to the ends
of the earth. 19And did they understand [that
God would give his salvation to others if they
refused to take it[d]]? Yes, for even back in the
time of Moses, God had said that he would
make his people jealous and try to wake them up
by giving his salvation to the foolish heathen
nations. 20And later on Isaiah said boldly that
God would be found by people who weren't
even looking for him.[e] 21 In the meantime, he

[b] Isaiah 52:7. [c] Isaiah 53:1. [d] Implied. [e] Isaiah 65:1.

Today's English Version

sengers are not sent out? As the scripture says,
"How wonderful is the coming of those who
bring good news!" 16 But they have not all accepted the Good News. Isaiah himself said,
"Lord, who believed our message?" 17 So then,
faith comes from hearing the message, and the
message comes through preaching Christ.
18 But I ask: Is it true that they did not hear
the message? Of course they did—as the scripture says:

"The sound of their voices went out to all the
world;
their words reached the ends of the earth."

19Again I ask: Did the people of Israel not
know? Moses himself is the first one to answer:

"I will make you jealous of a people who are
not a real nation;
I will make you angry with a nation of foolish people."

20And Isaiah is bolder when he says,

"I was found by those who were not looking
for me,
I appeared to those who were not asking
for me."

21 But concerning Israel he says, "I held out my

New International Version

they are sent? As it is written, "How beautiful
are the feet of those who bring good news!" [s]
16 But not all the Israelites responded to the
good news. For Isaiah says, "Lord, who has
believed our message?" [t] 17 Consequently, faith
comes from hearing the message, and the message is heard through the word of Christ. 18 But
I ask, did they not hear? Of course they did:
"Their voice has gone out into all the earth,
their words to the ends of the world." [u]
19Again I ask, did Israel not understand? First,
Moses says,
"I will make you envious by means of those
who are not a nation;
I will make you angry by a nation that has
no understanding." [v]
20 Then Isaiah boldly says,
"I was found by those who did not seek me;
I revealed myself to those who did not ask
for me." [w]
21 But concerning Israel he says, "All day long

[s] Isaiah 52:7. [t] Isaiah 53:1. [u] Psalm 19:4. [v] Deut. 32:21. [w] Isaiah 65:1.

Phillips Modern English

As the scripture puts it:

How beautiful are the feet of them that bring glad tidings of good things!

Yet not all have responded to the gospel. Isaiah asks, you remember,

Lord, who hath believed our report?

Faith, you see, can only come from hearing the message, and the message is the word of Christ.

But when I ask myself: "Did they never hear?" I have to answer that they *have* heard, for

Their sound went out into all the earth,
And their words unto the ends of the world.

Then I say to myself: "Did Israel not know?" And my answer must be that they did. For Moses says:

I will provoke you to jealousy with that which is no nation,
With a nation void of understanding will I anger you.

And Isaiah, more daring still, puts these words into the mouth of God:

I was found of them that sought me not.
I became manifest unto them that asked not of me.

And then, speaking to Israel:

Revised Standard Version

they are sent? As it is written, "How beautiful
are the feet of those who preach good news!"
16 But they have not all obeyed the gospel; for
Isaiah says, "Lord, who has believed what he
has heard from us?" 17 So faith comes from
what is heard, and what is heard comes by the
preaching of Christ.
18 But I ask, have they not heard? Indeed
they have; for
"Their voice has gone out to all the earth,
and their words to the ends of the world."
19 Again I ask, did Israel not understand? First
Moses says,
"I will make you jealous of those who are not
a nation;
with a foolish nation I will make you angry."
20 Then Isaiah is so bold as to say,
"I have been found by those who did not
seek me;
I have shown myself to those who did not
ask for me."
21 But of Israel he says, "All day long I have

Jerusalem Bible

sent, but as scripture says: *The footsteps of*
those who bring good news is a welcome sound.[l]
16 Not everyone, of course, listens to the Good
News. As Isaiah says: *Lord, how many believed*
what we proclaimed?[m] 17 So faith comes from
what is preached, and what is preached comes
from the word of Christ.
18 Let me put the question: is it possible that
they did not hear? Indeed they did; in the
words of the psalm, *their voice has gone out*
through all the earth, and their message to the
ends of the world.[n] 19 A second question: is it
possible that Israel did not understand? Moses
answered this long ago: *I will make you jealous*
of people who are not even a nation; I will
make you angry with an irreligious people.[o]
20 Isaiah said more clearly: *I have been found*
by those who did not seek me, and have revealed
myself to those who did not consult me[p]; 21 and
referring to Israel he goes on: *Each day I*

[l] Is. 52:7. [m] Is. 53:1. [n] Ps. 19:4. [o] Dt. 32:21.
[p] Is. 65:1,2.

New English Bible

to do so? And that is what Scripture affirms: 'How welcome are the feet of the messengers of good news!'

But not all have responded to the good news. For Isaiah says, 'Lord, who has believed our message?' We conclude that faith is awakened by the message, and the message that awakens it comes through the word of Christ.

But, I ask, can it be that they never heard it? Of course they did: 'Their voice has sounded all over the earth, and their words to the bounds of the inhabited world.' But, I ask again, can it be that Israel failed to recognize the message? In reply, I first cite Moses, who says, 'I will use a nation that is no nation to stir your envy, and a foolish nation to rouse your anger.' But Isaiah is still more daring: 'I was found', he says, 'by those who were not looking for me; I was clearly shown to those who never asked about me'; while to Israel he says, 'All day long I have

King James Version

long I have stretched forth my hands unto a
disobedient and gainsaying people.

11 I say then, Hath God cast away his people? God forbid. For I also am an Israelite,
of the seed of Abraham, *of* the tribe of Benjamin. 2 God hath not cast away his people which
he foreknew. Wot ye not what the Scripture
saith of Elias? how he maketh intercession to
God against Israel, saying, 3 Lord, they have
killed thy prophets, and digged down thine
altars; and I am left alone, and they seek my
life. 4 But what saith the answer of God unto
him? I have reserved to myself seven thousand
men, who have not bowed the knee to *the image
of* Baal. 5 Even so then at this present time also
there is a remnant according to the election of
grace. 6 And if by grace, then *is it* no more of
works: otherwise grace is no more grace. But if
it be of works, then is it no more grace: otherwise work is no more work. 7 What then? Israel
hath not obtained that which he seeketh for; but

Living Bible

keeps on reaching out his hands to the Jews,
but they keep arguing[f] and refusing to come.

11 I ask then, has God rejected and deserted
his people the Jews? Oh no, not at all. Remember that I myself am a Jew, a descendant
of Abraham and a member of Benjamin's family.
2, 3 No, God has not discarded his own people whom he chose from the very beginning. Do
you remember what the Scriptures say about
this? Elijah the prophet was complaining to
God about the Jews, telling God how they had
killed the prophets and torn down God's altars;
Elijah claimed that he was the only one left in
all the land who still loved God, and now they
were trying to kill him too.
4 And do you remember how God replied?
God said, "No, you are not the only one left.
I have seven thousand others besides you who
still love me and have not bowed down to
idols!"[a]
5 It is the same today. Not all the Jews have
turned away from God; there are a few being
saved as a result of God's kindness in choosing
them. 6 And if it is by God's kindness, then it is
not by their being good enough. For in that case
the free gift would no longer be free—it isn't
free when it is earned.
7 So this is the situation: Most of the Jews
have not found the favor of God they are look-

[*f*] Literally, "disobedient, obstinate." [*a*] I Kings 19:18.

Today's English Version

hands the whole day long to a disobedient and
rebellious people."

God's mercy on Israel

11 I ask, then: Did God reject his own people? Certainly not! I myself am an Israelite,
a descendant of Abraham, a member of the tribe
of Benjamin. 2 God has not rejected his people,
whom he chose from the beginning. You know
what the scripture says in the passage where Elijah
pleads with God against Israel: 3 "Lord, they
have killed your prophets and torn down your
altars; I am the only one left, and they are trying to kill me." 4 What answer did God give
him? "I have kept for myself seven thousand
men who have not worshiped the false god Baal."
5 It is the same way now at this time: there is a
small number of those whom God has chosen,
because of his mercy. 6 His choice is based on
his mercy, not on what they have done. For if
God's choice were based on what men do, then
his mercy would not be true mercy.
7 What then? The people of Israel did not find
what they were looking for. It was the small
group that God chose who found it; the rest

New International Version

I have held out my hands to a disobedient and
obstinate people."[x]

The remnant of Israel

11 I ask then, Did God reject his people? By
no means! I am an Israelite myself, a descendant of Abraham, from the tribe of Benjamin. 2 God did not reject his people, whom he
foreknew. Don't you know what the Scripture
says in the passage about Elijah—how he appealed to God against Israel: 3 "Lord, they have
killed your prophets and torn down your altars;
I am the only one left, and they are trying to
kill me"[y]? 4 And what was God's answer to
him? "I have reserved for myself seven thousand who have not bowed the knee to Baal."[z]
5 So too, at the present time there is a remnant
chosen by grace. 6 And if by grace, then it is no
longer by works; if it were, grace would no
longer be grace.[a]
7 What then? What Israel sought so earnestly
it did not obtain, but the elect did. The others

[*x*] Isaiah 65:2. [*y*] 1 Kings 19:10,14. [*z*] 1 Kings 19:18. [*a*] Some MSS add *But if by works, then it is no longer grace; if it were, work would no longer be work.*

Phillips Modern English

All the day long did I spread out my hands unto a disobedient and gainsaying people.

11.1 Israel's failure—yet remember the faithful few

This leads me to the question, "Has God then totally repudiated his people?" Certainly not! For I myself am an Israelite, a descendant of Abraham and of the tribe of Benjamin. It is unthinkable that God should have repudiated his own people, the people whose destiny he himself appointed. Don't you remember what the scripture says in the story of Elijah? How he pleaded with God on Israel's behalf:

Lord, they have killed thy prophets
They have digged down thine altars:
And I am left alone, and they seek my life.

And do you remember God's reply?

I have left for myself seven thousand men
Who have not bowed the knee to Baal.

In just the same way, there is at the present time a minority, chosen by the grace of God. And if it is a matter of the grace of God, it cannot be a question of their actions especially deserving God's favour, for that would make grace meaningless.

What conclusion do we reach now? That Israel did not, as a whole, obtain the object of

Revised Standard Version

held out my hands to a disobedient and contrary people."

11 I ask, then, has God rejected his people?
By no means! I myself am an Israelite, a
descendant of Abraham, a member of the tribe
of Benjamin. 2 God has not rejected his people
whom he foreknew. Do you not know what the
scripture says of Elijah, how he pleads with God
against Israel? 3 "Lord, they have killed thy
prophets, they have demolished thy altars, and
I alone am left, and they seek my life." 4 But
what is God's reply to him? "I have kept for
myself seven thousand men who have not bowed
the knee to Baal." 5 So too at the present time
there is a remnant, chosen by grace. 6 But if it
is by grace, it is no longer on the basis of works;
otherwise grace would no longer be grace.
7 What then? Israel failed to obtain what it
sought. The elect obtained it, but the rest were

Jerusalem Bible

stretched out my hand to a disobedient and rebellious people.

The remnant of Israel

11 Let me put a further question then: is it
possible that *God has rejected his people?* [q]
Of course not. I, an Israelite, descended from
Abraham through the tribe of Benjamin, 2 could
never agree that God had rejected his people,
the people he chose specially long ago. Do you
remember what scripture says of Elijah—how he
complained to God about Israel's behavior?
3 *Lord, they have killed your prophets and
broken down your altars. I, and I only, remain,
and they want to kill me.* [r] 4 What did God say
to that? *I have kept for myself seven thousand
men who have not bent the knee to Baal.* [s] 5 Today the same thing has happened: there is a
remnant, chosen by grace. 6 By grace, you notice, nothing therefore to do with good deeds, or
grace would not be grace at all!
7 What follows? It was not Israel as a whole
that found what it was seeking, but only the

[q] Ps. 94:14. [r] 1 K. 19:10,14. [s] 1 K. 19:18.

New English Bible

stretched out my hands to an unruly and defiant people.'

11 I ask then, has God rejected his people? I cannot believe it! I am an Israelite myself, of the stock of Abraham, of the tribe of Benjamin. No! God has not rejected the people which he acknowledged of old as his own. You know (do you not?) what Scripture says in the story of Elijah—how Elijah pleads with God against Israel: 'Lord, they have killed thy prophets, they have torn down thine altars, and I alone am left, and they are seeking my life.' But what does the divine voice say to him? 'I have left myself seven thousand men who have not knelt to Baal.' In just the same way at the present time a 'remnant' has come into being, selected by the grace of God. But if it is by grace, then it does not rest on deeds done, or grace would cease to be grace.

What follows? What Israel sought, Israel has not achieved, but the selected few have achieved

King James Version

the election hath obtained it, and the rest were
blinded 8 (According as it is written, God hath
given them the spirit of slumber, eyes that they
should not see, and ears that they should not
hear;) unto this day. 9 And David saith, Let
their table be made a snare, and a trap, and a
stumblingblock, and a recompense unto them:
10 Let their eyes be darkened, that they may not
see, and bow down their back alway. 11 I say
then, Have they stumbled that they should fall?
God forbid: but *rather* through their fall salvation *is come* unto the Gentiles, for to provoke
them to jealousy. 12 Now if the fall of them *be*
the riches of the world, and the diminishing of
them the riches of the Gentiles; how much more
their fulness? 13 For I speak to you Gentiles, inasmuch as I am the apostle of the Gentiles, I

Living Bible

ing for. A few have—the ones God has picked
out—but the eyes of the others have been
blinded. 8 This is what our Scriptures refer to
when they say that God has put them to sleep,
shutting their eyes and ears so that they do not
understand what we are talking about when we
tell them of Christ. And so it is to this very day.
9 King David spoke of this same thing when
he said, "Let their good food and other blessings
trap them into thinking all is well between themselves and God. Let these good things boomer-
ang on them and fall back upon their heads to
justly crush them. 10 Let their eyes be dim," he
said, "so that they cannot see, and let them
walk bent-backed forever with a heavy load."
11 Does this mean that God has rejected his
Jewish people forever? Of course not! His purpose was to make his salvation available to the
Gentiles, and then the Jews would be jealous
and begin to want God's salvation for themselves. 12 Now if the whole world became rich
as a result of God's offer of salvation, when the
Jews stumbled over it and turned it down, think
how much greater a blessing the world will share
in later on when the Jews, too, come to Christ.
13 As you know, God has appointed me as a
special messenger to you Gentiles. I lay great

Today's English Version

grew deaf to God's call. 8 As the scripture says,
"God made them dull of heart and mind; to this
very day they cannot see with their eyes or hear
with their ears." 9 And David says,

"May they be caught and trapped at their
feasts;
may they fall, may they be punished!
10 May their eyes be closed so that they cannot see;
and make them bend under their troubles at all times."

11 I ask, then: When the Jews stumbled, did
they fall to their ruin? By no means! Because
they sinned, salvation has come to the Gentiles,
to make the Jews jealous of them. 12 The sin of
the Jews brought rich blessings to the world,
and their spiritual poverty brought rich blessings
to the Gentiles. How much greater the blessings
will be, then, when the complete number of Jews
is included!

The salvation of the Gentiles

13 I am speaking now to you Gentiles: as long
as I am an apostle to the Gentiles I will take

New International Version

became hardened, 8 as it is written:
"God gave them a spirit of stupor,
eyes so that they could not see
and ears so that they could not hear,
to this very day." [b]
9 And David says:
"May their table become a snare and a trap,
a stumbling block and a retribution for
them.
10 "May their eyes be darkened so that they
cannot see,
and their backs be bent forever." [c]

Ingrafted branches

11 Again I ask, Did they stumble so as to fall
beyond recovery? Not at all! Rather, because of
their transgression, salvation has come to the
Gentiles to make Israel envious. 12 But if their
transgression means riches for the world, and
their loss means riches for the Gentiles, how
much greater riches will their fullness bring!
13 I am talking to you Gentiles. Inasmuch as
I am the apostle to the Gentiles, I make much

[*b*] Deut. 29:4; Isaiah 29:10. [*c*] Psalm 69:22,23.

Phillips Modern English

his striving, but a chosen few achieved it. The remainder became more and more insensitive to the righteousness of God. This is borne out by the scripture:

God gave them a spirit of stupor,
Eyes that they should not see,
And ears that they should not hear,
Unto this very day.

And David says of them:

Let their table be made a snare, and a trap,
And a stumbling-block, and a recompense unto them:
Let their eyes be darkened, that they may not see,
And bow thou down their back alway.

11.11 In the providence of God disaster has been turned to good account

Now I ask myself, "Was this fall of theirs an utter disaster?" It was not! For through their failure the benefit of salvation has passed to the gentiles, with the result that Israel is made to see and feel what they have missed. For if their failure has so enriched the world, and their defection proved such a benefit to the gentiles, think what tremendous advantages their fulfilling of God's plan could mean!

Now a word to you who are gentiles. I should like you to know that I make as much as I can

Revised Standard Version

hardened, 8 as it is written,
"God gave them a spirit of stupor,
eyes that should not see and ears that should not hear,
down to this very day."
9 And David says,
"Let their table become a snare and a trap,
a pitfall and a retribution for them;
10 let their eyes be darkened so that they cannot see,
and bend their backs for ever."
11 So I ask, have they stumbled so as to
fall? By no means! But through their trespass
salvation has come to the Gentiles, so as to make
Israel jealous. 12 Now if their trespass means
riches for the world, and if their failure means
riches for the Gentiles, how much more will
their full inclusion mean!
13 Now I am speaking to you Gentiles. Inasmuch then as I am an apostle to the Gentiles,

Jerusalem Bible

chosen few. The rest were not allowed to see the
truth; 8 as scripture says: *God has given them
a sluggish spirit, unseeing eyes and inattentive
ears, and they are still like that today.*[t] 9 And
David says: *May their own table prove a trap
for them, a snare and a pitfall—let that be their
punishment;* 10 *may their eyes be struck incur-
ably blind, their backs bend for ever.*[u]

The Jews to be restored in the future

11 Let me put another question then: have
the Jews fallen for ever, or have they just
stumbled? Obviously they have not fallen for
ever: their fall, though, has saved the pagans in
a way the Jews may now well emulate. 12 Think
of the extent to which the world, the pagan
world, has benefited from their fall and defection—then think how much more it will benefit
from the conversion of them all. 13 Let me tell
you pagans[v] this: I have been sent to the pagans

[*t*] Is. 29:10. [*u*] Ps. 69:22f. [*v*] Converts from paganism.

New English Bible

it. The rest were made blind to the truth, exactly as it stands written: 'God brought upon them a numbness of spirit; he gave them blind eyes and deaf ears, and so it is still.' Similarly David says:

'May their table be a snare and a trap,
both stumbling-block and retribution!
May their eyes become so dim that they lose their sight!
Bow down their backs unceasingly!'

I now ask, did their failure mean complete downfall? Far from it! Because they offended, salvation has come to the Gentiles, to stir Israel to emulation. But if their offence means the enrichment of the world, and if their falling-off means the enrichment of the Gentiles, how much more their coming to full strength!

But I have something to say to you Gentiles. I am a missionary to the Gentiles, and as such I

King James Version

magnify mine office: 14 If by any means I may provoke to emulation *them which are* my flesh, and might save some of them. 15 For if the casting away of them *be* the reconciling of the world, what *shall* the receiving *of them be*, but life from the dead? 16 For if the firstfruit *be* holy, the lump *is* also *holy:* and if the root *be* holy, so *are* the branches. 17 And if some of the branches be broken off, and thou, being a wild olive tree, wert graffed in among them, and with them partakest of the root and fatness of the olive tree; 18 Boast not against the branches. But if thou boast, thou bearest not the root, but the root thee. 19 Thou wilt say then, The branches were broken off, that I might be graffed in. 20 Well; because of unbelief they were broken off, and thou standest by faith. Be not highminded, but fear: 21 For if God spared not the natural branches, *take heed* lest he also spare not thee. 22 Behold therefore the good-

Living Bible

stress on this and remind the Jews about it as often as I can, 14 so that if possible I can make them want what you Gentiles have and in that way save some of them. 15And how wonderful it will be when they become Christians! When God turned away from them it meant that he turned to the rest of the world to offer his salvation; and now it is even more wonderful when the Jews come to Christ. It will be like dead people coming back to life. 16And since Abraham and the prophets are God's people, their children will be too. For if the roots of the tree are holy, the branches will be too.

17 But some of these branches from Abraham's tree, some of the Jews, have been broken off. And you Gentiles who were branches from, we might say, a wild olive tree, were grafted in. So now you, too, receive the blessing God has promised Abraham and his children, sharing in God's rich nourishment of his own special olive tree.

18 But you must be careful not to brag about being put in to replace the branches that were broken off. Remember that you are important only because you are now a part of God's tree; you are just a branch, not a root.

19 "Well," you may be saying, "those branches were broken off to make room for me so I must be pretty good."

20 Watch out! Remember that those branches, the Jews, were broken off because they didn't believe God, and you are there only because you do. Do not be proud; be humble and grateful—and careful. 21 For if God did not spare the branches he put there in the first place, he won't spare you either.

22 Notice how God is both kind and severe.

Today's English Version

pride in my work. 14 Perhaps I can make the people of my own race jealous, and so be able to save some of them. 15 For when they were rejected, the world was made friends with God. What will it be, then, when they are accepted? It will be life for the dead!

16 If the first piece of bread is given to God, then the whole loaf is his also; and if the roots of a tree are offered to God, the branches are his also. 17 Some of the branches of the cultivated olive tree have been broken off, and the branch of a wild olive tree has been joined to it. You Gentiles are like that wild olive tree, and now you share the strength and rich life of the Jews. 18 So then, you must not despise those who were broken off like branches. How can you be proud? You are just a branch; you don't support the root—the root supports you.

19 But you will say, "Yes, but the branches were broken off to make room for me." 20 This is true. They were broken off because they did not believe, while you remain in place because you believe. But do not have proud thoughts about it; instead, be afraid. 21 God did not spare the Jews, who were like natural branches; do you think he will spare you? 22 Here we see how

New International Version

of my ministry 14 in the hope that I may somehow arouse my own people to envy and save some of them. 15 For if their rejection is the reconciliation of the world, what will their acceptance be, but life from the dead? 16 If the part of the dough offered as firstfruits is holy, then the whole batch is holy; if the root is holy, so are the branches.

17 If some of the branches have been broken off, and you, though a wild olive shoot, have been grafted in among the others and now share in the nourishing sap from the olive root, 18 do not boast over those branches If you do, consider this: You do not support the root, but the root supports you. 19 You will say then, "Branches were broken off so that I could be grafted in." 20 Granted. But they were broken off because of unbelief, and you stand by faith. Do not be arrogant, but be afraid. 21 For if God did not spare the natural branches, he will not spare you either.

22 Consider therefore the kindness and stern-

Phillips Modern English

of my ministry as "God's messenger to the gentiles" so as to make my kinsfolk jealous and thus save some of them. For if their exclusion from the pale of salvation has meant the reconciliation of the rest of mankind to God, what would their inclusion mean? It would be nothing less than life from the dead! If the flour is consecrated to God so is the whole loaf, and if the roots of a tree are dedicated to God every branch will belong to him also.

11.17 A word of warning

But if some of the branches of the tree have been lopped off, while you, a shoot of wild-olive, have been grafted in, and share like a natural branch the rich nourishment of the root, don't let yourself feel superior to the former branches. If you feel inclined that way, remind yourself that you do not support the root, the root supports you. You may make the natural retort, "But the branches were lopped off to make room for my grafting!" Very well, then. They lost their position because they failed to believe; you only maintain yours because you do believe. The situation does not call for conceit but for a certain wholesome fear. If God removed the natural branches for a good reason, take care that you don't give him the same reason for removing you. You must try to ap-

Revised Standard Version

I magnify my ministry 14 in order to make my
fellow Jews jealous, and thus save some of
them. 15 For if their rejection means the reconciliation of the world, what will their acceptance
mean but life from the dead? 16 If the dough
offered as first fruits is holy, so is the whole
lump; and if the root is holy, so are the
branches.
17 But if some of the branches were broken
off, and you, a wild olive shoot, were grafted
in their place to share the richness[o] of the olive
tree, 18 do not boast over the branches. If you
do boast, remember it is not you that support
the root, but the root that supports you. 19 You
will say, "Branches were broken off so that I
might be grafted in." 20 That is true. They were
broken off because of their unbelief, but you
stand fast only through faith. So do not become
proud, but stand in awe. 21 For if God did not
spare the natural branches, neither will he spare
you. 22 Note then the kindness and the severity

[o] Other ancient authorities read *rich root*.

Jerusalem Bible

as their apostle, and I am proud of being sent,
14 but the purpose of it is to make my own people envious of you, and in this way save some
of them. 15 Since their rejection meant the reconciliation of the world, do you know what their
admission will mean? Nothing less than a resurrection from the dead!

The Jews are still the chosen people

16 A whole batch of bread is made holy if
the first handful of dough is made holy; all the
branches are holy if the root is holy. 17 No doubt
some of the branches have been cut off, and,
like shoots of wild olive, you have been grafted
among the rest to share with them the rich sap
provided by the olive tree itself, 18 but still,
even if you think yourself superior to the other
branches, remember that you do not support the
root; it is the root that supports you. 19 You
will say, "Those branches were cut off on purpose to let me be grafted in!" True, 20 they were
cut off, but through their unbelief; if you still
hold firm, it is only thanks to your faith. Rather
than making you proud, that should make you
afraid. 21 God did not spare the natural
branches, and he is not likely to spare you.
22 Do not forget that God can be severe as well

New English Bible

give all honour to that ministry when I try to stir emulation in the men of my own race, and so to save some of them. For if their rejection has meant the reconciliation of the world, what will their acceptance mean? Nothing less than life from the dead! If the first portion of dough is consecrated, so is the whole lump. If the root is consecrated, so are the branches. But if some of the branches have been lopped off, and you, a wild olive, have been grafted in among them, and have come to share the same root and sap as the olive, do not make yourself superior to the branches. If you do so, remember that it is not you who sustain the root: the root sustains you.

You will say, 'Branches were lopped off so that I might be grafted in.' Very well: they were lopped off for lack of faith, and by faith you hold your place. Put away your pride, and be on your guard; for if God did not spare the native branches, no more will he spare you. Observe the

King James Version

ness and severity of God: on them which fell, **severity; but toward thee, goodness, if thou** continue in *his* goodness: otherwise thou also shalt be cut off. 23And they also, if they abide not still in unbelief, shall be graffed in: for God is able to graff them in again. 24 For if thou wert cut out of the olive tree which is wild by nature, and wert graffed contrary to nature into a good olive tree; how much more shall these, which be the natural *branches,* be graffed into their own olive tree? 25 For I would not, brethren, that ye should be ignorant of this mystery, lest ye should be wise in your own conceits, that blindness in part is happened to Israel, until the fulness of the Gentiles be come in. 26And so all Israel shall be saved: as it is written, There shall come out of Sion the Deliverer, and shall turn away ungodliness from Jacob: 27 For this *is* my covenant unto them, when I shall take away their sins. 28As concerning the gospel, *they are* enemies for your sakes: but as touching the election, *they are* beloved for the fathers' sakes. 29 For the gifts and calling of God *are*

Living Bible

He is very hard on those who disobey, but very good to you if you continue to love and trust him. But if you don't, you too will be cut off. 23 On the other hand, if the Jews leave their unbelief behind them and come back to God, God will graft them back into the tree again. He has the power to do it.

24 For if God was willing to take you who were so far away from him—being part of a wild olive tree—and graft you into his own good tree—a very unusual thing to do—don't you see that he will be far more ready to put the Jews back again, who were there in the first place?

25 I want you to know about this truth from God, dear brothers, so that you will not feel proud and start bragging. Yes, it is true that some of the Jews have set themselves against the Gospel now, but this will last only until all of you Gentiles have come to Christ—those of you who will. 26And then all Israel will be saved.

Do you remember what the prophets said about this? "There shall come out of Zion a Deliverer, and he shall turn the Jews from all ungodliness. 27At that time I will take away their sins, just as I promised."

28 Now many of the Jews are enemies of the Gospel. They hate it. But this has been a benefit to you, for it has resulted in God's giving his gifts to you Gentiles. Yet the Jews are still beloved of God because of his promises to Abraham, Isaac, and Jacob. 29 For God's gifts and

Today's English Version

kind and how severe God is. He is severe toward those who have fallen, but kind to you—if you continue in his kindness; but if you do not, you too will be broken off. 23And the Jews, if they abandon their unbelief, will be put back in the place where they were, because God is able to put them back again. 24 You Gentiles are like the branch of a wild olive tree that is broken off, and then, contrary to nature, is joined to the cultivated olive tree. The Jews are like this cultivated tree; and it will be much easier, then, for God to join these broken-off branches back to their own tree.

God's mercy on all

25 There is a secret truth, my brothers, which I want you to know. It will keep you from thinking how wise you are. It is this: the stubbornness of the people of Israel is not permanent, but will last only until the complete number of Gentiles comes to God. 26And this is how all Israel will be saved. As the scripture says,

"The Savior will come from Zion,
and remove all wickedness from the descendants of Jacob.
27 I will make this covenant with them,
when I take away their sins."

28 Because they reject the Good News, the Jews are God's enemies for the sake of you, the Gentiles. But because of God's choice, they are his friends for the sake of the patriarchs. 29 For

New International Version

ness of God: sternness to those who fell, but kindness to you, provided that you continue in his kindness. Otherwise, you also will be cut off. 23And if they do not persist in unbelief, they will be grafted in, for God is able to graft them in again. 24After all, if you were cut out of an olive tree that is wild by nature, and contrary to nature were grafted into a cultivated olive tree, how much more readily will these, the natural branches, be grafted into their own olive tree?

All Israel will be saved

25 I do not want you to be ignorant of this mystery, brothers, so that you may not be conceited: Israel has experienced a hardening in part until the full number of the Gentiles has come in. 26And so all Israel will be saved, as it is written:

"The deliverer will come from Zion;
he will turn godlessness away from Jacob.
27And this is[d] my covenant with them
when I take away their sins."[e]

28 As far as the gospel is concerned, they are enemies on your account; but as far as election is concerned, they are loved on account of the patriarchs, 29 for God's gifts and his call are

[*d*] Or *will be.* [*e*] Isaiah 59:20,21; 27:9.

Phillips Modern English

preciate both the kindness and the strict justice of God. Those who fell experienced his justice, while you are experiencing his kindness, and will continue to do so as long as you do not abuse that kindness. Otherwise you too will be cut off from the tree. And as for the fallen branches, unless they are obstinate in their unbelief, they will be grafted in again. Such a restoration is by no means beyond the power of God. And, in any case, if you who were, so to speak, a cutting from a wild-olive, were grafted in against the natural order, is it not a far simpler matter for the natural branches to be grafted back into the parent stem?

11.25 God still has a plan for Israel

Now I don't want you, my brothers, to be totally ignorant of God's secret plan. And I should not wish you to have ideas of your own which may be false. No, the partial insensibility which has come to Israel is only to last until the full number of the gentiles has been called in. Once this has happened, all Israel will be saved, as the scripture says:

There shall come out of Zion the deliverer;
He shall turn away ungodliness from Jacob:
And this is my covenant unto them,
When I shall take away their sins.

As far as the gospel goes, they are at present God's enemies—which is to your advantage. But as far as God's purpose in choosing is concerned, they are still beloved for their fathers' sakes.

Revised Standard Version

of God: severity toward those who have fallen,
but God's kindness to you, provided you continue in his kindness; otherwise you too will be
cut off. 23 And even the others, if they do not
persist in their unbelief, will be grafted in, for
God has the power to graft them in again.
24 For if you have been cut from what is by
nature a wild olive tree, and grafted, contrary
to nature, into a cultivated olive tree, how much
more will these natural branches be grafted back
into their own olive tree.
25 Lest you be wise in your own conceits, I
want you to understand this mystery, brethren:
a hardening has come upon part of Israel, until
the full number of the Gentiles come in, 26 and
so all Israel will be saved; as it is written,
"The Deliverer will come from Zion,
he will banish ungodliness from Jacob";
27 "and this will be my covenant with them
when I take away their sins."
28 As regards the gospel they are enemies of God,
for your sake; but as regards election they are
beloved for the sake of their forefathers. 29 For

Jerusalem Bible

as kind: he is severe to those who fell, and he
is kind to you, but only for as long as he chooses
to be, otherwise you will find yourself cut off
too, 23 and the Jews, if they give up their unbelief, grafted back in your place. God is perfectly able to graft them back again; 24 after all,
if you were cut from your natural wild olive to
be grafted unnaturally on to a cultivated olive,
it will be much easier for them, the natural
branches, to be grafted back on the tree they
came from.

The conversion of the Jews

25 There is a hidden reason for all this, brothers, of which I do not want you to be ignorant,
in case you think you know more than you do.
One section of Israel has become blind, but this
will last only until the whole pagan world has
entered, 26 and then after this the rest of Israel
will be saved as well. As scripture says: *The
liberator will come from Zion, he will banish
godlessness from Jacob.* 27 *And this is the covenant I will make with them when I take their
sins away.*[w]
28 The Jews are enemies of God only with
regard to the Good News, and enemies only for
your sake; but as the chosen people, they are
still loved by God, loved for the sake of their
ancestors. 29 God never takes back his gifts or

[*w*] Is. 27:9.

New English Bible

kindness and the severity of God—severity to those who fell away, divine kindness to you, if only you remain within its scope; otherwise you too will be cut off, whereas they, if they do not continue faithless, will be grafted in; for it is in God's power to graft them in again. For if you were cut from your native wild olive and against all nature grafted into the cultivated olive, how much more readily will they, the natural olive-branches, be grafted into their native stock!

For there is a deep truth here, my brothers, of which I want you to take account, so that you may not be complacent about your own discernment: this partial blindness has come upon Israel only until the Gentiles have been admitted in full strength; when that has happened, the whole of Israel will be saved, in agreement with the text of Scripture:

'From Zion shall come the Deliverer;
he shall remove wickedness from Jacob.
And this is the covenant I will grant them,
when I take away their sins.'

In the spreading of the Gospel they are treated as God's enemies for your sake; but God's choice stands, and they are his friends for the sake of the patriarchs. For the gracious gifts of God and

King James Version

without repentance. 30 For as ye in times past have not believed God, yet have now obtained mercy through their unbelief: 31 Even so have these also now not believed, that through your mercy they also may obtain mercy. 32 For God hath concluded them all in unbelief, that he might have mercy upon all. 33 O the depth of the riches both of the wisdom and knowledge of God! how unsearchable *are* his judgments, and his ways past finding out! 34 For who hath known the mind of the Lord? or who hath been his counsellor? 35 Or who hath first given to him, and it shall be recompensed unto him again? 36 For of him, and through him, and to him, *are* all things: to whom *be* glory for ever. Amen.

Living Bible

his call can never be withdrawn; he will never go back on his promises. 30 Once you were rebels against God, but when the Jews refused his gifts God was merciful to you instead. 31 And now the Jews are the rebels, but some day they, too, will share in God's mercy upon you. 32 For God has given them all up to sin[b] so that he could have mercy upon all alike.

33 Oh, what a wonderful God we have! How great are his wisdom and knowledge and riches! How impossible it is for us to understand his decisions and his methods! 34 For who among us can know the mind of the Lord? Who knows enough to be his counselor and guide? 35 And who could ever offer to the Lord enough to induce him to act? 36 For everything comes from God alone. Everything lives by his power, and everything is for his glory. To him be glory evermore.

[b] Literally, "shut up all unto disobedience."

Today's English Version

God does not change his mind about whom he chooses and blesses. 30 As for you Gentiles, you disobeyed God in the past; but now you have received God's mercy because the Jews disobeyed. 31 In the same way, because of the mercy that you have received, the Jews now disobey God, in order that they also may now receive God's mercy. 32 For God has made all men prisoners of disobedience, that he might show mercy to them all.

Praise to God

33 How great are God's riches! How deep are his wisdom and knowledge! Who can explain his decisions? Who can understand his ways? 34 As the scripture says,

"Who knows the mind of the Lord?
Who is able to give him advice?
35 Who has ever given him anything,
so that he had to pay it back?"

36 For all things were created by him, and all things exist through him and for him. To God be the glory forever! Amen.

New International Version

irrevocable. 30 Just as you who were at one time disobedient to God have now received mercy as a result of their disobedience, 31 so they too, as a result of God's mercy to you, have now become disobedient in order that they too may now receive mercy. 32 For God has bound all men over to disobedience so that he may have mercy on them all.

Doxology

33 Oh the depth of the riches, the wisdom
and the knowledge of God!
How unsearchable his judgments,
and his paths beyond tracing out!
34 "Who has known the mind of the Lord?
Or who has been his adviser?"[f]
35 "Who has ever given to God,
that God should repay him?"[g]
36 For from him and through him and to him
are all things.
To him be the glory forever! Amen.

[f] Isaiah 40:13; Jer. 23:18. [g] Job 41:11.

Phillips Modern English

For once they are made, God does not withdraw his gifts or his calling.

11.30 The whole scheme looks topsy-turvy, until we see the amazing wisdom of God!

Just as in the past you were disobedient to God but have found that mercy which might have been theirs but for their disobedience, so they, who at the present moment are disobedient, will eventually share the mercy which has been extended to you. God has all men penned together in the prison of disobedience, that he may have mercy upon them all.

I stand amazed at the fathomless wealth of God's wisdom and God's knowledge. How could man ever understand his reasons for action, or explain his methods of working? For:

Who hath known the mind of the Lord?
Or who hath been his counsellor?
Or who hath first given to him, and it shall be recompensed unto him again?
For everything began with him, continues its existence because of him, and ends in him.
To him be the glory for ever, amen.

Revised Standard Version

the gifts and the call of God are irrevocable. 30 Just as you were once disobedient to God but now have received mercy because of their disobedience, 31 so they have now been disobedient in order that by the mercy shown to you they also may[p] receive mercy. 32 For God has consigned all men to disobedience, that he may have mercy upon all.

33 O the depth of the riches and wisdom and knowledge of God! How unsearchable are his judgments and how inscrutable his ways!

34 "For who has known the mind of the Lord,
or who has been his counselor?"
35 "Or who has given a gift to him
that he might be repaid?"

36 For from him and through him and to him are all things. To him be glory for ever. Amen.

[p] Other ancient authorities add *now*.

Jerusalem Bible

revokes his choice.

30 Just as you changed from being disobedient to God, and now enjoy mercy because of their disobedience, 31 so those who are disobedient now—and only because of the mercy shown to you—will also enjoy mercy eventually. 32 God has imprisoned all men in their own disobedience only to show mercy to all mankind.

A hymn to God's mercy and wisdom

33 How rich are the depths of God—how deep his wisdom and knowledge—and how impossible to penetrate his motives or understand his methods! 34 *Who could ever know the mind of the Lord? Who could ever be his counselor?* 35 *Who could ever give him anything or lend him anything?* [x] 36 All that exists comes from him; all is by him and for him. To him be glory for ever! Amen.

[x] Is. 40:13.

New English Bible

his calling are irrevocable. Just as formerly you were disobedient to God, but now have received mercy in the time of their disobedience, so now, when you receive mercy, they have proved disobedient, but only in order that they too may receive mercy. For in making all mankind prisoners to disobedience, God's purpose was to show mercy to all mankind.

O depth of wealth, wisdom, and knowledge in God! How unsearchable his judgements, how untraceable his ways! Who knows the mind of the Lord? Who has been his counsellor? Who has ever made a gift to him, to receive a gift in return? Source, Guide, and Goal of all that is—to him be glory for ever! Amen.

King James Version

12 I beseech you therefore, brethren, by the
mercies of God, that ye present your bodies
a living sacrifice, holy, acceptable unto God,
which is your reasonable service. 2 And be not
conformed to this world: but be ye transformed
by the renewing of your mind, that ye may
prove what *is* that good, and acceptable, and
perfect will of God. 3 For I say, through the
grace given unto me, to every man that is
among you, not to think *of himself* more highly
than he ought to think; but to think soberly,
according as God hath dealt to every man the
measure of faith. 4 For as we have many members in one body, and all members have not the
same office: 5 So we, *being* many, are one body
in Christ, and every one members one of another. 6 Having then gifts differing according
to the grace that is given to us, whether
prophecy, *let us prophesy* according to the proportion of faith; 7 Or ministry, *let us wait* on
our ministering; or he that teacheth, on teaching; 8 Or he that exhorteth, on exhortation: he
that giveth, *let him do it* with simplicity; he

Living Bible

12 And so, dear brothers, I plead with you
to give your bodies to God. Let them be a
living sacrifice, holy—the kind he can accept.
When you think of what he has done for you,
is this too much to ask? 2 Don't copy the behavior
and customs of this world, but be a new and
different person with a fresh newness in all you
do and think. Then you will learn from your
own experience how his ways will really satisfy
you.
3 As God's messenger I give each of you
God's warning: Be honest in your estimate of
yourselves, measuring your value by how much
faith God has given you. 4, 5 Just as there are
many parts to our bodies, so it is with Christ's
body. We are all parts of it, and it takes every
one of us to make it complete, for we each have
different work to do. So we belong to each other,
and each needs all the others.
6 God has given each of us the ability to do
certain things well. So if God has given you the
ability to prophesy, then prophesy whenever you
can—as often as your faith is strong enough to
receive a message from God. 7 If your gift is
that of serving others, serve them well. If you
are a teacher, do a good job of teaching. 8 If
you are a preacher, see to it that your sermons
are strong and helpful. If God has given you
money, be generous in helping others with it. If
God has given you administrative ability and
put you in charge of the work of others, take
the responsibility seriously. Those who offer

Today's English Version

Life in God's service

12 So then, my brothers, because of God's
great mercy to us, I make this appeal to
you: Offer yourselves as a living sacrifice to
God, dedicated to his service and pleasing to
him. This is the true worship that you should
offer. 2 Do not conform outwardly to the standards of this world, but let God transform you
inwardly by a complete change of your mind.
Then you will be able to know the will of God—
what is good, and is pleasing to him, and is
perfect.
3 And because of God's gracious gift to me,
I say to all of you: Do not think of yourselves
more highly than you should. Instead, be modest in your thinking, and each one of you judge
himself according to the amount of faith that
God has given him. 4 We have many parts in
the one body, and all these parts have different
functions. 5 In the same way, though we are
many, we are one body in union with Christ
and we are all joined to each other as different
parts of one body. 6 So we are to use our different gifts in accordance with the grace that
God has given us. If our gift is to speak God's
message, we must do it according to the faith
that we have. 7 If it is to serve, we must serve.
If it is to teach, we must teach. 8 If it is to encourage others, we must do so. Whoever shares
with others what he has, must do it generously;
whoever has authority, must work hard; who-

New International Version

Living sacrifices

12 Therefore, I urge you, brothers, in view
of God's mercy, to offer yourselves as living sacrifices, holy and pleasing to God—which
is your spiritual worship. 2 Do not conform any
longer to the pattern of this world, but be transformed by the renewing of your mind. Then you
will be able to test and approve what God's will
is—his good, pleasing and perfect will.
3 For by the grace given to me I say to every
one of you: Do not think of yourself more
highly than you ought, but rather think of yourself with sober judgment, in accordance with the
measure of faith God has given you. 4 Just as
each of us has one body with many members,
and these members do not all have the same
function, 5 so in Christ we who are many form
one body, and each member belongs to all the
others. 6 We have different gifts, according to
the grace given us. If a man's gift is prophesying, let him use it in proportion to his faith. 7 If
it is serving, let him serve; if it is teaching, let
him teach; 8 if it is encouraging, let him encourage; if it is contributing to the needs of
others, let him give generously; if it is leadership,

Phillips Modern English

12.1 We have seen God's mercy and wisdom: how shall we respond?

With eyes wide open to the mercies of God, I beg you, my brothers, as an act of intelligent worship, to give him your bodies, as a living sacrifice, consecrated to him and acceptable by him. Don't let the world around you squeeze you into its own mould, but let God re-make you so that your whole attitude of mind is changed. Thus you will prove in practice that the will of God's good, acceptable to him and perfect.

As your spiritual teacher I, by the grace God gave me, give this advice to each one of you. Don't cherish exaggerated ideas of yourself or your importance, but try to have a sane estimate of your capabilities by the light of the faith that God has given to you all. For just as you have many members in one physical body and those members differ in their functions, so we, though many in number, compose one body in Christ and are all members to one another. Through the grace of God we have different gifts. If our gift is preaching, let us preach to the limit of our vision. If it is serving others let us concentrate on our service; if it is teaching let us give all we have to our teaching; and if our gift be the stimulating of the faith of others let us set ourselves to it. Let the man who is called to give, give freely; let the man in authority work with enthusiasm; and

Revised Standard Version

12 I appeal to you therefore, brethren, by the mercies of God, to present your bodies as a living sacrifice, holy and acceptable to God, which is your spiritual worship. 2 Do not be conformed to this world [q] but be transformed by the renewal of your mind, that you may prove what is the will of God, what is good and acceptable and perfect.[r]

3 For by the grace given to me I bid every one among you not to think of himself more highly than he ought to think, but to think with sober judgment, each according to the measure of faith which God has assigned him. 4 For as in one body we have many members, and all the members do not have the same function, 5 so we, though many, are one body in Christ, and individually members one of another. 6 Having gifts that differ according to the grace given to us, let us use them: if prophecy, in proportion to our faith; 7 if service, in our serving; he who teaches, in his teaching; 8 he who exhorts, in his exhortation; he who contributes, in liberality; he

[q] Greek *age.* [r] Or *what is the good and acceptable and perfect will of God.*

Jerusalem Bible

Exhortation

Spiritual worship

12 Think of God's mercy, my brothers, and worship him, I beg you, in a way that is worthy of thinking beings, by offering your living bodies as a holy sacrifice, truly pleasing to God. 2 Do not model yourselves on the behavior of the world around you, but let your behavior change, modeled by your new mind. This is the only way to discover the will of God and know what is good, what it is that God wants, what is the perfect thing to do.

Humility and charity

3 In the light of the grace I have received I want to urge each one among you not to exaggerate his real importance. Each of you must judge himself soberly by the standard of the faith God has given him. 4 Just as each of our bodies has several parts and each part has a separate function, 5 so all of us, in union with Christ, form one body, and as parts of it we belong to each other. 6 Our gifts differ according to the grace given us. If your gift is prophecy, then use it as your faith suggests; 7 if administration, then use it for administration; if teaching, then use it for teaching. 8 Let the preachers deliver sermons, the almsgivers give freely, the

New English Bible

Christian behaviour

12 Therefore, my brothers, I implore you by God's mercy to offer your very selves to him: a living sacrifice, dedicated and fit for his acceptance, the worship offered by mind and heart.[a] Adapt yourselves no longer to the pattern of this present world, but let your minds be remade and your whole nature thus transformed. Then you will be able to discern the will of God, and to know what is good, acceptable, and perfect.

In virtue of the gift that God in his grace has given me I say to everyone among you: do not be conceited or think too highly of yourself; but think your way to a sober estimate based on the measure of faith that God has dealt to each of you. For just as in a single human body there are many limbs and organs, all with different functions, so all of us, united with Christ, form one body, serving individually as limbs and organs to one another.

The gifts we possess differ as they are allotted to us by God's grace, and must be exercised accordingly: the gift of inspired utterance, for example, in proportion to a man's faith; or the gift of administration, in administration. A teacher should employ his gift in teaching, and one who has the gift of stirring speech should use it to stir his hearers. If you give to charity, give with all your heart; if you are a leader, exert

[a] *Or* . . . acceptance, for such is the worship which you, as rational creatures, should offer.

King James Version

that ruleth, with diligence; he that sheweth
mercy, with cheerfulness. 9 *Let* love be without
dissimulation. Abhor that which is evil; cleave
to that which is good. 10 *Be* kindly affectioned
one to another with brotherly love; in honour
preferring one another; 11 Not slothful in business; fervent in spirit; serving the Lord; 12 Rejoicing in hope; patient in tribulation; continuing instant in prayer; 13 Distributing to the
necessity of saints; given to hospitality. 14 Bless
them which persecute you: bless, and curse not.
15 Rejoice with them that do rejoice, and weep
with them that weep. 16 *Be* of the same mind
one toward another. Mind not high things, but
condescend to men of low estate. Be not wise
in your own conceits. 17 Recompense to no man
evil for evil. Provide things honest in the sight
of all men. 18 If it be possible, as much as lieth
in you, live peaceably with all men. 19 Dearly
beloved, avenge not yourselves, but *rather* give
place unto wrath: for it is written, Vengeance

Living Bible

comfort to the sorrowing should do so with
Christian cheer.
9 Don't just pretend that you love others:
really love them. Hate what is wrong. Stand on
the side of the good. 10 Love each other with
brotherly affection and take delight in honoring
each other. 11 Never be lazy in your work but
serve the Lord enthusiastically.
12 Be glad for all God is planning for you.
Be patient in trouble, and prayerful always.
13 When God's children are in need, you be the
one to help them out. And get into the habit of
inviting guests home for dinner or, if they need
lodging, for the night.
14 If someone mistreats you because you are
a Christian, don't curse him; pray that God
will bless him. 15 When others are happy, be
happy with them. If they are sad, share their
sorrow. 16 Work happily together. Don't try to
act big. Don't try to get into the good graces
of important people, but enjoy the company of
ordinary folks. And don't think you know it all!
17 Never pay back evil for evil. Do things
in such a way that everyone can see you are
honest clear through. 18 Don't quarrel with anyone. Be at peace with everyone, just as much as
possible.
19 Dear friends, never avenge yourselves.
Leave that to God, for he has said that he will
repay those who deserve it. [Don't take the law

Today's English Version

ever shows kindness to others, must do it
cheerfully.
9 Love must be completely sincere. Hate what
is evil, hold on to what is good. 10 Love one another warmly as brothers in Christ, and be eager
to show respect for one another. 11 Work hard,
and do not be lazy. Serve the Lord with a heart
full of devotion. 12 Let your hope keep you joyful, be patient in your troubles, and pray at all
times. 13 Share your belongings with your needy
brothers, and open your homes to strangers.
14 Ask God to bless those who persecute you;
yes, ask him to bless, not to curse. 15 Be happy
with those who are happy, weep with those who
weep. 16 Have the same concern for all alike. Do
not be proud, but accept humble duties. Do not
think of yourselves as wise.
17 If someone does evil to you, do not pay
him back with evil. Try to do what all men consider to be good. 18 Do everything possible, on
your part, to live at peace with all men. 19 Never
take revenge, my friends, but instead let God's
wrath do it. For the scripture says, "I will take

New International Version

let him govern diligently; if it is showing mercy,
let him do it cheerfully.

Love

9 Love must be sincere. Hate what is evil;
cling to what is good. 10 Be devoted to one another in brotherly love. Honor one another above
yourselves. 11 Never be lacking in zeal, but keep
your spiritual fervor, serving the Lord. 12 Be joyful in hope, patient in affliction, faithful in
prayer. 13 Share with God's people who are in
need. Practice hospitality.
14 Bless those who persecute you; bless and
do not curse. 15 Rejoice with those who rejoice;
mourn with those who mourn. 16 Live in harmony with one another. Don't be proud, but be
willing to associate with people of low position.[h]
Don't be conceited.
17 Do not repay anyone evil for evil. Be
careful to do what is right in the sight of everybody. 18 If it is possible, as far as it depends on
you, live at peace with everyone. 19 Do not take
revenge, my friends, but leave room for God's
wrath, for it is written: "It is mine to avenge, I

[*h*] Or *willing to do menial work.*

Phillips Modern English

let the man who feels sympathy for his fellows in distress help them cheerfully.

12.9 *Let us have real Christian behaviour*

Let us have no imitation Christian love. Let us have a genuine hatred for evil and a real devotion to good. Let us have real warm affection for one another as between brothers, and a willingness to let the other man have the credit. Let us not allow slackness to spoil our work and let us keep the fires of the spirit burning, as we do our work for the Lord. Base your happiness on your hope in Christ. When trials come endure them patiently; steadfastly maintain the habit of prayer. Give freely to fellow-Christians in want, never grudging a meal or a bed to those who need them. And as for those who try to make your life a misery, bless them. Don't curse, bless. Share the happiness of those who are happy, and the sorrow of those who are sad. Live in harmony with each other. Don't become snobbish but take a real interest in ordinary people. Don't become set in your own opinions. Don't pay back a bad turn by a bad turn, to anyone. See that your public behaviour is above criticism. As far as your responsibility goes, livc at peace with everyone. Never take vengeance into your own hands, my dear friends: stand back and let God punish if he will. For it is written:

Vengeance belongeth unto me: I will recompense, saith the Lord.

Revised Standard Version

who gives aid, with zeal; he who does acts of mercy, with cheerfulness.
9 Let love be genuine; hate what is evil, hold
fast to what is good; 10 love one another with
brotherly affection; outdo one another in showing honor. 11 Never flag in zeal, be aglow with
the Spirit, serve the Lord. 12 Rejoice in your
hope, be patient in tribulation, be constant in
prayer. 13 Contribute to the needs of the saints,
practice hospitality.
14 Bless those who persecute you; bless and
do not curse them. 15 Rejoice with those who
rejoice, weep with those who weep. 16 Live in
harmony with one another; do not be haughty,
but associate with the lowly;[s] never be conceited. 17 Repay no one evil for evil, but take
thought for what is noble in the sight of all. 18 If
possible, so far as it depends upon you, live
peaceably with all. 19 Beloved, never avenge
yourselves, but leave it[t] to the wrath of God;
for it is written, "Vengeance is mine, I will repay,

[*s*] Or *give yourselves to humble tasks.* [*t*] Greek *give place.*

Jerusalem Bible

officials be diligent, and those who do works of mercy do them cheerfully.
9 Do not let your love be a pretense, but
sincerely prefer good to evil. 10 Love each other
as much as brothers should, and have a profound respect for each other. 11 Work for the
Lord with untiring effort and with great earnestness of spirit. 12 If you have hope, this will make
you cheerful. Do not give up if trials come; and
keep on praying. 13 If any of the saints are in
need you must share with them; and you should
make hospitality your special care.

Charity to everyone, including enemies

14 Bless those who persecute you: never curse
them, bless them. 15 Rejoice with those who rejoice and be sad with those in sorrow. 16 Treat
everyone with equal kindness; never be con-
descending but make real friends with the poor.
Do not allow yourself to become self-satisfied.
17 Never repay evil with evil but let everyone
see that you are interested only in the highest
ideals. 18 Do all you can to live at peace with
everyone. 19 Never try to get revenge; leave that,
my friends, to God's anger. As scripture says:
Vengeance is mine—I will pay them back,[y] the

[*y*] Dt. 32:35.

New English Bible

yourself to lead; if you are helping others in distress, do it cheerfully.

Love in all sincerity, loathing evil and clinging to the good. Let love for our brotherhood breed warmth of mutual affection. Give pride of place to one another in esteem.

With unflagging energy, in ardour of spirit, serve the Lord.[a]

Let hope keep you joyful; in trouble stand firm; persist in prayer.

Contribute to the needs of God's people, and practise hospitality.

Call down blessings on your persecutors—blessings, not curses.

With the joyful be joyful, and mourn with the mourners.

Care as much about each other as about yourselves. Do not be haughty, but go about with humble folk. Do not keep thinking how wise you are.

Never pay back evil for evil. Let your aims be such as all men count honourable. If possible, so far as it lies with you, live at peace with all men. My dear friends, do not seek revenge, but leave a place for divine retribution; for there is a text which reads, 'Justice is mine, says the Lord,

[*a*] *Some witnesses read* meet the demands of the hour.

King James Version

is mine; I will repay, saith the Lord. 20 Therefore if thine enemy hunger, feed him; if he thirst, give him drink: for in so doing thou shalt heap coals of fire on his head. 21 Be not overcome of evil, but overcome evil with good.

13 Let every soul be subject unto the higher powers. For there is no power but of God: the powers that be are ordained of God. 2 Whosoever therefore resisteth the power, resisteth the ordinance of God: and they that resist shall receive to themselves damnation. 3 For rulers are not a terror to good works, but to the evil. Wilt thou then not be afraid of the power? do that which is good, and thou shalt have praise of the same: 4 For he is the minister of God to thee for good. But if thou do that which is evil, be afraid; for he beareth not the sword in vain: for he is the minister of God, a revenger to *execute* wrath upon him that doeth evil. 5 Wherefore *ye* must needs be subject, not only for wrath, but also for conscience' sake. 6 For, for this cause pay ye tribute also: for they are God's ministers, attending continually upon this very thing. 7 Render therefore to all their dues: tribute to whom tribute *is due;* custom to whom

Living Bible

into your own hands.[a]] 20 Instead, feed your enemy if he is hungry. If he is thirsty give him something to drink and you will be "heaping coals of fire on his head." In other words, he will feel ashamed of himself for what he has done to you. 21 Don't let evil get the upper hand but conquer evil by doing good.

13 Obey the government, for God is the one who has put it there. There is no government anywhere that God has not placed in power. 2 So those who refuse to obey the laws of the land are refusing to obey God, and punishment will follow. 3 For the policeman does not frighten people who are doing right; but those doing evil will always fear him. So if you don't want to be afraid, keep the laws and you will get along well. 4 The policeman is sent by God to help you. But if you are doing something wrong, of course you should be afraid, for he will have you punished. He is sent by God for that very purpose. 5 Obey the laws, then, for two reasons: first, to keep from being punished, and second, just because you know you should.

6 Pay your taxes too, for these same two reasons. For government workers need to be paid so that they can keep on doing God's work, serving you. 7 Pay everyone whatever he ought to have: pay your taxes and import duties gladly,

[a] Implied.

Today's English Version

revenge, I will pay back, says the Lord." 20 Instead, as the scripture says: "If your enemy is hungry, feed him; if he is thirsty, give him a drink; for by doing this you will heap burning coals on his head." 21 Do not let evil defeat you; instead, conquer evil with good.

Duties toward the state authorities

13 Everyone must obey the state authorities, because no authority exists without God's permission, and the existing authorities have been put there by God. 2 Whoever opposes the existing authority opposes what God has ordered; and anyone who does so will bring judgment on himself. 3 For rulers are not to be feared by those who do good but by those who do evil. Would you like to be unafraid of the man in authority? Then do what is good, and he will praise you. 4 For he is God's servant working for your own good. But if you do evil, be afraid of him, because his power to punish is real. He is God's servant and carries out God's wrath on those who do evil. 5 For this reason you must obey the authorities—not just because of God's wrath, but also as a matter of conscience.

6 This is also the reason that you pay taxes, because the authorities are working for God when they fulfill their duties. 7 Pay, then, what you owe them; pay them your personal and

New International Version

will repay," [i] says the Lord. 20 On the contrary: "If your enemy is hungry, feed him; if he is thirsty, give him something to drink. In doing this, you will heap burning coals on his head." [j] 21 Do not be overcome by evil, but overcome evil with good.

Submission to the authorities

13 Everyone must submit himself to the governing authorities, for there is no authority except that which God has established. The authorities that exist have been established by God. 2 Consequently, he who rebels against the authority is rebelling against what God has instituted, and those who do so will bring judgment on themselves. 3 For rulers hold no terror for those who do right, but for those who do wrong. Do you want to be free from fear of the one in authority? Then do what is right and he will commend you. 4 For he is God's servant to do you good. But if you do wrong, be afraid, for he does not bear the sword for nothing. He is God's servant, an agent of justice to bring punishment on the wrongdoer. 5 Therefore, it is necessary to submit to the authorities, not only because of possible punishment but also because of conscience.

6 This is also why you pay taxes, for the authorities are God's servants, who give their full time to governing. 7 Give everyone what you owe him: If you owe taxes, pay taxes; if revenue,

[i] Deut. 32:35. [j] Prov. 25:21,22.

Phillips Modern English

And it is also written:

If thine enemy hunger, feed him;
If he thirst, give him to drink:
For in so doing thou shalt heap coals of fire
upon his head.

Don't allow yourself to be overpowered by evil. Take the offensive—overpower evil with good!

13.1 The Christian and the civil law

Everyone ought to obey the civil authorities, for all legitimate authority is derived from God's authority, and the existing authority is appointed under God. To oppose authority then is to oppose God, and such opposition is bound to be punished.

The honest citizen has no need to fear the keepers of law and order, but the dishonest man will always be afraid of them. If you want to avoid this anxiety just lead a law-abiding life, and all that can come your way is a word of approval. The officer is God's servant for your protection. But if you are leading a wicked life you have reason to be alarmed. The "power of the law" which is vested in every legitimate officer, is no empty phrase. He is, in fact, divinely appointed to inflict God's punishment upon evil-doers.

You must, therefore, obey the authorities, not simply because it is the safest, but because it is the right thing to do. It is right, too, for you to pay taxes for the civil authorities are appointed by God for the constant maintenance of pub-

Revised Standard Version

says the Lord." 20 No, "if your enemy is hungry,
feed him; if he is thirsty, give him drink; for by
so doing you will heap burning coals upon his
head." 21 Do not be overcome by evil, but overcome evil with good.

13 Let every person be subject to the governing authorities. For there is no authority except from God, and those that exist have
been instituted by God. 2 Therefore he who resists the authorities resists what God has appointed, and those who resist will incur judgment. 3 For rulers are not a terror to good
conduct, but to bad. Would you have no fear
of him who is in authority? Then do what is
good, and you will receive his approval, 4 for
he is God's servant for your good. But if you do
wrong, be afraid, for he does not bear the sword
in vain; he is the servant of God to execute his
wrath on the wrongdoer. 5 Therefore one must
be subject, not only to avoid God's wrath but
also for the sake of conscience. 6 For the same
reason you also pay taxes, for the authorities
are ministers of God, attending to this very
thing. 7 Pay all of them their dues, taxes to
whom taxes are due, revenue to whom revenue

Jerusalem Bible

Lord promises. 20 But there is more: *If your
enemy is hungry, you should give him food, and
if he is thirsty, let him drink. Thus you heap
red-hot coals on his head.*[z] 21 Resist evil and
conquer it with good.

Submission to civil authority

13 You must all obey the governing authorities. Since all government comes from God,
the civil authorities were appointed by God,
2 and so anyone who resists authority is rebelling
against God's decision, and such an act is bound
to be punished. 3 Good behavior is not afraid
of magistrates; only criminals have anything to
fear. If you want to live without being afraid of
authority, you must live honestly and authority
may even honor you. 4 The state is there to
serve God for your benefit. If you break the
law, however, you may well have fear: the
bearing of the word has its significance. The
authorities are there to serve God: they carry
out God's revenge by punishing wrongdoers.
5 You must obey, therefore, not only because
you are afraid of being punished, but also for
conscience' sake. 6 This is also the reason why
you must pay taxes, since all government officials are God's officers. They serve God by collecting taxes. 7 Pay every government official

[z] Pr. 25:21-22.

New English Bible

I will repay.' But there is another text: 'If your enemy is hungry, feed him; if he is thirsty, give him a drink; by doing this you will heap live coals on his head.' Do not let evil conquer you, but use good to defeat evil.

13 Every person must submit to the supreme authorities. There is no authority but by act of God, and the existing authorities are instituted by him; consequently anyone who rebels against authority is resisting a divine institution, and those who so resist have themselves to thank for the punishment they will receive. For government, a terror to crime, has no terrors for good behaviour. You wish to have no fear of the authorities? Then continue to do right and you will have their approval, for they are God's agents working for your good. But if you are doing wrong, then you will have cause to fear them; it is not for nothing that they hold the power of the sword, for they are God's agents of punishment, for retribution on the offender. That is why you are obliged to submit. It is an obligation imposed not merely by fear of retribution but by conscience. That is also why you pay taxes. The authorities are in God's service and to these duties they devote their energies.

Discharge your obligations to all men; pay

King James Version

custom; fear to whom fear; honour to whom
honour. 8 Owe no man any thing, but to love
one another: for he that loveth another hath
fulfilled the law. 9 For this, Thou shalt not
commit adultery, Thou shalt not kill, Thou
shalt not steal, Thou shalt not bear false witness, Thou shalt not covet; and if *there be* any
other commandment, it is briefly comprehended
in this saying, namely, Thou shalt love thy
neighbour as thyself. 10 Love worketh no ill to
his neighbour: therefore love *is* the fulfilling of
the law. 11 And that, knowing the time, that now
it is high time to awake out of sleep: for now
is our salvation nearer than when we believed.
12 The night is far spent, the day is at hand:
let us therefore cast off the works of darkness,
and let us put on the armour of light. 13 Let us
walk honestly, as in the day; not in rioting and
drunkenness, not in chambering and wantonness, not in strife and envying: 14 But put ye on
the Lord Jesus Christ, and make not provision
for the flesh, to *fulfil* the lusts *thereof*.

Living Bible

obey those over you, and give honor and respect
to all those to whom it is due. 8 Pay all your
debts except the debt of love for others—never
finish paying that! For if you love them, you
will be obeying all of God's laws, fulfilling all
his requirements. 9 If you love your neighbor as
much as you love yourself you will not want
to harm or cheat him, or kill him or steal from
him. And you won't sin with his wife or want
what is his, or do anything else the Ten Commandments say is wrong. All ten are wrapped
up in this one, to love your neighbor as you
love yourself. 10 Love does no wrong to anyone.
That's why it fully satisfies all of God's requirements. It is the only law you need.
11 Another reason for right living is this: you
know how late it is; time is running out. Wake
up, for the coming of the Lord [a] is nearer now
than when we first believed. 12, 13 The night is
far gone, the day of his return[a] will soon be
here. So quit the evil deeds of darkness and put
on the armor of right living, as we who live in
the daylight should! Be decent and true in everything you do so that all can approve your behavior. Don't spend your time in wild parties
and getting drunk or in adultery and lust, or
fighting, or jealousy. 14 But ask the Lord Jesus
Christ to help you live as you should, and don't
make plans to enjoy evil.

[*13a*] Literally, "our salvation."

Today's English Version

property taxes, and show respect and honor for
them all.

Duties toward one another

8 Be in debt to no one—the only debt you
should have is to love one another. Whoever
loves his fellow-man has obeyed the Law. 9 The
commandments, "Do not commit adultery; do
not murder; do not steal; do not covet"—all
these, and any others besides, are summed up in
the one command, "Love your fellow-man as
yourself." 10 Whoever loves his fellow-man will
never do him wrong. To love, then, is to obey
the whole Law.
11 You must do this, because you know what
hour it is: the time has come for you to wake
up from your sleep. For the moment when we
will be saved is closer now than it was when we
first believed. 12 The night is nearly over, day is
almost here. Let us stop doing the things that
belong to the dark, and take up the weapons for
fighting in the light. 13 Let us conduct ourselves
properly, as people who live in the light of day;
no orgies or drunkenness, no immorality or indecency, no fighting or jealousy. 14 But take up
the weapons of the Lord Jesus Christ, and stop
giving attention to your sinful nature, to satisfy
its desires.

New International Version

then revenue; if respect, then respect; if honor,
then honor.

Love, for the day is near

8 Let no debt remain outstanding, except the
continuing debt to love one another, for he who
loves his fellow man has fulfilled the law. 9 The
commandments, "Do not commit adultery," "Do
not murder," "Do not steal," "Do not covet," [k]
and whatever other commandment there may be,
are summed up in this one rule: "Love your neighbor as yourself." [l] 10 Love does no harm to its
neighbor. Therefore love is the fulfillment of the
law.
11 And do this, understanding the present
time. The hour has come for you to wake up
from your slumber, because our salvation is
nearer now than when we first believed. 12 The
night is nearly over; the day is almost here. So
let us put aside the deeds of darkness and put
on the armor of light. 13 Let us behave decently,
as in the daytime, not in orgies and drunkenness,
not in sexual immorality and debauchery, not in
dissension and jealousy. 14 Rather, clothe yourselves with the Lord Jesus Christ, and do not
think about how to gratify the desires of your
sinful nature.

[*k*] Exodus 20:13-15,17; Deut. 5:17-19,21. [*l*] Lev. 19:18.

Phillips Modern English

lic order. Give everyone his legitimate due, whether it be toll, or taxes, or reverence, or honour.

13.8 To love others is the highest conduct

Keep out of debt altogether, except that perpetual debt of love which we owe one another. The man who loves his neighbour has obeyed the whole Law in regard to his neighbour. For the commandments, "Thou shalt not commit adultery", "Thou shalt not kill", "Thou shalt not steal", "Thou shalt not covet" and all other commandments are summed up in this one rule: "Thou shalt love thy neighbour as thyself." Love hurts nobody: therefore love is the answer to the Law's commands.

13.11 Wake up and live!

Why all this stress on behaviour? Because, as I think you have realised the present time is of the highest importance—it is time to wake up to reality. Every day brings God's salvation nearer than the day in which we took the first step of faith.

The night is nearly over, the day has almost dawned. Let us therefore fling away the things that men do in the dark, let us arm ourselves for the fight of the day! Let us live cleanly, as in the daylight, not in the delights of getting drunk or playing with sex, nor yet in quarrelling or jealousies. Let us be Christ's men from head to foot, and give no chances to the flesh to have its fling.

Revised Standard Version

is due, respect to whom respect is due, honor to whom honor is due.
8 Owe no one anything, except to love one
another; for he who loves his neighbor has fulfilled the law. 9 The commandments, "You shall
not commit adultery, You shall not kill, You shall not steal, You shall not covet," and any other commandment, are summed up in this sentence, "You shall love your neighbor as yourself." 10 Love does no wrong to a neighbor;
therefore love is the fulfilling of the law.
11 Besides this you know what hour it is,
how it is full time now for you to wake from sleep. For salvation is nearer to us now than
when we first believed; 12 the night is far gone,
the day is at hand. Let us then cast off the works
of darkness and put on the armor of light; 13 let
us conduct ourselves becomingly as in the day, not in reveling and drunkenness, not in debauchery and licentiousness, not in quarreling and
jealousy. 14 But put on the Lord Jesus Christ,
and make no provision for the flesh, to gratify its desires.

Jerusalem Bible

what he has a right to ask—whether it be direct tax or indirect, fear or honor.

Love and law

8 Avoid getting into debt, except the debt of mutual love. If you love your fellow men you have carried out your obligations. 9 All the commandments: *You shall not commit adultery, you shall not kill, you shall not steal, you shall not covet,*[a] and so on, are summed up in this single command: *You must love your neighbor as yourself.*[b] 10 Love is the one thing that cannot hurt your neighbor; that is why it is the answer to every one of the commandments.

Children of the light

11 Besides, you know "the time" has come: you must wake up now: our salvation is even nearer than it was when we were converted.
12 The night is almost over, it will be daylight soon—let us give up all the things we prefer to do under cover of the dark; let us arm ourselves and appear in the light. 13 Let us live decently as people do in the daytime: no drunken orgies, no promiscuity or licentiousness, and no wrangling or jealousy. 14 Let your armor be the Lord Jesus Christ; forget about satisfying your bodies with all their cravings.

[a] From the commandments in Ex. 20 and Dt. 17.
[b] Lv. 19:18.

New English Bible

tax and toll, reverence and respect, to those to whom they are due. Leave no claim outstanding against you, except that of mutual love. He who loves his neighbour has satisfied every claim of the law. For the commandments, 'Thou shalt not commit adultery, thou shalt not kill, thou shalt not steal, thou shalt not covet', and any other commandment there may be, are all summed up in the one rule, 'Love your neighbour as yourself.' Love cannot wrong a neighbour; therefore the whole law is summed up in love.[a]

In all this, remember how critical the moment is. It is time for you to wake out of sleep, for deliverance is nearer to us now than it was when first we believed. It is far on in the night; day is near. Let us therefore throw off the deeds of darkness and put on our armour as soldiers of the light. Let us behave with decency as befits the day: no revelling or drunkenness, no debauchery or vice, no quarrels or jealousies! Let Christ Jesus himself be the armour that you wear; give no more thought to satisfying the bodily appetites.

[a] *Or* the whole law is fulfilled by love.

King James Version

14 Him that is weak in the faith receive ye, *but* not to doubtful disputations. 2 For one believeth that he may eat all things: another, who is weak, eateth herbs. 3 Let not him that eateth despise him that eateth not; and let not him which eateth not judge him that eateth: for God hath received him. 4 Who art thou that judgest another man's servant? to his own master he standeth or falleth; yea, he shall be holden up: for God is able to make him stand. 5 One man esteemeth one day above another: another esteemeth every day *alike*. Let every man be fully persuaded in his own mind. 6 He that regardeth the day, regardeth *it* unto the

Living Bible

14 Give a warm welcome to any brother who wants to join you, even though his faith is weak. Don't criticize him for having different ideas from yours about what is right and wrong.[a] 2 For instance, don't argue with him about whether or not to eat meat that has been offered to idols. You may believe there is no harm in this, but the faith of others is weaker; they think it is wrong, and will go without any meat at all and eat vegetables rather than eat that kind of meat. 3 Those who think it is all right to eat such meat must not look down on those who won't. And if you are one of those who won't, don't find fault with those who do. For God has accepted them to be his children. 4 They are God's servants, not yours. They are responsible to him, not to you. Let him tell them whether they are right or wrong. And God is able to make them do as they should.

5 Some think that Christians should observe the Jewish holidays as special days to worship God, but others say it is wrong and foolish to go to all that trouble, for every day alike belongs to God. On questions of this kind everyone must decide for himself. 6 If you have special days for worshiping the Lord, you are trying

[*14a*] Literally, "Receive him that is weak in faith, not for decisions of scruples." Perhaps the meaning is, "Receive those whose consciences hurt them when they do things others have no doubts about." Accepting them might cause discord in the church, but Paul says to welcome them anyway.

Today's English Version

Do not judge your brother

14 Accept among you the man who is weak in the faith, but do not argue with him about his personal opinions. 2 One man's faith allows him to eat anything, but the man who is weak in the faith eats only vegetables. 3 The man who will eat anything is not to despise the man who doesn't; while the one who eats only vegetables is not to pass judgment on the one who eats anything, because God has accepted him. 4 Who are you to judge the servant of someone else? It is his own Master who will decide whether he succeeds or fails. And he will suceed, because the Lord is able to make him succeed.

5 One man thinks that a certain day is more important than the others, while another man thinks that all days are the same. Each one should have his own mind firmly made up. 6 Whoever thinks highly of a certain day does it in honor of the Lord; whoever eats anything

New International Version

The weak and the strong

14 Accept him whose faith is weak, without passing judgment on disputable matters. 2 One man's faith allows him to eat everything, but another man, whose faith is weak, eats only vegetables. 3 The man who eats everything must not look down on him who does not, and the man who does not eat everything must not condemn the man who does, for God has accepted him. 4 Who are you to judge someone else's servant? To his own master he stands or falls. And he will stand, for the Lord is able to make him stand.

5 One man considers one day more sacred than another; another man considers every day alike. Each one should be fully convinced in his own mind. 6 He who regards one day as special, does so to the Lord. He who eats meat, eats to

Phillips Modern English

14.1 Don't criticise each other's convictions

Welcome a man whose faith is weak, but not with the idea of arguing over his scruples. One man believes that he may eat anything, another man, without this strong conviction, is a vegetarian. The meat-eater should not despise the vegetarian, nor should the vegetarian condemn the meat-eater—they should reflect that God has accepted them both. After all, who are you to criticise the servant of somebody else? It is to his own master that he stands or falls. And he will stand for the Lord is well able to make him do so.

14.5 People are different—make allowances

Again, one man thinks one day of more importance than others. Another man considers them all alike. Let every one be definite in his own convictions. If a man specially observes one particular day, he does so for the Lord's sake.

Revised Standard Version

14 As for the man who is weak in faith, welcome him, but not for disputes over opinions. 2 One believes he may eat anything, while the weak man eats only vegetables. 3 Let not him who eats despise him who abstains, and let not him who abstains pass judgment on him who eats; for God has welcomed him. 4 Who are you to pass judgment on the servant of another? It is before his own master that he stands or falls. And he will be upheld, for the Master is able to make him stand.

5 One man esteems one day as better than another, while another man esteems all days alike. Let every one be fully convinced in his own mind. 6 He who observes the day, observes it in honor of the Lord. He also who eats, eats

Jerusalem Bible

Charity toward the scrupulous

14 If a person's faith is not strong enough, welcome him all the same without starting an argument. 2 People range from those who believe they may eat any sort of meat to those whose faith is so weak they dare not eat anything except vegetables. 3 Meat eaters must not despise the scrupulous. On the other hand, the scrupulous must not condemn those who feel free to eat anything they choose, since God has welcomed them. 4 It is not for you to condemn someone else's servant: whether he stands or falls it is his own master's business; he will stand, you may be sure, because the Lord has power to make him stand. 5 If one man keeps certain days as holier than others, and another considers all days to be equally holy, each must be left free to hold his own opinion. 6 The one who observes special days does so in honor of

New English Bible

14 If a man is weak in his faith you must accept him without attempting to settle doubtful points. For instance, one man will have faith enough to eat all kinds of food, while a weaker man eats only vegetables. The man who eats must not hold in contempt the man who does not, and he who does not eat must not pass judgement on the one who does; for God has accepted him. Who are you to pass judgement on someone else's servant? Whether he stands or falls is his own Master's business; and stand he will, because his Master has power to enable him to stand.

Again, this man regards one day more highly than another, while that man regards all days alike. On such a point everyone should have reached conviction in his own mind. He who respects the day has the Lord in mind in doing so,

King James Version

Lord; and he that regardeth not the day, to the
Lord he doth not regard *it*. He that eateth, eateth to the Lord, for he giveth God thanks; and
he that eateth not, to the Lord he eateth not,
and giveth God thanks. 7 For none of us liveth
to himself, and no man dieth to himself. 8 For
whether we live, we live unto the Lord; and
whether we die, we die unto the Lord: whether
we live therefore, or die, we are the Lord's.
9 For to this end Christ both died, and rose, and
revived, that he might be Lord both of the dead
and living. 10 But why dost thou judge thy
brother? or why dost thou set at nought thy
brother? for we shall all stand before the judgment seat of Christ. 11 For it is written, *As* I
live, saith the Lord, every knee shall bow to
me, and every tongue shall confess to God.
12 So then every one of us shall give account
of himself to God. 13 Let us not therefore judge
one another any more: but judge this rather,
that no man put a stumblingblock or an occasion to fall in *his* brother's way. 14 I know, and
am persuaded by the Lord Jesus, that *there is*
nothing unclean of itself: but to him that esteemeth any thing to be unclean, to him *it is* unclean. 15 But if thy brother be grieved with *thy*
meat, now walkest thou not charitably. Destroy
not him with thy meat, for whom Christ died.

Living Bible

to honor him; you are doing a good thing. So
is the person who eats meat that has been offered to idols; he is thankful to the Lord for it;
he is doing right. And the person who won't
touch such meat, he, too, is anxious to please
the Lord, and is thankful. 7 We are not our own
bosses to live or die as we ourselves might
choose. 8 Living or dying we follow the Lord.
Either way we are his. 9 Christ died and rose
again for this very purpose, so that he can be
our Lord both while we live and when we die.

10 You have no right to criticize your brother
or look down on him. Remember, each of us
will stand personally before the Judgment Seat
of God. 11 For it is written, "As I live," says
the Lord, "every knee shall bow to me and
every tongue confess to God." 12 Yes, each of us
will give an account of himself to God. 13 So
don't criticize each other any more. Try instead
to live in such a way that you will never make
your brother stumble by letting him see you
doing something he thinks is wrong.

14 As for myself, I am perfectly sure on the
authority of the Lord Jesus that there is nothing
really wrong with eating meat that has been
offered to idols. But if someone believes it is
wrong, then he shouldn't do it because for him
it is wrong. 15 And if your brother is bothered
by what you eat, you are not acting in love if
you go ahead and eat it. Don't let your eating

Today's English Version

does it in honor of the Lord, because he gives
thanks to God for the food. Whoever refuses to
eat certain things does so in honor of the Lord,
and he gives thanks to God. 7 None of us lives
for himself only, none of us dies for himself
only; 8 if we live, it is for the Lord that we live,
and if we die, it is for the Lord that we die.
Whether we live or die, then, we belong to the
Lord. 9 For Christ died and rose to life in order
to be the Lord of the living and of the dead.
10 You, then—why do you pass judgment on
your brother? And you—why do you despise
your brother? All of us will stand before God,
to be judged by him. 11 For the scripture says,

"As I live, says the Lord,
everyone will kneel before me,
and everyone will confess that I am God."

12 Every one of us, then, will have to give an
account of himself to God.

Do not make your brother fall

13 So then, let us stop judging one another.
Instead, this is what you should decide: not to
do anything that would make your brother
stumble, or fall into sin. 14 My union with the
Lord Jesus makes me know for certain that
nothing is unclean of itself; but if a man believes that something is unclean, then it becomes unclean for him. 15 If you hurt your
brother because of something you eat, then you
are no longer acting from love. Do not let the
food that you eat ruin the man for whom Christ

New International Version

the Lord, for he gives thanks to God; and he
who abstains, does so to the Lord, and gives
thanks to God. 7 For none of us lives to himself
alone and none of us dies to himself alone. 8 If
we live, we live to the Lord; and if we die, we
die to the Lord. So, whether we live or die, we
belong to the Lord.

9 For this very reason, Christ died and returned to life so that he might be the Lord of
both the dead and the living. 10 You, then, why
do you judge your brother? Or why do you look
down on your brother? For we will all stand before God's judgment seat. 11 It is written:

" 'As I live,' says the Lord,
'Every knee will bow before me;
every tongue will confess to God.' " [m]

12 So then, each of us will give an account of
himself to God.

13 Therefore, let us stop passing judgment on
one another. Instead, make up your mind not to
put any stumbling block or obstacle in your
brother's way. 14 As one who is in the Lord
Jesus, I am fully convinced that no food is unclean in itself. But if anyone regards something
as unclean, then for him it is unclean. 15 If your
brother is distressed because of what you eat, you
are no longer acting in love. Do not by your eating destroy your brother for whom Christ died.

[*m*] Isaiah 49:18; 45:23.

Phillips Modern English

The man who eats, eats for the Lord's sake, for he thanks God for the food. The man who fasts also does it for the Lord's sake, for he thanks God for the benefits of fasting. The truth is that we neither live nor die as self-contained units. At every turn life links us to the Lord and when we die we come face to face with him. In life or death we are in the hands of the Lord. Christ lived and died that he might be the Lord in both life and death.

Why, then, do you criticise your brother's actions, why do you try to make him look small? We shall all be judged one day, not by each other's standards or even by our own, but by the judgment of God. It is written:

As I live, saith the Lord, to me every knee
shall bow,
And every tongue shall confess to God.

It is to God alone that we shall have to answer for our actions.

14.13 This should be our attitude

Let us therefore stop turning critical eyes on one another. Let us rather be critical of our own conduct and see that we do nothing to make a brother stumble or fall.

I am convinced, and I say this as in the presence of the Lord Jesus, that nothing is intrinsically unholy. But none the less it is unholy to the man who thinks it is. If your habit of unrestricted diet seriously upsets your brother, you are no longer living in love towards him. And surely you wouldn't let food mean ruin to a man

Revised Standard Version

in honor of the Lord, since he gives thanks to
God; while he who abstains, abstains in honor
of the Lord and gives thanks to God. 7 None of
us lives to himself, and none of us dies to himself. 8 If we live, we live to the Lord, and if we
die, we die to the Lord; so then, whether we live
or whether we die, we are the Lord's. 9 For to
this end Christ died and lived again, that he
might be Lord both of the dead and of the
living.
10 Why do you pass judgment on your
brother? Or you, why do you despise your
brother? For we shall all stand before the judgment seat of God; 11 for it is written,
"As I live, says the Lord, every knee shall
bow to me,
and every tongue shall give praise[u] to God."
12 So each of us shall give account of himself
to God.
13 Then let us no more pass judgment on one
another, but rather decide never to put a stumbling block or hindrance in the way of a brother.
14 I know and am persuaded in the Lord Jesus
that nothing is unclean in itself; but it is unclean
for any one who thinks it unclean. 15 If your
brother is being injured by what you eat, you
are no longer walking in love. Do not let what
you eat cause the ruin of one for whom Christ

[u] Or *confess*.

Jerusalem Bible

the Lord. The one who eats meat also does so
in honor of the Lord, since he gives thanks to
God; but then the man who abstains does that
too in honor of the Lord, and so he also gives
God thanks. 7 The life and death of each of us
has its influence on others; 8 if we live, we live
for the Lord; and if we die, we die for the
Lord, so that alive or dead we belong to the
Lord. 9 This explains why Christ both died and
came to life, it was so that he might be Lord
both of the dead and of the living. 10 This is
also why you should never pass judgment on a
brother or treat him with contempt, as some of
you have done. We shall have to stand before
the judgment seat of God; 11 as scripture says:
*By my life—it is the Lord who speaks—every
knee shall bend before me, and every tongue
shall praise God.*[c] 12 It is to God, therefore, that
each of us must give an account of himself.
13 Far from passing judgment on each other,
therefore, you should make up your mind never
to be the cause of your brother tripping or
falling. 14 Now I am perfectly well aware, of
course, and I speak for the Lord Jesus, that no
food is unclean in itself; however, if someone
thinks that a particular food is unclean, then it
is unclean for him. 15And indeed if your attitude to food is upsetting your brother, then
you are hardly being guided by charity. You are
certainly not free to eat what you like if that
means the downfall of someone for whom Christ
died.

[c] Is. 45:23.

New English Bible

and he who eats meat has the Lord in mind when he eats, since he gives thanks to God; and he who abstains has the Lord in mind no less, since he too gives thanks to God.

For no one of us lives, and equally no one of us dies, for himself alone. If we live, we live for the Lord; and if we die, we die for the Lord. Whether therefore we live or die, we belong to the Lord. This is why Christ died and came to life again, to establish his lordship over dead and living. You, sir, why do you pass judgement on your brother? And you, sir, why do you hold your brother in contempt? We shall all stand before God's tribunal. For Scripture says, 'As I live, says the Lord, to me every knee shall bow and every tongue acknowledge God.' So, you see, each of us will have to answer for himself.

Let us therefore cease judging one another, but rather make this simple judgement: that no obstacle or stumbling-block be placed in a brother's way. I am absolutely convinced, as a Christian,[a] that nothing is impure in itself; only, if a man considers a particular thing impure, then to him it is impure. If your brother is outraged by what you eat, then your conduct is no longer guided by love. Do not by your eating bring disaster to a man for whom Christ died!

[a] *Or* on the authority of the Lord Jesus.

King James Version

16 Let not then your good be evil spoken of: 17 For the kingdom of God is not meat and drink; but righteousness, and peace, and joy in the Holy Ghost. 18 For he that in these things serveth Christ *is* acceptable to God, and approved of men. 19 Let us therefore follow after the things which make for peace, and things wherewith one may edify another. 20 For meat destroy not the work of God. All things indeed *are* pure; but *it is* evil for that man who eateth with offence. 21 *It is* good neither to eat flesh, nor to drink wine, nor *any thing* whereby thy brother stumbleth, or is offended, or is made weak. 22 Hast thou faith? have *it* to thyself before God. Happy *is* he that condemneth not himself in that thing which he alloweth. 23 And he that doubteth is damned if he eat, because *he eateth* not of faith: for whatsoever *is* not of faith is sin.

15 We then that are strong ought to bear the infirmities of the weak, and not to please ourselves. 2 Let every one of us please

Living Bible

ruin someone for whom Christ died. 16 Don't do anything that will cause criticism against yourself even though you know that what you do is right. 17 For, after all, the important thing for ns as Christians is not what we eat or drink but stirring up goodness and peace and joy from the Holy Spirit. 18 If you let Christ be Lord in these affairs, God will be glad; and so will others. 19 In this way aim for harmony in the church and try to build each other up.

20 Don't undo the work of God for a chunk of meat. Remember, there is nothing wrong with the meat, but it is wrong to eat it if it makes another stumble. 21 The right thing to do is to quit eating meat or drinking wine or doing anything else that offends your brother or makes him sin. 22 You may know that there is nothing wrong with what you do, even from God's point of view, but keep it to yourself; don't flaunt your faith in front of others who might be hurt by it. In this situation, happy is the man who does not sin by doing what he knows is right. 23 But anyone who believes that something he wants to do is wrong shouldn't do it. He sins if he does, for he thinks it is wrong, and so for him it *is* wrong. Anything that is done apart from what he feels is right is sin.

15 Even if we believe that it makes no difference to the Lord whether we do these things, still we cannot just go ahead and do them to please ourselves; for we must bear the "burden" of being considerate of the doubts and fears of others—of those who feel these things are wrong. Let's please the other fellow, not

Today's English Version

died! 16 Do not let what you regard as good acquire a bad name. 17 For God's Kingdom is not a matter of eating and drinking, but of the righteousness, peace, and joy that the Holy Spirit gives. 18 And whoever serves Christ in this way wins God's pleasure and man's approval.

19 So then, we must always aim at those things that bring peace, and that help strengthen one another. 20 Do not, because of food, destroy what God has done. All foods may be eaten, but it is wrong to eat anything that will cause someone else to fall into sin. 21 The right thing to do is to keep from eating meat, drinking wine, or doing anything else that will make your brother fall. 22 Keep what you believe about this matter, then, between yourself and God. Happy is the man who does not feel himself condemned when he does what he approves of! 23 But if he has doubts about what he eats, God condemns him when he eats it, because his action is not based on faith. And anything that is not based on faith is sin.

Please others, not yourselves

15 We who are strong in the faith ought to help the weak to carry their burdens. We should not please ourselves. 2 Instead, each of

New International Version

16 Do not allow what you consider good to be spoken of as evil. 17 For the kingdom of God is not a matter of eating and drinking, but of righteousness, peace and joy in the Holy Spirit, 18 because anyone who serves Christ in this way is pleasing to God and approved by men.

19 Let us therefore make every effort to do what leads to peace and to mutual edification. 20 Do not destroy the work of God for the sake of food. All food is clean, but it is wrong for a man to eat anything that causes someone else to stumble. 21 It is better not to eat meat or drink wine or to do anything else that will cause your brother to fall.

22 So whatever you believe about these things keep between yourself and God. Blessed is the man who does not condemn himself by what he approves. 23 But the man who has doubts is condemned if he eats, because his eating is not from faith; and everything that does not come from faith is sin.

15 We who are strong ought to bear with the failings of the weak, and not to please ourselves. 2 Each of us should please his neigh-

Phillips Modern English

for whom Christ died. You mustn't let something that is all right for you look like an evil practice to somebody else. After all, the kingdom of Heaven is not a matter of whether you get what you like to eat and drink, but of righteousness and peace and joy in the Holy Spirit. If you put these things first in serving Christ you will please God and are not likely to offend men. So let us concentrate on the things which make for harmony, and on the growth of our fellowship together. Surely we shouldn't wish to undo God's work for the sake of a plate of meat!

I freely admit that all food is, in itself, harmless, but it can be harmful for the man who eats it and so upsets the faith of others. We should be willing to be both vegetarians and teetotallers or abstain from anything else if by doing otherwise we should impede a brother's progress in the faith. Your personal convictions are a matter of faith between yourself and God, and you are happy if you have no qualms about what you allow yourself to eat. Yet if a man eats meat with an uneasy conscience, you may be sure he is wrong to do so. For his action does not spring from his faith, and when we act apart from our faith we sin.

15.1 Christian behaviour to one another

We who have strong faith ought to shoulder the burden of the doubts and qualms of the weak and not just go our own sweet way. We

Revised Standard Version

died. 16 So do not let your good be spoken of
as evil. 17 For the kingdom of God is not food
and drink but righteousness and peace and joy
in the Holy Spirit; 18 he who thus serves Christ
is acceptable to God and approved by men.
19 Let us then pursue what makes for peace and
for mutual upbuilding. 20 Do not, for the sake
of food, destroy the work of God. Everything is
indeed clean, but it is wrong for any one to make
others fall by what he eats; 21 it is right not to
eat meat or drink wine or do anything that
makes your brother stumble.[v] 22 The faith that
you have, keep between yourself and God; happy
is he who has no reason to judge himself for
what he approves. 23 But he who has doubts is
condemned, if he eats, because he does not act
from faith; for whatever does not proceed from
faith is sin.[w]

15 We who are strong ought to bear with
the failings of the weak, and not to please
ourselves; 2 let each of us please his neighbor

[v] Other ancient authorities add *or be upset or be weakened.* [w] Other authorities, some ancient, insert here Ch 16.25–27.

Jerusalem Bible

16 In short, you must not compromise your
privilege, 17 because the kingdom of God does
not mean eating or drinking this or that, it
means righteousness and peace and joy brought
by the Holy Spirit. 18 If you serve Christ in
this way you will please God and be respected
by men. 19 So let us adopt any custom that
leads to peace and our mutual improvement;
20 do not wreck God's work over a question of
food. Of course all food is clean, but it becomes evil if by eating it you make somebody
else fall away. 21 In such cases the best course
is to abstain from meat and wine and anything
else that would make your brother trip or fall
or weaken in any way.
22 Hold on to your own belief, as between
yourself and God—and consider the man fortunate who can make his decision without going
against his conscience. 23 But anybody who eats
in a state of doubt is condemned, because he is
not in good faith; and every act done in bad
faith is a sin.

15 We who are strong have a duty to put
up with the qualms of the weak without
thinking of ourselves. 2 Each of us should think

New English Bible

What for you is a good thing must not become an occasion for slanderous talk; for the kingdom of God is not eating and drinking, but justice, peace, and joy, inspired by the Holy Spirit. He who thus shows himself a servant of Christ is acceptable to God and approved by men.

Let us then pursue the things that make for peace and build up the common life. Do not ruin the work of God for the sake of food. Everything is pure in itself, but anything is bad for the man who by his eating causes another to fall. It is a fine thing to abstain from eating meat or drinking wine, or doing anything which causes your brother's downfall. If you have a clear conviction, apply it to yourself in the sight of God. Happy is the man who can make his decision with a clear conscience![a] But a man who has doubts is guilty if he eats, because his action does not arise from his conviction, and anything which does not arise from conviction is sin.[b]

15 Those of us who have a robust conscience must accept as our own burden the tender scruples of weaker men, and not consider ourselves. Each of us must consider his neighbour

[a] *Or* who does not bring judgement upon himself by what he approves! [b] *See p. 1175, note g.*

King James Version

his neighbour for *his* good to edification. 3 For
even Christ pleased not himself; but, as it is
written, The reproaches of them that reproached
thee fell on me. 4 For whatsoever things were
written aforetime were written for our learning, that we through patience and comfort of
the Scriptures might have hope. 5 Now the God
of patience and consolation grant you to be like-
minded one toward another according to Christ
Jesus: 6 That ye may with one mind *and* one
mouth glorify God, even the Father of our
Lord Jesus Christ. 7 Wherefore receive ye one
another, as Christ also received us, to the glory
of God. 8 Now I say that Jesus Christ was a
minister of the circumcision for the truth of
God, to confirm the promises *made* unto the
fathers: 9And that the Gentiles might glorify
God for *his* mercy; as it is written, For this
cause I will confess to thee among the Gentiles,
and sing unto thy name. 10And again he saith,

Living Bible

ourselves, and do what is for his good and thus
build him up in the Lord. 3 Christ didn't please
himself. As the Psalmist said, "He came for the
very purpose of suffering under the insults of
those who were against the Lord." 4 These things
that were written in the Scriptures so long ago
are to teach us patience and to encourage us, so
that we will look forward expectantly to the
time when God will conquer sin and death.
5 May God who gives patience, steadiness,
and encouragement help you to live in complete
harmony with each other—each with the attitude
of Christ toward the other. 6And then all of us
can praise the Lord together with one voice,
giving glory to God, the Father of our Lord
Jesus Christ.
7 So, warmly welcome each other into the
church, just as Christ has warmly welcomed
you; then God will be glorified. 8 Remember
that Jesus Christ came to show that God is true
to his promises and to help the Jews. 9And remember that he came also that the Gentiles
might be saved and give glory to God for his
mercies to them. That is what the Psalmist
meant when he wrote: "I will praise you among
the Gentiles, and sing to your name."
10 And in another place, "Be glad, O you

Today's English Version

us should please his brother for his own good,
in order to build him up in the faith. 3 For Christ
did not please himself. Instead, as the scripture
says, "The insults spoken by those who insulted
you have fallen on me." 4 Everything written in
the Scriptures was written to teach us, in order
that we might have hope through the patience
and encouragement the Scriptures give us. 5And
may God, the source of patience and encouragement, enable you to have the same point of view
among yourselves by following the example of
Christ Jesus, 6 so that all of you together, with
one voice, may praise the God and Father of
our Lord Jesus Christ.

The gospel to the Gentiles

7 Accept one another, then, for the glory of
God, as Christ has accepted you. 8 Because I tell
you that Christ became a servant of the Jews to
show that God is faithful, to make God's promises to the patriarchs come true, 9 and also to
enable the Gentiles to praise God for his mercy.
As the scripture says,

"And so I will give thanks to you among the
Gentiles,
I will sing praises to your name."

10Again it says,

New International Version

bor for his good, to build him up. 3 For even
Christ did not please himself but, as it is written:
"The insults of those who insult you have fallen
on me." [n] 4 For everything that was written in
the past was written to teach us, so that through
endurance and the encouragement of the Scriptures we might have hope.
5 May the God who gives endurance and
encouragement give you a spirit of unity among
yourselves as you follow Christ Jesus, 6 so that
with one heart and mouth you may glorify the
God and Father of our Lord Jesus Christ.
7 Accept one another, then, just as Christ accepted you, in order to bring praise to God.
8 For I tell you that Christ has become a servant
of the Jews[o] on behalf of God's truth, to confirm the promises made to the patriarchs 9 so
that the Gentiles may glorify God for his mercy,
as it is written:
"For this reason I will praise you among the
Gentiles;
I will sing hymns to your name." [p]
10Again, it says,

[*n*] Psalm 69:9. [*o*] Greek *circumcision*. [*p*] Psalm 18:49.

Phillips Modern English

should consider the good of our neighbour and help to build up his character. For even Christ did not choose his own pleasure, but as it is written:

The reproaches of them that reproached thee fell upon me.

For all those words which were written long ago are meant to teach us today; so that we may be encouraged to endure and to go on hoping in our own time. May the God who inspires men to endure, and gives them constant encouragement, give you a mind united with one another in your common loyalty to Christ Jesus. And then, as one man, you will sing from the heart the praises of God the Father of our Lord Jesus Christ. So open your hearts to one another as Christ has opened his heart to you, and God will be glorified.

15.8 A reminder—Christ the universal saviour

Christ was made a servant of the Jews to prove God's trustworthiness, since he implemented the promises made long ago to the fathers, and also that the gentiles might bring glory to God for his mercy to them. It is written:

Therefore will I give praise unto thee among the gentiles
And sing unto thy name.

And again:

Revised Standard Version

for his good, to edify him. 3 For Christ did not
please himself; but, as it is written, "The reproaches of those who reproached thee fell on
me." 4 For whatever was written in former days
was written for our instruction, that by steadfastness and by the encouragement of the scriptures we might have hope. 5 May the God of
steadfastness and encouragement grant you to
live in such harmony with one another, in accord
with Christ Jesus, 6 that together you may with
one voice glorify the God and Father of our
Lord Jesus Christ.
7 Welcome one another, therefore, as Christ
has welcomed you, for the glory of God. 8 For I
tell you that Christ became a servant to the circumcised to show God's truthfulness, in order to
confirm the promises given to the patriarchs,
9 and in order that the Gentiles might glorify
God for his mercy. As it is written,
"Therefore I will praise thee among the Gentiles,
and sing to thy name";
10 and again it is said,

Jerusalem Bible

of his neighbors and help them to become
stronger Christians. 3 Christ did not think of
himself: the words of scripture—*the insults of those who insult you fall on me*[d]—apply to him.
4 And indeed everything that was written long
ago in the scriptures was meant to teach us
something about hope from the examples scripture gives of how people who did not give up
were helped by God. 5 And may he who helps
us when we refuse to give up, help you all to
be tolerant with each other, following the example of Christ Jesus, 6 so that united in mind
and voice you may give glory to the God and
Father of our Lord Jesus Christ.

An appeal for unity

7 It can only be to God's glory, then, for you
to treat each other in the same friendly way as
Christ treated you. 8 The reason Christ became
the servant of circumcised Jews was not only
so that God could faithfully carry out the
promises made to the patriarchs, 9 it was also to
get the pagans to give glory to God for his
mercy, as scripture says in one place: *For this I shall praise you among the pagans and sing to your name.*[e] 10 And in another place: *Rejoice,*

[d] Ps. 69:9. [e] Ps. 18:50.

New English Bible

and think what is for his good and will build up the common life. For Christ too did not consider himself, but might have said, in the words of Scripture, 'The reproaches of those who reproached thee fell upon me.' For all the ancient scriptures were written for our own instruction, in order that through the encouragement they give us we may maintain our hope with fortitude. And may God, the source of all fortitude and all encouragement, grant that you may agree with one another after the manner of Christ Jesus, so that with one mind and one voice you may praise the God and Father of our Lord Jesus Christ.

In a word, accept one another as Christ accepted us, to the glory of God. I mean that Christ became a servant of the Jewish people to maintain the truth of God by making good his promises to the patriarchs, and at the same time to give the Gentiles cause to glorify God for his mercy. As Scripture says, 'Therefore I will praise thee among the Gentiles and sing hymns to thy name'; and again, 'Gentiles, make

King James Version

Rejoice, ye Gentiles, with his people. 11And
again, Praise the Lord, all ye Gentiles; and laud
him, all ye people. 12 And again, Esaias saith,
There shall be a root of Jesse, and he that shall
rise to reign over the Gentiles; in him shall the
Gentiles trust. 13 Now the God of hope fill you
with all joy and peace in believing, that ye may
abound in hope, through the power of the Holy
Ghost. 14And I myself also am persuaded of
you, my brethren, that ye also are full of goodness, filled with all knowledge, able also to admonish one another. 15 Nevertheless, brethren, I
have written the more boldly unto you in some
sort, as putting you in mind, because of the
grace that is given to me of God, 16 That I
should be the minister of Jesus Christ to the
Gentiles, ministering the gospel of God, that
the offering up of the Gentiles might be acceptable, being sanctified by the Holy Ghost.
17 I have therefore whereof I may glory through
Jesus Christ in those things which pertain to
God. 18 For I will not dare to speak of any of
those things which Christ hath not wrought by

Living Bible

Gentiles, along with his people the Jews."

11 And yet again, "Praise the Lord, O you Gentiles, let everyone praise him."

12 And the prophet Isaiah said, "There shall be an Heir in the house of Jesse, and he will be King over the Gentiles; they will pin their hopes on him alone."

13 So I pray for you Gentiles that God who gives you hope will keep you happy and full of peace as you believe in him. I pray that God will help you overflow with hope in him through the Holy Spirit's power within you.

14 I know that you are wise and good, my
brothers, and that you know these things so well
that you are able to teach others all about them.
15, 16 But even so I have been bold enough to
emphasize some of these points, knowing that
all you need is this reminder from me; for I
am, by God's grace, a special messenger from
Jesus Christ to you Gentiles, bringing you the
Gospel and offering you up as a fragrant sacrifice to God; for you have been made pure and
pleasing to him by the Holy Spirit. 17 So it is
right for me to be a little proud of all Christ
Jesus has done through me. 18 I dare not judge
how effectively he has used others, but I know
this: he has used me to win the Gentiles to

Today's English Version

"Rejoice, Gentiles, with God's chosen people!"

11And again,

"Praise the Lord, all Gentiles;
praise him, all peoples!"

12And again, Isaiah says,

"A descendant of Jesse will come;
he will be raised to rule the Gentiles,
and they will put their hope in him."

13 May God, the source of hope, fill you with all joy and peace by means of your faith in him, so that your hope will continue to grow by the power of the Holy Spirit.

Paul's reason for writing so boldly

14 My brothers: I myself feel sure that you
are full of goodness, that you are filled with all
knowledge and are able to teach one another.
15 But in this letter I have been quite bold about
certain subjects of which I have reminded you. I
have been bold because of the privilege God has
given me 16 of being a servant of Christ Jesus to
work for the Gentiles. I serve like a priest in
preaching the Good News from God, in order
that the Gentiles may be an offering acceptable
to God, dedicated to him by the Holy Spirit.
17 In union with Christ Jesus, then, I can be
proud of my service for God. 18 I will be bold
and speak only of what Christ has done through

New International Version

"Rejoice,[q] Gentiles, with his people."

11And again,

"Praise the Lord, all you Gentiles,
and sing praises to him, all you peoples."[r]

12And again, Isaiah says,

"The root of Jesse will spring up,
one who will arise to rule over the nations;
the Gentiles will hope in him."[s]

13 May the God of hope fill you with great joy and peace as you trust in him, so that you may overflow with hope by the power of the Holy Spirit.

Paul the minister to the Gentiles

14 I myself am convinced, my brothers, that
you yourselves are full of goodness, complete in
knowledge and competent to instruct one another. 15 I have written you quite boldly on some
points, as if to remind you of them again, because of the grace God gave me 16 to be a minister of Christ Jesus to the Gentiles with the
priestly duty of proclaiming the gospel of God,
so that the Gentiles might become an offering
acceptable to God, sanctified by the Holy Spirit.
17 Therefore, I glory in Christ Jesus in my
service to God. 18 I will not venture to speak of
anything except what Christ has accomplished

[q] Deut. 32:43. [r] Psalm 117:1. [s] Isaiah 11:10.

Phillips Modern English

Rejoice, ye gentiles, with his people.

And yet again:

Praise the Lord, all ye gentiles;
And let all the peoples praise him.

And then Isaiah says:

There shall be the root of Jesse,
And he that ariseth to rule over the gentiles:
On him shall the gentiles hope.

May the God of hope fill you with all joy and peace in your faith, that by the power of the Holy Spirit, your whole life and outlook may be radiant with hope.

15.14 What I have tried to do

For myself I feel certain that you, my brothers, have real Christian character and experience, and that you are capable of keeping each other on the right road. Nevertheless I have in some places written to you with a greater frankness, to refresh your minds with truths that you already know. It is by virtue of the commission given to me by God that I am the minister of Christ to the gentiles. This makes it my priestly duty to tell them the gospel of God, and thus to present them as an offering which he can accept, because they are sanctified by the Holy Spirit. And I think I have something to be proud of through Jesus Christ in my work for God. I am not competent to speak of the work Christ has

Revised Standard Version

"Rejoice, O Gentiles, with his people";
11 and again,
"Praise the Lord, all Gentiles,
and let all the peoples praise him";
12 and further Isaiah says,
"The root of Jesse shall come,
he who rises to rule the Gentiles;
in him shall the Gentiles hope."
13 May the God of hope fill you with all joy and peace in believing, so that by the power of the Holy Spirit you may abound in hope.

14 I myself am satisfied about you, my brethren, that you yourselves are full of goodness, filled with all knowledge, and able to instruct one another. 15 But on some points I have written to you very boldly by way of reminder, because of the grace given me by God 16 to be a minister of Christ Jesus to the Gentiles in the priestly service of the gospel of God, so that the offering of the Gentiles may be acceptable, sanctified by the Holy Spirit. 17 In Christ Jesus, then, I have reason to be proud of my work for God. 18 For I will not venture to speak of anything except what Christ has wrought through me

Jerusalem Bible

pagans, with his people,[f] 11 and in a third place: *Let all the pagans praise the Lord, let all the peoples sing his praises.*[g] 12 Isaiah too has this to say: *The root of Jesse will appear, rising up to rule the pagans, and in him the pagans will put their hope.*[h]

13 May the God of hope bring you such joy and peace in your faith that the power of the Holy Spirit will remove all bounds to hope.

Epilogue

Paul's ministry

14 It is not because I have any doubts about you, my brothers; on the contrary I am quite certain that you are full of good intentions, perfectly well instructed and able to advise each other. 15 The reason why I have written to you, and put some things rather strongly, is to refresh your memories, since God has given me this special position. 16 He has appointed me as a priest of Jesus Christ, and I am to carry out my priestly duty by bringing the Good News from God to the pagans, and so make them acceptable as an offering, made holy by the Holy Spirit.

17 I think I have some reason to be proud of what I, in union with Christ Jesus, have been able to do for God. 18 What I am presuming to speak of, of course, is only what Christ him-

[f] Dt. 32:43 (LXX). [g] Ps. 117:1. [h] Is. 11:10; 11:1.

New English Bible

merry together with his own people'; and yet again, 'All Gentiles, praise the Lord; let all peoples praise him.' Once again, Isaiah says, 'There shall be the Scion of Jesse, the one raised up to govern the Gentiles; on him the Gentiles shall set their hope.' And may the God of hope fill you with all joy and peace by your faith in him, until, by the power of the Holy Spirit, you overflow with hope.

My friends, I have no doubt in my own mind that you yourselves are quite full of goodness and equipped with knowledge of every kind, well able to give advice to one another; nevertheless I have written to refresh your memory, and written somewhat boldly at times, in virtue of the gift I have from God. His grace has made me a minister of Christ Jesus to the Gentiles; my priestly service is the preaching of the gospel of God, and it falls to me to offer the Gentiles to him as[a] an acceptable sacrifice, consecrated by the Holy Spirit.

Thus in the fellowship of Christ Jesus I have ground for pride in the service of God. I will venture to speak of those things alone in which

[a] *Or* . . . of God, so that the worship which the Gentiles offer may be . . .

King James Version

me, to make the Gentiles obedient, by word and deed, 19 Through mighty signs and wonders, by the power of the Spirit of God; so that from Jerusalem, and round about unto Illyricum, I have fully preached the gospel of Christ. 20 Yea, so have I strived to preach the gospel, not where Christ was named, lest I should build upon another man's foundation: 21 But as it is written, To whom he was not spoken of, they shall see: and they that have not heard shall understand. 22 For which cause also I have been much hindered from coming to you. 23 But now having no more place in these parts, and having a great desire these many years to come unto you; 24 Whensoever I take my journey into Spain, I will come to you: for I trust to see you in my journey, and to be brought on my way thitherward by you, if first I be somewhat filled with your *company*. 25 But now I go unto Jerusalem to minister unto the saints. 26 For it hath pleased them of Macedonia and Achaia to make a certain contribution for the poor saints which are at Jerusalem. 27 It hath pleased them verily; and their debtors they are. For if the Gentiles have been made partakers of their spiritual

Living Bible

God. 19 I have won them by my message and by the good way I have lived before them, and by the miracles done through me as signs from God—all by the Holy Spirit's power. In this way I have preached the full [a] Gospel of Christ all the way from Jerusalem clear over into Illyricum.

20 But all the while my ambition has been to go still farther, preaching where the name of Christ has never yet been heard, rather than where a church has already been started by someone else. 21 I have been following the plan spoken of in the Scriptures where Isaiah says that those who have never heard the name of Christ before will see and understand. 22 In fact that is the very reason I have been so long in coming to visit you.

23 But now at last I am through with my work here, and I am ready to come after all these long years of waiting. 24 For I am planning to take a trip to Spain, and when I do, I will stop off there in Rome; and after we have had a good time together for a little while, you can send me on my way again.

25 But before I come, I must go down to Jerusalem to take a gift to the Jewish Christians there. 26 For you see, the Christians in Macedonia and Achaia have taken up an offering for those in Jerusalem who are going through such hard times. 27 They were very glad to do this, for they feel that they owe a real debt to the Jerusalem Christians. Why? Because the news about Christ came to these Gentiles from the church in Jerusalem. And since they received this wonderful spiritual gift of the Gospel from

[a] Or, "I have fully accomplished my Gospel ministry."

Today's English Version

me to lead the Gentiles to obey God, by means of words and deeds, 19 by the power of signs and miracles, and by the power of the Spirit. And so, in traveling all the way from Jerusalem to Illyricum, I have proclaimed fully the Good News about Christ. 20 My ambition has always been to proclaim the Good News in places where Christ has not been heard of, so as not to build on the foundation laid by someone else. 21 As the scripture says,

"Those who were not told about him will see,
and those who have not heard will understand."

Paul's plan to visit Rome

22 For this reason I have been prevented many times from coming to you. 23 But now that I have finished my work in these regions, and since I have been wanting for so many years to come to see you, 24 I hope to do so now. I would like to see you on my way to Spain, and be helped by you to go there, after I have enjoyed visiting you for a while. 25 Right now, however, I am going to Jerusalem in the service of God's people there. 26 For the churches in Macedonia and Greece have freely decided to give an offering to help the poor among God's people in Jerusalem. 27 They themselves decided to do it. But, as a matter of fact, they have an obligation to help those poor; the Jews shared their spiritual blessings with the Gentiles, and so the Gentiles

New International Version

through me in leading the Gentiles to obey God by what I have said and done—19 by the power of signs and miracles, through the power of the Spirit. So from Jerusalem all the way around to Illyricum, I have fully proclaimed the gospel of Christ. 20 It has always been my ambition to preach the gospel where Christ was not known, so that I would not be building on someone else's foundation. 21 Rather, as it is written:

"Those who were not told about him will see,
and those who have not heard will understand." [t]

22 This is why I have often been hindered from coming to you.

Paul's plan to visit Rome

23 But now that there is no more place for me to work in these regions, and since I have been longing for many years to see you, 24 I plan to do so when I go to Spain. I hope to visit you while passing through and to have you assist me on my journey there, after I have enjoyed your company for a while. 25 Now, however, I am on my way to Jerusalem in the service of the saints there. 26 For Macedonia and Achaia were pleased to make a contribution for the poor among the saints in Jerusalem. 27 They were pleased to do it, and indeed they owe it to them. For if the Gentiles have shared in the

[t] Isaiah 52:15.

Phillips Modern English

done through others, but I do know that through me he has secured the obedience of gentiles in word and deed, working by sign and miracle and all the power of the Holy Spirit. Thus I have been able to complete the preaching of the gospel of Christ from Jerusalem as far round as Illyricum. My constant ambition has been to preach the gospel where the name of Christ was previously unknown, and to avoid building on another man's foundation, as Scripture says:

They shall see, to whom no tidings of him came,
And they who have not heard shall understand.

15.22 My future plans

Perhaps this will explain why I have so frequently been prevented from coming to see you. But now, since my work in these places no longer needs my presence, and since for many years I have had a great desire to see you, I hope to visit you on my way to Spain. I hope to see you on my way through, and I hope also that you will speed me on my journey, after I have had the satisfaction of seeing you all. At the moment my next call is to Jerusalem, to look after the welfare of the Christians there. The churches in Macedonia and Achaia, you see, have thought it a good thing to make a contribution towards the poor Christians in Jerusalem. They have decided to do this, and indeed they owe it to them. For if the gentiles have had a share in the Jews' spiritual good things it is only

Revised Standard Version

to win obedience from the Gentiles, by word and
deed, 19 by the power of signs and wonders, by
the power of the Holy Spirit, so that from Jerusalem and as far round as Illyricum I have fully
preached the gospel of Christ, 20 thus making it
my ambition to preach the gospel, not where
Christ has already been named, lest I build on
another man's foundation, 21 but as it is written,
"They shall see who have never been told of him,
and they shall understand who have never heard of him."
22 This is the reason why I have so often been
hindered from coming to you. 23 But now, since
I no longer have any room for work in these
regions, and since I have longed for many years
to come to you, 24 I hope to see you in passing
as I go to Spain, and to be sped on my journey
there by you, once I have enjoyed your company for a little. 25 At present, however, I am
going to Jerusalem with aid for the saints. 26 For
Macedonia and Achaia have been pleased to
make some contribution for the poor among the
saints at Jerusalem; 27 they were pleased to do
it, and indeed they are in debt to them, for if
the Gentiles have come to share in their spiritual

Jerusalem Bible

self has done to win the allegiance of the pagans, using what I have said and done 19 by the
power of signs and wonders, by the power of the
Holy Spirit. Thus, all the way along, from Jerusalem to Illyricum,[i] I have preached Christ's
Good News to the utmost of my capacity. 20 I
have always, however, made it an unbroken rule
never to preach where Christ's name has already
been heard. The reason for that was that I had
no wish to build on other men's foundations;
21 on the contrary, my chief concern has been
to fulfill the text: *Those who have never been told about him will see him, and those who have never heard about him will understand.*[j]

Paul's plans

22 That is the reason why I have been kept
from visiting you so long, 23 though for many
years I have been longing to pay you a visit.
Now, however, having no more work to do here,
24 I hope to see you on my way to Spain and,
after enjoying a little of your company, to complete the rest of the journey with your good
wishes. 25 First, however, I must take a present
of money to the saints in Jerusalem, 26 since
Macedonia and Achaia have decided to send a
generous contribution to the poor among the
saints at Jerusalem. 27 A generous contribution
as it should be, since it is really repaying a debt:
the pagans who share the spiritual possessions

[i] The two extremes of Paul's missionary journeys.
[j] Is. 52:15.

New English Bible

I have been Christ's instrument to bring the Gentiles into his allegiance, by word and deed, by the force of miraculous signs and by the power of the Holy Spirit. As a result I have completed the preaching of the gospel of Christ from Jerusalem as far round as Illyricum. It is my ambition to bring the Gospel to places where the very name of Christ has not been heard, for I do not want to build on another man's foundation; but, as Scripture says,

'They who had no news of him shall see,
and they who never heard of him shall understand.'

That is why I have been prevented all this time from coming to you. But now I have no further scope in these parts, and I have been longing for many years to visit you on my way to Spain; for I hope to see you as I travel through, and to be sent there with your support after having enjoyed your company for a while. But at the moment I am on my way to Jerusalem, on an errand to God's people there. For Macedonia and Achaia have resolved to raise a common fund for the benefit of the poor among God's people at Jerusalem. They have resolved to do so, and indeed they are under an obligation to them. For if the Jewish Christians shared their spiritual treasures with the Gentiles, the Gentiles

King James Version

things, their duty is also to minister unto them in carnal things. 28 When therefore I have performed this, and have sealed to them this fruit, I will come by you into Spain. 29 And I am sure that, when I come unto you, I shall come in the fullness of the blessing of the gospel of Christ. 30 Now I beseech you, brethren, for the Lord Jesus Christ's sake, and for the love of the Spirit, that ye strive together with me in *your* prayers to God for me; 31 That I may be delivered from them that do not believe in Judea; and that my service which *I have* for Jerusalem may be accepted of the saints; 32 That I may come unto you with joy by the will of God, and may with you be refreshed. 33 Now the God of peace *be* with you all. Amen.

16 I commend unto you Phebe our sister, which is a servant of the church which is at Cenchrea: 2 That ye receive her in the Lord, as becometh saints, and that ye assist her in whatsoever business she hath need of you: for she hath been a succourer of many, and of myself also. 3 Greet Priscilla and Aquila, my helpers in Christ Jesus: 4 Who have for my life laid down their own necks: unto whom not only I give thanks, but also all the churches of the

Living Bible

there, they feel that the least they can do in return is to give some material aid.[b] 28 As soon as I have delivered this money and completed this good deed of theirs, I will come to see you on my way to Spain. 29 And I am sure that when I come the Lord will give me a great blessing for you.

30 Will you be my prayer partners? For the Lord Jesus Christ's sake, and because of your love for me—given to you by the Holy Spirit—pray much with me for my work. 31 Pray that I will be protected in Jerusalem from those who are not Christians. Pray also that the Christians there will be willing to accept the money I am bringing them. 32 Then I will be able to come to you with a happy heart by the will of God, and we can refresh each other.

33 And now may our God, who gives peace, be with you all. Amen.

16 Phoebe, a dear Christian woman from the town of Cenchreae, will be coming to see you soon. She has worked hard in the church there. Receive her as your sister in the Lord, giving her a warm Christian welcome. Help her in every way you can, for she has helped many in their needs, including me. 3 Tell Priscilla and Aquila "hello." They have been my fellow workers in the affairs of Christ Jesus. 4 In fact, they risked their lives for me; and I am not the only one who is thankful to them: so

[b] Literally, "For if the Gentiles have come to share in their spiritual blessings, they ought also to be of service to them in material blessings."

Today's English Version

ought to serve the Jews with their material blessings. 28 When I have finished this task, and have turned over to them the full amount of money that has been raised for them, I shall leave for Spain and visit you on my way there. 29 When I come to you, I know that I shall come with a full measure of the blessing of Christ.

30 I urge you, brothers, by our Lord Jesus Christ and by the love that the Spirit gives: join me in praying fervently to God for me. 31 Pray that I may be kept safe from the unbelievers in Judea, and that my service in Jerusalem may be acceptable to God's people there. 32 And so I will come to you full of joy, if it is God's will, and enjoy a refreshing visit with you. 33 May God, our source of peace, be with all of you. Amen.

Personal greetings

16 I recommend to you our sister Phoebe, who serves the church at Cenchreae. 2 Receive her in the Lord's name, as God's people should, and give her any help she may need from you; for she herself has been a good friend to many people and also to me.

3 I send greetings to Priscilla and Aquila, my fellow workers in the service of Christ Jesus, 4 who risked their lives for me. I am grateful to them—not only I, but all the Gentile churches as

New International Version

Jews' spiritual blessings, they owe it to the Jews to share with them their material blessings. 28 So after I have completed this task and have made sure that they have received this fruit, I will go to Spain and visit you on the way. 29 I know that when I come to you, I will come in the full measure of the blessing of Christ.

30 I urge you, brothers, by our Lord Jesus Christ and by the love of the Spirit, to join me in my struggle by praying to God for me. 31 Pray that I may be rescued from the unbelievers in Judea and that my service in Jerusalem may be acceptable to the saints there. 32 Then by God's will I can come to you with joy and together with you be refreshed. 33 The God of peace be with all. Amen.

Personal greetings

16 I commend to you our sister Phoebe, a servant[u] of the church in Cenchreae. 2 I ask you to receive her in the Lord in a way worthy of the saints and to give her any help she may need from you, for she has been a great help to many people, including me.

3 Greet Priscilla[v] and Aquila, my fellow workers in Christ Jesus. 4 They risked their lives for me. Not only I but all the churches of the

[u] Or *deaconess.* [v] Greek *Prisca.*

Phillips Modern English

fair that they should look after the Jews as far as the good things of this world are concerned.

When I have completed this task, then, and put this gift safely into their hands, I shall come to you *en route* for Spain. I feel sure that in this visit I shall bring with me the full blessing of Christ.

Now, my brothers, I am going to ask you, for the sake of our Lord Jesus Christ and for the love we bear each other in the Spirit, to stand behind me in earnest prayer to God on my behalf—that I may not fall into the hands of the unbelievers in Judaea, and that the Jerusalem Christians may welcome the gift I am taking to them. Then I shall come to you, in the purpose of God, with a happy heart, and may even enjoy with you a little holiday.

The God of peace be with you all, amen.

16.1 Personal greetings and messages

I want this letter to introduce to you Phoebe, our sister, a deaconess of the church at Cenchrea. Please give her a Christian welcome, and any assistance with her work that she may need. She has herself been of great assistance to many, not excluding myself.

Give my good wishes to Prisca and Aquila. They have not only worked with me for Christ Jesus, but have risked their necks to save my life. Not only I, but all the gentile churches, owe

Revised Standard Version

blessings, they ought also to be of service to them
in material blessings. 28 When therefore I have
completed this, and have delivered to them what
has been raised,[x] I shall go on by way of you to
Spain; 29 and I know that when I come to you
I shall come in the fulness of the blessing[y] of
Christ.
30 I appeal to you, brethren, by our Lord
Jesus Christ and by the love of the Spirit, to
strive together with me in your prayers to God
on my behalf, 31 that I may be delivered from
the unbelievers in Judea, and that my service
for Jerusalem may be acceptable to the saints,
32 so that by God's will I may come to you with
joy and be refreshed in your company. 33 The
God of peace be with you all. Amen.

16 I commend to you our sister Phoebe, a
deaconess of the church at Cenchreae,
2 that you may receive her in the Lord as befits
the saints, and help her in whatever she may
require from you, for she has been a helper of
many and of myself as well.
3 Greet Prisca and Aquila, my fellow workers
in Christ Jesus, 4 who risked their necks for my
life, to whom not only I but also all the churches

[x] Greek *sealed to them this fruit.* [y] Other ancient authorities insert *of the gospel.*

Jerusalem Bible

of these poor people have a duty to help them
with temporal possessions. 28 So when I have
done this and officially handed over what has
been raised, I shall set out for Spain and visit
you on the way. 29 I know that when I reach
you I shall arrive with rich blessings from
Christ.
30 But I beg you, brothers, by our Lord Jesus
Christ and the love of the Spirit, to help me
through my dangers by praying to God for me.
31 Pray that I may escape the unbelievers in
Judaea, and that the aid I carry to Jerusalem
may be accepted by the saints. 32 Then, if God
wills, I shall be feeling very happy when I come
to enjoy a period of rest among you. 33 May the
God of peace be with you all! Amen.

Greetings and good wishes

16 I commend to you our sister Phoebe,[k] a
deaconness of the church at Cenchreae.
2 Give her, in union with the Lord, a welcome
worthy of saints, and help her with anything she
needs: she has looked after a great many people,
myself included.
3 My greetings to Prisca and Aquila, my fellow workers in Christ Jesus, 4 who risked death
to save my life[l]: I am not the only one to owe
them a debt of gratitude, all the churches among

[k] Probably the bearer of the letter. [l] Probably in Ephesus, either at the time of the riot described in Ac. 19 or during Paul's imprisonment there.

New English Bible

have a clear duty to contribute to their material needs. So when I have finished this business and delivered the proceeds under my own seal, I shall set out for Spain by way of your city, and I am sure that when I arrive I shall come to you with a full measure of the blessing of Christ.

I implore you by our Lord Jesus Christ and by the love that the Spirit inspires, be my allies in the fight; pray to God for me that I may be saved from unbelievers in Judaea and that my errand to Jerusalem may find acceptance with God's people, so that by his will I may come to you in a happy frame of mind and enjoy a time of rest with you. The God of peace be with you all. Amen.[b]

16 I commend to you Phoebe, a fellow-Christian who holds office in the congregation at Cenchreae. Give her, in the fellowship of the Lord, a welcome worthy of God's people, and stand by her in any business in which she may need your help, for she has herself been a good friend to many, including myself.

Give my greetings to Prisca and Aquila, my fellow-workers in Christ Jesus. They risked their necks to save my life, and not I alone but all

[b] *See p. 1175, note g.*

King James Version

Gentiles. 5 Likewise *greet* the church that is in
their house. Salute my well beloved Epenetus,
who is the firstfruits of Achaia unto Christ.
6 Greet Mary, who bestowed much labour on us.
7 Salute Andronicus and Junia, my kinsmen,
and my fellow prisoners, who are of note among
the apostles, who also were in Christ before me.
8 Greet Amplias, my beloved in the Lord. 9 Salute Urbane, our helper in Christ, and Stachys
my beloved. 10 Salute Apelles approved in
Christ. Salute them which are of Aristobulus'
household. 11 Salute Herodion my kinsman.
Greet them that be of the *household* of Narcissus, which are in the Lord. 12 Salute Tryphena
and Tryphosa, who labour in the Lord. Salute
the beloved Persis, which laboured much in the
Lord. 13 Salute Rufus chosen in the Lord, and
his mother and mine. 14 Salute Asyncritus,
Phlegon, Hermas, Patrobas, Hermes, and the
brethren which are with them. 15 Salute Philologus, and Julia, Nereus, and his sister, and
Olympas, and all the saints which are with
them. 16 Salute one another with a holy kiss. The
churches of Christ salute you. 17 Now I beseech you, brethren, mark them which cause

Living Bible

are all the Gentile churches.
5 Please give my greetings to all those who
meet to worship in their home. Greet my good
friend Epaenetus. He was the very first person
to become a Christian in Asia. 6 Remember me
to Mary, too, who has worked so hard to help
us. 7 Then there are Andronicus and Junias, my
relatives who were in prison with me. They are
respected by the apostles, and became Christians
before I did. Please give them my greetings.
8 Say "hello" to Ampliatus, whom I love as one
of God's own children, 9 and Urbanus, our fellow worker, and beloved Stachys.
10 Then there is Apelles, a good man whom
the Lord approves; greet him for me. And give
my best regards to those working at the house
of Aristobulus. 11 Remember me to Herodion
my relative. Remember me to the Christian
slaves over at Narcissus House. 12 Say "hello"
to Tryphaena and Tryphosa, the Lord's workers,
and to dear Persis, who has worked so hard for
the Lord. 13 Greet Rufus for me, whom the Lord
picked out to be his very own; and also his dear
mother who has been such a mother to me.
14 And please give my greetings to Asyncritus,
Phlegon, Hermes, Patrobas, Hermas, and the
other brothers who are with them. 15 Give my
love to Philologus, Julia, Nereus and his sister,
and to Olympas, and all the Christians who are
with them. 16 Shake hands warmly with each
other. All the churches here send you their
greetings.
17 And now there is one more thing to say
before I end this letter. Stay away from those

Today's English Version

well. 5 Greetings also to the church that meets
in their house.
Greetings to my dear friend Epaenetus, who
was the first man in the province of Asia to believe in Christ. 6 Greetings to Mary, who has
worked so hard for you. 7 Greetings to Andronicus and Junias, fellow Jews who were in prison
with me; they are well known among the apostles,
and they became Christians before I did.
8 My greetings to Ampliatus, my dear friend
in the fellowship of the Lord. 9 Greetings to Urbanus, our fellow worker in Christ's service, and
to Stachys, my dear friend. 10 Greetings to Apelles, whose loyalty to Christ has been proved.
Greetings to those who belong to the family of
Aristobulus. 11 Greetings to Herodion, a fellow
Jew, and to the Christian brothers in the family
of Narcissus.
12 My greetings to Tryphaena and Tryphosa,
who work in the Lord's service, and to my dear
friend Persis, who has done so much work for
the Lord. 13 I send greetings to Rufus, that outstanding worker in the Lord's service, and to his
mother, who has always treated me like a son.
14 My greetings to Asyncritus, Phlegon, Hermes,
Patrobas, Hermas, and all the other Christian
brothers with them. 15 Greetings to Philologus
and Julia, to Nereus and his sister, to Olympas
and to all of God's people who are with them.
16 Greet one another with a brotherly kiss. All
the churches of Christ send you their greetings.

Final instructions

17 I urge you, my brothers: watch out for
those who cause divisions and upset people's

New International Version

Gentiles are grateful to them.
5 Greet also the church that meets at their house.
Greet my dear friend Epaenetus, who was the
first convert to Christ in the province of
Asia.
6 Greet Mary, who worked very hard for you.
7 Greet Andronicus and Junias, my relatives who
have been in prison with me. They are outstanding among the apostles, and they were
in Christ before I was.
8 Greet Ampliatus, whom I love in the Lord.
9 Greet Urbanus, our fellow worker in Christ,
and my dear friend Stachys.
10 Greet Apelles, tested and approved in Christ.
Greet those who belong to the household of
Aristobulus.
11 Greet Herodion, my relative.
Greet those in the household of Narcissus who
are in the Lord.
12 Greet Tryphaena and Tryphosa, those women
who work hard in the Lord.
Greet my dear friend Persis, another woman
who has worked very hard in the Lord.
13 Greet Rufus, chosen in the Lord, and his
mother, who has been a mother to me, too.
14 Greet Asyncritus, Phlegon, Hermes, Patrobas,
Hermas and the brothers with them.
15 Greet Philologus, Julia, Nereus and his sister,
and Olympas and all the saints with them.
16 Greet one another with a holy kiss.
All the churches of Christ send greetings.
17 I urge you, brothers, to watch out for those
who cause divisions and put obstacles in your

Phillips Modern English

them a great debt. Give my love to the church that meets in their house.

My good wishes also to dear Epaenetus, Asia's first man to be won for Christ, and of course greet Mary who has worked so hard for you. A warm greeting, too, for Andronicus and Junias my fellow-countrymen and fellow-prisoners; they are outstanding men among the messengers and were Christians before I was.

Another warm greeting for Ampliatus, dear Christian that he is, and also for Urbanus, who has worked with me for Christ, and dear Stachys, too.

More greetings from me, please, to:
Apelles, the man who has proved his faith,
The household of Aristobulus,
Herodion, my fellow-countryman,
Narcissus' household, who are Christians.

Remember me to Tryphena and Tryphosa, who work so hard for the Lord, and to my dear Persis who has also done great work for him.

My greetings also to Rufus—that splendid Christian, and greet his mother, who has been a mother to me too. Greetings to Asyncritus, Phlegon, Hermes, Patrobas, Hermas and their Christian group: also to Philologus and Julia, Nereus and his sister, and Olympas and the Christians who are with them.

Give each other a hearty handshake all round in Christian love. The greetings of all the churches come to you with this letter.

16.17 A final warning

And now I implore you, my brothers, to keep a watchful eye on those who cause trouble and

Revised Standard Version

of the Gentiles give thanks; 5 greet also the
church in their house. Greet my beloved Epaenetus, who was the first convert in Asia for
Christ. 6 Greet Mary, who has worked hard
among you. 7 Greet Andronicus and Junias, my
kinsmen and my fellow prisoners; they are men
of note among the apostles, and they were in
Christ before me. 8 Greet Ampliatus, my beloved
in the Lord. 9 Greet Urbanus, our fellow worker
in Christ, and my beloved Stachys. 10 Greet
Apelles, who is approved in Christ. Greet those
who belong to the family of Aristobulus.
11 Greet my kinsman Herodion. Greet those in
the Lord who belong to the family of Narcissus.
12 Greet those workers in the Lord, Tryphaena
and Tryphosa. Greet the beloved Persis, who has
worked hard in the Lord. 13 Greet Rufus, eminent in the Lord, also his mother and mine.
14 Greet Asyncritus, Phlegon, Hermes, Patrobas,
Hermas, and the brethren who are with them.
15 Greet Philologus, Julia, Nereus and his sister,
and Olympas, and all the saints who are with
them. 16 Greet one another with a holy kiss. All
the churches of Christ greet you.

17 I appeal to you, brethren, to take note of
those who create dissensions and difficulties, in

Jerusalem Bible

the pagans do as well. 5 My greetings also to
the church that meets at their house.
6 Greetings to my friend Epaenetus, the first
of Asia's gifts to Christ; greetings to Mary who
worked so hard for you; 7 to those outstanding
apostles Andronicus and Junias, my compatriots
and fellow prisoners who became Christians before me; 8 to Ampliatus, my friend in the Lord;
9 to Urban, my fellow worker in Christ; to my
friend Stachys; 10 to Apelles who has gone
through so much for Christ; to everyone who
belongs to the houschold of Aristobulus; 11 to
my compatriot Herodion; to those in the household of Narcissus who belong to the Lord; 12 to
Tryphaena and Tryphosa, who work hard for the
Lord; to my friend Persis who has done so
much for the Lord; 13 to Rufus, a chosen servant of the Lord, and to his mother who has
been a mother to me too. 14 Greetings to Asyncritus, Phlegon, Hermes, Patrobas, Hermas, and
all the brothers who are with them; 15 to Philologus and Julia, Nereus and his sister, and
Olympas and all the saints who are with them.
16 Greet each other with a holy kiss. All the
churches of Christ send greetings.

A warning and first postscript

17 I implore you, brothers, be on your guard
against anybody who encourages trouble or puts

New English Bible

the gentile congregations are grateful to them. Greet also the congregation at their house.

Give my greetings to my dear friend Epaenetus, the first convert to Christ in Asia, and to Mary, who toiled hard for you. Greet Andronicus and Junias[a] my fellow-countrymen and comrades in captivity. They are eminent among the apostles, and they were Christians before I was.

Greetings to Ampliatus, my dear friend in the fellowship of the Lord, to Urban my comrade in Christ, and to my dear Stachys. My greetings to Apelles, well proved in Christ's service, to the household of Aristobulus, and my countryman Herodion, and to those of the household of Narcissus who are in the Lord's fellowship. Greet Tryphaena and Tryphosa, who toil in the Lord's service, and dear Persis who has toiled in his service so long. Give my greetings to Rufus, an outstanding follower of the Lord, and to his mother, whom I call mother too. Greet Asyncritus, Phlegon, Hermes, Patrobas, Hermas, and all friends in their company. Greet Philologus and Julia,[b] Nereus and his sister, and Olympas, and all God's people associated with them.

Greet one another with the kiss of peace. All Christ's congregations send you their greetings.

I implore you, my friends, keep your eye on those who stir up quarrels and lead others astray,

[a] *Or* Junia; *some witnesses read* Julia, *or* Julias.
[b] *Or* Julias; *some witnesses read* Junia, *or* Junias.

King James Version

divisions and offences contrary to the doctrine
which ye have learned; and avoid them. 18 For
they that are such serve not our Lord Jesus
Christ, but their own belly; and by good words
and fair speeches deceive the hearts of the simple. 19 For your obedience is come abroad unto
all *men*. I am glad therefore on your behalf: but
yet I would have you wise unto that which is
good, and simple concerning evil. 20 And the
God of peace shall bruise Satan under your feet
shortly. The grace of our Lord Jesus Christ *be*
with you. Amen. 21 Timotheus my workfellow,
and Lucius, and Jason, and Sosipater, my kinsmen, salute you. 22 I Tertius, who wrote *this*
epistle, salute you in the Lord. 23 Gaius mine
host, and of the whole church, saluteth you.
Erastus the chamberlain of the city saluteth you,
and Quartus a brother. 24 The grace of our Lord
Jesus Christ *be* with you all. Amen. 25 Now to
him that is of power to stablish you according
to my gospel, and the preaching of Jesus Christ,
according to the revelation of the mystery, which
was kept secret since the world began, 26 But
now is made manifest, and by the Scriptures of
the prophets, according to the commandment of
the everlasting God, made known to all nations for the obedience of faith: 27 To God only
wise, *be* glory through Jesus Christ for ever.
Amen.

Written to the Romans from Corinthus, *and sent* by Phebe servant of the church at Cenchrea.

Living Bible

who cause divisions and are upsetting people's
faith, teaching things about Christ that are contrary to what you have been taught. 18 Such
teachers are not working for our Lord Jesus, but
only want gain for themselves. They are good
speakers, and simple-minded people are often
fooled by them. 19 But everyone knows that you
stand loyal and true. This makes me very happy.
I want you always to remain very clear about
what is right, and to stay innocent of any wrong.
20 The God of peace will soon crush Satan under your feet. The blessings from our Lord Jesus
Christ be upon you.

21 Timothy my fellow-worker, and Lucius and
Jason and Sosipater, my relatives, send you their
good wishes. 22 I, Tertius, the one who is writing
this letter for Paul, send my greetings too, as a
Christian brother. 23 Gaius says to say "hello" to
you for him. I am his guest, and the church
meets here in his home. Erastus, the city treasurer, sends you his greetings and so does Quartus, a Christian brother. 24 Good-bye. May the
grace of our Lord Jesus Christ be with you all.

25, 26, 27 I commit you to God, who is able
to make you strong and steady in the Lord, just
as the Gospel says, and just as I have told you.
This is God's plan of salvation for you Gentiles,
kept secret from the beginning of time. But now
as the prophets foretold and as God commands,
this message is being preached everywhere, so
that people all around the world will have faith
in Christ and obey him. To God, who alone is
wise, be the glory forever through Jesus Christ
our Lord. Amen.

Sincerely,
Paul

Today's English Version

faith, who go against the teaching which you
have received; keep away from them. 18 For
those who do such things are not serving Christ
our Lord, but their own appetites. By their fine
words and flattering speech they deceive the
minds of innocent people. 19 Everyone has heard
of your loyalty to the gospel, and for this reason
I am happy about you. I want you to be wise
about what is good, but innocent in what is
evil. 20 And God, our source of peace, will soon
crush Satan under your feet.

The grace of our Lord Jesus be with you.

21 Timothy, my fellow worker, sends you his
greetings; and so do Lucius, Jason, and Sosipater,
fellow Jews.

22 I, Tertius, the writer of this letter, send
you Christian greetings.

23 My host Gaius, in whose house the church
meets, sends you his greetings; Erastus, the city
treasurer, and our brother Quartus, send you
their greetings.

[24 The grace of our Lord Jesus Christ be with
you all. Amen.]

Concluding prayer of praise

25 Let us give glory to God! He is able to
make you stand firm in your faith, according to
the Good News I preach, the message about Jesus Christ, and according to the revelation of the
secret truth which was hidden for long ages in
the past. 26 Now, however, that truth has been
brought out into the open through the writings
of the prophets; and by the command of the
eternal God it is made known to all nations, so
that all may believe and obey.

27 To the only God, who alone is all-wise, be
the glory through Jesus Christ forever! Amen.

New International Version

way, contrary to the teaching you have learned.
Keep away from them. 18 For such people are
not serving our Lord Christ, but their own appetites. By smooth talk and flattery they deceive
the minds of naive people. 19 Everyone has heard
about your obedience, so I am full of joy over
you; but I want you to be wise about what is
good, and innocent about what is evil.

20 The God of peace will soon crush Satan
under your feet.

The grace of our Lord Jesus be with you.

21 Timothy, my fellow worker, sends his
greetings to you, as do Lucius, Jason and Sosipater, my relatives.

22 I, Tertius, who wrote down this letter, greet
you in the Lord.

23 Gaius, whose hospitality I and the whole
church here enjoy, sends you his greetings.

Erastus, who is the city's director of public
works, and our brother Quartus send you their
greetings.[w]

25 Now to him who is able to establish you by
my gospel and the proclamation of Jesus Christ,
according to the revelation of the mystery hidden for long ages past, 26 but now revealed and
made known through the prophetic writings by
the command of the eternal God, so that all nations might believe and obey him—27 to the only
wise God be glory forever through Jesus Christ!
Amen.

[w] Some MSS add verse 24: *May the grace of our Lord Jesus Christ be with all of you. Amen.*

Phillips Modern English

make difficulties among you, in plain opposition to the teaching you have been given, and steer clear of them. Such men do not really serve our Lord Christ at all but their own ambitions. Yet with their plausible and attractive arguments they deceive those who are too simple-hearted to see through them.

Your loyalty to the gospel is known everywhere, and that gives me great joy. I want to see you experts in good, and not even beginners in evil. It will not be long before the God of peace will crush Satan under your feet. May the grace of our Lord Jesus be with you.

Timothy, who works with me, sends his greetings, and so do Lucius and Jason and Sosipater my fellow-countrymen. I, Tertius, who have been taking down this epistle from Paul's dictation, send you my Christian greetings too. Gaius, my host (and the host as a matter of fact of the whole church here), sends you his greetings. Erastus, our city treasurer, and Quartus, another Christian brother, send greetings too.

Now to him who is able to set you firmly on your feet—according to my gospel, according to the preaching of Jesus Christ himself, and in accordance with the disclosing of that secret purpose which, after long ages of silence, has now been made known (in full agreement with the writings of the prophets long ago), by the command of the everlasting God to all the gentiles, that they might turn to him in the obedience of faith—to him, I say, the God who alone is wise, be glory for ever through Jesus Christ, amen!

Revised Standard Version

opposition to the doctrine which you have been taught; avoid them. 18 For such persons do not serve our Lord Christ, but their own appetites,[z] and by fair and flattering words they deceive the hearts of the simple-minded. 19 For while your obedience is known to all, so that I rejoice over you, I would have you wise as to what is good and guileless as to what is evil; 20 then the God of peace will soon crush Satan under your feet. The grace of our Lord Jesus Christ be with you.[a]

21 Timothy, my fellow worker, greets you; so do Lucius and Jason and Sosipater, my kinsmen.

22 I Tertius, the writer of this letter, greet you in the Lord.

23 Gaius, who is host to me and to the whole church, greets you. Erastus, the city treasurer, and our brother Quartus, greet you.[b]

25 Now to him who is able to strengthen you according to my gospel and the preaching of Jesus Christ, according to the revelation of the mystery which was kept secret for long ages 26 but is now disclosed and through the prophetic writings is made known to all nations, according to the command of the eternal God, to bring about the obedience of faith—27 to the only wise God be glory for evermore through Jesus Christ! Amen.

[z] Greek *their own belly* (Phil 3.19). [a] Other ancient authorities omit this sentence. [b] Other ancient authorities insert verse 24, *The grace of our Lord Jesus Christ be with you all. Amen.*

Jerusalem Bible

difficulties in the way of the doctrine you have been taught. Avoid them. 18 People like that are not slaves of Jesus Christ, they are slaves of their own appetites, confusing the simple-minded with their pious and persuasive arguments. 19 Your fidelity to Christ, anyway, is famous everywhere, and that makes me very happy about you. I only hope that you are also wise in what is good and innocent of what is bad. 20 The God of peace will soon crush Satan beneath your feet. The grace of our Lord Jesus Christ be with you.

Last greetings and second postscript

21 Timothy, who is working with me, sends his greetings; so do my compatriots, Jason and Sosipater. 22 I, Tertius, who wrote out this letter, greet you in the Lord. 23 Greetings from Gaius, who is entertaining me and from the whole church that meets in his house. Erastus, the city treasurer, sends his greetings; so does our brother Quartus.

Doxology

25 Glory to him who is able to give you the strength to live according to the Good News I preach, and in which I proclaim Jesus Christ, the revelation of a mystery kept secret for endless ages, 26 but now so clear that it must be broadcast to pagans everywhere to bring them to the obedience of faith. This is only what scripture has predicted, and it is all part of the way the eternal God wants things to be. 27 He alone is wisdom; give glory therefore to him through Jesus Christ for ever and ever. Amen.

New English Bible

contrary to the teaching you received. Avoid them, for such people are servants not of Christ our Lord but of their own appetites, and they seduce the minds of innocent people with smooth and specious words. The fame of your obedience has spread everywhere. This makes me happy about you; yet I should wish you to be experts in goodness but simpletons in evil; and the God of peace will soon crush Satan beneath your feet. The grace of our Lord Jesus be with you![c]

Greetings to you from my colleague Timothy, and from Lucius, Jason, and Sosipater my fellow-countrymen. (I Tertius, who took this letter down, add my Christian greetings.) Greetings also from Gaius, my host and host of the whole congregation, and from Erastus, treasurer of this city, and our brother Quartus.[d]

To him who has power to make your standing sure, according to the Gospel I brought you and the proclamation of Jesus Christ, according to the revelation of that divine secret kept in silence for long ages but now disclosed, and through prophetic scriptures by eternal God's command made known to all nations, to bring them to faith and obedience—to God who alone is wise, through Jesus Christ,[e] be glory for endless ages! Amen.[f] [g]

[c] *The words* The grace . . . with you *are omitted at this point in some witnesses; in some, these or similar words are given as verse 24, and in some others after verse 27 (see note on verse 23).* [d] *Some witnesses add* (24) The grace of our Lord Jesus Christ be with you all! Amen. [e] Some witnesses insert to whom [f] *Here some witnesses add* The grace of our Lord Jesus Christ be with you! [g] Some witnesses *place verses 25-27 at the end of chapter 14, one other places them at the end of chapter 15, and others omit them altogether.*

King James Version

THE FIRST EPISTLE OF PAUL THE APOSTLE TO THE CORINTHIANS

1 Paul, called *to be* an apostle of Jesus Christ through the will of God, and Sosthenes *our* brother, 2 Unto the church of God which is at Corinth, to them that are sanctified in Christ Jesus, called *to be* saints, with all that in every place call upon the name of Jesus Christ our Lord, both theirs and ours: 3 Grace *be* unto you, and peace, from God our Father, and *from*

Living Bible

1 CORINTHIANS

1 From: Paul, chosen by God to be Jesus Christ's missionary, and from brother Sosthenes.

2 *To:* The Christians in Corinth, invited by God to be his people and made acceptable[a] to him by Christ Jesus. *And to:* All Christians everywhere—whoever calls upon the name of Jesus Christ, our Lord and theirs.

3 May God our Father and the Lord Jesus Christ give you all of his blessings, and great peace of heart and mind.

[*a*] Or, "chosen by Christ Jesus." Literally, "sanctified in Christ Jesus."

Today's English Version

PAUL'S FIRST LETTER TO THE CORINTHIANS

1 From Paul, who by the will of God was called to be an apostle of Christ Jesus, and from our brother Sosthenes—

2 To the church of God which is in Corinth, to all who are called to be God's holy people, who belong to him in union with Christ Jesus, together with all people everywhere who call on the name of our Lord Jesus Christ, their Lord and ours:

3 May God our Father and the Lord Jesus Christ give you grace and peace.

New International Version

1 CORINTHIANS

1 Paul, called to be an apostle of Christ Jesus by the will of God, and our brother Sosthenes,

2 To the church of God in Corinth, to those sanctified in Christ Jesus and called to be holy, together with all those everywhere who call on the name of our Lord Jesus Christ—their Lord and ours:

3 Grace and peace to you from God our Father and the Lord Jesus Christ.

Phillips Modern English

THE FIRST LETTER TO THE CHRISTIANS AT CORINTH

Paul, commissioned by the will of God as a messenger of Christ Jesus, and Sosthenes, a Christian brother, to the church of God at Corinth—to those whom Christ Jesus has made holy, who are called to be God's men and women, to all true believers in Jesus Christ, their Lord and ours—grace and peace be to you from God the Father and the Lord, Jesus Christ!

Revised Standard Version

THE FIRST LETTER OF PAUL TO THE CORINTHIANS

1 Paul, called by the will of God to be an apostle of Christ Jesus, and our brother Sosthenes,

2 To the church of God which is at Corinth, to those sanctified in Christ Jesus, called to be saints together with all those who in every place call on the name of our Lord Jesus Christ, both their Lord and ours:

3 Grace to you and peace from God our Father and the Lord Jesus Christ.

Jerusalem Bible

THE FIRST LETTER OF PAUL TO THE CHURCH AT CORINTH 1 CORINTHIANS

Introduction

Address and greetings. Thanksgiving

1 I, Paul, appointed by God to be an apostle, together with brother Sosthenes, send greetings 2 to the church of God in Corinth, to the holy people of Jesus Christ, who are called to take their place among all the saints everywhere who pray to our Lord Jesus Christ; for he is their Lord no less than ours. 3 May God our Father and the Lord Jesus Christ send you grace and peace.

New English Bible

THE FIRST LETTER OF PAUL TO THE CORINTHIANS

Unity and order in the church

1 From Paul, apostle of Jesus Christ at God's call and by God's will, together with our colleague Sosthenes, to the congregation of God's people at Corinth, dedicated to him in Christ Jesus, claimed by him as his own, along with all men everywhere who invoke the name of our Lord Jesus Christ—their Lord as well as ours.

Grace and peace to you from God our Father and the Lord Jesus Christ.

King James Version

the Lord Jesus Christ. 4 I thank my God always on your behalf, for the grace of God which is given you by Jesus Christ; 5 That in every thing ye are enriched by him, in all utterance, and *in* all knowledge; 6 Even as the testimony of Christ was confirmed in you: 7 So that ye come behind in no gift; waiting for the coming of our Lord Jesus Christ: 8 Who shall also confirm you unto the end, *that ye may be* blameless in the day of our Lord Jesus Christ. 9 God *is* faithful, by whom ye were called unto the fellowship of his Son Jesus Christ our Lord. 10 Now I beseech you, brethren, by the name of our Lord Jesus Christ, that ye all speak the same thing, and *that* there be no divisions among you; but *that* ye be perfectly joined together in the same mind and in the same judgment. 11 For it hath been declared unto me of you, my brethren, by them *which are of the house* of Chloe, that there are contentions among you. 12 Now this I say, that every one of you saith, I am of Paul; and I of

Living Bible

4 I can never stop thanking God for all the wonderful gifts he has given you, now that you are Christ's: 5 he has enriched your whole life. He has helped you speak out for him and has given you a full understanding of the truth; 6 what I told you Christ could do for you has happened! 7 Now you have every grace and blessing; every spiritual gift and power for doing his will are yours during this time of waiting for the return of our Lord Jesus Christ. 8 And he guarantees right up to the end that you will be counted free from all sin and guilt on that day when he returns. 9 God will surely do this for you, for he always does just what he says, and he is the one who invited you into this wonderful friendship with his Son, even Christ our Lord.

10 But, dear brothers, I beg you in the name of the Lord Jesus Christ to stop arguing among yourselves. Let there be real harmony so that there won't be splits in the church. I plead with you to be of one mind, united in thought and purpose. 11 For some of those who live at Chloe's house have told me of your arguments and quarrels, dear brothers. 12 Some of you are saying, "I am a follower of Paul"; and others

Today's English Version

Blessings in Christ

4 I always give thanks to my God for you, because of the grace he has given you through Christ Jesus. 5 For in union with Christ you have become rich in all things, including all speech and all knowledge. 6 The message about Christ has become so firmly fixed in you, 7 that you have not failed to receive a single blessing, as you wait for our Lord Jesus Christ to be revealed. 8 He will also keep you firm to the end, so that you will be found without fault in the Day of our Lord Jesus Christ. 9 God is to be trusted, the God who called you to have fellowship with his Son Jesus Christ, our Lord.

Divisions in the church

10 I appeal to you, brothers, by the authority of our Lord Jesus Christ: agree, all of you, in what you say, so that there will be no divisions among you. Be completely united, with only one thought and one purpose. 11 For some people from Chloe's family have told me quite plainly, my brothers, that there are quarrels among you. 12 Let me put it this way: each one of you says something different. One says, "I am with Paul";

New International Version

Thankgiving

4 I always thank God for you because of his grace given you in Christ Jesus. 5 For in him you have been enriched in every way—in all your speaking and in all your knowledge—6 because our testimony about Christ was confirmed in you. 7 Therefore you do not lack any spiritual gift as you eagerly wait for our Lord Jesus Christ to be revealed. 8 He will keep you strong to the end, so that you will be blameless on the day of our Lord Jesus Christ. 9 God, who has called you into fellowship with his Son Jesus Christ our Lord, is faithful.

Divisions in the church

10 I appeal to you, brothers, in the name of our Lord Jesus Christ, that all of you agree with one another so that there may be no divisions among you and that you may be perfectly united in mind and thought. 11 My brothers, some from Chloe's household have informed me that there are quarrels among you. 12 What I mean is this: One of you says, "I follow Paul"; another, "I

Phillips Modern English

1.4 I am thankful for your faith

I am always thankful to God for what the gift of his grace in Christ Jesus has meant to you. For, as the Christian message has become established among you, he has enriched your whole lives, from the words on your lips to the understanding in your hearts. And you have been eager to receive his gifts during this time of waiting for his final appearance. He will keep you steadfast in the faith to the end, so that when his day comes you need fear no condemnation. God is utterly dependable, and it is he who has called you into fellowship with his Son Jesus Christ, our Lord.

1.10 But I am anxious over your "divisions"

Now I do beg you, my brothers, by all that our Lord Jesus Christ means to you, to speak with one voice, and not allow yourselves to be split up into parties. All together you should be achieving a unity in thought and judgment. For I know, from what some of Chloe's people have told me, that you are each making different claims—"I am one of Paul's men," says one; "I

Revised Standard Version

4 I give thanks to God[a] always for you because of the grace of God which was given you
in Christ Jesus, 5 that in every way you were
enriched in him with all speech and all knowledge—6 even as the testimony to Christ was confirmed among you—7 so that you are not lacking in any spiritual gift, as you wait for the
revealing of our Lord Jesus Christ; 8 who will
sustain you to the end, guiltless in the day of
our Lord Jesus Christ. 9 God is faithful, by
whom you were called into the fellowship of
his Son, Jesus Christ our Lord.
10 I appeal to you, brethren, by the name of
our Lord Jesus Christ, that all of you agree and
that there be no dissensions among you, but that
you be united in the same mind and the same
judgment. 11 For it has been reported to me by
Chloe's people that there is quarreling among
you, my brethren. 12 What I mean is that each
one of you says, "I belong to Paul," or "I belong

[a] Other ancient authorities read *my God*.

Jerusalem Bible

4 I never stop thanking God for all the graces
you have received through Jesus Christ. 5 I
thank him that you have been enriched in so
many ways, especially in your teachers and
preachers; 6 the witness to Christ has indeed
been strong among you 7 so that you will not
be without any of the gifts of the Spirit while
you are waiting for our Lord Jesus Christ to be
revealed; 8 and he will keep you steady and
without blame until the last day, the day of our
Lord Jesus Christ, 9 because God by calling you
has joined you to his Son, Jesus Christ; and
God is faithful.

I. Divisions and scandals

A. Factions in the Corinthian church

Dissensions among the faithful

10 All the same, I do appeal to you, brothers,
for the sake of our Lord Jesus Christ, to make
up the differences between you, and instead of
disagreeing among yourselves, to be united again
in your belief and practice. 11 From what
Chloe's people have been telling me, my dear
brothers, it is clear that there are serious differences among you. 12 What I mean are all
these slogans that you have, like: "I am for

New English Bible

I am always thanking God for you. I thank him for his grace given to you in Christ Jesus. I thank him for all the enrichment that has come to you in Christ. You possess full knowledge and you can give full expression to it, because in you the evidence for the truth of Christ has found confirmation. There is indeed no single gift you lack, while you wait expectantly for our Lord Jesus Christ to reveal himself. He will keep you firm to the end, without reproach on the Day of our Lord Jesus. It is God himself who called you to share in the life of his Son Jesus Christ our Lord; and God keeps faith.

I appeal to you, my brothers, in the name of our Lord Jesus Christ: agree among yourselves, and avoid divisions; be firmly joined in unity of mind and thought. I have been told, my brothers, by Chloe's people that there are quarrels among you. What I mean is this: each of you is saying,

King James Version

Apollos; and I of Cephas; and I of Christ. 13 Is
Christ divided? was Paul crucified for you? or
were ye baptized in the name of Paul? 14 I thank
God that I baptized none of you, but Crispus
and Gaius; 15 Lest any should say that I had
baptized in mine own name. 16 And I baptized
also the household of Stephanas: besides, I
know not whether I baptized any other. 17 For
Christ sent me not to baptize, but to preach the
gospel: not with wisdom of words, lest the cross
of Christ should be made of none effect. 18 For
the preaching of the cross is to them that perish,
foolishness; but unto us which are saved, it is the
power of God. 19 For it is written, I will destroy

Living Bible

say that they are for Apollos or for Peter; and
some that they alone are the true followers of
Christ. 13 And so, in effect, you have broken
Christ into many pieces.

But did I, Paul, die for your sins? Were any
of you baptized in my name? 14 I am so thankful now that I didn't baptize any of you except
Crispus and Gaius. 15 For now no one can think
that I have been trying to start something new,
beginning a "Church of Paul." 16 Oh, yes, and I
baptized the family of Stephanas. I don't remember ever baptizing anyone else. 17 For Christ
didn't send me to baptize, but to preach the
Gospel; and even my preaching sounds poor,
for I do not fill my sermons with profound
words and high sounding ideas, for fear of di-
luting the mighty power there is in the simple
message of the cross of Christ.

18 I know very well how foolish it sounds to
those who are[b] lost, when they hear that Jesus
died to save them. But we who are[b] saved recognize this message as the very power of God.
19 For God says, "I will destroy all human plans

[b] Or, "are being . . ."

Today's English Version

another, "I am with Apollos"; another, "I am
with Peter"; and another, "I am with Christ."
13 Christ has been divided into groups! Was it
Paul who died on the cross for you? Were you
baptized as Paul's disciples?

14 I thank God that I did not baptize any of
you except Crispus and Gaius. 15 No one can
say, then, that you were baptized as my disciples.
16 (Oh yes, I also baptized Stephanas and his
family; but I can't remember whether I baptized
anyone else.) 17 Christ did not send me to baptize. He sent me to tell the Good News, and to
tell it without using the language of men's wisdom, to keep Christ's death on the cross from
being robbed of its power.

Christ the power and the wisdom of God

18 For the message about Christ's death on the
cross is nonsense to those who are being lost; but
for us who are being saved, it is God's power.
19 The scripture says,

"I will destroy the wisdom of the wise,

New International Version

follow Apollos"; another, "I follow Cephas[a]";
still another, "I follow Christ."

13 Is Christ divided? Was Paul crucified for
you? Were you baptized into[b] the name of Paul?
14 I am thankful that I did not baptize any of
you except Crispus and Gaius, 15 so no one can
say that you were baptized into[b] my name.
16 (Yes, I also baptized the household of
Stephanas; beyond that, I don't remember if I
baptized anyone else.) 17 For Christ did not
send me to baptize, but to preach the gospel—
not with words of human wisdom, lest the cross
of Christ be emptied of its power.

Christ the wisdom and power of God

18 For the message of the cross is foolishness
to those who are perishing, but to us who are
being saved it is the power of God. 19 For it is
written:

"I will destroy the wisdom of the wise;

[a] That is, Peter. [b] Or *in*.

Phillips Modern English

am one of Apollos'," says another; or "I am one of Cephas',"; while someone else says, "I owe my faith to Christ alone."

1.13 *Do consider how serious these divisions are!*

What *are* you saying? Is there more than one Christ? Was it Paul who died on the cross for you? Were you baptised in the name of Paul? It makes me thankful that I didn't actually baptise any of you (except Crispus and Gaius), or perhaps someone would be saying I did it in my own name. (Oh yes, I did baptise Stephanas' family, but I can't remember anyone else.) For Christ did not send me primarily to baptise, but to proclaim the gospel. And I have not done this by the persuasiveness of clever words, for I have no desire to rob the cross of its power. The preaching of the cross is, I know, nonsense to those who are involved in this dying world, but to us who are being saved from that death it is nothing less than the power of God.

1.19 *The cross shows that God's wisdom is not man's wisdom by any means*

It is written:

I will destroy the wisdom of the wise,

Revised Standard Version

to Apollos," or "I belong to Cephas," or "I belong to Christ." 13 Is Christ divided? Was Paul crucified for you? Or were you baptized in the name of Paul? 14 I am thankful [b] that I baptized none of you except Crispus and Gaius; 15 lest any one should say that you were baptized in my name. 16 (I did baptize also the household of Stephanas. Beyond that, I do not know whether I baptized any one else.) 17 For Christ did not send me to baptize but to preach the gospel, and not with eloquent wisdom, lest the cross of Christ be emptied of its power.

18 For the word of the cross is folly to those who are perishing, but to us who are being saved it is the power of God. 19 For it is written,

"I will destroy the wisdom of the wise,

[b] Other ancient authorities read *I thank God*.

Jerusalem Bible

Paul," "I am for Apollos," "I am for Cephas,"[a] "I am for Christ." 13 Has Christ been parceled out? Was it Paul that was crucified for you? Were you baptized in the name of Paul? 14 I am thankful that I never baptized any of you after Crispus and Gaius 15 so none of you can say he was baptized in my name. 16 Then there was the family of Stephanas, of course, that I baptized too, but no one else as far as I can remember.

The true wisdom and the false

17 For Christ did not send me to baptize, but to preach the Good News, and not to preach that in the terms of philosophy[b] in which the crucifixion of Christ cannot be expressed. 18 The language of the cross may be illogical to those who are not on the way to salvation, but those of us who are on the way see it as God's power to save. 19As scripture says: *I shall destroy the*

[a] Peter. [b] "wisdom," the term used by Paul for the human wisdom of philosophy and rhetoric.

New English Bible

'I am Paul's man', or 'I am for Apollos'; 'I follow Cephas', or 'I am Christ's.' Surely Christ has not been divided among you! Was it Paul who was crucified for you? Was it in the name of Paul that you were baptized? Thank God, I never baptized one of you—except Crispus and Gaius. So no one can say you were baptized in my name.—Yes, I did baptize the household of Stephanas; I cannot think of anyone else. Christ did not send me to baptize, but to proclaim the Gospel; and to do it without relying on the language of worldly wisdom, so that the fact of Christ on his cross might have its full weight.

This doctrine of the cross is sheer folly to those on their way to ruin, but to us who are on the way to salvation it is the power of God. Scripture says, 'I will destroy the wisdom of the

King James Version

the wisdom of the wise, and will bring to nothing the understanding of the prudent. 20 Where *is* the wise? where *is* the scribe? where *is* the disputer of this world? hath not God made foolish the wisdom of this world? 21 For after that in the wisdom of God the world by wisdom knew not God, it pleased God by the foolishness of preaching to save them that believe. 22 For the Jews require a sign, and the Greeks seek after wisdom: 23 But we preach Christ crucified, unto the Jews a stumblingblock, and unto the Greeks foolishness; 24 But unto them which are called, both Jews and Greeks, Christ the power of God, and the wisdom of God. 25 Because the foolishness of God is wiser than men; and the weakness of God is stronger than men. 26 For ye see your calling, brethren, how that not many wise men after the flesh, not many mighty, not many noble, *are called:* 27 But God hath chosen the foolish things of the world to confound the wise; and God hath chosen the weak things of the world to confound the things which are mighty; 28 And base things of the world, and things which are despised, hath God

Living Bible

of salvation no matter how wise they seem to be, and ignore the best ideas of men, even the most brilliant of them."

20 So what about these wise men, these scholars, these brilliant debaters of this world's great affairs? God has made them all look foolish, and shown their wisdom to be useless nonsense. 21 For God in his wisdom saw to it that the world would never find God through human brilliance, and then he stepped in and saved all those who believed his message, which the world calls foolish and silly. 22 It seems foolish to the Jews because they want a sign from heaven as proof that what is preached is true; and it is foolish to the Gentiles because they believe only what agrees with their philosophy and seems wise to them. 23 So when we preach about Christ dying to save them, the Jews are offended and the Gentiles say it's all nonsense. 24 But God has opened the eyes of those called to salvation, both Jews and Gentiles, to see that Christ is the mighty power of God to save them; Christ himself is the center of God's wise plan for their salvation. 25 This so-called "foolish" plan of God is far wiser than the wisest plan of the wisest man, and God in his weakness—Christ dying on the cross—is far stronger than any man.

26 Notice among yourselves, dear brothers, that few of you who follow Christ have big names or power or wealth. 27 Instead, God has deliberately chosen to use ideas the world considers foolish and of little worth in order to shame those people considered by the world as wise and great. 28 He has chosen a plan despised by the world, counted as nothing at all, and used

Today's English Version

and set aside the understanding of the scholars."

20 So then, where does that leave the wise men? Or the scholars? Or the skillful debaters of this world? God has shown that this world's wisdom is foolishness!

21 For God, in his wisdom, made it impossible for men to know him by means of their own wisdom. Instead, God decided to save those who believe, by means of the "foolish" message we preach. 22 Jews want miracles for proof, and Greeks look for wisdom. 23 As for us, we proclaim Christ on the cross, a message that is offensive to the Jews and nonsense to the Gentiles; 24 but for those whom God has called, both Jews and Gentiles, this message is Christ, who is the power of God and the wisdom of God. 25 For what seems to be God's foolishness is wiser than men's wisdom, and what seems to be God's weakness is stronger than men's strength.

26 Now remember what you were, brothers, when God called you. Few of you were wise, or powerful, or of high social standing, from the human point of view. 27 God purposely chose what the world considers nonsense in order to put wise men to shame, and what the world considers weak in order to put powerful men to shame. 28 He chose what the world looks down on, and despises, and thinks is nothing, in order

New International Version

the intelligence of the intelligent I will frustrate." [c]

20 Where is the wise man? Where is the scholar? Where is the philosopher of this age? Has not God made foolish the wisdom of the world? 21 For since in the wisdom of God the world through its wisdom did not know him, God was pleased through the foolishness of what was preached to save those who believe. 22 Jews demand miraculous signs and Greeks look for wisdom, 23 but we preach Christ crucified: a stumbling block to Jews and foolishness to Gentiles, 24 but to those whom God has called, both Jews and Greeks, Christ the power of God and the wisdom of God. 25 For the foolishness of God is wiser than man's wisdom, and the weakness of God is stronger than man's strength.

26 Brothers, think of what you were when you were called. Not many of you were wise by human standards; not many were influential; not many were of noble birth. 27 But God chose the foolish things of the world to shame the wise; God chose the weak things of the world to shame the strong. 28 He chose the lowly things of this world and the despised things—and the things

[c] Isaiah 29:14.

Phillips Modern English

And the prudence of the prudent will I reject.

For consider, what have the philosopher, the writer and the critic of this world to show for all their wisdom? Has not God made the wisdom of this world look foolish? For it was after the world in its wisdom had failed to know God, that he in his wisdom chose to save all who would believe by the "simple-mindedness" of the gospel message. For the Jews ask for miraculous proofs and the Greeks an intellectural panacea, but all we preach is Christ crucified—a stumbling-block to the Jews and sheer nonsense to the gentiles, but for those who are called, whether Jews or Greeks, Christ the power of God and the wisdom of God. And this is really only natural, for God's "foolishness" is wiser than men, and his "weakness" is stronger than men.

1.26 Nor are God's values the same as man's

For look at your own calling as Christians, my brothers. You don't see among you many of the wise (according to this world's judgment) nor many of the ruling class, nor many from the noblest families. But God has chosen what the world calls foolish to shame the wise; he has chosen what the world calls weak to shame the strong. He has chosen things of little strength and small repute, yes and even things which have

Revised Standard Version

and the cleverness of the clever I will thwart."
20 Where is the wise man? Where is the scribe?
Where is the debater of this age? Has not God
made foolish the wisdom of the world? 21 For
since, in the wisdom of God, the world did not
know God through wisdom, it pleased God
through the folly of what we preach to save
those who believe. 22 For Jews demand signs and
Greeks seek wisdom, 23 but we preach Christ
crucified, a stumbling block to Jews and folly
to Gentiles, 24 but to those who are called, both
Jews and Greeks, Christ the power of God and
the wisdom of God. 25 For the foolishness of
God is wiser than men, and the weakness of
God is stronger than men.
26 For consider your call, brethren; not many
of you were wise according to worldly standards,
not many were powerful, not many were of
noble birth; 27 but God chose what is foolish in
the world to shame the wise, God chose what
is weak in the world to shame the strong, 28 God
chose what is low and despised in the world,

Jerusalem Bible

wisdom of the wise and bring to nothing all the
learning of the learned. 20 *Where are the phi-*
losophers now? Where are the scribes? [c] Where
are any of our thinkers today? Do you see now
how God has shown up the foolishness of human wisdom? 21 If it was God's wisdom that
human wisdom should not know God, it was
because God wanted to save those who have
faith through the foolishness of the message that
we preach. 22 And so, while the Jews demand
miracles and the Greeks look for wisdom, 23 here
are we preaching a crucified Christ; to the Jews
an obstacle that they cannot get over, to the
pagans madness, 24 but to those who have been
called, whether they are Jews or Greeks, a Christ
who is the power and the wisdom of God. 25 For
God's foolishness is wiser than human wisdom,
and God's weakness is stronger than human
strength.
26 Take yourselves for instance, brothers, at
the time when you were called: how many of
you were wise in the ordinary sense of the word,
how many were influential people, or came from
noble families? 27 No, it was to shame the wise
that God chose what is foolish by human reckoning, and to shame what is strong that he chose
what is weak by human reckoning; 28 those
whom the world thinks common and contempti-

[c] Quotations from Is. 29:14, Ps. 33:10 and Is. 33:18 (LXX).

New English Bible

wise, and bring to nothing the cleverness of the clever.' Where is your wise man now, your man of learning, or your subtle debater—limited, all of them, to this passing age? God has made the wisdom of this world look foolish. As God in his wisdom ordained, the world failed to find him by its wisdom, and he chose to save those who have faith by the folly of the Gospel. Jews call for miracles, Greeks look for wisdom; but we proclaim Christ—yes, Christ nailed to the cross; and though this is a stumbling-block to Jews and folly to Greeks, yet to those who have heard his call, Jews and Greeks alike, he is the power of God and the wisdom of God.

Divine folly is wiser than the wisdom of man, and divine weakness stronger than man's strength. My brothers, think what sort of people you are, whom God has called. Few of you are men of wisdom, by any human standard; few are powerful or highly born. Yet, to shame the wise, God has chosen what the world counts folly, and to shame what is strong, God has chosen what the world counts weakness. He has chosen things low and contemptible, mere noth-

King James Version

chosen, *yea,* and things which are not, to bring
to nought things that are: 29 That no flesh
should glory in his presence. 30 But of him are
ye in Christ Jesus, who of God is made unto us
wisdom, and righteousness, and sanctification,
and redemption: 31 That, according as it is written, He that glorieth, let him glory in the Lord.

2 And I, brethren, when I came to you, came
not with excellency of speech or of wisdom,
declaring unto you the testimony of God. 2 For
I determined not to know any thing among you,
save Jesus Christ, and him crucified. 3 And I was
with you in weakness, and in fear, and in much
trembling. 4 And my speech and my preaching
was not with enticing words of man's wisdom,
but in demonstration of the Spirit and of power:
5 That your faith should not stand in the wisdom

Living Bible

it to bring down to nothing those the world
considers great, 29 so that no one anywhere can
ever brag in the presence of God.
30 For it is from God alone that you have
your life through Christ Jesus. He showed us
God's plan of salvation; he was the one who
made us acceptable to God; he made us pure
and holy[c] and gave himself to purchase our
salvation.[d] 31 As it says in the Scriptures, "If
anyone is going to boast, let him boast only of
what the Lord has done."

2 Dear brothers, even when I first came to
you I didn't use lofty words and brilliant
ideas to tell you God's message. 2 For I decided
that I would speak only of Jesus Christ and his
death on the cross. 3 I came to you in weakness
—timid and trembling. 4 And my preaching was
very plain, not with a lot of oratory and human
wisdom, but the Holy Spirit's power was in my
words, proving to those who heard them that
the message was from God. 5 I did this because
I wanted your faith to stand firmly upon God,
not on man's great ideas.

[*c*] Or, "he brought us near to God." [*d*] Or, "to free us from slavery to sin."

Today's English Version

to destroy what the world thinks is important.
29 This means that no one can boast in God's
presence. 30 But God has brought you into union
with Christ Jesus, and God has made Christ to
be our wisdom; by him we are put right with
God, we become God's holy people, and are set
free. 31 So then, as the scripture says, "Whoever wants to boast must boast of what the Lord
has done."

The message about Christ on the cross

2 When I came to you, my brothers, to
preach God's secret truth to you, I did not
use long words and great learning. 2 For I made
up my mind to forget everything while I was
with you except Jesus Christ, and especially his
death on the cross. 3 So when I came to you I
was weak and trembled all over with fear, 4 and
my teaching and message were not delivered with
skillful words of human wisdom, but with convincing proof of the power of God's Spirit.
5 Your faith, then, does not rest on man's wisdom, but on God's power.

New International Version

that are not—to nullify the things that are, 29 so
that no man may boast before him. 30 It is because of him that you are in Christ Jesus, who
has become for us wisdom from God—that is,
our righteousness, holiness and redemption.
31 Therefore, as it is written: "Let him who
boasts boast in the Lord."[d]

2 When I came to you, brothers, I did not
come with eloquence or superior wisdom as
I proclaimed to you the testimony about God.[e]
2 For I resolved to know nothing while I was
with you except Jesus Christ and him crucified.
3 I came to you in weakness and fear, and with
much trembling. 4 My message and my preaching were not with wise and persuasive words,
but with a demonstration of the Spirit's power,
5 so that your faith might not rest on men's wisdom, but on God's power.

[*d*] Jer. 9:24. [*e*] Some MSS read *proclaimed to you God's mystery.*

Phillips Modern English

no real existence, to explode the pretensions of the things that are—that no man may boast in the presence of God. Yet from this same God you have received your standing in Jesus Christ, and he has become for us the true wisdom, a matter, in practice, of being made righteous and holy, in fact, of being redeemed. And this makes us see the truth of the scripture:

He that glorieth, let him glory in the Lord.

2.1 *I came to you in God's strength not my own*

In the same way, my brothers, when I came to proclaim to you God's secret purpose, I did not come equipped with any brilliance of speech or intellect. You may as well know now that it was my secret determination to concentrate entirely on Jesus Christ himself and the fact of his death upon the cross. As a matter of fact, in myself I was feeling far from strong; I was nervous and rather shaky. What I said and preached had none of the attractiveness of the clever mind, but it was a demonstration of the power of the Spirit! Plainly God's purpose was that your faith should rest not upon man's cleverness but upon the power of God.

Revised Standard Version

even things that are not, to bring to nothing
things that are, 29 so that no human being might
boast in the presence of God. 30 He is the
source of your life in Christ Jesus, whom God
made our wisdom, our righteousness and sanctification and redemption; 31 therefore, as it is
written, "Let him who boasts, boast of the
Lord."

2 When I came to you, brethren, I did not
come proclaiming to you the testimony[c] of
God in lofty words or wisdom. 2 For I decided
to know nothing among you except Jesus Christ
and him crucified. 3 And I was with you in
weakness and in much fear and trembling; 4 and
my speech and my message were not in plausible
words of wisdom, but in demonstration of the
Spirit and of power, 5 that your faith might not
rest in the wisdom of men but in the power of
God.

[c] Other ancient authorities read *mystery* (or *secret*).

Jerusalem Bible

ble are the ones that God has chosen—those
who are nothing at all to show up those who
are everything. 29 The human race has nothing
to boast about to God, 30 but God has made
you members of Christ Jesus and by God's doing he has become our wisdom, and our virtue,
and our holiness, and our freedom. 31 As scripture says: *if anyone wants to boast, let him
boast about the Lord.*[d]

2 As for me, brothers, when I came to you,
it was not with any show of oratory or
philosophy, but simply to tell you what God
has guaranteed. 2 During my stay with you, the
only knowledge I claimed to have was about
Jesus, and only about him as the crucified
Christ. 3 Far from relying on any power of my
own, I came among you in great "fear and
trembling"[e] 4 and in my speeches and the sermons that I gave, there were none of the arguments that belong to philosophy; only a demonstration of the power of the Spirit. 5 And I
did this so that your faith should not depend
on human philosophy but on the power of God.

[d] Jr. 9:22-23. [e] A scriptural cliché frequently used by Paul.

New English Bible

ings, to overthrow the existing order. And so there is no place for human pride in the presence of God. You are in Christ Jesus by God's act, for God has made him our wisdom; he is our righteousness; in him we are consecrated and set free. And so (in the words of Scripture), 'If a man must boast, let him boast of the Lord.'

2 As for me, brothers, when I came to you, I declared the attested truth of God[a] without display of fine words or wisdom. I resolved that while I was with you I would think of nothing but Jesus Christ—Christ nailed to the cross. I came before you weak, nervous, and shaking with fear. The word I spoke, the gospel I proclaimed, did not sway you with subtle arguments; it carried conviction by spiritual power, so that your faith might be built not upon human wisdom but upon the power of God.

[a] *Some witnesses read* I declared God's secret purpose . . .

King James Version

of men, but in the power of God. 6 Howbeit we
speak wisdom among them that are perfect: yet
not the wisdom of this world, nor of the princes
of this world, that come to nought: 7 But we
speak the wisdom of God in a mystery, *even*
the hidden *wisdom,* which God ordained before
the world unto our glory: 8 Which none of the
princes of this world knew: for had they known
it, they would not have crucified the Lord of
glory. 9 But as it is written, Eye hath not seen,
nor ear heard, neither have entered into the
heart of man, the things which God hath prepared for them that love him. 10 But God hath
revealed *them* unto us by his Spirit: for the
Spirit searcheth all things, yea, the deep things
of God. 11 For what man knoweth the things of
a man, save the spirit of man which is in him?
even so the things of God knoweth no man, but
the Spirit of God. 12 Now we have received, not
the spirit of the world, but the Spirit which is
of God; that we might know the things that are

Living Bible

6 Yet when I am among mature Christians I
do speak with words of great wisdom, but not
the kind that comes from here on earth, and
not the kind that appeals to the great men of
this world, who are doomed to fall. 7 Our words
are wise because they are from God, telling of
God's wise plan to bring us into the glories of
heaven. This plan was hidden in former times,
though it was made for our benefit before the
world began. 8 But the great men of the world
have not understood it; if they had, they never
would have crucified the Lord of Glory.
9 That is what is meant by the Scriptures
which say that no mere man has ever seen,
heard or even imagined what wonderful things
God has ready for those who love the Lord.
10 But we know about these things because God
has sent his Spirit to tell us, and his Spirit
searches out and shows us all of God's deepest
secrets. 11 No one can really know what anyone else is thinking, or what he is really like,
except that person himself. And no one can
know God's thoughts except God's own Spirit.
12 And God has actually given us his Spirit (not
the world's spirit) to tell us about the wonderful free gifts of grace and blessing that God has

Today's English Version

God's wisdom

6 Yet I do speak wisdom to those who are
spiritually mature. But it is not the wisdom that
belongs to this world, or to the powers that rule
this world—powers that are losing their power.
7 The wisdom I speak is God's secret wisdom,
hidden from men, which God had already chosen
for our glory even before the world was made.
8 None of the rulers of this world knew this
wisdom. If they had known it, they would not
have nailed the Lord of glory to the cross.
9 However, as the scripture says,

"What no man ever saw or heard,
what no man ever thought could happen,
is the very thing God prepared for those
who love him."

10 But it was to us that God made known his
secret, by means of his Spirit. The Spirit searches
everything, even the hidden depths of God's
purposes. 11 As for a man, it is his own spirit
within him that knows all about him; in the
same way, only God's Spirit knows all about
God. 12 We have not received this world's spirit;
we have received the Spirit sent by God, so that
we may know all that God has given us.

New International Version

Wisdom from the Spirit

6 We do, however, speak a message of wisdom
among the mature, but not the wisdom of this
age or of the rulers of this age, who are coming
to nothing. 7 No, we speak of God's secret wisdom, a wisdom that has been hidden and that
God destined for our glory before time began.
8 None of the rulers of this age understood it,
for if they had, they would not have crucified
the Lord of glory. 9 However, as it is written:

"No eye has seen,
no ear has heard,
no mind has conceived
what God has prepared for those who love
him" [f]—

10 but God has revealed it to us by his Spirit.
The Spirit searches all things, even the deep
things of God. 11 For who among men knows
the thoughts of a man except the man's spirit
within him? In the same way no one knows the
thoughts of God except the Spirit of God. 12 We
have not received the spirit of the world but the
Spirit who is from God, that we may under-

[*f*] Isaiah 64:4.

Phillips Modern English

2.6 There is, of course, a real wisdom, which God allows us to share with him

We do, of course, speak "wisdom" among those who are spiritually mature, but it is not what is called wisdom by this world, nor by the powers-that-be, who soon will be only the powers that have been. The wisdom we speak of is that mysterious secret wisdom of God which he planned before the creation for our glory today. None of the powers of this world have known this wisdom—if they had they would never have crucified the Lord of glory! But, as it is written:

Things which eye saw not, and ear heard not,
And which entered not into the heart of man,
Whatsoever things God prepared for them
that love him.

Thus God has, through the Spirit, let us share his secret. For nothing is hidden from the Spirit, not even the deep wisdom of God. For who could really understand a man's inmost thoughts except the spirit of the man himself? How much less could anyone understand the thoughts of God except the very Spirit of God? We have now received not the spirit of the world but the Spirit of God himself, so that we can understand something of God's generosity towards us.

Revised Standard Version

6 Yet among the mature we do impart wisdom, although it is not a wisdom of this age
or of the rulers of this age, who are doomed to
pass away. 7 But we impart a secret and hidden
wisdom of God, which God decreed before the
ages for our glorification. 8 None of the rulers
of this age understood this; for if they had, they
would not have crucified the Lord of glory.
9 But, as it is written,
"What no eye has seen, nor ear heard,
nor the heart of man conceived,
what God has prepared for those who love
him,"
10 God has revealed to us through the Spirit.
For the Spirit searches everything, even the
depths of God. 11 For what person knows a
man's thoughts except the spirit of the man
which is in him? So also no one comprehends the
thoughts of God except the Spirit of God.
12 Now we have received not the spirit of the
world, but the Spirit which is from God, that
we might understand the gifts bestowed on us

Jerusalem Bible

6 But still we have a wisdom to offer those
who have reached maturity: not a philosophy of
our age, it is true, still less of the masters of
our age, which are coming to their end. 7 The
hidden wisdom of God which we teach in our
mysteries is the wisdom that God predestined
to be for our glory before the ages began. 8 It
is a wisdom that none of the masters of this age
have ever known, or they would not have crucified the Lord of Glory; 9 we teach what scripture calls: *the things that no eye has seen and*
no ear has heard, things beyond the mind of
man, all that God has prepared for those who
love him.[f]
10 These are the very things that God has
revealed to us through the Spirit, for the Spirit
reaches the depths of everything, even the depths
of God. 11 After all, the depths of a man can
only be known by his own spirit, not by any
other man, and in the same way the depths of
God can only be known by the Spirit of God.
12 Now instead of the spirit of the world, we
have received the Spirit that comes from God,
to teach us to understand the gifts that he has

[f] A free combination of Is. 64:3 and Jr. 3:16.

New English Bible

And yet I do speak words of wisdom to those who are ripe for it, not a wisdom belonging to this passing age, nor to any of its governing powers, which are declining to their end; I speak God's hidden wisdom, his secret purpose framed from the very beginning to bring us to our full glory. The powers that rule the world have never known it; if they had, they would not have crucified the Lord of glory. But, in the words of Scripture, 'Things beyond our seeing, things beyond our hearing, things beyond our imagining, all prepared by God for those who love him', these it is that God has revealed to us through the Spirit.

For the Spirit explores everything, even the depths of God's own nature. Among men, who knows what a man is but the man's own spirit within him? In the same way, only the Spirit of God knows what God is. This is the Spirit that we have received from God, and not the spirit of the world, so that we may know all that God

King James Version

freely given to us of God. 13 Which things also
we speak, not in the words which man's wisdom
teacheth, but which the Holy Ghost teacheth;
comparing spiritual things with spiritual. 14 But
the natural man receiveth not the things of the
Spirit of God: for they are foolishness unto him:
neither can he know *them,* because they are
spiritually discerned. 15 But he that is spiritual
judgeth all things, yet he himself is judged of
no man. 16 For who hath known the mind of
the Lord, that he may instruct him? But we have
the mind of Christ.

3 And I, brethren, could not speak unto you
as unto spiritual, but as unto carnal, *even*

Living Bible

given us. 13 In telling you about these gifts we
have even used the very words given to us by
the Holy Spirit, not words that we as men might
choose. So we use the Holy Spirit's words to
explain the Holy Spirit's facts.[a] 14 But the man
who isn't a Christian can't understand and can't
accept these thoughts from God, which the Holy
Spirit teaches us. They sound foolish to him, because only those who have the Holy Spirit within
them can understand what the Holy Spirit means.
Others just can't take it in. 15 But the spiritual
man has insight into everything, and that bothers
and baffles the man of the world, who can't understand him at all. 16 How could he? For certainly he has never been one to know the Lord's
thoughts, or to discuss them with him, or to
move the hands of God by prayer.[b] But, strange
as it seems, we Christians actually do have
within us a portion of the very thoughts and
mind of Christ.

3 Dear brothers, I have been talking to you
as though you were still just babies in the
Christian life, who are not following the Lord,
but your own desires; I cannot talk to you as I
would to healthy Christians, who are filled with

[a] Or, "interpreting spiritual truth in spiritual language." [b] Or, "who can advise him?"

Today's English Version

13 So then, we do not speak in words taught
by human wisdom, but in words taught by the
Spirit, as we explain spiritual truths to those
who have the Spirit. 14 But the man who does
not have the Spirit cannot receive the gifts that
come from God's Spirit. He really does not
understand them; they are nonsense to him, because their value can be judged only on a spiritual basis. 15 The man who has the Spirit is able
to judge the value of everything, but no one is
able to judge him. 16 As the scripture says,

"Who knows the mind of the Lord?
Who is able to give him advice?"

We, however, have the mind of Christ.

Servants of God

3 As a matter of fact, brothers, I could not
talk to you as I talk to men who have the
Spirit; I had to talk to you as men of this

New International Version

stand what God has freely given us. 13 This is
what we speak, not in words taught us by human
wisdom but in words taught by the Spirit, expressing spiritual truths in spiritual words.[g]
14 The man without the Spirit does not accept
the things that come from the Spirit of God, for
they are foolishness to him, and he cannot understand them, because they are spiritually discerned. 15 The spiritual man makes judgments
about all things, but he himself is not subject to
any man's judgment:

16 "For who has known the mind of the Lord
that he may instruct him?"[h]
But we have the mind of Christ.

On divisions in the church

3 Brothers, I could not address you as spiritual but as worldly—mere infants in Christ.

[g] Or *Spirit, interpreting spiritual truths to spiritual men.* [h] Isaiah 40:13.

Phillips Modern English

2.13 This wisdom is only understood by the spiritual

It is these things that we talk about, not using the expressions of the human intellect but those which the Holy Spirit teaches us, explaining spiritual things to those who are spiritual.

But the unspiritual man simply cannot accept the matters which the Spirit deals with—they just don't make sense to him, for, after all, you must be spiritual to see spiritual things. The spiritual man, on the other hand, has an insight into the meaning of everything, though his insight may baffle the man of the world. This is because the former is sharing in God's wisdom, and

Who hath known the mind of the Lord,
That he should instruct him?

Nevertheless, we who are spiritual have the very thoughts of Christ!

3.1 But I cannot yet call you spiritual

I, my brothers, was unable to talk to you as spiritual men: I had to talk to you as unspiri-

Revised Standard Version

by God. 13And we impart this in words not taught by human wisdom but taught by the Spirit, interpreting spiritual truths to those who possess the Spirit.[d]

14 The unspiritual[e] man does not receive the gifts of the Spirit of God, for they are folly to him, and he is not able to understand them because they are spiritually discerned. 15 The spiritual man judges all things, but is himself to be judged by no one. 16 "For who has known the mind of the Lord so as to instruct him?" But we have the mind of Christ.

3 But I, brethren, could not address you as spiritual men, but as men of the flesh, as

[d] Or *interpreting spiritual truths in spiritual language;* or *comparing spiritual things with spiritual.*
[e] Or *natural.*

Jerusalem Bible

given us. 13 Therefore we teach, not in the way in which philosophy is taught, but in the way that the Spirit teaches us: we teach spiritual things spiritually. 14An unspiritual person is one who does not accept anything of the Spirit of God: he sees it all as nonsense; it is beyond his understanding because it can only be understood by means of the Spirit. 15A spiritual man, on the other hand, is able to judge the value of everything, and his own value is not to be judged by other men. 16As scripture says: *Who can know the mind of the Lord, so who can teach him?*[g] But we are those who have the mind of Christ.

3 Brothers, I myself was unable to speak to you as people of the Spirit: I treated you

[g] Is. 40:13.

New English Bible

of his own grace has given us; and, because we are interpreting spiritual truths to those who have the Spirit, we speak of these gifts of God in words found for us not by our human wisdom but by the Spirit. A man who is unspiritual refuses what belongs to the Spirit of God; it is folly to him; he cannot grasp it, because it needs to be judged in the light of the Spirit. A man gifted with the Spirit can judge the worth of everything, but is not himself subject to judgement by his fellow-men. For (in the words of Scripture) 'who knows the mind of the Lord? Who can advise him?' We, however, possess the mind of Christ.

3 For my part, my brothers, I could not speak to you as I should speak to people who have the Spirit. I had to deal with you on the merely

King James Version

as unto babes in Christ. 2 I have fed you with
milk, and not with meat: for hitherto ye were
not able *to bear it,* neither yet now are ye able.
3 For ye are yet carnal: for whereas *there is*
among you envying, and strife, and divisions,
are ye not carnal, and walk as men? 4 For
while one saith, I am of Paul; and another, I
am of Apollos; are ye not carnal? 5 Who then
is Paul, and who *is* Apollos, but ministers by
whom ye believed, even as the Lord gave to
every man? 6 I have planted, Apollos watered;
but God gave the increase. 7 So then neither is
he that planteth any thing, neither he that watereth; but God that giveth the increase. 8 Now
he that planteth and he that watereth are one:
and every man shall receive his own reward according to his own labour. 9 For we are labourers together with God: ye are God's husbandry,
ye are God's building. 10 According to the grace
of God which is given unto me, as a wise mas-
terbuilder, I have laid the foundation, and another buildeth thereon. But let every man take
heed how he buildeth thereupon. 11 For other
foundation can no man lay than that is laid,

Living Bible

the Spirit. 2 I have had to feed you with milk
and not with solid food, because you couldn't
digest anything stronger. And even now you still
have to be fed on milk. 3 For you are still only
baby Christians, controlled by your own desires,
not God's. When you are jealous of one another
and divide up into quarreling groups, doesn't
that prove you are still babies, wanting your
own way? In fact, you are acting like people
who don't belong to the Lord at all. 4 There
you are, quarreling about whether I am greater
than Apollos, and dividing the church. Doesn't
this show how little you have grown in the
Lord? [a]

5 Who am I, and who is Apollos, that we
should be the cause of a quarrel? Why, we're
just God's servants, each of us with certain special abilities, and with our help you believed.
6 My work was to plant the seed in your hearts,
and Apollos' work was to water it, but it was
God, not we, who made the garden grow in your
hearts. 7 The person who does the planting or
watering isn't very important, but God is important because he is the one who makes things
grow. 8 Apollos and I are working as a team,
with the same aim, though each of us will be
rewarded for his own hard work. 9 We are only
God's co-workers. You are *God's* garden, not
ours; you are *God's* building, not ours.

10 God, in his kindness, has taught me how
to be an expert builder. I have laid the foundation and Apollos has built on it. But he who
builds on the foundation must be very careful.
11 And no one can ever lay any other real foundation than that one we already have—Jesus

[*a*] Literally, "Are you not (mere) men?"

Today's English Version

world, as children in the Christian faith. 2 I had
to feed you milk, not solid food, because you
were not ready for it. And even now you are
not ready for it, 3 because you still live as men
of this world. When there is jealousy among you,
and you quarrel with one another, doesn't this
prove that you are men of this world, living by
this world's standards? 4 When one of you says,
"I am with Paul," and another, "I am with
Apollos"—aren't you acting like worldly men?

5 After all, who is Apollos? And who is Paul?
We are simply God's servants, by whom you
were led to believe. Each one of us does the
work the Lord gave him to do: 6 I planted the
seed, Apollos watered the plant, but it was God
who made the plant grow. 7 The one who plants
and the one who waters really do not matter. It
is God who matters, because he makes the plant
grow. 8 There is no difference between the man
who plants and the man who waters; God will
reward each one according to the work he has
done. 9 For we are partners working together
for God, and you are God's field.

You are also God's building. 10 Using the gift
that God gave me, I did the work of an expert
builder and laid the foundation, and another
man is building on it. But each one must be
careful how he builds. 11 For God has already
placed Jesus Christ as the one and only foundation, and no other foundation can be laid.

New International Version

2 I gave you milk, not solid food, for you were
not yet ready for it. Indeed, you are still not
ready. 3 You are still worldly. For since there is
jealousy and quarreling among you, are you not
worldly? Are you not acting like mere men?
4 For when one says, "I follow Paul," and another, "I follow Apollos," are you not mere
men?

5 What, after all, is Apollos? And what is
Paul? Only servants, through whom you came to
believe—as the Lord has assigned to each his
task. 6 I planted the seed, Apollos watered it, but
God made it grow. 7 So neither he who plants
nor he who waters is anything, but only God,
who makes things grow. 8 The man who plants
and the man who waters have one purpose, and
each will be rewarded according to his own
labor. 9 For we are God's fellow workers; you
are God's field, God's building.

10 By the grace God has given me, I laid a
foundation as an expert builder, and others are
building on it. But each one should be careful
how he builds. 11 For no one can lay any foundation other than the one already laid, which is

Phillips Modern English

tual, as yet babies in the Christian life. And my practice has been to feed you, as it were, with "milk" and not with "meat". You were unable to digest "meat" in those days, and I don't believe you can do it now. For you are still unspiritual; all the time that there is jealousy and squabbling among you you show that you are —you are living just like men of the world. While one of you says, "I am one of Paul's converts" and another says, "I am one of Apollos' ", are you not plainly unspiritual?

After all, who is Apollos? Who is Paul? No more than servants through whom you came to believe as the Lord gave each man his opportunity. I may have done the planting and Apollos the watering, but it was God who made the seed grow! The planter and the waterer are nothing compared with him who gives life to the seed. Planter and waterer are alike insignificant, though each shall be rewarded according to his particular work.

3.9 We work on God's foundation

In this work, we work with God, and that means that you are a field under God's cultivation, or, if you like, a house being built to his plan. I, like a master-builder who knows his job, by the grace God has given me, lay the foundation; someone else builds upon it. I only say this, let the builder be careful how he builds! The foundation is laid already, and no one can lay

Revised Standard Version

babes in Christ. 2 I fed you with milk, not solid
food; for you were not ready for it; and even yet
you are not ready, 3 for you are still of the flesh.
For while there is jealousy and strife among you,
are you not of the flesh, and behaving like ordinary men? 4 For when one says, "I belong to
Paul," and another, "I belong to Apollos," are
you not merely men?
5 What then is Apollos? What is Paul? Servants through whom you believed, as the Lord
assigned to each. 6 I planted, Apollos watered,
but God gave the growth. 7 So neither he who
plants nor he who waters is anything, but only
God who gives the growth. 8 He who plants and
he who waters are equal, and each shall receive his wages according to his labor. 9 For
we are God's fellow workers; you are God's
field, God's building.
10 According to the grace of God given to
me, like a skilled master builder I laid a foundation, and another man is building upon it. Let
each man take care how he builds upon it. 11 For
no other foundation can any one lay than that

Jerusalem Bible

as sensual men, still infants in Christ. 2 What
I fed you with was milk, not solid food, for you
were not ready for it; and indeed, you are still
not ready for it 3 since you are still unspiritual.
Isn't that obvious from all the jealousy and
wrangling that there is among you, from the
way that you go on behaving like ordinary people? 4 What could be more unspiritual than
your slogans, "I am for Paul" and "I am for
Apollos"?

The place of the Christian preacher

5 After all, what is Apollos and what is Paul?
They are servants who brought the faith to you.
Even the different ways in which they brought
it were assigned to them by the Lord. 6 I did
the planting, Apollos did the watering, but God
made things grow. 7 Neither the planter nor the
waterer matters: only God, who makes things
grow. 8 It is all one who does the planting and
who does the watering, and each will duly be
paid according to his share in the work. 9 We
are fellow workers with God; you are God's
farm, God's building.
10 By the grace God gave me, I succeeded as
an architect and laid the foundations, on which
someone else is doing the building. Everyone
doing the building must work carefully. 11 For
the foundation, nobody can lay any other than
the one which has already been laid, that is

New English Bible

natural plane, as infants in Christ. And so I gave you milk to drink, instead of solid food, for which you were not yet ready. Indeed, you are still not ready for it, for you are still on the merely natural plane. Can you not see that while there is jealousy and strife among you, you are living on the purely human level of your lower nature? When one says, 'I am Paul's man', and another, 'I am for Apollos', are you not all too human?

After all, what is Apollos? What is Paul? We are simply God's agents in bringing you to the faith. Each of us performed the task which the Lord allotted to him: I planted the seed, and Apollos watered it; but God made it grow. Thus it is not the gardeners with their planting and watering who count, but God, who makes it grow. Whether they plant or water, they work as a team,[a] though each will get his own pay for his own labour. We are God's fellow-workers;[b] and you are God's garden.

Or again, you are God's building. I am like a skilled master-builder who by God's grace laid the foundation, and someone else is putting up the building. Let each take care how he builds. There can be no other foundation beyond that which is already laid; I mean Jesus Christ him-

[a] *Or* Whether they plant or water, it is all the same. [b] *Or* We are fellow-workers in God's service.

King James Version

which is Jesus Christ. 12 Now if any man build
upon this foundation gold, silver, precious stones,
wood, hay, stubble; 13 Every man's work shall
be made manifest: for the day shall declare it,
because it shall be revealed by fire; and the fire
shall try every man's work of what sort it is.
14 If any man's work abide which he hath built
thereupon, he shall receive a reward. 15 If any
man's work shall be burned, he shall suffer loss:
but he himself shall be saved; yet so as by fire.
16 Know ye not that ye are the temple of God,
and *that* the Spirit of God dwelleth in you? 17 If
any man defile the temple of God, him shall
God destroy; for the temple of God is holy,
which *temple* ye are. 18 Let no man deceive himself. If any man among you seemeth to be wise
in this world, let him become a fool, that he may
be wise. 19 For the wisdom of this world is foolishness with God: for it is written, He taketh
the wise in their own craftiness. 20 And again,
The Lord knoweth the thoughts of the wise, that

Living Bible

Christ. 12 But there are various kinds of materials that can be used to build on that foundation. Some use gold and silver and jewels; and
some build with sticks, and hay, or even straw!
13 There is going to come a time of testing at
Christ's Judgment Day to see what kind of material each builder has used. Everyone's work
will be put through the fire so that all can see
whether or not it keeps its value, and what was
really accomplished. 14 Then every workman
who has built on the foundation with the right
materials, and whose work still stands, will get
his pay. 15 But if the house he has built burns
up, he will have a great loss. He himself will
be saved, but like a man escaping through a
wall of flames.

16 Don't you realize that all of you together
are the house of God, and that the Spirit of
God lives among you in his house? 17 If anyone
defiles and spoils God's home, God will destroy
him. For God's home is holy and clean, and you
are that home.

18 Stop fooling yourselves. If you count yourself above average in intelligence, as judged by
this world's standards, you had better put this
all aside and be a fool rather than let it hold
you back from the true wisdom from above.
19 For the wisdom of this world is foolishness
to God. As it says in the book of Job, God uses
man's own brilliance to trap him; he stumbles
over his own "wisdom" and falls. 20 And again,
in the book of Psalms, we are told that the
Lord knows full well how the human mind reasons, and how foolish and futile it is.

Today's English Version

12 Some will use gold, or silver, or precious
stones in building on the foundation; others will
use wood, or grass, or straw. 13 And the quality
of each man's work will be seen when the Day
of Christ exposes it. For that Day's fire will
reveal every man's work; the fire will test it and
show its real quality. 14 If what a man built on
the foundation survives the fire, he will receive
a reward. 15 But if any man's work is burnt up,
then he will lose it; but he himself will be saved,
as if he had escaped through the fire.

16 Surely you know that you are God's temple, and that God's Spirit lives in you! 17 So if
anyone destroys God's temple, God will destroy
him. For God's temple is holy, and you yourselves are his temple.

18 No one should fool himself. If anyone
among you thinks that he is a wise man by this
world's standards, he should become a fool, in
order to be really wise. 19 For what this world
considers to be wisdom is nonsense in God's
sight. As the scripture says, "God traps the wise
men in their cleverness"; 20 and another scripture says, "The Lord knows that the thoughts

New International Version

Jesus Christ. 12 If any man builds on this foundation using gold, silver, costly stones, wood, hay
or straw, 13 his work will be shown for what it
is, because the Day will bring it to light. It will
be revealed with fire, and the fire will test the
quality of each man's work. 14 If what he has
built survives, he will receive his reward. 15 If it
is burned up, he will suffer loss; he himself will
be saved, but only as one escaping through the
flames.

16 Don't you know that you yourselves are
God's temple and that God's Spirit lives in you?
17 If anyone destroys God's temple, God will
destroy him; for God's temple is sacred, and you
are that temple.

18 Do not deceive yourselves. If any one of
you thinks he is wise by the standards of this
age, he should become a "fool" so that he may
become wise. 19 For the wisdom of this world
is foolishness in God's sight. As it is written:
"He catches the wise in their craftiness" [i];
20 and again, "The Lord knows that the thoughts

[*i*] Job 5:13.

Phillips Modern English

another, for it is Jesus Christ himself. But any man who builds on the foundation using as his material gold, silver, precious stones, wood, hay or straw, must know that each man's work will one day be shown for what it is. The day will show it plainly enough, for the day will arise in a blaze of fire, and that fire will prove the value of each man's work. If the work which a man has built upon the foundation stands this test, he will be rewarded. But if his work is burnt down, he loses it all. He personally will be safe, though rather like a man rescued from a fire.

3.16 *Make no mistake: you are God's holy building*

Don't you realise that you yourselves are the temple of God, and that God's Spirit lives in you? God will destroy anyone who defiles his temple, for his temple is holy—*and that is exactly what you are!*

Let no one be under any illusion over this. If any man among you thinks himself one of the world's clever ones, let him discard his cleverness that he may learn to be truly wise. For this world's cleverness is stupidity to God. It is written:

He that taketh the wise in their craftiness.

And again:
The Lord knoweth the reasonings of the wise,
that they are vain.

Revised Standard Version

which is laid, which is Jesus Christ. 12 Now if
any one builds on the foundation with gold,
silver, precious stones, wood, hay, straw—
13 each man's work will become manifest; for
the Day will disclose it, because it will be revealed with fire, and the fire will test what sort
of work each one has done. 14 If the work
which any man has built on the foundation
survives, he will receive a reward. 15 If any man's
work is burned up, he will suffer loss, though he
himself will be saved, but only as through fire.
16 Do you not know that you are God's temple and that God's Spirit dwells in you? 17 If
any one destroys God's temple, God will destroy him. For God's temple is holy, and that
temple you are.
18 Let no one deceive himself. If any one
among you thinks that he is wise in this age, let
him become a fool that he may become wise.
19 For the wisdom of this world is folly with
God. For it is written, "He catches the wise in
their craftiness," 20 and again, "The Lord knows

Jerusalem Bible

Jesus Christ. 12 On this foundation you can
build in gold, silver and jewels, or in wood,
grass and straw, 13 but whatever the material,
the work of each builder is going to be clearly
revealed when the day comes. That day will
begin with fire, and the fire will test the quality
of each man's work. 14 If his structure stands
up to it, he will get his wages; 15 if it is burned
down, he will be the loser, and though he is
saved himself, it will be as one who has gone
through fire.
16 Didn't you realize that you were God's
temple and that the Spirit of God was living
among you? 17 If anybody should destroy the
temple of God, God will destroy him, because
the temple of God is sacred; and you are that
temple.

Conclusions

18 Make no mistake about it: if any one of
you thinks of himself as wise, in the ordinary
sense of the word, then he must learn to be a
fool before he really can be wise. 19 Why? Because the wisdom of this world is foolishness
to God. As scripture says: *The Lord knows wise
men's thoughts: he knows how useless they are*[h]:
20 or again: *God is not convinced by the argu-*

[h] Jb. 5:13.

New English Bible

self. If anyone builds on that foundation with gold, silver, and fine stone, or with wood, hay, and straw, the work that each man does will at last be brought to light; the day of judgement will expose it. For that day dawns in fire, and the fire will test the worth of each man's work. If a man's building stands, he will be rewarded; if it burns, he will have to bear the loss; and yet he will escape with his life, as one might from a fire. Surely you know that you are God's temple, where the Spirit of God dwells. Anyone who destroys God's temple will himself be destroyed[c] by God, because the temple of God is holy; and that temple you are.

Make no mistake about this: if there is anyone among you who fancies himself wise—wise, I mean, by the standards of this passing age—he must become a fool to gain true wisdom. For the wisdom of this world is folly in God's sight. Scripture says, 'He traps the wise in their own cunning', and again, 'The Lord knows that the

[c] *Some witnesses read* is himself destroyed.

King James Version

they are vain. 21 Therefore let no man glory in
men: for all things are yours; 22 Whether Paul,
or Apollos, or Cephas, or the world, or life, or
death, or things present, or things to come; all
are yours; 23 And ye are Christ's; and Christ *is*
God's.

4 Let a man so account of us, as of the ministers of Christ, and stewards of the mysteries
of God. 2 Moreover it is required in stewards,
that a man be found faithful. 3 But with me it
is a very small thing that I should be judged
of you, or of man's judgment: yea, I judge not
mine own self. 4 For I know nothing by myself;
yet am I not hereby justified: but he that judgeth
me is the Lord. 5 Therefore judge nothing before
the time, until the Lord come, who both will
bring to light the hidden things of darkness, and
will make manifest the counsels of the hearts:
and then shall every man have praise of God.
6 And these things, brethren, I have in a figure
transferred to myself and *to* Apollos for your

Living Bible

21 So don't be proud of following the wise
men of this world.[b] For God has already given
you everything you need. 22 He has given you
Paul and Apollos and Peter as your helpers. He
has given you the whole world to use, and life
and even death are your servants. He has given
you all of the present and all of the future. All
are yours, 23 and you belong to Christ, and
Christ is God's.

4 So Apollos and I should be looked upon
as Christ's servants who distribute God's
blessings by explaining God's secrets. 2 Now the
most important thing about a servant is that he
does just what his master tells him to. 3 What
about me? Have I been a good servant? Well,
I don't worry over what you think about this,
or what anyone else thinks. I don't even trust
my own judgment on this point. 4 My conscience
is clear, but even that isn't final proof. It is the
Lord himself who must examine me and decide.
5 So be careful not to jump to conclusions
before the Lord returns as to whether someone
is a good servant or not. When the Lord comes,
he will turn on the light so that everyone can
see exactly what each one of us is really like,
deep down in our hearts. Then everyone will
know why we have been doing the Lord's work.
At that time God will give to each one whatever
praise is coming to him.
6 I have used Apollos and myself as examples
to illustrate what I have been saying: that you

[b] Literally, "Let no one glory in men."

Today's English Version

of the wise are worthless." 21 No one, then,
should boast about what men can do. Actually
everything belongs to you: 22 Paul, Apollos, and
Peter; this world, life, and death, the present
and the future; all of these are yours, 23 and
you belong to Christ, and Christ belongs to
God.

Apostles of Christ

4 You should look on us as Christ's servants
who have been put in charge of God's secret
truths. 2 The one thing required of the man in
charge is that he be faithful to his master.
3 Now, I am not at all concerned about being
judged by you, or by any human standard; I
don't even pass judgment on myself. 4 My conscience is clear, but that does not prove that I
am really innocent. The Lord is the one who
passes judgment on me. 5 So you should not
pass judgment on anyone before the right time
comes. Final judgment must wait until the Lord
comes; he will bring to light the dark secrets
and expose the hidden purposes of men's hearts.
And then every man will receive from God the
praise he deserves.
6 For your sake, brothers, I have applied all
this to Apollos and me. I have used us as an

New International Version

of the wise are futile."[j] 21 So then, no more
boasting about men! All things are yours,
22 whether Paul or Apollos or Cephas[k] or the
world or life or death or the present or the
future—all are yours, 23 and you are of Christ,
and Christ is of God.

Apostles of Christ

4 So then, men ought to regard us as servants of Christ and as those entrusted with
the secret things of God. 2 Now it is required
that those who have been given a trust must
prove faithful. 3 I care very little if I am judged
by you or by any human court; indeed, I do not
even judge myself. 4 My conscience is clear, but
that does not make me innocent. It is the Lord
who judges me. 5 Therefore, judge nothing before the appointed time; wait till the Lord comes.
He will bring to light what is hidden in darkness
and will expose the motives of men's hearts. At
that time each will receive his praise from God.
6 Now, brothers, I have applied these things
to myself and Apollos for your benefit, so that

[j] Psalm 94:11. [k] That is, Peter.

Phillips Modern English

So let no one boast of men. Everything belongs to you! Paul, Apollos or Cephas; the world, life, death, the present or the future, everything is yours! For you belong to Christ, and Christ belongs to God.

4.1 Trust us, but make no hasty judgments

You should look upon us as ministers of Christ, as trustees of the secrets of God. And it is a prime requisite in a trustee that he should prove worthy of his trust. But, as a matter of fact, it matters very little to me what you, or any man, thinks of me—I don't even value my opinion of myself. For I might be quite ignorant of any fault in myself—but that doesn't justify me before God. My only true judge is the Lord.

The moral of this is that we should make no hasty or premature judgments. When the Lord comes he will bring into the light of day all that at present is hidden in darkness, and he will expose the secret motives of men's hearts. Then shall God himself give each man his share of praise.

4.6 Having your favourite teacher is not only silly but wrong

I have used myself and Apollos above as an illustration, so that you might learn from what

Revised Standard Version

that the thoughts of the wise are futile."
21 So
let no one boast of men. For all things are
yours, 22 whether Paul or Apollos or Cephas or
the world or life or death or the present or the
future, all are yours; 23 and you are Christ's; and
Christ is God's.

4 This is how one should regard us, as servants of Christ and stewards of the mysteries of God.
2 Moreover it is required of stewards that they be found trustworthy.
3 But with
me it is a very small thing that I should be
judged by you or by any human court. I do not
even judge myself.
4 I am not aware of anything
against myself, but I am not thereby acquitted.
It is the Lord who judges me.
5 Therefore do not
pronounce judgment before the time, before the
Lord comes, who will bring to light the things
now hidden in darkness and will disclose the
purposes of the heart. Then every man will receive his commendation from God.
6 I have applied all this to myself and Apollos for your benefit, brethren, that you may

Jerusalem Bible

ments of the wise.[i]
21 So there is nothing to
boast about in anything human:
22 Paul, Apollos, Cephas, the world, life and death, the present and the future, are all your servants;
23 but
you belong to Christ and Christ belongs to God.

4 People must think of us as Christ's servants, stewards entrusted with the mysteries
of God.
2 What is expected of stewards is that
each one should be found worthy of his trust.
3 Not that it makes the slightest difference to
me whether you, or indeed any human tribunal,
find me worthy or not. I will not even pass
judgment on myself.
4 True, my conscience does
not reproach me at all, but that does not prove
that I am acquitted: the Lord alone is my judge.
5 There must be no passing of premature judgment. Leave that until the Lord comes: he will
light up all that is hidden in the dark and reveal the secret intentions of men's hearts. Then
will be the time for each one to have whatever
praise he deserves from God.
6 Now in everything I have said here, brothers, I have taken Apollos and myself as an

New English Bible

arguments of the wise are futile.' So never make mere men a cause for pride. For though everything belongs to you—Paul, Apollos, and Cephas, the world, life, and death, the present and the future, all of them belong to you—yet you belong to Christ, and Christ to God.

4 We must be regarded as Christ's subordinates and as stewards of the secrets of God. Well then, stewards are expected to show themselves trustworthy. For my part, if I am called to account by you or by any human court of judgement, it does not matter to me in the least. Why, I do not even pass judgement on myself, for I have nothing on my conscience; but that does not mean I stand acquitted. My judge is the Lord. So pass no premature judgement; wait until the Lord comes. For he will bring to light what darkness hides, and disclose men's inward motives; then will be the time for each to receive from God such praise as he deserves.

Into this general picture, my friends, I have brought Apollos and myself on your account, so

[i] Ps. 94:11.

King James Version

sakes; that ye might learn in us not to think *of*
men above that which is written, that no one
of you be puffed up for one against another.
7 For who maketh thee to differ *from another?*
and what hast thou that thou didst not receive?
now if thou didst receive *it,* why dost thou glory,
as if thou hadst not received *it?* 8 Now ye are
full, now ye are rich, ye have reigned as kings
without us: and I would to God ye did reign,
that we also might reign with you. 9 For I think
that God hath set forth us the apostles last,
as it were appointed to death: for we are made
a spectacle unto the world, and to angels, and
to men. 10 We *are* fools for Christ's sake, but
ye *are* wise in Christ; we *are* weak, but ye *are*
strong; ye *are* honourable, but we *are* despised.
11 Even unto this present hour we both hunger,
and thirst, and are naked, and are buffeted, and
have no certain dwellingplace; 12And labour,
working with our own hands: being reviled, we
bless; being persecuted, we suffer it: 13 Being

Living Bible

must not have favorites. You must not be proud
of one of God's teachers more than another.
7 What are you so puffed up about? What do
you have that God hasn't given you? And if all
you have is from God, why act as though you
are so great, and as though you have accomplished something on your own?
8 You seem to think you already have all the
spiritual food you need. You are full and spiritually contented, rich kings on your thrones,
leaving us far behind! I wish you really were
already on your thrones, for when that time
comes you can be sure that we will be there,
too, reigning with you. 9 Sometimes I think God
has put us apostles at the very end of the line,
like prisoners soon to be killed, put on display
at the end of a victor's parade, to be stared at
by men and angels alike.
10 Religion has made us foolish, you say, but
of course you are all such wise and sensible
Christians! We are weak, but not you! You are
well thought of, while we are laughed at. 11 To
this very hour we have gone hungry and thirsty,
without even enough clothes to keep us warm.
We have been kicked around without homes of
our own. 12 We have worked wearily with our
hands to earn our living. We have blessed those
who cursed us. We have been patient with those
who injured us. 13 We have replied quietly when

Today's English Version

example, so that you may learn what the saying
means, "Observe the proper rules." None of you
should be proud of one man and despise the
other. 7 Who made you superior to the others?
Didn't God give you everything you have? Well,
then, how can you brag, as if what you have
were not a gift?
8 Already you have everything you need! Already you are rich! You have become kings,
even though we are not! Well, I wish you really
were kings, so that we could be kings together
with you. 9 For it seems to me that God has
given us apostles the very last place, like men
condemned to die in public, as a spectacle for
the whole world of angels and of men. 10 For
Christ's sake we are fools; but you are wise in
Christ! We are weak, but you are strong! We
are despised, but you are honored! 11 To this
very hour we go hungry and thirsty; we are
clothed in rags; we are beaten; we wander from
place to place; 12 we work hard to support ourselves. When we are cursed, we bless; when
we are persecuted, we endure; 13 when we are

New International Version

you may learn from us the meaning of the saying, "Do not go beyond what is written." Then
you will not take pride in one man over against
another. 7 For who makes you different from
anyone else? What do you have that you did
not receive? And if you did receive it, why do
you boast as though you did not?
8 Already you have all you want! Already you
have become rich! You have become kings—
and that without us! How I wish that you really
had become kings so that we might be kings with
you! 9 For it seems to me that God has put us
apostles on display at the end of the procession,
like men condemned to die in the arena. We
have been made a spectacle to the whole universe, to angels as well as to men. 10 We are
fools for Christ, but you are so wise in Christ!
We are weak, but you are strong! You are honored, we are dishonored! 11 To this very hour
we go hungry and thirsty, we are in rags, we are
brutally treated, we are homeless. 12 We work
hard with our own hands. When we are cursed,
we bless; when we are persecuted, we endure it;
13 when we are slandered, we answer kindly. Up

Phillips Modern English

I have said about us not to assess man above his value in God's sight, and may thus avoid the pride which comes from making one teacher more important than another. For who makes you different from anybody else, and what have you got that was not given to you? And if anything has been given to you, why boast of it as if you had achieved it yourself?

4.8 Think sometimes of what your happiness has cost us!

Oh, I know you are rich and flourishing! You've been living like kings, haven't you, while we've been away? I would to God you were really kings in God's sight so that we might reign with you!

I sometimes think that God means us, the messengers, to appear last in the procession of mankind, like the men who are to die in the arena. For indeed we are made a public spectacle before the angels of Heaven and the eyes of men. We are looked upon as fools, for Christ's sake, but you are wise in the Christian faith. We are considered weak, but you have become strong: you have found honour, we little but contempt. Up to this very hour we are hungry and thirsty, ill-clad, knocked about and practically homeless. We still have to work for our living by manual labour. Men curse us, but we return a blessing: they make our lives miserable but we take it patiently. They ruin our reputa-

Revised Standard Version

learn by us not to go beyond what is written, that none of you may be puffed up in favor of one against another. 7 For who sees anything different in you? What have you that you did not receive? If then you received it, why do you boast as if it were not a gift?

8 Already you are filled! Already you have become rich! Without us you have become kings! And would that you did reign, so that we might share the rule with you! 9 For I think that God has exhibited us apostles as last of all, like men sentenced to death; because we have become a spectacle to the world, to angels and to men. 10 We are fools for Christ's sake, but you are wise in Christ. We are weak, but you are strong. You are held in honor, but we in disrepute. 11 To the present hour we hunger and thirst, we are ill-clad and buffeted and homeless, 12 and we labor, working with our own hands. When reviled, we bless; when persecuted, we endure; 13 when slandered, we try to conciliate; we

Jerusalem Bible

example (remember the maxim: "Keep to what is written"); it is not for you, so full of your own importance, to go taking sides for one man against another. 7 In any case, brother, has anybody given you some special right? What do you have that was not given to you? And if it was given, how can you boast as though it were not? 8 Is it that you have everything you want—that you are rich already, in possession of your kingdom, with us left outside? Indeed I wish you were really kings, and we could be kings with you! 9 But instead, it seems to me, God has put us apostles at the end of his parade, with the men sentenced to death; it is true—we have been put on show in front of the whole universe, angels as well as men. 10 Here we are, fools for the sake of Christ, while you are the learned men in Christ; we have no power, but you are influential; you are celebrities, we are nobodies. 11 To this day, we go without food and drink and clothes; we are beaten and have no homes; 12 we work for our living with our own hands. When we are cursed, we answer with a blessing; when we are hounded, we put up with it; 13 we are insulted and we answer politely.

New English Bible

that you may take our case as an example, and learn to 'keep within the rules', as they say, and may not be inflated with pride as you patronize one and flout the other. Who makes you, my friend, so important? What do you possess that was not given you? If then you really received it all as a gift, why take the credit to yourself?

All of you, no doubt, have everything you could desire. You have come into your fortune already. You have come into your kingdom—and left us out. How I wish you had indeed won your kingdom; then you might share it with us! For it seems to me God has made us apostles the most abject of mankind. We are like men condemned to death in the arena, a spectacle to the whole universe—angels as well as men. We are fools for Christ's sake, while you are such sensible Christians. We are weak; you are so powerful. We are in disgrace; you are honoured. To this day we go hungry and thirsty and in rags; we are roughly handled; we wander from place to place; we wear ourselves out working with our own hands. They curse us, and we bless; they persecute us, and we submit to it; they slander us, and we humbly make our ap-

King James Version

defamed, we entreat: we are made as the filth
of the world, *and are* the offscouring of all things
unto this day. 14 I write not these things to
shame you, but as my beloved sons I warn *you.*
15 For though ye have ten thousand instructors
in Christ, yet *have ye* not many fathers: for in
Christ Jesus I have begotten you through the
gospel. 16 Wherefore I beseech you, be ye followers of me. 17 For this cause have I sent unto
you Timotheus, who is my beloved son, and
faithful in the Lord, who shall bring you into
remembrance of my ways which be in Christ, as
I teach every where in every church. 18 Now
some are puffed up, as though I would not come
to you. 19 But I will come to you shortly, if the
Lord will, and will know, not the speech of
them which are puffed up, but the power. 20 For
the kingdom of God *is* not in word, but in
power. 21 What will ye? shall I come unto you
with a rod, or in love, and *in* the spirit of meekness?

Living Bible

evil things have been said about us. Yet right
up to the present moment we are like dirt under
foot, like garbage.

14 I am not writing about these things to
make you ashamed, but to warn and counsel
you as beloved children. 15 For although you
may have ten thousand others to teach you
about Christ, remember that you have only me
as your father. For I was the one who brought
you to Christ when I preached the Gospel to
you. 16 So I beg you to follow my example, and
do as I do.

17 That is the very reason why I am sending
Timothy—to help you do this. For he is one of
those I won to Christ, a beloved and trustworthy
child in the Lord. He will remind you of what I
teach in all the churches wherever I go.

18 I know that some of you will have become
proud, thinking that I am afraid to come to deal
with you. 19 But I will come, and soon, if the
Lord will let me, and then I'll find out whether
these proud men are just big talkers or whether
they really have God's power. 20 The Kingdom
of God is not just talking; it is living by God's
power. 21 Which do you choose? Shall I come
with punishment and scolding, or shall I come
with quiet love and gentleness?

Today's English Version

insulted, we answer back with kind words. We
are no more than this world's garbage; we are
the scum of the earth to this very hour!

14 I write this to you, not because I want to
make you feel ashamed; I do it to instruct you
as my own dear children. 15 For even if you
have ten thousand guardians in your life in
Christ, you have only one father. For in your
life in Christ Jesus I have become your father,
by bringing the Good News to you. 16 I beg
you, then, follow my example. 17 For this purpose I am sending Timothy to you. He is my
own dear and faithful son in the Lord. He will
remind you of the principles which I follow in
the new life in Christ Jesus, and which I teach
in all the churches everywhere.

18 Some of you have become proud, thinking that I would not be coming to visit you.
19 If the Lord is willing, however, I will come
to you soon, and then I will find out for myself what these proud ones can do, and not just
what they can say. 20 For the Kingdom of God
is not a matter of words, but of power.
21 Which do you prefer? Shall I come to you
with a whip, or with a heart of love and gentleness?

New International Version

to this moment we have become the scum of the
earth, the refuse of the world.

14 I am not writing this to shame you, but to
warn you, as my dear children. 15 Even though
you have ten thousand guardians in Christ, you
do not have many fathers, for in Christ Jesus I
became your father through the gospel. 16 Therefore I urge you to imitate me. 17 For this reason
I am sending to you Timothy, my son whom I
love, who is faithful in the Lord. He will remind
you of my way of life in Christ Jesus, which
agrees with what I teach everywhere in every
church.

18 Some of you have become arrogant, as if
I were not coming to you. 19 But I will come to
you very soon, if the Lord is willing, and then I
will find out not only how these arrogant people are talking, but what power they have. 20 For
the kingdom of God is not a matter of talk but
of power. 21 What do you prefer? Shall I come
to you with punishment, or in love and with a
gentle spirit?

Phillips Modern English

tions but we go on trying to win them for God. We are the world's rubbish, the scum of the earth, yes, up to this very day.

4.14 A personal plea

I don't write these things merely to make you feel uncomfortable, but that you may realise facts, as my dear children. After all, you may have ten thousand teachers in the Christian faith, but you cannot have many fathers! For in Christ Jesus I am your spiritual father through the gospel; that is why I implore you to follow the footsteps of me your father. I have sent Timothy to you to help you in this. For he himself is my much-loved and faithful son in the Lord, and he will remind you of those ways of living in Christ which I teach in every church to which I go.

Some of you have apparently grown conceited since I did not visit you. But please God it will not be long before I do come to you in person. Then I shall be able to see what power, apart from their words, these pretentious ones among you really possess. For the kingdom of God is not a matter of a spate of words but of the power of Christian living.

Now it's up to you to choose! Shall I come to you ready to chastise you, or in love and gentleness?

Revised Standard Version

have become, and are now, as the refuse of the
world, the offscouring of all things.
14 I do not write this to make you ashamed,
but to admonish you as my beloved children.
15 For though you have countless guides in
Christ, you do not have many fathers. For I
became your father in Christ Jesus through
the gospel. 16 I urge you, then, be imitators of
me. 17 Therefore I sent [g] to you Timothy, my
beloved and faithful child in the Lord, to remind
you of my ways in Christ, as I teach them everywhere in every church. 18 Some are arrogant, as
though I were not coming to you. 19 But I will
come to you soon, if the Lord wills, and I will
find out not the talk of these arrogant people
but their power. 20 For the kingdom of God does
not consist in talk but in power. 21 What do you
wish? Shall I come to you with a rod, or with
love in a spirit of gentleness?

[g] Or *am sending*.

Jerusalem Bible

We are treated as the offal of the world, still to this day, the scum of the earth.

An appeal

14 I am saying all this not just to make you
ashamed but to bring you, as my dearest children, to your senses. 15 You might have thousands of guardians in Christ, but not more than
one father and it was I who begot you in Christ
Jesus by preaching the Good News. 16 That is
why I beg you to copy me 17 and why I have
sent you Timothy, my dear and faithful son in
the Lord: he will remind you of the way that I
live in Christ, as I teach it everywhere in all
the churches.
18 When it seemed that I was not coming to
visit you, some of you became self-important,
19 but I will be visiting you soon, the Lord willing, and then I shall want to know not what
these self-important people have to say, but
what they can do, 20 since the kingdom of God
is not just words, it is power. 21 It is for you
to decide: do I come with a stick in my hand
or in a spirit of love and good will?

New English Bible

peal. We are treated as the scum of the earth, the dregs of humanity, to this very day.

I am not writing thus to shame you, but to bring you to reason; for you are my dear children. You may have ten thousand tutors in Christ, but you have only one father. For in Christ Jesus you are my offspring, and mine alone, through the preaching of the Gospel. I appeal to you therefore to follow my example. That is the very reason why I have sent Timothy, who is a dear son to me and a most trustworthy Christian; he will remind you of the way of life in Christ which I follow, and which I teach everywhere in all our congregations. There are certain persons who are filled with self-importance because they think I am not coming to Corinth. I shall come very soon, if the Lord will; and then I shall take the measure of these self-important people, not by what they say, but by what power is in them. The kingdom of God is not a matter of talk, but of power. Choose, then: am I to come to you with a rod in my hand, or in love and a gentle spirit?

King James Version

5 It is reported commonly *that there is* fornication among you, and such fornication as is not so much as named among the Gentiles, that one should have his father's wife. 2 And ye are puffed up, and have not rather mourned, that he that hath done this deed might be taken away from among you. 3 For I verily, as absent in body, but present in spirit, have judged already, as though I were present, *concerning* him that hath so done this deed, 4 In the name of our Lord Jesus Christ, when ye are gathered together, and my spirit, with the power of our Lord Jesus Christ, 5 To deliver such a one unto Satan for the destruction of the flesh, that the spirit may be saved in the day of the Lord Jesus. 6 Your glorying *is* not good. Know ye not that a little leaven leaveneth the whole lump? 7 Purge out therefore the old leaven, that ye may be a new lump, as ye are unleavened. For even Christ our passover is sacrificed for us: 8 Therefore let us keep the feast, not with old leaven, neither with the leaven of malice and wickedness; but with the unleavened *bread* of sincerity and truth.

Living Bible

5 Everyone is talking about the terrible thing that has happened there among you, something so evil that even the heathen don't do it: you have a man in your church who is living in sin with his father's wife.[a] 2 And are you still so conceited, so "spiritual"? Why aren't you mourning in sorrow and shame, and seeing to it that this man is removed from your membership?

3, 4 Although I am not there with you, I have been thinking a lot about this, and in the name of the Lord Jesus Christ I have already decided what to do, just as though I were there. You are to call a meeting of the church—and the power of the Lord Jesus will be with you as you meet, and I will be there in spirit—5 and cast out this man from the fellowship of the church and into Satan's hands, to punish him,[b] in the hope that his soul will be saved when our Lord Jesus Christ returns.

6 What a terrible thing it is that you are boasting about your purity, and yet you let this sort of thing go on. Don't you realize that if even one person is allowed to go on sinning, soon all will be affected? 7 Remove this evil cancer—this wicked person—from among you, so that you can stay pure. Christ, God's Lamb, has been slain for us. 8 So let us feast upon him and grow strong in the Christian life, leaving entirely behind us the cancerous old life with all its hatreds and wickedness. Let us feast instead upon the pure bread of honor and sincerity and truth.

[*a*] Possibly his stepmother. [*b*] Literally, "for the destruction of the flesh."

Today's English Version

Immorality in the church

5 Now, it is actually being said that there is sexual immorality among you so terrible that not even the heathen would be guilty of it. I am told that a man is living with his stepmother! 2 How then, can you be proud? On the contrary, you should be filled with sadness, and the man who has done such a thing should be put out of your group. 3 As for me, even though I am far away from you in body, still I am there with you in spirit; and in the name of our Lord Jesus I have already passed judgment on the man who has done this terrible thing, as though I were there with you. 4 As you meet together, and I meet with you in my spirit, by the power of our Lord Jesus present with us, 5 you are to hand this man over to Satan for his body to be destroyed, so that his spirit may be saved in the Day of the Lord.

6 It is not right for you to be proud! You know the saying, "A little bit of yeast makes the whole batch of dough rise." 7 You must take out this old yeast of sin so that you will be entirely pure. Then you will be like a new batch of dough without any yeast, as indeed I know you actually are. For our Passover feast is ready, now that Christ, our Passover lamb, has been sacrificed. 8 Let us celebrate our feast, then, not with bread having the old yeast, the yeast of sin and wickedness, but with the bread that has no yeast, the bread of purity and truth.

New International Version

Expel the immoral brother!

5 It is actually reported that there is sexual immorality among you, and of a kind that does not occur even among pagans: A man has his father's wife. 2 And you are proud! Shouldn't you rather have been filled with grief and have put out of your fellowship the man who did this? 3 Even though I am not physically present, I am with you in spirit. And I have already passed judgment on the one who did this, just as if I were present. 4 When you are assembled in the name of our Lord Jesus and I am with you in spirit, and the power of our Lord Jesus is present, 5 hand this man over to Satan, so that his sinful nature[l] may be destroyed and his spirit saved on the day of the Lord.

6 Your boasting is not good. Don't you know that a little yeast works through the whole batch of dough? 7 Get rid of the old yeast that you may be a new batch without yeast—as you really are. For Christ, our Passover lamb, has been sacrificed. 8 Therefore, let us keep the Festival, not with the old yeast, the yeast of malice and wickedness, but with bread without yeast, the bread of sincerity and truth.

[*l*] Or *his body*.

Phillips Modern English

5.1 *A horrible sin and a stern remedy*

It is actually reported that there is sexual immorality among you, and immorality of a kind that even pagans condemn—a man has apparently taken his father's wife! Are you still proud of yourselves? Shouldn't you be overwhelmed with sorrow? The man who has done such a thing should certainly be expelled from your fellowship!

I know I am not with you physically but I am with you in spirit, and I assure you as though I were actually with you that I have already pronounced judgment in the name of the Lord Jesus on the man who has done this thing. As one present in spirit when you are assembled, I say by the power of the Lord Jesus that the man should be left to the mercy of Satan so that while his body will experience the destructive powers of sin his spirit may yet be saved in the day of the Lord.

Your pride in yourselves is lamentably out of place. Don't you know how a little yeast can permeate the whole lump? Clear out every bit of the old yeast that you may be new unleavened bread! We Christians have had a Passover lamb sacrificed for us—none other than Christ himself! So let us "keep the feast" with no trace of the yeast of the old life, nor the yeast of vice and wickedness, but with the unleavened bread of unadulterated truth!

Revised Standard Version

5 It is actually reported that there is immorality among you, and of a kind that is not found even among pagans; for a man is living with his father's wife. 2 And you are arrogant! Ought you not rather to mourn? Let him who has done this be removed from among you.

3 For though absent in body I am present in spirit, and as if present, I have already pronounced judgment 4 in the name of the Lord Jesus on the man who has done such a thing. When you are assembled, and my spirit is present, with the power of our Lord Jesus, 5 you are to deliver this man to Satan for the destruction of the flesh, that his spirit may be saved in the day of the Lord Jesus.[h]

6 Your boasting is not good. Do you not know that a little leaven leavens the whole lump? 7 Cleanse out the old leaven that you may be a new lump, as you really are unleavened. For Christ, our paschal lamb, has been sacrificed. 8 Let us, therefore, celebrate the festival, not with the old leaven, the leaven of malice and evil, but with the unleavened bread of sincerity and truth.

[h] Other ancient authorities omit *Jesus*.

Jerusalem Bible

B. Incest in Corinth

5 I have been told as an undoubted fact that one of you is living with his father's wife.[j] This is a case of sexual immorality among you that must be unparalleled even among pagans. 2 How can you be so proud of yourselves? You should be in mourning. A man who does a thing like that ought to have been expelled from the community. 3 Though I am far away in body, I am with you in spirit, and have already condemned the man who did this thing as if I were actually present. 4 When you are assembled together in the name of the Lord Jesus, and I am spiritually present with you, then with the power of our Lord Jesus 5 he is to be handed over to Satan so that his sensual body may be destroyed and his spirit saved on the day of the Lord.

6 The pride that you take in yourselves is hardly to your credit. You must know how even a small amount of yeast is enough to leaven all the dough, 7 so get rid of all the old yeast, and make yourselves into a completely new batch of bread, unleavened as you are meant to be. Christ, our passover, has been sacrificed; 8 let us celebrate the feast, then, by getting rid of all the old yeast of evil and wickedness, having only the unleavened bread of sincerity and truth.[k]

[j] Stepmother. Lv. 18:8 forbids sexual relations with "your father's wife." [k] See note *a* to Jn. 19, on the Passover practice.

New English Bible

5 I actually hear reports of sexual immorality among you, immorality such as even pagans do not tolerate: the union of a man with his father's wife. And you can still be proud of yourselves! You ought to have gone into mourning; a man who has done such a deed should have been rooted out of your company. For my part, though I am absent in body, I am present in spirit, and my judgement upon the man who did this thing is already given, as if I were indeed present: you all being assembled in the name of our Lord Jesus, and I with you in spirit, with the power of our Lord Jesus over us, this man is to be consigned to Satan for the destruction of the body, so that his spirit may be saved on the Day of the Lord.

Your self-satisfaction ill becomes you. Have you never heard the saying, 'A little leaven leavens all the dough'? The old leaven of corruption is working among you. Purge it out, and then you will be bread of a new baking. As Christians you are unleavened Passover bread; for indeed our Passover has begun; the sacrifice is offered—Christ himself. So we who observe the festival must not use the old leaven, the leaven of corruption and wickedness, but only the unleavened bread which is sincerity and truth.

King James Version

9 I wrote unto you in an epistle not to company
with fornicators: 10 Yet not altogether with the
fornicators of this world, or with the covetous,
or extortioners, or with idolaters; for then must
ye needs go out of the world. 11 But now I have
written unto you not to keep company, if any
man that is called a brother be a fornicator, or
covetous, or an idolater, or a railer, or a drunkard, or an extortioner; with such a one no not
to eat. 12 For what have I to do to judge them
also that are without? do not ye judge them
that are within? 13 But them that are without
God judgeth. Therefore put away from among
yourselves that wicked person.

6 Dare any of you, having a matter against
another, go to law before the unjust, and not
before the saints? 2 Do ye not know that the
saints shall judge the world? and if the world
shall be judged by you, are ye unworthy to judge
the smallest matters? 3 Know ye not that we
shall judge angels? how much more things that
pertain to this life? 4 If then ye have judgments

Living Bible

9 When I wrote to you before I said not to
mix with evil people. 10 But when I said that I
wasn't talking about unbelievers who live in
sexual sin, or are greedy cheats and thieves and
idol worshipers. For you can't live in this world
without being with people like that. 11 What I
meant was that you are not to keep company
with anyone who claims to be a brother Christian but indulges in sexual sins, or is greedy, or
is a swindler, or worships idols, or is a drunkard,
or abusive. Don't even eat lunch with such a
person.

12 It isn't our job to judge outsiders. But it
certainly is our job to judge and deal strongly
with those who are members of the church, and
who are sinning in these ways. 13 God alone is
the Judge of those on the outside. But you yourselves must deal with this man and put him out
of your church.

6 How is it that when you have something
against another Christian, you "go to law"
and ask a heathen court to decide the matter
instead of taking it to other Christians to decide
which of you is right? 2 Don't you know that
some day we Christians are going to judge and
govern the world? So why can't you decide even
these little things among yourselves? 3 Don't you
realize that we Christians will judge and reward
the very angels in heaven? So you should be
able to decide your problems down here on
earth easily enough. 4 Why then go to outside

[i] Or *now I write*.

Today's English Version

9 In the letter that I wrote you I told you
not to associate with immoral people. 10 Now,
I did not mean pagans who are immoral, or
greedy, or thieves, or who worship idols. To
avoid them you would have to get out of the
world completely. 11 What I meant was that
you should not associate with a man who calls
himself a brother but is immoral, or greedy, or
worships idols, or is a slanderer, or a drunkard,
or a thief. Don't even sit down to eat with such
a person.

12, 13 After all, it is none of my business to
judge outsiders. God will judge them. But should
you not judge the members of your own fellowship? As the scripture says, "Take the evil man
out of your group."

Lawsuits against brothers

6 If one of you has a dispute with a brother,
how dare he go before heathen judges, instead of letting God's people settle the matter?
2 Don't you know that God's people will judge
the world? Well, then, if you are to judge the
world, aren't you capable of judging small matters? 3 Do you not know that we shall judge the
angels? How much more, then, the things of this
life! 4 If, then, such matters come up, are you

New International Version

9 I have written you in my letter not to associate with sexually immoral people—10 not at all
meaning the people of this world who are immoral, or the greedy and swindlers, or idolaters.
In that case you would have to leave this world.
11 But now I am writing you that you must not
associate with anyone who calls himself a brother
but is sexually immoral or greedy, an idolater or
a slanderer, a drunkard or a swindler. With such
a man do not even eat.

12 What business is it of mine to judge those
outside the church? Are you not to judge those
inside? 13 God will judge those outside. "Expel
the wicked man from your number." [m]

Lawsuits among believers

6 If any of you has a dispute with another,
dare he take it before the ungodly for judgment instead of before the saints? 2 Do you not
know that God's people will judge the world?
And if you are to judge the world, are you not
competent to judge trivial cases? 3 Do you not
know that we will judge angels? How much more
the things of this life! 4 Therefore, if you have

[m] Deut. 17:7, 19:19; 22:21,24; 24:7.

Phillips Modern English

In my previous letter I said, "Don't mix with the immoral." I didn't mean, of course, that you were to have no contact at all with the immoral of this world, nor with any cheats or thieves or idolaters—for that would mean going out of the world altogether! But in this letter I tell you not to associate with any professing Christian who is known to be an impure man or a swindler, an idolater, a man with a foul tongue, a drunkard or a thief. My instruction is: "Don't even eat with such a man." Those outside the church it is not my business to judge. But surely it is your business to judge those who are inside the church—God alone can judge those who are outside. It is your plain duty to expel this wicked man from your fellowship!

6.1 Don't go to law in pagan courts

When any of you has a grievance against another, aren't you ashamed to bring the matter to be settled before a pagan court instead of before the church? Don't you know that Christians will one day judge the world? And if you are to judge the world do you consider yourselves incapable of settling such infinitely smaller matters? Don't you also know that we shall judge the very angels themselves—how much more then matters of this world only! In any case, if

Revised Standard Version

9 I wrote to you in my letter not to associate
with immoral men; 10 not at all meaning the
immoral of this world, or the greedy and robbers, or idolaters, since then you would need to
go out of the world. 11 But rather I wrote[t] to
you not to associate with any one who bears
the name of brother if he is guilty of immorality
or greed, or is an idolater, reviler, drunkard, or
robber—not even to eat with such a one. 12 For
what have I to do with judging outsiders? Is it
not those inside the church whom you are to
judge? 13 God judges those outside. "Drive out
the wicked person from among you."

6 When one of you has a grievance against
a brother, does he dare go to law before the
unrighteous instead of the saints? 2 Do you
not know that the saints will judge the world?
And if the world is to be judged by you, are you
incompetent to try trivial cases? 3 Do you not
know that we are to judge angels? How much
more, matters pertaining to this life! 4 If then

Jerusalem Bible

9 When I wrote in my letter to you not to
associate with people living immoral lives, 10 I
was not meaning to include all the people in
the world who are sexually immoral, any more
than I meant to include all usurers and swindlers
or idol worshipers. To do that, you would have
to withdraw from the world altogether. 11 What
I wrote was that you should not associate with
a brother Christian who is leading an immoral
life, or is a usurer, or idolatrous, or a slanderer,
or a drunkard, or is dishonest; you should not
even eat a meal with people like that. 12 It is
not my business to pass judgment on those outside. Of those who are inside, you can surely
be the judges. 13 But of those who are outside,
God is the judge.

You must drive out this evildoer from among you.[l]

C. Recourse to the pagan courts

6 How dare one of your members take up a
complaint against another in the law courts
of the unjust[m] instead of before the saints? 2 As
you know, it is the saints who are to "judge
the world"; and if the world is to be judged by
you, how can you be unfit to judge trifling
cases? 3 Since we are also to judge angels, it follows that we can judge matters of everyday life;
4 but when you have had cases of that kind, the

[l] Dt. 13:6. [m] The pagan magistrates of Corinth.

New English Bible

In my letter I wrote that you must have nothing to do with loose livers. I was not, of course, referring to pagans who lead loose lives or are grabbers and swindlers or idolaters. To avoid them you would have to get out of the world altogether. I now write that you must have nothing to do with any so-called Christian who leads a loose life, or is grasping, or idolatrous, a slanderer, a drunkard, or a swindler. You should not even eat with any such person. What business of mine is it to judge outsiders? God is their judge. You are judges within the fellowship. Root out the evil-doer from your community.

6 If one of your number has a dispute with another, has he the face to take it to pagan law-courts instead of to the community of God's people? It is God's people who are to judge the world; surely you know that. And if the world is to come before you for judgement, are you incompetent to deal with these trifling cases? Are you not aware that we are to judge angels? How much more, mere matters of business! If there-

King James Version

of things pertaining to this life, set them to judge who are least esteemed in the church. 5 I speak to your shame. Is it so, that there is not a wise man among you? no, not one that shall be able to judge between his brethren? 6 But brother goeth to law with brother, and that before the unbelievers. 7 Now therefore there is utterly a fault among you, because ye go to law one with another. Why do ye not rather take wrong? Why do ye not rather *suffer yourselves to* be defrauded? 8 Nay, ye do wrong, and defraud, and that *your* brethren. 9 Know ye not that the unrighteous shall not inherit the kingdom of God? Be not deceived: neither fornicators, nor idolaters, nor adulterers, nor effeminate, nor abusers of themselves with mankind, 10 Nor thieves, nor covetous, nor drunkards, nor revilers, nor extortioners, shall inherit the kingdom of God. 11 And such were some of you: but ye are washed, but ye are sanctified, but ye are justified in the name of the Lord Jesus, and by the Spirit of our God. 12 All things are lawful unto me, but all things are not expedient: all things are lawful for me, but I will not be brought under the power of any. 13 Meats for

Living Bible

judges who are not even Christians?[a] 5 I am trying to make you ashamed. Isn't there anyone in all the church who is wise enough to decide these arguments? 6 But, instead, one Christian sues another and accuses his Christian brother in front of unbelievers.

7 To have such lawsuits at all is a real defeat for you as Christians. Why not just accept mistreatment and leave it at that? It would be far more honoring to the Lord to let yourselves be cheated. 8 But, instead, you yourselves are the ones who do wrong, cheating others, even your own brothers.

9, 10 Don't you know that those doing such things have no share in the Kingdom of God? Don't fool yourselves. Those who live immoral lives, who are idol worshipers, adulterers or homosexuals—will have no share in his kingdom. Neither will thieves or greedy people, drunkards, slanderers, or robbers. 11 There was a time when some of you were just like that but now your sins are washed away, and you are set apart for God, and he has accepted you because of what the Lord Jesus Christ and the Spirit of our God have done for you. 12 I can do anything I want to if Christ has not said no,[b] but some of these things aren't good for me. Even if I am allowed to do them, I'll refuse to if I think they might get such a grip on me that I can't easily stop when I want to. 13 For instance, take the matter

[a] Or, "Even the least capable people in the church should be able to decide these things for you." Both interpretations are possible. [b] Literally, "All things are lawful for me." Obviously, Paul is not here permitting sins such as have just been expressly prohibited in verses 8 and 9. He is apparently quoting some in the church of lustful Corinth who were excusing their sins.

Today's English Version

going to take them to be settled by people who have no standing in the church? 5 Shame on you! Surely there is at least one wise man in your fellowship who can settle a dispute between the brothers. 6 Instead, one brother goes to court against another, and lets unbelievers judge the case!

7 The very fact that you have legal disputes among yourselves shows that you have failed completely. Would it not be better for you to be wronged? Would it not be better for you to be robbed? 8 Instead, you yourselves wrong one another, and rob one another, even your very brothers! 9 Surely you know that the wicked will not receive God's Kingdom. Do not fool yourselves; people who are immoral, or worship idols, or are adulterers, or homosexual perverts, 10 or who rob, or are greedy, or are drunkards, or who slander others, or are thieves—none of these will receive God's Kingdom. 11 Some of you were like that. But you have been cleansed from sin; you have been dedicated to God; you have been put right with God through the name of the Lord Jesus Christ and by the Spirit of our God.

Use your bodies for God's glory

12 Someone will say, "I am allowed to do anything." Yes; but not everything is good for you. I could say, "I am allowed to do anything"; but I am not going to let anything make a slave of me. 13 Someone else will say, "Food is for

New International Version

disputes about such matters, appoint as judges even men of little account in the church![n] 5 I say this to shame you. Is it possible that there is nobody among you wise enough to judge a dispute between believers? 6 But instead, one brother goes to law against another—and this in front of unbelievers!

7 The very fact that you have lawsuits among you means you have been completely defeated already. Why not rather be wronged? Why not rather be cheated? 8 Instead, you yourselves cheat and do wrong, and you do this to your brothers.

9 Don't you know that the wicked will not inherit the kingdom of God? Do not be deceived: Neither the sexually immoral nor idolaters nor adulterers nor male prostitutes nor homosexual offenders 10 nor thieves nor the greedy nor drunkards nor slanderers nor swindlers will inherit the kingdom of God. 11 And that is what some of you were. But you were washed, you were sanctified, you were justified in the name of the Lord Jesus Christ and by the Spirit of our God.

Sexual immorality

12 "Everything is permissible for me"—but not everything is beneficial. "Everything is permissible for me"—but I will not be mastered by anything. 13 "Food for the stomach and the

[n] Or *matters, do you appoint as judges men of little account in the church?*

Phillips Modern English

you find you have to judge matters of this world, why choose as judges those who count for nothing in the church? I say this deliberately to rouse your sense of shame. Are you really unable to find among your number one man with enough sense to decide a dispute between one and another of you, or must one brother resort to law against another and that before those who have no faith in Christ! It is surely obvious that something must be seriously wrong in your church for you to be having lawsuits at all. Why not *let* yourself be wronged or cheated? Instead of that you cheat and wrong your own brothers.

Have you forgotten that the kingdom of God will never belong to the wicked? Don't be under any illusion—neither the impure, the idolater or the adulterer; neither the effeminate, the pervert or the thief; neither the swindler, the drunkard, the foul-mouthed or the rapacious shall have any share in the kingdom of God. *And such were some of you!* But you have cleansed yourselves from all that, you have been made whole in spirit, you have been justified in the name of the Lord Jesus and in the Spirit of our God.

6.12 Christian liberty does not mean moral licence

As a Christian I *may* do anything, but that does not mean that everything is good for me. I may do everything, but I must not be a slave of anything. Food was meant for the stomach

Revised Standard Version

you have such cases, why do you lay them before
those who are least esteemed by the church? 5 I
say this to your shame. Can it be that there is
no man among you wise enough to decide between members of the brotherhood, 6 but
brother goes to law against brother, and that
before unbelievers?
7 To have lawsuits at all with one another is
defeat for you. Why not rather suffer wrong?
Why not rather be defrauded? 8 But you yourselves wrong and defraud, and that even your
own brethren.
9 Do you not know that the unrighteous will
not inherit the kingdom of God? Do not be deceived; neither the immoral, nor idolaters, nor
adulterers, nor sexual perverts, 10 nor thieves,
nor the greedy, nor drunkards, nor revilers, nor
robbers will inherit the kingdom of God. 11 And
such were some of you. But you were washed, you were sanctified, you were justified in the name of the Lord Jesus Christ and in the Spirit of our God.
12 "All things are lawful for me," but not all
things are helpful. "All things are lawful for me,"
but I will not be enslaved by anything. 13 "Food

Jerusalem Bible

people you appointed to try them were not even
respected in the Church. 5 You should be
ashamed: is there really not one reliable man
among you to settle differences between brothers
6 and so one brother brings a court case against
another in front of unbelievers? 7 It is bad
enough for you to have lawsuits at all against one another: oughtn't you to let yourselves be
wronged, and let yourselves be cheated? 8 But
you are doing the wronging and the cheating, and to your own brothers.
9 You know perfectly well that people who
do wrong will not inherit the kingdom of God: people of immoral lives, idolaters, adulterers,
catamites, sodomites, 10 thieves, usurers, drunkards, slanderers and swindlers will never inherit
the kingdom of God. 11 These are the sort of
people some of you were once, but now you have been washed clean, and sanctified, and justified through the name of the Lord Jesus Christ and through the Spirit of our God.

D. Fornication

12 "For me there are no forbidden things"[n];
maybe, but not everything does good. I agree there are no forbidden things for me, but I am
not going to let anything dominate me. 13 Food

[n] Probably one of Paul's own sayings which has been misapplied by false teachers: this section of the letter is directed against the libertines, who had been teaching that sexual intercourse was as necessary for the body as food and drink.

New English Bible

fore you have such business disputes, how can you entrust jurisdiction to outsiders, men who count for nothing in our community? I write this to shame you. Can it be that there is not a single wise man among you able to give a decision in a brother-Christian's cause? Must brother go to law with brother—and before unbelievers? Indeed, you already fall below your standard in going to law with one another at all. Why not rather suffer injury? Why not rather let yourself be robbed? So far from this, you actually injure and rob—injure and rob your brothers! Surely you know that the unjust will never come into possession of the kingdom of God. Make no mistake: no fornicator or idolater, none who are guilty either of adultery or of homosexual perversion, no thieves or grabbers or drunkards or slanderers or swindlers, will possess the kingdom of God. Such were some of you. But you have been through the purifying waters; you have been dedicated to God and justified through the name of the Lord Jesus and the Spirit of our God.

'I am free to do anything', you say. Yes, but not everything is for my good. No doubt I am free to do anything, but I for one will not let anything make free with me. 'Food is for the

King James Version

the belly, and the belly for meats: but God shall
destroy both it and them. Now the body *is* not
for fornication, but for the Lord; and the Lord
for the body. 14And God hath both raised up
the Lord, and will also raise up us by his own
power. 15 Know ye not that your bodies are the
members of Christ? shall I then take the members of Christ, and make *them* the members of
a harlot? God forbid. 16 What! know ye not
that he which is joined to a harlot is one body?
for two, saith he, shall be one flesh. 17 But he
that is joined unto the Lord is one spirit. 18 Flee
fornication. Every sin that a man doeth is without the body; but he that committeth fornication sinneth against his own body. 19 What!
know ye not that your body is the temple of
the Holy Ghost *which is* in you, which ye have
of God, and ye are not your own? 20 For ye are
bought with a price: therefore glorify God in
your body, and in your spirit, which are God's.

Living Bible

of eating. God has given us an appetite for food
and stomachs to digest it. But that doesn't mean
we should eat more than we need. Don't think
of eating as important, because some day God
will do away with both stomachs and food.

But sexual sin is never right: our bodies were
not made for that, but for the Lord, and the
Lord wants to fill our bodies with himself. 14And
God is going to raise our bodies from the dead
by his power just as he raised up the Lord Jesus
Christ. 15 Don't you realize that your bodies are
actually parts and members of Christ? So should
I take part of Christ and join him to a prostitute? Never! 16And don't you know that if a
man joins himself to a prostitute she becomes
a part of him and he becomes a part of her?
For God tells us in the Scripture that in his
sight the two become one person. 17 But if you
give yourself to the Lord, you and Christ are
joined together as one person.

18 That is why I say to run from sex sin. No
other sin affects the body as this one does.
When you sin this sin it is against your own
body. 19 Haven't you yet learned that your body
is the home of the Holy Spirit God gave you,
and that he lives within you? Your own body
does not belong to you. 20 For God has bought
you with a great price. So use every part of
your body to give glory back to God, because
he owns it.

Today's English Version

the stomach, and the stomach is for food." Yes;
but God will put an end to both. A man's body
is not to be used for immoral purposes, but to
serve the Lord; and the Lord serves the body.
14 God raised the Lord from death, and he will
also raise us by his power.

15 You know that your bodies are parts of
the body of Christ. Shall I take a part of Christ's
body and make it part of the body of a prostitute? Impossible! 16 Or perhaps you don't know
that the man who joins his body to a prostitute
becomes physically one with her? The scripture
says quite plainly, "The two will become one
body." 17 But he who joins himself to the Lord
becomes spiritually one with him.

18 Avoid immorality. Any other sin a man
commits does not affect his body; but the man
who commits immorality sins against his own
body. 19 Don't you know that your body is the
temple of the Holy Spirit, who lives in you, and
was given to you by God? You do not belong
to yourselves but to God; 20 he bought you for
a price. So use your bodies for God's glory.

New International Version

stomach for food"—but God will destroy them
both. The body is not meant for sexual immorality, but for the Lord, and the Lord for the
body. 14 By his power God raised the Lord from
the dead, and he will raise us also. 15 Do you
not know that your bodies are members of
Christ himself? Shall I then take the members
of Christ and unite them with a prostitute?
Never! 16 Do you not know that he who unites
himself with a prostitute is one with her in
body? For it is said, "The two will become one
flesh." [o] 17 But he who unites himself with the
Lord is one with him in spirit.

18 Flee from sexual immorality. All other sins
a man commits are outside his body, but he who
sins sexually sins against his own body. 19 Do
you not know that your body is a temple of
the Holy Spirit, who is in you, whom you have
received from God? You are not your own;
20 you were bought at a price. Therefore honor
God with your body.

[*o*] Gen. 2:24.

Phillips Modern English

and the stomach for food; but God has no permanent purpose for either. But you cannot say that our physical body was made for sexual promiscuity; it was made for the Lord, and in the Lord is the answer to its needs. The God who raised the Lord from the dead will also raise us mortal men by his power. Have you not realised that your bodies are integral parts of Christ himself? Am I then to take parts of Christ and join them to a prostitute? Never! Don't you realise that when a man joins himself to a prostitute he makes with her a physical unity? For, God says, "the two shall be one flesh". On the other hand the man who joins himself to the Lord is one with him in spirit.

Avoid sexual looseness like the plague! Every other sin that a man commits is done outside his own body, but this is an offence against his own body. Have you forgotten that your body is the temple of the Holy Spirit, who lives in you and is God's gift to you, and that you are not the owner of your own body? You have been bought, and at a price! Therefore bring glory to God in your body.

Revised Standard Version

is meant for the stomach and the stomach for
food"—and God will destroy both one and the
other. The body is not meant for immorality, but
for the Lord, and the Lord for the body. 14 And
God raised the Lord and will also raise us up
by his power. 15 Do you not know that your
bodies are members of Christ? Shall I therefore
take the members of Christ and make them
members of a prostitute? Never! 16 Do you not
know that he who joins himself to a prostitute
becomes one body with her? For, as it is written,
"The two shall become one flesh." 17 But he who
is united to the Lord becomes one spirit with
him. 18 Shun immorality. Every other sin which
a man commits is outside the body; but the
immoral man sins against his own body. 19 Do
you not know that your body is a temple of the
Holy Spirit within you, which you have from
God? You are not your own; 20 you were bought
with a price. So glorify God in your body.

Jerusalem Bible

is only meant for the stomach, and the stomach
for food; yes, and God is going to do away
with both of them. But the body—this is not
meant for fornication; it is for the Lord, and
the Lord for the body. 14 God, who raised the
Lord from the dead, will by his power raise us
up too.
15 You know, surely, that your bodies are
members making up the body of Christ; do you
think I can take parts of Christ's body and join
them to the body of a prostitute? Never! 16 As
you know, a man who goes with a prostitute is
one body with her, since *the two*, as it is said,
become one flesh. 17 But anyone who is joined
to the Lord is one spirit with him.
18 Keep away from fornication. All the other
sins are committed outside the body; but to for-
nicate is to sin against your own body. 19 Your
body, you know, is the temple of the Holy Spirit,
who is in you since you received him from God.
You are not your own property; 20 you have
been bought and paid for. That is why you
should use your body for the glory of God.

New English Bible

belly and the belly for food', you say. True; and one day God will put an end to both. But it is not true that the body is for lust; it is for the Lord—and the Lord for the body. God not only raised our Lord from the dead; he will also raise us by his power. Do you not know that your bodies are limbs and organs of Christ? Shall I then take from Christ his bodily parts and make them over to a harlot? Never! You surely know that anyone who links himself with a harlot becomes physically one with her (for Scripture says, 'The pair shall become one flesh'); but he who links himself with Christ is one with him, spiritually. Shun fornication. Every other sin that a man can commit is outside the body; but the fornicator sins against his own body. Do you not know that your body is a shrine of the indwelling Holy Spirit, and the Spirit is God's gift to you? You do not belong to yourselves; you were bought at a price. Then honour God in your body.

King James Version

7 Now concerning the things whereof ye wrote unto me: *It is* good for a man not to touch a woman. 2 Nevertheless, *to avoid* fornication, let every man have his own wife, and let every woman have her own husband. 3 Let the husband render unto the wife due benevolence: and likewise also the wife unto the husband. 4 The wife hath not power of her own body, but the husband: and likewise also the husband hath not power of his own body, but the wife. 5 Defraud ye not one the other, except *it be* with consent for a time, that ye may give yourselves to fasting and prayer; and come together again, that Satan tempt you not for your incontinency. 6 But I speak this by permission, *and* not of commandment. 7 For I would that all men were even as I myself. But every man hath his proper gift of God, one after this manner, and another after that. 8 I say therefore to the unmarried and widows, It is good for them if they abide even as I. 9 But if they cannot contain, let them

Living Bible

7 Now about those questions you asked in your last letter: my answer is that if you do not marry, it is good. 2 But usually it is best to be married, each man having his own wife, and each woman having her own husband, because otherwise you might fall back into sin.

3 The man should give his wife all that is her right as a married woman, and the wife should do the same for her husband: 4 for a girl who marries no longer has full right to her own body, for her husband then has his rights to it, too; and in the same way the husband no longer has full right to his own body, for it belongs also to his wife. 5 So do not refuse these rights to each other. The only exception to this rule would be the agreement of both husband and wife to refrain from the rights of marriage for a limited time, so that they can give themselves more completely to prayer. Afterwards, they should come together again so that Satan won't be able to tempt them because of their lack of self-control.

6 I'm not saying you *must* marry; but you certainly *may* if you wish. 7 I wish everyone could get along without marrying, just as I do. But we are not all the same. God gives some the gift of a husband or wife, and others he gives the gift of being able to stay happily unmarried. 8 So I say to those who aren't married, and to widows—better to stay unmarried if you can, just as I am. 9 But if you can't control

Today's English Version

Questions about marriage

7 Now, to deal with the matters you wrote about.

A man does well not to marry. 2 But because there is so much immorality, every man should have his own wife, and every woman should have her own husband. 3 A man should fulfill his duty as a husband and a woman should fulfill her duty as a wife, and each should satisfy the other's needs. 4 The wife is not the master of her own body, but the husband is; in the same way the husband is not the master of his own body, but the wife is. 5 Do not deny yourselves to each other, unless you first agree to do so for a while, in order to spend your time in prayer; but then resume normal marital relations, to keep you from giving in to Satan's temptation because of your lack of self-control.

6 I tell you this not as an order, but simply as a permission. 7 Actually I would prefer that all were as I am; but each one has the special gift that God has given him, one man this gift, another man that.

8 Now, I say this to the unmarried and to the widows: it would be better for you to continue to live alone, as I do. 9 But if you cannot re-

New International Version

Marriage

7 Now for the matters you wrote about: It is good for a man not to marry. 2 But since there is so much immorality, each man should have his own wife, and each woman her own husband. 3 The husband should fulfill his marital duty to his wife, and likewise the wife to her husband. 4 The wife's body does not belong to her alone but also to her husband. In the same way, the husband's body does not belong to him alone but also to his wife. 5 Do not deprive each other except by mutual consent and for a time, so that you may devote yourselves to prayer. Then come together again so that Satan will not tempt you because of your lack of self-control. 6 I say this as a concession, not as a command. 7 I wish that all men were as I am. But each man has his own gift from God; one has this gift, another has that.

8 Now to the unmarried and the widows I say: It is good for them to stay unmarried, as I am. 9 But if they cannot control themselves, they

Phillips Modern English

7.1 The question of marriage in present circumstances

Now let me deal with the questions raised in your letter.

It is a good principle for a man to have no physical contact with women. Nevertheless, because casual liaisons are so prevalent, let every man have his own wife and every woman her own husband. The husband should give his wife what is due to her as his wife, and the wife should be as fair to her husband. The wife has no longer full rights over her own person, but shares them with her husband. In the same way the husband shares his personal rights with his wife. Do not cheat each other of normal sexual intercourse, unless of course you both decide to abstain temporarily to make special opportunity for prayer. But afterwards you should resume relations as before, or you will expose yourselves to the obvious temptation of Satan.

I give the advice above more as a concession than as a command. I wish that all men were like myself, but I realise that everyone has his own particular gift from God, some one thing and some another. Yet to those who are unmarried or widowed, I say definitely that it is a good thing to remain unattached, as I am. But

Revised Standard Version

7 Now concerning the matters about which you wrote. It is well for a man not to touch a woman. 2 But because of the temptation to immorality, each man should have his own wife and each woman her own husband. 3 The husband should give to his wife her conjugal rights, and likewise the wife to her husband. 4 For the wife does not rule over her own body, but the husband does; likewise the husband does not rule over his own body, but the wife does. 5 Do not refuse one another except perhaps by agreement for a season, that you may devote yourselves to prayer; but then come together again, lest Satan tempt you through lack of self-control. 6 I say this by way of concession, not of command. 7 I wish that all were as I myself am. But each has his own special gift from God, one of one kind and one of another.

8 To the unmarried and the widows I say that it is well for them to remain single as I do. 9 But if they cannot exercise self-control, they

Jerusalem Bible

II. Answers to various questions

A. Marriage and virginity

7 Now for the questions about which you wrote. Yes, it is a good thing for a man not to touch a woman; 2 but since sex is always a danger, let each man have his own wife and each woman her own husband. 3 The husband must give his wife what she has the right to expect, and so too the wife to the husband. 4 The wife has no rights over her own body; it is the husband who has them. In the same way, the husband has no rights over his body; the wife has them. 5 Do not refuse each other except by mutual consent, and then only for an agreed time, to leave yourselves free for prayer; then come together again in case Satan should take advantage of your weakness to tempt you. 6 This is a suggestion, not a rule: 7 I should like everyone to be like me, but everybody has his own particular gifts from God, one with a gift for one thing and another with a gift for the opposite.

8 There is something I want to add for the sake of widows and those who are not married: it is a good thing for them to stay as they are, like me, 9 but if they cannot control the sexual

New English Bible

The Christian in a pagan society

7 And now for the matters you wrote about. It is a good thing for a man to have nothing to do with women;[a] but because there is so much immorality, let each man have his own wife and each woman her own husband. The husband must give the wife what is due to her, and the wife equally must give the husband his due. The wife cannot claim her body as her own; it is her husband's. Equally, the husband cannot claim his body as his own; it is his wife's. Do not deny yourselves to one another, except when you agree upon a temporary abstinence in order to devote yourselves to prayer; afterwards you may come together again; otherwise, for lack of self-control, you may be tempted by Satan.

All this I say by way of concession, not command. I should like you all to be as I am myself; but everyone has the gift God has granted him, one this gift and another that.

To the unmarried and to widows I say this: it is a good thing if they stay as I am myself; but if they cannot control themselves, they

[a] *Or* You say, 'It is a good thing . . . women'; . . .

King James Version

marry: for it is better to marry than to burn.
10And unto the married I command, *yet* not I,
but the Lord, Let not the wife depart from *her*
husband: 11 But and if she depart, let her remain unmarried, or be reconciled to *her* husband: and let not the husband put away *his*
wife. 12 But to the rest speak I, not the Lord:
If any brother hath a wife that believeth not,
and she be pleased to dwell with him, let him
not put her away. 13And the woman which hath
a husband that believeth not, and if he be
pleased to dwell with her, let her not leave him.
14 For the unbelieving husband is sanctified by
the wife, and the unbelieving wife is sanctified
by the husband: else were your children unclean; but now are they holy. 15 But if the
unbelieving depart, let him depart. A brother or
a sister is not under bondage in such *cases:* but
God hath called us to peace. 16 For what knowest thou, O wife, whether thou shalt save *thy*

Living Bible

yourselves, go ahead and marry. It is better to
marry than to burn with lust.
10 Now, for those who are married I have a
command, not just a suggestion. And it is not
a command from me, for this is what the Lord
himself has said: A wife must not leave her
husband. 11 But if she is separated from him,
let her remain single or else go back to him.
And the husband must not divorce his wife.
12 Here I want to add some suggestions of
my own. These are not direct commands from
the Lord, but they seem right to me: If a Christian has a wife who is not a Christian, but she
wants to stay with him anyway, he must not
leave her or divorce her. 13And if a Christian
woman has a husband who isn't a Christian, and
he wants her to stay with him, she must not
leave him. 14 For perhaps the husband who isn't
a Christian may become a Christian with the
help of his Christian wife. And the wife who
isn't a Christian may become a Christian with
the help of her Christian husband. Otherwise, if
the family separates, the children might never
come to know the Lord; whereas a united family
may, in God's plan, result in the children's
salvation.
15 But if the husband or wife who isn't a
Christian is eager to leave, it is permitted. In
such cases the Christian husband or wife should
not insist that the other stay, for God wants his
children to live in peace and harmony. 16 For,
after all, there is no assurance to you wives that
your husbands will be converted if they stay; and

Today's English Version

strain your desires, go on and marry—it is better
to marry than to burn with passion.
10 For married people I have a command,
not my own but the Lord's: a wife must not
leave her husband; 11 if she does, she must remain single or else be reconciled to her husband;
and a husband must not divorce his wife.
12 To the others I say (I, myself, not the
Lord): if a Christian man has a wife who is
an unbeliever and she agrees to go on living
with him, he must not divorce her. 13And if a
Christian woman is married to a man who is an
unbeliever, and he agrees to go on living with
her, she must not divorce him. 14 For the unbelieving husband is made acceptable to God by
being united to his wife, and the unbelieving
wife is made acceptable to God by being united
to her Christian husband. If this were not so,
their children would be like pagan children; but
as it is, they are acceptable to God. 15 However,
if the one who is not a believer wishes to leave
the Christian partner, let it be so. In such cases
the Christian partner, whether husband or wife,
is free to act. God has called you to live in
peace. 16 How can you be sure, Christian wife,
that you will not save your husband? Or how

New International Version

should marry, for it is better to marry than to
burn with passion.
10 To the married I give this command (not
I, but the Lord): A wife must not separate from
her husband. 11 But if she does, she must remain
unmarried or else be reconciled to her husband.
And a husband must not divorce his wife.
12 To the rest I say this (I, not the Lord):
If any brother has a wife who is not a believer
and she is willing to live with him, he must not
divorce her. 13And if a woman has a husband
who is not a believer and he is willing to live
with her, she must not divorce him. 14 For the
unbelieving husband has been sanctified through
his wife, and the unbelieving wife has been sanctified through her believing husband. Otherwise
your children would be "unclean," but as it is,
they are holy.
15 But if the unbeliever leaves, let him do so.
A believing man or woman is not bound in
such circumstances; God has called us to live in
peace. 16 How do you know, wife, whether you
will save your husband? Or, how do you know,

Phillips Modern English

if they have not the gift of self-control in such matters, by all means let them get married. It is better for them to be married than to be tortured by unsatisfied desire.

To those who are already married my command, or rather, the Lord's command, is that the wife should not be separated from her husband. But if she is separated from him she should either remain unattached or else be reconciled to her husband. A husband must not desert his wife.

7.12 Advice over marriage between Christian and pagan

To other people my advice (though this is not a divine command) is this. If a brother has a non-Christian wife who is willing to live with him he should not leave her. A wife in a similar position should not leave her husband. For the unbelieving husband is consecrated by being joined to the person of his wife; the unbelieving wife is similarly consecrated by the Christian brother she has married. If this were not so then your children would bear the stains of paganism, whereas they are actually consecrated to God.

But if the unbelieving partner decides to separate, then let there be a separation. The Christian partner need not consider himself bound in such cases. Yet God has called us to live in peace, and after all how can you, who are a wife, know whether you will be able to save

Revised Standard Version

should marry. For it is better to marry than to be aflame with passion.
10 To the married I give charge, not I but the Lord, that the wife should not separate from her husband
11 (but if she does, let her remain single or else be reconciled to her husband)—and that the husband should not divorce his wife.
12 To the rest I say, not the Lord, that if any brother has a wife who is an unbeliever, and she consents to live with him, he should not divorce her.
13 If any woman has a husband who is an unbeliever, and he consents to live with her, she should not divorce him.
14 For the unbelieving husband is consecrated through his wife, and the unbelieving wife is consecrated through her husband. Otherwise, your children would be unclean, but as it is they are holy.
15 But if the unbelieving partner desires to separate, let it be so; in such a case the brother or sister is not bound. For God has called us[l] to peace.
16 Wife, how do you know whether you will save your hus-

[l] Other ancient authorities read *you*.

Jerusalem Bible

urges, they should get married, since it is better to be married than to be tortured.
10 For the married I have something to say, and this is not from me but from the Lord: a wife must not leave her husband—
11 or if she does leave him, she must either remain unmarried or else make it up with her husband—nor must a husband send his wife away.
12 The rest is from me and not from the Lord. If a brother has a wife who is an unbeliever, and she is content to live with him, he must not send her away;
13 and if a woman has an unbeliever for her husband, and he is content to live with her, she must not leave him.
14 This is because the unbelieving husband is made one with the saints through his wife, and the unbelieving wife is made one with the saints through her husband. If this were not so, your children would be unclean, whereas in fact they are holy.
15 However, if the unbelieving partner does not consent, they may separate; in these circumstances, the brother or sister is not tied: God has called you to a life of peace.
16 If you are a wife, it may be your part to save your husband, for

New English Bible

should marry. Better be married than burn with vain desire.

To the married I give this ruling, which is not mine but the Lord's: a wife must not separate herself from her husband; if she does, she must either remain unmarried or be reconciled to her husband; and the husband must not divorce his wife.

To the rest I say this, as my own word, not as the Lord's: if a Christian has a heathen wife, and she is willing to live with him, he must not divorce her; and a woman who has a heathen husband willing to live with her must not divorce her husband. For the heathen husband now belongs to God through his Christian wife, and the heathen wife through her Christian husband. Otherwise your children would not belong to God, whereas in fact they do. If on the other hand the heathen partner wishes for a separation, let him have it. In such cases the Christian husband or wife is under no compulsion; but God's call is a call to live in peace. Think of it: as a wife you may be your husband's salvation; as a

King James Version

husband? or how knowest thou, O man, whether
thou shalt save *thy* wife? 17 But as God hath
distributed to every man, as the Lord hath called
every one, so let him walk. And so ordain I in
all churches. 18 Is any man called being circumcised? let him not become uncircumcised. Is any
called in uncircumcision? let him not be circumcised. 19 Circumcision is nothing, and uncircumcision is nothing, but the keeping of the commandments of God. 20 Let every man abide in
the same calling wherein he was called. 21 Art
thou called *being* a servant? care not for it: but
if thou mayest be made free, use *it* rather. 22 For
he that is called in the Lord, *being* a servant,
is the Lord's freeman: likewise also he that is
called, *being* free, is Christ's servant. 23 Ye are
bought with a price; be not ye the servants of
men. 24 Brethren, let every man, wherein he is
called, therein abide with God. 25 Now concerning virgins I have no commandment of the Lord:

Living Bible

the same may be said to you husbands concerning your wives.

17 But be sure in deciding these matters that
you are living as God intended, marrying or
not marrying in accordance with God's direction
and help, and accepting whatever situation God
has put you into. This is my rule for all the
churches.

18 For instance, a man who already has gone
through the Jewish ceremony of circumcision
before he became a Christian shouldn't worry
about it; and if he hasn't been circumcised, he
shouldn't do it now. 19 For it doesn't make any
difference at all whether a Christian has gone
through this ceremony or not. But it makes a
lot of difference whether he is pleasing God
and keeping God's commandments. That is the
important thing.

20 Usually a person should keep on with
the work he was doing when God called him.
21 Are you a slave? Don't let that worry you—
but of course, if you get a chance to be free,
take it. 22 If the Lord calls you, and you are a
slave, remember that Christ has set you free
from the awful power of sin; and if he has
called you and you are free, remember that you
are now a slave of Christ. 23 You have been
bought and paid for by Christ, so you belong to
him—be free now from all these earthly prides
and fears.[a] 24 So, dear brothers, whatever situation a person is in when he becomes a Christian,
let him stay there, for now the Lord is there to
help him.

25 Now I will try to answer your other question. What about girls who are not yet married?

[a] Literally, "Become not bondservants of men."

Today's English Version

can you be sure, Christian husband, that you
will not save your wife?

Live as God called you

17 Each one should go on living according to
the Lord's gift to him, and as he was when God
called him. This is the rule I teach in all the
churches. 18 If a circumcised man has accepted
God's call, he should not try to remove the
marks of circumcision; if an uncircumcised man
has accepted God's call, he should not get circumcised. 19 Because being circumcised or not
means nothing. What matters is to obey God's
commandments. 20 Every man should remain as
he was when he accepted God's call. 21 Were
you a slave when God called you? Well, never
mind; but if you do have a chance to become
a free man, use it. 22 For a slave who has been
called by the Lord is the Lord's free man; in
the same way a free man who has been called
by Christ is his slave. 23 God bought you for a
price; so do not become men's slaves. 24 Brothers, each one should remain in fellowship with
God in the same condition he was when he was
called.

Questions about the unmarried and the widows

25 Now, the matter about the unmarried: I
do not have a command from the Lord, but I

New International Version

husband, whether you will save your wife?

17 Nevertheless, each one should retain the
place in life that the Lord assigned to him and
to which God has called him. This is the rule I
lay down in all the churches. 18 Was a man already circumcised when he was called? He
should not become uncircumcised. Was a man
uncircumcised when he was called? He should
not be circumcised. 19 Circumcision is nothing
and uncircumcision is nothing. Keeping God's
commands is what counts. 20 Each one should
remain in the situation which he was in when
God called him. 21 Were you a slave when you
were called? Don't let it trouble you—although
if you can gain your freedom, do so. 22 For he
who was a slave when he was called by the Lord
is the Lord's freedman; similarly, he who was a
free man when he was called is Christ's slave.
23 You were bought at a price; do not become
slaves of men. 24 Brothers, each man, as responsible to God, should remain in the situation God
called him to.

25 Now about virgins: I have no command
from the Lord, but I give a judgment as one

Phillips Modern English

your husband or not? And the same applies to you who are a husband.

I merely add to the above that each man should live his life with the gifts that the Lord has given him and in the condition in which God has called him. This is the rule I lay down in all the churches.

For example, if a man was circumcised when God called him he should not attempt to remove the signs of his circumcision. If on the other hand he was uncircumcised he should not become circumcised. Being circumcised or not being circumcised, what do they matter? The great thing is to obey the orders of God. Everyone should continue in the state in which he heard the call of God. Were you a slave when you heard the call? Don't let that worry you, though if you find an opportunity to become free you had better take it. But a slave who is called to life in Christ is set free in the eyes of the Lord. Similarly a man who was free when God called him becomes a slave— to Christ himself! You have been redeemed, at tremendous cost; don't therefore sell yourselves as slaves to men! My brothers, let every one of us continue to live his life with God in the state in which he was when he was called.

7.25 In present circumstances it is really better not to marry

Now as far as young unmarried women are concerned, I must confess that I have no direct commands from the Lord. Nevertheless, I give

Revised Standard Version

band? Husband, how do you know whether you
will save your wife?
17 Only, let every one lead the life which the
Lord has assigned to him, and in which God has
called him. This is my rule in all the churches.
18 Was any one at the time of his call already
circumcised? Let him not seek to remove the
marks of circumcision. Was any one at the time
of his call uncircumcised? Let him not seek circumcision. 19 For neither circumcision counts
for anything nor uncircumcision, but keeping
the commandments of God. 20 Every one should
remain in the state in which he was called.
21 Were you a slave when called? Never mind.
But if you can gain your freedom, avail yourself of the opportunity.[x] 22 For he who was
called in the Lord as a slave is a freedman of
the Lord. Likewise he who was free when called
is a slave of Christ. 23 You were bought with a
price; do not become slaves of men. 24 So,
brethren, in whatever state each was called,
there let him remain with God.
25 Now concerning the unmarried,[y] I have
no command of the Lord, but I give my opinion

[x] Or *make use of your present condition instead.*
[y] Greek *virgins.*

Jerusalem Bible

all you know; if a husband, for all you know, it
may be your part to save your wife.
17 For the rest, what each one has is what the
Lord has given him and he should continue as
he was when God's call reached him. This is the
ruling that I give in all the churches. 18 If anyone had already been circumcised at the time
of his call, he need not disguise it, and anyone
who was uncircumcised at the time of his call
need not be circumcised; 19 because to be circumcised or uncircumcised means nothing: what
does matter is to keep the commandments of
God. 20 Let everyone stay as he was at the time
of his call. 21 If, when you were called, you
were a slave, do not let this bother you; but if
you should have the chance of being free, accept it. 22 A slave, when he is called in the Lord,
becomes the Lord's freedman, and a freeman
called in the Lord becomes Christ's slave. 23 You
have all been bought and paid for; do not be
slaves of other men. 24 Each one of you, my
brothers, should stay as he was before God at
the time of his call.
25 About remaining celibate, I have no directions from the Lord but give my own opinion

New English Bible

husband you may be your wife's salvation.

However that may be, each one must order his life according to the gift the Lord has granted him and his condition when God called him. That is what I teach in all our congregations. Was a man called with the marks of circumcision on him? Let him not remove them. Was he uncircumcised when he was called? Let him not be circumcised. Circumcision or uncircumcision is neither here nor there; what matters is to keep God's commands. Every man should remain in the condition in which he was called. Were you a slave when you were called? Do not let that trouble you; but if a chance of liberty should come, take it.[a] For the man who as a slave received the call to be a Christian is the Lord's freedman, and, equally, the free man who received the call is a slave in the service of Christ. You were bought at a price; do not become slaves of men. Thus each one, my friends, is to remain before God in the condition in which he received his call.

On the question of celibacy, I have no instructions from the Lord, but I give my judgement as

[a] *Or* but even if a chance of liberty should come, choose rather to make good use of your servitude.

King James Version

yet I give my judgment, as one that hath obtained mercy of the Lord to be faithful. 26 I suppose therefore that this is good for the present distress, *I say*, that *it is* good for a man so to be. 27 Art thou bound unto a wife? seek not to be loosed. Art thou loosed from a wife? seek not a wife. 28 But and if thou marry, thou hast not sinned; and if a virgin marry, she hath not sinned. Nevertheless such shall have trouble in the flesh: but I spare you. 29 But this I say, brethren, the time *is* short: it remaineth, that both they that have wives be as though they had none; 30 And they that weep, as though they wept not; and they that rejoice, as though they rejoiced not; and they that buy, as though they possessed not; 31 And they that use this world, as not abusing *it*: for the fashion of this world passeth away. 32 But I would have you without carefulness. He that is unmarried careth for the things that belong to the Lord, how he may please the Lord: 33 But he that is married careth for the things that are of the world, how he may please *his* wife. 34 There is difference *also* between a wife and a virgin. The unmarried

Living Bible

Should they be permitted to do so? In answer to this question, I have no special command for them from the Lord. But the Lord in his kindness has given me wisdom that can be trusted, and I will be glad to tell you what I think.

26 Here is the problem: We Christians are facing great dangers to our lives at present. In times like these I think it is best for a person to remain unmarried. 27 Of course, if you already are married, don't separate because of this. But if you aren't, don't rush into it at this time. 28 But if you men decide to go ahead anyway and get married now, it is all right; and if a girl gets married in times like these, it is no sin. However, marriage will bring extra problems that I wish you didn't have to face right now.

29 The important thing to remember is that our remaining time is very short, [and so are our opportunities for doing the Lord's work[b]]. For that reason those who have wives should stay as free as possible for the Lord;[c] 30 happiness or sadness or wealth should not keep anyone from doing God's work. 31 Those in frequent contact with the exciting things the world offers should make good use of their opportunities without stopping to enjoy them; for the world in its present form will soon be gone.

32 In all you do, I want you to be free from worry. An unmarried man can spend his time doing the Lord's work and thinking how to please him. 33 But a married man can't do that so well; he has to think about his earthly responsibilities and how to please his wife. 34 His interests are divided. It is the same with a girl

[*b*] Implied. [*c*] Literally, "(that) those who have wives may be as though they didn't."

Today's English Version

give my opinion as one who by the Lord's mercy is worthy of trust.

26 Considering the present distress, I think it is better for a man to stay as he is. 27 Do you have a wife? Then don't try to get rid of her. Are you unmarried? Then don't look for a wife. 28 But if you do marry, you haven't committed a sin; and if an unmarried woman marries, she hasn't committed a sin. But I would rather spare you the everyday troubles that such people will have.

29 What I mean, brothers, is this: there is not much time left, and from now on married men should live as though they were not married; 30 those who weep, as though they were not sad; those who laugh, as though they were not happy; those who buy, as though they did not own what they bought; 31 those who deal in worldly goods, as though they were not fully occupied with them. For this world, as it is now, will not last much longer.

32 I would like you to be free from worry. An unmarried man concerns himself with the Lord's work, because he is trying to please the Lord; 33 but a married man concerns himself with worldly matters, because he wants to please his wife, 34 and so he is pulled in two directions. An unmarried woman or a virgin concerns her-

New International Version

who by the Lord's mercy is trustworthy. 26 Because of the present crisis, I think that it is good for you to remain as you are. 27 Are you married? Do not seek a divorce. Are you unmarried? Do not look for a wife. 28 But if you do marry, you have not sinned; and if a virgin marries, she has not sinned. But those who marry will face many troubles in this life, and I want to spare you this.

29 What I mean, brothers, is that the time is short. From now on those who have wives should live as if they had none; 30 those who mourn, as if they did not; those who are happy, as if they were not; those who buy something, as if it were not theirs to keep; 31 those who use the things of the world, as if not engrossed in them. For this world in its present form is passing away.

32 I would like you to be free from concern. An unmarried man is concerned about the Lord's affairs—how he can please the Lord. 33 But a married man is concerned about the affairs of this world—how he can please his wife—34 and his interests are divided. An unmarried woman or virgin is concerned about the

Phillips Modern English

you my considered opinion as of one who is, I think, to be trusted after all his experience of God's mercy.

My opinion is this, that amid all the difficulties of the present time you would do best to remain just as you are. Are you married? Well, don't try to be separated. Are you separated? Then don't try to get married. But if you, a man, should marry, don't think that you have done anything sinful. And the same applies to a young woman. Yet I do believe that those who take this step are bound to find the married state an extra burden in these critical days, and I should like to spare you that. All our futures are so foreshortened, indeed, that those who have wives should live, so to speak, as though they had none! There is no time to indulge in sorrow, no time for enjoying our joys; those who buy have no time to enjoy their possessions, and indeed their every contact with the world must be as light as possible, for the present scheme of things is rapidly passing away. That is why I should like you to be free from worldly anxieties. The unmarried man is free to concern himself with the Lord's affairs, and how he may please him. But the married man is sure to be concerned also with matters of this world, that he may please his wife—his interests are divided. You find the same difference in the case of the

Revised Standard Version

as one who by the Lord's mercy is trustworthy.
26 I think that in view of the present [m] distress
it is well for a person to remain as he is. 27 Are
you bound to a wife? Do not seek to be free.
Are you free from a wife? Do not seek marriage. 28 But if you marry, you do not sin, and if
a girl [z] marries she does not sin. Yet those who
marry will have worldly troubles, and I would
spare you that. 29 I mean, brethren, the appointed time has grown very short; from now
on, let those who have wives live as though they
had none, 30 and those who mourn as though
they were not mourning, and those who rejoice
as though they were not rejoicing, and those
who buy as though they had no goods, 31 and
those who deal with the world as though they
had no dealings with it. For the form of this
world is passing away.
32 I want you to be free from anxieties. The
unmarried man is anxious about the affairs of
the Lord, how to please the Lord; 33 but the
married man is anxious about worldly affairs,
how to please his wife, 34 and his interests are
divided. And the unmarried woman or girl [z] is

[*m*] Or *impending*. [*z*] Greek *virgin*.

Jerusalem Bible

as one who, by the Lord's mercy, has stayed
faithful. 26 Well then, I believe that in these
present times of stress this is right: that it is
good for a man to stay as he is. 27 If you are
tied to a wife, do not look for freedom; if you
are free of a wife, then do not look for one.
28 But if you marry, it is no sin, and it is not a
sin for a young girl to get married. They will
have their troubles, though, in their married life,
and I should like to spare you that.
29 Brothers, this is what I mean: our time
is growing short. Those who have wives should
live as though they had none, 30 and those who
mourn should live as though they had nothing
to mourn for; those who are enjoying life should
live as though there were nothing to laugh about;
those whose life is buying things should live as
though they had nothing of their own; 31 and
those who have to deal with the world should
not become engrossed in it. I say this because
the world as we know it is passing away.
32 I would like to see you free from all worry.
An unmarried man can devote himself to the
Lord's affairs, all he need worry about is pleasing
the Lord; 33 but a married man has to bother
about the world's affairs and devote himself to
pleasing his wife: 34 he is torn two ways. In the
same way an unmarried woman, like a young

New English Bible

one who by God's mercy is fit to be trusted.

It is my opinion, then, that in a time of stress like the present this is the best way for a man to live—it is best for a man to be as he is. Are you bound in marriage? Do not seek a dissolution. Has your marriage been dissolved? Do not seek a wife. If, however, you do marry, there is nothing wrong in it; and if a virgin marries, she has done no wrong. But those who marry will have pain and grief in this bodily life, and my aim is to spare you.

What I mean, my friends, is this. The time we live in will not last long. While it lasts, married men should be as if they had no wives; mourners should be as if they had nothing to grieve them, the joyful as if they did not rejoice; buyers must not count on keeping what they buy, nor those who use the world's wealth on using it to the full. For the whole frame of this world is passing away.

I want you to be free from anxious care. The unmarried man cares for the Lord's business; his aim is to please the Lord. But the married man cares for worldly things; his aim is to please his wife; and he has a divided mind. The unmarried or celibate woman cares[b] for the Lord's busi-

[*b*] *Some witnesses read* . . . his wife. And there is a difference between the wife and the virgin. The unmarried woman cares . . .

King James Version

woman careth for the things of the Lord, that she may be holy both in body and in spirit: but she that is married careth for the things of the world, how she may please *her* husband. 35 And this I speak for your own profit; not that I may cast a snare upon you, but for that which is comely, and that ye may attend upon the Lord without distraction. 36 But if any man think that he behaveth himself uncomely toward his virgin, if she pass the flower of *her* age, and need so require, let him do what he will, he sinneth not: let them marry. 37 Nevertheless he that standeth steadfast in his heart, having no necessity, but hath power over his own will, and hath so decreed in his heart that he will keep his virgin, doeth well. 38 So then he that giveth *her* in marriage doeth well; but he that giveth *her* not in marriage doeth better. 39 The wife is bound by the law as long as her husband liveth; but if her husband be dead, she is at liberty to be married to whom she will; only in the Lord. 40 But she is happier if she so abide, after my judgment: and I think also that I have the Spirit of God.

Living Bible

who marries. She faces the same problem. A girl who is not married is anxious to please the Lord in all she is and does.[d] But a married woman must consider other things such as housekeeping and the likes and dislikes of her husband.

35 I am saying this to help you, not to try to keep you from marrying. I want you to do whatever will help you serve the Lord best, with as few other things as possible to distract your attention from him.

36 But if anyone feels he ought to marry because he has trouble controlling his passions, it is all right, it is not a sin; let him marry. 37 But if a man has the willpower not to marry and decides that he doesn't need to and won't, he has made a wise decision. 38 So the person who marries does well, and the person who doesn't marry does even better.

39 The wife is part of her husband as long as he lives; if her husband dies, then she may marry again, but only if she marries a Christian. 40 But in my opinion she will be happier if she doesn't marry again; and I think I am giving you counsel from God's Spirit when I say this.

[*d*] Literally, "pure in body and in spirit."

Today's English Version

self with the Lord's work, because she wants to be dedicated both in body and spirit; but a married woman concerns herself with worldly matters, because she wants to please her husband.

35 I am saying this because I want to help you. I am not trying to put restrictions on you. Instead, I want you to do what is right and proper, and give yourselves completely to the Lord's service without any reservation.

36 In the case of an engaged couple who have decided not to marry: if the man feels that he is not acting properly toward the girl; if his passions are too strong, and he feels that they ought to marry, then they should get married, as he wants to. There is no sin in this. 37 But if a man, without being forced to do so, has firmly made up his mind not to marry; if he has his will under complete control, and has already decided in his own mind what to do—then he does well not to marry the girl. 38 So the man who marries his girl does well, but the one who does not marry his girl will do even better.

39 A married woman is not free as long as her husband lives; but if her husband dies, then she is free to be married to the man she wants; but it must be a Christian marriage. 40 She will be happier, however, if she stays as she is. That is my opinion, and I think that I too have God's Spirit.

New International Version

Lord's affairs: Her aim is to be devoted to the Lord in both body and spirit. But a married woman is concerned about the affairs of this world—how she can please her husband. 35 I am saying this for your own good, not to restrict you. I want you to live in a right way in undivided devotion to the Lord.

36 If anyone thinks he is acting improperly toward the virgin he is engaged to, and if she is getting along in years and he feels he ought to marry, he should do as he wants. He is not sinning. They should get married. 37 But the man who has settled the matter in his own mind, who is under no compulsion but has control over his own will, and who has made up his mind not to marry the virgin—this man also does the right thing. 38 So then, he who marries the virgin does right, but he who does not marry her does even better.[p]

39 A woman is bound to her husband as long as he lives. But if her husband dies, she is free to marry anyone she wishes, but he must belong to the Lord. 40 In my judgment, she is happier if she stays as she is—and I think that I have the Spirit of God.

[*p*] Or *36 If anyone thinks he is not treating his daughter properly, and if she is getting along in years, and he feels she ought to marry, he should do as he wants. He is not sinning. They should get married. 37 But the man who has settled the matter in his own mind, who is under no compulsion but has control over his own will, and who has made up his mind to keep the virgin unmarried—this man also does the right thing. 38 So then, he who gives his virgin in marriage does right, but he who does not give her in marriage does even better.*

Phillips Modern English

unmarried and the married woman. The unmarried concerns herself with the Lord's affairs, and her aim in life is to make herself holy, in body and in spirit. But the married woman must concern herself with the things of this world, and her aim will be please her husband.

I tell you these things to help you; I am not putting difficulties in your path but setting before you an ideal, so that your service of God may be as far as possible free from worldly distractions.

7.36 But marriage is not wrong

But if any man feels he is not behaving honourably towards the woman he loves, especially as she is beginning to lose her first youth and the emotional strain is considerable, let him do what his heart tells him to do—let them be married, there is no sin in that. Yet for the man of steadfast purpose who is able to bear the strain and has his own desires well under control, if he decides not to marry the young woman, he too will be doing the right thing. Both of them are right, one in choosing marriage and the other in refraining from marriage, but the latter has chosen the better of two right courses.

A woman is bound to her husband while he is alive, but if he dies she is free to marry whom she likes—but let her be guided by the Lord. In my opinion she would be happier to remain as she is, unmarried. And I think I am here expressing not only my opinion, but the will of the Spirit as well.

Revised Standard Version

anxious about the affairs of the Lord, how to be
holy in body and spirit; but the married woman
is anxious about worldly affairs, how to please
her husband. 35 I say this for your own benefit,
not to lay any restraint upon you, but to promote good order and to secure your undivided
devotion to the Lord.
36 If any one thinks that he is not behaving
properly toward his betrothed,[z] if his passions
are strong, and it has to be, let him do as he
wishes: let them marry—it is no sin. 37 But whoever is firmly established in his heart, being under no necessity but having his desire under control, and has determined this in his heart, to keep
her as his betrothed,[z] he will do well. 38 So that
he who marries his betrothed[z] does well; and
he who refrains from marriage will do better.
39 A wife is bound to her husband as long
as he lives. If the husband dies, she is free to be
married to whom she wishes, only in the Lord.
40 But in my judgment she is happier if she
remains as she is. And I think that I have the
Spirit of God.

[z] Greek *virgin*.

Jerusalem Bible

girl, can devote herself to the Lord's affairs; all
she need worry about is being holy in body and
spirit. The married woman, on the other hand,
has to worry about the world's affairs and devote
herself to pleasing her husband. 35 I say this
only to help you, not to put a halter around your
necks, but simply to make sure that everything
is as it should be, and that you give your undivided attention to the Lord.
36 Still, if there is anyone who feels that it
would not be fair to his daughter to let her grow
too old for marriage, and that he should do
something about it, he is free to do as he likes:
he is not sinning if there is a marriage. 37 On
the other hand, if someone has firmly made his
mind up, without any compulsion and in complete freedom of choice, to keep his daughter
as she is, he will be doing a good thing. 38 In
other words, the man who sees that his daughter
is married has done a good thing but the man
who keeps his daughter unmarried has done
something even better.[o]
39 A wife is tied as long as her husband is
alive. But if the husband dies, she is free to
marry anybody she likes, only it must be in the
Lord. 40 She would be happier, in my opinion,
if she stayed as she is—and I too have the Spirit
of God, I think.

[o] "daughter" is not the only possible word; this passage has been read as alluding to the practice of a man and a woman living together under vows of chastity, a practice for which there is evidence from a later date.

New English Bible

ness; her aim is to be dedicated to him in body as in spirit; but the married woman cares for worldly things; her aim is to please her husband.

In saying this I have no wish to keep you on a tight rein. I am thinking simply of your own good, of what is seemly, and of your freedom to wait upon the Lord without distraction.

But if a man has a partner in celibacy[c] and feels that he is not behaving properly towards her, if, that is, his instincts are too strong for him,[d] and something must be done, he may do as he pleases; there is nothing wrong in it; let them marry.[e] But if a man is steadfast in his purpose, being under no compulsion, and has complete control of his own choice; and if he has decided in his own mind to preserve his partner[a] in her virginity, he will do well. Thus, he who marries his partner[b] does well, and he who does not will do better.

A wife is bound to her husband as long as he lives. But if the husband die, she is free to marry whom she will, provided the marriage is within the Lord's fellowship. But she is better off as she is; that is my opinion, and I believe that I too have the Spirit of God.

[c] *Or* a virgin daughter (*or* ward). [d] *Or* if she is ripe for marriage. [e] *Or* let the girl and her lover marry. [a] *Or* his daughter. [b] *Or* gives his daughter in marriage.

King James Version

8 Now as touching things offered unto idols,
we know that we all have knowledge. Knowledge puffeth up, but charity edifieth. 2 And if
any man think that he knoweth any thing, he
knoweth nothing yet as he ought to know. 3 But
if any man love God, the same is known of him.
4 As concerning therefore the eating of those
things that are offered in sacrifice unto idols,
we know that an idol *is* nothing in the world,
and that *there is* none other God but one. 5 For
though there be that are called gods, whether
in heaven or in earth, (as there be gods many,
and lords many,) 6 But to us *there is but* one
God, the Father, of whom *are* all things, and
we in him; and one Lord Jesus Christ, by whom
are all things, and we by him. 7 Howbeit *there*
is not in every man that knowledge: for some
with conscience of the idol unto this hour eat
it as a thing offered unto an idol; and their con-

Living Bible

8 Next is your question about eating food
that has been sacrificed to idols. On this
question everyone feels that only his answer is
the right one! But although being a "know-it-
all" makes us feel important, what is really
needed to build the church is love. 2 If anyone
thinks he knows all the answers, he is just showing his ignorance. 3 But the person who truly
loves God is the one who is open to God's
knowledge.

4 So now, what about it? Should we eat meat
that has been sacrificed to idols? Well, we all
know that an idol is not really a god, and that
there is only one God, and no other. 5 According to some people, there are a great many gods,
both in heaven and on earth. 6 But we know
that there is only one God, the Father, who
created all things[a] and made us to be his own;
and one Lord Jesus Christ, who made everything and gives us life.

7 However, some Christians don't realize this.
All their lives they have been used to thinking
of idols as alive, and have believed that food
offered to the idols is really being offered to
actual gods. So when they eat such food it
bothers them and hurts their tender consciences.

[*a*] Literally, "of whom are all things."

Today's English Version

The question about food offered to idols

8 Now, the matter about food offered to
idols.

It is true, of course, that "all of us have
knowledge," as they say. Such knowledge, however, puffs a man up with pride; but love builds
up. 2 The person who thinks he knows something really doesn't know as he ought to know.
3 But the man who loves God is known by him.

4 So then, about eating the food offered to
idols: we know that an idol stands for something
that does not really exist; we know that there is
only the one God. 5 Even if there are so-called
"gods," whether in heaven or on earth, and even
though there are many of these "gods" and
"lords," 6 yet there is for us only one God, the
Father, who is the creator of all things, and for
whom we live; and there is only one Lord, Jesus
Christ, through whom all things were created,
and through whom we live.

7 But not everyone knows this truth. Some
people are so used to idols that to this very day
when they eat such food they still think of it
as food that belongs to an idol; their conscience
is weak and they feel they are defiled by the

New International Version

Meat sacrificed to idols

8 Now about meat sacrificed to idols: We
know that we all possess knowledge.[q] Knowledge puffs up, but love builds up. 2 The man who
thinks he knows something does not yet know as
he ought to know. 3 But the man who loves God
is known by God.

4 So then, about eating meat sacrificed to
idols: We know that an idol is nothing at all
in the world, and that there is no God but one.
5 For even if there are so-called gods, whether
in heaven or on earth (as indeed there are many
"gods" and many "lords"), 6 yet for us there is
but one God, the Father, from whom all things
came and for whom we live; and there is but
one Lord, Jesus Christ, through whom all things
came and through whom we live.

7 But not everyone knows this. Some people
are still so accustomed to idols that when they
eat such meat, they think of it as having been
sacrificed to an idol, and since their conscience

[*q*] Or *"We all possess knowledge," as you say.*

Phillips Modern English

8.1 A practical problem: shall we be guided by superior knowledge or love?

Now to deal with the matter of food which has been sacrificed to idols. It is easy to think that we "know" over problems like this, but we should remember that while this "knowing" may make a man look big, it is only love that can make him grow to his full stature. For if a man thinks he "knows" he may still be quite ignorant of what he ought to know. But if he loves God he is the man who is known to God.

In this matter, then, of eating food which has been offered to idols, we are sure that no idol has any real existence, and that there is no God but one. For though there are so-called gods both in heaven and earth, gods and lords galore in fact, for us there is only one God, the Father, from whom everything comes, and for whom we live. And there is one Lord, Jesus Christ, through whom everything exists, and through whom we ourselves are alive. But this knowledge of ours is not shared by all men. For some, who until now have been used to idols, eat the food as food really sacrificed to a god, and their delicate

Revised Standard Version

8 Now concerning food offered to idols: we know that "all of us possess knowledge." "Knowledge" puffs up, but love builds up. 2 If any one imagines that he knows something, he does not yet know as he ought to know. 3 But if one loves God, one is known by him.

4 Hence, as to the eating of food offered to idols, we know that "an idol has no real existence," and that "there is no God but one." 5 For although there may be so-called gods in heaven or on earth—as indeed there are many "gods" and many "lords"—6 yet for us there is one God, the Father, from whom are all things and for whom we exist, and one Lord, Jesus Christ, through whom are all things and through whom we exist.

7 However, not all possess this knowledge. But some, through being hitherto accustomed to idols, eat food as really offered to an idol; and

Jerusalem Bible

B. Food offered to idols

General principles

8 Now about food sacrificed to idols. "We all have knowledge"; yes, that is so, but knowledge gives self-importance—it is love that makes the building grow. 2A man may imagine he understands something, but still not understand anything in the way that he ought to. 3 But any man who loves God is known by him. 4 Well then, about eating food sacrificed to idols[p]: we know that idols do not really exist in the world and that there is no god but the One. 5And even if there were things called gods, either in the sky or on earth—where there certainly seem to be "gods" and "lords" in plenty—6 still for us there is one God, the Father, from whom all things come and for whom we exist; and there is one Lord, Jesus Christ, through whom all things come and through whom we exist.

The claims of love

7 Some people, however, do not have this knowledge. There are some who have been so long used to idols that they eat this food as though it really had been sacrificed to the idol, and their conscience, being weak, is defiled by it.

[p] At feasts and public ceremonies, portions of the food were "sacrificed" and went to the gods, the priests and the donors; the whole of the food was regarded as dedicated, whether it was eaten at a ceremonial meal or part of it sold in the markets.

New English Bible

8 Now about food consecrated to heathen deities.

Of course we all 'have knowledge', as you say. This 'knowledge' breeds conceit; it is love that builds. If anyone fancies that he knows, he knows nothing yet, in the true sense of knowing. But if a man loves,[c] he is acknowledged by God.[d]

Well then, about eating this consecrated food: of course, as you say, 'a false god has no existence in the real world. There is no god but one.' For indeed, if there be so-called gods, whether in heaven or on earth—as indeed there are many 'gods' and many 'lords'—yet for us there is one God, the Father, from whom all being comes, towards whom we move; and there is one Lord, Jesus Christ, through whom all things came to be, and we through him.

But not everyone knows this. There are some who have been so accustomed to idolatry[e] that even now they eat this food with a sense of its heathen consecration, and their conscience, be-

[c] *Some witnesses read* loves God. [d] *Or* his is recognized. [e] *Some witnesses read* in whom the consciousness of the false god is so persistent . . .

King James Version

science being weak is defiled. 8 But meat commendeth us not to God: for neither, if we eat, are we the better; neither, if we eat not, are we the worse. 9 But take heed lest by any means this liberty of yours become a stumblingblock to them that are weak. 10 For if any man see thee which hast knowledge sit at meat in the idol's temple, shall not the conscience of him which is weak be emboldened to eat those things which are offered to idols; 11 And through thy knowledge shall the weak brother perish, for whom Christ died? 12 But when ye sin so against the brethren, and wound their weak conscience, ye sin against Christ. 13 Wherefore, if meat make my brother to offend, I will eat no flesh while the world standeth, lest I make my brother to offend.

9 Am I not an apostle? am I not free? have I not seen Jesus Christ our Lord? are not ye my work in the Lord? 2 If I be not an apostle unto others, yet doubtless I am to you: for the seal of mine apostleship are ye in the Lord. 3 Mine answer to them that do examine me is

Living Bible

8 Just remember that God doesn't care whether we eat it or not. We are no worse off if we don't eat it, and no better off if we do. 9 But be careful not to use your freedom to eat it, lest you cause some Christian brother to sin whose conscience[b] is weaker than yours.

10 You see, this is what may happen: Someone who thinks it is wrong to eat this food will see you eating at a temple restaurant, for you know there is no harm in it. Then he will become bold enough to do it too, although all the time he still feels it is wrong. 11 So because you "know it is all right to do it," you will be responsible for causing great spiritual damage to a brother with a tender conscience for whom Christ died. 12 And it is a sin against Christ to sin against your brother by encouraging him to do something he thinks is wrong. 13 So if eating meat offered to idols is going to make my brother sin, I'll not eat any of it as long as I live, because I don't want to do this to him.

9 I am an apostle, God's messenger, responsible to no mere man. I am one who has actually seen Jesus our Lord with my own eyes. And your changed lives are the result of my hard work for him. 2 If in the opinion of others, I am not an apostle, I certainly am to you, for you have been won to Christ through me. 3 This is my answer to those who question my rights.

[b] Implied. Literally, "faith."

Today's English Version

food. 8 Food, however, will not improve our relation with God; we shall not lose anything if we do not eat, nor shall we gain anything if we do eat.

9 Be careful, however, and do not let your freedom of action make those who are weak in the faith fall into sin. 10 Suppose a man whose conscience is weak in this matter sees you, who have "knowledge," eating in the temple of an idol; will not this encourage him to eat food offered to idols? 11 And so this weak man, your brother for whom Christ died, will perish because of your "knowledge"! 12 And in this way you will be sinning against Christ by sinning against your brothers and wounding their weak conscience. 13 So then, if food makes my brother sin, I will never eat meat again, so as not to make my brother fall into sin.

Rights and duties of an apostle

9 Am I not a free man? Am I not an apostle? Haven't I seen Jesus our Lord? And aren't you the result of my work for the Lord? 2 Even if others do not accept me as an apostle, surely you do! You yourselves, because of your life in the Lord, are proof of the fact that I am an apostle.

3 When people criticize me, this is how I

New International Version

is weak, it is defiled. 8 But food does not bring us near to God; we are no worse if we do not eat, and no better if we do.

9 Be careful, however, that the exercise of your freedom does not become a stumbling block to the weak. 10 For if anyone with a weak conscience sees you who have this knowledge eating in an idol's temple, won't he be emboldened to eat what has been sacrificed to idols? 11 So this weak brother, for whom Christ died, is destroyed by your knowledge. 12 When you sin against your brothers in this way and wound their weak conscience, you sin against Christ. 13 Therefore, if what I eat causes my brother to fall into sin, I will never eat meat again, so that I will not cause him to fall.

The rights of an apostle

9 Am I not free? Am I not an apostle? Have I not seen Jesus our Lord? Are you not the result of my work in the Lord? 2 Even though I may not be an apostle to others, surely I am to you! For you are the seal of my apostleship in the Lord.

3 This is my defense to those who sit in judg-

Phillips Modern English

conscience is thereby injured. Now our acceptance by God is not a matter of food. If we eat it, that does not make us better men, nor are we the worse if we do not eat it. You must be careful that your freedom to eat food does not in any way hinder anyone whose faith is not as robust as yours. For suppose you with your knowledge of God should be observed eating food in an idol's temple, are you not encouraging the man with a delicate conscience to do the same? Surely you would not want your superior knowledge to bring spiritual disaster to a weaker brother for whom Christ died? And when you sin like this and damage the weak consciences of your brethren you really sin against Christ. This makes me determined that, if there is any possibility of food injuring my brother, I will never eat food as long as I live, for fear I might do him harm.

9.1 A word of personal defence to my critics

Is there any doubt that I am a free man, any doubt that I am a genuine messenger? Have I not seen Jesus our Lord with my own eyes? Are not you yourselves samples of my work for the Lord? Even if other people should refuse to recognise my divine commission, yet to you at any rate I shall always be a true messenger, for you are a living proof of the Lord's call to me. This is my real ground of defense to those who cross-examine me.

Revised Standard Version

their conscience, being weak, is defiled. 8 Food will not commend us to God. We are no worse off if we do not eat, and no better off if we do. 9 Only take care lest this liberty of yours somehow become a stumbling block to the weak. 10 For if any one sees you, a man of knowledge, at table in an idol's temple, might he not be encouraged, if his conscience is weak, to eat food offered to idols? 11 And so by your knowledge this weak man is destroyed, the brother for whom Christ died. 12 Thus, sinning against your brethren and wounding their conscience when it is weak, you sin against Christ. 13 Therefore, if food is a cause of my brother's falling, I will never eat meat, lest I cause my brother to fall.

9 Am I not free? Am I not an apostle? Have I not seen Jesus our Lord? Are not you my workmanship in the Lord? 2 If to others I am not an apostle, at least I am to you; for you are the seal of my apostleship in the Lord.

3 This is my defense to those who would ex-

Jerusalem Bible

8 Food, of course, cannot bring us in touch with God: we lose nothing if we refuse to eat, we gain nothing if we eat. 9 Only be careful that you do not make use of this freedom in a way that proves a pitfall for the weak. 10 Suppose someone sees you, a man who understands, eating in some temple of an idol; his own conscience, even if it is weak, may encourage him to eat food which has been offered to idols. 11 In this way your knowledge could become the ruin of someone weak, of a brother for whom Christ died. 12 By sinning in this way against your brothers, and injuring their weak consciences, it would be Christ against whom you sinned. 13 That is why, since food can be the occasion of my brother's downfall, I shall never eat meat again in case I am the cause of a brother's downfall.

Paul invokes his own example

9 I, personally, am free: I am an apostle and I have seen Jesus our Lord. You are all my work in the Lord. 2 Even if I were not an apostle to others, I should still be an apostle to you who are the seal of my apostolate in the Lord. 3 My answer to those who want to interrogate me is

New English Bible

ing weak, is polluted by the eating. Certainly food will not bring us into God's presence: if we do not eat, we are none the worse, and if we eat, we are none the better. But be careful that this liberty of yours does not become a pitfall for the weak. If a weak character sees you sitting down to a meal in a heathen temple—you, who 'have knowledge'—will not his conscience be emboldened to eat food consecrated to the heathen deity? This 'knowledge' of yours is utter disaster to the weak, the brother for whom Christ died. In thus sinning against your brothers and wounding their conscience,[f] you sin against Christ. And therefore, if food be the downfall of my brother, I will never eat meat any more, for I will not be the cause of my brother's downfall.

9 Am I not a free man? Am I not an apostle? Did I not see Jesus our Lord? Are not you my own handiwork, in the Lord? If others do not accept me as an apostle, you at least are bound to do so, for you are yourselves the very seal of my apostolate, in the Lord.

To those who put me in the dock this is my

[f] *Some witnesses insert* weak as it is.

King James Version

this: 4 Have we not power to eat and to drink? 5 Have we not power to lead about a sister, a wife, as well as other apostles, and *as* the brethren of the Lord, and Cephas? 6 Or I only and Barnabas, have not we power to forbear working? 7 Who goeth a warfare any time at his own charges? who planteth a vineyard, and eateth not of the fruit thereof? or who feedeth a flock, and eateth not of the milk of the flock? 8 Say I these things as a man? or saith not the law the same also? 9 For it is written in the law of Moses, Thou shalt not muzzle the mouth of the ox that treadeth out the corn. Doth God take care for oxen? 10 Or saith he *it* altogether for our sakes? For our sakes, no doubt, *this* is written: that he that plougheth should plough in hope; and that he that thresheth in hope should be partaker of his hope. 11 If we have sown unto you spiritual things, *is it* a great thing if we shall reap your carnal things? 12 If others be partakers of *this* power over you, *are* not we rather? Nevertheless we have not used this

Living Bible

4 Or don't I have any rights at all? Can't I claim the same privilege the other apostles have of being a guest in your homes? 5 If [a] I had a wife, and if [a] she were a believer, couldn't I bring her along on these trips just as the other disciples do, and as the Lord's brothers do, and as Peter does? 6 And must Barnabas and I alone keep working for our living, while you supply these others? 7 What soldier in the army has to pay his own expenses? And have you ever heard of a farmer who harvests his crop and doesn't have the right to eat some of it? What shepherd takes care of a flock of sheep and goats and isn't allowed to drink some of the milk? 8 And I'm not merely quoting the opinions of men as to what is right. I'm telling you what God's law says. 9 For in the law God gave to Moses he said that you must not put a muzzle on an ox to keep it from eating when it is treading out the wheat. Do you suppose God was thinking only about oxen when he said this? 10 Wasn't he also thinking about us? Of course he was. He said this to show us that Christian workers should be paid by those they help. Those who do the plowing and threshing should expect some share of the harvest.

11 We have planted good spiritual seed in your souls. Is it too much to ask, in return, for mere food and clothing? 12 You give them to others who preach to you, and you should. But shouldn't we have an even greater right to them? Yet we have *never* used this right, but supply

[*a*] Implied. Literally, "Have we no right to lead about a wife that is a believer?"

Today's English Version

defend myself: 4 Don't I have the right to be given food and drink for my work? 5 Don't I have the right to do what the other apostles do, and the Lord's brothers, and Peter, and take a Christian wife with me on my trips? 6 Or are Barnabas and I the only ones who have to work for our living? 7 What soldier ever has to pay his own expenses in the army? What farmer does not eat the grapes from his own vineyard? What shepherd does not use the milk from his own sheep?

8 I don't have to limit myself to these everyday examples, because the Law says the same thing. 9 We read in the Law of Moses, "Do not tie up the mouth of the ox when it treads out the grain." Now, is God concerned about oxen? 10 Or did he not really mean us when he said this? Of course this was written for us. The man who plows and the man who reaps should do their work in the hope of getting a share of the crop. 11 We have sown spiritual seed among you. Is it too much if we reap material benefits from you? 12 If others have the right to expect this from you, don't we have an even greater right?

But we haven't made use of this right. In-

New International Version

ment on me. 4 Don't we have the right to food and drink? 5 Don't we have the right to take a believing wife along with us, as do the other apostles and the Lord's brothers and Cephas? [r] 6 Or is it only I and Barnabas who must work for a living?

7 Who serves as a soldier at his own expense? Who plants a vineyard and does not eat of its grapes? Who tends a flock and does not drink of the milk? 8 Do I say this merely from a human point of view? Doesn't the Law say the same thing? 9 For it is written in the Law of Moses: "Do not muzzle an ox when it is treading out the grain." [s] Is it about oxen that God is concerned? 10 Surely he says this for us, doesn't he? Yes, this was written for us, because when the plowman plows and the thresher threshes, they ought to do so in the hope of sharing in the harvest. 11 If we have sown spiritual seed among you, is it too much if we reap a material harvest from you? 12 If others have this right of support from you, shouldn't we have it all the more?

But we did not use this right. On the con-

[*r*] That is, Peter. [*s*] Deut. 25:4.

Phillips Modern English

Aren't we allowed to eat and drink? May we not travel with a Christian wife like the other messengers, like other Christian brothers, and like Cephas? Are Barnabas and I the only ones not allowed to leave their ordinary work to give time to the ministry?

9.7 *Even a preacher of the gospel has some rights!*

Just think for a moment. Does any soldier ever go to war at his own expense? Does any man plant a vineyard and have no share in its fruits? Does the shepherd who tends the flock never taste the milk? This is, I know an argument from everyday life, but it is a principle endorsed by the Law. For is it not written in the Law of Moses:

> Thou shalt not muzzle the ox when he treadeth out the corn?

Now does this imply merely God's care for oxen, or does it include his care for us too? Surely we are included! You might even say that the words were written for us. For both the ploughman as he ploughs, and the thresher as he threshes should have some hope of an ultimate share in the harvest. If we have sown for you the seed of spiritual things need you be greatly perturbed because we reap some of your material things? And if there are others with the right to have these things from you, have not we an even greater right? Yet we have never

Revised Standard Version

amine me. 4 Do we not have the right to our
food and drink? 5 Do we not have the right to
be accompanied by a wife,[n] as the other apostles
and the brothers of the Lord and Cephas? 6 Or
is it only Barnabas and I who have no right to
refrain from working for a living? 7 Who serves
as a soldier at his own expense? Who plants a
vineyard without eating any of its fruit? Who
tends a flock without getting some of the milk?
8 Do I say this on human authority? Does not
the law say the same? 9 For it is written in the
law of Moses, "You shall not muzzle an ox when
it is treading out the grain." Is it for oxen that
God is concerned? 10 Does he not speak entirely
for our sake? It was written for our sake, because the plowman should plow in hope and the
thresher thresh in hope of a share in the crop.
11 If we have sown spiritual good among you,
is it too much if we reap your material benefits?
12 If others share this rightful claim upon you,
do not we still more?
Nevertheless, we have not made use of this

[n] Greek *a sister as wife.*

Jerusalem Bible

this: 4 Have we not every right to eat and
drink?[q] 5 And the right to take a Christian
woman around with us, like all the other apostles and the brothers of the Lord and Cephas?
6 Are Barnabas and I the only ones who are not
allowed to stop working? 7 Nobody ever paid
money to stay in the army, and nobody ever
planted a vineyard and refused to eat the fruit
of it. Who has there ever been that kept a flock
and did not feed on the milk from his flock?
8 These may be only human comparisons, but
does not the Law itself say the same thing? 9 It
is written in the Law of Moses: *You must not
put a muzzle on the ox when it is treading out
the corn.*[r] Is it about oxen that God is concerned, 10 or is there not an obvious reference
to ourselves? Clearly this was written for our
sake to show that the plowman ought to plow
in expectation, and the thresher to thresh in the
expectation of getting his share. 11 If we have
sown spiritual things for you, why should you be
surprised if we harvest your material things?
12 Others are allowed these rights over you and
our right is surely greater? In fact we have never

[q] At the expense of the Christian congregations.
[r] Dt. 25:4.

New English Bible

answer: Have I no right to eat and drink? Have I no right to take a Christian wife about with me, like the rest of the apostles and the Lord's brothers, and Cephas? Or are Barnabas and I alone bound to work for our living? Did you ever hear of a man serving in the army at his own expense? or planting a vineyard without eating the fruit of it? or tending a flock without using its milk? Do not suppose I rely on these human analogies, for the law says the same; in the Law of Moses we read, 'You shall not muzzle a threshing ox.' Do you suppose God's concern is with oxen? Or is the reference clearly to ourselves? Of course it refers to us, in the sense that the ploughman should plough and the thresher thresh in the hope of getting some of the produce. If we have sown a spiritual crop for you, is it too much to expect from you a material harvest? If you allow others these rights, have not we a stronger claim?

On the contrary, I put up with all that comes

King James Version

power; but suffer all things, lest we should hinder
the gospel of Christ. 13 Do ye not know that
they which minister about holy things live *of*
the things of the temple? and they which wait
at the altar are partakers with the altar? 14 Even
so hath the Lord ordained that they which preach
the gospel should live of the gospel. 15 But I have
used none of these things: neither have I written
these things, that it should be so done unto me:
for *it were* better for me to die, than that any
man should make my glorying void. 16 For
though I preach the gospel, I have nothing to
glory of: for necessity is laid upon me; yea,
woe is unto me, if I preach not the gospel!
17 For if I do this thing willingly, I have a reward: but if against my will, a dispensation *of*
the gospel is committed unto me. 18 What is my
reward then? *Verily* that, when I preach the gos-

Living Bible

our own needs without your help. We have never
demanded payment of any kind for fear that,
if we did, you might be less interested in our
message to you from Christ.
13 Don't you realize that God told those
working in his temple to take for their own
needs some of the food brought there as gifts
to him? And those who work at the altar of
God get a share of the food that is brought by
those offering it to the Lord. 14 In the same way
the Lord has given orders that those who preach
the Gospel should be supported by those who
accept it. 15 Yet I have never asked you for
one penny. And I am not writing this to hint
that I would like to start now. In fact, I would
rather die of hunger than lose the satisfaction
I get from preaching to you without charge.
16 For just preaching the Gospel isn't any special
credit to me—I couldn't keep from preaching
it if I wanted to. I would be utterly miserable.
Woe unto me if I don't.
17 If I were volunteering my services of my
own free will, then the Lord would give me a
special reward; but that is not the situation, for
God has picked me out and given me this sacred
trust and I have no choice. 18 Under this circumstance, what is my pay? It is the special

Today's English Version

stead, we have endured everything in order not
to put any obstacle in the way of the Good
News about Christ. 13 Surely you know that the
men who work in the temple get their food from
the temple, and that those who offer the sacrifices on the altar get a share of the sacrifices.
14 In the same way, the Lord has ordered that
those who preach the gospel should get their
living from it.
15 But I haven't made use of any of these
rights, nor am I writing this now in order to
claim such rights for myself. I would rather die
first! Nobody is going to turn my rightful boast
into empty words! 16 I have no right to boast
just because I preach the gospel. After all, I am
under orders to do so. And how terrible it
would be for me if I did not preach the gospel!
17 If I did my work as a matter of free choice,
then I could expect to be paid; but since I do
it as a matter of duty, it is because God has
entrusted me with this task. 18 What pay do I
get, then? It is the privilege of preaching the

New International Version

trary, we put up with anything rather than hinder
the gospel of Christ. 13 Don't you know that
those who work in the temple get their food from
the temple, and those who serve at the altar
share in what is offered on the altar? 14 In the
same way, the Lord has commanded that those
who preach the gospel should receive their living from the gospel.
15 But I have not used any of these rights.
And I am not writing this in the hope that you
will do such things for me. I would rather die
than have anyone deprive me of this boast.
16 Yet when I preach the gospel, I cannot boast,
for I am compelled to preach. Woe to me if I
do not preach the gospel! 17 If I preach voluntarily, I have a reward; if not voluntarily, I am
simply discharging the trust committed to me.
18 What then is my reward? Just this: that in
preaching the gospel I may offer it free of

Phillips Modern English

exercised this right and have put up with all sorts of things, so that we might not hinder the spread of the gospel.

9.13 *I am entitled to a reward, yet I have not taken it*

Are you ignorant of the fact that those who minister sacred things take part of the sacred food of the Temple for their own use, and those who attend the altar have their share of what is placed on the altar? On the same principle the Lord has ordered that those who proclaim the gospel should receive their livelihood from those who accept the gospel.

But I have never used any of these privileges, nor am I writing now to suggest that I should be given them. Indeed I would rather die than have anyone make this boast of mine an empty one!

9.16 *My reward is to make the gospel free to all men*

For I take no special pride in the fact that I preach the gospel. I feel compelled to do so; I should be utterly miserable if I failed to preach it. If I do this work because I choose to do so then I am entitled to a reward. But if it is no choice of mine, but a sacred responsibility put upon me, what can I expect in the way of reward? This, that when I preach the gospel, I can

Revised Standard Version

right, but we endure anything rather than put
an obstacle in the way of the gospel of Christ.
13 Do you not know that those who are employed in the temple service get their food from
the temple, and those who serve at the altar
share in the sacrificial offerings? 14 In the same
way, the Lord commanded that those who proclaim the gospel should get their living by the
gospel.
15 But I have made no use of any of these
rights, nor am I writing this to secure any such
provision. For I would rather die than have any
one deprive me of my ground for boasting.
16 For if I preach the gospel, that gives me no
ground for boasting. For necessity is laid upon
me. Woe to me if I do not preach the gospel!
17 For if I do this of my own will, I have a
reward; but if not of my own will, I am entrusted with a commission. 18 What then is my
reward? Just this: that in my preaching I may

Jerusalem Bible

exercised this right. On the contrary we have
put up with anything rather than obstruct the
Good News of Christ in any way. 13 Remember
that the ministers serving in the Temple get their
food from the Temple and those serving at the
altar can claim their share from the altar itself.
14 In the same sort of way the Lord directed
that those who preach the gospel should get their
living from the gospel.
15 However, I have not exercised any of
these rights, and I am not writing all this to
secure this treatment for myself. I would rather
die than let anyone take away something that I
can boast of. 16 Not that I do boast of preaching the gospel, since it is a duty which has been
laid on me; I should be punished if I did not
preach it! 17 If I had chosen this work myself,
I might have been paid for it, but as I have not,
it is a responsibility which has been put into my
hands. 18 Do you know what my reward is? It
is this: in my preaching, to be able to offer the

New English Bible

my way rather than offer any hindrance to the gospel of Christ. You know (do you not?) that those who perform the temple service eat the temple offerings, and those who wait upon the altar claim their share of the sacrifice. In the same way the Lord gave instructions that those who preach the Gospel should earn their living by the Gospel. But I have never taken advantage of any such right, nor do I intend to claim it in this letter. I had rather die! No one shall make my boast an empty boast. Even if I preach the Gospel, I can claim no credit for it; I cannot help myself; it would be misery to me not to preach. If I did it of my own choice, I should be earning my pay; but since I do it apart from my own choice, I am simply discharging a trust.[a] Then what is my pay? The satisfaction of preaching the Gospel without expense to anyone;

[a] *Or* If I do it willingly I am earning my pay; if I did it unwillingly I should still have a trust laid upon me.

King James Version

pel, I may make the gospel of Christ without
charge, that I abuse not my power in the gospel.
19 For though I be free from all *men,* yet have
I made myself servant unto all, that I might
gain the more. 20And unto the Jews I became
as a Jew, that I might gain the Jews; to them
that are under the law, as under the law, that I
might gain them that are under the law; 21 To
them that are without law, as without law, (being not without law to God, but under the law
to Christ,) that I might gain them that are without law. 22 To the weak became I as weak, that
I might gain the weak: I am made all things to
all *men,* that I might by all means save some.
23And this I do for the gospel's sake, that I
might be partaker thereof with *you.* 24 Know ye
not that they which run in a race run all, but
one receiveth the prize? So run, that ye may
obtain. 25And every man that striveth for the
mastery is temperate in all things. Now they *do*

Living Bible

joy I get from preaching the Good News without expense to anyone, never demanding my
rights.
19 And this has a real advantage: I am not
bound to obey anyone just because he pays my
salary; yet I have freely and happily become a
servant of any and all so that I can win them
to Christ. 20 When I am with the Jews I seem
as one of them so that they will listen to the
Gospel and I can win them to Christ. When I
am with Gentiles who follow Jewish customs and
ceremonies I don't argue, even though I don't
agree, because I want to help them. 21 When
with the heathen I agree with them as much as I
can, except of course that I must always do what
is right as a Christian. And so, by agreeing, I can
win their confidence[b] and help them too.
22 When I am with those whose consciences
bother them easily, I don't act as though I
know it all and don't say they are foolish; the
result is that they are willing to let me help
them. Yes, whatever a person is like, I try to
find common ground with him so that he will
let me tell him about Christ and let Christ save
him. 23 I do this to get the Gospel to them and
also for the blessing I myself receive when I
see them come to Christ.
24 In a race, everyone runs but only one
person gets first prize. So run your race to win.
25 To win the contest you must deny yourselves
many things that would keep you from doing
your best. An athlete goes to all this trouble
just to win a blue ribbon or a silver cup,[c] but we

[*b*] Implied. [*c*] Literally, "a wreath that quickly fades," given to the winners of the original Olympic races of Paul's time.

Today's English Version

Good News without charging for it, without
claiming my rights in my work for the gospel.
19 I am a free man, nobody's slave; but I
make myself everybody's slave in order to win
as many as possible. 20 While working with the
Jews, I live like a Jew in order to win them;
and even though I myself am not subject to the
Law of Moses, I live as though I were, when
working with those who are, in order to win
them. 21 In the same way, when with Gentiles
I live like a Gentile, outside the Jewish Law, in
order to win Gentiles. This does not mean that
I don't obey God's law; I am really under
Christ's law. 22Among the weak in faith I become weak like one of them, in order to win
them. So I become all things to all men, that I
may save some of them by any means possible.
23 All this I do for the gospel's sake, in
order to share in its blessings. 24 Surely you
know that in a race all the runners take part in
it, but only one of them wins the prize. Run,
then, in such a way as to win the prize. 25 Every
athlete in training submits to strict discipline;
he does so in order to be crowned with a wreath

New International Version

charge, and so not make use of my rights in
preaching it.
19 Though I am free and belong to no man, I
make myself a slave to everyone, to win as many
as possible. 20 To the Jews I became like a
Jew, to win the Jews. To those under the law
I became like one under the law (though I myself am not under the law), so as to win those
under the law. 21 To those not having the law
I became like one not having the law (though I
am not free from God's law but am under
Christ's law), so as to win those not having the
law. 22 To the weak I became weak, to win the
weak. I have become all things to all men so
that by all possible means I might save some.
23 I do all this for the sake of the gospel, that
I may share in its blessings.
24 Do you not know that in a race all the
runners run, but only one gets the prize? Run in
such a way as to get the prize. 25 Everyone who
competes in the games goes into strict training.
They do it to get a crown of laurel that will not

Phillips Modern English

make it absolutely free of charge, and need not claim what is my rightful due as a preacher. For though I am no man's slave, yet I have made myself everyone's slave, that I might win more men to Christ. To the Jews I was a Jew that I might win the Jews. To those who were under the Law I put myself in the position of being under the Law (although in fact I stand free of it), that I might win those who are under the Law. To those who had no Law I myself became like a man without the Law (even though in fact I cannot be a lawless man for I am bound by the law of Christ), so that I might win the men who have no Law. To the weak I became a weak man, that I might win the weak. I have, in short, been all things to all sorts of men that by every possible means I might win some to God. I do all this for the sake of the gospel; I want to play my part properly.

9.24 To preach the gospel faithfully is my set purpose

Do you remember how, on a racing-track, every competitor runs, but only one wins the prize? Well, you ought to run with your minds fixed on winning the prize! Every competitor in athletic events goes into serious training. Athletes will take tremendous pains—for a fading crown of leaves. But our contest is for a crown

Revised Standard Version

make the gospel free of charge, not making full
use of my right in the gospel.
19 For though I am free from all men, I have
made myself a slave to all, that I might win
the more. 20 To the Jews I became as a Jew,
in order to win Jews; to those under the law I
became as one under the law—though not being myself under the law—that I might win those
under the law. 21 To those outside the law I became as one outside the law—not being without law toward God but under the law of
Christ—that I might win those outside the law.
22 To the weak I became weak, that I might win
the weak. I have become all things to all men,
that I might by all means save some. 23 I do it
all for the sake of the gospel, that I may share
in its blessings.
24 Do you not know that in a race all the
runners compete, but only one receives the prize?
So run that you may obtain it. 25 Every athlete
exercises self-control in all things. They do it

Jerusalem Bible

Good News free, and not insist on the rights
which the gospel gives me.
19 So though I am not a slave of any man I
have made myself the slave of everyone so as to
win as many as I could. 20 I made myself a Jew
to the Jews, to win the Jews; that is, I who am
not a subject of the Law made myself a subject
of the Law to those who are the subjects of the
Law, to win those who are subject to the Law.
21 To those who have no Law, I was free of the
Law myself (though not free from God's law,
being under the law of Christ) to win those who
have no Law. 22 For the weak I made myself
weak. I made myself all things to all men in
order to save some at any cost; 23 and I still do
this, for the sake of the gospel, to have a share
in its blessings.
24 All the runners at the stadium are trying
to win, but only one of them gets the prize. You
must run in the same way, meaning to win. 25 All
the fighters at the games go into strict training;
they do this just to win a wreath that will wither

New English Bible

in other words, of waiving the rights which my preaching gives me.

I am a free man and own no master; but I have made myself every man's servant, to win over as many as possible. To Jews I became like a Jew, to win Jews; as they are subject to the Law of Moses, I put myself under that law to win them although I am not myself subject to it. To win Gentiles, who are outside the Law, I made myself like one of them, although I am not in truth outside God's law, being under the law of Christ. To the weak I became weak, to win the weak. Indeed, I have become everything in turn to men of every sort, so that in one way or another I may save some. All this I do for the sake of the Gospel, to bear my part in proclaiming it.

You know (do you not?) that at the sports all the runners run the race, though only one wins the prize. Like them, run to win! But every athlete goes into strict training. They do it to

King James Version

it to obtain a corruptible crown; but we an incorruptible. 26 I therefore so run, not as uncer-
tainly; so fight I, not as one that beateth the
air: 27 But I keep under my body, and bring *it*
into subjection: lest that by any means, when I
have preached to others, I myself should be a
castaway.

10 Moreover, brethren, I would not that ye
should be ignorant, how that all our fathers were under the cloud, and all passed
through the sea; 2 And were all baptized unto
Moses in the cloud and in the sea; 3 And did all
eat the same spiritual meat; 4 And did all drink
the same spiritual drink; for they drank of that
spiritual Rock that followed them: and that
Rock was Christ. 5 But with many of them God
was not well pleased: for they were overthrown
in the wilderness. 6 Now these things were our
examples, to the intent we should not lust after
evil things, as they also lusted. 7 Neither be ye
idolaters, as *were* some of them; as it is written,

Living Bible

do it for a heavenly reward that never disappears. 26 So I run straight to the goal with purpose in every step. I fight to win. I'm not just
shadow-boxing or playing around. 27 Like an
athlete I punish my body, treating it roughly,
training it to do what it should, not what it
wants to. Otherwise I fear that after enlisting
others for the race, I myself might be declared
unfit and ordered to stand aside.

10 For we must never forget, dear brothers,
what happened to our people in the wilderness long ago. God guided them by sending a
cloud that moved along ahead of them; and he
brought them all safely through the waters of
the Red Sea. 2 This might be called their "baptism"—baptized both in sea and cloud!—as followers of Moses—their commitment to him as
their leader. 3, 4 And by a miracle[a] God sent
them food to eat and water to drink there in the
desert; they drank the water that Christ gave
them.[b] He was there with them as a mighty
Rock of spiritual refreshment. 5 Yet after all
this most of them did not obey God, and he
destroyed them in the wilderness.
6 From this lesson we are warned that we
must not desire evil things as they did, 7 nor
worship idols as they did. (The Scriptures tell
us, "The people sat down to eat and drink and

[*a*] Implied. Literally, "all ate the same supernatural food and drink." [*b*] Literally, "For they drank of a spiritual Rock that followed them, and the Rock was Christ."

Today's English Version

that will not last; but we do it for one that will
last forever. 26 That is why I run straight for
the finish line; that is why I am like a boxer,
who does not waste his punches. 27 I harden my
body with blows and bring it under complete
control, to keep from being rejected myself after
having called others to the contest.

Warning against idols

10 I want you to remember, brothers, what
happened to our ancestors who followed
Moses. They were all under the protection of
the cloud, and all passed safely through the Red
Sea. 2 In the cloud and in the sea they were all
baptized as followers of Moses. 3 All ate the
same spiritual bread, 4 and all drank the same
spiritual drink. They drank from that spiritual
rock that went along with them; and that rock
was Christ himself. 5 But even then God was not
pleased with most of them, and so their dead
bodies were scattered over the desert.
6 Now, all these things are examples for us,
to warn us not to desire evil things, as they did,
7 nor to worship idols, as some of them did. As

New International Version

last; but we do it to get a crown that will last
forever. 26 Therefore, I do not run like a man
running aimlessly; I do not fight like a man
shadow boxing. 27 No, I beat my body and make
it my slave so that after I have preached to
others, I myself will not be disqualified for the
prize.

Warnings from Israel's history

10 For I do not want you to be ignorant of
the fact, brothers, that our forefathers were
all under the cloud and that they all passed
through the sea. 2 They were all baptized into
Moses in the cloud and in the sea. 3 They all
ate the same spiritual food 4 and drank the same
spiritual drink; for they drank from the spiritual
rock that accompanied them, and that rock was
Christ. 5 Nevertheless, God was not pleased
with most of them, so their bodies were scattered over the desert.
6 Now these things occurred as examples,[t] to
keep us from setting our hearts on evil things as
they did. 7 Do not be idolaters, as some of them
were; as it is written: "The people sat down to

[*t*] Or *types*.

Phillips Modern English

that will never fade.

I run the race then with determination. I am no shadow-boxer, I really fight! I am my body's sternest master, for fear that when I have preached to others I should myself be disqualified.

10.1 *Spiritual experience does not guarantee infallibility*

For I should like to remind you, my brothers, that our ancestors all had the experience of being guided by the cloud in the desert and of crossing the sea dry-shod. They were all, so to speak, "baptised" into Moses by these experiences. They all shared the same spiritual food and drank the same spiritual drink (for they drank from the spiritual rock which followed them, and that rock was Christ). Yet in spite of all these experiences most of them failed to please God, and left their bones in the desert. Now in these events our ancestors stand as examples to us, warning us not to crave after evil things as they did. Nor are you to worship false gods as they did. The scripture says—

Revised Standard Version

to receive a perishable wreath, but we an imperishable. 26 Well, I do not run aimlessly, I do not box as one beating the air; 27 but I pommel my body and subdue it, lest after preaching to others I myself should be disqualified.

10 I want you to know, brethren, that our fathers were all under the cloud, and all passed through the sea, 2 and all were baptized into Moses in the cloud and in the sea, 3 and all ate the same supernatural [o] food 4 and all drank the same supernatural [o] drink. For they drank from the supernatural [o] Rock which followed them, and the Rock was Christ. 5 Nevertheless with most of them God was not pleased; for they were overthrown in the wilderness.

6 Now these things are warnings for us, not to desire evil as they did. 7 Do not be idolaters as some of them were; as it is written, "The

[*o*] Greek *spiritual.*

Jerusalem Bible

away, but we do it for a wreath that will never wither. 26 That is how I run, intent on winning; that is how I fight, not beating the air. 27 I treat my body hard and make it obey me, for, having been an announcer myself, I should not want to be disqualified.

A warning, and the lessons of Israel's history

10 I want to remind you, brothers, how our fathers were all guided by a cloud above them and how they all passed through the sea. 2 They were all baptized into Moses in this cloud and in this sea; 3 all ate the same spiritual food 4 and all drank the same spiritual drink, since they all drank from the spiritual rock that followed them as they went, and that rock was Christ. 5 In spite of this, most of them failed to please God and their corpses littered the desert.

6 These things all happened as warnings[s] for us, not to have the wicked lusts for forbidden things that they had. 7 Do not become idolaters as some of them did, for scripture says: *After*

[*s*] Literally, "types"; events prefiguring in the history of Israel the spiritual realities of the Messianic age.

New English Bible

win a fading wreath; we, a wreath that never fades. For my part, I run with a clear goal before me; I am like a boxer who does not beat the air; I bruise my own body and make it know its master, for fear that after preaching to others I should find myself rejected.

10 You should understand, my brothers, that our ancestors were all under the pillar of cloud, and all of them passed through the Red Sea; and so they all received baptism into the fellowship of Moses in cloud and sea. They all ate the same supernatural food, and all drank the same supernatural drink; I mean, they all drank from the supernatural rock that accompanied their travels—and that rock was Christ. And yet, most of them were not accepted by God, for the desert was strewn with their corpses.

These events happened as symbols to warn us not to set our desires on evil things, as they did. Do not be idolaters, like some of them; as Scrip-

King James Version

The people sat down to eat and drink, and rose up to play. 8 Neither let us commit fornication, as some of them committed, and fell in one day three and twenty thousand. 9 Neither let us tempt Christ, as some of them also tempted, and were destroyed of serpents. 10 Neither murmur ye, as some of them also murmured, and were destroyed of the destroyer. 11 Now all these things happened unto them for ensamples: and they are written for our admonition, upon whcm the ends of the world are come. 12 Wherefore let him that thinketh he standeth take heed lest he fall. 13 There hath no temptation taken you but such as is common to man: but God *is* faithful, who will not suffer you to be tempted above that ye are able; but will with the temptation also make a way to escape, that ye may

Living Bible

then got up to dance" in worship of the golden calf.)

8 Another lesson for us is what happened when some of them sinned with other men's wives, and 23,000 fell dead in one day. 9And don't try the Lord's patience—they did, and died from snake bites. 10And don't murmur against God and his dealings with you, as some of them did, for that is why God sent his Angel to destroy them.

11 All these things happened to them as examples—as object lessons to us—to warn us against doing the same things; they were written down so that we could read about them and learn from them in these last days as the world nears its end.

12 So be careful. If you are thinking, "Oh, I would never behave like that"—let this be a warning to you. For you too may fall into sin. 13 But remember this—the wrong desires that come into your life aren't anything new and different. Many others have faced exactly the same problems before you. And no temptation is irresistible. You can trust God to keep the temptation from becoming so strong that you can't stand up against it, for he has promised this and will do what he says. He will show you how to escape temptation's power so that you

Today's English Version

the scripture says, "The people sat down to eat and drink, and got up to dance." 8 We must not commit sexual immorality, as some of them did—and in one day twenty-three thousand of them fell dead. 9 We must not put the Lord to the test, as some of them did—and they were killed by the snakes. 10 You must not complain, as some of them did—and they were destroyed by the Angel of Death.

11 All these things happened to them as examples for others, and they were written down as a warning for us. For we live at the time when the end is about to come.

12 Whoever thinks he is standing up had better be careful that he does not fall. 13 Every temptation that has come your way is the kind that normally comes to people. But God keeps his promise, and he will not allow you to be tempted beyond your power to resist; at the time you are tempted he will give you the strength to endure it, and so provide you with a way out.

New International Version

eat and drink and got up to indulge in pagan revelry."[u] 8 We should not commit sexual immorality, as some of them did—and in one day twenty-three thousand of them died. 9 We should not test the Lord, as some of them did—and were killed by snakes. 10And do not grumble, as some of them did—and were killed by the destroying angel.

11 These things happened to them as examples[t] and were written down as warnings for us, on whom the fulfillment of the ages has come. 12 So, if you think you are standing firm, be careful that you don't fall! 13 No temptation has seized you except what is common to man. And God is faithful; he will not let you be tempted beyond what you can bear. But when you are tempted, he will also provide a way out so that you can stand up under it.

[u] Exodus 32:6.

Phillips Modern English

The people sat down to eat and drink, and rose up to play.

Neither should we give way to sexual immorality as did some of them, for we read that twenty-three thousand fell in a single day! Nor should we dare to exploit the goodness of God as some of them did, and fell victims to poisonous snakes. Nor yet must you curse the lot that God has appointed to you as some of them did, and met their end at the hand of the angel of death.

Now these things which happened to our ancestors are illustrations of the way in which God works, and they were written down to be a warning to us who are living in the final days of the present order.

So let the man who feels sure of his standing today be careful that he does not fall tomorrow.

10.13 God still governs human experience

No temptation has come your way that is too hard for flesh and blood to bear. But God can be trusted not to allow you to suffer any temptation beyond your powers of endurance. He will see to it that every temptation has its way out, so that it will be possible for you to bear it.

Revised Standard Version

people sat down to eat and drink and rose up
to dance." 8 We must not indulge in immorality
as some of them did, and twenty-three thousand
fell in a single day. 9 We must not put the
Lord [p] to the test, as some of them did and
were destroyed by serpents; 10 nor grumble, as
some of them did and were destroyed by the
Destroyer. 11 Now these things happened to
them as a warning, but they were written down
for our instruction, upon whom the end of the
ages has come. 12 Therefore let any one who
thinks that he stands take heed lest he fall.
13 No temptation has overtaken you that is not
common to man. God is faithful, and he will not
let you be tempted beyond your strength, but
with the temptation will also provide the way
of escape, that you may be able to endure it.

[p] Other ancient authorities read *Christ*.

Jerusalem Bible

sitting down to eat and drink, the people got up
to amuse themselves.[t] 8 We must never fall into
sexual immorality: some of them did, and
twenty-three thousand met their downfall in one
day. 9 We are not to put the Lord to the test:
some of them did, and they were killed by
snakes. 10 You must never complain: some of
them did, and they were killed by the Destroyer.
11 All this happened to them as a warning,
and it was written down to be a lesson for us
who are living at the end of the age. 12 The
man who thinks he is safe must be careful that
he does not fall. 13 The trials that you have
had to bear are no more than people normally
have. You can trust God not to let you be
tried beyond your strength, and with any trial
he will give you a way out of it and the strength
to bear it.

[t] Ex. 32:6.

New English Bible

ture has it, 'the people sat down to feast and rose up to revel'. Let us not commit fornication, as some of them did—and twenty-three thousand died in one day. Let us not put the power of the Lord [a] to the test, as some of them did—and were destroyed by serpents. Do not grumble against God, as some of them did—and were destroyed by the Destroyer.

All these things that happened to them were symbolic, and were recorded for our benefit as a warning. For upon us the fulfilment of the ages has come. If you feel sure that you are standing firm, beware! You may fall. So far you have faced no trial beyond what man can bear. God keeps faith, and he will not allow you to be tested above your powers, but when the test comes he will at the same time provide a way out, by enabling you to sustain it.

[a] *Some witnesses read* of Christ.

King James Version

be able to bear *it.* 14 Wherefore, my dearly beloved, flee from idolatry. 15 I speak as to wise
men; judge ye what I say. 16 The cup of blessing
which we bless, is it not the communion of the
blood of Christ? The bread which we break, is
it not the communion of the body of Christ?
17 For we *being* many are one bread, *and* one
body: for we are all partakers of that one bread.
18 Behold Israel after the flesh: are not they
which eat of the sacrifices partakers of the altar?
19 What say I then? that the idol is any thing,
or that which is offered in sacrifice to idols is
any thing? 20 But *I say,* that the things which
the Gentiles sacrifice, they sacrifice to devils,
and not to God: and I would not that ye should
have fellowship with devils. 21 Ye cannot drink
the cup of the Lord, and the cup of devils: ye
cannot be partakers of the Lord's table, and
of the table of devils. 22 Do we provoke the
Lord to jealousy? are we stronger than he? 23 All
things are lawful for me, but all things are not

Living Bible

can bear up patiently against it. 14 So, dear
friends, carefully avoid idol-worship of every
kind.

15 You are intelligent people. Look now and
see for yourselves whether what I am about to
say is true. 16 When we ask the Lord's blessing
upon our drinking from the cup of wine at the
Lord's Table, this means, doesn't it, that all who
drink it are sharing together the blessing of
Christ's blood? And when we break off pieces
of the bread from the loaf to eat there together,
this shows that we are sharing together in the
benefits of his body. 17 No matter how many of
us there are, we all eat from the same loaf,
showing that we are all parts of the one body
of Christ. 18 And the Jewish people, all who eat
the sacrifices, are united by that act.

19 What am I trying to say? Am I saying
that the idols to whom the heathen bring sacrifices are really alive and are real gods, and that
these sacrifices are of some value? No, not at
all. 20 What I am saying is that those who offer
food to these idols are united together in sacrificing to demons, certainly not to God. And I
don't want any of you to be partners with demons when you eat the same food, along with
the heathen, that has been offered to these idols.
21 You cannot drink from the cup at the Lord's
Table and at Satan's table, too. You cannot
eat bread both at the Lord's Table and at Satan's
table.

22 What? Are you tempting the Lord to be
angry with you? Are you stronger than he is?
23 You are certainly free to eat food offered to
idols if you want to; it's not against God's laws
to eat such meat, but that doesn't mean that

Today's English Version

14 So then, my dear friends, keep away from
the worship of idols. 15 I speak to you as sensible people; judge for yourselves what I say.
16 The cup of blessing for which we give thanks
to God: do we not share in the blood of Christ
when we drink from this cup? And the bread
we break: do we not share in the body of Christ
when we eat this bread? 17 Because there is the
one bread, all of us, though many, are one body,
because we all share the same loaf.

18 Consider the Hebrew people; those who
eat what is offered in sacrifice share in the altar's
service to God. 19 What do I mean? That an
idol or the food offered to it really amounts to
anything? 20 No! What I am saying is that what
is sacrificed on pagan altars is offered to demons,
not to God. And I do not want you to be partners with demons. 21 You cannot drink from
the Lord's cup and also from the cup of demons; you cannot eat at the Lord's table and
also at the table of demons. 22 Or do we want
to make the Lord jealous? Do we think that
we are stronger than he?

23 "We are allowed to do anything," so they
say. Yes, but not everything is good. "We are

New International Version

Idol feasts and the Lord's supper

14 Therefore, my dear friends, flee from
idolatry. 15 I speak to sensible people; judge for
yourselves what I say. 16 Is not the cup of
thanksgiving for which we give thanks a participation in the blood of Christ? And is not the
bread that we break a participation in the body
of Christ? 17 Because there is one loaf, we, who
are many, are one body, for we all partake of
the one loaf.

18 Consider the people of Israel: Do not those
who eat the sacrifices participate in the altar?
19 Do I mean then that a sacrifice offered to
an idol is anything, or that an idol is anything?
20 No, but the sacrifices of pagans are offered to
demons, not to God, and I do not want you to
be participants with demons. 21 You cannot
drink the cup of the Lord and the cup of demons
too; you cannot have a part in both the Lord's
table and the table of demons. 22 Are we trying
to arouse the Lord's jealousy? Are we stronger
than he?

The believer's freedom

23 "Everything is permissible"—but not every-

Phillips Modern English

10.14 We have great spiritual privileges: let us live up to them

The lesson we must learn, my brothers, is at all costs to avoid worshipping a false god. I am speaking to you as intelligent men: use your judgment over what I am saying.

The cup of blessing which we bless, is it not a very sharing in the blood of Christ? When we break the bread do we not actually share in the body of Christ? The very fact that we, many as we are, share one bread makes us all one body. Look at the Jewish people. Isn't there a fellowship between all those who eat the altar sacrifices?

Now am I implying that a false god really exists, or that sacrifices made to any god have some value? Not at all! I say emphatically that gentile sacrifices are made to evil spiritual powers and not to God at all. I don't want you to have any fellowship with such powers. You cannot drink both the cup of the Lord and the cup of devils. You cannot be a guest at the Lord's table and at the table of devils. Are we trying to arouse the wrath of the Lord? Do we think we are stronger than he?

10.23 The Christian's guiding principle is love not knowledge

As I have said before, the Christian position is this: I may do anything, but everything is not

Revised Standard Version

14 Therefore, my beloved, shun the worship of idols. 15 I speak as to sensible men; judge for yourselves what I say. 16 The cup of blessing which we bless, is it not a participation[q] in the blood of Christ? The bread which we break, is it not a participation[q] in the body of Christ? 17 Because there is one bread, we who are many are one body, for we all partake of the one bread. 18 Consider the people of Israel;[a] are not those who eat the sacrifices partners in the altar? 19 What do I imply then? That food offered to idols is anything, or that an idol is anything? 20 No, I imply that what pagans sacrifice they offer to demons and not to God. I do not want you to be partners with demons. 21 You cannot drink the cup of the Lord and the cup of demons. You cannot partake of the table of the Lord and the table of demons. 22 Shall we provoke the Lord to jealousy? Are we stronger than he?

23 "All things are lawful," but not all things

[q] Or *communion.* [a] Greek *Israel according to the flesh.*

Jerusalem Bible

Sacrificial feasts. No compromise with idolatry

14 This is the reason, my dear brothers, why you must keep clear of idolatry. 15 I say to you as sensible people: judge for yourselves what I am saying. 16 The blessing cup that we bless is a communion with the blood of Christ, and the bread that we break is a communion with the body of Christ. 17 The fact that there is only one loaf means that, though there are many of us, we form a single body because we all have a share in this one loaf. 18 Look at the other Israel, the race, where those who eat the sacrifices are in communion with the altar. 19 Does this mean that the food sacrificed to idols has a real value, or that the idol itself is real? 20 Not at all. It simply means that the sacrifices that they offer *they sacrifice to demons who are not God.*[u] I have no desire to see you in communion with demons. 21 You cannot drink the cup of the Lord and the cup of demons. You cannot take your share at the table of the Lord and at the table of demons. 22 Do we want to make the Lord angry; are we stronger than he is?

Food sacrificed to idols. Practical solutions

23 "For me there are no forbidden things," but not everything does good. True, there are

[u] Dt. 32:17.

New English Bible

So then, dear friends, shun idolatry. I speak to you as men of sense. Form your own judgement on what I say. When we bless 'the cup of blessing', is it not a means of sharing in the blood of Christ? When we break the bread, is it not a means of sharing in the body of Christ? Because there is one loaf, we, many as we are, are one body;[a] for it is one loaf of which we all partake.

Look at the Jewish people. Are not those who partake in the sacrificial meal sharers in the altar? What do I imply by this? that an idol is anything but an idol? or food offered to it anything more than food? No; but the sacrifices the heathen offer are offered (in the words of Scripture) 'to demons and to that which is not God'; and I will not have you become partners with demons. You cannot drink the cup of the Lord and the cup of demons. You cannot partake of the Lord's table and the table of demons. Can we defy the Lord? Are we stronger than he?

'We are free to do anything', you say. Yes, but is everything good for us? 'We are free to do

[a] *Or* For we, many as we are, are one loaf, one body.

King James Version

expedient: all things are lawful for me, but all things edify not. 24 Let no man seek his own, but every man another's *wealth.* 25 Whatsoever is sold in the shambles, *that* eat, asking no question for conscience' sake: 26 For the earth *is* the Lord's, and the fulness thereof. 27 If any of them that believe not bid you *to a feast,* and ye be disposed to go; whatsoever is set before you, eat, asking no question for conscience' sake. 28 But if any man say unto you, This is offered in sacrifice unto idols, eat not for his sake that shewed it, and for conscience' sake: for the earth *is* the Lord's, and the fulness thereof: 29 Conscience, I say, not thine own, but of the other: for why is my liberty judged of another *man's* conscience? 30 For if I by grace be a partaker, why am I evil spoken of for that for which I give thanks? 31 Whether therefore ye eat, or drink, or whatsoever ye do, do all to the glory of God. 32 Give none offence, neither to the Jews, nor to the Gentiles, nor to the church of God: 33 Even as I please all *men* in all *things,* not seeking mine own profit, but the *profit* of many, that they may be saved.

Living Bible

you should go ahead and do it. It may be perfectly legal, but it may not be best and helpful. 24 Don't think only of yourself. Try to think of the other fellow, too, and what is best for him.

25 Here's what you should do. Take any meat you want that is sold at the market. Don't ask whether or not it was offered to idols, lest the answer hurt your conscience. 26 For the earth and every good thing in it belongs to the Lord and is yours to enjoy.

27 If someone who isn't a Christian asks you out to dinner, go ahead; accept the invitation if you want to. Eat whatever is on the table and don't ask any questions about it. Then you won't know whether or not it has been used as a sacrifice to idols, and you won't risk having a bad conscience over eating it. 28 But if someone warns you that this meat has been offered to idols, then don't eat it for the sake of the man who told you, and of his conscience. 29 In this case *his* feeling about it is the important thing, not yours.

But why, you may ask, must I be guided and limited by what someone else thinks? 30 If I can thank God for the food and enjoy it, why let someone spoil everything just because he thinks I am wrong? 31 Well, I'll tell you why. It is because you must do everything for the glory of God, even your eating and drinking. 32 So don't be a stumbling block to anyone, whether they are Jews or Gentiles or Christians. 33 That is the plan I follow, too. I try to please everyone in everything I do, not doing what I like or what is best for me, but what is best for them, so that they may be saved.

Today's English Version

allowed to do anything"—but not everything is helpful. 24 No one should be looking out for his own interests, but for the interests of others.

25 You are free to eat anything sold in the meat market, without asking any questions because of conscience. 26 For, as the scripture says, "The earth and everything in it belong to the Lord."

27 If an unbeliever invites you to a meal and you decide to go, eat what is set before you without asking any questions because of conscience. 28 But if someone tells you, "This is food that was offered to idols," then do not eat that food, for the sake of the one who told you so and for conscience' sake—29 that is, not your own conscience, but the other man's conscience.

"Well, then," someone asks, "why should my freedom to act be limited by another person's conscience? 30 If I thank God for my food, why should anyone criticize me about food for which I give thanks?"

31 Well, whatever you do, whether you eat or drink, do it all for God's glory. 32 Live in such a way as to cause no trouble either to Jews, or Gentiles, or to the church of God. 33 Just do as I do; I try to please everyone in all that I do, with no thought of my own good, but for the good of all, so that they might be saved.

New International Version

thing is beneficial. "Everything is permissible" —but not everything is constructive. 24 Nobody should seek his own good, but the good of others.

25 Eat anything sold in the meat market without raising questions of conscience, 26 for, "The earth is the Lord's, and everything in it." [v]

27 If some unbeliever invites you to a meal and you want to go, eat whatever is put before you without raising questions of conscience. 28 But if anyone says to you, "This has been offered in sacrifice," then do not eat it, both for the sake of the man who told you and for conscience' sake[w]—29 the other man's conscience, I mean, not yours. For why should my freedom be judged by another's conscience? 30 If I take part in the meal with thankfulness, why am I denounced because of something I thank God for?

31 So whether you eat or drink or whatever you do, do it all for the glory of God. 32 Do not cause anyone to stumble, whether Jews, Greeks or the church of God—33 even as I try to please everybody in every way. For I am not seeking my own good but the good of many, so that they may be saved.

[v] Psalm 24:1. [w] Some MSS add *for "the earth is the Lord's and everything in it."*

Phillips Modern English

useful. Yes, I may do anything, but everything is not constructive. Let no man, then, set his own advantage as his objective, but rather the good of his neighbour.

Eat whatever is sold in the meat-market without any question of conscience. The whole earth and all that is in it belongs to the Lord.

If a pagan asks you to dinner and you want to go, feel free to eat whatever is set before you, without asking any questions through conscientious scruples. But if someone should say straight out, "This has been offered to an idol", then don't eat it, for his sake—I mean for the sake of conscience, not yours but his.

Now why should my freedom to eat be at the mercy of someone else's conscience? Or why should any evil be said of me when I have eaten food with gratitude, and have thanked God for it? Because, whatever you do, eating or drinking or anything else, everything should be done to bring glory to God.

Do nothing that might make men stumble, whether they are Jews or Greeks or members of the church of God. I myself try to be agreeable to all men without considering my own advantage but that of the majority, that if possible they may be saved.

Revised Standard Version

are helpful. "All things are lawful," but not all
things build up. 24 Let no one seek his own good,
but the good of his neighbor. 25 Eat whatever
is sold in the meat market without raising any
question on the ground of conscience. 26 For
"the earth is the Lord's, and everything in it."
27 If one of the unbelievers invites you to dinner
and you are disposed to go, eat whatever is set
before you without raising any question on the
ground of conscience. 28 (But if some one says
to you, "This has been offered in sacrifice," then
out of consideration for the man who informed
you, and for conscience' sake—29 I mean his
conscience, not yours—do not eat it.) For why
should my liberty be determined by another
man's scruples? 30 If I partake with thankfulness, why am I denounced because of that for
which I give thanks?
31 So, whether you eat or drink, or whatever you do, do all to the glory of God. 32 Give
no offense to jews or to Greeks or to the church
of God, 33 just as I try to please all men in
everything I do, not seeking my own advantage,
but that of many, that they may be saved.

Jerusalem Bible

no forbidden things, but it is not everything
that helps the building to grow. 24 Nobody
should be looking for his own advantage, but
everybody for the other man's. 25 Do not hesitate to eat anything that is sold in butchers'
shops: there is no need to raise questions of
conscience; 26 for *the earth and everything that*
is in it belong to the Lord.[v] 27 If an unbeliever
invites you to his house, go if you want to, and
eat whatever is put in front of you, without asking questions just to satisfy conscience. 28 But
if someone says to you, "This food was offered
in sacrifice," then, out of consideration for the
man that told you, you should not eat it, for
the sake of his scruples; 29 his scruples, you see,
not your own. Why should my freedom depend
on somebody else's conscience? 30 If I take my
share with thankfulness, why should I be blamed
for food for which I have thanked God?

Conclusion

31 Whatever you eat, whatever you drink,
whatever you do at all, do it for the glory of
God. 32 Never do anything offensive to anyone
—to Jews or Greeks or to the Church of God;
33 just as I try to be helpful to everyone at all
times, not anxious for my own advantage but
for the advantage of everybody else, so that they
may be saved.

[v] Ps. 24:1.

New English Bible

anything', but does everything help the building of the community? Each of you must regard, not his own interests, but the other man's.

You may eat anything sold in the meat-market without raising questions of conscience; for the earth is the Lord's and everything in it.

If an unbeliever invites you to a meal and you care to go, eat whatever is put before you, without raising questions of conscience. But if somebody says to you, 'This food has been offered in sacrifice', then, out of consideration for him, and for conscience' sake, do not eat it—not your conscience, I mean, but the other man's.

'What?' you say, 'is my freedom to be called in question by another man's conscience? If I partake with thankfulness, why am I blamed for eating food over which I have said grace?' Well, whether you eat or drink, or whatever you are doing, do all for the honour of God: give no offence to Jews, or Greeks, or to the church of God. For my part I always try to meet everyone half-way, regarding not my own good but the good of the many, so that they may be saved.

King James Version

11 Be ye followers of me, even as I also *am*
of Christ. 2 Now I praise you, brethren, that
ye remember me in all things, and keep the
ordinances, as I delivered *them* to you. 3 But I
would have you know, that the head of every
man is Christ; and the head of the woman *is*
the man; and the head of Christ *is* God. 4 Every
man praying or prophesying, having *his* head
covered, dishonoureth his head. 5 But every
woman that prayeth or prophesieth with *her*
head uncovered dishonoureth her head: for that
is even all one as if she were shaven. 6 For if
the woman be not covered, let her also be shorn:
but if it be a shame for a woman to be shorn
or shaven, let her be covered. 7 For a man indeed ought not to cover *his* head, forasmuch as
he is the image and glory of God: but the
woman is the glory of the man. 8 For the man
is not of the woman; but the woman of the man.
9 Neither was the man created for the woman;
but the woman for the man. 10 For this cause
ought the woman to have power on *her* head

Living Bible

11 And you should follow my example, just
as I follow Christ's. 2 I am so glad, dear
brothers, that you have been remembering and
doing everything I taught you. 3 But there is
one matter I want to remind you about: that a
wife is responsible to her husband, her husband
is responsible to Christ, and Christ is responsible to God. 4 That is why, if a man refuses to
remove his hat while praying or preaching, he
dishonors Christ. 5 And that is why a woman
who publicly prays or prophesies without a covering on her head dishonors her husband [for
her covering is a sign of her subjection to him[a]].
6 Yes, if she refuses to wear a head covering,
then she should cut off all her hair. And if it
is shameful for a woman to have her head
shaved, then she should wear a covering. 7 But
a man should not wear anything on his head
[when worshiping, for his hat is a sign of subjection to men[b]].
God's glory is man made in his image, and
man's glory is the woman. 8 The first man didn't
come from woman, but the first woman came
out of man.[c] 9 And Adam, the first man, was not
made for Eve's benefit, but Eve was made for
Adam. 10 So a woman should wear a covering
on her head as a sign that she is under man's
authority,[d] a fact for all the angels to notice and
rejoice in.[e]

[*a*] Implied in verses 7, 10. [*b*] Implied. [*c*] Genesis 2:21-22. [*d*] Literally, "For this cause ought the woman to have power on (her) head." [*e*] Literally, "because of the angels."

Today's English Version

11 Imitate me, then, just as I imitate Christ.

Covering the head in worship

2 I praise you, because you always remember
me and follow the teachings that I have handed
on to you. 3 But I want you to understand that
Christ is supreme over every man, the husband
is supreme over his wife, and God is supreme
over Christ. 4 So a man who prays or speaks
God's message in public worship with his head
covered disgraces Christ. 5 And any woman who
prays or speaks God's message in public worship with nothing on her head disgraces her
husband; there is no difference between her and
a woman whose head has been shaved. 6 If the
woman does not cover her head, she might as
well cut her hair. And since it is a shameful
thing for a woman to shave her head or cut her
hair, she should cover her head. 7 A man has no
need to cover his head, because he reflects the
image and glory of God. But woman reflects
the glory of man; 8 for man was not created
from woman, but woman from man. 9 Nor was
man created for woman's sake, but woman was
created for man's sake. 10 On account of the
angels, then, a woman should have a covering
over her head to show that she is under her

New International Version

11 Follow my example, as I follow the example of Christ.

Propriety in worship

2 I praise you for remembering me in everything and for holding to the teachings,[x] just as
I passed them on to you.
3 Now I want you to realize that the head of
every man is Christ, and the head of the woman
is man, and the head of Christ is God. 4 Every
man who prays or prophesies with his head
covered dishonors his head. 5 And every woman
who prays or prophesies with her head uncovered
dishonors her head—it is just as though her head
were shaved. 6 If a woman does not cover her
head, she should have her hair cut off; and if it
is a disgrace for a woman to have her hair cut
or shaved off, she should cover her head. 7 A man
ought not to cover his head,[y] since he is the
image and glory of God; but the woman is the
glory of man. 8 For man did not come from
woman, but woman from man; 9 neither was
man created for woman, but woman for man.
10 For this reason, and because of the angels, the
woman ought to have a sign of authority on her
head.

[*x*] Or *traditions.* [*y*] Or *4 Every man who prays or prophesies with long hair dishonors his head. 5 And every woman who prays or prophesies with no covering [of hair] on her head dishonors her head—she is just like one of the "shorn women." 6 If a woman has no covering, let her be for now with short hair, but since it is a disgrace for a woman to have her hair shorn or shaved, she should grow it again. 7 A man ought not to have long hair.*

Phillips Modern English

Copy me, my brothers, as I copy Christ himself.

11.2 The reasons that lie behind some of the traditions

I must give you credit for remembering what I taught you and adhering to the traditions I passed on to you. But I want you to know that Christ is the head of every individual man, just as a man is the "head" of the woman and God is the head of Christ. If a man prays or preaches with his head covered, he is dishonouring his own head. But in the case of a woman, if she prays or preaches with her head uncovered it is just as much a disgrace as if she had had it closely shaved. For if a woman does not cover her head she might just as well have her hair cropped. And if to be cropped or closely shaven is a sign of disgrace to women, then that is all the more reason for her to cover her head. A man ought not to cover his head, for he represents the very person and glory of God, while the woman reflects the glory of the man. For man does not exist because woman exists, but vice versa. Man was not created originally for the sake of woman, but woman was created for the sake of man. For this reason a woman ought to bear on her head an outward sign of man's authority for all the angels to see.

Revised Standard Version

11 Be imitators of me, as I am of Christ.
2 I commend you because you remember me
in everything and maintain the traditions even
as I have delivered them to you. 3 But I want
you to understand that the head of every man
is Christ, the head of a woman is her husband,
and the head of Christ is God. 4 Any man who
prays or prophesies with his head covered dishonors his head, 5 but any woman who prays or
prophesies with her head unveiled dishonors her
head—it is the same as if her head were shaven.
6 For if a woman will not veil herself, then she
should cut off her hair; but if it is disgraceful
for a woman to be shorn or shaven, let her wear
a veil. 7 For a man ought not to cover his head,
since he is the image and glory of God; but
woman is the glory of man. 8 (For man was not
made from woman, but woman from man.
9 Neither was man created for woman, but
woman for man.) 10 That is why a woman
ought to have a veil [r] on her head, because of

[r] Greek *authority* (the veil being a symbol of this).

Jerusalem Bible

11 Take me for your model, as I take Christ.

C. Decorum in public worship

Women's behavior at services

2 You have done well in remembering me so
constantly and in maintaining the traditions just
as I passed them on to you. 3 However, what I
want you to understand is that Christ is the
head of every man, man is the head of woman,
and God is the head of Christ. 4 For a man to
pray or prophesy with his head covered is a sign
of disrespect to his head.[w] 5 For a woman, however, it is a sign of disrespect to her head [x] if
she prays or prophesies unveiled; she might as
well have her hair shaved off. 6 In fact, a woman
who will not wear a veil ought to have her hair
cut off. If a woman is ashamed to have her hair
cut off or shaved, she ought to wear a veil.
7 A man should certainly not cover his head,
since he is the image of God and reflects God's
glory; but woman is the reflection of man's
glory. 8 For man did not come from woman; no,
woman came from man; 9 and man was not
created for the sake of woman, but woman was
created for the sake of man. 10 That is the argument for women's covering their heads with a
symbol of the authority over them, out of re-

[w] His leader, a Greek pun. [x] Her husband, who is her head; she is claiming equality.

New English Bible

11 Follow my example as I follow Christ's.

I commend you for always keeping me in mind, and maintaining the tradition I handed on to you. But I wish you to understand that, while every man has Christ for his Head, woman's head is man,[a] as Christ's Head is God. A man who keeps his head covered when he prays or prophesies brings shame on his head; a woman, on the contrary, brings shame on her head if she prays or prophesies bare-headed; it is as bad as if her head were shaved. If a woman is not to wear a veil she might as well have her hair cut off; but if it is a disgrace for her to be cropped and shaved, then she should wear a veil. A man has no need to cover his head, because man is the image of God, and the mirror of his glory, whereas woman reflects the glory of man.[b] For man did not originally spring from woman, but woman was made out of man; and man was not created for woman's sake, but woman for the sake of man; and therefore it is woman's duty to have a sign of authority[c] on her head, out of

[a] *Or* a woman's head is her husband. [b] *Or* a woman reflects her husband's glory. [c] *Some witnesses read* to have a veil.

King James Version

because of the angels. 11 Nevertheless neither is the man without the woman, neither the woman without the man, in the Lord. 12 For as the woman *is* of the man, even so *is* the man also by the woman; but all things of God. 13 Judge in yourselves: is it comely that a woman pray unto God uncovered? 14 Doth not even nature itself teach you, that, if a man have long hair, it is a shame unto him? 15 But if a woman have long hair, it is a glory to her: for *her* hair is given her for a covering. 16 But if any man seem to be contentious, we have no such custom, neither the churches of God. 17 Now in this that I declare *unto you* I praise *you* not, that ye come together not for the better, but for the worse. 18 For first of all, when ye come together in the church, I hear that there be divisions among you; and I partly believe it. 19 For there must be also heresies among you, that they which are approved may be made manifest among you. 20 When ye come together therefore into one place, *this* is not to eat the Lord's supper. 21 For in eating every one taketh before *other* his own supper: and one is hungry, and another is drunken. 22 What! have ye not houses to eat and to drink in? or despise ye the church of

Living Bible

11 But remember that in God's plan men and women need each other. 12 For although the first woman came out of man, all men have been born from women ever since, and both men and women come from God their Creator.

13 What do you yourselves really think about this? Is it right for a woman to pray in public without covering her head? 14, 15 Doesn't even instinct itself teach us that women's heads should be covered? For women are proud of their long hair, while a man with long hair tends to be ashamed. 16 But if anyone wants to argue about this, all I can say is that we never teach anything else than this—that a woman should wear a covering when prophesying or praying publicly in the church, and all the churches feel the same way about it.

17 Next on my list of items to write you about is something else I cannot agree with. For it sounds as if more harm than good is done when you meet together for your communion services. 18 Everyone keeps telling me about the arguing that goes on in these meetings, and the divisions developing among you, and I can just about believe it. 19 But I suppose you feel this is necessary so that you who are always right will become known and recognized!

20 When you come together to eat, it isn't the Lord's Supper you are eating, 21 but your own. For I am told that everyone hastily gobbles all the food he can without waiting to share with the others, so that one doesn't get enough and goes hungry while another has too much to drink and gets drunk. 22 What? Is this really true? Can't you do your eating and drinking at

Today's English Version

husband's authority. 11 In our life in the Lord, however, woman is not independent of man, nor is man independent of woman. 12 For as woman was made from man, in the same way man is born of woman; and all things come from God.

13 Judge for yourselves: is it proper for a woman to pray to God in public worship with nothing on her head? 14 Why, nature itself teaches you that long hair is a disgraceful thing for a man, 15 but is a woman's pride. Her long hair has been given her to serve as a covering. 16 But if anyone wants to argue about it, all I have to say is that neither we nor the churches of God have any other custom in worship.

The Lord's Supper

17 In the following instructions, however, I do not praise you; because your church meetings actually do more harm than good. 18 In the first place, I have been told that there are opposing groups in your church meetings; and this I believe is partly true. 19 (No doubt there must be divisions among you so that the ones who are in the right may be clearly seen.) 20 When you meet together as a group, you do not come to eat the Lord's Supper. 21 For as you eat, each one goes ahead with his own meal, so that some are hungry while others get drunk. 22 Don't you have your own homes in which to eat and

New International Version

11 In the Lord, however, woman is not independent of man, nor is man independent of woman. 12 For as woman came from man, so also man is born of woman. But everything comes from God. 13 Judge for yourselves: Is it proper for a woman to pray to God with her head uncovered? 14 Does not the very nature of things teach you that if a man has long hair, it is a disgrace to him, 15 but that if a woman has long hair, it is her glory? For long hair is given to her as a covering. 16 If anyone wants to be contentious about this, we have no other practice —nor do the churches of God.

The Lord's Supper

17 In the following directives I have no praise for you, for your meetings do more harm than good. 18 In the first place, I hear that when you come together as a church, there are divisions among you, and to some extent I believe it. 19 No doubt there have to be differences among you to show which of you have God's approval. 20 When you come together, it is not the Lord's Supper you eat, 21 for as you eat, each of you goes ahead without waiting for anybody else. One remains hungry, another gets drunk. 22 Don't you have homes to eat and drink in? Or do you despise the church of God and hu-

[y] The guardians of due order in public worship.
[z] The *agapē*, or love feast, preceding the liturgical meal.

Phillips Modern English

Of course, in the sight of the Lord neither "man" nor "woman" has any separate existence. For if woman was made originally from man, no man is now born except by a woman, and both man and woman, like everything else, owe their existence to God. But use your own judgment: do you think it right and proper for a woman to pray to God bare-headed? Isn't there a natural principle here, that makes us feel that long hair is disgraceful to a man, but of glorious beauty to a woman? We feel this because the long hair is the cover provided by nature for the woman's head. But if anyone wants to be argumentative about it, I can only say that we and the churches of God generally hold this ruling on the matter.

11.17 I must mention serious faults in your Church

But in giving you the following rules, I cannot commend your conduct, for it seems that your church meetings do you more harm than good! For first, when you meet for worship I hear that you split up into small groups, and I think there must be truth in what I hear. (I grant that you must be able to make choices or your best men might go unrecognised.) But, as it is, when you are assembled in one place you do not eat the *Lord's* supper. For everyone tries to grab his food before anyone else, with the result that one goes hungry and another has too much to drink! Haven't you houses of your own to have your meals in, or are you showing con-

Revised Standard Version

the angels. 11 (Nevertheless, in the Lord woman
is not independent of man nor man of woman;
12 for as woman was made from man, so man
is now born of woman. And all things are from
God.) 13 Judge for yourselves; is it proper for
a woman to pray to God with her head uncovered? 14 Does not nature itself teach you
that for a man to wear long hair is degrading to
him, 15 but if a woman has long hair, it is her
pride? For her hair is given to her for a covering. 16 If any one is disposed to be contentious,
we recognize no other practice, nor do the
churches of God.

17 But in the following instructions I do not
commend you, because when you come together
it is not for the better but for the worse. 18 For,
in the first place, when you assemble as a church,
I hear that there are divisions among you; and
I partly believe it, 19 for there must be factions among you in order that those who are
genuine among you may be recognized. 20 When
you meet together, it is not the Lord's supper
that you eat. 21 For in eating, each one goes
ahead with his own meal, and one is hungry
and another is drunk. 22 What! Do you not have
houses to eat and drink in? Or do you despise

Jerusalem Bible

spect for the angels.[y] 11 However, though woman
cannot do without man, neither can man do
without woman, in the Lord; 12 woman may
come from man, but man is born of woman—
both come from God.

13 Ask yourselves if it is fitting for a woman
to pray to God without a veil; 14 and whether
nature itself does not tell you that long hair on
a man is nothing to be admired, 15 while a
woman, who was given her hair as a covering,
thinks long hair her glory?

16 To anyone who might still want to argue:
it is not the custom with us, nor in the churches
of God.

The Lord's Supper

17 Now that I am on the subject of instructions, I cannot say that you have done well in
holding meetings that do you more harm than
good. 18 In the first place, I hear that when
you all come together as a community, there
are separate factions among you, and I half
believe it—19 since there must no doubt be
separate groups among you, to distinguish those
who are to be trusted. 20 The point is, when you
hold these meetings, it is not the Lord's Supper[z]
that you are eating, 21 since when the time
comes to eat, everyone is in such a hurry to start
his own supper that one person goes hungry
while another is getting drunk. 22 Surely you
have homes for eating and drinking in? Surely

New English Bible

regard for the angels.[d] And yet, in Christ's fellowship woman is as essential to man as man to woman. If woman was made out of man, it is through woman that man now comes to be; and God is the source of all.

Judge for yourselves: is it fitting for a woman to pray to God bare-headed? Does not Nature herself teach you that while flowing locks disgrace a man, they are a woman's glory? For her locks were given for covering.

However, if you insist on arguing, let me tell you, there is no such custom among us, or in any of the congregations of God's people.

In giving you these injunctions I must mention a practice which I cannot commend: your meetings tend to do more harm than good. To begin with, I am told that when you meet as a congregation you fall into sharply divided groups; and I believe there is some truth in it (for dissensions are necessary if only to show which of your members are sound). The result is that when you meet as a congregation, it is impossible for you to eat the Lord's Supper, because each of you is in such a hurry to eat his own, and while one goes hungry another has too much to drink. Have you no homes of your own to eat and drink in? Or are you so contemptuous of the

[*d*] *Or* and therefore a woman should keep her dignity on her head, for fear of the angels.

King James Version

God, and shame them that have not? What shall
I say to you? shall I praise you in this? I praise
you not. 23 For I have received of the Lord that
which also I delivered unto you, That the Lord
Jesus, the *same* night in which he was betrayed,
took bread: 24 And when he had given thanks,
he brake *it*, and said, Take, eat; this is my body,
which is broken for you: this do in remembrance of me. 25 After the same manner also *he
took* the cup, when he had supped, saying, This
cup is the new testament in my blood: this do
ye, as oft as ye drink *it*, in remembrance of me.
26 For as often as ye eat this bread, and drink
this cup, ye do shew the Lord's death till he
come. 27 Wherefore whosoever shall eat this
bread, and drink *this* cup of the Lord, unworthily, shall be guilty of the body and blood
of the Lord. 28 But let a man examine himself,
and so let him eat of *that* bread, and drink of
that cup. 29 For he that eateth and drinketh
unworthily, eateth and drinketh damnation to

Living Bible

home, to avoid disgracing the church and sham-
ing those who are poor and can bring no food?
What am I supposed to say about these things?
Do you want me to praise you? Well, I certainly
do not!

23 For this is what the Lord himself has said
about his Table, and I have passed it on to you
before: That on the night when Judas betrayed
him, the Lord Jesus took bread, 24 and when
he had given thanks to God for it, he broke it
and gave it to his disciples and said, "Take this
and eat it. This is my body, which is given[f] for
you. Do this to remember me." 25 In the same
way, he took the cup of wine after supper, saying, "This cup is the new agreement between
God and you that has been established and set
in motion by my blood. Do this in remembrance
of me whenever you drink it." 26 For every time
you eat this bread and drink this cup you are
re-telling the message of the Lord's death, that
he has died for you. Do this until he comes
again.

27 So if anyone eats this bread and drinks
from this cup of the Lord in an unworthy manner, he is guilty of sin against the body and the
blood of the Lord. 28 That is why a man should
examine himself carefully before eating the bread
and drinking from the cup. 29 For if he eats the
bread and drinks from the cup unworthily, not
thinking about the body of Christ and what it
means, he is eating and drinking God's judgment
upon himself; for he is trifling with the death of

[f] Some ancient manuscripts read, "broken."

Today's English Version

drink? Or would you rather despise the church
of God and put to shame the people who are
in need? What do you expect me to say to you
about this? Should I praise you? Of course I do
not praise you!

23 For from the Lord I received the teaching
that I passed on to you: that the Lord Jesus, on
the night he was betrayed, took the bread,
24 gave thanks to God, broke it, and said, "This
is my body, which is for you. Do this in memory
of me." 25 In the same way, he took the cup
after the supper and said, "This cup is God's
new covenant, sealed with my blood. Whenever
you drink it, do it in memory of me." 26 For
until the Lord comes, you proclaim his death
whenever you eat this bread and drink from
this cup.

27 It follows, then, that if anyone eats the
Lord's bread or drinks from his cup in a way
that dishonors him, he is guilty of sin against
the Lord's body and blood. 28 So then, everyone
should examine himself first, and then eat the
bread and drink from the cup. 29 For if he does
not recognize the meaning of the Lord's body
when he eats the bread and drinks from the
cup, he brings judgment on himself as he eats

New International Version

miliate those who have nothing? What shall I
say to you? Shall I praise you for this? Certainly not!

23 For I received from the Lord what I also
passed on to you: The Lord Jesus, on the night
he was betrayed, took bread, 24 and when he had
given thanks, he broke it and said, "This is my
body, which is for you; do this in remembrance
of me." 25 In the same way, after supper he took
the cup, saying, "This cup is the new covenant
in my blood; do this, whenever you drink it, in
remembrance of me." 26 For whenever you eat
this bread and drink this cup, you proclaim the
Lord's death until he comes.

27 Therefore, whoever eats the bread or drinks
the cup of the Lord in an unworthy manner will
be guilty of sinning against the body and blood
of the Lord. 28 A man ought to examine himself
before he eats of the bread and drinks of the
cup. 29 For anyone who eats and drinks without
recognizing the body of the Lord eats and drinks

Phillips Modern English

tempt for the church of God and causing acute embarrassment to those who have no other home?

What do you expect from me? Compliments? Certainly not on this!

11.23 To partake of the Lord's supper is a supremely serious thing

The teaching I gave you was given me personally by the Lord himself, and it was this: the Lord Jesus, in the same night in which he was betrayed, took bread and when he had given thanks he broke it and said, "This is my body—and it is for you. Do this in remembrance of me." Similarly, when supper was ended, he took the cup saying, "This cup is the new agreement made by my blood: do this, whenever you drink it, in remembrance of me."

This can only mean that whenever you eat this bread and drink this cup, you are proclaiming the Lord's death until he comes again. So that, whoever eats the bread or drinks the cup of the Lord without proper reverence is sinning against the body and blood of the Lord.

No, a man should thoroughly examine himself, and only then should he eat the bread or drink of the cup. He that eats and drinks carelessly is eating and drinking a condemnation of himself, for he is blind to the presence of the Body.

Revised Standard Version

the church of God and humiliate those who have nothing? What shall I say to you? Shall I commend you in this? No, I will not.

23 For I received from the Lord what I also delivered to you, that the Lord Jesus on the night when he was betrayed took bread, 24 and when he had given thanks, he broke it, and said, "This is my body which is for[s] you. Do this in remembrance of me." 25 In the same way also the cup, after supper, saying, "This cup is the new covenant in my blood. Do this, as often as you drink it, in remembrance of me." 26 For as often as you eat this bread and drink the cup, you proclaim the Lord's death until he comes.

27 Whoever, therefore, eats the bread or drinks the cup of the Lord in an unworthy manner will be guilty of profaning the body and blood of the Lord. 28 Let a man examine himself, and so eat of the bread and drink of the cup. 29 For any one who eats and drinks without discerning the body eats and drinks judg-

[s] Other ancient authorities read *broken for.*

Jerusalem Bible

you have enough respect for the community of God not to make poor people embarrassed? What am I to say to you? Congratulate you? I cannot congratulate you on this.

23 For this is what I received from the Lord, and in turn passed on to you: that on the same night that he was betrayed, the Lord Jesus took some bread, 24 and thanked God for it and broke it, and he said, "This is my body, which is for you; do this as a memorial of me." 25 In the same way he took the cup after supper, and said, "This cup is the new covenant in my blood. Whenever you drink it, do this as a memorial of me." 26 Until the Lord comes, therefore, every time you eat this bread and drink this cup, you are proclaiming his death, 27 and so anyone who eats the bread or drinks the cup of the Lord unworthily will be behaving unworthily toward the body and blood of the Lord.

28 Everyone is to recollect himself before eating this bread and drinking this cup; 29 because a person who eats and drinks without recognizing the Body is eating and drinking his

New English Bible

church of God that you shame its poorer members? What am I to say? Can I commend you? On this point, certainly not!

For the tradition which I handed on to you came to me from the Lord himself: that the Lord Jesus, on the night of his arrest, took bread and, after giving thanks to God, broke it and said: 'This is my body, which is for you; do this as a memorial of me.' In the same way, he took the cup after supper, and said: 'This cup is the new covenant sealed by my blood. Whenever you drink it, do this as a memorial of me.' For every time you eat this bread and drink the cup, you proclaim the death of the Lord, until he comes.

It follows that anyone who eats the bread or drinks the cup of the Lord unworthily will be guilty of desecrating the body and blood of the Lord. A man must test himself before eating his share of the bread and drinking from the cup. For he who eats and drinks eats and drinks judgement on himself if he does not discern the

King James Version

himself, not discerning the Lord's body. 30 For this cause many *are* weak and sickly among you, and many sleep. 31 For if we would judge ourselves, we should not be judged. 32 But when we are judged, we are chastened of the Lord, that we should not be condemned with the world. 33 Wherefore, my brethren, when ye come together to eat, tarry one for another. 34 And if any man hunger, let him eat at home; that ye come not together unto condemnation. And the rest will I set in order when I come.

12 Now concerning spiritual *gifts,* brethren, I would not have you ignorant. 2 Ye know that ye were Gentiles, carried away unto these dumb idols, even as ye were led. 3 Wherefore I give you to understand, that no man speaking

Living Bible

Christ. 30 That is why many of you are weak and sick, and some have even died.

31 But if you carefully examine yourselves before eating you will not need to be judged and punished. 32 Yet, when we are judged and punished by the Lord, it is so that we will not be condemned with the rest of the world. 33 So, dear brothers, when you gather for the Lord's Supper—the communion service—wait for each other; 34 if anyone is really hungry he should eat at home so that he won't bring punishment upon himself when you meet together.

I'll talk to you about the other matters after I arrive.

12 And now, brothers, I want to write about the special abilities the Holy Spirit gives to each of you, for I don't want any misunderstanding about them. 2 You will remember that before you became Christians you went around from one idol to another, not one of which could speak a single word. 3 But now you are meeting people who claim to speak messages from the Spirit of God. How can you know whether they

Today's English Version

and drinks. 30 That is why many of you are sick and weak, and several have died. 31 If we would examine ourselves first, we would not come under God's judgment. 32 But we are judged and punished by the Lord, so that we shall not be condemned together with the world.

33 So then, my brothers, when you gather together to eat the Lord's meal, wait for one another. 34 And if anyone is hungry, he should eat at home, so that you will not come under God's judgment as you meet together. As for the other matters, I will settle them when I come.

Gifts from the Holy Spirit

12 Now, the matter about the gifts from the Holy Spirit.

I want you to know the truth about them, my brothers. 2 You know that while you were still heathen you were controlled by dead idols, who always led you astray. 3 You must realize, then, that no one who is led by God's Spirit can

New International Version

judgment on himself. 30 That is why many among you are weak and sick, and a number of you have fallen asleep. 31 But if we judged ourselves, we would not come under judgment. 32 When we are judged by the Lord, we are being disciplined so that we will not be condemned with the world.

33 So then, my brothers, when you come together to eat, wait for each other. 34 If anyone is hungry, he should eat at home, so that when you meet together it may not result in judgment.

And when I come I will give further directions.

Spiritual gifts

12 Now about spiritual gifts, brothers, I do not want you to be ignorant. 2 You know that when you were pagans, somehow or other you were influenced and led astray to dumb idols. 3 Therefore I tell you that no one who is speaking by the Spirit of God says, "Jesus be

Phillips Modern English

11.30 Careless communion means spiritual weakness: let us take due care

It is this careless participation which is the reason for the many feeble and sickly Christians in your church, and the explanation of the fact that many of you are spiritually asleep.

If we were closely to examine ourselves beforehand, we should avoid the judgment of God. But when God does judge us, he disciplines us as his own sons, that we may not be involved in the general condemnation of the world.

Now, my brothers, when you come together to eat this bread, wait your proper turn. If a man is really hungry let him satisfy his appetite at home. Don't let your communions be God's judgment upon you!

The other matters I will settle in person, when I come.

12.1 The Holy Spirit inspires men's faith and imparts spiritual gifts

Now, my brothers, I want to give you some further information in spiritual matters. You have not forgotten that you are gentiles, following dumb idols just as your impulses led you. Now I want you to understand, as Christians, that no one speaking by the Spirit of God could

Revised Standard Version

ment upon himself. 30 That is why many of
you are weak and ill, and some have died.[t]
31 But if we judged ourselves truly, we should
not be judged. 32 But when we are judged by
the Lord, we are chastened[u] so that we may
not be condemned along with the world.
33 So then, my brethren, when you come together to eat, wait for one another—34 if any
one is hungry, let him eat at home—lest you
come together to be condemned. About the other
things I will give directions when I come.

12 Now concerning spiritual gifts,[x] brethren,
I do not want you to be uninformed. 2 You
know that when you were heathen, you were led
astray to dumb idols, however you may have
been moved. 3 Therefore I want you to understand that no one speaking by the Spirit of God

[t] Greek *have fallen asleep* (as in 15.6, 20). [u] Or *when we are judged we are being chastened by the Lord.* [x] Or *spiritual persons.*

Jerusalem Bible

own condemnation. 30 In fact that is why many
of you are weak and ill and some of you have
died. 31 If only we recollected ourselves, we
should not be punished like that. 32 But when
the Lord does punish us like that, it is to correct
us and stop us from being condemned with the
world.
33 So to sum up, my dear brothers, when you
meet for the Meal, wait for one another. 34 Anyone who is hungry should eat at home, and then
your meeting will not bring your condemnation.
The other matters I shall adjust when I come.

Spiritual gifts

12 Now my dear brothers, I want to clear
up a wrong impression about spiritual gifts.
2 You remember that, when you were pagans,
whenever you felt irresistibly drawn, it was toward dumb idols? 3 It is for that reason that I
want you to understand that on the one hand
no one can be speaking under the influence of

New English Bible

Body. That is why many of you are feeble and sick, and a number have died. But if we examined ourselves, we should not thus fall under judgement. When, however, we do fall under the Lord's judgement, he is disciplining us, to save us from being condemned with the rest of the world.

Therefore, my brothers, when you meet for a meal, wait for one another. If you are hungry, eat at home, so that in meeting together you may not fall under judgement. The other matters I will arrange when I come.

Spiritual gifts

12 About gifts of the Spirit, there are some things of which I do not wish you to remain ignorant.

You know how, in the days when you were still pagan, you were swept off to those dumb heathen gods, however you happened to be led.[a] For this reason I must impress upon you that no one who says 'A curse on Jesus!' can be speaking

[a] *Or* . . . pagan, you would be seized by some power which drove you to those dumb heathen gods.

King James Version

by the Spirit of God calleth Jesus accursed: and *that* no man can say that Jesus is the Lord, but by the Holy Ghost. 4 Now there are diversities of gifts, but the same Spirit. 5And there are differences of administrations, but the same Lord. 6And there are diversities of operations, but it is the same God which worketh all in all. 7 But the manifestation of the Spirit is given to every man to profit withal. 8 For to one is given by the Spirit the word of wisdom; to another the word of knowledge by the same Spirit; 9 To another faith by the same Spirit; to another the gifts of healing by the same Spirit; 10 To another the working of miracles; to another prophecy; to another discerning of spirits; to another *divers* kinds of tongues; to another the interpretation of tongues: 11 But all these worketh that one and the selfsame Spirit, dividing to every man severally as he will. 12 For as the body is one, and hath many members, and all the members of that one body, being many, are one body:

Living Bible

are really inspired by God or whether they are fakes? Here is the test: no one speaking by the power of the Spirit of God can curse Jesus, and no one can say, "Jesus is Lord," and really mean it, unless the Holy Spirit is helping him.

4 Now God gives us many kinds of special abilities, but it is the same Holy Spirit who is the source of them all. 5 There are different kinds of service to God, but it is the same Lord we are serving. 6 There are many ways in which God works in our lives, but it is the same God who does the work in and through all of us who are his. 7 The Holy Spirit displays God's power through each of us as a means of helping the entire church.

8 To one person the Spirit gives the ability to give wise advice; someone else may be especially good at studying and teaching, and this is his gift from the same Spirit. 9 He gives special faith to another, and to someone else the power to heal the sick. 10 He gives power for doing miracles to some, and to others power to prophesy and preach. He gives someone else the power to know whether evil spirits are speaking through those who claim to be giving God's messages—or whether it is really the Spirit of God who is speaking. Still another person is able to speak in languages he never learned; and others, who do not know the language either, are given power to understand what he is saying. 11 It is the same and only Holy Spirit who gives all these gifts and powers, deciding which each one of us should have.

12 Our bodies have many parts, but the many parts make up only one body when they are all put together. So it is with the "body" of Christ.

Today's English Version

say, "A curse on Jesus!", and no one can confess "Jesus is Lord," unless he is guided by the Holy Spirit.

4 There are different kinds of spiritual gifts, but the same Spirit gives them. 5 There are different ways of serving, but the same Lord is served. 6 There are different abilities to perform service, but the same God gives ability to everyone for their service. 7 The Spirit's presence is shown in some way in each one, for the good of all. 8 The Spirit gives one man a message of wisdom, while to another man the same Spirit gives a message of knowledge. 9 One and the same Spirit gives faith to one man, while to another man he gives the power to heal. 10 The Spirit gives one man the power to work miracles; to another, the gift of speaking God's message; and to yet another, the ability to tell the difference between gifts that come from the Spirit and those that do not. To one man he gives the ability to speak in strange tongues, and to another he gives the ability to explain what is said. 11 But it is one and the same Spirit who does all this; he gives a different gift to each man, as he wishes.

One body with many parts

12 Christ is like a single body, which has many parts; it is still one body, even though it

New International Version

cursed," and no one can say, "Jesus is Lord," except by the Holy Spirit.

4 There are different kinds of spiritual gifts, but the same Spirit. 5 There are different kinds of service, but the same Lord. 6 There are different kinds of working, but the same God works all of them in all men.

7 Now to each man the manifestation of the Spirit is given for the common good. 8 To one there is given through the Spirit the ability to speak with wisdom, to another the ability to speak with knowledge by means of the same Spirit, 9 to another faith by the same Spirit, to another gifts of healing by that one Spirit, 10 to another miraculous powers, to another prophecy, to another the ability to distinguish between spirits, to another the ability to speak in different kinds of tongues,[z] and to still another the interpretation of tongues.[z] 11All these are the work of one and the same Spirit, and he gives them to each man, just as he determines.

One body, many parts

12 The body is a unit, though it is made up of many parts; and though all its parts are many,

[z] Or *languages*.

Phillips Modern English

say, "a curse on Jesus", and no one could say, "Jesus is Lord", except by the Holy Spirit.

Men have different gifts, but it is the same Spirit who gives them. There are different ways of serving God, but it is the same Lord who is served. God works through different men in different ways, but it is the same God who achieves his purposes through them all. The Spirit openly makes his gift to each man, so that he may use it for the common good.

One man's gift by the Spirit is to speak with wisdom, another's to speak with knowledge. The same Spirit gives to another man faith, to another the ability to heal, to another the use of spiritual powers. The same Spirit gives to another man the gift of preaching the word of God, to another the ability to discriminate in spiritual matters, to another speech in different tongues and to yet another the power to interpret the tongues. Behind all these gifts is the operation of the same Spirit, who distributes to each individual man, as he wills.

12.12 The human body is an example of organic unity

As the human body, which has many parts, is a unity, and those parts, despite their multiplicity, constitute one single body, so it is with Christ.

Revised Standard Version

ever says "Jesus be cursed!" and no one can say "Jesus is Lord" except by the Holy Spirit.

4 Now there are varieties of gifts, but the same Spirit; 5 and there are varieties of service, but the same Lord; 6 and there are varieties of working, but it is the same God who inspires them all in every one. 7 To each is given the manifestation of the Spirit for the common good. 8 To one is given through the Spirit the utterance of wisdom, and to another the utterance of knowledge according to the same Spirit, 9 to another faith by the same Spirit, to another gifts of healing by the one Spirit, 10 to another the working of miracles, to another prophecy, to another the ability to distinguish between spirits, to another various kinds of tongues, to another the interpretation of tongues. 11 All these are inspired by one and the same Spirit, who apportions to each one individually as he wills.

12 For just as the body is one and has many members, and all the members of the body, though many, are one body, so it is with Christ.

Jerusalem Bible

the Holy Spirit and say, "Curse Jesus," and on the other hand, no one can say, "Jesus is Lord," unless he is under the influence of the Holy Spirit.

The variety and the unity of gifts

4 There is a variety of gifts but always the same Spirit; 5 there are all sorts of service to be done, but always to the same Lord; 6 working in all sorts of different ways in different people, it is the same God who is working in all of them. 7 The particular way in which the Spirit is given to each person is for a good purpose. 8 One may have the gift of preaching with wisdom given him by the Spirit; another may have the gift of preaching instruction given him by the same Spirit; 9 and another the gift of faith given by the same Spirit; another again the gift of healing, through this one Spirit; 10 one, the power of miracles; another, prophecy; another the gift of recognizing spirits; another the gift of tongues and another the ability to interpret them. 11 All these are the work of one and the same Spirit, who distributes different gifts to different people just as he chooses.

The analogy of the body

12 Just as a human body, though it is made up of many parts, is a single unit because all these parts, though many, make one body, so it

New English Bible

under the influence of the Spirit of God. And no one can say 'Jesus is Lord!' except under the influence of the Holy Spirit.

There are varieties of gifts, but the same Spirit. There are varieties of service, but the same Lord. There are many forms of work, but all of them, in all men, are the work of the same God. In each of us the Spirit is manifested in one particular way, for some useful purpose. One man, through the Spirit, has the gift of wise speech, while another, by the power of the same Spirit, can put the deepest knowledge into words. Another, by the same Spirit, is granted faith; another, by the one Spirit, gifts of healing, and another miraculous powers; another has the gift of prophecy, and another ability to distinguish true spirits from false; yet another has the gift of ecstatic utterance of different kinds, and another the ability to interpret it. But all these gifts are the work of one and the same Spirit, distributing them separately to each individual at will.

For Christ is like a single body with its many limbs and organs, which, many as they are, to-

King James Version

so also *is* Christ. 13 For by one Spirit are we
all baptized into one body, whether *we be* Jews
or Gentiles, whether *we be* bond or free; and
have been all made to drink into one Spirit.
14 For the body is not one member, but many.
15 If the foot shall say, Because I am not the
hand, I am not of the body; is it therefore not
of the body? 16And if the ear shall say, Because I am not the eye, I am not of the body;
is it therefore not of the body? 17 If the whole
body *were* an eye, where *were* the hearing? If
the whole *were* hearing, where *were* the smelling?
18 But now hath God set the members every
one of them in the body, as it hath pleased him.
19And if they were all one member, where *were*
the body? 20 But now *are they* many members,
yet but one body. 21And the eye cannot say unto
the hand, I have no need of thee: nor again
the head to the feet, I have no need of you.
22 Nay, much more those members of the body,
which seem to be more feeble, are necessary:
23And those *members* of the body, which we
think to be less honourable, upon these we bestow more abundant honour; and our uncomely
parts have more abundant comeliness. 24 For
our comely *parts* have no need: but God hath
tempered the body together, having given more

Living Bible

13 Each of us is a part of the one body of Christ.
Some of us are Jews, some are Gentiles, some
are slaves and some are free. But the Holy
Spirit has fitted us all together into one body.
We have been baptized into Christ's body by
the one Spirit, and have all been given that same
Holy Spirit.
14 Yes, the body has many parts, not just
one part. 15 If the foot says, "I am not a part
of the body because I am not a hand," that does
not make it any less a part of the body. 16And
what would you think if you heard an ear say,
"I am not part of the body because I am only
an ear, and not an eye"? Would that make it
any less a part of the body? 17 Suppose the
whole body were an eye—then how would you
hear? Or if your whole body were just one big
ear, how could you smell anything?
18 But that isn't the way God has made us.
He has made many parts for our bodies and
has put each part just where he wants it. 19 What
a strange thing a body would be if it had only
one part! 20 So he has made many parts, but
still there is only one body.
21 The eye can never say to the hand, "I
don't need you." The head can't say to the
feet, "I don't need you."
22 And some of the parts that seem weakest
and least important are really the most necessary. 23 Yes, we are especially glad to have
some parts that seem rather odd! And we carefully protect from the eyes of others those parts
that should not be seen, 24 while of course the
parts that may be seen do not require this special care. So God has put the body together in
such a way that extra honor and care are given

Today's English Version

is made up of different parts. 13 In the same
way, all of us, Jews and Gentiles, slaves and
free men, have been baptized into the one body
by the same Spirit, and we have all been given
the one Spirit to drink.
14 For the body itself is not made up of
only one part, but of many parts. 15 If the foot
were to say, "Because I am not a hand, I don't
belong to the body," that would not make it
stop being a part of the body. 16And if the ear
were to say, "Because I am not an eye, I don't
belong to the body," that would not make it
stop being a part of the body. 17 If the whole
body were just an eye, how could it hear? And
if it were only an ear, how could it smell? 18As
it is, however, God put every different part in
the body just as he wished. 19 There would not
be a body if it were all only one part! 20As it
is, there are many parts, and one body.
21 So then, the eye cannot say to the hand,
"I don't need you!" Nor can the head say to the
feet, "Well, I don't need you!" 22 On the contrary, we cannot do without the parts of the
body that seem to be weaker; 23 and those parts
that we think aren't worth very much are the
ones which we treat with greater care; while the
parts of the body which don't look very nice
receive special attention, 24 which the more
beautiful parts of our body do not need. God
himself has put the body together in such a way

New International Version

they form one body. So it is with Christ. 13 For
we were all baptized by one Spirit into one
body—whether Jews or Greeks, slave or free—
and we were all given the one Spirit to drink.
14 Now the body is not made up of one part
but of many. 15 If the foot should say, "Because
I am not a hand, I do not belong to the body,"
it would not for that reason cease to be part of
the body. 16And if the ear should say, "Because
I am not an eye, I do not belong to the body,"
it would not for that reason cease to be part of
the body. 17 If the whole body were an eye,
where would the sense of hearing be? If the
whole body were an ear, where would the sense
of smell be? 18 But in fact God has arranged the
parts in the body, every one of them, just as he
wanted them to be. 19 If they were all one part,
where would the body be? 20As it is, there are
many parts, but one body.
21 The eye cannot say to the hand, "I don't
need you!" And the head cannot say to the feet,
"I don't need you!" 22 On the contrary, those
parts of the body that seem to be weaker are indispensable, 23 and the parts that we think are
less honorable we treat with special honor. And
the parts that are unpresentable are treated with
special modesty, 24 while our presentable parts
need no special treatment. But God has com-

Phillips Modern English

For we were all baptised by the one Spirit into one body, whether we were Jews, Greeks, slaves or free men, and we have all had experience of the same Spirit.

Now the body is not one part but many. If the foot should say, "Because I am not a hand I don't belong to the body," does that alter the fact that the foot *is* a part of the body? Or if the ear should say, "Because I am not an eye I don't belong to the body," does that mean that the ear really is no part of the body? After all, if the body were all one eye, for example, where would be the sense of hearing? Or if it were all one ear, where would be the sense of smell? But God has arranged all the parts in the one body according to his design. For if everything were concentrated in one part, how could there be a body at all? The fact is there are many parts, but only one body. So that the eye cannot say to the hand, "I don't need you!" nor, again, can the head say to the feet, "I don't need you!" On the contrary, those parts of the body which seem to have less strength are more essential to health: and to those parts of the body which seem to us to be less admirable we have to allow the highest honour of function. The parts which do not look beautiful have a deeper beauty in the work they do, while the parts which look beautiful may not be at all essential to life! But God has harmonised the whole body by giving importance of

Revised Standard Version

13 For by one Spirit we were all baptized into
one body—Jews or Greeks, slaves or free—and
all were made to drink of one Spirit.
14 For the body does not consist of one member but of many. 15 If the foot should say, "Because I am not a hand, I do not belong to the
body," that would not make it any less a part
of the body. 16 And if the ear should say, "Because I am not an eye, I do not belong to the
body," that would not make it any less a part
of the body. 17 If the whole body were an eye,
where would be the hearing? If the whole body
were an ear, where would be the sense of smell?
18 But as it is, God arranged the organs in the
body, each one of them, as he chose. 19 If all
were a single organ, where would the body be?
20 As it is, there are many parts, yet one body.
21 The eye cannot say to the hand, "I have no
need of you," nor again the head to the feet,
"I have no need of you." 22 On the contrary,
the parts of the body which seem to be weaker
are indispensable, 23 and those parts of the body
which we think less honorable we invest with the
greater honor, and our unpresentable parts are
treated with greater modesty, 24 which our more
presentable parts do not require. But God has so

Jerusalem Bible

is with Christ. 13 In the one Spirit we were all
baptized, Jews as well as Greeks, slaves as well
as citizens, and one Spirit was given to us all to
drink.
14 Nor is the body to be identified with any
one of its many parts. 15 If the foot were to say,
"I am not a hand and so I do not belong to the
body," would that mean that it stopped being
part of the body? 16 If the ear were to say, "I am
not an eye, and so I do not belong to the body,"
would that mean that it was not a part of the
body? 17 If your whole body was just one eye,
how would you hear anything? If it was just one
ear, how would you smell anything?
18 Instead of that, God put all the separate
parts into the body on purpose. 19 If all the parts
were the same, how could it be a body? 20 As it
is, the parts are many but the body is one. 21 The
eye cannot say to the hand, "I do not need you,"
nor can the head say to the feet, "I do not need
you."
22 What is more, it is precisely the parts of
the body that seem to be the weakest which are
the indispensable ones; 23 and it is the least
honorable parts of the body that we clothe with
the greatest care. So our more improper parts
get decorated 24 in a way that our more proper
parts do not need. God has arranged the body

New English Bible

gether make up one body. For indeed we were all brought into one body by baptism, in the one Spirit, whether we are Jews or Greeks, whether slaves or free men, and that one Holy Spirit was poured out for all of us to drink.

A body is not one single organ, but many. Suppose the foot should say, 'Because I am not a hand, I do not belong to the body', it does belong to the body none the less. Suppose the ear were to say, 'Because I am not an eye, I do not belong to the body', it does still belong to the body. If the body were all eye, how could it hear? If the body were all ear, how could it smell? But, in fact, God appointed each limb and organ to its own place in the body, as he chose. If the whole were one single organ, there would not be a body at all; in fact, however, there are many different organs, but one body. The eye cannot say to the hand, 'I do not need you'; nor the head to the feet, 'I do not need you.' Quite the contrary: those organs of the body which seem to be more frail than others are indispensable, and those parts of the body which we regard as less honourable are treated with special honour. To our unseemly parts is given a more than ordinary seemliness, whereas our seemly parts need no adorning. But God has

King James Version

abundant honour to that *part* which lacked: 25 That there should be no schism in the body; but *that* the members should have the same care one for another. 26And whether one member suffer, all the members suffer with it; or one member be honoured, all the members rejoice with it. 27 Now ye are the body of Christ, and members in particular. 28And God hath set some in the church, first apostles, secondarily prophets, thirdly teachers, after that miracles, then gifts of healings, helps, governments, diversities of tongues. 29*Are* all apostles? *are* all prophets? *are* all teachers? *are* all workers of miracles? 30 Have all the gifts of healing? do all speak with tongues? do all interpret? 31 But covet earnestly the best gifts: and yet shew I unto you a more excellent way.

Living Bible

to those parts that might otherwise seem less important. 25 This makes for happiness among the parts, so that the parts have the same care for each other that they do for themselves. 26 If one part suffers, all parts suffer with it, and if one part is honored, all the parts are glad.

27 Now here is what I am trying to say: All of you together are the one body of Christ and each one of you is a separate and necessary part of it. 28 Here is a list of some of the parts he has placed in his church, which is his body:

Apostles,
Prophets—those who preach God's Word,
Teachers,
Those who do miracles,
Those who have the gift of healing;
Those who can help others,
Those who can get others to work together,
Those who speak in languages they have never learned.

29 Is everyone an apostle? Of course not. Is everyone a preacher? No. Are all teachers? Does everyone have the power to do miracles? 30 Can everyone heal the sick? Of course not. Does God give all of us the ability to speak in languages we've never learned? Can just anyone understand and translate what those are saying who have that gift of foreign speech? 31 No, but try your best to have the more important of these gifts.

First, however, let me tell you about something else that is better than any of them!

Today's English Version

as to give greater honor to those parts that lack it. 25And so there is no division in the body, but all its different parts have the same concern for one another. 26 If one part of the body suffers, all the other parts suffer with it; if one part is praised, all the other parts share its happiness.

27 All of you, then, are Christ's body, and each one is a part of it. 28 In the church, then, God has put all in place: in the first place, apostles, in the second place, prophets, and in the third place, teachers; then those who perform miracles, followed by those who are given the power to heal, or to help others, or to direct them, or to speak in strange tongues. 29 They are not all apostles, or prophets, or teachers. Not all have the power to work miracles, 30 or to heal diseases, or to speak in strange tongues, or to explain what is said. 31 Set your hearts, then, on the more important gifts.

Best of all, however, is the following way.

New International Version

bined the members of the body and has given greater honor to the parts that lacked it, 25 so that there should be no division in the body, but that its parts should have equal concern for each other. 26 If one part suffers, every part suffers with it; if one part is honored, every part rejoices with it.

27 Now you are the body of Christ, and each one of you is a part of it. 28And in the church God has appointed first of all apostles, second prophets, third teachers, then workers of miracles, also those having gifts of healing, those able to help others, those with gifts of administration, and finally those speaking in different kinds of tongues.[a] 29Are all apostles? Are all prophets? Are all teachers? Do all work miracles? 30 Do all have gifts of healing? Do all speak in tongues?[b] Do all interpret? 31 But eagerly desire the greater gifts.

Love

And now I will show you the most excellent way.

[*a*] Or *languages*. [*b*] Or *other languages*.

Phillips Modern English

function to the parts which lack apparent importance, that the body should work together as a whole with all the members in sympathetic relationship with one another. So it happens that if one member suffers all the other members suffer with it, and if one member is honoured all the members share a common joy.

Now you are together the body of Christ, and each of you is a part of it. And in the Church God has appointed first some to be his messengers, secondly, some to be preachers of power, thirdly teachers. After them he has appointed workers of spiritual power, men with the gift of healing, helpers, counsellors and those with the gift of speaking various "tongues".

As we look at the body of Christ do we find all are his messengers, all are preachers, or all teachers? Do we find all wielders of spiritual power, all able to heal, all able to speak with tongues, or all able to interpret the tongues?

You should set your hearts on the best spiritual gifts, but I will show you a way which surpasses them all.

Revised Standard Version

composed the body, giving the greater honor to the inferior part, 25 that there may be no discord in the body, but that the members may have the same care for one another. 26 If one member suffers, all suffer together; if one member is honored, all rejoice together.

27 Now you are the body of Christ and individually members of it. 28 And God has appointed in the church first apostles, second prophets, third teachers, then workers of miracles, then healers, helpers, administrators, speakers in various kinds of tongues. 29 Are all apostles? Are all prophets? Are all teachers? Do all work miracles? 30 Do all possess gifts of healing? Do all speak with tongues? Do all interpret? 31 But earnestly desire the higher gifts.

And I will show you a still more excellent way.

Jerusalem Bible

so that more dignity is given to the parts which are without it, 25 and so that there may not be disagreements inside the body, but that each part may be equally concerned for all the others. 26 If one part is hurt, all parts are hurt with it. If one part is given special honor, all parts enjoy it.

27 Now you together are Christ's body; but each of you is a different part of it. 28 In the Church, God has given the first place to apostles, the second to prophets, the third to teachers; after them, miracles, and after them the gift of healing; helpers, good leaders, those with many languages. 29 Are all of them apostles, or all of them prophets, or all of them teachers? Do they all have the gift of miracles, 30 or all have the gift of healing? Do all speak strange languages, and all interpret them?

The order of importance in spiritual gifts. Love

31 Be ambitious for the higher gifts. And I am going to show you a way that is better than any of them.

New English Bible

combined the various parts of the body, giving special honour to the humbler parts, so that there might be no sense of division in the body, but that all its organs might feel the same concern for one another. If one organ suffers, they all suffer together. If one flourishes, they all rejoice together.

Now you are Christ's body, and each of you a limb or organ of it. Within our community God has appointed, in the first place apostles, in the second place prophets, thirdly teachers; then miracle-workers, then those who have gifts of healing, or ability to help others or power to guide them, or the gift of ecstatic utterance of various kinds. Are all apostles? all prophets? all teachers? Do all work miracles? Have all gifts of healing? Do all speak in tongues of ecstasy? Can all interpret them? The higher gifts are those you should aim at.

And now I will show you the best way of all.

King James Version

13 Though I speak with the tongues of men and of angels, and have not charity, I am become *as* sounding brass, or a tinkling cymbal. 2 And though I have *the gift of* prophecy, and understand all mysteries, and all knowledge; and though I have all faith, so that I could remove mountains, and have not charity, I am nothing. 3 And though I bestow all my goods to feed *the poor,* and though I give my body to be burned, and have not charity, it profiteth me nothing. 4 Charity suffereth long, *and* is kind; charity envieth not; charity vaunteth not itself, is not puffed up, 5 Doth not behave itself unseemly, seeketh not her own, is not easily provoked, thinketh no evil; 6 Rejoiceth not in iniquity, but rejoiceth in the truth; 7 Beareth all things, believeth all things, hopeth all things, endureth all things. 8 Charity never faileth: but whether *there be* prophecies, they shall fail; whether *there*

Living Bible

13 If I had the gift of being able to speak in other languages without learning them, and could speak in every language there is in all of heaven and earth, but didn't love others, I would only be making noise. 2 If I had the gift of prophecy and knew all about what is going to happen in the future, knew everything about *everything,* but didn't love others, what good would it do? Even if I had the gift of faith so that I could speak to a mountain and make it move, I would still be worth nothing at all without love. 3 If I gave everything I have to poor people, and if I were burned alive for preaching the Gospel but didn't love others, it would be of no value whatever.

4 Love is very patient and kind, never jealous or envious, never boastful or proud, 5 never haughty or selfish or rude. Love does not demand its own way. It is not irritable or touchy. It does not hold grudges and will hardly even notice when others do it wrong. 6 It is never glad about injustice, but rejoices whenever truth wins out. 7 If you love someone you will be loyal to him no matter what the cost. You will always believe in him, always expect the best of him, and always stand your ground in defending him.

8 All the special gifts and powers from God will someday come to an end, but love goes on forever. Someday prophecy, and speaking in

Today's English Version

Love

13 I may be able to speak the languages of men and even of angels, but if I have not love, my speech is no more than a noisy gong or a clanging bell. 2 I may have the gift of inspired preaching; I may have all knowledge and understand all secrets; I may have all the faith needed to move mountains—but if I have not love, I am nothing. 3 I may give away everything I have, and even give up my body to be burned—but if I have not love, it does me no good.

4 Love is patient and kind; love is not jealous, or conceited, or proud; 5 love is not ill-mannered, or selfish, or irritable; love does not keep a record of wrongs; 6 love is not happy with evil, but is happy with the truth. 7 Love never gives up: its faith, hope, and patience never fail.

8 Love is eternal. There are inspired messages, but they are temporary; there are gifts of speak-

New International Version

13 If I speak in the tongues[c] of men and of angels, but have not love, I am only a resounding gong or a clanging cymbal. 2 If I have the gift of prophecy, and can fathom all mysteries and all knowledge, and if I have a faith that can move mountains, but have not love, I am nothing. 3 If I give all I possess to the poor and surrender my body to the flames,[d] but have not love, I gain nothing.

4 Love is patient, love is kind. It does not envy, it does not boast, it is not proud. 5 It is not rude, it is not self-seeking, it is not easily angered, it keeps no record of wrongs. 6 Love does not delight in evil but rejoices in the truth. 7 It always protects, always trusts, always hopes, always perseveres.

8 Love never fails. But where there are prophecies, they will cease; where there are

[c] Or *languages.* [d] Some early MSS read *body that I may boast.*

Phillips Modern English

13.1 Christian love—the highest and best gift

If I speak with the eloquence of men and of angels, but have no love, I become no more than blaring brass or crashing cymbal. If I have the gift of foretelling the future and hold in my mind not only all human knowledge but the very secrets of God, and if I also have that absolute faith which can move mountains, but have no love, I amount to nothing at all. If I dispose of all that I possess, yes, even if I give my own body to be burned, but have no love, I achieve precisely nothing.

This love of which I speak is slow to lose patience—it looks for a way of being constructive. It is not possessive: it is neither anxious to impress nor does it cherish inflated ideas of its own importance.

Love has good manners and does not pursue selfish advantage. It is not touchy. It does not keep account of evil or gloat over the wickedness of other people. On the contrary, it shares the joy of those who live by the truth.

Love knows no limit to its endurance, no end to its trust, no fading of its hope; it can outlast anything. Love never fails.

13.9 All gifts except love will be superseded one day

For if there are prophecies they will be fulfilled and done with, if there are "tongues" the

Revised Standard Version

13 If I speak in the tongues of men and of
angels, but have not love, I am a noisy
gong or a clanging cymbal. 2And if I have
prophetic powers, and understand all mysteries
and all knowledge, and if I have all faith, so as
to remove mountains, but have not love, I am
nothing. 3 If I give away all I have, and if I deliver my body to be burned,[v] but have not love,
I gain nothing.
4 Love is patient and kind; love is not jealous
or boastful; 5 it is not arrogant or rude. Love
does not insist on its own way; it is not irritable
or resentful; 6 it does not rejoice at wrong, but
rejoices in the right. 7 Love bears all things, believes all things, hopes all things, endures all
things.
8 Love never ends; as for prophecies, they will
pass away; as for tongues, they will cease; as for

[v] Other ancient authorities read *body that I may glory.*

Jerusalem Bible

13 If I have all the eloquence of men or of
angels, but speak without love, I am simply
a gong booming or a cymbal clashing. 2 If I
have the gift of prophecy, understanding all the
mysteries there are, and knowing everything, and
if I have faith in all its fullness, to move mountains, but without love, then I am nothing at all.
3 If I give away all that I possess, piece by piece,
and if I even let them take my body to burn it,
but am without love, it will do me no good whatever.
4 Love is always patient and kind; it is never
jealous; love is never boastful or conceited; 5 it
is never rude or selfish; it does not take offense,
and is not resentful. 6 Love takes no pleasure in
other people's sins but delights in the truth; 7 it
is always ready to excuse, to trust, to hope, and
to endure whatever comes.
8 Love does not come to an end. But if there
are gifts of prophecy, the time will come when
they must fail; or the gift of languages, it will

New English Bible

13 I may speak in tongues of men or of angels, but if I am without love, I am a sounding gong or a clanging cymbal. I may have the gift of prophecy, and know every hidden truth; I may have faith strong enough to move mountains; but if I have no love, I am nothing. I may dole out all I possess, or even give my body to be burnt,[a] but if I have no love, I am none the better.

Love is patient; love is kind and envies no one. Love is never boastful, nor conceited, nor rude; never selfish, not quick to take offence. Love keeps no score of wrongs; does not gloat over other men's sins, but delights in the truth. There is nothing love cannot face; there is no limit to its faith, its hope, and its endurance.

Love will never come to an end. Are there prophets? their work will be over. Are there

[a] *Some witnesses read* even seek glory by self-sacrifice.

King James Version

be tongues, they shall cease; whether *there be*
knowledge, it shall vanish away. 9 For we know
in part, and we prophesy in part. 10 But when
that which is perfect is come, then that which
is in part shall be done away. 11 When I was a
child, I spake as a child, I understood as a
child, I thought as a child: but when I became
a man, I put away childish things. 12 For now
we see through a glass, darkly; but then face to
face: now I know in part; but then shall I know
even as also I am known. 13 And now abideth
faith, hope, charity, these three; but the greatest of these *is* charity.

14 Follow after charity, and desire spiritual
gifts, but rather that ye may prophesy.
2 For he that speaketh in an *unknown* tongue
speaketh not unto men, but unto God: for no
man understandeth *him;* howbeit in the spirit
he speaketh mysteries. 3 But he that prophesieth

Living Bible

unknown languages, and special knowledge—
these gifts will disappear. 9 Now we know so
little, even with our special gifts, and the preaching of those most gifted is still so poor. 10 But
when we have been made perfect and complete,
then the need for these inadequate special gifts
will come to an end, and they will disappear.
11 It's like this: when I was a child I spoke
and thought and reasoned as a child does. But
when I became a man my thoughts grew far beyond those of my childhood, and now I have
put away the childish things. 12 In the same
way, we can see and understand only a little
about God now, as if we were peering at his
reflection in a poor mirror; but someday we are
going to see him in his completeness, face to
face. Now all that I know is hazy and blurred,
but then I will see everything clearly, just as
clearly as God sees into my heart right now.
13 There are three things that remain—faith,
hope, and love—and the greatest of these is love.

14 Let love be your greatest aim; nevertheless, ask also for the special abilities the
Holy Spirit gives, and especially the gift of
prophecy, being able to preach the messages of
God.
2 But if your gift is that of being able to
"speak in tongues," that is, to speak in languages
you haven't learned, you will be talking to God
but not to others, since they won't be able to
understand you. You will be speaking by the
power of the Spirit but it will all be a secret.
3 But one who prophesies, preaching the mes-

Today's English Version

ing in strange tongues, but they will cease; there
is knowledge, but it will pass. 9 For our gifts of
knowledge and of inspired messages are only
partial; 10 but when what is perfect comes, then
what is partial will disappear.
11 When I was a child, my speech, feelings,
and thinking were all those of a child; now that
I am a man, I have no more use for childish
ways. 12 What we see now is like the dim image
in a mirror; then we shall see face to face. What
I know now is only partial; then it will be complete, as complete as God's knowledge of me.
13 Meanwhile these three remain: faith, hope,
and love; and the greatest of these is love.

More about gifts from
the Spirit

14 It is love, then, that you should strive for.
Set your hearts on spiritual gifts, especially
the gift of speaking God's message. 2 The one
who speaks in strange tongues does not speak to
men but to God, because no one understands
him. He is speaking secret truths by the power of
the Spirit. 3 But the one who speaks God's mes-

New International Version

tongues, they will be stilled; where there is knowledge, it will pass away. 9 For we know in part
and we prophesy in part, 10 but when perfection
comes, the imperfect disappears. 11 When I was
a child, I talked like a child, I thought like a
child, I reasoned like a child. When I became a
man, I put childish ways behind me. 12 Now we
see but a poor reflection; then we shall see face
to face. Now I know in part; then I shall know
fully, even as I am fully known.
13 And now these three remain: faith, hope
and love. But the greatest of these is love.

Gifts of prophecy and tongues

14 Follow the way of love and eagerly desire
spiritual gifts, especially the gift of prophecy. 2 For anyone who speaks in a tongue[e] does
not speak to men but to God. Indeed, no one
understands him; he utters mysteries with his
spirit.[f] 3 But everyone who prophesies speaks to

[e] Or *another language.* Also in verses 4, 13, 14, 19, 26 and 27. [f] Or *by the Spirit.*

Phillips Modern English

need for them will disappear, if there is knowledge it will be swallowed up in truth. For our knowledge is always incomplete and our prophecy is always incomplete, and when the complete comes, that is the end of the incomplete.

When I was a little child I talked and felt and thought like a little child. Now that I am a man I have finished with childish things.

At present we are men looking at puzzling reflections in a mirror. The time will come when we shall see reality whole and face to face! At present all I know is a little fraction of the truth, but the time will come when I shall know it as fully as God has known me!

In this life we have three lasting qualities—faith, hope and love. But the greatest of them is love.

14.1 "Tongues" are not the greatest gift

Follow, then, the way of love, while you set your heart on the gifts of the Spirit. The highest gift you can wish for is to be able to speak the messages of God. The man who speaks in a "tongue" addresses not men (for no one understands a word he says) but God: and only in his spirit is he speaking spiritual secrets. But he who preaches the word of God is using his

Revised Standard Version

knowledge, it will pass away. 9 For our knowledge is imperfect and our prophecy is imperfect;
10 but when the perfect comes, the imperfect will
pass away. 11 When I was a child, I spoke like a
child, I thought like a child, I reasoned like a
child; when I became a man, I gave up childish
ways. 12 For now we see in a mirror dimly, but
then face to face. Now I know in part; then I
shall understand fully, even as I have been fully
understood. 13 So faith, hope, love abide, these
three; but the greatest of these is love.

14 Make love your aim, and earnestly desire
the spiritual gifts, especially that you may
prophesy. 2 For one who speaks in a tongue
speaks not to men but to God; for no one understands him, but he utters mysteries in the Spirit.
3 On the other hand, he who prophesies speaks

Jerusalem Bible

not continue for ever; and knowledge—for this,
too, the time will come when it must fail. 9 For
our knowledge is imperfect and our prophesying
is imperfect; 10 but once perfection comes, all
imperfect things will disappear. 11 When I was
a child, I used to talk like a child, and think
like a child, and argue like a child, but now I
am a man, all childish ways are put behind me.
12 Now we are seeing a dim reflection in a
mirror; but then we shall be seeing face to face.
The knowledge that I have now is imperfect;
but then I shall know as fully as I am known.
13 In short, there are three things that last:
faith, hope and love; and the greatest of these
is love.

Spiritual gifts: their respective importance in the community

14 You must want love more than anything
else; but still hope for the spiritual gifts as
well, especially prophecy. 2 Anybody with the
gift of tongues speaks to God, but not to other
people; because nobody understands him when
he talks in the spirit about mysterious things.
3 On the other hand, the man who prophesies

New English Bible

tongues of ecstasy? they will cease. Is there knowledge? it will vanish away; for our knowledge and our prophecy alike are partial, and the partial vanishes when wholeness comes. When I was a child, my speech, my outlook, and my thoughts were all childish. When I grew up, I had finished with childish things. Now we see only puzzling reflections in a mirror, but then we shall see face to face. My knowledge now is partial; then it will be whole, like God's knowledge of me. In a word, there are three things that last for ever: faith, hope, and love; but the greatest of them all is love.

14 Put love first; but there are other gifts of the Spirit at which you should aim also, and above all prophecy. When a man is using the language of ecstasy he is talking with God, not with men, for no man understands him; he is no doubt inspired, but he speaks mysteries. On the other hand, when a man prophesies, he

King James Version

speaketh unto men *to* edification, and exhortation, and comfort. 4 He that speaketh in an *unknown* tongue edifieth himself; but he that
prophesieth edifieth the church. 5 I would that
ye all spake with tongues, but rather that ye
prophesied: for greater *is* he that prophesieth
than he that speaketh with tongues, except he
interpret, that the church may receive edifying.
6 Now, brethren, if I come unto you speaking
with tongues, what shall I profit you, except I
shall speak to you either by revelation, or by
knowledge, or by prophesying, or by doctrine?
7 And even things without life giving sound,
whether pipe or harp, except they give a distinction in the sounds, how shall it be known
what is piped or harped? 8 For if the trumpet
give an uncertain sound, who shall prepare himself to the battle? 9 So likewise ye, except ye
utter by the tongue words easy to be understood,
how shall it be known what is spoken? for ye
shall speak into the air. 10 There are, it may be,
so many kinds of voices in the world, and none

Living Bible

sages of God, is helping others grow in the Lord,
encouraging and comforting them. 4 So a person
"speaking in tongues" helps himself grow spiritually, but one who prophesies, preaching messages from God, helps the entire church grow
in holiness and happiness.

5 I wish you all had the gift of "speaking in
tongues" but, even more, I wish you were all
able to prophesy, preaching God's messages, for
that is a greater and more useful power than to
speak in unknown languages—unless, of course,
you can tell everyone afterwards what you were
saying, so that they can get some good out of it
too.

6 Dear friends, even if I myself should come
to you talking in some language you don't understand, how would that help you? But if I
speak plainly what God has revealed to me, and
tell you the things I know, and what is going
to happen, and the great truths of God's Word
—that is what you need; that is what will help
you. 7 Even musical instruments—the flute, for
instance, or the harp—are examples of the need
for speaking in plain, simple English[a] rather
than in unknown languages. For no one will
recognize the tune the flute is playing unless
each note is sounded clearly. 8 And if the army
bugler doesn't play the right notes, how will
the soldiers know that they are being called to
battle? 9 In the same way, if you talk to a person in some language he doesn't understand,
how will he know what you mean? You might
as well be talking to an empty room.

10 I suppose that there are hundreds of different languages in the world, and all are ex-

[*a*] The local language, whatever it is.

Today's English Version

sage speaks to men, and gives them help, encouragement, and comfort. 4 The man who speaks in
strange tongues helps only himself, but the one
who speaks God's message helps the whole
church.

5 I would like for all of you to speak in
strange tongues; but I would rather that all of
you had the gift of speaking God's message. For
the man who speaks God's message is of greater
value than the one who speaks in strange tongues
—unless there is someone present who can explain what he says, so that the whole church may
be helped. 6 So when I come to you, brothers,
what use will I be to you if I speak in strange
tongues? Not a bit, unless I bring you some
revelation from God, or some knowledge, or
some inspired message, or some teaching.

7 Even such lifeless musical instruments as the
flute and the harp—how will anyone know the
tune that is being played unless the notes are
sounded distinctly? 8 And if the man who plays
the bugle does not sound a clear call, who will
prepare for battle? 9 In the same way, how will
anyone understand what you are talking about if
your message by means of strange tongues is not
clear? Your words will vanish in the air! 10 There
are many different languages in the world, yet

New International Version

men for their strengthening, encouragement and
comfort. 4 He who speaks in a tongue edifies himself, but he who prophesies edifies the church.
5 I would like every one of you to speak in
tongues,[g] but I would rather have you prophesy.
He who prophesies is greater than one who
speaks in tongues,[g] unless he interprets, so that
the church may be edified.

6 Now, brothers, if I come to you and speak
in tongues, what good will I be to you, unless I
bring you some revelation or knowledge or
prophecy or teaching? 7 Even in the case of lifeless things that make sounds, such as the flute or
harp, how will anyone know what tune is being
played unless there is a distinction in the notes?
8 Again, if the trumpet does not sound a clear call,
who will get ready for battle? 9 So it is with you.
Unless you speak intelligible words with your
tongue, how will anyone know what you are saying? You will just be speaking into the air. 10 Undoubtedly there are all sorts of languages in the

[*g*] Or *other languages.* Also in verses 6, 18, 22, 23
and 39.

Phillips Modern English

speech for the building up of the faith of one man, the encouragement of another or the consolation of another. The speaker in a "tongue" builds up his own soul, but the preacher builds up the Church.

I should indeed like you all to speak with "tongues", but I would much rather that you all preached the word of God. For the preacher of the word does a greater work than the speaker with "tongues", unless of course the latter interprets his words for the benefit of the Church.

14.6 Unless "tongues" are interpreted do they help the Church?

For suppose I came to you, my brothers, speaking with "tongues", what good could I do you unless I could give you some revelation of truth, some knowledge in spiritual things, some message from God, or some teaching about the Christian life?

Even in the case of inanimate objects which are capable of making sound, such as a flute or harp, unless their notes have the proper intervals, who can tell what tune is being played on them? Unless the bugle-notes are clear who will be called to arms? So, in your case, unless you make intelligible sounds with your "tongue" how can anyone know what you are talking about? You might just as well be addressing an empty room!

There may be in the world a great variety of

Revised Standard Version

to men for their upbuilding and encouragement
and consolation. 4 He who speaks in a tongue
edifies himself, but he who prophesies edifies the
church. 5 Now I want you all to speak in
tongues, but even more to prophesy. He who
prophesies is greater than he who speaks in
tongues, unless some one interprets, so that the
church may be edified.
6 Now, brethren, if I come to you speaking
in tongues, how shall I benefit you unless I bring
you some revelation or knowledge or prophecy
or teaching? 7 If even lifeless instruments, such
as the flute or the harp, do not give distinct
notes, how will any one know what is played?
8 And if the bugle gives an indistinct sound, who
will get ready for battle? 9 So with yourselves;
if you in a tongue utter speech that is not intelligible, how will any one know what is said?
For you will be speaking into the air. 10 There
are doubtless many different languages in the

Jerusalem Bible

does talk to other people, to their improvement,
their encouragement and their consolation. 4 The
one with the gift of tongues talks for his own
benefit, but the man who prophesies does so for
the benefit of the community. 5 While I should
like you all to have the gift of tongues, I would
much rather you could prophesy, since the man
who prophesies is of greater importance than
the man with the gift of tongues, unless of course
the latter offers an interpretation so that the
church may get some benefit.
6 Now suppose, my dear brothers, I am someone with the gift of tongues, and I come to
visit you, what use shall I be if all my talking
reveals nothing new, tells you nothing, and
neither inspires you nor instructs you? 7 Think
of a musical instrument, a flute or a harp: if one
note on it cannot be distinguished from another,
how can you tell what tune is being played?
8 Or if no one can be sure which call the trumpet has sounded, who will be ready for the attack? 9 It is the same with you: if your tongue
does not produce intelligible speech, how can
anyone know what you are saying? You will be
talking to the air. 10 There are any number of
different languages in the world, and not one of

New English Bible

is talking to men, and his words have power to build; they stimulate and they encourage. The language of ecstasy is good for the speaker himself, but it is prophecy that builds up a Christian community. I should be pleased for you all to use the tongues of ecstasy, but better pleased for you to prophesy. The prophet is worth more than the man of ecstatic speech—unless indeed he can explain its meaning, and so help to build up the community. Suppose, my friends, that when I come to you I use ecstatic language: what good shall I do you, unless what I say contains something by way of revelation, or enlightenment, or prophecy, or instruction?

Even with inanimate things that produce sounds—a flute, say, or a lyre—unless their notes mark definite intervals, how can you tell what tune is being played? Or again, if the trumpet-call is not clear, who will prepare for battle? In the same way if your ecstatic utterance yields no precise meaning, how can anyone tell what you are saying? You will be talking into the air. How many different kinds of sound there are, or may be, in the world! Nothing is alto-

King James Version

of them *is* without signification. 11 Therefore if I know not the meaning of the voice, I shall be unto him that speaketh a barbarian, and he that speaketh *shall be* a barbarian unto me. 12 Even so ye, forasmuch as ye are zealous of spiritual *gifts,* seek that ye may excel to the edifying of the church. 13 Wherefore let him that speaketh in an *unknown* tongue pray that he may interpret. 14 For if I pray in an *unknown* tongue, my spirit prayeth, but my understanding is unfruitful. 15 What is it then? I will pray with the spirit, and I will pray with the understanding also: I will sing with the spirit, and I will sing with the understanding also. 16 Else, when thou shalt bless with the spirit, how shall he that occupieth the room of the unlearned say Amen at thy giving of thanks, seeing he understandeth not what thou sayest? 17 For thou verily givest thanks well, but the other is not edified. 18 I thank my God, I speak with tongues more than ye all: 19 Yet in the church I had rather speak five words with my understanding, that *by my voice* I might teach others also, than ten thousand words in an *unknown* tongue. 20 Brethren, be not children in understanding: howbeit in

Living Bible

cellent for those who understand them, 11 but to me they mean nothing. A person talking to me in one of these languages will be a stranger to me and I will be a stranger to him. 12 Since you are so anxious to have special gifts from the Holy Spirit, ask him for the very best, for those that will be of real help to the whole church.

13 If someone is given the gift of speaking in unknown tongues, he should pray also for the gift of knowing what he has said, so that he can tell people afterwards, plainly. 14 For if I pray in a language I don't understand, my spirit is praying but I don't know what I am saying. 15 Well, then, what shall I do? I will do both. I will pray in unknown tongues and also in ordinary language that everyone understands. I will sing in unknown tongues and also in ordinary language, so that I can understand the praise I am giving; 16 for if you praise and thank God with the spirit alone, speaking in another language, how can those who don't understand you be praising God along with you? How can they join you in giving thanks when they don't know what you are saying? 17 You will be giving thanks very nicely, no doubt, but the other people present won't be helped.

18 I thank God that I "speak in tongues" privately[b] more than any of the rest of you. 19 But in public worship I would much rather speak five words that people can understand and be helped by, than ten thousand words while "speaking in tongues" in an unknown language.

20 Dear brothers, don't be childish in your understanding of these things. Be innocent babies when it comes to planning evil, but be men

[*b*] Implied. See verses 19 and 28.

Today's English Version

none of them is without meaning. 11 But if I do not know the language being spoken, the man who uses it will be a foreigner to me and I will be a foreigner to him. 12 Since you are eager to have the gifts of the Spirit, above everything else you must try to make greater use of those which help build up the church.

13 The man who speaks in strange tongues, then, must pray for the gift to explain what he says. 14 For if I pray in this way, my spirit prays indeed, but my mind has no part in it. 15 What should I do, then? I will pray with my spirit, but I will pray also with my mind; I will sing with my spirit, but I will sing also with my mind. 16 When you give thanks to God in spirit only, how can an ordinary man taking part in the meeting say "Amen" to your prayer of thanksgiving? He has no way of knowing what you are saying. 17 Even if your prayer of thanks to God is quite good, the other man is not helped at all.

18 I thank God that I speak in strange tongues much more than any of you. 19 But in church worship I would rather speak five words that can be understood, in order to teach others, than speak thousands of words in strange tongues.

20 Do not be like children in your thinking, brothers; be children so far as evil is concerned,

New International Version

world, yet none of them is without meaning. 11 If then I do not grasp the meaning of what someone is saying, I am a foreigner to the speaker, and he is a foreigner to me. 12 So it is with you. Since you are eager to have spiritual gifts, try to excel in gifts that build up the church.

13 For this reason the man who speaks in a tongue should pray that he may interpret what he says. 14 For if I pray in a tongue, my spirit prays, but my mind is unfruitful. 15 So what shall I do? I will pray with my spirit, but I will also pray with my mind; I will sing with my spirit, but I will also sing with my mind. 16 If you are praising God with your spirit, how can one who finds himself among those who do not understand[h] say "Amen" to your thanksgiving, since he does not know what you are saying? 17 You may be giving thanks well enough, but the other man is not edified.

18 I thank God that I speak in tongues more than all of you. 19 But in the church I would rather speak five intelligible words to instruct others than ten thousand words in a tongue.

20 Brothers, stop thinking like children. In re-

[*h*] Or *among the inquirers.*

Phillips Modern English

spoken sounds and none is without meaning. But if the sounds of the speaker's voice mean nothing to me I am bound to sound like a foreigner to him, and he like a foreigner to me.

So, with yourselves, since you are so eager to possess spiritual gifts, concentrate your ambition upon receiving those which make for the real growth of your church. And that means if one of your number speaks with a "tongue", he should pray that he may be able to interpret what he says.

If I pray in a "tongue" my spirit is praying but my mind is inactive. I am therefore determined to pray with my spirit *and* my mind, and if I sing I will sing with both spirit and mind. Otherwise, if you are praising God with your spirit, how can the uninstructed man say amen to your thanksgiving, since he does not know what you are talking about? You may be thanking God splendidly, but it doesn't help the other man at all. I thank God that I have a greater gift of "tongues" than any of you, yet when I am in church I would rather speak five words with my mind (which might teach something to other people) than ten thousand words in a "tongue" which nobody understands.

14.20 You must use your minds in this matter of tongues

My brothers, don't be children but use your intelligence! By all means be innocent as babes

Revised Standard Version

world, and none is without meaning; 11 but if
I do not know the meaning of the language, I
shall be a foreigner to the speaker and the
speaker a foreigner to me. 12 So with yourselves;
since you are eager for manifestations of the
Spirit, strive to excel in building up the church.
13 Therefore, he who speaks in a tongue
should pray for the power to interpret. 14 For
if I pray in a tongue, my spirit prays but my
mind is unfruitful. 15 What am I to do? I will
pray with the spirit and I will pray with the
mind also; I will sing with the spirit and I will
sing with the mind also. 16 Otherwise, if you
bless[w] with the spirit, how can any one in the
position of an outsider[x] say the "Amen" to your
thanksgiving when he does not know what you
are saying? 17 For you may give thanks well
enough, but the other man is not edified. 18 I
thank God that I speak in tongues more than
you all; 19 nevertheless, in church I would rather
speak five words with my mind, in order to instruct others, than ten thousand words in a
tongue.
20 Brethren, do not be children in your think-

[w] That is, ***give thanks to God.*** [x] Or ***him that is without gifts.***

Jerusalem Bible

them is meaningless, 11 but if I am ignorant of
what the sounds mean, I am a savage to the
man who is speaking, and he is a savage to me.
12 It is the same in your own case: since you
aspire to spiritual gifts, concentrate on those
which will grow to benefit the community.
13 That is why anybody who has the gift of
tongues must pray for the power of interpreting
them. 14 For if I use this gift in my prayers, my
spirit may be praying but my mind is left barren. 15 What is the answer to that? Surely I
should pray not only with the spirit but with the
mind as well? And sing praises not only with
the spirit but with the mind as well? 16 Any uninitiated person will never be able to say Amen to
your thanksgiving, if you only bless God with the
spirit, for he will have no idea what you are saying. 17 However well you make your thanksgiving, the other gets no benefit from it. 18 I thank
God that I have a greater gift of tongues than all
of you, 19 but when I am in the presence of the
community I would rather say five words that
mean something than ten thousand words in a
tongue.
20 Brothers, you are not to be childish in
your outlook. You can be babies as far as wick-

New English Bible

gether soundless. Well then, if I do not know the meaning of the sound the speaker makes, his words will be gibberish to me, and mine to him. You are, I know, eager for gifts of the Spirit; then aspire above all to excel in those which build up the church.

I say, then, that the man who falls into ecstatic utterance should pray for the ability to interpret. If I use such language in my prayer, the Spirit in me prays, but my intellect lies fallow. What then? I will pray as I am inspired to pray, but I will also pray intelligently. I will sing hymns as I am inspired to sing, but I will sing intelligently too. Suppose you are praising God in the language of inspiration: how will the plain man who is present be able to say 'Amen' to your thanksgiving, when he does not know what you are saying? Your prayer of thanksgiving may be all that could be desired, but it is no help to the other man. Thank God, I am more gifted in ecstatic utterance than any of you,[a] but in the congregation I would rather speak five intelligible words, for the benefit of others as well as myself, than thousands of words in the language of ecstasy.

Do not be childish, my friends. Be as innocent

[a] *Or* . . . man. I say the thanksgiving; I use ecstatic speech more than any of you.

King James Version

malice be ye children, but in understanding be
men. 21 In the law it is written, With *men of*
other tongues and other lips will I speak unto
this people; and yet for all that will they not
hear me, saith the Lord. 22 Wherefore tongues
are for a sign, not to them that believe, but to
them that believe not: but prophesying *serveth*
not for them that believe not, but for them
which believe. 23 If therefore the whole church
be come together into one place, and all speak
with tongues, and there come in *those that are*
unlearned, or unbelievers, will they not say that
ye are mad? 24 But if all prophesy, and there
come in one that believeth not, or *one* unlearned, he is convinced of all, he is judged of
all: 25 And thus are the secrets of his heart made
manifest; and so falling down on *his* face he will
worship God, and report that God is in you of
a truth. 26 How is it then, brethren? when ye
come together, every one of you hath a psalm,
hath a doctrine, hath a tongue, hath a revelation, hath an interpretation. Let all things be
done unto edifying. 27 If any man speak in an

Living Bible

of intelligence in understanding matters of this
kind. 21 We are told in the ancient Scriptures
that God would send men from other lands to
speak in foreign languages to his people, but
even then they would not listen. 22 So you see
that being able to "speak in tongues" is not a
sign to God's children concerning his power,
but is a sign to the unsaved. However, prophecy
(preaching the deep truths of God) is what the
Christians need, and unbelievers aren't yet ready
for it. 23 Even so, if an unsaved person, or
someone who doesn't have these gifts, comes to
church and hears you all talking in other languages, he is likely to think you are crazy.
24 But if you prophesy, preaching God's Word,
[even though such preaching is mostly for believers[c]] and an unsaved person or a new Christian comes in who does not understand about
these things, all these sermons will convince him
of the fact that he is a sinner, and his conscience
will be pricked by everything he hears. 25 As he
listens, his secret thoughts will be laid bare and
he will fall down on his knees and worship God,
declaring that God is really there among you.
26 Well, my brothers, let's add up what I am
saying. When you meet together some will sing,
another will teach, or tell some special information God has given him, or speak in an unknown
language, or tell what someone else is saying
who is speaking in the unknown language, but
everything that is done must be useful to all,
and build them up in the Lord. 27 No more than

[*c*] Implied.

Today's English Version

but be mature in your thinking. 21 In the Scriptures it is written,

"By means of men of strange languages
I will speak to this people, says the Lord.
I will speak through lips of foreigners,
but even then they will not listen to me."

22 So then, the gift of speaking in strange tongues
is proof for unbelievers, not for believers, while
the gift of speaking God's message is proof for
believers, not for unbelievers.
23 If, then, the whole church meets together
and everyone starts speaking in strange tongues
—if some ordinary people or unbelievers come
in, won't they say that you are all crazy? 24 But
if all speak God's message, when some unbeliever
or ordinary person comes in he will be convinced
of his sin by what he hears. He will be judged by
all he hears, 25 his secret thoughts will be brought
into the open, and he will bow down and worship
God, confessing, "Truly God is here with you!"

Order in the church

26 What do I mean, my brothers? When you
meet for worship, one man has a hymn, another
a teaching, another a revelation from God, another a message in strange tongues, and still
another the explanation of what is said. Everything must be of help to the church. 27 If some-

New International Version

gard to evil be infants, but in your thinking be
adults. 21 In the Law it is written:
"Through men of strange tongues
and through the lips of foreigners
I will speak to this people,
but even then they will not listen to me,"[i]
says the Lord.
22 Tongues, then, are a sign, not for believers
but for unbelievers; prophecy, however, is for believers, not for unbelievers. 23 So if the whole
church comes together and everyone speaks in
tongues, and some who do not understand[j] or
some unbelievers come in, will they not say that
you are out of your mind? 24 But if an unbeliever
or someone who does not understand[k] comes in
while everybody is prophesying, he will be convinced by all that he is a sinner and will be
judged by all, 25 and the secrets of his heart will
be laid bare. So he will fall down and worship
God, exclaiming, "God is really among you!"

Orderly worship

26 What then shall we say, brothers? When
you come together, everyone has a hymn, or a
word of instruction, a revelation, a tongue, or an
interpretation. All of these must be done for the
strengthening of the church. 27 If anyone speaks

[*i*] Isaiah 28:11,12; Deut. 28:49. [*j*] Or *some inquirers.* [*k*] Or *some inquirer.*

Phillips Modern English

as far as evil is concerned, but where your minds are concerned be full-grown men! In the Law it is written:

> By men of strange tongues and by the lips of strangers will I speak unto this people: and not even thus will they hear me, saith the Lord.

That means that tongues are a sign of God's power, not for those who are unbelievers but for those who already believe. Preaching the word of God, on the other hand, is a sign of God's power to those who do not believe rather than to believers. So that, if at a full church meeting you are all speaking with tongues and men come in who are uninstructed or without faith, will they not say that you are insane? But if you are preaching God's word and such a man should come in to your meeting, he is convicted and challenged by your united speaking of the truth. His secrets are exposed and he will fall on his knees acknowledging God and saying that God is truly among you!

14.26 Some practical regulations for the exercise of spiritual gifts

Well then, my brothers, whenever you meet let everyone be ready to contribute a psalm, a piece of teaching, a spiritual truth, or a "tongue" with an interpreter. Everything should be done to make your church strong in the faith.

If the question of speaking with a "tongue"

Revised Standard Version

ing; be babes in evil, but in thinking be mature. 21 In the law it is written, "By men of
strange tongues and by the lips of foreigners
will I speak to this people, and even then they
will not listen to me, says the Lord." 22 Thus,
tongues are a sign not for believers but for unbelievers, while prophecy is not for unbelievers
but for believers. 23 If, therefore, the whole
church assembles and all speak in tongues, and
outsiders or unbelievers enter, will they not say
that you are mad? 24 But if all prophesy, and
an unbeliever or outsider enters, he is convicted
by all, he is called to account by all, 25 the secrets of his heart are disclosed; and so, falling
on his face, he will worship God and declare
that God is really among you.
26 What then, brethren? When you come together, each one has a hymn, a lesson, a revelation, a tongue, or an interpretation. Let all
things be done for edification. 27 If any speak

Jerusalem Bible

edness is concerned, but mentally you must be
adult. 21 In the written Law it says: *Through
men speaking strange languages and through the
lips of foreigners, I shall talk to the nation, and
still they will not listen to me, says the Lord.*[a]
22 You see then, that the strange languages are
meant to be a sign not for believers but for unbelievers, while on the other hand, prophecy is a
sign not for unbelievers but for believers. 23 So
that any uninitiated people or unbelievers, coming into a meeting of the whole church where
everybody was speaking in tongues, would say
you were all mad; 24 but if you were all prophesying and an unbeliever or uninitiated person
came in, he would find himself analyzed and
judged by everyone speaking; 25 he would find
his secret thoughts laid bare, and then fall on
his face and worship God, declaring that *God
is among you indeed.*[b]

Regulating spiritual gifts

26 So, my dear brothers, what conclusion is
to be drawn? At all your meetings, let everyone
be ready with a psalm or a sermon or a revelation, or ready to use his gift of tongues or to give
an interpretation; but it must always be for the
common good. 27 If there are people present

[a] A free version of Is. 28:11-12. [b] Is. 45:14.

New English Bible

of evil as babes, but at least be grown-up in your thinking. We read in the Law: 'I will speak to this nation through men of strange tongues, and by the lips of foreigners; and even so they will not heed me, says the Lord.' Clearly then these 'strange tongues' are not intended as a sign for believers, but for unbelievers, whereas prophecy is designed not for unbelievers but for those who hold the faith. So if the whole congregation is assembled and all are using the 'strange tongues' of ecstasy, and some uninstructed persons or unbelievers should enter, will they not think you are mad? But if all are uttering prophecies, the visitor, when he enters, hears from everyone something that searches his conscience and brings conviction, and the secrets of his heart are laid bare. So he will fall down and worship God, crying, 'God is certainly among you!'

To sum up, my friends: when you meet for worship, each of you contributes a hymn, some instruction, a revelation, an ecstatic utterance, or the interpretation of such an utterance. All of these must aim at one thing: to build up the church. If it is a matter of ecstatic utterance,

King James Version

unknown tongue, *let it be* by two, or at the
most *by* three, and *that* by course; and let one
interpret. 28 But if there be no interpreter, let
him keep silence in the church; and let him
speak to himself, and to God. 29 Let the prophets speak two or three, and let the other judge.
30 If *any thing* be revealed to another that sitteth by, let the first hold his peace. 31 For ye
may all prophesy one by one, that all may learn,
and all may be comforted. 32 And the spirits of
the prophets are subject to the prophets. 33 For
God is not *the author* of confusion, but of peace,
as in all churches of the saints. 34 Let your
women keep silence in the churches: for it is
not permitted unto them to speak; but *they are
commanded* to be under obedience, as also saith
the law. 35 And if they will learn any thing, let
them ask their husbands at home: for it is a
shame for women to speak in the church.

Living Bible

two or three should speak in an unknown language, and they must speak one at a time, and
someone must be ready to interpret what they
are saying. 28 But if no one is present who can
interpret, they must not speak out loud. They
must talk silently to themselves and to God in
the unknown language but not publicly.

29, 30 Two or three may prophesy, one at a
time, if they have the gift, while all the others
listen. But if, while someone is prophesying,
someone else receives a message or idea from
the Lord, the one who is speaking should stop.
31 In this way all who have the gift of prophecy
can speak, one after the other, and everyone
will learn and be encouraged and helped. 32 Remember that a person who has a message from
God has the power to stop himself or wait
his turn.[d] 33 God is not one who likes things to
be disorderly and upset. He likes harmony, and
he finds it in all the other churches.

34 Women should be silent during the church
meetings. They are not to take part in the discussion, for they are subordinate to men[e] as the
Scriptures also declare. 35 If they have any questions to ask, let them ask their husbands at
home, for it is improper for women to express
their opinions in church meetings.

[*d*] Literally, "The spirits of the prophets are subject to the prophets." [*e*] Literally, "They are not authorized to speak." They are permitted to pray and prophesy (1 Cor. 11:5), apparently in public meetings, but not to teach men (1 Tim. 2:12).

Today's English Version

one is going to speak in strange tongues, two or
three at the most should speak, one after the
other, and someone else must explain what is
being said. 28 But if no one is there who can explain, then the one who speaks in strange tongues
must be quiet in the meeting, and speak only to
himself and to God. 29 Two or three who are
given God's message should speak, while the
others judge what they say. 30 But if someone
sitting in the meeting receives a message from
God, the one who is speaking should stop. 31 All
of you may speak God's message, one by one, so
that all will learn and be encouraged. 32 The gift
of speaking God's message should be under the
speaker's control, 33 because God has not called
us to be disorderly, but peaceful.

As in all the churches of God's people, 34 the
women should keep quiet in the church meetings.
They are not allowed to speak; as the Jewish
Law says, they must not be in charge. 35 If they
want to find out about something, they should
ask their husbands at home. It is a disgraceful
thing for a woman to speak in a church meeting.

New International Version

in a tongue, two—or at the most three—should
speak, one at a time, and someone must interpret.
28 If there is no interpreter, the speaker should
keep quiet in the church and speak to himself and
God.

29 Two or three prophets should speak, and
the others should weigh carefully what is said.
30 And if a revelation comes to someone who is
sitting down, the first speaker should stop. 31 For
you can all prophesy in turn so that everyone
may be instructed and encouraged. 32 The spirits
of prophets are subject to the control of prophets.
33 For God is not a God of disorder but of
peace.

As in all the congregations of the saints,
34 women should remain silent in the churches.
They are not allowed to speak, but must be in
submission, as the Law says. 35 If they want to
inquire about something, they should ask their
own husbands at home; for it is disgraceful for

Phillips Modern English

arises, confine the speaking to two or three at the most. They must speak in turn and have someone to interpret what is said. If you have no interpreter then let the speaker with a "tongue" keep silent in the church and speak only to himself and God. Don't have more than two or three preachers either, while the others think over what has been said. But should a message of truth come to one who is seated, then the original speaker should stop talking. For in this way you can all have the opportunity to give a message, one after the other, and everyone will learn something and everyone will have his faith stimulated. The spirit of a true preacher is under that preacher's control, for God is not a God of disorder but of harmony, as is plain in all the churches.

14.34 The speaking of women in church is forbidden

Let women be silent in church; they are not to be allowed to speak. They must submit to this regulation, as the Law itself instructs. If they have questions to ask they must ask their husbands at home, for there is something improper about a woman's speaking in church.

Revised Standard Version

in a tongue, let there be only two or at most three, and each in turn; and let one interpret. 28 But if there is no one to interpret, let each of them keep silence in church and speak to himself and to God. 29 Let two or three prophets speak, and let the others weigh what is said. 30 If a revelation is made to another sitting by, let the first be silent. 31 For you can all prophesy one by one, so that all may learn and all be encouraged; 32 and the spirits of prophets are subject to prophets. 33 For God is not a God of confusion but of peace.

As in all the churches of the saints, 34 the women should keep silence in the churches. For they are not permitted to speak, but should be subordinate, as even the law says. 35 If there is anything they desire to know, let them ask their husbands at home. For it is shameful for

Jerusalem Bible

with the gift of tongues, let only two or three, at the most, be allowed to use it, and only one at a time, and there must be someone to interpret. 28 If there is no interpreter present, they must keep quiet in church and speak only to themselves and to God. 29 As for prophets, let two or three of them speak, and the others attend to them. 30 If one of the listeners receives a revelation, then the man who is already speaking should stop. 31 For you can all prophesy in turn, so that everybody will learn something and everybody will be encouraged. 32 Prophets can always control their prophetic spirits, 33 since God is not a God of disorder but of peace.

As in all the churches of the saints, 34 women are to remain quiet at meetings since they have no permission to speak; they must keep in the background as the Law itself lays it down. 35 If they have any questions to ask, they should ask their husbands at home: it does not seem right for a woman to raise her voice at meetings.

New English Bible

only two should speak, or at most three, one at a time, and someone must interpret. If there is no interpreter, the speaker had better not address the meeting at all, but speak to himself and to God. Of the prophets, two or three may speak, while the rest exercise their judgement upon what is said. If someone else, sitting in his place, receives a revelation, let the first speaker stop. You can all prophesy, one at a time, so that the whole congregation may receive instruction and encouragement. It is for prophets to control prophetic inspiration, for the God who inspires them is not a God of disorder but of peace.

As in all congregations of God's people, women[a] should not address the meeting. They have no licence to speak, but should keep their place as the law directs. If there is something they want to know, they can ask their own husbands at home. It is a shocking thing that a woman should address the congregation.

[a] *Or* of peace, as in all communities of God's people. Women . . .

King James Version

36 What! came the word of God out from you? or came it unto you only? 37 If any man think himself to be a prophet, or spiritual, let him acknowledge that the things that I write unto you are the commandments of the Lord. 38 But if any man be ignorant, let him be ignorant. 39 Wherefore, brethren, covet to prophesy, and forbid not to speak with tongues. 40 Let all things be done decently and in order.

15 Moreover, brethren, I declare unto you the gospel which I preached unto you, which also ye have received, and wherein ye stand; 2 By which also ye are saved, if ye keep in memory what I preached unto you, unless ye have believed in vain. 3 For I delivered unto you first of all that which I also received, how

Living Bible

36 You disagree? And do you think that the knowledge of God's will begins and ends with you Corinthians? Well, you are mistaken! 37 You who claim to have the gift of prophecy or any other special ability from the Holy Spirit should be the first to realize that what I am saying is a commandment from the Lord himself. 38 But if anyone still disagrees—well, we will leave him in his ignorance.[f]

39 So, my fellow believers, long to be prophets so that you can preach God's message plainly; and never say it is wrong to "speak in tongues"; 40 however, be sure that everything is done properly in a good and orderly way.

15 Now let me remind you, brothers, of what the Gospel really is, for it has not changed—it is the same Good News I preached to you before. You welcomed it then and still do now, for your faith is squarely built upon this wonderful message; 2 and it is this Good News that saves you if you still firmly believe it, unless of course you never really believed it in the first place.

3 I passed on to you right from the first what had been told to me, that Christ died for our

[f] Or, "If he disagrees, ignore his opinion."

Today's English Version

36 Or could it be that the word of God came from you? Or are you the only ones to whom it came? 37 If anyone supposes he is God's messenger or has a spiritual gift, he must realize that what I am writing you is the Lord's command. 38 But if he does not pay attention to this, pay no attention to him.

39 So then, my brothers, set your heart on speaking God's message, but do not forbid the speaking in strange tongues. 40 Everything must be done in a proper and orderly way.

The resurrection of Christ

15 And now I want to remind you, brothers, of the Good News which I preached to you, which you received, and on which your faith stands firm. 2 That is the gospel, the message that I preached to you. You are saved by the gospel if you hold firmly to it—unless it was for nothing that you believed.

3 I passed on to you what I received, which is of the greatest importance: that Christ died for

New International Version

a woman to speak in the church. 36 Did the word of God originate with you? Or are you the only people it has reached?

37 If anybody thinks he is a prophet or spiritually gifted, let him acknowledge that what I am writing to you is the Lord's command. 38 If he ignores this, he himself will be ignored.[l]

39 Therefore, my brothers, be eager to prophesy, and do not forbid speaking in tongues. 40 But everything should be done in a fitting and orderly way.

The resurrection of Christ

15 Now, brothers, I want to remind you of the gospel I preached to you, which you received and on which you have taken your stand. 2 By this gospel you are saved, if you hold firmly to the word I preached to you. Otherwise, you have believed in vain.

3 For what I received I passed on to you as of first importance[m]: that Christ died for our sins

[l] Some MSS read *If he ignores this, let him ignore this.* [m] Or *you at the first.*

Phillips Modern English

14.36 You must accept the rules I have given by authority

Are you beginning to imagine that the Word of God originated in your church, or that you have a monopoly of God's truth? If any of your number think himself a true preacher and a spiritually-minded man, let him realise that what I have written is by divine command! If a man does not recognise this he himself should not be recognised.

In conclusion then, my brothers, set your heart on preaching the word of God, while not forbidding the use of "tongues". Let everything be done decently and in order.

15.1 A reminder of the gospel message: the resurrection is an integral part of our faith

Now, my brothers, I want to remind you of the gospel which I have previously preached to you, which you accepted, on which you have taken your stand and by which, if you remain faithful to the message I gave you, your salvation is being worked out—unless, of course, your faith had no meaning behind it at all.

For I passed on to you,—as essential, the message I had myself received—that Christ died for

Revised Standard Version

a woman to speak in church. 36 What! Did the word of God originate with you, or are you the only ones it has reached?

37 If any one thinks that he is a prophet, or spiritual, he should acknowledge that what I am writing to you is a command of the Lord. 38 If any one does not recognize this, he is not recognized. 39 So, my brethren, earnestly desire to prophesy, and do not forbid speaking in tongues; 40 but all things should be done decently and in order.

15 Now I would remind you, brethren, in what terms I preached to you the gospel, which you received, in which you stand, 2 by which you are saved, if you hold it fast—unless you believed in vain.

3 For I delivered to you as of first importance what I also received, that Christ died for our

Jerusalem Bible

36 Do you think the word of God came out of yourselves? Or that it has come only to you? 37 Anyone who claims to be a prophet or inspired ought to recognize that what I am writing to you is a command from the Lord. 38 Unless he recognizes this, you should not recognize him.

39 And so, my dear brothers, by all means be ambitious to prophesy, do not suppress the gift of tongues, 40 but let everything be done with propriety and in order.

III. The resurrection of the dead

The fact of the resurrection

15 Brothers, I want to remind you of the gospel I preached to you, the gospel that you received and in which you are firmly established; 2 because the gospel will save you only if you keep believing exactly what I preached to you—believing anything else will not lead to anything.

3 Well then, in the first place, I taught you what I had been taught myself, namely that

New English Bible

Did the word of God originate with you? Or are you the only people to whom it came? If anyone claims to be inspired or a prophet, let him recognize that what I write has the Lord's authority. If he does not acknowledge this, God does not acknowledge him.[b]

In short, my friends, be eager to prophesy; do not forbid ecstatic utterance; but let all be done decently and in order.

Life after death

15 And now, my brothers, I must remind you of the gospel that I preached to you; the gospel which you received, on which you have taken your stand, and which is now bringing you salvation. Do you still hold fast the Gospel as I preached it to you? If not, your conversion was in vain.[a]

First and foremost, I handed on to you the facts which had been imparted to me: that Christ

[b] *Some witnesses read* If he refuses to recognize this, let him refuse! [a] *Or* Do you remember the terms in which I preached the Gospel to you?—for I assume you did not accept it thoughtlessly.

King James Version

that Christ died for our sins according to the Scriptures; 4And that he was buried, and that he rose again the third day according to the Scriptures: 5And that he was seen of Cephas, then of the twelve: 6After that, he was seen of above five hundred brethren at once; of whom the greater part remain unto this present, but some are fallen asleep. 7After that, he was seen of James; then of all the apostles. 8And last of all he was seen of me also, as of one born out of due time. 9 For I am the least of the apostles, that am not meet to be called an apostle, because I persecuted the church of God. 10 But by the grace of God I am what I am: and his grace which *was bestowed* upon me was not in vain; but I laboured more abundantly than they all: yet not I, but the grace of God which was with me. 11 Therefore whether *it were* I or they, so we preach, and so ye believed. 12 Now if Christ be preached that he rose from the dead, how say some among you that there is no resurrection of the dead? 13 But if there be no resurrection of the dead, then is Christ not risen: 14And if Christ be not risen, then *is* our preaching vain, and your faith *is* also vain. 15 Yea, and we are found false witnesses of God; because we have testified of God that he raised up Christ: whom he raised not up, if so

Living Bible

sins just as the Scriptures said he would, 4 and that he was buried, and that three days afterwards he arose from the grave just as the prophets foretold. 5 He was seen by Peter and later by the rest of "the Twelve." [a] 6After that he was seen by more than five hundred Christian brothers at one time, most of whom are still alive, though some have died by now. 7 Then James saw him and later all the apostles. 8 Last of all I saw him too, long after the others, as though I had been born almost too late for this. 9 For I am the least worthy of all the apostles, and I shouldn't even be called an apostle at all after the way I treated the church of God.

10 But whatever I am now it is all because God poured out such kindness and grace upon me—and not without results: for I have worked harder than all the other apostles, yet actually I wasn't doing it, but God working in me, to bless me. 11 It makes no difference who worked the hardest, I or they; the important thing is that we preached the Gospel to you, and you believed it.

12 But tell me this! Since you believe what we preach, that *Christ* rose from the dead, why are some of you saying that dead people will never come back to life again? 13 For if there is no resurrection of the dead, then Christ must still be dead. 14And if he is still dead, then all our preaching is useless and your trust in God is empty, worthless, hopeless; 15 and we apostles are all liars because we have said that God raised Christ from the grave, and of course that isn't true if the dead do not come back to life

[*a*] The name given to Jesus' twelve disciples, and still used after Judas was gone from among them.

Today's English Version

our sins, as written in the Scriptures; 4 that he was buried, and was raised to life on the third day, as written in the Scriptures; 5 that he appeared to Peter, and then to all twelve apostles. 6 Then he appeared to more than five hundred of his followers at once, most of whom are still alive, although some have died. 7 Then he appeared to James, and then to all the apostles.

8 Last of all he appeared also to me—even though I am like one who was born in a most unusual way. 9 For I am the least of all the apostles—I do not even deserve to be called an apostle, because I persecuted God's church. 10 But by God's grace I am what I am, and the grace that he gave me was not without effect. On the contrary, I have worked harder than all the other apostles, although it was not really my own doing, but God's grace working with me. 11 So then, whether it came from me or from them, this is what we all preach, this is what you believe.

Our resurrection

12 Now, since our message is that Christ has been raised from death, how can some of you say that the dead will not be raised to life? 13 If that is true, it means that Christ was not raised; 14 and if Christ has not been raised from death, then we have nothing to preach and you have nothing to believe. 15 More than that, we are shown to be lying against God, because we said of him that he raised Christ from death—but he did not raise him, if it is true that the dead are

New International Version

according to the Scriptures, 4 that he was buried, that he was raised on the third day according to the Scriptures, 5 and that he appeared to Peter,[n] and then to the Twelve. 6After that, he appeared to more than five hundred of the brothers at the same time, most of whom are still living, though some have fallen asleep. 7 Then he appeared to James, then to all the apostles, 8 and last of all he appeared to me also, as to one abnormally born.

9 For I am the least of the apostles and do not even deserve to be called an apostle, because I persecuted the church of God. 10 But by the grace of God I am what I am, and his grace to me was not without effect. No, I worked harder than all of them—yet not I, but the grace of God that was with me. 11 Whether, then, it was I or they, this is what we preach, and this is what you believed.

The resurrection of the dead

12 But if it is preached that Christ has been raised from the dead, how can some of you say that there is no resurrection of the dead? 13 If there is no resurrection of the dead, then not even Christ has been raised. 14And if Christ has not been raised, our preaching is useless and so is your faith. 15 More than that, we are then found to be false witnesses about God, for we have testified about God that he raised Christ from the dead. But he did not raise him if in fact

[*n*] Greek *Cephas.*

Phillips Modern English

our sins, as the scriptures said he would; that he was buried and rose again on the third day, again as the scriptures foretold. He was seen by Cephas, then by the twelve, and subsequently he was seen simultaneously by over five hundred Christians, of whom the majority are still alive, though some have since died. He was then seen by James, then by all the messengers. And last of all, as to one born abnormally late, he appeared even to me! I am the least of the messengers, and indeed I do not deserve that title at all, because I persecuted the Church of God. But what I am now I am by the grace of God. The grace he gave me has not proved a barren gift. I have worked harder than any of the others—and yet it was not I but this same grace of God within me. In any event, whoever has done the work, whether I or they, this has been our message and this has been your faith.

15.12 If the resurrection is the heart of the gospel how can any Christian deny life after death?

Now if the rising of Christ from the dead is the very heart of our message, how can some of you deny that there is any resurrection? For if there is no such thing as the resurrection of the dead, then Christ was never raised. And if Christ was not raised then neither our preaching nor your faith has any meaning at all. Further it would mean that we are lying in our witness for God, for we have given our solemn testimony

Revised Standard Version

sins in accordance with the scriptures, 4 that he
was buried, that he was raised on the third day
in accordance with the scriptures, 5 and that he
appeared to Cephas, then to the twelve. 6 Then
he appeared to more than five hundred brethren
at one time, most of whom are still alive, though
some have fallen asleep. 7 Then he appeared to
James, then to all the apostles. 8 Last of all, as
to one untimely born, he appeared also to me.
9 For I am the least of the apostles, unfit to be
called an apostle, because I persecuted the
church of God. 10 But by the grace of God I
am what I am, and his grace toward me was
not in vain. On the contrary, I worked harder
than any of them, though it was not I, but the
grace of God which is with me. 11 Whether
then it was I or they, so we preach and so you
believed.
12 Now if Christ is preached as raised from
the dead, how can some of you say that there
is no resurrection of the dead? 13 But if there is
no resurrection of the dead, then Christ has not
been raised; 14 if Christ has not been raised,
then our preaching is in vain and your faith is
in vain. 15 We are even found to be misrep-
resenting God, because we testified of God that
he raised Christ, whom he did not raise if it is

Jerusalem Bible

Christ died for our sins, in accordance with the
scriptures; 4 that he was buried; and that he was
raised to life on the third day, in accordance
with the scriptures; 5 that he appeared first to
Cephas and secondly to the Twelve. 6 Next he
appeared to more than five hundred of the
brothers at the same time, most of whom are still
alive, though some have died; 7 then he appeared
to James, and then to all the apostles; 8 and last
of all he appeared to me too; it was as though I
was born when no one expected it.
9 I am the least of the apostles; in fact, since
I persecuted the Church of God, I hardly deserve the name apostle; 10 but by God's grace
that is what I am, and the grace that he gave me
has not been fruitless. On the contrary, I, or
rather the grace of God that is with me, have
worked harder than any of the others; 11 but
what matters is that I preach what they preach,
and this is what you all believed.
12 Now if Christ raised from the dead is what
has been preached, how can some of you be
saying that there is no resurrection of the dead?
13 If there is no resurrection of the dead, Christ
himself cannot have been raised, 14 and if
Christ has not been raised then our preaching
is useless and your believing it is useless; 15 indeed, we are shown up as witnesses who have
committed perjury before God, because we swore
in evidence before God that he raised Christ to

New English Bible

died for our sins, in accordance with the scriptures; that he was buried; that he was raised to life on the third day, according to the scriptures; and that he appeared to Cephas, and afterwards to the Twelve. Then he appeared to over five hundred of our brothers at once, most of whom are still alive, though some have died. Then he appeared to James, and afterwards to all the apostles.

In the end he appeared even to me. It was like an abnormal birth; I had persecuted the church of God and am therefore inferior to all other apostles—indeed not fit to be called an apostle. However, by God's grace I am what I am, nor has his grace been given to me in vain; on the contrary, in my labours I have outdone them all—not I, indeed, but the grace of God working with me. But what matter, I or they? This is what we all proclaim, and this is what you believed.

Now if this is what we proclaim, that Christ was raised from the dead, how can some of you say there is no resurrection of the dead? If there be no resurrection, then Christ was not raised; and if Christ was not raised, then our gospel is null and void, and so is your faith; and we turn out to be lying witnesses for God, because we bore witness that he raised Christ to life, whereas, if the dead are not raised, he did not

King James Version

be that the dead rise not. 16 For if the dead rise not, then is not Christ raised: 17 And if Christ be not raised, your faith *is* vain; ye are yet in your sins. 18 Then they also which are fallen asleep in Christ are perished. 19 If in this life only we have hope in Christ, we are of all men most miserable. 20 But now is Christ risen from the dead, *and* become the firstfruits of them that slept. 21 For since by man *came* death, by man *came* also the resurrection of the dead. 22 For as in Adam all die, even so in Christ shall all be made alive. 23 But every man in his own order: Christ the firstfruits; afterward they that are Christ's at his coming. 24 Then *cometh* the end, when he shall have delivered up the kingdom to God, even the Father; when he shall have put down all rule, and all authority and power. 25 For he must reign, till he hath put all enemies under his feet. 26 The last enemy *that* shall be destroyed *is* death. 27 For he hath put all things under his feet. But when he saith, All things are

Living Bible

again. 16 If they don't, then Christ is still dead, 17 and you are very foolish to keep on trusting God to save you, and you are still under condemnation for your sins; 18 in that case all Christians who have died are lost! 19 And if being a Christian is of value to us only now in this life, we are the most miserable of creatures.

20 But the fact is that Christ did actually rise from the dead, and has become the first of millions[b] who will come back to life again some day.

21 Death came into the world because of what one man (Adam) did, and it is because of what this other man (Christ) has done that now there is the resurrection from the dead. 22 Everyone dies because all of us are related to Adam, being members of his sinful race, and wherever there is sin, death results. But all who are related to Christ will rise again. 23 Each, however, in his own turn: Christ rose first; then when Christ comes back, all his people will become alive again.

24 After that the end will come when he will turn the kingdom over to God the Father, having put down all enemies of every kind. 25 For Christ will be King until he has defeated all his enemies, 26 including the last enemy—death. This too must be defeated and ended. 27 For the rule and authority over all things has been given

[*b*] Literally, "the first-fruits of them that are asleep."

Today's English Version

not raised to life. 16 For if the dead are not raised, neither has Christ been raised. 17 And if Christ has not been raised, then your faith is a delusion and you are still lost in your sins. 18 It would also mean that the believers in Christ who have died are lost. 19 If our hope in Christ is good for this life only, and no more, then we deserve more pity than anyone else in all the world.

20 But the truth is that Christ has been raised from death, as the guarantee that those who sleep in death will also be raised. 21 For just as death came by means of a man, in the same way the rising from death comes by means of a man. 22 For just as all men die because of their union to Adam, in the same way all will be raised to life because of their union to Christ. 23 But each one in his proper order: Christ, the first of all; then those who belong to Christ, at the time of his coming. 24 Then the end will come; Christ will overcome all spiritual rulers, authorities, and powers, and hand over the Kingdom to God the Father. 25 For Christ must rule until God defeats all enemies and puts them under his feet. 26 The last enemy to be defeated will be death. 27 For the scripture says, "God put *all* things un-

New International Version

the dead are not raised. 16 For if the dead are not raised, then Christ has not been raised either. 17 And if Christ has not been raised, your faith is futile; you are still in your sins. 18 Then those also who have fallen asleep in Christ are lost. 19 If only for this life we have hope in Christ, we are to be pitied more than all men.

20 But Christ has indeed been raised from the dead, the firstfruits of those who have fallen asleep. 21 For since death came through a man, the resurrection of the dead comes also through a man. 22 For as in Adam all die, so in Christ all will be made alive. 23 But each in his own turn: Christ, the firstfruits; then, when he comes, those who belong to him. 24 Then the end will come, when he hands over the kingdom to God the Father after he has destroyed all dominion, authority and power. 25 For he must reign until God has put all his enemies under his feet. 26 The last enemy to be destroyed is death. 27 For God

Phillips Modern English

that he did raise up Christ—and that is utterly false if it should be true that the dead do not, in fact, rise again! For if the dead do not rise neither did Christ rise, and if Christ did not rise your faith is futile and your sins have never been forgiven. Moreover those who have died believing in Christ are utterly dead and gone. Truly, if our hope in Christ were limited to this life only we should, of all mankind, be the most to be pitied!

15.20 But Christianity rests on a fact —Christ did rise

But the glorious fact is that Christ was raised from the dead: he has become the very first to rise of all who sleep the sleep of death. As death entered the world through a man, so has rising from the dead come to us through a man! As members of a sinful race all men die; as members of Christ all men shall be raised to life, each in his proper order, with Christ the very first and after him all who belong to him when he comes.

Then, and not till then, comes the end when Christ, having abolished all other rule, authority and power, hands over the kingdom to God the Father. Christ's reign will and must continue until every enemy has been conquered. The last enemy of all to be destroyed is death itself. The scripture says:

> He hath put all things in subjection under his feet.

Revised Standard Version

true that the dead are not raised. 16 For if the
dead are not raised, then Christ has not been
raised. 17 If Christ has not been raised, your
faith is futile and you are still in your sins.
18 Then those also who have fallen asleep in
Christ have perished. 19 If for this life only we
have hoped in Christ, we are of all men most to
be pitied.
20 But in fact Christ has been raised from
the dead, the first fruits of those who have fallen
asleep. 21 For as by a man came death, by a
man has come also the resurrection of the dead.
22 For as in Adam all die, so also in Christ
shall all be made alive. 23 But each in his own
order: Christ the first fruits, then at his coming
those who belong to Christ. 24 Then comes the
end, when he delivers the kingdom to God the
Father after destroying every rule and every
authority and power. 25 For he must reign until
he has put all his enemies under his feet. 26 The
last enemy to be destroyed is death. 27 "For
God [z] has put all things in subjection under his

Jerusalem Bible

life. 16 For if the dead are not raised, Christ
has not been raised, 17 and if Christ has not been
raised, you are still in your sins. 18And what is
more serious, all who have died in Christ have
perished. 19 If our hope in Christ has been for
this life only, we are the most unfortunate of
all people.
20 But Christ has in fact been raised from the
dead, the first fruits of all who have fallen asleep.
21 Death came through one man and in the same
way the resurrection of the dead has come
through one man. 22 Just as all men die in Adam,
so all men will be brought to life in Christ;
23 but all of them in their proper order: Christ
as the first fruits and then, after the coming of
Christ, those who belong to him. 24After that
will come the end, when he hands over the kingdom to God the Father, having done away with
every sovereignty, authority and power. 25 For he
must be king *until he has put all his enemies*
under his feet[c] 26 and the last of the enemies
to be destroyed is death, for everything is to be
put under his feet.—27 Though when it is said

[c] Ps. 110:1.

New English Bible

raise him. For if the dead are not raised, it follows that Christ was not raised; and if Christ was not raised, your faith has nothing in it and you are still in your old state of sin. It follows also that those who have died within Christ's fellowship are utterly lost. If it is for this life only that Christ has given us hope,[b] we of all men are most to be pitied.

But the truth is, Christ was raised to life—the firstfruits of the harvest of the dead. For since it was a man who brought death into the world, a man also brought resurrection of the dead. As in Adam all men die, so in Christ all will be brought to life; but each in his own proper place: Christ the firstfruits, and afterwards, at his coming, those who belong to Christ. Then comes the end, when he delivers up the kingdom to God the Father, after abolishing every kind of domination, authority, and power. For he is destined to reign until God has put all enemies under his feet; and the last enemy to be abolished is death.[a] Scripture says, 'He has put

[*b*] *Or* If it is only an uncertain hope that our life in Christ has given us . . . [*a*] *Or* Then at the end, when . . . power (for he . . . feet), the last enemy, death, will be abolished.

King James Version

put under *him, it is* manifest that he is excepted,
which did put all things under him. 28And when
all things shall be subdued unto him, then shall
the Son also himself be subject unto him that
put all things under him, that God may be all in
all. 29 Else what shall they do which are baptized for the dead, if the dead rise not at all?
why are they then baptized for the dead?
30 And why stand we in jeopardy every hour?
31 I protest by your rejoicing which I have in
Christ Jesus our Lord, I die daily. 32 If after
the manner of men I have fought with beasts
at Ephesus, what advantageth it me, if the dead
rise not? let us eat and drink; for to morrow we
die. 33 Be not deceived: evil communications
corrupt good manners. 34Awake to righteous-

Living Bible

to Christ by his Father; except, of course, Christ
does not rule over the Father himself, who gave
him this power to rule. 28 When Christ has finally won the battle against all his enemies, then
he, the Son of God, will put himself also under
his Father's orders, so that God who has given
him the victory over everything else will be
utterly supreme.
29 If the dead will not come back to life
again, then what point is there in people being
baptized for those who are gone? Why do it unless you believe that the dead will some day rise
again?
30 And why should we ourselves be continually risking our lives, facing death hour by
hour? 31 For it is a fact that I face death daily;
that is as true as my pride in your growth in the
Lord. 32And what value was there in fighting
wild beasts—those men of Ephesus—if it was
only for what I gain in this life down here? If
we will never live again after we die, then we
might as well go and have ourselves a good time:
let us eat, drink, and be merry. What's the difference? For tomorrow we die, and that ends
everything!
33 Don't be fooled by those who say such
things. If you listen to them you will start acting
like them. 34 Get some sense and quit your sin-

Today's English Version

der his feet." It is clear, of course, that the words
"all things" do not include God himself, who puts
all things under Christ. 28 But when all things
have been placed under Christ's rule, then he
himself, the Son, will place himself under God,
who placed all under him; and God will rule
completely over all.
29 Now, what of those people who are baptized for the dead? What do they hope to accomplish? If it is true, as they claim, that the
dead are not raised to life, why are they being
baptized for the dead? 30And as for us—why
would we run the risk of danger every hour?
31 Brothers, I face death every day! The pride
I have in you in our life in Christ Jesus our
Lord makes me declare this. 32 If, as it were, I
have fought "wild beasts" here in Ephesus, simply from human motives, what have I gained?
But if the dead are not raised to life, then "Let
us eat and drink, for tomorrow we will die," as
the saying goes.
33 Do not be fooled. "Bad companions ruin
good character." 34 Come back to your right

New International Version

"has put everything under his feet." [o] Now when
it says that "everything" has been put under him,
it is clear that this does not include God himself, who put everything under Christ. 28 When
he has done this, then the Son himself will be
made subject to him who put everything under
him, so that God may be all in all.
29 Now if there is no resurrection, what will
those do who are baptized for the dead? If the
dead are not raised at all, why are people baptized for them? 30And as for us, why do we en-
danger ourselves every hour? 31 I die every day
—I mean that, brothers—just as surely as I glory
over you in Christ Jesus our Lord. 32 If I fought
wild beasts in Ephesus for merely human reasons,
what have I gained? If the dead are not raised,
"Let us eat and drink,
for tomorrow we die." [p]
33 Do not be misled: "Bad company corrupts
good character." 34 Come back to your senses

[*o*] Psalm 8:6. [*p*] Isaiah 22:13.

Phillips Modern English

But in the term "all things" it is quite obvious that God, who brings them all under subjection to Christ, is himself excepted. Nevertheless, when everything has been made subject to God, then shall the Son himself be subject to God, who gave him power over all things. Thus, in the end, shall God be wholly and absolutely God.

15.29 To refuse to believe in the resurrection is both foolish and wicked

Further, you should consider this, that if there is to be no resurrection what is the point of some of you being baptised for the dead by proxy? Why should you be baptised for *dead bodies?* And why should we live a life of such hourly danger? I assure you, by the proud certainty which we share in Christ Jesus our Lord, that I face death every day of my life! And if, to use the popular expression, I have "fought with wild beasts" here in Ephesus, what is the good of an ordeal like that if there is no life after this one? Let us rather eat, drink and be merry, for tomorrow we die!

Don't let yourselves be deceived. It is true that "evil communication corrupt good manners".* Come back to your right senses, and stop sin-

* This is a direct quotation from the Greek dramatist Menander (c. 342–291 B.C.). It must have been a proverbial saying throughout the Greek-speaking Mediterranean countries, and it is still a proverb in English.

Revised Standard Version

feet." But when it says, "All things are put in subjection under him," it is plain that he is excepted who put all things under him. 28 When all things are subjected to him, then the Son himself will also be subjected to him who put all things under him, that God may be everything to every one.
29 Otherwise, what do people mean by being baptized on behalf of the dead? If the dead are not raised at all, why are people baptized on their behalf? 30 Why am I in peril every hour?
31 I protest, brethren, by my pride in you which I have in Christ Jesus our Lord, I die every day!
32 What do I gain if, humanly speaking, I fought with beasts at Ephesus? If the dead are not raised, "Let us eat and drink, for tomorrow we die." 33 Do not be deceived: "Bad company ruins good morals." 34 Come to your right mind,

[z] Greek *he*.

Jerusalem Bible

that *everything is subjected,* this clearly cannot include the One who subjected everything to him. 28 And when everything is subjected to him, then the Son himself will be subject in his turn to the One who subjected all things to him, so that God may be all in all.
29 If this were not true, what do people hope to gain by being baptized for the dead? If the dead are not ever going to be raised, why be baptized on their behalf? 30 What about ourselves? Why are we living under a constant threat? 31 I face death every day, brothers, and I can swear it by the pride that I take in you in Christ Jesus our Lord. 32 If my motives were only human ones, what good would it do me to fight the wild animals at Ephesus? 33 You say: *Let us eat and drink today; tomorrow we shall be dead.*[d] You must stop being led astray: "Bad friends ruin the noblest people."[e] 34 Come to

[d] Is. 22:13. [e] This quotation from Menander's *Thais* may have become a proverb.

New English Bible

all things in subjection under his feet.' But in saying 'all things', it clearly means to exclude God who subordinates them; and when all things are thus subject to him, then the Son himself will also be made subordinate to God who made all things subject to him, and thus God will be all in all.

Again, there are those who receive baptism on behalf of the dead. Why should they do this? If the dead are not raised to life at all, what do they mean by being baptized on their behalf? And we ourselves—why do we face these dangers hour by hour? Every day I die: I swear it by my pride in you, my brothers—for in Christ Jesus our Lord I am proud of you. If, as the saying is, I 'fought wild beasts' at Ephesus, what have I gained by it?[b] If the dead are never raised to life, 'let us eat and drink, for tomorrow we die'.

Make no mistake: 'Bad company is the ruin of a good character.' Come back to a sober and

[b] *Or* If, as men do, I had fought wild beasts at Ephesus, what good would it be to me? *or* If I had been in no better case than one fighting beasts in the arena at Ephesus, what good would it be to me?

King James Version

ness, and sin not; for some have not the knowledge of God: I speak *this* to your shame. 35 But
some *man* will say, How are the dead raised up?
and with what body do they come? 36 *Thou*
fool, that which thou sowest is not quickened,
except it die: 37And that which thou sowest,
thou sowest not that body that shall be, but bare
grain, it may chance of wheat, or of some other
grain: 38 But God giveth it a body as it hath
pleased him, and to every seed his own body.
39All flesh *is* not the same flesh: but *there is* one
kind of flesh of men, another flesh of beasts,
another of fishes, *and* another of birds. 40 *There
are* also celestial bodies, and bodies terrestrial:
but the glory of the celestial *is* one, and the
glory of the terrestrial *is* another. 41 *There is*
one glory of the sun, and another glory of the
moon, and another glory of the stars; for *one*
star differeth from *another* star in glory. 42 So
also *is* the resurrection of the dead. It is sown in
corruption, it is raised in incorruption: 43 It is
sown in dishonour, it is raised in glory: it is

Living Bible

ning. For to your shame I say it, some of you are not even Christians at all and have never really known God.[c]

35 But someone may ask, "How will the dead
be brought back to life again? What kind of
bodies will they have?" 36 What a foolish question! You will find the answer in your own
garden! When you put a seed into the ground it
doesn't grow into a plant unless it "dies" first.
37And when the green shoot comes up out of
the seed, it is very different from the seed you
first planted. For all you put into the ground is
a dry little seed of wheat, or whatever it is you
are planting, 38 then God gives it a beautiful
new body—just the kind he wants it to have; a
different kind of plant grows from each kind of
seed. 39And just as there are different kinds of
seeds and plants, so also there are different kinds
of flesh. Humans, animals, fish, and birds are
all different.

40 The angels[d] in heaven have bodies far
different from ours, and the beauty and the
glory of their bodies is different from the beauty
and the glory of ours. 41 The sun has one kind
of glory while the moon and stars have another
kind. And the stars differ from each other in
their beauty and brightness.

42 In the same way, our earthly bodies which
die and decay are different from the bodies we
shall have when we come back to life again, for
they will never die. 43 The bodies we have now
embarrass us for they become sick and die; but
they will be full of glory when we come back

[c] Or, "there are some who know nothing of God."
[d] Literally, "There are celestial bodies." But perhaps this may refer to the sun, moon, planets, and stars.

Today's English Version

senses and stop your sinful ways. I say this to your shame: some of you do not know God.

The resurrection body

35 Someone will ask, "How can the dead be
raised to life? What kind of body will they have?"
36 You fool! When you plant a seed in the
ground it does not sprout to life unless it dies.
37And what you plant in the ground is a bare
seed, perhaps a grain of wheat, or of some other
kind, not the full-bodied plant that will grow up.
38 God provides that seed with the body he
wishes; he gives each seed its own proper body.

39 And the flesh of living beings is not all the
same kind of flesh; men have one kind of flesh,
animals another, birds another, and fish another.

40 And there are heavenly bodies and earthly
bodies; there is a beauty that belongs to heavenly
bodies, and another kind of beauty that belongs
to earthly bodies. 41 The sun has its own beauty,
the moon another beauty, and the stars a different
beauty; and even among stars there are different
kinds of beauty.

42 This is how it will be when the dead are
raised to life. When the body is buried it is
mortal; when raised, it will be immortal. 43 When
buried, it is ugly and weak; when raised, it will

New International Version

as you ought, and stop sinning; for there are some who are ignorant of God—I say this to your shame.

The resurrection body

35 But someone may ask, "How are the dead
raised? With what kind of body will they come?"
36 How foolish! What you sow does not come to
life unless it dies. 37 When you sow, you do not
plant the body that will be, but just a seed, perhaps of wheat or of something else. 38 But God
gives it a body as he has determined, and to
each kind of seed he gives its own body. 39All
flesh is not the same: Men have one kind of
flesh, animals have another, birds another and
fish another. 40 There are also heavenly bodies
and there are earthly bodies; but the splendor
of the heavenly bodies is one kind, and the
splendor of the earthly bodies is another. 41 The
sun has one kind of splendor, the moon another
and the stars another; and star differs from star
in splendor.

42 So it will be with the resurrection of the
dead. The body that is sown is perishable, it is
raised imperishable; 43 it is sown in dishonor, it
is raised in glory; it is sown in weakness, it is

Phillips Modern English

ning like this! Remember that there are men who have no knowledge of God. You should be ashamed that I have to write like this!

15.35 Parallels in nature help us to grasp the truths of the resurrection

But perhaps someone will ask, "How is the resurrection achieved? With what sort of body do the dead arrive?" Now that is a silly question! In your own experience you know that a seed does not germinate without itself "dying". When you sow a seed you do not sow the "body" that will eventually be produced, but bare grain, of wheat, for example, or one of the other seeds. God gives the seed a "body" according to his laws—a different "body" to each kind of seed.

Then again, all flesh is not identical. There is a difference in the flesh of human beings, animals, birds and fish.

There are bodies which exist in the heavens, and bodies which exist in this world. The splendour of an earthly body is quite a different thing from the splendour of a heavenly body. The sun, the moon and the stars all have their own particular splendour; and one star differs from another in splendour.

There are illustrations here of the raising of the dead. The body is "sown" in corruption; it is raised beyond the reach of corruption. It is "sown" in dishonour; it is raised in splendour.

Revised Standard Version

and sin no more. For some have no knowledge
of God. I say this to your shame.
35 But some one will ask, "How are the dead
raised? With what kind of body do they come?"
36 You foolish man! What you sow does not
come to life unless it dies. 37 And what you
sow is not the body which is to be, but a bare
kernel, perhaps of wheat or of some other grain.
38 But God gives it a body as he has chosen,
and to each kind of seed its own body. 39 For
not all flesh is alike, but there is one kind for
men, another for animals, another for birds, and
another for fish. 40 There are celestial bodies
and there are terrestrial bodies; but the glory of
the celestial is one, and the glory of the terrestrial is another. 41 There is one glory of the sun,
and another glory of the moon, and another
glory of the stars; for star differs from star in
glory.
42 So is it with the resurrection of the dead.
What is sown is perishable, what is raised is imperishable. 43 It is sown in dishonor, it is raised
in glory. It is sown in weakness, it is raised in

Jerusalem Bible

your senses, behave properly, and leave sin alone; there are some of you who seem not to know God at all; you should be ashamed.

The manner of the resurrection

35 Someone may ask, "How are dead people
raised, and what sort of body do they have when
they come back?" 36 They are stupid questions.
Whatever you sow in the ground has to die before it is given new life 37 and the thing that
you sow is not what is going to come; you sow
a bare grain, say of wheat or something like
that, 38 and then God gives it the sort of body
that he has chosen: each sort of seed gets its own
sort of body.
39 Everything that is flesh is not the same
flesh: there is human flesh, animals' flesh, the
flesh of birds and the flesh of fish. 40 Then there
are heavenly bodies and there are earthly bodies;
but the heavenly bodies have a beauty of their
own and the earthly bodies a different one.
41 The sun has its brightness, the moon a different brightness, and the stars a different brightness, and the stars differ from each other in
brightness. 42 It is the same with the resurrection
of the dead: the thing that is sown is perishable
but what is raised is imperishable; 43 the thing
that is sown is contemptible but what is raised

New English Bible

upright life and leave your sinful ways. There are some who know nothing of God; to your shame I say it.

But, you may ask, how are the dead raised? In what kind of body? How foolish! The seed you sow does not come to life unless it has first died; and what you sow is not the body that shall be, but a naked grain, perhaps of wheat, or of some other kind; and God clothes it with the body of his choice, each seed with its own particular body. All flesh is not the same flesh: there is flesh of men, flesh of beasts, of birds, and of fishes—all different. There are heavenly bodies and earthly bodies; and the splendour of the heavenly bodies is one thing, the splendour of the earthly, another. The sun has a splendour of its own, the moon another splendour, and the stars another, for star differs from star in brightness. So it is with the resurrection of the dead. What is sown in the earth as a perishable thing is raised imperishable. Sown in humiliation, it is raised in glory; sown in weak-

King James Version

sown in weakness, it is raised in power: 44 It is
sown a natural body, it is raised a spiritual
body. There is a natural body, and there is a
spiritual body. 45 And so it is written, The first
man Adam was made a living soul; the last
Adam *was made* a quickening spirit. 46 Howbeit
that *was* not first which is spiritual, but that
which is natural; and afterward that which is
spiritual. 47 The first man *is* of the earth, earthy:
the second man *is* the Lord from heaven. 48 As
is the earthy, such *are* they also that are earthy:
and as *is* the heavenly, such *are* they also that
are heavenly. 49 And as we have borne the image
of the earthy, we shall also bear the image of
the heavenly. 50 Now this I say, brethren, that
flesh and blood cannot inherit the kingdom of
God; neither doth corruption inherit incorruption. 51 Behold, I shew you a mystery; We shall
not all sleep, but we shall all be changed, 52 In
a moment, in the twinkling of an eye, at the last
trump: for the trumpet shall sound, and the
dead shall be raised incorruptible, and we shall
be changed. 53 For this corruptible must put on

Living Bible

to life again. Yes, they are weak, dying bodies
now, but when we live again they will be full of
strength. 44 They are just human bodies at death,
but when they come back to life they will be
superhuman bodies. For just as there are natural,
human bodies, there are also supernatural, spiritual bodies.

45 The Scriptures tell us that the first man,
Adam, was given a natural, human body[e] but
Christ[f] is more[g] than that, for he was life-giving
Spirit.

46 First, then, we have these human bodies
and later on God gives us spiritual, heavenly
bodies. 47 Adam was made from the dust of the
earth, but Christ came from heaven above.
48 Every human being has a body just like
Adam's, made of dust, but all who became
Christ's will have the same kind of body as his
—a body from heaven. 49 Just as each of us now
has a body like Adam's, so we shall some day
have a body like Christ's.

50 I tell you this, my brothers: an earthly
body made of flesh and blood cannot get into
God's kingdom. These perishable bodies of ours
are not the right kind to live forever. 51 But I
am telling you this strange and wonderful secret:
we shall not all die, but we shall all be given
new bodies! 52 It will all happen in a moment,
in the twinkling of an eye, when the last trumpet
is blown. For there will be a trumpet blast from
the sky[g] and all the Christians who have died
will suddenly become alive, with new bodies that
will never, never die; and then we who are still
alive shall suddenly have new bodies too. 53 For

[e] Literally, "was made a living soul." [f] Literally, "the last Adam." [g] Implied.

Today's English Version

be beautiful and strong. 44 When buried, it is a
physical body; when raised, it will be a spiritual
body. There is, of course, a physical body, so
there has to be a spiritual body. 45 For the scripture says, "The first man, Adam, was created a
living being"; but the last Adam is the life-giving
Spirit. 46 It is not the spiritual that comes first,
but the physical, and then the spiritual. 47 The
first Adam was made of the dust of the earth; the
second Adam came from heaven. 48 Those who
belong to the earth are like the one who was
made of earth; those who are of heaven are like
the one who came from heaven. 49 Just as we
wear the likeness of the man made of earth, so
we will wear the likeness of the Man from
heaven.

50 What I mean, brothers, is this: what is
made of flesh and blood cannot share in God's
Kingdom, and what is mortal cannot possess
immortality.

51 Listen to this secret: we shall not all die,
but in an instant we shall all be changed, 52 as
quickly as the blinking of an eye, when the last
trumpet sounds. For when it sounds, the dead
will be raised immortal beings, and we shall all
be changed. 53 For what is mortal must clothe

New International Version

raised in power; 44 it is sown a natural body, it
is raised a spiritual body.

If there is a natural body, there is also a spiritual body. 45 So it is written: "The first man
Adam became a living being"[q]; the last Adam,
a life-giving spirit. 46 The spiritual did not come
first, but the natural, and after that the spiritual.
47 The first man was of the dust of the earth,
the second man from heaven. 48 As was the earthly
man, so are those who are of the earth; and as
is the man from heaven, so also are those who
are of heaven. 49 And just as we have borne the
likeness of the earthly man, so we shall bear[r]
the likeness of the man from heaven.

50 I declare to you, brothers, that flesh and
blood cannot inherit the kingdom of God, nor
does the perishable inherit the imperishable.
51 Listen, I tell you a mystery: We shall not all
sleep, but we shall all be changed—52 in a flash,
in the twinkling of an eye, at the last trumpet.
For the trumpet will sound, the dead will be
raised imperishable, and we shall be changed.
53 For the perishable must clothe itself with the

[q] Gen. 2:7. [r] Some early MSS read *so let us bear.*

Phillips Modern English

It is sown in weakness; it is raised in power. It is sown a natural body; it is raised a spiritual body. As there is a natural body so will there be a spiritual body.

It is written, moreover, that:

The first man Adam became a living soul.

So the last Adam is a life-giving Spirit. But we should notice that the "spiritual" does not come first: the order is "natural" first and then "spiritual". The first man came out of the earth, a material creature; the second man came from heaven. For the life of this world men are made like the material man; but for the life that is to come they are made like the one from heaven. So that just as we have been made like the material pattern, so we shall be made like the heavenly pattern. For I assure you, my brothers, it is utterly impossible for flesh and blood to possess the kingdom of God. The transitory could never possess the everlasting.

15.51 The dead and the living will be fitted for immortality

Listen, and I will tell you a secret. We shall not all die, but suddenly, in the twinkling of an eye, every one of us will be changed as the last trumpet sounds! For the trumpet will sound and the dead shall be raised beyond the reach of corruption, and we shall be changed. For this

Revised Standard Version

power. 44 It is sown a physical body, it is raised a spiritual body. If there is a physical body, there is also a spiritual body. 45 Thus it is written, "The first man Adam became a living being"; the last Adam became a life-giving spirit. 46 But it is not the spiritual which is first but the physical, and then the spiritual. 47 The first man was from the earth, a man of dust; the second man is from heaven. 48 As was the man of dust, so are those who are of the dust; and as is the man of heaven, so are those who are of heaven. 49 Just as we have borne the image of the man of dust, we shall[a] also bear the image of the man of heaven. 50 I tell you this, brethren: flesh and blood cannot inherit the kingdom of God, nor does the perishable inherit the imperishable.

51 Lo! I tell you a mystery. We shall not all sleep, but we shall all be changed, 52 in a moment, in the twinkling of an eye, at the last trumpet. For the trumpet will sound, and the dead will be raised imperishable, and we shall be changed. 53 For this perishable nature must

[a] Other ancient authorities read *let us*.

Jerusalem Bible

is glorious; the thing that is sown is weak but what is raised is powerful; 44 when it is sown it embodies the soul, when it is raised it embodies the spirit.

If the soul has its own embodiment, so does the spirit have its own embodiment. 45 The first *man,* Adam, as scripture says, *became a living soul;* but the last Adam has become a life-giving spirit. 46 That is, first the one with the soul, not the spirit, and after that, the one with the spirit. 47 The first man, being from the earth, is earthly by nature; the second man is from heaven. 48 As this earthly man was, so are we on earth; and as the heavenly man is, so are we in heaven. 49 And we, who have been modeled on the earthly man, will be modeled on the heavenly man.

50 Or else, brothers, put it this way: flesh and blood cannot inherit the kingdom of God: and the perishable cannot inherit what lasts for ever. 51 I will tell you something that has been secret: that we are not all going to die, but we shall all be changed. 52 This will be instantaneous, in the twinkling of an eye, when the last trumpet sounds. It will sound, and the dead will be raised, imperishable, and we shall be changed as well, 53 because our present perishable nature must

New English Bible

ness, it is raised in power; sown as an animal body, it is raised as a spiritual body.

If there is such a thing as an animal body, there is also a spiritual body. It is in this sense that Scripture says, 'The first man, Adam, became an animate being', whereas the last Adam has become a life-giving spirit. Observe, the spiritual does not come first; the animal body comes first, and then the spiritual. The first man was made 'of the dust of the earth': the second man is from heaven. The man made of dust is the pattern of all men of dust, and the heavenly man is the pattern of all the heavenly. As we have worn the likeness of the man made of dust, so we shall wear the likeness of the heavenly man.

What I mean, my brothers, is this: flesh and blood can never possess the kingdom of God, and the perishable cannot possess immortality. Listen! I will unfold a mystery: we shall not all die, but we shall all be changed in a flash, in the twinkling of an eye, at the last trumpet-call. For the trumpet will sound, and the dead will rise immortal, and we shall be changed. This

King James Version

incorruption, and this mortal *must* put on immortality. 54 So when this corruptible shall have put on incorruption, and this mortal shall have put on immortality, then shall be brought to pass the saying that is written, Death is swallowed up in victory. 55 O death, where *is* thy sting? O grave, where *is* thy victory? 56 The sting of death *is* sin; and the strength of sin *is* the law. 57 But thanks *be* to God, which giveth us the victory through our Lord Jesus Christ. 58 Therefore, my beloved brethren, be ye steadfast, unmoveable, always abounding in the work of the Lord, forasmuch as ye know that your labour is not in vain in the Lord.

16 Now concerning the collection for the saints, as I have given order to the churches of Galatia, even so do ye. 2 Upon the first *day* of the week let every one of you lay by him in

Living Bible

our earthly bodies, the ones we have now that can die, must be transformed into heavenly bodies that cannot perish but will live forever.

54 When this happens, then at last this Scripture will come true—"Death is swallowed up in victory." 55, 56 O death, where then your victory? Where then your sting? For sin—the sting that causes death—will all be gone; and the law, which reveals our sins, will no longer be our judge. 57 How we thank God for all of this! It is he who makes us victorious through Jesus Christ our Lord!

58 So, my dear brothers, since future victory is sure, be strong and steady, always abounding in the Lord's work, for you know that nothing you do for the Lord is ever wasted as it would be if there were no resurrection.

16 Now here are the directions about the money you are collecting to send to the Christians in Jerusalem;[a] (and, by the way, these are the same directions I gave to the churches in Galatia). 2 On every Lord's Day each of you should put aside something from what you have

[*a*] Implied.

Today's English Version

itself with what is immortal; what will die must clothe itself with what cannot die. 54 So when what is mortal has been clothed with what is immortal, and when what will die has been clothed with what cannot die, then the scripture will come true: "Death is destroyed; victory is complete!"

55 "Where, Death, is your victory?
Where, Death, is your power to hurt?"

56 Death gets its power to hurt from sin, and sin gets its power from the Law. 57 But thanks be to God who gives us the victory through our Lord Jesus Christ!

58 So then, my dear brothers, stand firm and steady. Keep busy always in your work for the Lord, since you know that nothing you do in the Lord's service is ever without value.

The offering for fellow believers

16 Now the matter about the money to be raised to help God's people in Judea: you must do what I told the churches in Galatia to do. 2 Every Sunday each of you must put aside some money, in proportion to what he has

New International Version

imperishable, and the mortal with immortality. 54 When the perishable has been clothed with the imperishable, and the mortal with immortality, then the saying that is written will come true: "Death has been swallowed up in victory."[s]

55 "Where, O death, is your victory?
Where, O death, is your sting?"[t]

56 The sting of death is sin, and the power of sin is the law. 57 But thanks be to God! He gives us the victory through our Lord Jesus Christ.

58 Therefore, my dear brothers, stand firm. Let nothing move you. Always give yourselves fully to the work of the Lord, because you know that your labor in the Lord is not in vain.

The collection for God's people

16 Now about the collection for God's people: Do what I told the Galatian churches to do. 2 On the first day of every week, each one of you should set aside a sum of money in keep-

[*s*] Isaiah 25:8. [*t*] Hosea 13:14.

Phillips Modern English

perishable nature of ours must be wrapped in imperishability, these bodies which are mortal must be wrapped in immortality. So when the perishable is lost in the imperishable, the mortal lost in the immortal, this scripture will come true:

Death is swallowed up in victory.

Where now, O death, is your victory; where now is your stinging power? It is sin which gives death its sting, and it is the Law which gives sin its power. All thanks to God, then, who gives us the victory over these things through our Lord Jesus Christ!

And so, brothers of mine, stand firm! Let nothing move you as you busy yourselves in the Lord's work. Be sure that nothing you do for him is ever lost or ever wasted.

16.1 The matter of the fund: my own immediate plans

Now as far as the fund for Christians in need is concerned, I should like you to follow the same rule that I gave to the Galatian church.

On the first day of the week let everyone put so much by him, according to his financial pros-

Revised Standard Version

put on the imperishable, and this mortal nature
must put on immortality. 54 When the perishable puts on the imperishable, and the mortal
puts on immortality, then shall come to pass the
saying that is written:
"Death is swallowed up in victory."
55 "O death, where is thy victory?
O death, where is thy sting?"
56 The sting of death is sin, and the power of
sin is the law. 57 But thanks be to God, who
gives us the victory through our Lord Jesus
Christ.
58 Therefore, my beloved brethren, be steadfast, immovable, always abounding in the work
of the Lord, knowing that in the Lord your
labor is not in vain.

16 Now concerning the contribution for the
saints: as I directed the churches of
Galatia, so you also are to do. 2 On the first day
of every week, each of you is to put something

Jerusalem Bible

put on imperishability and this mortal nature must put on immortality.

A hymn of triumph. Conclusion

54 When this perishable nature has put on imperishability, and when this mortal nature has
put on immortality, then the words of scripture
will come true: *Death is swallowed up in victory.*
55 *Death, where is your* victory? *Death, where is*
your sting? [f] 56 Now the sting of death is sin, and
sin gets its power from the Law. 57 So let us
thank God for giving us the victory through our
Lord Jesus Christ.
58 Never give in then, my dear brothers, never
admit defeat; keep on working at the Lord's
work always, knowing that, in the Lord, you
cannot be laboring in vain.

Conclusion

Commendations. Greetings

16 Now about the collection made for the
saints: you are to do as I told the churches
in Galatia to do. 2 Every Sunday, each one of
you must put aside what he can afford, so that

[f] A free version; see Ho. 13:14.

New English Bible

perishable being must be clothed with the imperishable, and what is mortal must be clothed with immortality. And when[a] our mortality has been clothed with immortality, then the saying of Scripture will come true: 'Death is swallowed up; victory is won!' 'O Death, where is your victory? O Death, where is your sting?' The sting of death is sin, and sin gains its power from the law; but, God be praised, he gives us the victory through our Lord Jesus Christ.

Therefore, my beloved brothers, stand firm and immovable, and work for the Lord always, work without limit, since you know that in the Lord your labour cannot be lost.

Christian giving

16 And now about the collection in aid of God's people: you should follow my directions to our congregations in Galatia. Every Sunday each of you is to put aside and keep by

[a] *Some witnesses insert* our perishable nature has been clothed with the imperishable, and . . .

King James Version

store, as *God* hath prospered him, that there be no gatherings when I come. 3And when I come, whomsoever ye shall approve by *your* letters, them will I send to bring your liberality unto Jerusalem. 4And if it be meet that I go also, they shall go with me. 5 Now I will come unto you, when I shall pass through Macedonia: for I do pass through Macedonia. 6And it may be that I will abide, yea, and winter with you, that ye may bring me on my journey whithersoever I go. 7 For I will not see you now by the way; but I trust to tarry a while with you, if the Lord permit. 8 But I will tarry at Ephesus until Pentecost. 9 For a great door and effectual is opened unto me, and *there are* many adversaries. 10 Now if Timotheus come, see that he may be with you without fear: for he worketh the work of the Lord, as I also *do*. 11 Let no man therefore despise him: but conduct him forth in peace, that he may come unto me: for I look for him with the brethren. 12As touching *our* brother Apollos, I greatly desired him to come unto you with the brethren: but his will was not at all to come at this time; but he will come

Living Bible

earned during the week, and use it for this offering. The amount depends on how much the Lord has helped you earn. Don't wait until I get there and then try to collect it all at once. 3 When I come I will send your loving gift with a letter to Jerusalem, to be taken there by trustworthy messengers you yourselves will choose. 4And if it seems wise for me to go along too, then we can travel together.

5 I am coming to visit you after I have been to Macedonia first, but I will be staying there only for a little while. 6 It could be that I will stay longer with you, perhaps all winter, and then you can send me on to my next destination. 7 This time I don't want to make just a passing visit and then go right on; I want to come and stay awhile, if the Lord will let me. 8 I will be staying here at Ephesus until the holiday of Pentecost, 9 for there is a wide open door for me to preach and teach here. So much is happening, but there are many enemies.

10 If Timothy comes make him feel at home, for he is doing the Lord's work just as I am. 11 Don't let anyone despise or ignore him [because he is young[b]], but send him back to me happy with his time among you; I am looking forward to seeing him soon, along with the others who are returning. 12 I begged Apollos to visit you along with the others, but he thought that it was not at all God's will for him to go now; he will be seeing you later on when he has the opportunity.

[*b*] Implied in 1 Timothy 4:12.

Today's English Version

earned, and save it up, so there will be no need to collect money when I come. 3After I come I shall send the men you have approved, with letters of introduction, to take your gift to Jerusalem. 4 If it seems worthwhile for me to go, then they will go along with me.

Paul's plans

5 I shall come to you after I have gone through Macedonia—because I am going through Macedonia. 6 I shall probably spend some time with you, perhaps the whole winter, and then you can help me to continue my trip, wherever it is I shall go next. 7 I do not want to see you just briefly in passing. I hope to spend quite a long time with you, if the Lord allows.

8 But I will stay here in Ephesus until the day of Pentecost. 9 There is a real opportunity here for great and worthwhile work, even though there are many opponents.

10 If Timothy comes your way, however, be sure to make him feel welcome among you, because he is working for the Lord, just as I am. 11 No one is to look down on him, but you must help him continue his trip in peace, so that he will come back to me; for I am expecting him back with the brothers.

12 Now, about brother Apollos. I have often encouraged him to visit you with the other brothers, but he is not completely convinced that he should go right now. When he gets the chance, however, he will go.

New International Version

ing with his income, saving it up, so that when I come no collections will have to be made. 3 Then, when I arrive, I will give letters of introduction to the men you approve and send them with your gift to Jerusalem. 4 If it seems advisable for me to go also, they will accompany me.

Personal requests

5 After I go through Macedonia, I will come to you—for I will be going through Macedonia. 6 Perhaps I will stay with you awhile, or even spend the winter, so that you can help me on my journey, wherever I go. 7 I do not want to see you now and make only a passing visit; I hope to spend some time with you, if the Lord permits. 8 But I will stay on at Ephesus until Pentecost, 9 because a great door for effective work has opened to me, and there are many who oppose me.

10 If Timothy comes, see to it that he has nothing to fear while he is with you, for he is carrying on the work of the Lord, just as I am. 11 No one, then, should refuse to accept him. Send him on his way in peace so that he may return to me. I am expecting him along with the brothers.

12 Now about our brother Apollos: I strongly urged him to go to you with the brothers. He was quite unwilling to go now, but he will go when he has the opportunity.

Phillips Modern English

perity, so that there will be no need for collections when I come. Then, on my arrival, I will send whomever you approve to take your gift, with my written recommendation, to Jerusalem. If it seems right for me to go as well, we will make up a party together. I shall come to you after my intended journey through Macedonia and I may stay with you awhile or even spend the winter with you. Then you can see me on my way—wherever it is that I go next. I don't wish to see you now, for it would merely be in passing, and I hope to spend some time with you, if it is the Lord's will. I shall stay here in Ephesus until the feast of Pentecost, for I have been given a great opportunity of doing useful work, and there are many against me.

16.10 News of Timothy and Apollos

If Timothy comes to you, put him at his ease. He is as genuine a worker for the Lord as I am, and there is therefore no reason to look down on him. Send him on his way in peace, for I am expecting him to come to me here with the other Christian brothers. As for our brother Apollos I pressed him strongly to go to you with the rest, but it was definitely not God's will for him to do so then. However, he will come to you as soon as an opportunity occurs.

Revised Standard Version

aside and store it up, as he may prosper, so that
contributions need not be made when I come.
3 And when I arrive, I will send those whom
you accredit by letter to carry your gift to Jerusalem. 4 If it seems advisable that I should go
also, they will accompany me.
5 I will visit you after passing through Macedonia, for I intend to pass through Macedonia,
6 and perhaps I will stay with you or even spend
the winter, so that you may speed me on my
journey, wherever I go. 7 For I do not want to
see you now just in passing; I hope to spend
some time with you, if the Lord permits. 8 But
I will stay in Ephesus until Pentecost, 9 for a
wide door for effective work has opened to me,
and there are many adversaries.
10 When Timothy comes, see that you put
him at ease among you, for he is doing the work
of the Lord, as I am. 11 So let no one despise
him. Speed him on his way in peace, that he
may return to me; for I am expecting him with
the brethren.
12 As for our brother Apollos, I strongly
urged him to visit you with the other brethren,
but it was not at all his will [b] to come now. He
will come when he has opportunity.

[b] Or *God's will for him.*

Jerusalem Bible

collections need not be made after I have come.
3 When I am with you, I will send your offering
to Jerusalem by the hand of whatever men you
give letters of reference to; 4 if it seems worth
while for me to go too, they can travel with me.
5 I shall be coming to you after I have passed
through Macedonia—and I am doing no more
than pass through Macedonia—6 and I may be
staying with you, perhaps even passing the
winter, to make sure that it is you who send me
on my way wherever my travels take me. 7 As
you see, I do not want to make it only a passing
visit to you and I hope to spend some time with
you, the Lord permitting. 8 In any case I shall
be staying at Ephesus until Pentecost 9 because
a big and important door has opened for my
work and there is a great deal of opposition.
10 If Timothy comes, show him that he has
nothing to be afraid of in you: like me, he is
doing the Lord's work, 11 and nobody is to be
scornful of him. Send him happily on his way
to come back to me; the brothers and I are waiting for him. 12 As for our brother Apollos, I
begged him to come to you with the brothers but
he was quite firm that he did not want to go yet
and he will come as soon as he can.

New English Bible

him a sum in proportion to his gains, so that there may be no collecting when I come. When I arrive, I will give letters of introduction to persons approved by you, and send them to carry your gift to Jerusalem. If it should seem worth while for me to go as well, they shall go with me.

I shall come to Corinth after passing through Macedonia—for I am travelling by way of Macedonia—and I may stay with you, perhaps even for the whole winter, and then you can help me on my way wherever I go next. I do not want this to be a flying visit; I hope to spend some time with you, if the Lord permits. But I shall remain at Ephesus until Whitsuntide, for a great opportunity has opened for effective work, and there is much opposition.

If Timothy comes, see that you put him at his ease; for it is the Lord's work that he is engaged upon, as I am myself; so no one must slight him. Send him happily on his way to join me, since I am waiting for him with our friends. As for our friend Apollos, I urged him strongly to go to Corinth with the others, but he was quite determined not to go[a] at present; he will go when opportunity offers.

[a] *Or* but it was by no means the will of God that he should go . . .

King James Version

when he shall have convenient time. 13 Watch
ye, stand fast in the faith, quit you like men, be
strong. 14 Let all your things be done with
charity. 15 I beseech you, brethren, (ye know
the house of Stephanas, that it is the firstfruits
of Achaia, and *that* they have addicted themselves to the ministry of the saints,) 16 That ye
submit yourselves unto such, and to every one
that helpeth with *us*, and laboureth. 17 I am glad
of the coming of Stephanas and Fortunatus and
Achaicus: for that which was lacking on your
part they have supplied. 18 For they have refreshed my spirit and yours: therefore acknowledge ye them that are such. 19 The churches of
Asia salute you. Aquila and Priscilla salute you
much in the Lord, with the church that is in
their house. 20 All the brethren greet you. Greet
ye one another with a holy kiss. 21 The salutation of *me* Paul with mine own hand. 22 If any
man love not the Lord Jesus Christ, let him be
Anathema, Maran atha. 23 The grace of our
Lord Jesus Christ *be* with you. 24 My love *be*
with you all in Christ Jesus. Amen.

The first *epistle* to the Corinthians was written from Philippi by Stephanas, and Fortunatus, and Achaicus, and Timotheus.

Living Bible

13 Keep your eyes open for spiritual danger;
stand true to the Lord; act like men; be strong;
14 and whatever you do, do it with kindness and
love.
15 Do you remember Stephanas and his family? They were the first to become Christians in
Greece and they are spending their lives helping
and serving Christians everywhere. 16 Please follow their instructions and do everything you can
to help them as well as all others like them who
work hard at your side with such real devotion.
17 I am so glad that Stephanas, Fortunatus, and
Achaicus have arrived here for a visit. They
have been making up for the help you aren't
here to give me. 18 They have cheered me greatly
and have been a wonderful encouragement to
me, as I am sure they were to you, too. I hope
you properly appreciate the work of such men
as these.
19 The churches here in Asia send you their
loving greetings. Aquila and Priscilla send you
their love and so do all the others who meet in
their home for their church service. 20 All the
friends here have asked me to say "hello" to
you for them. And give each other a loving handshake when you meet.
21 I will write these final words of this letter
with my own hand: 22 if anyone does not love
the Lord, that person is cursed. Lord Jesus,
come! 23 May the love and favor of the Lord
Jesus Christ rest upon you. 24 My love to all
of you, for we all belong to Christ Jesus.

Sincerely,
Paul

Today's English Version

Final words

13 Be alert, stand firm in the faith, be brave,
be strong. 14 Do all your work in love.
15 You know about Stephanas and his family; they are the first Christian converts in
Greece, and have given themselves to the
service of God's people. I beg you, my brothers, 16 to follow the leadership of such people
as these, and of anyone else who works and
serves with them.
17 I am happy over the coming of Stephanas,
Fortunatus, and Achaicus; they have made up
for your absence, 18 and have cheered me up,
just as they cheered you up. Such men as these
deserve notice.
19 The churches in the province of Asia send
you their greetings; Aquila and Priscilla and the
church that meets in their house send warm
Christian greetings. 20 All the brothers here send
greetings.
Greet one another with a brotherly kiss.
21 With my own hand I write this: *Greetings
from Paul.*
22 Whoever does not love the Lord—a curse
on him!
Marana tha—Our Lord, come!
23 The grace of the Lord Jesus be with you.
24 My love be with you all in Christ Jesus.

New International Version

13 Be on your guard; stand firm in the faith;
be men of courage; be strong. 14 Do everything
in love.
15 You know that the household of Stephanas
were the first converts in Achaia, and they have
devoted themselves to the service of the saints.
I urge you, brothers, 16 to submit to such as
these and to everyone who joins in the work and
labors at it. 17 I was glad when Stephanas, Fortunatus and Achaicus arrived, because they have
supplied what was lacking from you. 18 For
they refreshed my spirit and yours also. Such
men deserve recognition.

Final greetings

19 The churches in the province of Asia send
you greetings. Aquila and Priscilla[u] greet you
warmly in the Lord, and so does the church
that meets at their house. 20 All the brothers
here send you greetings. Greet one another with
a holy kiss.
21 I, Paul, write this greeting in my own hand.
22 If anyone does not love the Lord—a curse
be on him. Come, O Lord! [v]
23 The grace of the Lord Jesus be with you.
24 My love to all of you in Christ Jesus.

[u] Greek *Prisca.* [v] The expression *Come, O Lord!* is in Aramaic *Marana tha!*

Phillips Modern English

16.13 A little sermon in a nutshell!

Be on your guard, stand firm in the faith, live like men, be strong! Let everything that you do be done in love.

16.15 A request, and final greetings

Now I have a request to make of you, my brothers.

You remember the household of Stephanas, the first men of Achaia to be won for Christ? Well, they have made up their minds to devote their lives to looking after Christian brothers. I do beg you to recognise such men, and to extend your recognition to anyone who works and labours with them.

I am very glad that Stephanas, Fortunatus and Achaicus have arrived. They have made up for what you were unable to do. They have relieved my anxiety and yours. You should appreciate having men like that!

Greetings from the churches of Asia. Aquila and Prisca send you their warmest Christian greetings and so does the church that meets in their house. All the Christians here send greetings. I should like you to shake hands all round as a sign of Christian love.

Here is my own greeting, written by me, Paul. "If any man does not love the Lord, a curse be on him; may the Lord soon come!"

The grace of the Lord Jesus be with you and my love be with you all in Christ Jesus.

Revised Standard Version

13 Be watchful, stand firm in your faith, be
courageous, be strong. 14 Let all that you do be
done in love.
15 Now, brethren, you know that the household of Stephanas were the first converts in
Achaia, and they have devoted themselves to
the service of the saints; 16 I urge you to be
subject to such men and to every fellow worker
and laborer. 17 I rejoice at the coming of
Stephanas and Fortunatus and Achaicus, because they have made up for your absence;
18 for they refreshed my spirit as well as yours.
Give recognition to such men.
19 The churches of Asia send greetings.
Aquila and Prisca, together with the church in
their house, send you hearty greetings in the
Lord. 20 All the brethren send greetings. Greet
one another with a holy kiss.

21 I, Paul, write this greeting with my own
hand. 22 If any one has no love for the Lord,
let him be accursed. Our Lord, come! [c] 23 The
grace of the Lord Jesus be with you. 24 My love
be with you all in Christ Jesus. Amen.

[c] Greek *Maranatha.*

Jerusalem Bible

13 Be awake to all the dangers; stay firm in
the faith; be brave and be strong. 14 Let everything you do be done in love.
15 There is something else to ask you, brothers. You know how the Stephanas family, who
were the first fruits of Achaia, have really
worked hard to help the saints. 16 Well, I want
you in your turn to put yourselves at the service
of people like this, and anyone who helps and
works with them. 17 I am delighted that Stephanas, Fortunatus and Achaicus have arrived; they
make up for your absence. 18 They have settled
my mind, and yours too; I hope you appreciate
men like this.
19 All the churches of Asia send you greetings. Aquila and Prisca, with the church that
meets at their house, send you their warmest
wishes, in the Lord. 20 All the brothers send you
their greetings. Greet one another with a holy
kiss.
21 This greeting is in my own hand—Paul.
22 If anyone does not love the Lord, a curse
on him. *"Maran atha."* [g]
23 The grace of the Lord Jesus be with you.
24 My love is with you all in Christ Jesus.

[g] Aramaic. "The Lord is coming" or "Lord, come."

New English Bible

Be alert; stand firm in the faith; be valiant and strong. Let all you do be done in love.

I have a request to make of you, my brothers. You know that the Stephanas family were the first converts in Achaia, and have laid themselves out to serve God's people. I wish you to give their due position to such persons, and indeed to everyone who labours hard at our common task. It is a great pleasure to me that Stephanas, Fortunatus, and Achaicus have arrived, because they have done what you had no chance to do; they have relieved my mind—and no doubt yours too. Such men deserve recognition.

Greetings from the congregations in Asia. Many greetings in the Lord from Aquila and Prisca and the congregation at their house. Greetings from all the brothers. Greet one another with the kiss of peace.

This greeting is in my own hand—PAUL.

If anyone does not love the Lord, let him be outcast.

Marana tha—Come, O Lord!

The grace of the Lord Jesus Christ be with you.

My love to you all in Christ Jesus. Amen.

King James Version

THE SECOND EPISTLE OF PAUL THE APOSTLE TO THE CORINTHIANS

1 Paul, an apostle of Jesus Christ by the will of God, and Timothy *our* brother, unto the church of God which is at Corinth, with all the saints which are in all Achaia: 2 Grace *be* to you, and peace, from God our Father, and

Living Bible

2 CORINTHIANS

1 Dear friends,
This letter is from me, Paul, appointed by God to be Jesus Christ's messenger; and from our dear brother Timothy. We are writing to all of you Christians there in Corinth and throughout Greece.[a] 2 May God our Father and the Lord Jesus Christ mightily bless each one of you, and give you peace.

[a] Or, "throughout Achaia."

Today's English Version

PAUL'S SECOND LETTER TO THE CORINTHIANS

1 From Paul, apostle of Christ Jesus by God's will, and from our brother Timothy—
To the church of God in Corinth, and to all God's people in all Greece:
2 May God our Father and the Lord Jesus Christ give you grace and peace.

New International Version

2 CORINTHIANS

1 Paul, an apostle of Christ Jesus by the will of God, and Timothy our brother,
To the church of God in Corinth, together with all the saints throughout Achaia:
2 Grace and peace to you from God our Father and the Lord Jesus Christ.

Phillips Modern English

THE SECOND LETTER TO THE CHRISTIANS AT CORINTH

This letter comes to you from Paul, God's messenger for Christ Jesus by the will of God, and from brother Timothy, and is addressed to the church of God in Corinth and all Christians throughout Achaia.

May grace and peace come to you from God our Father and from the Lord Jesus Christ.

Revised Standard Version

THE SECOND LETTER OF PAUL TO THE CORINTHIANS

1 Paul, an apostle of Christ Jesus by the will of God, and Timothy our brother.

To the church of God which is at Corinth, with all the saints who are in the whole of Achaia:

2 Grace to you and peace from God our Father and the Lord Jesus Christ.

Jerusalem Bible

THE SECOND LETTER OF PAUL TO THE CHURCH AT CORINTH

2 CORINTHIANS

Introduction

Address and greetings. Thanksgiving

1 From Paul, appointed by God to be an apostle of Christ Jesus, and from Timothy, one of the brothers, to the church of God at Corinth and to all the saints in the whole of Achaia. 2 Grace and peace to you from God our Father and the Lord Jesus Christ.

New English Bible

THE SECOND LETTER OF PAUL TO THE CORINTHIANS

Personal religion and the ministry

1 From Paul, apostle of Christ Jesus by God's will, and our colleague Timothy, to the congregation of God's people at Corinth, together with all who are dedicated to him throughout the whole of Achaia.

Grace and peace to you from God our Father and the Lord Jesus Christ.

King James Version

from the Lord Jesus Christ. 3 Blessed *be* God,
even the Father of our Lord Jesus Christ, the
Father of mercies, and the God of all comfort;
4 Who comforteth us in all our tribulation, that
we may be able to comfort them which are in
any trouble, by the comfort wherewith we ourselves are comforted of God. 5 For as the sufferings of Christ abound in us, so our consolation also aboundeth by Christ. 6 And whether we
be afflicted, *it is* for your consolation and salvation, which is effectual in the enduring of the
same sufferings which we also suffer: or whether
we be comforted, *it is* for your consolation and
salvation. 7 And our hope of you *is* steadfast,
knowing, that as ye are partakers of the sufferings, so *shall ye be* also of the consolation. 8 For
we would not, brethren, have you ignorant of
our trouble which came to us in Asia, that we
were pressed out of measure, above strength,
insomuch that we despaired even of life: 9 But
we had the sentence of death in ourselves, that
we should not trust in ourselves, but in God
which raiseth the dead: 10 Who delivered us

Living Bible

3, 4 What a wonderful God we have—he is
the Father of our Lord Jesus Christ, the source
of every mercy, and the one who so wonderfully comforts and strengthens us in our hardships and trials. And why does he do this? So
that when others are troubled, needing our sympathy and encouragement, we can pass on to
them this same help and comfort God has given
us. 5 You can be sure that the more we undergo
sufferings for Christ, the more he will shower
us with his comfort and encouragement. 6, 7 We
are in deep trouble for bringing you God's comfort and salvation. But in our trouble God has
comforted us—and this, too, to help you: to
show you from our personal experience how
God will tenderly comfort you when you undergo
these same sufferings. He will give you the
strength to endure.

8 I think you ought to know, dear brothers,
about the hard time we went through in Asia.
We were really crushed and overwhelmed, and
feared we would never live through it. 9 We felt
we were doomed to die and saw how powerless
we were to help ourselves; but that was good,
for then we put everything into the hands of
God, who alone could save us, for he can even
raise the dead. 10 And he did help us, and saved

Today's English Version

Paul gives thanks to God

3 Let us give thanks to the God and Father
of our Lord Jesus Christ, the merciful Father,
the God from whom all help comes! 4 He helps
us in all our troubles, so that we are able to
help those who have all kinds of troubles, using
the same help that we ourselves have received
from God. 5 Just as we have a share in Christ's
many sufferings, so also through Christ we share
in his great help. 6 If we suffer, it is for your
help and salvation; if we are helped, then you
too are helped and given the strength to endure
with patience the same sufferings that we also
endure. 7 So our hope in you is never shaken;
we know that just as you share in our sufferings,
you also share in the help we receive.

8 We want to remind you, brothers, of the
trouble we had in the province of Asia. The
burdens laid upon us were so great and so
heavy, that we gave up all hope of living. 9 We
felt that the sentence of death had been passed
against us. But this happened so that we should
rely, not on ourselves, but only on God, who
raises the dead. 10 From such terrible dangers

New International Version

The God of all comfort

3 Praise be to the God and Father of our
Lord Jesus Christ, the Father of compassion and
the God of all comfort, 4 who comforts us in all
our troubles, so that we can comfort those in any
trouble with the comfort we ourselves have received from God. 5 For just as the sufferings of
Christ flow over into our lives, so also through
Christ our comfort overflows. 6 If we are distressed, it is for your comfort and salvation; if
we are comforted, it is for your comfort, which
produces in you patient endurance of the same
sufferings we suffer. 7 And our hope for you is
firm, because we know that just as you share in
our sufferings, so also you share in our comfort.

8 We do not want you to be uninformed,
brothers, about the hardships we suffered in the
province of Asia. We were under great pressure,
far beyond our ability to endure, so that we
despaired even of life. 9 Indeed, in our hearts
we felt the sentence of death. But this happened
that we might not rely on ourselves but on God,
who raises the dead. 10 He has delivered us from

Phillips Modern English

1.3 God's encouragements are adequate for all life's troubles

Thank God, the Father of our Lord Jesus Christ, that he is our Father and the source of all mercy and comfort. For he gives us comfort in all our trials so that we in turn may be able to give the same sort of strong sympathy to others in their troubles that we receive from God. Indeed, experience shows that the more we share in Christ's immeasurable suffering the more we are able to give of his encouragement. This means that if we experience trouble it is for your comfort and spiritual protection; for if we ourselves have been comforted we know how to encourage you to endure patiently the same sort of troubles that we ourselves endure. We are quite confident that if you have to suffer troubles as we have done, then, like us, you will find the comfort and encouragement of God.

1.8 Man's extremity is God's opportunity

We should like you, our brothers, to know something of the trouble we went through in Asia. At that time we were completely overwhelmed, the burden was more than we could bear, in fact we told ourselves that this was the end. Yet we believe now that we had this sense of impending disaster so that we might learn to trust, not in ourselves, but in God who can raise the dead. It was God who preserved us from such

Revised Standard Version

3 Blessed be the God and Father of our Lord
Jesus Christ, the Father of mercies and God of
all comfort, 4 who comforts us in all our affliction, so that we may be able to comfort those
who are in any affliction, with the comfort with
which we ourselves are comforted by God. 5 For
as we share abundantly in Christ's sufferings, so
through Christ we share abundantly in comfort
too.[a] 6 If we are afflicted, it is for your comfort
and salvation; and if we are comforted, it is for
your comfort, which you experience when you
patiently endure the same sufferings that we
suffer. 7 Our hope for you is unshaken; for we
know that as you share in our sufferings, you
will also share in our comfort.
8 For we do not want you to be ignorant,
brethren, of the affliction we experienced in
Asia; for we were so utterly, unbearably crushed
that we despaired of life itself. 9 Why, we felt
that we had received the sentence of death; but
that was to make us rely not on ourselves but
on God who raises the dead; 10 he delivered us

[a] Or *For as the sufferings of Christ abound for us, so also our comfort abounds through Christ.*

Jerusalem Bible

3 Blessed be the God and Father of our Lord
Jesus Christ, a gentle Father and the God of
all consolation, 4 who comforts us in all our
sorrows, so that we can offer others, in their
sorrows, the consolation that we have received
from God ourselves. 5 Indeed, as the sufferings
of Christ overflow to us, so, through Christ, does
our consolation overflow. 6 When we are made
to suffer, it is for your consolation and salvation.
When, instead, we are comforted, this should be
a consolation to you, supporting you in patiently
bearing the same sufferings as we bear. 7 And our
hope for you is confident, since we know that,
sharing our sufferings, you will also share our
consolations.
8 For we should like you to realize, brothers,
that the things we had to undergo in Asia were
more of a burden than we could carry, so that
we despaired of coming through alive. 9 Yes, we
were carrying our own death warrant with us,
and it has taught us not to rely on ourselves but
only on God, who raises the dead to life. 10 And
he saved us from dying, as he will save us again;

New English Bible

Praise be to the God and Father of our Lord Jesus Christ, the all-merciful Father, the God whose consolation never fails us! He comforts us in all our troubles, so that we in turn may be able to comfort others in any trouble of theirs and to share with them the consolation we ourselves receive from God. As Christ's cup of suffering overflows, and we suffer with him, so also through Christ our consolation overflows. If distress be our lot, it is the price we pay for your consolation, for your salvation; if our lot be consolation, it is to help us to bring you comfort, and strength to face with fortitude the same sufferings we now endure. And our hope for you is firmly grounded;[a] for we know that if you have part in the suffering, you have part also in the divine consolation.

In saying this, we should like you to know, dear friends, how serious was the trouble that came upon us in the province of Asia. The burden of it was far too heavy for us to bear, so heavy that we even despaired of life. Indeed, we felt in our hearts that we had received a death-sentence. This was meant to teach us not to place reliance on ourselves, but on God who raises the dead. From such mortal peril God

[a] *Some witnesses give these clauses* If distress . . . firmly grounded *in different sequence.*

King James Version

from so great a death, and doth deliver: in
whom we trust that he will yet deliver *us;* 11 Ye
also helping together by prayer for us, that for
the gift *bestowed* upon us by the means of many
persons thanks may be given by many on our
behalf. 12 For our rejoicing is this, the testimony of our conscience, that in simplicity and
godly sincerity, not with fleshly wisdom, but by
the grace of God, we have had our conversation in the world, and more abundantly to you-
ward. 13 For we write none other things unto
you, than what ye read or acknowledge; and I
trust ye shall acknowledge even to the end;
14 As also ye have acknowledged us in part, that
we are your rejoicing, even as ye also *are* ours
in the day of the Lord Jesus. 15 And in this
confidence I was minded to come unto you before, that ye might have a second benefit;
16 And to pass by you into Macedonia, and to
come again out of Macedonia unto you, and of

Living Bible

us from a terrible death; yes, and we expect
him to do it again and again. 11 But you must
help us too, by praying for us. For much thanks
and praise will go to God from you who see his
wonderful answers to your prayers for our safety!
12 We are so glad that we can say with utter
honesty that in all our dealings we have been
pure and sincere, quietly depending upon the
Lord for his help, and not on our own skills.
And that is even more true, if possible, about
the way we have acted toward you. 13, 14 My letters have been straightforward and sincere; nothing is written between the lines! And even
though you don't know me very well (I hope
someday you will), I want you to try to accept me and be proud of me, as you already
are to some extent; just as I shall be of you on
that day when our Lord Jesus comes back again.
15, 16 It was because I was so sure of your understanding and trust that I planned to stop and
see you on my way to Macedonia, as well as
afterwards when I returned, so that I could be

Today's English Version

of death he saved us, and will save us; and we
have placed our hope in him that he will save us
again, 11 as you help us by means of your prayers for us. So it will be that the many prayers
for us will be answered, and God will bless us;
and many will raise their voices to him in
thanksgiving for us.

The change in Paul's plans

12 This is what we are proud of: our conscience assures us that our lives in this world,
and especially our relations with you, have been
ruled by God-given frankness and sincerity, by
the power of God's grace, and not by human
wisdom. 13 We write to you only what you can
read and understand. And I hope that you will
come to understand completely 14 what you
now understand only in part, so that in the Day
of the Lord Jesus you can be as proud of us as
we shall be of you.
15 I was so sure of all this that I made plans
at first to visit you in order that you might be
blessed twice. 16 For I planned to visit you on
my way to Macedonia and again on my way

New International Version

such a deadly peril, and he will deliver us. On
him we have set our hope that he will continue
to deliver us, 11 as you help us by your prayers.
Then many will give thanks on our[a] behalf for
the gracious favor granted us in answer to the
prayers of many.

Paul's change of plans

12 Now this is our boast: Our conscience
testifies that we have conducted ourselves in the
world, and especially in our relations with you,
in the holiness and sincerity that are from God.
We have done so not according to worldly wisdom but according to God's grace. 13 For we
do not write you anything you cannot read or
understand. And I hope that, 14 as you have
understood us in part, you will come to understand fully that you can boast of us just as we
will boast of you in the day of the Lord Jesus.
15 Because I was confident of this, I planned
to visit you first so that you might benefit twice.
16 I planned to visit you on my way to Macedonia and to come back to you from Macedonia,

[a] Many MSS read *your*.

Phillips Modern English

deadly perils, and it is he who still preserves us. We put our full trust in him and he will keep us safe in the future. Here you can co-operate by praying for us, so that the help that is given to us in answer to many prayers will mean that many will thank God for our preservation.

1.12 Our dealings with you have always been straightforward

Now it is a matter of pride to us—endorsed by our conscience—that our activities in this world, particularly our dealings with you, have been absolutely above-board and sincere before God. They have not been marked by any worldly wisdom, but by the grace of God. Our letters to you have no double meaning—they mean just what you understand them to mean when you read them. I hope you will always understand these letters. Just as I believe that you have partially understood me, so you will come to realise that you can be as honestly proud of us, as we are of you, on the day of the Lord Jesus.

1.15 Change of plan does not necessarily mean fickleness of heart

Trusting you, and believing that you trusted us, our original plan was to pay you a visit first, and give you a double "treat". We meant to come here to Macedonia after first visiting you, and then to visit you again on leaving here. You

Revised Standard Version

from so deadly a peril, and he will deliver us; on
him we have set our hope that he will deliver
us again. 11 You also must help us by prayer,
so that many will give thanks on our behalf for
the blessing granted us in answer to many
prayers.
12 For our boast is this, the testimony of our
conscience that we have behaved in the world,
and still more toward you, with holiness and
godly sincerity, not by earthly wisdom but by
the grace of God. 13 For we write you nothing
but what you can read and understand; I hope
you will understand fully, 14 as you have understood in part, that you can be proud of us as
we can be of you, on the day of the Lord Jesus.
15 Because I was sure of this, I wanted to
come to you first, so that you might have a
double pleasure;[b] 16 I wanted to visit you on
my way to Macedonia, and to come back to you

[b] Other ancient authorities read *favor*.

Jerusalem Bible

yes, that is our firm hope in him, that in the
future he will save us again. 11 You must all
join in the prayers for us; the more people there
are asking for help for us, the more will be giving thanks when it is granted to us.

I. Some recent events reviewed

Why Paul changed his plans

12 There is one thing we are proud of, and
our conscience tells us it is true: that we have
always treated everybody, and especially you,
with the reverence and sincerity which come
from God, and by the grace of God we have
done this without ulterior motives. 13 There are
no hidden meanings in our letters besides what
you can read for yourselves and understand.
14 And I hope that, although you do not know
us very well yet, you will have to come to recognize, when the day of our Lord Jesus comes,
that you can be as proud of us as we are of you.
15 Because I was so sure of this, I had meant
to come to you first, so that you would benefit
doubly; 16 staying with you before going to
Macedonia and coming back to you again on

New English Bible

delivered us; and he will deliver us again,[s] he on whom our hope is fixed. Yes, he will continue to deliver us, if you will co-operate by praying for us. Then, with so many people praying for our deliverance, there will be many to give thanks on our behalf for the gracious favour God has shown towards us.

There is one thing we are proud of: our conscience assures us that in our dealings with our fellow-men, and above all in our dealings with you, our conduct has been governed by a devout and godly sincerity,[t] by the grace of God and not by worldly wisdom. There is nothing in our letters to you but what you can read for yourselves, and understand too. Partial as your present knowledge of us is, you will I hope come to understand fully that you have as much reason to be proud of us, as we of you, on the Day of our Lord Jesus.

It was because I felt so confident about all this that I had intended to come first of all to you[u] and give you the benefit of a double visit: I meant to visit you on my way to Macedonia, and after leaving Macedonia, to return to you,

[s] *Some witnesses read* and he still delivers us. [t] *Some witnesses read* by sincere and godly singleness of mind. [u] *Or* had originally intended to come to you . . .

King James Version

you to be brought on my way toward Judea.
17 When I therefore was thus minded, did I use
lightness? or the things that I purpose, do I
purpose according to the flesh, that with me
there should be yea, yea, and nay, nay? 18 But
as God *is* true, our word toward you was not
yea and nay. 19 For the Son of God, Jesus
Christ, who was preached among you by us,
even by me and Silvanus and Timotheus, was
not yea and nay, but in him was yea. 20 For all
the promises of God in him *are* yea, and in him
Amen, unto the glory of God by us. 21 Now he
which stablisheth us with you in Christ, and
hath anointed us, *is* God; 22 Who hath also
sealed us, and given the earnest of the Spirit in
our hearts. 23 Moreover I call God for a record
upon my soul, that to spare you I came not as
yet unto Corinth. 24 Not for that we have
dominion over your faith, but are helpers of
your joy: for by faith ye stand.

Living Bible

a double blessing to you and so that you could
send me on my way to Judea.

17 Then why, you may be asking, did I change
my plan? Hadn't I really made up my mind
yet? Or am I like a man of the world who says
"yes" when he really means "no"? 18 Never! As
surely as God is true, I am not that sort of
person. My "yes" means "yes."

19 Timothy and Silvanus and I have been
telling you about Jesus Christ the Son of God.
He isn't one to say "yes" when he means "no."
He always does exactly what he says. 20 He
carries out and fulfills all of God's promises,
no matter how many of them there are; and
we have told everyone how faithful he is, giving
glory to his name. 21 It is this God who has
made you and me into faithful Christians and
commissioned us apostles to preach the Good
News. 22 He has put his brand upon us—his
mark of ownership—and given us his Holy
Spirit in our hearts as guarantee that we belong
to him, and as the first installment of all that
he is going to give us.

23 I call upon this God to witness against
me if I am not telling the absolute truth: the
reason I haven't come to visit you yet is that
I don't want to sadden you with a severe rebuke.
24 When I come, although I can't do much to
help your faith, for it is strong already, I want
to be able to do something about your joy: I
want to make you happy, not sad.

Today's English Version

back, to get help from you for my trip to Judea.
17 In planning this did I appear fickle? When I
make my plans, do I make them from selfish
motives, ready to say "Yes, yes" and "No, no"
at the same time? 18 As God is true, my promise
to you was not a "Yes" and a "No." 19 For Jesus Christ, the Son of God, who was preached
among you by Silas, Timothy, and myself, is not
one who is "Yes" and "No." On the contrary, he
is God's "Yes"; 20 for it is he who is the "Yes"
to all of God's promises. This is the reason that
through Jesus Christ our "Amen" is said, to the
glory of God. 21 It is God himself who makes
us sure, with you, of our life in Christ; it is God
himself who has set us apart, 22 who placed his
mark of ownership upon us, and who gave the
Holy Spirit in our hearts as the guarantee of all
that he has for us.

23 I call God as my witness—he knows my
heart! It was in order to spare you that I decided
not to go to Corinth. 24 We are not trying to
dictate to you what you must believe; because
you stand firm in the faith. Instead, we are
working with you for your own happiness.

New International Version

and then to have you send me on my way to
Judea. 17 When I planned this, did I do it lightly?
Or do I make my plans in a worldly manner so
that in the same breath I say, "Yes, yes" and
"No, no"?

18 But as surely as God is faithful, our message to you is not "Yes" and "No." 19 For the
Son of God, Jesus Christ, who was preached
among you by me and Silas[b] and Timothy, was
not "Yes" and "No," but in him it has always
been "Yes." 20 For no matter how many promises God has made, they are "Yes" in Christ.
And so through him the "Amen" is spoken by
us to the glory of God. 21 Now it is God who
makes both us and you stand firm in Christ. He
anointed us, 22 set his seal of ownership on us,
and put his Spirit in our hearts as a deposit,
guaranteeing what is to come.

23 I call God as my witness that it was in
order to spare you that I did not return to
Corinth. 24 Not that we lord it over your faith,
but we work with you for your joy, because it is

[b] Greek *Silvanus*.

Phillips Modern English

could thus have helped us on our way towards Judaea. Because we had to change this plan, does it mean that we are fickle? Do you think I plan with my tongue in my cheek, saying "yes" and "no" to suit my own wishes? We solemnly assure you that as certainly as God is faithful so we have never given you a message meaning "yes" and "no". Jesus Christ, the Son of God, whom Silvanus, Timothy and I have preached to you, was himself no doubtful quantity, he is the divine "yes". Every promise of God finds its affirmative in him, and through him can be said the final amen, to the glory of God. Both you and we owe our position in Christ to this God of positive promise: it is he who has consecrated us to this special work, he who has given us the living guarantee of the Spirit in our hearts.

1.23 I have never wanted to hurt you

No, I declare before God—and I would stake my life on it—that it was to avoid hurting you that I did not come to Corinth. We are not trying to dominate you and your faith—your faith is firm enough—but we can work with you to increase your joy.

Revised Standard Version

from Macedonia and have you send me on my way to Judea. 17 Was I vacillating when I wanted to do this? Do I make my plans like a worldly man, ready to say Yes and No at once? 18 As surely as God is faithful, our word to you has not been Yes and No. 19 For the Son of God, Jesus Christ, whom we preached among you, Silvanus and Timothy and I, was not Yes and No; but in him it is always Yes. 20 For all the promises of God find their Yes in him. That is why we utter the Amen through him, to the glory of God. 21 But it is God who establishes us with you in Christ, and has commissioned us; 22 he has put his seal upon us and given us his Spirit in our hearts as a guarantee.

23 But I call God to witness against me—it was to spare you that I refrained from coming to Corinth. 24 Not that we lord it over your faith; we work with you for your joy, for you stand firm

Jerusalem Bible

the way back from Macedonia, for you to see me on my way to Judaea. 17 Do you think I was not sure of my own intentions when I planned this? Do you really think that when I am making my plans, my motives are ordinary human ones, and that I say Yes, yes, and No, no, at the same time? 18 I swear by God's truth, there is no Yes and No about what we say to you. 19 The Son of God, the Christ Jesus that we proclaimed among you—I mean Silvanus and Timothy and I—was never Yes and No: with him it was always Yes, 20 and however many the promises God made, the Yes to them all is in him. That is why it is "through him" that we answer Amen to the praise of God. 21 Remember it is God himself who assures us all, and you, of our standing in Christ, and has anointed us, 22 marking us with his seal and giving us the pledge, the Spirit, that we carry in our hearts.

23 By my life, I call God to witness that the reason why I did not come to Corinth after all was to spare your feelings. 24 We are not dictators over your faith, but are fellow workers with you for your happiness; in the faith you are steady enough.

New English Bible

and you would then send me on my way to Judaea. That was my intention; did I lightly change my mind?[c] Or do I, when I frame my plans, frame them as a worldly man might, so that it should rest with me to say 'yes' and 'yes', or 'no' and 'no'? As God is true, the language in which we address you is not an ambiguous blend of Yes and No. The Son of God, Christ Jesus, proclaimed among you by us (by Silvanus and Timothy, I mean, as well as myself), was never a blend of Yes and No. With him it was, and is, Yes. He is the Yes pronounced upon God's promises, every one of them. That is why, when we give glory to God, it is through Christ Jesus that we say 'Amen'. And if you and we belong to Christ, guaranteed as his and anointed, it is all God's doing; it is God also who has set his seal upon us, and as a pledge of what is to come has given the Spirit to dwell in our hearts.

I appeal to God to witness what I am going to say; I stake my life upon it: it was out of consideration for you that I did not after all come to Corinth. Do not think we are dictating the terms of your faith; your hold on the faith is secure enough. We are working with you for your own happiness.

[c] *Or* in forming this intention, did I act irresponsibly?

King James Version

2 But I determined this with myself, that I
would not come again to you in heaviness.
2 For if I make you sorry, who is he then that
maketh me glad, but the same which is made
sorry by me? 3 And I wrote this same unto you,
lest, when I came, I should have sorrow from
them of whom I ought to rejoice; having confidence in you all, that my joy is *the joy* of you
all. 4 For out of much affliction and anguish of
heart I wrote unto you with many tears; not that
ye should be grieved, but that ye might know
the love which I have more abundantly unto
you. 5 But if any have caused grief, he hath not
grieved me, but in part: that I may not over-
charge you all. 6 Sufficient to such a man *is* this
punishment, which *was inflicted* of many. 7 So
that contrariwise ye *ought* rather to forgive
him, and comfort *him*, lest perhaps such a one
should be swallowed up with overmuch sorrow.
8 Wherefore I beseech you that ye would confirm *your* love toward him. 9 For to this end
also did I write, that I might know the proof of
you, whether ye be obedient in all things. 10 To
whom ye forgive any thing, I *forgive* also: for if
I forgave any thing, to whom I forgave *it*, for
your sakes *forgave I it* in the person of Christ;

Living Bible

2 "No," I said to myself, "I won't do it. I'll
not make them unhappy with another painful visit." 2 For if I make you sad, who is going
to make me happy? You are the ones to do it,
and how can you if I cause you pain? 3 That is
why I wrote as I did in my last letter, so that
you will get things straightened out before I
come.[a] Then, when I do come, I will not be
made sad by the very ones who ought to give
me greatest joy. I felt sure that your happiness
was so bound up in mine that you would not
be happy either, unless I came with joy.
4 Oh, how I hated to write that letter! It almost broke my heart and I tell you honestly
that I cried over it. I didn't want to hurt you,
but I had to show you how very much I loved
you and cared about what was happening to you.
5, 6 Remember that the man I wrote about,
who caused all the trouble, has not caused sorrow to me as much as to all the rest of you—
though I certainly have my share in it too. I
don't want to be harder on him than I should.
He has been punished enough by your united
disapproval. 7 Now it is time to forgive him and
comfort him. Otherwise he may become so bitter
and discouraged that he won't be able to recover. 8 Please show him now that you still do
love him very much.
9 I wrote to you as I did so that I could
find out how far you would go in obeying me.
10 When you forgive anyone, I do too. And
whatever I have forgiven (to the extent that this
affected me too) has been by Christ's authority,

[a] Implied.

Today's English Version

2 So I made up my mind about this: I would
not come to you again to make you sad.
2 For if I were to make you sad, who would
be left to cheer me up? Only the very persons I
had saddened. 3 That is why I wrote that letter
to you—I did not want to come to you and be
made sad by the very people who should make
me glad. For I am convinced that when I am
happy, then all of you are happy too. 4 I wrote
you with a greatly troubled and distressed heart,
and with many tears, not to make you sad, but
to make you realize how much I love you all.

Forgiveness for the offender

5 Now, if anyone has made somebody sad,
he has not done it to me but to you; or to some
of you, at least, since I do not want to be too
hard on him. 6 It is enough for this person that
he has been punished in this way by most of
you. 7 Now, however, you should forgive him
and encourage him, to keep him from becoming
so sad as to give up completely. 8 Let him know,
then, I beg you, that you really do love him.
9 I wrote you that letter for this very reason: I
wanted to find out how well you had stood the
test, and whether you are always ready to obey
my instructions. 10 When you forgive someone
for what he has done, I forgive him too. For
when I forgive—if, indeed, I need to forgive
anything—I do it because of you, in Christ's

New International Version

2 by faith you stand firm. 1 So I made up my
mind that I would not make another painful
visit to you. 2 For if I grieve you, who is left to
make me glad but you whom I have grieved?
3 I wrote as I did so that when I came I should
not be distressed by those who ought to make
me rejoice. I had confidence in all of you, that
you would all share my joy. 4 For I wrote you
out of great distress and anguish of heart and
with many tears, not to grieve you but to let you
know the depth of my love for you.

Forgiveness for the sinner

5 If anyone has caused grief, he has not so
much grieved me as he has grieved all of you,
to some extent—not to put it too severely. 6 The
punishment inflicted on him by the majority is
sufficient for him. 7 Now instead, you ought to
forgive and comfort him, so that he will not be
overwhelmed by excessive sorrow. 8 I urge you,
therefore, to reaffirm your love for him. 9 The
reason I wrote you was to see if you would stand
the test and be obedient in everything. 10 If you
forgive anyone, I also forgive him. And what I
have forgiven—if there was anything to forgive
—I have forgiven in the sight of Christ for your

Phillips Modern English

And I made up my mind that I would not pay you another painful visit. For what point is there in my depressing the very people who can give me such joy? The real purpose of my previous letter was in fact to save myself from being saddened by those whom I might reasonably expect to bring me joy. I felt sure that my happiness was also yours! I wrote to you in deep distress and out of a most unhappy heart (I don't mind telling you I shed tears over that letter), not, believe me, to cause you pain, but to show you how very deep is my love for you.

2.5 A word of explanation

If the behaviour of a certain person has caused distress, it does not mean so much that he has injured me, but that to some extent (I do not wish to exaggerate), he has injured all of you. But now I think that the punishment which most of you inflicted on such a man has been sufficient. Now is the time to offer him forgiveness and comfort, so that a man in his position is not completely overwhelmed by remorse. I ask you to assure him now that you love him. My previous letter was something of a test—I wanted to make sure that you would follow my orders implicitly. If you forgive a certain person for anything, I forgive him too. Insofar as I had anything personally to forgive, I do

Revised Standard Version

2 in your faith. 1 For I made up my mind not
to make you another painful visit. 2 For if I
cause you pain, who is there to make me glad
but the one whom I have pained? 3And I wrote
as I did, so that when I came I might not suffer
pain from those who should have made me rejoice, for I felt sure of all of you, that my joy
would be the joy of you all. 4 For I wrote you
out of much affliction and anguish of heart and
with many tears, not to cause you pain but to
let you know the abundant love that I have for
you.
5 But if any one has caused pain, he has
caused it not to me, but in some measure—not
to put it too severely—to you all. 6 For such
a one this punishment by the majority is enough;
7 so you should rather turn to forgive and comfort him, or he may be overwhelmed by excessive sorrow. 8 So I beg you to reaffirm your
love for him. 9 For this is why I wrote, that I
might test you and know whether you are obedient in everything. 10Any one whom you forgive, I also forgive. What I have forgiven, if I
have forgiven anything, has been for your sake

Jerusalem Bible

2 Well then, I made up my mind not to pay
you a second distressing visit. 2 I may have
hurt you, but if so I have hurt the only people
who could give me any pleasure. 3 I wrote as I
did to make sure that, when I came, I should not
be distressed by the very people who should
have made me happy. I am sure you all know
that I could never be happy unless you were.
4 When I wrote to you, in deep distress and
anguish of mind, and in tears, it was not to make
you feel hurt but to let you know how much love
I have for you.
5 Someone has been the cause of pain; and
the cause of pain not to me, but to some degree
—not to overstate it—to all of you. 6 The punishment already imposed by the majority on the man
in question is enough; 7 and the best thing now
is to give him your forgiveness and encouragement, or he might break down from so much
misery. 8 So I am asking you to give some definite proof of your love for him. 9 What I really
wrote for, after all, was to test you and see
whether you are completely obedient. 10Anybody
that you forgive, I forgive; and as for my forgiving anything—if there has been anything to
be forgiven, I have forgiven it for your sake in

New English Bible

2 So I made up my mind that my next visit to you must not be another painful one. If I cause pain to you, who is left to cheer me up, except you, whom I have offended? This is precisely the point I made in my letter: I did not want, I said, to come and be made miserable by the very people who ought to have made me happy; and I had sufficient confidence in you all to know that for me to be happy is for all of you to be happy. That letter I sent you came out of great distress and anxiety; how many tears I shed as I wrote it! But I never meant to cause you pain; I wanted you rather to know the love, the more than ordinary love, that I have for you.

Any injury that has been done, has not been done to me; to some extent, not to labour the point, it has been done to you all. The penalty on which the general meeting has agreed has met the offence well enough. Something very different is called for now: you must forgive the offender and put heart into him; the man's sorrow must not be made so severe as to overwhelm him. I urge you therefore to assure him of your love for him by a formal act. I wrote, I may say, to see how you stood the test, whether you fully accepted my authority. But anyone who has your forgiveness has mine too; and when I speak of forgiving (so far as there is anything for me to forgive), I mean that as the representative of

King James Version

11 Lest Satan should get an advantage of us:
for we are not ignorant of his devices. 12 Furthermore, when I came to Troas to *preach*
Christ's gospel, and a door was opened unto me
of the Lord, 13 I had no rest in my spirit, because I found not Titus my brother; but taking
my leave of them, I went from thence into
Macedonia. 14 Now thanks *be* unto God, which
always causeth us to triumph in Christ, and
maketh manifest the savour of his knowledge
by us in every place. 15 For we are unto God a
sweet savour of Christ, in them that are saved,
and in them that perish: 16 To the one *we are*
the savour of death unto death; and to the
other the savour of life unto life. And who *is*
sufficient for these things? 17 For we are not as
many, which corrupt the word of God: but as
of sincerity, but as of God, in the sight of God
speak we in Christ.

Living Bible

and for your good. 11 A further reason for forgiveness is to keep from being outsmarted by
Satan; for we know what he is trying to do.
12 Well, when I got as far as the city of
Troas, the Lord gave me tremendous opportunities to preach the Gospel. 13 But Titus, my dear
brother, wasn't there to meet me and I couldn't
rest, wondering where he was and what had
happened to him. So I said good-bye and went
right on to Macedonia to try to find him.
14 But thanks be to God! For through what
Christ has done, he has triumphed over us so
that now wherever we go he uses us to tell
others about the Lord and to spread the Gospel
like a sweet perfume. 15 As far as God is concerned there is a sweet, wholesome fragrance in
our lives. It is the fragrance of Christ within
us, an aroma to both the saved and the unsaved
all around us. 16 To those who are not being
saved, we seem a fearful smell of death and
doom, while to those who know Christ we are
a life-giving perfume. But who is adequate for
such a task as this? 17 Only those who, like ourselves, are men of integrity, sent by God, speaking with Christ's power, with God's eye upon
us. We are not like those hucksters—and there
are many of them—whose idea in getting out
the Gospel is to make a good living out of it.

Today's English Version

presence, 11 in order to keep Satan from getting
the upper hand over us; for we know what his
plans are.

Paul's anxiety in Troas

12 When I arrived in Troas to preach the
Good News about Christ, I found that the Lord
had opened the way for the work there. 13 But
I was deeply worried because I could not find
our brother Titus. So I said good-bye to the
people there, and went on to Macedonia.

Victory through Christ

14 But thanks be to God! For in union with
Christ we are always led by God as prisoners
in Christ's victory procession. God uses us to
make the knowledge about Christ spread everywhere like a sweet smell. 15 For we are like a
sweet-smelling incense offered by Christ to God,
which spreads among those who are being saved
and those who are being lost. 16 For those who
are being lost, it is a deadly stench that kills;
for those who are being saved, it is a fragrance
that brings life. Who, then, is capable for such
a task? 17 We are not like so many others, who
handle God's message as if it were cheap merchandise; but because God has sent us, we speak
with sincerity in his presence, as servants of
Christ.

New International Version

sake, 11 in order that Satan might not outwit
us. For we are not unaware of his schemes.

Ministers of the new covenant

12 Now when I went to Troas to preach the
gospel of Christ and found that the Lord had
opened a door for me, 13 I still had no peace of
mind, because I did not find my brother Titus
there. So I said good-by and went on to Macedonia.
14 But thanks be to God, who always leads
us in triumphal procession in Christ and through
us spreads everywhere the fragrance of the
knowledge of him. 15 For we are to God the
aroma of Christ among those who are being
saved and those who are perishing. 16 To the
one we are the stench of death; to the other,
the fragrance of life. And who is equal to such
a task? 17 Unlike so many, we do not peddle the
word of God for profit. On the contrary, in
Christ we speak before God with sincerity, like
men sent from God.

Phillips Modern English

forgive him for your sake, as before Christ. We don't want Satan to win any victory here, and well we know his methods!

2.12 And a further confidence

Well, when I came to Troas to preach the gospel of Christ, although there was an obvious God-given opportunity, I must confess I was on edge the whole time because there was no sign of brother Titus. So I said good-bye and went from there to Macedonia. Thanks be to God who leads us, wherever we are, on Christ's triumphant way and makes our knowledge of him spread throughout the world like a lovely perfume! We Christians have the unmistakable "scent" of Christ, discernible alike to those who are being saved and to those who are heading for death. To the latter it seems like the deathly smell of doom, to the former it has the refreshing fragrance of life itself.

Who is fit for such a task! We are not like that large number who corrupt the Word of God. No, we speak in utter sincerity as men sent by God, Christ's ministers under the eyes of God.

Revised Standard Version

in the presence of Christ, 11 to keep Satan from
gaining the advantage over us; for we are not
ignorant of his designs.
12 When I came to Troas to preach the gospel of Christ, a door was opened for me in the
Lord; 13 but my mind could not rest because I
did not find my brother Titus there. So I took
leave of them and went on to Macedonia.
14 But thanks be to God, who in Christ always leads us in triumph, and through us
spreads the fragrance of the knowledge of him
everywhere. 15 For we are the aroma of Christ
to God among those who are being saved and
among those who are perishing, 16 to one a fragrance from death to death, to the other a
fragrance from life to life. Who is sufficient for
these things? 17 For we are not, like so many,
peddlers of God's word; but as men of sincerity,
as commissioned by God, in the sight of God
we speak in Christ.

Jerusalem Bible

the presence of Christ. 11And so we will not be
outwitted by Satan—we know well enough what
his intentions are.

From Troas to Macedonia.
The apostolate: its importance

12 When I went up to Troas to preach the
Good News of Christ, and the door was wide open
for my work there in the Lord, 13 I was so continually uneasy in mind at not meeting brother
Titus there, I said good-by to them and went on
to Macedonia.
14 Thanks be to God who, wherever he goes,
makes us, in Christ, partners of his triumph,[a]
and through us is spreading the knowledge of
himself, like a sweet smell, everywhere. 15 We
are Christ's incense to God for those who are
being saved and for those who are not; 16 for the
last, the smell of death that leads to death, for
the first the sweet smell of life that leads to life.
And who could be qualified for work like this?
17At least we do not go around offering the
word of God for sale, as many other people do.
In Christ, we speak as men of sincerity, as envoys of God and in God's presence.

[a] Like a victorious general making his ceremonial entry into Rome.

New English Bible

Christ I have forgiven him for your sake.[a] For Satan must not be allowed to get the better of us; we know his wiles all too well.

Then when I came to Troas, where I was to preach the gospel of Christ, and where an opening awaited me for the Lord's work, I still found no relief of mind, for my colleague Titus was not there to meet me; so I took leave of the people there and went off to Macedonia. But thanks be to God, who continually leads us about, captives in Christ's triumphal procession, and everywhere uses us to reveal and spread abroad the fragrance of the knowledge of himself! We are indeed the incense offered by Christ to God, both for those who are on the way to salvation, and for those who are on the way to perdition: to the latter it is a deadly fume that kills, to the former a vital fragrance that brings life. Who is equal to such a calling? At least we do not go hawking the word of God about, as so many do; when we declare the word we do it in sincerity, as from God and in God's sight, as members of Christ.

[a] *Or* that I have forgiven him for your sake, in the presence of Christ.

King James Version

3 Do we begin again to commend ourselves?
or need we, as some *others*, epistles of commendation to you, or *letters* of commendation
from you? 2 Ye are our epistle written in our
hearts, known and read of all men: 3 *Forasmuch*
as ye are manifestly declared to be the epistle
of Christ ministered by us, written not with ink,
but with the Spirit of the living God; not in
tables of stone, but in fleshly tables of the heart.
4 And such trust have we through Christ to
God-ward: 5 Not that we are sufficient of ourselves to think any thing as of ourselves; but
our sufficiency *is* of God; 6 Who also hath made
us able ministers of the new testament; not of
the letter, but of the spirit: for the letter killeth,
but the spirit giveth life. 7 But if the ministration of death, written *and* engraven in stones,
was glorious, so that the children of Israel could
not steadfastly behold the face of Moses for the

Living Bible

3 Are we beginning to be like those false
teachers of yours who must tell you all
about themselves and bring long letters of recommendation with them? I think you hardly need
someone's letter to tell you about us, do you?
And we don't need a recommendation from you,
either! 2 The only letter I need is you yourselves!
By looking at the good change in your hearts,
everyone can see that we have done a good
work among you. 3 They can see that you are
a letter from Christ, written by us. It is not a
letter written with pen and ink, but by the Spirit
of the living God; not one carved on stone,
but in human hearts.
4 We dare to say these good things about
ourselves only because of our great trust in God
through Christ, that he will help us to be true
to what we say, 5 and not because we think we
can do anything of lasting value by ourselves.
Our only power and success comes from God.
6 He is the one who has helped us tell others
about his new agreement to save them. We do
not tell them that they must obey every law of
God or die; but we tell them there is life for
them from the Holy Spirit. The old way, trying
to be saved by keeping the Ten Commandments,
ends in death; in the new way, the Holy Spirit
gives them life.
7 Yet that old system of law that led to death
began with such glory that people could not
bear to look at Moses' face. For as he gave
them God's law to obey, his face shone out with

Today's English Version

Servants of the new covenant

3 Does this sound as if we were again boasting about ourselves? Could it be that, like
some other people, we need letters of recommendation to you or from you? 2 You yourselves are the letter we have, written on our
hearts, for everyone to know and read. 3 It is
clear that Christ himself wrote this letter and
sent it by us. It is written not with ink on stone
tablets, but on human hearts, with the Spirit of
the living God.
4 We say this because we have confidence in
God through Christ. 5 There is nothing in us that
allows us to claim that we are capable of doing
this work. The capacity we have comes from
God; 6 it is he who made us capable of serving
the new covenant, which consists not of a written law, but of the Spirit. The written law brings
death, but the Spirit gives life.
7 The Law was carved in letters on stone tablets, and God's glory appeared when it was
given. Even though the brightness on Moses' face
faded away, it was so strong that the people of
Israel could not keep their eyes fixed on him. If

New International Version

3 Are we beginning to commend ourselves
again? Or do we need, like some people,
letters of recommendation to you or from you?
2 You yourselves are our letter, written on our
hearts, known and read by everybody. 3 You
show that you are a letter from Christ, the result
of our ministry, written not with ink but with
the Spirit of the living God, not on tablets of
stone but on tablets of human hearts.
4 Such confidence as this is ours through
Christ before God. 5 Not that we are competent
of ourselves to judge anything we do, but our
competence comes from God. 6 He has enabled
us to be ministers of a new covenant—not of the
letter but of the Spirit; for the letter kills, but
the Spirit gives life.

The glory of the new covenant

7 Now if the ministry that brought death,
which was engraved in letters on stone, came
with glory, so that the Israelites could not look

Phillips Modern English

3.1 *You yourselves are the proof of our ministry*

Does this mean yet another production of credentials? Do we need, as some apparently do, to exchange testimonials before we can be friends? You yourselves are our testimonial, written in our hearts and yet open for anyone to inspect and read. You are an open letter about Christ delivered by us and written, not with pen and ink but with the Spirit of the living God, engraved not on stone, but on human hearts.

We dare to say such things because of the confidence we have in God through Christ. Not that we are in any way confident of doing anything by our own resources—our ability comes from God. It is he who makes us competent administrators of the new agreement, concerned not with the letter but with the Spirit. The letter of the Law leads to the death of the soul; the Spirit alone can give it life.

3.7 *The splendour of our ministry outshines that of Moses*

The administration of the Law which was engraved in stone (and which led in fact to spiritual death) was so magnificent that the Israelites were unable to look unflinchingly at Moses' face,

Revised Standard Version

3 Are we beginning to commend ourselves
again? Or do we need, as some do, letters of
recommendation to you, or from you? 2 You
yourselves are our letter of recommendation,
written on your[c] hearts, to be known and read
by all men; 3 and you show that you are a letter
from Christ delivered by us, written not with
ink but with the Spirit of the living God, not
on tablets of stone but on tablets of human
hearts.
4 Such is the confidence that we have through
Christ toward God. 5 Not that we are competent
of ourselves to claim anything as coming from
us; our competence is from God, 6 who has
made us competent to be ministers of a new
covenant, not in a written code but in the Spirit;
for the written code kills, but the Spirit gives
life.
7 Now if the dispensation of death, carved
in letters on stone, came with such splendor that

[c] Other ancient authorities read *our*.

Jerusalem Bible

3 Does this sound like a new attempt to
commend ourselves to you? Unlike other
people, we need no letters of recommendation
either to you or from you, 2 because you are
yourselves our letter, written in our hearts, that
anybody can see and read, 3 and it is plain that
you are a letter from Christ, drawn up by us,
and written not with ink but with the Spirit of
the living God, not on stone tablets but on the
tablets of your living hearts.
4 Before God, we are confident of this through
Christ: 5 not that we are qualified in ourselves
to claim anything as our own work: all our
qualifications come from God. 6 He is the one
who has given us the qualifications to be the
administrators of this new covenant, which is
not a covenant of written letters but of the
Spirit: the written letters bring death, but the
Spirit gives life. 7 Now if the administering of
death, in the written letters engraved on stones,
was accompanied by such a brightness that the
Israelites could not bear looking at the face of

New English Bible

3 Are we beginning all over again to produce our credentials? Do we, like some people, need letters of introduction to you, or from you? No, you are all the letter we need, a letter written on our heart; any man can see it for what it is and read it for himself. And as for you, it is plain that you are a letter that has come from Christ, given to us to deliver: a letter written not with ink but with the Spirit of the living God, written not on stone tablets but on the pages of the human heart.

It is in full reliance upon God, through Christ, that we make such claims. There is no question of our being qualified in ourselves: we cannot claim anything as our own. The qualification we have comes from God; it is he who has qualified us to dispense his new covenant—a covenant expressed not in a written document, but in a spiritual bond; for the written law condemns to death, but the Spirit gives life.

The law, then, engraved letter by letter upon stone, dispensed death, and yet it was inaugurated with divine splendour. That splendour, though it was soon to fade, made the face of Moses so

King James Version

glory of his countenance; which *glory* was to be done away; 8 How shall not the ministration of the spirit be rather glorious? 9 For if the ministration of condemnation *be* glory, much more doth the ministration of righteousness exceed in glory. 10 For even that which was made glorious had no glory in this respect, by reason of the glory that excelleth. 11 For if that which is done away *was* glorious, much more that which remaineth *is* glorious. 12 Seeing then that we have such hope, we use great plainness of speech: 13 And not as Moses, *which* put a vail over his face, that the children of Israel could not stedfastly look to the end of that which is abolished: 14 But their minds were blinded: for until this day remaineth the same vail untaken away in the reading of the old testament; which *vail* is done away in Christ. 15 But even unto this day, when Moses is read, the vail is upon their heart. 16 Nevertheless, when it shall turn to the Lord, the vail shall be taken away. 17 Now the Lord is that Spirit: and where the Spirit of the Lord *is*, there *is* liberty. 18 But we all, with open face beholding as in a glass the glory of the Lord, are

Living Bible

the very glory of God—though the brightness was already fading away. 8 Shall we not expect far greater glory in these days when the Holy Spirit is giving life? 9 If the plan that leads to doom was glorious, much more glorious is the plan that makes men right with God. 10 In fact, that first glory as it shone from Moses' face is worth nothing at all in comparison with the overwhelming glory of the new agreement. 11 So if the old system that faded into nothing was full of heavenly glory, the glory of God's new plan for our salvation[a] is certainly far greater, for it is eternal.

12 Since we know that this new glory will never go away, we can preach with great boldness, 13 and not as Moses did, who put a veil over his face so that the Israelis could not see the glory fade away.

14 Not only Moses' face was veiled, but his people's minds and understanding were veiled and blinded too. Even now when the Scripture is read it seems as though Jewish hearts and minds are covered by a thick veil, because they cannot see and understand the real meaning of the Scriptures. For this veil of misunderstanding can be removed only by believing in Christ. 15 Yes, even today when they read Moses' writings their hearts are blind and they think that obeying the Ten Commandments is the way to be saved.

16 But whenever anyone turns to the Lord from his sins, then the veil is taken away. 17 The Lord is the Spirit who gives them life, and where he is there is freedom [from trying to be saved by keeping the laws of God [a]]. 18 But we Christians have no veil over our faces; we can

[*a*] Implied.

Today's English Version

the Law, whose service was to bring death, came with such glory, 8 how much greater is the glory that belongs to the service of the Spirit! 9 The service by which men are condemned was glorious; how much more glorious is the service by which men are declared innocent! 10 We may say that, because of the far brighter glory now, the glory that was so bright in the past is gone. 11 For if there was glory in that which lasted for a while, how much more glory is there in that which lasts forever!

12 Because we have this hope, we are very bold. 13 We are not like Moses, who had to put a veil over his face, so that the people of Israel would not see the brightness fade and disappear. 14 Their minds, indeed, were closed; and to this very day their minds are covered with the same veil, as they read the books of the old covenant. The veil is removed only when a man is joined to Christ. 15 Even today, whenever they read the Law of Moses, the veil still covers their minds. 16 But it is removed, as the scripture says, "Moses' veil was removed when he turned to the Lord." 17 Now, "the Lord" in this passage is the Spirit; and where the Spirit of the Lord is present, there is freedom. 18 All of us, then, reflect the glory of the Lord with uncovered

New International Version

steadily at the face of Moses because of its glory, fading though it was, 8 will not the ministry of the Spirit be even more glorious? 9 If the ministry that condemns men is glorious, how much more glorious is the ministry that brings righteousness! 10 For what was glorious has no glory now in comparison with the surpassing glory. 11 And if what was fading away came with glory, how much greater is the glory of that which lasts!

12 Therefore, since we have such a hope, we are very bold. 13 We are not like Moses, who veiled his face to keep the Israelites from gazing at it while the radiance was fading away. 14 But their minds were made dull, for to this day the same veil remains when the old covenant is read. It has not been removed, because only in Christ is it taken away. 15 Even to this day when Moses is read, a veil covers their hearts. 16 But when ever anyone turns to the Lord, "the veil is taken away."[c] 17 Now the Lord is the Spirit, and where the Spirit of the Lord is, there is freedom. 18 And we, who with unveiled faces all reflect[d] the Lord's glory, are being transformed into his

[*c*] Exodus 34:34. [*d*] Or ***contemplate***.

Phillips Modern English

for it was alight with heavenly splendour. Now if the old administration held such heavenly, even though transitory, splendour, can we not see what a much more glorious thing is the new administration of the Spirit of life? If to administer a system which is to end in condemning men had its glory, how infinitely more splendid is it to administer a system which ends in making men right with God! And while it is true that the former glory has been eclipsed by the latter, we do well to remember that it is eclipsed because the present and permanent is so much more glorious than the old and transient.

3.12 Our ministry is an open and splendid thing

With this hope in our hearts we are quite frank and open in our ministry. We are not like Moses, who veiled his face to prevent the Israelites from seeing its fading glory. But it was their minds really which were blinded, for even today when the old agreement is read to them there is still a veil over their minds—though the veil has actually been lifted by Christ. Yes even to this day there is still a veil over their hearts when the writings of Moses are read. Yet if they "turned to the Lord" the veil would disappear. For the Lord to whom they could turn is the Spirit, and wherever the Spirit of the Lord is, men's souls are set free.

But all of us who are Christians have no veils on our faces, but reflect like mirrors the glory

Revised Standard Version

the Israelites could not look at Moses' face because of its brightness, fading as this was, 8 will not the dispensation of the Spirit be attended with greater splendor? 9 For if there was splendor in the dispensation of condemnation, the dispensation of righteousness must far exceed it in splendor. 10 Indeed, in this case, what once had splendor has come to have no splendor at all, because of the splendor that surpasses it. 11 For if what faded away came with splendor, what is permanent must have much more splendor.

12 Since we have such a hope, we are very bold, 13 not like Moses, who put a veil over his face so that the Israelites might not see the end of the fading splendor. 14 But their minds were hardened; for to this day, when they read the old covenant, that same veil remains unlifted, because only through Christ is it taken away. 15 Yes, to this day whenever Moses is read a veil lies over their minds; 16 but when a man turns to the Lord the veil is removed. 17 Now the Lord is the Spirit, and where the Spirit of the Lord is, there is freedom. 18 And we all, with unveiled face, beholding[d] the glory

[d] Or *reflecting.*

Jerusalem Bible

Moses, though it was a brightness that faded, 8 then how much greater will be the brightness that surrounds the administering of the Spirit! 9 For if there was any splendor in administering condemnation, there must be very much greater splendor in administering justification. 10 In fact, compared with this greater splendor, the thing that used to have such splendor now seems to have none; 11 and if what was so temporary had any splendor, there must be much more in what is going to last for ever.

12 Having this hope, we can be quite confident; 13 not like Moses, who put a veil over his face so that the Israelites would not notice the ending of what had to fade.[b] 14 And anyway, their minds had been dulled; indeed, to this very day, that same veil is still there when the old covenant is being read, a veil never lifted, since Christ alone can remove it. 15 Yes, even today, whenever Moses is read, the veil is over their minds. 16 It will not be removed until they turn to the Lord. 17 Now this Lord is the Spirit, and where the Spirit of the Lord is, there is freedom. 18 And we, with our unveiled faces reflecting like mirrors the brightness of the Lord,

[b] See Ex. 34:33.

New English Bible

bright that the Israelites could not gaze steadily at him. But if so, must not even greater splendour rest upon the divine dispensation of the Spirit? If splendour accompanied the dispensation under which we are condemned, how much richer in splendour must that one be under which we are acquitted! Indeed, the splendour that once was is now no splendour at all; it is outshone by a splendour greater still. For if that which was soon to fade had its moment of splendour, how much greater is the splendour of that which endures!

With such a hope as this we speak out boldly; it is not for us to do as Moses did: he put a veil over his face to keep the Israelites from gazing on that fading splendour until it was gone. But in any case their minds had been made insensitive, for that same veil is there to this very day when the lesson is read from the old covenant; and it is never lifted, because only in Christ is the old covenant abrogated. But to this very day, every time the Law of Moses is read, a veil lies over the minds of the hearers. However, as Scripture says of Moses, 'whenever he turns to the Lord the veil is removed'.[b] **Now the Lord of whom this passage speaks is the Spirit; and where the Spirit of the Lord is, there is liberty. And because for us there is no veil over the face, we all reflect as in a mirror the splendour of the**

[a] *Or* in Christ is it abolished. [b] *Or* as Scripture says, when one turns to the Lord the veil is removed.

King James Version

changed into the same image from glory to glory, *even* as by the Spirit of the Lord.

4 Therefore, seeing we have this ministry, as we have received mercy, we faint not; 2 But have renounced the hidden things of dishonesty, not walking in craftiness, nor handling the word of God deceitfully; but, by manifestation of the truth, commending ourselves to every man's conscience in the sight of God. 3 But if our gospel be hid, it is hid to them that are lost: 4 In whom the god of this world hath blinded the minds of them which believe not, lest the light of the glorious gospel of Christ, who is the image of God, should shine unto them. 5 For we preach not ourselves, but Christ Jesus the Lord; and ourselves your servants for Jesus' sake. 6 For God, who commanded the light to shine out of darkness, hath shined in our hearts, to *give* the light of the knowledge of the glory of God in the

Living Bible

be mirrors that brightly reflect the glory of the Lord. And as the Spirit of the Lord works within us, we become more and more like him.

4 It is God himself, in his mercy, who has given us this wonderful work [of telling his Good News to others[a]], and so we never give up. 2 We do not try to trick people into believing—we are not interested in fooling anyone. We never try to get anyone to believe that the Bible teaches what it doesn't. All such shameful methods we forego. We stand in the presence of God as we speak and so we tell the truth, as all who know us will agree.

3 If the Good News we preach is hidden to anyone, it is hidden from the one who is on the road to eternal death. 4 Satan, who is the god of this evil world, has made him blind, unable to see the glorious light of the Gospel that is shining upon him, or to understand the amazing message we preach about the glory of Christ, who is God.[b] 5 We don't go around preaching about ourselves, but about Christ Jesus as Lord. All we say of ourselves is that we are your slaves because of what Jesus has done for us. 6 For God, who said, "Let there be light in the darkness," has made us understand that it is the brightness of his glory that is seen in the face of Jesus Christ.

(4) [*a*] Implied. [*b*] Literally, "who is the image of God."

Today's English Version

faces; and that same glory, coming from the Lord who is the Spirit, transforms us into his very likeness, in an ever greater degree of glory.

Spiritual treasure in clay pots

4 God, in his mercy, has given us this service, and so we do not become discouraged. 2 We put aside all secret and shameful deeds; we do not act with deceit, nor do we falsify the word of God. In the full light of truth, we live in God's sight and try to commend ourselves to everyone's good conscience. 3 For if the gospel we preach is hidden, it is hidden only to those who are being lost. 4 They do not believe because their minds have been kept in the dark by the evil god of this world. He keeps them from seeing the light shining on them, the light that comes from the Good News about the glory of Christ, who is the exact likeness of God. 5 For it is not ourselves that we preach; we preach Jesus Christ as Lord, and ourselves as your servants for Jesus' sake. 6 The God who said, "Out of darkness the light shall shine!" is the same God who made his light shine in our hearts, to bring us the light of the knowledge of God's glory, shining in the face of Christ.

New International Version

likeness with ever-increasing glory, which comes from the Lord, who is the Spirit.

Treasures in jars of clay

4 Therefore, since through God's mercy we have this ministry, we do not lose heart. 2 Rather, we have renounced secret and shameful ways; we do not use deception, nor do we distort the word of God. On the contrary, by setting forth the truth plainly we commend ourselves to every man's conscience in the sight of God. 3 And even if our gospel is veiled, it is veiled to those who are perishing. 4 The god of this age has blinded the minds of unbelievers, so that they cannot see the light of the gospel of the glory of Christ, who is the image of God. 5 For we do not preach ourselves, but Jesus Christ as Lord, and ourselves as your servants for Jesus' sake. 6 For God who said, "Let light shine out of darkness,"[e] made his light shine in our hearts to give us the light of the knowledge of the glory of God in the face of Christ.

[*e*] Gen. 1:3.

Phillips Modern English

of the Lord. We are transformed in ever-increasing splendour into his own image, and this is the work of the Lord who is the Spirit.

4.1 ***Ours is a straightforward ministry bringing light into darkness***

This is the ministry which God in his mercy has given us and nothing can daunt us. We have set our faces against all shameful secret practices; we use no clever tricks, no dishonest manipulation of the Word of God. We speak the plain truth and so commend ourselves to every man's conscience in the sight of God. If our gospel is "veiled", the veil must be in the minds of those who are spiritually dying. The god of this world has blinded the minds of those who do not believe, and prevents the light of the glorious gospel of Christ, the image of God, from shining on them. For it is Christ Jesus as Lord whom we preach, not ourselves; we are your servants for Jesus' sake. God, who first ordered light to shine in darkness, has flooded our hearts with his light, so that we can enlighten men with the knowledge of the glory of God, as we see it in the face of Christ.

Revised Standard Version

of the Lord, are being changed into his likeness from one degree of glory to another; for this comes from the Lord who is the Spirit.

4 Therefore, having this ministry by the mercy
of God,[e] we do not lose heart. 2 We have
renounced disgraceful, underhanded ways; we
refuse to practice cunning or to tamper with
God's word, but by the open statement of the
truth we would commend ourselves to every
man's conscience in the sight of God. 3 And
even if our gospel is veiled, it is veiled only to
those who are perishing. 4 In their case the god
of this world has blinded the minds of the unbelievers, to keep them from seeing the light of
the gospel of the glory of Christ, who is the
likeness of God. 5 For what we preach is not
ourselves, but Jesus Christ as Lord, with ourselves as your servants[f] for Jesus' sake. 6 For
it is the God who said, "Let light shine out of
darkness," who has shone in our hearts to give
the light of the knowledge of the glory of God
in the face of Christ.

[e] Greek *as we have received mercy.* [f] Or *slaves.*

Jerusalem Bible

all grow brighter and brighter as we are turned into the image that we reflect; this is the work of the Lord who is Spirit.

4 Since we have by an act of mercy been entrusted with this work of administration,
there is no weakening on our part. 2 On the contrary, we will have none of the reticence of those
who are ashamed, no deceitfulness or watering
down the word of God; but the way we commend ourselves to every human being with a
conscience is by stating the truth openly in the
sight of God. 3 If our gospel does not penetrate
the veil, then the veil is on those who are not
on the way to salvation; 4 the unbelievers whose
minds the god of this world has blinded, to stop
them seeing the light shed by the Good News of
the glory of Christ, who is the image of God.
5 For it is not ourselves that we are preaching,
but Christ Jesus as the Lord, and ourselves as
your servants for Jesus' sake. 6 It is the same
God that said, "Let there be light shining out
of darkness," who has shone in our minds to
radiate the light of the knowledge of God's glory,
the glory on the face of Christ.

New English Bible

Lord; thus we are transfigured into his likeness, from splendour to splendour; such is the influence of the Lord who is Spirit.

4 Seeing then that we have been entrusted with this commission, which we owe entirely to God's mercy, we never lose heart. We have renounced the deeds that men hide for very shame; we neither practise cunning nor distort the word of God; only by declaring the truth openly do we recommend ourselves, and then it is to the common conscience of our fellow-men and in the sight of God. And if indeed our gospel be found veiled, the only people who find it so are those on the way to perdition. Their unbelieving minds are so blinded by the god of this passing age, that the gospel of the glory of Christ, who is the very image of God, cannot dawn upon them and bring them light. It is not ourselves that we proclaim; we proclaim Christ Jesus as Lord, and ourselves as your servants, for Jesus' sake. For the same God who said, 'Out of darkness let light shine', has caused his light to shine within us, to give the light of revelation—the revelation of the glory of God in the face of Jesus Christ.

King James Version

face of Jesus Christ. 7 But we have this treasure
in earthen vessels, that the excellency of the
power may be of God, and not of us. 8 *We are*
troubled on every side, yet not distressed; *we*
are perplexed, but not in despair; 9 Persecuted,
but not forsaken; cast down, but not destroyed;
10Always bearing about in the body the dying of
the Lord Jesus, that the life also of Jesus might
be made manifest in our body. 11 For we which
live are alway delivered unto death for Jesus'
sake, that the life also of Jesus might be made
manifest in our mortal flesh. 12 So then death
worketh in us, but life in you. 13 We having the
same spirit of faith, according as it is written, I
believed, and therefore have I spoken; we also
believe, and therefore speak; 14 Knowing that
he which raised up the Lord Jesus shall raise up
us also by Jesus, and shall present *us* with you.
15 For all things *are* for your sakes, that the
abundant grace might through the thanksgiving

Living Bible

7 But this precious treasure—this light and
power that now shine within us[a]—is held in a
perishable container, that is, in our weak bodies.
Everyone can see that the glorious power within
must be from God and is not our own.

8 We are pressed on every side by troubles,
but not crushed and broken. We are perplexed
because we don't know why things happen as
they do, but we don't give up and quit. 9 We
are hunted down, but God never abandons us.
We get knocked down, but we get up again and
keep going. 10 These bodies of ours are constantly facing death just as Jesus did; so it is
clear to all that it is only the living Christ within
[who keeps us safe[a]].

11 Yes, we live under constant danger to our
lives because we serve the Lord, but this gives us
constant opportunities to show forth the power
of Jesus Christ within our dying bodies. 12 Because of our preaching we face death, but it has
resulted in eternal life for you.

13 We boldly say what we believe [trusting
God to care for us[c]], just as the Psalm writer
did when he said, "I believe and therefore I
speak." 14 We know that the same God who
brought the Lord Jesus back from death will
also bring us back to life again with Jesus, and
present us to him along with you. 15 These sufferings of ours are for your benefit. And the
more of you who are won to Christ, the more
there are to thank him for his great kindness,
and the more the Lord is glorified.

[*a*] Implied.

Today's English Version

7 Yet we who have this spiritual treasure are
like common clay pots, to show that the supreme
power belongs to God, not to us. 8 We are often
troubled, but not crushed; sometimes in doubt,
but never in despair; 9 there are many enemies,
but we are never without a friend; and though
badly hurt at times, we are not destroyed. 10At
all times we carry in our mortal bodies the death
of Jesus, so that his life also may be seen in
our bodies. 11 Throughout our lives we are always in danger of death for Jesus' sake, in order
that his life may be seen in this mortal body of
ours. 12 This means that death is at work in us;
but life is at work in you.

13 The scripture says, "I spoke because I
believed." In the same spirit of faith, we also
speak because we believe. 14 We know that God,
who raised the Lord Jesus to life, will also raise
us up with Jesus and bring us, together with you,
into his presence. 15 All this is for your sake;
and as God's grace reaches more and more
people, they will offer more prayers of thanksgiving, to the glory of God.

New International Version

7 But we have this treasure in jars of clay
to show that this all-surpassing power is from
God and not from us. 8 We are hard pressed
on every side, but not crushed; perplexed, but
not in despair; 9 persecuted, but not abandoned;
struck down, but not destroyed. 10 We always
carry around in our body the death of Jesus, so
that the life of Jesus may also be revealed in
our body. 11 For we who are alive are always
being given over to death for Jesus' sake, so
that his life may be revealed in our mortal body.
12 So then, death is at work in us, but life is
at work in you.

13 It is written: "I believed; therefore I have
spoken."[f] With that same spirit of faith we also
believe and therefore speak, 14 because we know
that the one who raised the Lord Jesus from
the dead will also raise us with Jesus and present
us with you in his presence. 15All this is for your
benefit, so that the grace that is reaching more
and more people may cause thanksgiving to
overflow to the glory of God.

[*f*] Psalm 116:10.

Phillips Modern English

4.7 We experience death—we give life, by the power of God

This priceless treasure we hold, so to speak, in common earthenware—to show that the splendid power of it belongs to God and not to us. We are hard-pressed on all sides, but we are never frustrated; we are puzzled, but never in despair. We are persecuted, but are never deserted: we may be knocked down but we are never knocked out! Every day we experience something of the death of Jesus, so that we may also show the power of the life of Jesus in these bodies of ours. Yes, we who are living are always being exposed to death for Jesus' sake, so that the life of Jesus may be plainly seen in our mortal lives. We are always facing physical death, so that you may know spiritual life. Our faith is like that mentioned in the scripture:

I believed and therefore did I speak.

For we too speak because we believe, and we know for certain that he who raised the Lord Jesus from death shall also raise us with Jesus. We shall all stand together before him.

4.15 We live a transitory life with our eyes on the life eternal

All this is indeed working out for your benefit, for as more grace is given to more and more people so will the thanksgiving to the glory of

Revised Standard Version

7 But we have this treasure in earthen vessels, to show that the transcendent power belongs to God and not to us. 8 We are afflicted
in every way, but not crushed; perplexed, but
not driven to despair; 9 persecuted, but not forsaken; struck down, but not destroyed; 10 always carrying in the body the death of Jesus,
so that the life of Jesus may also be manifested
in our bodies. 11 For while we live we are always being given up to death for Jesus' sake, so
that the life of Jesus may be manifested in our
mortal flesh. 12 So death is at work in us, but
life in you.

13 Since we have the same spirit of faith as
he had who wrote, "I believed, and so I spoke,"
we too believe, and so we speak, 14 knowing
that he who raised the Lord Jesus will raise us
also with Jesus and bring us with you into his
presence. 15 For it is all for your sake, so that
as grace extends to more and more people it
may increase thanksgiving, to the glory of God.

Jerusalem Bible

The trials and hopes of the apostolate

7 We are only the earthenware jars that hold
this treasure, to make it clear that such an overwhelming power comes from God and not from
us. 8 We are in difficulties on all sides, but never
cornered; we see no answer to our problems, but
never despair; 9 we have been persecuted, but
never deserted; knocked down, but never killed;
10 always, wherever we may be, we carry with
us in our body the death of Jesus, so that the
life of Jesus, too, may always be seen in our
body. 11 Indeed, while we are still alive, we are
consigned to our death every day, for the sake
of Jesus, so that in our mortal flesh the life of
Jesus, too, may be openly shown. 12 So death
is at work in us, but life in you.

13 But as we have the same spirit of faith
that is mentioned in scripture—*I believed, and
therefore I spoke*[c]—we too believe and therefore
we too speak, 14 knowing that he who raised
the Lord Jesus to life will raise us with Jesus in
our turn, and put us by his side and you with us.
15 You see, all this is for your benefit, so that
the more grace is multiplied among people, the
more thanksgiving there will be, to the glory
of God.

[*c*] Ps. 116:10.

New English Bible

We are no better than pots of earthenware to contain this treasure, and this proves that such transcendent power does not come from us, but is God's alone. Hard-pressed on every side, we are never hemmed in; bewildered, we are never at our wits' end; hunted, we are never abandoned to our fate; struck down, we are not left to die. Wherever we go we carry death with us in our body, the death that Jesus died, that in this body also life may reveal itself, the life that Jesus lives. For continually, while still alive, we are being surrendered into the hands of death, for Jesus' sake, so that the life of Jesus also may be revealed in this mortal body of ours. Thus death is at work in us, and life in you.

But Scripture says, 'I believed, and therefore I spoke out', and we too, in the same spirit of faith, believe and therefore speak out; for we know that he who raised the Lord Jesus to life will with Jesus raise us too, and bring us to his presence, and you with us. Indeed, it is for your sake that all things are ordered, so that, as the abounding grace of God is shared by more and more, the greater may be the chorus of thanksgiving that ascends to the glory of God.

King James Version

of many redound to the glory of God. 16 For which cause we faint not; but though our outward man perish, yet the inward *man* is renewed day by day. 17 For our light affliction, which is but for a moment, worketh for us a far more exceeding *and* eternal weight of glory; 18 While we look not at the things which are seen, but at the things which are not seen: for the things which are seen *are* temporal; but the things which are not seen *are* eternal.

5 For we know that, if our earthly house of *this* tabernacle were dissolved, we have a building of God, a house not made with hands, eternal in the heavens. 2 For in this we groan, earnestly desiring to be clothed upon with our house which is from heaven: 3 If so be that being clothed we shall not be found naked. 4 For we that are in *this* tabernacle do groan, being burdened: not for that we would be unclothed, but clothed upon, that mortality might be swallowed up of life. 5 Now he that hath wrought us for the selfsame thing *is* God, who also hath

Living Bible

16 That is why we never give up. Though our bodies are dying, our inner strength in the Lord is growing every day. 17 These troubles and sufferings of ours are, after all, quite small and won't last very long. Yet this short time of distress will result in God's richest blessing upon us forever and ever! 18 So we do not look at what we can see right now, the troubles all around us, but we look forward to the joys in heaven which we have not yet seen. The troubles will soon be over, but the joys to come will last forever.

5 For we know that when this tent we live in now is taken down—when we die and leave these bodies—we will have wonderful new bodies in heaven, homes that will be ours forevermore, made for us by God himself, and not by human hands. 2 How weary we grow of our present bodies. That is why we look forward eagerly to the day when we shall have heavenly bodies which we shall put on like new clothes. 3 For we shall not be merely spirits without bodies. 4 These earthly bodies make us groan and sigh, but we wouldn't like to think of dying and having no bodies at all. We want to slip into our new bodies so that these dying bodies will, as it were, be swallowed up by everlasting life. 5 This is what God has prepared for us and, as a guarantee, he has given us his Holy Spirit.

Today's English Version

Living by faith

16 For this reason we never become discouraged. Even though our physical being is gradually decaying, yet our spiritual being is renewed day after day. 17 And this small and temporary trouble we suffer will bring us a tremendous and eternal glory, much greater than the trouble. 18 For we fix our attention, not on things that are seen, but on things that are unseen. What can be seen lasts only for a time; but what cannot be seen lasts forever.

5 For we know that when this tent we live in—our body here on earth—is torn down, God will have a house in heaven for us to live in, a home he himself made, which will last forever. 2 And now we sigh, so great is our desire to have our home which is in heaven put on over us; 3 by being clothed with it we shall not be found without a body. 4 While we live in this earthly tent we groan with a feeling of oppression; it is not that we want to get rid of our earthly body, but that we want to have the heavenly one put on over us, so that what is mortal will be swallowed up by life. 5 God is the one who has prepared us for this change, and he gave us his Spirit as the guarantee of all that he has for us.

New International Version

16 Therefore we do not lose heart. Though outwardly we are wasting away, yet inwardly we are being renewed day by day. 17 For our light and momentary troubles are achieving for us an eternal glory that far outweighs them all. 18 So we fix our eyes not on what is seen, but on what is unseen. For what is seen is temporary, but what is unseen is eternal.

Our heavenly dwelling

5 Now we know that if the earthly tent we live in is destroyed, we have a building from God, an eternal house in heaven, not built by human hands. 2 Meanwhile we groan, longing to be clothed with our heavenly dwelling, 3 since when we are clothed, we will not be found naked. 4 For while we are in this tent, we groan and are burdened, because we do not wish to be unclothed but to be clothed with our heavenly dwelling, so that what is mortal may be swallowed up by life. 5 Now it is God who has made us for this very purpose and has given us the Spirit as a deposit, guaranteeing what is to come.

Phillips Modern English

God be increased. This is the reason why we never lose heart. The outward man does indeed suffer wear and tear, but every day the inward man receives fresh strength. These little troubles (which are really so transitory) are winning for us a permanent, glorious and solid reward out of all proportion to our pain. For we are looking all the time not at the visible things but at the invisible. The visible things are transitory: it is the invisible things that are really permanent.

We know, for instance, that if our earthly dwelling were taken down, like a tent, we have a permanent house in Heaven, made, not by man, but by God. In this present frame we sigh with deep longing for our heavenly house, for we do not want to face utter nakedness. So long as we are clothed in this temporary dwelling we have a painful longing, not because we want just to get rid of these "clothes" but because we want to know the full cover of the permanent. We want our transitory life to be absorbed into the life that is eternal.

5.5 *Death can have no terrors, for it means being with God*

Now the power that has planned this experience for us is God, and he has given us the

Revised Standard Version

16 So we do not lose heart. Though our outer
nature is wasting away, our inner nature is being
renewed every day. 17 For this slight momentary
affliction is preparing for us an eternal weight of
glory beyond all comparison, 18 because we look
not to the things that are seen but to the things
that are unseen; for the things that are seen
are transient, but the things that are unseen are
eternal.

5 For we know that if the earthly tent we live
in is destroyed, we have a building from
God, a house not made with hands, eternal in
the heavens. 2 Here indeed we groan, and long
to put on our heavenly dwelling, 3 so that by
putting it on we may not be found naked. 4 For
while we are still in this tent, we sigh with anxiety; not that we would be unclothed, but that
we would be further clothed, so that what is
mortal may be swallowed up by life. 5 He who
has prepared us for this very thing is God, who
has given us the Spirit as a guarantee.

Jerusalem Bible

16 That is why there is no weakening on our
part, and instead, though this outer man of ours
may be falling into decay, the inner man is renewed day by day. 17 Yes, the troubles which
are soon over, though they weigh little, train us
for the carrying of a weight of eternal glory
which is out of all proportion to them. 18 And so
we have no eyes for things that are visible, but
only for things that are invisible; for visible
things last only for a time, and the invisible
things are eternal.

5 For we know that when the tent that we
live in on earth is folded up, there is a house
built by God for us, an everlasting home not
made by human hands, in the heavens. 2 In this
present state, it is true, we groan as we wait with
longing to put on our heavenly home over the
other; 3 we should like to be found wearing
clothes and not without them. 4 Yes, we groan
and find it a burden being still in this tent, not
that we want to strip it off, but to put the second
garment over it and to have what must die taken
up into life. 5 This is the purpose for which God
made us, and he has given us the pledge of the
Spirit.

New English Bible

No wonder we do not lose heart! Though our outward humanity is in decay, yet day by day we are inwardly renewed. Our troubles are slight and short-lived; and their outcome an eternal glory which outweighs them far. Meanwhile our eyes are fixed, not on the things that are seen, but on the things that are unseen: for what is seen passes away; what is unseen is eternal.

5 For we know that if the earthly frame that houses us today should be demolished, we possess a building which God has provided—a house not made by human hands, eternal, and in heaven. In this present body we do indeed groan; we yearn to have our heavenly habitation put on over this one—in the hope that, being thus clothed, we shall not find ourselves naked. We groan indeed, we who are enclosed within this earthly frame; we are oppressed because we do not want to have the old body stripped off. Rather our desire is to have the new body put on over it, so that our mortal part may be absorbed into life immortal. God himself has shaped us for this very end; and as a pledge of it he has given us the Spirit.

King James Version

given unto us the earnest of the Spirit. 6 Therefore *we are* always confident, knowing that,
whilst we are at home in the body, we are absent
from the Lord: 7 (For we walk by faith, not by
sight:) 8 We are confident, *I say,* and willing
rather to be absent from the body, and to be
present with the Lord. 9 Wherefore we labour,
that, whether present or absent, we may be accepted of him. 10 For we must all appear before
the judgment seat of Christ; that every one may
receive the things *done* in his *body,* according
to that he hath done, whether *it be* good or bad.
11 Knowing therefore the terror of the Lord, we
persuade men; but we are made manifest unto
God; and I trust also are made manifest in
your consciences. 12 For we commend not ourselves again unto you, but give you occasion to
glory on our behalf, that ye may have somewhat
to *answer* them which glory in appearance, and
not in heart. 13 For whether we be beside ourselves, *it is* to God: or whether we be sober, *it
is* for your cause. 14 For the love of Christ con-
straineth us; because we thus judge, that if one
died for all, then were all dead: 15And *that* he

Living Bible

6 Now we look forward with confidence to
our heavenly bodies, realizing that every moment we spend in these earthly bodies is time
spent away from our eternal home in heaven
with Jesus. 7 We know these things are true by
believing, not by seeing. 8And we are not afraid,
but are quite content to die, for then we will be
at home with the Lord. 9 So our aim is to please
him always in everything we do, whether we are
here in this body or away from this body and
with him in heaven. 10 For we must all stand
before Christ to be judged and have our lives
laid bare—before him. Each of us will receive
whatever he deserves for the good or bad things
he has done in his earthly body.

11 It is because of this solemn fear of the
Lord, which is ever present in our minds, that
we work so hard to win others. God knows our
hearts, that they are pure in this matter, and I
hope that, deep within, you really know it too.

12 Are we trying to pat ourselves on the back
again? No, I am giving you some good am-
munition! You can use this on those preachers
of yours who brag about how well they look
and preach, but don't have true and honest
hearts. You can boast about us that we, at least,
are well intentioned and honest. 13, 14Are we insane [to say such things about ourselves[a]]? If
so, it is to bring glory to God. And if we are in
our right minds, it is for your benefit. Whatever we do, it is certainly not for our own
profit, but because Christ's love controls us now.
Since we believe that Christ died for all of us,
we should also believe that we have died to the
old life we used to live. 15 He died for all so

[a] Implied.

Today's English Version

6 So we are always full of courage. We know
that as long as we are at home in this body we are
away from the Lord's home. 7 For our life is a
matter of faith, not of sight. 8 We are full of
courage, and would much prefer to leave our
home in this body and be at home with the
Lord. 9 More than anything else, however, we
want to please him, whether in our home here or
there. 10 For all of us must appear before
Christ, to be judged by him. Each one will receive what he deserves, according to what he
has done, good or bad, in his bodily life.

Friendship with God through Christ

11 We know what it means to fear the Lord,
and so we try to persuade men. God knows us
completely, and I hope that in your hearts you
know me as well. 12 We are not trying again to
recommend ourselves to you; rather, we are trying to give you a good reason to be proud of
us, so that you will be able to answer those who
boast about a man's appearance, and not about
his character. 13Are we really insane? It is for
God's sake. Or are we sane? It is for your sake.
14 We are ruled by Christ's love for us, now that
we recognize that one man died for all men,
which means that all men take part in his death.
15 He died for all men so that those who live

New International Version

6 Therefore we are always confident and know
that as long as we are at home in the body we
are away from the Lord. 7 We live by faith, not
by sight. 8 We are confident, I say, and would
prefer to be away from the body and at home
with the Lord. 9 So we make it our goal to
please him, whether we are at home in the body
or away from it. 10 For we must all appear before the judgment seat of Christ, that each one
may receive what is due him for the things done
while in the body, whether good or bad.

The ministry of reconciliation

11 Since, then, we know what it is to fear
the Lord, we try to persuade men. What we are
is plain to God, and I hope it is also plain to
your conscience. 12 We are not trying to commend ourselves to you again, but are giving you
an opportunity to take pride in us, so that you
can answer those who take pride in what is seen
rather than in what is in the heart. 13 If we are
out of our mind, it is for the sake of God; if
we are in our right mind, it is for you. 14 For
Christ's love compels us, because we are convinced that one died for all, and therefore all
died. 15And he died for all that those who live

Phillips Modern English

Spirit as a guarantee of its truth. This makes us confident, whatever happens. We realise that being "at home" in the body means that to some extent we are "away" from the Lord, for we have to live by trusting him without seeing him. We are so sure of this that we would really rather be "away" from the body and be "at home with the Lord.

It is our aim, therefore, to please him, whether we are "at home" or "away". For every one of us will have to stand without pretence before Christ our judge, and we shall each receive our due for what we did when we lived in our bodies, whether it was good or bad.

5.11 Our ministry is based on solemn convictions

All our persuading of men, then, is with this solemn fear of God in our minds. What we are is utterly plain to God—and I hope to your consciences as well. No, we are not recommending ourselves to you again, but we can give you grounds for legitimate pride in us—if that is what you need to meet those who are so proud of the outward rather than the inward qualification. If we are "mad" it is for God's glory; if we are perfectly sane it is for your benefit. The very spring of our actions is the love of Christ. We look at it like this: if one died for all men, then, in a sense, they all died, and his pur-

Revised Standard Version

6 So we are always of good courage; we know
that while we are at home in the body we are
away from the Lord, 7 for we walk by faith,
not by sight. 8 We are of good courage, and we
would rather be away from the body and at
home with the Lord. 9 So whether we are at
home or away, we make it our aim to please
him. 10 For we must all appear before the
judgment seat of Christ, so that each one may
receive good or evil, according to what he has
done in the body.

11 Therefore, knowing the fear of the Lord,
we persuade men; but what we are is known to
God, and I hope it is known also to your conscience. 12 We are not commending ourselves to
you again but giving you cause to be proud of
us, so that you may be able to answer those
who pride themselves on a man's position and
not on his heart. 13 For if we are beside ourselves, it is for God; if we are in our right mind,
it is for you. 14 For the love of Christ controls
us, because we are convinced that one has died
for all; therefore all have died. 15 And he died

Jerusalem Bible

6 We are always full of confidence, then, when
we remember that to live in the body means to
be exiled from the Lord, 7 going as we do by
faith and not by sight—8 we are full of confidence, I say, and actually want to be exiled from
the body and make our home with the Lord.
9 Whether we are living in the body or exiled
from it, we are intent on pleasing him. 10 For all
the truth about us will be brought out in the
law court of Christ, and each of us will get
what he deserves for the things he did in the
body, good or bad.

The apostolate in action

11 And so it is with the fear of the Lord in
mind that we try to win people over. God knows
us for what we really are, and I hope that in
your consciences you know us too. 12 This is
not another attempt to commend ourselves to
you: we are simply giving you reasons to be
proud of us, so that you will have an answer
ready for the people who can boast more about
what they seem than what they are. 13 If we
seemed out of our senses, it was for God; but
if we are being reasonable now, it is for your
sake. 14 And this is because the love of Christ
overwhelms us when we reflect that if one man
has died for all, then all men should be dead;
15 and the reason he died for all was so that

New English Bible

Therefore we never cease to be confident. We know that so long as we are at home in the body we are exiles from the Lord; faith is our guide, we do not see him.[a] We are confident, I repeat, and would rather leave our home in the body and go to live with the Lord. We therefore make it our ambition, wherever we are, here or there, to be acceptable to him. For we must all have our lives laid open before the tribunal of Christ, where each must receive what is due to him for his conduct in the body, good or bad.

With this fear of the Lord before our eyes we address our appeal to men. To God our lives lie open, as I hope they also lie open to you in your heart of hearts. This is not another attempt to recommend ourselves to you: we are rather giving you a chance to show yourselves proud of us; then you will have something to say to those whose pride is all in outward show and not in inward worth. It may be we are beside ourselves, but it is for God; if we are in our right mind, it is for you. For the love of Christ leaves us no choice, when once we have reached the conclusion that one man died for all and therefore all mankind has died. His purpose in

[a] *Or* faith is our guide and not the things we see.

King James Version

died for all, that they which live should not
henceforth live unto themselves, but unto him
which died for them, and rose again. 16 Wherefore henceforth know we no man after the
flesh: yea, though we have known Christ after
the flesh, yet now henceforth know we *him* no
more. 17 Therefore if any man *be* in Christ, *he*
is a new creature: old things are passed away;
behold, all things are become new. 18 And all
things *are* of God, who hath reconciled us to
himself by Jesus Christ, and hath given to us
the ministry of reconciliation; 19 To wit, that
God was in Christ, reconciling the world unto
himself, not imputing their trespasses unto them;
and hath committed unto us the word of reconciliation. 20 Now then we are ambassadors for
Christ, as though God did beseech *you* by us:
we pray *you* in Christ's stead, be ye reconciled
to God. 21 For he hath made him *to be* sin for
us, who knew no sin; that we might be made the
righteousness of God in him.

Living Bible

that all who live—having received eternal life
from him—might live no longer for themselves,
to please themselves, but to spend their lives
pleasing Christ who died and rose again for
them. 16 So stop evaluating Christians by what
the world thinks about them or by what they
seem to be like on the outside. Once I mis-
takenly thought of Christ that way, merely as a
human being like myself. How differently I feel
now! 17 When someone becomes a Christian he
becomes a brand new person inside. He is not
the same any more. A new life has begun!

18 All these new things are from God who
brought us back to himself through what Christ
Jesus did. And God has given us the privilege
of urging everyone to come into his favor and
be reconciled to him. 19 For God was in Christ,
restoring the world to himself, no longer counting men's sins against them but blotting them
out. This is the wonderful message he has given
us to tell others. 20 We are Christ's ambassadors.
God is using us to speak to you: we beg you,
as though Christ himself were here pleading with
you, receive the love he offers you—be reconciled to God. 21 For God took the sinless Christ
and poured into him our sins. Then, in exchange,
he poured God's goodness into us! [b]

[*b*] Literally, "Him who knew no sin, he made sin on our behalf, that we might become the righteousness of God in him."

Today's English Version

should no longer live for themselves, but only
for him who died and was raised to life for their
sake.

16 No longer, then, do we judge anyone by
human standards. Even if at one time we judged
Christ according to human standards, we no
longer do so. 17 When anyone is joined to
Christ he is a new being; the old is gone, the
new has come. 18 All this is done by God, who
through Christ changed us from enemies into his
friends, and gave us the task of making others
his friends also. 19 Our message is that God was
making friends of all men through Christ. God
did not keep an account of their sins against
them, and he has given us the message of how
he makes them his friends.

20 Here we are, then, speaking for Christ,
as though God himself were appealing to you
through us: on Christ's behalf, we beg you, let
God change you from enemies into friends!
21 Christ was without sin, but for our sake God
made him share our sin in order that we, in
union with him, might share the righteousness
of God.

New International Version

should no longer live for themselves, but for
him who died for them and was raised again.

16 So from now on we regard no one from
a worldly point of view. Though we once regarded Christ in this way, we do so no longer.
17 Therefore, if anyone is in Christ, he is a new
creation; the old has gone, the new has come!
18 All this is from God, who reconciled us to
himself through Christ and gave us the ministry
of reconciliation: 19 that God was reconciling
the world to himself in Christ, not counting
men's sins against them. And he has committed
to us the message of reconciliation. 20 We are
therefore Christ's ambassadors, as though God
were making his appeal through us. We implore
you on Christ's behalf: Be reconciled to God.
21 God made him who had no sin to be sin[g] for
us, so that in him we might become the righteousness of God.

[*g*] Or *a sin offering.*

Phillips Modern English

pose in dying for them is that their lives should now be no longer lived for themselves but for him who died and was raised to life for them. This means that our knowledge of men can no longer be based on their outward lives (indeed, even though we knew Christ as a man we do not know him like that any longer). For if a man is in Christ he becomes a new person altogether—the past is finished and gone, everything has become fresh and new. All this is God's doing, for he has reconciled us to himself through Christ; and he has made us agents of the reconciliation. God was in Christ personally reconciling the world to himself—not counting their sins against them—and has commissioned us with the message of reconciliation. We are now Christ's ambassadors, as though God were appealing direct to you through us. For Christ's sake we beg you, "Make your peace with God." For God caused Christ, who himself knew nothing of sin, actually to *be* sin for our sakes, so that in Christ we might be made good with the goodness of God.

Revised Standard Version

for all, that those who live might live no longer for themselves but for him who for their sake died and was raised.

16 From now on, therefore, we regard no one from a human point of view; even though we once regarded Christ from a human point of view, we regard him thus no longer. 17 Therefore, if any one is in Christ, he is a new creation;[g] the old has passed away, behold, the new has come. 18 All this is from God, who through Christ reconciled us to himself and gave us the ministry of reconciliation; 19 that is, in Christ God was reconciling[h] the world to himself, not counting their trespasses against them, and entrusting to us the message of reconciliation. 20 So we are ambassadors for Christ, God making his appeal through us. We beseech you on behalf of Christ, be reconciled to God. 21 For our sake he made him to be sin who knew no sin, so that in him we might become the righteousness of God.

[g] Or *creature*. [h] Or *God was in Christ reconciling*.

Jerusalem Bible

living men should live no longer for themselves, but for him who died and was raised to life for them.

16 From now onward, therefore, we do not judge anyone by the standards of the flesh. Even if we did once know Christ in the flesh, that is not how we know him now. 17 And for anyone who is in Christ, there is a new creation; the old creation has gone, and now the new one is here. 18 It is all God's work. It was God who reconciled us to himself through Christ and gave us the work of handing on this reconciliation. 19 In other words, God in Christ was reconciling the world to himself, not holding men's faults against them, and he has entrusted to us the news that they are reconciled. 20 So we are ambassadors for Christ; it is as though God were appealing through us, and the appeal that we make in Christ's name is: be reconciled to God. 21 For our sake God made the sinless one into sin, so that in him we might become the goodness of God.

New English Bible

dying for all was that men, while still in life, should cease to live for themselves, and should live for him who for their sake died and was raised to life. With us therefore worldly standards have ceased to count in our estimate of any man; even if once they counted in our understanding of Christ, they do so now no longer. When anyone is united to Christ, there is a new world;[a] the old order has gone, and a new order has already begun.[b]

From first to last this has been the work of God. He has reconciled us men to himself through Christ, and he has enlisted us in this service of reconciliation. What I mean is, that God was in Christ reconciling the world to himself,[c] no longer holding men's misdeeds against them, and that he has entrusted us with the message of reconciliation. We come therefore as Christ's ambassadors. It is as if God were appealing to you through us: in Christ's name, we implore you, be reconciled to God! Christ was innocent of sin, and yet for our sake God made him one with the sinfulness of men,[d] so that in him we might be made one with the goodness of God himself.

[a] *Or* a new act of creation. [b] *Or* when anyone is united to Christ he is a new creature: his old life is over; a new life has already begun. [c] *Or* God was reconciling the world to himself by Christ. [d] *Or* and yet God made him a sin-offering for us.

King James Version

6 We then, *as* workers together *with him,* beseech *you* also that ye receive not the grace
of God in vain. 2 (For he saith, I have heard
thee in a time accepted, and in the day of salvation have I succoured thee: behold, now *is* the
accepted time; behold, now *is* the day of salvation.) 3 Giving no offence in any thing, that the
ministry be not blamed: 4 But in all *things* approving ourselves as the ministers of God, in
much patience, in afflictions, in necessities, in
distresses, 5 In stripes, in imprisonments, in tumults, in labours, in watchings, in fastings; 6 By
pureness, by knowledge, by longsuffering, by
kindness, by the Holy Ghost, by love unfeigned,
7 By the word of truth, by the power of God,
by the armour of righteousness on the right
hand and on the left, 8 By honour and dishonour, by evil report and good report: as deceivers, and *yet* true; 9 As unknown, and *yet*

Living Bible

6 As God's partners we beg you not to toss
aside this marvelous message of God's great
kindness. 2 For God says, "Your cry came to me
at a favorable time, when the doors of welcome
were wide open. I helped you on a day when
salvation was being offered." Right now God is
ready to welcome you. Today he is ready to
save you.
3 We try to live in such a way that no one
will ever be offended or kept back from finding
the Lord by the way we act, so that no one can
find fault with us and blame it on the Lord.
4 In fact, in everything we do we try to show
that we are true ministers of God.
We patiently endure suffering and hardship
and trouble of every kind. 5 We have been
beaten, put in jail, faced angry mobs, worked to
exhaustion, stayed awake through sleepless nights
of watching, and gone without food. 6 We have
proved ourselves to be what we claim by our
wholesome lives and by our understanding of
the Gospel and by our patience. We have been
kind and truly loving and filled with the Holy
Spirit. 7 We have been truthful, with God's
power helping us in all we do. All of the godly
man's arsenal—weapons of defense, and weapons
of attack—have been ours.
8 We stand true to the Lord whether others
honor us or despise us, whether they criticize
us or commend us. We are honest, but they call
us liars.
9 The world ignores us, but we are known to

Today's English Version

6 In our work together with God, then, we
beg of you; you have received God's grace,
and you must not let it be wasted. 2 Hear what
God says:

"I heard you in the hour to show you favor,
I helped you on the day to save you."

Listen! This is the hour to receive God's favor,
today is the day to be saved!
3 We do not want anyone to find fault with
our work, so we try not to put obstacles in
anyone's way. 4 Instead, in everything we do we
show that we are God's servants, by enduring
troubles, hardships, and difficulties with great
patience. 5 We have been beaten, jailed, and
mobbed; we have been overworked and have
gone without sleep or food. 6 By our purity,
knowledge, patience, and kindness we have
shown ourselves to be God's servants; by the
Holy Spirit, by our true love, 7 by our message
of truth, and by the power of God. We have
righteousness as our weapon, both to attack and
to defend ourselves. 8 We are honored and disgraced; we are insulted and praised. We are
treated as liars, yet we speak the truth; 9 as un-

New International Version

6 As God's fellow workers we urge you not
to receive God's grace in vain. 2 For he says,
"At the time of my favor I heard you,
and on the day of salvation I helped you."[h]
I tell you, now is the time of God's favor, now
is the day of salvation.

Paul's hardships

3 We put no stumbling block in anyone's
path, so that our ministry will not be discredited.
4 Rather, in every way we show ourselves to be
servants of God: in great endurance; in troubles,
hardships and distresses; 5 in beatings, imprisonments and riots; in hard work, sleepless nights
and hunger; 6 in purity, understanding, patience
and kindness; in the Holy Spirit and in sincere
love; 7 in truthful speech and in the power of
God; with weapons of righteousness in the right
hand and in the left; 8 through glory and dishonor, praise and blame; genuine, yet regarded
as impostors; 9 known, yet regarded as unknown;

[*h*] Isaiah 49:8.

Phillips Modern English

6.1 The hard but glorious life of God's ministers

As co-operators with God himself we beg you, then, not to fail to use the grace of God which you have received. For God's word is—

At an acceptable time I hearkened unto thee,
And in a day of salvation did I succour thee.

Now *is* the "acceptable time", and this very day *is* the "day of salvation".

As far as we are concerned we do not wish to stand in anyone's way, nor do we wish to bring discredit on the ministry God has given us. Indeed we want to prove ourselves genuine ministers of God whatever we have to go through—patient endurance of troubles, hardship, desperate situations, being flogged or imprisoned; being mobbed, overworked, sleepless and starving; with sincerity, with insight and patience; by sheer kindness and the Holy Spirit; with genuine love, speaking the plain truth, and living by the power of God. Our sole defence, our only weapon, is a life of integrity, whether we meet honour or dishonour, praise or blame. Called "imposters" we must be true, called "nobodies" we

Revised Standard Version

6 Working together with him, then, we entreat you not to accept the grace of God in
vain. 2 For he says,
"At the acceptable time I have listened to you,
and helped you on the day of salvation."
Behold, now is the acceptable time; behold,
now is the day of salvation. 3 We put no obstacle in any one's way, so that no fault may be
found with our ministry, 4 but as servants of
God we commend ourselves in every way:
through great endurance, in afflictions, hardships, calamities, 5 beatings, imprisonments, tumults, labors, watching, hunger; 6 by purity,
knowledge, forbearance, kindness, the Holy
Spirit, genuine love, 7 truthful speech, and the
power of God; with the weapons of righteousness for the right hand and for the left; 8 in
honor and dishonor, in ill repute and good repute. We are treated as impostors, and yet are
true; 9 as unknown, and yet well known; as dy-

Jerusalem Bible

6 As his fellow workers, we beg you once
again not to neglect the grace of God that
you have received. 2 For he says: *At the favorable time, I have listened to you; on the day
of salvation I came to your help.*[d] Well, now is
the favorable time; this is the day of salvation.
3 We do nothing that people might object to,
so as not to bring discredit on our function as
God's servants. 4 Instead, we prove we are servants of God by great fortitude in times of suffering: in times of hardship and distress; 5 when
we are flogged, or sent to prison, or mobbed;
laboring, sleepless, starving. 6 We prove we are
God's servants by our purity, knowledge, patience and kindness; by a spirit of holiness, by
a love free from affectation; 7 by the word of
truth and by the power of God; by being armed
with the weapons of righteousness in the right
hand and in the left, 8 prepared for honor or
disgrace, for blame or praise; taken for impostors while we are genuine; 9 obscure yet fa-

[*d*] Is. 49:8.

New English Bible

6 Sharing in God's work, we urge this appeal upon you: you have received the grace of God; do not let it go for nothing. God's own words are:

'In the hour of my favour I gave heed to you;
on the day of deliverance I came to your aid.'

The hour of favour has now come; now, I say, has the day of deliverance dawned.

In order that our service may not be brought into discredit, we avoid giving offence in anything. As God's servants, we try to recommend ourselves in all circumstances by our steadfast endurance: in distress, hardships, and dire straits; flogged, imprisoned, mobbed; overworked, sleepless, starving. We recommend ourselves by the innocence of our behaviour, our grasp of truth, our patience and kindliness; by gifts of the Holy Spirit, by sincere love, by declaring the truth, by the power of God. We wield the weapons of righteousness in right hand and left. Honour and dishonour, praise and blame, are alike our lot: we are the impostors who speak the truth, the

King James Version

well known; as dying, and, behold, we live; as
chastened, and not killed; 10 As sorrowful, yet
alway rejoicing; as poor, yet making many rich;
as having nothing, and *yet* possessing all things.
11 O *ye* Corinthians, our mouth is open unto
you, our heart is enlarged. 12 Ye are not straitened in us, but ye are straitened in your own
bowels. 13 Now for a recompense in the same,
(I speak as unto *my* children,) be ye also enlarged. 14 Be ye not unequally yoked together
with unbelievers: for what fellowship hath righteousness with unrighteousness? and what communion hath light with darkness? 15 And what
concord hath Christ with Belial? or what part
hath he that believeth with an infidel? 16 And
what agreement hath the temple of God with
idols? for ye are the temple of the living God;

Living Bible

God; we live close to death, but here we are,
still very much alive. We have been injured but
kept from death. 10 Our hearts ache, but at the
same time we have the joy of the Lord. We are
poor, but we give rich spiritual gifts to others.
We own nothing, and yet we enjoy everything.
11 Oh, my dear Corinthian friends! I have
told you all my feelings; I love you with all my
heart. 12 Any coldness still between us is not
because of any lack of love on my part, but because your love is too small and does not reach
out to me and draw me in. 13 I am talking to
you now as if you truly were my very own children. Open your hearts to us! Return our love!
14 Don't be teamed with those who do not
love the Lord, for what do the people of God
have in common with the people of sin? How
can light live with darkness? 15 And what harmony can there be between Christ and the devil?
How can a Christian be a partner with one who
doesn't believe? 16 And what union can there be
between God's temple and idols? For you are
God's temple, the home of the living God, and

Today's English Version

known, yet we are known by all; as though we
were dead, but, as you see, we live on. Although
punished, we are not killed; 10 although saddened, we are always glad; we seem poor, but
we make many people rich; we seem to have
nothing, yet we really possess everything.
11 Dear friends in Corinth! We have spoken
frankly to you, we have opened wide our hearts.
12 We have not closed our hearts to you; it is
you who have closed your hearts to us. 13 I
speak now as though you were my children:
show us the same feelings that we have for you.
Open wide your hearts!

Warning against pagan influences

14 Do not try to work together as equals with
unbelievers, for it cannot be done. How can
right and wrong be partners? How can light and
darkness live together? 15 How can Christ and
the Devil agree? What does a believer have in
common with an unbeliever? 16 How can God's
temple come to terms with pagan idols? For we
are the temple of the living God! As God himself has said,

New International Version

dying, and yet we live on; beaten, and yet not
killed; 10 sorrowful, yet always rejoicing; poor,
yet making many rich; having nothing, and yet
possessing everything.
11 We have spoken freely to you, Corinthians,
and opened wide our hearts to you. 12 We are
not withholding our affection from you, but you
are withholding yours from us. 13 As a fair exchange—I speak as to my children—open wide
your hearts also.

Do not be yoked with unbelievers

14 Do not be yoked together with unbelievers.
For what do righteousness and wickedness have
in common? Or what fellowship can light have
with darkness? 15 What harmony is there between Christ and Belial? [i] What does a believer
have in common with an unbeliever? 16 What
agreement is there between the temple of God
and idols? For we are the temple of the living
God. As God has said:

[i] Greek *Beliar*.

Phillips Modern English

must be in the public eye. Never far from death, yet here we are alive, always "going through it" yet never "going under". We know sorrow, yet our joy is inextinguishable. We have "nothing to bless ourselves with" yet we bless many others with true riches. We are penniless, and yet we possess everything.

6.11 We have used utter frankness, won't you do the same?

Dear friends in Corinth, we are hiding nothing from you and our hearts are absolutely open to you. Any restraint between us must be on your side, for we assure you there is none on ours. Do reward me (I talk to you as though you were my own children) with the same complete candour!

6.14 We must warn you against entanglement with pagans

Don't link up with unbelievers and try to work with them. What common interest can there be between goodness and evil? How can light and darkness share life together? How can there be harmony between Christ and the devil? What can a believer have in common with an unbeliever? What common ground can idols hold with the temple of God? For we, remember, are ourselves temples of the living God, as God has said:

Revised Standard Version

ing, and behold we live; as punished, and yet not killed; 10 as sorrowful, yet always rejoicing; as poor, yet making many rich; as having nothing, and yet possessing everything.

11 Our mouth is open to you, Corinthians; our heart is wide. 12 You are not restricted by us, but you are restricted in your own affections. 13 In return—I speak as to children—widen your hearts also.

14 Do not be mismated with unbelievers. For what partnership have righteousness and iniquity? Or what fellowship has light with darkness? 15 What accord has Christ with Belial?[i] Or what has a believer in common with an unbeliever? 16 What agreement has the temple of God with idols? For we are the temple of the living God; as God said,

[*i*] Greek *Beliar*.

Jerusalem Bible

mous; said to be dying and here are we alive; rumored to be executed before we are sentenced; 10 thought most miserable and yet we are always rejoicing; taken for paupers though we make others rich, for people having nothing though we have everything.

Paul opens his heart. A warning

11 Corinthians, we have spoken to you very frankly; our mind has been opened in front of you. 12 Any constraint that you feel is not on our side; the constraint is in your own selves. 13 I speak as if to children of mine: as a fair exchange, open your minds in the same way.

14 Do not harness yourselves in an uneven team with unbelievers. Virtue is no companion for crime. Light and darkness have nothing in common. 15 Christ is not the ally of Beliar, nor has a believer anything to share with an unbeliever. 16 The temple of God has no common ground with idols, and that is what we are—the temple of the living God. We have God's

New English Bible

unknown men whom all men know; dying we still live on; disciplined by suffering, we are not done to death; in our sorrows we have always cause for joy; poor ourselves, we bring wealth to many; penniless, we own the world.

Men of Corinth, we have spoken very frankly to you; we have opened our heart wide to you all. On our part there is no constraint; any constraint there may be is in yourselves. In fair exchange then (may a father speak so to his children?) open wide your hearts to us.

Problems of church life and discipline

Do not unite yourselves with unbelievers; they are no fit mates for you. What has righteousness to do with wickedness? Can light consort with darkness? Can Christ agree with Belial, or a believer join hands with an unbeliever? Can there be a compact between the temple of God and the idols of the heathen? And the temple of the living God is what we are. God's own words are:

King James Version

as God hath said, I will dwell in them, and walk
in *them;* and I will be their God, and they shall
be my people. 17 Wherefore come out from
among them, and be ye separate, saith the Lord,
and touch not the unclean *thing;* and I will receive you, 18 And will be a Father unto you,
and ye shall be my sons and daughters, saith the
Lord Almighty.

7 Having therefore these promises, dearly beloved, let us cleanse ourselves from all filthiness of the flesh and spirit, perfecting holiness
in the fear of God. 2 Receive us; we have
wronged no man, we have corrupted no man,
we have defrauded no man. 3 I speak not *this*
to condemn *you:* for I have said before, that ye
are in our hearts to die and live with *you.*
4 Great *is* my boldness of speech toward you,
great *is* my glorying of you: I am filled with

Living Bible

God has said of you, "I will live in them and
walk among them, and I will be their God and
they shall be my people." 17 That is why the
Lord has said, "Leave them; separate yourselves
from them; don't touch their filthy things, and
I will welcome you, 18 and be a Father to you,
and you will be my sons and daughters."

7 Having such great promises as these, dear
friends, let us turn away from everything
wrong, whether of body or spirit, and purify
ourselves, living in the wholesome fear of God,
giving ourselves to him alone. 2 Please open
your hearts to us again, for not one of you has
suffered any wrong from us. Not one of you
was led astray. We have cheated no one nor
taken advantage of anyone. 3 I'm not saying this
to scold or blame you, for, as I have said before, you are in my heart forever and I live and
die with you. 4 I have the highest confidence in
you, and my pride in you is great. You have

Today's English Version

"I will make my home with my people
and live among them;
I will be their God,
and they shall be my people."

17 And so the Lord says,

"You must leave them,
and separate yourselves from them.
Have nothing to do with what is unclean,
and I will accept you.
18 I will be your father,
and you shall be my sons and daughters,
says the Lord Almighty."

7 All these promises are made to us, my dear
friends. So then, let us purify ourselves from
everything that makes body or soul unclean, and
let us be completely holy, by living in the fear
of God.

Paul's joy

2 Make room for us in your hearts. We have
done wrong to no one, we have ruined no one,
nor tried to take advantage of anyone. 3 I do
not say this to condemn you; for, as I have
said before, you are so dear to us that we are
together always, whether we live or die. 4 I am
so sure of you, I take such pride in you! In all

New International Version

"I will live with them and walk among them,
and I will be their God,
and they will be my people."[j]
17 "Therefore come out from them
and be separate,
says the Lord.

Touch no unclean thing,
and I will receive you."[k]
18 "I will be a Father to you,
and you will be my sons and daughters,
says the Lord Almighty."[l]

7 Since we have these promises, dear friends,
let us purify ourselves from everything that
contaminates body and spirit, and let us strive
for perfection out of reverence for God.

Paul's joy

2 Make room for us in your hearts. We have
wronged no one, we have corrupted no one, we
have exploited no one. 3 I do not say this to
condemn you; I have said before that you have
such a place in our hearts that we would live or
die with you. 4 I have great confidence in you;
I take great pride in you. I am greatly en-

[*j*] Lev. 26:12; Jer. 32:38; Ezek. 37:27. [*k*] Isaiah 52:11; Ezek. 20:34,41. [*l*] 2 Samuel 7:14; 7:8.

Phillips Modern English

I will dwell in them and walk in them:
And I will be their God, and they shall be my people.
Therefore
Come ye out from among them and be ye separate, saith the Lord,
And touch no unclean thing;
And I will receive you,
And will be to you a Father,
And ye shall be to me sons and daughters,
Saith the Lord Almighty.

With these promises ringing in our ears, dear friends, let us cleanse ourselves from anything that pollutes body or soul. Let us prove our reverence for God by consecrating ourselves to him completely.

7.2 Does "that letter" still rankle? Hear my explanation

Do make room in your hearts for us! Not one of you has ever been wronged or ruined or cheated by us. I don't say this to condemn your attitude, but simply because, as I said before, whether we meet death or life together you live in our hearts. I talk to you with utter frankness; I think of you with deepest pride. Whatever troubles I have gone through, the thought of

Revised Standard Version

"I will live in them and move among them,
and I will be their God,
and they shall be my people.
17 Therefore come out from them,
and be separate from them, says the Lord,
and touch nothing unclean;
then I will welcome you,
18 and I will be a father to you,
and you shall be my sons and daughters,
says the Lord Almighty."

7 Since we have these promises, beloved, let us cleanse ourselves from every defilement of body and spirit, and make holiness perfect in the fear of God.

2 Open your hearts to us; we have wronged no one, we have corrupted no one, we have taken advantage of no one. 3 I do not say this to condemn you, for I said before that you are in our hearts, to die together and to live together. 4 I have great confidence in you; I have

Jerusalem Bible

word for it: *I will make my home among them and live with them; I will be their God and they shall be my people.*[e] 17 Then *come away from them and keep aloof, says the Lord. Touch nothing that is unclean,*[f] *and I will welcome you* 18 *and be your father, and you shall be my sons and daughters, says the Almighty Lord.*[g]

7 With promises like these made to us, dear brothers, let us wash off all that can soil either body or spirit, to reach perfection of holiness in the fear of God.

2 Keep a place for us in your hearts. We have not injured anyone, or ruined anyone, or exploited anyone. 3 I am not saying this to put any blame on you; as I have already told you, you are in our hearts—together we live or together we die. 4 I have the very greatest confidence in you, and I am so proud of you that

[e] Lv. 26:11-12. [f] Is. 52:11. [g] Is. 43:6.

New English Bible

'I will live and move about among them; I will be their God, and they shall be my people.' And therefore, 'come away and leave them, separate yourselves, says the Lord; touch nothing unclean. Then I will accept you, says the Lord, the Ruler of all being; I will be a father to you, and you shall be my sons and daughters.'

7 Such are the promises that have been made to us, dear friends. Let us therefore cleanse ourselves from all that can defile flesh or spirit, and in the fear of God complete our consecration.

Do make a place for us in your hearts! We have wronged no one, ruined no one, taken advantage of no one. I do not want to blame you. Why, as I have told you before, the place you have in our heart is such that, come death, come life, we meet it together. I am perfectly frank with you. I have great pride in you. In all our

King James Version

comfort, I am exceeding joyful in all our tribulation. 5 For, when we were come into Macedonia, our flesh had no rest, but we were
troubled on every side; without *were* fightings,
within *were* fears. 6 Nevertheless God, that comforteth those that are cast down, comforted us
by the coming of Titus; 7 And not by his coming
only, but by the consolation wherewith he was
comforted in you, when he told us your earnest
desire, your mourning, your fervent mind toward me; so that I rejoiced the more. 8 For
though I made you sorry with a letter, I do not
repent, though I did repent: for I perceive that
the same epistle hath made you sorry, though *it*
were but for a season. 9 Now I rejoice, not that
ye were made sorry, but that ye sorrowed to
repentance: for ye were made sorry after a
godly manner, that ye might receive damage by
us in nothing. 10 For godly sorrow worketh
repentance to salvation not to be repented of:
but the sorrow of the world worketh death.
11 For behold this selfsame thing, that ye sorrowed after a godly sort, what carefulness it
wrought in you, yea, *what* clearing of yourselves, yea, *what* indignation, yea, *what* fear,
yea, *what* vehement desire, yea, *what* zeal, yea,

Living Bible

greatly encouraged me; you have made me so
happy in spite of all my suffering.
5 When we arrived in Macedonia there was
no rest for us; outside, trouble was on every
hand and all around us; within us, our hearts
were full of dread and fear. 6 Then God who
cheers those who are discouraged refreshed us
by the arrival of Titus. 7 Not only was his
presence a joy, but also the news that he brought
of the wonderful time he had with you. When
he told me how much you were looking forward
to my visit, and how sorry you were about what
had happened, and about your loyalty and warm
love for me, well, I overflowed with joy!
8 I am no longer sorry that I sent that letter
to you, though I was very sorry for a time,
realizing how painful it would be to you. But it
hurt you only for a little while. 9 Now I am
glad I sent it, not because it hurt you, but because the pain turned you to God. It was a
good kind of sorrow you felt, the kind of sorrow God wants his people to have, so that I
need not come to you with harshness. 10 For
God sometimes uses sorrow in our lives to help
us turn away from sin and seek eternal life.
We should never regret his sending it. But the
sorrow of the man who is not a Christian is not
the sorrow of true repentance and does not prevent eternal death.
11 Just see how much good this grief from
the Lord did for you! You no longer shrugged
your shoulders, but became earnest and sincere,
and very anxious to get rid of the sin that I
wrote you about. You became frightened about
what had happened, and longed for me to come
and help. You went right to work on the prob-

Today's English Version

our troubles I am still full of courage, I am
running over with joy.
5 Even after we arrived in Macedonia we did
not have any rest. There were troubles everywhere, quarrels with others, fears in our hearts.
6 But God, who encourages the downhearted,
encouraged us with the coming of Titus. 7 It
was not only his coming, but also his report of
how you encouraged him. He told us how much
you want to see me, how sorry you are, how
ready you are to defend me; and so I am even
happier now.
8 For even if that letter of mine made you
sad, I am not sorry I wrote it. I could have
been sorry about it when I saw that the letter
made you sad for a while. 9 But now I am
happy—not because I made you sad, but because your sadness made you change your ways.
That sadness was used by God, and so we caused
you no harm. 10 For the sadness that is used by
God brings a change of heart that leads to salvation—and there is no regret in that! But
worldly sadness causes death. 11 See what God
did with this sadness of yours: how earnest it
has made you, how eager to prove your innocence! Such indignation, such alarm, such feelings, such devotion, such readiness to punish

New International Version

couraged; in all our troubles my joy knows no
bounds.
5 For when we came into Macedonia, this
body of ours had no rest, but we were harassed
at every turn—conflicts on the outside, fears
within. 6 But God, who comforts the downcast,
comforted us by the coming of Titus, 7 and not
only by his coming but also by the comfort
you had given him. He told us about your affection, your deep sorrow, your ardent concern
for me, so that my joy was greater than ever.
8 Even if I caused you sorrow by my letter,
I do not regret it. Though I did regret it—I see
that my letter hurt you, but only for a little
while—9 yet now I am happy, not because you
were made sorry, but because your sorrow led
you to repentance. For you became sorrowful
as God intended and so were not harmed in any
way by us. 10 Godly sorrow brings repentance
that leads to salvation and leaves no regret, but
worldly sorrow brings death. 11 See what this
godly sorrow has produced in you: what earnestness, what eagerness to clear yourselves, what
indignation, what alarm, what affection, what

Phillips Modern English

you has filled me with comfort and deep happiness.

For even when we arrived in Macedonia we found no rest but trouble all round us—wrangling outside and anxiety within. Not but what God, who cheers the depressed, gave us the comfort of the arrival of Titus. And it wasn't merely his coming that cheered us, but the comfort you had given him, for he could tell us of your eagerness to see me, your deep sorrow and keen interest on my behalf. All that made me doubly glad to see him. For although my letter had hurt you I don't regret it now (even if I did at one time). I can see that the letter did upset you, though only for a time, and now I am glad I sent it, not because I want to hurt you but because it made you grieve for things that were wrong. In other words, the result was to make you sorry as God would have had you sorry, and not to make you feel injured by what we said. The sorrow which God uses means a change of heart and leads to salvation without regret—it is the world's sorrow that is such a deadly thing. You can look back now and see how the hand of God was in that sorrow. Look how seriously it made you think, how eager it made you to prove your innocence, how indignant it made you and how afraid! Look how it made you long for my presence, how it stirred

Revised Standard Version

great pride in you; I am filled with comfort.
With all our affliction, I am overjoyed.
5 For even when we came into Macedonia,
our bodies had no rest but we were afflicted at
every turn—fighting without and fear within.
6 But God, who comforts the downcast, comforted us by the coming of Titus, 7 and not only
by his coming but also by the comfort with
which he was comforted in you, as he told us
of your longing, your mourning, your zeal for
me, so that I rejoiced still more. 8 For even if
I made you sorry with my letter, I do not regret it (though I did regret it), for I see that
that letter grieved you, though only for a while.
9 As it is, I rejoice, not because you were grieved,
but because you were grieved into repenting;
for you felt a godly grief, so that you suffered
no loss through us. 10 For godly grief produces
a repentance that leads to salvation and brings
no regret, but worldly grief produces death.
11 For see what earnestness this godly grief has
produced in you, what eagerness to clear yourselves, what indignation, what alarm, what longing, what zeal, what punishment! At every point

Jerusalem Bible

in all our trouble I am filled with consolation and my joy is overflowing.

Paul in Macedonia; he is joined by Titus

5 Even after we had come to Macedonia,
however, there was no rest for this body of
ours. Far from it; we found trouble on all sides:
quarrels outside, misgivings inside. 6 But God
comforts the miserable, and he comforted us, by
the arrival of Titus, 7 and not only by his arrival but also by the comfort which he had
gained from you. He has told us all about how
you want to see me, how sorry you were, and
how concerned for me, and so I am happier now
than I was before.
8 But to tell the truth, even if I distressed
you by my letter, I do not regret it. I did regret
it before, and I see that that letter did distress
you, at least for a time; 9 but I am happy now
—not because I made you suffer, but because
your suffering led to your repentance. Yours
has been a kind of suffering that God approves,
and so you have come to no kind of harm from
us. 10 To suffer in God's way means changing
for the better and leaves no regrets, but to suffer as the world knows suffering brings death.
11 Just look at what suffering in God's way has
brought you: what keenness, what explanations,
what indignation, what alarm! Yes, and what
aching to see me, what concern for me, and

New English Bible

many troubles my cup is full of consolation, and overflows with joy.

Even when we reached Macedonia there was still no relief for this poor body of ours; instead, there was trouble at every turn, quarrels all round us, forebodings in our heart. But God, who brings comfort to the downcast, has comforted us by the arrival of Titus, and not merely by his arrival, but by his being so greatly comforted about you. He has told us how you long for me, how sorry you are, and how eager to take my side; and that has made me happier still.

Even if I did wound you by the letter I sent, I do not now regret it. I may have been sorry for it when I saw that the letter had caused you pain, even if only for a time; but now I am happy, not that your feelings were wounded but that the wound led to a change of heart. You bore the smart as God would have you bear it, and so you are no losers by what we did. For the wound which is borne in God's way brings a change of heart too salutary to regret; but the hurt which is borne in the world's way brings death. You bore your hurt in God's way, and see what its results have been! It made you take the matter seriously and vindicate yourselves. How angered you were, how apprehensive! How your longing for me awoke, yes, and

King James Version

what revenge! In all *things* ye have approved yourselves to be clear in this matter. 12 Wherefore, though I wrote unto you, *I did it* not for his cause that had done the wrong, nor for his cause that suffered wrong, but that our care for you in the sight of God might appear unto you. 13 Therefore we were comforted in your comfort: yea, and exceedingly the more joyed we for the joy of Titus, because his spirit was refreshed by you all. 14 For if I have boasted any thing to him of you, I am not ashamed; but as we spake all things to you in truth, even so our boasting, which *I made* before Titus, is found a truth. 15 And his inward affection is more abundant toward you, whilst he remembereth the obedience of you all, how with fear and trembling ye received him. 16 I rejoice therefore that I have confidence in you in all *things*.

8 Moreover, brethren, we do you to wit of the grace of God bestowed on the churches of Macedonia; 2 How that in a great trial of affliction, the abundance of their joy and their

Living Bible

lem and cleared it up [punishing the man who sinned [a]]. You have done everything you could to make it right.

12 I wrote as I did so the Lord could show how much you really do care for us. That was my purpose even more than to help the man[a] who sinned, or his father[a] to whom he did the wrong.

13 In addition to the encouragement you gave us by your love, we were made happier still by Titus' joy when you gave him such a fine welcome and set his mind at ease. 14 I told him how it would be—told him before he left me of my pride in you—and you didn't disappoint me. I have always told you the truth and now my boasting to Titus has also proved true! 15 He loves you more than ever when he remembers the way you listened to him so willingly and received him so anxiously and with such deep concern. 16 How happy this makes me, now that I am sure all is well between us again. Once again I can have perfect confidence in you.

8 Now I want to tell you what God in his grace has done for the churches in Macedonia.

2 Though they have been going through much trouble and hard times, they have mixed their wonderful joy with their deep poverty, and the

[a] Implied.

Today's English Version

wrongdoing! You have shown yourselves to be without fault in the whole matter.

12 So, even though I wrote that letter, it was not because of the one who did wrong, or the one who was wronged. Instead, I wrote it to make plain to you, in God's sight, how deep is your devotion to us. 13 That is why we were encouraged.

Not only were we encouraged; how happy Titus made us with his happiness over the way in which all of you helped to cheer him up. 14 I did boast of you to him, and you have not disappointed me. We have always spoken the truth to you. In the same way, the boast we made to Titus has proved true. 15 And so his love for you grows stronger, as he remembers how all of you were ready to obey, how you welcomed him with fear and trembling. 16 How happy I am that I can depend on you completely!

Christian giving

8 We want you to know, brothers, what God's grace has done in the churches in Macedonia. 2 They have been severely tested by the troubles they went through; but their joy was so

New International Version

concern, what readiness to see justice done. At every point you have proved yourselves to be innocent in this matter. 12 So even though I wrote to you, it was not on account of the one who did the wrong or of the injured party, but rather that before God you could see for yourselves how devoted to us you are. 13 By all this we are encouraged.

In addition to our own encouragement, we were especially delighted to see how happy Titus was, because all of you helped put his mind at ease. 14 I had boasted to him about you, and you have not embarrassed me. But just as everything we said to you was true, so our boasting about you to Titus has proved to be true as well. 15 And his affection for you is all the greater when he remembers that you were all obedient, receiving him with fear and trembling. 16 I am glad I can have complete confidence in you.

Generosity encouraged

8 And now, brothers, we want you to know about the grace that God has given the Macedonian churches. 2 Out of the most severe trial, their overflowing joy and their extreme

Phillips Modern English

up your keenness for the faith, how ready it made you to punish the offender! You have completely cleared yourselves in this matter.

Now I did not write that letter really for the sake of the man who sinned, or even for the sake of the one who was sinned against, but to let you see for yourselves, in the sight of God, how deeply you really do care for us. That is why we now feel so encouraged, and, in addition, our sense of joy was greatly enhanced by knowing what happiness you all gave to Titus by setting his mind at rest. You see, I had told him of my pride in you, and you have not let me down. I have always spoken the truth *to* you, and this proves that my proud words *about* you were true as well. Titus himself has a much greater love for you, now that he has seen for himself the obedience you gave him, and the respect and reverence with which you treated him. I am profoundly glad to have my confidence in you so fully proved.

8.1 *The Macedonian churches have given magnificently: will you not do so too?*

Now, my brothers, we must tell you about the grace that God has given to the Macedonian churches. Somehow, in most difficult circumstances, their overflowing joy and the fact of being down to their last penny themselves, pro-

Revised Standard Version

you have proved yourselves guiltless in the matter. 12 So although I wrote to you, it was not on account of the one who did the wrong, nor on account of the one who suffered the wrong, but in order that your zeal for us might be revealed to you in the sight of God. 13 Therefore we are comforted.

And besides our own comfort we rejoiced still more at the joy of Titus, because his mind has been set at rest by you all. 14 For if I have expressed to him some pride in you, I was not put to shame; but just as everything we said to you was true, so our boasting before Titus has proved true. 15 And his heart goes out all the more to you, as he remembers the obedience of you all, and the fear and trembling with which you received him. 16 I rejoice, because I have perfect confidence in you.

8 We want you to know, brethren, about the grace of God which has been shown in the churches of Macedonia, 2 for in a severe test of affliction, their abundance of joy and their ex-

Jerusalem Bible

what justice done! In every way you have shown yourselves blameless in this affair. 12 So then, though I wrote the letter to you, it was not written for the sake either of the offender or of the one offended; it was to make you realize, in the sight of God, your own concern for us.
13 That is what we have found so encouraging.

With this encouragement, too, we had the even greater happiness of finding Titus so happy; thanks to you all, he has no more worries; 14 I had rather boasted to him about you, and now I have not been made to look foolish; in fact, our boasting to Titus has proved to be as true as anything that we ever said to you. 15 His own personal affection for you is all the greater when he remembers how willing you have all been, and with what deep respect you welcomed him. 16 I am very happy knowing that I can rely on you so completely.

II. Organization of the collection

Why the Corinthians should be generous

8 Now here, brothers, is the news of the grace of God which was given in the churches in Macedonia; 2 and of how, throughout great trials by suffering, their constant cheer-

New English Bible

your devotion and your eagerness to see justice done! At every point you have cleared yourselves of blame in this trouble. And so, although I did send you that letter, it was not the offender or his victim that most concerned me. My aim in writing was to help to make plain to you, in the sight of God, how truly you are devoted to us. That is why we have been so encouraged.

But besides being encouraged ourselves we have also been delighted beyond everything by seeing how happy Titus is: you have all helped to set his mind completely at rest. Anything I may have said to him to show my pride in you has been justified. Every word we ever addressed to you bore the mark of truth; and the same holds of the proud boast we made in the presence of Titus: that also has proved true. His heart warms all the more to you as he recalls how ready you all were to do what he asked, meeting him as you did in fear and trembling. How happy I am now to have complete confidence in you!

Trials of a Christian missionary

8 We must tell you, friends, about the grace of generosity which God has imparted to[a] our congregations in Macedonia. The troubles they have been through have tried them hard, yet in all this they have been so exuberantly

[a] *Or* how gracious God has been to . . .

King James Version

deep poverty abounded unto the riches of their
liberality. 3 For to *their* power, I bear record,
yea, and beyond *their* power *they were* willing
of themselves; 4 Praying us with much entreaty
that we would receive the gift, and *take upon us*
the fellowship of the ministering to the saints.
5 And *this they did,* not as we hoped, but first
gave their own selves to the Lord, and unto us
by the will of God. 6 Insomuch that we desired
Titus, that as he had begun, so he would also
finish in you the same grace also. 7 Therefore,
as ye abound in every *thing, in* faith, and utterance, and knowledge, and *in* all diligence, and
in your love to us, *see* that ye abound in this
grace also. 8 I speak not by commandment, but
by occasion of the forwardness of others, and
to prove the sincerity of your love. 9 For ye
know the grace of our Lord Jesus Christ, that,
though he was rich, yet for your sakes he became poor, that ye through his poverty might be
rich. 10 And herein I give *my* advice: for this is
expedient for you, who have begun before, not

Living Bible

result has been an overflow of giving to others.
3 They gave not only what they could afford, but
far more; and I can testify that they did it because they wanted to, and not because of nagging on my part. 4 They begged us to take the
money so they could share in the joy of helping
the Christians in Jerusalem. 5 Best of all, they
went beyond our highest hopes, for their first
action was to dedicate themselves to the Lord
and to us, for whatever directions God might
give to them through us. 6 They were so enthusiastic about it that we have urged Titus, who
encouraged your giving in the first place, to visit
you and encourage you to complete your share
in this ministry of giving. 7 You people there
are leaders in so many ways—you have so much
faith, so many good preachers, so much learning,
so much enthusiasm, so much love for us. Now
I want you to be leaders also in the spirit of
cheerful giving. 8 I am not giving you an order;
I am not saying you must do it, but others are
eager for it. This is one way to prove that your
love is real, that it goes beyond mere words.

9 You know how full of love and kindness
our Lord Jesus was: though he was so very rich,
yet to help you he became so very poor, so that
by being poor he could make you rich.

10 I want to suggest that you finish what you
started to do a year ago, for you were not only

Today's English Version

great that they were extremely generous in their
giving, even though they were very poor. 3 I assure you, they gave as much as they could, and
even more than they could. Of their own free
will 4 they begged us and insisted on the privilege of having a part in helping God's people
in Judea. 5 It was more than we could have
hoped for! First they gave themselves to the
Lord; and then, by God's will, they gave themselves to us as well. 6 So we urged Titus, who
began this work, to continue it and help you
complete this special service of love. 7 You are
so rich in all you have: in faith, speech, and
knowledge, in your eagerness to help, and in
your love for us. And so we want you to be
generous also in this service of love.

8 I am not laying down any rules. But by
showing how eager others are to help, I am trying to find out how real your own love is. 9 For
you know the grace of our Lord Jesus Christ;
rich as he was, he made himself poor for your
sake, in order to make you rich by means of his
poverty.

10 This is my opinion on the matter: it is
better for you to finish now what you began

New International Version

poverty welled up in rich generosity. 3 For I
testify that they gave as much as they were able,
and even beyond their ability. Entirely on their
own, 4 they urgently pleaded with us for the
privilege of sharing in this service to the saints.
5 And they did not do as we expected, but they
gave themselves first to the Lord and then to
us in keeping with God's will. 6 So we urged
Titus, since he had earlier made a beginning, to
bring also to completion this act of grace on
your part. 7 But just as you excel in everything
—in faith, in speech, in knowledge, in complete
earnestness and in your love for us[m]—see that
you also excel in this grace of giving.

8 I am not commanding you, but I want to
test the sincerity of your love by comparing it
with the earnestness of others. 9 For you know
the grace of our Lord Jesus Christ, that though
he was rich, yet for your sakes he became poor,
so that you through his poverty might become
rich.

10 And here is my advice about what is best
for you in this matter: Last year you were the

[m] Many MSS read *our love for you.*

Phillips Modern English

duced a magnificent concern for other people. I can guarantee that they were willing to give to the limit of their means, yes and beyond their means, without the slightest urging from me or anyone else. In fact they simply begged us to accept their gifts and so let them share the honour of supporting their brothers in Christ. Nor was their gift, as I must confess I had expected, a mere cash payment. Instead they made a complete dedication of themselves first to the Lord and then to us, because God willed it.

Now this has made us ask Titus, who began this task, to complete it by arranging for you to share in this work of generosity. Already you are well to the fore in every good quality—you have faith, you can express that faith in words; you have knowledge, enthusiasm and your love for us. Could you not add generosity to your virtues? I don't give you this as an order. It is only my suggestion, prompted by what I have seen in others of eagerness to help, that here is a way to prove the reality of your love. Do you remember the generosity of Jesus Christ, the Lord of us all? He was rich, yet he became poor for your sakes so that his poverty might make you rich.

8.10 *I merely suggest that you finish your original generous gesture*

Here is my opinion in the matter. I think it would be a good thing for you, who were the first a year ago to think of helping, as well as

Revised Standard Version

treme poverty have overflowed in a wealth of
liberality on their part. 3 For they gave according to their means, as I can testify, and beyond their means, of their own free will, 4 begging us earnestly for the favor of taking part in
the relief of the saints—5 and this, not as we
expected, but first they gave themselves to the
Lord and to us by the will of God. 6 Accordingly we have urged Titus that as he had already
made a beginning, he should also complete
among you this gracious work. 7 Now as you
excel in everything—in faith, in utterance, in
knowledge, in all earnestness, and in your love
for us—see that you excel in this gracious work
also.
8 I say this not as a command, but to prove
by the earnestness of others that your love also
is genuine. 9 For you know the grace of our
Lord Jesus Christ, that though he was rich, yet
for your sake he became poor, so that by his
poverty you might become rich. 10 And in this
matter I give my advice: it is best for you now

Jerusalem Bible

fulness and their intense poverty have overflowed
in a wealth of generosity. 3 I can swear that
they gave not only as much as they could afford, but far more, and quite spontaneously,
4 begging and begging us for the favor of sharing in this service to the saints 5 and, what was
quite unexpected, they offered their own selves
first to God and, under God, to us.
6 Because of this, we have asked Titus, since
he has already made a beginning, to bring this
work of mercy to the same point of success
among you. 7 You always have the most of
everything—of faith, of eloquence, of understanding, of keenness for any cause, and the
biggest share of our affection—so we expect
you to put the most into this work of mercy
too. 8 It is not an order that I am giving you;
I am just testing the genuineness of your love
against the keenness of others. 9 Remember how
generous the Lord Jesus was: he was rich, but
he became poor for your sake, to make you
rich out of his poverty. 10 As I say, I am only
making a suggestion; it is only fair to you, since

New English Bible

happy that from the depths of their poverty they have shown themselves lavishly open-handed. Going to the limit of their resources, as I can testify, and even beyond that limit, they begged us most insistently, and on their own initiative, to be allowed to share in this generous service to their fellow-Christians. And their giving surpassed our expectations; for they gave their very selves, offering them in the first instance to the Lord, but also, under God, to us. The upshot is that we have asked Titus, who began it all, to visit you and bring this work of generosity also to completion. You are so rich in everything—in faith, speech, knowledge, and zeal of every kind, as well as in the loving regard you have for us[a]—surely you should show yourselves equally lavish in this generous service! This is not meant as an order; by telling you how keen others are I am putting your love to the test. For you know how generous our Lord Jesus Christ has been: he was rich, yet for your sake he became poor, so that through his poverty you might become rich.

Here is my considered opinion on the matter. What I ask you to do is in your own interests. You made a good beginning last year both in

[a] *Some witnesses read* the love we have for you, *or* the love which we have kindled in your hearts.

King James Version

only to do, but also to be forward a year ago.
11 Now therefore perform the doing *of it;* that as *there was* a readiness to will, so *there may be* a performance also out of that which ye have.
12 For if there be first a willing mind, *it is* accepted according to that a man hath, *and* not according to that he hath not. 13 For *I mean* not that other men be eased, and ye burdened:
14 But by an equality, *that* now at this time your abundance *may be a supply* for their want, that their abundance also may be *a supply* for your want; that there may be equality: 15As it is written, He that *had gathered* much had nothing over; and he that *had gathered* little had no lack. 16 But thanks *be* to God, which put the same earnest care into the heart of Titus for you.
17 For indeed he accepted the exhortation; but being more forward, of his own accord he went unto you. 18And we have sent with him the brother, whose praise *is* in the gospel throughout all the churches; 19And not *that* only, but who was also chosen of the churches to travel with us with this grace, which is administered by us to the glory of the same Lord, and *declaration of* your ready mind: 20Avoiding this, that

Living Bible

the first to propose this idea, but the first to begin doing something about it. 11 Having started the ball rolling so enthusiastically, you should carry this project through to completion just as gladly, giving whatever you can out of whatever you have. Let your enthusiastic idea at the start be equalled by your realistic action now. 12 If you are really eager to give, then it isn't important how much you have to give. God wants you to give what you have, not what you haven't.

13 Of course, I don't mean that those who receive your gifts should have an easy time of it at your expense, 14 but you should divide with them. Right now you have plenty and can help them; then at some other time they can share with you when you need it. In this way each will have as much as he needs. 15 Do you remember what the Scriptures say about this? "He that gathered much had nothing left over, and he that gathered little had enough." So you also should share with those in need.

16 I am thankful to God that he has given Titus the same real concern for you that I have.
17 He is glad to follow my suggestion that he visit you again—but I think he would have come anyway, for he is very eager to see you! 18 I am sending another well-known brother with him, who is highly praised as a preacher of the Good News in all the churches. 19 In fact, this man was elected by the churches to travel with me to take the gift to Jerusalem. This will glorify the Lord and show our eagerness to help each other. 20 By traveling together we will guard

Today's English Version

last year. You were the first, not only to act, but also to be willing to act. 11 On with it, then, and finish the job! Be as eager to finish it as you were to plan it, and do it with what you have. 12 If you are eager to give, God will accept your gift on the basis of what you have to give, not on what you don't have.

13, 14 I am not trying to relieve others by putting a burden on you; but since you have plenty at this time, it is only fair that you should help those who are in need. Then, when you are in need and they have plenty, they will help you. In this way both are treated equally. 15As the scripture says,

"The man who gathered much
did not have too much,
and the man who gathered little
did not have too little."

Titus and his companions

16 How we thank God for making Titus as eager as we are to help you! 17 Not only did he welcome our request; he was so eager to help that of his own free will he decided to go to you.
18 With him we are sending the brother who is highly respected in all the churches for his work in preaching the gospel. 19And besides that, he has been chosen and appointed by the churches to travel with us as we carry out this service of love for the Lord's glory, and to show that we want to help.

20 We are being careful not to stir up any

New International Version

first not only to give but also to have the desire to do so. 11 Now finish the work, so that your eager willingness to do it may be matched by your completion of it, according to your means.
12 For if the willingness is there, the gift is acceptable according to what one has, not according to what he does not have.

13 Our desire is not that others might be relieved while you are hard pressed, but that there might be equality. 14At the present time your plenty will supply what they need, so that in turn their plenty will supply what you need. Then there will be equality, 15 as it is written:

"He that gathered much did not have too much,
and he that gathered little did not have too little." [n]

Titus sent to Corinth

16 I thank God, who put into the heart of Titus the same concern I have for you. 17 For Titus not only welcomed our appeal, but he is coming to you with much enthusiasm and on his own initiative. 18And we are sending along with him the brother who is praised by all the churches for his service to the gospel. 19 What is more, he was chosen by the churches to accompany us as we carry the offering, which we administer in order to honor the Lord himself and to show our eagerness to help. 20 We want

[*n*] Exodus 16:18.

Phillips Modern English

the first to give, to carry through what you then intended to do. Finish it, then, as well as your means allow, and show that you can complete what you set out to do with as much readiness as you showed eagerness to begin. The important thing is to be willing to give as much as we can—that is what God accepts, and no one is asked to give what he has not got. Of course, I don't mean that others should be relieved to an extent that leaves you in distress. It is a matter of share and share alike. At present your plenty should supply their need, and then at some future date their plenty may supply your need. In that way we share with each other, as the scripture says,

He that gathered much had nothing over,
And he that gathered little had no lack.

8.16 Titus is bringing you this letter personally

Thank God Titus feels the same deep concern for you as we do! He accepts the suggestion outlined above, and in his enthusiasm comes to you personally at his own request. We are sending with him that brother whose services to the gospel are universally praised in the churches. He has moreover been chosen to travel with us in this work of administering this generous gift. It is a task that brings glory to God and demonstrates also our willingness to help. Naturally we

Revised Standard Version

to complete what a year ago you began not only
to do but to desire, 11 so that your readiness in
desiring it may be matched by your completing
it out of what you have. 12 For if the readiness
is there, it is acceptable according to what a
man has, not according to what he has not. 13 I
do not mean that others should be eased and
you burdened, 14 but that as a matter of equality
your abundance at the present time should supply their want, so that their abundance may
supply your want, that there may be equality.
15As it is written, "He who gathered much had
nothing over, and he who gathered little had no
lack."

16 But thanks be to God who puts the same
earnest care for you into the heart of Titus.
17 For he not only accepted our appeal, but
being himself very earnest he is going to you of
his own accord. 18 With him we are sending the
brother who is famous among all the churches
for his preaching of the gospel; 19 and not only
that, but he has been appointed by the churches
to travel with us in this gracious work which
we are carrying on, for the glory of the Lord
and to show our good will. 20 We intend that

Jerusalem Bible

you were the first, a year ago, not only in taking
action but even in deciding to. 11 So now finish
the work and let the results be worthy, as far
as you can afford it, of the decision you made
so promptly. 12As long as the readiness is there,
a man is acceptable with whatever he can afford;
never mind what is beyond his means. 13 This
does not mean that to give relief to others you
ought to make things difficult for yourselves: it
is a question of balancing 14 what happens to
be your surplus now against their present need,
and one day they may have something to spare
that will supply your own need. That is how
we strike a balance: 15 as scripture says: *The
man who gathered much had none too much,
the man who gathered little did not go short.*[h]

The delegates recommended to the Corinthians

16 I thank God for putting into Titus' heart
the same concern for you that I have myself.
17 He did what we asked him; indeed he is more
concerned than ever, and is visiting you on his
own initiative. 18As his companion we are sending the brother who is famous in all the churches
for spreading the gospel. 19 More than that, he
happens to be the same brother who has been
elected by the churches to be our companion
on this errand of mercy that, for the glory of
God, we have undertaken to satisfy our impa-
tience to help. 20 We hope that in this way

[*h*] Ex. 16:18.

New English Bible

the work you did and in your willingness to undertake it. Now I want you to go on and finish it: be as eager to complete the scheme as you were to adopt it, and give according to your means. Provided there is an eager desire to give, God accepts what a man has; he does not ask for what he has not. There is no question of relieving others at the cost of hardship to yourselves; it is a question of equality. At the moment your surplus meets their need, but one day your need may be met from their surplus. The aim is equality; as Scripture has it, 'The man who got much had no more than enough, and the man who got little did not go short.'

I thank God that he has made Titus as keen on your behalf as we are! For Titus not only welcomed our request; he is so eager that by his own desire he is now leaving to come to you. With him we are sending one of our company whose reputation is high among our congregations everywhere for his services to the Gospel. Moreover they have duly appointed him to travel with us and help in this beneficent work, by which we do honour to the Lord himself and show our own eagerness to serve. We want to

King James Version

no man should blame us in this abundance which is administered by us: 21 Providing for honest things, not only in the sight of the Lord, but also in the sight of men. 22And we have sent with them our brother, whom we have oftentimes proved diligent in many things, but now much more diligent, upon the great confidence which *I have* in you. 23 Whether *any do inquire* of Titus, *he is* my partner and fellow helper concerning you: or our brethren *be inquired of, they are* the messengers of the churches, *and* the glory of Christ. 24 Wherefore shew ye to them, and before the churches, the proof of your love, and of our boasting on your behalf.

9 For as touching the ministering to the saints, it is superfluous for me to write to you: 2 For I know the forwardness of your mind, for which I boast of you to them of Macedonia, that Achaia was ready a year ago; and your zeal hath provoked very many. 3 Yet have I sent the brethren, lest our boasting of you should be in vain in this behalf; that, as I said, ye may be ready: 4 Lest haply if they of Macedonia come with me, and find you unprepared, we (that we say not, ye) should be ashamed in this same confident boasting.

Living Bible

against any suspicion, for we are anxious that no one should find fault with the way we are handling this large gift. 21 God knows we are honest, but I want everyone else to know it too. That is why we have made this arrangement.

22 And I am sending you still another brother, whom we know from experience to be an earnest Christian. He is especially interested, as he looks forward to this trip, because I have told him all about your eagerness to help.

23 If anyone asks who Titus is, say that he is my partner, my helper in helping you, and you can also say that the other two brothers represent the assemblies here and are splendid examples of those who belong to the Lord.

24 Please show your love for me to these men and do for them all that I have publicly boasted you would.

9 I realize that I really don't even need to mention this to you, about helping God's people. 2 For I know how eager you are to do it, and I have boasted to the friends in Macedonia that you were ready to send an offering a year ago. In fact, it was this enthusiasm of yours that stirred up many of them to begin helping. 3 But I am sending these men just to be sure that you really are ready, as I told them you would be, with your money all collected; I don't want it to turn out that this time I was wrong in my boasting about you. 4 I would be very much ashamed—and so would you—if some of these Macedonian people come with me, only to find that you still aren't ready after all I have told them!

Today's English Version

complaints about the way we handle this generous gift. 21 Our purpose is to do what is right, not only in the sight of the Lord, but also in the sight of men.

22 So we are sending our brother with them; we have tested him many times, and found him always very eager to help. And now that he has so much confidence in you, he is all the more eager to help. 23As for Titus, he is my partner who works with me to help you; as for the other brothers who are going with him, they represent the churches and bring glory to Christ. 24 Show your love to them, so that all the churches will be sure of it and know that we are right in boasting of you.

Help for fellow Christians

9 There is really no need for me to write you about the help being sent to God's people in Judea. 2 I know that you are willing to help, and I have boasted of you to the people in Macedonia. "The brothers in Greece," I said, "have been ready to help since last year." Your eagerness has stirred up most of them. 3 Now I am sending these brothers, so that our boasting of you in this matter may not turn out to be empty words. But, just as I said, you will be ready with your help. 4 Or else, if the people from Macedonia should come with me and find out that you are not ready, how ashamed we would be—not to speak of your shame—for

New International Version

to avoid any criticism of the way we administer this liberal gift. 21 For we are taking pains to do what is right, not only in the eyes of the Lord but also in the eyes of men.

22 In addition, we are sending with them our brother who has often proved to us in many ways that he is zealous, and now even more so because of his great confidence in you. 23As for Titus, he is my partner and fellow worker among you; as for our brothers, they are representatives of the churches and an honor to Christ. 24 Therefore, show these men the proof of your love and the reason for our pride in you, so that all the churches can see it.

9 There is no need for me to write to you about this service to the saints. 2 For I know your eagerness to help, and I have been boasting about it to the Macedonians, telling them that since last year you in Achaia were ready to give; and your enthusiasm has stirred most of them to action. 3 But I am sending the brothers in order that our boasting about you in this matter should not prove hollow, but that you may be ready, as I said you would be. 4 For if any Macedonians come with me and find you unprepared, we—not to say anything about you—would be ashamed of having been so confident.

Phillips Modern English

want to avoid the slightest breath of criticism in the distribution of their gifts, and to be absolutely above-board not only in the sight of God but in the eyes of men.

With these two we are also sending our brother, of whose keenness we have ample proof and whose interest is especially aroused on this occasion as he has such confidence in you. As for Titus, he is my partner and colleague in your affairs, and both the brothers are official messengers of the churches, a credit to Christ. So do let them see how genuine is your love, and justify my pride in you, so that all the churches may see it.

9.1 A word in confidence about this gift of yours

Of course I know it is really quite superfluous for me to be writing to you about this matter of giving to fellow Christians, for I know how willing you are. Indeed I have told the Macedonians with some pride that "Achaia was ready to undertake this service twelve months ago". Your enthusiasm has consequently stimulated most of them. I am, however, sending the brothers just to make sure that our pride in you is not unjustified and that you are ready, as I said you were. For it would never do if some of the Macedonians were to accompany me on my visit to you and find you unprepared! We (not to speak of you) should be acutely embarrassed, just because we had been so confident in you.

Revised Standard Version

no one should blame us about this liberal gift
which we are administering, 21 for we aim at
what is honorable not only in the Lord's sight
but also in the sight of men. 22 And with them
we are sending our brother whom we have often
tested and found earnest in many matters, but
who is now more earnest than ever because of
his great confidence in you. 23 As for Titus, he
is my partner and fellow worker in your service;
and as for our brethren, they are messengers[j] of
the churches, the glory of Christ. 24 So give
proof, before the churches, of your love and of
our boasting about you to these men.

9 Now it is superfluous for me to write to
you about the offering for the saints, 2 for
I know your readiness, of which I boast about
you to the people of Macedonia, saying that
Achaia has been ready since last year; and your
zeal has stirred up most of them. 3 But I am
sending the brethren so that our boasting about
you may not prove vain in this case, so that you
may be ready, as I said you would be; 4 lest if
some Macedonians come with me and find that
you are not ready, we be humiliated—to say

[j] Greek *apostles*.

Jerusalem Bible

there will be no accusations made about our
administering such a large fund; 21 for *we are
trying* to *do right* not only *in the sight of God*
but *also* in the sight of *men.*[i] 22 To accompany
these, we are sending a third brother, of whose
keenness we have often had proof in many different ways, and who is particularly keen about
this, because he has great confidence in you.
23 Titus, perhaps I should add, is my own colleague and fellow worker in your interests; the
other two brothers, who are delegates of the
churches, are a real glory to Christ. 24 So then,
in front of all the churches, give them a proof
of your love, and prove to them that we are
right to be proud of you.

9 There is really no need for me to write to
you on the subject of offering your services
to the saints, 2 since I know how anxious you
are to help; in fact, I boast about you to the
Macedonians, telling them, "Achaia has been
ready since last year." So your zeal has been
a spur to many more. 3 I am sending the brothers all the same, to make sure that our boasting
about you does not prove to have been empty
this time, and that you really are ready as I
said you would be. 4 If some of the Macedonians who are coming with me found you
unprepared, we should be humiliated—to say
nothing of yourselves—after being so confident.

[i] Pr. 3:4 (LXX).

New English Bible

guard against any criticism of our handling of this generous gift; for our aims are entirely honourable, not only in the Lord's eyes, but also in the eyes of men.

With these men we are sending another of our company whose enthusiasm we have had many opportunities of testing, and who is now all the more earnest because of the great confidence he has in you. If there is any question about Titus, he is my partner and my associate in dealings with you; as for the others, they are delegates of our congregations, an honour to Christ.[b] Then give them clear expression of your love and justify our pride in you; justify it to them, and through them to the congregations.

9 About the provision of aid for God's people, it is superfluous for me to write to you. I know how eager you are to help; I speak of it with pride to the Macedonians: I tell them that Achaia had everything ready last year; and most of them have been fired by your zeal. My purpose in sending these friends is to ensure that what we have said about you in this matter should not prove to be an empty boast. By that I mean, I want you to be prepared, as I told them you were; for if I bring with me men from Macedonia and they find you are not prepared, what a disgrace it will be to us, let alone to you,

[b] *Or* they are . . . congregations; they reflect Christ.

King James Version

5 Therefore I thought it necessary to exhort the
brethren, that they would go before unto you,
and make up beforehand your bounty, whereof
ye had notice before, that the same might be
ready, as *a matter of* bounty, and not as *of*
covetousness. 6 But this *I say,* He which soweth
sparingly shall reap also sparingly; and he which
soweth bountifully shall reap also bountifully.
7 Every man according as he purposeth in his
heart, *so let him give;* not grudgingly, or of
necessity: for God loveth a cheerful giver. 8 And
God *is* able to make all grace abound toward
you; that ye, always having all sufficiency in all
things, may abound to every good work: 9 (As
it is written, He hath dispersed abroad; he hath
given to the poor: his righteousness remaineth
for ever. 10 Now he that ministereth seed to the
sower both minister bread for *your* food, and
multiply your seed sown, and increase the fruits
of your righteousness:) 11 Being enriched in
every thing to all bountifulness, which causeth
through us thanksgiving to God. 12 For the administration of this service not only supplieth
the want of the saints, but is abundant also by
many thanksgivings unto God; 13 While by the

Living Bible

5 So I have asked these other brothers to arrive ahead of me to see that the gift you promised is on hand and waiting. I want it to be a
real gift and not look as if it were being given
under pressure. 6 But remember this—if you give
little, you will get little. A farmer who plants
just a few seeds will get only a small crop, but
if he plants much, he will reap much. 7 Every
one must make up his own mind as to how
much he should give. Don't force anyone to give
more than he really wants to, for cheerful givers
are the ones God prizes. 8 God is able to make
it up to you by giving you everything you need
and more, so that there will not only be enough
for your own needs, but plenty left over to give
joyfully to others. 9 It is as the Scriptures say:
"The godly man gives generously to the poor.
His good deeds will be an honor to him forever."

10 For God, who gives seed to the farmer to
plant, and later on, good crops to harvest and
eat, will give you more and more seed to plant
and will make it grow so that you can give away
more and more fruit from your harvest.

11 Yes, God will give you much so that you
can give away much, and when we take your
gifts to those who need them they will break
out into thanksgiving and praise to God for your
help. 12 So, two good things happen as a result
of your gifts—those in need are helped, and
they overflow with thanks to God. 13 Those you

Today's English Version

feeling so sure of you! 5 So I thought it necessary to urge these brothers to go to you ahead
of me and get ready in advance the gift you
promised to make. Then it will be ready when
I arrive, and it will show that you give because
you want to, not because you have to.

6 Remember this: the man who plants few
seeds will have a small crop; the one who plants
many seeds will have a large crop. 7 Each one
should give, then, as he has decided, not with
regret or out of a sense of duty; for God loves
the one who gives gladly. 8 And God is able to
give you more than you need, so that you will
always have all you need for yourselves and
more than enough for every good cause. 9 As
the scripture says,

"He gives generously to the poor;
his kindness lasts forever."

10 And God, who supplies seed for the sower
and bread to eat, will also supply you with all
the seed you need and make it grow, to produce
a rich harvest from your generosity. 11 He will
always make you rich enough to be generous at
all times, so that many will thank God for your
gifts they receive from us. 12 For this service
you perform not only meets the needs of God's
people, but also produces an outpouring of
grateful thanks to God. 13 And because of the

New International Version

5 So I thought it necessary to urge the brothers
to visit you in advance and finish the arrangements for the generous gift you had promised.
Then it will be ready as a generous gift, not as
one grudgingly given.

Sowing generously

6 Remember this: Whoever sows sparingly will
also reap sparingly, and whoever sows generously will also reap generously. 7 Each man
should give what he has decided in his heart to
give, not reluctantly or under compulsion, for
God loves a cheerful giver. 8 And God is able
to make all grace abound to you, so that in all
things at all times, having all that you need, you
will abound in every good work. 9 As it is written:

"He has scattered abroad his gifts to the poor;
his righteousness endures for ever." [o]

10 Now he who supplies seed to the sower and
bread for food will also supply and increase
your store of seed and will enlarge the harvest
of your righteousness. 11 You will be made rich
in every way so that you can be generous on
every occasion, and through us your generosity
will result in thanksgiving to God.

12 This service that you perform is not only
supplying the needs of God's people but is also
overflowing in many expressions of thanks to
God. 13 Because of the service by which you

[o] Psalm 112:9.

Phillips Modern English

This is my reason, then, for urging the brothers to visit you before I come myself, so that they can get your promised gift ready in good time. For I should like it to be a spontaneous gift, and not money squeezed out of you. All I will say is that poor sowing means a poor harvest, and generous sowing means a generous harvest.

9.7 Giving does not only help the one who receives

Let everyone give as his heart tells him, neither grudgingly nor under compulsion, for God loves the man who gives cheerfully. God can give you more than you can ever need, so that you may always have sufficient for yourselves and enough left over to give to every good cause. As the scripture says:

He hath scattered abroad, he hath given to the poor;
His righteousness abidith for ever.

He who gives the seed to the sower and bread to eat, will give you the seed of generosity to sow and will make it grow into a harvest of good deeds done. The more you are enriched the more scope will there be for generous giving, and your gifts, administered through us, will mean that many will thank God. For your giving does not end in meeting the wants of your fellow-Christians. It also results in an overflowing tide of thanksgiving to God. Moreover, your very

Revised Standard Version

nothing of you—for being so confident. 5 So I
thought it necessary to urge the brethren to go
on to you before me, and arrange in advance for
this gift you have promised, so that it may be
ready not as an exaction but as a willing gift.
6 The point is this: he who sows sparingly
will also reap sparingly, and he who sows bountifully will also reap bountifully. 7 Each one
must do as he has made up his mind, not reluctantly or under compulsion, for God loves a
cheerful giver. 8 And God is able to provide
you with every blessing in abundance, so that
you may always have enough of everything and
may provide in abundance for every good work.
9 As it is written,

"He scatters abroad, he gives to the poor;
his righteousness[k] endures for ever."

10 He who supplies seed to the sower and bread
for food will supply and multiply your resources[l] and increase the harvest of your righteousness.[k] 11 You will be enriched in every way
for great generosity, which through us will produce thanksgiving to God; 12 for the rendering
of this service not only supplies the wants of the
saints but also overflows in many thanksgivings
to God. 13 Under the test of this service, you[m]

[k] Or *benevolence*. [l] Greek *sowing*. [m] Or *they*.

Jerusalem Bible

5 That is why I have thought it necessary to
ask these brothers to go on to you ahead of us,
and make sure in advance that the gift you
promised is all ready, and that it all comes as a
gift out of your generosity and not by being
extorted from you.

Blessings to be expected from the collection

6 Do not forget: thin sowing means thin
reaping; the more you sow, the more you reap.
7 Each one should give what he has decided
in his own mind, not grudgingly or because he
is made to, for *God loves a cheerful giver.*[j]
8 And there is no limit to the blessings which
God can send you—he will make sure that you
will always have all you need for yourselves in
every possible circumstance, and still have something to spare for all sorts of good works. 9 As
scripture says: *He was free in almsgiving, and
gave to the poor: his good deeds will never be
forgotten.*[k]
10 "The one who provides *seed for the sower
and bread for food* will provide you with all the
seed you want and make *the harvest of your
good deeds* a larger one, 11 and, made richer
in every way, you will be able to do all the generous things which, through us, are the cause
of thanksgiving to God. 12 For doing this holy
service is not only supplying all the needs of the
saints, but it is also increasing the amount of
thanksgiving that God receives. 13 By offering

[j] Pr. 22:8 (LXX). [k] Ps. 112.9.

New English Bible

after all the confidence we have shown! I have accordingly thought it necessary to ask these friends to go on ahead to Corinth, to see that your promised bounty is in order before I come; it will then be awaiting me as a bounty indeed, and not as an extortion.

Remember: sparse sowing, sparse reaping; sow bountifully, and you will reap bountifully. Each person should give as he has decided for himself; there should be no reluctance, no sense of compulsion; God loves a cheerful giver. And it is in God's power to provide you richly with every good gift; thus you will have ample means in yourselves to meet each and every situation, with enough and to spare for every good cause. Scripture says of such a man: 'He has lavished his gifts on the needy, his benevolence stands fast for ever.' Now he who provides seed for sowing and bread for food will provide the seed for you to sow; he will multiply it and swell the harvest of your benevolence, and you will always be rich enough to be generous. Through our action such generosity will issue in thanksgiving to God, for as a piece of willing service this is not only a contribution towards the needs of God's people; more than that, it overflows in a flood of thanksgiving to God. For through the proof which this

King James Version

experiment of this ministration they glorify God
for your professed subjection unto the gospel of
Christ, and for *your* liberal distribution unto
them, and unto all *men;* 14And by their prayer
for you, which long after you for the exceeding
grace of God in you. 15 Thanks *be* unto God
for his unspeakable gift.

10 Now I Paul myself beseech you by the
meekness and gentleness of Christ, who in
presence *am* base among you, but being absent
am bold toward you: 2 But I beseech *you,* that
I may not be bold when I am present with that
confidence, wherewith I think to be bold against
some, which think of us as if we walked according to the flesh. 3 For though we walk in the
flesh, we do not war after the flesh: 4 (For the
weapons of our warfare *are* not carnal, but
mighty through God to the pulling down of
strong holds;) 5 Casting down imaginations, and
every high thing that exalteth itself against the
knowledge of God, and bringing into captivity

Living Bible

help will be glad not only because of your
generous gifts to themselves and to others, but
they will praise God for this proof that your
deeds are as good as your doctrine. 14And they
will pray for you with deep fervor and feeling
because of the wonderful grace of God shown
through you.

15 Thank God for his Son—his Gift too
wonderful for words.

10 I plead with you—yes, I, Paul—and I
plead gently, as Christ himself would do.
Yet some of you are saying, "Paul's letters are
bold enough when he is far away, but when he
gets here he will be afraid to raise his voice!"

2 I hope I won't need to show you when I
come how harsh and rough I can be. I don't
want to carry out my present plans against some
of you who seem to think my deeds and words
are merely those of an ordinary man. 3 It is true
that I am an ordinary, weak human being, but I
don't use human plans and methods to win my
battles. 4 I use God's mighty weapons, not those
made by men, to knock down the devil's strongholds. 5 These weapons can break down every
proud argument against God and every wall that
can be built to keep men from finding him. With
these weapons I can capture rebels and bring
them back to God, and change them into men

Today's English Version

proof which this service of yours brings, many
will give glory to God for your loyalty to the
gospel of Christ, which you profess, and for
your generosity in sharing with them and all
others. 14And so they will pray for you with
great affection for you because of the extraordinary grace God has shown you. 15 Let us
thank God for his priceless gift!

Paul defends his ministry

10 I, Paul, make a personal appeal to you—
I who am said to be meek and mild when
I am with you, but bold toward you when I am
away from you. I beg of you, by the gentleness
and kindness of Christ: 2 Do not force me to be
bold with you when I come; for I am sure I can
be bold with those who say that we act from
worldly motives. 3 It is true that we live in the
world; but we do not fight from worldly motives. 4 The weapons we use in our fight are not
the world's weapons, but God's powerful weapons, with which to destroy strongholds. We destroy false arguments; 5 we pull down every
proud obstacle that is raised against the knowledge of God; we take every thought captive and

New International Version

have proved yourselves, men will praise God for
the obedience that accompanies your confession
of the gospel of Christ, and for your generosity
in sharing with them and with everyone else.
14And in their prayers for you their hearts will
go out to you, because of the surpassing grace
God has given you. 15 Thanks be to God for his
indescribable gift!

Paul's defense of his ministry

10 By the meekness and gentleness of Christ,
I appeal to you—I, Paul, who am "timid"
when face to face with you, but "bold" when
away! 2 I beg you that when I come I may not
have to be as bold as I expect to be toward
some people who think that we live by the
standards of this world. 3 For though we live
in the world, we do not wage war as the world
does. 4 The weapons we fight with are not the
weapons of the world. On the contrary, they
have divine power to tear down strongholds.
5 We demolish arguments and every pretension
that sets itself up against the knowledge of God,
and we take captive every thought to make it

Phillips Modern English

giving proves the reality of your faith, and that means that men thank God that you practise the gospel of Christ that you profess to believe in, as well as for the actual gifts your fellowship makes to them and to others. And yet further, men will pray for you and feel drawn to you because you have obviously received a generous measure of the grace of God.

Thank God, then, for his indescribable generosity to you!

10.1 We are not merely human agents but God-appointed ministers

Now I am going to appeal to you personally, by the gentleness and kindness of Christ himself. Yes, I, Paul, the one who is "humble enough in our presence but outspoken when away from us", am begging you to make it unnecessary for me to be outspoken and stern in your presence. For I am afraid otherwise that I think I shall have to do some plain speaking to those of you who will persist in reckoning that our activities are on the purely human level. The truth is that, although we lead normal human lives, the battle we are fighting is on the spiritual level. The very weapons we use are not human but powerful in God's warfare for the destruction of the enemy's strongholds. Our battle is to break down every deceptive argument and every imposing defence that men erect against the true knowledge of God. We fight to capture every thought until it

Revised Standard Version

will glorify God by your obedience in acknowledging the gospel of Christ, and by the generosity of your contribution for them and for all
others; 14 while they long for you and pray for you, because of the surpassing grace of God in
you. 15 Thanks be to God for his inexpressible gift!

10 I, Paul, myself entreat you, by the meekness and gentleness of Christ—I who am humble when face to face with you, but bold to
you when I am away!—2 I beg of you that when I am present I may not have to show boldness with such confidence as I count on showing against some who suspect us of acting
in worldly fashion. 3 For though we live in the world we are not carrying on a worldly war,
4 for the weapons of our warfare are not worldly but have divine power to destroy strongholds. 5 We destroy arguments and every proud obstacle to the knowledge of God, and take

Jerusalem Bible

this service, you show them what you are, and that makes them give glory to God for the way you accept and profess the gospel of Christ, and for your sympathetic generosity to them and to
all. 14 And their prayers for you, too, show how they are drawn to you on account of all the
grace that God has given you. 15 Thanks be to God for his inexpressible gift!

III. Paul's apologia

Paul's reply to accusations of weakness

10 This is a personal matter; this is Paul himself appealing to you by the gentleness and patience of Christ—I, the man who is so humble when he is facing you, but bullies you
when he is at a distance. 2 I only ask that I do not have to bully you when I come, with all the confident assurance I mean to show when I come face to face with people I could name who think we go by ordinary human motives.
3 We live in the flesh, of course, but the muscles that we fight with are not flesh.
4 Our war is not fought with weapons of flesh, yet they are strong enough, in God's cause, to demolish fortresses. We demolish sophistries,
5 and the arrogance that tries to resist the knowledge of God; every thought is our prisoner, captured to

New English Bible

affords, many will give honour to God when they see how humbly you obey him and how faithfully you confess the gospel of Christ; and will thank him for your liberal contribution to their need and to the general good. And as they join in prayer on your behalf, their hearts will go out to you because of the richness of the grace which God has imparted to you. Thanks be to God for his gift beyond words!

Trials of a Christian Missionary

10 But I, Paul, appeal to you by the gentleness and magnanimity of Christ—I, so feeble (you say) when I am face to face with you, so brave when I am away. Spare me, I beg you, the necessity of such bravery when I come, for I reckon I could put on as bold a face as you please against those who charge us with moral weakness. Weak men we may be, but it is not as such that we fight our battles. The weapons we wield are not merely human,[a] but divinely potent to demolish strongholds; we demolish sophistries and all that rears its proud head against the knowledge of God; we compel every human thought to surrender in obedience to

[a] *Or* charge us with worldly standards. We live, no doubt, in the world; but it is not on that level that we fight our battles. The weapons we wield are not those of the world . . .

King James Version

every thought to the obedience of Christ; 6 And having in a readiness to revenge all disobedience, when your obedience is fulfilled. 7 Do ye look on things after the outward appearance? If any man trust to himself that he is Christ's, let him of himself think this again, that, as he *is* Christ's, even so *are* we Christ's. 8 For though I should boast somewhat more of our authority, which the Lord hath given us for edification, and not for your destruction, I should not be ashamed: 9 That I may not seem as if I would terrify you by letters. 10 For *his* letters, say they, *are* weighty and powerful; but *his* bodily presence *is* weak, and *his* speech contemptible. 11 Let such a one think this, that, such as we are in word by letters when we are absent, such *will we* be also in deed when we are present. 12 For we dare not make ourselves of the number, or compare ourselves with some that commend themselves: but they, measuring them-

Living Bible

whose hearts' desire is obedience to Christ. 6 I will use these weapons against every rebel who remains after I have first used them on you yourselves, and you surrender to Christ.

7 The trouble with you is that you look at me and I seem weak and powerless, but you don't look beneath the surface. Yet if anyone can claim the power and authority of Christ, I certainly can. 8 I may seem to be boasting more than I should about my authority over you—authority to help you, not to hurt you—but I shall make good every claim. 9 I say this so that you will not think I am just blustering when I scold you in my letters.

10 "Don't bother about his letters," some say. "He sounds big, but it's all noise. When he gets here you will see that there is nothing great about him, and you have never heard a worse preacher!" 11 This time my personal presence is going to be just as rough on you as my letters are!

12 Oh, don't worry, I wouldn't dare say that I am as wonderful as these other men who tell you how good they are! Their trouble is that they are only comparing themselves with each

Today's English Version

make it obey Christ. 6 And after you have proved your complete loyalty, we will be ready to punish any act of disloyalty.

7 You are looking at things as they are on the outside. Is there someone there who reckons himself to belong to Christ? Well, let him think again about himself, because we belong to Christ just as much as he does. 8 For I am not ashamed, even if I have boasted somewhat too much of the authority that the Lord has given us—authority to build you up, that is, not to tear you down. 9 I do not want it to appear that I am trying to frighten you with my letters. 10 Someone will say, "Paul's letters are severe and strong, but when he is with us in person he is weak, and his words are nothing!" 11 Such a person must understand that there is no difference between what we write in our letters when we are away, and what we will do when we are there with you.

12 Of course we would not dare classify ourselves or compare ourselves with those who rate themselves so highly. How stupid they are! They make up their own standards to measure them-

New International Version

obedient to Christ. 6 And we will be ready to punish every act of disobedience, once your obedience is complete.

7 You are looking only on the surface of things.[p] If anyone is confident that he belongs to Christ, he should consider again that we belong to Christ just as much as he. 8 For even if I boast somewhat freely about the authority the Lord gave us for building you up rather than pulling you down, I will not be ashamed of it. 9 I do not want to seem to be trying to frighten you with my letters. 10 For some say, "His letters are weighty and forceful, but in person he is unimpressive and his speaking amounts to nothing." 11 Such people should realize that what we are in our letters when we are absent, we will be in our actions when we are present.

12 We do not dare to classify or compare ourselves with some who commend themselves. When they measure themselves by themselves

[p] Or *Look at the obvious facts.*

Phillips Modern English

acknowledges the authority of Christ. Once we are sure of your obedience we are ready to punish every disobedience.

10.7 I really am a Christian, you know!

Do look at things which stare you in the face! So-and-so considers himself to belong to Christ. All right; but let him think again about himself, for we belong to Christ every bit as much as he. You may think that I have boasted unduly of my authority (which the Lord gave me, remember, to build you up not to break you down), but I don't think I have done anything which will make me ashamed. Yet I don't want you to think of me merely as the man who writes you terrifying letters. I know my critics say, "His letters are impressive and moving, but his actual presence is feeble and his speaking beneath contempt." Let them realise that we can be just as "impressive and moving" in person as we are in our letters.

10.12 God's appointment means more than self-recommendation

Of course we shouldn't dare include ourselves in the same class as those who write their own testimonials, or even to compare ourselves with them! All they are doing, of course, is to measure themselves by their own standards or by com-

Revised Standard Version

every thought captive to obey Christ, 6 being
ready to punish every disobedience, when your
obedience is complete.
7 Look at what is before your eyes. If any
one is confident that he is Christ's, let him remind himself that as he is Christ's, so are we.
8 For even if I boast a little too much of our
authority, which the Lord gave for building you
up and not for destroying you, I shall not be
put to shame. 9 I would not seem to be fright-
ening you with letters. 10 For they say, "His
letters are weighty and strong, but his bodily
presence is weak, and his speech of no account." 11 Let such people understand that what
we say by letter when absent, we do when present. 12 Not that we venture to class or compare
ourselves with some of those who commend
themselves. But when they measure themselves
by one another, and compare themselves with

Jerusalem Bible

be brought into obedience to Christ. 6 Once you
have given your complete obedience, we are
prepared to punish any disobedience.
7 Face plain facts. Anybody who is convinced
that he belongs to Christ must go on to reflect
that we all belong to Christ no less than he
does. 8 Maybe I do boast rather too much
about our authority, but the Lord gave it to me
for building you up and not for pulling you
down, and I shall not be ashamed of it. 9 I
do not want you to think of me as someone
who only frightens you by letter. 10 Someone
said, "He writes powerful and strongly worded
letters but when he is with you you see only
half a man and no preacher at all." 11 The man
who said that can remember this: whatever we
are like in the words of our letters when we are
absent, that is what we shall be like in our actions when we are present.

His reply to the accusation of ambition

12 We are not being so bold as to rank ourselves, or invite comparison, with certain people who write their own references. Measuring themselves against themselves, and comparing them-

New English Bible

Christ; and we are prepared to punish all rebellion when once you have put yourselves in our hands.

Look facts in the face.[b] Someone is convinced, is he, that he belongs to Christ? Let him think again, and reflect that we belong to Christ as much as he does. Indeed, if I am somewhat overboastful about our authority—an authority given by the Lord to build you up, not pull you down—I shall make my boast good. So you must not think of me as one who scares you by the letters he writes. 'His letters', so it is said, 'are weighty and powerful; but when he appears he has no presence, and as a speaker he is beneath contempt.' People who talk in that way should reckon with this: when I come, my actions will show the same man as my letters showed in my absence.

We should not dare to class ourselves or compare ourselves with any of those who put forward their own claims. What fools they are to measure

[b] *Or* You are looking only at what catches the eye.

King James Version

selves by themselves, and comparing themselves among themselves, are not wise. 13 But we will not boast of things without *our* measure, but according to the measure of the rule which God hath distributed to us, a measure to reach even unto you. 14 For we stretch not ourselves beyond *our measure,* as though we reached not unto you; for we are come as far as to you also in *preaching* the gospel of Christ: 15 Not boasting of things without *our* measure, *that is,* of other men's labours; but having hope, when your faith is increased, that we shall be enlarged by you according to our rule abundantly, 16 To preach the gospel in the *regions* beyond you, *and* not to boast in another man's line of things made ready to our hand. 17 But he that glorieth, let him glory in the Lord. 18 For not he that commendeth himself is approved, but whom the Lord commendeth.

11 Would to God ye could bear with me a little in *my* folly: and indeed bear with me. 2 For I am jealous over you with godly jealousy: for I have espoused you to one husband, that I may present *you as* a chaste virgin to Christ.

Living Bible

other, and measuring themselves against their own little ideas. What stupidity!

13 But we will not boast of authority we do not have. Our goal is to measure up to God's plan for us, and this plan includes our working there with you. 14 We are not going too far when we claim authority over you, for we were the first to come to you with the Good News concerning Christ. 15 It is not as though we were trying to claim credit for the work someone else has done among you. Instead, we hope that your faith will grow and that, still within the limits set for us, our work among you will be greatly enlarged.

16 After that, we will be able to preach the Good News to other cities that are far beyond you, where no one else is working; then there will be no question about being in someone else's field. 17 As the Scriptures say, "If anyone is going to boast, let him boast about what the Lord has done and not about himself." 18 When someone boasts about himself and how well he has done, it doesn't count for much. But when the Lord commends him, that's different!

11 I hope you will be patient with me as I keep on talking like a fool. Do bear with me and let me say what is on my heart. 2 I am anxious for you with the deep concern of God himself—anxious that your love should be for Christ alone, just as a pure maiden saves her love for one man only, for the one who will be

Today's English Version

selves by, and judge themselves by their own standards! 13 As for us, however, our boasting will not go beyond certain limits; it will stay within the limits of the work which God has set for us, which includes our work among you. 14 And since you are within those limits, we did not go beyond them when we came to you, bringing the Good News about Christ. 15 So we do not boast of the work that others have done beyond the limits God set for us. Instead, we hope that your faith may grow, and that we may be able to do a much greater work among you, always within the limits that God has set. 16 Then we can preach the Good News in other countries beyond you, and shall not have to boast of work already done in another man's field.

17 But as the scripture says, "Whoever wants to boast, must boast of what the Lord has done." 18 Because a man is really approved when the Lord thinks well of him, not when he thinks well of himself.

Paul and the false apostles

11 I wish you would tolerate me, even when I am a bit foolish. Please do! 2 I am jealous for you just as God is; you are like a pure virgin whom I have promised in marriage to one man

New International Version

and compare themselves with themselves, they are not wise. 13 We, however, will not boast beyond proper limits, but will confine our boasting to the field God has assigned to us, a field that reaches even to you. 14 We are not going too far in our boasting, as would be the case if we had not come to you, for we did get as far as you with the gospel of Christ. 15 Neither do we go beyond our limits by boasting of work done by others.[q] Our hope is that, as your faith continues to grow, our area of activity among you will greatly expand, 16 so that we can preach the gospel in the regions beyond you. For we do not want to boast about work already done in another man's territory. 17 But, "Let him who boasts, boast in the Lord."[r] 18 For it is not the man who commends himself who is approved, but the man whom the Lord commends.

Paul and the false apostles

11 I hope you will put up with a little of my foolishness; but you are already doing that. 2 I am jealous for you with a godly jealousy. I promised you to one husband, to Christ, so that I might present you as a pure virgin to him.

[q] Or *13We, however, will not boast about things that cannot be measured, but we will boast according to the standard of measurement that the God of measure has assigned us—a measurement that relates even to you. 14. . . . 15Neither do we boast about things that cannot be measured in regard to the work done by others.* [r] Jer. 9:24.

Phillips Modern English

parisons within their own circle, and that doesn't make for accurate estimation, you may be sure. No, we shall not make any wild claims, but simply judge ourselves by that line of duty which God has marked out for us, and that line includes our work on your behalf. We do not exceed our duty when we embrace your interests, for it was our preaching of the gospel which brought us into contact with you. Our pride is not in matters beyond our proper sphere nor in the labours of other men. No, our hope is that your growing faith will mean the expansion of our proper sphere of action, so that before long we shall be preaching the gospel in districts beyond you, instead of being proud of work that has already been done in someone else's province.

But,

He that glorieth let him glory in the Lord.

It is not self-commendation that matters, it is winning the approval of God.

11.1 Why do you so readily accept the false and reject the true?

I wish you could put up with a little of my foolishness—please try! My jealousy over you is the right sort of jealousy, for in my eyes you are like a fresh unspoiled girl whom I am presenting as fiancée to your only husband, Christ

Revised Standard Version

one another, they are without understanding.
13 But we will not boast beyond limit, but
will keep to the limits God has apportioned us,
to reach even to you. 14 For we are not over-
extending ourselves, as though we did not reach
you; we were the first to come all the way to
you with the gospel of Christ. 15 We do not
boast beyond limit, in other men's labors; but
our hope is that as your faith increases, our
field among you may be greatly enlarged, 16 so
that we may preach the gospel in lands beyond
you, without boasting of work already done in
another's field. 17 "Let him who boasts, boast of
the Lord." 18 For it is not the man who commends himself that is accepted, but the man
whom the Lord commends.

11 I wish you would bear with me in a little
foolishness. Do bear with me! 2 I feel a
divine jealousy for you, for I betrothed you to
Christ to present you as a pure bride to her one

Jerusalem Bible

selves to themselves, they are simply foolish.
13 We, on the other hand, are not going to
boast without a standard to measure against:
taking for our measure the yardstick which
God gave us to measure with, which is long
enough to reach to you. 14 We are not stretching further than we ought; otherwise we should
not have reached you, as we did come all the
way to you with the gospel of Christ. 15 So we
are not boasting without any measure, about
work that was done by other people; in fact,
we trust that, as your faith grows, we shall get
taller and taller, when judged by our own standard. 16 I mean, we shall be carrying the gospel
to places far beyond you, without encroaching
on anyone else's field, not boasting of the work
already done. 17 *If anyone wants to boast, let
him boast of the Lord.*[l] 18 It is not the man
who commends himself that can be accepted,
but the man who is commended by the Lord.

Paul is driven to sound his own praises

11 I only wish you were able to tolerate a
little foolishness from me. But of course:
you are tolerant toward me. 2 You see, the
jealousy that I feel for you is God's own jealousy: I arranged for you to marry Christ so
that I might give you away as a chaste virgin

[l] Jr. 9:23.

New English Bible

themselves by themselves, to find in themselves their own standard of comparison![c] With us there will be no attempt to boast beyond our proper sphere; and our sphere is determined by the limit God laid down for us, which permitted us to come as far as Corinth. We are not overstretching our commission, as we should be if it did not extend to you, for we were the first to reach Corinth in preaching the gospel of Christ. And we do not boast of work done where others have laboured, work beyond our proper sphere. Our hope is rather that, as your faith grows, we may attain a position among you greater than ever before, but still within the limits of our sphere. Then we can carry the Gospel to lands that lie beyond you, never priding ourselves on work already done in another man's sphere. If a man must boast, let him boast of the Lord. Not the man who recommends himself, but the man whom the Lord recommends—he and he alone is to be accepted.

11 I wish you would bear with me in a little of my folly; please do bear with me. I am jealous for you, with a divine jealousy; for I betrothed you to Christ, thinking to present you as a chaste virgin to her true and only husband.

[c] *Some witnesses read* On the contrary we measure ourselves by ourselves, by our own standard of comparison.

King James Version

3 But I fear, lest by any means, as the serpent beguiled Eve through his subtilty, so your minds should be corrupted from the simplicity that is in Christ. 4 For if he that cometh preacheth another Jesus, whom we have not preached, or *if* ye receive another spirit, which ye have not received, or another gospel, which ye have not accepted, ye might well bear with *him*. 5 For I suppose I was not a whit behind the very chiefest apostles. 6 But though *I be* rude in speech, yet not in knowledge; but we have been thoroughly made manifest among you in all things. 7 Have I committed an offence in abasing myself that ye might be exalted, because I have preached to you the gospel of God freely? 8 I robbed other churches, taking wages *of them*, to do you service. 9 And when I was present with you, and wanted, I was chargeable to no man: for that which was lacking to me the brethren which came from Macedonia supplied: and in all *things* I have kept myself from being burdensome unto you, and *so* will I keep *myself*. 10 As the truth of Christ is in me, no man shall stop me of this boasting in the regions of Achaia. 11 Wherefore? because I love you not? God knoweth. 12 But what I do, that I will do, that I may cut off occasion from them which desire occasion; that wherein they glory, they may be found even as we. 13 For such *are* false apostles, deceitful workers, transforming themselves into

Living Bible

her husband. 3 But I am frightened, fearing that in some way you will be led away from your pure and simple devotion to our Lord, just as Eve was deceived by Satan in the Garden of Eden. 4 You seem so gullible: you believe whatever anyone tells you even if he is preaching about another Jesus than the one we preach, or a different spirit than the Holy Spirit you received, or shows you a different way to be saved. You swallow it all.

5 Yet I don't feel that these marvelous "messengers from God," as they call themselves, are any better than I am. 6 If I am a poor speaker, at least I know what I am talking about, as I think you realize by now, for we have proved it again and again.

7 Did I do wrong and cheapen myself and make you look down on me because I preached God's Good News to you without charging you anything? 8, 9 Instead I "robbed" other churches by taking what they sent me, and using it up while I was with you, so that I could serve you without cost. And when that was gone[a] and I was getting hungry I still didn't ask you for anything, for the Christians from Macedonia brought me another gift. I have never yet asked you for one cent, and I never will. 10 I promise this with every ounce of truth I possess—that I will tell everyone in Greece about it! 11 Why? Because I don't love you? God knows I do. 12 But I will do it to cut out the ground from under the feet of those who boast that they are doing God's work in just the same way we are.

13 God never sent those men at all; they are "phonies" who have fooled you into thinking

[a] Implied.

Today's English Version

only, who is Christ. 3 I am afraid that your minds will be corrupted and that you will abandon your full and pure devotion to Christ—in the same way that Eve was deceived by the snake's clever lies. 4 For you gladly tolerate anyone who comes to you and preaches a different Jesus, not the one we preached; and you accept a spirit and a gospel completely different from the Spirit and the gospel you received from us!

5 I do not think that I am the least bit inferior to those very special "apostles" of yours! 6 Perhaps I am an amateur in speaking, but certainly not in knowledge; we have made this clear to you at all times and in all conditions.

7 I did not charge you a thing when I preached the Good News of God to you; I humbled myself in order to make you important. Was that wrong of me? 8 While I was working among you I was paid by other churches. I was robbing them, so to speak, to help you. 9 And during the time I was with you I did not bother you for help when I needed money; the brothers who came from Macedonia brought me everything I needed. As in the past, so in the future: I will never be a burden to you! 10 By Christ's truth in me, I promise that this boast of mine will not be silenced anywhere in all of Greece. 11 Why do I say this? Because I don't love you? God knows I do!

12 I will go on doing what I am doing now, in order to keep those other "apostles" from having any reason for boasting and saying that they work in the same way that we do. 13 Those men are not true apostles—they are false apostles, who lie about their work and change themselves to look like real apostles of Christ.

New International Version

3 But I am afraid that just as Eve was deceived by the serpent's cunning, your minds may somehow be led astray from your sincere and pure devotion to Christ. 4 For if someone comes to you and preaches a Jesus other than the Jesus we preached, or if you receive a different spirit from the one you received, or a different gospel from the one you accepted, you put up with it easily enough. 5 But I do not think I am in the least inferior to those "super-apostles." 6 I may not be a trained speaker, but I do have knowledge. We have made this perfectly clear to you in every way.

7 Was it a sin for me to lower myself in order to elevate you by preaching the gospel of God to you free of charge? 8 I robbed other churches by receiving support from them so as to serve you. 9 And when I was with you and needed something, I was not a burden to anyone, for the brothers who came from Macedonia supplied what I needed. I have kept myself from being a burden to you in any way, and will continue to do so. 10 As surely as the truth of Christ is in me, nobody in the regions of Achaia will stop this boasting of mine. 11 Why? Because I do not love you? God knows I do! 12 And I will keep on doing what I am doing in order to cut the ground from under those who want an opportunity to be considered equal with us in the things they boast about.

13 For such men are false apostles, deceitful workmen, masquerading as apostles of Christ.

Phillips Modern English

himself. I am afraid that your minds may be seduced from a single-hearted devotion to him by the same subtle means that the serpent used towards Eve. For apparently you cheerfully accept a man who comes to you preaching a different Jesus from the one we told you about, and you readily receive a spirit and a gospel quite different from the ones you originally accepted. Yet I cannot believe I am in the least inferior to these extra-special messengers. Perhaps I am not a polished speaker, but I do know what I am talking about, and both what I am and what I say is well known to you. Perhaps I made a mistake in lowering myself (though I did it to raise you up) by preaching the gospel of God without a fee? As a matter of fact I was only able to do this by "robbing" other churches, for it was what they paid me that made it possible to minister to you. Even when I was with you and was hard up, I did not bother any of you. It was the brothers who came from Macedonia who brought me all that I needed. Yes, I kept myself from being a burden to you then, and so I intend to do in the future. By the truth of Christ within me, no one shall stop my being proud of this independence through all Achaia!

Does this mean that I do not love you? God knows it doesn't, but I am determined to go on doing as I am doing, so as to cut the ground from under the feet of those who would dearly love to be thought of as God's messengers on the same terms as I am. *God's* messengers? They are counterfeits of the real thing, dishonest practitioners masquerading as the messengers of

Revised Standard Version

husband. 3 But I am afraid that as the serpent deceived Eve by his cunning, your thoughts will be led astray from a sincere and pure devotion to Christ. 4 For if some one comes and preaches another Jesus than the one we preached, or if you receive a different spirit from the one you received, or if you accept a different gospel from the one you accepted, you submit to it readily enough. 5 I think that I am not in the least inferior to these superlative apostles. 6 Even if I am unskilled in speaking, I am not in knowledge; in every way we have made this plain to you in all things.

7 Did I commit a sin in abasing myself so that you might be exalted, because I preached God's gospel without cost to you? 8 I robbed other churches by accepting support from them in order to serve you. 9 And when I was with you and was in want, I did not burden any one, for my needs were supplied by the brethren who came from Macedonia. So I refrained and will refrain from burdening you in any way. 10 As the truth of Christ is in me, this boast of mine shall not be silenced in the regions of Achaia. 11 And why? Because I do not love you? God knows I do!

12 And what I do I will continue to do, in order to undermine the claim of those who would like to claim that in their boasted mission they work on the same terms as we do. 13 For such men are false apostles, deceitful workmen, disguising themselves as apostles of Christ.

Jerusalem Bible

to this one husband. 3 But the serpent, with his cunning, seduced Eve, and I am afraid that in the same way your ideas may get corrupted and turned away from simple devotion to Christ. 4 Because any newcomer has only to proclaim a new Jesus, different from the one that we preached, or you have only to receive a new spirit, different from the one you have already received, or a new gospel, different from the one you have already accepted—and you welcome it with open arms. 5 As far as I can tell, these archapostles have nothing more than I have. 6 I may not be a polished speechmaker, but as for knowledge, that is a different matter; surely we have made this plain, speaking on every subject in front of all of you.

7 Or was I wrong, lowering myself so as to lift you high, by preaching the gospel of God to you and taking no fee for it? 8 I was robbing other churches, living on them so that I could serve you. 9 When I was with you and ran out of money, I was no burden to anyone; the brothers who came from Macedonia provided me with everything I wanted. I was very careful, and I always shall be, not to be a burden to you in any way, 10 and by Christ's truth in me, this cause of boasting will never be taken from me in the regions of Achaia. 11 Would I do that if I did not love you? God knows I do. 12 I intend to go on doing what I am doing now—leaving no opportunity for those people who are looking for an opportunity to claim equality with us in what they boast of. 13 These people are counterfeit apostles, they are dishonest work-

New English Bible

But as the serpent in his cunning seduced Eve, I am afraid that your thoughts may be corrupted and you may lose your[a] single-hearted devotion to Christ. For if someone comes who proclaims another Jesus, not the Jesus whom we proclaimed, or if you then receive a spirit different from the Spirit already given to you, or a gospel different from the gospel you have already accepted, you manage to put up with that well enough. Have I in any way come short of those superlative apostles? I think not. I may be no speaker, but knowledge I have; at all times we have made known to you the full truth.

Or was this my offence, that I made no charge for preaching the gospel of God, lowering myself to help in raising you? It is true that I took toll of other congregations, accepting[b] support from them to serve you. Then, while I was with you, if I ran short I sponged on no one; anything I needed was fully met by our friends who came from Macedonia; I made it a rule, as I always shall, never to be a burden to you. As surely as the truth of Christ is in me, I will preserve my pride in this matter throughout Achaia, and nothing shall stop me. Why? Is it that I do not love you? God knows I do.

And I shall go on doing as I am doing now, to cut the ground from under those who would seize any chance to put their vaunted apostleship on the same level as ours. Such men are sham-apostles, crooked in all their practices, mas-

[a] *Some witnesses insert* purity and . . . [b] *Or* Did I take toll of other congregations by accepting . . . ?

King James Version

the apostles of Christ. 14And no marvel; for
Satan himself is transformed into an angel of
light. 15 Therefore *it is* no great thing if his ministers also be transformed as the ministers of
righteousness; whose end shall be according to
their works. 16 I say again, Let no man think me
a fool; if otherwise, yet as a fool receive me, that
I may boast myself a little. 17 That which I
speak, I speak *it* not after the Lord, but as it
were foolishly, in this confidence of boasting.
18 Seeing that many glory after the flesh, I will
glory also. 19 For ye suffer fools gladly, seeing ye
yourselves are wise. 20 For ye suffer, if a man
bring you into bondage, if a man devour *you*, if
a man take *of you*, if a man exalt himself, if a
man smite you on the face. 21 I speak as concerning reproach, as though we had been weak.
Howbeit, whereinsoever any is bold, (I speak
foolishly,) I am bold also. 22Are they Hebrews?
so *am* I. Are they Israelites? so *am* I. Are they
the seed of Abraham? so *am* I. 23Are they ministers of Christ? (I speak as a fool,) I *am* more;
in labours more abundant, in stripes above meas-

Living Bible

they are Christ's apostles. 14 Yet I am not surprised! Satan can change himself into an angel
of light, 15 so it is no wonder his servants can
do it too, and seem like godly ministers. In the
end they will get every bit of punishment their
wicked deeds deserve.

16 Again I plead, don't think that I have
lost my wits to talk like this; but even if you
do, listen to me anyway—a witless man, a fool—
while I also boast a little as they do. 17 Such
bragging isn't something the Lord commanded
me to do, for I am acting like a brainless fool.
18 Yet those other men keep telling you how
wonderful they are, so here I go: 19, 20 (You
think you are so wise—yet you listen gladly to
those fools; you don't mind at all when they
make you their slaves and take everything you
have, and take advantage of you, and put on
airs, and slap you in the face. 21 I'm ashamed
to say that I'm not strong and daring like that!
But whatever they can boast about—I'm talking
like a fool again—I can boast about it, too.)

22 They brag that they are Hebrews, do they?
Well, so am I. And they say that they are Israelites, God's chosen people? So am I. And they
are descendants of Abraham? Well, I am too.

23 They say they serve Christ? But I have
served him far more! (Have I gone mad to
boast like this?) I have worked harder, been

Today's English Version

14 Well, no wonder! Even Satan can change himself to look like an angel of light! 15 So it is no
great thing if his servants change themselves to
look like servants of right. In the end they will
get exactly what they deserve for the things they
do.

Paul's sufferings as an apostle

16 I repeat: no one should think that I am a
fool. But if you do, at least accept me as a
fool, just so I will have a little to boast of. 17 Of
course what I am saying now is not what the
Lord would have me say; in this matter of boasting I am really talking like a fool. 18 But since
there are so many who boast for merely human
reasons, I will do the same. 19 You yourselves
are so wise, and so you gladly tolerate fools!
20 You tolerate anyone who orders you around,
or takes advantage of you, or traps you, or looks
down on you, or slaps you in the face. 21 I am
ashamed to admit it: we were too timid to do
that!

But if anyone dares to boast of something—I
am talking like a fool—I will be just as daring.
22Are they Hebrews? So am I. Are they Israelites? So am I. Are they Abraham's descendants? So am I. 23Are they Christ's servants? I
sound like a madman—but I am a better servant
than they are! I have worked much harder, I

New International Version

14And no wonder, for Satan himself masquerades as an angel of light. 15 It is not surprising,
then, if his servants masquerade as servants of
righteousness. Their end will be what their actions deserve.

Paul boasts about his sufferings

16 I repeat: Let no one take me for a fool.
But if you do, then receive me just as you would
a fool, so that I may do a little boasting. 17 In
this self-confident boasting I am not talking as
the Lord would, but as a fool. 18 Since many are
boasting in the way the world does, I too will
boast. 19 You gladly put up with fools since you
are so wise! 20 In fact, you even put up with
anyone who enslaves you or exploits you or takes
advantage of you or pushes himself forward or
slaps you in the face. 21 To my shame I admit
that we were too weak for that!

What anyone else dares to boast about—I am
speaking as a fool—I also dare to boast about.
22Are they Hebrews? So am I. Are they Israelites? So am I. Are they Abraham's descendants? So am I. 23Are they servants of Christ?
(I am out of my mind to talk like this.) I am
more. I have worked much harder, been in

Phillips Modern English

Christ. Nor do their tactics surprise me when I consider how Satan himself masquerades as an angel of light. It is only to be expected that his agents shall have the appearance of ministers of righteousness—but they will get what they deserve in the end.

11.16 If you like self-commendations, listen to mine!

Once more, let me advise you not to look upon me as a fool. Yet if you do, then listen to what this "fool" has to make his little boast about.

I am not now speaking as the Lord commands me but as a fool in this business of boasting. Since all the others are so proud of themselves, let me do a little boasting as well. From your heights of wisdom I am sure you can smile tolerantly on a fool. Oh, you're tolerant all right! You don't mind, do you, if a man takes away your liberty, spends your money, takes advantage of you, puts on airs or even smacks your face? I am almost ashamed to say that I never did brave strong things like that to you. Yet in whatever particular they parade such confidence I (speaking as a fool, remember) can do the same.

Are they Hebrews? So am I.
Are they Israelites? So am I.
Are they descendants of Abraham? So am I.
Are they ministers of Christ? I have more claim to this title than they. This is a silly game but look at this list:

I have worked harder than any of them.

Revised Standard Version

14And no wonder, for even Satan disguises himself as an angel of light. 15 So it is not strange
if his servants also disguise themselves as servants of righteousness. Their end will correspond
to their deeds.
16 I repeat, let no one think me foolish; but
even if you do, accept me as a fool, so that I
too may boast a little. 17 (What I am saying I
say not with the Lord's authority but as a fool,
in this boastful confidence; 18 since many boast
of worldly things, I too will boast.) 19 For you
gladly bear with fools, being wise yourselves!
20 For you bear it if a man makes slaves of you,
or preys upon you, or takes advantage of you,
or puts on airs, or strikes you in the face. 21 To
my shame, I must say, we were too weak for
that!
But whatever any one dares to boast of—I am
speaking as a fool—I also dare to boast of that.
22Are they Hebrews? So am I. Are they Israelites? So am I. Are they descendants of Abraham? So am I. 23Are they servants of Christ? I
am a better one—I am talking like a madman—
with far greater labors, far more imprisonments,

Jerusalem Bible

men disguised as apostles of Christ. 14 There
is nothing unexpected about that; if Satan himself goes disguised as an angel of light, 15 there
is no need to be surprised when his servants,
too, disguise themselves as the servants of righteousness. They will come to the end that they
deserve.
16 As I said before, let no one take me for
a fool; but if you must, then treat me as a fool
and let me do a little boasting of my own.
17 What I am going to say now is not prompted
by the Lord, but said as if in a fit of folly, in
the certainty that I have something to boast
about. 18 So many others have been boasting
of their worldly achievements, that I will boast
myself. 19 You are all wise men and can cheerfully tolerate fools, 20 yes, even to tolerating
somebody who makes slaves of you, makes you
feed him, imposes on you, orders you about and
slaps you in the face. 21 I hope you are ashamed
of us for being weak with you instead!
But if anyone wants some brazen speaking—
I am still talking as a fool—then I can be as
brazen as any of them, and about the same
things. 22 Hebrews, are they? So am I. Israelites? So am I. Descendants of Abraham? So am
I. 23 The servants of Christ? I must be mad to
say this, but so am I, and more than they: more,
because I have worked harder, I have been sent

New English Bible

querading as apostles of Christ. There is nothing surprising about that; Satan himself masquerades as an angel of light. It is therefore a simple thing for his agents to masquerade as agents of good. But they will meet the end their deeds deserve.

I repeat: let no one take me for a fool; but if you must, then give me the privilege of a fool, and let me have my little boast like others. I am not speaking here as a Christian, but like a fool, if it comes to bragging. So many people brag of their earthly distinctions that I shall do so too. How gladly you bear with fools, being yourselves so wise! If a man tyrannizes over you, exploits you, gets you in his clutches, puts on airs, and hits you in the face, you put up with it. And we, you say, have been weak! I admit the reproach.

But if there is to be bravado (and here I speak as a fool), I can indulge in it too. Are they Hebrews? So am I. Israelites? So am I. Abraham's descendants? So am I. Are they servants of Christ? I am mad to speak like this, but I can outdo them. More overworked than they,

King James Version

ure, in prisons more frequent, in deaths oft.
24 Of the Jews five times received I forty *stripes*
save one. 25 Thrice was I beaten with rods, once
was I stoned, thrice I suffered shipwreck, a night
and a day I have been in the deep; 26 *In* journey-
ings often, *in* perils of waters, *in* perils of robbers, *in* perils by *mine own* countrymen, *in* perils
by the heathen, *in* perils in the city, *in* perils in
the wilderness, *in* perils in the sea, *in* perils
among false brethren; 27 In weariness and pain-
fulness, in watchings often, in hunger and thirst,
in fastings often, in cold and nakedness. 28 Beside those things that are without, that which
cometh upon me daily, the care of all the
churches. 29 Who is weak, and I am not weak?
who is offended, and I burn not? 30 If I must
needs glory, I will glory of the things which concern mine infirmities. 31 The God and Father of
our Lord Jesus Christ, which is blessed for evermore, knoweth that I lie not. 32 In Damascus
the governor under Aretas the king kept the city
of the Damascenes with a garrison, desirous to
apprehend me: 33 And through a window in a
basket was I let down by the wall, and escaped
his hands.

Living Bible

put in jail oftener, been whipped times without
number, and faced death again and again and
again. 24 Five different times the Jews gave me
their terrible thirty-nine lashes. 25 Three times I
was beaten with rods. Once I was stoned. Three
times I was shipwrecked. Once I was in the open
sea all night and the whole next day. 26 I have
traveled many weary miles and have been often
in great danger from flooded rivers, and from
robbers, and from my own people, the Jews, as
well as from the hands of the Gentiles. I have
faced grave dangers from mobs in the cities and
from death in the deserts and in the stormy seas
and from men who claim to be brothers in Christ
but are not. 27 I have lived with weariness and
pain and sleepless nights. Often I have been
hungry and thirsty and have gone without food;
often I have shivered with cold, without enough
clothing to keep me warm.

28 Then, besides all this, I have the constant worry of how the churches are getting
along: 29 Who makes a mistake and I do not
feel his sadness? Who falls without my longing
to help him? Who is spiritually hurt without my
fury rising against the one who hurt him?

30 But if I must brag, I would rather brag
about the things that show how weak I am.
31 God, the Father of our Lord Jesus Christ,
who is to be praised forever and ever, knows I
tell the truth. 32 For instance, in Damascus the
governor under King Aretas kept guards at the
city gates to catch me; 33 but I was let down by
rope and basket from a hole in the city wall,
and so I got away! [What popularity! [b]]

[*b*] Implied.

Today's English Version

have been in prison more times, I have been
whipped much more, and I have been near
death more often. 24 Five times I was given the
thirty-nine lashes by the Jews; 25 three times I
was whipped by the Romans, and once I was
stoned; I have been in three shipwrecks, and
once I spent twenty-four hours in the water.
26 In my many travels I have been in danger
from floods and from robbers, in danger from
fellow Jews and from Gentiles; there have been
dangers in the cities, dangers in the wilds,
dangers on the high seas, and dangers from false
friends. 27 There has been work and toil; often
I have gone without sleep; I have been hungry
and thirsty; I have often been without enough
food, shelter, or clothing. 28 And, not to mention other things, every day I am under the
pressure of my concern for all the churches.
29 When someone is weak, then I feel weak too;
when someone is led into sin, I am filled with
distress.

30 If I must boast, I will boast of things that
show how weak I am. 31 The God and Father
of the Lord Jesus—blessed be his name forever!—knows that I am not lying. 32 When I
was in Damascus, the governor under King
Aretas placed guards at the city gates to arrest
me. 33 But I was let down in a basket, through
an opening in the wall, and escaped from him.

New International Version

prison more frequently, been flogged more severely, and been exposed to death again and
again. 24 Five times I received from the Jews
the forty lashes minus one. 25 Three times I was
beaten with rods, once I was stoned, three times
I was shipwrecked, I spent a night and a day in
the open sea, 26 I have been constantly on the
move. I have been in danger from rivers, in
danger from bandits, in danger from my own
countrymen, in danger from Gentiles; in danger
in the city, in danger in the country, in danger at
sea; and in danger from false brothers. 27 I have
labored and toiled and have often gone without
sleep; I have known hunger and thirst and have
often gone without food; I have been cold and
naked. 28 Besides everything else, I face daily
the pressure of my concern for all the churches.
29 Who is weak, and I do not feel weak? Who is
led into sin, and I do not inwardly burn?

30 If I must boast, I will boast of the things
that show my weakness. 31 The God and Father of the Lord Jesus, who is to be praised forever, knows that I am not lying. 32 In Damascus
the governor under King Aretas had the city of
the Damascenes guarded in order to arrest me.
33 But I was lowered in a basket from a window
in the wall and slipped through his hands.

Phillips Modern English

I have served more prison sentences!
I have been beaten times without number.
I have faced death again and again.
I have been beaten the regulation thirty-nine stripes by the Jews five times.
I have been beaten with rods three times.
I have been stoned once.
I have been shipwrecked three times.
I have been twenty-four hours in the open sea.
In my travels I have been in constant danger from rivers, from bandits, from my own countrymen, and from pagans. I have faced danger in city streets, danger in the desert, danger on the high seas, danger among false Christians. I have known drudgery, exhaustion, many sleepless nights, hunger and thirst, fasting, cold and exposure.

Apart from all external trials I have the daily burden of responsibility for all the churches. Do you think anyone is weak without my feeling his weakness? Does anyone have his faith upset without my burning with indignation?

Oh, if I am going to boast, let me boast of the things which have shown up my weakness! The God and Father of the Lord Jesus, he who is blessed for ever, knows that I speak the simple truth.

In Damascus, the town governor, acting by King Aretas' order, had his patrols out to arrest me. I escaped through a window and was let down the wall in a basket.

Revised Standard Version

with countless beatings, and often near death.
24 Five times I have received at the hands of the
Jews the forty lashes less one. 25 Three times I
have been beaten with rods; once I was stoned.
Three times I have been shipwrecked; a night
and a day I have been adrift at sea; 26 on frequent journeys, in danger from rivers, danger
from robbers, danger from my own people,
danger from Gentiles, danger in the city, danger
in the wilderness, danger at sea, danger from
false brethren; 27 in toil and hardship, through
many a sleepless night, in hunger and thirst,
often without food, in cold and exposure. 28 And,
apart from other things, there is the daily pressure upon me of my anxiety for all the churches.
29 Who is weak, and I am not weak? Who is
made to fall, and I am not indignant?
30 If I must boast, I will boast of the things
that show my weakness. 31 The God and Father
of the Lord Jesus, he who is blessed for ever,
knows that I do not lie. 32 At Damascus, the
governor under King Aretas guarded the city of
Damascus in order to seize me, 33 but I was let
down in a basket through a window in the wall,
and escaped his hands.

Jerusalem Bible

to prison more often, and whipped so many
times more, often almost to death. 24 Five times
I had the thirty-nine lashes from the Jews;
25 three times I have been beaten with sticks;
once I was stoned; three times I have been
shipwrecked and once adrift in the open sea for
a night and a day. 26 Constantly traveling, I
have been in danger from rivers and in danger
from brigands, in danger from my own people
and in danger from pagans; in danger in the
towns, in danger in the open country, danger at
sea and danger from so-called brothers. 27 I
have worked and labored, often without sleep;
I have been hungry and thirsty and often starving; I have been in the cold without clothes.
28 And, to leave out much more, there is my
daily preoccupation: my anxiety for all the
churches. 29 When any man has had scruples,
I have had scruples with him; when any man is
made to fall, I am tortured.
30 If I am to boast, then let me boast of my
own feebleness. 31 The God and Father of the
Lord Jesus—bless him for ever—knows that I
am not lying. 32 When I was in Damascus, the
ethnarch of King Aretas put guards around the
city to catch me, 33 and I had to be let down
over the wall in a hamper, through a window,
in order to escape.

New English Bible

scourged more severely, more often imprisoned, many a time face to face with death. Five times the Jews have given me the thirty-nine strokes; three times I have been beaten with rods; once I was stoned; three times I have been shipwrecked, and for twenty-four hours I was adrift on the open sea. I have been constantly on the road; I have met dangers from rivers, dangers from robbers, dangers from my fellow-countrymen, dangers from foreigners, dangers in towns, dangers in the country, dangers at sea, dangers from false friends. I have toiled and drudged, I have often gone without sleep; hungry and thirsty, I have often gone fasting; and I have suffered from cold and exposure.

Apart from these external things,[a] there is the responsibility that weighs on me every day, my anxious concern for all our congregations. If anyone is weak, do I not share his weakness? If anyone is made to stumble, does my heart not blaze with indignation? If boasting there must be, I will boast of the things that show up my weakness. The God and Father of the Lord Jesus (blessed be his name for ever!) knows that what I say is true. When I was in Damascus, the commissioner of King Aretas kept the city under observation so as to have me arrested; and I was let down in a basket, through a window in the wall, and so escaped his clutches.

[a] *Or* Apart from things which I omit.

King James Version

12 It is not expedient for me doubtless to
glory. I will come to visions and revelations
of the Lord. 2 I knew a man in Christ above
fourteen years ago, (whether in the body, I cannot tell; or whether out of the body, I cannot
tell: God knoweth;) such a one caught up to the
third heaven. 3 And I knew such a man, (whether
in the body, or out of the body, I cannot tell:
God knoweth;) 4 How that he was caught up
into paradise, and heard unspeakable words,
which it is not lawful for a man to utter. 5 Of
such a one will I glory: yet of myself I will not
glory, but in mine infirmities. 6 For though I
would desire to glory, I shall not be a fool; for
I will say the truth: but *now* I forbear, lest any
man should think of me above that which he
seeth me *to be*, or *that* he heareth of me. 7 And
lest I should be exalted above measure through
the abundance of the revelations, there was given
to me a thorn in the flesh, the messenger of
Satan to buffet me, lest I should be exalted
above measure. 8 For this thing I besought the
Lord thrice, that it might depart from me. 9 And
he said unto me, My grace is sufficient for thee:
for my strength is made perfect in weakness.
Most gladly therefore will I rather glory in my

Living Bible

12 This boasting is all so foolish, but let me
go on. Let me tell about the visions I've
had, and revelations from the Lord.
2, 3 Fourteen years ago I[a] was taken up to
heaven[b] for a visit. Don't ask me whether my
body was there or just my spirit, for I don't
know; only God can answer that. But anyway,
there I was in paradise, 4 and heard things so
astounding that they are beyond a man's power
to describe or put in words (and anyway I am
not allowed to tell them to others). 5 That experience is something worth bragging about, but
I am not going to do it. I am going to boast
only about how weak I am and how great God
is to use such weakness for his glory. 6 I have
plenty to boast about and would be no fool in
doing it, but I don't want anyone to think more
highly of me than he should from what he can
actually see in my life and my message.
7 I will say this: because these experiences I
had were so tremendous, God was afraid I might
be puffed up by them; so I was given a physical
condition which has been a thorn in my flesh, a
messenger from Satan to hurt and bother me,
and prick my pride. 8 Three different times I
begged God to make me well again.
9 Each time he said, "No. But I am with
you; that is all you need. My power shows up
best in weak people." Now I am glad to boast
about how weak I am; I am glad to be a liv-

[*a*] Literally, "A man in Christ." [*b*] Literally, "the third heaven."

Today's English Version

Paul's visions and revelations

12 I have to boast, even though it doesn't do
any good. But I will now talk about visions and revelations given me by the Lord. 2 I
know a certain Christian man who fourteen
years ago was snatched up to the highest heaven
(I do not know whether this actually happened,
or whether he had a vision—only God knows).
3 I repeat, I know that this man was snatched
to Paradise (again, I do not know whether this
actually happened, or whether it was a vision—
only God knows), 4 and there he heard things
which cannot be put into words, things that human lips may not speak. 5 So I will boast of
this man—but I will not boast about myself,
except the things that show how weak I am.
6 If I wanted to boast, I would not be a fool,
because I would be telling the truth. But I will
not boast, because I do not want anyone to have
a higher opinion of me than he has from what
he has seen me do and heard me say.
7 But to keep me from being puffed up with
pride because of the many wonderful things I
saw, I was given a painful physical ailment,
which acts as Satan's messenger to beat me and
keep me from being proud. 8 Three times I
prayed to the Lord about this, and asked him
to take it away. 9 His answer was, "My grace is
all you need; for my power is strongest when
you are weak." I am most happy, then, to be

New International Version

Paul's vision and his thorn

12 I must go on boasting. Although there is
nothing to be gained, I will go on to visions
and revelations from the Lord. 2 I know a man
in Christ who fourteen years ago was caught up
to the third heaven. Whether it was in the body
or out of the body I do not know—God knows.
3 And I know that this man—whether in the
body or apart from the body I do not know, but
God knows—4 was caught up to Paradise. He
heard inexpressible things, things that man is
not permitted to tell. 5 I will boast about a
man like that, but I will not boast about myself,
except about my weaknesses. 6 Even if I should
choose to boast, I would not be a fool, because
I would be speaking the truth. But I refrain, so
no one will think more of me than is warranted
by what I do or say.
7 To keep me from becoming conceited because of these surpassingly great revelations,
there was given me a thorn in my flesh, a messenger of Satan, to torment me. 8 Three times
I pleaded with the Lord to take it away from
me. 9 But he said to me, "My grace is sufficient
for you, for my power is made perfect in weakness." Therefore, I will boast all the more gladly

Phillips Modern English

12.1 I have real grounds for "boasting", but I will only hint at them

I don't think it's really a good thing for me to boast at all, but if I must I will go on to visions and revelations of the Lord himself. I know a man in Christ who, fourteen years ago, had the experience of being caught up into the third Heaven. I don't know whether it was an actual physical experience, only God knows that. All I know is that this man was caught up into paradise. (I repeat, I do not know whether this was a physical happening or not, God alone knows.) This man heard words that cannot, and indeed must not, be put into human speech. I am proud of an experience like that, but I have made up my mind not to boast of anything personal, except of my weaknesses. If I should want to boast I should certainly be no fool, for I should be speaking nothing but the truth. Yet I am not going to do so, for I don't want anyone to think more highly of me than is warranted by what he sees of me and hears from me. So tremendous, however, were the revelations that God gave me that, in order to prevent my becoming absurdly conceited, I was given a stabbing pain—one of Satan's angels—to plague me and effectually stop any conceit. Three times I begged the Lord for it to leave me, but his reply has been, "My grace is enough for you: for where there is weakness, my power is shown the more completely." Therefore, I have cheerfully made up my mind to be proud of my weak-

Revised Standard Version

12 I must boast; there is nothing to be
gained by it, but I will go on to visions and
revelations of the Lord. 2 I know a man in Christ
who fourteen years ago was caught up to the
third heaven—whether in the body or out of the
body I do not know, God knows. 3 And I know
that this man was caught up into Paradise—
whether in the body or out of the body I do not
know, God knows—4 and he heard things that
cannot be told, which man may not utter. 5 On
behalf of this man I will boast, but on my own
behalf I will not boast, except of my weaknesses.
6 Though if I wish to boast, I shall not be a fool,
for I shall be speaking the truth. But I refrain
from it, so that no one may think more of me
than he sees in me or hears from me. 7 And to
keep me from being too elated by the abundance
of revelations, a thorn was given me in the flesh,
a messenger of Satan, to harass me, to keep me
from being too elated. 8 Three times I besought
the Lord about this, that it should leave me;
9 but he said to me, "My grace is sufficient for
you, for my power is made perfect in weakness."
I will all the more gladly boast of my weak-

Jerusalem Bible

12 Must I go on boasting, though there is
nothing to be gained by it? But I will move
on to the visions and revelations I have had
from the Lord. 2 I know a man in Christ who,
fourteen years ago, was caught up—whether
still in the body or out of the body, I do not
know; God knows—right into the third heaven.[m]
3 I do know, however, that this same person—
whether in the body or out of the body, I do
not know; God knows—4 was caught up into
paradise and heard things which must not and
cannot be put into human language. 5 I will
boast about a man like that, but not about anything of my own except my weaknesses. 6 If I
should decide to boast, I should not be made
to look foolish, because I should only be speaking the truth; but I am not going to, in case
anyone should begin to think I am better than
he can actually see and hear me to be.
7 In view of the extraordinary nature of these
revelations, to stop me from getting too proud
I was given a thorn in the flesh, an angel of
Satan to beat me and stop me from getting too
proud! 8 About this thing, I have pleaded with
the Lord three times for it to leave me, 9 but he
has said, "My grace is enough for you: my
power is at its best in weakness." So I shall be
very happy to make my weaknesses my special

[m] I.e., the highest heaven.

New English Bible

12 I am obliged to boast. It does no good; but I shall go on to tell of visions and revelations granted by the Lord. I know a Christian man who fourteen years ago (whether in the body or out of it, I do not know—God knows) was caught up as far as the third heaven. And I know that this same man (whether in the body or out of it, I do not know—God knows) was caught up into paradise, and heard words so secret that human lips may not repeat them. About such a man as that I am ready to boast; but I will not boast on my own account, except of my weaknesses. If I should choose to boast, it would not be the boast of a fool, for I should be speaking the truth. But I refrain, because I should not like anyone to form an estimate of me which goes beyond the evidence of his own eyes and ears. And so, to keep me from being unduly elated by the magnificence of such revelations, I was given[b] a sharp physical pain[c] which came as Satan's messenger to bruise me; this was to save me from being unduly elated. Three times I begged the Lord to rid me of it, but his answer was: 'My grace is all you need; power comes to its full strength in weakness.' I shall therefore prefer to find my joy and pride in the very things that are my weakness; and then the

[b] *Some witnesses read* . . . ears, and because of the magnificence of the revelations themselves. Therefore to keep me from being unduly elated I was given . . . [c] *Or* a painful wound to my pride (*literally* a stake, *or* thorn, for the flesh).

King James Version

infirmities, that the power of Christ may rest upon me. 10 Therefore I take pleasure in infirmities, in reproaches, in necessities, in persecutions, in distresses for Christ's sake: for when I am weak, then am I strong. 11 I am become a fool in glorying; ye have compelled me: for I ought to have been commended of you: for in nothing am I behind the very chiefest apostles, though I be nothing. 12 Truly the signs of an apostle were wrought among you in all patience, in signs, and wonders, and mighty deeds. 13 For what is it wherein ye were inferior to other churches, except *it be* that I myself was not burdensome to you? forgive me this wrong. 14 Behold, the third time I am ready to come to you; and I will not be burdensome to you: for I seek not yours, but you: for the children ought not to lay up for the parents, but the parents for the children. 15 And I will very gladly spend and be

Living Bible

ing demonstration of Christ's power, instead of showing off my own power and abilities. 10 Since I know it is all for Christ's good, I am quite happy about "the thorn," and about insults and hardships, persecutions and difficulties; for when I am weak, then I am strong—the less I have, the more I depend on him.

11 You have made me act like a fool—boasting like this—for you people ought to be writing about me and not making me write about myself. There isn't a single thing these other marvelous fellows have that I don't have too, even though I am really worth nothing at all. 12 When I was there I certainly gave you every proof that I was truly an apostle, sent to you by God himself: for I patiently did many wonders and signs and mighty works among you. 13 The only thing I didn't do for you, that I do everywhere else in all other churches, was to become a burden to you—I didn't ask you to give me food to eat and a place to stay. Please forgive me for this wrong!

14 Now I am coming to you again, the third time; and it is still not going to cost you anything, for I don't want your money. I want *you!* And anyway, you are my children, and little children don't pay for their father's and mother's food—it's the other way around; parents supply food for their children. 15 I am glad to give

Today's English Version

proud of my weaknesses, in order to feel the protection of Christ's power over me. 10 I am content with weaknesses, insults, hardships, persecutions, and difficulties for Christ's sake. For when I am weak, then I am strong.

Paul's concern for the Corinthians

11 I am acting like a fool—but you have made me do it. You are the ones who ought to show your approval of me. For even if I am nothing, I am in no way inferior to those very special "apostles" of yours. 12 The things that prove that I am an apostle were done with all patience among you; there were signs and wonders and miracles. 13 How were you treated any worse than the other churches, except that I did not bother you for help? Please forgive me for being so unfair!

14 This is now the third time that I am ready to come to visit you—and I will not make any demands on you. It is you I want, not your money. After all, children should not have to provide for their parents, but parents should provide for their children. 15 I will be glad to spend

New International Version

about my weaknesses, so that Christ's power may rest on me. 10 That is why, for Christ's sake, I delight in weaknesses, in insults, in hardships, in persecutions, in difficulties. For when I am weak, then I am strong.

Paul's concern for the Corinthians

11 I have made a fool of myself, but you drove me to it. I ought to have been commended by you, for I am not in the least inferior to the "super-apostles," even though I am nothing. 12 The things that mark an apostle—signs, wonders and miracles—were done among you with great perseverance. 13 How were you inferior to the other churches, except that I was never a burden to you? Forgive me this wrong!

14 Now I am ready to visit you for the third time, and I will not be a burden to you, because what I want is not your possessions but you. After all, children should not have to save up for their parents, but parents for their children. 15 So I will very gladly spend for you

Phillips Modern English

nesses, because they mean a deeper experience of the power of Christ. I can even enjoy weaknesses, insults, privations, persecutions and difficulties for Christ's sake. For my very weakness makes me strong in him.

12.11 This boasting is silly, but you made it necessary

I have made a fool of myself in this "boasting" business, but you forced me to do it. If only you had had a better opinion of me it would have been quite unnecessary. For I am not really in the least inferior, nobody as I am, to these extra-special messengers. You have had a demonstration of the power God gives to a genuine messenger by his sheer endurance as well as the miracles, signs and works of spiritual power that you saw with your own eyes. What makes you feel so inferior to other churches? Is it because I have not allowed you to support me financially? My humblest apologies for this great wrong!

12.14 What can be your grounds for suspicion of me?

Now I am all ready to visit you for the third time, and I am still not going to be a burden to you. It is you I want—not your money. Children don't have to put by their savings for their parents; parents do that for their children. Con-

Revised Standard Version

nesses, that the power of Christ may rest upon
me. 10 For the sake of Christ, then, I am content with weaknesses, insults, hardships, persecutions, and calamities; for when I am weak,
then I am strong.
11 I have been a fool! You forced me to it,
for I ought to have been commended by you.
For I was not at all inferior to these superlative
apostles, even though I am nothing. 12 The signs
of a true apostle were performed among you in
all patience, with signs and wonders and mighty
works. 13 For in what were you less favored than
the rest of the churches, except that I myself
did not burden you? Forgive me this wrong!
14 Here for the third time I am ready to
come to you. And I will not be a burden, for I
seek not what is yours but you; for children
ought not to lay up for their parents, but parents
for their children. 15 I will most gladly spend

Jerusalem Bible

boast so that the power of Christ may stay over
me, 10 and that is why I am quite content with
my weaknesses, and with insults, hardships, persecutions, and the agonies I go through for
Christ's sake. For it is when I am weak that I
am strong.
11 I have been talking like a fool, but you
forced me to do it: you are the ones who
should have been commending me. Though I
am a nobody, there is not a thing these archapostles have that I do not have as well. 12 You
have seen done among you all the things that
mark the true apostle, unfailingly produced: the
signs, the marvels, the miracles. 13 Is there anything of which you have had less than the other
churches have had, except that I have not myself
been a burden on you? For this unfairness,
please forgive me. 14 I am all prepared now to
come to you for the third time, and I am not
going to be a burden on you: it is you I want,
not your possessions. Children are not expected
to save up for their parents, but parents for
children. 15 I am perfectly willing to spend what

New English Bible

power of Christ will come and rest upon me. Hence I am well content, for Christ's sake, with weakness, contempt, persecution, hardship, and frustration; for when I am weak, then I am strong.

I am being very foolish, but it was you who drove me to it; my credentials should have come from you. In no respect did I fall short of these superlative apostles, even if I am a nobody. The marks of a true apostle were there, in the work I did among you, which called for such constant fortitude, and was attended by signs, marvels, and miracles. Is there anything in which you were treated worse than the other congregations—except this, that I never sponged upon you? How unfair of me! I crave forgiveness.

Here am I preparing to pay you a third visit; and I am not going to sponge upon you. It is you I want, not your money; parents should make provision for their children, not children for their parents. As for me, I will gladly spend

King James Version

spent for you; though the more abundantly I
love you, the less I be loved. 16 But be it so, I
did not burden you: nevertheless, being crafty,
I caught you with guile. 17 Did I make a gain
of you by any of them whom I sent unto you?
18 I desired Titus, and with *him* I sent a brother.
Did Titus make a gain of you? walked we not
in the same spirit? *walked we* not in the same
steps? 19 Again, think ye that we excuse ourselves unto you? we speak before God in Christ:
but *we do* all things, dearly beloved, for your
edifying. 20 For I fear, lest, when I come, I shall
not find you such as I would, and *that* I shall be
found unto you such as ye would not: lest *there
be* debates, envyings, wraths, strifes, backbit-
ings, whisperings, swellings, tumults: 21 *And* lest,
when I come again, my God will humble me
among you, and *that* I shall bewail many which
have sinned already, and have not repented of
the uncleanness and fornication and lasciviousness which they have committed.

Living Bible

you myself and all I have for your spiritual
good, even though it seems that the more I love
you, the less you love me.
16 Some of you are saying, "It's true that his
visits didn't seem to cost us anything, but he is
a sneaky fellow, that Paul, and he fooled us. As
sure as anything he must have made money
from us some way."
17 But how? Did any of the men I sent to
you take advantage of you? 18 When I urged
Titus to visit you, and sent our other brother
with him, did they make any profit? No, of
course not. For we have the same Holy Spirit,
and walk in each other's steps, doing things the
same way.
19 I suppose you think I am saying all this to
get back into your good graces. That isn't it at
all. I tell you, with God listening as I say it, that
I have said this to help *you,* dear friends—to
build you up spiritually and not to help myself.
20 For I am afraid that when I come to visit you
I won't like what I find, and then you won't
like the way I will have to act. I am afraid that
I will find you quarreling, and envying each
other, and being angry with each other, and acting big, and saying wicked things about each
other and whispering behind each other's backs,
filled with conceit and disunity. 21 Yes, I am
afraid that when I come God will humble me
before you and I will be sad and mourn because
many of you who have sinned became sinners
and don't even care about the wicked, impure
things you have done: your lust and immorality,
and the taking of other men's wives.

Today's English Version

all I have, and myself as well, in order to help
you. Will you love me less because I love you
so much?
16 You will agree, then, that I was not a
burden to you. But, someone will say, I was
tricky and trapped you with lies. 17 How? Did
I take advantage of you through any of the messengers I sent? 18 I begged Titus to go, and I
sent the other Christian brother with him. Would
you say that Titus took advantage of you? Do
not he and I act from the very same motives
and behave in the same way?
19 Perhaps you think that all along we have
been trying to defend ourselves before you. No!
We speak as Christ would have us speak, in
the presence of God, and everything we do, dear
friends, is done to help you. 20 I am afraid that
when I get there I will find you different from
what I would like you to be and you will find
me different from what you would like me to
be. I am afraid that I will find quarreling and
jealousy, hot tempers and selfishness, insults and
gossip, pride and disorder. 21 I am afraid that
the next time I come my God will humiliate me
in your presence, and I shall weep over many
who sinned in the past and have not repented
of the immoral things they have done, their
sexual sins and lustful deeds.

New International Version

everything I have and expend myself as well. If
I love you more, will you love me less? 16 Be
that as it may, I have not been a burden to
you. Yet, crafty fellow that I am, I caught you
by trickery! 17 Did I exploit you through any of
the men I sent you? 18 I urged Titus to go to
you and I sent our brother with him. Titus did
not exploit you, did he? Did we not act in the
same spirit and follow the same course?
19 Have you been thinking all along that we
have been defending ourselves to you? We have
been speaking in the sight of God as those in
Christ; and everything we do, dear friends, is for
your strengthening. 20 For I am afraid that when
I come I may not find you as I want you to be,
and you may not find me as you want me to
be. I fear that there may be quarreling, jealousy,
outbursts of anger, factions, slander, gossip, arrogance and disorder. 21 I am afraid that when
I come again my God will humble me before
you, and I will be grieved over many who have
sinned earlier and have not repented of the impurity, sexual sin and debauchery in which they
have indulged.

Phillips Modern English

sequently I will most gladly spend and be spent for your good utterly. Does that mean that the more I love you the less you love me?

"All right then," I hear you say, "we agree that he himself had none of our money." But are you thinking that I nevertheless was rogue enough to catch you by some trick? Just think. Did I make any profit out of the messengers I sent you? I asked Titus to go, and sent the brother with him. You don't think Titus made anything out of you, do you? Yet didn't I act in the same spirit as he, and take the same line as he did?

12.19 Remember what I really am, and whose authority I have

Are you thinking all this time that I am trying to justify myself in your eyes? Actually I am speaking in Christ before God himself, and my only reason for so doing, my dear friends, is to help you in your spiritual life.

For I must confess that I am afraid that when I come I shall not perhaps find you as I should like to find you, and that you will not find me quite as you would like me to be. I am afraid of finding arguments, jealousy, ill-feeling, divided loyalties, slander, whispering, pride and disharmony. When I come again, will God make me feel ashamed of you as I stand among you? Shall I have to grieve over many who have sinned already and are not yet sorry for the impurity, the immorality and the lustfulness of which they are guilty?

Revised Standard Version

and be spent for your souls. If I love you the
more, am I to be loved the less? 16 But granting
that I myself did not burden you, I was crafty,
you say, and got the better of you by guile.
17 Did I take advantage of you through any of
those whom I sent to you? 18 I urged Titus to
go, and sent the brother with him. Did Titus
take advantage of you? Did we not act in the
same spirit? Did we not take the same steps?

19 Have you been thinking all along that we
have been defending ourselves before you? It is
in the sight of God that we have been speaking
in Christ, and all for your upbuilding, beloved.
20 For I fear that perhaps I may come and find
you not what I wish, and that you may find me
not what you wish; that perhaps there may be
quarreling, jealousy, anger, selfishness, slander,
gossip, conceit, and disorder. 21 I fear that when
I come again my God may humble me before
you, and I may have to mourn over many of
those who sinned before and have not repented
of the impurity, immorality, and licentiousness
which they have practiced.

Jerusalem Bible

I have, and to be expended, in the interests of
your souls. Because I love you more, must I
be loved the less?

16 All very well, you say: I personally put
no pressure on you, but like the cunning fellow
that I am, I took you in by a trick. 17 So we
exploited you, did we, through one of the men
that I have sent to you? 18 Well, Titus went at
my urging, and I sent the brother that came
with him. Can Titus have exploited you? You
know that he and I have always been guided
by the same spirit and trodden in the same
tracks.

Paul's fears and anxieties

19 All this time you have been thinking that
our defense is addressed to you, but it is before
God that we, in Christ, are speaking; and it is
all, my dear brothers, for your benefit. 20 What
I am afraid of is that when I come I may find
you different from what I want you to be, and
you may find that I am not as you would like
me to be; and then there will be wrangling,
jealousy, and tempers roused, intrigues and backbiting and gossip, obstinacies and disorder. 21 I
am afraid that on my next visit, my God may
make me ashamed on your account and I shall
be grieving over all those who sinned before
and have still not repented of the impurities,
fornication and debauchery they committed.

New English Bible

what I have for you—yes, and spend myself to the limit. If I love you overmuch, am I to be loved the less? But, granted that I did not prove a burden to you, still I was unscrupulous enough, you say, to use a trick to catch you. Who, of the men I have sent to you, was used by me to defraud you? I begged Titus to visit you, and I sent our friend with him. Did Titus defraud you? Have we not both been guided by the same Spirit, and followed the same course?

Perhaps you think that all this time we have been addressing our defence to you. No; we are speaking in God's sight, and as Christian men. Our whole aim, my own dear people, is to build you up. I fear that when I come I may perhaps find you different from what I wish you to be, and that you may find me also different from what you wish. I fear I may find quarrelling and jealousy, angry tempers and personal rivalries, backbiting and gossip, arrogance and general disorder. I am afraid that, when I come again, my God may humiliate me in your presence, that I may have tears to shed over many of those who have sinned in the past and have not repented of their unclean lives, their fornication and sensuality.

King James Version

13 This *is* the third *time* I am coming to you.
In the mouth of two or three witnesses
shall every word be established. 2 I told you
before, and foretell you, as if I were present,
the second time; and being absent now I write
to them which heretofore have sinned, and to
all other, that, if I come again, I will not spare:
3 Since ye seek a proof of Christ speaking in
me, which to you-ward is not weak, but is
mighty in you. 4 For though he was crucified
through weakness, yet he liveth by the power of
God. For we also are weak in him, but we shall
live with him by the power of God toward you.
5 Examine yourselves, whether ye be in the faith;
prove your own selves. Know ye not your own
selves, how that Jesus Christ is in you, except ye
be reprobates? 6 But I trust that ye shall know
that we are not reprobates. 7 Now I pray to God
that ye do no evil; not that we should appear
approved, but that ye should do that which is
honest, though we be as reprobates. 8 For we

Living Bible

13 This is the third time I am coming to
visit you. The Scriptures tell us that if two
or three have seen a wrong, it must be punished.
[Well, this is my third warning, as I come now
for this visit.[a]] 2 I have already warned those
who had been sinning when I was there last;
now I warn them again, and all others, just as
I did then, that this time I come ready to punish severely and I will not spare them.

3 I will give you all the proof you want that
Christ speaks through me. Christ is not weak in
his dealings with you, but is a mighty power
within you. 4 His weak, human body died on
the cross, but now he lives by the mighty power
of God. We, too, are weak in our bodies, as he
was, but now we live and are strong, as he is,
and have all of God's power to use in dealing
with you.

5 Check up on yourselves. Are you really
Christians? Do you pass the test? Do you feel
Christ's presence and power more and more
within you? Or are you just pretending to be
Christians when actually you aren't at all? 6 I
hope you can agree that I have stood that test
and truly belong to the Lord.

7 I pray that you will live good lives, not because that will be a feather in our caps[b], proving that what we teach is right; no, for we want
you to do right even if we ourselves are despised. 8 Our responsibility is to encourage the

[a] Implied. [b] Literally, "not that we may appear approved."

Today's English Version

Final warnings and greetings

13 This is now the third time that I am
coming to visit you. "Any accusation must
be upheld by the evidence of two or three witnesses"—as the scripture says. 2 I want to tell
you who have sinned in the past, and all the
others; I said it before, during my second visit
to you, but I will say it again now that I am
away: the next time I come nobody will escape
punishment. 3 You will have all the proof you
want that Christ speaks through me. When he
deals with you he is not weak; instead he shows
his power among you. 4 For even though it was
in weakness that he was put to death on the
cross, it is by God's power that he lives. In
union with him we also are weak; but in our
relations with you, we shall live with him by
God's power.

5 Put yourselves to the test and judge yourselves, to find out whether you are living in
faith. Surely you know that Christ Jesus is in
you?—unless you have completely failed. 6 I
trust you will know that we are not failures.
7 We pray to God that you will do no wrong—
not in order to show that we are a success, but
that you may do what is right, even though we
may seem to be failures. 8 For we cannot do a

New International Version

Final warnings

13 This will be my third visit to you. "Every
matter must be established by the testimony of two or three witnesses." [a] 2 I already
gave you a warning when I was with you the
second time. I now repeat it while absent: On
my return I will not spare those who sinned
earlier or any of the others, 3 since you are
demanding proof that Christ is speaking through
me. He is not weak in dealing with you, but is
powerful among you. 4 For to be sure, he was
crucified in weakness, yet he lives by God's
power. Likewise, we are weak in him, yet by
God's power we will live with him to serve you.

5 Examine yourselves to see whether you are
in the faith; test yourselves. Do you not realize
that Christ Jesus is in you—unless, of course,
you fail the test? 6And I trust that you will discover that we have not failed the test. 7 Now
we pray to God that you will not do anything
wrong. Not that people will see that we have
stood the test but that you will do what is right
even though we may seem to have failed. 8 For

[a] Deut. 19:15.

Phillips Modern English

This will be my third visit to you. Remember the ancient Law: "In the mouth of two or three witnesses shall every word be established." My previous warning, given on my second visit, still stands and, though absent, I repeat it now as though I were present to those who had sinned before and to all the others, that my coming will not mean leniency. That will be the proof you seek that I speak by the power of Christ. The Christ you have to deal with is not a weak person outside you, but a tremendous power inside you. He was "weak" enough to be crucified, yes, but he lives now by the power of God. We are weak as he was weak, but we are strong enough to deal with you for we share his life by the power of God.

13.5 Why not test yourselves instead of me?

You should be looking at yourselves to make sure that you are really Christ's. It is yourselves that you should be testing. You ought to know by this time that Christ Jesus is in you, unless you are not real Christians at all. And when you have applied your test, I am confident that you will find that I myself am a genuine Christian. I pray God that you may make no mistake, not because I have any need of your approval, but because I earnestly want you to find the right answer, even if that should make me no real Christian. For we can make no progress

Revised Standard Version

13 This is the third time I am coming to you.
Any charge must be sustained by the evidence of two or three witnesses. 2 I warned
those who sinned before and all the others, and
I warn them now while absent, as I did when
present on my second visit, that if I come again
I will not spare them—3 since you desire proof
that Christ is speaking in me. He is not weak in
dealing with you, but is powerful in you. 4 For
he was crucified in weakness, but lives by the
power of God. For we are weak in him, but in
dealing with you we shall live with him by the
power of God.
5 Examine yourselves, to see whether you are
holding to your faith. Test yourselves. Do you
not realize that Jesus Christ is in you?—unless
indeed you fail to meet the test! 6 I hope you
will find out that we have not failed. 7 But we
pray God that you may not do wrong—not that
we may appear to have met the test, but that
you may do what is right, though we may seem
to have failed. 8 For we cannot do anything

Jerusalem Bible

13 This will be the third time I have come
to you. *The evidence of three, or at least
two, witnesses is necessary to sustain the charge.*[n]
2 I gave warning when I was with you the
second time and I give warning now, too, before I come, to those who sinned before and
to any others, that when I come again, I shall
have no mercy. 3 You want proof, you say, that
it is Christ speaking in me: you have known
him not as a weakling, but as a power among
you? 4 Yes, but he was crucified through weakness, and still he lives now through the power
of God. So then, we are weak, as he was, but
we shall live with him, through the power of
God, for your benefit.
5 Examine yourselves to make sure you are
in the faith; test yourselves. Do you acknowledge that Jesus Christ is really in you? If not,
you have failed the test, 6 but we, as I hope
you will come to see, have not failed it. 7 We
pray to God that you will do nothing wrong:
not that we want to appear as the ones who
have been successful—we would rather that you
did well even though we failed. 8 We have no

New English Bible

13 This will be my third visit to you; and all facts must be established by the evidence of two or three witnesses. To those who have sinned in the past, and to everyone else, I repeat the warning I gave before; I gave it in person on my second visit, and I give it now in absence. It is that when I come this time, I will show no leniency. Then you will have the proof you seek of the Christ who speaks through me, the Christ who, far from being weak with you, makes his power felt among you. True, he died on the cross in weakness, but he lives by the power of God; and we who share his weakness shall by the power of God live with him in your service.

Examine yourselves: are you living the life of faith? Put yourselves to the test. Surely you recognize that Jesus Christ is among you?—unless of course you prove unequal to the test. I hope you will come to see that we are not unequal to it. Our prayer to God is that you may do no wrong; we are not concerned to be vindicated ourselves; we want you to do what is right, even if we should seem to be discredited. For we

[n] Dt. 19:15.

King James Version

can do nothing against the truth, but for the
truth. 9 For we are glad, when we are weak, and
ye are strong: and this also we wish, *even* your
perfection. 10 Therefore I write these things being absent, lest being present I should use sharpness, according to the power which the Lord hath given me to edification, and not to destruction. 11 Finally, brethren, farewell. Be perfect, be of good comfort, be of one mind, live in peace; and the God of love and peace shall be with
you. 12 Greet one another with a holy kiss. 13 All
the saints salute you. 14 The grace of the Lord
Jesus Christ, and the love of God, and the communion of the Holy Ghost, *be* with you all. Amen.

The second *epistle* to the Corinthians was written from Philippi, *a city* of Macedonia, by Titus and Lucas.

Living Bible

right at all times, not to hope for evil.[c] 9 We are
glad to be weak and despised if you are really strong. Our greatest wish and prayer is that you will become mature Christians.

10 I am writing this to you now in the hope that I won't need to scold and punish when I come; for I want to use the Lord's authority which he has given me, not to punish you but to make you strong.

11 I close my letter with these last words:

Be happy.
Grow in Christ.
Pay attention to what I have said.
Live in harmony and peace.

And may the God of love and peace be with you.

12 Greet each other warmly in the Lord.
13 All the Christians here send you their best regards.
14 May the grace of our Lord Jesus Christ be with you all. May God's love and the Holy Spirit's friendship be yours.

Paul

[c] Literally, "For we can do nothing against the truth, but for the truth."

Today's English Version

thing against the truth, but only for it. 9 We are
glad when we are weak but you are strong. And so we also pray that you will become perfect.
10 That is why I write this while I am away from you; it is so that when I arrive I will not have to deal harshly with you in using the authority that the Lord gave me—authority to build you up, not to tear you down.

11 And now, brothers, good-bye! Strive for perfection; listen to my appeals; agree with one another, and live in peace. And the God of love and peace will be with you.

12 Greet one another with a brotherly kiss.

All God's people send you their greetings.

13 The grace of the Lord Jesus Christ, the love of God, and the fellowship of the Holy Spirit be with you all.

New International Version

we cannot do anything against the truth, but
only for the truth. 9 We are glad whenever we
are weak but you are strong; and our prayer is
for your perfection. 10 This is why I write these things when I am absent, that when I come I may not have to be harsh in my use of authority —the authority the Lord gave me for building you up, not for tearing you down.

Final greetings

11 Finally, brothers, good-by. Aim for perfection, listen to my appeal, be of one mind, live in peace. And the God of love and peace will be with you.

12 Greet one another with a holy kiss. 13 All
the saints send their greetings.

14 May the grace of the Lord Jesus Christ, and the love of God, and the fellowship of the Holy Spirit be with you all.

Phillips Modern English

against the truth; we can only work for it.

We are always quite happy to be weak if it means that you are strong. Our prayer for you is true Christian maturity. Hence the tone of this letter, so that when I do come I shall not be obliged to use with severity that power which the Lord has given me—though even that is not meant to break you down but to build you up.

13.11 Finally, Farewell

Finally, then, my brothers, cheer up! Aim at perfection and accept my encouragement, agree with one another and live at peace. So shall the God of love and peace be ever with you.

A handshake all round, please! All the Christians here send greeting.

The grace of the Lord Jesus Christ, the love of God, and the fellowship that is ours in the Holy Spirit be with you all!

Revised Standard Version

against the truth, but only for the truth. 9 For we are glad when we are weak and you are strong. What we pray for is your improvement. 10 I write this while I am away from you, in order that when I come I may not have to be severe in my use of the authority which the Lord has given me for building up and not for tearing down.

11 Finally, brethren, farewell. Mend your ways, heed my appeal, agree with one another, live in peace, and the God of love and peace will be with you. 12 Greet one another with a holy kiss. 13 All the saints greet you.

14 The grace of the Lord Jesus Christ and the love of God and the fellowship of [n] the Holy Spirit be with you all.

[n] Or *and participation in.*

Jerusalem Bible

power to resist the truth; only to further it. 9 We are only too glad to be weak provided you are strong. What we ask in our prayers is for you to be made perfect. 10 That is why I am writing this from a distance, so that when I am with you I shall not need to be strict, with the authority which the Lord gave me for building up and not for destroying.

Conclusion

Recommendations. Greetings. Final good wishes

11 In the meantime, brothers, we wish you happiness; try to grow perfect; help one another. Be united; live in peace, and the God of love and peace will be with you.

12 Greet one another with the holy kiss. All the saints send you greetings.

13 The grace of the Lord Jesus Christ, the love of God and the fellowship of the Holy Spirit be with you all.

New English Bible

have no power to act against the truth, but only for it. We are well content to be weak at any time if only you are strong. Indeed, my whole prayer is that all may be put right with you. My purpose in writing this letter before I come, is to spare myself, when I come, any sharp exercise of authority—authority which the Lord gave me for building up and not for pulling down.

And now, my friends, farewell. Mend your ways; take our appeal to heart; agree with one another; live in peace; and the God of love and peace will be with you. Greet one another with the kiss of peace. All God's people send you greetings.

The grace of the Lord Jesus Christ, and the love of God, and fellowship in the Holy Spirit, be with you all.

King James Version

THE EPISTLE OF PAUL THE APOSTLE TO THE GALATIANS

1 Paul, an apostle, (not of men, neither by
man, but by Jesus Christ, and God the Father, who raised him from the dead;) 2 And
all the brethren which are with me, unto the
churches of Galatia: 3 Grace *be* to you, and
peace, from God the Father, and *from* our Lord
Jesus Christ, 4 Who gave himself for our sins,
that he might deliver us from this present evil
world, according to the will of God and our
Father: 5 To whom *be* glory for ever and ever.

Living Bible

GALATIANS

1 *From:* Paul the missionary and all the other
Christians here.
To: The churches of Galatia.[a]
I was not called to be a missionary by any
group or agency. My call is from Jesus Christ
himself, and from God the Father who raised
him from the dead. 3 May peace and blessing be
yours from God the Father and from the Lord
Jesus Christ. 4 He died for our sins just as God
our Father planned, and rescued us from this
evil world in which we live. 5 All glory to God
through all the ages of eternity. Amen.

[a] Galatia was a province in what is now called Turkey.

Today's English Version

PAUL'S LETTER TO THE GALATIANS

1 From Paul, whose call to be an apostle did
not come from man or by means of man,
but from Jesus Christ and God the Father, who
raised him from death. 2 All the brothers who
are here join me in sending greetings to the
churches of Galatia:
3 May God our Father and the Lord Jesus
Christ give you grace and peace.
4 In order to set us free from this present
evil age, Christ gave himself for our sins, in
obedience to the will of our God and Father.
5 To God be the glory forever and ever! Amen.

New International Version

GALATIANS

1 Paul, an apostle—sent not from men nor by
man, but by Jesus Christ and God the Father,
who raised him from the dead—2 and all the
brothers with me,
To the churches in Galatia:
3 Grace and peace to you from God our Father and the Lord Jesus Christ, 4 who gave himself for our sins to rescue us from the present
evil age, according to the will of our God and
Father, 5 to whom be glory for ever and ever.
Amen.

Phillips Modern English

THE LETTER TO THE CHRISTIANS IN GALATIA

I, Paul, who am appointed and commissioned a messenger not by man but by Jesus Christ and God the Father (who raised him from the dead), I and all the brothers with me send greetings to the churches in Galatia. Grace and peace to you from God our Father and the Lord Jesus Christ, who according to the will of our God and Father gave himself for our sins and thereby rescued us from the present evil world-order. To him be glory for ever and ever. Amen.

Revised Standard Version

THE LETTER OF PAUL TO THE GALATIANS

1 Paul an apostle—not from men nor through
man, but through Jesus Christ and God the
Father, who raised him from the dead—2 and
all the brethren who are with me,
To the churches of Galatia:
3 Grace to you and peace from God the
Father and our Lord Jesus Christ, 4 who gave
himself for our sins to deliver us from the present evil age, according to the will of our God
and Father; 5 to whom be the glory for ever
and ever. Amen.

Jerusalem Bible

THE LETTER OF PAUL TO THE CHURCH IN GALATIA GALATIANS

Address

1 From Paul to the churches of Galatia, 2 and
from all the brothers who are here with me,
an apostle who does not owe his authority to
men or his appointment to any human being but
who has been appointed by Jesus Christ and by
God the Father who raised Jesus from the dead.
3 We wish you the grace and peace of God our
Father and of the Lord Jesus Christ, 4 who in
order to rescue us from this present wicked
world sacrificed himself for our sins, in accordance with the will of God our Father, 5 to whom
be glory for ever and ever. Amen.

New English Bible

THE LETTER OF PAUL TO THE GALATIANS

Faith and freedom

1 From Paul, an apostle, not by human appointment or human commission, but by commission from Jesus Christ and from God the Father who raised him from the dead. I and the group of friends now with me send greetings to the Christian congregations of Galatia.

Grace and peace to you from God the Father and our Lord Jesus Christ,[a] who sacrificed himself for our sins, to rescue us out of this present age of wickedness, as our God and Father willed; to whom be glory for ever and ever. Amen.

[a] *Some witnesses read* God our Father and the Lord Jesus Christ.

King James Version

Amen. 6 I marvel that ye are so soon removed
from him that called you into the grace of Christ
unto another gospel: 7 Which is not another; but
there be some that trouble you, and would pervert the gospel of Christ. 8 But though we, or
an angel from heaven, preach any other gospel
unto you than that which we have preached
unto you, let him be accursed. 9 As we said before, so say I now again, If any *man* preach
any other gospel unto you than that ye have
received, let him be accursed. 10 For do I now
persuade men, or God? or do I seek to please
men? for if I yet pleased men, I should not be
the servant of Christ. 11 But I certify you, brethren, that the gospel which was preached of me
is not after man. 12 For I neither received it of

Living Bible

6 I am amazed that you are turning away so
soon from God who, in his love and mercy, invited you to share the eternal life he gives
through Christ; you are already following a different "way to heaven," which really doesn't go
to heaven at all. 7 For there is no other way
than the one we showed you; you are being
fooled by those who twist and change the truth
concerning Christ.

8 Let God's curses fall on anyone, including
myself, who preaches any other way to be saved
than the one we told you about; yes, if an angel
comes from heaven and preaches any other message, let him be forever cursed. 9 I will say it
again: if anyone preaches any other Gospel than
the one you welcomed, let God's curse fall upon
him.

10 You can see that I am not trying to please
you by sweet talk and flattery; no, I am trying
to please God. If I were still trying to please
men I could not be Christ's servant.

11 Dear friends, I solemnly swear that the
way to heaven which I preach is not based on
some mere human whim or dream. 12 For my

Today's English Version

The one gospel

6 I am surprised at you! In no time at all
you are deserting the one who called you by the
grace of Christ, and are going to another gospel.
7 Actually, there is no "other gospel," but I say
it because there are some people who are upsetting you and trying to change the gospel of
Christ. 8 But even if we, or an angel from
heaven, should preach to you a gospel that is
different from the one we preached to you, may
he be condemned to hell! 9 We have said it before, and now I say it again: if anyone preaches
to you a gospel that is different from the one
you accepted, may he be condemned to hell!

10 Does this sound as if I am trying to win
men's approval? No! I want God's approval! Am
I trying to be popular with men? If I were still
trying to do so, I would not be a servant of
Christ.

How Paul became an apostle

11 Let me tell you, my brothers, that the gospel I preach was not made by man. 12 I did not

New International Version

No other gospel

6 I am astonished that you are so quickly
deserting the one who called you by the grace
of Christ and are turning to a different gospel—
7 which is really no gospel at all. Evidently some
people are throwing you into confusion and are
trying to pervert the gospel of Christ. 8 But even
if we or an angel from heaven should preach a
gospel other than the one we preached to you,
let him be eternally condemned! 9 As we have
already said, so now I say again: If anybody is
preaching to you a gospel other than what you
accepted, let him be eternally condemned!

10 Am I now trying to win the approval of
men, or of God? Or am I trying to please men?
If I were still trying to please men, I would not
be a servant of Christ.

Paul called by God

11 I want you to know, brothers, that the
gospel I preached is not something that man
made up. 12 I did not receive it from any man,

Phillips Modern English

1.6 The gospel is God's truth: men must not dare to pervert it

I am amazed that you have so quickly transferred your allegiance from him who called you by the grace of Christ to another "gospel"! Not that it is another gospel, but there are men who are upsetting your faith with a travesty of the gospel of Christ. Yet I say that if I, or an angel from Heaven, were to preach to you any other gospel than the one you have heard, may he be damned! You have heard me say it before and now I say it again—may anybody who preaches any other gospel than the one you have already heard be a damned soul! (Does that make you think now that I am seeking man's approval or God's? Am I trying to please men? If I were trying to win human approval I should never be Christ's servant.)

1.11 The gospel was given to me by Christ himself, and not by any human agency, as my story will show

I do assure you, my brothers, that the gospel I preached to you is no human invention. No

Revised Standard Version

6 I am astonished that you are so quickly deserting him who called you in the grace of Christ and turning to a different gospel—7 not that there is another gospel, but there are some who trouble you and want to pervert the gospel of Christ. 8 But even if we, or an angel from heaven, should preach to you a gospel contrary to that which we preached to you, let him be accursed. 9 As we have said before, so now I say again, If any one is preaching to you a gospel contrary to that which you received, let him be accursed.

10 Am I now seeking the favor of men, or of God? Or am I trying to please men? If I were still pleasing men, I should not be a servant[a] of Christ.

11 For I would have you know, brethren, that the gospel which was preached by me is not man's[b] gospel. 12 For I did not receive it from

[a] Or *slave*. [b] Greek *according to man*.

Jerusalem Bible

A warning

6 I am astonished at the promptness with which you have turned away from the one who called you and have decided to follow a different version of the Good News. 7 Not that there can be more than one Good News; it is merely that some troublemakers among you want to change the Good News of Christ; 8 and let me warn you that if anyone preaches a version of the Good News different from the one we have already preached to you, whether it be ourselves or an angel from heaven, he is to be condemned. 9 I am only repeating what we told you before: if anyone preaches a version of the Good News different from the one you have already heard, he is to be condemned. 10 So now whom am I trying to please—man, or God? Would you say it is men's approval I am looking for?[a] If I still wanted that, I should not be what I am—a servant of Christ.

I. Paul's apologia

God's call

11 The fact is, brothers, and I want you to realize this, the Good News I preached is not a human message 12 that I was given by men, it

[a] Probably a rejoinder to an accusation by the Judaizers that Paul was trying to make the pagans' conversion easy by not insisting on circumcision.

New English Bible

I am astonished to find you turning so quickly away from him who called you by grace,[b] and following a different gospel. Not that it is in fact another gospel; only there are persons who unsettle your minds by trying to distort the gospel of Christ. But if anyone, if we ourselves or an angel from heaven, should preach a gospel at variance with the gospel we preached to you, he shall be held outcast. I now repeat what I have said before: if anyone preaches a gospel at variance with the gospel which you received, let him be outcast!

Does my language now sound as if I were canvassing for men's support? Whose support do I want but God's alone? Do you think I am currying favour with men? If I still sought men's favour, I should be no servant of Christ.

I must make it clear to you, my friends, that the gospel you heard me preach is no human invention. I did not take it over from any man; no

[b] *Some witnesses read* from Christ who called you by grace, *or* from him who called you by grace of Christ.

King James Version

man, neither was I taught *it,* but by the revelation of Jesus Christ. 13 For ye have heard of my
conversation in time past in the Jews' religion,
how that beyond measure I persecuted the
church of God, and wasted it: 14 And profited in
the Jews' religion above many my equals in
mine own nation, being more exceedingly zealous of the traditions of my fathers. 15 But when
it pleased God, who separated me from my
mother's womb, and called *me* by his grace,
16 To reveal his Son in me, that I might preach
him among the heathen; immediately I conferred
not with flesh and blood: 17 Neither went I up
to Jerusalem to them which were apostles before
me; but I went into Arabia, and returned again
unto Damascus. 18 Then after three years I went
up to Jerusalem to see Peter, and abode with
him fifteen days. 19 But other of the apostles
saw I none, save James the Lord's brother.
20 Now the things which I write unto you, behold, before God, I lie not. 21 Afterwards I came
into the regions of Syria and Cilicia; 22 And was
unknown by face unto the churches of Judea
which were in Christ: 23 But they had heard
only, That he which persecuted us in times past

Living Bible

message comes from no less a person than Jesus
Christ himself, who told me what to say. No
one else has taught me.
13 You know what I was like when I followed the Jewish religion—how I went after the
Christians mercilessly, hunting them down and
doing my best to get rid of them all. 14 I was
one of the most religious Jews of my own age
in the whole country, and tried as hard as I possibly could to follow all the old, traditional rules
of my religion.
15 But then something happened! For even
before I was born God had chosen me to be his,
and called me—what kindness and grace—16 to
reveal his Son within me so that I could go to
the Gentiles and show them the Good News
about Jesus.
When all this happened to me I didn't go at
once and talk it over with anyone else; 17 I
didn't go up to Jerusalem to consult with those
who were apostles before I was. No, I went
away into the deserts of Arabia, and then came
back to the city of Damascus. 18 It was not until three years later that I finally went to Jerusalem for a visit with Peter, and stayed there
with him for fifteen days. 19 And the only other
apostle I met at that time was James, our Lord's
brother. 20 (Listen to what I am saying, for I
am telling you this in the very presence of God.
This is exactly what happened—I am not lying
to you.) 21 Then after this visit I went to Syria
and Cilicia. 22 And still the Christians in Judea
didn't even know what I looked like. 23 All they
knew was what people were saying, that "our

Today's English Version

receive it from any man, nor did anyone teach
it to me. Instead, it was Jesus Christ himself
who revealed it to me.
13 You have been told of the way I used to
live when I was devoted to the Jewish religion,
how I persecuted without mercy the church of
God and did my best to destroy it. 14 I was
ahead of most fellow Jews of my age in my
practice of the Jewish religion. I was much more
devoted to the traditions of our ancestors.
15 But God, in his grace, chose me even before I was born, and called me to serve him.
And when he decided 16 to reveal his Son to
me, so that I might preach the Good News
about him to the Gentiles, I did not go to anyone for advice, 17 nor did I go to Jerusalem to
see those who were apostles before me. Instead,
I went at once to Arabia, and then I returned
to Damascus. 18 It was three years later that I
went to Jerusalem to get information from Peter,
and I stayed with him for two weeks. 19 I did
not see any other apostle except James, the
Lord's brother.
20 What I write is true. I am not lying, so
help me God!
21 Afterward I went to places in Syria and
Cilicia. 22 At that time the members of the
Christian churches in Judea did not know me
personally. 23 They knew only what others said,
"The man who used to persecute us is now

New International Version

nor was I taught it; rather, I received it by
revelation from Jesus Christ.
13 For you have heard of my previous way
of life in Judaism, how I violently persecuted
the church of God and tried to destroy it. 14 I
was advancing in Judaism beyond many Jews
of my own age and was extremely zealous for
the traditions of my ancestors. 15 But when God,
who set me apart from birth[a] and called me by
his grace, was pleased 16 to reveal his Son in
me so that I might preach him among the Gentiles, I did not consult any man. 17 I did not go
up to Jerusalem to see those who were apostles
before I was. Instead, I went immediately into
Arabia and later returned to Damascus.
18 Then after three years, I went up to Jerusalem to get acquainted with Peter[b] and stayed
with him fifteen days. 19 I saw none of the other
apostles—only James, the Lord's brother. 20 I
assure you before God that what I am writing
you is no lie. 21 Later I went to Syria and Cilicia.
22 I was personally unknown to the churches of
Judea that are in Christ. 23 They only heard the
report: "The man who formerly persecuted us

[a] Or *from my mother's womb.* [b] Greek *Cephas.*

Phillips Modern English

man gave it to me, no man taught it to me; it came to me as a direct revelation from Jesus Christ. For you have heard of my past career in the Jewish religion, how I persecuted the Church of God with fanatical zeal and, in fact, did my best to destroy it. I was ahead of most of my contemporaries in the Jewish religion, and had a boundless enthusiasm for the old traditions. But when it pleased God (who had chosen me from the moment of my birth, and called me by his grace) to reveal his Son to me so that I might proclaim him to the non-Jewish world, I did not at once talk over the matter with any human being. I did not even go to Jerusalem to meet those who were God's messengers before me—no, I went away to Arabia and later came back to Damascus. It was not until three years later that I went up to Jerusalem to see Cephas, and I stayed with him just over two weeks. I did not see any of the other messengers, except James, the Lord's brother.

All this that I am telling you is, I assure you before God, the plain truth. Later, I visited districts in Syria and Cilicia, but I was still unknown by sight to the churches of Judaea. All they knew of me, in fact, was the saying: "The

Revised Standard Version

man, nor was I taught it, but it came through a
revelation of Jesus Christ. 13 For you have heard
of my former life in Judaism, how I persecuted
the church of God violently and tried to destroy
it; 14 and I advanced in Judaism beyond many
of my own age among my people, so extremely
zealous was I for the traditions of my fathers.
15 But when he who had set me apart before I
was born, and had called me through his grace,
16 was pleased to reveal his Son to[c] me, in
order that I might preach him among the Gentiles, I did not confer with flesh and blood,
17 nor did I go up to Jerusalem to those who
were apostles before me, but I went away into
Arabia; and again I returned to Damascus.
18 Then after three years I went up to Jerusalem to visit Cephas, and remained with him
fifteen days. 19 But I saw none of the other apostles except James the Lord's brother. 20 (In what
I am writing to you, before God, I do not lie!)
21 Then I went into the regions of Syria and
Cilicia. 22And I was still not known by sight to
the churches of Christ in Judea; 23 they only
heard it said, "He who once persecuted us is now

[c] Greek *in*.

Jerusalem Bible

is something I learned only through a revelation
of Jesus Christ. 13 You must have heard of my
career as a practicing Jew, how merciless I was
in persecuting the Church of God, how much
damage I did to it, 14 how I stood out among
other Jews of my generation, and how enthusiastic I was for the traditions of my ancestors.
15 Then God, who had specially *chosen* me
while I was *still in my mother's womb*,[b] called
me through his grace and chose 16 to reveal his
Son in me, so that I might preach the Good
News about him to the pagans. I did not stop
to discuss this with any human being, 17 nor
did I go up to Jerusalem to see those who were
already apostles before me, but I went off to
Arabia[c] at once and later went straight back
from there to Damascus. 18 Even when after
three years I went up to Jerusalem to visit
Cephas and stayed with him for fifteen days,
19 I did not see any of the other apostles; I only
saw James, the brother of the Lord, 20 and I
swear before God that what I have just written
is the literal truth. 21After that I went to Syria
and Cilicia, 22 and was still not known by sight
to the churches of Christ in Judaea, 23 who had
heard nothing except that their onetime perse-

[b] Is. 49:1. [c] Probably the kingdom of the Nabataean Arabs, to the south of Damascus.

New English Bible

man taught it me; I received it through a revelation of Jesus Christ.

You have heard what my manner of life was when I was still a practising Jew: how savagely I persecuted the church of God, and tried to destroy it; and how in the practice of our national religion I was outstripping many of my Jewish contemporaries in my boundless devotion to the traditions of my ancestors. But then in his good pleasure God, who had set me apart from birth and called me through his grace, chose to reveal his Son to me and through me, in order that I might proclaim him among the Gentiles. When that happened, without consulting any human being, without going up to Jerusalem to see those who were apostles before me, I went off at once to Arabia, and afterwards returned to Damascus.

Three years later I did go up to Jerusalem to get to know Cephas. I stayed with him for a fortnight, without seeing any other of the apostles, except[a] James the Lord's brother. What I write is plain truth; before God I am not lying.

Next I went to the regions of Syria and Cilicia, and remained unknown by sight[b] to Christ's congregations in Judaea. They only heard it said, 'Our former persecutor is preaching the good

[a] *Or* but only. [b] *Or* unknown personally.

King James Version

now preacheth the faith which once he destroyed. 24 And they glorified God in me.

2 Then fourteen years after I went up again to Jerusalem with Barnabas, and took Titus with *me* also. 2 And I went up by revelation, and communicated unto them that gospel which I preach among the Gentiles, but privately to them which were of reputation, lest by any means I should run, or had run, in vain. 3 But neither Titus, who was with me, being a Greek, was compelled to be circumcised: 4 And that because of false brethren unawares brought in, who came in privily to spy out our liberty which we have in Christ Jesus, that they might bring us into bondage: 5 To whom we gave place by subjection, no, not for an hour; that the truth of the gospel might continue with you. 6 But of those who seemed to be somewhat, whatsoever they

Living Bible

former enemy is now preaching the very faith he tried to wreck." 24 And they gave glory to God because of me.

2 Then fourteen years later I went back to Jerusalem again, this time with Barnabas; and Titus came along too. 2 I went there with definite orders from God to confer with the brothers there about the message I was preaching to the Gentiles. I talked privately to the leaders of the church so that they would all understand just what I had been teaching and, I hoped, agree that it was right. 3 And they did agree; they did not even demand that Titus, my companion, should be circumcised, though he was a Gentile.

4 Even that question wouldn't have come up except for some so-called "Christians" there—false ones, really—who came to spy on us and see what freedom we enjoyed in Christ Jesus, as to whether we obeyed the Jewish laws or not. They tried to get us all tied up in their rules, like slaves in chains. 5 But we did not listen to them for a single moment, for we did not want to confuse you into thinking that salvation can be earned by being circumcised and by obeying Jewish laws.

6 And the great leaders of the church who were there had nothing to add to what I was

Today's English Version

preaching the faith that he once tried to destroy!" 24 And so they praised God because of me.

Paul and the other apostles

2 Fourteen years later I went back to Jerusalem with Barnabas; I also took Titus along with me. 2 I went because God revealed to me that I should go. In a private meeting with the leaders, I explained to them the gospel message that I preach to the Gentiles. I did not want my work in the past or in the present to go for nothing. 3 My companion Titus, even though he is Greek, was not forced to be circumcised, 4 although some men, who had pretended to be brothers and joined the group, wanted to circumcise him. These people had slipped in as spies, to find out about the freedom we have through our union with Christ Jesus. They wanted to make slaves of us. 5 We did not give in to them for a minute, in order to keep the truth of the gospel safe for you.

6 But those who seemed to be the leaders—I say this because it makes no difference to me

New International Version

is now preaching the faith he once tried to destroy." 24 And they praised God because of me.

Paul accepted by the apostles

2 Fourteen years later I went up again to Jerusalem, this time with Barnabas. I took Titus along also. 2 I went in response to a revelation and set before them the gospel that I preach among the Gentiles. But I did this privately to those who seemed to be leaders, for fear that I was running or had run my race in vain. 3 Yet not even Titus, who was with me, was compelled to be circumcised, even though he was a Greek. 4 [This matter arose] because some false brothers had infiltrated our ranks to spy on the freedom we have in Christ Jesus and to make us slaves. 5 We did not give in to them for a moment, so that the truth of the gospel might remain with you.

6 As for those who seemed to be important—whatever they were makes no difference to me;

Phillips Modern English

man who used to persecute us is now preaching the faith he once tried to destroy." And they thanked God for what had happened to me.

2.1 *Years later I met church leaders in Jerusalem: no criticism of my gospel was made*

Fourteen years later, I went up to Jerusalem again, this time with Barnabas, and we took Titus with us. My visit on this occasion was by divine command, and I gave a full exposition of the gospel which I preach among the gentiles. I did this in private conference with the Church leaders, to make sure that what I had done and proposed doing was sound. But no one insisted that my companion Titus, though he was a Greek, should be circumcised. In fact, the suggestion would never have arisen but for the presence of some pseudo-Christians, who wormed their way into our meeting to spy on the liberty we enjoy in Christ Jesus, and then attempted to tie us up with rules and regulations. We did not give in to those men for a moment, for the truth of the gospel for you and all gentiles was at stake. And as far as their reputed leaders were concerned (I neither know nor care what their

Revised Standard Version

preaching the faith he once tried to destroy."
24 And they glorified God because of me.

2 Then after fourteen years I went up again
to Jerusalem with Barnabas, taking Titus
along with me. 2 I went up by revelation; and I
laid before them (but privately before those who
were of repute) the gospel which I preach
among the Gentiles, lest somehow I should be
running or had run in vain. 3 But even Titus,
who was with me, was not compelled to be circumcised, though he was a Greek. 4 But because
of false brethren secretly brought in, who slipped
in to spy out our freedom which we have in
Christ Jesus, that they might bring us into bondage—5 to them we did not yield submission even
for a moment, that the truth of the gospel might
be preserved for you. 6 And from those who were
reputed to be something (what they were makes

Jerusalem Bible

cutor was now preaching the faith he had previously tried to destroy; 24 and they gave glory to
God for me.

The meeting at Jerusalem

2 It was not till fourteen years had passed
that I went up to Jerusalem again. I went
with Barnabas and took Titus with me. 2 I went
there as the result of a revelation, and privately
I laid before the leading men the Good News
as I proclaim it among the pagans; I did so for
fear the course I was adopting or had already
adopted would not be allowed. 3 And what happened? Even though Titus who had come with
me is a Greek, he was not obliged to be circumcised. 4 The question came up only because some
who do not really belong to the brotherhood
have furtively crept in to spy on the liberty we
enjoy in Christ Jesus, and want to reduce us all
to slavery. 5 I was so determined to safeguard
for you the true meaning of the Good News,
that I refused even out of deference to yield to
such people for one moment. 6 As a result, these
people who are acknowledged leaders—not that

New English Bible

news of the faith which once he tried to destroy'; and they praised God for me.

2 Next, fourteen years later, I went again[c] to Jerusalem with Barnabas, taking Titus with us. I went up because it had been revealed by God that I should do so. I laid before them—but at a private interview with the men of repute—the gospel which I am accustomed to preach to the Gentiles, to make sure that the race I had run, and was running, should not be run in vain. Yet even my companion Titus, Greek though he is, was not compelled to be circumcised. That course was urged only as a concession to certain[d] sham-Christians, interlopers who had stolen in to spy upon the liberty we enjoy in the fellowship of Christ Jesus. These men wanted to bring us into bondage, but not for one moment did I yield to their dictation; I was determined that the full truth of the Gospel should be maintained for you.[e]

But as for the men of high reputation (not that their importance matters to me: God does

[c] *Some witnesses omit* again. [d] *Or* The question was later raised because of certain . . . [e] *Or, following the reading of some witnesses,* Yet even . . . is, was under no absolute compulsion to be circumcised, but for the sake of certain . . . of Christ Jesus, with the intention of bringing us into bondage, I yielded to their demand for the moment, to ensure that gospel truth should not be prevented from reaching you.

King James Version

were, it maketh no matter to me: God accepteth no man's person: for they who seemed *to be somewhat* in conference added nothing to me: 7 But contrariwise, when they saw that the gospel of the uncircumcision was committed unto me, as *the gospel* of the circumcision *was* unto Peter; 8 (For he that wrought effectually in Peter to the apostleship of the circumcision, the same was mighty in me toward the Gentiles;) 9 And when James, Cephas, and John, who seemed to be pillars, perceived the grace that was given unto me, they gave to me and Barnabas the right hands of fellowship; that we *should go* unto the heathen, and they unto the circumcision. 10 Only *they would* that we should remember the poor; the same which I also was forward to do. 11 But when Peter was come to Antioch, I withstood him to the face, because he was to be blamed. 12 For before that certain came from James, he did eat with the Gentiles: but when they were come, he withdrew and separated himself, fearing them which were of the circumcision. 13 And the other Jews dissembled likewise with him; insomuch that Barnabas also was carried away with their dissimulation. 14 But when I saw that they walked not uprightly

Living Bible

preaching. (By the way, their being great leaders made no difference to me, for all are the same to God.) 7, 8, 9 In fact, when Peter, James, and John, who were known as the pillars of the church, saw how greatly God had used me in winning the Gentiles, just as Peter had been blessed so greatly in his preaching to the Jews —for the same God gave us each our special gifts—they shook hands with Barnabas and me and encouraged us to keep right on with our preaching to the Gentiles while they continued their work with the Jews. 10 The only thing they did suggest was that we must always remember to help the poor, and I, too, was eager for that.

11 But when Peter came to Antioch I had to oppose him publicly, speaking strongly against what he was doing for it was very wrong. 12 For when he first arrived he ate with the Gentile Christians [who don't bother with circumcision and the many other Jewish laws[a]]. But afterwards when some Jewish friends of James came, he wouldn't eat with the Gentiles anymore because he was afraid of what these Jewish legalists, who insisted that circumcision was necessary for salvation, would say; 13 and then all the other Jewish Christians and even Barnabas became hypocrites too, following Peter's example, though they certainly knew better. 14 When

[*a*] Implied.

Today's English Version

what they were; God does not judge by outward appearances—those leaders, I say, made no new suggestions to me. 7 On the contrary, they saw that God had given me the task of preaching the gospel to the Gentiles, just as he had given Peter the task of preaching the gospel to the Jews. 8 For by God's power I was made an apostle to the Gentiles, just as Peter was made an apostle to the Jews. 9 James, Peter, and John, who seemed to be the leaders, recognized that God had given me this special task; so they shook hands with Barnabas and me. As partners we all agreed that we would work among the Gentiles and they among the Jews. 10 All they asked was that we should remember the needy in their group, the very thing I have worked hard to do.

Paul rebukes Peter at Antioch

11 When Peter came to Antioch, I opposed him in public, because he was clearly wrong. 12 Before some men who had been sent by James arrived there, Peter had been eating with the Gentile brothers. But after these men arrived, he drew back and would not eat with them, because he was afraid of those who were in favor of circumcising the Gentiles. 13 The other Jewish brothers started acting like cowards, along with Peter; and even Barnabas was swept along by their cowardly action. 14 When I saw that

New International Version

God does not judge by external appearance—those men added nothing to my message. 7 On the contrary, they saw that I had been given the task of preaching the gospel to the Gentiles,[c] just as Peter had been given the task of preaching the gospel to the Jews.[d] 8 For God, who was at work in the ministry of Peter as an apostle to the Jews,[d] was also at work in my ministry as an apostle to the Gentiles. 9 James, Peter[e] and John, those reputed to be pillars, gave me and Barnabas the right hand of fellowship when they recognized the grace given to me. They agreed that we should go to the Gentiles, and they to the Jews.[d] 10 All they asked was that we should continue to remember the poor, the very thing I was eager to do.

Paul opposes Peter

11 When Peter[c] came to Antioch, I opposed him to his face, because he was in the wrong. 12 Before certain men came from James, he used to eat with the Gentiles. But when they arrived, he began to draw back and separate himself from the Gentiles because he was afraid of those who belonged to the circumcision group. 13 The other Jews joined him in his hypocrisy, so that by their hypocrisy even Barnabas was led astray.

14 When I saw that they were not acting in

[*c*] Greek *uncircumcised.* [*d*] Greek *circumcised.* [*e*] Greek *Cephas.*

Phillips Modern English

exact position was: God is not impressed with a man's office), they had nothing to add to my gospel. In fact they recognised that the gospel for the uncircumcised was as much my commission as the gospel for the circumcised was Peter's. For the God who had done such great work in Peter's ministry for the Jews was plainly doing the same in my ministry for the gentiles. When, therefore, James, Cephas and John (who were the recognised "pillars" of the Church there) saw how God had given me his grace, they held out to Barnabas and me the right hand of fellowship, in full agreement that our mission was to the gentiles and theirs to the Jews. The only suggestion they made was that we should not forget the poor—and with this I was, of course, only too ready to agree.

2.11 *I had once to defend the truth of the gospel even against a church leader*

Later, however, when Cephas came to Antioch I had to oppose him publicly, for he was then plainly in the wrong. It happened like this. Until the arrival of some of James' men, he, Cephas was in the habit of eating his meals with the gentiles. After they came, however, he withdrew and began to separate himself from them—out of sheer fear of the Jews. The other Jewish Christians carried out a similar piece of discrimination, and the force of their bad example was so great that even Barnabas was infected by it. But when I saw that this behaviour was a

Revised Standard Version

no difference to me; God shows no partiality)—
those, I say, who were of repute added nothing
to me; 7 but on the contrary, when they saw
that I had been entrusted with the gospel to the
uncircumcised, just as Peter had been entrusted
with the gospel to the circumcised 8 (for he who
worked through Peter for the mission to the circumcised worked through me also for the Gentiles), 9 and when they perceived the grace that
was given to me, James and Cephas and John,
who were reputed to be pillars, gave to me and
Barnabas the right hand of fellowship, that we
should go to the Gentiles and they to the circumcised; 10 only they would have us remember
the poor, which very thing I was eager to do.
11 But when Cephas came to Antioch I opposed him to his face, because he stood condemned. 12 For before certain men came from
James, he ate with the Gentiles; but when they
came he drew back and separated himself, fearing the circumcision party. 13 And with him the
rest of the Jews acted insincerely, so that even
Barnabas was carried away by their insincerity.
14 But when I saw that they were not straight-

Jerusalem Bible

their importance matters to me, since God has no favorites—these leaders, as I say, had nothing to add to the Good News as I preach it.
7 On the contrary, they recognized that I had
been commissioned to preach the Good News to the uncircumcised just as Peter had been commissioned to preach it to the circumcised. 8 The
same person whose action had made Peter the apostle of the circumcised had given me a similar mission to the pagans. 9 So, James, Cephas
and John, these leaders, these pillars, shook hands with Barnabas and me as a sign of partnership: we were to go to the pagans and they
to the circumcised.[d] 10 The only thing they insisted on was that we should remember to help the poor, as indeed I was anxious to do.

Peter and Paul at Antioch

11 When Cephas came to Antioch, however,
I opposed him to his face, since he was manifestly in the wrong. 12 His custom had been to
eat with the pagans,[e] but after certain friends of James arrived he stopped doing this and kept away from them altogether for fear of the group that insisted on circumcision. 13 The other
Jews joined him in this pretense, and even Barnabas felt himself obliged to copy their behavior.
14 When I saw they were not respecting the

[d] The distinction is geographical rather than racial; when Paul went among the Gentiles the resident Jews were his first concern. [e] Converts from paganism.

New English Bible

not recognize these personal distinctions)—these men of repute, I say, did not prolong the consultation,[f] but on the contrary acknowledged that I had been entrusted with the Gospel for Gentiles as surely as Peter had been entrusted with the Gospel for Jews. For God whose action made Peter an apostle to the Jews, also made me an apostle to the Gentiles.

Recognizing, then, the favour thus bestowed upon me, those reputed pillars of our society, James, Cephas, and John, accepted Barnabas and myself as partners, and shook hands upon it, agreeing that we should go to the Gentiles while they went to the Jews. All they asked was that we should keep their poor in mind, which was the very thing I made[g] it my business to do.

But when Cephas came to Antioch, I opposed him to his face, because he was clearly in the wrong. For until certain persons[h] came from James he was taking his meals with gentile Christians; but when they[i] came he drew back and began to hold aloof, because he was afraid of the advocates of circumcision. The other Jewish Christians showed the same lack of principle; even Barnabas was carried away and played false like the rest. But when I saw that their conduct

[f] *Or* gave me no further instructions. [g] *Or* had made, *or* have made. [h] *Some witnesses read* a certain person. [i] *Some witnesses read* he.

King James Version

according to the truth of the gospel, I said unto Peter before *them* all, If thou, being a Jew, livest after the manner of Gentiles, and not as do the Jews, why compellest thou the Gentiles to live as do the Jews? 15 We *who are* Jews by nature, and not sinners of the Gentiles, 16 Knowing that a man is not justified by the works of the law, but by the faith of Jesus Christ, even we have believed in Jesus Christ, that we might be justified by the faith of Christ, and not by the works of the law: for by the works of the law shall no flesh be justified. 17 But if, while we seek to be justified by Christ, we ourselves also are found sinners, *is* therefore Christ the minister of sin? God forbid. 18 For if I build again the things which I destroyed, I make myself a transgressor. 19 For I through the law am dead to the law, that I might live unto God. 20 I am crucified with Christ: nevertheless I live; yet not I, but Christ liveth in me: and the life

Living Bible

I saw what was happening and that they weren't being honest about what they really believed, and weren't following the truth of the Gospel, I said to Peter in front of all the others, "Though you are a Jew by birth, you have long since discarded the Jewish laws; so why, all of a sudden, are you trying to make these Gentiles obey them? 15 You and I are Jews by birth, not mere Gentile sinners, 16 and yet we Jewish Christians know very well that we cannot become right with God by obeying our Jewish laws, but only by faith in Jesus Christ to take away our sins. And so we, too, have trusted Jesus Christ, that we might be accepted by God because of faith—and not because we have obeyed the Jewish laws. For no one will ever be saved by obeying them."

17 But what if we trust Christ to save us and then find that we are wrong, and that we cannot be saved without being circumcised and obeying all the other Jewish laws? Wouldn't we need to say that faith in Christ had ruined us? God forbid that anyone should dare to think such things about our Lord. 18 Rather, we are sinners if we start rebuilding the old systems I have been destroying, of trying to be saved by keeping Jewish laws, 19 for it was through reading the Scripture that I came to realize that I could never find God's favor by trying—and failing—to obey the laws. I came to realize that acceptance with God comes by believing in Christ.[b]

20 I have been crucified with Christ: and I myself no longer live, but Christ lives in me.

[*b*] Literally, "For I through the law died unto the law, that I might live unto God."

Today's English Version

they were not walking a straight path in line with the truth of the gospel, I said to Peter, in front of them all, "You are a Jew, yet you have been living like a Gentile, not like a Jew. How, then, can you try to force Gentiles to live like Jews?"

Jews and Gentiles are saved by faith

15 Indeed, we are Jews by birth, and not Gentile sinners. 16 Yet we know that a man is put right with God only through faith in Jesus Christ, never by doing what the Law requires. We, too, have believed in Christ Jesus in order to be put right with God through our faith in Christ, and not by doing what the Law requires. For no man is put right with God by doing what the Law requires. 17 If, then, as we try to be put right with God by our union with Christ, it is found that we are sinners as much as the Gentiles are—does this mean that Christ has served the interests of sin? By no means! 18 If I start to build up again what I have torn down, it proves that I am breaking the Law. 19 So far as the Law is concerned, however, I am dead—killed by the Law itself—in order that I might live for God. I have been put to death with Christ on his cross, 20 so that it is no longer I who live, but it is Christ who lives in me. This

New International Version

line with the truth of the gospel, I said to Peter[e] in front of them all, "You are a Jew, yet you live like a Gentile and not like a Jew. How is it, then, that you force Gentiles to follow Jewish customs?

15 "We who are Jews by birth and not 'Gentile sinners' 16 know that a man is not justified by observing the law, but by faith in Jesus Christ. So we, too, have put our faith in Christ Jesus that we may be justified by faith in Christ and not by observing the law, because by observing the law no one will be justified.

17 "If, while we seek to be justified in Christ, it becomes evident that we ourselves are sinners, does that mean that Christ promotes sin? Absolutely not! 18 If I rebuild what I destroyed, I prove that I am a lawbreaker. 19 For through the law I died to the law so that I might live for God. 20 I have been crucified with Christ and I no longer live, but Christ lives in me. The life

[*e*] Greek *Cephas*.

Phillips Modern English

contradiction of the truth of the gospel, I said to Cephas so that everyone could hear, "If you, who are a Jew, do not live like a Jew but like a gentile, why do you try to make gentiles live like Jews?" And then I went on to explain that we, who are Jews by birth and not gentile sinners, know that a man is justified not by performing what the Law commands but only by faith in Jesus Christ. We ourselves have believed in Christ Jesus, so that we may be made right with God by faith in Christ and not by obeying the Law's commands. For we have recognised that no one can achieve justification by doing the "works of Law". Now if, as we seek justification in Christ, we find that we are ourselves as much sinners as the gentiles, does that mean that Christ is a producer of sin? Of course not! But if I attempt to build again the whole structure of justification by the Law which I have demolished then I do, in earnest, prove myself a sinner. For under the Law I "died", and I am dead to the Law's demands so that I may live for God. I died on the cross with Christ. And my present life is not that of the old "I", but the living Christ within me. The

Revised Standard Version

forward about the truth of the gospel, I said to Cephas before them all, "If you, though a Jew, live like a Gentile and not like a Jew, how can you compel the Gentiles to live like Jews?" 15 We ourselves, who are Jews by birth and not Gentile sinners, 16 yet who know that a man is not justified [d] by works of the law but through faith in Jesus Christ, even we have believed in Christ Jesus, in order to be justified by faith in Christ, and not by works of the law, because by works of the law shall no one be justified. 17 But if, in our endeavor to be justified in Christ, we ourselves were found to be sinners, is Christ then an agent of sin? Certainly not! 18 But if I build up again those things which I tore down, then I prove myself a transgressor. 19 For I through the law died to the law, that I might live to God. 20 I have been crucified with Christ; it is no longer I who live, but Christ who lives in

[d] Or *reckoned righteous;* and so elsewhere.

Jerusalem Bible

true meaning of the Good News, I said to Cephas in front of everyone, "In spite of being a Jew, you live like the pagans and not like the Jews, so you have no right to make the pagans copy Jewish ways."

The Good News as proclaimed by Paul

15 Though we were born Jews and not pagan sinners, 16 we acknowledge that what makes a man righteous is not obedience to the Law, but faith in Jesus Christ. We had to become believers in Christ Jesus no less than you had, and now we hold that faith in Christ rather than fidelity to the Law is what justifies us, and that *no one can be justified* [f] by keeping the Law. 17 Now if we were to admit that the result of looking to Christ to justify us is to make us sinners like the rest, it would follow that Christ had induced us to sin, which would be absurd. 18 If I were to return to a position I had already abandoned, I should be admitting I had done something wrong. 19 In other words, through the Law I am dead to the Law, so that now I can live for God. I have been crucified with Christ, 20 and I live now not with my own life but with the life of Christ who lives in me. The life I

[f] Ps. 143:2.

New English Bible

did not square with[a] the truth of the Gospel, I said to Cephas, before the whole congregation, 'If you, a Jew born and bred, live like a Gentile, and not like a Jew, how can you insist that Gentiles must live like Jews?'

We ourselves are Jews by birth, not Gentiles and sinners. But we know that no man is ever justified by doing what the law demands, but only through faith in Christ Jesus; so we too have put our faith in Jesus Christ, in order that we might be justified through this faith, and not through deeds dictated by law; for by such deeds, Scripture says, no mortal man shall be justified.

If now, in seeking to be justified in Christ, we ourselves no less than the Gentiles turn out to be sinners against the law[b] does that mean that Christ is an abettor of sin? No, never! No, if I start building up again a system which I have pulled down, then it is that I show myself up as a transgressor of the law. For through the law I died to law—to live for God. I have been crucified with Christ: the life I now live is not my

[a] *Or* I saw that they were not making progress towards . . . [b] *Or* no less than the Gentiles have accepted the position of sinners against the law.

King James Version

which I now live in the flesh I live by the faith of the Son of God, who loved me, and gave himself for me. 21 I do not frustrate the grace of God: for if righteousness *come* by the law, then Christ is dead in vain.

3 O foolish Galatians, who hath bewitched you, that ye should not obey the truth, before whose eyes Jesus Christ hath been evidently set forth, crucified among you? 2 This only would I learn of you, Received ye the Spirit by the works of the law, or by the hearing of faith? 3 Are ye so foolish? having begun in the Spirit, are ye now made perfect by the flesh? 4 Have ye suffered so many things in vain? if *it be* yet in vain. 5 He therefore that ministereth to you the Spirit, and worketh miracles among you,

Living Bible

And the real life I now have within this body is a result of my trusting in the Son of God, who loved me and gave himself for me. 21 I am not one of those who treats Christ's death as meaningless. For if we could be saved by keeping Jewish laws, then there was no need for Christ to die.

3 Oh, foolish Galatians! What magician has hypnotized you and cast an evil spell upon you? For you used to see the meaning of Jesus Christ's death as clearly as though I had waved a placard before you with a picture on it of Christ dying on the cross. 2 Let me ask you this one question: Did you receive the Holy Spirit by trying to keep the Jewish laws? Of course not, for the Holy Spirit came upon you only after you heard about Christ and trusted him to save you. 3 Then have you gone completely crazy? For if trying to obey the Jewish laws never gave you spiritual life in the first place, why do you think that trying to obey them now will make you stronger Christians? 4 You have suffered so much for the Gospel. Now are you going to just throw it all overboard? I can hardly believe it!

5 I ask you again, does God give you the power of the Holy Spirit and work miracles among you as a result of your trying to obey

Today's English Version

life that I live now, I live by faith in the Son of God, who loved me and gave his life for me. 21 I do not reject the grace of God. If a man is put right with God through the Law, it means that Christ died for nothing!

Law or faith

3 You foolish Galatians! Who put a spell on you? Right before your eyes you had a plain description of the death of Jesus Christ on the cross! 2 Tell me just this one thing: did you receive God's Spirit by doing what the Law requires, or by hearing and believing the gospel? 3 How can you be so foolish! You began by God's Spirit; do you now want to finish by your own power? 4 Did all your experience mean nothing at all? Surely it meant something! 5 Does God give you the Spirit and work miracles among you because you do what the Law re-

New International Version

I live in the body, I live by faith in the Son of God, who loved me and gave himself for me. 21 I do not set aside the grace of God, for if righteousness could be gained through the law, Christ died for nothing!" [f]

Faith or observance of the law

3 You foolish Galatians! Who has bewitched you? Before your very eyes Jesus Christ was clearly portrayed as crucified. 2 I would like to learn just one thing from you: Did you receive the Spirit by observing the law, or by believing what you heard? 3 Are you so foolish? After beginning with the Spirit, are you now trying to attain perfection by human effort? 4 Have you suffered so much for nothing—if it really was for nothing? 5 Does God give you his Spirit and work miracles among you because you observe

[f] Some interpreters end the quotation after verse 14.

Phillips Modern English

bodily life I now live, I live believing in the Son of God who loved me and sacrificed himself for me. I refuse to make nonsense of the grace of God! For if righteousness were possible under the Law then Christ died for nothing.

3.1 *What has happened to your life of faith?*

O you dear idiots of Galatia, who saw Jesus Christ the crucified so plainly, who has been casting a spell over you? I will ask you one simple question: did you receive the Spirit by trying to keep the Law or by believing the message of the gospel? Surely you can't be so stupid as to think that you begin your spiritual life in the Spirit and then complete it by reverting to physical observances? Has all your painful experience brought you nowhere? I simply cannot believe it! Does God, who gives you his Spirit and works miracles among you, do these things

Revised Standard Version

me; and the life I now live in the flesh I live by faith in the Son of God, who loved me and gave himself for me. 21 I do not nullify the grace of God; for if justification[e] were through the law, then Christ died to no purpose.

3 O foolish Galatians! Who has bewitched you, before whose eyes Jesus Christ was publicly portrayed as crucified? 2 Let me ask you only this: Did you receive the Spirit by works of the law, or by hearing with faith? 3 Are you so foolish? Having begun with the Spirit, are you now ending with the flesh? 4 Did you experience so many things in vain?—if it really is in vain. 5 Does he who supplies the Spirit to you and works miracles among you do so by

[e] Or *righteousness.*

Jerusalem Bible

now live in this body I live in faith: faith in the Son of God who loved me and who sacrificed himself for my sake. 21 I cannot bring myself to give up God's gift: if the Law can justify us, there is no point in the death of Christ.

II. Doctrinal matters

Justification by faith

3 Are you people in Galatia mad? Has someone put a spell on you, in spite of the plain explanation you have had of the crucifixion of Jesus Christ? 2 Let me ask you one question: was it because you practiced the Law that you received the Spirit, or because you believed what was preached to you? 3 Are you foolish enough to end in outward observances what you began in the Spirit? 4 Have all the favors you received been wasted? And if this were so, they would most certainly have been wasted. 5 Does God give you the Spirit so freely and work miracles

New English Bible

life, but the life which Christ lives in me; and my present bodily life is lived by faith in the Son of God, who loved me and gave himself up for me. I will not nullify the grace of God; if righteousness comes by law, then Christ died for nothing.

3 You stupid Galatians! You must have been bewitched—you before whose eyes Jesus Christ was openly displayed upon his cross! Answer me one question: did you receive the Spirit by keeping the law or by believing the gospel message[c]? Can it be that you are so stupid? You started with the spiritual; do you now look to the material to make you perfect? Have all your great experiences been in vain—if vain indeed they should be? I ask then: when God gives you the Spirit and works miracles among you, why is

[c] *Or* or by the message of faith, *or* or by hearing and believing.

King James Version

doeth he it by the works of the law, or by the
hearing of faith? 6 Even as Abraham believed
God, and it was accounted to him for righteousness. 7 Know ye therefore that they which are of
faith, the same are the children of Abraham.
8 And the Scripture, foreseeing that God would
justify the heathen through faith, preached before the gospel unto Abraham, *saying,* In thee
shall all nations be blessed. 9 So then they which
be of faith are blessed with faithful Abraham.
10 For as many as are of the works of the law
are under the curse: for it is written, Cursed *is*
every one that continueth not in all things which
are written in the book of the law to do them.
11 But that no man is justified by the law in the
sight of God, *it is* evident: for, The just shall
live by faith. 12 And the law is not of faith: but,

Living Bible

the Jewish laws? No, of course not. It is when
you believe in Christ and fully trust him.
6 Abraham had the same experience—God
declared him fit for heaven only because he believed God's promises. 7 You can see from this
that the real children of Abraham are all the
men of faith who truly trust in God.
8, 9 What's more, the Scriptures looked forward to this time when God would save the
Gentiles also, through their faith. God told
Abraham about this long ago when he said, "I
will bless those in every nation who trust in me
as you do." And so it is: all who trust in Christ
share the same blessing Abraham received.
10 Yes, and those who depend on the Jewish
laws to save them are under God's curse, for
the Scriptures point out very clearly, "Cursed is
everyone who at any time breaks a single one
of these laws that are written in God's Book of
the Law." 11 Consequently, it is clear that no
one can ever win God's favor by trying to keep
the Jewish laws, because God has said that the
only way we can be right in his sight is by
faith. As the prophet Habakkuk says it, "The
man who finds life will find it through trusting
God." 12 How different from this way of faith

Today's English Version

quires, or because you hear and believe the gospel?
6 It is just as the scripture says about Abraham, "He believed God, and because of his faith
God accepted him as righteous." 7 You should
realize, then, that the people who have faith are
the real descendants of Abraham. 8 The scripture saw ahead of time that God would put the
Gentiles right with himself through faith. And
so the scripture preached the Good News to
Abraham ahead of time: "Through you God
will bless all the people on earth." 9 Abraham
believed and was blessed; so all who believe are
blessed as he was.
10 Those who depend on obeying the Law
live under a curse. For the scripture says, "Whoever does not always obey everything that is
written in the book of the Law is under God's
curse!" 11 Now, it is clear that no man is put
right with God by means of the Law; because
the scripture says, "He who is put right with
God through faith shall live." 12 But the Law
does not depend on faith. Instead, as the scrip-

New International Version

the law, or because you believe what you heard?
6 Consider Abraham: "He believed God, and
it was credited to him as righteousness." [g] 7 Understand, then, that those who believe are children of Abraham. 8 The Scripture foresaw that
God would justify the Gentiles by faith, and announced the gospel in advance to Abraham: "All
nations will be blessed in you." [h] 9 So those who
have faith are blessed along with Abraham, the
man of faith.
10 All who rely on observing the law are under a curse, for it is written: "Cursed is everyone who does not continue to do everything
written in the book of the Law." [i] 11 Clearly no
one is justified before God by the law, because,
"The righteous will live by faith." [j] 12 The law

[g] Gen. 15:6. [h] Gen. 12:3; 18:18; 22:18. [i] Deut.
27:26. [j] Hab. 2:4.

Phillips Modern English

because you have obeyed the Law or because you have believed the gospel?

3.6 *The futility of trying to be justified by the Law: the promises to men of faith*

You can go right back to Abraham to see the principle of faith in God. He, we are told, "believed God and it was counted unto him for righteousness." You may be certain, then, that all those who "believe God" are the real "sons of Abraham". The scripture, foreseeing that God would justify the gentiles "by faith", proclaimed the gospel in the words spoken to Abraham, "In thee shall all nations be blessed." All men of faith share the blessing of Abraham who "believed God".

Everyone, however, who is involved in trying to keep the Law's demands falls under a curse, for it is written:

> Cursed is everyone which continueth not
> In *all things* which are written in the book of the Law,
> To do them.

It is clear that no one is justified in God's sight by obeying the Law, for:

> The righteous shall live by *faith*.

And the Law is not a matter of faith at all but of doing, as, for example, in the scripture:

Revised Standard Version

works of the law, or by hearing with faith?
6 Thus Abraham "believed God, and it was
reckoned to him as righteousness." 7 So you
see that it is men of faith who are the sons of
Abraham. 8 And the scripture, foreseeing that
God would justify the Gentiles by faith, preached
the gospel beforehand to Abraham, saying, "In
you shall all the nations be blessed." 9 So then,
those who are men of faith are blessed with
Abraham who had faith.
10 For all who rely on works of the law are
under a curse; for it is written, "Cursed be every
one who does not abide by all things written in
the book of the law, and do them." 11 Now it
is evident that no man is justified before God
by the law; for "He who through faith is righteous shall live";[f] 12 but the law does not rest

[f] Or *the righteous shall live by faith.*

Jerusalem Bible

among you because you practice the Law, or
because you believed what was preached to you?
6 Take Abraham for example: *he put his faith
in God, and this faith was considered as justifying him.*[g] 7 Don't you see that it is those who
rely on faith who are the sons of Abraham?
8 Scripture foresaw that God was going to use
faith to justify the pagans, and proclaimed the
Good News long ago when Abraham was told:
In you all the pagans will be blessed.[h] 9 Those
therefore who rely on faith receive the same
blessing as Abraham, the man of faith.

The curse brought by the Law

10 On the other hand, those who rely on the
keeping of the Law are under a curse, since
scripture says: *Cursed be everyone who does
not persevere in observing everything prescribed
in the book of the Law.*[i] 11 The Law will not
justify anyone in the sight of God, because we
are told: *the righteous man finds life through
faith.*[j] 12 The Law is not even based on faith,

[g] Gn. 15:6. [h] Gn. 12:3. [i] Dt. 27:26. [j] Hab. 2:4.

New English Bible

this? Is it because you keep the law, or is it because you have faith in the gospel message? Look at Abraham: he put his faith in God, and that faith was counted to him as righteousness.

You may take it, then, that it is the men of faith who are Abraham's sons. And Scripture, foreseeing that God would justify the Gentiles through faith, declared the Gospel to Abraham beforehand: 'In you all nations shall find blessing.' Thus it is the men of faith who share the blessing with faithful Abraham.

On the other hand those who rely on obedience to the law are under a curse; for Scripture says, 'A curse is on all who do not persevere in doing everything that is written in the Book of the Law.' It is evident that no one is ever justified before God in terms of law; because we read, 'he shall gain life who is justified through faith'. Now law is not at all a matter of having

King James Version

The man that doeth them shall live in them.
13 Christ hath redeemed us from the curse of
the law, being made a curse for us: for it is
written, Cursed *is* every one that hangeth on a
tree: 14 That the blessing of Abraham might
come on the Gentiles through Jesus Christ; that
we might receive the promise of the Spirit
through faith. 15 Brethren, I speak after the
manner of men; Though *it be* but a man's covenant, yet *if it be* confirmed, no man disannulleth,
or addeth thereto. 16 Now to Abraham and his
seed were the promises made. He saith not, And
to seeds, as of many; but as of one, And to thy
seed, which is Christ. 17 And this I say, *that* the
covenant, that was confirmed before of God in
Christ, the law, which was four hundred and
thirty years after, cannot disannul, that it should
make the promise of none effect. 18 For if the
inheritance *be* of the law, *it is* no more of promise: but God gave *it* to Abraham by promise.

Living Bible

is the way of law which says that a man is
saved by obeying every law of God, without one
slip. 13 But Christ has bought us out from under
the doom of that impossible system by taking
the curse for our wrongdoing upon himself. For
it is written in the Scripture, "Anyone who is
hanged on a tree is cursed" [as Jesus was hung
upon a wooden cross[a]].

14 Now God can bless the Gentiles, too, with
this same blessing he promised to Abraham; and
all of us as Christians can have the promised
Holy Spirit through this faith. 15 Dear brothers,
even in everyday life a promise made by one
man to another, if it is written down and signed,
cannot be changed. He cannot decide afterward
to do something else instead.

16 Now, God gave some promises to Abraham
and his Child. And notice that it doesn't say the
promises were to his *children*, as it would if all
his sons—all the Jews—were being spoken of,
but to his *Child*—and that, of course, means
Christ. 17 Here's what I am trying to say: God's
promise to save through faith—and God wrote
this promise down and signed it—could not be
canceled or changed four hundred and thirty
years later when God gave the Ten Commandments. 18 If *obeying those laws* could save us,
then it is obvious that this would be a different
way of gaining God's favor than Abraham's way,
for he simply accepted God's promise.

[*a*] Implied.

Today's English Version

ture says, "The man who does everything the
Law requires will live by it."

13 But Christ has redeemed us from the curse
that the Law brings, by becoming a curse for
us; because the scripture says, "Anyone who is
hanged on a tree is under God's curse." 14 Christ
did this in order that the blessing God promised
Abraham might be given to the Gentiles by
means of Christ Jesus, so that we, through faith,
might receive the Spirit promised by God.

The Law and the promise

15 Brothers, I am going to use an everyday
example: when two men agree on a matter and
sign a covenant, no one can break that covenant
or add anything to it. 16 Now, God made his
promises to Abraham and to his descendant.
The scripture does not say, "and to your descendants," meaning many people. It says, "and
to your descendant," meaning one person only,
who is Christ. 17 What I mean is this: God
made a covenant and promised to keep it. The
Law, which came four hundred and thirty years
later, cannot break that covenant and cancel
God's promise. 18 For if what God gives depends on the Law, then it no longer depends
on his promise. However, it was because God
had promised it that he gave it to Abraham.

New International Version

is not based on faith; on the contrary, "The man
who does these things will live by them."[k]
13 Christ redeemed us from the curse of the law
by becoming a curse for us, for it is written:
"Cursed is everyone who is hanged on a tree."[l]
14 He redeemed us in order that the blessing
given to Abraham might come to the Gentiles
through Christ Jesus, so that by faith we might
receive the promise of the Spirit.

The law and the promise

15 Brothers, let me take an example from
everyday life. Just as no one can set aside or
add to a human covenant that has been duly
established, so it is in this case. 16 The promises
were spoken to Abraham and to his seed. The
Scripture does not say "and to seeds," meaning
many people, but "and to your seed,"[m] meaning
one person, who is Christ. 17 What I mean is
this: The law, introduced 430 years later, does
not set aside the covenant previously established
by God and thus do away with the promise.
18 For if the inheritance depends on the law,
then it no longer depends on a promise; but
God in his grace gave it to Abraham through a
promise.

[*k*] Lev. 18:5. [*l*] Deut. 21:23. [*m*] Gen. 13:15; 24:7.

Phillips Modern English

He that *doeth* them shall live in them.

Now Christ has redeemed us from the curse of the Law by himself becoming a curse for us. For the scripture is plain:

Cursed is every one that hangeth on a tree.

God's purpose is therefore plain: that the blessing given to Abraham might reach the gentiles through Christ Jesus, and the promise of the Spirit might become ours by faith.

3.15 The Law cannot interfere with the original promise

Let me give you an everyday illustration, my brothers. Once a contract has been properly drawn up and signed, it is honoured by both parties, and can neither be disregarded nor modified by a third party.

Now the promises were made to Abraham and his seed. (Note in passing that the scripture says not "seeds" but uses the singular "seed", meaning Christ.) I say then that the Law, which came into existence four hundred and thirty years later, cannot render null and void the original "contract" which God had made, and thus rob the promise of its value. For if the receiving of the inheritance were to depend on the Law, then it does not depend on promise. But God gave it to Abraham by promise.

Revised Standard Version

on faith, for "He who does them shall live by
them." 13 Christ redeemed us from the curse of
the law, having become a curse for us—for it is
written, "Cursed be every one who hangs on a
tree"—14 that in Christ Jesus the blessing of
Abraham might come upon the Gentiles, that
we might receive the promise of the Spirit
through faith.

15 To give a human example, brethren: no
one annuls even a man's will,[g] or adds to it, once
it has been ratified. 16 Now the promises were
made to Abraham and to his offspring. It does
not say, "And to offsprings," referring to many;
but, referring to one, "And to your offspring,"
which is Christ. 17 This is what I mean: the law,
which came four hundred and thirty years afterward, does not annul a covenant previously ratified by God, so as to make the promise void.
18 For if the inheritance is by the law, it is no
longer by promise; but God gave it to Abraham
by a promise.

[g] Or *covenant* (as in verse 17).

Jerusalem Bible

since we are told: *The man who practices these precepts finds life through practicing them.*[k]
13 Christ redeemed us from the curse of the Law
by being cursed for our sake, since scripture
says: *Cursed be everyone who is hanged on a
tree.*[l] 14 This was done so that in Christ Jesus
the blessing of Abraham might include the pagans, and so that through faith we might receive the promised Spirit.

The Law did not cancel the promise

15 Compare this, brothers, with what happens
in ordinary life. If a will has been drawn up in
due form, no one is allowed to disregard it or
add to it. 16 Now the promises were addressed
to Abraham *and to his descendants*—notice, in
passing, that scripture does not use a plural word
as if there were several descendants, it uses the
singular: to his posterity, which is Christ. 17 But
my point is this: once God had expressed his
will in due form, no law that came four hundred
and thirty years later could cancel that and
make the promise meaningless. 18 If you inherit
something as a legal right, it does not come to
you as the result of a promise, and it was precisely in the form of a promise that God made his gift to Abraham.

[k] Lv. 18:5. [l] Dt. 21:23.

New English Bible

faith: we read, 'he who does this shall gain life by what he does'.

Christ bought us freedom from the curse of the law by becoming for our sake an accursed thing; for Scripture says, 'A curse is on everyone who is hanged on a gibbet.' And the purpose of it all was that the blessing of Abraham should in Jesus Christ be extended to the Gentiles, so that we might receive the promised Spirit through faith.

My brothers, let me give you an illustration. Even in ordinary life, when a man's will and testament has been duly executed, no one else can set it aside or add a codicil. Now the promises were pronounced to Abraham and to his 'issue'. It does not say 'issues' in the plural, but in the singular, 'and to your issue'; and the 'issue' intended is Christ. What I am saying is this: a testament, or covenant, had already been validated by God; it cannot be invalidated, and its promises rendered ineffective, by a law made four hundred and thirty years later. If the inheritance is by legal right, then it is not by promise; but it was by promise that God bestowed it as a free gift on Abraham.

King James Version

19 Wherefore then *serveth* the law? It was added
because of transgressions, till the seed should
come to whom the promise was made; *and it
was* ordained by angels in the hand of a mediator. 20 Now a mediator is not *a mediator*
of one, but God is one. 21 *Is* the law then against
the promises of God? God forbid: for if there
had been a law given which could have given
life, verily righteousness should have been by
the law. 22 But the Scripture hath concluded all
under sin, that the promise by faith of Jesus
Christ might be given to them that believe.
23 But before faith came, we were kept under
the law, shut up unto the faith which should
afterwards be revealed. 24 Wherefore the law
was our schoolmaster *to bring us* unto Christ,
that we might be justified by faith. 25 But after
that faith is come, we are no longer under a
schoolmaster. 26 For ye are all the children of
God by faith in Christ Jesus. 27 For as many of

Living Bible

19 Well then, why were the laws given? They
were added after the promise was given, to show
men how guilty they are of breaking God's laws.
But this system of law was to last only until the
coming of Christ, the Child to whom God's
promise was made. (And there is this further
difference. God gave his laws to angels to give
to Moses, who then gave them to the people;
20 but when God gave his promise to Abraham,
he did it by himself alone, without angels or
Moses as go-betweens.)

21, 22 Well then, are God's laws and God's
promises against each other? Of course not! If
we could be saved by his laws, then God would
not have had to give us a different way to get
out of the grip of sin—for the Scriptures insist
we are all its prisoners. The only way out is
through faith in Jesus Christ; the way of escape
is open to all who believe him.

23 Until Christ came we were guarded by
the law, kept in protective custody, so to speak,
until we could believe in the coming Savior.

24 Let me put it another way. The Jewish
laws were our teacher and guide until Christ
came to give us right standing with God through
our faith. 25 But now that Christ has come, we
don't need those laws any longer to guard us
and lead us to him. 26 For now we are all children of God through faith in Jesus Christ,
27 and we who have been baptized into union

Today's English Version

19 What was the purpose of the Law, then? It
was added in order to show what wrongdoing
is, and was meant to last until the coming of
Abraham's descendant, to whom the promise
was made. The Law was handed down by angels,
with a man acting as a go-between. 20 But a
go-between is not needed when there is only one
person; and God is one.

The purpose of the Law

21 Does this mean that the Law is against
God's promises? No, not at all! For if a law
had been given that could bring life to men, then
man could be put right with God through law.
22 But the scripture has said that the whole
world is under the power of sin, so that the gift
which is promised on the basis of faith in Jesus
Christ might be given to those who believe.

23 Before the time for faith came, however,
the Law kept us all locked up as prisoners, until
this coming faith should be revealed. 24 So the
Law was in charge of us until Christ came, so
that we might be put right with God through
faith. 25 Now that the time of faith is here, the
Law is no longer in charge of us.

26 It is through faith that all of you are God's
sons in union with Christ Jesus. 27 You were

New International Version

19 What, then, was the purpose of the law?
It was added because of transgressions until the
Seed to whom the promise referred had come.
The law was put into effect through angels by a
mediator. 20 A mediator, however, does not rep-
resent just one party; but God is one.

21 Is the law, therefore, opposed to the promises of God? Absolutely not! For if a law had
been given that could impart life, then righteousness would certainly have come by the law.
22 But the Scripture declares that the whole
world is a prisoner of sin, so that what was
promised, being given through faith in Jesus
Christ, might be given to those who believe.

23 Before this faith came, we were held prisoners by the law, locked up until faith should
be revealed. 24 So the law was put in charge to
lead us to Christ that we might be justified by
faith. 25 Now that faith has come, we are no
longer under the supervision of the law.

Sons of God

26 You are all sons of God through faith in
Christ Jesus, 27 for all of you who were united

Phillips Modern English

Where then lies the point of the Law? It was an addition made to underline the existence and extent of sin but only until the arrival of the "seed" to whom the promise referred. The Law was appointed by means of angels, by the hand of an intermediary. The very fact that there was an intermediary is enough to show that this was not the fulfilling of the promise. For the promise of God needs neither angelic witness nor any intermediary but depends on him alone.

Is the Law then to be looked upon as a contradiction of the promises? Certainly not, for if there could have been a law which gave men spiritual life then that law would have produced righteousness. But, as things are, the scripture has all men "imprisoned" under the power of sin, so that to men in such condition the promise might be given to all who believe in Jesus Christ.

3.23 By faith we are rescued from the Law and become sons of God

Before the coming of this faith we were all imprisoned under the power of the Law, with our only hope of deliverance the faith that was to be shown to us. The Law was like a strict tutor in charge of us until we went to the school of Christ and learned to be justified by faith in him. Once we have that faith we are completely free from the tutor's authority. For now that you have faith in Christ Jesus you are all sons of God. All of you who were baptised "into"

Revised Standard Version

19 Why then the law? It was added because of transgressions, till the offspring should come to whom the promise had been made; and it was ordained by angels through an intermediary. 20 Now an intermediary implies more than one; but God is one.

21 Is the law then against the promises of God? Certainly not; for if a law had been given which could make alive, then righteousness would indeed be by the law. 22 But the scripture consigned all things to sin, that what was promised to faith in Jesus Christ might be given to those who believe.

23 Now before faith came, we were confined under the law, kept under restraint until faith should be revealed. 24 So that the law was our custodian until Christ came, that we might be justified by faith. 25 But now that faith has come, we are no longer under a custodian; 26 for in Christ Jesus you are all sons of God, through faith. 27 For as many of you as were baptized

Jerusalem Bible

The purpose of the Law

19 What then was the purpose of adding the Law? This was done to specify crimes, until the posterity came to whom the promise was addressed. The Law was promulgated by angels,[m] assisted by an intermediary. 20 Now there can only be an intermediary between two parties, yet God is one. 21 Does this mean that there is opposition between the Law and the promises of God? Of course not. We could have been justified by the Law if the Law we were given had been capable of giving life, 22 but it is not: scripture makes no exceptions when it says that sin is master everywhere. In this way the promise can only be given through faith in Jesus Christ and can only be given to those who have this faith.

The coming of faith

23 Before faith came, we were allowed no freedom by the Law; we were being looked after till faith was revealed. 24 The Law was to be our guardian until the Christ came and we could be justified by faith. 25 Now that that time has come we are no longer under that guardian, 26 and you are, all of you, sons of God through faith in Christ Jesus. 27 All baptized in Christ,

[m] In Jewish tradition angels were present at Sinai; the "intermediary" is Moses.

New English Bible

Then what of the law? It was added to make wrongdoing a legal offence.[q] It was a temporary measure pending the arrival of the 'issue' to whom the promise was made. It was promulgated through angels, and there was an intermediary; but an intermediary is not needed for one party acting alone, and God is one.

Does the law, then, contradict the promises? No, never! If a law had been given which had power to bestow life, then indeed righteousness would have come from keeping the law. But Scripture has declared the whole world to be prisoners in subjection to sin, so that faith in Jesus Christ may be the ground on which the promised blessing is given, and given to those who have such faith.

Before this faith came, we were close prisoners in the custody of law, pending the revelation of faith. Thus the law was a kind of tutor in charge of us until Christ should come,[r] when we should be justified through faith; and now that faith has come, the tutor's charge is at an end.

For through faith you are all sons of God in union with Christ Jesus. Baptized into union

[q] Or added because of offences. [r] Or a kind of tutor to conduct us to Christ.

King James Version

you as have been baptized into Christ have put on Christ. 28 There is neither Jew nor Greek, there is neither bond nor free, there is neither male nor female: for ye are all one in Christ Jesus. 29And if ye *be* Christ's, then are ye Abraham's seed, and heirs according to the promise.

4 Now I say, *That* the heir, as long as he is a child, differeth nothing from a servant, though he be lord of all; 2 But is under tutors and governors until the time appointed of the father. 3 Even so we, when we were children, were in bondage under the elements of the world: 4 But when the fulness of the time was come, God sent forth his Son, made of a woman, made under the law, 5 To redeem them that were under the law, that we might receive the adoption of sons. 6And because ye are sons, God hath sent forth the Spirit of his Son into your hearts, crying, Abba, Father. 7 Wherefore thou art no more a servant, but a son; and if a son,

Living Bible

with Christ are enveloped by him. 28 We are no longer Jews or Greeks or slaves or free men or even merely men or women, but we are all the same—we are Christians; we are one in Christ Jesus. 29And now that we are Christ's we are the true descendants of Abraham, and all of God's promises to him belong to us.

4 But remember this, that if a father dies and leaves great wealth for his little son, that child is not much better off than a slave until he grows up, even though he actually owns everything his father had. 2 He has to do what his guardians and managers tell him to, until he reaches whatever age his father set.

3 And that is the way it was with us before Christ came. We were slaves to Jewish laws and rituals for we thought they could save us. 4 But when the right time came, the time God decided on, he sent his Son, born of a woman, born as a Jew, 5 to buy freedom for us who were slaves to the law so that he could adopt us as his very own sons. 6And because we are his sons God has sent the Spirit of his Son into our hearts, so now we can rightly speak of God as our dear Father. 7 Now we are no longer slaves, but God's own sons. And since we are his sons, everything he has belongs to us, for that is the way God planned.

Today's English Version

baptized into union with Christ, and so have taken upon yourselves the qualities of Christ himself. 28 So there is no difference between Jews and Gentiles, between slaves and free men, between men and women; you are all one in union with Christ Jesus. 29 If you belong to Christ, then you are the descendants of Abraham, and will receive what God has promised.

4 But to continue: the son who will receive his father's property is treated just like a slave while he is young even though he really owns everything. 2 While he is young, there are men who take care of him and manage his affairs until the time set by his father. 3 In the same way, we too were slaves of the ruling spirits of the universe, before we reached spiritual maturity. 4 But when the right time finally came, God sent his own Son. He came as the son of a human mother, and lived under the Jewish Law, 5 to redeem those who were under the Law, so that we might become God's sons.

6 To show that you are his sons, God sent the Spirit of his Son into our hearts, the Spirit who cries, "Father, my Father." 7 So then, you are no longer a slave, but a son. And since you are his son, God will give you all he has for his sons.

New International Version

with Christ in baptism have been clothed with Christ. 28 There is neither Jew nor Greek, slave nor free, male nor female, for you are all one in Christ Jesus. 29 If you belong to Christ, then you are Abraham's seed, and heirs according to the promise.

4 What I am saying is that as long as the heir is a child, he is no different from a slave, although he owns the whole estate. 2 He is subject to guardians and trustees until the time set by his father. 3 So also, when we were children, we were enslaved by the basic principles of the world. 4 But when the time had fully come, God sent his Son, born of a woman, born under law, 5 to redeem those under law, that we might receive the full rights of sons. 6 Because you are sons, God sent the Spirit of his Son into our hearts, the Spirit who calls out, "*Abba*,[n] Father." 7 So you are no longer a slave, but a son; and since you are a son, God has made you also an heir.

[n] Aramaic for *Father*.

Phillips Modern English

Christ have put on the family likeness of Christ. Gone is the distinction between Jew and Greek, slave and free man, male and female—you are all one in Christ Jesus. And if you belong to Christ, you are true descendants of Abraham, you are true heirs of his promise.

What I am saying is that so long as an heir is a child, though he is destined to be master of everything, he is, in practice, no different from a servant. He has to obey guardians or trustees until the time which his father has chosen for him to receive his inheritance. So is it with us: while we were "children" we lived under the authority of basic moral principles. But when the proper time came God sent his own Son, born of a human mother and born under the jurisdiction of the Law, that he might redeem those who were under the authority of the Law, so that we might become sons of God. It is because you really are his sons that God has sent the Spirit of his Son into our hearts to cry "Father, dear Father". You are not a servant any longer; through God you are a *son;* and, if you are a son, then you are certainly an heir.

Revised Standard Version

into Christ have put on Christ. 28 There is
neither Jew nor Greek, there is neither slave nor free, there is neither male nor female; for you are all one in Christ Jesus. 29And if you are
Christ's, then you are Abraham's offspring, heirs according to promise.

4 I mean that the heir, as long as he is a child, is no better than a slave, though he is the owner of all the estate; 2 but he is under
guardians and trustees until the date set by the
father. 3 So with us; when we were children, we were slaves to the elemental spirits of the uni-
verse. 4 But when the time had fully come, God sent forth his Son, born of woman, born under the law, 5 to redeem those who were under the law, so that we might receive adoption as sons.
6And because you are sons, God has sent the Spirit of his Son into our hearts, crying, "Abba!
Father!" 7 So through God you are no longer a slave but a son, and if a son then an heir.

Jerusalem Bible

you have all clothed yourselves in Christ, 28 and
there are no more distinctions between Jew and Greek, slave and free, male and female, but all of you are one in Christ Jesus. 29 Merely by belonging to Christ you are the posterity of Abraham, the heirs he was promised.

Sons of God

4 Let me put this another way: an heir, even if he has actually inherited everything, is no different from a slave for as long as he re-
mains a child. 2 He is under the control of guardians and administrators until he reaches the age fixed by his father. 3 Now before we came of age we were as good as slaves to the elemental principles of this world,[n] 4 but when the appointed time came, God sent his Son, born of a woman, born a subject of the Law, 5 to redeem the subjects of the Law and to enable us to be adopted as sons. 6 The proof that you are sons is that God has sent the Spirit of his Son into our hearts: the Spirit that cries, "Abba, Father,"
7 and it is this that makes you a son, you are not a slave any more; and if God has made you son, then he has made you heir.

[n] The principles that make up the physical universe; Paul has related the Law to "outward observances," 3:3.

New English Bible

with him, you have all put on Christ as a garment. There is no such thing as Jew and Greek, slave and freeman, male and female; for you are all one person in Christ Jesus. But if you thus belong to Christ, you are the 'issue' of Abraham, and so heirs by promise.

4 This is what I mean: so long as the heir is a minor, he is no better off than a slave, even though the whole estate is his; he is under guardians and trustees until the date fixed by his father. And so it was with us. During our minority we were slaves to the elemental spirits of the universe,[b] but when the term was completed, God sent his own Son, born of a woman, born under the law, to purchase freedom for the subjects of the law, in order that we might attain the status of sons.

To prove that you are sons, God has sent into our hearts the Spirit of his Son, crying 'Abba! Father!' You are therefore no longer a slave but a son, and if a son, then also by God's own act an heir.

[b] *Or* the elements of the natural world, *or* elementary ideas belonging to this world.

King James Version

then an heir of God through Christ. 8 Howbeit
then, when ye knew not God, ye did service unto
them which by nature are no gods. 9 But now,
after that ye have known God, or rather are
known of God, how turn ye again to the weak
and beggarly elements, whereunto ye desire again
to be in bondage? 10 Ye observe days, and
months, and times, and years. 11 I am afraid of
you, lest I have bestowed upon you labour in
vain. 12 Brethren, I beseech you, be as I *am;*
for I *am* as ye *are:* ye have not injured me at
all. 13 Ye know how through infirmity of the
flesh I preached the gospel unto you at the first.
14 And my temptation which was in my flesh ye
despised not, nor rejected; but received me as
an angel of God, *even* as Christ Jesus. 15 Where
is then the blessedness ye spake of? for I bear
you record, that, if *it had been* possible, ye
would have plucked out your own eyes, and
have given them to me. 16 Am I therefore become your enemy, because I tell you the truth?
17 They zealously affect you, *but* not well; yea,
they would exclude you, that ye might affect

Living Bible

8 Before you Gentiles knew God you were
slaves to so-called gods that did not even exist.
9 And now that you have found God (or I should
say, now that God has found you) how can it
be that you want to go back again and become
slaves once more to another poor, weak, useless
religion of trying to get to heaven by obeying
God's laws? 10 You are trying to find favor
with God by what you do or don't do on certain
days or months or seasons or years. 11 I fear for
you. I am afraid that all my hard work for you
was worth nothing.

12 Dear brothers, please feel as I do about
these things, for I am as free from these chains
as you used to be. You did not despise me then
when I first preached to you, 13 even though I
was sick when I first brought you the Good
News of Christ. 14 But even though my sickness
was revolting to you, you didn't reject me and
turn me away. No, you took me in and cared
for me as though I were an angel from God, or
even Jesus Christ himself.

15 Where is that happy spirit that we felt together then? For in those days I know you would
gladly have taken out your own eyes and given
them to replace mine[a] if that would have helped
me.

16 And now have I become your enemy because I tell you the truth?

17 Those false teachers who are so anxious to
win your favor are not doing it for your good.

[a] It is traditional to suppose that Paul was handicapped by a disease of the eyes.

Today's English Version

Paul's concern for the Galatians

8 In the past you did not know God, and so
you were slaves of beings who are not gods.
9 But now that you know God—or, I should say,
now that God knows you—how is it that you
want to turn back to those weak and pitiful
ruling spirits? Why do you want to become their
slaves all over again? 10 You pay special attention to certain days, months, seasons, and
years. 11 I am afraid for you! Can it be that all
my work for you has been for nothing?

12 I beg you, my brothers, be like me. After
all, I am like you. You have not done me any
wrong. 13 You remember why I preached the
gospel to you the first time; it was because I
was sick. 14 But you did not despise or reject
me, even though my physical condition was a
great trial to you. Instead, you received me as
you would God's angel; you received me as you
would Christ Jesus. 15 You were so happy! What
has happened? I myself can say this about you:
you would have taken out your own eyes, if
you could, and given them to me. 16 Have I now
become your enemy by telling you the truth?

17 Those other people show a deep concern
for you, but their intentions are not good. All

New International Version

Paul's concern for the Galatians

8 Formerly, when you did not know God, you
were slaves to those who by nature are not gods.
9 But now that you know God—or rather are
known by God—how is it that you are turning
back to those weak and miserable principles?
Do you wish to be enslaved by them all over
again? 10 You are observing special days and
months and seasons and years! 11 I fear for you,
that somehow I have wasted my efforts on you.

12 I plead with you, brothers, become like
me, for I became like you. You have done me
no wrong. 13 As you know, it was because of an
illness that I first preached the gospel to you.
14 Even though my illness was a trial to you,
you did not treat me with contempt or scorn.
Instead, you welcomed me as if I were an angel
of God, as if I were Christ Jesus himself. 15 What
has happened to all your joy? I can testify that,
if you could have done so, you would have torn
out your eyes and given them to me. 16 Have I
now become your enemy by telling you the truth?

17 Those people are zealous to win you over,
but for no good. What they want is to alienate

Phillips Modern English

4.8 *Consider your own progress: do you want to go backwards?*

At one time when you had no knowledge of God, you were under the authority of gods who had no real existence. But now that you have come to know God, or rather are known by him, how can you revert to the weakness and poverty of such principles and consent to be under their power all over again? Your religion is beginning to be a matter of observing special days and months and seasons and years. You make me wonder if all my efforts over you have been wasted!

4.12 *I appeal to you by our past friendship, don't be misled*

I do beg you to put yourselves in my place, my brothers, as I have put myself in yours. I have nothing against you personally. You know that it was physical illness which was the cause of my first preaching the gospel to you. You didn't despise me or let yourself be revolted by my disease. No, you welcomed me as though I were an angel of God, or even as though I were Christ Jesus himself! What has happened to that fine spirit of yours? I guarantee that in those days you would, if you could, have plucked out your eyes and given them to me. Have I now become your enemy because I continue to tell you the truth? Oh, I know how keen these men are to win you over, but their motives are all

Revised Standard Version

8 Formerly, when you did not know God, you
were in bondage to beings that by nature are no
gods; 9 but now that you have come to know
God, or rather to be known by God, how can
you turn back again to the weak and beggarly
elemental spirits, whose slaves you want to be
once more? 10 You observe days, and months,
and seasons, and years! 11 I am afraid I have
labored over you in vain.

12 Brethren, I beseech you, become as I am,
for I also have become as you are. You did me
no wrong; 13 you know it was because of a
bodily ailment that I preached the gospel to
you at first; 14 and though my condition was a
trial to you, you did not scorn or despise me,
but received me as an angel of God, as Christ
Jesus. 15 What has become of the satisfaction
you felt? For I bear you witness that, if possible,
you would have plucked out your eyes and given
them to me. 16 Have I then become your enemy
by telling you the truth? [h] 17 They make much
of you, but for no good purpose; they want to

[*h*] Or *by dealing truly with you.*

Jerusalem Bible

8 Once you were ignorant of God, and enslaved to "gods" who are not really gods at all;
9 but now that you have come to acknowledge
God—or rather, now that God has acknowledged
you—how can you want to go back to elemental
things like these, that can do nothing and give
nothing, and be their slaves? 10 You and your
special days and months and seasons and years!
11 You make me feel I have wasted my time
with you.

A personal appeal

12 Brothers, all I ask is that you should copy
me as I copied you. You have never treated me
in an unfriendly way before; 13 even at the beginning, when that illness gave me the opportunity to preach the Good News to you, 14 you
never showed the least sign of being revolted or
disgusted by my disease that was such a trial to
you; instead you welcomed me as an angel of
God, as if I were Christ Jesus himself. 15 What
has become of this enthusiasm you had? I swear
that you would even have gone so far as to
pluck out your eyes and give them to me. 16 Is
it telling you the truth that has made me your
enemy? 17 The blame lies in the way they have
tried to win you over: by separating you from

New English Bible

Formerly, when you did not acknowledge God, you were the slaves of beings which in their nature are no gods.[c] But now that you do acknowledge God—or rather, now that he has acknowledged you—how can you turn back to the mean and beggarly spirits of the elements?[d] Why do you propose to enter their service all over again? You keep special days and months and seasons and years. You make me fear that all the pains I spent on you may prove to be labour lost.

Put yourselves in my place, my brothers, I beg you, for I have put myself in yours. It is not that you did me any wrong. As you know, it was bodily illness that originally[e] led to my bringing you the Gospel, and you resisted any temptation to show scorn or disgust at the state of my poor body,[f] you welcomed me as if I were an angel of God, as you might have welcomed Christ Jesus himself. Have you forgotten how happy you thought yourselves in having me with you? I can say this for you: you would have torn out your very eyes, and given them to me, had that been possible! And have I now made myself your enemy by being frank with you?

The persons I have referred to are envious of you, but not with an honest envy:[g] what they really want is to bar the door to you so that you

[*c*] *Or* were slaves to 'gods' which in reality do not exist. [*d*] *See note on 4.3.* [*e*] *Or* formerly, *or* on the first of my two visits. [*f*] *Or* you showed neither scorn nor disgust at the trial my poor body was enduring. [*g*] *Or* paying court to you, but not with honest intentions.

King James Version

them. 18 But *it is* good to be zealously affected always in *a* good *thing,* and not only when I am present with you. 19 My little children, of whom I travail in birth again until Christ be formed in you, 20 I desire to be present with you now, and to change my voice; for I stand in doubt of you. 21 Tell me, ye that desire to be under the law, do ye not hear the law? 22 For it is written, that Abraham had two sons, the one by a bondmaid, the other by a free woman. 23 But he *who was* of the bondwoman was born after the flesh; but he of the free woman *was* by promise. 24 Which things are an allegory: for these are the two covenants; the one from the mount Sinai, which gendereth to bondage, which is Agar. 25 For this Agar is mount Sinai in Arabia, and answereth to Jerusalem which now is, and is in bondage with her children. 26 But Jerusalem which is above is free, which is the mother

Living Bible

What they are trying to do is to shut you off from me so that you will pay more attention to them. 18 It is a fine thing when people are nice to you with good motives and sincere hearts, especially if they aren't doing it just when I am with you! 19 Oh, my children, how you are hurting me! I am once again suffering for you the pains of a mother waiting for her child to be born—longing for the time when you will finally be filled with Christ. 20 How I wish I could be there with you right now and not have to reason with you like this, for at this distance I frankly don't know what to do.

21 Listen to me, you friends who think you have to obey the Jewish laws to be saved: Why don't you find out what those laws really mean? 22 For it is written that Abraham had two sons, one from his slave-wife and one from his freeborn wife. 23 There was nothing unusual about the birth of the slave-wife's baby. But the baby of the freeborn wife was born only after God had especially promised he would come.

24, 25 Now this true story is an illustration of God's two ways of helping people. One way was by giving them his laws to obey. He did this on Mount Sinai, when he gave the Ten Commandments to Moses. Mount Sinai, by the way, is called "Mount Hagar" by the Arabs—and in my illustration Abraham's slave-wife Hagar represents Jerusalem, the mother-city of the Jews, the center of that system of trying to please God by trying to obey the Commandments; and the Jews, who try to follow that system, are her slave children. 26 But our mother-city is the heavenly Jerusalem, and she is not a slave to Jewish laws.

Today's English Version

they want is to separate you from me, so that you will have the same concern for them as they have for you. 18 Now, it is good to have such a deep concern for a good purpose—this is true always, and not only when I am with you. 19 My dear children! Once again, just like a mother in childbirth, I feel the same kind of pain for you, until Christ's nature is formed in you. 20 How I wish I were with you now, so that I could take a different attitude toward you. I am so worried about you!

The example of Hagar and Sarah

21 Let me ask those of you who want to be subject to the Law: do you not hear what the Law says? 22 It says that Abraham had two sons, one by a slave woman, the other by a free woman. 23 His son by the slave woman was born in the usual way, but his son by the free woman was born as a result of God's promise. 24 This can be taken as a figure: the two women are two covenants, one of which (Hagar, that is) comes from Mount Sinai, whose children are born in slavery. 25 Hagar stands for Mount Sinai in Arabia, and she is a figure of the present city of Jerusalem, a slave with all its people. 26 But the heavenly Jerusalem is free, and she is

New International Version

you [from us], so that you may be zealous for them. 18 It is fine to be zealous, provided the purpose is good, and to be so always and not just when I am with you. 19 My dear children, for whom I am again in the pains of childbirth until Christ is formed in you, 20 how I wish I could be with you now and change my tone, because I am perplexed about you!

Hagar and Sarah

21 Tell me, you who want to be under the law, are you not aware of what the law says? 22 For it is written that Abraham had two sons, one by the slave woman and the other by the free woman. 23 His son by the slave woman was born in the ordinary way; but his son by the free woman was born as the result of a promise.

24 These things may be taken figuratively, for the women represent two covenants. One covenant is from Mount Sinai and bears children who are to be slaves: This is Hagar. 25 Now Hagar stands for Mount Sinai in Arabia and corresponds to the present city of Jerusalem, because she is in slavery with her children. 26 But the Jerusalem that is above is free, and she is

Phillips Modern English

wrong. They would like to see you and me separated altogether, and have you all to themselves. It is always a fine thing that men should take an interest in you, whether I'm there or not, provided their motives are good. Oh, my dear children, I feel the pangs of childbirth all over again till Christ be formed within you, and how I long to be with you now! Perhaps I could then alter my tone. As it is, I honestly don't know how to deal with you.

4.21 *Let us see what the Law itself has to say*

Now tell me, you who want to be under the Law, have you heard what the Law says?

It is written that Abraham had two sons, one by the slave and one by the free woman. The child of the slave was born in the ordinary course of nature, but the child of the free woman was born in accordance with God's promise. This can be regarded as an allegory. Here are the two agreements represented by the two women: the one from Mount Sinai bearing children into slavery, typified by Hagar (Mount Sinai being in Arabia, the land of the descendants of Ishmael, Hagar's son), and corresponding to present-day Jerusalem—for the Jews are still, spiritually speaking, "slaves". But the free woman typifies the heavenly Jerusalem, who is the

Revised Standard Version

shut you out, that you may make much of them.
18 For a good purpose it is always good to be
made much of, and not only when I am present with you. 19 My little children, with whom I
am again in travail until Christ be formed in you!
20 I could wish to be present with you now and
to change my tone, for I am perplexed about
you.

21 Tell me, you who desire to be under law,
do you not hear the law? 22 For it is written
that Abraham had two sons, one by a slave and
one by a free woman. 23 But the son of the
slave was born according to the flesh, the son of
the free woman through promise. 24 Now this is
an allegory: these women are two covenants.
One is from Mount Sinai, bearing children for
slavery; she is Hagar. 25 Now Hagar is Mount
Sinai in Arabia;[i] she corresponds to the present
Jerusalem, for she is in slavery with her children.
26 But the Jerusalem above is free, and she is

[*i*] Other ancient authorities read *For Sinai is a mountain in Arabia.*

Jerusalem Bible

me, they want to win you over to themselves.
18 It is always a good thing to win people over
—and I do not have to be there with you—but it
must be for a good purpose, 19 my children! I
must go through the pain of giving birth to you
all over again, until Christ is formed in you. 20 I
wish I were with you now so that I could know
exactly what to say; as it is, I have no idea what
to do for the best.

The two covenants: Hagar and Sarah

21 You want to be subject to the Law? Then
listen to what the Law says. 22 It says, if you
remember, that Abraham had two sons, one by
the slave girl, and one by his freeborn wife.
23 The child of the slave girl was born in the
ordinary way; the child of the free woman was
born as the result of a promise. 24 This can be
regarded as an allegory: the women stand for
the two covenants. The first who comes from
Mount Sinai, and whose children are slaves, is
Hagar—25 since Sinai is in Arabia—and she
corresponds to the present Jerusalem that is a
slave like her children. 26 The Jerusalem above,

New English Bible

may come to envy[h] them. It is always a fine thing to deserve an honest envy[i]—always, and not only when I am present with you, dear children. For my children you are, and I am in travail with you over again until you take the shape of Christ. I wish I could be with you now; then I could modify my tone;[a] as it is, I am at my wits' end about you.

Tell me now, you who are so anxious to be under law, will you not listen to what the Law says? It is written there that Abraham had two sons, one by his slave and the other by his free-born wife. The slave-woman's son was born in the course of nature, the free woman's through God's promise. This is an allegory. The two women stand for two covenants. The one bearing children into slavery is the covenant that comes from Mount Sinai: that is Hagar. Sinai is a mountain in Arabia and it represents the Jerusalem of today, for she and her children are in slavery. But the heavenly Jerusalem is the free

[*h*] *Or* pay court to. [*i*] *Or* to be honourably wooed.
[*a*] *Or* now, and could exchange words with you.

King James Version

of us all. 27 For it is written, Rejoice, thou barren that bearest not; break forth and cry, thou that travailest not: for the desolate hath many more children than she which hath a husband. 28 Now we, brethren, as Isaac was, are the children of promise. 29 But as then he that was born after the flesh persecuted him *that was born* after the Spirit, even so *it is* now. 30 Nevertheless what saith the Scripture? Cast out the bondwoman and her son: for the son of the bondwoman shall not be heir with the son of the free woman. 31 So then, brethren, we are not children of the bondwoman, but of the free.

5 Stand fast therefore in the liberty wherewith Christ hath made us free, and be not entangled again with the yoke of bondage. 2 Behold, I Paul say unto you, that if ye be circumcised, Christ shall profit you nothing. 3 For I

Living Bible

27 That is what Isaiah meant when he prophesied, "Now you can rejoice, O childless woman; you can shout with joy though you never before had a child. For I am going to give you many children—more children than the slave-wife has."

28 You and I, dear brothers, are the children that God promised, just as Isaac was. 29And so we who are born of the Holy Spirit are persecuted now by those who want us to keep the Jewish laws, just as Isaac the child of promise was persecuted by Ishmael the slave-wife's son.

30 But the Scriptures say that God told Abraham to send away the slave-wife and her son, for the slave-wife's son could not inherit Abraham's home and lands along with the free woman's son. 31 Dear brothers, we are not slave children, obligated to the Jewish laws, but children of the free woman, acceptable to God because of our faith.

5 So Christ has made us free. Now make sure that you stay free and don't get all tied up again in the chains of slavery to Jewish laws and ceremonies. 2 Listen to me, for this is serious: *if you are counting on circumcision and keeping the Jewish laws to make you right with God, then Christ cannot save you.* 3 I'll say it again.

Today's English Version

our mother. 27 For the scripture says,

"Be happy, woman who never had children!
Shout and cry with joy, you who never felt the pains of childbirth!
For the woman who was deserted will have more children
than the woman living with her husband."

28 Now, you, my brothers, are God's children as a result of his promise, just as Isaac was. 29At that time the son who was born in the usual way persecuted the one who was born because of God's Spirit; and it is the same now. 30 But what does the scripture say? It says, "Throw out the slave woman and her son; for the son of the slave woman will not share the father's property with the son of the free woman." 31 So then, my brothers, we are not the children of a slave woman, but of the free woman.

Preserve your freedom

5 Freedom is what we have—Christ has set us free! Stand, then, as free men, and do not allow yourselves to become slaves again.

2 Listen! I, Paul, tell you this: if you allow yourselves to be circumcised, it means that Christ is of no use to you at all. 3 Once more I

New International Version

our mother. 27 For it is written:

"Be glad, O barren woman,
who bears no children;
break forth and cry aloud,
you who have no labor pains;
there are more children of the desolate woman
than of her who has a husband."[o]

28 Now you, brothers, like Isaac, are children of promise. 29At that time the son born in the ordinary way persecuted the son born by the power of the Spirit. It is the same now. 30 But what does the Scripture say? "Get rid of the slave woman and her son, for the slave woman's son will never share in the inheritance with the free woman's son."[p] 31 Therefore, brothers, we are not children of the slave woman, but of the free woman.

Freedom in Christ

5 It is for freedom that Christ has set us free. Stand firm, then, and do not let yourselves be burdened again by a yoke of slavery.

2 Mark my words! I, Paul, tell you that if you let yourselves be circumcised, Christ will be of no value to you at all. 3Again I declare to every

[*o*] Isaiah 54:1. [*p*] Gen. 21:10.

Phillips Modern English

mother of us all, and is spiritually "free". It is written:

Rejoice, thou barren that bearest not;
Break forth and cry, thou that travailest not:
For more are the children of the desolate
Than of her which hath the husband.

Now you, my brothers, are like Isaac, children born "by promise". But just as in those far-off days the natural son persecuted the "spiritual" son, so it is today. Yet what is the scriptural instruction?

Cast out the handmaid and her son:
For the son of the handmaid shall not inherit
With the son of the free woman.

So then, my brothers, we are not to look upon ourselves as the sons of the slave woman but of the free, not sons of slavery under the Law but sons of freedom under grace.

5.1 Do not lose your freedom by giving in to those who urge circumcision

Plant your feet firmly therefore within the freedom that Christ has won for us, and do not let yourselves be caught again in the shackles of slavery. Listen! I, Paul, say this to you: if you consent to be circumcised then Christ will be of no use to you at all. I say this solemnly

Revised Standard Version

our mother. 27 For it is written,
"Rejoice, O barren one who does not bear;
break forth and shout, you who are not in travail;
for the children of the desolate one are many more
than the children of her that is married."
28 Now we,[j] brethren, like Isaac, are children
of promise. 29 But as at that time he who was
born according to the flesh persecuted him who
was born according to the Spirit, so it is now.
30 But what does the scripture say? "Cast out
the slave and her son; for the son of the slave
shall not inherit with the son of the free woman."
31 So, brethren, we are not children of the slave
but of the free woman.

5 For freedom Christ has set us free; stand
fast therefore, and do not submit again to a
yoke of slavery.
2 Now I, Paul, say to you that if you receive
circumcision, Christ will be of no advantage to
you. 3 I testify again to every man who receives

[j] Other ancient authorities read *you*.

Jerusalem Bible

however, is free and is our mother, 27 since scrip-
ture says: *Shout for joy, you barren women who bore no children! Break into shouts of joy and gladness, you who were never in labor. For there are more sons of the forsaken one than sons of the wedded wife.*[o] 28 Now you, my brothers, like Isaac, are children of the promise,
29 and as at that time the child born in the or-
dinary way persecuted the child born in the Spirit's way, so also now. 30 Does not scripture
say: *Drive away that slave girl and her son; this slave girl's son is not to share the inheritance with the son*[p] of the free woman? 31 So,
my brothers, we are the children, not of the slave girl, but of the freeborn wife.

III. Exhortation

Christian liberty

5 When Christ freed us, he meant us to remain free. Stand firm, therefore, and do not
submit again to the yoke of slavery. 2 It is I,
Paul, who tell you this: if you allow yourselves to be circumcised, Christ will be of no benefit
to you at all. 3 With all solemnity I repeat my

[o] Is. 54:1. [p] Gn. 21:10.

New English Bible

woman; she is our mother. For Scripture says, 'Rejoice, O barren woman who never bore child; break into a shout of joy, you who never knew a mother's pangs; for the deserted wife shall have more children than she who lives with the husband.'

And you, my brothers, like Isaac, are children of God's promise. But just as in those days the natural-born son persecuted the spiritual son, so it is today. But what does Scripture say? 'Drive out the slave-woman and her son, for the son of the slave shall not share the inheritance with the free woman's son.' You see, then, my brothers, we are no slave-woman's children; our mother is the free woman.

5 Christ set us free, to be free men.[b] Stand firm, then, and refuse to be tied to the yoke of slavery again.

Mark my words: I, Paul, say to you that if you receive circumcision Christ will do you no good at all. Once again, you can take it from

[b] *Or* What Christ has done is to set us free.

King James Version

testify again to every man that is circumcised,
that he is a debtor to do the whole law. 4 Christ
is become of no effect unto you, whosoever of
you are justified by the law; ye are fallen from
grace. 5 For we through the Spirit wait for the
hope of righteousness by faith. 6 For in Jesus
Christ neither circumcision availeth any thing,
nor uncircumcision; but faith which worketh by
love. 7 Ye did run well; who did hinder you that
ye should not obey the truth? 8 This persuasion
cometh not of him that calleth you. 9A little
leaven leaveneth the whole lump. 10 I have confidence in you through the Lord, that ye will be
none otherwise minded: but he that troubleth
you shall bear his judgment, whosoever he be.
11And I, brethren, if I yet preach circumcision,
why do I yet suffer persecution? then is the of-

Living Bible

Anyone trying to find favor with God by being circumcised must always obey every other Jewish law or perish. 4 Christ is useless to you if you are counting on clearing your debt to God by keeping those laws; you are lost from God's grace.

5 But we by the help of the Holy Spirit are
counting on Christ's death to clear away our sins
and make us right with God. 6And we to whom
Christ has given eternal life don't need to worry about whether we have been circumcised or not, or whether we are obeying the Jewish ceremonies or not; for all we need is faith working through love.

7 You were getting along so well. Who has
interfered with you to hold you back from
following the truth? 8 It certainly isn't God who
has done it, for he is the one who has called you
to freedom in Christ. 9 But it takes only one
wrong person among you to infect all the others.

10 I am trusting the Lord to bring you back to believing as I do about these things. God will deal with that person, whoever he is, who has been troubling and confusing you.

11 Some people even say that I myself am preaching that circumcision and Jewish laws are necessary to the plan of salvation. Well, if I preached that, I would be persecuted no more—for that message doesn't offend anyone. The fact that I am still being persecuted proves that I am still preaching salvation through faith in the cross of Christ alone.

Today's English Version

warn any man who allows himself to be circumcised that he is obliged to obey the whole Law.
4 Those of you who try to be put right with
God by obeying the Law have cut yourselves off
from Christ. You are outside God's grace. 5As
for us, our hope is that God will put us right with him; and this is what we wait for, by the
power of God's Spirit working through our faith.
6 For when we are in union with Christ Jesus,
neither circumcision nor the lack of it makes any difference at all; what matters is faith that works through love.

7 You were doing so well! Who made you
stop obeying the truth? How did he persuade
you? 8 It was not done by God, who calls you.
9 "It takes only a little yeast to raise the whole
batch of dough," as they say. 10 But I still feel
sure about you. Our union in the Lord makes me confident that you will not take a different view, and that the man who is upsetting you, whoever he is, will be punished by God.

11 But as for me, brothers, why am I still persecuted if I continue to preach that circumcision is necessary? If that were true, then my preaching about the cross of Christ would cause

New International Version

man who lets himself be circumcised that he is
obligated to obey the whole law. 4 You who are
trying to be justified by law have been alienated
from Christ; you have fallen away from grace.
5 But by faith we eagerly await through the
Spirit the righteousness for which we hope. 6 For
in Christ Jesus neither circumcision nor uncircumcision has any value. The only thing that counts is faith expressing itself through love.

7 You were running a good race. Who cut in
on you and kept you from obeying the truth?
8 That kind of persuasion does not come from
the one who calls you. 9 "A little yeast works
through the whole batch of dough." 10 I am
confident in the Lord that you will take no other view. The one who is throwing you into confusion will pay the penalty, whoever he may be.
11 Brothers, if I am still preaching circumcision,
why am I still being persecuted? In that case

Phillips Modern English

again to every one of you: every man who consents to be circumcised is bound to obey all the rest of the Law! If you try to be justified by the Law you automatically cut yourself off from the power of Christ, you put yourself outside the range of his grace. For it is *by faith* that we await in his Spirit the righteousness we hope to see. In Christ Jesus there is no validity in either circumcision or uncircumcision; it is a matter of faith, faith which expresses itself in love.

You were making splendid progress; who stopped you from obeying the truth? That sort of persuasion does not come from the One who is calling you. Alas, it takes only a little leaven to affect the whole lump! I feel confident in the Lord that you will not take any fatal step. But whoever it is who is worrying you will have a serious charge to answer.

And as for me, my brothers, if I were still advocating circumcision, why am I still suffering persecution? I suppose if only I would recommend this little rite all the hostility which the preaching of the cross provokes would dis-

Revised Standard Version

circumcision that he is bound to keep the whole
law. 4 You are severed from Christ, you who
would be justified by the law; you have fallen
away from grace. 5 For through the Spirit, by
faith, we wait for the hope of righteousness.
6 For in Christ Jesus neither circumcision nor
uncircumcision is of any avail, but faith working[x] through love. 7 You were running well;
who hindered you from obeying the truth? 8 This
persuasion is not from him who calls you. 9 A
little leaven leavens the whole lump. 10 I have
confidence in the Lord that you will take no
other view than mine; and he who is troubling
you will bear his judgment, whoever he is. 11 But
if I, brethren, still preach circumcision, why am
I still persecuted? In that case the stumbling

[x] Or *made effective.*

Jerusalem Bible

warning: Everyone who accepts circumcision is
obliged to keep the whole Law. 4 But if you do
look to the Law to make you justified, then you
have separated yourselves from Christ, and have
fallen from grace. 5 Christians are told by the
Spirit to look to faith for those rewards that
righteousness hopes for, 6 since in Christ Jesus
whether you are circumcised or not makes no
difference—what matters is faith that makes its
power felt through love.
7 You began your race well: who made you
less anxious to obey the truth? 8 You were not
prompted by him who called you! 9 The yeast
seems to be spreading through the whole batch
of you. 10 I feel sure that, united in the Lord,
you will agree with me, and anybody who troubles you in future will be condemned, no matter who he is. 11 As for me, my brothers, if I
still preach circumcision,[q] why am I still persecuted? If I did that now, would there be any

[q] As Paul's enemies were apparently claiming.

New English Bible

me that every man who receives circumcision is under obligation to keep the entire law. When you seek to be justified by way of law, your relation with Christ is completely severed: you have fallen out of the domain of God's grace. For to us, our hope of attaining that righteousness which we eagerly await is the work of the Spirit through faith. If we are in union with Christ Jesus circumcision makes no difference at all, nor does the want of it; the only thing that counts is faith active in love.[c]

You were running well; who was it hindered you from following the truth? Whatever persuasion he used, it did not come from God who is calling you; 'a little leaven', remember, 'leavens all the dough'. United with you in the Lord, I am confident that you will not take the wrong view; but the man who is unsettling your minds, whoever he may be, must bear God's judgement. And I, my friends, if I am still advocating circumcision, why is it I am still persecuted? In that case, my preaching of the cross is a stum-

[c] *Or* inspired by love.

King James Version

fence of the cross ceased. 12 I would they were even cut off which trouble you. 13 For, brethren, ye have been called unto liberty; only *use* not liberty for an occasion to the flesh, but by love serve one another. 14 For all the law is fulfilled in one word, *even* in this; Thou shalt love thy neighbour as thyself. 15 But if ye bite and devour one another, take heed that ye be not consumed one of another. 16 *This* I say then, Walk in the Spirit, and ye shall not fulfil the lust of the flesh. 17 For the flesh lusteth against the Spirit, and the Spirit against the flesh: and these are contrary the one to the other; so that ye cannot do the things that ye would. 18 But if ye be led of the Spirit, ye are not under the law. 19 Now the works of the flesh are manifest, which are *these,* Adultery, fornication, uncleanness, lasciviousness, 20 Idolatry, witchcraft, hatred, variance, emulations, wrath, strife, seditions, heresies,

Living Bible

12 I only wish these teachers who want you to cut yourselves by being circumcised would cut themselves off from you and leave you alone! [a]

13 For, dear brothers, you have been given freedom: not freedom to do wrong, but freedom to love and serve each other. 14 For the whole Law can be summed up in this one command: "Love others as you love yourself." 15 But if instead of showing love among yourselves you are always critical and catty, watch out! Beware of ruining each other.

16 I advise you to obey only the Holy Spirit's instructions. He will tell you where to go and what to do, and then you won't always be doing the wrong things your evil nature wants you to. 17 For we naturally love to do evil things that are just the opposite from the things that the Holy Spirit tells us to do; and the good things we want to do when the Spirit has his way with us are just the opposite of our natural desires. These two forces within us are constantly fighting each other to win control over us, and our wishes are never free from their pressures. 18 When you are guided by the Holy Spirit you need no longer force yourself to obey Jewish laws.

19 But when you follow your own wrong inclinations your lives will produce these evil results: impure thoughts, eagerness for lustful pleasure, 20 idolatry, spiritism (that is, encouraging the activity of demons), hatred and fighting, jealousy and anger, constant effort to get the best for yourself, complaints and criticisms, the feeling that everyone else is wrong except

[*a*] Or, "Would that those disturbing you would go and castrate themselves."

Today's English Version

no trouble. 12 I wish that the people who are upsetting you would go all the way; let them go on and castrate themselves!

13 As for you, my brothers, you were called to be free. But do not let this freedom become an excuse for letting your physical desires rule you. Instead, let love make you serve one another. 14 For the whole Law is summed up in one commandment: "Love your fellowman as yourself." 15 But if you act like animals, hurting and harming each other, then watch out, or you will completely destroy one another.

The Spirit and human nature

16 What I say is this: let the Spirit direct your lives, and do not satisfy the desires of the human nature. 17 For what our human nature wants is opposed to what the Spirit wants, and what the Spirit wants is opposed to what human nature wants. The two are enemies, and this means that you cannot do what you want to do. 18 If the Spirit leads you, then you are not subject to the Law.

19 What human nature does is quite plain. It shows itself in immoral, filthy, and indecent actions; 20 in worship of idols and witchcraft. People become enemies, they fight, become jealous, angry, and ambitious. They separate into parties

New International Version

the offense of the cross has been abolished. 12 As for those agitators, I wish they would go the whole way and emasculate themselves!

Life by the Spirit

13 You, my brothers, were called to be free. But do not use your freedom to indulge your sinful nature; rather, serve one another in love. 14 The entire law is summed up in a single command: "Love your neighbor as yourself." [q] 15 If you keep on biting and devouring each other, watch out or you will be destroyed by each other.

16 So I say, live by the Spirit, and you will not gratify the desires of your sinful nature. 17 For the sinful nature desires what is contrary to the Spirit, and the Spirit what is contrary to the sinful nature. They are in conflict with each other, so that you do not do what you want. 18 But if you are led by the Spirit, you are not under law.

19 The acts of the sinful nature are obvious: sexual immorality, impurity and debauchery; 20 idolatry and witchcraft; hatred, discord, jealousy, fits of rage, selfish ambition, dissensions,

[*q*] Lev. 19:18.

Phillips Modern English

appear! I wish those who are unsettling you would cut themselves off from you altogether!

It is to freedom that you have been called, my brothers. Only be careful that freedom does not become mere opportunity for your lower nature. You should be free to serve each other in love. For after all, the whole Law toward others is summed up by this one command, "Thou shalt love thy neighbour as thyself."

But if freedom means merely that you are free to attack and tear each other to pieces, be careful that it doesn't mean that between you you destroy your fellowship altogether!

5.16 The way to live in freedom is by the Spirit

Here is my advice. Live your whole life in the Spirit and you will not satisfy the desires of your lower nature. For the whole energy of the lower nature is set against the Spirit, while the whole power of the Spirit is contrary to the lower nature. Here is the conflict, and that is why you are not able to do what you want to do. But if you follow the leading of the Spirit, you stand clear of the Law.

The activities of the lower nature are obvious. Here is a list: sexual immorality, impurity of mind, sensuality, worship of false gods, witchcraft, hatred, strife, jealousy, bad temper, rivalry,

Revised Standard Version

block of the cross has been removed.
12 I wish
those who unsettle you would mutilate themselves!

13 For you were called to freedom, brethren; only do not use your freedom as an opportunity for the flesh, but through love be servants of one another.
14 For the whole law is fulfilled in one word, "You shall love your neighbor as yourself."
15 But if you bite and devour one another take heed that you are not consumed by one another.

16 But I say, walk by the Spirit, and do not gratify the desires of the flesh.
17 For the desires of the flesh are against the Spirit, and the desires of the Spirit are against the flesh; for these are opposed to each other, to prevent you from doing what you would.
18 But if you are led by the Spirit you are not under the law.
19 Now the works of the flesh are plain: fornication, impurity, licentiousness,
20 idolatry, sorcery, enmity, strife, jealousy, anger, selfishness,

Jerusalem Bible

scandal of the cross?
12 Tell those who are disturbing you I would like to see the knife slip.

Liberty and charity

13 My brothers, you were called, as you know, to liberty; but be careful, or this liberty will provide an opening for self-indulgence. Serve one another, rather, in works of love,
14 since the whole of the Law is summarized in a single command: *Love your neighbor as yourself.*[r]
15 If you go snapping at each other and tearing each other to pieces, you had better watch or you will destroy the whole community.

16 Let me put it like this: if you are guided by the Spirit you will be in no danger of yielding to self-indulgence,
17 since self-indulgence is the opposite of the Spirit, the Spirit is totally against such a thing, and it is precisely because the two are so opposed that you do not always carry out your good intentions.
18 If you are led by the Spirit, no law can touch you.
19 When self-indulgence is at work the results are obvious: fornication, gross indecency and sexual irresponsibility;
20 idolatry and sorcery; feuds and wrangling, jealousy, bad temper and quarrels;

[r] Lv. 19:18.

New English Bible

bling-block no more. As for these agitators, they had better go the whole way and make eunuchs of themselves!

You, my friends, were called to be free men; only do not turn your freedom into licence for your lower nature, but be servants to one another in love. For the whole law can be summed up in a single commandment: 'Love your neighbour as yourself.' But if you go on fighting one another, tooth and nail, all you can expect is mutual destruction.

I mean this: if you are guided by the Spirit you will not fulfil the desires of your lower nature. That nature sets its desires against the Spirit, while the Spirit fights against it. They are in conflict with one another so that what you will to do you cannot do. But if you are led by the Spirit, you are not under law.

Anyone can see the kind of behaviour that belongs to the lower nature: fornication, impurity, and indecency; idolatry and sorcery; quarrels,

King James Version

21 Envyings, murders, drunkenness, revellings,
and such like: of the which I tell you before,
as I have also told *you* in time past, that they
which do such things shall not inherit the kingdom of God. 22 But the fruit of the Spirit is
love, joy, peace, longsuffering, gentleness, goodness, faith, 23 Meekness, temperance: against
such there is no law. 24 And they that are Christ's
have crucified the flesh with the affections and
lusts. 25 If we live in the Spirit, let us also walk
in the Spirit. 26 Let us not be desirous of vain-
glory, provoking one another, envying one another.

6 Brethren, if a man be overtaken in a fault,
ye which are spiritual, restore such a one in
the spirit of meekness; considering thyself, lest
thou also be tempted. 2 Bear ye one another's
burdens, and so fulfil the law of Christ. 3 For if
a man think himself to be something, when he
is nothing, he deceiveth himself. 4 But let every
man prove his own work, and then shall he have
rejoicing in himself alone, and not in another.
5 For every man shall bear his own burden.

Living Bible

those in your own little group—and there will be
wrong doctrine, 21 envy, murder, drunkenness,
wild parties, and all that sort of thing. Let me
tell you again as I have before, that anyone living that sort of life will not inherit the kingdom
of God.

22 But when the Holy Spirit controls our lives
he will produce this kind of fruit in us: love, joy,
peace, patience, kindness, goodness, faithfulness,
23 gentleness and self-control; and here there is
no conflict with Jewish laws.

24 Those who belong to Christ have nailed
their natural evil desires to his cross and crucified them there.

25 If we are living now by the Holy Spirit's
power, let us follow the Holy Spirit's leading in
every part of our lives. 26 Then we won't need
to look for honors and popularity, which lead to
jealousy and hard feelings.

6 Dear brothers, if a Christian is overcome by
some sin, you who are godly should gently
and humbly help him back onto the right path,
remembering that next time it might be one of
you who is in the wrong. 2 Share each other's
troubles and problems, and so obey our Lord's
command. 3 If anyone thinks he is too great to
stoop to this, he is fooling himself. He is really
a nobody.

4 Let everyone be sure that he is doing his
very best, for then he will have the personal satisfaction of work well done, and won't need to
compare himself with someone else. 5 Each of

Today's English Version

and groups; 21 they are envious, get drunk, have
orgies, and do other things like these. I warn
you now as I have before: those who do these
things will not receive the Kingdom of God.

22 But the Spirit produces love, joy, peace,
patience, kindness, goodness, faithfulness, 23 humility, and self-control. There is no law against
such things as these. 24 And those who belong to
Christ Jesus have put to death their human nature, with all its passions and desires. 25 The
Spirit has given us life; he must also control our
lives. 26 We must not be proud, or irritate one
another, or be jealous of one another.

Bear one another's burdens

6 My brothers, if someone is caught in any
kind of wrongdoing, those of you who are
spiritual should set him right; but you must do
it in a gentle way. And keep an eye on yourself,
so that you will not be tempted, too. 2 Help
carry one another's burdens, and in this way
you will obey the law of Christ. 3 If someone
thinks he is something, when he really is nothing, he is only fooling himself. 4 Each one should
judge his own conduct for himself. If it is good,
then he can be proud of what he himself has
done, without having to compare it with what
someone else has done. 5 For everyone has to
carry his own load.

New International Version

factions 21 and envy; drunkenness, orgies, and
the like. I warn you, as I did before, that those
who live like this will not inherit the kingdom
of God.

22 But the fruit of the Spirit is love, joy,
peace, patience, kindness, goodness, faithfulness,
23 gentleness and self-control. Against such things
there is no law. 24 Those who belong to Christ
Jesus have crucified their sinful nature with its
passions and desires. 25 Since we live by the
Spirit, let us keep in step with the Spirit. 26 Let
us not become conceited, provoking and envying
each other.

Doing good to all

6 Brothers, if a man is trapped in some sin,
you who are spiritual should restore him
gently. But watch yourself; you also may be
tempted. 2 Carry each other's burdens, and in
this way you will fulfill the law of Christ. 3 If
anyone thinks he is something when he is nothing, he deceives himself. 4 Each man should test
his own actions. Then he can take pride in himself, without comparing himself to somebody else,
5 for each man should carry his own load.

Phillips Modern English

factions, party-spirit, envy, drunkenness, orgies and things like that. I solemnly assure you, as I did before, that those who indulge in such things will never inherit God's kingdom. The Spirit, however, produces in human life fruits such as these: love, joy, peace, patience, kindness, generosity, fidelity, tolerance and self-control—and no law exists against any of them.

Those who belong to Christ Jesus have crucified their lower nature with all that it loved and lusted for. If our lives are centred in the Spirit, let us be guided by the Spirit. Let us not be ambitious for our own reputations, for that only means making each other jealous.

6.1 Some practical wisdom

Even if a man should be detected in some sin, my brothers, the spiritual ones among you should quietly set him back on the right path, not with any feeling of superiority but being yourselves on guard against temptation. Carry each other's burdens and so live out the law of Christ.

If a man thinks he is "somebody" when he is nobody, he is deceiving himself. Let every man learn to assess properly the value of his own work and he can then be rightly proud when he has done something worth doing, without depending on the approval of others. For every

Revised Standard Version

dissension, party spirit, 21 envy,[k] drunkenness, carousing, and the like. I warn you, as I warned you before, that those who do such things shall not inherit the kingdom of God. 22 But the fruit of the Spirit is love, joy, peace, patience, kindness, goodness, faithfulness, 23 gentleness, self-control; against such there is no law. 24 And those who belong to Christ Jesus have crucified the flesh with its passions and desires.

25 If we live by the Spirit, let us also walk by the Spirit. 26 Let us have no self-conceit, no provoking of one another, no envy of one another.

6 Brethren, if a man is overtaken in any trespass, you who are spiritual should restore him in a spirit of gentleness. Look to yourself, lest you too be tempted. 2 Bear one another's burdens, and so fulfil the law of Christ. 3 For if any one thinks he is something, when he is nothing, he deceives himself. 4 But let each one test his own work, and then his reason to boast will be in himself alone and not in his neighbor. 5 For each man will have to bear his own load.

[k] Other ancient authorities add *murder*.

Jerusalem Bible

disagreements, factions, 21 envy; drunkenness, orgies and similar things. I warn you now, as I warned you before: those who behave like this will not inherit the kingdom of God. 22 What the Spirit brings is very different: love, joy, peace, patience, kindness, goodness, trustfulness, 23 gentleness and self-control. There can be no law against things like that, of course. 24 You cannot belong to Christ Jesus unless you crucify all self-indulgent passions and desires.

25 Since the Spirit is our life, let us be directed by the Spirit. 26 We must stop being conceited, provocative and envious.

On kindness and perseverance

6 Brothers, if one of you misbehaves, the more spiritual of you who set him right should do so in a spirit of gentleness, not forgetting that you may be tempted yourselves. 2 You should carry each other's troubles and fulfill the law of Christ. 3 It is the people who are not important who often make the mistake of thinking that they are. 4 Let each of you examine his own conduct; if you find anything to boast about, it will at least be something of your own, not just something better than your neighbor has. 5 Everyone has his own burden to carry.

New English Bible

a contentious temper, envy, fits of rage, selfish ambitions, dissensions, party intrigues, and jealousies; drinking bouts, orgies, and the like. I warn you, as I warned you before, that those who behave in such ways will never inherit the kingdom of God.

But the harvest of the Spirit is love, joy, peace, patience, kindness, goodness, fidelity, gentleness, and self-control. There is no law dealing with such things as these. And those who belong to Christ Jesus have crucified the lower nature with its passions and desires. If the Spirit is the source of our life, let the Spirit also direct our course.

We must not be conceited, challenging one another to rivalry, jealous of one another.

6 If a man should do something wrong, my brothers, on a sudden impulse,[a] you who are endowed with the Spirit must set him right again very gently. Look to yourself, each one of you: you may be tempted too. Help one another to carry these heavy loads, and in this way you will fulfil the law of Christ.

For if a man imagines himself to be somebody, when he is nothing, he is deluding himself. Each man should examine his own conduct for himself; then he can measure his achievement by comparing himself with himself and not

[a] *Or* If a man is caught doing something wrong, my brothers, . . .

King James Version

6 Let him that is taught in the word communicate unto him that teacheth in all good things.
7 Be not deceived; God is not mocked: for whatsoever a man soweth, that shall he also reap.
8 For he that soweth to his flesh shall of the
flesh reap corruption; but he that soweth to the
Spirit shall of the Spirit reap life everlasting.
9 And let us not be weary in well doing: for in
due season we shall reap, if we faint not. 10 As
we have therefore opportunity, let us do good
unto all *men,* especially unto them who are of
the household of faith. 11 Ye see how large a
letter I have written unto you with mine own
hand. 12 As many as desire to make a fair shew
in the flesh, they constrain you to be circum-

Living Bible

us must bear some faults and burdens of his own.
For none of us is perfect!
6 Those who are taught the Word of God
should help their teachers by paying them.
7 Don't be misled; remember that you can't
ignore God and get away with it: a man will always reap just the kind of crop he sows! 8 If he
sows to please his own wrong desires, he will be
planting seeds of evil and he will surely reap a
harvest of spiritual decay and death; but if he
plants the good things of the Spirit, he will reap
the everlasting life which the Holy Spirit gives
him. 9 And let us not get tired of doing what is
right, for after a while we will reap a harvest of
blessing if we don't get discouraged and give up.
10 That's why whenever we can we should always
be kind to everyone, and especially to our Christian brothers.
11 I will write these closing words in my own
handwriting. See how large I have to make the
letters! 12 Those teachers of yours who are trying to convince you to be circumcised are doing

Today's English Version

6 The man who is being taught the Christian
message should share all the good things he has
with his teacher.
7 Do not deceive yourselves; no one makes a
fool of God. A man will reap exactly what he
plants. 8 If he plants in the field of his natural
desires, from it he will gather the harvest of
death; if he plants in the field of the Spirit, from
the Spirit he will gather the harvest of eternal
life. 9 So let us not become tired of doing good;
for if we do not give up, the time will come
when we will reap the harvest. 10 So then, as
often as we have the chance, we should do good
to everyone, but especially to those who belong
to our family in the faith.

Final warning and greeting

11 See what big letters I make as I write to
you now with my own hand! 12 Those who want
to show off and brag about external matters are

New International Version

6 Anyone who receives instruction in the word
must share all good things with his instructor.
7 Do not be deceived: God cannot be
mocked. A man reaps what he sows. 8 The one
who sows to please his sinful nature, from that
nature will reap destruction; the one who sows
to please the Spirit, from the Spirit will reap
eternal life. 9 Let us not become weary in doing
good, for at the proper time we will reap a
harvest if we do not give up. 10 Therefore, as we
have opportunity, let us do good to all people,
especially to those who belong to the family of
believers.

Not circumcision but a new creation

11 See what large letters I use as I write to
you with my own hand!
12 Those who want to make a good impression outwardly are trying to compel you to be

Phillips Modern English

man must "shoulder his own pack".

The man under Christian instruction should be willing to share the good things of life with his teacher.

6.7 The inevitability of life's harvest

Don't be under any illusion: you cannot make a fool of God! A man's harvest in life will depend entirely on what he sows. If he sows for his own lower nature his harvest will be the decay and death of his own nature. But if he sows for the Spirit he will reap the harvest of everlasting life from that Spirit. Let us not grow tired of doing good, for, unless we throw in our hand, the ultimate harvest is assured. Let us then do good to all men as opportunity offers, especially to those who belong to the Christian household.

6.11 A final appeal, in my own handwriting

Look at these huge letters I am making in writing these words to you with my own hand! *

These men who are always urging you to be circumcised—what are they after? They want to

* According to centuries-old Eastern usage, this could easily mean, "Note how heavily I have pressed upon the pen in writing this." Thus it could be translated, "Notice how heavily I have underlined these words to you."

Revised Standard Version

6 Let him who is taught the word share all
good things with him who teaches.
7 Do not be deceived; God is not mocked, for
whatever a man sows, that he will also reap.
8 For he who sows to his own flesh will from the
flesh reap corruption; but he who sows to the
Spirit will from the Spirit reap eternal life. 9 And
let us not grow weary in well-doing, for in due
season we shall reap, if we do not lose heart.
10 So then, as we have opportunity, let us do
good to all men, and especially to those who are
of the household of faith.

11 See with what large letters I am writing to
you with my own hand. 12 It is those who want
to make a good showing in the flesh that would

Jerusalem Bible

6 People under instruction should always contribute something to the support of the man
who is instructing them.
7 Don't delude yourself into thinking God
can be cheated: where a man sows, there he
reaps: 8 if he sows in the field of self-indulgence
he will get a harvest of corruption out of it;
if he sows in the field of the Spirit he will get
from it a harvest of eternal life. 9 We must
never get tired of doing good because if we
don't give up the struggle we shall get our
harvest at the proper time. 10 While we have
the chance, we must do good to all, and especially to our brothers in the faith.

Epilogue

11 Take good note of what I am adding in
my own handwriting and in large letters. 12 It
is only self-interest that makes them want to

New English Bible

with anyone else. For everyone has his own proper burden to bear.

When anyone is under instruction in the faith, he should give his teacher a share of all good things he has.

Make no mistake about this: God is not to be fooled; a man reaps what he sows. If he sows seed in the field of his lower nature, he will reap from it a harvest of corruption, but if he sows in the field of the Spirit, the Spirit will bring him a harvest of eternal life. So let us never tire of doing good, for if we do not slacken our efforts we shall in due time reap our harvest. Therefore, as opportunity offers, let us work for the good of all, especially members of the household of the faith.

You see these big letters? I am now writing to you in my own hand. It is all those who want to make a fair outward and bodily show who

King James Version

cised; only lest they should suffer persecution for the cross of Christ. 13 For neither they themselves who are circumcised keep the law; but desire to have you circumcised, that they may glory in your flesh. 14 But God forbid that I should glory, save in the cross of our Lord Jesus Christ, by whom the world is crucified unto me, and I unto the world. 15 For in Christ Jesus neither circumcision availeth any thing, nor uncircumcision, but a new creature. 16 And as many as walk according to this rule, peace *be* on them, and mercy, and upon the Israel of God. 17 From henceforth let no man trouble me: for I bear in my body the marks of the Lord Jesus. 18 Brethren, the grace of our Lord Jesus Christ *be* with your spirit. Amen.

Unto the Galatians written from Rome.

Living Bible

it for just one reason: so that they can be popular and avoid the persecution they would get if they admitted that the cross of Christ alone can save. 13 And even those teachers who submit to circumcision don't try to keep the other Jewish laws; but they want you to be circumcised in order that they can boast that you are their disciples.

14 As for me, God forbid that I should boast about anything except the cross of our Lord Jesus Christ. Because of that cross my interest in all the attractive things of the world was killed long ago, and the world's interest in me is also long dead. 15 It doesn't make any difference now whether we have been circumcised or not; what counts is whether we really have been changed into new and different people.

16 May God's mercy and peace be upon all of you who live by this principle and upon those everywhere who are really God's own. 17 From now on please don't argue with me about these things, for I carry on my body the scars of the whippings and wounds from Jesus' enemies that mark me as his slave.

18 Dear brothers, may the grace of our Lord Jesus Christ be with you all.

Sincerely,
Paul

Today's English Version

the ones who are trying to force you to be circumcised. They do it, however, only that they may not be persecuted for the cross of Christ. 13 Even those who practice circumcision do not obey the Law; they want you to be circumcised so they can boast that you submitted to this physical ceremony. 14 As for me, however, I will boast only of the cross of our Lord Jesus Christ; for by means of his cross the world is dead to me, and I am dead to the world. 15 It does not matter at all whether or not one is circumcised. What does matter is being a new creature. 16 As for those who follow this rule in their lives, may peace and mercy be with them—with them and with all God's people!

17 To conclude: let no one give me any more trouble, because the scars I have on my body show that I am the slave of Jesus.

18 May the grace of our Lord Jesus Christ be with you all, my brothers. Amen.

New International Version

circumcised. The only reason they do this is to avoid being persecuted for the cross of Christ. 13 Not even those who are circumcised obey the law, yet they want you to be circumcised that they may boast about your flesh. 14 May I never boast except in the cross of our Lord Jesus Christ, through which the world has been crucified to me, and I to the world. 15 Neither circumcision nor uncircumcision means anything; what counts is a new creation. 16 Peace and mercy to all who follow this rule, even to the Israel of God.

17 Finally, let no one cause me trouble, for I bear on my body the marks of Jesus.

18 The grace of our Lord Jesus Christ be with your spirit, brothers. Amen.

Phillips Modern English

present a pleasing front to the world and they want to avoid being persecuted for the cross of Christ. For even those who have been circumcised do not themselves keep the Law. But they want you circumcised so that they may be able to boast about your submission to their ruling. Yet God forbid that I should boast about anything or anybody except the cross of our Lord Jesus Christ, which means that the world is a dead thing to me and I am a dead man to the world. But in Christ it is not circumcision or uncircumcision that counts but the power of new birth. To all who live by this principle, to the true Israel of God, may there be peace and mercy!

Let no one interfere with me after this. I carry on my scarred body the marks of Jesus.

The grace of our Lord Jesus Christ, my brothers, be with your spirit. Amen.

Revised Standard Version

compel you to be circumcised, and only in order
that they may not be persecuted for the cross of
Christ. 13 For even those who receive circumcision do not themselves keep the law, but they
desire to have you circumcised that they may
glory in your flesh. 14 But far be it from me to
glory except in the cross of our Lord Jesus
Christ, by which[l] the world has been crucified
to me, and I to the world. 15 For neither circumcision counts for anything, nor uncircumcision, but a new creation. 16 Peace and mercy be
upon all who walk by this rule, upon the Israel
of God.

17 Henceforth let no man trouble me; for I
bear on my body the marks of Jesus.

18 The grace of our Lord Jesus Christ be with
your spirit, brethren. Amen.

[l] Or *through whom.*

Jerusalem Bible

force circumcision on you—they want to escape
persecution for the cross of Christ—13 they accept circumcision but do not keep the Law
themselves; they only want you to be circumcised so that they can boast of the fact. 14 As
for me, the only thing I can boast about is the
cross of our Lord Jesus Christ, through whom
the world is crucified to me, and I to the world.
15 It does not matter if a person is circumcised
or not; what matters is for him to become an
altogether new creature. 16 Peace and mercy to
all who follow this rule, who form the Israel of
God.

17 I want no more trouble from anybody
after this; the marks on my body are those of
Jesus. 18 The grace of our Lord Jesus Christ
be with your spirit, my brothers. Amen.

New English Bible

are trying to force circumcision upon you; their sole object is to escape persecution for the cross of Christ. For even those who do receive circumcision are not thoroughgoing observers of the law; they only want you to be circumcised in order to boast of your having submitted to that outward rite. But God forbid that I should boast of anything but the cross of our Lord Jesus Christ, through which[a] the world is crucified to me and I to the world! Circumcision is nothing; uncircumcision is nothing; the only thing that counts is new creation! Whoever they are who take this principle for their guide, peace and mercy be upon them, and upon the whole Israel of God!

In future let no one make trouble for me, for I bear the marks of Jesus branded on my body.

The grace of our Lord Jesus Christ be with your spirit, my brothers. Amen.

[a] *Or* whom.

King James Version

THE EPISTLE OF PAUL THE APOSTLE TO THE EPHESIANS

1 Paul, an apostle of Jesus Christ by the will
of God, to the saints which are at Ephesus,
and to the faithful in Christ Jesus: 2 Grace *be*
to you, and peace, from God our Father, and

Living Bible

EPHESIANS

1 Dear Christian friends at Ephesus, ever loyal
to the Lord: This is Paul writing to you,
chosen by God to be Jesus Christ's messenger.
2 May his blessings and peace be yours, sent to
you from God our Father and Jesus Christ our

Today's English Version

PAUL'S LETTER TO THE EPHESIANS

1 From Paul, who by God's will is an apostle
of Christ Jesus—
To God's people who live in Ephesus, those
who are faithful in their life in Christ Jesus:
2 May God our Father and the Lord Jesus
Christ give you grace and peace.

New International Version

EPHESIANS

1 Paul, an apostle of Christ Jesus by the will
of God,
To the saints in Ephesus,[a] the faithful in
Christ Jesus:
2 Grace and peace to you from God our Father and the Lord Jesus Christ.

[a] Some early MSS omit *in Ephesus.*

Phillips Modern English

THE LETTER TO THE CHRISTIANS AT EPHESUS AND IN OTHER PLACES

Paul, messenger of Christ Jesus by God's will, to all faithful Christians at Ephesus: grace and peace be to you from God our Father and the Lord Jesus Christ.

Revised Standard Version

THE LETTER OF PAUL TO THE EPHESIANS

1 Paul, an apostle of Christ Jesus by the will of God,
To the saints who are also faithful [a] in Christ Jesus:
2 Grace to you and peace from God our Father and the Lord Jesus Christ.

[a] Other ancient authorities read *who are at Ephesus and faithful.*

Jerusalem Bible

THE LETTER OF PAUL TO THE CHURCH AT EPHESUS EPHESIANS

Address and greetings

1 From Paul, appointed by God to be an apostle of Christ Jesus, to the saints who are faithful to Christ Jesus: 2 Grace and peace to you from God our Father and from the Lord Jesus Christ.

New English Bible

THE LETTER OF PAUL TO THE EPHESIANS

The glory of Christ in the church

1 From Paul, apostle of Christ Jesus, commissioned by the will of God, to God's people at Ephesus,[a] believers incorporate in Christ Jesus.
Grace to you and peace from God our Father and the Lord Jesus Christ.

[a] *Some witnesses omit* at Ephesus.

King James Version

from the Lord Jesus Christ. 3 Blessed *be* the God and Father of our Lord Jesus Christ, who hath blessed us with all spiritual blessings in heavenly *places* in Christ: 4 According as he hath chosen us in him before the foundation of the world, that we should be holy and without blame before him in love: 5 Having predestinated us unto the adoption of children by Jesus Christ to himself, according to the good pleasure of his will,. 6 To the praise of the glory of his grace, wherein he hath made us accepted in the beloved: 7 In whom we have redemption through his blood, the forgiveness of sins, according to the riches of his grace; 8 Wherein he hath abounded toward us in all wisdom and prudence; 9 Having made known unto us the mystery of his will, according to his good pleasure which he hath purposed in himself: 10 That in the dispensation of the fulness of times he might gather together in one all things in Christ, both which are in heaven, and which are on earth; *even* in him: 11 In whom also we have obtained

Living Bible

Lord. 3 How we praise God, the Father of our Lord Jesus Christ, who has blessed us with every blessing in heaven because we belong to Christ.

4 Long ago, even before he made the world, God chose us to be his very own, through what Christ would do for us; he decided then to make us holy in his eyes, without a single fault—we who stand before him covered with his love. 5 His unchanging plan has always been to adopt us into his own family by sending Jesus Christ to die for us. And he did this because he wanted to!

6 Now all praise to God for his wonderful kindness to us and his favor that he has poured out upon us, because we belong to his dearly loved Son. 7 So overflowing is his kindness towards us that he took away all our sins through the blood of his Son, by whom we are saved; 8 and he has showered down upon us the richness of his grace—for how well he understands us and knows what is best for us at all times.

9 God has told us his secret reason for sending Christ, a plan he decided on in mercy long ago; 10 and this was his purpose: that when the time is ripe he will gather us all together from wherever we are—in heaven or on earth—to be with him in Christ, forever. 11 Moreover, because

Today's English Version

Spiritual blessings in Christ

3 Let us give thanks to the God and Father of our Lord Jesus Christ! For he has blessed us, in our union with Christ, by giving us every spiritual gift in the heavenly world. 4 Before the world was made, God had already chosen us to be his in Christ, so that we would be holy and without fault before him. Because of his love, 5 God had already decided that through Jesus Christ he would bring us to himself as his sons —this was his pleasure and purpose. 6 Let us praise God for his glorious grace, for the free gift he gave us in his dear Son!

7 For by the death of Christ we are set free, that is, our sins are forgiven. How great is the grace of God, 8 which he gave to us in such large measure! In all his wisdom and insight 9 God did what he had purposed, and made known to us the secret plan he had already decided to complete by means of Christ. 10 God's plan, which he will complete when the time is right, is to bring all creation together, everything in heaven and on earth, with Christ as head.

11 All things are done according to God's

New International Version

Spiritual blessings in Christ

3 Praise be to the God and Father of our Lord Jesus Christ, who has blessed us in the heavenly realms with every spiritual blessing in Christ. 4 For he chose us in him before the creation of the world to be holy and blameless in his sight. In love 5 he[b] predestined us to be adopted as sons through Jesus Christ, in accordance with his pleasure and will—6 to the praise of his glorious grace, which he has freely given us in the One he loves. 7 In him we have redemption through his blood, the forgiveness of sins, in accordance with the riches of God's grace 8 that he lavished on us with all wisdom and understanding. 9 And he[c] made known to us the mystery of his will according to his good pleasure, which he purposed in Christ, 10 to be put into effect when the times will have reached their fulfillment—to bring all things in heaven and on earth together under one head, even Christ.

11 In him we were also chosen, having been

[*b*] Or *sight in love.* [5]*He.* [*c*] Or *us. With all wisdom and understanding,* [9]*he.*

Phillips Modern English

1.3 Praise God for what he has done for us Christians!

Praise be to God and Father of our Lord Jesus Christ for giving us through Christ every spiritual benefit as citizens of Heaven! For consider what he has done—before the foundation of the world he chose us to be, in Christ, his children, holy and blameless in his sight. He planned, in his love, that we should be adopted as his own children through Jesus Christ—this was his will and pleasure that we might praise that glorious generosity of his which he granted to us in his Beloved. It is through him, at the cost of his own blood, that we are redeemed, freely forgiven through that free and generous grace which has overflowed into our lives and given us wisdom and insight. For God has allowed us to know the secret of his plan, and it is this: he purposed long ago in his sovereign will that all human history should be consummated in Christ, that everything that exists in Heaven or earth should find its perfection and fulfilment in him. In Christ we have been given

Revised Standard Version

3 Blessed be the God and Father of our Lord
Jesus Christ, who has blessed us in Christ with
every spiritual blessing in the heavenly places,
4 even as he chose us in him before the foundation of the world, that we should be holy and
blameless before him. 5 He destined us in love[b]
to be his sons through Jesus Christ, according
to the purpose of his will, 6 to the praise of his
glorious grace which he freely bestowed on us
in the Beloved. 7 In him we have redemption
through his blood, the forgiveness of our trespasses, according to the riches of his grace
8 which he lavished upon us. 9 For he has made
known to us in all wisdom and insight the mystery of his will, according to his purpose which
he set forth in Christ 10 as a plan for the fulness
of time, to unite all things in him, things in
heaven and things on earth.
11 In him, according to the purpose of him

[b] Or *before him in love, having destined us.*

Jerusalem Bible

I. The mystery of salvation and of the church

God's plan of salvation

3 Blessed be God the Father of our Lord Jesus Christ,
who has blessed us with all the spiritual blessings of heaven in Christ.
4 Before the world was made, he chose us, chose us in Christ,
to be holy and spotless, and to live through love in his presence,
5 determining that we should become his adopted sons, through Jesus Christ
for his own kind purposes,
6 to make us praise the glory of his grace,
his free gift to us in the Beloved,
7 in whom, through his blood, we gain our freedom, the forgiveness of our sins.
Such is the richness of the grace
8 which he has showered on us
in all wisdom and insight.
9 He has let us know the mystery of his purpose,
the hidden plan he so kindly made in Christ from the beginning
10 to act upon when the times had run their course to the end:
that he would bring everything together under Christ, as head,
everything in the heavens and everything on earth.
11 And it is in him that we were claimed as

New English Bible

Praise be to the God and Father of our Lord Jesus Christ, who has bestowed on us in Christ every spiritual blessing in the heavenly realms. In Christ he chose us before the world was founded, to be dedicated, to be without blemish in his sight, to be full of love; and he[b] destined us—such was his will and pleasure—to be accepted as his sons through Jesus Christ, in order that the glory of his gracious gift, so graciously bestowed on us in his Beloved, might redound to his praise. For in Christ our release is secured and our sins are forgiven through the shedding of his blood. Therein lies the richness of God's free grace lavished upon us, imparting full wisdom and insight. He has made known to us his hidden purpose—such was his will and pleasure determined beforehand in Christ—to be put into effect when the time was ripe: namely, that the universe, all in heaven and on earth, might be brought into a unity in Christ.

In Christ indeed we have been given our share

[b] *Or* . . . sight. In his love he . . .

King James Version

an inheritance, being predestinated according to the purpose of him who worketh all things after the counsel of his own will: 12 That we should be to the praise of his glory, who first trusted in Christ. 13 In whom ye also *trusted,* after that ye heard the word of truth, the gospel of your salvation: in whom also, after that ye believed, ye were sealed with that Holy Spirit of promise, 14 Which is the earnest of our inheritance until the redemption of the purchased possession, unto the praise of his glory. 15 Wherefore I also, after I heard of your faith in the Lord Jesus, and love unto all the saints, 16 Cease not to give thanks for you, making mention of you in my prayers; 17 That the God of our Lord Jesus Christ, the Father of glory, may give unto you the spirit of wisdom and revelation in the knowledge of him: 18 The eyes of your understanding being enlightened; that ye may know what is the hope of his calling, and what the riches of the glory of his inheritance in the saints, 19 And

Living Bible

of what Christ has done we have become gifts to God that he delights in, for as part of God's sovereign plan we were chosen from the beginning to be his, and all things happen just as he decided long ago. 12 God's purpose in this was that we should praise God and give glory to him for doing these mighty things for us, who were the first to trust in Christ.

13 And because of what Christ did, all you others too, who heard the Good News about how to be saved, and trusted Christ, were marked as belonging to Christ by the Holy Spirit, who long ago had been promised to all of us Christians. 14 His presence within us is God's guarantee that he really will give us all that he promised; and the Spirit's seal upon us means that God has already purchased us and that he guarantees to bring us to himself. This is just one more reason for us to praise our glorious God.

15 That is why, ever since I heard of your strong faith in the Lord Jesus and of the love you have for Christians everywhere, 16, 17 I have never stopped thanking God for you. I pray for you constantly, asking God, the glorious Father of our Lord Jesus Christ, to give you wisdom to see clearly and really understand who Christ is and all that he has done for you. 18 I pray that your hearts will be flooded with light so that you can see something of the future he has called you to share. I want you to realize that God has been made rich because we who are Christ's have been given to him! 19 I pray that you will begin to

Today's English Version

plan and decision; and God chose us to be his own people in union with Christ because of his own purpose, based on what he had decided from the very beginning. 12 Let us, then, who were the first to hope in Christ, praise God's glory!

13 And so it was with you also: when you heard the true message, the Good News that brought you salvation, you believed in Christ, and God put his stamp of ownership on you by giving you the Holy Spirit he had promised. 14 The Spirit is the guarantee that we shall receive what God has promised his people, and assures us that God will give complete freedom to those who are his. Let us praise his glory!

Paul's prayer

15 For this reason, ever since I heard of your faith in the Lord Jesus and your love for all God's people, 16 I have not stopped giving thanks to God for you. I remember you in my prayers, 17 and ask the God of our Lord Jesus Christ, the glorious Father, to give you the Spirit, who will make you wise and reveal God to you, so that you will know him. 18 I ask that your minds may be opened to see his light, so that you will know what is the hope to which he has called you, how rich are the wonderful blessings he promises his people, 19 and how very great

New International Version

predestined according to the plan of him who works out everything in conformity with the purpose of his will, 12 in order that we, who were the first to hope in Christ, might be for the praise of his glory. 13 And you also were included in Christ when you heard the word of truth, the gospel of your salvation. In him, when you believed, you were marked with a seal, the promised Holy Spirit, 14 who is a deposit guaranteeing our inheritance until the redemption of those who are God's possession—to the praise of his glory.

Thanksgiving and prayer

15 For this reason, I, since I heard about your faith in the Lord Jesus and your love for all the saints, 16 have never stopped giving thanks for you, remembering you in my prayers. 17 I keep asking that the God of our Lord Jesus Christ, the glorious Father, may give you the Spirit[d] of wisdom and revelation, so that you may know him better. 18 I pray also that the eyes of your heart may be enlightened in order that you may know the hope to which he has called you, the riches of his glorious inheritance in the saints, 19 and his incomparably great power for us who

[d] Or *a spirit.*

Phillips Modern English

an inheritance, since we were destined for this, by the One who works out all his purposes according to the design of his own will. So that we, in due time, as the first to put our hope in Christ, may bring praise to his glory! And you too trusted him, when you had heard the message of truth, the gospel of your salvation. And after you gave your confidence to him you were, so to speak, stamped with the promised Holy Spirit as a pledge of our inheritance, until the day when God completes the redemption of what is his own; and that will again be to the praise of his glory.

1.15 I thank God for you, and pray for you

This is why since I heard of this faith of yours in the Lord Jesus and the love which you bear towards fellow-Christians, I thank God continually for you and I never give up praying for you; and this is my prayer. That the God of our Lord Jesus Christ, the all-glorious Father, will give you spiritual wisdom and the insight to know more of him: that you may receive that inner illumination of the spirit which will make you realise how great is the hope to which he is calling you—the magnificence and splendour of the inheritance promised to Christians—and how

Revised Standard Version

who accomplishes all things according to the
counsel of his will, 12 we who first hoped in
Christ have been destined and appointed to live
for the praise of his glory. 13 In him you also,
who have heard the word of truth, the gospel of
your salvation, and have believed in him, were
sealed with the promised Holy Spirit, 14 which is
the guarantee of our inheritance until we acquire
possession of it, to the praise of his glory.
15 For this reason, because I have heard of
your faith in the Lord Jesus and your love[c]
toward all the saints, 16 I do not cease to give
thanks for you, remembering you in my prayers,
17 that the God of our Lord Jesus Christ, the
Father of glory, may give you a spirit of wisdom
and of revelation in the knowledge of him,
18 having the eyes of your hearts enlightened,
that you may know what is the hope to which
he has called you, what are the riches of his
glorious inheritance in the saints, 19 and what is

[c] Other ancient authorities omit *your love*.

Jerusalem Bible

God's own,
chosen from the beginning,
under the predetermined plan of the one
who guides all things
as he decides by his own will;
12 chosen to be,
for his greater glory,
the people who would put their hopes in
Christ before he came.
13 Now you too, in him,
have heard the message of the truth and the
good news of your salvation,
and have believed it;
and you too have been stamped with the
seal of the Holy Spirit of the Promise,
14 the pledge of our inheritance
which brings freedom for those whom God
has taken for his own,
to make his glory praised.

The triumph and the supremacy of Christ

15 That will explain why I, having once heard
about your faith in the Lord Jesus, and the love
that you show toward all the saints, 16 have
never failed to remember you in my prayers
and to thank God for you. 17 May the God of
our Lord Jesus Christ, the Father of glory, give
you a spirit of wisdom and perception of what
is revealed, to bring you to full knowledge of
him. 18 May he enlighten the eyes of your mind
so that you can see what hope his call holds for
you, what rich glories he has promised the saints
will inherit 19 and how infinitely great is the

New English Bible

in the heritage, as was decreed in his design whose purpose is everywhere at work. For it was his will that we, who were the first to set our hope on Christ,[c] should cause his glory to be praised. And you too, when you had heard the message of the truth, the good news of your salvation, and had believed it, became incorporate in Christ and received the seal of the promised Holy Spirit; and that Spirit is the pledge that we shall enter upon our heritage, when God has redeemed what is his own, to his praise and glory.

Because of all this, now that I have heard of the faith you have in the Lord Jesus and of the love you bear towards all God's people, I never cease to give thanks for you when I mention you in my prayers. I pray that the God of our Lord Jesus Christ, the all-glorious Father, may give you the spiritual powers of wisdom and vision, by which there comes the knowledge of him. I pray that your inward eyes may be illumined, so that you may know what is the hope to which he calls you, what the wealth and glory of the share he offers you among his people in their heritage, and how vast the resources of his power

[c] *Or* who already enjoyed the hope of Christ, *or* whose expectation and hope are in Christ.

King James Version

what *is* the exceeding greatness of his power to
us-ward who believe, according to the working
of his mighty power, 20 Which he wrought in
Christ, when he raised him from the dead, and
set *him* at his own right hand in the heavenly
places, 21 Far above all principality, and power,
and might, and dominion, and every name that
is named, not only in this world, but also in
that which is to come: 22And hath put all *things*
under his feet, and gave him *to be* the head over
all *things* to the church, 23 Which is his body,
the fulness of him that filleth all in all.

2 And you *hath he quickened,* who were dead
in trespasses and sins; 2 Wherein in time past
ye walked according to the course of this world,
according to the prince of the power of the air,
the spirit that now worketh in the children of
disobedience: 3Among whom also we all had
our conversation in times past in the lusts of our
flesh, fulfilling the desires of the flesh and of the
mind; and were by nature the children of wrath,
even as others. 4 But God, who is rich in mercy,
for his great love wherewith he loved us, 5 Even
when we were dead in sins, hath quickened us

Living Bible

understand how incredibly great his power is to
help those who believe him. It is that same
mighty power 20 that raised Christ from the dead
and seated him in the place of honor at God's
right hand in heaven, 21 far, far above any other
king or ruler or dictator or leader. Yes, his honor
is far more glorious than that of anyone else
either in this world or in the world to come.
22And God has put all things under his feet and
made him the supreme Head of the church—
23 which is his body, filled with himself, the Author and Giver of everything everywhere.

2 Once you were under God's curse, doomed
forever for your sins. 2 You went along with
the crowd and were just like all the others, full
of sin, obeying Satan, the mighty prince of the
power of the air, who is at work right now in
the hearts of those who are against the Lord.
3All of us used to be just as they are, our lives
expressing the evil within us, doing every wicked
thing that our passions or our evil thoughts
might lead us into. We started out bad, being
born with evil natures, and were under God's
anger just like everyone else.

4 But God is so rich in mercy; he loved us so
much 5 that even though we were spiritually
dead and doomed by our sins, he gave us back

Today's English Version

is his power at work in us who believe. This
power in us is the same as the mighty strength
20 which he used when he raised Christ from
death, and seated him at his right side in the
heavenly world. 21 Christ rules there above all
heavenly rulers, authorities, powers, and lords;
he is above all titles of power in this world and
in the next. 22 God put all things under Christ's
feet, and gave him to the church as supreme
Lord over all things. 23 The church is Christ's
body, the completion of him who himself completes all things everywhere.

From death to life

2 In the past you were spiritually dead because of your disobedience and sins. 2At that
time you followed the world's evil way; you
obeyed the ruler of the spiritual powers in space,
the spirit who now controls the people who disobey God. 3Actually all of us were like them,
and lived according to our natural desires, and
did whatever suited the wishes of our own bodies
and minds. Like everyone else, we too were
naturally bound to suffer God's wrath.

4 But God's mercy is so abundant, and his
love for us is so great, 5 that while we were
spiritually dead in our disobedience he brought

New International Version

believe. That power is like the working of his
mighty strength, 20 which he exerted in Christ
when he raised him from the dead and seated
him at his right hand in the heavenly realms,
21 far above all rule and authority, power and
dominion, and every title that can be given, not
only in the present age but also in the one to
come. 22And God placed all things under his
feet and appointed him to be head over everything for the church, 23 which is his body, the
fullness of him who fills everything in every way.

Made alive in Christ

2 As for you, you were dead in your transgressions and sins, 2 in which you used to
live when you followed the ways of this world
and of the ruler of the kingdom of the air, the
spirit who is now at work in those who are disobedient. 3All of us also lived among them at
one time, gratifying the cravings of our sinful
nature and following its desires and thoughts.
Like the rest, we were by nature objects of wrath.
4 But because of his great love for us, God, who
is rich in mercy, 5 made us alive with Christ
even when we were dead in transgressions—it is

Phillips Modern English

tremendous is the power available to us who believe in God. That power is the same divine energy which was demonstrated in Christ when he raised him from the dead and gave him the place of highest honour in Heaven—a place that is infinitely superior to any command, authority, power or control, and which carries with it a name far beyond any name that could ever be used in this world or the world to come.

God has placed everything under the power of Christ and has set him up as supreme head to the Church. For the Church is his body, and in that body lives fully the One who fills the whole wide universe.

2.1 *We were all dead: God gave us life through Christ*

You were spiritually dead through your sins and failures, all the time that you followed this world's ideas of living, and obeyed the evil ruler of the spiritual realm—who is indeed fully operative today in those who disobey God. We all lived like that in the past, and followed the desires and imaginings of our lower nature, being in fact under the wrath of God by nature, like everyone else. But even though we were dead in our sins God, who is rich in mercy, because of the great love he had for us, gave us life to-

Revised Standard Version

the immeasurable greatness of his power in us
who believe, according to the working of his
great might 20 which he accomplished in Christ
when he raised him from the dead and made
him sit at his right hand in the heavenly places,
21 far above all rule and authority and power
and dominion, and above every name that is
named, not only in this age but also in that
which is to come; 22 and he has put all things
under his feet and has made him the head over
all things for the church, 23 which is his body,
the fulness of him who fills all in all.

2 And you he made alive, when you were
dead through the trespasses and sins 2 in
which you once walked, following the course of
this world, following the prince of the power of
the air, the spirit that is now at work in the sons
of disobedience. 3 Among these we all once lived
in the passions of our flesh, following the desires of body and mind, and so we were by nature children of wrath, like the rest of mankind.
4 But God, who is rich in mercy, out of the great
love with which he loved us, 5 even when we
were dead through our trespasses, made us alive

Jerusalem Bible

power that he has exercised for us believers.
This you can tell from the strength of his power
20 at work in Christ, when he used it to raise
him from the dead and to make him sit at his
right hand, in heaven, 21 far above every Sovereignty, Authority, Power, or Domination,[a] or
any other name that can be named, not only
in this age but also in the age to come. 22 *He
has put all things under his feet,*[b] and made him,
as the ruler of everything, the head of the
Church; 23 which is his body, the fullness of
him who fills the whole creation.

Salvation in Christ a free gift

2 And you were dead, through the crimes
and the sins 2 in which you used to live
when you were following the way of this world,
obeying the ruler who governs the air,[c] the spirit
who is at work in the rebellious. 3 We all were
among them too in the past, living sensual lives,
ruled entirely by our own physical desires and
our own ideas; so that by nature we were as
much under God's anger as the rest of the world.
4 But God loved us with so much love that he
was generous with his mercy: 5 when we were
dead through our sins, he brought us to life

[*a*] Orders of the angelic hierarchy in Jewish literature. [*b*] Ps. 8:6. [*c*] Satan.

New English Bible

open to us who trust in him. They are measured by his strength and the might which he exerted in Christ when he raised him from the dead, when he enthroned him at his right hand in the heavenly realms, far above all government and authority, all power and dominion, and any title of sovereignty that can be named, not only in this age but in the age to come. He put everything in subjection beneath his feet, and appointed him as supreme head to the church, which is his body and as such holds within it the fullness of him who himself receives the entire fullness of God.[a]

2 Time was when you were dead in your sins and wickedness, when you followed the evil ways of this present age, when you obeyed the commander of the spiritual powers of the air, the spirit now at work among God's rebel subjects. We too were once of their number: we all lived our lives in sensuality, and obeyed the promptings of our own instincts and notions. In our natural condition we, like the rest, lay under the dreadful judgement of God. But God, rich in mercy, for the great love he bore us, brought us to life with Christ even when we were dead in

[*a*] *Or* as supreme head to the church, which is his body and as such holds within it the fullness of him who fills the universe in all its parts; *or* as supreme head to the church which is his body, and to be all that he himself is who fills the universe in all its parts.

King James Version

together with Christ, (by grace ye are saved;)
6And hath raised *us* up together, and made *us*
sit together in heavenly *places* in Christ Jesus:
7 That in the ages to come he might shew the
exceeding riches of his grace, in *his* kindness
toward us, through Christ Jesus. 8 For by grace
are ye saved through faith; and that not of yourselves: *it is* the gift of God: 9 Not of works,
lest any man should boast. 10 For we are his
workmanship, created in Christ Jesus unto good
works, which God hath before ordained that we
should walk in them. 11 Wherefore remember,
that ye *being* in time past Gentiles in the flesh,
who are called Uncircumcision by that which
is called the Circumcision in the flesh made by
hands; 12 That at that time ye were without
Christ, being aliens from the commonwealth of
Israel, and strangers from the covenants of
promise, having no hope, and without God in
the world: 13 But now, in Christ Jesus, ye who
sometime were far off are made nigh by the
blood of Christ. 14 For he is our peace, who hath

Living Bible

our lives again[a] when he raised Christ from the
dead—only by his undeserved favor have we ever
been saved—6 and lifted us up from the grave
into glory along with Christ, where we sit with
him in the heavenly realms—all because of what
Christ Jesus did. 7And now God can always
point to us as examples of how very, very rich
his kindness is, as shown in all he has done for
us through Jesus Christ.

8 Because of his kindness you have been saved
through trusting Christ. And even trusting[b] is
not of yourselves; it too is a gift from God.
9 Salvation is not a reward for the good we have
done, so none of us can take any credit for it.
10 It is God himself who has made us what we
are and given us new lives from Christ Jesus;
and long ages ago he planned that we should
spend these lives in helping others.

11 Never forget that once you were heathen,
and that you were called godless and "unclean"
by the Jews. (But their hearts, too, were still unclean, even though they were going through the
ceremonies and rituals of the godly, for they circumcised themselves as a sign of godliness.)
12 Remember that in those days you were living
utterly apart from Christ; you were enemies of
God's children and he had promised you no
help. You were lost, without God, without hope.

13 But now you belong to Christ Jesus, and
though you once were far away from God, now
you have been brought very near to him because
of what Jesus Christ has done for you with his
blood.

14 For Christ himself is our way of peace. He

[*a*] Literally, "he made us alive." [*b*] Or, "Salvation is not of yourselves."

Today's English Version

us to life with Christ. It is by God's grace that
you have been saved. 6 In our union with Christ
Jesus he raised us up with him to rule with him
in the heavenly world. 7 He did this to demonstrate for all time to come the extraordinary
greatness of his grace in the love he showed us
in Christ Jesus. 8 For it is by God's grace that
you have been saved, through faith. It is not
your own doing, but God's gift. 9 There is nothing here to boast of, since it is not the result of
your own efforts. 10 God is our Maker, and in
our union with Christ Jesus he has created us
for a life of good works, which he has already
prepared for us to do.

One in Christ

11 You Gentiles by birth—who are called the
uncircumcised by the Jews, who call themselves
the circumcised (which refers to what men themselves do on their bodies)—remember what you
were in the past. 12At that time you were apart
from Christ. You were foreigners, and did not
belong to God's chosen people. You had no part
in the covenants, which were based on God's
promises to his people. You lived in this world
without hope and without God. 13 But now, in
union with Christ Jesus, you who used to be
far away have been brought near by the death
of Christ. 14 For Christ himself has brought us

New International Version

by grace you have been saved. 6And God raised
us up with Christ and seated us with him in the
heavenly realms in Christ Jesus, 7 in order that
in the coming ages he might show the incompa-
rable riches of his grace, expressed in his kindness to us in Christ Jesus. 8 For it is by grace
you have been saved, through faith—and this
not from yourselves, it is the gift of God—
9 not by works, so that no one can boast. 10 For
we are God's workmanship, created in Christ
Jesus to do good works, which God prepared
in advance for us to do.

One in Christ

11 Therefore, remember that formerly you
who are Gentiles by birth and called "uncircumcised" by those who call themselves "the circumcision" (that done in the body by the hands
of men)—12 remember that at that time you
were separate from Christ, excluded from citizenship in Israel and foreigners to the covenants of
the promise, without hope and without God in
the world. 13 But now in Christ Jesus you who
once were far away have been brought near
through the blood of Christ.

14 For he himself is our peace, who has made

Phillips Modern English

gether with Christ—it is, remember, by grace that you are saved—and has lifted us to take our place with him in Christ Jesus in the Heavens. Thus he shows for all the ages to come the tremendous generosity of the grace and kindness he has expressed towards us in Christ Jesus. For it is by grace that you are saved, through faith. This does not depend on anything you have achieved, it is the free gift of God; and because it is not earned no man can boast about it. For God has made us what we are, created in Christ Jesus to do those good deeds which he planned for us to do.

2.11 You were gentiles: we were Jews. God has made us fellow-Christians

Do not lose sight of the fact that you were born "gentiles", known by those whose bodies were circumcised by the hand of man as "the uncircumcised". You were then without Christ, you were utter strangers to God's chosen community, Israel, and you had no knowledge of, or right to, the promised agreements. You had nothing to look forward to and no God to whom you could turn. But now, in Christ Jesus, you who were once far off are brought near through the shedding of Christ's blood. For

Revised Standard Version

together with Christ (by grace you have been saved), 6 and raised us up with him, and made us sit with him in the heavenly places in Christ Jesus, 7 that in the coming ages he might show the immeasurable riches of his grace in kindness toward us in Christ Jesus. 8 For by grace you have been saved through faith; and this is not your own doing, it is the gift of God—9 not because of works, lest any man should boast. 10 For we are his workmanship, created in Christ Jesus for good works, which God prepared beforehand, that we should walk in them.

11 Therefore remember that at one time you Gentiles in the flesh, called the uncircumcision by what is called the circumcision, which is made in the flesh by hands—12 remember that you were at that time separated from Christ, alienated from the commonwealth of Israel, and strangers to the covenants of promise, having no hope and without God in the world. 13 But now in Christ Jesus you who once were far off have been brought near in the blood of Christ. 14 For he is our peace, who has made us both

Jerusalem Bible

with Christ—it is through grace that you have been saved—6 and raised us up with him and gave us a place with him in heaven, in Christ Jesus.

7 This was to show for all ages to come, through his goodness toward us in Christ Jesus, how infinitely rich he is in grace. 8 Because it is by grace that you have been saved, through faith; not by anything of your own, but by a gift from God; 9 not by anything that you have done, so that nobody can claim the credit. 10 We are God's work of art, created in Christ Jesus to live the good life as from the beginning he had meant us to live it.

Reconciliation of the Jews and the pagans with each other and with God

11 Do not forget, then, that there was a time when you who were pagans physically, termed the Uncircumcised by those who speak of themselves as the Circumcision by reason of a physical operation, 12 do not forget, I say, that you had no Christ and were excluded from membership of Israel, aliens with no part in the covenants with their Promise; you were immersed in this world, without hope and without God. 13 But now in Christ Jesus, you that used to be so far apart from us have been brought very close, by the blood of Christ. 14 For he is the

New English Bible

our sins; it is by his grace you are saved. And in union with Christ Jesus he raised us up and enthroned us with him in the heavenly realms, so that he might display in the ages to come how immense are the resources of his grace, and how great his kindness to us in Christ Jesus. For it is by his grace you are saved, through trusting him; it is not your own doing. It is God's gift, not a reward for work done. There is nothing for anyone to boast of. For we are God's handiwork, created in Christ Jesus to devote ourselves to the good deeds for which God has designed us.

Remember then your former condition: you, Gentiles as you are outwardly,[b] you, 'the uncircumcised' so called by those who are called 'the circumcised' (but only with reference to an outward rite)—you were at that time separate from Christ, strangers to the community of Israel, outside God's covenants and the promise that goes with them. Your world was a world without hope and without God. But now in union with Christ Jesus you who once were far off have been brought near through the shedding of Christ's blood. For he is himself our peace.

[b] *Or* by birth.

King James Version

made both one, and hath broken down the middle wall of partition *between us;* 15 Having abolished in his flesh the enmity, *even* the law of
commandments *contained* in ordinances; for to
make in himself of twain one new man, *so* making peace; 16 And that he might reconcile both
unto God in one body by the cross, having slain
the enmity thereby: 17 And came and preached
peace to you which were afar off, and to them
that were nigh. 18 For through him we both have
access by one Spirit unto the Father. 19 Now
therefore ye are no more strangers and foreigners, but fellow citizens with the saints, and of
the household of God; 20 And are built upon the
foundation of the apostles and prophets, Jesus
Christ himself being the chief corner *stone;* 21 In
whom all the building fitly framed together
groweth unto a holy temple in the Lord: 22 In
whom ye also are builded together for a habitation of God through the Spirit.

Living Bible

has made peace between us Jews and you Gentiles by making us all one family,[c] breaking down
the wall of contempt[d] that used to separate us.
15 By his death he ended the angry resentment between us, caused by the Jewish laws which favored the Jews and excluded the Gentiles, for
he died to annul that whole system of Jewish
laws. Then he took the two groups that had been
opposed to each other and made them parts of
himself; thus he fused us together to become
one new person, and at last there was peace.
16 As parts of the same body, our anger against
each other has disappeared, for both of us have
been reconciled to God. And so the feud ended
at last at the cross. 17 And he has brought this
Good News of peace to you Gentiles who were
very far away from him, and to us Jews who
were near. 18 Now all of us, whether Jews or
Gentiles, may come to God the Father with the
Holy Spirit's help because of what Christ has
done for us.

19 Now you are no longer strangers to God
and foreigners to heaven, but you are members
of God's very own family, citizens of God's
country, and you belong in God's household with
every other Christian.

20 What a foundation you stand on now: the
apostles and the prophets; and the cornerstone
of the building is Jesus Christ himself! 21 We
who believe are carefully joined together with
Christ as parts of a beautiful, constantly growing temple for God. 22 And you also are joined
with him and with each other by the Spirit, and
are part of this dwelling place of God.

[*c*] Literally, "by making us one." [*d*] Implied.

Today's English Version

peace, by making the Jews and Gentiles one
people. With his own body he broke down the
wall that separated them and kept them enemies. 15 He abolished the Jewish Law, with its
commandments and rules, in order to create out
of the two races one new people in union with
himself, in this way making peace. 16 By his
death on the cross Christ destroyed the enmity;
by means of the cross he united both races into
one body and brought them back to God. 17 So
Christ came and preached the Good News of
peace to all—to you Gentiles, who were far
away from God, and to the Jews, who were near
to him. 18 It is through Christ that all of us,
Jews and Gentiles, are able to come in the one
Spirit into the presence of the Father.

19 So then, you Gentiles are not foreigners or
strangers any longer; you are now fellow-citizens
with God's people, and members of the family
of God. 20 You, too, are built upon the foundation laid by the apostles and prophets, the cornerstone being Christ Jesus himself. 21 He is the
one who holds the whole building together and
makes it grow into a sacred temple in the Lord.
22 In union with him you too are being built
together with all the others into a house where
God lives through his Spirit.

New International Version

the two one and has destroyed the barrier, the
dividing wall of hostility, 15 by abolishing in his
flesh the law with its commandments and regulations. His purpose was to create in himself one
new man out of the two, thus making peace,
16 and in this one body to reconcile both of
them to God through the cross, by which he
put to death their hostility. 17 He came and
preached peace to you who were far away and
peace to those who were near. 18 For through
him we both have access to the Father by one
Spirit.

19 Consequently, you are no longer foreigners
and aliens, but fellow citizens with God's people
and members of God's household, 20 built on the
foundation of the apostles and prophets, with
Christ Jesus himself as the chief cornerstone.
21 In him the whole building is joined together
and rises to become a holy temple in the Lord.
22 And in him you too are being built together
to become a dwelling in which God lives by his
Spirit.

Phillips Modern English

Christ is our living peace. He has made us both one by breaking down the barrier and enmity which lay between us. By his sacrifice he removed the hostility of the Law, with all its commandments and rules, and made in himself out of the two, Jew and gentile, one new man, thus producing peace. For he reconciled both to God by the sacrifice of one body on the cross, and by his act killed the enmity between them. Then he came and brought the good news of peace to you who were far from God and to us who were near. And it is through him that both of us now can approach the Father in the one Spirit.

So you are no longer outsiders or aliens, but fellow-citizens with every other Christian—you belong now to the household of God. Firmly beneath you is the foundation, God's messengers and prophets, the corner-stone being Christ Jesus himself. In him each separate piece of building, properly fitting into its neighbour, grows together into a temple consecrated to the Lord. You are all part of this building in which God himself lives by his Spirit.

Revised Standard Version

one, and has broken down the dividing wall of
hostility, 15 by abolishing in his flesh the law of
commandments and ordinances, that he might
create in himself one new man in place of the
two, so making peace, 16 and might reconcile
us both to God in one body through the cross,
thereby bringing the hostility to an end. 17 And
he came and preached peace to you who were
far off and peace to those who were near; 18 for
through him we both have access in one Spirit
to the Father. 19 So then you are no longer
strangers and sojourners, but you are fellow
citizens with the saints and members of the
household of God, 20 built upon the foundation
of the apostles and prophets, Christ Jesus himself being the cornerstone, 21 in whom the whole
structure is joined together and grows into a
holy temple in the Lord; 22 in whom you also
are built into it for a dwelling place of God in
the Spirit.

Jerusalem Bible

peace between us, and has made the two into
one and broken down the barrier which used to
keep them apart, actually destroying in his own
person the hostility 15 caused by the rules and
decrees of the Law. This was to create one single New Man in himself out of the two of them
and by restoring peace 16 through the cross, to
unite them both in a single Body and reconcile
them with God. In his own person he killed the
hostility. 17 Later he came to bring the good
news of peace, *peace to you who were far away
and peace to those who were near at hand.*[d]
18 Through him, both of us have in the one
Spirit our way to come to the Father.
19 So you are no longer aliens or foreign
visitors: you are citizens like all the saints, and
part of God's household. 20 You are part of a
building that has the apostles and prophets[e] for
its foundations, and Christ Jesus himself for its
main cornerstone. 21 As every structure is aligned
on him, all grow into one holy temple in the
Lord; 22 and you too, in him, are being built
into a house where God lives, in the Spirit.

[d] Is. 57:19. [e] The New Testament prophets.

New English Bible

Gentiles and Jews, he has made the two one, and in his own body of flesh and blood has broken down the enmity which stood like a dividing wall between them; for he annulled the law with its rules and regulations, so as to create out of the two a single new humanity in himself, thereby making peace. This was his purpose, to reconcile the two in a single body to God through the cross, on which he killed the enmity.

So he came and proclaimed the good news: peace to you who were far off, and peace to those who were near by; for through him we both alike have access to the Father in the one Spirit. Thus you are no longer aliens in a foreign land, but fellow-citizens with God's people, members of God's household. You are built upon the foundation laid by the apostles and prophets, and Christ Jesus himself is the foundation-stone.[b] In him the whole building[c] is bonded together and grows into a holy temple in the Lord. In him you too are being built with all the rest into a spiritual dwelling for God.

[a] *Or* . . . cross. Thus in his own person he put the enmity to death. [b] *Or* built upon the foundation of the apostles and prophets, and Christ Jesus himself is the keystone. [c] *Or* every structure.

King James Version

3 For this cause I Paul, the prisoner of Jesus
Christ for you Gentiles, 2 If ye have heard
of the dispensation of the grace of God which
is given me to you-ward: 3 How that by revelation he made known unto me the mystery; (as
I wrote afore in few words; 4 Whereby, when ye
read, ye may understand my knowledge in the
mystery of Christ,) 5 Which in other ages was
not made known unto the sons of men, as it is
now revealed unto his holy apostles and prophets by the Spirit; 6 That the Gentiles should be
fellow heirs, and of the same body, and partakers of his promise in Christ by the gospel:
7 Whereof I was made a minister, according to
the gift of the grace of God given unto me by
the effectual working of his power. 8 Unto me,
who am less than the least of all saints, is this
grace given, that I should preach among the
Gentiles the unsearchable riches of Christ; 9 And
to make all *men* see what *is* the fellowship of
the mystery, which from the beginning of the
world hath been hid in God, who created all

Living Bible

3 I Paul, the servant of Christ, am here in
jail because of you—for preaching that you
Gentiles are a part of God's house. 2, 3 No doubt
you already know that God has given me this
special work of showing God's favor to you Gentiles, as I briefly mentioned before in one of my
letters. God himself showed me this secret plan
of his, that the Gentiles, too, are included in his
kindness. 4 I say this to explain to you how I
know about these things. 5 In olden times God
did not share this plan with his people, but now
he has revealed it by the Holy Spirit to his
apostles and prophets.

6 And this is the secret: that the Gentiles
will have their full share with the Jews in all the
riches inherited by God's sons; both are invited
to belong to his church, and all of God's promises of mighty blessings through Christ apply to
them both when they accept the Good News
about Christ and what he has done for them.
7 God has given me the wonderful privilege of
telling everyone about this plan of his; and he
has given me his power and special ability to do
it well.

8 Just think! Though I did nothing to deserve
it, and though I am the most useless Christian
there is, yet I was the one chosen for this special
joy of telling the Gentiles the Glad News of the
endless treasures available to them in Christ;
9 and to explain to everyone that God is the
Savior of the Gentiles too, just as he who made
all things had secretly planned from the very beginning.

Today's English Version

Paul's work for the Gentiles

3 For this reason I, Paul, the prisoner of
Christ Jesus for the sake of you Gentiles,
pray to God. 2 Surely you have heard that God,
in his grace, has given me this work to do for
your good. 3 God revealed his secret plan and
made it known to me. (I have written briefly
about this, 4 and if you will read what I have
written you can learn my understanding of the
secret of Christ.) 5 In past times men were not
told this secret, but God has revealed it now by
the Spirit to his holy apostles and prophets.
6 The secret is this: by means of the gospel the
Gentiles have a part with the Jews in God's
blessings; they are members of the same body,
and share in the promise that God made in
Christ Jesus.

7 I was made a servant of the gospel by God's
special gift, which he gave me through the working of his power. 8 I am less than the least of
all God's people; yet God gave me this privilege
of taking to the Gentiles the Good News of the
infinite riches of Christ, 9 and to make all men
see how God's secret plan is to be put into effect. God, who is the Creator of all things, kept

New International Version

Paul the preacher to the Gentiles

3 For this reason I, Paul, the prisoner of
Christ Jesus for the sake of you Gentiles—
2 Surely you have heard about the administration of God's grace that was given to me for
you, 3 that is, the mystery made known to me
by revelation, as I have already written briefly.
4 In reading this, then, you will be able to understand my insight into the mystery of Christ,
5 which was not made known to men in other
generations as it has now been revealed by the
Spirit to God's holy apostles and prophets. 6 This
mystery is that through the gospel the Gentiles
are heirs together with Israel, members together
of one body, and sharers together in the promise
in Christ Jesus.

7 I became a servant of this gospel by the
gift of God's grace given me through the working of his power. 8 Although I am less than the
least of all God's people, this grace was given
me: to preach to the Gentiles the unsearchable
riches of Christ, 9 and to make plain to everyone
my administration of this mystery, which for
ages past was kept hidden in God, who created

Phillips Modern English

3.1 God has made me minister to you gentiles

It is in this great cause that I, Paul, have become a prisoner of Christ Jesus for you gentiles. For you must have heard how God gave me grace to become your minister, and how he allowed me to understand his secret by giving me a direct revelation. What I have written briefly of this above will explain to you my knowledge of the mystery of Christ. This secret was hidden to past generations of mankind, but it has now, by the Spirit, been made plain to God's consecrated messengers and prophets. It is simply this: that the gentiles are to be equal heirs with his chosen people, equal members and equal partners in God's promise given by Christ Jesus through the gospel. And I was made a minister of that gospel by the grace he freely gave me, and by the action within me of his own power. Yes, to me, less than the least of all Christians, has God given this grace, to enable me to proclaim to the gentiles the gospel of the incalculable riches of Christ, and to make plain to all men the meaning of that divine secret which he who created everything has kept

Revised Standard Version

3 For this reason I, Paul, a prisoner for
Christ Jesus on behalf of you Gentiles—2 assuming that you have heard of the stewardship
of God's grace that was given to me for you,
3 how the mystery was made known to me by
revelation, as I have written briefly. 4 When you
read this you can perceive my insight into the
mystery of Christ, 5 which was not made known
to the sons of men in other generations as it
has now been revealed to his holy apostles and
prophets by the Spirit; 6 that is, how the Gentiles
are fellow heirs, members of the same body, and
partakers of the promise in Christ Jesus through
the gospel.
7 Of this gospel I was made a minister according to the gift of God's grace which was
given me by the working of his power. 8 To me,
though I am the very least of all the saints, this
grace was given, to preach to the Gentiles the
unsearchable riches of Christ, 9 and to make
all men see what is the plan of the mystery hidden for ages in[d] God who created all things;

[d] Or *by*.

Jerusalem Bible

Paul, a servant of the mystery

3 So I, Paul, a prisoner of Christ Jesus for
the sake of you pagans . . . 2 You have
probably heard how I have been entrusted by
God with the grace he meant for you, 3 and
that it was by a revelation that I was given the
knowledge of the mystery, as I have just described it very shortly. 4 If you read my words,
you will have some idea of the depths that I see
in the mystery of Christ. 5 This mystery that has
now been revealed through the Spirit to his holy
apostles and prophets was unknown to any men
in past generations; 6 it means that pagans
now share the same inheritance, that they are
parts of the same body, and that the same
promise has been made to them, in Christ Jesus,
through the gospel. 7 I have been made the servant of that gospel by a gift of grace from God
who gave it to me by his own power. 8 I, who
am less than the least of all the saints, have
been entrusted with this special grace, not only
of proclaiming to the pagans the infinite treasure
of Christ 9 but also of explaining how the mystery is to be dispensed. Through all the ages,
this has been kept hidden in God, the creator

New English Bible

3 With this in mind I make my prayer, I, Paul, who in the cause of you Gentiles am now the prisoner of Christ Jesus—for surely you have heard how God has assigned the gift of his grace to me for your benefit. It was by a revelation that his secret was made known to me. I have already written a brief account of this, and by reading it you may perceive that I understand the secret of Christ. In former generations this was not disclosed to the human race; but now it has been revealed by inspiration to his dedicated apostles and prophets, that through the Gospel the Gentiles are joint heirs with the Jews, part of the same body, sharers together in the promise made in Christ Jesus. Such is the gospel of which I was made a minister, by God's gift, bestowed unmerited on me in the working of his power. To me, who am less than the least of all God's people, he has granted of his grace the privilege of proclaiming to the Gentiles the good news of the unfathomable riches of Christ, and of bringing to light how this hidden purpose was to be put into effect. It was hidden for long

King James Version

things by Jesus Christ: 10 To the intent that now
unto the principalities and powers in heavenly
places might be known by the church the manifold wisdom of God, 11 According to the eternal
purpose which he purposed in Christ Jesus our
Lord: 12 In whom we have boldness and access
with confidence by the faith of him. 13 Wherefore I desire that ye faint not at my tribulations
for you, which is your glory. 14 For this cause
I bow my knees unto the Father of our Lord
Jesus Christ, 15 Of whom the whole family in
heaven and earth is named, 16 That he would
grant you, according to the riches of his glory,
to be strengthened with might by his Spirit in
the inner man; 17 That Christ may dwell in your
hearts by faith; that ye, being rooted and
grounded in love, 18 May be able to comprehend
with all saints what *is* the breadth, and length,
and depth, and height; 19 And to know the love
of Christ, which passeth knowledge, that ye
might be filled with all the fulness of God.
20 Now unto him that is able to do exceeding
abundantly above all that we ask or think, according to the power that worketh in us, 21 Unto

Living Bible

10 And his reason? To show to all the rulers
in heaven how perfectly wise he is when all of
his family—Jews and Gentiles alike—are seen
to be joined together in his church, 11 in just the
way he had always planned it through Jesus
Christ our Lord.
12 Now we can come fearlessly right into
God's presence, assured of his glad welcome
when we come with Christ and trust in him.
13 So please don't lose heart at what they are
doing to me here. It is for you I am suffering and
you should feel honored and encouraged.
14, 15 When I think of the wisdom and scope of
his plan I fall down on my knees and pray to
the Father of all the great family of God—some
of them already in heaven and some down here
on earth—16 that out of his glorious, unlimited
resources he will give you the mighty inner
strengthening of his Holy Spirit. 17 And I pray
that Christ will be more and more at home in
your hearts, living within you as you trust in
him. May your roots go down deep into the soil
of God's marvelous love; 18, 19 and may you be
able to feel and understand, as all God's children
should, how long, how wide, how deep, and how
high his love really is; and to experience this love
for yourselves, though it is so great that you will
never see the end of it or fully know or understand it. And so at last you will be filled up with
God himself.
20 Now glory be to God who by his mighty
power at work within us is able to do far more
than we would ever dare to ask or even dream
of—infinitely beyond our highest prayers, desires, thoughts, or hopes. 21 May he be given

Today's English Version

his secret hidden through all the past ages, 10 in
order that at the present time, by means of the
church, the angelic rulers and powers in the
heavenly world might know God's wisdom, in
all its different forms. 11 God did this according
to his eternal purpose, which he achieved through
Christ Jesus our Lord. 12 In union with him, and
through our faith in him, we have the freedom
to enter into God's presence with all confidence.
13 I beg you, then, do not be discouraged because I am suffering for you; it is all for your
benefit.

The love of Christ

14 For this reason, then, I fall on my knees
before the Father, 15 from whom every family
in heaven and on earth receives its true name.
16 I ask God, from the wealth of his glory, to
give you power through his Spirit to be strong in
your inner selves, 17 and that Christ will make
his home in your hearts, through faith. I pray
that you may have your roots and foundations
in love, 18 so that you, together with all God's
people, may have the power to understand how
broad and long and high and deep is Christ's
love. 19 Yes, may you come to know his love—
although it can never be fully known—and so
be completely filled with the perfect fulness of
God.
20 To him who is able to do so much more
than we can ever ask for, or even think of, by
means of the power working in us: 21 to God

New International Version

all things. 10 His intent was that now, through
the church, the manifold wisdom of God should
be made known to the rulers and authorities in
the heavenly realms, 11 according to his eternal
purpose which he accomplished in Christ Jesus
our Lord. 12 In him and through faith in him
we may approach God with freedom and confidence. 13 I ask you, therefore, not to be discouraged because of my sufferings for you, which
are your glory.

A prayer for the Ephesians

14 For this reason I kneel before the Father,
15 from whom the whole family of believers[e] in
heaven and on earth derives its name. 16 I pray
that out of his glorious riches he may strengthen
you with power through his Spirit in your inner
being, 17 so that Christ may dwell in your hearts
through faith. And I pray that you, being rooted
and established in love, 18 may have power, together with all the saints, to grasp how wide and
long and high and deep is the love of Christ,
19 and to know this love that surpasses knowledge—that you may be filled to the measure of
all the fullness of God.
20 Now to him who is able to do immeasurably more than all we ask or imagine, according
to his power that is at work within us, 21 to him

[e] Or *from whom all fatherhood.*

Phillips Modern English

hidden from the creation until now. The purpose is that all the angelic powers should now see the complex wisdom of God's plan being worked out through the Church, in conformity to that timeless purpose which he centred in Christ Jesus, our Lord. It is in this same Jesus, because we have faith in him, that we dare, even with confidence, to approach God. So then I beg you not to lose heart because I am now suffering on your behalf. Indeed, you should be honoured.

3.14 I pray that you may know God's power in practice

As I think of this great plan I fall on my knees before the Father (from whom all fatherhood, earthly or heavenly, derives its name), and I pray that out of the glorious richness of his resources he will enable you to know the strength of the Spirit's inner re-inforcement—that Christ may actually live in your hearts by your faith. And I pray that you, rooted and founded in love yourselves, may be able to grasp (with all Christians) how wide and long and deep and high is the love of Christ—and to know for yourselves that love so far above our understanding. So will you be filled through all your being with God himself!

Now to him who by his power within us is able to do infinitely more than we ever dare to ask or imagine—to him be glory in the Church

Revised Standard Version

10 that through the church the manifold wisdom
of God might now be made known to the principalities and powers in the heavenly places.
11 This was according to the eternal purpose
which he has realized in Christ Jesus our Lord,
12 in whom we have boldness and confidence of
access through our faith in him. 13 So I ask
you not to[e] lose heart over what I am suffering
for you, which is your glory.
14 For this reason I bow my knees before
the Father, 15 from whom every family in heaven
and on earth is named, 16 that according to the
riches of his glory he may grant you to be
strengthened with might through his Spirit in
the inner man, 17 and that Christ may dwell in
your hearts through faith; that you, being rooted
and grounded in love, 18 may have power to
comprehend with all the saints what is the
breadth and length and height and depth, 19 and
to know the love of Christ which surpasses
knowledge, that you may be filled with all the
fulness of God.
20 Now to him who by the power at work
within us is able to do far more abundantly than
all that we ask or think, 21 to him be glory in

[e] Or *I ask that I may not.*

Jerusalem Bible

of everything. Why? 10 So that the Sovereignties
and Powers should learn only now, through the
Church, how comprehensive God's wisdom really
is, 11 exactly according to the plan which he
had had from all eternity in Christ Jesus our
Lord. 12 This is why we are bold enough to
approach God in complete confidence, through
our faith in him; 13 so, I beg you, never lose
confidence just because of the trials that I go
through on your account: they are your glory.

Paul's prayer

14 This, then, is what I pray, kneeling before
the Father, 15 from whom every family,[f] whether
spiritual or natural, takes its name:
16 Out of his infinite glory, may he give you
the power through his Spirit for your hidden
self to grow strong, 17 so that Christ may live
in your hearts through faith, and then, planted
in love and built on love, 18 you will with all
the saints have strength to grasp the breadth
and the length, the height and the depth; 19 until, knowing the love of Christ, which is beyond
all knowledge, you are filled with the utter fullness of God.
20 Glory be to him whose power, working in
us, can do infinitely more than we can ask or
imagine; 21 glory be to him from generation to

[*f*] A pun on the words "Father" and "family" (clan or tribe) is lost in translation; traces of it survive in *paternity* and *patriotism*.

New English Bible

ages in God the creator of the universe, in order that now, through the church, the wisdom of God in all its varied forms might be made known to the rulers and authorities in the realms of heaven. This is in accord with his age-long purpose, which he achieved in Christ Jesus our Lord. In him we have access to God with freedom, in the confidence born of trust in him. I beg you, then, not to lose heart over my sufferings for you; indeed, they are your glory.

With this in mind, then, I kneel in prayer to the Father, from whom every family[d] in heaven and on earth takes its name, that out of the treasures of his glory he may grant you strength and power through his Spirit in your inner being, that through faith Christ may dwell in your hearts in love. With deep roots and firm foundations, may you be strong to grasp, with all God's people, what is the breadth and length and height and depth of the love of Christ, and to know it, though it is beyond knowledge. So may you attain to fullness of being, the fullness of God himself.[e]

Now to him who is able to do immeasurably more than all we can ask or conceive, by the power which is at work among us, to him be

[*d*] *Or* his whole family. [*e*] *Or* the fullness which God requires.

King James Version

him *be* glory in the church by Christ Jesus
throughout all ages, world without end. Amen.

4 I therefore, the prisoner of the Lord, beseech you that ye walk worthy of the vocation wherewith ye are called, 2 With all lowliness
and meekness, with longsuffering, forbearing one
another in love; 3 Endeavouring to keep the
unity of the Spirit in the bond of peace. 4 *There
is* one body, and one Spirit, even as ye are called
in one hope of your calling; 5 One Lord, one
faith, one baptism, 6 One God and Father of all,
who *is* above all, and through all, and in you
all. 7 But unto every one of us is given grace
according to the measure of the gift of Christ.
8 Wherefore he saith, When he ascended up on
high, he led captivity captive, and gave gifts

Living Bible

glory forever and ever through endless ages because of his master plan of salvation for the
church through Jesus Christ.

4 I beg you—I, a prisoner here in jail for serving the Lord—to live and act in a way
worthy of those who have been chosen for such
wonderful blessings as these. 2 Be humble and
gentle. Be patient with each other, making allowance for each other's faults because of your
love. 3 Try always to be led along together by
the Holy Spirit, and so be at peace with one
another.

4 We are all parts of one body, we have the
same Spirit, and we have all been called to the
same glorious future. 5 For us there is only one
Lord, one faith, one baptism, 6 and we all have
the same God and Father who is over us all and
in us all, and living through every part of us.
7 However, Christ has given each of us special
abilities—whatever he wants us to have out of
his rich storehouse of gifts.

8 The Psalmist tells us about this, for he says
that when Christ returned triumphantly to
heaven after his resurrection and victory over

Today's English Version

be the glory in the church and in Christ Jesus,
for all time, forever and ever! Amen.

The unity of the body

4 I urge you, then—I who am a prisoner because I serve the Lord: live a life that measures up to the standard God set when he called
you. 2 Be humble, gentle, and patient always.
Show your love by being helpful to one another.
3 Do your best to preserve the unity which the
Spirit gives, by the peace that binds you together. 4 There is one body and one Spirit, just
as there is one hope to which God has called
you. 5 There is one Lord, one faith, one baptism;
6 there is one God and Father of all men, who
is Lord of all, works through all, and is in all.
7 Each one of us has been given a special
gift, in proportion to what Christ has given. 8 As
the scripture says,

"When he went up to the very heights
he took many captives with him;
he gave gifts to men."

New International Version

be glory in the church and in Christ Jesus
throughout all generations, for ever and ever!
Amen.

Unity in the body of Christ

4 As a prisoner for the Lord, then, I urge you to live a life worthy of the calling you
have received. 2 Be completely humble and gentle; be patient, bearing with one another in love.
3 Make every effort to keep the unity of the
Spirit through the bond of peace. 4 There is one
body and one Spirit—just as you were called to
one hope when you were called—5 one Lord,
one faith, one baptism; 6 one God and Father
of all, who is over all and through all and in all.
7 But to each one of us grace has been given
as Christ apportioned it. 8 This is why it[f] says:
"When he ascended on high,
he led captives in his train
and gave gifts to men." [g]

[f] Or *God.* [g] Psalm 68:18.

Phillips Modern English

and in Christ Jesus for ever and ever, amen!

4.1 Christians should be at one, as God is one

As the Lord's prisoner, then, I beg you to live lives worthy of your high calling. Accept life with humility and patience, generously making allowances for each other because you love each other. Make it your aim to be at one in the Spirit, and you will be bound together in peace. There is one Body and one Spirit, just as it was to one hope that you were called. There is one Lord, one faith, one baptism, one God and Father of all, who is the one over all, the one working through all and the one living in all.

4.7 God's gifts vary, but it is the same God who gives

To each one of us is given his measure of grace from the richness of Christ's gift. Thus the scripture says:

When he ascended on high, he led captivity captive,
And gave gifts unto men.

Revised Standard Version

the church and in Christ Jesus to all generations, for ever and ever. Amen.

4 I therefore, a prisoner for the Lord, beg you to lead a life worthy of the calling to
which you have been called, 2 with all lowliness
and meekness, with patience, forbearing one another in love, 3 eager to maintain the unity of the
Spirit in the bond of peace. 4 There is one body
and one Spirit, just as you were called to the one
hope that belongs to your call, 5 one Lord, one
faith, one baptism, 6 one God and Father of us
all, who is above all and through all and in all.
7 But grace was given to each of us according
to the measure of Christ's gift. 8 Therefore it is
said,

"When he ascended on high he led a host of captives,
and he gave gifts to men."

Jerusalem Bible

generation in the Church and in Christ Jesus for ever and ever. Amen.

II. Exhortation

A call to unity

4 I, the prisoner in the Lord, implore you therefore to lead a life worthy of your vocation. 2 Bear with one another charitably, in
complete selflessness, gentleness and patience.
3 Do all you can to preserve the unity of the
Spirit by the peace that binds you together.
4 There is one Body, one Spirit, just as you were
all called into one and the same hope when
you were called. 5 There is one Lord, one faith,
one baptism, 6 and one God who is Father of
all, over all, through all and within all.
7 Each one of us, however, has been given
his own share of grace, given as Christ allotted
it. 8 It was said that he would:

When he ascended to the height, he captured prisoners,
he gave gifts to men.[g]

[g] Ps. 68:18.

New English Bible

glory in the church and in Christ Jesus from generation to generation evermore! Amen.

4 I entreat you, then—I, a prisoner for the Lord's sake: as God has called you, live up to your calling. Be humble always and gentle, and patient too. Be forbearing with one another and charitable. Spare no effort to make fast with bonds of peace the unity which the Spirit gives. There is one body and one Spirit, as there is also one hope held out in God's call to you; one Lord, one faith, one baptism; one God and Father of all, who is over all and through all and in all.

But each of us has been given his gift, his due portion of Christ's bounty. Therefore Scripture says:

'He ascended into the heights
with captives in his train;
he gave gifts to men.'

King James Version

unto men. 9 (Now that he ascended, what is it but that he also descended first into the lower parts of the earth? 10 He that descended is the same also that ascended up far above all heavens, that he might fill all things.) 11 And he gave some, apostles; and some, prophets; and some, evangelists; and some, pastors and teachers; 12 For the perfecting of the saints, for the work of the ministry, for the edifying of the body of Christ: 13 Till we all come in the unity of the faith, and of the knowledge of the Son of God, unto a perfect man, unto the measure of the stature of the fulness of Christ: 14 That we *henceforth* be no more children, tossed to and fro, and carried about with every wind of doctrine, by the sleight of men, *and* cunning craftiness, whereby they lie in wait to deceive; 15 But speaking the truth in love, may grow up into him in all things, which is the head, *even* Christ: 16 From whom the whole body fitly joined to-

Living Bible

Satan, he gave generous gifts to men. 9 Notice that it says he returned to heaven. This means that he had first come down from the heights of heaven, far down to the lowest parts of the earth. 10 The same one who came down is the one who went back up, that he might fill all things everywhere with himself, from the very lowest to the very highest.[a]

11 Some of us have been given special ability as apostles; to others he has given the gift of being able to preach well; some have special ability in winning people to Christ, helping them to trust him as their Savior; still others have a gift for caring for God's people as a shepherd does his sheep, leading and teaching them in the ways of God.

12 Why is it that he gives us these special abilities to do certain things best? It is that God's people will be equipped to do better work for him, building up the church, the body of Christ, to a position of strength and maturity; 13 until finally we all believe alike about our salvation and about our Savior, God's Son, and all become full-grown in the Lord—yes, to the point of being filled full with Christ.

14 Then we will no longer be like children, forever changing our minds about what we believe because someone has told us something different, or has cleverly lied to us and made the lie sound like the truth. 15, 16 Instead, we will lovingly follow the truth at all times—speaking truly, dealing truly, living truly[b]—and so become more and more in every way like Christ who is the Head of his body, the church. Under his

[a] Literally, "that he might fill all things." [b] Amplified New Testament.

Today's English Version

9 Now, what does "he went up" mean? It means that first he came down—that is, down to the lower depths of the earth. 10 So he who came down is the same one who went up, above and beyond the heavens, to fill the whole universe with his presence. 11 It was he who "gave gifts to men"; he appointed some to be apostles, others to be prophets, others to be evangelists, others to be pastors and teachers. 12 He did this to prepare all God's people for the work of Christian service, to build up the body of Christ. 13 And so we shall all come together to that oneness in our faith and in our knowledge of the Son of God; we shall become mature men, reaching to the very height of Christ's full stature. 14 Then we shall no longer be children, carried by the waves and blown about by every shifting wind of the teaching of deceitful men, who lead others to error by the tricks they invent. 15 Instead, by speaking the truth in a spirit of love, we must grow up in every way to Christ, who is the head. 16 Under his control all the

New International Version

9 (What does "he ascended" mean except that he also descended to the lower, earthly regions? 10 He who descended is the very one who ascended higher than all the heavens, in order to fill the whole universe.) 11 It was he who gave some to be apostles, some to be prophets, some to be evangelists, and some to be pastors and teachers, 12 to prepare God's people for works of service, so that the body of Christ may be built up 13 until we all reach unity in the faith and in the knowledge of the Son of God and become mature, attaining the full measure of perfection found in Christ.

14 Then we will no longer be infants, tossed back and forth by the waves, and blown here and there by every wind of teaching and by the cunning and craftiness of men in their deceitful scheming. 15 Instead, speaking the truth in love, we will in all things grow up into him who is the Head, that is, Christ. 16 From him the whole

Phillips Modern English

Note the implication here—to say that Christ "ascended" means that he must previously have "descended", that is to the depth of this world. The one who made this descent is the same person as he who has now ascended high above the very Heavens—that he might fill the whole universe.

His "gifts unto men" were varied. Some he made his messengers, some prophets, some preachers of the gospel; to some he gave the power to guide and teach his people. His gifts were made that Christians might be properly equipped for their service, that the whole body might be built up until the time comes when, in the unity of common faith and common knowledge of the Son of God, we arrive at real maturity—that measure of development which is meant by "the fulness of Christ".

4.14 True maturity means growing up "into" Christ

We are not meant to remain as children at the mercy of every chance wind of teaching, and of the jockeying of men who are expert in the crafty presentation of lies. But we are meant to speak the truth in love, and to grow up in every way into Christ, the head. For it is from the head

Revised Standard Version

9 (In saying, "He ascended," what does it mean
but that he had also descended into the lower
parts of the earth? 10 He who descended is he
who also ascended far above all the heavens, that
he might fill all things.) 11 And his gifts were
that some should be apostles, some prophets,
some evangelists, some pastors and teachers,
12 to equip the saints for the work of ministry,
for building up the body of Christ, 13 until we
all attain to the unity of the faith and of the
knowledge of the Son of God, to mature manhood, to the measure of the stature of the fulness of Christ; 14 so that we may no longer be
children, tossed to and fro and carried about
with every wind of doctrine, by the cunning of
men, by their craftiness in deceitful wiles.
15 Rather, speaking the truth in love, we are to
grow up in every way into him who is the head,
into Christ, 16 from whom the whole body,

Jerusalem Bible

9 When it says, "he ascended," what can it
mean if not that he descended right down to
the lower regions of the earth? 10 The one who
rose higher than all the heavens to fill all things
is none other than the one who descended.
11 And to some, his gift was that they should
be apostles; to some, prophets; to some, evangelists; to some, pastors and teachers; 12 so that
the saints together make a unity in the work of
service, building up the body of Christ. 13 In
this way we are all to come to unity in our
faith and in our knowledge of the Son of God,
until we become the perfect Man, fully mature
with the fullness of Christ himself.
14 Then we shall not be children any longer,
or tossed one way and another and carried
along by every wind of doctrine, at the mercy
of all the tricks men play and their cleverness
in practicing deceit. 15 If we live by the truth
and in love, we shall grow in all ways into
Christ, who is the head 16 by whom the whole

New English Bible

Now, the word 'ascended' implies that he also descended to the lowest level, down to the very earth.[a] He who descended is no other than he who ascended far above all heavens, so that he might fill the universe. And these were his gifts: some to be apostles, some prophets, some evangelists, some pastors and teachers, to equip God's people for work in his service, to the building up of the body of Christ. So shall we all at last attain to the unity inherent in our faith and our knowledge of the Son of God—to mature manhood, measured by nothing less than the full stature of Christ. We are no longer to be children, tossed by the waves and whirled about by every fresh gust of teaching, dupes of crafty rogues and their deceitful schemes. No, let us speak the truth in love; so shall we fully grow up into Christ. He is the head, and on him the

[a] *Or* descended to the regions beneath the earth.

King James Version

gether and compacted by that which every joint supplieth, according to the effectual working in the measure of every part, maketh increase of the body unto the edifying of itself in love. 17 This I say therefore, and testify in the Lord, that ye henceforth walk not as other Gentiles walk, in the vanity of their mind, 18 Having the understanding darkened, being alienated from the life of God through the ignorance that is in them, because of the blindness of their heart: 19 Who being past feeling have given themselves over unto lasciviousness, to work all uncleanness with greediness. 20 But ye have not so learned Christ; 21 If so be that ye have heard him, and have been taught by him, as the truth is in Jesus: 22 That ye put off concerning the former conversation the old man, which is corrupt according to the deceitful lusts; 23 And be renewed in the spirit of your mind; 24 And that ye put on the new man, which after God is created in righteousness and true holiness. 25 Wherefore putting away lying, speak every man truth with his neighbour: for we are members one of another. 26 Be ye angry, and sin not: let not the sun go down upon your wrath: 27 Neither give place

Living Bible

direction the whole body is fitted together perfectly, and each part in its own special way helps the other parts, so that the whole body is healthy and growing and full of love.

17, 18 Let me say this, then, speaking for the Lord: Live no longer as the unsaved do, for they are blinded and confused. Their closed hearts are full of darkness; they are far away from the life of God because they have shut their minds against him, and they cannot understand his ways. 19 They don't care anymore about right and wrong and have given themselves over to impure ways. They stop at nothing, being driven by their evil minds and reckless lusts.

20 But that isn't the way Christ taught you! 21 If you have really heard his voice and learned from him the truths concerning himself, 22 then throw off your old evil nature—the old you that was a partner in your evil ways—rotten through and through, full of lust and sham.

23 Now your attitudes and thoughts must all be constantly changing for the better. 24 Yes, you must be a new and different person, holy and good. Clothe yourself with this new nature.

25 Stop lying to each other; tell the truth, for we are parts of each other and when we lie to each other we are hurting ourselves. 26 If you are angry, don't sin by nursing your grudge. Don't let the sun go down with you still angry—get over it quickly; 27 for when you are angry you give a mighty foothold to the devil.

Today's English Version

different parts of the body fit together, and the whole body is held together by every joint with which it is provided. So when each separate part works as it should, the whole body grows and builds itself up through love.

The new life in Christ

17 In the Lord's name, then, I say this and warn you: do not live any longer like the heathen, whose thoughts are worthless, 18 and whose minds are in the dark. They have no part in the life that God gives, because they are completely ignorant and stubborn. 19 They have lost all feeling of shame; they give themselves over to vice, and do all sorts of indecent things without restraint.

20 That was not what you learned about Christ! 21 You certainly heard about him, and as his followers you were taught the truth that is in Jesus. 22 So get rid of your old self, which made you live as you used to—the old self that was being destroyed by its deceitful desires. 23 Your hearts and minds must be made completely new. 24 You must put on the new self, which is created in God's likeness, and reveals itself in the true life that is upright and holy.

25 No more lying, then! Everyone must tell the truth to his brother, because we are all members together in the body of Christ. 26 If you become angry, do not let your anger lead you into sin; and do not stay angry all day. 27 Don't

New International Version

body, joined and held together by every supporting ligament, grows and builds itself up in love, as each part does its work.

Living as children of light

17 So I tell you this, and insist on it in the Lord, that you must no longer live as the Gentiles do, in the futility of their thinking. 18 They are darkened in their understanding and separated from the life of God because of the ignorance that is in them due to the hardening of their hearts. 19 Having lost all sensitivity, they have given themselves over to sensuality so as to indulge in every kind of impurity, with a continual lust for more.

20 You, however, did not come to know Christ that way. 21 Surely you heard of him and were taught in him in accordance with the truth that is in Jesus. 22 You were taught, with regard to your former way of life, to put off your old self, which is being corrupted by its deceitful desires; 23 to be made new in the attitude of your minds; 24 and to put on the new self, created to be like God in true righteousness and holiness.

25 Therefore, each of you must put off falsehood and speak truthfully to his neighbor, for we are all members of one body. 26 In your anger do not sin: Do not let the sun go down while you are still angry, 27 and do not give the

Phillips Modern English

that the whole body, as a harmonious structure knit together by the joints with which it is provided, grows by the proper functioning of individual parts, and so builds itself up in love.

4.17 *Have no more to do with the old life! Learn the new*

This is my instruction, then, which I give you in the Lord's name. Do not live any longer the futile lives of gentiles. For they live in a world of shadows, and are cut off from the life of God through their deliberate ignorance of mind and sheer hardness of heart. They have lost all decent feelings and abandoned themselves to sensuality, practising any form of impurity which lust can suggest. But you have learned nothing like that from Christ, if you have really heard his voice and understood the truth that Jesus has taught you. No, what you learned was to fling off the dirty clothes of the old way of living, which were rotted through and through with lust's illusions, and, with yourselves mentally and spiritually re-made, to put on the clean fresh clothes of the new life which was made by God's design for righteousness and the holiness which is no illusion.

Finish, then, with lying and let each man tell his neighbour the truth, for we are all parts of the same body. If you are angry, be sure that it is not a sinful anger. Never go to bed angry—don't give the devil that sort of foothold.

Revised Standard Version

joined and knit together by every joint with which it is supplied, when each part is working properly, makes bodily growth and upbuilds itself in love.

17 Now this I affirm and testify in the Lord, that you must no longer live as the Gentiles do, in the futility of their minds; 18 they are darkened in their understanding, alienated from the life of God because of the ignorance that is in them, due to their hardness of heart; 19 they have become callous and have given themselves up to licentiousness, greedy to practice every kind of uncleanness. 20 You did not so learn Christ!—21 assuming that you have heard about him and were taught in him, as the truth is in Jesus. 22 Put off your old nature which belongs to your former manner of life and is corrupt through deceitful lusts, 23 and be renewed in the spirit of your minds, 24 and put on the new nature, created after the likeness of God in true righteousness and holiness.

25 Therefore, putting away falsehood, let every one speak the truth with his neighbor, for we are members one of another. 26 Be angry but do not sin; do not let the sun go down on your anger, 27 and give no opportunity to the devil.

Jerusalem Bible

body is fitted and joined together, every joint adding its own strength, for each separate part to work according to its function. So the body grows until it has built itself up, in love.

The new life in Christ

17 In particular, I want to urge you in the name of the Lord, not to go on living the aimless kind of life that pagans live. 18 Intellectually they are in the dark, and they are estranged from the life of God, without knowledge because they have shut their hearts to it. 19 Their sense of right and wrong once dulled, they have abandoned themselves to sexuality and eagerly pursue a career of indecency of every kind. 20 Now that is hardly the way you have learned from Christ, 21 unless you failed to hear him properly when you were taught what the truth is in Jesus. 22 You must give up your old way of life; you must put aside your old self, which gets corrupted by following illusory desires. 23 Your mind must be renewed by a spiritual revolution 24 so that you can put on the new self that has been created in God's way, in the goodness and holiness of the truth.

25 So from now on, there must be no more lies: *You must speak the truth to one another,*[h] since we are all parts of one another. 26 *Even if you are angry, you must not sin*[i]*:* never let the sun set on your anger 27 or else you will

[*h*] Zc. 8:16. [*i*] Ps. 4:4 (LXX).

New English Bible

whole body depends. Bonded and knit together by every constituent joint, the whole frame grows through the due activity of each part, and builds itself up in love.

This then is my word to you, and I urge it upon you in the Lord's name. Give up living like pagans with their good-for-nothing notions. Their wits are beclouded, they are strangers to the life that is in God, because ignorance prevails among them and their minds have grown hard as stone. Dead to all feeling, they have abandoned themselves to vice, and stop at nothing to satisfy their foul desires. But that is not how you learned Christ. For were you not told of him, were you not as Christians taught the truth as it is in Jesus?—that, leaving your former way of life, you must lay aside that old human nature which, deluded by its lusts, is sinking towards death. You must be made new in mind and spirit, and put on the new nature of God's creating, which shows itself in the just and devout life called for by the truth.

Then throw off falsehood; speak the truth to each other, for all of us are the parts of one body.

If you are angry, do not let anger lead you into sin; do not let sunset find you still nursing it; leave no loop-hole for the devil.

King James Version

to the devil. 28 Let him that stole steal no more: but rather let him labour, working with *his* hands the thing which is good, that he may have to give to him that needeth. 29 Let no corrupt communication proceed out of your mouth, but that which is good to the use of edifying, that it may minister grace unto the hearers. 30And grieve not the Holy Spirit of God, whereby ye are sealed unto the day of redemption. 31 Let all bitterness, and wrath, and anger, and clamour, and evil speaking, be put away from you, with all malice: 32And be ye kind one to another, tenderhearted, forgiving one another, even as God for Christ's sake hath forgiven you.

5 Be ye therefore followers of God, as dear children; 2And walk in love, as Christ also hath loved us, and hath given himself for us an offering and a sacrifice to God for a sweet-smelling savour. 3 But fornication, and all uncleanness, or covetousness, let it not be once named among you, as becometh saints; 4 Nei-

Living Bible

28 If anyone is stealing he must stop it and begin using those hands of his for honest work so he can give to others in need. 29 Don't use bad language. Say only what is good and helpful to those you are talking to, and what will give them a blessing.

30 Don't cause the Holy Spirit sorrow by the way you live. Remember, he is the one who marks you to be present[c] on that day when salvation from sin will be complete.

31 Stop being mean, bad-tempered and angry. Quarreling, harsh words, and dislike of others should have no place in your lives. 32 Instead, be kind to each other, tenderhearted, forgiving one another, just as God has forgiven you because you belong to Christ.

5 Follow God's example in everything you do just as a much loved child imitates his father. 2 Be full of love for others, following the example of Christ who loved you and gave himself to God as a sacrifice to take away your sins. And God was pleased, for Christ's love for you was like sweet perfume to him.

3 Let there be no sex sin, impurity or greed among you. Let no one be able to accuse you of any such things. 4 Dirty stories, foul talk and

[c] Literally, "in whom you were sealed unto the day of redemption."

Today's English Version

give the Devil a chance. 28 The man who used to rob must stop robbing and start working, to earn an honest living for himself, and to be able to help the poor. 29 Do not use harmful words in talking. Use only helpful words, the kind that build up and provide what is needed, so that what you say will do good to those who hear you. 30And do not make God's Holy Spirit sad; for the Spirit is God's mark of ownership on you, a guarantee that the Day will come when God will set you free. 31 Get rid of all bitterness, passion, and anger. No more shouting or insults. No more hateful feelings of any sort. 32 Instead, be kind and tender-hearted to one another, and forgive one another, as God has forgiven you in Christ.

Living in the light

5 Since you are God's dear children, you must try to be like him. 2 Your life must be controlled by love, just as Christ loved us and gave his life for us, as a sweet-smelling offering and sacrifice that pleases God.

3 Since you are God's people, it is not right that any questions of immorality, or indecency, or greed should even be mentioned among you. 4 Nor is it fitting for you to use obscene, fool-

New International Version

devil a foothold. 28 He who has been stealing must steal no longer, but must work, doing something useful with his own hands, that he may have something to share with those in need.

29 Do not let any unwholesome talk come out of your mouths, but only what is helpful for building others up according to their needs, that it may benefit those who listen. 30And do not grieve the Holy Spirit of God, with whom you were sealed for the day of redemption. 31Get rid of all bitterness, rage and anger, brawling and slander, along with every form of malice. 32 Be kind and compassionate to one another, forgiving each other, just as in Christ God forgave you.

5 Be imitators of God, therefore, as dearly loved children 2 and live a life of love, just as Christ loved us and gave himself up for us as a fragrant offering and sacrifice to God.

3 But among you there must not be even a hint of sexual immorality, or of any kind of impurity, or of greed, because these are improper for God's holy people. 4 Nor should there

Phillips Modern English

4.28 *The new life means positive good*

The man who used to be a thief must give up stealing, and do an honest day's work with his own hands, so that he may be able to give to those in need.

Let there be no more foul language, but good words instead—words suitable for the occasion, which God can use to help other people. Never wound the Holy Spirit. He is, remember, the seal upon you of your eventual full redemption.

Let there be no more bitter resentment or anger, no more shouting or slander, and let there be no bad feeling of any kind among you. Be kind to each other, be compassionate. Be as ready to forgive others as God for Christ's sake has forgiven you.

So then you should try to become like God, for you are his children and he loves you. Live your lives in love—the same sort of love which Christ gave us and which he perfectly expressed when he gave himself up for us as an offering and a sacrifice well-pleasing to God. But as for sexual immorality in all its forms, and the itch to get your hands on what belongs to other people—don't even talk about such things; they are no fit subjects for Christians to talk about. The

Revised Standard Version

28 Let the thief no longer steal, but rather let him labor, doing honest work with his hands, so that he may be able to give to those in need. 29 Let no evil talk come out of your mouths, but only such as is good for edifying, as fits the occasion, that it may impart grace to those who hear. 30 And do not grieve the Holy Spirit of God, in whom you were sealed for the day of redemption. 31 Let all bitterness and wrath and anger and clamor and slander be put away from you, with all malice, 32 and be kind to one another, tenderhearted, forgiving one another, as God in Christ forgave you.

5 Therefore be imitators of God, as beloved children. 2 And walk in love, as Christ loved us and gave himself up for us, a fragrant offering and sacrifice to God.

3 But fornication and all impurity or covetousness must not even be named among you, as is fitting among saints. 4 Let there be no filthiness,

Jerusalem Bible

give the devil a foothold. 28 Anyone who was a thief must stop stealing; he should try to find some useful manual work instead, and be able to do some good by helping others that are in need. 29 Guard against foul talk; let your words be for the improvement of others, as occasion offers, and do good to your listeners, 30 otherwise you will only be grieving the Holy Spirit of God who has marked you with his seal for you to be set free when the day comes. 31 Never have grudges against others, or lose your temper, or raise your voice to anybody, or call each other names, or allow any sort of spitefulness. 32 Be friends with one another, and kind, forgiving each other as readily as God forgave you in Christ.

5 Try, then, to imitate God, as children of his that he loves, 2 and follow Christ by loving as he loved you, giving himself up in our place *as a fragrant offering and a sacrifice to God.*[j] 3 Among you there must be not even a mention of fornication or impurity in any of its forms, or promiscuity: this would hardly become the saints! 4 There must be no coarseness

[j] Ex. 29:18.

New English Bible

The thief must give up stealing, and instead work hard and honestly with his own hands, so that he may have something to share with the needy.

No bad language must pass your lips, but only what is good and helpful to the occasion, so that it brings a blessing to those who hear it. And do not grieve the Holy Spirit of God, for that Spirit is the seal with which you were marked for the day of our final liberation. Have done with spite and passion, all angry shouting and cursing, and bad feeling of every kind.

Be generous to one another, tender-hearted, forgiving one another as God in Christ forgave you.

5 In a word, as God's dear children, try to be like him, and live in love as Christ loved you, and gave himself up on your behalf as an offering and sacrifice whose fragrance is pleasing to God.

Fornication and indecency of any kind, or ruthless greed, must not be so much as mentioned among you, as befits the people of God. No coarse, stupid, or flippant talk; these things

King James Version

ther filthiness, nor foolish talking, nor jesting, which are not convenient: but rather giving of thanks. 5 For this ye know, that no whoremonger, nor unclean person, nor covetous man, who is an idolater, hath any inheritance in the kingdom of Christ and of God. 6 Let no man deceive you with vain words: for because of these things cometh the wrath of God upon the children of disobedience. 7 Be not ye therefore partakers with them. 8 For ye were sometime darkness, but now *are ye* light in the Lord: walk as children of light; 9 (For the fruit of the Spirit *is* in all goodness and righteousness and truth;) 10 Proving what is acceptable unto the Lord. 11 And have no fellowship with the unfruitful works of darkness, but rather reprove *them.* 12 For it is a shame even to speak of those things which are done of them in secret. 13 But all things that are reproved are made manifest by the light: for whatsoever doth make manifest is light. 14 Wherefore he saith, Awake thou that sleepest, and arise from the dead, and Christ

Living Bible

coarse jokes—these are not for you. Instead, remind each other of God's goodness and be thankful.

5 You can be sure of this: The kingdom of Christ and of God will never belong to anyone who is impure or greedy, for a greedy person is really an idol worshiper—he loves and worships the good things of this life more than God. 6 Don't be fooled by those who try to excuse these sins, for the terrible wrath of God is upon all those who do them. 7 Don't even associate with such people. 8 For though once your heart was full of darkness, now it is full of light from the Lord, and your behavior should show it! 9 Because of this light within you, you should do only what is good and right and true.

10 Learn as you go along what pleases the Lord.[a] 11 Take no part in the worthless pleasures of evil and darkness, but instead, rebuke and expose them. 12 It would be shameful even to mention here those pleasures of darkness which the ungodly do. 13 But when you expose them, the light shines in upon their sin and shows it up, and when they see how wrong they really are, some of them may even become children of light! 14 That is why God says in the Scriptures, "Awake, O sleeper, and rise up from the dead; and Christ shall give you light."

[*a*] Or, "your lives should be an example."

Today's English Version

ish, or dirty words. Rather you should give thanks to God. 5 You may be sure of this: no man who is immoral, indecent, or greedy (for greediness is a form of idol worship) will ever receive a share in the Kingdom of Christ and of God.

6 Do not let anyone deceive you with foolish words; it is because of these very things that God's wrath will come upon those who do not obey him. 7 So have nothing at all to do with such people. 8 You yourselves used to be in the darkness, but since you have become the Lord's people you are in the light. So you must live like people who belong to the light. 9 For it is the light that brings a rich harvest of every kind of goodness, righteousness, and truth. 10 Try to learn what pleases the Lord. 11 Have nothing to do with the worthless things that people do, that belong to the darkness. Instead, bring them out to the light. 12 (It is really too shameful even to talk about the things they do in secret.) 13 And when all things are brought out to the light, then their true nature is clearly revealed; 14 for anything that is clearly revealed becomes light. That is why it is said,

"Wake up, sleeper,
and rise from the dead!
And Christ will shine on you."

New International Version

be obscenity, foolish talk or coarse joking, which are out of place, but rather thanksgiving. 5 For of this you can be sure: No immoral, impure, or greedy person—such a man is an idolater—has any inheritance in the kingdom of Christ and of God. 6 Let no one deceive you with empty words, for because of such things God's wrath comes on those who are disobedient. 7 Therefore do not be partners with them.

8 For you were once darkness, but now you are light in the Lord. Live as children of light 9 (for the fruit of the light consists in all goodness, righteousness and truth) 10 and find out what pleases the Lord. 11 Have nothing to do with the fruitless deeds of darkness, but rather expose them. 12 For it is shameful even to mention what is done in secret. 13 But everything exposed by the light becomes visible, 14 for it is light that makes everything visible. This is why it is said:

"Wake up, O sleeper,
rise from the dead,
and Christ will shine on you."

Phillips Modern English

key-note of your conversation should not be coarseness or silliness or flippancy—which are quite out of place, but a sense of all that we owe to God.

5.5 *Evil is as utterly different from good as light from darkness*

For of this you can be quite certain: that neither the immoral nor the dirty-minded nor the covetous man (whose greed makes him worship gain) has any inheritance in the kingdom of Christ and of God. Don't let anyone fool you with empty words. It is these very things which bring down the wrath of God upon the disobedient. Have nothing to do with men like that—once you were "darkness" but now as Christians you are "light". Live then as children of the light. The light produces in men all that is good and right and true. Let your lives by living proofs of the things which please God. Steer clear of the fruitless activities of darkness; let your lives expose their futility. (You know the sort of things I mean—to detail their secret doings is too shameful to mention.) For light is capable of showing up everything for what it really is. It is even possible for light to turn the thing it shines upon into light also. Thus it is said:

Awake thou that sleepest, and arise from the dead,
And Christ shall shine upon thee.

Revised Standard Version

nor silly talk, nor levity, which are not fitting;
but instead let there be thanksgiving. 5 Be sure
of this, that no fornicator or impure man, or one
who is covetous (that is, an idolater), has any
inheritance in the kingdom of Christ and of God.
6 Let no one deceive you with empty words, for
it is because of these things that the wrath of
God comes upon the sons of disobedience.
7 Therefore do not associate with them, 8 for
once you were darkness, but now you are light
in the Lord; walk as children of light 9 (for the
fruit of light is found in all that is good and
right and true), 10 and try to learn what is pleasing to the Lord. 11 Take no part in the unfruitful
works of darkness, but instead expose them.
12 For it is a shame even to speak of the things
that they do in secret; 13 but when anything is
exposed by the light it becomes visible, for anything that becomes visible is light. 14 Therefore
it is said,

"Awake, O sleeper, and arise from the dead,
and Christ shall give you light."

Jerusalem Bible

or salacious talk and jokes—all this is wrong
for you; raise your voices in thanksgiving instead. 5 For you can be quite certain that nobody
who actually indulges in fornication or impurity
or promiscuity—which is worshiping a false god
—can inherit anything of the kingdom of God.
6 Do not let anyone deceive you with empty
arguments: it is for this loose living that God's
anger comes down on those who rebel against
him. 7 Make sure that you are not included with
them. 8 You were darkness once, but now you
are light in the Lord; be like children of light,
9 for the effects of the light are seen in complete
goodness and right living and truth. 10 Try to
discover what the Lord wants of you, 11 having
nothing to do with the futile works of darkness
but exposing them by contrast. 12 The things
which are done in secret are things that people
are ashamed even to speak of; 13 but anything
exposed by the light will be illuminated 14 and
anything illuminated turns into light. That is
why it is said [k]:

Wake up from your sleep,
rise from the dead,
and Christ will shine on you.

[k] Presumably a quotation from a Christian hymn.

New English Bible

are out of place; you should rather be thanking God. For be very sure of this: no one given to fornication or indecency, or the greed which makes an idol of gain, has any share in the kingdom of Christ and of God.

Let no one deceive you with shallow arguments; it is for all these things that God's dreadful judgement is coming upon his rebel subjects. Have no part or lot with them. For though you were once all darkness, now as Christians you are light. Live like men who are at home in daylight, for where light is, there all goodness springs up, all justice and truth. Try to find out what would please the Lord; take no part in the barren deeds of darkness, but show them up for what they are. The things they do in secret it would be shameful even to mention. But everything, when once the light has shown it up, is illumined, and everything thus illumined is all light. And so the hymn says:

'Awake, sleeper,
rise from the dead,
and Christ will shine upon you.'

King James Version

shall give thee light. 15 See then that ye walk
circumspectly, not as fools, but as wise, 16 Redeeming the time, because the days are evil.
17 Wherefore be ye not unwise, but understanding what the will of the Lord *is.* 18 And be not
drunk with wine, wherein is excess; but be filled
with the Spirit; 19 Speaking to yourselves in
psalms and hymns and spiritual songs, singing
and making melody in your heart to the Lord;
20 Giving thanks always for all things unto God
and the Father in the name of our Lord Jesus
Christ; 21 Submitting yourselves one to another
in the fear of God. 22 Wives, submit yourselves
unto your own husbands, as unto the Lord.
23 For the husband is the head of the wife, even
as Christ is the head of the church: and he is
the Saviour of the body. 24 Therefore as the
church is subject unto Christ, so *let* the wives
be to their own husbands in every thing. 25 Husbands, love your wives, even as Christ also loved

Living Bible

15, 16 So be careful how you act; these are
difficult days. Don't be fools; be wise: make the
most of every opportunity you have for doing
good. 17 Don't act thoughtlessly, but try to find
out and do whatever the Lord wants you to.
18 Don't drink too much wine, for many evils lie
along that path; be filled instead with the Holy
Spirit, and controlled by him.
19 Talk with each other much about the Lord,
quoting psalms and hymns and singing sacred
songs, making music in your hearts to the Lord.
20 Always give thanks for everything to our God
and Father in the name of our Lord Jesus Christ.
21 Honor Christ by submitting to each other.
22 You wives must submit to your husbands'
leadership in the same way you submit to the
Lord. 23 For a husband is in charge of his wife
in the same way Christ is in charge of his body
the church. (He gave his very life to take care
of it and be its Savior!) 24 So you wives must
willingly obey your husbands in everything, just
as the church obeys Christ.
25 And you husbands, show the same kind of
love to your wives as Christ showed to the

Today's English Version

15 So pay close attention to how you live.
Don't live like ignorant men, but like wise men.
16 Make good use of every opportunity you get,
because these are bad days. 17 Don't be fools,
then, but try to find out what the Lord wants
you to do.
18 Do not get drunk with wine, which will
only ruin you; instead, be filled with the Spirit.
19 Speak to one another in the words of psalms,
hymns, and sacred songs; sing hymns and psalms
to the Lord, with praise in your hearts. 20 Always give thanks for everything to God the
Father, in the name of our Lord Jesus Christ.

Wives and husbands

21 Submit yourselves to one another, because
of your reverence for Christ.
22 Wives, submit yourselves to your husbands, as to the Lord. 23 For a husband has
authority over his wife in the same way that
Christ has authority over the church; and Christ
is himself the Savior of the church, his body.
24 And so wives must submit themselves completely to their husbands, in the same way that
the church submits itself to Christ.
25 Husbands, love your wives in the same
way that Christ loved the church and gave his

New International Version

15 Be very careful, then, how you live—not
as unwise but as wise, 16 making the most of
every opportunity, because the days are evil.
17 Therefore do not be foolish, but understand
what the Lord's will is. 18 Do not get drunk on
wine, which leads to debauchery. Instead, be
filled with the Spirit. 19 Speak to one another
with psalms, hymns and spiritual songs. Sing
and make music in your heart to the Lord,
20 always giving thanks to God the Father for
everything, in the name of our Lord Jesus Christ.

Wives and husbands

21 Submit to one another out of reverence
for Christ.
22 Wives, submit to your husbands as to the
Lord. 23 For the husband is the head of the
wife as Christ is the head of the church, his
body, of which he is the Savior. 24 Now as the
church submits to Christ, so also wives should
submit to their husbands in everything.
25 Husbands, love your wives, just as Christ
loved the church and gave himself up for her

Phillips Modern English

5.15 You know the truth—let your life show it!

Live life, then, with a due sense of responsibility, not as men who do not know the meaning of life but as *those who do.* Make the best use of your time, despite all the evils of these days. Don't be vague but grasp firmly what you know to be the will of the Lord. Don't get your stimulus from wine (for there is always the danger of excessive drinking), but let the Spirit stimulate your souls. Sing among yourselves psalms and hymns and spiritual songs, your voices making music in your hearts for the ears of the Lord! Thank God the Father at all times for everything, in the name of our Lord Jesus Christ. And "fit in with" each other, because of your common reverence for Christ.

5.22 Christ and the Church the pattern relationship for husband and wife

You wives must learn to adapt yourselves to your husbands, as you submit yourselves to the Lord, for the husband is the "head" of the wife in the same way that Christ is head of the Church and saviour of the Body. The willing subjection of the Church to Christ should be reproduced in the submission of wives to their husbands in everything. The husband must give his wife the same sort of love that Christ gave to the Church, when he sacrificed himself for

Revised Standard Version

15 Look carefully then how you walk, not as
unwise men but as wise, 16 making the most of
the time, because the days are evil. 17 Therefore
do not be foolish, but understand what the will
of the Lord is. 18 And do not get drunk with
wine, for that is debauchery; but be filled with
the Spirit, 19 addressing one another in psalms
and hymns and spiritual songs, singing and
making melody to the Lord with all your heart,
20 always and for everything giving thanks in
the name of our Lord Jesus Christ to God the
Father.
21 Be subject to one another out of reverence
for Christ. 22 Wives, be subject to your husbands,
as to the Lord. 23 For the husband is the head
of the wife as Christ is the head of the church, his
body, and is himself its Savior. 24 As the church
is subject to Christ, so let wives also be subject
in everything to their husbands. 25 Husbands,
love your wives, as Christ loved the church and

Jerusalem Bible

15 So be very careful about the sort of lives you
lead, like intelligent and not like senseless people.
16 This may be a wicked age, but your lives
should redeem it. 17 And do not be thoughtless
but recognize what is the will of the Lord. 18 Do
not drug yourselves with wine; this is simply
dissipation; be filled with the Spirit. 19 Sing the
words and tunes of the psalms and hymns when
you are together, and go on singing and chanting to the Lord in your hearts,
20 so that always
and everywhere you are giving thanks to God
who is our Father in the name of our Lord
Jesus Christ.

The morals of the home

21 Give way to one another in obedience to
Christ. 22 Wives should regard their husbands
as they regard the Lord, 23 since as Christ is
head of the Church and saves the whole body,
so is a husband the head of his wife; 24 and as
the Church submits to Christ, so should wives
to their husbands, in everything. 25 Husbands
should love their wives just as Christ loved the

New English Bible

Be most careful then how you conduct yourselves: like sensible men, not like simpletons. Use the present opportunity to the full, for these are evil days. So do not be fools, but try to understand what the will of the Lord is. Do not give way to drunkenness and the dissipation that goes with it, but let the Holy Spirit fill you: speak to one another in psalms, hymns, and [a] songs; sing and make music in your hearts to the Lord; and in the name of our Lord Jesus Christ give thanks every day for everything to our God and Father.

Be subject to one another out of reverence for Christ.

Wives, be subject to your husbands as to the Lord; for the man is the head of the woman, just as Christ also is the head of the church. Christ is, indeed, the Saviour of the body; but just as the church is subject to Christ, so must women be to their husbands in everything.

Husbands, love your wives, as Christ also

[a] *Some witnesses insert* spiritual, *as in Colossians 3. 16.*

King James Version

the church, and gave himself for it; 26 That he
might sanctify and cleanse it with the washing
of water by the word, 27 That he might present
it to himself a glorious church, not having spot,
or wrinkle, or any such thing; but that it should
be holy and without blemish. 28 So ought men
to love their wives as their own bodies. He that
loveth his wife loveth himself. 29 For no man
ever yet hated his own flesh; but nourisheth and
cherisheth it, even as the Lord the church:
30 For we are members of his body, of his flesh,
and of his bones. 31 For this cause shall a man
leave his father and mother, and shall be joined
unto his wife, and they two shall be one flesh.
32 This is a great mystery: but I speak concerning Christ and the church. 33 Nevertheless, let
every one of you in particular so love his wife
even as himself; and the wife *see* that she reverence *her* husband.

Living Bible

church when he died for her, 26 to make her
holy and clean, washed by baptism[b] and God's
Word; 27 so that he could give her to himself as
a glorious church without a single spot or wrinkle
or any other blemish, being holy and without a
single fault. 28 That is how husbands should
treat their wives, loving them as parts of themselves. For since a man and his wife are now one,
a man is really doing himself a favor and loving himself when he loves his wife! 29, 30 No
one hates his own body but lovingly cares for it,
just as Christ cares for his body the church, of
which we are parts.

31 (That the husband and wife are one body
is proved by the Scripture which says, "A man
must leave his father and mother when he marries, so that he can be perfectly joined to his
wife, and the two shall be one.") 32 I know this
is hard to understand, but it is an illustration of
the way we are parts of the body of Christ.

33 So again I say, a man must love his wife
as a part of himself; and the wife must see to it
that she deeply respects her husband—obeying,
praising and honoring him.

[*b*] Literally, "having cleansed it by washing of water with the word."

Today's English Version

life for it. 26 He did this to dedicate the church
to God, by his word, after making it clean by
the washing in water, 27 in order to present the
church to himself, in all its beauty, pure and
faultless, without spot or wrinkle, or any other
imperfection. 28 Men ought to love their wives
just as they love their own bodies. A man who
loves his wife loves himself. 29 (No one ever
hates his own body. Instead, he feeds it and
takes care of it, just as Christ does the church;
30 for we are members of his body.) 31 As the
scripture says, "For this reason, a man will leave
his father and mother, and unite with his wife,
and the two will become one." 32 There is a
great truth revealed in this scripture, and I understand it applies to Christ and the church.
33 But it also applies to you: every husband
must love his wife as himself, and every wife
must respect her husband.

New International Version

26 to make her holy, cleansing her by the washing with water through the word, 27 and to present her to himself as a radiant church, without
stain or wrinkle or any other blemish, but holy
and blameless. 28 In this same way, husbands
ought to love their wives as their own bodies.
He who loves his wife loves himself. 29 After all,
no one ever hated his own body, but he feeds
and cares for it, just as Christ does the church—
30 for we are members of his body. 31 "For this
reason a man will leave his father and mother
and will be united to his wife, and the two
will become one flesh."[h] 32 This is a profound
mystery—but I am talking about Christ and the
church. 33 However, each one of you also must
love his wife as he loves himself, and the wife
must respect her husband.

[*h*] Gen. 2:24.

Phillips Modern English

her. Christ gave himself to make her holy, having cleansed her through the baptism of his Word—to make her an altogether glorious Church in his eyes. She is to be free from spots, wrinkles or any other disfigurement—a Church holy and perfect.

So men ought to give their wives the love they naturally have for their own bodies. The love a man gives his wife is the extending of his love for himself to enfold her. Nobody ever hated his own body; he feeds it and looks after it. And that is what Christ does for his Body, the Church. And we are all members of that Body.

For this cause shall a man leave his father and mother,
And shall cleave to his wife; and the twain shall become one flesh.

The marriage relationship is a great mystery, but I see it as a symbol of the marriage of Christ and his Church.

In practice what I have said amounts to this: let every one of you who is a husband love his wife as he loves himself, and let every wife respect her husband.

Revised Standard Version

gave himself up for her, 26 that he might sanctify
her, having cleansed her by the washing of water
with the word, 27 that he might present the
church to himself in splendor, without spot or
wrinkle or any such thing, that she might be
holy and without blemish. 28 Even so husbands
should love their wives as their own bodies. He
who loves his wife loves himself. 29 For no man
ever hates his own flesh, but nourishes and cher-
ishes it, as Christ does the church, 30 because
we are members of his body. 31 "For this reason
a man shall leave his father and mother and be
joined to his wife, and the two shall become one
flesh." 32 This mystery is a profound one, and
I am saying that it refers to Christ and the
church; 33 however, let each one of you love his
wife as himself, and let the wife see that she respects her husband.

Jerusalem Bible

Church and sacrificed himself for her 26 to make
her holy. He made her clean by washing her
in water with a form of words, 27 so that when
he took her to himself she would be glorious,
with no speck or wrinkle or anything like that,
but holy and faultless. 28 In the same way, husbands must love their wives as they love their
own bodies; for a man to love his wife is for
him to love himself. 29 A man never hates his
own body, but he feeds it and looks after it; and
that is the way Christ treats the Church, 30 because it is his body—and we are its living parts.
31 *For this reason, a man must leave his father
and mother and be joined to his wife, and the
two will become one body.*[l] 32 This mystery has
many implications; but I am saying it applies to
Christ and the Church. 33 To sum up; you too,
each one of you, must love his wife as he loves
himself; and let every wife respect her husband.

New English Bible

loved the church and gave himself up for it, to consecrate it, cleansing it by water and word, so that he might present the church to himself all glorious, with no stain or wrinkle or anything of the sort, but holy and without blemish. In the same way men also are bound to love their wives, as they love their own bodies. In loving his wife a man loves himself. For no one ever hated his own body: on the contrary, he provides and cares for it; and that is how Christ treats the church, because it is his body, of which we are living parts. Thus it is that (in the words of Scripture) 'a man shall leave his father and mother and shall be joined to his wife, and the two shall become one flesh'. It is a great truth that is hidden here. I for my part refer it to Christ and to the church, but it applies also individually: each of you must love his wife as his very self; and the woman must see to it that she pays her husband all respect.

[l] Gn. 2:24.

King James Version

6 Children, obey your parents in the Lord: for this is right. 2 Honour thy father and mother; which is the first commandment with promise; 3 That it may be well with thee, and thou mayest live long on the earth. 4 And, ye fathers, provoke not your children to wrath: but bring them up in the nurture and admonition of the Lord. 5 Servants, be obedient to them that are *your* masters according to the flesh, with fear and trembling, in singleness of your heart, as unto Christ; 6 Not with eyeservice, as menpleasers; but as the servants of Christ, doing the will of God from the heart; 7 With good will doing service, as to the Lord, and not to men: 8 Knowing that whatsoever good thing any man doeth, the same shall he receive of the Lord, whether *he be* bond or free. 9 And, ye masters, do the same things unto them, forbearing threatening: knowing that your Master also is in heaven; neither is there respect of persons with

Living Bible

6 Children, obey your parents; this is the right thing to do because God has placed them in authority over you. 2 Honor your father and mother. This is the first of God's Ten Commandments that ends with a promise. 3 And this is the promise: that if you honor your father and mother, yours will be a long life, full of blessing.

4 And now a word to you parents. Don't keep on scolding and nagging your children, making them angry and resentful. Rather, bring them up with the loving discipline the Lord himself approves, with suggestions and godly advice.

5 Slaves, obey your masters; be eager to give them your very best. Serve them as you would Christ. 6, 7 Don't work hard only when your master is watching and then shirk when he isn't looking; work hard and with gladness all the time, as though working for Christ, doing the will of God with all your hearts. 8 Remember, the Lord will pay you for each good thing you do, whether you are slave or free.

9 And you slave owners must treat your slaves right, just as I have told them to treat you. Don't keep threatening them; remember, you yourselves are slaves to Christ; you have the same Master they do, and he has no favorites.

Today's English Version

Children and parents

6 Children, it is your Christian duty to obey your parents, for this is the right thing to do. 2 "Honor your father and mother" is the first commandment that has a promise added: 3 "so that all may be well with you, and you may live a long time in the land."

4 Parents, do not treat your children in such a way as to make them angry. Instead, raise them with Christian discipline and instruction.

Slaves and masters

5 Slaves, obey your human masters, with fear and trembling; and do it with a sincere heart, as though you were serving Christ. 6 Do this not only when they are watching you, to gain their approval; but with all your heart do what God wants, as slaves of Christ. 7 Do your work as slaves cheerfully, then, as though you served the Lord, and not merely men. 8 Remember that the Lord will reward every man, whether slave or free, for the good work he does.

9 Masters, behave in the same way toward your slaves; and stop using threats. Remember that you and your slaves belong to the same Master in heaven, who judges everyone by the same standard.

New International Version

Children and parents

6 Children, obey your parents in the Lord, for this is right. 2 "Honor your father and mother"—which is the first commandment with a promise—3 "that it may go well with you and that you may enjoy long life on the earth." [i]

4 Fathers, do not exasperate your children; instead, bring them up in the training and instruction of the Lord.

Slaves and masters

5 Slaves, obey your earthly masters with respect and fear, and with sincerity of heart, just as you would obey Christ. 6 Obey them not only to win their favor when their eye is on you, but like slaves of Christ, doing the will of God from your heart. 7 Serve wholeheartedly, as if you were serving the Lord, not men, 8 because you know that the Lord will reward everyone for whatever good he does, whether he is slave or free.

9 And masters, treat your slaves in the same way. Do not threaten them, since you know that he who is both their Master and yours is in heaven, and there is no favoritism with him.

[*i*] Deut. 5:16.

Phillips Modern English

6.1 Children and parents: servants and masters

Children, the right thing for you to do is to obey your parents as those whom the Lord has set over you. The first commandment to contain a promise was:

Honour thy father and thy mother
That it may be well with thee, and that thou mayest live long on the earth.

Fathers, don't over-correct your children or make it difficult for them to obey the commandment. Bring them up with Christian teaching in Christian discipline.

Slaves, obey your human masters loyally with a proper sense of respect and responsibility, as service rendered to Christ; not only working when you are being watched, as if looking for human approval, but as servants of Christ conscientiously doing what you believe to be the will of God. Work cheerfully as if it were for the Lord and not for a man. You may be sure that the Lord will reward each man for good work irrespectively of whether he be slave or free. And as for you employers, act towards those who serve you in the same way. Do not threaten them, but remember that both you and they have the same Lord in Heaven, who makes no distinction between master and man.

Revised Standard Version

6 Children, obey your parents in the Lord,
for this is right. 2 "Honor your father and
mother" (this is the first commandment with a
promise), 3 "that it may be well with you and
that you may live long on the earth." 4 Fathers,
do not provoke your children to anger, but bring
them up in the discipline and instruction of the
Lord.
5 Slaves, be obedient to those who are your
earthly masters, with fear and trembling, in singleness of heart, as to Christ; 6 not in the way of
eyeservice, as men-pleasers, but as servants[f] of
Christ, doing the will of God from the heart,
7 rendering service with a good will as to the
Lord and not to men, 8 knowing that whatever
good any one does, he will receive the same
again from the Lord, whether he is a slave or
free. 9 Masters, do the same to them, and forbear threatening, knowing that he who is both
their Master and yours is in heaven, and that
there is no partiality with him.

[f] Or *slaves*.

Jerusalem Bible

6 Children, be obedient to your parents in
the Lord—that is your duty. 2 The first
commandment that has a promise attached to it
is: *Honor your father and mother,* 3 and the
promise is: *and you will prosper and have a
long life in the land.*[m] 4 And parents, never drive
your children to resentment but in bringing them
up correct them and guide them as the Lord
does.
5 Slaves, be obedient to the men who are
called your masters in this world, with deep
respect and sincere loyalty, as you are obedient
to Christ: 6 not only when you are under their
eye, as if you had only to please men, but because you are slaves of Christ and wholeheartedly do the will of God. 7 Work hard and
willingly, but do it for the sake of the Lord
and not for the sake of men. 8 You can be sure
that everyone, whether a slave or a free man,
will be properly rewarded by the Lord for whatever work he has done well. 9 And those of you
who are employers, treat your slaves in the same
spirit; do without threats, remembering that they
and you have the same Master in heaven and
he is not impressed by one person more than
by another.

[m] Ex. 20:12.

New English Bible

6 Children, obey your parents, for it is right that you should. 'Honour your father and mother' is the first commandment with a promise attached, in the words: 'that it may be well with you and that you may live long in the land'.

You fathers, again, must not goad your children to resentment, but give them the instruction, and the correction, which belong to a Christian upbringing.

Slaves, obey your earthly masters with fear and trembling, single-mindedly, as serving Christ. Do not offer merely the outward show of service, to curry favour with men, but, as slaves of Christ, do whole-heartedly the will of God. Give the cheerful service of those who serve the Lord, not men. For you know that whatever good each man may do, slave or free, will be repaid him by the Lord.

You masters, also, must do the same by them. Give up using threats; remember you both have the same Master in heaven, and he has no favourites.

King James Version

him. 10 Finally, my brethren, be strong in the Lord, and in the power of his might. 11 Put on the whole armour of God, that ye may be able to stand against the wiles of the devil. 12 For we wrestle not against flesh and blood, but against principalities, against powers, against the rulers of the darkness of this world, against spiritual wickedness in high *places.* 13 Wherefore take unto you the whole armour of God, that ye may be able to withstand in the evil day, and having done all, to stand. 14 Stand therefore, having your loins girt about with truth, and having on the breastplate of righteousness; 15 And your feet shod with the preparation of the gospel of peace; 16 Above all, taking the shield of faith, wherewith ye shall be able to quench all the fiery darts of the wicked. 17 And take the helmet of salvation, and the sword of the Spirit, which is the word of God: 18 Praying always with all prayer and supplication in the Spirit, and watching thereunto with all perseverance and supplication for all saints; 19 And for me, that utterance may be given unto me, that I may open my mouth boldly, to make known the mystery of the gospel, 20 For which I am an ambassador in bonds; that therein I may speak boldly,

Living Bible

10 Last of all I want to remind you that your strength must come from the Lord's mighty power within you. 11 Put on all of God's armor so that you will be able to stand safe against all strategies and tricks of Satan. 12 For we are not fighting against people made of flesh and blood, but against persons without bodies—the evil rulers of the unseen world, those mighty satanic beings and great evil princes of darkness who rule this world; and against huge numbers of wicked spirits in the spirit world.

13 So use every piece of God's armor to resist the enemy whenever he attacks, and when it is all over, you will still be standing up. ,

14 But to do this, you will need the strong belt of truth and the breastplate of God's approval. 15 Wear shoes that are able to speed you on as you preach the Good News of peace with God. 16 In every battle you will need faith as your shield to stop the fiery arrows aimed at you by Satan. 17 And you will need the helmet of salvation and the sword of the Spirit—which is the Word of God.

18 Pray all the time. Ask God for anything in line with the Holy Spirit's wishes. Plead with him, reminding him of your needs, and keep praying earnestly for all Christians everywhere. 19 Pray for me, too, and ask God to give me the right words as I boldly tell others about the Lord, and as I explain to them that his salvation is for the Gentiles too. 20 I am in chains now for preaching this message from God. But pray that I will keep on speaking out boldly for him even here in prison, as I should.

Today's English Version

The whole armor of God

10 Finally, build up your strength in union with the Lord, and by means of his mighty power. 11 Put on all the armor that God gives you, so that you will stand up against the Devil's evil tricks. 12 For we are not fighting against human beings, but against the wicked spiritual forces in the heavenly world, the rulers, authorities, and cosmic powers of this dark age. 13 So take up God's armor now! Then when the evil day comes, you will be able to resist the enemy's attacks, and after fighting to the end, you will still hold your ground.

14 So stand ready: have truth for a belt tight around your waist; put on righteousness for your breastplate, 15 and the readiness to announce the Good News of peace as shoes for your feet. 16 At all times carry faith as a shield; with it you will be able to put out all the burning arrows shot by the Evil One. 17 And accept salvation for a helmet, and the word of God as the sword that the Spirit gives you. 18 Do all this in prayer, asking for God's help. Pray on every occasion, as the Spirit leads. For this reason keep alert and never give up; pray always for all God's people. 19 And pray also for me, that God will give me a message, when I am ready to speak, that I may speak boldly and make known the gospel's secret. 20 For the sake of this gospel I am an ambassador, though now I am in prison. Pray that I may be bold in speaking of it, as I should.

New International Version

The armor of God

10 Finally, be strong in the Lord and in his mighty power. 11 Put on the full armor of God so that you can take your stand against the devil's schemes. 12 For our struggle is not against flesh and blood, but against the rulers, against the authorities, against the powers of this dark world and against the spiritual forces of evil in the heavenly realms. 13 Therefore put on the full armor of God, so that when the day of evil comes, you may be able to stand your ground, and after you have done everything, to stand. 14 Stand firm then, with the belt of truth buckled around your waist, with the breastplate of righteousness in place, 15 and with your feet fitted with the gospel of peace as a firm footing. 16 In addition to all this, take up the shield of faith, with which you can extinguish all the flaming arrows of the evil one. 17 Take the helmet of salvation and the sword of the Spirit, which is the word of God. 18 And pray in the Spirit on all occasions with all kinds of prayers and requests. With this in mind, be alert and always keep on praying for all the saints.

19 Pray also for me, that whenever I open my mouth, words may be given me so that I will fearlessly make known the mystery of the gospel, 20 for which I am an ambassador in chains. Pray that I may declare it fearlessly, as I should.

Phillips Modern English

6.10 Be forewarned and forearmed in your spiritual conflict

In conclusion be strong—not in yourselves but in the Lord, in the power of his boundless strength. Put on God's complete armour so that you can successfully resist all the devil's craftiness. For our fight is not against any physical enemy: it is against organisations and powers that are spiritual. We are up against the unseen power that controls this dark world, and spiritual agents from the very headquarters of evil. Therefore you must wear the whole armour of God that you may be able to resist evil in its day of power, and that even when you have fought to a standstill you may still stand your ground. Take your stand then with truth as your belt, integrity your breastplate, the gospel of peace firmly on your feet, salvation as your helmet and in your hand the sword of the Spirit, the Word of God. Above all be sure you take faith as your shield, for it can quench every burning missile the enemy hurls at you. In all your petitions pray at all times with every kind of spiritual prayer, keeping alert and persistent as you pray for all Christ's men and women. And pray for me, too, that I may be able to speak the message here boldly, to make known the secret of that gospel for which I am an ambassador in chains. Pray that I may speak out about it as is my plain and obvious duty.

Revised Standard Version

10 Finally, be strong in the Lord and in the
strength of his might. 11 Put on the whole armor
of God, that you may be able to stand against
the wiles of the devil. 12 For we are not contending against flesh and blood, but against the principalities, against the powers, against the world
rulers of this present darkness, against the spiritual hosts of wickedness in the heavenly places.
13 Therefore take the whole armor of God, that
you may be able to withstand in the evil day, and
having done all, to stand. 14 Stand therefore, having girded your loins with truth, and having put
on the breastplate of righteousness, 15 and having shod your feet with the equipment of the
gospel of peace; 16 besides all these, taking the
shield of faith, with which you can quench all
the flaming darts of the evil one. 17 And take the
helmet of salvation, and the sword of the Spirit,
which is the word of God. 18 Pray at all times
in the Spirit, with all prayer and supplication.
To that end keep alert with all perseverance,
making supplication for all the saints, 19 and also
for me, that utterance may be given me in opening my mouth boldly to proclaim the mystery of
the gospel, 20 for which I am an ambassador in
chains; that I may declare it boldly, as I ought
to speak.

Jerusalem Bible

The spiritual war

10 Finally, grow strong in the Lord, with the
strength of his power. 11 Put God's armor on so
as to be able to resist the devil's tactics. 12 For
it is not against human enemies that we have
to struggle, but against the Sovereignties and
the Powers who originate the darkness in this
world, the spiritual army of evil in the heavens.
13 That is why you must rely on God's armor,
or you will not be able to put up any resistance
when the worst happens, or have enough resources to hold your ground.
14 So stand your ground, with *truth buckled
around your waist,* and *integrity for a breastplate,*[n] 15 wearing for shoes on your feet *the
eagerness to spread the gospel of peace*[o] 16 and
always carrying the shield of faith so that you
can use it to put out the burning arrows of the
evil one. 17 And then you must accept *salvation
from God to be your helmet* and receive the
word of God from the Spirit to use as a sword.
18 Pray all the time, asking for what you
need, praying in the Spirit on every possible
occasion. Never get tired of staying awake to
pray for all the saints; 19 and pray for me to be
given an opportunity to open my mouth and
speak without fear and give out the mystery of
the gospel 20 of which I am an ambassador in
chains; pray that in proclaiming it I may speak
as boldly as I ought to.

[*n*] Is. 59:17. [*o*] Is. 40:9.

New English Bible

Finally then, find your strength in the Lord, in his mighty power. Put on all the armour which God provides, so that you may be able to stand firm against the devices of the devil. For our fight is not against human foes, but against cosmic powers, against the authorities and potentates of this dark world, against the superhuman forces of evil in the heavens. Therefore, take up God's armour; then you will be able to stand your ground when things are at their worst, to complete every task and still to stand. Stand firm, I say. Fasten on the belt of truth; for coat of mail put on integrity; let the shoes on your feet be the gospel of peace, to give you firm footing; and, with all these, take up the great shield of faith, with which you will be able to quench all the flaming arrows of the evil one. Take salvation for helmet; for sword, take that which the Spirit gives you—the words that come from God. Give yourselves wholly to prayer and entreaty; pray on every occasion in the power of the Spirit. To this end keep watch and persevere, always interceding for all God's people; and pray for me, that I may be granted the right words when I open my mouth, and may boldly and freely make known his hidden purpose, for which I am an ambassador—in chains. Pray that I may speak of it boldly, as it is my duty to speak.

King James Version

as I ought to speak. 21 But that ye also may
know my affairs, *and* how I do, Tychicus, a beloved brother and faithful minister in the Lord,
shall make known to you all things: 22 Whom
I have sent unto you for the same purpose, that
ye might know our affairs, and *that* he might
comfort your hearts. 23 Peace *be* to the brethren,
and love with faith, from God the Father and
the Lord Jesus Christ. 24 Grace *be* with all them
that love our Lord Jesus Christ in sincerity.
Amen.

Written from Rome unto the Ephesians by Tychicus.

Living Bible

21 Tychicus, who is a much loved brother and
faithful helper in the Lord's work, will tell you
all about how I am getting along. 22 I am sending him to you for just this purpose, to let you
know how we are and be encouraged by his
report.

23 May God give peace to you, my Christian
brothers, and love, with faith from God the
Father and the Lord Jesus Christ. 24 May God's
grace and blessing be upon all who sincerely love
our Lord Jesus Christ.

Sincerely,
Paul

Today's English Version

Final greetings

21 Tychicus, our dear brother and faithful
servant in the Lord's work, will give you all the
news about me, so that you may know how I am
getting along. 22 That is why I am sending him
to you—to tell you how all of us are getting
along, and so bring courage to your hearts.

23 May God the Father and the Lord Jesus
Christ give peace and love to all the brothers,
with faith. 24 May God's grace be with all those
who love our Lord Jesus Christ with undying
love.

New International Version

Final greetings

21 Tychicus, the dear brother and faithful
servant in the Lord, will tell you everything, so
that you also may know how I am and what I
am doing. 22 I am sending him to you for this
very purpose, that you may know how we are,
and that he may encourage you.

23 Peace to the brothers, and love with faith
from God the Father and the Lord Jesus Christ.
24 Grace to all who love our Lord Jesus Christ
with an undying love.

Phillips Modern English

Tychicus, beloved brother and faithful Christian minister, will tell you personally about my affairs and how I am getting on. I am sending him to you bringing this letter for that purpose, so that you will know exactly how we are and may take fresh heart.

Peace be to all Christian brothers, and love with faith from God the Father and the Lord Jesus Christ!

Grace be with all those who love our Lord Jesus Christ with unfailing love.

Revised Standard Version

21 Now that you also may know how I am and what I am doing, Tychicus the beloved brother and faithful minister in the Lord will tell you everything. 22 I have sent him to you for this very purpose, that you may know how we are, and that he may encourage your hearts.
23 Peace be to the brethren, and love with faith, from God the Father and the Lord Jesus Christ. 24 Grace be with all who love our Lord Jesus Christ with love undying.

Jerusalem Bible

Personal news and final salutation

21 I should like you to know, as well, what is happening to me and what I am doing; my dear brother Tychicus, my loyal helper in the Lord, will tell you everything. 22 I am sending him to you precisely for this purpose, to give you news about us and reassure you.
23 May God the Father and the Lord Jesus Christ grant peace, love and faith to all the brothers. 24 May grace and eternal life be with all who love our Lord Jesus Christ.

New English Bible

You will want to know about my affairs, and how I am; Tychicus will give you all the news. He is our dear brother and trustworthy helper in the Lord's work. I am sending him to you on purpose to let you know all about us, and to put fresh heart into you.

Peace to the brotherhood and love, with faith, from God the Father and the Lord Jesus Christ. God's grace be with all who love our Lord Jesus Christ, grace and immortality.[a]

[*a*] *Or* who love . . . Christ with love imperishable.

King James Version

THE EPISTLE OF PAUL THE APOSTLE TO THE PHILIPPIANS

1 Paul and Timotheus, the servants of Jesus Christ, to all the saints in Christ Jesus which are at Philippi, with the bishops and deacons:
2 Grace *be* unto you, and peace, from God our

Living Bible

PHILIPPIANS

1 *From:* Paul and Timothy, slaves of Jesus Christ.
To: The pastors and deacons and all the Christians in the city of Philippi.
2 May God bless you all. Yes, I pray that God our Father and the Lord Jesus Christ will give each of you his fullest blessings, and his peace

Today's English Version

PAUL'S LETTER TO THE PHILIPPIANS

1 From Paul and Timothy, servants of Christ Jesus—
To all God's people living in Philippi who are in union with Christ Jesus, and to the church leaders and helpers:
2 May God our Father and the Lord Jesus Christ give you grace and peace.

New International Version

PHILIPPIANS

1 Paul and Timothy, servants of Christ Jesus,
To all the saints in Christ Jesus at Philippi, together with the overseers[a] and deacons:
2 Grace and peace to you from God our Father and the Lord Jesus Christ.

[a] Or *bishops*.

Phillips Modern English

THE LETTER
TO THE CHRISTIANS AT

PHILIPPI

Paul and Timothy, servants of Jesus Christ, to all true Christians at Philippi and to their bishops and deacons, grace and peace from God our Father and Jesus Christ the Lord!

Revised Standard Version

THE
LETTER OF PAUL TO THE

PHILIPPIANS

1 Paul and Timothy, servants[a] of Christ Jesus,
To all the saints in Christ Jesus who are at
Philippi, with the bishops[b] and deacons:
2 Grace to you and peace from God our
Father and the Lord Jesus Christ.

[a] Or *slaves*. [b] Or *overseers*.

Jerusalem Bible

THE LETTER OF PAUL
TO THE CHURCH
AT PHILIPPI

PHILIPPIANS

Address

1 From Paul and Timothy, servants of Christ
Jesus, to all the saints in Christ Jesus, together with their presiding elders and deacons.
2 We wish you the grace and peace of God our
Father and of the Lord Jesus Christ.

New English Bible

THE
LETTER OF PAUL TO THE

PHILIPPIANS

The apostle and his friends

1 From Paul and Timothy, servants of Christ Jesus, to all those of God's people, incorporate in Christ Jesus, who live at Philippi, including their bishops and deacons.

Grace to you and peace from God our Father and the Lord Jesus Christ.

King James Version

Father and *from* the Lord Jesus Christ. 3 I thank
my God upon every remembrance of you, 4Al-
ways in every prayer of mine for you all making
request with joy, 5 For your fellowship in the
gospel from the first day until now; 6 Being confident of this very thing, that he which hath
begun a good work in you will perform *it* until
the day of Jesus Christ: 7 Even as it is meet for
me to think this of you all, because I have you
in my heart; inasmuch as both in my bonds, and
in the defence and confirmation of the gospel,
ye all are partakers of my grace. 8 For God is
my record, how greatly I long after you all in
the bowels of Jesus Christ. 9And this I pray,
that your love may abound yet more and more
in knowledge and *in* all judgment; 10 That ye
may approve things that are excellent; that ye
may be sincere and without offence till the day
of Christ; 11 Being filled with the fruits of righteousness, which are by Jesus Christ, unto the
glory and praise of God. 12 But I would ye
should understand, brethren, that the things
which happened unto me have fallen out rather
unto the furtherance of the gospel; 13 So that

Living Bible

in your hearts and your lives. 3All my prayers
for you are full of praise to God! 4 When I pray
for you, my heart is full of joy, 5 because of all
your wonderful help in making known the Good
News about Christ from the time you first heard
it until now. 6And I am sure that God who began the good work within you will keep right
on helping you grow in his grace until his task
within you is finally finished on that day when
Jesus Christ returns.
7 How natural it is that I should feel as I do
about you, for you have a very special place in
my heart. We have shared together the blessings
of God, both when I was in prison and when I
was out, defending the truth and telling others
about Christ. 8 Only God knows how deep is my
love and longing for you—with the tenderness
of Jesus Christ. 9 My prayer for you is that you
will overflow more and more with love for others, and at the same time keep on growing in
spiritual knowledge and insight, 10 for I want
you always to see clearly the difference between
right and wrong, and to be inwardly clean, no
one being able to criticize you from now until
our Lord returns. 11 May you always be doing
those good, kind things which show that you are
a child of God, for this will bring much praise
and glory to the Lord.
12 And I want you to know this, dear brothers: Everything that has happened to me here
has been a great boost in getting out the Good
News concerning Christ. 13 For everyone around

Today's English Version

Paul's prayer for his readers

3 I thank my God for you every time I think
of you; 4 and every time I pray for you all, I
pray with joy, 5 because of the way in which
you have helped me in the work of the gospel,
from the very first day until now. 6And so I am
sure of this: that God, who began this good
work in you, will carry it on until it is finished
in the Day of Christ Jesus. 7 You are always
in my heart! And so it is only right for me to
feel this way about you. For you have all shared
with me in this privilege that God has given
me, both now that I am in prison and also while
I was free to defend and firmly establish the
gospel. 8 God knows that I tell the truth when
I say that my deep feeling for you all comes
from the heart of Christ Jesus himself.
9 This is my prayer for you: I pray that your
love will keep on growing more and more, together with true knowledge and perfect judgment, 10 so that you will be able to choose what
is best. Then you will be free from all impurity
and blame on the Day of Christ. 11 Your lives
will be filled with the truly good qualities which
Jesus Christ alone can produce, for the glory
and praise of God.

To live is Christ

12 I want you to know, my brothers, that the
things that have happened to me have really
helped the progress of the gospel. 13As a result,

New International Version

Thanksgiving and prayer

3 I thank my God every time I remember
you. 4 In all my prayers for all of you, I always
pray with joy 5 because of your partnership in
the gospel from the first day until now, 6 being
confident of this, that he who began a good work
in you will carry it on to completion until the
day of Christ Jesus.
7 It is right for me to feel this way about all
of you, since I have you in my heart; for whether
I am in chains or defending and confirming the
gospel, all of you share in God's grace with me.
8 God can testify how I long for all of you
with the affection of Christ Jesus.
9 And this is my prayer: that your love may
abound more and more in knowledge and depth
of insight, 10 so that you may be able to discern
what is best and may be pure and blameless
until the day of Christ, 11 filled with the fruit of
righteousness that comes through Jesus Christ—
to the glory and praise of God.

Paul's chains advance the gospel

12 Now I want you to know, brothers, that
what has happened to me has really served to
advance the gospel. 13As a result, it has become

Phillips Modern English

1.3 I have the most pleasant memories of you all

I thank my God for you whenever I think of you. My constant prayers for you are a real joy, because we have worked together for the gospel from the first day until the present. I am confident of this: that the One who has begun his good work in you will go on developing it until the day of Jesus Christ.

It is only natural that I should feel like this about you all—you are very dear to me. For during the time I was in prison as well as when I was defending and proving the authority of the gospel we shared together the grace of God. God knows how much I long, with the deep love and affection of Christ Jesus, for your companionship. My prayer for you is that you may have still more love—a love that is full of knowledge and every wise insight. I want you to be able always to recognise the highest and the best, and to live sincere and blameless lives until the day of Christ. I want to see your lives full of true goodness, produced by the power that Jesus Christ gives you to the glory and praise of God.

1.12 My imprisonment has turned out to be no bad thing

Now I want you to know, my brothers, that what has happened to me has, in effect, turned out to the advantage of the gospel. For, first of

Revised Standard Version

3 I thank my God in all my remembrance of
you, 4 always in every prayer of mine for you
all making my prayer with joy, 5 thankful for
your partnership in the gospel from the first
day until now. 6 And I am sure that he who began a good work in you will bring it to completion at the day of Jesus Christ. 7 It is right
for me to feel thus about you all, because I
hold you in my heart, for you are all partakers
with me of grace, both in my imprisonment and
in the defense and confirmation of the gospel.
8 For God is my witness, how I yearn for you
all with the affection of Christ Jesus. 9 And it is
my prayer that your love may abound more and
more, with knowledge and all discernment, 10 so
that you may approve what is excellent, and
may be pure and blameless for the day of Christ,
11 filled with the fruits of righteousness which
come through Jesus Christ, to the glory and
praise of God.
12 I want you to know, brethren, that what
has happened to me has really served to advance
the gospel, 13 so that it has become known

Jerusalem Bible

Thanksgiving and prayer

3 I thank my God whenever I think of you;
and 4 every time I pray for all of you, I pray
with joy, 5 remembering how you have helped
to spread the Good News from the day you
first heard it right up to the present. 6 I am quite
certain that the One who began this good work
in you will see that it is finished when the Day
of Christ Jesus comes. 7 It is only natural that
I should feel like this toward you all, since you
have shared the privileges which have been
mine: both my chains and my work defending
and establishing the gospel. You have a permanent place in my heart, 8 and God knows how
much I miss you all, loving you as Christ Jesus
loves you. 9 My prayer is that your love for
each other may increase more and more and
never stop improving your knowledge and deepening your perception 10 so that you can always
recognize what is best. This will help you to
become pure and blameless, and prepare you for
the Day of Christ, 11 when you will reach the
perfect goodness which Jesus Christ produces
in us for the glory and praise of God.

Paul's own circumstances

12 I am glad to tell you, brothers, that the
things that happened to me have actually been
a help to the Good News.
13 My chains, in Christ, have become famous

New English Bible

I thank my God whenever I think of you; and when I pray for you all, my prayers are always joyful, because of the part you have taken in the work of the Gospel from the first day until now. Of one thing I am certain: the One who started the good work in you will bring it to completion by the Day of Christ Jesus. It is indeed only right that I should feel like this about you all, because you hold me in such affection, and because, when I lie in prison or appear in the dock to vouch for the truth of the Gospel, you all share in the privilege that is mine.[a] God knows how I long for you all, with the deep yearning of Christ Jesus himself. And this is my prayer, that your love may grow ever richer and richer in knowledge and insight of every kind, and may thus bring you the gift of true discrimination.[b] Then on the Day of Christ you will be flawless and without blame, reaping the full harvest of righteousness that comes through Jesus Christ, to the glory and praise of God.

Friends, I want you to understand that the work of the Gospel has been helped on, rather than hindered, by this business of mine. My im-

[a] *Or* I am justified in taking this view about you all, because I hold you in closest union, as those who, when I lie . . . of the Gospel, all share in the privilege that is mine. [b] *Or* may teach you by experience what things are most worth while.

King James Version

my bonds in Christ are manifest in all the palace,
and in all other *places;* 14 And many of the
brethren in the Lord, waxing confident by my
bonds, are much more bold to speak the word
without fear. 15 Some indeed preach Christ even
of envy and strife; and some also of good will:
16 The one preach Christ of contention, not sincerely, supposing to add affliction to my bonds:
17 But the other of love, knowing that I am set
for the defence of the gospel. 18 What then? notwithstanding, every way, whether in pretence, or
in truth, Christ is preached; and I therein do
rejoice, yea, and will rejoice. 19 For I know that
this shall turn to my salvation through your
prayer, and the supply of the Spirit of Jesus
Christ, 20 According to my earnest expectation
and *my* hope, that in nothing I shall be ashamed,
but *that* with all boldness, as always, *so* now
also Christ shall be magnified in my body,
whether *it be* by life, or by death. 21 For to me
to live *is* Christ, and to die *is* gain. 22 But if I
live in the flesh, this *is* the fruit of my labour:
yet what I shall choose I wot not. 23 For I am
in a strait betwixt two, having a desire to depart,

Living Bible

here, including all the soldiers over at the barracks, knows that I am in chains simply because
I am a Christian. 14 And because of my imprisonment many of the Christians here seem to
have lost their fear of chains! Somehow my patience has encouraged them and they have become more and more bold in telling others about
Christ.

15 Some, of course, are preaching the Good
News because they are jealous of the way God
has used me. They want reputations as fearless
preachers! But others have purer motives,
16, 17 preaching because they love me, for they
know that the Lord has brought me here to use
me to defend the Truth. And some preach to
make me jealous, thinking that their success will
add to my sorrows here in jail! 18 But whatever
their motive for doing it, the fact remains that
the Good News about Christ is being preached
and I am glad.

19 I am going to keep on being glad, for I
know that as you pray for me, and as the Holy
Spirit helps me, this is all going to turn out for
my good. 20 For I live in eager expectation and
hope that I will never do anything that will cause
me to be ashamed of myself but that I will always be ready to speak out boldly for Christ
while I am going through all these trials here,
just as I have in the past; and that I will always
be an honor to Christ, whether I live or whether
I must die. 21 For to me, living means opportunities for Christ, and dying—well, that's better
yet! 22 But if living will give me more opportunities to win people to Christ, then I really don't
know which is better, to live or die! 23 Sometimes
I want to live and at other times I don't, for I

Today's English Version

the whole palace guard and all the others here
know that I am in prison because I am a servant
of Christ. 14 And my being in prison has given
most of the brothers more confidence in the
Lord, so that they grow bolder all the time in
preaching the message without fear.

15 Of course some of them preach Christ
because they are jealous and quarrelsome, but
others preach him with all good will. 16 These
do so from love, because they know that God
has given me the work of defending the gospel.
17 The others do not proclaim Christ sincerely,
but from a spirit of selfish ambition; they think
that they will make more trouble for me while
I am in prison.

18 It does not matter! I am happy about it—
just so Christ is preached in every way possible,
whether from wrong or right motives. And I
will continue to be happy, 19 because I know
that by means of your prayers and the help
which comes from the Spirit of Jesus Christ, I
shall be set free. 20 My deep desire and hope
is that I shall never fail my duty, but that at all
times, and especially right now, I shall be full
of courage, so that with my whole being I shall
bring honor to Christ, whether I live or die.
21 For what is life? To me, it is Christ. Death,
then, will bring more. 22 But if by living on I
can do more worthwhile work, then I am not
sure which I should choose. 23 I am caught
from both sides. I want very much to leave this

New International Version

clear throughout the whole palace guard [b] and
to everyone else that I am in chains for Christ.
14 Because of my chains, most of the brothers
in the Lord have been encouraged to speak the
word of God more courageously and fearlessly.

15 It is true that some preach Christ out of
envy and rivalry, but others out of good will.
16 The latter do so in love, knowing that I am
put here for the defense of the gospel. 17 The
former preach Christ out of selfish ambition, not
sincerely, supposing that they can stir up trouble
for me while I am in chains. 18 But what does it
matter? The important thing is that in every way,
whether from false motives or true, Christ is
preached. And because of this I rejoice.

Yes, and I will continue to rejoice, 19 for I
know that through your prayers and the help
given by the Spirit of Jesus Christ, what has
happened to me will turn out for my deliverance.
20 I eagerly expect and hope that I will in no
way be ashamed, but will have sufficient courage so that now as always Christ will be exalted
in my body, whether by life or by death. 21 For
to me, to live is Christ and to die is gain. 22 If I
am to go on living in the body, this will mean
fruitful labor for me. Yet, what shall I choose?
I do not know! 23 I am torn between the two: I
desire to depart and be with Christ, which is

[b] Or *whole palace.*

Phillips Modern English

all, my imprisonment means a personal witness
for Christ before the palace guards, not to mention others who come and go. Then, it means
that most of our brothers, taking fresh heart in
the Lord from the very fact that I am a prisoner
for Christ's sake, have shown far more courage
in boldly proclaiming the Word of God. I know
that some are preaching Christ out of jealousy,
in order to annoy me, but some are preaching
him in good faith. These latter are preaching
out of their love for me. For they know that
I am here to defend the gospel. The motive of
the former is questionable—they preach in a
partisan spirit, hoping to make my chains even
more galling than they are. But what does it
matter? However they may look at it, the fact
remains that Christ *is* being preached, whether
sincerely or not, and that fact makes me very
happy. Yes, and I shall go on being happy, for I
know that what is happening will result in my
release, thanks to your prayers and the resources
of the Spirit of Jesus Christ. It all accords with
my own earnest wishes and hopes, which are
that I should never be in any way ashamed, but
that now, as always, I should honour Christ with
the utmost boldness by the way I live, whether
that means I am to face death or to go on living.
For living to me means simply "Christ", and if
I die I should merely gain more of him. For me
to go on living in this world may serve some
good purpose. I should find it very hard to make
a choice. I am torn in two directions—on the
one hand I long to leave this world and live with

Revised Standard Version

throughout the whole praetorian guard [c] and to
all the rest that my imprisonment is for Christ;
14 and most of the brethren have been made
confident in the Lord because of my imprisonment, and are much more bold to speak the
word of God without fear.
15 Some indeed preach Christ from envy and
rivalry, but others from good will. 16 The latter
do it out of love, knowing that I am put here
for the defense of the gospel; 17 the former proclaim Christ out of partisanship, not sincerely
but thinking to afflict me in my imprisonment.
18 What then? Only that in every way, whether
in pretense or in truth, Christ is proclaimed; and
in that I rejoice.
19 Yes, and I shall rejoice. For I know that
through your prayers and the help of the Spirit
of Jesus Christ this will turn out for my deliverance, 20 as it is my eager expectation and hope
that I shall not be at all ashamed, but that with
full courage now as always Christ will be honored in my body, whether by life or by death.
21 For to me to live is Christ, and to die is
gain. 22 If it is to be life in the flesh, that means
fruitful labor for me. Yet which I shall choose
I cannot tell. 23 I am hard pressed between the
two. My desire is to depart and be with Christ,

[c] Greek *in the whole praetorium.*

Jerusalem Bible

not only all over the Praetorium but everywhere,
14 and most of the brothers have taken courage
in the Lord from these chains of mine and are
getting more and more daring in announcing
the Message without any fear. 15 It is true that
some of them are doing it just out of rivalry
and competition, but the rest preach Christ with
the right intention, 16 out of nothing but love,
as they know that this is my invariable way of
defending the gospel. 17 The others, who proclaim Christ for jealous or selfish motives, do
not mind if they make my chains heavier to
bear. 18 But does it matter? Whether from dishonest motives or in sincerity, Christ is proclaimed; and that makes me happy; 19 and I
shall continue being happy, because I know *this
will help to save me,*[a] thanks to your prayers
and to the help which will be given to me by
the Spirit of Jesus. 20 My one hope and trust is
that I shall never have to admit defeat, but that
now as always I shall have the courage for
Christ to be glorified in my body, whether by
my life or by my death. 21 Life to me, of course,
is Christ, but then death would bring me something more; 22 but then again, if living in this
body means doing work which is having good
results—I do not know what I should choose.
23 I am caught in this dilemma: I want to be
gone and be with Christ, which would be very

[*a*] Jb. 13:16 (LXX).

New English Bible

prisonment in Christ's cause has become common knowledge to all at headquarters[c] here, and
indeed among the public at large; and it has
given confidence to most of our fellow-Christians to speak the word of God fearlessly and
with extraordinary courage.
Some, indeed, proclaim Christ in a jealous and
quarrelsome spirit; others proclaim him in true
goodwill, and these are moved by love for me;
they know that it is to defend the Gospel that I
am where I am. But the others, moved by personal rivalry, present Christ from mixed motives,
meaning to stir up fresh trouble for me as I lie
in prison.[d] What does it matter? One way or
another, in pretence or sincerity, Christ is set
forth, and for that I rejoice.
Yes, and rejoice I will, knowing well that the
issue of it all will be my deliverance, because
you are praying for me and the Spirit of Jesus
Christ is given me for support.[a] For, as I passion-
ately hope, I shall have no cause to be ashamed,
but shall speak so boldly that now as always the
greatness of Christ will shine out clearly in my
person, whether through my life or through my
death. For to me life is Christ, and death gain;
but what if my living on in the body may serve
some good purpose? Which then am I to choose?
I cannot tell. I am torn two ways: what I should
like is to depart and be with Christ; that is better

[*c*] *Or* to all the imperial guard, *or* to all at the
Residency (*Greek* Praetorium). [*d*] *Or* meaning to
make use of my imprisonment to stir up fresh trouble. [*a*] *Or* supplies me with all I need.

King James Version

and to be with Christ; which is far better:
24 Nevertheless to abide in the flesh *is* more
needful for you. 25 And having this confidence,
I know that I shall abide and continue with you
all for your furtherance and joy of faith; 26 That
your rejoicing may be more abundant in Jesus
Christ for me by my coming to you again.
27 Only let your conversation be as it becometh
the gospel of Christ: that whether I come and
see you, or else be absent, I may hear of your
affairs, that ye stand fast in one spirit, with one
mind striving together for the faith of the gospel;
28 And in nothing terrified by your adversaries:
which is to them an evident token of perdition,
but to you of salvation, and that of God. 29 For
unto you it is given in the behalf of Christ, not
only to believe on him, but also to suffer for his
sake; 30 Having the same conflict which ye saw
in me, and now hear *to be* in me.

Living Bible

long to go and be with Christ. How much happier for *me* than being here! 24 But the fact is
that I can be of more help to *you* by staying!
25 Yes, I am still needed down here and so
I feel certain I will be staying on earth a little
longer, to help you grow and become happy in
your faith; 26 my staying will make you glad
and give you reason to glorify Christ Jesus for
keeping me safe, when I return to visit you again.
27 But whatever happens to me, remember
always to live as Christians should, so that,
whether I ever see you again or not, I will keep
on hearing good reports that you are standing
side by side with one strong purpose—to tell the
Good News 28 fearlessly, no matter what your
enemies may do. They will see this as a sign of
their downfall, but for you it will be a clear sign
from God that he is with you, and that he has
given you eternal life with him. 29 For to you
has been given the privilege not only of trusting
him but also of suffering for him. 30 We are in
this fight together. You have seen me suffer for
him in the past; and I am still in the midst of a
great and terrible struggle now, as you know so
well.

Today's English Version

life and be with Christ, which is a far better
thing; 24 but it is much more important, for
your sake, that I remain alive. 25 I am sure of
this, and so I know that I will stay. I will stay
on with you all, to add to your progress and
joy in the faith. 26 So when I am with you
again you will have even more reason to be
proud of me, in your life in Christ Jesus.
27 Now, the important thing is that your
manner of life be as the gospel of Christ requires, so that, whether or not I am able to go
to see you, I will hear that you stand firm with
one common purpose, and fight together, with
only one wish, for the faith of the gospel.
28 Don't be afraid of your enemies; always be
courageous, and this will prove to them that
they will lose, and that you will win, because it
is God who gives you the victory. 29 For you
have been given the privilege of serving Christ,
not only by believing in him, but also by suffering for him. 30 Now you can take part with
me in the fight. It is the same one you saw me
fighting in the past and the same one I am still
fighting, as you hear.

New International Version

better by far; 24 but it is more necessary for
you that I remain in the body. 25 Convinced of
this, I know that I will remain, and I will continue with all of you for your progress and joy
in the faith, 26 so that through my being with
you again your joy in Christ Jesus will overflow
on account of me. .
27 Whatever happens, conduct yourselves in
a manner worthy of the gospel of Christ. Then,
whether I come and see you or only hear about
you in my absence, I will know that you stand
firm in one spirit, contending as one man for
the faith of the gospel 28 without being frightened in any way by those who oppose you. This
is a sign to them that they will be destroyed, but
that you will be saved—and that by God. 29 For
it has been granted to you on behalf of Christ
not only to believe on him, but also to suffer for
him, 30 since you are going through the same
struggle you saw I had, and now hear that I
still have.

Phillips Modern English

Christ, and that is obviously the best thing for me. Yet, on the other hand, it is probably more necessary for you that I should stay here on earth. Because I am sure of this, I know that I shall remain and continue to stand by you all, to help you forward in Christian living and to find increasing joy in your faith. So that you may feel great pride in me as your minister in Christ when I come and see you again!

But whatever happens, make sure that your everyday life is worthy of the gospel of Christ. So that whether I do come and see you, or merely hear about you from a distance, I may know that you are standing fast in a united spirit, battling with a single mind for the faith of the gospel and not caring two straws for your enemies. The fact that they are your enemies is plain proof that they are lost to God, while the fact that you have such men as enemies is plain proof that you yourselves are being saved by God. You are given the privilege not merely of believing in Christ but also of suffering for his sake. Now you are taking part in that battle you once saw me fight, and which, as you hear, I am still fighting.

Revised Standard Version

for that is far better. 24 But to remain in the flesh is more necessary on your account. 25 Convinced of this, I know that I shall remain and continue with you all, for your progress and joy in the faith, 26 so that in me you may have ample cause to glory in Christ Jesus, because of my coming to you again.

27 Only let your manner of life be worthy of the gospel of Christ, so that whether I come and see you or am absent, I may hear of you that you stand firm in one spirit, with one mind striving side by side for the faith of the gospel, 28 and not frightened in anything by your opponents. This is a clear omen to them of their destruction, but of your salvation, and that from God. 29 For it has been granted to you that for the sake of Christ you should not only believe in him but also suffer for his sake, 30 engaged in the same conflict which you saw and now hear to be mine.

Jerusalem Bible

much the better, 24 but for me to stay alive in this body is a more urgent need for your sake. 25 This weighs with me so much that I feel sure I shall survive and stay with you all, and help you to progress in the faith and even increase your joy in it; 26 and so you will have another reason to give praise to Christ Jesus on my account when I am with you again.

Fight for the faith

27 Avoid anything in your everyday lives that would be unworthy of the gospel of Christ, so that, whether I come to you and see for myself, or stay at a distance and only hear about you, I shall know that you are unanimous in meeting the attack with firm resistance, united by your love for the faith of the gospel 28 and quite unshaken by your enemies. This would be the sure sign that they will lose and you will be saved. It would be a sign from God 29 that he has given you the privilege not only of believing in Christ, but of suffering for him as well. 30 You and I are together in the same fight as you saw me fighting before and, as you will have heard, I am fighting still.

New English Bible

by far; but for your sake there is greater need for me to stay on in the body. This indeed I know for certain: I shall stay, and stand by you all to help you forward and to add joy to your faith, so that when I am with you again, your pride in me may be unbounded in Christ Jesus.

Only, let your conduct be worthy of the gospel of Christ, so that whether I come and see you for myself or hear about you from a distance, I may know that you are standing firm, one in spirit, one in mind, contending as one man for the gospel faith, meeting your opponents without so much as a tremor. This is a sure sign to them that their doom is sealed, but a sign of your salvation, and one afforded by God himself; for you have been granted the privilege not only of believing in Christ but also of suffering for him. You and I are engaged in the same contest; you saw me in it once, and, as you hear, I am in it still.

King James Version

2 If *there be* therefore any consolation in
Christ, if any comfort of love, if any fellowship of the Spirit, if any bowels and mercies,
2 Fulfil ye my joy, that ye be likeminded, having
the same love, *being* of one accord, of one mind.
3 *Let* nothing *be done* through strife or vain-
glory; but in lowliness of mind let each esteem
other better than themselves. 4 Look not every
man on his own things, but every man also on
the things of others. 5 Let this mind be in you,
which was also in Christ Jesus: 6 Who, being in
the form of God, thought it not robbery to be
equal with God: 7 But made himself of no reputation, and took upon him the form of a servant,
and was made in the likeness of men: 8 And being found in fashion as a man, he humbled himself, and became obedient unto death, even the
death of the cross. 9 Wherefore God also hath
highly exalted him, and given him a name which
is above every name: 10 That at the name of

Living Bible

2 Is there any such thing as Christians cheering each other up? Do you love me enough
to want to help me? Does it mean anything to
you that we are brothers in the Lord, sharing the
same Spirit? Are your hearts tender and sympathetic at all? 2 Then make me truly happy by
loving each other and agreeing wholeheartedly
with each other, working together with one heart
and mind and purpose.
3 Don't be selfish; don't live to make a good
impression on others. Be humble, thinking of
others as better than yourself. 4 Don't just think
about your own affairs, but be interested in
others, too, and in what they are doing.
5 Your attitude should be the kind that was
shown us by Jesus Christ, 6 who, though he was
God, did not demand and cling to his rights as
God, 7 but laid aside his mighty power and
glory, taking the disguise of a slave and becoming like men.[a] 8 And he humbled himself even
further, going so far as actually to die a criminal's death on a cross.[b]
9 Yet it was because of this that God raised
him up to the heights of heaven and gave him
a name which is above every other name, 10 that

[*a*] Literally, "was made in the likeness of men."
[*b*] Literally, "became obedient unto death, even the death of the cross."

Today's English Version

Christ's humility and greatness

2 Does your life in Christ make you strong?
Does his love comfort you? Do you have
fellowship with the Spirit? Do you feel kindness
and compassion for one another? 2 I urge you,
then, make me completely happy by having the
same thoughts, sharing the same love, and being one in soul and mind. 3 Don't do anything
from selfish ambition, or from a cheap desire
to boast; but be humble toward each other,
never thinking you are better than others. 4 And
look out for each other's interests, not just for
your own. 5 The attitude you should have is the
one that Christ Jesus had:

6 He always had the very nature of God,
but he did not think that by force he
should try to become equal with God.
7 Instead, of his own free will he gave it all up,
and took the nature of a servant.
He became like man,
and appeared in human likeness.
8 He was humble and walked the path of obedience to death—
his death on the cross.
9 For this reason God raised him to the highest place above,
and gave him the name that is greater than any other name.
10 And so, in honor of the name of Jesus,

New International Version

Imitating Christ's humility

2 If you have any encouragement from being
united with Christ, if any comfort from his
love, if any fellowship with the Spirit, if any
tenderness and compassion, 2 then make my joy
complete by being like-minded, having the same
love, being one in spirit and purpose. 3 Do
nothing out of selfish ambition or vain conceit,
but in humility consider others better than yourselves. 4 Each of you should look not only to
your own interests, but also to the interests of
others.
5 Your attitude should be the same as that of
Christ Jesus:

6 Who, being in very nature[c] God,
did not consider equality with God
something to be grasped,
7 but made himself nothing,
taking the very nature[d] of a servant,
being made in human likeness.
8 And being found in appearance as a man,
he humbled himself
and became obedient to death—
even death on a cross!
9 Therefore God exalted him to the highest place
and gave him the name that is above every name,
10 that at the name of Jesus every knee should

[*c*] Or *in the form of.* [*d*] Or *the form.*

Phillips Modern English

2.1 *Above all things be loving, humble, united*

Now if you have known anything of Christ's encouragement and of his reassuring love; if you have known something of the fellowship of his Spirit, and of compassion and deep sympathy, do make my joy complete—live together in harmony, live together in love, as though you had only one mind and one spirit between you. Never act from motives of rivalry or personal vanity, but in humility think more of each other than you do of yourselves. None of you should think only of his own affairs, but consider other people's interests also.

2.5 *Let Christ be your example of humility*

Let your attitude to life be that of Christ Jesus himself. For he, who had always been God by nature, did not cling to his privileges as God's equal, but stripped himself of every advantage by consenting to be a slave by nature and being born a man. And, plainly seen as a human being, he humbled himself by living a life of utter obedience, to the point of death, and the death he died was the death of a common criminal. That is why God has now lifted him to the heights, and has given him the name beyond all names, so that at the name of Jesus "every knee shall

Revised Standard Version

2 So if there is any encouragement in Christ,
any incentive of love, any participation in
the Spirit, any affection and sympathy, 2 complete my joy by being of the same mind, having
the same love, being in full accord and of one
mind. 3 Do nothing from selfishness or conceit,
but in humility count others better than yourselves. 4 Let each of you look not only to his
own interests, but also to the interests of others.
5 Have this mind among yourselves, which is
yours in Christ Jesus, 6 who, though he was in
the form of God, did not count equality with
God a thing to be grasped, 7 but emptied himself, taking the form of a servant,[d] being born
in the likeness of men. 8 And being found in
human form he humbled himself and became
obedient unto death, even death on a cross.
9 Therefore God has highly exalted him and
bestowed on him the name which is above every
name, 10 that at the name of Jesus every knee

[d] Or *slave*.

Jerusalem Bible

Preserve unity in humility

2 If our life in Christ means anything to
you, if love can persuade at all, or the
Spirit that we have in common, or any tenderness and sympathy, 2 then be united in your
convictions and united in your love, with a
common purpose and a common mind. That is
the one thing which would make me completely
happy. 3 There must be no competition among
you, no conceit; but everybody is to be self-
effacing. Always consider the other person to
be better than yourself, 4 so that nobody thinks
of his own interests first but everybody thinks
of other people's interest instead. 5 In your
minds you must be the same as Christ Jesus[b]:

6 His state was divine,
yet he did not cling
to his equality with God
7 but emptied himself
to assume the condition of a slave,
and became as men are;
and being as all men are,
8 he was humbler yet,
even to accepting death,
death on a cross.
9 But God raised him high
and gave him the name
which is above all other names
10 so that *all beings*

[*b*] Vv. 6-11 are a hymn, though whether composed or only quoted by Paul is uncertain.

New English Bible

2 If then our common life in Christ yields anything to stir the heart, any loving consolation, any sharing of the Spirit, any warmth of affection or compassion, fill up my cup of happiness by thinking and feeling alike, with the same love for one another, the same turn of mind, and a common care for unity. There must be no room for rivalry and personal vanity among you, but you must humbly reckon others better than yourselves. Look to each other's interest and not merely to your own.

Let your bearing towards one another arise out of your life in Christ Jesus.[b] For the divine nature was his from the first; yet he did not think to snatch at equality with God,[c] but made himself nothing, assuming the nature of a slave. Bearing the human likeness, revealed in human shape, he humbled himself, and in obedience accepted even death—death on a cross. Therefore God raised him to the heights and bestowed on him the name above all names, that at the

[*b*] *Or* Have that bearing towards one another which was also found in Christ Jesus. [*c*] *Or* yet he did not prize his equality with God.

King James Version

Jesus every knee should bow, of *things* in heaven,
and *things* in earth, and *things* under the earth;
11 And *that* every tongue should confess that
Jesus Christ *is* Lord, to the glory of God the
Father. 12 Wherefore, my beloved, as ye have
always obeyed, not as in my presence only, but
now much more in my absence, work out your
own salvation with fear and trembling: 13 For it
is God which worketh in you both to will and to
do of *his* good pleasure. 14 Do all things without murmurings and disputings: 15 That ye may
be blameless and harmless, the sons of God,
without rebuke, in the midst of a crooked and
perverse nation, among whom ye shine as lights
in the world; 16 Holding forth the word of life;
that I may rejoice in the day of Christ, that I
have not run in vain, neither laboured in vain.
17 Yea, and if I be offered upon the sacrifice
and service of your faith, I joy, and rejoice with
you all. 18 For the same cause also do ye joy,

Living Bible

at the name of Jesus every knee shall bow in
heaven and on earth and under the earth, 11 and
every tongue shall confess that Jesus Christ is
Lord, to the glory of God the Father.
12 Dearest friends, when I was there with you,
you were always so careful to follow my instructions. And now that I am away you must be even
more careful to do the good things that result
from being saved, obeying God with deep reverence, shrinking back from all that might displease him. 13 For God is at work within you,
helping you want to obey him, and then helping
you do what he wants.
14 In everything you do, stay away from complaining and arguing, 15 so that no one can
speak a word of blame against you. You are to
live clean, innocent lives as children of God in
a dark world full of people who are crooked
and stubborn. Shine out among them like beacon
lights, 16 holding out to them the Word of Life.
Then when Christ returns how glad I will be
that my work among you was so worthwhile.
17 And if my lifeblood is, so to speak, to be
poured out over your faith which I am offering
up to God as a sacrifice—that is, if I am to die
for you—even then I will be glad, and will share
my joy with each of you. 18 For you should be
happy about this, too, and rejoice with me for
having this privilege of dying for you.

Today's English Version

all beings in heaven, on earth, and in the
world below
will fall on their knees,
11 and all will openly proclaim that Jesus
Christ is the Lord,
to the glory of God the Father.

Shining as lights in the world

12 So then, dear friends, as you always obeyed
me when I was with you, it is even more important that you obey me now, while I am away
from you. Keep on working, with fear and
trembling, to complete your salvation, 13 because God is always at work in you to make
you willing and able to obey his own purpose.
14 Do everything without complaining or arguing, 15 so that you may be innocent and pure,
as God's perfect children who live in a world
of corrupt and sinful people. You must shine
among them like stars lighting up the sky, 16 as
you offer them the message of life. If you do
so, I shall have reason to be proud of you on
the Day of Christ, because it will show that all
my effort and work have not been wasted.
17 Perhaps my life's blood is to be poured
out like an offering on the sacrifice that your
faith offers to God. If that is so, I am glad, and
share my joy with you all. 18 In the same way,
you too must be glad and share your joy with
me.

New International Version

bow,
in heaven and on earth and under the
earth,
11 and every tongue confess that Jesus Christ
is Lord,
to the glory of God the Father.

Shining as stars

12 Therefore, my dear friends, as you have
always obeyed—not only in my presence, but
now much more in my absence—continue to
work out your salvation with fear and trembling,
13 for it is God who works in you to will and do
what pleases him.
14 Do everything without complaining or arguing, 15 so that you may become blameless
and pure, children of God without fault in a
crooked and depraved generation, in which you
shine like stars in the universe 16 as you hold
out[e] the word of life—in order that I may boast
on the day of Christ that I did not run or labor
for nothing. 17 But even if I am being poured
out like a drink offering on the sacrifice and
service coming from your faith, I am glad and
rejoice with all of you. 18 So you too should be
glad and rejoice with me.

[e] Or *hold on to*.

Phillips Modern English

bow", whether in Heaven or earth or under the earth. And that is why "every tongue shall confess" that Jesus Christ is Lord, to the glory of God the Father.

2.12 God is himself at work within you

So then, my dear friends, as you have always obeyed me—and that not only when I was with you—now, even more in my absence, complete the salvation that God has given you with a proper sense of awe and responsibility. For it is God who is at work within you, giving you the will and the power to achieve his purpose.

Do all you have to do without grumbling or arguing, so that you may be blameless and harmless, faultless children of God, living in a warped and diseased age, and shining like lights in a dark world. For you hold up in your hands the very word of life. Thus can you give me something to be proud of in the day of Christ, for I shall know then that I did not spend my energy in vain. Yes, and if it should happen that my life-blood is, so to speak, poured out upon the sacrifice and offering which your faith means to God, then I can still be very happy, and I can share my happiness with you all. You should be glad about this too, and share this happiness with me.

Revised Standard Version

should bow, in heaven and on earth and under
the earth, 11 and every tongue confess that Jesus Christ is Lord, to the glory of God the
Father.
12 Therefore, my beloved, as you have always
obeyed, so now, not only as in my presence but
much more in my absence, work out your own
salvation with fear and trembling; 13 for God
is at work in you, both to will and to work for
his good pleasure.
14 Do all things without grumbling or questioning, 15 that you may be blameless and innocent, children of God without blemish in the
midst of a crooked and perverse generation,
among whom you shine as lights in the world,
16 holding fast the word of life, so that in the
day of Christ I may be proud that I did not run
in vain or labor in vain. 17 Even if I am to be
poured as a libation upon the sacrificial offering of your faith, I am glad and rejoice with
you all. 18 Likewise you also should be glad
and rejoice with me.

Jerusalem Bible

in the heavens, on earth and in the underworld,
should bend the knee[c] at the name of Jesus
11 and that every tongue should acclaim
Jesus Christ as Lord,
to the glory of God the Father.

Work for salvation

12 So then, my dear friends, continue to do
as I tell you, as you always have; not only as
you did when I was there with you, but even
more now that I am no longer there; and work
for your salvation "in fear and trembling." 13 It
is God, for his own loving purpose, who puts
both the will and the action into you. 14 Do
all that has to be done without complaining or
arguing 15 and then you will be innocent and
genuine, *perfect children of God among a deceitful and underhand brood,*[d] and you will
shine in the world like bright stars 16 because
you are offering it the word of life. This would
give me something to be proud of for the Day
of Christ, and would mean that I had not run
in the race and exhausted myself for nothing.
17 And then, if my blood has to be shed as part
of your own sacrifice and offering—which is
your faith[e]—I shall still be happy and rejoice
with all of you, 18 and you must be just as
happy and rejoice with me.

[c] Is. 45:23. [d] Dt. 32:5. [e] Libations were common to Greek and Jewish sacrifices.

New English Bible

name of Jesus every knee should bow—in heaven, on earth, and in the depths—and every tongue confess, 'Jesus Christ is Lord', to the glory of God the Father.

So you too, my friends, must be obedient, as always; even more, now that I am away, than when I was with you. You must work out your own salvation in fear and trembling; for it is God who works in you, inspiring both the will and the deed, for his own chosen purpose.

Do all you have to do without complaint or wrangling. Show yourselves guileless and above reproach, faultless children of God in a warped and crooked generation, in which you shine[a] like stars in a dark world[b] and proffer the word of life.[c] Thus you will be my pride on the Day of Christ, proof that I did not run my race in vain, or work in vain. But if my life-blood is to crown that sacrifice which is the offering up of your faith, I am glad of it, and I share my gladness with you all. Rejoice, you no less than I, and let us share our joy.

[a] *Or* . . . generation. Shine out among them . . .
[b] *Or* in the firmament. [c] *Or* as the very principle of its life.

King James Version

and rejoice with me. 19 But I trust in the Lord
Jesus to send Timotheus shortly unto you, that
I also may be of good comfort, when I know
your state. 20 For I have no man likeminded,
who will naturally care for your state. 21 For all
seek their own, not the things which are Jesus
Christ's. 22 But ye know the proof of him, that,
as a son with the father, he hath served with me
in the gospel. 23 Him therefore I hope to send
presently, so soon as I shall see how it will go
with me. 24 But I trust in the Lord that I also
myself shall come shortly. 25 Yet I supposed it
necessary to send to you Epaphroditus, my
brother, and companion in labour, and fellow
soldier, but your messenger, and he that ministered to my wants. 26 For he longed after you
all, and was full of heaviness, because that ye
had heard that he had been sick. 27 For indeed
he was sick nigh unto death: but God had mercy
on him; and not on him only, but on me also,
lest I should have sorrow upon sorrow. 28 I sent
him therefore the more carefully, that, when ye
see him again, ye may rejoice, and that I may
be the less sorrowful. 29 Receive him therefore
in the Lord with all gladness; and hold such in
reputation: 30 Because for the work of Christ he
was nigh unto death, not regarding his life, to
supply your lack of service toward me.

Living Bible

19 If the Lord is willing, I will send Timothy
to see you soon. Then when he comes back he
can cheer me up by telling me all about you and
how you are getting along. 20 There is no one
like Timothy for having a real interest in you;
21 everyone else seems to be worrying about his
own plans and not those of Jesus Christ. 22 But
you know Timothy. He has been just like a son
to me in helping me preach the Good News.
23 I hope to send him to you just as soon as I
find out what is going to happen to me here.
24 And I am trusting the Lord that soon I myself may come to see you.

25 Meanwhile, I thought I ought to send
Epaphroditus back to you. You sent him to help
me in my need; well, he and I have been real
brothers, working and battling side by side.
26 Now I am sending him home again, for he
has been homesick for all of you and upset
because you heard that he was ill. 27 And he
surely was; in fact, he almost died. But God had
mercy on him, and on me too, not allowing me
to have this sorrow on top of everything else.

28 So I am all the more anxious to get him
back to you again, for I know how thankful you
will be to see him, and that will make me happy
and lighten all my cares. 29 Welcome him in the
Lord with great joy, and show your appreciation, 30 for he risked his life for the work of
Christ and was at the point of death while trying to do for me the things you couldn't do because you were far away.

Today's English Version

Timothy and Epaphroditus

19 I trust in the Lord Jesus that I will be
able to send Timothy to you soon, so that I
may be encouraged by news of you. 20 He is
the only one who shares my feelings, and who
really cares about you. 21 Everyone else is concerned only about his own affairs, not about the
cause of Jesus Christ. 22 And you yourselves
know how he has proved his worth, how he and
I, like a son and his father, have worked together for the sake of the gospel. 23 I hope to
send him to you, then, as soon as I know how
things are going to turn out for me. 24 And I
trust in the Lord that I myself will be able to
come to you soon.

25 I have thought it necessary to send you
our brother Epaphroditus, who has worked and
fought by my side, and who has served as your
messenger in helping me. 26 He is anxious to
see you all, and is very upset because you heard
that he was sick. 27 Indeed he was sick, and
almost died. But God had pity on him, and not
only on him but on me, too, and spared me
even greater sorrow. 28 I am all the more eager,
then, to send him to you, so that you will be
glad again when you see him, and my own sorrow will disappear. 29 Receive him, then, with all
joy, as a brother in the Lord. Show respect to
all such men as he, 30 because he risked his
life and nearly died, for the sake of the work of
Christ, in order to give me the help that you
yourselves could not give.

New International Version

Timothy and Epaphroditus

19 I hope in the Lord Jesus to send Timothy
to you soon, that I also may be cheered when
I receive news about you. 20 I have no one else
like him, who takes a genuine interest in your
welfare. 21 For everyone looks out for his own
interests, not those of Jesus Christ. 22 But you
know that Timothy has proved himself, because
as a son with his father he has served with me
in the work of the gospel. 23 I hope, therefore,
to send him as soon as I see how things go with
me. 24 And I am confident in the Lord that I
myself will come soon.

25 But I think it is necessary to send back to
you Epaphroditus, my brother, fellow worker
and fellow soldier, who is also your messenger,
whom you sent to take care of my needs. 26 For
he longs for all of you and is distressed because
you heard he was ill. 27 Indeed he was ill, and
almost died. But God had mercy on him, and not
on him only but also on me, to spare me sorrow
upon sorrow. 28 Therefore I am all the more
eager to send him, so that when you see him
again you may be glad and I may have less
anxiety. 29 Welcome him in the Lord with great
joy, and honor men like him, 30 because he
almost died for the work of Christ, risking his
life to make up for the help you could not give
me.

Phillips Modern English

2.19 I am sending Epaphroditus with this letter, and Timothy later

But I hope in the Lord Jesus that it will not be long before I send Timothy to you, and then I shall be cheered by news of you and your doings. I have nobody else here who shares my genuine concern for you. They are all wrapped up in their own affairs and do not really care for the cause of Jesus Christ. But you know Timothy's worth, how he has worked with me for the gospel like a son with his father. This is the man I hope to send to you as soon as I can tell how things will work out for me, but God gives me hope that it will not be long before I am able to come myself. I have considered it desirable, however, to send you Epaphroditus. He has been to me brother, fellow-worker and comrade-in-arms, as well as being the messenger you sent to see to my wants. He has been homesick for you all, and was worried because he knew that you had heard that he was ill. Indeed he was ill, dangerously ill, but God had mercy on him—and incidentally on me as well, so that I did not have the sorrow of losing him to add to my sufferings. I am particularly anxious, therefore, to send him to you so that when you see him again you may be glad, and this will lighten my own sorrows. Welcome him in the Lord with great joy! You should hold men like him in highest honour, for his loyalty to Christ brought him very near death—he risked his life to do for me in person what distance prevented you from doing.

Revised Standard Version

19 I hope in the Lord Jesus to send Timothy
to you soon, so that I may be cheered by news
of you. 20 I have no one like him, who will be
genuinely anxious for your welfare. 21 They all
look after their own interests, not those of Jesus
Christ. 22 But Timothy's worth you know, how
as a son with a father he has served with me
in the gospel. 23 I hope therefore to send him
just as soon as I see how it will go with me;
24 and I trust in the Lord that shortly I myself
shall come also.

25 I have thought it necessary to send to you
Epaphroditus my brother and fellow worker
and fellow soldier, and your messenger and
minister to my need, 26 for he has been longing
for you all, and has been distressed because you
heard that he was ill. 27 Indeed he was ill, near
to death. But God had mercy on him, and not
only on him but on me also, lest I should have
sorrow upon sorrow. 28 I am the more eager to
send him, therefore, that you may rejoice at
seeing him again, and that I may be less anxious. 29 So receive him in the Lord with all joy;
and honor such men, 30 for he nearly died for
the work of Christ, risking his life to complete
your service to me.

Jerusalem Bible

The mission of Timothy and Epaphroditus

19 I hope, in the Lord Jesus, to send Timothy
to you soon, and I shall be reassured by having
news of you. 20 I have nobody else like him
here, as wholeheartedly concerned for your welfare: 21 all the rest seem more interested in
themselves than in Jesus Christ. 22 But you know
how he has proved himself by working with me
on behalf of the Good News like a son helping
his father. 23 That is why he is the one that I
am hoping to send you, as soon as I know something definite about my fate. 24 But I continue
to trust, in the Lord, that I shall be coming
soon myself.

25 It is essential, I think, to send brother
Epaphroditus back to you. He was sent as your
representative to help me when I needed someone to be my companion in working and battling, 26 but he misses you all and is worried
because you heard about his illness. 27 It is true
that he has been ill, and almost died, but God
took pity on him, and on me as well as him,
and spared me what would have been one grief
on top of another. 28 So I shall send him back
as promptly as I can; you will be happy to see
him again, and that will make me less sorry.
29 Give him a most hearty welcome, in the Lord;
people like him are to be honored. 30 It was
for Christ's work that he came so near to dying, and he risked his life to give me the help
that you were not able to give me yourselves.

New English Bible

I hope (under the Lord Jesus) to send Timothy to you soon; it will cheer me to hear news of you. There is no one else here who sees things as I do, and takes[d] a genuine interest in your concerns; they are all bent on their own ends, not on the cause of Christ Jesus. But Timothy's record is known to you: you know that he has been at my side in the service of the Gospel like a son working under his father. Timothy, then, I hope to send as soon as ever I can see how things are going with me; and I am confident, under the Lord, that I shall myself be coming before long.

I feel also I must send our brother Epaphroditus, my fellow-worker and comrade, whom you commissioned to minister to my needs. He has been missing all of you sadly, and has been distressed that you heard he was ill. (He was indeed dangerously ill, but God was merciful to him, and merciful no less to me, to spare me sorrow upon sorrow.) For this reason I am all the more eager to send him, to give you the happiness of seeing him again, and to relieve my sorrow. Welcome him then in the fellowship of the Lord with whole-hearted delight. You should honor men like him; in Christ's cause he came near to death, risking his life to render me the service you could not give.

[*d*] *Or* no one else here like him, who takes . . .

King James Version

3 Finally, my brethren, rejoice in the Lord.
To write the same things to you, to me indeed
is not grievous, but for you *it is* safe. 2 Beware
of dogs, beware of evil workers, beware of the
concision. 3 For we are the circumcision, which
worship God in the spirit, and rejoice in Christ
Jesus, and have no confidence in the flesh.
4 Though I might also have confidence in the
flesh. If any other man thinketh that he hath
whereof he might trust in the flesh, I more:
5 Circumcised the eighth day, of the stock of
Israel, *of* the tribe of Benjamin, a Hebrew of the
Hebrews; as touching the law, a Pharisee; 6 Con-

Living Bible

3 Whatever happens, dear friends, be glad
in the Lord. I never get tired of telling you
this and it is good for you to hear it again and
again.
2 Watch out for those wicked men—dangerous dogs, I call them—who say you must be
circumcised to be saved. 3 For it isn't the *cutting
of our bodies* that makes us children of God; it is
worshiping him with our spirits. That is the only
true "circumcision." We Christians glory in what
Christ Jesus has done for us and realize that we
are helpless to save ourselves.
4 Yet if anyone ever had reason to hope that
he could save himself, it would be I. If others
could be saved by what they are, certainly I
could! 5 For I went through the Jewish initiation ceremony when I was eight days old, having been born into a pure-blooded Jewish home
that was a branch of the old original Benjamin
family. So I was a real Jew if there ever was
one! What's more, I was a member of the
Pharisees who demand the strictest obedience to
every Jewish law and custom. 6And sincere? Yes,

Today's English Version

The true righteousness

3 In conclusion, my brothers, may the Lord
give you much joy. It doesn't bother me to
repeat what I have written before, and it will
add to your safety. 2 Watch out for those who
do evil things, those dogs, men who insist on
cutting the body. 3 For we, not they, are the
ones who have received the true circumcision,
because we worship God by his Spirit, and rejoice in our life in Christ Jesus. We do not put
any trust in external ceremonies. 4 I could, of
course, put my trust in such things. If anyone
thinks he can trust in external ceremonies, I
have even more reason to feel that way. 5 I was
circumcised when I was a week old. I am an
Israelite by birth, of the tribe of Benjamin, a
pure-blooded Hebrew. So far as keeping the
Jewish Law is concerned, I was a Pharisee,
6 and I was so zealous that I persecuted the

New International Version

No confidence in the flesh

3 Finally, my brothers, rejoice in the Lord!
It is no trouble for me to write the same
things to you again, and it is a safeguard for you.
2 Watch out for those dogs, those men who
do evil, those mutilators of the flesh. 3 For it is
we who are the circumcision, we who worship by
the Spirit of God, who glory in Christ Jesus, and
who put no confidence in the flesh—4 though I
myself have reasons for such confidence.
If anyone else thinks he has reasons to put
confidence in the flesh, I have more: 5 circumcised on the eighth day, of the people of Israel,
of the tribe of Benjamin, a Hebrew of Hebrews;
in regard to the law, a Pharisee; 6 as for zeal,

Phillips Modern English

Finally, my brothers, delight yourselves in the Lord! It doesn't bore me to repeat a piece of advice like this, and you will find it a safeguard to your souls.

3.2 The "circumcision" party are the enemies of your faith and freedom

Be on your guard against these curs, these wicked workmen, these would-be mutilators of your bodies! We are truly circumcised when we worship God by the Spirit; we pride ourselves in Jesus Christ and put no confidence in the flesh.

3.4 I was even more of a Jew than these Jews, yet knowing Christ has changed my whole life

If it were right to have such confidence, I could certainly have it, and if any of these men thinks he has grounds for such confidence I can assure him I have more. I was born from the people of Israel, I was circumcised on the eighth day, I was a member of the tribe of Benjamin. I was in fact a full-blooded Jew. As far as keeping the Law is concerned I was a Pharisee, and you can judge my enthusiasm for

Revised Standard Version

3 Finally, my brethren, rejoice in the Lord.
To write the same things to you is not irksome to me, and is safe for you.
2 Look out for the dogs, look out for the
evil-workers, look out for those who mutilate
the flesh. 3 For we are the true circumcision,
who worship God in spirit,[e] and glory in Christ
Jesus, and put no confidence in the flesh.
4 Though I myself have reason for confidence
in the flesh also. If any other man thinks he
has reason for confidence in the flesh, I have
more: 5 circumcised on the eighth day, of the
people of Israel, of the tribe of Benjamin, a
Hebrew born of Hebrews; as to the law a Pharisee, 6 as to zeal a persecutor of the church, as

[e] Other ancient authorities read *worship by the Spirit of God.*

Jerusalem Bible

3 Finally, my brothers, rejoice in the Lord.[f]

The true way of Christian salvation

It is no trouble to me to repeat what I have
already written to you, and as far as you are
concerned, it will make for safety. 2 Beware of
dogs! Watch out for the people who are making mischief. Watch out for the cutters.[g] 3 We
are the real people of the circumcision, we who
worship in accordance with the Spirit of God;
we have our own glory from Christ Jesus without having to rely on a physical operation. 4 If
it came to relying on physical evidence, I should
be fully qualified myself. Take any man who
thinks he can rely on what is physical: I am
even better qualified. 5 I was born of the race
of Israel and of the tribe of Benjamin, a Hebrew born of Hebrew parents, and I was circumcised when I was eight days old. As for the
Law, I was a Pharisee; 6 as for working for

[f] Paul's conclusion is interrupted by a long postscript. [g] A contemptuous reference to the circumcisers comparing circumcision with self-inflicted gashes in pagan cults.

New English Bible

3 And now, friends, farewell; I wish you joy in the Lord.

To repeat what I have written to you before is no trouble to me, and it is a safeguard for you. Beware of those dogs and their malpractices. Beware of those who insist on mutilation—'circumcision' I will not call it; we are the circumcised, we whose worship is spiritual,[a] whose pride is in Christ Jesus, and who put no confidence in anything external. Not that I am without grounds myself even for confidence of that kind. If anyone thinks to base his claims on externals, I could make a stronger case for myself: circumcised on my eighth day, Israelite by race, of the tribe of Benjamin, a Hebrew born and bred;[b] in my attitude to the law, a Pharisee; in pious zeal, a persecutor of the church; in legal

[a] *Some witnesses read* who worship God in the spirit; *others read* who worship by the Spirit of God. [b] *Or* a Hebrew-speaking Jew of a Hebrew-speaking family.

King James Version

cerning zeal, persecuting the church; touching
the righteousness which is in the law, blameless.
7 But what things were gain to me, those I
counted loss for Christ. 8 Yea doubtless, and I
count all things *but* loss for the excellency of
the knowledge of Christ Jesus my Lord: for
whom I have suffered the loss of all things, and
do count them *but* dung, that I may win Christ,
9 And be found in him, not having mine own
righteousness, which is of the law, but that which
is through the faith of Christ, the righteousness
which is of God by faith: 10 That I may know
him, and the power of his resurrection, and the
fellowship of his sufferings, being made con-
formable unto his death; 11 If by any means I
might attain unto the resurrection of the dead.
12 Not as though I had already attained, either
were already perfect: but I follow after, if that
I may apprehend that for which also I am apprehended of Christ Jesus. 13 Brethren, I count not
myself to have apprehended: but *this* one thing
I do, forgetting those things which are behind,
and reaching forth unto those things which are
before, 14 I press toward the mark for the prize

Living Bible

so much so that I greatly persecuted the church;
and I tried to obey every Jewish rule and regulation right down to the very last point.

7 But all these things that I once thought
very worthwhile—now I've thrown them all away
so that I can put my trust and hope in Christ
alone. 8 Yes, everything else is worthless when
compared with the priceless gain of knowing
Christ Jesus my Lord. I have put aside all else,
counting it worth less than nothing, in order that
I can have Christ, 9 and become one with him,
no longer counting on being saved by being
good enough or by obeying God's laws, but by
trusting Christ to save me; for God's way of
making us right with himself depends on faith
—counting on Christ alone. 10 Now I have given
up everything else—I have found it to be the
only way to really know Christ and to experience
the mighty power that brought him back to life
again, and to find out what it means to suffer
and to die with him. 11 So, whatever it takes, I
will be one who lives in the fresh newness of
life of those who are alive from the dead.

12 I don't mean to say I am perfect. I haven't
learned all I should even yet, but I keep working toward that day when I will finally be all
that Christ saved me for and wants me to be.

13 No, dear brothers, I am still not all I
should be but I am bringing all my energies to
bear on this one thing: Forgetting the past and
looking forward to what lies ahead, 14 I strain
to reach the end of the race and receive the prize
for which God is calling us up to heaven because
of what Christ Jesus did for us.

Today's English Version

church. So far as a man can be righteous by
obeying the commands of the Law, I was without fault. 7 But all those things that I might
count as profit I now reckon as loss, for Christ's
sake. 8 Not only those things; I reckon everything as complete loss for the sake of what is so
much more valuable, the knowledge of Christ
Jesus my Lord. For his sake I have thrown
everything away; I consider it all as mere garbage, so that I might gain Christ, 9 and be completely united with him. No longer do I have a
righteousness of my own, the kind to be gained
by obeying the Law. I now have the righteousness that is given through faith in Christ, the
righteousness that comes from God, and is
based on faith. 10 All I want is to know Christ
and to experience the power of his resurrection;
to share in his sufferings and become like him
in his death, 11 in the hope that I myself will
be raised from death to life.

Running toward the goal

12 I do not claim that I have already succeeded or have already become perfect. I keep
going on to try to win the prize for which
Christ Jesus has already won me to himself.
13 Of course, brothers, I really do not think
that I have already won it; the one thing I do,
however, is to forget what is behind me and do
my best to reach what is ahead. 14 So I run
straight toward the goal in order to win the
prize, which is God's call through Christ Jesus
to the life above.

New International Version

persecuting the church; as for legalistic righteousness, faultless.

7 But whatever was to my profit I now consider loss for the sake of Christ. 8 What is more,
I consider everything a loss compared to the surpassing greatness of knowing Christ Jesus my
Lord, for whose sake I have lost all things. I
consider them rubbish, that I may gain Christ
9 and be found in him, not having a righteousness of my own that comes from the law, but
that which is through faith in Christ—the righteousness that comes from God and is by faith.
10 I want to know Christ and the power of his
resurrection and the fellowship of sharing in his
sufferings, becoming like him in his death, 11 and
so, somehow, to attain to the resurrection from
the dead.

Pressing on toward the goal

12 Not that I have already obtained all this,
or have already been made perfect, but I press
on to take hold of that for which Christ Jesus
took hold of me. 13 Brothers, I do not consider myself yet to have taken hold of it. But
one thing I do: Forgetting what is behind and
straining toward what is ahead, 14 I press on
toward the goal to win the prize for which God
has called me heavenward in Christ Jesus.

Phillips Modern English

the Jewish faith by my active persecution of the Church. As far as the Law's righteousness is concerned, I don't think anyone could have found fault with me. Yet every advantage that I had gained I considered lost for Christ's sake. Yes, and I look upon everything as loss compared with the overwhelming gain of knowing Christ Jesus my Lord. For his sake I did in fact suffer the loss of everything, but I considered it mere garbage compared with being able to win Christ. For now my place is in him, and I am not dependent upon any of the self-achieved righteousness of the Law; God has given me that genuine righteousness which comes from faith in Christ. Now I long to know Christ and the power shown by his resurrection; now I long to share his sufferings, even to die as he died, so that I may somehow attain the resurrection from the dead. Not that I claim to have achieved all this, nor to have reached perfection already. But I keep going on, trying to grasp that purpose for which Christ Jesus grasped me. My brothers, I do not consider myself to have grasped it fully even now. But I do concentrate on this: I forget all that lies behind me and with hands outstretched to whatever lies ahead I go straight for the goal—my reward the honour of my high calling by God in Christ Jesus.

Revised Standard Version

to righteousness under the law blameless. 7 But whatever gain I had, I counted as loss for the sake of Christ. 8 Indeed I count everything as loss because of the surpassing worth of knowing Christ Jesus my Lord. For his sake I have suffered the loss of all things, and count them as refuse, in order that I may gain Christ 9 and be found in him, not having a righteousness of my own, based on law, but that which is through faith in Christ, the righteousness from God that depends on faith; 10 that I may know him and the power of his resurrection, and may share his sufferings, becoming like him in his death, 11 that if possible I may attain the resurrection from the dead.

12 Not that I have already obtained this or am already perfect; but I press on to make it my own, because Christ Jesus has made me his own. 13 Brethren, I do not consider that I have made it my own; but one thing I do, forgetting what lies behind and straining forward to what lies ahead, 14 I press on toward the goal for the prize of the upward call of God in Christ

Jerusalem Bible

religion, I was a persecutor of the Church; as far as the Law can make you perfect, I was faultless. 7 But because of Christ, I have come to consider all these advantages that I had as disadvantages. 8 Not only that, but I believe nothing can happen that will outweigh the supreme advantage of knowing Christ Jesus my Lord. For him I have accepted the loss of everything, and I look on everything as so much rubbish if only I can have Christ 9 and be given a place in him. I am no longer trying for perfection by my own efforts, the perfection that comes from the Law, but I want only the perfection that comes through faith in Christ, and is from God and based on faith. 10 All I want is to know Christ and the power of his resurrection and to share his sufferings by reproducing the pattern of his death. 11 That is the way I can hope to take my place in the resurrection of the dead. 12 Not that I have become perfect yet: I have not yet won, but I am still running, trying to capture the prize for which Christ Jesus captured me. 13 I can assure you my brothers, I am far from thinking that I have already won. All I can say is that I forget the past and I strain ahead for what is still to come; 14 I am racing for the finish, for the prize to which God calls us upward to receive in Christ

New English Bible

rectitude, faultless. But all such assets I have written off because of Christ. I would say more: I count everything sheer loss, because all is far outweighed by the gain of knowing Christ Jesus my Lord, for whose sake I did in fact lose everything. I count it so much garbage,[c] for the sake of gaining Christ and finding myself incorporate in him, with no righteousness of my own, no legal rectitude, but the righteousness which comes[d] from faith in Christ, given by God in response to faith. All I care for is to know Christ, to experience the power of his resurrection, and to share his sufferings, in growing conformity with his death, if only I may finally arrive at the resurrection from the dead.

It is not to be thought that I have already achieved all this. I have not yet reached perfection, but I press on, hoping to take hold of that for which Christ once took hold of me. My friends, I do not reckon myself to have got hold of it yet. All I can say is this: forgetting what is behind me, and reaching out for that which lies ahead, I press towards the goal to win the prize which is God's call to the life above, in Christ Jesus.

[c] *Or* dung. [d] *Or* and in him finding that, though I have no righteousness of my own, no legal rectitude, I have the righteousness which comes . . .

King James Version

of the high calling of God in Christ Jesus. 15 Let
us therefore, as many as be perfect, be thus
minded: and if in any thing ye be otherwise
minded, God shall reveal even this unto you.
16 Nevertheless, whereto we have already attained, let us walk by the same rule, let us mind
the same thing. 17 Brethren, be followers together of me, and mark them which walk so as
ye have us for an ensample. 18 (For many walk,
of whom I have told you often, and now tell you
even weeping, *that they are* the enemies of the
cross of Christ: 19 Whose end *is* destruction,
whose God *is their* belly, and *whose* glory *is* in
their shame, who mind earthly things.) 20 For
our conversation is in heaven; from whence also
we look for the Saviour, the Lord Jesus Christ:
21 Who shall change our vile body, that it may
be fashioned like unto his glorious body, according to the working whereby he is able even to
subdue all things unto himself.

4 Therefore, my brethren dearly beloved and
longed for, my joy and crown, so stand fast

Living Bible

15 I hope all of you who are mature Christians will see eye-to-eye with me on these things,
and if you disagree on some point, I believe that
God will make it plain to you—16 if you fully
obey the truth you have.

17 Dear brothers, pattern your lives after
mine and notice who else lives up to my example.
18 For I have told you often before, and I say it
again now with tears in my eyes, there are many
who walk along the Christian road who are really
enemies of the cross of Christ. 19 Their future is
eternal loss, for their god is their appetite: they
are proud of what they should be ashamed of;
and all they think about is this life here on earth.
20 But our homeland is in heaven, where our
Savior the Lord Jesus Christ is; and we are looking forward to his return from there. 21 When
he comes back he will take these dying bodies
of ours and change them into glorious bodies
like his own, using the same mighty power that
he will use to conquer all else everywhere.

4 Dear brother Christians, I love you and long
to see you, for you are my joy and my reward for my work. My beloved friends, stay true
to the Lord.

Today's English Version

15 All of us who are spiritually mature should
have this same attitude. If, however, some of
you have a different attitude, God will make
this clear to you. 16 However that may be, let us
go forward according to the same rules we have
followed until now.

17 Keep on imitating me, my brothers. We
have set the right example for you, so pay
attention to those who follow it. 18 I have told
you this many times before, and now I repeat
it, with tears: there are many whose lives make
them enemies of Christ's death on the cross.
19 They are going to end up in hell, because
their god is their bodily desires, they are proud
of what they should be ashamed of, and they
think only of things that belong to this world.
20 We, however, are citizens of heaven, and we
eagerly wait for our Savior to come from
heaven, the Lord Jesus Christ. 21 He will change
our weak mortal bodies and make them like his
own glorious body, using that power by which
he is able to bring all things under his rule.

Instructions

4 So, then, my brothers—and how dear you
are to me, and how I miss you! how happy
you make me, and how proud I am of you!—
this, dear brothers, is how you should stand
firm in your life in the Lord.

New International Version

15 All of us who are mature should take such
a view of things. And if on some point you think
differently, that too God will make clear to you.
16 Only let us live up to what we have already
attained.

17 Join with others in following my example,
brothers, and take note of those who live according to the pattern we gave you. 18 For, as
I have often told you before and now say again
even with tears, many live as enemies of the
cross of Christ. 19 Their destiny is destruction,
their god is their stomach, and their glory is in
their shame. Their mind is on earthly things.
20 But our citizenship is in heaven. And we
eagerly await a Savior from there, the Lord Jesus Christ, 21 who, by the power that enables
him to bring everything under his control, will
transform our lowly bodies so that they will be
like his glorious body.

4 Therefore, my brothers, you whom I love
and long for, my joy and crown, that is how
you should stand firm in the Lord, dear friends!

Phillips Modern English

3.15 My ambition is the true goal of the spiritually adult: make it yours too

All of us who are spiritually adult should think like this, and if at present you think otherwise, yet you will find that God will make even this clear to you. It is important that we go forward in the light of such truth as we have already learned.

My brothers I should like you all to imitate me and observe those whose lives are based on the pattern that we give you. For there are many, of whom I have told you before and tell you again now, even with tears, whose lives make them the enemies of the cross of Christ. These men are heading for utter destruction—their god is their own appetite, they glory in their shame, and this world is the limit of their horizon. But we are citizens of Heaven; we eagerly wait for the saviour who will come from Heaven, the Lord Jesus Christ. He will change these wretched bodies of ours so that they resemble his own glorious body, by that power of his which makes him in command of everything.

So, my brothers whom I love and long for, my joy and my crown, do stand firmly in the Lord, and remember how much I love you.

Revised Standard Version

Jesus. 15 Let those of us who are mature be thus minded; and if in anything you are otherwise minded, God will reveal that also to you. 16 Only let us hold true to what we have attained.

17 Brethren, join in imitating me, and mark those who so live as you have an example in us. 18 For many, of whom I have often told you and now tell you even with tears, live as enemies of the cross of Christ. 19 Their end is destruction, their god is the belly, and they glory in their shame, with minds set on earthly things. 20 But our commonwealth is in heaven, and from it we await a Savior, the Lord Jesus Christ, 21 who will change our lowly body to be like his glorious body, by the power which enables him even to subject all things to himself.

4 Therefore, my brethren, whom I love and long for, my joy and crown, stand firm thus in the Lord, my beloved.

Jerusalem Bible

Jesus. 15 We who are called "perfect" must all think in this way. If there is some point on which you see things differently, God will make it clear to you; 16 meanwhile, let us go forward on the road that has brought us to where we are.

17 My brothers, be united in following my rule of life. Take as your models everybody who is already doing this and study them as you used to study us. 18 I have told you often, and I repeat it today with tears, there are many who are behaving as the enemies of the cross of Christ. 19 They are destined to be lost. They make foods into their god and they are proudest of something they ought to think shameful; the things they think important are earthly things. 20 For us, our homeland is in heaven, and from heaven comes the Savior we are waiting for, the Lord Jesus Christ, 21 and he will transfigure these wretched bodies of ours into copies of his glorious body. He will do that by the same power with which he can subdue the whole universe.

4 So then, my brothers and dear friends, do not give way but remain faithful in the Lord. I miss you very much, dear friends; you are my joy and my crown.

New English Bible

Let us then keep to this way of thinking, those of us who are mature. If there is any point on which you think differently, this also God will make plain to you. Only let our conduct be consistent with the level we have already reached.

Agree together, my friends, to follow my example. You have us for a model; watch those whose way of life conforms to it. For, as I have often told you, and now tell you with tears in my eyes, there are many whose way of life makes them enemies of the cross of Christ. They are heading for destruction, appetite is their god, and they glory in their shame. Their minds are set on earthly things. We, by contrast, are citizens of heaven, and from heaven we expect our deliverer to come, the Lord Jesus Christ. He will transfigure the body belonging to our humble state, and give it a form like that of his own resplendent body, by the very power which enables him to make all things subject to himself.

4 Therefore, my friends, beloved friends whom I long for, my joy, my crown, stand thus firm in the Lord, my beloved!

King James Version

in the Lord, *my* dearly beloved. 2 I beseech
Euodias, and beseech Syntyche, that they be of
the same mind in the Lord. 3 And I entreat thee
also, true yokefellow, help those women which
laboured with me in the gospel, with Clement
also, and *with* other my fellow labourers, whose
names *are* in the book of life. 4 Rejoice in the
Lord always: *and* again I say, Rejoice. 5 Let your
moderation be known unto all men. The Lord
is at hand. 6 Be careful for nothing; but in every
thing by prayer and supplication with thanksgiving let your requests be made known unto God.
7 And the peace of God, which passeth all understanding, shall keep your hearts and minds
through Christ Jesus. 8 Finally, brethren, whatsoever things are true, whatsoever things *are*
honest, whatsoever things *are* just, whatsoever
things *are* pure, whatsoever things *are* lovely,
whatsoever things *are* of good report; if *there be*
any virtue, and if *there be* any praise, think on
these things. 9 Those things, which ye have both
learned, and received, and heard, and seen in me,
do: and the God of peace shall be with you.

Living Bible

2 And now I want to plead with those two
dear women, Euodias and Syntyche. Please,
please, with the Lord's help, quarrel no more—
be friends again. 3 And I ask you, my true team-
mate, to help these women, for they worked
side by side with me in telling the Good News
to others; and they worked with Clement, too,
and the rest of my fellow workers whose names
are written in the Book of Life.

4 Always be full of joy in the Lord; I say it
again, rejoice! 5 Let everyone see that you are
unselfish and considerate in all you do. Remember that the Lord is coming soon. 6 Don't worry
about anything; instead, pray about everything;
tell God your needs and don't forget to thank
him for his answers. 7 If you do this you will experience God's peace, which is far more wonderful than the human mind can understand. His
peace will keep your thoughts and your hearts
quiet and at rest as you trust in Christ Jesus.

8 And now, brothers, as I close this letter let
me say this one more thing: Fix your thoughts
on what is true and good and right. Think about
things that are pure and lovely, and dwell on the
fine, good things in others. Think about all you
can praise God for and be glad about. 9 Keep
putting into practice all you learned from me
and saw me doing, and the God of peace will be
with you.

Today's English Version

2 Euodia and Syntyche, please, I beg you, try
to agree as sisters in the Lord. 3 And you too,
my faithful partner, I want you to help these
women; for they have worked hard with me to
spread the gospel, together with Clement and
all my other fellow workers, whose names are
in God's book of the living.

4 May you always be joyful in your life in the
Lord. I say it again: rejoice!

5 Show a gentle attitude toward all. The Lord
is coming soon. 6 Don't worry about anything,
but in all your prayers ask God for what you
need, always asking him with a thankful heart.
7 And God's peace, which is far beyond human
understanding, will keep your hearts and minds
safe, in union with Christ Jesus.

8 In conclusion, my brothers, fill your minds
with those things that are good and deserve
praise: things that are true, noble, right, pure,
lovely, and honorable. 9 Put into practice what
you learned and received from me, both from
my words and from my deeds. And the God
who gives us peace will be with you.

New International Version

Exhortations

2 I plead with Euodia and I plead with Syntyche to agree with each other in the Lord. 3 Yes,
and I ask you, loyal yokefellow,[f] help these
women who have contended at my side in the
cause of the gospel, along with Clement and the
rest of my fellow workers, whose names are in
the book of life.

4 Rejoice in the Lord always. I will say it
again: Rejoice! 5 Let your gentleness be evident
to all. The Lord is near. 6 Do not be anxious
about anything, but in everything, by prayer and
petition, with thanksgiving, present your requests to God. 7 And the peace of God, which
transcends all understanding, will guard your
hearts and your minds in Christ Jesus.

8 Finally, brothers, whatever is true, whatever is noble, whatever is right, whatever is
pure, whatever is lovely, whatever is admirable
—if anything is excellent or praiseworthy—
think about such things. 9 Whatever you have
learned or received or heard from me, or seen
in me—put it into practice. And the God of
peace will be with you.

[f] Or *loyal Syzygus.*

Phillips Modern English

4.2 *Be united, be joyful, be at peace*

Euodia and Syntyche, I beg you by name to make up your differences as Christians should! And you, my true fellow-worker, I ask you to help these women. They both worked hard with me for the gospel, as did Clement and all my other fellow-workers whose names are in the book of life.

Delight yourselves in the Lord, yes, find your joy in him at all times. Have a reputation for being reasonable, and never forget the nearness of your Lord.

Don't worry over anything whatever; whenever you pray tell God every detail of your needs in thankful prayer, and the peace of God, which surpasses human understanding, will keep constant guard over your hearts and minds as they rest in Christ Jesus.

My brothers I need only add this. If you believe in goodness and if you value the approval of God, fix your minds on whatever is true and honourable and just and pure and lovely and admirable. Put into practice what you have learned from me and what I passed on to you, both what you heard from me and what you saw in me, and the God of peace will be with you.

Revised Standard Version

2 I entreat Euodia and I entreat Syntyche to
agree in the Lord. 3 And I ask you also, true
yokefellow, help these women, for they have
labored side by side with me in the gospel together with Clement and the rest of my fellow
workers, whose names are in the book of life.
4 Rejoice in the Lord always; again I will
say, Rejoice. 5 Let all men know your forbearance. The Lord is at hand. 6 Have no anxiety
about anything, but in everything by prayer and
supplication with thanksgiving let your requests
be made known to God. 7 And the peace of God,
which passes all understanding, will keep your
hearts and your minds in Christ Jesus.

8 Finally, brethren, whatever is true, whatever is honorable, whatever is just, whatever is
pure, whatever is lovely, whatever is gracious,
if there is any excellence, if there is anything
worthy of praise, think about these things.
9 What you have learned and received and
heard and seen in me, do; and the God of peace
will be with you.

Jerusalem Bible

Last advice

2 I appeal to Evodia and I appeal to Syntyche
to come to agreement with each other, in the
Lord; 3 and I ask you, Syzygus,[h] to be truly a
"companion" and to help them in this. These
women were a help to me when I was fighting
to defend the Good News—and so, at the same
time, were Clement and the others who worked
with me. Their names are written in the book
of life.
4 I want you to be happy, always happy in
the Lord; I repeat, what I want is your happiness. 5 Let your tolerance be evident to everyone: the Lord is very near. 6 There is no need
to worry; but if there is anything you need,
pray for it, asking God for it with prayer and
thanksgiving, 7 and that peace of God, which
is so much greater than we can understand,
will guard your hearts and your thoughts, in
Christ Jesus. 8 Finally, brothers, fill your minds
with everything that is true, everything that is
noble, everything that is good and pure, everything that we love and honor, and everything
that can be thought virtuous or worthy of praise.
9 Keep doing all the things that you learned
from me and have been taught by me and have
heard or seen that I do. Then the God of peace
will be with you.

[h] "Companion" is the meaning of the proper name Syzygus.

New English Bible

I beg Euodia, and I beg Syntyche, to agree together in the Lord's fellowship. Yes, and you too, my loyal comrade, I ask you to help these women, who shared my struggles in the cause of the Gospel, with Clement and my other fellow-workers, whose[a] names are in the roll of the living.

Farewell; I wish you all joy in the Lord. I will say it again: all joy be yours.

Let your magnanimity be manifest to all.

The Lord is near; have no anxiety, but in everything make your requests known to God in prayer and petition with thanksgiving. Then the peace of God, which is beyond our utmost understanding,[b] will keep guard over your hearts and your thoughts, in Christ Jesus.

And now, my friends, all that is true, all that is noble, all that is just and pure, all that is lovable and gracious,[c] whatever is excellent and admirable—fill all your thoughts with these things.

The lessons I taught you, the tradition I have passed on, all that you heard me say or saw me do, put into practice; and the God of peace will be with you.

[a] *Some witnesses read* my fellow-workers, and the others whose . . . [b] *Or* of far more worth than human reasoning. [c] *Or* of good repute.

King James Version

10 But I rejoiced in the Lord greatly, that now
at the last your care of me hath flourished again;
wherein ye were also careful, but ye lacked opportunity. 11 Not that I speak in respect of want:
for I have learned, in whatsoever state I am,
therewith to be content. 12 I know both how to
be abased, and I know how to abound: every
where and in all things I am instructed both to
be full and to be hungry, both to abound and
to suffer need. 13 I can do all things through
Christ which strengtheneth me. 14 Notwithstanding, ye have well done, that ye did communicate with my affliction. 15 Now ye Philippians
know also, that in the beginning of the gospel,
when I departed from Macedonia, no church
communicated with me as concerning giving and
receiving, but ye only. 16 For even in Thessalonica ye sent once and again unto my necessity.
17 Not because I desire a gift: but I desire fruit
that may abound to your account. 18 But I have
all, and abound: I am full, having received of
Epaphroditus the things *which were sent* from
you, an odour of a sweet smell, a sacrifice acceptable, well pleasing to God. 19 But my God
shall supply all your need according to his riches
in glory by Christ Jesus. 20 Now unto God and
our Father *be* glory for ever and ever. Amen.

Living Bible

10 How grateful I am and how I praise the
Lord that you are helping me again. I know you
have always been anxious to send what you
could, but for a while you didn't have the
chance. 11 Not that I was ever in need, for I
have learned how to get along happily whether
I have much or little. 12 I know how to live on
almost nothing or with everything. I have learned
the secret of contentment in every situation,
whether it be a full stomach or hunger, plenty
or want; 13 for I can do everything God asks me
to with the help of Christ who gives me the
strength and power. 14 But even so, you have
done right in helping me in my present difficulty.
15 As you well know, when I first brought the
Gospel to you and then went on my way, leaving
Macedonia, only you Philippians became my
partners in giving and receiving. No other church
did this. 16 Even when I was over in Thessalonica
you sent help twice. 17 But though I appreciate
your gifts, what makes me happiest is the well-
earned reward you will have because of your
kindness.
18 At the moment I have all I need—more
than I need! I am generously supplied with the
gifts you sent me when Epaphroditus came. They
are a sweet-smelling sacrifice that pleases God
well. 19And it is he who will supply all your
needs from his riches in glory, because of what
Christ Jesus has done for us. 20 Now unto God
our Father be glory forever and ever. Amen.

Sincerely,
Paul

Today's English Version

Thanks for the gift

10 How great is the joy I have in my life in
the Lord! After so long a time, you once more
had the chance of showing that you care for me.
I don't mean that you had quit caring for me—
you did not have a chance to show it. 11And I
am not saying this because I feel neglected; for
I have learned to be satisfied with what I have.
12 I know what it is to be in need, and what it is
to have more than enough. I have learned this
secret, so that anywhere, at any time, I am content, whether I am full or hungry, whether I
have too much or too little. 13 I have the
strength to face all conditions by the power that
Christ gives me.
14 But it was very good of you to help me
in my troubles. 15 You Philippians yourselves
know very well that when I left Macedonia,
in the early days of preaching the Good News,
you were the only church to help me; you were
the only ones who shared my profits and losses.
16 More than once, when I needed help in
Thessalonica, you sent it to me. 17 It is not that
I just want to receive gifts; rather, I want to see
profit added to your account. 18 Here, then, is
my receipt for everything you have given me—
and it has been more than enough! I have all I
need, now that Epaphroditus has brought me all
your gifts. These are like a sweet-smelling offering to God, a sacrifice which is acceptable and
pleasing to him. 19And my God, with all his
abundant wealth in Christ Jesus, will supply all
your needs. 20 To our God and Father be the
glory forever and ever. Amen.

New International Version

Thanks for the gifts

10 I rejoice greatly in the Lord that at last
you have renewed your concern for me. Indeed,
you have been concerned, but you had no opportunity to show it. 11 I am not saying this because I am in need, for I have learned to be content whatever the circumstances. 12 I know what
it is to be in need, and I know what it is to have
plenty. I have learned the secret of being content in any and every situation, whether well-fed
or hungry, whether living in plenty or in want.
13 I can do everything through him who gives me
strength.
14 Yet it was good of you to share in my
troubles. 15 Moreover, as you Philippians know,
in the early days of your acquaintance with the
gospel, when I set out from Macedonia, not one
church shared with me in the matter of giving
and receiving, except you only; 16 for even when
I was in Thessalonica, you sent me aid again
and again when I was in need. 17 Not that I am
looking for a gift, but I am looking for what may
be credited to your account. 18 I have received
full payment and even more; I am amply supplied, now that I have received from Epaphroditus the gifts you sent. They are a fragrant offering, an acceptable sacrifice, pleasing to God.
19And my God will meet all your needs according to his glorious riches in Christ Jesus.
20 To our God and Father be glory for ever
and ever. Amen.

Phillips Modern English

4.10 The memory of your generosity is an abiding joy to me

It is a great and truly Christian joy to me that after all this time you have shown such renewed interest in my welfare. I don't mean that you had forgotten me, but up till now you had no opportunity of expressing your concern. Nor do I mean that I have been in actual need, for I have learned to be content, whatever the circumstances may be. I know now how to live when things are difficult and I know how to live when things are prosperous. In general and in particular I have learned the secret of eating well or going hungry—of facing either plenty or poverty. I am ready for anything through the strength of the One who lives within me. Nevertheless I am very grateful for the way in which you were willing to share my troubles. You Philippians will remember that in the early days of the gospel when I left Macedonia, you were the only church who shared with me the fellowship of giving and receiving. Even in Thessalonica you sent me help when I was in need, not once but twice. It isn't the value of the gift that I am keen on, it is the reward that will be credited to you.

Now I have everything I want—in fact I am rich. Yes, I am quite content, thanks to your gifts received through Epaphroditus. Such generosity is like a lovely fragrance, a sacrifice that pleases the very heart of God. My God will supply all that you need from his glorious resources in Christ Jesus. And may glory be to our God and our Father for ever and ever, amen!

Revised Standard Version

10 I rejoice in the Lord greatly that now at length you have revived your concern for me; you were indeed concerned for me, but you had no opportunity. 11 Not that I complain of want; for I have learned, in whatever state I am, to be content. 12 I know how to be abased, and I know how to abound; in any and all circumstances I have learned the secret of facing plenty and hunger, abundance and want. 13 I can do all things in him who strengthens me.

14 Yet it was kind of you to share my trouble. 15 And you Philippians yourselves know that in the beginning of the gospel, when I left Macedonia, no church entered into partnership with me in giving and receiving except you only; 16 for even in Thessalonica you sent me help[f] once and again. 17 Not that I seek the gift; but I seek the fruit which increases to your credit. 18 I have received full payment, and more; I am filled, having received from Epaphroditus the gifts you sent, a fragrant offering, a sacrifice acceptable and pleasing to God. 19 And my God will supply every need of yours according to his riches in glory in Christ Jesus. 20 To our God and Father be glory for ever and ever. Amen.

[f] Other ancient authorities read *money for my needs.*

Jerusalem Bible

Thanks for help received

10 It is a great joy to me, in the Lord, that at last you have shown some concern for me again; though of course you were concerned before, and only lacked an opportunity. 11 I am not talking about shortage of money: I have learned to manage on whatever I have, 12 I know how to be poor and I know how to be rich too. I have been through my initiation and now I am ready for anything anywhere: full stomach or empty stomach, poverty or plenty. 13 There is nothing I cannot master with the help of the One who gives me strength. 14 All the same, it was good of you to share with me in my hardships. 15 In the early days of the Good News, as you people of Philippi well know, when I left Macedonia, no other church helped me with gifts of money. You were the only ones; 16 and twice since my stay in Thessalonika you have sent me what I needed. 17 It is not your gift that I value; what is valuable to me is the interest that is mounting up in your account. 18 Now for the time being I have everything that I need and more: I am fully provided now that I have received from Epaphroditus the offering that you sent, *a sweet fragrance*—the sacrifice that God accepts and finds pleasing. 19 In return my God will fulfill all your needs, in Christ Jesus, as lavishly as only God can. 20 Glory to God, our Father, for ever and ever. Amen.

New English Bible

It is a great joy to me, in the Lord, that after so long your care for me has now blossomed afresh. You did care about me before for that matter; it was opportunity that you lacked. Not that I am alluding to want, for I have learned to find resources in myself whatever my circumstances. I know what it is to be brought low, and I know what it is to have plenty. I have been very thoroughly initiated into the human lot with all its ups and downs—fullness and hunger, plenty and want. I have strength for anything through him who gives me power. But it was kind of you to share the burden of my troubles.

As you know yourselves, Philippians, in the early days of my mission, when I set out from Macedonia, you alone of all our congregations were my partners in payments and receipts; for even at Thessalonica you contributed to my needs, not once but twice over. Do not think I set my heart upon the gift; all I care for is the profit accruing to you. However, here I give you my receipt for everything—for more than everything; I am paid in full, now that I have received from Epaphroditus what you sent. It is a fragrant offering, an acceptable sacrifice, pleasing to God. And my God will supply all your wants out of the magnificence of his riches in Christ Jesus. To our God and Father be glory for endless ages! Amen.

King James Version

21 Salute every saint in Christ Jesus. The brethren which are with me greet you. 22All the saints salute you, chiefly they that are of Cesar's household. 23 The grace of our Lord Jesus Christ *be* with you all. Amen.

It was written to the Philippians from Rome by Epaphroditus.

Living Bible

P.S.

21 Say "hello" for me to all the Christians there; the brothers with me send their greetings too. 22And all the other Christians here want to be remembered to you, especially those who work in Caesar's palace. 23 The blessings of our Lord Jesus Christ be upon your spirits.

Today's English Version

Final greetings

21 Greetings to all God's people who belong to Christ Jesus. The brothers here with me send you their greetings. 22All God's people here send greetings, especially those who belong to the Emperor's palace.

23 May the grace of the Lord Jesus Christ be with you all.

New International Version

Final greetings

21 Greet all the saints in Christ Jesus. The brothers who are with me send greetings. 22All the saints send you greetings, especially those who belong to Caesar's household.

23 The grace of the Lord Jesus Christ be with your spirit.

Phillips Modern English

4.21 Farewell messages

Give my greetings in Christian fellowship to every one of God's people. The brothers here with me also send greetings. All the Christians here would like to send their best wishes, particularly those who belong to the emperor's household.

The grace of the Lord Jesus Christ be with your spirit.

Revised Standard Version

21 Greet every saint in Christ Jesus. The brethren who are with me greet you. 22 All the saints greet you, especially those of Caesar's household.
23 The grace of the Lord Jesus Christ be with your spirit.

Jerusalem Bible

Greetings and final wish

21 My greetings to every one of the saints in Christ Jesus. The brothers who are with me send their greetings. 22 All the saints send their greetings, especially those of the imperial household.[i]
23 May the grace of the Lord Jesus Christ be with your spirit.

[i] I.e., in the service of the emperor.

New English Bible

Give my greetings, in the fellowship of Christ Jesus, to each one of God's people. The brothers who are now with me send their greetings to you, and so do all God's people here, particularly those who belong to the imperial establishment.

The grace of our Lord Jesus Christ be with your spirit.

King James Version

THE EPISTLE OF PAUL THE APOSTLE TO THE COLOSSIANS

1 Paul, an apostle of Jesus Christ by the will
of God, and Timotheus *our* brother, 2 To the
saints and faithful brethren in Christ which are
at Colosse: Grace *be* unto you, and peace, from
God our Father and the Lord Jesus Christ. 3 We
give thanks to God and the Father of our Lord
Jesus Christ, praying always for you, 4 Since we
heard of your faith in Christ Jesus, and of the
love *which ye have* to all the saints, 5 For the
hope which is laid up for you in heaven, whereof
ye heard before in the word of the truth of the
gospel; 6 Which is come unto you, as *it is* in all

Living Bible

COLOSSIANS

1 *From:* Paul, chosen by God to be Jesus
Christ's messenger, and from Brother Timothy.
2 *To:* The faithful Christian brothers—God's
people—in the city of Colosse.
May God our Father shower you with blessings and fill you with his great peace. 3 Whenever we pray for you we always begin by giving
thanks to God the Father of our Lord Jesus
Christ, 4 for we have heard how much you trust
the Lord, and how much you love his people.
5 And you are looking forward to the joys of
heaven, and have been ever since the Gospel
first was preached to you. 6 The same Good

Today's English Version

PAUL'S LETTER TO THE COLOSSIANS

1 From Paul, who by God's will is an apostle of Christ Jesus, and from our brother
Timothy—
2 To God's people in Colossae, those who are
faithful brothers in Christ:
May God our Father give you grace and
peace.

Prayer of thanksgiving

3 We always give thanks to God, the Father
of our Lord Jesus Christ, when we pray for you.
4 For we have heard of your faith in Christ Jesus, and of your love for all God's people.
5 When the true message, the Good News, first
came to you, you heard of the hope it offers.
So your faith and love are based on what you
hope for, which is kept safe for you in heaven.
6 The gospel is bringing blessings and spreading

New International Version

COLOSSIANS

1 Paul, an apostle of Christ Jesus by the will
of God, and Timothy our brother,
2 To the holy and faithful brothers in Christ
at Colosse:
Grace and peace to you from God our
Father.[a]

Thanksgiving and prayer

3 We always thank God, the Father of our
Lord Jesus Christ, when we pray for you, 4 because we have heard of your faith in Christ Jesus
and of the love you have for all the saints—5 the
faith and love that spring from the hope stored
up for you in heaven, and which you have already heard about in the word of truth, the
gospel 6 that has come to you. All over the

[a] Some MSS add *and the Lord Jesus Christ.*

Phillips Modern English

THE LETTER TO THE CHRISTIANS AT COLOSSAE

Paul, a messenger of Christ Jesus by God's will, and our brother Timothy send this greeting to all faithful Christian brothers at Colossae: grace and peace be to you from God our Father!

1.3 *We thank God for you and pray constantly for you*

We here are constantly praying for you, and whenever we do we thank God the Father of our Lord Jesus Christ for you because we have heard that you believe in Christ Jesus and because you are showing true Christian love towards other Christians. We know that you are showing these qualities because you have grasped the hope reserved for you in Heaven—that hope which first became yours when you heard the message of truth. This is the gospel itself, which

Revised Standard Version

THE LETTER OF PAUL TO THE COLOSSIANS

1 Paul, an apostle of Christ Jesus by the will of God, and Timothy our brother,
2 To the saints and faithful brethren in Christ at Colossae:
Grace to you and peace from God our Father.

3 We always thank God, the Father of our
Lord Jesus Christ, when we pray for you, 4 because we have heard of your faith in Christ
Jesus and of the love which you have for all
the saints, 5 because of the hope laid up for
you in heaven. Of this you have heard before
in the word of the truth, the gospel 6 which has

Jerusalem Bible

THE LETTER OF PAUL TO THE CHURCH AT COLOSSAE COLOSSIANS

Preface

Address

1 From Paul, appointed by God to be apostle of Christ Jesus, and from our brother Timothy 2 to the saints in Colossae, our faithful
brothers in Christ: Grace and peace to you from God our Father.

Thanksgiving and prayer

3 We have never failed to remember you in
our prayers and to give thanks for you to God,
the Father of our Lord Jesus Christ, 4 ever since
we heard about your faith in Christ Jesus and
the love that you show toward all the saints
5 because of the hope which is stored up for
you in heaven. It is only recently that you heard
of this, when it was announced in the message
of the truth. The Good News 6 which has

New English Bible

THE LETTER OF PAUL TO THE COLOSSIANS

The centre of Christian belief

1 From Paul, apostle of Christ Jesus commissioned by the will of God, and our colleague Timothy, to God's people at Colossae, brothers in the faith, incorporate in Christ.

Grace to you and peace from God our Father.

In all our prayers to God, the Father of our Lord Jesus Christ, we thank him for you, because we have heard of the faith you hold in Christ Jesus, and the love you bear towards all God's people. Both spring from the hope stored up for you in heaven—that hope of which you learned when the message of the true Gospel first came to you. In the same way it is coming

King James Version

the world; and bringeth forth fruit, as *it doth*
also in you, since the day ye heard *of it*, and
knew the grace of God in truth: 7 As ye also
learned of Epaphras our dear fellow servant,
who is for you a faithful minister of Christ;
8 Who also declared unto us your love in the
Spirit. 9 For this cause we also, since the day
we heard *it*, do not cease to pray for you, and
to desire that ye might be filled with the knowledge of his will in all wisdom and spiritual understanding; 10 That ye might walk worthy of
the Lord unto all pleasing, being fruitful in every
good work, and increasing in the knowledge of
God; 11 Strengthened with all might, according
to his glorious power, unto all patience and
longsuffering with joyfulness; 12 Giving thanks
unto the Father, which hath made us meet to
be partakers of the inheritance of the saints in
light: 13 Who hath delivered us from the power
of darkness, and hath translated *us* into the kingdom of his dear Son: 14 In whom we have redemption through his blood, *even* the forgive-

Living Bible

News that came to you is going out all over the
world and changing lives everywhere, just as it
changed yours that very first day you heard it
and understood about God's great kindness to
sinners.
7 Epaphras, our much-loved fellow worker,
was the one who brought you this Good News.
He is Jesus Christ's faithful slave, here to help
us in your place. 8 And he is the one who has
told us about the great love for others which
the Holy Spirit has given you. 9 So ever since we
first heard about you we have kept on praying
and asking God to help you understand what he
wants you to do; asking him to make you wise
about spiritual things; 10 and asking that the
way you live will always please the Lord and
honor him, so that you will always be doing
good, kind things for others, while all the time
you are learning to know God better and better.
11 We are praying, too, that you will be filled
with his mighty, glorious strength so that you can
keep going no matter what happens—always full
of the joy of the Lord, 12 and always thankful
to the Father who has made us fit to share all
the wonderful things that belong to those who
live in the kingdom of light. 13 For he has rescued us out of the darkness and gloom of Satan's
kingdom and brought us into the kingdom of his
dear Son, 14 who bought our freedom with his
blood and forgave us all our sins.

Today's English Version

through the whole world, just as it has among
you ever since the day you first heard of the
grace of God and came to know it as it really
is. 7 You learned this from Epaphras, our dear
fellow servant, who is a faithful worker for
Christ on our behalf. 8 He told us of the love
that the Spirit has given you.
9 For this reason we always pray for you,
ever since we heard about you. We ask God to
fill you with the knowledge of his will, with all
the wisdom and understanding that his Spirit
gives. 10 Then you will be able to live as the
Lord wants, and always do what pleases him.
Your lives will be fruitful in all kinds of good
works, and you will grow in your knowledge of
God. 11 May you be made strong with all the
strength which comes from his glorious might,
so that you may be able to endure everything
with patience. 12 And give thanks, with joy, to
the Father, who has made you fit to have your
share of what God has reserved for his people
in the kingdom of light. 13 He rescued us from
the power of darkness and brought us safe into
the kingdom of his dear Son, 14 by whom we
are set free, that is, our sins are forgiven.

New International Version

world this gospel is producing fruit and growing, just as it has been doing among you since
the day you heard it and understood God's grace
in all its truth. 7 You learned it from Epaphras,
our dear fellow servant, who is a faithful minister of Christ on our[b] behalf, 8 and who also told
us of your love in the Spirit.
9 For this reason, since the day we heard
about you, we have not stopped praying for you
and asking God to fill you with the knowledge
of his will through all spiritual wisdom and understanding. 10 And we pray this in order that
you may live a life worthy of the Lord and may
please him in every way: bearing fruit in every
good work, growing in the knowledge of God,
11 being strengthened with all power according
to his glorious might so that you may have great
endurance and patience, and joyfully 12 giving
thanks to the Father, who has qualified you[c] to
share in the inheritance of the saints in the kingdom of light. 13 For he has rescued us from the
dominion of darkness and brought us into the
kingdom of the Son he loves, 14 in whom we
have redemption,[d] the forgiveness of sins.

[*b*] Some MSS read *your*. [*c*] Some MSS read *us*.
[*d*] A few late MSS add *through his blood*.

Phillips Modern English

has reached you as it spreads all over the world. Wherever that gospel goes, it produces Christian character, and develops it, as it has done in your own case from the time you first heard and realised the truth of God's grace.

You learned these things, we understand, from Epaphras, who is in the same service as we are. He is a faithful and well-loved minister of Christ, and has your well-being at heart. It was from him that we heard about your growth in Christian love, so you will understand that since we heard about you we have never missed you in our prayers. We are asking God that you may be filled with such wisdom and that you may understand his purpose. We also pray that your outward lives, which men see, may bring credit to your master's name, and that you may bring joy to his heart by bearing genuine Christian fruit in all that you do, and that your knowledge of God may grow yet deeper.

1.11 We pray for you to have real Christian experience

We pray that you will be strengthened from God's glorious power, so that you may be able to pass through any experience and endure it with joy. You will be able to thank the Father because you are privileged to share the lot of the saints who are living in the light. For he rescued us from the power of darkness, and re-established us in the kingdom of his beloved Son. For it is by him that we have been redeemed and have had our sins forgiven.

Revised Standard Version

come to you, as indeed in the whole world it is
bearing fruit and growing—so among yourselves,
from the day you heard and understood the
grace of God in truth, 7 as you learned it from
Epaphras our beloved fellow servant. He is a
faithful minister of Christ on our[a] behalf 8 and
has made known to us your love in the Spirit.
9 And so, from the day we heard of it, we
have not ceased to pray for you, asking that you
may be filled with the knowledge of his will in
all spiritual wisdom and understanding, 10 to
lead a life worthy of the Lord, fully pleasing to
him, bearing fruit in every good work and increasing in the knowledge of God. 11 May you
be strengthened with all power, according to his
glorious might, for all endurance and patience
with joy, 12 giving thanks to the Father, who
has qualified us[b] to share in the inheritance of
the saints in light. 13 He has delivered us from
the dominion of darkness and transferred us to
the kingdom of his beloved Son, 14 in whom we
have redemption, the forgiveness of sins.

[a] Other ancient authorities read *your*. [b] Other ancient authorities read *you*.

Jerusalem Bible

reached you is spreading all over the world and
producing the same results as it has among you
ever since the day when you heard about God's
grace and understood what this really is. 7 Epaphras, who taught you, is one of our closest fellow workers and a faithful deputy for us as
Christ's servant, 8 and it was he who told us all
about your love in the Spirit.
9 That will explain why, ever since the day
he told us, we have never failed to pray for you,
and what we ask God is that through perfect wisdom and spiritual understanding you should
reach the fullest knowledge of his will. 10 So you
will be able to lead the kind of life which the
Lord expects of you, a life acceptable to him in
all its aspects; showing the results in all the good
actions you do and increasing your knowledge
of God. 11 You will have in you the strength,
based on his own glorious power, never to give
in, but to bear anything joyfully, 12 thanking the
Father who has made it possible for you to join
the saints and with them to inherit the light.
13 Because that is what he has done: he has
taken us out of the power of darkness and created a place for us in the kingdom of the Son
that he loves, 14 and in him, we gain our freedom, the forgiveness of our sins.

New English Bible

to men the whole world over; everywhere it is growing and bearing fruit as it does among you, and has done since the day when you heard of the graciousness of God and recognized it for what in truth it is. You were taught this by Epaphras, our dear fellow-servant, a trusted worker for Christ on our[a] behalf, and it is he who has brought us the news of your God-given love.[b]

For this reason, ever since the day we heard of it, we have not ceased to pray for you. We ask God that you may receive from him all wisdom and spiritual understanding for full insight into his will, so that your manner of life may be worthy of the Lord and entirely pleasing to him. We pray that you may bear fruit in active goodness of every kind, and grow in the knowledge of God. May he strengthen you, in his glorious might, with ample power to meet whatever comes with fortitude, patience, and joy; and to give thanks[c] to the Father who has made you fit to share the heritage of God's people in the realm of light.

He rescued us from the domain of darkness and brought us away into the kingdom of his dear Son, in whom our release is secured and

[a] *Some witnesses read* your. [b] *Or* your love within the fellowship of the Spirit. [c] *Or* with fortitude and patience, and to give joyful thanks . . .

King James Version

ness of sins: 15 Who is the image of the invisible God, the firstborn of every creature: 16 For by him were all things created, that are in heaven, and that are in earth, visible and invisible, whether *they be* thrones, or dominions, or principalities, or powers: all things were created by him, and for him: 17 And he is before all things, and by him all things consist: 18 And he is the head of the body, the church: who is the beginning, the firstborn from the dead; that in all things he might have the preeminence. 19 For it pleased *the Father* that in him should all fulness dwell; 20 And, having made peace through the blood of his cross, by him to reconcile all things unto himself; by him, *I say,* whether *they be* things in earth, or things in heaven 21 And you, that were sometime alienated and enemies in *your* mind by wicked works, yet now hath he

Living Bible

15 Christ is the exact likeness of the unseen God. He existed before God made anything at all,[a] and, in fact, 16 Christ himself is the Creator who made everything in heaven and earth, the things we can see and the things we can't; the spirit world with its kings and kingdoms, its rulers and authorities; all were made by Christ for his own use and glory. 17 He was before all else began and it is his power that holds everything together. 18 He is the Head of the body made up of his people—that is, his church—which he began; and he is the Leader of all those who arise from the dead,[b] so that he is first in everything; 19 for God wanted all of himself to be in his Son.

20 It was through what his Son did that God cleared a path for everything to come to him—all things in heaven and on earth—for Christ's death on the cross has made peace with God for all by his blood. 21 This includes you who were once so far away from God. You were his enemies and hated him and were separated from him by your evil thoughts and actions, yet now

[a] Literally, "he is the firstborn of all creation."
[b] Literally, "he is the Beginning, the firstborn from the dead."

Today's English Version

The person and work of Christ

15 Christ is the visible likeness of the invisible God. He is the firstborn Son, superior to all created things. 16 For by him God created everything in heaven and on earth, the seen and the unseen things, including spiritual powers, lords, rulers, and authorities. God created the whole universe through him and for him. 17 He existed before all things, and in union with him all things have their proper place. 18 He is the head of his body, the church; he is the source of the body's life; he is the firstborn Son who was raised from death, in order that he alone might have the first place in all things. 19 For it was by God's own decision that the Son has in himself the full nature of God. 20 Through the Son, then, God decided to bring the whole universe back to himself. God made peace through his Son's death on the cross, and so brought back to himself all things, both on earth and in heaven.

21 At one time you were far away from God and were his enemies because of the evil things

New International Version

The supremacy of Christ

15 He is the image of the invisible God, the firstborn over all creation. 16 For by him all things were created: things in heaven and on earth, visible and invisible, whether thrones or powers or rulers or authorities; all things were created by him and for him. 17 He is before all things, and in him all things hold together. 18 And he is the head of the body, the church; he is the beginning and the firstborn from among the dead, so that in everything he might have the supremacy. 19 For God was pleased to have all his fullness dwell in him, 20 and through him to reconcile to himself all things, whether things on earth or things in heaven, by making peace through his blood, shed on the cross.

21 Once you were alienated from God and were enemies in your minds because of your

Phillips Modern English

1.15 *Who Christ is, and what he has done*

Now Christ is the visible expression of the invisible God. He was born before creation began, for it was through him that everything was made, whether heavenly or earthly, seen or unseen. Through him, and for him, also, were created power and dominion, ownership and authority. In fact, all things were created through, and for, him. He is both the first principle and the upholding principle of the whole scheme of creation. And now he is the head of the Body which is the Church. He is the Beginning, the first to be born from the dead, which gives him pre-eminence over all things. It was in him that the full nature of God chose to live, and through him God planned to reconcile to his own person everything on earth and everything in Heaven, making peace by virtue of Christ's death on the cross.

And you yourselves, who were strangers to God, and, in fact, through the evil things you

Revised Standard Version

15 He is the image of the invisible God, the
first-born of all creation; 16 for in him all things
were created, in heaven and on earth, visible
and invisible, whether thrones or dominions or
principalities or authorities—all things were created through him and for him. 17 He is before
all things, and in him all things hold together.
18 He is the head of the body, the church; he
is the beginning, the first-born from the dead,
that in everything he might be pre-eminent.
19 For in him all the fulness of God was pleased
to dwell, 20 and through him to reconcile to
himself all things, whether on earth or in heaven,
making peace by the blood of his cross.
21 And you, who once were estranged and

Jerusalem Bible

1. Formal instruction

Christ is the head of all creation

15 He is the image of the unseen God
and the first-born of all creation,
16 for in him were created
all things in heaven and on earth:
everything visible and everything invisible,
Thrones, Dominations, Sovereignties, Powers—
all things were created through him and for him.
17 Before anything was created, he existed,
and he holds all things in unity.
18 Now the Church is his body,
he is its head.

As he is the Beginning,
he was first to be born from the dead,
so that he should be first in every way;
19 because God wanted all perfection
to be found in him
20 and all things to be reconciled through him and for him,
everything in heaven and everything on earth,
when he made peace
by his death on the cross.

The Colossians have their share in salvation

21 Not long ago, you were foreigners and enemies, in the way that you used to think and

New English Bible

our sins forgiven. He is the image of the invisible God; his is the primacy over[a] all created things. In him everything in heaven and on earth was created, not only things visible but also the invisible orders of thrones, sovereignties, authorities, and powers: the whole universe has been created through him and for him. And he exists before everything, and all things are held together in him. He is, moreover, the head of the body, the church. He is its origin, the first to return from the dead, to be in all things alone supreme. For in him the complete being of God, by God's own choice, came to dwell. Through him God chose to reconcile the whole universe to himself, making peace through the shedding of his blood upon the cross—to reconcile all things, whether on earth or in heaven, through him alone.

Formerly you were yourselves estranged from God; you were his enemies in heart and mind,

[a] *Or* image of the invisible God, born before . . .

King James Version

reconciled 22 In the body of his flesh through
death, to present you holy and unblameable and
unreproveable in his sight: 23 If ye continue in
the faith grounded and settled, and *be* not moved
away from the hope of the gospel, which ye have
heard, *and* which was preached to every creature
which is under heaven; whereof I Paul am made
a minister; 24 Who now rejoice in my sufferings
for you, and fill up that which is behind of the
afflictions of Christ in my flesh for his body's
sake, which is the church: 25 Whereof I am made
a minister, according to the dispensation of
God which is given to me for you, to fulfil the
word of God; 26 *Even* the mystery which hath
been hid from ages and from generations, but
now is made manifest to his saints: 27 To whom
God would make known what *is* the riches of
the glory of this mystery among the Gentiles;
which is Christ in you, the hope of glory:

Living Bible

he has brought you back as his friends. 22 He has
done this through the death on the cross of
his own human body, and now as a result Christ
has brought you into the very presence of God,
and you are standing there before him with nothing left against you—nothing left that he could
even chide you for; 23 the only condition is that
you fully believe the Truth, standing in it steadfast and firm, strong in the Lord, convinced of
the Good News that Jesus died for you, and
never shifting from trusting him to save you.
This is the wonderful news that came to each
of you and is now spreading all over the world.
And I, Paul, have the joy of telling it to others.

24 But part of my work is to suffer for you;
and I am glad, for I am helping to finish up the
remainder of Christ's sufferings for his body, the
church.

25 God has sent me to help his church and
to tell his secret plan to you Gentiles. 26, 27 He
has kept this secret for centuries and generations
past, but now at last it has pleased him to tell it
to those who love him and live for him, and the
riches and glory of his plan are for you Gentiles
too. And this is the secret: *that Christ in your
hearts is your only hope of glory.*

Today's English Version

you did and thought. 22 But now, by means of
the physical death of his Son, God has made
you his friends, in order to bring you, holy,
pure, and faultless, into his presence. 23 You
must, of course, continue faithful on a firm and
sure foundation, and not allow yourselves to
be shaken from the hope you gained when you
heard the gospel. It is of this gospel that I,
Paul, became a servant—this gospel which has
been preached to everybody in the world.

Paul's ministry to the church

24 And now I am happy about my sufferings
for you. For by means of my physical sufferings
I help complete what still remains of Christ's
sufferings on behalf of his body, which is the
church. 25And I have been made a servant of
the church by God, who gave me this task to
perform for your good. It is the task of fully
proclaiming his message, 26 which is the secret
he hid through all past ages from all mankind,
but has now revealed to his people. 27 God's
plan is this: to make known his secret to his
people, this rich and glorious secret which he has
for all peoples. And the secret is this: Christ is
in you, which means that you will share the glory

New International Version

evil behavior. 22 But now he has reconciled you
by Christ's physical body through death to present you holy in his sight, without blemish and
free from accusation—23 if you continue in your
faith, established and firm, not moved from the
hope held out in the gospel. This is the gospel
that you heard and that has been proclaimed to
every creature under heaven, and of which I,
Paul, have become a servant.

Paul's labor for the church

24 Now I rejoice in what was suffered for you,
and I fill up in my flesh what is still lacking in
regard to Christ's afflictions, for the sake of his
body, which is the church. 25 I have become its
servant by the commission God gave me to
present to you the word of God in its fullness—
26 the mystery that has been kept hidden for
ages and generations, but is now disclosed to
the saints. 27 To them God has chosen to make
known among the Gentiles the glorious riches
of this mystery, which is Christ in you, the hope
of glory.

Phillips Modern English

had done, his spiritual enemies, he has now reconciled through the death of Christ's body on the cross, so that he might welcome you to his presence clean and pure, without blame or reproach. This reconciliation assumes that you maintain a firm position in the faith, and do not allow yourselves to be shifted away from the hope of the gospel, which you have heard, and which, indeed, has been proclaimed to the whole created world under heaven. I, Paul, have become a minister of this same gospel.

1.23b My divine commission

It is true at this moment that I am suffering on behalf of you who have heard the gospel, yet I am glad, because it gives me a chance to contribute my own sufferings something to the uncompleted pains which Christ suffers on behalf of his Body, the Church. For I am a minister of the Church by divine commission, a commission granted to me for your benefit, and for a special purpose: that I might fully declare God's Word—that sacred mystery which up till now has been hidden in every age and every generation, but which is now as clear as daylight to those who love God. They are those to whom God has planned to give a vision of the wonder and splendour of his secret plan for the nations. And the secret is simply this: Christ *in you!* Yes, Christ *in you* bringing with him the hope of all the glorious things to come.

Revised Standard Version

hostile in mind, doing evil deeds, 22 he has now
reconciled in his body of flesh by his death, in
order to present you holy and blameless and irreproachable before him, 23 provided that you
continue in the faith, stable and steadfast, not
shifting from the hope of the gospel which you
heard, which has been preached to every creature
under heaven, and of which I, Paul, became a
minister.
24 Now I rejoice in my sufferings for your
sake, and in my flesh I complete what is lacking in Christ's afflictions for the sake of his
body, that is, the church, 25 of which I became
a minister according to the divine office which
was given to me for you, to make the word of
God fully known, 26 the mystery hidden for ages
and generations[c] but now made manifest to his
saints. 27 To them God chose to make known
how great among the Gentiles are the riches of
the glory of this mystery, which is Christ in you,

[c] Or *from angels and men.*

Jerusalem Bible

the evil things that you did; 22 but now he has
reconciled you, by his death and in that mortal
body. Now you are able to appear before him
holy, pure and blameless—23 as long as you
persevere and stand firm on the solid base of
the faith, never letting yourselves drift away
from the hope promised by the Good News,
which you have heard, which has been preached
to the whole human race, and of which I, Paul,
have become the servant.

Paul's labors in the service of the pagans

24 It makes me happy to suffer for you, as I
am suffering now, and in my own body to do
what I can to make up all that has still to be
undergone by Christ for the sake of his body,
the Church. 25 I became the servant of the
Church when God made me responsible for
delivering God's message to you, 26 the message which was a mystery hidden for generations
and centuries and has now been revealed to his
saints. 27 It was God's purpose to reveal it to
them and to show all the rich glory of this mystery to pagans. The mystery is Christ among

New English Bible

and your deeds were evil. But now by Christ's death in his body of flesh and blood God has reconciled you to himself, so that he may present you before himself as dedicated men, without blemish and innocent in his sight. Only you must continue in your faith, firm on your foundations, never to be dislodged from the hope offered in the gospel which you heard. This is the gospel which has been proclaimed in the whole creation under heaven; and I, Paul, have become its minister.

It is now my happiness to suffer for you. This is my way of helping to complete, in my poor human flesh, the full tale of Christ's afflictions still to be endured, for the sake of his body which is the church. I became its servant by virtue of the task assigned to me by God for your benefit: to deliver his message in full; to announce the secret hidden for long ages and through many generations, but now disclosed to God's people, to whom it was his will to make it known—to make known how rich and glorious it is among all nations. The secret is this: Christ in[b] you, the hope of a glory to come.

[b] *Or* among.

King James Version

28 Whom we preach, warning every man, and
teaching every man in all wisdom; that we may
present every man perfect in Christ Jesus:
29 Whereunto I also labour, striving according
to his working, which worketh in me mightily.

2 For I would that ye knew what great conflict I have for you, and *for* them at Laodicea, and *for* as many as have not seen my
face in the flesh; 2 That their hearts might be
comforted, being knit together in love, and unto
all riches of the full assurance of understanding, to the acknowledgment of the mystery of
God, and of the Father, and of Christ; 3 In
whom are hid all the treasures of wisdom and
knowledge. 4 And this I say, lest any man should
beguile you with enticing words. 5 For though I
be absent in the flesh, yet am I with you in the
spirit, joying and beholding your order, and the
steadfastness of your faith in Christ. 6 As ye have
therefore received Christ Jesus the Lord, *so* walk

Living Bible

28 So everywhere we go we talk about Christ
to all who will listen, warning them and teaching them as well as we know how. We want to
be able to present each one to God, perfect because of what Christ has done for each of them.
29 This is my work, and I can do it only because
Christ's mighty energy is at work within me.

2 I wish you could know how much I have
struggled in prayer for you and for the
church at Laodicea, and for my many other
friends who have never known me personally.
2 This is what I have asked of God for you: that
you will be encouraged and knit together by
strong ties of love, and that you will have the
rich experience of knowing Christ with real certainty and clear understanding. *For God's secret
plan, now at last made known, is Christ himself.* 3 In him lie hidden all the mighty, untapped
treasures of wisdom and knowledge.
4 I am saying this because I am afraid that
someone may fool you with smooth talk. 5 For
though I am far away from you my heart is with
you, happy because you are getting along so well,
happy because of your strong faith in Christ.
6 And now just as you trusted Christ to save you,
trust him, too, for each day's problems; live in

Today's English Version

of God. 28 So we preach Christ to all men. We
warn and teach everyone, with all possible wisdom, in order to bring each one into God's
presence as a mature individual in union with
Christ. 29 To get this done I toil and struggle,
using the mighty strength that Christ supplies,
which is at work in me.

2 Let me tell you how hard I have worked for
you, and for the people in Laodicea, and for
all those who do not know me personally. 2 I do
so that their hearts may be filled with courage,
and that they may be drawn together in love and
have the full wealth of assurance which true
understanding brings. And so they will know
God's secret, which is Christ himself. 3 He is the
key that opens all the hidden treasures of God's
wisdom and knowledge.
4 I tell you, then, do not let anyone fool you
with false arguments, no matter how good they
seem to be. 5 For even though I am absent in
body, yet I am with you in spirit, and I am glad
as I see the resolute firmness with which you
stand together in your faith in Christ.

Fulness of life in Christ

6 Since you have accepted Christ Jesus as

New International Version

28 We proclaim him, counseling and teaching
everyone with all wisdom, so that we may present everyone perfect in Christ. 29 To this end
I labor, struggling with all the energy he so
powerfully works in me.

2 I want you to know how strenuously I
am exerting myself for you and for those at
Laodicea, and for all who have not met me personally. 2 My purpose is that they may be encouraged in heart and united in love, so that they
may have the full riches of complete understanding, in order that they may know the mystery of
God, namely, Christ,[e] 3 in whom are hidden all
the treasures of wisdom and knowledge. 4 I tell
you this so that no one may deceive you by fine-
sounding arguments. 5 For though I am absent
from you in body, I am present with you in
spirit and delight to see how orderly you are and
how firm your faith in Christ is.

Freedom from human regulations through life with Christ

6 So then, just as you received Christ Jesus

[e] Some MSS read *know the mystery of God, even the Father, and of Christ.*

Phillips Modern English

1.28 To preach and teach Christ is everything to us

So, naturally, we proclaim Christ! We warn everyone we meet, and we teach everyone we can, all that we know about him, so that we may bring every man up to his full maturity in Christ. This is what I am working and struggling at, with all the strength that God puts into me.

I wish you could understand how deep is my anxiety for you, nd for those at Laodicea, and for all who hav never met me personally. How I long that they may be encouraged, and find out more and more how strong are the bonds of Christian love. How I long for them to experience the wealth of conviction which is brought by understanding—that they may come to know more fully God's great secret, Christ himself! For it is *in him*, and in him alone, that all the treasures of wisdom and knowledge lie hidden.

2.4 Let me warn you against "intellectuals"

I write like this to prevent you from being led astray by someone or other's attractive arguments. For though I am a long way away from you in body, in spirit I am by your side, rejoicing as I see the solid steadfastness of your faith in Christ. Just as you received Christ Jesus the Lord, so go on living in him—in simple

Revised Standard Version

the hope of glory. 28 Him we proclaim, warning every man and teaching every man in all wisdom, that we may present every man mature in Christ. 29 For this I toil, striving with all the energy which he mightily inspires within me.

2 For I want you to know how greatly I strive for you, and for those at Laodicea, and for all who have not seen my face, 2 that their hearts may be encouraged as they are knit together in love, to have all the riches of assured understanding and the knowledge of God's mystery, of Christ, 3 in whom are hid all the treasures of wisdom and knowledge. 4 I say this in order that no one may delude you with beguiling speech. 5 For though I am absent in body, yet I am with you in spirit, rejoicing to see your good order and the firmness of your faith in Christ.

6 As therefore you received Christ Jesus the

Jerusalem Bible

you, your hope of glory: 28 this is the Christ we proclaim, this is the wisdom in which we thoroughly train everyone and instruct everyone, to make them all perfect in Christ. 29 It is for this I struggle wearily on, helped only by his power driving me irresistibly.

Paul's concern for the Colossians' faith

2 Yes, I want you to know that I do have to struggle hard for you, and for those in Laodicea, and for so many others who have never seen me face to face. 2 It is all to bind you together in love and to stir your minds, so that your understanding may come to full development, until you really know God's secret 3 in which all the jewels of wisdom and knowledge are hidden.

4 I say this to make sure that no one deceives you with specious arguments. 5 I may be absent in body, but in spirit I am there among you, delighted to find you all in harmony and to see how firm your faith in Christ is.

II. A warning against some errors

Live according to the true faith in Christ, not according to false teaching

6 You must live your whole life according to the Christ you have received—Jesus the Lord;

New English Bible

He it is whom we proclaim. We admonish everyone without distinction, we instruct everyone in all the ways of wisdom, so as to present each one of you as a mature member of Christ's body. To this end I am toiling strenuously with all the energy and power of Christ at work in me.

2 For I want you to know how strenuous are my exertions for you and the Laodiceans and all who have never set eyes on me. I want them to continue in good heart and in the unity of love, and to come to the full wealth of conviction which understanding brings, and grasp God's secret. That secret is Christ himself; in him lie hidden all God's treasures of wisdom and knowledge. I tell you this to save you from being talked [a] into error by specious arguments. For though absent in body, I am with you in spirit, and rejoice to see your orderly array and the firm front which your faith in Christ presents.

Therefore, since Jesus was delivered to you as Christ and Lord, live your lives in union with

[a] *Or* What I mean is this: no one must talk you . . .

King James Version

ye in him: 7 Rooted and built up in him, and
stablished in the faith, as ye have been taught,
abounding therein with thanksgiving. 8 Beware
lest any man spoil you through philosophy and
vain deceit, after the tradition of men, after the
rudiments of the world, and not after Christ.
9 For in him dwelleth all the fulness of the Godhead bodily. 10 And ye are complete in him,
which is the head of all principality and power:
11 In whom also ye are circumcised with the
circumcision made without hands, in putting off
the body of the sins of the flesh by the circumcision of Christ: 12 Buried with him in baptism,
wherein also ye are risen with *him* through the
faith of the operation of God, who hath raised
him from the dead. 13 And you, being dead in
your sins and the uncircumcision of your flesh,
hath he quickened together with him, having forgiven you all trespasses; 14 Blotting out the handwriting of ordinances that was against us, which
was contrary to us, and took it out of the way,
nailing it to his cross; 15 *And* having spoiled prin-

Living Bible

vital union with him. 7 Let your roots grow down
into him and draw up nourishment from him.
See that you go on growing in the Lord, and become strong and vigorous in the truth you were
taught. Let your lives overflow with joy and
thanksgiving for all he has done.
8 Don't let others spoil your faith and joy
with their philosophies, their wrong and shallow
answers built on men's thoughts and ideas, instead of on what Christ has said. 9 For in Christ
there is all of God in a human body; 10 *so you
have everything when you have Christ,* and you
are filled with God through your union with
Christ. He is the highest Ruler, with authority
over every other power.
11 When you came to Christ he set you free
from your evil desires, not by a bodily operation of circumcision but by a spiritual operation,
the baptism of your souls. 12 For in baptism you
see how your old, evil nature died with him and
was buried with him; and then you came up out
of death with him into a new life because you
trusted the Word of the mighty God who raised
Christ from the dead.
13 You were dead in sins, and your sinful
desires were not yet cut away. Then he gave you
a share in the very life of Christ, for he forgave all your sins, 14 and blotted out the charges
proved against you, the list of his commandments which you had not obeyed. He took this
list of sins and destroyed it by nailing it to
Christ's cross. 15 In this way God took away
Satan's power to accuse you of sin, and God
openly displayed to the whole world Christ's

Today's English Version

Lord, live in union with him. 7 Keep your roots
deep in him, build your lives on him, and become ever stronger in your faith, as you were
taught. And be filled with thanksgiving.
8 See to it, then, that no one makes a captive of you with the worthless deceit of human
wisdom, which comes from the teachings handed
down by men, and from the ruling spirits of the
universe, and not from Christ. 9 For the full
content of divine nature lives in Christ, in his
humanity, 10 and you have been given full life
in union with him. He is supreme over every
spiritual ruler and authority.
11 In union with him you were circumcised,
not with the circumcision that is made by men,
but with Christ's own circumcision, which consists of being freed from the power of this sinful
body. 12 For when you were baptized, you were
buried with Christ, and in baptism you were also
raised with Christ through your faith in the
active power of God, who raised him from
death. 13 You were at one time spiritually dead
because of your sins, and because you were Gentiles without the Law. But God has now brought
you to life with Christ; God forgave us all our
sins. 14 He canceled the unfavorable record of
our debts, with its binding rules, and did away
with it completely by nailing it to the cross.
15 And on that cross Christ freed himself from
the power of the spiritual rulers and authorities;

New International Version

as Lord, continue to live in him, 7 rooted and
built up in him, strengthened in the faith as you
were taught, and overflowing with thankfulness.
8 See to it that no one takes you captive
through hollow and deceptive philosophy, which
depends on human tradition and the basic principles of this world rather than on Christ.
9 For in Christ all the fullness of the Deity
lives in bodily form, 10 and you have this fullness in Christ, who is the head over every power
and authority. 11 In him you were also circumcised, in the putting off of your sinful nature,
not with a circumcision done by the hands of
men but with the circumcision done by Christ.
12 In baptism you were buried with him and
raised with him through your faith in the power
of God, who raised him from the dead.
13 When you were dead in your sins and in
the uncircumcision of your sinful nature, God
made you alive with Christ. He forgave us all
our sins, 14 having canceled the written code,
with its regulations, that was against us and that
stood opposed to us; he took it away, nailing it
to the cross. 15 And having disarmed the powers

Phillips Modern English

faith. Yes, be rooted in him and founded upon him, continually strengthened by the faith as you were taught it and your lives will overflow with joy and thankfulness.

Be careful that nobody spoils your faith through intellectualism or high-sounding nonsense. Such stuff is at best founded on men's ideas of the nature of the world and disregards Christ! Yet it is in him that God gives a full and complete expression of himself in bodily form. Moreover, your own completeness is realised in him, who is the ruler over all authorities, and the supreme head over all powers.

2.11 *The old Law can't condemn you now*

In Christ, you were circumcised, not by any physical act, but by being set free from the sins of the flesh by virtue of Christ's circumcision. You shared in that, just as in baptism you shared in his death, and in him shared the rising again to life—and all this because you have faith in the tremendous power of God, who raised Christ from the dead. You, who were spiritually dead because of your sins and your uncircumcision, God has now made to share in the very life of Christ! He has forgiven you all your sins: he has utterly wiped out the written evidence of broken commandments which always hung over our heads, and has completely annulled it by nailing it to the cross. And then, having drawn the sting of all the powers and authorities ranged against us, he exposed them,

Revised Standard Version

Lord, so live in him, 7 rooted and built up in him and established in the faith, just as you were taught, abounding in thanksgiving.

8 See to it that no one makes a prey of you by philosophy and empty deceit, according to human tradition, according to the elemental spirits of the universe, and not according to Christ. 9 For in him the whole fulness of deity dwells bodily, 10 and you have come to fulness of life in him, who is the head of all rule and authority. 11 In him also you were circumcised with a circumcision made without hands, by putting off the body of flesh in the circumcision of Christ; 12 and you were buried with him in baptism, in which you were also raised with him through faith in the working of God, who raised him from the dead. 13 And you, who were dead in trespasses and the uncircumcision of your flesh, God made alive together with him, having forgiven us all our trespasses, 14 having canceled the bond which stood against us with its legal demands; this he set aside, nailing it to the cross. 15 He disarmed the principalities and

Jerusalem Bible

7 you must be rooted in him and built on him and held firm by the faith you have been taught, and full of thanksgiving.

8 Make sure that no one traps you and deprives you of your freedom by some secondhand, empty, rational philosophy based on the principles of this world instead of on Christ.

Christ alone is the true head of men and angels

9 In his body lives the fullness of divinity, and in him you too find your own fulfillment, 10 in the one who is the head of every Sovereignty and Power.[a]

11 In him you have been circumcised, with a circumcision not performed by human hand, but by the complete stripping of your body of flesh. This is circumcision according to Christ. 12 You have been buried with him, when you were baptized; and by baptism, too, you have been raised up with him through your belief in the power of God who raised him from the dead. 13 You were dead, because you were sinners and had not been circumcised: he[b] has brought you to life with him, he has forgiven us all our sins.

14 He has overriden the Law, and canceled every record of the debt that we had to pay; he has done away with it by nailing it to the cross[c]; 15 and so he got rid of the Sovereignties and the

[*a*] I.e., over the highest orders of angels. [*b*] God the Father. [*c*] Destroying our death warrant.

New English Bible

him. Be rooted in him; be built in him; be consolidated in the faith you were taught;[b] let your hearts overflow with thankfulness. Be on your guard; do not let your minds be captured by hollow and delusive speculations, based on traditions of man-made teaching and centred on the elemental spirits of the universe[c] and not on Christ.

For it is in Christ that the complete being of the Godhead dwells embodied,[d] and in him you have been brought to completion. Every power and authority in the universe is subject to him as Head. In him also you were circumcised, not in a physical sense, but by being divested of the lower nature; this is Christ's way of circumcision. For in baptism[e] you were buried with him, in baptism also you were raised to life with him through your faith in the active power of God who raised him from the dead. And although you were dead because of your sins and because you were morally uncircumcised, he has made you alive with Christ. For he has forgiven us all our sins; he has cancelled the bond which pledged us to the decrees of the law. It stood against us, but he has set it aside, nailing it to the cross. On that cross he discarded the cosmic powers and authorities like a garment; he made

[*b*] *Or* by your faith, as you were taught. [*c*] *Or* the elements of the natural world, *or* elementary ideas belonging to this world. [*d*] *Or* corporately. [*e*] *Or* . . . nature, in the very circumcision of Christ himself; for in baptism . . .

King James Version

cipalities and powers, he made a shew of them openly, triumphing over them in it. 16 Let no man therefore judge you in meat, or in drink, or in respect of a holyday, or of the new moon, or of the sabbath *days:* 17 Which are a shadow of things to come; but the body *is* of Christ. 18 Let no man beguile you of your reward in a voluntary humility and worshipping of angels, intruding into those things which he hath not seen, vainly puffed up by his fleshly mind, 19 And not holding the Head, from which all the body by joints and bands having nourishment ministered, and knit together, increaseth with the increase of God. 20 Wherefore if ye be dead with Christ from the rudiments of the world, why, as though living in the world, are ye subject to ordinances, 21 (Touch not; taste not; handle not; 22 Which all are to perish with the using;) after the commandments and doctrines of men? 23 Which things have indeed a shew of wisdom in will-worship, and humility, and neglecting of the body; not in any honour to the satisfying of the flesh.

Living Bible

triumph at the cross where your sins were all taken away.

16 So don't let anyone criticize you for what you eat or drink, or for not celebrating Jewish holidays and feasts or new moon ceremonies or Sabbaths. 17 For these were only temporary rules that ended when Christ came. They were only shadows of the real thing—of Christ himself. 18 Don't let anyone declare you lost when you refuse to worship angels, as they say you must. They have seen a vision, they say, and know you should. These proud men (though they claim to be so humble) have a very clever imagination. 19 But they are not connected to Christ, the Head to which all of us who are his body are joined; for we are joined together by his strong sinews and we grow only as we get our nourishment and strength from God.

20 Since you died, as it were, with Christ and this has set you free from following the world's ideas of how to be saved—by doing good and obeying various rules[a]—why do you keep right on following them anyway, still bound by such rules as 21 not eating, tasting, or even touching certain foods? 22 Such rules are mere human teachings, for food was made to be eaten and used up. 23 These rules may seem good, for rules of this kind require strong devotion and are humiliating and hard on the body, but they have no effect when it comes to conquering a person's evil thoughts and desires. They only make him proud.

[a] Literally, "by the rudiments of the world."

Today's English Version

he made a public spectacle of them by leading them as captives in his victory procession.

16 So let no one make rules about what you eat or drink, or about the subject of holy days, or the new moon festival, or the Sabbath. 17 All such things are only a shadow of things in the future; the reality is Christ. 18 Do not allow yourselves to be condemned by anyone who claims to be superior because of special visions, and insists on false humility and the worship of angels. Such a person is all puffed up, for no reason at all, by his human way of thinking, 19 and has stopped holding on to Christ, who is the head. Under Christ's control the whole body is nourished and held together by its joints and ligaments, and grows as God wants it to grow.

Dying and living with Christ

20 You have died with Christ and are set free from the ruling spirits of the universe. Why, then, do you live as though you belonged to this world? Why do you obey such rules as 21 "Don't handle this," "Don't taste that," "Don't touch the other"? 22 All these things become useless, once they are used. They are only man-made rules and teachings. 23 Of course they appear to have wisdom in their forced worship of angels, and false humility, and severe treatment of the body; but they have no real value in controlling physical passions.

New International Version

and authorities, he made a public spectacle of them, triumphing over them by the cross.

16 Therefore do not let anyone judge you by what you eat or drink, or with regard to a religious festival, a new moon celebration, or a sabbath day. 17 These are a shadow of the things that were to come; the reality, however, is found in Christ. 18 Do not let anyone who delights in false humility and the worship of angels disqualify you for the prize. Such a person goes into great detail about what he has seen, and his unspiritual mind puffs him up with idle notions. 19 He has lost connection with the Head, from whom the whole body, supported and held together by its ligaments and sinews, grows as God causes it to grow.

20 If you died with Christ to the basic principles of this world, why, as though you still belonged to it, do you submit to its rules: 21 "Do not handle! Do not taste! Do not touch!"? 22 These are all destined to perish with use, because they are based on human commands and teachings. 23 Such regulations indeed have an appearance of wisdom, with their self-imposed worship, their false humility and their harsh treatment of the body, but they lack any value in restraining sensual indulgence.

Phillips Modern English

shattered, empty and defeated, in his own triumphant victory!

2.16 *It is the spiritual, not the material, attitude which matters*

In view of these tremendous facts, don't let anyone worry you by criticising what you eat or drink, or what holy days you ought to observe, or bothering you over new moons or sabbaths. All these things are no more than foreshadowings: the reality belongs to Christ. Let no man cheat you out of your joy by wanting you to join him in his false humility and worship of angels. Such a man, presuming on the little he has seen, by using an unspiritual imagination, entirely forgets the head. It is from the head alone that the body, through its joints and ligaments, is nourished and built up and grows as God meant it to grow.

So if, through your faith in Christ, you are dead to the principles of this world's life, why, as if you were still part and parcel of this world-wide system, do you take the slightest notice of these purely human prohibitions—"Don't touch this," "Don't taste that" and "Don't handle the other"? "This", "that" and "the other" will all pass away after use! I know that these regulations look wise with their self-inspired efforts at piety, their policy of self-humbling, and their studied neglect of the body. But in actual practice they are of no moral value, but simply pamper the flesh.

Revised Standard Version

powers and made a public example of them, triumphing over them in him.[d]
16 Therefore let no one pass judgment on you in questions of food and drink or with regard to a festival or a new moon or a sabbath.
17 These are only a shadow of what is to come; but the substance belongs to Christ.
18 Let no one disqualify you, insisting on self-abasement and worship of angels, taking his stand on visions, puffed up without reason by his sensuous mind,
19 and not holding fast to the Head, from whom the whole body, nourished and knit together through its joints and ligaments, grows with a growth that is from God.
20 If with Christ you died to the elemental spirits of the universe, why do you live as if you still belonged to the world? Why do you submit to regulations,
21 "Do not handle, Do not taste, Do not touch"
22 (referring to things which all perish as they are used), according to human precepts and doctrines?
23 These have indeed an appearance of wisdom in promoting rigor of devotion and self-abasement and severity to the body, but they are of no value in checking the indulgence of the flesh.[e]

[d] Or *in it* (that is, the cross). [e] Or *are of no value, serving only to indulge the flesh.*

Jerusalem Bible

Powers, and paraded them in public, behind him in his triumphal procession.[d]

Against the false asceticism based on "the principles of this world"

16 From now onward, never let anyone else decide what you should eat or drink, or whether you are to observe annual festivals. New Moons or sabbaths.
17 These were only pale reflections of what was coming: the reality is Christ.
18 Do not be taken in by people who like groveling to angels and worshiping them; people like that are always going on about some vision they have had, inflating themselves to a false importance with their worldly outlook.
19 A man of this sort is not united to the head, and it is the head that adds strength and holds the whole body together, with all its joints and sinews—and this is the only way in which it can reach its full growth in God.
20 If you have really died with Christ to the principles of this world, why do you still let rules dictate to you, as though you were still living in the world?
21 "It is forbidden to pick up this, it is forbidden to taste that, it is forbidden to touch something else";
22 all these prohibitions are only concerned with things that perish by their very use—an example of *human doctrines and regulations!*[e]
23 It may be argued that true wisdom is to be found in these, with their self-imposed devotions, their self-abasement, and their severe treatment of the body; but once the flesh starts to protest, they are no use at all.

[d] The tradition was that the Law was brought down to Moses by angels. [e] Is. 29:13

New English Bible

a public spectacle of them and led them[f] as captives in his triumphal procession.

Allow no one therefore to take you to task about what you eat or drink, or over the observance of festival, new moon, or sabbath. These are no more than a shadow of what was to come; the solid reality is Christ's. You are not to be disqualified by the decision of people who go in for self-mortification and angel-worship, and try to enter into some vision of their own. Such people, bursting with the futile conceit of worldly minds, lose hold upon the Head; yet it is from the Head that the whole body, with all its joints and ligaments, receives its supplies, and thus knit together grows according to God's design.

Did you not die with Christ and pass beyond reach of the elemental spirits of the universe[a]? Then why behave as though you were still living the life of the world? Why let people dictate to you: 'Do not handle this, do not taste that, do not touch the other'—all of them things that must perish as soon as they are used? That is to follow merely human injunctions and teaching. True, it has an air of wisdom, with its forced piety, its self-mortification, and its severity to the body; but it is of no use at all in combating sensuality.

[f] *Or* he stripped himself of his physical body, and thereby boldly made a spectacle of the cosmic powers and authorities, and led them . . . ; *or* he despoiled the cosmic powers and authorities, and boldly made a spectacle of them, leading them . . . [a] *Or* the elements of the natural world, *or* elementary ideas belonging to this world.

King James Version

3 If ye then be risen with Christ, seek those things which are above, where Christ sitteth on the right hand of God. 2 Set your affection on things above, not on things on the earth. 3 For ye are dead, and your life is hid with Christ in God. 4 When Christ, *who is* our life, shall appear, then shall ye also appear with him in glory. 5 Mortify therefore your members which are upon the earth; fornication, uncleanness, inordinate affection, evil concupiscence, and covetousness, which is idolatry: 6 For which things' sake the wrath of God cometh on the children of disobedience: 7 In the which ye also walked sometime, when ye lived in them. 8 But now ye also put off all these; anger, wrath, malice, blasphemy, filthy communication out of your mouth. 9 Lie not one to another, seeing that ye have put off the old man with his deeds; 10 And have put

Living Bible

3 Since you became alive again, so to speak, when Christ arose from the dead, now set your sights on the rich treasures and joys of heaven where he sits beside God in the place of honor and power. 2 Let heaven fill your thoughts; don't spend your time worrying about things down here. 3 You should have as little desire for this world as a dead person does. Your real life is in heaven with Christ and God. 4 And when Christ who is our real life comes back again, you will shine with him and share in all his glories.

5 Away then with sinful, earthly things; deaden the evil desires lurking within you; have nothing to do with sexual sin, impurity, lust and shameful desires; don't worship the good things of life, for that is idolatry. 6 God's terrible anger is upon those who do such things. 7 You used to do them when your life was still part of this world; 8 but now is the time to cast off and throw away all these rotten garments of anger, hatred, cursing, and dirty language.

9 Don't tell lies to each other; it was your old life with all its wickedness that did that sort of thing; now it is dead and gone. 10 You are liv-

Today's English Version

3 You have been raised to life with Christ. Set your hearts, then, on the things that are in heaven, where Christ sits on his throne at the right side of God. 2 Keep your minds fixed on things there, not on things here on earth. 3 For you have died, and your life is hidden with Christ in God. 4 Your real life is Christ, and when he appears, then you too will appear with him and share his glory!

The old life and the new

5 You must put to death, then, the earthly desires at work in you, such as immorality, indecency, lust, evil passions, and greed (for greediness is a form of idol worship). 6 Because of such things God's wrath will come upon those who do not obey him. 7 And you yourselves at one time used to live according to such desires, when your life was dominated by them.

8 But now you must get rid of all these things: anger, passion, and hateful feelings. No insults or obscene talk must ever come from your lips. 9 Do not lie to one another, because you have put off the old self with its habits, 10 and have put on the new self. This is the

New International Version

Rules for holy living

3 Since, then, you have been raised with Christ, set your hearts on things above, where Christ is seated at the right hand of God. 2 Set your minds on things above, not on earthly things. 3 For you died, and your life is now hidden with Christ in God. 4 When Christ, who is your life, appears, then you also will appear with him in glory.

5 Put to death, therefore, whatever belongs to your earthly nature: sexual immorality, impurity, lust, evil desires and greed, which is idolatry. 6 Because of these, the wrath of God is coming.[f] 7 You used to walk in these ways, in the life you once lived. 8 But now you must rid yourselves of all such things as these: anger, rage, malice, slander, filthy language. 9 Do not lie to each other, since you have taken off your old self with its practices 10 and have put on the

[f] Some early MSS add *on those who are disobedient*.

Phillips Modern English

3.1 *Live a new life by the power of the risen Christ*

If you are then raised up with Christ, reach out for the highest gifts of Heaven, where Christ reigns in power. Be concerned with the heavenly things, not with the passing things of earth. For, as far as this world is concerned, you are already dead, and your true life is a hidden one in God, through Christ. One day, Christ, who is your life, will show himself openly, and you will all share in that magnificent revelation.

Consider yourselves dead to worldly contacts: have nothing to do with sexual immorality, dirty-mindedness, uncontrolled passion, evil desire, and the lust for other people's goods, which amounts to idolatry. It is because of these very things that the holy anger of God falls upon those who refuse to obey him. And never forget that you had your part in those dreadful things when you lived that old life.

But now you must put away all these things: evil temper, furious rage, malice, insults and shouted abuse! Don't deceive each other with lies any more, for you have discarded the old nature and all that it did, and you have put on

Revised Standard Version

3 If then you have been raised with Christ,
seek the things that are above, where Christ
is, seated at the right hand of God. 2 Set your
minds on things that are above, not on things
that are on earth. 3 For you have died, and
your life is hid with Christ in God. 4 When
Christ who is our life appears, then you also will
appear with him in glory.
5 Put to death therefore what is earthly in
you: fornication, impurity, passion, evil desire,
and covetousness, which is idolatry. 6 On account of these the wrath of God is coming.[f] 7 In
these you once walked, when you lived in them.
8 But now put them all away: anger, wrath,
malice, slander, and foul talk from your mouth.
9 Do not lie to one another, seeing that you
have put off the old nature with its practices
10 and have put on the new nature, which is

[f] Other ancient authorities add *upon the sons of disobedience*.

Jerusalem Bible

Life-giving union with the glorified Christ

3 Since you have been brought back to true
life with Christ, you must look for the
things that are in heaven, where Christ is, sitting
at God's right hand. 2 Let your thoughts be on
heavenly things, not on the things that are on the
earth, 3 because you have died, and now the life
you have is hidden with Christ in God. 4 But
when Christ is revealed—and he is your life—
you too will be revealed in all your glory with
him.

III. Exhortation

General rules of Christian behavior

5 That is why you must kill everything in you
that belongs only to earthly life: fornication,
impurity, guilty passion, evil desires and especially greed, which is the same thing as worshiping a false god; 6 all this is the sort of behavior
that makes God angry. 7 And it is the way in
which you used to live when you were surrounded by people doing the same thing, 8 but
now you, of all people, must give all these things
up: getting angry, being bad-tempered, spitefulness, abusive language and dirty talk; 9 and never
tell each other lies. You have stripped off your
old behavior with your old self, 10 and you have

New English Bible

3 Were you not raised to life with Christ? Then aspire to the realm above, where Christ is, seated at the right hand of God, and let your thoughts dwell on that higher realm, not on this earthly life. I repeat, you died; and now your life lies hidden with Christ in God. When Christ, who is our life, is manifested, then you too will be manifested with him in glory.

Then put to death those parts of you which belong to the earth—fornication, indecency, lust, foul cravings, and the ruthless greed which is nothing less than idolatry. Because of these, God's dreadful judgement is impending; and in the life you once lived these are the ways you yourselves followed. But now you must yourselves lay aside all anger, passion, malice, cursing, filthy talk—have done with them! Stop lying to one another, now that you have discarded the old nature with its deeds and have put on the

King James Version

on the new *man*, which is renewed in knowledge
after the image of him that created him:
11 Where there is neither Greek nor Jew, circumcision nor uncircumcision, Barbarian, Scythian,
bond *nor* free: but Christ *is* all, and in all. 12 Put
on therefore, as the elect of God, holy and beloved, bowels of mercies, kindness, humbleness
of mind, meekness, longsuffering; 13 Forbearing
one another, and forgiving one another, if any
man have a quarrel against any: even as Christ
forgave you, so also *do* ye. 14 And above all these
things *put on* charity, which is the bond of per-
fectness. 15 And let the peace of God rule in your
hearts, to the which also ye are called in one
body; and be ye thankful. 16 Let the word of
Christ dwell in you richly in all wisdom; teaching and admonishing one another in psalms and
hymns and spiritual songs, singing with grace in
your hearts to the Lord. 17 And whatsoever ye
do in word or deed, *do* all in the name of the
Lord Jesus, giving thanks to God and the Father

Living Bible

ing a brand new kind of life that is continually
learning more and more of what is right, and
trying constantly to be more and more like Christ
who created this new life within you. 11 In this
new life one's nationality or race or education
or social position is unimportant; such things
mean nothing. Whether a person has Christ is
what matters, and he is equally available to all.
12 Since you have been chosen by God who
has given you this new kind of life, and because
of his deep love and concern for you, you should
practice tenderhearted mercy and kindness to
others. Don't worry about making a good impression on them but be ready to suffer quietly
and patiently. 13 Be gentle and ready to forgive;
never hold grudges. Remember, the Lord forgave
you, so you must forgive others.
14 Most of all, let love guide your life, for
then the whole church will stay together in perfect harmony. 15 Let the peace of heart which
comes from Christ be always present in your
hearts and lives, for this is your responsibility
and privilege as members of his body. And always be thankful.
16 Remember what Christ taught and let his
words enrich your lives and make you wise; teach
them to each other and sing them out in psalms
and hymns and spiritual songs, singing to the
Lord with thankful hearts. 17 And whatever you
do or say, let it be as a representative of the
Lord Jesus, and come with him into the presence of God the Father to give him your thanks.

Today's English Version

new man which God, its creator, is constantly
renewing in his own image, to bring you to a
full knowledge of himself. 11 As a result, there
are no Gentiles and Jews, circumcised and uncircumcised, barbarians, savages, slaves, or free
men, but Christ is all, Christ is in all.
12 You are the people of God; he loved you
and chose you for his own. So then; you must
put on compassion, kindness, humility, gentleness, and patience. 13 Be helpful to one another,
and forgive one another, whenever any of you
has a complaint against someone else. You must
forgive each other in the same way that the
Lord has forgiven you. 14 And to all these add
love, which binds all things together in perfect
unity. 15 The peace that Christ gives is to be the
judge in your hearts; for to this peace God has
called you together in the one body. And be
thankful. 16 Christ's message, in all its richness,
must live in your hearts. Teach and instruct
each other with all wisdom. Sing psalms, hymns,
and sacred songs; sing to God, with thanksgiving in your hearts. 17 Everything you do or say,
then, should be done in the name of the Lord
Jesus, as you give thanks through him to God
the Father.

New International Version

new self, which is being renewed in knowledge
in the image of its Creator. 11 Here there is no
Greek or Jew, circumcised or uncircumcised,
barbarian, Scythian, slave or free, but Christ is
all, and is in all.
12 Therefore, as God's chosen people, holy
and dearly loved, clothe yourselves with compassion, kindness, humility, gentleness and patience. 13 Bear with each other and forgive
whatever grievances you may have against one
another. Forgive as the Lord forgave you. 14 And
over all these virtues put on love, which binds
them all together in perfect unity.
15 Let the peace of Christ rule in your hearts,
since, as members of one body, you were called
to peace. And be thankful. 16 Let the word of
Christ dwell in you richly as you teach and counsel one another with all wisdom, and as you
sing psalms, hymns and spiritual songs with
gratitude in your hearts to God. 17 And whatever
you do, whether in word or deed, do it all in the
name of the Lord Jesus, giving thanks to God
the Father through him.

Phillips Modern English

the new nature which, by constant renewal in the likeness of its Creator, leads to a fuller knowledge of God. In this new man there is no distinction between Greek and Jew, circumcised or uncircumcised, foreigner or savage, slave or free man. Christ is all that matters for Christ lives in all.

3.12 *The expression of the new life (i)*

As, therefore, God's picked representatives, purified and beloved, put on that nature which is merciful in action, kindly in heart, and humble in mind. Accept life, and be most patient and tolerant with one another, always ready to forgive if you have a difference with anyone. Forgive as freely as the Lord has forgiven you. And, above everything else, be truly loving, for love binds all the virtues together in perfection.

Let the peace of Christ guide all your decisions, for you were called to live as one united body; and always be thankful. Let the full richness of Christ's teaching find its home among you. Teach and advise one another wisely. Use psalms and hymns and Christian songs, singing God's praises from joyful hearts. And whatever work you have to do, either in speech or action, do everything in the name of the Lord Jesus, thanking God the Father through him.

Revised Standard Version

being renewed in knowledge after the image of
its creator. 11 Here there cannot be Greek and
Jew, circumcised and uncircumcised, barbarian,
Scythian, slave, free man, but Christ is all, and
in all.
12 Put on then, as God's chosen ones, holy
and beloved, compassion, kindness, lowliness,
meekness, and patience, 13 forbearing one another and, if one has a complaint against another, forgiving each other; as the Lord has
forgiven you, so you also must forgive. 14 And
above all these put on love, which binds everything together in perfect harmony. 15 And let the
peace of Christ rule in your hearts, to which
indeed you were called in the one body. And
be thankful. 16 Let the word of Christ dwell in
you richly, teach and admonish one another in
all wisdom, and sing psalms and hymns and
spiritual songs with thankfulness in your hearts
to God. 17 And whatever you do, in word or
deed, do everything in the name of the Lord
Jesus, giving thanks to God the Father through
him.

Jerusalem Bible

put on a new self which will progress toward
true knowledge the more it is renewed in the
image of its creator; 11 and in that image there
is no room for distinction between Greek and
Jew, between the circumcised or the uncircumcised, or between barbarian and Scythian, slave
and free man. There is only Christ: he is everything and he is in everything.
12 You are God's chosen race, his saints; he
loves you, and you should be clothed in sincere
compassion, in kindness and humility, gentleness and patience. 13 Bear with one another;
forgive each other as soon as a quarrel begins.
The Lord has forgiven you; now you must do
the same. 14 Over all these clothes, to keep them
together and complete them, put on love. 15 And
may the peace of Christ reign in your hearts,
because it is for this that you were called together as parts of one body. Always be thankful.
16 Let the message of Christ, in all its richness, find a home with you. Teach each other,
and advise each other, in all wisdom. With
gratitude in your hearts sing psalms and hymns
and inspired songs to God; 17 and never say or
do anything except in the name of the Lord
Jesus, giving thanks to God the Father through
him.

New English Bible

new nature, which is being constantly renewed in the image of its Creator and brought to know God. There is no question here of Greek and Jew, circumcised and uncircumcised, barbarian, Scythian, slave and freeman; but Christ is all, and is in all.

Then put on the garments that suit God's chosen people, his own, his beloved: compassion, kindness, humility, gentleness, patience. Be forbearing with one another, and forgiving, where any of you has cause for complaint: you must forgive as the Lord forgave you. To crown all, there must be love, to bind all together and complete the whole. Let Christ's peace be arbiter in your hearts: to this peace you were called as members of a single body. And be filled with gratitude. Let the message of Christ dwell among you in all its richness. Instruct and admonish each other with the utmost wisdom. Sing thankfully in your hearts to God,[a] with psalms and hymns and spiritual songs. Whatever you are doing, whether you speak or act, do everything in the name of the Lord Jesus, giving thanks to God the Father through him.

[a] *Some witnesses read* the Lord.

King James Version

by him. 18 Wives, submit yourselves unto your
own husbands, as it is fit in the Lord. 19 Husbands, love *your* wives, and be not bitter against
them. 20 Children, obey *your* parents in all
things: for this is well pleasing unto the Lord.
21 Fathers, provoke not your children *to anger*,
lest they be discouraged. 22 Servants, obey in all
things *your* masters according to the flesh; not
with eyeservice, as menpleasers; but in singleness
of heart, fearing God: 23 And whatsoever ye do,
do *it* heartily, as to the Lord, and not unto men;
24 Knowing that of the Lord ye shall receive the
reward of the inheritance: for ye serve the Lord
Christ. 25 But he that doeth wrong shall receive
for the wrong which he hath done: and there is
no respect of persons.

4 Masters, give unto *your* servants that which
is just and equal; knowing that ye also have

Living Bible

18 You wives, submit yourselves to your husbands, for that is what the Lord has planned for you.
19 And you husbands must be loving and
kind to your wives and not bitter against them,
nor harsh.

20 You children must always obey your fathers and mothers, for that pleases the Lord.
21 Fathers, don't scold your children so much
that they become discouraged and quit trying.

22 You slaves must always obey your earthly masters, not only trying to please them when they are watching you but all the time; obey them willingly because of your love for the Lord and because you want to please him.
23 Work hard and cheerfully at all you do, just
as though you were working for the Lord and
not merely for your masters, 24 remembering that
it is the Lord Christ who is going to pay you,
giving you your full portion of all he owns. He
is the one you are really working for. 25 And if
you don't do your best for him, he will pay you
in a way that you won't like—for he has no
special favorites who can get away with shirking.

4 You slave owners must be just and fair to all your slaves. Always remember that you, too, have a Master in heaven who is closely watching you.

Today's English Version

Personal relations in the new life

18 Wives, be obedient to your husbands, for that is what you should do as Christians.

19 Husbands, love your wives, and do not be harsh with them.

20 Children, it is your Christian duty to obey your parents always, for that is what pleases God.

21 Parents, do not irritate your children, so that they will become discouraged.

22 Slaves, obey your human masters in all things, and do it not only when they are watching you, just to gain their approval, but do it with a sincere heart, because of your reverence
for the Lord. 23 Whatever you do, work at it
with all your heart, as though you were working for the Lord, and not for men. 24 Remember
that the Lord will reward you; you will receive
what he has kept for his people. For Christ is
the real Master you serve. 25 And the wrongdoer, whoever he is, will be paid for the wrong
things he does; for God judges everyone by the
same standard.

4 Masters, be right and fair in the way you treat your slaves. Remember that you too have a Master in heaven.

New International Version

Rules for christian households

18 Wives, submit to your husbands, as is fitting in the Lord.

19 Husbands, love your wives and do not be harsh with them.

20 Children, obey your parents in everything, for this pleases the Lord.

21 Fathers, do not embitter your children, or they will become discouraged.

22 Slaves, obey your masters in everything; and do it, not only when their eye is on you and to win their favor, but with sincerity of heart
and reverence for the Lord. 23 Whatever you do,
work at it with all your heart, as working for the
Lord, not for men, 24 since you know that you
will receive an inheritance from the Lord as a
reward. It is the Lord Christ you are serving.
25 Anyone who does wrong will be repaid for
his wrong, and there is no favoritism.

4 Masters, provide your slaves with what is right and fair, because you know that you also have a Master in heaven.

Phillips Modern English

3.18 The expression of the new life (ii)

Wives, adapt yourselves to your husbands; that is your Christian duty. Husbands, give your wives much love; never treat them harshly. As for you children, obey your parents in everything, for this is the right and Christian thing to do. Fathers, don't over-correct your children, or you will take all the heart out of them. Slaves, your job is to obey your human masters, not with the idea of catching their eye or currying favour, but as a sincere expression of your devotion to the Lord. Whatever your task is, put your whole heart and soul into it, as into work done for the Lord and not merely for men—knowing that your real reward will come from him. You are actually slaves of the Lord Christ Jesus.

But the dishonest man will be paid back for his dishonesty, and no favouritism will be shown.

Remember, then, you employers, to be just and fair to those whom you employ, never forgetting that you yourselves have a heavenly Employer.

Revised Standard Version

18 Wives, be subject to your husbands, as is fitting in the Lord. 19 Husbands, love your wives, and do not be harsh with them. 20 Children, obey your parents in everything, for this pleases the Lord. 21 Fathers, do not provoke your children, lest they become discouraged. 22 Slaves, obey in everything those who are your earthly masters, not with eyeservice, as men-pleasers, but in singleness of heart, fearing the Lord. 23 Whatever your task, work heartily, as serving the Lord and not men, 24 knowing that from the Lord you will receive the inheritance as your reward; you are serving the Lord Christ. 25 For the wrongdoer will be paid back for the wrong he has done, and there is no partiality.

4 Masters, treat your slaves justly and fairly, knowing that you also have a Master in heaven.

Jerusalem Bible

The morals of the home and household

18 Wives, give way to your husbands, as you should in the Lord. 19 Husbands, love your wives and treat them with gentleness. 20 Children, be obedient to your parents always, because that is what will please the Lord. 21 Parents, never drive your children to resentment or you will make them feel frustrated.

22 Slaves, be obedient to the men who are called your masters in this world; not only when you are under their eye, as if you had only to please men, but wholeheartedly, out of respect for the Master. 23 Whatever your work is, put your heart into it as if it were for the Lord and not for men, 24 knowing that the Lord will repay you by making you his heirs. It is Christ the Lord that you are serving; 25 anyone who does wrong will be repaid in kind and he does not favor one person more than another.

4 Masters, make sure that your slaves are given what is just and fair, knowing that you too have a Master in heaven.

New English Bible

Wives, be subject to your husbands; that is your Christian duty. Husbands, love your wives and do not be harsh with them. Children, obey your parents in everything, for that is pleasing to God and is the Christian way. Fathers, do not exasperate your children, for fear they grow disheartened. Slaves, give entire obedience to your earthly masters, not merely with an outward show of service, to curry favour with men, but with single-mindedness, out of reverence for the Lord. Whatever you are doing, put your whole heart into it, as if you were doing it for the Lord and not for men, knowing that there is a Master who will give you your heritage as a reward for your service. Christ is the Master whose slaves you must be. Dishonesty will be requited, and he has no favourites.

4 Masters, be just and fair to your slaves, knowing that you too have a Master in heaven.

King James Version

a Master in heaven. 2 Continue in prayer, and
watch in the same with thanksgiving; 3 Withal
praying also for us, that God would open unto
us a door of utterance, to speak the mystery of
Christ, for which I am also in bonds: 4 That I
may make it manifest, as I ought to speak.
5 Walk in wisdom toward them that are without,
redeeming the time. 6 Let your speech *be* always
with grace, seasoned with salt, that ye may know
how ye ought to answer every man. 7 All my state
shall Tychicus declare unto you, *who is* a beloved brother, and a faithful minister and fellow
servant in the Lord: 8 Whom I have sent unto
you for the same purpose, that he might know
your estate, and comfort your hearts; 9 With
Onesimus, a faithful and beloved brother, who is
one of you. They shall make known unto you all

Living Bible

2 Don't be weary in prayer; keep at it; watch
for God's answers and remember to be thankful
when they come. 3 Don't forget to pray for us
too, that God will give us many chances to
preach the Good News of Christ for which I am
here in jail. 4 Pray that I will be bold enough to
tell it freely and fully, and make it plain, as, of
course, I should.
5 Make the most of your chances to tell others
the Good News. Be wise in all your contacts
with them. 6 Let your conversation be gracious
as well as sensible, for then you will have the
right answer for everyone.
7 Tychicus, our much loved brother, will tell
you how I am getting along. He is a hard worker
and serves the Lord with me. 8 I have sent him
on this special trip just to see how you are, and
to comfort and encourage you. 9 I am also sending Onesimus, a faithful and much loved brother,
one of your own people. He and Tychicus will
give you all the latest news.

Today's English Version

Instructions

2 Be persistent in prayer, and keep alert as
you pray, with thanks to God. 3 At the same
time pray also for us, so that God will give us
a good opportunity to preach his message, to tell
the secret of Christ. For that is why I am now
in prison. 4 Pray, then, that I may speak in
such a way as to make it clear, as I should.
5 Be wise in the way you act toward those
who are not believers, making good use of every
opportunity you have. 6 Your speech should always be pleasant and interesting, and you should
know how to give the right answer to everyone.

Final greetings

7 Our dear brother Tychicus, who is a faithful
worker and fellow servant in the Lord's work,
will give you all the news about me. 8 That is
why I am sending him to you, to cheer you up
by telling you how all of us are getting along.
9 With him goes Onesimus, the dear and faithful
brother, who belongs to your group. They will
tell you everything that is happening here.

New International Version

Further instructions

2 Devote yourselves to prayer, being watchful
and thankful. 3 And pray for us, too, that God
may open a door for our message, so that we
may proclaim the mystery of Christ, for which
I am in chains. 4 Pray that I may proclaim it
clearly, as I should. 5 Be wise in the way you act
toward outsiders; make the most of every opportunity. 6 Let your conversation be always full of
grace, seasoned with salt, so that you may know
how to answer everyone.

Final greetings

7 Tychicus will tell you all the news about me.
He is a dear brother, a faithful minister and fellow servant in the Lord. 8 I am sending him to
you for the express purpose that you may know
about our circumstances and that he may encourage your hearts. 9 He is coming with Onesimus, our faithful and dear brother, who is one
of you. They will tell you everything that is happening here.

Phillips Modern English

4.2 Some simple, practical advice

Always maintain the habit of prayer: be both alert and thankful as you pray. Include us in your prayers, please, that God may open for us a door for the entrance of the gospel. Pray that we may speak of the mystery of Christ (for which speaking I am at present in chains), and that I may make that mystery plain to men, which I know is my duty.

Be wise in your behaviour towards non-Christians, and make the best possible use of your time. Speak pleasantly to them, but never sentimentally, and learn how to give the proper answer to every questioner.

4.7 Greetings and farewell

Tychicus (a well-loved brother, a faithful minister and a fellow-servant of the Lord) will tell you all about my present circumstances. I am sending him to you so that you may find out how we are all getting on, and that he may put new heart into you. With him is Onesimus, one of your own congregation (well-loved and faithful, too). Between them they will tell you of all that goes on here.

Revised Standard Version

2 Continue steadfastly in prayer, being watchful in it with thanksgiving;
3 and pray for us also, that God may open to us a door for the word, to declare the mystery of Christ, on account of which I am in prison,
4 that I may make it clear, as I ought to speak.

5 Conduct yourselves wisely toward outsiders, making the most of the time.
6 Let your speech always be gracious, seasoned with salt, so that you may know how you ought to answer every one.

7 Tychicus will tell you all about my affairs; he is a beloved brother and faithful minister and fellow servant in the Lord.
8 I have sent him to you for this very purpose, that you may know how we are and that he may encourage your hearts,
9 and with him Onesimus, the faithful and beloved brother, who is one of yourselves. They will tell you of everything that has taken place here.

Jerusalem Bible

The apostolic spirit

2 Be persevering in your prayers and be thankful as you stay awake to pray.
3 Pray for us especially, asking God to show us opportunities for announcing the message and proclaiming the mystery of Christ, for the sake of which I am in chains;
4 pray that I may proclaim it as clearly as I ought.

5 Be tactful with those who are not Christians and be sure you make the best use of your time with them.
6 Talk to them agreeably and with a flavor of wit, and try to fit your answers to the needs of each one.

Personal news

7 Tychicus will tell you all the news about me. He is a brother I love very much, and a loyal helper and companion in the service of the Lord.
8 I am sending him to you precisely for this purpose: to give you news about us and to reassure you.
9 With him I am sending Onesimus, that dear and faithful brother who is a fellow citizen of yours. They will tell you everything that is happening here.

New English Bible

Persevere in prayer, with mind awake and thankful heart; and include a prayer for us, that God may give us an opening for preaching, to tell the secret of Christ; that indeed is why I am now in prison. Pray that I may make the secret plain, as it is my duty to do.

Behave wisely towards those outside your own number; use the present opportunity to the full. Let your conversation be always gracious, and never insipid; study how best to talk with each person you meet.

You will hear all about my affairs from Tychicus, our dear brother and trustworthy helper and fellow-servant in the Lord's work. I am sending him to you on purpose to let you know all about us and to put fresh heart into you. With him comes Onesimus, our trustworthy and dear brother, who is one of yourselves. They will tell you all the news here.

King James Version

things which *are done* here. 10Aristarchus my
fellow prisoner saluteth you, and Marcus, sister's
son to Barnabas, (touching whom ye received
commandments: if he come unto you, receive
him;) 11And Jesus, which is called Justus, who
are of the circumcision. These only *are my* fellow
workers unto the kingdom of God, which have
been a comfort unto me. 12 Epaphras, who is
one of you, a servant of Christ, saluteth you, always labouring fervently for you in prayers, that
ye may stand perfect and complete in all the
will of God. 13 For I bear him record, that he
hath a great zeal for you, and them *that are* in
Laodicea, and them in Hierapolis. 14 Luke,
the beloved physician, and Demas, greet you.
15 Salute the brethren which are in Laodicea,
and Nymphas, and the church which is in his
house. 16And when this epistle is read among
you, cause that it be read also in the church of
the Laodiceans; and that ye likewise read the
epistle from Laodicea. 17And say to Archippus,
Take heed to the ministry which thou hast received in the Lord, that thou fulfil it. 18 The salutation by the hand of me Paul. Remember my
bonds. Grace *be* with you. Amen.

Written from Rome to the Colossians by Tychicus and Onesimus.

Living Bible

10 Aristarchus, who is with me here as a
prisoner, sends you his love, and so does Mark,
a relative of Barnabas. And as I said before, give
Mark a hearty welcome[a] if he comes your way.
11 Jesus Justus also sends his love. These are the
only Jewish Christians working with me here,
and what a comfort they have been!

12 Epaphras, from your city, a servant of
Christ Jesus, sends you his love. He is always
earnestly praying for you, asking God to make
you strong and perfect and to help you know his
will in everything you do. 13 I can assure you
that he has worked hard for you with his prayers,
and also for the Christians in Laodicea and
Hierapolis.

14 Dear doctor Luke sends his love, and so
does Demas.

15 Please give my greeting to the Christian
friends at Laodicea, and to Nymphas, and to
those who meet in his home. 16 By the way, after
you have read this letter will you pass it on to
the church at Laodicea? And read the letter I
wrote to them. 17And say to Archippus, "Be sure
that you do all the Lord has told you to."

18 Here is my own greeting in my own handwriting: Remember me here in jail. May God's
blessings surround you.

Sincerely,
Paul

[a] Literally, "receive him."

Today's English Version

10 Aristarchus, who is in prison with me,
sends you greetings, and so does Mark, the
cousin of Barnabas. (You have already received
instructions about him, to welcome him if he
comes your way.) 11 Joshua, called Justus, also
sends greetings. These three are the only Jewish
converts who work with me for the Kingdom of
God, and they have been a great help to me.

12 Greetings from Epaphras, another member
of your group, and a servant of Christ Jesus. He
always prays fervently for you, asking God to
make you stand firm, mature, and fully convinced, in complete obedience to his will. 13 I
can personally testify to his hard work for you,
and for the people in Laodicea and Hierapolis.
14 Luke, our dear doctor, and Demas send you
their greetings.

15 Give our best wishes to the brothers in
Laodicea, and to Nympha and the church that
meets in her house. 16 After you read this letter, make sure that it is read also in the church
at Laodicea. At the same time, you are to read
the letter Laodicea will send you. 17And tell
Archippus, "Be sure to finish the task you were
given in the Lord's service."

18 With my own hand I write this: *Greetings
from Paul.* Do not forget my chains!

May God's grace be with you.

New International Version

10 My fellow prisoner Aristarchus sends you
his greetings, as does Mark, the cousin of Barnabas. (You have received instructions about him;
if he comes to you, welcome him.) 11 Jesus, who
is called Justus, also sends greetings. These are
the only Jews among my fellow workers for the
kingdom of God, and they have proved a comfort to me. 12 Epaphras, who is one of you and
a servant of Christ Jesus, sends greetings. He is
always wrestling in prayer for you, that you may
stand firm in all the will of God, mature and
fully assured. 13 I vouch for him that he is
working hard for you and for those at Laodicea
and Hierapolis. 14 Our dear friend Luke, the
doctor, and Demas send greetings. 15 Give my
greetings to the brothers at Laodicea, and to
Nympha and the church in her house.

16 After this letter has been read to you, see
that it is also read in the church of the Laodiceans and that you in turn read the letter from
Laodicea.

17 Tell Archippus: "See to it that you complete the work you have received in the Lord."

18 I, Paul, write this greeting in my own hand.
Remember my chains. Grace be with you.

Phillips Modern English

Aristarchus, who is also in prison here, sends greetings, and so does Barnabas' cousin, Mark. I gave you instructions before about him; if he comes to you, make him welcome. Jesus Justus is here too. Only these few fellow-Jews are working with me for the kingdom, but what a help they have been!

Epaphras, another member of your Church, and a real servant of Christ Jesus, sends his greeting. He works hard for you even here, for he prays constantly and earnestly for you, that you may become mature Christians, and may fulfil God's will for you. From my own observation I can tell you that he has a real passion for your welfare, and for that of the churches at Laodicea and Hierapolis.

Luke, our beloved doctor, and Demas send their best wishes. My own greetings to the Christians in Laodicea, and to Nympha and the congregation who meet in her house.

When you have had this letter read in your church, see that the Laodiceans have it read in their church too; and see that you in turn read the letter to Laodicea.

A brief message to Archippus: remember the Lord ordained you to your ministry—see that you carry it out!

My personal greeting to you written by myself, Paul.

Don't forget I'm in prison. Grace be with you.

Revised Standard Version

10 Aristarchus my fellow prisoner greets you, and Mark the cousin of Barnabas (concerning whom you have received instructions—if he comes to you, receive him), 11 and Jesus who is called Justus. These are the only men of the circumcision among my fellow workers for the kingdom of God, and they have been a comfort to me. 12 Epaphras, who is one of yourselves, a servant[g] of Christ Jesus, greets you, always remembering you earnestly in his prayers, that you may stand mature and fully assured in all the will of God. 13 For I bear him witness that he has worked hard for you and for those in Laodicea and in Hierapolis. 14 Luke the beloved physician and Demas greet you. 15 Give my greetings to the brethren at Laodicea, and to Nympha and the church in her house. 16 And when this letter has been read among you, have it read also in the church of the Laodiceans; and see that you read also the letter from Laodicea. 17 And say to Archippus, "See that you fulfil the ministry which you have received in the Lord."

18 I, Paul, write this greeting with my own hand. Remember my fetters. Grace be with you.

[g] Or *slave*.

Jerusalem Bible

Greetings and final wishes

10 Aristarchus, who is here in prison with me, sends his greetings, and so does Mark, the cousin of Barnabas—you were sent some instructions about him; if he comes to you, give him a warm welcome—11 and Jesus Justus adds his greetings. Of all those who have come over from the Circumcision, these are the only ones actually working with me for the kingdom of God. They have been a great comfort to me. 12 Epaphras, your fellow citizen, sends his greetings; this servant of Christ Jesus never stops battling for you, praying that you will never lapse but always hold perfectly and securely to the will of God. 13 I can testify for him that he works hard for you, as well as for those at Laodicea and Hierapolis. 14 Greetings from my dear friend Luke, the doctor, and also from Demas.

15 Please give my greetings to the brothers at Laodicea and to Nympha and the church which meets in her house. 16 After this letter has been read among you, send it on to be read in the church of the Laodiceans; and get the letter from Laodicea for you to read yourselves. 17 Give Archippus this message, "Remember the service that the Lord wants you to do, and try to carry it out."

18 Here is a greeting in my own handwriting—PAUL. Remember the chains I wear. Grace be with you.

New English Bible

Aristarchus, Christ's captive like myself, sends his greetings; so does Mark, the cousin of Barnabas (you have had instructions about him; if he comes, make him welcome), and Jesus Justus. Of the Jewish Christians, these are the only ones who work with me for the kingdom of God, and they have been a great comfort to me. Greetings from Epaphras, servant of Christ, who is one of yourselves. He prays hard for you all the time, that you may stand fast, ripe in conviction[a] and wholly devoted to doing God's will. For I can vouch for him, that he works tirelessly for you and the people at Laodicea and Hierapolis. Greetings to you from our dear friend Luke, the doctor, and from Demas. Give our greetings to the brothers at Laodicea, and Nympha and the congregation at her house.[b] And when this letter is read among you, see that it is also read to the congregation at Laodicea, and that you in return read the one from Laodicea. This special word to Archippus: 'Attend to the duty entrusted to you in the Lord's service, and discharge it to the full.'

This greeting is in my own hand—PAUL. Remember I am in prison. God's grace be with you.

[a] *Or* stand fast, mature and complete . . . [b] *Some witnesses read* Nymphas and the congregation at his house.

King James Version

THE FIRST EPISTLE OF PAUL THE APOSTLE TO THE THESSALONIANS

1 Paul, and Silvanus, and Timotheus, unto the
church of the Thessalonians *which is* in God
the Father, and *in* the Lord Jesus Christ: Grace
be unto you, and peace, from God our Father,
and the Lord Jesus Christ. 2 We give thanks to
God always for you all, making mention of you
in our prayers; 3 Remembering without ceasing
your work of faith, and labour of love, and patience of hope in our Lord Jesus Christ, in the
sight of God and our Father; 4 Knowing, breth-

Living Bible

1 THESSALONIANS

1 *From:* Paul, Silas and Timothy.
To: The Church at Thessalonica—to you who belong to God the Father and the Lord Jesus Christ: May blessing and peace of heart be your rich gifts from God our Father, and from Jesus Christ our Lord.

2 We always thank God for you and pray for
you constantly. 3 We never forget your loving
deeds as we talk to our God and Father about you, and your strong faith and steady looking forward to the return of our Lord Jesus Christ.
4 We know that God has chosen you, dear

Today's English Version

PAUL'S FIRST LETTER TO THE THESSALONIANS

1 From Paul, Silas, and Timothy—
To the people of the church in Thessalonica, who belong to God the Father and the Lord Jesus Christ:
May grace and peace be yours.

The life and faith of the Thessalonians

2 We always thank God for you all, and always mention you in our prayers. 3 For we remember before our God and Father how you
put your faith into practice, how your love made you work so hard, and how your hope in our Lord Jesus Christ is firm. 4 We know, brothers,

New International Version

1 THESSALONIANS

1 Paul, Silas[a] and Timothy,
To the church of the Thessalonians, who are in God the Father and the Lord Jesus Christ:
Grace and peace to you.

Thanksgiving for the Thessalonians' faith

2 We always thank God for all of you, mentioning you in our prayers. 3 We continually remember before our God and Father your work produced by faith, your labor prompted by love, and your endurance inspired by hope in our Lord Jesus Christ.
4 Brothers loved by God, we know that he

[a] Greek *Silvanus.*

Phillips Modern English

THE FIRST LETTER TO THE CHRISTIANS IN THESSALONICA

To the church of the Thessalonians, founded on God the Father and the Lord Jesus Christ, grace and peace from Paul, Silvanus and Timothy.

1.2 *Your faith cheers us and encourages many others*

We are always thankful to God as we pray for you all, for we never forget that your faith has meant solid achievement, your love has meant hard work, and the hope that you have in our Lord Jesus Christ means sheer dogged endurance in the life that you live before God, the Father of us all.

We know, brothers, that God not only loves

Revised Standard Version

THE FIRST LETTER OF PAUL TO THE THESSALONIANS

1 Paul, Silvanus, and Timothy,
To the church of the Thessalonians in God the Father and the Lord Jesus Christ:
Grace to you and peace.

2 We give thanks to God always for you all,
constantly mentioning you in our prayers, 3 remembering before our God and Father your
work of faith and labor of love and steadfastness of hope in our Lord Jesus Christ. 4 For

Jerusalem Bible

THE FIRST LETTER OF PAUL TO THE CHURCH IN THESSALONIKA

1 THESSALONIANS

Address

1 From Paul, Silvanus and Timothy, to the Church in Thessalonika which is in God the Father and the Lord Jesus Christ; wishing you grace and peace.

Thanksgiving and congratulations

2 We always mention you in our prayers and
thank God for you all, 3 and constantly remember before God our Father how you have shown
your faith in action, worked for love and persevered through hope, in our Lord Jesus Christ.
4 We know, brothers, that God loves you and

New English Bible

THE FIRST LETTER OF PAUL TO THE THESSALONIANS

Hope and discipline

1 From Paul, Silvanus, and Timothy to the congregation of Thessalonians who belong to God the Father and the Lord Jesus Christ.

Grace to you and peace.

We always thank God for you all, and mention you in our prayers continually. We call to mind, before our God and Father, how your faith has shown itself in action, your love in labour, and your hope of our Lord Jesus Christ in fortitude. We are certain, brothers beloved

King James Version

ren beloved, your election of God. 5 For our gospel came not unto you in word only, but also in power, and in the Holy Ghost, and in much assurance; as ye know what manner of men we were among you for your sake. 6And ye became followers of us, and of the Lord, having received the word in much affliction, with joy of the Holy Ghost: 7 So that ye were ensamples to all that believe in Macedonia and Achaia. 8 For from you sounded out the word of the Lord not only in Macedonia and Achaia, but also in every place your faith to God-ward is spread abroad; so that we need not to speak any thing. 9 For they themselves shew of us what manner of entering in we had unto you, and how ye turned to God from idols to serve the living and true God; 10And to wait for his Son from heaven, whom he raised from the dead, *even* Jesus, which delivered us from the wrath to come.

2 For yourselves, brethren, know our entrance in unto you, that it was not in vain: 2 But even after that we had suffered before, and were shamefully entreated, as ye know, at Philippi, we were bold in our God to speak unto you the gospel of God with much contention. 3 For our exhortation *was* not of deceit, nor of unclean-

Living Bible

brothers, much beloved of God. 5 For when we brought you the Good News, it was not just meaningless chatter to you; no, you listened with great interest. What we told you produced a powerful effect upon you, for the Holy Spirit gave you great and full assurance that what we said was true. And you know how our very lives were further proof to you of the truth of our message. 6 So you became our followers and the Lord's; for you received our message with joy from the Holy Spirit in spite of the trials and sorrows it brought you.

7 Then you yourselves became an example to all the other Christians in Greece. 8And now the Word of the Lord has spread out from you to others everywhere, far beyond your boundaries, for wherever we go we find people telling us about your remarkable faith in God. We don't need to tell *them* about it, 9 for *they* keep telling *us* about the wonderful welcome you gave us, and how you turned away from your idols to God so that now the living and true God only is your Master. 10And they speak of how you are looking forward to the return of God's Son from heaven—Jesus, whom God brought back to life—and he is our only Savior from God's terrible anger against sin.

2 You yourselves know, dear brothers, how worthwhile that visit was. 2 You know how badly we have been treated at Philippi just before we came to you, and how much we suffered there. Yet God gave us the courage to boldly repeat the same message to you, even though we were surrounded by enemies. 3 So you can see that we were not preaching with

Today's English Version

that God loves you and has chosen you to be his own. 5 For we brought the Good News to you, not with words only, but also with power and the Holy Spirit, and with complete conviction of its truth. You know how we lived when we were with you; it was for your own good. 6 You imitated us and the Lord; and even though you suffered much, you received the message with the joy that comes from the Holy Spirit. 7 So you became an example to all believers in Macedonia and Greece. 8 For the message about the Lord went out from you not only to Macedonia and Greece, but, the news of your faith in God has gone everywhere. There is nothing, then, that we need to say. 9All those people speak of how you received us when we visited you, and how you turned away from idols to God, to serve the true and living God 10 and to wait for his Son to come from heaven—his Son Jesus, whom he raised from death, and who rescues us from God's wrath that is to come.

Paul's work in Thessalonica

2 You yourselves know, brothers, that our visit to you was not a failure. 2 You know how we had already been mistreated and insulted in Philippi before we came to you in Thessalonica. Yet our God gave us courage to tell you the Good News that comes from him, even though there was much opposition. 3 The appeal we make to you is not based on error or

New International Version

has chosen you, 5 because our gospel came to you not simply with words, but also with power, with the Holy Spirit and with deep conviction. You know how we lived among you for your sake. 6 You became imitators of us and of the Lord; in spite of severe suffering, you welcomed the message with the joy given by the Holy Spirit. 7And so you became a model to all the believers in Macedonia and Achaia. 8 The Lord's message rang out from you not only in Macedonia and Achaia—your faith in God has become known everywhere. Therefore we do not need to say anything about it, 9 for they themselves report what kind of reception you gave us. They tell how you turned to God from idols to serve the living and true God, 10 and to wait for his Son from heaven, whom he raised from the dead—Jesus, who rescues us from the coming wrath.

Paul's ministry in Thessalonica

2 You know, brothers, that our visit to you was not a failure. 2 We had previously suffered and been insulted in Philippi, as you know, but with the help of our God we dared to tell you his gospel in spite of strong opposition. 3 For the appeal we make does not spring from

Phillips Modern English

you but has selected you for a special purpose. For we remember how our gospel came to you not as mere words, but as a message with power behind it—the convincing power of the Holy Spirit. You know what sort of men we were when we lived among you. You set yourselves to copy us, and indeed, the Lord himself. You remember how, although accepting the message meant serious trouble, yet you experienced the joy of the Holy Spirit. You thus became an example to all who believe in Macedonia and Achaia. You have become a sort of sounding-board from which the Word of the Lord has rung out, not only in Macedonia and Achaia but everywhere where the story of your faith in God has become known. We find we don't have to tell people about it. They tell *us* the story of our coming to you: how you turned from idols to serve the true living God, and how your whole lives now look forward to the coming of his Son from Heaven—the Son Jesus, whom God raised from the dead, and who delivered us from the judgment which hung over our heads.

2.1 The spirit of our visit to you is well known to you all

My brothers, you know from your own experience that our visit to you was no failure. We had, as you also know, suffered and been treated with insults at Philippi, and we came on to you only because God gave us courage. Whatever the strain we came to tell you the gospel of God.

Our message to you is true, our motives are

Revised Standard Version

we know, brethren beloved by God, that he has
chosen you; 5 for our gospel came to you not
only in word, but also in power and in the Holy
Spirit and with full conviction. You know what
kind of men we proved to be among you for
your sake. 6 And you became imitators of us
and of the Lord, for you received the word in
much affliction, with joy inspired by the Holy
Spirit; 7 so that you became an example to all
the believers in Macedonia and in Achaia. 8 For
not only has the word of the Lord sounded
forth from you in Macedonia and Achaia, but
your faith in God has gone forth everywhere,
so that we need not say anything. 9 For they
themselves report concerning us what a welcome
we had among you, and how you turned to God
from idols, to serve a living and true God, 10 and
to wait for his Son from heaven, whom he raised
from the dead, Jesus who delivers us from the
wrath to come.

2 For you yourselves know, brethren, that
our visit to you was not in vain; 2 but
though we had already suffered and been shamefully treated at Philippi, as you know, we had
courage in our God to declare to you the gospel
of God in the face of great opposition. 3 For
our appeal does not spring from error or un-

Jerusalem Bible

that you have been chosen, 5 because when we
brought the Good News to you, it came to you
not only as words, but as power and as the
Holy Spirit and as utter conviction. And you
observed the sort of life we lived when we were
with you, which was for your instruction, 6 and
you were led to become imitators of us, and of
the Lord; and it was with the joy of the Holy
Spirit that you took to the gospel, in spite of
the great opposition all around you. 7 This has
made you the great example to all believers in
Macedonia and Achaia 8 since it was from you
that the word of the Lord started to spread—
and not only throughout Macedonia and Achaia,
for the news of your faith in God has spread
everywhere. We do not need to tell other people about it: 9 other people tell us how we
started the work among you, how you broke
with idolatry when you were converted to God
and became servants of the real, living God;
10 and how you are now waiting for Jesus, his
Son, whom he raised from the dead, to come
from heaven to save us from the retribution
which is coming.

Paul's example in Thessalonika

2 You know yourselves, my brothers, that
our visit to you has not proved ineffectual.
2 We had, as you know, been given rough
treatment and been grossly insulted at Philippi,
and it was our God who gave us the courage to
proclaim his Good News to you in the face of
great opposition. 3 We have not taken to preaching because we are deluded or immoral or

New English Bible

by God, that he has chosen you and that[a] when we brought you the Gospel, we brought it not in mere words but in the power of the Holy Spirit, and with strong conviction, as you know well. That is the kind of men we were at Thessalonica, and it was for your sake.

And you, in your turn, followed the example set by us and by the Lord; the welcome you gave the message meant grave suffering for you, yet you rejoiced in the Holy Spirit; thus you have become a model for all believers in Macedonia and in Achaia. From Thessalonica the word of the Lord rang out; and not in Macedonia and Achaia alone, but everywhere your faith in God has reached men's ears. No words of ours are needed, for they themselves spread the news of our visit to you and its effect: how you turned from idols, to be servants of the living and true God, and to wait expectantly for the appearance from heaven of his Son Jesus, whom he raised from the dead, Jesus our deliverer from the terrors of judgement to come.

2 You know for yourselves, brothers, that
our visit to you was not fruitless. Far from it; after all the injury and outrage which to your knowledge we had suffered at Philippi, we declared the gospel of God to you frankly and fearlessly, by the help of our God. A hard struggle it was. Indeed, the appeal we make never springs from error or base motive; there

[a] *Or* . . . chosen you, because . . .

King James Version

ness, nor in guile: 4 But as we were allowed of God to be put in trust with the gospel, even so we speak; not as pleasing men, but God, which trieth our hearts. 5 For neither at any time used we flattering words, as ye know, nor a cloak of covetousness; God *is* witness: 6 Nor of men sought we glory, neither of you, nor *yet* of others, when we might have been burdensome, as the apostles of Christ. 7 But we were gentle among you, even as a nurse cherisheth her children: 8 So being affectionately desirous of you, we were willing to have imparted unto you, not the gospel of God only, but also our own souls, because ye were dear unto us. 9 For ye remember, brethren, our labour and travail: for labouring night and day, because we would not be chargeable unto any of you, we preached unto you the gospel of God. 10 Ye *are* witnesses, and God *also*, how holily and justly and unblameably we behaved ourselves among you that believe: 11 As ye know how we exhorted and comforted and charged every one of you, as a father *doth* his children, 12 That ye would walk worthy of God, who hath called you unto his kingdom and glory. 13 For this cause also thank we God without ceasing, because, when ye received the word

Living Bible

any false motives or evil purposes in mind; we were perfectly straightforward and sincere.

4 For we speak as messengers from God, trusted by him to tell the truth; we change his message not one bit to suit the taste of those who hear it; for we serve God alone, who examines our hearts' deepest thoughts. 5 Never once did we try to win you with flattery, as you very well know, and God knows we were not just pretending to be your friends so that you would give us money! 6 As for praise, we have never asked for it from you or anyone else, although as apostles of Christ we certainly had a right to some honor from you. 7 But we were as gentle among you as a mother feeding and caring for her own children. 8 We loved you dearly—so dearly that we gave you not only God's message, but our own lives too.

9 Don't you remember, dear brothers, how hard we worked among you? Night and day we toiled and sweated to earn enough to live on so that our expenses would not be a burden to anyone there, as we preached God's Good News among you. 10 You yourselves are our witnesses—as is God—that we have been pure and honest and faultless toward every one of you. 11 We talked to you as a father to his own children—don't you remember?—pleading with you, encouraging you and even demanding 12 that your daily lives should not embarrass God, but bring joy to him who invited you into his kingdom to share his glory.

13 And we will never stop thanking God for this: that when we preached to you, you didn't

Today's English Version

impure motives, nor do we try to trick anyone. 4 Instead, we always speak as God wants us to, because he approved us and entrusted the Good News to us. We do not try to please men, but to please God, who tests our motives. 5 You know very well that we did not come to you with flattering talk, nor did we use words to cover up greed—God is our witness! 6 We did not try to get praise from anyone, either from you or from others, 7 even though we could have made demands on you as apostles of Christ. But we were gentle when we were with you, as gentle as a mother taking care of her children. 8 Because of our love for you we were ready to share with you not only the Good News from God but even our own lives. You were so dear to us! 9 Surely you remember, brothers, how we worked and toiled! We worked day and night so we would not be any trouble to you as we preached to you the Good News from God.

10 You are our witnesses, and so is God: our conduct toward you who believe was pure, right, and without fault. 11 You know that we treated each one of you just as a father treats his own children. 12 We encouraged you, we comforted you, and we kept urging you to live the kind of life that pleases God, who calls you to share his own Kingdom and glory.

13 And for this other reason, also, we always give thanks to God. When we brought you

New International Version

error or impure motives, nor are we trying to trick you. 4 On the contrary, we speak as men approved by God to be entrusted with the gospel. We are not trying to please men but God, who tests our hearts. 5 You know we never used flattery, nor did we put on a mask to cover up greed—God is our witness. 6 We were not looking for praise from men, not from you or anyone else.

7 As apostles of Christ we could have been a burden to you, but we were gentle among you, like a mother caring for her little children. 8 We loved you so much that we were delighted to share with you not only the gospel of God but our lives as well, because you had become so dear to us. 9 Surely you remember, brothers, our toil and hardship; we worked night and day in order not be a burden to anyone while we preached the gospel of God to you.

10 You are witnesses, and so is God, of how holy, righteous and blameless we were among you who believed. 11 For you know that we dealt with each of you as a father deals with his own children, 12 encouraging, comforting and urging you to live lives worthy of God, who calls you into his kingdom and glory.

13 And we also thank God continually because, when you received the word of God,

Phillips Modern English

pure, our conduct is absolutely above board. We speak under the solemn sense of being entrusted by God with the gospel. We do not aim to please men, but to please God who knows us through and through. No one could say, as again you know, that we used flattery to conceal greed, and God himself is our witness. We made no attempt to win honour from men, either from you or from anybody else, though I suppose as Christ's own messengers we might have used the weight of our authority. Our attitude among you was one of tenderness, rather like a nurse caring for her babies. Because we loved you, it was a joy to us to give you not only the gospel of God but our very hearts—so dear had you become to us. Our struggles and hard work, my brothers, must be still fresh in your minds. Day and night we worked so that our preaching of the gospel to you might not be a burden to any of you. You are witnesses, as is God himself, that our life among you believers was devoted, straightforward and above criticism. You will remember how we dealt with each one of you personally, like a father with his own children, comforting and encouraging. We told you from our own experience how to live lives worthy of the God who is calling you to share the splendour of his own kingdom.

And so we are continually thankful to God that when you heard the Word of God from

Revised Standard Version

cleanness, nor is it made with guile; 4 but just
as we have been approved by God to be entrusted with the gospel, so we speak, not to
please men, but to please God who tests our
hearts. 5 For we never used either words of
flattery, as you know, or a cloak for greed, as
God is witness; 6 nor did we seek glory from
men, whether from you or from others, though
we might have made demands as apostles of
Christ. 7 But we were gentle[a] among you, like
a nurse taking care of her children. 8 So, being
affectionately desirous of you, we were ready
to share with you not only the gospel of God
but also our own selves, because you had become very dear to us.
9 For you remember our labor and toil,
brethren; we worked night and day, that we
might not burden any of you, while we preached
to you the gospel of God. 10 You are witnesses,
and God also, how holy and righteous and
blameless was our behavior to you believers;
11 for you know how, like a father with his
children, we exhorted each one of you and encouraged you and charged you 12 to lead a life
worthy of God, who calls you into his own kingdom and glory.
13 And we also thank God constantly for
this, that when you received the word of God

[a] Other ancient authorities read *babes*.

Jerusalem Bible

trying to deceive anyone; 4 it was God who decided that we were fit to be entrusted with the
Good News, and when we are speaking, we are
not trying to please men but God, *who can read*
our *inmost thoughts.*[a] 5 You know very well,
and we can swear it before God, that never at
any time have our speeches been simply flattery
or a cover for trying to get money; 6 nor have
we ever looked for any special honor from men,
either from you or anybody else, 7 when we
could have imposed ourselves on you with full
weight, as apostles of Christ.
Instead, we were unassuming. Like a mother
feeding and looking after her own children,
8 we felt so devoted and protective toward you,
and had come to love you so much, that we
were eager to hand over to you not only the
Good News but our whole lives as well. 9 Let
me remind you, brothers, how hard we used to
work, slaving night and day so as not to be a
burden on any one of you while we were proclaiming God's Good News to you. 10 You are
witnesses, and so is God, that our treatment of
you, since you became believers, has been impeccably right and fair. 11 You can remember
how we treated every one of you as a father
treats his children, 12 teaching you what was
right, encouraging you and appealing to you to
live a life worthy of God, who is calling you to
share the glory of his kingdom.

The faith and the patience of the Thessalonians

13 Another reason why we constantly thank
God for you is that as soon as you heard the

[a] Jr. 11:20.

New English Bible

is no attempt to deceive; but God has approved us as fit to be entrusted with the Gospel, and on those terms we speak. We do not curry favour with men; we seek only the favour of God, who is continually testing our hearts. Our words have never been flattering words, as you have cause to know; nor, as God is our witness, have they ever been a cloak for greed. We have never sought honour from men, from you or from anyone else, although as Christ's own envoys we might have made our weight felt; but we were as gentle with you as a nurse caring fondly for her children. With such yearning love we chose to impart to you not only the gospel of God but our very selves, so dear had you become to us. Remember, brothers, how we toiled and drudged. We worked for a living night and day, rather than be a burden to anyone, while we proclaimed before you the good news of God.

We call you to witness, yes and God himself, how devout and just and blameless was our behaviour towards you who are believers. As you well know, we dealt with you one by one, as a father deals with his children, appealing to you by encouragement, as well as by solemn injunctions, to live lives worthy of the God who calls you into his kingdom and glory.

This is why we thank God continually, because when we handed on God's message, you

King James Version

of God which ye heard of us, ye received *it* not
as the word of men, but, as it is in truth, the
word of God, which effectually worketh also in
you that believe. 14 For ye, brethren, became followers of the churches of God which in Judea
are in Christ Jesus: for ye also have suffered
like things of your own countrymen, even as they
have of the Jews: 15 Who both killed the Lord
Jesus, and their own prophets, and have persecuted us; and they please not God, and are contrary to all men: 16 Forbidding us to speak to
the Gentiles that they might be saved, to fill up
their sins always: for the wrath is come upon
them to the uttermost. 17 But we, brethren, being
taken from you for a short time in presence, not
in heart, endeavoured the more abundantly to
see your face with great desire. 18 Wherefore we
would have come unto you, even I Paul, once
and again; but Satan hindered us. 19 For what *is*
our hope, or joy, or crown of rejoicing? *Are* not

Living Bible

think of the words we spoke as being just our
own, but you accepted what we said as the very
Word of God—which, of course, it was—and it
changed your lives when you believed it.
14 And then, dear brothers, you suffered what
the churches in Judea did, persecution from your
own countrymen, just as they suffered from their
own people the Jews. 15After they had killed
their own prophets, they even executed the Lord
Jesus; and now they have brutally persecuted us
and driven us out. They are against both God
and man, 16 trying to keep us from preaching to
the Gentiles for fear some might be saved; and
so their sins continue to grow. But the anger of
God has caught up with them at last.
17 Dear brothers, after we left you and had
been away from you but a very little while
(though our hearts never left you), we tried
hard to come back to see you once more. 18 We
wanted very much to come and I, Paul, tried
again and again, but Satan stopped us. 19 For
what is it we live for, that gives us hope and
joy and is our proud reward and crown? It is

Today's English Version

God's message, you heard it and accepted it, not
as man's message but as God's message, which
indeed it is. For God is at work in you who
believe. 14 You, my brothers, had the same
things happen to you that happened to the
churches of God in Judea, to the people there
who belong to Christ Jesus. You suffered the
same persecutions from your own countrymen
that they suffered from the Jews, 15 who killed
the Lord Jesus and the prophets, and persecuted us. How displeasing they are to God! How
hostile they are to all men! 16 They even tried
to stop us from preaching to the Gentiles the
message that would bring them salvation. This
is the last full measure of the sins they have
always committed. And now God's wrath has
at last fallen upon them!

Paul's desire to visit them again

17 As for us, brothers, when we were separated from you for a little while—not in our
thoughts, of course, but only in body—how
we missed you and how hard we tried to see
you again! 18 We wanted to go back to you.
I, Paul, tried to go back more than once, but
Satan would not let us. 19After all, it is you—
you, no less than others!—who are our hope,
our joy, and our reason for boasting of our vic-

New International Version

which you heard from us, you accepted it not
as the word of men, but as it actually is, the
word of God, which is at work in you who believe. 14 For you, brothers, became imitators of
God's churches in Judea, which are in Christ
Jesus. You suffered from your own countrymen
the same things those churches suffered from
the Jews, 15 who killed the Lord Jesus and the
prophets and also drove us out. They displease
God and are hostile to all men 16 in their effort
to keep us from speaking to the Gentiles so
that they may be saved. In this way they always
heap up their sins to the limit. The wrath of
God has come upon them at last.[b]

Paul's longing to see the Thessalonians

17 But, brothers, when we were torn away
from you for a short time (in person, not in
thought), out of our intense longing we made
every effort to see you. 18 For we wanted to
come to you—certainly I, Paul, did, again and
again—but Satan stopped us. 19 For what is our
hope, our joy, or the crown in which we will

[b] Or *fully*.

Phillips Modern English

us you accepted it, not as a mere human message, but as it really is, God's Word, a power in the lives of you who believe.

2.14 *You have experienced persecution like your Jewish brothers*

For you, my brothers, followed the example of the churches of God which have come into being through Christ Jesus in Judaea. For when you suffered at the hands of your fellow-countrymen you were sharing the experience of the Judaean Christian churches, who suffered persecution by the Jews. It was the Jews who killed their own prophets, the Jews who killed the Lord Jesus, and the Jews who drove us out. They do not please God, and are in opposition to all mankind. They refused to let us speak to the gentiles to tell them the message by which they could be saved. All these years they have been adding to the full record of their sins and finally the wrath of God has fallen upon them.

2.17 *Absence has indeed made our hearts grow fonder*

Since we have been physically separated from you, my brothers (though never for a moment separated in heart), we have longed all the more to see you face to face. Yes, I, Paul, have longed to come and see you more than once—but somehow Satan prevented our coming.

For who could take your place as our hope and joy and pride when our Lord Jesus comes?

Revised Standard Version

which you heard from us, you accepted it not as
the word of men but as what it really is, the
word of God, which is at work in you believers.
14 For you, brethren, became imitators of the
churches of God in Christ Jesus which are in
Judea; for you suffered the same things from
your own countrymen as they did from the
Jews, 15 who killed both the Lord Jesus and the
prophets, and drove us out, and displease God
and oppose all men 16 by hindering us from
speaking to the Gentiles that they may be saved
—so as always to fill up the measure of their
sins. But God's wrath has come upon them at
last! [b]
17 But since we were bereft of you, brethren,
for a short time, in person not in heart, we endeavored the more eagerly and with great desire to see you face to face; 18 because we
wanted to come to you—I, Paul, again and again
—but Satan hindered us. 19 For what is our
hope or joy or crown of boasting before our

[*b*] Or *completely*, or *for ever*.

Jerusalem Bible

message that we brought you as God's message,
you accepted it for what it really is, God's message and not some human thinking; and it is still
a living power among you who believe it. 14 For
you, my brothers, have been like the churches
of God in Christ Jesus which are in Judaea, in
suffering the same treatment from your own
countrymen as they have suffered from the Jews,
15 the people who put the Lord Jesus to death,
and the prophets too. And now they have been
persecuting us, and acting in a way that cannot
please God and makes them the enemies of
the whole human race, 16 because they are hindering us from preaching to the pagans and trying to save them. They never stop trying *to finish*
off the sins they have begun,[b] but retribution is
overtaking them at last.

Paul's anxiety

17 A short time after we had been separated
from you—in body but never in thought, brothers—we had an especially strong desire and longing to see you face to face again, 18 and we
tried hard to come and visit you; I, Paul, tried
more than once, but Satan prevented us. 19 What
do you think is our pride and our joy? You are;
and you will be *the crown* of which we shall be

[*b*] 2 M. 6:14.

New English Bible

received it, not as the word of men, but as what it truly is, the very word of God at[a] work in you who hold the faith. You have fared like the congregations in Judaea, God's people in Christ Jesus. You have been treated by your countrymen as they are treated by the Jews, who killed the Lord Jesus and the prophets[b] and drove us out, the Jews who are heedless of God's will and enemies of their fellow-men, hindering us from speaking to the Gentiles to lead them to salvation. All this time they have been making up the full measure of their guilt, and now retribution has overtaken them for good and all.[c]

My friends, when for a short spell you were lost to us—lost to sight, not to our hearts—we were exceedingly anxious to see you again. So we did propose to come to Thessalonica—I, Paul, more than once—but Satan thwarted us. For after all, what hope or joy or crown of pride is

[*a*] *Or* word of God who is at . . . [*b*] *Some witnesses read* their own prophets. [*c*] *Or* now at last retribution has overtaken them.

King James Version

even ye in the presence of our Lord Jesus Christ at his coming? 20 For ye are our glory and joy.

3 Wherefore when we could no longer forbear, we thought it good to be left at Athens alone; 2And sent Timotheus, our brother, and minister of God, and our fellow labourer in the gospel of Christ, to establish you, and to comfort you concerning your faith: 3 That no man should be moved by these afflictions: for yourselves know that we are appointed thereunto. 4 For verily, when we were with you, we told you before that we should suffer tribulation; even as it came to pass, and ye know. 5 For this cause, when I could no longer forbear, I sent to know your faith, lest by some means the tempter have tempted you, and our labour be in vain. 6 But now when Timotheus came from you unto us, and brought us good tidings of your faith and charity, and that ye have good remembrance of us always, desiring greatly to see us, as we also *to see* you: 7 Therefore, brethren, we were comforted over you in all our affliction and distress by your faith: 8 For now we live, if ye stand

Living Bible

you! Yes, you will bring us much joy as we stand together before our Lord Jesus Christ when he comes back again. 20 For you are our trophy and joy.

3 Finally, when I could stand it no longer, I decided to stay alone in Athens 2, 3 and send Timothy, our brother and fellow worker, God's minister, to visit you to strengthen your faith and encourage you, and to keep you from becoming fainthearted in all the troubles you were going through. (But of course you know that such troubles are a part of God's plan for us Christians. 4 Even while we were still with you we warned you ahead of time that suffering would soon come—and it did.)

5 As I was saying, when I could bear the suspense no longer I sent Timothy to find out whether your faith was still strong. I was afraid that perhaps Satan had gotten the best of you and that all our work had been useless. 6And now Timothy has just returned and brings the welcome news that your faith and love are as strong as ever, and that you remember our visit with joy and want to see us just as much as we want to see you. 7 So we are greatly comforted, dear brothers, in all of our own crushing troubles and suffering here, now that we know you are standing true to the Lord. 8 We can bear any-

Today's English Version

tory in the presence of our Lord Jesus when he comes. 20 Indeed, you are our pride and our joy!

3 Finally, we could not bear it any longer. So we decided to stay on alone in Athens 2 while we sent Timothy, our brother who works with us for God in preaching the Good News about Christ. We sent him to strengthen you and help your faith, 3 so that none of you should turn back because of these persecutions. You yourselves know that such persecutions are part of God's will for us. 4 For while we were still with you, we told you ahead of time that we were going to be persecuted; and, as you well know, that is exactly what happened. 5 That is why I had to send Timothy. I could not bear it any longer, so I sent him to find out about your faith. Surely it could not be that the Devil had tempted you, and all our work had been for nothing!

6 Now Timothy has come back to us from you, and he has brought the welcome news about your faith and love. He has told us that you always think well of us, and that you want to see us just as much as we want to see you. 7 So, in all our trouble and suffering we have been encouraged about you, brothers. It was your faith that encouraged us, 8 because now we

New International Version

glory in the presence of our Lord Jesus Christ when he comes? Is it not you? 20 Indeed, you are our glory and joy.

3 So when we could stand it no longer, we thought it best to be left by ourselves in Athens. 2 We sent Timothy, who is our brother and God's fellow worker[c] in spreading the gospel of Christ, to strengthen and encourage you in your faith, 3 so that no one would be unsettled by these trials. You know quite well that we were destined for them. 4 In fact, when we were with you, we kept telling you that we would be persecuted. And it turned out that way, as you well know. 5 For this reason, when I could stand it no longer, I sent to find out about your faith. I was afraid that in some way the tempter might have tempted you and our efforts might have been useless.

Timothy's encouraging report

6 But Timothy has just now come to us from you and has brought good news about your faith and love. He has told us that you always have pleasant memories of us and that you long to see us, just as we also long to see you. 7 Therefore, brothers, in all our distress and persecution we were encouraged about you because of your faith. 8 For now we really live, since you are

[c] Some textual sources read *brother and fellow worker;* others, *brother and God's servant.*

Phillips Modern English

Who but you, as you will stand before him at his coming? Yes, you are indeed our pride and our joy!

And so, when the separation became intolerable, we thought the best plan was for us to stay at Athens alone, while we sent Timothy, our brother and God's fellow-worker in the gospel of Christ, to strengthen and encourage you in your faith. We did not want any of you to lose heart at the troubles you were going through, but to realise that we must expect such things. Actually we did warn you what to expect, when we were with you, and our words have come true, as you know. You will understand that, when the suspense became unbearable, I sent to find out how your faith was standing the strain, and to make sure that the tempter's activities had not destroyed our work.

3.6 The good news about you is a tonic to us

Timothy has just come straight from you to us, with a glowing account of your faith and love, and definite news that you cherish happy memories of us and long to see us as much as we to see you. This has cheered us, my brothers, in all the miseries and troubles we ourselves are going through. To know that you are standing

Revised Standard Version

Lord Jesus at his coming? Is it not you? 20 For you are our glory and joy.

3 Therefore when we could bear it no longer, we were willing to be left behind at Athens alone, 2 and we sent Timothy, our brother and God's servant in the gospel of Christ, to establish you in your faith and to exhort you, 3 that no one be moved by these afflictions. You yourselves know that this is to be our lot. 4 For when we were with you, we told you beforehand that we were to suffer affliction; just as it has come to pass, and as you know. 5 For this reason, when I could bear it no longer, I sent that I might know your faith, for fear that somehow the tempter had tempted you and that our labor would be in vain.

6 But now that Timothy has come to us from you, and has brought us the good news of your faith and love and reported that you always remember us kindly and long to see us, as we long to see you—7 for this reason, brethren, in all our distress and affliction we have been comforted about you through your faith; 8 for now

Jerusalem Bible

proudest in the presence of our Lord Jesus when he comes; 20 you are our pride and our joy.

Timothy's mission to Thessalonika

3 When we could not bear the waiting any longer, we decided it would be best to be left without a companion at Athens, and 2 sent our brother Timothy, who is God's helper in spreading the Good News of Christ, to keep you firm and strong in the faith 3 and prevent any of you from being unsettled by the present troubles. As you know, these are bound to come our way: 4 when we were with you, we warned you that we must expect to have persecutions to bear, and that is what has happened now, as you have found out. 5 That is why, when I could not stand waiting any longer, I sent to assure myself of your faith: I was afraid the Tempter[c] might have tried you too hard, and all our work might have been wasted.

Paul thanks God for good reports of the Thessalonians

6 However, Timothy is now back from you and he has given us good news of your faith and your love, telling us that you always remember us with pleasure and want to see us quite as much as we want to see you. 7 And so, brothers, your faith has been a great comfort to us in the middle of our own troubles and sorrows; 8 now

[c] I.e., "the one who puts you to the test."

New English Bible

there for us, what indeed but you, when we stand before our Lord Jesus at his coming? It is you who are indeed our glory and our joy.

3 So when we could bear it no longer, we decided to remain alone at Athens, and sent Timothy, our brother and God's fellow-worker[a] in the service of the gospel of Christ, to encourage you to stand firm for the faith and, under all these hardships, not to be shaken;[b] for you know that this is our appointed lot. When we were with you we warned you that we were bound to suffer hardship; and so it has turned out, as you know. And thus it was that when I could bear it no longer, I sent to find out about your faith, fearing that the tempter might have tempted you and my labour might be lost.

But now Timothy has just arrived from Thessalonica, bringing good news of your faith and love. He tells us that you always think kindly of us, and are as anxious to see us as we are to see you. And so in all our difficulties and hardships your faith reassures us about you. It is the

[a] *Or* and fellow-worker for God; *one witness has simply* and fellow-worker. [b] *Or* beguiled away.

King James Version

fast in the Lord. 9 For what thanks can we
render to God again for you, for all the joy
wherewith we joy for your sakes before our God;
10 Night and day praying exceedingly that we
might see your face, and might perfect that
which is lacking in your faith? 11 Now God himself and our Father, and our Lord Jesus Christ,
direct our way unto you. 12 And the Lord make
you to increase and abound in love one toward
another, and toward all *men*, even as we *do* toward you: 13 To the end he may stablish your
hearts unblameable in holiness before God, even
our Father, at the coming of our Lord Jesus
Christ with all his saints.

4 Furthermore then we beseech you, brethren,
and exhort *you* by the Lord Jesus, that as ye
have received of us how ye ought to walk and
to please God, *so* ye would abound more and
more. 2 For ye know what commandments we
gave you by the Lord Jesus. 3 For this is the
will of God, *even* your sanctification, that ye
should abstain from fornication; 4 That every
one of you should know how to possess his
vessel in sanctification and honour; 5 Not in the
lust of concupiscence, even as the Gentiles which
know not God: 6 That no *man* go beyond and

Living Bible

thing as long as we know that you remain strong
in him.
9 How can we thank God enough for you
and for the joy and delight you have given us in
our praying for you? 10 For night and day we
pray on and on for you, asking God to let us
see you again, to fill up any little cracks there
may yet be in your faith. 11 May God our
Father himself and our Lord Jesus send us back
to you again. 12 And may the Lord make your
love to grow and overflow to each other and to
everyone else, just as our love does toward you.
13 This will result in your hearts being made
strong, sinless and holy by God our Father, so
that you may stand before him guiltless on that
day when our Lord Jesus Christ returns with all
those who belong to him.[a]

4 Let me add this, dear brothers: You already know how to please God in your daily
living, for you know the commands we gave
you from the Lord Jesus himself. Now we beg
you—yes, we demand of you in the name of
the Lord Jesus—that you live more and more
closely to that ideal. 3, 4 For God wants you to
be holy and pure, and to keep clear of all sexual
sin so that each of you will marry in holiness
and honor—5 not in lustful passion as the heathen do, in their ignorance of God and his ways.
6 And this also is God's will: that you never

[a] Literally, "with all his saints. Amen."

Today's English Version

really live if you stand firm in your life in the
Lord. 9 Now we can give thanks to God for
you. We thank him for the joy we have before
our God because of you. 10 Day and night we
ask him with all our heart to let us see you
personally and supply what is needed in your
faith.
11 May our God and Father himself, and our
Lord Jesus, prepare the way for us to come to
you! 12 May the Lord make your love for one
another and for all people grow more and more
and become as great as our love for you. 13 In
this way he will make your hearts strong, and
you will be perfect and holy in the presence of
our God and Father when our Lord Jesus comes
with all who belong to him.

A life that pleases God

4 Finally, brothers, you learned from us how
you should live in order to please God. This
is, of course, the way you have been living. And
now we beg and urge you, in the name of the
Lord Jesus, to do even more. 2 For you know
the instructions we gave you, by the authority of
the Lord Jesus. 3 This is God's will for you: he
wants you to be holy and completely free from
immorality. 4 Each of you men should know
how to take a wife in a holy and honorable way,
5 not with a lustful desire, like the heathen who
do not know God. 6 In this matter, then, no

New International Version

standing firm in the Lord. 9 How can we thank
God enough for you in return for all the joy we
have in the presence of our God because of you?
10 Night and day we pray most earnestly that
we may see you again and supply what is lacking in your faith.
11 Now may our God and Father himself and
our Lord Jesus clear the way for us to come to
you. 12 May the Lord make your love increase
and overflow for each other and for everyone
else, just as ours does for you. 13 May he give
you inner strength that you may be blameless
and holy in the presence of our God and Father
when our Lord Jesus comes with all his holy
ones.

Living to please God

4 Finally, brothers, we instructed you how
to live in order to please God, as in fact you
are living. Now we ask you and urge you in the
Lord Jesus to do this more and more. 2 You
know what instructions we gave you by the
authority of the Lord Jesus.
3 It is God's will that you should be holy;
that you should avoid sexual immorality; 4 that
each of you should learn to control his own
body[d] in a way that is holy and honorable, 5 not
in passionate lust like the heathen, who do not
know God; 6 and that in this matter no one

[d] Or *learn to live with his own wife*.

Phillips Modern English

fast in the Lord is indeed a breath of life to us. How can we thank our God enough for you, and for all the joy you have brought in the presence of our God, as we pray earnestly day and night to see you face to face again, and to complete whatever is imperfect in your faith?

3.11 *This is our prayer for you*

So may God our Father himself and our Lord Jesus guide our steps to you. May the Lord give you the same increasing and overflowing love for each other and towards all men as we have towards you. May he establish you, holy and blameless in heart and soul, before God, the Father of us all, when our Lord Jesus comes with all who belong to him.

4.1 *Purity, love and hard work are good rules for life*

To sum up, my brothers, we beg and pray you by the Lord Jesus, that as you have learned from us the way of life that pleases God, you may continue in it, as indeed you are doing, and deepen your experience of it. You will remember the instructions we gave you then in the name of the Lord Jesus. God's plan is to make you holy, and that means a clean cut with sexual immorality. Every one of you should learn to control his body, keeping it pure and treating it with respect, and never allowing it to fall victim to lust, as do pagans with no knowledge of God. You cannot break this rule without

Revised Standard Version

we live, if you stand fast in the Lord. 9 For
what thanksgiving can we render to God for
you, for all the joy which we feel for your sake
before our God, 10 praying earnestly night and
day that we may see you face to face and supply
what is lacking in your faith?
11 Now may our God and Father himself,
and our Lord Jesus, direct our way to you;
12 and may the Lord make you increase and
abound in love to one another and to all men,
as we do to you, 13 so that he may establish
your hearts unblamable in holiness before our
God and Father, at the coming of our Lord
Jesus with all his saints.

4 Finally, brethren, we beseech and exhort
you in the Lord Jesus, that as you learned
from us how you ought to live and to please
God, just as you are doing, you do so more and
more. 2 For you know what instructions we
gave you through the Lord Jesus. 3 For this is
the will of God, your sanctification: that you
abstain from unchastity; 4 that each one of you
know how to take a wife for himself[x] in holiness and honor, 5 not in the passion of lust like
heathen who do not know God; 6 that no man

[x] Or *how to control his own body.*

Jerusalem Bible

we can breathe again, as you are still holding
firm in the Lord. 9 How can we thank God
enough for you, for all the joy we feel before our
God on your account? 10 We are earnestly praying night and day to be able to see you face to
face again and make up any shortcomings in
your faith.
11 May God our Father himself, and our
Lord Jesus Christ, make it easy for us to come
to you. 12 May the Lord be generous in increasing your love and make you love one another
and the whole human race as much as we love
you. 13 And may he so confirm your hearts in
holiness that you may be blameless in the sight
of our God and Father when our Lord Jesus
Christ comes *with all his saints.*

Live in holiness and charity

4 Finally, brothers, we urge you and appeal
to you in the Lord Jesus to make more and
more progress in the kind of life that you are
meant to live: the life that God wants, as you
learned from us, and as you are already living
it. 2 You have not forgotten the instructions we
gave you on the authority of the Lord Jesus.
3 What God wants is for you all to be holy.
He wants you to keep away from fornication,
4 and each one of you to know how to use the
body that belongs to him[d] in a way that is holy
and honorable, 5 not giving way to selfish lust
like *the pagans who do not know God.*[e] 6 He

[d] Literally, "the vessel that is his": either his own body or his wife's. [e] Jr. 10:25; Ps. 79:6.

New English Bible

breath of life to us that you stand firm in the Lord. What thanks can we return to God for you? What thanks for all the joy you have brought us, making us rejoice before our God while we pray most earnestly night and day to be allowed to see you again and to mend your faith where it falls short?

May our God and Father himself, and our Lord Jesus, bring us direct to you; and may the Lord make your love mount and overflow towards one another and towards all, as our love does towards you. May he make your hearts firm, so that you may stand before our God and Father holy and faultless when our Lord Jesus comes with all those who are his own.

4 And now, my friends, we have one thing to beg and pray of you, by our fellowship with the Lord Jesus. We passed on to you the tradition of the way we must live to please God; you are indeed already following it, but we beg you to do so yet more thoroughly.

For you know what orders we gave you, in the name of the Lord Jesus. This is the will of God, that you should be holy: you must abstain from fornication; each one of you must learn to gain mastery over his body, to hallow and honour it, not giving way to lust like the pagans who are ignorant of God; and no man must do his

King James Version

defraud his brother in *any* matter: because that the Lord *is* the avenger of all such, as we also have forewarned you and testified. 7 For God hath not called us unto uncleanness, but unto holiness. 8 He therefore that despiseth, despiseth not man, but God, who hath also given unto us his Holy Spirit. 9 But as touching brotherly love ye need not that I write unto you: for ye yourselves are taught of God to love one another. 10 And indeed ye do it toward all the brethren which are in all Macedonia: but we beseech you, brethren, that ye increase more and more; 11 And that ye study to be quiet, and to do your own business, and to work with your own hands, as we commanded you; 12 That ye may walk honestly toward them that are without, and *that* ye may have lack of nothing. 13 But I would not have you to be ignorant, brethren, concerning them which are asleep, that ye sorrow not, even as others which have no hope. 14 For if we believe that Jesus died and rose again, even so them also which sleep in Jesus will God bring with him. 15 For this we say unto you by the word of the Lord, that we which are alive *and* remain unto the coming of the Lord shall not

Living Bible

cheat in this matter by taking another man's wife, because the Lord will punish you terribly for this, as we have solemnly told you before. 7 For God has not called us to be dirty-minded and full of lust, but to be holy and clean. 8 If anyone refuses to live by these rules he is not disobeying the rules of men but of God who gives his *Holy* Spirit to you.

9 But concerning the pure brotherly love that there should be among God's people, I don't need to say very much, I'm sure! For God himself is teaching you to love one another. 10 Indeed, your love is already strong toward all the Christian brothers throughout your whole nation. Even so, dear friends, we beg you to love them more and more. 11 This should be your ambition: to live a quiet life, minding your own business and doing your own work, just as we told you before. 12 As a result, people who are not Christians will trust and respect you, and you will not need to depend on others for enough money to pay your bills.

13 And now, dear brothers, I want you to know what happens to a Christian when he dies so that when it happens, you will not be full of sorrow, as those are who have no hope. 14 For since we believe that Jesus died and then came back to life again, we can also believe that when Jesus returns, God will bring back with him all the Christians who have died.

15 I can tell you this directly from the Lord: that we who are still living when the Lord returns will not rise to meet him ahead of those

Today's English Version

man should do wrong to his brother or take advantage of him. We have told you this before, we strongly warned you, that the Lord will punish those who do such wrongs. 7 God did not call us to live in immorality, but in holiness. 8 So then, whoever rejects this teaching is not rejecting man, but God, who gives you his Holy Spirit.

9 There is no need to write you about love for your fellow believers. You yourselves have been taught by God how you should love one another. 10 And you have behaved in this way toward all the brothers in all of Macedonia. So we beg you, brothers, to do even more. 11 Make it your aim to live a quiet life, to mind your own business, and earn your own living, just as we told you before. 12 In this way you will win the respect of those who are not believers, and will not have to depend on anyone for what you need.

The Lord's coming

13 Brothers, we want you to know the truth about those who have died, so that you will not be sad, as are those who have no hope. 14 We believe that Jesus died and rose again; so we believe that God will bring with Jesus those who have died believing in him.

15 This is the Lord's teaching that we tell you: we who are alive on the day the Lord comes will not go ahead of those who have died.

New International Version

should wrong his brother or take advantage of him. The Lord will punish men for all such sins, as we have already told you and warned you. 7 For God did not call us to be impure, but to live a holy life. 8 Therefore, he who rejects this instruction does not reject man but God, who gives you his Holy Spirit.

9 Now about brotherly love we do not need to write to you, for you yourselves have been taught by God to love each other. 10 And in fact, you do love all the brothers throughout Macedonia. Yet we urge you, brothers, to do so more and more.

11 Make it your ambition to lead a quiet life, to mind your own business and to work with your hands, just as we told you, 12 so that your daily life may win the respect of outsiders and so that you will not be dependent on anybody.

The coming of the Lord

13 Brothers, we do not want you to be ignorant about those who sleep, or to grieve like the rest of men, who have no hope. 14 We believe that Jesus died and rose again and so we believe that God will bring with Jesus those who sleep in him. 15 According to the Lord's own word, we tell you that we who are still alive, who are left till the coming of the Lord, will certainly not precede those who have fallen asleep.

Phillips Modern English

cheating and exploiting your fellow-men. Indeed God will punish all who do offend in this matter, as we have plainly told you and warned you. The calling of God is not to impurity but to the most thorough purity, and anyone who makes light of the matter is not making light of a man's ruling but of God's command. It is not for nothing that the Spirit God gives us is called the *Holy* Spirit.

Next, as regards brotherly love, you don't need any written instructions. God himself is teaching you to love each other, and you are already extending your love to all the Macedonians. Yet we urge you to have more and more of this love, and to make it your ambition to have, in a sense, no ambition! Be busy with your own affairs and do your work yourselves, as we instructed you. Then the world outside will respect your life, and you will never be in want.

4.13 God's message regarding those who have died

Now we don't want you, my brothers, to be in any doubt about those who "fall asleep" in death, or to grieve over them like the rest of men who have no hope. If we believe that Jesus died and rose again, then we can believe that God will just as surely bring with Jesus all who are "asleep" in him. Here we have a definite message from the Lord. It is that those who are still living when he comes will not in any way precede those who have previously fallen asleep.

Revised Standard Version

transgress, and wrong his brother in this matter,[c] because the Lord is an avenger in all these
things, as we solemnly forewarned you. 7 For
God has not called us for uncleanness, but in
holiness. 8 Therefore whoever disregards this,
disregards not man but God, who gives his
Holy Spirit to you.
9 But concerning love of the brethren you
have no need to have any one write to you, for
you yourselves have been taught by God to love
one another; 10 and indeed you do love all the
brethren throughout Macedonia. But we exhort
you, brethren, to do so more and more, 11 to
aspire to live quietly, to mind your own affairs,
and to work with your hands, as we charged
you; 12 so that you may command the respect
of outsiders, and be dependent on nobody.
13 But we would not have you ignorant,
brethren, concerning those who are asleep, that
you may not grieve as others do who have no
hope. 14 For since we believe that Jesus died
and rose again, even so, through Jesus, God will
bring with him those who have fallen asleep.
15 For this we declare to you by the word of
the Lord, that we who are alive, who are left
until the coming of the Lord, shall not precede

[c] Or *defraud his brother in business.*

Jerusalem Bible

wants nobody at all ever to sin by taking advantage of a brother in these matters; the Lord
always punishes sins of that sort, as we told you
before and assured you. 7 We have been called
by God to be holy, not to be immoral; 8 in other
words, anyone who objects is not objecting to a
human authority, but to God, *who gives you his*
Holy *Spirit.*[f]
9 As for loving our brothers, there is no need
for anyone to write to you about that, since you
have learned from God yourselves to love one
another, 10 and in fact this is what you are doing
with all the brothers throughout the whole of
Macedonia. However, we do urge you, brothers,
to go on making even greater progress 11 and to
make a point of living quietly, attending to your
own business and earning your living, just as we
told you to, 12 so that you are seen to be respectable by those outside the Church, though
you do not have to depend on them.

The dead and the living at the time of the Lord's coming

13 We want you to be quite certain, brothers,
about those who have died,[g] to make sure that
you do not grieve about them, like the other
people who have no hope. 14 We believe that
Jesus died and rose again, and that it will be the
same for those who have died in Jesus: God will
bring them with him. 15 We can tell you this
from the Lord's own teaching, that any of us
who are left alive until the Lord's coming will
not have any advantage over those who have

[f] Ezk. 37:14 [g] Literally, "those who are sleeping."

New English Bible

brother wrong in this matter,[c] or invade his rights, because, as we told you before with all emphasis, the Lord punishes all such offences. For God called us to holiness, not to impurity. Anyone therefore who flouts these rules is flouting, not man, but God who bestows upon you his Holy Spirit.

About love for our brotherhood you need no words of mine, for you are yourselves taught by God to love one another, and you are in fact practising this rule of love towards all your fellow-Christians throughout Macedonia. Yet we appeal to you, brothers, to do better still. Let it be your ambition to keep calm and look after your own business, and to work with your hands, as we ordered you, so that you may command the respect of those outside your own number, and at the same time may never be in want.

We wish you not to remain in ignorance, brothers, about those who sleep in death; you should not grieve like the rest of men, who have no hope. We believe that Jesus died and rose again; and so it will be for those who died as Christians; God will bring them to life with Jesus.[a]

For this we tell you as the Lord's word: we who are left alive until the Lord comes shall not

[c] *Or* must overreach his brother in his business (*or* in lawsuits). [a] *Or* will bring them in company with Jesus.

King James Version

prevent them which are asleep. 16 For the Lord himself shall descend from heaven with a shout, with the voice of the archangel, and with the trump of God: and the dead in Christ shall rise first: 17 Then we which are alive *and* remain shall be caught up together with them in the clouds, to meet the Lord in the air: and so shall we ever be with the Lord. 18 Wherefore comfort one another with these words.

5 But of the times and the seasons, brethren, ye have no need that I write unto you. 2 For yourselves know perfectly that the day of the Lord so cometh as a thief in the night. 3 For when they shall say, Peace and safety; then sudden destruction cometh upon them, as travail upon a woman with child; and they shall not escape. 4 But ye, brethren, are not in darkness, that that day should overtake you as a thief. 5 Ye are all the children of light, and the children of the day: we are not of the night, nor of darkness. 6 Therefore let us not sleep, as *do* others; but let us watch and be sober. 7 For they that sleep sleep in the night; and they that be drunken are drunken in the night. 8 But let us, who are of the day, be sober, putting on the breastplate of faith and love; and for a helmet,

Living Bible

who are in their graves. 16 For the Lord himself will come down from heaven with a mighty shout and with the soul-stirring cry of the archangel and the great trumpet-call of God. And the believers who are dead will be the first to rise to meet the Lord. 17 Then we who are still alive and remain on the earth will be caught up with them in the clouds to meet the Lord in the air and remain with him forever. 18 So comfort and encourage each other with this news.

5 When is all this going to happen?

I really don't need to say anything about that, dear brothers, 2 for you know perfectly well that no one knows. That day of the Lord will come unexpectedly like a thief in the night. 3 When people are saying, "All is well, everything is quiet and peaceful"—then, all of a sudden, disaster will fall upon them as suddenly as a woman's birth pains begin when her child is born. And these people will not be able to get away anywhere—there will be no place to hide.

4 But, dear brothers, you are not in the dark about these things, and you won't be surprised as by a thief when that day of the Lord comes. 5 For you are all children of the light and of the day, and do not belong to darkness and night. 6 So be on your guard, not asleep like the others. Watch for his return and stay sober. 7 Night is the time for sleep and the time when people get drunk. 8 But let us who live in the light keep sober, protected by the armor of faith and love, and wearing as our helmet the happy hope of salvation.

Today's English Version

16 There will be the shout of command, the archangel's voice, the sound of God's trumpet, and the Lord himself will come down from heaven. Those who have died believing in Christ will rise to life first; 17 then we who are living at that time will all be gathered up along with them in the clouds to meet the Lord in the air. And so we will always be with the Lord. 18 So then, cheer each other up with these words.

Be ready for the Lord's coming

5 There is no need to write you, brothers, about the times and occasions when these things will happen. 2 For you yourselves know very well that the Day of the Lord will come as a thief comes at night. 3 When people say, "Everything is quiet and safe," then suddenly destruction will hit them! They will not escape —it will be like the pains that come upon a woman who is about to give birth. 4 But you, brothers, are not in the darkness, and the Day should not take you by surprise like a thief. 5 All of you are people who belong to the light, who belong to the day. We are not of the night or of the darkness. 6 So then, we should not be sleeping, like the others; we should be awake and sober. 7 It is at night when people sleep; it is at night when people get drunk. 8 But we belong to the day, and we should be sober. We must wear faith and love as a breastplate, and

New International Version

16 For the Lord himself will come down from heaven, with a loud command, with the voice of the archangel and with the trumpet call of God, and the dead in Christ will rise first. 17 After that, we who are still alive and are left will be caught up with them in the clouds to meet the Lord in the air. And so we will be with the Lord forever. 18 Therefore encourage each other with these words.

5 Now, brothers, about times and dates we do not need to write to you, 2 for you know very well that the day of the Lord will come like a thief in the night. 3 While people are saying, "Peace and safety," destruction will come on them suddenly, as labor pains on a pregnant woman, and they will not escape.

4 But you, brothers, are not in darkness so that this day should surprise you like a thief. 5 You are all sons of the light and sons of the day. We do not belong to the night or to the darkness. 6 So then, let us not be like others who are asleep, but let us be alert and self-controlled. 7 For those who sleep, sleep at night, and those who get drunk, get drunk at night. 8 But since we belong to the day, let us be self-controlled, putting on faith and love as a breastplate, and

Phillips Modern English

One word of command, one shout from the archangel, one blast from the trumpet of God and the Lord himself will come down from Heaven! Those who have died in Christ will be the first to rise, and then we who are still living will be swept up with them into the clouds to meet the Lord in the air. And after that we shall be with him for ever. So by all means use this message to encourage one another.

5.1 We must keep awake for his sudden coming

But as far as times and seasons go, my brothers, you don't need written instructions. You are well aware that the day of the Lord will come unexpectedly, like a thief in the night. When men are saying "Peace and security", catastrophe will sweep down upon them as suddenly and inescapably as birth-pangs to a pregnant woman.

But because you, my brothers, are not living in darkness the day cannot take you by surprise, like a burglar! You are all sons of light, sons of the day, and none of us belongs to darkness or the night. Let us then never fall asleep, like the rest of the world: let us keep awake, with our wits about us. Night is the time for sleep and the time when men get drunk, but we men of the daylight should be sober, with faith and love as our breastplate and the hope of our salvation

Revised Standard Version

those who have fallen asleep. 16 For the Lord himself will descend from heaven with a cry of command, with the archangel's call, and with the sound of the trumpet of God. And the dead in Christ will rise first; 17 then we who are alive, who are left, shall be caught up together with them in the clouds to meet the Lord in the air; and so we shall always be with the Lord. 18 Therefore comfort one another with these words.

5 But as to the times and the seasons, brethren, you have no need to have anything written to you. 2 For you yourselves know well that the day of the Lord will come like a thief in the night. 3 When people say, "There is peace and security," then sudden destruction will come upon them as travail comes upon a woman with child, and there will be no escape. 4 But you are not in darkness, brethren, for that day to surprise you like a thief. 5 For you are all sons of light and sons of the day; we are not of the night or of darkness. 6 So then let us not sleep, as others do, but let us keep awake and be sober. 7 For those who sleep sleep at night, and those who get drunk are drunk at night. 8 But, since we belong to the day, let us be sober, and put on the breastplate of faith and love, and for a

Jerusalem Bible

died. 16 At the trumpet of God, the voice of the archangel will call out the command and the Lord himself will come down from heaven; those who have died in Christ will be the first to rise, 17 and then those of us who are still alive will be taken up in the clouds, together with them, to meet the Lord in the air. So we shall stay with the Lord for ever. 18 With such thoughts as these you should comfort one another.

Watchfulness while awaiting the coming of the Lord

5 You will not be expecting us to write anything to you, brothers, about "times and seasons," 2 since you know very well that the Day of the Lord is going to come like a thief in the night. 3 It is when people are saying, "How quiet and peaceful it is" that the worst suddenly happens, as suddenly as labor pains come on a pregnant woman; and there will be no way for anybody to evade it.

4 But it is not as if you live in the dark, my brothers, for that Day to overtake you like a thief. 5 No, you are all sons of light and sons of the day: we do not belong to the night or to darkness, 6 so we should not go on sleeping, as everyone else does, but stay wide awake and sober. 7 Night is the time for sleepers to sleep and drunkards to be drunk, 8 but we belong to the day and we should be sober; let us put on faith and love for a *breastplate,* and the hope of

New English Bible

forestall those who have died; because at the word of command, at the sound of the archangel's voice and God's trumpet-call, the Lord himself will descend from heaven; first the Christian dead will rise, then we who are left alive shall join them, caught up in clouds to meet the Lord in the air. Thus we shall always be with the Lord. Console one another, then, with these words.

5 About dates and times, my friends, we need not write to you, for you know perfectly well that the Day of the Lord comes like a thief in the night. While they are talking of peace and security, all at once calamity is upon them, sudden as the pangs that come upon a woman with child; and there will be no escape. But you, my friends, are not in the dark, that the day should overtake you like a thief.[b] You are all children of light, children of day. We do not belong to night or darkness, and we must not sleep like the rest, but keep awake and sober. Sleepers sleep at night, and drunkards are drunk at night. but we, who belong to daylight, must keep sober, armed with faith and love for coat of mail, and the hope of salvation for helmet.

[b] *Some witnesses read* thieves.

King James Version

the hope of salvation. 9 For God hath not appointed us to wrath, but to obtain salvation by our Lord Jesus Christ, 10 Who died for us, that, whether we wake or sleep, we should live together with him. 11 Wherefore comfort yourselves together, and edify one another, even as also ye do. 12 And we beseech you, brethren, to know them which labour among you, and are over you in the Lord, and admonish you; 13 And to esteem them very highly in love for their work's sake. *And* be at peace among yourselves. 14 Now we exhort you, brethren, warn them that are unruly, comfort the feebleminded, support the weak, be patient toward all *men*. 15 See that none render evil for evil unto any *man;* but ever follow that which is good, both among yourselves, and to all *men*. 16 Rejoice evermore. 17 Pray without ceasing. 18 In every thing give thanks: for this is the will of God in Christ Jesus concerning you. 19 Quench not the Spirit. 20 Despise not prophesyings. 21 Prove all things; hold fast that which is good. 22 Abstain from all

Living Bible

9 For God has not chosen to pour out his anger upon us, but to save us through our Lord Jesus Christ; 10 he died for us so that we can live with him forever, whether we are dead or alive at the time of his return. 11 So encourage each other to build each other up, just as you are already doing.

12 Dear brothers, honor the officers of your church who work hard among you and warn you against all that is wrong. 13 Think highly of them and give them your whole-hearted love because they are straining to help you. And remember, no quarreling among yourselves.

14 Dear brothers, warn those who are lazy; comfort those who are frightened; take tender care of those who are weak; and be patient with everyone. 15 See that no one pays back evil for evil, but always try to do good to each other and to everyone else. 16 Always be joyful. 17 Always keep on praying. 18 No matter what happens, always be thankful, for this is God's will for you who belong to Christ Jesus.

19 Do not smother the Holy Spirit. 20 Do not scoff at those who prophesy, 21 but test everything that is said to be sure it is true, and if it is, then accept it. 22 Keep away from every kind

Today's English Version

our hope of salvation as a helmet. 9 God did not choose us to suffer his wrath, but to possess salvation through our Lord Jesus Christ, 10 who died for us in order that we might live together with him, whether we are alive or dead when he comes. 11 For this reason encourage one another, and help one another, just as you are now doing.

Final instructions and greetings

12 We beg you, brothers, to pay proper respect to those who work among you, those whom the Lord has chosen to guide and instruct you. 13 Treat them with the greatest respect and love, because of the work they do. Be at peace among yourselves.

14 We urge you brothers: warn the idle, encourage the timid, help the weak, be patient with all. 15 See that no one pays back wrong for wrong, but at all times make it your aim to do good to one another and to all people.

16 Be joyful always, 17 pray at all times, 18 be thankful in all circumstances. This is what God wants of you, in your life in Christ Jesus.

19 Do not restrain the Holy Spirit; 20 do not despise inspired messages. 21 Put all things to the test: keep what is good, 22 and avoid every kind of evil.

New International Version

the hope of salvation as a helmet. 9 For God did not appoint us to suffer wrath but to receive salvation through our Lord Jesus Christ. 10 He died for us so that, whether we are awake or asleep, we may live together with him. 11 Therefore, encourage one another and build each other up, just as in fact you are doing.

Final instructions

12 Now we ask you, brothers, to respect those who work hard among you, who are over you in the Lord and who admonish you. 13 Hold them in the highest regard in love because of their work. Live in peace with each other. 14 And we urge you, brothers, warn those who are idle, encourage the timid, help the weak. be patient with everyone. 15 Make sure that nobody pays back wrong for wrong, but always try to be kind to each other and to everyone else.

16 Be joyful always; 17 pray continually; 18 give thanks in all circumstances, for this is God's will for you in Christ Jesus. 19 Do not put out the Spirit's fire; 20 do not treat prophecies with contempt. 21 Test everything. Hold on to the good. 22 Avoid every kind of evil.

Phillips Modern English

as our helmet. For God did not choose us to condemn us, but that we might secure his salvation through Jesus Christ our Lord. He died for us, so that whether we are "awake" or "asleep" we share our life with him. So go on cheering and strengthening each other, as I have no doubt you are doing.

5.12 Reverence your ministers: regulate the conduct of church members

We ask you too, my brothers, to recognise those who work so hard among you. They are your leaders in the Lord, to give you good advice. Because of this task of theirs, hold them in respect and affection.

Live together in peace, brothers, and we appeal to you to warn the unruly, encourage the timid, help the weak and be very patient with all men. Be sure that no one repays a bad turn with a bad turn; good should be your objective always, among yourselves and in the world at large.

Be happy in your faith at all times. Never stop praying. Be thankful, whatever the circumstances may be.

For this is the will of God for you in Christ Jesus.

5.19 Final advice and farewell

Never damp the fire of the Spirit, and never despise what is spoken in the name of the Lord. By all means use your judgment, and hold on to whatever is good. Steer clear of evil in any form.

Revised Standard Version

helmet the hope of salvation. 9 For God has
not destined us for wrath, but to obtain salvation through our Lord Jesus Christ, 10 who died
for us so that whether we wake or sleep we
might live with him. 11 Therefore encourage one
another and build one another up, just as you
are doing.
12 But we beseech you, brethren, to respect
those who labor among you and are over you
in the Lord and admonish you, 13 and to esteem them very highly in love because of their
work. Be at peace among yourselves. 14 And we
exhort you, brethren, admonish the idlers, encourage the fainthearted, help the weak, be patient with them all. 15 See that none of you
repays evil for evil, but always seek to do good
to one another and to all. 16 Rejoice always,
17 pray constantly, 18 give thanks in all circumstances; for this is the will of God in Christ
Jesus for you. 19 Do not quench the Spirit,
20 do not despise prophesying, 21 but test everything; hold fast what is good, 22 abstain from
every form of evil.

Jerusalem Bible

salvation for a *helmet.* 9 God never meant us to
experience the Retribution, but to win salvation
through our Lord Jesus Christ, 10 who died for
us so that, alive or dead, we should still live
united to him. 11 So give encouragement to each
other, and keep strengthening one another, as
you do already.

Some demands made by life in community

12 We appeal to you, my brothers, to be considerate to those who are working among you
and are above you in the Lord as your teachers.
13 Have the greatest respect and affection for
them because of their work.
Be at peace among yourselves. 14 And this is
what we ask you to do, brothers: warn the idlers,
give courage to those who are apprehensive, care
for the weak and be patient with everyone.
15 Make sure that people do not try to take revenge; you must all think of what is best for
each other and for the community. 16 Be happy
at all times; 17 pray constantly; 18 and for all
things give thanks to God, because this is what
God expects you to do in Christ Jesus.
19 Never try to suppress the Spirit 20 or treat
the gift of prophecy with contempt; 21 think before you do anything—hold on to what is good
22 and *avoid every* form of *evil.*

New English Bible

For God has not destined us to the terrors of judgement, but to the full attainment of salvation through our Lord Jesus Christ. He died for us so that we, awake or asleep, might live in company with him. Therefore hearten one another, fortify one another—as indeed you do.

We beg you, brothers, to acknowledge those who are working so hard among you, and in the Lord's fellowship are your leaders and counsellors. Hold them in the highest possible esteem and affection for the work they do.

You must live at peace among yourselves. And we would urge you, brothers, to admonish the careless, encourage the faint-hearted, support the weak, and to be very patient with them all.

See to it that no one pays back wrong for wrong, but always aim at doing the best you can for each other and for all men.

Be always joyful; pray continually; give thanks whatever happens; for this is what God in Christ wills for you.

Do not stifle inspiration, and do not despise prophetic utterances, but bring them all to the test and then keep what is good in them and avoid the bad of whatever kind.[a]

[a] *Or* . . . utterances. Put everything to the test; keep hold of what is good and avoid every kind of evil.

King James Version

appearance of evil. 23And the very God of peace
sanctify you wholly; and *I pray God* your whole
spirit and soul and body be preserved blameless
unto the coming of our Lord Jesus Christ.
24 Faithful *is* he that calleth you, who also will
do *it*. 25 Brethren, pray for us. 26 Greet all the
brethren with a holy kiss. 27 I charge you by the
Lord, that this epistle be read unto all the holy
brethren. 28 The grace of our Lord Jesus Christ
be with you. Amen.

The first *epistle* unto the Thessalonians was written from Athens.

Living Bible

of evil. 23 May the God of peace himself make
you entirely pure and devoted to God; and may
your spirit and soul and body be kept strong and
blameless until that day when our Lord Jesus
Christ comes back again. 24 God, who called you
to become his child, will do all this for you, just
as he promised. 25 Dear brothers, pray for us.
26 Shake hands for me with all the brothers
there. 27 I command you in the name of the Lord
to read this letter to all the Christians. 28And
may rich blessings from our Lord Jesus Christ
be with you, every one.

Sincerely,
Paul

Today's English Version

23 May the God who gives us peace make you holy in every way, and keep your whole being, spirit, soul, and body, free from all fault at the coming of our Lord Jesus Christ.
24 He who calls you will do it, because he is faithful.

25 Pray also for us, brothers.

26 Greet all the brothers with a brotherly kiss.

27 I urge you, by the authority of the Lord, to read this letter to all the brothers.

28 The grace of our Lord Jesus Christ be with you.

New International Version

23 May God himself, the God of peace, sanctify you through and through. May your whole
spirit, soul and body be kept blameless at the
coming of our Lord Jesus Christ. 24 The one
who calls you is faithful and he will do it.

25 Brothers, pray for us. 26 Greet all the
brothers with a holy kiss. 27 I charge you before the Lord to have this letter read to all the
brothers.

28 The grace of our Lord Jesus Christ be with you.

Phillips Modern English

May the God of peace make you holy through and through. May you be kept sound in spirit, mind and body, blameless until the coming of our Lord Jesus Christ. He who calls you is utterly faithful and he will finish what he has set out to do.

Pray for us, my brothers. Give a handshake all round among the brotherhood. The Lord's command, which I give you now, is that this letter should be read to all the brothers.

The grace of our Lord Jesus Christ be with you.

Revised Standard Version

23 May the God of peace himself sanctify you wholly; and may your spirit and soul and body be kept sound and blameless at the coming of our Lord Jesus Christ. 24 He who calls you is faithful, and he will do it.
25 Brethren, pray for us.
26 Greet all the brethren with a holy kiss.
27 I adjure you by the Lord that this letter be read to all the brethren.
28 The grace of our Lord Jesus Christ be with you.

Jerusalem Bible

Closing prayer and farewell

23 May the God of peace make you perfect and holy; and may you all be kept safe and blameless, spirit, soul and body, for the coming of our Lord Jesus Christ. 24 God has called you and he will not fail you.
25 Pray for us, my brothers.
26 Greet all the brothers with the holy kiss.
27 My orders, in the Lord's name, are that this letter is to be read to all the brothers.
28 The grace of our Lord Jesus Christ be with you.

New English Bible

May God himself, the God of peace, make you holy in every part, and keep you sound in spirit, soul, and body, without fault when our Lord Jesus Christ comes. He who calls you is to be trusted; he will do it.

Brothers, pray for us also.

Greet all our brothers with the kiss of peace.

I adjure you by the Lord to have this letter read to the whole brotherhood.

The grace of our Lord Jesus Christ be with you!

King James Version

THE SECOND EPISTLE OF PAUL THE APOSTLE TO THE THESSALONIANS

1 Paul, and Silvanus, and Timotheus, unto
the church of the Thessalonians in God our
Father and the Lord Jesus Christ: 2 Grace unto
you, and peace, from God our Father and the
Lord Jesus Christ. 3 We are bound to thank God
always for you, brethren, as it is meet, because
that your faith groweth exceedingly, and the
charity of every one of you all toward each other
aboundeth; 4 So that we ourselves glory in you
in the churches of God, for your patience and
faith in all your persecutions and tribulations

Living Bible

2 THESSALONIANS

1 *From:* Paul, Silas and Timothy.
To: The church of Thessalonica—kept safe
in God our Father and in the Lord Jesus Christ.
2 May God the Father and the Lord Jesus
Christ give you rich blessings and peace-filled
hearts and minds.
3 Dear brothers, giving thanks to God for you
is not only the right thing to do, but it is our
duty to God, because of the really wonderful
way your faith has grown, and because of your
growing love for each other. 4 We are happy to
tell other churches about your patience and complete faith in God, in spite of all the crushing
troubles and hardships you are going through.

Today's English Version

PAUL'S SECOND LETTER TO THE THESSALONIANS

1 From Paul, Silas, and Timothy—
To the people of the church in Thessa-
lonica, who belong to God our Father and the
Lord Jesus Christ:
2 May God the Father and the Lord Jesus
Christ give you grace and peace.

The judgment at Christ's coming

3 We must thank God at all times for you,
brothers. It is right for us to do so, because
your faith is growing so much and the love each
of you has for the others is becoming greater.
4 That is why we ourselves boast about you in
the churches of God. We boast about the way
you continue to endure and believe, through all
the persecutions and sufferings you are experiencing.

New International Version

2 THESSALONIANS

1 Paul, Silas[a] and Timothy,
To the church of the Thessalonians, who
are in God our Father and the Lord Jesus
Christ:
2 Grace and peace to you from God the
Father and the Lord Jesus Christ.

Thanksgiving and prayer

3 We ought always to thank God for you,
brothers, and rightly so, because your faith is
growing more and more, and the love every
one of you has for each other is increasing.
4 Therefore, among God's churches we boast
about your perseverance and faith in all the
persecutions and trials you are enduring.

[a] Greek *Silvanus.*

Phillips Modern English

THE SECOND LETTER TO THE CHRISTIANS IN THESSALONICA

To the church of the Thessalonians, founded on God our Father and Jesus Christ the Lord, from Paul, Silvanus and Timothy; grace to you and peace from God the Father and the Lord Jesus Christ.

1.3 ***Your sufferings are a guarantee of great joy one day***

My brothers, nowadays I always thank God for you not only in common fairness but as a moral obligation! Your faith has made such strides, and your love, each for all and all for each, has reached such proportions that we actually boast about you in the churches of God, because you have shown such endurance and faith in all the persecutions and troubles which you are now enduring.

Revised Standard Version

THE SECOND LETTER OF PAUL TO THE THESSALONIANS

1 Paul, Silvanus, and Timothy,
To the church of the Thessalonians in God our Father and the Lord Jesus Christ:
2 Grace to you and peace from God the Father and the Lord Jesus Christ.

3 We are bound to give thanks to God always for you, brethren, as is fitting, because your faith is growing abundantly, and the love of every one of you for one another is increasing.
4 Therefore we ourselves boast of you in the churches of God for your steadfastness and faith in all your persecutions and in the afflictions which you are enduring.

Jerusalem Bible

THE SECOND LETTER OF PAUL TO THE CHURCH IN THESSALONIKA

2 THESSALONIANS

Address

1 From Paul, Silvanus and Timothy, to the Church in Thessalonika which is in God our Father and the Lord Jesus Christ; 2 wishing you grace and peace from God the Father and the Lord Jesus Christ.

Thanksgiving and encouragement. The Last Judgment

3 We feel we must be continually thanking God for you, brothers; quite rightly, because your faith is growing so wonderfully and the love that you have for one another never stops increasing; 4 and among the churches of God we can take special pride in you for your constancy and faith under all the persecutions and troubles

New English Bible

THE SECOND LETTER OF PAUL TO THE THESSALONIANS

Hope and discipline

1 From Paul, Silvanus, and Timothy to the congregation of Thessalonians who belong to God our Father and the Lord Jesus Christ.

Grace to you and peace from God the Father and the Lord Jesus Christ.

Our thanks are always due to God for you, brothers. It is right that we should thank him, because your faith increases mightily, and the love you have, each for all and all for each, grows ever greater. Indeed we boast about you ourselves among the congregations of God's people, because your faith remains so steadfast under all your persecutions, and all the troubles

King James Version

that ye endure: 5 *Which is* a manifest token of the righteous judgment of God, that ye may be counted worthy of the kingdom of God, for which ye also suffer: 6 Seeing *it is* a righteous thing with God to recompense tribulation to them that trouble you; 7 And to you who are troubled rest with us, when the Lord Jesus shall be revealed from heaven with his mighty angels, 8 In flaming fire taking vengeance on them that know not God, and that obey not the gospel of our Lord Jesus Christ: 9 Who shall be punished with everlasting destruction from the presence of the Lord, and from the glory of his power; 10 When he shall come to be glorified in his saints, and to be admired in all them that believe (because our testimony among you was believed) in that day. 11 Wherefore also we pray always for you, that our God would count you worthy of *this* calling, and fulfil all the good pleasure of *his* goodness, and the work of faith with power: 12 That the name of our Lord Jesus Christ may be glorified in you, and ye in him, according to the grace of our God and the Lord Jesus Christ.

2 Now we beseech you, brethren, by the coming of our Lord Jesus Christ, and *by* our gathering together unto him, 2 That ye be not

Living Bible

5 This is only one example of the fair, just way God does things, for he is using your sufferings to make you ready for his kingdom, 6 while at the same time he is preparing judgment and punishment for those who are hurting you.

7 And so I would say to you who are suffering, God will give you rest along with us when the Lord Jesus appears suddenly from heaven in flaming fire with his mighty angels, 8 bringing judgment on those who do not wish to know God, and who refuse to accept his plan to save them through our Lord Jesus Christ. 9 They will be punished in everlasting hell, forever separated from the Lord, never to see the glory of his power, 10 when he comes to receive praise and admiration because of all he has done for his people, his saints. And you will be among those praising him, because you have believed what we told you about him.

11 And so we keep on praying for you that our God will make you the kind of children he wants to have—will make you as good as you wish you could be!—rewarding your faith with his power. 12 Then everyone will be praising the name of the Lord Jesus Christ because of the results they see in you; and your greatest glory will be that you belong to him. The tender mercy of our God and of the Lord Jesus Christ has made all this possible for you.

2 And now, what about the coming again of our Lord Jesus Christ, and our being gathered together to meet him? Please don't be upset

Today's English Version

5 Here is the proof of God's righteous judgment, because as a result of all this you will become worthy of his Kingdom, for which you are suffering. 6 God will do what is right: he will bring suffering on those who make you suffer, 7 and he will give relief to you who suffer, and to us as well. He will do this when the Lord Jesus appears from heaven with his mighty angels, 8 with a flaming fire, to punish those who do not know God and those who do not obey the Good News about our Lord Jesus. 9 They will suffer the punishment of eternal destruction, separated from the presence of the Lord and from his glorious might, 10 when he comes on that Day to receive glory from all his people and honor from all who believe. You too will be among them, because you have believed the message that we told you.

11 This is why we always pray for you. We ask our God to make you worthy of the life he called you to live. May he, by his power, fulfill all your desire for goodness and complete your work of faith. 12 In this way the name of our Lord Jesus will receive glory from you, and you from him, by the grace of our God and the Lord Jesus Christ.

The Wicked One

2 Concerning the coming of our Lord Jesus Christ and our being gathered together to be with him: I beg you, brothers, 2 do not be

New International Version

5 All this is evidence that God's judgment is right, and as a result you will be counted worthy of the kingdom of God, for which you are suffering. 6 God is just: He will pay back trouble to those who trouble you 7 and give relief to you who are troubled, and to us as well. This will happen when the Lord Jesus is revealed from heaven in blazing fire with his powerful angels. 8 He will punish those who do not know God and do not obey the gospel of our Lord Jesus. 9 They will be punished with everlasting destruction and shut out from the presence of the Lord and from the majesty of his power 10 on the day he comes to be glorified in his holy people and to be marveled at among all those who have believed. This includes you, because you believed our testimony to you.

11 With this in mind, we constantly pray for you, that our God may count you worthy of his calling, and that by his power he may fulfill every good purpose of yours and every act prompted by your faith. 12 We pray this so that the name of our Lord Jesus may be glorified in you, and you in him, according to the grace of our God and the Lord Jesus Christ.[b]

The man of lawlessness

2 Concerning the coming of our Lord Jesus Christ and our being gathered to him, we ask you, brothers, 2 not to become easily unset-

[*b*] Or *our God and Lord Jesus Christ.*

Phillips Modern English

See how justly the judgment of God works out! He intends to use your suffering to prove you worthy of his kingdom. For God's justice will repay trouble to those who have troubled you, and give relief to all of us who, like you, have suffered. This judgment will issue in the final appearance of the Lord Jesus from Heaven with the angels of his power. He will bring full justice in dazzling flame upon those who have refused to recognise God or to obey the gospel of our Lord Jesus. Their punishment will be eternal loss—exclusion from the radiance of the face of the Lord, and the glorious majesty of his power. But to those whom he has made holy his coming will mean splendour unimaginable. It will be a breath-taking wonder to all who believe—including you, for you have believed the message that we have given you.

In view of this we pray for you constantly, that God will count you worthy of his calling, and by his power may fulfil all your good intentions and every effort of faith. We pray that the name of our Lord Jesus may become more glorious through you, and that you may thus share something of his glory—all through the grace of our God and the Lord Jesus Christ.

2.1 *Before Christ's coming there will be certain signs*

Now we implore you, brothers, by the certainty of the coming of our Lord Jesus Christ and of our meeting him together, to keep your heads

Revised Standard Version

5 This is evidence of the righteous judgment
of God, that you may be made worthy of the
kingdom of God, for which you are suffering—
6 since indeed God deems it just to repay with
affliction those who afflict you, 7 and to grant
rest with us to you who are afflicted, when the
Lord Jesus is revealed from heaven with his
mighty angels in flaming fire, 8 inflicting vengeance upon those who do not know God and
upon those who do not obey the gospel of our
Lord Jesus. 9 They shall suffer the punishment
of eternal destruction and exclusion from the
presence of the Lord and from the glory of his
might, 10 when he comes on that day to be
glorified in his saints, and to be marveled at in
all who have believed, because our testimony to
you was believed. 11 To this end we always pray
for you, that our God may make you worthy
of his call, and may fulfil every good resolve and
work of faith by his power, 12 so that the name
of our Lord Jesus may be glorified in you, and
you in him, according to the grace of our God
and the Lord Jesus Christ.

2 Now concerning the coming of our Lord
Jesus Christ and our assembling to meet
him, we beg you, brethren, 2 not to be quickly

Jerusalem Bible

you have to bear. 5 It all shows that God's judgment is just, and the purpose of it is that you
may be found worthy of the kingdom of God; it
is for the sake of this that you are suffering now.
6 God will very rightly repay with injury those
who are injuring you, 7 and reward you, who are
suffering now, with the same peace as he will
give us, when the Lord Jesus appears from
heaven with the angels of his power. 8 He will
come *in flaming fire* to impose the penalty on
all who do not acknowledge God[a] and *refuse
to accept* the Good News of our Lord Jesus.
9 It will be their punishment to be lost eternally,
excluded *from the presence of the Lord and from
the glory of his strength* 10 *on that day* when
he comes *to be glorified among his saints and
seen in his glory*[b] by all who believe in him; and
you are believers, through our witness.
11 Knowing this, we pray continually that our
God will make you worthy of his call, and by
his power fulfill all your desires for goodness
and complete all that you have been doing
through faith; 12 because in this way *the name*
of our Lord Jesus Christ *will be glorified* in you
and you in him, by the grace of our God and
the Lord Jesus Christ.

The coming of the Lord and the prelude to it

2 To turn now, brothers, to the coming of
our Lord Jesus Christ and how we shall all
be gathered around him: 2 please do not get

[a] God's *coming in fire* is quoted from Is. 66:15; the penalty on *those who do not acknowledge him* is a quotation from Jr. 10:25. [b] Quotations from Is. 2:10-17; 49:3; 66:5.

New English Bible

you endure. See how this brings out the justice of God's judgement. It will prove you worthy of the kingdom of God, for which indeed you are suffering.

It is surely just that God should balance the account by sending trouble to those who trouble you, and relief to you who are troubled, and to us as well, when our Lord Jesus Christ is revealed from heaven with his mighty angels in blazing fire. Then he will do justice upon those who refuse to acknowledge God and upon those who will not obey[a] the gospel of our Lord Jesus. They will suffer the punishment of eternal ruin, cut off from the presence of the Lord and the splendour of his might, when on that great Day he comes to be glorified among his own and adored among all believers; for you did indeed believe the testimony we brought you.

With this in mind we pray for you always, that our God may count you worthy of his calling, and mightily bring to fulfilment every good purpose and every act inspired by faith, so that the name of our Lord Jesus may be glorified in you, and you in him, according to the grace of our God and the Lord Jesus Christ.

2 And now, brothers, about the coming of our
Lord Jesus Christ and his gathering of us to
himself: I beg you, do not suddenly lose your

[a] *Or* justice upon those who refuse . . . and will not obey . . .

King James Version

soon shaken in mind, or be troubled, neither by
spirit, nor by word, nor by letter as from us, as
that the day of Christ is at hand. 3 Let no man
deceive you by any means: for *that day shall not
come,* except there come a falling away first, and
that man of sin be revealed, the son of perdition;
4 Who opposeth and exalteth himself above all
that is called God, or that is worshipped; so that
he as God sitteth in the temple of God, shewing
himself that he is God. 5 Remember ye not,
that, when I was yet with you, I told you
these things? 6 And now ye know what with-
holdeth that he might be revealed in his time.
7 For the mystery of iniquity doth already
work: only he who now letteth *will let,* until he
be taken out of the way. 8 And then shall that
Wicked be revealed, whom the Lord shall consume with the spirit of his mouth, and shall
destroy with the brightness of his coming: 9 *Even
him,* whose coming is after the working of Satan
with all power and signs and lying wonders,
10 And with all deceivableness of unrighteousness
in them that perish; because they received not
the love of the truth, that they might be saved.
11 And for this cause God shall send them strong
delusion, that they should believe a lie: 12 That
they all might be damned who believed not the

Living Bible

and excited, dear brothers, by the rumor that this
day of the Lord has already begun. If you hear
of people having visions and special messages
from God about this, or letters that are supposed
to have come from me, don't believe them.
3 Don't be carried away and deceived regardless
of what they say.

For that day will not come until two things
happen: first, there will be a time of great rebellion against God, and then the man of rebellion will come—the son of hell. 4 He will defy
every god there is, and tear down every other
object of adoration and worship. He will go in
and sit as God in the temple of God, claiming
that he himself is God. 5 Don't you remember
that I told you this when I was with you? 6 And
you know what is keeping him from being here
already; for he can come only when his time is
ready.

7 As for the work this man of rebellion and
hell will do when he comes, it is already going
on,[a] but he himself will not come until the one
who is holding him back steps out of the way.
8 Then this wicked one will appear, whom the
Lord Jesus will burn up with the breath of his
mouth and destroy by his presence when he returns. 9 This man of sin will come as Satan's
tool, full of satanic power, and will trick everyone with strange demonstrations, and will do
great miracles. 10 He will completely fool those
who are on their way to hell because they have
said "no" to the Truth; they have refused to believe it and love it, and let it save them, 11 so
God will allow them to believe lies with all their
hearts, 12 and all of them will be justly judged
for believing falsehood, refusing the Truth, and

[*a*] Literally, "the mystery of lawlessness is already at work."

Today's English Version

so easily confused in your thinking or upset by
the claim that the Day of the Lord has come.
Perhaps this was said by someone prophesying,
or by someone preaching. Or it may have been
said that we wrote this in a letter. 3 Do not let
anyone fool you in any way. For the Day will
not come until the final Rebellion takes place
and the Wicked One appears, who is destined to
hell. 4 He will oppose everything which men
worship and everything which men consider divine. He will put himself above them all, and
even go in and sit down in God's temple and
claim to be God.

5 Don't you remember? I told you all this
while I was with you. 6 Yet there is something
that keeps this from happening now, and you
know what it is. At the proper time, then, the
Wicked One will appear. 7 The Mysterious Wickedness is already at work, but what is going to
happen will not happen until the one who holds
it back is taken out of the way. 8 Then the
Wicked One will appear, and the Lord Jesus will
kill him with the breath from his mouth and
destroy him with his glorious appearing, when
he comes. 9 The Wicked One will come with the
power of Satan and perform all kinds of miracles and false signs and wonders, 10 and use
every kind of wicked deceit on those who will
perish. They will perish because they did not
welcome and love the truth so as to be saved.
11 For this reason God sends the power of error
to work in them so that they believe what is
false. 12 The result is that all who have not believed the truth, but have taken pleasure in sin,
will be condemned.

New International Version

tled or alarmed by some prophecy, report or
letter supposed to have come from us, saying
that the day of the Lord has already come.
3 Don't let anyone deceive you in any way, for
[that day will not come] until the rebellion occurs and the man of lawlessness[c] is revealed,
the man doomed to destruction. 4 He opposes and
exalts himself over everything that is called God
or is worshiped, and even sets himself up in
God's temple, proclaiming himself to be God.

5 Don't you remember that when I was with
you I used to tell you these things? 6 And now
you know what is holding him back, so that he
may be revealed at the proper time. 7 For the
secret power of lawlessness is already at work;
but the one who now holds it back will continue to do so till he is taken out of the way.
8 And then the lawless one will be revealed, whom
the Lord Jesus will overthrow with the breath of
his mouth and destroy by the splendor of his
coming. 9 The coming of the lawless one will be
in accordance with the work of Satan displayed
in all kinds of counterfeit miracles, signs and
wonders, 10 and in every sort of evil that deceives those who are perishing. They perish because they refused to love the truth and so be
saved. 11 For this reason God sends them a
powerful delusion so that they will believe the lie
and 12 so that all will be condemned who have
not believed the truth but have delighted in
wickedness.

[*c*] Many early MSS read *man of sin.*

Phillips Modern English

and not be thrown off your balance by any prediction or message or letter purporting to come from us, and saying that the day of the Lord has already come. Don't let anyone deceive you by any means whatever. That day will not come before there first arises a definite rejection of God and the appearance of the lawless man. He is the product of all that leads to death, and he sets himself up in opposition to every religion. He even takes his seat in the Sanctuary of God, to show that he really claims to be God.

You must surely remember how I talked about this when I was with you. You now know about the "restraining power" which prevents him from being revealed until the proper time. Evil is already insidiously at work but its activities are secret until what I have called the "restraining power" is removed. When that happens the lawless man will be plainly seen—though the words from the mouth of the Lord Jesus spell his doom, and the radiance of his coming will be his utter destruction. The lawless man is produced by the power of Satan and armed with all the force, wonders and signs that falsehood can devise. To those doomed to perish he will come with evil's undiluted power to deceive, for they have refused to love the truth which could have saved them. God sends upon them, therefore, the full force of evil's delusion, so that they put their faith in an utter fraud and meet the inevitable judgment of all who have refused to believe the truth and who have made evil their pleasure.

Revised Standard Version

shaken in mind or excited, either by spirit or
by word, or by letter purporting to be from us,
to the effect that the day of the Lord has come.
3 Let no one deceive you in any way; for that
day will not come, unless the rebellion comes
first, and the man of lawlessness[a] is revealed,
the son of perdition, 4 who opposes and exalts
himself against every so-called god or object of
worship, so that he takes his seat in the temple
of God, proclaiming himself to be God. 5 Do
you not remember that when I was still with you
I told you this? 6 And you know what is restraining him now so that he may be revealed
in his time. 7 For the mystery of lawlessness is
already at work; only he who now restrains it
will do so until he is out of the way. 8 And
then the lawless one will be revealed, and the
Lord Jesus will slay him with the breath of his
mouth and destroy him by his appearing and
his coming. 9 The coming of the lawless one by
the activity of Satan will be with all power and
with pretended signs and wonders, 10 and with
all wicked deception for those who are to perish,
because they refused to love the truth and so
be saved. 11 Therefore God sends upon them a
strong delusion, to make them believe what is
false, 12 so that all may be condemned who did
not believe the truth but had pleasure in unrighteousness.

[a] Other ancient authorities read *sin*.

Jerusalem Bible

excited too soon or alarmed by any prediction
or rumor or any letter claiming to come from
us, implying that the Day of the Lord has already arrived. 3 Never let anyone deceive you
in this way.

It cannot happen until the Great Revolt has
taken place and the Rebel, the Lost One, has
appeared. 4 This is the Enemy, the one who
claims to be so much *greater than all* that men
call "god," so much greater than anything that
is worshiped, that *he enthrones himself* in
God's sanctuary and claims that he is God.
5 Surely you remember me telling you about this
when I was with you? 6 And you know, too, what
is still holding him back from appearing before
his appointed time. 7 Rebellion is at its work
already, but in secret, and the one who is holding it back has first to be removed 8 before the
Rebel appears openly. The Lord *will kill him*
with the breath of his mouth[c] and will annihilate
him with his glorious appearance at his coming.
9 But when the Rebel comes, Satan will set
to work: there will be all kinds of miracles and
a deceptive show of signs and portents, 10 and
everything evil that can deceive those who are
bound for destruction because they would not
grasp the love of the truth which could have
saved them. 11 The reason why God is sending
a power to delude them and make them believe
what is untrue 12 is to condemn all who refused
to believe in the truth and chose wickedness
instead.

[c] Is. 11:4.

New English Bible

heads or alarm yourselves, whether at some oracular utterance, or pronouncement, or some letter purporting to come from us, alleging that the Day of the Lord is already here. Let no one deceive you in any way whatever. That day cannot come before the final rebellion against God, when wickedness will be revealed in human form, the man doomed to perdition. He is the Enemy. He rises in his pride against every god, so called, every object of men's worship, and even takes his seat in the temple of God claiming to be a god himself.

You cannot but remember that I told you this while I was still with you; you must now be aware of the restraining hand which ensures that he shall be revealed only at the proper time. For already the secret power of wickedness is at work, secret only for the present until the Restrainer disappears from the scene. And then he will be revealed, that wicked man whom the Lord Jesus will destroy with the breath of his mouth, and annihilate by the radiance of his coming. But the coming of that wicked man is the work of Satan. It will be attended by all the powerful signs and miracles of the Lie, and all the deception that sinfulness can impose on those doomed to destruction. Destroyed they shall be, because they did not open their minds to love of the truth, so as to find salvation. Therefore God puts them under a delusion, which works upon them to believe the lie, so that they may all be brought to judgement, all who do not believe the truth but make sinfulness their deliberate choice.

King James Version

truth, but had pleasure in unrighteousness. 13 But we are bound to give thanks always to God for you, brethren beloved of the Lord, because God hath from the beginning chosen you to salvation through sanctification of the Spirit and belief of the truth: 14 Whereunto he called you by our gospel, to the obtaining of the glory of our Lord Jesus Christ. 15 Therefore, brethren, stand fast, and hold the traditions which ye have been taught, whether by word, or our epistle. 16 Now our Lord Jesus Christ himself, and God, even our Father, which hath loved us, and hath given *us* everlasting consolation and good hope through grace, 17 Comfort your hearts, and stablish you in every good word and work.

3 Finally, brethren, pray for us, that the word of the Lord may have *free* course, and be glorified, even as *it is* with you: 2 And that we may be delivered from unreasonable and wicked men: for all *men* have not faith. 3 But the Lord is faithful, who shall stablish you, and keep *you* from evil. 4 And we have confidence in the Lord

Living Bible

enjoying their sins. 13 But we must forever give thanks to God for you, our brothers loved by the Lord, because God chose from the very first to give you salvation,[b] cleansing you by the work of the Holy Spirit and by your trusting in the Truth. 14 Through us he told you the Good News. Through us he called you to share in the glory of our Lord Jesus Christ.

15 With all these things in mind, dear brothers, stand firm and keep a strong grip on the truth that we taught you in our letters and during the time we were with you.

16 May our Lord Jesus Christ himself and God our Father, who has loved us and given us everlasting comfort and hope which we don't deserve, 17 comfort your hearts with all comfort, and help you in every good thing you say and do.

3 Finally, dear brothers, as I come to the end of this letter I ask you to pray for us. Pray first that the Lord's message will spread rapidly and triumph wherever it goes, winning converts everywhere as it did when it came to you. 2 Pray too that we will be saved out of the clutches of evil men, for not everyone loves the Lord. 3 But the Lord is faithful; he will make you strong and guard you from satanic attacks of every kind. 4 And we trust the Lord that you are putting

[*b*] Or, "because God chose you to be among the first to believe."

Today's English Version

You are chosen for salvation

13 We must thank God at all times for you, brothers, you whom the Lord loves. For God chose you as the first to be saved, by the Spirit's power to make you God's holy people, and by your faith in the truth. 14 God called you to this through the Good News we preached to you; he called you to possess your share of the glory of our Lord Jesus Christ. 15 So then, brothers, stand firm and hold on to those truths which we taught you, both in our preaching and in our letter.

16 May our Lord Jesus Christ himself, and God our Father, who loved us and in his grace gave us eternal courage and a good hope, 17 fill your hearts with courage and make you strong to do and say all that is good.

Pray for us

3 Finally, brothers, pray for us, that the Lord's message may continue to spread rapidly and receive glory, just as it did among you. 2 Pray also that God will rescue us from wicked and evil men. For not all people believe the message.

3 But the Lord is faithful. He will make you strong and keep you safe from the Evil One. 4 And the Lord gives us confidence in you; we

New International Version

Stand firm

13 But we ought always to thank God for you, brothers loved by the Lord, because from the beginning God chose you[d] to be saved through the sanctifying work of the Spirit and through belief in the truth. 14 He called you to this through our gospel, that you might share in the glory of our Lord Jesus Christ. 15 So then, brothers, stand firm and hold to the teachings[e] we passed on to you, whether by word of mouth or by letter.

16 May our Lord Jesus Christ himself and God our Father, who loved us and by his grace gave us eternal encouragement and good hope, 17 encourage and strengthen you in every good deed and word.

Request for prayer

3 Finally, brothers, pray for us that the message of the Lord may spread rapidly and be honored, just as it was with you. 2 And pray that we may be delivered from wicked and evil men, for not everyone has faith. 3 But the Lord is faithful, and he will strengthen and protect you from the evil one. 4 We have confidence in

[*d*] Some early textual sources read *because God chose you as his firstfruits.* [*e*] Or *traditions.*

Phillips Modern English

2.13 You, thank God, belong to those who believe the truth

But we must thank God continually for you, brothers, whom the Lord loves. He has chosen you as the first to be saved, to make you holy by the work of his Spirit and your own belief in the truth. It was for this that he called you when we preached the gospel to you, and he wanted you to possess the glory of our Lord Jesus Christ. So stand firm, and hold fast to the teachings we passed on to you, whether by word of mouth or by letter.

May our Lord Jesus Christ himself and God our Father (who has loved us and given us unending encouragement and unfailing hope by his grace) inspire you with courage and confidence in every good thing you say or do.

3.1 We ask your prayers for God's work here

Finally, my brothers, do pray for us, that the Lord's message may go forward unhindered and may bring him glory, as it has with you. Pray, too, that we may be rescued from bigoted and wicked men; for all men, alas, have not faith. Yet the Lord is utterly to be depended upon and he will give you stability and protection against the evil one. It is he who makes us feel

Revised Standard Version

13 But we are bound to give thanks to God always for you, brethren beloved by the Lord, because God chose you from the beginning[b] to be saved, through sanctification by the Spirit[c] and belief in the truth. 14 To this he called you through our gospel, so that you may obtain the glory of our Lord Jesus Christ. 15 So then, brethren, stand firm and hold to the traditions which you were taught by us, either by word of mouth or by letter.

16 Now may our Lord Jesus Christ himself, and God our Father, who loved us and gave us eternal comfort and good hope through grace, 17 comfort your hearts and establish them in every good work and word.

3 Finally, brethren, pray for us, that the word of the Lord may speed on and triumph, as it did among you, 2 and that we may be delivered from wicked and evil men; for not all have faith. 3 But the Lord is faithful; he will strengthen you and guard you from evil.[d] 4And

[b] Other ancient authorities read *as the first converts.* [c] Or *of spirit.* [d] Or *the evil one.*

Jerusalem Bible

Encouragement to persevere

13 But we feel that we must be continually thanking God for you, brothers whom the Lord loves, because God chose you from the beginning to be saved by the sanctifying Spirit and by faith in the truth. 14 Through the Good News that we brought he called you to this so that you should share the glory of our Lord Jesus Christ. 15 Stand firm, then, brothers, and keep the traditions that we taught you, whether by word of mouth or by letter. 16 May our Lord Jesus Christ himself, and God our Father who has given us his love and, through his grace, such inexhaustible comfort and such sure hope, 17 comfort you and strengthen you in everything good that you do or say.

3 Finally, brothers, pray for us; pray that the Lord's message may spread quickly and be received with honor as it was among you; 2 and pray that we may be preserved from the interference of bigoted and evil people, for faith is not given to everyone. 3 But the Lord is faithful, and he will give you strength and guard you from the evil one, 4 and we, in the Lord, have

New English Bible

But we are bound to thank God always for you, brothers beloved by the Lord, because from the beginning of time God chose you[a] to find salvation in the Spirit that consecrates you, and in the truth that you believe. It was for this that he called you through the gospel we brought, so that you might possess for your own the splendour of our Lord Jesus Christ.

Stand firm, then, brothers, and hold fast to the traditions which you have learned from us by word or by letter. And may our Lord Jesus Christ himself and God our Father, who has shown us such love, and in his grace has given us such unfailing encouragement and such bright hopes, still encourage and fortify you in every good deed and word!

3 And now, brothers, pray for us, that the word of the Lord may have everywhere the swift and glorious course that it has had among you, and that we may be rescued from wrong-headed and wicked men; for it is not all who have faith. But the Lord is to be trusted, and he will fortify you and guard you from the evil one. We feel perfect confidence about you, in the

[a] *Some witnesses read* because God chose you as his firstfruits . . .

King James Version

touching you, that ye both do and will do the
things which we command you. 5 And the Lord
direct your hearts into the love of God, and
into the patient waiting for Christ. 6 Now we
command you, brethren, in the name of our
Lord Jesus Christ, that ye withdraw yourselves
from every brother that walketh disorderly, and
not after the tradition which he received of us.
7 For yourselves know how ye ought to follow
us: for we behaved not ourselves disorderly
among you; 8 Neither did we eat any man's
bread for nought; but wrought with labour and
travail night and day, that we might not be
chargeable to any of you: 9 Not because we have
not power, but to make ourselves an ensample
unto you to follow us. 10 For even when we were
with you, this we commanded you, that if any
would not work, neither should he eat. 11 For
we hear that there are some which walk among
you disorderly, working not at all, but are busybodies. 12 Now them that are such we command
and exhort by our Lord Jesus Christ, that with
quietness they work, and eat their own bread.

Living Bible

into practice the things we taught you, and that
you always will. 5 May the Lord bring you into
an ever deeper understanding of the love of God
and of the patience that comes from Christ.
6 Now here is a command, dear brothers,
given in the name of our Lord Jesus Christ by
his authority: Stay away from any Christian who
spends his days in laziness and does not follow
the ideal of hard work we set up for you. 7 For
you well know that you ought to follow our example: you never saw us loafing; 8 we never accepted food from anyone without buying it; we
worked hard day and night for the money we
needed to live on, in order that we would not be
a burden to any of you. 9 It wasn't that we didn't
have the right to ask you to feed us, but we
wanted to show you, firsthand, how you should
work for your living. 10 Even while we were still
there with you we gave you this rule: "He who
does not work shall not eat."
11 Yet we hear that some of you are living in
laziness, refusing to work, and wasting your time
in gossiping. 12 In the name of the Lord Jesus
Christ we appeal to such people—we command
them—to quiet down, get to work, and earn their

Today's English Version

are sure that you are doing and will continue
to do what we tell you.
5 May the Lord lead your hearts to the love
for God and to the endurance that is given by
Christ.

The obligation to work

6 In the name of the Lord Jesus Christ we
command you, brothers: keep away from all
brothers who are living a lazy life, who do not
follow the instructions that we gave them. 7 You
yourselves know very well that you should do
just what we did. We were not lazy when we
were with you. 8 We did not accept anyone's
support without paying for it. Instead, we
worked and toiled; day and night we kept working so as not to be an expense to any of you.
9 We did this, not because we do not have the
right to demand our support; we did it to be an
example for you to follow. 10 While we were
with you we told you, "Whoever does not want
to work is not allowed to eat."
11 We say this because we hear that there are
some people among you who live lazy lives, who
do nothing except meddle in other people's business. 12 In the name of the Lord Jesus Christ
we command these people and warn them: they
must lead orderly lives and work to earn their
own living.

New International Version

the Lord that you are doing and will continue
to do the things we command. 5 May the Lord
direct your hearts into God's love and Christ's
perseverance.

Warning against idleness

6 In the name of the Lord Jesus Christ, we
command you, brothers, to keep away from
every brother who is idle and does not live according to the teaching[f] you received from us.
7 For you yourselves know how you ought to
follow our example. We were not idle when we
were with you, 8 nor did we eat anyone's food
without paying for it. On the contrary, we
worked night and day, laboring and toiling so
that we would not be a burden to any of you.
9 We did this, not because we do not have the
right to such help, but in order to make ourselves a model for you to follow. 10 For even
when we were with you, we gave you this rule:
"If a man will not work, he shall not eat."
11 We hear that some among you are idle.
They are not busy; they are busybodies. 12 In
the name of the Lord Jesus Christ, we command and urge such people to settle down and

[f] Or *tradition*.

Phillips Modern English

confident about you, that you are acting and will act in accordance with our commands. May the Lord guide your hearts into deeper understanding of God's love and of the patient suffering of Christ.

3.6 Remember our example: everyone should do his fair share of work

One order, brothers, we must give you in the name of our Lord Jesus Christ: don't associate with the brother whose life is undisciplined, and not in accordance with the tradition which you received from us. You know well that we ourselves are your examples here, and that our lives among you were never undisciplined. We did not eat anyone's food without paying for it. In fact we toiled and laboured night and day to avoid being the slightest expense to any of you. This was not because we had no right to ask our necessities of you, but because we wanted to set you an example to imitate. When we were actually with you we gave you this principle to work on: "If a man will not work, he shall not eat." Now we hear that you have some among you living quite undisciplined lives, never doing a stroke of work, and busy only in other people's affairs. Our order to such men, indeed our appeal by the Lord Jesus Christ, is to settle down to work and eat the food they have earned themselves.

Revised Standard Version

we have confidence in the Lord about you, that
you are doing and will do the things which we
command. 5 May the Lord direct your hearts
to the love of God and to the steadfastness of
Christ.
6 Now we command you, brethren, in the
name of our Lord Jesus Christ, that you keep
away from any brother who is living in idleness
and not in accord with the tradition that you
received from us. 7 For you yourselves know
how you ought to imitate us; we were not idle
when we were with you, 8 we did not eat any
one's bread without paying, but with toil and
labor we worked night and day, that we might
not burden any of you. 9 It was not because we
have not that right, but to give you in our conduct an example to imitate. 10 For even when
we were with you, we gave you this command:
If any one will not work, let him not eat. 11 For
we hear that some of you are living in idleness,
mere busybodies, not doing any work. 12 Now
such persons we command and exhort in the
Lord Jesus Christ to do their work in quietness

Jerusalem Bible

every confidence that you are doing and will go
on doing all that we tell you. 5 May the Lord
turn your hearts toward the love of God and the
fortitude of Christ.

Against idleness and disunity

6 In the name of the Lord Jesus Christ, we
urge you, brothers, to keep away from any of the
brothers who refuses to work or to live according to the tradition we passed on to you.
7 You know how you are supposed to imitate
us: now we were not idle when we were with
you, 8 nor did we ever have our meals at anyone's table without paying for them; no, we
worked night and day, slaving and straining, so
as not to be a burden on any of you. 9 This was
not because we had no right to be, but in order
to make ourselves an example for you to follow.
10 We gave you a rule when we were with
you: not to let anyone have any food if he
refused to do any work. 11 Now we hear that
there are some of you who are living in idleness,
doing no work themselves but interfering with
everyone else's. 12 In the Lord Jesus Christ, we
order and call on people of this kind to go on
quietly working and earning the food that they
eat.

New English Bible

Lord, that you are doing and will continue to do what we order. May the Lord direct your hearts towards God's love and the steadfastness of Christ!

These are our orders to you, brothers, in the name of our Lord Jesus Christ: hold aloof from every Christian brother who falls into idle habits, and does not follow the tradition you received from us. You know yourselves how you ought to copy our example: we were no idlers among you; we did not accept board and lodging from anyone without paying for it; we toiled and drudged, we worked for a living night and day, rather than be a burden to any of you—not because we have not the right to maintenance, but to set an example for you to imitate. For even during our stay with you we laid down the rule: the man who will not work shall not eat. We mention this because we hear that some of your number are idling their time away, minding everybody's business but their own. To all such we give these orders, and we appeal to them in the name of the Lord Jesus Christ to work quietly for their living.

King James Version

13 But ye, brethren, be not weary in well doing. 14And if any man obey not our word by this epistle, note that man, and have no company with him, that he may be ashamed. 15 Yet count *him* not as an enemy, but admonish *him* as a brother. 16 Now the Lord of peace himself give you peace always by all means. The Lord *be* with you all. 17 The salutation of Paul with mine own hand, which is the token in every epistle: so I write. 18 The grace of our Lord Jesus Christ *be* with you all. Amen.

The second *epistle* to the Thessalonians was written from Athens.

Living Bible

own living. 13And to the rest of you I say, dear brothers, never be tired of doing right.

14 If anyone refuses to obey what we say in this letter, notice who he is and stay away from him, that he may be ashamed of himself. 15 Don't think of him as an enemy, but speak to him as you would to a brother who needs to be warned. 16 May the Lord of peace himself give you his peace no matter what happens. The Lord be with you all.

17 Now here is my greeting which I am writing with my own hand, as I do at the end of all my letters, for proof that it really is from me. This is in my own handwriting. 18 May the blessing of our Lord Jesus Christ be upon you all.

Sincerely,
Paul

Today's English Version

13 But you, brothers, must not get tired of doing good. 14 There may be someone there who will not obey the message we send you in this letter. If so, take note of him and have nothing to do with him, so that he will be ashamed. 15 But do not treat him as an enemy; instead, warn him as a brother.

Final words

16 May the Lord himself, who is our source of peace, give you peace at all times and in every way. The Lord be with you all.

17 With my own hand I write this: *Greetings from Paul.* This is the way I sign every letter; this is how I write.

18 May the grace of our Lord Jesus Christ be with you all.

New International Version

earn the bread they eat. 13And as for you, brothers, never tire of doing what is right.

14 If anyone does not obey our instruction in this letter, take special note of him. Do not associate with him, in order that he may feel ashamed. 15 Yet do not regard him as an enemy, but warn him as a brother.

Final greetings

16 Now may the Lord of peace himself give you peace at all times and in every way. The Lord be with all of you.

17 I, Paul, write this greeting in my own hand, which is the distinguishing mark in all my letters. This is how I write.

18 The grace of our Lord Jesus Christ be with you all.

Phillips Modern English

And the rest of you, my brothers—don't get tired of honest work! If anyone refuses to obey the command given in this letter, mark that man, do not associate with him until he is ashamed of himself. I don't mean, of course, treat him as an enemy, but reprimand him as a brother.

3.16 My blessing on you all!

Now may the Lord of peace personally give you peace at all times and in all ways. The Lord be with you all.

This is the greeting of PAUL, written by my own hand—my "mark" on all my letters. This is how I write.

The grace of our Lord Jesus Christ be with you all.

Revised Standard Version

and to earn their own living. 13 Brethren, do not be weary in well-doing.

14 If any one refuses to obey what we say in this letter, note that man, and have nothing to do with him, that he may be ashamed. 15 Do not look on him as an enemy, but warn him as a brother.

16 Now may the Lord of peace himself give you peace at all times in all ways. The Lord be with you all.

17 I, Paul, write this greeting with my own hand. This is the mark in every letter of mine; it is the way I write. 18 The grace of our Lord Jesus Christ be with you all.

Jerusalem Bible

13 My brothers, never grow tired of doing what is right. 14 If anyone refuses to obey what I have written in this letter, take note of him and have nothing to do with him, so that he will feel that he is in the wrong; 15 though you are not to regard him as an enemy but as a brother in need of correction.

Prayer and farewell wishes

16 May the Lord of peace himself give you peace all the time and in every way. The Lord be with you all.

17 From me, PAUL, these greetings in my own handwriting, which is the mark of genuineness in every letter; this is my own writing. 18 May the grace of our Lord Jesus Christ be with you all.

New English Bible

But you, my friends, must never tire of doing right. If anyone disobeys our instructions given by letter, mark him well, and have no dealings with him until he is ashamed of himself. I do not mean treat him as an enemy, but give him friendly advice, as one of the family. May the Lord of peace himself give you peace at all times and in all ways.[a] The Lord be with you all.

The greeting is in my own hand, signed with my name, PAUL; this authenticates all my letters; this is how I write. The grace[b] of our Lord Jesus Christ be with you all.

[a] *Some witnesses read* at all times, wherever you may be. [b] *Or* . . . letters. My message is this: the grace . . .

King James Version

THE FIRST EPISTLE OF PAUL THE APOSTLE TO TIMOTHY

1 Paul, an apostle of Jesus Christ by the commandment of God our Saviour, and Lord Jesus Christ, *which is* our hope; 2 Unto Timothy, *my* own son in the faith: Grace, mercy, *and* peace, from God our Father, and Jesus Christ

Living Bible

1 TIMOTHY

1 *From:* Paul, a missionary of Jesus Christ, sent out by the direct command of God our Savior and by Jesus Christ our Lord—our only hope.

2 *To:* Timothy.

Timothy, you are like a son to me in the things of the Lord. May God our Father and Jesus Christ our Lord show you his kindness and mercy and give you great peace of heart and mind.

Today's English Version

PAUL'S FIRST LETTER TO TIMOTHY

1 From Paul, an apostle of Christ Jesus by order of God our Savior and Christ Jesus our hope—

2 To Timothy, my true son in the faith:

May God the Father and Christ Jesus our Lord give you grace, mercy, and peace.

New International Version

1 TIMOTHY

1 Paul, an apostle of Christ Jesus by the command of God our Savior and of Christ Jesus our hope,

2 To Timothy my true son in the faith:

Grace, mercy and peace from God the Father and Christ Jesus our Lord.

Phillips Modern English

THE FIRST LETTER TO TIMOTHY

Paul, Jesus Christ's messenger by command of God our saviour and Christ Jesus our hope, to Timothy my true son in the faith: grace, mercy and peace be to you from God the Father and Christ Jesus our Lord.

Revised Standard Version

THE FIRST LETTER OF PAUL TO TIMOTHY

1 Paul, an apostle of Christ Jesus by command of God our Savior and of Christ Jesus our hope,
2 To Timothy, my true child in the faith:
Grace, mercy, and peace from God the Father and Christ Jesus our Lord.

Jerusalem Bible

THE FIRST LETTER FROM PAUL TO TIMOTHY

1 TIMOTHY

Address

1 From Paul, apostle of Christ Jesus appointed by the command of God our savior and of Christ Jesus our hope, 2 to Timothy, true child of mine in the faith; wishing you grace, mercy and peace from God the Father and from Christ Jesus our Lord.

New English Bible

THE FIRST LETTER OF PAUL TO TIMOTHY

Church order

1 From Paul, apostle of Christ Jesus by command of God our Saviour and Christ Jesus our hope, to Timothy his true-born son in the faith.

Grace, mercy, and peace to you from God the Father and Christ Jesus our Lord.

King James Version

our Lord. 3 As I besought thee to abide still at Ephesus, when I went into Macedonia, that thou mightest charge some that they teach no other doctrine, 4 Neither give heed to fables and endless genealogies, which minister questions, rather than godly edifying which is in faith: *so do.* 5 Now the end of the commandment is charity out of a pure heart, and *of* a good conscience, and *of* faith unfeigned: 6 From which some having swerved have turned aside unto vain jangling; 7 Desiring to be teachers of the law; understanding neither what they say, nor whereof they affirm. 8 But we know that the law *is* good, if a man use it lawfully; 9 Knowing this, that the law is not made for a righteous man, but for the lawless and disobedient, for the ungodly and for sinners, for unholy and profane, for murderers of fathers and murderers of mothers, for manslayers, 10 For whoremongers, for them that defile themselves with mankind, for menstealers, for liars, for perjured persons, and if there be any other thing that is contrary to sound doctrine; 11 According to the glorious gospel of the blessed God, which was committed

Living Bible

3, 4 As I said when I left for Macedonia, please stay there in Ephesus and try to stop the men who are teaching such wrong doctrine. Put an end to their myths and fables, and their idea of being saved by finding favor with an endless chain of angels leading up to God—wild ideas that stir up questions and arguments instead of helping people accept God's plan of faith. 5 What I am eager for is that all the Christians there will be filled with love that comes from pure hearts, and that their minds will be clean and their faith strong.

6 But these teachers have missed this whole idea and spend their time arguing and talking foolishness. 7 They want to become famous as teachers of the laws of Moses when they haven't the slightest idea what those laws really show us. 8 Those laws are good when used as God intended. 9 But they were not made for us, whom God has saved; they are for sinners who hate God, have rebellious hearts, curse and swear, attack their fathers and mothers, and murder. 10, 11 Yes, these laws are made to identify as sinners all who are immoral and impure: homosexuals, kidnappers, liars, and all others who do things that contradict the glorious Good News of our blessed God, whose messenger I am.

Today's English Version

Warnings against false teaching

3 I want you to stay in Ephesus, just as I urged you when I was on my way to Macedonia. Some people there are teaching false doctrines, and you must order them to stop. 4 Tell them to give up those legends and those long lists of names of ancestors, because these only produce arguments; they do not serve God's plan, which is known by faith. 5 The purpose of this order is to arouse the love that comes from a pure heart, a clear conscience, and a genuine faith. 6 Some men have turned away from these and have lost their way in foolish discussions. 7 They want to be teachers of God's law, but they do not understand their own words or the matters about which they speak with so much confidence.

8 We know that the Law is good, if it is used as it should be used. 9 It must be remembered, of course, that laws are made, not for good people, but for lawbreakers and criminals, for the godless and sinful, for those who are not religious or spiritual, for men who kill their fathers or mothers, for murderers, 10 for the immoral, for sexual perverts, for kidnappers, for those who lie and give false testimony or do anything else contrary to the true teaching. 11 That teaching is found in the gospel that was entrusted to me to announce, the Good News from the glorious and blessed God.

New International Version

Warning against false teachers of the law

3 As I urged you when I went into Macedonia, stay there in Ephesus so that you may command certain men not to teach false doctrines any longer 4 nor to devote themselves to myths and endless genealogies. These promote controversies rather than God's work—which is by faith. 5 The goal of this command is love, which comes from a pure heart, a good conscience and a sincere faith. 6 Some have wandered away from these and turned to meaningless talk. 7 They want to be teachers of the law, but they do not know what they are talking about or what they so confidently affirm.

8 We know that the law is good if a man uses it properly. 9 We also know that law is made not for good men, but for lawbreakers and rebels, the ungodly and sinful, the unholy and irreligious; for those who kill their fathers or mothers, for murderers, 10 for adulterers and perverts, for slave traders and liars and perjurers—and for whatever else is contrary to the sound doctrine 11 that conforms to the glorious gospel of the blessed God, which he entrusted to me.

Phillips Modern English

1.3 A reminder

I am repeating in this letter the advice I gave you just before I went to Macedonia and urged you to stay at Ephesus. I wanted you to do this so that you could order certain persons to stop inventing new doctrines and to leave hoary old myths and interminable genealogies alone. Such things lead men to speculation rather than to the ordered living which results from faith in God. The ultimate aim of the Christian ministry, after all, is to produce the love which springs from a pure heart, a good conscience and a genuine faith. Some seem to have forgotten this and to have lost themselves in endless words. They want a reputation as teachers of the Law, yet they fail to realise the meaning of their own words still less of the subject they are so dogmatic about. We know, of course, that the Law is good in itself and has a legitimate function. Yet we also know that the Law is not really meant for the good man, but for the man who has neither principles nor self-control; for the man who is really wicked, who has neither scruples nor reverence. Yes, the Law is directed against the sort of people who attack their own parents, who kill their fellows, who are sexually uncontrolled or perverted, or who traffic in the bodies of others. It is against liars and perjurers—in fact it is against any and every action which contradicts the wholesome teaching of the glorious gospel which the blessed God has given and entrusted to me.

Revised Standard Version

3 As I urged you when I was going to Macedonia, remain at Ephesus that you may charge
certain persons not to teach any different doctrine, 4 nor to occupy themselves with myths
and endless genealogies which promote speculations rather than the divine training[a] that is in
faith; 5 whereas the aim of our charge is love
that issues from a pure heart and a good conscience and sincere faith. 6 Certain persons by
swerving from these have wandered away into
vain discussion, 7 desiring to be teachers of the
law, without understanding either what they are
saying or the things about which they make
assertions.
8 Now we know that the law is good, if any
one uses it lawfully, 9 understanding this, that
the law is not laid down for the just but for
the lawless and disobedient, for the ungodly and
sinners, for the unholy and profane, for murderers of fathers and murderers of mothers, for
manslayers, 10 immoral persons, sodomites, kid-
napers, liars, perjurers, and whatever else is
contrary to sound doctrine, 11 in accordance
with the glorious gospel of the blessed God with
which I have been entrusted.

[a] Or *stewardship*, or *order*.

Jerusalem Bible

Suppress the false teachers

3 As I asked you when I was leaving for
Macedonia, please stay at Ephesus, to insist that
certain people stop teaching strange doctrines
4 and taking notice of myths and endless genealogies; these things are only likely to raise ir-
relevant doubts instead of furthering the design
of God which are revealed in faith. 5 The only
purpose of this instruction is that there should
be love, coming out of a pure heart, a clear conscience and a sincere faith. 6 There are some
people who have gone off the straight course and
taken a road that leads to empty speculation;
7 they claim to be doctors of the Law but they
understand neither the arguments they are using
nor the opinions they are upholding.

The purpose of the Law

8 We know, of course, that the Law is good,
but only provided it is treated like any law,
9 in the understanding that laws are not framed
for people who are good. On the contrary, they
are for criminals and revolutionaries, for the irreligious and the wicked, for the sacrilegious and
the irreverent; they are for people who kill their
fathers or mothers and for murderers, 10 for
those who are immoral with women or with
boys or with men, for liars and for perjurers—
and for everything else that is contrary to the
sound teaching 11 that goes with the Good
News of the glory of the blessed God, the gospel
that was entrusted to me.

New English Bible

When I was starting for Macedonia, I urged you to stay on at Ephesus. You were to command certain persons to give up teaching erroneous doctrines and studying those interminable myths and genealogies, which issue in mere speculation and cannot make known God's plan for us, which works through faith.[a]

The aim and object of this command is the love which springs from a clean heart, from a good conscience, and from faith that is genuine. Through falling short of these, some people have gone astray into a wilderness of words. They set out to be teachers of the moral law, without understanding either the words they use or the subjects about which they are so dogmatic.

We all know that the law is an excellent thing, provided we treat it as law, recognizing that it is not aimed at good citizens, but at the lawless and unruly, the impious and sinful, the irreligious and worldly; at parricides and matricides, murderers and fornicators, perverts, kidnappers, liars, perjurers—in fact all whose behaviour flouts the wholesome teaching which conforms with the gospel entrusted to me, the gospel which tells of the glory of God in his eternal felicity.

[a] *Or* cannot promote the faithful discharge of God's stewardship.

King James Version

to my trust. 12 And I thank Christ Jesus our Lord, who hath enabled me, for that he counted me faithful, putting me into the ministry; 13 Who was before a blasphemer, and a persecutor, and injurious: but I obtained mercy, because I did *it* ignorantly in unbelief. 14 And the grace of our Lord was exceeding abundant with faith and love which is in Christ Jesus. 15 This *is* a faithful saying, and worthy of all acceptation, that Christ Jesus came into the world to save sinners; of whom I am chief. 16 Howbeit for this cause I obtained mercy, that in me first Jesus Christ might shew forth all longsuffering, for a pattern to them which should hereafter believe on him to life everlasting. 17 Now unto the King eternal, immortal, invisible, the only wise God, *be* honour and glory for ever and ever. Amen. 18 This charge I commit unto thee, son Timothy, according to the prophecies which went before on thee, that thou by them mightest war a good warfare; 19 Holding faith, and a good conscience; which some having put away, concern-

Living Bible

12 How thankful I am to Christ Jesus our Lord for choosing me as one of his messengers, and giving me the strength to be faithful to him, 13 even though I used to scoff at the name of Christ. I hunted down his people, harming them in every way I could. But God had mercy on me because I didn't know what I was doing, for I didn't know Christ at that time. 14 Oh, how kind our Lord was, for he showed me how to trust him and become full of the love of Christ Jesus.

15 How true it is, and how I long that everyone should know it, that Christ Jesus came into the world to save sinners—and I was the greatest of them all. 16 But God had mercy on me so that Christ Jesus could use me as an example to show everyone how patient he is with even the worst sinners, so that others will realize that they, too, can have everlasting life. 17 Glory and honor to God forever and ever. He is the King of the ages, the unseen one who never dies; he alone is God, and full of wisdom. Amen.

18 Now, Timothy, my son, here is my command to you: Fight well in the Lord's battles, just as the Lord told us through his prophets that you would. 19 Cling tightly to your faith in Christ and always keep your conscience clear, doing what you know is right. For some people have disobeyed their consciences and have deliberately done what they knew was wrong. It isn't surprising that soon they lost their faith in Christ

Today's English Version

Gratitude for God's mercy

12 I give thanks to Christ Jesus our Lord, who has given me strength for my work. I thank him for considering me worthy, and appointing me to serve him, 13 even though in the past I spoke evil of him, and persecuted and insulted him. But God was merciful to me, because I did not believe and so did not know what I was doing. 14 And our Lord poured out his abundant grace on me and gave me the faith and love which are ours in union with Christ Jesus. 15 This is a true saying, to be completely accepted and believed: Christ Jesus came into the world to save sinners. I am the worst of them, 16 but it was for this very reason that God was merciful to me, in order that Christ Jesus might show his full patience in dealing with me, the worst of sinners, as an example for all those who would later believe in him and receive eternal life. 17 To the eternal King, immortal and invisible, the only God—to him be honor and glory forever and ever! Amen.

18 Timothy, my child, I entrust this command to you. It is according to the words of prophecy spoken long ago about you. Let those words be your weapons as you fight the good fight, 19 and keep your faith and clear conscience. Some men have not listened to their conscience, and have

New International Version

The Lord's grace to Paul

12 I thank Christ Jesus our Lord, who has given me strength, that he considered me faithful, appointing me to his service. 13 Even though I was once a blasphemer and a persecutor and a violent man, I was shown mercy because I acted in ignorance and unbelief. 14 The grace of our Lord was poured out on me abundantly, along with the faith and love that are in Christ Jesus.

15 Here is a trustworthy saying that deserves full acceptance: Christ Jesus came into the world to save sinners—of whom I am the worst. 16 But for that very reason I was shown mercy so that in me, the worst of sinners, Christ Jesus might display his unlimited patience as an example for those who would believe on him and receive eternal life. 17 Now to the King eternal, immortal, invisible, the only God, be honor and glory for ever and ever. Amen.

18 Timothy, my son, I give you this instruction in keeping with the prophecies once made about you, so that by following them you may fight the good fight, 19 holding on to faith and a good conscience. Some have rejected these and

Phillips Modern English

1.12 My debt to Jesus Christ

I am deeply grateful to Christ Jesus our Lord (to whom I owe all that I have accomplished) for trusting me enough to appoint me his minister, despite the fact that I had previously blasphemed his name, persecuted and insulted him. I believe he was merciful to me because what I did was done in the ignorance of a man without faith. Our Lord poured out his grace upon me, giving me faith in, and love for, Christ Jesus himself. This statement is completely reliable and should be universally accepted:—"Christ Jesus entered the world to rescue sinners". I realise that I was the worst of them all, and that because of this very fact God was particularly merciful to me. It was a demonstration of the extent of Christ's patience towards the worst of men, to serve as an example to all who in the future should trust him for eternal life.

So to the king of all the ages, the immortal, invisible, and only God, be honour and glory for ever and ever, amen!

1.18 My personal charge to you

Timothy my son, I give you the following charge. It is in full accord with those prophecies made about you, which sent you out to battle for the right armed only with your faith and a clear conscience. Some have laid these simple weapons contemptuously aside and, as far as their faith is concerned, have run their ships on

Revised Standard Version

12 I thank him who has given me strength
for this, Christ Jesus our Lord, because he
judged me faithful by appointing me to his
service, 13 though I formerly blasphemed and
persecuted and insulted him; but I received
mercy because I had acted ignorantly in unbelief, 14 and the grace of our Lord overflowed
for me with the faith and love that are in Christ
Jesus. 15 The saying is sure and worthy of full
acceptance, that Christ Jesus came into the
world to save sinners. And I am the foremost
of sinners; 16 but I received mercy for this
reason, that in me, as the foremost, Jesus Christ
might display his perfect patience for an example to those who were to believe in him for
eternal life. 17 To the King of ages, immortal,
invisible, the only God, be honor and glory for
ever and ever.[b] Amen.
18 This charge I commit to you, Timothy,
my son, in accordance with the prophetic utterances which pointed to you, that inspired by
them you may wage the good warfare, 19 holding faith and a good conscience. By rejecting
conscience, certain persons have made shipwreck

[b] Greek *to the ages of ages.*

Jerusalem Bible

Paul on his own calling

12 I thank Christ Jesus our Lord, who has
given me strength, and who judged me faithful
enough to call me into his service 13 even though
I used to be a blasphemer and did all I could to
injure and discredit the faith. Mercy, however,
was shown me, because until I became a believer
I had been acting in ignorance; 14 and the grace
of our Lord filled me with faith and with the
love that is in Christ Jesus. 15 Here is a saying
that you can rely on and nobody should doubt:
that Christ Jesus came into the world to save
sinners. I myself am the greatest of them; 16 and
if mercy has been shown to me, it is because
Jesus Christ meant to make me the greatest
evidence of his inexhaustible patience for all the
other people who would later have to trust in
him to come to eternal life. 17 To the eternal
King, the undying, invisible and only God, be
honor and glory for ever and ever. Amen.

Timothy's responsibility

18 Timothy, my son, these are the instructions that I am giving you: I ask you to remember the words once spoken over you by the
prophets, and taking them to heart to fight like
a good soldier 19 with faith and a good conscience for your weapons. Some people have
put conscience aside and wrecked their faith in

New English Bible

I thank him who has made me equal to the task, Christ Jesus our Lord; I thank him for judging me worthy of this trust and appointing me to his service—although in the past I had met him with abuse and persecution and outrage. But because I acted ignorantly in unbelief I was dealt with mercifully; the grace of our Lord was lavished upon me, with the faith and love which are ours in Christ Jesus.

Here are words you may trust, words that merit full acceptance: 'Christ Jesus came into the world to save sinners'; and among them I stand first. But I was mercifully dealt with for this very purpose, that Jesus Christ might find in me the first occasion for displaying all his patience, and that I might be typical of all who were in future to have faith in him and gain eternal life. Now to the King of all worlds, immortal, invisible, the only God, be honour and glory for ever and ever! Amen.

This charge, son Timothy, I lay upon you, following that prophetic utterance which first pointed you out to me. So fight gallantly, armed with faith and a good conscience. It was through spurning conscience that certain persons made

King James Version

ing faith have made shipwreck: 20 Of whom is Hymeneus and Alexander; whom I have delivered unto Satan, that they may learn not to blaspheme.

2 I exhort therefore, that, first of all, supplications, prayers, intercessions, *and* giving of thanks, be made for all men; 2 For kings, and *for* all that are in authority; that we may lead a quiet and peaceable life in all godliness and honesty. 3 For this *is* good and acceptable in the sight of God our Saviour; 4 Who will have all men to be saved, and to come unto the knowledge of the truth. 5 For *there is* one God, and one mediator between God and men, the man Christ Jesus; 6 Who gave himself a ransom for all, to be testified in due time. 7 Whereunto I am ordained a preacher, and an apostle, (I speak the truth in Christ, *and* lie not,) a teacher of the Gentiles in faith and verity. 8 I will therefore that men pray every where, lifting up

Living Bible

after defying God like that. 20 Hymenaeus and Alexander are two examples of this. I had to give them over to Satan to punish them until they could learn not to bring shame to the name of Christ.

2 Here are my directions: Pray much for others; plead for God's mercy upon them; give thanks for all he is going to do for them.

2 Pray in this way for kings and all others who are in authority over us, or are in places of high responsibility, so that we can live in peace and quietness, spending our time in godly living and thinking much about the Lord.[a] 3 This is good and pleases God our Savior, 4 for he longs for all to be saved and to understand this truth: 5 *That God is on one side and all the people on the other side, and Christ Jesus, himself man, is between them to bring them together,* 6 *by giving his life for all mankind.*

This is the message which at the proper time God gave to the world. 7 And I have been chosen —this is the absolute truth—as God's minister and missionary to teach this truth to the Gentiles, and to show them God's plan of salvation through faith. 8 So I want men everywhere to pray with holy hands lifted up to God, free from

[a] Literally, "in gravity."

Today's English Version

made a ruin of their faith. 20 Among them are Hymenaeus and Alexander, whom I have handed over to the power of Satan, so that they will be taught to stop speaking evil of God.

Church worship

2 First of all, then, I urge that petitions, prayers, requests, and thanksgivings be offered to God for all men; 2 for kings and all others who are in authority, that we may live a quiet and peaceful life, in entire godliness and proper conduct. 3 This is good and it pleases God our Savior, 4 who wants all men to be saved and to come to know the truth. 5 For there is one God, and there is one who brings God and men together, the man Christ Jesus, 6 who gave himself to redeem all men. That was the proof, at the right time, that God wants all men to be saved, 7 and this is why I was sent as an apostle and teacher of the Gentiles, to proclaim the message of faith and truth. I am not lying, I am telling the truth!

8 I want men everywhere to pray, men who are dedicated to God and can lift up their hands in prayer without anger or argument.

New International Version

so have shipwrecked their faith. 20 Among them are Hymenaeus and Alexander, whom I have handed over to Satan to be taught not to blaspheme.

Instructions on worship

2 I urge, then, first of all, that requests, prayers, intercession and thanksgiving be made for everyone—2 for kings and all those in authority, that we may live peaceful and quiet lives in all godliness and holiness. 3 This is good, and pleases God our Savior, 4 who wants all men to be saved and to come to a knowledge of the truth. 5 For there is one God and one mediator between God and men, the man Christ Jesus, 6 who gave himself as a ransom for all men— the testimony given in its proper time. 7 And for this purpose I was appointed a herald and an apostle—I am telling the truth, I am not lying —and a teacher of the true faith to the Gentiles.

8 I want men everywhere to lift up holy hands in prayer, without anger or disputing.

Phillips Modern English

the rocks. Hymenaeus and Alexander are men of this sort, and as a matter of fact I had to hand them over to Satan to teach them not to blaspheme.

Here then is my charge:

First, supplications, prayers, intercessions and thanksgivings should be made on behalf of all men: for kings and rulers in positions of responsibility, so that our common life may be lived in peace and quiet, with a proper sense of God and of our responsibility to him for what we do with our lives. In the sight of God our saviour this is undoubtedly the right way to pray; for his purpose is that all men should be saved and come to know the truth. For there is only one God, and only one intermediary between God and men, the Man Christ Jesus. He gave himself as a ransom for all men—an act of redemption which stands at all times as a witness to what he is. I was appointed proclaimer and messenger of this to teach (I speak the sober truth; I do not lie) the gentile world to believe and know the truth.

2.8 *My views on men and women in the Church*

Therefore, I want the men to pray in all the churches with sincerity, without resentment or

Revised Standard Version

of their faith, 20 among them Hymenaeus and
Alexander, whom I have delivered to Satan
that they may learn not to blaspheme.

2 First of all, then, I urge that supplications, prayers, intercessions, and thanksgivings be made for all men, 2 for kings and all
who are in high positions, that we may lead a
quiet and peaceable life, godly and respectful
in every way. 3 This is good, and it is acceptable in the sight of God our Savior, 4 who desires all men to be saved and to come to the
knowledge of the truth. 5 For there is one God,
and there is one mediator between God and
men, the man Christ Jesus, 6 who gave himself
as a ransom for all, the testimony to which was
borne at the proper time. 7 For this I was appointed a preacher and apostle (I am telling the
truth, I am not lying), a teacher of the Gentiles in faith and truth.
8 I desire then that in every place the men
should pray, lifting holy hands without anger or

Jerusalem Bible

consequence. 20 I mean men like Hymenaeus
and Alexander, whom I have handed over to
Satan to teach them not to be blasphemous.

Liturgical prayer

2 My advice is that, first of all, there should
be prayers offered for everyone—petitions,
intercessions and thanksgiving—2 and especially
for kings and others in authority, so that we may
be able to live religious and reverent lives in
peace and quiet. 3 To do this is right, and will
please God our Savior: 4 he wants everyone to
be saved and reach full knowledge of the truth.
5 For there is only one God, and there is only
one mediator between God and mankind, himself a man, Christ Jesus, 6 who sacrificed himself
as a ransom for them all. He is the evidence of
this, sent at the appointed time, and 7 I have
been named a herald and apostle of it and—I
am telling the truth and no lie—a teacher of the
faith and the truth to the pagans.
8 In every place, then, I want the men to lift
their hands up reverently in prayer, with no
anger or argument.

New English Bible

shipwreck of their faith, among them Hymenaeus and Alexander, whom I consigned to Satan, in the hope that through this discipline they might learn not to be blasphemous.

2 First of all, then, I urge that petitions, prayers, intercessions, and thanksgivings be offered for all men; for sovereigns and all in high office, that we may lead a tranquil and quiet life in full observance of religion and high standards of morality. Such prayer is right, and approved by God our Saviour, whose will it is that all men should find salvation and come to know the truth. For there is one God, and also one mediator between God and men, Christ Jesus, himself man, who sacrificed himself to win freedom for all mankind, so providing, at the fitting time, proof of the divine purpose; of this I was appointed herald and apostle (this is no lie, but the truth), to instruct the nations in the true faith.

It is my desire, therefore, that everywhere prayers be said by the men of the congregation, who shall lift up their hands with a pure intention, excluding angry or quarrelsome thoughts.

King James Version

holy hands, without wrath and doubting. 9 In
like manner also, that women adorn themselves
in modest apparel, with shamefacedness and sobriety; not with braided hair, or gold, or pearls,
or costly array; 10 But (which becometh women
professing godliness) with good works. 11 Let
the woman learn in silence with all subjection.
12 But I suffer not a woman to teach, nor to
usurp authority over the man, but to be in silence. 13 For Adam was first formed, then Eve.
14 And Adam was not deceived, but the woman
being deceived was in the transgression. 15 Notwithstanding she shall be saved in childbearing,
if they continue in faith and charity and holiness
with sobriety.

3 This *is* a true saying, If a man desire the
office of a bishop, he desireth a good work.
2 A bishop then must be blameless, the husband
of one wife, vigilant, sober, of good behaviour,
given to hospitality, apt to teach; 3 Not given
to wine, no striker, not greedy of filthy lucre;
but patient, not a brawler, not covetous; 4 One
that ruleth well his own house, having his chil-

Living Bible

sin and anger and resentment. 9, 10 And the
women should be the same way, quiet and sensible in manner and clothing. Christian women
should be noticed for being kind and good, not
for the way they fix their hair or because of their
jewels or fancy clothes. 11 Women should listen
and learn quietly and humbly.

12 I never let women teach men or lord it over
them. Let them be silent in your church meetings.
13 Why? Because God made Adam first, and afterwards he made Eve. 14 And it was not Adam
who was fooled by Satan, but Eve, and sin was
the result. 15 So God sent pain and suffering to
women when their children are born, but he will
save their souls if they trust in him, living quiet,
good, and loving lives.

3 It is a true saying that if a man wants to
be a pastor[a] he has a good ambition. 2 For
a pastor must be a good man whose life cannot
be spoken against. He must have only one wife,
and he must be hard working and thoughtful,
orderly, and full of good deeds. He must enjoy
having guests in his home, and must be a good
Bible teacher. 3 He must not be a drinker or
quarrelsome, but he must be gentle and kind, and
not be one who loves money. 4 He must have a
well-behaved family, with children who obey

[a] More literally, "church leader" or "presiding elder."

Today's English Version

9 I also want women to be modest and sensible about their clothes and to dress properly;
not with fancy hair styles, or with gold ornaments or pearls or expensive dresses, 10 but with
good deeds, as is proper for women who claim
to be religious. 11 Women should learn in silence and all humility. 12 I do not allow women
to teach or to have authority over men; they
must keep quiet. 13 For Adam was created first,
and then Eve. 14 And it was not Adam who was
deceived; it was the woman who was deceived
and broke God's law. 15 But a woman will be
saved through having children, if she perseveres
in faith and love and holiness, with modesty.

Leaders in the church

3 This is a true saying: If a man is eager to be
a church leader he desires an excellent work.
2 A church leader must be a man without fault;
he must have only one wife, be sober, self-
controlled, and orderly; he must welcome strangers in his home; he must be able to teach; 3 he
must not be a drunkard or a violent man, but
gentle and peaceful; he must not love money;
4 he must be able to manage his own family
well, and make his children obey him with all

New International Version

9 I also want women to dress modestly, with
decency and propriety, not with braided hair or
gold or pearls or expensive clothes, 10 but with
good deeds, appropriate for women who profess
to worship God.

11 A woman should learn in quietness and
full submission. 12 I do not permit a woman to
teach or to have authority over a man; she must
be silent. 13 For Adam was formed first, then
Eve. 14 And Adam was not the one deceived; it
was the woman who was deceived and became
a sinner. 15 But women will be kept safe[a]
through childbirth, if they continue in faith, love
and holiness with propriety.

Overseers and deacons

3 Here is a trustworthy saying: If anyone
sets his heart on being an overseer,[b] he desires a noble task. 2 Now the overseer[b] must be
above reproach, the husband of but one wife,
temperate, self-controlled, respectable, hospitable,
able to teach, 3 not given to much wine, not
violent but gentle, not quarrelsome, not a lover
of money. 4 He must manage his own family
well and see that his children obey him with

[a] Or *be saved.* [b] Or *bishop.*

Phillips Modern English

doubt in their minds. Similarly, the women should be dressed neatly, their adornment being modesty and serious-mindedness. It is not for them to have an elaborate hair-style, jewellery of gold or pearls, or expensive clothes, but, as becomes women who profess to believe in God, it is for them to show their faith by the way they live. A woman should learn quietly and humbly. Personally, I don't allow women to teach, nor do I ever put them in authority over men—I believe they should be quiet. (My reasons are that man was created before woman. Further, it was Eve and not Adam who was first deceived and fell into sin. Nevertheless I believe that women will come safely through child-birth if they maintain a life of faith, love, holiness and modesty.)

3.1 The sort of men to bear office: bishops

It is quite true to say that a man who sets his heart on leadership has laudable ambition. Well, for the office of a bishop a man must be of blameless reputation, he must be married to one wife only, and be a man of self-control and discretion. He must be a man of disciplined life; he must be hospitable and have the gift of teaching. He must be neither intemperate nor violent, but gentle. He must not be a controversialist nor must he be greedy for money. He must have proper authority in his own household, and be

Revised Standard Version

quarreling; 9 also that women should adorn
themselves modestly and sensibly in seemly apparel, not with braided hair or gold or pearls
or costly attire 10 but by good deeds, as befits
women who profess religion. 11 Let a woman
learn in silence with all submissiveness. 12 I permit no woman to teach or to have authority
over men; she is to keep silent. 13 For Adam
was formed first, then Eve; 14 and Adam was
not deceived, but the woman was deceived and
became a transgressor. 15 Yet woman will be
saved through bearing children,[c] if she continues[d] in faith and love and holiness, with modesty.

3 The saying is sure: If any one aspires to the office of bishop, he desires a noble task.
2 Now a bishop must be above reproach, the
husband of one wife, temperate, sensible, dignified, hospitable, an apt teacher, 3 no drunkard,
not violent but gentle, not quarrelsome, and no
lover of money. 4 He must manage his own
household well, keeping his children submissive

[c] Or *by the birth of the child.* [d] Greek *they continue.*

Jerusalem Bible

Women in the assembly

9 Similarly, I direct that women are to wear
suitable clothes and to be dressed quietly and
modestly, without braided hair or gold and jewelry or expensive clothes; their adornment is
10 to do the sort of good works that are proper
for women who profess to be religious. 11 During instruction, a woman should be quiet and
respectful. 12 I am not giving permission for a
woman to teach or to tell a man what to do. A
woman ought not to speak, 13 because Adam was
formed first and Eve afterward, 14 and it was not
Adam who was led astray but the woman who
was led astray and fell into sin. 15 Nevertheless,
she will be saved by childbearing, provided she
lives a modest life and is constant in faith and
love and holiness.

The elder in charge

3 Here is a saying that you can rely on: To want to be a presiding elder[a] is to want to
do a noble work. 2 That is why the president
must have an impeccable character. He must
not have been married more than once, and he
must be temperate, discreet and courteous, hospitable and a good teacher; 3 not a heavy
drinker, not hot-tempered, but kind and peaceable. He must not be a lover of money. 4 He
must be a man who manages his own family well

[a] The word *episcopos* used here by Paul had not yet acquired the same meaning as "bishop."

New English Bible

Women again must dress in becoming manner, modestly and soberly, not with elaborate hair-styles, not decked out with gold or pearls, or expensive clothes, but with good deeds, as befits women who claim to be religious. A woman must be a learner, listening quietly and with due submission. I do not permit a woman to be a teacher, nor must woman domineer over man; she should be quiet. For Adam was created first, and Eve afterwards; and it was not Adam who was deceived; it was the woman who, yielding to deception, fell into sin. Yet she will be saved through motherhood[q]—if only women continue in faith,[r] love, and holiness, with a sober mind.

3 There is a popular saying:[s] 'To aspire to leadership is an honourable ambition.' Our leader, therefore, or bishop, must be above reproach, faithful to his one wife,[t] sober, temperate, courteous, hospitable, and a good teacher; he must not be given to drink, or a brawler, but of a forbearing disposition, avoiding quarrels, and no lover of money. He must be one who manages his own household well and wins obedi-

[q] *Or* saved through the Birth of the Child, *or* brought safely through childbirth. [r] *Or* if only husband and wife continue in mutual fidelity . . . [s] *Some witnesses read* Here are words you may trust, *which some interpreters attach to the end of the preceding paragraph.* [t] *Or* married to one wife, *or* married only once.

King James Version

dren in subjection with all gravity; 5 (For if a
man know not how to rule his own house, how
shall he take care of the church of God?) 6 Not
a novice, lest being lifted up with pride he fall
into the condemnation of the devil. 7 Moreover
he must have a good report of them which are
without; lest he fall into reproach and the snare
of the devil. 8 Likewise *must* the deacons *be*
grave, not double-tongued, not given to much
wine, not greedy of filthy lucre; 9 Holding the
mystery of the faith in a pure conscience. 10 And
let these also first be proved; then let them use
the office of a deacon, being *found* blameless.
11 Even so *must their* wives *be* grave, not slanderers, sober, faithful in all things. 12 Let the
deacons be the husbands of one wife, ruling their
children and their own houses well. 13 For they
that have used the office of a deacon well purchase to themselves a good degree, and great
boldness in the faith which is in Christ Jesus.

Living Bible

quickly and quietly. 5 For if a man can't make
his own little family behave, how can he help
the whole church?
6 The pastor must not be a new Christian, because he might be proud of being chosen so soon,
and pride comes before a fall. (Satan's downfall
is an example.) 7 Also, he must be well spoken
of by people outside the church—those who
aren't Christians—so that Satan can't trap him
with many accusations, and leave him without
freedom to lead his flock.
8 The deacons must be the same sort of good,
steady men as the pastors. They must not be
heavy drinkers and must not be greedy for
money. 9 They must be earnest, wholehearted
followers of Christ who is the hidden Source of
their faith. 10 Before they are asked to be
deacons they should be given other jobs in the
church as a test of their character and ability,
and if they do well, then they may be chosen as
deacons.
11 Their wives must be thoughtful, not heavy
drinkers, not gossipers, but faithful in everything
they do. 12 Deacons should have only one wife
and they should have happy, obedient families.
13 Those who do well as deacons will be well rewarded both by respect from others and also by
developing their own confidence and bold trust
in the Lord.

Today's English Version

respect. 5 For if a man does not know how to
manage his own family, how can he take care
of the church of God? 6 He must not be a man
who has been recently converted; else he will
swell up with pride and be condemned, as the
Devil was. 7 He should be a man who is respected by the people outside the church, so
that he will not be disgraced and fall into the
Devil's trap.

Helpers in the church

8 Church helpers must also be of a good character and sincere; they must not drink too much
wine or be greedy; 9 they should hold to the
revealed truth of the faith with a clear conscience. 10 They should be tested first, and then,
if they pass the test, they should serve. 11 Their
wives also must be of good character, and not
gossip; they must be sober and honest in everything. 12 A church helper must have only one
wife, and be able to manage his children and
family well. 13 Those who do a good work win
for themselves a good standing and are able to
speak boldly about their faith in Christ Jesus.

New International Version

proper respect. 5 (If anyone does not know
how to manage his own family, how can he
take care of God's church?) 6 He must not be
a recent convert, or he may become conceited
and fall under the same judgment as the devil.
7 He must also have a good reputation with
outsiders, so that he will not fall into disgrace
and into the devil's trap.
8 Deacons, likewise, are to be men worthy of
respect, sincere, not indulging in much wine, and
not pursuing dishonest gain. 9 They must keep
hold of the deep truths of the faith with a clear
conscience. 10 They must first be tested; and then
if there is nothing against them, let them serve
as deacons.
11 In the same way, their wives[c] are to be
women worthy of respect, not malicious talkers
but temperate and trustworthy in everything.
12 A deacon must be the husband of but one
wife and must manage his children and his
household well. 13 Those who have served well
gain an excellent standing and great assurance
in their faith in Christ Jesus.

[c] Or *way, deaconesses.*

Phillips Modern English

able to control and command the respect of his children. (For if a man cannot rule in his own house how can he look after a church of God?) He must not be a beginner in the faith, for fear of his becoming conceited and sharing the devil's downfall. He should, in addition to the above qualifications, have a good reputation with the outside world, in case his good name is attacked and he is caught by the devil that way.

3.8 Deacons

Deacons, similarly, should be men of serious outlook and sincere conviction. They too should be temperate and not sordidly greedy for profit. They should hold the mystery of the faith with complete sincerity.

Let them serve a period of probation first, and only serve as deacons if they prove satisfactory. Their wives should share their serious outlook, and must be women of discretion and self-control—women who can be thoroughly trusted. Deacons should be men with only one wife, able to control their children and manage their own households properly. Those who do well as deacons earn for themselves a proper standing, as well as the ability to speak freely on matters of the Christian faith.

Revised Standard Version

and respectful in every way; 5 for if a man does
not know how to manage his own household,
how can he care for God's church? 6 He must
not be a recent convert, or he may be puffed
up with conceit and fall into the condemnation
of the devil;[f] 7 moreover he must be well
thought of by outsiders, or he may fall into
reproach and the snare of the devil.[f]
8 Deacons likewise must be serious, not
double-tongued, not addicted to much wine, not
greedy for gain; 9 they must hold the mystery of
the faith with a clear conscience. 10 And let them
also be tested first; then if they prove themselves
blameless let them serve as deacons. 11 The
women likewise must be serious, no slanderers,
but temperate, faithful in all things. 12 Let deacons be the husband of one wife, and let them
manage their children and their households well;
13 for those who serve well as deacons gain a
good standing for themselves and also great confidence in the faith which is in Christ Jesus.

[*f*] Or *slanderer*.

Jerusalem Bible

and brings his children up to obey him and be
well-behaved: 5 how can any man who does
not understand how to manage his own family
have responsibility for the church of God? 6 He
should not be a new convert, in case pride might
turn his head and then he might be condemned
as the devil was condemned. 7 It is also necessary that people outside the Church should
speak well of him, so that he never gets a bad
reputation and falls into the devil's trap.

Deacons

8 In the same way, deacons must be respectable men whose word can be trusted, moderate
in the amount of wine they drink and with no
squalid greed for money. 9 They must be conscientious believers in the mystery of the faith.
10 They are to be examined first, and only admitted to serve as deacons if there is nothing
against them. 11 In the same way, the women
must be respectable, not gossips but sober and
quite reliable. 12 Deacons must not have been
married more than once, and must be men who
manage their children and families well. 13 Those
of them who carry out their duties well as
deacons will earn a high standing for themselves
and be rewarded with great assurance in their
work for the faith in Christ Jesus.

New English Bible

ence from his children, and a man of the highest principles. If a man does not know how to control his own family, how can he look after a congregation of God's people? He must not be a convert newly baptized, for fear the sin of conceit should bring upon him a judgement contrived by the devil.[c] He must moreover have a good reputation with the non-Christian public, so that he may not be exposed to scandal and get caught in the devil's snare.

Deacons, likewise, must be men of high principle, not indulging in double talk, given neither to excessive drinking nor to money-grubbing. They must be men who combine a clear conscience with a firm hold on the deep truths of our faith. No less than bishops, they must first undergo a scrutiny, and if there is no mark against them, they may serve. Their wives,[d] equally, must be women of high principle, who will not talk scandal, sober and trustworthy in every way. A deacon must be faithful to his one wife,[b] and good at managing his children and his own household. For deacons with a good record of service may claim a high standing and the right to speak openly on matters of the Christian faith.

[*c*] *Or* the judgement once passed on the devil. [*d*] *Or* . . . serve. Deaconesses . . . [*b*] *Or* married to one wife, *or* married only once.

King James Version

14 These things write I unto thee, hoping to come
unto thee shortly: 15 But if I tarry long, that
thou mayest know how thou oughtest to behave
thyself in the house of God, which is the church
of the living God, the pillar and ground of the
truth. 16 And without controversy great is the
mystery of godliness: God was manifest in
the flesh, justified in the Spirit, seen of angels,
preached unto the Gentiles, believed on in the
world, received up into glory.

4 Now the Spirit speaketh expressly, that in
the latter times some shall depart from the
faith, giving heed to seducing spirits, and doctrines of devils; 2 Speaking lies in hypocrisy;
having their conscience seared with a hot iron;
3 Forbidding to marry, *and commanding* to abstain from meats, which God hath created to be
received with thanksgiving of them which believe

Living Bible

14 I am writing these things to you now, even
though I hope to be with you soon, 15 so that
if I don't come for awhile you will know what
kind of men you should choose as officers for
the church of the living God, which contains and
holds high the truth of God.

16 It is quite true that the way to live a godly
life is not an easy matter. But the answer lies in
Christ, who came to earth as a man, was proved
spotless and pure in his Spirit, was served by
angels, was preached among the nations, was accepted by men everywhere and was received up
again to his glory in heaven.

4 But the Holy Spirit tells us clearly that in
the last times some in the church will turn
away from Christ and become eager followers of
teachers with devil-inspired ideas. 2 These teachers will tell lies with straight faces and do it so
often that their consciences won't even bother
them. 3 They will say it is wrong to be married
and wrong to eat meat, even though God gave
these things to well-taught Christians to enjoy and

Today's English Version

The great secret

14 As I write this letter to you, I hope to
come and see you soon. 15 But if I delay, this
letter will let you know how we should conduct
ourselves in God's household, which is the church
of the living God, the pillar and support of the
truth. 16 No one can deny how great is the
secret of our religion.

He appeared in human form,
was shown to be right by the Spirit, and
was seen by angels.
He was preached among the nations,
was believed in the world, and was taken
up to heaven.

False teachers

4 The Spirit says clearly that some men will
abandon the faith in later times; they will
obey lying spirits and follow the teachings of
demons. 2 These teachings come from the deceit
of men who are liars, and whose consciences are
dead, as if burnt with a hot iron. 3 Such men
teach that it is wrong to marry and to eat certain
foods. But God created these foods to be eaten,
after a prayer of thanks, by those who are believers and have come to know the truth.

New International Version

14 Although I hope to come to you soon, I am
writing you these instructions so that, 15 if I am
delayed, you will know how people ought to
conduct themselves in God's household, which
is the church of the living God, the pillar and
foundation of the truth. 16 Beyond all question,
the mystery of godliness is great:

He[d] appeared in a body,
was vindicated by the Spirit,
was seen by angels,
was preached among the nations,
was believed on in the world,
was taken up in glory.

Instructions to Timothy

4 The Spirit clearly says that in later times
some will abandon the faith and follow deceiving spirits and things taught by demons.
2 Such teachings come through hypocritical liars,
whose consciences have been seared as with a
hot iron. 3 They forbid people to marry and
order them to abstain from certain foods, which
God created to be received with thanksgiving by
those who believe and who know the truth.

[d] Some MSS read *God*.

Phillips Modern English

3.14 The tremendous responsibility of being God's minister

At the moment of writing I hope to be with you soon, but if there should be any delay then what I have written will show you the sort of character men of God's household ought to have. It is, remember, the Church of the living God, the pillar and the foundation of the truth. No one would deny that this religion of ours is a tremendous mystery, resting as it does on the one who appeared in human flesh, was vindicated in the spirit, seen by angels; proclaimed among the nations, believed in throughout the world, taken back to Heaven in glory.

4.1 Beware of false teachers: warn your people

God's Spirit specifically tells us that in later days there will be men who abandon the true faith and allow themselves to be spiritually seduced by teachings of demons, teachings given by men who are lying hypocrites, whose consciences are as dead as seared flesh. These men forbid marriage and command abstinence from foods—good things which God created to be thankfully enjoyed by those who believe in him

Revised Standard Version

14 I hope to come to you soon, but I am writing these instructions to you so that, 15 if I am
delayed, you may know how one ought to behave in the household of God, which is the church of the living God, the pillar and bulwark of the
truth. 16 Great indeed, we confess, is the mystery of our religion:

He[h] was manifested in the flesh,
vindicated[i] in the Spirit,
seen by angels,
preached among the nations,
believed on in the world,
taken up in glory.

4 Now the Spirit expressly says that in later times some will depart from the faith by giving heed to deceitful spirits and doctrines of demons,
2 through the pretensions of liars whose consciences are seared,
3 who forbid marriage and enjoin abstinence from foods which God created to be received with thanksgiving by those

[*h*] Greek *Who;* other ancient authorities read *God;* others, *Which.* [*i*] Or *justified.*

Jerusalem Bible

The Church and the mystery of the spiritual life

14 At the moment of writing to you, I am hoping that I may be with you soon;
15 but in case I should be delayed, I wanted you to know how people ought to behave in God's family—that is, in the Church of the living God, which upholds the truth and keeps it safe.
16 Without any doubt, the mystery of our religion is very deep indeed:

He was made visible in the flesh,
attested by the Spirit,
seen by angels,
proclaimed to the pagans,
believed in by the world,
taken up in glory.

False teachers

4 The Spirit has explicitly said that during the last times there will be some who will desert the faith and choose to listen to deceitful spirits and doctrines that come from the devils;
2 and the cause of this is the lies told by hypocrites whose consciences are branded as though with a red-hot iron[b]:
3 they will say marriage is forbidden, and lay down rules about abstaining from foods which God created to be accepted with thanksgiving by all who believe and who

[*b*] Like runaway slaves.

New English Bible

I am hoping to come to you before long, but I write this in case I am delayed, to let you know how men ought to conduct themselves in God's household, that is, the church of the living God, the pillar and bulwark of the truth. And great beyond all question is the mystery of our religion:

'He who was manifested in the body,
vindicated in the spirit,
seen by angels;
who was proclaimed among the nations,
believed in throughout the world,
glorified in high heaven.'

4 The Spirit says expressly that in after times some will desert from the faith and give their minds to subversive doctrines inspired by devils, through the specious falsehoods of men whose own conscience is branded with the devil's sign. They forbid marriage and inculcate abstinence from certain foods, though God created them to be enjoyed with thanksgiving by believers who

King James Version

and know the truth. 4 For every creature of God
is good, and nothing to be refused, if it be received with thanksgiving: 5 For it is sanctified
by the word of God and prayer. 6 If thou put
the brethren in remembrance of these things,
thou shalt be a good minister of Jesus Christ,
nourished up in the words of faith and of good
doctrine, whereunto thou hast attained. 7 But refuse profane and old wives' fables, and exercise
thyself *rather* unto godliness. 8 For bodily exercise profiteth little: but godliness is profitable
unto all things, having promise of the life that
now is, and of that which is to come. 9 This *is*
a faithful saying, and worthy of all acceptation.
10 For therefore we both labour and suffer reproach, because we trust in the living God, who
is the Saviour of all men, specially of those that
believe. 11 These things command and teach.
12 Let no man despise thy youth; but be thou
an example of the believers, in word, in conversation, in charity, in spirit, in faith, in purity.
13 Till I come, give attendance to reading, to
exhortation, to doctrine. 14 Neglect not the gift

Living Bible

be thankful for. 4 For everything God made is
good, and we may eat it gladly if we are thankful
for it, 5 and if we ask God to bless it, for it is
made good by the Word of God and prayer.
6 If you explain this to the others you will be
doing your duty as a worthy pastor who is fed
by faith and by the true teaching you have followed.
7 Don't waste time arguing over foolish ideas
and silly myths and legends. Spend your time
and energy in the exercise of keeping spiritually
fit. 8 Bodily exercise is all right, but spiritual exercise is much more important and is a tonic for
all you do. So exercise yourself spiritually and
practice being a better Christian, because that
will help you not only now in this life, but in the
next life too. 9, 10 This is the truth and everyone
should accept it. We work hard and suffer much
in order that people will believe it, for our hope
is in the living God who died for all, and particularly for those who have accepted his salvation.
11 Teach these things and make sure everyone
learns them well. 12 Don't let anyone think little
of you because you are young. Be their ideal; let
them follow the way you teach and live; be a
pattern for them in your love, your faith, and
your clean thoughts. 13 Until I get there, read
and explain the Scriptures to the church; preach
God's Word.
14 Be sure to use the abilities God has given

Today's English Version

4 Everything that God has created is good; nothing is to be rejected, but all is to be received with
a prayer of thanks; 5 because the word of God
and the prayer make it acceptable to God.

A good servant of Christ Jesus

6 If you give these instructions to the brothers
you will be a good servant of Christ Jesus, as
you feed yourself spiritually on the words of
faith and of the true teaching which you have
followed. 7 But keep away from those godless
legends, which are not worth telling. Keep
yourself in training for a godly life. 8 Physical
exercise has some value in it, but spiritual exercise is valuable in every way, because it promises life both for now and for the future. 9 This
is a true saying, to be completely accepted and
believed. 10 That is why we struggle and work
hard, because we have placed our hope in the
living God, who is Savior of all men, and especially of those who believe.
11 Command and teach these things. 12 Do
not let anyone look down on you because you are
young, but be an example for the believers, in
your speech, your conduct, your love, faith, and
purity. 13 Give your time and effort, until I
come, to the public reading of the Scriptures,
and to preaching and teaching. 14 Do not neglect

New International Version

4 For everything God created is good, and nothing is to be rejected if it is received with thanksgiving, 5 because it is consecrated by the word
of God and prayer.
6 If you point these things out to the brothers,
you will be a good minister of Christ Jesus,
brought up in the truths of the faith and of the
good teaching that you have followed. 7 Have
nothing to do with godless myths and old wives'
tales; rather, train yourself to be godly. 8 For
physical training is of some value, but godliness
has value for all things, holding promise for
both the present life and the life to come.
9 This is a trustworthy saying that deserves
full acceptance 10 (and for this we labor and
strive), that we have put our hope in the living
God, who is the Savior of all men, and especially
of those who believe.
11 Command and teach these things. 12 Don't
let anyone look down on you because you are
young, but set an example for the believers in
speech, in life, in love, in faith and in purity.
13 Until I come, devote yourself to the public
reading of Scripture, to preaching and to teaching. 14 Do not neglect your gift, which was

Phillips Modern English

and know the truth. Everything God made is good, and is meant to be gratefully used, not despised. The holiness or otherwise of a certain food, for instance, depends not on its nature but on whether it is eaten thankfully or not. It is consecrated by the word of God and by prayer.

You will be a faithful minister of Christ Jesus if you remind your church members of these things. You will show yourself as a man nourished by the message of the true faith and by the sound teaching he has followed. But steer clear of all these heathen old-wives' tales.

Take time and trouble to keep yourself spiritually fit. Bodily fitness has a limited value, but spiritual fitness is of unlimited value, for it holds promise both for this present life and for the life to come. There is no doubt about this at all; it is a truth that you can accept completely. It is because we realise the paramount importance of the spiritual that we labour and struggle. We place all our hopes upon the living God, the Saviour of all men, and especially of those who believe in him. These convictions should be the basis of your instruction and teaching.

4.12 A little personal advice

Don't let anyone look down on you because you are young: see that they look up to you because you are an example to believers in your speech and behaviour, in your love and faith and sincerity. Concentrate until my arrival on your reading and on your preaching and teaching. Do not neglect the special gift that was given to

Revised Standard Version

who believe and know the truth. 4 For everything created by God is good, and nothing is to
be rejected if it is received with thanksgiving;
5 for then it is consecrated by the word of God
and prayer.
6 If you put these instructions before the
brethren, you will be a good minister of Christ
Jesus, nourished on the words of the faith and
of the good doctrine which you have followed.
7 Have nothing to do with godless and silly
myths. Train yourself in godliness; 8 for while
bodily training is of some value, godliness is of
value in every way, as it holds promise for the
present life and also for the life to come. 9 The
saying is sure and worthy of full acceptance.
10 For to this end we toil and strive,[j] because
we have our hope set on the living God, who is
the Savior of all men, especially of those who
believe.
11 Command and teach these things. 12 Let no
one despise your youth, but set the believers an
example in speech and conduct, in love, in faith,
in purity. 13 Till I come, attend to the public
reading of scripture, to preaching, to teaching.
14 Do not neglect the gift you have, which was

[j] Other ancient authorities read *suffer reproach*.

Jerusalem Bible

know the truth.[c] 4 Everything God has created is
good, and no food is to be rejected, provided
grace is said for it: 5 the word of God and the
prayer make it holy. 6 If you put all this to the
brothers, you will be a good servant of Christ
Jesus and show that you have really digested the
teaching of the faith and the good doctrine
which you have always followed. 7 Have nothing
to do with godless myths and old wives' tales.
Train yourself spiritually. 8 "Physical exercises
are useful enough, but the usefulness of spiritual-
ity is unlimited, since it holds out the reward
of life here and now and of the future life as
well"; 9 that is a saying that you can rely on and
nobody should doubt it. 10 I mean that the point
of all our toiling and battling is that we have
put our trust in the living God and he is the
savior of the whole human race but particularly
of all believers. 11 This is what you are to en-
force in your teaching.
12 Do not let people disregard you because
you are young, but be an example to all the
believers in the way you speak and behave, and
in your love, your faith and your purity. 13 Make
use of the time until I arrive by reading to the
people, preaching and teaching. 14 You have in

[c] The rejection of marriage was to be one of the hallmarks of Gnosticism; dietary regulations were more specifically Jewish.

New English Bible

have inward knowledge of the truth. For everything that God created is good, and nothing is to be rejected when it is taken with thanksgiving, since it is hallowed by God's own word and by prayer.

By offering such advice as this to the brotherhood you will prove a good servant of Christ Jesus, bred in the precepts of our faith and of the sound instruction which you have followed. Have nothing to do with those godless myths, fit only for old women. Keep yourself in training for the practice of religion. The training of the body does bring limited benefit, but the benefits of religion are without limit, since it holds promise not only for this life but for the life to come. Here are words you may trust, words that merit full acceptance: 'With this before us we labour and struggle,[a] because[b] we have set our hope on the living God, who is the Saviour of all men'—the Saviour, above all, of believers.

Pass on these orders and these teachings. Let no one slight you because you are young, but make yourself an example to believers in speech and behaviour, in love, fidelity, and purity. Until I arrive devote your attention to the public reading of the scriptures, to exhortation, and to teaching. Do not neglect the spiritual endow-

[a] *Some witnesses read* suffer reproach. [b] *Or* since 'It holds promise . . . to come.' These are words . . . acceptance. For this is the aim of all our labour and struggle, since . . .

King James Version

that is in thee, which was given thee by prophecy, with the laying on of the hands of the presbytery. 15 Meditate upon these things; give thyself wholly to them; that thy profiting may appear to all. 16 Take heed unto thyself, and unto the doctrine; continue in them: for in doing this thou shalt both save thyself, and them that hear thee.

5 Rebuke not an elder, but entreat *him* as a father; *and* the younger men as brethren; 2 The elder women as mothers; the younger as sisters, with all purity. 3 Honour widows that are widows indeed. 4 But if any widow have children or nephews, let them learn first to shew piety at home, and to requite their parents: for that is good and acceptable before God. 5 Now she that is a widow indeed, and desolate, trusteth in God, and continueth in supplications and prayers night and day. 6 But she that liveth in

Living Bible

you through his prophets when the elders of the church laid their hands upon your head. 15 Put these abilities to work; throw yourself into your tasks so that everyone may notice your improvement and progress. 16 Keep a close watch on all you do and think. Stay true to what is right and God will bless you and use you to help others.

5 Never speak sharply to an older man, but plead with him respectfully just as though he were your own father. Talk to the younger men as you would to much loved brothers. 2 Treat the older women as mothers, and the girls as your sisters, thinking only pure thoughts about them.

3 The church should take loving care of women whose husbands have died, if they don't have anyone else to help them. 4 But if they have children or grandchildren, these are the ones who should take the responsibility, for kindness should begin at home, supporting needy parents. This is something that pleases God very much.

5 The church should care for widows who are poor and alone in the world, if they are looking to God for his help and spending much time in prayer; 6 but not if they are spending their time

Today's English Version

the spiritual gift that is in you, which was given to you when the prophets spoke and the elders laid their hands on you. 15 Practice these things and give yourself to them, in order that your progress may be seen by all. 16 Watch yourself, and watch your teaching. Keep on doing these things, because if you do you will save both yourself and those who hear you.

Responsibilities toward believers

5 Do not rebuke an older man, but appeal to him as if he were your father. Treat the younger men as your brothers, 2 the older women as mothers, and the younger women as sisters, with all purity.

3 Show respect for widows who really are widows. 4 But if a widow has children or grandchildren, they should learn first to carry out their religious duties toward their own family and in this way repay their parents and grandparents, because that is what pleases God. 5 The woman who is a true widow, with no one to take care of her, has placed her hope in God and continues to pray and ask him for his help night and day. 6 But the widow who gives

New International Version

given you through a prophetic message when the body of elders laid their hands on you.

15 Be diligent in these matters; give yourself wholly to them, so that everyone may see your progress. 16 Watch your life and doctrine closely. Persevere in them, because if you do, you will save both yourself and your hearers.

Advice about widows, elders and slaves

5 Do not rebuke an older man harshly, but exhort him as if he were your father. Treat younger men as brothers, 2 older women as mothers, and younger women as sisters, with absolute purity.

3 Give proper recognition to widows who are left all alone. 4 But if a widow has children or grandchildren, these should learn first of all to put their religion into practice by caring for their own family and so repaying their parents and grandparents, for this is pleasing to God. 5 The widow who is all alone puts her hope in God and continues night and day to pray and to ask God for help. 6 But the widow who lives

Phillips Modern English

you through prophecy at the time when the assembled elders laid their hands on you. Give your whole attention, all your energies, to these things, so that your progress is plain for all to see. Keep a critical eye both upon your own life and on the teaching you give, and if you continue to follow the line I have indicated you will not only save your own soul but the souls of your hearers as well.

Don't reprimand a senior member of your church, appeal to him as a father. Treat the young men as brothers, and the older women as mothers. Treat the younger women as sisters, and no more.

5.3 How to deal with widows in the church

You should treat with great consideration widows who are really alone in the world. But remember that if a widow has children or grandchildren it is primarily their duty to show the genuineness of their religion in their own homes by repaying their parents for what has been done for them, and God readily accepts such service. But the widow who is really alone and desolate can only hope in God, and she will pray earnestly to him night and day. The widow who

Revised Standard Version

given you by prophetic utterance when the council of elders laid their hands upon you. 15 Practice these duties, devote yourself to them, so that all may see your progress. 16 Take heed to yourself and to your teaching; hold to that, for by so doing you will save both yourself and your hearers.

5 Do not rebuke an older man but exhort him as you would a father; treat younger men like brothers, 2 older women like mothers, younger women like sisters, in all purity.

3 Honor widows who are real widows. 4 If a widow has children or grandchildren, let them first learn their religious duty to their own family and make some return to their parents; for this is acceptable in the sight of God. 5 She who is a real widow, and is left all alone, has set her hope on God and continues in supplications and prayers night and day; 6 whereas she

Jerusalem Bible

you a spiritual gift which was given to you when the prophets spoke and the body of elders laid their hands on you; do not let it lie unused.
15 Think hard about all this, and put it into practice, and everyone will be able to see how you are advancing. 16 Take great care about what you do and what you teach; always do this, and in this way you will save both yourself and those who listen to you.

Pastoral practice

5 Do not speak harshly to a man older than yourself, but advise him as you would your own father; treat the younger men as brothers
2 and older women as you would your mother. Always treat young women with propriety, as if they were sisters.

Widows

3 Be considerate to widows; I mean those who are truly widows. 4 If a widow has children or grandchildren, they are to learn first of all to do their duty to their own families and repay their debt to their parents, because this is what pleases God. 5 But a woman who is really widowed and left without anybody can give herself up to God and consecrate all her days and nights to petitions and prayer. 6 The one

New English Bible

ment you possess, which was given you, under the guidance of prophecy, through the laying on of the hands of the elders as a body.[c]

Make these matters your business and your absorbing interest, so that your progress may be plain to all. Persevere in them, keeping close watch on yourself and your teaching; by doing so you will further the salvation of yourself and your hearers.

5 Never be harsh with an elder; appeal to him as if he were your father. Treat the younger men as brothers, the older women as mothers, and the younger as your sisters, in all purity.

The status of widow is to be granted only to widows who are such in the full sense. But if a widow has children or grandchildren, then they should learn as their first duty to show loyalty to the family and to repay what they owe to their parents and grandparents; for this God approves. A widow, however, in the full sense, one who is alone in the world, has all her hope set on God, and regularly attends the meetings for prayer and worship night and day. But a

[c] *Or* through your ordination as an elder.

King James Version

pleasure is dead while she liveth. 7And these things give in charge, that they may be blameless. 8 But if any provide not for his own, and specially for those of his own house, he hath denied the faith, and is worse than an infidel. 9 Let not a widow be taken into the number under threescore years old, having been the wife of one man, 10 Well reported of for good works; if she have brought up children, if she have lodged strangers, if she have washed the saints' feet, if she have relieved the afflicted, if she have diligently followed every good work. 11 But the younger widows refuse: for when they have begun to wax wanton against Christ, they will marry; 12 Having damnation, because they have cast off their first faith. 13And withal they learn *to be* idle, wandering about from house to house; and not only idle, but tattlers also and busybodies, speaking things which they ought not. 14 I will therefore that the younger women marry, bear children, guide the house, give none occasion to the adversary to speak reproachfully. 15 For some are already turned aside after Satan. 16 If any man or woman that believeth have

Living Bible

running around gossiping, seeking only pleasure and thus ruining their souls. 7 This should be your church rule so that the Christians will know and do what is right.

8 But anyone who won't care for his own relatives when they need help, especially those living in his own family, has no right to say he is a Christian. Such a person is worse than the heathen.

9 A widow who wants to become one of the special church workers[a] should be at least sixty years old and have been married only once. 10 She must be well thought of by everyone because of the good she has done. Has she brought up her children well? Has she been kind to strangers as well as to other Christians? Has she helped those who are sick and hurt? Is she always ready to show kindness?

11 The younger widows should not become members of this special group because after awhile they are likely to disregard their vow to Christ and marry again. 12And so they will stand condemned because they broke their first promise. 13 Besides, they are likely to be lazy and spend their time gossiping around from house to house, getting into other people's business. 14 So I think it is better for these younger widows to marry again and have children, and take care of their own homes; then no one will be able to say anything against them. 15 For I am afraid that some of them have already turned away from the church and been led astray by Satan.

16 Let me remind you again that a widow's

[a] Literally, "enrolled as a widow."

Today's English Version

herself to pleasure has already died, even though she lives. 7 Give them this command, so that no one will find fault with them. 8 But if someone does not take care of his relatives, especially the members of his own family, he has denied the faith and is worse than an unbeliever.

9 Do not add any widow to the list of widows unless she is more than sixty years old. In addition, she must have been married only once, 10 and have a reputation for good deeds: a woman who brought up her children well, received strangers in her home, washed the feet of God's people, helped those in trouble, and gave herself to all kinds of good works.

11 But do not include the younger widows in the list; because when their desires make them want to marry, they turn away from Christ, 12 and so become guilty of breaking their first promise to him. 13 They also learn to waste their time in going around from house to house; but even worse, they learn to be gossips and busybodies, talking of things they should not. 14 So I would rather that the younger widows get married, have children, and take care of their homes, so as to give our enemies no chance of speaking evil of us. 15 For some widows have already turned away to follow Satan. 16 But if any

New International Version

for pleasure is dead even while she lives. 7 Give the people these instructions, too, so that no one may be open to blame. 8 If anyone does not provide for his relatives, and especially for his immediate family, he has denied the faith and is worse than an unbeliever.

9 No widow may be put on the list of widows unless she is over sixty, has been faithful to her husband,[e] 10 and is well-known for her good deeds, such as bringing up children, showing hospitality, washing the feet of the saints, helping those in trouble and devoting herself to all kinds of good deeds.

11 As for younger widows, do not put them on such a list. For when their sensual desires overcome their dedication to Christ, they want to marry. 12 Thus they bring judgment on themselves, because they have broken their first pledge. 13 Besides, they get into the habit of being idle and going about from house to house. And not only do they become idlers, but also gossips and busybodies, saying things they ought not to. 14 So I counsel younger widows to marry, to have children, to manage their homes and to give the enemy no opportunity for slander. 15 Some have in fact already turned away to follow Satan.

16 If any woman who is a believer has widows

[e] Or *has had but one husband.*

Phillips Modern English

plunges into all the pleasure that the world can give her is killing her own soul.

You should therefore make the following rules for the widows, to avoid abuses:

1. You should make it clear that for a man to refuse to look after his own relations, especially those actually living in his house, is a denial of the faith he professes. He is worse than a man who makes no profession.

2. Widows for your church list should be at least sixty years of age, should have had only one husband and have a well-founded reputation for having lived a good life. Some such questions as these should be asked:—has she brought up her children well, has she been hospitable to strangers, has she been willing to serve fellow-Christians in menial ways, has she relieved those in distress, has she, in a word, conscientiously done all the good she can?

3. Don't put the younger widows on your list. My experience is that when their natural desires grow stronger than their spiritual devotion to Christ they want to marry again, thus proving themselves unfaithful to their first loyalty. Moreover, they get into habits of slackness by being so much in and out of other people's houses. In fact they easily become worse than lazy, and degenerate into gossips and busybodies with dangerous tongues.

4. My advice is that the younger widows should, normally, marry again, bear children and run their own households. They should certainly not provide the means for lowering the reputation of the church in the sight of our enemies. Some have already played into their hands.

5. As a general rule it should be taken for

Revised Standard Version

who is self-indulgent is dead even while she lives.
7 Command this, so that they may be without
reproach. 8 If any one does not provide for his
relatives, and especially for his own family, he
has disowned the faith and is worse than an
unbeliever.
9 Let a widow be enrolled if she is not less
than sixty years of age, having been the wife of
one husband; 10 and she must be well attested
for her good deeds, as one who has brought up
children, shown hospitality, washed the feet of
the saints, relieved the afflicted, and devoted herself to doing good in every way. 11 But refuse
to enrol younger widows; for when they grow
wanton against Christ they desire to marry,
12 and so they incur condemnation for having
violated their first pledge. 13 Besides that, they
learn to be idlers, gadding about from house to
house, and not only idlers but gossips and busybodies, saying what they should not. 14 So I
would have younger widows marry, bear children, rule their households, and give the enemy
no occasion to revile us. 15 For some have already strayed after Satan. 16 If any believing

Jerusalem Bible

who thinks only of pleasure is already dead
while she is still alive: 7 remind them of all this,
too, so that their lives may be blameless. 8 Anyone who does not look after his own relations,
especially if they are living with him, has rejected
the faith and is worse than an unbeliever.
9 Enrollment as a widow is permissible only
for a woman at least sixty years old who has had
only one husband. 10 She must be a woman
known for her good works and for the way in
which she has brought up her children, shown
hospitality to strangers and washed the saints'
feet, helped people who are in trouble and been
active in all kinds of good work. 11 Do not
accept young widows because if their natural
desires get stronger than their dedication to
Christ, they want to marry again, 12 and then
people condemn them for being unfaithful to
their original promise. 13 Besides, they learn how
to be idle and go around from house to house;
and then, not merely idle, they learn to be gossips and meddlers in other people's affairs, and
to chatter when they would be better keeping
quiet. 14 I think it is best for young widows to
marry again and have children and a home to
look after, and not give the enemy any chance
to raise a scandal about them; 15 there are
already some who have left us to follow Satan.
16 If a Christian woman has widowed relatives,

New English Bible

widow given over to self-indulgence is as good as dead. Add these orders to the rest, so that the widows may be above reproach. But if anyone does not make provision for his relations, and especially for members of his own household, he has denied the faith and is worse than an unbeliever.

A widow should not be put on the roll under sixty years of age. She must have been faithful in marriage to one man, and must produce evidence of good deeds performed, showing whether she has had the care of children, or given hospitality, or washed the feet of God's people, or supported those in distress—in short, whether she has taken every opportunity of doing good.

Younger widows may not be placed on the roll. For when their passions draw them away from Christ, they hanker after marriage and stand condemned for breaking their troth with him. Moreover, in going round from house to house they learn to be idle, and worse than idle, gossips and busybodies, speaking of things better left unspoken. It is my wish, therefore, that young widows shall marry again, have children, and preside over a home; then they will give no opponent occasion for slander. For there have in fact been some who have taken the wrong turning and gone to the devil.

If a Christian man or woman has widows in

King James Version

widows, let them relieve them, and let not the church be charged; that it may relieve them that are widows indeed. 17 Let the elders that rule well be counted worthy of double honour, especially they who labour in the word and doctrine. 18 For the Scripture saith, Thou shalt not muzzle the ox that treadeth out the corn. And, The labourer *is* worthy of his reward. 19 Against an elder receive not an accusation, but before two or three witnesses. 20 Them that sin rebuke before all, that others also may fear. 21 I charge *thee* before God, and the Lord Jesus Christ, and the elect angels, that thou observe these things without preferring one before another, doing nothing by partiality. 22 Lay hands suddenly on no man, neither be partaker of other men's sins:

Living Bible

relatives must take care of her, and not leave this to the church to do. Then the church can spend its money for the care of widows who are all alone and have nowhere else to turn.

17 Pastors who do their work well should be paid well and should be highly appreciated, especially those who work hard at both preaching and teaching. 18 For the Scriptures say, "Never tie up the mouth of an ox when it is treading out the grain—let him eat as he goes along!" And in another place, "Those who work deserve their pay!"

19 Don't listen to complaints against the pastor unless there are two or three witnesses to accuse him. 20 If he has really sinned, then he should be rebuked in front of the whole church so that no one else will follow his example.

21 I solemnly command you in the presence of God and the Lord Jesus Christ and of the holy angels to do this whether the pastor is a special friend of yours or not. All must be treated exactly the same. 22 Never be in a hurry about choosing a pastor; you may overlook his sins and it will look as if you approve of them. Be sure that you yourself stay away from all sin.

Today's English Version

woman who is a believer has widows in her family, she must take care of them, and not put the burden on the church, so that it may take care of the widows who are all alone.

17 The elders who do good work as leaders should be considered worthy of receiving double pay, especially those who work hard at preaching and teaching. 18 For the scripture says, "Do not tie up the mouth of the ox when it is treading out the grain," and, "The worker deserves his wages." 19 Do not listen to an accusation against an elder unless it is brought by two or three witnesses. 20 Rebuke publicly all those who commit sins, so that the rest may be afraid.

21 In the presence of God, and of Christ Jesus, and of the holy angels, I solemnly call upon you to obey these instructions without showing any prejudice or favor to anyone in anything you do. 22 Be in no hurry to lay hands on anyone for the Lord's service. Take no part in the sins of others; keep yourself pure.

New International Version

in her family, she should help them and not let the church be burdened with them, so that the church can help those widows who are all alone.

17 The elders who direct the affairs of the church well are worthy of double honor, especially those whose work is preaching and teaching. 18 For the Scripture says, "Do not muzzle the ox while it is treading out the grain," [f] and "The worker deserves his wages." [g] 19 Do not entertain an accusation against an elder unless it is brought by two or three witnesses. 20 Those who sin are to be rebuked publicly, so that the others may take warning.

21 I charge you, in the sight of God and Christ Jesus and the elect angels, to keep these instructions without partiality, and to do nothing out of favoritism.

22 Do not be hasty in the laying on of hands, and do not share in the sins of others. Keep yourself pure.

[*f*] Deut. 25:4. [*g*] Luke 10:7.

Phillips Modern English

granted that any Christians who have widows in the family circle should do everything possible for them and not allow them to become the church's responsibility. The church will then be free to look after those widows who are alone in the world.

5.17 You and your elders

Elders with a gift of leadership should be considered worthy of respect, and of adequate salary, particularly if they work hard at their preaching and teaching. Remember the scriptural principle:

Thou shalt not muzzle the ox when he treadeth out the corn,

and

The labourer is worthy of his hire.

Take no notice of charges brought against an elder unless they can be substantiated by proper witnesses. If sin is actually proved, then the offenders should be publicly rebuked as a salutary warning to others.

I solemnly charge you in the sight of God and Christ Jesus and the holy angels to follow these orders with the strictest impartiality and to have no favourites.

Never be in a hurry to ordain a man by laying your hands upon him, or you may be making yourself responsible for the sins of others. Be

Revised Standard Version

woman[l] has relatives who are widows, let her assist them; let the church not be burdened, so that it may assist those who are real widows.
17 Let the elders who rule well be considered worthy of double honor, especially those who labor in preaching and teaching; 18 for the scripture says, "You shall not muzzle an ox when it is treading out the grain," and, "The laborer deserves his wages." 19 Never admit any charge against an elder except on the evidence of two or three witnesses. 20 As for those who persist in sin, rebuke them in the presence of all, so that the rest may stand in fear. 21 In the presence of God and of Christ Jesus and of the elect angels I charge you to keep these rules without favor, doing nothing from partiality. 22 Do not be hasty in the laying on of hands, nor participate in another man's sins; keep yourself pure.

[*l*] Other ancient authorities read *man or woman;* others, simply *man.*

Jerusalem Bible

she should support them and not make the Church bear the expense but enable it to support those who are genuinely widows.

The elders

17 The elders who do their work well while they are in charge are to be given double consideration, especially those who are assiduous in preaching and teaching. 18 As scripture says: *You must not muzzle an ox when it is treading out the corn*[d]; and again: *The worker deserves his pay.*[e] 19 Never accept any accusation brought against an elder unless it is supported *by two or three witnesses.* 20 If any of them are at fault, reprimand them publicly, as a warning to the rest. 21 Before God, and before Jesus Christ and the angels he has chosen, I put it to you as a duty to keep these rules impartially and never to be influenced by favoritism. 22 Do not be too quick to lay hands on any man, and never make yourself an accomplice in anybody else's sin; keep yourself pure.

[*d*] Dt. 25:4. [*e*] Not traceable in the Old Testament; but this is also to be found in Lk. 10:7 where, again, it may be a quotation.

New English Bible

the family, he must support them himself;[a] the congregation must be relieved of the burden, so that it may be free to support those who are widows in the full sense of the term.

Elders who do well as leaders should be reckoned worthy of a double stipend, in particular those who labour at preaching and teaching. For Scripture says, 'You shall not muzzle a threshing ox'; and besides, 'the worker earns his pay'.

Do not entertain a charge against an elder unless it is supported by two or three witnesses. Those who commit sins you must expose publicly, to put fear into the others. Before God and Christ Jesus and the angels who are his chosen, I solemnly charge you, maintain these rules, and never pre-judge the issue, but act with strict impartiality. Do not be over-hasty in laying on hands in ordination,[b] or you may find yourself responsible for other people's misdeeds; keep your own hands clean.

[*a*] *Some witnesses read* If a Christian woman has widows in her family, she must support them herself. [*b*] *Or* in restoring an offender by the laying on of hands.

King James Version

keep thyself pure. 23 Drink no longer water, but use a little wine for thy stomach's sake and thine often infirmities. 24 Some men's sins are open beforehand, going before to judgment; and some *men* they follow after. 25 Likewise also the good works *of some* are manifest beforehand; and they that are otherwise cannot be hid.

6 Let as many servants as are under the yoke count their own masters worthy of all honour, that the name of God and *his* doctrine be not blasphemed. 2 And they that have believing masters, let them not despise *them*, because they are brethren; but rather do *them* service, because they are faithful and beloved, partakers of the benefit. These things teach and exhort. 3 If any man teach otherwise, and consent not to wholesome words, *even* the words of our Lord Jesus Christ, and to the doctrine which is according

Living Bible

23 (By the way, this doesn't mean you should completely give up drinking wine. You ought to take a little sometimes as medicine for your stomach because you are sick so often.)

24 Remember that some men, even pastors, lead sinful lives and everyone knows it. In such situations you can do something about it. But in other cases only the judgment day will reveal the terrible truth. 25 In the same way, everyone knows how much good some pastors do, but sometimes their good deeds aren't known until long afterward.

6 Christian slaves should work hard for their owners and respect them; never let it be said that Christ's people are poor workers. Don't let the name of God or his teaching be laughed at because of this. 2 If their owner is a Christian, that is no excuse for slowing down; rather they should work all the harder because a brother in the faith is being helped by their efforts.

Teach these truths, Timothy, and encourage all to obey them. 3 Some may deny these things, but they are the sound, wholesome teachings of the Lord Jesus Christ and are the foundation

Today's English Version

23 Do not drink water only, but take a little wine to help your digestion, since you are sick so often.

24 The sins of some men are plain to see, and their sins go ahead of them to judgment; but the sins of others are seen only later. 25 In the same way good deeds are plainly seen, and even those that are not so plain cannot be hidden.

6 All who are slaves must consider their masters worthy of all respect, so that no one will speak evil of the name of God and of our teaching. 2 Slaves belonging to masters who are believers must not despise them because they are their brothers. Instead, they are to serve them even better, because those who benefit from their work are believers whom they love.

False teaching and true riches

You must teach and preach these things. 3 Whoever teaches a different doctrine and does not agree with the true words of our Lord Jesus Christ and with the teaching of our religion

New International Version

23 Stop drinking only water, and use a little wine because of your stomach and your frequent illnesses.

24 The sins of some men are obvious, reaching the place of judgment ahead of them; the sins of others trail behind them. 25 In the same way, good deeds are obvious, and even those that are not cannot be hidden.

6 All who are under the yoke of slavery should consider their masters worthy of full respect, so that God's name and our teaching may not be slandered. 2 Those who have believing masters are not to show less respect for them because they are brothers. Instead, they are to serve them even better, because those who benefit from their service are believers, and dear to them. These are the things you are to teach and urge on them.

Love of money

3 If anyone teaches false doctrines and does not agree to the sound instruction of our Lord

Phillips Modern English

careful that your own life is pure. (By the way, I should advise you to drink wine in moderation, instead of water. It will do your stomach good and help you to get over your frequent spells of illness.) Remember that some men's sins are obvious, and are equally obviously bringing them to judgment. The sins of other men are not apparent, but are dogging them, nevertheless, under the surface. Similarly some virtues are plain to see, while others, though not at all conspicuous, will eventually become known.

6.1 The behaviour of slaves in the church

Christian slaves should treat their masters with respect, and avoid causing dishonour to the name of God and our teaching. If they have Christian masters they should not despise them because they work for brothers in the faith. Indeed they should serve them all the better because they are thereby benefiting those who have the some faith and love as themselves.

6.3 The dangers of false doctrine and the love of money

This is the sort of thing you should teach and preach, and if anyone tries to teach some doctrinal novelty and does not follow sound teaching (which we base on our Lord Jesus Christ's own words and which leads to Christ-like liv-

Revised Standard Version

23 No longer drink only water, but use a little wine for the sake of your stomach and your frequent ailments.
24 The sins of some men are conspicuous, pointing to judgment, but the sins of others appear later. 25 So also good deeds are conspicuous; and even when they are not, they cannot remain hidden.

6 Let all who are under the yoke of slavery regard their masters as worthy of all honor, so that the name of God and the teaching may not be defamed. 2 Those who have believing masters must not be disrespectful on the ground that they are brethren; rather they must serve all the better since those who benefit by their service are believers and beloved.

Teach and urge these duties. 3 If any one teaches otherwise and does not agree with the sound words of our Lord Jesus Christ and the

Jerusalem Bible

23 You should give up drinking only water and have a little wine for the sake of your digestion and the frequent bouts of illness that you have.
24 The faults of some people are obvious long before anyone makes any complaint about them, while others have faults that are not discovered until afterward. 25 In the same way, the good that people do can be obvious; but even when it is not, it cannot be hidden for ever.

Slaves

6 All slaves "under the yoke" must have unqualified respect for their masters, so that the name of God and our teaching are not brought into disrepute. 2 Slaves whose masters are believers are not to think any the less of them because they are brothers; on the contrary, they should serve them all the better, since those who have the benefit of their services are believers and dear to God.

The true teacher and the false teacher

This is what you are to teach them to believe and persuade them to do. 3 Anyone who teaches anything different, and does not keep to the sound teaching which is that of our Lord Jesus Christ, the doctrine which is in accordance with

New English Bible

Stop drinking nothing but water; take a little wine for your digestion, for your frequent ailments.
While there are people whose offences are so obvious that they run before them into court, there are others whose offences have not yet overtaken them. Similarly, good deeds are obvious, or even if they are not, they cannot be concealed for ever.

6 All who wear the yoke of slavery must count their own masters worthy of all respect, so that the name of God and the Christian teaching are not brought into disrepute. If the masters are believers, the slaves must not respect them any less for being their Christian brothers. Quite the contrary; they must be all the better servants because those who receive the benefit of their service are one with them in faith and love.

This is what you are to teach and preach. If anyone is teaching otherwise, and will not give his mind to wholesome precepts—I mean those of our Lord Jesus Christ—and to good religious

King James Version

to godliness; 4 He is proud, knowing nothing,
but doting about questions and strifes of words,
whereof cometh envy, strife, railings, evil sur-
misings, 5 Perverse disputings of men of corrupt
minds, and destitute of the truth, supposing that
gain is godliness: from such withdraw thyself.
6 But godliness with contentment is great gain.
7 For we brought nothing into *this* world, *and*
it is certain we can carry nothing out. 8 And
having food and raiment, let us be therewith
content. 9 But they that will be rich fall into
temptation and a snare, and *into* many foolish
and hurtful lusts, which drown men in destruction and perdition. 10 For the love of money is
the root of all evil: which while some coveted
after, they have erred from the faith, and pierced
themselves through with many sorrows. 11 But
thou, O man of God, flee these things; and follow after righteousness, godliness, faith, love,
patience, meekness. 12 Fight the good fight of
faith, lay hold on eternal life, whereunto thou
art also called, and hast professed a good pro-

Living Bible

for a godly life. 4 Anyone who says anything different is both proud and stupid. He is quibbling
over the meaning of Christ's words and stirring
up arguments ending in jealousy and anger,
which only lead to name-calling, accusations, and
evil suspicions. 5 These arguers—their minds
warped by sin—don't know how to tell the
truth; to them the Good News is just a means
of making money. Keep away from them.
6 Do you want to be truly rich? You already
are if you are happy and good. 7 After all, we
didn't bring any money with us when we came
into the world, and we can't carry away a single
penny when we die. 8 So we should be well satisfied without money if we have enough food
and clothing. 9 But people who long to be rich
soon begin to do all kinds of wrong things to
get money, things that hurt them and make them
evil-minded and finally send them to hell itself.
10 For the love of money is the first step toward
all kinds of sin. Some people have even turned
away from God because of their love for it, and
as a result have pierced themselves with many
sorrows.
11 Oh, Timothy, you are God's man. Run
from all these evil things and work instead at
what is right and good, learning to trust him
and love others, and to be patient and gentle.
12 Fight on for God. Hold tightly to the eternal
life which God has given you, and which you
have confessed with such a ringing confession
before many witnesses.

Today's English Version

4 is swollen with pride and knows nothing. He
has an unhealthy desire to argue and quarrel about
words, and this brings on jealousy, dissension,
insults, evil suspicions, 5 and constant arguments from men whose minds do not function
and who no longer have the truth. They think
that religion is a way to become rich.
6 Well, religion does make a man very rich,
if he is satisfied with what he has. 7 What did
we bring into the world? Nothing! What can we
take out of the world? Nothing! 8 So then, if
we have food and clothes, that should be
enough for us. 9 But those who want to get
rich fall into temptation and are caught in the
trap of many foolish and harmful desires, which
pull men down to ruin and destruction. 10 For
the love of money is a source of all kinds of evil.
Some have been so eager to have it that they
have wandered away from the faith and have
broken their hearts with many sorrows.

Personal instructions

11 But you, man of God, avoid all these
things. Strive for righteousness, godliness, faith,
love, endurance, and gentleness. 12 Run your
best in the race of faith, and win eternal life
for yourself; for it was to this life that God
called you when you made your good profession

New International Version

Jesus Christ and to godly teaching, 4 he is conceited and understands nothing. He has an unhealthy interest in controversies and arguments
that result in envy, quarreling, malicious talk,
evil suspicions 5 and constant friction between
men of corrupt mind, who have been robbed of
the truth and who think that godliness is a means
to financial gain.
6 But godliness with contentment is great gain.
7 For we brought nothing into the world, and
we can take nothing out of it. 8 But if we have
food and clothing, we will be content with that.
9 People who want to get rich fall into temptation and a trap and into many foolish and harmful desires that plunge men into ruin and destruction. 10 For the love of money is a root of all
kinds of evil. Some people, eager for money,
have wandered from the faith and pierced themselves with many griefs.

Paul's charge to Timothy

11 But you, man of God, flee from all this,
and pursue righteousness, godliness, faith, love,
endurance and gentleness. 12 Fight the good fight
of the faith. Take hold of the eternal life to
which you were called when you made your good
confession in the presence of many witnesses.

Phillips Modern English

ing), then he is a conceited idiot! His mind is a morbid jumble of disputation and argument, things which lead to nothing but jealousy, quarrelling, insults and malicious innuendoes—continual wrangling, in fact, among men of warped minds who have lost their real hold on the truth but hope to make some profit out of the Christian religion. There is a real profit, of course. It is peace of heart for those who live as God would have them live. We brought nothing with us when we entered this world and we can be sure we shall take nothing with us when we leave it. Surely then, as far as physical things are concerned, it is sufficient for us to keep our bodies fed and clothed. For men who set their hearts on being wealthy expose themselves to temptation. They fall into a trap and lay themselves open to all sorts of silly and wicked desires, which are quite capable of utterly ruining and destroying their souls. For loving money leads to all kinds of evil, and some men in the struggle to be rich have lost their faith and caused themselves untold agonies of mind.

6.11 Maintain a fearless witness until the last day

But you, the man of God, keep clear of such things. Set your heart on integrity, true piety, faithfulness, love, endurance and gentleness. Fight the worthwhile battle of the faith, keep your grip on that life eternal to which you have been called, and to which you boldly professed

Revised Standard Version

teaching which accords with godliness, 4 he is
puffed up with conceit, he knows nothing; he
has a morbid craving for controversy and for
disputes about words, which produce envy, dissension, slander, base suspicions, 5 and wrangling
among men who are depraved in mind and bereft
of the truth, imagining that godliness is a means
of gain. 6 There is great gain in godliness with
contentment; 7 for we brought nothing into the
world, and [m] we cannot take anything out of the
world; 8 but if we have food and clothing, with
these we shall be content. 9 But those who desire
to be rich fall into temptation, into a snare, into
many senseless and hurtful desires that plunge
men into ruin and destruction. 10 For the love
of money is the root of all evils; it is through
this craving that some have wandered away from
the faith and pierced their hearts with many
pangs.
11 But as for you, man of God, shun all this;
aim at righteousness, godliness, faith, love,
steadfastness, gentleness. 12 Fight the good fight
of the faith; take hold of the eternal life to
which you were called when you made the good
confession in the presence of many witnesses.

[m] Other ancient authorities insert *it is certain that.*

Jerusalem Bible

true religion, 4 is simply ignorant and must be
full of self-conceit—with a craze for questioning
everything and arguing about words. All that
can come of this is jealousy, contention, abuse and
wicked mistrust of one another; 5 and unending
disputes by people who are neither rational nor
informed and imagine that religion is a way of
making a profit. 6 Religion, of course, does bring
large profits, but only to those who are content
with what they have. 7 We brought nothing into
the world, and we can take nothing out of it;
8 but as long as we have food and clothing, let
us be content with that. 9 People who long to
be rich are a prey to temptation; they get trapped
into all sorts of foolish and dangerous ambitions
which eventually plunge them into ruin and destruction. 10 "The love of money is the root of
all evils" and there are some who, pursuing it,
have wandered away from the faith, and so given
their souls any number of fatal wounds.

Timothy's vocation recalled

11 But, as a man dedicated to God, you must
avoid all that. You must aim to be saintly and
religious, filled with faith and love, patient and
gentle. 12 Fight the good fight of the faith and
win for yourself the eternal life to which you
were called when you made your profession and
spoke up for the truth in front of many wit-

New English Bible

teaching, I call him a pompous ignoramus. He is morbidly keen on mere verbal questions and quibbles, which give rise to jealousy, quarrelling, slander, base suspicions, and endless wrangles: all typical of men who have let their reasoning powers become atrophied and have lost grip of the truth. They think religion should yield dividends; and of course religion does yield high dividends, but only to the man whose resources are within him. We brought nothing into the world; for that matter we cannot take anything with us when we leave, but if we have food and covering we may rest content. Those who want to be rich fall into temptations and snares and many foolish harmful desires which plunge men into ruin and perdition. The love of money is the root of all evil things, and there are some who in reaching for it have wandered from the faith and spiked themselves on many thorny griefs.

But you, man of God, must shun all this, and pursue justice, piety, fidelity, love, fortitude, and gentleness. Run the great race of faith and take hold of eternal life. For to this you were called; and you confessed your faith nobly before many

King James Version

fession before many witnesses. 13 I give thee
charge in the sight of God, who quickeneth all
things, and *before* Christ Jesus, who before Pontius Pilate witnessed a good confession; 14 That
thou keep *this* commandment without spot, un-
rebukeable, until the appearing of our Lord
Jesus Christ: 15 Which in his times he shall
shew, *who is* the blessed and only Potentate, the
King of kings, and Lord of lords; 16 Who only
hath immortality, dwelling in the light which no
man can approach unto; whom no man hath
seen, nor can see: to whom *be* honour and
power everlasting. Amen. 17 Charge them that
are rich in this world, that they be not highminded, nor trust in uncertain riches, but in the
living God, who giveth us richly all things to enjoy; 18 That they do good, that they be rich in
good works, ready to distribute, willing to communicate; 19 Laying up in store for themselves
a good foundation against the time to come, that

Living Bible

13 I command you before God who gives
life to all, and before Christ Jesus who gave a
fearless testimony before Pontius Pilate, 14 that
you fulfill all he has told you to do, so that no
one can find fault with you from now until our
Lord Jesus Christ returns. 15 For in due season
Christ will be revealed from heaven by the
blessed and only Almighty God, the King of
kings and Lord of lords, 16 who alone can never
die, who lives in light so terrible that no human
being can approach him. No mere man has ever
seen him, nor ever will. Unto him be honor and
everlasting power and dominion forever and
ever. Amen.

17 Tell those who are rich not to be proud
and not to trust in their money, which will soon
be gone, but their pride and trust should be in
the living God who always richly gives us all
we need for our enjoyment. 18 Tell them to use
their money to do good. They should be rich in
good works and should give happily to those in
need, always being ready to share with others
whatever God has given them. 19 By doing this
they will be storing up real treasure for themselves in heaven—it is the only safe investment
for eternity! And they will be living a fruitful
Christian life down here as well.

Today's English Version

of faith before many witnesses. 13 Before God,
who gives life to all things, and before Christ
Jesus, who made the good profession before
Pontius Pilate, I command you: 14 Obey the
commandment and keep it pure and faultless,
until the Day our Lord Jesus Christ will appear.
15 His appearing will be brought about at the
right time by God, the blessed and only Ruler,
the King of kings and the Lord of lords. 16 He
alone is immortal; he lives in the light that no
one can approach. No one has ever seen him,
no one can ever see him. To him be honor and
eternal might! Amen.

17 Command those who are rich in the things
of this life not to be proud, and to place their
hope, not in such an uncertain thing as riches,
but in God, who generously gives us everything
for us to enjoy. 18 Command them to do good,
to be rich in good works, to be generous and
ready to share with others. 19 In this way they
will store up for themselves a treasure which will
be a solid foundation for the future. And then
they will be able to win the life which is true
life.

New International Version

13 In the sight of God, who gives life to everything, and of Christ Jesus, who while testifying
before Pontius Pilate made the good confession,
I charge you 14 to keep this commandment
without spot or blame until the appearing of our
Lord Jesus Christ, 15 which God will bring
about in his own time—God, the blessed and
only Ruler, the King of kings and Lord of lords,
16 who alone is immortal and who lives in unapproachable light, whom no one has seen or can
see. To him be honor and might forever. Amen.

17 Command those who are rich in this present world not to be arrogant nor to put their
hope in wealth, which is so uncertain, but to
put their hope in God, who richly provides us
with everything for our enjoyment. 18 Command them to do good, to be rich in good deeds,
and to be generous and willing to share. 19 In
this way they will lay up treasure for themselves
as a firm foundation for the coming age, so that
they may take hold of the life that is truly life.

Phillips Modern English

your loyalty before many witnesses. I charge you in the sight of God who gives life to all things and Christ Jesus who fearlessly witnessed to the truth before Pontius Pilate, to keep your commission clean and above reproach until the final coming of Christ. This will be, in his own time, the final dénouement of God, who is the blessed controller of all things, the king over all kings and the master of all masters, the only source of immortality, the One who lives in unapproachable light, the One whom no mortal eye has even seen or ever can see. To him be acknowledged all honour and power for ever, amen!

6.17 Have a word for the rich

Tell those who are rich in this present world not to be contemptuous of others, and not to rest the weight of their confidence on the transitory power of wealth but on the living God, who generously gives us everything for our enjoyment. Tell them to do good, to be rich in kindly actions, to be ready to give to others and to sympathise with those in distress. Their security should be invested in the life to come, so that they may be sure of holding a share in the life which is real and permanent.

Revised Standard Version

13 In the presence of God who gives life to all
things, and of Christ Jesus who in his testimony
before Pontius Pilate made the good confession,
14 I charge you to keep the commandment unstained and free from reproach until the appearing of our Lord Jesus Christ; 15 and this
will be made manifest at the proper time by the
blessed and only Sovereign, the King of kings
and Lord of lords, 16 who alone has immortality
and dwells in unapproachable light, whom no
man has ever seen or can see. To him be honor
and eternal dominion. Amen.

17 As for the rich in this world, charge them
not to be haughty, nor to set their hopes on uncertain riches but on God who richly furnishes
us with everything to enjoy. 18 They are to do
good, to be rich in good deeds, liberal and generous, 19 thus laying up for themselves a good
foundation for the future, so that they may take
hold of the life which is life indeed.

Jerusalem Bible

nesses. 13 Now, before God the source of all life
and before Jesus Christ, who spoke up as a witness for the truth in front of Pontius Pilate, I
put to you the duty 14 of doing all that you have
been told, with no faults or failures, until the
Appearing of our Lord Jesus Christ,

15 who at the due time will be revealed
by God, the blessed and only Ruler of all,
the King of kings and the Lord of lords,
16 who alone is immortal,
whose home is in inaccessible light,
whom no man has seen and no man is able to see:
to him be honor and everlasting power. Amen.

Rich Christians

17 Warn those who are rich in this world's
goods that they are not to look down on other
people; and not to set their hopes on money,
which is untrustworthy, but on God who, out
of his riches, gives us all that we need for our
happiness. 18 Tell them that they are to do good,
and be rich in good works, to be generous and
willing to share—19 this is the way they can
save up a good capital sum for the future if
they want to make sure of the only life that is
real.

New English Bible

witnesses. Now in the presence of God, who gives life to all things, and of Jesus Christ, who himself made the same noble confession and gave his testimony to it before Pontius Pilate, I charge you to obey your orders irreproachably and without fault until our Lord Jesus Christ appears. That appearance God will bring to pass in his own good time—God who in eternal felicity alone holds sway. He is King of kings and Lord of lords; he alone possesses immortality, dwelling in unapproachable light. No man has ever seen or ever can see him. To him be honour and might for ever! Amen.

Instruct those who are rich in this world's goods not to be proud, and not to fix their hopes on so uncertain a thing as money, but upon God, who endows us richly with all things to enjoy. Tell them to do good and to grow rich in noble actions, to be ready to give away and to share, and so acquire a treasure which will form a good foundation for the future. Thus they will grasp the life which is life indeed.

King James Version

they may lay hold on eternal life. 20 O Timothy, keep that which is committed to thy trust, avoiding profane *and* vain babblings, and oppositions of science falsely so called: 21 Which some professing have erred concerning the faith. Grace *be* with thee. Amen.

The first to Timothy was written from Laodicea, which is the chiefest city of Phrygia Pacatiana.

Living Bible

20 Oh, Timothy, don't fail to do these things that God entrusted to you. Keep out of foolish arguments with those who boast of their "knowledge" and thus prove their lack of it. 21 Some of these people have missed the most important thing in life—they don't know God. May God's mercy be upon you.

Sincerely,
Paul

Today's English Version

20 Timothy, keep safe what has been turned over to your care. Avoid the godless talk and foolish arguments of "Knowledge," as some people wrongly call it. 21 For some have claimed to possess it, and as a result they have lost the way of faith.

God's grace be with you all.

New International Version

20 Timothy, guard what has been entrusted to your care. Turn away from godless chatter and the opposition of what is falsely called knowledge, 21 which some have professed and in so doing have wandered from the faith.

Grace be with you.

Phillips Modern English

6.20 My final appeal

Timothy, guard most carefully your divine commission. Avoid the Godless mixture of contradictory notions which is falsely known as "knowledge"—some have followed it *and lost their faith.*
Grace be with you all.

Revised Standard Version

20 O Timothy, guard what has been entrusted to you. Avoid the godless chatter and contradictions of what is falsely called knowledge,
21 for by professing it some have missed the mark as regards the faith.
Grace be with you.

Jerusalem Bible

Final warning and conclusion

20 My dear Timothy, take great care of all that has been entrusted to you. Have nothing to do with the pointless philosophical discussions and antagonistic beliefs of the "knowledge" which is not knowledge at all;
21 by adopting this, some have gone right away from the faith.
Grace be with you.

New English Bible

Timothy, keep safe that which has been entrusted to you. Turn a deaf ear to empty and worldly chatter, and the contradictions of so-called 'knowledge', for many who lay claim to it have shot far wide of the faith.
Grace be with you all!

King James Version

THE SECOND EPISTLE OF PAUL THE APOSTLE TO TIMOTHY

1 Paul, an apostle of Jesus Christ by the will of God, according to the promise of life which is in Christ Jesus, 2 To Timothy, *my* dearly beloved son: Grace, mercy, *and* peace, from God the Father and Christ Jesus our Lord.

Living Bible

2 TIMOTHY

1 *From:* Paul, Jesus Christ's missionary, sent out by God to tell men and women everywhere about the eternal life he has promised them through faith in Jesus Christ.

2 *To:* Timothy, my dear son. May God the Father and Christ Jesus our Lord shower you with his kindness, mercy and peace.

Today's English Version

PAUL'S SECOND LETTER TO TIMOTHY

1 From Paul, an apostle of Christ Jesus by God's will, sent to proclaim the promised life which we have in union with Christ Jesus—

2 To Timothy, my dear son:

May God the Father and Christ Jesus our Lord give you grace, mercy, and peace.

New International Version

2 TIMOTHY

1 Paul, an apostle of Christ Jesus by the will of God, according to the promise of life that is in Christ Jesus,

2 To Timothy, my dear son:

Grace, mercy and peace from God the Father and Christ Jesus our Lord.

Phillips Modern English

THE SECOND LETTER TO TIMOTHY

Paul, messenger by God's appointment in the promised life of Christ Jesus, to Timothy, my own dearly loved son: grace, mercy and peace be to you from God the Father and Christ Jesus, our Lord.

Revised Standard Version

THE SECOND LETTER OF PAUL TO TIMOTHY

1 Paul, an apostle of Christ Jesus by the will of God according to the promise of the life which is in Christ Jesus,
2 To Timothy, my beloved child:
Grace, mercy, and peace from God the Father and Christ Jesus our Lord.

Jerusalem Bible

THE SECOND LETTER FROM PAUL TO TIMOTHY

2 TIMOTHY

Greeting and thanksgiving

1 From Paul, appointed by God to be an apostle of Christ Jesus in his design to promise life in Christ Jesus; 2 to Timothy, dear child of mine, wishing you grace, mercy and peace from God the Father and from Christ Jesus our Lord.

New English Bible

THE SECOND LETTER OF PAUL TO TIMOTHY

Character of a Christian minister

1 From Paul, apostle of Jesus Christ by the will of God, whose promise of life is fulfilled in Christ Jesus, to Timothy his dear son.
Grace, mercy, and peace to you from God the Father and our Lord Jesus Christ.

King James Version

3 I thank God, whom I serve from *my* forefathers with pure conscience, that without ceasing I have remembrance of thee in my prayers night and day; 4 Greatly desiring to see thee, being mindful of thy tears, that I may be filled with joy; 5 When I call to remembrance the unfeigned faith that is in thee, which dwelt first in thy grandmother Lois, and thy mother Eunice; and I am persuaded that in thee also. 6 Wherefore I put thee in remembrance, that thou stir up the gift of God, which is in thee by the putting on of my hands. 7 For God hath not given us the spirit of fear; but of power, and of love, and of a sound mind. 8 Be not thou therefore ashamed of the testimony of our Lord, nor of me his prisoner: but be thou partaker of the afflictions of the gospel according to the power of God; 9 Who hath saved us, and called *us* with a holy calling, not according to our works, but according to his own purpose and grace, which was given us in Christ Jesus before the world began; 10 But is now made manifest by the appearing of our Saviour Jesus Christ, who hath abolished death, and hath brought life and immortality to light through the gospel: 11 Whereunto I am appointed a preacher, and

Living Bible

3 How I thank God for you, Timothy. I pray for you every day, and many times during the long nights I beg my God to bless you richly. He is my fathers' God, and mine, and my only purpose in life is to please him.

4 How I long to see you again. How happy I would be, for I remember your tears as we left each other.

5 I know how much you trust the Lord, just as your mother Eunice and your grandmother Lois do; and I feel sure you are still trusting him as much as ever.

6 This being so, I want to remind you to stir into flame the strength and boldness[a] that is in you, that entered into you when I laid my hands upon your head and blessed you. 7 For the Holy Spirit, God's gift, does not want you to be afraid of people, but to be wise and strong, and to love them and enjoy being with them. 8 If you will stir up this inner power, you will never be afraid to tell others about our Lord, or to let them know that I am your friend even though I am here in jail for Christ's sake. You will be ready to suffer with me for the Lord, for he will give you strength in suffering.

9 It is he who saved us and chose us for his holy work, not because we deserved it but because that was his plan long before the world began—to show his love and kindness to us through Christ. 10 And now he has made all of this plain to us by the coming of our Savior Jesus Christ, who broke the power of death and showed us the way of everlasting life through trusting him. 11 And God has chosen me to be his missionary, to preach to the Gentiles and teach them.

[*a*] Implied. Literally, "stir up the gift of God."

Today's English Version

Thanksgiving and encouragement

3 I give thanks to God, whom I serve with a clear conscience, as my ancestors did. I thank him as I remember you always in my prayers, night and day. 4 I remember your tears, and I want to see you very much, so that I may be filled with joy. 5 I remember the sincere faith you have, the kind of faith that your grandmother Lois and your mother Eunice also had. I am sure that you have it also. 6 For this reason I remind you to keep alive the gift that God gave to you when I laid my hands on you. 7 For the Spirit that God has given us does not make us timid; instead, his Spirit fills us with power, love, and self-control.

8 Do not be ashamed, then, of witnessing for our Lord; neither be ashamed of me, his prisoner. Instead, take your part in suffering for the Good News, as God gives you the strength for it. 9 He saved us and called us to be his own people, not because of what we have done, but because of his own purpose and grace. He gave us this grace by means of Christ Jesus before the beginning of time, 10 but now it has been revealed to us through the coming of our Savior, Christ Jesus. He has ended the power of death, and through the Good News has revealed immortal life.

11 God has appointed me to proclaim the

New International Version

Encouragement to be faithful

3 I thank God, whom I serve, as my forefathers did, with a clear conscience, as night and day I constantly remember you in my prayers. 4 Recalling your tears, I long to see you, so that I may be filled with joy. 5 I have been reminded of your sincere faith, which first lived in your grandmother Lois and in your mother Eunice, and I am persuaded, now lives in you also. 6 For this reason I remind you to fan into flame the gift of God, which is in you through the laying on of my hands. 7 For God did not give us a spirit of timidity, but a spirit of power, of love and of self-discipline.

8 So do not be ashamed to testify about our Lord, or ashamed of me his prisoner. But join with me in suffering for the gospel, by the power of God, 9 who has saved us and called us to a holy life—not because of anything we have done but because of his own purpose and grace. This grace was given us in Christ Jesus before the beginning of time, 10 but it has now been revealed through the appearing of our Savior, Christ Jesus, who has destroyed death and has brought life and immortality to light through the gospel. 11 And of this gospel I was appointed

Phillips Modern English

1.3 I thank God for your faith: guard it well

I thank the God of my forefathers, whom I also serve with a clear conscience, as I remember you constantly in my prayers night and day. I am longing to see you, for I can't forget how moved you were when I left you, and to have you with me again would be the greatest possible joy. I often think of that genuine faith of yours—a faith that first appeared in your grandmother Lois, then in Eunice your mother, and is now, I am convinced, in you as well. Because of this faith, I now remind you to stir up that inner fire which God gave you at your ordination through my hands. For God has not given us a spirit of cowardice, but a spirit of power and love and a sound mind. So never be ashamed of bearing witness to our Lord, nor of me, his prisoner. Accept your share of the hardship that faithfulness to the gospel entails in the strength that God gives you. For he has saved us from all that is evil and called us to a life of holiness—not because of any of our achievements but for his own purpose. Before time began he planned to give us in Christ Jesus the grace to achieve this purpose, but it is only since our saviour Christ Jesus has been revealed that the method has become apparent. For Christ has completely abolished death, and has now, through the gospel, opened to us men the shining possibilities of the life that is eternal. It is this gospel that I am commissioned to proclaim; it is of this gospel that I am appointed

Revised Standard Version

3 I thank God whom I serve with a clear
conscience, as did my fathers, when I remember
you constantly in my prayers. 4 As I remember
your tears, I long night and day to see you, that
I may be filled with joy. 5 I am reminded of
your sincere faith, a faith that dwelt first in
your grandmother Lois and your mother Eunice
and now, I am sure, dwells in you. 6 Hence I
remind you to rekindle the gift of God that is
within you through the laying on of my hands;
7 for God did not give us a spirit of timidity but
a spirit of power and love and self-control.
8 Do not be ashamed then of testifying to our
Lord, nor of me his prisoner, but share in suffering for the gospel in the power of God, 9 who
saved us and called us with a holy calling, not
in virtue of our works but in virtue of his own
purpose and the grace which he gave us in
Christ Jesus ages ago, 10 and now has manifested
through the appearing of our Savior Christ Jesus,
who abolished death and brought life and immortality to light through the gospel. 11 For this
gospel I was appointed a preacher and apostle

Jerusalem Bible

3 Night and day I thank God, keeping my
conscience clear and remembering my duty to
him as my ancestors did, and always I remember
you in my prayers; I remember your tears 4 and
long to see you again to complete my happiness.
5 Then I am reminded of the sincere faith which
you have; it came first to live in your grandmother Lois, and your mother Eunice, and I have
no doubt that it is the same faith in you as well.

The gifts that Timothy has received

6 This is why I am reminding you now to fan
into a flame the gift that God gave you when I
laid my hands on you. 7 God's gift was not a
spirit of timidity, but the Spirit of power and
love and self-control. 8 So you are never to be
ashamed of witnessing to the Lord or ashamed of
me for being his prisoner; but with me bear the
hardships for the sake of the Good News, relying on the power of God 9 who has saved us and
called us to be holy—not because of anything we
ourselves have done but for his own purpose and
by his own grace. This grace had already been
granted to us, in Christ Jesus, before the beginning of time, 10 but it has only been revealed
by the Appearing of our Savior Christ Jesus. He
abolished death, and he has proclaimed life and
immortality through the Good News; 11 and I
have been named its herald, its apostle and its
teacher.

New English Bible

I thank God—whom I, like my forefathers, worship with a pure intention—when I mention you in my prayers; this I do constantly night and day. And when I remember the tears you shed, I long to see you again to make my happiness complete. I am reminded of the sincerity of your faith, a faith which was alive in Lois your grandmother and Eunice your mother before you, and which, I am confident, lives in you also. That is why I now remind you to stir into flame the gift of God which is within you through the laying on of my hands. For the spirit that God gave us is no craven spirit, but one to inspire strength, love, and self-discipline. So never be ashamed of your testimony to our Lord, nor of me his prisoner, but take your share of suffering for the sake of the Gospel, in the strength that comes from God. It is he who brought us salvation and called us to a dedicated life, not for any merit of ours but of his own purpose and his own grace, which was granted to us in Christ Jesus from all eternity, but has now at length been brought fully into view by the appearance on earth of our Saviour Jesus Christ. For he has broken the power of death and brought life and immortality to light through the Gospel.

Of this Gospel I, by his appointment, am

King James Version

an apostle, and a teacher of the Gentiles. 12 For
the which cause I also suffer these things: nevertheless I am not ashamed; for I know whom I
have believed, and am persuaded that he is able
to keep that which I have committed unto him
against that day. 13 Hold fast the form of sound
words, which thou hast heard of me, in faith
and love which is in Christ Jesus. 14 That good
thing which was committed unto thee keep by
the Holy Ghost which dwelleth in us. 15 This
thou knowest, that all they which are in Asia
be turned away from me; of whom are Phygellus
and Hermogenes. 16 The Lord give mercy unto
the house of Onesiphorus; for he oft refreshed
me, and was not ashamed of my chain: 17 But,
when he was in Rome, he sought me out very
diligently, and found *me*. 18 The Lord grant unto
him that he may find mercy of the Lord in that
day: and in how many things he ministered unto
me at Ephesus, thou knowest very well.

2 Thou therefore, my son, be strong in the
grace that is in Christ Jesus. 2 And the things

Living Bible

12 That is why I am suffering here in jail and
I am certainly not ashamed of it, for I know the
one in whom I trust, and I am sure that he is
able to safely guard all that I have given him until the day of his return.
13 Hold tightly to the pattern of truth I taught
you, especially concerning the faith and love
Christ Jesus offers you.[b] 14 Guard well the
splendid, God-given ability you received as a gift
from the Holy Spirit who lives within you.
15 As you know, all the Christians who came
here from Asia have deserted me; even Phygellus
and Hermogenes are gone. 16 May the Lord bless
Onesiphorus and all his family, because he visited
me and encouraged me often. His visits revived
me like a breath of fresh air, and he was never
ashamed of my being in jail. 17 In fact, when he
came to Rome he searched everywhere trying to
find me, and finally did. 18 May the Lord give
him a special blessing at the day of Christ's return. And you know better than I can tell you
how much he helped me at Ephesus.

2 Oh, Timothy, my son, be strong with the
strength Christ Jesus gives you. 2 For you

[b] Literally, "and love that is in Christ Jesus."

Today's English Version

Good News as an apostle and teacher, 12 and it
is for this reason that I suffer these things. But
I am still full of confidence, because I know
whom I have trusted, and I am sure that he is
able to keep safe until that Day what he has
entrusted to me. 13 Hold to the true words that
I taught you, as the example for you to follow,
and stay in the faith and love that are ours in
union with Christ Jesus. 14 Keep the good things
that have been entrusted to you, through the
power of the Holy Spirit, who lives in us.
15 You know that everyone in the province
of Asia deserted me, including Phygelus and
Hermogenes. 16 May the Lord show mercy to
the family of Onesiphorus, because he cheered
me up many times. He was not ashamed that I
am in prison, 17 but as soon as he arrived in
Rome he started looking for me until he found
me. 18 May the Lord grant him to receive mercy
from the Lord on that Day! And you know very
well how much he did for me in Ephesus.

A loyal soldier of Christ Jesus

2 As for you, my son, be strong through the
grace that is ours in union with Christ Jesus. 2 Take the words that you heard me preach

New International Version

a herald and an apostle and a teacher. 12 That
is why I am suffering as I am. Yet I am not
ashamed, because I know whom I have believed,
and am convinced that he is able to guard what
I have entrusted to him for that day.
13 What you heard from me, keep as the
pattern of sound teaching, with faith and love
in Christ Jesus. 14 Guard the good deposit that
was entrusted to you—guard it with the help
of the Holy Spirit who lives in us.
15 You know that everyone in the province of
Asia has deserted me, including Phygelus and
Hermogenes.
16 May the Lord show mercy to the household of Onesiphorus, because he often refreshed
me and was not ashamed of my chains. 17 On
the contrary, when he was in Rome, he searched
hard for me until he found me. 18 May the
Lord grant that he will find mercy from the
Lord on that day! You know very well in how
many ways he helped me in Ephesus.

2 You then, my son, be strong in the grace
that is in Christ Jesus. 2 And the things you

Phillips Modern English

both messenger and teacher, and it is for this gospel that I am now suffering these things. Yet I am not in the least ashamed. For I know the one in whom I have placed my confidence, and I am perfectly certain that the work he has committed to me is safe in his hands until that day.

So keep my words in your mind as the pattern of sound teaching, given to you in the faith and love of Christ Jesus. Take the greatest care of the treasures which were entrusted to you by the Holy Spirit who lives within us.

1.15 Deserters—and a friend

You will know, I expect, that all those who are in Asia have deserted me, Phygelus and Hermogenes among them. But may the Lord have mercy on the household of Onesiphorus. Many times did that man put fresh heart into me, and he was not in the least ashamed of my being a prisoner in chains. Indeed, when he was in Rome he went to a great deal of trouble to find me—may the Lord grant he finds his mercy in that day!—and you well know in how many ways he helped me at Ephesus as well.

2.1 Above all things be faithful

So, my son, be strong in the grace that Christ Jesus gives. Everything that you have heard me teach in public you should in turn entrust to

Revised Standard Version

and teacher, 12 and therefore I suffer as I do.
But I am not ashamed, for I know whom I have
believed, and I am sure that he is able to guard
until that Day what has been entrusted to me.[a]
13 Follow the pattern of the sound words which
you have heard from me, in the faith and love
which are in Christ Jesus; 14 guard the truth that
has been entrusted to you by the Holy Spirit who
dwells within us.
15 You are aware that all who are in Asia
turned away from me, and among them Phygelus
and Hermogenes. 16 May the Lord grant mercy
to the household of Onesiphorus, for he often
refreshed me; he was not ashamed of my chains,
17 but when he arrived in Rome he searched for
me eagerly and found me—18 may the Lord
grant him to find mercy from the Lord on that
Day—and you well know all the service he
rendered at Ephesus.

2 You then, my son, be strong in the grace
that is in Christ Jesus, 2 and what you have

[a] Or *what I have entrusted to him.*

Jerusalem Bible

12 It is only on account of this that I am experiencing fresh hardships here now[a]; but I
have not lost confidence, because I know who it
is that I have put my trust in, and I have no
doubt at all that he is able to take care of all
that I have entrusted to him until that Day.
13 Keep as your pattern the sound teaching
you have heard from me, in the faith and love
that are in Christ Jesus. 14 You have been
trusted to look after something precious; guard
it with the help of the Holy Spirit who lives in
us.
15 As you know, Phygelus and Hermogenes
and all the others from Asia refuse to have
anything more to do with me. 16 I hope the
Lord will be kind to all the family of Onesiphorus, because he has often been a comfort to
me and has never been ashamed of my chains.
17 On the contrary, as soon as he reached Rome,
he really searched hard for me and found out
where I was. 18 May it be the Lord's will that
he shall find the Lord's mercy on that Day. You
know better than anyone else how much he
helped me at Ephesus.

How Timothy should face hardships

2 Accept the strength, my dear son, that comes
from the grace of Christ Jesus. 2 You have

[a] The second imprisonment at Rome.

New English Bible

herald, apostle, and teacher. That is the reason for my present plight; but I am not ashamed of it, because I know who it is in whom[a] I have trusted. and am confident of his power to keep safe what he has put into my charge,[b] until the great Day. Keep before you an outline of the sound teaching which[c] you heard from me, living by the faith and love which are ours in Christ Jesus. Guard the treasure put into our charge, with the help of the Holy Spirit dwelling within us.

As you know, everyone in the province of Asia deserted me, including Phygelus and Hermogenes. But may the Lord's mercy rest on the house of Onesiphorus! He has often relieved me in my troubles. He was not ashamed to visit a prisoner, but took pains to search me out when he came to Rome, and found me. I pray that the Lord may grant him to find mercy from the Lord on the great Day. The many services he rendered at Ephesus you know better than I could tell you.

2 Now therefore, my son, take strength from
the grace of God which is ours in Christ
Jesus. You heard my teaching in the presence of

[a] *Or* I know the one whom . . . [b] *Or* what I have put into his charge. [c] *Or* Keep before you as a model of sound teaching that which . . .

King James Version

that thou hast heard of me among many witnesses, the same commit thou to faithful men,
who shall be able to teach others also. 3 Thou
therefore endure hardness, as a good soldier of
Jesus Christ. 4 No man that warreth entangleth
himself with the affairs of *this* life; that he may
please him who hath chosen him to be a soldier.
5And if a man also strive for masteries, *yet* is
he not crowned, except he strive lawfully. 6 The
husbandman that laboureth must be first partaker of the fruits. 7 Consider what I say; and
the Lord give thee understanding in all things.
8 Remember that Jesus Christ of the seed of
David was raised from the dead, according to
my gospel: 9 Wherein I suffer trouble, as an evil
doer, *even* unto bonds; but the word of God is
not bound. 10 Therefore I endure all things for
the elect's sake, that they may also obtain the
salvation which is in Christ Jesus with eternal
glory. 11 *It is* a faithful saying: For if we be
dead with *him,* we shall also live with *him:*
12 If we suffer, we shall also reign with *him:* if
we deny *him,* he also will deny us: 13 If we
believe not, *yet* he abideth faithful: he cannot

Living Bible

must teach others those things you and many others have heard me speak about. Teach these great
truths to trustworthy men who will, in turn, pass
them on to others.
3 Take your share of suffering as a good soldier of Jesus Christ, just as I do, 4 and as Christ's
soldier do not let yourself become tied up in
worldly affairs, for then you cannot satisfy the
one who has enlisted you in his army. 5 Follow
the Lord's rules for doing his work, just as an
athlete either follows the rules or is disqualified
and wins no prize. 6 Work hard, like a farmer
who gets paid well if he raises a large crop.
7 Think over these three illustrations, and may
the Lord help you to understand how they apply
to you.
8 Don't ever forget the wonderful fact that
Jesus Christ was a Man, born into King David's
family; and that he was God, as shown by the
fact that he rose again from the dead. 9 It is because I have preached these great truths that I
am in trouble here and have been put in jail like
a criminal. But the Word of God is not chained,
even though I am. 10 I am more than willing to
suffer if that will bring salvation and eternal
glory in Christ Jesus to those God has chosen.
11 I am comforted by this truth, that when we
suffer and die for Christ it only means that we
will begin living with him in heaven. 12And if we
think that our present service for him is hard,
just remember that some day we are going to
sit with him and rule with him. But if we give
up when we suffer, and turn against Christ, then
he must turn against us. 13 Even when we are too
weak to have any faith left, he remains faithful
to us and will help us, for he cannot disown us

Today's English Version

in the presence of many witnesses, and give them
into the keeping of men you can trust, men who
will be able to teach others also.
3 Take your part in suffering, as a loyal soldier of Christ Jesus. 4A soldier in active service
wants to please his commanding officer, and so
does not get mixed up in the affairs of civilian
life. 5An athlete who runs in a race cannot win
the prize unless he obeys the rules. 6 The farmer
who has done the hard work should have the
first share of the harvest. 7 Think about what I
am saying, because the Lord will enable you to
understand all things.
8 Remember Jesus Christ, who was raised
from death, who was a descendant of David, as
told in the Good News I preach. 9 Because I
preach the Good News I suffer, and I am even
chained like a criminal. But the word of God is
not in chains, 10 and for this reason I endure
everything for the sake of God's chosen people,
in order that they too may obtain the salvation
that is in Christ Jesus, together with eternal
glory. 11 This is a true saying:

"If we have died with him,
we shall also live with him.
12 If we continue to endure,
we shall also rule with him.
If we deny him,
he also will deny us.
13 If we are not faithful,
he remains faithful,

New International Version

have heard me say in the presence of many witnesses entrust to reliable men who will also be
qualified to teach others. 3 Endure hardship with
us like a good soldier of Christ Jesus. 4 No one
serving as a soldier gets involved in civilian affairs—he wants to please his commanding officer.
5 Similarly, if anyone competes as an athlete, he
does not receive the victor's crown unless he
competes according to the rules. 6 The hard-
working farmer should be the first to receive a
share of the crops. 7 Reflect on what I am saying, for the Lord will give you insight into all
this.
8 Remember Jesus Christ, raised from the
dead, descended from David. This is my gospel,
9 for which I am suffering even to the point of
being chained like a criminal. But God's word
is not chained. 10 Therefore I endure everything
for the sake of the elect, that they too may obtain the salvation that is in Christ Jesus, with
eternal glory.
11 Here is a trustworthy saying:
If we died with him,
we will also live with him;
12 if we endure,
we will also reign with him.
If we disown him,
he will also disown us;
13 if we are faithless,
he will remain faithful,

Phillips Modern English

reliable men, who will be able to pass it on to others.

Put up with your share of hardship as a loyal soldier in Christ's army. Remember: 1. That no soldier on active service gets himself entangled in business, or he will not please his commanding officer. 2. A man who enters an athletic contest wins no prize unless he keeps the rules laid down. 3. Only the man who works on the land has the right to the first share of its produce. Consider these three illustrations of mine and the Lord will help you to understand all that I mean.

Remember always, as the centre of everything, Jesus Christ, a descendant of David, yet raised by God from the dead according to my gospel. For preaching this I am having to endure being chained in prison as if I were some sort of a criminal. But they cannot chain the Word of God, and I can endure all these things for the sake of those whom God is calling, so that they too may receive the salvation of Christ Jesus, and its complement of glory after the world of time. I rely on this saying: *If we died with him we shall also live with him: if we endure we shall also reign with him. If we deny him he will also deny us: yet if we are faithless*

Revised Standard Version

heard from me before many witnesses entrust
to faithful men who will be able to teach others
also. 3 Share in suffering as a good soldier of
Christ Jesus. 4 No soldier on service gets entangled in civilian pursuits, since his aim is to
satisfy the one who enlisted him. 5 An athlete is
not crowned unless he competes according to
the rules. 6 It is the hard-working farmer who
ought to have the first share of the crops.
7 Think over what I say, for the Lord will grant
you understanding in everything.
8 Remember Jesus Christ, risen from the dead,
descended from David, as preached in my gospel,
9 the gospel for which I am suffering and wearing fetters like a criminal. But the word of God
is not fettered. 10 Therefore I endure everything
for the sake of the elect, that they also may obtain salvation in Christ Jesus with its eternal
glory.
11 The saying is sure:
If we have died with him, we shall also live
with him;
12 if we endure, we shall also reign with him;
if we deny him, he also will deny us;
13 if we are faithless, he remains faithful—

Jerusalem Bible

heard everything that I teach in public; hand it
on to reliable people so that they in turn will be
able to teach others.
3 Put up with your share of difficulties, like a
good soldier of Christ Jesus. 4 In the army, no
soldier gets himself mixed up in civilian life,
because he must be at the disposal of the man
who enlisted him; 5 or take an athlete—he cannot win any crown unless he has kept all the
rules of the contest; 6 and again, it is the working farmer who has the first claim on any crop
that is harvested. 7 Think over what I have said,
and the Lord will show you how to understand
it all.
8 Remember the Good News that I carry,
"Jesus Christ risen from the dead, sprung from
the race of David"; 9 it is on account of this that
I have my own hardships to bear, even to being
chained like a criminal—but they cannot chain
up God's news. 10 So I bear it all for the sake of
those who are chosen, so that in the end they
may have the salvation that is in Christ Jesus and
the eternal glory that comes with it. 11 Here is
a saying that you can rely on:

If we have died with him, then we shall
live with him.
12 If we hold firm, then we shall reign with
him.
If we disown him, then he will disown us.
13 We may be unfaithful, but he is always
faithful,

New English Bible

many witnesses; put that teaching into the charge of men you can trust, such men as will be competent to teach others.

Take your share of hardship, like a good soldier of Christ Jesus. A soldier on active service will not let himself be involved in civilian affairs; he must be wholly at his commanding officer's disposal. Again, no athlete can win a prize unless he has kept the rules. The farmer who gives his labour has first claim on the crop. Reflect on what I say, for the Lord will help you to full understanding.

Remember Jesus Christ, risen from the dead, born of David's line. This is the theme of my gospel, in whose service I am exposed to hardship, even to the point of being shut up like a common criminal; but the word of God is not shut up. And I endure it all for the sake of God's chosen ones, with this end in view, that they too may attain the glorious and eternal salvation which is in Christ Jesus.

Here are words you may trust:

'If we died with him, we shall live with him;
if we endure, we shall reign with him.
If we deny him, he will deny us.
If we are faithless, he keeps faith,

King James Version

deny himself. 14 Of these things put *them* in remembrance, charging *them* before the Lord that they strive not about words to no profit, *but* to the subverting of the hearers. 15 Study to shew thyself approved unto God, a workman that needeth not to be ashamed, rightly dividing the word of truth. 16 But shun profane *and* vain babblings: for they will increase unto more ungodliness. 17 And their word will eat as doth a canker: of whom is Hymeneus and Philetus; 18 Who concerning the truth have erred, saying that the resurrection is past already; and overthrow the faith of some. 19 Nevertheless the foundation of God standeth sure, having this seal, The Lord knoweth them that are his. And, Let every one that nameth the name of Christ depart from iniquity. 20 But in a great house there are not only vessels of gold and of silver, but also of wood and of earth; and some to honour, and some to dishonour. 21 If a man therefore purge himself from these, he shall be

Living Bible

who are part of himself, and he will always carry out his promises to us.

14 Remind your people of these great facts, and command them in the name of the Lord not to argue over unimportant things. Such arguments are confusing and useless, and even harmful. 15 Work hard so God can say to you, "Well done." Be a good workman, one who does not need to be ashamed when God examines your work. Know what his Word says and means. 16 Steer clear of foolish discussions which lead people into the sin of anger with each other. 17 Things will be said that will burn and hurt for a long time to come. Hymenaeus and Philetus, in their love of argument, are men like that. 18 They have left the path of truth, preaching the lie that the resurrection of the dead has already occurred; and they have weakened the faith of some who believe them.

19 But God's truth stands firm like a great rock, and nothing can shake it. It is a foundation stone with these words written on it: "The Lord knows those who are really his," and "A person who calls himself a Christian should not be doing things that are wrong."

20 In a wealthy home there are dishes made of gold and silver as well as some made from wood and clay. The expensive dishes are used for guests, and the cheap ones are used in the kitchen or to put garbage in. 21 If you stay away from sin you will be like one of these

Today's English Version

because he cannot be false to himself."

An approved worker

14 Remind your people of this, and give them solemn warning in God's presence not to fight over words. It does no good, but only ruins the people who listen. 15 Do your best to win full approval in God's sight, as a worker who is not ashamed of his work, one who correctly teaches the message of God's truth. 16 Keep away from godless and foolish discussions, which only drive people farther away from God. 17 What they teach will be like an open sore that eats away the flesh. Two of these teachers are Hymenaeus and Philetus. 18 They have left the way of truth and are upsetting the faith of some believers by saying that our resurrection has already taken place. 19 But the solid foundation that God has laid cannot be shaken; and these words are written on it: "The Lord knows those who are his"; and, "Whoever says that he belongs to the Lord must turn away from wrongdoing."

20 In a large house there are dishes and bowls of all kinds: some are made of silver and gold, others of wood and clay; some are for special occasions, others for ordinary use. 21 If anyone makes himself clean from all these evil things,

New International Version

for he cannot disown himself.

A workman approved by God

14 Keep reminding them of these things. Warn them before God against quarreling about words; it is of no value, and only ruins those who listen. 15 Do your best to present yourself to God as one approved, a workman who does not need to be ashamed and who correctly handles the word of truth. 16 Avoid godless chatter, because those who indulge in it will become more and more ungodly. 17 Their teaching will spread like gangrene. Among them are Hymenaeus and Philetus, 18 who have wandered away from the truth. They say that the resurrection has already taken place, and they destroy the faith of some. 19 Nevertheless, God's solid foundation stands firm, sealed with this inscription: "The Lord knows those who are his,"[a] and, "Everyone who confesses the name of the Lord must turn away from wickedness."

20 In a large house there are not only articles of gold and silver, but also of wood and clay; some are for noble purposes and some for ignoble. 21 If a man cleanses himself from the latter, he will be an instrument for noble pur-

[a] Num. 16:5.

Phillips Modern English

he always remains faithful. He cannot deny his own nature.

2.14 *Hold fast to the true: avoid dangerous error*

Remind your people of things like this, and tell them as before God not to fight wordy battles, which help no one and may undermine the faith of those who hear them.

For yourself, concentrate on winning God's approval, on being a workman with nothing to be ashamed of, and who knows how to use the word of truth to the best advantage. But steer clear of these unchristian babblings, which in practice lead further and further away from Christian living. For their teachings are as dangerous as blood-poisoning to the body, and spread like sepsis from a wound. Hymenaeus and Philetus are responsible for this sort of thing, and they are men who are palpable traitors to the truth, for they say that the resurrection has already happened and, of course, badly upset some people's faith.

God's solid foundation still stands, however, with this double inscription: *The Lord knows those who belong to him,* and *Let every true Christian have no dealings with evil.*

In any big household there are naturally not only gold and silver vessels but wooden and earthenware utensils as well. Some are used for the highest purposes and some for the lowest. If a man keeps himself clean from the contaminations of evil he will be a vessel used for

Revised Standard Version

for he cannot deny himself.
14 Remind them of this, and charge them
before the Lord [b] to avoid disputing about words,
which does no good, but only ruins the hearers.
15 Do your best to present yourself to God as
one approved, a workman who has no need to
be ashamed, rightly handling the word of truth.
16 Avoid such godless chatter, for it will lead
people into more and more ungodliness, 17 and
their talk will eat its way like gangrene. Among
them are Hymenaeus and Philetus, 18 who have
swerved from the truth by holding that the
resurrection is past already. They are upsetting
the faith of some. 19 But God's firm foundation
stands, bearing this seal: "The Lord knows those
who are his," and, "Let everyone who names the
name of the Lord depart from iniquity."
20 In a great house there are not only vessels
of gold and silver but also of wood and earthenware, and some for noble use, some for ignoble.
21 If any one purifies himself from what is ignoble, then he will be a vessel for noble use,

[b] Other ancient authorities read *God*.

Jerusalem Bible

for he cannot disown his own self.

The struggle against the immediate danger from false teachers

14 Remind them of this; and tell them in the
name of God that there is to be no wrangling
about words: all that this ever achieves is the
destruction of those who are listening. 15 Do all
you can to present yourself in front of God as a
man who has come through his trials, and a man
who has no cause to be ashamed of his life's
work and has kept a straight course with the
message of the truth. 16 Have nothing to do with
pointless philosophical discussions—they only
lead further and further away from true religion.
17 Talk of this kind corrodes like gangrene, as in
the case of Hymenaeus and Philetus, 18 the men
who have gone right away from the truth and
claim that the resurrection has already taken
place. Some people's faith cannot stand up to
them.
19 However, God's solid foundation stone is
still in position, and this is the inscription on it:
"The Lord knows those who are his own" [b] and
"All who *call on the name of the Lord* [c] must
avoid sin."
20 Not all the dishes in a large house are
made of gold and silver; some are made of wood
or earthenware: some are kept for special occasions and others are for ordinary purposes.
21 Now, to avoid these faults that I am speaking
about is the way for anyone to become a ves-

[b] Nb. 16:5,26. [c] Is. 26:13.

New English Bible

for he cannot deny himself.'

Go on reminding people of this, and charge them solemnly before God to stop disputing about mere words; it does no good, and is the ruin of those who listen. Try hard to show yourself worthy of God's approval, as a labourer who need not be ashamed; be straightforward in your proclamation of the truth. Avoid empty and worldly chatter; those who indulge in it will stray further and further into godless courses, and the infection of their teaching will spread like a gangrene. Such are Hymenaeus and Philetus; they have shot wide of the truth in saying that our resurrection has already taken place, and are upsetting people's faith. But God has laid a foundation, and it stands firm, with this inscription: 'The Lord knows his own', and, 'Everyone who takes the Lord's name upon his lips must forsake wickedness.' Now in any great house there are not only utensils of gold and silver, but also others of wood or earthenware; the former are valued, the latter held cheap. To be among those which are valued and dedicated, a

King James Version

a vessel unto honour, sanctified, and meet for the master's use, *and* prepared unto every good work. 22 Flee also youthful lusts: but follow righteousness, faith, charity, peace, with them that call on the Lord out of a pure heart. 23 But foolish and unlearned questions avoid, knowing that they do gender strifes. 24 And the servant of the Lord must not strive; but be gentle unto all *men,* apt to teach, patient; 25 In meekness instructing those that oppose themselves; if God peradventure will give them repentance to the acknowledging of the truth; 26 And *that* they may recover themselves out of the snare of the devil, who are taken captive by him at his will.

3 This know also, that in the last days perilous times shall come. 2 For men shall be lovers of their own selves, covetous, boasters, proud, blasphemers, disobedient to parents, unthankful, unholy, 3 Without natural affection, trucebreakers, false accusers, incontinent, fierce,

Living Bible

dishes made of purest gold—the very best in the house—so that Christ himself can use you for his highest purposes.

22 Run from anything that gives you the evil thoughts that young men often have, but stay close to anything that makes you want to do right. Have faith and love, and enjoy the companionship of those who love the Lord and have pure hearts.

23 Again I say, don't get involved in foolish arguments which only upset people and make them angry. 24 God's people must not be quarrelsome; they must be gentle, patient teachers of those who are wrong. 25 Be humble when you are trying to teach those who are mixed up concerning the truth. For if you talk meekly and courteously to them they are more likely, with God's help, to turn away from their wrong ideas and believe what is true. 26 Then they will come to their senses and escape from Satan's trap of slavery to sin which he uses to catch them whenever he likes, and then they can begin doing the will of God.

3 You may as well know this too, Timothy, that in the last days it is going to be very difficult to be a Christian. 2 For people will love only themselves and their money; they will be proud and boastful, sneering at God, disobedient to their parents, ungrateful to them, and thoroughly bad. 3 They will be hardheaded and never give in to others; they will be constant liars and

Today's English Version

he will be used for special purposes, because he is dedicated and useful to his Master, ready to be used for every good work. 22 Avoid the passions of youth, and strive for righteousness, faith, love, and peace, together with those who with a pure heart call for the Lord to help them. 23 But stay away from foolish and ignorant arguments; you know that they end up in quarrels. 24 The Lord's servant must not quarrel. He must be kind toward all, a good and patient teacher, 25 who is gentle as he corrects his opponents. It may be that God will give them the opportunity to repent and come to know the truth. 26 And then they will return to their senses and escape from the trap of the Devil, who had caught them and made them obey his will.

The last days

3 Remember this! There will be difficult times in the last days. 2 Men will be selfish, greedy, boastful, and conceited; they will be insulting, disobedient to their parents, ungrateful, and irreligious; 3 they will be unkind, merciless, slanderers, violent, and fierce; they will hate the

New International Version

poses, made holy, useful to the Master and prepared to do any good work.

22 Flee the evil desires of youth, and pursue righteousness, faith, love and peace, along with those who call on the Lord out of a pure heart. 23 Don't have anything to do with foolish and stupid arguments, because you know they produce quarrels. 24 And the Lord's servant must not quarrel; instead, he must be kind to everyone, able to teach, not resentful. 25 Those who oppose him he must gently instruct, in the hope that God will give them a change of heart leading them to a knowledge of the truth, 26 and that they will come to their senses and escape from the trap of the devil, who has taken them captive to do his will.

Godlessness in the last days

3 But mark this: There will be terrible times in the last days. 2 People will be lovers of themselves, lovers of money, boastful, proud, abusive, disobedient to their parents, ungrateful, unholy, 3 without love, unforgiving, slanderous, without self-control, brutal, not lovers of the

Phillips Modern English

honourable purposes, dedicated and serviceable for the use of the master of the household, all ready, in fact, for any good purpose.

2.22 *Be positively good—and patient*

Turn your back on the turbulent desires of youth and give your positive attention to goodness, integrity, love and peace in company with all those who approach the Lord in sincerity. But have nothing to do with silly and ill-informed controversies which lead inevitably, as you know, to strife. And the Lord's servant must not be a man of strife: he must be kind to all, ready and able to teach: he must be tolerant and have the ability gently to correct those who oppose his message. For God may give them a different outlook, and they may come to know the truth. They may come to their senses and be rescued from the snare of the devil and caught by God for his purposes.

3.1 *A warning of what to expect*

But you must realise that in the last days the times will be full of danger. Men will become utterly self-centred, greedy for money, full of big words. They will be proud and abusive, without any regard for what their parents taught them. They will be utterly lacking in gratitude, reverence and normal human affections. They will be remorseless, scandal-mongers, uncon-

Revised Standard Version

consecrated and useful to the master of the house,
ready for any good work. 22 So shun youthful
passions and aim at righteousness, faith, love,
and peace, along with those who call upon the
Lord from a pure heart. 23 Have nothing to do
with stupid, senseless controversies; you know
that they breed quarrels. 24 And the Lord's
servant must not be quarrelsome but kindly to
every one, an apt teacher, forbearing, 25 correcting his opponents with gentleness. God may perhaps grant that they will repent and come to
know the truth, 26 and they may escape from
the snare of the devil, after being captured by
him to do his will.[c]

3 But understand this, that in the last days
there will come times of stress. 2 For men
will be lovers of self, lovers of money, proud,
arrogant, abusive, disobedient to their parents,
ungrateful, unholy, 3 inhuman, implacable, slan-

[c] Or *by him, to do his* (that is, God's) *will.*

Jerusalem Bible

sel for special occasions, fit for the Master himself to use, and kept ready for any good work.
22 Instead of giving in to your impulses like
a young man, fasten your attention on holiness,
faith, love and peace, in union with all those who
call on the Lord with pure minds. 23 Avoid these
futile and silly speculations, understanding that
they only give rise to quarrels; 24 and a servant
of the Lord is not to engage in quarrels, but has
to be kind to everyone, a good teacher, and patient. 25 He has to be gentle when he corrects
people who dispute what he says, never forgetting that God may give them a change of mind
so that they recognize the truth and 26 come to
their senses, once out of the trap where the devil
caught them and kept them enslaved.

The dangers of the last days

3 You may be quite sure that in the last days
there are going to be some difficult times.
2 People will be self-centered and grasping;
boastful, arrogant and rude; disobedient to their
parents, ungrateful, irreligious; 3 heartless and
unappeasable; they will be slanderers, profligates,

New English Bible

thing of use to the Master of the house, a man must cleanse himself from all those evil things;[a] then he will be fit for any honourable purpose.

Turn from the wayward impulses of youth, and pursue justice, integrity, love, and peace with all who invoke the Lord in singleness of mind. Have nothing to do with foolish and ignorant speculations. You know they breed quarrels, and the servant of the Lord must not be quarrelsome, but kindly towards all. He should be a good teacher, tolerant, and gentle when discipline is needed for the refractory. The Lord may grant them a change of heart and show them the truth, and thus they may come to their senses and escape from the devil's snare, in which they have been caught and held at his will.[b]

3 You must face the fact: the final age of this
world is to be a time of troubles. Men will
love nothing but money and self; they will be
arrogant, boastful, and abusive; with no respect
for parents, no gratitude, no piety, no natural
affection; they will be implacable in their ha-

[a] *Or* must separate himself from these persons.
[b] *Or* escape from the devil's snare, caught now by God and made subject to his will.

King James Version

despisers of those that are good, 4 Traitors,
heady, highminded, lovers of pleasures more
than lovers of God; 5 Having a form of godliness, but denying the power thereof: from such
turn away. 6 For of this sort are they which
creep into houses, and lead captive silly women
laden with sins, led away with divers lusts, 7 Ever
learning, and never able to come to the knowledge of the truth. 8 Now as Jannes and Jambres
withstood Moses, so do these also resist the
truth: men of corrupt minds, reprobate concerning the faith. 9 But they shall proceed no further:
for their folly shall be manifest unto all *men,* as
theirs also was. 10 But thou hast fully known
my doctrine, manner of life, purpose, faith, longsuffering, charity, patience, 11 Persecutions, afflictions, which came unto me at Antioch, at
Iconium, at Lystra; what persecutions I endured:
but out of *them* all the Lord delivered me.
12 Yea, and all that will live godly in Christ
Jesus shall suffer persecution. 13 But evil men

Living Bible

troublemakers and will think nothing of immorality. They will be rough and cruel, and sneer at
those who try to be good. 4 They will betray
their friends; they will be hotheaded, puffed up
with pride, and prefer good times to worshiping
God. 5 They will go to church,[a] yes, but they
won't really believe anything they hear. Don't be
taken in by people like that.
6 They are the kind who craftily sneak into
other people's homes and make friendships with
silly, sin-burdened women and teach them their
new doctrines. 7 Women of that kind are forever following new teachers, but they never understand the truth. 8 And these teachers fight
truth just as Jannes and Jambres fought against
Moses. They have dirty minds, warped and
twisted, and have turned against the Christian
faith.
9 But they won't get away with all this forever. Some day their deceit will be well known
to everyone, as was the sin of Jannes and Jambres.
10 But you know from watching me that I am
not that kind of person. You know what I believe and the way I live and what I want. You
know my faith in Christ and how I have suffered.
You know my love for you, and my patience.
11 You know how many troubles I have had as
a result of my preaching the Good News. You
know about all that was done to me while I was
visiting in Antioch, Iconium and Lystra, but the
Lord delivered me. 12 Yes, and those who decide to please Christ Jesus by living godly lives
will suffer at the hands of those who hate him.
13 In fact, evil men and false teachers will be-

[*a*] Literally, "having a form of godliness."

Today's English Version

good; 4 they will be treacherous, reckless, and
swollen with pride; they will love pleasure rather
than God; 5 they will hold to the outward form
of our religion, but reject its real power. Keep
away from these men. 6 Some of them go into
homes and get control over weak women who
are burdened by the guilt of their sins and driven
by all kinds of desires, 7 women who are always
trying to learn but who never can come to know
the truth. 8 As Jannes and Jambres were opposed
to Moses, so also these men are opposed to the
truth—men whose minds do not function and
who are failures in the faith. 9 But they will not
get very far, because everyone will see how
stupid they are, just as it happened to Jannes and
Jambres.

Last instructions

10 But you have followed my teaching, my
conduct, and my purpose in life; you have observed my faith, my patience, my love, my endurance, 11 my persecutions, and my sufferings.
You know all the things that happened to me
in Antioch, Iconium, and Lystra, the terrible
persecutions I endured! But the Lord rescued
me from them all. 12 All who want to live a
godly life in union with Christ Jesus will be
persecuted; 13 but evil men and impostors will

New International Version

good, 4 treacherous, rash, conceited, lovers of
pleasure rather than lovers of God—5 having a
form of godliness but denying its power. Have
nothing to do with them.
6 They are the kind who worm their way into
homes and gain control over weak-willed women,
who are loaded down with sins and are swayed
by all kinds of evil desires, 7 always learning but
never able to acknowledge the truth. 8 Just as
Jannes and Jambres opposed Moses, so also
these men oppose the truth—men of depraved
minds, who, as far as the faith is concerned, are
rejected. 9 But they will not get very far because, as in the case of those men, their folly
will be clear to everyone.

Paul's charge to Timothy

10 You, however, know all about my teaching,
my way of life, my purpose, faith, patience,
love, endurance, 11 persecutions, sufferings—what
kinds of things happened to me in Antioch,
Iconium and Lystra, the persecutions I endured.
Yet the Lord rescued me from all of them.
12 In fact, everyone who wants to live a godly
life in Christ Jesus will be persecuted, 13 while

Phillips Modern English

trolled and violent and haters of all that is good. They will be treacherous, reckless and arrogant, loving what gives them pleasure instead of loving God. They will maintain a façade of "religion" but their life denies its truth. Keep clear of people like that.

From their number come those creatures who worm their way into people's houses, and find easy prey in silly women with an exaggerated sense of sin and assorted desires—who are always anxious to learn and yet never able to grasp the truth. These men are as much enemies to the truth as Jannes and Jambres were to Moses. Their minds are distorted, and they are traitors to the faith. But in the long run they won't get very far. Their folly will become as obvious to everybody as did that of Moses' opponents.

3.10 *Your knowledge of the truth should be your safeguard*

But you, Timothy, have closely followed my teaching and my way of life, my purpose, my faith, my endurance; my love and courage in all those persecutions and difficulties at Antioch, Iconium and Lystra. And you know how the Lord brought me safely through them all. Persecution is inevitable for those who are determined to live really Christian lives, while wicked

Revised Standard Version

derers, profligates, fierce, haters of good, 4 treacherous, reckless, swollen with conceit, lovers of
pleasure rather than lovers of God, 5 holding the
form of religion but denying the power of it.
Avoid such people. 6 For among them are those
who make their way into households and capture weak women, burdened with sins and
swayed by various impulses, 7 who will listen to
anybody and can never arrive at a knowledge of
the truth. 8 As Jannes and Jambres opposed
Moses, so these men also oppose the truth, men
of corrupt mind and counterfeit faith; 9 but they
will not get very far, for their folly will be plain
to all, as was that of those two men.
10 Now you have observed my teaching, my
conduct, my aim in life, my faith, my patience,
my love, my steadfastness, 11 my persecutions,
my sufferings, what befell me at Antioch, at
Iconium, and at Lystra, what persecutions I
endured; yet from them all the Lord rescued me.
12 Indeed all who desire to live a godly life in
Christ Jesus will be persecuted, 13 while evil

Jerusalem Bible

savages and enemies of everything that is good;
4 they will be treacherous and reckless and de-
mented by pride, preferring their own pleasure to
God. 5 They will keep up the outward appearance of religion but will have rejected the inner
power of it. Have nothing to do with people
like that.
6 Of the same kind, too, are those men who
insinuate themselves into families in order to
get influence over silly women who are obsessed
with their sins and follow one craze after another 7 in the attempt to educate themselves, but
can never come to knowledge of the truth. 8 Men
like this defy the truth just as Jannes and Jambres defied Moses[d]: their minds are corrupt and
their faith spurious. 9 But they will not be able
to go on any longer: their foolishness, like that of
the other two, must become obvious to everybody.
10 You know, though, what I have taught,
how I have lived, what I have aimed at; you
know my faith, my patience and my love; my
constancy 11 and the persecutions and hardships that came to me in places like Antioch,
Iconium and Lystra—all the persecutions I have
endured; and the Lord has rescued me from
every one of them. 12 You are well aware, then,
that anybody who tries to live in devotion to
Christ is certain to be attacked; 13 while these

[d] In Jewish tradition, the leaders of the Egyptian magicians and disciples of Balaam.

New English Bible

treds, scandal-mongers, intemperate and fierce, strangers to all goodness, traitors, adventurers, swollen with self-importance. They will be men who put pleasure in the place of God, men who preserve the outward form of religion, but are a standing denial of its reality. Keep clear of men like these. They are the sort that insinuate themselves into private houses and there get miserable women into their clutches, women burdened with a sinful past, and led on by all kinds of desires, who are always wanting to be taught, but are incapable of reaching a knowledge of the truth. As Jannes and Jambres defied Moses, so these men defy the truth; they have lost the power to reason, and they cannot pass the tests of faith. But their successes will be short-lived, for, like those opponents of Moses, they will come to be recognized by everyone for the fools they are.

But you, my son, have followed, step by step, my teaching and my manner of life, my resolution, my faith, patience, and spirit of love, and my fortitude under persecutions and sufferings—all that I went through at Antioch, at Iconium, at Lystra, all the persecutions I endured; and the Lord rescued me out of them all. Yes, persecution will come to all who want to live a godly life as Christians, whereas wicked men

King James Version

and seducers shall wax worse and worse, deceiving, and being deceived. 14 But continue thou in the things which thou hast learned and hast been assured of, knowing of whom thou hast learned *them;* 15 And that from a child thou hast known the holy Scriptures, which are able to make thee wise unto salvation through faith which is in Christ Jesus. 16 All Scripture is given by inspiration of God, and *is* profitable for doctrine, for reproof, for correction, for instruction in righteousness: 17 That the man of God may be perfect, thoroughly furnished unto all good works.

4 I charge *thee* therefore before God, and the Lord Jesus Christ, who shall judge the quick and the dead at his appearing and his kingdom; 2 Preach the word; be instant in season, out of season; reprove, rebuke, exhort with all long-suffering and doctrine. 3 For the time will come when they will not endure sound doctrine; but after their own lusts shall they heap to themselves teachers, having itching ears; 4 And they

Living Bible

come worse and worse, deceiving many, they themselves having been deceived by Satan.

14 But you must keep on believing the things you have been taught. You know they are true for you know that you can trust those of us who have taught you. 15 You know how, when you were a small child, you were taught the holy Scriptures; and it is these that make you wise to accept God's salvation by trusting in Christ Jesus. 16 The whole Bible[b] was given to us by inspiration from God and is useful to teach us what is true and to make us realize what is wrong in our lives; it straightens us out and helps us do what is right. 17 It is God's way of making us well prepared at every point, fully equipped to do good to everyone.

4 And so I solemnly urge you before God and before Christ Jesus—who will some day judge the living and the dead when he appears to set up his kingdom—2 to preach the Word of God urgently at all times, whenever you get the chance, in season and out, when it is convenient and when it is not. Correct and rebuke your people when they need it, encourage them to do right, and all the time be feeding them patiently with God's Word.

3 For there is going to come a time when people won't listen to the truth, but will go around looking for teachers who will tell them just what they want to hear. 4 They won't listen

[*b*] Literally, "Every Scripture."

Today's English Version

keep on going from bad to worse, deceiving others and being deceived themselves. 14 But as for you, continue in the truths that you were taught and firmly believe. You know who your teachers were, 15 and you remember that ever since you were a child you have known the Holy Scriptures, which are able to give you the wisdom that leads to salvation through faith in Christ Jesus. 16 All Scripture is inspired by God and is useful for teaching the truth, rebuking error, correcting faults, and giving instruction for right living, 17 so that the man who serves God may be fully qualified and equipped to do every kind of good work.

4 I solemnly urge you in the presence of God and of Christ Jesus, who will judge all men, living and dead: because of his coming and of his Kingdom, I command you 2 to preach the message, to insist upon telling it, whether the time is right or not; to convince, reproach, and encourage, teaching with all patience. 3 The time will come when men will not listen to the true teaching, but will follow their own desires, and will collect for themselves more and more teachers who will tell them what they are itching to hear. 4 They will turn away from listening to

New International Version

evil men and impostors will go from bad to worse, deceiving and being deceived. 14 But as for you, continue in what you have learned and have become convinced of, because you know those from whom you learned it, 15 and how from infancy you have known the holy Scriptures, which are able to make you wise for salvation through faith in Christ Jesus. 16 All Scripture is God-breathed and is useful for teaching, rebuking, correcting and training in righteousness, 17 so that the man of God may be thoroughly equipped for every good work.

4 In the presence of God and of Christ Jesus, who will judge the living and the dead, and in view of his appearing and his kingdom, I give you this charge: 2 Preach the Word; be prepared in season and out of season; correct, rebuke and encourage—with great patience and careful instruction. 3 For the time will come when men will not put up with sound doctrine. Instead, to suit their own desires, they will gather around them a great number of teachers to say what their itching ears want to hear. 4 They will

Phillips Modern English

and deceitful men will go from bad to worse, deluding others and deluding themselves.

Yet you must go on steadily in those things that you have learned and which you know are true. Remember from whom your knowledge has come, and how from early childhood your mind has been familiar with the holy scriptures, which can open the mind to the salvation which comes through believing in Christ Jesus. All scripture is inspired by God and is useful for teaching the faith and correcting error, for resetting the direction of a man's life and training him in good living. The scriptures are the comprehensive equipment of the man of God, and fit him fully for all branches of his work.

4.1 My time is nearly over: you must carry on

I solemnly charge you, Timothy, in the presence of God and of Christ Jesus who will judge the living and the dead, by his appearing and his kingdom, to preach the Word. Never lose your sense of urgency, in season or out of season. Reprove, correct, and encourage, using the utmost patience in your teaching. For the time is coming when men will not tolerate wholesome teaching. They will want something to tickle their own fancies, and they will collect teachers who will speak what they want to hear. They will no longer listen to the truth, but will

Revised Standard Version

men and impostors will go on from bad to worse, deceivers and deceived. 14 But as for you, continue in what you have learned and have firmly believed, knowing from whom you learned it 15 and how from childhood you have been acquainted with the sacred writings which are able to instruct you for salvation through faith in Christ Jesus. 16 All scripture is inspired by God and[d] profitable for teaching, for reproof, for correction, and for training in righteousness, 17 that the man of God may be complete, equipped for every good work.

4 I charge you in the presence of God and of Christ Jesus who is to judge the living and the dead, and by his appearing and his kingdom: 2 preach the word, be urgent in season and out of season, convince, rebuke, and exhort, be unfailing in patience and in teaching. 3 For the time is coming when people will not endure sound teaching, but having itching ears they will accumulate for themselves teachers to suit their own likings, 4 and will turn away from

[d] Or *Every scripture inspired by God is also.*

Jerusalem Bible

wicked impostors will go from bad to worse, deceiving others and deceived themselves.

14 You must keep to what you have been taught and know to be true; remember who your teachers were, 15 and how, ever since you were a child, you have known the holy scriptures—from these you can learn the wisdom that leads to salvation through faith in Christ Jesus. 16 All scripture is inspired by God and can profitably be used for teaching, for refuting error, for guiding people's lives and teaching them to be holy. 17 This is how the man who is dedicated to God becomes fully equipped and ready for any good work.

A solemn charge

4 Before God and before Christ Jesus who is to be judge of the living and the dead, I put this duty to you, in the name of his Appearing and of his kingdom: 2 proclaim the message and, welcome or unwelcome, insist on it. Refute falsehood, correct error, call to obedience—but do all with patience and with the intention of teaching. 3 The time is sure to come when, far from being content with sound teaching, people will be avid for the latest novelty and collect themselves a whole series of teachers according to their own tastes; 4 and then, instead

New English Bible

and charlatans will make progress from bad to worse, deceiving and deceived. But for your part, stand by the truths you have learned and are assured of. Remember from whom you learned them; remember that from early childhood you have been familiar with the sacred writings which have power to make you wise and lead you to salvation through faith in Christ Jesus. Every inspired scripture has its use for teaching the truth and refuting error, or for reformation of manners and discipline in right living, so that the man who belongs to God may be efficient and equipped for good work of every kind.

4 Before God, and before Christ Jesus who is to judge men living and dead, I charge you solemnly by his coming appearance and his reign, proclaim the message, press it home on all occasions,[a] convenient or inconvenient, use argument, reproof, and appeal, with all the patience that the work of teaching requires. For the time will come when they will not stand wholesome teaching, but will follow their own fancy and gather a crowd of teachers to tickle their ears. They will stop their ears to the truth

[a] *Or* be on duty at all times.

King James Version

shall turn away *their* ears from the truth, and
shall be turned unto fables. 5 But watch thou
in all things, endure afflictions, do the work of
an evangelist, make full proof of thy ministry.
6 For I am now ready to be offered, and the
time of my departure is at hand. 7 I have fought
a good fight, I have finished *my* course, I have
kept the faith: 8 Henceforth there is laid up for
me a crown of righteousness, which the Lord,
the righteous judge, shall give me at that day:
and not to me only, but unto all them also that
love his appearing. 9 Do thy diligence to come
shortly unto me: 10 For Demas hath forsaken
me, having loved this present world, and is departed unto Thessalonica; Crescens to Galatia,
Titus unto Dalmatia. 11 Only Luke is with me.
Take Mark, and bring him with thee: for he is
profitable to me for the ministry. 12 And Tychicus
have I sent to Ephesus. 13 The cloak that I left
at Troas with Carpus, when thou comest, bring
with thee, and the books, *but* especially the
parchments. 14 Alexander the coppersmith did
me much evil: the Lord reward him according

Living Bible

to what the Bible says but will blithely follow
their own misguided ideas.

5 Stand steady, and don't be afraid of suffering for the Lord. Bring others to Christ. Leave
nothing undone that you ought to do.

6 I say this because I won't be around to help
you very much longer. My time has almost run
out. Very soon now I will be on my way to
heaven. 7 I have fought long and hard for my
Lord, and through it all I have kept true to him.
And now the time has come for me to stop fighting and rest. 8 In heaven a crown is waiting for
me which the Lord, the righteous Judge, will
give me on that great day of his return. And not
just to me, but to all those whose lives show
that they are eagerly looking forward to his coming back again.

9 Please come as soon as you can, 10 for
Demas has left me. He loved the good things of
this life and went to Thessalonica. Crescens has
gone to Galatia, Titus to Dalmatia. 11 Only Luke
is with me. Bring Mark with you when you come,
for I need him. 12 (Tychicus is gone too, as I
sent him to Ephesus.) 13 When you come, be
sure to bring the coat I left at Troas with
Brother Carpus, and also the books, but especially the parchments.

14 Alexander the coppersmith has done me

Today's English Version

the truth and give their attention to legends.
5 But you must keep control of yourself in all
circumstances; endure suffering, do the work of
a preacher of the Good News, and perform your
whole duty as a servant of God.

6 As for me, the hour has come for me to be
sacrificed; the time is here for me to leave this
life. 7 I have done my best in the race, I have
run the full distance, I have kept the faith. 8 And
now the prize of victory is waiting for me, the
crown of righteousness which the Lord, the
righteous Judge, will give me on that Day—
and not only to me, but to all those who wait
with love for him to appear.

Personal words

9 Do your best to come to me soon. 10 Demas
fell in love with this present world and has deserted me; he has gone off to Thessalonica.
Crescens went to Galatia, and Titus to Dalmatia. 11 Only Luke is with me. Get Mark and
bring him with you, because he can help me in
the work. 12 I sent Tychicus to Ephesus.
13 When you come, bring my coat that I left in
Troas with Carpus; bring the books too, and
especially the ones made of parchment.

14 Alexander the metalworker did me great
harm; the Lord will reward him according to

New International Version

turn their ears away from the truth and turn
aside to myths. 5 But you, keep your head in all
situations, endure hardship, do the work of an
evangelist, discharge all the duties of your ministry.

6 For I am already being poured out as a
drink offering, and the time has come for my
departure. 7 I have fought the good fight, I have
finished the race, I have kept the faith. 8 Now
there is in store for me the crown of righteousness, which the Lord, the righteous Judge, will
award to me on that day—and not only to me,
but also to all who have longed for his appearing.

Personal remarks

9 Do your best to come to me quickly, 10 for
Demas, because he loved this world, has deserted me and has gone to Thessalonica. Crescens has gone to Galatia, and Titus to Dalmatia. 11 Only Luke is with me. Get Mark and
bring him with you, because he is helpful to me
in my ministry. 12 I sent Tychicus to Ephesus.
13 When you come, bring the cloak that I left
with Carpus at Troas, and my scrolls, especially
the parchments.

14 Alexander the metalworker did me a great
deal of harm. The Lord will repay him for what

Phillips Modern English

wander off after man-made myths.

For yourself, keep your mind sane and balanced, meeting whatever suffering this may involve. Go on steadily preaching the gospel and carry out to the full the commission that God gave you.

As for me, I feel that the last drops of my life are being poured out for God. The time for my departure has arrived. The glorious fight that God gave me I have fought, the course that I was set I have finished, and I have kept the faith. The future for me holds the crown of righteousness which the Lord, the true judge, will give to me in that day—and not, of course, only to me but to all those who have loved what they have seen of him.

4.9 Personal messages

Do your best to come to me as soon as you can. Demas, loving this present world, I fear, has left me and gone to Thessalonica. Crescens has gone to Galatia, and Titus is away in Dalmatia. Only Luke is with me now.

When you come, pick up Mark and bring him with you. I can certainly find a ministry for him here. (I had to send Tychicus off to Ephesus.) And please bring with you the cloak I left with Carpus at Troas, and the books, especially the manuscripts. Alexander the coppersmith did me a great deal of harm—the Lord

Revised Standard Version

listening to the truth and wander into myths.
5 As for you, always be steady, endure suffering,
do the work of an evangelist, fulfil your ministry.
6 For I am already on the point of being
sacrificed; the time of my departure has come.
7 I have fought the good fight, I have finished
the race, I have kept the faith. 8 Henceforth
there is laid up for me the crown of righteousness, which the Lord, the righteous judge, will
award to me on that Day, and not only to me
but also to all who have loved his appearing.
9 Do your best to come to me soon. 10 For
Demas, in love with this present world, has deserted me and gone to Thessalonica; Crescens
has gone to Galatia,[e] Titus to Dalmatia. 11 Luke
alone is with me. Get Mark and bring him with
you; for he is very useful in serving me. 12 Tychicus I have sent to Ephesus. 13 When you come,
bring the cloak that I left with Carpus at Troas,
also the books, and above all the parchments.
14 Alexander the coppersmith did me great harm;

[e] Other ancient authorities read *Gaul*.

Jerusalem Bible

of listening to the truth, they will turn to myths.
5 Be careful always to choose the right course;
be brave under trials; make the preaching of the
Good News your life's work, in thoroughgoing
service.

Paul in the evening of his life

6 As for me, my life is already being poured
away as a libation, and the time has come for
me to be gone. 7 I have fought the good fight
to the end; I have run the race to the finish; I
have kept the faith; 8 all there is to come now
is the crown of righteousness reserved for me,
which the Lord, the righteous judge, will give to
me on that Day; and not only to me but to all
those who have longed for his Appearing.

Final advice

9 Do your best to come and see me as soon as
you can. 10 As it is, Demas has deserted me for
love of this life and gone to Thessalonika,
Crescens has gone to Galatia and Titus to Dalmatia; 11 only Luke is with me. Get Mark to
come and bring him with you; I find him a useful
helper in my work. 12 I have sent Tychicus to
Ephesus. 13 When you come, bring the cloak I
left with Carpus in Troas, and the scrolls, especially the parchment ones. 14 Alexander the
coppersmith has done me a lot of harm; *the*

New English Bible

and turn to mythology. But you yourself must keep calm and sane at all times; face hardship, work to spread the Gospel, and do all the duties of your calling.

As for me, already my life is being poured out on the altar, and the hour for my departure is upon me. I have run the great race, I have finished the course, I have kept faith. And now the prize awaits me, the garland of righteousness which the Lord, the all-just Judge, will award me on that great Day; and it is not for me alone, but for all who have set their hearts on his coming appearance.

Do your best to join me soon; for Demas has deserted me because his heart was set on this world; he has gone to Thessalonica, Crescens to Galatia,[b] Titus to Dalmatia; I have no one with me but Luke. Pick up Mark and bring him with you, for I find him a useful assistant. Tychicus I have sent to Ephesus. When you come, bring the cloak I left with Carpus at Troas, and the books, above all my notebooks.

Alexander the copper-smith did me a great deal of harm. Retribution will fall upon him

[b] *Or* Gaul; *some witnesses read* Gallia.

King James Version

to his works: 15 Of whom be thou ware also; for he hath greatly withstood our words. 16 At my first answer no man stood with me, but all *men* forsook me: *I pray God* that it may not be laid to their charge. 17 Notwithstanding the Lord stood with me, and strengthened me; that by me the preaching might be fully known, and *that* all the Gentiles might hear: and I was delivered out of the mouth of the lion. 18 And the Lord shall deliver me from every evil work, and will preserve *me* unto his heavenly kingdom: to whom *be* glory for ever and ever. Amen. 19 Salute Prisca and Aquila, and the household of Onesiphorus. 20 Erastus abode at Corinth: but Trophimus have I left at Miletum sick. 21 Do thy diligence to come before winter. Eubulus greeteth thee, and Pudens, and Linus, and Claudia, and all the brethren. 22 The Lord Jesus Christ *be* with thy spirit. Grace *be* with you. Amen.

The second *epistle* unto Timotheus, ordained the first bishop of the church of the Ephesians, was written from Rome, when Paul was brought before Nero the second time.

Living Bible

much harm. The Lord will punish him, 15 but be careful of him, for he fought against everything we said.

16 The first time I was brought before the judge no one was here to help me. Everyone had run away. I hope that they will not be blamed for it. 17 But the Lord stood with me and gave me the opportunity to boldly preach a whole sermon for all the world to hear. And he saved me from being thrown to the lions.[a] 18 Yes, and the Lord will always deliver me from all evil and will bring me into his heavenly kingdom. To God be the glory forever and ever. Amen.

19 Please say "hello" for me to Priscilla and Aquila and those living at the home of Onesiphorus. 20 Erastus stayed at Corinth, and I left Trophimus sick at Miletus.

21 Do try to be here before winter. Eubulus sends you greetings, and so do Pudens, Linus, Claudia, and all the others. 22 May the Lord Jesus Christ be with your spirit.

Farewell,
Paul

[a] Literally, "I was delivered out of the mouth of the lion."

Today's English Version

what he has done. 15 Be on your guard against him yourself, because he was violently opposed to our message.

16 No one stood by me the first time I defended myself; all deserted me. May God not count it against them! 17 But the Lord stayed with me and gave me strength, so that I was able to proclaim the full message for all the Gentiles to hear; and I was rescued from the lion's mouth. 18 And the Lord will rescue me from all evil, and take me safely into his heavenly Kingdom. To him be the glory forever and ever! Amen.

Final greetings

19 I send greetings to Priscilla and Aquila, and to the family of Onesiphorus. 20 Erastus stayed in Corinth, and I left Trophimus in Miletus, because he was sick. 21 Do your best to come before winter.

Eubulus, Pudens, Linus, and Claudia send their greetings, and so do all the other brothers.

22 The Lord be with your spirit.

God's grace be with you all.

New International Version

he has done. 15 You too should be on your guard against him, because he strongly opposed our message.

16 At my first defense, no one came to my support, but everyone deserted me. May it not be held against them. 17 But the Lord stood at my side and gave me strength, so that through me the message might be fully proclaimed and all the Gentiles might hear it. And I was delivered from the lion's mouth. 18 The Lord will rescue me from every evil attack and will bring me safely to his heavenly kingdom. To him be glory for ever and ever. Amen.

Final greetings

19 Greet Priscilla[b] and Aquila and the household of Onesiphorus. 20 Erastus stayed in Corinth, and I left Trophimus sick in Miletus. 21 Do your best to get here before winter. Eubulus greets you, and so do Pudens, Linus, Claudia and all the brothers.

22 The Lord be with your spirit. Grace be with you.

[b] Greek *Prisca*.

Phillips Modern English

will reward him for what he did—and I should be very careful of him if I were you. He has been a bitter opponent of our teaching.

The first time I had to defend myself no one was on my side—they all deserted me, God forgive them! Yet the Lord himself stood by me and gave me the strength to proclaim the message clearly and fully, so that the gentiles could hear it, and I was rescued "from the lion's mouth". I am sure the Lord will rescue me from every evil plot, and will keep me safe until I reach his heavenly kingdom. Glory be to him for ever and ever, amen!

4.19 Closing greetings

Give my love to Prisca and Aquila and Onesiphorus and his family. Erastus is still staying on at Corinth, and Trophimus I had to leave sick at Miletus.

Do your best to get here before the winter. Eubulus, Pudens, Linus, Claudia and all here send their greetings to you. The Lord be with your spirit. Grace be with you all.

Revised Standard Version

the Lord will requite him for his deeds. 15 Beware of him yourself, for he strongly opposed
our message. 16 At my first defense no one took
my part; all deserted me. May it not be charged
against them! 17 But the Lord stood by me and
gave me strength to proclaim the message fully,
that all the Gentiles might hear it. So I was
rescued from the lion's mouth. 18 The Lord will
rescue me from every evil and save me for his
heavenly kingdom. To him be the glory for
ever and ever. Amen.

19 Greet Prisca and Aquila, and the household of Onesiphorus. 20 Erastus remained at
Corinth; Trophimus I left ill at Miletus. 21 Do
your best to come before winter. Eubulus sends
greetings to you, as do Pudens and Linus and
Claudia and all the brethren.
22 The Lord be with your spirit. Grace be
with you.

Jerusalem Bible

Lord will repay him for what he has done.[e]
15 Be on your guard against him yourself, because he has been bitterly contesting everything
that we say.
16 The first time I had to present my defense,
there was not a single witness to support me.
Every one of them deserted me—may they not
be held accountable for it. 17 But the Lord stood
by me and gave me power, so that through me
the whole message might be proclaimed for all
the pagans to hear; and so I was *rescued from*
the lion's mouth.[f] 18 The Lord will rescue me
from all evil attempts on me, and bring me
safely to his heavenly kingdom. To him be glory
for ever and ever. Amen.

Farewells and final good wishes

19 Greetings to Prisca and Aquila, and the
family of Onesiphorus. 20 Erastus remained at
Corinth, and I left Trophimus ill at Miletus.
21 Do your best to come before the winter.
Greetings to you from Eubulus, Pudens, Linus,
Claudia and all the brothers.
22 The Lord be with your spirit. Grace be
with you.

[*e*] Ps. 28:4 and 62:12; Pr. 24:12. [*f*] Ps. 22:21.

New English Bible

from the Lord. You had better be on your guard against him too, for he violently opposed everything I said. At the first hearing of my case no one came into court to support me; they all left me in the lurch; I pray that it may not be held against them. But the Lord stood by me and lent me strength, so that I might be his instrument in making the full proclamation of the Gospel for the whole pagan world to hear; and thus I was rescued out of the lion's jaws. And the Lord will rescue me from every attempt to do me harm, and keep me safe until his heavenly reign begins.[a] Glory to him for ever and ever! Amen.

Greetings to Prisca and Aquila, and the household of Onesiphorus.

Erastus stayed behind at Corinth, and I left Trophimus ill at Miletus. Do try to get here before winter.

Greetings from Eubulus, Pudens, Linus, and Claudia, and from all the brotherhood here.

The Lord be with your spirit. Grace be with you all!

[*a*] *Or* from all that evil can do, and bring me safely into his heavenly kingdom.

King James Version

THE EPISTLE OF PAUL TO TITUS

1 Paul, a servant of God, and an apostle of Jesus Christ, according to the faith of God's elect, and the acknowledging of the truth which is after godliness; 2 In hope of eternal life, which God, that cannot lie, promised before the world began; 3 But hath in due times manifested his word through preaching, which is committed unto me according to the commandment of God

Living Bible

TITUS

1 *From:* Paul, the slave of God and the messenger of Jesus Christ.

I have been sent to bring faith to those God has chosen and to teach them to know God's truth—the kind of truth that changes lives—so that they can have eternal life, which God promised them before the world began—and he cannot lie. 3And now in his own good time he has revealed this Good News and permits me to tell it to everyone. By command of God our Savior I have been trusted to do this work for him.

Today's English Version

PAUL'S LETTER TO TITUS

1 From Paul, a servant of God and an apostle of Jesus Christ.

I was chosen and sent to help the faith of God's chosen people and lead them to the truth taught by our religion, 2 which is based on the hope for eternal life. God, who does not lie, promised us this life before the beginning of time, 3 and at the right time he revealed it in his message. This was entrusted to me, and I proclaim it by order of God our Savior.

New International Version

TITUS

1 Paul, a servant of God and an apostle of Jesus Christ for the faith of God's elect and the knowledge of the truth that leads to godliness—2 a faith and knowledge resting on the hope of eternal life, which God, who does not lie, promised before the beginning of time, 3 and at his appointed season he brought his word to light through the preaching entrusted to me by the command of God our Savior,

Phillips Modern English

THE LETTER TO TITUS

From Paul, a servant of God and messenger of Jesus Christ in the faith God gives to his chosen, in the knowledge of the truth that comes from a God-fearing life, and in the hope of the everlasting life which God, who cannot lie, promised before the beginning of time. At the moment of his choice he made his Word known in the declaration which has been entrusted to me by the

Revised Standard Version

THE LETTER OF PAUL TO TITUS

1 Paul, a servant[a] of God and an apostle of Jesus Christ, to further the faith of God's elect and their knowledge of the truth which accords with godliness, 2 in hope of eternal life which God, who never lies, promised ages ago 3 and at the proper time manifested in his word through the preaching with which I have been entrusted by command of God our Savior;

[a] Or *slave*.

Jerusalem Bible

THE LETTER FROM PAUL TO TITUS

Address

1 From Paul, servant of God, an apostle of Jesus Christ to bring those whom God has chosen to faith and to the knowledge of the truth that leads to true religion; 2 and to give them the hope of the eternal life that was promised so long ago by God. He does not lie 3 and so, at the appointed time, he revealed his decision, and, by the command of God our savior, I have been

New English Bible

THE LETTER OF PAUL TO TITUS

Training for the Christian life

1 From Paul, servant of God and apostle of Jesus Christ, marked as such by faith and knowledge and hope—the faith of God's chosen people, knowledge of the truth as our religion has it, and the hope of eternal life.[a] Yes, it is eternal life that God, who cannot lie, promised long ages ago, and now in his own good time he has openly declared himself in the proclamation which was entrusted to me by ordinance of God our Saviour.

[a] *Or* apostle of Jesus Christ, to bring God's chosen people to faith and to a knowledge of the truth as our religion has it, with its hope for eternal life.

King James Version

our Saviour; 4 To Titus, *mine* own son after the common faith: Grace, mercy, *and* peace, from God the Father and the Lord Jesus Christ our Saviour. 5 For this cause left I thee in Crete, that thou shouldest set in order the things that are wanting, and ordain elders in every city, as I had appointed thee: 6 If any be blameless, the husband of one wife, having faithful children not accused of riot or unruly. 7 For a bishop must be blameless, as the steward of God; not selfwilled, not soon angry, not given to wine, no striker, not given to filthy lucre; 8 But a lover of hospitality, a lover of good men, sober, just, holy, temperate; 9 Holding fast the faithful word as he hath been taught, that he may be able by sound doctrine both to exhort and to convince

Living Bible

4 *To:* Titus, who is truly my son in the affairs of the Lord.

May God the Father and Christ Jesus our Savior give you his blessings and his peace.

5 I left you there on the island of Crete so that you could do whatever was needed to help strengthen each of its churches, and I asked you to appoint pastors[a] in every city who would follow the instructions I gave you. 6 The men you choose must be well thought of for their good lives; they must have only one wife and their children must love the Lord and not have a reputation for being wild or disobedient to their parents.

7 These pastors[a] must be men of blameless lives because they are God's ministers. They must not be proud or impatient; they must not be drunkards or fighters or greedy for money. 8 They must enjoy having guests in their homes and must love all that is good. They must be sensible men, and fair. They must be clean minded and level headed. 9 Their belief in the truth which they have been taught must be strong and steadfast, so that they will be able to teach it to others and show those who disagree with them where they are wrong.

[*a*] More literally, "elders."

Today's English Version

4 I write to Titus, my true son in the faith that we share:

May God the Father and Christ Jesus our Savior give you grace and peace.

Titus' work in Crete

5 I left you in Crete for you to put in order the things that still needed doing, and to appoint church elders in every town. Remember my instructions: 6 an elder must be without fault; he must have only one wife, and his children must be believers and not have the reputation of being wild or disobedient. 7 For since he is in charge of God's work, the church leader should be without fault. He must not be arrogant or quick-tempered, or a drunkard, or violent, or greedy. 8 He must be hospitable and love what is good. He must be self-controlled, upright, holy, and disciplined. 9 He must hold firmly to the message which can be trusted and which agrees with the doctrine. In this way he will be able to encourage others with the true teaching, and also show the error of those who are opposed to it.

New International Version

4 To Titus, my true son in our common faith:

Grace and peace from God the Father and Christ Jesus our Savior.

Titus' task on Crete

5 The reason I left you in Crete was that you might straighten out what was left unfinished and appoint[a] elders in every town, as I directed you. 6 An elder must be blameless, the husband of but one wife, a man whose children believe and are not open to the charge of being wild and disobedient. 7 Since an overseer[b] is entrusted with God's work, he must be blameless—not overbearing, not quick-tempered, not given to much wine, not violent, not pursuing dishonest gain. 8 Rather he must be hospitable, one who loves what is good, who is self-controlled, upright, holy and disciplined. 9 He must hold firmly to the trustworthy message as it has been taught, so that he can encourage others by sound doctrine and refute those who oppose it.

[*a*] Or *ordain.* [*b*] Or *bishop.*

Phillips Modern English

command of the God who saves us. To Titus, my true son in our common faith, be grace and peace from God the Father and Christ Jesus our saviour.

1.5 Men who are appointed to the ministry must be of the highest character

I left you in Crete to set right matters which needed attention, and told you to appoint elders in every city according to my direction. They were to be men of unquestioned integrity with only one wife, and with children brought up as Christians and not likely to be accused of loose living or law-breaking. To exercise spiritual oversight a man must be of unimpeachable virtue, for he is God's agent in the affairs of his household. He must not be aggressive or hot-tempered or over-fond of wine; nor must he be violent or greedy for financial gain. On the contrary, he must be hospitable, a genuine lover of what is good, a man who is discreet, fair-minded, holy and self-controlled: a man who takes his stand on the true faith, so that he can by sound teaching both stimulate faith and confute opposition.

Revised Standard Version

4 To Titus, my true child in a common faith: Grace and peace from God the Father and Christ Jesus our Savior.

5 This is why I left you in Crete, that you might amend what was defective, and appoint elders in every town as I directed you, 6 if any man is blameless, the husband of one wife, and his children are believers and not open to the charge of being profligate or insubordinate. 7 For a bishop, as God's steward, must be blameless; he must not be arrogant or quick-tempered or a drunkard or violent or greedy for gain, 8 but hospitable, a lover of goodness, master of himself, upright, holy, and self-controlled; 9 he must hold firm to the sure word as taught, so that he may be able to give instruction in sound doctrine and also to confute those who contradict it.

Jerusalem Bible

commissioned to proclaim it. 4 To Titus, true child of mine in the faith that we share, wishing you grace and peace from God the Father and from Christ Jesus our savior.

The appointment of elders

5 The reason I left you behind in Crete was for you to get everything organized there and appoint elders in every town, in the way that I told you: 6 that is, each of them must be a man of irreproachable character; he must not have been married more than once, and his children must be believers and not uncontrollable or liable to be charged with disorderly conduct. 7 Since, as president, he will be God's representative, he must be irreproachable: never an arrogant or hot-tempered man, nor a heavy drinker or violent, nor out to make money; 8 but a man who is hospitable and a friend of all that is good; sensible, moral, devout and self-controlled; 9 and he must have a firm grasp of the unchanging message of the tradition, so that he can be counted on for both expounding the sound doctrine and refuting those who argue against it.

New English Bible

To Titus, my true-born son in the faith which we share, grace and peace from God our Father and Christ Jesus our Saviour.

My intention in leaving you behind in Crete was that you should set in order what was left over, and in particular should institute elders in each town. In doing so, observe the tests I prescribed: is he a man of unimpeachable character, faithful to his one wife,[b] the father of children who are believers, who are under no imputation of loose living, and are not out of control? For as God's steward a bishop must be a man of unimpeachable character. He must not be overbearing or short-tempered; he must be no drinker, no brawler, no money-grubber, but hospitable, right-minded, temperate, just, devout, and self-controlled. He must adhere to the true doctrine, so that he may be well able both to move his hearers with wholesome teaching and to confute objectors.

[*b*] *See note on 1 Timothy 3. 2.*

King James Version

the gainsayers. 10 For there are many unruly
and vain talkers and deceivers, specially they
of the circumcision; 11 Whose mouths must be
stopped, who subvert whole houses, teaching
things which they ought not, for filthy lucre's
sake. 12 One of themselves, *even* a prophet of
their own, said, The Cretians *are* always liars,
evil beasts, slow bellies. 13 This witness is true.
Wherefore rebuke them sharply, that they may
be sound in the faith; 14 Not giving heed to Jewish fables, and commandments of men, that turn
from the truth. 15 Unto the pure all things *are*
pure: but unto them that are defiled and unbelieving *is* nothing pure; but even their mind and
conscience is defiled. 16 They profess that they
know God; but in works they deny *him,* being
abominable, and disobedient, and unto every
good work reprobate.

Living Bible

10 For there are many who refuse to obey;
this is especially true among those who say that
all Christians must obey the Jewish laws. But
this is foolish talk; it blinds people to the truth,
11 and it must be stopped. Already whole families have been turned away from the grace of
God. Such teachers are only after your money.
12 One of their own men, a prophet from Crete,
has said about them, "These men of Crete are
all liars; they are like lazy animals, living only
to satisfy their stomachs." 13 And this is true. So
speak to the Christians there as sternly as necessary to make them strong in the faith, 14 and to
stop them from listening to Jewish folk tales and
the demands of men who have turned their backs
on the truth.

15 A person who is pure of heart sees goodness and purity in everything; but a person whose
own heart is evil and untrusting finds evil in
everything, for his dirty mind and rebellious
heart color all he sees and hears. 16 Such persons claim they know God, but from seeing the
way they act, one knows they don't. They are
rotten and disobedient, worthless so far as doing
anything good is concerned.

Today's English Version

10 For there are many who rebel and deceive
others with their nonsense, especially the converts from Judaism. 11 It is necessary to stop
their talking, because they are upsetting whole
families by teaching what they should not, for
the shameful purpose of making money. 12 It
was a Cretan himself, one of their own prophets,
who said, "Cretans are always liars, wicked
beasts, and lazy gluttons." 13 And what he said
is true. For this reason you must rebuke them
sharply, so that they may have a healthy faith,
14 and no longer hold on to Jewish legends and
to human commandments which come from men
who have rejected the truth. 15 Everything is
pure to those who are themselves pure; but nothing is pure to those who are defiled and unbelieving, because their minds and consciences have
been defiled. 16 They claim that they know God,
but their actions deny it. They are hateful and
disobedient, not fit to do anything good.

New International Version

10 For there are many rebellious people, mere
talkers and deceivers, especially those of the
circumcision group. 11 They must be silenced,
because they are ruining whole households by
teaching things they ought not to teach—and
that for the sake of dishonest gain. 12 Even one
of their own prophets has said, "Cretans are
always liars, evil brutes, lazy gluttons." 13 This
testimony is true. Therefore, rebuke them
sharply, so that they will be sound in the faith
14 and will pay no attention to Jewish myths or
to the commands of those who reject the truth.
15 To the pure, all things are pure, but to those
who are corrupted and do not believe, nothing
is pure. In fact, both their minds and consciences
are corrupted. 16 They claim to know God, but
by their actions they deny him. They are detestable, disobedient and unfit for doing anything
good.

Phillips Modern English

1.10 Be on your guard against counterfeit Christians

For there are many, especially among the Jews, who will not recognise authority, who talk nonsense and yet in so doing have managed to deceive men's minds. They must be silenced, for they upset the faith of whole households, teaching what they have no business to teach for the sake of what they can get. One of them, yes, one of their own prophets, has said: "Men of Crete were always liars, evil and beastly, lazy and greedy." There is truth in this testimonial! Don't hesitate therefore to reprimand them sharply, for you want them to be sound and healthy Christians, with a proper contempt for Jewish fairy tales and orders issued by men who have forsaken the path of truth. Everything is clean to those who have clean minds. But nothing is wholesome to those who are themselves corrupt and who have no faith in God—their very minds and consciences are diseased. They profess to know God, but their behaviour contradicts their profession. They are vile and disobedient and when it comes to doing any real good they are palpable frauds.

Revised Standard Version

10 For there are many insubordinate men, empty
talkers and deceivers, especially the circumcision
party; 11 they must be silenced, since they are
upsetting whole families by teaching for base
gain what they have no right to teach. 12 One
of themselves, a prophet of their own, said,
"Cretans are always liars, evil beasts, lazy gluttons." 13 This testimony is true. Therefore rebuke them sharply, that they may be sound in
the faith, 14 instead of giving heed to Jewish
myths or to commands of men who reject the
truth. 15 To the pure all things are pure, but
to the corrupt and unbelieving nothing is pure;
their very minds and consciences are corrupted.
16 They profess to know God, but they deny him
by their deeds; they are detestible, disobedient,
unfit for any good deed.

Jerusalem Bible

Opposing the false teachers

10 And in fact you have there a great many
people who need to be disciplined, who talk
nonsense and try to make others believe it, particularly among those of the Circumcision.
11 They have got to be silenced: men of this
kind ruin whole families, by teaching things that
they ought not to, and doing it with the vile
motive of making money. 12 It was one of themselves, one of their own prophets, who said,[a]
"Cretans were never anything but liars, dangerous animals and lazy": 13 and that is a true
statement. So you will have to be severe in correcting them, and make them sound in the faith
14 so that they stop taking notice of Jewish
myths and doing what they are told to do by
people who are no longer interested in the truth.
15 To all who are pure themselves, everything
is pure; but to those who have been corrupted
and lack faith, nothing can be pure—the corruption is both in their minds and in their consciences. 16 They claim to have knowledge of
God but the things they do are nothing but a
denial of him; they are outrageously rebellious
and quite incapable of doing good.

[a] Attributed to the Cretan poet Epimenides of Knossos.

New English Bible

There are all too many, especially among Jewish converts, who are out of all control; they talk wildly and lead men's minds astray. Such men must be curbed, because they are ruining whole families by teaching things they should not, and all for sordid gain. It was a Cretan prophet, one of their own countrymen, who said, 'Cretans were always liars, vicious brutes, lazy gluttons'—and he told the truth! All the more reason why you should pull them up sharply, so that they may come to a sane belief, instead of lending their ears to Jewish myths and commandments of merely human origin, the work of men who turn their backs upon the truth.

To the pure all things are pure; but nothing is pure to the tainted minds of disbelievers, tainted alike in reason and conscience. They profess to acknowledge God, but deny him by their actions. Their detestable obstinacy disqualifies them for any good work.

King James Version

2 But speak thou the things which become
sound doctrine: 2 That the aged men be sober, grave, temperate, sound in faith, in charity,
in patience. 3 The aged women likewise, that
they be in behaviour as becometh holiness, not
false accusers, not given to much wine, teachers
of good things; 4 That they may teach the young
women to be sober, to love their husbands, to
love their children, 5 *To be* discreet, chaste,
keepers at home, good, obedient to their own
husbands, that the word of God be not blasphemed. 6 Young men likewise exhort to be
soberminded. 7 In all things shewing thyself a
pattern of good works: in doctrine *shewing* un-
corruptness, gravity, sincerity, 8 Sound speech,
that cannot be condemned; that he that is of
the contrary part may be ashamed, having no
evil thing to say of you. 9 *Exhort* servants to be
obedient unto their own masters, *and* to please
them well in all things; not answering again;
10 Not purloining, but shewing all good fidelity;
that they may adorn the doctrine of God our

Living Bible

2 But as for you, speak up for the right living that goes along with true Christianity.
2 Teach the older men to be serious and unruf-
fled; they must be sensible, knowing and believing the truth and doing everything with love and
patience.
3 Teach the older women to be quiet and respectful in everything they do. They must not
go around speaking evil of others and must not
be heavy drinkers, but they should be teachers
of goodness. 4 These older women must train
the younger women to live quietly, to love their
husbands and their children, 5 and to be sensible and clean minded, spending their time in
their own homes, being kind and obedient to
their husbands, so that the Christian faith can't
be spoken against by those who know them.
6 In the same way, urge the young men to
behave carefully, taking life seriously. 7 And
here you yourself must be an example to them
of good deeds of every kind. Let everything you
do reflect your love of the truth and the fact
that you are in dead earnest about it. 8 Your
conversation should be so sensible and logical
that anyone who wants to argue will be ashamed
of himself because there won't be anything to
criticize in anything you say!
9 Urge slaves to obey their masters and to
try their best to satisfy them. They must not talk
back, 10 nor steal, but must show themselves to
be entirely trustworthy. In this way they will

Today's English Version

Sound doctrine

2 But you must teach what is required by
sound doctrine. 2 Tell the older men to be
sober, sensible, and self-controlled; to be sound
in their faith, love, and endurance. 3 In the same
way tell the older women to behave as women
who live a holy life should. They must not be
slanderers, or slaves to wine. They must teach
what is good, 4 in order to train the younger
women to love their husbands and children, 5 to
be self-controlled and pure, and to be good
housewives, who obey their husbands, so that no
one will speak evil of the message from God.
6 In the same way urge the young men to be
self-controlled. 7 You yourself, in all things, must
be an example in good works. Be sincere and
serious in your teaching. 8 Use sound words that
cannot be criticized, so that your enemies may
be put to shame by not having anything bad to
say about us.
9 Slaves are to obey their masters and please
them in all things. They must not talk back to
them, 10 or steal from them. Instead, they must
show that they are always good and faithful,

New International Version

What must be taught to various groups

2 You must teach what is in accord with
sound doctrine. 2 Teach the older men to be
temperate, worthy of respect, self-controlled, and
sound in faith, in love and in endurance.
3 Likewise, teach the older women to be reverent in the way they live, not to be slanderers
or addicted to much wine, but to teach what is
good. 4 Then they can train the younger women
to love their husbands and children, 5 to be self-
controlled and pure, to be busy at home, to be
kind, and to be subject to their husbands, so
that no one will malign the word of God.
6 Similarly, encourage the young men to be
self-controlled. 7 In everything set them an example by doing what is good. In your teaching
show integrity, seriousness 8 and soundness of
speech that cannot be condemned, so that those
who oppose you may be ashamed because they
have nothing bad to say about us.
9 Teach slaves to be subject to their masters
in everything, to try to please them, not to talk
back to them, 10 and not to steal from them,
but to show that they can be fully trusted, so that

Phillips Modern English

2.1 Good character should follow good teaching

Now you must tell them the sort of character which should spring from sound teaching. The old men should be temperate, serious, wise—spiritually healthy through their faith and love and patience. Similarly the old women should be reverent in their behaviour, should not make unfounded complaints and should not be addicted to wine. They should be examples of the good life, so that the younger women may learn to love their husbands and their children, to be sensible and chaste, home-lovers, kind-hearted and willing to adapt themselves to their husbands—a good advertisement for the Christian faith. The young men, too, you should urge to take life seriously, letting your own life stand as a pattern of good living. In all your teaching show the strictest regard for truth, and show that you appreciate the seriousness of the matters you are dealing with. Your speech should be unaffected and above criticism, so that your opponent may feel ashamed at finding nothing with which to discredit us.

2.9 The duty of slaves—and of us all

Slaves should be told that it is their duty as Christians to obey their masters and to give them satisfactory service in every way. They are not to answer back or to be light-fingered, but

Revised Standard Version

2 But as for you, teach what befits sound
doctrine. 2 Bid the older men be temperate,
serious, sensible, sound in faith, in love, and in
steadfastness. 3 Bid the older women likewise
to be reverent in behavior, not to be slanderers
or slaves to drink; they are to teach what is
good, 4 and so train the young women to love
their husbands and children, 5 to be sensible,
chaste, domestic, kind, and submissive to their
husbands, that the word of God may not be
discredited. 6 Likewise urge the younger men to
control themselves. 7 Show yourself in all respects a model of good deeds, and in your teaching show integrity, gravity, 8 and sound speech
that cannot be censured, so that an opponent
may be put to shame, having nothing evil to say
of us. 9 Bid slaves to be submissive to their
masters and to give satisfaction in every respect;
they are not to be refractory, 10 nor to pilfer,
but to show entire and true fidelity, so that in

Jerusalem Bible

Some specific moral instruction

2 It is for you, then, to preach the behavior
which goes with healthy doctrine. 2 The
older men should be reserved, dignified, moderate, sound in faith and love and constancy.
3 Similarly, the older women should behave as
though they were religious, with no scandal-
mongering and no habitual wine drinking—they
are to be the teachers of the right behavior
4 and show the younger women how they should
love their husbands and love their children,
5 how they are to be sensible and chaste, and
how to work in their homes, and be gentle and
do as their husbands tell them, so that the message of God is never disgraced. 6 In the same
way, you have got to persuade the younger men
to be moderate 7 and in everything you do make
yourself an example to them of working for
good: when you are teaching, be an example to
them in your sincerity and earnestness 8 and
in keeping all that you say so wholesome that
nobody can make objections to it; and then any
opponent will be at a loss, with no accusation
to make against us. 9 Tell the slaves that they
are to be obedient to their masters and always
do what they want without any argument; 10 and
there must be no petty thieving—they must show

New English Bible

2 For your own part, what you say must be in keeping with wholesome doctrine. Let the older men know that they should be sober, high-principled, and temperate, sound in faith, in love, and in endurance. The older women, similarly, should be reverent in their bearing, not scandal-mongers or slaves to strong drink; they must set a high standard, and school the younger women to be loving wives and mothers, temperate, chaste, and kind, busy at home, respecting the authority of their own husbands. Thus the Gospel will not be brought into disrepute.

Urge the younger men, similarly, to be temperate in all things, and set them a good example yourself. In your teaching, you must show integrity and high principle, and use wholesome speech to which none can take exception. This will shame any opponent, when he finds not a word to say to our discredit.

Tell slaves to respect their masters' authority in everything, and to comply with their demands without answering back; not to pilfer, but to show themselves strictly honest and trustworthy;

King James Version

Saviour in all things. 11 For the grace of God
that bringeth salvation hath appeared to all men,
12 Teaching us that, denying ungodliness and
worldly lusts, we should live soberly, righteously,
and godly, in this present world; 13 Looking for
that blessed hope, and the glorious appearing
of the great God and our Saviour Jesus Christ;
14 Who gave himself for us, that he might redeem us from all iniquity, and purify unto himself a peculiar people, zealous of good works.
15 These things speak, and exhort, and rebuke
with all authority. Let no man despise thee.

Living Bible

make people want to believe in our Savior and
God.
11 For the free gift of eternal salvation is now
being offered to everyone; 12 and along with this
gift comes the realization that God wants us to
turn from godless living and sinful pleasures and
to live good, God-fearing lives day after day,
13 looking forward to that wonderful time we've
been expecting, when his glory shall be seen—the
glory of our great God and Savior Jesus Christ.
14 He died under God's judgment against our
sins, so that he could rescue us from constant
falling into sin and make us his very own people,
with cleansed hearts and real enthusiasm for doing kind things for others. 15 You must teach
these things and encourage your people to do
them, correcting them when necessary as one
who has every right to do so. Don't let anyone
think that what you say is not important.

Today's English Version

so as to bring credit to the teaching about God
our Savior in all they do.
11 For God has revealed his grace for the
salvation of all men. 12 That grace instructs us
to give up ungodly living and worldly passions,
and to live self-controlled, upright, and godly
lives in this world, 13 as we wait for the blessed
Day we hope for, when the glory of our great
God and Savior Jesus Christ will appear. 14 He
gave himself for us, to rescue us from all wickedness and make us a pure people who belong to
him alone and are eager to do good.
15 Teach these things, and use your full authority as you encourage and rebuke your
hearers. Let none of them look down on you.

New International Version

in every way they will make the teaching about
God our Savior attractive.
11 For the grace of God that brings salvation
has appeared to all men. 12 It teaches us to say
"No" to ungodliness and worldly passions, and
to live self-controlled, upright and godly lives in
this present age, 13 while we wait for the blessed
hope—the glorious appearing of our great God
and Savior, Jesus Christ, 14 who gave himself
for us to redeem us from all wickedness and
to purify for himself a people that are his very
own, eager to do what is good.
15 These, then, are the things you should
teach. Encourage and rebuke with all authority.
Do not let anyone despise you.

Phillips Modern English

they are to show themselves utterly trustworthy, a shining testimonial to the teaching of God our saviour. For the grace of God, which can save every man, has now been shown for all men, and it teaches us to have no more to do with godlessness or the desires of this world but to live, here and now, responsible, honourable and God-fearing lives. And while we live this life we hope and wait for the glorious dénouement of the great God and of Christ Jesus our saviour. For he gave himself for us, that he might set us free from all our evil ways and make for himself a people of his own, clean and pure, with our hearts set upon living a life that is good.

Tell men of these things. Plead with them, prove the truth to them with full authority—and let no one treat you with contempt.

Revised Standard Version

everything they may adorn the doctrine of God our Savior.

11 For the grace of God has appeared for the salvation of all men, 12 training us to renounce irreligion and worldly passions, and to live sober, upright, and godly lives in this world, 13 awaiting our blessed hope, the appearing of the glory of our great God and Savior[c] Jesus Christ, 14 who gave himself for us to redeem us from all iniquity and to purify for himself a people of his own who are zealous for good deeds.

15 Declare these things; exhort and reprove with all authority. Let no one disregard you.

[c] Or *of the great God and our Savior.*

Jerusalem Bible

complete honesty at all times, so that they are in every way a credit to the teaching of God our savior.

The basis of the Christian moral life

11 You see, God's grace has been revealed, and it has made salvation possible for the whole human race 12 and taught us that what we have to do is to give up everything that does not lead to God, and all our worldly ambitions; we must be self-restrained and live good and religious lives here in this present world, 13 while we are waiting in hope for the blessing which will come with the Appearing of the glory of our great God and savior Christ Jesus.[b] 14 He sacrificed himself for us in order to *set us free from all wickedness*[c] and *to purify a people so that it could be his very own*[d] and would have no ambition except to do good.

15 Now this is what you are to say, whether you are giving instruction or correcting errors; you can do so with full authority, and no one is to question it.

[b] Or "our great God and our savior, Christ Jesus."
[c] Ps. 130:8. [d] Ex. 19:5.

New English Bible

for in all such ways they will add lustre to the doctrine of God our Saviour.

For the grace of God has dawned upon the world with healing for all mankind; and by it we are disciplined to renounce godless ways and worldly desires, and to live a life of temperance, honesty, and godliness in the present age, looking forward to the happy fulfilment of our hope when the splendour of our great God and Saviour[a] Christ Jesus will appear. He it is who sacrificed himself for us, to set us free from all wickedness and to make us a pure people marked out for his own, eager to do good.

These, then, are your themes; urge them and argue them. And speak with authority: let no one slight you.

[a] *Or* of the great God and our Saviour . . .

King James Version

3 Put them in mind to be subject to principalities and powers, to obey magistrates, to be ready to every good work, 2 To speak evil of no man, to be no brawlers, *but* gentle, shewing all meekness unto all men. 3 For we ourselves also were sometime foolish, disobedient, deceived, serving divers lusts and pleasures, living in malice and envy, hateful, *and* hating one another. 4 But after that the kindness and love of God our Saviour toward man appeared, 5 Not by works of righteousness which we have done, but according to his mercy he saved us, by the washing of regeneration, and renewing of the Holy Ghost; 6 Which he shed on us abundantly through Jesus Christ our Saviour; 7 That being justified by his grace, we should be made heirs according to the hope of eternal life. 8 *This is* a faithful saying, and these things I will that thou affirm constantly, that they which have believed in God might be careful to maintain good works. These things are good and profitable

Living Bible

3 Remind your people to obey the government and its officers, and always to be obedient and ready for any honest work. 2 They must not speak evil of anyone, nor quarrel, but be gentle and truly courteous to all.

3 Once we, too, were foolish and disobedient; we were misled by others and became slaves to many evil pleasures and wicked desires. Our lives were full of resentment and envy. We hated others and they hated us.

4 But when the time came for the kindness and love of God our Savior to appear, 5 then he saved us—not because we were good enough to be saved, but because of his kindness and pity —by washing away our sins and giving us the new joy of the indwelling Holy Spirit 6 whom he poured out upon us with wonderful fullness—and all because of what Jesus Christ our Savior did 7 so that he could declare us good in God's eyes—all because of his great kindness; and now we can share in the wealth of the eternal life he gives us, and we are eagerly looking forward to receiving it. 8 These things I have told you are all true. Insist on them so that Christians will be careful to do good deeds all the time, for this is not only right, but it brings results.

Today's English Version

Christian conduct

3 Remind your people to submit to rulers and authorities, to obey them, to be ready to do every good thing. 2 Tell them not to speak evil of anyone, but to be peaceful and friendly, and always show a gentle attitude toward all men. 3 For we ourselves were once foolish, disobedient, and wrong. We were slaves to passions and pleasures of all kinds. We spent our lives in malice and envy; others hated us and we hated them. 4 But when the kindness and love of God our Savior appeared, 5 he saved us. It was not because of any good works that we ourselves had done, but because of his own mercy that he saved us through the washing by which the Holy Spirit gives us new birth and new life. 6 God poured out the Holy Spirit abundantly on us, through Jesus Christ our Savior, 7 so that by his grace we might be put right with God and come into possession of the eternal life we hope for. 8 This is a true saying.

I want you to give special emphasis to these matters, so that those who believe in God may be concerned with giving their time to doing good works. These are good and useful for men.

New International Version

Doing what is good

3 Remind the people to be subject to rulers and authorities, to be obedient, to be ready to do whatever is good, 2 to slander no one, to be peaceable and considerate, and to show true humility toward all men.

3 At one time we too were foolish, disobedient, deceived and enslaved by all kinds of passions and pleasures. We lived in malice and envy, being hated and hating one another. 4 But when the kindness and love of God our Savior appeared, 5 he saved us, not because of righteous things we had done, but because of his mercy. He saved us through the washing of rebirth and renewal by the Holy Spirit, 6 whom he poured out on us generously through Jesus Christ our Savior, 7 so that, having been justified by his grace, we might become heirs having the hope of eternal life. 8 This is a trustworthy saying. And I want you to stress these things, so that those who have trusted in God may be careful to devote themselves to doing what is good. These things are excellent and profitable for everyone.

Phillips Modern English

3.1 *Instructions for the Christians of Crete*

Remind your people to recognise the power of those who rule and bear authority. They must obey them and be prepared to render whatever good service they can. They are not to speak evil of any man, they must not be quarrelsome but reasonable, showing every consideration to all men. For we ourselves have known what it is to be ignorant, disobedient and deceived, the slaves of various desires and pleasures, while our lives were spent in malice and jealousy—we were hateful and we hated each other. But when the kindness and love of God our saviour dawned upon us, he saved us in his mercy—not by virtue of any moral achievement of ours, but by the cleansing power of a new birth and the renewal of the Holy Spirit, which he poured upon us through Jesus Christ our Saviour. The result is that we are acquitted by his grace, and can look forward in hope to inheriting life eternal. This is solid truth: I want you to speak about these matters with absolute certainty, so that those who have believed in God may concentrate upon a life of goodness. Good work is good in itself and is also useful to mankind.

Revised Standard Version

3 Remind them to be submissive to rulers
and authorities, to be obedient, to be ready
for any honest work, 2 to speak evil of no one,
to avoid quarreling, to be gentle, and to show
perfect courtesy toward all men. 3 For we ourselves were once foolish, disobedient, led astray,
slaves to various passions and pleasures, passing
our days in malice and envy, hated by men and
hating one another; 4 but when the goodness and
loving kindness of God our Savior appeared,
5 he saved us, not because of deeds done by us
in righteousness, but in virtue of his own mercy,
by the washing of regeneration and renewal in
the Holy Spirit, 6 which he poured out upon us
richly through Jesus Christ our Savior, 7 so that
we might be justified by his grace and become
heirs in hope of eternal life. 8 The saying is sure.
I desire you to insist on these things, so that
those who have believed in God may be careful
to apply themselves to good deeds;[d] these are

[*d*] Or *enter honorable occupations.*

Jerusalem Bible

General instruction for believers

3 Remind them that it is their duty to be
obedient to the officials and representatives
of the government; to be ready to do good at
every opportunity; 2 not to go slandering other
people or picking quarrels, but to be courteous
and always polite to all kinds of people. 3 Remember, there was a time when we too were
ignorant, disobedient, and misled and enslaved
by different passions and luxuries; we lived then
in wickedness and ill-will, hating each other and
hateful ourselves.
4 But when the kindness and love of God our
savior for mankind were revealed, 5 it was not
because he was concerned with any righteous
actions we might have done ourselves; it was for
no reason except his own compassion that he
saved us, by means of the cleansing water of
rebirth and by renewing us with the Holy Spirit
6 which he has so generously poured over us
through Jesus Christ our savior. 7 He did this
so that we should be justified by his grace, to
become heirs looking forward to inheriting eternal life. 8 This is doctrine that you can rely on.

Personal advice to Titus

I want you to be quite uncompromising in teaching all this, so that those who now believe in God may keep their minds constantly occupied in doing good works. All this is good, and

New English Bible

3 Remind them to be submissive to the government and the authorities, to obey them, and to be ready for any honourable form of work;[b] to slander no one, not to pick quarrels, to show forbearance and a consistently gentle disposition towards all men.

For at one time we ourselves in our folly and obstinacy were all astray. We were slaves to passions and pleasures of every kind. Our days were passed in malice and envy; we were odious ourselves and we hated one another. But when the kindness and generosity of God our Saviour dawned upon the world, then, not for any good deeds of our own, but because he was merciful, he saved us through the water of rebirth and the renewing power of[a] the Holy Spirit. For he sent down the Spirit upon us plentifully through Jesus Christ our Saviour, so that, justified by his grace, we might in hope become heirs to eternal life. These are words you may trust.

Such are the points I should wish you to insist on. Those who have come to believe in God should see that they engage in honourable occupations, which are not only honourable in them-

[*b*] *Or* ready always to do good. [*a*] *Or* the water of rebirth and of renewal by . . .

King James Version

unto men. 9 But avoid foolish questions, and genealogies, and contentions, and strivings about the law; for they are unprofitable and vain. 10 A man that is a heretic, after the first and second admonition, reject; 11 Knowing that he that is such is subverted, and sinneth, being condemned of himself. 12 When I shall send Artemas unto thee, or Tychicus, be diligent to come unto me to Nicopolis: for I have determined there to winter. 13 Bring Zenas the lawyer and Apollos on their journey diligently, that nothing be wanting unto them. 14 And let ours also learn to maintain good works for necessary uses, that they be not unfruitful. 15 All that are with me salute thee. Greet them that love us in the faith. Grace *be* with you all. Amen.

It was written to Titus, ordained the first bishop of the church of the Cretians, from Nicopolis of Macedonia.

Living Bible

9 Don't get involved in arguing over unanswerable questions and controversial theological ideas; keep out of arguments and quarrels about obedience to Jewish laws, for this kind of thing isn't worthwhile; it only does harm. 10 If anyone is causing divisions among you, he should be given a first and second warning. After that have nothing more to do with him, 11 for such a person has a wrong sense of values. He is sinning, and he knows it.

12 I am planning to send either Artemas or Tychicus to you. As soon as one of them arrives, please try to meet me at Nicopolis as quickly as you can, for I have decided to stay there for the winter. 13 Do everything you can to help Zenas the lawyer and Apollos with their trip; see that they are given everything they need. 14 For our people must learn to help all who need their assistance, that their lives will be fruitful.

15 Everybody here sends greetings. Please say "hello" to all of the Christian friends there. May God's blessings be with you all.

Sincerely,
Paul

Today's English Version

9 But avoid stupid arguments, long lists of names of ancestors, quarrels, and fights about the Law. They are useless and worthless. 10 Give at least two warnings to the man who causes divisions, and then have nothing more to do with him. 11 You know that such a person is corrupt, and his sins prove that he is wrong.

Final instructions

12 When I send Artemas or Tychicus to you, do your best to come to me in Nicopolis, because I have decided to spend the winter there. 13 Do your best to help Zenas the lawyer and Apollos to get started on their travels, and see to it that they have everything they need. 14 Have our people learn to give their time in doing good works, to provide for real needs; they should not live useless lives.

15 All who are with me send you greetings. Give our greetings to our friends in the faith.

God's grace be with you all.

New International Version

9 But avoid foolish controversies and genealogies and arguments and quarrels about the law, because these are unprofitable and useless. 10 Warn a divisive person once, and then warn him a second time. After that, have nothing to do with him. 11 You may be sure that such a man is warped and sinful; he is self-condemned.

Final remarks

12 As soon as I send Artemas or Tychicus to you, do your best to come to me at Nicopolis, because I have decided to winter there. 13 Do everything you can to help Zenas the lawyer and Apollos on their way and see that they have everything they need. 14 Our people must learn to devote themselves to doing what is good, in order that they may provide for daily necessities and not live unproductive lives.

15 Everyone with me sends you greetings. Greet those who love us in the faith.

Grace be with you all.

Phillips Modern English

But steer clear of stupid speculations, genealogies, controversies and quarrels over the Law. They settle nothing and lead nowhere. If a man is self-opinionated, warn him. But after the second warning you should reject him. You can be sure that he has a moral twist, and he is self-condemned.

3.12 Final messages

As soon as I send Artemas to you (or perhaps it will be Tychicus), do your best to come to me at Nicopolis, for I have made up my mind to spend the winter there. See that Zenas the lawyer and Apollos have what they require and give them a good send-off. And our people should learn to earn what they need by honest work and so be self-supporting.

All those here with me send you greetings. Please give our greetings to all who love us in the faith. Grace be with you all.

Revised Standard Version

excellent and profitable to men. 9 But avoid
stupid controversies, genealogies, dissensions, and
quarrels over the law, for they are unprofitable
and futile. 10 As for a man who is factious, after
admonishing him once or twice, have nothing
more to do with him, 11 knowing that such a
person is perverted and sinful; he is self-condemned.

12 When I send Artemas or Tychicus to you,
do your best to come to me at Nicopolis, for I
have decided to spend the winter there. 13 Do
your best to speed Zenas the lawyer and Apollos on their way; see that they lack nothing.
14 And let our people learn to apply themselves
to good deeds,[d] so as to help cases of urgent
need, and not to be unfruitful.

15 All who are with me send greetings to you.
Greet those who love us in the faith.

Grace be with you all.

[d] Or *enter honorable occupations.*

Jerusalem Bible

will do nothing but good to everybody. 9 But
avoid pointless speculations, and those genealogies, and the quibbles and disputes about the
Law—these are useless and can do no good to
anyone. 10 If a man disputes what you teach,
then after a first and a second warning, have
no more to do with him: 11 you will know that
any man of that sort has already lapsed and
condemned himself as a sinner.

Practical recommendations, farewells and good wishes

12 As soon as I have sent Artemas or
Tychicus to you, lose no time in joining me at
Nicopolis, where I have decided to spend the
winter. 13 See to all the traveling arrangements
for Zenas the lawyer and Apollos, and make
sure they have everything they need. 14 All our
people are to learn to occupy themselves in doing good works for their practical needs as well,
and not to be entirely unproductive.

15 All those who are with me send their
greetings. Greetings to those who love us in the
faith. Grace be with you all.

New English Bible

selves, but also useful to their fellow-men.[b] But steer clear of foolish speculations, genealogies, quarrels, and controversies over the Law; they are unprofitable and pointless.

A heretic should be warned once, and once again; after that, have done with him, recognizing that a man of that sort has a distorted mind and stands self-condemned in his sin.

When I send Artemas to you, or Tychicus, make haste to join me at Nicopolis, for that is where I have determined to spend the winter. Do your utmost to help Zenas the lawyer and Apollos on their travels, and see that they are not short of anything. And our own people must be taught to engage in honest employment to produce the necessities of life; they must not be unproductive.

All who are with me send you greetings. My greetings to those who are our friends in truth.[c] Grace be with you all!

[b] *Or* should make it their business to practise virtue. These precepts are good in themselves and useful to society. [c] *Or* our friends in the faith.

King James Version

THE EPISTLE OF PAUL TO PHILEMON

Paul, a prisoner of Jesus Christ, and Timothy
our brother, unto Philemon our dearly beloved, and fellow labourer, 2And to *our* beloved
Apphia, and Archippus our fellow soldier, and
to the church in thy house: 3 Grace to you, and
peace, from God our Father and the Lord Jesus

Living Bible

PHILEMON

1 *From:* Paul, in jail for preaching the Good
News about Jesus Christ, and from Brother
Timothy.
To: Philemon, our much loved fellow worker,
and to the church that meets in your home, and
to Apphia our sister, and to Archippus who like
myself is a soldier of the cross.
3 May God our Father and the Lord Jesus
Christ give you his blessings and his peace.

Today's English Version

PAUL'S LETTER TO PHILEMON

1 From Paul, a prisoner for the sake of Christ
Jesus, and from our brother Timothy—
To our friend and fellow worker Philemon,
2 and the church that meets in your house, and
our sister Apphia, and our fellow soldier Archippus:
3 May God our Father and the Lord Jesus
Christ give you grace and peace.

New International Version

PHILEMON

1 Paul, a prisoner of Christ Jesus, and Timothy
our brother,
To Philemon our dear friend and fellow
worker, 2 to Apphia our sister, to Archippus our
fellow soldier, and to the church that meets in
your home:
3 Grace to you and peace from God our Father and the Lord Jesus Christ.

Phillips Modern English

THE LETTER TO

PHILEMON

Paul, a prisoner of Christ Jesus, and brother Timothy to Philemon our much-loved fellow-worker, to Apphia our sister and Archippus who is with us in the fight; to the church that meets in your house—grace and peace be to you from God our Father and from the Lord Jesus Christ.

Revised Standard Version

THE LETTER OF PAUL TO

PHILEMON

1 Paul, a prisoner for Christ Jesus, and Timothy our brother,

To Philemon our beloved fellow worker 2 and Apphia our sister and Archippus our fellow soldier, and the church in your house:

3 Grace to you and peace from God our Father and the Lord Jesus Christ.

Jerusalem Bible

THE LETTER FROM PAUL TO PHILEMON

PHILEMON

Address

1 From Paul, a prisoner of Christ Jesus and from our brother Timothy; to our dear fellow worker Philemon, 2 our sister Apphia, our fellow soldier Archippus and the church that meets in your house; 3 wishing you the grace and the peace of God our Father and the Lord Jesus Christ.

New English Bible

THE LETTER OF PAUL TO

PHILEMON

A runaway slave

From Paul, a prisoner of Christ Jesus, and our colleague Timothy, to Philemon our dear friend and fellow-worker, and Apphia our sister, and Archippus our comrade-in-arms, and the congregation at your house.

Grace to you and peace from God our Father and the Lord Jesus Christ.

King James Version

Christ. 4 I thank my God, making mention of
thee always in my prayers, 5 Hearing of thy love
and faith, which thou hast toward the Lord
Jesus, and toward all saints; 6 That the communication of thy faith may become effectual
by the acknowledging of every good thing which
is in you in Christ Jesus. 7 For we have great
joy and consolation in thy love, because the
bowels of the saints are refreshed by thee,
brother. 8 Wherefore, though I might be much
bold in Christ to enjoin thee that which is convenient, 9 Yet for love's sake I rather beseech
thee, being such a one as Paul the aged, and
now also a prisoner of Jesus Christ. 10 I beseech
thee for my son Onesimus, whom I have begotten in my bonds: 11 Which in time past was
to thee unprofitable, but now profitable to thee
and to me: 12 Whom I have sent again: thou
therefore receive him, that is, mine own bowels:
13 Whom I would have retained with me, that
in thy stead he might have ministered unto me
in the bonds of the gospel: 14 But without thy
mind would I do nothing; that thy benefit should
not be as it were of necessity, but willingly.

Living Bible

4 I always thank God when I am praying for
you, dear Philemon, 5 because I keep hearing of
your love and trust in the Lord Jesus and in his
people. 6And I pray that as you share your faith
with others it will grip their lives too, as they
see the wealth of good things in you that come
from Christ Jesus. 7 I myself have gained much
joy and comfort from your love, my brother, because your kindness has so often refreshed the
hearts of God's people.

8, 9 Now I want to ask a favor of you. I
could demand it of you in the name of Christ
because it is the right thing for you to do, but I
love you and prefer just to ask you—I, Paul, an
old man now, here in jail for the sake of Jesus
Christ. 10 My plea is that you show kindness to
my child Onesimus, whom I won to the Lord
while here in my chains. 11 Onesimus (whose
name means "Useful") hasn't been of much use
to you in the past, but now he is going to be of
real use to both of us. 12 I am sending him back
to you, and with him comes my own heart.

13 I really wanted to keep him here with me
while I am in these chains for preaching the
Good News, and you would have been helping
me through him, 14 but I didn't want to do it
without your consent. I didn't want you to be
kind because you had to but because you wanted

Today's English Version

Philemon's love and faith

4 Every time I pray, brother Philemon, I
mention you and give thanks to my God. 5 For
I hear of your love for all God's people and the
faith you have in the Lord Jesus. 6 My prayer is
that our fellowship with you as believers will
bring about a deeper understanding of every
blessing which we have in our life in Christ.
7 Your love, dear brother, has brought me great
joy and much encouragement! You have cheered
the hearts of all God's people.

A request for Onesimus

8 For this reason I could be bold enough, as
your brother in Christ, to order you to do what
should be done. 9 But love compels me to make
a request instead. I do this even though I am
Paul, the ambassador of Christ Jesus and at
present also a prisoner for his sake. 10 So I
make a request to you on behalf of Onesimus,
who is my own son in Christ; for while in prison
I have become his spiritual father. 11At one
time he was of no use to you, but now he is
useful both to you and to me.

12 I am sending him back to you now, and
with him goes my heart. 13 I would like to keep
him here with me, while I am in prison for the
gospel's sake, so that he could help me in your
place. 14 However, I do not want to force you
to help me; rather, I would like for you to do
it of your own free will. So I will not do a
thing unless you agree.

New International Version

Thanksgiving and prayer

4 I always thank my God as I remember you
in my prayers, 5 because I hear about your love
and faith in the Lord Jesus and your love for
all the saints. 6 I pray that you may be active
in sharing your faith, so that you will have a
full understanding of every good thing we have
in Christ. 7 Your love has given me great joy
and encouragement, because you, brother, have
refreshed the hearts of the saints.

Paul's plea for Onesimus

8 Therefore, although in Christ I could be
bold and order you to do what you ought to do,
9 yet I appeal to you on the basis of love. I
then, as Paul—an old man and now also a
prisoner of Christ Jesus—10 I appeal to you for
my son Onesimus,[a] who became my son while
I was in chains. 11 Formerly he was useless to
you, but now he has become useful both to you
and to me.

12 I am sending him—who is my very heart—
back to you. 13 I would have liked to keep him
with me so that he could take your place in
helping me while I am in chains for the gospel.
14 But I did not want to do anything without
your consent, so that any favor you do will be

[a] *Onesimus* means *useful.*

Phillips Modern English

4 *A personal appeal*

I always thank God for you, Philemon, in my constant prayers for you, for I have heard how you love and trust both the Lord Jesus himself and those who believe in him. And I pray that those who share your faith may be led into the knowledge of all the good things that believing in Christ Jesus means to us. It is your love, my brother, that gives us such comfort and happiness, and it cheers the hearts of your fellow-Christians. And although I could rely on my authority in Christ and dare to *order* you to do what I consider right, I am not doing that. No, I am appealing in love, a simple personal appeal from Paul the old man, in prison for Christ Jesus' sake. I am appealing for my child. Yes I have become a father though I have been under lock and key, and the child's name is—Onesimus! Oh, I know you have found him useless in the past but he is going to be useful now, to both of us. I am sending him back to you—part of my very heart. I should have dearly loved to have kept him with me: he could have done what you would have done—looked after me here in prison for the gospel's sake. But I would do nothing without consulting you first, for if you have a favour to give me, let it be spontaneous and not forced from you by circumstances!

Revised Standard Version

4 I thank my God always when I remember
you in my prayers, 5 because I hear of your love
and of the faith which you have toward the
Lord Jesus and all the saints, 6 and I pray that
the sharing of your faith may promote the
knowledge of all the good that is ours in Christ.
7 For I have derived much joy and comfort from
your love, my brother, because the hearts of the
saints have been refreshed through you.
8 Accordingly, though I am bold enough in
Christ to command you to do what is required,
9 yet for love's sake I prefer to appeal to you
—I, Paul, an ambassador[a] and now a prisoner
also for Christ Jesus—10 I appeal to you for
my child, Onesimus, whose father I have become
in my imprisonment. 11 (Formerly he was useless to you, but now he is indeed useful [b] to you
and to me.) 12 I am sending him back to you,
sending my very heart. 13 I would have been glad
to keep him with me, in order that he might
serve me on your behalf during my imprisonment
for the gospel; 14 but I preferred to do nothing
without your consent in order that your goodness
might not be by compulsion but of your own free
will.

[a] Or *an old man*. [b] The name Onesimus means *useful* or (compare verse 20) *beneficial*.

Jerusalem Bible

Thanksgiving and prayer

4 I always mention you in my prayers and
thank God for you, 5 because I hear of the love
and the faith which you have for the Lord Jesus
and for all the saints. 6 I pray that this faith
will give rise to a sense of fellowship that will
show you all the good things that we are able to
do for Christ. 7 I am so delighted, and comforted, to know of your love; they tell me,
brother, how you have put new heart into the
saints.

The request about Onesimus

8 Now, although in Christ I can have no diffi-
dence about telling you to do whatever is your
duty, 9 I am appealing to your love instead, reminding you that this is Paul writing, an old
man now and, what is more, still a prisoner of
Christ Jesus. 10 I am appealing to you for a
child of mine, whose father I became while
wearing these chains: I mean Onesimus. 11 He
was of no use to you before, but he will be useful[a] to you now, as he has been to me. 12 I
am sending him back to you, and with him—I
could say—a part of my own self. 13 I should
have liked to keep him with me; he could have
been a substitute for you, to help me while I
am in the chains that the Good News has
brought me. 14 However, I did not want to do
anything without your consent; it would have
been forcing your act of kindness, which should

[a] A pun—"Onesimus" means "useful."

New English Bible

I thank my God always when I mention you in my prayers, for I hear of your love and faith towards the Lord Jesus and towards all God's people. My prayer is that your fellowship with us in our common faith may deepen the understanding of all the blessings that our union with Christ brings us.[a] For I am delighted and encouraged by your love; through you, my brother, God's people have been much refreshed.

Accordingly, although in Christ I might make bold to point out your duty, yet, because of that same love, I would rather appeal to you. Yes, I, Paul, ambassador as I am of Christ Jesus—and now his prisoner—appeal to you about my child, whose father I have become in this prison.

I mean Onesimus, once so little use to you, but now useful indeed, both to you and to me. I am sending him back to you, and in doing so I am sending a part of myself. I should have liked to keep him with me, to look after me as you would wish, here in prison for the Gospel. But I would rather do nothing without your consent, so that your kindness may be a matter not of com-

[a] *Or* that bring us to Christ.

King James Version

15 For perhaps he therefore departed for a season, that thou shouldest receive him for ever;
16 Not now as a servant, but above a servant,
a brother beloved, specially to me, but how much
more unto thee, both in the flesh, and in the
Lord? 17 If thou count me therefore a partner,
receive him as myself. 18 If he hath wronged
thee, or oweth *thee* aught, put that on mine account; 19 I Paul have written *it* with mine own
hand, I will repay *it:* albeit I do not say to thee
how thou owest unto me even thine own self
besides. 20 Yea, brother, let me have joy of thee
in the Lord: refresh my bowels in the Lord.
21 Having confidence in thy obedience I wrote
unto thee, knowing that thou wilt also do more
than I say. 22 But withal prepare me also a
lodging: for I trust that through your prayers I
shall be given unto you. 23 There salute thee
Epaphras, my fellow prisoner in Christ Jesus;
24 Marcus, Aristarchus, Demas, Lucas, my fellow
labourers. 25 The grace of our Lord Jesus Christ
be with your spirit. Amen.

Written from Rome to Philemon, by Onesimus a servant.

Living Bible

to. 15 Perhaps you could think of it this way:
that he ran away from you for a little while so
that now he can be yours forever, 16 no longer
only a slave, but something much better—a beloved brother, especially to me. Now he will
mean much more to you too, because he is not
only a servant but also your brother in Christ.

17 If I am really your friend, give him the
same welcome you would give to me if I were
the one who was coming. 18 If he has harmed
you in any way or stolen anything from you,
charge me for it. 19 I will pay it back (I, Paul,
personally guarantee this by writing it here with
my own hand) but I won't mention how much
you owe me! The fact is, you even owe me your
very soul! 20 Yes, dear brother, give me joy with
this loving act and my weary heart will praise the
Lord.

21 I've written you this letter because I am positive that you will do what I ask and even more!

22 Please keep a guest room ready for me, for I am hoping that God will answer your prayers and let me come to you soon.

23 Epaphras my fellow prisoner, who is also
here for preaching Christ Jesus, sends you his
greetings. 24 So do Mark, Aristarchus, Demas
and Luke, my fellow workers.

25 The blessings of our Lord Jesus Christ be upon your spirit.

Paul

Today's English Version

15 It may be that Onesimus was away from
you for a short time so that you might have him
back for all time. 16 And now he is not just a
slave, but much more than a slave: he is a dear
brother in Christ. How much he means to me!
And how much more he will mean to you, both
as a slave and as a brother in the Lord!

17 So, if you think of me as your partner,
welcome him back just as you would welcome
me. 18 If he has done you any wrong, or owes
you anything, charge it to my account. 19 Here,
I will write this with my own hand: ***I, Paul, will***
pay you back. (I should not have to remind you,
of course, that you owe your very life to me.)
20 So, my brother, please do me this favor, for
the Lord's sake; cheer up my heart, as a brother
in Christ!

21 I am sure, as I write this, that you will do
what I ask—in fact I know that you will do
even more. 22 At the same time, get a room ready
for me, because I hope that God will answer
the prayers of all of you and give me back to
you.

Final greetings

23 Epaphras, who is in prison with me for the
sake of Christ Jesus, sends you his greetings,
24 and so do my fellow workers Mark, Aristarchus, Demas, and Luke.

25 May the grace of the Lord Jesus Christ be with you all.

New International Version

spontaneous and not forced. 15 Perhaps the reason he was separated from you for a little while
was that you might have him back for good—
16 no longer as a slave, but better than a slave,
as a dear brother. He is very dear to me but
even dearer to you, both as a man and as a
brother in the Lord.

17 So if you consider me a partner, welcome
him as you would welcome me. 18 If he has
done you any wrong or owes you anything,
charge it to me. 19 I, Paul, am writing this with
my own hand. I will pay it back—not to mention that you owe me your very self. 20 I do
wish, brother, that I may have some benefit from
you in the Lord; refresh my heart in Christ.
21 Confident of your obedience, I write to you,
knowing that you will do even more than I ask.

22 And one thing more: Prepare a guest room for me, because I hope to be restored to you in answer to your prayers.

23 Epaphras, my fellow prisoner for Christ
Jesus, sends you greetings. 24 And so do Mark,
Aristarchus, Demas and Luke, my fellow work-
ers.

25 The grace of the Lord Jesus Christ be with your spirit.

Phillips Modern English

It occurs to me that there has been a purpose in your losing him. You lost him, a slave for a time; now you are having him back for good, not merely as a slave, but as a beloved brother. He is already especially dear to me—how much more will you be able to love him, both as a man and as a fellow-Christian! You and I have been true friends, haven't we? Then do welcome him as you would welcome me. If he has wronged or cheated you put it down to my account. I've written this with my own hand: I, Paul, hereby promise to repay you. (Of course I'm not stressing the fact that you might be said to owe me your very soul!) Now do grant me this favour, my brother—such a Christian act would set my heart at rest. As I send you this letter I know you'll do what I ask—I believe, in fact, you'll do more.

Will you do something else? Get the guest-room ready for me, for I have great hopes that through your prayers I myself will be returned to you as well!

Epaphras, here in prison with me for Christ Jesus' sake, sends his greetings; so do Mark, Aristarchus, Demas and Luke, all fellow-workers of mine.

The grace of our Lord Jesus Christ be with your spirit, amen.

Revised Standard Version

15 Perhaps this is why he was parted from you
for a while, that you might have him back for
ever, 16 no longer as a slave but more than a
slave, as a beloved brother, especially to me but
how much more to you, both in the flesh and in
the Lord. 17 So if you consider me your partner, receive him as you would receive me. 18 If
he has wronged you at all, or owes you anything,
charge that to my account. 19 I, Paul, write this
with my own hand, I will repay it—to say nothing of your owing me even your own self. 20 Yes,
brother, I want some benefit from you in the
Lord. Refresh my heart in Christ.

21 Confident of your obedience, I write to
you, knowing that you will do even more than I
say. 22 At the same time, prepare a guest room
for me, for I am hoping through your prayers to
be granted to you.

23 Epaphras, my fellow prisoner in Christ
Jesus, sends greetings to you, 24 and so do Mark,
Aristarchus, Demas, and Luke, my fellow work-
ers.

25 The grace of the Lord Jesus Christ be with
your spirit.

Jerusalem Bible

be spontaneous. 15 I know you have been deprived of Onesimus for a time, but it was only
so that you could have him back for ever, 16 not
as a slave any more, but something much better
than a slave, a dear brother; especially dear to
me, but how much more to you, as a blood
brother as well as a brother in the Lord. 17 So
if all that we have in common means anything
to you, welcome him as you would me; 18 but
if he has wronged you in any way or owes you
anything, then let me pay for it. 19 I am writing
this in my own handwriting: I, Paul, shall pay
it back—I will not add any mention of your
own debt to me, which is yourself. 20 Well then,
brother, I am counting on you, in the Lord;
put new heart into me, in Christ. 21 I am writing with complete confidence in your compli-
ance, sure that you will do even more than I ask.

A personal request. Good wishes

22 There is another thing: will you get a place
ready for me to stay in? I am hoping through
your prayers to be restored to you.

23 Epaphras, a prisoner with me in Christ
Jesus, sends his greetings; 24 so do my colleagues
Mark, Aristarchus, Demas and Luke.

25 May the grace of our Lord Jesus Christ
be with your spirit.

New English Bible

pulsion, but of your own free will. For perhaps this is why you lost him for a time, that you might have him back for good, no longer as a slave, but as more than a slave—as a dear brother, very dear indeed to me and how much dearer to you, both as man and as Christian.

If, then, you count me partner in the faith, welcome him as you would welcome me. And if he has done you any wrong or is in your debt, put that down to my account. Here is my signature, PAUL; I undertake to repay—not to mention that you owe your very self to me as well. Now brother, as a Christian, be generous with me, and relieve my anxiety; we are both in Christ!

I write to you confident that you will meet my wishes; I know that you will in fact do better than I ask. And one thing more: have a room ready for me, for I hope that, in answer to your prayers, God will grant me to you.

Epaphras, Christ's captive like myself, sends you greetings. So do Mark, Aristarchus, Demas, and Luke, my fellow-workers.

The grace of the Lord Jesus Christ be with your spirit!

King James Version

THE EPISTLE OF PAUL THE APOSTLE TO THE HEBREWS

1 God, who at sundry times and in divers manners spake in time past unto the fathers by the prophets, 2 Hath in these last days spoken unto us by *his* Son, whom he hath appointed heir of all things, by whom also he made the worlds; 3 Who being the brightness of *his* glory, and the express image of his person, and upholding all things by the word of his power, when he had by himself purged our sins, sat down

Living Bible

HEBREWS

1 Long ago God spoke in many different ways to our fathers through the prophets [in visions, dreams, and even face to face[a]], telling them little by little about his plans.

2 But now in these days he has spoken to us through his Son to whom he has given everything, and through whom he made the world and everything there is.

3 God's Son shines out with God's glory, and all that God's Son is and does marks him as God. He regulates the universe by the mighty power of his command. He is the one who died to cleanse us and clear our record of all sin, and then sat down in highest honor beside the great God of heaven.

[*a*] Implied.

Today's English Version

THE LETTER TO THE HEBREWS

God's word through his Son

1 In the past God spoke to our ancestors many times and in many ways through the prophets, 2 but in these last days he has spoken to us through his Son. He is the one through whom God created the universe, the one whom God has chosen to possess all things at the end. 3 He shines with the brightness of God's glory; he is the exact likeness of God's own being, and sustains the universe with his powerful word. After he had made men clean from their sins, he sat down in heaven at the right side of God, the Supreme Power.

New International Version

HEBREWS

The Son superior to angels

1 In the past God spoke to our forefathers through the prophets at many times and in various ways, 2 but in these last days he has spoken to us by his Son, whom he appointed heir of all things, and through whom he made the universe. 3 The Son is the radiance of God's glory and the exact representation of his being, sustaining all things by his powerful word. After he had provided purification for sins, he sat down at the right hand of the Majesty in

Phillips Modern English

THE LETTER TO JEWISH CHRISTIANS (THE EPISTLE TO THE HEBREWS)

God, who gave to our forefathers many different glimpses of the truth in the words of the prophets, has now, at the end of the present age, given us the truth in the Son. Through the Son God made the whole universe, and to the Son he has ordained that all creation shall ultimately belong. This Son, radiance of the glory of God, flawless expression of the nature of God, himself the upholding power of all that is, having effected in person the cleansing of men's sin, took his seat at the right hand of the majesty on

Revised Standard Version

THE LETTER TO THE HEBREWS

1 In many and various ways God spoke of
old to our fathers by the prophets; 2 but in
these last days he has spoken to us by a Son,
whom he appointed the heir of all things,
through whom also he created the world. 3 He
reflects the glory of God and bears the very
stamp of his nature, upholding the universe by
his word of power. When he had made purification for sins, he sat down at the right hand of

Jerusalem Bible

THE LETTER TO THE HEBREWS

Prologue

The greatness of the incarnate Son of God

1 At various times in the past and in various
different ways, God spoke to our ancestors
through the prophets; but 2 in our own time, the
last days, he has spoken to us through his Son,
the Son that he has appointed to inherit everything and through whom he made everything
there is. 3 He is the radiant light of God's glory
and the perfect copy of his nature, sustaining
the universe by his powerful command; and now
that he has destroyed the defilement of sin, he
has gone to take his place in heaven at the

New English Bible

A LETTER TO HEBREWS

Christ divine and human

1 When in former times God spoke to our forefathers, he spoke in fragmentary and varied fashion through the prophets. But in this the final age he has spoken to us in the Son whom he has made heir to the whole universe, and through whom he created all orders of existence: the Son who is the effulgence of God's splendour and the stamp of God's very being, and sustains[a] the universe by his word of power. When he had brought about the purgation of sins, he took his

[a] *Or* bears along.

King James Version

on the right hand of the Majesty on high; 4 Being made so much better than the angels, as he
hath by inheritance obtained a more excellent
name than they. 5 For unto which of the angels
said he at any time, Thou art my Son, this day
have I begotten thee? And again, I will be to
him a Father, and he shall be to me a Son?
6 And again, when he bringeth in the firstbegot-
ten into the world, he saith, And let all the
angels of God worship him. 7 And of the angels
he saith, Who maketh his angels spirits, and his
ministers a flame of fire. 8 But unto the Son *he
saith,* Thy throne, O God, *is* for ever and ever:
a sceptre of righteousness *is* the sceptre of thy
kingdom. 9 Thou hast loved righteousness, and

Living Bible

4 Thus he became far greater than the angels,
as proved by the fact that his name "Son of
God," which was passed on to him from his
Father, is far greater than the names and titles
of the angels. 5, 6 For God never said to any
angel, "You are my Son, and today I have given
you the honor that goes with that name." [b] But
God said it about Jesus. Another time he said,
"I am his Father and he is my Son." And still
another time—when his firstborn Son came to
earth—God said, "Let all the angels of God
worship him."
7 God speaks of his angels as messengers
swift as the wind and as servants made of flaming fire; 8 but of his Son he says, "Your kingdom, O God, will last forever and ever; its commands are always just and right. 9 You love right

[b] Literally, "this day I have begotten you."

Today's English Version

The Son greater than the angels

4 The Son was made greater than the angels,
just as the name that God gave him is greater
than theirs. 5 For God never said to any of his
angels,

"You are my Son;
today I have become your Father."

Nor did God say to any angel,

"I will be his Father,
and he shall be my Son."

6 When God was about to send his firstborn Son
into the world, he also said,

"All of God's angels must worship him."

7 This is what God said about the angels,

"God makes his angels winds,
and his servants flames of fire."

8 About the Son, however, God said:

"Your throne, O God, will last forever and ever!
You rule over your kingdom with justice.
9 You love the right and hate the wrong;

New International Version

heaven. 4 So he became as much superior to
the angels as the name he has inherited is superior to theirs.
5 For to which of the angels did God ever
say,
"You are my Son;
today I have become your Father[a]"? [b]
Or again,
"I will be his Father,
and he will be my Son"? [c]
6 And again, when God brings his firstborn into
the world, he says,
"Let all God's angels worship him." [d]
7 In speaking of the angels he says,
"He makes his angels winds,
his servants flames of fire." [e]
8 But about the Son he says,
"Your throne, O God, will last for ever and ever,
and righteousness will be the scepter of your kingdom.
9 You have loved righteousness and hated wickedness;

[a] Or *have begotten you.* [b] Psalm 2:7. [c] 2 Samuel 7:14. [d] Deut. 32:43 (Septuagint, Dead Sea Scrolls); Psalm 97:7. [e] Psalm 104:4.

Phillips Modern English

high—thus proving himself, by the more glorious name that he had been given, far greater than all the angels of God.

1.5 Scripture endorses this superiority

For to which of the angels did he ever say such words as these:

Thou art my Son,
This day have I begotten thee?

Or, again:

I will be to him a Father,
And he shall be to me a Son?

Further, when he brings his first-born into this world of men, he says:

Let all the angels of God worship him.

This is what he says of the angels:

Who maketh his angels winds
And his ministers a flame of fire.

But when he speaks of the Son, he says:

Thy throne, O God, is for ever and ever;
And the sceptre of uprightness is the sceptre of thy kingdom.
Thou hast loved righteousness and hated iniquity;

Revised Standard Version

the Majesty on high, 4 having become as much
superior to angels as the name he has obtained
is more excellent than theirs.
5 For to what angel did God ever say,
"Thou art my Son,
today I have begotten thee"?
Or again,
"I will be to him a father,
and he shall be to me a son"?
6 And again, when he brings the first-born into
the world, he says,
"Let all God's angels worship him."
7 Of the angels he says,
"Who makes his angels winds,
and his servants flames of fire."
8 But of the Son he says,
"Thy throne, O God,[a] is for ever and ever,
the righteous scepter is the scepter of thy[b] kingdom.
9 Thou hast loved righteousness and hated lawlessness;

[a] Or *God is thy throne*. [b] Other ancient authorities read *his*.

Jerusalem Bible

right hand of divine Majesty. 4 So he is now
as far above the angels as the title which he has
inherited is higher than their own name.

1. The Son is greater than the angels

Proof from the scriptures

5 God has never said to any angel: *You are
my Son, today I have become your father*[a]; or:
I will be a father to him and he a son to me.[b]
6 Again, when he brings the First-born into the
world, he says: *Let all the angels of God worship him.*[c]
7 About the angels, he says: *He makes
his angels winds and his servants flames of fire,*[d]
8 but to his Son he says: *God, your throne shall
last for ever and ever;* and: *his royal scepter is
the scepter of virtue;* 9 *virtue you love as much*

[a] Ps. 2:7. [b] 2 S. 7:14. [c] Dt. 32:43. [d] Ps. 104:4.

New English Bible

seat at the right hand of Majesty on high, raised as far above the angels, as the title he has inherited is superior to theirs.

For God never said to any angel, 'Thou art my Son; today I have begotten thee', or again, 'I will be father to him, and he shall be my son.' Again, when he presents the first-born to the world, he says, 'Let all the angels of God pay him homage.' Of the angels he says,

'He who makes his angels winds,
and his ministers a fiery flame';

but of the Son,

'Thy throne, O God, is for ever and ever,
and the sceptre[b] of justice is the sceptre of his kingdom.
Thou hast loved right and hated wrong;

[b] *Or* God is thy throne for ever and ever, and thy sceptre . . .

King James Version

hated iniquity; therefore God, *even* thy God,
hath anointed thee with the oil of gladness above
thy fellows. 10And, Thou, Lord, in the beginning
hast laid the foundation of the earth; and the
heavens are the works of thine hands. 11 They
shall perish, but thou remainest: and they all
shall wax old as doth a garment; 12And as a
vesture shalt thou fold them up, and they shall
be changed: but thou art the same, and thy
years shall not fail. 13 But to which of the angels
said he at any time, Sit on my right hand, until
I make thine enemies thy footstool? 14Are they
not all ministering spirits, sent forth to minister
for them who shall be heirs of salvation?

2 Therefore we ought to give the more earnest
heed to the things which we have heard, lest
at any time we should let *them* slip. 2 For if the

Living Bible

and hate wrong; so God, even your God, has
poured out more gladness upon you than on
anyone else."
10 God also called him "Lord" when he said,
"Lord, in the beginning you made the earth, and
the heavens are the work of your hands. 11 They
will disappear into nothingness, but you will remain forever. They will become worn out like
old clothes, 12 and some day you will fold them
up and replace them. But you yourself will never
change, and your years will never end."
13 And did God ever say to an angel, as he
does to his Son, "Sit here beside me in honor
until I crush all your enemies beneath your
feet"?
14 No, for the angels are only spirit-messengers
sent out to help and care for those who are to
receive his salvation.

2 So we must listen very carefully to the
truths we have heard, or we may drift away
from them. 2 For since the messages from angels

Today's English Version

that is why God, your God, chose you
and gave you the joy of an honor far
greater
than he gave to your companions."

10 He also said,

"You, Lord, in the beginning created the
earth,
and with your own hands you made the
heavens.
11 They will all disappear, but you will remain;
they will all grow old like clothes.
12 You will fold them up like a coat,
and they will be changed like clothes.
But you are always the same,
and you will never grow old."

13 God never did say to any of his angels:

"Sit here at my right side,
until I put your enemies
as a footstool under your feet."

14 What are the angels, then? They are all
spirits who serve God and are sent by him to
help those who are to receive salvation.

The great salvation

2 That is why we must hold on all the more
firmly to the truths we have heard, so that
we will not be carried away. 2 The message given

New International Version

therefore God, your God, has set you
above your companions
by anointing you with the oil of joy." [f]
10 He also says,
"In the beginning, O Lord, you laid the
foundations of the earth,
and the heavens are the work of your
hands.
11 They will perish, but you remain;
they will all wear out like a garment.
12 You will roll them up like a robe;
like a garment they will be changed.
But you remain the same,
and your years will never end." [g]
13 To which of the angels did God ever say,
"Sit at my right hand
until I make your enemies your footstool"? [h]
14Are not all angels ministering spirits sent to
serve those who will inherit salvation?

Warning to pay attention

2 We must pay more careful attention, therefore, to what we have heard, so that we do
not drift away. 2 For if the message spoken by

[*f*] Psalm 45:6,7. [*g*] Psalm 102:25-27. [*h*] Psalm 110:1.

Phillips Modern English

Therefore God, thy God, hath anointed thee
With the oil of gladness above thy fellows.

He also says:

Thou, *Lord*, in the beginning hast laid the foundation of the earth,
And the heavens are the work of thy hands:
They shall perish, but thou continuest:
And they all shall wax old as doth a garment;
And as a mantle shalt thou roll them up,
As a garment, and they shall be changed:
But thou art the same,
And thy years shall not fail.

But does he ever say this to any of the angels:

Sit thou on my right hand,
Till I make thine enemies the footstool of thy feet?

Surely the angels are no more than spirits in the service of God, commissioned to serve the heirs of God's salvation.

2.1 *The angels had authority in past ages: today the Son is the authority*

We ought, therefore, to pay the greatest attention to the truth that we have heard and not allow ourselves to drift away from it. For if the

Revised Standard Version

therefore God, thy God, has anointed thee
with the oil of gladness beyond thy comrades."
10And,
"Thou, Lord, didst found the earth in the beginning,
and the heavens are the work of thy hands;
11 they will perish, but thou remainest;
they will all grow old like a garment,
12 like a mantle thou wilt roll them up,
and they will be changed.[c]
But thou art the same,
and thy years will never end."
13 But to what angel has he ever said,
"Sit at my right hand,
till I make thy enemies
a stool for thy feet"?
14Are they not all ministering spirits sent forth to serve, for the sake of those who are to obtain salvation?

2 Therefore we must pay the closer attention to what we have heard, lest we drift away
from it. 2 For if the message declared by angels

[c] Other ancient authorities add *like a garment*.

Jerusalem Bible

as you hate wickedness. This is why God, your God, has anointed you with the oil of gladness, above all your rivals.[e] 10And again: *It is you, Lord, who laid earth's foundations in the beginning, the heavens are the work of your hands;*
11 *all will vanish, though you remain, all wear out like a garment;* 12 *you will roll them up like a cloak, and like a* garment *they will be changed. But yourself, you never change and your years are unending.*[f] 13 God has never said to any
angel: *Sit at my right hand and I will make your enemies a footstool for you.*[g] 14 The truth is
they are all spirits whose work is service, sent to help those who will be the heirs of salvation.

An exhortation

2 We ought, then, to turn our minds more attentively than before to what we have been taught, so that we do not drift away. 2 If a

[e] Ps. 45:6-7. [f] Ps. 102:25-27. [g] Ps. 110:1.

New English Bible

therefore, O God, thy God[c] has set thee above thy fellows,
by anointing with the oil of exultation.'

And again,

'By thee, Lord, were earth's foundations laid of old,
and the heavens are the work of thy hands.
They shall pass away, but thou endurest;
like clothes they shall all grow old;
thou shalt fold them up like a cloak;
yes, they shall be changed like any garment.
But thou art the same, and thy years shall have no end.'

To which of the angels has he ever said, 'Sit at my right hand until I make thy enemies thy footstool'? What are they all but ministrant spirits, sent out to serve, for the sake of those who are to inherit salvation?

2 Thus we are bound to pay all the more heed to what we have been told, for fear of drifting from our course. For if the word spoken

[c] *Or* therefore God who is thy God . . .

King James Version

word spoken by angels was steadfast, and every
transgression and disobedience received a just
recompense of reward; 3 How shall we escape,
if we neglect so great salvation; which at the
first began to be spoken by the Lord, and was
confirmed unto us by them that heard *him;*
4 God also bearing *them* witness, both with signs
and wonders, and with divers miracles, and gifts
of the Holy Ghost, according to his own will?
5 For unto the angels hath he not put in subjection the world to come, whereof we speak.
6 But one in a certain place testified, saying,
What is man, that thou art mindful of him? or
the son of man, that thou visitest him? 7 Thou
madest him a little lower than the angels; thou
crownedst him with glory and honour, and didst
set him over the works of thy hands: 8 Thou
hast put all things in subjection under his feet.
For in that he put all in subjection under him,
he left nothing *that is* not put under him. But
now we see not yet all things put under him.
9 But we see Jesus, who was made a little lower
than the angels for the suffering of death,

Living Bible

have always proved true and people have always
been punished for disobeying them, 3 what makes
us think that we can escape if we are indifferent
to this great salvation announced by the Lord
Jesus himself, and passed on to us by those who
heard him speak?
4 God always has shown us that these messages are true by signs and wonders and various
miracles and by giving certain special abilities
from the Holy Spirit to those who believe; yes,
God has assigned such gifts to each of us.
5 And the future world we are talking about
will not be controlled by angels. 6 No, for in the
book of Psalms David says to God, "What is
mere man that you are so concerned about him?
And who is this Son of Man you honor so
highly? 7 For though you made him lower than
the angels for a little while, now you have
crowned him with glory and honor. 8 And you
have put him in complete charge of everything
there is. Nothing is left out."
We have not yet seen all of this take place,
9 but we do see Jesus—who for awhile was a
little lower than the angels—crowned now by

Today's English Version

by the angels was shown to be true, and anyone
who did not follow it or obey it received the
punishment he deserved. 3 How, then, shall we
escape if we pay no attention to such a great
salvation? The Lord himself first announced this
salvation, and those who heard him proved to
us that it is true. 4 At the same time God added
his witness to theirs by doing signs of power,
wonders, and many kinds of miracles. He also
distributed the gifts of the Holy Spirit according
to his will.

The leader to salvation

5 God did not place the angels as rulers over
the world he was about to create—the world of
which we speak. 6 Instead, as it is said somewhere in the Scriptures:

"God, what is man, that you should think of
him;
mere man, that you should care for him?
7 You made him for a little while lower than
the angels;
you crowned him with glory and honor,
8 and made him ruler over all things."

It says that God made man "ruler over all
things"; this clearly includes everything. But we
do not see man ruling over all things now. 9 But
we do see Jesus! For a little while he was made
lower than the angels, so that through God's

New International Version

angels was binding, and every violation and disobedience received its just punishment, 3 how
shall we escape if we ignore such a great salvation? This salvation, which was first announced
by the Lord, was confirmed to us by those who
heard him. 4 God also testified to it by signs,
wonders and various miracles, and gifts of the
Holy Spirit distributed according to his will.

Jesus made like his brothers

5 It is not to angels that he has subjected the
world to come, about which we are speaking.
6 But there is a place where someone has testified:
"What is man that you are concerned about
him,
or the son of man that you should care for
him?
7 You made him a little lower than the angels;
you crowned him with glory and honor
8 and put everything under his feet." [i]
In putting everything under him, God left nothing that is not subject to him. Yet at present we
do not see everything subject to him. 9 But we
see Jesus, who was made a little lower than the
angels, now crowned with glory and honor be-

[i] Psalm 8:4-6.

Phillips Modern English

message given through angels proved authentic, so that defiance of it and disobedience to it received appropriate retribution, how shall we escape if we refuse to pay proper attention to that greater salvation which is offered us? For this salvation came first through the words of the Lord himself: it was confirmed for us by men who had heard him speak, and God moreover has plainly endorsed their witness by signs and miracles, by all kinds of spiritual power, and by gifts of the Holy Spirit, distributed as he pleased.

For God did not put the future world of men under the control of angels, and it is this world that we are now talking about.

But someone has truly said:

What is man, that thou art mindful of him?
Or the son of man, that thou visitest him?
Thou madest him a little lower than the angels;
Thou crownedst him with glory and honour,
And didst set him over the works of thy hands;
Thou didst put all things in subjection under
his feet.

Notice that the writer puts "all things" under the sovereignty of man: he left nothing outside his control. But we do not yet see "all things" under his control.

2.9 *Christ became man, not angel, to save mankind*

What we see is Jesus, after being made temporarily inferior to the angels and so subject to

Revised Standard Version

was valid and every transgression or disobedience received a just retribution, 3 how shall we
escape if we neglect such a great salvation? It
was declared at first by the Lord, and it was attested to us by those who heard him, 4 while God
also bore witness by signs and wonders and
various miracles and by gifts of the Holy Spirit
distributed according to his own will.
5 For it was not to angels that God subjected
the world to come, of which we are speaking.
6 It has been testified somewhere,
"What is man that thou art mindful of him,
or the son of man, that thou carest for him?
7 Thou didst make him for a little while lower
than the angels,
thou hast crowned him with glory and
honor,[d]
8 putting everything in subjection under his
feet."
Now in putting everything in subjection to him,
he left nothing outside his control. As it is, we
do not yet see everything in subjection to him.
9 But we see Jesus, who for a little while was
made lower than the angels, crowned with glory

[d] Other ancient authorities insert *and didst set him over the works of thy hands.*

Jerusalem Bible

promise that was made through angels[h] proved
to be so true that every infringement and disobedience brought its own proper punishment,
3 then we shall certainly not go unpunished if
we neglect this salvation that is promised to us.
The promise was first announced by the Lord
himself, and is guaranteed to us by those who
heard him; 4 God himself confirmed their witness with signs and marvels and miracles of all
kinds, and by freely giving the gifts of the Holy
Spirit.

Redemption brought by Christ, not by angels

5 He did not appoint angels to be rulers of
the world to come, and that world is what we
are talking about. 6 Somewhere there is a passage that shows us this. It runs: *What is man
that you should spare a thought for him, the
son of man that you should care for him?* 7 *For
a short while you made him lower than the
angels; you crowned him with glory and splendor.* 8 *You have put him in command of everything.*[i] Well then, if he has *put him in command
of everything,* he has left nothing which is not
under his command. At present, it is true, we
are not able to see that *everything has been put
under his command,* 9 but we do see in Jesus
one who was *for a short while made lower than*

[h] The Law. [i] Ps. 8:4-6 (LXX).

New English Bible

through angels had such force that any transgression or disobedience met with due retribution, what escape can there be for us if we ignore a deliverance so great? For this deliverance was first announced through the lips of the Lord himself; those who heard him confirmed it to us, and God added his testimony by signs, by miracles, by manifold works of power, and by distributing the gifts of the Holy Spirit at his own will.

For it is not to angels that he has subjected the world to come, which is our theme. But there is somewhere a solemn assurance which runs:

'What is man, that thou rememberest him,
or the son of man, that thou hast regard to
him?
Thou didst make him for a short while lower
than the angels;
thou didst crown him with glory and honour;
thou didst put all things in subjection beneath
his feet.'

For in subjecting all things to him, he left nothing that is not subject. But in fact we do not yet see all things in subjection to man. In Jesus, however, we do see one who[a] for a short while was made lower than the angels, crowned now

[a] *Or* in subjection to him. But we see Jesus, who . . .

King James Version

crowned with glory and honour; that he by the
grace of God should taste death for every man.
10 For it became him, for whom *are* all things,
and by whom *are* all things, in bringing many
sons unto glory, to make the captain of their
salvation perfect through sufferings. 11 For both
he that sanctifieth and they who are sanctified
are all of one: for which cause he is not ashamed
to call them brethren, 12 Saying, I will declare
thy name unto my brethren, in the midst of the
church will I sing praise unto thee. 13 And again,
I will put my trust in him. And again, Behold
I and the children which God hath given me.
14 Forasmuch then as the children are partakers
of flesh and blood, he also himself likewise took
part of the same; that through death he might
destroy him that had the power of death, that
is, the devil; 15 And deliver them, who through
fear of death were all their lifetime subject to
bondage. 16 For verily he took not on *him the
nature of* angels; but he took on *him* the seed
of Abraham. 17 Wherefore in all things it be-
hooved him to be made like unto *his* brethren,
that he might be a merciful and faithful high

Living Bible

God with glory and honor because he suffered
death for us. Yes, because of God's great kindness, Jesus tasted death for everyone in all the
world. 10 And it was right and proper that God,
who made everything for his own glory, should
allow Jesus to suffer, for in doing this he was
bringing vast multitudes of God's people to
heaven; for his suffering made Jesus a perfect
Leader, one fit to bring them into their salvation.

11 We who have been made holy by Jesus,
now have the same Father he has. That is why
Jesus is not ashamed to call us his brothers.
12 For he says in the book of Psalms, "I will
talk to my brothers about God my Father, and
together we will sing his praises." 13 At another
time he said, "I will put my trust in God along
with my brothers." And at still another time,
"See, here am I and the children God gave me."

14 Since we, God's children, are human beings
—made of flesh and blood—he became flesh and
blood too by being born in human form; for
only as a human being could he die and in dying
break the power of the devil who had the power
of death. 15 Only in that way could he deliver
those who through fear of death have been
living all their lives as slaves to constant dread.

16 We all know he did not come as an angel
but as a human being—yes, a Jew. 17 And it was
necessary for Jesus to be like us, his brothers,
so that he could be our merciful and faithful
High Priest before God, a Priest who would be

Today's English Version

grace he should die for all men. We see him
crowned with glory and honor now because of
the death he suffered. 10 It was only right that
God, who creates and preserves all things, should
make Jesus perfect through suffering, in order
to bring many sons to share his glory. For Jesus
is the one who leads them to salvation.

11 He makes men pure from their sins, and
both he and those who are made pure all have
the same Father. That is why Jesus is not
ashamed to call them his brothers. 12 As he says,

"God, I will speak about you to my brothers;
I will praise you before the whole gathering."

13 He also says, "I will put my trust in God."
And he also says, "Here I am with the children
that God has given me."

14 Since the children, as he calls them, are
people of flesh and blood, Jesus himself became
like them and shared their human nature. He
did so that through his death he might destroy
the Devil, who has the power over death, 15 and
so set free those who were slaves all their lives
because of their fear of death. 16 For it is clear
that it is not the angels that he helps. Instead, as
the scripture says, "He helps the descendants of
Abraham." 17 This means that he had to become
like his brothers in every way, in order to be
their faithful and merciful high priest in his serv-

New International Version

cause he suffered death, so that by the grace of
God he might taste death for everyone.

10 In bringing many sons to glory, it was
fitting that God, for whom and through whom
everything exists, should make the Pioneer[j] of
their salvation perfect through suffering. 11 Both
the one who makes men holy and those who are
made holy are of the same family. So Jesus is
not ashamed to call them brothers. 12 He says,

"I will declare your name to my brothers;
in the presence of the congregation I will
sing your praises."[k]

13 And again,

"I will put my trust in him."[l]

And again he says,

"Here am I, and the children God has given
me."[m]

14 Since the children have flesh and blood,
he too shared in their humanity so that by his
death he might destroy him who holds the power
of death—that is, the devil—15 and free those
who all their lives were held in slavery by their
fear of death. 16 For surely it is not angels he
helps, but Abraham's descendants. 17 For this
reason he had to be made like his brothers in
every way, in order that he might become a
merciful and faithful high priest in service to

[*j*] Or *Originator*. [*k*] Psalm 22:22. [*l*] Isaiah 8:17.
[*m*] Isaiah 8:18.

Phillips Modern English

death, in order that he should, by God's grace, taste death for every man, now crowned with glory and honour. It was right and proper that in bringing many sons to glory, God (from whom and by whom everything exists) should make the leader of their salvation perfect through his sufferings. For the one who makes men holy and the men who are made holy share a common humanity. So that he is not ashamed to call them his brothers, for he says:

I will declare thy name unto my brethren,
In the midst of the congregation will I sing thy praise.

And again, speaking as a man, he says:

I will put my trust in him.

And, one more instance, in these words:

Behold, I and the children which God hath given me.

Since, then, "the children" have a common physical nature as human beings, he also became a human being, so that by going through death as a man he might destroy him who had the power of death, that is, the devil; and might also set free those who lived their whole lives a prey to the fear of death. It is plain that for this purpose his concern is not for angels but for men, the sons of Abraham. It was imperative that he should be made like his brothers in every respect, if he were to become a High Priest both compassionate and faithful in the things of

Revised Standard Version

and honor because of the suffering of death, so that by the grace of God he might taste death for every one.
10 For it was fitting that he, for whom and by whom all things exist, in bringing many sons to glory, should make the pioneer of their salvation perfect through suffering.
11 For he who sanctifies and those who are sanctified have all one origin. That is why he is not ashamed to call them brethren,
12 saying,
"I will proclaim thy name to my brethren,
in the midst of the congregation I will praise thee."
13 And again,
"I will put my trust in him."
And again,
"Here am I, and the children God has given me."
14 Since therefore the children share in flesh and blood, he himself likewise partook of the same nature, that through death he might destroy him who has the power of death, that is, the devil,
15 and deliver all those who through fear of death were subject to lifelong bondage.
16 For surely it is not with angels that he is concerned but with the descendants of Abraham.
17 Therefore he had to be made like his brethren in every respect, so that he might become a merciful and faithful high priest in the service

Jerusalem Bible

the angels and is now *crowned with glory and splendor* because he submitted to death; by God's grace he had to experience death for all mankind.
10 As it was his purpose to bring a great many of his sons into glory, it was appropriate that God, for whom everything exists and through whom everything exists, should make perfect, through suffering, the leader who would take them to their salvation.
11 For the one who sanctifies, and the ones who are sanctified, are of the same stock; that is why he openly calls them *brothers*
12 in the text: *I shall announce your name to my brothers, praise you in full assembly*[j]; or the text:
13 *In him I hope;* or the text: *Here I am with the children whom God has given me.*[k]
14 Since all the *children* share the same blood and flesh, he too shared equally in it, so that by his death he could take away all the power of the devil, who had power over death,
15 and set free all those who had been held in slavery all their lives by the fear of death.
16 For it was not the angels that he took to himself; he took to himself *descent from Abraham.*[l]
17 It was essential that he should in this way become completely like his brothers so that he could be a compassionate and trustworthy high priest

[j] Ps. 22:22. [k] This, and the previous text, are from Is. 8:17-18. [l] Is. 41:8-9.

New English Bible

with glory and honour because he suffered death, so that, by God's gracious will, in tasting death he should stand[b] for us all.

It was clearly fitting that God for whom and through whom all things exist should, in bringing many sons to glory, make the leader who delivers them perfect through sufferings. For a consecrating priest and those whom he consecrates are all of one stock; and that is why the Son does not shrink from calling men his brothers, when he says, 'I will proclaim thy name to my brothers; in full assembly I will sing thy praise'; and again, 'I will keep my trust fixed on him'; and again, 'Here am I, and the children whom God has given me.' The children of a family share the same flesh and blood; and so he too shared ours, so that through death he might break the power of him who had death at his command, that is, the devil; and might liberate those who, through fear of death, had all their lifetime been in servitude. It is not angels, mark you, that he takes to himself, but the sons of Abraham. And therefore he had to be made like these brothers of his in every way, so that he might be merciful and faithful as their high

[b] *Some witnesses read* so that apart from God he should taste death . . .

King James Version

priest in things *pertaining* to God, to make reconciliation for the sins of the people. 18 For in that he himself hath suffered being tempted, he is able to succour them that are tempted.

3 Wherefore, holy brethren, partakers of the heavenly calling, consider the Apostle and High Priest of our profession, Christ Jesus; 2 Who was faithful to him that appointed him, as also Moses *was faithful* in all his house. 3 For this *man* was counted worthy of more glory than Moses, inasmuch as he who hath builded the house hath more honour than the house. 4 For every house is builded by some *man;* but he that built all things *is* God. 5 And Moses verily *was* faithful in all his house as a servant, for a testimony of those things which were to be spoken after; 6 But Christ as a son over his own house; whose house are we, if we hold fast the confidence and the rejoicing of the hope firm unto

Living Bible

both merciful to us and faithful to God in dealing with the sins of the people. 18 For since he himself has now been through suffering and temptation, he knows what it is like when we suffer and are tempted, and he is wonderfully able to help us.

3 Therefore, dear brothers whom God has set apart for himself—you who are chosen for heaven—I want you to think now about this Jesus who is God's Messenger and the High Priest of our faith.

2 For Jesus was faithful to God who appointed him High Priest, just as Moses also faithfully served in God's house. 3 But Jesus has far more glory than Moses, just as a man who builds a fine house gets more praise than his house does. 4 And many people can build houses, but only God made everything.

5 Well, Moses did a fine job working in God's house, but he was only a servant; and his work was mostly to illustrate and suggest those things that would happen later on. 6 But Christ, God's faithful Son, is in complete charge of God's house. And we Christians are God's house—he lives in us!—if we keep up our courage firm to the end, and our joy and our trust in the Lord.

Today's English Version

ice to God, so that the people's sins would be forgiven. 18 And now he can help those who are tempted, because he himself was tempted and suffered.

Jesus greater than Moses

3 My Christian brothers, who also have been called by God! Think of Jesus, whom God sent to be the High Priest of the faith we profess. 2 He was faithful to God, who chose him to do this work, just as Moses was faithful in his work in God's whole house. 3 A man who builds a house receives more honor than the house itself. In the same way, Jesus is worthy of much more glory than Moses. 4 Every house, of course, is built by someone—and God is the one who has built all things. 5 Moses was faithful in God's whole house as a servant, and spoke of the things that God would say in the future. 6 But Christ is faithful as the Son in charge of God's house. We are his house, if we keep our courage and our confidence in what we hope for.

New International Version

God, and that he might make atonement for the sins of the people. 18 Because he himself suffered when he was tempted, he is able to help those who are being tempted.

Jesus greater than Moses

3 Therefore, holy brothers, who share in the heavenly calling, fix your thoughts on Jesus, the apostle and high priest whom we confess. 2 He was faithful to the one who appointed him, just as Moses was faithful in all God's house. 3 Jesus has been found worthy of greater honor than Moses, just as the builder of a house has greater honor than the house itself. 4 For every house is built by someone, but God is the builder of everything. 5 Moses was faithful as a servant in all God's house, testifying to what would be said in the future. 6 But Christ is faithful as a son over God's house. And we are his house, if we hold on to our courage and the hope of which we boast.

Phillips Modern English

God, and at the same time able to make atonement for the sins of the people. For by virtue of his own suffering under temptation he is able to help those who are exposed to temptation.

3.1 Moses was a faithful servant: Christ a faithful son

So then, my brothers in holiness who share a heavenly calling, I want you to think of Christ Jesus the Apostle and High Priest of the faith we hold. See him as faithful to the charge God gave him, and compare him with Moses who also faithfully discharged his duty in the household of God. For this man Jesus has been considered worthy of greater honour than Moses, just as the founder of a house may be truly said to have more honour than the house itself. Every house is founded by someone, but the founder of everything is God himself. Moses was certainly faithful in all his duties in God's household, but he was faithful as a servant and his work was only a foreshadowing of the truth that would be known later. But Christ was faithful as a son in the household of his own Father. And we are members of this household if we hold on to the end, with confidence and pride in our hope.

Revised Standard Version

of God, to make expiation for the sins of the
people. 18 For because he himself has suffered
and been tempted, he is able to help those who
are tempted.

3 Therefore, holy brethren, who share in a
heavenly call, consider Jesus, the apostle and
high priest of our confession. 2 He was faithful
to him who appointed him, just as Moses also
was faithful in[e] God's house. 3 Yet Jesus has
been counted worthy of as much more glory than
Moses as the builder of a house has more honor
than the house. 4 (For every house is built by
some one, but the builder of all things is God.)
5 Now Moses was faithful in all God's house as
a servant, to testify to the things that were to
be spoken later, 6 but Christ was faithful over
God's[f] house as a son. And we are his house if
we hold fast our confidence and pride in our
hope.[g]

[e] Other ancient authorities insert *all*. [f] Greek *his*.
[g] Other ancient authorities insert *firm to the end*.

Jerusalem Bible

of God's religion, able to atone for human sins.
18 That is, because he has himself been through
temptation he is able to help others who are
tempted.

II. Jesus the faithful and merciful high priest

Christ higher than Moses

3 That is why all you who are holy brothers
and have had the same heavenly call should
turn your minds to Jesus, the apostle and the
high priest of our religion. 2 He was *faithful* to
the one who appointed him, just like *Moses,*
who stayed faithful *in all his house;* 3 but he
has been found to deserve a greater glory than
Moses. It is the difference between the honor
given to the man that built the house and to
the house itself. 4 Every house is built by someone, of course; but God built everything that
exists. 5 It is true that Moses was *faithful in the*
house of God, as a servant, acting as witness
to the things which were to be divulged later;
6 but Christ was faithful as a son, and as the
master in the house. And we are his house, as
long as we cling to our hope with the confidence that we glory in.

New English Bible

priest before God, to expiate the sins of the people. For since he himself has passed through the test of suffering, he is able to help those who are meeting their test now.

3 Therefore, brothers in the family of God, who share a heavenly calling, think of the Apostle and High Priest of the religion we profess,[a] who was faithful to God who appointed him. Moses also was faithful in God's household; and Jesus, of whom I speak, has been deemed worthy of greater honour than Moses, as the founder of a house enjoys more honour than his household. For every house has its founder; and the founder of all is God. Moses, then, was faithful as a servitor in God's whole household; his task was to bear witness to the words that God would speak; but Christ is faithful as a son, set over his household. And we are that household of his, if only we are fearless and keep our hope high.

[a] *Or* of him whom we confess as God's Envoy and High Priest.

King James Version

the end. 7 Wherefore as the Holy Ghost saith,
To day if ye will hear his voice, 8 Harden not
your hearts, as in the provocation, in the day of
temptation in the wilderness: 9 When your fathers tempted me, proved me, and saw my works
forty years. 10 Wherefore I was grieved with
that generation, and said, They do always err in
their heart; and they have not known my ways.
11 So I sware in my wrath, They shall not enter
into my rest. 12 Take heed, brethren, lest there
be in any of you an evil heart of unbelief, in
departing from the living God. 13 But exhort one
another daily, while it is called To day; lest any
of you be hardened through the deceitfulness
of sin. 14 For we are made partakers of Christ,
if we hold the beginning of our confidence steadfast unto the end; 15 While it is said, To day if
ye will hear his voice, harden not your hearts,

Living Bible

7, 8 And since Christ is so much superior, the
Holy Spirit warns us to listen to him, to be careful to hear his voice today and not let our hearts
become set against him, as the people of Israel
did. They steeled themselves against his love and
complained against him in the desert while he
was testing them. 9 But God was patient with
them forty years, though they tried his patience
sorely; he kept right on doing his mighty miracles
for them to see. 10 "But," God says, "I was very
angry with them, for their hearts were always
looking somewhere else instead of up to me, and
they never found the paths I wanted them to follow."

11 Then God, full of this anger against them,
bound himself with an oath that he would never
let them come to his place of rest.

12 Beware then of your hearts, dear brothers,
lest you find that they, too, are evil and unbelieving and are leading you away from the living
God. 13 Speak to each other about these things
every day while there is still time, so that none
of you will become hardened against God, being blinded by the glamor[a] of sin. 14 For if we
are faithful to the end, trusting God just as we
did when we first became Christians, we will
share in all that belongs to Christ.

15 But *now* is the time. Never forget the
warning, "*Today* if you hear God's voice speaking to you, do not harden your hearts against
him, as the people of Israel did when they rebelled against him in the desert."

[a] Literally, "deceitfulness."

Today's English Version

A rest for God's people

7 So then, as the Holy Spirit says,

"If you hear God's voice today,
8 do not be stubborn as you were when you
rebelled against God,
as you were that day in the desert when
you put him to the test.
9 There your ancestors put me to the test and
tried me, says God,
even though they saw what I did for forty
years.
10 For that reason I was angry with those people and said,
'They are always disloyal,
and refuse to obey my commands.'
11 I was angry and made a solemn promise:
'They shall never come in and rest with
me!'"

12 My brothers, be careful that no one among
you has a heart so bad and unbelieving that he
will turn away from the living God. 13 Instead,
in order that none of you be deceived by sin
and become stubborn, you must help one another every day, as long as the "Today" in the
scripture applies to us. 14 For we are all partners
with Christ, if we hold on firmly to the end the
confidence we had at the beginning.
15 This is what the scripture says:

"If you hear God's voice today,
do not be stubborn as you were
when you rebelled against God."

New International Version

Warning against unbelief

7 So, as the Holy Spirit says:
"Today, if you hear his voice,
8 do not harden your hearts
as you did in the rebellion,
during the time of testing in the desert,
9 where your fathers tested and tried me,
and for forty years saw what I did.
10 That is why I was angry with that generation,
and I said, 'Their hearts are always going
astray,
and they have not known my ways.'
11 So I declared on oath in my anger,
'They shall never enter my rest.'"[n]
12 See to it, brothers, that none of you has a
sinful, unbelieving heart that turns away from
the living God. 13 But encourage one another
daily, as long as it is called Today, so that none
of you may be hardened by sin's deceitfulness.
14 We have come to share in Christ if we hold
firmly till the end the confidence we had at
first. 15 As has just been said:
"Today, if you hear his voice,
do not harden your hearts
as you did in the rebellion."[o]

[n] Psalm 95:7-11. [o] Psalm 95:7,8.

Phillips Modern English

3.7 *Let us be on our guard that unbelief does not creep in*

We ought to take note of these words in which the Holy Spirit says:

Today if ye shall hear his voice,
Harden not your hearts, as in the provocation,
Like as in the day of the temptation in the wilderness,
Wherewith your fathers tempted me by proving me,
And saw my works forty years.
Wherefore I was displeased with this generation,
And said, they do alway err in their heart:
But they did not know my ways;
As I sware in my wrath,
They shall not enter into my rest.

You should therefore be most careful, my brothers, that there should not be in any of you that wickedness of heart which refuses to trust, and deserts the cause of the living God. Encourage each other every day, while it is still called "today", and beware that none of you becomes deaf and blind to God through the delusive glamour of sin. For we continue to share in all that Christ has for us so long as we steadily maintain until the end the trust with which we began. These words are still being said for our ears to hear:

Today if ye shall hear his voice,
Harden not your hearts, as in the provocation.

Revised Standard Version

7 Therefore, as the Holy Spirit says,
"Today, when you hear his voice,
8 do not harden your hearts as in the rebellion,
on the day of testing in the wilderness,
9 where your fathers put me to the test
and saw my works for forty years.
10 Therefore I was provoked with that generation,
and said, 'They always go astray in their hearts;
they have not known my ways.'
11 As I swore in my wrath,
'They shall never enter my rest.'"
12 Take care, brethren, lest there be in any of
you an evil, unbelieving heart, leading you to
fall away from the living God. 13 But exhort one
another every day, as long as it is called "today,"
that none of you may be hardened by the deceitfulness of sin. 14 For we share in Christ, if
only we hold our first confidence firm to the
end. 15 while it is said,
"Today, when you hear his voice,
do not harden your hearts as in the rebellion."

Jerusalem Bible

How to reach God's land of rest

7 The Holy Spirit says: *If only you would
listen to him today; 8 do not harden your hearts,
as happened in the Rebellion, on the Day of
Temptation in the wilderness, 9 when your ancestors challenged me and tested me, though
they had seen what I could do 10 for forty
years. That was why I was angry with that generation and said: How unreliable these people
who refuse to grasp my ways! 11 And so, in
anger, I swore that not one would reach the
place of rest I had for them.*[m] 12 Take care,
brothers, that there is not in any one of your
community a wicked mind, so unbelieving as to
turn away from the living God. 13 Every day,
as long as this "today" lasts, keep encouraging
one another so that none of you is *hardened*
by the lure of sin, 14 because we shall remain
co-heirs with Christ only if we keep a grasp on
our first confidence right to the end. 15 In this
saying: *If only you would listen to him today;
do not harden your hearts, as happened in the*

[*m*] Ps. 95.

New English Bible

'Today', therefore, as the Holy Spirit says—

'Today if you hear his voice,
do not grow stubborn as in those days of rebellion,
at that time of testing in the desert,
where your forefathers tried me and tested me,
and saw[b] the things I did for forty years.
And so, I was indignant with that generation
and I said, Their hearts are for ever astray;
they would not discern my ways;
as I vowed in my anger, they shall never enter my rest.'

See to it, brothers, that no one among you has the wicked, faithless heart of a deserter from the living God; but day by day, while that word 'Today' still sounds in your ears, encourage one another, so that no one of you is made stubborn by the wiles of sin. For we have become Christ's partners[a] if only we keep our original confidence firm to the end.

When Scripture says, 'Today if you hear his voice, do not grow stubborn as in those days of

[*b*] *Or* though they saw . . . [*a*] *Or* have been given a share in Christ.

King James Version

as in the provocation. 16 For some, when they had heard, did provoke: howbeit not all that came out of Egypt by Moses. 17 But with whom was he grieved forty years? *was it* not with them that had sinned, whose carcasses fell in the wilderness? 18 And to whom sware he that they should not enter into his rest, but to them that believed not? 19 So we see that they could not enter in because of unbelief.

4 Let us therefore fear, lest, a promise being left *us* of entering into his rest, any of you should seem to come short of it. 2 For unto us was the gospel preached, as well as unto them: but the word preached did not profit them, not being mixed with faith in them that heard *it*. 3 For we which have believed do enter into rest, as he said, As I have sworn in my wrath, if they shall enter into my rest: although the works were finished from the foundation of the world. 4 For he spake in a certain place of the seventh *day* on this wise, And God did rest the seventh

Living Bible

16 And who were those people I speak of, who heard God's voice speaking to them but then rebelled against him? They were the ones who came out of Egypt with Moses their leader. 17 And who was it who made God angry for all those forty years? These same people who sinned and as a result died in the wilderness. 18 And to whom was God speaking when he swore with an oath that they could never go into the land he had promised his people? He was speaking to all those who disobeyed him. 19 And why couldn't they go in? Because they didn't trust him.

4 Although God's promise still stands—his promise that all may enter his place of rest—we ought to tremble with fear because some of you may be on the verge of failing to get there after all. 2 For this wonderful news—the message that God wants to save us—has been given to us just as it was to those who lived in the time of Moses. But it didn't do them any good because they didn't believe it. They didn't mix it with faith. 3 For only we who believe God can enter into his place of rest. He has said, "I have sworn in my anger that those who don't believe me will never get in," even though he has been ready and waiting for them since the world began.

4 We know he is ready and waiting because it is written that God rested on the seventh day

Today's English Version

16 Who heard God's voice and rebelled against him? All the people who were led out of Egypt by Moses. 17 With whom was God angry for forty years? With the people who sinned, who fell down dead in the desert. 18 When God made his solemn promise, "They shall never come in and rest with me"—of whom was he speaking? Of those who rebelled. 19 We see, then, that they were not able to go in because they did not believe.

4 Now, God has left us the promise that we may go in and rest with him. Let us fear, then, so that none of you will be found to have failed to go in to that rest. 2 For we have heard the Good News, just as they did. They heard the message but it did them no good, because when they heard it they did not receive it with faith. 3 We who believe, then, do go in and rest with God. It is just as he said,

"I was angry and made a solemn promise:
'They shall never come in and rest with me!'"

He said this even though his work was finished from the time he created the world. 4 For somewhere in the Scriptures this is said about the

New International Version

16 Who were they who heard and rebelled? Were they not all those Moses led out of Egypt? 17 And with whom was he angry for forty years? Was it not with those who sinned, whose bodies fell in the desert? 18 And to whom did God swear that they would never enter his rest if not to those who disobeyed?[p] 19 So we see that they were not able to enter, because of their unbelief.

A Sabbath-rest for the people of God

4 Therefore, since the promise of entering his rest still stands, let us be careful that none of you be found to have fallen short of it. 2 For we also have had the gospel preached to us, just as they did; but the message they heard was of no value to them, because those who heard did not combine it with faith.[q] 3 Now we who have believed enter that rest, just as God has said,

"So I declared on oath in my anger,
'They shall never enter my rest.'"[r]

And yet his work has been finished since the creation of the world. 4 For somewhere he has spoken about the seventh day in these words:

[p] Or *disbelieved*. [q] Many MSS read *because they did not share in the faith of those who obeyed*. [r] Psalm 95:11.

Phillips Modern English

For who was it who heard the Word of God and yet provoked his indignation? Was it not all who left Egypt under the leadership of Moses? And who was it with whom God was displeased for forty long years? Was it not those who, after all their hearing of God's Word, fell into sin, and left their bones in the desert? And to whom did God swear that they should never enter into his rest? Was it not these very men who refused to trust him?

Yes, it is all too plain that it was refusal to trust God that prevented these men from entering his rest.

4.1 Men failed in the past to find God's rest: let us not fail!

Now since the same promise of rest is offered to us today, let us be continually on our guard that none of us even looks like failing to attain it. For we too have had a gospel preached to us, as those men had. Yet the message proclaimed to them did them no good, because they only heard and did not believe as well. It is only as a result of our faith and trust that we experience that rest. For he said:

As I sware in my wrath,
They shall not enter into my rest:

not because the rest was not prepared—it had been ready since the work of creation was completed, as he says elsewhere in the scriptures, speaking of the seventh day of creation,

Revised Standard Version

16 Who were they that heard and yet were rebellious? Was it not all those who left Egypt
under the leadership of Moses? 17 And with
whom was he provoked forty years? Was it not
with those who sinned, whose bodies fell in the
wilderness? 18 And to whom did he swear that
they should never enter his rest, but to those who
were disobedient? 19 So we see that they were
unable to enter because of unbelief.

4 Therefore, while the promise of entering his
rest remains, let us fear lest any of you be
judged to have failed to reach it. 2 For good
news came to us just as to them; but the message
which they heard did not benefit them, because
it did not meet with faith in the hearers.[h] 3 For
we who have believed enter that rest, as he has
said,

"As I swore in my wrath,
'They shall never enter my rest,' "

although his works were finished from the foundation of the world. 4 For he has somewhere
spoken of the seventh day in this way, "And

[h] Other manuscripts read *they were not united in faith with the hearers.*

Jerusalem Bible

Rebellion, 16 those who *rebelled* after they had
listened were all the people who were brought
out of Egypt by Moses. 17 And those who made
God *angry for forty years* were the ones who
sinned and whose *dead bodies were left lying in*
the wilderness.[n] 18 Those that he *swore would*
never reach the place of rest he had for them
were those who had been disobedient. 19 We see,
then, that it was because they were unfaithful
that they were not able to reach it.

4 Be careful, then: the promise of *reaching*
the place of rest he had for them still holds
good, and none of you must think that he has
come too late for it. 2 We received the Good
News exactly as they did; but hearing the message did them no good because they did not
share the faith of those who listened. 3 We,
however, who have faith, shall reach a place of
rest, as in the text: *And so, in anger, I swore*
that not one would reach the place of rest I had
for them. God's work was undoubtedly all finished at the beginning of the world; 4 as one
text says, referring to the seventh day: *After all*

[n] Nb. 14:29.

New English Bible

rebellion', who, I ask, were those who heard and rebelled? All those, surely, whom Moses had led out of Egypt. And with whom was God indignant for forty years? With those, surely, who had sinned, whose bodies lay where they fell in the desert. And to whom did he vow that they should not enter his rest, if not to those who had refused to believe? We perceive that it was unbelief which prevented their entering.

4 Therefore we must have before us the fear that while the promise of entering his rest remains open, one or another among you should be found to have missed his chance. For indeed we have heard the good news, as they did. But in them the message they heard did no good, because it met with no faith in those who heard it. It is we, we who have become believers, who enter the rest referred to in the words, 'As I vowed in my anger, they shall never enter my rest.' Yet God's work has been finished ever since the world was created; for does not Scripture somewhere speak thus of the seventh

King James Version

day from all his works. 5 And in this *place* again, If they shall enter into my rest. 6 Seeing therefore it remaineth that some must enter therein, and they to whom it was first preached entered not in because of unbelief: 7 Again, he limiteth a certain day, saying in David, To day, after so long a time; as it is said, To day if ye will hear his voice, harden not your hearts. 8 For if Jesus had given them rest, then would he not afterward have spoken of another day. 9 There remaineth therefore a rest to the people of God. 10 For he that is entered into his rest, he also hath ceased from his own works, as God *did* from his. 11 Let us labour therefore to enter into that rest, lest any man fall after the same example of unbelief. 12 For the word of God *is* quick, and powerful, and sharper than any two-edged sword, piercing even to the dividing asunder of soul and spirit, and of the joints and marrow, and *is* a discerner of the thoughts and intents of the heart. 13 Neither is there any creature that is not manifest in his sight: but all things *are* naked and opened unto the eyes of

Living Bible

of creation, having finished all that he had planned to make.

5 Even so they didn't get in, for God finally said, "They shall never enter my rest." 6 Yet the promise remains and some get in—but not those who had the first chance, for they disobeyed God and failed to enter.

7 But he has set another time for coming in, and that time is now. He announced this through King David long years after man's first failure to enter, saying in the words already quoted, "Today when you hear him calling, do not harden your hearts against him."

8 This new place of rest he is talking about does not mean the land of Israel that Joshua led them into. If that were what God meant, he would not have spoken long afterwards about "today" being the time to get in. 9 So there is a full complete rest *still waiting* for the people of God. 10 Christ has already entered there. He is resting from his work, just as God did after the creation. 11 Let us do our best to go into that place of rest, too, being careful not to disobey God as the children of Israel did, thus failing to get in.

12 For whatever God says to us is full of living power: it is sharper than the sharpest dagger, cutting swift and deep into our innermost thoughts and desires with all their parts, exposing us for what we really are. 13 He knows about everyone, everywhere. Everything about us is bare and wide open to the all-seeing eyes of our living God; nothing can be hidden from him to whom we must explain all that we have done.

Today's English Version

seventh day, "God rested on the seventh day from all his works." 5 This same matter is spoken of again: "They shall never come in and rest with me." 6 Those who first heard the Good News did not go in and rest with God because they did not believe. There are, then, others who are allowed to go in and rest with God. 7 This is shown by the fact that God sets another day, which is called "Today." He spoke of it many years later by means of David, in the scripture already quoted,

"If you hear God's voice today,
do not be stubborn."

8 If Joshua had led the people into God's rest, God would not have spoken later about another day. 9 As it is, however, there still remains for God's people a rest like God's resting on the seventh day. 10 For whoever goes in and rests with God will rest from his own works, just as God rested from his. 11 Let us, then, do our best to go in and rest with God. We must not, any of us, disobey as they did and fail to go in.

12 The word of God is alive and active. It is sharper than any double-edged sword. It cuts all the way through, to where soul and spirit meet, to where joints and marrow come together. It judges the desires and thoughts of men's hearts. 13 There is nothing that can be hid from God. Everything in all creation is exposed and lies open before his eyes; and it is to him that we must all give account of ourselves.

New International Version

"And on the seventh day God rested from all his work." [s] 5 And again in the passage above he says, "They shall never enter my rest." [r]

6 It still remains that some will enter that rest, and those who formerly had the gospel preached to them did not go in, because of their disobedience. 7 Therefore God again set a certain day, calling it Today, when a long time later he spoke through David, as was said before:

"Today, if you hear his voice,
do not harden your hearts." [t]

8 For if Joshua had given them rest, God would not have spoken later about another day. 9 There remains, then, a Sabbath-rest for the people of God; 10 for anyone who enters God's rest also rests from his own work, just as God did from his. 11 Let us, therefore, make every effort to enter that rest, so that no one will fall by following their example of disobedience.

12 The word of God is living and active. Sharper than any double-edged sword, it penetrates even to dividing soul and spirit, joints and marrow; it judges the thoughts and attitudes of the heart. 13 Nothing in all creation is hidden from God's sight. Everything is uncovered and laid bare before the eyes of him to whom we must give account.

[s] Gen. 2:2. [r] Psalm 95:11. [t] Psalm 95:7,8.

Phillips Modern English

And God rested on the seventh day from all his works.

In the passage above he says, "They shall not enter into my rest." It is clear that some were intended to experience this rest and, since the previous hearers of the message failed to attain to it because they would not believe God, he proclaims a further opportunity when he says through David, many years later, "today", just as he had said "today" before.

Today if ye shall hear his voice,
Harden not your hearts.

For if Joshua had given them the rest, we should not find God saying, at a much later date, "today". There still exists, therefore, a full and complete rest for the people of God. And he who experiences his rest is resting from his own work as fully as God from his.

Let us then be eager to know this rest for ourselves, and let us beware that no one misses it through falling into the same kind of unbelief as those we have mentioned. For the Word that God speaks is alive and active; it cuts more keenly than any two-edged sword: it strikes through to the place where soul and spirit meet, to the innermost intimacies of a man's being: it examines the very thoughts and motives of a man's heart. No creature has any cover from the sight of God; everything lies naked and exposed before the eyes of him with whom we have to deal.

Revised Standard Version

God rested on the seventh day from all his
works." 5 And again in this place he said,
"They shall never enter my rest."
6 Since therefore it remains for some to enter it,
and those who formerly received the good news
failed to enter because of disobedience, 7 again
he sets a certain day, "Today," saying through
David so long afterward, in the words already
quoted,
"Today, when you hear his voice,
do not harden your hearts."
8 For if Joshua had given them rest, God [i]
would not speak later of another day. 9 So then,
there remains a sabbath rest for the people of
God; 10 for whoever enters God's rest also ceases
from his labors as God did from his.
11 Let us therefore strive to enter that rest,
that no one fall by the same sort of disobedience.
12 For the word of God is living and active,
sharper than any two-edged sword, piercing to
the division of soul and spirit, of joints and
marrow, and discerning the thoughts and intentions of the heart. 13 And before him no creature is hidden, but all are open and laid bare to
the eyes of him with whom we have to do.

[i] Greek *he*.

Jerusalem Bible

his work God rested on the seventh day.[o] 5 The
text we are considering says: *They shall not
reach the place of rest I had for them.* 6 It is
established, then, that there would be some people who would reach it, and since those who
first heard the Good News failed to reach it
through their disobedience, 7 God fixed another
day when, much later, he said "today" through
David in the text already quoted: *If only you
would listen to him today; do not harden your
hearts.* 8 If Joshua had led them into this place
of rest, God would not later on have spoken so
much of another day. 9 There must still be,
therefore, a place of rest reserved for God's
people, the seventh-day rest, 10 since to *reach
the place of rest* is to *rest after your work,* as
God did after his. 11 We must therefore do
everything we can to *reach this place of rest,* or
some of you might copy this example of disobedience and be lost.

The word of God and Christ the priest

12 The word of God is something alive and
active: it cuts like any double-edged sword but
more finely: it can slip through the place where
the soul is divided from the spirit, or joints
from the marrow; it can judge the secret emotions and thoughts. 13 No created thing can
hide from him; everything is uncovered and
open to the eyes of the one to whom we must
give account of ourselves.

[o] Gn. 2:2.

New English Bible

day: 'God rested from all his work on the seventh day'?—and once again in the passage above we read, 'They shall never enter my rest.' The fact remains that someone must enter it, and since those who first heard the good news failed to enter through unbelief, God fixes another day. Speaking through the lips of David after many long years, he uses the words already quoted: 'Today if you hear his voice, do not grow stubborn.' If Joshua had given them rest, God would not thus have spoken of another day after that. Therefore, a sabbath rest still awaits the people of God; for anyone who enters God's rest, rests from his own work as God did from his. Let us then make every effort to enter that rest, so that no one may fall by following this evil example of unbelief.

For the word of God is alive and active. It cuts more keenly than any two-edged sword, piercing as far as the place where life and spirit, joints and marrow, divide. It sifts the purposes and thoughts of the heart. There is nothing in creation that can hide from him; everything lies naked and exposed to the eyes of the One with whom we have to reckon.

King James Version

him with whom we have to do. 14 Seeing then that we have a great high priest, that is passed into the heavens, Jesus the Son of God, let us hold fast *our* profession. 15 For we have not a high priest which cannot be touched with the feeling of our infirmities; but was in all points tempted like as *we are, yet* without sin. 16 Let us therefore come boldly unto the throne of grace, that we may obtain mercy, and find grace to help in time of need.

5 For every high priest taken from among men is ordained for men in things *pertaining* to God, that he may offer both gifts and sacrifices for sins: 2 Who can have compassion on the ignorant, and on them that are out of the way; for that he himself also is compassed with infirmity. 3 And by reason hereof he ought, as for the people, so also for himself, to offer for sins. 4 And no man taketh this honour unto himself, but he that is called of God, as *was* Aaron. 5 So also Christ glorified not himself to be made a high priest; but he that said unto him, Thou

Living Bible

14 But Jesus the Son of God is our great High Priest who has gone to heaven itself to help us; therefore let us never stop trusting him. 15 This High Priest of ours understands our weaknesses, since he had the same temptations we do, though he never once gave way to them and sinned. 16 So let us come boldly to the very throne of God and stay there to receive his mercy and to find grace to help us in our times of need.

5 The Jewish high priest is merely a man like anyone else, but he is chosen to speak for all other men in their dealings with God. He presents their gifts to God and offers to him the blood of animals that are sacrificed to cover the sins of the people and his own sins too. And because he is a man he can deal gently with other men, though they are foolish and ignorant, for he, too, is surrounded with the same temptations and understands their problems very well.

4 Another thing to remember is that no one can be a high priest just because he wants to be. He has to be called by God for this work in the same way God chose Aaron.

5 That is why Christ did not elect himself to the honor of being High Priest; no, he was chosen by God. God said to him, "My Son, to-

Today's English Version

Jesus the great high priest

14 Let us, then, hold firmly to the faith we profess. For we have a great high priest who has gone into the very presence of God—Jesus, the Son of God. 15 Our high priest is not one who cannot feel sympathy with our weaknesses. On the contrary, we have a high priest who was tempted in every way that we are, but did not sin. 16 Let us be brave, then, and come forward to God's throne, where there is grace. There we will receive mercy and find grace to help us just when we need it.

5 Every high priest is chosen from his fellowmen and appointed to serve God on their behalf, to offer gifts and sacrifices for sins. 2 Since he himself is weak in many ways, he is able to be gentle with those who are ignorant and make mistakes. 3 And because he is himself weak, he must offer sacrifices not only for the sins of the people but also for his own sins. 4 No one chooses for himself the honor of being a high priest. It is only by God's call that a man is made a high priest—just as Aaron was called.

5 In the same way, Christ did not take upon himself the honor of being a high priest. Instead, God said to him,

New International Version

Jesus the great high priest

14 Therefore, since we have a great high priest who has gone into heaven, Jesus the Son of God, let us hold firmly to the faith we profess. 15 For we do not have a high priest who is unable to sympathize with our weaknesses, but we have one who has been tempted in every way, just as we are—yet was without sin. 16 Let us then approach the throne of grace with confidence, so that we may receive mercy and find grace to help us in our time of need.

5 Every high priest is selected from among men and is appointed to represent them in matters related to God, to offer gifts and sacrifices for sins. 2 He is able to deal gently with those who are ignorant and are going astray, since he himself is subject to weakness. 3 This is why he has to offer sacrifices for his own sins, as well as for the sins of the people.

4 No one takes this honor upon himself; he must be called by God, just as Aaron was. 5 So Christ also did not take upon himself the glory of becoming a high priest. But God said to him,

Phillips Modern English

4.14 For our help and comfort—Jesus the great High Priest

Seeing that we have a great High Priest who has passed through the heavens, Jesus the Son of God, let us hold firmly to our faith. For ours is no High Priest who cannot sympathise with our weaknesses—he himself has shared fully in all our experience of temptation, except that he never sinned.

Let us therefore approach the throne of grace with fullest confidence, that we may receive mercy for our failures and grace to help in the hour of need.

5.1 A High Priest must be duly qualified and divinely appointed

Note that when a man is chosen as High Priest he is appointed on men's behalf as their representative in the things of God—he offers gifts to God and makes the necessary sacrifices for sins on behalf of his fellow-men. He must be able to deal sympathetically with the ignorant and foolish because he realises that he is himself prone to human weakness. This means that the offering which he makes for sin is made on his own behalf as well as on behalf of those whom he represents.

Note also that nobody chooses for himself the honour of being a High Priest, but he is called by God to the work, as was Aaron, the first High Priest in ancient times.

Thus we see that the Christ did not choose for himself the glory of being High Priest, but he was honoured by the one who said:

Revised Standard Version

14 Since then we have a great high priest who
has passed through the heavens, Jesus, the Son
of God, let us hold fast our confession. 15 For
we have not a high priest who is unable to sympathize with our weaknesses, but one who in
every respect has been tempted as we are, yet
without sin. 16 Let us then with confidence draw
near to the throne of grace, that we may receive
mercy and find grace to help in time of need.

5 For every high priest chosen from among
men is appointed to act on behalf of men in
relation to God, to offer gifts and sacrifices for
sins. 2 He can deal gently with the ignorant and
wayward, since he himself is beset with weakness.
3 Because of this he is bound to offer sacrifice
for his own sins as well as for those of the people. 4 And one does not take the honor upon himself, but he is called by God, just as Aaron was.
5 So also Christ did not exalt himself to be
made a high priest, but was appointed by him
who said to him,

Jerusalem Bible

14 Since in Jesus, the Son of God, we have
the supreme high priest who has gone through
to the highest heaven, we must never let go of
the faith that we have professed. 15 For it is not
as if we had a high priest who was incapable
of feeling our weaknesses with us; but we have
one who has been tempted in every way that
we are, though he is without sin. 16 Let us be
confident, then, in approaching the throne of
grace, that we shall have mercy from him and
find grace when we are in need of help.

Jesus the compassionate high priest

5 Every high priest has been taken out of
mankind and is appointed to act for men in
their relations with God, to offer gifts and sacrifices for sins; and so 2 he can sympathize with
those who are ignorant or uncertain because he
too lives in the limitations of weakness. 3 That
is why he has to make sin offerings for himself
as well as for the people. 4 No one takes this
honor on himself, but each one is called by
God, as Aaron was. 5 Nor did Christ give himself the glory of becoming high priest, but he
had it from the one who said to him: *You are*

New English Bible

Since therefore we have a great high priest who has passed through the heavens, Jesus the Son of God, let us hold fast to the religion we profess. For ours is not a high priest unable to sympathize with our weaknesses, but one who, because of his likeness to us, has been tested every way,[a] only without sin. Let us therefore boldly approach the throne of our gracious God, where we may receive mercy and in his grace find timely help.

The shadow and the real

5 For every high priest is taken from among men and appointed their representative before God, to offer gifts and sacrifices for sins. He is able to bear patiently with the ignorant and erring, since he too is beset by weakness; and because of this he is bound to make sin-offerings for himself no less than for the people. And nobody arrogates the honour to himself: he is called by God, as indeed Aaron was. So it is with Christ: he did not confer upon himself the glory of becoming high priest; it was granted by God, who said to him, 'Thou art my Son; today

[a] *Or* who has been tested every way, as we are.

King James Version

art my Son, to day have I begotten thee. 6As
he saith also in another *place*, Thou *art* a priest
for ever after the order of Melchisedec. 7 Who
in the days of his flesh, when he had offered
up prayers and supplications with strong crying
and tears unto him that was able to save him
from death, and was heard in that he feared;
8 Though he were a Son, yet learned he obedience by the things which he suffered; 9And being
made perfect, he became the author of eternal
salvation unto all them that obey him; 10 Called
of God a high priest after the order of Mel-

Living Bible

day I have honored [a] you." 6And another time
God said to him, "You have been chosen to be
a priest forever, with the same rank as Melchizedek."

7 Yet while Christ was here on earth he
pleaded with God, praying with tears and agony
of soul to the only one who would save him
from [premature[b]] death. And God heard his
prayers because of his strong desire to obey
God at all times.

8 And even though Jesus was God's Son, he
had to learn from experience what it was like
to obey, when obeying meant suffering. 9 It was
after he had proved himself perfect in this experience that Jesus became the Giver of eternal
salvation to all those who obey him. 10 For remember that God has chosen him to be a High
Priest with the same rank as Melchizedek.

[*a*] Literally, "begotten you." Probably the reference is to the day of Christ's resurrection. [*b*] Implied. Christ's longing was to live until he could die on the cross for all mankind. There is a strong case to be made that Satan's great desire was that Christ should die prematurely, before the mighty work at the cross could be performed. Christ's body, being human, was frail and weak like ours (except that his was sinless). He had said just a few moments before, "My soul is exceeding sorrowful *unto death*." And can a human body live long under such pressure of spirit as he underwent in the Garden, that caused sweating of great drops of blood? But God graciously heard and answered his anguished cry in Gethsemane ("Let this cup pass from me") and preserved him from seemingly imminent and premature death: for an angel was sent to strengthen him so that he could live to accomplish God's perfect will at the cross. . . . But some readers may prefer the explanation that Christ's plea was that he be saved *out from* death, at the Resurrection.

Today's English Version

"You are my Son;
today I have become your Father."

6 He also said in another place,

"You will be a priest forever,
in the priestly order of Melchizedek."

7 In his life on earth Jesus made his prayers
and requests with loud cries and tears to God,
who could save him from death. Because he was
humble and devoted, God heard him. 8 But even
though he was God's Son he learned to be obedient by means of his sufferings. 9 When he was
made perfect, he became the source of eternal
salvation for all those who obey him, 10 and
God declared him to be high priest, in the
priestly order of Melchizedek.

New International Version

"You are my Son;
today I have become your Father.[u]" [v]
6And he says in another place,
"You are a priest forever,
just like Melchizedek." [w]
7 During the days of Jesus' life on earth, he
offered up prayers and petitions with loud cries
and tears to the One who could save him from
death, and he was heard because of his reverent
submission. 8Although he was a son, he learned
obedience from what he suffered, 9 and once
made perfect, he became the source of eternal
salvation for all who obey him 10 and was designated by God to be high priest, just like Melchizedek.

[*u*] Or *have begotten you.* [*v*] Psalm 2:7. [*w*] Psalm 110:4.

Phillips Modern English

Thou art my Son,
This day have I begotten thee.

And he says in another passage:

Thou art a priest for ever
After the order of Melchizedek.

5.7 Christ, the perfect High Priest, was the perfect Son

Christ, in the days when he was a man on earth, appealed to the One who could save him from death in desperate prayer and the agony of tears. His prayers were heard because of his willingness to obey. But, Son though he was, he had to prove the meaning of obedience through all that he suffered. Then, when he had been proved the perfect Son, he became the source of eternal salvation to all who should obey him, being designated by God himself as High Priest "after the order of Melchizedek".

Revised Standard Version

"Thou art my Son,
today I have begotten thee";
6 as he says also in another place,
"Thou art a priest for ever,
after the order of Melchizedek."
7 In the days of his flesh, Jesus[j] offered up
prayers and supplications, with loud cries and
tears, to him who was able to save him from
death, and he was heard for his godly fear.
8 Although he was a Son, he learned obedience
through what he suffered; 9 and being made perfect he became the source of eternal salvation
to all who obey him, 10 being designated by
God a high priest after the order of Melchizedek.

[j] Greek *he*.

Jerusalem Bible

my son, today I have become your father,[p]
6 and in another text: *You are a priest of the*
order of Melchizedek, and for ever.[q] 7 During
his life on earth, he offered up prayer and entreaty, aloud and in silent tears, to the one who
had the power to save him out of death, and
he submitted so humbly that his prayer was
heard. 8 Although he was Son, he learned to
obey through suffering; 9 but having been made
perfect, he became for all who obey him the
source of eternal salvation 10 and was acclaimed
by God with the title of high priest *of the order*
of Melchizedek.

[p] Ps. 2:7. [q] Ps. 110:4.

New English Bible

I have begotten thee'; as also in another place he says, 'Thou art a priest for ever, in the succession of Melchizedek.' In the days of his earthly life he offered up prayers and petitions, with loud cries and tears, to God who was able to deliver him from the grave. Because of his humble submission his prayer was heard: son though he was, he learned obedience in the school of suffering, and, once perfected, became the source of eternal salvation for all who obey him, named by God high priest in the succession of Melchizedek.

King James Version

chisedec. 11 Of whom we have many things to say, and hard to be uttered, seeing ye are dull of hearing. 12 For when for the time ye ought to be teachers, ye have need that one teach you again which *be* the first principles of the oracles of God; and are become such as have need of milk, and not of strong meat. 13 For every one that useth milk *is* unskilful in the word of righteousness: for he is a babe. 14 But strong meat belongeth to them that are of full age, *even* those who by reason of use have their senses exercised to discern both good and evil.

6 Therefore leaving the principles of the doctrine of Christ, let us go on unto perfection; not laying again the foundation of repentance from dead works, and of faith toward God, 2 Of

Living Bible

11 There is much more I would like to say along these lines, but you don't seem to listen, so it's hard to make you understand.

12, 13 You have been Christians a long time now, and you ought to be teaching others, but instead you have dropped back to the place where you need someone to teach you all over again the very first principles in God's Word. You are like babies who can drink only milk, not old enough for solid food. And when a person is still living on milk it shows he isn't very far along in the Christian life, and doesn't know much about the difference between right and wrong. He is still a baby-Christian! 14 You will never be able to eat solid spiritual food and understand the deeper things of God's Word until you become better Christians and learn right from wrong by practicing doing right.

6 Let us stop going over the same old ground again and again, always teaching those first lessons about Christ. Let us go on instead to other things and become mature in our understanding, as strong Christians ought to be. Surely we don't need to speak further about the foolishness of trying to be saved by being good, or about the necessity of faith in God; 2 you don't

Today's English Version

Warning against falling away

11 There is much we have to say about this matter, but it is hard to explain to you, because you are so slow to understand. 12 There has been enough time for you to be teachers—yet you still need someone to teach you the first lessons of God's message. Instead of eating solid food, you still have to drink milk. 13 Anyone who has to drink milk is still a child, without any experience in the matter of right and wrong. 14 Solid food, on the other hand, is for adults, who have trained and used their tastes to know the difference between good and evil.

6 Let us go forward, then, to mature teaching and leave behind us the first lessons of the Christian message. We should not lay again the foundation of turning away from useless works and believing in God; 2 of the teaching about

New International Version

Warning against falling away

11 We have much to say about this, but it is hard to explain because you are slow to learn. 12 In fact, though by this time you ought to be teachers, you need someone to teach you the elementary truths of God's word all over again. You need milk, not solid food! 13 Anyone who lives on milk, being still an infant, is not acquainted with the teaching about righteousness. 14 But solid food is for the mature, who by constant use have trained themselves to distinguish good from evil.

6 Therefore let us leave the elementary teachings about Christ and go on to maturity. Let us not lay again the foundation of repentance from acts that lead to death, and of faith in God, 2 instruction about baptisms, the laying

Phillips Modern English

5.11 There is much food for thought here—but only for the mature Christian

There is a great deal that we should like to say about this high priesthood, but it is not easy to explain to you since you seem so slow to grasp spiritual truth. At a time when you should be teaching others, you need teachers yourselves to repeat to you the ABC of God's revelation to men. You have become people who need a milk diet and cannot face solid food! For anyone who continues to live on "milk" is unable to digest what is right—he simply has not grown up. "Solid food" is only for the adult, that is, for the man who has developed by experience his power to discriminate between what is good and what is evil.

6.1 Can we not leave spiritual babyhood behind—and go on to maturity?

Let us leave behind the elementary teaching about Christ and go forward to adult understanding. Let us not lay over and over again the foundation truths—repentance from the deeds which led to death, believing in God, the teach-

Revised Standard Version

11 About this we have much to say which is hard to explain, since you have become dull of hearing. 12 For though by this time you ought to be teachers, you need some one to teach you again the first principles of God's word. You need milk, not solid food; 13 for every one who lives on milk is unskilled in the word of righteousness, for he is a child. 14 But solid food is for the mature, for those who have their faculties trained by practice to distinguish good from evil.

6 Therefore let us leave the elementary doctrine of Christ and go on to maturity, not laying again a foundation of repentance from dead works and of faith toward God, 2 with in-

Jerusalem Bible

III. The authentic priesthood of Jesus Christ

Christian life and theology

11 On this subject we have many things to say, and they are difficult to explain because you have grown so slow at understanding. 12 Really, when you should by this time have become masters, you need someone to teach you all over again the elementary principles of interpreting God's oracles; you have gone back to needing milk and not solid food. 13 Truly, anyone who is still living on milk cannot digest the doctrine of righteousness because he is still a baby. 14 Solid food is for mature men with minds trained by practice to distinguish between good and bad.

The author explains his intention

6 Let us leave behind us then all the elementary teaching about Christ and concentrate on its completion, without going over the fundamental doctrines again: the turning away from dead actions and toward faith in God; 2 the teaching about baptisms and the laying on

New English Bible

About Melchizedek we have much to say, much that is difficult to explain, now that you have grown so dull of hearing. For indeed, though by this time you ought to be teachers, you need someone to teach you the ABC of God's oracles over again; it has come to this, that you need milk instead of solid food. Anyone who lives on milk, being an infant, does not know[a] what is right. But grown men can take solid food; their perceptions are trained by long use to discriminate between good and evil.

6 Let us then stop discussing the rudiments of Christianity. We ought not to be laying over again the foundations of faith in God and of repentance from the deadness of our former ways, by instruction[b] about cleansing rites and

[a] *Or* is incompetent to speak of . . . [b] *Or, according to some witnesses,* laying the foundations over again: repentance from the deadness of our former ways and faith in God, instruction . . .

King James Version

the doctrine of baptisms, and of laying on of
hands, and of resurrection of the dead, and
of eternal judgment. 3 And this will we do, if
God permit. 4 For *it is* impossible for those who
were once enlightened, and have tasted of the
heavenly gift, and were made partakers of the
Holy Ghost, 5 And have tasted the good word
of God, and the powers of the world to come,
6 If they shall fall away, to renew them again
unto repentance; seeing they crucify to themselves the Son of God afresh, and put *him* to
an open shame. 7 For the earth which drinketh
in the rain that cometh oft upon it, and bringeth
forth herbs meet for them by whom it is dressed,
receiveth blessing from God: 8 But that which
beareth thorns and briers *is* rejected, and *is* nigh
unto cursing; whose end *is* to be burned. 9 But,
beloved, we are persuaded better things of you,

Living Bible

need further instruction about baptism and spiritual gifts[a] and the resurrection of the dead and
eternal judgment.
3 The Lord willing, we will go on now to
other things.
4 There is no use trying to bring you back to
the Lord again if you have once understood the
Good News and tasted for yourself the good
things of heaven and shared in the Holy Spirit,
5 and know how good the Word of God is, and
felt the mighty powers of the world to come,
6 and then have turned against God. You cannot bring yourself to repent again if you have
nailed the Son of God to the cross again by rejecting him, holding him up to mocking and to
public shame.
7 When a farmer's land has had many showers
upon it and good crops come up, that land has
experienced God's blessing upon it. 8 But if it
keeps on having crops of thistles and thorns,
the land is considered no good and is ready for
condemnation and burning off.
9 Dear friends, even though I am talking like

[a] Literally, "the laying on of hands."

Today's English Version

baptisms and the laying on of hands; of the
raising of the dead and the eternal judgment.
3 Let us go forward! And this is what we will
do, if God allows.
4 For how can those who fall away be brought
back to repent again? They were once in God's
light. They tasted heaven's gift and received
their share of the Holy Spirit. 5 They knew from
experience that God's word is good, and they
had felt the powers of the coming age. 6 And
then they fell away! It is impossible to bring
them back to repent again, because they are
nailing the Son of God to the cross once more
and exposing him to public shame.
7 God blesses the ground that drinks in the
rain that often falls on it, and that grows plants
that are useful to those for whom it is cultivated.
8 But if it grows thorns and weeds it is worth
nothing; it is in danger of being cursed by God,
and will be destroyed by fire.
9 But even if we speak like this, dear friends,

New International Version

on of hands, the resurrection of the dead, and
eternal judgment. 3 And God permitting, we will
do so.
4 It is impossible for those who have once
been enlightened, who have tasted the heavenly
gift, who have shared in the Holy Spirit, 5 who
have tasted the goodness of the word of God
and the powers of the coming age, 6 if they fall
away, to be brought back to repentance, because[x] to their loss they are crucifying the Son
of God all over again and subjecting him to
public disgrace.
7 Land that drinks in the rain often falling
on it and that produces a crop useful to those
who farm it receives the blessing of God. 8 But
land that produces thorns and thistles is worthless and is in danger of being cursed. In the
end it will be burned.
9 Even though we speak like this, dear friends,

[x] Or *repentance while*.

Phillips Modern English

ing of baptism and laying-on of hands, belief in the resurrection of the dead and the final judgment. No, if God allows, let us go on.

6.4 Going back to the foundations will not help those who have deliberately turned away from God

When you find men who have been enlightened, who have tasted the heavenly gift and received the Holy Spirit, who have known the wholesome nourishment of the Word of God and touched the spiritual resources of the eternal world and who then fall away, it proves impossible to make them repent as they did at first. For they are re-crucifying the Son of God in their own souls, and exposing him to contempt. Ground which absorbs the rain that often falls on it and produces plants which are useful to those who cultivate it, is ground which has the blessing of God. But ground which produces nothing but thorns and thistles is of no value and is bound sooner or later to be condemned —the only thing to do is to burn it.

6.9 We want you to make God's promise real through your faith, hope and patience

But although we give these words of warn-

Revised Standard Version

struction[k] about ablutions, the laying on of
hands, the resurrection of the dead, and eternal
judgment. 3 And this we will do if God permits.[l]
4 For it is impossible to restore again to repentance those who have once been enlightened, who
have tasted the heavenly gift, and have become
partakers of the Holy Spirit, 5 and have tasted
the goodness of the word of God and the powers of the age to come, 6 if they then commit
apostasy, since they crucify the Son of God on
their own account and hold him up to contempt.
7 For land which has drunk the rain that often
falls upon it, and brings forth vegetation useful
to those for whose sake it is cultivated, receives
a blessing from God. 8 But if it bears thorns
and thistles, it is worthless and near to being
cursed; its end is to be burned.
9 Though we speak thus, yet in your case, be-

[k] Other ancient manuscripts read *of instruction.*
[l] Other ancient manuscripts read *let us do this if God permits.*

Jerusalem Bible

of hands; the teaching about the resurrection of
the dead and eternal judgment. 3 This, God
willing, is what we propose to do.
4 As for those people who were once brought
into the light, and tasted the gift from heaven,
and received a share of the Holy Spirit, 5 and
appreciated the good message of God and the
powers of the world to come 6 and yet in spite
of this have fallen away—it is impossible for
them to be renewed a second time. They cannot
be repentant if they have willfully crucified the
Son of God and openly mocked him. 7 A field
that has been well watered by frequent rain,
and gives the crops that are wanted by the owners who grew them, is given God's blessing;
8 but one that grows brambles and thistles is
abandoned, and practically cursed. It will end
by being burned.

Words of hope and encouragement

9 But you, my dear people, in spite of what

New English Bible

the laying-on-of-hands, about the resurrection of the dead and eternal judgement. Instead, let us advance towards maturity; and so we shall, if God permits.

For when men have once been enlightened, when they have had a taste of the heavenly gift and a share in the Holy Spirit, when they have experienced the goodness of God's word and the spiritual energies of the age to come, and after all this have fallen away, it is impossible to bring them again to repentance; for with their own hands they are crucifying[c] the Son of God and making mock of his death. When the earth drinks in the rain that falls upon it from time to time, and yields a useful crop to those for whom it is cultivated, it is receiving its share of blessing from God; but if it bears thorns and thistles, it is worthless and God's curse hangs over it; the end of that is burning. But although we speak as we do, we are convinced that you,

[c] *Or* crucifying again.

King James Version

and things that accompany salvation, though we thus speak. 10 For God *is* not unrighteous to forget your work and labour of love, which ye have shewed toward his name, in that ye have ministered to the saints, and do minister. 11 And we desire that every one of you do shew the same diligence to the full assurance of hope unto the end: 12 That ye be not slothful, but followers of them who through faith and patience inherit the promises. 13 For when God made promise to Abraham, because he could swear by no greater, he sware by himself, 14 Saying, Surely blessing I will bless thee, and multiplying I will multiply thee. 15 And so, after he had patiently endured, he obtained the promise. 16 For men verily swear by the greater: and an oath for confirmation *is* to them an end of all strife. 17 Wherein God, willing more abundantly to shew unto the heirs of promise the immutability of his counsel, confirmed *it* by an oath: 18 That by two immutable things, in which *it was* impossible for God to

Living Bible

this I really don't believe that what I am saying applies to you. I am confident you are producing the good fruit that comes along with your salvation. 10 For God is not unfair. How can he forget your hard work for him, or forget the way you used to show your love for him—and still do—by helping his children? 11 And we are anxious that you keep right on loving others as long as life lasts, so that you will get your full reward.

12 Then, knowing what lies ahead for you, you won't become bored with being a Christian, nor become spiritually dull and indifferent, but you will be anxious to follow the example of those who receive all that God has promised them because of their strong faith and patience.

13 For instance, there was God's promise to Abraham: God took an oath in his own name, since there was no one greater to swear by, 14 that he would bless Abraham again and again, and give him a son and make him the father of a great nation of people. 15 Then Abraham waited patiently until finally God gave him a son, Isaac, just as he had promised.

16 When a man takes an oath, he is calling upon someone greater than himself to force him to do what he has promised, or to punish him if he later refuses to do it; the oath ends all argument about it. 17 God also bound himself with an oath, so that those he promised to help would be perfectly sure and never need to wonder whether he might change his plans.

18 He has given us both his promise and his oath, two things we can completely count on, for it is impossible for God to tell a lie. Now all those who flee to him to save them can take new

Today's English Version

we feel sure about you. We know that you have the better blessings that belong to your salvation. 10 God is not unfair. He will not forget the work you did, or the love you showed for him in the help you gave and still give your fellow Christians. 11 Our great desire is that each one of you keep up his eagerness to the end, so that the things you hope for will come true. 12 We do not want you to become lazy, but to be like those who believe and are patient, and so receive what God has promised.

God's sure promise

13 When God made the promise to Abraham, he made a vow to do what he had promised. Since there was no one greater than himself, he used his own name when he made his vow. 14 He said, "I promise you that I will bless you and give you many descendants." 15 Abraham was patient, and so he received what God had promised. 16 When a man makes a vow he uses the name of someone greater than himself, and a vow settles all arguments between men. 17 God wanted to make it very clear to those who were to receive what he promised that he would never change his purpose; so he added his vow to the promise. 18 There are these two things, then, that cannot change and about which God cannot lie.

New International Version

we are confident of better things in your case—things that accompany salvation. 10 God is not unjust; he will not forget your work and the love you have shown him as you have helped his people and continue to help them. 11 We want each of you to show this same diligence to the very end, in order to make your hope sure. 12 We do not want you to become lazy, but to imitate those who through faith and patience inherit what has been promised.

The certainty of God's promise

13 When God made his promise to Abraham, since there was no one greater for him to swear by, he swore by himself, 14 saying, "I will surely bless you and give you many descendants."[y] 15 And so after waiting patiently, Abraham received what was promised.

16 Men swear by someone greater than themselves, and the oath confirms what is said and puts an end to all argument. 17 Because God wanted to make the unchanging nature of his purpose very clear to the heirs of what was promised, he confirmed it with an oath. 18 God did this so that, by two unchangeable things in

[y] Gen. 22:17.

Phillips Modern English

ing we feel sure that you, whom we love, are capable of better things and will enjoy the full experience of salvation. God is not unfair: he will not lose sight of all that you have done nor of the loving labour which you have shown for his sake in looking after fellow-Christians (as you are still doing). It is our earnest wish that every one of you should show a similar keenness in fully grasping the hope that is within you, until the end. We do not want any of you to grow slack, but to follow the example of those who through sheer patient faith came to possess the promises.

When God made his promise to Abraham he swore by himself, for there was no one greater by whom he could swear, and he said:

Surely blessing I will bless thee
And multiplying I will multiply thee.

And then Abraham, after patient endurance, found the promise true.

Among men it is customary to swear by something greater than themselves. And if a statement is confirmed by an oath, that is the end of all quibbling. So in this matter, God, wishing to show the heirs of his promise even more clearly that his plan was unchangeable, confirmed it with an oath. So that by two utterly immutable things, the word of God and the oath of God, who cannot lie, we who are refu-

Revised Standard Version

loved, we feel sure of better things that belong to
salvation. 10 For God is not so unjust as to overlook your work and the love which you showed
for his sake in serving the saints, as you still
do. 11 And we desire each one of you to show the
same earnestness in realizing the full assurance
of hope until the end, 12 so that you may not be
sluggish, but imitators of those who through faith
and patience inherit the promises.
13 For when God made a promise to Abraham, since he had no one greater by whom to
swear, he swore by himself, 14 saying, "Surely
I will bless you and multiply you." 15 And thus
Abraham,[m] having patiently endured, obtained
the promise. 16 Men indeed swear by a greater
than themselves, and in all their disputes an
oath is final for confirmation. 17 So when God
desired to show more convincingly to the heirs
of the promise the unchangeable character of
his purpose, he interposed with an oath, 18 so
that through two unchangeable things, in which
it is impossible that God should prove false, we

[m] Greek *he*.

Jerusalem Bible

we have just said, we are sure you are in a better
state and on the way to salvation. 10 God would
not be so unjust as to forget all you have done,
the love that you have for his name or the services you have done, and are still doing, for the
saints.[r] 11 Our one desire is that every one of
you should go on showing the same earnestness
to the end, to the perfect fulfillment of our
hopes, 12 never growing careless, but imitating
those who have the faith and the perseverance
to inherit the promises.
13 When God made the promise to Abraham,
he *swore by his own self*, since it was impossible for him to swear by anyone greater: 14 *I
will shower blessings on you and give you many
descendants.*[s] 15 Because of that, Abraham persevered and saw the promise fulfilled. 16 Men,
of course, swear an oath by something greater
than themselves, and between men, confirmation
by an oath puts an end to all dispute. 17 In the
same way, when God wanted to make the heirs
to the promise thoroughly realize that his purpose was unalterable, he conveyed this by an
oath; 18 so that there would be two unalterable
things in which it was impossible for God to be

[r] The same phrase is used in Rm. and 2 Co. about a collection of money made for the church in Jerusalem. [s] Gn. 22.

New English Bible

my friends, are in the better case, and this makes for your salvation. For God would not be so unjust as to forget all that you did for love of his name, when you rendered service to his people, as you still do. But we long for every one of you to show the same eager concern, until your hope is finally realized. We want you not to become lazy, but to imitate those who, through faith and patience, are inheriting the promises.

When God made his promise to Abraham, he swore by himself, because he had no one greater to swear by: 'I vow that I will bless you abundantly and multiply your descendants.' Thus it was that Abraham, after patient waiting, attained the promise. Men swear by a greater than themselves, and the oath provides a confirmation to end all dispute; and so God, desiring to show even more clearly to the heirs of his promise how unchanging was his purpose, guaranteed it by oath. Here, then, are two irrevocable acts in which God could not possibly play us false, to

King James Version

lie, we might have a strong consolation, who
have fled for refuge to lay hold upon the hope
set before us: 19 Which *hope* we have as an anchor of the soul, both sure and steadfast, and
which entereth into that within the vail;
20 Whither the forerunner is for us entered, *even*
Jesus, made a high priest for ever after the order
of Melchisedec.

7 For this Melchisedec, king of Salem, priest
of the most high God, who met Abraham returning from the slaughter of the kings, and
blessed him; 2 To whom also Abraham gave a
tenth part of all; first being by interpretation
King of righteousness, and after that also King
of Salem, which is, King of peace; 3 Without
father, without mother, without descent, having
neither beginning of days, nor end of life; but

Living Bible

courage when they hear such assurances from
God; now they can know without doubt that he
will give them the salvation he has promised
them.
19 This certain hope of being saved is a
strong and trustworthy anchor for our souls,
connecting us with God himself behind the sacred curtains of heaven, 20 where Christ has
gone ahead to plead for us from his position as[b]
our High Priest, with the honor and rank of
Melchizedek.

7 This Melchizedek was king of the city of
Salem, and also a priest of the Most High
God. When Abraham was returning home after
winning a great battle against many kings, Melchizedek met him and blessed him; 2 then Abraham took a tenth of all he had won in the battle
and gave it to Melchizedek.
Melchizedek's name means "Justice," so he is
the King of Justice; and he is also the King of
Peace because of the name of his city, Salem,
which means "Peace." 3 Melchizedek had no father or mother[a] and there is no record of any
of his ancestors. He was never born and he

[b] Literally, "having become our High Priest."
[a] No one can be sure whether this means that Melchizedek was Christ appearing to Abraham in human form, or simply that there is no *record* of who Melchizedek's father or mother were, no *record* of his birth or death.

Today's English Version

So we who have found safety with him are
greatly encouraged to hold firmly to the hope
that is placed before us. 19 We have this hope
as an anchor for our hearts. It is safe and sure,
and goes through the curtain of the heavenly
temple into the inner sanctuary. 20 Jesus has
gone in there before us, on our behalf. He has
become a high priest forever, in the priestly
order of Melchizedek.

The priest Melchizedek

7 This Melchizedek was king of Salem and a
priest of the Most High God. As Abraham
was coming back from the battle in which he
killed the kings, Melchizedek met him and
blessed him. 2 Abraham gave him one tenth of
all he had taken. (The first meaning of Melchizedek's name is "King of Righteousness." And
because he was king of Salem, his name also
means "King of Peace.") 3 There is no record
of Melchizedek's father or mother, or of any of
his ancestors; no record of his birth or of his

New International Version

which it is impossible for God to lie, we who
have fled to take hold of the hope offered to us
may be greatly encouraged. 19 We have this hope
as an anchor for the soul, firm and secure. It
enters the inner sanctuary behind the curtain,
20 where Jesus, who went before us, has entered
on our behalf. He has become a high priest forever, just like Melchizedek.

Melchizedek the priest

7 This Melchizedek was king of Salem and a
priest of God Most High. He met Abraham
returning from the defeat of the kings and
blessed him, 2 and Abraham gave him a tenth
of everything. First, his name means "king of
righteousness"; then also, "king of Salem" means
"king of peace." 3 Without father or mother,

Phillips Modern English

gees from this dying world might have a powerful source of strength, and might grasp the hope that he holds out to us. This hope we hold as an utterly reliable anchor for our souls, fixed in the innermost shrine of Heaven, where Jesus has already entered on our behalf, having become, as we have seen, "High Priest for ever after the order of Melchizedek".

7.1 The mysterious Melchizedek: his superiority to Abraham and the Levites

Now this Melchizedek was king of Salem and priest of God Most High. He met Abraham when the latter was returning from the defeat of the kings, and blessed him. Abraham gave him a tribute of a tenth part of all the spoils of battle.

Melchizedek means first "king of righteousness," and his other title is "king of peace", for Salem means peace. He had no father or mother and no family tree. He was not born nor did he

Revised Standard Version

who have fled for refuge might have strong encouragement to seize the hope set before us. 19 We have this as a sure and steadfast anchor of the soul, a hope that enters into the inner shrine behind the curtain, 20 where Jesus has gone as a forerunner on our behalf, having become a high priest for ever after the order of Melchizedek.

7 For this Melchizedek, king of Salem, priest of the Most High God, met Abraham returning from the slaughter of the kings and blessed him; 2 and to him Abraham apportioned a tenth part of everything. He is first, by translation of his name, king of righteousness, and then he is also king of Salem, that is, king of peace. 3 He is without father or mother or genealogy, and has neither beginning of days nor end of life, but re-

Jerusalem Bible

lying, and so that we, now we have found safety, should have a strong encouragement to take a firm grip on the hope that is held out to us. 19 Here we have an anchor for our soul, as sure as it is firm, and reaching right *through beyond the veil* [t] 20 where Jesus has entered before us and on our behalf, to become a high *priest of the order of Melchizedek, and for ever.*

A. Christ's priesthood higher than Levitical priesthood

Melchizedek[u]

7 You remember that *Melchizedek, king of Salem, a priest of God Most High, went to meet Abraham who was on his way back after defeating the kings,* and *blessed him;* 2 and also that it was to him that Abraham gave *a tenth of all that he had.* By the interpretation of his name, he is, first, "king of righteousness" and also *king of Salem,* that is, "king of peace"; 3 he has no father, no mother or ancestry, and

[*t*] Lv. 16:2. [*u*] Gn. 14, from which the following quotation is made, is silent about any ancestors or descendants of Melchizedek, and about "the beginning and ending" of his life.

New English Bible

give powerful encouragement to us, who have claimed his protection by grasping[a] the hope set before us. That hope we hold. It is like an anchor for our lives, an anchor safe and sure. It enters in through the veil, where Jesus has entered on our behalf as forerunner, having become a high priest for ever in the succession of Melchizedek.

7 This Melchizedek, king of Salem, priest of God Most High, met Abraham returning from the rout of the kings and blessed him; and Abraham gave him a tithe of everything as his portion. His name, in the first place, means 'king of righteousness'; next he is king of Salem, that is, 'king of peace'. He has no father, no mother, no lineage; his years have no beginning, his life

[*a*] *Or* to give to us, who have claimed his protection, a powerful incentive to grasp . . .

King James Version

made like unto the Son of God; abideth a priest
continually. 4 Now consider how great this man
was, unto whom even the patriarch Abraham
gave the tenth of the spoils. 5 And verily they
that are of the sons of Levi, who receive the
office of the priesthood, have a commandment
to take tithes of the people according to the law,
that is, of their brethren, though they come out of
the loins of Abraham: 6 But he whose descent is
not counted from them received tithes of Abraham, and blessed him that had the promises.
7 And without all contradiction the less is blessed
of the better. 8 And here men that die receive
tithes; but there he *receiveth them,* of whom it is
witnessed that he liveth. 9 And as I may so say,
Levi also, who receiveth tithes, paid tithes in
Abraham. 10 For he was yet in the loins of his
father, when Melchisedec met him. 11 If therefore perfection were by the Levitical priesthood,

Living Bible

never died but his life is like that of the Son of
God—a priest forever.
4 See then how great this Melchizedek is:
(*a*) Even Abraham, the first and most honored of all God's chosen people, gave Melchizedek a tenth of the spoils he took from the
kings he had been fighting. 5 One could understand why Abraham would do this if Melchizedek had been a Jewish priest, for later on God's
people were required by law to give gifts to help
their priests because the priests were their relatives. 6 But Melchizedek was not a relative, and
yet Abraham paid him.
(*b*) Melchizedek placed a blessing upon
mighty Abraham, 7 and as everyone knows, a
person who has the power to bless is always
greater than the person he blesses.
8 (*c*) The Jewish priests, though mortal, received tithes; but we are told that Melchizedek
lives on.
9 (*d*) One might even say that Levi himself
(the ancestor of all Jewish priests, of all who receive tithes), paid tithes to Melchizedek through
Abraham. 10 For although Levi wasn't born yet,
the seed from which he came was in Abraham
when Abraham paid the tithes to Melchizedek.
11 (*e*) If the Jewish priests and their laws

Today's English Version

death. He is like the Son of God; he remains a
priest forever.
4 You see, then, how great he was. Abraham,
the patriarch, gave him one tenth of all he got
in the battle. 5 And those descendants of Levi
who are priests are commanded by the Law to
collect one tenth from the people of Israel—
that is, they collect it from their own countrymen, even though they too are descendants of
Abraham. 6 Melchizedek was not descended from
Levi, but he collected one tenth from Abraham
and blessed him who received God's promises.
7 There is no doubt that the one who blesses is
greater than the one who is blessed. 8 In the
case of the priests, the tenth is collected by men
who die; but as for Melchizedek, the tenth was
collected by one who lives, as the scripture says.
9 And, so to speak, when Abraham paid the
tenth, Levi (whose descendants collect the tenth)
also paid it. 10 For Levi had not yet been born,
but was, so to speak, in the body of his ancestor Abraham when Melchizedek met him.
11 It was on the basis of the Levitical priest-

New International Version

without beginning of days or end of life, like
the Son of God he remains a priest forever.
4 Just think how great he was: Even the
patriarch Abraham gave him a tenth of the
plunder! 5 Now the law requires the descendants
of Levi who become priests to collect a tenth
from the people—that is, their brothers—even
though their brothers are descended from Abraham. 6 This man, however, did not trace his
descent from Levi, yet he collected a tenth from
Abraham and blessed him who had the promises. 7 And without doubt the lesser person is
blessed by the greater. 8 In the one case, the
tenth is collected by men who die; but in the
other case, by him who is declared to be living.
9 One might even say that Levi, who collects the
tenth, paid the tenth through Abraham, 10 because when Melchizedek met Abraham, Levi was
still in the body of his ancestor.

Jesus like Melchizedek

11 If perfection could have been attained

Phillips Modern English

die, but, being like the Son of God, is a perpetual priest.

Now notice the greatness of this man. Even Abraham the patriarch pays him a tribute of a tenth part of the spoils. Further, we know that, according to the Law, the descendants of Levi who accept the office of priest have the right to demand a "tenth" from the people, that is from their brothers, despite the fact that the latter are descendants of Abraham. But here we have one who is quite independent of Levitic ancestry taking a "tenth" from Abraham, and giving a blessing to Abraham, the holder of God's promises! And no one can deny that the receiver of a blessing is inferior to the one who gives it. Again, in the one case it is mortal men who receive the "tenths", and in the other it is one who, we are assured, is alive. One might say that even Levi, the proper receiver of "tenths", has paid his tenth to this man, for in a sense he already existed in the body of his father Abraham when Melchizedek met him.

7.11 *The revival of the Melchizedek priesthood means that the Levitical priesthood is superseded*

We may go further. If it were possible to

Revised Standard Version

sembling the Son of God he continues a priest for ever.

4 See how great he is! Abraham the patriarch gave him a tithe of the spoils. 5 And those descendants of Levi who receive the priestly office have a commandment in the law to take tithes from the people, that is, from their brethren, though these also are descended from Abraham.
6 But this man who has not their genealogy received tithes from Abraham and blessed him who had the promises. 7 It is beyond dispute that the inferior is blessed by the superior.
8 Here tithes are received by mortal men; there, by one of whom it is testified that he lives. 9 One might even say that Levi himself, who receives tithes, paid tithes through Abraham, 10 for he was still in the loins of his ancestor when Melchizedek met him.

11 Now if perfection had been attainable

Jerusalem Bible

his life has no beginning or ending; he is like the Son of God. He remains a priest for ever.

Melchizedek accepted tithes from Abraham

4 Now think how great this man must have been, if the patriarch *Abraham paid him a tenth of the treasure he had captured.*[v] 5 We know that any of the descendants of Levi who are admitted to the priesthood are obliged by the Law to take tithes from the people, and this is taking them from their own brothers although they too are descended from Abraham. 6 But this man, who was not of the same descent, took his tenth from Abraham, and he gave his blessing to the holder of the promises. 7 Now it is indisputable that a blessing is given by a superior to an inferior. 8 Further, in the one case it is ordinary mortal men who receive the tithes, and in the other, someone who is declared to be still alive. 9 It could be said that Levi himself, who receives tithes, actually paid them, in the person of Abraham, 10 because he was still in the loins of his ancestor when *Melchizedek came to meet him.*

From levitical priesthood to the priesthood of Melchizedek

11 Now if perfection had been reached

[v] The regular tithe paid to levitical priests was a tenth.

New English Bible

no end. He is like the Son of God: he remains a priest for all time.

Consider now how great he must be for Abraham the patriarch to give him a tithe of the finest of the spoil. The descendants of Levi who take the priestly office are commanded by the Law to tithe the people, that is, their kinsmen, although they too are descendants of Abraham. But Melchizedek, though he does not trace his descent from them, has tithed Abraham himself, and given his blessing to the man who received the promises; and beyond all dispute the lesser is always blessed by the greater. Again, in the one instance tithes are received by men who must die; but in the other, by one whom Scripture affirms to be alive. It might even be said that Levi, who receives tithes, has himself been tithed through Abraham; for he was still in his ancestor's loins when Melchizedek met him.

Now if perfection had been attainable through

King James Version

(for under it the people received the law,) what
further need *was there* that another priest should
rise after the order of Melchisedec, and not be
called after the order of Aaron? 12 For the
priesthood being changed, there is made of necessity a change also of the law. 13 For he of
whom these things are spoken pertaineth to another tribe, of which no man gave attendance at
the altar. 14 For *it is* evident that our Lord
sprang out of Juda; of which tribe Moses spake
nothing concerning priesthood. 15 And it is yet
far more evident: for that after the similitude of
Melchisedec there ariseth another priest, 16 Who
is made, not after the law of a carnal commandment, but after the power of an endless life.
17 For he testifieth, Thou *art* a priest for ever
after the order of Melchisedec. 18 For there is
verily a disannulling of the commandment going
before for the weakness and unprofitableness
thereof. 19 For the law made nothing perfect,
but the bringing in of a better hope *did;* by the

Living Bible

had been able to save us, why then did God
need to send Christ as a priest with the rank of
Melchizedek, instead of sending someone with
the rank of Aaron the same rank all other
priests had?

12, 13, 14 And when God sends a new kind
of priest, his law must be changed to permit it.
As we all know, Christ did not belong to the
priest-tribe of Levi, but came from the tribe of
Judah, which had not been chosen for priesthood; Moses had never given them that work.
15 So we can plainly see that God's method
changed, for Christ, the new High Priest who
came with the rank of Melchizedek, 16 did not
become a priest by meeting the old requirement
of belonging to the tribe of Levi, but on the
basis of power flowing from a life that cannot
end. 17 And the Psalmist points this out when
he says of Christ, "You are a priest forever with
the rank of Melchizedek."

18 Yes, the old system of priesthood based on
family lines was canceled because it didn't work.
It was weak and useless for saving people. 19 It
never made anyone really right with God. But
now we have a far better hope, for Christ makes
us acceptable to God, and now we may draw
near to him.

Today's English Version

hood that the Law was given to the people of
Israel. Now, if the work of the Levitical priests
had been perfect, there would have been no need
for a different kind of priest to appear, one who
is in the priestly order of Melchizedek, not in
Aaron's order. 12 For when the priesthood is
changed, there also has to be a change of the
law. 13 And our Lord, of whom these things are
said, belonged to a different tribe; and no member of his tribe ever served as a priest at the
altar. 14 It is well known that he was born a
member of the tribe of Judah; and Moses did
not mention this tribe when he spoke of priests.

Another priest, like Melchizedek

15 The matter becomes even plainer; a different priest has appeared, who is like Melchizedek. 16 He was not made a priest by human rules
and regulations; he became a priest through the
power of a life which has no end. 17 For the
scripture says, "You will be a priest forever, in
the priestly order of Melchizedek." 18 The old
rule, then, is set aside, because it was weak and
useless. 19 For the Law of Moses could not
make anything perfect. And now a better hope
has been brought in, through which we come
near to God.

New International Version

through the Levitical priesthood (for on the
basis of it the law was given to the people), why
was there still need for another priest to come—
one like Melchizedek, not like Aaron? 12 For
when there is a change of the priesthood, there
must also be a change of the law. 13 He of whom
these things are said belonged to a different tribe,
and no one from that tribe has ever served at
the altar. 14 For it is clear that our Lord descended from Judah, and in regard to that tribe
Moses said nothing about priests. 15 And what
we have said is even more clear if another priest
like Melchizedek appears, 16 one who has become a priest not on the basis of a regulation
as to his ancestry but on the basis of the power
of an indestructible life. 17 For it is declared:

"You are a priest forever,
just like Melchizedek." [z]

18 The former regulation is set aside because
it was weak and useless 19 (for the law made
nothing perfect), and a better hope is introduced, by which we draw near to God.

[z] Psalm 110:4.

Phillips Modern English

bring men to spiritual maturity through the Levitical priestly system (for that is the system under which the people were given the Law), why does the necessity arise for another priest to make his appearance *after the order of Melchizedek,* instead of following the normal priestly calling of Aaron? For if there is a transference of priestly powers, there will necessarily follow an alteration of the Law regarding priesthood. He who is described as our High Priest belongs to another tribe, no member of which had ever attended the altar! For it is a matter of history that our Lord was a descendant of Judah, and Moses made no mention of priesthood in connection with that tribe.

How fundamental is this change becomes all the more apparent when we see this other priest appearing according to the Melchizedek pattern, and deriving his priesthood not by virtue of a command imposed from outside, but from the power of indestructible life within. For the witness to him, as we have seen, is:

Thou are a priest for ever
After the order of Melchizedek.

Quite plainly, then, there is a definite cancellation of the previous commandment because of its ineffectiveness and uselessness—the Law was incapable of bringing anyone to real maturity—followed by the introduction of a better hope, through which we approach God.

Revised Standard Version

through the Levitical priesthood (for under it
the people received the law), what further need
would there have been for another priest to
arise after the order of Melchizedek, rather than
one named after the order of Aaron? 12 For
when there is a change in the priesthood, there
is necessarily a change in the law as well. 13 For
the one of whom these things are spoken belonged to another tribe, from which no one has
ever served at the altar. 14 For it is evident that
our Lord was descended from Judah, and in
connection with that tribe Moses said nothing
about priests.

15 This becomes even more evident when another priest arises in the likeness of Melchizedek,
16 who has become a priest, not according to a
legal requirement concerning bodily descent but
by the power of an indestructible life. 17 For it
is witnessed of him,

"Thou art a priest for ever,
after the order of Melchizedek."

18 On the one hand, a former commandment is
set aside because of its weakness and uselessness
19 (for the law made nothing perfect); on the
other hand, a better hope is introduced, through
which we draw near to God.

Jerusalem Bible

through the levitical priesthood because the Law
given to the nation rests on it; why was it still
necessary for a new priesthood to arise, one *of
the same order as Melchizedek*[w] not counted as
being "of the same order as" Aaron? 12 But
any change in the priesthood must mean a
change in the Law as well.

13 So our Lord, of whom these things were
said, belonged to a different tribe, the members
of which have never done service at the altar;
14 everyone knows he came from Judah, a tribe
which Moses did not even mention when dealing with priests.

The abrogation of the old Law

15 This[x] becomes even more clearly evident
when there appears a second Melchizedek, who
is a priest 16 not by virtue of a law about physical descent, but by the power of an indestructible life. 17 For it was about him that the prophecy was made: *You are a priest of the order of
Melchizedek, and for ever.* 18 The earlier commandment is thus abolished, because it was
neither effective nor useful, 19 since the Law
could not make anyone perfect; but now this
commandment is replaced by something better
—the hope that brings us nearer to God.

New English Bible

the Levitical priesthood (for it is on this basis that the people were given the Law), what further need would there have been to speak of another priest arising, in the succession of Melchizedek, instead of the succession of Aaron? For a change of priesthood must mean a change of law. And the one here spoken of belongs to a different tribe, no member of which has ever had anything to do with the altar. For it is very evident that our Lord is sprung from Judah, a tribe to which Moses made no reference in speaking of priests.

The argument becomes still clearer, if the new priest who arises is one like Melchizedek, owing his priesthood not to a system of earth-bound rules but to the power of a life that cannot be destroyed. For here is the testimony: 'Thou art a priest for ever, in the succession of Melchizedek.' The earlier rules are cancelled as impotent and useless, since the Law brought nothing to perfection; and a better hope is introduced, through which we draw near to God.

[w] Ps. 110:4. [x] What has been said in v. 12.

King James Version

which we draw nigh unto God. 20And inasmuch as not without an oath *he was made priest:*
21 (For those priests were made without an oath;
but this with an oath by him that said unto him,
The Lord sware and will not repent, Thou *art*
a priest for ever after the order of Melchisedec:)
22 By so much was Jesus made a surety of a
better testament. 23And they truly were many
priests, because they were not suffered to continue by reason of death: 24 But this *man,* because he continueth ever, hath an unchangeable
priesthood. 25 Wherefore he is able also to save
them to the uttermost that come unto God by
him, seeing he ever liveth to make intercession
for them. 26 For such a high priest became us,
who is holy, harmless, undefiled, separate from
sinners, and made higher than the heavens;
27 Who needeth not daily, as those high priests,
to offer up sacrifice, first for his own sins, and
then for the people's: for this he did once, when

Living Bible

20 God took an oath that Christ would always be a Priest, 21 although he never said that
of other priests. Only to Christ he said, "The
Lord has sworn and will never change his mind:
You are a Priest forever, with the rank of
Melchizedek." 22 Because of God's oath, Christ
can guarantee forever the success of this new
and better arrangement.

23 Under the old arrangement there had to
be many priests, so that when the older ones
died off, the system could still be carried on by
others who took their places.

24 But Jesus lives forever and continues to
be a Priest so that no one else is needed. 25 He
is able to save completely all who come to God
through him. Since he will live forever, he will
always be there to remind God that he has paid
for their sins with his blood.

26 He is, therefore, exactly the kind of High
Priest we need; for he is holy and blameless,
unstained by sin, undefiled by sinners, and to
him has been given the place of honor in heaven.
27 He never needs the daily blood of animal
sacrifices, as other priests did, to cover over first
their own sins and then the sins of the people; for
he finished all sacrifices, once and for all, when

Today's English Version

20 In addition, there is also God's vow. There
was no such vow when the others were made
priests. 21 But Jesus became a priest by means
of a vow, when God said to him,

"The Lord has made a vow;
and will not change his mind:
'You will be a priest forever.' "

22 This difference, then, makes Jesus the guarantee also of a better covenant.

23 There is another difference: those other
priests were many because they died and could
not continue their work. 24 But Jesus lives on
forever, and his work as priest does not pass
on to someone else. 25And so he is able, now
and always, to save those who come to God
through him, because he lives forever to plead
with God for them.

26 Jesus, then, is the High Priest that meets
our needs. He is holy; he has no fault or sin
in him; he has been set apart from sinful men
and raised above the heavens. 27 He is not like
other high priests; he does not need to offer
sacrifices every day, for his own sins first, and
then for the sins of the people. He offered one
sacrifice, once and for all, when he offered him-

New International Version

20 And it was not without an oath! Others
became priests without any oath, 21 but he became a priest with an oath when God said to
him:

"The Lord has sworn
and will not change his mind,
'You are a priest forever.' "[a]

22 Because of this oath, Jesus has become the
guarantee of a better covenant.

23 Now there were many of those priests,
since death prevented them from continuing in
office; 24 but because Jesus lives forever, he has
a permanent priesthood. 25 Therefore he is able
to save completely[b] those who come to God
through him, because he always lives to intercede for them.

26 Such a high priest meets our need—one
who is holy, blameless, pure, set apart from
sinners, exalted above the heavens. 27 Unlike the
other high priests, he does not need to offer
sacrifices day after day, first for his own sins,
and then for the sins of the people. He sacrificed
for their sins once for all when he offered him-

[a] Psalm 110:4. [b] Or *forever.*

Phillips Modern English

7.20 The High Priesthood of Christ rests upon the oath of God

This means a far better hope for us because Jesus has become our priest by the oath of God. Other men have been priests without any sworn guarantee, but Jesus has the oath of him that said of him:

The Lord sware and will not repent himself,
Thou art a priest for ever.

And he is, by virtue of this fact, himself the living guarantee of a better agreement. Human High Priests have always been changing, for death made a permanent appointment impossible. But Christ, because he lives for ever, possesses a priesthood that needs no successor. This means that he can save fully and completely those who approach God through him, for he is always living to intercede on their behalf.

7.26 Christ the perfect High Priest, who meets our need

Here is the High Priest we need. A man who is holy, faultless, unstained, separated from sinners and lifted above the very Heavens. There is no need for him, like the High Priests we know, to offer up daily sacrifices, first for his own sins and then for the people's. He made one sacrifice, once for all, when he offered up himself.

Revised Standard Version

20 And it was not without an oath.
21 Those who formerly became priests took their office without an oath, but this one was addressed with an oath,
"The Lord has sworn
and will not change his mind,
'Thou art a priest forever.' "
22 This makes Jesus the surety of a better covenant.
23 The former priests were many in number, because they were prevented by death from continuing in office;
24 but he holds his priesthood permanently, because he continues for ever.
25 Consequently he is able for all time to save those who draw near to God through him, since he always lives to make intercession for them.
26 For it was fitting that we should have such a high priest, holy, blameless, unstained, separated from sinners, exalted above the heavens.
27 He has no need, like those high priests, to offer sacrifices daily, first for his own sins and then for those of the people; he did this once

Jerusalem Bible

Christ's priesthood is unchanging

20 What is more, this was not done without the taking of an oath. The others, indeed, were made priests without any oath;
21 but he with an oath sworn by the one who declared to him: *The Lord has sworn an oath which he will never retract: you are a priest, and for ever.*[y]
22 And it follows that it is a greater covenant for which Jesus has become our guarantee.
23 Then there used to be a great number of those other priests, because death put an end to each one of them;
24 but this one, because he remains *for ever*, can never lose his priesthood.
25 It follows, then, that his power to save is utterly certain, since he is living for ever to intercede for all who come to God through him.

The perfection of the heavenly high priest

26 To suit us, the ideal high priest would have to be holy, innocent and uncontaminated, beyond the influence of sinners, and raised up above the heavens;
27 one who would not need to offer sacrifices every day, as the other high priests do for their own sins and then for those of the people, because he has done this once and

[y] Ps. 110:4.

New English Bible

How great a difference it makes that an oath was sworn! There was no oath sworn when those others were made priests; but for this priest an oath was sworn, as Scripture says of him: 'The Lord has sworn and will not go back on his word, "Thou art a priest for ever."' How far superior must the covenant also be of which Jesus is the guarantor! Those other priests are appointed in numerous succession, because they are prevented by death from continuing in office; but the priesthood which Jesus holds is perpetual, because he remains for ever. That is why he is also able to save absolutely those who approach God through him; he is always living to plead on their behalf.

Such a high priest does indeed fit our condition—devout, guileless, undefiled, separated from sinners, raised high above the heavens. He has no need to offer sacrifices daily, as the high priests do, first for his own sins and then for those of the people; for this he did once and for all when

King James Version

he offered up himself. 28 For the law maketh men high priests which have infirmity; but the word of the oath, which was since the law, *maketh* the Son, who is consecrated for evermore.

8 Now of the things which we have spoken *this is* the sum: We have such a high priest, who is set on the right hand of the throne of the Majesty in the heavens; 2 A minister of the sanctuary, and of the true tabernacle, which the Lord pitched, and not man. 3 For every high priest is ordained to offer gifts and sacrifices: wherefore *it is* of necessity that this man have somewhat also to offer. 4 For if he were on earth, he should not be a priest, seeing that there are priests that offer gifts according to the law: 5 Who serve unto the example and shadow of heavenly things, as Moses was admonished of God when he was

Living Bible

he sacrificed himself on the cross. 28 Under the old system, even the high priests were weak and sinful men who could not keep from doing wrong, but later God appointed by his oath his Son who is perfect forever.

8 What we are saying is this: Christ, whose priesthood we have just described, is our High Priest, and is in heaven at the place of greatest honor next to God himself. 2 He ministers in the temple in heaven, the true place of worship built by the Lord and not by human hands.

3 And since every high priest is appointed to offer gifts and sacrifices, Christ must make an offering too. 4 The sacrifice he offers is far better than those offered by the earthly priests. (But even so, if he were on earth he wouldn't even be permitted to be a priest, because down here the priests still follow the old Jewish system of sacrifices.) 5 Their work is connected with a mere earthly model of the real tabernacle in heaven; for when Moses was getting ready to build the

Today's English Version

self. 28 The Law of Moses appoints men who are imperfect to be high priests; but God's promise with the vow, which came later than the Law, appoints the Son, who has been made perfect forever.

Jesus our high priest

8 Here is the whole point of what we are saying: we have such a high priest as this, who sits at the right of the throne of the Divine Majesty in heaven. 2 He serves as high priest in the Most Holy Place, that is, in the real tent which was put up by the Lord, not by man.

3 Every high priest is appointed to offer gifts and animal sacrifices to God; and so our high priest must also have something to offer. 4 If he were on earth, he would not be a priest at all, since there are priests who offer the gifts according to the Jewish Law. 5 The work they do as priests is really only a copy and a shadow of what is in heaven. It is the same as it was with Moses. When he was about to put up the tent,

New International Version

self. 28 For the law appoints as high priests men who are weak; but the oath, which came after the law, appointed the Son, who has been made perfect forever.

The high priest of a new covenant

8 The point of what we are saying is this: We do have such a high priest, who sat down at the right hand of the throne of the Majesty in heaven, 2 and who serves in the sanctuary, the true tabernacle set up by the Lord, not by man.

3 Every high priest is appointed to offer both gifts and sacrifices, and so it was necessary for this one also to have something to offer. 4 If he were on earth, he would not be a priest, for there are already men who offer the gifts prescribed by the law. 5 They serve at a sanctuary that is a copy and shadow of what is in heaven. This is why Moses was warned when he was about to

Phillips Modern English

The Law makes for its High Priests men of human weakness. But the word of the oath, which came after the Law, makes for High Priest the Son. who is perfect for ever!

8.1 Christ our High Priest in Heaven is High Priest of a new agreement

Now to sum up—we have an ideal High Priest such as has been described above. He has taken his seat at the right hand of the throne of Heavenly majesty. He is the minister of the sanctuary and of the real tabernacle—that is the one which the Lord has set up and not man. Every High Priest is appointed to offer gifts and make sacrifices. It follows, therefore, that in these holy places this man must have something to offer.

Now if he were still living on earth he would not be a priest at all, for there are already priests offering the gifts prescribed by the Law. These men are serving what is only a pattern or reproduction of things that exist in Heaven. Moses, you will remember, when he was going to construct the tabernacle, was cautioned by God in these words:

Revised Standard Version

for all when he offered up himself. 28 Indeed, the law appoints men in their weakness as high priests, but the word of the oath, which came later than the law, appoints a Son who has been made perfect for ever.

8 Now the point in what we are saying is
this: we have such a high priest, one who
is seated at the right hand of the throne of the
Majesty in heaven, 2 a minister in the sanctuary and the true tent[n] which is set up not by
man but by the Lord. 3 For every high priest is
appointed to offer gifts and sacrifices; hence it
is necessary for this priest also to have something to offer. 4 Now if he were on earth, he
would not be a priest at all, since there are
priests who offer gifts according to the law.
5 They serve a copy and shadow of the heavenly sanctuary; for when Moses was about to
erect the tent,[n] he was instructed by God, say-

[n] Or *tabernacle*.

Jerusalem Bible

for all by offering himself. 28 The Law appoints
high priests who are men subject to weakness;
but the promise on oath, which came after the
Law, appointed the Son who is made perfect *for ever.*

B. The superiority of the worship, the sanctuary and the mediation provided by Christ the priest

The new priesthood and the new sanctuary

8 The great point of all that we have said is
that we have a high priest of exactly this
kind. He has his place *at the right* of the throne
of divine Majesty in the heavens, 2 and he is
the minister of the sanctuary and of the true
Tent of Meeting which *the Lord,* and not any
man, *set up.*[z] 3 It is the duty of every high priest
to offer gifts and sacrifices, and so this one too
must have something to offer. 4 In fact, if he
were on earth, he would not be a priest at all,
since there are others who make the offerings
laid down by the Law 5 and these only maintain
the service of a model or a reflection of the
heavenly realities. For Moses, when he had the
Tent to build, was warned by God who said:

[z] Nb. 24:6 (LXX).

New English Bible

he offered up himself. The high priests made by the Law are men in all their frailty; but the priest appointed by the words of the oath which supersedes the Law is the Son, made perfect now for ever.

8 Now this is my main point: just such a high priest we have, and he has taken his seat at the right hand of the throne of Majesty in the heavens, a ministrant in the real sanctuary, the tent pitched by the Lord and not by man. Every high priest is appointed to offer gifts and sacrifices; hence, this one too must have[a] something to offer. Now if he had been on earth, he would not even have been a priest, since there are already priests who offer the gifts which the Law prescribes, though they minister in a sanctuary which is only a copy and shadow of the heavenly. This is implied when Moses, about to erect

[a] *Or* must have had.

King James Version

about to make the tabernacle: for, See, saith he,
that thou make all things according to the pattern shewed to thee in the mount. 6 But now hath
he obtained a more excellent ministry, by how
much also he is the mediator of a better covenant, which was established upon better promises. 7 For if that first *covenant* had been faultless, then should no place have been sought for
the second. 8 For finding fault with them, he
saith, Behold, the days come, saith the Lord,
when I will make a new covenant with the house
of Israel and with the house of Judah: 9 Not according to the covenant that I made with their
fathers, in the day when I took them by the hand
to lead them out of the land of Egypt; because
they continued not in my covenant, and I regarded them not, saith the Lord. 10 For this *is*
the covenant that I will make with the house of
Israel after those days, saith the Lord; I will put
my laws into their mind, and write them in

Living Bible

tabernacle, God warned him to follow exactly
the pattern of the heavenly tabernacle as shown
to him on Mount Sinai. 6 But Christ, as a Minister in heaven, has been rewarded with a far
more important work than those who serve under the old laws, because the new agreement
which he passes on to us from God contains far
more wonderful promises.

7 The old agreement didn't even work. If it
had, there would have been no need for another
to replace it. 8 But God himself found fault with
the old one, for he said, "The day will come
when I will make a new agreement with the
people of Israel and the people of Judah. 9 This
new agreement will not be like the old one I
gave to their fathers on the day when I took
them by the hand to lead them out of the land
of Egypt; they did not keep their part in that
agreement, so I had to cancel it. 10 But this is
the new agreement I will make with the people
of Israel, says the Lord: I will write my laws in
their minds so that they will know what I want
them to do without my even telling them, and
these laws will be in their hearts so that they

Today's English Version

God told him, "Be sure to make everything like
the pattern you were shown on the mountain."
6 But, as it is, Jesus has been given priestly work
which is much greater than theirs, just as the
covenant which he arranged between God and
men is a better one, because it is based on promises of better things.

7 If there had been nothing wrong with the
first covenant, there would have been no need
for a second one. 8 But God finds fault with his
people when he says,

"The days are coming, says the Lord,
when I will draw up a new covenant
with the people of Israel,
and with the tribe of Judah.
9 It will not be like the covenant that I made
with their ancestors
on the day I took them by the hand to
lead them out of the land of Egypt.
They were not faithful to the covenant I
made with them,
and so I paid no attention to them, says
the Lord.
10 Now, this is the covenant that I will make
with the people of Israel
in the days to come, says the Lord:
I will put my laws in their minds,
and write them on their hearts.

New International Version

build the tabernacle: "See to it that you make
everything according to the pattern shown you
on the mountain." [c] 6 But the ministry Jesus has
received is as superior to theirs as the covenant
of which he is mediator is superior to the old
one, and it is founded on better promises.

7 For if there had been nothing wrong with
that first covenant, no place would have been
sought for another. 8 But God found fault with
the people and said:[d]

"The time is coming, says the Lord,
when I will make a new covenant
with the house of Israel
and with the house of Judah.
9 It will not be like the covenant I made with
their forefathers
when I took them by the hand to lead
them out of Egypt,
because they did not remain faithful to my
covenant,
and I turned away from them,
says the Lord.
10 This is the covenant I will make with the
house of Israel
after that time, says the Lord.
I will put my laws in their minds
and write them on their hearts.

[c] Exodus 25:40. [d] Some MSS allow *fault and said to the people.*

Phillips Modern English

See that thou make all things
According to the pattern that was showed thee in the mount.

But our High Priest has been given a far higher ministry for he mediates a higher agreement, which in turn rests upon higher promises. If the first agreement had proved satisfactory there would have been no need to look for a second. Actually, however, God does show himself dissatisfied for he says:

Behold the days come, saith the Lord,
That I will make a new covenant with the house of Israel and with the house of Judah;
Not according to the covenant that I made with their fathers
In the day that I took them by the hand to lead them forth out of the land of Egypt;
For they continued not in my covenant,
And I regarded them not, saith the Lord.
For this is the covenant that I will make with the house of Israel
After those days, saith the Lord;
I will put my laws into their mind,
And on their heart also will I write them:

Revised Standard Version

ing, "See that you make everything according to the pattern which was shown you on the mountain." 6 But as it is, Christ[o] has obtained a ministry which is as much more excellent than the old as the covenant he mediates is better, since it is enacted on better promises. 7 For if that first covenant had been faultless, there would have been no occasion for a second.
8 For he finds fault with them when he says:
"The days will come, says the Lord,
when I will establish a new covenant with the house of Israel
and with the house of Judah;
9 not like the covenant that I made with their fathers
on the day when I took them by the hand
to lead them out of the land of Egypt;
for they did not continue in my covenant,
and so I paid no heed to them, says the Lord.
10 This is the covenant that I will make with the house of Israel
after those days, says the Lord:
I will put my laws into their minds,
and write them on their hearts,

[o] Greek *he*.

Jerusalem Bible

See that you make everything according to the pattern shown you on the mountain.[a]

Christ is the mediator of a greater covenant

6 We have seen that he has been given a ministry of a far higher order, and to the same degree it is a better covenant of which he is the mediator, founded on better promises. 7 If that first covenant had been without a fault, there would have been no need for a second one to replace it. 8And in fact God does find fault with them; he says:

See, the days are coming—it is the Lord who speaks—
when I will establish a new covenant
with the House of Israel and the House of Judah,
9 *but not a covenant like the one I made with their ancestors*
on the day I took them by the hand
to bring them out of the land of Egypt.
They abandoned that covenant of mine,
and so I on my side deserted them. It is the Lord who speaks.
10 *No, this is the covenant I will make*
with the House of Israel
when those days arrive—it is the Lord who speaks.
I will put my laws into their minds
and write them on their hearts.

[a] Ex. 25:40..

New English Bible

the tent, is instructed by God: 'See to it that you make everything according to the pattern shown you on the mountain.' But in fact the ministry which has fallen to Jesus is as far superior to theirs as are the covenant he mediates and the promises upon which it is legally secured.

Had that first covenant been faultless, there would have been no need to look for a second in its place. But God, finding fault with them, says, 'The days are coming, says the Lord, when I will conclude a new covenant with the house of Israel and the house of Judah. It will not be like the covenant I made with their forefathers when I took them by the hand to lead them out of Egypt; because they did not abide by the terms of that covenant, and I abandoned them, says the Lord. For the covenant I will make with the house of Israel after those days, says the Lord, is this: I will set my laws in their understanding and write them on their hearts;

King James Version

their hearts: and I will be to them a God, and
they shall be to me a people: 11And they shall
not teach every man his neighbour, and every
man his brother, saying, Know the Lord: for
all shall know me, from the least to the greatest.
12 For I will be merciful to their unrighteousness, and their sins and their iniquities will I
remember no more. 13 In that he saith, A new
covenant, he hath made the first old. Now that
which decayeth and waxeth old *is* ready to vanish away.

9 Then verily the first *covenant* had also ordinances of divine service, and a worldly
sanctuary. 2 For there was a tabernacle made;
the first, wherein *was* the candlestick, and the
table, and the shewbread; which is called the
sanctuary. 3And after the second vail, the tabernacle which is called the holiest of all; 4 Which
had the golden censer, and the ark of the covenant overlaid round about with gold, wherein
was the golden pot that had manna, and Aaron's
rod that budded, and the tables of the covenant;

Living Bible

will want to obey them, and I will be their God
and they shall be my people. 11And no one
then will need to speak to his friend or neighbor or brother, saying, 'You, too, should know
the Lord,' because everyone, great and small,
will know me already. 12And I will be merciful
to them in their wrongdoings, and I will remember their sins no more."

13 God speaks of these new promises, of this
new agreement, as taking the place of the old
one; for the old one is out of date now and has
been put aside forever.

9 Now in that first agreement between God
and his people there were rules for worship
and there was a sacred tent down here on earth.
Inside this place of worship there were two
rooms. The first one contained the golden candlestick and a table with special loaves of holy
bread upon it; this part was called the Holy
Place. 3 Then there was a curtain and behind the
curtain was a room called the Holy of Holies.
4 In that room there were a golden incense-altar
and the golden chest, called the ark of the
covenant, completely covered on all sides with
pure gold. Inside the ark were the tablets of
stone with the Ten Commandments written on
them, and a golden jar with some manna in it,

Today's English Version

I will be their God,
and they shall be my people.
11 None of them will have to teach his fellow-citizen,
or tell his fellow-countryman,
'Know the Lord.'
Because they will all know me,
from the least to the greatest.
12 I will have mercy on their transgressions,
and will no longer remember their sins."

13 By speaking of a new covenant, God has
made the first one old; and anything that is
getting old and worn-out will soon disappear.

Earthly and heavenly worship

9 The first covenant had rules for worship
and a man-made place for worship as well.
2A tent was put up, the outside one, which was
called the Holy Place. In it were the lamp, the
table, and the bread offered to God. 3 Behind
the second curtain was the tent called the Most
Holy Place. 4 In it were the gold altar for the
burning of incense, and the box of the covenant, all covered with gold. The box contained
the gold jar with the manna in it, Aaron's rod
that had sprouted leaves, and the two stone
tablets with the commandments written on them.

New International Version

I will be their God,
and they will be my people.
11 No longer will a man teach his neighbor,
or a man his brother, saying, 'Know the Lord'
because they will all know me,
from the least of them to the greatest.
12 I will forgive their wickedness,
and will remember their sins no more." [e]

13 By calling this covenant "new," he has
made the first one obsolete; and what is obsolete and aging will soon disappear.

Worship in the earthly tabernacle

9 Now the first covenant had regulations for
worship and also an earthly sanctuary. 2A
tabernacle was set up. In its first room were the
lampstand, the table and the consecrated bread;
this was called the Holy Place. 3 Behind the
second curtain was a room called the Most Holy
Place, 4 which had the golden altar of incense
and the gold-covered chest of the covenant. This
chest contained the golden jar of manna, Aaron's
rod that had budded, and the stone tablets of

[*e*] Jer. 31:31-34.

Phillips Modern English

And I will be to them a God,
And they shall be to me a people:
And they shall not teach every man his fellow-citizen,
And every man his brother, saying, Know the Lord:
For all shall know me,
From the least to the greatest of them.
For I will be merciful to their iniquities.
And their sins will I remember no more.

The mere fact that God speaks of a new covenant or agreement makes the old one out of date. And when a thing grows weak and out of date it is obviously soon going to disappear.

9.1 The sanctuary under the old agreement

Now the first agreement had certain rules for the service of God, and it had a sanctuary, a holy place in this world for the eternal God. A tent was erected: in the outer compartment were placed the lamp-standard, the table and the sacred loaves. Inside, beyond the curtain, was the inner tent called the holy place, in which were the golden incense-altar and the gold-covered ark of the agreement, containing the golden jar of manna. Aaron's budding staff and the stone tablets inscribed with the words

Revised Standard Version

and I will be their God,
and they shall be my people.
11 And they shall not teach every one his fellow
or every one his brother, saying, 'Know the Lord,'
for all shall know me,
from the least of them to the greatest.
12 For I will be merciful toward their iniquities,
and I will remember their sins no more."
13 In speaking of a new covenant he treats the
first as obsolete. And what is becoming obsolete and growing old is ready to vanish away.

9 Now even the first covenant had regulations for worship and an earthly sanctuary.
2 For a tent[p] was prepared, the outer one, in
which were the lampstand and the table and the
bread of the Presence;[q] it is called the Holy
Place. 3 Behind the second curtain stood a tent[p]
called the Holy of Holies, 4 having the golden
altar of incense and the ark of the covenant
covered on all sides with gold, which contained
a golden urn holding the manna, and Aaron's
rod that budded, and the tables of the covenant;

[p] Or *tabernacle*. [q] Greek *the presentation of the loaves*.

Jerusalem Bible

Then I will be their God
and they shall be my people.
11 *There will be no further need for neighbor to try to teach neighbor,*
or brother to say to brother,
"Learn to know the Lord."
No, they will all know me,
the least no less than the greatest,
12 *since I will forgive their iniquities*
and never call their sins to mind.[b]

13 By speaking of a *new* covenant, he implies that the first one is already old. Now anything old only gets more antiquated until in the end it disappears.

Christ enters the heavenly sanctuary

9 The first covenant also had its laws governing worship, and its sanctuary, a sanctuary on this earth. 2 There was a tent which
comprised two compartments: the first, in which
the lampstand, the table and the presentation
loaves were kept, was called the Holy Place;
3 then beyond the second veil, an innermost
part which was called the Holy of Holies 4 to
which belonged the gold altar of incense, and
the ark of the covenant, plated all over with
gold. In this were kept the gold jar containing
the manna, Aaron's branch that grew the buds,

[b] Jr. 31:31-34.

New English Bible

and I will be their God, and they shall be my people. And they shall not teach one another, saying to brother and fellow-citizen,[b] "Know the Lord!" For all of them, high and low, shall know me; I will be merciful to their wicked deeds, and I will remember their sins no more.' By speaking of a new covenant, he has pronounced the first one old; and anything that is growing old and ageing will shortly disappear.

9 The first covenant indeed had its ordinances of divine service and its sanctuary, but a material sanctuary. For a tent was prepared—the first tent—in which was the lamp-stand, and the table with the bread of the Presence; this is called the Holy Place. Beyond the second curtain was the tent called the Most Holy Place. Here was a golden altar of incense, and the ark of the covenant plated all over with gold, in which were a golden jar containing the manna, and Aaron's staff which once budded, and the

[b] *Some witnesses read* brother and neighbour.

King James Version

5And over it the cherubim of glory shadowing
the mercy seat; of which we cannot now speak
particularly. 6 Now when these things were thus
ordained, the priests went always into the first
tabernacle, accomplishing the service *of God.*
7 But into the second *went* the high priest alone
once every year, not without blood, which he
offered for himself, and *for* the errors of the
people: 8 The Holy Ghost this signifying, that
the way into the holiest of all was not yet made
manifest, while as the first tabernacle was yet
standing: 9 Which *was* a figure for the time then
present, in which were offered both gifts and
sacrifices, that could not make him that did the
service perfect, as pertaining to the conscience;
10 *Which stood* only in meats and drinks, and
divers washings, and carnal ordinances, imposed
on them until the time of reformation. 11 But
Christ being come a high priest of good things
to come, by a greater and more perfect tabernacle, not made with hands, that is to say, not
of this building; 12 Neither by the blood of
goats and calves, but by his own blood he en-

Living Bible

and Aaron's wooden cane that budded. 5Above
the golden chest were statues of angels called
the cherubim—the guardians of God's glory—
with their wings stretched out over the ark's
golden cover, called the mercy seat. But enough
of such details.
6 Well, when all was ready the priests went in
and out of the first room whenever they wanted
to, doing their work. 7 But only the high priest
went into the inner room, and then only once a
year, all alone, and always with blood which he
sprinkled on the mercy seat as an offering to
God to cover his own mistakes and sins, and the
mistakes and sins of all the people.
8 And the Holy Spirit uses all this to point
out to us that under the old system the common
people could not go into the Holy of Holies as
long as the outer room and the entire system it
represents were still in use.
9 This has an important lesson for us today.
For under the old system, gifts and sacrifices
were offered, but these failed to cleanse the
hearts of the people who brought them. 10 For
the old system dealt only with certain rituals—
what foods to eat and drink, rules for washing
themselves, and rules about this and that. The
people had to keep these rules to tide them over
until Christ came with God's new and better
way.
11 He came as High Priest of this better system which we now have. He went into that
greater, perfect tabernacle in heaven, not made
by men nor part of this world, 12 and once for
all took blood into that inner room, the Holy
of Holies, and sprinkled it on the mercy seat;
but it was not the blood of goats and calves.

Today's English Version

5Above the box were the glorious creatures representing the Divine Presence, with their wings
spread over the place where sins were forgiven.
But now is not the time to explain everything
in detail.
6 This is how those things were arranged. The
priests go into the outside tent every day to perform their duties; 7 but only the High Priest
goes into the inside tent, and he does so only
once a year. He takes blood with him which he
offers to God on behalf of himself and for the
sins which the people have committed without
knowing they were sinning. 8 The Holy Spirit
clearly teaches from all these arrangements that
the way into the Most Holy Place has not yet
been opened as long as the outside tent still
stands. 9 This is a figure which refers to the
present time. It means that the gifts and animal
sacrifices offered to God cannot make the worshiper's heart perfect. 10 They have to do only
with food, drink, and various cleansing ceremonies. These are all outward rules, which apply
only until the time when God will reform all
things.
11 But Christ has already come as the High
Priest of the good things that are already here.
The tent in which he serves is greater and more
perfect; it is not made by men, that is, it is not
a part of this created world. 12 When Christ
went through the tent and entered once and for
all into the Most Holy Place, he did not take
the blood of goats and calves to offer as sacri-

New International Version

the covenant. 5Above the chest were the cherubim of the Glory, overshadowing the place of
atonement. But we cannot discuss these things
in detail now.
6 When everything had been arranged like
this, the priests entered regularly into the outer
room to carry on their ministry. 7 But only the
high priest entered the inner room, and that
only once a year, and never without blood, which
he offered for himself and for the sins the people had committed in ignorance. 8 The Holy
Spirit was showing by this that the way into the
Most Holy Place had not yet been disclosed as
long as the first tabernacle was still standing.
9 This is an illustration for the present time, indicating that the gifts and sacrifices being offered
were not able to clear the conscience of the worshiper. 10 They are only a matter of food and
drink and various ceremonial washings—external
regulations applying until the time of the new
order.

The blood of Christ

11 When Christ came as high priest of the
good things that are already here,[f] he went
through the greater and more perfect tabernacle
that is not man-made, that is to say, not a part
of this creation. 12 He did not enter by means
of the blood of goats and calves; but he entered

[*f*] Some early MSS read *are to come.*

Phillips Modern English

of the actual agreement. Above these things were fixed representations of the cherubim of glory, casting their shadow over the mercy seat. (All this is full of meaning but we cannot enter now into a detailed explanation.)

Under this arrangement the outer tent was habitually used by the priests in the regular discharge of their religious duties. But the inner tent was entered once a year only, by the High Priest, alone, bearing a sacrifice of shed blood to be offered for himself and for the sins of the people which they had committed unwittingly.

9.8 *The old arrangements stood as symbols until Christ, the truth, came*

By these things the Holy Spirit means us to understand that the way to the holy place was not yet open, that is, so long as the first tent and all that it stands for still exist. For in this outer tent we see a picture of the present time, in which both gifts and sacrifices are offered and yet are incapable of cleansing the soul of the worshipper. The ceremonies are concerned with food and drink, various washings and rules for bodily conduct, and were only intended to be valid until the time when the new order should be established. For now Christ has come among us, the High Priest of the good things which were to come, and has passed through a greater and more perfect tent which no human hand had made (for it was no part of this world of ours). It was not with goats' or calves' blood

Revised Standard Version

5 above it were the cherubim of glory overshadowing the mercy seat. Of these things we cannot now speak in detail.
6 These preparations having thus been made, the priests go continually into the outer tent,[p] performing their ritual duties; 7 but into the second only the high priest goes, and he but once a year, and not without taking blood which he offers for himself and for the errors of the people. 8 By this the Holy Spirit indicates that the way into the sanctuary is not yet opened as long as the outer tent[p] is still standing 9 (which is symbolic for the present age). According to this arrangement, gifts and sacrifices are offered which cannot perfect the conscience of the worshiper, 10 but deal only with food and drink and various ablutions, regulations for the body imposed until the time of reformation.
11 But when Christ appeared as a high priest of the good things that have come,[r] then through the greater and more perfect tent[p] (not made with hands, that is, not of this creation) 12 he entered once for all into the Holy Place, taking[s] not the blood of goats and calves but his own

[p] Or *tabernacle*. [r] Other manuscripts read *good things to come*. [s] Greek *through*.

Jerusalem Bible

and the stone tablets of the covenant. 5 On top of it was the throne of mercy, and outspread over it were the glorious cherubs. This is not the time to go into greater detail about this.
6 Under these provisions, priests are constantly going into the outer tent to carry out their acts of worship, 7 but the second tent is entered only once a year, and then only by the high priest who must go in by himself and take the blood to offer for his own faults and the people's. 8 By this, the Holy Spirit is showing that no one has the right to go into the sanctuary as long as the outer tent remains standing;
9 it is a symbol for this present time. None of the gifts and sacrifices offered under these regulations can possibly bring any worshiper to perfection in his inner self; 10 they are rules about the outward life, connected with foods and drinks and washing at various times, intended to be in force only until it should be time to reform them.
11 But now Christ has come, as the high priest of all the blessings which were to come. He has passed through the greater, the more perfect tent, which is better than the one made by men's hands because it is not of this created order;
12 and he has entered the sanctuary once and for all, taking with him not the blood of goats

New English Bible

tablets of the covenant; and above it the cherubim of God's glory, overshadowing the place of expiation. On these we cannot now enlarge.

Under this arrangement, the priests are always entering the first tent in the discharge of their duties; but the second is entered only once a year, and by the high priest alone, and even then he must take with him the blood which he offers on his own behalf and for the people's sins of ignorance. By this the Holy Spirit signifies that so long as the earlier tent still stands, the way into the sanctuary remains unrevealed. All this is symbolic, pointing to the present time. The offerings and sacrifices there prescribed cannot give the worshipper inward perfection. It is only a matter of food and drink and various rites of cleansing—outward ordinances in force until the time of reformation.

But now Christ has come, high priest of good things already in being.[a] The tent of his priesthood is a greater and more perfect one, not made by men's hands, that is, not belonging to this created world; the blood of his sacrifice is his own blood, not the blood of goats and calves;

[a] *Some witnesses read* good things which were (*or* are) to be.

King James Version

tered in once into the holy place, having obtained eternal redemption *for us.* 13 For if the blood of bulls and of goats, and the ashes of a heifer sprinkling the unclean, sanctifieth to the purifying of the flesh; 14 How much more shall the blood of Christ, who through the eternal Spirit offered himself without spot to God, purge your conscience from dead works to serve the living God? 15 And for this cause he is the mediator of the new testament, that by means of death, for the redemption of the transgressions *that were* under the first testament, they which are called might receive the promise of eternal inheritance. 16 For where a testament *is,* there must also of necessity be the death of the testator. 17 For a testament *is* of force after men are dead: otherwise it is of no strength at all while the testator liveth. 18 Whereupon neither the first *testament* was dedicated without blood. 19 For when Moses had spoken every precept to all the people according to the law, he took the blood of calves and of goats, with water, and scarlet wool, and hyssop, and sprinkled both the book and all the people, 20 Saying, This *is* the blood

Living Bible

No, he took his own blood, and with it he, by himself, made sure of our eternal salvation.

13 And if under the old system the blood of bulls and goats and the ashes of young cows could cleanse men's bodies from sin, 14 just think how much more surely the blood of Christ will transform our lives and hearts. His sacrifice frees us from the worry of having to obey the old rules, and makes us want to serve the living God. For by the help of the eternal Holy Spirit, Christ willingly gave himself to God to die for our sins—he being perfect, without a single sin or fault. 15 Christ came with this new agreement so that all who are invited may come and have forever all the wonders God has promised them. For Christ died to rescue them from the penalty of the sins they had committed while still under that old system.

16 Now, if someone dies and leaves a will—a list of things to be given away to certain people when he dies—no one gets anything until it is proved that the person who wrote the will is dead. 17 The will goes into effect only after the death of the person who wrote it. While he is still alive no one can use it to get any of those things he has promised them.

18 That is why blood was sprinkled [as proof of Christ's death[a]] before even the first agreement could go into effect. 19 For after Moses had given the people all of God's laws, he took the blood of calves and goats, along with water, and sprinkled the blood over the book of God's laws and over all the people, using branches of hyssop bushes and scarlet wool to sprinkle with. 20 Then he said, "This is the blood that marks

[a] Implied.

Today's English Version

fice; rather, he took his own blood and obtained eternal salvation for us. 13 The blood of goats and bulls and the ashes of the burnt calf are sprinkled on the people who are ritually unclean, and make them clean by taking away their ritual impurity. 14 Since this is true, how much more is accomplished by the blood of Christ! Through the eternal Spirit he offered himself as a perfect sacrifice to God. His blood will make our consciences clean from useless works, so that we may serve the living God.

15 For this reason Christ is the one who arranges a new covenant, so that those who have been called by God may receive the eternal blessings that God has promised. This can be done because there has been a death which sets men free from the wrongs they did while they were under the first covenant.

16 Where there is a will, it has to be proved that the man who made it has died. 17 For a will means nothing while the man who made it is alive; it goes into effect only after his death. 18 That is why even the first covenant was made good only with the use of blood. 19 First, Moses told the people all the commandments, as set forth in the Law. Then he took the blood of calves, together with water, and sprinkled both the book of the Law and all the people with hyssop and scarlet wool. 20 He said, "This is the

New International Version

the Most Holy Place once for all by his own blood, having obtained eternal redemption. 13 The blood of goats and bulls and the ashes of a heifer sprinkled on those who are ceremonially unclean sanctify them so that they are outwardly clean. 14 How much more, then, will the blood of Christ, who through the eternal Spirit offered himself unblemished to God, cleanse our consciences from acts that lead to death, so that we may serve the living God!

15 For this reason Christ is the mediator of a new covenant, that those who are called may receive the promised eternal inheritance—now that he has died as a ransom to set them free from the sins committed under the first covenant.

16 In the case of a will,[g] it is necessary to prove the death of the one who made it, 17 because a will [g] is in force only when somebody has died; it never takes effect while the one who made it is living. 18 This is why even the first covenant was not put into effect without blood. 19 When Moses had proclaimed every commandment of the law to all the people, he took the blood of calves, together with water, scarlet wool and branches of hyssop, and sprinkled the scroll and all the people. 20 He said, "This is the blood

[g] Same Greek word as *covenant.*

Phillips Modern English

but with his own blood that he entered once and for all into the holy place, having won for us men eternal reconciliation with God. For if the blood of bulls and goats and the ashes of a burnt heifer were, when sprinkled on the unholy, sufficient to make the body pure, then how much more will the blood of Christ himself, who in the eternal spirit offered himself to God as the perfect sacrifice, purify our conscience from the deeds of death, that we may serve the living God!

9.15 The death of Christ gives him power to administer the new agreement

Christ is consequently the administrator of an entirely new agreement, having the power, by virtue of his death, to redeem transgressions committed under the first agreement: to enable those who obey God's call to enjoy the promises of the eternal inheritance. For, as in the case of a will, the agreement is only valid after death. While the testator lives, a will has no legal power. And indeed we find that even the first agreement of God's will was not put into force without the shedding of blood. For when Moses had told the people every command of the Law he took calves' and goats' blood with water and scarlet wool, and sprinkled both the book and all the people with a sprig of hyssop, saying: "This is the blood of the agreement

Revised Standard Version

blood, thus securing an eternal redemption.
13 For if the sprinkling of defiled persons with
the blood of goats and bulls and with the ashes
of a heifer sanctifies for the purification of the
flesh, 14 how much more shall the blood of
Christ, who through the eternal Spirit offered
himself without blemish to God, purify your[t]
conscience from dead works to serve the living
God.
15 Therefore he is the mediator of a new
covenant, so that those who are called may receive
the promised eternal inheritance, since a
death has occurred which redeems them from
the transgressions under the first covenant.[u]
16 For where a will[u] is involved, the death of
the one who made it must be established. 17 For
a will[u] takes effect only at death, since it is not
in force as long as the one who made it is alive.
18 Hence even the first covenant was not ratified
without blood. 19 For when every commandment
of the law had been declared by Moses to all
the people, he took the blood of calves and
goats, with water and scarlet wool and hyssop,
and sprinkled both the book itself and all the
people, 20 saying, "This is the blood of the cove-

[*t*] Other manuscripts read *our*. [*u*] The Greek word here used means both *covenant* and *will*.

Jerusalem Bible

and bull calves, but his own blood, having won
an eternal redemption for us. 13 The blood of
goats and bulls and the ashes of a heifer are
sprinkled on those who have incurred defilement
and they restore the holiness of their outward
lives; 14 how much more effectively the
blood of Christ, who offered himself as the perfect
sacrifice to God through the eternal Spirit,
can purify our inner self from dead actions so
that we do our service to the living God.

Christ seals the new covenant with his blood

15 He brings a new covenant, as the mediator,
only so that the people who were called to an
eternal inheritance may actually receive what
was promised: his death took place to cancel
the sins that infringed the earlier covenant.
16 Now wherever a will is in question, the death
of the testator must be established; 17 indeed, it
only becomes valid with that death, since it is
not meant to have any effect while the testator
is still alive. 18 That explains why even the
earlier covenant needed something to be killed
in order to take effect, 19 and why, after Moses
had announced all the commandments of the
Law to the people, he took the calves' blood,
the goats' blood and some water, and with these
he sprinkled the book itself and all the people,
using scarlet wool and hyssop; 20 saying as he

New English Bible

and thus he has entered the sanctuary once and for all and secured an eternal deliverance. For if the blood of goats and bulls and the sprinkled ashes of a heifer have power to hallow those who have been defiled and restore their external purity, how much greater is the power of the blood of Christ; he offered himself without blemish to God, a spiritual and eternal sacrifice; and his blood will cleanse our conscience from the deadness of our former ways and fit us for the service of the living God.

And therefore he is the mediator of a new covenant, or testament, under which, now that there has been a death to bring deliverance from sins committed under the former covenant, those whom God has called may receive the promise of the eternal inheritance. For where there is a testament it is necessary for the death of the testator to be established. A testament is operative only after a death: it cannot possibly have force while the testator is alive. Thus we find that the former covenant itself was not inaugurated without blood. For when, as the Law directed, Moses had recited all the commandments to the people, he took the blood of the calves, with water, scarlet wool, and marjoram, and sprinkled the law-book itself and all the people, saying, 'This is the blood of the cove-

King James Version

of the testament which God hath enjoined unto
you. 21 Moreover he sprinkled likewise with
blood both the tabernacle, and all the vessels of
the ministry. 22And almost all things are by the
law purged with blood; and without shedding of
blood is no remission. 23 *It was* therefore necessary that the patterns of things in the heavens
should be purified with these; but the heavenly
things themselves with better sacrifices than
these. 24 For Christ is not entered into the holy
places made with hands, *which are* the figures of
the true; but into heaven itself, now to appear in
the presence of God for us: 25 Nor yet that he
should offer himself often, as the high priest
entereth into the holy place every year with
blood of others; 26 For then must he often have
suffered since the foundation of the world: but
now once in the end of the world hath he appeared to put away sin by the sacrifice of himself. 27And as it is appointed unto men once to
die, but after this the judgment: 28 So Christ
was once offered to bear the sins of many; and

Living Bible

the beginning of the agreement between you and God, the agreement God commanded me to make with you." 21And in the same way he sprinkled blood on the sacred tent and on whatever instruments were used for worship. 22 In fact we can say that under the old agreement almost everything was cleansed by sprinkling it with blood, and without the shedding of blood there is no forgiveness of sins.

23 That is why the sacred tent down here on earth, and everything in it—all copied from things in heaven—all had to be made pure by Moses in this way, by being sprinkled with the blood of animals. But the real things in heaven, of which these down here are copies, were made pure with far more precious offerings.

24 For Christ has entered into heaven itself, to appear now before God as our Friend. It was not in the earthly place of worship that he did this, for that was merely a copy of the real temple in heaven. 25 Nor has he offered himself again and again, as the high priest down here on earth offers animal blood in the Holy of Holies each year. 26 If that had been necessary, then he would have had to die again and again, ever since the world began. But no! He came once for all, at the end of the age, to put away the power of sin forever by dying for us.

27 And just as it is destined that men die only once, and after that comes judgment, 28 so also Christ died only once as an offering for the sins of many people; and he will come again, but not to deal again with our sins.

Today's English Version

blood which seals the covenant that God has commanded you to obey." 21 In the same way, Moses also sprinkled the blood on the tent and over all the things used in worship. 22 Indeed, according to the Law, almost everything is made clean by blood; and sins are forgiven only if blood is poured out.

Christ's sacrifice takes away sins

23 These things, which are copies of the heavenly originals, had to be made clean in this way. But the heavenly things themselves require much better sacrifices. 24 For Christ did not go into a holy place made by men, a copy of the real one. He went into heaven itself, where he now appears on our behalf in the presence of God. 25 The Jewish High Priest goes into the Holy Place every year with the blood of an animal. But Christ did not go in to offer himself many times; 26 for then he would have had to suffer many times ever since the creation of the world. Instead, he has now appeared once and for all, when all ages of time are nearing the end, to remove sin through the sacrifice of himself. 27 Everyone must die once, and after that be judged by God. 28 In the same manner, Christ also was offered in sacrifice once to take

New International Version

of the covenant, which God has commanded you to keep."[h] 21 In the same way, he sprinkled with the blood both the tabernacle and everything used in its ceremonies. 22 In fact, the law requires that nearly everything be cleansed with blood, and without the shedding of blood there is no forgiveness.

23 It was necessary, then, for the copies of the heavenly things to be purified with these sacrifices, but the heavenly things themselves with better sacrifices than these. 24 For Christ did not enter a man-made sanctuary that was only a copy of the true one; he entered heaven itself, now to appear for us in God's presence. 25 Nor did he enter heaven to offer himself again and again, the way the high priest enters the Most Holy Place every year with blood that is not his own. 26 Then Christ would have had to suffer many times since the creation of the world. But now he has appeared once for all at the end of the ages to do away with sin by the sacrifice of himself. 27 Just as man is destined to die once, and after that to face judgment, 28 so Christ was sacrificed once to take away the sins of many

[h] Exodus 24:8.

Phillips Modern English

God makes with you." Moses also sprinkled with blood the tent itself and all the sacred vessels. And you will find that in the Law almost all cleansing is made by means of blood—it implies again and again: "No shedding of blood, no remission of sin."

9.23 *Christ has achieved the real appearance before God for us*

It was necessary for the earthly reproductions of heavenly realities to be purified by such methods, but the actual heavenly things could only be made pure in God's sight by higher sacrifices than these. Christ did not therefore enter into any holy places made by human hands (however truly these may represent heavenly realities), but he entered Heaven itself to make his appearance before God on our behalf. There is no intention that he should offer himself over and over again, like the High Priest entering the holy place year after year with the blood of another creature. For that would mean that he would have to suffer death every time he entered Heaven from the beginning of the world! No, the fact is that now, at this point in time, the end of the present age, he has appeared once and for all to abolish sin by the sacrifice of himself. And just as surely as it is appointed for all men to die once, and after that pass to their judgment, so it is certain that Christ was offered once to bear the sins of many and after that, to those who look for him, he will appear

Revised Standard Version

nant which God commanded you." 21 And in the same way he sprinkled with the blood both the tent[p] and all the vessels used in worship. 22 Indeed, under the law almost everything is purified with blood, and without the shedding of blood there is no forgiveness of sins.

23 Thus it was necessary for the copies of the heavenly things to be purified with these rites, but the heavenly things themselves with better sacrifices than these. 24 For Christ has entered, not into a sanctuary made with hands, a copy of the true one, but into heaven itself, now to appear in the presence of God on our behalf. 25 Nor was it to offer himself repeatedly, as the high priest enters the Holy Place yearly with blood not his own; 26 for then he would have had to suffer repeatedly since the foundation of the world. But as it is, he has appeared once for all at the end of the age to put away sin by the sacrifice of himself. 27 And just as it is appointed for men to die once, and after that comes judgment, 28 so Christ, having been offered once to bear the sins of many, will appear

Jerusalem Bible

did so: *This is the blood of the covenant that God has laid down for you.*[c] 21 After that, he sprinkled the tent and all the liturgical vessels with blood in the same way. 22 In fact, according to the Law almost everything has to be purified[d] with blood; and if there is no shedding of blood, there is no remission. 23 Obviously, only the copies of heavenly things can be purified in this way, and the heavenly things themselves have to be purified by a higher sort of sacrifice than this. 24 It is not as though Christ had entered a man-made sanctuary which was only modeled on the real one; but it was heaven itself, so that he could appear in the actual presence of God on our behalf. 25 And he does not have to offer himself again and again, like the high priest going into the sanctuary year after year with the blood that is not his own, 26 or else he would have had to suffer over and over again since the world began. Instead of that, he has made his appearance once and for all, now at the end of the last age, to do away with sin by sacrificing himself. 27 Since men only die once, and after that comes judgment, 28 so Christ, too, offers himself only once *to take the faults of many on himself,*[e] and

[c] Ex. 24:8. [d] Many instances are given in Lv. [e] Is. 53:12.

New English Bible

nant which God has enjoined upon you.' In the same way he also sprinkled the tent and all the vessels of divine service with blood. Indeed, according to the Law, it might almost be said, everything is cleansed by blood and without the shedding of blood there is no forgiveness.

If, then, these sacrifices cleanse the copies of heavenly things, those heavenly things themselves require better sacrifices to cleanse them. For Christ has entered, not that sanctuary made by men's hands which is only a symbol of the reality, but heaven itself, to appear now before God on our behalf. Nor is he there to offer himself again and again, as the high priest enters the sanctuary year by year with blood not his own. If that were so, he would have had to suffer many times since the world was made. But as it is, he has appeared once and for all at the climax of history to abolish sin by the sacrifice of himself. And as it is the lot of men to die once, and after death comes judgement, so Christ was offered once to bear the burden of men's sins,[a] and will appear a second time, sin

[a] *Or* to remove men's sins.

King James Version

unto them that look for him shall he appear the second time without sin unto salvation.

10 For the law having a shadow of good things to come, *and* not the very image of the things, can never with those sacrifices, which they offered year by year continually, make the comers thereunto perfect. 2 For then would they not have ceased to be offered? because that the worshippers once purged should have had no more conscience of sins. 3 But in those *sacrifices there is* a remembrance again *made* of sins every year. 4 For *it is* not possible that the blood of bulls and of goats should take away sins.

Living Bible

This time he will come bringing salvation to all those who are eagerly and patiently waiting for him.

10 The old system of Jewish laws gave only a dim foretaste of the good things Christ would do for us. The sacrifices under the old system were repeated again and again, year after year, but even so they could never save those who lived under their rules. 2 If they could have, one offering would have been enough; the worshipers would have been cleansed once for all, and their feeling of guilt would be done.

3 But just the opposite happened: those yearly sacrifices reminded them of their disobedience and guilt instead of relieving their minds. 4 For it is not possible for the blood of bulls and goats really to take away sins.[a]

[*a*] The blood of bulls and goats merely covered over the sins, taking them out of sight for hundreds of years until Jesus Christ came to die on the cross. There he gave his own blood which forever took those sins away.

Today's English Version

away the sins of many. He will appear a second time, not to deal with sin, but to save those who are waiting for him.

10 The Jewish Law is not a full and faithful model of the real things. It is only a faint outline of the good things to come. The same sacrifices are offered forever, year after year. How can the Law, then, by means of these sacrifices, make perfect the people who come to God? 2 If the people worshiping God had been made really clean from their sins, they would not feel guilty of sin any more, and all sacrifices would stop. 3 As it is, however, the sacrifices serve to remind people of their sins, year after year. 4 For the blood of bulls and goats can never take sins away.

New International Version

people; and he will appear a second time, not to bear sin, but to bring salvation to those who are waiting for him.

Christ's sacrifice once for all

10 The law is only a shadow of the good things that are coming—not the realities themselves. For this reason it can never, by the same sacrifices repeated endlessly year after year, make perfect those who draw near to worship. 2 If it could, would they not have stopped being offered? For the worshipers would have been cleansed once for all, and would no longer have felt guilty for their sins. 3 But those sacrifices are an annual reminder of sins, 4 because it is impossible for the blood of bulls and goats to take away sins.

Phillips Modern English

a second time, not this time to deal with sin, but to bring to full salvation those who eagerly await him.

10.1 Sacrifices under the Law were "typical" not final

The Law possessed only a dim outline of the benefits Christ would bring and did not actually reproduce them. Consequently it was incapable of perfecting the souls of those who offered their regular annual sacrifices. For if it had, surely the sacrifices would have been discontinued—on the grounds that the worshippers, having been really cleansed, would have had no further consciousness of sin. In practice, however, the sacrifices amounted to an annual reminder of sins; for the blood of bulls and goats cannot really remove the guilt of sin.

Revised Standard Version

a second time, not to deal with sin but to save those who are eagerly waiting for him.

10 For since the law has but a shadow of
the good things to come instead of the
true form of these realities, it can never, by the
same sacrifices which are continually offered year
after year, make perfect those who draw near.
2 Otherwise, would they not have ceased to be offered? If the worshipers had once been cleansed,
they would no longer have any consciousness of
sin. 3 But in these sacrifices there is a reminder
of sin year after year. 4 For it is impossible that
the blood of bulls and goats should take away
sins.

Jerusalem Bible

when he appears a second time, it will not be to deal with sin but to reward with salvation those who are waiting for him.

Summary: Christ's sacrifice superior to the sacrifices of the Mosaic Law

The old sacrifices ineffective

10 So, since the Law has no more than a
reflection of these realities, and no finished picture of them, it is quite incapable of
bringing the worshipers to perfection, with the
same sacrifices repeatedly offered year after year.
2 Otherwise, the offering of them would have
stopped, because the worshipers, when they had
been purified once, would have no awareness of
sins. 3 Instead of that, the sins are recalled year
after year in the sacrifices. 4 Bulls' blood and
goats' blood are useless for taking away sins,

New English Bible

done away, to bring salvation to those who are watching for him.

10 For the Law contains but a shadow, and no true image,[b] of the good things which were to come; it provides for the same sacrifices year after year, and with these it can never bring the worshippers to perfection for all time.[c] If it could, these sacrifices would surely have ceased to be offered, because the worshippers, cleansed once for all, would no longer have any sense of sin. But instead, in these sacrifices year after year sins are brought to mind, because sins can never be removed by the blood of bulls and goats.

[b] *One witness reads* a shadow and likeness . . .
[c] *Or* bring to perfection the worshippers who come continually.

King James Version

5 Wherefore, when he cometh into the world, he
saith, Sacrifice and offering thou wouldest not,
but a body hast thou prepared me: 6 In burnt
offerings and *sacrifices* for sin thou hast had no
pleasure. 7 Then said I, Lo, I come (in the volume of the book it is written of me) to do thy
will, O God. 8 Above when he said, Sacrifice and
offering and burnt offerings and *offering* for sin
thou wouldest not, neither hadst pleasure *therein;*
which are offered by the law; 9 Then said he, Lo,
I come to do thy will, O God. He taketh away
the first, that he may establish the second. 10 By
the which will we are sanctified through the offering of the body of Jesus Christ once *for all.*
11 And every priest standeth daily ministering and
offering oftentimes the same sacrifices, which can
never take away sins: 12 But this man, after he
had offered one sacrifice for sins for ever, sat
down on the right hand of God; 13 From henceforth expecting till his enemies be made his foot-

Living Bible

5 That is why Christ said, as he came into
the world, "O God, the blood of bulls and goats
cannot satisfy you, so you have made ready this
body of mine for me to lay as a sacrifice upon
your altar. 6 You were not satisfied with the
animal sacrifices, slain and burnt before you as
offerings for sin. 7 Then I said, 'See, I have
come to do your will, to lay down my life, just
as the Scriptures said that I would.' "

8 After Christ said this, about not being satisfied with the various sacrifices and offerings required under the old system, 9 he then added,
"Here I am. I have come to give my life."

He cancels the first system in favor of a far
better one. 10 Under this new plan we have been
forgiven and made clean by Christ's dying for
us once and for all. 11 Under the old agreement
the priests stood before the altar day after day
offering sacrifices that could never take away
our sins. 12 But Christ gave himself to God for
our sins as one sacrifice for all time, and then
sat down in the place of highest honor at God's
right hand, 13 waiting for his enemies to be laid

Today's English Version

5 For this reason, when Christ was about to
come into the world, he said to God:

"You do not want sacrifices and offerings,
but you have prepared a body for me.
6 You are not pleased with animals burned
whole on the altar,
or with sacrifices to take away sins.
7 Then I said, 'Here I am, God,
to do what you want me to,
just as it is written of me in the book of
the Law.' "

8 First he said, "You neither want nor are you
pleased with sacrifices and offerings, or with animals burned on the altar and the sacrifices to
take away sins." He said this even though all
these sacrifices are offered according to the Law.
9 Then he said, "Here I am, God, to do what
you want me to do." So God does away with all
the old sacrifices and puts the sacrifice of Christ
in their place. 10 Because Jesus Christ did what
God wanted him to do, we are all made clean
from sin by the offering that he made of his own
body, once and for all.

11 Every Jewish priest stands and performs
his services every day and offers the same sacrifices many times. But these sacrifices can never
take away sins. 12 Christ, however, offered one
sacrifice for sins, an offering that is good forever, and then sat down at the right side of
God. 13 There he now waits until God puts his

New International Version

5 Therefore, when Christ came into the world,
he said:
"Sacrifice and offering you did not desire,
but a body you prepared for me;
6 with burnt offerings and sin offerings
you were not pleased.
7 Then I said, 'Here I am—it is written about
me in the scroll—
I have come to do your will, O God.' " [i]
8 First he said, "Sacrifices and offerings, burnt
offerings and sin offerings you did not desire,
nor were you pleased with them" (although the
law required them to be made). 9 Then he said,
"Here I am, I have come to do your will." He
sets aside the first to establish the second. 10 And
by that will, we have been made holy through
the sacrifice of the body of Jesus Christ once for
all.

11 Day after day every priest stands and performs his religious duties; again and again he
offers the same sacrifices, which can never take
away sins. 12 But when this priest had offered
for all time one sacrifice for sins, he sat down
at the right hand of God. 13 Since that time he
waits for his enemies to be made his footstool,

[i] Psalm 40:6-8.

Phillips Modern English

10.5 *Christ, however, makes the old order obsolete and makes the perfect sacrifice*

Therefore, when Christ enters the world, he says:

Sacrifice and offering thou wouldest not,
But a body didst thou prepare for me;
In whole burnt offerings and sacrifices for sin
thou hadst no pleasure:
Then said I, Lo, I am come
(In the roll of the book it is written of me)
To do thy will, O God.

After saying that God has "no pleasure in sacrifice, offering and burnt-offering" (which are made according to the Law), Christ then says, "Lo, I am come to do thy will." That means that he is dispensing with the old order of sacrifices, and establishing a new order of obedience to the will of God, and in that will we have been made holy by the single unique offering of the body of Jesus Christ.

Every human priest stands day by day performing his religious duties and offering time after time the same sacrifices—which can never actually remove sins. But this man, after offering one sacrifice for sins for ever, took his seat at God's right hand, from that time offering no more sacrifice, but waiting until "his enemies be

Revised Standard Version

5 Consequently, when Christ[v] came into the world, he said,
"Sacrifices and offerings thou hast not desired,
but a body hast thou prepared for me;
6 in burnt offerings and sin offerings thou hast taken no pleasure.
7 Then I said, 'Lo, I have come to do thy will, O God,'
as it is written of me in the roll of the book."
8 When he said above, "Thou hast neither desired nor taken pleasure in sacrifices and offerings and burnt offerings and sin offerings" (these are offered according to the law), 9 then he
added, "Lo, I have come to do thy will." He abolishes the first in order to establish the second.
10 And by that will we have been sanctified through the offering of the body of Jesus Christ once for all.
11 And every priest stands daily at his service, offering repeatedly the same sacrifices, which can never take away sins.
12 But when Christ[w] had offered for all time a single sacrifice for sins, he sat down at the right hand of God,
13 then to wait until his enemies should be

[v] Greek *he*. [w] Greek *this one*.

Jerusalem Bible

5 and this is what he said, on coming into the world:

You who wanted no sacrifice or oblation,
prepared a body for me.
6 *You took no pleasure in holocausts or sacrifices for sin;*
7 *then I said,*
just as I was commanded in the scroll of the book,
"*God, here I am! I am coming to obey your will.*" [f]

8 Notice that he says first: *You did not want* what the Law lays down as the things to be offered, that is: *the sacrifices, the oblations, the holocausts and the sacrifices for sin,* and *you took no pleasure* in them;
9 and then he says: *Here I am! I am coming to obey your will.* He is abolishing the first sort to replace it with the second.
10 And this *will* was for us to be made holy by the *offering* of his *body* made once and for all by Jesus Christ.

The efficacy of Christ's sacrifice

11 All the priests stand at their duties every day, offering over and over again the same sacrifices which are quite incapable of taking sins away.
12 He, on the other hand, has offered one single sacrifice for sins, and then taken his place for ever, *at the right hand of God,*
13 where he is now waiting *until his enemies are made into a*

[f] Ps. 40:6-8 (LXX).

New English Bible

That is why, at his coming into the world, he says:

'Sacrifice and offering thou didst not desire,
but thou hast prepared a body for me.
Whole-offerings and sin-offerings thou didst not
delight in.
Then I said, "Here am I: as it is written of me
in the scroll,
I have come, O God, to do thy will." '

First he says, 'Sacrifices and offerings, whole-offerings and sin-offerings, thou didst not desire nor delight in'—although the Law prescribes them—and then he says, 'I have come to do thy will.' He thus annuls the former to establish the latter. And it is by the will of God that we have been consecrated, through the offering of the body of Jesus Christ once and for all.

Every priest stands performing his service daily and offering time after time the same sacrifices, which can never remove sins. But Christ offered for all time one sacrifice for sins, and took his seat at the right hand of God, where he waits henceforth until his enemies are made his foot-

King James Version

stool. 14 For by one offering he hath perfected
for ever them that are sanctified. 15 *Whereof* the
Holy Ghost also is a witness to us: for after that
he had said before, 16 This *is* the covenant that I
will make with them after those days, saith the
Lord; I will put my laws into their hearts, and
in their minds will I write them; 17 And their sins
and iniquities will I remember no more. 18 Now
where remission of these *is, there is* no more
offering for sin. 19 Having therefore, brethren,
boldness to enter into the holiest by the blood of
Jesus, 20 By a new and living way, which he
hath consecrated for us, through the vail, that
is to say, his flesh; 21 And *having* a high priest
over the house of God; 22 Let us draw near with
a true heart in full assurance of faith, having our

Living Bible

under his feet. 14 For by that one offering he
made forever perfect in the sight of God all
those whom he is making holy.

15 And the Holy Spirit testifies that this is
so, for he has said, 16 "This is the agreement I
will make with the people of Israel, though they
broke their first agreement: I will write my laws
into their minds so that they will always know
my will, and I will put my laws in their hearts
so that they will want to obey them." 17 And
then he adds, "I will never again remember their
sins and lawless deeds."

18 Now, when sins have once been forever
forgiven and forgotten, there is no need to offer
more sacrifices to get rid of them. 19 And so,
dear brothers, now we may walk right into the
very Holy of Holies where God is, because of
the blood of Jesus. 20 This is the fresh, new,
life-giving way which Christ has opened up for
us by tearing the curtain—his human body—to
let us into the holy presence of God.

21 And since this great High Priest of ours
rules over God's household, 22 let us go right
in, to God himself, with true hearts fully trusting

Today's English Version

enemies as a footstool under his feet. 14 With
one sacrifice, then, he has made perfect forever
those who are clean from sin.

15 And the Holy Spirit also gives us his witness. First he says,

16 "This is the covenant that I will make with
them
in the days to come, says the Lord:
I will put my laws in their hearts,
and write them on their minds."

17 And then he says, "I will not remember their
sins and wicked deeds any longer." 18 So when
these have been forgiven, an offering to take
away sins is no longer needed.

Let us come near to God

19 We have, then, brothers, complete freedom
to go into the Most Holy Place by means of
the death of Jesus. 20 He opened for us a new
way, a living way, through the curtain—that is,
through his own body. 21 We have a great priest
in charge of the house of God. 22 Let us come
near to God, then, with a sincere heart and a

New International Version

14 because by one sacrifice he has made perfect
forever those who are being made holy.

15 The Holy Spirit also testifies to us about
this. First he says:

16 "This is the covenant I will make with them
after that time, says the Lord.
I will put my laws in their hearts,
and I will write them on their minds." [j]

17 Then he adds:
"Their sins and lawless acts
I will remember no more." [k]

18 And where these have been forgiven, there is
no longer any sacrifice for sin.

A call to persevere

19 Therefore, brothers, since we have confidence to enter the Most Holy Place by the
blood of Jesus, 20 by a new and living way
opened for us through the curtain, that is, his
body, 21 and since we have a great priest over
the house of God, 22 let us draw near to God
with a sincere heart in full assurance of faith,

[*j*] Jer. 31:33. [*k*] Jer. 31:34.

Phillips Modern English

made his footstool". For by virtue of that one offering he has perfected for all time every one whom he makes holy. The Holy Spirit himself endorses this truth for us, when he says, first:

This is the covenant that I will make with them
After those days, saith the Lord;
I will put my laws on their heart,
And upon their mind also will I write them.

And then, he adds:

And their sins and their iniquities will I remember no more.

Where God grants remission of sin there can be no question of making further atonement.

10.19 Through Christ we can confidently approach God

So, by virtue of the blood of Jesus, you and I, my brothers, may now have confidence to enter the holy place by a fresh and living way, which he has opened up for us by himself passing through the curtain, that is, his own human nature. Further, since we have a great High Priest set over the household of God, let us draw near with true hearts and fullest confi-

Revised Standard Version

made a stool for his feet. 14 For by a single
offering he has perfected for all time those who
are sanctified. 15 And the Holy Spirit also bears
witness to us; for after saying,
16 "This is the covenant that I will make with
them
after those days, says the Lord:
I will put my laws on their hearts,
and write them on their minds,"
17 then he adds,
"I will remember their sins and their misdeeds no more."
18 Where there is forgiveness of these, there is
no longer any offering for sin.
19 Therefore, brethren, since we have confidence to enter the sanctuary by the blood of
Jesus, 20 by the new and living way which he
opened for us through the curtain, that is,
through his flesh, 21 and since we have a great
priest over the house of God, 22 let us draw near
with a true heart in full assurance of faith, with

Jerusalem Bible

footstool for him.[g] 14 By virtue of that one single offering, he has achieved the eternal perfection of all whom he is sanctifying. 15 The Holy
Spirit assures us of this; for he says, first:

16 *This is the covenant I will make with them*
when those days arrive[h];

and the Lord then goes on to say:

I will put my laws into their hearts
and write them on their minds.
17 *I will never call their sins to mind,*
or their offenses.

18 When all sins have been forgiven, there can
be no more sin offerings.

IV. Persevering faith

The Christian opportunity

19 In other words, brothers, through the
blood of Jesus we have the right to enter the
sanctuary, 20 by a new way which he has opened
for us, a living opening through the curtain,
that is to say, his body. 21 And we have the
supreme high priest over all *the house of God.*
22 So as we go in, let us be sincere in heart and
filled with faith, our minds sprinkled and free

[g] Ps. 110. [h] From the long quotation from Jr. 31 made in ch. 8.

New English Bible

stool. For by one offering he has perfected for all time those who are thus consecrated. Here we have also the testimony of the Holy Spirit: he first says, 'This is the covenant which I will make with them after those days, says the Lord: I will set my laws in their hearts and write them on their understanding'; then he adds, 'and their sins and wicked deeds I will remember no more at all.' And where these have been forgiven, there are offerings for sin no longer.

So now, my friends, the blood of Jesus makes us free to enter boldly into the sanctuary by the new, living way which he has opened for us through the curtain, the way of his flesh.[a] We have, moreover, a great priest set over the household of God; so let us make our approach in sincerity of heart and full assurance of faith, our

[a] *Or* through the curtain of his flesh.

King James Version

hearts sprinkled from an evil conscience, and our bodies washed with pure water. 23 Let us hold fast the profession of *our* faith without wavering, for he *is* faithful that promised; 24 And let us consider one another to provoke unto love and to good works: 25 Not forsaking the assembling of ourselves together, as the manner of some *is;* but exhorting *one another:* and so much the more, as ye see the day approaching. 26 For if we sin wilfully after that we have received the knowledge of the truth, there remaineth no more sacrifice for sins, 27 But a certain fearful looking for of judgment and fiery indignation, which shall devour the adversaries. 28 He that despised Moses' law died without mercy under two or three witnesses: 29 Of how much sorer punishment, suppose ye, shall he be thought worthy, who hath trodden under foot the Son of God, and hath counted the blood of the covenant, wherewith he was sanctified, an unholy thing, and hath done despite unto the Spirit of grace? 30 For we know him that hath said, Vengeance *belongeth* unto me, I will recompense, saith the

Living Bible

him to receive us, because we have been sprinkled with Christ's blood to make us clean, and because our bodies have been washed with pure water.

23 Now we can look forward to the salvation God has promised us. There is no longer any room for doubt, and we can tell others that salvation is ours, for there is no question that he will do what he says.

24 In response to all he has done for us, let us outdo each other in being helpful and kind to each other and in doing good.

25 Let us not neglect our church meetings, as some people do, but encourage and warn each other, especially now that the day of his coming back again is drawing near.

26 If anyone sins deliberately by rejecting the Savior after knowing the truth of forgiveness, this sin is not covered by Christ's death; there is no way to get rid of it. 27 There will be nothing to look forward to but the terrible punishment of God's awful anger which will consume all his enemies. 28 A man who refused to obey the laws given by Moses was killed without mercy if there were two or three witnesses to his sin. 29 Think how much more terrible the punishment will be for those who have trampled underfoot the Son of God and treated his cleansing blood as though it were common and unhallowed, and insulted and outraged the Holy Spirit who brings God's mercy to his people.

30 For we know him who said, "Justice belongs to me; I will repay them"; who also said,

Today's English Version

sure faith, with hearts that have been made clean from a guilty conscience, and bodies washed with pure water. 23 Let us hold on firmly to the hope we profess, because we can trust God to keep his promise. 24 Let us be concerned with one another, to help one another to show love and to do good. 25 Let us not give up the habit of meeting together, as some are doing. Instead, let us encourage one another, all the more since you see that the Day of the Lord is coming near.

26 For there is no longer any sacrifice that will take away sins if we purposely go on sinning after the truth has been made known to us. 27 Instead, all that is left is to be afraid of what will happen: the Judgment and the fierce fire which will destroy those who oppose God! 28 Anyone who disobeys the Law of Moses is put to death, without any mercy, when judged guilty from the evidence of two or three witnesses. 29 What, then, of the man who despises the Son of God? who treats as a cheap thing the blood of God's covenant which cleansed him from sin? who insults the Spirit of grace? Just think how much worse is the punishment he will deserve! 30 For we know who said, "I will take revenge, I will repay"; and who also said,

New International Version

having our hearts sprinkled to cleanse us from a guilty conscience and having our bodies washed with pure water. 23 Let us hold unswervingly to the hope we profess, for he who promised is faithful. 24 And let us consider how we may spur one another on toward love and good deeds. 25 Let us not give up meeting together, as some are in the habit of doing, but let us encourage one another—and all the more as you see the Day approaching.

26 If we deliberately keep on sinning after we have received the knowledge of the truth, no sacrifice for sins is left, 27 but only a fearful expectation of judgment and of raging fire that will consume the enemies of God. 28 Anyone who rejected the law of Moses died without mercy on the testimony of two or three witnesses. 29 How much more severely do you think a man deserves to be punished who has trampled the Son of God under foot, who has treated as an unholy thing the blood of the covenant that sanctified him, and who has insulted the Spirit of grace? 30 For we know him who said, "It is mine to avenge; I will repay," [l] and again, "The

[l] Deut. 32:35.

Phillips Modern English

dence, knowing that our inmost souls have been purified by the sprinkling of his blood just as our bodies are cleansed by the washing of clean water. In this confidence let us hold on to the hope that we profess without the slightest hesitation—for he is utterly dependable—and let us think of one another and how we can encourage each other to love and do good deeds. And let us not hold aloof from our church meetings, as some do. Let us do all we can to help one another's faith, and this the more earnestly as we see the final day drawing nearer.

10.26 *A warning: let us not abuse the great sacrifice*

Now if we sin deliberately after we have known and accepted the truth, there can be no further sacrifice for sin for us but only a terrifying expectation of judgment and the fire of God's indignation, which will consume all that sets itself against him. The man who showed contempt for Moses' Law died without hope of appeal on the evidence of two or three witnesses. How much more dreadful a punishment will he be thought to deserve who has poured scorn on the Son of God, treated like dirt the blood of the agreement which had once made him holy, and insulted the very Spirit of grace? For we know the one who said:

> Vengeance belongeth unto me, I will recompense.

Revised Standard Version

our hearts sprinkled clean from an evil conscience and our bodies washed with pure water. 23 Let us hold fast the confession of our hope without wavering, for he who promised is faithful; 24 and let us consider how to stir up one another to love and good works, 25 not neglecting to meet together, as is the habit of some, but encouraging one another, and all the more as you see the Day drawing near.

26 For if we sin deliberately after receiving the knowledge of the truth, there no longer remains a sacrifice for sins, 27 but a fearful prospect of judgment, and a fury of fire which will consume the adversaries. 28 A man who has violated the law of Moses dies without mercy at the testimony of two or three witnesses. 29 How much worse punishment do you think will be deserved by the man who has spurned the Son of God, and profaned the blood of the covenant by which he was sanctified, and outraged the Spirit of grace? 30 For we know him who said, "Vengeance is mine, I will repay." And again,

Jerusalem Bible

from any trace of bad conscience and our bodies washed with pure water. 23 Let us keep firm in the hope we profess, because the one who made the promise is faithful. 24 Let us be concerned for each other, to stir a response in love and good works. 25 Do not stay away from the meetings of the community, as some do, but encourage each other to go; the more so as you see the Day drawing near.

The danger of apostasy

26 If, after we have been given knowledge of the truth, we should deliberately commit any sins, then there is no longer any sacrifice for them. 27 There will be left only the dread prospect of judgment and of *the raging fire* that is to *burn rebels.*[i] 28 Anyone who disregards the Law of Moses is ruthlessly *put to death on the word of two witnesses or three*[j]; 29 and you may be sure that anyone who tramples on the Son of God, and who treats *the blood of the covenant* which sanctified him as if it were not holy, and who insults the Spirit of grace, will be condemned to a far severer punishment. 30 We are all aware who it was that said: *Vengeance is mine; I will repay.*[k] And again:

[*i*] Is. 26:11 (LXX). [*j*] Dt. 17:6. [*k*] Dt. 32:35-36.

New English Bible

guilty hearts sprinkled clean, our bodies washed with pure water. Let us be firm and unswerving in the confession of our hope, for the Giver of the promise may be trusted. We ought to see how each of us may best arouse others to love and active goodness, not staying away from our meetings, as some do, but rather encouraging one another, all the more because you see the Day drawing near.

For if we wilfully persist in sin after receiving the knowledge of the truth, no sacrifice for sins remains: only a terrifying expectation of judgement and a fierce fire which will consume God's enemies. If a man disregards the Law of Moses, he is put to death without pity on the evidence of two or three witnesses. Think how much more severe a penalty that man will deserve who has trampled under foot the Son of God, profaned the blood of the covenant by which he was consecrated, and affronted God's gracious Spirit! For we know who it is that has said, 'Justice is mine:

King James Version

Lord. And again, The Lord shall judge his people.
31 *It is* a fearful thing to fall into the hands of
the living God. 32 But call to remembrance the
former days, in which, after ye were illuminated,
ye endured a great fight of afflictions; 33 Partly,
whilst ye were made a gazingstock both by reproaches and afflictions; and partly, whilst ye
became companions of them that were so used.
34 For ye had compassion of me in my bonds,
and took joyfully the spoiling of your goods,
knowing in yourselves that ye have in heaven a
better and an enduring substance. 35 Cast not
away therefore your confidence, which hath great
recompense of reward. 36 For ye have need of
patience, that, after ye have done the will of
God, ye might receive the promise. 37 For yet
a little while, and he that shall come will come,
and will not tarry. 38 Now the just shall live by
faith: but if *any man* draw back, my soul shall

Living Bible

"The Lord himself will handle these cases."
31 It is a fearful thing to fall into the hands
of the living God.

32 Don't ever forget those wonderful days
when you first learned about Christ. Remember
how you kept right on with the Lord even
though it meant terrible suffering. 33 Sometimes
you were laughed at and beaten, and sometimes
you watched and sympathized with others suffering the same things. 34 You suffered with
those thrown into jail, and you were actually
joyful when all you owned was taken from you,
knowing that better things were awaiting you in
heaven, things that would be yours forever.

35 Do not let this happy trust in the Lord
die away, no matter what happens. Remember
your reward! 36 You need to keep on patiently
doing God's will if you want him to do for you
all that he has promised. 37 His coming will not
be delayed much longer. 38 And those whose
faith has made them good in God's sight must
live by faith, trusting him in everything. Otherwise, if they shrink back, God will have no
pleasure in them.

Today's English Version

"The Lord will judge his people." 31 It is a terrible thing to fall into the hands of the living
God!

32 Remember how it was with you in the
past. In those days, after God's light had shone
on you, you suffered many things, yet were not
defeated by the struggle. 33 You were at times
publicly insulted and mistreated, and at other
times you were ready to join those who were
being treated in this way. 34 You shared the sufferings of prisoners, and when all your belongings were seized you endured your loss gladly,
because you knew that you still had for yourselves something much better, which would last
forever. 35 Do not lose your courage, then, because it brings with it a great reward. 36 You
need to be patient, in order to do the will of
God and receive what he promises. 37 For, as
the scripture says,

> "Just a little while longer,
> and he who is coming will come;
> he will not delay.
> 38 My righteous people, however, will believe
> and live;
> but if any of them turns back, I will not
> be pleased with him."

New International Version

Lord will judge his people." [m] 31 It is a dreadful
thing to fall into the hands of the living God.

32 Remember those earlier days after you had
received the light, when you stood your ground
in a great contest in the face of suffering.
33 Sometimes you were publicly exposed to insult and persecution; at other times you stood
side by side with those who were so treated.
34 You sympathized with those in prison and
joyfully accepted the confiscation of your property, because you knew that you yourselves had
better and lasting possessions.

35 So do not throw away your confidence; it
will be richly rewarded. 36 You need to persevere so that when you have done the will of
God, you will receive what he has promised.
37 For in just a very little while,

> "He who is coming will come and will not be
> late.
> 38 But my righteous one[n] will live by faith.
> And if he shrinks back,
> I will not be pleased with him." [o]

[m] Deut. 32:36; Psalm 135:14. [n] One early MS reads *But the righteous.* [o] Hab. 2:3,4.

Phillips Modern English

And, again:

The Lord shall judge his people.

Truly it is a terrible thing for a man who has done this to fall into the hands of the living God!

10.32 Recollect your former faith, and stand firm today!

You must never forget those past days when you had received the light and endured such a great and painful struggle. It was partly because everyone's eye was on you as you suffered harsh words and hard experiences, partly because you threw in your lot with those who suffered much the same. You sympathised with those who were put in prison and you were cheerful when your own goods were confiscated, for you knew that you had a much more solid and lasting treasure. Don't throw away your trust now—it carries with it a rich reward. Patient endurance is what you need if, after doing God's will, you are to receive what he has promised.

For yet a very little while,
He that cometh shall come, and shall not tarry.
But my righteous one shall live by faith;
And if he shrink back, my soul hath no pleasure in him.

Revised Standard Version

"The Lord will judge his people." 31 It is a fearful thing to fall into the hands of the living God.
32 But recall the former days when, after you
were enlightened, you endured a hard struggle
with sufferings, 33 sometimes being publicly exposed to abuse and affliction, and sometimes
being partners with those so treated. 34 For you
had compassion on the prisoners, and you joyfully accepted the plundering of your property,
since you knew that you yourselves had a better
possession and an abiding one. 35 Therefore do
not throw away your confidence, which has a
great reward. 36 For you have need of endurance, so that you may do the will of God and
receive what is promised.
37 "For yet a little while,
and the coming one shall come and shall not tarry;
38 but my righteous one shall live by faith,
and if he shrinks back,
my soul has no pleasure in him."

Jerusalem Bible

The Lord will judge his people. 31 It is a dreadful thing to fall into the hands of the living God.

Motives for perseverance

32 Remember all the sufferings that you had
to meet after you received the light, in earlier
days; 33 sometimes by being yourselves publicly
exposed to insults and violence, and sometimes
as associates of others who were treated in the
same way. 34 For you not only shared in the
sufferings of those who were in prison, but you
happily accepted being stripped of your belongings, knowing that you owned something that
was better and lasting. 35 Be as confident now,
then, since the reward is so great. 36 You will
need endurance to do God's will and gain what
he has promised.

37 *Only a little while now, a very little while,*
and the one that is coming will have come;
he will not delay.[l]
38 *The righteous man will live by faith,*
but if he draws back, my soul will take no pleasure in him.[m]

[*l*] Is. 26:20 (LXX). [*m*] Hab. 2:3-4 (LXX).

New English Bible

I will repay'; and again, 'The Lord will judge his people.' It is a terrible thing to fall into the hands of the living God.

Remember the days gone by, when, newly enlightened, you met the challenge of great sufferings and held firm. Some of you were abused and tormented to make a public show, while others stood loyally by those who were so treated. For indeed you shared the sufferings of the prisoners, and you cheerfully accepted the seizure of your possessions, knowing that you possessed something better and more lasting. Do not then throw away your confidence, for it carries a great reward. You need endurance, if you are to do God's will and win what he has promised. For 'soon, very soon' (in the words of Scripture), 'he who is to come will come; he will not delay; and by faith my righteous servant shall find life; but if a

King James Version

have no pleasure in him. 39 But we are not of them who draw back unto perdition; but of them that believe to the saving of the soul.

11 Now faith is the substance of things hoped for, the evidence of things not seen. 2 For by it the elders obtained a good report. 3 Through faith we understand that the worlds were framed by the word of God, so that things which are seen were not made of things which do appear. 4 By faith Abel offered unto God a more excellent sacrifice than Cain, by which he obtained witness that he was righteous, God testifying of his gifts: and by it he being dead yet speaketh. 5 By faith Enoch was translated that he should not see death; and was not found, because God had translated him: for before his translation he had this testimony, that he pleased

Living Bible

39 But we have never turned our backs on God and sealed our fate. No, our faith in him assures our souls' salvation.

11 What is faith? It is the confident assurance that something we want is going to happen. It is the certainty that what we hope for is waiting for us, even though we cannot see it up ahead. 2 Men of God in days of old were famous for their faith.

3 By faith—by believing God—we know that the world and the stars—in fact, all things—were made at God's command; and that they were all made from things that can't be seen.[a]

4 It was by faith that Abel obeyed God and brought an offering that pleased God more than Cain's offering did. God accepted Abel and proved it by accepting his gift; and though Abel is long dead, we can still learn lessons from him about trusting God.

5 Enoch trusted God too, and that is why God took him away to heaven without dying; suddenly he was gone because God took him. Before this happened God had said [b] how pleased

[a] Perhaps the reference is to atoms, electrons, etc.
[b] Implied.

Today's English Version

39 We are not people who turn back and are lost. Instead, we have faith and are saved.

Faith

11 To have faith is to be sure of the things we hope for, to be certain of the things we cannot see. 2 It was by their faith that the men of ancient times won God's approval.

3 It is by faith that we understand that the universe was created by God's word, so that what can be seen was made out of what cannot be seen.

4 It was faith that made Abel offer to God a better sacrifice than Cain's. Through his faith he won God's approval as a righteous man, because God himself approved his gifts. By means of his faith Abel still speaks, even though he is dead.

5 It was faith that kept Enoch from dying. Instead, he was taken up to God, and nobody could find him, because God had taken him up. The scripture says that before Enoch was taken

New International Version

39 But we are not of those who shrink back and are destroyed, but of those who believe and are saved.

By faith

11 Now faith is being sure of what we hope for and certain of what we do not see. 2 This is what the ancients were commended for.

3 By faith we understand that the universe was formed at God's command, so that what is seen was not made out of what was visible.

4 By faith Abel offered God a better sacrifice than Cain did. By faith he was commended as a righteous man, when God spoke well of his offerings. And by faith he still speaks, even though he is dead.

5 By faith Enoch was taken from this life, so that he did not experience death; he could not be found, because God had taken him away. For before he was taken, he was commended as one

Phillips Modern English

Surely we are not going to be men who cower back and are lost, but men who maintain their faith for the salvation of their souls!

Now faith means that we have full confidence in the things we hope for, it means being certain of things we cannot see. It was this faith that won their reputation for the saints of old. And it is only by faith that our minds accept as fact that the whole universe was formed by God's command—that the world which we can see has come into being through what is invisible.

11.4 *Faith is the distinctive mark of the saints of the old agreement*

ABEL

It was because of his faith that Abel made a better sacrifice to God than Cain, and he had evidence that God looked upon him as a righteous man, whose gifts he could accept. And though Cain killed him, yet by his faith he still speaks to us today.

ENOCH

It was because of his faith that Enoch was taken to the eternal world without experiencing death. He disappeared from this world because God had taken him, and before that happened

Revised Standard Version

39 But we are not of those who shrink back and are destroyed, but of those who have faith and keep their souls.

11 Now faith is the assurance of things hoped
for, the conviction of things not seen. 2 For
by it the men of old received divine approval.
3 By faith we understand that the world was
created by the word of God, so that what is seen
was made out of things which do not appear.
4 By faith Abel offered to God a more acceptable sacrifice than Cain, through which he
received approval as righteous, God bearing witness by accepting his gifts; he died, but through
his faith he is still speaking. 5 By faith Enoch
was taken up so that he should not see death;
and he was not found, because God had taken
him. Now before he was taken he was attested

Jerusalem Bible

39 You and I are not the sort of people who *draw back,* and are lost by it; we are the sort who keep *faithful* until our souls are saved.

The exemplary faith of our ancestors

11 Only faith can guarantee the blessings that
we hope for, or prove the existence of the
realities that at present remain unseen. 2 It was
for faith that our ancestors were commended.
3 It is by faith that we understand that the
world was created by one word from God, so
that no apparent cause can account for the
things we can see.
4 It was because of his faith that Abel offered
God a better sacrifice than Cain, and for that
he was declared to be righteous when *God* made
acknowledgment *of his offerings.* Though he is
dead, he still speaks by faith.
5 It was because of his faith that Enoch was
taken up and did not have to experience death:
he was not to be found because God had taken
him.[n] This was because before his assumption

[n] Gn. 5:24.

New English Bible

man shrinks back, I take no pleasure in him.' But we are not among those who shrink back and are lost; we have the faith to make life our own.

A call to faith

11 And what is faith? Faith gives substance[a] to our hopes, and makes us certain of realities we do not see.

It is for their faith that the men of old stand on record.

By faith we perceive that the universe was fashioned by the word of God, so that the visible came forth from the invisible.

By faith Abel offered a sacrifice greater than Cain's, and through faith his goodness was attested, for his offerings had God's approval; and through faith he continued to speak after his death.

By faith Enoch was carried away to another life without passing through death; he was not to be found, because God had taken him. For it is the testimony of Scripture that before he was

[a] *Or* assurance.

King James Version

God. 6 But without faith *it is* impossible to please *him:* for he that cometh to God must believe that he is, and *that* he is a rewarder of them that diligently seek him. 7 By faith Noah, being warned of God of things not seen as yet, moved with fear, prepared an ark to the saving of his house; by the which he condemned the world, and became heir of the righteousness which is by faith. 8 By faith Abraham, when he was called to go out into a place which he should after receive for an inheritance, obeyed; and he went out, not knowing whither he went. 9 By faith he sojourned in the land of promise, as *in* a strange country, dwelling in tabernacles with Isaac and Jacob, the heirs with him of the same promise: 10 For he looked for a city which hath foundations, whose builder and maker *is* God. 11 Through faith also Sarah herself received strength to conceive seed, and was delivered of a child when she was past age, because she judged him faithful who had promised. 12 Therefore sprang there even of one, and him as good

Living Bible

he was with Enoch. 6 You can never please God without faith, without depending on him. Anyone who wants to come to God must believe that there is a God and that he rewards those who sincerely look for him.

7 Noah was another who trusted God. When he heard God's warning about the future, Noah believed him even though there was then no sign of a flood, and wasting no time, he built the ark and saved his family. Noah's belief in God was in direct contrast to the sin and disbelief of the rest of the world—which refused to obey—and because of his faith he became one of those whom God has accepted.

8 Abraham trusted God, and when God told him to leave home and go far away to another land which he promised to give him, Abraham obeyed. Away he went, not even knowing where he was going. 9And even when he reached God's promised land, he lived in tents like a mere visitor, as did Isaac and Jacob, to whom God gave the same promise. 10Abraham did this because he was confidently waiting for God to bring him to that strong heavenly city whose designer and builder is God.

11 Sarah, too, had faith, and because of this she was able to become a mother in spite of her old age, for she realized that God, who gave her his promise, would certainly do what he said. 12And so a whole nation came from Abraham, who was too old to have even one child—a na-

Today's English Version

up he had pleased God. 6 No man can please God without faith. For whoever comes to God must have faith that God exists and rewards those who seek him.

7 It was faith that made Noah hear God's warnings about things in the future that he could not see. He obeyed God, and built an ark in which he and his family were saved. In this way he condemned the world, and received from God the righteousness that comes by faith.

8 It was faith that made Abraham obey when God called him, and go out to a country which God had promised to give him. He left his own country without knowing where he was going. 9 By faith he lived in the country that God had promised him, as though he were a foreigner. He lived in tents with Isaac and Jacob, who received the same promise from God. 10 For Abraham was waiting for the city which God has designed and built, the city with permanent foundations.

11 It was faith that made Abraham able to become a father even though he was too old and Sarah herself was unable to have children. He trusted God to keep his promise. 12 Though he was practically dead, from this one man

New International Version

who pleased God. 6And without faith it is impossible to please God, because anyone who comes to him must believe that he exists and that he rewards those who earnestly seek him.

7 By faith Noah, when warned about things not yet seen, in holy fear built an ark to save his family. By his faith he condemned the world and became heir of the righteousness that comes by faith.

8 By faith Abraham, when called to go to a place he would later receive as his possession, obeyed and went, even though he did not know where he was going. 9 By faith he made his home in the promised land like a stranger in a foreign country; he lived in tents, as did Isaac and Jacob, who were heirs with him of the same promise. 10 For he was looking forward to the city with foundations, whose architect and builder is God.

11 By faith Abraham, even though he was past age—and Sarah herself was barren—was enabled to become a father because he[p] considered him faithful who had made the promise. 12And so from this one man, and he as good as dead, came descendants as numerous as

[*p*] Or *By faith even Sarah, who was past age, was enabled to bear children because she.*

Phillips Modern English

his reputation was that "he pleased God". And without faith it is impossible to please him. The man who approaches God must have faith in two things, first that God exists and secondly that God rewards those who search for him.

NOAH

It was through his faith that Noah, on receiving God's warning of impending disaster with reverence, constructed an ark to save his household. This action of faith condemned the unbelief of the rest of the world, and won for Noah the righteousness before God which follows such a faith.

ABRAHAM

It was by faith that Abraham obeyed the summons to go out to a place which he would eventually possess, and he set out in complete ignorance of his destination. It was faith that kept him journeying like a foreigner through the land of promise, with no more home than the tents which he shared with Isaac and Jacob, co-heirs with him of the promise. For Abraham's eyes were looking forward to that city with solid foundations of which God himself is both architect and builder.

SARAH

It was by faith that even Sarah gained the physical vitality to conceive despite her great age, and she gave birth to a child when far beyond the normal years of child-bearing. She did this because she believed that the One who had given the promise was utterly trustworthy. So it happened that from one man, who as a poten-

Revised Standard Version

as having pleased God. 6 And without faith it is
impossible to please him. For whoever would
draw near to God must believe that he exists
and that he rewards those who seek him. 7 By
faith Noah, being warned by God concerning
events as yet unseen, took heed and constructed
an ark for the saving of his household; by this
he condemned the world and became an heir of
the righteousness which comes by faith.
8 By faith Abraham obeyed when he was
called to go out to a place which he was to receive as an inheritance; and he went out, not
knowing where he was to go. 9 By faith he
sojourned in the land of promise, as in a foreign
land, living in tents with Isaac and Jacob, heirs
with him of the same promise. 10 For he looked
forward to the city which has foundations, whose
builder and maker is God. 11 By faith Sarah
herself received power to conceive, even when
she was past the age, since she considered him
faithful who had promised. 12 Therefore from
one man, and him as good as dead, were born

Jerusalem Bible

it is attested that *he had pleased God.* 6 Now
it is impossible to please God without faith,
since anyone who comes to him must believe that
he exists and rewards those who try to find him.
7 It was through his faith that Noah, when he
had been warned by God of something that had
never been seen before, felt a holy fear and built
an ark to save his family. By his faith the world
was convicted, and he was able to claim the
righteousness which is the reward of faith.
8 It was by faith that Abraham obeyed the
call to *set out* for a country that was the inheritance given to him and his descendants, and that
he set out without knowing where he was going.
9 By faith he arrived, *as a foreigner,* in the Promised Land, and lived there as if in a strange
country, with Isaac and Jacob, who were heirs
with him of the same promise. 10 They lived
there in tents while he looked forward to a city
founded, designed and built by God.
11 It was equally by faith that Sarah, in spite
of being past the age, was made able to conceive,
because she believed that he who had made the
promise would be faithful to it. 12 Because of
this, there came from one man, and one who was

New English Bible

taken he had pleased God, and without faith it is impossible to please him; for anyone who comes to God must believe that he exists and that he rewards those who search for him.

By faith Noah, divinely warned about the unseen future, took good heed and built an ark to save his household. Through his faith he put the whole world in the wrong, and made good his own claim to the righteousness which comes of faith.

By faith Abraham obeyed the call to go out to a land destined for himself and his heirs, and left home without knowing where he was to go. By faith he settled as an alien in the land promised him, living in tents, as did Isaac and Jacob, who were heirs to the same promise. For he was looking forward to the city with firm foundations, whose architect and builder is God.

By faith even Sarah herself received strength to conceive, though she was past the age, because she judged that he who had promised would keep faith; and therefore from one man, and one as good as dead, there sprang descend-

King James Version

as dead, *so many* as the stars of the sky in multitude, and as the sand which is by the sea shore innumerable. 13 These all died in faith, not having received the promises, but having seen them afar off, and were persuaded of *them,* and embraced *them,* and confessed that they were strangers and pilgrims on the earth. 14 For they that say such things declare plainly that they seek a country. 15 And truly, if they had been mindful of that *country* from whence they came out, they might have had opportunity to have returned. 16 But now they desire a better *country,* that is, a heavenly: wherefore God is not ashamed to be called their God: for he hath prepared for them a city. 17 By faith Abraham, when he was tried, offered up Isaac: and he that had received the promises offered up his only begotten *son,* 18 Of whom it was said, That in Isaac shall thy seed be called: 19 Accounting that God *was* able to raise *him* up, even from the

Living Bible

tion with so many millions of people that, like the stars of the sky and the sand on the ocean shores, there is no way to count them.

13 These men of faith I have mentioned died without ever receiving all that God had promised them; but they saw it all awaiting them on ahead and were glad, for they agreed that this earth was not their real home but that they were just strangers visiting down here. 14 And quite obviously when they talked like that, they were looking forward to their real home in heaven.

15 If they had wanted to, they could have gone back to the good things of this world. 16 But they didn't want to. They were living for heaven. And now God is not ashamed to be called their God, for he has made a heavenly city for them.

17 While God was testing him, Abraham still trusted in God and his promises, and so he offered up his son Isaac, and was ready to slay him on the altar of sacrifice; 18 yes, to slay even Isaac, through whom God had promised to give Abraham a whole nation of descendants! 19 He believed that if Isaac died God would bring him back to life again; and that is just about what happened, for as far as Abraham was concerned,

Today's English Version

there came as many descendants as there are stars in the sky, as many as the numberless grains of sand on the seashore.

13 It was in faith that all these persons died. They did not receive the things God had promised, but from a long way off they saw and welcomed them, and admitted openly that they were foreigners and refugees on earth. 14 Those who say such things make it clear that they are looking for a country of their own. 15 They did not think back to the country they had left; if they had, they would have had the chance to return. 16 Instead, it was a better country they longed for, the heavenly country. And so God is not ashamed to have them call him their God, because he has prepared a city for them.

17 It was faith that made Abraham offer his son Isaac as a sacrifice, when God put Abraham to the test. Abraham was the one to whom God had made the promise, yet he was ready to offer his only son as a sacrifice. 18 God had said to him, "It is through Isaac that you will have descendants." 19 Abraham reckoned that God was able to raise Isaac back from death—and, so to

New International Version

the stars in the sky and as countless as the sand of the seashore.

13 All these people were still living by faith when they died. They did not receive the things promised; they only saw them and welcomed them from a distance. And they admitted that they were foreigners and strangers on earth. 14 People who say such things show that they are looking for a country of their own. 15 If they had been thinking of the country they had left, they would have had opportunity to return. 16 Instead, they were longing for a better country—a heavenly one. Therefore God is not ashamed to be called their God, for he has prepared a city for them.

17 By faith Abraham, when God tested him, offered Isaac as a sacrifice. He who had received the promises was about to sacrifice his one and only son, 18 even though God had said to him, "Through Isaac shall your promised offspring[q] come."[r] 19 Abraham reasoned that God

[q] Greek *seed.* [r] Gen. 21:12.

Phillips Modern English

tial father was already considered dead, there arose a race "as numerous as the stars", as "countless as the sands of the sea-shore".

11.13 All the heroes of faith looked forward to their true country

All these whom we have mentioned maintained their faith but died without actually receiving God's promises, though they had seen them in the distance, had hailed them as true. They freely admitted that they lived on this earth as exiles and foreigners. Men who say that mean, of course, that their eyes are fixed upon their true home-land. If they had meant the particular country they had left behind, they had ample opportunity to return. No, the fact is that they longed for a better country altogether, nothing less than a heavenly one. And because of this faith of theirs, God is not ashamed to be called their God for he has prepared for them a city.

11.17 Abraham's faith once more

It was by faith that Abraham, when put to the test, offered Isaac for sacrifice. Yes, the man who had heard God's promises was prepared to offer up his only son of whom it had been said "In Isaac shall thy seed be called." He believed that God could raise his son up, even if he were

Revised Standard Version

descendants as many as the stars of heaven and as the innumerable grains of sand by the seashore.
13 These all died in faith, not having received what was promised, but having seen it and greeted it from afar, and having acknowledged that they were strangers and exiles on the earth.
14 For people who speak thus make it clear
that they are seeking a homeland. 15 If they
had been thinking of that land from which they had gone out, they would have had opportunity
to return. 16 But as it is, they desire a better
country, that is, a heavenly one. Therefore God is not ashamed to be called their God, for he has prepared for them a city.
17 By faith Abraham, when he was tested, offered up Isaac, and he who had received the promises was ready to offer up his only son,
18 of whom it was said, "Through Isaac shall
your descendants be named." 19 He considered
that God was able to raise men even from the

Jerusalem Bible

already as good as dead himself, *more descendants than could be counted, as many as the stars of heaven or the grains of sand on the seashore.*[o]
13 All these died in faith, before receiving any of the things that had been promised, but they saw them in the far distance and welcomed them, recognizing that they were only *strangers and nomads on earth.*
14 People who use such
terms about themselves make it quite plain that they are in search of their real homeland.
15 They can hardly have meant the country they came from, since they had the opportunity to
go back to it; 16 but in fact they were longing
for a better homeland, their heavenly homeland. That is why God is not ashamed to be called their God, since he has founded the city for them.
17 It was by faith that Abraham, *when put to the test, offered up Isaac.*[p] He offered to sacrifice his only son even though the promises had
been made to him 18 and he had been told: *It
is through Isaac that your name will be carried
on.*[q] 19 He was confident that God had the power

[o] Gn. 22:17, also quoted in Ex. 32. [p] Gn. 22:1-14. [q] Gn. 21:12.

New English Bible

ants numerous as the stars or as the countless grains of sand on the sea-shore.

All these persons died in faith. They were not yet in possession of the things promised, but had seen them far ahead and hailed them, and confessed themselves no more than strangers or passing travellers on earth. Those who use such language show plainly that they are looking for a country of their own. If their hearts had been in the country they had left, they could have found opportunity to return. Instead, we find them longing for a better country—I mean, the heavenly one. That is why God is not ashamed to be called their God; for he has a city ready for them.

By faith Abraham, when the test came, offered up Isaac: he had received the promises, and yet he was on the point of offering his only son, of whom he had been told, 'Through the line of Isaac your descendants shall be traced.'[a] For he reckoned that God had power even to raise from

[a] *Or* God's call shall be for your descendants in the line of Isaac.

King James Version

dead; from whence also he received him in a figure. 20 By faith Isaac blessed Jacob and Esau concerning things to come. 21 By faith Jacob, when he was a dying, blessed both the sons of Joseph; and worshipped, *leaning* upon the top of his staff. 22 By faith Joseph, when he died, made mention of the departing of the children of Israel; and gave commandment concerning his bones. 23 By faith Moses, when he was born, was hid three months of his parents, because they saw *he was* a proper child; and they were not afraid of the king's commandment. 24 By faith Moses, when he was come to years, refused to be called the son of Pharaoh's daughter; 25 Choosing rather to suffer affliction with the people of God, than to enjoy the pleasures of sin for a season; 26 Esteeming the reproach of Christ greater riches than the treasures in Egypt: for he had respect unto the recompense of the reward. 27 By faith he forsook Egypt, not fearing the wrath of the king: for he endured, as seeing him who is invisible. 28 Through faith he kept

Living Bible

Isaac was doomed to death, but he came back again alive! 20 It was by faith that Isaac knew God would give future blessings to his two sons, Jacob and Esau.

21 By faith Jacob, when he was old and dying, blessed each of Joseph's two sons as he stood and prayed, leaning on the top of his cane.

22 And it was by faith that Joseph, as he neared the end of his life, confidently spoke of God bringing the people of Israel out of Egypt; and he was so sure of it that he made them promise to carry his bones with them when they left!

23 Moses' parents had faith too. When they saw that God had given them an unusual child, they trusted that God would save him from the death the king commanded, and they hid him for three months, and were not afraid.

24, 25 It was by faith that Moses, when he grew up, refused to be treated as the grandson of the king, but chose to share ill-treatment with God's people instead of enjoying the fleeting pleasures of sin. 26 He thought that it was better to suffer for the promised Christ than to own all the treasures of Egypt, for he was looking forward to the great reward that God would give him. 27 And it was because he trusted God that he left the land of Egypt and wasn't afraid of the king's anger. Moses kept right on going; it seemed as though he could see God right there with him. 28 And it was because he be-

Today's English Version

speak, Abraham did receive Isaac back from death.

20 It was faith that made Isaac promise blessings for the future to Jacob and Esau.

21 It was faith that made Jacob bless each of the sons of Joseph just before he died; he leaned on the top of his walking stick and worshiped God.

22 It was faith that made Joseph, when he was about to die, speak of the departure of the Israelites from Egypt, and leave instructions about what should be done with his body.

23 It was faith that made the parents of Moses hide him for three months after he was born. They saw that he was a beautiful child, and they were not afraid to disobey the king's order.

24 It was faith that made Moses, when he was grown, refuse to be called the son of Pharaoh's daughter. 25 He preferred to suffer with God's people rather than to enjoy sin for a little while. 26 He reckoned that to suffer scorn for the Messiah was worth far more than all the treasures of Egypt; because he kept his eyes on the future reward.

27 It was faith that made Moses leave Egypt without being afraid of the king's anger; he would not turn back, as though he saw the invisible God. 28 It was faith that made him

New International Version

could raise the dead, and figuratively speaking, he did receive Isaac back from death.

20 By faith Isaac blessed Jacob and Esau in regard to their future.

21 By faith Jacob, when he was dying, blessed each of Joseph's sons, and worshiped as he leaned on the top of his staff.

22 By faith Joseph, when his end was near, spoke about the exodus of the Israelites from Egypt and gave instructions about his bones.

23 By faith Moses' parents hid him for three months after he was born, because they saw he was no ordinary child, and they were not afraid of the king's edict.

24 By faith Moses, when he had grown up, refused to be known as the son of Pharaoh's daughter. 25 He chose to be mistreated along with the people of God rather than to enjoy the pleasures of sin for a short time. 26 He regarded disgrace for the sake of Christ as of greater value than the treasures of Egypt, because he was looking ahead to his reward. 27 By faith he left Egypt, not fearing the king's anger; he persevered because he saw him who is invisible. 28 By faith he kept the Passover and the sprin-

Phillips Modern English

dead. And he did, in a manner of speaking, receive him back from death.

11.20 The faith of Isaac, Jacob and Joseph

It was by faith that Isaac gave Jacob and Esau his blessing, for his words dealt with what should happen in the future. It was by faith that the dying Jacob blessed each of Joseph's sons as he bowed in prayer over his staff. It was by faith that Joseph on his death-bed spoke of the exodus of the Israelites, and gave orders about the disposal of his own mortal remains.

11.23 Moses

It was by faith that Moses was hidden by his parents for three months after his birth, for they saw that he was a beautiful child and refused to be daunted by the king's decree. It was also by faith that Moses himself when grown up refused to be called the son of Pharaoh's daughter. He preferred sharing the burden of God's people to enjoying the temporary advantages of sin. He considered the "reproach of Christ" more precious than all the wealth of Egypt, for he looked steadily at the ultimate reward.

By faith he left Egypt; he defied the king's anger with the strength that came from obedience to the invisible king.

By faith Moses kept the first Passover and

Revised Standard Version

dead; hence, figuratively speaking, he did receive
him back. 20 By faith Isaac invoked future blessings on Jacob and Esau. 21 By faith Jacob, when
dying, blessed each of the sons of Joseph, bowing in worship over the head of his staff. 22 By
faith Joseph, at the end of his life, made mention of the exodus of the Israelites and gave directions concerning his burial.[x]
23 By faith Moses, when he was born, was
hid for three months by his parents, because
they saw that the child was beautiful; and they
were not afraid of the king's edict. 24 By faith
Moses, when he was grown up, refused to be
called the son of Pharaoh's daughter, 25 choosing rather to share ill-treatment with the people
of God than to enjoy the fleeting pleasures of
sin. 26 He considered abuse suffered for the
Christ greater wealth than the treasures of
Egypt, for he looked to the reward. 27 By faith
he left Egypt, not being afraid of the anger of
the king; for he endured as seeing him who is
invisible. 28 By faith he kept the Passover and

[x] Greek *bones*.

Jerusalem Bible

even to raise the dead; and so, figuratively speaking, he was given back Isaac from the dead.
20 It was by faith that this same Isaac gave
his blessing to Jacob and Esau for the still distant future. 21 By faith Jacob, when he was dying, blessed each of Joseph's sons, *leaning on*
the end of his stick as though bowing to pray.[r]
22 It was by faith that, when he was about to
die, Joseph recalled the Exodus of the Israelites
and made the arrangements for his own burial.
23 It was by faith that Moses, when he was
born, *was hidden by his parents for three*
months; they defied the royal edict when they
saw he was such a *fine* child. 24 It was by faith
that, *when he grew to manhood,* Moses refused
to be known as the son of Pharaoh's daughter
25 and chose to be ill-treated in company with
God's people rather than to enjoy for a time the
pleasures of sin. 26 He considered that the insults
offered to the Anointed were something more
precious than all the treasures of Egypt, because
he had his eyes fixed on the reward. 27 It was by
faith that he left Egypt and was not afraid of the
king's anger; he held to his purpose like a man
who could see the Invisible. 28 It was by faith

[r] Gn. 47:31.

New English Bible

the dead—and from the dead, he did, in a sense, receive him back.

By faith Isaac blessed Jacob and Esau and spoke of things to come. By faith Jacob, as he was dying, blessed each of Joseph's sons, and worshipped God, leaning on the top of his staff. By faith Joseph, at the end of his life, spoke of the departure of Israel from Egypt, and instructed them what to do with his bones.

By faith, when Moses was born, his parents hid him for three months, because they saw what a fine child he was; they were not afraid of the king's edict. By faith Moses, when he grew up, refused to be called the son of Pharaoh's daughter, preferring to suffer hardship with the people of God rather than enjoy the transient pleasures of sin. He considered the stigma that rests on God's Anointed greater wealth than the treasures of Egypt, for his eyes were fixed upon the coming day of recompense. By faith he left Egypt, and not because he feared the king's anger; for he was resolute, as one who saw the invisible God.

By faith he celebrated the Passover and sprin-

King James Version

the passover, and the sprinkling of blood, lest
he that destroyed the firstborn should touch
them. 29 By faith they passed through the Red
sea as by dry *land:* which the Egyptians assay-
ing to do were drowned. 30 By faith the walls of
Jericho fell down, after they were compassed
about seven days. 31 By faith the harlot Rahab
perished not with them that believed not, when
she had received the spies with peace. 32And
what shall I more say? for the time would fail
me to tell of Gideon, and *of* Barak, and *of* Samson, and *of* Jephthah; *of* David also, and Samuel,
and *of* the prophets: 33 Who through faith subdued kingdoms, wrought righteousness, obtained
promises, stopped the mouths of lions,
34 Quenched the violence of fire, escaped the
edge of the sword, out of weakness were made
strong, waxed valiant in fight, turned to flight
the armies of the aliens. 35 Women received their

Living Bible

lieved God would save his people that he commanded them to kill a lamb as God had told
them to and sprinkle the blood on the door-
posts of their homes, so that God's terrible
Angel of Death could not touch the oldest child
in those homes, as he did among the Egyptians.
29 The people of Israel trusted God and went
right through the Red Sea as though they were
on dry ground. But when the Egyptians chasing
them tried it, they all were drowned.
30 It was faith that brought the walls of
Jericho tumbling down after the people of Israel
had walked around them seven days, as God had
commanded them. 31 By faith—because she believed in God and his power—Rahab the harlot
did not die with all the others in her city when
they refused to obey God, for she gave a friendly
welcome to the spies.
32 Well, how much more do I need to say?
It would take too long to recount the stories
of the faith of Gideon and Barak and Samson
and Jephthah and David and Samuel and all the
other prophets. 33 These people all trusted God
and as a result won battles, overthrew kingdoms,
ruled their people well, and received what God
had promised them; they were kept from harm
in a den of lions, 34 and in a fiery furnace. Some,
through their faith, escaped death by the sword.
Some were made strong again after they had
been weak or sick. Others were given great
power in battle; they made whole armies turn
and run away. 35And some women, through

Today's English Version

establish the Passover and order the blood
sprinkled on the doors, so that the Angel of
Death would not kill the firstborn sons of the
Israelites.
29 It was faith that enabled the Israelites to
cross the Red Sea as if on dry land; when the
Egyptians tried to do it, the water swallowed
them up.
30 It was faith that made the walls of Jericho
fall down, after the Israelites had marched
around them for seven days. 31 It was faith that
kept the harlot Rahab from being killed with
those who disobeyed God, because she gave the
spies a friendly welcome.
32 Should I go on? There isn't enough time
for me to speak of Gideon, Barak, Samson,
Jephthah, David, Samuel, and the prophets.
33 Through faith they fought whole countries
and won. They did what was right and received
what God had promised. They shut the mouths
of lions, 34 put out fierce fires, escaped being
killed by the sword. They were weak but became strong; they were mighty in battle and
defeated the armies of foreigners. 35 Through

New International Version

kling of blood, so that the destroyer of the first-
born would not touch the firstborn of Israel.
29 By faith the people passed through the
Red Sea[s] as on dry land; but when the Egyptians
tried to do so, they were drowned.
30 By faith the walls of Jericho fell, after the
people had marched around them for seven days.
31 By faith the prostitute Rahab, because she
welcomed the spies, was not killed with those
who were disobedient.[t]
32 And what more shall I say? I do not have
time to tell about Gideon, Barak, Samson,
Jephthah, David, Samuel and the prophets, 33 who
by faith conquered kingdoms, administered justice, and gained what was promised; who shut
the mouths of lions, 34 quenched the fury of
the flames, and escaped the edge of the sword;
whose weakness was turned to strength; and
who became powerful in battle and routed foreign armies. 35 Women received back their dead,

[s] That is, Sea of Reeds. [t] Or *unbelieving.*

Phillips Modern English

made the blood-sprinkling, so that the angel of death which killed the first-born should not touch those of his people.

By faith the people walked through the Red Sea as though it were dry land, and the Egyptians who tried to do the same thing were drowned.

11.30 *Rahab*

It was by faith that the walls of Jericho collapsed, for the people had obeyed God's command to encircle them for seven days. It was because of her faith that Rahab the prostitute did not share the fate of the disobedient, for she welcomed the Israelites sent out to reconnoitre.

11.32 *The Old Testament is full of examples of faith*

And what other examples shall I give? There is not time to continue by telling the stories of Gideon, Barak, Samson and Jeptha; of David, Samuel and the prophets. Through their faith these men conquered kingdoms, ruled in justice and proved the truth of God's promises. They shut the mouths of lions, they quenched the furious blaze of fire, they escaped death by the sword. From being weaklings they became strong men and mighty warriors; they routed whole armies of foreigners. Women received

Revised Standard Version

sprinkled the blood, so that the Destroyer of
the first-born might not touch them.
29 By faith the people crossed the Red Sea as
if on dry land; but the Egyptians, when they attempted to do the same, were drowned. 30 By
faith the walls of Jericho fell down after they
had been encircled for seven days. 31 By faith
Rahab the harlot did not perish with those who
were disobedient, because she had given friendly
welcome to the spies.
32 And what more shall I say? For time
would fail me to tell of Gideon, Barak, Samson, Jephthah, of David and Samuel and the
prophets—33 who through faith conquered kingdoms, enforced justice, received promises,
stopped the mouths of lions, 34 quenched raging fire, escaped the edge of the sword, won
strength out of weakness, became mighty in war,
put foreign armies to flight. 35 Women received

Jerusalem Bible

that he kept *the Passover* and sprinkled *the
blood* to prevent *the Destroyer* from touching
any of the first-born sons of Israel. 29 It was by
faith they crossed the Red Sea as easily as dry
land, while the Egyptians, trying to do the same,
were drowned.
30 It was through faith that the walls of
Jericho fell down when the people had been
around them for seven days. 31 It was by faith
that Rahab the prostitute welcomed the spies
and so was not killed with the unbelievers.
32 Is there any need to say more? There is
not time for me to give an account of Gideon,
Barak, Samson, Jephthah, or of David, Samuel
and the prophets. 33 These were men who
through faith conquered kingdoms, did what is
right and earned the promises. They could keep
a lion's mouth shut, 34 put out blazing fires and
emerge unscathed from battle. They were weak
people who were given strength, to be brave in
war and drive back foreign invaders. 35 Some

New English Bible

kled the blood, so that the destroying angel might not touch the first-born of Israel. By faith they crossed the Red Sea as though it were dry land, whereas the Egyptians, when they attempted the crossing, were drowned.

By faith the walls of Jericho fell down after they had been encircled on seven successive days. By faith the prostitute Rahab escaped the doom of the unbelievers, because she had given the spies a kindly welcome.

Need I say more? Time is too short for me to tell the stories of Gideon, Barak, Samson, and Jephthah, of David and Samuel and the prophets. Through faith they overthrew kingdoms, established justice, saw God's promises fulfilled. They muzzled ravening lions, quenched the fury of fire, escaped death by the sword. Their weakness was turned to strength, they grew powerful in war, they put foreign armies to rout. Women

King James Version

dead raised to life again: and others were tortured, not accepting deliverance; that they might
obtain a better resurrection: 36And others had
trial of *cruel* mockings and scourgings, yea,
moreover of bonds and imprisonment: 37 They
were stoned, they were sawn asunder, were
tempted, were slain with the sword: they wandered about in sheepskins and goatskins; being
destitute, afflicted, tormented; 38 Of whom the
world was not worthy: they wandered in deserts,
and *in* mountains, and *in* dens and caves of the
earth. 39And these all, having obtained a good
report through faith, received not the promise:
40 God having provided some better thing for
us, that they without us should not be made
perfect.

12 Wherefore, seeing we also are compassed
about with so great a cloud of witnesses, let
us lay aside every weight, and the sin which doth
so easily beset *us,* and let us run with patience
the race that is set before us, 2 Looking unto

Living Bible

faith, received their loved ones back again from
death. But others trusted God and were beaten
to death, preferring to die rather than turn from
God and be free—trusting that they would rise
to a better life afterwards.
36 Some were laughed at and their backs cut
open with whips, and others were chained in
dungeons. 37, 38 Some died by stoning and some
by being sawed in two; others were promised
freedom if they would renounce their faith, then
were killed with the sword. Some went about in
skins of sheep and goats, wandering over deserts
and mountains, hiding in dens and caves. They
were hungry and sick and ill-treated—too good
for this world. 39And these men of faith, though
they trusted God and won his approval, none
of them received all that God had promised
them; 40 for God wanted them to wait and share
the even better rewards that were prepared for
us.

12 Since we have such a huge crowd of men
of faith watching us from the grandstands,
let us strip off anything that slows us down or
holds us back, and especially those sins that
wrap themselves so tightly around our feet and
trip us up; and let us run with patience the
particular race that God has set before us.
2 Keep your eyes on Jesus, our leader and in-

Today's English Version

faith women received their dead raised back to
life.
Others, refusing to accept freedom, died under
torture in order to be raised to a better life.
36 Some were mocked and whipped, and others
were tied up and put in prison. 37 They were
stoned, they were sawn in two, they were killed
with the sword. They went around clothed in
skins of sheep or goats, poor,. persecuted, and
mistreated. 38 The world was not good enough
for them! They wandered like refugees in the
deserts and hills, living in caves and holes in the
ground.
39 What a record all of these have won by
their faith! Yet they did not receive what God
had promised, 40 because God had decided on
an even better plan for us. His purpose was that
they would be made perfect only with us.

God our Father

12 As for us, we have this large crowd of
witnesses around us. Let us rid ourselves,
then, of everything that gets in the way, and the
sin which holds on to us so tightly, and let us
run with determination the race that lies before
us. 2 Let us keep our eyes fixed on Jesus, on

New International Version

raised to life again. Others were tortured and
refused to be released, so that they might gain
a better resurrection. 36 Some faced jeers and
flogging, while still others were chained and put
in prison. 37 They were stoned;[u] they were sawed
in two; they were put to death by the sword.
They went about in sheepskins and goatskins,
destitute, persecuted and mistreated—38 the
world was not worthy of them. They wandered
in deserts and mountains, and in caves and holes
in the ground.
39 These were all commended for their faith,
yet none of them received what had been promised. 40 God had planned something better for
us so that only together with us would they be
made perfect.

God disciplines his sons

12 Therefore, since we are surrounded by
such a great cloud of witnesses, let us
throw off everything that hinders and the sin
that so easily entangles, and let us run with
perseverance the race marked out for us. 2 Let

[u] Some early MSS add *they were put to the test.*

Phillips Modern English

their dead raised to life again, while others were tortured to death and refused to be ransomed, because they wanted a more honourable resurrection. Others were exposed to the test of public mockery and flogging, and to being left bound in prison. They were killed by stoning, by being sawn in two; they were murdered by the sword. They went about with nothing but sheepskins or goatskins to cover them. They lost everything and yet were spurned and ill-treated by a world too evil to see their worth. They lived as vagrants in the desert, on the mountains, or in caves or holes in the ground.

All these won a glowing testimony to their faith, but they did not then and there receive the fulfilment of the promise. God had something better planned for our day, and it was not his plan that they should reach perfection without us.

12.1 We should consider these examples and Christ the perfect example

Surrounded then as we are by these serried ranks of witnesses, let us strip off everything that hinders us, as well as the sin which dogs our feet, and let us run the race that we have to run with patience, our eyes fixed on Jesus

Revised Standard Version

their dead by resurrection. Some were tortured,
refusing to accept release, that they might rise
again to a better life. 36 Others suffered mocking and scourging, and even chains and imprisonment. 37 They were stoned, they were sawn
in two,[y] they were killed with the sword; they
went about in skins of sheep and goats, destitute, afflicted, ill-treated—38 of whom the world
was not worthy—wandering over deserts and
mountains, and in dens and caves of the earth.
39 And all these, though well attested by
their faith, did not receive what was promised,
40 since God had foreseen something better for
us, that apart from us they should not be made
perfect.

12 Therefore, since we are surrounded by so great a cloud of witnesses, let us also lay aside every weight, and sin which clings so closely, and let us run with perseverance the
race that is set before us, 2 looking to Jesus the

[y] Other manuscripts add *they were tempted.*

Jerusalem Bible

came back to their wives from the dead, by resurrection; and others submitted to torture, refusing release so that they would rise again to a
better life. 36 Some had to bear being pilloried
and flogged, or even chained up in prison.
37 They were stoned, or sawn in half,[s] or beheaded; they were homeless, and dressed in the skins of sheep and goats; they were penniless and were given nothing but ill-treatment. 38 They
were too good for the world and they went out to live in deserts and mountains and in caves
and ravines. 39 These are all heroes of faith, but
they did not receive what was promised, 40 since
God had made provision for us to have something better, and they were not to reach perfection except with us.

The example of Jesus Christ

12 With so many witnesses in a great cloud on every side of us, we too, then, should throw off everything that hinders us, especially the sin that clings so easily, and keep running
steadily in the race we have started. 2 Let us not

[s] Some apocryphal books say that this was how King Manasseh had Isaiah executed.

New English Bible

received back their dead raised to life. Others were tortured to death, disdaining release, to win a better resurrection. Others, again, had to face jeers and flogging, even fetters and prison bars. They were stoned,[a] they were sawn in two, they were put to the sword, they went about dressed in skins of sheep or goats, in poverty, distress, and misery. They were too good for a world like this. They were refugees in deserts and on the hills, hiding in caves and holes in the ground. These also, one and all, are commemorated for their faith; and yet they did not enter upon the promised inheritance, because, with us in mind, God had made a better plan, that only in company with us should they reach their perfection.

12 And what of ourselves? With all these witnesses to faith around us like a cloud, we must throw off every encumbrance, every sin to which we cling,[b] and run with resolution the race for which we are entered, our eyes fixed on

[a] *Some witnesses insert* they were put to the question. [b] *Or* every clinging sin; *one witness reads* the sin which all too readily distracts us.

King James Version

Jesus the author and finisher of *our* faith; who
for the joy that was set before him endured the
cross, despising the shame, and is set down at
the right hand of the throne of God. 3 For consider him that endured such contradiction of
sinners against himself, lest ye be wearied and
faint in your minds. 4 Ye have not yet resisted
unto blood, striving against sin. 5 And ye have
forgotten the exhortation which speaketh unto
you as unto children, My son, despise not thou
the chastening of the Lord, nor faint when thou
art rebuked of him: 6 For whom the Lord loveth
he chasteneth, and scourgeth every son whom he
receiveth. 7 If ye endure chastening, God deal-
eth with you as with sons; for what son is
he whom the father chasteneth not? 8 But if
ye be without chastisement, whereof all are partakers, then are ye bastards, and not sons. 9 Furthermore, we have had fathers of our flesh which
corrected *us*, and we gave *them* reverence: shall
we not much rather be in subjection unto the

Living Bible

structor. He was willing to die a shameful death
on the cross because of the joy he knew would
be his afterwards; and now he sits in the place
of honor by the throne of God. 3 If you want to
keep from becoming fainthearted and weary,
think about his patience as sinful men did such
terrible things to him. 4 After all, you have never
yet struggled against sin and temptation until
you sweat great drops of blood.

5 And have you quite forgotten the encouraging words God spoke to you, his child? He
said, "My son, don't be angry when the Lord
punishes you. Don't be discouraged when he has
to show you where you are wrong. 6 For when
he punishes you, it proves that he loves you.
When he whips you it proves you are really his
child."

7 Let God train you, for he is doing what any
loving father does for his children. Whoever
heard of a son who was never corrected? 8 If
God doesn't punish you when you need it, as
other fathers punish their sons, then it means
that you aren't really God's son at all—that you
don't really belong in his family. 9 Since we respect our fathers here on earth, though they
punish us, should we not all the more cheerfully
submit to God's training so that we can begin
really to live?

Today's English Version

whom our faith depends from beginning to end.
He did not give up because of the cross! On
the contrary, because of the joy that was waiting for him, he thought nothing of the disgrace
of dying on the cross, and is now seated at the
right side of God's throne.

3 Think of what he went through, how he put
up with so much hatred from sinful men! So
do not let yourselves become discouraged and
give up. 4 For in your struggle against sin you
have not yet had to fight to the point of being
killed. 5 Have you forgotten the encouraging
words which God speaks to you as his sons?

"My son, pay attention when the Lord punishes you,
and do not be discouraged when he rebukes you.
6 Because the Lord punishes everyone he
loves,
and chastises everyone he accepts as a
son."

7 Endure what you suffer as being a father's
punishment; because your suffering shows that
God is treating you as his sons. Was there ever
a son who was not punished by his father? 8 If
you are not punished as all his sons are, it means
you are not real sons, but bastards. 9 In the case
of our human fathers, they punished us and we
respected them. How much more, then, should
we submit to our spiritual Father and live!

New International Version

us fix our eyes on Jesus, the Pioneer[v] and Perfecter of our faith, who for the joy set before
him endured the cross, scorning its shame, and
sat down at the right hand of the throne of God.
3 Consider him who endured such opposition
from sinful men, so that you will not grow weary
and lose heart.

4 In your struggle against sin, you have not
yet resisted to the point of shedding your blood.
5 And you have forgotten that word of encouragement that addresses you as sons:

"My son, do not make light of the Lord's
discipline,
and do not lose heart when he rebukes
you,
6 because the Lord disciplines those whom he
loves,
and he punishes everyone he accepts as a
son."[w]

7 Endure hardship as discipline; God is treating you as sons. For what son is not disciplined
by his father? 8 If you are not disciplined (and
everyone undergoes discipline), then you are illegitimate children and not true sons. 9 Moreover, we have all had human fathers who disciplined us and we respected them for it. How
much more should we submit to the Father of

[v] Or *Originator*. [w] Prov. 3:11,12.

Phillips Modern English

the source and the goal of our faith. For he himself endured a cross and thought nothing of its shame because of the joy he knew would follow his suffering; and he is now seated at the right hand of God's throne. Think constantly of him enduring all that sinful men could say against him and you will not lose your purpose or your courage.

12.4 Look upon suffering as heavenly discipline

After all, your fight against sin has not yet meant the shedding of blood, and you have perhaps lost sight of that piece of advice which reminds you of your sonship in God:

My son, regard not lightly the chastening of the Lord,
Nor faint when thou art reproved of him;
For whom the Lord loveth he chasteneth,
And scourgeth every son whom he receiveth.

Bear what you have to bear as "chastening"—as God's dealing with you as sons. No true son ever grows up uncorrected by his father. For if you had no experience of the correction which all sons have to bear you might well doubt the legitimacy of your sonship. After all, when we were children we had fathers who corrected us, and we respected them for it. Can we not much more readily submit to the discipline of the Father of men's souls, and learn how to live?

Revised Standard Version

pioneer and perfecter of our faith, who for the joy that was set before him endured the cross, despising the shame, and is seated at the right hand of the throne of God.
3 Consider him who endured from sinners
such hostility against himself, so that you may
not grow weary or faint-hearted. 4 In your struggle against sin you have not yet resisted to the
point of shedding your blood. 5 And have you
forgotten the exhortation which addresses you
as sons?—
"My son, do not regard lightly the discipline of the Lord,
nor lose courage when you are punished by him.
6 For the Lord disciplines him whom he loves,
and chastises every son whom he receives."
7 It is for discipline that you have to endure.
God is treating you as sons; for what son is
there whom his father does not discipline? 8 If
you are left without discipline, in which all have
participated, then you are illegitimate children
and not sons. 9 Besides this, we have had earthly
fathers to discipline us and we respected them.
Shall we not much more be subject to the Fa-

Jerusalem Bible

lose sight of Jesus, who leads us in our faith and brings it to perfection: for the sake of the joy which was still in the future, he endured the cross, disregarding the shamefulness of it, and *from now on has taken his place at the right* of
God's throne. 3 Think of the way he stood such
opposition from sinners and then you will not
give up for want of courage. 4 In the fight
against sin, you have not yet had to keep fighting
to the point of death.

God's fatherly instruction

5 Have you forgotten that encouraging text in
which you are addressed as sons? *My son, when the Lord corrects you, do not treat it lightly; but do not get discouraged when he reprimands you.*
6 *For the Lord trains the ones that he loves and he punishes all those that he acknowledges as his sons.*[t] 7 Suffering is part of your *training;*
God is treating you as his *sons.* Has there ever
been any *son* whose father did not *train* him?
8 If you were not getting this training, as all of
you are, then you would not be *sons* but bastards.
9 Besides, we have all had our human fathers
who punished us, and we respected them for it;
we ought to be even more willing to submit ourselves to our spiritual Father, to be given life.

[t] Ps. 3:11-12 (LXX).

New English Bible

Jesus, on whom faith depends from start to finish: Jesus who, for the sake of the joy that lay ahead of him,[c] endured the cross, making light of its disgrace, and has taken his seat at the right hand of the throne of God.

Think of him who submitted to such opposition from sinners: that will help you not to lose heart and grow faint. In your struggle against sin, you have not yet resisted to the point of shedding your blood. You have forgotten the text of Scripture which addresses you as sons and appeals to you in these words:

'My son, do not think lightly of the Lord's discipline,
nor lose heart when he corrects you;
for the Lord disciplines those whom he loves;
he lays the rod on every son whom he acknowledges.'

You must endure it as discipline: God is treating you as sons. Can anyone be a son, who is not disciplined by his father? If you escape the discipline in which all sons share, you must be bastards and no true sons. Again, we paid due respect to the earthly fathers who disciplined us; should we not submit even more readily to our

[c] *Or* who, in place of the joy that was open to him, . . .

King James Version

Father of spirits, and live? 10 For they verily for
a few days chastened *us* after their own pleasure;
but he for *our* profit, that *we* might be partakers
of his holiness. 11 Now no chastening for the
present seemeth to be joyous, but grievous:
nevertheless, afterward it yieldeth the peaceable
fruit of righteousness unto them which are exercised thereby. 12 Wherefore lift up the hands
which hang down, and the feeble knees; 13 And
make straight paths for your feet, lest that which
is lame be turned out of the way; but let it
rather be healed. 14 Follow peace with all *men*,
and holiness, without which no man shall see
the Lord: 15 Looking diligently lest any man
fail of the grace of God; lest any root of bitterness springing up trouble *you*, and thereby many
be defiled; 16 Lest there *be* any fornicator, or
profane person, as Esau, who for one morsel of
meat sold his birthright. 17 For ye know how that
afterward, when he would have inherited the
blessing, he was rejected: for he found no place
of repentance, though he sought it carefully with

Living Bible

10 Our earthly fathers trained us for a few
brief years, doing the best for us that they knew
how, but God's correction is always right and
for our best good, that we may share his holiness. 11 Being punished isn't enjoyable while it is
happening—it hurts! But afterwards we can
see the result, a quiet growth in grace and character.

12 So take a new grip with your tired hands,
stand firm on your shaky legs, 13 and mark out
a straight, smooth path for your feet so that
those who follow you, though weak and lame,
will not fall and hurt themselves, but become
strong.

14 Try to stay out of all quarrels and seek to
live a clean and holy life, for one who is not
holy will not see the Lord. 15 Look after each
other so that not one of you will fail to find
God's best blessings. Watch out that no bitterness takes root among you, for as it springs up
it causes deep trouble, hurting many in their
spiritual lives. 16 Watch out that no one becomes involved in sexual sin or becomes careless
about God as Esau did: he traded his rights as
the oldest son for a single meal. 17 And afterwards, when he wanted those rights back again,
it was too late, even though he wept bitter tears
of repentance. So remember, and be careful.

Today's English Version

10 Our human fathers punished us for a short
time, as it seemed right to them. But God does
it for our own good, so that we may share his
holiness. 11 When we are punished, it seems to
us at the time something to make us sad, not
glad. Later, however, those who have been disciplined by such punishment reap the peaceful
reward of a righteous life.

Instructions and warnings

12 Lift up your limp hands, then, and
strengthen your weak knees! 13 Keep walking
on straight paths, so that the lame foot may not
be disabled, but instead be healed.

14 Try to be at peace with all men, and try
to live a holy life, because no one will see the
Lord without it. 15 Be careful that no one turns
back from the grace of God. Be careful that no
one becomes like a bitter plant that grows up
and troubles many with its poison. 16 Be careful
that no one becomes immoral or unspiritual like
Esau, who for a single meal sold his rights
as the older son. 17 Afterward, you know, he
wanted to receive his father's blessing; but he
was turned back, because he could not find a
way to change what he had done, even though
he looked for it with tears.

New International Version

our spirits and live! 10 Our fathers disciplined
us for a little while as they thought best; but
God disciplines us for our good, that we may
share in his holiness. 11 No discipline seems
pleasant at the time, but painful. Later on, however, it produces a harvest of righteousness and
peace for those who have been trained by it.

12 Therefore, strengthen your feeble arms and
weak knees. 13 Make level paths for your feet,
so that the lame may not be disabled, but rather
healed.

Warning against refusing God

14 Make every effort to live in peace with all
men and to be holy; without holiness no will see
the Lord. 15 See to it that no one misses the
grace of God and that no bitter root grows up
to cause trouble and defile many. 16 See that
no one is sexually immoral, or is godless like
Esau, who for a single meal sold his inheritance
rights as the oldest son. 17 Afterward, as you
know, when he wanted to inherit this blessing,
he was rejected. He could bring about no
change of mind, though he sought the blessing
with tears.

Phillips Modern English

For our fathers used to correct us according to their own ideas during the brief days of childhood. But God corrects us for our own benefit, so that we may share in his holiness. Now obviously no "chastening" seems pleasant at the time: it is in fact most unpleasant. Yet when it is all over we can see that it has quietly produced the fruit of real goodness in the characters of those who have accepted it. So tighten your loosening grip and steady your trembling knees. Keep your feet on a steady path, so that the limping foot does not collapse but recovers strength.

12.14 *In times of testing be especially on your guard against certain sins*

Let it be your ambition to live at peace with all men and to achieve holiness "without which no man shall see the Lord". Be careful that none of you fails to respond to the grace of God, for if he does there can spring up in him a bitter spirit which can poison the lives of many others. Be careful, too, that none of you falls into impurity or loses his reverence for the things of God like Esau, who sold his birthright for a single meal. Remember how afterwards, when he wanted to have the blessing which was his birthright, he was refused. He never afterwards found the way of repentance though he sought it desperately and with tears.

Revised Standard Version

ther of spirits and live? 10 For they disciplined
us for a short time at their pleasure, but he
disciplines us for our good, that we may share
his holiness. 11 For the moment all discipline
seems painful rather than pleasant; later it yields
the peaceful fruit of righteousness to those who
have been trained by it.
12 Therefore lift your drooping hands and
strengthen your weak knees, 13 and make
straight paths for your feet, so that what is lame
may not be put out of joint but rather be healed.
14 Strive for peace with all men, and for the
holiness without which no one will see the Lord.
15 See to it that no one fail to obtain the grace
of God; that no "root of bitterness" spring up
and cause trouble, and by it the many become
defiled; 16 that no one be immoral or irreligious
like Esau, who sold his birthright for a single
meal. 17 For you know that afterward, when he
desired to inherit the blessing, he was rejected,
for he found no chance to repent, though he
sought it with tears.

Jerusalem Bible

10 Our human fathers were thinking of this
short life when they punished us, and could
only do what they thought best; but he does it
all for our own good, so that we may share his
own holiness. 11 Of course, any punishment is
most painful at the time, and far from pleasant;
but later, in those on whom it has been used, it
bears fruit in peace and goodness. 12 So *hold up
your limp arms and steady your trembling knees*[u]
13 and *smooth out the path you tread*[v]; then
the injured limb will not be wrenched, it will
grow strong again.

Unfaithfulness is punished

14 *Always be wanting peace*[w] with all people,
and the holiness without which no one can ever
see the Lord. 15 Be careful that no one is deprived of the grace of God and that no *root of
bitterness should begin to grow and make trouble*[x]; this can poison a whole community. 16 And
be careful that there is no immorality, or that
any of you does not degrade religion like Esau,
who sold his birthright for one single meal. 17 As
you know, when he wanted to obtain the blessing
afterward, he was rejected and, though he
pleaded for it with tears, he was unable to elicit
a change of heart.

[*u*] Is. 35:3. [*v*] Pr. 4:26 (LXX). [*w*] Ps. 34:14. [*x*] Dt. 29:17.

New English Bible

spiritual Father, and so attain life? They disciplined us for this short life according to their lights; but he does so for our true welfare, so that we may share his holiness. Discipline, no doubt, is never pleasant; at the time it seems painful, but in the end it yields for those who have been trained by it the peaceful harvest of an honest life. Come, then, stiffen your drooping arms and shaking knees, and keep your steps from wavering. Then the disabled limb will not be put out of joint, but regain its former powers.

Aim at peace with all men, and a holy life, for without that no one will see the Lord. Look to it that there is no one among you who forfeits the grace of God, no bitter, noxious weed growing up to poison the whole, no immoral person, no one worldly-minded like Esau. He sold his birth-right for a single meal, and you know that although he wanted afterwards to claim the blessing, he was rejected; though he begged for it to the point of tears, he found no way open for second thoughts.

King James Version

tears. 18 For ye are not come unto the mount that might be touched, and that burned with fire, nor unto blackness, and darkness, and tempest, 19And the sound of a trumpet, and the voice of words; which *voice* they that heard entreated that the word should not be spoken to them any more: 20 (For they could not endure that which was commanded, And if so much as a beast touch the mountain, it shall be stoned, or thrust through with a dart: 21And so terrible was the sight, *that* Moses said, I exceedingly fear and quake:) 22 But ye are come unto mount Sion, and unto the city of the living God, the heavenly Jerusalem, and to an innumerable company of angels, 23 To the general assembly and church of the firstborn, which are written in heaven, and to God the Judge of all, and to the spirits of just men made perfect, 24And to Jesus the mediator of the new covenant, and to the blood of sprinkling, that speaketh better things than *that of* Abel. 25 See that ye refuse not him that speaketh: for if they escaped not who refused him that spake on earth, much more *shall not* we *escape,* if we turn away from him that *speaketh* from heaven: 26 Whose voice then shook the earth: but now he hath promised, say-

Living Bible

18 You have not had to stand face to face with terror, flaming fire, gloom, darkness and a terrible storm, as the Israelites did at Mount Sinai when God gave them his laws. 19 For there was an awesome trumpet blast, and a voice with a message so terrible that the people begged God to stop speaking. 20 They staggered back under God's command that if even an animal touched the mountain it must die. 21 Moses himself was so frightened at the sight that he shook with terrible fear.

22 But you have come right up into Mount Zion, to the city of the living God, the heavenly Jerusalem, and to the gathering of countless happy angels; 23 and to the church, composed of all those registered in heaven; and to God who is Judge of all; and to the spirits of the redeemed in heaven, already made perfect; 24 and to Jesus himself, who has brought us his wonderful new agreement; and to the sprinkled blood which graciously forgives instead of crying out for vengeance as the blood of Abel did.

25 So see to it that you obey him who is speaking to you. For if the people of Israel did not escape when they refused to listen to Moses, the earthly messenger, how terrible our danger if we refuse to listen to God who speaks to us from heaven! 26 When he spoke from Mount Sinai his voice shook the earth,. but, "Next

Today's English Version

18 You have not come, as the people of Israel came, to what you can feel, to Mount Sinai with its blazing fire, the darkness and the gloom, the storm, 19 the noise of a trumpet, and the sound of a voice. When the people heard the voice they begged not to have to hear another word, 20 because they could not bear the order which said, "If even an animal touches the mountain it must be stoned to death." 21 The sight was so terrible that Moses said, "I am trembling and afraid!"

22 Instead, you have come to Mount Zion and to the city of the living God, the heavenly Jerusalem, with its thousands of angels. 23 You have come to the joyful gathering of God's oldest sons, whose names are written in heaven. You have come to God, who is the judge of all men, and to the spirits of righteous men made perfect. 24 You have come to Jesus, who arranged the new covenant, and to the sprinkled blood that tells of much better things than Abel's blood.

25 Be careful, then, and do not refuse to hear him who speaks. Those who refused to hear him who gave the divine message on earth did not escape. How much less shall we escape, then, if we turn away from him who speaks from heaven! 26 His voice shook the earth at that time, but now he has promised, "I will once

New International Version

18 You have not come to a mountain that can be touched and that is burning with fire; to darkness, gloom and storm; 19 to a trumpet blast or to such a voice speaking words, so that those who heard it begged that no further word be spoken to them, 20 because they could not bear what was commanded: "If even an animal touches the mountain, it must be stoned."[x] 21 The sight was so terrifying that Moses said, "I am trembling with fear."[y]

22 But you have come to Mount Zion, to the heavenly Jerusalem, the city of the living God. You have come to thousands upon thousands of angels in joyful assembly, 23 to the church of the firstborn, whose names are written in heaven. You have come to God, the judge of all men, to the spirits of righteous men made perfect, 24 to Jesus the mediator of a new covenant, and to the sprinkled blood that speaks a better word than the blood of Abel.

25 See to it that you do not refuse him who speaks. If they did not escape when they refused him who warned them on earth, how much less will we, if we turn away from him who warns us from heaven? 26At that time his voice shook the earth, but now he has promised, "Once more

[*x*] Exodus 19:12,13. [*y*] Deut. 9:19.

Phillips Modern English

12.18 Your experience is not that of the old agreement but of the new

You have not had to approach things which your senses could experience as they did in the old days—flaming fire, black darkness, rushing wind and out of it a trumpet-blast, a voice speaking human words. So terrible was that voice that those who heard it begged and prayed that it might say no more. For what it had already commanded was more than they could bear—that "if even a beast touch this mountain it must be stoned". So fearful was the spectacle that Moses cried out, "I am terrified and tremble!"

No, you have been allowed to approach the true Mount Zion, the city of the living God, the heavenly Jerusalem. You have drawn near to the countless angelic army, the assembly of the Church of the first-born whose names are written in Heaven. You have drawn near to God, the judge of all, to the souls of good men made perfect, and to Jesus, mediator of a new agreement, to that cleansing blood which tells a better story than the blood of Abel.

So be sure you do not refuse to hear the voice that speaks. For if they who refused to hear those who spoke to them on earth did not escape, how little chance of escape is there for us if we refuse to hear the One who speaks from Heaven. Then his voice shook, the earth, but now he promises:

Revised Standard Version

18 For you have not come to what may be
touched, a blazing fire, and darkness, and gloom,
and a tempest, 19 and the sound of a trumpet,
and a voice whose words made the hearers entreat that no further messages be spoken to
them. 20 For they could not endure the order
that was given, "If even a beast touches the
mountain, it shall be stoned." 21 Indeed, so terrifying was the sight that Moses said, "I tremble
with fear." 22 But you have come to Mount Zion
and to the city of the living God, the heavenly
Jerusalem, and to innumerable angels in festal
gathering, 23 and to the assembly[z] of the first-
born who are enrolled in heaven, and to a judge
who is God of all, and to the spirits of just
men made perfect, 24 and to Jesus, the mediator
of a new covenant, and to the sprinkled blood
that speaks more graciously than the blood of
Abel.
25 See that you do not refuse him who is
speaking. For if they did not escape when they
refused him who warned them on earth, much
less shall we escape if we reject him who warns
from heaven. 26 His voice then shook the earth;
but now he has promised, "Yet once more I will

[z] Or *angels, and to the festal gathering and assembly.*

Jerusalem Bible

The two covenants

18 What you have come to is nothing known
to the senses: not a *blazing fire,*[y] or a *gloom*
turning to *total darkness,* or a *storm;* 19 or
trumpeting thunder or the *great voice speak-*
ing which made everyone that heard it beg that
no more should be said to them. 20 They were
appalled at the order that was given: *If even an*
animal touches the mountain, it must be stoned.
21 The whole scene was so terrible that Moses
said: *I am afraid,*[z] and was trembling with fright.
22 But what you have come to is Mount Zion
and the city of the living God, the heavenly
Jerusalem where the millions of angels have
gathered for the festival, 23 with the whole
Church in which everyone is a "first-born son"
and a citizen of heaven. You have come to God
himself, the supreme Judge, and been placed with
the spirits of the saints who have been made perfect; 24 and to Jesus, the mediator who brings a
new covenant and a blood for purification which
pleads more insistently than Abel's. 25 Make
sure that you never refuse to listen when he
speaks. The people who refused to listen to the
warning from a voice on earth could not escape
their punishment, and how shall we escape if we
turn away from a voice that warns us from
heaven? 26 That time his voice made the earth
shake, but now he has given us this promise: *I*

[y] The quotations in vv. 18-20 are from Ex. 19 (recalled in Dt. 4). [z] Dt. 9:19.

New English Bible

Remember where you stand: not before the palpable, blazing fire of Sinai, with the darkness, gloom, and whirlwind, the trumpet-blast and the oracular voice, which they heard, and begged to hear no more; for they could not bear the command, 'If even an animal touches the mountain, it must be stoned.' So appalling was the sight, that Moses said, 'I shudder with fear.'

No, you stand before Mount Zion and the city of the living God, heavenly Jerusalem, before myriads of angels, the full concourse and assembly of the first-born citizens of heaven, and God the judge of all, and the spirits of good men made perfect, and Jesus the mediator of a new covenant, whose sprinkled blood has better things to tell than the blood of Abel. See that you do not refuse to hear the voice that speaks. Those who refused to hear the oracle speaking on earth found no escape; still less shall we escape if we refuse to hear the One who speaks from heaven. Then indeed his voice shook the earth, but now he has promised, 'Yet once again

King James Version

ing, Yet once more I shake not the earth only, but also heaven. 27 And this *word*, Yet once more, signifieth the removing of those things that are shaken, as of things that are made, that those things which cannot be shaken may remain. 28 Wherefore we receiving a kingdom which cannot be moved, let us have grace, whereby we may serve God acceptably with reverence and godly fear: 29 For our God *is* a consuming fire.

13 Let brotherly love continue. 2 Be not forgetful to entertain strangers: for thereby some have entertained angels unawares. 3 Remember them that are in bonds, as bound with them; *and* them which suffer adversity, as being yourselves also in the body. 4 Marriage *is* honourable in all, and the bed undefiled: but whoremongers and adulterers God will judge. 5 *Let your* conversation *be* without covetousness; *and be* content with such things as ye have: for he hath said, I will never leave thee, nor forsake

Living Bible

time," he says, "I will not only shake the earth, but the heavens too." 27 By this he means that he will sift out everything without solid foundations, so that only unshakable things will be left.

28 Since we have a kingdom nothing can destroy, let us please God by serving him with thankful hearts, and with holy fear and awe. 29 For our God is a consuming fire.

13 Continue to love each other with true brotherly love. 2 Don't forget to be kind to strangers, for some who have done this have entertained angels without realizing it! 3 Don't forget about those in jail. Suffer with them as though you were there yourself. Share the sorrow of those being mistreated, for you know what they are going through.

4 Honor your marriage and its vows, and be pure; for God will surely punish all those who are immoral or commit adultery.

5 Stay away from the love of money; be satisfied with what you have. For God has said, "I will never, *never* fail you nor forsake you."

Today's English Version

more shake not only the earth but heaven as well." 27 The words "once more" plainly show that the created things will be shaken and removed, so that the things that are not shaken will remain.

28 Let us be thankful, then, because we receive a kingdom that cannot be shaken. Let us be grateful and worship God in a way that will please him, with reverence and fear; 29 because our God is indeed a destroying fire.

How to please God

13 Keep on loving one another as brothers in Christ. 2 Remember to welcome strangers in your homes. There were some who did it and welcomed angels without knowing it. 3 Remember those who are in prison, as though you were in prison with them. Remember those who are suffering, as though you were suffering as they are.

4 Marriage should be honored by all, and husbands and wives must be faithful to each other. God will judge those who are immoral and those who commit adultery.

5 Keep your lives free from the love of money, and be satisfied with what you have. For God has said, "I will never leave you; I will never

New International Version

I will shake not only the earth but also the heavens."[z] 27 The words "once more" indicate the removing of what can be shaken—that is, created things—so that what cannot be shaken may remain.

28 Therefore, since we are receiving a kingdom that cannot be shaken, let us be thankful, and so worship God acceptably with reverence and awe, 29 for our God is a consuming fire.

Concluding exhortations

13 Keep on loving each other as brothers. 2 Do not forget to entertain strangers, for by so doing some people have entertained angels without knowing it. 3 Remember those in prison as if you were their fellow prisoners, and those who are mistreated as if you yourselves were suffering.

4 Marriage should be honored by all, and the marriage bed kept pure, for God will judge the adulterer and all the sexually immoral. 5 Keep your lives free from the love of money and be content with what you have, because God has said,

"Never will I leave you;
never will I forsake you."[a]

[z] Haggai 2:6. [a] Deut. 31:6.

Phillips Modern English

Yet once more will I make to tremble
Not the earth only, but also the heaven.

This means that in this final "shaking" all that is impermanent will be removed, that is, everything that is merely "made", and only the unshakable things will remain. Since then we have been given a kingdom that is "unshakable", let us serve God with thankfulness in the ways which please him, but always with reverence and holy fear. For it is perfectly true that our God is a burning fire.

13.1 Some practical instructions for Christian living

Never let your brotherly love fail, nor refuse to extend your hospitality to strangers—sometimes men have entertained angels unawares. Think constantly of those in prison as if you were prisoners at their side. Think too of all who suffer for you still live in this world.

Marriage is honourable and faithfulness should be respected by you all. God himself will judge those who traffic in the bodies of others or defile the relationship of marriage. Keep your lives free from the lust for money: be content with what you have.

God has said:

I will in no wise fail thee,
Neither will I in any wise forsake thee.

Revised Standard Version

shake not only the earth but also the heaven."
27 This phrase, "Yet once more," indicates the
removal of what is shaken, as of what has been
made, in order that what cannot be shaken may
remain. 28 Therefore let us be grateful for receiving a kingdom that cannot be shaken, and
thus let us offer to God acceptable worship,
with reverence and awe; 29 for our God is a
consuming fire.

13 Let brotherly love continue. 2 Do not
neglect to show hospitality to strangers,
for thereby some have entertained angels unawares. 3 Remember those who are in prison,
as though in prison with them; and those who
are ill-treated, since you also are in the body.
4 Let marriage be held in honor among all, and
let the marriage bed be undefiled; for God will
judge the immoral and adulterous. 5 Keep your
life free from love of money, and be content
with what you have; for he has said, "I will

Jerusalem Bible

shall make the earth shake once more and not
only the earth but *heaven as well.*[a] 27 The words
once more show that since the things being
shaken are created things, they are going to be
changed, so that the unshakable things will be
left. 28 We have been given possession of an unshakable kingdom. Let us therefore hold on to
the grace that we have been given and use it to
worship God in the way that he finds acceptable,
in reverence and fear. 29 For our *God* is a *consuming fire.*[b]

Appendix

Final recommendations

13 Continue to love each other like brothers,
2 and remember always to welcome strangers, for by doing this, some people have entertained angels without knowing it. 3 Keep in mind
those who are in prison, as though you were in
prison with them; and those who are being badly
treated, since you too are in the one body.
4 Marriage is to be honored by all, and marriages
are to be kept undefiled, because fornicators and
adulterers will come under God's judgment.
5 Put greed out of your lives and be content with
whatever you have; God himself has said: *I will*

[a] Hg. 2:6, probably influenced also by Ps. 68:8. [b] Dt. 4:24.

New English Bible

I will shake not earth alone, but the heavens also.' The words 'once again'—and only once—imply that the shaking of these created things means their removal, and then what is not shaken will remain. The kingdom we are given is unshakable; let us therefore give thanks to God, and so worship him as he would be worshipped, with reverence and awe; for our God is a devouring fire.

13 Never cease to love your fellow-Christians. Remember to show hospitality. There are some who, by so doing, have entertained angels without knowing it.

Remember those in prison as if you were there with them; and those who are being maltreated, for you like them are still in the world.

Marriage is honourable; let us all keep it so, and the marriage-bond inviolate; for God's judgement will fall on fornicators and adulterers.

Do not live for money; be content with what you have; for God himself has said, 'I will never

King James Version

thee. 6 So that we may boldly say, The Lord *is* my helper, and I will not fear what man shall do unto me. 7 Remember them which have the rule over you, who have spoken unto you the word of God: whose faith follow, considering the end of *their* conversation. 8 Jesus Christ the same yesterday, and to day, and for ever. 9 Be not carried about with divers and strange doctrines: for *it is* a good thing that the heart be established with grace; not with meats, which have not profited them that have been occupied therein. 10 We have an altar, whereof they have no right to eat which serve the tabernacle. 11 For the bodies of those beasts, whose blood is brought into the sanctuary by the high priest for sin, are burned without the camp. 12 Wherefore Jesus also, that he might sanctify the people with his own blood, suffered without the gate. 13 Let us go forth therefore unto him without the camp, bearing his reproach. 14 For here have we no continuing city, but we seek one to come. 15 By him therefore let us offer the sacrifice of praise to God continually, that is, the fruit of *our* lips, giving thanks to his name. 16 But to

Living Bible

6 That is why we can say without any doubt or fear, "The Lord is my Helper and I am not afraid of anything that mere man can do to me."

7 Remember your leaders who have taught you the Word of God. Think of all the good that has come from their lives, and try to trust the Lord as they do.

8 Jesus Christ is the same yesterday, today, and forever. 9 So do not be attracted by strange, new ideas. Your spiritual strength comes as a gift from God, not from ceremonial rules about eating certain foods—a method which, by the way, hasn't helped those who have tried it!

10 We have an altar—the cross where Christ was sacrificed—where those who continue to seek salvation by obeying Jewish laws can never be helped. 11 Under the system of Jewish laws the high priest brought the blood of the slain animals into the sanctuary as a sacrifice for sin, and then the bodies of the animals were burned outside the city. 12 That is why Jesus suffered and died outside the city, where his blood washed our sins away.

13 So let us go out to him beyond the city walls [that is, outside the interests of this world, being willing to be despised [a]] to suffer with him there, bearing his shame. 14 For this world is not our home; we are looking forward to our everlasting home in heaven.

15 With Jesus' help we will continually offer our sacrifice of praise to God by telling others of the glory of his name. 16 Don't forget to do

[*a*] Implied.

Today's English Version

abandon you." 6 Let us be bold, then, and say,

"The Lord is my helper,
I will not be afraid.
What can man do to me?"

7 Remember your former leaders, who spoke God's message to you. Think back on how they lived and died, and imitate their faith. 8 Jesus Christ is the same yesterday, today, and forever. 9 Do not let all kinds of strange teachings lead you from the right way. It is good for our souls to be made strong by God's grace, not by obeying rules about foods; those who obey these rules have not been helped by them.

10 The priests who serve in the Jewish tent have no right to eat of the sacrifice on our altar. 11 The Jewish High Priest brings the blood of the animals into the Most Holy Place to offer it as a sacrifice for sins; but the bodies of the animals are burned outside the camp. 12 For this reason Jesus also died outside the city gate, in order to cleanse the people from sin with his own blood. 13 Let us, then, go to him outside the camp and share his shame. 14 For there is no permanent city for us here on earth; we are looking for the city which is to come. 15 Let us, then, always offer praise to God as our sacrifice through Jesus, which is the offering presented by lips that confess his name. 16 Do not forget to

New International Version

6 So we say with confidence,
"The Lord is my helper;
I will not be afraid.
What can man do to me?" [b]

7 Remember your leaders, who spoke the word of God to you. Consider the outcome of their way of life and imitate their faith. 8 Jesus Christ is the same yesterday and today and forever.

9 Do not be carried away by all kinds of strange teachings. It is good for our hearts to be strengthened by grace, not by ceremonial foods, which are of no value to those who eat them. 10 We have an altar from which those who minister at the tabernacle have no right to eat.

11 The high priest carries the blood of animals into the Most Holy Place as a sin offering, but the bodies are burned outside the camp. 12 And so Jesus also suffered outside the city gate to make his people holy through his own blood. 13 Let us, then, go to him outside the camp, bearing the disgrace he bore. 14 For here we do not have an enduring city, but we are looking for the city that is to come.

15 Through Jesus, therefore, let us continually offer to God a sacrifice of praise—the fruit of lips that confess his name. 16 And do not for-

[*b*] Psalm 118:6.

Phillips Modern English

We, therefore, can confidently say:

The Lord is my helper; I will not fear:
What shall man do unto me?

13.7 Be loyal to your leaders and, above all, to Christ

Never forget your leaders, who first spoke to you the Word of God. Remember the result of their lives, and imitate their faith.

Jesus Christ is always the same, yesterday, today and for ever. Do not be carried away by various peculiar teachings. It is good to depend on the grace of God for inward strength, and not on rules of diet—which have not spiritually benefited those who followed them. We have an Altar from which those who still serve the tabernacle have no right to eat.

When the blood of animals was presented as a sin-offering by the High Priest in the sanctuary, their bodies were burned outside the precincts of the camp. That is why Jesus, when he sanctified men by the shedding of his own blood, suffered and died outside the city gates. Let us go out to him, then, beyond the boundaries of the camp, proudly bearing his "disgrace". For we have no permanent city here on earth, we are looking for one in the world to come. Through him, therefore, let us offer a constant sacrifice of praise to God—the tribute of lips which openly acknowledge his name. Yet we should not for-

Revised Standard Version

never fail you nor forsake you." 6 Hence we can confidently say,

"The Lord is my helper,
I will not be afraid;
what can man do to me?"

7 Remember your leaders, those who spoke to you the word of God; consider the outcome of their life, and imitate their faith. 8 Jesus Christ is the same yesterday and today and for ever. 9 Do not be led away by diverse and strange teachings; for it is well that the heart be strengthened by grace, not by foods, which have not benefited their adherents. 10 We have an altar from which those who serve the tent[a] have no right to eat. 11 For the bodies of those animals whose blood is brought into the sanctuary by the high priest as a sacrifice for sin are burned outside the camp. 12 So Jesus also suffered outside the gate in order to sanctify the people through his own blood. 13 Therefore let us go forth to him outside the camp, and bear the abuse he endured. 14 For here we have no lasting city, but we seek the city which is to come. 15 Through him then let us continually offer up a sacrifice of praise to God, that is, the fruit of lips that acknowledge his name. 16 Do not neglect to do good and to share what

[*a*] Or *tabernacle*.

Jerusalem Bible

not fail you or desert you,[c] 6 and so we can say with confidence: *With the Lord to help me, I fear nothing: what can man do to me?* [d]

Faithfulness

7 Remember your leaders, who preached the word of God to you, and as you reflect on the outcome of their lives, imitate their faith. 8 Jesus Christ is the same today as he was yesterday and as he will be for ever. 9 Do not let yourselves be led astray by all sorts of strange doctrines: it is better to rely on grace for inner strength than on dietary laws which have done no good to those who kept them. 10 We have our own altar from which those who serve the tabernacle have no right to eat. 11 The bodies of the animals *whose blood is brought into the sanctuary* by the high priest *for the atonement of sin are burned outside the camp,*[e] 12 and so Jesus too suffered outside the gate to sanctify the people with his own blood. 13 Let us go to him, then, *outside the camp,* and share his degradation. 14 For there is no eternal city for us in this life but we look for one in the life to come. 15 Through him, *let us offer God* an unending *sacrifice of praise,*[f] a verbal sacrifice that is offered every time we acknowledge his name. 16 Keep doing good works

[*c*] Dt. 31:6. [*d*] Ps. 118:6; Ps. 27:1. [*e*] Lv. 16:27. [*f*] Ps. 50:14.

New English Bible

leave you or desert you'; and so we can take courage and say, 'The Lord is my helper, I will not fear; what can man do to me?'

Remember your leaders, those who first spoke God's message to you; and reflecting upon the outcome of their life and work, follow the example of their faith.

Jesus Christ is the same yesterday, today, and for ever. So do not be swept off your course by all sorts of outlandish teachings; it is good that our souls should gain their strength from the grace of God, and not from scruples about what we eat, which have never done any good to those who were governed by them.

Our altar is one from which[a] the priests of the sacred tent have no right to eat. As you know, those animals whose blood is brought as a sin-offering by the high priest into the sanctuary, have their bodies burnt outside the camp, and therefore Jesus also suffered outside the gate, to consecrate the people by his own blood. Let us then go to him outside the camp, bearing the stigma that he bore. For here we have no permanent home, but we are seekers after the city which is to come. Through Jesus, then, let us continually offer up to God the sacrifice of praise, that is, the tribute of lips which acknowledge his name, and never forget to show kind-

[*a*] *Or* one like that from which . . .

King James Version

do good and to communicate forget not: for
with such sacrifices God is well pleased. 17 Obey
them that have the rule over you, and submit
yourselves: for they watch for your souls, as
they that must give account, that they may do it
with joy, and not with grief: for that *is* unprofitable for you. 18 Pray for us: for we trust we
have a good conscience, in all things willing to
live honestly. 19 But I beseech *you* the rather to
do this, that I may be restored to you the sooner.
20 Now the God of peace, that brought again
from the dead our Lord Jesus, that great Shepherd of the sheep, through the blood of the
everlasting covenant, 21 Make you perfect in
every good work to do his will, working in you
that which is well pleasing in his sight, through
Jesus Christ; to whom *be* glory for ever and ever.

Living Bible

good and to share what you have with those in
need, for such sacrifices are very pleasing to
him. 17 Obey your spiritual leaders and be willing to do what they say. For their work is to
watch over your souls, and God will judge them
on how well they do this. Give them reason to
report joyfully about you to the Lord and not
with sorrow, for then you will suffer for it too.
18 Pray for us, for our conscience is clear and
we want to keep it that way. 19 I especially need
your prayers right now so that I can come back
to you sooner.

20, 21 And now may the God of peace, who
brought again from the dead our Lord Jesus,
equip you with all you need for doing his will.
May he who became the great Shepherd of the
sheep by an everlasting agreement between God
and you, signed with his blood, produce in you
through the power of Christ all that is pleasing
to him. To him be glory forever and ever.
Amen.

Today's English Version

do good and to help one another, because these
are the sacrifices that please God.

17 Obey your leaders and follow their orders.
They watch over your souls without resting,
since they must give an account of their service
to God. If you obey them, they will do their
work gladly; else they will do it with sadness,
and that would not be of any help to you.

18 Keep on praying for us. We are sure we
have a clear conscience, because we want to do
the right thing at all times. 19 And I beg you all
the more to pray that God will send me back to
you the sooner.

Prayer

20 God has raised from the dead our Lord
Jesus, who is the Great Shepherd of the sheep
because of his death, by which the eternal covenant is sealed. 21 May the God of peace provide
you with every good thing you need in order
to do his will, and may he, through Jesus Christ,
do in us what pleases him. And to Christ be
the glory forever and ever! Amen.

New International Version

get to do good and to share with others, for with
such sacrifices God is pleased.

17 Obey your leaders and submit to their
authority. They keep watch over you as men
who must give an account. Obey them so that
their work will be a joy, not a burden, for that
would be of no advantage to you.

18 Pray for us. We are sure that we have a
clear conscience and desire to live honorably in
every way. 19 I particularly urge you to pray so
that I may be restored to you soon.

20 May the God of peace, who through the
blood of the eternal covenant brought back from
the dead our Lord Jesus, that great Shepherd of
the sheep, 21 equip you with everything good for
doing his will, and may he work in us what is
pleasing to him, through Jesus Christ, to whom
be glory for ever and ever. Amen.

Phillips Modern English

get to do good and to share our good things with others, for these too are the sort of sacrifices God will accept.

Obey your rulers and recognise their authority. They keep constant watch over your welfare, and they have great responsibility. Try to make their work a pleasure and not a painful burden —that would be no advantage to you.

13.18 Personal: our blessing and our greetings

Pray for us. Our conscience is clear before God, and our great desire is to lead a life that is good in every way. Please pray earnestly that I may be restored to you the sooner.

Now the God of peace, who brought back from the dead that great shepherd of the sheep, our Lord Jesus, by the blood of the everlasting agreement, equip you thoroughly for the doing of his will! May he effect in us everything that pleases him through Jesus Christ, to whom be glory for ever and ever. Amen.

Revised Standard Version

you have, for such sacrifices are pleasing to God.

17 Obey your leaders and submit to them; for they are keeping watch over your souls, as men who will have to give account. Let them do this joyfully, and not sadly, for that would be of no advantage to you.

18 Pray for us, for we are sure that we have a clear conscience, desiring to act honorably in all things. 19 I urge you the more earnestly to do this in order that I may be restored to you the sooner.

20 Now may the God of peace who brought again from the dead our Lord Jesus, the great shepherd of the sheep, by the blood of the eternal covenant, 21 equip you with everything good that you may do his will, working in you[b] that which is pleasing in his sight, through Jesus Christ; to whom be glory for ever and ever. Amen.

[*b*] Other ancient authorities read *us*.

Jerusalem Bible

and sharing your resources, for these are sacrifices that please God.

Obedience to religious leaders

17 Obey your leaders and do as they tell you, because they must give an account of the way they look after your souls; make this a joy for them to do, and not a grief—you yourselves would be the losers. 18 We are sure that our own conscience is clear and we are certainly determined to behave honorably in everything we do; pray for us. 19 I ask you very particularly to pray that I may come back to you all the sooner.

Epilogue

News, good wishes and greetings

20 I pray that the God of peace, *who brought* our Lord Jesus *back*[g] from the dead *to become the great Shepherd of the sheep*[h] *by the blood that sealed an eternal covenant,*[i] 21 may make you ready to do his will in any kind of good action; and turn us all into whatever is acceptable to himself through Jesus Christ, to whom be glory for ever and ever, Amen.

[*g*] Is. 63:11. [*h*] Ezk. 34:23. [*i*] Ezk. 37:26.

New English Bible

ness and to share what you have with others; for such are the sacrifices which God approves.

Obey your leaders and defer to them; for they are tireless in their concern for you, as men who must render an account. Let it be a happy task for them, and not pain and grief, for that would bring you no advantage.

Pray for us; for we are convinced that our conscience is clear; our one desire is always to do what is right. All the more earnestly I ask for your prayers, that I may be restored to you the sooner.

May the God of peace, who brought up from the dead our Lord Jesus, the great Shepherd of the sheep, by the blood of the eternal covenant, make you perfect in all goodness so that you may do his will; and may he make of us what he would have us be through Jesus Christ, to whom be glory for ever and ever! Amen.

King James Version

Amen. 22 And I beseech you, brethren, suffer the word of exhortation: for I have written a letter unto you in few words. 23 Know ye that *our* brother Timothy is set at liberty; with whom, if he come shortly, I will see you. 24 Salute all them that have the rule over you, and all the saints. They of Italy salute you. 25 Grace *be* with you all. Amen.

Written to the Hebrews from Italy by Timothy.

Living Bible

22 Brethren, please listen patiently to what I have said in this letter, for it is a short one. 23 I want you to know that Brother Timothy is now out of jail; if he comes here soon, I will come with him to see you. 24, 25 Give my greetings to all your leaders and to the other believers there. The Christians from Italy who are here with me send you their love. God's grace be with you all.

Good-bye.

Today's English Version

Final words

22 I beg you, my brothers, to listen patiently to this message of encouragement; for this letter I have written you is not very long. 23 I want you to know that our brother Timothy has been let out of prison. If he comes soon enough, I will have him with me when I see you.

24 Give our greetings to all your leaders and to all God's people. The brothers from Italy send you their greetings.

25 May God's grace be with you all.

New International Version

22 Brothers, I urge you to bear with my word of exhortation, for I have written you only a short letter.

23 I want you to know that our brother Timothy has been released. If he arrives soon, I will come with him to see you.

24 Greet all your leaders and all God's people. Those from Italy send you their greetings.

25 Grace be with you all.

Phillips Modern English

My brothers, I ask you to bear with this message of encouragement, for I have indeed compressed it into this short letter!

You will be glad to know that brother Timothy is now at liberty. If he comes here in time, he and I will see you together.

Greetings to all your leaders and all your church members. The Christians of Italy send their greetings.

Grace be with you all.

Revised Standard Version

22 I appeal to you, brethren, bear with my word of exhortation, for I have written to you
briefly. 23 You should understand that our
brother Timothy has been released, with whom
I shall see you if he comes soon. 24 Greet all
your leaders and all the saints. Those who come
from Italy send you greetings. 25 Grace be with
all of you. Amen.

Jerusalem Bible

22 I do ask you, brothers, to take these words of advice kindly; that is why I have written to you so briefly.

23 I want you to know that our brother Timothy has been set free. If he arrives in time, he
will be with me when I see you. 24 Greetings to
all your leaders and to all the saints. The saints
of Italy send you greetings. 25 Grace be with
you all.

New English Bible

I beg you, brothers, bear with this exhortation; for it is after all a short letter. I have news for you: our friend Timothy has been released; and if he comes in time he will be with me when I see you.

Greet all your leaders and all God's people. Greetings to you from our Italian friends.

God's grace be with you all!

King James Version

THE GENERAL EPISTLE OF JAMES

1 James, a servant of God and of the Lord
Jesus Christ, to the twelve tribes which are
scattered abroad, greeting. 2 My brethren, count
it all joy when ye fall into divers temptations;
3 Knowing *this,* that the trying of your faith
worketh patience. 4 But let patience have *her*
perfect work, that ye may be perfect and entire,

Living Bible

JAMES

1 *From:* James, a servant of God and of the
Lord Jesus Christ.
To: Jewish Christians scattered everywhere.
Greetings!
2 Dear brothers, is your life full of difficulties and temptations? Then be happy, 3 for when
the way is rough, your patience has a chance to
grow. 4 So let it grow, and don't try to squirm
out of your problems. For when your patience
is finally in full bloom, then you will be ready
for anything, strong in character, full and complete.

Today's English Version

THE LETTER FROM JAMES

1 From James, a servant of God and of the
Lord Jesus Christ:
Greetings to all God's people, scattered over
the whole world.

Faith and wisdom

2 My brothers! Consider yourselves fortunate
when all kinds of trials come your way, 3 because you know that when your faith succeeds
in facing such trials, the result is the ability to
endure. 4 Be sure that your endurance carries
you all the way, without failing, so that you may

New International Version

JAMES

1 James, a servant of God and of the Lord
Jesus Christ,
To the twelve tribes scattered among the nations:
Greetings.

Trials and temptations

2 Consider it pure joy, my brothers, whenever
you face trials of many kinds, 3 because you
know that the testing of your faith develops
perseverance. 4 Perseverance must finish its work
so that you may be mature and complete, not

Phillips Modern English

THE LETTER OF JAMES

James, a servant of God and of the Lord Jesus Christ, sends greeting to the twelve dispersed tribes.

1.2 *The Christian can even welcome trouble*

When all kinds of trials and temptations crowd into your lives, my brothers, don't resent them as intruders, but welcome them as friends! Realise that they come to test your faith and to produce in you the quality of endurance. But let the process go on until that endurance is fully developed, and you will find you have become men of mature character, men of integrity with

Revised Standard Version

THE LETTER OF JAMES

1 James, a servant of God and of the Lord Jesus Christ,
To the twelve tribes in the Dispersion:
Greeting.

2 Count it all joy, my brethren, when you
meet various trials, 3 for you know that the testing of your faith produces steadfastness. 4 And
let steadfastness have its full effect, that you may be perfect and complete, lacking in nothing.

Jerusalem Bible

THE LETTER OF JAMES

Address and greetings

1 From James, servant of God and of the Lord Jesus Christ. Greetings to the twelve tribes of the Dispersion.[a]

Trials a privilege

2 My brothers, you will always have your trials but, when they come, try to treat them as a
happy privilege[b]; 3 you understand that your
faith is only put to the test to make you patient,
4 but patience too is to have its practical results so that you will become fully developed, complete, with nothing missing.

[a] In Old Testament days the "Dispersion" (*diaspora*) meant the Jews who had emigrated from their own country. The writer is using it here to mean the Jewish Christians, living in the Graeco-Roman world. [b] "happy privilege" is a pun on the greeting formula in v. 1.

New English Bible

A LETTER OF JAMES

Practical religion

1 From James, a servant of God and the Lord Jesus Christ.
Greetings to the Twelve Tribes dispersed throughout the world.
My brothers, whenever you have to face trials of many kinds, count yourselves supremely happy, in the knowledge that such testing of your faith breeds fortitude, and if you give fortitude full play you will go on to complete a balanced

King James Version

wanting nothing. 5 If any of you lack wisdom, let him ask of God, that giveth to all *men* liberally, and upbraideth not; and it shall be given him. 6 But let him ask in faith, nothing wavering: for he that wavereth is like a wave of the sea driven with the wind and tossed. 7 For let not that man think that he shall receive any thing of the Lord. 8 A doubleminded man *is* unstable in all his ways. 9 Let the brother of low degree rejoice in that he is exalted: 10 But the rich, in that he is made low: because as the flower of the grass he shall pass away. 11 For the sun is no sooner risen with a burning heat, but it withereth the grass, and the flower thereof falleth, and the grace of the fashion of it perisheth: so also shall the rich man fade away in his ways. 12 Blessed *is* the man that endureth temptation: for when he is tried, he shall receive

Living Bible

5 If you want to know what God wants you to do, ask him, and he will gladly tell you, for he is always ready to give a bountiful supply of wisdom to all who ask him; he will not resent it. 6 But when you ask him, be sure that you really expect him to tell you, for a doubtful mind will be as unsettled as a wave of the sea that is driven and tossed by the wind; 7, 8 and every decision you then make will be uncertain, as you turn first this way, and then that. If you don't ask with faith, don't expect the Lord to give you any solid answer.

9 A Christian who doesn't amount to much in this world should be glad, for he is great in the Lord's sight. 10, 11 But a rich man should be glad that his riches mean nothing to the Lord, for he will soon be gone, like a flower that has lost its beauty and fades away, withered —killed by the scorching summer sun. So it is with rich men. They will soon die and leave behind all their busy activities.

12 Happy is the man who doesn't give in and do wrong when he is tempted, for afterwards he

Today's English Version

be perfect and complete, lacking nothing. 5 But if any of you lacks wisdom, he should pray to God, who will give it to him; because God gives generously and graciously to all. 6 But you must believe when you pray, and not doubt at all. Whoever doubts is like a wave in the sea that is driven and blown about by the wind. 7, 8 Such a person is a hypocrite, undecided in all he does, and he must not think that he will receive anything from the Lord.

Poverty and riches

9 The poor brother must be glad when God lifts him up, 10 and the rich brother when God brings him down. For the rich will pass away like the bloom of a wild plant. 11 The sun rises with its blazing heat and burns the plant; its bloom falls off, and its beauty is destroyed. In the same way the rich man will be destroyed while busy conducting his affairs.

Testing and tempting

12 Happy is the man who remains faithful under trials, because when he succeeds in pass-

New International Version

lacking anything. 5 If any of you lacks wisdom, he should ask God, who gives generously to all without finding fault, and it will be given to him. 6 But when he asks, he must believe and not doubt, because he who doubts is like a wave of the sea, blown and tossed by the wind. 7 That man should not think he will receive anything from the Lord; 8 he is a double-minded man, unstable in all he does.

9 The brother in humble circumstances ought to take pride in his high position. 10 But the one who is rich should take pride in his low position, because he will pass away like a wild flower. 11 For the sun rises with scorching heat and withers the plant; its blossom falls and its beauty is destroyed. In the same way, the rich man will fade away even while he goes about his business.

12 Blessed is the man who perseveres under trial, because when he has stood the test, he will

Phillips Modern English

no weak spots. And if, in the process, any of you does not know how to meet any particular problem he has only to ask God—who gives generously to all men without making them feel guilty—and he may be quite sure that the necessary wisdom will be given him. But he must ask in sincere faith without secret doubts. For the man who doubts is like a wave of the sea, carried forward by the wind one moment and driven back the next. That sort of man cannot hope to receive anything from the Lord, and the life of a man of divided loyalty will reveal instability at every turn.

1.9 ***Rich and poor can be glad—for different reasons!***

The brother who is poor may be proud because God has raised him to the true riches. The rich may be proud that God has shown him his spiritual poverty. For the rich man will wither away like summer flowers. One day the sunrise brings a scorching wind; the grass withers at once and so do all the flowers—all that lovely sight is destroyed. Just as surely will the rich man and all his ways fall into the blight of decay.

1.12 ***No temptation comes from God, only highest good***

The man who patiently endures the temptations and trials that come to him is the truly

Revised Standard Version

5 If any of you lacks wisdom, let him ask
God, who gives to all men generously and without reproaching, and it will be given him. 6 But
let him ask in faith, with no doubting, for he
who doubts is like a wave of the sea that is
driven and tossed by the wind. 7,8 For that person must not suppose that a double-minded
man, unstable in all his ways, will receive anything from the Lord.
9 Let the lowly brother boast in his exaltation,
10 and the rich in his humiliation, because like
the flower of the grass he will pass away. 11 For
the sun rises with its scorching heat and withers
the grass; its flower falls, and its beauty perishes. So will the rich man fade away in the
midst of his pursuits.
12 Blessed is the man who endures trial, for
when he has stood the test he will receive the

Jerusalem Bible

5 If there is any one of you who needs wisdom,
he must ask God, who gives to all freely and
ungrudgingly; it will be given to him. 6 But he
must ask with faith, and no trace of doubt, because a person who has doubts is like the
7 waves thrown up in the sea when the wind
drives. 8 That sort of person, in two minds,
wavering between going different ways, must not
expect that the Lord will give him anything.
9 It is right for the poor brother to be proud
of his high rank, 10 and the rich one to be thankful that he has been humbled, because riches
last no longer than *the flowers in the grass;*
11 the scorching sun comes up, and *the grass*
withers, the flower falls[c]; what looked so beautiful now disappears. It is the same with the rich
man: his business goes on; he himself perishes.
12 *Happy the man who stands firm*[d] when
trials come. He has proved himself, and will win

[c] Is. 40:6-7. [d] Dn. 12:12.

New English Bible

character that will fall short in nothing. If any of you falls short in wisdom, he should ask God for it and it will be given him, for God is a generous giver who neither refuses nor reproaches anyone. But he must ask in faith, without a doubt in his mind; for the doubter is like a heaving sea ruffled by the wind. A man of that kind must not expect the Lord to give him anything; he is double-minded, and never can keep[a] a steady course.

The brother in humble circumstances may well be proud that God lifts him up; and the wealthy brother must find his pride in being brought low. For the rich man will disappear like the flower of the field; once the sun is up with its scorching heat the flower withers, its petals fall, and what was lovely to look at is lost for ever. So shall the rich man wither away as he goes about his business.

Happy the man who remains steadfast under trial, for having passed that test he will receive

[a] *Or* anything; a double-minded man never keeps . . .

King James Version

the crown of life, which the Lord hath promised
to them that love him. 13 Let no man say when
he is tempted, I am tempted of God: for God
cannot be tempted with evil, neither tempteth
he any man: 14 But every man is tempted, when
he is drawn away of his own lust, and enticed.
15 Then when lust hath conceived, it bringeth
forth sin; and sin, when it is finished, bringeth
forth death. 16 Do not err, my beloved brethren.
17 Every good gift and every perfect gift is from
above, and cometh down from the Father of
lights, with whom is no variableness, neither
shadow of turning. 18 Of his own will begat he
us with the word of truth, that we should be a
kind of firstfruits of his creatures. 19 Wherefore,
my beloved brethren, let every man be swift to
hear, slow to speak, slow to wrath: 20 For the
wrath of man worketh not the righteousness of
God. 21 Wherefore lay apart all filthiness and
superfluity of naughtiness, and receive with meekness the engrafted word, which is able to save

Living Bible

will get as his reward the crown of life that God
has promised those who love him. 13 And remember, when someone wants to do wrong it is
never God who is tempting him, for God never
wants to do wrong and never tempts anyone
else to do it. 14 Temptation is the pull of man's
own evil thoughts and wishes. 15 These evil
thoughts lead to evil actions and afterwards to
the death penalty from God. 16 So don't be misled, dear brothers.

17 But whatever is good and perfect comes to
us from God, the Creator of all light, and he
shines forever without change or shadow. 18 And
it was a happy day for him[a] when he gave us
our new lives, through the truth of his Word,
and we became, as it were, the first children in
his new family.

19 Dear brothers, don't ever forget that it is
best to listen much, speak little, and not become
angry; 20 for anger doesn't make us good, as
God demands that we must be.

21 So get rid of all that is wrong in your life,
both inside and outside, and humbly be glad for
the wonderful message we have received, for it
is able to save our souls as it takes hold of our
hearts.

[a] Literally, "Of his own free will he gave us, etc."

Today's English Version

ing the test he will receive as his reward the life
which God has promised to those who love him.
13 If a man is tempted by such testing, he must
not say, "This temptation comes from God."
For God cannot be tempted by evil, and he himself tempts no one. 14 But a person is tempted
when he is drawn away and trapped by his own
evil desire. 15 Then his evil desire conceives and
gives birth to sin; and sin, when it is full-grown,
gives birth to death.

16 Do not be deceived, my dear brothers!
17 Every good gift and every perfect present
comes from heaven; it comes down from God,
the Creator of the heavenly lights. He himself
does not change or cause darkness by turning.
18 By his own will he brought us into being
through the word of truth, so that we should
have first place among all his creatures.

Hearing and doing

19 Remember this, my dear brothers! Everyone must be quick to listen, but slow to speak,
and slow to become angry. 20 Man's anger does
not achieve God's righteous purpose. 21 Rid
yourselves, then, of every filthy habit and all
wicked conduct. Submit to God and accept the
word that he plants in your hearts, which is
able to save you.

New International Version

receive the victor's crown, the life God has
promised to those who love him.

13 When tempted, no one should say, "God
is tempting me." For God cannot be tempted by
evil, nor does he tempt anyone; 14 but each one
is tempted when, by his own evil desire, he is
dragged away and enticed. 15 Then, after desire
has conceived, it gives birth to sin; and sin,
when it is full-grown, gives birth to death.

16 Don't be deceived, my dear brothers.
17 Every good and perfect gift is from above,
coming down from the Father of the heavenly
lights, who does not change like shifting shadows. 18 He chose to give us birth through the
word of truth, that we might be a kind of firstfruits of all he created.

Listening and doing

19 My dear brothers, take note of this: Everyone should be quick to listen, slow to speak, and
slow to become angry, 20 for man's anger does
not bring about the righteous life that God desires. 21 Therefore, get rid of all moral filth and
the evil that is so prevalent, and humbly accept
the word planted in you, which can save you.

Phillips Modern English

happy man. For once his testing is complete he will receive the crown of life which the Lord has promised to all who love him.

A man must not say when he is tempted, "God is tempting me." For God cannot be tempted by evil, and does not himself tempt anyone. No, a man's temptation is due to the pull of his own inward desires, which greatly attract him. It is his own desire which conceives and gives birth to sin. And sin when fully grown produces death—make no mistake about that, brothers of mine! But every good endowment and every complete gift must come from above, from the Father of all lights, with whom there is never the slightest variation or shadow of inconsistency. By his own wish he made us his own sons through the Word of truth, that we might be, so to speak, the first specimens of his new creation.

1.19 Hear God's Word and put it into practice: that is real religion

Knowing this, then, dear brothers, let every man be quick to listen but slow to use his tongue, and slow to lose his temper. For man's temper is never the means of achieving God's true goodness.

Have done, then, with impurity and every other evil which overflows into the lives of others, and humbly accept the message that God has planted in your hearts, and which can save

Revised Standard Version

crown of life which God has promised to those who love him. 13 Let no one say when he is tempted, "I am tempted by God"; for God cannot be tempted with evil and he himself tempts no one; 14 but each person is tempted when he is lured and enticed by his own desire. 15 Then desire when it has conceived gives birth to sin; and sin when it is full-grown brings forth death.

16 Do not be deceived, my beloved brethren. 17 Every good endowment and every perfect gift is from above, coming down from the Father of lights with whom there is no variation or shadow due to change.[a] 18 Of his own will he brought us forth by the word of truth that we should be a kind of first fruits of his creatures.

19 Know this, my beloved brethren. Let every man be quick to hear, slow to speak, slow to anger, 20 for the anger of man does not work the righteousness of God. 21 Therefore put away all filthiness and rank growth of wickedness and receive with meekness the implanted word, which is able to save your souls.

[a] Other ancient authorities read *variation due to a shadow of turning.*

Jerusalem Bible

the prize of life, the crown that the Lord has promised to those who love him.

Temptation

13 Never, when you have been tempted, say, "God sent the temptation"; God cannot be tempted to do anything wrong, and he does not tempt anybody. 14 Everyone who is tempted is attracted and seduced by his own wrong desire. 15 Then the desire conceives and gives birth to sin, and when sin is fully grown, it too has a child, and the child is death.

16 Make no mistake about this, my dear brothers: 17 it is all that is good, everything that is perfect, which is given us from above; it comes down from the Father of all light; with him there is no such thing as alteration, no shadow of a change. 18 By his own choice he made us his children by the message of the truth so that we should be a sort of first fruits of all that he had created.

True religion

19 Remember this, my dear brothers: be *quick to listen*[e] but *slow* to speak and slow to rouse your temper; 20 God's righteousness is never served by man's anger; 21 so do away with all the impurities and bad habits that are still left in you—accept and submit to the word which has been planted in you and can save your souls.

[e] Ecclesiasticus 5:11.

New English Bible

for his prize the gift of life promised to those who love God. No one under trial or temptation should say, 'I am being tempted by God'; for God is untouched by evil,[a] and does not himself tempt anyone. Temptation arises when a man is enticed and lured away by his own lust; then lust conceives, and gives birth to sin; and sin full-grown breeds death.

Make no mistake, my friends. All good giving, every perfect gift, comes[b] from above, from the Father of the lights of heaven. With him there is no variation, no play of passing shadows.[c] Of his set purpose, by declaring the truth, he gave us birth to be a kind of first fruits of his creatures.

Of that you may be certain, my friends. But each of you must be quick to listen, slow to speak, and slow to be angry. For a man's anger cannot promote the justice of God. Away then with all that is sordid, and the malice that hurries to excess, and quietly accept the message planted in your hearts, which can bring you salvation.

[a] *Or* God cannot be tempted by evil. [b] *Or* All giving is good, and every perfect gift comes . . . [c] *Some witnesses read* no variation, or shadow caused by change.

King James Version

your souls. 22 But be ye doers of the word, and
not hearers only, deceiving your own selves.
23 For if any be a hearer of the word, and not a
doer, he is like unto a man beholding his natural
face in a glass: 24 For he beholdeth himself, and
goeth his way, and straightway forgetteth what
manner of man he was. 25 But whoso looketh
into the perfect law of liberty, and continueth
therein, he being not a forgetful hearer, but a
doer of the work, this man shall be blessed in
his deed. 26 If any man among you seem to be
religious, and bridleth not his tongue, but deceiveth his own heart, this man's religion *is* vain.
27 Pure religion and undefiled before God and
the Father is this, To visit the fatherless and
widows in their affliction, *and* to keep himself
unspotted from the world.

2 My brethren, have not the faith of our Lord
Jesus Christ, *the Lord* of glory, with respect
of persons. 2 For if there come unto your assembly a man with a gold ring, in goodly apparel,
and there come in also a poor man in vile raiment; 3 And ye have respect to him that weareth
the gay clothing, and say unto him, Sit thou here
in a good place; and say to the poor, Stand thou

Living Bible

22 And remember, it is a message to obey,
not just to listen to. So don't fool yourselves.
23 For if a person just listens and doesn't obey,
he is like a man looking at his face in a mirror;
24 as soon as he walks away, he can't see himself anymore or remember what he looks like.
25 But if anyone keeps looking steadily into
God's law for free men, he will not only remember it but he will do what it says, and God will
greatly bless him in everything he does.
26 Anyone who says he is a Christian but
doesn't control his sharp tongue is just fooling
himself, and his religion isn't worth much.
27 The Christian who is pure and without fault,
from God the Father's point of view, is the one
who takes care of orphans and widows, and who
remains true to the Lord—not soiled and dirtied
by his contacts with the world.

2 Dear brothers, how can you claim that you
belong to the Lord Jesus Christ, the Lord
of glory, if you show favoritism to rich people
and look down on poor people?
2 If a man comes into your church dressed in
expensive clothes and with valuable gold rings
on his fingers, and at the same moment another
man comes in who is poor and dressed in thread-
bare clothes, 3 and you make a lot of fuss over
the rich man and give him the best seat in the
house and say to the poor man, "You can stand
over there if you like, or else sit on the floor"—

Today's English Version

22 Do not fool yourselves by just listening to
his word. Instead, put it into practice. 23 Whoever listens to the word but does not put it into
practice is like a man who looks in a mirror
and sees himself as he is. 24 He takes a good
look at himself and then goes away, and at once
forgets what he looks like. 25 But whoever looks
closely into the perfect law that sets men free,
who keeps on paying attention to it, and does
not simply listen and then forget it, but puts it
into practice—that person will be blessed by
God in what he does.
26 Does anyone think he is a religious man?
If he does not control his tongue his religion is
worthless and he deceives himself. 27 What God
the Father considers to be pure and genuine
religion is this: to take care of orphans and
widows in their suffering, and to keep oneself
from being corrupted by the world.

Warning against prejudice

2 My brothers! As believers in our Lord Jesus Christ, the Lord of glory, you must never
treat people in different ways, according to their
outward appearance. 2 Suppose a rich man wearing a gold ring and fine clothes comes to your
meeting, and a poor man in ragged clothes also
comes. 3 If you show more respect to the well-
dressed man and say to him, "Have this best
seat here," but say to the poor man, "Stand, or

New International Version

22 Do not merely listen to the word, and so
deceive yourselves. Do what it says. 23 Anyone
who listens to the word but does not do what
it says is like a man who looks at his face in a
mirror 24 and, after looking at himself, goes
away and immediately forgets what he looks
like. 25 But the man who looks intently into the
perfect law that gives freedom, and continues to
do this, not forgetting what he has heard, but
doing it—he will be blessed in what he does.
26 If anyone considers himself religious and
yet does not keep a tight rein on his tongue, he
deceives himself and his religion is worthless.
27 Religion that God our Father accepts as
pure and faultless is this: to look after orphans
and widows in their distress and to keep oneself
from being polluted by the world.

Favoritism forbidden

2 My brothers, as believers in our glorious
Lord Jesus Christ, don't show favoritism.
2 Suppose a man comes into your meeting wearing a gold ring and fine clothes, and a poor man
in shabby clothes also comes in. 3 If you show
special attention to the man wearing fine clothes
and say, "Here's a good seat for you," but say
to the poor man, "You stand there," or, "Sit

Phillips Modern English

your souls. Don't only hear the message, but put it into practice; otherwise you are merely deluding yourselves. The man who simply hears and does nothing about it is like a man catching the reflection of his natural face in a mirror. He sees himself, it is true, but he goes off without the slightest recollection of what sort of person he saw in the mirror. But the man who looks into the perfect law, the law of liberty, and makes a habit of so doing, is not the man who hears and forgets. He puts that law into practice and he wins true happiness.

If anyone appears to be "religious" but cannot control his tongue, he deceives himself and we may be sure that his religion is useless. Religion that is pure and genuine in the sight of God the Father will show itself by such things as visiting orphans and widows in their distress and keeping oneself uncontaminated by the world.

2.1 *Avoid snobbery: keep the royal law*

Don't ever attempt, my brothers, to combine snobbery with faith in our glorious Lord Jesus Christ! Suppose one man comes into your meeting well-dressed and with a gold ring on his finger, and another man, obviously poor, arrives in shabby clothes. If you pay special attention to the well-dressed man by saying, "Please sit here—it's an excellent seat", and say to the poor man, "You stand over there, or if you must sit,

Revised Standard Version

22 But be doers of the word, and not hearers only, deceiving yourselves. 23 For if any one is a hearer of the word and not a doer, he is like a man who observes his natural face in a mirror; 24 for he observes himself and goes away and at once forgets what he was like. 25 But he who looks into the perfect law, the law of liberty, and perseveres, being no hearer that forgets but a doer that acts, he shall be blessed in his doing.

26 If any one thinks he is religious, and does not bridle his tongue but deceives his heart, this man's religion is vain. 27 Religion that is pure and undefiled before God and the Father is this: to visit orphans and widows in their affliction, and to keep oneself unstained from the world.

2 My brethren, show no partiality as you hold the faith of our Lord Jesus Christ, the Lord of glory. 2 For if a man with gold rings and in fine clothing comes into your assembly, and a poor man in shabby clothing also comes in, 3 and you pay attention to the one who wears the fine clothing and say, "Have a seat here, please," while you say to the poor man,

Jerusalem Bible

22 But you must do what the word tells you, and not just listen to it and deceive yourselves. 23 To listen to the word and not obey is like looking at your own features in a mirror and then, 24 after a quick look, going off and immediately forgetting what you looked like. 25 But the man who looks steadily at the perfect law of freedom and makes that his habit—not listening and then forgetting, but actively putting it into practice—will be happy in all that he does.

26 Nobody must imagine that he is religious while he still goes on deceiving himself and not keeping control over his tongue; anyone who does this has the wrong idea of religion. 27 Pure, unspoiled religion, in the eyes of God our Father is this: coming to the help of orphans and widows when they need it, and keeping oneself uncontaminated by the world.

Respect for the poor

2 My brothers, do not try to combine faith in Jesus Christ, our glorified Lord, with the making of distinctions between classes of people. 2 Now suppose a man comes into your synagogue,[f] beautifully dressed and with a gold ring on, and at the same time a poor man comes in, in shabby clothes, 3 and you take notice of the well-dressed man, and say, "Come this way to the best seats"; then you tell the poor man, "Stand over there" or "You can sit on the floor

[f] Jewish Christians may still have been attending synagogues, or the writer may have adopted this word for the Christian assembly.

New English Bible

Only be sure that you act on the message and do not merely listen; for that would be to mislead yourselves. A man who listens to the message but never acts upon it is like one who looks in a mirror at the face nature gave him. He glances at himself and goes away, and at once forgets what he looked like. But the man who looks closely into the perfect law, the law that makes us free, and who lives in its company, does not forget what he hears, but acts upon it; and that is the man who by acting will find happiness.

A man may think he is religious, but if he has no control over his tongue, he is deceiving himself; that man's religion is futile. The kind of religion which is without stain or fault in the sight of God our Father is this: to go to the help of orphans and widows in their distress and keep oneself untarnished by the world.

2 My brothers, believing as you do in our Lord Jesus Christ, who reigns in glory, you must never show snobbery. For instance, two visitors may enter your place of worship, one a well-dressed man with gold rings, and the other a poor man in shabby clothes. Suppose you pay special attention to the well-dressed man and say to him, 'Please take this seat', while to the poor man you say, 'You can stand; or you may sit

King James Version

there, or sit here under my footstool: 4 Are ye
not then partial in yourselves, and are become
judges of evil thoughts? 5 Hearken, my beloved
brethren, Hath not God chosen the poor of this
world rich in faith, and heirs of the kingdom
which he hath promised to them that love him?
6 But ye have despised the poor. Do not rich
men oppress you, and draw you before the judgment seats? 7 Do not they blaspheme that worthy name by the which ye are called? 8 If ye
fulfil the royal law according to the Scripture,
Thou shalt love thy neighbour as thyself, ye do
well: 9 But if ye have respect to persons, ye
commit sin, and are convinced of the law as
transgressors. 10 For whosoever shall keep the
whole law, and yet offend in one *point*, he is
guilty of all. 11 For he that said, Do not commit
adultery, said also, Do not kill. Now if thou
commit no adultery, yet if thou kill, thou art
become a transgressor of the law. 12 So speak
ye, and so do, as they that shall be judged by
the law of liberty. 13 For he shall have judgment
without mercy, that hath shewed no mercy; and

Living Bible

well, 4 judging a man by his wealth shows that
you are guided by wrong motives.

5 Listen to me, dear brothers: God has
chosen poor people to be rich in faith, and the
Kingdom of Heaven is theirs, for that is the gift
God has promised to all those who love him.
6 And yet, of the two strangers, you have despised the poor man. Don't you realize that it is
usually the rich men who pick on you and drag
you into court? 7 And all too often they are the
ones who laugh at Jesus Christ, whose noble
name you bear.

8 Yes indeed, it is good when you truly obey
our Lord's command, "You must love and help
your neighbors just as much as you love and
take care of yourself." 9 But you are breaking
this law of our Lord's when you favor the rich
and fawn over them; it is sin.

10 And the person who keeps every law of
God, but makes one little slip, is just as guilty
as the person who has broken every law there
is. 11 For the God who said you must not marry
a woman who already has a husband, also said
you must not murder, so even though you have
not broken the marriage laws by committing
adultery, but have murdered someone, you have
entirely broken God's laws and stand utterly
guilty before him.

12 You will be judged on whether or not you
are doing what Christ wants you to. So watch
what you do and what you think; 13 for there
will be no mercy to those who have shown no
mercy. But if you have been merciful, then God's
mercy toward you will win out over his judgment against you.

Today's English Version

sit down here on the floor by my feet," 4 then
you are guilty of creating distinctions among
yourselves and of making judgments based on
evil motives.

5 Listen, my dear brothers! God chose the
poor people of this world to be rich in faith
and to possess the Kingdom which he promised
to those who love him. 6 But you dishonor the
poor! Who are the ones who oppress you and
drag you before the judges? The rich! 7 They
are the ones who speak evil of that good name
which has been given to you.

8 You will be doing the right thing if you
obey the law of the Kingdom, which is found
in the scripture, "Love your fellow-man as
yourself." 9 But if you treat people according to
their outward appearance, you are guilty of sin,
and the Law condemns you as a lawbreaker.
10 Whoever breaks one command of the Law is
guilty of breaking them all. 11 For the same
one who said, "Do not commit adultery," also
said, "Do not murder." Even if you do not
commit adultery, you have become a lawbreaker
if you murder. 12 Speak and act as people who
will be judged by the law that sets men free.
13 For God will not show mercy when he judges
the man who has not been merciful; but mercy
triumphs over judgment.

New International Version

on the floor by my feet," 4 have you not discriminated among yourselves and become judges
with evil thoughts?

5 Listen, my dear brothers: Has not God
chosen those who are poor in the eyes of the
world to be rich in faith and to inherit the kingdom he promised those who love him? 6 But you
have insulted the poor. Is it not the rich who are
exploiting you? Are they not the ones who are
dragging you into court? 7 Are they not the ones
who are slandering the noble name of him to
whom you belong?

8 If you really keep the royal law found in
Scripture, "Love your neighbor as yourself," [a]
you are doing right. 9 But if you show favoritism,
you sin and are convicted by the law as lawbreakers. 10 For whoever keeps the whole law,
and yet stumbles at just one point, is guilty of
breaking all of it. 11 For he who said, "Do not
commit adultery," [b] also said, "Do not murder." [c]
If you do not commit adultery but do commit
murder, you have become a lawbreaker.

12 Speak and act as those who are going to
be judged by the law that gives freedom, 13 because judgment without mercy will be shown
to anyone who has not been merciful. Mercy
triumphs over judgment!

[*a*] Lev. 19:18. [*b*] Exodus 20:14; Deut. 5:18. [*c*] Exodus 20:13; Deut. 5:17.

Phillips Modern English

sit on the floor by my feet", doesn't that prove that you are making class-distinctions in your mind, and setting yourselves up to assess a man's quality from wrong motives? For do notice, my dear brothers, that God chose poor men, whose only wealth was their faith, and made them heirs to the kingdom promised to those who love him. And if you behave as I have suggested, it is the poor man that you are insulting. Look around you. Isn't it the rich who are always trying to rule your lives, isn't it the rich who drag you into litigation? Isn't it usually the rich who blaspheme the glorious name by which you are known?

If you obey the royal Law, expressed by the scripture, "Thou shalt love thy neighbour as thyself", all is well. But once you allow any invidious distinctions to creep in, you are sinning, you stand condemned by that Law. Remember that a man who keeps the whole Law but for a single exception is none the less a law-breaker. The one who said, "Thou shalt not commit adultery" also said, "Thou shalt do no murder". If you were to keep clear of adultery but were to murder a man you would have become a breaker of the whole Law.

Anyway, you should speak and act as men who will be judged by the law of freedom. The man who makes no allowances for others will find none made for him. Mercy may laugh in the face of judgment.

Revised Standard Version

"Stand there," or, "Sit at my feet," 4 have you
not made distinctions among yourselves, and become judges with evil thoughts? 5 Listen, my
beloved brethren. Has not God chosen those
who are poor in the world to be rich in faith
and heirs of the kingdom which he has promised
to those who love him? 6 But you have dishonored the poor man. Is it not the rich who
oppress you, is it not they who drag you into
court? 7 Is it not they who blaspheme the honorable name which was invoked over you?
8 If you really fulfil the royal law, according
to the scripture, "You shall love your neighbor
as yourself," you do well. 9 But if you show partiality, you commit sin, and are convicted by
the law as transgressors. 10 For whoever keeps
the whole law but fails in one point has become
guilty of all of it. 11 For he who said, "Do not
commit adultery," said also, "Do not kill." If
you do not commit adultery but do kill, you
have become a transgressor of the law. 12 So
speak and so act as those who are to be judged
under the law of liberty. 13 For judgment is
without mercy to one who has shown no mercy;
yet mercy triumphs over judgment.

Jerusalem Bible

by my footrest." 4 Can't you see that you have
used two different standards in your mind, and
turned yourselves into judges, and corrupt judges
at that?
5 Listen, my dear brothers: it was those who
are poor according to the world that God chose,
to be rich in faith and to be the heirs to the
kingdom which he promised to those who love
him. 6 In spite of this, you have no respect for
anybody who is poor. Isn't it always the rich
who are against you? Isn't it always their doing
when you are dragged before the court? 7 Aren't
they the ones who insult the honorable name to
which you have been dedicated? 8 Well, the right
thing to do is to keep the supreme law of scripture: *you must love your neighbor as yourself* [g];
9 but as soon as you make distinctions between
classes of people, you are committing sin, and
under condemnation for breaking the Law.
10 You see, if a man keeps the whole of the
Law, except for one small point at which he
fails, he is still guilty of breaking it all. 11 It was
the same person who said, *"You must not commit adultery"* and *"you must not kill."* [h] Now
if you commit murder, you do not have to commit adultery as well to become a breaker of the
Law. 12 Talk and behave like people who are
going to be judged by the law of freedom, 13 because there will be judgment without mercy for
those who have not been merciful themselves;
but the merciful need have no fear of judgment.

[g] Lv. 19:18. [h] Ex. 20:13-14.

New English Bible

here[d] on the floor by my footstool', do you not see that you are inconsistent and judge by false standards?

Listen, my friends. Has not God chosen those who are poor in the eyes of the world to be rich in faith and to inherit the kingdom he has promised to those who love him? And yet you have insulted the poor man. Moreover, are not the rich your oppressors? Is it not they who drag you into court and pour contempt on the honoured name by which God has claimed you?

If, however, you are observing the sovereign law laid down in Scripture, 'Love your neighbour as yourself', that is excellent. But if you show snobbery, you are committing a sin and you stand convicted by that law as transgressors. For if a man keeps the whole law apart from one single point, he is guilty of breaking all of it. For the One who said, 'Thou shalt not commit adultery', said also, 'Thou shalt not commit murder.' You may not be an adulterer, but if you commit murder you are a law-breaker all the same. Always speak and act as men who are to be judged under a law of freedom. In that judgement there will be no mercy for the man who has shown no mercy. Mercy triumphs over judgement.

[d] *Some witnesses read* Stand where you are or sit here . . . : *others read* Stand where you are or sit . . .

King James Version

mercy rejoiceth against judgment. 14 What *doth*
it profit, my brethren, though a man say he hath
faith, and have not works? can faith save him?
15 If a brother or sister be naked, and destitute
of daily food, 16 And one of you say unto them,
Depart in peace, be *ye* warmed and filled; notwithstanding ye give them not those things which
are needful to the body; what *doth it* profit?
17 Even so faith, if it hath not works, is dead,
being alone. 18 Yea, a man may say, Thou hast
faith, and I have works: shew me thy faith without thy works, and I will shew thee my faith
by my works. 19 Thou believest that there is one
God; thou doest well: the devils also believe,
and tremble. 20 But wilt thou know, O vain man,
that faith without works is dead? 21 Was not
Abraham our father justified by works, when
he had offered Isaac his son upon the altar?
22 Seest thou how faith wrought with his works,
and by works was faith made perfect? 23 And
the Scripture was fulfilled which saith, Abraham

Living Bible

14 Dear brothers, what's the use of saying
that you have faith and are Christians if you
aren't proving it by helping others? Will *that*
kind of faith save anyone? 15 If you have a
friend who is in need of food and clothing,
16 and you say to him, "Well, good-bye and God
bless you; stay warm and eat hearty," and then
don't give him clothes or food, what good does
that do?

17 So you see, it isn't enough just to have
faith. You must also do good to prove that you
have it. Faith that doesn't show itself by good
works is no faith at all—it is dead and useless.

18 But someone may well argue, "You say
the way to God is by faith alone, plus nothing;
well, I say that good works are important too,
for without good works you can't prove whether
you have faith or not; but anyone can see that
I have faith by the way I act."

19 Are there still some among you who hold
that "only believing" is enough? Believing in
one God? Well, remember that the demons believe this too—so strongly that they tremble in
terror! 20 Fool! When will you ever learn that
"believing" is useless without *doing* what God
wants you to? Faith that does not result in good
deeds is not real faith.

21 Don't you remember that even our father
Abraham was declared good because of what he
did, when he was willing to obey God, even if it
meant offering his son Isaac to die on the altar?
22 You see, he was trusting God so much that
he was willing to do whatever God told him to;
his faith was made complete by what he did,
by his actions, his good deeds. 23 And so it happened just as the Scriptures say, that Abraham

Today's English Version

Faith and actions

14 My brothers! What good is it for someone
to say, "I have faith," if his actions do not prove
it? Can that faith save him? 15 Suppose there
are brothers or sisters who need clothes and
don't have enough to eat. 16 What good is there
in your saying to them, "God bless you! Keep
warm and eat well!"—if you don't give them
the necessities of life? 17 So it is with faith: if
it is alone and has no actions with it, then it is
dead.

18 But someone will say, "One person has
faith, another has actions." My answer is, "Show
me how anyone can have faith without actions.
I will show you my faith by my actions." 19 Do
you believe that there is only one God? Good!
The demons also believe—and tremble with fear.
20 You fool! Do you want to be shown that
faith without actions is useless? 21 How was our
ancestor Abraham put right with God? It was
through his actions, when he offered his son
Isaac on the altar. 22 Can't you see? His faith
and his actions worked together; his faith was
made perfect through his actions. 23 And the
scripture came true that said, "Abraham be-

New International Version

Faith and deeds

14 What good is it, my brothers, if a man
claims to have faith but has no deeds? Can such
faith save him? 15 Suppose a brother or sister is
without clothes and daily food. 16 If one of you
says to him, "Go, I wish you well; keep warm
and well fed," but does nothing about his physical needs, what good is it? 17 In the same way,
faith by itself, if it is not accompanied by action,
is dead.

18 But someone will say, "You have faith; I
have deeds."

Show me your faith without deeds, and I will
show you my faith by what I do. 19 You believe
that there is one God. Good! Even the demons
believe that—and shudder.

20 You foolish man, do you want evidence
that faith without deeds is useless?[d] 21 Was not
our ancestor Abraham considered righteous for
what he did when he offered his son Isaac on
the altar? 22 You see that his faith and his actions were working together, and his faith was
made complete by what he did. 23 And the
scripture was fulfilled that says, "Abraham be-

[*d*] Some early MSS read *dead.*

Phillips Modern English

2.14 The relation between faith and action

Now what use is it, my brothers, for a man to say he "has faith" if his actions do not correspond with it? Could that sort of faith save anyone's soul? If a fellow man or woman has no clothes to wear and nothing to eat, and one of you say, "Good luck to you I hope you'll keep warm and find enough to eat", and yet give them nothing to meet their physical needs, what on earth is the good of that? Yet that is exactly what a bare faith without a corresponding life is like—quite dead. A man could challenge us by saying, "You have faith and I have merely good actions. Well, all you can do is to show me a faith without corresponding actions, but I can show you by my actions that I have faith as well."

So you believe that there is one God? That's fine. So do all the devils in hell, and shudder in terror! For, my dear short-sighted man, can't you see far enough to realise that faith without the right actions is dead and useless? Think of Abraham, our ancestor. Wasn't it his action which really justified him in God's sight when his faith led him to offer his son Isaac on the altar? Can't you see that his faith and his actions were, so to speak, partners—that his faith was implemented by his deed? That is what the scripture means when it says:

And Abraham believed God,

Revised Standard Version

14 What does it profit, my brethren, if a man
says he has faith but has not works? Can his
faith save him? 15 If a brother or sister is ill-
clad and in lack of daily food, 16 and one of you
says to them, "Go in peace, be warmed and
filled," without giving them the things needed
for the body, what does it profit? 17 So faith by
itself, if it has no works, is dead.
18 But some one will say, "You have faith
and I have works." Show me your faith apart
from your works, and I by my works will show
you my faith. 19 You believe that God is one;
you do well. Even the demons believe—and
shudder. 20 Do you want to be shown, you shallow man, that faith apart from works is barren?
21 Was not Abraham our father justified by
works, when he offered his son Isaac upon the
altar? 22 You see that faith was active along
with his works, and faith was completed by
works, 23 and the scripture was fulfilled which
says, "Abraham believed God, and it was reck-

Jerusalem Bible

Faith and good works

14 Take the case, my brothers, of someone
who has never done a single good act but claims
that he has faith. Will that faith save him? 15 If
one of the brothers or one of the sisters is in
need of clothes and has not enough food to live
on, 16 and one of you says to them, "I wish
you well; keep yourself warm and eat plenty,"
without giving them these bare necessities of life,
then what good is that? 17 Faith is like that: if
good works do not go with it, it is quite dead.
18 This is the way to talk to people of that
kind: "You say you have faith and I have good
deeds; I will prove to you that I have faith by
showing you my good deeds—now you prove to
me that you have faith without any good deeds
to show. 19 You believe in the one God—that is
creditable enough, but the demons have the
same belief, and they tremble with fear. 20 Do
realize, you senseless man, that faith without
good deeds is useless. 21 You surely know that
Abraham our father was justified by his deed,
because he *offered his son Isaac on the altar?* [i]
22 There you see it: faith and deeds were working together; his faith became perfect by what
he did. 23 This is what scripture really means
when it says: *Abraham put his faith in God,*

[i] Gn. 22:9.

New English Bible

My brothers, what use is it for a man to say he has faith when he does nothing to show it? Can that faith save him? Suppose a brother or a sister is in rags with not enough food for the day, and one of you says, 'Good luck to you, keep yourselves warm, and have plenty to eat', but does nothing to supply their bodily needs, what is the good of that? So with faith; if it does not lead to action, it is in itself a lifeless thing.

But someone may object: 'Here is one who claims to have faith and another who points to his deeds.' To which I reply: 'Prove to me that this faith you speak of is real though not accompanied by deeds, and by my deeds I will prove to you my faith.' You have faith enough to believe that there is one God. Excellent! The devils have faith like that, and it makes them tremble. But can you not see, you quibbler, that faith divorced from deeds is barren? Was it not by his action, in offering his son Isaac upon the altar, that our father Abraham was justified? Surely you can see that faith was at work in his actions, and that by these actions the integrity of his faith was fully proved. Here was fulfilment of the words of Scripture: 'Abraham put his

King James Version

believed God, and it was imputed unto him for
righteousness: and he was called the Friend of
God. 24 Ye see then how that by works a man
is justified, and not by faith only. 25 Likewise
also was not Rahab the harlot justified by works,
when she had received the messengers, and had
sent *them* out another way? 26 For as the body
without the spirit is dead, so faith without works
is dead also.

3 My brethren, be not many masters, knowing that we shall receive the greater condemnation. 2 For in many things we offend all. If
any man offend not in word, the same *is* a
perfect man, *and* able also to bridle the whole
body. 3 Behold, we put bits in the horses' mouths,
that they may obey us; and we turn about their
whole body. 4 Behold also the ships, which
though *they be* so great, and *are* driven of fierce

Living Bible

trusted God, and the Lord declared him good
in God's sight, and he was even called "the
friend of God." 24 So you see, a man is saved
by what he does, as well as by what he believes.
25 Rahab, the prostitute, is another example
of this. She was saved because of what she did
when she hid those messengers and sent them
safely away by a different road. 26 Just as the
body is dead when there is no spirit in it, so
faith is dead if it is not the kind that results in
good deeds.

3 Dear brothers, don't be too eager to tell
others their faults,[a] for we all make many
mistakes; and when we teachers of religion,
who should know better, do wrong, our punishment will be greater than it would be for others.
If anyone can control his tongue, it proves that
he has perfect control over himself in every
other way. 3 We can make a large horse turn
around and go wherever we want by means of
a small bit in his mouth. 4 And a tiny rudder
makes a huge ship turn wherever the pilot wants

[a] Literally, "Not many (of you) should become masters (teachers)."

Today's English Version

lieved God, and because of his faith God accepted him as righteous." And so Abraham was
called God's friend. 24 You see, then, that a
man is put right with God by what he does, and
not because of his faith alone.
25 It was the same with the prostitute Rahab.
She was put right with God through her actions,
by welcoming the Jewish messengers and helping them escape by a different road.
26 So then, as the body without the spirit is
dead, also faith without actions is dead.

The tongue

3 My brothers! Not many of you should
become teachers, because you know that we
teachers will be judged with greater strictness
than others. 2 All of us often make mistakes.
The person who never makes a mistake in what
he says is perfect, able also to control his whole
being. 3 We put a bit into the mouth of a horse
to make it obey us, and we are able to make it
go where we want. 4 Or think of a ship: big as
it is, and driven by such strong winds, it can be

New International Version

lieved God, and it was credited to him as
righteousness,"[e] and he was called God's friend.
24 You see that a person is justified by what he
does and not by faith alone.
25 In the same way, was not even Rahab the
prostitute considered righteous for what she did
when she gave lodging to the spies and sent them
off in a different direction? 26 As the body without the spirit is dead, so faith without deeds is
dead.

Taming the tongue

3 Not many of you should act as teachers,
my brothers, because you know that we who
teach will be judged more strictly. 2 We all
stumble in many ways. If anyone is never at
fault in what he says, he is a perfect man, able
to keep his whole body in check.
3 When we put bits into the mouths of horses
to make them obey us, we can turn the whole
animal. 4 Or take ships as an example. Although
they are so large and are driven by strong winds,

[e] Gen. 15:6.

Phillips Modern English

And it was reckoned unto him for righteousness;
And he was called the friend of God.

A man is justified before God by what he does as well as by what he believes. Rahab, who was a prostitute, has been quoted as an example of faith, yet surely it was her action that pleased God, when she welcomed Joshua's reconnoitring party and sent them safely back by a different route.

Yes, faith without action is as dead as a body without a soul.

3.1 The responsibility of a teacher's position

Don't aim at adding to the number of teachers, my brothers, I beg you! Remember that we who are teachers will be judged by a much higher standard.

3.2 The danger of the tongue

We all make mistakes in all kinds of ways, but the man who can claim that he never says the wrong thing can consider himself perfect, for if he can control his tongue he can control every other part of his personality! Men control the movements of a large animal like the horse with a tiny bit placed in its mouth. Ships too, for all their size and the momentum they have with a

Revised Standard Version

oned to him as righteousness"; and he was called
the friend of God. 24 You see that a man is
justified by works and not by faith alone. 25 And
in the same way was not also Rahab the harlot
justified by works when she received the messengers and sent them out another way? 26 For
as the body apart from the spirit is dead, so
faith apart from works is dead.

3 Let not many of you become teachers, my
brethren, for you know that we who teach
shall be judged with greater strictness. 2 For we
all make many mistakes, and if any one makes
no mistakes in what he says he is a perfect man,
able to bridle the whole body also. 3 If we put
bits into the mouths of horses that they may
obey us, we guide their whole bodies. 4 Look at
the ships also; though they are so great and are

Jerusalem Bible

and this was counted as making him justified [j]; and that is why he was called "the friend of God."

24 You see now that it is by doing something
good, and not only by believing, that a man is
justified. 25 There is another example of the
same kind: Rahab the prostitute, justified by her
deeds because she welcomed the messengers and
showed them a different way to leave. 26 A body
dies when it is separated from the spirit, and in
the same way faith is dead if it is separated
from good deeds.

Uncontrolled language

3 Only a few of you, my brothers, should be teachers, bearing in mind that those of us who teach can expect a stricter judgment.

2 After all, every one of us does something
wrong, over and over again; the only man who
could reach perfection would be someone who
never said anything wrong—he would be able to
control every part of himself. 3 Once we put a
bit into the horse's mouth, to make it do what
we want, we have the whole animal under our
control. 4 Or think of ships: no matter how
big they are, even if a gale is driving them, the

[j] Gn. 15:6.

New English Bible

faith in God, and that faith was counted to him as righteousness'; and elsewhere he is called 'God's friend'. You see then that a man is justified by deeds and not by faith in itself. The same is true of the prostitute Rahab also. Was not she justified by her action in welcoming the messengers into her house and sending them away by a different route? As the body is dead when there is no breath left in it, so faith divorced from deeds is lifeless as a corpse.

3 My brothers, not many of you should become teachers, for you may be certain that we who teach shall ourselves be judged with greater strictness. All of us often go wrong; the man who never says a wrong thing is a perfect character, able to bridle his whole being. If we put bits into horses' mouths to make them obey our will, we can direct their whole body. Or think of ships: large they may be, yet even when

King James Version

winds, yet are they turned about with a very
small helm, whithersoever the governor listeth.
5 Even so the tongue is a little member, and
boasteth great things. Behold, how great a matter a little fire kindleth! 6And the tongue *is* a
fire, a world of iniquity: so is the tongue among
our members, that it defileth the whole body,
and setteth on fire the course of nature; and it
is set on fire of hell. 7 For every kind of beasts,
and of birds, and of serpents, and of things in
the sea, is tamed, and hath been tamed of mankind: 8 But the tongue can no man tame; *it is*
an unruly evil, full of deadly poison. 9 Therewith bless we God, even the Father; and therewith curse we men, which are made after the
similitude of God. 10 Out of the same mouth
proceedeth blessing and cursing. My brethren,
these things ought not so to be. 11 Doth a fountain send forth at the same place sweet *water*
and bitter? 12 Can the fig tree, my brethren, bear
olive berries? either a vine, figs? so *can* no fountain both yield salt water and fresh. 13 Who *is*
a wise man and endued with knowledge among
you? let him shew out of a good conversation
his works with meekness of wisdom. 14 But if ye
have bitter envying and strife in your hearts,

Living Bible

it to go, even though the winds are strong.
5 So also the tongue is a small thing, but what
enormous damage it can do. A great forest can
be set on fire by one tiny spark. 6And the tongue
is a flame of fire. It is full of wickedness, and
poisons every part of the body. And the tongue
is set on fire by hell itself, and can turn our
whole lives into a blazing flame of destruction
and disaster.
7 Men have trained, or can train, every kind
of animal or bird that lives and every kind of
reptile and fish, 8 but no human being can tame
the tongue. It is always ready to pour out its
deadly poison. 9 Sometimes it praises our heavenly Father, and sometimes it breaks out into
curses against men who are made like God.
10And so blessing and cursing come pouring out
of the same mouth. Dear brothers, surely this
is not right! 11 Does a spring of water bubble
out first with fresh water and then with bitter
water? 12 Can you pick olives from a fig tree,
or figs from a grape vine? No, and you can't
draw fresh water from a salty pool.
13 If you are wise, live a life of steady goodness, so that only good deeds will pour forth.
And if you don't brag about them, then you
will be truly wise! 14And by all means don't brag
about being wise and good if you are bitter and

Today's English Version

steered by a very small rudder, and goes wherever the pilot wants it to go. 5 So it is with the
tongue: small as it is, it can boast about great
things.
Just think how large a forest can be set on
fire by a tiny flame! 6And the tongue is like a
fire. It is a world of wrong, occupying its place
in our bodies and spreading evil through our
whole being. It sets on fire the entire course of
our existence with the fire that comes to it from
hell itself. 7 Man is able to tame, and has tamed,
all other creatures—wild animals and birds, reptiles and fish. 8 But no man has ever been able
to tame the tongue. It is evil and uncontrollable,
full of deadly poison. 9 We use it to give thanks
to our Lord and Father, and also to curse our
fellow-men, created in the likeness of God.
10 Words of thanksgiving and cursing pour out
from the same mouth. My brothers! This should
not happen! 11 No spring of water pours out
sweet and bitter water from the same opening.
12A fig tree, my brothers, cannot bear olives; a
grapevine cannot bear figs; nor can salty water
produce fresh water.

The wisdom from above

13 Is there someone among you who is wise
and understanding? He is to prove it by his
good life, by his good deeds performed with
humility and wisdom. 14 But if in your heart
you are jealous, bitter, and selfish, then you

New International Version

they are steered by a very small rudder wherever the pilot wants to go. 5 Likewise the tongue
is a small part of the body, but it makes great
boasts. Consider what a great forest is set on
fire by a small spark. 6 The tongue also is a
fire, a world of evil among the parts of the body.
It corrupts the whole person, sets the whole
course of his life on fire, and is itself set on
fire by hell.
7 All kinds of animals, birds, reptiles and
creatures of the sea are being tamed and have
been tamed by man, 8 but no man can tame the
tongue. It is a restless evil, full of deadly
poison.
9 With the tongue we praise our Lord and
Father, and with it we curse men, who have
been made in God's likeness. 10 Out of the
same mouth come praise and cursing. My brothers, this should not be. 11 Can both fresh water
and salt water flow from the same spring? 12 My
brothers, can a fig tree bear olives, or a grapevine bear figs? Neither can a salt spring produce fresh water.

Two kinds of wisdom

13 Who is wise and understanding among
you? Let him show it by his good life, by deeds
done in the humility that comes from wisdom.
14 But if you harbor bitter envy and selfish ambition in your hearts, do not boast about it or

Phillips Modern English

strong wind behind them, are controlled by a very small rudder according to the course chosen by the helmsman. The human tongue is physically small, but what tremendous effects it can boast of! A whole forest can be set ablaze by a tiny spark of fire, and the tongue is a fire, a whole world of evil. It is set within our bodily members but it can poison the whole body, it can set the whole of life ablaze, fed with the fires of hell.

Beasts, birds, reptiles and all kinds of sea-creatures can be, and in fact are, tamed by man, but no one can tame the human tongue. It is an evil always liable to break out, and the poison it spreads is deadly. We use the tongue to bless our Lord and Father and we use the same tongue to curse our fellow-men, who are all created in God's likeness. Blessing and curses come out of the same mouth—surely, my brothers, this is the sort of thing that never ought to happen! Have you ever known a spring to give sweet and bitter water from the same source? Have you ever seen a fig-tree with a crop of olives, or seen figs growing on a vine? It is just as impossible for salt water to produce fresh.

3.13 *Real, spiritual, wisdom means humility, not rivalry*

Is there some wise and understanding man among you? Then let his life be a shining example of the humility that is born of true wisdom. But if your heart is full of bitter jealousy and rivalry, then do not boast and do not deny the

Revised Standard Version

driven by strong winds, they are guided by a very small rudder wherever the will of the pilot directs. 5 So the tongue is a little member and boasts of great things. How great a forest is set ablaze by a small fire!

6 And the tongue is a fire. The tongue is an unrighteous world among our members, staining the whole body, setting on fire the cycle of nature,[b] and set on fire by hell.[c] 7 For every kind of beast and bird, of reptile and sea creature, can be tamed and has been tamed by humankind, 8 but no human being can tame the tongue—a restless evil, full of deadly poison. 9 With it we bless the Lord and Father, and with it we curse men, who are made in the likeness of God. 10 From the same mouth come blessing and cursing. My brethren, this ought not to be so. 11 Does a spring pour forth from the same opening fresh water and brackish? 12 Can a fig tree, my brethren, yield olives, or a grapevine figs? No more can salt water yield fresh.

13 Who is wise and understanding among you? By his good life let him show his works in the meekness of wisdom. 14 But if you have bitter jealousy and selfish ambition in your

[b] Or *wheel of birth.* [c] Greek *Gehenna.*

Jerusalem Bible

man at the helm can steer them anywhere he likes by controlling a tiny rudder. 5 So is the tongue only a tiny part of the body, but it can proudly claim that it does great things. Think how small a flame can set fire to a huge forest; 6 the tongue is a flame like that. Among all the parts of the body, the tongue is a whole wicked world in itself: it infects the whole body; catching fire itself from hell, it sets fire to the whole wheel of creation. 7 Wild animals and birds, reptiles and fish can all be tamed by man, and often are; 8 but nobody can tame the tongue—it is a pest that will not keep still, full of deadly poison. 9 We use it to bless the Lord and Father, but we also use it to curse men who are made in God's image: 10 the blessing and the curse come out of the same mouth. My brothers, this must be wrong—11 does any water supply give a flow of fresh water and salt water out of the same pipe? 12 Can a fig tree give you olives, my brothers, or a vine give figs? No more can sea water give you fresh water.

Real wisdom and its opposite

13 If there are any wise or learned men among you, let them show it by their good lives, with humility and wisdom in their actions. 14 But if at heart you have the bitterness of jealousy, or

New English Bible

driven by strong gales they can be directed by a tiny rudder on whatever course the helmsman chooses. So with the tongue. It is a small member but it can make huge claims.[a]

What an immense stack of timber[b] can be set ablaze by the tiniest spark! And the tongue is in effect a fire. It represents among our members the world with all its wickedness; it pollutes our whole being; it keeps the wheel of our existence red-hot, and its flames are fed by hell. Beasts and birds of every kind, creatures that crawl on the ground or swim in the sea, can be subdued and have been subdued by mankind; but no man can subdue the tongue. It is an intractable evil, charged with deadly venom. We use it to sing the praises of our Lord and Father, and we use it to invoke curses upon our fellow-men who are made in God's likeness. Out of the same mouth come praises and curses. My brothers, this should not be so. Does a fountain gush with both fresh and brackish water from the same opening? Can a fig-tree, my brothers, yield olives, or a vine figs? No more does salt water yield fresh.

Who among you is wise or clever? Let his right conduct give practical proof of it, with the modesty that comes of wisdom. But if you are harbouring bitter jealousy and selfish ambition

[a] *Or* it is a great boaster. [b] *Or* What a huge forest . . .

King James Version

glory not, and lie not against the truth. 15 This
wisdom descendeth not from above, but *is*
earthly, sensual, devilish. 16 For where envying
and strife *is,* there *is* confusion and every evil
work. 17 But the wisdom that is from above is
first pure, then peaceable, gentle, *and* easy to be
entreated, full of mercy and good fruits, without
partiality, and without hypocrisy. 18 And the fruit
of righteousness is sown in peace of them that
make peace.

4 From whence *come* wars and fightings
among you? *come they* not hence, *even* of
your lusts that war in your members? 2 Ye lust,
and have not: ye kill, and desire to have, and
cannot obtain: ye fight and war, yet ye have
not, because ye ask not. 3 Ye ask, and receive
not, because ye ask amiss, that ye may consume
it upon your lusts. 4 Ye adulterers and adulter-
esses, know ye not that the friendship of the
world is enmity with God? whosoever therefore
will be a friend of the world is the enemy of

Living Bible

jealous and selfish; that is the worst sort of lie.
15 For jealousy and selfishness are not God's
kind of wisdom. Such things are earthly, unspiritual, inspired by the devil. 16 For wherever
there is jealousy or selfish ambition, there will
be disorder and every other kind of evil.

17 But the wisdom that comes from heaven
is first of all pure and full of quiet gentleness.
Then it is peace-loving and courteous. It allows
discussion and is willing to yield to others; it is
full of mercy and good deeds. It is wholehearted
and straightforward and sincere. 18 And those
who are peacemakers will plant seeds of peace
and reap a harvest of goodness.

4 What is causing the quarrels and fights
among you? Isn't it because there is a whole
army of evil desires within you? 2 You want
what you don't have, so you kill to get it. You
long for what others have, and can't afford it,
so you start a fight to take it away from them.
And yet the reason you don't have what you
want is that you don't ask God for it. 3 And
even when you do ask you don't get it because
your whole aim is wrong—you want only what
will give *you* pleasure.

4 You are like an unfaithful wife who loves
her husband's enemies. Don't you realize that
making friends with God's enemies—the evil
pleasures of this world—makes you an enemy
of God? I say it again, that if your aim is to
enjoy the evil pleasure of the unsaved world,

Today's English Version

must not be proud and tell lies against the
truth. 15 This kind of wisdom does not come
down from heaven; it belongs to the world, it is
unspiritual and demonic. 16 Where there is jealousy and selfishness, there is also disorder and
every kind of evil. 17 But the wisdom from
above is pure, first of all; it is also peaceful,
gentle, and friendly; it is full of compassion
and produces a harvest of good deeds; it is free
from prejudice and hypocrisy. 18 And goodness
is the harvest that is produced from the seeds
the peacemakers plant in peace.

Friendship with the world

4 Where do all the fights and quarrels among
you come from? They come from your desires for pleasure, which are constantly fighting
within your bodies. 2 You want things, but you
cannot have them, so you are ready to kill; you
strongly desire things, but you cannot get them,
so you quarrel and fight. You do not have what
you want because you do not ask God for it.
3 And when you ask you do not receive it, because your motives are bad; you ask for things
to use for your own pleasures. 4 Unfaithful people! Don't you know that to be the world's
friend means to be God's enemy? Whoever
wants to be the world's friend makes himself

New International Version

deny the truth. 15 Such "wisdom" does not
come down from heaven but is earthly, unspiritual, of the devil. 16 For where you have
envy and selfish ambition, there you find disorder and every evil practice.

17 But the wisdom that comes from heaven
is first of all pure; then peace-loving, considerate,
submissive, full of mercy and good fruit, impartial and sincere. 18 Peacemakers who sow in
peace raise a harvest of righteousness.

Submit yourselves to God

4 What causes fights and quarrels among
you? Don't they come from your desires that
battle within you? 2 You want something but
don't get it. You kill and covet, but you cannot
have what you want. You quarrel and fight. You
do not have, because you do not ask God.
3 When you ask, you do not receive, because
you ask with wrong motives, that you may spend
what you get on your pleasures.

4 You adulterous people, don't you know that
friendship with the world is hatred toward God?
Anyone who chooses to be a friend of the world

Phillips Modern English

truth. You may acquire a certain wisdom, but it does not come from above—it comes from this world, from your own lower nature, even from the devil. For wherever you find jealousy and rivalry you also find disharmony and all other kinds of evil. The wisdom that comes from above is first pure, then peace-loving, gentle, approachable, full of merciful thoughts and kindly actions, straightforward, with no hint of hypocrisy. And the peacemakers go on quietly sowing for a harvest of righteousness.

4.1 *Your jealousies spring from love of what the world can give*

But what about the feuds and struggles that exist among you—where do you suppose they come from? Can't you see that they arise from conflicting desires for pleasure within yourselves? You crave for something and don't get it; you are murderously jealous of what you can't possess yourselves; you struggle and fight with one another. You don't get what you want because you don't ask God for it. And when you do ask he doesn't give it to you, for you ask in quite the wrong spirit—you only want to satisfy your own desires.

You are like unfaithful wives, never realising that to be the world's lover means becoming the enemy of God! Anyone who chooses to be the world's friend is thereby making himself

Revised Standard Version

hearts, do not boast and be false to the truth.
15 This wisdom is not such as comes down from
above, but is earthly, unspiritual, devilish. 16 For
where jealousy and selfish ambition exist, there
will be disorder and every vile practice. 17 But
the wisdom from above is first pure, then peaceable, gentle, open to reason, full of mercy and
good fruits, without uncertainty or insincerity.
18 And the harvest of righteousness is sown in
peace by those who make peace.

4 What causes wars, and what causes fightings among you? Is it not your passions
that are at war in your members? 2 You desire
and do not have; so you kill. And you covet[d]
and cannot obtain; so you fight and wage war.
You do not have, because you do not ask.
3 You ask and do not receive, because you ask
wrongly, to spend it on your passions. 4 Unfaithful creatures! Do you not know that friendship with the world is enmity with God? Therefore whoever wishes to be a friend of the world

[d] Or *you kill and you covet.*

Jerusalem Bible

a self-seeking ambition, never make any claims
for yourself or cover up the truth with lies—
15 principles of this kind are not the wisdom
that comes down from above: they are only
earthly, animal and devilish. 16 Wherever you
find jealousy and ambition, you find disharmony,
and wicked things of every kind being done;
17 whereas the wisdom that comes down from
above is essentially something pure; it also makes
for peace, and is kindly and considerate; it is
full of compassion and shows itself by doing
good; nor is there any trace of partiality or hypocrisy in it. 18 Peacemakers, when they work
for peace, sow the seeds which will bear fruit
in holiness.

Disunity among Christians

4 Where do these wars and battles between
yourselves first start? Isn't it precisely in the
desires fighting inside your own selves? 2 You
want something and you haven't got it; so you
are prepared to kill. You have an ambition that
you cannot satisfy; so you fight to get your way
by force. Why you don't have what you want is
because you don't pray for it; 3 when you do
pray and don't get it, it is because you have not
prayed properly, you have prayed for something
to indulge your own desires.
4 You are as unfaithful as adulterous wives;
don't you realize that making the world your
friend is making God your enemy? Anyone who
chooses the world for his friend turns himself

New English Bible

in your hearts, consider whether your claims are not false, and a defiance of the truth. This is not the wisdom that comes from above; it is earthbound, sensual, demonic. For with jealousy and ambition come disorder and evil of every kind. But the wisdom from above is in the first place pure; and then peace-loving, considerate, and open to reason; it is straightforward and sincere, rich in mercy and in the kindly deeds that are its fruit. True justice is the harvest reaped by peacemakers from seeds sown in a spirit of peace.

4 What causes conflicts and quarrels among you? Do they not spring from the aggressiveness of your bodily desires? You want something which you cannot have, and so you are bent on murder; you are envious, and cannot attain your ambition, and so you quarrel and fight. You do not get what you want, because you do not pray for it. Or, if you do, your requests are not granted because you pray from wrong motives, to spend what you get on your pleasures. You false, unfaithful creatures! Have you never learned that love of the world is enmity to God? Whoever chooses to be the world's friend makes

King James Version

God. 5 Do ye think that the Scripture saith in
vain, The spirit that dwelleth in us lusteth to
envy? 6 But he giveth more grace. Wherefore he
saith, God resisteth the proud, but giveth grace
unto the humble. 7 Submit yourselves therefore
to God. Resist the devil, and he will flee from
you. 8 Draw nigh to God, and he will draw nigh
to you. Cleanse *your* hands, *ye* sinners; and
purify *your* hearts, *ye* doubleminded. 9 Be afflicted, and mourn, and weep: let your laughter
be turned to mourning, and *your* joy to heaviness. 10 Humble yourselves in the sight of the
Lord, and he shall lift you up. 11 Speak not evil
one of another, brethren. He that speaketh evil
of *his* brother, and judgeth his brother, speaketh
evil of the law, and judgeth the law: but if thou
judge the law, thou art not a doer of the law,

Living Bible

you cannot also be a friend of God. 5 Or what
do you think the Scripture means when it says
that the Holy Spirit, whom God has placed
within us, watches over us with tender jealousy?
6 But he gives us more and more strength to
stand against all such evil longings. As the Scripture says, God gives strength to the humble, but
sets himself against the proud and haughty.
7 So give yourselves humbly to God. Resist
the devil and he will flee from you. 8 And when
you draw close to God, God will draw close to
you. Wash your hands, you sinners, and let your
hearts be filled with God alone to make them
pure and true to him. 9 Let there be tears for
the wrong things you have done. Let there be
sorrow and sincere grief. Let there be sadness
instead of laughter, and gloom instead of joy.
10 Then when you realize your worthlessness before the Lord, he will lift you up, encourage
and help you.
11 Don't criticize and speak evil about each
other, dear brothers. If you do, you will be
fighting against God's law of loving one another,
declaring it is wrong. But your job is not to
decide whether this law is right or wrong, but to

Today's English Version

God's enemy. 5 Do not think that the scripture
means nothing that says, "The spirit that God
placed in us is filled with fierce desires." 6 But
the grace that God gives is even stronger. As
the scripture says, "God resists the proud, but
gives grace to the humble."
7 So then, submit yourselves to God. Resist
the Devil, and he will run away from you.
8 Come near to God, and he will come near to
you. Wash your hands, you sinners! Cleanse
your hearts, you hypocrites! 9 Be sorrowful, cry,
and weep; change your laughter into crying,
your joy into gloom! 10 Humble yourselves before the Lord, and he will lift you up.

Warning against judging a brother

11 Do not criticize one another, my brothers.
Whoever criticizes his brother, or judges him,
criticizes the Law and judges it. If you judge
the Law, then you are no longer one who obeys

New International Version

becomes an enemy of God. 5 Or do you think
Scripture says without reason that the spirit he
caused to live in us tends toward envy,[f] 6 but he
gives us more grace? That is why Scripture says;
"God opposes the proud,
but gives grace to the humble."[g]
7 Submit yourselves, then, to God. Resist the
devil, and he will flee from you. 8 Come near
to God and he will come near to you. Wash your
hands, you sinners, and purify your hearts, you
double-minded. 9 Grieve, mourn and wail.
Change your laughter to mourning and your joy
to gloom. 10 Humble yourselves before the Lord,
and he will lift you up.
11 Brothers, do not slander one another. Anyone who speaks against his brother, or judges
him, speaks against the law and judges it. When
you judge the law, you are not keeping it, but

[f] Or *that God jealously longs for the spirit that he made to live in us;* or *that the Spirit he caused to live in us longs jealously.* [g] Prov. 3:34.

Phillips Modern English

God's enemy. Or do you think what the scriptures have to say about this is a mere formality? Do you imagine that this spirit of passionate jealousy is the Spirit he has caused to live in us? Yet he gives us grace which is stronger. That is why he says:

God resisteth the proud,
But giveth grace to the humble.

4.7 You should be humble, not proud

Be humble then before God. But resist the devil and you'll find he'll run away from you. Come close to God and he will come close to you. You are sinners: get your hands clean again. Your loyalty is divided: get your hearts made true once more. You should be deeply sorry, you should be grieved, you should even be in tears. Your laughter will have to become mourning, your high spirits will have to become dejection. You must humble yourselves in the sight of the Lord before he will lift you up.

4.11 It is for God to judge, not for us

Never pull each other to pieces, my brothers. If you criticise your brother and judge your brother you have become in fact a critic and judge of the Law. Yet if you start to criticise the Law instead of obeying it you are setting your-

Revised Standard Version

makes himself an enemy of God. 5 Or do you
suppose it is in vain that the scripture says, "He
yearns jealously over the spirit which he has
made to dwell in us"? 6 But he gives more grace;
therefore it says, "God opposes the proud, but
gives grace to the humble." 7 Submit yourselves
therefore to God. Resist the devil and he will
flee from you. 8 Draw near to God and he will
draw near to you. Cleanse your hands, you sinners, and purify your hearts, you men of double
mind. 9 Be wretched and mourn and weep. Let
your laughter be turned to mourning and your
joy to dejection. 10 Humble yourselves before
the Lord and he will exalt you.
11 Do not speak evil against one another,
brethren. He that speaks evil against a brother
or judges his brother, speaks evil against the law
and judges the law. But if you judge the law,
you are not a doer of the law but a judge.

Jerusalem Bible

into God's enemy. 5 Surely you don't think scripture is wrong when it says: the spirit which he
sent to live in us wants us for himself alone?
6 But he has been even more generous to us, as
scripture says: *God opposes the proud but he
gives generously to the humble.*[k] 7 Give in to
God, then; resist the devil, and he will run
away from you. 8 The nearer you go to God, the
nearer he will come to you. Clean your hands,
you sinners, and clear your minds, you waverers.
9 Look at your wretched condition, and weep
for it in misery; be miserable instead of laughing, gloomy instead of happy. 10 Humble yourselves before the Lord and he will lift you up.
11 Brothers, do not slander one another. Anyone who slanders a brother, or condemns him,
is speaking against the Law and condemning the
Law. But if you condemn the Law, you have
stopped keeping it and become a judge over it.

New English Bible

himself God's enemy. Or do you suppose that Scripture has no meaning when it says that the spirit which God implanted in man turns towards envious desires? And yet the grace he gives is stronger. Thus Scripture says, 'God opposes the arrogant and gives grace to the humble.' Be submissive then to God. Stand up to the devil and he will turn and run. Come close to God, and he will come close to you. Sinners, make your hands clean; you who are double-minded, see that your motives are pure. Be sorrowful, mourn and weep. Turn your laughter into mourning and your gaiety into gloom. Humble yourselves before God and he will lift you high.

Brothers, you must never disparage one another. He who disparages a brother or passes judgement on his brother disparages the law and judges the law. But if you judge the law, you are not keeping it but sitting in judgement upon it.

[k] Pr. 3:34 (LXX).

King James Version

but a judge. 12 There is one lawgiver, who is able to save and to destroy: who art thou that judgest another? 13 Go to now, ye that say, To day or to morrow we will go into such a city, and continue there a year, and buy and sell, and get gain: 14 Whereas ye know not what *shall be* on the morrow. For what *is* your life? It is even a vapour, that appeareth for a little time, and then vanisheth away. 15 For that ye *ought* to say, If the Lord will, we shall live, and do this, or that. 16 But now ye rejoice in your boastings: all such rejoicing is evil. 17 Therefore to him that knoweth to do good, and doeth *it* not, to him it is sin.

5 Go to now, *ye* rich men, weep and howl for your miseries that shall come upon *you*. 2 Your riches are corrupted, and your garments are motheaten. 3 Your gold and silver is cankered; and the rust of them shall be a witness

Living Bible

obey it. 12 Only he who made the law can rightly judge among us. He alone decides to save us or destroy. So what right do you have to judge or criticize others?

13 Look here, you people who say, "Today or tomorrow we are going to such and such a town, stay there a year, and open up a profitable business." 14 How do you know what is going to happen tomorrow? For the length of your lives is as uncertain as the morning fog—now you see it; soon it is gone. 15 What you ought to say is, "If the Lord wants us to, we shall live and do this or that." 16 Otherwise you will be bragging about your own plans, and such self-confidence never pleases God.

17 Remember, too, that knowing what is right to do and then not doing it is sin.

5 Look here, you rich men, now is the time to cry and groan with anguished grief because of all the terrible troubles ahead of you. 2 Your wealth is even now rotting away, and your fine clothes are becoming mere moth-eaten rags. 3 The value of your gold and silver is dropping fast, yet it will stand as evidence against

Today's English Version

the Law, but one who judges it. 12 God is the only lawgiver and judge. He alone can save and destroy. Who do you think you are, to judge your fellow-man?

Warning against boasting

13 Now listen to me, you that say, "Today or tomorrow we will travel to a certain city, where we will stay a year, and go into business and make a lot of money." 14 You don't even know what your life tomorrow will be! You are like a thin fog, which appears for a moment and then disappears. 15 What you should say is this, "If the Lord is willing, we will live and do this or that." 16 But now you are proud, and you boast; all such boasting is wrong.

17 So then, the person who does not do the good he knows he should do is guilty of sin.

Warning to the rich

5 And now, you rich people, listen to me! Weep and wail over the miseries that are coming upon you! 2 Your riches have rotted away, and your clothes have been eaten by moths. 3 Your gold and silver are covered with rust, and this rust will be a witness against you,

New International Version

sitting in judgment on it. 12 There is only one Lawgiver and Judge, the one who is able to save and destroy. But you—who are you to judge your neighbor?

Boasting about tomorrow

13 Now listen, you who say, "Today or tomorrow we will go to this or that city, spend a year there, carry on business and make money." 14 Why, you do not even know what will happen tomorrow. What is your life? You are a mist that appears for a little while and then vanishes. 15 Instead, you ought to say, "If it is the Lord's will, we will live and do this or that." 16 As it is, you boast and brag. All such boasting is evil. 17 Anyone, then, who knows the good he ought to do and doesn't do it, sins.

Warning to rich oppressors

5 Now listen, you rich people, weep and wail because of the misery that is coming upon you. 2 Your wealth has rotted, and moths have eaten your clothes. 3 Your gold and silver are corroded. Their corrosion will testify against you

Phillips Modern English

self up as judge. There is only one judge, the One who gave the Law, to whom belongs absolute power of life and death. How can you then be your neighbour's judge?

4.13 It is still true that man proposes, but God disposes

Just a moment, now, you who say, "We are going to such-and-such a city today or tomorrow. We shall stay there a year doing business and make a profit"! How do you know what will happen tomorrow? What, after all, is your life? It is like a puff or smoke visible for a little while and then dissolving into thin air. Your remarks should be prefaced with, "If it is the Lord's will, we shall still be alive and will do so-and-so." As it is, you take a certain pride in planning with such confidence. That sort of pride is all wrong. Well then, if a man knows what is right and fails to do it, his failure is a real sin.

5.1 Riches are going to prove a liability, not an asset, to the selfish

And now, you men of affluence, is the time for you to weep and wail because of the miseries in store for you! Your riches are ruined, your fine clothes are moth-eaten, your gold and silver are tarnished. Yes, their very tarnish will be

Revised Standard Version

12 There is one lawgiver and judge, he who is
able to save and to destroy. But who are you
that you judge your neighbor?

13 Come now, you who say, "Today or tomorrow we will go into such and such a town
and spend a year there and trade and get gain";
14 whereas you do not know about tomorrow.
What is your life? For you are a mist that appears for a little time and then vanishes. 15 Instead you ought to say, "If the Lord wills, we
shall live and we shall do this or that." 16 As
it is, you boast in your arrogance. All such
boasting is evil. 17 Whoever knows what is right
to do and fails to do it, for him it is sin.

5 Come now, you rich, weep and howl for
the miseries that are coming upon you.
2 Your riches have rotted and your garments
are moth-eaten. 3 Your gold and silver have
rusted, and their rust will be evidence against

Jerusalem Bible

12 There is only one lawgiver and he is the only
judge and has the power to acquit or to sentence.
Who are you to give a verdict on your neighbor?

A warning for the rich and self-confident

13 Here is the answer for those of you who
talk like this: "Today or tomorrow, we are off
to this or that town; we are going to spend a
year there, trading, and make some money."
14 You never know what will happen tomorrow:
you are no more than a mist that is here for
a little while and then disappears. 15 The most
you should ever say is: "If it is the Lord's will,
we shall still be alive to do this or that." 16 But
how proud and sure of yourselves you are now!
Pride of this kind is always wicked. 17 Everyone
who knows what is the right thing to do and
doesn't do it commits a sin.

5 Now an answer for the rich. Start crying,
weep for the miseries that are coming to
you. 2 Your wealth is all rotting, your clothes
are all eaten up by moths. 3 All your gold and
your silver are corroding away, and the same

New English Bible

There is only one lawgiver and judge, the One who is able to save life and destroy it. So who are you to judge your neighbour?

A word with you, you who say, 'Today or tomorrow we will go off to such and such a town and spend a year there trading and making money.' Yet you have no idea what tomorrow will bring. Your life, what is it? You are no more than a mist, seen for a little while and then dispersing. What you ought to say is: 'If it be the Lord's will, we shall live to do this or that.' But instead, you boast and brag, and all such boasting is wrong. Well then, the man who knows the good he ought to do and does not do it is a sinner.

5 Next a word to you who have great possessions. Weep and wail over the miserable fate descending on you. Your riches have rotted; your fine clothes are moth-eaten; your silver and gold have rusted away, and their very rust will

King James Version

against you, and shall eat your flesh as it were
fire. Ye have heaped treasure together for the
last days. 4 Behold, the hire of the labourers
who have reaped down your fields, which is of
you kept back by fraud, crieth: and the cries
of them which have reaped are entered into the
ears of the Lord of Sabaoth. 5 Ye have lived in
pleasure on the earth, and been wanton; ye have
nourished your hearts, as in a day of slaughter.
6 Ye have condemned *and* killed the just; *and*
he doth not resist you. 7 Be patient therefore,
brethren, unto the coming of the Lord. Behold,
the husbandman waiteth for the precious fruit
of the earth, and hath long patience for it, until
he receive the early and latter rain. 8 Be ye also
patient; stablish your hearts: for the coming of
the Lord draweth nigh. 9 Grudge not one against
another, brethren, lest ye be condemned: behold,
the judge standeth before the door. 10 Take, my
brethren, the prophets, who have spoken in the
name of the Lord, for an example of suffering
affliction, and of patience. 11 Behold, we count
them happy which endure. Ye have heard of
the patience of Job, and have seen the end of

Living Bible

you, and eat your flesh like fire. That is what
you have stored up for yourselves, to receive on
that coming day of judgment. 4 For listen! Hear
the cries of the field workers whom you have
cheated of their pay. Their cries have reached
the ears of the Lord of Hosts.

5 You have spent your years here on earth
having fun, satisfying your every whim, and
now your fat hearts are ready for the slaughter.
6 You have condemned and killed good men
who had no power to defend themselves against
you.

7 Now as for you, dear brothers who are
waiting for the Lord's return, be patient, like
a farmer who waits until the autumn for his
precious harvest to ripen. 8 Yes, be patient. And
take courage, for the coming of the Lord is near.

9 Don't grumble about each other, brothers.
Are you yourselves above criticism? For see! The
great Judge is coming. He is almost here. [Let
him do whatever criticizing must be done[a].]

10 For examples of patience in suffering, look
at the Lord's prophets. 11 We know how happy
they are now because they stayed true to him
then, even though they suffered greatly for it.
Job is an example of a man who continued to
trust the Lord in sorrow; from his experiences

[*a*] Implied.

Today's English Version

and eat up your flesh like fire. You have piled
up riches in these last days. 4 You have not paid
the wages to the men who work in your fields.
Hear their complaints! The cries of those who
gather in your crops have reached the ears of
God, the Lord Almighty. 5 Your life here on
earth has been full of luxury and pleasure. You
have made yourselves fat for the day of slaughter. 6 You have condemned and murdered the
innocent man, and he does not resist you.

Patience and prayer

7 Be patient, then, my brothers, until the Lord
comes. See how the farmer is patient as he
waits for his land to produce precious crops.
He waits patiently for the autumn and spring
rains. 8 You also must be patient. Keep your
hopes high, for the day of the Lord's coming is
near.

9 Do not complain against one another, my
brothers, so that God will not judge you. The
Judge is near, ready to come in. 10 My brothers,
remember the prophets who spoke in the name
of the Lord. Take them as examples of patient
endurance under suffering. 11 We call them
happy because they endured. You have heard of
Job's patience, and you know how the Lord

New International Version

and eat your flesh like fire. You have hoarded
wealth in the last days. 4 Look! The wages you
failed to pay the workmen who mowed your
fields are crying out against you. The cries of the
harvesters have reached the ears of the Lord
All-powerful. 5 You have lived on earth in
luxury and self-indulgence. You have fattened
yourselves in the day of slaughter. 6 You have
condemned and murdered innocent men, who
were not opposing you.

Patience and suffering

7 Be patient, then, brothers, until the Lord's
coming. See how the farmer waits for the land
to yield its valuable crop and how patient he is
for the fall and spring rains. 8 You too, be patient and stand firm, because the Lord's coming
is near. 9 Don't grumble against each other,
brothers, or you will be judged. The Judge is
standing at the door!

10 Brothers, as an example of patience in the
face of suffering, take the prophets who spoke in
the name of the Lord. 11 As you know, we consider blessed those who have persevered. You

Phillips Modern English

evidence against you, and they will burn your flesh like fire. You have made a fine pile in these last days, haven't you? But look, here is the pay of the reaper you hired and whom you never paid, and it cries out against you! And the cries of the harvesters have reached the ears of the Lord of Hosts himself. Yes, you have had a magnificent time on this earth, and have indulged yourselves to the full. You have picked out just what you wanted like soldiers looting after battle. You have condemned and ruined innocent men, and they are powerless to stop you.

5.7 Ultimate justice will surely come: be patient meanwhile

But be patient, my brothers, as you wait for the Lord to come. Look at the farmer quietly awaiting the precious harvest of his land. See how he has to possess his soul in patience till the early and late rains have fallen. So must you be patient, resting your hearts on the ultimate certainty. The Lord's coming is very near.

Don't make complaints against each other in the meantime, my brothers—you may be the one at fault yourself. The judge himself is already at the door.

For our example of the patient endurance of suffering we can take the prophets who have spoken in the Lord's name. Remember that it is those who have patiently endured to whom we accord the word "blessed". You have heard of Job's patient endurance and how the Lord dealt with him in the end, and therefore you have seen

Revised Standard Version

you and will eat your flesh like fire. You have
laid up treasure[e] for the last days. 4 Behold,
the wages of the laborers who mowed your
fields, which you kept back by fraud, cry out;
and the cries of the harvesters have reached the
ears of the Lord of hosts. 5 You have lived on
the earth in luxury and in pleasure; you have
fattened your hearts in a day of slaughter. 6 You
have condemned, you have killed the righteous
man; he does not resist you.
7 Be patient, therefore, brethren, until the
coming of the Lord. Behold, the farmer waits
for the precious fruit of the earth, being patient
over it until it receives the early and the late
rain. 8 You also be patient. Establish your hearts,
for the coming of the Lord is at hand. 9 Do not
grumble, brethren, against one another, that you
may not be judged; behold, the Judge is standing
at the doors. 10 As an example of suffering and
patience, brethren, take the prophets who spoke
in the name of the Lord. 11 Behold, we call those
happy who were steadfast. You have heard of
the steadfastness of Job, and you have seen the

[*e*] Or *will eat your flesh, since you have stored up fire.*

Jerusalem Bible

corrosion will be your own sentence, and eat
into your body. It was a burning fire that you
stored up as your treasure for the last days.
4 Laborers mowed your fields, and you cheated
them—listen to the wages that you kept back,
calling out; realize that the cries of the reapers
have reached the ears of the Lord of hosts. 5 On
earth you have had a life of comfort and luxury;
in the time of slaughter you went on eating to
your heart's content. 6 It was you who condemned the innocent and killed them; they offered you no resistance.

A final exhortation

7 Now be patient, brothers, until the Lord's
coming. Think of a farmer: how patiently he
waits for the precious fruit of the ground until
it has had the autumn rains and the spring rains!
8 You too have to be patient; do not lose heart,
because the Lord's coming will be soon. 9 Do
not make complaints against one another, brothers, so as not to be brought to judgment yourselves; the Judge is already to be seen waiting
at the gates. 10 For your example, brothers, in
submitting with patience, take the prophets who
spoke in the name of the Lord; 11 remember it
is those who had endurance that we say are the
blessed ones. You have heard of the patience of

New English Bible

be evidence against you and consume your flesh like fire. You have piled up wealth in an age that is near its close. The wages you never paid to the men who mowed your fields are loud against you, and the outcry of the reapers has reached the ears of the Lord of Hosts. You have lived on earth in wanton luxury, fattening yourselves like cattle—and the day for slaughter has come. You have condemned the innocent and murdered him: he offers no resistance.

Be patient, my brothers, until the Lord comes. The farmer looking for the precious crop his land may yield can only wait in patience, until the autumn and spring rains have fallen. You too must be patient and stout-hearted, for the coming of the Lord is near. My brothers, do not blame your troubles on one another, or you will fall under judgement; and there stands the Judge, at the door. If you want a pattern of patience under ill-treatment, take the prophets who spoke in the name of the Lord; remember: 'We count those happy who stood firm.' You have all heard how Job stood firm, and you have seen how the Lord treated him in the end. For the Lord is

King James Version

the Lord; that the Lord is very pitiful, and of tender mercy. 12 But above all things, my brethren, swear not, neither by heaven, neither by the earth, neither by any other oath: but let your yea be yea; and *your* nay, nay; lest ye fall into condemnation. 13 Is any among you afflicted? let him pray. Is any merry? let him sing psalms. 14 Is any sick among you? let him call for the elders of the church; and let them pray over him, anointing him with oil in the name of the Lord: 15 And the prayer of faith shall save the sick, and the Lord shall raise him up; and if he have committed sins, they shall be forgiven him. 16 Confess *your* faults one to another, and pray one for another, that ye may be healed. The effectual fervent prayer of a righteous man availeth much. 17 Elias was a man subject to like passions as we are, and he prayed earnestly that it might not rain: and it rained not on the earth by the space of three years and six months. 18 And he prayed again, and the heaven gave rain, and the earth brought forth

Living Bible

we can see how the Lord's plan finally ended in good, for he is full of tenderness and mercy.

12 But most of all, dear brothers, do not swear either by heaven or earth or anything else; just say a simple yes or no, so that you will not sin and be condemned for it.

13 Is anyone among you suffering? He should keep on praying about it. And those who have reason to be thankful should continually be singing praises to the Lord.

14 Is anyone sick? He should call for the elders of the church and they should pray over him and pour a little oil upon him, calling on the Lord to heal him. 15 And their prayer, if offered in faith, will heal him, for the Lord will make him well; and if his sickness was caused by some sin, the Lord will forgive him.

16 Admit your faults to one another and pray for each other so that you may be healed. The earnest prayer of a righteous man has great power and wonderful results. 17 Elijah was as completely human as we are, and yet when he prayed earnestly that no rain would fall, none fell for the next three and one half years! 18 Then he prayed again, this time that it *would* rain, and down it poured and the grass turned green and the gardens began to grow again.

Today's English Version

provided for him in the end. For the Lord is full of mercy and compassion.

12 Above all, my brothers, do not use an oath when you make a promise; do not swear by heaven, or by earth, or by anything else. Say only "Yes" when you mean yes, and "No" when you mean no, so that you will not come under God's judgment.

13 Is anyone among you in trouble? He should pray. Is anyone happy? He should sing praises. 14 Is there anyone who is sick? He should call the church elders, who will pray for him and rub oil on him in the name of the Lord. 15 This prayer, made in faith, will heal the sick man; the Lord will restore him to health, and the sins he has committed will be forgiven. 16 So then, confess your sins to one another, and pray for one another, so that you will be healed. The prayer of a good man has a powerful effect. 17 Elijah was the same kind of person that we are. He prayed earnestly that there would be no rain, and no rain fell on the land for three and a half years. 18 Once again he prayed, and the sky poured out its rain and the earth produced its crops.

New International Version

have heard of Job's perseverance and have seen what the Lord finally brought about. The Lord is full of compassion and mercy.

12 Above all, my brothers, do not swear—not by heaven or by earth or by anything else. Let your "Yes" be yes, and your "No," no, or you will be condemned.

The prayer of faith

13 Is any one of you in trouble? He should pray. Is anyone happy? Let him sing songs of praise. 14 Is any one of you sick? He should call the elders of the church to pray over him and anoint him with oil in the name of the Lord. 15 And the prayer offered in faith will make the sick person well; the Lord will raise him up. If he has sinned, he will be forgiven. 16 Therefore, confess your sins to each other and pray for each other so that you may be healed. The prayer of a righteous man is powerful and effective.

17 Elijah was a man just like us. He prayed earnestly that it would not rain, and it did not rain on the land for three and a half years. 18 Again he prayed, and the heavens gave rain, and the earth produced its crops.

Phillips Modern English

that the Lord is merciful and full of understanding pity.

5.12 Don't emphasise with oaths: speak the plain truth

It is of the highest importance, my brothers, that your speech should be free from oaths (whether they are "by" heaven or earth or anything else). Your yes should be a plain yes, and your no a plain no, and then you cannot go wrong in the matter.

5.13 Prayer is a great weapon

If any of you is in trouble let him pray. If anyone is flourishing let him sing praises to God. If anyone is ill he should send for the church elders. They should pray over him, anointing him with oil in the Lord's name. Believing prayer will save the sick man; the Lord will restore him and any sins that he has committed will be forgiven. You should get into the habit of admitting your sins to each other, and praying for each other, so that you may be healed.

Tremendous power is made available through a good man's earnest prayer. Do you remember Elijah? He was a man as human as we are but he prayed earnestly that it should not rain. In fact, not a drop fell on the land for three and a half years. Then he prayed again, the heavens gave the rain and the earth sprouted with vegetation again.

Revised Standard Version

purpose of the Lord, how the Lord is compassionate and merciful.

12 But above all, my brethren, do not swear, either by heaven or by earth or with any other oath, but let your yes be yes and your no be no, that you may not fall under condemnation.

13 Is any one among you suffering? Let him pray. Is any cheerful? Let him sing praise. 14 Is any among you sick? Let him call for the elders of the church, and let them pray over him, anointing him with oil in the name of the Lord; 15 and the prayer of faith will save the sick man, and the Lord will raise him up; and if he has committed sins, he will be forgiven. 16 Therefore confess your sins to one another, and pray for one another, that you may be healed. The prayer of a righteous man has great power in its effects. 17 Elijah was a man of like nature with ourselves and he prayed fervently that it might not rain, and for three years and six months it did not rain on the earth. 18 Then he prayed again and the heaven gave rain, and the earth brought forth its fruit.

Jerusalem Bible

Job, and understood the Lord's purpose, realizing that *the Lord is kind and compassionate.*[l]

12 Above all, my brothers, do not swear by heaven or by the earth, or use any oaths at all. If you mean "yes," you must say "yes"; if you mean "no," say "no." Otherwise you make yourselves liable to judgment.

13 If any one of you is in trouble, he should pray; if anyone is feeling happy, he should sing a psalm. 14 If one of you is ill, he should send for the elders of the church, and they must anoint him with oil in the name of the Lord and pray over him. 15 The prayer of faith will save the sick man and the Lord will raise him up again; and if he has committed any sins, he will be forgiven. 16 So confess your sins to one another, and pray for one another, and this will cure you; the heartfelt prayer of a good man works very powerfully. 17 Elijah was a human being like ourselves—he prayed hard for it not to rain, and no rain fell for three and a half years; 18 then he prayed again and the sky gave rain and the earth gave crops.

New English Bible

full of pity and compassion.

Above all things, my brothers, do not use oaths, whether 'by heaven' or 'by earth' or by anything else. When you say yes or no, let it be plain 'Yes' or 'No', for fear that you expose yourselves to judgement.

Is anyone among you in trouble? He should turn to prayer. Is anyone in good heart? He should sing praises. Is one of you ill? He should send for the elders of the congregation to pray over him and anoint him with oil in the name of the Lord. The prayer offered in faith will save the sick man, the Lord will raise him from his bed, and any sins he may have committed will be forgiven. Therefore confess your sins to one another, and pray for one another, and then you will be healed. A good man's prayer is powerful and effective. Elijah was a man with human frailties like our own; and when he prayed earnestly that there should be no rain, not a drop fell on the land for three years and a half; then he prayed again, and down came the rain and the land bore crops once more.

[*l*] Ps. 103:8.

King James Version

her fruit. 19 Brethren, if any of you do err from the truth, and one convert him; 20 Let him know, that he which converteth the sinner from the error of his way shall save a soul from death, and shall hide a multitude of sins.

Living Bible

19 Dear brothers, if anyone has slipped away from God and no longer trusts the Lord, and someone helps him understand the Truth again, 20 that person who brings him back to God will have saved a wandering soul from death, bringing about the forgiveness of his many sins.

Sincerely,
James

Today's English Version

19 My brothers! If one of you wanders away from the truth, and another one brings him back again, 20 remember this: whoever turns a sinner back from his wrong way will save that sinner's soul from death, and bring about the forgiveness of many sins.

New International Version

19 My brothers, if one of you should wander from the truth and someone should bring him back, 20 remember this: Whoever turns a sinner away from his error will save him from death and cover many sins.

Phillips Modern English

5.19 A concluding hint

My brothers, if any of you should wander away from the truth and another should turn him back on to the right path, then the latter may be sure that in turning a man back from his wandering course he has rescued a soul from death, and in so doing will "cover a multitude of sins".

Revised Standard Version

19 My brethren, if any one among you wanders from the truth and some one brings him
back, 20 let him know that whoever brings back a sinner from the error of his way will save his soul from death and will cover a multitude of sins.

Jerusalem Bible

19 My brothers, if one of you strays away from the truth, and another brings him back to
it, 20 he may be sure that anyone who can bring back a sinner from the wrong way that he has taken will be saving a soul from death and *covering up a great number of sins.*[m]

New English Bible

My brothers, if one of your number should stray from the truth and another succeed in bringing him back, be sure of this: any man who brings a sinner back from his crooked ways will be rescuing his soul from death and cancelling innumerable sins.

[*m*] Pr. 10:12.

King James Version

THE FIRST EPISTLE GENERAL OF

PETER

1 Peter, an apostle of Jesus Christ, to the
strangers scattered throughout Pontus, Galatia, Cappadocia, Asia, and Bithynia, 2 Elect according to the foreknowledge of God the Father,
through sanctification of the Spirit, unto obedience and sprinkling of the blood of Jesus Christ:
Grace unto you, and peace, be multiplied.
3 Blessed *be* the God and Father of our Lord
Jesus Christ, which according to his abundant
mercy hath begotten us again unto a lively hope
by the resurrection of Jesus Christ from the

Living Bible

1 PETER

1 *From:* Peter, Jesus Christ's missionary.
To: The Jewish Christians driven out of Jerusalem and scattered throughout Pontus, Galatia, Cappadocia, Ausia, and Bithynia.
2 Dear friends, God the Father chose you
long ago and knew you would become his children. And the Holy Spirit has been at work in
your hearts, cleansing you with the blood of Jesus Christ and making you to please him. May
God bless you richly and grant you increasing
freedom from all anxiety and fear.
3 All honor to God, the God and Father of
our Lord Jesus Christ; for it is his boundless
mercy that has given us the privilege of being
born again, so that we are now members of
God's own family. Now we live in the hope of
eternal life because Christ rose again from the

Today's English Version

THE FIRST LETTER FROM

PETER

1 From Peter, apostle of Jesus Christ—
To God's chosen people who live as refugees scattered throughout the provinces of Pontus, Galatia, Cappadocia, Asia, and Bithynia.
2 You were chosen according to the purpose of
God the Father, and were made a holy people
by his Spirit, to obey Jesus Christ and be
cleansed by his blood.
May grace and peace be yours in full measure.

A living hope

3 Let us give thanks to the God and Father
of our Lord Jesus Christ! Because of his great
mercy, he gave us new life by raising Jesus
Christ from the dead. This fills us with a living

New International Version

1 PETER

1 Peter, an apostle of Jesus Christ,
To God's elect, strangers in the world, scattered throughout Pontus, Galatia, Cappadocia,
Asia and Bithynia, 2 who have been chosen
according to the foreknowledge of God the Father, by the sanctifying work of the Spirit, for
obedience to Jesus Christ and sprinkling by his
blood:
Grace and peace be yours in abundance.

Praise to God for a living hope

3 Praise be to the God and Father of our
Lord Jesus Christ! In his great mercy he has
given us new birth into a living hope through
the resurrection of Jesus Christ from the dead,

Phillips Modern English

THE FIRST LETTER OF PETER

Peter, a messenger of Jesus Christ, sends this letter to God's people now dispersed in Pontus, Galatia, Cappadocia, Asia and Bithynia, whom God the Father knew and chose long ago to be made holy by his Spirit, that they might obey Jesus Christ and be cleansed by his blood: may you know more and more of God's grace and peace.

1.3 ***Your faith is being tested, but your future is magnificent***

Thank God, the God and Father of our Lord Jesus Christ, that in his great mercy we have been born again into a life full of hope, through

Revised Standard Version

THE FIRST LETTER OF PETER

1 Peter, an apostle of Jesus Christ, To the exiles of the Dispersion in Pontus, Galatia, Cappadocia, Asia, and Bithynia, 2 chosen and destined by God the Father and sanctified by the Spirit for obedience to Jesus Christ and for sprinkling with his blood:

May grace and peace be multiplied to you.

3 Blessed be the God and Father of our Lord Jesus Christ! By his great mercy we have been born anew to a living hope through the resurrec-

Jerusalem Bible

THE FIRST LETTER OF PETER

1 PETER

Address. Greetings

1 Peter, apostle of Jesus Christ, sends greetings to all those living among foreigners in the Dispersion of Pontus, Galatia, Cappadocia, Asia and Bithynia, who have been chosen, 2 by the provident purpose of God the Father, to be made holy by the Spirit, obedient to Jesus Christ and sprinkled with his blood. Grace and peace be with you more and more.

Introduction. The salvation of Christians

3 Blessed be God the Father of our Lord Jesus Christ, who in his great mercy has given us a new birth as his sons, by raising Jesus Christ from the dead, so that we have a sure hope

New English Bible

THE FIRST LETTER OF PETER

The calling of a Christian

1 From Peter, apostle of Jesus Christ, to those of God's scattered people who lodge for a while in Pontus, Galatia, Cappadocia, Asia, and Bithynia—chosen of old in the purpose of God the Father, hallowed to his service by the Spirit, and consecrated with the sprinkled blood of Jesus Christ.

Grace and peace to you in fullest measure.

Praise be to the God and Father of our Lord Jesus Christ, who in his great mercy gave us new birth into a living hope by the resurrection

King James Version

dead, 4 To an inheritance incorruptible, and undefiled, and that fadeth not away, reserved in
heaven for you, 5 Who are kept by the power
of God through faith unto salvation ready to be
revealed in the last time. 6 Wherein ye greatly
rejoice, though now for a season, if need be,
ye are in heaviness through manifold temptations: 7 That the trial of your faith, being much
more precious than of gold that perisheth,
though it be tried with fire, might be found unto
praise and honour and glory at the appearing of
Jesus Christ: 8 Whom having not seen, ye love;
in whom, though now ye see *him* not, yet believing, ye rejoice with joy unspeakable and full
of glory: 9 Receiving the end of your faith, *even*
the salvation of *your* souls. 10 Of which salvation the prophets have inquired and searched
diligently, who prophesied of the grace *that*
should come unto you: 11 Searching what, or
what manner of time the Spirit of Christ which
was in them did signify, when it testified beforehand the sufferings of Christ, and the glory that
should follow. 12 Unto whom it was revealed,
that not unto themselves, but unto us they did

Living Bible

dead. 4And God has reserved for his children
the priceless gift of eternal life; it is kept in
heaven for you, pure and undefiled, beyond the
reach of change and decay. 5And God, in his
mighty power, will make sure that you get there
safely to receive it, because you are trusting
him. It will be yours in that coming last day
for all to see. 6 So be truly glad! There is wonderful joy ahead, even though the going is rough
for a while down here.

7 These trials are only to test your faith, to
see whether or not it is strong and pure. It is
being tested as fire tests gold and purifies it—
and your faith is far more precious to God than
mere gold; so if your faith remains strong after
being tried in the test tube of fiery trials, it will
bring you much praise and glory and honor on
the day of his return.

8 You love him even though you have never
seen him; though not seeing him, you trust him;
and even now you are happy with the inexpressible joy that comes from heaven itself. 9And your
further reward for trusting him will be the salvation of your souls.

10 This salvation was something the prophets
did not fully understand. Though they wrote
about it, they had many questions as to what it
all could mean. 11 They wondered what the
Spirit of Christ within them was talking about,
for he told them to write down the events which,
since then, have happened to Christ: his suffering, and his great glory afterwards. And they
wondered when and to whom all this would
happen.

12 They were finally told that these things
would not occur during their lifetime, but long

Today's English Version

hope, 4 and so we look forward to possess the
rich blessings that God keeps for his people. He
keeps them for you in heaven, where they cannot decay or spoil or fade away. 5 They are for
you, who through faith are kept safe by God's
power for the salvation which is ready to be
revealed at the end of time.

6 Be glad about this, even though it may now
be necessary for you to be sad for a while because of the many kinds of trials you suffer.
7 Their purpose is to prove that your faith is
genuine. Even gold, which can be destroyed, is
tested by fire; and so your faith, which is much
more precious than gold, must also be tested,
that it may endure. Then you will receive praise
and glory and honor on the Day when Jesus
Christ is revealed. 8 You love him, although you
have not seen him. You believe in him, although
you do not now see him. And so you rejoice
with a great and glorious joy, which words cannot express, 9 because you are receiving the purpose of your faith, the salvation of your souls.

10 It was concerning this salvation that the
prophets made careful search and investigation;
and they prophesied about this gift that God
would give you. 11 They tried to find out when
the time would be and how it would come. This
was the time to which Christ's Spirit in them
pointed as the Spirit predicted the sufferings
that Christ would have to endure and the glory
that would follow. 12 God revealed to these
prophets that their work was not for their own

New International Version

4 and into an inheritance that can never perish,
spoil or fade—kept in heaven for you. 5 Through
faith you are shielded by God's power until the
coming of the salvation that is ready to be revealed in the last time. 6 In this you greatly
rejoice, though now for a little while you may
have suffered grief in all kinds of trials. 7 These
have come so that your faith—of greater worth
than gold, which perishes even though refined
by fire—may be proved genuine and may result
in praise, glory and honor when Jesus Christ is
revealed. 8 Though you have not seen him, you
love him; and even though you do not see him
now, you believe in him and are filled with an
inexpressible and glorious joy, 9 for you are
receiving the goal of your faith, the salvation
of your souls.

10 Concerning this salvation, the prophets,
who spoke of the grace that was to come to you,
searched intently and with the greatest care,
11 trying to find out the time and circumstances
to which the Spirit of Christ in them was pointing when he predicted the sufferings of Christ
and the glories that would follow. 12 It was revealed to them that they were not serving them-

Phillips Modern English

Christ's rising again from the dead! You can now hope for a perfect inheritance beyond the reach of change and decay, reserved in Heaven for you. And in the meantime you are guarded by the power of God operating through your faith, till you enter fully into the salvation which is all ready to be revealed at the last. This means tremendous joy to you, even though at present you may be temporarily harassed by all kinds of trials. This is no accident—it happens to prove your faith, which is infinitely more valuable than gold, and gold, as you know, even though it is ultimately perishable, must be purified by fire. This proving of your faith is planned to result in praise and glory and honour in the day when Jesus Christ reveals himself. And though you have never seen him, yet you love him. At present you trust him without being able to see him, and even now he brings you a joy that words cannot express and which has in it a hint of the glories of Heaven; and all the time you are receiving the result of your faith in him—the salvation of your own souls. The prophets of old did their utmost to discover and obtain this salvation. They prophesied of this grace that has now come to you. They tried hard to discover to what time and to what sort of circumstances the Spirit of Christ working in them was referring. For he foretold the sufferings of Christ and the glories that should follow them. It was then made clear to them that they were dealing with matters not meant for themselves, but for you. It is these very matters which have been made plain to you by those who

Revised Standard Version

tion of Jesus Christ from the dead, 4 and to an
inheritance which is imperishable, undefiled, and
unfading, kept in heaven for you, 5 who by
God's power are guarded through faith for a
salvation ready to be revealed in the last time.
6 In this you rejoice,[a] though now for a little
while you may have to suffer various trials, 7 so
that the genuineness of your faith, more precious
than gold which though perishable is tested by
fire, may redound to praise and glory and honor
at the revelation of Jesus Christ. 8 Without having seen[b] him you[c] love him; though you do not
now see him you[c] believe in him and rejoice
with unutterable and exalted joy. 9 As the outcome of your faith you obtain the salvation of
your souls.
10 The prophets who prophesied of the grace
that was to be yours searched and inquired about
this salvation; 11 they inquired what person or
time was indicated by the Spirit of Christ within
them when predicting the sufferings of Christ
and the subsequent glory. 12 It was revealed to
them that they were serving not themselves but

[a] Or *Rejoice in this*. [b] Other ancient authorities read *known*. [c] Or omit *you*.

Jerusalem Bible

4 and the promise of an inheritance that can
never be spoiled or soiled and never fade away,
because it is being kept for you in the heavens.
5 Through your faith, God's power will guard
you until the salvation which has been prepared
is revealed at the end of time. 6 This is a cause
of great joy for you, even though you may for
a short time have to bear being plagued by all
sorts of trials; 7 so that, when Jesus Christ is
revealed, your faith will have been tested and
proved like gold—only it is more precious than
gold, which is corruptible even though it bears
testing by fire—and then you will have praise
and glory and honor. 8 You did not see him, yet
you love him; and still without seeing him, you
are already filled with a joy so glorious that it
cannot be described, because you believe; 9 and
you are sure of the end to which your faith
looks forward, that is, the salvation of your
souls.

The hope of the prophets

10 It was this salvation that the prophets were
looking and searching so hard for; their prophecies were about the grace which was to come
to you. 11 The Spirit of Christ which was in them
foretold the sufferings of Christ and the glories
that would come after them, and they tried to
find out at what time and in what circumstances
all this was to be expected. 12 It was revealed to
them that the news they brought of all the

New English Bible

of Jesus Christ from the dead! The inheritance to which we are born is one that nothing can destroy or spoil or wither. It is kept for you in heaven, and you, because you put your faith in God, are under the protection of his power until salvation comes—the salvation which is even now in readiness and will be revealed at the end of time.

This is cause for great joy, even though now you smart for a little while, if need be, under trials of many kinds. Even gold passes through the assayer's fire, and more precious than perishable gold is faith which has stood the test. These trials come so that your faith may prove itself worthy of all praise, glory, and honour when Jesus Christ is revealed.

You have not seen him, yet you love him; and trusting in him now without seeing him, you are transported with a joy too great for words, while you reap the harvest of your faith, that is, salvation for your souls. This salvation was the theme which the prophets pondered and explored, those who prophesied about the grace of God awaiting you. They tried to find out what was the time,[a] and what the circumstances, to which the spirit of Christ in them pointed, foretelling the sufferings in store for Christ and the splendours to follow; and it was disclosed to them that the matter they treated of was not for their time but for yours. And now it has been openly announced to you through preachers who brought

[a] *Or* who was the person . . .

King James Version

minister the things, which are now reported unto
you by them that have preached the gospel unto
you with the Holy Ghost sent down from
heaven; which things the angels desire to look
into. 13 Wherefore gird up the loins of your
mind, be sober, and hope to the end for the
grace that is to be brought unto you at the
revelation of Jesus Christ; 14 As obedient children, not fashioning yourselves according to the
former lusts in your ignorance: 15 But as he
which hath called you is holy, so be ye holy in
all manner of conversation; 16 Because it is written, Be ye holy; for I am holy. 17 And if ye call
on the Father, who without respect of persons
judgeth according to every man's work, pass the
time of your sojourning *here* in fear: 18 Forasmuch as ye know that ye were not redeemed
with corruptible things, *as* silver and gold, from
your vain conversation *received* by tradition
from your fathers; 19 But with the precious
blood of Christ, as of a lamb without blemish
and without spot: 20 Who verily was foreordained before the foundation of the world, but
was manifest in these last times for you, 21 Who
by him do believe in God, that raised him up

Living Bible

years later, during yours. And now at last this
Good News has been plainly announced to all
of us. It was preached to us in the power of
the same heaven-sent Holy Spirit who spoke to
them; and it is all so strange and wonderful
that even the angels in heaven would give a
great deal to know more about it. 13 So now
you can look forward soberly and intelligently
to more of God's kindness to you when Jesus
Christ returns.

14 Obey God because you are his children;
don't slip back into your old ways—doing evil
because you knew no better. 15 But be holy now
in everything you do, just as the Lord is holy,
who invited you to be his child. 16 He himself
has said, "You must be holy, for I am holy."

17 And remember that your heavenly Father
to whom you pray has no favorites when he
judges. He will judge you with perfect justice
for everything you do; so act in reverent fear
of him from now on until you get to heaven.
18 God paid a ransom to save you from the
impossible road to heaven which your fathers
tried to take, and the ransom he paid was not
mere gold or silver, as you very well know.
19 But he paid for you with the precious life-
blood of Christ, the sinless, spotless Lamb of
God. 20 God chose him for this purpose long
before the world began, but only recently was
he brought into public view, in these last days,
as a blessing to you.

21 Because of this, your trust can be in God
who raised Christ from the dead and gave him

Today's English Version

good, but for yours, as they spoke about those
things which you have now heard from the messengers of the Good News, who announced
them by the power of the Holy Spirit sent from
heaven. These are things which even the angels
would like to understand.

A call to holy living

13 So then, have your minds ready for action. Keep alert, and set your hope completely
on the blessing which will be given you when
Jesus Christ is revealed. 14 Be obedient to God,
and do not allow your lives to be shaped by
those desires you had when you were still ignorant. 15 Instead, be holy in all that you do, just
as God who called you is holy. 16 The scripture
says, "You must be holy, because I am holy."

17 You call him Father, when you pray to
God, who judges all men by the same standard,
according to what each one has done; so then,
spend the rest of your lives here on earth in
reverence for him. 18 For you know what was
paid to set you free from the worthless manner
of life you received from your ancestors. It was
not something that loses its value, such as silver
or gold; 19 you were set free by the costly sacrifice of Christ, who was like a lamb without
defect or spot. 20 He had been chosen by God
before the creation of the world, and was
revealed in these last days for your sake.
21 Through him you believe in God, who raised
him from death and gave him glory; and so

New International Version

selves but you, when they spoke of the things
that have now been told you by those who have
preached the gospel to you by the Holy Spirit
sent from heaven. Even angels long to look into
these things.

Be holy

13 Therefore, prepare your minds for action;
be self-controlled; set your hope fully on the
grace to be given you when Jesus Christ is revealed. 14 As obedient children, do not conform
to the evil desires you had when you lived in ignorance. 15 But just as he who called you is holy,
so be holy in all you do; 16 for it is written: "Be
holy, because I am holy." [a]

17 Since you call on a Father who judges each
man's work impartially, live your lives as strangers here in reverent fear. 18 For you know that
it was not with perishable things such as silver
or gold that you were redeemed from the empty
way of life handed down to you from your forefathers, 19 but with the precious blood of Christ,
a lamb without blemish or defect. 20 He was
chosen before the creation of the world, but was
revealed in these last times for your sake.
21 Through him you believe in God, who raised
him from the dead and glorified him, and so

[*a*] Lev. 11:44,45; 19:2; 20:7.

Phillips Modern English

preached the gospel to you by the Holy Spirit sent from Heaven—and these are facts to command the interest of the very angels!

1.13 Consider soberly what God has done for you

So brace up your minds, and, as men who know what they are doing, rest the full weight of your hopes on the grace that will be yours when Jesus Christ reveals himself. Live as obedient children before God. Don't let your character be moulded by the desires of your ignorant days, but be holy in every part of your lives, for the one who has called you is himself holy. The scripture says:

Ye shall be holy; for I am holy

If you pray to a Father who judges men by their actions without the slightest favouritism, then you should spend the time of your stay here on earth with reverent fear. For you must realise that you have been ransomed from the futile way of living passed on to you by your traditions, but not by any money payment of this passing world. No, the price was in fact the life-blood of Christ, the unblemished and unstained lamb of sacrifice. It is true that he was destined for this purpose before the world was founded, but it was for your benefit that he was revealed in these last days—for you who found your faith in God through him. And God raised him from the dead and gave him heavenly

Revised Standard Version

you, in the things which have now been announced to you by those who preached the good
news to you through the Holy Spirit sent from
heaven, things into which angels long to look.
13 Therefore gird up your minds, be sober,
set your hope fully upon the grace that is coming to you at the revelation of Jesus Christ. 14 As
obedient children, do not be conformed to the
passions of your former ignorance, 15 but as he
who called you is holy, be holy yourselves in all
your conduct; 16 since it is written, "You shall
be holy, for I am holy." 17 And if you invoke as
Father him who judges each one impartially
according to his deeds, conduct yourselves with
fear throughout the time of your exile. 18 You
know that you were ransomed from the futile
ways inherited from your fathers, not with
perishable things such as silver or gold, 19 but
with the precious blood of Christ, like that of
a lamb without blemish or spot. 20 He was destined before the foundation of the world but
was made manifest at the end of the times for
your sake. 21 Through him you have confidence
in God, who raised him from the dead and gave

Jerusalem Bible

things which have now been announced to you, by those who preached to you the Good News through the Holy Spirit sent from heaven, was for you and not for themselves. Even the angels long to catch a glimpse of these things.

A call to sanctity and watchfulness

13 Free your minds, then, of encumbrances;
control them, and put your trust in nothing but
the grace that will be given you when Jesus
Christ is revealed. 14 Do not behave in the way
that you liked to before you learned the truth;
make a habit of obedience: 15 be holy in all
you do, since it is the Holy One who has called
you, 16 and scripture says: *Be holy, for I am
holy.*[a]
17 If you are acknowledging as your Father
one who has no favorites and judges everyone
according to what he has done, you must be
scrupulously careful as long as you are living
away from your home. 18 Remember, the ransom that was *paid to free you*[b] from the useless
way of life your ancestors handed down was not
paid in anything corruptible, neither in *silver* nor
gold, 19 but in the precious blood of a lamb
without spot or stain, namely Christ; 20 who,
though known since before the world was made,
has been revealed only in our time, the end of
the ages, for your sake. 21 Through him you
now have faith in God, who raised him from
the dead and gave him glory for that very rea-

[a] Lv. 19:2. [b] Is. 52:3.

New English Bible

you the Gospel in the power of the Holy Spirit sent from heaven. These are things that angels long to see into.

You must therefore be mentally stripped for action, perfectly self-controlled. Fix your hopes on the gift of grace which is to be yours when Jesus Christ is revealed. As obedient children, do not let your characters be shaped any longer by the desires you cherished in your days of ignorance. The One who called you is holy; like him, be holy in all your behaviour, because Scripture says, 'You shall be holy, for I am holy.'

If you say 'our Father' to the One who judges every man impartially on the record of his deeds, you must stand in awe of him while you live out your time on earth. Well you know that it was no perishable stuff, like gold or silver, that bought your freedom from the empty folly of your traditional ways. The price was paid in precious blood, as it were of a lamb without mark or blemish—the blood of Christ. Predestined before the foundation of the world, he was made manifest in this last period of time for your sake. Through him you have come to trust in God who raised him from the dead and

King James Version

from the dead, and gave him glory; that your
faith and hope might be in God. 22 Seeing ye
have purified your souls in obeying the truth
through the Spirit unto unfeigned love of the
brethren, *see that ye* love one another with a
pure heart fervently: 23 Being born again, not
of corruptible seed, but of incorruptible, by the
word of God, which liveth and abideth for ever.
24 For all flesh *is* as grass, and all the glory of
man as the flower of grass. The grass withereth,
and the flower thereof falleth away: 25 But the
word of the Lord endureth for ever. And this
is the word which by the gospel is preached unto
you.

2 Wherefore laying aside all malice, and all
guile, and hypocrisies, and envies, and all evil
speakings, 2As newborn babes, desire the sincere
milk of the word, that ye may grow thereby:
3 If so be ye have tasted that the Lord *is* gra-

Living Bible

great glory. Now your faith and hope can rest
in him alone. 22 Now you can have real love
for everyone because your souls have been
cleansed from selfishness and hatred when you
trusted Christ to save you; so see to it that you
really do love each other warmly, with all your
hearts.
23 For you have a new life. It was not passed
on to you from your parents, for the life they
gave you will fade away. This new one will last
forever, for it comes from Christ, God's ever-
living Message to men. 24 Yes, our natural lives
will fade as grass does when it becomes all
brown and dry. All our greatness is like a flower
that droops and falls; 25 but the Word of the
Lord will last forever. And his message is the
Good News that was preached to you.

2 So get rid of your feelings of hatred. Don't
just pretend to be good! Be done with dishonesty and jealousy and talking about others
behind their backs. 2, 3 [a] Now that you realize
how kind the Lord has been to you, put away
all evil, deception, envy, and fraud. Long to
grow up into the fullness of your salvation; cry

[*a*] An alternative paraphrase of these verses could read: "If you have tasted the Lord's goodness and kindness, cry for more, as a baby cries for milk. Eat God's Word—read it, think about it—and grow strong in the Lord and be saved."

Today's English Version

your faith and hope are fixed on God.
22 Now that by your obedience to the truth
you have purified yourselves and have come to
have a sincere love for your fellow believers,
love one another earnestly with all your hearts.
23 For through the living and eternal word of
God you have been born again as the children
of a parent who is immortal, not mortal. 24As
the scripture says,

"All men are like the wild grass,
and all their glory is like its flower.
The grass dies, and its flower falls off,
25 but the word of the Lord remains forever."

This is the word that the Good News brought
to you.

The living stone and the holy nation

2 Rid yourselves, therefore, of all evil; no
more lying, or hypocrisy, or jealousy, or insulting language. 2 Be like newborn babies, always thirsty for the pure spiritual milk, so that
by drinking it you may grow up and be saved.
3As the scripture says, "You have tasted the
Lord's kindness."

New International Version

your faith and hope are in God.
22 Now that you have purified yourselves by
obeying the truth so that you have sincere love
for your brothers, love one another deeply, with
all your hearts.[b] 23 For you have been born
again, not of perishable seed, but of imperishable, through the living and enduring word of
God. 24 For,
"All men are like grass,
and all their glory is like the wild flower;
the grass withers,
and the flower falls,
25 but the word of the Lord stands forever." [c]
And this is the word that was preached to you.

2 Therefore, rid yourselves of all malice and
all deceit, hypocrisy, jealousy, and slander of
every kind. 2 Like newborn babies, crave pure
spiritual milk, so that by it you may grow up in
your salvation, 3 now that you have tasted that
the Lord is good.

[*b*] Some early MSS read *from a pure heart*. [*c*] Isaiah 40:6-8.

Phillips Modern English

splendour, so that all your faith and hope might be centred in God.

1.22 Let your life match your high calling

Now that you have, by obeying the truth, made your souls clean enough for a genuine love of your fellows, see that you do love each other, fervently and from the heart. For you are not just mortals now but sons of God; the live, permanent Word of the living God has given you his own indestructible heredity. It is true that:

All flesh is as grass,
And all the glory thereof as the flower of grass.
The grass withereth, and the flower falleth:
But the word of the Lord abideth for ever.

The Word referred to is the message of the gospel that was preached to you.

Have done, then, with all evil and deceit, all pretence and jealousy and slander. You are babies, new-born in God's family, and you should be crying out for unadulterated spiritual milk to make you grow up to salvation! And so you will, if you have already tasted the goodness of the Lord.

Revised Standard Version

him glory, so that your faith and hope are in God.[d]
22 Having purified your souls by your obedience to the truth for a sincere love of the brethren, love one another earnestly from the heart. 23 You have been born anew, not of perishable seed but of imperishable, through the living and abiding word of God; 24 for
"All flesh is like grass
and all its glory like the flower of grass.
The grass withers, and the flower falls,
25 but the word of the Lord abides for ever."
That word is the good news which was preached to you.

2 So put away all malice and all guile and insincerity and envy and all slander. 2 Like
newborn babes, long for the pure spiritual milk,
that by it you may grow up to salvation; 3 for
you have tasted the kindness of the Lord.

[d] Or *so that your faith is hope in God.*

Jerusalem Bible

son—so that you would have faith and hope in God.

Love

22 You have been obedient to the truth and
purified your souls until you can love like brothers, in sincerity; let your love for each other
be real and from the heart—23 your new birth
was not from any mortal seed but from the
everlasting word of the living and eternal God.
24*All flesh is grass and its glory like the wild flower's. The grass withers, the flower falls,*
25 *but the word of the Lord remains for ever.*[c]
What is this word? It is the Good News that has been brought to you.

Integrity

2 Be sure, then, you are never spiteful, or deceitful, or hypocritical, or envious and
critical of each other. 2 You are newborn, and,
like babies, you should be hungry for nothing
but milk—the spiritual honesty which will help
you to grow up to salvation—3 now that you
have *tasted the goodness of the Lord.*[d]

[c] Is. 40:6-8. [d] Ps. 34:8.

New English Bible

gave him glory, and so your faith and hope are fixed on God.

Now that by obedience to the truth you have purified your souls until you feel sincere affection towards your brother Christians, love one another whole-heartedly with all your strength. You have been born anew, not of mortal parentage but of immortal, through the living and enduring word of God.[a] For (as Scripture says)

'All mortals are like grass;
all their splendour like the flower of the field;
the grass withers, the flower falls;
but the word of the Lord endures for evermore.'

And this 'word' is the word of the Gospel preached to you.

2 Then away with all malice and deceit, away with all pretence and jealousy and recrimination of every kind! Like the new-born infants you are, you must crave for pure milk (spiritual milk, I mean), so that you may thrive upon it to your souls' health. Surely you have tasted that the Lord is good.

[a] *Or* through the word of the living and enduring God.

King James Version

cious. 4 To whom coming, *as unto* a living
stone, disallowed indeed of men, but chosen of
God, *and* precious, 5 Ye also, as lively stones,
are built up a spiritual house, a holy priesthood,
to offer up spiritual sacrifices, acceptable to God
by Jesus Christ. 6 Wherefore also it is contained
in the Scripture, Behold, I lay in Sion a chief
corner stone, elect, precious: and he that believeth on him shall not be confounded. 7 Unto
you therefore which believe *he is* precious: but
unto them which be disobedient, the stone which
the builders disallowed, the same is made the
head of the corner, 8 And a stone of stumbling,
and a rock of offence, *even to them* which stumble at the word, being disobedient: whereunto
also they were appointed. 9 But ye *are* a chosen
generation, a royal priesthood, a holy nation, a
peculiar people; that ye should shew forth the
praises of him who hath called you out of darkness into his marvellous light: 10 Which in time
past *were* not a people, but *are* now the people
of God: which had not obtained mercy, but now

Living Bible

for this as a baby cries for his milk. 4 Come to
Christ, who is the living Foundation of Rock
upon which God builds; though men have
spurned him, he is very precious to God who
has chosen him above all others.
5 And now you have become living building-
stones for God's use in building his house. What's
more, you are his holy priests; so come to him
—[you who are acceptable to him because of
Jesus Christ[b]]—and offer to God those things
that please him. 6 As the Scriptures express it,
"See, I am sending Christ to be the carefully
chosen, precious Cornerstone of my church, and
I will never disappoint those who trust in him."
7 Yes, he is very precious to you who believe;
and to those who reject him, well—"The same
Stone that was rejected by the builders has become the Cornerstone, the most honored and
important part of the building." 8 And the Scriptures also say, "He is the Stone that some will
stumble over, and the Rock that will make them
fall." They will stumble because they will not
listen to God's Word, nor obey it, and so this
punishment must follow—that they will fall.
9 But you are not like that, for you have
been chosen by God himself—you are priests of
the King, you are holy and pure, you are God's
very own—all this so that you may show to
others how God called you out of the darkness
into his wonderful light. 10 Once you were less
than nothing; now you are God's own. Once you

[*b*] Implied.

Today's English Version

4 Come to the Lord, the living stone rejected
as worthless by men, but chosen as valuable by
God. 5 Come as living stones, and let yourselves
be used in building the spiritual temple, where
you will serve as holy priests to offer spiritual
and acceptable sacrifices to God through Jesus
Christ. 6 For the scripture says,

"I chose a valuable stone,
which now I place for the cornerstone in Zion;
and whoever believes in him will never be disappointed."

7 This stone is of great value for you that believe; but for those who do not believe:

"The very stone which the builders rejected
turned out to be the most important stone."

8 And another scripture says,

"This is the stone that will make people stumble,
the rock that will make them fall."

They stumbled because they did not believe in
the word; such was God's will for them.
9 But you are the chosen race, the King's
priests, the holy nation, God's own people,
chosen to proclaim the wonderful acts of God,
who called you from the darkness into his own
marvelous light. 10 At one time you were not
God's people, but now you are his people; at

New International Version

The living stone and a chosen people

4 As you come to him, the living Stone—rejected by men but chosen by God and precious
to him—5 you also, like living stones, are being
built into a spiritual house to be a holy priesthood, offering spiritual sacrifices acceptable to
God through Jesus Christ. 6 For in Scripture it
says:

"See, I lay a stone in Zion,
a chosen and precious cornerstone,
and the one who trusts in him will never be put to shame."[d]

7 Now to you who believe, this stone is precious.
But to those who do not believe:

"The stone the builders rejected
has become the capstone,"[e]

8 and,

"A stone that causes men to stumble
and a rock that makes them fall."[f]

They stumble because they disobey the message
—which is also what they were destined for.
9 But you are a chosen people, a royal priesthood, a holy nation, a people belonging to God,
that you may declare the praises of him who
called you out of darkness into his wonderful
light. 10 Once you were not a people, but now
you are the people of God; once you had not

[*d*] Isaiah 28:16. [*e*] Psalm 118:22. [*f*] Isaiah 8:14.

Phillips Modern English

You have come to the living Stone despised indeed by men but chosen and greatly honoured by God. So you yourselves, as living stones, must be built up into a spiritual House of God, in which you become a holy priesthood, able to offer those spiritual sacrifices which are acceptable to God by Jesus Christ. There is a passage to this effect in scripture, and it runs like this:

Behold I lay in Zion a chief corner stone, elect, precious:
And he that believeth on him shall not be put to shame.

It is to you who believe in him that he is "precious", but to those who disobey God, it is true that:

The stone which the builders rejected,
The same was made the head of the corner.

And he is, to them,

A stone of stumbling and a rock of offence.

Yes, they stumble at the Word of God for in their hearts they are unwilling to obey it—which makes stumbling a foregone conclusion. But you are God's "chosen generation", his "royal priesthood", his "holy nation", his "peculiar people"—all the old titles of God's people now belong to you. It is for you now to demonstrate the goodness of him who has called you out of darkness into his amazing light. In the past you were not "a people" at all: now you are the people of God. In the past you had

Revised Standard Version

4 Come to him, to that living stone, rejected
by men but in God's sight chosen and precious;
5 and like living stones be yourselves built into
a spiritual house, to be a holy priesthood, to
offer spiritual sacrifices acceptable to God
through Jesus Christ. 6 For it stands in scripture:
"Behold, I am laying in Zion a stone, a corner-
stone chosen and precious,
and he who believes in him will not be put
to shame."
7 To you therefore who believe, he is precious,
but for those who do not believe,
"The very stone which the builders rejected
has become the head of the corner,"
8 and
"A stone that will make men stumble,
a rock that will make them fall";
for they stumble because they disobey the word,
as they were destined to do.
9 But you are a chosen race, a royal priesthood, a holy nation, God's own people,[e] that
you may declare the wonderful deeds of him
who called you out of darkness into his marvelous light. 10 Once you were no people but now
you are God's people; once you had not received

[e] Greek *a people for his possession.*

Jerusalem Bible

The new priesthood

4 He is the living stone, rejected by men but
chosen by God and precious to him; set yourselves close to him 5 so that you too, the holy
priesthood that offers the spiritual sacrifices which
Jesus Christ has made acceptable to God, may
be living stones making a spiritual house. 6 As
scripture says: *See how I lay in Zion a precious
cornerstone that I have chosen* and *the man who
rests his trust on it will not be disappointed.*[e]
7 That means that for you who are believers, it
is precious; but for unbelievers, *the stone rejected by the builders has proved to be the keystone,*[f] 8 *a stone to stumble over, a rock to bring
men down.*[g] They stumble over it because they
do not believe in the word; it was the fate in
store for them.
9 But you are *a chosen race, a royal priesthood, a consecrated nation, a people set apart*[h]
to sing the praises of God who called you out of
the darkness into his wonderful light. 10 Once
you were *not a people*[i] at all and now you are
the People of God; once you were *outside the*

[e] Is. 28:16. [f] Ps. 18:22. [g] Is. 8:14. [h] Is. 43: 20-21. [i] Ho. 1:9; the two other quotations in this sentence are allusive references to Ho. 2.

New English Bible

So come to him, our living Stone—the stone rejected by men but choice and precious in the sight of God. Come, and let yourselves be built, as living stones, into a spiritual temple; become a holy priesthood,[b] to offer spiritual sacrifices acceptable to God through Jesus Christ. For it stands written:

'I lay in Zion a choice corner-stone of great worth.
The man who has faith in it will not be put to shame.'

The great worth of which it speaks is for you who have faith. For those who have no faith, the stone which the builders rejected has become not only the corner-stone,[a] but also 'a stone to trip over, a rock to stumble against'. They fall when they disbelieve the Word. Such was their appointed lot!

But you are a chosen race, a royal priesthood, a dedicated nation, and a people claimed by God for his own, to proclaim the triumphs of him who has called you out of darkness into his marvellous light. You are now the people of God, who once were not his people; outside

[b] *Or* a spiritual temple for the holy work of priesthood. [a] *Or* the apex of the building.

King James Version

have obtained mercy. 11 Dearly beloved, I beseech *you* as strangers and pilgrims, abstain from fleshly lusts, which war against the soul; 12 Having your conversation honest among the Gentiles: that, whereas they speak against you as evil doers, they may by *your* good works, which they shall behold, glorify God in the day of visitation. 13 Submit yourselves to every ordinance of man for the Lord's sake: whether it be to the king, as supreme; 14 Or unto governors, as unto them that are sent by him for the punishment of evil doers, and for the praise of them that do well. 15 For so is the will of God, that with well doing ye may put to silence the ignorance of foolish men: 16 As free, and not using *your* liberty for a cloak of maliciousness, but as the servants of God. 17 Honour all *men.* Love the brotherhood. Fear God. Honour the king.

Living Bible

knew very little of God's kindness; now your very lives have been changed by it.

11 Dear brothers, you are only visitors here. Since your real home is in heaven I beg you to keep away from the evil pleasures of this world; they are not for you, for they fight against your very souls.

12 Be careful how you behave among your unsaved neighbors; for then, even if they are suspicious of you and talk against you, they will end up praising God for your good works when Christ returns. 13 For the Lord's sake, obey every law of your government: those of the king as head of the state, 14 and those of the king's officers, for he has sent them to punish all who do wrong, and to honor those who do right.

15 It is God's will that your good lives should silence those who foolishly condemn the Gospel without knowing what it can do for them, having never experienced its power. 16 You are free from the law, but that doesn't mean you are free to do wrong. Live as those who are free to do only God's will at all times.

17 Show respect for everyone. Love Christians everywhere. Fear God and honor the government.

Today's English Version

one time you did not know God's mercy, but now you have received his mercy.

Slaves of God

11 I appeal to you, my friends, as strangers and refugees in this world! Do not give in to bodily passions, which are always at war against the soul. 12 Your conduct among the heathen should be so good that when they accuse you of being evildoers they will have to recognize your good deeds, and so praise God on the Day of his coming.

13 Submit yourselves, for the Lord's sake, to every human authority: to the Emperor, who is the supreme authority, 14 and to the governors, who have been sent by him to punish the evildoers and praise those who do good. 15 For God's will is this: he wants you to silence the ignorant talk of foolish men by the good things you do. 16 Live as free men; do not use your freedom, however, to cover up any evil, but live as God's slaves. 17 Respect all men, love your fellow believers, fear God, and respect the Emperor.

New International Version

received mercy, but now you have received mercy.

11 Dear friends, I urge you, as foreigners and strangers in the world, to abstain from sinful desires, which war against your soul. 12 Live such good lives among the pagans that, though they accuse you of doing wrong, they may see your good deeds and glorify God on the day he visits us.

Submission to rulers and masters

13 Submit yourselves for the Lord's sake to every authority instituted among men: whether to the king, as the supreme authority, 14 or to governors, who are sent by him to punish those who do wrong and to commend those who do right. 15 For it is God's will that by doing good you should silence the ignorant talk of foolish men. 16 Live as free men, but do not use your freedom as a cover-up for evil; live as servants of God. 17 Show proper respect to everyone: Love the brotherhood of believers, fear God, honor the king.

Phillips Modern English

no experience of his mercy, but now it is intimately yours.

2.11 Your behaviour to the outside world

I beg you, as those whom I love, to live in this world as strangers and "temporary residents", to keep clear of the desires of your lower natures, for they are always at war with your souls. Your conduct among the surrounding peoples in your different countries should always be good and right, so that although they may slander you as evil-doers yet when troubles come, they may glorify God when they see how well you conduct yourselves.

Obey every man-made authority for the Lord's sake—whether it is the emperor, as the supreme ruler, or the governors whom he has appointed to punish evil-doers and reward those who do good service. It is the will of God that you may thus silence the ill-informed criticisms of the foolish. As free men you should never use your freedom as a screen for doing wrong, but live as servants of God. You should have respect for everyone, you should love our brotherhood, fear God and honour the emperor.

Revised Standard Version

mercy but now you have received mercy.

11 Beloved, I beseech you as aliens and exiles to abstain from the passions of the flesh that wage war against your soul. 12 Maintain good conduct among the Gentiles, so that in case they speak against you as wrongdoers, they may see your good deeds and glorify God on the day of visitation.

13 Be subject for the Lord's sake to every human institution,[f] whether it be to the emperor as supreme, 14 or to governors as sent by him to punish those who do wrong and to praise those who do right. 15 For it is God's will that by doing right you should put to silence the ignorance of foolish men. 16 Live as free men, yet without using your freedom as a pretext for evil; but live as servants of God. 17 Honor all men. Love the brotherhood. Fear God. Honor the emperor.

[f] Or *every institution ordained for men.*

Jerusalem Bible

mercy and now *you have been given mercy.*

The obligations of Christians: toward pagans

11 I urge you, my dear people, while you are *visitors and pilgrims*[j] to keep yourselves free from the selfish passions that attack the soul. 12Always behave honorably among pagans so that they can see your good works for themselves and, when the day of reckoning comes, give thanks to God for the things which now make them denounce you as criminals.

Toward civil authority

13 For the sake of the Lord, accept the authority of every social institution: the emperor, as the supreme authority, 14 and the governors as commissioned by him to punish criminals and praise good citizenship. 15 God wants you to be good citizens, so as to silence what fools are saying in their ignorance. 16 You are slaves of no one except God, so behave like free men, and never use your freedom as an excuse for wickedness. 17 Have respect for everyone and love for our community; fear God and honor the emperor.

[j] Ps. 39:12.

New English Bible

his mercy once, you have now received his mercy.

Dear friends, I beg you, as aliens in a foreign land, to abstain from the lusts of the flesh which are at war with the soul. Let all your behaviour be such as even pagans can recognize as good, and then, whereas they malign you as criminals now, they will come to see for themselves that you live good lives, and will give glory to God on the day when he comes to hold assize.

Submit yourselves to every human institution for the sake of the Lord, whether to the sovereign as supreme, or to the governor as his deputy for the punishment of criminals and the commendation of those who do right. For it is the will of God that by your good conduct you should put ignorance and stupidity to silence.

Live as free men; not however as though your freedom were there to provide a screen for wrongdoing, but as slaves in God's service. Give due honour to everyone: love to the brotherhood, reverence to God, honour to the sovereign.

King James Version

18 Servants, *be* subject to *your* masters with all
fear; not only to the good and gentle, but also
to the froward. 19 For this *is* thankworthy, if
a man for conscience toward God endure grief,
suffering wrongfully. 20 For what glory *is it*, if,
when ye be buffeted for your faults, ye shall take
it patiently? but if, when ye do well, and suffer
for it, ye take it patiently, this *is* acceptable with
God. 21 For even hereunto were ye called: because Christ also suffered for us, leaving us an
example, that ye should follow his steps: 22 Who
did no sin, neither was guile found in his mouth:
23 Who, when he was reviled, reviled not again;
when he suffered, he threatened not; but committed *himself* to him that judgeth righteously:
24 Who his own self bare our sins in his own
body on the tree, that we, being dead to sins,
should live unto righteousness: by whose stripes
ye were healed. 25 For ye were as sheep going
astray; but are now returned unto the Shepherd
and Bishop of your souls.

3 Likewise, ye wives, *be* in subjection to your
own husbands; that, if any obey not the
word, they also may without the word be won

Living Bible

18 Servants, you must respect your masters
and do whatever they tell you—not only if they
are kind and reasonable, but even if they are
tough and cruel. 19 Praise the Lord if you are
punished for doing right! 20 Of course, you get
no credit for being patient if you are beaten for
doing wrong; but if you do right and suffer for
it, and are patient beneath the blows, God is
well pleased.

21 This suffering is all part of the work God
has given you. Christ, who suffered for you, is
your example. Follow in his steps: 22 He never
sinned, never told a lie, 23 never answered back
when insulted; when he suffered he did not
threaten to get even; he left his case in the
hands of God who always judges fairly. 24 He
personally carried the load of our sins in his
own body when he died on the cross, so that
we can be finished with sin and live a good life
from now on. For his wounds have healed ours!
25 Like sheep you wandered away from God,
but now you have returned to your Shepherd,
the Guardian of your souls who keeps you safe
from all attacks.

3 Wives, fit in with your husbands' plans;
for then if they refuse to listen when you talk
to them about the Lord, they will be won by

Today's English Version

The example of Christ's suffering

18 You servants must submit yourselves to
your masters and show them complete respect,
not only to those who are kind and considerate,
but also to those who are harsh. 19 God will
bless you for this, if you endure the pain of undeserved suffering because you are conscious of
his will. 20 For what credit is there if you endure the beatings you deserve for having done
wrong? But if you endure suffering even when
you have done right, God will bless you for it.
21 It was to this that God called you; because
Christ himself suffered for you and left you an
example, so that you would follow in his steps.
22 He committed no sin; no one ever heard a
lie come from his lips. 23 When he was insulted
he did not answer back with an insult; when he
suffered he did not threaten, but placed his hopes
in God, the righteous Judge. 24 Christ himself
carried our sins in his body to the cross, so that
we might die to sin and live for righteousness.
By his wounds you have been healed. 25 You
were like sheep that had lost their way; but now
you have been brought back to follow the Shepherd and Keeper of your souls.

Wives and husbands

3 In the same way you wives must submit
yourselves to your husbands, so that if some
of them do not believe God's word, they will be

New International Version

18 Slaves, submit yourselves to your masters
with all respect, not only to those who are good
and considerate, but also to those who are harsh.
19 For it is commendable if a man bears up under the pain of unjust suffering because he is
conscious of God. 20 But how is it to your credit
if you receive a beating for doing wrong and
endure it? But if you suffer for doing good and
you endure it, this is commendable before God.
21 To this you were called, because Christ suffered for you, leaving you an example, that you
should follow in his steps.

22 "He committed no sin,
and no deceit was found in his mouth." [g]

23 When they hurled their insults at him, he did
not retaliate; when he suffered, he made no
threats. Instead, he entrusted himself to him who
judges justly. 24 He himself bore our sins in his
body on the cross, so that we might die to sins
and live for righteousness; by his wounds you
have been healed. 25 For you were like sheep
going astray, but now you have returned to the
Shepherd and Overseer of your souls.

Wives and husbands

3 Wives, in the same way be submissive to
your husbands so that, if any of them do not
believe the word, they may be won over with-

[g] Isaiah 53:9.

Phillips Modern English

2.18 A word to household servants

You who are servants should submit to your masters with proper respect—not only to the good and kind, but also to the difficult. A man does a fine thing when he endures pain, with a clear conscience towards God, though he knows he is suffering unjustly. After all, it is no credit to you if you are patient in bearing a punishment which you have richly deserved! But if you do your duty and are punished for it and can still accept it patiently, you are doing something worthwhile in God's sight. Indeed this is your calling. For Christ suffered for you and left you a personal example, so that you might follow in his footsteps. He was guilty of no sin nor of the slightest prevarication. Yet when he was insulted he offered no insult in return. When he suffered he made no threats of revenge. He simply committed his cause to the One who judges fairly. And he personally bore our sins in his own body on the cross, so that we might be dead to sin and be alive to all that is good. It was the suffering that he bore which has healed you. You had wandered away like so many sheep, but now you have returned to the shepherd and guardian of your souls.

3.1 A word to married Christians

In the same spirit you married women should adapt yourselves to your husbands, so that even if they do not obey the Word of God they may

Revised Standard Version

18 Servants, be submissive to your masters
with all respect, not only to the kind and gentle
but also to the overbearing. 19 For one is approved if, mindful of God, he endures pain while
suffering unjustly. 20 For what credit is it, if
when you do wrong and are beaten for it you
take it patiently? But if when you do right and
suffer for it you take it patiently, you have God's
approval. 21 For to this you have been called,
because Christ also suffered for you, leaving you
an example, that you should follow in his steps.
22 He committed no sin; no guile was found on
his lips. 23 When he was reviled, he did not
revile in return; when he suffered, he did not
threaten; but he trusted to him who judges
justly. 24 He himself bore our sins in his body on
the tree,[g] that we might die to sin and live to
righteousness. By his wounds you have been
healed. 25 For you were straying like sheep, but
have now returned to the Shepherd and Guardian of your souls.

3 Likewise you wives, be submissive to your husbands, so that some, though they do not obey the word, may be won without a word by

[g] Or *carried up . . . to the tree.*

Jerusalem Bible

Toward masters

18 Slaves must be respectful and obedient to
their masters, not only when they are kind and
gentle but also when they are unfair. 19 You see,
there is some merit in putting up with the pains
of unearned punishment if it is done for the sake
of God 20 but there is nothing meritorious in
taking a beating patiently if you have done something wrong to deserve it. The merit, in the sight
of God, is in bearing it patiently when you are
punished after doing your duty.
21 This, in fact, is what you were called to
do, because Christ suffered for you and left an
example for you to follow the way he took.
22 He had not done anything wrong, and *there
had been no perjury in his mouth.*[k] 23 He was
insulted and did not retaliate with insults; when
he was tortured he made no threats but he put
his trust in the righteous judge. 24 He was *bearing our faults* in his own body on the cross, so
that we might die to our faults and live for
holiness; *through his wounds you have been
healed.* 25 You had *gone astray like sheep* but
now you have come back to the shepherd and
guardian[l] of your souls.

In marriage

3 In the same way, wives should be obedient to their husbands. Then, if there are some husbands who have not yet obeyed the word,

[k] This quotation, and the others in this paragraph, are from Is. 53. [l] *episcopos.*

New English Bible

Servants, accept the authority of your masters with all due submission, not only when they are kind and considerate, but even when they are perverse. For it is a fine[b] thing if a man endure the pain of undeserved suffering because God is in his thoughts. What credit is there in fortitude when you have done wrong and are beaten for it? But when you have behaved well and suffer for it, your fortitude is a fine thing[c] in the sight of God. To that you were called, because Christ suffered [d] on your behalf, and thereby left you an example; it is for you to follow in his steps. He committed no sin, he was convicted of no falsehood; when he was abused he did not retort with abuse, when he suffered he uttered no threats, but committed his cause to the One who judges justly. In his own person he carried our sins to[a] the gibbet, so that we might cease to live for sin and begin to live for righteousness. By his wounds you have been healed. You were straying like sheep, but now you have turned towards the Shepherd and Guardian of your souls.

3 In the same way you women must accept the authority of your husbands, so that if there are any of them who disbelieve the Gospel they

[b] *Or* creditable. [c] *Or* is creditable. [d] *Some witnesses read* died. [a] *Or* on.

King James Version

by the conversation of the wives; 2 While they behold your chaste conversation *coupled* with fear. 3 Whose adorning, let it not be that outward *adorning* of plaiting the hair, and of wearing of gold, or of putting on of apparel; 4 But *let it be* the hidden man of the heart, in that which is not corruptible, *even the ornament* of a meek and quiet spirit, which is in the sight of God of great price. 5 For after this manner in the old time the holy women also, who trusted in God, adorned themselves, being in subjection unto their own husbands: 6 Even as Sarah obeyed Abraham, calling him lord: whose daughters ye are, as long as ye do well, and are not afraid with any amazement. 7 Likewise, ye husbands, dwell with *them* according to knowledge, giving honour unto the wife, as unto the weaker vessel, and as being heirs together of the grace of life; that your prayers be not hindered. 8 Finally, *be ye* all of one mind, having compassion one of another; love as brethren, *be* pitiful, *be* courteous: 9 Not rendering evil for evil, or railing for railing: but contrariwise blessing; knowing that ye are thereunto called, that ye should inherit a blessing. 10 For he that will love life, and

Living Bible

your respectful, pure behavior. Your godly lives will speak to them better than any words.

3 Don't be concerned about the outward beauty that depends on jewelry, or beautiful clothes, or hair arrangement. 4 Be beautiful inside, in your hearts, with the lasting charm of a gentle and quiet spirit which is so precious to God. 5 That kind of deep beauty was seen in the saintly women of old, who trusted God and fitted in with their husbands' plans.

6 Sarah, for instance, obeyed her husband Abraham, honoring him as head of the house. And if you do the same, you will be following in her steps like good daughters and doing what is right; then you will not need to fear [offending your husbands[a]].

7 You husbands must be careful of your wives, being thoughtful of their needs and honoring them as the weaker sex. Remember that you and your wife are partners in receiving God's blessings, and if you don't treat her as you should, your prayers will not get ready answers.

8 And now this word to all of you: You should be like one big happy family, full of sympathy toward each other, loving one another with tender hearts and humble minds. 9 Don't repay evil for evil. Don't snap back at those who say unkind things about you. Instead, pray for God's help for them, for we are to be kind to others, and God will bless us for it.

10 If you want a happy, good life, keep con-

[a] Implied.

Today's English Version

won over to believe by your conduct. It will not be necessary for you to say a word, 2 because they will see how pure and reverent your conduct is. 3 You should not use outward aids to make yourselves beautiful, such as the way you fix your hair, or the jewelry you put on, or the dresses you wear. 4 Instead, your beauty should consist of your true inner self, the ageless beauty of a gentle and quiet spirit, which is of the greatest value in God's sight. 5 For the devout women of the past, who hoped in God, used to make themselves beautiful in this way, by submitting themselves to their husbands. 6 Sarah was like that; she obeyed Abraham and called him "My master." You are now her daughters if you do good and are not afraid of anything.

7 You husbands, also, in living with your wives you must recognize that they are the weaker sex. So you must treat them with respect, because they also will receive, together with you, God's gift of life. Do this so that nothing will interfere with your prayers.

Suffering for doing right

8 To conclude: you must all have the same thoughts and the same feelings; love one another as brothers, and be kind and humble with one another. 9 Do not pay back evil with evil, or cursing with cursing; instead pay back with a blessing, because a blessing is what God promised to give you when he called you. 10 As the scripture says,

New International Version

out talk by the behavior of their wives, 2 when they see the purity and reverence of your lives. 3 Your beauty should not come from outward adornment, such as braided hair and the wearing of gold jewelry and fine clothes. 4 Instead, it should be that of your inner self, the unfading beauty of a gentle and quiet spirit, which is of great worth in God's sight. 5 For this is the way the holy women of the past who put their hope in God used to make themselves beautiful. They were submissive to their own husbands, 6 like Sarah, who obeyed Abraham and called him her master. You are her daughters if you do what is right and do not give way to fear.

7 Husbands, in the same way be considerate as you live with your wives, and treat them with respect as the weaker partner and as heirs with you of the gracious gift of life, so that nothing will hinder your prayers.

Suffering for doing good

8 Finally, all of you, live in harmony with one another; be sympathetic, love as brothers, be compassionate and humble. 9 Do not repay evil with evil or insult with insult, but with blessing, because to this you were called so that you may inherit a blessing. 10 For,

Phillips Modern English

be won to God without any word being spoken, simply by seeing the pure and reverent conduct of you, their wives. Your beauty should not be dependent on an elaborate coiffure, or on the wearing of jewellery or fine clothes, but on the inner personality—the unfading loveliness of a calm and gentle spirit, a thing very precious in the eyes of God. This was the beauty of the holy women of ancient times who trusted in God and were submissive to their husbands. Sarah, you will remember, obeyed Abraham and called him her lord. And you have become her true descendants today as long as you too live good lives and do not give way to hysterical fears.

Similarly, you husbands should try to understand the wives you live with, honouring them as physically weaker yet equally heirs with you of the grace of life. If you don't do this, you will find it impossible to pray together properly.

3.8 Be good to each other—and to all men

To sum up, you should all be of one mind living like brothers with true love and sympathy for each other, compassionate and humble. Never pay back a bad turn with a bad turn or an insult with another insult, but on the contrary pay back with good. For this is your calling—to do good and to inherit the goodness of God. For:

Revised Standard Version

the behavior of their wives, 2 when they see your
reverent and chaste behavior. 3 Let not yours be
the outward adorning with braiding of hair,
decoration of gold, and wearing of fine clothing,
4 but let it be the hidden person of the heart
with the imperishable jewel of a gentle and quiet
spirit, which in God's sight is very precious. 5 So
once the holy women who hoped in God used
to adorn themselves and were submissive to their
husbands, 6 as Sarah obeyed Abraham, calling
him lord. And you are now her children if you
do right and let nothing terrify you.

7 Likewise you husbands, live considerately
with your wives, bestowing honor on the woman
as the weaker sex, since you are joint heirs of the
grace of life, in order that your prayers may not
be hindered.

8 Finally, all of you, have unity of spirit, sympathy, love of the brethren, a tender heart and
a humble mind. 9 Do not return evil for evil or
reviling for reviling; but on the contrary bless,
for to this you have been called, that you may
obtain a blessing. 10 For

Jerusalem Bible

they may find themselves won over, without a
word spoken, by the way their wives behave,
2 when they see how faithful and conscientious
they are. 3 Do not dress up for show: doing up
your hair, wearing gold bracelets and fine
clothes; 4 all this should be inside, in a person's
heart, imperishable: the ornament of a sweet and
gentle disposition—this is what is precious in
the sight of God. 5 That was how the holy
women of the past dressed themselves attractively
—they hoped in God and were tender and obedient to their husbands; 6 like Sarah, who was
obedient to Abraham, and called him her *lord*.
You are now her children, as long as you live
good lives and do not give way to fear or worry.

7 In the same way, husbands must always
treat their wives with consideration in their life
together, respecting a woman as one who, though
she may be the weaker partner, is equally an
heir to the life of grace. This will stop anything
from coming in the way of your prayers.

Toward the brothers

8 Finally: you should all agree among yourselves and be sympathetic; love the brothers,
have compassion and be self-effacing. 9 Never pay
back one wrong with another, or an angry word
with another one; instead, pay back with a
blessing. That is what you are called to do, so
that you inherit a blessing yourself. 10 Remem-

New English Bible

may be won over, without a word being said, by observing the chaste and reverent behaviour of their wives. Your beauty should reside, not in outward adornment—the braiding of the hair, or jewellery, or dress—but in the inmost centre of your being, with its imperishable ornament, a gentle, quiet spirit, which is of high value in the sight of God. Thus it was among God's people in days of old: the women who fixed their hopes on him adorned themselves by submission to their husbands. Such was Sarah, who obeyed Abraham and called him 'my master'. Her children you have now become, if you do good and show no fear.

In the same way, you husbands must conduct your married life with understanding: pay honour to the woman's body, not only because it is weaker, but also because you share together in the grace of God which gives you life. Then your prayers will not be hindered.

To sum up: be one in thought and feeling, all of you; be full of brotherly affection, kindly and humble-minded. Do not repay wrong with wrong, or abuse with abuse; on the contrary, retaliate with blessing, for a blessing is the inheritance to which you yourselves have been called.

King James Version

see good days, let him refrain his tongue from
evil, and his lips that they speak no guile: 11 Let
him eschew evil, and do good; let him seek
peace, and ensue it. 12 For the eyes of the Lord
are over the righteous, and his ears *are open*
unto their prayers: but the face of the Lord *is*
against them that do evil. 13 And who *is* he that
will harm you, if ye be followers of that which
is good? 14 But and if ye suffer for righteousness' sake, happy *are ye:* and be not afraid of
their terror, neither be troubled; 15 But sanctify
the Lord God in your hearts: and *be* ready
always to *give* an answer to every man that asketh you a reason of the hope that is in you, with
meekness and fear: 16 Having a good conscience;
that, whereas they speak evil of you, as of evil
doers, they may be ashamed that falsely accuse
your good conversation in Christ. 17 For *it is*
better, if the will of God be so, that ye suffer
for well doing, than for evil doing. 18 For Christ
also hath once suffered for sins, the just for the
unjust, that he might bring us to God, being put

Living Bible

trol of your tongue, and guard your lips from
telling lies. 11 Turn away from evil and do good.
Try to live in peace even if you must run after
it to catch and hold it! 12 For the Lord is
watching his children, listening to their prayers;
but the Lord's face is hard against those who
do evil.

13 Usually no one will hurt you for wanting
to do good. 14 But even if they should, you are
to be envied, for God will reward you for it.
15 Quietly trust yourself to Christ your Lord
and if anybody asks why you believe as you do,
be ready to tell him, and do it in a gentle and
respectful way.

16 Do what is right; then if men speak against
you, calling you evil names, they will become
ashamed of themselves for falsely accusing you
when you have only done what is good. 17 Remember, if God wants you to suffer, it is better
to suffer for doing good than for doing wrong!

18 Christ also suffered. He died once for the
sins of all us guilty sinners, although he himself
was innocent of any sin at any time, that he
might bring us safely home to God. But though

Today's English Version

"Whoever wants to enjoy life
and wishes to see good times,
must keep from speaking evil
and stop telling lies.
11 He must turn away from evil and do good;
he must seek peace and pursue it.
12 For the Lord keeps his eyes on the righteous
and always listens to their prayers;
but he turns against those who do evil."

13 Who will harm you if you are eager to do
what is good? 14 But even if you should suffer
for doing what is right, how happy you are! Do
not be afraid of men, and do not worry. 15 But
have reverence for Christ in your hearts, and
make him your Lord. Be ready at all times to
answer anyone who asks you to explain the
hope you have in you. 16 But do it with gentleness and respect. Keep your conscience clear,
so that when you are insulted, those who speak
evil of your good conduct as followers of
Christ will be made ashamed of what they say.
17 Because it is better to suffer for doing good,
if this should be God's will, than for doing
wrong. 18 For Christ himself died for you; once
and for all he died for sins, a good man for
bad men, in order to lead you to God. He was

New International Version

"Whoever would love life
and see good days
must keep his tongue from evil
and his lips from deceitful speech.
11 He must turn from evil and do good;
he must seek peace and pursue it.
12 For the eyes of the Lord are on the righteous,
and his ears are attentive to their prayer,
but the face of the Lord is against those
who do evil." [h]

13 Who is going to harm you if you are eager
to do good? 14 But even if you should suffer for
what is right, you are blessed. "Do not fear what
they fear[i]; do not be frightened." [j] 15 But in
your hearts acknowledge Christ as the holy Lord.
Always be prepared to give an answer to everyone who asks you to give the reason for the hope
that you have. 16 But do this with gentleness and
respect, keeping a clear conscience, so that those
who speak maliciously against your good behavior in Christ may be ashamed of their slander.
17 It is better, if it is God's will, to suffer for doing good than for doing evil. 18 For Christ died
for your sins once for all, the righteous for the
unrighteous, to bring you to God. He was put

[*h*] Psalm 34:12-16. [*i*] Or *fear their threats.* [*j*]
Isaiah 8:12.

Phillips Modern English

He that would love life,
And see good days,
Let him refrain his tongue from evil,
And his lips that they speak no guile:
And let him turn away from evil, and do good;
Let him seek peace and pursue it.
For the eyes of the Lord are upon the righteous,
And his ears unto their supplication:
But the face of the Lord is against them that do evil.

3.13 Do good, even if you suffer for it

After all, who is likely to injure you for being devoted to what is good? And if it should happen that you suffer for living a good life you are fortunate. You need neither fear men's threats nor worry about them; simply concentrate on being completely devoted to Christ in your hearts. Be ready at any time to give a quiet and reverent answer to any man who wants a reason for the hope that you have within you. Make sure that your conscience is perfectly clear, so that if men should speak slanderously of you as rogues they máy come to feel ashamed of themselves for abusing you for your good Christian behaviour.

If it is the will of God that you should suffer it is better to suffer for doing good than for doing wrong. Remember that Christ the just suffered for us the unjust, to bring us to God. That

Revised Standard Version

"He that would love life
and see good days,
let him keep his tongue from evil
and his lips from speaking guile;
11 let him turn away from evil and do right;
let him seek peace and pursue it.
12 For the eyes of the Lord are upon the righteous,
and his ears are open to their prayer.
But the face of the Lord is against those that do evil."

13 Now who is there to harm you if you are
zealous for what is right? 14 But even if you do
suffer for righteousness' sake, you will be blessed.
Have no fear of them, nor be troubled, 15 but
in your hearts reverence Christ as Lord. Always
be prepared to make a defense to any one who
calls you to account for the hope that is in you,
yet do it with gentleness and reverence; 16 and
keep your conscience clear, so that, when you
are abused, those who revile your good behavior
in Christ may be put to shame. 17 For it is better
to suffer for doing right, if that should be
God's will, than for doing wrong. 18 For
Christ also died[h] for sins once for all, the righteous
for the unrighteous, that he might bring us

[h] Other ancient authorities read *suffered*.

Jerusalem Bible

ber: *Anyone who wants to have a happy life and to enjoy prosperity must banish malice from his tongue, deceitful conversation from his lips;*
11 *he must never yield to evil but must practice good; he must seek peace and pursue it.* 12 *Because the face of the Lord frowns on evil men, but the eyes of the Lord are turned toward the virtuous.*[m]

In persecution

13 No one can hurt you if you are determined
to do only what is right; 14 if you do have to
suffer for being good, you will count it a blessing.
*There is no need to be afraid or to worry
about them.*[n] 15 Simply *reverence the Lord*[o]
Christ in your hearts, and always have your answer
ready for people who ask you the reason
for the hope that you all have. 16 But give it
with courtesy and respect and with a clear conscience,
so that those who slander you when you
are living a good life in Christ may be proved
wrong in the accusations that they bring. 17 And
if it is the will of God that you should suffer, it
is better to suffer for doing right than for doing
wrong.

The resurrection and "the descent into hell"

18 Why, Christ himself, innocent though he
was, had died once for sins, died for the guilty,

[m] Ps. 34:12-16. [n] Is. 8:12-13 (LXX). [o] Pr. 3:25.

New English Bible

'Whoever loves life and would see good days
must restrain his tongue from evil
and his lips from deceit;
must turn from wrong and do good,
seek peace and pursue it.
For the Lord's eyes are turned towards the righteous,
his ears are open to their prayers;
but the Lord's face is set against wrong-doers.'

Who is going to do you wrong if you are devoted to what is good? And yet if you should suffer for your virtues, you may count yourselves happy. Have no fear of them:[b] do not be perturbed, but hold the Lord Christ in reverence in your hearts.[c] Be always ready with your defence whenever you are called to account for the hope that is in you, but make that defence with modesty and respect. Keep your conscience clear, so that when you are abused, those who malign your Christian conduct may be put to shame. It is better to suffer for well-doing, if such should be the will of God, than for doing wrong. For Christ also died[d] for our sins[e] once and for all. He, the just, suffered for the unjust, to bring us to God.

[b] Or Do not fear what they fear. [c] *Or* hold Christ in reverence in your hearts, as Lord. [d] *Some witnesses read* suffered. [e] *Some witnesses read* for sins; others read for sins on our behalf.

King James Version

to death in the flesh, but quickened by the Spirit: 19 By which also he went and preached unto the spirits in prison; 20 Which sometime were disobedient, when once the longsuffering of God waited in the days of Noah, while the ark was a preparing, wherein few, that is, eight souls were saved by water. 21 The like figure whereunto *even* baptism doth also now save us, (not the putting away of the filth of the flesh, but the answer of a good conscience toward God,) by the resurrection of Jesus Christ: 22 Who is gone into heaven, and is on the right hand of God; angels and authorities and powers being made subject unto him.

4 Forasmuch then as Christ hath suffered for us in the flesh, arm yourselves likewise with the same mind: for he that hath suffered in the flesh hath ceased from sin; 2 That he no longer should live the rest of *his* time in the flesh to the lusts of men, but to the will of God. 3 For the time past of *our* life may suffice us to have wrought the will of the Gentiles, when we walked in lasciviousness, lusts, excess of wine, revellings, banquetings, and abominable idola-

Living Bible

his body died, his spirit lived on, 19 and it was in the spirit that he visited the spirits in prison, and preached to them—20 spirits of those who, long before in the days of Noah, had refused to listen to God, though he waited patiently for them while Noah was building the ark. Yet only eight persons were saved from drowning in that terrible flood. 21 (That, by the way, is what baptism pictures for us: In baptism we show that we have been saved from death and doom by the resurrection of Christ;[b] not because our bodies are washed clean by the water, but because in being baptized we are turning to God and asking him to cleanse our *hearts* from sin.) 22 And now Christ is in heaven, sitting in the place of honor next to God the Father, with all the angels and powers of heaven bowing before him and obeying him.

4 Since Christ suffered and underwent pain, you must have the same attitude he did; you must be ready to suffer, too. For remember, when your body suffers, sin loses its power, 2 and you won't be spending the rest of your life chasing after evil desires, but will be anxious to do the will of God. 3 You have had enough in the past of the evil things the godless enjoy—sex sin, lust, getting drunk, wild parties, drinking bouts, and the worship of idols, and other terrible sins.[a]

[*b*] Or, "Baptism, which corresponds to this, now saves you through the Resurrection." [*a*] Literally, "lawless idolatries."

Today's English Version

put to death physically, but made alive spiritually, 19 and in his spiritual existence he went and preached to the imprisoned spirits. 20 These were the spirits of those who had not obeyed God, when he waited patiently during the days that Noah was building the ark. The few people in the ark—eight in all—were saved by the water, 21 which was a figure pointing to baptism, which now saves you. It is not the washing off of bodily dirt, but the promise made to God from a good conscience. It saves you through the resurrection of Jesus Christ, 22 who has gone to heaven and is at the right side of God, ruling over all angels and heavenly authorities and powers.

Changed lives

4 Since Christ suffered physically, you too must strengthen yourselves with the same way of thinking; because whoever suffers physically is no longer involved with sin. 2 From now on, then, you must live the rest of your earthly lives controlled by God's will, not by human desires. 3 You have spent enough time in the past doing what the heathen like to do. Your lives were spent in indecency, lust, drunkenness, orgies, drinking parties, and the disgusting wor-

New International Version

to death in the body but made alive by the Spirit, 19 through whom also he went and preached to the spirits in prison 20 who disobeyed long ago when God waited patiently in the days of Noah while the ark was being built. In it only a few people, eight in all, were saved through water, 21 and this water symbolizes baptism that now saves you also—not the removal of dirt from the body but the pledge of a good conscience toward God. It saves you by the resurrection of Jesus Christ, 22 who has gone into heaven and is at God's right hand—with angels, authorities and powers in submission to him.

Living for God

4 Therefore, since Christ suffered in his body, arm yourselves also with the same attitude, because he who has suffered in his body is done with sin. 2 As a result, he does not live the rest of his earthly life for evil human desires, but rather for the will of God. 3 For you have spent enough time in the past doing what pagans choose to do —living in debauchery, lust, drunkenness, orgies,

Phillips Modern English

meant the death of his body, but he was brought to life again in the spirit. It was in the spirit that he went and preached to the imprisoned souls of those who had been disobedient in the days of Noah—the days of God's great patience during the period of the building of the ark, in which eventually only eight souls were saved from the water. That water was a kind of prophetic parable of the water of baptism which now saves you. Baptism does not merely mean the washing of a dirty body; it is the appeal of a clear conscience towards God—a thing made possible by the power of Christ's resurrection. For he has now entered Heaven and sits at God's right hand, with all angels, authorities and powers made subject to him.

4.1 *Following Christ will mean pain*

Since Christ suffered physical pain you must arm yourselves with the same inner conviction that he had. To be free from sin means bodily suffering, and the man who accepts this will spend the rest of his time here on earth, not in being led by human desires, but in doing the will of God. Your past life may have been good enough for pagan purposes, though it meant sensuality, lust, drunkenness, orgies, carousals

Revised Standard Version

to God, being put to death in the flesh but made
alive in the spirit; 19 in which he went and
preached to the spirits in prison, 20 who formerly
did not obey, when God's patience waited in the
days of Noah, during the building of the ark, in
which a few, that is, eight persons, were saved
through water. 21 Baptism, which corresponds to
this, now saves you, not as a removal of dirt
from the body but as an appeal to God for a
clear conscience, through the resurrection of
Jesus Christ, 22 who has gone into heaven and
is at the right hand of God, with angels, authorities, and powers subject to him.

4 Since therefore Christ suffered in the flesh,[i]
arm yourselves with the same thought, for
whoever has suffered in the flesh has ceased
from sin, 2 so as to live for the rest of the time
in the flesh no longer by human passions but
by the will of God. 3 Let the time that is past
suffice for doing what the Gentiles like to do,
living in licentiousness, passions, drunkenness,

[i] Other ancient authorities add *for us;* some *for you.*

Jerusalem Bible

to lead us to God. In the body he was put to
death, in the spirit he was raised to life, 19 and,
in the spirit, he went to preach to the spirits in
prison. 20 Now it was long ago, when Noah was
still building that ark which saved only a small group of eight people "by water," and when God was still waiting patiently, that these spirits
refused to believe. 21 That water is a type of the
baptism which saves you now, and which is not the washing off of physical dirt but a pledge made to God from a good conscience, through
the resurrection of Jesus Christ, 22 who has entered heaven and is at God's right hand, now that he has made the angels and Dominations and Powers his subjects.

4 Think of what Christ suffered in this life, and then arm yourselves with the same resolution that he had: anyone who in this life has
bodily suffering has broken with sin, 2 because
for the rest of his life on earth he is not ruled
by human passions but only by the will of God.
3 You spent quite long enough in the past living
the sort of life that pagans live, behaving indecently, giving way to your passions, drinking all the time, having wild parties and drunken orgies and degrading yourselves by following

New English Bible

In the body he was put to death; in the spirit he was brought to life. And in the spirit he went and made his proclamation to the imprisoned spirits. They had refused obedience long ago, while God waited patiently in the days of Noah and the building of the ark, and in the ark a few persons, eight in all, were brought to safety through the water. This water prefigured the water of baptism through which you are now brought to safety. Baptism is not the washing away of bodily pollution, but the appeal made to God by a good conscience; and it brings salvation through the resurrection of Jesus Christ, who entered heaven after receiving the submission of angelic authorities and powers, and is now at the right hand of God.

4 Remembering that Christ endured bodily suffering, you must arm yourselves with a temper of mind like his. When a man has thus endured bodily suffering he has finished with sin, and for the rest of his days on earth he may live, not for the things that men desire, but for what God wills. You had time enough in the past to do all the things that men want to do in the pagan world. Then you lived in licence and debauchery, drunkenness, revelry, and tippling, and

King James Version

tries: 4 Wherein they think it strange that ye run
not with *them* to the same excess of riot, speaking evil of *you:* 5 Who shall give account to him
that is ready to judge the quick and the dead.
6 For, for this cause was the gospel preached
also to them that are dead, that they might be
judged according to men in the flesh, but live
according to God in the spirit. 7 But the end of
all things is at hand: be ye therefore sober, and
watch unto prayer. 8 And above all things have
fervent charity among yourselves: for charity
shall cover the multitude of sins. 9 Use hospitality one to another without grudging. 10 As every
man hath received the gift, *even so* minister the
same one to another, as good stewards of the
manifold grace of God. 11 If any man speak,
let him speak as the oracles of God; if any
man minister, *let him do it* as of the ability
which God giveth; that God in all things may be
glorified through Jesus Christ: to whom be praise

Living Bible

4 Of course, your former friends will be very
surprised when you don't eagerly join them any
more in the wicked things they do, and they
will laugh at you in contempt and scorn. 5 But
just remember that they must face the Judge of
all, living and dead; they will be punished for
the way they have lived. 6 That is why the Good
News was preached even to those who were dead
—killed by the flood [b]—so that although their
bodies were punished with death, they could still
live in their spirits as God lives.

7 The end of the world is coming soon. Therefore be earnest, thoughtful men of prayer.
8 Most important of all, continue to show deep
love for each other, for love makes up for many
of your faults.[c] 9 Cheerfully share your home
with those who need a meal or a place to stay
for the night.

10 God has given each of you some special
abilities; be sure to use them to help each
other, passing on to others God's many kinds
of blessings. 11 Are you called to preach? Then
preach as though God himself were speaking
through you. Are you called to help others?
Do it with all the strength and energy that God
supplies, so that God will be glorified through
Jesus Christ—to him be glory and power forever and ever. Amen.

[*b*] Implied. See 1 Peter 3:19,20. [*c*] Or, "love over-looks each other's many faults."

Today's English Version

ship of idols. 4 And now the heathen are surprised when you do not join them in the same
wild and reckless living, and so they insult you.
5 But they will give an account of themselves
to God, who is ready to judge the living and the
dead. 6 That is why the Good News was
preached also to the dead, to those who had
been judged in their physical existence as all
men are judged; it was preached to them so
that in their spiritual existence they may live as
God lives.

Good managers of God's gifts

7 The end of all things is near. You must be
self-controlled and alert, to be able to pray.
8 Above everything, love one another earnestly,
because love covers over many sins. 9 Open
your homes to each other, without complaining.
10 Each one, as a good manager of God's different gifts, must use for the good of others the
special gift he has received from God. 11 Whoever preaches, must preach God's words; whoever serves, must serve with the strength that
God gives him, so that in all things praise may
be given to God through Jesus Christ, to whom
belong glory and power forever and ever. Amen.

New International Version

carousing and detestable idolatry. 4 They think
it strange that you do not plunge with them into
the same flood of dissipation, and they heap
abuse on you. 5 But they will have to give account to him who is ready to judge the living
and the dead. 6 For this is the reason the gospel
was preached even to those who are now dead,
so that they might be judged according to men
in regard to the body, but live according to God
in regard to the spirit.

7 The end of all things is near. Therefore be
clear-minded and self-controlled so that you can
pray. 8 Above all, love each other deeply, because
love covers over a multitude of sins. 9 Offer hospitality to one another without grumbling.
10 Each one should use whatever spiritual gift
he has received to serve others, faithfully administering God's grace in its various forms. 11 If
anyone speaks, he should do it as one speaking
the very words of God. If anyone serves, he
should do it with the strength God provides, so
that in all things God may be praised through
Jesus Christ. To him be the glory and the
power for ever and ever. Amen.

Phillips Modern English

and worshipping forbidden gods. Indeed your
former companions may think it very strange
that you no longer join with them in their
riotous excesses, and accordingly say all sorts
of abusive things about you. They are the ones
who will have to answer for their behaviour before the One who is prepared to judge all men,
living or dead. That is why the dead also had
the gospel preached to them. For although they
must be condemned for the life they lived in
the body of men, they might find life in the
spirit by obeying God's will.

4.7 *Your attitude in these last days*

We are near the end of all things now, and
you should therefore be calm, self-controlled
men of prayer. Above everything else be sure
that you have real deep love for each other, remembering how love can cover a multitude of
sins. Be hospitable to each other without secretly wishing you hadn't got to be! Serve one
another with the particular gifts God has given
each of you, as faithful dispensers of the wonderfully varied grace of God. If any of you is a
preacher then he should preach his message as
from God. And in whatever way a man serves
the Church he should do it recognising the fact
that God gives him his ability, so that God may
be glorified in everything through Jesus Christ.
To him belong glory and power for ever, amen!

Revised Standard Version

revels, carousing, and lawless idolatry. 4 They
are surprised that you do not now join them in
the same wild profligacy, and they abuse you;
5 but they will give account to him who is ready
to judge the living and the dead. 6 For this is
why the gospel was preached even to the dead,
that though judged in the flesh like men, they
might live in the spirit like God.
7 The end of all things is at hand; therefore
keep sane and sober for your prayers. 8 Above
all hold unfailing your love for one another,
since love covers a multitude of sins. 9 Practice
hospitality ungrudgingly to one another. 10 As
each has received a gift, employ it for one another, as good stewards of God's varied grace:
11 whoever speaks, as one who utters oracles of
God; whoever renders service, as one who renders it by the strength which God supplies; in
order that in everything God may be glorified
through Jesus Christ. To him belong glory and
dominion for ever and ever. Amen.

Jerusalem Bible

false gods. 4 So people cannot understand why
you no longer hurry off with them to join this
flood which is rushing down to ruin, and then
they begin to spread libels about you. 5 They
will have to answer for it in front of the judge
who is ready to judge the living and the dead.
6 And because he is their judge too, the dead had
to be told the Good News as well, so that
though, in their life on earth, they had been
through the judgment that comes to all humanity, they might come to God's life in the spirit.

The revelation of Christ is close

7 Everything will soon come to an end, so, to
pray better, keep a calm and sober mind. 8 Above
all, never let your love for each other grow in-
sincere, since *love covers over many a sin.*[p]
9 Welcome each other into your houses without
grumbling. 10 Each one of you has received a
special grace, so, like good stewards responsible
for all these different graces of God, put yourselves at the service of others. 11 If you are a
speaker, speak in words which seem to come
from God; if you are a helper, help as though
every action was done at God's orders; so that
in everything God may receive the glory, through
Jesus Christ, since to him alone belong all glory
and power for ever and ever. Amen.

[p] Pr. 10:12.

New English Bible

the forbidden worship of idols. Now, when you
no longer plunge with them into all this reckless
dissipation, they cannot understand it, and they
vilify you accordingly; but they shall answer for
it to him who stands ready to pass judgement on
the living and the dead. Why was the Gospel
preached to those who are dead? In order that,
although in the body they received the sentence
common to men, they might in the spirit be
alive with the life of God.
The end of all things is upon us, so you must
lead an ordered and sober life, given to prayer.
Above all, keep your love for one another at full
strength, because love cancels innumerable sins.
Be hospitable to one another without complaining. Whatever gift each of you may have received, use it in service to one another, like good
stewards dispensing the grace of God in its
varied forms. Are you a speaker? Speak as if
you uttered oracles of God. Do you give service?
Give it as in the strength which God supplies. In
all things so act that the glory may be God's
through Jesus Christ; to him belong glory and
power for ever and ever. Amen.

King James Version

and dominion for ever and ever. Amen. 12 Beloved, think it not strange concerning the fiery
trial which is to try you, as though some strange
thing happened unto you: 13 But rejoice, inasmuch as ye are partakers of Christ's sufferings;
that, when his glory shall be revealed, ye may be
glad also with exceeding joy. 14 If ye be reproached for the name of Christ, happy *are ye;*
for the Spirit of glory and of God resteth upon
you: on their part he is evil spoken of, but on
your part he is glorified. 15 But let none of you
suffer as a murderer, or *as* a thief, or *as* an evil
doer, or as a busybody in other men's matters.
16 Yet if *any man suffer* as a Christian, let him
not be ashamed; but let him glorify God on this
behalf. 17 For the time *is come* that judgment
must begin at the house of God: and if *it* first
begin at us, what shall the end *be* of them that
obey not the gospel of God? 18 And if the righteous scarcely be saved, where shall the ungodly
and the sinner appear? 19 Wherefore, let them
that suffer according to the will of God commit
the keeping of their souls *to him* in well doing,
as unto a faithful Creator.

Living Bible

12 Dear friends, don't be bewildered or surprised when you go through the fiery trials
ahead, for this is no strange, unusual thing that
is going to happen to you. 13 Instead, be really
glad—because these trials will make you partners with Christ in his suffering, and afterwards
you will have the wonderful joy of sharing his
glory in that coming day when it will be displayed.

14 Be happy if you are cursed and insulted for
being a Christian, for when that happens the
Spirit of God will come upon you with great
glory.[d] 15 Don't let me hear of your suffering
for murdering or stealing or making trouble or
being a busybody and prying into other people's affairs. 16 But it is no shame to suffer for
being a Christian. Praise God for the privilege
of being in Christ's family and being called by
his wonderful name! 17 For the time has come
for judgment, and it must begin first among
God's own children. And if even we who are
Christians must be judged, what terrible fate
awaits those who have never believed in the
Lord? 18 If the righteous are barely saved, what
chance will the godless have?

19 So if you are suffering according to God's
will, keep on doing what is right and trust yourself to the God who made you, for he will never
fail you.

[*d*] Or, "the glory of the Spirit of God is being seen in you."

Today's English Version

Suffering as a Christian

12 My dear friends, do not be surprised at
the painful test you are suffering, as though
something unusual were happening to you.
13 Rather be glad that you are sharing Christ's
sufferings, so that you may be full of joy when
his glory is revealed. 14 Happy are you if you
are insulted because you are Christ's followers;
this means that the glorious Spirit, the Spirit of
God, is resting on you. 15 None of you should
suffer because he is a murderer, or a thief, or
a criminal, or tries to manage other people's
business. 16 But if you suffer because you are a
Christian, don't be ashamed of it, but thank
God that you bear Christ's name.

17 The time has come for the judgment to
begin, and God's own people are the first to be
judged. If it starts with us, how will it end with
those who do not believe the Good News from
God? 18 As the scripture says,

"It is difficult for good men to be saved;
what, then, will become of the godless and sinful?"

19 So then, those who suffer because it is God's
will for them, should by their good actions trust
themselves completely to their Creator, who always keeps his promise.

New International Version

Suffering for being a Christian

12 Dear friends, do not be surprised at the
painful trial you are suffering, as though something strange were happening to you. 13 But rejoice that you participate in the sufferings of
Christ, so that you may be overjoyed when his
glory is revealed. 14 If you are insulted because
of the name of Christ, you are blessed, for the
Spirit of glory and of God rests on you. 15 If
you suffer, it should not be as a murderer or
thief or any other kind of criminal, or even as a
meddler. 16 However, if you suffer as a Christian,
do not be ashamed, but praise God that you bear
that name. 17 For it is time for judgment to begin with the family of God; and if it begins with
us, what will the outcome be for those who do
not obey the gospel of God? 18 And,

"If it is hard for the righteous to be saved,
what will become of the ungodly and the sinner?"[k]

19 So then, those who suffer according to
God's will should commit themselves to their
faithful Creator and continue to do good.

[*k*] Prov. 11:31.

Phillips Modern English

4.12 Your attitude to persecution

And now, dear friends of mine, I beg you not to be unduly alarmed at the fiery ordeals which come to test your faith, as though this were some abnormal experience. You should be glad, because it means that you are sharing in Christ's sufferings. One day, when he shows himself in full splendour, you will be filled with the most tremendous joy. If you are reproached for being Christ's followers, that is a cause for joy, for you can be sure that God's Spirit of glory is resting upon you. But take care that none of your number suffers as a murderer, or a thief, a rogue or a busy-body! If he suffers as a Christian he has nothing to be ashamed of and may glorify God by confessing Christ's name.

The time has evidently arrived for God's judgment to begin, and it is beginning at his own household. And if it starts with us, what is it going to mean to those who refuse to obey the gospel of God? If even the good man is only just saved, what will be the fate of the wicked and the sinner? Therefore those who suffer according to God's will can safely commit their souls to their faithful Creator, and go on doing all the good they can.

Revised Standard Version

12 Beloved, do not be surprised at the fiery ordeal which comes upon you to prove you, as though something strange were happening to you. 13 But rejoice in so far as you share Christ's sufferings, that you may also rejoice and be glad when his glory is revealed. 14 If you are reproached for the name of Christ, you are blessed, because the spirit of glory[j] and of God rests upon you. 15 But let none of you suffer as a murderer, or a thief, or a wrongdoer, or a mischief-maker; 16 yet if one suffers as a Christian, let him not be ashamed, but under that name let him glorify God. 17 For the time has come for judgment to begin with the household of God; and if it begins with us, what will be the end of those who do not obey the gospel of God? 18 And

"If the righteous man is scarcely saved,
where will the impious and sinner appear?"

19 Therefore let those who suffer according to God's will do right and entrust their souls to a faithful Creator.

[j] Other ancient authorities insert *and of power.*

Jerusalem Bible

Recapitulation

12 My dear people, you must not think it unaccountable that you should be tested by fire. There is nothing extraordinary in what has happened to you. 13 If you can have some share in the sufferings of Christ, be glad, because you will enjoy a much greater gladness when his glory is revealed. 14 It is a blessing for you when they insult you for bearing the name of Christ, because it means that you have the Spirit of glory, the Spirit of God resting on you. 15 None of you should ever deserve to suffer for being a murderer, a thief, a criminal or an informer; 16 but if anyone of you should suffer for being a Christian, then he is not to be ashamed of it; he should thank God that he has been called one. 17 The time has come for the judgment to begin at the household of God; and if what we know now is only the beginning, what will it be when it comes down to those who refuse to believe God's Good News? 18 *If it is hard for a good man to be saved, what will happen to the wicked and to sinners?*[q] 19 So even those whom God allows to suffer must trust themselves to the constancy of the creator and go on doing good.

[q] Pr. 11:31 (LXX).

New English Bible

My dear friends, do not be bewildered by the fiery ordeal that is upon you, as though it were something extraordinary. It gives you a share in Christ's sufferings, and that is cause for joy; and when his glory is revealed, your joy will be triumphant. If Christ's name is flung in your teeth as an insult, count yourselves happy, because then that glorious Spirit which is the Spirit of God is resting upon you. If you suffer, it must not be for murder, theft, or sorcery,[a] nor for infringing the rights of others. But if anyone suffers as a Christian, he should feel it no disgrace, but confess that name to the honour of God.

The time has come for the judgement to begin: it is beginning with God's own household. And if it is starting with you, how will it end for those who refuse to obey the gospel of God? It is hard enough for the righteous to be saved; what then will become of the impious and sinful? So even those who suffer, if it be according to God's will, should commit their souls to him —by doing good; their Maker will not fail them.

[a] *Or* other crime.

King James Version

5 The elders which are among you I exhort,
who am also an elder, and a witness of the
sufferings of Christ, and also a partaker of the
glory that shall be revealed: 2 Feed the flock of
God which is among you, taking the oversight
thereof, not by constraint, but willingly; not for
filthy lucre, but of a ready mind; 3 Neither as
being lords over *God's* heritage, but being ensamples to the flock. 4 And when the chief Shepherd shall appear, ye shall receive a crown of
glory that fadeth not away. 5 Likewise, ye
younger, submit yourselves unto the elder. Yea,
all *of you* be subject one to another, and be
clothed with humility: for God resisteth the
proud, and giveth grace to the humble. 6 Humble yourselves therefore under the mighty hand
of God, that he may exalt you in due time:
7 Casting all your care upon him; for he careth

Living Bible

5 And now, a word to you elders of the
church. I, too, am an elder; with my own
eyes I saw Christ dying on the cross; and I,
too, will share his glory and his honor when he
returns. Fellow elders, this is my plea to you:
2 Feed the flock of God; care for it willingly,
not grudgingly; not for what you will get out of
it, but because you are eager to serve the Lord.
3 Don't be tyrants, but lead them by your good
example, 4 and when the Head Shepherd comes,
your reward will be a never-ending share in his
glory and honor.

5 You younger men, follow the leadership of
those who are older. And all of you serve each
other with humble spirits, for God gives special
blessings to those who are humble, but sets himself against those who are proud. 6 If you will
humble yourselves under the mighty hand of
God, in his good time he will lift you up.

7 Let him have all your worries and cares,
for he is always thinking about you and watching everything that concerns you.

Today's English Version

The flock of God

5 I appeal to the church elders among you,
I who am an elder myself. I am a witness of
Christ's sufferings, and I will share in the glory
that will be revealed. I appeal to you: 2 be
shepherds of the flock that God gave you, and
look after it willingly, as God wants you to, and
not unwillingly. Do your work, not for mere
pay, but from a real desire to serve. 3 Do not
try to rule over those who have been given into
your care, but be examples to the flock. 4 And
when the Chief Shepherd appears, you will receive the glorious crown which will never lose
its brightness.

5 In the same way, you younger men must
submit yourselves to the older men. And all of
you must put on the apron of humility, to serve
one another; for the scripture says, "God resists
the proud, but gives grace to the humble."
6 Humble yourselves, then, under God's mighty
hand, so that he will lift you up in his own
good time. 7 Throw all your worries on him,
because he cares for you.

New International Version

To elders and young men

5 To the elders among you, I appeal as a
fellow elder, a witness of Christ's sufferings
and one who also will share in the glory to be
revealed: 2 Be shepherds of God's flock that is
under your care, serving as overseers—not because you must, but because you are willing, as
God wants you to be; not greedy for money, but
eager to serve; 3 not lording it over those entrusted to you, but being examples to the flock.
4 And when the Chief Shepherd appears, you will
receive the crown of glory that will never fade
away.

5 Young men, in the same way be submissive
to those who are older. Clothe yourselves with
humility toward one another, because,

"God opposes the proud
but gives grace to the humble." [l]

6 Humble yourselves, therefore, under God's
mighty hand, that he may lift you up in due
time. 7 Cast all your anxiety on him because he
cares for you.

[*l*] Prov. 3:34.

Phillips Modern English

5.1 *A word to your leaders*

Now may I who am myself an elder say a word to you my fellow-elders? I speak as one who actually saw Christ suffer, and as one who will share with you the glories that are to be unfolded. Shepherd your flock of God, looking after them not because you feel compelled to, but willingly, as God would wish. Never do this work thinking of your personal gain but with true compassion. You should aim not at being dictators but examples of Christian living in the eyes of the flock committed to your charge. And then, when the Chief Shepherd reveals himself, you will receive that crown of glory which cannot fade.

5.5 *Learn to be humble and to trust*

You younger members must also accept the authority of the elders. Indeed all of you should defer to one another and wear the "overall" of humility in serving each other. God is always against the proud, but he is always ready to give grace to the humble. So, humble yourselves under God's strong hand, and in his own good time he will lift you up. You can throw the whole weight of your anxieties upon him, for you are his personal concern.

Revised Standard Version

5 So I exhort the elders among you, as a fellow elder and a witness of the sufferings of
Christ as well as a partaker in the glory that is
to be revealed. 2 Tend the flock of God that is
your charge,[k] not by constraint but willingly,[l]
not for shameful gain but eagerly, 3 not as domi-
neering over those in your charge but being
examples to the flock. 4 And when the chief
Shepherd is manifested you will obtain the unfading crown of glory. 5 Likewise you that are
younger be subject to the elders. Clothe yourselves, all of you, with humility toward one another, for "God opposes the proud, but gives
grace to the humble."
6 Humble yourselves therefore under the
mighty hand of God, that in due time he may
exalt you. 7 Cast all your anxieties on him, for

[k] Other ancient authorities add *exercising the oversight.* [l] Other ancient authorities add *as God would have you.*

Jerusalem Bible

Instructions: to the elders

5 Now I have something to tell your elders:
I am an elder myself, and a witness to the
sufferings of Christ, and with you I have a share
in the glory that is to be revealed. 2 Be the
shepherds of the flock of God that is entrusted
to you: watch over it, not simply as a duty but
gladly, because God wants it; not for sordid
money, but because you are eager to do it.
3 Never be a dictator over any group that is
put in your charge, but be an example that the
whole flock can follow. 4 When the chief shepherd appears, you will be given the crown of unfading glory.

To the faithful

5 To the rest of you I say: do what the elders
tell you, and all wrap yourselves in humility to
be servants of each other, because *God refuses
the proud and will always favor the humble.*[r]
6 Bow down, then, before the power of God
now, and he will raise you up on the appointed
day; 7 *unload* all *your worries on to him,*[s] since

[r] Pr. 3:34 (LXX). [s] Ps. 55:22.

New English Bible

5 And now I appeal to the elders of your community, as a fellow-elder and a witness of Christ's sufferings, and also a partaker in the splendour that is to be revealed. Tend that flock of God whose shepherds you are, and do it, not under compulsion, but of your own free will, as God would have it; not for gain but out of sheer devotion; not tyrannizing over those who are allotted to your care, but setting an example to the flock. And then, when the Head Shepherd appears, you will receive for your own the unfading garland of glory.

In the same way you younger men must be subordinate to your elders. Indeed, all of you should wrap yourselves in the garment of humility towards each other, because God sets his face against the arrogant but favours the humble. Humble yourselves then under God's mighty hand, and he will lift you up in due time. Cast all your cares on him, for you are his charge.

King James Version

for you. 8 Be sober, be vigilant; because your adversary the devil, as a roaring lion, walketh about, seeking whom he may devour: 9 Whom resist steadfast in the faith, knowing that the same afflictions are accomplished in your brethren that are in the world. 10 But the God of all grace, who hath called us unto his eternal glory by Christ Jesus, after that ye have suffered a while, make you perfect, stablish, strengthen, settle *you.* 11 To him *be* glory and dominion for ever and ever. Amen. 12 By Silvanus, a faithful brother unto you, as I suppose, I have written briefly, exhorting, and testifying that this is the true grace of God wherein ye stand. 13 The *church that is* at Babylon, elected together with *you,* saluteth you; and *so doth* Marcus my son. 14 Greet ye one another with a kiss of charity. Peace *be* with you all that are in Christ Jesus. Amen.

Living Bible

8 Be careful—watch out for attacks from Satan, your great enemy. He prowls around like a hungry, roaring lion, looking for some victim to tear apart. 9 Stand firm when he attacks. Trust the Lord; and remember that other Christians all around the world are going through these sufferings too.

10 After you have suffered a little while, our God, who is full of kindness through Christ, will give you his eternal glory. He personally will come and pick you up, and set you firmly in place, and make you stronger than ever. 11 To him be all power over all things, forever and ever. Amen.

12 I am sending this note to you through the courtesy of Silvanus who is, in my opinion, a very faithful brother. I hope I have encouraged you by this letter for I have given you a true statement of the way God blesses. What I have told you here should help you to stand firmly in his love.

13 The church here in Rome[a]—she is your sister in the Lord—sends you her greetings; so does my son Mark. 14 Give each other the handshake of Christian love. Peace be to all of you who are in Christ.

Peter

[a] Literally, "She who is at Babylon is likewise chosen"; but Babylon was the Christian nickname for Rome, and the "she" is thought by many to be Peter's wife to whom reference is made in Matthew 8:14, 1 Corinthians 9:5, etc. Others believe this should read: "Your sister church here in Babylon salutes you, and so does my son Mark."

Today's English Version

8 Be alert, be on watch! Your enemy, the Devil, roams around like a roaring lion, looking for someone to devour. 9 Be firm in your faith and resist him, because you know that your fellow believers in all the world are going through the same kind of sufferings. 10 But after you have suffered for a little while, the God of all grace, who calls you to share his eternal glory in union with Christ, will himself perfect you, and give you firmness, strength, and a sure foundation. 11 To him be the power forever! Amen.

Final greetings

12 I write you this brief letter with the help of Silas, whom I regard as a faithful brother. I want to encourage you and give my testimony that this is the true grace of God. Stand firm in it.

13 Your sister church in Babylon, also chosen by God, sends you greetings, and so does my son Mark. 14 Greet each other with the kiss of Christian love.

May peace be with all of you who belong to Christ.

New International Version

8 Be self-controlled and alert. Your enemy the devil prowls around like a roaring lion looking for someone to devour. 9 Resist him, standing firm in the faith, because you know that your brothers throughout the world are undergoing the same kind of sufferings.

10 And the God of all grace, who called you to his eternal glory in Christ, after you have suffered a little while, will himself restore you and make you strong, firm and steadfast. 11 To him be the power for ever and ever. Amen.

Final greetings

12 With the help of Silas,[m] whom I regard as a faithful brother, I have written to you briefly, encouraging you and testifying that this is the true grace of God. Stand fast in it.

13 She who is in Babylon, chosen together with you, sends you her greetings, and so does my son Mark. 14 Greet one another with a kiss of love.

Peace to all of you who are in Christ.

[m] Greek *Silvanus.*

Phillips Modern English

5.8 *Resist the devil: you are in God's hands*

Be self-controlled and vigilant always, for your enemy the devil is always about, prowling like a lion roaring for its prey. Resist him, standing firm in your faith, remembering that the strain is the same for all your fellow-Christians in other parts of the world. And after you have borne these sufferings a very little while, the God of all grace, who has called you to share his eternal splendour through Christ, will himself make you whole and secure and strong. All power is his for ever and ever, amen!

5.12 *Final greetings*

I am sending this short letter by Silvanus, whom I know to be a faithful brother, to stimulate your faith and assure you that the above words represent the true grace of God. See that you stand fast in that grace!

Your sister-church here in "Babylon" sends you greetings, and so does my son Mark. Give each other a handshake all round as a sign of love.

Peace be to all true Christians.

Revised Standard Version

he cares about you. 8 Be sober, be watchful.
Your adversary the devil prowls around like a
roaring lion, seeking some one to devour. 9 Resist him, firm in your faith, knowing that the
same experience of suffering is required of your
brotherhood throughout the world. 10 And after
you have suffered a little while, the God of all
grace, who has called you to his eternal glory in
Christ, will himself restore, establish, and
strengthen[m] you. 11 To him be the dominion for
ever and ever. Amen.

12 By Silvanus, a faithful brother as I regard
him, I have written briefly to you, exhorting and
declaring that this is the true grace of God;
stand fast in it. 13 She who is at Babylon, who
is likewise chosen, sends you greetings; and so
does my son Mark. 14 Greet one another with
the kiss of love.

Peace to all of you that are in Christ.

[*m*] Other ancient authorities read *restore, establish, strengthen and settle.*

Jerusalem Bible

he is looking after you. 8 *Be calm but vigilant,*
because your enemy the devil is prowling around
like a roaring lion, looking for someone to eat.
9 Stand up to him, strong in faith and in the
knowledge that your brothers all over the world
are suffering the same things. 10 You will have
to suffer only for a little while: the God of all
grace who called you to eternal glory in Christ
will see that all is well again: he will confirm,
strengthen and support you. 11 His power lasts
for ever and ever. Amen.

Last words. Greetings

12 I write these few words to you through Silvanus, who is a brother I know I can trust, to encourage you never to let go this true grace of God to which I bear witness.

13 Your sister in Babylon, who is with you among the chosen, sends you greetings; so does my son, Mark.

14 Greet one another with a kiss of love.

Peace to you all who are in Christ.

New English Bible

Awake! be on the alert! Your enemy the devil, like a roaring lion, prowls round looking for someone to devour. Stand up to him, firm in faith, and remember that your brother Christians are going through the same kinds of suffering while they are in the world. And the God of all grace, who called you into his eternal glory in Christ, will himself, after your brief suffering, restore, establish, and strengthen you on a firm foundation. He holds dominion for ever and ever. Amen.

I write you this brief appeal through Silvanus, our trusty brother as I hold him, adding my testimony that this is the true grace of God. In this stand fast.

Greetings from her who dwells in Babylon, chosen by God like you, and from my son Mark. Greet one another with the kiss of love.

Peace to you all who belong to Christ!

King James Version

THE SECOND EPISTLE GENERAL OF PETER

1 Simon Peter, a servant and an apostle of
Jesus Christ, to them that have obtained like
precious faith with us through the righteousness
of God and our Saviour Jesus Christ: 2 Grace
and peace be multiplied unto you through the
knowledge of God, and of Jesus our Lord, 3 According as his divine power hath given unto us
all things that *pertain* unto life and godliness,
through the knowledge of him that hath called
us to glory and virtue: 4 Whereby are given unto
us exceeding great and precious promises; that

Living Bible

2 PETER

1 *From:* Simon Peter, a servant and missionary of Jesus Christ.
To: All of you who have our kind of faith.
The faith I speak of is the kind that Jesus Christ
our God and Savior gives to us. How precious
it is, and how just and good he is to give this
same faith to each of us.
2 Do you want more and more of God's kindness and peace? Then learn to know him better
and better. 3 For as you know him better, he will
give you, through his great power, everything
you need for living a truly good life: he even
shares his own glory and his own goodness with
us! 4 And by that same mighty power he has
given us all the other rich and wonderful bless-

Today's English Version

THE SECOND LETTER FROM PETER

1 From Simon Peter, a servant and apostle of
Jesus Christ—
To those who through the righteousness of
our God and Savior Jesus Christ have been
given a faith as precious as ours:
2 May grace and peace be yours in full measure, through your knowledge of God and of
Jesus our Lord.

God's call and choice

3 God's divine power has given us everything
we need to live a godly life through our knowledge of the one who called us to share his own
glory and goodness. 4 In this way he has given
us the very great and precious gifts he promised,

New International Version

2 PETER

1 Simon Peter, a servant and apostle of Jesus
Christ,
To those who through the righteousness of our
God and Savior Jesus Christ have received a
faith as precious as ours:
2 Grace and peace be yours in abundance
through the knowledge of God and of Jesus our
Lord.

Making one's calling and election sure

3 His divine power has given us everything we
need for life and godliness through our knowledge of him who called us by his own glory
and goodness. 4 Through these he has given us
his very great and precious promises, so that

Phillips Modern English

THE SECOND LETTER OF PETER

Simon Peter, a servant and messenger of Jesus Christ, sends this letter to those who have been given a faith as valuable as ours in the righteousness of our God, and saviour Jesus Christ. May you know more and more of grace and peace as your knowledge of God and Jesus our Lord grows deeper.

1.3 God has done his part: see that you do yours

He has by his own action given us everything that is necessary for living the truly good life, in allowing us to know the one who has called us to him, through his own glorious goodness. It is through this generosity that God's greatest and most precious promises have become availa-

Revised Standard Version

THE SECOND LETTER OF PETER

1 Simeon[x] Peter, a servant and apostle of Jesus Christ,
To those who have obtained a faith of equal standing with ours in the righteousness of our God and Savior Jesus Christ:[a]
2 May grace and peace be multiplied to you in the knowledge of God and of Jesus our Lord.

3 His divine power has granted to us all things that pertain to life and godliness, through the knowledge of him who called us to[b] his own glory and excellence, 4 by which he has granted to us his precious and very great promises, that

[x] Other authorities read *Simon*. [a] Or *of our God and the Savior Jesus Christ*. [b] Or *by*.

Jerusalem Bible

THE SECOND LETTER OF PETER

2 PETER

Greetings

1 From Simeon Peter, servant and apostle of Jesus Christ; to all who treasure the same faith as ourselves, given through the righteousness of our God and Savior Jesus Christ. 2 May you have more and more grace and peace as you come to know our Lord more and more.

A call to Christian living, and its reward

3 By his divine power, he has given us all the things that we need for life and for true devotion, bringing us to know God himself, who has called us by his own glory and goodness. 4 In making these gifts, he has given us the guarantee

New English Bible

THE SECOND LETTER OF PETER

The remedy for doubt

1 From Simeon Peter, servant and apostle of Jesus Christ, to those who through the justice of our God and Saviour Jesus Christ share our faith and enjoy equal privilege with ourselves.
Grace and peace be yours in fullest measure, through the knowledge of God and Jesus our Lord.
His divine power has bestowed on us everything that makes for life and true religion, enabling us to know the One who called us by his own splendour and might. Through this might and splendour he has given us his promises, great

King James Version

by these ye might be partakers of the divine
nature, having escaped the corruption that is in
the world through lust. 5And besides this, giving
all diligence, add to your faith virtue; and to
virtue, knowledge; 6And to knowledge, temperance; and to temperance, patience; and to patience, godliness; 7And to godliness, brotherly
kindness; and to brotherly kindness, charity.
8 For if these things be in you, and abound, they
make *you that ye shall* neither *be* barren nor
unfruitful in the knowledge of our Lord Jesus
Christ. 9 But he that lacketh these things is blind,
and cannot see afar off, and hath forgotten that
he was purged from his old sins. 10 Wherefore
the rather, brethren, give diligence to make your
calling and election sure: for if ye do these
things, ye shall never fall: 11 For so an entrance
shall be ministered unto you abundantly into the
everlasting kingdom of our Lord and Saviour
Jesus Christ. 12 Wherefore I will not be negligent
to put you always in remembrance of these
things, though ye know *them,* and be established
in the present truth. 13 Yea, I think it meet, as

Living Bible

ings he promised; for instance, the promise to
save us from the lust and rottenness all around
us, and to give us his own character.
5 But to obtain these gifts, you need more
than faith; you must also work hard to be good,
and even that is not enough. For then you must
learn to know God better and discover what he
wants you to do. 6 Next, learn to put aside your
own desires so that you will become patient and
godly, gladly letting God have his way with you.
7 This will make possible the next step, which is
for you to enjoy other people and to like them,
and finally you will grow to love them deeply.
8 The more you go on in this way, the more you
will grow strong spiritually and become fruitful
and useful to our Lord Jesus Christ. 9 But anyone who fails to go after these additions to faith
is blind indeed, or at least very shortsighted,
and has forgotten that God delivered him from
the old life of sin so that now he can live a
strong, good life for the Lord.

10 So, dear brothers, work hard to prove that
you really are among those God has called and
chosen, and then you will never stumble or fall
away. 11And God will open wide the gates of
heaven for you to enter into the eternal kingdom of our Lord and Savior Jesus Christ.

12 I plan to keep on reminding you of these
things even though you already know them and
are really getting along quite well! 13, 14 But the

Today's English Version

so that by means of these gifts you may escape
from the destructive lust that is in the world,
and come to share the divine nature. 5 For this
very reason do your best to add goodness to
your faith; to your goodness add knowledge;
6 to your knowledge add self-control; to your
self-control add endurance; to your endurance
add godliness; 7 to your godliness add brotherly
love; and to your brotherly love add love.
8 These are the qualities you need, and if you
have them in abundance they will make you
active and effective in your knowledge of our
Lord Jesus Christ. 9 But whoever does not have
them is so shortsighted that he cannot see, and
has forgotten that his past sins have been
washed away.

10 So then, my brothers, try even harder to
make God's call and his choice of you a permanent experience; if you do so, you will never
fall away. 11 In this way you will be given the
full right to enter the eternal Kingdom of our
Lord and Savior Jesus Christ.

12 For this reason I will always remind you
of these matters, even though you already know
them and are firmly fixed in the truth you have
received. 13 I think it only right for me to stir

New International Version

through them you may participate in the divine
nature and escape the corruption in the world
caused by evil desires.

5 For this very reason, make every effort to
add to your faith goodness; and to goodness,
knowledge; 6 and to knowledge, self-control; and
to self-control, perseverance; and to perseverance, godliness; 7 and to godliness, brotherly
kindness; and to brotherly kindness, love. 8 For
if you possess these qualities in increasing measure, they will keep you from being ineffective
and unproductive in your knowledge of our Lord
Jesus Christ. 9 But if anyone does not have them,
he is nearsighted and blind, and has forgotten
that he has been cleansed from his past sins.

10 Therefore, my brothers, be all the more
eager to make your calling and election sure. For
if you do these things, you will never fall, 11 and
you will receive a rich welcome into the eternal
kingdom of our Lord and Savior Jesus Christ.

Prophecy of scripture

12 So I will always remind you of these things,
even though you know them and are firmly established in the truth you now have. 13 I think it

Phillips Modern English

ble to us men, making it possible for you to escape the inevitable disintegration that lust produces in the world and to share in God's essential nature. For this very reason you must do your utmost from your side, and see that your faith carries with it real goodness of life. Your goodness must be accompanied by knowledge, your knowledge by self-control, your self-control by the ability to endure. Your endurance too must always be accompanied by devotion to God; that in turn must have in it the quality of brotherliness, and your brotherliness must lead on to Christian love. If you have these qualities existing and growing in you then it means that knowing our Lord Jesus Christ has not made your lives either complacent or unproductive. The man whose life fails to exhibit these qualities is blind—his eyes so closed that he has forgotten that he was cleansed from his former sins.

Set your minds, then, on endorsing by your conduct the fact that God has called and chosen you. If you go along these lines there is no reason why you should stumble. Indeed if you live this sort of life a rich welcome awaits you as you enter the eternal kingdom of our Lord and saviour Jesus Christ.

1.12 Truth will bear repetition

Therefore I shall not fail to remind you again and again of things like this although you know them and are already established in the truth which has come to you. I consider it my duty,

Revised Standard Version

through these you may escape from the corruption that is in the world because of passion, and
become partakers of the divine nature. 5 For this
very reason make every effort to supplement
your faith with virtue, and virtue with knowledge,
6 and knowledge with self-control, and self-
control with steadfastness, and steadfastness with
godliness, 7 and godliness with brotherly affection, and brotherly affection with love. 8 For if
these things are yours and abound, they keep
you from being ineffective or unfruitful in the
knowledge of our Lord Jesus Christ. 9 For whoever lacks these things is blind and shortsighted
and has forgotten that he was cleansed from his
old sins. 10 Therefore, brethren, be the more zealous to confirm your call and election, for if you
do this you will never fall; 11 so there will be
richly provided for you an entrance into the
eternal kingdom of our Lord and Savior Jesus
Christ.
12 Therefore I intend always to remind you
of these things, though you know them and are
established in the truth that you have. 13 I think

Jerusalem Bible

of something very great and wonderful to come:
through them you will be able to share the divine
nature and to escape corruption in a world that
is sunk in vice. 5 But to attain this, you will
have to do your utmost yourselves, adding goodness to the faith that you have, understanding to
your goodness, 6 self-control to your understanding, patience to your self-control, true devotion
to your patience, 7 kindness toward your fellow
men to your devotion, and, to this kindness,
love. 8 If you have a generous supply of these,
they will not leave you ineffectual or unproductive: they will bring you to a real knowledge of
our Lord Jesus Christ. 9 But without them a
man is blind or else shortsighted; he has forgotten how his past sins were washed away.
10 Brothers, you have been called and chosen:
work all the harder to justify it. If you do all
these things there is no danger that you will ever
fall away. 11 In this way you will be granted
admittance into the eternal kingdom of our
Lord and savior Jesus Christ.

The apostolic witness

12 That is why I am continually recalling the
same truths to you, even though you already
know them and firmly hold them. 13 I am sure

New English Bible

beyond all price, and through them you may escape the corruption with which lust has infected the world, and come to share in the very being of God.

With all this in view, you should try your hardest to supplement your faith with virtue, virtue with knowledge, knowledge with self-control, self-control with fortitude, fortitude with piety, piety with brotherly kindness, and brotherly kindness with love.

These are gifts which, if you possess and foster them, will keep you from being either useless or barren in the knowledge of our Lord Jesus Christ. The man who lacks them is short-sighted and blind; he has forgotten how he was cleansed from his former sins. All the more then, my friends, exert yourselves to clinch God's choice and calling of you. If you behave so, you will never come to grief. Thus you will be afforded full and free admission into the eternal kingdom of our Lord and Saviour Jesus Christ.

And so I will not hesitate to remind you of this again and again, although you know it and are well grounded in the truth that has already reached you. Yet I think it right to keep refresh-

King James Version

long as I am in this tabernacle, to stir you up by putting *you* in remembrance; 14 Knowing that shortly I must put off *this* my tabernacle, even as our Lord Jesus Christ hath shewed me. 15 Moreover I will endeavour that ye may be able after my decease to have these things always in remembrance. 16 For we have not followed cunningly devised fables, when we made known unto you the power and coming of our Lord Jesus Christ, but were eyewitnesses of his majesty. 17 For he received from God the Father honour and glory, when there came such a voice to him from the excellent glory, This is my beloved Son, in whom I am well pleased. 18 And this voice which came from heaven we heard, when we were with him in the holy mount. 19 We have also a more sure word of prophecy; whereunto ye do well that ye take heed, as unto a light that shineth in a dark place, until the day dawn, and the daystar arise in your hearts: 20 Knowing this first, that no prophecy of the Scripture is of any private interpretation. 21 For the prophecy came not in old time by the will of man: but holy men of God spake *as they were* moved by the Holy Ghost.

Living Bible

Lord Jesus Christ has showed me that my days here on earth are numbered, and I am soon to die. As long as I am still here I intend to keep sending these reminders to you, 15 hoping to impress them so clearly upon you that you will remember them long after I have gone.

16 For we have not been telling you fairy tales when we explained to you the power of our Lord Jesus Christ and his coming again. My own eyes have seen his splendor and his glory: 17, 18 I was there on the holy mountain when he shone out with honor given him by God his Father; I heard that glorious, majestic voice calling down from heaven, saying, "This is my much-loved Son; I am well pleased with him."

19 So we have seen and proved that what the prophets said came true. You will do well to pay close attention to everything they have written, for, like lights shining into dark corners, their words help us to understand many things that otherwise would be dark and difficult. But when you consider the wonderful truth of the prophets' words, then the light will dawn in your souls and Christ the Morning Star will shine in your hearts. 20, 21 For no prophecy recorded in Scripture was ever thought up by the prophet himself. It was the Holy Spirit within these godly men who gave them true messages from God.

Today's English Version

up your memory of these matters, as long as I am still alive. 14 I know that I shall soon put off this mortal body, as our Lord Jesus Christ plainly told me. 15 I will do my best, then, to provide a way for you to remember these matters at all times after my death.

Eyewitnesses of Christ's glory

16 We have not depended on made-up legends in making known to you the mighty coming of our Lord Jesus Christ. With our own eyes we saw his greatness. 17 We were there when he was given honor and glory by God the Father, when the voice came to him from the Supreme Glory, saying, "This is my own dear Son, with whom I am well pleased!" 18 We ourselves heard this voice coming from heaven, when we were with him on the sacred mountain.

19 So we are even more confident of the message proclaimed by the prophets. You will do well to pay attention to it, because it is like a lamp shining in a dark place, until the Day dawns and the light of the morning star shines in your hearts. 20 Above all else, however, remember this: no one can explain, by himself, a prophecy in the Scriptures. 21 For no prophetic message ever came just from the will of man, but men were carried along by the Holy Spirit as they spoke the message that came from God.

New International Version

is right to refresh your memory as long as I live in the tent of this body, 14 because I know that I will soon put it aside, as our Lord Jesus Christ has made clear to me. 15 And I will make every effort to see that after my departure you will always be able to remember these things.

16 We did not follow cleverly invented stories when we told you about the power and coming of our Lord Jesus Christ, but we were eyewitnesses of his majesty. 17 For he received honor and glory from God the Father when the voice came to him from the Majestic Glory, saying, "This is my Son, whom I love; with him I am well-pleased." 18 We ourselves heard this voice that came from heaven when we were with him on the sacred mountain.

19 And we have the word of the prophets made more certain, and you will do well to pay attention to it, as to a light shining in a dark place, until the day dawns and the morning star rises in your hearts. 20 Above all, you must understand that no prophecy of Scripture came about by the prophet's own interpretation. 21 For prophecy never had its origin in the will of man, but men spoke from God as they were carried along by the Holy Spirit.

Phillips Modern English

as long as I live in the temporary dwelling of this body, to stimulate you by these reminders. I know that I shall have to leave this body at very short notice, as our Lord Jesus Christ made clear to me. Consequently I shall make the most of every opportunity, so that after I am gone you will remember these things.

We were not following a cleverly written-up story when we told you about the power and presence of our Lord Jesus Christ—we actually saw his majesty with our own eyes. He received honour and glory from God the Father himself when that voice said to him, out of the sublime glory of Heaven, "This is my beloved Son, in whom I am well pleased." We actually heard that voice speaking from Heaven while we were with him on the sacred mountain. Thus we hold the word of prophecy to be more certain than ever. You should give that word your closest attention, for it shines like a lamp amidst the darkness of the world, until the day dawns, and the morning star rises in your hearts.

1.20 False prophets will flourish, but only for a time

But you must understand that this is of the highest importance: no prophecy of scripture can be interpreted by a single human mind. No prophecy came because a man wanted it to: men of God spoke because they were inspired by the Holy Spirit.

Revised Standard Version

it right, as long as I am in this body,[c] to arouse
you by way of reminder, 14 since I know that the
putting off of my body[c] will be soon, as our Lord
Jesus Christ showed me. 15And I will see to it
that after my departure you may be able at any
time to recall these things.
16 For we did not follow cleverly devised
myths when we made known to you the power
and coming of our Lord Jesus Christ, but we
were eyewitnesses of his majesty. 17 For when
he received honor and glory from God the
Father and the voice was borne to him by the
Majestic Glory, "This is my beloved Son,[d] with
whom I am well pleased," 18 we heard this voice
borne from heaven, for we were with him on the
holy mountain. 19And we have the prophetic
word made more sure. You will do well to pay
attention to this as to a lamp shining in a dark
place, until the day dawns and the morning star
rises in your hearts. 20 First of all you must
understand this, that no prophecy of scripture
is a matter of one's own interpretation, 21 because no prophecy ever came by the impulse of
man, but men moved by the Holy Spirit spoke
from God.

[*c*] Greek *tent*. [*d*] Or *my Son, my* (or *the*) *Beloved*. [*e*] Other authorities read *moved by the Holy Spirit holy men of God spoke*.

Jerusalem Bible

it is my duty, as long as I am in this tent, to keep
stirring you up with reminders, 14 since I know
the time for taking off this tent is coming soon,
as our Lord Jesus Christ foretold to me. 15And
I shall take great care that after my own departure you will still have a means to recall these
things to memory.
16 It was not any cleverly invented myths that
we were repeating when we brought you the
knowledge of the power and the coming of our
Lord Jesus Christ; we had seen his majesty for
ourselves. 17 He was honored and glorified by
God the Father, when the Sublime Glory itself
spoke to him and said, "This is my Son, the
Beloved; he enjoys my favor." 18 We heard this
ourselves, spoken from heaven, when we were
with him on the holy mountain.[a]

The value of prophecy

19 So we have confirmation of what was said
in prophecies; and you will be right to depend
on prophecy and take it as a lamp for lighting a
way through the dark until the dawn comes and
the morning star rises in your minds. 20At the
same time, we must be most careful to remember
that the interpretation of scriptural prophecy is
never a matter for the individual. 21 Why? Because no prophecy ever came from man's initiative. When men spoke for God it was the Holy
Spirit that moved them.

[*a*] At the transfiguration; Mt. 17; Mk. 9; Lk. 9.

New English Bible

ing your memory so long as I still lodge in this body. I know that very soon I must leave it; indeed our Lord Jesus Christ has told me so.[q] But I will see to it that after I am gone you will have means of remembering these things at all times.

It was not on tales artfully spun that we relied when we told you of the power of our Lord Jesus Christ and his coming; we saw him with our own eyes in majesty, when at the hands of God the Father he was invested with honour and glory, and there came to him from the sublime Presence a voice which said: 'This is my Son, my Beloved,[r] on whom my favour rests.' This voice from heaven we ourselves heard; when it came, we were with him on the sacred mountain.

All this only confirms for us the message of the prophets,[s] to which you will do well to attend, because it is like a lamp shining in a murky place, until the day breaks and the morning star rises to illuminate your minds.

But first note this: no one can interpret any prophecy of Scripture by himself. For it was not through any human whim that men prophesied of old; men they were, but, impelled by the Holy Spirit, they spoke the words of God.

[*q*] *Or* I must leave it, as our Lord Jesus Christ told me. [*r*] *Or* This is my only Son. [*s*] *Or* And in the message of the prophets we have something still more certain.

King James Version

2 But there were false prophets also among the people, even as there shall be false teachers among you, who privily shall bring in damnable heresies, even denying the Lord that bought them, and bring upon themselves swift destruction. 2And many shall follow their pernicious ways; by reason of whom the way of truth shall be evil spoken of. 3And through covetousness shall they with feigned words make merchandise of you: whose judgment now of a long time lingereth not, and their damnation slumbereth not. 4 For if God spared not the angels that sinned, but cast *them* down to hell, and delivered *them* into chains of darkness, to be reserved unto judgment; 5And spared not the old world, but saved Noah the eighth *person,* a preacher of righteousness, bringing in the flood upon the world of the ungodly; 6And turning the cities of Sodom and Gomorrah into ashes condemned *them* with an overthrow, making *them* an ensample unto those that after should live ungodly; 7And delivered just Lot, vexed with the filthy conversation of the wicked: 8 (For that righteous man dwelling among them, in seeing and hearing, vexed *his* righteous soul from day to day with *their* unlawful deeds:) 9 The Lord knoweth how to deliver the godly out of temptation, and to reserve the unjust unto the

Living Bible

2 But there were false prophets, too, in those days, just as there will be false teachers among you. They will cleverly tell their lies about God, turning against even their Master who bought them; but theirs will be a swift and terrible end. 2 Many will follow their evil teaching that there is nothing wrong with sexual sin. And because of them Christ and his way will be scoffed at.

3 These teachers in their greed will tell you anything to get hold of your money. But God condemned them long ago and their destruction is on the way. 4 For God did not spare even the angels who sinned, but threw them into hell, chained in gloomy caves and darkness until the judgment day. 5And he did not spare any of the people who lived in ancient times before the flood except Noah, the one man who spoke up for God, and his family of seven. At that time God completely destroyed the whole world of ungodly men with the vast flood. 6 Later, he turned the cities of Sodom and Gomorrah into heaps of ashes and blotted them off the face of the earth, making them an example for all the ungodly in the future to look back upon and fear.

7, 8 But at the same time the Lord rescued Lot out of Sodom because he was a good man, sick of the terrible wickedness he saw everywhere around him day after day. 9 So also the Lord can rescue you and me from the temptations that surround us, and continue to punish the ungodly until the day of final judgment

Today's English Version

False teachers

2 False prophets appeared in the past among the people, and in the same way false teachers will appear among you. They will bring in destructive, untrue doctrines, and deny the Master who redeemed them, and so bring upon themselves sudden destruction. 2 Even so, many will follow their immoral ways; and, because of what they do, people will speak evil of the Way of truth. 3 In their greed these false teachers will make a profit out of telling you made-up stories. For a long time now their Judge has been ready, and their Destroyer has been wide awake!

4 God did not spare the angels who sinned, but threw them into hell, where they are kept chained in darkness, waiting for the Day of Judgment. 5 God did not spare the ancient world, but brought the Flood on the world of godless men; the only ones he saved were Noah, who preached righteousness, and seven other people. 6 God condemned the cities of Sodom and Gomorrah, destroying them with fire, and made them an example of what will happen to the godless. 7 He rescued Lot, a good man, who was troubled by the immoral conduct of lawless men. 8 That good man lived among them and day after day saw and heard such things that his good heart was tormented by their evil actions. 9And so the Lord knows how to rescue godly men from their trials, and how to keep the wicked under punishment for the Day of Judg-

New International Version

False teachers and their destruction

2 But there were also false prophets among the people, just as there will be false teachers among you. They will secretly introduce destructive heresies, even denying the sovereign Lord who bought them—bringing swift destruction on themselves. 2 Many will follow their shameful ways and will bring the way of truth into disrepute. 3 In their greed these teachers will exploit you with stories they have made up. Their condemnation has long been hanging over them, and their destruction has not been sleeping.

4 For if God did not spare angels when they sinned, but sent them to hell,[a] putting them into gloomy dungeons[b] to be held for judgment; 5 if he did not spare the ancient world when he brought the flood on its ungodly people, but protected Noah, a preacher of righteousness, and seven others; 6 if he condemned the cities of Sodom and Gomorrah by burning them to ashes, and made them an example of what is going to happen to the ungodly; 7 and if he rescued Lot, a righteous man, who was distressed by the filthy lives of lawless men 8 (for that righteous man, living among them day after day, was tormented by the lawless deeds he saw and heard)—9 if this is so, then the Lord knows how to rescue godly men from trials and to hold the unrighteous for the day of judgment, while

[a] Greek *Tartarus.* [b] Some early MSS read *int chains of darkness.*

Phillips Modern English

But even in those days there were false prophets among the people, just as there will be false teachers among you today. They will be men who will subtly introduce dangerous heresies. They will thereby deny the Lord who redeemed them, and it will not be long before they bring on themselves their own downfall. Many will follow their flagrant immorality and thereby bring discredit on the way of truth. In their lust to make converts these men will try to exploit you too with their bogus arguments. But judgment has been for some time hard on their heels and their downfall is inevitable. For if God did not spare angels who sinned against him, but banished them to the dark imprisonment of hell till judgment day; if he did not spare the ancient world but only saved Noah, the solitary voice that cried out for righteousness, and his seven companions when he brought the flood upon the world in its wickedness; and if God reduced the entire cities of Sodom and Gomorrah to ashes, when he sentenced them to destruction as a fearful example to those who wanted to live in defiance of his laws, and yet saved Lot the righteous man, in acute mental distress at the filthy lives of the godless—Lot, remember, was a good man suffering spiritual agonies day after day at what he saw and heard of their lawlessness—then you may be absolutely certain that the Lord knows how to rescue good men surrounded by temptation, and how to reserve his punishment for the wicked until their day comes.

Revised Standard Version

2 But false prophets also arose among the
people, just as there will be false teachers
among you, who will secretly bring in destructive heresies, even denying the Master who
bought them, bringing upon themselves swift
destruction. 2 And many will follow their licentiousness, and because of them the way of truth
will be reviled. 3 And in their greed they will exploit you with false words; from of old their
condemnation has not been idle, and their destruction has not been asleep.
4 For if God did not spare the angels when
they sinned, but cast them into hell [f] and committed them to pits of nether gloom to be kept
until the judgment; 5 if he did not spare the
ancient world, but preserved Noah, a herald of
righteousness, with seven other persons, when
he brought a flood upon the world of the ungodly; 6 if by turning the cities of Sodom and
Gomorrah to ashes he condemned them to ex-
tinction and made them an example to those
who were to be ungodly; 7 and if he rescued
righteous Lot, greatly distressed by the licentiousness of the wicked 8 (for by what that
righteous man saw and heard as he lived among
them, he was vexed in his righteous soul day
after day with their lawless deeds), 9 then the
Lord knows how to rescue the godly from trial,
and to keep the unrighteous under punishment

[f] Greek *Tartarus*.

Jerusalem Bible

False teachers

2 As there were false prophets in the past
history of our people, so you too will have
your false teachers, who will insinuate their own
disruptive views and disown the Master who
purchased their freedom. They will destroy themselves very quickly; 2 but there will be many who
copy their shameful behavior and the Way of
Truth will be brought into disrepute on their
account. 3 They will eagerly try to buy you
for themselves with insidious speeches, but for
them the Condemnation, pronounced so long
ago, is at its work already, and Destruction is
not asleep. 4 When angels sinned, God did not
spare them: he sent them down to the underworld and consigned them to the dark under-
ground caves to be held there till the day of
Judgment. 5 Nor did he spare the world in ancient times: it was only Noah he saved, the
preacher of righteousness, along with seven others, when he sent the Flood over a disobedient
world. 6 The cities of Sodom and Gomorrah,
these too he condemned and reduced to ashes;
he destroyed them completely, as a warning to
anybody lacking reverence in the future; 7 he
rescued Lot, however, a holy man who had been
sickened by the shameless way in which these vile
people behaved—8 for that holy man, living
among them, was outraged in his good soul by
the crimes that he saw and heard of every day.
9 These are all examples of how the Lord can
rescue the good from the ordeal, and hold the
wicked for their punishment until the day of

New English Bible

2 But Israel had false prophets as well as true; and you likewise will have false teachers among you. They will import disastrous heresies, disowning the very Master who bought them, and bringing swift disaster on their own heads. They will gain many adherents to their dissolute practices, through whom the true way will be brought into disrepute. In their greed for money they will trade on your credulity with sheer fabrications.

But the judgement long decreed for them has not been idle; perdition waits for them with unsleeping eyes. God did not spare the angels who sinned, but consigned them to the dark pits of hell,[c] where they are reserved for judgement. He did not spare the world of old (except for Noah, preacher of righteousness, whom he preserved with seven others), but brought the deluge upon that world of godless men. The cities of Sodom and Gomorrah God burned to ashes, and condemned them to total destruction, making them an object-lesson for godless men in future days. But he rescued Lot, who was a good man, shocked by the dissolute habits of the lawless society in which he lived; day after day every sight, every sound, of their evil courses tortured that good man's heart. Thus the Lord is well able to rescue the godly out of trials, and to reserve the wicked under punishment until the day of judgement.

[c] *Some witnesses read* consigned them to darkness and chains in hell.

King James Version

day of judgment to be punished: 10 But chiefly
them that walk after the flesh in the lust of uncleanness, and despise government. Presumptuous *are they,* selfwilled, they are not afraid to
speak evil of dignities. 11 Whereas angels, which
are greater in power and might, bring not railing accusation against them before the Lord.
12 But these, as natural brute beasts made to be
taken and destroyed, speak evil of the things
that they understand not; and shall utterly perish in their own corruption; 13 And shall receive
the reward of unrighteousness, *as* they that count
it pleasure to riot in the daytime. Spots *they are*
and blemishes, sporting themselves with their own
deceivings while they feast with you; 14 Having
eyes full of adultery, and that cannot cease
from sin; beguiling unstable souls: a heart they
have exercised with covetous practices; cursed
children: 15 Which have forsaken the right way,
and are gone astray, following the way of Balaam *the son* of Bosor, who loved the wages
of unrighteousness; 16 But was rebuked for his
iniquity: the dumb ass speaking with man's voice

Living Bible

comes. 10 He is especially hard on those who
follow their own evil, lustful thoughts, and those
who are proud and willful, daring even to scoff
at the Glorious Ones[a] without so much as trembling, 11 although the angels in heaven who
stand in the very presence of the Lord, and are
far greater in power and strength than these false
teachers, never speak out disrespectfully against
these evil Mighty Ones.
12 But false teachers are fools—no better
than animals. They do whatever they feel like;
born only to be caught and killed, they laugh at
the terrifying powers of the underworld[b] which
they know so little about; and they will be destroyed along with all the demons and powers
of hell.[c]
13 That is the pay these teachers will have
for their sin. For they live in evil pleasures day
after day. They are a disgrace and a stain
among you, deceiving you by living in foul sin
on the side while they join your love feasts as
though they were honest men. 14 No woman can
escape their sinful stare, and of adultery they
never have enough. They make a game of luring
unstable women. They train themselves to be
greedy; and are doomed and cursed. 15 They
have gone off the road and become lost like
Balaam, the son of Beor, who fell in love with
the money he could make by doing wrong;
16 but Balaam was stopped from his mad course
when his donkey spoke to him with a human
voice, scolding and rebuking him.

[*a*] Or, "the glories of the unseen world." [*b*] Literally, "the things they do not understand." [*c*] Implied. Literally, "will be destroyed in the same destruction with them."

Today's English Version

ment, 10 especially those who follow their filthy
bodily lusts and despise God's authority.
These false teachers are bold and arrogant,
and show no respect for the glorious beings
above; instead, they insult them. 11 Even the
angels, who are so much stronger and mightier
than these false teachers, do not accuse them
with insults in the presence of the Lord. 12 But
these men act by instinct, like wild animals born
to be captured and killed; they insult things they
do not understand. They will be destroyed like
wild animals; 13 they will be paid with suffering for the suffering they caused. Pleasure for
them is to do anything in broad daylight that
will satisfy their bodily appetites; they are a
shame and a disgrace as they join you in your
meals, all the while enjoying their deceitful
ways! 14 They want to look at nothing else but
immoral women; their appetite for sin is never
satisfied. They lead weak people into a trap.
Their hearts are trained to be greedy. They are
under God's curse! 15 They have left the straight
path and have lost their way; they have followed the path taken by Balaam the son of
Bosor, who loved the money he would get for
doing wrong, 16 and was rebuked for his sin. His
donkey spoke with a human voice and stopped
the prophet's insane action.

New International Version

continuing their punishment. 10 This is especially
true of those who follow the corrupt desire of
their sinful natures and despise authority.
Bold and arrogant, these men are not afraid
to slander celestial beings; 11 yet even angels,
although they are stronger and more powerful,
do not bring slanderous accusations against such
beings in the presence of the Lord. 12 But these
men blaspheme in matters they do not understand. They are like brute beasts, creatures of
instinct, born only to be caught and destroyed,
and like beasts they too will perish.
13 They will be paid back with harm for the
harm they have done. Their idea of pleasure is
to carouse in broad daylight. They are blots and
blemishes, reveling in their pleasures while they
feast with you.[c] 14 With eyes full of adultery,
they never stop sinning; they seduce the unstable;
they are experts in greed—an accursed brood!
15 They have left the straight way and wandered
off to follow the way of Balaam son of Beor,
who loved the wages of wickedness. 16 But he
was rebuked for his wrongdoing by a donkey—
a beast without speech—who spoke with a
man's voice and restrained the prophet's madness.

[*c*] Some MSS read *in their love feasts.*

Phillips Modern English

2.10 Let me show you what these men are really like

His judgment is chiefly reserved for those who have indulged all the foulness of their lower natures, and have nothing but contempt for authority. These men are arrogant and presumptuous—they think nothing of scoffing at the glories of the unseen world. Yet even angels, who are their superiors in strength and power, do not bring insulting criticisms of such things before the Lord.

But these men, with no more sense than the unreasoning brute beasts which are born to be caught and killed, scoff at things outside their own experience, and will most certainly be destroyed in their own corruption. Their wickedness has earned them an evil end and they will be paid in full.

These are the men who delight in daylight self-indulgence; they are foul spots and blots, playing their tricks at your very dinner-tables. Their eyes cannot look at a woman without lust, and they miss no opportunity for sin. They captivate the unstable ones, and their technique of getting what they want is, through long practice, highly developed. They are born under a curse, for they have abandoned the right road and wandered off to follow the old trail of Balaam, son of Beor, the man who had no objection to wickedness as long as he was paid for it. But he, you remember, was sharply reprimanded for his wickedness—by a donkey, of all things, speaking with a human voice to check the prophet's wicked infatuation!

Revised Standard Version

until the day of judgment, 10 and especially those
who indulge in the lust of defiling passion and
despise authority.
Bold and wilful, they are not afraid to revile
the glorious ones, 11 whereas angels, though
greater in might and power, do not pronounce
a reviling judgment upon them before the Lord.
12 But these, like irrational animals, creatures of
instinct, born to be caught and killed, reviling in
matters of which they are ignorant, will be destroyed
in the same destruction with them, 13 suffering wrong for their wrongdoing. They count
it pleasure to revel in the daytime. They are blots
and blemishes, reveling in their dissipation,[g]
carousing with you. 14 They have eyes full of
adultery, insatiable for sin. They entice unsteady
souls. They have hearts trained in greed. Accursed
children! 15 Forsaking the right way they
have gone astray; they have followed the way
of Balaam, the son of Beor, who loved gain from
wrong-doing, 16 but was rebuked for his own
transgression; a dumb ass spoke with human
voice and restrained the prophet's madness.

[g] Other ancient authorities read *love feasts*.

Jerusalem Bible

Judgment, 10 especially those who are governed
by their corrupt bodily desires and have no respect
for authority.

The punishment to come

Such self-willed people with no reverence are
not afraid of offending against the glorious
ones, 11 but the angels in their greater strength
and power make no complaint or accusation
against them in front of the Lord. 12 All the
same, these people who only insult anything that
they do not understand are not reasoning beings,
but simply animals born to be caught and killed,
and they will quite certainly destroy themselves
by their own work of destruction, 13 and get
their reward of evil for the evil that they do.
They are unsightly blots on your society: men
whose only object is dissipation all day long, and
they amuse themselves deceiving you even when
they are your guests at a meal; 14 with their
eyes always looking for adultery, men with an
infinite capacity for sinning, they will seduce any
soul which is at all unstable. Greed is the one
lesson their minds have learned. They are under
a curse. 15 They have left the right path and
wandered off to follow the path of Balaam son
of Beor, who thought he could profit best by sinning,
16 until he was called to order for his
faults. The dumb donkey put a stop to that
prophet's madness when it talked like a man.

New English Bible

Above all he will punish those who follow their abominable lusts. They flout authority; reckless and headstrong, they are not afraid to insult celestial beings, whereas angels, for all their superior strength and might, employ no insults in seeking judgement against them before the Lord.

These men are like brute beasts, born in the course of nature to be caught and killed. They pour abuse upon things they do not understand; like the beasts they will perish, suffering hurt for the hurt they have inflicted. To carouse in broad daylight is their idea of pleasure; while they sit with you at table they are an ugly blot on your company, because they revel in their own deceptions.[a]

They have eyes for nothing but women, eyes never at rest from sin. They lure the unstable to their ruin; past masters in mercenary greed, God's curse is on them! They have abandoned the straight road and lost their way. They have followed in the steps of Balaam son of Beor, who consented to take pay for doing wrong, but had his offence brought home to him when the dumb beast spoke with a human voice and put a stop to the prophet's madness.

[a] *Some witnesses read* in their love-feasts.

King James Version

forbade the madness of the prophet. 17 These are wells without water, clouds that are carried with a tempest; to whom the mist of darkness is reserved for ever. 18 For when they speak great swelling *words* of vanity, they allure through the lusts of the flesh, *through much* wantonness, those that were clean escaped from them who live in error. 19 While they promise them liberty, they themselves are the servants of corruption: for of whom a man is overcome, of the same is he brought in bondage. 20 For if after they have escaped the pollutions of the world through the knowledge of the Lord and Saviour Jesus Christ, they are again entangled therein, and overcome, the latter end is worse with them than the beginning. 21 For it had been better for them not to have known the way of righteousness, than, after they have known *it*, to turn from the holy commandment delivered unto them. 22 But it is happened unto them according to the true proverb, The dog *is* turned to his own vomit again; and, The sow that was washed to her wallowing in the mire.

3 This second epistle, beloved, I now write unto you; in *both* which I stir up your pure minds by way of remembrance: 2 That ye may

Living Bible

17 These men are as useless as dried-up springs of water, promising much and delivering nothing; they are as unstable as clouds driven by the storm winds. They are doomed to the eternal pits of darkness. 18 They proudly boast about their sins and conquests, and, using lust as their bait, they lure back into sin those who have just escaped from such wicked living.

19 "You aren't saved by being good," they say, "so you might as well be bad. Do what you like, be free."

But these very teachers who offer this "freedom" from law are themselves slaves to sin and destruction. For a man is a slave to whatever controls him. 20 And when a person has escaped from the wicked ways of the world by learning about our Lord and Savior Jesus Christ, and then gets tangled up with sin and becomes its slave again, he is worse off than he was before. 21 It would be better if he had never known about Christ at all than to learn of him and then afterwards turn his back on the holy commandments that were given to him. 22 There is an old saying that "A dog comes back to what he has vomited, and a pig is washed only to come back and wallow in the mud again." That is the way it is with those who turn again to their sin.

3 This is my second letter to you, dear brothers, and in both of them I have tried to remind you—if you will let me—about facts you already know: facts you learned from the holy

Today's English Version

17 These men are like dried-up springs, like clouds blown along by a storm; God has reserved a place for them in the deepest darkness. 18 They make proud and stupid statements, and use immoral bodily lusts to trap those who are just beginning to escape from among people who live in error. 19 They promise them freedom, while they themselves are slaves of destructive habits—for a man is a slave of anything that has conquered him. 20 If men have escaped from the corrupting forces of the world through their knowledge of our Lord and Savior Jesus Christ, and then are again caught and conquered by them, such men are in worse condition at the end than they were at the beginning. 21 It would have been much better for them never to have known the way of righteousness than to know it and then turn away from the sacred command that was given them. 22 What happened to them shows that the proverb is true, "A dog goes back to what it has vomited," and, "A pig that has been washed goes back to roll in the mud."

The promise of the Lord's coming

3 My dear friends! This is now the second letter I have written you. In both letters I have tried to arouse pure thoughts in your minds by reminding you of these things. 2 I want

New International Version

17 These men are springs without water and mists driven by a storm. Blackest darkness is reserved for them. 18 For they mouth empty, boastful words and, by appealing to the lustful desires of sinful human nature, they entice people who are just escaping from those who live in error. 19 They promise them freedom, while they themselves are slaves of depravity—for a man is a slave to whatever has mastered him. 20 If they have escaped the corruption of the world by knowing our Lord and Savior Jesus Christ and are again entangled in it and overcome, they are worse off at the end than they were at the beginning. 21 It would have been better for them not to have known the way of righteousness, than to have known it and then to turn their backs on the sacred commandment that was passed on to them. 22 Of them the proverbs are true: "A dog returns to its vomit,"[d] and, "A sow that is washed goes back to her wallowing in the mud."

The day of the Lord

3 Dear friends, this is now my second letter to you. I have written both of them as reminders to stimulate you to wholesome thinking. 2 I

[*d*] Prov 26:11.

Phillips Modern English

These men are like wells without a drop of water in them, like the changing shapes of whirling storm-clouds, and their fate will be the black night of utter darkness. With their high-sounding nonsense they use the sensual pull of the lower passions to attract those who were just on the point of cutting loose from their companions in evil. They promise them liberty. Liberty!—when they themselves are bound hand and foot to utter depravity. For a man is the slave of whatever masters him. If men have escaped from the world's contaminations through knowing our Lord and saviour Jesus Christ, and then become entangled and defeated by them all over again, their last position is worse than their first. For it would be better for them not to have known the way of goodness at all, than after knowing it to turn their backs on the sacred commandments given to them. For them, the old proverbs have come true about the "dog returning to his vomit", and "the sow that had been washed going back to wallow in the muck".

3.1 God delays the last day, in his mercy

This is the second letter I have written to you, dear friends of mine, and in both of them I have tried to stimulate you, as men with minds uncontaminated by error, by reminding you of what you really know already. This means re-

Revised Standard Version

17 These are waterless springs and mists
driven by a storm; for them the nether gloom of
darkness has been reserved. 18 For, uttering
loud boasts of folly, they entice with licentious
passions of the flesh men who have barely escaped from those who live in error. 19 They
promise them freedom, but they themselves are
slaves of corruption; for whatever overcomes a
man, to that he is enslaved. 20 For if, after they
have escaped the defilements of the world
through the knowledge of our Lord and Savior
Jesus Christ, they are again entangled in them
and overpowered, the last state has become
worse for them than the first. 21 For it would
have been better for them never to have known
the way of righteousness than after knowing it
to turn back from the holy commandment delivered to them. 22 It has happened to them according to the true proverb, The dog turns back
to his own vomit, and the sow is washed only
to wallow in the mire.

3 This is now the second letter that I have
written to you, beloved, and in both of them
I have aroused your sincere mind by way of
reminder; 2 that you should remember the pre-

Jerusalem Bible

17 People like this are dried-up rivers, fogs
swirling in the wind, and the dark underworld
is the place reserved for them. 18 With their
high-flown talk, which is all hollow, they tempt
back the ones who have only just escaped from
paganism, playing on their bodily desires with
debaucheries. 19 They may promise freedom but
they themselves are slaves, slaves to corruption;
because if anyone lets himself be dominated by
anything, then he is a slave to it; 20 and anyone
who has escaped the pollution of the world once
by coming to know our Lord and savior Jesus
Christ, and who then allows himself to be entangled by it a second time and mastered, will
end up in a worse state than he began in. 21 It
would even have been better for him never to
have learned the way of holiness, than to know
it and afterward desert the holy rule that was
entrusted to him. 22 What he has done is exactly
as the proverb rightly says: *The dog goes back
to his own vomit*[b] and: When the sow has been
washed, it wallows in the mud.

The Day of the Lord; the prophets and the apostles

3 My friends, this is my second letter to you,
and in both of them I have tried to awaken
a true understanding in you by giving you a reminder: 2 recalling to you what was said in the

[b] Pr. 26:11.

New English Bible

These men are springs that give no water, mists driven by a storm; the place reserved for them is blackest darkness. They utter big, empty words, and make of sensual lusts and debauchery a bait to catch those who have barely begun to escape from their heathen environment. They promise them freedom, but are themselves slaves of corruption; for a man is the slave of whatever has mastered him. They had once escaped the world's defilements through the knowledge of our Lord and Saviour Jesus Christ; yet if they have entangled themselves in these all over again, and are mastered by them, their plight in the end is worse than before. How much better never to have known the right way, than, having known it, to turn back and abandon the sacred commandments delivered to them! For them the proverb has proved true: 'The dog returns to its own vomit', and, 'The sow after a wash rolls in the mud again.'

3 This is now my second letter to you, my friends. In both of them I have been recalling to you what you already know, to rouse you to honest thought. Remember the predictions made

King James Version

be mindful of the words which were spoken
before by the holy prophets, and of the commandment of us the apostles of the Lord and
Saviour: 3 Knowing this first, that there shall
come in the last days scoffers, walking after
their own lusts, 4 And saying, Where is the promise of his coming? for since the fathers fell
asleep, all things continue as *they were* from
the beginning of the creation. 5 For this they
willingly are ignorant of, that by the word of
God the heavens were of old, and the earth
standing out of the water and in the water:
6 Whereby the world that then was, being overflowed with water, perished: 7 But the heavens
and the earth, which are now, by the same word
are kept in store, reserved unto fire against the
day of judgment and perdition of ungodly men.
8 But, beloved, be not ignorant of this one thing,
that one day *is* with the Lord as a thousand
years, and a thousand years as one day. 9 The
Lord is not slack concerning his promise, as
some men count slackness; but is longsuffering
to us-ward, not willing that any should perish,
but that all should come to repentance. 10 But
the day of the Lord will come as a thief in the
night; in the which the heavens shall pass away
with a great noise, and the elements shall melt
with fervent heat, the earth also and the works

Living Bible

prophets and from us apostles who brought you
the words of our Lord and Savior.
3 First, I want to remind you that in the last
days there will come scoffers who will do every
wrong they can think of, and laugh at the truth.
4 This will be their line of argument: "So Jesus
promised to come back, did he? Then where is
he? He'll never come! Why, as far back as anyone can remember everything has remained exactly as it was since the first day of creation."
5, 6 They deliberately forget this fact: that
God did destroy the world with a mighty flood,
long after he had made the heavens by the word
of his command, and had used the waters to
form the earth and surround it. 7 And God has
commanded that the earth and the heavens be
stored away for a great bonfire at the judgment
day, when all ungodly men will perish.
8 But don't forget this, dear friends, that a
day or a thousand years from now is like tomorrow to the Lord. 9 He isn't really being slow
about his promised return, even though it sometimes seems that way. But he is waiting, for the
good reason that he is not willing that any
should perish, and he is giving more time for
sinners to repent. 10 The day of the Lord is
surely coming, as unexpectedly as a thief, and
then the heavens will pass away with a terrible
noise and the heavenly bodies will disappear in
fire, and the earth and everything on it will be
burned up.

Today's English Version

you to remember the words that were spoken
long ago by the holy prophets, and the command
from the Lord and Savior which was given you
by your apostles. 3 First of all, you must understand that in the last days some men will appear
whose lives are controlled by their own lusts.
They will make fun of you 4 and say, "He promised to come, didn't he? Where is he? Our fathers
have already died, but everything is still the
same as it was since the creation of the world!"
5 They purposely ignore the fact that long ago
God spoke, and the heavens and earth were
created. The earth was formed out of water, and
by water, 6 and it was by water also, the water
of the Flood, that the old world was destroyed.
7 But the heavens and earth that now exist are
being preserved, by the same word of God, for
destruction by fire. They are being kept for the
day when godless men will be judged and destroyed.
8 But do not forget this one thing, my dear
friends! There is no difference in the Lord's
sight between one day and a thousand years; to
him the two are the same. 9 The Lord is not
slow to do what he has promised, as some think.
Instead, he is patient with you, because he does
not want anyone to be destroyed, but wants all
to turn away from their sins.
10 But the Day of the Lord will come as a
thief. On that Day the heavens will disappear
with a shrill noise, the heavenly bodies will burn
up and be destroyed, and the earth with every-

New International Version

want you to recall the words spoken in the past
by the holy prophets and the command given by
our Lord and Savior through your apostles.
3 First of all, you must understand that in
the last days scoffers will come, scoffing and following their own evil desires. 4 They will say,
"Where is this 'coming' he promised? Ever since
our fathers died, everything goes on as it has
since the beginning of creation." 5 But they deliberately forget that long ago by God's word
the heavens existed and the earth was formed
out of water and with water. 6 By water also the
world of that time was deluged and destroyed.
7 By the same word the present heavens and
earth are reserved for fire, being kept for the day
of judgment and destruction of ungodly men.
8 But do not forget this one thing, dear
friends: With the Lord a day is like a thousand
years, and a thousand years are like a day. 9 The
Lord is not slow in keeping his promise, as
some understand slowness. He is patient with
you, not wanting anyone to perish, but everyone
to come to repentance.
10 But the day of the Lord will come like a
thief. The heavens will disappear with a roar;
the elements will be destroyed by fire, and the
earth and everything in it will be laid bare.[e]

[e] Some early MSS read *will be burned up*.

Phillips Modern English

calling the words spoken of old by the holy prophets as well as the commands of our Lord and saviour given to you through his messengers.

First of all you must realise that in the last days cynical mockers will undoubtedly come—men whose only guide in life is what they want for themselves—and they will say, "Where is his promised coming? Since our fathers fell asleep, everything remains exactly as it was since the beginning of creation!" They are deliberately shutting their eyes to the fact that there were heavens in the old days and an earth formed by God's command out of water and by water. It was by water that the world of those days was deluged and destroyed, but the present heavens and earth are, also by God's command, being carefully kept and maintained for the fire of the day of judgment and the destruction of wicked men.

But you should never lose sight of this fact, dear friends, that with the Lord a day may be a thousand years, and a thousand years only a day. It is not that he is dilatory about keeping his own promise as some men seem to think; the fact is that he is very patient with you. He has no wish that any man should be destroyed; he wishes that all men should find the way to repentance. Yet the day of the Lord will come as unexpectedly as a thief. In that day the heavens will vanish in a tearing blast, the very elements will disintegrate in heat and the earth and all its works will disappear.

Revised Standard Version

dictions of the holy prophets and the commandment of the Lord and Savior through your apostles. 3 First of all you must understand this, that scoffers will come in the last days with scoffing, following their own passions 4 and saying, "Where is the promise of his coming? For ever since the fathers fell asleep, all things have continued as they were from the beginning of creation." 5 They deliberately ignore this fact, that by the word of God heavens existed long ago, and an earth formed out of water and by means of water, 6 through which the world that then existed was deluged with water and perished. 7 But by the same word the heavens and earth that now exist have been stored up for fire, being kept until the day of judgment and destruction of ungodly men.

8 But do not ignore this one fact, beloved, that with the Lord one day is as a thousand years, and a thousand years as one day. 9 The Lord is not slow about his promise as some count slowness, but is forbearing toward you,[h] not wishing that any should perish, but that all should reach repentance. 10 But the day of the Lord will come like a thief, and then the heavens will pass away with a loud noise, and the elements will be dissolved with fire, and the earth and the works that are upon it will be burned up.

[h] Other ancient authorities read *on your account*.

Jerusalem Bible

past by the holy prophets and the commandments of the Lord and savior which you were given by the apostles.

3 We must be careful to remember that during the last days there are bound to be people who will be scornful, the kind who always please themselves in what they do, and they will make fun of the promise 4 and ask, "Well, where is this coming? Everything goes on as it has since the Fathers died, as it has since it began at the creation." 5 They are choosing to forget that there were heavens at the beginning, and that the earth was formed by the word of God out of water and between the waters, 6 so that the world of that time was destroyed by being flooded by water. 7 But by the same word, the present sky and earth are destined for fire, and are only being reserved until Judgment day so that all sinners may be destroyed.

8 But there is one thing, my friends, that you must never forget: that with the Lord, "a day" can mean a thousand years, and *a thousand years is like a day.*[c] 9 The Lord is not being slow to carry out his promises, as anybody else might be called slow; but he is being patient with you all, wanting nobody to be lost and everybody to be brought to change his ways. 10 The Day of the Lord will come like a thief, and then with a roar the sky will vanish, the elements will catch fire and fall apart, the earth and all that it contains will be burned up.

[c] Pr. 90:4

New English Bible

by God's own prophets, and the commands given by the Lord and Saviour through your apostles.

Note this first: in the last days there will come men who scoff at religion and live self-indulgent lives, and they will say: 'Where now is the promise of his coming? Our fathers have been laid to their rest, but still everything continues exactly as it has always been since the world began.'

In taking this view they lose sight of the fact[b] that there were heavens and earth long ago, created by God's word out of water and with water; and by water that first world was destroyed, the water of the deluge. And the present heavens and earth, again by God's word, have been kept in store for burning; they are being reserved until the day of judgement when the godless will be destroyed.

And here is one point, my friends, which you must not lose sight of: with the Lord one day is like a thousand years and a thousand years like one day. It is not that the Lord is slow in fulfilling his promise, as some suppose, but that he is very patient with you, because it is not his will for any to be lost, but for all to come to repentance.

But the Day of the Lord will come; it will come, unexpected as a thief. On that day the heavens will disappear with a great rushing sound, the elements will disintegrate in flames, and the earth with all that is in it will be laid bare.[a]

[b] *Or* They choose to overlook the fact . . . [a] *Some witnesses read* will be burnt up.

King James Version

that are therein shall be burned up. 11 *Seeing*
then *that* all these things shall be dissolved, what
manner *of persons* ought ye to be in *all* holy
conversation and godliness, 12 Looking for and
hasting unto the coming of the day of God,
wherein the heavens being on fire shall be dissolved, and the elements shall melt with fervent
heat? 13 Nevertheless we, according to his promise, look for new heavens and a new earth,
wherein dwelleth righteousness. 14 Wherefore, beloved, seeing that ye look for such things, be
diligent that ye may be found of him in peace,
without spot, and blameless. 15 And account
that the longsuffering of our Lord *is* salvation;
even as our beloved brother Paul also according to the wisdom given unto him hath written
unto you; 16 As also in all *his* epistles, speaking
in them of these things; in which are some things
hard to be understood, which they that are unlearned and unstable wrest, as *they do* also the
other Scriptures, unto their own destruction.
17 Ye therefore, beloved, seeing ye know *these*
things before, beware lest ye also, being led
away with the error of the wicked, fall from
your own steadfastness. 18 But grow in grace,
and *in* the knowledge of our Lord and Saviour
Jesus Christ. To him *be* glory both now and
for ever. Amen.

Living Bible

11 And so since everything around us is going to melt away, what holy, godly lives we
should be living! 12 You should look forward to
that day and hurry it along—the day when
God will set the heavens on fire, and the heavenly bodies will melt and disappear in flames.
13 But we are looking forward to God's promise of new heavens and a new earth afterwards,
where there will be only goodness.[a]

14 Dear friends, while you are waiting for
these things to happen and for him to come, try
hard to live without sinning; and be at peace
with everyone so that he will be pleased with
you when he returns.

15, 16 And remember why he is waiting. He
is giving us time to get his message of salvation
out to others. Our wise and beloved brother
Paul has talked about these same things in many
of his letters. Some of his comments are not
easy to understand, and there are people who
are deliberately stupid, and always demand some
unusual interpretation—they have twisted his letters around to mean something quite different
from what he meant, just as they do the other
parts of the Scripture—and the result is disaster
for them.

17 I am warning you ahead of time, dear
brothers, so that you can watch out and not
be carried away by the mistakes of these wicked
men, lest you yourselves become mixed up too.
18 But grow in spiritual strength and become
better acquainted with our Lord and Savior Jesus Christ. To him be all glory and splendid
honor, both now and and forevermore. Good-
bye.

Peter

[a] Literally, "wherein righteousness dwells."

Today's English Version

thing in it will vanish. 11 Since all these things
will be destroyed in this way, what kind of people should you be? Your lives should be holy
and dedicated to God, 12 as you wait for the
Day of God, and do your best to make it come
soon—the Day when the heavens will burn up
and be destroyed, and the heavenly bodies will
be melted by the heat. 13 But we wait for what
God has promised: new heavens and a new
earth, where righteousness will be at home.

14 And so, my friends, as you wait for that
Day, do your best to be pure and faultless in
God's sight and to be at peace with him. 15 Look
on our Lord's patience as the opportunity he
gives you to be saved, just as our dear brother
Paul wrote to you, using the wisdom God gave
him. 16 This is what he says in all his letters,
when he writes on this subject. There are some
difficult things in his letters which ignorant and
unstable people explain falsely, as they do with
other passages of the Scriptures. So they bring
on their own destruction.

17 But you, my friends, already know this.
Be on your guard, then, so that you will not be
led away by the errors of lawless men and fall
from your safe position. 18 But continue to grow
in the grace and knowledge of our Lord and
Savior Jesus Christ. To him be the glory, now
and forever! Amen.

New International Version

11 Since everything will be destroyed in this
way, what kind of people ought you to be? You
ought to live holy and godly lives 12 as you look
forward to the day of God and speed its coming.[f] That day will bring about the destruction
of the heavens by fire, and the elements will melt
in the heat. 13 But in keeping with his promise
we are looking forward to a new heaven and a
new earth, the home of righteousness.

14 So then, dear friends, since you are looking forward to this, make every effort to be
found spotless, blameless and at peace with him.
15 Bear in mind that our Lord's patience means
salvation, just as our dear brother Paul also
wrote you with the wisdom that God gave him.
16 He writes the same way in all his letters,
speaking in them of these matters. His letters
contain some things that are hard to understand,
which ignorant and unstable people distort, as
they do the other Scriptures, to their own destruction.

17 Therefore, dear friends, since you already
know this, be on your guard so that you may not
be carried away by the error of lawless men and
fall from your secure position. 18 But grow in
the grace and knowledge of our Lord and Savior
Jesus Christ. To him be glory both now and forever! Amen.

[f] Or *as you wait eagerly for the day of God to come.*

Phillips Modern English

3.11 *Never lose sight of the eternal world*

In view of the fact that all these things are to be dissolved, what sort of people ought you to be? Surely men of good and holy character, who live expecting and working for the coming of the day of God. This day will mean that the heavens will disintegrate in fire and the burning elements will melt, but our hopes are set on new heavens and a new earth which he has promised us, in which justice will make its home.

Because, my dear friends, you have a hope like this before you, I urge you to make certain that the day will find you at peace with God, flawless and blameless in his sight. Meanwhile, consider that our Lord's patience for man's salvation, as our dear brother Paul pointed out in his letter to you, written out of the wisdom God gave him. This is how he writes in all his letters when he refers to these things. There are some points in his letters which are difficult to understand, and which ill-informed and unbalanced people distort (as they do the other scriptures), and bring disaster on their own heads.

But you, my friends whom I love, are forewarned, and should therefore be very careful not to be carried away by the errors of unprincipled men and so lose your proper foothold. On the contrary, you should grow in grace and in knowledge of our Lord and saviour Jesus Christ—to him be glory now and until the day of eternity!

Revised Standard Version

11 Since all these things are thus to be dissolved, what sort of persons ought you to be in lives of holiness and godliness, 12 waiting for and hastening[i] the coming of the day of God, because of which the heavens will be kindled and dissolved, and the elements will melt with fire! 13 But according to his promise we wait for new heavens and a new earth in which righteousness dwells.

14 Therefore, beloved, since you wait for these, be zealous to be found by him without spot or blemish, and at peace. 15 And count the forbearance of our Lord as salvation. So also our beloved brother Paul wrote to you according to the wisdom given him, 16 speaking of this as he does in all his letters. There are some things in them hard to understand, which the ignorant and unstable twist to their own destruction, as they do the other scriptures. 17 You therefore, beloved, knowing this beforehand, beware lest you be carried away with the error of lawless men and lose your own stability. 18 But grow in the grace and knowledge of our Lord and Savior Jesus Christ. To him be the glory both now and to the day of eternity. Amen.

[i] Or *earnestly desiring*.

Jerusalem Bible

Conclusion and doxology

11 Since everything is coming to an end like this, you should be living holy and saintly lives 12 while you wait and long for the Day of God to come, when the sky will dissolve in flames and the elements melt in the heat. 13 What we are waiting for is what he promised: the new heavens and new earth, the place where righteousness will be at home. 14 So then, my friends, while you are waiting, do your best to live lives without spot or stain so that he will find you at peace. 15 Think of our Lord's patience as your opportunity to be saved: our brother Paul, who is so dear to us, told you this when he wrote to you with the wisdom that is his special gift. 16 He always writes like this when he deals with this sort of subject, and this makes some points in his letter hard to understand; these are the points that uneducated and unbalanced people distort, in the same way as they distort the rest of scripture—a fatal thing for them to do. 17 You have been warned about this, my friends; be careful not to get carried away by the errors of unprincipled people, from the firm ground that you are standing on. 18 Instead, go on growing in the grace and in the knowledge of our Lord and savior Jesus Christ. To him be glory, in time and in eternity. Amen.

New English Bible

Since the whole universe is to break up in this way, think what sort of people you ought to be, what devout and dedicated lives you should live! Look eagerly for the coming of the Day of God and work to hasten it on; that day will set the heavens ablaze until they fall apart, and will melt the elements in flames. But we have his promise, and look forward to new heavens and a new earth, the home of justice.

With this to look forward to, do your utmost to be found at peace with him, unblemished and above reproach in his sight. Bear in mind that our Lord's patience with us is our salvation, as Paul, our friend and brother, said when he wrote to you with his inspired wisdom. And so he does in all his other letters, wherever he speaks of this subject, though they contain some obscure passages, which the ignorant and unstable misinterpret to their own ruin, as they do the other scripture.[b]

But you, my friends, are forewarned. Take care, then, not to let these unprincipled men seduce you with their errors; do not lose your own safe foothold. But grow in the grace and in the knowledge of our Lord and Saviour Jesus Christ.[c] To him be glory now and for all eternity!

[b] *Or* his other writings. [c] *Or* But grow up, by the grace of our Lord and Savior Jesus Christ, and by knowing him.

King James Version

THE FIRST EPISTLE GENERAL OF JOHN

1 That which was from the beginning, which
we have heard, which we have seen with our
eyes, which we have looked upon, and our
hands have handled, of the Word of life; 2 (For
the life was manifested, and we have seen *it*,
and bear witness, and shew unto you that eternal life, which was with the Father, and was
manifested unto us;) 3 That which we have seen
and heard declare we unto you, that ye also may
have fellowship with us: and truly our fellowship *is* with the Father, and with his Son Jesus
Christ. 4 And these things write we unto you,

Living Bible

1 JOHN

1 Christ was alive when the world began, yet
I myself have seen him with my own eyes
and listened to him speak. I have touched him
with my own hands. He is God's message of
Life. 2 This one who is Life from God has been
shown to us and we guarantee that we have seen
him; I am speaking of Christ, who is eternal
Life. He was with the Father and then was
shown to us. 3 Again I say, we are telling you
about what we ourselves have actually seen and
heard, so that you may share the fellowship
and the joys we have with the Father and with
Jesus Christ his Son. 4 And if you do as I say in
this letter, then you, too, will be full of joy, and
so will we.

Today's English Version

THE FIRST LETTER OF JOHN

The Word of life

1 We write to you about the Word of life,
which has existed from the very beginning:
we have heard it, and we have seen it with our
eyes; yes, we have seen it, and our hands have
touched it. 2 When this life became visible, we
saw it; so we speak of it and tell you about the
eternal life which was with the Father and was
made known to us. 3 What we have seen and
heard we tell to you also, so that you will join
with us in the fellowship that we have with the
Father and with his Son Jesus Christ. 4 We write
this in order that our joy may be complete.

New International Version

1 JOHN

The word of life

1 That which was from the beginning, which
we have heard, which we have seen with our
eyes, which we have looked at and our hands
have touched—this we proclaim concerning the
Word of life. 2 The life appeared; we have seen
it and testify to it, and we proclaim to you the
eternal life, which was with the Father and has
appeared to us. 3 We proclaim to you what we
have seen and heard, so that you also may have
fellowship with us. And our fellowship is with
the Father and with his Son, Jesus Christ. 4 We
write this to make our[a] joy complete.

[a] Some early MSS read *your*.

Phillips Modern English

THE FIRST LETTER OF JOHN

We are writing to you about something which has always existed yet which we ourselves actually heard and saw with our own eyes: something which we had opportunity to observe closely and even to hold in our hands, something of the Word of life! For it was *life* which appeared before us: we saw it, we are eye-witnesses of it, and are now writing to you about it. It was the very life of all ages, the life that has always existed with the Father, which actually became visible in person to us. We repeat, we really saw and heard what we are now writing to you about. We want you to be with us in this—in this fellowship with the Father, and Jesus Christ his Son. We write and tell you about it, so that our joy may be complete.

Revised Standard Version

THE FIRST LETTER OF JOHN

1 That which was from the beginning, which
we have heard, which we have seen with our
eyes, which we have looked upon and touched
with our hands, concerning the word of life—
2 the life was made manifest, and we saw it, and
testify to it, and proclaim to you the eternal life
which was with the Father and was made manifest to us—3 that which we have seen and heard
we proclaim also to you, so that you may have
fellowship with us; and our fellowship is with
the Father and with his Son Jesus Christ. 4 And
we are writing this that our[a] joy may be complete.

[a] Other ancient authorities read *your*.

Jerusalem Bible

THE FIRST LETTER OF JOHN

1 JOHN

Introduction

The incarnate Word

1 Something which has existed since the beginning,
that we have heard,
and we have seen with our own eyes;
that we have watched
and touched with our hands:
the Word, who is life—
this is our subject.
2 That life was made visible:
we saw it and we are giving our testimony,
telling you of eternal life
which was with the Father and has been made visible to us.
3 What we have seen and heard
we are telling you
so that you too may be in union with us,
as we are in union
with the Father
and with his Son Jesus Christ.
4 We are writing this to you to make our own joy complete.

New English Bible

THE FIRST LETTER OF JOHN

Recall to fundamentals

1 It was there from the beginning; we have heard it; we have seen it with our own eyes; we looked upon it, and felt it with our own hands; and it is of this we tell. Our theme is the word of life. This life was made visible; we have seen it and bear our testimony; we here declare to you the eternal life which dwelt with the Father and was made visible to us. What we have seen and heard we declare to you, so that you and we together may share in a common life, that life which we share with the Father and his Son Jesus Christ. And we write this in order that the joy of us all may be complete.

King James Version

that your joy may be full. 5 This then is the message which we have heard of him, and declare unto you, that God is light, and in him is no darkness at all. 6 If we say that we have fellowship with him, and walk in darkness, we lie, and do not the truth: 7 But if we walk in the light, as he is in the light, we have fellowship one with another, and the blood of Jesus Christ his Son cleanseth us from all sin. 8 If we say that we have no sin, we deceive ourselves, and the truth is not in us. 9 If we confess our sins, he is faithful and just to forgive us *our* sins, and to cleanse us from all unrighteousness. 10 If we say that we have not sinned, we make him a liar, and his word is not in us.

Living Bible

5 This is the message God has given us to pass on to you: that God is Light and in him is no darkness at all. 6 So if we say we are his friends, but go on living in spiritual darkness and sin, we are lying. 7 But if we are living in the light of God's presence, just as Christ does, then we have wonderful fellowship and joy with each other, and the blood of Jesus his Son cleanses us from every sin.

8 If we say that we have no sin, we are only fooling ourselves, and refusing to accept the truth. 9 But if we confess our sins to him,[a] he can be depended on to forgive us and to cleanse us from every wrong. [And it is perfectly proper for God to do this for us because Christ died to wash away our sins.[b]] 10 If we claim we have not sinned, we are lying and calling God a liar, *for he says we have sinned.*

[*a*] Implied. Literally, "if we confess our sins." [*b*] Literally, "he is . . . just."

Today's English Version

God is light

5 Now this is the message that we have heard from his Son and announce to you: God is light and there is no darkness at all in him. 6 If, then, we say that we have fellowship with him, yet at the same time live in the darkness, we are lying both in our words and in our actions. 7 But if we live in the light—just as he is in the light—then we have fellowship with one another, and the blood of Jesus, his Son, makes us clean from every sin.

8 If we say that we have no sin, we deceive ourselves and there is no truth in us. 9 But if we confess our sins to God, he will keep his promise and do what is right: he will forgive us our sins and make us clean from all our wrongdoing. 10 If we say that we have not sinned, we make a liar out of God, and his word is not in us.

New International Version

Walking in the light

5 This is the message we have heard from him and declare to you: God is light; in him there is no darkness at all. 6 If we claim to have fellowship with him yet walk in the darkness, we lie and do not put the truth into practice. 7 But if we walk in the light, as he is in the light, we have fellowship with one another, and the blood of Jesus, his Son, purifies us from every sin.

8 If we claim to be without sin, we deceive ourselves and the truth is not in us. 9 If we confess our sins, he is faithful and just and will forgive us our sins and purify us from all unrighteousness. 10 If we claim we have not sinned, we make him out to be a liar, and his word has no place in our lives.

Phillips Modern English

1.5 Experience of living "in the light"

Here, then, is the message which we heard from him, and now proclaim to you: GOD IS LIGHT and no shadow of darkness can exist in him. Consequently, if we were to say that we enjoyed fellowship with him and still went on living in darkness, we should be both telling and living a lie. But if we really are living in the same light in which he eternally exists, then we have true fellowship with each other, and the blood which his son Jesus shed for us keeps us clean from all sin. If we refuse to admit that we are sinners, then we live in a world of illusion and truth becomes a stranger to us. But if we freely admit that we have sinned, we find him reliable and just—he forgives our sins and makes us thoroughly clean from all that is evil. For if we say "we have not sinned", we are making him a liar and cut ourselves off from what he has to say to us.

Revised Standard Version

5 This is the message we have heard from
him and proclaim to you, that God is light and
in him is no darkness at all. 6 If we say we have
fellowship with him while we walk in darkness,
we lie and do not live according to the truth;
7 but if we walk in the light, as he is in the light,
we have fellowship with one another, and the
blood of Jesus his Son cleanses us from all sin.
8 If we say we have no sin, we deceive ourselves, and the truth is not in us. 9 If we confess our sins, he is faithful and just, and will
forgive our sins and cleanse us from all unrighteousness. 10 If we say we have not sinned, we
make him a liar, and his word is not in us.

Jerusalem Bible

I. Walk in the light

5 This is what we have heard from him,
and the message that we are announcing to you:
God is light; there is no darkness in him at all.
6 If we say that we are in union with God [a]
while we are living in darkness,
we are lying because we are not living the truth.
7 But if we live our lives in the light,
as he is in the light,
we are in union with one another,
and the blood of Jesus, his Son,
purifies us from all sin.

First condition: break with sin

8 If we say we have no sin in us,
we are deceiving ourselves
and refusing to admit the truth;
9 but if we acknowledge our sins,
then God who is faithful and just
will forgive our sins and purify us
from everything that is wrong.
10 To say that we have never sinned
is to call God a liar
and to show that his word is not in us.

[a] In the translation, "God" or "Christ" has been used in several places, where the Greek has a simple pronoun, in order to make the writer's meaning clear.

New English Bible

Here is the message we heard from him and pass on to you: that God is light, and in him there is no darkness at all. If we claim to be sharing in his life while we walk in the dark, our words and our lives are a lie; but if we walk in the light as he himself is in the light, then we share together a common life, and we are being cleansed from every sin by the blood of Jesus his Son.

If we claim to be sinless, we are self-deceived and strangers to the truth. If we confess our sins, he is just, and may be trusted to forgive our sins and cleanse us from every kind of wrong; but if we say we have committed no sin, we make him out to be a liar, and then his word has no place in us.

King James Version

2 My little children, these things write I unto
you, that ye sin not. And if any man sin, we
have an advocate with the Father, Jesus Christ
the righteous: 2And he is the propitiation for
our sins: and not for ours only, but also for
the sins of the whole world. 3And hereby we do
know that we know him, if we keep his commandments. 4 He that saith, I know him, and
keepeth not his commandments, is a liar, and
the truth is not in him. 5 But whoso keepeth his
word, in him verily is the love of God perfected:
hereby know we that we are in him. 6 He that
saith he abideth in him ought himself also so to
walk, even as he walked. 7 Brethren, I write no
new commandment unto you, but an old com-

Living Bible

2 My little children, I am telling you this so
that you will stay away from sin. But if you
sin, there is someone to plead for you before
the Father. His name is Jesus Christ, the one
who is all that is good and who pleases God
completely. 2 He is the one who took God's
wrath against our sins upon himself, and brought
us into fellowship with God; and he is the forgiveness[a] for our sins, and not only ours but all
the world's.
3 And how can we be sure that we belong to
him? By looking within ourselves: are we really
trying to do what he wants us to?
4 Someone may say, "I am a Christian; I am
on my way to heaven; I belong to Christ." But
if he doesn't do what Christ tells him to, he is
a liar. 5 But those who do what Christ tells
them will learn to love God more and more.
That is the way to know whether or not you are
a Christian. 6Anyone who says he is a Christian
should live as Christ did.
7 Dear brothers, I am not writing out a new
rule for you to obey, for it is an old one you

[*a*] Or, "atoning sacrifice."

Today's English Version

Christ our helper

2 I write you this, my children, so that you
will not sin; but if anyone does sin, we have
Jesus Christ, the righteous, who pleads for us
with the Father. 2And Christ himself is the
means by which our sins are forgiven, and not
our sins only, but also the sins of all men.
3 If we obey God's commands, then we are
sure that we know him. 4 If someone says, "I
do know him," but does not obey his commands, such a person is a liar and there is no
truth in him. 5 But whoever obeys his word is
the one whose love for God has really been
made perfect. This is how we can be sure that
we live in God: 6 whoever says that he lives in
God should live just as Jesus Christ did.

The new command

7 My dear friends, this command I write you
is not new; it is the old command, the one you

New International Version

2 My dear children, I write this to you so
that you will not sin. But if anybody does
sin, we have one who speaks to the Father in our
defense—Jesus Christ, the Righteous One. 2 He
is the atoning sacrifice for our sins, and not only
for ours but also for the sins of the whole world.
3 We can be sure we know him if we obey
his commands. 4 The man who says, "I know
him," but does not do what he commands is a
liar, and the truth is not in him. 5 But if anyone obeys his word, God's love is truly made
complete in him. This is how we know we are
in him: 6 Whoever claims to live in him must
walk as Jesus did.
7 Dear friends, I am not writing you a new
command but an old one, which you have had

Phillips Modern English

2.1 Love and obedience are essentials for living in the light

I write these things to you, my children, to help you to avoid sin. But if a man should sin, remember that our advocate before the Father is Jesus Christ and he is just, the one who made personal atonement for our sins (and for those of the rest of the world as well). It is only when we obey God's laws that we can be quite sure that we really know him. The man who claims to know God but does not obey his laws is not only a liar but lives in self-delusion. But the more a man obeys God's laws the more truly and fully does he show his love for him. Obedience is the test of whether we really live "in God" or not. The life of a man who professes to be living in him must live as Christ lived.

I am not writing to tell you of any new command, brothers of mine. It is the old command

Revised Standard Version

2 My little children, I am writing this to you
so that you may not sin; but if any one does
sin, we have an advocate with the Father, Jesus
Christ the righteous; 2 and he is the expiation for
our sins, and not for ours only but also for the
sins of the whole world. 3 And by this we may
be sure that we know him, if we keep his commandments. 4 He who says "I know him" but
disobeys his commandments is a liar, and the
truth is not in him; 5 but whoever keeps his
word, in him truly love for God is perfected. By
this we may be sure that we are in him: 6 he
who says he abides in him ought to walk in the
same way in which he walked.
7 Beloved, I am writing you no new commandment, but an old commandment which you

Jerusalem Bible

2 I am writing this, my children,
to stop you sinning;
but if anyone should sin,
we have our advocate with the Father,
Jesus Christ, who is just;
2 he is the sacrifice that takes our sins away,
and not only ours,
but the whole world's.

Second condition: keep the commandments, especially the law of love

3 We can be sure that we know God
only by keeping his commandments.
4 Anyone who says, "I know him,"
and does not keep his commandments,
is a liar,
refusing to admit the truth.
5 But when anyone does obey what he has said,
God's love comes to perfection in him.
We can be sure
that we are in God
6 only when the one who claims to be living in him
is living the same kind of life as Christ lived.
7 My dear people,
this is not a new commandment that I am writing to tell you,

New English Bible

2 My children, in writing thus to you my purpose is that you should not commit sin. But should anyone commit a sin, we have one to plead our cause[a] with the Father, Jesus Christ, and he is just. He is himself the remedy for the defilement of our sins, not our sins only but the sins of all the world.

Here is the test by which we can make sure that we know him: do we keep his commands? The man who says, 'I know him', while he disobeys his commands, is a liar and a stranger to the truth; but in the man who is obedient to his word, the divine love has indeed come to its perfection.

Here is the test by which we can make sure that we are in him: whoever claims to be dwelling in him, binds himself to live as Christ himself lived. Dear friends, I give you no new command. It is the old command which you

[a] *Literally* we have an advocate . . .

King James Version

mandment which ye had from the beginning.
The old commandment is the word which ye
have heard from the beginning. 8Again, a new
commandment I write unto you, which thing
is true in him and in you: because the darkness
is past, and the true light now shineth. 9 He
that saith he is in the light, and hateth his
brother, is in darkness even until now. 10 He
that loveth his brother abideth in the light, and
there is none occasion of stumbling in him.
11 But he that hateth his brother is in darkness,
and walketh in darkness, and knoweth not
whither he goeth, because that darkness hath
blinded his eyes. 12 I write unto you, little children, because your sins are forgiven you for his
name's sake. 13 I write unto you, fathers, because ye have known him *that is* from the
beginning. I write unto you, young men, because
ye have overcome the wicked one. I write unto
you, little children, because ye have known the

Living Bible

have always had, right from the start. You have
heard it all before. 8 Yet it is always new, and
works for you just as it did for Christ; and as
we obey this commandment, *to love one another*,
the darkness in our lives disappears and the new
light of life in Christ shines in.
9 Anyone who says he is walking in the light
of Christ but dislikes his fellow man, is still in
darkness. 10 But whoever loves his fellow man
is "walking in the light" and can see his way
without stumbling around in darkness and sin.
11 For he who dislikes his brother is wandering
in spiritual darkness and doesn't know where he
is going, for the darkness has made him blind
so that he cannot see the way.
12 I am writing these things to all of you,
my little children, because your sins have been
forgiven in the name of Jesus our Savior. 13 I
am saying these things to you older men because
you really know Christ, the one who has been
alive from the beginning. And you young men,
I am talking to you because you have won your
battle with Satan. And I am writing to you
younger boys and girls because you, too, have
learned to know God our Father.

Today's English Version

have had from the very beginning. The old
command is the message you have already heard.
8 However, the command I write you is new,
and its truth is seen in Christ and also in you.
For the darkness is passing away, and the real
light is already shining.
9 Whoever says that he is in the light, yet
hates his brother, is in the darkness to this very
hour. 10 Whoever loves his brother stays in the
light, and so there is nothing in him that will
cause someone else to sin. 11 But whoever hates
his brother is in the darkness; he walks in it and
does not know where he is going, because the
darkness has made him blind.
12 I write to you, my children, because your
sins are forgiven for the sake of Christ's name.
13 I write to you, fathers, because you know
him who has existed from the beginning. I write
to you, young men, because you have defeated
the Evil One.
14 I write to you, children, because you know

New International Version

since the beginning. This old command is the
message you have heard. 8 Yet I am writing you
a new command; its truth is seen in him and
you, because the darkness is passing and the
true light is already shining.
9 Anyone who claims to be in the light but
hates his brother is still in the darkness. 10 Whoever loves his brother lives in the light, and there
is nothing in him[b] to make him stumble. 11 But
whoever hates his brother is in the darkness and
walks around in the darkness; he does not know
where he is going, because the darkness has
blinded him.

12 I write to you, dear children,
because your sins have been forgiven on account of his name.
13 I write to you, fathers,
because you have known him who is from the beginning.
I write to you, young men,
because you have overcome the evil one.
I write to you, dear children,
because you have known the Father.

[b] Or *it*.

Phillips Modern English

which you had at the beginning; it is the old message which you have heard before. And yet as I write it to you again I know that it is true—in your life as it was in his. For the darkness is beginning to lift and the true light is already shining. Anyone who claims to be "in the light" and hates his brother is, in fact, still in complete darkness. The man who loves his brother lives in the light, and has no reason to stumble. But the man who hates his brother is shut off from the light and gropes his way in the dark without knowing where he is going. For the darkness has made him blind.

2.12 As I write I visualise you, my children

I write this letter to you all, as my dear children, because your sins are forgiven for his name's sake. I write to you, fathers, because you have known him who has always existed. And to you young men I am writing because you have defeated the evil one. I have written to you, dear children, because you have known the Father;

Revised Standard Version

had from the beginning; the old commandment
is the word which you have heard. 8 Yet I am
writing you a new commandment, which is true
in him and in you, because[b] the darkness is
passing away and the true light is already shining. 9 He who says he is in the light and hates
his brother is in the darkness still. 10 He who
loves his brother abides in the light, and in it[c]
there is no cause for stumbling. 11 But he who
hates his brother is in the darkness and walks
in the darkness, and does not know where he is
going, because the darkness has blinded his eyes.
12 I am writing to you, little children, because
your sins are forgiven for his sake. 13 I am writing to you, fathers, because you know him who
is from the beginning. I am writing to you, young
men, because you have overcome the evil one. I
write to you, children, because you know the

[b] Or *that*. [c] Or *him*.

Jerusalem Bible

but an old commandment
that you were given from the beginning,
the original commandment which was the message brought to you.

8 Yet in another way, what I am writing to you,
and what is being carried out in your lives as it was in his,
is a new commandment;
because the night is over
and the real light is already shining.

9 Anyone who claims to be in the light
but hates his brother
is still in the dark.

10 But anyone who loves his brother is living in the light
and need not be afraid of stumbling;

11 unlike the man who hates his brother and is in the darkness,
not knowing where he is going,
because it is too dark to see.

Third condition: detachment from the world

12 I am writing to you, my own children,
whose sins have already been forgiven through his name;

13 I am writing to you, fathers,
who have come to know the one
who has existed since the beginning;
I am writing to you, young men,
who have already overcome the Evil One;

14 I have written to you, children,
because you already know the Father;

New English Bible

always had before you; the old command is the message which you heard at the beginning. And yet again it is a new command that I am giving you—new in the sense that the darkness is passing and the real light already shines. Christ has made this true, and it is true in your own experience.

A man may say, 'I am in the light'; but if he hates his brother, he is still in the dark. Only the man who loves his brother dwells in light: there is nothing to make him stumble. But one who hates his brother is in darkness; he walks in the dark and has no idea where he is going, because the darkness has made him blind.

I write to you, my children, because your sins have been forgiven for his sake.[a]
I write to you, fathers, because you know him who is and has been from the beginning.[b]
I write to you, young men, because you have mastered the evil one.

To you, children, I have written because you know the Father.

[a] *Or* forgiven, since you bear his name. [b] *Or* him whom we have known from the beginning.

King James Version

Father. 14 I have written unto you, fathers, because ye have known him *that is* from the beginning. I have written unto you, young men, because ye are strong, and the word of God abideth in you, and ye have overcome the wicked one. 15 Love not the world, neither the things *that are* in the world. If any man love the world, the love of the Father is not in him. 16 For all that *is* in the world, the lust of the flesh, and the lust of the eyes, and the pride of life, is not of the Father, but is of the world. 17 And the world passeth away, and the lust thereof: but he that doeth the will of God abideth for ever. 18 Little children, it is the last time: and as ye have heard that antichrist shall come, even now are there many antichrists; whereby we know that it is the last time. 19 They went out from us, but they were not of us; for if they

Living Bible

14 And so I say to you fathers who know the eternal God, and to you young men who are strong, with God's Word in your hearts, and have won your struggle against Satan: 15 Stop loving this evil world and all that it offers you, for when you love these things you show that you do not really love God; 16 for all these worldly things, these evil desires—the craze for sex, the ambition to buy everything that appeals to you, and the pride that comes from wealth and importance—these are not from God. They are from this evil world itself. 17 And this world is fading away, and these evil, forbidden things will go with it, but whoever keeps doing the will of God will live forever.

18 Dear children, this world's last hour has come. You have heard about the Anti-christ who is coming—the one who is against Christ—and already many such persons have appeared. This makes us all the more certain that the end of the world is near. 19 These "against-Christ" people used to be members of our churches, but

Today's English Version

the Father. I write to you, fathers, because you know him who has existed from the beginning. I write to you, young men, because you are strong; the word of God lives in you and you have defeated the Evil One.

15 Do not love the world or anything that belongs to the world. If you love the world, you do not have the love for the Father in you. 16 Everything that belongs to the world—what the sinful self desires, what people see and want, and everything in this world that people are so proud of—none of this comes from the Father; it all comes from the world. 17 The world and everything in it that men desire is passing away; but he who does what God wants lives forever.

The Enemy of Christ

18 My children, the end is near! You were told that the Enemy of Christ would come; and now many enemies of Christ have already appeared, and so we know that the end is near. 19 These people really did not belong to our group, and that is why they left us; if they had

New International Version

14 I write to you, fathers,
because you have known him who is from the beginning.
I write to you, young men,
because you are strong,
and the word of God lives in you,
and you have overcome the evil one.

Do not love the world

15 Do not love the world or anything in the world. If anyone loves the world, the love of the Father is not in him. 16 For everything in the world—the cravings of sinful man, the lust of his eyes and his pride in possessions—comes not from the Father but from the world. 17 The world and its desires pass away, but the man who does the will of God lives forever.

Warning against antichrists

18 Dear children, this is the last hour; and as you have heard that the antichrist is coming, even now many antichrists have come. This is how we know it is the last hour. 19 They went out from us, but they did not really belong to

Phillips Modern English

to you fathers because you have known the one who has always existed, and to you young men because you have all the vigour of youth, because God's truth is at home in you and because you have defeated the evil one.

2.15 See "the world" for what it is

Never give your hearts to this world or to any of the things in it. A man cannot love the Father and love the world at the same time. For the whole world-system, based as it is on men's desires, their greedy ambitions and the glamour of all that they think splendid, is not derived from the Father at all, but from the world itself. The world and all its passionate desires will one day disappear. But the man who is following God's will is part of the permanent and cannot die.

2.18 Little anti-christs are abroad already

Even now, dear children, we are getting near the last hour. You have heard about the coming of anti-Christ. Believe me, there are anti-christs about already, which confirms my belief that we are near the last hour. These men went out from our company, it is true, but they never

Revised Standard Version

Father. 14 I write to you, fathers, because you
know him who is from the beginning. I write to
you, young men, because you are strong, and
the word of God abides in you, and you have
overcome the evil one.
15 Do not love the world or the things in the
world. If any one loves the world, love for
the Father is not in him. 16 For all that is in the
world, the lust of the flesh and the lust of the
eyes and the pride of life, is not of the Father
but is of the world. 17 And the world passes
away, and the lust of it; but he who does the will
of God abides for ever.

18 Children, it is the last hour; and as you
have heard that antichrist is coming, so now
many antichrists have come; therefore we know
that it is the last hour. 19 They went out from us,
but they were not of us; for if they had been of

Jerusalem Bible

I have written to you, fathers,
because you have come to know the one
who has existed since the beginning;
I have written to you, young men,
because you are strong and God's word has made its home in you,
and you have overcome the Evil One.
15 You must not love this passing world
or anything that is in the world.
The love of the Father cannot be
in any man who loves the world,
16 because nothing the world has to offer
—the sensual body,
the lustful eye,
pride in possessions—
could ever come from the Father
but only from the world;
17 and the world, with all it craves for,
is coming to an end;
but anyone who does the will of God
remains for ever.

Fourth condition: be on guard against the enemies of Christ

18 Children, these are the last days;
you were told that an Antichrist must come,
and now several antichrists have already appeared;
we know from this that these are the last days.
19 Those rivals of Christ came out of our own number, but they had never really belonged;

New English Bible

To you, fathers, I have written because you know him who is and has been from the beginning.[b]
To you, young men, I have written because you are strong; God's word remains in you, and you have mastered the evil one.

Do not set your hearts on the godless world or anything in it. Anyone who loves the world is a stranger to the Father's love. Everything the world affords, all that panders to the appetites or entices the eyes, all the glamour of its life, springs not from the Father but from the godless world. And that world is passing away with all its allurements, but he who does God's will stands for evermore.

My children, this is the last hour! You were told that Antichrist was to come, and now many antichrists have appeared; which proves to us that this is indeed the last hour. They went out from our company, but never really belonged to

[b] *Or* him whom we have known from the beginning.

King James Version

had been of us, they would *no doubt* have continued with us: but *they went out,* that they
might be made manifest that they were not all
of us. 20 But ye have an unction from the Holy
One, and ye know all things. 21 I have not written unto you because ye know not the truth,
but because ye know it, and that no lie is of the
truth. 22 Who is a liar but he that denieth that
Jesus is the Christ? He is antichrist, that denieth
the Father and the Son. 23 Whosoever denieth
the Son, the same hath not the Father: [*but*] *he
that acknowledgeth the Son hath the Father
also.* 24 Let that therefore abide in you, which
ye have heard from the beginning. If that which
ye have heard from the beginning shall remain
in you, ye also shall continue in the Son, and
in the Father. 25 And this is the promise that he
hath promised us, *even* eternal life. 26 These
things have I written unto you concerning them
that seduce you. 27 But the anointing which ye
have received of him abideth in you, and ye

Living Bible

they never really belonged with us or else they
would have stayed. When they left us it proved
that they were not of us at all.
20 But you are not like that, for the Holy
Spirit has come upon you, and you know the
truth. 21 So I am not writing to you as to those
who need to know the truth, but I warn you as
those who can discern the difference between
true and false.
22 And who is the greatest liar? The one who
says that Jesus is not Christ. Such a person is
antichrist, for he does not believe in God the
Father and in his Son. 23 For a person who
doesn't believe in Christ, God's Son, can't have
God the Father either. But he who has Christ,
God's Son, has God the Father also.
24 So keep on believing what you have been
taught from the beginning. If you do, you will
always be in close fellowship with both God the
Father and his Son. 25 And he himself has promised us this: *eternal life.*
26 These remarks of mine about the Antichrist are pointed at those who would dearly
love to blindfold you and lead you astray. 27 But
you have received the Holy Spirit and he lives

Today's English Version

belonged to our group, they would have stayed
with us. But they left so that it might be clear
that none of them really belonged to our group.
20 But you have had the Holy Spirit poured
out on you by Christ, and so all of you know the
truth. 21 I write you, then, not because you do
not know the truth; instead, it is because you do
know it, and also know that no lie ever comes
from the truth.
22 Who, then, is the liar? It is he who says
that Jesus is not the Christ. This one is the
Enemy of Christ—he rejects both the Father
and the Son. 23 For whoever rejects the Son
also rejects the Father; whoever accepts the
Son has the Father also.
24 Be sure, then, to keep in your hearts the
message you heard from the beginning. If you
keep what you heard from the beginning, then
you will always live in union with the Son and
the Father. 25 And this is what Christ himself
promised to give us—eternal life.
26 I write you this about those who are trying to deceive you. 27 But as for you, Christ has
poured out his Spirit on you. As long as his

New International Version

us. For if they had belonged to us, they would
have remained with us; but their going showed
that none of them belonged to us.
20 But you have an anointing from the Holy
One, and all of you know the truth.[c] 21 I do
not write to you because you do not know the
truth, but because you do know it and because
no lie comes from the truth. 22 Who is the liar?
It is the man who denies that Jesus is the Christ.
Such a man is the antichrist—he denies the Father and the Son. 23 No one who denies the
Son has the Father; whoever acknowledges the
Son has the Father also.
24 See that what you have heard from the
beginning remains in you. If it does, you also
will remain in the Son and in the Father. 25 And
this is what he promised us—even eternal life.
26 I am writing these things to you about
those who are trying to lead you astray. 27 As
for you, the anointing you received from him

[*c*] Some MSS read *and you know all the truth.*

Phillips Modern English

really belonged to it. If they had really belonged to us they would have stayed. In fact, their going proves beyond doubt that men like that were not "our men" at all.

2.20, 21 Be on your guard against error

God has given you all a certain amount of spiritual insight, and indeed I have not written this warning as if I were writing to men who don't know what error is. I write because your eyes are clear enough to discern a lie when you come across it. And who, I ask you, is the real liar? Surely the one who denies that Jesus is the Christ. I say, therefore, that any man who refuses to acknowledge the Father and the Son is the anti-christ. The man who will not recognise the Son cannot possibly know the Father; yet the man who believes in the Son knows the Father as well.

For yourselves keep faithful to what you heard at the beginning. If you do, you will be living in fellowship with both the Father and the Son. And that means sharing his own life for ever, as he has promised.

I had to write to you about these men who try to lead you astray. Yet I know that the touch of his Spirit never leaves you, and you

Revised Standard Version

us, they would have continued with us; but they
went out, that it might be plain that they all are
not of us. 20 But you have been anointed by the
Holy One, and you all know.[d] 21 I write to you,
not because you do not know the truth, but
because you know it, and know that no lie is of
the truth. 22 Who is the liar but he who denies
that Jesus is the Christ? This is the antichrist,
he who denies the Father and the Son. 23 No one
who denies the Son has the Father. He who confesses the Son has the Father also. 24 Let what
you heard from the beginning abide in you. If
what you heard from the beginning abides in
you, then you will abide in the Son and in the
Father. 25 And this is what he has promised us,[e]
eternal life.

26 I write this to you about those who would
deceive you; 27 but the anointing which you received from him abides in you, and you have no

[*d*] Other ancient authorities read *you know everything*. [*e*] Other ancient authorities read *you*.

Jerusalem Bible

if they had belonged, they would have stayed with us;
but they left us, to prove that not one of them
ever belonged to us.
20 But you have been anointed by the Holy One,
and have all received the knowledge.
21 It is not because you do not know the truth that I am writing to you
but rather because you know it already
and know that no lie can come from the truth.
22 The man who denies that Jesus is the Christ—
he is the liar,
he is Antichrist;
and he is denying the Father as well as the Son,
23 because no one who has the Father can deny the Son,
and to acknowledge the Son is to have the Father as well.
24 Keep alive in yourselves what you were taught in the beginning:
as long as what you were taught in the beginning is alive in you,
you will live in the Son
and in the Father;
25 and what is promised to you by his own promise
is eternal life.
26 This is all that I am writing to you about the people who are trying to lead you astray.
27 But you have not lost the anointing that he gave you,

New English Bible

us; if they had, they would have stayed with us. They went out, so that it might be clear that not all in our company truly belong to it.[c]

You, no less than they, are among the initiated;[a] this is the gift of the Holy One, and by it you all have knowledge.[b] It is not because you are ignorant of the truth that I have written to you, but because you know it, and because lies, one and all, are alien to the truth.

Who is the liar? Who but he that denies that Jesus is the Christ? He is Antichrist, for he denies both the Father and the Son: to deny the Son is to be without the Father; to acknowledge the Son is to have the Father too. You therefore must keep in your hearts that which you heard at the beginning; if what you heard then still dwells in you, you will yourselves dwell in the Son and also in the Father. And this is the promise that he himself gave us, the promise of eternal life.

So much for those who would mislead you. But as for you, the initiation[c] which you received from him stays with you; you need no

[*c*] *Or* that none of them truly belong to us. [*a*] *Literally* have an anointing (*Greek* chrism). [*b*] *Some witnesses read* you have all knowledge. [*c*] *Literally* the anointing.

King James Version

need not that any man teach you: but as the same anointing teacheth you of all things, and is truth, and is no lie, and even as it hath taught you, ye shall abide in him.
28And now, little children, abide in him; that, when he shall appear, we may have confidence, and not be ashamed before him at his coming.
29 If ye know that he is righteous, ye know that every one that doeth righteousness is born of him.

3 Behold, what manner of love the Father hath bestowed upon us, that we should be called the sons of God: therefore the world knoweth us not, because it knew him not.
2 Beloved, now are we the sons of God, and it doth not yet appear what we shall be: but we know that, when he shall appear, we shall be like him;

Living Bible

within you, in your hearts, so that you don't need anyone to teach you what is right. For he teaches you all things, and he is the Truth, and no liar; and so, just as he has said, you must live in Christ, never to depart from him.

28 And now, my little children, stay in happy fellowship with the Lord so that when he comes you will be sure that all is well, and will not have to be ashamed and shrink back from meeting him.
29 Since we know that God is always good and does only right, we may rightly assume that all those who do right are his children.

3 See how very much our heavenly Father loves us, for he allows us to be called his children—think of it—and we really *are!* But since most people don't know God, naturally they don't understand that we are his children.
2 Yes, dear friends, we are already God's children, right now, and we can't even imagine what it is going to be like later on. But we do know this, that when he comes we will be like him,

Today's English Version

Spirit remains in you, you do not need anyone to teach you. For his Spirit teaches you about everything, and what he teaches is true, not false. Obey the Spirit's teaching, then, and remain in Christ.

28 Yes, my children, remain in him, so that we may be full of courage when he appears and need not hide in shame from him on the Day he comes.
29 You know that Christ is righteous; you should know, then, that everyone who does what is right is God's child.

Children of God

3 See how much the Father has loved us! His love is so great that we are called God's children—and so, in fact, we are. This is why the world does not know us: it has not known God.
2 My dear friends, we are now God's children, but it is not yet clear what we shall become. But we know that when Christ appears, we shall become like him, because we

New International Version

remains in you, and you do not need anyone to teach you. But as his anointing teaches you about all things and as that anointing is real, not counterfeit—just as it has taught you, remain in him.

Children of God

28 And now, dear children, continue in him, so that when he appears we may be confident and unashamed before him at his coming.

29 If you know that he is righteous, you know that everyone who does what is right has been born of him.

3 How great is the love the Father has lavished on us, that we should be called children of God! And that is what we are! The reason the world does not know us is that it did not know him.
2 Dear friends, now we are children of God, and what we will be has not yet been made known. But we know that when he appears,[d] we shall be like him, for we shall see

[d] Or *when it is made known.*

Phillips Modern English

don't really need a human teacher. You know that his Spirit teaches you about all things, always telling you the truth and never telling you a lie. So, as he has taught you, live continually in him. Yes, now, little children remember to live continually in him. So that if he were to reveal himself we should have confidence, and not have to shrink away from his presence in shame.

2.29 *What it means to be sons of God*

You all know that God is really good. You may be just as sure that the man who leads a really good life is a true child of God.

Consider the incredible love that the Father has shown us in allowing us to be called "children of God"—and that is not just what we are called, but what we *are*. This explains why the world will no more recognise us than it recognised Christ.

Here and now, my dear friends, we *are* God's children. We don't know what we shall become in the future. We only know that when he appears we shall be like him, for we shall see him as he is!

Revised Standard Version

need that any one should teach you; as his anointing teaches you about everything, and is true, and is no lie, just as it has taught you, abide in him.
28 And now, little children, abide in him, so
that when he appears we may have confidence
and not shrink from him in shame at his coming.
29 If you know that he is righteous, you may be
sure that every one who does right is born of him.

3 See what love the Father has given us, that
we should be called children of God; and so
we are. The reason why the world does not know
us is that it did not know him. 2 Beloved, we are
God's children now; it does not yet appear what we shall be, but we know that when he appears we shall be like him, for we shall see him as he

Jerusalem Bible

and you do not need anyone to teach you;
the anointing he gave teaches you everything;
you are anointed with truth, not with a lie,
and as it has taught you, so you must stay in him.
28 Live in Christ, then, my children,
so that if he appears, we may have full confidence,
and not turn from him in shame
at his coming.
29 You know that God is righteous—
then you must recognize that everyone whose life is righteous
has been begotten by him.

II. Live as God's children

3 Think of the love that the Father has lavished on us,
by letting us be called God's children;
and that is what we are.
Because the world refused to acknowledge him,
therefore it does not acknowledge us.
2 My dear people, we are already the children of God
but what we are to be in the future has not yet been revealed;
all we know is, that when it is revealed
we shall be like him
because we shall see him as he really is.

New English Bible

other teacher, but learn all you need to know from his initiation, which is real and no illusion. As he taught you, then, dwell in him.

Even now, my children, dwell in him, so that when he appears we may be confident and unashamed before him at his coming. If you know that he is righteous, you must recognize that every man who does right is his child.

3 How great is the love that the Father has shown to us! We were called God's children, and such we are;[d] and the reason why the godless world does not recognize us is that it has not known him. Here and now, dear friends, we are God's children; what we shall be has not yet been disclosed, but we know that when it is disclosed[e] we shall be like him,[f] because we shall

[*d*] *Or* We are called children of God! Not only called, we really are his children. [*e*] *Or* when he appears. [*f*] *Or* we are God's children, though he has not yet appeared; what we shall be we know, for when he does appear we shall be like him.

King James Version

for we shall see him as he is. 3And every man
that hath this hope in him purifieth himself,
even as he is pure. 4 Whosoever committeth sin
transgresseth also the law: for sin is the transgression of the law. 5And ye know that he was
manifested to take away our sins; and in him is
no sin. 6 Whosoever abideth in him sinneth not:
whosoever sinneth hath not seen him, neither
known him. 7 Little children, let no man deceive you: he that doeth righteousness is righteous, even as he is righteous. 8 He that committeth sin is of the devil; for the devil sinneth
from the beginning. For this purpose the Son of
God was manifested, that he might destroy the
works of the devil. 9 Whosoever is born of God
doth not commit sin; for his seed remaineth in
him: and he cannot sin, because he is born of
God. 10 In this the children of God are manifest, and the children of the devil: whosoever

Living Bible

as a result of seeing him as he really is. 3And
everyone who really believes this will try to stay
pure because Christ is pure.
4 But those who keep on sinning are against
God, for every sin is done against the will of
God. 5And you know that he became a man so
that he could take away our sins, and that there
is no sin in him, no missing of God's will at any
time in any way. 6 So if we stay close to him,
obedient to him, we won't be sinning either; but
as for those who keep on sinning, they should
realize this: They sin because they have never
really known him or become his.
7 Oh, dear children, don't let anyone deceive
you about this: if you are constantly doing what
is good, it is because you *are* good, even as he
is. 8 But if you keep on sinning, it shows that
you belong to Satan, who since he first began
to sin has kept steadily at it. But the Son of
God came to destroy these works of the devil.
9 The person who has been born into God's
family does not make a practice of sinning, because now God's life is in him; so he can't keep
on sinning, for this new life has been born into
him and controls him—he has been *born again.*
10 So now we can tell who is a child of God
and who belongs to Satan. Whoever is living a

Today's English Version

shall see him as he really is. 3 Everyone who has
this hope in Christ keeps himself pure, just as
Christ is pure.
4 Whoever sins is guilty of breaking God's
law; because sin is a breaking of the law. 5 You
know that Christ appeared in order to take
away men's sins, and that there is no sin in
him. 6 So everyone who lives in Christ does not
continue to sin; but whoever continues to sin
has never seen him or known him.
7 Let no one deceive you, children! Whoever does what is right is righteous, just as Christ
is righteous. 8 Whoever continues to sin belongs
to the Devil, because the Devil has sinned from
the very beginning. The Son of God appeared
for this very reason, to destroy the Devil's works.
9 Whoever is a child of God does not continue to sin, because God's very nature is in
him; and because God is his Father, he cannot continue to sin. 10 Here is the clear difference between God's children and the Devil's

New International Version

him as he is. 3 Everyone who has this hope in
him purifies himself, just as he is pure.
4 Everyone who sins breaks the law; in fact,
sin is lawlessness. 5 But you know that he appeared so that he might take away our sins. And
in him is no sin. 6 No one who lives in him
keeps on sinning. No one who continues to sin
has either seen him or known him.
7 Dear children, do not let anyone lead you
astray. He who does what is right is righteous,
just as he is righteous. 8 He who does what is
sinful is of the devil, because the devil has been
sinning from the beginning. The reason the Son
of God appeared was to destroy the devil's work.
9 No one who is born of God will continue to
sin, because God's seed remains in him; he cannot sin, because he has been born of God. 10 This
is how we know who the children of God are
and who the children of the devil are: Anyone

Phillips Modern English

Everyone who has at heart a hope like that keeps himself pure, as Christ is pure.

3.4 *Conduct will show who is a man's spiritual father*

Everyone who commits sin breaks God's law, for that is what sin is—a breaking of God's law. You know, moreover, that Christ became man to take away sin, and that he himself was free from sin. The man who lives "in Christ" does not habitually sin. The regular sinner has never seen or known him. You, my children, should not let anyone deceive you. The man who lives a good life is a good man, as surely as Christ is good. But the man whose life is habitually sinful is spiritually a son of the devil, for the devil has been a sinner from the beginning. Now the Son of God came to earth with the express purpose of undoing the devil's work. The man who is really God's son does not practise sin, for God's nature is in him, for good, and such a heredity is incapable of sin.

Here we have a clear indication as to who are the children of God and who are the children of

Revised Standard Version

is. 3 And every one who thus hopes in him purifies himself as he is pure.
4 Every one who commits sin is guilty of lawlessness; sin is lawlessness. 5 You know that he
appeared to take away sins, and in him there is
no sin. 6 No one who abides in him sins; no
one who sins has either seen him or known
him. 7 Little children, let no one deceive you.
He who does right is righteous, as he is righteous. 8 He who commits sin is of the devil; for
the devil has sinned from the beginning. The
reason the Son of God appeared was to destroy
the works of the devil. 9 No one born of God
commits sin; for God's[f] nature abides in him,
and he cannot sin because he is[g] born of God.
10 By this it may be seen who are the children
of God, and who are the children of the devil:

[f] Greek *his.* [g] Or *for the offspring of God abide in him, and they cannot sin because they are.*

Jerusalem Bible

First condition: break with sin

3 Surely everyone who entertains this hope
must purify himself, must try to be as pure
as Christ.
4 Anyone who sins at all
breaks the law,
because to sin is to break the law.
5 Now you know that he appeared in order
to abolish sin,
and that in him there is no sin;
6 anyone who lives in God does not sin,
and anyone who sins
has never seen him or known him.
7 My children, do not let anyone lead you
astray:
to live a holy life
is to be holy just as he is holy;
8 to lead a sinful life is to belong to the devil,
since the devil was a sinner from the beginning.
It was to undo all that the devil has done
that the Son of God appeared.
9 No one who has been begotten by God sins;
because God's seed remains inside him,
he cannot sin when he has been begotten
by God.

Second condition: keep the commandments, especially the law of love

10 In this way we distinguish the children of
God
from the children of the devil:

New English Bible

see him as he is. Everyone who has this hope before him purifies himself, as Christ is pure.

To commit sin is to break God's law: sin, in fact, is lawlessness. Christ appeared, as you know, to do away with sins, and there is no sin in him. No man therefore who dwells in him is a sinner; the sinner has not seen him and does not know him.

My children, do not be misled: it is the man who does right who is righteous, as God is righteous; the man who sins is a child of the devil, for the devil has been a sinner from the first; and the Son of God appeared for the very purpose of undoing the devil's work.

A child of God does not commit sin, because the divine seed remains in him; he cannot be a sinner, because he is God's child. That is the distinction between the children of God and the children of the devil: no one who does not do

King James Version

doeth not righteousness is not of God, neither
he that loveth not his brother. 11 For this is the
message that ye heard from the beginning, that
we should love one another. 12 Not as Cain,
who was of that wicked one, and slew his
brother. And wherefore slew he him? Because
his own works were evil, and his brother's righteous. 13 Marvel not, my brethren, if the world
hate you. 14 We know that we have passed from
death unto life, because we love the brethren.
He that loveth not *his* brother abideth in death.
15 Whosoever hateth his brother is a murderer:
and ye know that no murderer hath eternal life
abiding in him. 16 Hereby perceive we the love
of God, because he laid down his life for us:
and we ought to lay down *our* lives for the
brethren. 17 But whoso hath this world's good,
and seeth his brother have need, and shutteth
up his bowels *of compassion* from him, how
dwelleth the love of God in him? 18 My little
children, let us not love in word, neither in

Living Bible

life of sin and doesn't love his brother shows
that he is not in God's family; 11 for the message
to us from the beginning has been that we should
love one another.
12 We are not to be like Cain, who belonged
to Satan and killed his brother. Why did he kill
him? Because Cain had been doing wrong and
he knew very well that his brother's life was
better than his. 13 So don't be surprised, dear
friends, if the world hates you.
14 If we love other Christians it proves that
we have been delivered from hell and given
eternal life. But a person who doesn't have love
for others is headed for eternal death. 15 Anyone
who hates his Christian brother is really a murderer at heart; and you know that no one
wanting to murder has eternal life within. 16 We
know what real love is from Christ's example
in dying for us. And so we also ought to lay
down our lives for our Christian brothers.
17 But if someone who is supposed to be a
Christian has money enough to live well, and
sees a brother in need, and won't help him—
how can God's love be within *him?* 18 Little
children, let us stop just *saying* we love people;
let us *really* love them, and *show it* by our *ac-*

Today's English Version

children: anyone who does not do what is right,
or does not love his brother, is not God's child.

Love one another

11 The message you heard from the very beginning is this: we must love one another. 12 We
must not be like Cain; he belonged to the Evil
One, and murdered his own brother. Why did
Cain murder him? Because the things he did
were wrong, but the things his brother did were
right.
13 So do not be surprised, my brothers, if
the people of the world hate you. 14 We know
that we have left death and come over into life;
we know it because we love our brothers. Whoever does not love is still in death. 15 Whoever
hates his brother is a murderer; and you know
that a murderer does not have eternal life in
him. 16 This is how we know what love is:
Christ gave his life for us. We too, then, ought
to give our lives for our brothers! 17 If a man
is rich and sees his brother in need, yet closes
his heart against his brother, how can he claim
that he has love for God in his heart? 18 My
children! Our love should not be just words and
talk; it must be true love, which shows itself in
action.

New International Version

who does not do what is right is not a child of
God; neither is anyone who does not love his
brother.

Love one another

11 This is the message you heard from the beginning: We should love one another. 12 Do not
be like Cain, who belonged to the evil one and
murdered his brother. And why did he murder
him? Because his own actions were evil and his
brother's were righteous. 13 Do not be surprised,
my brothers, if the world hates you. 14 We know
that we have passed from death to life, because
we love our brothers. Anyone who does not
love remains in death. 15 Anyone who hates his
brother is a murderer, and you know that no
murderer has eternal life in him.
16 This is how we know what love is: Jesus
Christ laid down his life for us. And we ought
to lay down our lives for our brothers. 17 If anyone has material possessions and sees his brother
in need but has no pity on him, how can the
love of God be in him? 18 Dear children, let
us not love with words or tongue but with ac-

Phillips Modern English

the devil. The man who does not lead a good life is no son of God, nor is the man who fails to love his brother. For the original command, as you know, is that we should love one another. We are none of us to have the spirit of Cain, who was a son of the evil one and murdered his brother. Have you realised his motive? It was because he realised the goodness of his brother's life and the evil of his own. Don't be surprised, my brothers, if the world hates you.

3.14 Love and life are interconnected

We know that we have crossed the frontier from death to life because we do love our brothers. The man without love for his brother is still living in death. The man who hates his brother is at heart a murderer, and you know that the eternal life of God cannot live in the heart of a murderer.

We know what love is because Christ laid down his life for us. We must in turn lay down our lives for our brothers. But as for the well-to-do man who sees his brother in want but shuts his heart against him, how could anyone believe that the love of God lives in him? My children, let us love not merely in theory or in words—let us love in sincerity and in practice!

Revised Standard Version

whoever does not do right is not of God, nor he
who does not love his brother.
11 For this is the message which you have
heard from the beginning, that we should love
one another, 12 and not be like Cain who was
of the evil one and murdered his brother. And
why did he murder him? Because his own deeds
were evil and his brother's righteous. 13 Do not
wonder, brethren, that the world hates you.
14 We know that we have passed out of death
into life, because we love the brethren. He who
does not love abides in death. 15 Any one who
hates his brother is a murderer, and you know
that no murderer has eternal life abiding in him.
16 By this we know love, that he laid down his
life for us; and we ought to lay down our lives
for the brethren. 17 But if any one has the
world's goods and sees his brother in need, yet
closes his heart against him, how does God's
love abide in him? 18 Little children, let us not
love in word or speech but in deed and in truth.

Jerusalem Bible

anybody not living a holy life
and not loving his brother
is no child of God's.

11 This is the message
as you heard it from the beginning:
that we are to love one another;

12 not to be like Cain, who belonged to the Evil One
and cut his brother's throat;
cut his brother's throat simply for this reason,
that his own life was evil and his brother lived a good life.

13 You must not be surprised, brothers, when the world hates you;

14 we have passed out of death and into life,
and of this we can be sure
because we love our brothers.

15 If you refuse to love, you must remain dead;
to hate your brother is to be a murderer,
and murderers, as you know, do not have eternal life in them.

16 This has taught us love—
that he gave up his life for us;
and we, too, ought to give up our lives for our brothers.

17 If a man who was rich enough in this world's goods
saw that one of his brothers was in need,
but closed his heart to him,
how could the love of God be living in him?

18 My children,
our love is not to be just words or mere talk,
but something real and active;

New English Bible

right is God's child, nor is anyone who does not love his brother. For the message you have heard from the beginning is this: that we should love one another; unlike Cain, who was a child of the evil one and murdered his brother. And why did he murder him? Because his own actions were wrong, and his brother's were right.

My brothers, do not be surprised if the world hates you. We for our part have crossed over from death to life; this we know, because we love our brothers. The man who does not love is still in the realm of death, for everyone who hates his brother is a murderer, and no murderer, as you know, has eternal life dwelling within him. It is by this that we know what love is: that Christ laid down his life for us. And we in our turn are bound to lay down our lives for our brothers. But if a man has enough to live on, and yet when he sees his brother in need shuts up his heart against him, how can it be said that the divine love[a] dwells in him?

My children, love must not be a matter of words or talk; it must be genuine, and show

[a] *Or* that love for God . . .

King James Version

tongue; but in deed and in truth. 19And hereby we know that we are of the truth, and shall assure our hearts before him. 20 For if our heart condemn us, God is greater than our heart, and knoweth all things. 21 Beloved, if our heart condemn us not, *then* have we confidence toward God. 22And whatsoever we ask, we receive of him, because we keep his commandments, and do those things that are pleasing in his sight. 23And this is his commandment, That we should believe on the name of his Son Jesus Christ, and love one another, as he gave us commandment. 24And he that keepeth his commandments dwelleth in him, and he in him. And hereby we know that he abideth in us, by the Spirit which he hath given us.

4 Beloved, believe not every spirit, but try the spirits whether they are of God: because many false prophets are gone out into the world.

Living Bible

tions. 19 Then we will know for sure, by our actions, that we are on God's side, and our consciences will be clear, even when we stand before the Lord. 20 But if we have bad consciences and feel that we have done wrong, the Lord will surely feel it even more,[a] for he knows everything we do.

21 But, dearly loved friends, if our consciences are clear, we can come to the Lord with perfect assurance and trust, 22 and get whatever we ask for because we are obeying him and doing the things that please him. 23And this is what God says we must do: Believe on the name of his Son Jesus Christ, and love one another. 24 Those who do what God says—they are living with God and he with them. We know this is true because the Holy Spirit he has given us tells us so.

4 Dearly loved friends, don't always believe everything you hear just because someone says it is a message from God: test it first to see if it really is. For there are many false teachers

[*a*] Or, perhaps, "the Lord will be merciful anyway." Literally, "If our heart condemns us, God is greater than our heart."

Today's English Version

Courage before God

19 This, then, is how we will know that we belong to the truth. This is how our hearts will be confident in God's presence. 20 If our heart condemns us, we know that God is greater than our heart, and that he knows everything. 21And so, my dear friends, if our heart does not condemn us, we have courage in God's presence. 22 We receive from him whatever we ask, because we obey his commands and do what pleases him. 23 This is what he commands: that we believe in the name of his Son Jesus Christ and love one another, just as Christ commanded us. 24 Whoever obeys God's commands lives in God and God lives in him. And this is how we know that God lives in us: we know it because of the Spirit he has given us.

The true and the false Spirit

4 My dear friends: do not believe all who claim to have the Spirit, but test them to find out if the spirit they have comes from God. For many false prophets have gone out every-

New International Version

tions and in truth. 19 This then is how we know that we belong to the truth, and how we set our hearts at rest in his presence 20 whenever our hearts condemn us. For God is greater than our hearts, and he knows everything.

21 Dear friends, if our hearts do not condemn us, we have confidence before God 22 and receive from him anything we ask, because we obey his commands and do what pleases him. 23And this is his command: to believe in the name of his Son, Jesus Christ, and to love one another as he commanded us. 24 Those who obey his commands live in him, and he in them. And this is how we know that he lives in us: We know it by the Spirit he gave us.

Test the spirits

4 Dear friends, do not believe every spirit, but test the spirits to see whether they are from God, because many false prophets have

Phillips Modern English

3.19 Living in love means confidence in God

This is how we shall know that we are children of the truth and can reassure ourselves in the sight of God, even if our own conscience makes us feel guilty. For God is greater than our conscience, and he knows everything. And if, dear friends of mine, our conscience no longer accuses us, we may have the utmost confidence in God's presence. We receive whatever we ask for, because we are obeying his orders and following his wishes. His orders are that we should put our trust in the name of his Son, Jesus Christ, and love one another—as he commanded us to do.

The man who does obey God's commands lives in God and God lives in him, and the guarantee of his presence within us is the Spirit he has given us.

4.1 I repeat my warning against false teaching

Don't trust every spirit, dear friends of mine, but test them to discover whether they come from God or not. For the world is full of false

Revised Standard Version

19 By this we shall know that we are of the
truth, and reassure our hearts before him
20 whenever our hearts condemn us; for God is
greater than our hearts, and he knows everything. 21 Beloved, if our hearts do not condemn
us, we have confidence before God; 22 and we
receive from him whatever we ask, because we
keep his commandments and do what pleases
him. 23 And this is his commandment, that we
should believe in the name of his Son Jesus
Christ and love one another, just as he has commanded us. 24 All who keep his commandments
abide in him, and he in them. And by this we
know that he abides in us, by the Spirit which
he has given us.

4 Beloved, do not believe every spirit, but test the spirits to see whether they are of God; for many false prophets have gone out into

Jerusalem Bible

19 only by this can we be certain
that we are children of the truth
and be able to quiet our conscience in his presence,
20 whatever accusations it may raise against us,
because God is greater than our conscience
and he knows everything.
21 My dear people,
if we cannot be condemned by our own conscience,
we need not be afraid in God's presence,
22 and whatever we ask him,
we shall receive,
because we keep his commandments
and live the kind of life that he wants.
23 His commandments are these:
that we believe in the name of his Son Jesus Christ
and that we love one another
as he told us to.
24 Whoever keeps his commandments
lives in God and God lives in him.
We know that he lives in us
by the Spirit that he has given us.

Third condition: be on guard against the enemies of Christ and against the world

4 It is not every spirit, my dear people, that you can trust;
test them, to see if they come from God;
there are many false prophets, now, in the world.

New English Bible

itself in action. This is how we may know that we belong to the realm of truth, and convince ourselves in his sight that even if our conscience condemns us, God is greater than our conscience[b] and knows all.

Dear friends, if our conscience does not condemn us, then we can approach God with confidence, and obtain from him whatever we ask, because we are keeping his commands and doing what he approves. This is his command: to give our allegiance to his Son Jesus Christ and love one another as he commanded. When we keep his commands we dwell in him and he dwells in us. And this is how we can make sure that he dwells within us: we know it from the Spirit he has given us.

4 But do not trust any and every spirit, my friends; test the spirits, to see whether they are from God, for among those who have gone

[*b*] *Or* and reassure ourselves in his sight in matters where our conscience condemns us, because God is greater than our conscience . . .; *Or* and yet we shall do well to convince ourselves that if even our own conscience condemns us, still more will God who is greater than conscience . . .

King James Version

2 Hereby know ye the Spirit of God: Every
spirit that confesseth that Jesus Christ is come
in the flesh is of God: 3 And every spirit that
confesseth not that Jesus Christ is come in the
flesh is not of God: and this is that *spirit* of
antichrist, whereof ye have heard that it should
come; and even now already is it in the world.
4 Ye are of God, little children, and have overcome them: because greater is he that is in you,
than he that is in the world. 5 They are of the
world: therefore speak they of the world, and
the world heareth them. 6 We are of God: he
that knoweth God heareth us; he that is not of
God heareth not us. Hereby know we the spirit

Living Bible

around, 2 and the way to find out if their message is from the Holy Spirit is to ask: Does it
really agree that Jesus Christ, God's Son, actually became man with a human body? If so,
then the message is from God. 3 If not, the
message is not from God but from one who is
against Christ, like the "Antichrist" you have
heard about who is going to come, and his attitude of enmity against Christ is already abroad
in the world.
4 Dear young friends, you belong to God and
have already won your fight with those who are
against Christ, because there is someone in your
hearts who is stronger than any evil teacher in
this wicked world. 5 These men belong to this
world, so, quite naturally, they are concerned
about worldly affairs and the world pays attention to them. 6 But we are children of God;
that is why only those who have walked and
talked with God will listen to us. Others won't.
That is another way to know whether a message
is really from God; for if it is, the world won't
listen to it.

Today's English Version

where. 2 This is how you will be able to know
whether it is God's Spirit: anyone who declares
that Jesus Christ came as a human being has
the Spirit who comes from God. 3 But anyone
who denies this about Jesus does not have the
Spirit from God. This spirit is from the Enemy
of Christ; you heard that it would come, and
now it is here in the world already.
4 But you belong to God, my children, and
have defeated the false prophets; because the
Spirit who is in you is more powerful than the
spirit in those who belong to the world. 5 They
speak about matters of the world and the world
listens to them because they belong to the
world. 6 But we belong to God. Whoever knows
God listens to us; whoever does not belong to
God does not listen to us. This is the way, then,
that we can tell the difference between the Spirit
of truth and the spirit of error.

New International Version

gone out into the world. 2 This is how you can
recognize the Spirit of God: Every spirit that
acknowledges that Jesus Christ has come in the
flesh is from God, 3 but every spirit that does
not acknowledge Jesus is not from God. This is
the spirit of the antichrist, which you have
heard is coming and even now is already in the
world.
4 You, dear children, are from God and have
overcome them, because the one who is in you
is greater than the one who is in the world.
5 They are from the world and therefore speak
from the viewpoint of the world, and the world
listens to them. 6 We are from God, and whoever knows God listens to us; but whoever is
not from God does not listen to us. This is how
we recognize the Spirit[e] of truth and the spirit
of falsehood.

[e] Or *spirit*.

Phillips Modern English

prophets. You can test whether they come from God in this simple way: every spirit that acknowledges the fact that Jesus Christ actually became man, comes from God, but the spirit which denies this fact does not come from God. The latter comes from the anti-Christ, which you were warned would come and which is already in the world.

You, my children, who belong to God have already defeated them, because the one who lives in you is stronger than the anti-Christ in the world. The agents of the anti-Christ are children of the world, they speak the world's language and the world pays attention to what they say. We are God's children and the man who knows God hears our message; what we say means nothing to the man who is not himself a child of God.

This gives us a ready means of distinguishing the spirit of truth from the spirit of falsehood.

Revised Standard Version

the world. 2 By this you know the Spirit of God:
every spirit which confesses that Jesus Christ has
come in the flesh is of God, 3 and every spirit
which does not confess Jesus is not of God. This
is the spirit of antichrist, of which you heard
that it was coming, and now it is in the world
already. 4 Little children, you are of God, and
have overcome them; for he who is in you is
greater than he who is in the world. 5 They are
of the world, therefore what they say is of the
world, and the world listens to them. 6 We are
of God. Whoever knows God listens to us, and
he who is not of God does not listen to us. By
this we know the spirit of truth and the spirit of
error.

Jerusalem Bible

2 You can tell the spirits that come from God by this:
every spirit which acknowledges that Jesus the Christ has come in the flesh
is from God;
3 but any spirit which will not say this of Jesus
is not from God,
but is the spirit of Antichrist,
whose coming you were warned about.
Well, now he is here, in the world.
4 Children,
you have already overcome these false prophets,
because you are from God and you have in you
one who is greater than anyone in this world;
5 as for them, they are of the world,
and so they speak the language of the world
and the world listens to them.
6 But we are children of God,
and those who know God listen to us;
those who are not of God refuse to listen to us.
This is how we can tell
the spirit of truth from the spirit of falsehood.

New English Bible

out into the world there are many prophets falsely inspired. This is how we may recognize the Spirit of God: every spirit which acknowledges that Jesus Christ has come in the flesh is from God, and every spirit which does not thus acknowledge Jesus is not from God. This is what is meant by 'Antichrist';[a] you have been told that he was to come, and here he is, in the world already!

But you, my children, are of God's family, and you have the mastery over these false prophets, because he who inspires you is greater than he who inspires the godless world. They are of that world, and so therefore is their teaching; that is why the world listens to them. But we belong to God, and a man who knows God listens to us, while he who does not belong to God refuses us a hearing. That is how we distinguish the spirit of truth from the spirit of error.

[a] *Or* This is the spirit of Antichrist.

King James Version

of truth, and the spirit of error. 7 Beloved, let us
love one another: for love is of God; and every
one that loveth is born of God, and knoweth
God. 8 He that loveth not, knoweth not God;
for God is love. 9 In this was manifested the
love of God toward us, because that God sent
his only begotten Son into the world, that we
might live through him. 10 Herein is love, not
that we loved God, but that he loved us, and
sent his Son *to be* the propitiation for our sins.
11 Beloved, if God so loved us, we ought also to
love one another. 12 No man hath seen God at
any time. If we love one another, God dwelleth
in us, and his love is perfected in us. 13 Hereby
know we that we dwell in him, and he in us,
because he hath given us of his Spirit. 14 And
we have seen and do testify that the Father sent
the Son *to be* the Saviour of the world. 15 Whosoever shall confess that Jesus is the Son of
God, God dwelleth in him, and he in God.

Living Bible

7 Dear friends, let us practice loving each
other, for love comes from God and those who
are loving and kind show that they are the
children of God, and that they are getting to
know him better. 8 But if a person isn't loving
and kind, it shows that he doesn't know God—
for God is love.

9 God showed how much he loved us by
sending his only Son into this wicked world to
bring to us eternal life through his death. 10 In
this act we see what real love is: it is not our
love for God, but his love for us when he sent
his Son to satisfy God's anger against our sins.

11 Dear friends, since God loved us as much
as that, we surely ought to love each other too.
12 For though we have never yet seen God,
when we love each other God lives in us and
his love within us grows ever stronger. 13 And
he has put his own Holy Spirit into our hearts
as a proof to us that we are living with him and
he with us. 14 And furthermore, we have seen
with our own eyes and now tell all the world
that God sent his Son to be their Savior. 15 Anyone who believes and says that Jesus is the Son
of God has God living in him, and he is living
with God.

Today's English Version

God is love

7 Dear friends! Let us love one another, because love comes from God. Whoever loves is
a child of God and knows God. 8 Whoever does
not love does not know God, because God is
love. 9 This is how God showed his love for us:
he sent his only Son into the world that we
might have life through him. 10 This is what
love is: it is not that we have loved God, but
that he loved us and sent his Son to be the
means by which our sins are forgiven.

11 Dear friends, if this is how God loved us,
then we should love one another. 12 No one has
ever seen God; if we love one another, God lives
in us and his love is made perfect in us.

13 This is how we are sure that we live in
God and he lives in us: he has given us his
Spirit. 14 And we have seen and tell others that
the Father sent his Son to be the Savior of the
world. 15 Whoever declares that Jesus is the
Son of God, God lives in him, and he lives in

New International Version

God's love and ours

7 Dear friends, let us love one another, for
love comes from God. Everyone who loves has
been born of God and knows God. 8 Whoever
does not love does not know God, because God
is love. 9 This is how God showed his love
among us: He sent his one and only Son[f] into
the world that we might live through him. 10 This
is love: not that we loved God, but that he
loved us and sent his Son as an atoning sacrifice
for our sins. 11 Dear friends, since God so loved
us, we also ought to love one another. 12 No one
has ever seen God; but if we love each other,
God lives in us and his love is made complete
in us.

13 We know that we live in him and he in us,
because he has given us of his Spirit. 14 And we
have seen and testify that the Father has sent
his Son to be the Savior of the world. 15 If anyone acknowledges that Jesus is the Son of God,

[f] Or *his only begotten Son.*

Phillips Modern English

4.7 *Let us love: God has shown us love at its highest*

To you whom I love I say, let us go on loving one another, for love comes from God. Every man who truly loves is God's son and knows him. But the man who does not love cannot know him at all, for God is love.

To us, the greatest demonstration of God's love for us has been his sending his only Son into the world to give us life through him. We see real love, not in the fact that we loved God, but that he loved us and sent his Son to make personal atonement for our sins. If God loved us as much as that, surely we, in our turn, should love each other!

It is true that no human being has ever had a direct vision of God. Yet if we love each other God does actually live within us, and his love grows in us towards perfection. And the guarantee of our living in him and his living in us is the share of his own Spirit which he gives us.

4.14 *Knowing Christ means more love and confidence, less and less fear*

We ourselves are eye-witnesses able and willing to testify to the fact that the Father did send the Son to save the world. Everyone who acknowledges that Jesus is the Son of God finds

Revised Standard Version

7 Beloved, let us love one another; for love
is of God, and he who loves is born of God and
knows God. 8 He who does not love does not
know God; for God is love. 9 In this the love of
God was made manifest among us, that God
sent his only Son into the world, so that we
might live through him. 10 In this is love, not
that we loved God but that he loved us and
sent his Son to be the expiation for our sins.
11 Beloved, if God so loved us, we also ought to
love one another. 12 No man has ever seen God;
if we love one another, God abides in us and his
love is perfected in us.
13 By this we know that we abide in him and
he in us, because he has given us of his own
Spirit. 14 And we have seen and testify that the
Father has sent his Son as the Savior of the
world. 15 Whoever confesses that Jesus is the
Son of God, God abides in him, and he in God.

Jerusalem Bible

III. Love and faith

Love

7 My dear people,
let us love one another
since love comes from God
and everyone who loves is begotten by God
and knows God.
8 Anyone who fails to love can never have
known God,
because God is love.
9 God's love for us was revealed
when God sent into the world his only Son
so that we could have life through him;
10 this is the love I mean:
not our love for God,
but God's love for us when he sent his Son
to be the sacrifice that takes our sins away.
11 My dear people,
since God has loved us so much,
we too should love one another.
12 No one has ever seen God;
but as long as we love one another
God will live in us
and his love will be complete in us.
13 We can know that we are living in him
and he is living in us
because he lets us share his Spirit.
14 We ourselves saw and we testify
that the Father sent his Son
as savior of the world.
15 If anyone acknowledges that Jesus is the
Son of God,
God lives in him, and he in God.

New English Bible

Dear friends, let us love one another, because love is from God. Everyone who loves is a child of God and knows God, but the unloving know nothing of God. For God is love; and his love was disclosed to us in this, that he sent his only Son into the world to bring us life. The love I speak of is not our love for God, but the love he showed to us in sending his Son as the remedy for the defilement of our sins. If God thus loved us, dear friends, we in turn are bound to love one another. Though God has never been seen by any man, God himself dwells in us if we love one another; his love is brought to perfection within us.

Here is the proof that we dwell in him and he dwells in us: he has imparted his Spirit to us. Moreover, we have seen for ourselves, and we attest, that the Father sent the Son to be the saviour of the world, and if a man acknowledges that Jesus is the Son of God, God dwells in him

King James Version

16And we have known and believed the love that God hath to us. God is love; and he that dwelleth in love dwelleth in God, and God in him. 17 Herein is our love made perfect, that we may have boldness in the day of judgment: because as he is, so are we in this world. 18 There is no fear in love; but perfect love casteth out fear: because fear hath torment. He that feareth is not made perfect in love. 19 We love him, because he first loved us. 20 If a man say, I love God, and hateth his brother, he is a liar: for he that loveth not his brother whom he hath seen, how can he love God whom he hath not seen? 21 And this commandment have we from him, That he who loveth God love his brother also.

5 Whosoever believeth that Jesus is the Christ is born of God: and every one that loveth him that begat loveth him also that is begotten of him. 2 By this we know that we love the chil-

Living Bible

16 We know how much God loves us because we have felt his love and because we believe him when he tells us that he loves us dearly. God is love, and anyone who lives in love is living with God and God is living in him. 17And as we live with Christ, our love grows more perfect and complete; so we will not be ashamed and embarrassed at the day of judgment, but can face him with confidence and joy, because he loves us and we love him too.

18 We need have no fear of someone who loves us perfectly; his perfect love for us eliminates all dread of what he might do to us. If we are afraid, it is for fear of what he might do to us, and shows that we are not fully convinced that he really loves us. 19 So you see, our love for him comes as a result of his loving us first.

20 If anyone says "I love God," but keeps on hating his brother, he is a liar; for if he doesn't love his brother who is right there in front of him, how can he love God whom he has never seen? 21And God himself has said that one must love not only God, but his brother too.

5 If you believe that Jesus is the Christ—that he is God's Son and your Savior—then you are a child of God. And all who love the Father love his children too. 2 So you can find

Today's English Version

God. 16And we ourselves know and believe the love which God has for us.

God is love, and whoever lives in love lives in God and God lives in him. 17 The purpose of love being made perfect in us is that we may have courage on Judgment Day; and we will have it because our life in this world is the same as Christ's. 18 There is no fear in love; perfect love drives out all fear. So then, love has not been made perfect in the one who fears, because fear has to do with punishment.

19 We love because God first loved us. 20 If someone says, "I love God," but hates his brother, he is a liar. For he cannot love God, whom he has not seen, if he does not love his brother, whom he has seen. 21 This, then, is the command that Christ gave us: he who loves God must love his brother also.

Our victory over the world

5 Whoever believes that Jesus is the Messiah is a child of God; and whoever loves a father loves his child also. 2 This is how we

New International Version

God lives in him and he in God. 16And so we know and rely on the love God has for us.

God is love. Whoever lives in love lives in God, and God in him. 17 Love is made complete among us so that we will have confidence on the day of judgment, because in this world we are like him. 18 There is no fear in love. But perfect love drives out fear, because fear has to do with punishment. The man who fears is not made perfect in love.

19 We love because he first loved us. 20 If anyone says, "I love God," yet hates his brother, he is a liar. For anyone who does not love his brother, whom he has seen, cannot love God, whom he has not seen. 21And he has given us this command: Whoever loves God must also love his brother.

Faith in the Son of God

5 Everyone who believes that Jesus is the Christ is born of God, and everyone who loves the father loves his child as well. 2 This is

Phillips Modern English

that God lives in him, and he lives in God. So have we come to know and trust the love God has for us. God *is* love, and the man whose life is lived in love does, in fact, live in God, and God does, in fact, live in him. So our love for him grows more and more, filling us with complete confidence for the day when he shall judge all men—for we realise that our life in this world is actually his life lived in us. Love contains no fear—indeed fully-developed love expels every particle of fear, for fear always contains some of the torture of feeling guilty. The man who lives in fear has not yet had his love perfected.

Yes, we love because he first loved us. If a man says, "I love God" and hates his brother, he is a liar. For if he does not love the brother before his eyes how can he love the one beyond his sight? And in any case it is his explicit command that the one who loves God must love his brother too.

5.1 *Only real faith in Christ as God's son can make a man confident, obedient and loving*

Everyone who really believes that Jesus is the Christ is himself one of God's family. The man who loves the Father cannot help loving the Father's sons.

The test of our love for God's family lies in

Revised Standard Version

16 So we know and believe the love God has
for us. God is love, and he who abides in love
abides in God, and God abides in him. 17 In this
is love perfected with us, that we may have confidence for the day of judgment, because as he is
so are we in this world. 18 There is no fear in
love, but perfect love casts out fear. For fear
has to do with punishment, and he who fears is
not perfected in love. 19 We love, because he
first loved us. 20 If any one says, "I love God,"
and hates his brother, he is a liar; for he who does
not love his brother whom he has seen, cannot[h]
love God whom he has not seen. 21 And this
commandment we have from him, that he who
loves God should love his brother also.

5 Every one who believes that Jesus is the
Christ is a child of God, and every one who
loves the parent loves the child. 2 By this we

[*h*] Other ancient authorities read *how can he.*

Jerusalem Bible

16 We ourselves have known and put our faith in
God's love toward ourselves.
God is love
and anyone who lives in love lives in God,
and God lives in him.
17 Love will come to its perfection in us
when we can face the day of Judgment without fear;
because even in this world
we have become as he is.
18 In love there can be no fear,
but fear is driven out by perfect love:
because to fear is to expect punishment,
and anyone who is afraid is still imperfect in love.
19 We are to love, then,
because he loved us first.
20 Anyone who says, "I love God,"
and hates his brother,
is a liar,
since a man who does not love the brother that he can see
cannot love God, whom he has never seen.
21 So this is the commandment that he has given us,
that anyone who loves God must also love his brother.

5 Whoever believes that Jesus is the Christ
has been begotten by God;
and whoever loves the Father that begot him
loves the child whom he begets.
2 We can be sure that we love God's children

New English Bible

and he dwells in God. Thus we have come to know and believe the love which God has for us.

God is love; he who dwells in love is dwelling in God, and God in him. This is for us the perfection of love, to have confidence on the day of judgement, and this we can have, because even in this world we are as he is. There is no room for fear in love; perfect love banishes fear. For fear brings with it the pains of judgement, and anyone who is afraid has not attained to love in its perfection. We love because he loved us first. But if a man says, 'I love God', while hating his brother, he is a liar. If he does not love the brother whom he has seen, it cannot be that he loves God whom he has not seen. And indeed this command comes to us from Christ himself: that he who loves God must also love his brother.

5 Everyone who believes that Jesus is the Christ is a child of God, and to love the parent means to love his child; it follows that

King James Version

dren of God, when we love God, and keep his
commandments. 3 For this is the love of God,
that we keep his commandments: and his commandments are not grievous. 4 For whatsoever
is born of God overcometh the world: and this
is the victory that overcometh the world, *even*
our faith. 5 Who is he that overcometh the
world, but he that believeth that Jesus is the Son
of God? 6 This is he that came by water and
blood, *even* Jesus Christ; not by water only, but
by water and blood. And it is the Spirit that
beareth witness, because the Spirit is truth. 7 For
there are three that bear record in heaven, the
Father, the Word, and the Holy Ghost: and
these three are one. 8 And there are three that
bear witness in earth, the spirit, and the water,
and the blood: and these three agree in one.
9 If we receive the witness of men, the witness
of God is greater: for this is the witness of
God which he hath testified of his Son. 10 He
that believeth on the Son of God hath the
witness in himself: he that believeth not God
hath made him a liar; because he believeth

Living Bible

out how much you love God's children—your
brothers and sisters in the Lord—by how much
you love and obey God. 3 Loving God means
doing what he tells us to do, and really, that
isn't hard at all; 4 for every child of God can
obey him, defeating sin and evil pleasure by
trusting Christ to help him.
5 But who could possibly fight and win this
battle except by believing that Jesus is truly the
Son of God? 6, 7, 8 And we know he is, because
God said so with a voice from heaven when
Jesus was baptized, and again as he was facing
death[a]—yes, not only at his baptism but also as
he faced death.[b] And the Holy Spirit, forever
truthful, says it too. So we have these three witnesses: the voice of the Holy Spirit in our hearts,
the voice from heaven at Christ's baptism, and
the voice before he died.[c] And they all say the
same thing: that Jesus Christ is the Son of God.[d]
9 We believe men who witness in our courts, and
so surely we can believe whatever God declares.
And God declares that Jesus is his Son. 10 All
who believe this know in their hearts that it is
true. If anyone doesn't believe this, he is actually calling God a liar, because he doesn't be-

[*a*] Literally, "This is he who came by water and blood." See Matthew 3:16,17; Luke 9:31,35; John 12:27,28,32,33. Other interpretations of this verse are equally possible. [*b*] Literally, "not by water only, but by water and blood." [*c*] Literally, "the Spirit, and the water, and the blood." [*d*] Implied.

Today's English Version

know that we love God's children: it is by loving God and obeying his commands. 3 For our
love for God means that we obey his commands.
And his commands are not too hard for us,
4 because every child of God is able to defeat
the world. This is how we win the victory over
the world: with our faith. 5 Who can defeat the
world? Only he who believes that Jesus is the
Son of God.

The witness about Jesus Christ

6 Jesus Christ is the one who came; he came
with the water of his baptism and the blood of
his death. He came not only with the water, but
with both the water and the blood. And the
Spirit himself testifies that this is true, because
the Spirit is truth. 7 There are three witnesses,
8 the Spirit, the water, and the blood; and all
three agree. 9 We believe the witness that men
give; the witness that God gives is much stronger,
and this is the witness that God has given about
his Son. 10 So whoever believes in the Son of
God has this witness in his heart; but whoever
does not believe God has made a liar out of

New International Version

how we know that we love the children of God:
by loving God and carrying out his commands.
3 This is love for God: to obey his commands.
And his commands are not burdensome, 4 for
everyone born of God has overcome the world.
This is the victory that has overcome the world,
even our faith. 5 Who is it that overcomes the
world? Only he who believes that Jesus is the
Son of God.
6 This is the one who came by water and
blood—Jesus Christ. He did not come by water
only, but by water and blood. And it is the
Spirit who testifies, because the Spirit is the
truth. 7 For there are three that testify:[g] 8 the
Spirit, the water, and the blood; and the three
are in agreement. 9 We accept man's testimony,
but God's testimony is greater because it is the
testimony of God, which he has given about his
Son. 10 Anyone who believes in the Son of God
has this testimony in his heart. Anyone who does
not believe God has made him out to be a liar,

[*g*] Late MSS of the Vulgate add *in heaven: the Father, the Word and the Holy Spirit, and these three are one. And there are three that testify on earth:*

Phillips Modern English

this question—do we love God himself and do we obey his commands? For loving God means obeying his commands, and these commands of his are not burdensome. In fact, this faith of ours is the only way in which the world can be conquered. For who could ever be said to conquer the world but the man who really believes that Jesus is God's Son? Jesus Christ himself is the one who came by water and by blood—not by the water only, but by the water and the blood. The Spirit bears witness to this, for the Spirit is the truth. The witness therefore is a triple one—the Spirit, the water of baptism and the blood of atonement—and they all say the same thing. If we accept human testimony, God's own testimony concerning his own Son carries far more weight. The man who really believes in the Son of God will find God's testimony in his own heart. The man who will not believe

Revised Standard Version

know that we love the children of God, when
we love God and obey his commandments. 3 For
this is the love of God, that we keep his commandments. And his commandments are not
burdensome. 4 For whatever is born of God
overcomes the world; and this is the victory that
overcomes the world, our faith. 5 Who is it that
overcomes the world but he who believes that
Jesus is the Son of God?
6 This is he who came by water and blood,
Jesus Christ, not with the water only but with
the water and the blood. 7 And the Spirit is the
witness, because the Spirit is the truth. 8 There
are three witnesses, the Spirit, the water, and the
blood; and these three agree. 9 If we receive the
testimony of men, the testimony of God is
greater; for this is the testimony of God that he
has borne witness to his Son. 10 He who believes
in the Son of God has the testimony in himself.
He who does not believe God has made him a

Jerusalem Bible

if we love God himself and do what he has
commanded us;
3 this is what loving God is—
keeping his commandments;
4 and his commandments are not difficult,
because anyone who has been begotten by
God
has already overcome the world;
this is the victory over the world—
our faith.

Faith

5 Who can overcome the world?
Only the man who believes that Jesus is the
Son of God:
6 Jesus Christ who came by water and blood,[b]
not with water only,
but with water and blood;
with the Spirit as another witness—
since the Spirit is the truth—
7 so that there are three witnesses,
8 the Spirit, the water and the blood,
and all three of them agree.
9 We accept the testimony of human witnesses,
but God's testimony is much greater,
and this is God's testimony,
given as evidence for his Son.
10 Everybody who believes in the Son of God
has this testimony inside him;
and anyone who will not believe God

[b] The water and the blood from the side of Jesus, Jn. 19:34, are here used as figures of his "coming" to all Christians, through the water of baptism and through his sacrificial death.

New English Bible

when we love God and obey his commands we love his children too. For to love God is to keep his commands; and they are not burdensome, because every child of God is victor over the godless world. The victory that defeats the world is our faith, for who is victor over the world but he who believes that Jesus is the Son of God?

This is he who came with water and blood: Jesus Christ. He came, not by water alone, but by water and blood; and there is the Spirit to bear witness, because the Spirit is truth. For there are three witnesses, the Spirit, the water, and the blood, and these three are in agreement. We accept human testimony, but surely divine testimony is stronger, and this threefold testimony is indeed that of God himself, the witness he has borne to his Son. He who believes in the Son of God has this testimony in his own heart, but he who disbelieves God, makes him out to

King James Version

not the record that God gave of his Son. 11 And
this is the record, that God hath given to us
eternal life, and this life is in his Son. 12 He
that hath the Son hath life; *and* he that hath not
the Son of God hath not life. 13 These things
have I written unto you that believe on the
name of the Son of God; that ye may know that
ye have eternal life, and that ye may believe on
the name of the Son of God. 14 And this is the
confidence that we have in him, that, if we ask
any thing according to his will, he heareth us:
15 And if we know that he hear us, whatsoever
we ask, we know that we have the petitions that
we desired of him. 16 If any man see his brother
sin a sin *which is* not unto death, he shall ask,

Living Bible

lieve what God has said about his Son.

11 And what is it that God has said? That
he has given us eternal life, and that this life
is in his Son. 12 So whoever has God's Son has
life; whoever does not have his Son, does not
have life.

13 I have written this to you who believe in
the Son of God so that you may know you have
eternal life. 14 And we are sure of this, that he
will listen to us whenever we ask him for anything in line with his will. 15 And if we really
know he is listening when we talk to him and
make our requests, then we can be sure that he
will answer us.

16 If you see a Christian sinning in a way
that does not end in death, you should ask God

Today's English Version

him, because he has not believed what God has
said as a witness about his Son. 11 This, then, is
the witness: God has given us eternal life, and
this life is in his Son. 12 Whoever has the Son
has this life; whoever does not have the Son of
God does not have life.

Eternal life

13 I write you this so that you may know
that you have eternal life—you that believe in
the name of the Son of God. 14 We have courage in God's presence because we are sure that
he hears us if we ask him for anything that is
according to his will. 15 He hears us whenever
we ask him; since we know this is true, we know
also that he gives us what we ask from him.

16 If anyone sees his brother commit a sin that
does not lead to death, he should pray to God,

New International Version

because he has not believed the testimony God
has given about his Son. 11 And this is the testimony: God has given us eternal life, and this
life is in his Son. 12 He who has the Son has life;
he who does not have the Son of God does not
have life.

Concluding remarks

13 I write these things to you who believe in
the name of the Son of God so that you may
know that you have eternal life. 14 We have this
assurance in approaching God, that if we ask
anything according to his will, he hears us.
15 And if we know that he hears us—whatever
we ask—we know that we have what we asked
of him.

16 If anyone sees his brother commit a sin
that does not lead to death, he should pray and

Phillips Modern English

God is making him out to be a liar, because he is refusing to accept the testimony that God has given concerning his own Son. This is, that God has given men eternal life and this real life is to be found only in his Son. It follows naturally that any man who has Christ has this life; and if he has not, then he does not possess this life at all.
I have written like this to you who already believe in the name of God's Son so that you may be quite sure that, here and now, you possess eternal life. We have such confidence in him that we are certain that he hears every request that is made in accord with his own plan. And since we know that he invariably gives his attention to our prayers, whatever they are, we can be quite sure that what we have asked for is already ours.

5.16 Help each other to live without sin

If any of you should see his brother committing a sin—not a deadly sin—he should pray

Revised Standard Version

liar, because he has not believed in the testimony
that God has borne to his Son. 11 And this is the
testimony, that God gave us eternal life, and this
life is in his Son. 12 He who has the Son has
life; he who has not the Son of God has not life.

13 I write this to you who believe in the name
of the Son of God, that you may know that you
have eternal life. 14 And this is the confidence
which we have in him, that if we ask anything
according to his will he hears us. 15 And if we
know that he hears us in whatever we ask, we
know that we have obtained the requests made
of him. 16 If any one sees his brother committing what is not a mortal sin, he will ask, and

Jerusalem Bible

is making God out to be a liar,
because he has not trusted
the testimony God has given about his Son.
11 This is the testimony:
God has given us eternal life
and this life is in his Son;
12 anyone who has the Son has life,
anyone who does not have the Son does not have life.

Conclusion

13 I have written all this to you
so that you who believe in the name of the Son of God
may be sure that you have eternal life.

Ending

Prayer for sinners

14 We are quite confident that if we ask him for anything,
and it is in accordance with his will,
he will hear us;
15 and, knowing that whatever we may ask, he hears us,
we know that we have already been granted what we asked of him.
16 If anybody sees his brother commit a sin
that is not a deadly sin,
he has only to pray, and God will give life

New English Bible

be a liar, by refusing to accept God's own witness to his Son. The witness is this: that God has given us eternal life, and that this life is found in his Son. He who possesses the Son has life indeed; he who does not possess the Son of God has not that life.

This letter is to assure you that you have eternal life. It is addressed to those who give their allegiance to the Son of God.

We can approach God with confidence for this reason: if we make requests which accord with his will he listens to us; and if we know that our requests are heard, we know also that the things we ask for are ours.

If a man sees his brother committing a sin which is not a deadly sin, he should pray to God

King James Version

and he shall give him life for them that sin not
unto death. There is a sin unto death: I do not
say that he shall pray for it. 17 All unrighteousness is sin: and there is a sin not unto death.
18 We know that whosoever is born of God
sinneth not; but he that is begotten of God
keepeth himself, and that wicked one toucheth
him not. 19 *And* we know that we are of God,
and the whole world lieth in wickedness. 20 And
we know that the Son of God is come, and hath
given us an understanding, that we may know
him that is true; and we are in him that is true,
even in his Son Jesus Christ. This is the true
God, and eternal life. 21 Little children, keep
yourselves from idols. Amen.

Living Bible

to forgive him and God will give him life. unless
he has sinned that one fatal sin. But there is
that one sin which ends in death and if he has
done that, there is no use praying for him.
17 Every wrong is a sin, of course. I'm not talking about these ordinary sins; I am speaking of
that one that ends in death.[e]
18 No one who has become part of God's
family makes a practice of sinning, for Christ,
God's Son, holds him securely and the devil
cannot get his hands on him. 19 We know that
we are children of God and that all the rest of
the world around us is under Satan's power and
control. 20 And we know that Christ, God's Son,
has come to help us understand and find the
true God. And now we are in God because we
are in Jesus Christ his Son, who is the only true
God; and he is eternal Life.
21 Dear children, keep away from anything
that might take God's place in your hearts.
Amen.

Sincerely,
John

[e] Commentators differ widely in their thoughts about what sin this is, and whether it causes physical death or spiritual death. Blasphemy against the Holy Spirit results in spiritual death (Mark 3:29) but can a Christian ever sin in such a way? Impenitence at the Communion Table sometimes ends in physical death (1 Cor. 11:30). And Hebrews 6:4-8 speaks of the terrible end of those who fall away.

Today's English Version

who will give him life. This applies to those
whose sins do not lead to death. But there is
sin which leads to death, and I do not say that
you should pray to God about that. 17 All
wrongdoing is sin, but there is sin which does
not lead to death.
18 We know that no child of God keeps on
sinning, because the Son of God keeps him safe,
and the Evil One cannot harm him.
19 We know that we belong to God even
though the whole world is under the rule of the
Evil One.
20 We know that the Son of God has come
and has given us understanding, so that we
know the true God. Our lives are in the true
God—in his Son Jesus Christ. This is the true
God, and this is eternal life.
21 My children, keep yourselves safe from
false gods!

New International Version

God will give him life. I refer to those whose
sin does not lead to death. There is a sin that
leads to death. I am not saying that he should
pray about that. 17 All wrongdoing is sin, and
there is sin that does not lead to death.
18 We know that anyone born of God does
not continue to sin; the one who was born of
God keeps him safe, and the evil one does not
touch him. 19 We know that we are children of
God, and that the whole world is under the
control of the evil one. 20 We know also that
the Son of God has come and has given us understanding, so that we may know him who is
true. And we are in him who is true—even in
his Son Jesus Christ. He is the true God and
eternal life.
21 Dear children, keep yourselves from idols.

Phillips Modern English

and God will give him life, provided the sin was not a deadly sin. I am not saying that you should pray about that; every act of wrong-doing is a sin, but not all sin is deadly.

5.18 Our certain knowledge

We know that the true child of God does not sin, he is in the charge of God's own Son and the evil one cannot touch him.

We know that we ourselves are children of God, and we also know that the world around us is under the power of the evil one. We know too that the Son of God has come, and has given us understanding to know the One who is true. We know that our life is in the true One —in his Son Jesus Christ. This is the real God and this is eternal life.

But be on your guard, my dear children, against every false god!

Revised Standard Version

God [i] will give him life for those whose sin
is not mortal. There is sin which is mortal; I
do not say that one is to pray for that. 17 All
wrongdoing is sin, but there is sin which is not
mortal.
18 We know that any one born of God does
not sin, but He who was born of God keeps him,
and the evil one does not touch him.
19 We know that we are of God, and the
whole world is in the power of the evil one.
20 And we know that the Son of God has
come and has given us understanding, to know
him who is true; and we are in him who is true,
in his Son Jesus Christ. This is the true God
and eternal life. 21 Little children, keep yourselves from idols.

[i] Greek *he*.

Jerusalem Bible

to the sinner
—not those who commit a deadly sin;
for there is a sin that is death,
and I will not say that you must pray about that.
17 Every kind of wrongdoing is sin,
but not all sin is deadly.

Summary of the letter

18 We know that anyone who has been begotten by God
does not sin,
because the begotten Son of God protects him,
and the Evil One does not touch him.
19 We know that we belong to God,
but the whole world lies in the power of the Evil One.
20 We know, too, that the Son of God has come,
and has given us the power
to know the true God.
We are in the true God,
as we are in his Son, Jesus Christ.
This is the true God,
this is eternal life.
21 Children, be on your guard against false gods.

New English Bible

for him, and he will grant him life—that is, when men are not guilty of deadly sin. There is such a thing as deadly sin, and I do not suggest that he should pray about that; but although all wrongdoing is sin, not all sin is deadly sin.

We know that no child of God is a sinner; it is the Son of God who keeps him safe, and the evil one cannot touch him.

We know that we are of God's family, while the whole godless world lies in the power of the evil one.

We know that the Son of God has come and given us understanding to know him who is real; indeed we are in him who is real, since we are in his Son Jesus Christ. This is the true God, this is eternal life. My children, be on the watch against false gods.

King James Version

THE SECOND EPISTLE OF JOHN

The elder unto the elect lady and her children, whom I love in the truth; and not I only,
but also all they that have known the truth;
2 For the truth's sake, which dwelleth in us, and
shall be with us for ever. 3 Grace be with you,
mercy, *and* peace, from God the Father, and
from the Lord Jesus Christ, the Son of the
Father, in truth and love. 4 I rejoiced greatly
that I found of thy children walking in truth,
as we have received a commandment from the
Father. 5 And now I beseech thee, lady, not as

Living Bible

2 JOHN

1 *From:* John, the old Elder of the church.
To: That dear woman Cyria, one of God's
very own, and to her children whom I love so
much, as does everyone else in the church.
2 Since the Truth is in our hearts forever, 3 God
the Father and Jesus Christ his Son will bless
us with great mercy and much peace, and with
truth and love.

4 How happy I am to find some of your children here, and to see that they are living as
they should, following the Truth, obeying God's
command.

5 And now I want to urgently remind you,

Today's English Version

THE SECOND LETTER OF JOHN

1 From the Elder—
To the dear Lady and to her children, whom
I truly love. I am not the only one, but all who
know the truth love you, 2 because the truth
remains in us and will be with us forever.

3 May God the Father and Jesus Christ, the
Father's Son, give us grace, mercy, and peace;
may they be ours in truth and love.

Truth and love

4 How happy I was to find that some of your
children live in the truth, just as the Father
commanded us. 5 And so I ask you, dear Lady:

New International Version

2 JOHN

1 The elder,
To the chosen lady and her children, whom I
love in the truth—and not I only, but also all
who know the truth—2 because of the truth,
which lives in us and will be with us forever:

3 Grace, mercy and peace from God the Father and from Jesus Christ, the Father's Son,
will be with us in truth and love.

4 It has given me great joy to find some of
your children living by the truth, just as the Father commanded us. 5 And now, dear lady, I am

Phillips Modern English

THE SECOND LETTER OF JOHN

This letter comes from the Elder to a lady chosen by God and her children, held in the highest affection not only by me but by all who know the truth. For that truth's sake (which even now we know and which will be our companion for ever) I wish you, in all love and sincerity, grace, mercy and peace from God the Father and the Lord Jesus Christ, the Father's Son.

4 *Let us love, but have no dealings with lies*

I was overjoyed to find some of your children living the life of truth, as the Father himself instructed us. I beg you now, dear lady, not as though I were issuing any new order but simply

Revised Standard Version

THE SECOND LETTER OF JOHN

1 The elder to the elect lady and her children,
whom I love in the truth, and not only I but also
all who know the truth, 2 because of the truth
which abides in us and will be with us for ever:
3 Grace, mercy, and peace will be with us,
from God the Father and from Jesus Christ the
Father's Son, in truth and love.

4 I rejoiced greatly to find some of your children following the truth, just as we have been
commanded by the Father. 5 And now I beg you,

Jerusalem Bible

THE SECOND LETTER OF JOHN

2 JOHN

1 From the Elder: my greetings to the Lady,
the chosen one,[a] and to her children, she whom
I love in the truth—and I am not the only one,
for so do all who have come to know the truth—
2 because of the truth that lives in us and will
be with us for ever. 3 In our life of truth and
love, we shall have grace, mercy and peace from
God the Father and from Jesus Christ, the Son
of the Father.

The law of love

4 It has given me great joy to find that your
children have been living the life of truth as we
were commanded by the Father. 5 I am writing

[a] The local church to which the letter is addressed.

New English Bible

THE SECOND LETTER OF JOHN

Truth and love

The elder to the Lady chosen by God, and her children, whom I love in truth—and not I alone but all who know the truth—for the sake of the truth that dwells among us and will be with us for ever.

Grace, mercy, and peace shall be with us from God the Father and from Jesus Christ the Son of the Father, in truth and love.

I was delighted to find that some of your children are living by the truth, as we were commanded by the Father. And now I have a

King James Version

though I wrote a new commandment unto thee,
but that which we had from the beginning, that
we love one another. 6And this is love, that we
walk after his commandments. This is the commandment, That, as ye have heard from the beginning, ye should walk in it. 7 For many deceivers are entered into the world, who confess
not that Jesus Christ is come in the flesh. This
is a deceiver and an antichrist. 8 Look to yourselves, that we lose not those things which we
have wrought, but that we receive a full reward. 9 Whosoever transgresseth, and abideth
not in the doctrine of Christ, hath not God. He
that abideth in the doctrine of Christ, he hath
both the Father and the Son. 10 If there come
any unto you, and bring not this doctrine, receive him not into *your* house, neither bid him
God speed: 11 For he that biddeth him God
speed is partaker of his evil deeds. 12 Having
many things to write unto you, I would not
write with paper and ink: but I trust to come
unto you, and speak face to face, that our joy
may be full. 13 The children of thy elect sister
greet thee. Amen.

Living Bible

dear friends, of the old rule God gave us right
from the beginning, that Christians should love
one another. 6 If we love God, we will do whatever he tells us to. And he has told us from the
very first to love each other.
7 Watch out for the false leaders—and there
are many of them around—who don't believe
that Jesus Christ came to earth as a human being with a body like ours. Such people are
against the truth and against Christ. 8 Beware
of being like them, and losing the prize that you
and I have been working so hard to get. See to
it that you win your full reward from the Lord.
9 For if you wander beyond the teaching of
Chirst, you will leave God behind; while if you
are loyal to Christ's teachings, you will have
God too. Then you will have both the Father
and the Son.
10 If anyone comes to teach you, and he
doesn't believe what Christ taught, don't even
invite him into your home. Don't encourage
him in any way. 11 If you do you will be a
partner with him in his wickedness.
12 Well, I would like to say much more, but
I don't want to say it in this letter, for I hope
to come to see you soon and then we can talk
over these things together and have a joyous
time.
13 Greetings from the children of your sister
—another choice child of God.

Sincerely,
John

Today's English Version

let us all love one another. This is no new
command I write you; it is the command which
we have had from the beginning. 6 This love I
speak of means that we must live in obedience
to God's commands. The command, as you have
all heard from the beginning, is this: you must
all live in love.
7 Many deceivers have gone out over the
world, men who do not declare that Jesus Christ
came as a human being. Such a person is a
deceiver and the Enemy of Christ. 8 Watch yourselves, then, so that you will not lose what you
have worked for, but will receive your reward
in full.
9 Anyone who does not stay with the teaching of Christ, but goes beyond it, does not
have God. Whoever does stay with the teaching
has both the Father and the Son. 10 If anyone
comes to you, then, who does not bring this
teaching, do not welcome him in your home; do
not even say, "Peace be with you." 11 For anyone who wishes him peace becomes his partner
in the evil things he does.

Final words

12 I have so much to tell you, but I would
rather not do it with paper and ink; instead, I
hope to visit you and talk with you personally,
so that we shall be completely happy.
13 The children of your dear Sister send you
their greetings.

New International Version

not writing you a new command but one we
have had from the beginning. I ask that we love
one another. 6And this is love: that we live in
obedience to his commands. As you have heard
from the beginning, his command is that you
live a life of love.
7 Many deceivers, who do not acknowledge
that Jesus Christ has come in the flesh, have
gone out into the world. Any such person is the
deceiver and the antichrist. 8 Watch out that you
do not lose what you have worked for, but that
you may be rewarded fully. 9Anyone who runs
ahead and does not continue in the teaching of
Christ does not have God; whoever continues in
the teaching has both the Father and the Son.
10 If anyone comes to you and does not bring
this teaching, do not take him into your house
or welcome him. 11Anyone who welcomes him
shares in his wicked work.
12 I have much to write to you, but I do not
want to use paper and ink. Instead, I hope to
visit you and talk with you face to face, so that
our joy may be complete.
13 The children of your chosen sister send
their greetings.

Phillips Modern English

reminding you of the original one, to see that we continue to love one another. Real love means obeying the Father's orders, and you have known from the beginning that you must live in obedience to him. For the world is becoming full of impostors—men who will not admit that Jesus the Christ really became man. Now this is the very spirit of deceit and is anti-Christ. Take care of yourselves; don't throw away all the labour that has been spent on you, but persevere till you receive your full reward.

9 Have nothing to do with false teachers

The man who is so "advanced" that he is not content with what Christ taught, has in fact no God. The man who bases his life on Christ's teaching, however, has both the Father and the Son. If any teacher comes to you who is disloyal to what Christ taught, don't have him inside your house; don't even greet him. For to greet such a man is to share in the evil that he is doing.

12 Personal

I have a lot that I could write to you, but I find it hard to put down on paper. I hope to come and see you personally, and we will have a heart-to-heart talk together—and how we shall enjoy that! The children of your sister, chosen by God, send their love.

Revised Standard Version

lady, not as though I were writing you a new
commandment, but the one we have had from
the beginning, that we love one another. 6 And
this is love, that we follow his commandments;
this is the commandment, as you have heard
from the beginning, that you follow love. 7 For
many deceivers have gone out into the world,
men who will not acknowledge the coming of
Jesus Christ in the flesh; such a one is the deceiver and the antichrist. 8 Look to yourselves,
that you may not lose what you[a] have worked
for, but may win a full reward. 9 Any one who
goes ahead and does not abide in the doctrine
of Christ does not have God; he who abides in
the doctrine has both the Father and the Son.
10 If any one comes to you and does not bring
this doctrine, do not receive him into the house
or give him any greeting; 11 for he who greets
him shares his wicked work.

12 Though I have much to write to you, I
would rather not use paper and ink, but I hope
to come to see you and talk with you face to
face, so that our joy may be complete.
13 The children of your elect sister greet you.

[a] Other ancient authorities read *we*.

Jerusalem Bible

now, dear lady, not to give you any new commandment, but the one which we were given at the beginning, and to plead: let us love one another.

6 To love is to live according to his commandments: this is the commandment which you have heard since the beginning, to live a life of love.

The enemies of Christ

7 There are many deceivers about in the
world, refusing to admit that Jesus Christ has
come in the flesh. They are the Deceiver; they
are the Antichrist. 8 Watch yourselves, or all our
work will be lost and not get the reward it deserves. 9 If anybody does not keep within the
teaching of Christ but goes beyond it, he cannot have God with him: only those who keep to
what he taught can have the Father and the Son
with them. 10 If anyone comes to you bringing
a different doctrine, you must not receive him in
your house or even give him a greeting. 11 To
greet him would make you a partner in his
wicked work.

12 There are several things I have to tell you, but I have thought it best not to trust them to paper and ink. I hope instead to visit you and talk to you personally, so that our joy may be complete.

13 Greetings to you from the children of your sister,[b] the chosen one.

[b] The local church from which the letter is sent.

New English Bible

request to make of you. Do not think I am giving a new command; I am recalling the one we have had before us from the beginning: let us love one another. And love means following the commands of God. This is the command which was given you from the beginning, to be your rule of life.

Many deceivers have gone out into the world, who do not acknowledge Jesus Christ as coming in the flesh. These are the persons described as the Antichrist, the arch-deceiver. Beware of them, so that you may not lose all that we worked for, but receive your reward in full.

Anyone who runs ahead too far, and does not stand by the doctrine of the Christ, is without God; he who stands by that doctrine possesses both the Father and the Son. If anyone comes to you who does not bring this doctrine, do not welcome him into your house or give him a greeting; for anyone who gives him a greeting is an accomplice in his wicked deeds.

I have much to write to you, but I do not care to put it down in black and white. But I hope to visit you and talk with you face to face, so that our joy may be complete. The children of your Sister, chosen by God, send their greetings.

King James Version

THE THIRD EPISTLE OF JOHN

The elder unto the well beloved Gaius, whom I love in the truth. 2 Beloved, I wish above all things that thou mayest prosper and be in health, even as thy soul prospereth. 3 For I rejoiced greatly, when the brethren came and testified of the truth that is in thee, even as thou walkest in the truth. 4 I have no greater joy than

Living Bible

3 JOHN

1 *From:* John, the Elder.
To: Dear Gaius, whom I truly love.
2 Dear friend, I am praying that all is well with you and that your body is as healthy as I know your soul is. 3 Some of the brothers traveling by have made me very happy by telling me that your life stays clean and true, and that you are living by the standards of the Gospel.
4 I could have no greater joy than to hear such things about my children.

Today's English Version

THE THIRD LETTER OF JOHN

1 From the Elder—
To my dear Gaius, whom I truly love.
2 My dear friend, I pray that everything may go well with you, and that you may be in good health—as I know you are well in spirit. 3 I was so happy when some brothers arrived and told how faithful you are to the truth—just as you always live in the truth. 4 Nothing makes me happier than to hear that my children live in the truth.

New International Version

3 JOHN

1 The elder,
To my dear friend Gaius, whom I love in the truth.
2 Dear friend, I pray that you may enjoy good health and that all may go well with you, even as your soul is getting along well. 3 It gave me great joy to have some brothers come and tell about your faithfulness to the truth and how you continue to live according to the truth. 4 I have no greater joy than to hear that my children are living according to the truth.

Phillips Modern English

THE
THIRD LETTER OF
JOHN

The elder sends this letter to my very dear friend Gaius whom I love sincerely.

2 *I thank God for you and pray for you*

My prayer for you, my very dear friend, is that you may be as healthy and prosperous in every way as you are in soul. I was delighted when the brothers arrived and spoke so highly of the sincerity of your life—obviously you are living in the truth. Nothing brings me greater joy than hearing that my children are living in the truth.

Revised Standard Version

THE
THIRD LETTER OF
JOHN

1 The elder to the beloved Gaius, whom I
love in the truth.
2 Beloved, I pray that all may go well with
you and that you may be in health; I know that
it is well with your soul. 3 For I greatly rejoiced
when some of the brethren arrived and testified
to the truth of your life, as indeed you do follow the truth. 4 No greater joy can I have than
this, to hear that my children follow the truth.

Jerusalem Bible

THE THIRD LETTER
OF JOHN
3 JOHN

1 From the Elder: greetings to my dear friend
Gaius, whom I love in the truth. 2 My dear
friend, I hope everything is going happily with
you and that you are as well physically as you
are spiritually. 3 It was a great joy to me when
some brothers came and told of your faithfulness to the truth, and of your life in the truth.
4 It is always my greatest joy to hear that my
children are living according to the truth.

New English Bible

THE
THIRD LETTER OF
JOHN

Trouble in the church

The elder to dear Gaius, whom I love in truth.
My dear Gaius, I pray that you may enjoy good health, and that all may go well with you, as I know it goes well with your soul. I was delighted when friends came and told me how true you have been; indeed you are true in your whole life. Nothing gives me greater joy than to hear that my children are living by the truth.

King James Version

to hear that my children walk in truth. 5 Beloved, thou doest faithfully whatsoever thou
doest to the brethren, and to strangers; 6 Which
have borne witness of thy charity before the
church: whom if thou bring forward on their
journey after a godly sort, thou shalt do well:
7 Because that for his name's sake they went
forth, taking nothing of the Gentiles. 8 We
therefore ought to receive such, that we might
be fellow helpers to the truth. 9 I wrote unto
the church: but Diotrephes, who loveth to have
the preeminence among them, receiveth us not.
10 Wherefore, if I come, I will remember his
deeds which he doeth, prating against us with
malicious words: and not content therewith,
neither doth he himself receive the brethren, and
forbiddeth them that would, and casteth *them*

Living Bible

5 Dear friend, you are doing a good work
for God in taking care of the traveling teachers
and missionaries who are passing through. 6 They
have told the church here of your friendship
and your loving deeds. I am glad when you send
them on their way with a generous gift. 7 For
they are traveling for the Lord, and take neither
food, clothing, shelter, nor money from those
who are not Christians, even though they have
preached to them. 8 So we ourselves should take
care of them in order that we may become
partners with them in the Lord's work.
9 I sent a brief letter to the church about
this, but proud Diotrephes, who loves to push
himself forward as the leader of the Christians
there, does not admit my authority over him
and refuses to listen to me. 10 When I come I
will tell you some of the things he is doing and
what wicked things he is saying about me and
what insulting language he is using. He not only
refuses to welcome the missionary travelers himself, but tells others not to, and when they do he
tries to put them out of the church.

Today's English Version

Gaius is praised

5 My dear friend, you are so faithful in the
work you do for the brothers, even when they
are strangers. 6 They have spoken of your love
to the church here. Please help them to continue their trip in a way that will please God.
7 For they set out on their trip in the service
of Christ without accepting any help from unbelievers. 8 We Christians, then, must help these
men, so that we may share in their work for the
truth.

Diotrephes and Demetrius

9 I wrote a short letter to the church; but
Diotrephes, who loves to be their leader, will
not pay any attention to what I say. 10 When I
come, then, I will bring up everything he has
done: the terrible things he says about us and
the lies he tells! But that is not enough for him;
he will not receive the brothers when they come,
and even stops those who want to receive them
and tries to drive them out of the church!

New International Version

5 Dear friend, you are faithful in what you
are doing for the brothers, even though they are
strangers to you. 6 They have told the church
about your love. You will do well to send them
on their way in a manner worthy of God. 7 It
was for the sake of the Name that they went
out, receiving no help from the pagans. 8 We
ought therefore to show hospitality to such men
so that we may work together for the truth.
9 I wrote to the church, but Diotrephes, who
loves to be first, will have nothing to do with
us. 10 So if I come, I will call attention to what
he is doing, gossiping maliciously about us. Not
satisfied with that, he refuses to welcome the
brothers. He also stops those who want to do
so and puts them out of the church.

Phillips Modern English

5 *Your actions have been just right*

You are doing a fine faithful piece of work, dear friend, in looking after the brothers who come your way, especially when you have never seen them before. They have testified to your love before the church here. It is a fine thing to help them on their way—you realise the importance of what they are doing for God. They set out on this work for the sake of "the name" and they accept no help from non-Christians. We ought to give such men every support and prove that we too are co-operating with the truth.

9 *I know about Diotrephes*

I did write a letter to the church, but Diotrephes, who wants to be head of everything, does not recognise us! If I do come to you, I shall not forget his actions nor the slanderous things he has said in spite against us. And it doesn't stop there, for he refuses to welcome the brothers himself, and stops those who would like to do so—he even excommunicates them!

Revised Standard Version

5 Beloved, it is a loyal thing you do when
you render any service to the brethren, especially
to strangers, 6 who have testified to your love
before the church. You will do well to send
them on their journey as befits God's service.
7 For they have set out for his sake and have
accepted nothing from the heathen. 8 So we
ought to support such men, that we may be fellow workers in the truth.
9 I have written something to the church; but
Diotrephes, who likes to put himself first, does
not acknowledge my authority. 10 So if I come,
I will bring up what he is doing, prating against
me with evil words. And not content with that,
he refuses himself to welcome the brethren, and
also stops those who want to welcome them and
puts them out of the church.

Jerusalem Bible

5 My friend, you have done faithful work in
looking after these brothers, even though they
were complete strangers to you. 6 They are a
proof to the whole Church of your charity and
it would be a very good thing if you could help
them on their journey in a way that God would
approve. 7 It was entirely for the sake of the
name that they set out, without depending on
the pagans for anything; 8 it is our duty to welcome men of this sort and contribute our share
to their work for the truth.

Beware of the example of Diotrephes

9 I have written a note for the members of
the church, but Diotrephes, who seems to enjoy
being in charge of it, refuses to accept us. 10 So
if I come, I shall tell everyone how he has behaved, and about the wicked accusations he has
been circulating against us. As if that were not
enough, he not only refuses to welcome our
brothers, but prevents the other people who
would have liked to from doing it, and expels

New English Bible

My dear friend, you show a fine loyalty in everything that you do for these our fellow-Christians, strangers though they are to you. They have spoken of your kindness before the congregation here. Please help them on their journey in a manner worthy of the God we serve. It was on Christ's work that they went out; and they would accept nothing from pagans. We are bound to support such men, and so play our part in spreading the truth.

I sent a letter to the congregation, but Diotrephes, their would-be leader,[a] will have nothing to do with us. If I come, I will bring up the things he is doing. He lays baseless and spiteful charges against us; not satisfied with that, he refuses to receive our friends, and he interferes with those who would do so, and tries to expel them from the congregation.

[a] *Or* who enjoys being their leader.

King James Version

out of the church. 11 Beloved, follow not that
which is evil, but that which is good. He that
doeth good is of God: but he that doeth evil
hath not seen God. 12 Demetrius hath good report of all *men,* and of the truth itself: yea, and
we *also* bear record; and ye know that our
record is true. 13 I had many things to write, but
I will not with ink and pen write unto thee:
14 But I trust I shall shortly see thee, and we
shall speak face to face. Peace *be* to thee. *Our*
friends salute thee. Greet the friends by name.

Living Bible

11 Dear friend, don't let this bad example
influence you. Follow only what is good. Remember that those who do what is right prove
that they are God's children; and those who
continue in evil prove that they are far from
God. 12 But everyone, including Truth itself,
speaks highly of Demetrius. I myself can say
the same for him, and you know I speak the
truth.

13 I have much to say but I don't want to
write it, 14 for I hope to see you soon and then
we will have much to talk about together. 15 So
good-bye for now. Friends here send their love,
and please give each of the folks there a special
greeting from me.

Sincerely,
John

Today's English Version

11 My dear friend, do not imitate what is bad,
but imitate what is good. Whoever does good
belongs to God; whoever does what is bad has
not seen God.

12 Everyone speaks well of Demetrius; truth
itself speaks well of him. And we add our witness, and you know that what we say is true.

Final greetings

13 I have so much to tell you, but I do not
want to do it with pen and ink. 14 I hope to see
you soon, and then we will talk personally.

15 Peace be with you.

All your friends send greetings. Greet all our
friends personally.

New International Version

11 Dear friend, do not imitate what is evil but
what is good. Anyone who does what is good
is from God. Anyone who does what is evil has
not seen God. 12 Demetrius is well spoken of
by everyone—and even by the truth itself. We
also speak well of him, and you know that our
testimony is true.

13 I have much to write you, but I do not
want to do so with pen and ink. 14 I hope to
see you soon, and we will talk face to face.

Peace to you. The friends here send their
greetings. Greet the friends there by name.

Phillips Modern English

11 *A little piece of advice: and I shall soon be seeing you personally*

Never let evil be your example, dear friend of mine, but good. The man who does good is God's man, but the man who does evil has never seen God.

Everyone has a good word to say for Demetrius, and the very truth speaks well of him. He has our warm recommendation also, and you know you can trust what we say about anyone.

There is a great deal I want to say to you but I can't put it down in black and white. I hope to see you before long, and we will have a heart-to-heart talk. Peace be with you. All our friends here send love: please give ours personally to all our friends.

Revised Standard Version

11 Beloved, do not imitate evil but imitate
good. He who does good is of God; he who does
evil has not seen God. 12 Demetrius has testimony from every one, and from the truth itself;
I testify to him too, and you know my testimony
is true.

13 I had much to write to you, but I would
rather not write with pen and ink; 14 I hope to
see you soon, and we will talk together face to
face.
15 Peace be to you. The friends greet you.
Greet the friends, every one of them.

Jerusalem Bible

them from the church. 11 My dear friend, never
follow such a bad example, but keep following
the good one; anyone who does what is right is
a child of God, but the person who does what
is wrong has never seen God.

Commendation of Demetrius

12 Demetrius has been approved by everyone, and indeed by the truth itself. We too will vouch for him and you know that our testimony is true.

Epilogue

13 There were several things I had to tell you
but I would rather not trust them to pen and
ink. 14 However, I hope to see you soon and
talk to you personally. 15 Peace be with you;
greetings from your friends; greet each of our
friends by name.

New English Bible

My dear friend, do not imitate bad examples, but good ones. The well-doer is a child of God; the evil-doer has never seen God.

Demetrius gets a good testimonial from everybody—yes, and from the truth itself. I add my testimony, and you know that my testimony is true.

I have much to write to you, but I do not care to set it down with pen and ink. I hope to see you very soon, and we will talk face to face. Peace be with you. Our friends send their greetings. Greet our friends one by one.

King James Version

THE GENERAL EPISTLE OF JUDE

Jude, the servant of Jesus Christ, and brother
of James, to them that are sanctified by God
the Father, and preserved in Jesus Christ, *and*
called: 2 Mercy unto you, and peace, and love,
be multiplied. 3 Beloved, when I gave all diligence to write unto you of the common salvation, it was needful for me to write unto you,
and exhort *you* that ye should earnestly contend
for the faith which was once delivered unto the
saints. 4 For there are certain men crept in unawares, who were before of old ordained to this
condemnation, ungodly men, turning the grace
of our God into lasciviousness, and denying the

Living Bible

JUDE

1 *From:* Jude, a servant of Jesus Christ, and
a brother of James.
To: Christians everywhere—beloved of God
and chosen by him. 2 May you be given more
and more of God's kindness, peace, and love.
3 Dearly loved friends, I had been planning
to write you some thoughts about the salvation
God has given us, but now I find I must write
of something else instead, urging you to stoutly
defend the truth which God gave, once for all,
to his people to keep without change through
the years. 4 I say this because some godless
teachers have wormed their way in among you,
saying that after we become Christians we can
do just as we like without fear of God's punishment. The fate of such people was written long
ago, for they have turned against our only
Master and Lord, Jesus Christ.

Today's English Version

THE LETTER FROM JUDE

1 From Jude, a servant of Jesus Christ, and
the brother of James—
To those who have been called by God, who
live in the love of God the Father and the protection of Jesus Christ:
2 May mercy, peace, and love be yours in
full measure.

False teachers

3 My dear friends! I was doing my best to
write to you about the salvation we share in
common, when I felt the need of writing you
now to encourage you to fight on for the faith
which once and for all God has given to his
people. 4 For some godless men have slipped in
unnoticed among us, who distort the message
about the grace of our God to excuse their immoral ways, and reject Jesus Christ, our only
Master and Lord. Long ago the Scriptures predicted this condemnation they have received.

New International Version

JUDE

1 Jude, a servant of Jesus Christ and a brother
of James,
To those who have been called, who are loved
by God the Father and kept by Jesus Christ:
2 Mercy, peace and love be yours in abundance.

The sin and doom of godless men

3 Dear friends, although I was very eager to
write to you about the salvation we share, I felt
I had to write and urge you to contend for the
faith that God has once for all entrusted to the
saints. 4 For certain men whose condemnation
was written about long ago have secretly slipped
in among you. They are godless men, who
change the grace of our God into a license for
immorality and deny Jesus Christ our only Sovereign and Lord.

Phillips Modern English

THE LETTER OF JUDE

Jude, a servant of Jesus Christ and brother of James, to those who have obeyed the call, who are loved by God the Father and kept in the faith by Jesus Christ—may you ever experience more and more of mercy, peace and love!

3 *The reason for this letter*

While I was fully engaged, dear friends, in writing to you about our common salvation, I felt compelled to make my letter to you an earnest appeal to put up a real fight for the faith which has been once and for all handed on to those who are committed to God. For there are men who have surreptitiously entered the Church but who have long ago been marked out for condemnation. They have no reverence for God, and they abuse his grace as an opportunity for immorality. They will not recognise the only master, Jesus Christ our Lord.

Revised Standard Version

THE LETTER OF JUDE

1 Jude, a servant of Jesus Christ and brother of James,
To those who are called, beloved in God the Father and kept for Jesus Christ:
2 May mercy, peace, and love be multiplied to you.

3 Beloved, being very eager to write to you of our common salvation, I found it necessary to write appealing to you to contend for the faith which was once for all delivered to the saints. 4 For admission has been secretly gained by some who long ago were designated for this condemnation, ungodly persons who pervert the grace of our God into licentiousness and deny our only Master and Lord, Jesus Christ.[a]

[a] Or *the only Master and our Lord Jesus Christ.*

Jerusalem Bible

THE LETTER OF JUDE

Address

1 From Jude, servant of Jesus Christ and brother of James; to those who are called, to those who are dear to God the Father and kept safe for Jesus Christ, 2 wishing you all mercy and peace and love.

The reason for this letter

3 My dear friends, at a time when I was eagerly looking forward to writing to you about the salvation that we all share, I have been forced to write to you now and appeal to you to fight hard for the faith which has been once and for all entrusted to the saints. 4 Certain people have infiltrated among you, and they are the ones you had a warning about, in writing, long ago, when they were condemned for denying all religion, turning the grace of our God into immorality, and rejecting our only Master and Lord, Jesus Christ.

New English Bible

A LETTER OF JUDE

The danger of false belief

From Jude, servant of Jesus Christ and brother of James, to those whom God has called, who live in the love of God the Father and in the safe keeping of Jesus Christ.

Mercy, peace, and love be yours in fullest measure.

My friends, I was fully engaged in writing to you about our salvation—which is yours no less than ours—when it became urgently necessary to write at once and appeal to you to join the struggle in defence of the faith, the faith which God entrusted to his people once and for all. It is in danger from certain persons who have wormed their way in, the very men whom Scripture long ago marked down for the doom they have incurred. They are the enemies of religion; they pervert the free favour of our God into licentiousness, disowning Jesus Christ, our only Master and Lord.[a]

[a] *Or* disowning our one and only Master, and Jesus Christ our Lord.

King James Version

only Lord God, and our Lord Jesus Christ. 5 I
will therefore put you in remembrance, though
ye once knew this, how that the Lord, having
saved the people out of the land of Egypt, afterward destroyed them that believed not. 6 And
the angels which kept not their first estate, but
left their own habitation, he hath reserved in
everlasting chains under darkness unto the judgment of the great day. 7 Even as Sodom and
Gomorrah, and the cities about them in like
manner, giving themselves over to fornication,
and going after strange flesh, are set forth for
an example, suffering the vengeance of eternal
fire. 8 Likewise also these *filthy* dreamers defile
the flesh, despise dominion, and speak evil of
dignities. 9 Yet Michael the archangel, when
contending with the devil he disputed about the
body of Moses, durst not bring against him a
railing accusation, but said, The Lord rebuke
thee. 10 But these speak evil of those things
which they know not: but what they know
naturally, as brute beasts, in those things they

Living Bible

5 My answer to them is: Remember this fact
—which you know already—that the Lord saved
a whole nation of people out of the land of
Egypt, and then killed every one of them who
did not trust and obey him. 6 And I remind you
of those angels who were once pure and holy,
but turned to a life of sin.[a] Now God has them
chained up in prisons of darkness, waiting for
the judgment day. 7 And don't forget the cities
of Sodom and Gomorrah and their neighboring
towns, all full of lust of every kind including
lust of men for other men. Those cities were
destroyed by fire and continue to be a warning
to us that there is a hell in which sinners are
punished.

8 Yet these false teachers carelessly go right
on living their evil, immoral lives, degrading
their bodies and laughing at those in authority
over them, even scoffing at the Glorious Ones.
9 Yet Michael, one of the mightiest of the
angels, when he was arguing with Satan about
Moses' body, did not dare to accuse even Satan,
or jeer at him, but simply said, "The Lord rebuke you." 10 But these men mock and curse at
anything they do not understand, and, like animals, they do whatever they feel like, thereby
ruining their souls.

[*a*] Or, "who abandoned their original rank and left their proper home."

Today's English Version

5 For even though you know all this, I want
to remind you of how the Lord saved the people of Israel from the land of Egypt, but afterward destroyed those who did not believe. 6 Remember the angels who did not stay within the
limits of their proper authority, but abandoned
their own dwelling place: they are bound with
eternal chains in the darkness below, where God
is keeping them for that great Day on which
they will be condemned. 7 Remember Sodom and
Gomorrah, and the nearby towns, whose people
acted as those angels did and committed sexual
immorality and perversion: they suffer the punishment of eternal fire as a plain warning to all.

8 In the same way also, these men have visions which make them sin against their own
bodies; they despise God's authority and insult
the glorious beings above. 9 Not even the chief
angel Michael has done this. In his quarrel with
the Devil, when they argued about who would
have the body of Moses, Michael did not dare
condemn the Devil with insulting words, but
said, "The Lord rebuke you!" 10 But these men
insult things they do not understand; and those
things that they know by instinct, like wild animals, are the very things that destroy them.

New International Version

5 Though you already know all this, I want
to remind you that the Lord[a] delivered his
people out of Egypt, but later destroyed those
who did not believe. 6 And the angels who did
not keep their positions of authority but abandoned their own home—these he has kept in
darkness, bound with everlasting chains for judgment on the great Day. 7 In a similar way,
Sodom and Gomorrah and the surrounding towns
gave themselves up to sexual immorality and
perversion. They serve as an example of those
who suffer the punishment of eternal fire.

8 In the very same way, these dreamers pollute their own bodies, reject authority, and
slander celestial beings. 9 But even the archangel
Michael, when he was disputing with the devil
about the body of Moses, did not dare to bring
a slanderous accusation against him, but said,
"The Lord rebuke you!" 10 Yet these men speak
abusively against whatever they do not understand; and what things they do understand by
instinct, like unreasoning animals—these are the
very things that destroy them.

[*a*] Some early MSS read *Jesus*.

Phillips Modern English

5 Past history warns us that the unfaithful have mingled with the faithful

I want to remind you of something that you really know already: that although the Lord saved all the people from the land of Egypt, yet afterwards he brought to their downfall those who would not trust him. And the very angels who failed in their high duties and abandoned their proper sphere have been deprived by God of both light and liberty until the judgment of the great day. Sodom and Gomorrah and the adjacent cities who, in the same way as these men today, gave themselves up to sexual immorality and perversion, stand in their punishment as a permanent warning of the fire of judgment. Yet these men are defiling their bodies by their filthy fantasies in just the same way; they show utter contempt for authority and make a jest of the heavenly glories. But I would remind you that even the archangel Michael when he was contending with the devil in the dispute over the body of Moses did not dare to condemn him with mockery. He simply said, the Lord rebuke you!

These fellows, however, are ready to mock at anything that is beyond their knowledge, while in the things that they know by instinct like

Revised Standard Version

5 Now I desire to remind you, though you
were once for all fully informed, that he[b] who
saved a people out of the land of Egypt, afterward destroyed those who did not believe. 6And
the angels that did not keep their own position
but left their proper dwelling have been kept by
him in eternal chains in the nether gloom until
the judgment of the great day; 7 just as Sodom
and Gomorrah and the surrounding cities, which
likewise acted immorally and indulged in unnatural lust, serve as an example by undergoing
a punishment of eternal fire.
8 Yet in like manner these men in their
dreamings defile the flesh, reject authority, and
revile the glorious ones.[c] 9 But when the archangel Michael, contending with the devil, disputed about the body of Moses, he did not presume to pronounce a reviling judgment upon
him, but said, "The Lord rebuke you." 10 But
these men revile whatever they do not understand, and by those things that they know by instinct as irrational animals do, they are de-

[b] Ancient authorities read *Jesus* or *the Lord* or *God*. [c] Greek *glories*.

Jerusalem Bible

The false teachers: the certainty of their punishment

5 I should like to remind you—though you
have already learned it once and for all—how
the Lord rescued the nation from Egypt, but
afterward he still destroyed the men who did not
trust him. 6 Next let me remind you of the
angels who had supreme authority but did not
keep it and left their appointed sphere[a]; he has
kept them down in the dark, in spiritual chains,
to be judged on the great day. 7 The fornication
of Sodom and Gomorrah and the other nearby
towns was equally unnatural, and it is a warning
to us that they are paying for their crimes in
eternal fire.

Their violent language

8 Nevertheless, these people are doing the
same: in their delusions they not only defile
their bodies and disregard authority, but abuse
the glorious angels as well. 9 Not even the archangel Michael, when he was engaged in argument with the devil about the corpse of Moses,
dared to denounce him in the language of abuse;
all he said was, "Let the Lord correct you."
10 But these people abuse anything they do not
understand; and the only things they do understand—just by nature like unreasoning animals
—will turn out to be fatal to them.

[a] Briefly mentioned in Gn. 6:1-2, but elaborated in *The Book of Enoch*.

New English Bible

You already know it all, but let me remind you how the Lord,[b] having once delivered the people of Israel out of Egypt, next time destroyed those who were guilty of unbelief. Remember too the angels, how some of them were not content to keep the dominion given to them but abandoned their proper home; and God has reserved them for judgement on the great Day, bound beneath the darkness in everlasting chains. Remember Sodom and Gomorrah and the neighbouring towns; like the angels, they committed fornication and followed unnatural lusts; and they paid the penalty in eternal fire, an example for all to see.

So too with these men today. Their dreams lead them to defile the body, to flout authority, and to insult celestial beings. In contrast, when the archangel Michael was in debate with the devil, disputing the possession of Moses's body, he did not presume to condemn him in insulting words,[c] but said, 'May the Lord rebuke you!'

But these men pour abuse upon things they do not understand; the things they do understand, by instinct like brute beasts, prove their

[b] *Some witnesses read* Jesus (*which might be understood as* Joshua). [c] *Or* to charge him with blasphemy.

King James Version

corrupt themselves. 11 Woe unto them! for they
have gone in the way of Cain, and ran greedily
after the error of Balaam for reward, and perished in the gainsaying of Core. 12 These are
spots in your feasts of charity, when they feast
with you, feeding themselves without fear:
clouds *they are* without water, carried about of
winds; trees whose fruit withereth, without fruit,
twice dead, plucked up by the roots; 13 Raging
waves of the sea, foaming out their own shame;
wandering stars, to whom is reserved the blackness of darkness for ever. 14 And Enoch also,
the seventh from Adam, prophesied of these,
saying, Behold, the Lord cometh with ten thousands of his saints, 15 To execute judgment upon
all, and to convince all that are ungodly among
them of all their ungodly deeds which they have
ungodly committed, and of all their hard
speeches which ungodly sinners have spoken
against him. 16 These are murmurers, com-
plainers, walking after their own lusts; and their

Living Bible

11 Woe upon them! For they follow the example of Cain who killed his brother; and, like
Balaam, they will do anything for money; and
like Korah, they have disobeyed God and will
die under his curse.
12 When these men join you at the love feasts
of the church, they are evil smears among you,
laughing and carrying on, gorging and stuffing
themselves without a thought for others. They
are like clouds blowing over dry land without
giving rain, promising much, but producing nothing. They are like fruit trees without any fruit
at picking time. They are not only dead, but
doubly dead, for they have been pulled out,
roots and all, to be burned.
13 All they leave behind them is shame and
disgrace like the dirty foam left along the beach
by the wild waves. They wander around looking
as bright as stars, but ahead of them is the
everlasting gloom and darkness that God has
prepared for them.
14 Enoch, who lived seven generations after
Adam, knew about these men and said this
about them: "See, the Lord is coming with millions of his holy ones. 15 He will bring the people of the world before him in judgment, to
receive just punishment, and to prove the terrible things they have done in rebellion against
God, revealing all they have said against him."
16 These men are constant gripers, never satisfied, doing whatever evil they feel like; they are

Today's English Version

11 How terrible for them! They have followed
the way that Cain took. For the sake of money
they have given themselves over to the error that
Balaam committed. They have rebelled as Korah
rebelled, and like him they are destroyed.
12 They are like dirty spots in your fellowship
meals, with their shameless carousing. They
take care of themselves only. They are like
clouds carried along by the wind and bringing
no rain. They are like trees that bear no fruit,
even in autumn, trees that have been pulled up
by the roots and are completely dead. 13 They
are like wild waves of the sea, with their shameful deeds showing up like foam. They are like
wandering stars, for whom God has reserved a
place forever in the deepest darkness.
14 It was Enoch, the sixth direct descendant
from Adam, who long ago prophesied this
about them: "Look! The Lord will come with
many thousands of his holy angels, 15 to bring
judgment on all, to condemn all godless sinners
for all the godless deeds they have performed,
and for all the terrible words these godless men
have spoken against God!"
16 These men are always grumbling and
blaming others; they follow their own evil de-

New International Version

11 Woe to them! They have taken the way of
Cain; they have rushed for profit into Balaam's
error; they have been destroyed in Korah's rebellion.
12 These men are blemishes at your love
feasts, eating with you without the slightest
qualm—shepherds who feed only themselves.
They are clouds without rain, blown along by
the wind; autumn trees, without fruit and uprooted—twice dead. 13 They are wild waves of
the sea, foaming up their shame; wandering
stars, for whom blackest darkness has been reserved forever.
14 Enoch, the seventh from Adam, prophesied
about these men: "See, the Lord is coming with
thousands upon thousands of his holy ones 15 to
judge everyone, and to convict all the ungodly
of all their ungodly acts they have done in their
ungodly way, and of all the harsh words ungodly sinners have spoken against him." 16 These
men are grumblers and faultfinders; they follow

Phillips Modern English

unreasoning beasts they are utterly depraved. I say, Woe to them! For they have taken the road of Cain; for what they could get they have rushed into the same error as Balaam; they have destroyed themselves by rebelling against God as did Korah long ago.

12 Be on your guard against these wicked men

These men are blots on the good-fellowship of your feasts, for they eat in your company without reverence, looking after no one but themselves. They are like clouds driven up by the wind, but they bring no rain. They are like trees in autumn without a single fruit—doubly dead for they have been pulled up by the roots. They are like raging waves of the sea producing only the spume of their own shameful deeds. They are like stars which follow no orbit, and their proper place is the everlasting blackness of the regions beyond the light. It was of these men that Enoch (seventh descendant from Adam) prophesied when he said:

> Behold, the Lord came with ten thousands of his holy ones, to execute judgment upon all, and to convict all the ungodly of all their works of ungodliness which they have ungodly wrought, and of all the hard things which ungodly sinners have spoken against him.

These are the men who complain and curse their fate while trying all the time to mould life ac-

Revised Standard Version

stroyed. 11 Woe to them! For they walk in the way of Cain, and abandon themselves for the sake of gain to Balaam's error, and perish in Korah's rebellion. 12 These are blemishes[d] on your love feasts, as they boldly carouse together, looking after themselves; waterless clouds, carried along by winds; fruitless trees in late autumn, twice dead, uprooted; 13 wild waves of the sea, casting up the foam of their own shame; wandering stars for whom the nether gloom of darkness has been reserved for ever.

14 It was of these also that Enoch in the seventh generation from Adam prophesied, saying, "Behold, the Lord came with his holy myriads, 15 to execute judgment on all, and to convict all the ungodly of all their deeds of ungodliness which they have committed in such an ungodly way, and of all the harsh things which ungodly sinners have spoken against him." 16 These are grumblers, malcontents, following their own passions, loud-mouthed boasters, flat-

[d] Or *reefs*.

Jerusalem Bible

Their vicious behavior

11 May they get what they deserve, because they have followed Cain; they have rushed to make the same mistake as Balaam and for the same reward; they have rebelled just as Korah did—and share the same fate. 12 They are a dangerous obstacle to your community meals, coming for the food and quite shamelessly only looking after themselves. They are like clouds blown about by the winds and bringing no rain, or like barren trees which are then uprooted in the winter and so are twice dead; 13 like wild sea waves capped with shame as if with foam; or like shooting stars bound for an eternity of black darkness. 14 It was with them in mind that Enoch, the seventh patriarch from Adam, made his prophecy when he said, "I tell you, the Lord will come with his saints in their tens of thousands, 15 to pronounce judgment on all mankind and to sentence the wicked for all the wicked things they have done, and for all the defiant things said against him by irreligious sinners." 16 They are mischief-makers, grumblers governed only by their own desires, with *mouths*

New English Bible

undoing. Alas for them! They have gone the way of Cain; they have plunged into Balaam's error for pay; they have rebelled like Korah, and they share his doom.

These men are a blot on your love-feasts, where they eat and drink without reverence. They are shepherds who take care only of themselves. They are clouds carried away by the wind without giving rain, trees that in season bear no fruit, dead twice over and pulled up by the roots. They are fierce waves of the sea, foaming shameful deeds; they are stars that have wandered from their course, and the place for ever reserved for them is blackest darkness.

It was to them that Enoch, the seventh in descent from Adam, directed his prophecy when he said: 'I saw the Lord come with his myriads of angels, to bring all men to judgement and to convict all the godless of all the godless deeds they had committed, and of all the defiant words which godless sinners had spoken against him.'

They are a set of grumblers and malcontents. They follow their lusts. Big words come rolling

King James Version

mouth speaketh great swelling *words,* having
men's persons in admiration because of advantage. 17 But, beloved, remember ye the words
which were spoken before of the apostles of our
Lord Jesus Christ; 18 How that they told you
there should be mockers in the last time, who
should walk after their own ungodly lusts.
19 These be they who separate themselves, sensual, having not the Spirit. 20 But ye, beloved,
building up yourselves on your most holy faith,
praying in the Holy Ghost, 21 Keep yourselves
in the love of God, looking for the mercy of our
Lord Jesus Christ unto eternal life. 22And of
some have compassion, making a difference:
23And others save with fear, pulling *them* out
of the fire; hating even the garment spotted by

Living Bible

loud-mouthed "show-offs," and when they show
respect for others, it is only to get something
from them in return.
17 Dear friends, remember what the apostles
of our Lord Jesus Christ told you, 18 that in the
last times there would come these scoffers whose
whole purpose in life is to enjoy themselves in
every evil way imaginable. 19 They stir up arguments; they love the evil things of the world;
they do not have the Holy Spirit living in them.
20 But you, dear friends, must build up your
lives ever more strongly upon the foundation of
our holy faith, learning to pray in the power
and strength of the Holy Spirit.
21 Stay always within the boundaries where
God's love can reach and bless you. Wait patiently for the eternal life that our Lord Jesus
Christ in his mercy is going to give you. 22 Try
to help those who argue against you. Be merciful to those who doubt. 23 Save some by snatching them as from the very flames of hell itself.
And as for others, help them to find the Lord
by being kind to them, but be careful that you
yourselves aren't pulled along into their sins.
Hate every trace of their sin while being merciful to them as sinners.

Today's English Version

sires; they brag about themselves, and flatter
others in order to get their own way.

Warnings and instructions

17 But remember, my friends! Remember
what you were told in the past by the apostles
of our Lord Jesus Christ. 18 They said to you,
"When the last days come, men will appear who
will make fun of you, men who follow their
own godless desires." 19 These are the men who
cause divisions, who are controlled by their
natural desires, who do not have the Spirit.
20 But you, my friends, keep on building yourselves up on your most sacred faith. Pray in the
power of the Holy Spirit, 21 and keep yourselves
in the love of God, as you wait for our Lord
Jesus Christ in his mercy to give you eternal
life.
22 Show mercy toward those who have
doubts: 23 save them, by snatching them out of
the fire. Show mercy also, mixed with fear, to
others as well, but hate their very clothes,
stained by their sinful lusts.

New International Version

their own evil desires; they boast about themselves and flatter others for their own advantage.

A call to persevere

17 But, dear friends, remember what the apostles of our Lord Jesus Christ foretold. 18 They
said to you, "In the last times there will be
scoffers who will follow their own ungodly desires." 19 These are the men who divide you,
who follow mere natural instincts and do not
have the Spirit.
20 But you, dear friends, build yourselves up
in your most holy faith and pray in the Holy
Spirit. 21 Keep yourselves in God's love as you
wait for the mercy of our Lord Jesus Christ to
bring you to eternal life. 22 Be merciful to those
who doubt; 23 snatch others from the fire and
save them; to others show mercy, mixed with
fear—hating even the clothing stained by corrupted flesh.

Phillips Modern English

cording to their own desires. They "talk big" but will pay men great respect if it is to their own advantage.

17 *Forewarned is forearmed*

Now do remember, dear friends, the words that the messengers of Jesus Christ gave us beforehand when they said "there will come in the last days mockers who live according to their own godless desires". These are the men who split communities, for they are led by human emotions and never by the Spirit of God.

20 *Look after your own faith: save whom you can*

But you, dear friends of mine, build yourselves up on the foundation of your most holy faith and by praying through the Holy Spirit keep yourselves within the love of God. Wait patiently for the mercy of our Lord Jesus Christ which will bring you to the life eternal. There are some whom you must pity because of their doubts; some you must save by snatching them out of the fire. But there are others for whom your pity must be mixed with caution, hating the very clothes which their deeds have soiled.

Revised Standard Version

tering people to gain advantage.

17 But you must remember, beloved, the predictions of the apostles of our Lord Jesus Christ; 18 they said to you, "In the last time there will be scoffers, following their own ungodly passions." 19 It is these who set up divisions, worldly people, devoid of the Spirit. 20 But you, beloved, build yourselves up on your most holy faith; pray in the Holy Spirit; 21 keep yourselves in the love of God; wait for the mercy of our Lord Jesus Christ unto eternal life. 22 And convince some, who doubt; 23 save some, by snatching them out of the fire; on some have mercy with fear, hating even the garment spotted by the flesh.[e]

[*e*] The Greek text in this sentence is uncertain at several points.

Jerusalem Bible

full of boastful talk, ready with flattery for other people when they see some advantage in it.

A warning

17 But remember, my dear friends, what the apostles of our Lord Jesus Christ told you to expect. 18 "At the end of time," they told you, "there are going to be people who sneer at religion and follow nothing but their own desires for wickedness." 19 These unspiritual and selfish people are nothing but mischief-makers.

The duties of love

20 But you, my dear friends, must use your most holy faith as your foundation and build on that, praying in the Holy Spirit; 21 keep yourselves within the love of God and wait for the mercy of our Lord Jesus Christ to give you eternal life. 22 When there are some who have doubts, reassure them; 23 when there are some to be saved from the fire, pull them out; but there are others to whom you must be kind with great caution, keeping your distance even from outside clothing which is contaminated by vice.

New English Bible

from their lips, and they court favour to gain their ends. But you, my friends, should remember the predictions made by the apostles of our Lord Jesus Christ. This was the warning they gave you: 'In the final age there will be men who pour scorn on religion, and follow their own godless lusts.'

These men draw a line between spiritual and unspiritual persons, although they are themselves[a] wholly unspiritual. But you, my friends, must fortify yourselves in your most sacred faith. Continue to pray in the power of the Holy Spirit. Keep yourselves in the love of God, and look forward to the day when our Lord Jesus Christ in his mercy will give eternal life.

There are some doubting souls who need your pity;[b] snatch them from the flames and save them.[c] There are others for whom your pity must be mixed with fear; hate the very clothing that is contaminated with sensuality.

[*a*] *Or* These men create divisions; they are . . .
[*b*] *Some witnesses read* There are some who raise disputes; these you should refute. [*c*] *So one witness; the rest read* some you should snatch from the flames and save.

King James Version

the flesh. 24 Now unto him that is able to keep you from falling, and to present *you* faultless before the presence of his glory with exceeding joy, 25 To the only wise God our Saviour, *be* glory and majesty, dominion and power, both now and ever. Amen.

Living Bible

24, 25 And now—all glory to him who alone is God, who saves us through Jesus Christ our Lord; yes, splendor and majesty, all power and authority are his from the beginning; his they are and his they evermore shall be. And he is able to keep you from slipping and falling away, and to bring you, sinless and perfect, into his glorious presence with mighty shouts of everlasting joy. Amen.

Jude

Today's English Version

Prayer of praise

24 To him who is able to keep you from falling and bring you faultless and joyful before his glorious presence—25 to the only God our Savior, through Jesus Christ our Lord, be glory, majesty, might, and authority, from all ages past, and now, and forever and ever! Amen.

New International Version

Doxology

24 To him who is able to keep you from falling and to present you before his glorious presence without fault and with great joy—25 to the only God our Savior be glory, majesty, power and authority, through Jesus Christ our Lord, before all ages, now and forevermore! Amen.

Phillips Modern English

24 Ascription

Now to him who is able to keep you from falling and to present you before his glory without fault and with unspeakable joy, to the only God, our saviour, be glory and majesty, power and authority, through Jesus Christ our Lord, before time was, now, and in all ages to come, amen.

Revised Standard Version

24 Now to him who is able to keep you from falling and to present you without blemish before the presence of his glory with rejoicing,
25 to the only God, our Savior through Jesus Christ our Lord, be glory, majesty, dominion, and authority, before all time and now and for ever. Amen.

Jerusalem Bible

Doxology

24 Glory be to him who can keep you from falling and bring you safe to his glorious presence, innocent and happy. 25 To God, the only God, who saves us through Jesus Christ our Lord, be the glory, majesty, authority and power, which he had before time began, now and for ever. Amen.

New English Bible

Now to the One who can keep you from falling and set you in the presence of his glory, jubilant and above reproach, to the only God our Saviour, be glory and majesty, might and authority, through Jesus Christ our Lord, before all time, now, and for evermore. Amen.

King James Version

THE REVELATION OF
St. JOHN the Divine

1 The Revelation of Jesus Christ, which God
gave unto him, to shew unto his servants things
which must shortly come to pass; and he sent
and signified *it* by his angel unto his servant
John: 2 Who bare record of the word of God,
and of the testimony of Jesus Christ, and of all
things that he saw. 3 Blessed *is* he that readeth,
and they that hear the words of this prophecy,
and keep those things which are written therein:
for the time *is* at hand.

Living Bible

THE REVELATION

1 This book unveils some of the future activities soon to occur in the life of Jesus
Christ.[a] God permitted him to reveal these things
to his servant John in a vision; and then an
angel was sent from heaven to explain the
vision's meaning. 2 John wrote it all down—the
words of God and Jesus Christ and everything
he heard and saw.
3 If you read this prophecy aloud to the
church, you will receive a special blessing from
the Lord. Those who listen to it being read and
do what it says will also be blessed. For the time
is near when these things will all come true.

[a] Literally, "the revelation of (*concerning*, or, *from*) Jesus Christ."

Today's English Version

THE REVELATION TO
JOHN

1 This book is about what Jesus Christ revealed, which God gave him, to show to
God's servants what must happen very soon.
Christ made these things known to his servant
John by sending his angel to him, 2 and John
has told all that he has seen. This is his report
concerning the message from God and the truth
revealed by Jesus Christ. 3 Happy is the one who
reads this book, and happy are those who listen
to the words of this prophetic message and obey
what is written in this book! For the time is
near when all this will happen.

New International Version

REVELATION

Prologue

1 The revelation of Jesus Christ, which God
gave him to show his servants what must
soon take place. He made it known by sending
his angel to his servant John, 2 who testifies to
everything he saw—that is, the word of God
and the testimony of Jesus Christ. 3 Blessed is
the one who reads the words of this prophecy,
and blessed are those who hear it and take to
heart what is written in it, because the time is
near.

Phillips Modern English

THE REVELATION OF JOHN

1.1 *Concerning this book*

This is a Revelation from Jesus Christ, which God gave him so that he might show his servants what must very soon take place. He made it known by sending his angel to his servant John, who is the witness of all that he saw—the message of God, and the testimony of Jesus Christ.

Happy is the man who reads this prophecy and happy are those who hear it read and pay attention to its message; for the time is near.

Revised Standard Version

THE REVELATION TO JOHN

(The Apocalypse)

1 The revelation of Jesus Christ, which God
gave him to show to his servants what must
soon take place; and he made it known by sending his angel to his servant John, 2 who bore
witness to the word of God and to the testimony of Jesus Christ, even to all that he saw.
3 Blessed is he who reads aloud the words of the
prophecy, and blessed are those who hear, and
who keep what is written therein; for the time
is near.

Jerusalem Bible

THE BOOK OF REVELATION

Prologue

1 This is the revelation given by God to Jesus Christ so that he could tell his servants
about the *things which are* now *to take place*[a]
very soon; he sent his angel to make it known
to his servant John, 2 and John has written down
everything he saw and swears it is the word of
God guaranteed by Jesus Christ. 3 Happy the
man who reads this prophecy, and happy those
who listen to him, if they treasure all that it
says, because the Time is close.

[a] Dn. 2:28.

New English Bible

THE REVELATION OF JOHN

1 This is the revelation given by God to Jesus Christ. It was given to him so that he might show his servants what must shortly happen. He made it known by sending his angel to his servant John, who, in telling all that he saw, has borne witness to the word of God and to the testimony of Jesus Christ.[a]

Happy is the man who reads, and happy those who listen to the words of this prophecy and heed what is written in it. For the hour of fulfilment is near.

[a] *Or* has borne his testimony to the word of God and to Jesus Christ.

King James Version

4 John to the seven churches which are in
Asia: Grace *be* unto you, and peace, from him
which is, and which was, and which is to come;
and from the seven Spirits which are before his
throne; 5 And from Jesus Christ, *who is* the faithful witness, *and* the first-begotten of the dead,
and the prince of the kings of the earth. Unto
him that loved us, and washed us from our sins
in his own blood, 6 And hath made us kings and
priests unto God and his Father; to him *be* glory
and dominion for ever and ever. Amen. 7 Behold,
he cometh with clouds; and every eye shall see
him, and they *also* which pierced him: and all
kindreds of the earth shall wail because of him.
Even so, Amen. 8 I am Alpha and Omega, the beginning and the ending, saith the Lord, which is,
and which was, and which is to come, the Al-

Living Bible

4 *From:* John
To: The seven churches in Turkey.[b]
Dear Friends:
May you have grace and peace from God
who is, and was, and is to come! and from the
seven-fold Spirit[c] before his throne; 5 and from
Jesus Christ who faithfully reveals all truth to
us. He was the first to rise from death, to die
no more.[d] He is far greater than any king in all
the earth. All praise to him who always loves
us and who set us free from our sins by pouring
out his life blood for us. 6 He has gathered us
into his kingdom and made us priests of God his
Father. Give to him everlasting glory! He rules
forever! Amen!
7 See! He is arriving, surrounded by clouds;
and every eye shall see him—yes, and those who
pierced him.[e] And the nations will weep in sorrow and in terror when he comes. Yes! Amen!
Let it be so!
8 "I am the A and the Z,[f] the Beginning and
the Ending of all things," says God, who is the
Lord, the All Powerful One who is, and was, and
is coming again![g]

[*b*] Literally, "in Asia." [*c*] Literally, "the seven spirits." But see Isaiah 11:2, where various aspects of the Holy Spirit are described, and Zechariah 4:2-6, giving probability to the paraphrase; also see Revelation 2:7. [*d*] Literally, "the First-born from the dead." Others (Lazarus, etc.) rose to die again. As used here the expression therefore implies "to die no more." [*e*] John saw this happen with his own eyes—the piercing of Jesus—and never forgot the horror of it. [*f*] Literally, I am Alpha and Omega"; these are the first and last letters of the Greek alphabet. [*g*] Literally, "who comes" or "who is to come."

Today's English Version

Greetings to the seven churches

4 From John to the seven churches in the
province of Asia:
Grace and peace be yours from God, who is,
who was, and who is to come, and from the
seven spirits in front of his throne, 5 and from
Jesus Christ, the faithful witness, the firstborn
Son who was raised from death, who is also the
ruler of the kings of earth.
He loves us, and by his death he has freed us
from our sins 6 and made us a kingdom of
priests to serve his God and Father. To Jesus
Christ be the glory and power forever and ever!
Amen.
7 Look, he is coming with the clouds! Everyone will see him, including those who pierced
him. All peoples of earth will mourn over him.
Certainly so! Amen.
8 "I am the Alpha and the Omega," says the
Lord God Almighty, who is, who was, and who
is to come.

New International Version

Greetings and doxology

4 John,
To the seven churches in the province of Asia:
Grace and peace to you from him who is, and
who was, and who is to come, and from the
seven spirits[a] before his throne, 5 and from Jesus Christ, who is the faithful witness, the first-
born from the dead, and the ruler of the kings
of the earth.
To him who loves us and has freed us from
our sins by his blood, 6 and has made us to be
a kingdom and priests to serve his God and
Father—to him be glory and power for ever
and ever! Amen.
7 Look, he is coming with the clouds,
and every eye will see him,
even those who pierced him;
and all the peoples of the earth will mourn
because of him.
So shall it be! Amen.
8 "I am the Alpha and the Omega," says the
Lord God, "who is, and who was, and who is
to come, the Almighty."

[*a*] Or *the sevenfold Spirit.*

Phillips Modern English

1.4 John's greeting and ascription

John, to the seven Churches in Asia:

Grace and peace be to you from him who is and who was and who is coming, from the seven Spirits before his throne, and from Jesus Christ the faithful witness, first-born of the dead, and ruler of kings upon earth. To him who loves us and has set us free from our sins through his own blood, who has made us a kingdom of priests to his God and Father, to him be glory and power for timeless ages, amen!

See, he is coming in the clouds and every eye shall see him, even those who pierced him, and his coming will mean bitter sorrow to every tribe upon the earth. So let it be!

"I am Alpha and Omega," says the Lord God, "who is and who was and who is coming, the Almighty."

Revised Standard Version

4 John to the seven churches that are in Asia:

Grace to you and peace from him who is and who was and who is to come, and from the seven spirits who are before his throne, 5 and from Jesus Christ the faithful witness, the first-born of the dead, and the ruler of kings on earth.

To him who loves us and has freed us from our sins by his blood 6 and made us a kingdom, priests to his God and Father, to him be glory and dominion for ever and ever. Amen. 7 Behold, he is coming with the clouds, and every eye will see him, every one who pierced him; and all tribes of the earth will wail on account of him. Even so. Amen.

8 "I am the Alpha and the Omega," says the Lord God, who is and who was and who is to come, the Almighty.

Jerusalem Bible

I. The letters to the churches of Asia

Address and greeting[b]

4 From John, to the seven churches of Asia: grace and peace to you from him who is, who was, and who is to come, from the seven spirits in his presence before his throne, 5 and from Jesus Christ, *the faithful witness, the First-born* from the dead, *the Ruler of the kings of the earth.* He loves us and has washed away our sins with his blood, 6 and made us a *line of kings, priests to serve* his God and Father; to him, then, be glory and power for ever and ever. Amen. 7 It is he who *is coming on the clouds;* everyone will see him, even *those who pierced him,* and *all the races of the earth will mourn over him.* This is the truth. Amen. 8 "I am the Alpha and the Omega," says the Lord God, who is, who was, and who is to come, the Almighty.

[*b*] This section contains many Old Testament allusions to the time of the Messiah. The five direct quotations printed in italic are from: Ps. 89:37,27; Is. 55:4; Ex. 19:6; Dn. 7:13; and Zc. 12:10,14.

New English Bible

A message from Christ to the churches

John to the seven churches in the province of Asia.

Grace be to you and peace, from him who is and who was and who is to come, from the seven spirits before his throne, and from Jesus Christ, the faithful witness, the first-born from the dead and ruler of the kings of the earth.

To him who loves us and freed us from our sins with his life's blood, who made of us a royal house, to serve as the priests of his God and Father—to him be glory and dominion for ever and ever! Amen.

Behold, he is coming with the clouds! Every eye shall see him, and among them those who pierced him; and all the peoples of the world shall lament in remorse. So it shall be. Amen.

'I am the Alpha and the Omega', says the Lord God, who is and who was and who is to come, the sovereign Lord of all.

King James Version

mighty. 9 I John, who also am your brother, and
companion in tribulation, and in the kingdom and
patience of Jesus Christ, was in the isle that is
called Patmos, for the word of God, and for the
testimony of Jesus Christ. 10 I was in the Spirit
on the Lord's day, and heard behind me a great
voice, as of a trumpet, 11 Saying, I am Alpha
and Omega, the first and the last: and, What
thou seest, write in a book, and send *it* unto the
seven churches which are in Asia; unto Ephesus,
and unto Smyrna, and unto Pergamos, and unto
Thyatira, and unto Sardis, and unto Philadelphia, and unto Laodicea. 12And I turned to see
the voice that spake with me. And being turned,
I saw seven golden candlesticks; 13And in the
midst of the seven candlesticks *one* like unto the
Son of man, clothed with a garment down to the
foot, and girt about the paps with a golden
girdle. 14 His head and *his* hairs *were* white like
wool, as white as snow; and his eyes *were* as a
flame of fire; 15And his feet like unto fine brass,
as if they burned in a furnace; and his voice as
the sound of many waters. 16And he had in his
right hand seven stars: and out of his mouth
went a sharp twoedged sword: and his countenance *was* as the sun shineth in his strength.
17And when I saw him, I fell at his feet as dead.
And he laid his right hand upon me, saying unto
me, Fear not; I am the first and the last: 18 I
am he that liveth, and was dead; and, behold, I

Living Bible

9 It is I, your brother John, a fellow sufferer
for the Lord's sake, who am writing this letter to
you. I, too, have shared the patience Jesus gives,
and we shall share his kingdom!
I was on the island of Patmos, exiled there
for preaching the Word of God, and for telling
what I knew about Jesus Christ. 10 It was the
Lord's Day and I was worshiping, when suddenly I heard a loud voice behind me, a voice
that sounded like a trumpet blast, 11 saying, "I
am A and Z, the First and Last!" And then I
heard him say, "Write down everything you see,
and send your letter to the seven churches in
Turkey:[h] to the church in Ephesus, the one in
Smyrna, and those in Pergamos, Thyatira, Sardis,
Philadelphia, and Laodicea."
12 When I turned to see who was speaking,
there behind me were seven candlesticks of gold.
13And standing among them was one who looked
like Jesus who called himself the Son of Man,[i]
wearing a long robe circled with a golden band
across his chest. 14 His hair[j] was white as wool
or snow, and his eyes penetrated like flames of
fire. 15 His feet gleamed like burnished bronze,
and his voice thundered like the waves against
the shore. 16 He held seven stars in his right
hand and a sharp, double-bladed sword in his
mouth,[k] and his face shone like the power of
the sun in unclouded brilliance.
17, 18 When I saw him, I fell at his feet as
dead; but he laid his right hand on me and said,
"Don't be afraid! Though I am the First and

[*h*] "The seven churches in Asia." [*i*] Literally, "like unto a Son of Man"; John recognizes him from having lived with him for three years, and from seeing him in glory at the Transfiguration. [*j*] Literally, "His head—the hair—was white like wool." [*k*] Literally, "coming out from his mouth."

Today's English Version

A vision of Christ

9 I am John, your brother, and in union with
Jesus I share with you in suffering, and in his
Kingdom, and in enduring. I was put on the
island named Patmos because I had proclaimed
God's word and the truth that Jesus revealed.
10 On the Lord's day the Spirit took control of
me, and I heard a loud voice, that sounded like
a trumpet, speaking behind me. 11 It said, "Write
down what you see, and send the book to these
seven churches: in Ephesus, Smyrna, Pergamum,
Thyatira, Sardis, Philadelphia, and Laodicea."
12 I turned around to see who was talking
to me. There I saw seven gold lampstands.
13Among them stood a being who looked like
a man, wearing a robe that reached to his feet,
and a gold band around his chest. 14 His hair
was white as wool, or as snow, and his eyes
blazed like fire; 15 his feet shone like brass
melted in the furnace and then polished, and
his voice sounded like a mighty waterfall. 16 He
held seven stars in his right hand, and a sharp
two-edged sword came out of his mouth. His
face was as bright as the midday sun. 17 When
I saw him I fell down at his feet like a dead
man. He placed his right hand on me and said,
"Don't be afraid! I am the first and the last.
18 I am the living one! I was dead, but look, I

New International Version

One like a son of man

9 I, John, your brother and companion in the
suffering and kingdom and patient endurance
that are ours in Jesus, was on the island of
Patmos because of the word of God and the
testimony of Jesus. 10 On the Lord's Day I was
in the Spirit, and I heard behind me a loud voice
like a trumpet, 11 which said: "Write on a scroll
what you see and send it to the seven churches:
to Ephesus, Smyrna, Pergamum, Thyatira, Sardis,
Philadelphia and Laodicea."
12 I turned around to see the voice that was
speaking to me. And when I turned I saw seven
golden lampstands, 13 and among the lampstands
was someone "like a son of man,"[b] dressed in
a robe reaching down to his feet and with a
golden sash around his chest. 14 His head and
hair were white like wool, as white as snow,
and his eyes were like blazing fire. 15 His feet
were like brass glowing in a furnace, and his
voice was like the sound of rushing waters. 16 In
his right hand he held seven stars, and out of
his mouth came a sharp double-edged sword. His
face was like the sun shining in all its brilliance.
17 When I saw him, I fell at his feet as
though dead. Then he placed his right hand on
me and said: "Do not be afraid. I am the First
and the Last. 18 I am the Living One; I was

[*b*] Daniel 7:13.

Phillips Modern English

1.9 *The message to the seven Churches*

I, John, who am your brother and your companion in distress, and in the kingdom and faithful endurance to which Jesus calls us, was on the island called Patmos because I had spoken God's message and borne witness to Jesus. On the Lord's day I knew myself inspired by the Spirit, and I heard from behind me a voice loud as a trumpet-call, saying,

"Write down in a book what you see, and send it to the seven Churches—to Ephesus, Smyrna, Pergamum, Thyatira, Sardis, Philadelphia and Laodicea!"

I turned to see whose voice it was that was speaking to me and when I had turned I saw seven golden lampstands, and among these lampstands I saw someone like a Son of Man. He was dressed in a long robe with a golden girdle around his breast; his head and his hair were white as snow-white wool, his eyes blazed like fire, and his feet shone as the finest bronze glows in the furnace. His voice had the sound of a great waterfall, and I saw that in his right hand he held seven stars. A sharp two-edged sword came out of his mouth, and his face was ablaze like the sun at its height.

When my eyes took in this sight I fell at his feet like a dead man. And then he placed his right hand upon me and said,

"Do not be afraid. I am the first and the last, the living one. I am he who was dead, and

Revised Standard Version

9 I John, your brother, who share with you in
Jesus the tribulation and the kingdom and the
patient endurance, was on the island called Patmos on account of the word of God and the
testimony of Jesus. 10 I was in the Spirit on the
Lord's day, and I heard behind me a loud voice
like a trumpet 11 saying, "Write what you see
in a book and send it to the seven churches, to
Ephesus and to Smyrna and to Pergamum and
to Thyatira and to Sardis and to Philadelphia
and to Laodicea."
12 Then I turned to see the voice that was
speaking to me, and on turning I saw seven
golden lampstands, 13 and in the midst of the
lampstands one like a son of man, clothed with a
long robe and with a golden girdle round his
breast; 14 his head and his hair were white as
white wool, white as snow; his eyes were like a
flame of fire, 15 his feet were like burnished
bronze, refined as in a furnace, and his voice
was like the sound of many waters; 16 in his right
hand he held seven stars, from his mouth issued
a sharp two-edged sword, and his face was like
the sun shining in full strength.
17 When I saw him, I fell at his feet as though
dead. But he laid his right hand upon me, saying,
"Fear not, I am the first and the last, 18 and the

Jerusalem Bible

The beginning of the vision

9 My name is John, and through our union
in Jesus I am your brother and share your sufferings, your kingdom, and all you endure. I
was on the island of Patmos[c] for having preached
God's word and witnessed for Jesus; 10 it was
the Lord's day and the Spirit possessed me, and
I heard a voice behind me, shouting like a trumpet, 11 "Write down all that you see in a book,
and send it to the seven churches of Ephesus,
Smyrna, Pergamum, Thyatira, Sardis, Philadelphia and Laodicea." 12 I turned around to see
who had spoken to me, and when I turned I
saw seven golden lampstands 13 and, surrounded
by them, a figure *like a Son of man,*[d] dressed
in a long robe tied at the waist with a *golden*
girdle. 14 *His head* and *his hair* were *white as*
white wool or as snow, *his eyes* like a *burning*
flame, 15 *his feet like burnished bronze* when it
has been refined in a furnace, and *his voice like*
the sound of the ocean.[e] 16 In his right hand he
was holding seven stars, out of his mouth came
a sharp sword, double-edged, and his face was
like the sun shining with all its force.
17 When I saw him, I fell in a dead faint at
his feet, but he touched me with his right hand
and said, "Do not be afraid; it is I, *the First*
and *the Last;* I am the Living One, 18 I was

[c] Patmos (ten miles by five miles) was used by the Romans as a penal colony. [*d*] The Messianic figure in Deuteronomy; the descriptive quotations which follow are from Dn. 7 and 10. [*e*] Ezk. 43:2.

New English Bible

I, John, your brother, who share with you in the suffering and the sovereignty and the endurance which is ours in Jesus—I was on the island called Patmos because I had preached God's word and borne my testimony to Jesus. It was on the Lord's day, and I was caught up by the Spirit; and behind me I heard a loud voice, like the sound of a trumpet, which said to me, 'Write down what you see on a scroll and send it to the seven churches: to Ephesus, Smyrna, Pergamum, Thyatira, Sardis, Philadelphia, and Laodicea.' I turned to see whose voice it was that spoke to me; and when I turned I saw seven standing lamps of gold, and among the lamps one like a son of man, robed down to his feet, with a golden girdle round his breast. The hair of his head was white as snow-white wool, and his eyes flamed like fire; his feet gleamed like burnished brass refined in a furnace, and his voice was like the sound of rushing waters. In his right hand he held seven stars, and out of his mouth came a sharp two-edged sword; and his face shone like the sun in full strength.

When I saw him, I fell at his feet as though dead. But he laid his right hand upon me and said, 'Do not be afraid. I am the first and the last, and I am the living one; for I was dead

King James Version

am alive for evermore, Amen; and have the keys of hell and of death. 19 Write the things which thou hast seen, and the things which are, and the things which shall be hereafter; 20 The mystery of the seven stars which thou sawest in my right hand, and the seven golden candlesticks. The seven stars are the angels of the seven churches: and the seven candlesticks which thou sawest are the seven churches.

2 Unto the angel of the church of Ephesus write; These things saith he that holdeth the seven stars in his right hand, who walketh in the midst of the seven golden candlesticks; 2 I know thy works, and thy labour, and thy patience, and how thou canst not bear them which are evil: and thou hast tried them which say they are apostles, and are not, and hast found them liars: 3 And hast borne, and hast patience, and for my name's sake hast laboured, and hast not fainted. 4 Nevertheless I have *somewhat* against thee, because thou hast left thy first love. 5 Remember therefore from whence thou art fallen, and repent, and do the first works; or

Living Bible

Last, the Living One who died, who is now alive forevermore, who has the keys of hell and death —don't be afraid! 19 Write down what you have just seen, and what will soon be shown to you. 20 This is the meaning of the seven stars you saw in my right hand, and the seven golden candlesticks: The seven stars are the leaders[l] of the seven churches, and the seven candlesticks are the churches themselves.

2 *"Write a letter to the leader[a] of the church at Ephesus and tell him this:*

"I write to inform you of a message from him who walks among the churches[b] and holds their leaders in his right hand.

"He says to you: 2 I know how many good things you are doing. I have watched your hard work and your patience; I know you don't tolerate sin among your members, and you have carefully examined the claims of those who say they are apostles but aren't. You have found out how they lie. 3 You have patiently suffered for me without quitting.

4 "Yet there is one thing wrong; you don't love me as at first! 5 Think about those times of your first love (how different now!) and turn back to me again and work as you did be-

[*l*] Literally, "angels." Some expositors (Origen, Jerome, etc.) believe from this that an angelic being is appointed by God to oversee each local church. [*a*] Literally, "angel," as in 1:20. [*b*] Literally, "from him who holds the seven stars in his right hand and walks among the golden candlesticks."

Today's English Version

am alive forever and ever. I have authority over death and the world of the dead. 19 Write, then, the things you see, both the things that are now, and the things that will happen afterward. 20 Here is the secret meaning of the seven stars that you see in my right hand, and of the seven gold lampstands: the seven stars are the angels of the seven churches, and the seven lampstands are the seven churches."

The message to Ephesus

2 "To the angel of the church in Ephesus write:

"This is the message from the one who holds the seven stars in his right hand, who walks among the seven gold lampstands. 2 I know what you have done; I know how hard you have worked and how patient you have been. I know that you cannot tolerate evil men, and that you have tested those who say they are apostles but are not, and have found out that they are liars. 3 You are patient, you have suffered troubles for my sake, and you have not given up. 4 But here is what I have against you: you do not love me now as you did at first. 5 Remember how far you have fallen! Turn from your sins and do what you did at first. If you don't turn from your sins,

New International Version

dead, and behold I am alive for ever and ever! And I hold the keys of death and Hades.

19 "Write, therefore, what you have seen, what is now and what will take place later. 20 The mystery of the seven stars that you saw in my right hand and of the seven golden lampstands is this: The seven stars are the angels[c] of the seven churches, and the seven lampstands are the seven churches.

To the church in Ephesus

2 "To the angel[d] of the church in Ephesus write:

These are the words of him who holds the seven stars in his right hand and walks among the seven golden lampstands: 2 I know your deeds, your hard work and your perseverance. I know that you cannot tolerate wicked men, that you have tested those who claim to be apostles but are not, and have found them false. 3 You have persevered and have endured hardships for my name, and have not grown weary.

4 Yet I hold this against you: You have forsaken your first love. 5 Remember the height from which you have fallen! Repent and do the things you did at first. If you do

[*c*] Or *messengers.* [*d*] Or *messenger* (and elsewhere in chapters 2 and 3).

Phillips Modern English

now you see me alive for timeless ages! I hold in my hand the keys of death and the grave. Therefore, write down what you have seen, both the things which are now, and the things which are to be hereafter. The secret meaning of the seven stars which you saw in my right hand, and of the seven golden lampstands is this: the seven stars are the angels of the seven Churches and the seven lampstands are the Churches themselves."

2.1 *(i) To the loveless Church*

"Write this to the angel of the Church in Ephesus:

These words are spoken by the one who holds the seven stars safe in his right hand, and who walks among the seven golden lampstands. I know what you have done; I know how hard you have worked and what you have endured. I know that you will not tolerate wicked men, that you have put to the test self-styled 'apostles', who are nothing of the sort, and have found them to be liars. I know your powers of endurance—how you have suffered for the sake of my name and have not grown weary. But I hold this against you, that you do not love as you did at first. Remember then how far you have fallen. Repent and live as you lived at first. Otherwise, if your heart remains unchanged, I

Revised Standard Version

living one; I died, and behold I am alive for evermore, and I have the keys of Death and Hades. 19 Now write what you see, what is and what is to take place hereafter. 20 As for the mystery of the seven stars which you saw in my right hand, and the seven golden lampstands, the seven stars are the angels of the seven churches and the seven lampstands are the seven churches.

2 "To the angel of the church in Ephesus write: 'The words of him who holds the seven stars in his right hand, who walks among the seven golden lampstands.

2 " 'I know your works, your toil and your patient endurance, and how you cannot bear evil men but have tested those who call themselves apostles but are not, and found them to be false; 3 I know you are enduring patiently and bearing up for my name's sake, and you have not grown weary. 4 But I have this against you, that you have abandoned the love you had at first. 5 Remember then from what you have fallen, repent and do the works you did at

Jerusalem Bible

dead and now I am to live for ever and ever, and I hold the keys of death and of the underworld. 19 Now write down all that you see of present happenings and *things that are still to come.*[f] 20 The secret of the seven stars you have seen in my right hand, and of the seven golden lampstands is this: the seven stars are the angels of the seven churches, and the seven lampstands are the seven churches themselves.

1. Ephesus

2 "Write to the angel of the church in Ephesus and say, 'Here is the message of the one who holds the seven stars in his right hand and who lives surrounded by the seven golden lampstands: 2 I know all about you: how hard you work and how much you put up with. I know you cannot stand wicked men, and how you tested the impostors who called themselves apostles and proved they were liars. 3 I know, too, that you have patience, and have suffered for my name without growing tired. 4 Nevertheless, I have this complaint to make; you have less love now than you used to. 5 Think where you were before you fell; repent, and do as you used to at first, or else, if you will not repent, I shall

[f] Dn. 2:28.

New English Bible

and now I am alive for evermore, and I hold the keys of Death and Death's domain. Write down therefore what you have seen, what is now, and what will be hereafter.

'Here is the secret meaning of the seven stars which you saw in my right hand, and of the seven lamps of gold: the seven stars are the angels of the seven churches, and the seven lamps are the seven churches.

2 'To the angel of the church at Ephesus write:

' "These are the words of the One who holds the seven stars in his right hand and walks among the seven lamps of gold: I know all your ways, your toil and your fortitude. I know you cannot endure evil men; you have put to the proof those who claim to be apostles but are not, and have found them false. Fortitude you have; you have borne up in my cause and never flagged. But I have this against you: you have lost your early love. Think from what a height you have fallen; repent, and do as you once did. Otherwise, if you do not repent, I shall come to

King James Version

else I will come unto thee quickly, and will remove thy candlestick out of his place, except
thou repent. 6 But this thou hast, that thou
hatest the deeds of the Nicolaitans, which I
also hate. 7 He that hath an ear, let him hear
what the Spirit saith unto the churches; To him
that overcometh will I give to eat of the tree of
life, which is in the midst of the paradise of God.
8 And unto the angel of the church in Smyrna
write; These things saith the first and the last,
which was dead, and is alive; 9 I know thy
works, and tribulation, and poverty, (but thou
art rich) and *I know* the blasphemy of them
which say they are Jews, and are not, but *are*
the synagogue of Satan. 10 Fear none of those
things which thou shalt suffer: behold, the devil
shall cast *some* of you into prison, that ye may
be tried; and ye shall have tribulation ten days:
be thou faithful unto death, and I will give thee
a crown of life. 11 He that hath an ear, let him
hear what the Spirit saith unto the churches; He
that overcometh shall not be hurt of the second
death. 12 And to the angel of the church in Pergamos write; These things saith he which hath

Living Bible

fore; or else I will come and remove your candlestick from its place among the churches.
6 "But there is this about you that is good:
You hate the deeds of the licentious Nicolaitans,[c] just as I do.
7 "Let this message sink into the ears of anyone who listens to what the Spirit is saying to
the churches: To everyone who is victorious, I
will give fruit from the Tree of Life in the Paradise of God.
8 "*To the leader[d] of the church in Smyrna
write this letter:*
"This message is from him who is the First
and Last, who was dead and then came back
to life.
9 "I know how much you suffer for the Lord,
and I know all about your poverty (but you
have heavenly riches!). I know the slander of
those opposing you, who say that they are Jews
—the children of God—but they aren't, for
they support the cause of Satan. 10 Stop being
afraid of what you are about to suffer—for the
devil will soon throw some of you into prison
to test you. You will be persecuted for 'ten days.'
Remain faithful even when facing death and I
will give you the crown of life—an unending,
glorious future.[e] 11 Let everyone who can hear,
listen to what the Spirit is saying to the churches:
He who is victorious shall not be hurt by the
Second Death.
12 "*Write this letter to the leader[d] of the
church in Pergamos:*

[*c*] Nicolaitans, when translated from Greek to Hebrew, becomes Balaamites; followers of the man who induced the Israelites to fall by lust. (See Revelation 2:14 and Numbers 31:15,16.) [*d*] Literally, "angel." See note on 1:20. [*e*] Implied.

Today's English Version

I will come to you and take your lampstand
from its place. 6 But here is what you have in
your favor: you hate what the Nicolaitans do, as
much as I.
7 "If you have ears, then, listen to what the
Spirit says to the churches!
"To those who have won the victory I will
give the right to eat the fruit of the tree of life
that grows in the Garden of God."

The message to Smyrna

8 "To the angel of the church in Smyrna
write:
"This is the message from the one who is the
first and the last, who died and lived again. 9 I
know your troubles; I know that you are poor—
but really you are rich! I know the evil things
said against you by those who claim to be Jews,
but are not; they are a group that belongs to
Satan! 10 Do not be afraid of anything you are
about to suffer. Listen! The Devil will put you
to the test by having some of you thrown into
prison; your troubles will last ten days. Be
faithful to me, even if it means death, and I
will give you the crown of life.
11 "If you have ears, then, listen to what the
Spirit says to the churches!
"Those who win the victory will not be hurt
by the second death."

The message to Pergamum

12 "To the angel of the church in Pergamum
write:

New International Version

not repent, I will come to you and remove
your lampstand from its place. 6 But you have
this in your favor: You hate the practices of
the Nicolaitans, which I also hate.
7 He who has an ear, let him hear what the
Spirit says to the churches. To him who overcomes, I will give the right to eat from the
tree of life, which is in the paradise of God.

To the church in Smyrna

8 "To the angel of the church in Smyrna write:

These are the words of him who is the First
and the Last, who died and came to life again.
9 I know your afflictions and your poverty—
yet you are rich! I know the slander of those
who say they are Jews and are not, but are a
synagogue of Satan. 10 Do not be afraid of
what you are about to suffer. I tell you, the
devil will put some of you in prison to test
you, and you will suffer persecution for ten
days. Be faithful, even to the point of death,
and I will give you the crown of life.
11 He who has an ear, let him hear what
the Spirit says to the churches. He who overcomes will not be hurt at all by the second
death.

To the church in Pergamum

12 "To the angel of the church in Pergamum
write:

Phillips Modern English

shall come to you and remove your lampstand from its place.

Yet you have this to your credit, that you hate the practices of the Nicolaitans, which I myself detest. Let every listener hear what the Spirit says to the Churches:

To the victorious I will give the right to eat from the tree of life which grows in the paradise of God.

2.8 (ii) To the persecuted Church

"Write this to the angel of the Church in Smyrna:

These words are spoken by the first and the last, who died and came to life again. I know of your tribulation and of your poverty—though in fact you are rich! I know how you are slandered by those who call themselves Jews, but in fact are no Jews but a synagogue of Satan. Have no fear of what you will suffer. I tell you now that the devil is going to cast some of your number into prison where your faith will be tested and your distress will last for ten days. Be faithful in the face of death and I will give you the crown of life. Let every listener hear what the Spirit says to the Churches:

The victorious cannot suffer the slightest hurt from the second death.

2.12 (iii) To the over-tolerant Church

"Write this to the angel of the Church in Pergamum:

Revised Standard Version

first. If not, I will come to you and remove
your lampstand from its place, unless you repent. 6 Yet this you have, you hate the works
of the Nicolaitans, which I also hate. 7 He who
has an ear, let him hear what the Spirit says
to the churches. To him who conquers I will
grant to eat of the tree of life, which is in the
paradise of God.'
8 "And to the angel of the church in Smyrna
write: 'The words of the first and the last, who
died and came to life.
9 " 'I know your tribulation and your poverty
(but you are rich) and the slander of those who
say that they are Jews and are not, but are a
synagogue of Satan. 10 Do not fear what you
are about to suffer. Behold, the devil is about
to throw some of you into prison, that you may
be tested, and for ten days you will have tribulation. Be faithful unto death, and I will give
you the crown of life. 11 He who has an ear,
let him hear what the Spirit says to the churches.
He who conquers shall not be hurt by the second death.'
12 "And to the angel of the church in Pergamum write: 'The words of him who has the

Jerusalem Bible

come to you and take your lampstand from its
place. 6 It is in your favor, nevertheless, that you
loathe as I do what the Nicolaitans are doing.
7 If anyone has ears to hear, let him listen to
what the Spirit is saying to the churches: those
who prove victorious I will feed *from the tree
of life set in* God's *paradise.*' [g]

2. Smyrna

8 "Write to the angel of the church in Smyrna
and say, 'Here is the message of *the First* and
the Last, who was dead and has come to life
again: 9 I know the trials you have had, and
how poor you are—though you are rich—and
the slanderous accusations that have been made
by the people who profess to be Jews but are
really members of the synagogue of Satan. 10 Do
not be afraid of the sufferings that are coming
to you: I tell you, the devil is going to send
some of you to prison *to test you,* and you must
face an ordeal for *ten days.*[h] Even if you have
to die, keep faithful, and I will give you the
crown of life for your prize. 11 If anyone has
ears to hear, let him listen to what the Spirit is
saying to the churches: for those who prove
victorious there is nothing to be afraid of in the
second death.'

3. Pergamum

12 "Write to the angel of the church in Pergamum and say, 'Here is the message of the one

[g] Gn. 2:9. [h] I.e., of short duration.

New English Bible

you and remove your lamp from its place. Yet you have this in your favour: you hate the practices of the Nicolaitans, as I do. Hear, you who have ears to hear, what the Spirit says to the churches! To him who is victorious I will give the right to eat from the tree of life that stands in the Garden of God."

'To the angel of the church at Smyrna write:

' "These are the words of the First and the Last, who was dead and came to life again: I know how hard pressed you are, and poor—and yet you are rich; I know how you are slandered by those who claim to be Jews but are not—they are Satan's synagogue. Do not be afraid of the suffering to come. The Devil will throw some of you into prison, to put you to the test; and for ten days you will suffer cruelly. Only be faithful till death, and I will give you the crown of life. Hear, you who have ears to hear, what the Spirit says to the churches! He who is victorious cannot be harmed by the second death."

'To the angel of the church at Pergamum write:

King James Version

the sharp sword with two edges; 13 I know thy
works, and where thou dwellest, *even* where
Satan's seat *is:* and thou holdest fast my name,
and hast not denied my faith, even in those days
wherein Antipas *was* my faithful martyr, who
was slain among you, where Satan dwelleth.
14 But I have a few things against thee, because
thou hast there them that hold the doctrine of
Balaam, who taught Balak to cast a stumbling-
block before the children of Israel, to eat things
sacrificed unto idols, and to commit fornication.
15 So hast thou also them that hold the doctrine
of the Nicolaitans, which thing I hate. 16 Repent;
or else I will come unto thee quickly, and will
fight against them with the sword of my mouth.
17 He that hath an ear, let him hear what the
Spirit saith unto the churches; To him that
overcometh will I give to eat of the hidden
manna, and will give him a white stone, and in
the stone a new name written, which no man
knoweth saving he that receiveth *it.* 18 And unto
the angel of the church in Thyatira write; These
things saith the Son of God, who hath his eyes
like unto a flame of fire, and his feet *are* like fine
brass; 19 I know thy works, and charity, and
service, and faith, and thy patience, and thy

Living Bible

"This message is from him who wields the
sharp and double-bladed sword. 13 I am fully
aware that you live in the city where Satan's
throne is, at the center of satanic worship; and
yet you have remained loyal to me, and refused
to deny me, even when Antipas, my faithful
witness, was martyred among you by Satan's
devotees.

14 "And yet I have a few things against you.
You tolerate some among you who do as Balaam
did when he taught Balak how to ruin the people of Israel by involving them in sexual sin
and encouraging them to go to idol feasts.
15 Yes, you have some of these very same followers of Balaam[f] among you!

16 "Change your mind and attitude, or else
I will come to you suddenly and fight against
them with the sword of my mouth.

17 "Let everyone who can hear, listen to what
the Spirit is saying to the churches: Every one
who is victorious shall eat of the hidden manna,
the secret nourishment from heaven; and I will
give to each a white stone, and on the stone will
be engraved a new name that no one else knows
except the one receiving it.

18 "*Write this letter to the leader[d] of the
church in Thyatira:*

"This is a message from the Son of God,
whose eyes penetrate like flames of fire, whose
feet are like glowing brass.

19 "I am aware of all your good deeds—your
kindness to the poor, your gifts and service to
them; also I know your love and faith and pa-

[*f*] Literally, "Nicolaitans," Greek form of "Balaamites." [*d*] Literally, "angel." See note on 1:20.

Today's English Version

"This is the message from the one who has the
sharp two-edged sword. 13 I know where you
live, there where Satan has his throne. You are
true to me, and you did not abandon your faith
in me even during the time when Antipas, a
faithful witness for me, was killed there where
Satan lives. 14 But here are a few things I have
against you: there with you are some who follow
the teaching of Balaam, who taught Balak how
to cause the people of Israel to sin by eating
food that had been offered to idols, and by committing immorality. 15 In the same way, you also
have people among you who follow the teaching of the Nicolaitans. 16 Turn from your sins,
then! If not, I will come to you soon and fight
against those people with the sword that comes
out of my mouth.

17 "If you have ears, then, listen to what the
Spirit says to the churches!

"To those who have won the victory I will
give some of the hidden manna. I will also give
each of them a white stone, on which a new
name is written, which no one knows except the
one who receives it."

The message to Thyatira

18 "To the angel of the church in Thyatira
write:

"This is the message from the Son of God,
whose eyes blaze like fire, whose feet shine like
polished brass. 19 I know what you do. I know
your love, your faithfulness, your service, and

New International Version

These are the words of him who has the
sharp, double-edged sword. 13 I know where
you live—where Satan has his throne. Yet you
remain true to my name. You did not renounce your faith in me, even in the days of
Antipas, my faithful witness, who was put to
death in your city—where Satan lives.

14 Nevertheless, I have a few things against
you: You have people there who hold to the
teaching of Balaam, who taught Balak to entice the Israelites to sin by eating food sacrificed to idols and by committing sexual immorality. 15 And you have others who hold to
the teaching of the Nicolaitans. 16 Repent therefore! Otherwise, I will soon come to you and
will fight against them with the sword of my
mouth.

17 He who has an ear, let him hear what
the Spirit says to the churches. To him who
overcomes, I will give some of the hidden
manna. I will also give him a white stone with
a new name written on it, known only to him
who receives it.

To the church in Thyatira

18 "To the angel of the church in Thyatira write:

These are the words of the Son of God,
whose eyes are like blazing fire and whose
feet are like burnished brass. 19 I know your
deeds, your love and faith, your service and

Phillips Modern English

These words are spoken by him who has the sharp two-edged sword. I know where you live—where Satan sits enthroned. I know that you hold fast to my name and that you never denied your faith in me even in the days when Antipas, my faithful witness, was killed before your eyes in the very house of Satan.

Yet I have a few things against you—some of your number cling to the teaching of Balaam, the man who taught Balak how to entice the children of Israel into eating meat sacrificed to idols and into sexual immorality. I have also against you the fact that among your number are some who hold just as closely to the teaching of the Nicolaitans. Repent then, or else I shall come to you quickly and make war upon them with the sword of my mouth. Let the listener hear what the Spirit says to the Churches:

I will give the victorious some of the hidden manna, and I will also give him a white stone with a new name written upon it which no man knows except the man who receives it.

2.18 (iv) To the compromising Church

"Write this to the angel of the Church in Thyatira:

These are the words of the Son of God whose eyes blaze like fire and whose feet shine like the finest bronze:

I know what you have done. I know of your love and your loyalty, your service and your

Revised Standard Version

sharp two-edged sword.
13 " 'I know where you dwell, where Satan's
throne is; you hold fast my name and you did
not deny my faith even in the days of Antipas
my witness, my faithful one, who was killed
among you, where Satan dwells. 14 But I have
a few things against you: you have some there
who hold the teaching of Balaam, who taught
Balak to put a stumbling block before the sons
of Israel, that they might eat food sacrificed to
idols and practice immorality. 15 So you also
have some who hold the teaching of the Nicolaitans.
16 Repent then. If not, I will come to
you soon and war against them with the sword
of my mouth. 17 He who has an ear, let him
hear what the Spirit says to the churches. To
him who conquers I will give some of the hidden
manna, and I will give him a white stone, with
a new name written on the stone which no one
knows except him who receives it.'
18 "And to the angel of the church in Thyatira
write: 'The words of the Son of God, who
has eyes like a flame of fire, and whose feet are
like burnished bronze.
19 " 'I know your works, your love and faith
and service and patient endurance, and that

Jerusalem Bible

who has the sharp sword, double-edged: 13 I
know where you live, in the place where Satan
is enthroned, and that you still hold firmly to
my name, and did not disown your faith in me
even when my faithful witness, Antipas, was
killed in your own town, where Satan lives.[i]
14 Nevertheless, I have one or two complaints
to make: some of you are followers of
Balaam, who taught Balak to set a trap for the
Israelites so that they committed adultery by
eating food that had been sacrificed to idols;
15 and among you, too, there are some as bad
who accept what the Nicolaitans teach. 16 You
must repent, or I shall soon come to you and
attack these people with the sword out of my
mouth. 17 If anyone has ears to hear, let him
listen to what the Spirit is saying to the churches:
to those who prove victorious I will give the
hidden manna and a white stone[j]—a stone with
a new name written on it, known only to the
man who receives it.'

4. Thyatira

18 "Write to the angel of the church in
Thyatira and say, 'Here is the message of the
Son of God who has eyes like a burning flame
and feet like burnished bronze: 19 I know all
about you and how charitable you are; I know
your faith and devotion and how much you put

[i] I.e., "where emperor-worship is practiced." [j] The manna hidden by Jeremiah (2 Maccabees 2:4-8), to be the food of those who are saved in the heavenly kingdom; the white stone is a badge or token of admittance or membership.

New English Bible

' "These are the words of the One who has the sharp two-edged sword: I know where you live; it is the place where Satan has his throne. And yet you are holding fast to my cause. You did not deny your faith in me even at the time when Antipas, my faithful witness, was killed in your city, the home of Satan. But I have a few matters to bring against you: you have in Pergamum some that hold to the teaching of Balaam, who taught Balak to put temptation in the way of the Israelites. He encouraged them to eat food sacrificed to idols and to commit fornication, and in the same way you also have some who hold the doctrine of the Nicolaitans. So repent! If you do not, I shall come to you soon and make war upon them with the sword that comes out of my mouth. Hear, you who have ears to hear, what the Spirit says to the churches! To him who is victorious I will give some of the hidden manna; I will give him also a white stone, and on the stone will be written a new name, known to none but him that receives it."

'To the angel of the church at Thyatira write:

' "These are the words of the Son of God, whose eyes flame like fire and whose feet gleam like burnished brass: I know all your ways, your love and faithfulness, your good

King James Version

works; and the last *to be* more than the first.
20 Notwithstanding I have a few things against
thee, because thou sufferest that woman Jezebel,
which calleth herself a prophetess, to teach and
to seduce my servants to commit fornication, and
to eat things sacrificed unto idols. 21 And I gave
her space to repent of her fornication; and she
repented not. 22 Behold, I will cast her into a
bed, and them that commit adultery with her
into great tribulation, except they repent of their
deeds. 23 And I will kill her children with death;
and all the churches shall know that I am he
which searcheth the reins and hearts: and I will
give unto every one of you according to your
works. 24 But unto you I say, and unto the rest
in Thyatira, as many as have not this doctrine,
and which have not known the depths of Satan,
as they speak; I will put upon you none other
burden. 25 But that which ye have *already,* hold
fast till I come. 26 And he that overcometh, and
keepeth my works unto the end, to him will I
give power over the nations: 27 And he shall rule
them with a rod of iron; as the vessels of a potter shall they be broken to shivers: even as I
received of my Father. 28 And I will give him
the morning star. 29 He that hath an ear, let him
hear what the Spirit saith unto the churches.

Living Bible

tience, and I can see your constant improvement in all these things.
20 "Yet I have this against you: You are
permitting that woman Jezebel, who calls herself a prophetess, to teach my servants that sex
sin is not a serious matter; she urges them to
practice immorality and to eat meat that has
been sacrificed to idols. 21 I gave her time to
change her mind and attitude, but she refused.
22 Pay attention now to what I am saying: I
will lay her upon a sickbed of intense affliction,
along with all her immoral followers,[g] unless
they turn again to me, repenting of their sin
with her; 23 and I will strike her children dead.
And all the churches shall know that I am he
who searches deep within men's hearts, and
minds; I will give to each of you whatever you
deserve.
24, 25 "As for the rest of you in Thyatira
who have not followed this false teaching
('deeper truths,' as they call them—depths of
Satan, really), I will ask nothing further of you;
only hold tightly to what you have until I come.
26 "To every one who overcomes—who to the
very end keeps on doing things that please me—
I will give power over the nations. 27 You will
rule them with a rod of iron just as my Father
gave me the authority to rule them; they will
be shattered like a pot of clay that is broken
into tiny pieces. 28 And I will give you the
Morning Star!
29 "Let all who can hear, listen to what the
Spirit says to the churches.

[g] Literally, "together with all those who commit adultery with her."

Today's English Version

your patience. I know that you are doing more
now than you did at first. 20 But here is what
I have against you: you tolerate that woman
Jezebel, who calls herself a messenger of God.
She teaches and misleads my servants into committing immorality and eating food that has
been offered to idols. 21 I have given her time
to turn from her sins, but she does not wish to
turn from her immorality. 22 And so I will throw
her on a bed where she and those who committed adultery with her will suffer terribly. I
will do this now, unless they repent from the
wicked things they did with her. 23 I will also
kill her followers, and then all the churches will
know that I am he who knows men's thoughts
and wishes. I will repay each one of you according to what you have done.
24 "But the rest of you in Thyatira have not
followed this evil teaching; you have not learned
what the others call 'the deep secrets of Satan.'
I say to you that I will not put any other burden
on you. 25 But you must hold firmly to what you
have until I come. 26, 28 To those who win the
victory, who continue to do what I want until
the very end, I will give the same authority
which I received from my Father: I will give
them authority over the nations, to rule them
with an iron rod and to break them to pieces
like clay pots. I will also give them the morning star.
29 "If you have ears, then, listen to what the
Spirit says to the churches!"

New International Version

perseverance, and that you are now doing
more than you did at first.
20 Nevertheless, I have this against you:
You tolerate that woman Jezebel, who calls
herself a prophetess. By her teaching she misleads my servants into sexual immorality and
the eating of food sacrificed to idols. 21 I have
given her time to repent of her immorality,
but she is unwilling. 22 So I will cast her on
a bed of suffering, and I will make those who
commit adultery with her suffer intensely, unless they repent of her ways. 23 I will strike
her children dead. Then all the churches will
know that I am he who searches hearts and
minds, and I will repay each of you according
to your deeds. 24 Now I say to the rest of you
in Thyatira, to you who do not hold to her
teaching and have not learned Satan's so-
called deep secrets (I will not impose any
other burden on you): 25 Only hold on to
what you have until I come.
26 To him who overcomes and does my
will to the end, I will give authority over the
nations—
27 'He will rule them with a rod of iron
and dash them to pieces like pottery'[e]—
just as I have received authority from my Father. 28 I will also give him the morning star.
29 He who has an ear, let him hear what the
Spirit says to the churches.

[e] Psalm 2:9.

Phillips Modern English

endurance. Moreover, I know that you are doing more than you did at first. But I have this against you, that you tolerate that woman Jezebel who calls herself a prophetess, but who by her teaching deceives my servants into sexual immorality and eating idols'-meat. I have given her time to repent but she has shown no desire to repent of her immorality. See, now, how I throw her into bed and her lovers with her, and I will send them terrible suffering unless they repent of what she has done. As for her children, I shall strike them dead. Then all the Churches will know that I am the one who searches men's hearts and minds, and that I will reward each one of you according to your deeds.

But for the rest of you at Thyatira, who do not hold this teaching, and have not learned what they call 'the deep things of Satan', I will lay no further burden upon you, except that you hold on to what you have until I come!

To the one who is victorious, who carries out my work to the end, I will give authority over the nations, just as I myself have received authority from my Father, and I will give him the morning star. He shall 'shepherd them with a rod of iron'; he shall 'dash them in pieces like a potter's vessel'. Let the listener hear what the Spirit says to the Churches.

Revised Standard Version

your latter works exceed the first. 20 But I have
this against you, that you tolerate the woman
Jezebel, who calls herself a prophetess and is
teaching and beguiling my servants to practice
immorality and to eat food sacrificed to idols.
21 I gave her time to repent, but she refuses to
repent of her immorality. 22 Behold, I will throw
her on a sickbed, and those who commit adultery with her I will throw into great tribulation,
unless they repent of her doings; 23 and I will
strike her children dead. And all the churches
shall know that I am he who searches mind
and heart, and I will give to each of you as
your works deserve. 24 But to the rest of you in
Thyatira, who do not hold this teaching, who
have not learned what some call the deep things
of Satan, to you I say, I do not lay upon you
any other burden; 25 only hold fast what you
have, until I come. 26 He who conquers and
who keeps my works until the end, I will give
him power over the nations, 27 and he shall rule
them with a rod of iron, as when earthen pots
are broken in pieces, even as I myself have received power from my Father; 28 and I will give
him the morning star. 29 He who has an ear, let
him hear what the Spirit says to the churches.'

Jerusalem Bible

up with, and I know how you are still making
progress. 20 Nevertheless, I have a complaint to
make: you are encouraging the woman Jezebel [k]
who claims to be a prophetess, and by her teaching she is luring my servants away to commit
the adultery of eating food which has been sacrificed to idols. 21 I have given her time to reform but she is not willing to change her adulterous life. 22 Now I am consigning her to bed,
and all her partners in adultery to troubles that
will test them severely, unless they repent of
their practices; 23 and I will see that her children
die, so that all the churches realize that it is
I who *search heart and loins and give each one
of you what your behavior deserves.*[l] 24 But on
the rest of you in Thyatira, all of you who have
not accepted this teaching or learned the secrets
of Satan, as they are called, I am not laying any
special duty; 25 but hold firmly on to what you
already have until I come. 26 To those who
prove victorious, and keep working for me until the end, *I will give* the authority over *the
pagans*[m] 27 which I myself have been given by
my Father, *to rule them with an iron scepter
and shatter them like earthenware.* 28And I will
give him the Morning Star.[n] 29 If anyone has
ears to hear, let him listen to what the Spirit is
saying to the churches.'

[k] By this name the writer is indicating a prophetess of the Nicolaitan sect. [l] Jr. 11:20. [m] Ps. 2:8-9. [n] Symbol of power and thus of the resurrection.

New English Bible

service and your fortitude; and of late you have done even better than at first. Yet I have this against you: you tolerate that Jezebel, the woman who claims to be a prophetess, who by her teaching lures my servants into fornication and into eating food sacrificed to idols. I have given her time to repent, but she refuses to repent of her fornication. So I will throw her on to a bed of pain,[a] and plunge her lovers into terrible suffering, unless they forswear what she is doing; and her children I will strike dead. This will teach all the churches that I am the searcher of men's hearts and thoughts, and that I will reward each one of you according to his deeds. And now I speak to you others in Thyatira, who do not accept this teaching and have had no experience of what they like to call the deep secrets of Satan; on you I will impose no further burden. Only hold fast to what you have, until I come. To him who is victorious, to him who perseveres in doing my will to the end, I will give authority over the nations—that same authority which I received from my Father—and he shall rule them with an iron rod, smashing them to bits like earthenware; and I will give him also the star of dawn. Hear, you who have ears to hear, what the Spirit says to the churches!"

[a] *One witness reads* into a furnace.

King James Version

3 And unto the angel of the church in Sardis write; These things saith he that hath the seven Spirits of God, and the seven stars; I know thy works, that thou hast a name that thou livest, and art dead. 2 Be watchful, and strengthen the things which remain, that are ready to die: for I have not found thy works perfect before God. 3 Remember therefore how thou hast received and heard, and hold fast, and repent. If therefore thou shalt not watch, I will come on thee as a thief, and thou shalt not know what hour I will come upon thee. 4 Thou hast a few names even in Sardis which have not defiled their garments; and they shall walk with me in white: for they are worthy. 5 He that overcometh, the same shall be clothed in white raiment; and I will not blot out his name out of the book of life, but I will confess his name before my Father, and before his angels. 6 He that hath an ear, let him hear what the Spirit saith unto the churches. 7And to the angel of the church in Philadelphia write; These things saith he that is holy, he that is true, he that hath the key of

Living Bible

3 "*To the leader*[a] *of the church in Sardis write this letter:*

"This message is sent to you by the one who has the seven-fold Spirit[b] of God and the seven stars.

"I know your reputation as a live and active church, but you are dead. 2 Now wake up! Strengthen what little remains—for even what is left is at the point of death. Your deeds are far from right in the sight of God. 3 Go back to what you heard and believed at first; hold to it firmly and turn to me again. Unless you do, I will come suddenly upon you, unexpected as a thief, and punish you.

4 "Yet even there in Sardis some haven't soiled their garments with the world's filth; they shall walk with me in white, for they are worthy. 5 Everyone who conquers will be clothed in white, and I will not erase his name from the Book of Life, but I will announce before my Father and his angels that he is mine.

6 "Let all who can hear, listen to what the Spirit is saying to the churches.

7 "*Write this letter to the leader*[a] *of the church in Philadelphia.*

"This message is sent to you by the one who is holy and true, and has the key of David to

[a] Literally, "angel." See note on 1:20. [b] Literally, "the seven spirits of God." See note on 1:4.

Today's English Version

The message to Sardis

3 "To the angel of the church in Sardis write:

"This is the message from the one who has the seven spirits of God and the seven stars. I know what you are doing; I know that you have the reputation of being alive, even though you are dead! 2 So wake up, and strengthen what you still have, before it dies completely. For I find that what you have done is not yet perfect in the sight of my God. 3 Remember, then, what you were taught and how you heard it; obey it, and turn from your sins. If you do not wake up, I will come upon you like a thief, and you will not even know the hour when I come. 4 But a few of you there in Sardis have kept your clothes clean. You will walk with me, clothed in white, because you are worthy to do so. 5 Those who win the victory will be clothed like this in white, and I will not remove their names from the book of the living. In the presence of my Father and of his angels I will declare openly that they belong to me.

6 "If you have ears, then, listen to what the Spirit says to the churches!"

The message to Philadelphia

7 "To the angel of the church in Philadelphia write:

"This is the message from the one who is holy and true, who holds the key that belonged to

New International Version

To the church in Sardis

3 "To the angel of the church in Sardis write:

These are the words of him who holds the seven spirits[f] of God and the seven stars. I know your deeds; you have a reputation of being alive, but you are dead. 2 Wake up! Strengthen what remains and is about to die, for I have not found your deeds complete in the sight of my God. 3 Remember, therefore, what you have received and heard; obey it, and repent. But if you do not wake up, I will come like a thief, and you will not know at what time I will come to you.

4 Yet you have a few people in Sardis who have not soiled their clothes. They will walk with me, dressed in white, for they are worthy. 5 He who overcomes will, like them, be dressed in white. I will never erase his name from the book of life, but will acknowledge his name before my Father and his angels. 6 He who has an ear, let him hear what the Spirit says to the churches.

To the church in Philadelphia

7 "To the angel of the church in Philadelphia write:

These are the words of him who is holy and true, who holds the key of David. What he

[f] Or *the sevenfold Spirit.*

Phillips Modern English

3.1 (*v*) *To the sleeping Church*

"Write this to the angel of the Church in Sardis:

These are the words of him who holds in his hand the seven Spirits of God and the seven stars:

I know what you have done, that you have a reputation for being alive, but that in fact you are dead. Now wake up! Strengthen what you still have before it dies! For I have not found any of your deeds complete in the sight of my God. Remember then what you were given and what you were taught. Hold to those things and repent. If you refuse to wake up, then I will come to you like a thief, and you will have no idea of the hour of my coming.

Yet you still have a few names in Sardis of people who have not soiled their garments. They shall walk with me in white, for they have deserved to do so. The victorious shall wear such white garments, and never will I erase his name from the book of life. Indeed, I will speak his name openly in the presence of my Father and of his angels. Let the listener hear what the Spirit says to the Churches.

3.7 (*vi*) *To the Church with opportunity*

"Then write this to the angel of the Church in Philadelphia:

These are the words of the Holy One and the true, who holds the key of David, who opens

Revised Standard Version

3 "And to the angel of the church in Sardis write: 'The words of him who has the seven spirits of God and the seven stars.

" 'I know your works; you have the name of being alive, and you are dead. 2 Awake, and strengthen what remains and is on the point of death, for I have not found your works perfect in the sight of my God. 3 Remember then what you received and heard; keep that, and repent. If you will not awake, I will come like a thief, and you will not know at what hour I will come upon you. 4 Yet you have still a few names in Sardis, people who have not soiled their garments; and they shall walk with me in white, for they are worthy. 5 He who conquers shall be clad thus in white garments, and I will not blot his name out of the book of life; I will confess his name before my Father and before his angels. 6 He who has an ear, let him hear what the Spirit says to the churches.'

7 "And to the angel of the church in Philadelphia write: 'The words of the holy one, the true one, who has the key of David, who opens

Jerusalem Bible

5. Sardis

3 "Write to the angel of the church in Sardis and say, 'Here is the message of the one who holds the seven spirits of God and the seven stars: I know all about you: how you are reputed to be alive and yet are dead. 2 Wake up; revive what little you have left: it is dying fast. So far I have failed to notice anything in the way you live that my God could possibly call perfect, 3 and yet do you remember how eager you were when you first heard the message? Hold on to that. Repent. If you do not wake up, I shall come to you like a thief, without telling you at what hour to expect me. 4 There are a few in Sardis, it is true, who have kept their robes from being dirtied, and they are fit to come with me, dressed in white. 5 Those who prove victorious will be dressed, like these, in white robes; I shall not blot their names out of the book of life, but acknowledge their names in the presence of my Father and his angels. 6 If anyone has ears to hear, let him listen to what the Spirit is saying to the churches.'

6. Philadelphia

7 "Write to the angel of the church in Philadelphia and say, 'Here is the message of the holy and faithful one who *has the key of David,* so

New English Bible

3 'To the angel of the church at Sardis write:

' "These are the words of the One who holds the seven spirits of God, the seven stars: I know all your ways; that though you have a name for being alive, you are dead. Wake up, and put some strength into what is left, which must otherwise die! For I have not found any work of yours completed in the eyes of my God. So remember the teaching you received; observe it, and repent. If you do not wake up, I shall come upon you like a thief, and you will not know the moment of my coming. Yet you have a few persons in Sardis who have not polluted their clothing. They shall walk with me in white, for so they deserve. He who is victorious shall thus be robed all in white; his name I will never strike off the roll of the living, for in the presence of my Father and his angels I will acknowledge him as mine. Hear, you who have ears to hear, what the Spirit says to the churches!"

'To the angel of the church at Philadelphia write:

' "These are the words of the holy one, the true one, who holds the key of David; when he

King James Version

David, he that openeth, and no man shutteth;
and shutteth, and no man openeth; 8 I know
thy works: behold, I have set before thee an
open door, and no man can shut it: for thou
hast a little strength, and hast kept my word,
and hast not denied my name. 9 Behold, I will
make them of the synagogue of Satan, which
say they are Jews, and are not, but do lie; behold, I will make them to come and worship before thy feet, and to know that I have loved
thee. 10 Because thou hast kept the word of my
patience, I also will keep thee from the hour of
temptation, which shall come upon all the world,
to try them that dwell upon the earth. 11 Behold, I come quickly: hold that fast which
thou hast, that no man take thy crown. 12 Him
that overcometh will I make a pillar in the temple of my God, and he shall go no more out:
and I will write upon him the name of my God,
and the name of the city of my God, *which is*
new Jerusalem, which cometh down out of
heaven from my God: and *I will write upon*
him my new name. 13 He that hath an ear, let
him hear what the Spirit saith unto the churches.
14 And unto the angel of the church of the
Laodiceans write; These things saith the Amen,

Living Bible

open what no one can shut and to shut what no
one can open.

8 "I know you well; you aren't strong, but
you have tried to obey[c] and have not denied my
Name. Therefore I have opened a door to you
that no one can shut.

9 "Note this: I will force those supporting
the causes of Satan while claiming to be mine[d]
(but they aren't—they are lying) to fall at your
feet and acknowledge that you are the ones I
love.

10 "Because you have patiently obeyed me
despite the persecution, therefore I will protect
you from[e] the time of Great Tribulation and
temptation, which will come upon the world to
test everyone alive. 11 Look, I am coming soon![f]
Hold tightly to the little strength you have—so
that no one will take away your crown.

12 "As for the one who conquers, I will make
him a pillar in the temple of my God; he will
be secure, and will go out no more; and I will
write my God's Name on him, and he will be a
citizen in the city of my God—the New Jerusalem, coming down from heaven from my God;
and he will have my new Name inscribed upon
him.

13 "Let all who can hear, listen to what the
Spirit is saying to the churches.

14 "*Write this letter to the leader*[a] *of the
church in Laodicea:*

[*c*] Literally, "you have kept my word." [*d*] Literally, "say they are Jews but are not." [*e*] Or, "I will keep you from failing in the hour of testing . . ." The inference is not clear in the Greek as to whether this means "kept from" or "kept through" the coming horror. [*f*] Or, "suddenly," "unexpectedly." [*a*] Literally, "angel." See note on 1:20.

Today's English Version

David, who opens so that none can close, who
closes so that none can open. 8 I know what you
do; I know that you have a little power; you
have followed my teaching and have been faithful to me. I have opened a door before you,
which no one can close. 9 Listen! As for that
group that belongs to Satan, those liars who
claim that they are Jews, but are not, I will make
them come before you and bow down at your
feet. They will all know that I love you. 10 Because you have kept my order to be patient, I
will also keep you safe from the time of trouble
which is coming upon the whole world, to test
all the people on earth. 11 I am coming soon.
Keep safe what you have, so that no one will
rob you of your victory prize. 12 I will make
him who is victorious a pillar in the temple of
my God, and he will never again leave it. I
will write on him the name of my God, and the
name of the city of my God, the new Jerusalem,
which will come down out of heaven from my
God. I will also write on him my new name.

13 "If you have ears, then, listen to what the
Spirit says to the churches!"

The message to Laodicea

14 "To the angel of the church in Laodicea
write:

New International Version

opens, no one can shut; and what he shuts,
no one can open. 8 I know your deeds. See, I
have placed before you an open door that no
one can shut. I know that you have little
strength, yet you have kept my word and have
not denied my name. 9 I will make those who
are of the synagogue of Satan, who claim to
be Jews though they are not, but are liars—I
will make them come and fall down at your
feet and acknowledge that I have loved you.
10 Since you have kept my command to endure patiently, I will also keep you from the
hour of trial that is going to come upon the
whole world to test those who live on the
earth.

11 I am coming soon. Hold on to what you
have, so that no one will take your crown.
12 Him who overcomes I will make a pillar in
the temple of my God. Never again will he
leave it. I will write on him the name of my
God and the name of the city of my God,
the new Jerusalem, which is coming down out
of heaven from my God; and I will also write
on him my new name. 13 He who has an ear,
let him hear what the Spirit says to the
churches.

To the church in Laodicea

14 "To the angel of the church in Laodicea write:

Phillips Modern English

and no man shall shut, and who shuts and no man shall open. I know what you have done. See, I have given you a door flung wide open, which no man can close! For you have some little power and have been faithful to my message and have not denied my name. See how I deal with those of Satan's synagogue, who claim to be Jews, yet are no Jews but liars! Watch how I make them come and bow down before your feet and acknowledge that I have loved you. Because you have obeyed my call to patient endurance I will keep you safe from the hour of trial which is to come upon the whole world, to test all who live upon the earth. I am coming soon; hold fast to what you have—let no one deprive you of your crown. As for the victorious, I will make him a pillar in the Temple of my God, and he will never leave it. I will write upon him the name of my God, and the name of the city of my God, the new Jerusalem which comes down out of Heaven from my God. And I will write upon him my own new name. Let the listener hear what the Spirit says to the Churches.

3.14 (*vii*) *To the complacent Church*

"Then write this to the angel of the Church in Laodicea:

Revised Standard Version

and no one shall shut, who shuts and no one opens.
8 " 'I know your works. Behold, I have set before you an open door, which no one is able to shut; I know that you have but little power, and yet you have kept my word and have not
denied my name. 9 Behold, I will make those of the synagogue of Satan who say that they are Jews and are not, but lie—behold, I will make them come and bow down before your feet, and
learn that I have loved you. 10 Because you have kept my word of patient endurance, I will keep you from the hour of trial which is coming on the whole world, to try those who
dwell upon the earth. 11 I am coming soon; hold fast what you have, so that no one may seize
your crown. 12 He who conquers, I will make him a pillar in the temple of my God; never shall he go out of it, and I will write on him the name of my God, and the name of the city of my God, the new Jerusalem which comes down from my God out of heaven, and my own
new name. 13 He who has an ear, let him hear what the Spirit says to the churches.'
14 "And to the angel of the church in Laodicea write: 'The words of the Amen, the faith-

Jerusalem Bible

that *when he opens, nobody can close, and when he closes, nobody can open*[o]: 8 I know all about you; and now I have opened in front of you a door that nobody will be able to close—and I know that though you are not very strong, you have kept my commandments and not disowned
my name. 9 Now I am going to make the synagogue of Satan—those who profess to be Jews, but are liars, because they are no such thing—I will make them come and *fall at your feet*[p] and admit that *you are* the people *that I love.*[q]
10 Because you have kept my commandment to endure trials, I will keep you safe in the time of trial which is going to come for the whole world, to test the people of the world. 11 Soon
I shall be with you: hold firmly to what you already have, and let nobody take your prize away
from you. 12 Those who prove victorious I will make into pillars in the sanctuary of my God, and they will stay there for ever; I will inscribe on them the name of my God and the name of the city of my God, the new Jerusalem which comes down from my God in heaven, and my own new name as well. 13 If anyone has ears
to hear, let him listen to what the Spirit is saying to the churches.'

7. Laodicea

14 "Write to the angel of the church in Laodicea and say, 'Here is the message of the

[*o*] Is. 22:22. [*p*] Is. 45:14. [*q*] Is. 43:4.

New English Bible

opens none may shut, when he shuts none may open: I know all your ways, and look, I have set before you an open door, which no one can shut. Your strength, I know, is small, yet you have observed my commands and have not disowned my name. So this is what I will do: I will make those of Satan's synagogue, who claim to be Jews but are lying frauds, come and fall down at your feet; and they shall know that you are my beloved people. Because you have kept my command and stood fast, I will also keep you from the ordeal that is to fall upon the whole world and test its inhabitants. I am coming soon; hold fast what you have, and let no one rob you of your crown. He who is victorious—I will make him a pillar in the temple of my God; he shall never leave it. And I will write the name of my God upon him, and the name of the city of my God, that new Jerusalem which is coming down out of heaven from my God, and my own new name. Hear, you who have ears to hear, what the Spirit says to the churches!"

'To the angel of the church at Laodicea write:

King James Version

the faithful and true witness, the beginning of
the creation of God; 15 I know thy works, that
thou art neither cold nor hot: I would thou
wert cold or hot. 16 So then because thou art
lukewarm, and neither cold nor hot, I will spew
thee out of my mouth. 17 Because thou sayest, I
am rich, and increased with goods, and have
need of nothing; and knowest not that thou art
wretched, and miserable, and poor, and blind,
and naked: 18 I counsel thee to buy of me gold
tried in the fire, that thou mayest be rich; and
white raiment, that thou mayest be clothed, and
that the shame of thy nakedness do not appear;
and anoint thine eyes with eyesalve, that thou
mayest see. 19 As many as I love, I rebuke and
chasten: be zealous therefore, and repent. 20 Behold, I stand at the door, and knock: if any
man hear my voice, and open the door, I will
come in to him, and will sup with him, and he
with me. 21 To him that overcometh will I grant
to sit with me in my throne, even as I also overcame, and am set down with my Father in his
throne. 22 He that hath an ear, let him hear what
the Spirit saith unto the churches.

Living Bible

"This message is from the one who stands
firm,[g] the faithful and true Witness [of all that
is or was or evermore shall be[h]], the primeval
source of God's creation:

15 "I know you well—you are neither hot nor
cold; I wish you were one or the other! 16 But
since you are merely lukewarm, I will spit you
out of my mouth!

17 "You say, 'I am rich, with everything I
want; I don't need a thing!' And you don't realize that spiritually you are wretched and miserable and poor and blind and naked.

18 "My advice to you is to buy pure gold
from me, gold purified by fire—only then will
you truly be rich. And to purchase from me
white garments, clean and pure, so you won't be
naked and ashamed; and to get medicine from
me to heal your eyes and give you back your
sight. 19 I continually discipline and punish everyone I love; so I must punish you, unless you
turn from your indifference and become enthusiastic about the things of God.

20 "Look! I have been standing at the door
and I am constantly knocking. If anyone hears
me calling him and opens the door, I will come
in and fellowship with him and he with me. 21 I
will let every one who conquers sit beside me on
my throne, just as I took my place with my Father on his throne when I had conquered. 22 Let
those who can hear, listen to what the Spirit is
saying to the churches."

[g] Literally, "from the Amen." [h] Implied.

Today's English Version

"This is the message from the Amen, the
faithful and true witness, who is the origin of
all that God has created. 15 I know what you
have done; I know that you are neither cold
nor hot. How I wish you were either one or the
other! 16 But because you are barely warm,
neither hot nor cold, I am going to spit you
out of my mouth! 17 'I am rich and well off,' you
say, 'I have all I need.' But you do not know
how miserable and pitiful you are! You are
poor, naked, and blind. 18 I advise you, then, to
buy gold from me, pure gold, in order to be
rich. Buy also white clothing to dress yourself
and cover up your shameful nakedness. Buy also
some medicine to put on your eyes, so that you
may see. 19 I reprove and punish all whom I
love. Be in earnest, then, and turn from your
sins. 20 Listen! I stand at the door and knock; if
anyone hears my voice and opens the door, I
will come into his house and eat with him, and
he will eat with me. 21 To those who win the
victory I will give the right to sit by me on my
throne, just as I have been victorious, and now
sit by my Father on his throne.

22 "If you have ears, then, listen to what the
Spirit says to the churches!"

New International Version

These are the words of the Amen, the faithful and true witness, the ruler of God's creation. 15 I know your deeds, that you are neither
cold nor hot. I wish you were either one or
the other! 16 So, because you are lukewarm—
neither hot nor cold—I am about to spit you
out of my mouth. 17 You say, 'I am rich; I
have acquired wealth and do not need a thing.'
But you do not realize that you are wretched,
pitiful, poor, blind and naked. 18 I counsel you
to buy from me gold refined in the fire, so
you can become rich; and white clothes to
wear, so you can cover your shameful nakedness; and salve to put on your eyes, so you
can see.

19 Those whom I love I rebuke and discipline. So be earnest, and repent. 20 Here I
am! I stand at the door and knock. If anyone
hears my voice and opens the door, I will go
in and eat with him, and he with me.

21 To him who overcomes, I will give the
right to sit with me on my throne, just as I
overcame and sat down with my Father on
his throne. 22 He who has an ear, let him hear
what the Spirit says to the churches."

Phillips Modern English

These are the words of the Amen, the faithful and true witness, the beginning of God's creation:

I know what you have done, and that you are neither cold nor hot. I could wish that you were either cold or hot! But since you are lukewarm and neither hot nor cold, I intend to spit you out of my mouth! While you say, 'I am rich, I have prospered, and there is nothing that I need', you have no eyes to see that you are wretched, pitiable, poverty-stricken, blind and naked. My advice to you is to buy from me that gold which is refined in the furnace so that you may be rich, and white garments to wear so that you may hide the shame of your nakedness, and salve to put on your eyes to make you see. All those whom I love I correct and discipline. Therefore, shake off your complacency and repent. See, I stand knocking at the door. If anyone listens to my voice and opens the door, I will go into his house and dine with him, and he with me. As for the victorious, I will give him the honour of sitting beside me on my throne, just as I myself have won the victory and have taken my seat beside my Father on his throne. Let the listener hear what the Spirit says to the Churches."

Revised Standard Version

ful and true witness, the beginning of God's creation.

15 " 'I know your works: you are neither cold nor hot. Would that you were cold or hot! 16 So, because you are lukewarm, and neither cold nor hot, I will spew you out of my mouth. 17 For you say, I am rich, I have prospered, and I need nothing; not knowing that you are wretched, pitiable, poor, blind, and naked. 18 Therefore I counsel you to buy from me gold refined by fire, that you may be rich, and white garments to clothe you and to keep the shame of your nakedness from being seen, and salve to anoint your eyes, that you may see. 19 Those whom I love, I reprove and chasten; so be zealous and repent. 20 Behold, I stand at the door and knock; if any one hears my voice and opens the door, I will come in to him and eat with him, and he with me. 21 He who conquers, I will grant him to sit with me on my throne, as I myself conquered and sat down with my Father on his throne. 22 He who has an ear, let him hear what the Spirit says to the churches.' "

Jerusalem Bible

Amen, the faithful, the true witness, the ultimate source of God's creation: 15 I know all about you: how you are neither cold nor hot. I wish you were one or the other, 16 but since you are neither, but only lukewarm, I will spit you out of my mouth. 17 You say to yourself, "I am rich, I have made a fortune, and have everything I want," never realizing that you are wretchedly and pitiably poor, and blind and naked too. 18 I warn you, buy from me the gold that has been tested in the fire to make you really rich, and white robes to clothe you and cover your shameful nakedness, and eye ointment to put on your eyes so that you are able to see. 19 I *am the* one *who reproves and disciplines all those he loves*[r]: so repent in real earnest. 20 Look, I am standing at the door, knocking. If one of you hears me calling and opens the door, I will come in to share his meal, side by side with him. 21 Those who prove victorious I will allow to share my throne, just as I was victorious myself and took my place with my Father on his throne. 22 If anyone has ears to hear, let him listen to what the Spirit is saying to the churches.' "

[*r*] Pr. 3:12.

New English Bible

' "These are the words of the Amen, the faithful and true witness, the prime source of all God's creation: I know all your ways; you are neither hot nor cold. How I wish you were either hot or cold! But because you are lukewarm, neither hot nor cold, I will spit you out of my mouth. You say, 'How rich I am! And how well I have done! I have everything I want.' In fact, though you do not know it, you are the most pitiful wretch, poor, blind, and naked. So I advise you to buy from me gold refined in the fire, to make you truly rich, and white clothes to put on to hide the shame of your nakedness, and ointment for your eyes so that you may see. All whom I love I reprove and discipline. Be on your mettle therefore and repent. Here I stand knocking at the door; if anyone hears my voice and opens the door, I will come in and sit down to supper with him and he with me. To him who is victorious I will grant a place on my throne, as I myself was victorious and sat down with my Father on his throne. Hear, you who have ears to hear, what the Spirit says to the churches!" '

King James Version

4 After this I looked, and, behold, a door
was opened in heaven: and the first voice
which I heard *was* as it were of a trumpet talking with me; which said, Come up hither, and I
will shew thee things which must be hereafter.
2And immediately I was in the Spirit: and, behold, a throne was set in heaven, and *one* sat on
the throne. 3And he that sat was to look upon
like a jasper and a sardine stone: and *there was*
a rainbow round about the throne, in sight like
unto an emerald. 4And round about the throne
were four and twenty seats: and upon the seats
I saw four and twenty elders sitting, clothed in
white raiment; and they had on their heads
crowns of gold. 5And out of the throne proceeded lightnings and thunderings and voices:
and *there were* seven lamps of fire burning before the throne, which are the seven Spirits of
God. 6And before the throne *there was* a sea of
glass like unto crystal: and in the midst of the
throne, and round about the throne, *were* four
beasts full of eyes before and behind. 7And the
first beast *was* like a lion, and the second beast
like a calf, and the third beast had a face as a
man, and the fourth beast *was* like a flying

Living Bible

4 Then as I looked, I saw a door standing
open in heaven, and the same voice I had
heard before, that sounded like a mighty trumpet
blast, spoke to me and said, "Come up here and
I will show you what must happen in the future!"
2 And instantly I was, in spirit, there in
heaven and saw—oh, the glory of it!—a throne
and someone sitting on it! 3 Great bursts of light
flashed forth from him as from a glittering diamond, or from a shining ruby, and a rainbow
glowing like an emerald encircled his throne.
4 Twenty-four smaller thrones surrounded his,
with twenty-four Elders sitting on them; all were
clothed in white, with golden crowns upon their
heads. 5 Lightning and thunder issued from the
throne, and there were voices in the thunder.
Directly in front of his throne were seven lighted
lamps representing the seven-fold Spirit[a] of God.
6 Spread out before it was a shiny crystal sea.
Four Living Beings, dotted front and back with
eyes, stood at the throne's four sides. 7 The first
of these Living Beings was in the form of a lion;
the second looked like an ox; the third had the
face of a man; and the fourth, the form of an
eagle, with wings spread out as though in flight.

[*a*] Literally, "the seven spirits of God." But see Zechariah 4:2-6, where the lamps are equated with the one Spirit.

Today's English Version

Worship in heaven

4 At this point I had another vision, and
saw an open door in heaven.
And the voice that sounded like a trumpet,
which I had heard speaking to me before, said,
"Come up here, and I will show you what must
happen after this." 2At once the Spirit took
control of me. There in heaven was a throne,
with someone sitting on it. 3 His face gleamed
like such precious stones as jasper and carnelian;
all around the throne there was a rainbow the
color of an emerald. 4 In a circle around the
throne were twenty-four other thrones, on which
were seated twenty-four elders dressed in white
and wearing gold crowns. 5 From the throne
came flashes of lightning, sounds, and peals of
thunder. There were seven lighted torches burning before the throne; these are the seven spirits
of God. 6 In front of the throne there was what
looked like a sea of glass, clear as crystal.
Surrounding the throne, on each of its sides,
were four living creatures covered with eyes in
front and in back. 7 The first living creature
looked like a lion; the second looked like a calf;
the third had a face like a man's face; and the

New International Version

The throne in heaven

4 After this I looked, and there before me
was a door standing open in heaven. And
the voice I had first heard speaking to me like
a trumpet said, "Come up here, and I will
show you what must take place after this." 2At
once I was in the Spirit, and there before me was
a throne in heaven with someone sitting on it.
3And the one who sat there had the appearance
of jasper and carnelian. A rainbow, resembling
an emerald, encircled the throne. 4 Surrounding
the throne were twenty-four other thrones, and
seated on them were twenty-four elders. They
were dressed in white and had crowns of gold
on their heads. 5 From the throne came flashes
of lightning, rumblings and peals of thunder.
Before the throne, seven lamps were blazing.
These are the seven spirits[g] of God. 6Also before the throne there was what looked like a
sea of glass, clear as crystal.
In the center, around the throne, were four
living creatures, and they were covered with
eyes, in front and in back. 7 The first living
creature was like a lion, the second was like an
ox, the third had a face like a man, the fourth

[g] Or *the sevenfold Spirit.*

Phillips Modern English

4.1 The vision of Heaven

Later I looked again, and before my eyes a door stood open in Heaven, and in my ears was the voice with the ring of a trumpet, which I had heard at first, speaking to me and saying, "Come up here, and I will show you what must happen in the future."

Immediately I knew myself to be inspired by the Spirit, and in my vision I saw that a throne had been set up in Heaven, and there was someone seated upon the throne. His appearance blazed like jasper and cornelian, and all around the throne shone a halo like an emerald rainbow. In a circle around the throne there were twenty-four thrones and seated upon them twenty-four elders dressed in white with golden crowns upon their heads. From the central throne come flashes of lightning, noises and peals of thunder. Seven lamps are burning before the throne, and they are the seven Spirits of God. In front of the throne there appears a sea of glass as clear as crystal. On each side, encircling the throne, are four living creatures covered with eyes in front and behind. The first living creature is like a lion, the second is like a calf, the third has a face like a man, and the fourth living creature appears like an eagle in

Revised Standard Version

4 After this I looked, and lo, in heaven an open door! And the first voice, which I had heard speaking to me like a trumpet, said, "Come up hither, and I will show you what must take place after this." 2 At once I was in the Spirit, and lo, a throne stood in heaven, with one seated on the throne! 3 And he who sat there appeared like jasper and carnelian, and round the throne was a rainbow that looked like an emerald. 4 Round the throne were twenty-four thrones, and seated on the thrones were twenty-four elders, clad in white garments, with golden crowns upon their heads. 5 From the throne issue flashes of lightning, and voices and peals of thunder, and before the throne burn seven torches of fire, which are the seven spirits of God; 6 and before the throne there is as it were a sea of glass, like crystal.

And round the throne, on each side of the throne, are four living creatures, full of eyes in front and behind: 7 the first living creature like a lion, the second living creature like an ox, the third living creature with the face of a man, and the fourth living creature like a flying eagle.

Jerusalem Bible

II. The prophetic visions

A. The prelude to the great day

God entrusts the future of the world to the Lamb

4 Then, in my vision, I saw a door open in heaven and heard the same voice speaking to me, the voice like a trumpet, saying, "Come up here: I will show you *what is to come* in the future." 2 With that, the Spirit possessed me and I saw a throne standing in heaven, and the *One* who was *sitting on the throne,* 3 and the Person sitting there looked like a diamond and a ruby. There was a rainbow encircling the throne, and this looked like an emerald.[s] 4 Around the throne in a circle were twenty-four thrones, and on them I saw twenty-four elders sitting, dressed in white robes with golden crowns on their heads. 5 Flashes of lightning were coming from the throne, and the sound of peals of thunder, and in front of the throne there were seven flaming lamps burning, the seven Spirits of God. 6 Between the throne and myself was a sea that seemed to be made of glass, like crystal. *In the center,* grouped around the throne itself, were *four animals*[t] *with many eyes,* in front and behind. 7 *The first* animal was like *a lion, the second* like *a bull, the third* animal had *a human face,* and *the fourth* animal was like a flying

[s] For many of the descriptive details in this scene the writer draws on Ezk. 1, 10 and Is. 6. [t] The angels or "principles" which direct the physical world. Since Irenaeus, these four creatures have been used as symbols of the four evangelists.

New English Bible

The opening of the sealed book

4 After this I looked, and there before my eyes was a door opened in heaven; and the voice that I had first heard speaking to me like a trumpet said, 'Come up here, and I will show you what must happen hereafter.' At once I was caught up by the Spirit. There in heaven stood a throne, and on the throne sat one whose appearance was like the gleam of jasper and cornelian; and round the throne was a rainbow, bright as an emerald. In a circle about this throne were twenty-four other thrones, and on them sat twenty-four elders, robed in white and wearing crowns of gold. From the throne went out flashes of lightning and peals of thunder. Burning before the throne were seven flaming torches, the seven spirits of God, and in front of it stretched what seemed a sea of glass, like a sheet of ice.

In the centre, round the throne itself, were four living creatures, covered with eyes, in front and behind. The first creature was like a lion, the second like an ox, the third had a human

King James Version

eagle. 8 And the four beasts had each of them six wings about *him;* and *they were* full of eyes within: and they rest not day and night, saying, Holy, holy, holy, Lord God Almighty, which was, and is, and is to come. 9 And when those beasts give glory and honour and thanks to him that sat on the throne, who liveth for ever and ever, 10 The four and twenty elders fall down before him that sat on the throne, and worship him that liveth for ever and ever, and cast their crowns before the throne, saying, 11 Thou art worthy, O Lord, to receive glory and honour and power: for thou hast created all things, and for thy pleasure they are and were created.

5 And I saw in the right hand of him that sat on the throne a book written within and on the back side, sealed with seven seals. 2 And I saw a strong angel proclaiming with a loud voice, Who is worthy to open the book, and to

Living Bible

8 Each of these Living Beings had six wings, and the central sections of their wings were covered with eyes. Day after day and night after night they kept on saying, "Holy, holy, holy, Lord God Almighty—the one who was, and is, and is to come."

9 And when the Living Beings gave glory and honor and thanks to the one sitting on the throne, who lives forever and ever, 10 the twenty-four Elders fell down before him and worshiped him, the Eternal Living One, and cast their crowns before the throne, singing, 11 "O Lord, you are worthy to receive the glory and the honor and the power, for you have created all things. They were created and called into being by your act of will."

5 And I saw a scroll in the right hand of the one who was sitting on the throne, a scroll with writing on the inside and on the back, and sealed with seven seals. 2 A mighty angel with a loud voice was shouting out this question: "Who is worthy to break the seals on this scroll, and to

Today's English Version

fourth looked like a flying eagle. 8 Each one of the four living creatures had six wings, and they were covered over with eyes, inside and out. They never stop their singing day or night:

"Holy, holy, holy, is the Lord God Almighty,
who was, who is, and who is to come."

9 The four living creatures sing songs of glory and honor and thanks to the one who sits on the throne, who lives forever and ever. When they do so, 10 the twenty-four elders fall down before the one who sits on the throne, and worship him who lives forever and ever. They throw their crowns before the throne, and say,

11 "Our Lord and God! You are worthy
to receive glory, honor, and power.
For you created all things,
and by your will they were given existence and life."

The scroll and the Lamb

5 I saw a scroll in the right hand of the one who sat on the throne; it was covered with writing on both sides, and was sealed with seven seals. 2 And I saw a mighty angel, who announced in a loud voice, "Who is worthy to

New International Version

was like a flying eagle. 8 Each of the four living creatures had six wings and was covered with eyes all around, even under his wings. Day and night they never stop saying:

"Holy, holy, holy
is the Lord God Almighty,
who was, and is, and is to come."

9 Whenever the living creatures give glory, honor and thanks to him who sits on the throne and who lives for ever and ever, 10 the twenty-four elders fall down before him who sits on the throne, and worship him who lives for ever and ever. They lay their crowns before the throne and say:

11 "You are worthy, our Lord and God,
to receive glory and honor and power,
for you created all things,
and by your will they were created and have their being."

The scroll and the Lamb

5 Then I saw in the right hand of him who sat on the throne a scroll with writing on both sides and sealed with seven seals. 2 And I saw a mighty angel proclaiming in a loud voice, "Who is worthy to break the seals and open the

Phillips Modern English

flight. These four creatures have each of them six wings and are covered with eyes, all around them, and even within them. Day and night they never cease to say,

"Holy, holy, holy is the Lord God, the Almighty, who was and who is and who is coming."

4.9 The ceaseless worship of Heaven

And whenever the living creatures give glory and honour and thanksgiving to the one who sits upon the throne, who lives for timeless ages, the twenty-four elders prostrate themselves before him who is seated upon the throne and worship the One who lives for timeless ages. They cast their crowns before the throne and say,

"Thou art worthy, O Lord our God, to receive glory and honour and power, for thou didst create all things; by thy will they existed and were created."

5.1 The sealed book of future events

Then I noticed in the right hand of the One seated upon the throne a book filled with writing both inside and on its back, and it was sealed with seven seals. And I saw a mighty angel who called out in a loud voice,

"Who is fit to open the book and break its seals?"

Revised Standard Version

8And the four living creatures, each of them with six wings, are full of eyes all round and within, and day and night they never cease to sing,

"Holy, holy, holy, is the Lord God Almighty,
who was and is and is to come!"

9And whenever the living creatures give glory and honor and thanks to him who is seated on the throne, who lives for ever and ever, 10 the twenty-four elders fall down before him who is seated on the throne and worship him who lives for ever and ever; they cast their crowns before the throne, singing,

11 "Worthy art thou, our Lord and God,
to receive glory and honor and power,
for thou didst create all things,
and by thy will they existed and were created."

5 And I saw in the right hand of him who was seated on the throne a scroll written within and on the back, sealed with seven seals; 2 and I saw a strong angel proclaiming with a loud voice, "Who is worthy to open the scroll

Jerusalem Bible

eagle. 8 *Each* of the four animals had *six wings* and *had eyes all the way around* as well as inside; and day and night they never stopped singing:

"Holy, Holy, Holy
is the Lord God, the Almighty;
he was, he is and he is to come."

9 Every time the animals glorified and honored and gave thanks to the One sitting on the throne, *who lives for ever and ever,* 10 the twenty-four elders prostrated themselves before him to worship the One *who lives for ever and ever,* and threw down their crowns in front of the throne, saying, 11 "You are our Lord and our God, you are worthy of glory and honor and power, because you made all the universe and it was only by your will that everything was made and exists."

5 I saw that in the right hand of the One sitting on the throne there was *a scroll that had writing on back and front*[u] and was sealed with seven seals. 2 Then I saw a powerful angel who called with a loud voice, "Is there anything worthy to open the scroll and break the seals of

[u] Ezk. 2:9.

New English Bible

face, the fourth was like an eagle in flight. The four living creatures, each of them with six wings, had eyes all over, inside and out; and by day and by night without a pause they sang:

'Holy, holy, holy is God the sovereign Lord of all, who was, and is, and is to come!'

As often as the living creatures give glory and honour and thanks to the One who sits on the throne, who lives for ever and ever, the twenty-four elders fall down before the One who sits on the throne and worship him who lives for ever and ever; and as they lay their crowns before the throne they cry:

'Thou art worthy, O Lord our God, to receive glory and honour and power, because thou didst create all things; by thy will they were created, and have their being!'

5 Then I saw in the right hand of the One who sat on the throne a scroll, with writing inside and out, and it was sealed up with seven seals. And I saw a mighty angel proclaiming in a loud voice, 'Who is worthy to open the scroll

King James Version

loose the seals thereof? 3And no man in heaven,
nor in earth, neither under the earth, was able
to open the book, neither to look thereon. 4And
I wept much, because no man was found worthy
to open and to read the book, neither to look
thereon. 5And one of the elders saith unto me,
Weep not: behold, the Lion of the tribe of Juda,
the Root of David, hath prevailed to open the
book, and to loose the seven seals thereof. 6And
I beheld, and, lo, in the midst of the throne and
of the four beasts, and in the midst of the elders,
stood a Lamb, as it had been slain, having seven
horns and seven eyes, which are the seven Spirits
of God sent forth into all the earth. 7And he
came and took the book out of the right hand
of him that sat upon the throne. 8And when he
had taken the book, the four beasts and four
and twenty elders fell down before the Lamb,
having every one of them harps, and golden vials
full of odours, which are the prayers of saints.
9And they sung a new song, saying, Thou art
worthy to take the book, and to open the seals
thereof: for thou wast slain, and hast redeemed
us to God by thy blood out of every kindred,

Living Bible

unroll it?" 3 But no one in all heaven or earth
or from among the dead was permitted to open
and read it.
4 Then I wept with disappointment[a] because
no one anywhere was worthy; no one could tell
us what it said.
5 But one of the twenty-four Elders said to
me, "Stop crying, for look! The Lion of the tribe
of Judah, the Root of David, has conquered, and
proved himself worthy to open the scroll and to
break its seven seals."
6 I looked and saw a Lamb standing there
before the twenty-four Elders, in front of the
throne and the Living Beings, and on the Lamb
were wounds that once had caused his death. He
had seven horns and seven eyes, which represent
the seven-fold Spirit[b] of God, sent out into every
part of the world. 7 He stepped forward and
took the scroll from the right hand of the one
sitting upon the throne. 8And as he took the
scroll, the twenty-four Elders fell down before
the Lamb, each with a harp and golden vials
filled with incense—the prayers of God's people!
9 They were singing[c] him a new song with
these words: "You are worthy to take the scroll
and break its seals and open it; for you were
slain, and your blood has bought people from

[*a*] Implied. [*b*] Literally, "the seven spirits of God"; but see Zechariah 4:2-6,10, where the seven eyes are equated with the seven lamps and the one Spirit. [*c*] Literally, "saying" or "said."

Today's English Version

break the seals and open the scroll?" 3 But no
one was found in heaven, or on earth, or in the
world below, who could open the scroll and
look inside it. 4 I cried bitterly because no one
had been found who was worthy to open the
scroll or look inside it. 5 Then one of the elders
said to me, "Don't cry. Look! The Lion from
Judah's tribe, the great descendant of David,
has won the victory and can break the seven
seals and open the scroll."
6 Then I saw a Lamb standing in the center
of the throne, surrounded by the four living
creatures and the elders. The Lamb appeared to
have been killed. It had seven horns and seven
eyes, which are the seven spirits of God that
have been sent into all the world. 7 The Lamb
went and took the scroll from the right hand of
the one who sat on the throne. 8As he did so,
the four living creatures and the twenty-four
elders fell down before the Lamb. Each had a
harp, and gold bowls filled with incense, which
are the prayers of God's people. 9 They sang a
new song:

"You are worthy to take the scroll
and to break open its seals.
For you were killed, and by your death
you bought men for God,
from every tribe, language, nation, and
race.

New International Version

scroll?" 3 But no one in heaven or on earth or
under the earth could open the scroll or even
look inside it. 4 I wept and wept because no one
was found who was worthy to open the scroll or
look inside. 5 Then one of the elders said to me,
"Do not weep! See, the Lion of the tribe of
Judah, the Root of David, has triumphed. He is
able to open the scroll and its seven seals."
6 Then I saw a Lamb, looking as if it had
been slain, standing in the center of the throne,
encircled by the four living creatures and the
elders. He had seven horns and seven eyes,
which are the seven spirits[h] of God sent out into
all the earth. 7 He came and took the scroll from
the right hand of him who sat on the throne.
8And when he had taken it, the four living
creatures and the twenty-four elders fell down
before the Lamb. Each one had a harp and they
were holding golden bowls full of incense, which
are the prayers of the saints. 9And they sang a
new song:

"You are worthy to take the scroll
and to open its seals,
because you were slain,
and with your blood you purchased men
for God
from every tribe and language and people
and nation.

[*h*] Or *the sevenfold Spirit.*

Phillips Modern English

And no one in Heaven or upon earth or under the earth was able to open the book, or even to look at it. I began to weep bitterly because no one could be found fit to open the book, or even to look at it, when one of the elders said to me,

"Do not weep. See, the lion from the tribe of Judah, the root of David, has won the victory and is able to open the book and break its seven seals."

Then, standing in the very centre of the throne and of the four living creatures and of the elders, I saw a Lamb that seemed to have been slaughtered. He had seven horns and seven eyes, which are the seven Spirits of God and are sent out into every corner of the earth. Then he came and took the book from the right hand of him who was seated upon the throne.

5.8 *The new hymn of the created and of the redeemed*

When he had taken the book, the four living creatures and the twenty-four elders prostrated themselves before the Lamb. Each of them had a harp, and they had golden bowls full of incense, which are the prayers of the saints. They sang a new song and these are the words they sang,

"Worthy art thou to take the book and break its seals, for thou hast been slain and by thy blood hast purchased for God men from every

Revised Standard Version

and break its seals?"
3And no one in heaven or on earth or under the earth was able to open the scroll or to look into it,
4and I wept much that no one was found worthy to open the scroll or to look into it.
5Then one of the elders said to me, "Weep not; lo, the Lion of the tribe of Judah, the Root of David, has conquered, so that he can open the scroll and its seven seals."

6 And between the throne and the four living creatures and among the elders, I saw a Lamb standing, as though it had been slain, with seven horns and with seven eyes, which are the seven spirits of God sent out into all the earth;
7and he went and took the scroll from the right hand of him who was seated on the throne.
8And when he had taken the scroll, the four living creatures and the twenty-four elders fell down before the Lamb, each holding a harp, and with golden bowls full of incense, which are the prayers of the saints;
9and they sang a new song, saying,

"Worthy art thou to take the scroll and to open its seals,
for thou wast slain and by thy blood didst ransom men for God
from every tribe and tongue and people and nation,

Jerusalem Bible

it?"
3But there was no one, in heaven or on the earth or under the earth, who was able to open the scroll and read it.
4I wept bitterly because there was nobody fit to open the scroll and read it,
5but one of the elders said to me, "There is no need to cry: *the Lion* of the tribe *of Judah, the Root*[v] of David, has triumphed, and he will open the scroll and the seven seals of it."

6 Then I saw, standing between the throne with its four animals and the circle of the elders, a Lamb that seemed to have been sacrificed; it had seven horns, and it had seven eyes, which are the seven Spirits God has *sent out all over the world.*[w]
7The Lamb came forward to take the scroll from the right hand of the One sitting on the throne,
8and when he took it, the four animals prostrated themselves before him and with them the twenty-four elders; each one of them was holding a harp and had a golden bow full of incense made of the prayers of the saints.
9They sang a new hymn:

"You are worthy to take the scroll
and break the seals of it,
because you were sacrificed, and with your blood
you bought men for God
of every race, language, people and nation

[v] Gn. 49:9; Is. 11:10. [w] Zc. 4:10.

New English Bible

and to break its seals?' There was no one in heaven or on earth or under the earth able to open the scroll or to look inside it. I was in tears because no one was found who was worthy to open the scroll or to look inside it. But one of the elders said to me: 'Do not weep; for the Lion from the tribe of Judah, the Scion of David, has won the right to open the scroll and break its seven seals.'

Then I saw standing in the very middle of the throne, inside the circle of living creatures and the circle of elders,[a] a Lamb with the marks of slaughter upon him. He had seven horns and seven eyes, the eyes which are the seven spirits of God sent out over all the world. And the Lamb went up and took the scroll from the right hand of the One who sat on the throne. When he took it, the four living creatures and the twenty-four elders fell down before the Lamb. Each of the elders had a harp, and they held golden bowls full of incense, the prayers of God's people, and they were singing a new song:

'Thou art worthy to take the scroll and to break its seals, for thou wast slain and by thy blood didst purchase for God men of every tribe and language, people and nation;

[a] *Or* standing between the throne, with the four living creatures, and the elders . . .

King James Version

and tongue, and people, and nation; 10And hast
made us unto our God kings and priests: and
we shall reign on the earth. 11And I beheld, and
I heard the voice of many angels round about
the throne, and the beasts, and the elders: and
the number of them was ten thousand times ten
thousand, and thousands of thousands; 12 Saying with a loud voice, Worthy is the Lamb that
was slain to receive power, and riches, and wisdom, and strength, and honour, and glory, and
blessing. 13And every creature which is in
heaven, and on the earth, and under the earth,
and such as are in the sea, and all that are in
them, heard I saying, Blessing, and honour, and
glory, and power, *be* unto him that sitteth upon
the throne, and unto the Lamb for ever and
ever. 14And the four beasts said, Amen. And
the four *and* twenty elders fell down and worshipped him that liveth for ever and ever.

Living Bible

every nation as gifts for God. 10And you have
gathered them into a kingdom and made them
priests of our God; they shall reign upon the
earth."
11 Then in my vision I heard the singing[d] of
millions of angels surrounding the throne and
the Living Beings and the Elders: 12 "The Lamb
is worthy" (loudly they sang[d] it!) "—the Lamb
who was slain. He is worthy to receive the power,
and the riches, and the wisdom, and the strength,
and the honor, and the glory, and the blessing."
13 And then I heard everyone in heaven and
earth, and from the dead beneath the earth and
in the sea, exclaiming, "The blessing and the
honor and the glory and the power belong to the
one sitting on the throne, and to the Lamb forever and ever." 14And the four Living Beings
kept saying, "Amen!" And the twenty-four Elders fell down and worshiped him.

[*d*] Literally, "saying" or "said."

Today's English Version

10 You have made them a kingdom of priests
to serve our God,
and they shall rule on earth."

11 Again I looked, and I heard angels, thousands and millions of them! They stood around
the throne, the four living creatures, and the
elders, 12 and sang in a loud voice,

"The Lamb who was killed is worthy
to receive power, wealth, wisdom, and strength,
honor, glory, and praise!"

13And I heard every creature in heaven, on
earth, and in the world below, and every creature in the sea—all creatures in the whole universe—and they were singing,

"To him who sits on the throne, and to the Lamb,
be praise and honor, glory and might,
forever and ever!"

14 The four living creatures answered, "Amen!"
And the elders fell down and worshiped.

New International Version

10 You have made them to be a kingdom and
priests to serve our God,
and they will reign on the earth."
11 Then I looked and heard the voice of many
angels, numbering thousands upon thousands,
and ten thousand times ten thousand. They encircled the throne and the living creatures and
the elders. 12 In a loud voice they sang:
"Worthy is the Lamb, who was slain,
to receive power and wealth and wisdom and strength
and honor and glory and praise!"
13 Then I heard every creature in heaven and
on earth and under the earth and on the sea, and
all that is in them, singing:
"To him who sits on the throne and to the Lamb
be praise and honor and glory and power,
for ever and ever!"
14 The four living creatures said, "Amen," and
the elders fell down and worshiped.

Phillips Modern English

tribe, and tongue, and people, and nation! Thou hast made them a kingdom of priests for our God, and they shall reign as kings upon the earth."

5.11 The hymn of the whole company of Heaven

Then in my vision I heard the voices of many angels encircling the throne, the living creatures and the elders. There were myriads of myriads and thousands of thousands, crying in a great voice,

"Worthy is the Lamb who was slain, to receive power and riches and wisdom, and strength and honour and glory and blessing!"

Then I heard the voice of everything created in Heaven, upon earth, under the earth and upon the sea, and all that are in them saying, "Blessing and honour and glory and power be given to him who sits upon the throne, and to the Lamb, for timeless ages!"

The four living creatures said, "Amen", while the elders fell down and worshipped.

Revised Standard Version

10 and hast made them a kingdom and priests
to our God,
and they shall reign on earth."
11 Then I looked, and I heard around the throne
and the living creatures and the elders the voice
of many angels, numbering myriads of myriads
and thousands of thousands, 12 saying with a
loud voice, "Worthy is the Lamb who was slain,
to receive power and wealth and wisdom and
might and honor and glory and blessing!" 13 And
I heard every creature in heaven and on earth
and under the earth and in the sea, and all
therein, saying, "To him who sits upon the
throne and to the Lamb be blessing and honor
and glory and might for ever and ever!" 14 And
the four living creatures said, "Amen!" and the
elders fell down and worshiped.

Jerusalem Bible

10 and made them *a line of kings and priests,*[x]
to serve our God and to rule the world."

11 In my vision, I heard the sound of an immense number of angels gathered around the
throne and the animals and the elders; there
were *ten thousand times ten thousand of them*[y]
and *thousands upon thousands,* 12 shouting, "The
Lamb that was sacrificed is worthy to be given
power, riches, wisdom, strength, honor, glory and
blessing." 13 Then I heard all the living things
in creation—everything that lives in the air, and
on the ground, and under the ground, and in
the sea, crying, "To the One who is sitting on
the throne and to the Lamb, be all praise, honor,
glory and power, for ever and ever." 14 And the
four animals said, "Amen"; and the elders prostrated themselves to worship.

New English Bible

thou hast made of them a royal house, to serve our God as priests; and they shall reign upon earth.'

Then as I looked I heard the voices of countless angels. These were all round the throne and the living creatures and the elders. Myriads upon myriads there were, thousands upon thousands, and they cried aloud:

'Worthy is the Lamb, the Lamb that was slain, to receive all power and wealth, wisdom and might, honour and glory and praise!'

Then I heard every created thing in heaven and on earth and under the earth and in the sea, all that is in them, crying:

'Praise and honour, glory and might, to him who sits on the throne and to the Lamb for ever and ever!'

And the four living creatures said, 'Amen', and the elders fell down and worshipped.

[*x*] Is. 61:6. [*y*] Dn. 7:10.

King James Version

6 And I saw when the Lamb opened one of
the seals, and I heard, as it were the noise of
thunder, one of the four beasts saying, Come
and see. 2 And I saw, and behold a white horse:
and he that sat on him had a bow; and a crown
was given unto him: and he went forth conquering, and to conquer. 3 And when he had
opened the second seal, I heard the second beast
say, Come and see. 4 And there went out another
horse *that was* red: and *power* was given to him
that sat thereon to take peace from the earth,
and that they should kill one another: and there
was given unto him a great sword. 5 And when
he had opened the third seal, I heard the third
beast say, Come and see. And I beheld, and lo a

Living Bible

6 As I watched, the Lamb broke the first seal
and began to unroll the scroll. Then one of
the four Living Beings, with a voice that sounded
like thunder, said, "Come!"

2 I looked, and there in front of me was a
white horse. Its rider carried a bow, and a crown
was placed upon his head; he rode out to conquer in many battles and win the war.

3 Then he unrolled the scroll to the second
seal, and broke it open too. And I heard the
second Living Being say, "Come!"

4 This time a red horse rode out. Its rider
was given a long sword and the authority to
banish peace and bring anarchy to the earth;
war and killing broke out everywhere.

5 When he had broken the third seal, I heard
the third Living Being say, "Come!" And I saw

Today's English Version

The seals

6 Then I saw the Lamb break open the first
of the seven seals, and I heard one of the
four living creatures say in a voice that sounded
like thunder, "Come!" 2 I looked, and there was
a white horse. Its rider held a bow, and he was
given a crown. He went out as a conqueror to
conquer.

3 Then the Lamb broke open the second seal;
and I heard the second living creature say,
"Come!" 4 Another horse came out, a red one.
Its rider was given the power to bring war on
the earth, that men should kill each other; he
was given a large sword.

5 Then the Lamb broke open the third seal;
and I heard the third living creature say,
"Come!" I looked, and there was a black horse.

New International Version

The seals

6 I watched as the Lamb opened the first of
the seven seals. Then I heard one of the
four living creatures say in a voice like thunder,
"Come!" 2 I looked, and there before me was
a white horse! Its rider held a bow, and he was
given a crown, and he rode out as a conqueror
bent on conquest.

3 When the Lamb opened the second seal, I
heard the second living creature say, "Come!"
4 Then another horse came out, a fiery red one.
Its rider was given power to take peace from
the earth and to make men slay each other. To
him was given a large sword.

5 When the Lamb opened the third seal, I
heard the third living creature say, "Come!" I
looked, and there before me was a black horse!

Phillips Modern English

THE LAMB BREAKS THE SEALS

6.1 The first rider: Conquest

Then I watched while the Lamb broke one of the seven seals, and I heard one of the four living creatures say in a voice of thunder,
"Come out!"
I looked, and before my eyes was a white horse. Its rider carried a bow, and he was given a crown. He rode out conquering and bent on conquest.

6.3 The second rider: War

Then, when the Lamb broke the second seal, I heard the second living creature cry,
"Come out!"
And another horse came forth, red in colour. Its rider was given power to deprive the earth of peace, so that men should kill each other. A huge sword was put into his hand.

6.5 The third rider: Famine

When the Lamb broke the third seal, I heard the third living creature say,
"Come out!"
I looked again and there before my eyes was

Revised Standard Version

6 Now I saw when the Lamb opened one of
the seven seals, and I heard one of the four
living creatures say, as with a voice of thunder,
"Come!" 2And I saw, and behold, a white horse,
and its rider had a bow; and a crown was given
to him, and he went out conquering and to conquer.
3 When he opened the second seal, I heard
the second living creature say, "Come!" 4And
out came another horse, bright red; its rider
was permitted to take peace from the earth, so
that men should slay one another; and he was
given a great sword.
5 When he opened the third seal, I heard the
third living creature say, "Come!" And I saw,

Jerusalem Bible

The Lamb breaks the seven seals

6 Then I saw the Lamb break one of the
seven seals, and I heard one of the four animals shout in a voice like thunder, "Come."
2 Immediately a white horse appeared, and the
rider on it was holding a bow; he was given the
victor's crown and he went away, to go from
victory to victory.
3 When he broke the second seal, I heard the
second animal shout, "Come." 4And out came
another horse, bright red, and its rider was given
this duty: to take away peace from the earth
and set people killing each other. He was given
a huge sword.
5 When he broke the third seal, I heard the
third animal shout, "Come." Immediately a

New English Bible

6 Then I watched as the Lamb broke the first of the seven seals; and I heard one of the four living creatures say in a voice like thunder, 'Come!' And there before my eyes was a white horse, and its rider held a bow. He was given a crown, and he rode forth, conquering and to conquer.

When the Lamb broke the second seal, I heard the second creature say, 'Come!' And out came another horse, all red. To its rider was given power to take peace from the earth and make men slaughter one another; and he was given a great sword.

When he broke the third seal, I heard the third creature say, 'Come!' And there, as I looked, was

King James Version

black horse; and he that sat on him had a pair of balances in his hand. 6And I heard a voice in the midst of the four beasts say, A measure of wheat for a penny, and three measures of barley for a penny; and *see* thou hurt not the oil and the wine. 7And when he had opened the fourth seal, I heard the voice of the fourth beast say, Come and see. 8And I looked, and behold a pale horse: and his name that sat on him was Death, and Hell followed with him. And power was given unto them over the fourth part of the earth, to kill with sword, and with hunger, and with death, and with the beasts of the earth. 9And when he had opened the fifth seal, I saw under the altar the souls of them that were slain for the word of God, and for the testimony which they held: 10And they cried with a loud voice, saying, How long, O Lord, holy and true, dost thou not judge and avenge our blood on them that dwell on the earth? 11And white robes were given unto every one of them; and it was said unto them, that they should rest yet for a little season, until their fellow servants also and

Living Bible

a black horse, with its rider holding a pair of balances in his hand. 6And a voice from among the four Living Beings said, "A loaf of bread for $20, or three pounds of barley flour,[a] but there is no olive oil or wine." [b]

7 And when the fourth seal was broken, I heard the fourth Living Being say, "Come!" 8And now I saw a pale horse, and its rider's name was Death. And there followed after him another horse whose rider's name was Hell. They were given control of one-fourth of the earth, to kill with war and famine and disease and wild animals.

9 And when he broke open the fifth seal, I saw an altar, and underneath it all the souls of those who had been martyred for preaching the Word of God and for being faithful in their witnessing. 10 They called loudly to the Lord and said, "O Sovereign Lord, holy and true, how long will it be before you judge the people of the earth for what they've done to us? When will you avenge our blood against those living on the earth?" 11 White robes were given to each of them, and they were told to rest a little longer until their other brothers, fellow servants of Je-

[*a*] Literally, "A choenix of wheat for a denarius, and three choenix of barley for a denarius. . . ."
[*b*] Literally, "do not damage the oil and wine."

Today's English Version

Its rider held a pair of scales in his hand. 6 I heard what sounded like a voice coming from among the four living creatures. It said, "A quart of wheat for a day's wages, and three quarts of barley for a day's wages. But do not damage the olive oil and the wine!"

7 Then the Lamb broke open the fourth seal; and I heard the fourth living creature say, "Come!" 8 I looked, and there was a pale colored horse. Its rider was named Death, and Hades followed close behind. They were given authority over a fourth of the earth, to kill with war, famine, and disease, and with the wild animals of earth.

9 Then the Lamb broke open the fifth seal. I saw underneath the altar the souls of those who had been killed because they had proclaimed God's word and had been faithful in their witnessing. 10 They shouted in a loud voice, "Almighty Lord, holy and true! How long will it be until you judge the people of earth and punish them for killing us?" 11 Each of them was given a white robe; and they were told to rest a little while longer, until the total number was reached

New International Version

Its rider was holding a pair of scales in his hand. 6 Then I heard what sounded like a voice among the four living creatures, saying, "A quart of wheat for a day's wages,[i] and three quarts of barley for a day's wages,[i] and do not damage the oil and the wine!"

7 When the Lamb opened the fourth seal, I heard the voice of the fourth living creature say, "Come!" 8 I looked, and there before me was a pale horse! Its rider was named Death, and Hades was following close behind him. They were given power over a fourth of the earth to kill by sword, famine and plague, and by the wild beasts of the earth.

9 When he opened the fifth seal, I saw under the altar the souls of those who had been slain because of the word of God and the testimony they had maintained. 10 They called out in a loud voice, "How long, Sovereign Lord, holy and true, until you judge the inhabitants of the earth and avenge our blood?" 11 Then each of them was given a white robe, and they were told to wait a little longer, until the number of

[*i*] Greek *a denarius*.

Phillips Modern English

a black horse. Its rider had a pair of scales in his hand, and I heard a voice which seemed to come from the four living creatures, saying,

"A quart of wheat for a shilling, and three quarts of barley for a shilling—but no tampering with the oil or the wine!"

6.7 The fourth rider: Death

Then, when he broke the fourth seal I heard the voice of the fourth living creature cry,

"Come out!"

Again I looked, and there appeared a horse sickly green in colour. The name of its rider was death, and the grave followed close behind him. A quarter of the earth was put into their power, to kill with the sword, by famine, by violence, and through the wild beasts of the earth.

6.9 The cry of the martyrs in Heaven

When the Lamb broke the fifth seal, I could see, beneath the altar, the souls of those who had been killed for the sake of the Word of God and because of the faithfulness of their witness. They cried out in a loud voice, saying,

"How long shall it be, O Lord of all, holy and true, before thou shalt judge and avenge our blood upon the inhabitants of the earth?"

Then each of them was given a white robe, and they were told to be patient a little longer, until the number of their fellow-servants and of their

Revised Standard Version

and behold, a black horse, and its rider had a
balance in his hand; 6 and I heard what seemed
to be a voice in the midst of the four living
creatures saying, "A quart of wheat for a denarius,[a] and three quarts of barley for a denarius;[a] but do not harm oil and wine!"
7 When he opened the fourth seal, I heard
the voice of the fourth living creature say,
"Come!" 8 And I saw, and behold, a pale horse,
and its rider's name was Death, and Hades followed him; and they were given power over a
fourth of the earth, to kill with sword and with
famine and with pestilence and by wild beasts
of the earth.
9 When he opened the fifth seal, I saw under
the altar the souls of those who had been slain
for the word of God and for the witness they
had borne; 10 they cried out with a loud voice,
"O Sovereign Lord, holy and true, how long before thou wilt judge and avenge our blood on
those who dwell upon the earth?" 11 Then they
were each given a white robe and told to rest a
little longer, until the number of their fellow
servants and their brethren should be complete,

[a] The denarius was a day's wage for a laborer.

Jerusalem Bible

black horse appeared, and its rider was holding
a pair of scales; 6 and I seemed to hear a voice
shout from among the four animals and say,
"A ration of corn for a day's wages, and three
rations of barley for a day's wages, but do not
tamper with the oil or the wine."
7 When he broke the fourth seal, I heard the
voice of the fourth animal shout, "Come." 8 Immediately another horse appeared, deathly pale,
and its rider was called Plague, and Hades followed at his heels.
They were given authority over a quarter of
the earth, *to kill by the sword, by famine, by plague and wild beasts.*[z]
9 When he broke the fifth seal, I saw underneath the altar the souls of all the people who
had been killed on account of the word of God,
for witnessing to it. 10 They shouted aloud,
"Holy, faithful Master, how much longer will
you wait before you pass sentence and take
vengeance for our death on the inhabitants of
the earth?" 11 Each of them was given a white
robe, and they were told to be patient a little
longer, until the roll was complete and their fel-

[z] Ezk. 14:21.

New English Bible

a black horse; and its rider held in his hand a pair of scales. And I heard what sounded like a voice from the midst of the living creatures, which said, 'A whole day's wage for a quart of flour, a whole day's wage for three quarts of barley-meal! But spare the olive and the vine.'

When he broke the fourth seal, I heard the voice of the fourth creature say, 'Come!' And there, as I looked, was another horse, sickly pale; and its rider's name was Death, and Hades came close behind. To him was given power over a quarter of the earth, with the right to kill by sword and by famine, by pestilence and wild beasts.

When he broke the fifth seal, I saw underneath [a] the altar the souls of those who had been slaughtered for God's word and for the testimony they bore. They gave a great cry: 'How long, sovereign Lord, holy and true, must it be before thou wilt vindicate us and avenge our blood on the inhabitants of the earth?' Each of them was given a white robe; and they were told to rest a little while longer, until the tally should be complete of all their brothers in

[a] *Or* at the foot of . . .

King James Version

their brethren, that should be killed as they *were,* should be fulfilled. 12And I beheld when he had opened the sixth seal, and, lo, there was a great earthquake; and the sun became black as sackcloth of hair, and the moon became as blood. 13And the stars of heaven fell unto the earth, even as a fig tree casteth her untimely figs, when she is shaken of a mighty wind. 14And the heaven departed as a scroll when it is rolled together; and every mountain and island were moved out of their places. 15And the kings of the earth, and the great men, and the rich men, and the chief captains, and the mighty men, and every bond man, and every free man, hid themselves in the dens and in the rocks of the mountains; 16And said to the mountains and rocks, Fall on us, and hide us from the face of him that sitteth on the throne, and from the wrath of the Lamb: 17For the great day of his wrath is come; and who shall be able to stand?

7 And after these things I saw four angels standing on the four corners of the earth, holding the four winds of the earth, that the wind should not blow on the earth, nor on the

Living Bible

sus, had been martyred on the earth and joined them.

12 I watched as he broke the sixth seal, and there was a vast earthquake; and the sun became dark like black cloth, and the moon was blood-red. 13 Then the stars of heaven appeared to be falling to earth[c]—like green fruit from fig trees buffeted by mighty winds. 14And the starry heavens disappeared[d] as though rolled up like a scroll and taken away; and every mountain and island shook and shifted. 15 The kings of the earth, and world leaders and rich men, and high-ranking military officers, and all men great and small, slave and free, hid themselves in the caves and rocks of the mountains, 16 and cried to the mountains to crush them. "Fall on us," they pleaded, "and hide us from the face of the one sitting on the throne, and from the anger of the Lamb, 17 because the great day of their anger has come, and who can survive it?"

7 Then I saw four angels standing at the four corners of the earth, holding back the four winds from blowing, so that not a leaf rustled in the trees, and the ocean became as smooth as

[*c*] Literally, "the stars of heaven fell to the earth."
[*d*] Literally, "the sky departed."

Today's English Version

of their fellow servants and brothers who were to be killed, as they had been.

12 And I saw the Lamb break open the sixth seal. There was a violent earthquake, and the sun became black, like coarse black cloth, and the moon turned completely red, like blood. 13 The stars fell out of the sky to earth, like unripe figs falling from the tree when a strong wind shakes it. 14 The sky disappeared, like a scroll being rolled up, and every mountain and island was moved from its place. 15 Then the kings of the earth, the rulers and the military chiefs, the rich and the mighty, and all other men, slave and free, hid themselves in caves and under rocks on the mountains. 16 They called out to the mountains and to the rocks, "Fall on us and hide us from the eyes of the one who sits on the throne, and from the wrath of the Lamb! 17 The great day of their wrath is here, and who can stand up against it?"

The 144,000 people of Israel

7 After this I saw four angels standing at the four corners of the earth, holding back the four winds of the earth, so that no wind should

New International Version

their fellow servants and brothers who were to be killed as they had been was completed.

12 I watched as he opened the sixth seal. There was a great earthquake. The sun turned black like sackcloth made of goat hair, the whole moon turned blood-red, 13 and the stars in the sky fell to earth, as late figs drop from a fig tree when shaken by a strong wind. 14 The sky receded like a scroll, rolling up, and every mountain and island was removed from its place.

15 Then the kings of the earth, the princes, the generals, the rich, the mighty, and every slave and every free man hid in caves and among the rocks of the mountains. 16 They called to the mountains and the rocks, "Fall on us and hide us from the face of him who sits on the throne and from the wrath of the Lamb! 17 For the great day of their wrath has come, and who can stand?"

144,000 sealed

7 After this I saw four angels standing at the four corners of the earth, holding back the four winds of the earth to prevent any wind from blowing on the land or on the sea or on

Phillips Modern English

brethren, who were to die as they had died, should be complete.

6.12 *The awe-full wrath of God*

Then I watched while he broke the sixth seal. There was a tremendous earthquake, the sun turned dark like coarse black cloth, and the full moon was red as blood. The stars of the sky fell upon the earth, just as a fig-tree sheds unripe figs when shaken in a gale. The sky vanished as though it were a scroll being rolled up, and every mountain and island was jolted out of its place. Then the kings of the earth, and the great men, the captains, the wealthy, the powerful, and every man, whether slave or free, hid themselves in caves and among mountain rocks. They called out to the mountains and the rocks,

"Fall down upon us and hide us from the face of him who sits upon the throne, and from the wrath of the Lamb! For the great day of their wrath has come, and who can stand against it?"

7.1 *Judgment stayed for the sealing of God's people*

Later I saw four angels standing at the four corners of the earth holding in check the four winds of the earth that none should blow upon

Revised Standard Version

who were to be killed as they themselves had been.

12 When he opened the sixth seal, I looked, and behold, there was a great earthquake; and the sun became black as sackcloth, the full moon became like blood, 13 and the stars of the sky fell to the earth as the fig tree sheds its winter fruit when shaken by a gale; 14 the sky vanished like a scroll that is rolled up, and every mountain and island was removed from its place. 15 Then the kings of the earth and the great men and the generals and the rich and the strong, and every one, slave and free, hid in the caves and among the rocks of the mountains, 16 calling to the mountains and rocks, "Fall on us and hide us from the face of him who is seated on the throne, and from the wrath of the Lamb; 17 for the great day of their wrath has come, and who can stand before it?"

7 After this I saw four angels standing at the four corners of the earth, holding back the four winds of the earth, that no wind might blow

Jerusalem Bible

low servants and brothers had been killed just as they had been.

12 In my vision, when he broke the sixth seal, there was a violent earthquake and the sun went as black as coarse sackcloth; the moon turned red as blood all over, 13 and *the stars of the sky fell* [a] on to the earth *like figs* dropping from a fig tree when a high wind shakes it; 14 the *sky disappeared like a scroll rolling up* and all the mountains and islands were shaken from their places. 15 Then all the earthly rulers, the governors and the commanders, the rich people and the men of influence, the whole population, slaves and citizens, took to the mountains *to hide in caves and among the rocks.* [b] 16 *They said to the mountains* [c] and the rocks, *"Fall on us* and hide us away from the One who sits on the throne and from the anger of the Lamb. 17 For *the Great Day of his anger* has come, *and who can survive it?"* [d]

God's servants will be preserved

7 Next I saw four angels, standing at *the four corners of the earth,* [e] holding the four winds of the world back to keep them from blowing over the land or the sea or in the trees.

[a] Is. 34:4. [b] Ho. 10:8. [c] Is. 2:10,18,19. [d] Jl. 2:11; 3:4. [e] Ezk. 7:2.

New English Bible

Christ's service who were to be killed as they had been.

Then I watched as he broke the sixth seal. And there was a violent earthquake; the sun turned black as a funeral pall and the moon all red as blood; the stars in the sky fell to the earth, like figs shaken down by a gale; the sky vanished, as a scroll is rolled up, and every mountain and island was moved from its place. Then the kings of the earth, magnates and marshals, the rich and the powerful, and all men, slave or free, hid themselves in caves and mountain crags; and they called out to the mountains and the crags, 'Fall on us and hide us from the face of the One who sits on the throne and from the vengeance of the Lamb.' For the great day of their vengeance has come, and who will be able to stand?

7 After this I saw four angels stationed at the four corners of the earth, holding back the four winds so that no wind should blow on sea

King James Version

sea, nor on any tree. 2And I saw another angel
ascending from the east, having the seal of the
living God: and he cried with a loud voice to the
four angels, to whom it was given to hurt the
earth and the sea, 3 Saying, Hurt not the earth,
neither the sea, nor the trees, till we have sealed
the servants of our God in their foreheads. 4And
I heard the number of them which were sealed:
and there were sealed a hundred *and* forty *and*
four thousand of all the tribes of the children of
Israel. 5 Of the tribe of Juda *were* sealed twelve
thousand. Of the tribe of Reuben *were* sealed
twelve thousand. Of the tribe of Gad *were* sealed
twelve thousand. 6 Of the tribe of Aser *were*
sealed twelve thousand. Of the tribe of Nephthalim *were* sealed twelve thousand. Of the tribe
of Manasses *were* sealed twelve thousand. 7 Of
the tribe of Simeon *were* sealed twelve thousand. Of the tribe of Levi *were* sealed twelve
thousand. Of the tribe of Issachar *were* sealed
twelve thousand. 8 Of the tribe of Zabulon *were*
sealed twelve thousand. Of the tribe of Joseph
were sealed twelve thousand. Of the tribe of
Benjamin *were* sealed twelve thousand. 9After
this I beheld, and, lo, a great multitude, which
no man could number, of all nations, and kindreds, and people, and tongues, stood before
the throne, and before the Lamb, clothed with
white robes, and palms in their hands; 10And
cried with a loud voice, saying, Salvation to our

Living Bible

glass. 2And I saw another angel coming from
the east, carrying the Great Seal of the Living
God. And he shouted out to those four angels
who had been given power to injure earth and
sea, 3 "Wait! Don't do anything yet—hurt neither
earth nor sea nor trees—until we have placed
the Seal of God upon the foreheads of his servants."
4–8 How many were given this mark? I heard
the number—it was 144,000, out of all twelve
tribes of Israel, as listed here:

Judah	12,000
Reuben	12,000
Gad	12,000
Asher	12,000
Naphtali	12,000
Manasseh	12,000
Simeon	12,000
Levi	12,000
Issachar	12,000
Zebulun	12,000
Joseph	12,000
Benjamin	12,000

9 After this I saw a vast crowd, too great to
count, from all nations and provinces and languages, standing in front of the throne and before the Lamb, clothed in white, with palm
branches in their hands. 10And they were shouting with a mighty shout, "Salvation comes from

Today's English Version

blow on the earth, the sea, or any tree. 2And
I saw another angel coming up from the east
with the seal of the living God. He called out
in a loud voice to the four angels to whom God
had given the power to damage the earth and
the sea. 3 The angel said, "Do not harm the
earth, the sea, or the trees, until we mark the
servants of our God with a seal on their foreheads." 4And I was told the number of those
who were marked with God's seal on their foreheads: it was 144,000, from every tribe of the
people of Israel. 5 There were 12,000 from the
tribe of Judah marked with the seal; 12,000 from
the tribe of Reuben; 12,000 from the tribe of
Gad; 6 12,000 from the tribe of Asher; 12,000
from the tribe of Naphtali; 12,000 from the tribe
of Manasseh; 7 12,000 from the tribe of Simeon;
12,000 from the tribe of Levi; 12,000 from the
tribe of Issachar; 8 12,000 from the tribe of
Zebulun; 12,000 from the tribe of Joseph; and
12,000 from the tribe of Benjamin.

The great crowd

9 After this I looked, and there was a great
crowd—no one could count all the people! They
were from every race, tribe, nation, and language, and they stood in front of the throne and
of the Lamb, dressed in white robes, and holding
palm branches in their hands. 10 They called out
in a loud voice, "Our salvation comes from our

New International Version

any tree. 2 Then I saw another angel coming up
from the east, having the seal of the living God.
He called out in a loud voice to the four angels
who had been given power to harm the land and
the sea: 3 "Do not harm the land or the sea or
the trees until we put a seal on the foreheads of
the servants of our God." 4 Then I heard the
number of those who were sealed: 144,000 from
all the tribes of Israel.

5 From the tribe of Judah 12,000 were sealed,
from the tribe of Reuben 12,000,
from the tribe of Gad 12,000,
6 from the tribe of Asher 12,000,
from the tribe of Naphtali 12,000,
from the tribe of Manasseh 12,000,
7 from the tribe of Simeon 12,000,
from the tribe of Levi 12,000,
from the tribe of Issachar 12,000,
8 from the tribe of Zebulun 12,000,
from the tribe of Joseph 12,000,
from the tribe of Benjamin 12,000.

The great multitude in white robes

9 After this I looked and there before me was
a great multitude that no one could count, from
every nation, tribe, people and language, standing before the throne and in front of the Lamb.
They were wearing white robes and were holding
palm branches in their hands. 10And they cried
out in a loud voice:
"Salvation belongs to our God,

Phillips Modern English

the earth or upon the sea or upon any tree. Then I saw another angel ascending out of the east, holding the seal of the living God. He cried out in a loud voice to the four angels who had the power to harm the earth and the sea:

"Do no harm to the earth, nor to the sea, nor to the trees until we have sealed the servants of our God upon their foreheads."

I heard the number of those who were thus sealed and it was 144,000, from every tribe of the sons of Israel. Twelve thousand were sealed from the tribe of Judah; twelve thousand from the tribe of Reuben; twelve thousand from the tribe of Gad; twelve thousand from the tribe of Asher; twelve thousand from the tribe of Naphtali; twelve thousand from the tribe of Manasseh; twelve thousand from the tribe of Simeon; twelve thousand from the tribe of Levi; twelve thousand from the tribe of Issachar; twelve thousand from the tribe of Zebulun; twelve thousand from the tribe of Joseph; and twelve thousand were sealed from the tribe of Benjamin.

7.9 The countless host of the redeemed

When this was done I looked again, and before my eyes appeared a vast crowd beyond man's power to number. They came from every nation and tribe and people and language, and they stood before the throne of the Lamb, dressed in white robes with palm-branches in their hands. With a great voice they shouted these words:

"Salvation belongs to our God who sits upon

Revised Standard Version

on earth or sea or against any tree. 2 Then I
saw another angel ascend from the rising of the
sun, with the seal of the living God, and he
called with a loud voice to the four angels who
had been given power to harm earth and sea,
3 saying, "Do not harm the earth or the sea or
the trees, till we have sealed the servants of our
God upon their foreheads." 4 And I heard the
number of the sealed, a hundred and forty-four
thousand sealed, out of every tribe of the sons
of Israel, 5 twelve thousand sealed out of the
tribe of Judah, twelve thousand of the tribe of
Reuben, twelve thousand of the tribe of Gad,
6 twelve thousand of the tribe of Asher, twelve
thousand of the tribe of Naphtali, twelve thousand of the tribe of Manasseh, 7 twelve thousand
of the tribe of Simeon, twelve thousand of the
tribe of Levi, twelve thousand of the tribe of Issachar, 8 twelve thousand of the tribe of Zebulun, twelve thousand of the tribe of Joseph,
twelve thousand sealed out of the tribe of Benjamin.
9 After this I looked, and behold, a great
multitude which no man could number, from
every nation, from all tribes and peoples and
tongues, standing before the throne and before
the Lamb, clothed in white robes, with palm
branches in their hands, 10 and crying out with
a loud voice, "Salvation belongs to our God

Jerusalem Bible

2 Then I saw another angel rising where the sun
rises, carrying the seal of the living God; he
called in a powerful voice to the four angels
whose duty was to devastate land and sea,
3 "Wait before you do any damage on land or
at sea or to the trees, until we have put the *seal*
on the foreheads[f] of the servants of our God."
4 Then I heard how many were sealed: a hundred and forty-four thousand,[g] out of all the
tribes of Israel.
5 From the tribe of Judah, twelve thousand
had been sealed; from the tribe of Reuben,
twelve thousand; from the tribe of Gad, twelve
thousand; 6 from the tribe of Asher, twelve
thousand; from the tribe of Naphtali, twelve
thousand; from the tribe of Manasseh, twelve
thousand; 7 from the tribe of Simeon, twelve
thousand; from the tribe of Levi, twelve thousand; from the tribe of Issachar, twelve thousand; 8 from the tribe of Zebulun, twelve thousand; from the tribe of Joseph, twelve thousand;
and from the tribe of Benjamin, twelve thousand were sealed.

The rewarding of the saints

9 After that I saw a huge number, impossible
to count, of people from every nation, race, tribe
and language; they were standing in front of the
throne and in front of the Lamb, dressed in white
robes and holding palms in their hands. They
shouted aloud, 10 "Victory to our God, who sits

[*f*] Ezk. 9:4 (see also Is. 44:5). [*g*] Twelve (the sacred number) squared and multiplied by a thousand, representing the totality of the faithful.

New English Bible

or land or on any tree. Then I saw another angel rising out of the east, carrying the seal of the living God; and he called aloud to the four angels who had been given the power to ravage land and sea: 'Do no damage to sea or land or trees until we have set the seal of our God upon the foreheads of his servants.' And I heard the number of those who had received the seal. From all the tribes of Israel there were a hundred and forty-four thousand: twelve thousand from the tribe of Judah, twelve thousand from the tribe of Reuben, twelve thousand from the tribe of Gad, twelve thousand from the tribe of Asher, twelve thousand from the tribe of Naphtali, twelve thousand from the tribe of Manasseh, twelve thousand from the tribe of Simeon, twelve thousand from the tribe of Levi, twelve thousand from the tribe of Issachar, twelve thousand from the tribe of Zebulun, twelve thousand from the tribe of Joseph, and twelve thousand from the tribe of Benjamin.

After this I looked and saw a vast throng, which no one could count, from every nation, of all tribes, peoples, and languages, standing in front of the throne and before the Lamb. They were robed in white and had palms in their hands, and they shouted together:

'Victory to our God who sits on the throne,

King James Version

God which sitteth upon the throne, and unto
the Lamb. 11 And all the angels stood round
about the throne, and *about* the elders and the
four beasts, and fell before the throne on their
faces, and worshipped God, 12 Saying, Amen:
Blessing, and glory, and wisdom, and thanksgiving, and honour, and power, and might, *be*
unto our God for ever and ever. Amen. 13 And
one of the elders answered, saying unto me,
What are these which are arrayed in white
robes? and whence came they? 14 And I said unto
him, Sir, thou knowest. And he said to me,
These are they which came out of great tribulation, and have washed their robes, and made
them white in the blood of the Lamb. 15 Therefore are they before the throne of God, and
serve him day and night in his temple: and he
that sitteth on the throne shall dwell among
them. 16 They shall hunger no more, neither
thirst any more; neither shall the sun light on
them, nor any heat. 17 For the Lamb which is
in the midst of the throne shall feed them, and
shall lead them unto living fountains of waters:
and God shall wipe away all tears from their
eyes.

Living Bible

our God upon the throne, and from the Lamb."
11 And now all the angels were crowding around
the throne and around the Elders and the four
Living Beings, and falling face down before the
throne and worshiping God. 12 "Amen!" they
said. "Blessing, and glory, and wisdom, and
thanksgiving, and honor, and power, and might,
be to our God forever and forever. Amen!"

13 Then one of the twenty-four Elders asked
me, "Do you know who these are, who are
clothed in white, and where they come from?"

14 "No, sir," I replied. "Please tell me."

"These are the ones coming out of the Great
Tribulation," he said; "they washed their robes
and whitened them by the blood of the Lamb.
15 That is why they are here before the throne
of God, serving him day and night in his temple. The one sitting on the throne will shelter
them; 16 they will never be hungry again, nor
thirsty, and they will be fully protected from the
scorching noontime heat. 17 For the Lamb standing in front of [a] the throne will feed them and be
their Shepherd and lead them to the springs of
the Water of Life. And God will wipe their tears
away."

[*a*] Literally, "in the center of the throne": i.e., directly in front, not to one side. An alternate rendering might be, "at the heart of the throne."

Today's English Version

God, who sits on the throne, and from the
Lamb!" 11 All the angels stood around the throne,
the elders, and the four living creatures. Then
they fell down on their faces before the throne
and worshiped God, 12 saying, "Amen! Praise,
glory, wisdom, thanks, honor, power, and might
belong to our God forever and ever! Amen!"

13 One of the elders asked me, "Who are
these people dressed in white robes, and where
do they come from?"

14 "I don't know, sir. You do," I answered.

He said to me, "These are the people who
have come safely through the great persecution.
They washed their robes and made them white
with the blood of the Lamb. 15 That is why they
stand before God's throne and serve him day
and night in his temple. He who sits on the
throne will protect them with his presence.
16 Never again will they hunger or thirst; neither
sun nor any scorching heat will burn them;
17 because the Lamb, who is in the center of the
throne, will be their shepherd, and he will guide
them to springs of living water. And God will
wipe away every tear from their eyes."

New International Version

who sits on the throne,
and to the Lamb."

11 All the angels were standing around the throne
and around the elders and the four living creatures. They fell down on their faces before the
throne and worshiped God, 12 saying:

"Amen!
Praise and glory
and wisdom and thanks and honor
and power and strength
be to our God for ever and ever.
Amen!"

13 Then one of the elders asked me, "These
in white robes—who are they, and where did
they come from?"

14 I answered, "Sir, you know."

And he said, "These are they who have come
out of the great tribulation; they have washed
their robes and made them white in the blood
of the Lamb. 15 Therefore,

they are before the throne of God
and serve him day and night in his temple;
and he who sits on the throne will spread
his tent over them.
16 Never again will they hunger;
never again will they thirst.
The sun will not beat upon them,
nor any scorching heat.
17 For the Lamb at the center of the throne
will be their shepherd;
he will lead them to springs of living
water.
And God will wipe away every tear from
their eyes."

Phillips Modern English

the throne and to the Lamb!"

Then all the angels stood encircling the throne, the elders and the four living creatures, and prostrated themselves with heads bowed before the throne and worshipped God, saying,

"Amen! Blessing and glory and wisdom and thanksgiving and honour and power and strength be given to our God for timeless ages!"

7.13 *The countless host explained*

Then one of the elders addressed me and asked,

"These who are dressed in white robes—who are they, and where do they come from?"

"You know, my lord," I answered him.

Then he told me,

"These are those who have come through the great oppression: they have washed their robes and made them white in the blood of the Lamb. That is why they now have their place before the throne of God, and serve him day and night in his Temple. He who sits upon the throne will be their shelter. They will never again know hunger or thirst. The sun shall never beat upon them, neither shall there be any scorching heat, for the Lamb who is in the centre of the throne will be their shepherd and will lead them to springs of living water. And God will wipe away every tear from their eyes."

Revised Standard Version

who sits upon the throne, and to the Lamb!"
11 And all the angels stood round the throne
and round the elders and the four living creatures, and they fell on their faces before the
throne and worshiped God, 12 saying, "Amen!
Blessing and glory and wisdom and thanksgiving
and honor and power and might be to our God
for ever and ever! Amen."
13 Then one of the elders addressed me, saying, "Who are these, clothed in white robes, and
whence have they come?" 14 I said to him, "Sir,
you know." And he said to me, "These are they
who have come out of the great tribulation;
they have washed their robes and made them
white in the blood of the Lamb.

15 Therefore are they before the throne of God,
and serve him day and night within his temple;
and he who sits upon the throne will shelter them with his presence.
16 They shall hunger no more, neither thirst any more;
the sun shall not strike them, nor any scorching heat.
17 For the Lamb in the midst of the throne will be their shepherd,
and he will guide them to springs of living water;
and God will wipe away every tear from their eyes."

Jerusalem Bible

on the throne, and to the Lamb!" 11 And all the
angels who were standing in a circle around the
throne, surrounding the elders and the four
animals, prostrated themselves before the throne,
and touched the ground with their foreheads,
worshiping God 12 with these words, "Amen.
Praise and glory and wisdom and thanksgiving
and honor and power and strength to our God
for ever and ever. Amen."
13 One of the elders then spoke, and asked
me, "Do you know who these people are, dressed
in white robes, and where they have come from?"
14 I answered him, "You can tell me, my lord."
Then he said, "These are the people who have
been through the great persecution,[h] and because
they have washed their robes white again in the
blood of the Lamb, 15 they now stand in front of
God's throne and serve him day and night in
his sanctuary; and the One who sits on the
throne will spread his tent over them. 16 *They
will never hunger or thirst* again; *neither the sun
nor scorching wind will ever plague them,* 17 because the Lamb who is at the throne *will be their
shepherd and will lead them to springs of living
water*[i]; and God *will wipe away all tears from
their eyes."* [j]

New English Bible

and to the Lamb!'

And all the angels stood round the throne and the elders and the four living creatures, and they fell on their faces before the throne and worshipped God, crying:

'Amen! Praise and glory and wisdom, thanksgiving and honour, power and might, be to our God for ever and ever! Amen.'

Then one of the elders turned to me and said, 'These men that are robed in white—who are they and from where do they come?' But I answered, 'My lord, you know, not I.' Then he said to me, 'These are the men who have passed through the great ordeal; they have washed their robes and made them white in the blood of the Lamb. That is why they stand before the throne of God and minister to him day and night in his temple; and he who sits on the throne will dwell with them. They shall never again feel hunger or thirst, the sun shall not beat on them nor any scorching heat, because the Lamb who is at the heart of the throne will be their shepherd and will guide them to the springs of the water of life; and God will wipe all tears from their eyes.'

[*h*] Under Nero. [*i*] Is. 49:10. [*j*] Is. 25:8.

King James Version

8 And when he had opened the seventh seal,
there was silence in heaven about the space
of half an hour. 2And I saw the seven angels
which stood before God; and to them were
given seven trumpets. 3And another angel came
and stood at the altar, having a golden censer;
and there was given unto him much incense,
that he should offer *it* with the prayers of all
saints upon the golden altar which was before
the throne. 4And the smoke of the incense,
which came with the prayers of the saints,
ascended up before God out of the angel's hand.
5And the angel took the censer, and filled it
with fire of the altar, and cast *it* into the earth:
and there were voices, and thunderings, and
lightnings, and an earthquake. 6And the seven
angels which had the seven trumpets prepared
themselves to sound. 7 The first angel sounded,
and there followed hail and fire mingled with

Living Bible

8 When the Lamb had broken the seventh
seal, there was silence throughout all heaven
for what seemed like half an hour. 2And I saw
the seven angels that stand before God, and they
were given seven trumpets.
3 Then another angel with a golden censer
came and stood at the altar; and a great quantity of incense was given to him to mix with the
prayers of God's people, to offer upon the golden
altar before the throne. 4And the perfume of the
incense mixed with prayers ascended up to God
from the altar where the angel had poured them
out.
5 Then the angel filled the censer with fire
from the altar and threw it down upon the earth;
and thunder crashed and rumbled, lightning
flashed, and there was a terrible earthquake.
6 Then the seven angels with the seven trumpets prepared to blow their mighty blasts.
7 The first angel blew his trumpet, and hail
and fire mixed with blood were thrown down

Today's English Version

The seventh seal

8 When the Lamb broke open the seventh
seal, there was a silence in heaven for about
half an hour. 2 Then I saw the seven angels who
stand before God; they were given seven trumpets.
3 Another angel, who had a gold incense container, came and stood at the altar. He was given
much incense to add to the prayers of all God's
people and offer on the gold altar that stands
before the throne. 4 The smoke of the burning
incense went up with the prayers of God's people
from the hands of the angel standing before
God. 5 Then the angel took the incense container, filled it with fire from the altar, and
threw it on the earth. There were peals of thunder, sounds, flashes of lightning, and an earthquake.

The trumpets

6 Then the seven angels with the seven trumpets prepared to blow them.
7 The first angel blew his trumpet. Hail and
fire, mixed with blood, came pouring down on

New International Version

The seventh seal and the golden censer

8 When he opened the seventh seal, there was
silence in heaven for about half an hour.
2 And I saw the seven angels who stand before God, and to them were given seven trumpets.
3 Another angel, who had a golden censer,
came and stood at the altar. He was given much
incense to offer, with the prayers of all the saints,
on the golden altar before the throne. 4 The
smoke of the incense, together with the prayers
of the saints, went up before God from the
angel's hand. 5 Then the angel took the censer,
filled it with fire from the altar, and hurled it
on the earth; and there came peals of thunder,
rumblings, flashes of lightning and an earthquake.

The trumpets

6 Then the seven angels who had the seven
trumpets prepared to sound them.
7 The first angel sounded his trumpet, and
there came hail and fire mixed with blood, and

Phillips Modern English

8.1 The seventh seal: Complete silence

Then, when he had broken the seventh seal, there was utter silence in Heaven for what seemed to me half-an-hour.

8.2 The vision of the seven trumpeters

Then I saw the seven angels who stand in the presence of God, and seven trumpets were put into their hands.

Then another angel came and stood by the altar holding a golden censer. He was given a great quantity of incense to add to the prayers of all the saints, to be laid upon the golden altar before the throne. And the smoke of the incense rose up before God from the angel's hand, mingled with the prayers of the saints. Then the angel took the censer, filled it with fire from the altar, and hurled it upon the earth. And at that there were thunderings and noises, flashes of lightning and an earthquake.

Then the seven angels who were holding the seven trumpets prepared to blow them.

8.7 The first trumpet: Hail and fire

The first angel blew his trumpet. Hail and fire mingled with blood appeared, and were hurled

Revised Standard Version

8 When the Lamb opened the seventh seal,
there was silence in heaven for about half
an hour. 2 Then I saw the seven angels who
stand before God, and seven trumpets were
given to them. 3 And another angel came and
stood at the altar with a golden censer; and he
was given much incense to mingle with the prayers of all the saints upon the golden altar before
the throne; 4 and the smoke of the incense rose
with the prayers of the saints from the hand of
the angel before God. 5 Then the angel took
the censer and filled it with fire from the altar
and threw it on the earth; and there were peals
of thunder, voices, flashes of lightning, and an
earthquake.
6 Now the seven angels who had the seven
trumpets made ready to blow them.
7 The first angel blew his trumpet, and there
followed hail and fire, mixed with blood, which

Jerusalem Bible

The seventh seal

8 The Lamb then broke the seventh seal, and
there was silence in heaven for about half an
hour.[k]

The prayers of the saints bring the coming of the Great Day nearer

2 Next I saw seven trumpets being given to
the seven angels who stand in the presence of
God. 3 Another angel, who had a golden censer,[l]
came and stood at the altar.[m] A large quantity
of incense was given to him to offer with the
prayers of all the saints on the golden altar that
stood in front of the throne; 4 and so from the
angel's hand the smoke of the incense went up in
the presence of God and with it the prayers
of the saints. 5 Then the angel took the censer
and *filled it with the fire* from the altar, which
he then threw down on to the earth; immediately
there came peals of thunder and flashes of
lightning, and the earth shook.

The first four trumpets

6 The seven angels that had the seven trumpets now made ready to sound them. 7 The first
blew his trumpet and, with that, hail and fire,

[k] An awed silence; the "coming of Yahweh" is preceded by silence in the prophetic writings. [l] In the shape of a shovel: the flat incense vessel was also used for carrying live coals from the altar on which offerings were burned. [m] The altar of incense.

New English Bible

8 Now when the Lamb broke the seventh seal, there was silence in heaven for what seemed half an hour. Then I looked, and the seven angels that stand in the presence of God were given seven trumpets.

Then another angel came and stood at the altar, holding a golden censer; and he was given a great quantity of incense to offer with the prayers of all God's people upon the golden altar in front of the throne. And from the angel's hand the smoke of the incense went up before God with the prayers of his people. Then the angel took the censer, filled it from the altar fire, and threw it down upon the earth; and there were peals of thunder, lightning, and an earthquake.

The powers of darkness conquered

Then the seven angels that held the seven trumpets prepared to blow them.

The first blew his trumpet; and there came hail and fire mingled with blood, and this was hurled

King James Version

blood, and they were cast upon the earth: and
the third part of trees was burnt up, and all
green grass was burnt up. 8And the second
angel sounded, and as it were a great mountain
burning with fire was cast into the sea: and the
third part of the sea became blood; 9And the
third part of the creatures which were in the
sea, and had life, died; and the third part of
the ships were destroyed. 10And the third angel
sounded, and there fell a great star from heaven,
burning as it were a lamp, and it fell upon the
third part of the rivers, and upon the fountains
of waters; 11And the name of the star is called
Wormwood: and the third part of the waters
became wormwood; and many men died of the
waters, because they were made bitter. 12And
the fourth angel sounded, and the third part of
the sun was smitten, and the third part of the

Living Bible

upon the earth. One-third of the earth was set
on fire so that one-third of the trees were burned,
and all the green grass.

8, 9 Then the second angel blew his trumpet,
and what appeared to be a huge burning mountain was thrown into the sea, destroying a third
of all the ships; and a third of the sea turned
red as[a] blood; and a third of the fish were killed.

10 The third angel blew, and a great flaming
star fell from heaven upon a third of the rivers
and springs. 11 The star was called "Bitterness"[b]
because it poisoned a third of all the water on
the earth and many people died.

12 The fourth angel blew his trumpet and immediately a third of the sun was blighted and

[a] Literally, "became blood." [b] Literally, "Wormwood."

Today's English Version

the earth. A third of the earth was burned up,
a third of the trees, and every blade of green
grass.

8 Then the second angel blew his trumpet.
Something that looked like a large mountain
burning with fire was thrown into the sea. A
third of the sea was turned into blood, 9 a third
of the living creatures in the sea died, and a
third of the ships were destroyed.

10 Then the third angel blew his trumpet. A
large star, burning like a torch, dropped from
the sky and fell on a third of the rivers, and on
the springs of water. 11 (The name of the star
is Bitterness.) A third of the water turned bitter,
and many men died from drinking the water, because it had turned bitter.

12 Then the fourth angel blew his trumpet.
A third of the sun was struck, and a third of

New International Version

it was hurled down upon the earth. A third of
the earth was burned up, a third of the trees
were burned up, and all the green grass was
burned up.

8 The second angel sounded his trumpet, and
something like a huge mountain, all ablaze, was
thrown into the sea. A third of the sea turned
into blood, 9 a third of the living creatures in
the sea died, and a third of the ships were destroyed.

10 The third angel sounded his trumpet, and
a great star, blazing like a torch, fell from the
sky on a third of the rivers and on the springs
of water—11 the name of the star is Wormwood.[j] A third of the waters turned bitter, and
many people died from the waters that had become bitter.

12 The fourth angel sounded his trumpet, and
a third of the sun was struck, a third of the

[j] That is, Bitterness.

Phillips Modern English

upon the earth. One-third of the earth was burnt up, one-third of all the trees was burnt up, and every blade of green grass was burnt up.

8.8 The second trumpet: The blazing mountain

The second angel blew his trumpet, and something like a vast mountain blazing with fire was thrown into the sea. A third-part of the sea turned into blood, a third of all live creatures in the sea died, and a third-part of all shipping was destroyed.

8.10 The third trumpet: The poisonous star

Then the third angel blew his trumpet and there fell from the sky a huge star blazing like a torch. It fell upon a third of the rivers and springs of water. The name of the star is said to be Apsinthus (Wormwood). A third of all the waters turned into wormwood, and many people died because the waters had become so bitter.

8.12 The fourth trumpet: Light from the sky diminishes

The fourth angel blew his trumpet, and a third-part of the sun, a third-part of the moon

Revised Standard Version

fell on the earth; and a third of the earth was burnt up, and a third of the trees were burnt up, and all green grass was burnt up.
8 The second angel blew his trumpet, and something like a great mountain, burning with fire, was thrown into the sea; 9 and a third of the sea became blood, a third of the living creatures in the sea died, and a third of the ships were destroyed.
10 The third angel blew his trumpet, and a great star fell from heaven, blazing like a torch, and it fell on a third of the rivers and on the fountains of water. 11 The name of the star is Wormwood. A third of the waters became wormwood, and many men died of the water, because it was made bitter.
12 The fourth angel blew his trumpet, and a third of the sun was struck, and a third of the

Jerusalem Bible

mixed with blood, were dropped on the earth; a third of the earth was burned up, and a third of all trees, and every blade of grass was burned.
8 The second angel blew his trumpet, and it was as though a great mountain, all on fire, had been dropped into the sea: a third of the sea turned into blood, 9 a third of all the living things in the sea were killed, and a third of all ships were
destroyed. 10 The third angel blew his trumpet, and a huge star fell from the sky, burning like a ball of fire, and it fell on a third of all rivers
and springs; 11 this was the star called Wormwood, and a third of all water turned to bitter wormwood, so that many people died from
drinking it. 12 The fourth angel blew his trumpet, and a third of the sun and a third of the moon

New English Bible

upon the earth. A third of the earth was burnt, a third of the trees were burnt, all the green grass was burnt.

The second angel blew his trumpet; and what looked like a great blazing mountain was hurled into the sea. A third of the sea was turned to blood, a third of the living creatures in it died, and a third of the ships on it foundered.

The third angel blew his trumpet; and a great star shot from the sky, flaming like a torch; and it fell on a third of the rivers and springs. The name of the star was Wormwood; and a third of the water turned to wormwood, and men in great numbers died of the water because it had been poisoned.

The fourth angel blew his trumpet; and a third part of the sun was struck, a third of the

King James Version

moon, and the third part of the stars; so as the third part of them was darkened, and the day shone not for a third part of it, and the night likewise. 13 And I beheld, and heard an angel flying through the midst of heaven, saying with a loud voice, Woe, woe, woe, to the inhabiters of the earth by reason of the other voices of the trumpet of the three angels, which are yet to sound!

9 And the fifth angel sounded, and I saw a star fall from heaven unto the earth: and to him was given the key of the bottomless pit. 2 And he opened the bottomless pit; and there arose a smoke out of the pit, as the smoke of a great furnace; and the sun and the air were darkened by reason of the smoke of the pit. 3 And there came out of the smoke locusts upon the earth: and unto them was given power, as the scorpions of the earth have power. 4 And it was commanded them that they should not hurt the grass of the earth, neither any green thing, neither any tree; but only those men which have not the seal of God in their foreheads. 5 And to

Living Bible

darkened, and a third of the moon and the stars, so that the daylight was dimmed by a third, and the nighttime darkness deepened. 13 As I watched, I saw a solitary eagle flying through the heavens crying loudly, "Woe, woe, woe to the people of the earth because of the terrible things that will soon happen when the three remaining angels blow their trumpets."

9 Then the fifth angel blew his trumpet and I saw one[a] who was fallen to earth from heaven, and to him was given the key to the bottomless pit. 2 When he opened it, smoke poured out as though from some huge furnace, and the sun and air were darkened by the smoke.

3 Then locusts came from the smoke and descended onto the earth and were given power to sting like scorpions. 4 They were told not to hurt the grass or plants or trees, but to attack those people who did not have the mark of God on their foreheads. 5 They were not to kill them,

[a] Literally, "a star fallen from heaven"; it is unclear whether this person is of satanic origin, as most commentators believe, or whether the reference is to Christ.

Today's English Version

the moon, and a third of the stars, so that their light lost a third of its brightness; there was no light during a third of the day and during a third of the night also.

13 Then I looked, and I heard an eagle that was flying high in the air say in a loud voice, "O horror! horror! How horrible it will be for all who live on earth when the sound comes from the trumpets that the other three angels must blow!"

9 Then the fifth angel blew his trumpet. I saw a star which had fallen from the sky to earth; it was given the key to the abyss. 2 The star opened the abyss, and smoke poured out of it, like the smoke from a large furnace; the sunlight and the air were made dark by the smoke from the abyss. 3 Locusts came down out of the smoke upon the earth, and they were given power like that of scorpions. 4 They were told not to harm the grass, or the trees, or any other plant; they could harm only the men who did not have the mark of God's seal on their foreheads. 5 The locusts were not allowed to kill

New International Version

moon, and a third of the stars, so that a third of them turned dark. A third of the day was without light, and also a third of the night.

13 As I watched, I heard an eagle that was flying in midair call out in a loud voice: "Woe! Woe! Woe to the inhabitants of the earth, because of the trumpet blasts about to be sounded by the other three angels!"

9 The fifth angel sounded his trumpet, and I saw a star that had fallen from the sky to the earth. The star was given the key to the shaft of the Abyss. 2 When he opened the Abyss, smoke rose from it like the smoke from a gigantic furnace. The sun and sky were darkened by the smoke from the Abyss. 3 And out of the smoke locusts came down upon the earth and were given power like that of scorpions of the earth. 4 They were told not to harm the grass of the earth or any plant or tree, but only those people who did not have the seal of God on their foreheads. 5 They were not given power to kill

Phillips Modern English

and a third of the stars were struck. A third-part of the light of each of them was darkened, so that light by day and light by night were both diminished by a third-part.

8.13 The cry of pity from mid-heaven

Then in my vision I heard a solitary eagle flying in mid-heaven, crying in a loud voice, "Alas, alas, alas for the inhabitants of the earth for there are three more trumpet blasts which the three angels shall sound!"

9.1 The fifth trumpet: The fathomless pit

The fifth angel blew his trumpet. I saw a star that had fallen down from Heaven to earth, and to him was given the key to the shaft of the abyss. Then he opened the shaft and smoke like the smoke of a vast furnace rose out of it, so that the light of the sun and the air itself grew dark from the smoke of the shaft.

Then out of the smoke emerged locusts to descend upon the earth. They were given powers like those of earthly scorpions. They had orders to do no harm to any grass, green thing or tree upon the earth, but to injure only those human beings who did not bear the seal of God upon their foreheads. They were given no power to

Revised Standard Version

moon, and a third of the stars, so that a third of their light was darkened; a third of the day was kept from shining, and likewise a third of the night.

13 Then I looked, and I heard an eagle crying with a loud voice, as it flew in midheaven, "Woe, woe, woe to those who dwell on the earth, at the blasts of the other trumpets which the three angels are about to blow!"

9 And the fifth angel blew his trumpet, and I saw a star fallen from heaven to earth, and he was given the key of the shaft of the bottomless pit; 2 he opened the shaft of the bottomless pit, and from the shaft rose smoke like the smoke of a great furnace, and the sun and the air were darkened with the smoke from the shaft. 3 Then from the smoke came locusts on the earth, and they were given power like the power of scorpions of the earth; 4 they were told not to harm the grass of the earth or any green growth or any tree, but only those of mankind who have not the seal of God upon their foreheads; 5 they were allowed to torture them

Jerusalem Bible

and a third of the stars were blasted, so that the light went out of a third of them and for a third of the day there was no illumination, and the same with the night.

13 In my vision, I heard an eagle, calling aloud as it flew high overhead, "Trouble, trouble, trouble, for all the people on earth at the sound of the other three trumpets which the three angels are going to blow."

The fifth trumpet

9 Then the fifth angel blew his trumpet, and I saw a star[n] that had fallen from heaven on to the earth, and he was given the key to the shaft leading down to the Abyss.[o] 2 When he unlocked the shaft of the Abyss, *smoke poured up* out of the Abyss *like the smoke from a* huge *furnace*[p] so that the sun and the sky were darkened by it, 3 and out of the smoke dropped locusts which were given the powers that scorpions have on the earth: 4 they were forbidden to harm any fields or crops or trees and told only to attack any men who were without God's seal on their foreheads. 5 They were not to kill

[n] A fallen angel. [o] Where fallen angels were imprisoned, to be released only to their final punishment. [p] Ex. 19:18.

New English Bible

moon, and a third of the stars, so that the third part went dark and a third of the light of the day failed, and of the night.

Then I looked, and I heard an eagle calling with a loud cry as it flew in mid-heaven: 'Woe, woe, woe to the inhabitants of the earth when the trumpets sound which the three last angels must now blow!'

9 Then the fifth angel blew his trumpet; and I saw a star that had fallen from heaven to earth, and the star was given the key of the shaft of the abyss. With this he opened the shaft of the abyss; and from the shaft smoke rose like smoke from a great furnace, and the sun and the air were darkened by the smoke from the shaft. Then over the earth, out of the smoke, came locusts, and they were given the powers that earthly scorpions have. They were told to do no injury to the grass or to any plant or tree, but only to those men who had not received the seal of God on their foreheads. These

King James Version

them it was given that they should not kill them,
but that they should be tormented five months:
and their torment *was* as the torment of a
scorpion, when he striketh a man. 6And in those
days shall men seek death, and shall not find it;
and shall desire to die, and death shall flee from
them. 7And the shapes of the locusts *were* like
unto horses prepared unto battle; and on their
heads *were* as it were crowns like gold, and
their faces *were* as the faces of men. 8And they
had hair as the hair of women, and their teeth
were as *the teeth* of lions. 9And they had breastplates, as it were breastplates of iron; and the
sound of their wings *was* as the sound of
chariots of many horses running to battle. 10And
they had tails like unto scorpions, and there
were stings in their tails: and their power *was*
to hurt men five months. 11And they had a king
over them, *which is* the angel of the bottomless
pit, whose name in the Hebrew tongue *is* Abaddon, but in the Greek tongue hath *his* name
Apollyon. 12 One woe is past; *and,* behold, there
come two woes more hereafter. 13And the sixth
angel sounded, and I heard a voice from the
four horns of the golden altar which is before
God, 14 Saying to the sixth angel which had the
trumpet, Loose the four angels which are bound
in the great river Euphrates. 15And the four
angels were loosed, which were prepared for an
hour, and a day, and a month, and a year, for

Living Bible

but to torture them for five months with agony
like the pain of scorpion stings. 6 In those days
men will try to kill themselves but won't be able
to—death will not come. They will long to die—
but death will flee away!
7 The locusts looked like horses armored for
battle. They had what looked like golden crowns
on their heads, and their faces looked like men's.
8 Their hair was long like women's, and their
teeth were those of lions. 9 They wore breastplates that seemed to be of iron, and their wings
roared like an army of chariots rushing into battle. 10 They had stinging tails like scorpions, and
their power to hurt, given to them for five
months, was in their tails. 11 Their king is the
Prince of the bottomless pit whose name in Hebrew is Abaddon, and in Greek, Apollyon [and
in English, the Destroyer[b]].
12 One terror now ends, but there are two
more coming!
13 The sixth angel blew his trumpet and I
heard a voice speaking from the four horns of
the golden altar that stands before the throne of
God, 14 saying to the sixth angel, "Release the
four mighty demons[c] held bound at the great
River Euphrates." 15 They had been kept in
readiness for that year and month and day and
hour, and now they were turned loose to kill a

[*b*] Implied. [*c*] Literally, "(fallen) angels."

Today's English Version

these men, but only to torture them for five
months. The pain caused by their torture is like
the pain a man suffers when stung by a scorpion.
6 During the five months those men will seek
death, but will not find it; they will want to die,
but death will flee from them.
7 The locusts looked like horses ready for
battle; on their heads they had what seemed to
be gold crowns, and their faces were like men's
faces. 8 Their hair was like women's hair, their
teeth were like lions' teeth. 9 Their chests were
covered with what looked like iron breastplates,
and the sound made by their wings was like the
noise of many horse-drawn chariots rushing into
battle. 10 They have tails and stings, like those
of a scorpion, and it is with their tails that they
have the power to hurt men for five months.
11 They have a king ruling over them, who is
the angel in charge of the abyss. His name in
Hebrew is Abaddon; in Greek the name is
Apollyon (meaning "The Destroyer").
12 The first horror is over; after this there
are still two more horrors to come.
13 Then the sixth angel blew his trumpet. I
heard a voice coming from the corners of the
gold altar standing before God. 14 The voice
said to the sixth angel who had the trumpet,
"Release the four angels who are bound at the
great river Euphrates!" 15 The four angels were
released; they had been prepared for this very
hour of this very day of this very month and

New International Version

them, but only to torture them for five months.
And the agony they suffered was like that of
the sting of a scorpion when it strikes a man.
6 During those days men will seek death, but will
not find it; they will long to die, but death will
elude them.
7 The locusts looked like horses prepared for
battle. On their heads they wore something like
crowns of gold, and their faces resembled human
faces. 8 Their hair was like women's hair, and
their teeth were like lions' teeth. 9 They had
breastplates like breastplates of iron, and the
sound of their wings was like the thundering of
many horses and chariots rushing into battle.
10 They had tails and stings like scorpions, and
in their tails they had power to torment people for five months. 11 They had as king over
them the angel of the Abyss, whose name in
Hebrew is Abaddon[k] and in Greek, Apollyon.[k]
12 The first woe is past; two other woes are
yet to come.
13 The sixth angel blew his trumpet, and I
heard a voice coming from the horns[l] of the
golden altar that is before God. 14 It said to the
sixth angel who had the trumpet, "Release the
four angels who are bound at the great river
Euphrates." 15And the four angels who had been
kept ready for this very hour and day and month
and year were released to kill a third of man-

[*k*] That is, *Destroyer*. [*l*] That is, projections.

Phillips Modern English

kill men, but only to torture them for five months. The torture they could inflict was like the pain of a scorpion's sting.

In those days men will seek death but they will never find it; they will long to die but death will elude them. These locusts looked to me in my vision like horses prepared for battle. On their heads were what appeared to be crowns like gold; their faces were like human faces, and they had long hair like women. Their teeth were like lion's teeth, their breasts were like iron-breastplates, and the noise of their wings was like the noise of a host of chariots and horses charging into battle. They have tails and stings like scorpions, and it is in their tails that they possess the power to injure men for five months. They have as their king the angel of the pit, whose name in Hebrew is Abaddon and in Greek Apollyon, (meaning the destroyer).

The first disaster is now past, but I see two more approaching.

9.13 The sixth trumpet: The destroying angels

Then the sixth angel blew his trumpet, and I heard a solitary voice speaking from the four corners of the golden altar that stands in the presence of God. And it said to the sixth angel who held the trumpet,

"Release the four angels who are bound at the great river Euphrates!"

Then these four angels who had been held ready for the hour, the day, the month and the year, were set free to kill a third-part of all man-

Revised Standard Version

for five months, but not to kill them, and their
torture was like the torture of a scorpion, when
it stings a man. 6 And in those days men will
seek death and will not find it; they will long to
die, and death will fly from them.
7 In appearance the locusts were like horses
arrayed for battle; on their heads were what
looked like crowns of gold; their faces were like
human faces, 8 their hair like women's hair, and
their teeth like lions' teeth; 9 they had scales
like iron breastplates, and the noise of their
wings was like the noise of many chariots with
horses rushing into battle. 10 They have tails
like scorpions, and stings, and their power of
hurting men for five months lies in their tails.
11 They have as king over them the angel of
the bottomless pit; his name in Hebrew is Abaddon, and in Greek he is called Apollyon.[b]
12 The first woe has passed; behold, two woes
are still to come.
13 Then the sixth angel blew his trumpet, and
I heard a voice from the four horns of the
golden altar before God, 14 saying to the sixth
angel who had the trumpet, "Release the four
angels who are bound at the great river Euphrates." 15 So the four angels were released,
who had been held ready for the hour, the day,
the month, and the year, to kill a third of man-

[b] Or *Destroyer.*

Jerusalem Bible

them, but to give them pain for five months,
and the pain was to be the pain of a scorpion's
sting. 6 When this happens, *men will long for
death and not find it anywhere*[q]; they will want
to die and death will evade them.
7 To look at, these locusts were *like horses
armored for battle*[r]; they had things that looked
like gold crowns on their heads, and faces that
seemed human, 8 and hair like women's hair,
and *teeth like lions' teeth.* 9 They had body-
armor like iron breastplates, and the noise of
their wings sounded like a great charge of horses
and chariots into battle. 10 Their tails were like
scorpions', with stings, and it was with them
that they were able to injure people for five
months. 11 As their leader they had their emperor, the angel of the Abyss, whose name in
Hebrew is Abaddon, or Apollyon[s] in Greek.
12 That was the first of the troubles; there
are still two more to come.

The sixth trumpet

13 The sixth angel blew his trumpet, and I
heard a voice come out of the four horns of the
golden altar in front of God. 14 It spoke to the
sixth angel with the trumpet, and said, "Release
the four angels that are chained up at the great
river Euphrates." 15 These four angels had been
put there ready for this hour of this day of this
month of this year, and now they were released

[*q*] Jb. 3:21. [*r*] The descriptive details in vv. 7-9 owe much to Jl. 1 and 2. [*s*] "Destruction."

New English Bible

they were allowed to torment for five months, with torment like a scorpion's sting; but they were not to kill them. During that time these men will seek death, but they will not find it; they will long to die, but death will elude them.

In appearance the locusts were like horses equipped for battle. On their heads were what looked like golden crowns; their faces were like human faces and their hair like women's hair; they had teeth like lions' teeth, and wore breast-plates like iron; the sound of their wings was like the noise of horses and chariots rushing to battle; they had tails like scorpions, with stings in them, and in their tails lay their power to plague mankind for five months. They had for their king the angel of the abyss, whose name, in Hebrew, is Abaddon, and in Greek, Apollyon, or the Destroyer.

The first woe has now passed. But there are still two more to come.

The sixth angel then blew his trumpet; and I heard a voice coming from between the horns of the golden altar that stood in the presence of God. It said to the sixth angel, who held the trumpet: 'Release the four angels held bound at the great river Euphrates!' So the four angels were let loose, to kill a third of mankind. They had been held ready for this moment, for this

King James Version

to slay the third part of men. 16And the number of the army of the horsemen *were* two hundred thousand thousand: and I heard the number of them. 17And thus I saw the horses in the vision, and them that sat on them, having breastplates of fire, and of jacinth, and brimstone: and the heads of the horses *were* as the heads of lions; and out of their mouths issued fire and smoke and brimstone. 18 By these three was the third part of men killed, by the fire, and by the smoke, and by the brimstone, which issued out of their mouths. 19 For their power is in their mouth, and in their tails: for their tails *were* like unto serpents, and had heads, and with them they do hurt. 20And the rest of the men which were not killed by these plagues yet repented not of the works of their hands, that they should not worship devils, and idols of gold, and silver, and brass, and stone, and of wood; which neither can see, nor hear, nor walk: 21 Neither repented they of their murders, nor of their sorceries, nor of their fornication, nor of their thefts.

10 And I saw another mighty angel come down from heaven, clothed with a cloud: and a rainbow *was* upon his head, and his face *was* as it were the sun, and his feet as pillars of fire: 2And he had in his hand a little book open: and he set his right foot upon the sea, and *his*

Living Bible

third of all mankind. 16 They led an army of 200,000,000 [d] warriors[e]—I heard an announcement of how many there were.

17, 18 I saw their horses spread out before me in my vision; their riders wore fiery-red breastplates, though some were sky-blue and others yellow. The horses' heads looked much like lions', and smoke and fire and flaming sulphur billowed from their mouths, killing one-third of all mankind. 19 Their power of death was not only in their mouths, but in their tails as well, for their tails were similar to serpents' heads that struck and bit with fatal wounds.

20 But the men left alive after these plagues *still refused to worship God!* They would not renounce their demon-worship, nor their idols made of gold and silver, brass, stone, and wood —which neither see nor hear nor walk! 21 Neither did they change their mind and attitude about all their murders and witchcraft, their immorality and theft.

10 Then I saw another mighty angel coming down from heaven, surrounded by a cloud, with a rainbow over his head; his face shone like the sun and his feet flashed with fire. 2And he held open in his hand a small scroll. He set his right foot on the sea and his left foot on the

[*d*] If this is a literal figure, it is no longer incredible, in view of a world population of 6,000,000,000 in the near future. In China alone, in 1961, there were an "estimated 200,000,000 armed and organized militiamen" (Associated Press Release, April 24, 1964). [*e*] Literally, "horsemen."

Today's English Version

year, to kill a third of all mankind. 16 I was told the number of the mounted troops: it was 200 million. 17And in my vision I saw the horses and their riders: they had breastplates red as fire, blue as sapphire, and yellow as sulfur. The horses' heads were like lions' heads, and from their mouths came out fire, smoke, and sulfur. 18A third of mankind was killed by those three plagues: the fire, the smoke, and the sulfur coming out of the horses' mouths. 19 For the power of the horses is in their mouths, and also in their tails. Their tails are like snakes, with heads, and they use them to hurt people.

20 The rest of mankind, all those who had not been killed by these plagues, did not turn away from what they themselves had made. They did not stop worshiping the demons and the idols of gold, silver, bronze, stone, and wood, which cannot see, hear, or walk. 21 Nor did those men repent of their murders, their magic, their immorality, or their stealing.

The angel and the little scroll

10 Then I saw another mighty angel coming down out of heaven. He was dressed in a cloud, with a rainbow around his head; his face was like the sun, and his legs were like columns of fire. 2 He had a small scroll open in his hand. He put his right foot on the sea, his left foot on

New International Version

kind. 16 The number of the mounted troops was two hundred million. I heard their number.

17 The horses and riders I saw in my vision looked like this: Their breastplates were fiery red, dark blue, and yellow as sulfur. The heads of the horses resembled the heads of lions, and out of their mouths came fire, smoke and sulfur. 18A third of mankind was killed by the three plagues of fire, smoke and sulfur that came out of their mouths. 19 The power of the horses was in their mouths and in their tails; for their tails were like snakes, having heads with which they inflict injury.

20 The rest of mankind that were not killed by these plagues still did not repent of the work of their hands; they did not stop worshiping demons, and idols of gold, silver, bronze, stone and wood—idols that cannot see or hear or walk. 21 Nor did they repent of their murders, their magic arts, their sexual immorality or their thefts.

The angel and the little scroll

10 Then I saw another mighty angel coming down from heaven. He was robed in a cloud, with a rainbow above his head; his face was like the sun, and his legs were like fiery pillars. 2 He was holding a little scroll, which lay open in his hand. He planted his right foot

Phillips Modern English

kind. The number of their horsemen was two hundred million—I heard what their number was. In my vision I saw these horses and their riders, and their breastplates were fiery-red, blue and yellow. The horses' heads looked to me like the heads of lions, and out of their mouths poured fire and smoke and sulphur. A third of all mankind died from the fearful effects of these three, the fire, the smoke and the sulphur which pours out of their mouths. For the power of these horses lies in their mouths and in their tails. Indeed their tails are like serpents with heads, and with these they inflict injury.

The rest of mankind, who did not die in this fearful destruction, neither repented of the works of their own hands nor ceased to worship evil powers and idols of gold, silver, brass, stone or wood, which can neither see nor hear nor move. Neither did they repent of their murders, their sorceries, their sexual sins, nor of their thieving.

10.1 The angel with the little book

Then I saw another mighty angel descending from Heaven. He was clothed in a cloud, and there was a rainbow around his head. His face blazed like the sun, his legs like pillars of fire, and he had a little book lying open in his hand. He planted his right foot on the sea and his left

Revised Standard Version

kind. 16 The number of the troops of cavalry was twice ten thousand times ten thousand; I heard their number. 17 And this was how I saw the horses in my vision: the riders wore breastplates the color of fire and of sapphire[c] and of sulphur, and the heads of the horses were like lions' heads, and fire and smoke and sulphur issued from their mouths. 18 By these three plagues a third of mankind was killed, by the fire and smoke and sulphur issuing from their mouths. 19 For the power of the horses is in their mouths and in their tails; their tails are like serpents, with heads, and by means of them they wound.

20 The rest of mankind, who were not killed by these plagues, did not repent of the works of their hands nor give up worshiping demons and idols of gold and silver and bronze and stone and wood, which cannot either see or hear or walk; 21 nor did they repent of their murders or their sorceries or their immorality or their thefts.

10 Then I saw another mighty angel coming down from heaven, wrapped in a cloud, with a rainbow over his head, and his face was like the sun, and his legs like pillars of fire. 2 He had a little scroll open in his hand. And he set his right foot on the sea, and his left foot

[c] Greek *hyacinth*.

Jerusalem Bible

to destroy a third of the human race. 16 I learned how many there were in their army: twice ten thousand times ten thousand mounted men. 17 In my vision I saw the horses, and the riders with their breastplates of flame color, hyacinth blue and sulphur yellow; the horses had lions' heads, and fire, smoke and sulphur were coming out of their mouths. 18 It was by these three plagues, the fire, the smoke and the sulphur coming out of their mouths, that the one third of the human race was killed. 19 All the horses' power was in their mouths and their tails: their tails were like snakes, and had heads that were able to wound. 20 But the rest of the human race, who escaped these plagues, refused either to abandon *the things they had made with their own hands*[t]—the *idols made of gold, silver, bronze, stone and wood*[u] that can neither see nor hear nor move—or to stop worshiping devils. 21 Nor did they give up their murdering, or witchcraft, or fornication or stealing.

The imminence of the last punishment

10 Then I saw another powerful angel coming down from heaven, wrapped in a cloud, with a rainbow over his head; his face was like the sun, and his legs were pillars of fire. 2 In his hand he had a small scroll, unrolled; he put his right foot in the sea and his left foot on

[t] Is. 17:8. [u] Dn. 5:4.

New English Bible

very year and month, day and hour. And their squadrons of cavalry, whose count I heard, numbered two hundred million.

This was how I saw the horses and their riders in my vision: They wore breastplates, fiery red, blue, and sulphur-yellow; the horses had heads like lions' heads, and out of their mouths came fire, smoke, and sulphur. By these three plagues, that is, by the fire, the smoke, and the sulphur that came from their mouths, a third of mankind was killed. The power of the horses lay in their mouths, and in their tails also; for their tails were like snakes, with heads, and with them too they dealt injuries.

The rest of mankind who survived these plagues still did not abjure the gods their hands had fashioned, nor cease their worship of devils and of idols made from gold, silver, bronze, stone, and wood, which cannot see or hear or walk. Nor did they repent of their murders, their sorcery, their fornication, or their robberies.

10 Then I saw another mighty angel coming down from heaven. He was wrapped in cloud, with the rainbow round his head; his face shone like the sun and his legs were like pillars of fire. In his hand he held a little scroll unrolled. His right foot he planted on the sea, and

King James Version

left *foot* on the earth, 3And cried with a loud
voice, as *when* a lion roareth: and when he had
cried, seven thunders uttered their voices. 4And
when the seven thunders had uttered their voices,
I was about to write: and I heard a voice from
heaven saying unto me, Seal up those things
which the seven thunders uttered, and write
them not. 5And the angel which I saw stand
upon the sea and upon the earth lifted up his
hand to heaven, 6And sware by him that liveth
for ever and ever, who created heaven, and the
things that therein are, and the earth, and the
things that therein are, and the sea, and the
things which are therein, that there should be
time no longer: 7 But in the days of the voice
of the seventh angel, when he shall begin to
sound, the mystery of God should be finished,
as he hath declared to his servants the prophets. 8And the voice which I heard from heaven
spake unto me again, and said, Go *and* take the
little book which is open in the hand of the
angel which standeth upon the sea and upon
the earth. 9And I went unto the angel, and said
unto him, Give me the little book. And he said
unto me, Take *it*, and eat it up; and it shall
make thy belly bitter, but it shall be in thy
mouth sweet as honey. 10And I took the little
book out of the angel's hand, and ate it up; and
it was in my mouth sweet as honey: and as soon

Living Bible

earth, 3 and gave a great shout—it was like the
roar of a lion—and the seven thunders crashed
their reply.
4 I was about to write what the thunders said
when a voice from heaven called to me, "Don't
do it. Their words are not to be revealed."
5 Then the mighty angel standing on the sea
and land lifted his right hand to heaven, 6 and
swore by him who lives forever and ever, who
created heaven and everything in it and the earth
and all that it contains and the sea and its inhabitants, that there should be no more delay,
7 but that when the seventh angel blew his trumpet, then God's veiled plan—mysterious through
the ages ever since it was announced by his servants the prophets—would be fulfilled.
8 Then the voice from heaven spoke to me
again, "Go and get the unrolled scroll from the
mighty angel standing there upon the sea and
land."
9 So I approached him and asked him to give
me the scroll. "Yes, take it and eat it," he said.
"At first it will taste like honey, but when you
swallow it, it will make your stomach sour!"
10 So I took it from his hand, and ate it! And
just as he had said, it was sweet in my mouth
but it gave me a stomach ache when I swallowed
it.

Today's English Version

the land, 3 and called out in a loud voice that
sounded like the roar of lions. After he had
called out, the seven thunders answered back
with a roar. 4As soon as they spoke, I was about
to write. But I heard a voice speak from heaven,
"Keep secret what the seven thunders said; do
not write it down!"
5 Then the angel that I saw standing on the
sea and on the land raised his right hand to
heaven 6 and made a vow in the name of God,
who lives forever and ever, who created heaven
and all things in it, the earth and all things in
it, and the sea and all things in it. The angel
said, "There will be no more delay! 7 But when
the seventh angel blows his trumpet, then God
will accomplish his secret plan, as he announced
to his servants, the prophets."
8 Then the voice that I had heard speaking
from heaven spoke to me again, saying, "Go and
take the open scroll which is in the hand of the
angel standing on the sea and on the land."
9 I went to the angel and asked him to give
me the little scroll. He said to me, "Take it and
eat it; it will turn sour in your stomach, but in
your mouth it will be sweet as honey."
10 I took the little scroll from his hand and
ate it, and it tasted sweet as honey in my mouth.
But after I had swallowed it, it turned sour in

New International Version

on the sea and his left foot on the land, 3 and
he gave a loud shout like the roar of a lion.
When he shouted, the voices of the seven thunders spoke. 4And when the seven thunders spoke,
I was about to write; but I heard a voice from
heaven say, "Seal up what the seven thunders
have said and do not write it down."
5 Then the angel I had seen standing on the
sea and on the land raised his right hand to
heaven. 6And he swore by him who lives for
ever and ever, who created the heavens and all
that is in them, the earth and all that is in it,
and the sea and all that is in it, and said, "There
will be no more delay! 7 But in the days when
the seventh angel is about to sound his trumpet,
the mystery of God will be accomplished, just
as he announced to his servants the prophets."
8 Then the voice that I had heard from
heaven spoke to me once more: "Go, take the
scroll that lies open in the hand of the angel
who is standing on the sea and on the land."
9 So I went to the angel and asked him to
give me the little scroll. He said to me, "Take it
and eat it. It will turn your stomach sour, but in
your mouth it will be as sweet as honey." 10 I
took the little scroll from the angel's hand and
ate it. It tasted as sweet as honey in my mouth,
but when I had eaten it, my stomach turned

Phillips Modern English

foot on the land, and then shouted with a loud voice like the roar of a lion. And when he shouted the seven thunders lifted their voices. When the seven thunders had rolled I was on the point of writing but I heard a voice from Heaven, saying,

"Seal up what the seven thunders said, but do not write it down!"

Then the angel whom I had seen bestriding the sea and the land raised his right hand to Heaven and swore by the living one of the timeless ages, who created Heaven, earth and sea and all that is in them:

"There shall be no more delay! In the days which shall soon be announced by the trumpet-blast of the seventh angel the mysterious purpose of God shall be completed, as he assured his servants the prophets."

Then the voice which I had heard from Heaven was again in my ears, saying,

"Go and take the little book which lies open in the hand of the angel whose feet are planted on both sea and land."

So I went off towards the angel, asking him to give me the little book.

"Take it," he said to me, "and eat it up. It will be bitter to your stomach, but sweet as honey in your mouth."

Then I took the little book from the angel's hand and swallowed it. It was as sweet as honey to the taste but when I had eaten it up it was bitter to my stomach.

Revised Standard Version

on the land, 3 and called out with a loud voice,
like a lion roaring; when he called out, the
seven thunders sounded. 4 And when the seven
thunders had sounded, I was about to write, but
I heard a voice from heaven saying, "Seal up
what the seven thunders have said, and do not
write it down." 5 And the angel whom I saw
standing on sea and land lifted up his right hand
to heaven 6 and swore by him who lives for
ever and ever, who created heaven and what is
in it, the earth and what is in it, and the sea
and what is in it, that there should be no more
delay, 7 but that in the days of the trumpet call
to be sounded by the seventh angel, the mystery
of God, as he announced to his servants the
prophets, should be fulfilled.
8 Then the voice which I had heard from
heaven spoke to me again, saying, "Go, take the
scroll which is open in the hand of the angel
who is standing on the sea and on the land."
9 So I went to the angel and told him to give
me the little scroll; and he said to me, "Take it
and eat; it will be bitter to your stomach, but
sweet as honey in your mouth." 10 And I took
the little scroll from the hand of the angel and
ate it; it was sweet as honey in my mouth, but
when I had eaten it my stomach was made bit-

Jerusalem Bible

the land 3 and he shouted so loud, it was *like
a lion roaring.* At this, seven claps of thunder
made themselves heard 4 and when the seven
thunderclaps had spoken, I was preparing to
write, when I heard a voice from heaven say to
me, "Keep the words of the seven thunderclaps
secret and do not write them down." 5 Then
the angel that I had seen, standing on the sea
and the land, *raised his right hand to heaven,*[v]
6 and *swore by the One who lives for ever* and
ever, *and made heaven and all that is in it,* and
earth and all it bears, and *the sea and all it
holds,*[w] "The time of waiting is over; 7 at the
time when the seventh angel is heard sounding
his trumpet, God's secret intention will be fulfilled, just as he announced in the Good News
told to *his servants the prophets.*"

The seer eats the small scroll

8 Then I heard the voice I had heard from
heaven speaking to me again. "Go," it said,
"and take that open scroll out of the hand of
the angel standing on sea and land." 9 I went
to the angel and asked him to give me the
small scroll, and he said, "Take it and eat it;
it will turn your stomach sour, but in your
mouth it will taste as sweet as honey." 10 So I
took it out of the angel's hand, and swallowed
it; it was as sweet as honey in my mouth, but
when I had eaten it my stomach turned sour.

[v] Dt. 32:40. [w] Ne. 9:6.

New English Bible

his left on the land. Then he gave a great shout, like the roar of a lion; and when he shouted, the seven thunders spoke. I was about to write down what the seven thunders had said; but I heard a voice from heaven saying, 'Seal up what the seven thunders have said; do not write it down.' Then the angel that I saw standing on the sea and the land raised his right hand to heaven and swore by him who lives for ever and ever, who created heaven and earth and the sea and everything in them: 'There shall be no more delay; but when the time comes for the seventh angel to sound his trumpet, the hidden purpose of God will have been fulfilled, as he promised to his servants the prophets.'

Then the voice which I heard from heaven was speaking to me again, and it said, 'Go and take the open scroll in the hand of the angel that stands on the sea and the land.' So I went to the angel and asked him to give me the little scroll. He said to me, 'Take it, and eat it. It will turn your stomach sour, although in your mouth it will taste sweet as honey.' So I took the little scroll from the angel's hand and ate it, and in my mouth it did taste sweet as honey; but when I swallowed it my stomach turned sour.

King James Version

as I had eaten it, my belly was bitter. 11 And he said unto me, Thou must prophesy again before many peoples, and nations, and tongues, and kings.

11 And there was given me a reed like unto a rod: and the angel stood, saying, Rise, and measure the temple of God, and the altar, and them that worship therein. 2 But the court which is without the temple leave out, and measure it not; for it is given unto the Gentiles: and the holy city shall they tread under foot forty *and* two months. 3 And I will give *power* unto my two witnesses, and they shall prophesy a thousand two hundred *and* threescore days, clothed in sackcloth. 4 These are the two olive trees, and the two candlesticks standing before the God of the earth. 5 And if any man will hurt them, fire proceedeth out of their mouth, and devoureth their enemies: and if any man will hurt them, he must in this manner be killed. 6 These have power to shut heaven, that it rain not in the days of their prophecy: and have power over waters to turn them to blood, and to smite the earth

Living Bible

11 Then he told me, "You must prophesy further about many peoples, nations, tribes, and kings."

11 Now I was given a measuring stick and told to go and measure the temple of God, including the inner court where the altar stands, and to count the number of worshipers.[a] 2 "But do not measure the outer court," I was told, "for it has been turned over to the nations. They will trample the Holy City for forty-two months.[b] 3 And I will give power to my two witnesses to prophesy 1,260 days[b] clothed in sackcloth."

4 These two prophets are the two olive trees,[c] and two candlesticks standing before the God of all the earth. 5 Anyone trying to harm them will be killed by bursts of fire shooting from their mouths. 6 They have power to shut the skies so that no rain will fall during the three and a half years they prophesy, and to turn rivers and oceans to blood, and to send every kind of plague upon the earth as often as they wish.

[a] Literally, "Rise and measure the temple of God, and the altar, and them that worship therein." [b] 3½ years, as in Daniel 12:7. [c] Zechariah 4:3,4,11.

Today's English Version

my stomach. 11 Then I was told, "Once again you must speak God's message about many nations, races, languages, and kings."

The two witnesses

11 I was then given a measuring stick, like a rod, and told, "Get up and measure the temple of God and the altar, and count those who are worshiping in the temple. 2 But omit the outer courts of the temple. Do not measure them, because they have been given to the heathen, who will trample on the Holy City for 42 months. 3 I will send my two witnesses, dressed in sackcloth; and they will proclaim God's message during those 1,260 days."

4 The two witnesses are the two olive trees and the two lamps that stand before the Lord of the earth. 5 If anyone tries to harm them, fire comes out of their mouths and destroys their enemies; and in this way whoever shall try to harm them will be killed. 6 They have authority to shut up the sky so that there will be no rain during the time they proclaim God's message. They have authority also over the springs of water, to turn them into blood; they have authority also to strike the earth with every kind of plague as often as they wish.

New International Version

sour. 11 Then I was told, "You must prophesy again about many peoples, nations, languages and kings."

The two witnesses

11 I was given a reed like a measuring rod and was told, "Go and measure the temple of God and the altar, and count the worshipers there. 2 But exclude the outer court; do not measure it, because it has been given to the Gentiles. They will trample on the holy city for 42 months. 3 And I will give power to my two witnesses, and they will prophesy for 1,260 days, clothed in sackcloth." 4 These are the two olive trees and the two lampstands that stand before the Lord of the earth. 5 If anyone tries to harm them, fire comes from their mouths and devours their enemies. This is how anyone who wants to harm them must die. 6 These men have power to shut up the sky so that it will not rain during the time they are prophesying; and they have power to turn the waters into blood and to strike the earth with every kind of plague as often as they want.

Phillips Modern English

10.11 John is instructed to prophesy

Then they said to me, "It is again your duty to prophesy about peoples, nations, languages and many kings."

And I was given a measuring rod like a staff, and was I told, "Get up and measure the Sanctuary of God, and the altar, and count those who worship there. But leave out of your measurement the courtyard outside the Sanctuary—do not measure that at all. For it has been given over to the nations, and they will trample over the holy city for forty-two months."

11.3 God's two witnesses

"And I will give authority to my two witnesses to proclaim the message, clothed in sackcloth for twelve hundred and sixty days."

These are the two olive trees and the two lampstands which stand before the Lord of the earth. If anyone tries to harm them, fire issues from their mouths and consumes their enemies. Indeed, if anyone should try to hurt them, this is the way in which he will certainly meet his death. These witnesses have power to shut up the sky and stop any rain from falling during the time of their preaching. Moreover, they have power to turn the waters into blood, and to strike the earth with any plague as often as they wish.

Revised Standard Version

ter. 11And I was told, "You must again prophesy about many peoples and nations and tongues
and kings."

11 Then I was given a measuring rod like a
staff, and I was told: "Rise and measure the
temple of God and the altar and those who
worship there, 2 but do not measure the court
outside the temple; leave that out, for it is given
over to the nations, and they will trample over
the holy city for forty-two months. 3And I will
grant my two witnesses power to prophesy for
one thousand two hundred and sixty days,
clothed in sackcloth."
4 These are the two olive trees and the two
lampstands which stand before the Lord of the
earth. 5And if any one would harm them, fire
pours from their mouth and consumes their
foes; if any one would harm them, thus he is
doomed to be killed. 6 They have power to shut
the sky, that no rain may fall during the days
of their prophesying, and they have power over
the waters to turn them into blood, and to smite
the earth with every plague, as often as they

Jerusalem Bible

11 Then I was told, "You are to prophesy again,
this time about many different nations and countries and languages and emperors."

The two witnesses

11 Then I was given a long cane as a measuring rod, and I was told, "Go and measure
God's sanctuary, and the altar, and the people
who worship there; 2 but leave out the outer
court and do not measure it, because it has been
handed over to pagans—they will trample on
the holy city for forty-two months.[x] 3 But I
shall send my two witnesses to prophesy for
those twelve hundred and sixty days, wearing
sackcloth. 4 These are the *two olive trees*[y] and
the two lamps *that stand before the Lord of the
world.*[z] 5 Fire can come from their mouths and
consume their enemies if anyone tries to harm
them; and if anybody does try to harm them he
will certainly be killed in this way. 6 They are
able to lock up the sky so that it does not rain
as long as they are prophesying; they are able
to turn water into blood and strike the whole
world with any plague as often as they like.

[*x*] This period, taken from Deuteronomy, is used as the symbol for any time of persecution. [*y*] Zc. 4:3,14, where they symbolize Joshua and Zerubbabel; here they probably represent Peter and Paul. [*z*] 2 K. 1:10.

New English Bible

Then they said to me, 'Once again you must utter prophecies over peoples and nations and languages and many kings.'

11 I was given a long cane, a kind of measuring-rod, and told: 'Now go and measure the temple of God, the altar, and the number of the worshippers. But have nothing to do with the outer court of the temple; do not measure that; for it has been given over to the Gentiles, and they will trample the Holy City underfoot for forty-two months. And I have two witnesses, whom I will appoint to prophesy, dressed in sackcloth, all through those twelve hundred and sixty days.' These are the two olive-trees and the two lamps that stand in the presence of the Lord of the earth. If anyone seeks to do them harm, fire pours from their mouths and consumes their enemies; and thus shall the man die who seeks to do them harm. These two have the power to shut up the sky, so that no rain may fall during the time of their prophesying; and they have the power to turn water to blood and to strike the earth at will with every kind of

King James Version

with all plagues, as often as they will. 7And
when they shall have finished their testimony, the
beast that ascendeth out of the bottomless pit
shall make war against them, and shall overcome them, and kill them. 8And their dead
bodies *shall lie* in the street of the great city,
which spiritually is called Sodom and Egypt,
where also our Lord was crucified. 9And they of
the people and kindreds and tongues and nations shall see their dead bodies three days and
a half, and shall not suffer their dead bodies to
be put in graves. 10And they that dwell upon
the earth shall rejoice over them, and make
merry, and shall send gifts one to another; because these two prophets tormented them that
dwelt on the earth. 11And after three days and
a half the Spirit of life from God entered into
them, and they stood upon their feet; and great
fear fell upon them which saw them. 12And they
heard a great voice from heaven saying unto
them, Come up hither. And they ascended up
to heaven in a cloud; and their enemies beheld
them. 13And the same hour was there a great
earthquake, and the tenth part of the city fell,
and in the earthquake were slain of men seven

Living Bible

7 When they complete the three and a half
years of their solemn testimony, the tyrant who
comes out of the bottomless pit[d] will declare
war against them and conquer and kill them;
8, 9 and for three and a half days their bodies
will be exposed in the streets of Jerusalem (the
city fittingly described as "Sodom" or "Egypt")
—the very place where their Lord was crucified.
No one will be allowed to bury them, and people from many nations will crowd around to
gaze at them. 10And there will be a worldwide
holiday—people everywhere will rejoice and give
presents to each other and throw parties to celebrate the death of the two prophets who had
tormented them so much!
11 But after three and a half days, the spirit
of life from God will enter them and they will
stand up! And great fear will fall on everyone.
12 Then a loud voice will shout from heaven,
"Come up!" And they will rise to heaven in a
cloud as their enemies watch.
13 The same hour there will be a terrible
earthquake that levels a tenth of the city, leaving

[*d*] Revelation 9:11.

Today's English Version

7 When they finish proclaiming their message,
the beast that comes up out of the abyss will
fight against them. He will defeat them and kill
them, 8 and their bodies will lie on the street of
the great city, where their Lord was nailed to
the cross. The symbolic name of that city is
Sodom, or Egypt. 9 People from all nations,
tribes, languages, and races will look at their
bodies for three and a half days, and will not
allow them to be buried. 10 The people of earth
will be happy over the death of these two. They
will celebrate, and send presents to one another,
because those two prophets brought much suffering upon the people of earth. 11After three
and a half days a life-giving breath came from
God and entered them, and they stood up; all
who saw them were terribly afraid. 12 Then the
two prophets heard a loud voice say to them
from heaven, "Come up here!" As their enemies
watched, they went up into heaven in a cloud.
13At that very moment there was a violent earthquake; a tenth of the city was destroyed, and
7,000 people were killed in the earthquake. The

New International Version

7 Now when they have finished their testimony, the beast that comes up from the Abyss
will attack them, and overpower and kill them.
8 Their bodies will lie in the street of the great
city, which is figuratively called Sodom and
Egypt, where also their Lord was crucified. 9 For
three and a half days men from every people,
tribe, language and nation will gaze on their
bodies and refuse them burial. 10 The inhabitants
of the earth will gloat over them and will celebrate by sending each other gifts, because these
two prophets had tormented those who live on
the earth.
11 But after the three and a half days a
breath of life from God entered them, and they
stood on their feet, and terror struck those who
saw them. 12 Then they heard a loud voice from
heaven saying to them, "Come up here." And
they went up to heaven in a cloud, while their
enemies looked on.
13 At that very hour there was a severe earthquake and a tenth of the city collapsed. Seven
thousand people were killed in the earthquake,

Phillips Modern English

11.7 *The emergence of the animal*

Then, when their work of witness is complete, the animal will come up out of the pit and go to war with them. It will conquer and kill them, and their bodies will lie in the street of the great city, which is called by those with spiritual understanding, "Sodom" and "Egypt"—the very place where their Lord himself was crucified. For three and a half days men from all peoples and tribes and languages and nations will gaze upon their bodies and will not allow them to be buried. The inhabitants of the earth will gloat over them and will hold celebrations and send one another presents, because these two prophets had brought such misery to the inhabitants of the earth.

11.11 *The resurrection and ascension of the two witnesses*

But after three and a half days the Spirit of life from God entered them and they stood upright on their feet. This struck terror into the hearts of those who were watching them, and they heard a tremendous voice speaking to these two from Heaven, saying,

"Come up here!"

And they went up to Heaven in a cloud in full view of their enemies. And at that moment there was a great earthquake, a tenth-part of the city fell in ruins and seven thousand people were known to have been killed in the earthquake.

Revised Standard Version

desire. 7 And when they have finished their testimony, the beast that ascends from the bottomless pit will make war upon them and conquer
them and kill them, 8 and their dead bodies
will lie in the street of the great city which is
allegorically[d] called Sodom and Egypt, where
their Lord was crucified. 9 For three days and
a half men from the peoples and tribes and
tongues and nations gaze at their dead bodies
and refuse to let them be placed in a tomb,
10 and those who dwell on the earth will rejoice
over them and make merry and exchange presents, because these two prophets had been a
torment to those who dwell on the earth. 11 But
after the three and a half days a breath of life
from God entered them, and they stood up on
their feet, and great fear fell on those who saw
them. 12 Then they heard a loud voice from
heaven saying to them, "Come up hither!" And
in the sight of their foes they went up to heaven
in a cloud. 13 And at that hour there was a great
earthquake, and a tenth of the city fell; seven
thousand people were killed in the earthquake,

[d] Greek *spiritually*.

Jerusalem Bible

7 When they have completed their witnessing,
the beast that comes out of the Abyss *is going
to make war on them and overcome them*[a] and
kill them. 8 Their corpses will lie in the main
street of the Great City known by the symbolic
names Sodom and Egypt, in which their Lord
was crucified.[b] 9 Men out of every people, race,
language and nation will stare at their corpses,
for three and a half days, not letting them be
buried, 10 and the people of the world will be
glad about it and celebrate the event by giving
presents to each other, because these two prophets have been a plague to the people of the
world."
11 After the three and a half days, *God
breathed life into them and they stood up,*[c] and
everybody who saw it happen was terrified;
12 then they heard a loud voice from heaven
say to them, "Come up here," and while their
enemies were watching, they went up to heaven
in a cloud. 13 Immediately, there was a violent
earthquake, and a tenth of the city collapsed;
seven thousand persons[d] were killed in the earth-

[a] Dn. 7:21. [b] The "Great City" or "Babylon" in this book is Rome, whose actions were identified with Sodom's rejection of God's messengers and Egypt's oppression of God's people. The words "in which their Lord was crucified" may be a gloss, or may be justified by the responsibility of the Roman authority for the crucifixion. [c] Ezk. 37:5,10. [d] That is, a great number of all classes.

New English Bible

plague. But when they have completed their testimony, the beast that comes up from the abyss will wage war upon them and will defeat and kill them. Their corpses will lie in the street of the great city, whose name in allegory is Sodom, or Egypt, where also their Lord was crucified. For three days and a half men from every people and tribe, of every language and nation, gaze upon their corpses and refuse them burial. All men on earth gloat over them, make merry, and exchange presents; for these two prophets were a torment to the whole earth. But at the end of the three days and a half the breath of life from God came into them; and they stood up on their feet to the terror of all who saw it. Then a loud voice was heard speaking to them from heaven, which said, 'Come up here!' And they went up to heaven in a cloud, in full view of their enemies. At that same moment there was a violent earthquake, and a tenth of the city fell. Seven thousand people

King James Version

thousand: and the remnant were affrighted, and
gave glory to the God of heaven. 14 The second
woe is past; *and,* behold, the third woe cometh
quickly. 15 And the seventh angel sounded; and
there were great voices in heaven, saying, The
kingdoms of this world are become *the kingdoms* of our Lord, and of his Christ; and he
shall reign for ever and ever. 16 And the four and
twenty elders, which sat before God on their
seats, fell upon their faces, and worshipped God,
17 Saying, We give thee thanks, O Lord God
Almighty, which art, and wast, and art to come;
because thou hast taken to thee thy great power,
and hast reigned. 18 And the nations were angry,
and thy wrath is come, and the time of the dead,
that they should be judged, and that thou
shouldest give reward unto thy servants the
prophets, and to the saints, and them that fear
thy name, small and great; and shouldest destroy
them which destroy the earth. 19 And the temple
of God was opened in heaven, and there was
seen in his temple the ark of his testament: and
there were lightnings, and voices, and thunderings, and an earthquake, and great hail.

Living Bible

7,000 dead. Then everyone left will, in their terror, give glory to the God of heaven.
14 The second woe is past, but the third
quickly follows:
15 For just then the seventh angel blew his
trumpet, and there were loud voices shouting
down from heaven, "The kingdom of this world
now belongs to our Lord, and to his Christ; and
he shall reign forever and ever." [e]
16 And the twenty-four Elders sitting on their
thrones before God threw themselves down in
worship, saying, 17 "We give thanks, Lord God
Almighty, who is and was, for now you have assumed your great power and have begun to
reign. 18 The nations were angry with you, but
now it is your turn to be angry with them. It is
time to judge the dead, and reward your servants
—prophets and people alike, all who fear your
Name, both great and small—and to destroy
those who have caused destruction upon the
earth."
19 Then, in heaven, the temple of God was
opened and the ark of his covenant could be
seen inside. Lightning flashed and thunder
crashed and roared, and there was a great hailstorm and the world was shaken by a mighty
earthquake.

[*e*] Or, "The Lord and his Anointed shall now rule the world from this day to eternity."

Today's English Version

rest of the people were terrified and praised the
greatness of the God of heaven.
14 The second horror is over; but look! The
third horror will come soon.

The seventh trumpet

15 Then the seventh angel blew his trumpet,
and there were loud voices in heaven, saying,
"The power to rule over the world belongs now
to our Lord and his Messiah, and he will rule
forever and ever!" 16 Then the twenty-four elders
who sit on their thrones before God fell down
on their faces and worshiped God, 17 saying:

"Lord God Almighty, who is and who was!
We thank you that you have used your
great power
and have begun to rule!
18 The heathen were filled with rage,
because it is the time for your wrath to
come,
and for the dead to be judged.
It is the time to reward your servants, the
prophets,
and all your people, all who fear you,
great and small alike.
It is the time to destroy those who destroy
the earth!"

19 God's temple in heaven was opened, and
the box holding the covenant was seen in his
temple. Then there were flashes of lightning,
sounds, peals of thunder, an earthquake, and
heavy hail.

New International Version

and the survivors were terrified and gave glory
to the God of heaven.
14 The second woe has passed; the third woe
is coming soon.

The seventh trumpet

15 The seventh angel sounded his trumpet,
and there were loud voices in heaven, which
said:
"The kingdom of the world has become the
kingdom of our Lord and of his Christ,
and he will reign for ever and ever."
16 And the twenty-four elders, who were seated
on their thrones before God, fell on their faces
and worshiped God, 17 saying:
"We give thanks to you, Lord God Almighty,
who is and who was,
because you have taken your great power
and have begun to reign.
18 The nations were angry;
and your wrath has come.
The time has come for judging the dead,
and for rewarding your servants the
prophets
and your saints and those who reverence
your name,
both small and great—
and for destroying those who destroy the
earth."
19 Then God's temple in heaven was opened,
and within his temple was seen the sacred chest
of his covenant. And there came flashes of
lightning, rumblings, peals of thunder, an earthquake and a great hailstorm.

Phillips Modern English

The rest were terrified and acknowledged the glory of the God of Heaven.

11.14 The seventh trumpet: (i) The worship of Heaven

The second disaster is now past, and I see the third disaster following hard upon the heels of the second. The seventh angel blew his trumpet. There arose loud voices in Heaven and they were saying,

"The kingship of the world now belongs to our Lord and to his Christ, and he shall be king for timeless ages!"

Then the twenty-four elders, who sit upon their thrones in the presence of God, prostrated themselves and, with bowed heads, worshipped God, saying:

"We thank thee, O Lord who art God the Almighty, who art and who wast, that thou hast assumed thy great power and hast become king. The nations were full of fury, but now thy wrath has come and with it the time for the dead to be judged and for reward to be given to thy servants, the prophets and the saints, and all who fear thy name, both small and great. Now is the time for destroying the destroyers of the earth!"

Then the Sanctuary of God in Heaven was thrown open and the ark of his agreement within his Sanctuary could be clearly seen. Accompanying this sight were flashes of lightning, loud noises, peals of thunder, an earthquake and a violent storm of hail.

Revised Standard Version

and the rest were terrified and gave glory to the
God of heaven.
14 The second woe has passed; behold, the
third woe is soon to come.
15 Then the seventh angel blew his trumpet,
and there were loud voices in heaven, saying,
"The kingdom of the world has become the
kingdom of our Lord and of his Christ, and he
shall reign for ever and ever." 16 And the twenty-
four elders who sit on their thrones before God
fell on their faces and worshiped God, 17 saying,
"We give thanks to thee, Lord God Almighty, who art and who wast,
that thou hast taken thy great power and begun to reign.
18 The nations raged, but thy wrath came,
and the time for the dead to be judged,
for rewarding thy servants, the prophets and saints,
and those who fear thy name, both small and great,
and for destroying the destroyers of the earth."
19 Then God's temple in heaven was opened,
and the ark of his covenant was seen within his
temple; and there were flashes of lightning,
voices, peals of thunder, an earthquake, and
heavy hail.

Jerusalem Bible

quake, and the survivors, overcome with fear, could only praise the God of heaven.

The seventh trumpet

14 That was the second of the troubles; the
third is to come quickly after it.
15 Then the seventh angel blew his trumpet,
and voices could be heard shouting in heaven,
calling, "The kingdom of the world has become
the kingdom of our Lord and his Christ, and
he will reign for ever and ever." 16 The twenty-
four elders, enthroned in the presence of God,
prostrated themselves and touched the ground
with their foreheads worshiping God 17 with
these words, "We give thanks to you, Almighty
Lord God, He-Is-and-He-Was, for using your
great power and beginning your reign. 18 *The
nations were seething with rage*[e] and now the
time has come for your own anger, and for
the dead to be judged, and for your servants
the prophets, for the saints and for all who
worship you, small or great, to be rewarded.
The time has come to destroy those who are
destroying the earth."
19 Then the sanctuary of God in heaven
opened, and the ark of the covenant could be
seen inside it. Then came flashes of lightning,
peals of thunder and an earthquake, and violent
hail.

[e] Ps. 2:1,5.

New English Bible

were killed in the earthquake; the rest in terror did homage to the God of heaven.

The second woe has now passed. But the third is soon to come.

Then the seventh angel blew his trumpet; and voices were heard in heaven shouting:

'The sovereignty of the world has passed to our Lord and his Christ, and he shall reign for ever and ever!'

And the twenty-four elders, seated on their thrones before God, fell on their faces and worshipped God, saying:

'We give thee thanks, O Lord God, sovereign over all, who art and who wast, because thou hast taken thy great power into thy hands and entered upon thy reign. The nations raged, but thy day of retribution has come. Now is the time for the dead to be judged; now is the time for recompense to thy servants the prophets, to thy dedicated people, and all who honour thy name, both great and small, the time to destroy those who destroy the earth.'

Then God's temple in heaven was laid open, and within the temple was seen the ark of his covenant. There came flashes of lightning and peals of thunder, an earthquake, and a storm of hail.

King James Version

12 And there appeared a great wonder in
heaven; a woman clothed with the sun, and
the moon under her feet, and upon her head a
crown of twelve stars: 2And she being with
child cried, travailing in birth, and pained to be
delivered. 3And there appeared another wonder
in heaven; and behold a great red dragon,
having seven heads and ten horns, and seven
crowns upon his heads. 4And his tail drew the
third part of the stars of heaven, and did cast
them to the earth: and the dragon stood before
the woman which was ready to be delivered, for
to devour her child as soon as it was born. 5And
she brought forth a man child, who was to rule
all nations with a rod of iron: and her child was
caught up unto God, and *to* his throne. 6And
the woman fled into the wilderness, where she
hath a place prepared of God, that they should
feed her there a thousand two hundred *and*

Living Bible

12 Then a great pageant appeared in heaven,
portraying things to come. I saw a woman
clothed with the sun, with the moon beneath her
feet, and a crown of twelve stars on her head.
2 She was pregnant and screamed in the pain of
her labor, awaiting her delivery.

3 Suddenly a red Dragon appeared, with seven
heads and ten horns, and seven crowns on his
heads. 4 His tail drew along behind him a third
of the stars, which he plunged to the earth. He
stood before the woman as she was about to give
birth to her child, ready to eat the baby as soon
as it was born. 5 She gave birth to a boy who
was to rule all nations with a heavy hand, and
he was caught up to God and to his throne.
6 The woman fled into the wilderness, where God
had prepared a place for her, to take care of her
for 1,260 days.

Today's English Version

The woman and the dragon

12 Then a great mysterious sight appeared
in the sky. There was a woman, whose
dress was the sun and who had the moon under
her feet and a crown of twelve stars on her head.
2 She was soon to give birth, and the pains and
suffering of childbirth made her cry out.

3 Another mysterious sight appeared in the
sky. There was a huge red dragon with seven
heads and ten horns, and a crown on each of
his heads. 4 With his tail he dragged a third of
the stars out of the sky and threw them to earth.
He stood in front of the woman who was about
to give birth, in order to eat her child as soon
as it was born. 5 Then the woman gave birth to
a son, who will rule over all nations with an
iron rod. But the child was snatched away and
taken to God and his throne. 6 The woman fled
to the desert, to a place God had prepared for
her, where she will be taken care of for 1,260
days.

New International Version

The woman and the dragon

12 A great and wondrous sign appeared in
heaven: a woman clothed with the sun,
with the moon under her feet and a crown of
twelve stars on her head. 2 She was pregnant
and cried out in pain as she was about to give
birth. 3 Then another sign appeared in heaven:
an enormous red dragon with seven heads and
ten horns and seven crowns on his heads. 4 His
tail swept a third of the stars out of the sky and
flung them to the earth. The dragon stood in
front of the woman who was about to give birth,
so that he might devour her child the moment it
was born. 5 She gave birth to a son, a male
child, who will rule all the nations with a rod
of iron. And her child was snatched up to God
and to his throne. 6 The woman fled into the
desert to a place prepared for her by God, where
she might be taken care of for 1,260 days.

Phillips Modern English

12.1 The seventh trumpet: (ii) The sign of the woman

Then a huge sign became visible in the sky—the figure of a woman clothed with the sun, with the moon under her feet, and a crown of twelve stars upon her head. She was pregnant, and cried out in her labour and in the pains of bringing forth her child.

12.3 The seventh trumpet: (iii) The dragon, the enemy of the woman

Then another sign became visible in the sky, and I saw that it was a huge red dragon with seven heads and ten horns, with a diadem upon each of his heads. His tail swept down a third of the stars in the sky and hurled them upon the earth. The dragon took his place in front of the woman who was about to give birth to a child, so that as soon as she did so he might devour it. She gave birth to a male child who is to shepherd all the nations "with a rod of iron". Her child was snatched up to God and to his throne, while the woman fled into the desert where she has a place prepared for her by God's command. There they will take care of her for twelve hundred and sixty days.

Revised Standard Version

12 And a great portent appeared in heaven,
a woman clothed with the sun, with the
moon under her feet, and on her head a crown
of twelve stars; 2 she was with child and she
cried out in her pangs of birth, in anguish for
delivery. 3 And another portent appeared in
heaven; behold, a great red dragon, with seven
heads and ten horns, and seven diadems upon
his heads. 4 His tail swept down a third of the
stars of heaven, and cast them to the earth.
And the dragon stood before the woman who
was about to bear a child, that he might devour
her child when she brought it forth; 5 she
brought forth a male child, one who is to rule
all the nations with a rod of iron, but her child
was caught up to God and to his throne, 6 and
the woman fled into the wilderness, where she
has a place prepared by God, in which to be
nourished for one thousand two hundred and
sixty days.

Jerusalem Bible

The vision of the woman and the dragon

12 Now a great sign appeared in heaven: a
woman, adorned with the sun, standing on
the moon, and with the twelve stars on her head
for a crown. 2 She was pregnant, and in labor,
crying aloud in the pangs of childbirth. 3 Then
a second sign appeared in the sky, a huge red
dragon which had seven heads and ten horns,
and each of the seven heads crowned with a
coronet. 4 Its tail dragged a third of *the stars
from the sky and dropped them to the earth,*[f]
and the dragon stopped in front of the woman
as she was having the child, so that he could
eat it as soon as it was born from its mother.
5 The woman brought *a male child into the
world,* the son who was *to rule all the nations
with an iron scepter,*[g] and the child was taken
straight up to God and to his throne, 6 while
the woman escaped into the desert, where God
had made a place of safety ready, for her to be
looked after in the twelve hundred and sixty
days.

[f] Dn. 8:10. [g] Ps. 2:9.

New English Bible

12 Next appeared a great portent in heaven, a woman robed with the sun, beneath her feet the moon, and on her head a crown of twelve stars. She was pregnant, and in the anguish of her labour she cried out to be delivered. Then a second portent appeared in heaven: a great red dragon with seven heads and ten horns; on his heads were seven diadems, and with his tail he swept down a third of the stars in the sky and flung them to the earth. The dragon stood in front of the woman who was about to give birth, so that when her child was born he might devour it. She gave birth to a male child, who is destined to rule all nations with an iron rod. But her child was snatched up to God and his throne; and the woman herself fled into the wilds, where she had a place prepared for her by God, there to be sustained for twelve hundred and sixty days.

King James Version

threescore days. 7And there was war in heaven:
Michael and his angels fought against the
dragon; and the dragon fought and his angels,
8And prevailed not; neither was their place
found any more in heaven. 9And the great
dragon was cast out, that old serpent, called the
Devil, and Satan, which deceiveth the whole
world: he was cast out into the earth, and his
angels were cast out with him. 10And I heard a
loud voice saying in heaven, Now is come salvation, and strength, and the kingdom of our God,
and the power of his Christ: for the accuser of
our brethren is cast down, which accused them
before our God day and nig' t. 11And they overcame him by the blood of the Lamb, and by
the word of their testimony; and they loved not
their lives unto the death. 12 Therefore rejoice,
ye heavens, and ye that dwell in them. Woe to
the inhabiters of the earth and of the sea! for
the devil is come down unto you, having great
wrath, because he knoweth that he hath but a

Living Bible

7 Then there was war in heaven; Michael and
the angels under his command fought the Dragon
and his hosts of fallen angels. 8And the Dragon
lost the battle and was forced from heaven.
9 This great Dragon—the ancient serpent called
the devil, or Satan, the one deceiving the whole
world—was thrown down onto the earth with
all his army.
10 Then I heard a loud voice shouting across
the heavens, "It has happened at last! God's
salvation and the power and the rule, and the
authority of his Christ are finally here; for the
Accuser of our brothers has been thrown down
from heaven onto earth—he accused them day
and night before our God. 11 They defeated him
by the blood of the Lamb, and by their testimony; for they did not love their lives but laid
them down for him. 12 Rejoice, O heavens! You
citizens of heaven, rejoice! Be glad! But woe to
you people of the world, for the devil has come
down to you in great anger, knowing that he has
little time."

Today's English Version

7 Then war broke out in heaven. Michael and
his angels fought against the dragon, who fought
back with his angels; 8 but the dragon was defeated, and he and his angels were not allowed
to stay in heaven any longer. 9 The huge dragon
was thrown out! He is that old serpent, named
the Devil, or Satan, that deceived the whole
world. He was thrown down to earth, and all
his angels with him.
10 Then I heard a loud voice in heaven saying, "Now God's salvation has come! Now God
has shown his power as King! Now his Messiah
has shown his authority! For the accuser of our
brothers, who stood before God accusing them
day and night, has been thrown out of heaven.
11 Our brothers won the victory over him by
the blood of the Lamb, and by the truth which
they proclaimed; and they were willing to give
up their lives and die. 12And so be glad, you
heavens, and all you that live there! But how
terrible for the earth and the sea! For the Devil
has come down to you, and he is filled with
rage, because he knows that he has only a little
time left."

New International Version

7 And there was war in heaven. Michael and
his angels fought against the dragon, and the
dragon and his angels fought back. 8 But he
was not strong enough, and they lost their place
in heaven. 9 The great dragon was hurled down
—that ancient serpent called the devil or Satan,
who leads the whole world astray. He was hurled
to the earth, and his angels with him.
10 Then I heard a loud voice in heaven say:
"Now have come the salvation and the
power and the kingdom of our God,
and the authority of his Christ.
For the accuser of our brothers,
who accuses them before our God day
and night,
has been hurled down.
11 They overcame him
by the blood of the Lamb
and by the word of their testimony;
they did not love their lives so much
as to shrink from death.
12 Therefore rejoice, you heavens
and you who inhabit them!
But woe to the earth and the sea,
because the devil has gone down to you!
He is filled with fury,
because he knows that his time is short."

Phillips Modern English

12.7 War in Heaven

Then war broke out in Heaven. Michael and his angels battled with the dragon. The dragon and his angels fought back, but they did not prevail and they were expelled from Heaven. So the huge dragon, the serpent of ancient times, who is called the devil and Satan, the deceiver of the whole world, was hurled down upon the earth, and his angels were hurled down with him.

12.10 The victory of Heaven proclaimed

Then I heard a great voice in Heaven cry:
"Now the salvation and the power and kingdom of our God, and the authority of his Christ have come! For the accuser of our brethren has been thrown down from this place, where he stood before our God accusing them day and night. Now they have conquered him through the blood of the Lamb, and through the Word to which they bore witness. They did not cherish life even in the face of death!

"Therefore, rejoice, O Heavens, and all you who live in the Heavens! But alas for the earth and the sea, for the devil has come down to you in great fury, knowing that his time is short!"

Revised Standard Version

7 Now war arose in heaven, Michael and his
angels fighting against the dragon; and the
dragon and his angels fought, 8 but they were
defeated and there was no longer any place for
them in heaven. 9 And the great dragon was
thrown down, that ancient serpent, who is called
the Devil and Satan, the deceiver of the whole
world—he was thrown down to the earth, and
his angels were thrown down with him. 10 And
I heard a loud voice in heaven, saying, "Now
the salvation and the power and the kingdom
of our God and the authority of his Christ have
come, for the accuser of our brethren has been
thrown down, who accuses them day and night
before our God. 11 And they have conquered
him by the blood of the Lamb and by the word
of their testimony, for they loved not their lives
even unto death. 12 Rejoice then, O heaven and
you that dwell therein! But woe to you, O earth
and sea, for the devil has come down to you in
great wrath, because he knows that his time is
short!"

Jerusalem Bible

7 And now war broke out in heaven, when
Michael with his angels attacked the dragon.
The dragon fought back with his angels, 8 but
they were defeated and driven out of heaven.
9 The great dragon, the primeval serpent, known
as the devil or Satan, who had deceived all the
world, was hurled down to the earth and his
angels were hurled down with him. 10 Then I
heard a voice shout from heaven, "Victory and
power and empire for ever have been won by
our God, and all authority for his Christ, now
that the persecutor, who accused our brothers
day and night before our God, has been brought
down. 11 They have triumphed over him by the
blood of the Lamb and by the witness of their
martyrdom, because even in the face of death
they would not cling to life. 12 Let the heavens
rejoice and all who live there; but for you, earth
and sea, trouble is coming—because the devil
has gone down to you in a rage, knowing that
his days are numbered."

New English Bible

Then war broke out in heaven. Michael and his angels waged war upon the dragon. The dragon and his angels fought, but they had not the strength to win, and no foothold was left them in heaven. So the great dragon was thrown down, that serpent of old that led the whole world astray, whose name is Satan, or the Devil—thrown down to the earth, and his angels with him.

Then I heard a voice in heaven proclaiming aloud: 'This is the hour of victory for our God, the hour of his sovereignty and power, when his Christ comes to his rightful rule! For the accuser of our brothers is overthrown, who day and night accused them before our God. By the sacrifice of the Lamb they have conquered him, and by the testimony which they uttered;[a] for they did not hold their lives too dear to lay them down. Rejoice then, you heavens and you that dwell in them! But woe to you, earth and sea, for the Devil has come down to you in great fury, knowing that his time is short!'

[a] *Or* the word of God to which they bore witness.

King James Version

short time. 13And when the dragon saw that he was cast unto the earth, he persecuted the woman which brought forth the man *child.* 14And to the woman were given two wings of a great eagle, that she might fly into the wilderness, into her place, where she is nourished for a time, and times, and half a time, from the face of the serpent. 15And the serpent cast out of his mouth water as a flood after the woman, that he might cause her to be carried away of the flood. 16And the earth helped the woman; and the earth opened her mouth, and swallowed up the flood which the dragon cast out of his mouth. 17And the dragon was wroth with the woman, and went to make war with the remnant of her seed, which keep the commandments of God, and have the testimony of Jesus Christ.

13 And I stood upon the sand of the sea, and saw a beast rise up out of the sea, having seven heads and ten horns, and upon his horns ten crowns, and upon his heads the name of blasphemy. 2And the beast which I saw was like unto a leopard, and his feet were as *the feet* of a bear, and his mouth as the mouth of a lion: and the dragon gave him his power, and his seat, and great authority. 3And I saw one of his heads as it were wounded to death; and his

Living Bible

13 And when the Dragon found himself cast down to earth, he persecuted the woman who had given birth to the child. 14 But she was given two wings like those of a great eagle, to fly into the wilderness to the place prepared for her, where she was cared for and protected from the Serpent, the Dragon, for three and a half years.[a]

15 And from the Serpent's mouth a vast flood of water gushed out and swept toward the woman in an effort to get rid of her; 16 but the earth helped her by opening its mouth and swallowing the flood! 17 Then the furious Dragon set out to attack the rest of her children—all who were keeping God's commandments and confessing that they belong to Jesus. He stood waiting on an ocean beach.

13 And now, in my vision, I saw a strange Creature rising up out of the sea. It had seven heads and ten horns and ten crowns upon its horns. And written on each head were blasphemous names, each one defying and insulting God. 2 This Creature looked like a leopard but had bear's feet and a lion's mouth! And the Dragon gave him his own power and throne and great authority.

3 I saw that one of his heads seemed wounded beyond recovery—but the fatal wound was

[a] Literally, "a time and times and half a time."

Today's English Version

13 When the dragon realized that he had been thrown down to the earth, he began to pursue the woman who had given birth to the boy. 14 She was given the two wings of a large eagle in order to fly to her place in the desert, where she will be taken care of for three and a half years, safe from the serpent's attack. 15And then from his mouth the serpent poured out a flood of water after the woman, so that it would carry her away. 16 But the earth helped the woman; it opened its mouth and swallowed the water that had come from the dragon's mouth. 17 The dragon was furious with the woman, and went off to fight against the rest of her descendants, all those who obey God's commandments and are faithful to the truth revealed by Jesus. 18And the dragon stood on the seashore.

The two beasts

13 Then I saw a beast coming up out of the sea. It had ten horns and seven heads, with a crown on each of its horns, and a wicked name written on its heads. 2 The beast I saw looked like a leopard, with feet like a bear's feet, and a mouth like a lion's mouth. The dragon gave the beast his own power, his throne, and his vast authority. 3 One of the heads of the beast seemed to have been killed, but the fatal

New International Version

13 When the dragon saw that he had been hurled to the earth, he pursued the woman who had given birth to the male child. 14 The woman was given the two wings of a great eagle, so that she might fly to the place prepared for her in the desert, where she would be taken care of for a time, times, and half a time, out of the serpent's reach. 15 Then from his mouth the serpent spewed water like a river, to overtake the woman and sweep her away with the torrent. 16 But the earth helped the woman by opening its mouth and swallowing the river that the dragon had spewed out of his mouth. 17 Then the dragon was enraged at the woman, and went off to make war against the rest of her offspring—those who keep God's commandments and hold to the testimony of

13 Jesus. 1And the dragon[m] stood on the shore of the sea.

The beast out of the sea

And I saw a beast coming out of the sea. He had ten horns and seven heads, with ten crowns on his horns, and on each head a blasphemous name. 2 The beast I saw resembled a leopard, but had feet like those of a bear and a mouth like that of a lion. The dragon gave the beast his power and his throne and great authority. 3 One of the heads of the beast seemed to have had a

[m] Some late MSS read *And I.*

Phillips Modern English

12.13 The dragon's enmity against the woman

And when the dragon saw that he had been cast down upon the earth, he began to pursue the woman who had given birth to the male child. But she was given two great eagle's wings so that she could fly to her place in the desert, where she is kept safe from the serpent for a time and times and half a time. Then the serpent ejected water from his mouth, streaming like a river in pursuit of the woman, to drown her in its flood. But the earth came to the woman's rescue, opened its mouth and swallowed up the river which the dragon had emitted from his mouth. Then the dragon raged with fury against the woman and went off to make war against the rest of her children—those who keep the commandments of God and bear their witness to Jesus.

13.1 The animal from the sea

Then, as I stood on the sand of the sea-shore, there rose out of the sea before my eyes an animal with seven heads and ten horns. There were diadems upon its horns and blasphemous names upon its heads. The animal which I saw had the appearance of a leopard, though it had the feet of a bear and a mouth like the mouth of a lion. Then the dragon gave it his own power and throne and great authority. One of its heads appeared to have been wounded to death but the mortal wound had healed.

Revised Standard Version

13 And when the dragon saw that he had
been thrown down to the earth, he pursued the
woman who had borne the male child. 14 But
the woman was given the two wings of the
great eagle that she might fly from the serpent
into the wilderness, to the place where she is to
be nourished for a time, and times, and half a
time. 15 The serpent poured water like a river
out of his mouth after the woman, to sweep
her away with the flood. 16 But the earth came
to the help of the woman, and the earth opened
its mouth and swallowed the river which the
dragon had poured from his mouth. 17 Then
the dragon was angry with the woman, and
went off to make war on the rest of her offspring, on those who keep the commandments
of God and bear testimony to Jesus. And he
stood[e] on the sand of the sea.

13 And I saw a beast rising out of the sea,
with ten horns and seven heads, with ten
diadems upon its horns and a blasphemous name
upon its heads. 2 And the beast that I saw was
like a leopard, its feet were like a bear's, and
its mouth was like a lion's mouth. And to it the
dragon gave his power and his throne and great
authority. 3 One of its heads seemed to have a
mortal wound, but its mortal wound was healed,

[e] Other ancient authorities read *And I stood*, connecting the sentence with 13.1.

Jerusalem Bible

13 As soon as the devil found himself thrown
down to the earth, he sprang in pursuit of the
woman, the mother of the male child, 14 but
she was given a huge pair of eagle's wings to
fly away from the serpent into the desert, to the
place where she was to be looked after for *a
year and twice a year and half a year.*[h] 15 So
the serpent vomited water from his mouth, like
a river, after the woman, to sweep her away in
the current, 16 but the earth came to her rescue;
it opened its mouth and swallowed the river
thrown up by the dragon's jaws. 17 Then the
dragon was enraged with the woman and went
away to make war on the rest of her children,
that is, all who obey God's commandments and
bear witness for Jesus.

The dragon delegates his power to the beast

18 I was standing on the seashore.
13 Then I saw *a beast emerge from the sea*[i]:
it had seven heads and ten horns, with a
coronet on each of its ten horns, and its heads
were marked with blasphemous titles.[j] 2 I saw
that the beast *was like a leopard,* with paws like
a bear and a mouth like *a lion*[k]; the dragon had
handed over to it his own power and his throne
and his world-wide authority. 3 I saw that one
of its heads seemed to have had a fatal wound

[h] Dn. 7:25. Cf. 11:3. [i] Dn. 7:3. [j] Seven heads represent a succession of seven Roman emperors; ten crowned horns are ten subject kings. [k] Dn. 7:4-6.

New English Bible

When the dragon found that he had been thrown down to the earth, he went in pursuit of the woman who had given birth to the male child. But the woman was given two great eagle's wings, to fly to the place in the wilds where for three years and a half she was to be sustained, out of reach of the serpent. From his mouth the serpent spewed a flood of water after the woman to sweep her away with its spate. But the earth came to her rescue and opened its mouth and swallowed the river which the dragon spewed from his mouth. At this the dragon grew furious with the woman, and went off to wage war on the rest of her offspring, that is, on those who keep God's commandments and maintain their testimony to Jesus.

13 He took his stand on the sea-shore.
Then[a] out of the sea I saw a beast rising. It had ten horns and seven heads. On its horns were ten diadems, and on each head a blasphemous name. The beast I saw was like a leopard, but its feet were like a bear's and its mouth like a lion's mouth. The dragon conferred upon it his power and rule, and great authority. One of its heads appeared to have received a death-blow; but the mortal wound

[a] *Some witnesses read* . . . testimony to Jesus. Then I stood by the sea-shore and . . .

King James Version

deadly wound was healed: and all the world
wondered after the beast. 4And they worshipped
the dragon which gave power unto the beast:
and they worshipped the beast, saying, Who *is*
like unto the beast? who is able to make war
with him? 5And there was given unto him a
mouth speaking great things and blasphemies;
and power was given unto him to continue forty
and two months. 6And he opened his mouth in
blasphemy against God, to blaspheme his name,
and his tabernacle, and them that dwell in
heaven. 7And it was given unto him to make war
with the saints, and to overcome them: and
power was given him over all kindreds, and
tongues, and nations. 8And all that dwell upon
the earth shall worship him, whose names are
not written in the book of life of the Lamb
slain from the foundation of the world. 9 If any
man have an ear, let him hear. 10 He that leadeth
into captivity shall go into captivity: he that
killeth with the sword must be killed with the
sword. Here is the patience and the faith of the
saints. 11And I beheld another beast coming up

Living Bible

healed! All the world marveled at this miracle
and followed the Creature in awe. 4 They worshiped the Dragon for giving him such power,
and they worshiped the strange Creature. "Where
is there anyone as great as he?" they exclaimed.
"Who is able to fight against him?"

5 Then the Dragon encouraged the Creature
to speak great blasphemies against the Lord;
and gave him authority to control the earth for
forty-two months. 6All that time he blasphemed
God's Name and his temple and all those living
in heaven. 7 The Dragon gave him power to fight
against God's people[a] and to overcome them, and
to rule over all nations and language groups
throughout the world. 8And all mankind—whose
names were not written down before the founding of the world in the slain[b] Lamb's Book of
Life—worshiped the evil Creature.

9 Anyone who can hear, listen carefully:
10 The people of God who are destined for
prison will be arrested and taken away; those
destined for death will be killed.[c] But do not be
dismayed, for here is your opportunity for endurance and confidence.

11 Then I saw another strange animal, this

[*a*] Literally, "It was permitted to fight against God's people." [*b*] Or "those whose names were not written in the Book of Life of the Lamb slain before the founding of the world." That is, regarded as slain in the eternal plan and knowledge of God. [*c*] Or, "If anyone imprisons you, he will be imprisoned! If anyone kills you, he will be killed!"

Today's English Version

wound had healed. The whole earth was amazed
and followed after the beast. 4 All people worshiped the dragon because he had given his authority to the beast. They worshiped the beast
also, saying, "Who is like the beast? Who can
fight against it?"

5 The beast was allowed to say terribly wicked
things, and it was permitted to have authority
for 42 months. 6 It began to curse God, his
name, the place where he lives, and all those
who live in heaven. 7 It was allowed to fight
against God's people and to defeat them, and it
was given authority over every tribe, nation,
language, and race. 8All people living on earth
will worship it, that is, everyone whose name
has not been written, before the world was created, in the book of the living that belongs to
the Lamb that was killed.

9 "Listen, then, if you have ears to hear with!
10 Whoever is meant to be captured, will surely
be captured; whoever is meant to be killed by
the sword, will surely be killed by the sword.
This calls for endurance and faith on the part
of God's people."

11 Then I saw another beast coming up out

New International Version

fatal wound, but the fatal wound had been
healed. The whole world was astonished and
followed the beast. 4 Men worshiped the dragon
because he had given authority to the beast, and
they also worshiped the beast and asked, "Who
is like the beast? Who can make war against
him?"

5 The beast was given a mouth to utter proud
words and blasphemies and to exercise his authority for forty-two months. 6 He opened his
mouth to blaspheme God, and to slander his
name and his dwelling place and those who live
in heaven. 7 He was given power to make war
against the saints and to conquer them. And he
was given authority over every tribe, people,
language and nation. 8All inhabitants of the
earth will worship the beast—all whose names
have not been recorded in the book of life belonging to the Lamb that was slain from the
creation of the world.[n]

9 He who has an ear, let him hear.
10 If anyone is to go into captivity,
into captivity he will go.
If anyone is to be killed with the sword,
with the sword he will be killed.
This calls for patient endurance and faithfulness
on the part of the saints.

The beast out of the earth

11 Then I saw another beast, coming out of

[*n*] Or *recorded from the creation of the world in the book of life belonging to the Lamb that was slain.*

Phillips Modern English

The whole earth followed the animal with wonder, and they worshipped the dragon because he had given authority to the animal. Then they worshipped the animal, too, saying,

"Who is like the animal? Who could make war against it?"

It was allowed to speak monstrous blasphemies and to exert its authority for forty-two months. So it poured out blasphemies against God, blaspheming his name and his dwelling-place and those who live in Heaven. Moreover, it was permitted to make war upon the saints and to conquer them; the authority given to it extended over every tribe and people and language and nation. All the inhabitants of the earth will worship it—all those whose names have not been written in the book of life which belongs to the Lamb slain from the foundation of the world.

13.9 Parenthetical: a word to the reader

Let the listener hear this:

If any man is destined for captivity he will go into captivity. If any man kills with the sword he must himself be killed with the sword. Amid all this stands the endurance and faith of the saints.

13.11 The animal from the earth

Then I saw another animal rising out of the

Revised Standard Version

and the whole earth followed the beast with
wonder. 4 Men worshiped the dragon, for he
had given his authority to the beast, and they
worshiped the beast, saying, "Who is like the
beast, and who can fight against it?"
5 And the beast was given a mouth uttering haughty and blasphemous words, and it
was allowed to exercise authority for forty-two
months; 6 it opened its mouth to utter blasphemies against God, blaspheming his name and
his dwelling, that is, those who dwell in heaven.
7 Also it was allowed to make war on the saints
and to conquer them.[f] And authority was given
it over every tribe and people and tongue and
nation, 8 and all who dwell on earth will worship it, every one whose name has not been
written before the foundation of the world in
the book of life of the Lamb that was slain.
9 If any one has an ear, let him hear:
10 If any one is to be taken captive,
to captivity he goes;
if any one slays with the sword,
with the sword must he be slain.
Here is a call for the endurance and faith of the saints.
11 Then I saw another beast which rose out

[f] Other ancient authorities omit this sentence.

Jerusalem Bible

but that this deadly injury had healed and, after
that, the whole world had marveled and followed the beast. 4 They prostrated themselves in
front of the dragon because he had given the
beast his authority; and they prostrated themselves in front of the beast, saying, "Who can
compare with the beast? [l] How could anybody
defeat him?" 5 For forty-two months the beast
was allowed *to mouth its boasts*[m] and blasphemies and to do whatever it wanted; 6 and it
mouthed its blasphemies against God, against
his name, his heavenly Tent and all those who
are sheltered there. 7 It was allowed *to make
war against the saints and conquer them, and
given power* over every race, people, language
and nation; 8 and all people of the world will
worship it, that is, everybody whose name has
not been written down since the foundation of
the world in the book of life of the sacrificial
Lamb. 9 If anyone has ears to hear, let him
listen: 10 *Captivity for those who are destined
for captivity; the sword for those who are to die
by the sword.*[n] This is why the saints must have
constancy and faith.

The false prophet as the slave of the beast

11 Then I saw a second beast[o]; it emerged

[l] A parody of the name Michael, "who-can-compare-with-God?" [m] Dn. 7:8,11. [n] Jr. 15:2. [o] Also called "the false prophet," 16:13; 19:20; 20:10.

New English Bible

was healed. The whole world went after the beast in wondering admiration. Men worshipped the dragon because he had conferred his authority upon the beast; they worshipped the beast also, and chanted, 'Who is like the Beast? Who can fight against it?'

The beast was allowed to mouth bombast and blasphemy, and was given the right to reign for forty-two months. It opened its mouth in blasphemy against God, reviling his name and his heavenly dwelling.[b] It was also allowed to wage war on God's people and to defeat them, and was granted [c] authority over every tribe and people, language and nation. All on earth will worship it, except those whose names the Lamb that was slain keeps in his roll of the living, written there since the world was made.

Hear, you who have ears to hear! Whoever is to be made prisoner, a prisoner he shall be. Whoever takes the sword to kill, by the sword he is bound to be killed. This is where the fortitude and faithfulness of God's people have their place.

Then I saw another beast, which came up out

[b] *Some witnesses read* reviling his name and his dwelling place, that is, those that live in heaven. [c] *Some witnesses read* It was granted . . . (*omitting the words* was also . . . them, and).

King James Version

out of the earth; and he had two horns like a
lamb, and he spake as a dragon. 12 And he exer-
ciseth all the power of the first beast before him,
and causeth the earth and them which dwell
therein to worship the first beast, whose deadly
wound was healed. 13 And he doeth great wonders, so that he maketh fire come down from
heaven on the earth in the sight of men, 14 And
deceiveth them that dwell on the earth by *the*
means of those miracles which he had power to
do in the sight of the beast; saying to them that
dwell on the earth, that they should make an
image to the beast, which had the wound by a
sword, and did live. 15 And he had power to
give life unto the image of the beast, that the
image of the beast should both speak, and cause
that as many as would not worship the image
of the beast should be killed. 16 And he causeth
all, both small and great, rich and poor, free
and bond, to receive a mark in their right hand,
or in their foreheads: 17 And that no man might
buy or sell, save he that had the mark, or the
name of the beast, or the number of his name.
18 Here is wisdom. Let him that hath understanding count the number of the beast: for it
is the number of a man; and his number *is* Six
hundred threescore *and* six.

Living Bible

one coming up out of the earth, with two little
horns like those of a lamb but a fearsome voice
like the Dragon's. 12 He exercised all the authority of the Creature whose death-wound had been
healed, whom he required all the world to worship. 13 He did unbelievable miracles such as
making fire flame down to earth from the skies
while everyone was watching. 14 By doing these
miracles, he was deceiving people everywhere.
He could do these marvelous things whenever
the first Creature was there to watch him. And
he ordered the people of the world to make a
great statue of the first Creature, who was fatally
wounded and then came back to life. 15 He was
permitted to give breath to this statue and even
make it speak! Then the statue ordered that anyone refusing to worship it must die!

16 He required everyone—great and small,
rich and poor, slave and free—to be tattooed
with a certain mark on the right hand or on the
forehead. 17 And no one could get a job or even
buy in any store without the permit of that mark,
which was either the name of the Creature or
the code number of his name. 18 Here is a puzzle that calls for careful thought to solve it. Let
those who are able, interpret this code: the numerical values of the letters in his name add to
666! [d]

[d] Some manuscripts read "616."

Today's English Version

of the earth. It had two horns like a lamb's
horns, and it spoke like a dragon. 12 It used the
vast authority of the first beast in its presence.
It forced the earth and all who live on it to
worship the first beast, whose fatal wound had
been healed. 13 This second beast performed
great miracles; it made fire come down out of
heaven to earth, in the presence of all men.
14 And it deceived all the people living on earth
by means of the miracles which it was allowed
to perform in the presence of the first beast.
The beast told all the people of the world to
build an image in honor of the beast that had
been wounded by the sword, and yet lived.
15 The second beast was allowed to breathe life
into the image of the first beast, so that the
image could talk and put to death all those who
would not worship it. 16 The beast forced all
men, small and great, rich and poor, slave and
free, to have a mark placed on their right hands
and on their foreheads. 17 No one could buy or
sell unless he had this mark, that is, the beast's
name or the number that stands for the name.

18 This calls for wisdom. Whoever is intelligent can figure out the meaning of the number of the beast, because the number stands for
a man's name. Its number is 666.

New International Version

the earth. He had two horns like a lamb, but he
spoke like a dragon. 12 He exercised all the authority of the first beast on his behalf, and made
the earth and its inhabitants worship the first
beast, whose fatal wound had been healed. 13 And
he performed great and miraculous signs, even
causing fire to come down from heaven to earth
in full view of men. 14 Because of the signs he
was given power to do on behalf of the first
beast, he deceived the inhabitants of the earth.
He ordered them to set up an image in honor
of the beast who was wounded by the sword and
yet lived. 15 He was given power to give breath
to the image of the first beast, so that it could
speak and cause all who refused to worship the
image to be killed. 16 He also forced everyone,
small and great, rich and poor, free and slave,
to receive a mark on his right hand or on his
forehead, 17 so that no one could buy or sell
unless he had the mark, which is the name of
the beast or the number of his name.

18 This calls for wisdom. If anyone has insight, let him calculate the number of the beast,
for it is man's number. His number is 666.

Phillips Modern English

earth, and it had two horns like a lamb but it spoke in the voice of a dragon. It uses the full authority of the first animal in its presence. It compels the earth and all its inhabitants to worship the first animal—the one with the mortal wound which had healed. It performs great signs: before men's eyes it makes fire fall down from heaven to earth. It deceives the inhabitants of the earth by the signs which it is allowed to perform in the presence of the animal, and it tells them to make a statue in honour of the animal which received the sword-thrust and yet survived. Further, it was allowed to give the breath of life to the statue of the animal so that the statue could speak and condemn to death all those who do not worship its statue. Then it compels all, small and great, rich and poor, free men and slaves, to receive a mark on their right hands or on their foreheads. The purpose of this is that no one should be able to buy or sell unless he bears the mark of the name of the animal or the number of its name. Understanding is needed here: let every thinking man calculate the number of the animal. It is the number of a man, and its number is six hundred and sixty-six.

Revised Standard Version

of the earth; it had two horns like a lamb and
it spoke like a dragon. 12 It exercises all the
authority of the first beast in its presence, and
makes the earth and its inhabitants worship the
first beast, whose mortal wound was healed. 13 It
works great signs, even making fire come down
from heaven to earth in the sight of men; 14 and
by the signs which it is allowed to work in the
presence of the beast, it deceives those who
dwell on earth, bidding them make an image
for the beast which was wounded by the sword
and yet lived; 15 and it was allowed to give
breath to the image of the beast so that the
image of the beast should even speak, and to
cause those who would not worship the image
of the beast to be slain. 16 Also it causes all,
both small and great, both rich and poor, both
free and slave, to be marked on the right hand
or the forehead, 17 so that no one can buy or
sell unless he has the mark, that is, the name
of the beast or the number of its name. 18 This
calls for wisdom: let him who has understanding reckon the number of the beast, for it is a
human number, its number is six hundred and
sixty-six.[g]

[g] Other ancient authorities read *six hundred and sixteen.*

Jerusalem Bible

from the ground; it had two horns like a lamb,
but made a noise like a dragon. 12 This second
beast was servant to the first beast, and extended
its authority everywhere, making the world and
all its people worship the first beast, which had
had the fatal wound and had been healed. 13 And
it worked great miracles, even to calling down
fire from heaven on to the earth while people
watched. 14 Through the miracles which it was
allowed to do on behalf of the first beast, it was
able to win over the people of the world and
persuade them to put up a statue in honor of
the beast that had been wounded by the sword
and still lived. 15 It was allowed to breathe life
into this statue, so that the statue of the beast
was able to speak, and to have *anyone who re-*
fused to worship the statue of the beast[p] put to
death. 16 He compelled everyone—small and
great, rich and poor, slave and citizen—to be
branded on the right hand or on the forehead,
17 and made it illegal for anyone to buy or sell
anything unless he had been branded with the
name of the beast or with the number of its
name.
18 There is need for shrewdness here: if anyone is clever enough he may interpret the number of the beast: it is the number of a man, the number 666.[q]

[p] Dn. 3:5-7,15. [q] Codes and riddles were made in both Greek and Hebrew by using numbers for letters, according to their order in the alphabet. Some commentators have claimed that 666 is the total of the number values of "Nero Caesar."

New English Bible

of the earth; it had two horns like a lamb's, but spoke like a dragon. It wielded all the authority of the first beast in its presence, and made the earth and its inhabitants worship this first beast, whose mortal wound had been healed. It worked great miracles, even making fire come down from heaven to earth before men's eyes. By the miracles it was allowed to perform in the presence of the beast it deluded the inhabitants of the earth, and made them erect an image in honour of the beast that had been wounded by the sword and yet lived. It was allowed to give breath to the image of the beast, so that it could speak, and could cause all who would not worship the image to be put to death. Moreover, it caused everyone, great and small, rich and poor, slave and free, to be branded with a mark on his right hand or forehead, and no one was allowed to buy or sell unless he bore this beast's mark, either name or number. (Here is the key; and anyone who has intelligence may work out the number of the beast. The number represents a man's name, and the numerical value of its letters is six hundred and sixty-six.)

King James Version

14 And I looked, and, lo, a Lamb stood on
the mount Sion, and with him a hundred
forty *and* four thousand, having his Father's
name written in their foreheads. 2And I heard
a voice from heaven, as the voice of many
waters, and as the voice of a great thunder: and
I heard the voice of harpers harping with their
harps: 3And they sung as it were a new song
before the throne, and before the four beasts,
and the elders: and no man could learn that
song but the hundred *and* forty *and* four thousand, which were redeemed from the earth.
4 These are they which were not defiled with
women; for they are virgins. These are they
which follow the Lamb whithersoever he goeth.
These were redeemed from among men, *being*
the firstfruits unto God and to the Lamb. 5And
in their mouth was found no guile: for they are
without fault before the throne of God. 6And I
saw another angel fly in the midst of heaven,
having the everlasting gospel to preach unto
them that dwell on the earth, and to every nation, and kindred, and tongue, and people,
7 Saying with a loud voice, Fear God, and give
glory to him; for the hour of his judgment is

Living Bible

14 Then I saw a Lamb standing on Mount
Zion in Jerusalem, and with him were
144,000 who had his Name and his Father's
Name written on their foreheads. 2And I heard
a sound from heaven like the roaring of a great
waterfall or the rolling of mighty thunder. It was
the singing of a choir accompanied by harps.
3 This tremendous choir—144,000 strong—
sang a wonderful new song in front of the throne
of God and before the four Living Beings and
the twenty-four Elders; and no one could sing
this song except those 144,000 who had been redeemed from the earth. 4 For they are spiritually
undefiled, pure as virgins,[a] following the Lamb
wherever he goes. They have been purchased
from among the men on the earth as a consecrated offering to God and the Lamb. 5 No
falsehood can be charged against them; they are
blameless.
6 And I saw another angel flying through the
heavens, carrying the everlasting Good News to
preach to those on earth—to every nation, tribe,
language and people.
7 "Fear God," he shouted, "and extol his
greatness. For the time has come when he will

[*a*] Literally, "They have not defiled themselves with women, for they are virgins."

Today's English Version

The song of the redeemed

14 Then I looked, and there was the Lamb
standing on Mount Zion; with him were
144,000 people who have his name and his Father's name written on their foreheads. 2And I
heard a voice from heaven that sounded like the
roar of a mighty waterfall, like a loud peal of
thunder. The voice I heard sounded like the
music made by harpists playing their harps.
3 The 144,000 stood facing the throne, the four
living creatures, and the elders. They sang a
new song which only they, who had been redeemed from the earth, could learn. 4 They are
the men who have kept themselves pure by not
having sexual relations with women; they are
virgins. They follow the Lamb wherever he goes.
They have been redeemed from the rest of mankind and are the first ones to be offered to
God and to the Lamb. 5 They have never been
known to lie; they are faultless.

The three angels

6 Then I saw another angel flying high in the
air, with an eternal message of Good News to
announce to the peoples of the earth, to every
race, tribe, language, and nation. 7 He said in a
loud voice, "Fear God, and praise his greatness!

New International Version

The Lamb and the 144,000

14 Then I looked, and there before me was
the Lamb, standing on Mount Zion, and
with him 144,000 who had his name and his
Father's name written on their foreheads. 2And
I heard a sound from heaven like the roar of
rushing waters and like a loud peal of thunder.
The sound I heard was like that of harpists
playing their harps. 3And they sang a new song
before the throne and before the four living
creatures and the elders. No one could learn the
song except the 144,000 who had been redeemed
from the earth. 4 These are those who did not
defile themselves with women, for they kept
themselves pure. They follow the Lamb wherever he goes. They were purchased from among
men and offered as firstfruits to God and the
Lamb. 5 No lie was found in their mouths; they
are blameless.

The three angels

6 Then I saw another angel flying in midair,
and he had the eternal gospel to proclaim to
those who live on the earth—to every nation,
tribe, language and people. 7 He said in a loud
voice, "Fear God and give him glory, because the

Phillips Modern English

14.1 The vision of the Lamb and the first of the redeemed

Then I looked again and before my eyes the Lamb was standing on Mount Sion, and with him were a hundred and forty-four thousand who had his name and his Father's name written upon their foreheads. Then I heard a sound coming from Heaven like the roar of a great waterfall and the heavy rolling of thunder. Yet the sound which I heard was also like the music of harpists sweeping their strings. And they are singing a new song of praise before the throne, and before the four living creatures and the elders. No one could learn that song except the one hundred and forty-four thousand who had been redeemed from the earth. These are the men who have never defiled themselves with women, for they are celibate. These are the men who follow the Lamb wherever he may go; these men have been redeemed from among mankind as first-fruits to God and to the Lamb. They have never been guilty of any falsehood; they are beyond reproach.

14.6 The angel with the gospel

Then I saw another angel flying in mid-heaven, holding the everlasting gospel to proclaim to the inhabitants of the earth—to every nation and tribe and language and people. He was crying in a loud voice,

"Reverence God, and give glory to him; for

Revised Standard Version

14 Then I looked, and lo, on Mount Zion stood the Lamb, and with him a hundred and forty-four thousand who had his name and his Father's name written on their foreheads.
2And I heard a voice from heaven like the sound of many waters and like the sound of loud thunder; the voice I heard was like the sound of harpers playing on their harps, 3 and they sing a new song before the throne and before the four living creatures and before the elders. No one could learn that song except the hundred and forty-four thousand who had been redeemed from the earth. 4 It is these who have not defiled themselves with women, for they are chaste;[h] it is these who follow the Lamb wherever he goes; these have been redeemed from mankind as first fruits for God and the Lamb, 5 and in their mouth no lie was found, for they are spotless.
6 Then I saw another angel flying in midheaven, with an eternal gospel to proclaim to those who dwell on earth, to every nation and tribe and tongue and people; 7 and he said with a loud voice, "Fear God and give him glory,

[h] Greek *virgins*.

Jerusalem Bible

The companions of the Lamb

14 Next in my vision I saw Mount Zion, and standing on it a Lamb who had with him a hundred and forty-four thousand people, all with his name and his Father's name written on their foreheads. 2 I heard a sound coming out of the sky like the sound of the ocean or the roar of thunder; it seemed to be the sound of harpists playing their harps. 3 There in front of the throne they were singing a new hymn in the presence of the four animals and the elders, a hymn that could only be learned by the hundred and forty-four thousand who had been redeemed from the world. 4 These are the ones who have kept their virginity[r] and not been defiled with women; they *follow* the Lamb wherever he goes; they have been redeemed from among men to be *the first fruits for God*[s] and for the Lamb. 5 They never *allowed a lie to pass their lips*[t] and no fault can be found in them.

Angels announce the day of Judgment

6 Then I saw another angel, flying high overhead, sent to announce the Good News of eternity to all who live on the earth, every nation, race, language and tribe. 7 He was calling, "Fear God and praise him, because the time has come

[r] As so often in the Old Testament, "virginity" stands for faithfulness, and "adultery" or "fornication" for idolatry. [s] Jr. 2:2-3. [t] Zp. 3:13.

New English Bible

Visions of the end

14 Then I looked, and on Mount Zion stood the Lamb, and with him were a hundred and forty-four thousand who had his name and the name of his Father written on their foreheads. I heard a sound from heaven like the noise of rushing water and the deep roar of thunder; it was the sound of harpers playing on their harps. There before the throne, and the four living creatures and the elders, they were singing a new song. That song no one could learn except the hundred and forty-four thousand, who alone from the whole world had been ransomed. These are men who did not defile themselves with women, for they have kept themselves chaste, and they follow the Lamb wherever he goes. They have been ransomed as the firstfruits of humanity for God and the Lamb. No lie was found in their lips; they are faultless.

Then I saw an angel flying in mid-heaven, with an eternal gospel to proclaim to those on earth, to every nation and tribe, language and people. He cried in a loud voice, 'Fear God and pay him homage; for the hour of his judgement

King James Version

come: and worship him that made heaven, and
earth, and the sea, and the fountains of waters.
8And there followed another angel, saying, Babylon is fallen, is fallen, that great city, because
she made all nations drink of the wine of the
wrath of her fornication. 9And the third angel
followed them, saying with a loud voice, If any
man worship the beast and his image, and receive *his* mark in his forehead, or in his hand,
10 The same shall drink of the wine of the wrath
of God, which is poured out without mixture
into the cup of his indignation; and he shall be
tormented with fire and brimstone in the presence of the holy angels, and in the presence of
the Lamb: 11And the smoke of their torment
ascendeth up for ever and ever: and they have
no rest day nor night, who worship the beast
and his image, and whosoever receiveth the
mark of his name. 12 Here is the patience of the

Living Bible

sit as Judge. Worship him who made the heaven and the earth, the sea and all its sources."

8 Then another angel followed him through the skies, saying, "Babylon is fallen, is fallen—that great city—because she seduced the nations of the world and made them share the wine of her intense impurity and sin."

9 Then a third angel followed them shouting, "Anyone worshiping the Creature from the sea[b] and his statue and accepting his mark on the forehead or the hand, 10 must drink the wine of the anger of God; it is poured out undiluted into God's cup of wrath. And they will be tormented with fire and burning sulphur in the presence of the holy angels and the Lamb. 11 The smoke of their torture rises forever and ever, and they will have no relief day or night, for they have worshiped the Creature and his statue, and have been tattooed with the code of his name. 12 Let this

[b] Implied.

Today's English Version

For the time has come for him to judge mankind. Worship him who made heaven, earth, sea, and the springs of water!"

8 A second angel followed the first one, saying, "She has fallen! Great Babylon has fallen! She gave her wine to all peoples, and made them drink it—the strong wine of her immoral lust!"

9 A third angel followed the first two, saying in a loud voice, "Whoever worships the beast and its image, and receives the mark on his forehead or on his hand, 10 will himself drink God's wine, the wine of his anger, which he has poured at full strength into the cup of his wrath! All who do this will be tormented in fire and sulfur before the holy angels and the Lamb. 11 The smoke of the fire that torments them goes up forever and ever. There is no relief, day or night, for those who worship the beast and its image, for anyone who has the mark of its name."

12 This calls for endurance on the part of

New International Version

hour of his judgment has come. Worship him who made the heavens, the earth, the sea and the springs of water."

8 A second angel followed and said, "Fallen! Fallen is Babylon the Great, which made all the nations drink the maddening wine of her adulteries."

9 A third angel followed them and said in a loud voice: "If anyone worships the beast and his image and receives his mark on the forehead or on the hand, 10 he, too, will drink of the wine of God's fury, which has been poured full strength into the cup of his wrath. He will be tormented with burning sulfur in the presence of the holy angels and of the Lamb. 11And the smoke of their torment rises for ever and ever. There is no rest day or night for those who worship the beast and his image, or for anyone who receives the mark of his name." 12 This calls for

Phillips Modern English

the hour of his judgment has come! Worship him who made Heaven and earth, the sea and the springs of water."

14.8 The angel of doom

Then another, a second angel, followed him crying,

"Fallen, fallen is Babylon the great! She who made all nations drink the wine of her passionate unfaithfulness!"

14.9 The angel of judgment

Then a third angel followed these two, crying in a loud voice,

"If any man worships the animal and its statue and bears its mark upon his forehead or upon his hand, then that man shall drink the wine of God's passion, poured undiluted into the cup of his wrath. He shall be tortured by fire and sulphur in the presence of the holy angels and of the Lamb. The smoke of such men's torture ascends for timeless ages, and there is no respite from it day or night. Such are the worshippers of the animal and its statue and among their number are all who bear the mark of its name."

14.12 The call to stand fast

In all this stands the endurance of the saints

Revised Standard Version

for the hour of his judgment has come; and worship him who made heaven and earth, the sea and the fountains of water."
8 Another angel, a second, followed, saying, "Fallen, fallen is Babylon the great, she who made all nations drink the wine of her impure passion."
9 And another angel, a third, followed them, saying with a loud voice, "If any one worships the beast and its image, and receives a mark on his forehead or on his hand, 10 he also shall drink the wine of God's wrath, poured unmixed into the cup of his anger, and he shall be tormented with fire and sulphur in the presence of the holy angels and in the presence of the Lamb. 11 And the smoke of their torment goes up for ever and ever; and they have no rest, day or night, these worshipers of the beast and its image, and whoever receives the mark of its name."
12 Here is a call for the endurance of the

Jerusalem Bible

for him to sit in judgment; worship *the maker of heaven and earth and sea*[u] and every water spring."
8 A second angel followed him, calling, *"Babylon has fallen, Babylon the Great has fallen,*[v] Babylon which gave the whole world *the wine of* God's *anger* to drink."
9 A third angel followed, shouting aloud, "All those who worship the beast and his statue, or have had themselves branded on the hand or forehead, 10 will be made to drink the wine of God's fury which is ready, undiluted, in his cup of anger; in *fire and brimstone*[w] they will be tortured in the presence of the holy angels and the Lamb 11 and *the smoke* of their torture *will go up for ever*[x] and ever. There will be no respite, *night or day*, for those who worshiped the beast or its statue or accepted branding with its name." 12 This is why there must be constancy

[*u*] Ex. 20:11. [*v*] Is. 21:9. The *wine of* God's *anger* is a phrase from Is. 51:17, also used in Jr. 25:15f. [*w*] Gn. 19:28. [*x*] Is. 34:9-10.

New English Bible

has come! Worship him who made heaven and earth, the sea and the water-springs!'

Then another angel, a second, followed, and he cried, 'Fallen, fallen is Babylon the great, she who has made all nations drink the fierce wine of [a] her fornication!'

Yet a third angel followed, crying out loud, 'Whoever worships the beast and its image and receives its mark on his forehead or hand, he shall drink the wine of God's wrath, poured undiluted into the cup of his vengeance. He shall be tormented in sulphurous flames before the holy angels and before the Lamb. The smoke of their torment will rise for ever and ever, and there will be no respite day or night for those who worship the beast and its image or receive the mark of its name.' This is where the forti-

[*a*] *Or* drink the wine of God's wrath upon . . .

King James Version

saints: here *are* they that keep the commandments of God, and the faith of Jesus. 13And I
heard a voice from heaven saying unto me,
Write, Blessed *are* the dead which die in the
Lord from henceforth: Yea, saith the Spirit, that
they may rest from their labours; and their
works do follow them. 14And I looked, and behold a white cloud, and upon the cloud *one* sat
like unto the Son of man, having on his head a
golden crown, and in his hand a sharp sickle.
15And another angel came out of the temple,
crying with a loud voice to him that sat on the
cloud, Thrust in thy sickle, and reap: for the
time is come for thee to reap; for the harvest of
the earth is ripe. 16And he that sat on the cloud
thrust in his sickle on the earth; and the earth
was reaped. 17And another angel came out of
the temple which is in heaven, he also having
a sharp sickle. 18And another angel came out
from the altar, which had power over fire; and
cried with a loud cry to him that had the sharp

Living Bible

encourage God's people to endure patiently every
trial and persecution, for they are his saints who
remain firm to the end in obedience to his commands and trust in Jesus."
13 And I heard a voice in the heavens above
me saying, "Write this down: At last the time
has come for his martyrs[c] to enter into their full
reward. Yes, says the Spirit, they are blest indeed,
for now they shall rest from all their toils and
trials; for their good deeds follow them to
heaven!" 14 Then the scene changed and I saw
a white cloud, and someone sitting on it who
looked like Jesus, who was called "The Son of
Man," [d] with a crown of solid gold upon his head
and a sharp sickle in his hand.
15 Then an angel came from the temple and
called out to him, "Begin to use the sickle, for
the time has come for you to reap; the harvest
is ripe on the earth." 16 So the one sitting on
the cloud swung his sickle over the earth, and
the harvest was gathered in. 17After that another
angel came from the temple in heaven, and he
also had a sharp sickle.
18 Just then the angel who has power to
destroy the world with fire,[e] shouted to the angel

[*c*] Literally, "those who die in the faith of Jesus." Verse 12 implies death from persecution for Christ's sake. [*d*] Literally, "one like a Son of Man." [*e*] Literally, "who has power over fire."

Today's English Version

God's people, those who obey God's commandments and are faithful to Jesus.
13 Then I heard a voice from heaven saying,
"Write this: Happy are the dead who from now
on die in the service of the Lord!"
"Certainly so," answers the Spirit. "They will enjoy rest from their hard work, because the results of their service go with them."

The harvest of the earth

14 Then I looked, and there was a white
cloud, and sitting on the cloud was a being who
looked like a man, with a gold crown on his
head and a sharp sickle in his hand. 15 Then
another angel went out from the temple and
cried out in a loud voice to the one who was
sitting on the cloud, "Use your sickle and reap
the harvest, because the right time has come; the
earth is ripe for the harvest!" 16 Then the one
who sat on the cloud swung his sickle on the
earth, and the earth's harvest was reaped.
17 Then I saw another angel come out of the
temple in heaven, and he also had a sharp sickle.
18 Then another angel, who is in charge of
the fire, came from the altar. He shouted in a
loud voice to the angel who had the sharp sickle,

New International Version

patient endurance on the part of the saints who
keep God's commandments and remain faithful
to Jesus.
13 Then I heard a voice from heaven say,
"Write: Blessed are the dead who die in the
Lord from now on."
"Yes," says the Spirit, "they will rest from their labor, for their deeds will follow them."

The harvest of the earth

14 I looked, and there before me was a white
cloud, and seated on the cloud was one "like a
son of man" [o] with a crown of gold on his head
and a sharp sickle in his hand. 15 Then another
angel came out of the temple and called in a
loud voice to him who was sitting on the cloud,
"Take your sickle and reap, because the time to
reap has come, for the harvest of the earth is
ripe." 16 So he that was seated on the cloud
swung his sickle over the earth, and the earth
was harvested.
17 Another angel came out of the temple in
heaven, and he too had a sharp sickle. 18 Still
another angel, who had charge of the fire, came
from the altar and called in a loud voice to him

[*o*] Daniel 7:13.

Phillips Modern English

—those who keep the commandments of God and their faith in Jesus.

14.13 The security of the saints

Then I heard a voice from Heaven, saying, "Write this! From henceforth happy are the dead who die in the Lord!"

"Happy indeed," says the Spirit, "for they rest from their labours and their deeds go with them!"

14.14 The harvest of God's wrath

Once again I looked, and a white cloud appeared before me with someone sitting upon the cloud with the appearance of a man. He had a golden crown on his head, and held a sharp sickle in his hand. Then another angel came out from the Sanctuary, calling in a loud voice to the one sitting on the cloud,

"Thrust in your sickle and reap, for the time of reaping has come and the harvest of the earth is fully ripe!"

Then the one sitting upon the cloud swung his sickle upon the earth, and the reaping of the earth was done.

Then another angel came out from the Sanctuary in Heaven, and he also had a sharp sickle. Yet another angel came out from the altar where he has command over the fire, and called out in a loud voice to the angel with the sharp sickle,

Revised Standard Version

saints, those who keep the commandments of God and the faith of Jesus.
13 And I heard a voice from heaven saying, "Write this: Blessed are the dead who die in the Lord henceforth." "Blessed indeed," says the Spirit, "that they may rest from their labors, for their deeds follow them!"
14 Then I looked, and lo, a white cloud, and seated on the cloud one like a son of man, with a golden crown on his head, and a sharp sickle in his hand.
15 And another angel came out of the temple, calling with a loud voice to him who sat upon the cloud, "Put in your sickle, and reap, for the hour to reap has come, for the harvest of the earth is fully ripe."
16 So he who sat upon the cloud swung his sickle on the earth, and the earth was reaped.
17 And another angel came out of the temple in heaven, and he too had a sharp sickle.
18 Then another angel came out from the altar, the angel who has power over fire, and he called with a loud voice to him who had the sharp

Jerusalem Bible

in the saints who keep the commandments of God and faith in Jesus.
13 Then I heard a voice from heaven say to me, "Write down: Happy are those who die in the Lord! Happy indeed, the Spirit says; now they can rest for ever after their work, since their good deeds go with them."

The harvest and vintage of the pagans

14 Now in my vision I saw a white *cloud* and, *sitting on it, one like a son of man* with a gold crown on his head and a sharp sickle in his hand.
15 Then another angel came out of the sanctuary, and shouted aloud to the one sitting on the cloud, *"Put your sickle in* and reap: harvest time has come and *the harvest* of the earth *is ripe."* [y]
16 Then the one sitting on the cloud set his sickle to work on the earth, and the earth's harvest was reaped.
17 Another angel, who also carried a sharp sickle, came out of the temple in heaven,
18 and the angel in charge of the fire left the altar and shouted aloud to the one with the sharp sickle,

[y] Jl. 4:13; Am. 8:2.

New English Bible

tude of God's people has its place—in keeping God's commands and remaining loyal to Jesus.

Moreover, I heard a voice from heaven, saying, 'Write this: "Happy are the dead who die in the faith of Christ! Henceforth",[b] says the Spirit,[c] "they may rest from their labours; for they take with them the record of their deeds."'

Then as I looked there appeared a white cloud, and on the cloud sat one like a son of man. He had on his head a crown of gold and in his hand a sharp sickle. Another angel came out of the temple and called in a loud voice to him who sat on the cloud: 'Stretch out your sickle and reap; for harvest-time has come, and earth's crop is over-ripe.' So he who sat on the cloud put his sickle to the earth and its harvest was reaped.

Then another angel came out of the heavenly temple, and he also had a sharp sickle. Then from the altar came yet another, the angel who has authority over fire, and he shouted to the

[b] *Or* Assuredly. [c] *Some witnesses read* ". . . the dead who henceforth die in the faith of Christ!" "Yes," says the Spirit . . .

King James Version

sickle, saying, Thrust in thy sharp sickle, and
gather the clusters of the vine of the earth; for
her grapes are fully ripe. 19And the angel thrust
in his sickle into the earth, and gathered the
vine of the earth, and cast *it* into the great winepress of the wrath of God. 20And the winepress
was trodden without the city, and blood came
out of the winepress, even unto the horse bridles, by the space of a thousand *and* six hundred
furlongs.

15 And I saw another sign in heaven, great
and marvellous, seven angels having the
seven last plagues; for in them is filled up the
wrath of God. 2And I saw as it were a sea of
glass mingled with fire: and them that had gotten
the victory over the beast, and over his image,
and over his mark, *and* over the number of his
name, stand on the sea of glass, having the harps
of God. 3And they sing the song of Moses the
servant of God, and the song of the Lamb, saying, Great and marvellous *are* thy works, Lord
God Almighty; just and true *are* thy ways, thou
King of saints. 4 Who shall not fear thee, O

Living Bible

with the sickle, "Use your sickle now to cut off
the clusters of grapes from the vines of the earth,
for they are fully ripe for judgment." 19 So the
angel swung his sickle on the earth and loaded
the grapes into the great winepress of God's
wrath. 20And the grapes were trodden in the
winepress outside the city, and blood flowed out
in a stream 200 miles long and as a high as a
horse's bridle.

15 And I saw in heaven another mighty pageant showing things to come: Seven angels
were assigned to carry down to earth the seven
last plagues—and then at last God's anger will
be finished.

2 Spread out before me was what seemed to
be an ocean of fire and glass, and on it stood all
those who had been victorious over the Evil
Creature and his statue and his mark and number. All were holding harps of God, 3, 4 and they
were singing the song of Moses, the servant of
God, and the song of the Lamb:

"Great and marvelous
Are your doings,
Lord God Almighty.
Just and true
Are your ways,
O King of Ages.[a]
Who shall not fear,
O Lord,

[a] Some manuscripts read, "King of the Nations."

Today's English Version

"Use your sickle, and cut the grapes from the
vineyard of the earth, because the grapes are
ripe!" 19 So the angel swung his sickle on the
earth, cut the grapes from the vine, and threw
them into the winepress of God's great anger.
20 The grapes were squeezed out in the winepress outside the city, and blood came out of the
winepress in a flood 200 miles long and about
five feet deep.

The angels with the last plagues

15 Then I saw another mysterious sight in
the sky, great and amazing. There were
seven angels with seven plagues, which are the
last ones, because they are the final expression
of God's wrath.

2 Then I saw what looked like a sea of glass,
mixed with fire. I also saw those who had won
the victory over the beast and its image, and
over the one whose name is given by a number.
They were standing by the sea of glass, holding
harps that God had given them. 3 They were
singing the song of Moses, the servant of God,
and the song of the Lamb:

"Lord, God Almighty,
How great and wonderful are your deeds!
King of all nations,
how right and true are your ways!
4 Who will not fear you, Lord?

New International Version

who had the sharp sickle, "Take your sharp
sickle and gather the clusters of grapes from
the earth's vine, because its grapes are ripe."
19 The angel swung his sickle on the earth,
gathered its grapes and threw them into the great
winepress of God's wrath. 20 They were trampled
in the winepress outside the city, and blood
flowed out of the press, rising as high as the
horse's bridles for a distance of 1,600 stadia.[p]

Seven angels with seven plagues

15 I saw in heaven another great and marvelous sign: seven angels with the seven last
plagues—last, because with them God's wrath is
completed. 2And I saw what looked like a sea
of glass mixed with fire and, standing beside the
sea, those who had been victorious over the beast
and his image and over the number of his name.
They held harps given them by God 3 and sang
the song of Moses, the servant of God, and the
song of the Lamb:

"Great and marvelous are your deeds,
Lord God Almighty.
Just and true are your ways,
King of the ages.
4 Who will not fear you, O Lord,

[p] That is, about 200 miles.

Phillips Modern English

"Thrust in your sharp sickle and harvest the clusters from the vineyard of the earth for the grapes are fully ripe!"

Then the angel swung his sickle upon the earth and gathered the harvest of the earth's vineyard, and threw it into the great winepress of the wrath of God. The grapes were trodden outside the city, and out of the winepress flowed blood for two hundred miles in a stream as high as the horses' bridles.

15.1 The seven last plagues prepared

Then I saw another sign in Heaven, vast and awe-inspiring: seven angels are holding the seven last plagues, and with these the wrath of God is brought to an end.

15.2 The hymn of the redeemed

And I saw what appeared to be a sea of glass shot through with fire, and upon this glassy sea were standing those who had emerged victorious from the fight with the animal, its statue and the number which denotes its name. In their hands they hold harps which God has given them, and they are singing the song of Moses the servant of God, and the song of the Lamb, and these are the words they sing:

"Great and wonderful are thy works, O Lord God, the Almighty! Just and true are thy ways, thou king of the nations! Who should not rev-

Revised Standard Version

sickle, "Put in your sickle, and gather the clusters of the vine of the earth, for its grapes are ripe." 19 So the angel swung his sickle on the earth and gathered the vintage of the earth, and threw it into the great wine press of the wrath of God; 20 and the wine press was trodden outside the city, and blood flowed from the wine press, as high as a horse's bridle, for one thousand six hundred stadia.

15 Then I saw another portent in heaven, great and wonderful, seven angels with seven plagues, which are the last, for with them the wrath of God is ended.

2 And I saw what appeared to be a sea of glass mingled with fire, and those who had conquered the beast and its image and the number of its name, standing beside the sea of glass with harps of God in their hands. 3 And they sing the song of Moses, the servant of God, and the song of the Lamb, saying,

"Great and wonderful are thy deeds,
O Lord God the Almighty!
Just and true are thy ways,
O King of the ages! [j]
4 Who shall not fear and glorify thy name, O
Lord?

[i] About two hundred miles. [j] Other ancient authorities read *the nations*.

Jerusalem Bible

"Put your sickle in and cut all the bunches off the vine of the earth; all its grapes are ripe." 19 So the angel set his sickle to work on the earth and harvested the whole vintage of the earth and put it into a huge winepress, the winepress of God's anger, 20 outside the city, where it was trodden until the blood that came out of the winepress was up to the horses' bridles as far away as sixteen hundred furlongs.

The hymn of Moses and the Lamb

15 What I saw next, in heaven, was a great and wonderful sign: seven angels were bringing the seven plagues that are the last of all, because they exhaust the anger of God. 2 I seemed to see a glass lake suffused with fire, and standing by the lake of glass, those who had fought against the beast and won, and against his statue and the number which is his name. They all had harps from God, 3 and they were singing the hymn of Moses, the servant of God, and of the Lamb:

"How great and wonderful are all your works,
Lord God Almighty;
just and true are all your ways,
King of nations.
4 *Who would not revere* and *praise your*

New English Bible

one with the sharp sickle: 'Stretch out your sickle, and gather in earth's grape-harvest, for its clusters are ripe.' So the angel put his sickle to the earth and gathered in its grapes, and threw them into the great winepress of God's wrath. The winepress was trodden outside the city, and for two hundred miles around blood flowed from the press to the height of the horses' bridles.

15 Then I saw another great and astonishing portent in heaven: seven angels with seven plagues, the last plagues of all, for with them the wrath of God is consummated.

I saw what seemed a sea of glass shot with fire, and beside the sea of glass, holding the harps which God had given them, were those who had won the victory over the beast and its image and the number of its name.

They were singing the song of Moses, the servant of God, and the song of the Lamb, as they chanted:

'Great and marvellous are thy deeds, O Lord God, sovereign over all; just and true are thy ways, thou king of the ages.[a] Who shall not revere thee, Lord, and do homage to thy

[a] *Some witnesses read* king of the nations.

King James Version

Lord, and glorify thy name? for *thou* only *art*
holy: for all nations shall come and worship before thee; for thy judgments are made manifest.
5And after that I looked, and, behold, the temple of the tabernacle of the testimony in heaven
was opened: 6And the seven angels came out of
the temple, having the seven plagues, clothed in
pure and white linen, and having their breasts
girded with golden girdles. 7And one of the four
beasts gave unto the seven angels seven golden
vials full of the wrath of God, who liveth for
ever and ever. 8And the temple was filled with
smoke from the glory of God, and from his
power; and no man was able to enter into the
temple, till the seven plagues of the seven angels
were fulfilled.

16 And I heard a great voice out of the temple saying to the seven angels, Go your
ways, and pour out the vials of the wrath of

Living Bible

And glorify your Name?
For you alone are holy.
All nations will come
And worship before you,
For your righteous deeds
Have been disclosed."

5 Then I looked and saw that the Holy of
Holies of the temple in heaven was thrown
wide open!

6 The seven angels who were assigned to pour
out the seven plagues then came from the temple, clothed in spotlessly white linen, with golden
belts across their chests. 7And one of the four
Living Beings handed each of them a golden
flask filled with the terrible wrath of the Living
God who lives forever and forever. 8 The temple
was filled with smoke from his glory and power;
and no one could enter until the seven angels
had completed pouring out the seven plagues.

16 And I heard a mighty voice shouting from
the temple to the seven angels, "Now go
your ways and empty out the seven flasks of the
wrath of God upon the earth."

Today's English Version

Who will refuse to declare your greatness?
You alone are holy.
All the nations will come
and worship before you,
because your righteous deeds are seen by
all."

5 After this I saw the temple in heaven open,
with the tent of God's presence in it. 6 Then
seven angels who had the seven plagues came
out of the temple; they were dressed in
clean shining linen, and had gold bands tied
around their chests. 7 Then one of the four living
creatures gave the seven angels seven gold bowls
full of the wrath of God, who lives forever and
ever. 8 The temple was filled with smoke from
the glory and power of God, and no one could
go into the temple until the end of the seven
plagues brought by the seven angels.

The bowls of God's wrath

16 Then I heard a loud voice speaking from
the temple to the seven angels, "Go and
pour out the seven bowls of God's wrath on the
earth!"

New International Version

and bring glory to your name?
For you alone are holy.
All nations will come
and worship before you,
for your righteous acts have been revealed."

5 After this I looked and in heaven the temple, that is, the tabernacle of testimony, was
opened. 6 Out of the temple came the seven
angels with the seven plagues. They were dressed
in clean, shining linen and wore golden sashes
around their chests. 7 Then one of the four
living creatures gave to the seven angels seven
golden bowls filled with the wrath of God, who
lives for ever and ever. 8And the temple was
filled with smoke from the glory of God and
from his power, and no one could enter the
temple until the seven plagues of the seven angels
were completed.

The seven bowls of God's wrath

16 Then I heard a loud voice from the temple saying to the seven angels, "Go, pour
out the seven bowls of God's wrath on the
earth."

Phillips Modern English

erence thee, O Lord, and glorify thy name? For thou alone art holy; therefore all nations shall come and worship before thee, for thy just judgments have been made plain!"

15.5 The angels leave the Sanctuary of God—

Later in my vision I saw the Sanctuary of the tabernacle of testimony in Heaven wide open, and out of the Sanctuary came forth the seven angels who hold the seven plagues. They were dressed in spotless shining linen, and they were girded round their breasts with golden girdles.

Then one of the four living creatures gave to the seven angels seven golden bowls filled with the wrath of God who lives for timeless ages. The Sanctuary was filled with smoke from the glory and power of God, and no one could enter the Sanctuary until the seven plagues of the seven angels were past and over.

16.1 —and are ordered to pour out the bowls of his wrath

Then I heard a loud voice from the Sanctuary saying to the seven angels,

"Go and pour out upon the earth the seven bowls of the wrath of God!"

Revised Standard Version

For thou alone art holy.
All nations shall come and worship thee,
for thy judgments have been revealed."
5 After this I looked, and the temple of the
tent of witness in heaven was opened, 6 and
out of the temple came the seven angels with
the seven plagues, robed in pure bright linen,
and their breasts girded with golden girdles.
7 And one of the four living creatures gave the
seven angels seven golden bowls full of the
wrath of God who lives for ever and ever;
8 and the temple was filled with smoke from
the glory of God and from his power, and no
one could enter the temple until the seven
plagues of the seven angels were ended.

16 Then I heard a loud voice from the temple telling the seven angels, "Go and pour out on the earth the seven bowls of the wrath of God."

Jerusalem Bible

name, O Lord?
You alone are holy,
and all the pagans will come and adore you
for the many acts of justice you have shown." [z]

The seven bowls of plagues

5 After this, in my vision, the sanctuary, the
Tent of the Testimony, opened in heaven, 6 and
out came the seven angels with the seven
plagues, wearing pure white linen, fastened
around their waists with golden girdles. 7 One
of the four animals gave the seven angels seven
golden bowls filled with the anger of God who
lives for ever and ever. 8 *The smoke from the
glory* and the power *of God filled the temple so
that no one could go into it* [a] until the seven
plagues of the seven angels were completed.

16 Then I heard a voice from the sanctuary shouting to the seven angels, "Go, and empty the seven bowls of God's anger over the earth."

[z] This hymn is nearer to the Psalms than to the Song of Moses in Ex. 15. The two direct quotations are from Jr. 10 and Ps. 86; the opening of it is reminiscent of Ps. 92 and 98. [a] 1 K. 8:10-11.

New English Bible

name? For thou alone art holy. All nations shall come and worship in thy presence, for thy just dealings stand revealed.'

After this, as I looked, the sanctuary of the heavenly Tent of Testimony was thrown open, and out of it came the seven angels with the seven plagues. They were robed in fine linen, clean and shining, and had golden girdles round their breasts. Then one of the four living creatures gave the seven angels seven golden bowls full of the wrath of God who lives for ever and ever; and the sanctuary was filled with smoke from the glory of God and his power, so that no one could enter it until the seven plagues of the seven angels were completed.

16 Then from the sanctuary I heard a loud voice, and it said to the seven angels, 'Go and pour out the seven bowls of God's wrath on the earth.'

King James Version

God upon the earth. 2And the first went, and
poured out his vial upon the earth; and there
fell a noisome and grievous sore upon the men
which had the mark of the beast, and *upon*
them which worshipped his image. 3And the
second angel poured out his vial upon the sea;
and it became as the blood of a dead *man:* and
every living soul died in the sea. 4And the third
angel poured out his vial upon the rivers and
fountains of waters; and they became blood.
5And I heard the angel of the waters say, Thou
art righteous, O Lord, which art, and wast, and
shalt be, because thou hast judged thus. 6 For
they have shed the blood of saints and prophets,
and thou hast given them blood to drink; for
they are worthy. 7And I heard another out of
the altar say, Even so, Lord God Almighty, true

Living Bible

2 So the first angel left the temple and poured
out his flask over the earth, and horrible, malignant sores broke out on everyone who had the
mark of the Creature and was worshiping his
statue.

3 The second angel poured out his flask upon
the oceans, and they became like the watery
blood of a dead man; and everything in all the
oceans died.

4 The third angel poured out his flask upon
the rivers and springs and they became blood.
5And I heard this angel of the waters declaring,
"You are just in sending this judgment, O Holy
One, who is and was, 6 for your saints and
prophets have been martyred and their blood
poured out upon the earth; and now, in turn,
you have poured out the blood of those who
murdered them; it is their just reward."

7 And I heard the angel of the altar[a] say,
"Yes, Lord God Almighty, your punishments
are just and true."

[a] Literally, "I heard the altar cry. . . ."

Today's English Version

2 The first angel went and poured out his
bowl on the earth. Terrible and painful sores
appeared on those who had the mark of the
beast, and on those who had worshiped its image.

3 Then the second angel poured out his bowl
on the sea. The water became like the blood of
a dead person, and every living creature in the
sea died.

4 Then the third angel poured out his bowl
on the rivers and the springs of water, and they
turned into blood. 5 I heard the angel in charge
of the waters say, "You are righteous in these
judgments you have made, O Holy One, who is
and who was! 6 They poured out the blood of
God's people and of the prophets, and so you
have given them blood to drink. They are getting what they deserve!" 7 Then I heard a voice
from the altar saying, "Lord, God Almighty!
True and righteous indeed are your judgments!"

New International Version

2 The first angel went and poured out his
bowl on the land, and ugly and painful sores
broke out on the people who had the mark of
the beast and worshiped his image.

3 The second angel poured out his bowl on
the sea, and it turned into blood like that of a
dead man, and every living thing in the sea died.

4 The third angel poured out his bowl on the
rivers and springs of water, and they became
blood. 5 Then I heard the angel in charge of the
waters say:

"You are just in these judgments,
you who are and who were, the Holy One,
because you have so judged;
6 for they have shed the blood of your saints
and prophets,
and you have given them blood to drink
as they deserve."

7And I heard the altar respond:
"Yes, Lord God Almighty,
true and just are your judgments."

Phillips Modern English

16.2 The first bowl: Ulcers

The first angel went off and emptied his bowl upon the earth. Whereupon loathsome and malignant ulcers attacked all those who bore the mark of the animal and worshipped its statue.

16.3 The second bowl: Death in the sea

The second angel emptied his bowl into the sea, which turned into a fluid like the blood of a corpse, and every living thing in it died.

16.4 The third bowl: Water becomes blood

Then the third angel emptied his bowl into the rivers and springs of water, and they turned into blood. And I heard the angel of the waters say,

"Just art thou in these thy judgments, thou who art and wast the Holy One! For they have spilled the blood of saints and prophets, and now thou hast given them blood to drink. They have what they deserve."

And I heard the altar say,

"Yes, O Lord, God Almighty, thy judgments are true and right."

Revised Standard Version

2 So the first angel went and poured his bowl on the earth, and foul and evil sores came upon the men who bore the mark of the beast and worshiped its image.
3 The second angel poured his bowl into the sea, and it became like the blood of a dead man, and every living thing died that was in the sea.
4 The third angel poured his bowl into the rivers and the fountains of water, and they be-
came blood. 5 And I heard the angel of water say,

"Just art thou in these thy judgments,
thou who art and wast, O Holy One.
6 For men have shed the blood of saints and prophets,
and thou hast given them blood to drink.
It is their due!"

7 And I heard the altar cry,
"Yea, Lord God the Almighty,
true and just are thy judgments!"

Jerusalem Bible

2 The first angel went and emptied his bowl over the earth; at once, on all the people who had been branded with the mark of the beast and had worshiped its statue, there came disgusting and virulent sores.
3 The second angel emptied his bowl over the sea, and it turned to blood, like the blood of a corpse, and every living creature in the sea died.
4 The third angel emptied his bowl into the rivers and water springs and they turned into
blood. 5 Then I heard the angel of water say,
"You are the holy He-Is-and-He-Was, the Just
One, and this is a just punishment: 6 they spilled
the blood of the saints and the prophets, and blood is what you have given them to drink; it
is what they deserve." 7 And I heard the altar
itself say, "Truly, Lord God Almighty, the punishments you give are true and just."

New English Bible

So the first angel went and poured his bowl on the earth; and foul malignant sores appeared on those men that wore the mark of the beast and worshipped its image.

The second angel poured his bowl on the sea, and it turned to blood like the blood from a corpse; and every living thing in the sea died.

The third angel poured his bowl on the rivers and springs, and they turned to blood.

Then I heard the angel of the waters say, 'Just art thou in these thy judgements, thou Holy One who art and wast; for they shed the blood of thy people and of thy prophets, and thou hast given them blood to drink. They have their deserts!' And I heard the altar cry, 'Yes, Lord God, sovereign over all, true and just are thy judgements!'

King James Version

and righteous *are* thy judgments. 8And the fourth angel poured out his vial upon the sun; and power was given unto him to scorch men with fire. 9And men were scorched with great heat, and blasphemed the name of God, which hath power over these plagues: and they repented not to give him glory. 10And the fifth angel poured out his vial upon the seat of the beast; and his kingdom was full of darkness; and they gnawed their tongues for pain, 11And blasphemed the God of heaven because of their pains and their sores, and repented not of their deeds. 12And the sixth angel poured out his vial upon the great river Euphrates; and the water thereof was dried up, that the way of the kings of the east might be prepared. 13And I saw three unclean spirits like frogs *come* out of the mouth of the dragon, and out of the mouth of the beast, and out of the mouth of the false prophet. 14For they are the spirits of devils, working miracles, *which* go forth unto the kings of the earth and of the whole world, to gather them to the battle of that great day of God Almighty.

Living Bible

8 Then the fourth angel poured out his flask upon the sun, causing it to scorch all men with its fire. 9 Everyone was burned by this blast of heat, and they cursed the name of God who sent the plagues—they did not change their mind and attitude to give him glory.

10 Then the fifth angel poured out his flask upon the throne of the Creature from the sea,[b] and his kingdom was plunged into darkness. And his subjects gnawed their tongues in anguish, 11 and cursed the God of heaven for their pains and sores, but they refused to repent of all their evil deeds.

12 The sixth angel poured out his flask upon the great River Euphrates and it dried up so that the kings from the east could march their armies westward without hindrance. 13And I saw three evil spirts disguised as frogs leap from the mouth of the Dragon, the Creature, and his False Prophet.[c] 14 These miracle-working demons conferred with all the rulers of the world to gather them for battle against the Lord on that great

[*b*] Implied. [*c*] Described in 13:11-15 and 19:20.

Today's English Version

8 Then the fourth angel poured out his bowl on the sun, and it was allowed to burn men with its fiery heat. 9 Men were burned by the fierce heat, and they cursed the name of God, who has authority over these plagues. But they would not turn from their sins and praise his greatness.

10 Then the fifth angel poured out his bowl on the throne of the beast. Darkness fell over the beast's kingdom, and men bit their tongues because of their pain, 11 and they cursed the God of heaven for their pains and sores. But they did not turn from their evil ways.

12 Then the sixth angel poured out his bowl on the great river Euphrates. The river dried up, to provide a way for the kings who come from the east. 13 Then I saw three unclean spirits, that looked like frogs, coming out of the mouth of the dragon, the mouth of the beast, and the mouth of the false prophet. 14 They are the spirits of demons that perform miracles. These three spirits go out to the kings over the whole earth, to bring them together for the war

New International Version

8 The fourth angel poured out his bowl on the sun, and the sun was given power to scorch people with fire. 9 They were seared by the intense heat and they cursed the name of God, who had control over these plagues, but they refused to repent and glorify him.

10 The fifth angel poured out his bowl on the throne of the beast, and his kingdom was plunged into darkness. Men gnawed their tongues in agony 11 and cursed the God of heaven because of their pains and their sores, but they refused to repent of what they had done.

12 The sixth angel poured out his bowl on the great river Euphrates, and its water was dried up to prepare the way for the kings from the east. 13 Then I saw three evil [q] spirits that looked like frogs; they came out of the mouth of the dragon, out of the mouth of the beast and out of the mouth of the false prophet. 14 They are spirits of demons performing miraculous signs, and they go out to the kings of the whole world, to gather them for the battle on the great day of God

[*q*] Greek *unclean.*

Phillips Modern English

16.8 The fourth bowl: Scorching heat

The fourth angel emptied his bowl over the sun, and the sun was given power to scorch men in its fiery blaze. Then men were terribly burned in the heat, and they blasphemed the name of God who has power over these afflictions; but they neither repented nor gave him glory.

16.10 The fifth bowl: The plague of darkness

Then the fifth angel emptied his bowl upon the throne of the animal. Its kingdom was plunged into darkness; men gnawed their tongues in agony, cursed the God of Heaven for their pain and their ulcers, but refused to repent of what they had done.

16.12 The sixth bowl: The great river dried up

Then the sixth angel emptied his bowl upon the great river Euphrates. The waters of that river were dried up to prepare a road for the kings from the east. And then I noticed three foul spirits, looking like frogs, emerging from the mouths of the dragon, the animal and the false prophet. They are diabolical spirits performing wonders and they set out to muster all

Revised Standard Version

8 The fourth angel poured his bowl on the
sun, and it was allowed to scorch men with fire;
9 men were scorched by the fierce heat, and they
cursed the name of God who had power over
these plagues, and they did not repent and give
him glory.
10 The fifth angel poured his bowl on the
throne of the beast, and its kingdom was in darkness; men gnawed their tongues in anguish
11 and
cursed the God of heaven for their pain and
sores, and did not repent of their deeds.
12 The sixth angel poured his bowl on the
great river Euphrates, and its water was dried
up, to prepare the way for the kings from the
east.
13 And I saw, issuing from the mouth of the
dragon and from the mouth of the beast and
from the mouth of the false prophet, three foul
spirits like frogs;
14 for they are demonic spirits,
performing signs, who go abroad to the kings of
the whole world, to assemble them for battle on

Jerusalem Bible

8 The fourth angel emptied his bowl over the
sun and it was made to scorch people with its
flames;
9 but though people were scorched by
the fierce heat of it, they cursed the name of
God who had the power to cause such plagues,
and they would not repent and praise him.
10 The fifth angel emptied his bowl over the
throne of the beast and its whole empire was
plunged into darkness. Men were biting their
tongues for pain,
11 but instead of repenting for
what they had done, they cursed the God of
heaven because of their pains and sores.
12 The sixth angel emptied his bowl over the
great river Euphrates; all the water dried up so
that a way was made for the kings of the East [b]
to come in.
13 Then from the jaws of dragon
and beast and false prophet I saw three foul
spirits come; they looked like frogs
14 and in
fact were demon spirits, able to work miracles,
going out to all the kings of the world to call
them together for the war of the Great Day of

[b] Of Parthia, the savage enemy dreaded by the Roman world.

New English Bible

The fourth angel poured his bowl on the sun; and it was allowed to burn men with its flames. They were fearfully burned; but they only cursed the name of God who had the power to inflict such plagues, and they refused to repent or do him homage.

The fifth angel poured his bowl on the throne of the beast; and its kingdom was plunged in darkness. Men gnawed their tongues in agony, but they only cursed the God of heaven for their sores and pains, and would not repent of what they had done.

The sixth angel poured his bowl on the great river Euphrates; and its water was dried up, to prepare the way for the kings from the east.

Then I saw coming from the mouth of the dragon, the mouth of the beast, and the mouth of the false prophet, three foul spirits like frogs. These spirits were devils, with power to work miracles. They were sent out to muster all the kings of the world for the great day of battle of

King James Version

15 Behold, I come as a thief. Blessed *is* he that
watcheth, and keepeth his garments, lest he walk
naked, and they see his shame. 16And he gathered them together into a place called in the
Hebrew tongue Armageddon. 17And the seventh
angel poured out his vial into the air; and
there came a great voice out of the temple
of heaven, from the throne, saying, It is done.
18And there were voices, and thunders, and
lightnings; and there was a great earthquake,
such as was not since men were upon the earth,
so mighty an earthquake, *and* so great. 19And
the great city was divided into three parts, and
the cities of the nations fell: and great Babylon
came in remembrance before God, to give unto
her the cup of the wine of the fierceness of his
wrath. 20And every island fled away, and the
mountains were not found. 21And there fell upon
men a great hail out of heaven, *every stone*
about the weight of a talent: and men blasphemed God because of the plague of the hail;
for the plague thereof was exceeding great.

Living Bible

coming Judgment Day of God Almighty.
15 "Take note: I will come as unexpectedly
as a thief! Blessed are all who are awaiting me,
who keep their robes in readiness and will not
need to walk naked and ashamed."
16 And they gathered all the armies of the
world near a place called, in Hebrew, Armageddon—the Mountain of Megiddo.
17 Then the seventh angel poured out his flask
into the air; and a mighty shout came from the
throne of the temple in heaven, saying, "It is finished!" [d] 18 Then the thunder crashed and rolled,
and lightning flashed; and there was a great
earthquake of a magnitude unprecedented in human history. 19 The great city of "Babylon" split
into three sections, and cities around the world
fell in heaps of rubble; and so all of "Babylon's"
sins were remembered in God's thoughts, and
she was punished to the last drop of anger in the
cup of the wine of the fierceness of his wrath.
20And islands vanished, and mountains flattened
out, 21 and there was an incredible hailstorm
from heaven; hailstones weighing a hundred
pounds fell from the sky onto the people below,
and they cursed God because of the terrible
hail.

[d] Literally, "It has happened." An epoch of human history has come to an end.

Today's English Version

on the great day of Almighty God.
15 "Listen! I am coming like a thief! Happy
is he who stays awake and takes care of his
clothing, so that he will not walk around naked
and be ashamed in public!"
16 Then the spirits brought the kings together
in the place that in Hebrew is called Armageddon.
17 Then the seventh angel poured out his
bowl in the air. A loud voice came from the
throne in the temple, saying, "It is done!"
18 There were flashes of lightning, sounds, peals
of thunder, and a terrible earthquake. There
never has been such an earthquake since the
creation of man; this was the worst earthquake
of all! 19 The great city was split into three
parts, and the cities of all countries were destroyed. God remembered great Babylon, and
made her drink the wine from his cup—the wine
of his furious wrath. 20All the islands disappeared, all the mountains vanished. 21 Great
stones of hail, each weighing as much as a
hundred pounds, fell from the sky on men. And
men cursed God because of the plague of hail,
because it was such a terrible plague.

New International Version

Almighty.
15 "Behold, I come like a thief! Blessed is he
who stays awake and keeps his clothes with
him, so that he may not go naked and be shamefully exposed."
16 Then they gathered the kings together to
the place that in Hebrew is called Armageddon.
17 The seventh angel poured out his bowl into
the air, and out of the temple came a loud voice
from the throne, saying, "It is done!" 18 Then
there came flashes of lightning, rumblings, peals
of thunder and a severe earthquake. No earthquake like it has ever occurred since man has
been on earth, so tremendous was the quake.
19 The great city split into three parts, and the
cities of the nations collapsed. God remembered
Babylon the Great and gave her the cup filled
with the wine of the fury of his wrath. 20 Every
island fled away and the mountains could not be
found. 21 From the sky huge hailstones of about
a hundred pounds each fell upon men. And they
cursed God on account of the plague of hail,
because the plague was so terrible.

Phillips Modern English

the kings of the world for battle on the great day of God, the Almighty.

16.15 The words in the background

"See I am coming like a thief! Happy is the man who stays awake and keeps his clothes at his side, so that he will not have to walk naked and men see his shame."

So they brought them together to the place called, in Hebrew, Armageddon.

16.17 The seventh bowl: Devastation from the air

The seventh angel emptied his bowl into the air. A loud voice came out of the Sanctuary, from the throne, saying,

"The end has come!"

Then followed flashes of lightning, noises and peals of thunder. There was a terrific earthquake, the like of which no man has ever seen since mankind began to live upon the earth—so great and tremendous was this earthquake. The great city was split into three parts, and the cities of all the nations fell in ruins. And God called to mind Babylon the great and made her drink the cup of the wine of his furious wrath. Every island fled and the mountains vanished. Great hailstones like heavy weights fell from the sky, and men blasphemed God for the curse of the hail, for it fell upon them with savage and fearful blows.

Revised Standard Version

the great day of God the Almighty. 15 ("Lo, I am coming like a thief! Blessed is he who is awake, keeping his garments that he may not go naked and be seen exposed!") 16 And they assembled them at the place which is called in Hebrew Armageddon.

17 The seventh angel poured his bowl into the air, and a loud voice came out of the temple, from the throne, saying, "It is done!" 18 And there were flashes of lightning, voices, peals of thunder, and a great earthquake such as had never been since men were on the earth, so great was that earthquake. 19 The great city was split into three parts, and the cities of the nations fell, and God remembered great Babylon, to make her drain the cup of the fury of his wrath. 20 And every island fled away, and no mountains were to be found; 21 and great hailstones, heavy as a hundredweight, dropped on men from heaven, till men cursed God for the plague of the hail, so fearful was that plague.

Jerusalem Bible

God the Almighty.—15 This is how it will be: I shall come like a thief. Happy is the man who has stayed awake and not taken off his clothes so that he does not go out naked and expose his shame.—16 They called the kings together at the place called, in Hebrew, Armageddon.[c]

17 The seventh angel emptied his bowl into the air, and a voice shouted from the sanctuary, "The end has come." 18 Then there were flashes of lightning and peals of thunder and the most violent earthquake *that anyone has ever seen since there have been* men *on the earth.*[d] 19 The Great City was split into three parts and the cities of the world collapsed; Babylon the Great was not forgotten: God made her drink the full wine cup of his anger. 20 Every island vanished and the mountains disappeared; 21 and hail, with great hailstones weighing a talent each, fell from the sky on the people. They cursed God for sending a plague of hail; it was the most terrible plague.

[*c*] "Megiddo mountains"; Josiah's defeat at Megiddo, 2 K. 23:29f, made this place a symbol of military disaster, cf. Zc. 12:11. [*d*] Dn. 12:1.

New English Bible

God the sovereign Lord. ('That is the day when I come like a thief! Happy the man who stays awake and keeps on his clothes, so that he will not have to go naked and ashamed for all to see!') So they assembled the kings at the place called in Hebrew Armageddon.

Then the seventh angel poured his bowl on the air; and out of the sanctuary came a loud voice from the throne, which said, 'It is over!' And there followed flashes of lightning and peals of thunder, and a violent earthquake, like none before it in human history, so violent it was. The great city was split in three; the cities of the world fell in ruin; and God did not forget Babylon the great, but made her drink the cup which was filled with the fierce wine of his vengeance. Every island vanished; there was not a mountain to be seen. Huge hailstones, weighing perhaps a hundredweight, fell on men from the sky; and they cursed God for the plague of hail, because that plague was so severe.

King James Version

17 And there came one of the seven angels
which had the seven vials, and talked with
me, saying unto me, Come hither; I will shew
unto thee the judgment of the great whore that
sitteth upon many waters; 2 With whom the
kings of the earth have committed fornication,
and the inhabitants of the earth have been made
drunk with the wine of her fornication. 3 So he
carried me away in the spirit into the wilderness:
and I saw a woman sit upon a scarlet coloured
beast, full of names of blasphemy, having seven
heads and ten horns. 4And the woman was arrayed in purple and scarlet colour, and decked
with gold and precious stones and pearls, having
a golden cup in her hand full of abominations
and filthiness of her fornication: 5And upon her
forehead *was* a name written, MYSTERY, BAB-
YLON THE GREAT, THE MOTHER OF
HARLOTS AND ABOMINATIONS OF THE
EARTH. 6And I saw the woman drunken with
the blood of the saints, and with the blood of
the martyrs of Jesus: and when I saw her, I
wondered with great admiration. 7And the angel

Living Bible

17 One of the seven angels who had poured
out the plagues came over and talked with
me. "Come with me," he said, "and I will show
you what is going to happen to the Notorious
Prostitute, who sits upon the many waters of the
world. 2 The kings of the world have had immoral relations with her, and the people of the
earth have been made drunk by the wine of her
immorality."

3 So the angel took me in spirit into the
wilderness. There I saw a woman sitting on a
scarlet animal that had seven heads and ten
horns,[a] written all over with blasphemies against
God. 4 The woman wore purple and scarlet
clothing and beautiful jewelry made of gold and
precious gems and pearls, and held in her hand
a golden goblet full of obscenities:

5 A mysterious caption was written on her
forehead: "Babylon the Great, Mother of Prostitutes and of Idol Worship Everywhere around
the World."

6 I could see that she was drunk—drunk with
the blood of the martyrs of Jesus she had killed.
I stared at her in horror.

7 "Why are you so surprised?" the angel

[*a*] The Dragon—Satan—and the Creature from the sea are also described in 12:3,9 and 13:1.

Today's English Version

The great prostitute

17 Then one of the seven angels who had
the seven bowls came to me and said,
"Come, and I will show you how the great prostitute is to be punished, that great city that is
built near many rivers. 2 The kings of the earth
committed immorality with the great prostitute,
and the people of the world became drunk from
drinking the wine of her immorality."

3 The Spirit took control of me, and the angel
carried me to a desert. There I saw a woman
sitting on a red beast that had wicked names
written all over it; the beast had seven heads
and ten horns. 4 The woman was dressed in purple and scarlet, and covered with gold ornaments, precious stones, and pearls. In her hand
she held a gold cup full of obscene and filthy
things, the result of her immorality. 5 On her
forehead was written a name that has a secret
meaning: "The Great Babylon, mother of all
prostitutes and perverts of the world." 6And I
saw that the woman was drunk with the blood
of God's people, and the blood of those who
were killed because they had been loyal to Jesus.

When I saw her I was completely amazed.
7 "Why are you amazed?" the angel asked me.

New International Version

The woman on the beast

17 One of the seven angels who had the
seven bowls came and said to me, "Come,
I will show you the punishment of the great
prostitute, who sits on many waters. 2 With her
the kings of the earth committed adultery and
the inhabitants of the earth were intoxicated
with the wine of her adulteries."

3 Then the angel carried me away in the
Spirit into a desert. There I saw a woman sitting
on a scarlet beast that was covered with blasphemous names, and had seven heads and ten
horns. 4 The woman was dressed in purple and
scarlet, and was glittering with gold, precious
stones and pearls. She held a golden cup in her
hand, filled with abominable things and the filth
of her adulteries. 5 This title was written on her
forehead:

MYSTERY
BABYLON THE GREAT
THE MOTHER OF PROSTITUTES
AND OF THE ABOMINATIONS OF THE EARTH.

6 I saw that the woman was drunk with the
blood of the saints, the blood of those who bore
testimony to Jesus.

When I saw her, I was greatly astonished.
7 Then the angel said to me: "Why are you

Phillips Modern English

17.1 The judgment of the evil woman announced

Then came one of the seven angels who held the seven bowls, and said to me,

"Come, and I will show you the judgment passed upon the great harlot who is seated upon many waters. It is with her that the kings of the earth have debauched themselves and the inhabitants of the earth have become drunk on the wine of her filthiness."

17.3 The gorgeous mother of evil

Then he carried me away in spirit into the desert. There I saw a woman riding upon a scarlet animal, covered with blasphemous titles and having seven heads and ten horns. The woman herself was dressed in purple and scarlet, glittering with gold, jewels and pearls. In her hand she held a golden cup full of the earth's filthiness and her own foul impurity. On her forehead is written a name with a secret meaning—BABYLON THE GREAT, MOTHER OF ALL HARLOTS AND OF THE EARTH'S ABOMINATIONS.

17.6 The vision explained

Then I noticed that the woman was drunk with the blood of the saints and of the martyrs for Jesus. As I watched her, I was filled with utter amazement, but the angel said to me,

Revised Standard Version

17 Then one of the seven angels who had
the seven bowls came and said to me,
"Come, I will show you the judgment of the
great harlot who is seated upon many waters,
2 with whom the kings of the earth have committed fornication, and with the wine of whose
fornication the dwellers on earth have become
drunk." 3 And he carried me away in the Spirit
into a wilderness, and I saw a woman sitting on
a scarlet beast which was full of blasphemous
names, and it had seven heads and ten horns.
4 The woman was arrayed in purple and scarlet,
and bedecked with gold and jewels and pearls,
holding in her hand a golden cup full of abominations and the impurities of her fornication;
5 and on her forehead was written a name of
mystery: "Babylon the great, mother of harlots
and of earth's abominations." 6 And I saw the
woman, drunk with the blood of the saints and
the blood of the martyrs of Jesus.
When I saw her I marveled greatly. 7 But the

Jerusalem Bible

B. The punishment of Babylon

The famous prostitute

17 One of the seven angels that had the
seven bowls came to speak to me, and
said, "Come here and I will show you the punishment given to the famous prostitute[e] *who
rules enthroned beside abundant waters,*[f] 2 the
one with whom all the kings of the earth have
committed fornication, and who has made all
the population of the world drunk with the wine
of her adultery."[g] 3 He took me in spirit to a
desert, and there I saw a woman riding a scarlet
beast which had seven heads and ten horns and
had blasphemous titles written all over it. 4 The
woman was dressed in purple and scarlet, and
glittered with gold and jewels and pearls, and
she was holding a gold wine cup filled with the
disgusting filth of her fornication; 5 on her forehead was written a name, a cryptic name:
"Babylon the Great, the mother of all the
prostitutes and all the filthy practices on the
earth." 6 I saw that she was drunk, drunk with
the blood of the saints, and the blood of the
martyrs of Jesus; and when I saw her, I was
completely mystified. 7 The angel said to me,

[e] Rome. [f] Jr. 51:13, a literal description of Babylon, here applied metaphorically, as the author explains in v. 15. [g] I.e., the idolatry of emperor worship.

New English Bible

17 Then one of the seven angels that held the seven bowls came and spoke to me and said, 'Come, and I will show you the judgement on the great whore, enthroned above the ocean. The kings of the earth have committed fornication with her, and on the wine of her fornication men all over the world have made themselves drunk.' In the Spirit he carried me away into the wilds, and there I saw a woman mounted on a scarlet beast which was covered with blasphemous names and had seven heads and ten horns. The woman was clothed in purple and scarlet and bedizened with gold and jewels and pearls. In her hand she held a gold cup, full of obscenities and the foulness of her fornication; and written on her forehead was a name with a secret meaning: 'Babylon the great, the mother of whores and of every obscenity on earth.' The woman, I saw, was drunk with the blood of God's people and with the blood of those who had borne their testimony to Jesus.

As I looked at her I was greatly astonished. But the angel said to me, 'Why are you so aston-

King James Version

said unto me, Wherefore didst thou marvel? I
will tell thee the mystery of the woman, and of
the beast that carrieth her, which hath the seven
heads and ten horns. 8 The beast that thou sawest was, and is not; and shall ascend out of the
bottomless pit, and go into perdition: and they
that dwell on the earth shall wonder, whose
names were not written in the book of life from
the foundation of the world, when they behold
the beast that was, and is not, and yet is. 9And
here *is* the mind which hath wisdom. The seven
heads are seven mountains, on which the woman
sitteth. 10And there are seven kings: five are
fallen, and one is, *and* the other is not yet come;
and when he cometh, he must continue a short
space. 11And the beast that was, and is not, even
he is the eighth, and is of the seven, and goeth
into perdition. 12And the ten horns which thou
sawest are ten kings, which have received no
kingdom as yet; but receive power as kings one
hour with the beast. 13 These have one mind,
and shall give their power and strength unto the
beast. 14 These shall make war with the Lamb,

Living Bible

asked. "I'll tell you who she is and what the
animal she is riding represents. 8 He was alive
but isn't now. And yet, soon he will come up
out of the bottomless pit and go to eternal destruction;[b] and the people of earth, whose names
have not been written in the Book of Life before
the world began, will be dumbfounded at his
reappearance after being dead.[c]
9 "And now think hard: his seven heads represent a certain city[d] built on seven hills where
this woman has her residence. 10 They also represent seven kings. Five have already fallen, the
sixth now reigns, and the seventh is yet to come,
but his reign will be brief. 11 The scarlet animal that died is the eighth king, having reigned
before as one of the seven; after his second
reign, he too, will go to his doom. 12 His ten
horns are ten kings who have not yet risen to
power; they will be appointed to their kingdoms for one brief moment, to reign with him.
13 They will all sign a treaty giving their power
and strength to him. 14 Together they will wage

[*b*] Literally, "go to perdition." [*c*] Literally, "dumb-founded at the ruler who was, and is not, and will be present." [*d*] Implied in verse 18.

Today's English Version

"I will tell you the secret meaning of the woman
and of the beast that carries her, the beast with
seven heads and ten horns. 8 The beast you
saw was once alive, but lives no longer; it is
about to come up from the abyss and will go off
to be destroyed. The people living on earth
whose names have not been written, before the
world was created, in the book of the living,
will all be amazed as they look at the beast. It
was once alive; now it no longer lives, but it
will reappear.
9 "This calls for wisdom and understanding.
The seven heads are seven hills, the hills that
the woman sits on. They are also seven kings:
10 five of them have fallen, one still rules, and
the other one has not yet come; when he comes
he must remain only a little while. 11And the
beast that was once alive, but lives no longer,
is itself an eighth king who belongs to the first
seven and goes off to be destroyed.
12 "The ten horns you saw are ten kings who
have not yet begun to rule, but who will be
given authority to rule as kings for one hour
with the beast. 13 These ten all have the same
purpose, and they give their power and authority to the beast. 14 They will fight against the

New International Version

astonished? I will explain to you the mystery of
the woman and of the beast she rides, which has
the seven heads and ten horns. 8 The beast,
which you saw, once was, now is not, and will
come up out of the Abyss and go to his destruction. The inhabitants of the earth whose names
have not been written in the book of life from
the creation of the world will be astonished
when they see the beast, because he once was,
now is not, and yet will come.
9 "This calls for a mind with wisdom. The
seven heads are seven hills on which the woman
sits. They are also seven kings. 10 Five have fallen,
one is, the other has not yet come; but when he
does come, he must remain for a little while.
11 The beast who once was, and now is not, is
an eighth king. He belongs to the seven and is
going to his destruction.
12 "The ten horns you saw are ten kings who
have not yet received a kingdom, but who for
one hour will receive authority as kings along
with the beast. 13 They have one purpose and
will give their power and authority to the beast.
14 They will make war against the Lamb, but the

Phillips Modern English

"Why are you amazed? I will explain to you the mystery of the woman and of the animal with seven heads and ten horns which carries her. The animal, which you saw, once lived but now is no more—it will come up out of the abyss only to meet with destruction. The inhabitants of the earth, whose names have not been written in the book of life from the foundation of the world, will be utterly astonished when they see that the animal was, and is not, and yet is to come. (Here we need a mind with understanding.)

"The seven heads are seven hills on which the woman takes her seat. There are also seven kings; five have been dethroned, one reigns and the other has not yet appeared—when he comes he must remain only for a short time. As for the animal which once lived but now lives no longer, it is an eighth king which belongs to the seven, but it goes to utter destruction. The ten horns which you saw are ten kings who have not yet received their power to reign, but they will receive authority to be kings for one hour in company with the animal. They are of one mind, and they will hand over their power and authority to the animal. They will all go to war with the Lamb,

Revised Standard Version

angel said to me, "Why marvel? I will tell you
the mystery of the woman, and of the beast with
seven heads and ten horns that carries her. 8 The
beast that you saw was, and is not, and is to
ascend from the bottomless pit and go to perdition;
and the dwellers on earth whose names
have not been written in the book of life from
the foundation of the world, will marvel to behold
the beast, because it was and is not and is
to come. 9 This calls for a mind with wisdom:
the seven heads are seven mountains on which
the woman is seated; 10 they are also seven
kings, five of whom have fallen, one is, the other
has not yet come, and when he comes he must
remain only a little while. 11 As for the beast that
was and is not, it is an eighth but it belongs to
the seven, and it goes to perdition. 12 And the
ten horns that you saw are ten kings who have
not yet received royal power, but they are to
receive authority as kings for one hour, together
with the beast. 13 These are of one mind and
give over their power and authority to the beast;
14 they will make war on the Lamb, and the

Jerusalem Bible

"Don't you understand? Now I will tell you the meaning of this woman, and of the beast she is riding, with the seven heads and the ten horns.

The symbolism of the beast and the prostitute

8 "The beast you have seen once was and
now is not[h]; he is yet to come up from the
Abyss, but only to go to his destruction. And
the people of the world, whose names have not
been written since the beginning of the world in
the book of life, will think it miraculous when
they see how the beast once was and now is not
and is still to come. 9 Here there is need for
cleverness, for a shrewd mind; the seven heads
are the seven hills, and the woman is sitting on
them.
10 "The seven heads are also seven emperors.
Five of them have already gone, one is here
now, and one is yet to come; once here, he must
stay for a short while. 11 The beast, who once
was and now is not, is at the same time the
eighth and one of the seven, and he is going to
his destruction.
12 "*The ten horns are ten kings*[i] who have
not yet been given their royal power but will have
royal authority only for a single hour and in
association with the beast. 13 They are all of one
mind in putting their strength and their powers
at the beast's disposal, 14 and they will go to

[*h*] The popular belief that Nero would return from the dead at the head of a Parthian army accounts for this parody of the divine title. [*i*] Dn. 7:24; here they are the kings of the satellite nations.

New English Bible

ished? I will tell you the secret of the woman and of the beast she rides, with the seven heads and the ten horns. The beast you have seen is he who once was alive, and is alive no longer, but has yet to ascend out of the abyss before going to perdition. Those on earth whose names have not been inscribed in the roll of the living ever since the world was made will all be astonished to see the beast; for he once was alive, and is alive no longer, and has still to appear.

'But here is the clue for those who can interpret it. The seven heads are seven hills on which the woman sits. They represent also seven kings,[a] of whom five have already fallen, one is now reigning, and the other has yet to come; and when he does come he is only to last for a little while. As for the beast that once was alive and is alive no longer, he is an eighth—and yet he is one of the seven, and he is going to perdition. The ten horns you saw are ten kings who have not yet begun to reign, but who for one hour are to share with the beast the exercise of royal authority; for they have but a single purpose among them and will confer their power and authority upon the beast. They will wage war

[*a*] *Or* emperors.

King James Version

and the Lamb shall overcome them: for he is Lord of lords, and King of kings: and they that are with him *are* called, and chosen, and faithful. 15And he saith unto me, The waters which thou sawest, where the whore sitteth, are peoples, and multitudes, and nations, and tongues. 16And the ten horns which thou sawest upon the beast, these shall hate the whore, and shall make her desolate and naked, and shall eat her flesh, and burn her with fire. 17 For God hath put in their hearts to fulfil his will, and to agree, and give their kingdom unto the beast, until the words of God shall be fulfilled. 18And the woman which thou sawest is that great city, which reigneth over the kings of the earth.

18 And after these things I saw another angel come down from heaven, having great power; and the earth was lightened with his glory. 2And he cried mightily with a strong voice, saying, Babylon the great is fallen, is fallen, and is become the habitation of devils, and the hold of every foul spirit, and a cage of every unclean and hateful bird. 3 For all nations have drunk of the wine of the wrath of her fornication, and the kings of the earth have committed fornication with her, and the merchants

Living Bible

war against the Lamb, and the Lamb will conquer them; for he is Lord over all lords, and King of kings, and his people are the called and chosen and faithful ones.

15 "The oceans, lakes and rivers that the woman is sitting on represent masses of people of every race and nation.

16 "The scarlet animal and his ten horns—which represent ten kings who will reign with him—all hate the woman, and will attack her and leave her naked and ravaged by fire. 17 For God will put a plan into their minds, a plan that will carry out his purposes: They will mutually agree to give their authority to the scarlet animal, so that the words of God will be fulfilled. 18And this woman you saw in your vision represents the great city that rules over the kings of the earth."

18 After all this I saw another angel come down from heaven with great authority, and the earth grew bright with his splendor.

2 He gave a mighty shout, "Babylon the Great is fallen, is fallen; she has become a den of demons, a haunt of devils and every kind of evil spirit.[a] 3 For all the nations have drunk the fatal wine of her intense immorality. The rulers of earth have enjoyed themselves[b] with her, and

[*a*] Literally, "of every foul and hateful bird." [*b*] Literally, "have committed fornication with her."

Today's English Version

Lamb; but the Lamb, and his called, chosen, and faithful followers with him, will defeat them, because he is Lord of lords and King of kings."

15 The angel also said to me, "The waters you saw, on which the prostitute sits, are nations, peoples, races, and languages. 16 The ten horns you saw, and the beast, will hate the prostitute; they will take away everything she has and leave her naked; they will eat her flesh and destroy her with fire. 17 For God placed in their hearts the desire to carry out his purpose, by acting with one accord and giving to the beast their power to rule, until God's words come true.

18 "The woman you saw is the great city that rules over the kings of the earth."

The fall of Babylon

18 After this I saw another angel coming down out of heaven. He had great authority, and his splendor brightened the whole earth. 2 He cried out in a loud voice, "She has fallen! Great Babylon has fallen! She is now haunted by demons and unclean spirits; all kinds of filthy and hateful birds live in her. 3 For she gave her wine to all peoples and made them drink it—the strong wine of her immoral lust. The kings of the earth committed immorality with her,

New International Version

Lamb will overcome them because he is Lord of lords and King of kings—and with him will be his called, chosen and faithful followers."

15 Then the angel said to me, "The waters you saw, where the prostitute sits, are peoples, multitudes, nations and languages. 16 The beast and the ten horns you saw will hate the prostitute. They will bring her to ruin and leave her naked; they will eat her flesh and burn her with fire. 17 For God has put it into their hearts to accomplish his purpose by agreeing to give the beast their power to rule, until God's words are fulfilled. 18 The woman you saw is the great city that rules over the kings of the earth."

The fall of Babylon

18 After this I saw another angel coming down from heaven. He had great authority, and the earth was illuminated by his splendor. 2 With a mighty voice he shouted:

"Fallen! Fallen is Babylon the Great!
She has become a home for demons
and a haunt for every evil[r] spirit,
a haunt for every unclean and detestable bird.
3 For all the nations have drunk
the maddening wine of her adulteries.
The kings of the earth committed adultery with her,

[*r*] Greek *unclean*.

Phillips Modern English

and the Lamb, with his called, chosen and faithful followers, will conquer them. For he is Lord of lords and King of kings."

Then he said to me,

"As for the waters which you saw, on which the woman took her seat, they are peoples and vast crowds, nations and languages. The ten horns and the animal which you saw will loathe the harlot, and leave her deserted and naked. Moreover, they will devour her flesh, and then consume her with fire. For God has put it into their hearts to carry out his purpose by making them of one mind, and by handing over their authority to the animal, until the words of God have been fulfilled.

"The woman that you saw is the great city which dominates the kings of the earth."

18.1 The final overthrow of Babylon

Later I saw another angel coming down from Heaven, armed with great authority. The earth shone with the splendour of his presence, and he cried in a mighty voice,

"Fallen, fallen is Babylon* the great! She has become a haunt of devils, a prison for every unclean spirit, and a cage for every foul and hateful bird. For all nations have drunk the wine of her passionate unfaithfulness and have fallen thereby. The kings of the earth have debauched themselves with her, and the merchants

* Referring to Rome, but prophetically to any great prosperous but Godless city.

Revised Standard Version

Lamb will conquer them, or he is Lord of lords
and King of kings, and those with him are called
and chosen and faithful."
15 And he said to me, "The waters that you
saw, where the harlot is seated, are peoples and
multitudes and nations and tongues. 16 And the
ten horns that you saw, they and the beast will
hate the harlot; they will make her desolate and
naked, and devour her flesh and burn her up
with fire, 17 for God has put it into their hearts
to carry out his purpose by being of one mind
and giving over their royal power to the beast,
until the words of God shall be fulfilled. 18 And
the woman that you saw is the great city which
has dominion over the kings of the earth."

18 After this I saw another angel coming
down from heaven, having great authority;
and the earth was made bright with his splendor.
2 And he called out with a mighty voice,
"Fallen, fallen is Babylon the great!
It has become a dwelling place of demons,
a haunt of every foul spirit,
a haunt of every foul and hateful bird;
3 For all nations have drunk[k] the wine of her
impure passion,
and the kings of the earth have committed
fornication with her,

[k] Other ancient authorities read *fallen by*.

Jerusalem Bible

war against the Lamb; but the Lamb is *the Lord
of lords and the King of kings,*[j] and he will
defeat them and they will be defeated by his
followers, the called, the chosen, the faithful."
15 The angel continued, "The waters you
saw, beside which the prostitute was sitting, are
all the peoples, the populations, the nations and
the languages. 16 But the time will come when
the ten horns and the beast will turn against the
prostitute, and *strip off her clothes and leave
her naked*[k]; then they will eat her flesh and burn
the remains in the fire. 17 In fact, God influenced
their minds to do what he intended, to
agree together to put their royal powers at the
beast's disposal until the time when God's words
should be fulfilled. 18 The woman you saw is the
great city which has authority over all the rulers
on earth."

An angel announces the fall of Babylon

18 After this, I saw another angel come
down from heaven, with great authority
given to him; *the earth was lit up with his
glory.*[l] 2 At the top of his voice he shouted,
"*Babylon has fallen,* Babylon the Great has
fallen, and has become *the haunt of devils*[m] and
a lodging for every foul spirit and dirty, loathsome
bird. 3 All the nations have been intoxicated
by the wine of her prostitution; every king
in the earth has committed fornication with her,

[j] Dn. 10:17. [k] Ezk. 16:37f. [l] Ezk. 43:2. [m] Is. 34:11f.

New English Bible

upon the Lamb, but the Lamb will defeat them, for he is Lord of lords and King of kings, and his victory will be shared by his followers, called and chosen and faithful.'[a]

Then he said to me, 'The ocean you saw, where the great whore sat, is an ocean of peoples and populations, nations and languages. As for the ten horns you saw, they together with the beast will come to hate the whore; they will strip her naked and leave her desolate, they will batten on her flesh and burn her to ashes. For God has put it into their heads to carry out his purpose, by making common cause and conferring their sovereignty upon the beast until all that God has spoken is fulfilled. The woman you saw is the great city that holds sway over the kings of the earth.'

18 After this I saw another angel coming down from heaven; he came with great authority and the earth was lit up with his splendour. Then in a mighty voice he proclaimed, 'Fallen, fallen is Babylon the great! She has become a dwelling for demons, a haunt for every unclean spirit, for every vile and loathsome bird. For all nations have drunk deep of[b] the fierce wine of her fornication; the kings of the earth have committed fornication with her, and mer-

[a] *Or . . .* kings, and his followers are faithful men, called and selected for service. [b] *Other witnesses read* have been ruined by . . .

King James Version

of the earth are waxed rich through the abundance of her delicacies. 4 And I heard another voice from heaven, saying, Come out of her, my people, that ye be not partakers of her sins, and that ye receive not of her plagues. 5 For her sins have reached unto heaven, and God hath remembered her iniquities. 6 Reward her even as she rewarded you, and double unto her double according to her works: in the cup which she hath filled, fill to her double. 7 How much she hath glorified herself, and lived deliciously, so much torment and sorrow give her: for she saith in her heart, I sit a queen, and am no widow, and shall see no sorrow. 8 Therefore shall her plagues come in one day, death, and mourning, and famine; and she shall be utterly burned with fire: for strong *is* the Lord God who judgeth her. 9 And the kings of the earth, who have committed fornication and lived deliciously with her, shall bewail her, and lament for her, when they shall see the smoke of her burning, 10 Standing afar off for the fear of her

Living Bible

businessmen throughout the world have grown rich from all her luxurious living."

4 Then I heard another voice calling from heaven, "Come away from her, my people; do not take part in her sins, or you will be punished with her. 5 For her sins are piled as high as heaven and God is ready to judge her for her crimes. 6 Do to her as she has done to you, and more—give double penalty for all her evil deeds. She brewed many a cup of woe for others—give twice as much to her. 7 She has lived in luxury and pleasure—match it now with torments and with sorrows. She boasts, 'I am queen upon my throne. I am no helpless widow. I will not experience sorrow.' 8 Therefore the sorrows of death and mourning and famine shall overtake her in a single day, and she shall be utterly consumed by fire; for mighty is the Lord who judges her."

9 And the world leaders, who took part in her immoral acts and enjoyed her favors, will mourn for her as they see the smoke rising from her charred remains. 10 They will stand far off, trem-

Today's English Version

and the businessmen of the world grew rich from her unrestrained lust."

4 Then I heard another voice from heaven, saying,

"Come out, my people! Come out from her!
You must not take part in her sins;
you must not share her punishments!
5 For her sins are piled up as high as heaven,
and God remembers her wicked ways.
6 Treat her exactly as she has treated you;
pay her back twice as much as she has done.
Fill her cup with a drink twice as strong
as the drink she prepared for you.
7 Give her as much suffering and grief
as the glory and luxury she gave herself.
For she keeps telling herself:
'Here I sit, a queen!
I am no widow,
I will never know grief!'
8 Because of this her plagues will all strike her in one day,
disease, grief, and famine.
And she will be burned with fire,
because the Lord God, who judges her, is mighty."

9 The kings of the earth who shared her immorality and lust will cry and weep over the city when they see the smoke of her burning. 10 They stand a long way off, because they are

New International Version

and the merchants of the earth grew rich
from her excessive luxuries."

4 Then I heard another voice from heaven say:
"Come out of her, my people,
so that you will not share in her sins,
so that you will not receive any of her plagues;
5 for her sins are piled up to heaven,
and God has remembered her crimes.
6 Give back to her as she has given;
pay her back double for what she has done.
Mix her a double portion from her own cup.
7 Give her as much torture and grief
as the glory and luxury she gave herself.
In her heart she boasts,
'I sit as queen; I am not a widow,
and I will never mourn.'
8 Therefore in one day her plagues will overtake her:
death, mourning and famine.
She will be consumed by fire,
for mighty is the Lord God who judges her.

9 "When the kings of the earth who committed adultery with her and shared her luxury see the smoke of her burning, they will weep and mourn over her. 10 Terrified at her torment, they will stand far off and cry:

Phillips Modern English

of the earth have grown rich from the extravagance of her dissipation!"

Then I heard another voice from Heaven, crying,

"Come out from her, O my people, lest you become accomplices in her sins and must share in her punishment. For her sins have mounted up to the sky, and God has remembered the tale of her wickedness. Pay her back in her own coin—yes, pay her back double for all that she has done! Mix her a drink of double strength in the cup which she mixed for others! For the pride in which she flaunted herself give her torture and misery! Because she says to herself, 'Here I sit a queen on a throne; I am no woman who lacks a man and I shall never know sorrow!' So in a single day her punishments shall strike her—death, sorrow and famine and she shall be burned in the fire. For mighty is the Lord God who judges her!"

18.9 The lament over the city

Then the kings of the earth, who debauched and indulged themselves with her, will wail and lament over her. Standing at a safe distance through very fear of her torment, they will watch the smoke of her burning and cry,

Revised Standard Version

and the merchants of the earth have grown
rich with the wealth of her wantonness."
4 Then I heard another voice from heaven saying,
"Come out of her, my people,
lest you take part in her sins,
lest you share in her plagues;
5 for her sins are heaped high as heaven,
and God has remembered her iniquities.
6 Render to her as she herself has rendered,
and repay her double for her deeds;
mix a double draught for her in the cup she mixed.
7 As she glorified herself and played the wanton,
so give her a like measure of torment and mourning.
Since in her heart she says, 'A queen I sit,
I am no widow, mourning I shall never see,'
8 so shall her plagues come in a single day,
pestilence and mourning and famine,
and she shall be burned with fire;
for mighty is the Lord God who judges her."
9 And the kings of the earth, who committed
fornication and were wanton with her, will weep
and wail over her when they see the smoke of
her burning; 10 they will stand far off, in fear of
her torment, and say,

Jerusalem Bible

and every merchant grown rich through her debauchery."

The people of God summoned away

4 A new voice spoke from heaven; I heard
it say, "Come out, my people, away from her,
so that you do not share in her crimes and have
the same plagues to bear. 5 *Her sins have
reached up to heaven,*[n] and God has her crimes
in mind: 6 *she is to be paid in her own coin.*[o]
She must be paid double the amount she exacted. She is to have a doubly strong cup of her
own mixture. 7 Every one of her shows and
orgies is to be matched by a torture or a grief.
I am the queen on my throne, she says to herself,[p] and *I am no widow* and shall never be in
mourning. 8 For that, *within a single day,* the
plagues will fall on her: disease and mourning and famine. She will be burned right up. The Lord God has condemned her, and he has great power."

The people of the world mourn for Babylon

9 There will be mourning and weeping for
her by the kings of the earth who have fornicated with her and lived with her in luxury.
They see the smoke as she burns, 10 while they
keep at a safe distance from fear of her agony.
They will say:

[n] Jr. 51:9. [o] Jr. 50:15. [p] Is. 47:8.

New English Bible

chants the world over have grown rich on her bloated wealth.'

Then I heard another voice from heaven that said: 'Come out of her, my people, lest you take part in her sins and share in her plagues. For her sins are piled high as heaven, and God has not forgotten her crimes. Pay her back in her own coin, repay her twice over for her deeds! Double for her the strength of the potion she mixed! Mete out grief and torment to match her voluptuous pomp! She says in her heart, "I am a queen on my throne! No mourning for me, no widow's weeds!" Because of this her plagues shall strike her in a single day—pestilence, bereavement, famine, and burning—for mighty is the Lord God who has pronounced her doom!'

The kings of the earth who committed fornication with her and wallowed in her luxury will weep and wail over her, as they see the smoke of her conflagration. They will stand at a distance,

King James Version

torment, saying, Alas, alas, that great city Babylon, that mighty city! for in one hour is thy
judgment come. 11 And the merchants of the
earth shall weep and mourn over her; for no
man buyeth their merchandise any more: 12 The
merchandise of gold, and silver, and precious
stones, and of pearls, and fine linen, and purple,
and silk, and scarlet, and all thyine wood, and
all manner vessels of ivory, and all manner vessels of most precious wood, and of brass, and
iron, and marble. 13 And cinnamon, and odours,
and ointments, and frankincense, and wine, and
oil, and fine flour, and wheat, and beasts, and
sheep, and horses, and chariots, and slaves,
and souls of men. 14 And the fruits that thy soul
lusted after are departed from thee, and all
things which were dainty and goodly are departed from thee, and thou shalt find them no
more at all. 15 The merchants of these things,
which were made rich by her, shall stand afar
off for the fear of her torment, weeping and
wailing, 16 And saying, Alas, alas, that great city,
that was clothed in fine linen, and purple, and
scarlet, and decked with gold, and precious
stones, and pearls! 17 For in one hour so great
riches is come to nought. And every shipmaster,
and all the company in ships, and sailors, and
as many as trade by sea, stood afar off, 18 And
cried when they saw the smoke of her burning,
saying, What *city is* like unto this great city!
19 And they cast dust on their heads, and cried,

Living Bible

bling with fear and crying out, "Alas, Babylon,
that mighty city! In one moment her judgment
fell."

11 The merchants of the earth will weep and
mourn for her, for there is no one left to buy
their goods. 12 She was their biggest customer
for gold and silver, precious stones, pearls, finest
linens, purple silks, and scarlet; and every kind
of perfumed wood, and ivory goods and most
expensive wooden carvings, and brass and iron
and marble; 13 and spices and perfumes and incense, ointment and frankincense, wine, olive
oil, and fine flour; wheat, cattle, sheep, horses,
chariots, and slaves—and even the souls of men.

14 "All the fancy things you loved so much
are gone," they cry. "The dainty luxuries and
splendor that you prized so much will never be
yours again. They are gone forever."

15 And so the merchants who have become
wealthy by selling her these things shall stand at
a distance, fearing danger to themselves, weeping
and crying, 16 "Alas, that great city, so beautiful
—like a woman clothed in finest purple and
scarlet linens, decked out with gold and precious
stones and pearls! 17 In one moment, all the
wealth of the city is gone!"

And all the shipowners and captains of the
merchant ships and crews will stand a long way
off, 18 crying as they watch the smoke ascend,
and saying, "Where in all the world is there
another city such as this?" 19 And they will
throw dust on their heads in their sorrow and

Today's English Version

afraid of her suffering, and say, "How terrible!
How awful! This great and mighty city Babylon!
In just one hour you have been punished!"

11 The businessmen of the earth also cry and
mourn for her, because no one buys their goods
any longer; 12 no one buys their gold, silver,
precious stones, and pearls; their goods of linen,
purple cloth, silk, and scarlet; all kinds of rare
woods, and all kinds of objects made of ivory
and of expensive wood, of bronze, iron, and
marble; 13 and cinnamon, spice, incense, myrrh,
and frankincense; wine and oil, flour and wheat,
cattle and sheep, horses and carriages, slaves
and even men's souls. 14 The businessmen say
to her, "All the good things you longed to own
have disappeared, and all your wealth and
glamor are gone, and you will never find them
again!" 15 The businessmen, who became rich
from doing business in that city, will stand a
long way off, because they are afraid of her
suffering. They will cry and mourn, 16 and say,
"How terrible! How awful for the great city!
She used to dress herself in linen, purple, and
scarlet, and cover herself with gold ornaments,
precious stones, and pearls! 17 And in one hour
she has lost all this wealth!"

All the ship captains and passengers, the
sailors and all others who earn their living on
the sea, stood a long way off, 18 and cried out
as they saw the smoke of her burning, "There
never has been another city like the great city!"
19 They threw dust on their heads, they cried

New International Version

'Woe! Woe, O great city,
O Babylon, city of power!
In one hour your doom has come!'

11 "The merchants of the earth will weep and
mourn over her because no one buys their cargoes any more—12 cargoes of gold, silver,
precious stones and pearls; fine linen, purple,
silk and scarlet cloth; every sort of citron wood,
and articles of every kind made of ivory, costly
wood, bronze, iron and marble; 13 cargoes of
cinnamon and spice, of incense, myrrh and
frankincense, of wine and olive oil, of fine flour
and wheat; cattle and sheep; horses and carriages;
and bodies and souls of men.

14 "They will say, 'The fruit you longed for
is gone from you. All your riches and splendor
have vanished, never to be recovered.' 15 The
merchants who sold these things and gained their
wealth from her will stand far off, terrified at her
torment. They will weep and mourn 16 and cry
out:

'Woe! Woe, O great city,
dressed in fine linen, purple and scarlet,
and glittering with gold, precious stones
and pearls!
17 In one hour such great wealth has been
brought to ruin!'

"Every sea captain, and all who travel by ship,
the sailors, and all who earn their living from
the sea, will stand far off. 18 When they see the
smoke of her burning, they will exclaim, 'Was
there ever a city like this great city?' 19 They will
throw dust on their heads, and with weeping and
mourning cry out:

Phillips Modern English

"Alas, alas for the great city, Babylon the mighty city, that your judgment should come in a single hour."

The merchants of the earth shall also wail and lament over her, for there is no one left to buy their goods—cargoes of gold and silver, jewels and pearls, fine linen, purple, silk and scarlet, all kinds of scented wood, every sort of ivory vessel, every kind of vessel of precious wood, of bronze, iron and marble; cinnamon, spice, incense, myrrh, frankincense, wine, oil, fine flour and corn; cattle, sheep and horses; chariots, slaves, the very souls of men.*

Those who bought and sold these things, who had gained their wealth from her, will stand afar off through fear of her punishment, weeping and lamenting and saying,

"Alas, alas for the great city that was dressed in fine linen, purple and scarlet, and was bedecked with gold and jewels and pearls—alas that in a single hour all that wealth should be destroyed!"

Then every shipmaster and seafarer—sailors and all whose business is upon the sea—stood and watched the smoke of her burning from afar, and cried out,

"What city was ever like the great city?"

They even threw dust on their heads and cried aloud as they wept, saying,

* Verse 14 has been incorporated with verse 23, which seems to be its natural place.

Revised Standard Version

"Alas! alas! thou great city,
thou mighty city, Babylon!
In one hour has thy judgment come."
11 And the merchants of the earth weep and
mourn for her, since no one buys their cargo any
more, 12 cargo of gold, silver, jewels and pearls,
fine linen, purple, silk and scarlet, all kinds of
scented wood, all articles of ivory, all articles of
costly wood, bronze, iron and marble, 13 cinnamon, spice, incense, myrrh, frankincense, wine,
oil, fine flour and wheat, cattle and sheep, horses
and chariots, and slaves, that is, human souls.
14 "The fruit for which thy soul longed has
gone from thee,
and all thy dainties and thy splendor
are lost to thee, never to be found
again!"
15 The merchants of these wares, who gained
wealth from her, will stand far off, in fear of her
torment, weeping and mourning aloud,
16 "Alas, alas, for the great city
that was clothed in fine linen, in purple
and scarlet,
bedecked with gold, with jewels, and with
pearls!
17 In one hour all this wealth has been laid
waste."
And all shipmasters and seafaring men, sailors
and all whose trade is on the sea, stood far off
18 and cried out as they saw the smoke of her
burning,
"What city was like the great city?"
19 And they threw dust on their heads, as they
wept and mourned, crying out,

Jerusalem Bible

"Mourn, mourn for this great city,
Babylon, so powerful a city,
doomed as you are within a single hour."

11 There will be weeping and distress over her
among all the traders of the earth when there is
nobody left to buy their cargoes of goods;
12 their stocks of gold and silver, jewels and
pearls, linen and purple and silks and scarlet;
all the sandalwood, every piece in ivory or fine
wood, in bronze or iron or marble; 13 the cinnamon and spices, the myrrh and ointment and
incense; wine, oil, flour and corn; their stocks
of cattle, sheep, horses and chariots, their slaves,
their human cargo.
14 "All the fruits you had set your hearts on
have failed you; gone for ever, never to return,
is your life of magnificence and ease."
15 The traders who had made a fortune out
of her will be standing at a safe distance from
fear of her agony, mourning and weeping.
16 They will be saying:

"Mourn, mourn for this great city;
for all the linen and purple and scarlet that
you wore,
for all your finery of gold and jewels and
pearls;
17 your riches are all destroyed within a
single hour."

All the captains and seafaring men, sailors and
all those who make a living from the sea will
be keeping a safe distance, 18 watching the
smoke as she burns, and crying out, "Has there
ever been a city as great as this!" 19 They will
throw dust on their heads and say, with tears
and groans:

New English Bible

for horror at her torment, and will say, 'Alas, alas for the great city, the mighty city of Babylon! In a single hour your doom has struck!'

The merchants of the earth also will weep and mourn for her, because no one any longer buys their cargoes, cargoes of gold and silver, jewels and pearls, cloths of purple and scarlet, silks and fine linens; all kinds of scented woods, ivories, and every sort of thing made of costly woods, bronze, iron, or marble; cinnamon and spice, incense, perfumes and frankincense; wine, oil, flour and wheat, sheep and cattle, horses, chariots, slaves, and the lives of men. 'The fruit you longed for', they will say, 'is gone from you; all the glitter and the glamour are lost, never to be yours again!' The traders in all these wares, who gained their wealth from her, will stand at a distance for horror at her torment, weeping and mourning and saying, 'Alas, alas for the great city, that was clothed in fine linen and purple and scarlet, bedizened with gold and jewels and pearls! Alas that in one hour so much wealth should be laid waste!'

Then all the sea-captains and voyagers, the sailors and those who traded by sea, stood at a distance and cried out as they saw the smoke of her conflagration: 'Was there ever a city like the great city?' They threw dust on their heads,

King James Version

weeping and wailing, saying, Alas, alas, that
great city, wherein were made rich all that had
ships in the sea by reason of her costliness! for
in one hour is she made desolate. 20 Rejoice over
her, *thou* heaven, and *ye* holy apostles and
prophets; for God hath avenged you on her.
21And a mighty angel took up a stone like a
great millstone, and cast *it* into the sea, saying,
Thus with violence shall that great city Babylon
be thrown down, and shall be found no more
at all. 22And the voice of harpers, and musicians,
and of pipers, and trumpeters, shall be heard
no more at all in thee; and no craftsman, of
whatsoever craft *he be,* shall be found any more
in thee; and the sound of a millstone shall be
heard no more at all in thee; 23And the light
of a candle shall shine no more at all in thee;
and the voice of the bridegroom and of the bride
shall be heard no more at all in thee: for thy
merchants were the great men of the earth; for

Living Bible

say, "Alas, alas, for that great city! She made
us all rich from her great wealth. And now in a
single hour all is gone. . . ."
20 But you, O heaven, rejoice over her fate;
and you, O children of God and the prophets
and the apostles! For at last God has given judgment against her for you.
21 Then a mighty angel picked up a boulder
shaped like a millstone and threw it into the
ocean and shouted, "Babylon, that great city,
shall be thrown away as I have thrown away this
stone, and she shall disappear forever. 22 Never
again will the sound of music be there—no more
pianos, saxophones, and trumpets.[c] No industry
of any kind will ever again exist there, and there
will be no more milling of the grain. 23 Dark,
dark will be her nights; not even a lamp in a
window will ever be seen again. No more joyous
wedding bells and happy voices of the bride-
grooms and the brides. Her businessmen were
known around the world and she deceived all na-

[c] Literally, "harpers . . . pipers . . . and trumpet-ers."

Today's English Version

and mourned, saying, "How terrible! How awful
for the great city! She is the city where all who
have ships sailing the seas became rich on her
wealth! And in one hour she has lost everything!"
20 Be glad, heaven, because of her destruction! Be glad, God's people, and the apostles
and prophets! Because God has judged her for
what she did to you!
21 Then a mighty angel picked up a stone the
size of a large millstone and threw it into the
sea, saying, "This is how the great city Babylon
will be thrown down with violence, and will
never be seen again. 22 The music of harpists
and musicians, of players of the flute and the
trumpet, will never be heard in you again! No
workman in any trade will ever be found in you
again; and the sound of the millstone will be
heard no more! 23 Never again will the light of a
lamp be seen in you; no more will the voices of
bride and groom be heard in you. Your businessmen were the most powerful in all the world,
and with your false magic you deceived all the
peoples of the world!"

New International Version

'Woe! Woe, O great city,
where all who had ships on the sea
became rich through her wealth!
In one hour she has been brought to ruin!
20 Rejoice over her, O heaven!
Rejoice, saints and apostles and prophets!
God has judged her for the way she treated
you.' "
21 Then a mighty angel picked up a boulder
the size of a large millstone and threw it into
the sea, and said:
"With such violence
the great city of Babylon will be thrown
down,
never to be found again.
22 The music of harpists and musicians, flute-
players and trumpeters,
will never be heard in you again.
No workman of any trade
will ever be found in you again.
The sound of a millstone
will never be heard in you again.
23 The light of a lamp
will never shine in you again.
The voice of bridegroom and bride
will never be heard in you again.
Your merchants were the world's great men.
By your magic spell all the nations were
led astray.

Phillips Modern English

"Alas, alas for the great city where all who had ships on the sea grew wealthy through the richness of her treasure! Alas that in a single hour she should be ruined!"

18.20 A comment in the background

"Rejoice over her fate, O Heaven, and all you saints, apostles and prophets! For God has pronounced his judgment for you against her!"

18.21 The words of Babylon's doom

Then a mighty angel lifted up a stone like a huge mill-stone and hurled it into the sea, saying, "So shall Babylon the great city be sent hurtling down to disappear for ever! Never more shall the sound of harpists and musicians, flute-players and trumpeters be heard in you again! Never again shall a craftsman of any craft be found in you; never again will the sound of the mill-stone's grinding be heard in you! No light of a lamp shall ever shine in you again, and the voices of bridegroom and bride shall be heard in you no more! The fruit of your soul's desire is lost to you for ever. All your luxuries and brilliance are lost to you and men will never find them in you again!

"For your merchants were the great ones of the earth, and all nations were seduced by your witchery!"

Revised Standard Version

"Alas, alas, for the great city
where all who had ships at sea grew rich
by her wealth!
In one hour she has been laid waste.
20 Rejoice over her, O heaven,
O saints and apostles and prophets,
for God has given judgment for you against
her!"
21 Then a mighty angel took up a stone like
a great millstone and threw it into the sea, saying,
"So shall Babylon the great city be thrown
down with violence,
and shall be found no more;
22 and the sound of harpers and minstrels, of
flute players and trumpeters,
shall be heard in thee no more;
and a craftsman of any craft
shall be found in thee no more;
and the sound of the millstone
shall be heard in thee no more;
23 and the light of a lamp
shall shine in thee no more;
and the voice of bridegroom and bride
shall be heard in thee no more;
for thy merchants were the great men of the
earth,
and all nations were deceived by thy
sorcery.

Jerusalem Bible

"Mourn, mourn for this great city
whose lavish living has made a fortune
for every owner of a seagoing ship;
ruined within a single hour.

20 "Now heaven, celebrate her downfall, and all
you saints, apostles and prophets: God has given
judgment for you against her."
21 Then a powerful angel picked up a boulder like a great millstone, and as he hurled it
into the sea, he said, "That is how the great city
of Babylon is going to be hurled down, never
to be seen again.

22 "Never again in you, Babylon,
will be heard the song of harpists and
minstrels,
the music of flute and trumpet;
never again will craftsmen of every skill
be found
or *the sound of the mill* [q] be heard;
23 never again will shine *the light of the
lamp*,
never again will be heard
the voices of bridegroom and bride.
Your traders were the princes of the earth,
all the nations were under your spell.

[q] Jr. 25:10.

New English Bible

weeping and mourning and saying, 'Alas, alas for the great city, where all who had ships at sea grew rich on her wealth! Alas that in a single hour she should be laid waste!'

But let heaven exult over her; exult, apostles and prophets and people of God; for in the judgement against her he has vindicated your cause!

Then a mighty angel took up a stone like a great millstone and hurled it into the sea and said, 'Thus shall Babylon, the great city, be sent hurtling down, never to be seen again! No more shall the sound of harpers and minstrels, of flute-players and trumpeters, be heard in you; no more shall craftsmen of any trade be found in you; no more shall the sound of the mill be heard in you; no more shall the light of the lamp be seen in you; no more shall the voice of the bride and bridegroom be heard in you! Your traders were once the merchant princes of the world, and with your sorcery you deceived all the nations.'

King James Version

by thy sorceries were all nations deceived. 24And in her was found the blood of prophets, and of saints, and of all that were slain upon the earth.

19 And after these things I heard a great voice of much people in heaven, saying, Alleluia; Salvation, and glory, and honour, and power, unto the Lord our God: 2 For true and righteous *are* his judgments; for he hath judged the great whore, which did corrupt the earth with her fornication, and hath avenged the blood of his servants at her hand. 3And again they said, Alleluia. And her smoke rose up for ever and ever. 4And the four and twenty elders and the four beasts fell down and worshipped God that sat on the throne, saying, Amen; Alleluia. 5And a voice came out of the throne, saying, Praise our God, all ye his servants, and ye that fear him, both small and great. 6And I heard as it were the voice of a great multitude, and as the voice of many waters, and as the voice of mighty thunderings, saying, Alleluia: for the

Living Bible

tions with her sorceries. 24And she was responsible for the blood of all the martyred prophets and the saints."

19 After this I heard the shouting of a vast crowd in heaven, "Hallelujah! Praise the Lord! Salvation is from our God. Honor and authority belong to him alone; 2 for his judgments are just and true. He has punished the Great Prostitute who corrupted the earth with her sin;[a] and he has avenged the murder of his servants."

3 Again and again their voices rang, "Praise the Lord! The smoke from her burning ascends forever and forever!"

4 Then the twenty-four Elders and four Living Beings fell down and worshiped God, who was sitting upon the throne, and said, "Amen! Hallelujah! Praise the Lord!"

5 And out of the throne came a voice that said, "Praise our God, all you his servants, small and great, who fear him."

6 Then I heard again what sounded like the shouting of a huge crowd, or like the waves of a hundred oceans crashing on the shore, or like the mighty rolling of great thunder, "Praise the Lord. For the Lord our God, the Almighty,

[a] Literally, "fornication," the word used symbolically through the prophets for the worship of false gods.

Today's English Version

24 Babylon was punished because the blood of prophets and of God's people was found in the city; yes, the blood of all those who have been killed on earth.

19 After this I heard what sounded like the loud voice of a great crowd of people in heaven, saying, "Praise God! Salvation, glory, and power belong to our God! 2 True and righteous are his judgments! He has condemned the great prostitute who was corrupting the earth with her immorality. God has punished her because she killed his servants." 3Again they shouted, "Praise God! The smoke from the burning of the great city goes up forever and ever!" 4 The twenty-four elders and the four living creatures fell down and worshiped God who was seated on the throne, and said, "Amen! Praise God!"

The wedding feast of the Lamb

5 Then there came from the throne the sound of a voice, saying, "Praise our God, all his servants, and all men, both great and small, who fear him!" 6 Then I heard what sounded like the voice of a great crowd, like the roar of a mighty waterfall, like loud peals of thunder. I heard them say, "Praise God! For the Lord, our

New International Version

24 In her was found the blood of prophets and
of the saints,
and of all who have been killed on the
earth."

Hallelujah!

19 After this, I heard what sounded like the roar of a great multitude in heaven shouting:

"Hallelujah!
Salvation and glory and power belong to our
God,
2 for true and just are his judgments.
He has condemned the great prostitute
who corrupted the earth by her adulteries.
He has avenged on her the blood of his
servants."

3 And again they shouted:

"Hallelujah!
The smoke from her goes up for ever and
ever."

4 The twenty-four elders and the four living creatures fell down and worshiped God, who was seated on the throne. And they cried:

"Amen, Hallelujah!"

5 Then a voice came from the throne, saying:

"Praise our God,
all you his servants,
you who fear him,
both small and great!"

6 Then I heard what sounded like a great multitude, like the roar of rushing waters and like loud peals of thunder, shouting:

"Hallelujah!
For our Lord God Almighty reigns.

Phillips Modern English

For in her was discovered the blood of prophets and saints, indeed the blood of all who were ever slaughtered upon the earth.

19.1 Rejoicing in Heaven

Afterwards I heard what sounded like the mighty roar of a vast crowd in Heaven, crying, "Alleluia! Salvation and glory and power belong to our God, for his judgments are true and just. He has judged the great harlot who corrupted the earth with her wickedness, and he has avenged upon her the blood of his servants!"

Then they cried a second time,

"Alleluia! The smoke of her destruction ascends for timeless ages!"

Then the twenty-four elders and the four living creatures prostrated themselves and worshipped God who is seated upon the throne, saying,

"Amen, alleluia!"

Then out of the throne came a voice, saying,

"Praise our God, all you who serve him, all you who reverence him, both small and great!"

And then I heard a sound like the voices of a vast crowd, the roar of a great waterfall and the rolling of heavy thunder, and they were saying,

"Alleluia! For the Lord our God, the Al-

Revised Standard Version

24 And in her was found the blood of prophets and of saints,
and of all who have been slain on earth."

19 After this I heard what seemed to be the loud voice of a great multitude in heaven, crying,
"Hallelujah! Salvation and glory and power belong to our God,
2 for his judgments are true and just;
he has judged the great harlot who corrupted the earth with her fornication,
and he has avenged on her the blood of his servants."
3 Once more they cried,
"Hallelujah! The smoke from her goes up for ever and ever."
4And the twenty-four elders and the four living creatures fell down and worshiped God who is seated on the throne, saying, "Amen. Hallelujah!"
5And from the throne came a voice crying,
"Praise our God, all you his servants,
you who fear him, small and great."
6 Then I heard what seemed to be the voice of a great multitude, like the sound of many waters and like the sound of mighty thunderpeals, crying,
"Hallelujah! For the Lord our God the Almighty reigns.

Jerusalem Bible

24 In her you will find the blood of prophets and saints, and all the blood that was ever shed on earth."

Songs of victory in heaven

19 After this I seemed to hear the great sound of a huge crowd in heaven, singing,
"Alleluia! Victory and glory and power to our God!
2 He judges fairly, he punishes justly, and he has condemned the famous prostitute who corrupted the earth with her fornication; he has avenged his servants that she killed."
3 They sang again, "Alleluia! *The smoke* of her *will go up for ever* and ever."
4 Then the twenty-four elders and the four animals prostrated themselves and worshiped God seated there on his throne, and they cried, "Amen, Alleluia."
5 Then a voice came from the throne; it said, "Praise our God, you servants of his and *all who, great or small, revere him.*"
6And I seemed to hear the voices of a huge crowd, like the sound of the ocean or the great roar of thunder, answering, "Alleluia! The reign of the Lord our

New English Bible

For the blood of the prophets and of God's people was found in her, the blood of all who had been done to death on earth.

19 After this I heard what sounded like the roar of a vast throng in heaven; and they were shouting:

'Alleluia! Victory and glory and power belong to our God, for true and just are his judgements! He has condemned the great whore who corrupted the earth with her fornication, and has avenged upon her the blood of his servants.'

Then once more they shouted:

'Alleluia! The smoke goes up from her for ever and ever!'

And the twenty-four elders and the four living creatures fell down and worshipped God as he sat on the throne, and they too cried:

'Amen! Alleluia!'

Then a voice came from the throne which said: 'Praise our God, all you his servants, you that fear him, both great and small!'

Again I heard what sounded like a vast crowd, like the noise of rushing water and deep roars of thunder, and they cried:

King James Version

Lord God omnipotent reigneth. 7 Let us be glad and rejoice, and give honour to him: for the marriage of the Lamb is come, and his wife hath made herself ready. 8 And to her was granted that she should be arrayed in fine linen, clean and white: for the fine linen is the righteousness of saints. 9 And he saith unto me, Write, Blessed *are* they which are called unto the marriage supper of the Lamb. And he saith unto me, These are the true sayings of God. 10 And I fell at his feet to worship him. And he said unto me, See *thou do it* not: I am thy fellow servant, and of thy brethren that have the testimony of Jesus: worship God: for the testimony of Jesus is the spirit of prophecy. 11 And I saw heaven opened, and behold a white horse; and he that sat upon him *was* called Faithful and True, and in righteousness he doth judge and make war. 12 His eyes *were* as a flame of fire, and on his head *were* many crowns; and he had a name written, that no man knew, but he himself. 13 And he

Living Bible

reigns. 7 Let us be glad and rejoice and honor him; for the time has come for the wedding banquet of the Lamb, and his bride has prepared herself. 8 She is permitted to wear the cleanest and whitest and finest of linens." (Fine linen represents the good deeds done by the people of God.)

9 And the angel [b] dictated this sentence to me: "Blessed are those who are invited to the wedding feast of the Lamb." And he added, "God himself has stated this." [c]

10 Then I fell down at his feet to worship him, but he said, "No! Don't! For I am a servant of God just as you are, and as your brother Christians are, who testify of their faith in Jesus. The purpose of all prophecy and of all I have shown you is to tell about Jesus." [d]

11 Then I saw heaven opened and a white horse standing there; and the one sitting on the horse was named "Faithful and True"—the one who justly punishes and makes war. 12 His eyes were like flames, and on his head were many crowns. A name was written on his forehead,[e] and only he knew its meaning. 13 He was clothed

[*b*] Literally, "he"; the exact antecedent is unclear. [*c*] Literally, "These are the true words of God." [*d*] Literally, "The testimony of Jesus is the spirit of prophecy." [*e*] Implied.

Today's English Version

Almighty God, is King! 7 Let us rejoice and be glad; let us praise his greatness! For the time has come for the wedding of the Lamb, and his bride has prepared herself for it. 8 She has been given clean shining linen to dress herself with." (The linen is the righteous deeds of God's people.)

9 Then the angel said to me, "Write this: Happy are those who have been invited to the wedding feast of the Lamb." And the angel added, "These are the true words of God."

10 I fell down at his feet to worship him, but he said to me, "Don't do it! I am a fellow servant of yours, and of your brothers, all those who hold to the truth that Jesus revealed. Worship God!"

For the truth that Jesus revealed is what inspires the prophets.

The rider on the white horse

11 Then I saw heaven open, and there was a white horse. Its rider is called Faithful and True; it is with justice that he judges and fights his battles. 12 His eyes were like a flame of fire, and he wore many crowns on his head. He had a name written on him, but no one except himself knows what it is. 13 The robe he wore was

New International Version

7 Let us rejoice and be glad
and give him glory!
For the wedding of the Lamb has come,
and his bride has made herself ready.
8 Fine linen, bright and clean,
was given her to wear."

(Fine linen stands for the righteous acts of the saints.)

9 Then the angel said to me, "Write: 'Blessed are those who are invited to the wedding supper of the Lamb!'" And he added, "These are the true words of God."

10 At this I fell at his feet to worship him. But he said to me, "Do not do it! I am a fellow servant with you and with your brothers who hold to the testimony of Jesus. Worship God! For the testimony of Jesus is the spirit of prophecy."

The rider on the white horse

11 I saw heaven standing open and there before me was a white horse, whose rider is called Faithful and True. With justice he judges and makes war. 12 His eyes are like blazing fire, and on his head are many crowns. He has a name written on him that no one but he himself knows. 13 He is dressed in a robe dipped in

Phillips Modern English

mighty, has come into his kingdom! Let us rejoice, let us be glad with all our hearts. Let us give him the glory, for the wedding-day of the Lamb has come, and his bride has made herself ready. She may be seen dressed in linen, gleaming and spotless—for such linen is the righteous living of the saints!"

19.9 Instruction to John

Then he said to me,
"Write this down: Happy are those who are invited to the wedding-feast of the Lamb!"
Then he added,
"These are true words of God."
At that I fell at his feet to worship him, but he said to me,
"No! I am your fellow-servant and fellow-servant with your brothers who are holding fast their witness to Jesus. Give your worship to God!"
(This witness to Jesus inspires all prophecy.)

19.11 The Word of God on the white horse

Then I saw Heaven wide open, and before my eyes appeared a white horse, whose rider is called faithful and true, for his judgment and his warfare are just. His eyes are a flame of fire and there are many diadems upon his head. There is a name written upon him, known only to himself. He is dressed in a cloak dipped in blood,

Revised Standard Version

7 Let us rejoice and exult and give him the
glory,
for the marriage of the Lamb has come,
and his Bride has made herself ready;
8 it was granted her to be clothed with fine
linen, bright and pure"—
for the fine linen is the righteous deeds of the saints.
9 And the angel said[l] to me, "Write this:
Blessed are those who are invited to the marriage supper of the Lamb." And he said to me,
"These are true words of God." 10 Then I fell
down at his feet to worship him, but he said to
me, "You must not do that! I am a fellow servant with you and your brethren who hold the
testimony of Jesus. Worship God." For the testimony of Jesus is the spirit of prophecy.
11 Then I saw heaven opened, and behold, a
white horse! He who sat upon it is called Faithful and True, and in righteousness he judges and
makes war. 12 His eyes are like a flame of fire,
and on his head are many diadems; and he has
a name inscribed which no one knows but himself. 13 He is clad in a robe dipped in[m] blood,

[l] Greek *he said.* [m] Other ancient authorities read *sprinkled with.*

Jerusalem Bible

God Almighty has begun; 7 let us be glad and
joyful and give praise to God, because this is
the time for the marriage of the Lamb. 8 His
bride is ready, and she has been able to dress
herself in dazzling white linen, because her linen
is made of the good deeds of the saints." 9 The
angel said, "Write this: Happy are those who
are invited to the wedding feast of the Lamb,"
and he added, "All the things you have written
are true messages from God." 10 Then I knelt
at his feet to worship him, but he said to me,
"Don't do that: I am a servant just like you
and all your brothers who are witnesses to Jesus.
It is God that you must worship." The witness
Jesus gave is the same as the spirit of prophecy.

C. The destruction of the pagan nations

The first battle of the End

11 And now I saw heaven open, and a white
horse appear; its rider was called Faithful and
True; he is *a judge with integrity,*[r] a warrior
for justice. 12 His eyes were flames of fire, and
his head was crowned with many coronets; the
name written on him was known only to himself, 13 *his cloak was soaked in blood.*[s] He is

[r] Is. 11:4. [s] Is. 63:1.

New English Bible

'Alleluia! The Lord our God, sovereign over all, has entered on his reign! Exult and shout for joy and do him homage, for the wedding-day of the Lamb has come! His bride has made herself ready, and for her dress she has been given fine linen, clean and shining.'

(Now the fine linen signifies the righteous deeds of God's people.)

Then the angel said to me, 'Write this: "Happy are those who are invited to the wedding-supper of the Lamb!"' And he added, 'These are the very words of God.' At this I fell at his feet to worship him. But he said to me, 'No, not that! I am but a fellow-servant with you and your brothers who bear their testimony to Jesus. It is God you must worship. Those who bear testimony to Jesus are inspired like the prophets.'[a]

Then I saw heaven wide open, and there before me was a white horse; and its rider's name was Faithful and True, for he is just in judgement and just in war. His eyes flamed like fire, and on his head were many diadems. Written upon him was a name known to none but himself, and he was robed in a garment drenched in

[a] *Or* . . . worship. For testimony to Jesus is the spirit that inspires prophets.

King James Version

was clothed with a vesture dipped in blood: and
his name is called The Word of God. 14And the
armies *which were* in heaven followed him upon
white horses, clothed in fine linen, white and
clean. 15And out of his mouth goeth a sharp
sword, that with it he should smite the nations;
and he shall rule them with a rod of iron: and
he treadeth the winepress of the fierceness and
wrath of Almighty God. 16And he hath on *his*
vesture and on his thigh a name written, KING
OF KINGS, AND LORD OF LORDS. 17And
I saw an angel standing in the sun; and he
cried with a loud voice, saying to all the fowls
that fly in the midst of heaven, Come and gather
yourselves together unto the supper of the great
God; 18 That ye may eat the flesh of kings, and
the flesh of captains, and the flesh of mighty
men, and the flesh of horses, and of them that
sit on them, and the flesh of all *men, both* free
and bond, both small and great. 19And I saw
the beast, and the kings of the earth, and their
armies, gathered together to make war against
him that sat on the horse, and against his army.
20And the beast was taken, and with him the
false prophet that wrought miracles before him,
with which he deceived them that had received
the mark of the beast, and them that worshipped
his image. These both were cast alive into a
lake of fire burning with brimstone. 21And the
remnant were slain with the sword of him that
sat upon the horse, which *sword* proceeded out
of his mouth: and all the fowls were filled with
their flesh.

Living Bible

with garments dipped in blood, and his title was
"The Word of God." [f] 14 The armies of heaven,
dressed in finest linen, white and clean, followed
him on white horses.
15 In his mouth he held a sharp sword to
strike down the nations; he ruled them with an
iron grip; and he trod the winepress of the fierceness of the wrath of Almighty God. 16 On his
robe and thigh was written this title: "King of
Kings and Lord of Lords."
17 Then I saw an angel standing in the sunshine, shouting loudly to the birds, "Come!
Gather together for the supper of the Great
God! 18 Come and eat the flesh of kings, and
captains, and great generals; of horses and
riders; and of all humanity, both great and
small, slave and free."
19 Then I saw the Evil Creature gathering the
governments of the earth and their armies to
fight against the one sitting on the horse and
his army. 20And the Evil Creature was captured,
and with him the False Prophet,[g] who could do
mighty miracles when the Evil Creature was present—miracles that deceived all who had accepted
the Evil Creature's mark, and who worshiped
his statue. Both of them—the Evil Creature and
his False Prophet—were thrown alive into the
Lake of Fire that burns with sulphur. 21And
their entire army was killed with the sharp sword
in the mouth of the one riding the white horse,
and all the birds of heaven were gorged with
their flesh.

[*f*] Literally, "The Logos," as in John 1:1—the ultimate method of God's revealing himself to man. [*g*] See chapter 13, verses 11-16.

Today's English Version

covered with blood. The name by which he is
called is "The Word of God." 14 The armies of
heaven followed him, riding on white horses and
dressed in clean white linen. 15A sharp sword
came out of his mouth, with which he will defeat the nations. He will rule over them with a
rod of iron, and he will squeeze out the wine in
the winepress of the furious wrath of the Almighty God. 16 On his robe and on his leg was
written the name: "King of kings and Lord of
lords."
17 Then I saw an angel standing in the sun.
He shouted in a loud voice to all the birds flying in mid-air, "Come, and gather together for
God's great feast! 18 Come and eat the flesh of
kings, generals, and soldiers, the flesh of horses
and their riders, the flesh of all men, slave and
free, great and small!"
19 Then I saw the beast and the kings of the
earth and their armies gathered to fight against
the one who rides the horse, and against his
army. 20 The beast was taken prisoner, together
with the false prophet who had performed miracles in his presence. (It was by those miracles
that he had deceived those who had the mark
of the beast, and those who had worshiped the
image of the beast.) The beast and the false
prophet were both thrown alive into the lake of
fire that burns with sulfur. 21 Their armies were
killed by the sword that comes out of the mouth
of the one who rides the horse; and all the birds
ate all they could of their flesh.

New International Version

blood, and his name is the Word of God. 14 The
armies of heaven were following him, riding on
white horses and dressed in fine linen, white and
clean. 15 Out of his mouth comes a sharp sword
with which to strike down the nations. He will
rule them with a rod of iron. He treads the winepress of the fury of the wrath of God Almighty.
16 On his robe and on his thigh he has this name
written:

KING OF KINGS AND LORD OF LORDS.

17 And I saw an angel standing in the sun,
who cried in a loud voice to all the birds flying
in midair, "Come, gather together for the great
supper of God, 18 so that you may eat the flesh
of kings, generals, and mighty men, of horses
and their riders, and the flesh of all people, free
and slave, small and great."
19 Then I saw the beast and the kings of the
earth and their armies gathered together to make
war against the rider on the horse and his army.
20 But the beast was captured, and with him the
false prophet who had performed the miraculous
signs on his behalf. With these signs he had
deluded those who had received the mark of the
beast and worshiped his image. The two of them
were thrown alive into the fiery lake of burning
sulfur. 21 The rest of them were killed with the
sword that came out of the mouth of the rider
on the horse, and all the birds gorged themselves
on their flesh.

Phillips Modern English

and the name by which he is known is the Word of God.

The armies of Heaven follow him, riding upon white horses and clad in white and spotless linen. Out of his mouth there comes a sharp sword with which to strike the nations. He will shepherd them "with a rod of iron", and alone he will tread the winepress of the furious wrath of God the Almighty. Written upon his cloak and upon his thigh is the name, KING OF KINGS AND LORD OF LORDS.

19.17 The feast of death after battle

Then I saw an angel standing alone in the blazing light of the sun, and he shouted in a loud voice, calling to all the birds flying in mid-air,

"Come, flock together to God's great feast! Here you may eat the flesh of kings and captains, the flesh of strong men, of horses and their riders—the flesh of all men, free men and slaves, small and great!"

And I saw the animal with the kings of the earth and their armies massed together for battle against the rider upon the horse and his army. The animal was captured and with it the false prophet who had performed marvels in its presence, which he had used to deceive those who accepted the mark of the animal and worshipped its statue. These two were thrown alive into the lake of fire which burns with sulphur.

The rest were killed by the sword which issues from the mouth of the rider upon the horse; and all the birds gorged themselves on their flesh.

Revised Standard Version

and the name by which he is called is The Word
of God. 14 And the armies of heaven, arrayed in
fine linen, white and pure, followed him on white
horses. 15 From his mouth issues a sharp sword
with which to smite the nations, and he will rule
them with a rod of iron; he will tread the wine
press of the fury of the wrath of God the Almighty. 16 On his robe and on his thigh he has
a name inscribed, King of kings and Lord of
lords.
17 Then I saw an angel standing in the sun,
and with a loud voice he called to all the birds
that fly in mid-heaven, "Come, gather for the
great supper of God, 18 to eat the flesh of kings,
the flesh of captains, the flesh of mighty men, the
flesh of horses and their riders, and the flesh of
all men, both free and slave, both small and
great." 19 And I saw the beast and the kings of
the earth with their armies gathered to make war
against him who sits upon the horse and against
his army. 20 And the beast was captured, and
with it the false prophet who in its presence had
worked the signs by which he deceived those who
had received the mark of the beast and those
who worshiped its image. These two were thrown
alive into the lake of fire that burns with sulphur. 21 And the rest were slain by the sword of
him who sits upon the horse, the sword that issues from his mouth; and all the birds were
gorged with their flesh.

Jerusalem Bible

known by the name, The Word of God. 14 Behind him, dressed in linen of dazzling white,
rode the armies of heaven on white horses.
15 From his mouth came a sharp sword to strike
the pagans with; he is the one *who will rule
them with an iron scepter,*[t] and tread out the
wine of Almighty God's fierce anger. 16 On his
cloak and on his thigh[u] there was a name written: *The King of kings and the Lord of lords.*
17 I saw an angel standing in the sun, and
he shouted aloud to all the birds that were flying high overhead in the sky, "Come here.
Gather together at the great feast[v] that God is
giving. 18 *There will be the flesh* of kings for
you, and the flesh of great generals and heroes,
the flesh of horses and their riders and of all
kinds of men, citizens and slaves, small and
great."
19 Then I saw the beast, with all the kings
of the earth and their armies, gathered together
to fight the rider and his army. 20 But the beast
was taken prisoner, together with the false
prophet who had worked miracles on the beast's
behalf and by them had deceived all who had
been branded with the mark of the beast and
worshiped his statue. These two were thrown
alive into the fiery lake of burning sulphur.
21 All the rest were killed by the sword of the
rider, which came out of his mouth, and *all the
birds were gorged with their flesh.*

[t] Ps. 2:9. [u] I.e., the place where he wears his sword; so, perhaps, "on his sword." [v] Ezk. 39:17.

New English Bible

blood.[b] He was called the Word of God, and the armies of heaven followed him on white horses, clothed in fine linen, clean and shining. From his mouth there went a sharp sword with which to smite the nations; for he it is who shall rule them with an iron rod, and tread the winepress of the wrath and retribution of God the sovereign Lord. And on his robe and on his thigh there was written the name: 'King of kings and Lord of lords.'

Then I saw an angel standing in the sun, and he cried aloud to all the birds flying in mid-heaven: 'Come and gather for God's great supper, to eat the flesh of kings and commanders and fighting men, the flesh of horses and their riders, the flesh of all men, slave and free, great and small!' Then I saw the beast and the kings of the earth and their armies mustered to do battle with the Rider and his army. The beast was taken prisoner, and so was the false prophet who had worked miracles in its presence and deluded those that had received the mark of the beast and worshipped its image. The two of them were thrown alive into the lake of fire with its sulphurous flames. The rest were killed by the sword which went out of the Rider's mouth; and all the birds gorged themselves on their flesh.

[b] *Some witnesses read* spattered with blood.

King James Version

20 And I saw an angel come down from
heaven, having the key of the bottomless
pit and a great chain in his hand. 2And he laid
hold on the dragon, that old serpent, which is
the Devil, and Satan, and bound him a thousand
years, 3And cast him into the bottomless pit,
and shut him up, and set a seal upon him, that
he should deceive the nations no more, till the
thousand years should be fulfilled: and after that
he must be loosed a little season. 4And I saw
thrones, and they sat upon them, and judgment
was given unto them: and *I saw* the souls of
them that were beheaded for the witness of Jesus, and for the word of God, and which had
not worshipped the beast, neither his image, neither had received *his* mark upon their foreheads,
or in their hands; and they lived and reigned
with Christ a thousand years. 5 But the rest of
the dead lived not again until the thousand years
were finished. This *is* the first resurrection.
6 Blessed and holy *is* he that hath part in the
first resurrection: on such the second death hath
no power, but they shall be priests of God and
of Christ, and shall reign with him a thousand

Living Bible

20 Then I saw an angel come down from
heaven with the key to the bottomless pit
and a heavy chain in his hand. 2 He seized the
Dragon—that old Serpent, the devil, Satan—and
bound him in chains for 1,000 years, 3 and threw
him into the bottomless pit, which he then shut
and locked, so that he could not fool the nations
any more until the thousand years were finished.
Afterwards he would be released again for a little
while.
4 Then I saw thrones, and sitting on them
were those who had been given the right to judge.
And I saw the souls of those who had been beheaded for their testimony about Jesus, for proclaiming the Word of God, and who had not
worshiped the Creature or his statue, nor accepted his mark on their foreheads or their
hands. They had come to life again and now they
reigned with Christ for a thousand years.
5 This is the First Resurrection. (The rest of
the dead did not come back to life until the
thousand years had ended.) 6 Blessed and holy
are those who share in the First Resurrection.
For them the Second Death holds no terrors, for
they will be priests of God and of Christ, and
shall reign with him a thousand years.

Today's English Version

The thousand years

20 Then I saw an angel coming down from
heaven, holding in his hand the key of the
abyss and a heavy chain. 2 He seized the dragon,
that old serpent—that is, the Devil, or Satan—
and tied him up for a thousand years. 3 The
angel threw him into the abyss, locked it and
sealed it, so that he could not deceive the nations any more until the thousand years were
over. After that he must be set loose for a little
while.
4 Then I saw thrones, and those who sat on
them; they were given the power to judge. I also
saw the souls of those who had been executed
because they had proclaimed the truth that Jesus
revealed and the word of God. They had not
worshiped the beast or its image, nor had they
received the mark of the beast on their foreheads or hands. They came to life and ruled as
kings with Christ for a thousand years. 5 (The
rest of the dead did not come to life until the
thousand years were over.) This is the first raising of the dead. 6 Happy and greatly blessed are
those who are included in this first raising of
the dead. The second death has no power over
them; they shall be priests of God and of Christ,
and they will rule with him for a thousand years.

New International Version

The thousand years

20 And I saw an angel coming down out of
heaven, having the key to the Abyss
and holding in his hand a great chain. 2 He
seized the dragon, that ancient serpent, who is
the devil, or Satan, and bound him for a thousand years. 3 He threw him into the Abyss, and
locked and sealed it over him, to keep him from
deceiving the nations any more until the thousand years were ended. After that, he must be
set free for a short time.
4 I saw thrones on which were seated those
who had been given authority to judge. And I
saw the souls of those who had been beheaded
because of their testimony for Jesus and because
of the word of God. They had not worshiped the
beast or his image and had not received his mark
on their foreheads or their hands. They came to
life and reigned with Christ a thousand years.
5 (The rest of the dead did not come to life until the thousand years were ended.) This is the
first resurrection. 6 Blessed and holy are those
who have part in the first resurrection. The second death has no power over them, but they will
be priests of God and of Christ and will reign
with him for a thousand years.

Phillips Modern English

20.1 Satan bound for a thousand years

Then I saw an angel coming down from Heaven with the key of the pit and a huge chain in his hand. He seized the dragon, the serpent of ancient days, who is both the devil and Satan, and bound him fast for a thousand years. Then he hurled him into the pit, and locked and sealed it over his head, so that he could deceive the nations no more until the thousand years were past. But then he must be set free for a little while.

20.4 The first resurrection

And I saw thrones, with appointed judges seated upon them. Then I saw the souls of those who had been executed for their witness to Jesus and for proclaiming the Word of God—those who never worshipped the animal or its statue, and had not accepted its mark upon their foreheads or their hands. They came to life and reigned with Christ for a thousand years. (The rest of the dead did not come to life until the thousand years were over.) This is the first resurrection. Happy and holy is the one who shares in the first resurrection! The second death cannot touch such men; they shall be priests of God and of Christ, and shall reign with him for the thousand years.

Revised Standard Version

20 Then I saw an angel coming down from
heaven, holding in his hand the key of the
bottomless pit and a great chain. 2And he seized
the dragon, that ancient serpent, who is the Devil
and Satan, and bound him for a thousand years,
3 and threw him into the pit, and shut it and
sealed it over him, that he should deceive the
nations no more, till the thousand years were
ended. After that he must be loosed for a little
while.
4 Then I saw thrones, and seated on them
were those to whom judgment was committed.
Also I saw the souls of those who had been
beheaded for their testimony to Jesus and for the
word of God, and who had not worshiped the
beast or its image and had not received its mark
on their foreheads or their hands. They came to
life, and reigned with Christ a thousand years.
5 The rest of the dead did not come to life until
the thousand years were ended. This is the first
resurrection. 6 Blessed and holy is he who shares
in the first resurrection! Over such the second
death has no power, but they shall be priests of
God and of Christ, and they shall reign with him
a thousand years.

Jerusalem Bible

The reign of a thousand years

20 Then I saw an angel come down from
heaven with the key of the Abyss in his
hand and an enormous chain. 2 He overpowered
the dragon, that primeval serpent which is the
devil and Satan, and chained him up for a
thousand years. 3 He threw him into the Abyss,
and shut the entrance and sealed it over him, to
make sure he would not deceive the nations
again until the thousand years had passed. At
the end of that time he must be released, but
only for a short while.
4 Then I saw some thrones, and I saw *those
who are given the power to be judges*[w] take
their seats on them. I saw the souls of all who
had been beheaded for having witnessed for
Jesus and for having preached God's word, and
those who refused to worship the beast or his
statue and would not have the brand mark on
their foreheads or hands; they came to life, and
reigned with Christ for a thousand years. 5 This
is the first resurrection; the rest of the dead did
not come to life until the thousand years were
over. 6 Happy and blessed are those who share
in the first resurrection; the second death cannot
affect them but they will be priests of God and
of Christ and reign with him for a thousand
years.

[*w*] Dn. 7:22.

New English Bible

20 Then I saw an angel coming down from heaven with the key of the abyss and a great chain in his hands. He seized the dragon, that serpent of old, the Devil or Satan, and chained him up for a thousand years; he threw him into the abyss, shutting and sealing it over him, so that he might seduce the nations no more till the thousand years were over. After that he must be let loose for a short while.

Then I saw thrones, and upon them sat those to whom judgement was committed. I could see the souls of those who had been beheaded for the sake of God's word and their testimony to Jesus, those who had not worshipped the beast and its image or received its mark on forehead or hand. These came to life again and reigned with Christ for a thousand years, though the rest of the dead did not come to life until the thousand years were over. This is the first resurrection. Happy indeed, and one of God's own people, is the man who shares in this first resurrection! Upon such the second death has no claim; but they shall be priests of God and of Christ, and shall reign with him for the thousand years.

King James Version

years. 7And when the thousand years are expired, Satan shall be loosed out of his prison,
8And shall go out to deceive the nations which
are in the four quarters of the earth, Gog and
Magog, to gather them together to battle: the
number of whom *is* as the sand of the sea. 9And
they went up on the breadth of the earth, and
compassed the camp of the saints about, and
the beloved city: and fire came down from God
out of heaven, and devoured them. 10And the
devil that deceived them was cast into the lake
of fire and brimstone, where the beast and the
false prophet *are,* and shall be tormented day
and night for ever and ever. 11And I saw a
great white throne, and him that sat on it, from
whose face the earth and the heaven fled away;
and there was found no place for them. 12And
I saw the dead, small and great, stand before
God; and the books were opened: and another
book was opened, which is *the book* of life: and
the dead were judged out of those things which
were written in the books, according to their
works. 13And the sea gave up the dead which
were in it; and death and hell delivered up the
dead which were in them: and they were judged
every man according to their works. 14And death
and hell were cast into the lake of fire. This is
the second death. 15And whosoever was not

Living Bible

7 When the thousand years end, Satan will be
let out of his prison. 8 He will go out to deceive
the nations of the world and gather them together, with Gog and Magog, for battle—a
mighty host, numberless as sand along the shore.
9 They will go up across the broad plain of the
earth and surround God's people and the beloved
city of Jerusalem[a] on every side. But fire from
God in heaven will flash down on the attacking
armies and consume them.
10 Then the devil who had betrayed them will
again[b] be thrown into the Lake of Fire burning with sulphur where the Creature and False
Prophet are, and they will be tormented day and
night forever and ever.
11 And I saw a great white throne and the one
who sat upon it, from whose face the earth and
sky fled away, but they found no place to hide.[c]
12 I saw the dead, great and small, standing before God; and The Books were opened, including the Book of Life. And the dead were judged
according to the things written in The Books,
each according to the deeds he had done. 13 The
oceans surrendered the bodies buried in them;
and the earth and the underworld gave up the
dead in them. Each was judged according to his
deeds. 14And Death and Hell were thrown into
the Lake of Fire. This is the Second Death—the
Lake of Fire. 15 And if anyone's name was not

[*a*] Implied. [*b*] Implied; Revelation 20:3. [*c*] Literally, "There was no longer any place for them."

Today's English Version

The defeat of Satan

7 After the thousand years are over, Satan
will be set loose from his prison, 8 and he will
go out to deceive the nations scattered over all
the world, that is, Gog and Magog. Satan will
bring them all together for battle, as many as
the grains of sand on the seashore. 9 They
spread out over the earth and surrounded the
camp of God's people and the city that he loves.
But fire came down from heaven and destroyed
them. 10 Then the Devil, who deceived them,
was thrown into the lake of fire and sulfur,
where the beast and the false prophet had already been thrown; and they will be tormented
day and night, forever and ever.

The final judgment

11 Then I saw a large white throne and the
one who sits on it. Earth and heaven fled from
his presence, and were seen no more. 12And I
saw the dead, great and small alike, standing before the throne. Books were opened, and then
another book was opened, the book of the living. The dead were judged according to what
they had done, as was written in the books.
13 Then the sea gave up its dead. Death and the
world of the dead also gave up the dead they
held. And all were judged according to what
they had done. 14 Then death and the world of
the dead were thrown into the lake of fire. (This
lake of fire is the second death.) 15 Whoever

New International Version

Satan's doom

7 When the thousand years are over, Satan
will be released from his prison 8 and will go
out to deceive the nations in the four corners of
the earth—Gog and Magog—to gather them for
battle. In number they are like the sand on the
seashore. 9 They marched across the breadth of
the earth and surrounded the camp of God's
people, the city he loves. But fire came down
from heaven and devoured them. 10And the
devil, who deceived them, was thrown into the
lake of burning sulfur, where the beast and the
false prophet had been thrown. They will be tormented day and night for ever and ever.

The dead are judged

11 Then I saw a great white throne and him
who was seated on it. Earth and sky fled from
his presence, and there was no place for them.
12And I saw the dead, great and small, standing before the throne, and books were opened.
Another book was opened, which is the book
of life. The dead were judged according to
what they had done as recorded in the books.
13 The sea gave up the dead that were in it, and
death and Hades gave up the dead that were in
them, and each person was judged according to
what he had done. 14 Then death and Hades
were thrown into the lake of fire. The lake of
fire is the second death. 15 If anyone's name was

Phillips Modern English

20.7 Satan finally destroyed

Then, when the thousand years are over, Satan will be released from his prison, and will set out to deceive the nations in the four corners of the earth, Gog and Magog, and to lead them into battle. They will be as numerous as the sand of the seashore.

They came up and spread over the breadth of the earth; they encircled the army of the saints defending the beloved city. But fire came down from the sky and consumed them. The devil who deceived them was hurled into the lake of fire and sulphur to join the animal and the false prophet. And there they shall be tortured day and night for timeless ages.

20.11 The final judgment

And then I saw a great white throne, and One seated upon it from whose presence both earth and sky fled and vanished.

Then I saw the dead, great and small, standing before the throne and the books were opened. And another book was opened, which is the book of life. And the dead were judged by what was written in the books concerning what they had done. The sea gave up its dead, and death and the grave gave up the dead which were in them. And men were judged, each according to what he had done.

Then death and the grave were themselves hurled into the lake of fire, which is the second death. If anyone's name was not found written

Revised Standard Version

7 And when the thousand years are ended,
Satan will be loosed from his prison 8 and will
come out to deceive the nations which are at the
four corners of the earth, that is, Gog and Magog, to gather them for battle; their number is
like the sand of the sea. 9 And they marched up
over the broad earth and surrounded the
camp of the saints and the beloved city; but fire
came down from heaven[n] and consumed them,
10 and the devil who had deceived them was
thrown into the lake of fire and sulphur where
the beast and the false prophet were, and they
will be tormented day and night for ever and
ever.
11 Then I saw a great white throne and him
who sat upon it; from his presence earth and
sky fled away, and no place was found for them.
12 And I saw the dead, great and small, standing
before the throne, and books were opened. Also
another book was opened, which is the book of
life. And the dead were judged by what was
written in the books, by what they had done.
13 And the sea gave up the dead in it, Death and
Hades gave up the dead in them, and all were
judged by what they had done. 14 Then Death
and Hades were thrown into the lake of fire.
This is the second death, the lake of fire; 15 and

[n] Other ancient authorities read *from God, out of heaven,* or *out of heaven from God.*

Jerusalem Bible

The second battle of the End

7 When the thousand years are over, Satan
will be released from his prison 8 and will come
out to deceive all the nations in the four quarters of the earth, *Gog and Magog,*[x] and mobi-
lize them for war. His armies will be as many as
the sands of the sea; 9 they will come swarming
over the entire country and besiege the camp of
the saints, which is the city that God loves. But
fire will come down on them from heaven[y] and
consume them. 10 Then the devil, who misled
them, will be thrown into the lake of fire and
sulphur, where the beast and the false prophet
are, and their torture will not stop, day or night,
for ever and ever.

The punishment of the pagans

11 Then I saw a great white throne and the
One who was sitting on it. In his presence, earth
and sky vanished, leaving no trace. 12 I saw the
dead, both great and small, standing in front of
his throne, while the book of life was opened,
and *other books opened* which were the record
of what they had done in their lives, by which
the dead were judged.
13 The sea gave up all the dead who were in
it; 14 Death and Hades were emptied of the
dead that were in them; and every one was
judged according to the way in which he had
lived. Then Death and Hades were thrown into
the burning lake. This burning lake is the second
death; 15 and anybody whose name could not

[x] Ezk. 38:2. [y] Ezk. 38:22.

New English Bible

When the thousand years are over, Satan will be let loose from his dungeon; and he will come out to seduce the nations in the four quarters of the earth and to muster them for battle, yes, the hosts of Gog and Magog, countless as the sands of the sea. So they marched over the breadth of the land and laid siege to the camp of God's people and the city that he loves. But fire came down on them from heaven and consumed them; and the Devil, their seducer, was flung into the lake of fire and sulphur, where the beast and the false prophet had been flung, there to be tormented day and night for ever.

Then I saw a great white throne, and the One who sat upon it; from his presence earth and heaven vanished away, and no place was left for them. I could see the dead, great and small, standing before the throne; and books were opened. Then another book was opened, the roll of the living. From what was written in these books the dead were judged upon the record of their deeds. The sea gave up its dead, and Death and Hades gave up the dead in their keeping; they were judged, each man on the record of his deeds. Then Death and Hades were flung into the lake of fire. This lake of fire is the second

King James Version

found written in the book of life was cast into
the lake of fire.

21 And I saw a new heaven and a new earth:
for the first heaven and the first earth were
passed away; and there was no more sea. 2And
I John saw the holy city, new Jerusalem, coming
down from God out of heaven, prepared as a
bride adorned for her husband. 3And I heard
a great voice out of heaven saying, Behold, the
tabernacle of God *is* with men, and he will dwell
with them, and they shall be his people, and
God himself shall be with them, *and be* their
God. 4And God shall wipe away all tears from
their eyes; and there shall be no more death,
neither sorrow, nor crying, neither shall there
be any more pain: for the former things are
passed away. 5And he that sat upon the throne
said, Behold, I make all things new. And he
said unto me, Write: for these words are true
and faithful. 6And he said unto me, It is done.
I am Alpha and Omega, the beginning and the
end. I will give unto him that is athirst of the
fountain of the water of life freely. 7 He that
overcometh shall inherit all things; and I will be
his God, and he shall be my son. 8 But the fear-

Living Bible

found recorded in the Book of Life, he was
thrown into the Lake of Fire.

21 Then I saw a new earth (with no oceans!)
and a new sky, for the present earth and
sky had disappeared. 2And I, John, saw the Holy
City, the new Jerusalem, coming down from
God out of heaven. It was a glorious sight,
beautiful as a bride at her wedding.
3 I heard a loud shout from the throne saying, "Look, the home of God is now among men,
and he will live with them and they will be his
people; yes, God himself will be among them.[a]
4 He will wipe away all tears from their eyes,
and there shall be no more death, nor sorrow,
nor crying, nor pain. All of that has gone forever."
5 And the one sitting on the throne said, "See,
I am making all things new!" And then he said
to me, "Write this down, for what I tell you
is trustworthy and true: 6 It is finished! I
am the A and the Z—the Beginning and the
End. I will give to the thirsty the springs of the
Water of Life—as a gift! 7 Everyone who conquers will inherit all these blessings, and I will
be his God and he will be my son. 8 But cowards

[a] Some manuscripts add, "and be their God."

Today's English Version

did not have his name written in the book of
the living was thrown into the lake of fire.

The new heaven and the new earth

21 Then I saw a new heaven and a new
earth. The first heaven and the first earth
disappeared, and the sea vanished. 2And I saw
the Holy City, the new Jerusalem, coming down
out of heaven from God, prepared and ready,
like a bride dressed to meet her husband. 3 I
heard a loud voice speaking from the throne,
"Now God's home is with men! He will live
with them, and they shall be his people. God
himself will be with them, and he will be their
God. 4 He will wipe away all tears from their
eyes. There will be no more death, no more
grief, crying, or pain. The old things have disappeared."
5 Then the one who sits on the throne said,
"And now I make all things new!" He also said
to me, "Write this, because these words are true
and can be trusted." 6And he said, "It is done!
I am the Alpha and the Omega, the beginning
and the end. To anyone who is thirsty I will give
a free drink of water from the spring of the
water of life. 7 Whoever wins the victory will
receive this from me: I will be his God, and he
will be my son. 8 But the cowards, the traitors,

New International Version

not found written in the book of life, he was
thrown into the lake of fire.

The new Jerusalem

21 Then I saw a new heaven and a new
earth, for the first heaven and the first
earth had passed away, and there was no longer
any sea. 2 I saw the Holy City, the new Jerusalem, coming down out of heaven from God,
prepared as a bride beautifully dressed for her
husband. 3And I heard a loud voice from the
throne saying, "Now the dwelling of God is with
men, and he will live with them. They will be
his people, and God himself will be with them
and be their God. 4 He will wipe every tear
from their eyes. There will be no more death or
mourning or crying or pain, for the old order of
things has passed away."
He who was seated on the throne said, "I am
making everything new!" Then he said, "Write
this down, for these words are trustworthy and
true."
6 He said to me: "It is done. I am the Alpha
and the Omega, the Beginning and the End. To
him who is thirsty I will give to drink without
cost from the spring of the water of life. 7 He
who overcomes will inherit all this, and I will be
his God and he will be my son. 8 But the cow-

Phillips Modern English

in the book of life he was thrown into the lake of fire.

21.1 All things made new

Then I saw a new Heaven and a new earth, for the first Heaven and the first earth had disappeared and the sea was no more. I saw the holy city, the new Jerusalem, descending from God out of Heaven, prepared as a bride dressed in beauty for her husband. Then I heard a great voice from the throne crying,

"See! The home of God is with men, and he will live among them. They shall be his people, and God himself shall be with them, and will wipe away every tear from their eyes. Death shall be no more, and never again shall there be sorrow or crying or pain. For all those former things are past and gone."

Then he who is seated upon the throne said,

"See, I am making all things new!"

And he added,

"Write this down for my words are true and to be trusted."

Then he said to me,

"It is done! I am Alpha and Omega, the beginning and the end. I will give to the thirsty water without price from the fountain of life. The victorious shall inherit these things, and I will be God to him and he will be son to me. But as for the cowards, the faithless and the

Revised Standard Version

if any one's name was not found written in the book of life, he was thrown into the lake of fire.

21 Then I saw a new heaven and a new earth; for the first heaven and the first earth had passed away, and the sea was no more. 2And I saw the holy city, new Jerusalem, coming down out of heaven from God, prepared as a bride adorned for her husband; 3 and I heard a loud voice from the throne saying, "Behold, the dwelling of God is with men. He will dwell with them, and they shall be his people,[o] and God himself will be with them;[p] 4 he will wipe away every tear from their eyes, and death shall be no more, neither shall there be mourning nor crying nor pain any more, for the former things have passed away."

5 And he who sat upon the throne said, "Behold, I make all things new." Also he said, "Write this, for these words are trustworthy and true." 6And he said to me, "It is done! I am the Alpha and the Omega, the beginning and the end. To the thirsty I will give from the fountain of the water of life without payment. 7 He who conquers shall have this heritage, and I will be his God and he shall be my son. 8 But as for the

[o] Other ancient authorities read *peoples*. [p] Other ancient authorities add *and be their God*.

Jerusalem Bible

be found written in the book of life was thrown into the burning lake.

D. The Jerusalem of the future

The heavenly Jerusalem

21 Then I saw *a new heaven and a new earth*[z]; the first heaven and the first earth had disappeared now, and there was no longer any sea. 2 I saw the holy city, and the new Jerusalem, coming down from God out of heaven, as beautiful as a bride all dressed for her husband. 3 Then I heard a loud voice call from the throne, "You see this city? Here God lives among men. He will make *his home among them; they shall be his people*,[a] and he will be their God; his name is *God-with-them*. 4 *He will wipe away all tears from their eyes*[b]; there will be no more death, and no more mourning or sadness. The world of the past has gone."

5 Then the One sitting on the throne spoke: "Now I am making the whole of creation new," he said. "Write this: that what I am saying is sure and will come true." 6And then he said, "It is already done. I am the Alpha and the Omega, the Beginning and the End. I will give water from the well of life free to anybody who is thirsty; 7 it is the rightful inheritance of the one who proves victorious; and *I will be his God* and *he a son to me*.[c] 8 But the legacy for

[z] Is. 65:17. [a] Ezk. 37:27. [b] Is. 8:8 and 25:8. [c] 2 S. 7:14.

New English Bible

death; and into it were flung any whose names were not to be found in the roll of the living.

21 Then I saw a new heaven and a new earth, for the first heaven and the first earth had vanished, and there was no longer any sea. I saw the holy city, new Jerusalem, coming down out of heaven from God, made ready like a bride adorned for her husband. I heard a loud voice proclaiming from the throne: 'Now at last God has his dwelling among men! He will dwell among them and they shall be his people, and God himself will be with them.[a] He will wipe every tear from their eyes; there shall be an end to death, and to mourning and crying and pain; for the old order has passed away!'

Then he who sat on the throne said, 'Behold! I am making all things new!' (And he said to me, 'Write this down; for these words are trustworthy and true. Indeed they are already fulfilled.') 'I am the Alpha and the Omega, the beginning and the end. A draught from the water-springs of life will be my free gift to the thirsty. All this is the victor's heritage; and I will be his God and he shall be my son. But as for the

[a] *Some witnesses read* God-with-them shall himself be their God (*see Isaiah 7. 14; 8. 8*).

King James Version

ful, and unbelieving, and the abominable, and murderers, and whoremongers, and sorcerers, and idolaters, and all liars, shall have their part in the lake which burneth with fire and brimstone: which is the second death. 9And there came unto me one of the seven angels which had the seven vials full of the seven last plagues, and talked with me, saying, Come hither, I will shew thee the bride, the Lamb's wife. 10And he carried me away in the spirit to a great and high mountain, and shewed me that great city, the holy Jerusalem, descending out of heaven from God, 11 Having the glory of God: and her light *was* like unto a stone most precious, even like a jasper stone, clear as crystal; 12And had a wall great and high, *and* had twelve gates, and at the gates twelve angels, and names written thereon, which are *the names* of the twelve tribes of the children of Israel: 13 On the east three gates; on the north three gates; on the south three gates; and on the west three gates. 14And the wall of the city had twelve foundations, and in them the names of the twelve apostles of the Lamb. 15And he that talked with me had a golden

Living Bible

who turn back from following me, and those who are unfaithful to me, and the corrupt, and murderers, and the immoral, and those conversing with demons, and idol worshipers and all liars—their doom is in the Lake that burns with fire and sulphur. This is the Second Death."

9 Then one of the seven angels, who had emptied the flasks containing the seven last plagues, came and said to me, "Come with me and I will show you the bride, the Lamb's wife."

10 In a vision he took me to a towering mountain peak and from there I watched that wondrous city, the holy Jerusalem, descending out of the skies from God. 11 It was filled with the glory of God, and flashed and glowed like a precious gem, crystal clear like jasper. 12 Its walls were broad and high, with twelve gates guarded by twelve angels. And the names of the twelve tribes of Israel were written on the gates. 13 There were three gates on each side—north, south, east, and west. 14 The walls had twelve foundation stones, and on them were written the names of the twelve apostles of the Lamb.

15 The angel held in his hand a golden meas-

Today's English Version

and the perverts, the murderers and the immoral, those who practice magic and those who worship idols, and all liars—the place for them is the lake burning with fire and sulfur, which is the second death."

The new Jerusalem

9 One of the seven angels who had the seven bowls full of the seven last plagues came to me and said, "Come, and I will show you the Bride, the wife of the Lamb." 10 The Spirit took control of me, and the angel carried me to the top of a very high mountain. He showed me Jerusalem, the Holy City, coming down out of heaven from God, 11 shining with the glory of God. The city shone like a precious stone, like a jasper, clear as crystal. 12 It had a great, high wall, with twelve gates, and with twelve angels in charge of the gates. On the gates were written the names of the twelve tribes of the people of Israel. 13 There were three gates on each side: three on the east, three on the south, three on the north, and three on the west. 14 The city's wall was built on twelve stones, on which were written the names of the twelve apostles of the Lamb.

15 The angel who spoke to me had a gold

New International Version

ardly, the unbelieving, the vile, the murderers, the sexually immoral, those who practice magic arts, the idolators and all liars—their place will be in the fiery lake of burning sulfur. This is the second death."

9 One of the seven angels who had the seven bowls full of the seven last plagues came and said to me, "Come, I will show you the bride, the wife of the Lamb." 10And he carried me away in the Spirit to a mountain great and high, and showed me the Holy City, Jersualem, coming down out of heaven from God. 11 It shone with the glory of God, and its brilliance was like that of a very precious jewel, like a jasper, clear as crystal. 12 It had a great, high wall with twelve gates, and with twelve angels at the gates. On the gates were written the names of the twelve tribes of Israel. 13 There were three gates on the east, three on the north, three on the south and three on the west. 14 The wall of the city had twelve foundations, and on them were the names of the twelve apostles of the Lamb.

15 The angel who talked with me had a

Phillips Modern English

corrupt, the murderers, the traffickers in sex and sorcery, the worshippers of idols and all liars—their inheritance is in the lake which burns with fire and sulphur, which is the second death."

21.9 The vision of the New Jerusalem

Then one of the seven angels who hold the seven bowls which were filled with the seven last plagues, came to me and said,

"Come, and I will show you the bride, the wife of the Lamb."

Then he carried me away in spirit to the top of a vast mountain, and pointed out to me the city, the holy Jerusalem, descending from God out of Heaven, radiant with the glory of God. Her brilliance sparkled like a very precious jewel with the clear light of crystal. Around her she had a vast and lofty wall in which were twelve gateways with twelve angels at the gates. There were twelve names inscribed over the twelve gateways, and they are the names of the twelve tribes of the sons of Israel. On the east there were three gateways, on the north three gateways, on the south three gateways and on the west three gateways. The wall of the city had twelve foundation-stones, and on these were the names of the twelve apostles of the Lamb.

21.15 The measurement of the city

The one who was talking to me had a golden

Revised Standard Version

cowardly, the faithless, the polluted, as for murderers, fornicators, sorcerers, idolaters, and all liars, their lot shall be in the lake that burns with fire and sulphur, which is the second death."
9 Then came one of the seven angels who had
the seven bowls full of the seven last plagues, and
spoke to me, saying, "Come, I will show you the
Bride, the wife of the Lamb." 10 And in the Spirit
he carried me away to a great, high mountain,
and showed me the holy city Jerusalem coming down out of heaven from God, 11 having the
glory of God, its radiance like a most rare jewel,
like a jasper, clear as crystal. 12 It had a great,
high wall, with twelve gates, and at the gates
twelve angels, and on the gates the names of the
twelve tribes of the sons of Israel were inscribed;
13 on the east three gates, on the north three
gates, on the south three gates, and on the west
three gates. 14 And the wall of the city had
twelve foundations, and on them the twelve
names of the twelve apostles of the Lamb.
15 And he who talked to me had a measuring

Jerusalem Bible

cowards, for those who break their word, or worship obscenities, for murderers and fornicators, and for fortunetellers, idolaters or any other sort of liars, is the second death in the burning lake of sulphur."

The messianic Jerusalem

9 One of the seven angels that had the seven
bowls full of the seven last plagues came to
speak to me, and said, "Come here and I will
show you the bride that the Lamb has married."
10 *In the spirit, he took me to the top of an*
enormous high mountain[d] and showed me Jerusalem, the holy city, coming down from God
out of heaven. 11 It *had all the radiant glory*
of God[e] and glittered like some precious jewel
of crystal-clear diamond. 12 The walls of it
were of a great height, and had twelve gates;
at each of the twelve gates there was an angel,
and over the gates were written the names *of*
the twelve tribes of Israel; 13 *on the east there*
were three gates, on the north three gates, on
the south three gates, and on the west three
gates.[f] 14 The city walls stood on twelve foundation stones, each one of which bore the name
of one of the twelve apostles of the Lamb.
15 The angel that was speaking to me was

[d] Ezk. 40:2. [e] Is. 60:1-2. [f] Ezk. 48:31-35.

New English Bible

cowardly, the faithless, and the vile, murderers, fornicators, sorcerers, idolaters, and liars of every kind, their lot will be the second death, in the lake that burns with sulphurous flames.'

Then one of the seven angels that held the seven bowls full of the seven last plagues came and spoke to me and said, 'Come, and I will show you the bride, the wife of the Lamb.' So in the Spirit he carried me away to a great high mountain, and showed me the holy city of Jerusalem coming down out of heaven from God. It shone with the glory of God; it had the radiance of some priceless jewel, like a jasper, clear as crystal. It had a great high wall, with twelve gates, at which were twelve angels; and on the gates were inscribed the names of the twelve tribes of Israel. There were three gates to the east, three to the north, three to the south, and three to the west. The city wall had twelve foundation-stones, and on them were the names of the twelve apostles of the Lamb.

The angel who spoke with me carried a gold

King James Version

reed to measure the city, and the gates thereof,
and the wall thereof. 16And the city lieth foursquare, and the length is as large as the breadth:
and he measured the city with the reed, twelve
thousand furlongs. The length and the breadth
and the height of it are equal. 17And he measured the wall thereof, a hundred *and* forty
and four cubits, *according to* the measure of a
man, that is, of the angel. 18And the building
of the wall of it was *of* jasper: and the city *was*
pure gold, like unto clear glass. 19And the foundations of the wall of the city *were* garnished
with all manner of precious stones. The first
foundation *was* jasper; the second, sapphire; the
third, a chalcedony; the fourth, an emerald;
20 The fifth, sardonyx; the sixth, sardius; the
seventh, chrysolite; the eighth, beryl; the ninth,
a topaz; the tenth, a chrysoprasus; the eleventh,
a jacinth; the twelfth, an amethyst. 21And the
twelve gates *were* twelve pearls; every several
gate was of one pearl: and the street of the
city *was* pure gold, as it were transparent glass.
22And I saw no temple therein: for the Lord
God Almighty and the Lamb are the temple of
it. 23And the city had no need of the sun, nei-

Living Bible

uring stick to measure the city and its gates and
walls. 16 When he measured it, he found it was
a square as wide as it was long; in fact it was in
the form of a cube, for its height was exactly the
same as its other dimensions—1,500 miles each
way. 17 Then he measured the thickness of the
walls and found them to be 216 feet across (the
angel called out these measurements to me, using
standard units).[b]

18, 19, 20 The city itself was pure, transparent
gold like glass! The wall was made of jasper, and
was built on twelve layers of foundation stones
inlaid with gems:

The first layer[c] with jasper;
The second with sapphire;
The third with chalcedony;
The fourth with emerald;
The fifth with sardonyx;
The sixth layer with sardus;
The seventh with chrysolite;
The eighth with beryl;
The ninth with topaz;
The tenth with chrysoprase;
The eleventh with jacinth;
The twelfth with amethyst.

21 The twelve gates were made of pearls—each
gate from a single pearl! And the main street was
pure, transparent gold, like glass.

22 No temple could be seen in the city, for
the Lord God Almighty and the Lamb are worshiped in it everywhere.[d] 23And the city has no

[*b*] Literally, "144 cubits by human measurements." A cubit was the average length of a man's arm—not an angel's! The angel used normal units of measurement that John could understand. [*c*] Implied. [*d*] Literally, "are its temple."

Today's English Version

measuring stick, to measure the city, its gates,
and its wall. 16 The city was perfectly square, as
long as it was wide. The angel measured the
city with his measuring stick: it was 1,500 miles
long, and was as wide and as high as it was
long. 17 The angel also measured the wall, and
it was 216 feet high, according to the standard
unit of measure, which he was using. 18 The wall
was made of jasper, and the city itself was made
of pure gold, as clear as glass. 19 The foundation
stones of the city wall were adorned with all
kinds of precious stones. The first foundation
stone was jasper, the second sapphire, the third
agate, the fourth emerald, 20 the fifth onyx, the
sixth carnelian, the seventh yellow quartz, the
eighth beryl, the ninth topaz, the tenth chalcedony, the eleventh turquoise, the twelfth amethyst.
21 The twelve gates were twelve pearls; each gate
was made from a single pearl. The street of the
city was of pure gold, transparent as glass.

22 I did not see a temple in the city, because
its temple is the Lord God, the Almighty, and
the Lamb. 23 The city has no need of the sun

New International Version

measuring rod of gold to measure the city, its
gates and its wall. 16 The city was laid out like a
square, as long as it was wide. He measured the
city with the rod and found it to be 12,000
stadia[s] in length, and as wide and high as it is
long. 17 He measured its wall and it was 144
cubits[t] thick,[u] by man's measurement, which the
angel was using. 18 The wall was made of jasper,
and the city of pure gold, as pure as glass. 19 The
foundations of the city walls were decorated with
every kind of precious stone. The first foundation was jasper, the second sapphire, the third
chalcedony, the fourth emerald, 20 the fifth sardonyx, the sixth carnelian, the seventh chrysolite,
the eighth beryl, the ninth topaz, the tenth
chrysoprase, the eleventh jacinth, and the twelfth
amethyst. 21 The twelve gates were twelve pearls,
each gate made of a single pearl. The street of
the city was of pure gold, like transparent glass.

22 I did not see a temple in the city, because
the Lord God Almighty and the Lamb are its
temple. 23 The city does not need the sun or the

[*s*] That is, about 1500 miles. [*t*] That is, somewhat more than 200 feet. [*u*] Or *high*.

Phillips Modern English

rod in his hand with which to measure the city, its gateways and its wall. The city lies foursquare, its length equal to its breadth. He measured the city with his rod and it was twelve thousand furlongs in each direction, for its length, breadth and height are all equal. Then he measured its wall, and found that to be one hundred and forty-four half-yards high by human measurement, (which the angel was using).

21.18 The splendour of the city's building

The wall itself was built of translucent stone, while the city was of purest gold, with the brilliance of glass. The foundation stones of the wall of the city were fashioned out of every kind of precious stone. The first foundation-stone was jasper, the second sapphire, the third chalcedony, the fourth emerald, the fifth onyx, the sixth cornelian, the seventh goldstone, the eighth beryl, the ninth topaz, the tenth green goldstone, the eleventh turquoise, and the twelfth amethyst. The twelve gates were twelve pearls, each gate made of a single pearl. The street of the city was purest gold gleaming like glass.

21.22 The splendour within the city

I could see no Sanctuary in the city, for the Lord, the Almighty God, and the Lamb are themselves its Sanctuary. The city has no need

Revised Standard Version

rod of gold to measure the city and its gates and walls. 16 The city lies foursquare, its length the same as its breadth; and he measured the city with his rod, twelve thousand stadia;[q] its length and breadth and height are equal. 17 He also measured its wall, a hundred and forty-four cubits by a man's measure, that is, an angel's. 18 The wall was built of jasper, while the city was pure gold, clear as glass. 19 The foundations of the wall of the city were adorned with every jewel; the first was jasper, the second sapphire, the third agate, the fourth emerald, 20 the fifth onyx, the sixth carnelian, the seventh chrysolite, the eighth beryl, the ninth topaz, the tenth chrysoprase, the eleventh jacinth, the twelfth amethyst. 21 And the twelve gates were twelve pearls, each of the gates made of a single pearl, and the street of the city was pure gold, transparent as glass.

22 And I saw no temple in the city, for its temple is the Lord God the Almighty and the Lamb. 23 And the city has no need of sun or

[q] About fifteen hundred miles.

Jerusalem Bible

carrying a gold measuring rod to measure the city and its gates and wall. 16 The plan of the city is perfectly square, its length the same as its breadth. He measured the city with his rod and it was twelve thousand furlongs in length and in breadth, and equal in height. 17 He measured its wall, and this was a hundred and forty-four cubits high—the angel was using the ordinary cubit. 18 The wall was built of diamond, and the city of pure gold, like polished glass. 19 The foundations of the city wall were faced with all kinds of precious stone: the first with diamond, the second lapis lazuli, the third turquoise, the fourth crystal, 20 the fifth agate, the sixth ruby, the seventh gold quartz, the eighth malachite, the ninth topaz, the tenth emerald, the eleventh sapphire and the twelfth amethyst. 21 The twelve gates were twelve pearls, each gate being made of a single pearl, and the main street of the city was pure gold, transparent as glass. 22 I saw that there was no temple in the city since the Lord God Almighty and the Lamb were themselves the temple, 23 and the city did

New English Bible

measuring-rod, to measure the city, its wall, and its gates. The city was built as a square, and was as wide as it was long. It measured by his rod twelve thousand furlongs, its length and breadth and height being equal. Its wall was one hundred and forty-four cubits high, that is, by human measurements, which the angel was using. The wall was built of jasper, while the city itself was of pure gold, bright as clear glass. The foundations of the city wall were adorned with jewels of every kind, the first of the foundation-stones being jasper, the second lapis lazuli, the third chalcedony, the fourth emerald, the fifth sardonyx, the sixth cornelian, the seventh chrysolite, the eighth beryl, the ninth topaz, the tenth chrysoprase, the eleventh turquoise, and the twelfth amethyst. The twelve gates were twelve pearls, each gate being made from a single pearl. The streets of the city were of pure gold, like translucent glass.

I saw no temple in the city; for its temple was the sovereign Lord God and the Lamb. And the

King James Version

ther of the moon, to shine in it: for the glory of God did lighten it, and the Lamb *is* the light thereof. 24And the nations of them which are saved shall walk in the light of it: and the kings of the earth do bring their glory and honour into it. 25And the gates of it shall not be shut at all by day: for there shall be no night there. 26And they shall bring the glory and honour of the nations into it. 27And there shall in no wise enter into it any thing that defileth, neither *whatsoever* worketh abomination, or *maketh* a lie: but they which are written in the Lamb's book of life.

22 And he shewed me a pure river of water of life, clear as crystal, proceeding out of the throne of God and of the Lamb. 2 In the midst of the street of it, and on either side of the river, *was there* the tree of life, which bare twelve *manner of* fruits, *and* yielded her fruit every month: and the leaves of the tree *were* for the healing of the nations. 3And there shall be no more curse: but the throne of God and of the Lamb shall be in it; and his servants shall serve him: 4And they shall see his face; and his name *shall be* in their foreheads. 5And there shall be no night there; and they need no candle, neither light of the sun; for the Lord God giveth them light: and they shall reign for ever and

Living Bible

need of sun or moon to light it, for the glory of God and of the Lamb illuminate it. 24 Its light will light the nations of the earth, and the rulers of the world will come and bring their glory to it. 25 Its gates never close; they stay open all day long—and there is no night! 26And the glory and honor of all the nations shall be brought into it. 27 Nothing evil will be permitted in it—no one immoral or dishonest—but only those whose names are written in the Lamb's Book of Life.

22 And he pointed out to me a river of pure Water of Life, clear as crystal, flowing from the throne of God and the Lamb, 2 coursing down the center of the main street. On each side of the river grew Trees[a] of Life, bearing twelve crops of fruit, with a fresh crop each month; the leaves were used for medicine to heal the nations.

3 There shall be nothing in the city which is evil; for the throne of God and of the Lamb will be there, and his servants will worship him. 4And they shall see his face; and his name shall be written on their foreheads. 5And there will be no night there—no need for lamps or sun—for the Lord God will be their light; and they shall reign forever and ever.

[a] Literally, "the tree of life"—used here as a collective noun, implying plurality.

Today's English Version

or the moon to shine on it, because the glory of God shines on it, and the Lamb is its lamp. 24 The peoples of the world will walk by its light, and the kings of the earth will bring their wealth into it. 25 The gates of the city will stand open all day; they will never be closed, because there will be no night there. 26 The greatness and the wealth of the nations will be brought into the city. 27 But nothing that is impure will enter the city, nor anyone who does shameful things or tells lies. Only those whose names are written in the Lamb's book of the living will enter the city.

22 The angel also showed me the river of the water of life, sparkling like crystal, which comes from the throne of God and of the Lamb, 2 and flows down the middle of the city's street. On each side of the river was the tree of life, which bears fruit twelve times a year, once every month; and its leaves are for the healing of the nations. 3 Nothing that is under God's curse will be found in the city.

The throne of God and of the Lamb will be in the city, and his servants will worship him. 4 They will see his face, and his name will be written on their foreheads. 5 There shall be no more night, and they will not need lamps or sunlight, because the Lord God will be their light, and they will rule as kings forever and ever.

New International Version

moon to shine on it, for the glory of God gives it light, and the Lamb is its lamp. 24 The nations will walk by its light, and the kings of the earth will bring their splendor into it. 25 On no day will its gates ever be shut, for there will be no night there. 26 The glory and honor of the nations will be brought into it. 27 Nothing impure will ever enter it, nor will anyone who does what is shameful or deceitful, but only those whose names are written in the Lamb's book of life.

The river of life

22 Then the angel showed me the river of the water of life, as clear as crystal, flowing from the throne of God and of the Lamb 2 down the middle of the great street of the city. On each side of the river stood the tree of life, bearing twelve crops of fruit, yielding its fruit every month. And the leaves of the tree are for the healing of the nations. 3 No longer will there be any curse. The throne of God and of the Lamb will be in the city, and his servants will serve him. 4 They will see his face, and his name will be on their foreheads. 5 There will be no more night. They will not need the light of a lamp or the light of the sun, for the Lord God will give them light. And they will reign for ever and ever.

Phillips Modern English

for the light of sun or moon, for the splendour of God fills it with light and its radiance is the Lamb. The nations will walk by its light, and the kings of the earth will bring their glory into it. The city's gates shall stand open day after day—and there will be no night there. Into the city they will bring the splendours and honours of the nations.

But nothing unclean, no one who deals in filthiness and lies, shall ever at any time enter it—only those whose names are written in the Lamb's book of life.

22.1 A further glimpse of the city

Then he showed me the river of the water of life, sparkling like crystal as it flowed from the throne of God and of the Lamb. In the middle of the street of the city and on either bank of the river grew the tree of life, bearing twelve fruits, a different kind for each month. The leaves of the tree were for the healing of the nations.

Nothing that has cursed mankind shall exist any longer; the throne of God and of the Lamb shall be within the city. His servants shall worship him; they shall see his face, and his name will be upon their foreheads. Night shall be no more; they have no more need for either lamp-light or sunlight, for the Lord God will shed his light upon them and they shall reign as kings for timeless ages.

Revised Standard Version

moon to shine upon it, for the glory of God is
its light, and its lamp is the Lamb. 24 By its light
shall the nations walk; and the kings of the earth
shall bring their glory into it, 25 and its gates
shall never be shut by day—and there shall be
no night there; 26 they shall bring into it the
glory and the honor of the nations. 27 But nothing unclean shall enter it, nor any one who practices abomination or falsehood, but only those
who are written in the Lamb's book of life.

22 Then he showed me the river of the water
of life, bright as crystal, flowing from the
throne of God and of the Lamb 2 through the
middle of the street of the city; also, on either
side of the river, the tree of life[r] with its twelve
kinds of fruit, yielding its fruit each month; and
the leaves of the tree were for the healing of the
nations. 3 There shall no more be anything accursed, but the throne of God and of the Lamb
shall be in it, and his servants shall worship him;
4 they shall see his face, and his name shall be
on their foreheads. 5 And night shall be no more;
they need no light of lamp or sun, for the Lord
God will be their light, and they shall reign for
ever and ever.

[r] Or *the Lamb. In the midst of the street of the city, and on either side of the river, was the tree of life,* etc.

Jerusalem Bible

not need the sun or the moon for light, since it
was lit by the radiant glory of God and the
Lamb was a lighted torch for it. 24 *The pagan
nations will live by its light*[g] and the kings of
the earth will bring it their treasures. 25 *The
gates of it will never be shut by day*—and there
will be no night there—26 and *the nations will
come, bringing their treasure* and their wealth.
27 Nothing unclean may come into it: no one
who does what is loathsome or false, but only
those who are listed in the Lamb's book of life.

22 Then the angel showed me the river of
life, rising from the throne of God and
of the Lamb and flowing crystal-clear 2 down
the middle of the city street. *On either side of
the river were the trees of life, which bear
twelve crops of fruit in a year, one in each
month, and the leaves of which are the cure
for the pagans.*[h]
3 *The ban will be lifted.*[i] The throne of God
and of the Lamb will be in its place in the city;
his servants will worship him, 4 they will see
him face to face, and his name will be written
on their foreheads. 5 It will never be night again
and they will not need lamplight or sunlight,
because the Lord God will be shining on them.
They will reign for ever and ever.

[g] Is. 60:3. [h] Ezk. 47:12. [i] Zc. 14:11.

New English Bible

city had no need of sun or moon to shine upon it; for the glory of God gave it light, and its lamp was the Lamb. By its light shall the nations walk, and the kings of the earth shall bring into it all their splendour. The gates of the city shall never be shut by day—and there will be no night. The wealth and splendour of the nations shall be brought into it; but nothing unclean shall enter, nor anyone whose ways are false or foul, but only those who are inscribed in the Lamb's roll of the living.

22 Then he showed me the river of the water of life, sparkling like crystal, flowing from the throne of God and of the Lamb down the middle of the city's street. On either side of the river stood a tree of life, which yields twelve crops of fruit, one for each month of the year; the leaves of the trees serve for the healing of the nations. Every accursed thing shall disappear. The throne of God and of the Lamb will be there, and his servants shall worship him; they shall see him face to face, and bear his name on their foreheads. There shall be no more night, nor will they need the light of lamp or sun, for the Lord God will give them light; and they shall reign for evermore.

King James Version

ever. 6And he said unto me, These sayings *are*
faithful and true: and the Lord God of the
holy prophets sent his angel to shew unto his
servants the things which must shortly be done.
7 Behold, I come quickly: blessed *is* he that
keepeth the sayings of the prophecy of this book.
8And I John saw these things, and heard *them*.
And when I had heard and seen, I fell down to
worship before the feet of the angel which
shewed me these things. 9 Then saith he unto
me, See *thou do it* not: for I am thy fellow
servant, and of thy brethren the prophets, and
of them which keep the sayings of this book:
worship God. 10And he saith unto me, Seal not
the sayings of the prophecy of this book: for the
time is at hand. 11 He that is unjust, let him be
unjust still: and he which is filthy, let him be
filthy still: and he that is righteous, let him
be righteous still: and he that is holy, let him be

Living Bible

6, 7 Then the angel said to me, "These words
are trustworthy and true: 'I am coming soon!' [b]
God, who tells his prophets what the future
holds, has sent his angel to tell you this will happen
soon. Blessed are those who believe it and
all else written in the scroll."

8 I, John, saw and heard all these things, and
fell down to worship the angel who showed them
to me; 9 but again he said, "No, don't do anything
like that. I, too, am a servant of Jesus as
you are, and as your brothers the prophets are,
as well as all those who heed the truth stated in
this Book. Worship God alone."

10 Then he instructed me, "Do not seal up
what you have written, for the time of fulfillment
is near. 11And when that time comes, all doing
wrong will do it more and more; the vile will
become more vile; good men will be better; those
who are holy will continue on in greater holiness."

[b] Or, "suddenly," "unexpectedly."

Today's English Version

The coming of Jesus

6 Then the angel said to me, "These words
are true and can be trusted. And the Lord God,
who gives his Spirit to the prophets, sent his
angel to show his servants what must happen
very soon."

7 "Listen!" says Jesus. "I am coming soon!
Happy are those who obey the prophetic words
in this book!"

8 I, John, have heard and seen all these
things. And when I finished hearing and seeing
them, I fell down at the feet of the angel who
had shown me these things to worship him.
9 But he said to me, "Don't do it! I am a fellow
servant of yours, and of your brothers the
prophets, and of all those who obey the words
in this book. Worship God!" 10And he said to
me, "Do not keep the prophetic words of this
book a secret, because the time is near when
all this will happen. 11 Whoever is evil must go
on doing evil, and whoever is filthy must go on
being filthy; whoever is good must go on doing
good, and whoever is holy must go on being
holy."

New International Version

6 The angel said to me, "These words are
trustworthy and true. The Lord, the God of the
spirits of the prophets, sent his angel to show his
servants the things that must soon take place."

Jesus is coming

7 "Behold, I am coming soon! Blessed is he
who keeps the words of the prophecy in this
book."

8 I, John, am the one who heard and saw
these things. And when I had heard and seen
them, I fell down to worship at the feet of the
angel who had been showing them to me. 9 But
he said to me, "Do not do it! I am a fellow
servant with you and with your brothers the
prophets and of all who keep the words of this
book. Worship God!"

10 Then he told me, "Do not seal up the
words of the prophecy of this book, because
the time is near. 11 Let him who does wrong continue
to do wrong; let him who is vile continue
to be vile; let him who does right continue to do
right; and let him who is holy continue to be
holy."

Phillips Modern English

22.6 *The angel endorses the revelation*

Then the angel said to me,

"These words are true and to be trusted, for the Lord God, who inspired the prophets, has sent his angel to show his servants what must shortly happen."

"See, I come quickly! Happy is the man who pays heed to the words of the prophecy in this book."

22.8 *John's personal endorsement*

It is I, John, who have heard and seen these things. At the time when I heard and saw them I fell at the feet of the angel who showed them to me and I was about to worship him. But he said to me,

"No! I am fellow-servant to you and to your brothers, to the prophets and to those who keep the words of this book. Give your worship to God!"

Then he added,

"Do not seal up the words of the prophecy in this book, for the time of their fulfilment is near. Let the wicked man continue in his wickedness and the filthy man in his filthiness; let the good man continue his good deeds, and the holy man continue in holiness."

Revised Standard Version

6 And he said to me, "These words are trustworthy and true. And the Lord, the God of the
spirits of the prophets, has sent his angel to show
his servants what must soon take place. 7And
behold, I am coming soon."
Blessed is he who keeps the words of the
prophecy of this book.
8 I John am he who heard and saw these
things. And when I heard and saw them, I fell
down to worship at the feet of the angel who
showed them to me; 9 but he said to me, "You
must not do that! I am a fellow servant with you
and your brethren the prophets, and with those
who keep the words of this book. Worship God."
10 And he said to me, "Do not seal up the
words of the prophecy of this book, for the time
is near. 11 Let the evildoer still do evil, and the
filthy still be filthy, and the righteous still do
right, and the holy still be holy."

Jerusalem Bible

6 The angel said to me, "All that you have
written is sure and will come true: the Lord God
who gives the spirit to the prophets has sent his
angel to reveal to his servants *what is soon to
take place*. 7 Very soon now, I shall be with
you again." Happy are those who treasure the
prophetic message of this book.
8 I, John, am the one who heard and saw
these things. When I had heard and seen them
all, I knelt at the feet of the angel who had
shown them to me, to worship him; 9 but he
said, "Don't do that: I am a servant just like
you and like your brothers the prophets and
like those who treasure what you have written
in this book. It is God that you must worship."
10 This, too, he said to me, "Do not keep
the prophecies in this book a secret, because
the Time is close. 11 Meanwhile let the sinner
go on sinning, and the unclean continue to be
unclean; let those who do good go on doing
good, and those who are holy continue to be

New English Bible

Then he said to me, 'These words are trustworthy and true. The Lord God who inspires the prophets has sent his angel to show his servants what must shortly happen. And, remember, I am coming soon!'

Happy is the man who heeds the words of prophecy contained in this book! It is I, John, who heard and saw these things. And when I had heard and seen them, I fell in worship at the feet of the angel who had shown them to me. But he said to me, 'No, not that! I am but a fellow-servant with you and your brothers the prophets and those who heed the words of this book. It is God you must worship.' Then he told me, 'Do not seal up the words of prophecy in this book, for the hour of fulfilment is near. Meanwhile, let the evil-doer go on doing evil and the filthy-minded wallow in his filth, but let the good man persevere in his goodness and the dedicated man be true to his dedication.'

King James Version

holy still. 12And, behold, I come quickly; and
my reward *is* with me, to give every man according as his work shall be. 13 I am Alpha and
Omega, the beginning and the end, the first and
the last. 14 Blessed *are* they that do his commandments, that they may have right to the
tree of life, and may enter in through the gates
into the city. 15 For without *are* dogs, and sorcerers, and whoremongers, and murderers, and
idolaters, and whosoever loveth and maketh a
lie. 16 I Jesus have sent mine angel to testify
unto you these things in the churches. I am the
root and the offspring of David, *and* the bright
and morning star. 17And the Spirit and the bride
say, Come. And let him that heareth say, Come.
And let him that is athirst come. And whosoever

Living Bible

12 "See, I am coming soon,[b] and my reward
is with me, to repay everyone according to the
deeds he has done. 13 I am the A and the Z, the
Beginning and the End, the First and Last.
14 Blessed forever are all who are washing their
robes, to have the right to enter in through the
gates of the city, and to eat the fruit from the
Tree of Life.
15 "Outside the city are those who have
strayed away from God, and the sorcerers and
the immoral and murderers and idolaters, and all
who love to lie, and do so. 16 I, Jesus, have sent
my angel to you to tell the churches all these
things. I am both David's Root and his Descendant. I am the bright Morning Star. 17 The Spirit
and the bride say, 'Come.' Let each one who
hears them say the same, 'Come.' Let the thirsty
one come—anyone who wants to; let him come
and drink the Water of Life without charge.

[*b*] Or, "suddenly," "unexpectedly."

Today's English Version

12 "Listen!" says Jesus. "I am coming soon!
I will bring my rewards with me to give to each
one according to what he has done. 13 I am the
Alpha and the Omega, the first and the last,
the beginning and the end."
14 Happy are those who wash their robes
clean, and so have the right to eat the fruit from
the tree of life, and to go through the gates into
the city. 15 But outside the city are the perverts
and those who practice magic, the immoral and
the murderers, those who worship idols, and
those who are liars, both in words and deeds.
16 "I, Jesus, have sent my angel to announce
these things to you in the churches. I am the
descendant from the family of David; I am the
bright morning star."
17 The Spirit and the Bride say, "Come!"
Everyone who hears this must also say
"Come!"
Come, whoever is thirsty; accept the water of
life as a gift, whoever wants it.

New International Version

12 "Behold, I am coming soon! My reward
is with me, and I will give to everyone according
to what he has done. 13 I am the Alpha and the
Omega, the First and the Last, the Beginning and
the End.
14 "Blessed are those who wash their robes,
that they may have the right to the tree of life
and may go through the gates into the city.
15 Outside are the dogs, those who practice
magic arts, the sexually immoral, the murderers,
the idolaters and everyone who loves and practices falsehood.
16 "I, Jesus, have sent my angel to give you[v]
this testimony for the churches. I am the Root
and the Offspring of David, and the bright Morning Star."
17 The Spirit and the bride say, "Come!" And
let him who hears say, "Come!" Whoever is
thirsty, let him come; and whoever wishes, let
him take the free gift of the water of life.

[v] Greek *you* (plural).

Phillips Modern English

22.12 The interjected words of Christ

"See, I come quickly! I carry my reward with me, and repay every man according to his deeds. I am Alpha and Omega, the first and the last, the Beginning and the End. Happy are those who wash their robes, for they have the right to the tree of life and the freedom of the gates of the city. Shut out from the city shall be the depraved, the sorcerers, the impure, the murderers and the idolaters, and everyone who loves and practises a lie!

"I, Jesus, have sent my angel to you with this testimony for the Churches. I am both the root and stock of David, and the bright star of the morning!"

22.17 The invitation of the Church and the Spirit

The Spirit and the bride say, "Come!"
Let everyone who hears this also say, "Come!"
Let the thirsty man come, and let everyone who wishes take the water of life as a gift.

Revised Standard Version

12 "Behold, I am coming soon, bringing my recompense, to repay every one for what he has
done. 13 I am the Alpha and the Omega, the first and the last, the beginning and the end."
14 Blessed are those who wash their robes,[s] that they may have the right to the tree of life and that they may enter the city by the gates.
15 Outside are the dogs and sorcerers and fornicators and murderers and idolaters, and every one who loves and practices falsehood.
16 "I Jesus have sent my angel to you with this testimony for the churches. I am the root and the offspring of David, the bright morning star."
17 The Spirit and the Bride say, "Come." And let him who hears say, "Come." And let him who is thirsty come, let him who desires take the water of life without price.

[s] Other ancient authorities read *do his commandments.*

Jerusalem Bible

holy. 12 Very soon now, I shall be with you
again, *bringing the reward to be given to every man according to what he deserves.*[j] 13 I am the
Alpha and the Omega, *the First and the Last,*
the Beginning and the End. 14 Happy are those
who will have washed their robes clean, so that they will have the right to feed on the tree of life and can come through the gates into the
city. 15 These others must stay outside: dogs, fortunetellers, and fornicators, and murderers, and idolaters, and everyone of false speech and false life."

Epilogue

16 I, Jesus, have sent my angel to make these revelations to you for the sake of the churches. I am of David's line, the root of David and the bright star of the morning.
17 The Spirit and the Bride say, "Come." Let everyone who listens answer, "Come." *Then let all who are thirsty come*[k]*:* all who want it may *have the water* of life, *and have it free.*

[j] Ps. 62:12. [k] Is. 55:1.

New English Bible

'Yes, I am coming soon, and bringing my recompense with me, to requite everyone according to his deeds! I am the Alpha and the Omega, the first and the last, the beginning and the end.'

Happy are those who wash their robes clean! They will have the right to the tree of life and will enter by the gates of the city. Outside are dogs, sorcerers and fornicators, murderers and idolaters, and all who love and practise deceit.

'I, Jesus, have sent my angel to you with this testimony for the churches. I am the scion and offspring of David, the bright star of dawn."

'Come!' say the Spirit and the bride.
'Come!' let each hearer reply.
Come forward, you who are thirsty; accept the water of life, a free gift to all who desire it.

King James Version

will, let him take the water of life freely. 18 For
I testify unto every man that heareth the words
of the prophecy of this book, If any man shall
add unto these things, God shall add unto him
the plagues that are written in this book: 19And
if any man shall take away from the words of
the book of this prophecy, God shall take away
his part out of the book of life, and out of the
holy city, and *from* the things which are written
in this book. 20 He which testifieth these things
saith, Surely I come quickly: Amen. Even so,
come, Lord Jesus. 21 The grace of our Lord
Jesus Christ *be* with you all. Amen.

Living Bible

18And I solemnly declare to everyone who reads
this book: If anyone adds anything to what is
written here, God shall add to him the plagues
described in this book. 19And if anyone sub-
tracts any part of these prophecies, God shall
take away his share in the Tree of Life, and in
the Holy City just described.

20 "He who has said all these things declares:
Yes, I am coming soon!" [b]

Amen! Come, Lord Jesus!

21 The grace of our Lord Jesus Christ be with
you all. Amen!

[*b*] Or, "suddenly," "unexpectedly."

Today's English Version

Conclusion

18 I, John, solemnly warn everyone who hears
the prophetic words of this book: if anyone adds
anything to them, God will add to his punishment the plagues described in this book. 19And
if anyone takes away anything from the prophetic words of this book, God will take away
from him his share of the fruit of the tree of
life, and his share of the Holy City, which are
described in this book.

20 He who gives his testimony to all this,
says, "Certainly so! I am coming soon!"

So be it. Come, Lord Jesus!

21 May the grace of the Lord Jesus be with
all.

New International Version

18 I warn everyone who hears the words of
the prophecy of this book: If anyone adds anything to them, God will add to him the plagues
described in this book. 19And if anyone takes
words away from this book of prophecy, God
will take away from him his share in the tree of
life and in the holy city, which are described in
this book.

20 He who testifies to these things says, "Yes,
I am coming soon."

Amen. Come, Lord Jesus.

21 The grace of the Lord Jesus be with God's
people. Amen.

Phillips Modern English

22.18 John's testimony to this book

Now I bear solemn witness to every man who hears the words of prophecy in this book:

If anyone adds to these words God will add to him the disasters described in this book; if anyone takes away from the words of prophecy in this book, God will take away from him his share in the tree of life and in the holy city which are described in this book.

He, who is witness to all this, says,

"Yes, I am coming very quickly!"

"Amen, come, Lord Jesus!"

The grace of the Lord Jesus be with all his people.

Revised Standard Version

18 I warn every one who hears the words of the prophecy of this book: if any one adds to them, God will add to him the plagues described in this book, 19 and if any one takes away from the words of the book of this prophecy, God will take away his share in the tree of life and in the holy city, which are described in this book.

20 He who testifies to these things says, "Surely I am coming soon." Amen. Come, Lord Jesus!

21 The grace of the Lord Jesus be with all the saints.[t] Amen.

[t] Other ancient authorities omit *all;* others omit *the saints.*

Jerusalem Bible

18 This is my solemn warning to all who hear the prophecies in this book: if anyone adds anything to them, God will add to him every plague mentioned in the book; 19 if anyone cuts anything out of the prophecies in this book, God will cut off his share of the tree of life and of the holy city, which are described in the book.

20 The one who guarantees these revelations repeats his promise: I shall indeed *be with you* soon. Amen; come, Lord Jesus.

21 May the grace of the Lord Jesus be with you all. Amen.

New English Bible

For my part, I give this warning to everyone who is listening to the words of prophecy in this book: should anyone add to them, God will add to him the plagues described in this book; should anyone take away from the words in this book of prophecy, God will take away from him his share in the tree of life and the Holy City, described in this book.

He who gives this testimony speaks: 'Yes, I am coming soon!'

Amen. Come, Lord Jesus!

The grace of the Lord Jesus be with you all.[a]

[a] *Some witnesses read* with all; *others read* with all God's people; *others read* with God's people; *some add* Amen.